A Gale Ready Reference Handbook

Where to Go
Who to Ask

ISSN 1526-274X

A Gale Ready Reference Handbook

Where to Go Who to Ask

Carolyn A. Fischer, editor

GALE GROUP

Detroit
San Francisco
London
Boston
Woodbridge, CT

**Where to Go /
Who to Ask**
A Gale
Ready Reference
Handbook

Carolyn A. Fischer
Editor

Dawn Conzett DesJardins, Marc Faerber, Kristin Mallegg, Jeff Sumner
Contributing Editors

Amy L. Rance, *Associate Editor*
Kathleen Lopez Nolan, *Managing Editor*

Dorothy Maki, *Manufacturing Manager*
Wendy Blurton, *Senior Buyer*

Cindy Baldwin, *Product Design Manager*
Pamela A. E. Galbreath, *Senior Art Director*

©2000 Gale Group, Inc.
27500 Drake Road
Farmington Hills, MI 48331-3535

ISBN 0-7876-3951-6
0-7876-3946-X (complete set)

ISSN 1526-274X

Printed in the United States of America

Contents

A series of books designed to quickly answer questions on a number of subjects, the *Gale Ready Reference Handbooks* are a great addition to any library. The *Gale Ready Reference Handbooks* feature four task-specific references containing high-quality data, including essays, overviews, and contact information. Also featured are six related titles--sourcebooks which are industry targeted and contain a comprehensive cross-section of data, including information on associations, directories, periodicals, databases and online services, and leading companies and suppliers.

Fast Answers to Common Questions

Presented in a question and answer format, *Fast Answers to Common Questions (FACQ)* contains answers to 4,500 commonly asked ready-reference questions on a variety of subjects. For easier look-up, *FACQ* is arranged by subject and features a keyword index.

Fast Help for Major Medical Conditions

Fast Help for Major Medical Conditions (FHMMC) features essays about 100 common medical diseases and conditions, including an explanation of the disease/condition, symptoms, treatment, prognosis, prevention, and alternative treatments. For each disease, a list of association, agencies, clinics, and treatment centers is provided.

First Stop for Jobs and Industries

With information on more than 500 jobs and 1,100 industries, *First Stop for Jobs and Industries (FSJI)* is a great source for job seekers, career counselors, investors, and entrepreneurs alike. Researchers will gain valuable information on job duties, outlook and earnings, and industry trends, statistics, and leaders.

Where to Go / Who to Ask

Where to Go / Who to Ask (WGWA) contains contact information for approximately 4,900 associations, 8,600 publications, 1,600 databases, and 3,200 agencies and research centers and organizations. Arranged in a yellow pages-type format by keyword, *WGWA* will point you in the right direction whatever your need.

Related Titles

Gale's Guide to Genealogical and Historical Research
Contains associations, directories, periodicals, databases and online services, and leading companies relevant to genealogy.

Gale's Guide to Nonprofits
Contains associations, directories, periodicals, databases and online services, and leading companies relevant to the nonprofit industry.

Coming Soon

Gale's Guide to the Arts
Gale's Guide to the Government
Gale's Guide to Industry
Gale's Guide to the Media

Where to Go / Who to Ask is a handy directory to grab when you want to find out points of contact for commonly requested associations, databases, periodicals, research centers, organizations, and more. This useful product contains names, addresses, phone/fax numbers, and e-mail addresses/URLs for more than 18,000 listings.

Content and Arrangement

The information in this product is arranged in a yellow pages format by keyword for ease of use. There is also a title and keyword index which lists the names of all entries as well as important keywords within each name.

Descriptive Listings

There are nearly 500 keywords in *Where to Go / Who to Ask*. See the List of Keywords for more details.

Master Index

The index contains an alphabetical listing of all entry names and keywords mentioned within entry names. The numbers following the index citations refer to the page or pages on which the word or phrase can be found.

Comments and Suggestions

We invite comments and suggestions for improvement. Please contact:

Where to Go / Who to Ask

The Gale Group
27500 Drake Rd.
Farmington Hills, MI 48331-3535

Telephone: (248)699-4253
Toll-free: 800-347-4253
Fax: (248)699-8070

Where to Go / Who to Ask comprises descriptive listings of more than 18,000 associations, databases, publications, research centers, and organizations, as well as a keyword index. Each is fully explained below.

Descriptive Listings

● Association entries may contain the following elements: name of the association; address; phone, fax, and toll-free numbers; e-mail address; URL; names and titles of key personnel; and a brief description.

● Database entries may contain the following elements: name of the database; name of the company; address; phone, fax, and toll-free numbers; e-mail address; URL; names and titles of key personnel, including phone, fax, and e-mail if applicable; vendors; and a brief description.

● Publication entries (including directories, newsletters, and periodicals) may contain the following elements: publication titles; publishing company's name; address; phone, fax, and toll-free numbers; e-mail address; URL; names and titles of key personnel, including phone, fax, and e-mail if applicable; alternate contact information; and a brief description.

● Research centers may contain the following elements: name of the center; name of the organization which heads up the center; address; phone, fax, and toll-free numbers; e-mail address; URL; names and titles of key personnel; and a brief description.

● Government agencies, offices, or programs may contain the following elements: name of the agency, office or program; address; phone, fax, and toll-free numbers; e-mail address; URL; names and title s of key personnel; and a brief description.

Please note that although quite frequently there may appear to be duplicate entries, these entries are most likely not duplicates. Rather, one entry may be a periodical while the other entry of the same name is a database. (For example, the Dayton Daily News contains some of the same material but not all of the same material in its database form as it does in its print form.) Although these two entries may have the same name and the same basic contact information, more often than not there will be differences in what type of information each contains or what products or services each has to offer. Therefore, this book lists all of the different descriptions

of a product, to ensure that you find what you need.

In addition, some government agencies, offices, or programs may appear to have duplicate listings, such as the U.S. Department of Health and Human Services, National Institute of Allergy and Infectious Diseases, Division of Acquired Immunodeficiency Syndrome (AIDS), Basic Science Program. In this case, if you read the descriptions you will note that each entry, although appearing to be a duplicate, actually focuses on a distinct subject area or performs a specific function.

Index

The index provides alphabetical access by title and keywords within titles to all entries included in the book. Index references are to page numbers. On occasion, the same entry may be listed more than once with the same page number reference. This is because there is more than one entry on that page that contains that particular title or keyword.

Abortion
Accounting
Administration
Administrative Services
Advertising
Aerospace
Africa
Aging
Agriculture
AIDS
Alcoholic Beverages
Allergy
Alumni
Americas
Animal Welfare
Anthropology
Antiques
Apparel
Appraisers
Archaeology
Architecture
Armed Forces
Art
Arts and Sciences
Astrology
Astronomy
Atheist
Attorneys
Authors
Automobiles
Automotive
Aviation
Baking
Banking
Baptist
Baseball
Basketball
Beverages

Bible
Biographies
Biology
Boating
Books
Botany
Bowling
Boxing
Broadcasting
Building Industries
Building Trades
Business
Business Education
Cancer
Cardiology
Catholic
Cats
Cattle
Ceramics
Chambers of Commerce
Chemicals
Chemistry
Child Health
Child Welfare
Children
China
Chiropractic
Christianity
Civil Rights and Liberties
Clubs
Coaching
Collecting
Colleges and Universities
Commodities
Communications
Community Development
Computer Science
Computer Users

Computers
Concrete
Conservation
Conservative
Construction
Consumers
Contests
Contractors
Cooking
Copyright/Trademarks/Patents
Cosmetics/Hair
Crafts
Criminal Justice
Cycling
Dairy
Dance
Darts
Defense
Democratic Party
Dentistry
Dermatology
Diabetes
Disabilities
Diseases
Dogs
Donors
Ecology
Economics
Ecumenical
Education
Electrical
Electronics
Elks
Emergency
Emergency Medicine
Employee Benefits
Employment
Energy

Engineering
English
Entertainers
Entertainment
Environment
Ethnic Studies
Evangelism
Families
Family Planning
Farming
Federal Government
Feminism
Film
Finance
Fire Fighting
Firearms
Fish
Fishing
Florists
Food
Forest Industries
France/French
Free Enterprise
Friends
Fruits and Vegetables
Fuel
Fundraising
Furniture
Games
Gardening
Gay/Lesbian
Genealogy
Genetics
Geography
Geology
Germany/German
Gerontology
Glass
Golf
Government Employees
Graphic Arts/Design
Greece/Greek
Hardware
Health
Health Care
Health Care Products
Health Plans
Hearing Impaired
Heating and Cooling
Hispanic
Historic Preservation
History

Holocaust
Home Economics
Honor Societies
Horse Racing
Horseback Riding
Horses
Horticulture
Hospital
Hospitality Industries
Housing
Human Development
Human Rights
Humanities
Hunger
Immigration
Industrial Equipment
Industrial Workers
Information Management
Insurance
Interior Design
Internal Medicine
International Development
International Exchange
International Health
International Understanding
Internet
Investments
Israel
Italy/Italian
Japan/Japanese
Jewelry
Jewish
Journalism
Korea/Korean
Labor
Laboratory
Landscaping
Languages
Laundry
Law
Law Enforcement
Leadership
Legal Education
Libraries
Literacy
Literature
Livestock
Lutheran
Management
Manufacturing
Marine
Marketing

Marriage
Martial Arts
Masons
Mathematics
Medical
Medical Administration
Medical Education
Medical Technology
Medicine
Meeting Planners
Mennonite
Mental Health
Mentally Disabled
Metallurgy
Metals
Meteorology
Methodist
Middle East
Military
Minerals
Mining
Mission
Mortuary Services
Motorcycles
Municipal Government
Museums
Music
Native American
Natural Resources
Natural Sciences
Navy
Nephrology
Neurological Disorders
Nuclear Energy
Nuclear War and Weapons
Nursing
Nutrition
Nuts
Oceanography
Odd Fellows
Office Equipment
Oils and Fats
Ophthalmology
Optometry
Organizations
Ornithology
Orthopedics
Osteopathic Medicine
Outdoor Recreation
Packaging
Paper
Parents

Parks and Recreation
Pathology
Peace
Pediatrics
Performing Arts
Petroleum
Pets
Pharmaceuticals
Pharmacy
Philanthropy
Philately
Philosophy
Photography
Physical Fitness
Physics
Physiology
Plastics
Plumbing
Podiatry
Poetry
Poland/Polish
Political Action
Political Federations
Political Parties
Political Science
Politics
Pollution
Population
Postal Service
Postal Workers
Poverty
Psychiatry
Psychology
Psychotherapy
Public Policy
Public Relations
Public Speaking
Publishing
Purchasing
Radio
Radiology
Railroads
Reading
Real Estate
Recreation
Recreational Vehicles
Refugees
Rehabilitation
Relief
Religion
Renting and Leasing
Reproductive Rights

Republican Party
Research
Restaurants
Retailing
Retirement
Right to Life
Rubber
Russia
Safety
Sales
Science
Science Fiction
Scouting
Securities
Security
Seed
Seismology
Service
Service Clubs
Service Fraternities
Service Sororities
Sexual Abuse
Shipping
Shooting
Skating
Skiing
Small Business
Soccer
Social Clubs
Social Fraternities
Social Sciences
Social Sororities
Social Welfare
Social Work
Sociology
Softball
Spain/Spanish
Speech and Hearing
Sporting Goods
Sports
Standards
State Government
Statistics
Substance Abuse
Surgery
Taxation
Telecommunications
Television
Tennis
Testing
Textiles
Theater

Theology
Therapy
Thoracic Medicine
Tobacco
Tourism
Toxicology
Toys
Track and Field
Trade
Trails
Transportation
Travel
Trucks
United Church of Christ
United Nations
Urology
Utilities
Veterans
Veterinary
Vietnam
Vocational Education
Voluntarism
Waste
Water
Wildlife
Wildlife Conservation
Wine
Women
Wood
Woodmen
World Affairs
World Notables
Wrestling
Youth
Zoology

Abortion

NARRAL Newsletter

National Abortion and Reproductive Rights Action League (NARAL)

1156 15th St. NW, Ste. 700   Ph: (202)973-3000
Washington, DC 20005   Fax: (202)973-3099

Contact: Eugenia E. Gratto, Production Mgr.; Belle Taylor-McGhee, Director of Communications.

Desc: Monitors legislative news regarding the issue of abortion. Contains organizational news on various NARRAL affiliates and covers action taken by NARAL to help keep abortion safe and legal. *Type:* Newsletter.

National Abortion and Reproductive Action League

1156 15th St. NW, Ste. 700   Ph: (202)973-3000
Washington, DC 20005   Fax: (202)973-3096
E-mail: naral@newmedium.com
URL: http://www.naral.org

Contact: Kate Michelman, Pres.

Desc: To develop and sustain a pro-choice political constituency in order to maintain the right to legal abortion for all women. Initiates and coordinates political action of individuals and groups concerned with maintaining the 1973 Supreme Court abortion decision affirming the choice of abortion as a constitutional right. Maintains lobbyist; briefs members of Congress; testifies at hearings on abortion and related issues; organizes affiliates in states to build political awareness; trains field representatives. *Type:* Association.

ProLife News

Alliance Action, Inc.

B1-90 Garry St.   Ph: (204)943-5273
Winnipeg, MB, Canada R3C   Fax: (204)943-9283
4H1

Contact: Barbara LeBow, Senior Advisor.

Desc: Reports on developments in the areas of abortion, infanticide, and euthanasia in Canada. Recurring features include research news, interviews, reports of meetings, and book and video reviews. *Type:* Newsletter.

Accounting

ACAT ActionLetter

Accreditation Council for Accountancy and Taxation (ACAT)

1010 N. Fairfax St.   Ph: (703)549-2228
Alexandria, VA 22314-1574   Fax: (703)549-2984

Contact: Marianne M. Anderson, Editor.

Desc: Informs ACAT accredited individuals of Council activities relating to the improvement of professional standards in accountancy and taxation practices through accreditation and continuing education. Announces examination results and upcoming conferences and seminars. *Type:* Newsletter.

Accountant's Tax Weekly

Harcourt Brace Professional Publishing

525 B St., No. 1900   Ph: (619)699-6716
San Diego, CA 92101-4495   Free: 800-831-7799
   Fax: (619)699-6716

URL: http://www.hbpp.com; http://www.hbpp.com.

Desc: Provides tax-saving ideas and news on topics such as fringe benefits, company deductions, payroll taxes, travel and entertainment write-offs, and corporate tax returns. *Type:* Newsletter.

Accounting & Auditing Update Service

Warren, Gorham & Lamont, Inc.

RIA Group

PO Box 6159   Free: 800-950-1216
Carol Stream, IL 60197

Contact: S. Wasserman, Editor.

Desc: Provides straightforward analysis and interpretation of all new FASB and AICPA pronouncements as they're issues. *Type:* Newsletter.

Accounting Office Management and Administration Report

Institute of Management & Administration, Inc.

29 W. 35th St., 5th Fl.   Ph: (212)244-0360
New York, NY 10001-2299   Fax: (212)564-0465
E-mail: subserve@ioma.com
URL: http://www.ioma.com; http://www.ioma.com.

Contact: Ms. Susan F. Sandler, Editor.

Desc: Shows you how to operate your CPA firm at peak efficiency, improve firm pr ofitability, cut costs, update staffing ratios, and market and compete more eff ectively. Offers practical guidance on fees and billing rates, compensation lev els and benefits for CPAs and staff, firm performance, benchmarks and more. *Type:* Newsletter.

American Accounting Association

5717 Bessie Dr.   Ph: (941)921-7747
Sarasota, FL 34233-2399   Fax: (941)923-4093
E-mail: aaahg@packet.net
URL: http://www.aaa-edu.org

Desc: Professors and practitioners of accounting. Promotes worldwide excellence in accounting education, research and practice. *Type:* Association.

American Institute of Certified Public Accountants

1211 Avenue of the Americas   Ph: (212)596-6200
New York, NY 10036-8775   Free: 800-862-4272
   Fax: (212)596-6213

URL: http://www.aicpa.org

Desc: Professional society of accountants certified by the states and territories. *Type:* Association.

Assisted Housing Financial Management Insider

Brownstone Publishers, Inc.

149 Fifth Ave., 16th Fl.   Ph: (212)473-8200
New York, NY 10010-6801   Free: 800-643-8095
   Fax: (212)473-8786

E-mail: assisthous@aol.com.

Contact: John M. Striker, Publisher; Lynne Glass, Editor.

Desc: Explains how to comply with HUD regulatory requirements for accounting and auditing for federally-assisted housing. Includes accounting control policies, audit preparation checklists, model accounting book entries, forms, staff memoes, and model letters. *Type:* Newsletter.

Beta Alpha Psi

5717 Bessie Dr.
Sarasota, FL 34233

Contact: Nancy Harke, Exec.Dir.

Desc: Honorary and professional fraternity - men and women, accounting. *Type:* Association.

Bowman's Accounting Report

Hudson Sawyer Professional Services Marketing, Inc.

3445 Peachtree Rd. NE, Ste.   Ph: (404)264-9977
600   Free: 800-945-6462
Atlanta, GA 30326-1234   Fax: (404)264-9968
E-mail: mhsawyer@hs-bowmans.com

Contact: Arthur W. Bowman, Editor, awbowman@cris.com.

Desc: Contains articles on CPAs and CPA firms, provides news and analysis of management strategies, politics, marketing, computers, and personnel. Recurring features include interviews, commentary, reports of meetings, book reviews, and the columns titled Mergers, New Shareholders, Newsmakers, and Lawsuits. *Type:* Newsletter.

Business Matters

Canadian Institute of Chartered Accountants

277 Wellington St. W.   Ph: (416)977-3222
Toronto, ON, Canada M5V   Free: 800-268-3793
3H2   Fax: (416)977-8585
E-mail: andra.thurton@cica.ca.
URL: http://www.cica.ca

Contact: Kathleen Aldridge, Editor, fax: (416)204-3415, kathleen.aldridge@cica.ca.

Desc: Intended for distribution to clients of small- to medium-sized accounting firms. Covers accounting and auditing, general management, insurance and liability, computers, financial planning, and tax information. *Type:* Newsletter.

California Society of Certified Public Accountants

275 Shoreline Dr.
Redwood City, CA 94065-1412

Ph: (650)802-2600
Fax: (650)802-2225

URL: http://www.calcpa.org
Contact: James R. Kurtz, Exec.Dir.
Desc: Certified public accountants in business, education, government, industry, and private practice. Seeks to advance the profession, increase public awareness, and ensure high professional standards. *Type:* Association.

Cash Flow Management Strategies

Siefer Consultants, Inc.
PO Box 1384
Storm Lake, IA 50588

Ph: (712)732-7340
Free: 800-747-7342

E-mail: siefer@ncn.net
Contact: Steve Herron, Editor.
Desc: Features articles on what organizations are doing to increase cash flow. Topics include accounts receivables and collections, accounts payable, banking services, procurement, tax planning, capital financing, and new technology. *Type:* Newsletter.

Certified Management Accountants of British Columbia and Yukon—Update

Certified Management Accountants of British Columbia and Yukon
1575-650 W. Georgia St.
PO Box 11548
Vancouver, BC, Canada V6B 4W7

Ph: (604)687-5891
Free: 800-663-9646
Fax: (604)687-6688

E-mail: cmabc@cmabc.com
Contact: Heather Treleaven, Editor.
Desc: Promotes the aims of the Society, which are "to provide business advice and direction on strategic, tactical, and operational decisions." Recurring features include Interviews, news of research, a calendar of events, reports of meetings, news of educational opportunities, and job listings. *Type:* Newsletter.

CGA Manitoba Newsletter

Certified General Accountants' Association of Manitoba (CGA)
4 Donald St. S.
Winnipeg, MB, Canada R3L 2T7

Ph: (204)477-1256
Fax: (204)453-7176

Desc: Disseminates information of the Association. Offers announcements of continuing professional education, promotion brochures, and news of study groups. *Type:* Newsletter.

CPA Administrator's & Manager's Report

Harcourt Brace & Company
525 B St., Ste. 1900
San Diego, CA 92101-4495

Ph: (619)231-6616
Free: 800-831-7799
Fax: (619)699-6593

E-mail: propub@harcourtbrace.com; newsletters@hbpp.com.
Contact: Jayne Osborne, Editor; Sidney Bernstein, Esq., Sr. Acquisitions Editor; Lisa Dionne, Managing Editor, ldionne@harcourtbrace.com.
Desc: Covers management and administrative issues for CPA firms. Recurring features include calendar of events, reports of meetings, news of educational opportunities, book reviews, and a column titled News Briefs. *Type:* Newsletter.

CPA Associates—Outlook

CPA Associates International, Inc.
Meadows Office Complex
301 Rte. 17 N.
Rutherford, NJ 07070

Ph: (201)804-8686
Fax: (201)804-9222

Desc: Concerned with advancing and promoting the public accounting profession. Provides a forum for the discus-

sion and the exchange of information on such topics as government regulations, professional and ethical standards, practice management, and developments in accounting. *Type:* Newsletter.

CPA Client Bulletin

The American Institute of Certified Public Accountants
Harborside Financial Ctr.
201 Plaza 3
Jersey City, NJ 07311-3881

Ph: (201)938-3287
Free: 800-TOA-ICPA
Fax: (201)398-3741

Contact: Maria Luzarraga Albanese, Editor.
Desc: Discusses business-related topics, including taxes, management, and government regulation. Recurring features include news briefs on personal financial planning and taxes. *Type:* Newsletter.

CPA Construction Niche Builder

Harcourt Brace & Company
525 B St., Ste. 1900
San Diego, CA 92101-4495

Ph: (619)231-6616
Free: 800-831-7799
Fax: (619)699-6593

E-mail: propub@harcourtbrace.com; newsletters@hbpp.com.
Contact: John J. Corcoran, Editor; Dan Shiffrin, Editor.
Desc: Covers strategies and techniques for CPAs serving the construction industry. Recurring features include a calendar of events, reports of meetings, news of educational opportunities, and book reviews. *Type:* Newsletter.

CPA Government & Nonprofit Report

Harcourt Brace & Company
525 B St., Ste. 1900
San Diego, CA 92101-4495

Ph: (619)231-6616
Free: 800-831-7799
Fax: (619)699-6593

E-mail: propub@harcourtbrace.com; ldionne@harcourtbrace.com.
Contact: Rhett Harrell, Editor.
Desc: Covers advisory services on government and nonprofit accounting and auditing. Recurring features include calendar of events, reports of meetings, news of educational opportunities, book reviews, and a column titled Quick looks. *Type:* Newsletter.

CPA Internet Connection

Harcourt Brace Professional Publishing
525 B St., No. 1900
San Diego, CA 92101-4495

Ph: (619)699-6716
Free: 800-831-7799
Fax: (619)699-6716

URL: http://www.hbpp.com; http://www.hbpp.com.
Desc: Reports on methods and time-saving techniques on using the Internet to obtain research tips, marketing ideas, and communication strategies. *Type:* Newsletter.

The CPA Letter

American Institute of Certified Public Accountants
1211 Avenue of the Americas
New York, NY 10036

Ph: (212)596-6200
Free: 800-862-4272
Fax: (212)596-6213

Contact: Ellen J. Goldstein, Editor.
Desc: Presents "brief items on accounting and auditing developments, including new standards, Washington news of concern to the profession, AICPA professional activities," and related matters. *Type:* Newsletter.

CPA Litigation Service Counselor

Harcourt Brace & Company
525 B St., Ste. 1900
San Diego, CA 92101-4495

Ph: (619)231-6616
Free: 800-831-7799
Fax: (619)699-6593

E-mail: propub@harcourtbrace.com; newsletters@hbpp.com.

Contact: Jeffrey Salins, Editor, (619)231-6616, fax: (619)699-6593.
Desc: Covers strategies and techniques for maximizing profits in litigation support and engagements. Recurring features include calendar of events, reports of meetings, news of educational opportunities, book reviews, and a column titled Brief Cases. *Type:* Newsletter.

CPA Managing Partner Report

Strafford Publications, Inc.
590 Dutch Valley Rd., NE
PO Drawer 13729
Atlanta, GA 30324-0729

Ph: (404)881-1141
Free: 800-926-7926
Fax: (404)881-0074

E-mail: custserv@staffordpub.com
Contact: Jon McKenna, Executive Editor.
Desc: "Delivers successful tactics and methods CPA firm leaders may use to improve profits, growth, and professional relationships with partners and clients." *Type:* Newsletter.

CPA Marketing Report

Strafford Publications, Inc.
590 Dutch Valley Rd., NE
PO Drawer 13729
Atlanta, GA 30324-0729

Ph: (404)881-1141
Free: 800-926-7926
Fax: (404)881-0074

E-mail: custserv@staffordpub.com
Contact: Jon McKenna, Exec. Editor.
Desc: Presents integrated marketing strategies and techniques for accountants to excel in building and maintaining an outstanding practice development environment. *Type:* Newsletter.

The CPA Network

Jeffrey D. Halpern
1 Kendall Sq., Bldg. 600, Ste. 201
Cambridge, MA 02139

Fax: (617)494-1540

Contact: Candace C. Cline, Editor; Jeffrey D. Halpern, Publisher.
Desc: Lists job openings for certified public accountants. *Type:* Newsletter.

CPA Personnel Report

Strafford Publications, Inc.
590 Dutch Valley Rd., NE
PO Drawer 13729
Atlanta, GA 30324-0729

Ph: (404)881-1141
Free: 800-926-7926
Fax: (404)881-0074

E-mail: custserv@staffordpub.com
Contact: Jon McKenna, Editor.
Desc: Delivers guidelines and techniques for accountants to select, develop, train, and manage human resources for a productive firm environment. *Type:* Newsletter.

CPA Profitability Monthly

Harcourt Brace & Company
525 B St., Ste. 1900
San Diego, CA 92101-4495

Ph: (619)231-6616
Free: 800-831-7799
Fax: (619)699-6593

E-mail: propub@harcourtbrace.com; newsletters@hbpp.com.
Contact: Allan Boress, Editor.
Desc: Informs certified public accountants (CPAs) on techniques of quality service and marketing and how these techniques are working in actual CPA firms. Recurring features include interviews, calendar of events, reports of meetings, and book reviews. *Type:* Newsletter.

CPA Technology Advisor

Harcourt Brace & Company
525 B St., Ste. 1900
San Diego, CA 92101-4495

Ph: (619)231-6616
Free: 800-831-7799
Fax: (619)699-6593

E-mail: propub@harcourtbrace.com; newsletters@hbpp.com.

Contact: Robert Spencer, Editor.

Desc: Describes software and hardware tailored for use by certified public accountants. Offers recommendations on products and uses. *Type:* Newsletter.

Efficient Auditor

Audit/Watch, Inc.
PO Box 1181   Ph: (703)845-9204
Annandale, VA 22003-9181

Contact: Thomas Houck, Editor and Publisher.

Desc: Examines the auditing process and offers suggestions for efficiency. *Type:* Newsletter.

Emerson's Professional Services Review

Emerson Co.
12342 Northup Way   Ph: (425)869-0655
Bellevue, WA 98005   Fax: (425)869-0746
E-mail: emerson@emersoncompany.com

Contact: James C. Emerson, Editor.

Desc: Summarizes selected articles from major U.S. publications citing prominent professional services firms. *Type:* Newsletter.

Executive's Tax and Management Report

Harcourt Brace Professional Publishing
525 B St., No. 1900   Ph: (619)699-6716
San Diego, CA 92101-4495   Free: 800-831-7799
   Fax: (619)699-6716
URL: http://www.hbpp.com; http://www.hbpp.com.

Desc: Supplies information on how to obtain more tax-free cash from a company or business, cut a company's tax bill, increase personal deductions, and manage new crackdowns. *Type:* Newsletter.

Financial Accounting Foundation

401 Merritt 7   Ph: (203)847-0700
PO Box 5116   Fax: (203)849-9714
Norwalk, CT 06856
URL: http://www.gasb.org

Type: Association.

Forensic Accounting Review

Computer Protection Systems, Inc.
PO Box 6121   Ph: (313)459-8787
Plymouth, MI 48170

Contact: Jack Bologna, Editor.

Desc: Reports on accounting and auditing practices, bank scandals, laws, litigations, security leaks, white-collar crime, and corporate thievery. *Type:* Newsletter.

Foundation for Accounting Education

530 5th Ave., 5th Fl.   Ph: (212)719-8300
New York, NY 10036   Free: 800-537-3635
   Fax: (212)719-3365

Desc: Conducts educational and technical programs, seminars, workshops, and conferences for CPAs in private practice and industry. *Type:* Association.

Government Accounting and Auditing Update

Warren, Gorham & Lamont, Inc.
RIA Group
PO Box 6159   Free: 800-950-1216
Carol Stream, IL 60197

Contact: D. Cummings, Editor.

Desc: Provides information on changes taking place in government accounting and financial reporting. *Type:* Newsletter.

Horizons

Goldstein Golub Kessler & Co., P.C.
1185 Avenue of the Americas   Ph: (212)372-1000
New York, NY 10036-2602   Fax: (212)372-1001
URL: http://www.ggk.com.

Contact: Gerald L. Golub, Editor.

Desc: Features timely articles on topics of general and financial interest. Recurring features include a collection. *Type:* Newsletter.

Hospitality Financial and Technology Professionals

11709 Boulder Ln., Ste. 100   Ph: (512)249-5333
Austin, TX 78726   Free: 800-646-4387
   Fax: (512)249-1533
E-mail: hftp@hftp.org
URL: http://www.hitecshow.org

Desc: Accountants, financial officers and MIS managers in 50 countries working in hotels, resorts, casinos, restaurants, and clubs. Develops uniform system of accounts. *Type:* Association.

IFAC Quarterly Newsletter

International Federation of Accountants (IFAC)
535 5th Ave., 26th Fl.   Ph: (212)286-9344
New York, NY 10017   Fax: (212)286-9570
E-mail: mariahermann@ifac.org
URL: http://www.ifac.org.

Contact: Heline Kennedy, kencom@webspan.net.

Desc: Focuses on the activities of the Federation, whose goal is to coordinate efforts to achieve international, technical, ethical, and educational guidelines for the accountancy profession. Also reports on member accounting bodies and on regional groups with similar goals. *Type:* Newsletter.

IMA Focus

Institute of Management Accountants
10 Paragon Dr.   Ph: (201)573-9000
Montvale, NJ 07645-1760   Free: 800-638-4427
   Fax: (201)573-0639

Contact: Marie Gartshore, Editor, mgartsho@imanet.org.

Desc: Provides membership news; tips on publicity, promotion, and competition; and schedules of events. Aids volunteer leaders in chapter management and the planning of programs. *Type:* Newsletter.

Institute of Certified Management Accountants

10 Paragon Dr.   Ph: (201)573-9000
Montvale, NJ 07645   Free: 800-638-4427
   Fax: (201)573-8438

Desc: Persons who have earned or are in the process of earning Certified Management Accountant (CMA) designation. Evaluates credentials of CMA candidates; administers the CMA program; conducts examinations; grants certificates to those who qualify; ensures that CMAs continue to meet the professional development requirements necessary to retain their certificates. *Type:* Association.

Institute of Chartered Accountants of Alberta— CA Monthly Statement

Institute of Chartered Accountants of Alberta
580 Manulife Pl.   Ph: (780)424-7391
10180-101 St.   Free: 800-232-9406
Edmonton, AB, Canada T5J   Fax: (780)425-8766
4R2
E-mail: generaldelivery@icaa.ab.ca
URL: http://www.icaa.ab.ca; http://www.icaa.ab.ca.

Contact: Karin Holmgren, Editor, k.holmgren@icaa.ab.ca.

Desc: Covers business and accounting issues and Institute activities. Includes a calendar of events, news of members, news of meetings and educational opportunities, and columns titled President's Message, The Way You See It, PD Corner, Practice Review, A Matter of Discipline. *Type:* Newsletter.

Institute of Internal Auditors

249 Maitland Ave.   Ph: (407)830-7600
Altamonte Springs, FL 32701-   Fax: (407)831-5171
4201
E-mail: iia@theiia.org
URL: http://www.theiia.org

Desc: Members in internal auditing, governance, internal control, IT audit, education, and security. Leader in certification, education, research, and technological guidance for the profession. *Type:* Association.

Institute of Management Accountants

10 Paragon Dr.   Ph: (201)573-9000
Montvale, NJ 07645   Free: 800-638-4427
   Fax: (201)573-8483
E-mail: info@imanet.org
URL: http://www.imanet.org

Contact: Richard M. Swanson, Exec.Dir.

Desc: Management accountants in industry, public accounting, government, and academia; other persons interested in internal and management uses of accounting. Conducts research on accounting methods and procedures and the management purposes served. *Type:* Association.

Internal Auditing Alert

Warren, Gorham & Lamont, Inc.
RIA Group
PO Box 6159   Free: 800-950-1216
Carol Stream, IL 60197

Contact: Dorothy Cummings, Editor.

Desc: Presents unique coverage that includes reviews and explanations of current Institute of Internal Auditors releases, appraisals of new audit techniques, and highlights of successful audit management practices. *Type:* Newsletter.

International Affiliation of Independent Accounting Firms

9200 S. Dadeland Blvd., Ste.   Ph: (305)670-0580
510   Fax: (305)670-3818
Miami, FL 33156
E-mail: info@accountants.org
URL: http://www.accountants.org

Desc: Independent accounting firms in 85 countries. Promotes the benefits of group representation while retaining independence. *Type:* Association.

International Affiliation of Independent Accounting Firms—Update

International Affiliation of Independent Accounting Firms
9200 S. Dadeland Blvd., Ste.   Ph: (305)670-0580
510   Fax: (305)670-3818
Miami, FL 33156
URL: http://www.accountants.org.

Contact: Sufan Dent, Editor.

Desc: Advises independent accounting firms worldwide on management of accounting practices. Covers topics such as marketing, employee training, and office products and equipment. *Type:* Newsletter.

Journal of Accountancy

The American Institute of Certified Public Accountants
Harborside Financial Ctr.   Ph: (201)938-3287
201 Plaza 3   Free: 800-TOA-ICPA
Jersey City, NJ 07311-3881   Fax: (201)398-3741
URL: http://www.aicpa.org.

Contact: Colleen Katz, Editor; Robert P. Rainier, Publisher, (201)938-3283; Frank Brown, Assoc. Publisher, (212)596-6093, fax: (212)596-6038.

Desc: Accounting journal. *Alt. Contact:* Harborside Financial Center, 201 Plaza Three, Jersey City, NJ 07311-3881; telephone: (201)938-3292; fax: (201)938-3329. *Type:* Periodical.

Keep Up to Date on Accounts Payable

Progressive Business Publications
370 Technology Dr.   Ph: (610)695-8600
Malvern, PA 19355   Free: 800-220-5000
                                      Fax: (610)651-2981
URL: http://www.pbp.com.
Contact: Jennifer Azara, Editor.
Desc: Supplies updates on state and local sales use taxes, plus IRS 1099 regulations and best practices in accounts payable. Recurring features include interviews, news of research, a calendar of events, and a column titled Sharpen Your Judgment. *Type:* Newsletter.

Keep Up to Date on Payroll

Progressive Business Publications
370 Technology Dr.   Ph: (610)695-8600
Malvern, PA 19355   Free: 800-220-5000
                                      Fax: (610)651-2981
URL: http://www.pbp.com.
Contact: Jenny Weiss, Editor.
Desc: Presents the latest on federal and state tax laws and unemployment insurance. Recurring features include interviews, a calendar of events, news of educational opportunities, and a column titled Sharpen Your Judgment. *Type:* Newsletter.

Leader's Edge

Michigan Association of CPAs
28116 Orchard Lake Rd.   Ph: (248)855-2288
PO Box 9054   Fax: (248)855-9122
Farmington Hills, MI 48333
E-mail: macpa@michcpa.org.
Contact: Marla Janness, Editor, (248)528-2055, fax: (248)528-2055, mjanness@ix.netcom.com.
Desc: Contains professional and technical information for certified public accountants. *Type:* Newsletter.

Managing Accounts Payable

Institute of Management & Administration, Inc.
29 W. 35th St., 5th Fl.   Ph: (212)244-0360
New York, NY 10001-2299   Fax: (212)564-0465
E-mail: subserve@ioma.com
URL: http://www.ioma.com
Contact: Mary Ludwig, Editor, mludwig@ioma.com; Perry Patterson, Publisher, ppatterson@ioma.com.
Desc: Provides information on managing accounts payable departments. Remarks: Also available via e-mail. *Type:* Newsletter.

MicroView

Canadian Institute of Chartered Accountants
277 Wellington St. W.   Ph: (416)977-3222
Toronto, ON, Canada M5V   Free: 800-268-3793
    3H2   Fax: (416)977-8585
E-mail: microview@cica.ca.
URL: http://www.cica.ca
Contact: Robert Cuthbertson, Editor.
Desc: Concentrates on the application of PCs in the accounting and financial management professions. Offers in-depth articles exploring specific areas of technology, such as data communications and local area networks. *Type:* Newsletter.

National Association of Black Accountants— Chapter to Chapter

National Association of Black Accountants, Inc.
7249-A Hanover Pkwy.   Ph: (301)474-6222
Greenbelt, MD 20770-3653   Fax: (301)474-3114
URL: http://www.nabainc.org.
Desc: Serves as a means of communication among the Association's student chapters. Covers student programs and events sponsored by the Association. *Type:* Newsletter.

National Association of Black Accountants— News Plus

National Association of Black Accountants, Inc.
7249-A Hanover Pkwy.   Ph: (301)474-6222
Greenbelt, MD 20770-3653   Fax: (301)474-3114
URL: http://www.nabainc.org.
Desc: Addresses concerns of black business professionals, especially in the accounting profession. Reports on accounting education issues, developments affecting the profession, and the Association's activities on the behalf of minorities in the accounting profession. *Type:* Newsletter.

National Association of State Boards of Accountancy

150 Fourth Avenue, N, Ste.700   Ph: (615)880-4200
Nashville, TN 37219   Fax: (615)880-4290
E-mail: communications@nasba.org
URL: http://www.NASBA.org
Contact: David A. Costello, CPA, Pres. & CEO.
Desc: State and territorial boards of public accountancy. Serves as a forum for communication among state boards of accountancy. Assists member boards in obtaining services needed for the administration of public accountancy laws and the protection of the public interest. *Type:* Association.

National Society of Public Accountants

1010 N. Fairfax St.   Ph: (703)549-6400
Alexandria, VA 22314-1574   Free: 800-966-6679
                                    Fax: (703)549-2984
E-mail: nsa@wizard.net
URL: http://www.nsa.org
Contact: Bill Mathisen, EVP, Contact.
Desc: Professional orgnization for more than 17000 members who provide auditing, accounting, tax preparation, financial and estate planning and management servies to approximately 4 million individuals and business clients. Most members are sole practitioners or partners in small to mid-size accounting firms. *Type:* Association.

NewsAccount

Colorado Society of Certified Public Accountants
7979 E. Tufts Ave., Ste. 500   Ph: (303)773-2877
Denver, CO 80237-2845   Fax: (303)773-6344
E-mail: cpa-staff@cspa.denver.co.us
Contact: Liz Julin, Publisher.
Desc: Relays information on issues and trends affecting the Society, its members, and the accounting profession. Recurring features include letters to the editor, job listings, a calendar of events and columns titled Committees in Action, Student Corner, SEC Corner, and Technical Update. *Type:* Newsletter.

Nonprofit Tax Letter

Harcourt Brace Professional Publishing
525 B St., No. 1900   Ph: (619)699-6716
San Diego, CA 92101-4495   Free: 800-831-7799
                                    Fax: (619)699-6716
URL: http://www.hbpp.com; http://www.hbpp.com.
Desc: Contains tax law changes and rulings. Also includes techniques for building tax-free income for an organization. *Type:* Newsletter.

Partner to Partner Advisory

Harcourt Brace Professional Publishing
525 B St., No. 1900   Ph: (619)699-6716
San Diego, CA 92101-4495   Free: 800-831-7799
                                    Fax: (619)699-6716
URL: http://www.hbpp.com; http://www.hbpp.com.
Desc: Contains articles written by some of the accounting profession's top practitioners and consultants. Includes strategies for increasing profitability and expanding a client base. *Type:* Newsletter.

The Practical Accountant Alert

Warren, Gorham & Lamont R.I.A. Group
90 Fifth Ave., 10th Fl.   Ph: (212)807-2193
New York, NY 10011   Free: 800-950-1216
                                    Fax: (212)337-4183
Contact: Robert W. McGee, Editor.
Desc: Monitors developments in areas such as taxes, financial planning and reporting, accounting and auditing, Security and Exchange Commission (SEC) regulations, computers, practice management, and MAS as they affect accounting practices. Recurring features include columns titled Professional Societies, Accounting Firms, and ERISA. *Type:* Newsletter.

The Practicing CPA

The American Institute of Certified Public Accountants
Harborside Financial Ctr.   Ph: (201)938-3287
201 Plaza 3   Free: 800-TOA-ICPA
Jersey City, NJ 07311-3881   Fax: (201)398-3741
URL: http://www.aicpa.org.
Desc: Focuses on accounting practice management and the practical application of professional standards. Recurring features include letters to the editor, announcements of seminars and conferences, and bizsites. *Type:* Newsletter.

Public Accounting Report

Strafford Publications, Inc.
590 Dutch Valley Rd., NE   Ph: (404)881-1141
PO Drawer 13729   Free: 800-926-7926
Atlanta, GA 30324-0729   Fax: (404)881-0074
E-mail: custserv@staffordpub.com
Contact: Jon McKenna, Editor.
Desc: Supplies news and analysis of practices and trends in the international accounting profession. *Type:* Newsletter.

SEC Accounting Report

Warren, Gorham & Lamont, Inc.
RIA Group
PO Box 6159   Free: 800-950-1216
Carol Stream, IL 60197
Contact: J. Cursinella, Editor.
Desc: Offers timely coverage of the SEC, FASB and related financial reporting subjects. *Type:* Newsletter.

SEC Accounting & Reporting Update Service

Warren, Gorham & Lamont R.I.A. Group
90 Fifth Ave., 10th Fl.   Ph: (212)807-2193
New York, NY 10011   Free: 800-950-1216
                                    Fax: (212)337-4183
Contact: Allan B. Afterman, Editor.
Desc: Addresses issues related to accounting and reporting in consolidated financial statements. *Type:* Newsletter.

Single Audit Information Service

Thompson Publishing Group
1725 K St. NW, Ste. 700   Ph: (202)872-4000
Washington, DC 20006   Fax: (202)739-9578
Contact: Denise Lamoreaux, Sr. Pub. Mgr.; Elizabeth J. Sherfy, Editor.
Desc: Covers single audit developments. *Type:* Newsletter.

State Board Report

National Association of State Boards of Accountancy
150 Fourth Ave. N.   Ph: (615)880-4200
Nashville, TN 37219-2417   Fax: (615)880-4290
Contact: Louise Dratler Haberman, Editor.
Desc: Describes the activities and concerns of the National Association of State Boards of Accountancy. Recurring features include reports of meetings. *Type:* Newsletter.

Strategic Finance
Institute of Management Accountants
10 Paragon Dr.   Ph: (201)573-9000
Montvale, NJ 07645-1760   Free: 800-638-4427
                                  Fax: (201)573-0639
E-mail: mgtacct@ima.org.
URL: http://www.umi.com.
Contact: Rick Swanson, Publisher, rswanson@imanet.org;
Robert F. Randall, Asst. Publisher/Dir., brandall@imanet.
org; Kathy Williams, Editor/Dir., (201)573-6271, kwilliams@imanet.org.
Desc: Magazine reporting on corporate finance, accounting, cash management, and budgeting. *Type:* Periodical.

SumNews
Massachusetts Society of Certified Public Accountants, Inc.
105 Chauncey St., 10th Fl.   Ph: (617)556-4000
Boston, MA 02111-1742   Free: 800-392-6145
                                  Fax: (617)556-4126
URL: http://www.mscpaonline.org.
Contact: Cheryl McCloud, Managing Editor; Amy Kaiser, Editor; Erin Danehy, Editorial Assistant.
Desc: Covers issues of interest to members of the Massachusetts Society of Certified Public Accountants. *Type:* Newsletter.

Tax Management Compensation Planning Journal
Tax Management Inc.
1250 23rd St., N.W.   Ph: (202)833-7240
Washington, DC 20037-1166
E-mail: tm@bna.com
URL: http://www.taxmanagement.bna.com
Contact: tm@bna.com.
Desc: Reviews news developments which affect tax planning in major areas of specialized tax practice. Includes professional practitioners' commentary as well as reviews of actual or model benefit plans. *Available:* West Group, WESTLAW; LEXIS-NEXIS, LEXIS. *Type:* Database.

Tax Management Estates, Gifts, and Trusts Journal
Tax Management Inc.
1250 23rd St., N.W.   Ph: (202)833-7240
Washington, DC 20037-1166
E-mail: tm@bna.com
URL: http://www.taxmanagement.bna.com
Contact: tm@bna.com.
Desc: Reviews new developments which affect estate planning and planning opportunities. Includes professional practitioners' commentary. *Available:* West Group, WESTLAW; LEXIS-NEXIS, LEXIS. *Type:* Database.

Tax Management Memorandum
Tax Management Inc.
1250 23rd St., N.W.   Ph: (202)833-7240
Washington, DC 20037-1166
E-mail: tm@bna.com
URL: http://www.taxmanagement.bna.com
Contact: tm@bna.com.
Desc: Reviews current tax issues. Includes professional practitioners' commentary. *Available:* West Group, WESTLAW; LEXIS-NEXIS, LEXIS. *Type:* Database.

Tax Management Real Estate Journal
Tax Management Inc.
1250 23rd St., N.W.   Ph: (202)833-7240
Washington, DC 20037-1166
E-mail: tm@bna.com
URL: http://www.taxmanagement.bna.com
Contact: Glenn Davis, Managing Editor, tm@bna.com.

Desc: Reviews new developments which affect the taxation of real estate transactions. Includes professional practitioners' commentary. *Available:* West Group, WESTLAW; LEXIS-NEXIS, LEXIS. *Type:* Database.

Tax Return Preparer's Letter
Harcourt Brace Professional Publishing
525 B St., No. 1900   Ph: (619)699-6716
San Diego, CA 92101-4495   Free: 800-831-7799
                                 Fax: (619)699-6716
URL: http://www.hbpp.com; http://www.hbpp.com.
Desc: Discusses new tax developments. Also includes assistance with new tax forms and procedures and current ideas on increasing income and saving taxes for both individuals and corporations. *Type:* Newsletter.

What's Working in Credit & Collections
Progressive Business Publications
370 Technology Dr.   Ph: (610)695-8600
Malvern, PA 19355   Free: 800-220-5000
                                 Fax: (610)651-2981
URL: http://www.pbp.com.
Contact: Russell Case, Editor.
Desc: Teaches successful credit and collection techniques to build credit sales while avoiding losses. Recurring features include interviews, news of research, a calendar of events, and a column titled Sharpen Your Judgment. *Type:* Newsletter.

Administration

Administrative Assistant's Update
MPL Communications Inc.
133 Richmond St., Ste. 700   Ph: (416)869-1177
Toronto, ON, Canada M5H   Fax: (416)869-0616
   3M8
Contact: Audrey Greer, Editor.
Desc: Offers useful news, information, and suggestions to administrative assistants. Features articles on aspects of secretarial work, including items on problem-solving, office automation, computerization, and grammar and vocabulary development. *Type:* Newsletter.

American Society for Public Administration
1120 G St. NW, Ste. 700   Ph: (202)393-7878
Washington, DC 20005-3885   Fax: (202)638-4952
E-mail: info@aspanet.org
URL: http://www.aspanet.org
Contact: Mary Hamilton, Exec.Dir.
Desc: Professional society of public managers, public officials, educators, research workers, and others in related fields interested in public management as a career or profession. Maintains 19 sections. *Type:* Association.

Association of School Business Officials International
11401 N. Shore Dr.   Ph: (703)478-0405
Reston, VA 20190   Fax: (703)478-0205
E-mail: ditharpe@sprynet.com
Contact: Don I. Tharpe, Ed.D., Exec.Dir.
Desc: School business managers; assistant superintendents in charge of business; supervisors of accounting; directors of transportation, maintenance, food service, data processing, and operations; office managers; school business officials, school board members, and others interested in school business management. Business associates are vendors providing products and/or services to schools. Promotes improvement and advancement of school business management. *Type:* Association.

CAUSE
4840 Pearl East Cir., Ste. 302E   Ph: (303)449-4430
Boulder, CO 80301   Fax: (303)440-0461
E-mail: info@educause.org
URL: http://www.educause.edu
Contact: Jane N. Ryland, Pres.
Desc: College and university administrators engaged in the planning, evaluation, and management of information technology. Purpose is: to enhance the effectiveness of college and university delivery and administration through the use of computer-based information systems and related management techniques; to provide professional development opportunities for members; to serve as an information interchange. *Type:* Association.

National Academy of Public Administration
1120 G St. NW, Ste. 850   Ph: (202)347-3190
Washington, DC 20005   Fax: (202)393-0993
Contact: R. Scott Fosler, Pres.
Desc: Persons elected to the academy must have made significant scholarly contributions to public administration, or have had considerable administrative experience, exhibit interest and possess a reflective nature. Goals are to provide advice and assistance to governments at all levels on problems of public administration; help improve the policies, processes, and institutions of public administration through early identification of significant trends and problems; evaluate program performance and administrative progress; encourage education in and understanding of public administration and its critical role in the advancement of a democratic society. Conducts seminars and symposia. *Type:* Association.

National Association of College and University Business Officers
2501 M St., NW, Ste. 400   Ph: (202)861-2538
Washington, DC 20036   Fax: (202)861-2580
E-mail: dmanetta@nacubo.org
URL: http://www.nacubo.org
Contact: Damon Manetta, Contact.
Desc: Colleges, universities, and companies that are members of a regional association. Develops and maintains national interest in improving the principles and practices of business and financial administration in higher education. *Type:* Association.

National Association of Educational Office Professionals
PO Box 12619   Ph: (316)942-4822
Wichita, KS 67277   Fax: (316)942-7100
E-mail: naeop@naeop.org
URL: http://www.naeop.org
Contact: Sharon Daggett Manner, Contact.
Desc: Secretaries, stenographers, administrative assistants, bookkeepers, receptionists, and other office workers employed by schools, colleges and universities, educational associations, and county and state departments of education. Conducts professional standards program to measure the services of office personnel in education and awards certificates for achievements on five levels of education, experience, and professional activity. Maintains speakers' bureau. *Type:* Association.

National Association of Student Personnel Administrators
1875 Connecticut Ave. NW,   Ph: (202)265-7500
   Ste. 418   Fax: (202)797-1157
Washington, DC 20009
E-mail: office@nasp.org
URL: http://www.nasp.org
Contact: Gwendolyn J. Dungy, Exec.Dir.
Desc: Representatives of degree-granting institutions of higher education which have been fully accredited. Works

to enrich the educational experience of all students. Serves colleges and universities by providing leadership and professional growth opportunities for the chief student affairs officer and other professionals who consider higher education and student affairs issues from an institutional perspective. *Type:* Association.

Public Technology, Inc.
1301 Pennsylvania Ave. NW, Ph: (202)626-2400
Ste. 800 Fax: (202)626-2498
Washington, DC 20004
Contact: Dr. Costis Toregas, Pres.
Desc: Technical arm of International City/County Management Association and National League of Cities . Conducts research and development activities for cities and counties. Serves as vehicle for transferring new technologies and solutions to local government problems; provides technical assistance and management training to local governments. *Type:* Association.

Administrative Services

Administrative Assistant Adviser
Administrative Assistant Advisor
370 Technology Dr. Ph: (610)695-8600
Malvern, PA 19355 Fax: (610)647-8089
Contact: Karen Dawson, Editor.
Desc: Provides business and office information for business professionals. Recurring features include interviews, news of research, a calendar of events, and news of educational opportunities. *Type:* Newsletter.

American Society of Corporate Secretaries
521 5th Ave. Ph: (212)681-2000
New York, NY 10175-0003 Fax: (212)681-2005
URL: http://www.ascs.org
Contact: David W. Smith, Pres.
Desc: Corporate secretaries, assistant secretaries, officers and executives of corporations, and others interested in corporate practices and procedures. Conducts surveys and research. Sponsors educational programs for members. *Type:* Association.

American Society of Notaries
PO Box 5707 Ph: (850)671-5164
Tallahassee, FL 32314-5707 Free: 800-522-3392
 Fax: (850)671-5165
E-mail: mail@notaries.org
URL: http://www.notaries.org
Contact: Lisa K. Fisher, Exec.Dir.
Desc: Notaries Public. Provides members with educational services and technical support. *Type:* Association.

California Notary Bulletin
National Notary Association
9350 DeSoto Ave. Ph: (818)739-4000
Chatsworth, CA 91313-2402 Free: 800-876-6827
 Fax: (818)700-0920
E-mail: natlnotary@aol.com
Contact: Charles N. Faerber, Editor.
Desc: Reports on news affecting notaries in California and on a national level. Recurring features include letters to the editor, interviews, and legislative developments. *Type:* Newsletter.

Canadian Corporate Secretary's Guide
CCH Canadian Ltd.
90 Sheppard Ave., Ste. 300 Ph: (416)441-0086
North York, ON, Canada M2N Free: 800-268-4522
6X1 Fax: 800-461-4131
URL: http://www.ca.cch.com
Contact: Maria Yang, Editor.

Desc: Reference for administrators and corporate secretaries on duties and responsibilities. *Type:* Newsletter.

The Corporate Secretary
American Society of Corporate Secretaries, Inc.
521 5th Ave. Ph: (212)681-2000
New York, NY 10175 Fax: (212)681-2005
URL: http://www.ascs.org.
Contact: Michael E. Goodman, Editor, (212)681-2013, mgoodman@ascs.org.
Desc: Provides legal and legislative news involving corporate secretaries and their executive duties. Recurring features include columns titled SEC Update and Society Notes. *Type:* Newsletter.

Creative Secretary's Letter
Bureau of Business Practice
24 Rope Ferry Rd. Ph: (860)442-4365
Waterford, CT 06386 Free: 800-243-0876
 Fax: (860)437-3555
URL: http://www.bbpnews.com
Contact: Elaine Stattler, Editor, elaine_stattler@prenhall.com.
Desc: Offers tips to help office personnel perform their tasks more quickly, easily, and efficiently. *Type:* Newsletter.

Directorship
Directorship Inc.
8 Sound Shore Dr., Ste. 250 Ph: (203)618-7000
Greenwich, CT 06830 Fax: (203)618-7007
E-mail: editor@directorship.com
Contact: Bruce E. Beebe, beebe@directorship.com.
Desc: Covers issues of interest to directors and CEOs, including financial management, legal matters, compensation, and shareholders. *Type:* Newsletter.

The Executary
National Association of Executive Secretaries and Administrative Assistants
900 S. Washington St., No. Ph: (703)237-8616
G13 Fax: (703)533-1153
Falls Church, VA 22046-4020
E-mail: naesaa@erols.com
Contact: Ruth Ludeman, Director.
Desc: Provides information pertaining to the business and personal lives of administrative assistants and executive secretaries. Recurring features include Association news, and columns titled Wordperfect Tips and Jobline. *Type:* Newsletter.

Information Systems Audit and Control Association
3701 Algonquin Rd., Ste. 1010 Ph: (847)253-1545
Rolling Meadows, IL 60008 Fax: (847)253-1443
E-mail: webmaster@isaca.org
URL: http://www.isaca.org
Contact: Susan Caldwell, Exec.Dir.
Desc: Dedicated to the establishment of standards and systems of control designed to effectively organize and utilize information systems resources. Aids auditors, managers, and systems specialists in addressing problems related to controls in information systems. Offers Certified Information Systems Auditor Professional Designation Program. *Type:* Association.

International Association of Administrative Professionals
10502 NW Ambassador Dr. Ph: (816)891-6600
PO Box 20404 Fax: (816)891-9118
Kansas City, MO 64195-0404
E-mail: exec.director@iaap-hq.org
URL: http://www.gvi.net/psi

Contact: Thomas A. Watters, CAE.
Desc: Professional organization of secretaries. Monitors related legislative and governmental activities; sponsors audiovisual productions; provides group insurance plans. Sponsors Professional Secretaries' Day/Week. Has established the PSI Research and Educational Foundation to develop research and educational projects for secretaries, management, and educators. Has also established Professional Secretaries International Retirement Centers Trust to acquire and maintain a home in Albuquerque, NM for needy and elderly secretaries. Sponsors continuing education programs. *Type:* Association.

International Association for Human Resources Information Management
401 N. Michigan Ave. Ph: (312)321-5141
Chicago, IL 60611 Fax: (312)245-1080
URL: http://www.ihrim.org
Contact: John Hobart, CFO.
Desc: Human resource, payroll, and data processing professionals; others concerned with the development, maintenance, and operation of automated human resource systems. Provides a forum for exchanging experiences, acquiring information, and discussing common needs and problems relating to human resource systems. Works to enhance capabilities for effective and efficient human resource management. *Type:* Association.

International Data Base Management Association
10675 Treena St., Ste. 103 Ph: (619)578-3152
San Diego, CA 92131 Free: 800-767-SHOW
 Fax: (619)271-1032
Contact: Monica Giobbi, Pres.
Desc: Promotes the database management industry. Conducts hands-on computer workshops and seminars. Compiles statistics; conducts research programs. *Type:* Association.

Law Office Administrator
Ardmore Publishing Company
1800 Peachtree St. NW, Ste. Ph: (404)367-1991
335 Fax: (404)367-1995
Atlanta, GA 30355
E-mail: ardmore@mindspring.com
Contact: Bill Kimbro, Editor; Susan Crawford, Publisher.
Desc: Covers law practice management, including staff management, collections, facility management, human resources, information systems, marketing, and outsourcing. Recurring features include Interviews, news of research, notices of publications available, literature reviews, and a column titled This Month's Idea. *Type:* Newsletter.

National Notary Association
9350 De Soto Ave. Ph: (818)739-4000
PO Box 2402 Free: 800-876-6827
Chatsworth, CA 91313-2402 Fax: (818)700-0920
E-mail: nna@nationalnotary.org
URL: http://www.nationalnotary.org
Contact: Milton G. Valera, Pres.
Desc: Notaries public (officers empowered to witness the signing of documents, identify the signers, take acknowledgments, and administer oaths). Works to teach notaries public in the U.S. their duties, powers, limitations, liabilities, and obligations. *Type:* Association.

Notary Bulletin—National Edition
National Notary Association
9350 De Soto Ave. Ph: (818)739-4000
Chatsworth, CA 91313-2402 Free: 800-876-6827
 Fax: (818)700-0920
E-mail: natlnotary@aol.com
URL: http://www.nationalnotary.org.
Contact: Charles N. Faerber, Editor, (818)739-4015.

Desc: Reports on news and issues affecting notaries throughout the U.S. Recurring features include letters to the editor, interviews, and legislative developments. *Type:* Newsletter.

Office and Professional Employees International Union

265 W. 14th St., Ste. 610 Ph: (212)675-3210
New York, NY 10011 Free: 800-346-7348
Fax: (212)727-3466
E-mail: opeiu@opeiu.org
URL: http://www.opeiu.org
Contact: Michael Goodwin, Pres.
Desc: AFL-CIO. *Type:* Association.

Personal Report for the Professional Secretary

National Institute of Business Management
1750 Old Meadow Rd., Ste. Ph: (703)905-8000
302 Free: 800-543-2049
Mc Lean, VA 22102 Fax: (703)905-8042
Contact: Barry Lenson, Editor.
Desc: Advises secretaries and administrative assistants concerning career, workload, supervisors, coworkers, and personal life. Recurring features include letters to the editor, interviews, and Skills Check. *Type:* Newsletter.

Secretary's Letter

The Economic Press, Inc.
12 Daniel Rd. Ph: (973)227-1224
Fairfield, NJ 07004-2565 Free: 800-526-2554
Fax: (973)227-8360
E-mail: order@epinc.com; ino@epinc.com.
Contact: Susan Heybuer-O'Keefe, Editor.
Desc: Offers suggestions to secretaries on how to achieve more success on the job, such as: recognition, fewer routine tasks, and higher responsibilities. *Type:* Newsletter.

Advertising

AAF Government Report

American Advertising Federation (AAF)
1101 Vermont Ave. NW, Suite Ph: (202)898-0089
500 Free: 800-999-2231
Washington, DC 20005 Fax: (202)898-0159
E-mail: aaf@aaf.org
Contact: Jenny Pfalzgraf.
Desc: Supplies information on federal and state legislative and regulatory issues that affect the advertising industry. *Type:* Newsletter.

AD Business Report

Executive Communications, Inc.
185 E. 85th St., Ste. 11-C Ph: (212)831-3147
New York, NY 10028 Fax: (212)439-9109
Contact: Sue Fulton, Editor.
Desc: Contributes information to assist advertising agencies in business development and agency management. *Type:* Newsletter.

Ad Facs Directory—Eastern New York's Guide to Creative Resources, Production Facilities and Advertising Services

Ad Facs Communications Corp.
PO Box 585 Ph: (518)479-0433
East Greenbush, NY 12061
URL: http://www.adfacs.com.
Contact: R. F. Kessler, Editor.
Desc: About 1,500 advertising agencies, photographers, freelance writers, artists; film, video, and music production facilities; mail houses, and other companies, firms, and individuals involved in the advertising and marketing professions in New York. *Type:* Directory.

The Adcrafter

Adcraft Club of Detroit
3011 W. Grand Blvd., Ste. Ph: (313)872-7850
1715 Fax: (313)872-7858
Detroit, MI 48202
E-mail: adcraft@adcraft.org
Contact: Lee H. Wilson, Editor.
Desc: Presents information on opportunities and activities in the metropolitan Detroit advertising industry. Recurring features include a calendar of events. *Type:* Newsletter.

Admarks

Chicago Association of Direct Marketing
122 S. Michigan Ave., Ste. 1100 Fax: (312)541-1271
Chicago, IL 60603
Contact: Cynthia Quick, Editor.
Desc: Discusses news and activities of the Association, which "reaches out to men and women of all races, religions, and national origins who demonstrate an interest in direct marketing and commitment to the highest standards of business ethics." Recurring features include news of educational opportunities, a calendar of events, volunteer opportunities, and job listings. *Type:* Newsletter.

Advertiser & Agency Red Books Plus

National Register Publishing Co.
121 Chanlon Rd. Ph: (908)464-6800
New Providence, NJ 07974 Free: 800-521-8110
Fax: (908)508-7671
E-mail: info@renp.com
URL: http://www.reedref.com
Desc: CD-ROM. Covers 27,000 of the world's top advertisers, their products and what media they use, as well as 11,000 U.S. and international ad agencies and 107,000 corporate and agency personnel in management, creative, and media positions. *Type:* Directory.

Advertising Age

Crain Communications Inc.
740 N. Rush St. Ph: (312)649-5200
Chicago, IL 60611
URL: http://www.crain.com
Desc: Contains the complete text of Advertising Age, The International Newspaper of Marketing, covering developments and trends in advertising, marketing, media communications, and public relations. *Available:* LEXIS-NEXIS, NEXIS; Dow Jones Interactive Publishing; Prodigy Services Company, PRODIGY; Bell & Howell Information and Learning; NewsEdge Corporation; The Dialog Corporation, DIALOG; Reuters Information Services Inc.; The Gale Group, InfoTrac Web; The Dialog Corporation, DataStar. *Type:* Database.

Advertising Age

Crain Communications, Inc.
740 N. Rush St. Ph: (312)649-5200
Chicago, IL 60611-2590 Fax: (312)649-5360
Contact: David Klein, Editor; Joe Cappo, Senior VP; Ed Erhardt, Publisher.
Desc: Advertising trade publication covering agency, media, and advertiser news and trends. *Type:* Periodical.

Advertising Age—Advertising Agency Income Report Issue

Crain Communications, Inc.
740 N. Rush St. Ph: (312)649-5200
Chicago, IL 60611-2590 Fax: (312)649-5360
URL: http://www.adage.com.
Contact: Craig Endicott, Editor.
Desc: Ranked lists of about 650 U.S advertising agencies, 1,600 foreign agencies, and the world's Top 50 advertising organizations which reported billings and gross income, or whose billings and gross incomes were ascertained through research. *Type:* Directory.

Advertising Age—Leading National Advertisers Issue

Crain Communications, Inc.
740 N. Rush St. Ph: (312)649-5200
Chicago, IL 60611-2590 Fax: (312)649-5360
URL: http://www.adage.com.
Contact: Craig Endicott, Coordinating Editor.
Desc: List of the 100 leading U. S. advertisers in terms of the amount spent in national media advertising and below-the-line forms of spending. *Type:* Directory.

Advertising Career Directory

Gale Group Inc.
27500 Drake Rd. Ph: (248)699-4253
Farmington Hills, MI 48331- Free: 800-877-GALE
3535 Fax: (248)699-8070
E-mail: galeord@galegroup.com
URL: http://www.galegroup.com.
Contact: Bradley J. Morgan, Editor.
Desc: Approximately 150 companies and organizations offering job opportunities, internships, and training possibilities in account management, creative services, media, and research for those seeking a career in advertising; sources of help-wanted ads, professional associations, videos, databases, career guides, and professional guides and handbooks. *Type:* Directory.

Advertising Council

261 Madison Ave., 11th Fl. Ph: (212)922-1500
New York, NY 10016-2303 Fax: (212)922-1676
Contact: Ruth A. Wooden, Pres.
Desc: Founded and supported by American business, media, and advertising sectors to conduct public service advertising campaigns. Encourages advertising media to contribute time and space and advertising agencies to supply creative talent and facilities to further timely national causes. *Type:* Association.

Advertising Media Credit Executives Association—News & Views

Advertising Media Credit Executives Association
8815 Centre Park Dr., Ste. 200 Ph: (410)992-7609
Columbia, MD 21045-2158 Fax: (410)740-5574
Contact: Howard Wilson, Editor.
Desc: Carries news of the Association and of activities of its members, who are credit executives in advertising media. Recurring features include editorials, letters to the editor, news of research, book reviews, and a calendar of events. *Type:* Newsletter.

Advertising Topics

Council of Better Business Bureaus, Inc.
4200 Wilson Blvd., No. 800 Ph: (703)276-0100
Arlington, VA 22203-1838 Fax: (703)525-8277
Contact: Heather Durkin, Editor, (703)247-9316, hdurkin@cbbb.bbb.org.
Desc: Provides advice and cautions of the advertising industry, information on regulations, and deceptive advertisements made by corporations. *Type:* Newsletter.

Advertising Workshop

University of Alaska/JPC Ph: (907)786-4187
3211 Providence Dr. Fax: (907)786-4190
Anchorage, AK 99508
E-mail: afjra2@uaa.alaska.edu.
Contact: Jim Avery, Self-Syndicator.
Alt. Contact: University of Alaska/JPC, 3211 Providence Dr., Anchorage, AK 99508; telephone: (907)786-4187; fax: (907)786-4190. *Type:* Periodical.

American Advertising Federation

1101 Vermont Ave. NW, Ste.   Ph: (202)898-0089
500   Fax: (202)898-0159
Washington, DC 20005
E-mail: aaf@aaf.org
URL: http://www.aaf.org
Contact: Wally Snyder, Pres./CEO.

Desc: Works to advance the business of advertising as a vital and essential part of the American economy and culture through government and public relations; professional development and recognition; community service, social responsibility and high standards; and benefits and services to members. *Type:* Association.

American Association of Advertising Agencies

405 Lexington Ave., 18th Fl.   Ph: (212)682-2500
New York, NY 10174-1801   Fax: (212)682-8391
Contact: O. Burtch Drake, Pres. and CEO.

Desc: Fosters development of the advertising industry; assists member agencies to operate more efficiently and profitably. *Type:* Association.

Audit Bureau of Circulations

900 N. Meacham Rd.   Ph: (847)605-0909
Schaumburg, IL 60173-4968   Fax: (847)605-0483
URL: http://www.accessabvs.com
Contact: Michael J. Lavery, Pres. & Mng.Dir.

Desc: Advertisers, advertising agencies, and publishers of daily and weekly newspapers, farm publications, consumer magazines, and business publications in the United States and Canada. Issues standardized statements on the circulation of publisher members; verifies the figures shown in these statements by auditors' examination of publishers' records; disseminates circulation data. Provides academic associate support; conducts forums and seminars. *Type:* Association.

AWNY Matters

Advertising Women of New York
153 E. 57th St.   Ph: (212)593-1950
New York, NY 10022   Fax: (212)759-2865
E-mail: awny85@aol.com
Contact: Lana Bordolot, Editor.

Desc: Includes personnel movements and a calendar of events of interest to women in advertising in New York. *Type:* Newsletter.

BPA International

270 Madison Ave.   Ph: (212)779-3200
New York, NY 10016   Fax: (212)779-3615
Contact: Michael Marchesano, Pres. & CEO.

Desc: Publishers, advertisers, and advertising agencies. Audits all paid, all controlled, or any combination of paid and controlled circulation for business publications and consumer magazines. Conducts comparability programs through which publishers meet with advertising agencies to enhance cooperation in collecting and reporting circulation breakouts among similar publications in the same market or industry. *Type:* Association.

Business Exchange Network

Business Exchange Network
480 San Ramon Blvd., Ste. A   Ph: (510)831-9225
Danville, CA 94526   Fax: (510)831-8194
E-mail: staff@biz-exchange.com
URL: http://www.biz-exchange.com
Desc: The Business Exchange Network provides a listing of businesses for sale, and businesses wanted. A listing of contacts and service resources is available that may be searched by keyword, business name, or location. *Type:* Database.

Business Ideas Newsletter

Dan Newman Company
1051 Bloomfield Ave.   Ph: (201)778-6677
Clifton, NJ 07012
Contact: Dan Newman, Editor.

Desc: Publishes information for advertising and marketing executives to "increase results, returns, and profits." Reports on and interprets developments affecting the business community, including issues such as legislative and regulatory activities and tax reform. Covers new product developments, employment strategies, advertising techniques, and direct marketing potential. *Type:* Newsletter.

Business Marketing Association—Membership & Resource Directory

Business Marketing Association
150 N. Wacker Dr., 1760   Ph: (312)409-4262
Chicago, IL 60606   Free: 800-664-4262
   Fax: (312)409-4266
E-mail: bma@marketing.org.
URL: http://www.marketing.org.
Contact: Rick Kean, Editor.

Desc: Over 4,500 member business communications professionals in fields of advertising, marketing communications, and marketing; their service and supply companies are listed in the "Marketing Resources" section. *Type:* Directory.

The Canadian Direct Marketing Association—Communicator

The Canadian Direct Marketing Association
1 Concorde Gate, Ste. 607   Ph: (416)391-2362
Don Mills, ON, Canada M3C   Fax: (416)441-4062
3N6
Desc: Provides information about direct marketing in Canada. Recurring features include news of research, a calendar of events, reports of meetings, news of educational opportunities, book reviews, and notices of publications available. *Type:* Newsletter.

Canadian Direct Marketing Notes

MLS Computer Services
711 Directors Dr.   Ph: (817)640-7007
Arlington, TX 76011   Fax: (817)633-8008
E-mail: info@mlsc.com
Desc: Discusses issues relating to direct mailing to and within Canada. *Type:* Newsletter.

Card Talk

American Business Card Club
PO Box 460297-GL   Ph: (303)690-6496
Aurora, CO 80046-0297
Contact: Sue Pitzak, Editor; Avery N. Pitzak, Editor and Publisher.

Desc: Provides an international forum for exchange of design concepts, evaluation of card designs, applications, and strategies for producers, designers, users, and collectors. Encourages participation in scouting competitions. *Type:* Newsletter.

Cheap Relief

Jean Lawrence
734 W. El Alba Way   Ph: (602)899-8984
Chandler, AZ 85224   Fax: (602)899-1725
E-mail: jkellaw@aol.com.
Contact: Jean Lawrence, Editor.

Desc: Offers efficiency and money-saving advice in advertising, marketing, and public relations. Recurring features include news of research, news of educational opportunities, book reviews, and notices of publications available. *Type:* Newsletter.

Chip's Pre-Press Pointers

Communicolor
PO Box 400   Free: 800-848-7070
Newark, OH 43058-0400
Desc: Provides information about direct mail design. Topics include pre-production, tools, and scheduling. *Type:* Newsletter.

Communication Management, Inc.—The Yellow Sheet

The Yellow Sheet
13523 Barrett Pky., No. 221   Ph: (314)822-0555
Ballwin, MO 63021-3800
Contact: George Johnson, Editor.

Desc: Covers agency image, account management, client relations, campaign planning, competition, creative, finance, production and time management, computerization, new business, media relations, and merging and buying and selling. *Type:* Newsletter.

COMPMARK

Standard & Poor's
25 Broadway   Ph: (212)208-8363
New York, NY 10004-1064
URL: http://www.standardandpoors.com/ratings
Contact: Mary Maher, (212)208-8429, fax: (212)412-0459.

Desc: Contains information on U.S. companies and their executives. *Available:* Standard & Poor's; Standard & Poor's. *Type:* Database.

Computer Advertiser's Media Advisor

D & G Communications, Inc.
77 Ahlgren Circle   Ph: (508)481-9723
Marlborough, MA 01752   Fax: (508)229-0115
E-mail: camadg@aol.com.
URL: http://www.camaonline.com.
Contact: Mike D'Onofrio, Editor and Publisher.

Desc: Provides information for computer and high-technology advertisers. Includes media reviews and advice. *Type:* Newsletter.

Direct Mail Secrets

Lombardi Publishing Co.
51 Toro Rd.   Ph: (416)633-1600
North York, ON, Canada M3J   Fax: (416)633-6188
2A4
Contact: Adrian Newman, Editor.

Desc: Provides information on current trends in the direct mail industry. Includes recommendations on how to improve and revise direct mail pieces. *Type:* Newsletter.

Empa

Museum of Promotional Arts, Toronto
Box 400
Adelaide St. Sta.
Toronto, ON, Canada M5C 2J5
Contact: Frances E.M. Johnston, Editor.

Desc: "Devoted to furthering an appreciation of all the promotional arts and the work of the people involved in producing them." Serves to be a resource for persons studying the history of the promotional arts. *Type:* Newsletter.

Financial Advertising Review

The Business Word
5350 S. Roslyn St., Ste. 400   Ph: (303)967-0130
Englewood, CO 80111-2125   Free: 800-328-3211
   Fax: (303)290-9025
Contact: Tom Rees, Editor, tom.rees@businessword.com; Donald E.L. Johnson, Publisher; Jeannette Herreria, Editor.

Desc: Provides information for bank advertisers. Topics include print, radio, television, and direct mail advertising. *Type:* Newsletter.

FINDEX

Kalorama Information, LLC
7200 Wisconsin Ave., Ste. 601   Ph: 877-434-6339
Bethesda, MD 20814
E-mail: support@findexonline.com

Desc: Contains more than 14,000 citations, with abstracts, to publicly available market research reports, studies, and surveys on 55 industries. Includes consumer and product studies, surveys and polls, company and industry reports from investment firms, major multiclient industry studies, directories, and newsletters and databases relating to specific industries or products. *Available:* The Dialog Corporation, DIALOG; OCLC Online Computer Library Center, Inc., OCLC EPIC; OCLC Online Computer Library Center, Inc., OCLC FirstSearch Catalog; Kalorama Information, LLC. *Type:* Database.

The Flyer

Community Newspaper Company
254 Second Ave   Ph: (781)433-7800
Needham, MA 02192   Fax: (781)433-8202

Contact: Carlos Guzman, President.

Desc: Advertiser (English and Spanish). *Alt. Contact:* 11900 SW 128th St., Miami, FL 33186; telephone: (305)232-4115; fax: (305)251-5141. *Type:* Periodical.

Geiger Report

Geiger Report
Box 24248
Edina, MN 55424-0248

Contact: Bob Geiger, Editor and Publisher.

Desc: Provides information on advertising, marketing, and film production industries in the Minneapolis and St. Paul area. *Type:* Newsletter.

IAA World News

International Advertising Association
521 5th Ave., Ste. 1807   Ph: (212)557-1133
New York, NY 10175   Fax: (212)983-0455
E-mail: webmaster@iaaglobal.org
URL: http://www.iaaglobal.org.

Contact: Pamela Yaeger, Editor, pamela@iaaglobal.org; Kathleen Hahn, Editor.

Desc: Supplies information on Association policies and activities. Includes reviews of publications and reports from the 62 chapters worldwide. *Type:* Newsletter.

International Advertising Association

International Advertising Association
521 5th Ave., Ste. 1807   Ph: (212)557-1133
New York, NY 10175   Fax: (212)983-0455
E-mail: iaaglobal@worldnet.att.net
URL: http://www.iaaglobal.org

Contact: Norman Vale, Dir.General.

Desc: Global network of advertisers, advertising agencies, the media and related services, spanning 95 countries. Demonstrates to governments and consumers the benefits of advertising as the foundation of diverse, independent media. *Type:* Association.

International Sign Association—Perspectives

International Sign Association (ISA)
707 N. St. Asaph St.   Ph: (703)836-4012
Alexandria, VA 22314   Fax: (703)836-8353

Contact: Shane Artim, Editor, shane@signs.org.

Desc: Provides information on government-relations issues for the on-premise sign industry. Recurring features include interviews and a column titled View from the Hill. *Type:* Newsletter.

Kapitzky's Palm Tree Bugle

Kapitzky's Palm Tree Bugle
1715 E. Fowler Ave., Ste. 194   Ph: (813)914-0430
Tampa, FL 33612   Free: 877-530-5685
    Fax: (813)248-0289

Contact: Charles Kapitzky, Editor and Publisher.

Desc: Provides information on mail-order and multi-level marketing. Recurring features include letters to the editor, interviews, news of research, a calendar of events, reports of meetings, news of educational opportunities, job listings, book reviews, notices of publications available, and various columnists. *Type:* Newsletter.

Mail Advertising Service Association International

1421 Prince St.   Ph: (703)836-9200
Alexandria, VA 22314   Free: 800-333-6272
    Fax: (703)548-8204
E-mail: masa-mail@masa.org
URL: http://www.masa.org

Contact: David A. Weaver, Pres.

Desc: Commercial direct mail producers, lettershops, mailing list houses, fulfillment operations, and advertising agencies. *Type:* Association.

Mail Order Digest

National Mail Order Association, LLC
2807 Polk St. NE   Ph: (612)788-1673
Minneapolis, MN 55418-2954   Fax: (612)788-1147
E-mail: schulte@nmoa.org
URL: http://www.nmoa.org.

Contact: George Knotech, Editor.

Desc: Provides help for entrepreneurs small- and mid-size firms in the areas of mail order, direct mail, catalog sales, database marketing, television marketing, starting a mail order business, and exporting. Recurring features include letters to the editor, interviews, news of research, a calendar of events, reports of meetings, news of educational opportunities, job listings, book reviews, notices of publications available, and columns titled Beginner's Corner and Washington Newsletter. *Type:* Newsletter.

MarkIntel™

Thomson Financial Securities Data (TFSD)
Two Gateway Center   Ph: (973)622-3100
Newark, NJ 07102
URL: http://www.securitiesdata.com

Contact: John Webber, Marketing Communications Manager.

Desc: Contains the complete text of more than 45,000 market research reports covering 54 industries from 43 sources worldwide. Reports provide forecasts of market share and size, as well as evaluations of new products and technologies. *Available:* Thomson Financial Services, Inc., I/PLUS Direct; Thomson Financial Services, Inc., I/PLUS Direct. *Type:* Database.

The Mouser Report

Mouser Institute-School of Advertising
124 E. Carolina Ave.   Ph: (804)645-8200
Crewe, VA 23930   Free: 800-448-8595
    Fax: (804)645-8232

Contact: Charles Mouser, Editor, cmouser998@aol.com.

Desc: Concerned with retail advertising and marketing in newspapers. Offers suggestions for effective sales, advertising campaigns, selecting an intended audience, and planning successful retail ventures. *Type:* Newsletter.

The National Directory of Catalogs

Oxbridge Communications Inc.
150 5th Ave., Ste. 302   Ph: (212)741-0231
New York, NY 10011   Free: 800-955-0231
    Fax: (212)633-2938
E-mail: info@mediafinder.com
URL: http://www.mediafinder.com.

Contact: Savita Ali, Editor; Joy Goldstein, Editor.

Desc: Over 8,700 U.S. and Canadian catalogs. *Type:* Directory.

Newspaper Advertising Source

SRDS
1700 Higgins Rd.   Ph: (847)375-5000
Des Plaines, IL 60018-5605   Free: 800-851-7737
    Fax: (847)375-5001
E-mail: contact@srds.com
URL: http://www.srds.com.

Contact: Peter Spina, Editor.

Desc: More than 1,800 newspapers and newspaper groups, including newspaper-distributed magazines, comics, religious newspapers, Black newspapers, and specialized newspapers. *Type:* Directory.

Penton Executive Network

Penton Media Inc.
1100 Superior Ave.   Ph: (216)696-7000
Cleveland, OH 44114-2543   Fax: (216)931-9524
E-mail: corpcomm@penton.com

Contact: Rusty Pierson, Publisher.

Desc: Executive publications. *Type:* Periodical.

Philadelphia Advertising Club—Directory

Philadelphia Advertising Club
PO Box 11510   Ph: (610)874-8990
Philadelphia, PA 19116-0510   Fax: (610)874-5876
E-mail: phillyadclub@aol.com

Desc: About 800 member broadcasters and advertising and public relations personnel in the Greater Delaware Valley, including southeastern Pennsylvania, southern New Jersey, and Delaware. *Type:* Directory.

PIPELINE

Thomson Financial Securities Data (TFSD)
Two Gateway Center   Ph: (973)622-3100
Newark, NJ 07102
URL: http://www.securitiesdata.com

Contact: I/PLUS Direct Client Services.

Desc: Contains citations to more than 140,000 recently released investment, bond, and company research reports available for offline delivery by The Investext Group. Enables the user to request the hardcopy version of reports being prepared by The Investext Group for full-text online access from the Investext and Bondtext databases. *Available:* Thomson Financial Services, Inc., I/PLUS Direct. *Type:* Database.

Plus Business

Metro Creative Graphics Inc.
33 W. 34th St.   Ph: (212)947-5100
New York, NY 10001   Free: 800-223-1600
    Fax: (212)967-4602
E-mail: metrocserv@metrocreativegraphics.com; plusbusiness@metrocreativegraphics.com.
URL: http://www.metrocreativegraphics.com.

Contact: Alexandra Chang, Editor, alexachang@metrocreativegraphics.com.

Desc: Focuses on advertising ideas to make money and sell advertising space. Recurring features include interviews, a calendar of events, reports of meetings, and columns titled Inside Story, and Hunting Headlines. *Type:* Newsletter.

Prisoners of Advertising

San Francisco Advertising Club
150 Post St., Ste. 325   Ph: (415)986-3878
San Francisco, CA 94108-4707   Fax: (415)986-7457
Desc: Covers current club activities and events. Reports on the San Francisco advertising/communications community. *Type:* Newsletter.

Promotional Products Association International

3125 Skyway Cir. N.   Free: 888-492-6891
Irving, TX 75038-3526   Fax: (972)258-3004
E-mail: rayf@ppa.org
URL: http://www.ppa.org
Contact: Steven Slagle, Pres.
Desc: Suppliers and distributors of promotional products including calendars, imprinted ad specialties, premiums, and executive gifts. Promotes industry contacts in 40 countries. *Type:* Association.

Proof

Direct Marketing Club of New York
224 7th St.   Ph: (516)746-6700
Garden City, NY 11530   Fax: (516)294-8141
Contact: Loretta Schorr, Editorial Coord.
Desc: Provides information concerning direct marketing to members of the Direct Marketing Club of New York. Recurring features include a calendar of events, news of members, news of educational opportunities, book reviews, and various columns on direct marketing techniques and advancements. *Type:* Newsletter.

Radio Advertising Bureau

261 Madison Ave., 23rd. Fl.   Ph: (212)681-7200
New York, NY 10016   Free: 800-232-3131
                                Fax: (212)681-7223
URL: http://www.rab.com
Contact: Gary R. Fries, Pres. & CEO.
Desc: Includes radio stations, radio networks, station sales representatives, and allied industry services, such as producers, research firms, schools, and consultants. Calls on advertisers and agencies to promote the sale of radio time as an advertising medium. *Type:* Association.

Shelf Action

Better Homes and Gardens
125 Park Ave.   Ph: (212)557-6600
New York, NY 10017   Fax: (212)551-7114
Contact: Mary Rae, Editor.
Desc: Presents news and editorials on trends in the supermarket industry. Focuses on Better Homes and Gardens advertisers, with reproductions of the advertisements and explanations of the advertisers' strategies. *Type:* Newsletter.

Shopping Center Ad Trends

Phoenix Ventures Inc.
320 Valley   Ph: (319)752-5415
Burlington, IA 52601   Fax: (319)752-3421
Desc: Carries information on advertising campaigns for shopping centers. Recurring features include promotional calendars. *Type:* Newsletter.

Signals

International Sign Association (ISA)
707 N. St. Asaph St.   Ph: (703)836-4012
Alexandria, VA 22314   Fax: (703)836-8353
Contact: Shane Artim, Editor, shane@signs.org.
Desc: Disseminates information on the on-premise sign industry. Covers new technology, markets, laws, regulations, and upcoming trade shows. *Type:* Newsletter.

Signline

International Sign Association (ISA)
707 N. St. Asaph St.   Ph: (703)836-4012
Alexandria, VA 22314   Fax: (703)836-8353
Contact: Shane M. Artim, Editor.
Desc: Provides information about on-premise sign issues in communities, especially planning and zoning matters. Recurring features include interviews. *Type:* Newsletter.

Standard Directory of Advertisers

National Register Publishing Co.
121 Chanlon Rd.   Ph: (908)464-6800
New Providence, NJ 07974   Free: 800-521-8110
                                Fax: (908)508-7671
E-mail: info@renp.com
URL: http://www.reedref.com
Contact: Doug Edwards, Editor.
Desc: Over 20,000 U.S. and Canadian companies that place over $200,000 worth of national and/or regional advertising. *Type:* Directory.

Standard Directory of Advertising Agencies

National Register Publishing Co.
121 Chanlon Rd.   Ph: (908)464-6800
New Providence, NJ 07974   Free: 800-521-8110
                                Fax: (908)508-7671
E-mail: info@renp.com
URL: http://www.reedref.com
Contact: Doug Edwards, Editor.
Desc: Nearly 10,000 advertising agencies. *Type:* Directory.

Standard Directory of Advertising Agencies

National Register Publishing (NRP)
121 Chanlon Rd.   Ph: (908)464-6800
New Providence, NJ 07974
Desc: Contains information on approximately 8800 advertising agencies, their 59,000 personnel by title, and 75,000 accounts. For each agency, provides name, address, telephone number, year founded, number of employees, association memberships, area of specialization, annual billing, breakdown of gross billings by media, clients, executives, special markets, and new agencies. *Available:* LEXIS-NEXIS, NEXIS; The Dialog Corporation, DIALOG. *Type:* Database.

Television Bureau of Advertising

850 3rd Ave., 10th Fl.   Ph: (212)486-1111
New York, NY 10022   Fax: (212)935-5631
URL: http://www.tvb.org
Contact: Ave Butensky, Pres.
Desc: Television stations, station sales representatives, and program producers/syndicators. Strives to increase advertiser dollars to U.S. spot television. *Type:* Association.

Topline

McCollum Spielman Worldwide
235 Great Neck Rd.   Ph: (516)482-0310
Great Neck, NY 11021   Fax: (516)482-3228
Contact: Paula Kay Pierce, Editor.
Desc: Contains advertising research findings and analysis. Covers trends in advertising. *Type:* Newsletter.

Wadsworth Report on Mail Order

Bob E. Teague
PO Box 14689
Dayton, OH 45413
Contact: Bob E. Teague, Editor.
Desc: Provides information about mail order marketing. Topics include publishing, distribution, and legal issues. *Type:* Newsletter.

What's New in Advertising & Marketing

Advertising and Marketing Division
Special Libraries Association (SLA)
1700 18th St. NW   Ph: (202)234-4700
Washington, DC 20009   Fax: (202)265-9377
Desc: Consists of annotated bibliographic citations for free or inexpensive books, periodicals, and information services. Emphasizes the fields of advertising, marketing, marketing research, media, and customer surveys. *Type:* Newsletter.

Yellow Pages & Directory Report

SIMBA Information Inc.
11 Riverbend Dr. S.   Ph: (203)358-4100
PO Box 4234   Free: 800-307-2529
Stamford, CT 06907-0234   Fax: (203)358-5824
E-mail: info@simbanet.com
URL: http://www.simbanet.com
Contact: Tom Maguire, Managing Editor; Jessica Nutley, Editor.
Desc: Monitors the yellow pages publishing industry. Covers the activities of utility and independent yellow pages publishers, suppliers, certified marketing representatives, sales agents, and yellow pages associations. *Type:* Newsletter.

Aerospace

Academy of Model Aeronautics

5151 E. Memorial Dr.   Ph: (765)287-1256
Muncie, IN 47302   Free: 800-435-9262
                                Fax: (765)289-4248
E-mail: jhager@modelaircraft.org
Contact: Joyce Hager, Exec.Dir.
Desc: Persons interested in model aircraft. Membership includes model airplane flyer's sporting license which permits participation in officially sanctioned competitions and official recognition of national and world records when established. AMA is an autonomous division of the National Aeronautic Association of the U.S.A. *Type:* Association.

Aerospace Database

American Institute of Aeronautics and Astronautics (AIAA)
Technical Information Division
85 John St.   Ph: (212)349-1120
New York, NY 10038
E-mail: access@aiaa.org
URL: http://www.aiaa.org
Desc: Contains more than 1.9 million citations, with abstracts, to the worldwide published and unpublished literature on research and development in aerospace and related technological areas. Covers 76 subject areas, including aeronautics, astronautics, chemistry and materials (e.g., composite, metallic, nonmetallic), engineering, geosciences, life sciences, mathematical and computer sciences, physics, social sciences, and space sciences. *Available:* The Dialog Corporation, DIALOG; STN International; Cambridge Scientific Abstracts (CSA). *Type:* Database.

Aerospace/Defense Markets & Technology (A/DM&T)

The Gale Group
27500 Drake Rd.   Ph: (248)699-4253
Farmington Hills, MI 48331-3535
URL: http://www.galegroup.com
Contact: (650)378-5000, fax: (800)676-2345.
Desc: Contains more than 439,000 citations, with abstracts and selected full texts, to the worldwide literature

on the aerospace and defense industries. Covers companies, technologies, products, and shipments, as well as land, sea, and air defense systems. *Available:* The Dialog Corporation, DataStar; The Dialog Corporation, DIALOG. *Type:* Database.

Aerospace Education Foundation

1501 Lee Hwy.　　　　　Ph: (703)247-5839
Arlington, VA 22209-1198　Free: 800-727-3337
　　　　　　　　　　　　Fax: (703)247-5853
URL: http://www.aef.org
Contact: John Shaud, Exec.Dir.
Desc: Works to enhance public understanding of aerospace development; disseminate information concerning national defense and U.S. Air Force issues; encourage students to pursue higher education in scientific, mathematical, and technological fields. Sponsors annual contest for Air Force Junior ROTC students. *Type:* Association.

Aerospace Industries Association of America

1250 Eye St. NW　　　　Ph: (202)371-8400
Washington, DC 20005　　Fax: (202)371-8470
E-mail: aia@aia-aerospace.org
URL: http://www.aia-aerospace.org
Contact: Don Fuqua, Pres.
Desc: Trade association that represents the nation's manufacturers of commercial, military and business aircraft, helicopters, aircraft engines, missiles, spacecraft, and related components and equipment. *Type:* Association.

Aerospace News & Comment

Aerospace Industries Association of Canada
60 Queen St., Ste. 1200　Ph: (613)232-4297
Ottawa, ON, Canada K1P 5Y7　Fax: (613)232-1142
E-mail: aiac@fox.nstn.ca
Contact: Ray Windsor, Editor.
Desc: Provides information on news and issues affecting Canada's aerospace manufacturing sector. *Type:* Newsletter.

Aerospace Publishing Freelancer

Bernard Kovit
PO Box 364　　　　　　Ph: (516)295-0872
Woodmere, NY 11598-0364
Contact: Bernard Kovit, Editor and Publisher.
Desc: Provides information about creating a winning publications program for company newsletters, magazines, and annual reports. Examines using internal or external resources. *Type:* Newsletter.

Air, Inc.

1001 Rive　　　　　　　Ph: (770)996-5424
Atlanta, GA 30337　　　Free: 800-AIR-APPS
　　　　　　　　　　　　Fax: (770)996-5547
E-mail: airapps@aol.com
URL: http://www.airapps.com
Contact: Artemas K. Darby, Pres.
Desc: Career planning service for pilots. Services include reference publications for job hunting. *Type:* Association.

Air & Space Magazine

AIR&SPACE/Smithsonian
PO Box 420113
Palm Coast, FL 32142-0113
URL: http://airspacemag.com/
Desc: The online version of the Smithsonian publication, detailing the past, present, and future of flight. Science and technology as they pertain to flight is also covered. *Type:* Database.

Air Traffic Control Association

2300 Clarendon Blvd., Ste. 711　Ph: (703)522-5717
Arlington, VA 22201　　　　Fax: (703)527-7251
E-mail: Atca@worldnet.atc.net
URL: http://www.atca.org
Contact: Gabriel A. Hartl, Pres.
Desc: Air traffic controllers; private, commercial, and military pilots; private and business aircraft owners and operators; aircraft and electronics engineers; airlines, aircraft manufacturers, and electronic and human engineering firms. Promotes the establishment and maintenance of a safe and efficient air traffic control system. *Type:* Association.

Air Transport Association of America

1301 Pennsylvania Ave., Ste.　Ph: (202)626-4000
　1100　　　　　　　　　Fax: (202)626-4166
Washington, DC 20004-7017
E-mail: ata@air-transport.org
URL: http://www.air-transport.org
Contact: Carol B. Hallett, Pres. & CEO.
Desc: Airlines engaged in transporting persons, goods, and mail by aircraft between fixed terminals on regular schedules. *Type:* Association.

American Association of Airport Executives

4212 King St.　　　　　Ph: (703)824-0504
Alexandria, VA 22302　　Fax: (703)820-1395
E-mail: member.services@airportnet.org
URL: http://www.airportnet.org
Contact: Charles M. Barclay, Pres.
Desc: Airport management personnel; representatives of companies serving the civil airport industry. *Type:* Association.

American Institute of Aeronautics and Astronautics

Michael Lewis
1801 Alexander Bell Dr., Ste.　Ph: (703)264-7500
　500　　　　　　　　　Free: 800-NEW-AIAA
Reston, VA 20191-4344　　Fax: (703)264-7551
E-mail: customerserv@aiaa.org
URL: http://www.aiaa.org/
Contact: Anthony Lenti, Contact.
Desc: Scientists and engineers in the field of aeronautics and astronautics. Facilitates interchange of technological information through publications and technical meetings in order to foster overall technical progress in the field and increase the professional competence of members. Operates Public Policy program to provide federal decision-makers with the technical information and policy guidance needed to make effective policy on aerospace issues. *Type:* Association.

American Institute of Aeronautics and Astronautics Aeroplus Access

59 John St., 7th Fl.　　　Ph: (212)349-1120
New York, NY 10038　　Free: 800-348-7737
　　　　　　　　　　　　Fax: (212)349-1283
E-mail: access@aiaa.org
Contact: Anthony Lenti, Dir.
Desc: A division of the American Institute of Aeronautics and Astronautics (see separate entry) devoted to the acquisition, processing, and dissemination of technical and engineering information. *Type:* Association.

Aviation/Space Writers Association—Yearbook and Directory

Aviation/Space Writers Association
6540 50th St.,N.　　　　Ph: (612)779-9390
Oakdale, MN 55128-1708
Contact: Madeline Mohanco Field, Editor.
Desc: Member writers and communications specialists on aviation and space subjects for media, industry, and government. *Type:* Directory.

Aviation Week & Space Technology

McGraw-Hill Companies, Inc.
Aviation Week Group
1200 G Street, NW, Ste. 900　Ph: (202)383-2417
Washington, DC 20005
E-mail: rpickett@mcgraw-hill.com
URL: http://www.adaviation.com
Desc: Contains the complete text of Aviation Week & Space Technology, a magazine on technical and corporate developments in the aerospace industry. *Available:* LEXIS-NEXIS, NEXIS; The Dialog Corporation, DIALOG; Dow Jones Interactive Publishing; Bell & Howell Information and Learning. *Type:* Database.

Caterpillar Club

PO Box 1328　　　　　　Ph: (609)587-3300
Trenton, NJ 08607-1328　Fax: (609)586-6647
Contact: Richard Switlik, Sr., Pres.
Desc: Honorary club for airmen and individuals who have successfully used a parachute to save their lives. *Type:* Association.

Cessna Pilots Association

PO Box 5817　　　　　　Ph: (805)922-2580
Santa Maria, CA 93456　　Fax: (805)922-7249
E-mail: cpa@cessna.org
URL: http://www.cessna.org
Contact: John M. Frank, Jr., Dir.
Desc: Individuals who own, fly, or have an interest in Cessna aircraft. *Type:* Association.

EAA Aviation Foundation

EAA Aviation Center　　　Ph: (920)426-4800
PO Box 3065　　　　　　Fax: (920)426-4828
Oshkosh, WI 54903-3065
E-mail: communications@eaa.org
URL: http://www.eaa.org
Contact: Tom Poberezny, Pres.
Desc: Research and educational arm of the Experimental Aircraft Association dedicated to preserving and continuing the heritage of personal flight. *Type:* Association.

EAA Vintage Aircraft Association

EAA Aviation Center　　　Ph: (414)426-4800
PO Box 3086　　　　　　Fax: (414)426-4828
Oshkosh, WI 54903-3086
E-mail: vintage@eaa.org
URL: http://www.eaa.org
Contact: Espie Joyce, Pres.
Desc: A division of the Experimental Aircraft Association. Individuals interested in preserving and restoring Antique, Classic, and Contemporary aircraft. (Antique aircraft include airplanes made by the original manufacturer on or before August 31, 1945). *Type:* Association.

Experimental Aircraft Association

EAA Aviation Center　　　Ph: (414)426-4800
PO Box 3086
Oshkosh, WI 54903-3086
E-mail: webmaster@eaa.org
Contact: Tom Poberezny, Pres.
Desc: Individuals interested in sport and recreational flying. Mission is to make aviation accessible to all who wish to participate. *Type:* Association.

Flight Safety Foundation

601 Madison St., Ste. 300　Ph: (703)739-6700
Alexandria, VA 22314　　Fax: (703)739-6708
E-mail: fsf@radix.net
Contact: Stuart Matthews, Chm., CEO & Pres.
Desc: Aerospace manufacturers, domestic and foreign airlines, insurance companies, fuel and oil companies, schools, and miscellaneous organizations having an interest in the promotion of safety in flight. *Type:* Association.

Gay Airline and Travel Club

PO Box 69A04, Dept. NET   Ph: (213)650-5112
West Hollywood, CA 90069
E-mail: gayboylaca@writeme.com
URL: http://www.aa.org/stopp/contact.htm
Contact: Louis Wendruck, Publisher.
Desc: Gay men interested in travel, collecting airline memorabilia, or who work in or are interested in airlines and the travel industry. *Type:* Association.

Kennedy Space Center Home Page

NASA - John F. Kennedy Space Center
Kennedy Space Center, FL
    32899
URL: http://www.ksc.nasa.gov/ksc.html
Contact: webteam@news.ksc.nasa.gov.
Desc: The KSC Home Page provides a wealth of information including schedules and archives, photos, video files, technical data, general information, current project updates, historical data, and much more. New offerings include virtual tours/live video of the facilities and spacecraft, lots of images and news on recent missions such as the Mars Pathfinder expedition, and numerous links for additional information on present and future projects. *Type:* Database.

NASA Tech Briefs

U.S. National Aeronautics and Space
Administration (NASA)
Center for AeroSpace Information
800 Elkridge Landing Rd.   Ph: (301)621-0390
Linthicum Heights, MD 21090-
    2934
E-mail: help@STI.NASA.gov
URL: http://www.sti.nasa.gov
Desc: Contains approximately 18,000 citations, with abstracts, to articles taken from NASA Tech Briefs, published 12 times a year. Covers descriptions of new products and processes developed by NASA facilities and contractors. *Available:* U.S. National Aeronautics and Space Administration (NASA), Scientific and Technical Information, NASA/RECON; U.S. National Aeronautics and Space Administration (NASA), Scientific and Technical Information, NASA/RECON; Knowledge Express Data Systems, Knowledge Express. *Type:* Database.

NASA Tech Briefs

Associated Business Publications Co., Ltd.
317 Madison Ave.   Ph: (212)490-3999
New York, NY 10017   Fax: (212)986-7864
URL: http://www.nasatech.com.
Contact: Joseph Pramberger, Publisher, joe@abptuf.org; Bill Schnirring, Chairman, bill@abpinet.com; Domenic Mucchetti, President, dom@abptuf.org; Linda L. Bell, Chief Editor, linda@abptuf.org.
Desc: Publication covering technology for American industry and government in the fields of electronics, computers, physical sciences, materials, mechanics, machinery, fabrication technology, math and information sciences, and the life sciences. *Type:* Periodical.

National Aeronautic Association of the U.S.A.

1815 N. Fort Myer Dr., Ste.   Ph: (703)527-0226
    700   Free: 800-644-9777
Arlington, VA 22209-1805   Fax: (703)527-0229
E-mail: naa@naa.ycg.org
URL: http://www.naa.ycg.org
Contact: Steven J. Brown, Pres. & CEO.
Desc: Persons interested in the progress and development of American general and military aviation. Supervises sporting aviation competitions and official world records in aeronautics and astronautics, model flying, gliding, soaring, parachuting, hang gliding, ballooning, and helicopters. Directs and controls all official aircraft records of competitions conducted in the United States. *Type:* Association.

National Aeronautics and Space Administration
George C. Marshall Space Flight Center
Space Sciences Laboratory
Space Plasma Physics

Mailcode CO30
Huntsville, AL 35812
URL: http://wwwssl.msfc.nasa.gov/ssl/pad/sppb/
Desc: Physical processes that control the geospace plasma environment and its interaction with both banatural and man-made bodies in space. Emphases are on the plasma that originates in the ionosphere, and its heating in auroral light displays. *Type:* Research center.

National Aeronautics and Space Administration
Lyndon B. Johnson Space Center
Space and Life Sciences Directorate
Medical Sciences Division

Mail Code SD   Ph: (281)483-7108
2101 NASA Rd. 1   Fax: (281)483-2224
Houston, TX 77058
Contact: Dr. Jerry Homick, Dep.Chf.
Desc: Human response to microgravity and space flight. Emphasis is on medical care; vestibular, cardiovascular, and endocrine studies; toxicology; laboratory medicine hematology; and bioreactor development. *Type:* Research center.

National Space Society

600 Pennsylvania Ave. SE, Ste.   Ph: (202)543-1900
    201   Fax: (202)546-4189
Washington, DC 20003
E-mail: nsshq@nss.org
URL: http://www.nss.org/
Contact: Pat Dasch, Acting Exec.Dir.
Desc: Individuals dedicated "to convincing our nation and its leadership of the critical need for a growing progressive American technology for which a strong space program provides the thrust and momentum." Seeks to: provide a forum for public participation to help insure that the space program is responsive to public priorities; inspire space enthusiasts to elicit their responses to key issues on the space program; promote and create self-sustaining communities, large-scale industrialization, and private enterprise in space; support scholarships, lectureships, libraries, and museums which encourage the study of space and related technologies. *Type:* Association.

Order of Daedalians

PO Box 249   Ph: (210)945-2111
Randolph AFB, TX 78150   Fax: (210)945-2112
E-mail: daedalus@daedalians.org
URL: http://www.daedalians.org
Contact: Col. George G. Hull, USAF Ret. National Adjutant.
Desc: Military pilots of heavier-than-air powered aircraft who were commissioned as officers in the U.S. military services before November 12, 1918; descendants and designates of such pilots. Active duty, retired, or scheduled to draw title retired pay via reserve/guard duty. (Named for Daedalus who, in mythology, first accomplished heavier-than-air flight.). "To place nation above self and to be worthy of the trust and confidence of a fellow Daedalian." *Type:* Association.

Planetary Society

65 N. Catalina Ave.   Ph: (626)793-5100
Pasadena, CA 91106-2301   Free: 800-9-
    WORLDS
    Fax: (626)793-5528
E-mail: tps@mars.planetary.org
URL: http://www.planetary.org
Contact: Dr. Louis Friedman, Exec.Dir.

Desc: Individuals "devoted to a realistic continuing program of planetary exploration and the search for extraterrestrial life." Seeks to enhance public awareness and to stimulate fundamental research. Fosters communication among interested groups and individuals in the U.S. and 100 other countries; distributes information concerning the latest findings and discoveries in the field. *Type:* Association.

SAE Publications & Standards Database

Society of Automotive Engineers
Electronic Publishing Division
400 Commonwealth Dr.   Ph: (724)772-7144
Warrendale, PA 15096
E-mail: elecpubs@sae.org
URL: http://www.sae.org

Contact: Deb Tack, Marketing Communications Specialist, (724)772-7144, fax: (724)776-3087, elecpubs@sae.org.

Desc: Contains more than 66,000 document summaries (detailed abstracts and bibliographies) of Technology papers, journal articles, magazine articles, standards and specifications, Technology books, and research reports published by the Society of Automotive Engineers (SAE). *Available:* Society of Automotive Engineers, Electronic Publishing Division. *Type:* Database.

Scientific and Technical Aerospace Reports

U.S. National Aeronautics and Space
Administration (NASA)
Center for AeroSpace Information
800 Elkridge Landing Rd.   Ph: (301)621-0390
Linthicum Heights, MD 21090-
    2934
E-mail: help@STI.NASA.gov
URL: http://www.sti.nasa.gov

Desc: Provides citations and abstracts of unclassified technical reports in the field of aerospace science and technology issued by NASA and other organizations around the world. Data are derived from technical report literature from around the world comprised primarily of government reports and documents more than 3 million records in the database. *Available:* U.S. National Aeronautics and Space Administration (NASA), Scientific and Technical Information, NASA/RECON. *Type:* Database.

Soaring Society of America

PO Box E   Ph: (505)392-1177
Hobbs, NM 88241-7504   Fax: (505)392-8154
URL: http://www.ssa.org

Contact: Larry P. Sanderson, Pres.

Desc: Persons interested in the activity of soaring and gliding (building and flying of gliders and sailplanes). Promotes soaring in the U.S. *Type:* Association.

Space Calendar

Jet Propulsion Laboratory's New Products
Development (NPD) Group
4800 Oak Grove Dr.   Ph: (818)354-4321
Pasadena, CA 91109
URL: http://NewProducts.jpl.nasa.gov/calendar/

Contact: Ron Baalke, baalke@kelvin.jpl.nasa.gov.

Desc: The Space Calendar database provides a daily listing of space-related activities and anniversaries for the coming year. Listings include such items as: rocket launch dates, solar eclipses, meteor showers, historical anniversaries for space exploration events, etc. *Type:* Database.

U.S. Department of Defense

Air Force Materiel Command

Armstrong Laboratory

Aerospace Medicine Directorate

2509 Kennedy Circle   Ph: (210)536-3208
Brooks AFB, TX 78235-4119   Fax: (210)536-4103

Contact: Col. Gary L. Henriken, Dir.

Desc: Aerospace medicine and biomedicine. *Type:* Research center.

U.S. Department of Defense

Air Force Materiel Command

Human Systems Center

Air Force School of Aerospace Medicine

2602 W. Gate Rd.   Ph: (210)536-3500
USAFSAM   Fax: (210)536-2216
Brooks AFB, TX 78235

Contact: Col. Tommie G. Church, Comdr.

Desc: Science and technology divisions (Clinical Sciences, Crew Technology, and Radiation Sciences); operational support; and aeromedical education and training divisions (Education, Epidemiology, and Hyperbaric Medicine). Technical and Veterinary Sciences provide support. *Type:* Research center.

U.S. Department of Defense

Army Medical Research and Materiel Command

Army Aeromedical Research Laboratory

PO Box 620577   Ph: (334)255-6917
Fort Rucker, AL 36362-0577   Fax: (334)255-6937

Contact: Col. Dennis Shanahan, Contact.

Desc: Health hazards of Army aviation, tactical combat vehicles, and selected weapon systems; assessing stress and fatigue in personnel operating these systems and developing countermeasures; and assisting in the development of criteria upon which to base standards for entry and retention in Army aviation specialties. Principal areas of interest include medical study of visual/auditory functions, man-machine integration, physiological responses to operational environments, impact of continuous operations on individual and crew performance, testing of aeromedical evacuation life support equipment, development of improved means of patient evacuation, and airworthiness. *Type:* Research center.

U.S. Department of Transportation

Federal Aviation Administration

Civil Aeromedical Institute

PO Box 25082   Ph: (405)954-1000
AAM-3   Fax: (405)954-1010
Oklahoma City, OK 73125-
   5060
E-mail: william_collins@mmacmail.jccbi.gov
URL: http://www.cami.jccbi.gov/

Contact: Dr. William E. Collins, Dir.

Desc: Civil aviation medicine directed toward preventing aircraft accidents and increasing survival rates associated with aircraft accidents. Studies are primarily in the fields of human factors, psychology, physiology, toxicology, cabin safety, restraint, ditching, and protective breathing equipment. *Type:* Research center.

U.S. Department of Transportation

Federal Aviation Administration

Civil Aeromedical Institute

Aeromedical Research Division

Mail Code AAM-630   Ph: (405)954-5523
6500 S. MacArthur Blvd.   Fax: (405)954-0130
PO Box 25082
Oklahoma City, OK 73125
E-mail: jeff_marcus@mmacmail.jccbi.gov
URL: http://www.cami.jccbi.gov/research/index.html

Contact: Van Gowdy, Mgr.

Desc: Problems concerning civil airmen and equipment in emergency conditions, such as function of seat/restraint/interior crash injury protection, emergency evacuation, flotation, and cabin safety. Principal areas of research interest are biomechanics of impact, human factors, and breathing equipment. *Type:* Research center.

U.S. Department of Transportation

Federal Aviation Administration

Civil Aeromedical Institute

Aeromedical Research Division

6500 S. MacArthur Blvd.   Ph: (405)954-4866
PO Box 25082   Fax: (405)954-3705
Oklahoma City, OK 73125-
   5066
E-mail: dennis_canfield@mmacmail.jccbi.gov
URL: http://www.cami.jccbi.gov

Contact: Dennis Canfield, Mgr.

Desc: Human factor safety in civilian aviation. Studies are concerned with medical evidence available from aircraft accidents, including the genesis of the injuries experienced in those accidents; and effects of toxicants that may be present in post-crash fires or that may be otherwise introduced into the aviation environment. *Type:* Research center.

U.S. Department of Transportation

Federal Aviation Administration

Civil Aeromedical Institute

Aeromedical Research Division

Mail Code AAM-600   Ph: (405)954-4808
PO Box 25082   Fax: (405)954-0130
Oklahoma City, OK 73125-
   5066
E-mail: jerry_hordinsky@mmacmail.jccbi.gov
URL: http://www.cami.jccbi.gov

Contact: Dr. Jerry R. Hordinsky, Mgr.

Desc: Provides the Federal Aviation Administration (FAA) and the Federal Air Surgeon with the capability to: resolve operational, regulatory, and administrative problems related to medical certification of pilots; define and optimize workload and performance in aviation-related activities; and improve protection and survival in hostile and adverse aspects of general and commercial aviation. Division comprises the Toxicology and Accident Research Laboratory, Protection and Survival Laboratory, and Data Processing and Analysis Team. *Type:* Research center.

U.S. Department of Transportation

Federal Aviation Administration

Civil Aeromedical Institute

Aeromedical Research Division

Mail Code AAM-600   Ph: (405)954-4108
6500 S. MacArthur Blvd.   Fax: (405)954-1030
PO Box 25082
Oklahoma City, OK 73125
E-mail: bill_worner@mmacmail.jccbi.gov

Desc: Nonlinear models for toxicological data, probability models for identification of aircraft accident victims, and models of canine response to temperature and humidity factors; and analyses of data on various aspects of aviation and aviation safety (includes a cabin safety data bank and analyses of sled impact test data on various seat structures). *Type:* Research center.

U.S. Department of Transportation

Federal Aviation Administration

Civil Aeromedical Institute

Human Resources Research Division

Mail Code AAM-500   Ph: (405)954-4846
PO Box 25082   Fax: (405)954-4852
Oklahoma City, OK 73125
E-mail: david_schroeder@mmacmail.jccbi.gov

Contact: Dr. David J. Schroeder, Mgr.

Desc: Conducts an integrated program of applied field and laboratory performance research on organizational and human factors aspects of aviation work environments. Guidance for program development is obtained from the National Plan for Civil Aviation Human Factors, the FAA Strategic Plan, and senior agency management. *Type:* Research center.

U.S. Department of Transportation

Federal Aviation Administration

Office of Aviation Medicine

Medical Specialities Division

800 Independence Ave. SW   Ph: (202)267-8035
Washington, DC 20593   Fax: (202)493-5006

Contact: Dr. Robert S. Poole, Actg.Dir.

Desc: Program office for medical standards, certification policy, and aeromedical research and development. Principal area of research interest is clinical medicine. *Type:* Research center.

United States Ultralight Association

PO Box 667   Ph: (301)695-9100
Frederick, MD 21705   Fax: (301)695-0763
E-mail: usuahq@aol.com
URL: http://www.usua.com

Contact: John Ballantyne, Pres.

Desc: Ultralight aviation enthusiasts. Promotes the sport of ultralight and microlight aviation. (Ultralights and microlights are very light, slow planes used for recreational flight.) Represents members' interests on federal, state, and local levels; keeps members abreast of ultralight advancement. *Type:* Association.

Young Astronaut Council

1308 19th St. NW   Ph: (202)682-1985
Washington, DC 20036   Fax: (202)775-1773

Contact: T. Wendell Butler, Exec.Officer.

Desc: Administers the Young Astronaut Program, an educational program intended to encourage pre-school, elementary, and junior high school students to study science, mathematics, and technology, using the space program as a motivator. Provides updated information on the space program; develops and distributes curricular materials. Sponsors essay, art, math, and science competitions and awards prizes. *Type:* Association.

Africa

Africa-America Institute

Chanin Bldg.   Ph: (212)949-5666
380 Lexington Ave.   Free: 800-745-3899
New York, NY 10168-4298   Fax: (212)682-6174
E-mail: aai@aaionline.org
URL: http://www.aaionline.org

Contact: Mora McLean, Pres.

Desc: Works to further development in Africa, improve African-American understanding, and inform Americans about Africa. Engages in training, development assistance, and informational activities. Sponsors African-American conferences, media and congressional workshops, and regional seminars. *Type:* Association.

The Africa Fund

50 Braod St., Ste. 711
New York, NY 10004
Ph: (212)785-1024
Fax: (212)785-1078
E-mail: africafund@igc.org
URL: http://www.prairienet.org/acas/afund.html
Contact: Jennifer Davis, Exec.Dir.

Desc: Established by the American Committee on Africa. Works to support the struggle for democracy and economic justice. Defends human rights, including working for the release of political prisoners. *Type:* Association.

Africalink

Africalink Trade Bureau
2000 Hamilton St., Ste. 531
Philadelphia, PA 19130
Ph: (215)747-5905
Fax: (215)747-5598
E-mail: africalink1@mailcity.com; info@africalink.net.
URL: http://www.freeyellow.com/members2/africantrade/page1.html.
Contact: Muhammad Nassor Bey, Publisher.

Desc: Concentrates on import and export business, including nation profiles, currency exchange rates, and business leads. Recurring features include a calendar of events, news of educational opportunities, job listings, book reviews, and notices of publications available. *Type:* Newsletter.

Africana Libraries Newsletter

Africana Library
Michigan State University Libraries
East Lansing, MI 48824-1048
Ph: (517)432-2218
Fax: (517)432-1445
Contact: Joseph J. Lauer, Editor, lauer@pilot.msu.edu.

Desc: Concerned with librarianship in African studies. Recurring features include news of professionals in the field, reports from the African Studies Association's Africana Librarians Council, the Cooperative Africana Microform Project, notes on research on libraries, new reference sources, vendor announcements, and news about recent publications. *Type:* Newsletter.

Africare

440 R St. NW
Washington, DC 20001
Ph: (202)462-3614
Fax: (202)387-1034
Contact: C. Payne Lucas, Pres.

Desc: Seeks to improve the quality of life in rural Africa. Provides health and environmental protection services in rural areas of Africa; works to improve African water and agricultural resources; conducts public education programs in the U.S. on African development. *Type:* Association.

Guinea Development Foundation

140 W. End Ave., Ste. 176
New York, NY 10023
Ph: (212)874-2911
Fax: (212)496-9549
E-mail: guineadev@aol.org
URL: http://www.guineadev.com
Contact: Dr. Sekou Michael Sylla, MD,MPH, Pres.
Desc: Promotes health, culture, and education in the country of Guinea, Africa. *Type:* Association.

Operation Crossroads Africa

475 Riverside Dr., Ste. 1366
New York, NY 10115
Ph: (212)870-2106
Fax: (212)870-2644
E-mail: oca@igc.apc.org
URL: http://www.igc.org/oca
Contact: Willis Logan, Pres.

Desc: Students and professionals, mostly from the U.S., who live and work with African counterparts during July and August on selfhelp community development projects in Africa and Brazil Opportunities are provided for interaction with village elders, educators, and political and other community leaders. Emphasizes community growth from within a "Third World" structure. Before departure, participants make an intensive study of Africa; after their return, they give speeches about their experiences. *Type:* Association.

TransAfrica

1744 R St. NW
Washington, DC 20009
Ph: (202)797-2301
Fax: (202)797-2382
Contact: Randall Robinson, Pres.

Desc: Concerned with the political and human rights of people in Africa and the Caribbean, and those of African descent throughout the world. Attempts to influence U.S. foreign policy in these areas by informing the public of violations of social, political, and civil rights, and by advocating a more progressive attitude in the U.S. *Type:* Association.

Aging

AARP Bulletin

American Association of Retired Persons (AARP)
601 E St. NW
Washington, DC 20049
Ph: (202)434-2277
Fax: (202)434-6451
E-mail: aarp1@aol.com; bulletin@aarp.org.
URL: http://www.aarp.org.
Contact: Elliot Carlson, Editor; Martha Ramsey, Acting Pub. Dir., (202)434-6850; Patricia Mondello, Advertising Dir., (212)599-1880, fax: (212)986-8167.

Desc: Newspaper for mature Americans. *Alt. Contact:* 601 East St., NW, Washington, DC 20049; telephone: (202)434-3340; fax: 800-424-3410. *Type:* Periodical.

Administration on Aging - Information on Older Persons and Services for the Elderly

Department of Health and Human Services
Administration on Aging
330 Independence Ave. SW
Washington, DC 20201
Ph: (202)619-0724
E-mail: AoAInfo@ban-gate.aoa.dhhs.gov
URL: http://www.aoa.dhhs.gov/

Desc: As sure as we live, we face the prospect of growing older, and at this site you can find vast amounts of information and resources for persons with an aging spouse or relative - or who themselves are approaching their twilight. Available are fact sheets on issues facing the elderly; electronic books and booklets on such topics as health issues, retirement living, home modification, and other areas of concern to aging persons and their families; and dozens of links to other information repositories, state agencies, directories of elder care organizations, and associated resources. *Type:* Database.

Aging in America

1500 Pelham Pky. S
Bronx, NY 10461
Ph: (718)824-4004
Fax: (718)824-4242
Contact: William Smith, Pres.

Desc: Research and service organization for professionals in gerontology. Objectives are: to produce, implement, and share effective and affordable programs and services that improve the quality of life for the elderly community; to better prepare professionals and students interested in, or currently involved with, aging and the aged. Conducts research projects, educational and training seminars, and in-service curricula for long-term and acute care facilities. *Type:* Association.

Aging, Health and Society

Office of Gerontological Studies
McMaster University
DC-229
1280 Main St. West
Hamilton, ON, Canada L8S 4K1
Ph: (905)525-9140
Fax: (905)525-4198
E-mail: elliotg@mcmail.cis.mcmaster.ca.
Contact: Carolyn Rosenthal, Director, crosent@mcmail.cis.mcmaster.ca.

Desc: Reports on current issues in research, education, policy, and practice in gerontological studies. Provides information concerning activities in the field of aging within the community. *Type:* Newsletter.

Aging Research Institute

700 SW Harrison St., Ste. 1106
Topeka, KS 66603-3759
Ph: (913)233-0585
Fax: (913)233-9471
E-mail: jgrace@kahsa.org
URL: http://www.kahsa.org
Contact: John R. Grace, Dir.

Desc: Managed care and nursery facilities staff recruitment and retention. *Type:* Research center.

Alliance for Aging Research

2021 K St. NW, Ste. 305
Washington, DC 20006-1003
Ph: (202)293-2856
Free: 800-497-0360
Fax: (202)785-8574
E-mail: agecom@aol.com
Contact: Daniel Perry, Exec.Dir.

Desc: Gerontologists and other medical professionals, executives, and members of Congress are participants. Works to increase private and public research into aging. Supports policies concerning: productive aging; independence for older Americans; successful aging; human genome initiative. *Type:* Association.

American Association of Homes and Services for the Aging

901 E St. NW, Ste. 500
Washington, DC 20004-2037
Ph: (202)783-2242
Fax: (202)783-2255
E-mail: info@aahsa.org
URL: http://www.aahsa.org
Contact: Sheldon L. Goldberg, Pres.

Desc: Voluntary not-for-profit nursing homes, housing, retirement communities, and health-related facilities and services for the elderly; state associations; interested individuals. Provides a unified means of identifying and solving problems in order to protect and advance the interests of the residents served. Believes that long-term care should be geared toward individual needs and provided in a spectrum ranging from nursing care to independent living and community-based care. *Type:* Association.

American Federation for Aging Research

1414 Ave. of the Americas, 18th Fl.
New York, NY 10019
Ph: (212)752-2327
Fax: (212)832-2298
E-mail: amfedaging@aol.com
URL: http://www.afar.org
Contact: Odette Vanderwillik, Contact.
Desc: Aging and associated diseases. *Type:* Research center.

American Foundation for Aging Research

North Carolina State University
Biochemistry Dept.
140 Polk Hall
Raleigh, NC 27695-7622
Ph: (919)515-2011
Fax: (919)515-2047
E-mail: afar@bchserver.bch.ncsu.edu
URL: http://www4.ncsu.edu/unity/users/a/agris/afar/afar.htm
Contact: Paul F. Agris, Contact.

Desc: Age-related diseases and the biology of aging, focusing on modern biological, genetic, biochemical, and biophysical techniques and approaches to the problems of age-associated diseases and the understanding of aging. *Type:* Research center.

American Senior Citizens Association

PO Box 41
Fayetteville, NC 28302
Ph: (910)323-3641
Free: 800-323-6525
Fax: (910)323-4343
Contact: Ben Sutton, Exec.VP.

Desc: Senior citizens. Purpose is to promote the physical, mental, emotional, and economic well-being of senior citizens. Believes that senior citizens have a right to live with competence, security, and dignity. *Type:* Association.

American Society on Aging

833 Market St., Ste. 511
San Francisco, CA 94103-1824
Ph: (415)974-9600
Fax: (415)974-0300
E-mail: info@asa.asaging.org
URL: http://www.asaging.org
Contact: Gloria H. Cavanaugh, Exec.Dir.
Desc: Health care and social service professionals, educators, researchers, administrators, businesspersons, students, and senior citizens. Works to enhance the well-being of older individuals and to foster unity among those working with and for the elderly. *Type:* Association.

Baylor College of Medicine

Roy M. and Phyllis Gough Huffington Center on Aging

One Baylor Plaza, M-320
Houston, TX 77030-3498
Ph: (713)798-5804
Fax: (713)798-6688
E-mail: jsmith@bcm.tmc.edu
Contact: Robert J. Luchi, MD, Dir.
Desc: Cell and molecular biology of aging, cardiovascular disease, and ethics in long-term care. *Type:* Research center.

Bi-Folkal Times

Bi-Folkal Productions, Inc.
809 Williamson St.
Madison, WI 53703
Ph: (608)251-2818
Free: 800-568-5357
Fax: (608)251-2874
E-mail: bifolks@globaldialog.com
Contact: Lynne Martin Erickson, Editor.
Desc: Provides program ideas and resources for use with groups of older adults and mixed-age groups. Emphasizes multi-sensory and multi-media resources that focus on sharing the remembered past. *Type:* Newsletter.

The Brown University GeroPsych Report

Manisses Communications Group, Inc.
208 Governor St.
Providence, RI 02906-3246
Ph: (401)831-6020
Free: 800-333-7771
Fax: (401)861-6370
E-mail: manissescs@manisses.com
Contact: James McCartney, M.D., Editor.
Desc: Provides information on the use of psychotropic medications in elderly intervention strategies dealing with behavioral disorders from dementia to depression. *Type:* Newsletter.

Canadian Seniority Magazine

Retirement Lifestyle Publications, Inc.
2506 Linwood St.
Pickering, ON, Canada L1X
1E5
Ph: (416)283-2099
Contact: Sharon Buckingham, Publisher; David Todd, Editor; Eldrid Retief, Travel Ed.; Ursula Retief, Travel Ed.; Eric Buckingham, Sales Mgr.
Desc: Magazine featuring retirement issues. *Type:* Periodical.

Case Western Reserve University

University Center on Aging and Health

10900 Euclid Ave.
Cleveland, OH 44106-7131
Ph: (216)368-2692
Fax: (216)368-6389
E-mail: dxf5@po.cwru.edu
Contact: Dr. May L. Wykle, PhD,RN, Dir.
Desc: Conducts, supports, and facilitates research at the University Center on Aging and Health, including the effects of stress and strains, and elderly physical health in persons over 65 years of age. Emphasizes prevention, diagnosis, treatment, management of illness or disability, and service utilization of care giver. *Type:* Research center.

Center for Clinical and Aging Services Research

3330 Geary Blvd., 2nd Fl.
San Francisco, CA 94118
Ph: (415)750-4170
Fax: (415)750-4179
E-mail: mbrod@gioa.org
URL: http://www.careguide.net/careguide.cgi/ccasr/ccasrhome.html
Contact: Meryl Brod, PhD, Dir.
Desc: Geriatrics and gerontology, including testing and improvement of medical and social interventions; drug efficacy studies and medication compliance in the elderly; outcomes of long-term care interventions in the areas of Alzheimer's disease, respite care, and home care; and ethical issues arising from the extended life cycle. *Type:* Research center.

Center for the Study of Aging, Inc.

706 Madison Ave.
Albany, NY 12208-3604
Ph: (518)465-6927
Fax: (518)462-1339
E-mail: iapaas@aol.com
URL: http://members.aol.com/iapaas
Contact: Sara Harris, Exec.Dir.
Desc: Social and medical research on aging, including physical activity and aging, housing for the elderly, geriatric cardiology, nutrition, mental health, oral history, public policy, caregiving, prevention and respite care for the frail elderly. *Type:* Research center.

Children of Aging Parents

Woodbourne Office Campus,
Ste. 302A
1609 Woodbourne Rd.
Levittown, PA 19057-1511
Ph: (215)945-6900
Free: 800-227-7294
Fax: (215)945-8720
URL: http://www.careguide.net
Desc: National information and referral service for caregivers of the elderly. Provides a speakers bureau as part of its educational outreach mission to churches, service clubs, schools, hospitals, TV/radio and colleges. Conducts workshops, seminars, and conferences for lay individuals and professionals in the field of aging. *Type:* Association.

Christian Association of Primetimers

PO Box 777
St. Charles, IL 60174
Free: 800-443-0227
Fax: (630)444-0087
Contact: Roland Johnson, Pres.
Desc: Provides many benefits to the elderly including, health care coverage, hearing aids, automobile insurance, bargains, discounts on prescription drugs, and money management tips. *Type:* Association.

Coastline Elderly Services

1646 Purchase St.
New Bedford, MA 02740
Ph: (508)999-6400
Fax: (508)993-6510
E-mail: cesield@ici.net
URL: http://www.coastlineelderly.org
Contact: Charles Sisson, Dir.
Desc: Area agency on aging. Sponsors hot lunch program for seniors who are not homebound. *Type:* Association.

College of Maharishi Vedic Medicine

Center for Health and Aging Studies

DB 1134
Fairfield, IA 52557-1134
Ph: (515)472-1129
Fax: (515)472-1167
E-mail: rschneid@mum.edu
URL: http://www.mum.edu/CHAS
Contact: Robert H. Schneider, MD, Dir.
Desc: Behavioral cardiology, minority health, preventive cardiology, behavioral and preventive gerontology, and traditional and alternative medicine. Conducts controlled clinical trials on cardiovascular disease treatment and prevention in community settings with behavioral methods; research into methods to slow or retard aging processes; research and development in traditional natural medicine; and programs with African American populations. *Type:* Research center.

Columbia University

Stroud Center for Geriatrics and Gerontology

100 Haven Ave., Tower 3-30F
New York, NY 10032
Ph: (212)781-0600
Fax: (212)795-7696
Contact: Dr. Barry Gurland, Dir.
Desc: Methodological, epidemiological and clinical research in geriatrics/gerontology and long-term care. Specific studies are directed toward mental disorders, psychosocial problems, and funtional impairments of the elderly. *Type:* Research center.

Duke University

Center for the Study of Aging and Human Development

Medical Center
Box 3003
Durham, NC 27710
Ph: (919)660-7500
Fax: (919)684-8569
E-mail: ray00004@mc.duke.edu
URL: http://www.geri.duke.edu
Contact: Harvey Jay Cohen, MD, Dir.
Desc: Human and animal physiology, immunology, neuroendocrinology, pharmacology, carcinogenesis, enzyme biochemistry, free radical effects, membrane and receptor function, bone metabolism and osteoporosis, central nervous system structure and function, Alzheimer's disease, dementia, cognitive processes, psychometrics, human personality and behavior, family structure and intergenerational relationships, social factors and illness, epidemiology of aging and chronic illness, stress and coping, cell growth and differentiation, signal transduction, and the demographics and economics of aging populations. The Aging Center coordinates research, training, and clinical services in aging for the University. *Type:* Research center.

ElderCare Forum

ElderCare Financial Management, Inc.
170 Elaine Dr.
Roswell, GA 30075
Ph: (770)518-2767
E-mail: hwij87a@prodigy.com.
Contact: Laura Beller, Editor, lbeller301@aol.com.
Desc: Intended to help educate and inform caregivers about relevant issues related to aging and taking care of an aging parent. Provide practical information, useful tips, and guidance that caregivers need on a daily basis. *Type:* Newsletter.

Families U.S.A. Foundation

1334 G St. NW
Washington, DC 20005
Ph: (202)628-3030
Fax: (202)347-2417
E-mail: info@familiesusa.org
URL: http://www.familiesusa.org
Contact: Ronald F. Pollack, Exec.Dir.
Desc: Issues reports and other materials on health care and long term care for use by consumer organizations, policymakers, the media, and state-based coalitions working on health care and long term care reform. *Type:* Association.

Fifty Plus

Fifty Plus
PO Box 51277
Durham, NC 27717
Ph: (919)493-5900
Fax: (919)490-1925
E-mail: nc50plus@aol.comm.
Contact: Linda Scovill, Publisher; Paul Knechtel, Publisher.
Desc: Newspaper directed to persons fifty and over. *Type:* Periodical.

Gerontology and Geriatrics Research Centre

1036 Belvedere St.
Sherbrooke, PQ, Canada J1H
4C4
Ph: (819)829-7131
Fax: (819)829-7141
E-mail: rhebert@courrier.usherb.ca

URL: http://www.usherb.ca/cdrgg

Contact: Dr. Rejean Hebert, Dir.

Desc: Biology of aging, rehabilitation, Alzheimer's disease, diabetes, nutrition, epidemiology and prevention of functional decline, physical activity, gait and balance, psychosociology of aging, and sleep disorders. *Type:* Research center.

Good Times
Good Times

Robert Morris Bldg., 9th Fl.　　Ph: (215)496-0122
100 N. 17th St.　　Fax: (215)496-0463
Philadelphia, PA 19103

Contact: Karen Detwiler, (215)496-0122, fax: (215)496-0463; Marie-Therese Lacroix, (215)496-0122, fax: (215)496-0463.

Desc: The Lifestyle Magazine for Mature Pennsylvanians *Type:* Periodical.

Gray Panthers

733 15th St. NW, Ste. 437　　Ph: (202)737-6637
Washington, DC 20005　　Free: 800-280-5362
　　Fax: (202)737-1160

URL: http://www.graypanthers.com

Contact: Tim Fuller, Exec.Dir.

Desc: Consciousness-raising activist group of older adults and young people. Aims to combat ageism - the discrimination against persons on the basis of chronological age. Believes that both the old and the young have much to contribute to make our society more just and humane. *Type:* Association.

GRC News
Gerontology Research Centre
Simon Fraser University at Harbour Centre

515 W. Hastings St.　　Ph: (604)291-5062
Vancouver, BC, Canada V6B　　Fax: (604)291-5066
5K3

E-mail: gero@sfu.ca

URL: http://www.harbour.sfc.ca/gero/grcnews/; http://www.harbour.sfu.ca/gero/grcnews/.

Contact: Susannah Tredwell, Editor, (604)291-5064.

Desc: Describes current Centre projects and results of studies of the aged in British Columbia and Canada. *Type:* Newsletter.

Indiana University Bloomington
Center on Aging and Aged

Smith Research, Rm. 197　　Ph: (812)855-0815
Bloomington, IN 47405

E-mail: eklund@indiana.edu

URL: http://www.indiana.edu/~caa/

Contact: Susan J. Eklund, Dir.

Desc: Gerontology, including developmentally disabled, handicapped, minorities, rural-isolated, and mainstream aging populations. *Type:* Research center.

Institute of Developmental Neuroscience and Aging

PO Box 13076　　Ph: (303)333-0566
Denver, CO 80201-3276

Desc: Developmental neuroscience and aging, focusing on establishing neuroscience programs in developing and third world countries. *Type:* Research center.

J. Paul Sticht Center on Aging and Rehabilitation

North Carolina Baptist　　Ph: (336)716-4722
　Hospitals, Inc.　　Fax: (336)716-2067
Medical Center Blvd.
Winston Salem, NC 27157

E-mail: rtuttle@wfubmc.edu

URL: http://www.bgsm.edu

Contact: Robin Tuttle, Admin.Dir.

Desc: Metabolic and biomedical research in aging and rehabilitation, focusing on nutritional deficiencies and problems in the elderly. *Type:* Research center.

Jewish Association for Services for the Aged

132 W 31st St., 15th Fl.　　Ph: (212)273-5200
New York, NY 10001　　Fax: (212)695-4206

Contact: David J. Stern, Exec.VP.

Desc: Social welfare organization whose objective is to provide the services necessary to enable the older adult to remain in the community. Maintains 18 community service offices and 24 local senior citizens centers in New York City and Nassau and Suffolk Counties, NY. Services include: case management; information and referral to appropriate health, welfare, educational, social, recreational, and vacation services, and on government benefits and entitlements; personal counseling; financial assistance; health and medical service counsel; counsel on housing and long-term care; homemaker service; group educational and recreational activities through senior citizens centers; information and guidance for social action on legislative issues affecting the elderly; hot lunch programs; referral to summer camps; legal services; protective services; reaching out to the isolated; programs for independent senior clubs; volunteer service opportunities. *Type:* Association.

Jewish Council for the Aging
David Gamse

11820 Parklawn Dr., No. 200　　Ph: (301)881-8782
Rockville, MD 20852-2511　　Fax: (301)231-9360

E-mail: jca@jcagw.org

URL: http://www.jcagw.org

Contact: David N. Gamse, Exec.Dir.

Desc: Seeks to assist the elderly of all faiths lead independent lives. *Type:* Association.

Little Brothers - Friends of the Elderly

355 N. Ashland　　Ph: (312)455-1000
Chicago, IL 60607　　Fax: (312)455-9674

Contact: Tina Stretch, Exec.Dir.

Desc: Participants are individuals over 70 years old who live alone, have limited incomes, and do not receive emotional and physical support from relatives. Seeks to combat the isolation and loneliness often experienced by elderly people by providing friendship and special assistance. *Type:* Association.

Mature Life Features

PO Box 9642　　Ph: (619)483-3412
San Diego, CA 92169　　Fax: (619)483-0831

Contact: Igor Lobanov, Editor-in-Chief; Cecil Scaglione, VP Mktg.; Derwyn Christensen, VP Editorial.

Desc: Distributes book reviews, government affairs, health and fitness, lifestyles, personal finance, and travel columns; personality profiles of mature adults. *Alt. Contact:* PO Box 9642, San Diego, CA 92169; telephone: (619)483-3412; fax: (619)483-0831. *Type:* Periodical.

Mature Living
Lifeway Christian Resources of the Southern Baptist Convention, MSN 16

127 9th Ave. N.　　Ph: (615)251-2000
Nashville, TN 37234-0160　　Free: 800-458-2772

Contact: Al Shackleford, Editor.

Desc: Magazine for seniors featuring articles on cultivating strong relationships and improving communication skills, with emphasis on nostalgia. *Type:* Periodical.

Mature Market Editorial Services

10 Town Plz.　　Ph: (970)385-6999
Ste. 313
Durango, CO 81301

E-mail: lhansen@frontier.net.

Contact: Leonard J. Hansen, Columnist/Ed.

Alt. Contact: 10 Town Plz., Ste. 313, Durango, CO 81301; telephone: (970)385-6999. *Type:* Periodical.

Mature Outlook

PO Box 9390　　Free: 800-336-6330
Des Moines, IA 50306-9519　　Fax: (515)334-9247

Contact: Alison Poklop, Mktg.Mgr.

Desc: Individuals over 50 years of age. *Type:* Association.

The Maturing Marketplace
Business Publishers, Inc.

8737 Colesville Rd., Ste. 1100　　Ph: (301)589-5103
Silver Spring, MD 20910　　Free: 800-274-6737
　　Fax: (301)587-4530

E-mail: bpinews@bpinews.com

Contact: Sarah Spencer, Editor.

Desc: Provides information and techniques on marketing and advertising aimed at the older population of the United States. Includes articles on housing, stereotypes of 50-plus consumers, and retirement. *Type:* Newsletter.

Maturity
CYN Investments Ltd.

PO Box 397　　Ph: (604)540-7911
New Westminster, BC, Canada　　Fax: (604)540-7912
　V3L 4Y7

Contact: Donald A. Causton, Publisher; Audrey Gill, Editor; Alison Gardner, Assoc. Editor.

Desc: Mature market lifestyle magazine. *Type:* Periodical.

Maturity News Service

1101 Connecticut Ave. NW　　Ph: (202)662-8895
Ste. 310　　Fax: (202)662-8896
Washington, DC 20036-4303

Contact: Richard Bowers, Managing Editor.

Desc: Distributes news for and about mature Americans. *Alt. Contact:* 1101 Connecticut Ave. NW, Ste. 310, Washington, DC 20036-4303; telephone: (202)662-8895; fax: (202)662-8896. *Type:* Periodical.

McCall's Prime Time
G & J USA Publishing

375 Lexington Ave.　　Ph: (212)499-2000
New York, NY 10017　　Fax: (212)499-1778

Desc: Publication featuring articles for over 50 readers. *Type:* Periodical.

McGill University
McGill Centre for Studies in Aging

Douglas Hospital　　Ph: (514)766-2010
6825 La Salle Blvd.　　Fax: (514)888-4050
Verdun, PQ, Canada H4H 1R3

E-mail: mcmu@musica.mcgill.ca

URL: http://www.mcgill.ca/mcsa/mcsa/

Contact: Judes Poirier, PhD, Dir.

Desc: Alzheimer's disease, including diagnostic methods, drug trials, brain banking, and genetic studies; Parkinson's disease; prevention of falls and injuries; autonomous nervous dysfunction in aging; cellular models of aging; community health and epidemiology; bioethics; nutrition in aging; urologic dysfunction; and social gerontology. *Type:* Research center.

McMaster University

R. Samuel McLaughlin Centre for Gerontological Health Research

25 Main St. W. Ph: (905)546-3531
Hamilton, ON, Canada L8N Fax: (905)546-3645
3Z5
E-mail: everestb@fhs.csu.mcmaster.ca
Contact: Dr. Larry W. Chambers, Dir.
Desc: Encourages research to improve health and preventive care for seniors. *Type:* Research center.

MCP Hahnemann University of the Health Sciences

Institute on Aging

2900 Queen Ln. Ph: (215)991-8460
Philadelphia, PA 19129
URL: http://www.auhs.edu/institutes/instaging.html
Contact: Vincent J. Cristofalo, PhD, Dir.
Desc: Aging, gerontology, and geriatrics, including health care for people affected by age-related diseases. *Type:* Research center.

Modern Maturity

American Association of Retired Persons (AARP)
601 E St. NW Ph: (202)434-2277
Washington, DC 20049 Fax: (202)434-6451
E-mail: aarp1@aol.com
Contact: Henry Fenwick, Editor.
Desc: Magazine for persons fifty and older. *Type:* Periodical.

National Alliance of Senior Citizens

1700 18th St. NW, Ste. 401 Ph: (202)986-0117
Washington, DC 20009 Fax: (202)986-2974
Contact: Peter J. Luciano, CEO.
Desc: Persons advocating the advancement of senior Americans through sound fiscal policy and through belief in the American system of individuality and personal freedom. Purpose is to inform the membership and the American public of the needs of senior citizens and of the programs and policies being carried out by the government and other specified groups. Represents the views of senior Americans before Congress and state legislatures. *Type:* Association.

National Association of Area Agencies on Aging

927 15th St., 6th Fl. Ph: (202)296-8130
Washington, DC 20005 Fax: (202)296-8134
E-mail: jjfn4a@erols.com
Contact: Janice Jackson Fiegener, Exec.Dir.
Desc: Members are Area Agencies on Aging, established under the provisions of the Older Americans Act of 1965; also offers corporate and cooperating memberships. Promotes the achievement of a reasonable and realistic national policy on aging; assists the process of partnership and regular communication within a national network on aging. Acts as advocate for the needs of older persons at the national level. *Type:* Association.

National Caucus and Center on Black Aged

1424 K St. NW, Ste. 500 Ph: (202)637-8400
Washington, DC 20005 Fax: (202)347-0895
E-mail: ncba@aol.com
URL: http://www.ncba-blackaged.org
Contact: Samuel J. Simmons, Pres.
Desc: Seeks to improve living conditions for low-income elderly Americans, particularly blacks. Advocates changes in federal and state laws in improving the economic, health, and social status of low-income senior citizens. Promotes community awareness of problems and issues effecting low-income aging population. *Type:* Association.

National Council of Senior Citizens

8403 Colesville Rd. Ste 1200 Ph: (301)578-8800
Silver Spring, MD 20910 Fax: (301)578-8999
URL: http://www.ncscinc.org
Contact: Steve Protulis, Exec.Dir.
Desc: Organization of autonomous senior citizens clubs, associations, and councils. Educational and action group which supports the preservation of Medicare and Social Security, the enactment of a national health plan which includes long-term care, reduced costs on drugs, better housing, and other programs to aid senior citizens. Sponsors mass rallies, educational workshops and leadership training institutes; provides speakers on issues concerning senior citizens; helps organize and develop programs for local and state groups. *Type:* Association.

National Hispanic Council on Aging

2713 Ontario Rd. NW Ph: (202)265-1288
Washington, DC 20009 Fax: (202)745-2522
Contact: Marta Sotomayor, Ph.D., Pres.
Desc: Individuals and groups who work in administrative, planning, direct services, research, or educational areas who have a concern for the Hispanic elderly. Fosters the well-being of the Hispanic elderly through research, policy analysis, demonstration projects, development of educational resources, and training. *Type:* Association.

Nevada Senior World

Nevada Senior World
2340 Paseo Del Prado, Ste. 304 Ph: (702)367-6709
Las Vegas, NV 89102 Fax: (702)367-6883
Contact: Frank B. Fiedler, General Mgr.
Desc: Newspaper for senior citizens. *Type:* Periodical.

New Choices

Retirement Living Publishing Co.
28 W. 23rd St. Ph: (212)366-8800
New York, NY 10010-5204 Fax: (212)366-8899
E-mail: newchoices@readersdigest.com.
Desc: Magazine. *Type:* Periodical.

Nursing Home Advisory and Research Council

PO Box 18820 Ph: (216)321-4499
Cleveland Heights, OH 44118
Contact: Mary A. Mendelson, Dir.
Desc: Nursing homes, focusing on patient care, education, research, and improving conditions of nursing homes. *Type:* Research center.

Older American Support

Business Publishers, Inc.
8737 Colesville Rd., Ste. 1100 Ph: (301)589-5103
Silver Spring, MD 20910 Free: 800-274-6737
 Fax: (301)587-4530
E-mail: bpinews@bpinews.com
Contact: Sarah Spencer, Editor.
Desc: Covers a wide range of issues affecting managed care of the elderly, including legislation, regulations, cost-cutting measures, research findings and survey results. Also focuses on leading models in the managed care field. *Type:* Newsletter.

Orentreich Foundation for the Advancement of Science, Inc.

Biomedical Res. Stat. Ph: (914)265-4200
Rd. 2, Box 375 Fax: (914)265-4210
855 Rte. 201
Cold Spring, NY 10516
E-mail: ofas1@juno.com
Contact: Norman Orentreich, Pres./Dir.
Desc: Dermatology, aging, endocrinology, and serum markers for human diseases. *Type:* Research center.

Pennsylvania State University

Gerontology Center

S-105 Henderson Bldg. Ph: (814)865-1710
University Park, PA 16802 Fax: (814)863-9423
URL: http://geron.psu.edu
Contact: Dr. K. Warner Schaie, Dir.
Desc: Broad interdisciplinary approach to questions on aging. Major areas of research are cognition in aging, developmental methodology, family and informal supports, and animal models of aging. *Type:* Research center.

Prime Time

Westland Convelescent Center
36137 W. Warren Ph: (313)728-6100
Westland, MI 48185
Desc: Provides events, news, and information that pertains to residents and their family and friends and employees of Westland Convelescent Center. Recurring features include a calendar of events and columns titled Featured Resident, Birthdays, Featured Employee, and Gardener's Corner. *Type:* Newsletter.

Rehabilitation Research and Training Center on Aging With a Disability

Rancho Los Amigos Medical Ph: (310)401-7402
Center Fax: (310)401-7011
7601 E. Imperial Hwy.
Downey, CA 90242
URL: http://www.usc.edu/dept/gero/RRTConAging/
Contact: Bryan Kemp, PhD, Dir.
Desc: Problems people face as they age with disabilities, including those who are post-polio, have rheumatoid arthritis, cerebral palsy, or have suffered a stroke. *Type:* Research center.

Remedy

Rx Remedy, Inc.
120 Post Rd. W. Ph: (203)341-7000
Westport, CT 06880 Fax: (203)221-4913
E-mail: ldinerstein@rxremedy.com.
Contact: Joan Montgomery, National Sales Mgr.; Katherine G. Bell-Wills, Publisher; Valorie Weaver, Editor-in-Chief.
Desc: Consumer magazine covering health and wellness for individuals over 50 years in the U.S. *Type:* Periodical.

Retirement Income Association

PO Box 21957 Ph: (805)569-1363
Santa Barbara, CA 93121 Fax: (805)569-0861
Contact: James J. Maher, Pres.
Desc: Acts as a liaison between retired consumers and service and product providers. *Type:* Association.

Retirement Life

National Association of Retired Federal Employees
1533 New Hampshire Ave. NW Ph: (202)234-0832
Washington, DC 20036 Fax: (202)797-9698
Contact: Kathleen E. Delaney, Editor.
Desc: Magazine for federal civil service retirees and employees. *Type:* Periodical.

Rockefeller University

Zachary and Elizabeh M. Fisher Center for Research on Alzheimer's Disease

1230 York Ave. Ph: (212)327-8000
New York, NY 10021
URL: http://www.rockefeller.edu/graduate/cenzach.htm
Contact: Prof. Paul Greengard, Dir.
Desc: Alzheimer's disease, including how brain cells process the amyloid precursor phosphoprotein (APP) leading to the production of b-amyloid, a major component of the plaques that are a hallmark of Alzheimer's disease. *Type:* Research center.

Rush University

Rush Institute for Healthy Aging

1645 W. Jackson Blvd., Ste 675   Ph: (312)942-3350
Chicago, IL 60612   Fax: (312)942-2861
Contact: Dr. Denis A. Evans, MD, Co-Dir.
Desc: Epidemiology of Alzheimer's disease, community-based studies of Alzheimer's disease and other common problems of older persons, physical functions among older persons, and statistical methods in aging research. *Type:* Research center.

The Senior Advocate

Mar-Len Publications
131 Lincoln St.   Ph: (508)752-2512
Worcester, MA 01605   Fax: (508)752-9057
Contact: Sondra Shapiro, Editor; Philip Davis, Publisher; Philip Davis, Publisher.
Desc: Newspaper for senior citizens. *Type:* Periodical.

Senior Wire News Service

2377 Elm St.   Ph: (303)355-3882
Denver, CO 80207   Fax: (303)355-2720
E-mail: 72370.3520@compuserve.com.
Contact: Allison St. Claire, Pub./Ed.
Desc: Distributes Washington Watch; national news/analysis; Joking Around; political commentary; financial advice and commentary; food column; pet column; golf column; Grandparents Corner; Attic Antiques; Health Briefs; Beauty Beyond 50; puzzles; seasonal/holiday information columns; automotive/technical; computers/Internet; investment fraud; Pull Your Own Weight; RV Travel; Home Alone; humor columns. *Alt. Contact:* 2377 Elm St., Denver, CO 80207; telephone: (303)355-3882; fax: (303)355-2720. *Type:* Periodical.

Senior World Newsmagazine

Kendall Communications
PO Box 1565   Ph: (619)593-2900
El Cajon, CA 92022   Fax: (619)442-4043
Contact: Laura Impastato, Editor; Resa Trent, General Mgr.
Desc: Newspaper (tabloid) for active older adults. *Type:* Periodical.

Senior World Newsmagazine Orange County Edition

Kendell Communications, Inc.
26081 Merit Cir., Ste. 101   Ph: (714)898-2893
Laguna Hills, CA 92653-7017   Fax: (714)895-4322
Contact: Resa Trent, General Mgr.; Laura Impastato, Editor.
Desc: Magazine for mature adults. *Type:* Periodical.

Seniority

National Council of Senior Citizens, Inc.
8403 Colesville Rd., Ste. 1200   Ph: (301)578-8800
Silver Spring, MD 20910   Fax: (301)578-8999
Contact: Bette Cooper, Editor, (301)578-8837, fax: (301)578-8911.
Desc: Publishes news, information, activities and events of the Council. *Type:* Newsletter.

Seniors-Site.com

Writers Consortium
5443 Stag Mt. Rd.   Ph: (916)938-3163
Weed, CA 96094   Fax: (916)938-3850
URL: http://www.seniors-site.com/
Contact: Walter Cheney, Webmaster, writers@seniors-site.com.
Desc: Despite its name, this site is not for seniors only, unless of course anyone over 50 is to be considered a senior citizen these days. This site offers a vast library of information helpful to Americans over 50 years of age. *Type:* Database.

Southern California Senior Life

Senior Media Inc.
6022 W. Pico Blvd., Ste. 7   Ph: (213)933-9228
Los Angeles, CA 90035   Fax: (213)933-9261
E-mail: seniorlife@aol.com.
URL: seniorlife.com.
Contact: Jerry Beigel, Editor; Estelle Beigel, Publisher.
Desc: Newspaper (tabloid) for people over the age of fifty. *Type:* Periodical.

Temple University

Institute on Aging

1601 N. Broad St.   Ph: (215)204-6834
Philadelphia, PA 19122   Fax: (215)204-6733
E-mail: v2226a@vm.temple.edu
URL: http://www.temple.edu/aging
Contact: Kathy Segrist, PhD, Exec.Dir.
Desc: Changes in adaptive capabilities during aging, anti-aging effects of dehydroepiandrosterone (DHEA), the influences of characteristics of elderly disabled clients on their experiences in case management, minority/ethnic aging research, and service management and services to the frail elderly. *Type:* Research center.

ThirdAge

ThirdAge Media, Inc.
585 Howard St., First Fl.
San Francisco, CA 94105-3001
E-mail: feedback@thirdage.com
URL: http://www.thirdage.com/
Desc: Who said getting older was a drag? You'd have a hard time convincing the folks who operate this Web site. They see our later years, particularly when the kids have all flown the coop, as some of the most rewarding and challenging years of our lives. *Type:* Database.

United Seniors Association

3900 Jermantown Rd., Ste. 450   Ph: (703)359-6500
Fairfax, VA 22030-4900   Free: 800-8US-AUSA
   Fax: (703)359-6510
E-mail: usasenior@aol.com
URL: http://www.unitedseniors.org
Contact: Sandra L. Butler, Pres.
Desc: Seeks to educate senior citizens about Social Security, Medicare and other related issues. *Type:* Association.

United Seniors Health Cooperative

409 Third St. SW, 2nd Fl.   Ph: (202)479-6973
Washington, DC 20024   Free: 800-637-2604
   Fax: (202)783-0588
E-mail: 110226.2523@compuserve.com
URL: http://www.ushc-online.org
Contact: Eric Shulman, Pres. & CEO.
Desc: The elderly, their families, and interested others. *Type:* Association.

U.S. Department of Health and Human Services

Administration on Aging

330 Independence Ave. SW   Ph: (202)401-4541
Washington, DC 20201   Fax: (202)619-3759
URL: http://www.aoa.dhhs.gov/
Contact: Jeanette C. Takamura, Contact.
Desc: The Administration on Aging is the principal federal organization for identifying the needs, concerns, and interests of older persons; for promoting coordination of federal resources available to meet the needs of older persons; and for carrying out the programs of the Older Americans Act. Under this Act, AOA administers a program of formula grants to state agencies on aging to serve as advocates for the elderly and to assist in the establishment of comprehensive, coordinated service systems for older persons at the community level. *Type:* Government agency, office, or program.

U.S. Department of Health and Human Services

Administration on Aging

Office of Program Development

330 Independence Ave., S.W.   Ph: (202)619-3032
Washington, DC 20201   Fax: (202)260-1012
E-mail: aduncker@ban-gate.aoa.hhs.gov
Contact: Judy Satine, Dir.
Desc: Supports programs and activities which enhance the capacity of state, local and tribal governments and non-profit private agencies, organizations and institutions to develop and improve the quality and effectiveness of services and activities for older individuals. Meets its purposes through support of education and training, research and policy analysis, development of methods and practices, demonstrations, technical assistance and information dissemination activities. *Type:* Research center.

U.S. Department of Health and Human Services

National Institute on Aging

Public Information Office   Ph: (301)496-1752
Bldg. 31., Rm. 5C27   Fax: (301)496-1072
31 Center Dr., MSC 2292
Bethesda, MD 20892-2292
URL: http://www.nih.gov/nia
Contact: Dr. Richard J. Hodes, Dir.
Desc: Biomedical, social, and behavioral aspects of aging. The Intramural Research Program is primarily conducted at the Gerontology Research Center in Baltimore, MD. *Type:* Research center.

U.S. Department of Health and Human Services

National Institute on Aging

Behavioral and Social Research Program

Gateway Bldg., Rm 533   Ph: (301)496-3136
7201 Wisconsin Ave.   Fax: (301)402-0051
MSC 9205
Bethesda, MD 20892-9205
E-mail: BSRQUERY@
URL: http://www.nih.gov/nia/bsr/bsr.htm
Contact: Dr. Richard M. Suzman, Assoc.Dir.
Desc: Social, psychological, cultural, demographic, and economic factors that affect both the process of growing old and the place of older people in society, as well as the ways in which behavioral and social processes interacting with biomedical processes influence particular aspects of health and functioning as people age. Its goals are to prolong the productive, healthy, middle years of life and to prevent or reverse such decrements of old age as memory loss, chronic ill health, sensory deficits, low self-esteem, and withdrawal from active participation in social and economic roles. *Type:* Research center.

U.S. Department of Health and Human Services

National Institute on Aging

Biology of Aging Program

Biology Branch

Gateway Bldg., Ste. 2C231   Ph: (301)496-6402
7201 Wisconsin Ave., MSC   Fax: (301)402-0010
9205
Bethesda, MD 20892-9205
Contact: Francis L. Bellino, Actg.Dir.
Desc: Cellular aging research, which involves research using differentiated human cells in culture and the study of age-associated alterations in differentiated functions that are expressed by cells in vitro; fundamental molecular and genetics research and research training on the biology and mechanisms of aging at the cellular level and on vertebrate and invertebrate organisms, with particular interest in research that emphasizes the use of mammalian and human models; immunological research on the effects of aging on the various functions of the immune system; and research on age-related changes in endocrine function. *Type:* Research center.

U.S. Department of Health and Human Services
National Institute on Aging
Epidemiology, Demography, and Biometry Program
7201 Wisconsin Ave., Ste. 3C-309   Ph: (301)496-1178
Bethesda, MD 20892   Fax: (301)496-4006
URL: http://www.nih.gov/nia/edb
Contact: Richard J. Havlik, MD, Assoc.Dir.
Desc: Health and illness in older populations, including hip fractures and osteoporosis, dementia and other cognitive impairments, sleep disorders, predictive factors of mortality, bereavement behaviors, and events and conditions common among older persons prior to death. Gathers demographic information on the current and projected health, economic, social, and occupational status of older people. *Type:* Research center.

U.S. Department of Health and Human Services
National Institute on Aging
Geriatrics Program
7201 Wisconson Ave., St. 3E-327   Ph: (301)496-1033
Bethesda, MD 20892-9205   Fax: (301)402-1784
Contact: Dr. Evan Hadley, Chf.
Desc: Epidemiology, etiology, pathophysiology, diagnostic evaluation, and treatment of urinary incontinence in the elderly; studies on obesity, with particular interest in the effects of obesity on health and longevity, treatment of obesity, and contribution of overnutrition to aging of organ systems; research on infectious diseases in the elderly (cosponsored with the National Institute of Allergy and Infectious Diseases); studies on aspects of diabetes mellitus related to aging and the elderly and studies on the epidemiology of diabetes; and nutrition in relation to health of the aged and the aging process. Research also includes investigation of the function of the aging musculoskeletal system (including support for animal models or clinical studies in exercise physiology or orthopedic research); studies on enteral and parenteral nutritional support in elderly patients in acute and long-term care facilities (announced with five other institutes); research on the causes of age-related cardiovascular changes (and changes in risk factors for cardiovascular disease) and on the role of cardiovascular factors in age-related physiologic and pathologic changes; and studies on exercise physiology and aging. *Type:* Research center.

U.S. Department of Health and Human Services
National Institute on Aging
Intramural Research Program
Gerontology Research Center   Ph: (410)558-8114
5600 Nathan Shock Dr.   Fax: (410)558-8103
Baltimore, MD 21224
Contact: Dr. Dan L. Longo, Dir.
Desc: Process of aging in animals and man. Projects include the Baltimore Longitudinal Study of Aging, which involves the biennial observation of the same human subjects to determine changes and elucidate mechanisms underlying these changes. *Type:* Research center.

U.S. Department of Health and Human Services
National Institute on Aging
Intramural Research Program
Longitudinal Studies Section
Gerontology Research Center   Ph: (410)558-8364
5600 Nathan Shook Dr.   Fax: (410)558-8321
Baltimore, MD 21224
E-mail: jf72d@nih.gov
URL: http://www.grc.nia.nih.gov
Contact: Jerome L. Fleg, M.D., Interim Dir.
Desc: Longitudinal research on aging, particularly physiological and psychological aspects. *Type:* Research center.

U.S. Department of Health and Human Services
National Institute on Aging
Laboratory of Clinical Physiology
Gerontology Research Center   Ph: (410)558-8193
5600 Nathan Shock Dr.   Fax: (410)558-8113
Baltimore, MD 21224
Contact: Dr. Reubin Andres, Chf.
Desc: Physiologic changes occurring over the entire adult lifespan. The Laboratory comprises sections on Applied Physiology, Clinical Immunology, Endocrinology, and Metabolism. *Type:* Research center.

U.S. Department of Health and Human Services
National Institute on Aging
Laboratory of Personality and Cognition
Gerontology Research Center   Ph: (410)558-8216
5600 Nathan Shock Dr.   Fax: (410)558-8108
Baltimore, MD 21224
E-mail: ptc@nih.gov
URL: http://lpcwww.grc.nia.nih.gov/
Contact: Dr. Paul T. Costa, Chf.
Desc: Individual differences in cognitive and personality processes and traits. Also investigated are the influence of age on these variables and their reciprocal influence on health, well-being, and adaptation. *Type:* Research center.

U.S. Department of Health and Human Services
National Institute on Aging
Nathan W. Shock Laboratory
5600 Nathan-Shock Dr.   Ph: (410)558-8114
Baltimore, MD 21224   Fax: (410)558-8273
Contact: Dr. Edward Takatta, Actg.Sci.Dir.
Desc: Aging process. Analyzes changes in the capacities of aging individuals; and determines possible ways to prevent, slow down or compensate for loss of function associated with aging. *Type:* Research center.

U.S. Department of Health and Human Services
National Institute on Aging
Office of Extramural Affairs
Gateway Bldg. 2C218   Ph: (301)496-9373
7201 Wisconsin Ave.   Fax: (301)402-2945
Bethesda, MD 20892-9205
E-mail: mk46u@nih.gov
URL: http://www.nih.gov
Contact: Dr. Miriam F. Kelty, Assoc.Dir.
Desc: Administers the funding programs through which NIA supports research and research training. Specific NIA funding mechanisms include: Research Project Grants; Research Program Project Grants; Research Career Development Awards; Clinical Investigator Awards; Academic Awards; Special Emphasis Research Career Awards; National Research Service Awards; Physician Scientist Awards; Geriatric Leadership Academic Awards; Small Business Innovative Research Program; and Academic Research Enhancement Awards. *Type:* Research center.

U.S. Department of Health and Human Services
National Institutes of Health
National Institute on Aging
9000 Rockville Pike   Ph: (301)496-1752
Bethesda, MD 20892
URL: http://www.nih.gov/nia/
Contact: Richard J. Hodes, MD, Director.
Desc: The Institute conducts and supports biomedical and behavioral research to increase the knowledge of the aging process and associated physical, psychological, and social factors resulting from advanced age. Incontinence, menopause, susceptibility to diseases, and memory loss are among the areas of special concern. *Type:* Government agency, office, or program.

University of Akron
Institute for Life-Span Development and Gerontology
179 Simmons Hall   Ph: (330)972-7243
Akron, OH 44325-4307 Fax: (330)972-5174
E-mail: sterns%psychology%uakron@banyan.uakron.edu
URL: http://www.uakron.ilsdg.edu
Contact: Dr. Harvey L. Sterns, Dir.
Desc: Improving older adult cognitive functioning, aging and work, mental retardation and aging, training and retraining adult older workers, gender identity, human development, health and aging, and family and aging. Programs concentrate on aging changes in perception, perceptual style, selective attention, and learning and memory. *Type:* Research center.

University of Alabama at Birmingham
Center for Aging
201 Community Health Services Bldg.   Ph: (205)934-9261
                                        Fax: (205)934-7354
933 S. 19th St., Ste. 201
Birmingham, AL 35294-2041
E-mail: rallman@uab.edu
URL: http://www.aging.uab.edu
Contact: Richard M. Allman, MD, Dir.
Desc: Primary research areas include immobility and its complications, urinary incontinence, and the social-behavioral aspects of Alzheimer's disease. Collaborative research is conducted in the areas of atherosclerosis, muscoskeletal disease, and age-related cancer. *Type:* Research center.

University of Calgary
Vision and Aging Laboratory
Department of Psychology   Ph: (403)220-3600
Admin. 237   Fax: (403)282-8249
2500 University Dr. NW
Calgary, AB, Canada T2N 1N4
E-mail: donkline@.ucalgary.ca
URL: http://136.159.214.66
Contact: Prof. Donald Kline, PhD, Dir.
Desc: Effects of aging on vision, optical and neural aspects of visual aging, visual human factors, refractive surgery, visual tasks, vision change and quality-of-life, visual testing. *Type:* Research center.

University of California, Los Angeles
Alzheimer's Disease Center
Los Angeles, CA 90095-1769   Ph: (310)206-5238
                              Fax: (310)206-5287
E-mail: ccliff@ucla.edu
URL: http://neurology.medsch.ucla.edu/alzheime.htm
Contact: Jeffrey L. Cummings, MD, Dir.
Desc: Diagnosis, pathophysiology, and treatment of dementing illnesses, such as Alzheimer's disease. *Type:* Research center.

University of California, Los Angeles
Harbor-UCLA Medical Center
Center for Research on Aging Project
Department of Psychiatry, Box 498   Ph: (310)222-3137
                                      Fax: (310)328-5546
1000 W. Carson St.
Torrance, CA 90509
E-mail: ilesser@humc.edu
Contact: Ira Lesser, MD, Dir.
Desc: Neuroanatomic and neurophysiologic aspects of psychotic states of the elderly and ethnic differences in psychopharmacology in psychiatric patients. Conducts clinical evaluations of elderly psychiatric patients with neuroimaging techniques and performs comparisons of clinical course and blood levels of psychotropic drugs in Asian and Caucasian schizophrenic and depressed patients. *Type:* Research center.

University of California, San Diego

Sam and Rose Stein Institute for Research on Aging

0664 Sch. of Med.　　　　　Ph: (619)534-6299
9500 Gilman Dr.　　　　　　Fax: (619)534-5475
La Jolla, CA 92093-0664
E-mail: steininstitute@ucsd.edu

Contact: Dr. Dennis A. Carson, Dir.

Desc: Aging and Alzheimer's disease, arthritis, osteoporosis, cardiovascular disease, sleep disorders, genetics, and mind, body, and health relationships. Investigates the relationships between the deterioration of the central nervous system and speech, hearing, and sleep problems; studies the effects of aging on production of hormones; evaluates alternatives to nursing home confinement; investigates immune system deteriorations; and studies the genetic and biochemical basis for long and healthy lifespans and the genetic basis of human diseases of accelerated aging. *Type:* Research center.

University Center on Aging and Health Newsletter

University Center on Aging and Health
Case Western Reserve University
10900 Euclid Ave.　　　　　Ph: (216)368-2692
Cleveland, OH 44106-7131　　Fax: (216)368-6389
E-mail: mlw4@po.cwru.edu

Contact: May L. Wykle, Ph.D., Editor.

Desc: Contains descriptions of current research activities of gerontologists at the University and in the Northeast Ohio region. Features news items, articles, and a calendar of events and conferences. *Type:* Newsletter.

University of Florida

Center for the Neurobiology of Aging

Box 100 487　　　　　　　Fax: (352)392-6394
Hillis Miller Health Ctr.
Gainesville, FL 32610
E-mail: simpkins@cop.health.ufl.edu

Contact: Edwin M. Meyer, PhD, Co-Dir.

Desc: Alzheimer's disease studies, including evaluation of gene expression in Alzheimer's patients and evaluation of complex behaviors, especially memory. *Type:* Research center.

University of Illinois at Chicago

Rehabilitation Research and Training Center on Aging with Mental Retardation

Institute on Disability and　　Ph: (312)413-1520
　Human Development　　　Fax: (312)996-6942
1640 W. Roosevelt Rd.
Chicago, IL 60608-6904
URL: http://www.uic.edu/orgs/rrtcamr/index.html

Contact: Tamar Heller, PhD, Dir.

Desc: Older adults with mental retardation, especially increasing empowerment and self-advocacy through training in person-centered later life planning and leadership skills; understanding how age related changes affect medical and psychosocial well-being; developing service models for the needs of families from diverse cultures; enhancing coping techniques for changing capabilities through in-home interventions and assistive technologies; supporting individuals through life transitions including the death or incapacity of the caregiver; and expanding retirement, financial, health, and independent living options. *Type:* Research center.

University of Kansas

Center on Aging

Kansas Univ. Med. Ctr.　　Ph: (913)588-1265
3901 Rainbow Blvd.　　　　Fax: (913)588-1201
Kansas City, KS 66160-7117
E-mail: sstudens@kumc.edu

URL: http://www2.kumc.edu

Contact: Stephanie A. Studenski, MD, Dir.

Desc: Provides support for interdisciplinary research on issues of age and aging. *Type:* Research center.

University of Kentucky

Sanders-Brown Center on Aging

101 Sanders-Brown Bldg.　　Ph: (606)323-6040
Lexington, KY 40536-0230　　Fax: (606)323-2866

Contact: William R. Markesbery, MD, Dir.

Desc: Biology of aging, including studies on aging nervous systems, Alzheimer's disease, stroke, hypertension in the elderly, immunology, geriatrics, and social-behavioral science. *Type:* Research center.

University of Maryland

Center for the Study of Pharmacy and Therapeutics for the Elderly

Sch. of Pharmacy　　　　　Ph: (410)706-3011
20 N. Pine St.　　　　　　Fax: (410)706-5394
Baltimore, MD 21201-1180

Contact: Bruce C. Stuart, PhD, Dir.

Desc: Geriatrics and gerontology, focusing on drug use in the elderly and the development of artificial intelligence programs in support of optimal drug use. Also responsible for three elder care programs, the Parke-Davis Center for the Education of the Elderly, the Elder-Health Program, and the Maryland Caregiver Program. *Type:* Research center.

University of Maryland

Division of Infectious Diseases

Med. Sch. Teaching Facility　Ph: (410)706-7560
10 S. Pine St., Rm. 900　　Fax: (410)706-8700
Baltimore, MD 21201

Contact: John W. Warren, MD, Hd.

Desc: Infections in the elderly, including infection from urinary catheterization, epidemiology of nursing home patients, tests of antimicrobial agents, and pharmacokinetics and microbiology using animal models and clinical techniques. *Type:* Research center.

University of Miami

Center on Aging and Developmental Disabilities

1400 NW 10th Ave., Ste. 601　Ph: (305)243-6597
　(D305)　　　　　　　　Fax: (305)243-4804
Miami, FL 33136
E-mail: pbloom@mednet.med.miami.edu

Contact: Patricia Bloom, Dir.

Desc: Future planning needs of older parent caregivers of adults with developmental disabilities and the professionals who serve them. *Type:* Research center.

University of Michigan

Institute of Gerontology

300 N. Ingalls　　　　　　Ph: (734)764-3493
Ann Arbor, MI 48109-2007　Fax: (734)936-2116
E-mail: richard.c.adelman@uh.cc.uhich.edu

Contact: John A. Faulkner, PhD, Interim Dir.

Desc: Gerontological research studies in the behavioral, biological, clinical, and social sciences and the humanities. *Type:* Research center.

University of Michigan

Michigan Alzheimer's Disease Research Center

Department of Neurology　　Ph: (734)764-2190
300 NIB, Rm. 3C23 Box 0489　Fax: (734)936-8967
Ann Arbor, MI 48109-0489
E-mail: sgilman@umich.edu
URL: http://www.med.umich.edu/madrc/madrc.html

Contact: Sid Gilman, MD, Ch.

Desc: Alzheimer's disease and other neurodegenerative diseases associated with dementia, including Parkinson's disease, multiple system atrophy, progressive supranuclear palsy, and olivopontocerebellar atrophy. Studies involve positron emission tomography (PET) scanning of patients with neurological disorders, neuropathological studies of patients with neurodegenerative illnesses, animal models, and a statewide public opinion survey on Alzheimer's disease. *Type:* Research center.

University of Montreal

Geriatrics Institute Research Centre

4565, chemin de la Reine-Marie　Ph: (514)340-3540
Montreal, PQ, Canada H3W　Fax: (514)340-3548
　1W5

Contact: Yves Joanette, Dir.

Desc: Gerontology and geriatrics, including neuropsychology, neurolinguistics, and electrophysiology of normal and pathological aging; nutrition and epidemiology of illness in old age; and genetics, pathology, and epidemiology of Alzheimer's disease. *Type:* Research center.

University of North Texas Health Science Center at Fort Worth

Geriatrics Education and Research Institute

3500 Camp Bowie Blvd.　　Ph: (817)735-5440
Fort Worth, TX 76107-2699　Fax: (817)735-2486
E-mail: tfairchi@hsc.unt.edu
URL: http://www.hsc.unt.edu/research/aging.htm

Contact: Thomas J. Fairchild, PhD, Dir.

Desc: Biology of aging, including fundamental chemical and molecular biological changes that may cause aging; health promotion in older adults including health programs promoting physical, psychological, and social well being; geriatric care and practice including evaluation of new clinical programs, physical/mental functions, long term care system development focusing on case management, and in-home health screen/assessment of homebound elderly. *Type:* Research center.

University of Pennsylvania

Institute on Aging

3615 Chestnut St.　　　　　Ph: (215)898-3163
Philadelphia, PA 19104-6006　Fax: (215)573-8684
E-mail: lavimour@mail.med.upenn
URL: http://www.med.upenn.edu/~aging

Contact: Risa Lavizzo-Mourey, MD, Dir.

Desc: Biomedical and social science research on aging, including cellular mechanisms of aging, Alzheimer's disease, sleep disturbances, arthritis, osteoporosis, population demographics of aging, nursing home quality, organization and structure of life care communities, social security, and social support systems for the aged. *Type:* Research center.

University of Quebec at Trois-Rivieres

Departmental Laboratory on Gerontology

CP 500　　　　　　　　　Ph: (819)376-5085
Trois-Rivieres, PQ, Canada G9A　Fax: (819)376-5195
　5H7
E-mail: sylvie_lapierre@uqtr.uquebec.ca
URL: http://www.uqtr.uquebec.ca/psycho/gerontologie/

Contact: Sylvie Lapierre, Dir.

Desc: Gerontology and the elderly, including personal goals, suicidal ideas and behavior, self-actualization and well-being, grief and bereavement, and prevention of osteoporosis. *Type:* Research center.

University of Virginia

Center on Aging and Health

170 Rugby Rd.　　　　　　Ph: (804)979-9943
Charlottesville, VA 22903
E-mail: iabraham@uva.pcmail.virginia.edu

Contact: Ivo Abraham, PhD, Dir.

Desc: Aging, health, and quality of life of the elderly, focusing on health care needs of the elderly, causes and treatments of late life diseases, and the organization and delivery of specialized services. *Type:* Research center.

University of Western Ontario
Dementia Study Group
Univ. Hospital   Ph: (519)663-3035
London, ON, Canada N6A 5C1

Contact: Harold Merskey, Dir.

Desc: Clinical, pathological, and neurochemical analyses of normal aging in the human nervous system and in organic senile dementias, especially Alzheimer's disease. Clinical trials. *Type:* Research center.

USDA Human Nutrition Research Center on Aging
Tufts Univ.   Ph: (617)556-3330
711 Washington St.   Fax: (617)556-3295
Boston, MA 02111

Contact: Irwin H. Rosenberg, MD, Dir.

Desc: Investigates the relationship of nutrition to aging, including research programs in nutrient metabolism, nutrient requirements, nutritional epidemiology, functional systems, and drug-nutrient interactions. *Type:* Research center.

VANTAGE
The Signature Group
200 N. Martingale Rd.   Ph: (847)605-4601
Schaumburg, IL 60173   Fax: (847)605-4595

Contact: Paul Misniak, Publisher; Joanie Davies, Associate Publisher, fax: (847)605-4595.

Desc: Magazine for active consumers over 55 years of age. *Type:* Periodical.

Veterans Affairs Medical Center (Birmingham, AL)
Research and Development Service
700 S. 19th St.   Ph: (205)933-8101
Birmingham, AL 35233   Fax: (205)933-4471
E-mail: blackburn@birmingham.va.gov

Contact: Dr. Warren D. Blackburn, Jr., Assoc.Ch. of Staff.

Desc: Cancer, gastroenterology, rheumatology and arthritis, neurology, and spinal cord injury, repair systems, cardiology, nephrology, pulmonary disease, endocrinology, informatics and health services research. *Type:* Research center.

Veterans Affairs Medical Center (Gainesville, FL)
Geriatric Research, Education and Clinical Center
GRECC, (182)   Ph: (352)374-6077
1601 Archer Rd.   Fax: (352)374-6142
Gainesville, FL 32608-1197
E-mail: dlowenth@pharmacology.ufl.edu
URL: http://www.med.ufl.edu/pharm/facdata/GRECC

Contact: Dr. David T. Lowenthal, MD,PhD, Dir.

Desc: Geropharmacology, including mechanisms of drug action, pharmacokinetics, therapeutic uses, drug abuse, polypharmacy and drug compliance as it applies to geriatric patients. Clinical research is conducted in the areas of exercise in the healthy, frail, and elderly, cardiovascular function, and cognitive disorders in the elderly. *Type:* Research center.

Virginia Commonwealth University
Virginia Center on Aging
Med. College of Virginia   Ph: (804)828-1525
    Campus   Fax: (804)828-7905
Richmond, VA 23298-0229
E-mail: ccoogle@gems.vcu.edu

Contact: Edward F. Ansello, PhD, Dir.

Desc: Mental and physical health of the elderly, focusing on community-living and health-related factors of aging. Studies include: eldercare responsibilities of employed family caregivers, staffing requirements in residential care facilities, impact of aging of adults with developmental disabilities, minority healthcare utilization, caregiving of demented elders, research and documentation project on rural geropharmacy. *Type:* Research center.

Washington University in St. Louis
Alzheimer's Disease Research Center
4488 Forest Park Ave., Ste. 130   Ph: (314)286-2881
St. Louis, MO 63108   Fax: (314)286-2763
E-mail: adrcdir@neuro.wustl.edu
URL: http://www.adrc.wustl.edu/adrc

Contact: Eugene M. Johnson, PhD, Dir.

Desc: Aging and dementia, neurobiology of aging and cognition, Alzheimer's disease and related disorders, and the impact of dementia on the family or caregiver and the community. Studies include clinical research, clinical drug trials, neuropathological (autopsy) studies, genetic and other medical studies of persons with dementia, bench studies, behavioral/social research, and psychometric studies. *Type:* Research center.

Western Area Agency on Aging
465 Main St.   Ph: (207)795-4010
PO Box 659   Fax: (207)795-4009
Lewiston, ME 04243-0659

Contact: Eloise L. Moreau, Exec.Dir.

Desc: Provides services for the elderly. *Type:* Association.

Yeshiva University
Resnick Gerontology Center
Albert Einstein College of Med.   Ph: (718)430-3832
Bldg. R, Rm. 343   Fax: (718)430-3870
1300 Morris Park Ave.
Bronx, NY 10461
E-mail: crystal@aecom.yu.edu

Contact: Dr. Howard Crystal, Dir.

Desc: Alzheimer's disease and other dementia. Conducts the Bronx Aging Study, a ten-year longitudinal study of the Bronx elderly. *Type:* Research center.

Agriculture

Ag Executive
Ag Executive, Inc.
PO Box 180   Ph: (309)772-2166
Bushnell, IL 61422   Fax: (309)772-2167

Contact: Darrell L. Dunteman, Editor, darrellld@aol.com.

Desc: Focuses on financial, personnel, and risk management issues for commercial agriculture. Covers business analysis and practical management ideas for improving profitability. *Type:* Newsletter.

AgFocus
Cornell Cooperative Extension of Orange County
Community Campus   Ph: (914)344-1234
1 Ashley Ave.   Fax: (914)343-7471
Middletown, NY 10940

Contact: J. Sharon McCormick, Editor, jm115@cce.cornell.edu.

Desc: Furnishes information on Orange County's dairy, vegetable, horticulture, fruit, and livestock farms. Recurring features include a calendar of events, reports of meetings, news of educational opportunities, notices of publications available, and columns titled Focus on the Past, Focus on Home Living, DHI Tables, SCS News, Dairy Princess, and Farm Services News. *Type:* Newsletter.

AgraNews
3512 Porter St. NW   Ph: (202)363-1431
Washington, DC 20016   Fax: (202)363-1431

Desc: Distributes agricultural features. *Alt. Contact:* 3512 Porter St. NW, Washington, DC 20016; telephone: (202)363-1431; fax: (202)363-1431. *Type:* Periodical.

Agrarian Advocate
Community Alliance with Family Farmers
PO Box 363   Ph: (530)756-8518
Davis, CA 95617   Fax: (530)756-7857
E-mail: caff@caff.org
URL: http://www.caff.org; http://www.caff.org.

Contact: Karen Van Epen, Editor; Jill Klein, Associate Editor.

Desc: Educates on issues such as sustainable farming practices, the economic viability of family farming, and protection of farmland and water resources. Recurring features include reports on activities of CAFF, legislative updates, and book reviews. *Type:* Newsletter.

Agri-Food Research in Ontario
Ontario Ministry of Agriculture, Food and Rural Affairs
1 Stone Rd. W.   Ph: (519)826-4191
Guelph, ON, Canada N1G 4Y2   Free: 888-466-2372
    Fax: (519)826-4211
E-mail: research@omafra.gov.on.ca
URL: http://www.gov.on.ca/omafra/english/research/index.html; http://www.gov.on.ca/omafra.

Contact: Robyn Meerveld, Editor.

Desc: Provides information about agriculture research in Ontario, Canada. Recurring features include news of research. *Type:* Newsletter.

Agri Marketing—Farm Show Issue
Doane Agricultural Services
11701 Borman Dr., Ste. 100   Ph: (314)569-2700
St. Louis, MO 63146-4199   Fax: (314)569-1083
E-mail: agrimarketing@doane.com

Contact: Stephanie Wobbe, Editor, swobbe@primary.net; Keith Roberts, Editor, kroberts@primary.net.

Desc: List of about 200 agricultural trade shows, expositions, and fairs; coverage limited to the United States and Canada. *Type:* Directory.

Agri Marketing—Marketing Services Guide Issue
Doane Agricultural Services
11701 Borman Dr., Ste. 100   Ph: (314)569-2700
St. Louis, MO 63146-4199   Fax: (314)569-1083
E-mail: agrimarketing@doane.com

Contact: Bill Schuermann, Publisher; Stephanie Ohler-Wobbe, Editor; Keith Roberts, Editor.

Desc: Lists of top agricultural companies in the United States, leading agricultural advertisers (for past five years), marketing services firms (including public relations, photography, editorial, art and graphics, audiovisual, marketing research, marketing consultants), and United States and Canadian radio and television broadcasting stations, advertising and public relations agencies, network programming, and publications. Agriculture-related associations are included. *Type:* Directory.

Agri Marketing—The Top 50: Ag's Biggest Agencies Issue
Doane Agricultural Services
11701 Borman Dr., Ste. 100   Ph: (314)569-2700
St. Louis, MO 63146-4199   Fax: (314)569-1083
E-mail: agrimarketing@doane.com

Contact: Bill Schuermann, Publisher; Keith Roberts, News Editor; Stephanie Ohler-Wobbe, Editor.

Desc: List of the top 50 U.S. and Canadian advertising agencies and public relations firms, chosen on the basis of agricultural business income. *Type:* Directory.

Agri-News

Iowa Agricultural Statistics
833 Federal Bldg.   Ph: (515)284-4340
210 Walnut St.   Free: 800-772-0825
Des Moines, IA 50309-2103   Fax: (515)284-4342
E-mail: nass-ia@nass.usda.gov; nass-ia@nass.usda.gov.
URL: http://www.nass.udsa.gov/ia.
Contact: James K. Sands, Editor.
Desc: Features major crop, livestock, and price reports of concern to Iowa producers, including acreage, production, stocks, supply and demand, cattle, hogs, milk, poultry, and slaughter. Includes prices of various farm products. *Type:* Newsletter.

Agri-Plastics Report

American Society for Plasticulture
526 Brittany Dr.   Ph: (814)238-7045
State College, PA 16803-1420   Fax: (814)238-7051
E-mail: peh4@psu.edu; peh4@psu.edu.
Contact: Patricia E. Heuser, Editor.
Desc: Carries news of technical developments in the agricultural plastics industry and furthers the Association's goal to advance agriculture through the use of plastics. Reports on current research in the field as well as on the Association's educational program. *Type:* Newsletter.

Agri-Voice Network

Tribune Radio Networks
435 N. Michigan Ave.   Ph: (312)222-3342
Chicago, IL 60611   Fax: (312)222-4876
Contact: John Beebe, Agricultural Sales Mgr.
Desc: Agriculture and sports format. *Alt. Contact:* Tribune Radio Networks 435 N. Michigan Ave., Chicago, IL 60611; telephone: (312)222-3342; fax: (312)222-4876. *Type:* Periodical.

AgriAmerica Network

401 Pennsylvania Pkwy.   Ph: (317)848-4404
No. 300   Fax: (317)844-1243
Indianapolis, IN 46280
Contact: Gary Truitt, General Mgr.; Stacie Kiesle, Affiliate Relations; Darrin Johnston, Farm Dir.
Desc: Format comprises agricultural radio programming. *Alt. Contact:* 401 Pennsylvania Pkwy., No. 300, Indianapolis, IN 46280; telephone: (317)848-4404; fax: (317)844-1243. *Type:* Periodical.

AGRICOLA Database

U.S. National Agricultural Library
10301 Baltimore Ave., Rm. 013   Ph: (301)504-6813
Beltsville, MD 20705
E-mail: dgoldberg@nal.usda.gov
URL: http://www.ars.nal.usda.gov
Desc: Contains more than 3.3 million records from journal literature, government reports, serials, monographs, theses, patents, audiovisual resources, and technical reports in agriculture and related areas that have been acquired by the National Agricultural Library (NAL), as well as citations contributed by cooperating institutions. Covers agricultural economics and rural sociology, agricultural production, animal sciences, chemistry, entomology, food and human nutrition, forestry, natural resources, pesticides, plant science, soils and fertilizers, and water resources. *Available:* The Dialog Corporation, DIALOG; CompuServe Information Service, Knowledge Index; DIMDI (Deutsches Institut fuer Medizinische Dokumentation und Information); OCLC Online Computer Library Center, Inc., OCLC FirstSearch Catalog; OCLC Online Computer Library Center, Inc., OCLC EPIC; STN International; National Information Services Corporation (NISC), BiblioLine; Ovid Technologies, Inc. *Type:* Database.

Agricultural Division Newsletter

National Safety Council
1121 Spring Lake Dr.   Ph: (630)285-1121
Itasca, IL 60143-3201   Free: 800-539-7468
                                     Fax: (630)285-1315
URL: http://www.nsc.org; http://www.nsc.org.
Contact: Kathy Henderson, Editor.
Desc: Concerned with industrial and occupational safety in the agriculture industry. Focuses on safe work practices, conditions, precautions, and products. *Type:* Newsletter.

The Agricultural Law Letter

McLeod, Watkinson & Miller
One Massachusetts Ave. NW,   Ph: (202)842-2345
   Ste. 800   Fax: (202)408-7763
Washington, DC 20001
E-mail: aaci@erols.com.
Contact: Michael R. McLeod, Editor.
Desc: Highlights recent changes and developments in Agricultural Law and Legislation. Includes articles written by Agricultural Attorneys. *Type:* Newsletter.

Agricultural Letter

Federal Reserve Bank of Chicago
Public Affairs Department   Ph: (312)322-5111
230 S. LaSalle   Fax: (312)322-5515
Chicago, IL 60604
URL: http://www.frbchi.org.
Contact: Gary Benjamin, Editor.
Desc: Reports on agricultural developments in the nation and specifically in the seventh Federal Reserve district. Includes information on farmland values and examines selected agricultural economic indicators. *Type:* Newsletter.

Agricultural Libraries Information Notes

National Agricultural Library
U.S. Department of Agriculture (USDA)
10301 Baltimore Ave.   Ph: (301)504-6778
Beltsville, MD 20705-2351   Fax: (301)504-5472
URL: http://www.nal.usda.gov/alin/.
Contact: Joseph N. Swab, Editor, j.swab@nal.usda.gov.
Desc: Provides news of agricultural libraries and information centers. Features announcements of new publications, translations, bibliographies, and computerized services. *Type:* Newsletter.

Agriculture & Food

National Technical Information Service (NTIS)
U.S. Department of Commerce
5285 Port Royal Rd.   Ph: (703)605-6000
Springfield, VA 22161-0001   Free: 800-553-NTIS
                                     Fax: (703)605-6900
E-mail: orders@ntis.fedworld.gov
Desc: Publishes abstracts of reports on agricultural chemistry, agricultural equipment, facilities, and operations. Also covers agronomy, horticulture, and plant pathology; fisheries and aquaculture; animal husbandry and veterinary medicine; and food technology. *Type:* Newsletter.

Agriculture Newsletter Service—Weekly Outlook

University of Illinois
ACES Newsletter Service
69 Mumford Hall   Ph: (217)244-5166
1301 W. Gregory Dr.
Urbana, IL 61801
Contact: Darrel Good, Editor.
Desc: "Anticipates reports and interprets current market information," specifically, supply, demand, and price outlook for agricultural products. Remarks: Computer Purdue University. *Type:* Newsletter.

Agrinet Farm Radio Network

179 Lovers Lane   Ph: (919)335-7294
Ste. A
Elizabeth City, NC 27909
Contact: Bill Ray, Farm Dir.; Scott Fortenberry, Chief Engineer.
Desc: Format comprises news, weather, and short national and international events. *Alt. Contact:* 179 Lovers Lane, Ste. A, Elizabeth City, NC 27909; telephone: (919)335-7294. *Type:* Periodical.

Agroforestry Abstracts

CAB International
CABI Publishing
10 E. 40th St., Ste. 3203   Ph: (212)481-7018
New York, NY 10016
E-mail: cabi-nao@cabi.org
URL: http://www.cabi.org
Contact: Sue Hill, Product Manager, Crop Production and Natural Resources, s.hill@cabi.org.
Desc: Contains citations, with abstracts, to current periodical and other published literature relating to agroforestry. Corresponds to Agroforestry Abstracts and in part to the online CAB ABSTRACTS database and CAB ABSTRACTS on CD-ROM and the TREECD CD-ROM product. *Type:* Database.

Alberta Agrologist

Serecon
600 1st Edmonton Pl.   Ph: (403)448-7440
10665 Jasper Ave.   Fax: (403)421-1270
Edmonton, AB, Canada T5S
   3S9
E-mail: P.Ag.@aia.ab.ca.
Contact: Robert Burden, P.Ag., Editor; Cheryl Elder, Editor.
Desc: Provides news of events, nominations for the council and for awards, professional development seminars, and activities of the organization. Recurring features include letters to the editor, news of research, a calendar of events, reports of meetings, news of educational opportunities, job listings, and notices of publications available. *Type:* Newsletter.

Alberta Farm & Ranch Magazine

North Hill News Inc.
4000-19th St. NE   Ph: (403)250-6633
Calgary, AB, Canada T2E 6P8   Fax: (403)291-0502
Contact: Mike Steele, Editor; Dennis McCormack, Publisher; Ron Bergen, Advertising Mgr.
Type: Periodical.

Alfa News

ALFA/Alabama Farmers Federation
PO Box 11000   Ph: (334)288-3900
Montgomery, AL 36191-0001   Fax: (334)284-3957
Contact: Mark A. Morrison, Editor; Ronnie McKinney, Advertising Mgr., (334)263-6050, fax: (334)263-5933.
Desc: Fitness magazine with articles on diet and exercise. *Type:* Periodical.

Alpha Gamma Rho

10101 N. Executive Hills Blvd.   Ph: (816)891-9200
Kansas City, MO 64153
Contact: Philip Josephson, Exec.Dir.
Desc: Professional fraternity - agriculture. Conducts career development programs and individual chapter retreats and sessions. Compiles statistics. *Type:* Association.

Alpha Tau Alpha

Dr. Robert A. Martin
201 Curtiss Hall   Ph: (515)294-0896
Iowa State University   Fax: (515)294-0530
Ames, IA 50011

Contact: Dr. Robert A. Martin, Exec. Officer.

Desc: Honorary fraternity - agricultural education. *Type:* Association.

Alpha Zeta

PO Box 410260   Ph: (314)576-7730
St. Louis, MO 63141-0260   Free: 800-225-3629
                                    Fax: (314)576-7989

E-mail: info@alphazeta.org
URL: http://www.alphazeta.org

Contact: Steven C. Drake, Pres.

Desc: Honorary service and professional fraternity - agriculture. Maintains Alpha Zeta Foundation and National AZ Foundation of America, which provide scholarships, internships, and leadership and personal development conferences for students in agriculture. Maintains biographical archives. *Type:* Association.

Alternative Agriculture News

Henry A. Wallace Institute for Alternative Agriculture
9200 Edmonston Rd., Ste. 117   Ph: (301)441-8777
Greenbelt, MD 20770-1551   Fax: (301)220-0164
E-mail: hawiaa@access.digex.net; http://www.hawiaa.org.

Contact: Garth Youngberg, Editor.

Desc: Reports on scientific, legislative, and other developments involving alternative agriculture. Includes reports on activities of other organizations and actions taken by Congress and other federal agencies. *Type:* Newsletter.

American Ag Network

Box 1197   Ph: (605)224-9911
Pierre, SD 57501   Fax: (605)224-8984

Alt. Contact: Box 1197, Pierre, SD 57501; telephone: (605)224-9911; fax: (605)224-8984. *Type:* Periodical.

American Agri-Women Resource Center

Gail McPherson
251 E. Maple Lawn Rd.   Ph: (717)382-4878
New Park, PA 17352-9436   Fax: (717)382-4879
E-mail: maplelawn@cyberia.com
URL: http://www.americanagriwomen.com

Contact: Gail McPherson, Pres.

Desc: Farm women concerned with the advancement of agricultural production within the free enterprise system. Objectives are: to formulate and disseminate educational materials which accurately represent agripolitan America for use by teachers and the public; to initiate and promote educational program to advance the interests and welfare of agriculture. Provides training for women in leadership, public relations, and communications. *Type:* Association.

American Farmland Trust

1200 18th St. NW 800   Ph: (202)331-7300
Washington, DC 20036
URL: http://www.farmland.org

Contact: Ralph E. Grossi, Pres.

Desc: Dedicated to stopping the loss of productive farmland and promoting farming practices which lead to a healthy environment. Disseminates information on safeguarding farmlands, through conservation easements and other voluntary conservation programs. Encourages and assists policy makers to revise federal, state, and local policies on farmland preservation. *Type:* Association.

American Feed Industry Association

1501 Wilson Blvd., Ste. 1100   Ph: (703)524-0810
Arlington, VA 22209   Fax: (703)524-1921
E-mail: afia@afia.org
URL: http://www.afia.org

Contact: David A. Bossman, Pres.

Desc: Manufacturers of formula feed and pet food; suppliers to feed manufacturers; othher trade related associations. Compiles statistics. Maintains Equipment Manufacturing Council. *Type:* Association.

American Seed Trade Association

601 13th St. NW, Ste. 570 S.   Ph: (202)638-3128
Washington, DC 20005-3807   Free: 888-890-7333
                                    Fax: (202)638-3171

E-mail: durmston@ix.netcom.com
URL: http://www.amseed.com

Contact: Dean Urmston, Exec.VP.

Desc: Breeders, growers, assemblers, conditioners, wholesalers, and retailers of grain, grass, vegetable, flower, and other seed for planting purposes. *Type:* Association.

American Society of Agronomy

677 S. Segoe Rd.   Ph: (608)273-8080
Madison, WI 53711   Fax: (608)273-2021
URL: http://www.agronomy.org

Contact: Robert F. Barnes, Exec.VP.

Desc: Professional society of agronomists, plant breeders, physiologists, soil scientists, chemists, educators, technicians, and others concerned with crop production and soil management, and conditions affecting them. Sponsors fellowship program and student essay and speech contests. Provides placement service. *Type:* Association.

ANR Educator

Agricultural & Extension Education
Michigan State University
409 Agricultural Hall   Ph: (517)355-6580
East Lansing, MI 48824-1039   Fax: (517)353-4981
E-mail: anraee@msue.msu.edu; davisdia@pilot.msu.edu.

Contact: Kirk Heinze, Editor.

Desc: Covers issues in agriscience education. Recurring features include articles from instructors, a calendar of events, reports of meetings, and notices of workshops and audiovisual aids available. *Type:* Newsletter.

ARCLight

Agricultural Relations Council (ARC)
1629 K St. NW, Ste. 1100   Ph: (202)785-6710
Washington, DC 20006   Fax: (202)331-4212

Contact: Natalie Lutz, Editor.

Desc: Provides news of the Council and its members. Features public relations case studies. *Type:* Newsletter.

ARI Newsletter

Agricultural Research Institute (ARI)
236 Massachusetts Ave. NE   Ph: (202)544-5534
Washington, DC 20002   Fax: (202)544-5749
E-mail: ariherrett@aol.com

Contact: Richard A. Herrett, Editor.

Desc: Designed to keep members up-to-date on current work study panels, committees, and special task forces of the Institute. Provides a vehicle for exchange of professional information on agricultural research and related national policies and issues. *Type:* Newsletter.

Arizona Farm Bureau News

Arizona Farm Bureau Federation
3401 E. Elwood St.   Ph: (602)470-0088
Phoenix, AZ 85040-1625   Fax: (602)470-0178
Contact: Mike G. Shirra.

Desc: Covers the agricultural industry with an emphasis on Arizona. Specializes in issue specific and regulatory news. *Type:* Newsletter.

ASAC News

American Society of Agricultural Consultants (ASAC)
900 S. Cherry St., Ste. 508   Ph: (303)759-5091
Denver, CO 80246-2664   Fax: (303)758-0190
E-mail: asfmra@aol.com; asac@agrl-associations.org
Contact: Alan Yoder, Editor.

Desc: Focuses on the global economy, government decisions, and international trade of the agribusiness industry. Recurring features include news of members, news of research, and information on Society meetings and conferences. *Type:* Newsletter.

Association for Educating Agricultural Leaders

PO Box 20326   Ph: (334)288-0097
Montgomery, AL 36120-0326   Fax: (334)288-0097
Contact: Gordon Stone, Exec.VP.

Desc: Farmers and ranchers ages 18 to 40 involved in agricultural production. Seeks to encourage young farmers and to educate members on the latest production, management, and marketing techniques in farming. Promotes good urban-rural relations and provides information on agricultural issues affecting urban consumers. *Type:* Association.

Association of Farmworker Opportunity Programs

1611 N. Kent St., Ste. 910   Ph: (703)528-4141
Arlington, VA 22209-2111   Free: 800-543-AFOP
                                    Fax: (703)528-4145

E-mail: afop@afop.org
URL: http://www.afop.org
Contact: Lynda D. Mull, Exec.Dir.

Desc: Represents farmworker organizations in 49 states and Puerto Rico that operate employment, training, legalization, and related supportive service programs for migrant and seasonal farmworkers. Conducts research; issues policy statements and analyses on federal regulations and legislation affecting farmworkers. Provides consultation service; operates speakers' bureau; compiles statistics. *Type:* Association.

The Barley Grower

Western Barley Growers Association
2116 27th Ave. NE, Ste. 232   Ph: (403)291-3630
Calgary, AB, Canada T2E 7A6   Fax: (403)291-9841
Contact: Kathy Cooper, Editor.

Desc: Covers issues affecting barley growers in Canada, including government programs, economic developments, and marketing techniques. *Type:* Newsletter.

Bean Market News

Livestock and Seed Division
Agricultural Marketing Service
U.S. Department of Agriculture
711 O St.   Ph: (970)353-9750
Greeley, CO 80631
Contact: Brenda Shuklian, Editor.

Desc: Reviews California marketing trends for beans. Supplies statistics and analysis of sales for various types of beans. *Type:* Newsletter.

Biocontrol News and Information

CAB International
CABI Publishing
10 E. 40th St., Ste. 3203   Ph: (212)481-7018
New York, NY 10016
E-mail: cabi-nao@cabi.org
URL: http://www.cabi.org

Desc: Contains news items, review articles, and abstracts of journal articles related to agricultural entomology, plant pathology, weed science, and nematology. Corresponds to Biocontrol News and Information and in part to the on-line CAB ABSTRACTS and CAB PLANT PROTECTION databases and CAB ABSTRACTS on CD-ROM and the CABPESTCD product. *Type:* Database.

Biological & Agricultural Index

H.W. Wilson Company
950 University Ave.   Ph: (718)588-8400
Bronx, NY 10452
E-mail: custserv@hwwilson.com
URL: http://www.hwwilson.com
Contact: Technical Support Department., techmail@info. hwwilson.com.
Desc: Contains citations to articles, book reviews, reports of symposia and conferences, and selected letters to the editor in 258 English-language periodicals on biology and agriculture. Covers zoology, veterinary medicine, soil science, plant pathology, physiology, nutrition, microbiology, marine biology, limnology, genetics, cytology, horticulture, forestry, food science, entomology, environmental sciences, ecology, biology, biochemistry, botany, animal husbandry, agricultural research, agricultural engineering, agricultural economics, and agricultural chemicals. *Available:* Ovid Technologies, Inc.; OCLC Online Computer Library Center, Inc., OCLC EPIC; The Dialog Corporation, DIALOG; SilverPlatter Information, Inc.; H.W. Wilson Company, WilsonWeb. *Type:* Database.

Buckeye Farm News

Ohio Farm Bureau Federation
PO Box 479   Ph: (614)249-2483
Columbus, OH 43216   Fax: (614)249-2200
E-mail: glewis@ofbf.org'; lsnydedr@ofbf.org.
URL: http://www.ofbf.org.
Contact: Curt Dunham, Editor.
Desc: Official publication of Ohio Farm Bureau Federation. Magazine containing agricultural news. *Type:* Periodical.

The Byline

American Agricultural Editors Association
c/o Eddie Aldrete, Executive   Ph: (512)451-5000
   Secretary   Fax: (512)323-3503
4408-C Burnet Rd.
Austin, TX 78756-3319
E-mail: aaea@flash.net
Contact: Denise Clarke, Editor.
Desc: Presents news of interest to agricultural magazine editors. Recurring features include notices of job openings, reports from members, announcements of awards, Association news, and Professional Development. *Type:* Newsletter.

CAB ABSTRACTS

CAB International
CABI Publishing
10 E. 40th St., Ste. 3203
New York, NY 10016   Ph: (212)481-7018
E-mail: cabi-nao@cabi.org
URL: http://www.cabi.org
Contact: Chris Ison, ( )44 1491 832111, fax: ( )44 1491 829292, c.ison@cabi.org.
Desc: Contains more than 3 million citations, with abstracts, to worldwide literature in the agricultural sciences and related areas of applied biology. Covers crop production, protection, and postharvest technology; horticulture; soils and fertilizer technology; forestry and forest products; animal husbandry, nutrition, and breeding; dairy science and technology; animal health; agricultural engineering; agricultural biotechnology; agricultural economics; and rural development and sociology. *Available:* The Dialog Corporation, DataStar; The Dialog Corporation, DIALOG; DIMDI (Deutsches Institut fuer Medizinische Dokumentation und Information); CompuServe Information Service, Knowledge Index; STN International; Ovid Technologies, Inc.; European Information Network Services (EINS). *Type:* Database.

CAB ENGINEERING

CAB International
CABI Publishing
10 E. 40th St., Ste. 3203
New York, NY 10016   Ph: (212)481-7018
E-mail: cabi-nao@cabi.org
URL: http://www.cabi.org
Desc: Contains more than 52,000 citations, with abstracts, to current periodical and other published literature relating to agricultural engineering and allied topics. Corresponds to Agricultural Engineering Abstracts and in part to the online CAB ABSTRACTS database and the CAB ABSTRACTS on CD-ROM product. *Available:* DIMDI (Deutsches Institut fuer Medizinische Dokumentation und Information). *Type:* Database.

The Calavo News

Calavo Growers of California
PO Box 26081   Ph: (949)223-1111
Santa Ana, CA 92799-6081   Fax: (949)660-4232
Contact: James Wallace, Editor.
Desc: Contains news of avocado production, marketing, and the Calavo Growers of California. *Type:* Newsletter.

California Agri-Radio Network

1700 S. 1st Ave.   Free: 800-944-6077
Ste. 214   Fax: (520)782-1474
Yuma, AZ 85364
Contact: George G. Gatley, Pres./Dir.
Desc: Agricultural news format. *Alt. Contact:* 1700 S. 1st Ave., Ste. 214, Yuma, AZ 85364; fax: (520)782-1474; toll-free: 800-944-6077; Western Agri-Radio Networks. *Type:* Periodical.

California Agricultural Resource Directory

California Agricultural Statistics Service
U.S. Department of Agriculture (USDA)
PO Box 1258   Ph: (916)654-0895
Sacramento, CA 95812
Desc: Features information on California's agricultural commodities, principal crops, market value per acre, livestock and livestock prices, and cash farm receipts. List county agricultural commissioners. *Type:* Newsletter.

California Field Crop Review

California Agricultural Statistics Service
U.S. Department of Agriculture (USDA)
PO Box 1258   Ph: (916)654-0895
Sacramento, CA 95812
Desc: Reports on California's field production, prices, stocks, hired farm labor, and wage rates. *Type:* Newsletter.

California Grange News

California State Grange
2101 Stockton Blvd.   Ph: (916)454-5805
Sacramento, CA 95817   Fax: (916)739-8189
E-mail: grange@calweb.com.
URL: http://www.grange.org.
Contact: J.D. Hartz, Editor; John Felder, Publisher.
Desc: Features rural, agricultural, and fraternal news. *Type:* Newsletter.

California Grape Acreage

California Agricultural Statistics Service
U.S. Department of Agriculture (USDA)
PO Box 1258   Ph: (916)654-0895
Sacramento, CA 95812
Desc: Provides the current acreage statistics for the California grape industry. Covers new plantings, especially of premium varietals, and acreage increases in already established areas. *Type:* Newsletter.

Canada Agriculture

The WEFA Group
1110 Vermont Ave., NW   Ph: (202)775-0610
Washington, DC 20005
URL: http://www.fdic.gov
Desc: Contains quarterly historical regional and national agricultural data for Canada. Major catagories covered include crop acreage, yield, production, supply and disposition, and prices; livestock inventories, production and trade, including beef and pork supply and disposition, farm cash receipts, government program outlays, farm income, expenditures, and depreciation changes. *Available:* The WEFA Group. *Type:* Database.

Canadian Agriculture Forecast

The WEFA Group
1110 Vermont Ave., NW   Ph: (202)775-0610
Washington, DC 20005
URL: http://www.fdic.gov
Desc: Contains approximately 700 quarterly time series of historical and forecast data on a wide range of agricultural variables for Canada as a whole as well as for Eastern and Western Canada. Data are derived from Agriculture Canada, the Canadian Grain Commission, the Canadian Wheat Board, the Livestock Feed Board of Canada, and Statistics Canada. *Available:* The WEFA Group. *Type:* Database.

Canadian Federal Corporations and Directors

Infomart Dialog Limited
1450 Don Mills Rd.   Ph: (416)442-2198
Don Mills, ON, Canada M3B
   2X7
E-mail: helpdesk@infomart.ca
URL: http://www.infomart.com/
Contact: Client Services Consultants, (416)442-2198, fax: (416)442-2126, helpdesk@infomart.ca.
Desc: Contains descriptive and financial information on more than 225,000 federally incorporated Canadian companies. Includes company name, registered office mailing address, names of parent or subsidiary companies, reported revenues, assets, and earnings for the most recent 2 years, and the names and home addresses of corporate directors. *Available:* Infomart Online; Infomart Dialog Limited. *Type:* Database.

Canola Country

Saskatchewan Canola Growers Association
210-111 Research Dr.   Ph: (306)668-2380
Saskatoon, SK, Canada S7N   Fax: (306)975-1126
   3R2
E-mail: scga@innovplace.saskatoon.sk.ca
Contact: Holly Rask, Editor.
Desc: Provides information on the growing and marketing of canola. *Type:* Newsletter.

Canola Digest

Canola Council of Canada
400-167 Lombard Ave.   Ph: (204)982-2100
Winnipeg, MB, Canada R3B   Fax: (204)942-1841
   0T6
E-mail: admin@canada-council.org
URL: http://www.canola-council.org
Contact: Dave Wilkins, Manager of Information Services, wilkinsd@canola-council.org.
Desc: Provides information on canola and related interests. Recurring features include news of research, a calendar of events, reports of meetings, and news of educational opportunities. *Type:* Newsletter.

Capitol AgriBusiness

711 Hilsborough St.   Ph: (919)890-6046
Box 12800   Fax: (919)890-6213
Raleigh, NC 27605
Contact: George Habel, Vice President; Andy Roat, Sales Mgr.; Ken Tanner, Farm Ed.; Dan Wilkinson, Farm Dir.; Lisa Allen, Sales Rep.; Natalie Burgin, Sales Rep.
Desc: Agricultural format. *Alt. Contact:* 711 Hilsborough St., Box 12800, Raleigh, NC 27605; telephone: (919)890-6046; fax: (919)890-6213. *Type:* Periodical.

CARDreport

Center for Agricultural and Rural Development
Iowa State University   Ph: (515)294-6257
578 Heady Hall   Fax: (515)294-6336
Ames, IA 50011-1070
E-mail: card@card.iastate.edu
URL: http://www.card.iastate.edu.
Contact: Judith A. Pim, Manager, Communications and Information.
Desc: Includes articles on agricultural policy issues. Recurring features include news of research, notices of publications available, and columns titled From the Director. *Type:* Newsletter.

Center for Rural Affairs

PO Box 406   Ph: (402)846-5428
Walthill, NE 68067   Fax: (402)846-5420
E-mail: info@cfra.org
URL: http://www.cfra.org
Contact: Don Ralston, Adm.Dir.
Desc: Participants are farmers, ranchers, businesspersons, and educators concerned with the decline of the family farm. Purpose is to provoke public thought on social, economic, and environmental issues and government policies affecting rural America, especially the Midwest and Plains regions. Is dedicated to agricultural reform which will conserve human and natural resources, communities, and local farm ownership. *Type:* Association.

Center for Rural Affairs Newsletter

Center for Rural Affairs
PO Box 406   Ph: (402)846-5428
Walthill, NE 68067   Fax: (402)846-5420
E-mail: info@cfra.org; hn1721@handsnet.org.
Contact: Marie Powell, Editor, mariep@cfra.org.
Desc: Explores agricultural affairs at national and regional levels. Educates readers as to the issues facing family farms and rural communities, taking a "distinctly anti-corporate farming" attitude. *Type:* Newsletter.

Chautauqua County Agricultural News

Cornell Cooperative Extension Association of Chautauqua County
3542 Turner Rd., Ste. 1   Ph: (716)664-9502
Jamestown, NY 14701-9608   Fax: (716)664-6327
Contact: Andrew Dufresne, Editor.
Desc: Reports on agriculture and education in Chautauqua County, New York. *Type:* Newsletter.

CHEMNAME

The Dialog Corporation
DIALOG
11000 Regency Pkwy., Ste. 400   Ph: (919)462-8600
Cary, NC 27511
URL: http://www.dialog.com
Contact: Marketing.
Desc: Contains more than 9 million records covering chemical substances cited in Chemical Abstracts more than one time since 1967. Includes complete ring data for each substance, as well as additional search terms generated by DIALOG based on other chemical files. *Available:* The Dialog Corporation, DIALOG; The Dialog Corporation, DIALOG. *Type:* Database.

Co-op America

1612 K St. NW, Ste. 600   Ph: (202)872-5307
Washington, DC 20010   Free: 800-58-GREEN
   Fax: (202)331-8166
E-mail: info@coopamerica.org
URL: http://www.coopamerica.org
Contact: Elizabeth Elliott McGeveran, Mng.Dir.
Desc: Seeks to create a socially just and environmentally sustainable economy. *Type:* Association.

Colorado Hay Directory

Colorado Department of Agriculture
Markets Division
700 Kipling St., Ste. 4000   Ph: (303)239-4114
Lakewood, CO 80215-5894   Fax: (303)239-4125
Contact: Barbara High, Editor.
Desc: About 100 producers of hay in Colorado. *Type:* Directory.

Communicating for Agriculture

112 E. Lincoln Ave.   Ph: (218)739-3241
Fergus Falls, MN 56537   Free: 800-432-3276
   Fax: (218)739-3832
URL: http://www.cainc.org/
Contact: M. E. Smedsrud, Founder/Chmn. of the Bd.
Desc: Communicating for Agriculture, Inc. (CA) is a rural nonprofit group whose purpose is to promote the general health, well being and advancement of people in agriculture and agribusiness. CA is actively involved in federal and state issues that affect the quality of life in rural America and provides members with a variety of money-saving benefit programs. *Type:* Association.

Connecticut Weekly Agricultural Report

Connecticut Department of Agriculture
765 Asylum Ave.
Hartford, CT 06105
Desc: Provides agricultural news, pricing, and advertisements. *Type:* Newsletter.

Cornell Cooperative Extension of Allegany County—News & Views

Cornell Cooperative Extension Association of Allegany County
5435A County Rd., No. 48   Ph: (716)268-7644
Belmont, NY 14813
Contact: Paul W. Westfall, Editor.
Desc: Contains agriculture, home economics, and 4-H club news. Recurring features include news of research, a calendar of events, reports of meetings, and news of educational opportunities. *Type:* Newsletter.

Cotton Exchange News

New York Cotton Exchange
4 World Trade Center   Ph: (212)748-1000
New York, NY 10048
Contact: Ann P. Bruch, Editor.
Desc: Features information on the cotton industry. Recurring features include notices of publications available. *Type:* Newsletter.

CPM/Crop Protection Management

American Farm Network
197 W. 12th Ave.
Eugene, OR 97401-3408
URL: http://www.crop-net.com.
Contact: Jeff Powell, President/Publisher, jpowell@mpi-net.com.
Desc: Magazine covering crop information for large U.S. growers. *Type:* Periodical.

CRIS (Current Research Information System)

U.S. Department of Agriculture
Cooperative State Research, Education, and Extension
National Agricultural Library   Ph: (301)504-6846
   Bldg.
Beltsville, MD 20705
E-mail: cris@cris.nal.usda.gov
URL: http://cristel.nal.usda.gov:8080
Contact: Philip Dopkowski, Chief, Technical Products and Services, cris@cris.nalusda.gov.
Desc: Contains more than 52,000 descriptions of ongoing and completed research projects in agriculture, forestry, food and nutrition, biology, and related life sciences. Covers research sponsored or conducted by USDA research agencies, state land-grant institutions and agricultural experiment stations, state forestry and veterinary medicine schools, and other cooperating state institutions. *Available:* The Dialog Corporation, DIALOG. *Type:* Database.

Crop Advisory Team Alerts

Michigan State University Extension
c/o Joy N. Landis   Ph: (517)432-2203
IPM Programs   Fax: (517)353-4995
B18 Food Safety & Toxicology
East Lansing, MI 48824-1302
E-mail: catalert@msue.msu.edu.
URL: http://www.msue.msu.edu/ipm/aboutcat.htm.
Contact: Joy Neumann Landis.
Desc: Provides pest predictions and management recommendations in areas including vegetables, fruits, grains, ornamentals, turfgrass, and forestry. Supplies detailed maps and statistics. *Type:* Newsletter.

Crop Insurance Update

American Association of Crop Insurers
1 Massachusetts Ave. NW, Ste.   Ph: (202)789-4100
   800
Washington, DC 20001
Contact: Michael R. McLeod, Editor.
Desc: Highlights developments for agents in the multiple-peril crop insurance field. Monitors crop insurance legislation and reports on efforts to educate Congress on crop insurance issues. *Type:* Newsletter.

Crop Physiology Abstracts

CAB International
CABI Publishing
10 E. 40th St., Ste. 3203   Ph: (212)481-7018
New York, NY 10016
E-mail: cabi-nao@cabi.org
URL: http://www.cabi.org
Contact: Sue Hill, Product Manager, Crop Production and Natural Resources, s.hill@cabi.org.
Desc: Contains citations, with abstracts, to current periodical and other published literature related to the physiology of all higher plants of economic importance. Corresponds to Crop Physiology Abstracts and in part to the online CAB ABSTRACTS database and the CAB ABSTRACTS on CD-ROM product. *Type:* Database.

Crop Science Society of America

677 S. Segoe Rd.   Ph: (608)273-8086
Madison, WI 53711   Fax: (608)273-2021
E-mail: rbarnes@agronomy.org
URL: http://www.agronomy.org/asa.html
Contact: Robert F Barnes, Exec.VP.
Desc: Plant breeders, physiologists, ecologists, crop production specialists, seed technologists, turf grass specialists, and others interested in improvement, management, and use of field crops. Seeks to advance research, extension, and teaching of all basic and applied phases of the crop

sciences and to cooperate with all other organizations and societies similarly interested in the improvement, production, management, and utilization of field crops. Maintains numerous committees including Coordination of Resident Education Activities, Crop Registration, Crop Science Teaching Improvement, Crop Terminology, Intersociety Committee on Plant Terminology, and Preservation of Genetic Stocks; also supports various intersociety collaboration committees. *Type:* Association.

Crop Science—Soil Science—Agronomy News
American Society of Agronomy
677 S. Segoe Rd.   Ph: (608)273-8080
Madison, WI 53711   Fax: (608)273-2021
E-mail: general@agronomy.org
URL: http://www.soils.org
Contact: Jay Poster, Editor.
Desc: Publishes information on agronomy, crop science, soil science, and related topics. Provides news of the societies and members; reports of annual meetings; listings of publications; announcements of awards, retirements, and deaths; job listings; and a calendar of events. *Type:* Newsletter.

Crop Weather Report
California Agricultural Statistics Service
U.S. Department of Agriculture (USDA)
PO Box 1258   Ph: (916)654-0895
Sacramento, CA 95812
Desc: Reports on California's weather and how it affects livestock and fruit, nut, vegetable, and field crops. Features regional temperature and precipitation. *Type:* Newsletter.

Current Marketing
National Food & Energy Council, Inc.
601 Business Loop 70 W., Ste.   Ph: (573)875-7155
216 D   Fax: (573)449-5322
Columbia, MO 65203-2546
Desc: Focuses on electrical energy management and marketing ideas for the agricultural industry. *Type:* Newsletter.

Directory of California Agricultural Exporters
Database Publishing Co.
1590 S. Lewis St.   Ph: (714)778-6400
PO Box 70024   Free: 800-888-8434
Anaheim, CA 92825-0024   Fax: (714)778-6811
E-mail: sales@databasepublishing.com
URL: http://www.databasepublishing.com; http://www.databasepublishing.com.
Desc: Approximately 1,600 California companies in the growing, processing, and trading of food and fiber products in the worldwide market. *Type:* Directory.

Durum Wheat Report
Livestock and Seed Division
Agricultural Marketing Service
U.S. Department of Agriculture (USDA)
South Bldg., Rm. 2613   Ph: (202)720-6231
PO Box 96456   Fax: (202)690-3732
Washington, DC 20090-6456
Contact: Bob Brommer, Editor.
Desc: Reports on wheat statistics. Includes markets and prices. *Type:* Newsletter.

Earthkeeping Ontario
Jubilee Centre for Agricultural Research
115 Woolwich St., 2nd Fl.   Ph: (519)837-1620
Guelph, ON, Canada N1H 3V1   Fax: (519)824-1835
E-mail: ek-ont@christianfarmers.org
URL: http://www.christianfarmers.org.
Contact: Elbert van Donkersgoed, Editor and Publisher; Nellie van Donkersgoed, Story Editor.
Desc: Designed to "educate, challenge, and inspire farmers through stories that document how Christian faith and

values motivate the agricultural endeavour." Recurring features include interviews, notices of publications available, a calendar of events, occasional book reviews, occasional interviews and columns titled Cornerpost and Reflections. *Type:* Newsletter.

Equipment Manufacturers Institute
10 S. Riverside Plz., Ste. 1220   Ph: (312)321-1470
Chicago, IL 60606   Fax: (312)321-1480
E-mail: emi@emi.org
URL: http://www.emi.org
Contact: Emmett Barker, Pres.
Desc: Manufacturers of farm field machinery, farmstead equipment, construction equipment, utility equipment, forestry and materials handling equipment, industrial machinery and equipment; suppliers of materials, accessories, and services. *Type:* Association.

Fairs and Expos
International Association of Fairs and Expositions
3043 E. Cairo   Ph: (417)862-5771
PO Box 985   Free: 800-516-0313
Springfield, MO 65801   Fax: (417)862-0156
E-mail: iafe@iafenet.org
Contact: Max Willis, Editor.
Desc: Focuses on agricultural fairs and expositions as an industry. Recurring features include book reviews, a calendar of events, how-to items, and listings of fair dates and fair results. *Type:* Newsletter.

Farm Bureau News
American Farm Bureau Federation
600 Maryland Ave. SW, Ste.   Ph: (202)484-3600
800   Fax: (202)484-3602
Washington, DC 20024
E-mail: fbnews@fb.com.
URL: http://www.fb.com.
Contact: Joan Waldoch, Editor.
Desc: Discusses current legislation, court decisions, trade issues, and the use of innovative production methods. Recurring features include editorials, commentaries and the President's Column. *Type:* Newsletter.

Farm Economics
Pennsylvania State University
201 Armsby Bldg.   Ph: (814)863-0575
University Park, PA 16802   Fax: (814)865-3746
Contact: John C. Becker, Editor.
Desc: Summarizes agricultural topics and economic analysis of interest to farmers and those in agribusiness. Recurring features include news of research and news of educational opportunities. *Type:* Newsletter.

Farm Industry News
Webb Division, Intertec Publishing Corp.
7900 International Dr., 3rd Fl.   Ph: (612)851-9329
Minneapolis, MN 55425-1510   Free: 800-722-5334
    Fax: (612)851-4601
E-mail: fin@intertec.com
Contact: Kurt Lawton, Editor, kurt_lawton@intertec.com; Ron Sorensen, Publisher, ron_sorensen@intertec.com; Bob Moraczewski, Vice President, bob_moraczewski@intertec.com.
Desc: Agriculture trade magazine covering new products and technology. *Type:* Periodical.

Farm & Ranch Living
Reiman Publications, LLC
5400 S. 60th St.   Ph: (414)423-0100
Greendale, WI 53129-1404   Free: 800-682-9019
    Fax: (414)423-8463
URL: http://www.reimanpub.com.
Contact: Nick Pabst, Editor; Roy J. Reiman, Publisher.

Desc: Lifestyle magazine for farmers and ranchers. *Type:* Periodical.

Farm and Ranch Tax Letter
Ag Executive, Inc.
PO Box 180   Ph: (309)772-2166
Bushnell, IL 61422   Fax: (309)772-2167
Contact: Darrell L. Dunteman, Editor, darrellld@aol.com.
Desc: Provides information on agricultural taxation. *Type:* Newsletter.

Farm Show
Farm Show Publishing, Inc.
20088 Kenwood Trail   Ph: (612)469-5572
Box 1029
Lakeville, MN 55044
Contact: Mark Newhall, Editor and Publisher.
Desc: Magazine reporting on new products and product evaluations. *Type:* Periodical.

Farm Smart
FBS Systems, Inc.
1855 55th Ave.   Ph: (309)582-5628
Aledo, IL 61231-8610   Free: 800-437-7638
    Fax: (309)582-3423
E-mail: fbsmail@mcol.net
URL: http://www.fbssystems.com.
Contact: Wesley Prosser, Editor.
Desc: Informs and educates those involved in the business of farming about the latest state-of-the-art agricultural software products. Covers available FBS software, profiles agri-businesses using computers and agricultural software, reviews products, and provides accounting information. *Type:* Newsletter.

Farmers' Choice
Red Deer Advocate Ltd.
2950 Bremner Ave.   Ph: (403)343-2400
PO Bag 5200   Fax: (403)342-6560
Red Deer, AB, Canada T4N 5G3
Contact: Joe McLaughlin, Editor; Howard Janzen, Publisher; Bob Carey, Advertising Mgr.
Desc: Trade publication. *Type:* Periodical.

Farmers & Consumers Market Bulletin
Georgia Dept. of Agriculture
Agriculture Bldg., Capitol Sq.,   Ph: (404)656-3682
Rm. 226   Free: 800-282-5852
19 Martin Luther King Jr. Dr.   Fax: (404)651-7957
Atlanta, GA 30334-4250
URL: http://www.agr.state.ga.us.
Contact: Carlton Moore, Editor.
Desc: State agriculture and consumer newspaper. *Type:* Periodical.

Farmer's Voice
Minnesota Farm Bureau Federation
3080 Eagandale Place   Ph: (612)905-2118
PO Box 64370   Fax: (612)905-2159
St. Paul, MN 55164
E-mail: mfbf@aol.com; slengsfeld@aol.com.
Contact: Linda Hagan Kvanbeck, Editor.
Desc: Reports on issues related to farmers and farming in Minnesota. *Type:* Newsletter.

Farmland Industries
3315 N. Oak Trafficway   Ph: (816)459-6000
PO Box 7305   Fax: (816)241-6958
Dept. 16
Kansas City, MO 64116-0005
E-mail: hdcleberg@farmland.com

Contact: David Owens, Pres./CEO.

Desc: Regional federation of local cooperative organizations. Manufactures and sells petroleum products, fertilizer, feed, and other supplies to farmers. Processes and markets pork products through its subsidiary, Farmland Foods, Inc. *Type:* Association.

Farmland System News

Farmland Industries, Inc.
PO Box 7305, 3315 N. Oak   Ph: (816)459-6000
   Trafficway   Free: 800-821-8000
Kansas City, MO 64116   Fax: (816)459-6979
E-mail: fsneditor@farmland.com.
URL: http://www.farmland.com.
Contact: David Eaheart, Editor; Carolyn Riddle, Advertising & Circulation, (816)459-6896, fax: (816)459-6323, crriddle@farmland.com.
Desc: Magazine focusing on cooperative agriculture. *Alt. Contact:* fax: (816)459-6323. *Type:* Periodical.

Farmsafe

Farm Safety Association, Inc.
22-340 Woodlawn Rd. W.   Ph: (519)823-5600
Guelph, ON, Canada N1H 7K6   Free: 800-361-8855
     Fax: (519)823-8880
Contact: Ian Campbell, Editor.
Desc: Presents safety education for the agricultural/landscape industries. Recurring features include news of research and reports of meetings. *Type:* Newsletter.

Fastline--Dakota Farm Edition

Fastline
4900 Fox Run Rd.   Free: 800-626-6409
PO Box 248   Fax: (502)222-0615
Buckner, KY 40010
E-mail: fastpub@aol.com
Contact: William Howard, Publisher.
Desc: Trade magazine for the trucking and farming industry in North and South Dakota. *Type:* Periodical.

Federation of Southern Cooperatives Land Assistance Fund

2769 Church St.   Ph: (404)765-0991
East Point, GA 30344   Fax: (404)765-9178
Contact: Ralph Paige, Exec.Dir.
Desc: Cooperative associations chartered or doing business in the 17 southern states or the District of Columbia. Objectives are to assist people in building community-owned enterprises so they can control their own livelihood and to create housing, health care, and educational programs to complement economic development. *Type:* Association.

Feed Industry—Red Book

Moffatt Publishing, Inc.
200 Chestnut St., Ste. 100   Ph: (612)448-5402
Chaska, MN 55318   Fax: (612)448-6935
E-mail: seedtrade@skypoint.com.
Contact: Frank Zaworski, Editor.
Desc: List of over 200 firms involved in the large animal and pet food manufacturing and distribution business, including sources of feed ingredients and suppliers of feed materials handling equipment. *Type:* Directory.

FeedGram

American Feed Industry Association
1501 Wilson Blvd., No. 1100   Ph: (703)524-0810
Arlington, VA 22209   Fax: (703)524-1921
E-mail: mailafia@omco.net
URL: http://www.afia.org/FEEDGRAM.html.
Contact: Macky Hall, Editor.
Desc: Covers legislative news and regulatory developments affecting the feed industry. Focuses on association and member activities. *Type:* Newsletter.

FeedLine

American Feed Industry Association
1501 Wilson Blvd., No. 1100   Ph: (703)524-0810
Arlington, VA 22209   Fax: (703)524-1921
E-mail: mailafia@omco.net
URL: www.afic.org/feedline.html.
Contact: Macky Hall, Public Information Specialist.
Desc: Provides state-oriented news on the feed industry in Virginia. Recurring features include news of research and reports of meetings. *Type:* Newsletter.

The Fertilizer Institute

501 2nd St. NE   Ph: (202)675-8250
Washington, DC 20002   Fax: (202)544-8123
URL: http://www.tfi.org
Contact: Gary D. Myers, Pres.
Desc: Producers, manufacturers, retailers, trading firms, and equipment manufacturers. *Type:* Association.

FFA New Horizons

The National FFA Organization
6060 FFA Dr.   Ph: (317)802-6060
PO Box 68960   Fax: (317)802-6061
Indianapolis, IN 46268-0960
Contact: Erich Gaukel, Editor, egaukel@chilton.net; Jack Keller, Advertising Mgr.
Desc: Youth magazine. *Alt. Contact:* 191 S. Gary Ave., Carol Stream, IL 60188; telephone: (630)462-2342; fax: (630)462-2202. *Type:* Periodical.

Field Crop Abstracts

CAB International
CABI Publishing
10 E. 40th St., Ste. 3203   Ph: (212)481-7018
New York, NY 10016
E-mail: cabi-nao@cabi.org
URL: http://www.cabi.org
Contact: Sue Hill, Product Manager, Crop Production and Natural Resources, s.hill@cabi.org.
Desc: Contains citations, with abstracts, to current periodical and other published literature related to field crops. Corresponds to Field Crop Abstracts and in part to the on-line CAB ABSTRACTS database and the CAB ABSTRACTS on CD-ROM product. *Type:* Database.

FLAX Newsletter

Flax Growers Western Canada
PO Box 832   Ph: (306)781-7475
Regina, SK, Canada S4P 3B1   Fax: (306)525-4173
Desc: Reports on activity in the flax straw market. Provides market analyses, tips on machinery, and a column titled President's Report. *Type:* Newsletter.

Food & Drink Weekly

Sparks Companies, Inc.
6708 Whittier Ave.   Ph: (703)734-8787
Mc Lean, VA 22101   Fax: (703)556-7865
E-mail: editor@scipubs.com.
URL: http://www.scipubs.com.
Contact: Amie Chant, Editor.
Desc: International food and beverage business news, trends and policy. *Type:* Newsletter.

Food & Fiber Letter

Sparks Companies, Inc.
6708 Whittier Ave.   Ph: (703)734-8787
Mc Lean, VA 22101   Fax: (703)556-7865
E-mail: editor@scipubs.com.
URL: http://www.scipubs.com.
Contact: Barry Jenkins, Editor.
Desc: Provides current information on agricultural trade, economics, and policies. *Type:* Newsletter.

Fruit & Nut Statistics

California Agricultural Statistics Service
U.S. Department of Agriculture (USDA)
PO Box 1258   Ph: (916)654-0895
Sacramento, CA 95812
Desc: Reports on California's fruit and nut production, prices, farm labor, and wage rates. Included in California Agriculture. *Type:* Newsletter.

Good Earth Times

Good Earth Association, Inc.
202 E. Church St. at N. Bettis   Ph: (870)892-9545
Pocahontas, AR 72455-2899   Fax: (870)892-8329
E-mail: dwater@tcac.net.
Contact: Gladys Nelson, Editor, (870)647-2009, fax: (870)647-2009.
Desc: Discusses historical farm equipment, tools, skills, home sites, and farm operations. Recurring features include interviews, news of research, a calendar of events, reports of meetings, notices of publications available, and columns titled SOB: Save Our Barns and SOS: Save Our Seeds. *Type:* Newsletter.

Grain & Feed Market News

Livestock and Seed Division
Agricultural Marketing Service
U.S. Department of Agriculture (USDA)
South Bldg., Rm. 2613   Ph: (202)720-6231
PO Box 96456   Fax: (202)690-3732
Washington, DC 20090-6456
Contact: Kim Harmon, Editor.
Desc: Publishes weekly grain and feed marketing statistics. Includes narrative summaries of the grain and feed marketing situation in the U.S. *Type:* Newsletter.

Grain Matters

Canadian Wheat Board
423 Main St.   Ph: (204)983-3421
PO Box 816, Sta. Main   Fax: (204)983-4678
Winnipeg, MB, Canada R3C
   2P5
URL: http://www.cwb.ca.
Contact: Deanna Allen, Editor.
Desc: Contains articles related to the grain industry, with emphasis on CWB activities. Recurring features include columns titled Questions Farmers Are Asking. *Type:* Newsletter.

Grain Price Outlook

University of Illinois
ACES Newsletter Service
69 Mumford Hall   Ph: (217)244-5166
1301 W. Gregory Dr.
Urbana, IL 61801
Contact: Darrel Good, Editor.
Desc: Provides four issues each on corn and soybeans, analyzing areas of supply, demand, and price outlook. Discusses storage and pricing strategies for producers. *Type:* Newsletter.

Grain Stocks Report

Livestock and Seed Division
Agricultural Marketing Service
U.S. Department of Agriculture
1220 SW 3rd Ave., Rm. 1772   Ph: (503)326-2237
Portland, OR 97204   Fax: (503)326-5140
Contact: Lowell Serfling, Editor.
Desc: Reports on market summaries of grain stocks at selected terminal and elevator sites. *Type:* Newsletter.

The Grange Advocate

Pennsylvania State Grange
1604 N. 2nd St.
Harrisburg, PA 17102
Ph: (717)234-5001
Free: 800-552-3865
Contact: James C. Mentzer, Editor.
Desc: Provides Grange members and legislators with insights on current issues of interest to the Grange at national, state, and local levels. Supports the Grange in its efforts to represent rural Pennsylvania, including both rural citizens and the agricultural community. *Type:* Newsletter.

Grasslands and Forage Abstracts

CAB International
CABI Publishing
10 E. 40th St., Ste. 3203
New York, NY 10016
Ph: (212)481-7018
E-mail: cabi-nao@cabi.org
URL: http://www.cabi.org
Contact: Sue Hill, Product Manager, Crop Production and Natural Resources, s.hill@cabi.org.
Desc: Contains citations, with abstracts, to current periodical and other published literature relating to herbaceous vegetation. Corresponds to Grasslands and Forage Abstracts and in part to the online CAB ABSTRACTS database and the CAB ABSTRACTS on CD-ROM product. *Type:* Database.

Green Markets

Pike & Fischer, Inc.
1010 Wayne Ave., Ste. 1400
Silver Spring, MD 20910
Ph: (301)562-1530
Free: 800-255-8131
Fax: (301)562-1521
E-mail: pike@pf.com
Contact: Corriece Gwynn Perkins, Editor, cperkins@pf.com.
Desc: Reviews prices, politics, economics, and transportation developments affecting U.S. and international fertilizer markets. *Type:* Newsletter.

Green Markets Dealer Report

Pike & Fischer, Inc.
1010 Wayne Ave., Ste. 1400
Silver Spring, MD 20910
Ph: (301)562-1530
Free: 800-255-8131
Fax: (301)562-1521
E-mail: pike@pf.com
Contact: Carolyn Rhodes, Managing Editor.
Desc: Reviews prices, regulation, and company news affecting fertilizer and pesticide retailers in North America. *Type:* Newsletter.

Growing for Market

Fairplain Publications
Box 3747
Lawrence, KS 66046
Free: 800-307-8949
Fax: (785)748-0609
Contact: Lynn Byczynski, Editor and Publisher.
Desc: Provides information for small-scale produce and flower farmers. *Type:* Newsletter.

Hawaii Agriculture Research Center

99-193 Aiea Hieghts Dr.
Heights
Aiea, HI 96701-3911
Ph: (808)487-5561
Fax: (808)486-5020
E-mail: swhalen@harc-hspa.com
URL: http://www.hawaii.org/harc
Contact: Stephanie A. Whalen, Pres.
Desc: Sugar companies raising sugarcane and manufacturing sugar; individuals connected with these firms. Seeks to improve and protect the sugar industry of Hawaii; supports experiment station. Conducts training sessions for members of the sugar industry; compiles statistics. *Type:* Association.

Hay & Forage Grower

Webb Division, Intertec Publishing Corp.
7900 International Dr., 3rd Fl.
Minneapolis, MN 55425-1510
Ph: (612)851-9329
Free: 800-722-5334
Fax: (612)851-4601
URL: http://www.homefarm.com/.
Contact: Neil Tietz, Editor; Ron Sorensen, Publisher.
Desc: Trade magazine for large-acreage producers of forage crops. *Type:* Periodical.

Hay There!

National Hay Association, Inc.
102 Treasure Island Cswy., No. 201
St. Petersburg, FL 33706
Ph: (813)367-9702
Free: 800-707-0014
Fax: (813)367-9608
E-mail: haynha@aol.com
Contact: Donald F. Kieffer, Editor.
Desc: Reports current developments in the hay industry, including marketing and shipping information. *Type:* Newsletter.

The Herb Companion

Herb Companion Press, LLC
201 E. 4th St.
Loveland, CO 80537
Ph: (970)669-7672
Free: 800-272-2193
Fax: (970)667-8317
E-mail: herbcompanion@hcpress.com.
Contact: Robyn Griggs Lawrence, Editor; Suzanne De Atley, Advertising Mgr.
Desc: Magazine about the growing and using of herbs for food, fragrance, craft, and health. *Alt. Contact:* Herb Companion Press, L.L.C. 201 E. 4th St., Loveland, CO 80537. *Type:* Periodical.

Hops Market News

Livestock and Seed Division
Agricultural Marketing Service
U.S. Department of Agriculture
1220 SW 3rd Ave., Rm. 1772
Portland, OR 97204
Ph: (503)326-2237
Fax: (503)326-5140
Contact: Martha Hansen, Editor.
Desc: Reports on developments in the hops industry. Includes information on supplies available, price and markets, supply and distribution, and importing and exporting. *Type:* Newsletter.

Horizons

Rural Economic Analysis Program
Virginia Polytechnic Institute and State University
Department of Agricultural Economics
Blacksburg, VA 24061-0401
Ph: (540)231-9443
Fax: (540)231-7417
E-mail: reapo1@vt.edu
URL: http://www.reap.ut.edu/reap/reap/.
Contact: Karen Mundy, Editor.
Desc: Addresses issues affecting the economy of rural Virginia, such as rural development, feedgrain and agricultural industries, and groundwater protection. Recurring features include news of research, notices of publications available, and reports of events and elections. *Type:* Newsletter.

ICASA News

International Consortium for Agricultural Systems Applications (ICASA)
2500 Dole St., Krauss Hall 22
Honolulu, HI 96822-2332
Ph: (808)956-8858
Fax: (808)956-3421
E-mail: icasa@agrss.sherman.hawaii.edu
URL: http://www.agrss.sherman.hawaii.edu/icasa.
Contact: Gordon Y. Tsuji, Managing Editor.
Desc: Reports on the development and application of system simulation products and tools for agricultural production. Recurring features include news of research and a calendar of events. *Type:* Newsletter.

Illinois Grain and Livestock Market News

Division of Marketing and Agricultural Services
Illinois State Department of Agriculture
State Fairgrounds
PO Box 19281
Springfield, IL 62794-9281
Ph: (217)782-2172
Fax: (217)785-4505
Desc: Provides livestock and grain prices and related industry statistics. Includes data on direct feedlot sales, transportation movement, direct sales, terminal sales, meat trade prices, closing futures contract prices (grain), livestock futures, feedstuffs, rail car loadings, barge loads of grain and grain products, and barge movement. *Type:* Newsletter.

Interdimensional News

Interdimensional Sciences, Inc.
PO Box 128
Lakemont, GA 30552
Ph: (706)782-2524
Fax: (706)782-6127
Contact: Peter J. Kelly, Editor, petkell@stc.net.
Desc: Covers new technologies in agriculture radionics. *Type:* Newsletter.

International Fertilizer Development Center

PO Box 2040
Muscle Shoals, AL 35662
Ph: (205)381-6600
Fax: (205)381-7408
E-mail: general@ifdc.org
URL: http://www.ifdc.org
Contact: Dr. Amit H. Roy, Pres. & CEO.
Desc: Participants include scientists, engineers, economists, and specialists in market research and development, communications, and personnel development. To alleviate world hunger by increasing agricultural production in the tropics and subtropics through development of improved fertilizer and fertilizer use. Studies ways of processing indigenous resources of phosphate rock into efficient fertilizers; conducts nitrogen efficiency research; examines the agronomic efficiency of sulfur sources such as gypsum, anhydrite, and pyrites; sponsors studies of potassium, magnesium, and calcium use. *Type:* Association.

Iowa Crops & Weather

Iowa Agricultural Statistics
833 Federal Bldg.
210 Walnut St.
Des Moines, IA 50309-2103
Ph: (515)284-4340
Free: 800-772-0825
Fax: (515)284-4342
E-mail: nass-ia@nass.usda.gov; nass-ia@nass.usda.gov.
URL: http://www.nass.usda.gov/ia.
Contact: James K. Sands, Editor.
Desc: Provides a summary of crop and weather developments across Iowa, noting any possible effects on plant development. *Type:* Newsletter.

Irrigation Association

8260 Willow Oak Corporation Dr.
Fairfax, VA 22031
Ph: (703)573-3551
Fax: (703)573-1913
URL: http://www.irrigation.org
Contact: Thomas H. Kimmell, Exec.Dir.
Desc: Manufacturers, wholesalers, and contractors of irrigation equipment. Compiles statistics. Conducts Educations course (22) certifies Irrigation Designer, Contractors & Managers, and Government Relations. *Type:* Association.

Irrigation and Drainage Abstracts

CAB International
CABI Publishing
10 E. 40th St., Ste. 3203
New York, NY 10016
Ph: (212)481-7018
E-mail: cabi-nao@cabi.org
URL: http://www.cabi.org
Contact: Sue Hill, Product Manager, Crop Production and Natural Resources, s.hill@cabi.org.
Desc: Contains citations, with abstracts, to current worldwide periodical and other published scientific literature re-

lated to irrigation and drainage. Corresponds to Irrigation and Drainage Abstracts and in part to the online CAB ABSTRACTS database and the SOILCD and CAB ABSTRACTS on CD-ROM products. *Type:* Database.

Kansas Agriculture Network/Kansas Information Network

Box 1818 Ph: (913)272-3456
Topeka, KS 66601-1818 Fax: (913)272-3536
Contact: Al Lobeck, General Mgr.; Kathy Patton, Farm Dir.; Ed O'Donnell, Operations Dir.; Craig Colboch, Sales Mgr.
Desc: Format comprises adult Contemporary; Easy Listening; Goldies; Great American Country; Prime Demo. *Alt. Contact:* Box 1818, Topeka, KS 66601-1818; telephone: (913)272-3456; fax: (913)272-3536. *Type:* Periodical.

Kansas Crop Improvement Association—News Letter

Kansas Crop Improvement Association
2000 Kimball Ave. Ph: (913)532-6118
Manhattan, KS 66502 Fax: (913)532-6551
Contact: Daryl S. Srouts, Editor.
Desc: Serves persons and organizations concerned with certification standards for seeds, crop variety, production, and information on seed quality. Recurring features include news of research, statistics, advice on seed testing, and notices of meetings and staff activities. *Type:* Newsletter.

Kentucky Agri-News

Kentucky Agricultural Statistics
Kentucky State Department of Agriculture
PO Box 1120 Ph: (502)582-5293
Louisville, KY 40201 Fax: (502)582-5114
Contact: Leland Brown, Editor.
Desc: Features agricultural information about farm income, the trade balance, U.S. exports, and production figures for specific crops, livestock, or dairy products in Kentucky. *Type:* Newsletter.

King's Gulf Grain Guide

King Publishing Corporation
PO Box 52210 Ph: (423)584-6294
Knoxville, TN 37950 Free: 800-446-8214
Fax: (423)558-6101
Contact: M.I. Parker-O'Toole, Editor.
Desc: Contains a ship-by-ship report of grain exports. Includes port, country, shipper statistics and totals, vessel fixtures, and Department of Commerce tables. *Type:* Newsletter.

The Kiplinger Agriculture Letter

Kiplinger Washington Editors, Inc.
1729 H St. NW Ph: (202)887-6491
Washington, DC 20006 Free: 800-544-0155
Fax: (202)887-6542
Contact: Melissa S. Bristow, Editor.
Desc: Publishes information on actions and proposals by the administration, U.S. Department of Agriculture, and Congress affecting all aspects of agriculture. *Type:* Newsletter.

Kyloe Cry

Canadian Highland Cattle Society
307 Spicer Rd. Ph: (514)243-5543
Knowlton, PQ, Canada J0E Fax: (514)243-1150
1V0
E-mail: chcs@acbm.qc.ca
Contact: Margaret Badger, Editor.
Desc: Provides information on cattle breeds. *Type:* Newsletter.

The Leader for Agriculture

NYFEA—The Association for Educating Agricultural Leaders
PO Box 20326 Ph: (334)288-0097
Montgomery, AL 36120 Fax: (334)288-0097
Contact: Gordon Stone, Editor.
Desc: Serves as a communications link between state associations. Provides information on state and national educational programs, activities, and meetings. *Type:* Newsletter.

Louisiana Agri-News Network/Louisiana Network

263 Riverside Mall Ph: (504)383-8695
5th Fl. Fax: (504)342-9950
Baton Rouge, LA 70801
Contact: Bill Rigell, President; Mark Yearout, VP Sales and Mktg.; Rhett McMahon, VP Technology; Keith Stokes, Affiliate Mgr.; Don Molino, Farm Dir.; Jim Engster, News Dir.; Carolyn Bennett, Business Mgr.
Alt. Contact: 263 Riverside Mall, 5th Fl., Baton Rouge, LA 70801; telephone: (504)383-8695; fax: (504)342-9950. *Type:* Periodical.

Louisiana Country

Association of Louisiana Electric Cooperatives, Inc.
10725 Airline Hwy. Ph: (504)293-3450
Baton Rouge, LA 70816 Free: 800-355-3450
Fax: (504)296-0924
E-mail: alec@premier.net
Contact: Billy Gibson, Dir. of Communications; Randy Pierce, Associate Editor.
Desc: Electric cooperative membership magazine. *Type:* Periodical.

Maize Abstracts

CAB International
CABI Publishing
10 E. 40th St., Ste. 3203 Ph: (212)481-7018
New York, NY 10016
E-mail: cabi-nao@cabi.org
URL: http://www.cabi.org
Contact: Sue Hill, Product Manager, Crop Production and Natural Resources, s.hill@cabi.org.
Desc: Contains citations, with abstracts, to current periodical and other published literature related to maize. Corresponds to Maize Abstracts and in part to the online CAB ABSTRACTS database and the CAB ABSTRACTS on CD-ROM product. *Type:* Database.

Making a Difference

The National FFA Organization
6060 FFA Dr. Ph: (317)802-6060
PO Box 68960 Fax: (317)802-6061
Indianapolis, IN 46268-0960
URL: http://www.ffa.org.
Contact: Becky Meyer, Editor, bmeyer@ffa.org; Jeri Mattics, Managing Editor; Wes Ishmael, Asst. Editor; David Frazier, Contributing Editor.
Desc: Acts as an agriculture education publication for agriculture instructors. Recurring features include interviews, news of educational opportunities, and news of research. *Type:* Newsletter.

Michigan Country Lines

Michigan Electric Cooperative Association
2859 W. Jolly Rd. Ph: (517)351-6322
Okemos, MI 48864 Fax: (517)351-6396
URL: http://www.countrylines.com.
Contact: Michael F. Buda, Executive Editor, mbuda@countrylines.com; Gail Knudtson, Editor; Deena Carlson, Editorial Asst.; Alison Lahti, Advertising Asst.

Desc: Magazine on rural lifestyles and home energy use. *Type:* Periodical.

Mid-America Ag Network

1632 S. Maize Rd. Ph: (316)721-8484
Wichita, KS 67209 Fax: (316)721-8276
Contact: Larry Steckline, Pres./Owner.
Alt. Contact: 1632 S. Maize Rd., Wichita, KS 67209; telephone: (316)721-8484; fax: (316)721-8276. *Type:* Periodical.

Midwest Messenger

Plaindealer Publishing Co.
Box 239 Ph: (402)374-2226
Tekamah, NE 68061 Free: 800-888-1380
Fax: (402)374-2739
Contact: Joe Zink, Publisher; James Beaver, Sales Mgr.
Desc: Farm trade shopper. *Type:* Periodical.

Minnesota Agricultural Economist

Minnesota Extension Service
University of Minnesota
Department of Applied Ph: (612)625-3103
Economics Fax: (612)625-6245
1994 Buford Ave.
St. Paul, MN 55108-6040
Contact: Steven J. Taff, Editor.
Desc: Deals with agricultural and economic topics in Minnesota. Recurring features include news of research. *Type:* Newsletter.

Minnesota Pest Report

Ag Marketing and Development Division
Minnesota Department of Agriculture
90 W. Plato Blvd. Ph: (651)296-7686
St. Paul, MN 55107-2094 Fax: (651)297-7678
URL: http://www.mda.state.mn.us.
Contact: David D. Bartels, Ph.D., Entomologist, (651)296-6509, fax: (651)297-3631, david.bartels@state.mn.us.
Desc: Provides current information on pests that attack field crops, nursery stock and ornamental trees and shrubs in Minnesota. Collects survey data throughout the state and summarizes it in a non-technical style for interested individuals. *Type:* Newsletter.

Mississippi Farm Bureau News

Mississippi Farm Bureau Federation
6310 Interstate 55 North
PO Box 1972
Jackson, MS 39215
Contact: Glynda Phillips, Editor.
Desc: Farm news. *Type:* Periodical.

Molasses Market News

Livestock and Seed Division
Agricultural Marketing Service
U.S. Department of Agriculture (USDA)
South Bldg., Rm. 2613 Ph: (202)720-6231
PO Box 96456 Fax: (202)690-3732
Washington, DC 20090-6456
Contact: Keith Padgett, Editor.
Desc: Provides the market news on molasses and its import and export. *Type:* Newsletter.

Montana Farm Bureau Spokesman

Montana Farm Bureau Federation
502 S. 19th Ave. Ph: (406)587-3153
Bozeman, MT 59718 Fax: (406)587-0319
E-mail: mtfarmb@in-tch.com
Contact: Rebecca Colnar, Editor; J.T. Cummins, Editor.
Desc: Informs on issues effecting agriculture. Recurring features include letters to the editor, interviews, news of research, a calendar of events, reports of meetings, and news of educational opportunities. *Type:* Newsletter.

NASDA News

National Association of State Departments of Agriculture (NASDA)

1156 15th St. NW, Ste. 1020   Ph: (202)296-9680
Washington, DC 20005-1704   Fax: (202)296-9686
E-mail: nasda@patriot.net
Contact: Betsy Maixner, Editor.
Desc: Reports on legislative and regulatory developments in agriculture in Washington, D.C. Remarks: Available via e-mail or fax. *Type:* Newsletter.

National Association of State Departments of Agriculture

1156 15th St. NW, Ste. 1020   Ph: (202)296-9680
Washington, DC 20005   Fax: (202)296-9686
E-mail: nasda@patriot.net
URL: http://www.nasda-hq.org
Contact: Richard W. Kirchhoff, CEO.
Desc: Directors of state and territorial departments of agriculture. To coordinate policies, procedures, laws, and activities between the states and federal agencies and Congress. Conducts research. *Type:* Association.

National Association of Wheat Growers—Report From Washington

National Association of Wheat Growers

415 2nd St. NE, Ste. 300   Ph: (202)547-7800
Washington, DC 20002-4993   Fax: (202)546-2638
E-mail: wheatworld@wheatworld.com
URL: http://www.wheatworld.org.
Contact: Gina Hoback, Editor.
Desc: Provides updates on federal and state legislative and regulatory actions of interest to the nations's wheat growers. *Type:* Newsletter.

National Farmers Union News

National Farmers Union

11900 E. Cornell Ave.   Ph: (303)337-5500
Aurora, CO 80014-3194   Free: 800-347-1961
   Fax: (303)368-1390
E-mail: nfu.denver@ntu.org
URL: http://www.nfu.org.
Contact: Marilyn Wentz, Editor, marilyn.wentz@nfu.org.
Desc: Provides news, legislation, and tax information in relation to the farming industry. *Type:* Newsletter.

National FFA

1410 King St., Ste. 400   Ph: (703)838-5889
Alexandria, VA 22314   Free: 800-772-0939
   Fax: (703)838-5888
E-mail: info@ffa.org
URL: http://www.ffa.org
Contact: Dr. Larry Case, CEO.
Desc: Students of agriculture/agribusiness in public schools. Organized under the National Vocational Education Act to foster character development, agricultural leadership, and responsible citizenship and to supplement training opportunities for students preparing for over 200 careers agriculture National FFA Alumni Association is supportive group affiliated with the U.S. Department of Education. *Type:* Association.

National Grain and Feed Association

1201 New York Ave., NW, Ste.   Ph: (202)289-0873
830   Fax: (202)289-5388
Washington, DC 20005-3917
E-mail: ngfa@ngfa.org
URL: http://www.ngfa.org
Contact: Kendell W. Keith, Pres.
Desc: 1000 Grain, Feed and Processing firms. Terminal and export elevators; feed mills; cash grain and feed merchandisers; commodity futures brokers and commission merchants; processors; millers; and allied industries. Represents and provides services for grain and grain-related commercial businesses. *Type:* Association.

National Oilseed Processors Association

1255 23rd St. NW, Ste.220   Ph: (202)452-8040
Washington, DC 20037   Fax: (202)835-0400
E-mail: nopa@nopa.org
URL: http://www.nopa.org
Contact: Allen F. Johnson, Pres.
Desc: Processors of oilseeds. *Type:* Association.

National Pesticide Information Retrieval System

Purdue University

Entomology Hall   Ph: (765)494-6616
1231 Cumberland Ave., Ste A
West Lafayette, IN 47906-1317
E-mail: info@ceris.purdue.edu
URL: http://www.ceris.purdue.edu
Desc: Contains information on pesticides used in agriculture, industry, and general commerce. Corresponds to the online National Pesticide Information Retrieval System database. *Available:* Purdue University, Center for Environmental and Regulatory Information Systems (CERIS); SilverPlatter Information, Inc. *Type:* Database.

National Renderers Association

801 N. Fairfax St., Ste. 207   Ph: (703)683-0155
Alexandria, VA 22314   Fax: (703)683-2626
E-mail: renderers@aol.com
URL: http://www.renderers.org
Contact: Tom Cook, Exec.Dir.
Desc: Producers of tallow and grease products (for use in soap and lubricants), and meat meal (for use in animal feeds), obtained as by-products of the meat-packing industry. Conducts research and educational programs; provides international & domestic market development services and legislative representation. *Type:* Association.

NCPA Newsletter

National Cottonseed Products Association

1255 Lynnfield, Ste. 143   Ph: (901)682-0800
Memphis, TN 38119   Fax: (901)682-2856
E-mail: info@cottonseed.com
Contact: Ben Morgan, Editor.
Desc: Provides news and information on cottonseed and related products. Contains member news. *Type:* Newsletter.

Nebraska Pest Control Association Newsletter

Nebraska State Pest Control Association, Inc.

1111 Lincoln Mall, Ste. 308
Lincoln, NE 68508-3910
Contact: Robert L. Anderson, Editor; Alice L. Light, Managing Editor; Rebecca Barker, Advertising Editor.
Desc: Features news and information for those working in pest control. *Type:* Newsletter.

Neighbors

ALFA/Alabama Farmers Federation

PO Box 11000   Ph: (334)288-3900
Montgomery, AL 36191-0001   Fax: (334)284-3957
Contact: Mark Morrison, Editor; Ronnie McKinney, Advertising Mgr., (334)263-6050, fax: (334)263-5933.
Desc: Magazine covering agriculture, gardening, and rural lifestyles. *Type:* Periodical.

New Brunswick Institute of Agrologists Newsletter

New Brunswick Institute of Agrologists

c/o Agriculture Canada,
   Research Sta.
PO Box 20280
Fredericton, NB, Canada E3B
   4Z7
Contact: Dr. Warren K. Coleman, Editor.
Desc: Devoted to agricultural issues pertaining to the northern maritime environment. Remarks: Some articles in French. *Type:* Newsletter.

NewsCAST

Council for Agricultural Science & Technology (CAST)

4420 W. Lincoln Way   Ph: (515)292-2125
Ames, IA 50014   Fax: (515)292-4512
E-mail: cast@cast-science.org
URL: http://www.netins.net/showcase/cast/; http://www.cast-science.org.
Contact: Robert J. Ver Straeten, Editor, rverstraeten@cast-science.org.
Desc: Serves a consortium of 36 food and agricultural science societies, which promotes understanding by providing a background in agricultural science and technology. Carries features of interest to food and agricultural scientists and news of the organization's activities and programs. *Type:* Newsletter.

9N-2N-8N-NAA Newsletter

Robert R. Rinaldi Jr. and Gerard W. Rinaldi

PO Box 275   Ph: (802)439-6054
East Corinth, VT 05040   Fax: (802)439-6054
Contact: Gerard W. Rinaldi, Editor; Robert R. Rinaldi, Jr., Editor and Publisher.
Desc: Provides information about farm memorabilia and farm lifestyles. Recurring features include letters to the editor, interviews, and news. *Type:* Newsletter.

North American Equipment Dealers Association

10877 Watson Rd.   Ph: (314)821-7220
St. Louis, MO 63127   Fax: (314)821-0674
E-mail: naeda@naeda.com
URL: http://www.naeda.com
Contact: David G. Ottaway, Exec.VP/CEO.
Desc: Retailers of farm equipment, implements, light industrial equipment, outdoor power equipment, and related supplies. Conducts programs on management training, and governmental and trade relations. Sponsors group health and accident insurance program for members and their employees. *Type:* Association.

Northern Applicator

International Ag Aviation Foundation (IAAF)

PO Box 1607   Ph: (360)336-9737
Mt. Vernon, WA 98273   Fax: (360)336-2506
Contact: Tom J. Wood, Editor.
Desc: Reports on the agricultural pesticide spraying industry. Presents news of pilots, safety in the industry, new products, and the Environmental Protection Agency (EPA). *Type:* Newsletter.

Northwest Commodity Corner

Livestock & Grain Market News Branch
Agricultural Marketing Service
U.S. Department of Agriculture

1428 S. Pioneer Way   Ph: (509)765-3611
Moses Lake, WA 98837   Fax: (509)765-0454
Type: Newsletter.

Oklahoma Agrinet/Oklahoma News Network

Box 1000   Ph: (405)840-5271
Oklahoma City, OK 73101   Fax: (405)840-4025
Contact: Tim West, General Mgr.; Ron Hays, Farm Dir.; Jerry Vaughn, OPD.
Desc: State and agricultural news format. *Alt. Contact:* Box 1000, Oklahoma City, OK 73101; telephone: (405)840-5271; fax: (405)840-4025. *Type:* Periodical.

Olsen's Agribusiness Report

G.V. Olsen Associates

123 Picketts Ridge Rd.   Ph: (203)938-4188
West Redding, CT 06896   Fax: (203)938-4186
Contact: Gustav Olsen, Editor.
Desc: Monitors and evaluates agribusiness projects, products, technology, and research on a global basis. Analyzes the effects of current government policies on the agribusiness industry and reports on industry trends and personnel. *Type:* Newsletter.

The Organic Report

Organic Trade Association
PO Box 1078
Greenfield, MA 01302-1078   Ph: (413)774-7511
                             Fax: (413)774-6432
E-mail: ota@igc.org
Contact: Holly Givens, Editor; Katherine DiMatteo, Editor.
Desc: Provides news of interest to organic agricultural businesses. *Type:* Newsletter.

Pacific Northwest Christmas Tree Association Buy-Sell Directory

Pacific Northwest Christmas Tree Association
4093 12th St. SE   Ph: (503)364-2942
PO Box 3366   Fax: (503)581-6819
Salem, OR 97302
URL: http://www.nwtrees.com.
Contact: Wally Hunter, Editor.
Desc: Christmas tree sellers and buyers in Washington, Oregon, California, Idaho, and southwestern Canada. *Type:* Directory.

Pacific Northwest Feed Market News

Livestock and Seed Division
Agricultural Marketing Service
U.S. Department of Agriculture (USDA)
South Bldg., Rm. 2613   Ph: (202)720-6231
PO Box 96456   Fax: (202)690-3732
Washington, DC 20090-6456
Contact: Lowell Serfling, Editor.
Desc: Reports on prices and markets in the feed industry. Remarks: Also provides a 24-hour telephone report: (503) 326-5140. *Type:* Newsletter.

Pacific Northwest Grain and Feed Association—Official Directory

Pacific Northwest Grain and Feed Association
200 SW Market St., Ste. 1730   Ph: (503)227-0234
Portland, OR 97201   Fax: (503)227-0059
E-mail: pnwgfa@teleport.com
Contact: Jonathan Schlueter, Editor.
Desc: Grain, feed, milling and seed firms in Washington, Oregon, Montana, and Idaho. *Type:* Directory.

Pacific Northwest Grain Market News

Livestock and Seed Division
Agricultural Marketing Service
U.S. Department of Agriculture
1220 SW 3rd Ave., Rm. 1772   Ph: (503)326-2237
Portland, OR 97204   Fax: (503)326-5140
Contact: Lowell Serfling, Editor.
Desc: Reports on grain statistics in the Pacific Northwest region. Includes market summaries and prices. *Type:* Newsletter.

Partners

Illinois Farm Bureau
1701 Towanda Ave.   Ph: (309)557-2238
Bloomington, IL 61701   Free: 800-640-1995
E-mail: lgoltz@ilfb.org; lagoltz@aol.com.
Contact: Dave McClelland, Editor, fweditor@ilfb.org.
Desc: Publication for members of the Illinois Farm Bureau Assoc. *Type:* Periodical.

Peanut Industry Guide

Specialized Agricultural Publications, Inc.
3000 Highwoods Blvd., Ste. 300   Ph: (919)872-5040
Raleigh, NC 27604-1029   Fax: (919)876-6531
E-mail: publisher@peanutfarmer.com
URL: http://www.peanutfarmer.com.
Contact: Dayton Matlick, Publisher; Mary Evans, Editor; Pat Walston, Dir.Mgr.

Desc: Over 1,000 growers, associations, shellers, processors, brokers, government agencies, and other businesses associated with or serving the peanut industry. *Type:* Directory.

Pennsylvania Agriculture News

Pennsylvania Department of Agriculture
Bureau of Market Development
2301 N. Cameron St.   Ph: (717)787-4737
Harrisburg, PA 17110   Fax: (717)787-1039
Desc: Provides news and coverage of agricultural services, programs, and events. *Type:* Newsletter.

PENpages

Pennsylvania State University - College of Agricultural Sciences
405 Agricultural Administration   Ph: (814)863-3449
    Bldg.   Fax: (814)863-7209
University Park, PA 16802
E-mail: PENpages@email.cas.psu.edu
URL: http://www.penpages.psu.edu
Contact: Diann Leri, Training & Support Specialist, PENpages.
Desc: PENpages, run by Pennsylvania State University's College of Agricultural Sciences, provides weekly world weather and crop reports from the U.S. Department of Agriculture. *Type:* Database.

Pest Control Executive Reports

Pinto & Associates, Inc.
29839 Oak Rd.   Ph: (301)884-3020
Mechanicsville, MD 20659-   Fax: (301)884-4068
    2201
Contact: Lawrence J. Pinto, Publisher; Sandra K. Kraft, Editor.
Desc: Discusses topics of interest to the pest control industry. *Type:* Newsletter.

Pest Management and Crop Development Bulletin

University of Illinois
ACES Newsletter Service
69 Mumford Hall   Ph: (217)244-5166
1301 W. Gregory Dr.
Urbana, IL 61801
Contact: Kevin Steffey, Editor.
Desc: Reports on the current agricultural insect and plant disease situation, giving advice on control methods and covering new developments in pesticide application techniques. *Type:* Newsletter.

Plant Growth Regulator Abstracts

CAB International
CABI Publishing
10 E. 40th St., Ste. 3203   Ph: (212)481-7018
New York, NY 10016
E-mail: cabi-nao@cabi.org
URL: http://www.cabi.org
Desc: Contains citations, with abstracts, to current periodical and other published literature related to the role of chemicals in plant growth regulation and in beneficial modification of plant growth processes. Corresponds to Plant Growth Regulator Abstracts and in part to the online CAB ABSTRACTS database and the CAB ABSTRACTS on CD-ROM product. *Type:* Database.

Pool Today

Saskatchewan Wheat Pool
2625 Victoria Ave.
Regina, SK, Canada S4T 7T9
Contact: Doug Leask, Editor.
Desc: Discusses agricultural policy, company operations, and cooperative subjects. *Type:* Newsletter.

Postharvest News and Information

CAB International
CABI Publishing
10 E. 40th St., Ste. 3203   Ph: (212)481-7018
New York, NY 10016
E-mail: cabi-nao@cabi.org
URL: http://www.cabi.org
Contact: Sue Hill, Product Manager, Crop Production and Natural Resources, s.hill@cabi.org.
Desc: Contains citations, with abstracts, to current periodical and other published literature relating to the postharvest treatment of crops and the minimization of postharvest losses. Corresponds to Postharvest News and Information and in part to the online CAB ABSTRACTS database and the CAB ABSTRACTS on CD-ROM product. *Type:* Database.

Potato Abstracts

CAB International
CABI Publishing
10 E. 40th St., Ste. 3203   Ph: (212)481-7018
New York, NY 10016
E-mail: cabi-nao@cabi.org
URL: http://www.cabi.org
Contact: Sue Hill, Product Manager, Crop Production and Natural Resources, s.hill@cabi.org.
Desc: Contains citations, with abstracts, to current worldwide periodical and other published scientific literature related to Solanum tuberosum (potatoes). Corresponds to Potato Abstracts and in part to the online CAB ABSTRACTS database and the CAB ABSTRACTS on CD-ROM product. *Type:* Database.

Potato Country—Northwest Seed Potato Directory Issue

Columbia Publishing
PO Box 9036   Ph: (509)248-2452
Yakima, WA 98909-0036   Free: 800-900-2452
                            Fax: (509)248-4056
E-mail: management@freshcut.com; potatocountry@freshcut.com.
Contact: D. Brent Clement, Editor, brent@freshcut.com.
Desc: List of about 7,000 growers of seed potatoes and wholesale potato dealers in Arizona, California, Colorado, Idaho, Montana, Nevada, New Mexico, North Dakota, Oregon, Utah, Washington, and Wyoming. *Type:* Directory.

Progressive Farmer

Southern Progress
2100 Lakeshore Dr.   Ph: (205)877-6000
Birmingham, AL 35209-6721   Free: 888-737-3529
                            Fax: (205)877-6600
URL: http://www.progressivefarmer.com.
Contact: Jack Odle, Editor, jodle@progressivefarmer.com; Ed Dickinson, Publisher; Vicki A. Denmark, General Mgr.
Desc: Agricultural magazine, published in 18 editions, for farmers and ranchers. *Alt. Contact:* PO Box 2581, Birmingham, AL 35202. *Type:* Periodical.

Pulse Newsletter

Saskatchewan Pulse Corp.
PO Box 516   Ph: (306)781-7475
Regina, SK, Canada S4P 3A2 Fax: (306)525-4173
URL: http://www.vsource.com/saskpulse.
Contact: Donald Jaques, Administrator.
Desc: Provides information on the Saskatchewan pulse crop development board, as well as research and marketing of pulses. Recurring features include news of research, a calendar of events, and reports of meetings. *Type:* Newsletter.

Review of Agricultural Entomology

CAB International
CABI Publishing
10 E. 40th St., Ste. 3203   Ph: (212)481-7018
New York, NY 10016
E-mail: cabi-nao@cabi.org
URL: http://www.cabi.org

Desc: Contains citations, with abstracts, to current periodical and other published literature relatingto agricultural entomology. Covers insects and other pests of cultivated plants, forest trees, and stored products as well as beneficial arthropods such as parasites and predators. *Type:* Database.

Rice Abstracts

CAB International
CABI Publishing
10 E. 40th St., Ste. 3203   Ph: (212)481-7018
New York, NY 10016
E-mail: cabi-nao@cabi.org
URL: http://www.cabi.org

Contact: Sue Hill, Product Manager, Crop Production and Natural Resources, s.hill@cabi.org.

Desc: Contains citations, with abstracts, to current worldwide periodical and other published scientific literature related to rice. Corresponds to Rice Abstracts and in part to the online CAB ABSTRACTS database and the CAB ABSTRACTS on CD-ROM product. *Type:* Database.

Rice Market News

Livestock and Seed Division
Agricultural Marketing Service
U.S. Department of Agriculture
Box 391   Ph: (501)671-2200
Little Rock, AR 72203   Fax: (501)324-5870
Contact: Steve Cheney, Editor.

Desc: Reports on statistics and provides news of prices and markets, production, and sales in the rice industry. *Type:* Newsletter.

RiceGenes, a Rice Genome Database

Cornell University - Department of Plant Breeding
409 Bradfield   Ph: (607)225-9951
Ithaca, NY 14853   Fax: (607)255-6683
E-mail: epaul@nightshade.cit.cornell.edu
URL: http://probe.nalusda.gov:8000/plant/aboutricegenes.html
Contact: Marci Blinstrub, Curator, mab8@cornell.edu.

Desc: The RiceGenes database contains molecular and phenotypic information relating to rice, such as maps, probes, images, colleagues, references, etc. The full text of newsletters, instructions for use, and links to related sites are also available. *Type:* Database.

Rural Coalition

110 Maryland Ave., NE, Ste.   Ph: (202)544-9611
505
Washington, DC 20002
Contact: Lorette Hanson, Exec.Dir.

Desc: Organizations and individuals concerned with issues directly affecting low income and disadvantaged rural Americans. Objective is to work for effective public policies and to develop a strong rural constituency for progressive change to benefit rural people. Subscribes to the following principles: justice and equal opportunity regardless of sex, race, or place of residence; availability of goods and services essential to a decent quality of life; control and use of resources by rural people; development of rural, community-based organizations. *Type:* Association.

Rural Development Abstracts

CAB International
CABI Publishing
10 E. 40th St., Ste. 3203   Ph: (212)481-7018
New York, NY 10016
E-mail: cabi-nao@cabi.org
URL: http://www.cabi.org

Desc: Contains citations, with abstracts, to current periodical and other published literature relating to rural development and regional planning in the Third World. Corresponds to Rural Development Abstracts and in part to the online CAB ABSTRACTS and CAB: Economics, Development and Education databases. *Type:* Database.

SAGA

Sakatchewan Agricultural Graduates Association, Inc.
Box 320
RPO University
Saskatoon, SK, Canada S7N 4J8
E-mail: THESaga@home.com

Desc: Serves as the publication of the Saskatchwean Agricultural Graduates Assoc., Inc. Recurring features include news of research and a calendar of events. *Type:* Newsletter.

Saskatchewan Alfalfa Seed Producers Association Newsletter

Saskatchewan Alfalfa Seed Producers Association
107 Science Place   Ph: (306)956-7200
Saskatoon, SK, Canada S7N   Fax: (306)956-7247
0X2
Contact: Wayne Goerzen, Editor.

Desc: Features information on leafcutting bee propagation and alfalfa seed production. Recurring features include news of research, a calendar of events, reports of meetings, and notices of publications available. *Type:* Newsletter.

The Saskatchewan Pulse Grower

Saskatchewan Pulse Growers
210-111 Research Dr.   Ph: (306)668-5556
Saskatoon, SK, Canada S7N   Fax: (306)668-5557
3R2
URL: http://www.vsource.com/saskpulse/index.shtml.
Contact: Penny Sim, Editor; Garth Patterson, Editor.

Desc: Contains information about pulse crop agriculture. Recurring features include interviews and news of research. *Type:* Newsletter.

Seed Abstracts

CAB International
CABI Publishing
10 E. 40th St., Ste. 3203   Ph: (212)481-7018
New York, NY 10016
E-mail: cabi-nao@cabi.org
URL: http://www.cabi.org

Contact: Sue Hill, Product Manager, Crop Production and Natural Resources, s.hill@cabi.org.

Desc: Contains citations, with abstracts, to current periodical and other published literature related to seeds such as testing and storage, contamination of seeds by weed seeds, and seeds as carriers of pests and diseases. Corresponds to Seed Abstracts and in part to the online CAB ABSTRACTS database and the CAB ABSTRACTS on CD-ROM product. *Type:* Database.

Seed Scoop

Canadian Seed Growers Association
CPO Box 8455   Ph: (613)236-0497
Ottawa, ON, Canada K1G 3T1   Fax: (613)563-7855
E-mail: seeds@odo.eis.ca
Contact: Colleen Acres, Editor.

Desc: Discusses pure seed production in Canada. Provides news of association members. *Type:* Newsletter.

Seed Technologist News

Association of Official Seed Analysts, Inc. (AOSA)
201 N. 8th St., Ste. 400   Ph: (402)476-3852
PO Box 81152   Fax: (402)476-6547
Lincoln, NE 68501-1152
E-mail: assoc@navix.net

Contact: Diane Mesa, Editor.

Desc: Relates activities of the Society, with reports from various chapters across the U.S. and Canada. *Type:* Newsletter.

Shortliner

Farm Equipment Manufacturers Association
1000 Ececutive Parkway, Ste.   Ph: (314)878-2304
100   Fax: (314)878-1742
St. Louis, MO 63141
E-mail: fema@farmequip.org; vschmidt@farmequip.org.
URL: http://farmequip.org.

Contact: Robert K. Schnell, Editor.

Desc: Supplies news of trends, general industry information, equipment show dates, financial reports, and reviews of new industry innovations. Recurring features include editorials, news of research, and news of members. *Type:* Newsletter.

Soiless Grower

Hydroponic Society of America (HSA)
PO Box 1183   Ph: (510)232-2323
El Cerrito, CA 94530   Fax: (510)232-2384
URL: http://hsa.hydroponics.org.

Contact: Dan Lubkeman, Editor.

Desc: Covers issues and research in hydroponics. Recurring features include letters to the editor, a calendar of events, reports of meetings, news of educational opportunities, job listings, book reviews, and notices of publications available. *Type:* Newsletter.

Soils and Fertilizers

CAB International
CABI Publishing
10 E. 40th St., Ste. 3203   Ph: (212)481-7018
New York, NY 10016
E-mail: cabi-nao@cabi.org
URL: http://www.cabi.org

Contact: Sue Hill, Product Manager, Crop Production and Natural Resources, s.hill@cabi.org.

Desc: Contains citations, with abstracts, to current periodical and other published literature relating to soils and fertilizers. Corresponds to Soils and Fertilizers and in part to the online CAB ABSTRACTS database and the SOILCD and CAB ABSTRACTS CD-ROM products. *Type:* Database.

SolGenes, a Solanaceae Database

Cornell University - Department of Plant Breeding
409 Bradfield   Ph: (607)254-INFO
Ithaca, NY 14853
E-mail: info@cornell.edu
URL: http://probe.nalusda.gov:8000/plant/aboutsolgenes.html

Contact: Dr. Molly K. Jahn, Director, mmk9@cornell.edu.

Desc: The SolGenes database contains genetic information relating to the Solanaceae crops (tomato, potato, pepper), such as maps, probes, images, colleagues, references, and more. *Type:* Database.

Sorghum and Millets Abstracts

CAB International
CABI Publishing
10 E. 40th St., Ste. 3203   Ph: (212)481-7018
New York, NY 10016
E-mail: cabi-nao@cabi.org
URL: http://www.cabi.org

Contact: Sue Hill, Product Manager, Crop Production and Natural Resources, s.hill@cabi.org.

Desc: Contains citations, with abstracts, to current periodical and other published literature on sorghum, millet, and related crops. Corresponds in part to the online CAB ABSTRACTS database and the CAB ABSTRACTS on CD-ROM product. *Type:* Database.

South Dakota Department of Agriculture

523 E. Capitol   Ph: (605)773-3375
Pierre, SD 57501-3182   Free: 800-228-5254
     Fax: (605)773-5926
E-mail: leannen@doa.state.sd.us
URL: http://www.state.sd.us/state/executive/doa/doa.html

Contact: Darrell Cruea, Sec.

Desc: State government agency responsible for agricultural economic development in regulations of dairy, feed, fertilizers, pesticides, weeds, and pets; activities, forest health, and fire prevention and fire fighting. *Type:* Association.

Southeast Agrinet

3621 NW 10th St.   Ph: (904)629-7400
Ocala, FL 34475   Free: 800-944-6077
     Fax: (904)629-2139

Contact: Chuck Zimmerman, General Mgr.; Cindy Zimmerman, Farm Dir.

Alt. Contact: 3621 NW 10th St., Ocala, FL 34475; telephone: (904)629-7400; fax: (904)629-2139; toll-free: 800-944-6077. *Type:* Periodical.

Southern Farm Network

3012 Highwoods Blvd   Ph: (919)876-0674
Raleigh, NC 27604   Fax: (919)790-8369

Desc: Agricultural format. *Alt. Contact:* 3012 Highwoods Blvd, Raleigh, NC 27604; telephone: (919)876-0674; fax: (919)790-8369. *Type:* Periodical.

Southern U.S. Trade Association

World Trade Center, Ste. 1540   Ph: (504)568-5986
2 Canal St.   Fax: (504)568-6010
New Orleans, LA 70130
E-mail: susta@susta.org
URL: http://www.susta.org

Contact: Jim Ake, Exec.Dir.

Desc: Departments of agriculture of the Southern states; food and agricultural manufacturers and exporters operating in the southern United States. Promotes the export of high-value food and agricultural products of the South. *Type:* Association.

Southwest Agri-Radio Network

1700 S. 1st Ave.   Ph: 800-944-6077
Ste. 214   Fax: (520)782-1474
Yuma, AZ 85364

Contact: George G. Gatley, Pres./Dir.

Desc: Agricultural news format. *Alt. Contact:* 1700 S. 1st Ave., Ste. 214, Yuma, AZ 85364; telephone: 800-944-6077; fax: (520)782-1474; Western Agri-Radio Networks. *Type:* Periodical.

Soyabean Abstracts

CAB International
CABI Publishing
10 E. 40th St., Ste. 3203   Ph: (212)481-7018
New York, NY 10016
E-mail: cabi-nao@cabi.org
URL: http://www.cabi.org

Contact: Sue Hill, Product Manager, Crop Production and Natural Resources, s.hill@cabi.org.

Desc: Contains citations, with abstracts, to current periodical and other published literature related to soyabeans. Corresponds to Soyabean Abstracts and in part to the online CAB ABSTRACTS database and the CAB ABSTRACTS on CD-ROM product. *Type:* Database.

Spudletter

National Potato Council
5690 DTC Blvd., Ste. 230E   Ph: (303)773-9295
Englewood, CO 80111-3200   Fax: (303)773-9296
E-mail: npcspud@ix.netcom.com.
URL: http://www.npcspud.com.

Desc: Reports on the Council's efforts to influence national legislation and regulation on behalf of potato growers. Covers agricultural news and developments. *Type:* Newsletter.

Stat (Blaine)

Stat Publishing
Box 8110-361
Blaine, WA 98230
E-mail: publisher@statpub.com
URL: http://www.statpub.com; http://www.statpub.com.

Desc: Provides market analysis for pulses (edible seeds of various leguminous crops), dry legumes, and birdseeds. *Type:* Newsletter.

Sugar Industry Abstracts

CAB International
CABI Publishing
10 E. 40th St., Ste. 3203   Ph: (212)481-7018
New York, NY 10016
E-mail: cabi-nao@cabi.org
URL: http://www.cabi.org

Contact: Sue Hill, Product Manager, Crop Production and Natural Resources, s.hill@cabi.org.

Desc: Contains more than 9000 citations, with abstracts, to the worldwide literature on sugar production, properties, and uses. Covers cane and beet sugar manufacture, sugar refining, by-products, liquid sugar and sweeteners, and nutrition, health, and environmental issues. *Type:* Database.

Supima Newsletter

Supima Association of America
4141 E. Broadway Rd.   Ph: (602)437-1364
Phoenix, AZ 85040   Fax: (602)437-0143
E-mail: info@supimacotton.org; mlsupima@amug.org.
URL: http://www.supimacotton.org.

Contact: Matthew S. Laughlin, Editor, mattesupimacotton.org.

Desc: Provides information related to American Pima (extra-long staple) cotton. Covers Association activities. *Type:* Newsletter.

TecAgri News

Clark Consulting International, Inc.
PO Box 600   Ph: (847)836-5100
Dundee, IL 60118-0600
E-mail: Ag-PR@AgPR.com.

Contact: Warren E. Clark, Editor and Publisher.

Desc: Contains information for farmers who utilize and/or own computers. *Type:* Newsletter.

Techletter

Pinto & Associates, Inc.
29839 Oak Rd.   Ph: (301)884-3020
Mechanicsville, MD 20659-   Fax: (301)884-4068
2201

Contact: Lawrence J. Pinto, Publisher; Sandra K. Kraft, Editor.

Desc: Covers topics of interest to pest control technicians. *Type:* Newsletter.

Texas Agriculture

Texas Farm Bureau
Box 2689   Ph: (254)751-2244
Waco, TX 76702-2689   Fax: (254)772-1766

Contact: Mike Barnett, Editor; Gene Hall, Publisher; Drew Wenner, Advertising Mgr.

Desc: Farm newspaper (tabloid) containing legislative and commodity news, market trends, government regulatory updates, and feature articles on successful producers for members of the Texas Farm Bureau. *Type:* Periodical.

Two-Cylinder Club

PO Box 10   Ph: (319)345-6060
Grundy Center, IA 50638   Free: 800-782-2582
     Fax: (319)345-2662
URL: http://www.two-cylinder.com

Contact: Jack Bible, Dir.

Desc: Individuals interested in tractors manufactured by John Deere prior to 1973, collectors of John Deere memorabilia. Seeks to preserve and restore antique John Deere tractors and accessories. Assists members in obtaining technical information. *Type:* Association.

United Farm Workers of America

19700 Woodford-Tehachapi Rd.   Ph: (805)822-5571
Keene, CA 93531   Fax: (805)822-6103

Contact: Arturo S. Rodriguez, Pres.

Desc: AFL-CIO. Agricultural laborers. Chief purpose is to achieve collective bargaining rights for U.S. farm workers. Seeks to give farm laborers dignity and pride in their work by improving working and safety conditions and wages. *Type:* Association.

U.S. Agriculture

The WEFA Group
1110 Vermont Ave., NW   Ph: (202)775-0610
Washington, DC 20005
URL: http://www.fdic.gov

Desc: Contains more than 29,000 annual time series on the supply and disposition of crops, livestock, and meat commodities in more than 195 countries. Data include stocks; areas harvested, yield, production; domestic use broken down by food and industrial use; imports, exports, and imports from the United States. *Available:* The WEFA Group. *Type:* Database.

U.S. Department of Agriculture

Agricultural Research Service

6303 Ivy Ln., Rm. 450   Ph: (301)344-2340
Greenbelt, MD 20770

Desc: The Agricultural Research Service conducts research to develop and transfer solutions to agricultural problems of high national priority. It provides information access and dissemination to ensue high-quality, safe food and other agricultural products; assess the nutritional needs of Americans; sustain a competitive agricultural economy; enhance the natural resource base and the environment; and provide economic opportunities for rural citizens, communities, and society as a whole. *Type:* Government agency, office, or program.

U.S. Grains Council

1400 K St. NW, Ste. 1200   Ph: (202)789-0789
Washington, DC 20005   Fax: (202)898-0522
E-mail: grains@grains.org
URL: http://www.grains.org
Contact: Kenneth Hobbie, Pres.
Desc: Federation of feed grain producer organizations, seed trade associations, and organizations of grain processors, exporters, dealers, and related agribusiness manufacturers. Maintains 11 international offices for development of foreign markets in over 80 countries for corn, grain sorghum, barley, and related products. *Type:* Association.

U.S. Wheatletter

U.S. Wheat Associates
1620 I St. NW, Ste. 801   Ph: (202)463-0999
Washington, DC 20006   Fax: (202)785-1052
Desc: Presents information on U.S. wheat export credits, European Community (EC) subsidies, wheat production, and future markets. *Type:* Newsletter.

Universal Cooperatives

PO Box 460   Ph: (612)854-0800
Minneapolis, MN 55440-0460   Fax: (612)854-5744
Contact: Terrance J. Bohman, Pres./CEO.
Desc: Federation of regional agricultural cooperative associations. *Type:* Association.

U.S.A. Rice Federation

4301 N Fairfax Dr., Ste. 305   Ph: (703)351-8161
Arlington, VA 22203-1616   Fax: (703)351-8162
E-mail: info@va.com
URL: http://www.usarice.com
Contact: Ralph S. Newman, Jr., Admin.
Desc: Organizations comprising the U.S.A. Rice Council, U.S. Rice Producers' Group, and the Rice Millers' Association. *Type:* Association.

Vegetable Crops

California Agricultural Statistics Service
U.S. Department of Agriculture (USDA)
PO Box 1258   Ph: (916)654-0895
Sacramento, CA 95812
Desc: Provides forecasts and statistics concerning California vegetable crops. Remarks: Included in California Agriculture. *Type:* Newsletter.

Virginia Hay Clearing House

Virginia Department of Agriculture and Consumer Services
1100 Bank St., No. 805   Ph: (804)786-3947
Richmond, VA 23219-3638   Fax: (804)371-7787
E-mail: mktnews@vdacs.state.va.us; vamns@richmond.infi.net.
URL: http://www.state.va.us/~vdacs/divmkt/mktnews.htm.
Contact: J.P. Welch, Editor.
Desc: Provides information on the buying and selling of hay in Virginia. Listings are by geographic area of the state. *Type:* Newsletter.

The Washington Agricultural Record

Washington Agricultural Record
Box 25001, Georgetown Sta.   Ph: (202)333-8190
Washington, DC 20007   Free: 800-382-9989
   Fax: (202)337-3809
Contact: Matthew S. Strachorn, Editor.
Desc: Focuses on Washington farm issues and developments, reporting international congressional and United States Department of Agriculture (U.S.D.A.) news and international agricultural developments. *Type:* Newsletter.

The Webster Agricultural Letter

Webster Communications Corp.
1530 Key Blvd., Ste. 2   Ph: (703)525-4512
Arlington, VA 22209   Fax: (703)525-4917
E-mail: agletter@aol.com.
Contact: James C. Webster, Editor.
Desc: Covers agriculture, food, and politics. *Type:* Newsletter.

Weed Abstracts

CAB International
CABI Publishing
10 E. 40th St., Ste. 3203   Ph: (212)481-7018
New York, NY 10016
E-mail: cabi-nao@cabi.org
URL: http://www.cabi.org
Desc: Contains citations, with abstracts, to current periodical and other published literature relating to weed biology and control. Plants covered include annual field crops, vegetable crops, fruit crops, forests, grassland and herbage crops, ornamentals, plantation crops, aquatic weeds, woolly weeds, and parasitic weeds. *Type:* Database.

Weekly Market Bulletin

New Hampshire Department of Agriculture, Markets & Food
PO Box 2042   Ph: (603)271-2505
Concord, NH 03302-2042   Fax: (603)271-1109
E-mail: 103423.372@compuserve.com
Contact: Stephen H. Taylor, Editor.
Desc: Provides information on agriculture in New Hampshire. *Type:* Newsletter.

Weekly Market Summary

Missouri Department of Agriculture
PO Box 630   Ph: (573)751-7213
Jefferson City, MO 65102   Free: 800-877-4HAY
   Fax: (573)751-2868
Contact: Sam Shelton, Editor.
Desc: Features meat, livestock, egg, and grain prices; commodity futures; livestock slaughter; and the Missouri hay market. *Type:* Newsletter.

Weekly National Feed & Seed Summary

Livestock & Grain Market News Branch
Agricultural Marketing Service
U.S. Department of Agriculture
1428 S. Pioneer Way   Ph: (509)765-3611
Moses Lake, WA 98837   Fax: (509)765-0454
Type: Newsletter.

Weekly Outlook

University of Illinois
ACES Newsletter Service
69 Mumford Hall   Ph: (217)244-5166
1301 W. Gregory Dr.
Urbana, IL 61801
Contact: Darrel Good, Coordinator.
Desc: Anticipates, reports, and interprets current market information, supply, demand, and price outlook for agricultural products, including corn, soybeans, wheat, cattle, and hogs. *Type:* Newsletter.

Western Growers Association—Update

Western Growers Association
PO Box 2130   Ph: (949)863-1000
Newport Beach, CA 92658   Fax: (949)863-9028
E-mail: flower@wga.com
Contact: Heather Flower, Editor, flower@wga.com.
Desc: Serves the fresh produce industry in California and Arizona. Supplies current information on labor relations, transportation of fruit and vegetables, marketing, and legislation and regulations. *Type:* Newsletter.

The Western Stock Growers Newsletter

Garth Cochrane
2116 27th Ave. NE, Ste. 101   Ph: (403)250-9121
Calgary, AB, Canada T2E 7A6
Desc: Provides news and market reports of the agriculture industry. Recurring features include letters to the editor, interviews, news of research, and a calendar of events. *Type:* Newsletter.

Wheat, Barley and Triticale Abstracts

CAB International
CABI Publishing
10 E. 40th St., Ste. 3203   Ph: (212)481-7018
New York, NY 10016
E-mail: cabi-nao@cabi.org
URL: http://www.cabi.org
Contact: Sue Hill, Product Manager, Crop Production and Natural Resources, s.hill@cabi.org.
Desc: Contains citations, with abstracts, to current periodical and other published literature related to wheat, barley, and triticale. Corresponds to Wheat, Barley and Triticale Abstracts and in part to the online CAB ABSTRACTS database and the CAB ABSTRACTS on CD-ROM product. *Type:* Database.

Wheat Briefs

Wheat Quality Council
106 W. Capitol, Ste. 2   Ph: (605)224-5187
PO Box 966   Fax: (605)224-0517
Pierre, SD 57501-0966
E-mail: bhwqc@aol.com
Contact: Ben Handcock, Editor.
Desc: Serves as part of the educational and public relations effort of the agribusiness and baking industries to assure the protection and improvement of wheat. Provides information useful to the breadstuffs industry and other wheat users and producers, including crop reports, problem alerts, and selected data. *Type:* Newsletter.

World Agricultural Economics and Rural Sociology Abstracts

CAB International
CABI Publishing
10 E. 40th St., Ste. 3203   Ph: (212)481-7018
New York, NY 10016
E-mail: cabi-nao@cabi.org
URL: http://www.cabi.org
Desc: Contains citations, with abstracts, to current periodical and other published literature relating to world agricultural economics and rural sociology. Corresponds to World Agricultural Economics and Rural Sociology Abstracts and in part to the online CAB ABSTRACTS and CAB: Economics, Development and Education databases and the CAB ABSTRACTS on CD-ROM and AgE-CONCD products. *Type:* Database.

World Databases in Agriculture

National Register Publishing Co.
121 Chanlon Rd.   Ph: (908)464-6800
New Providence, NJ 07974   Free: 800-521-8110
   Fax: (908)508-7671
E mail: info@renp.com
URL: http://www.reedref.com
Contact: C.J. Armstrong, Editor.
Desc: Agricultural information on databases, including CD-ROM, magnetic tape, diskette, online, fax, or data-broadcast worldwide. *Type:* Directory.

AIDS

Aaron Diamond AIDS Research Center
455 1st Ave., 7th Fl. Ph: (212)725-0018
New York, NY 10016 Fax: (212)725-1126
URL: http://www.adarc.org
Contact: David D. Ho, MD, Dir.
Desc: Pathogenesis of HIV-1 in vivo, maternal-fetal transmission of HIV-1, antibody responses to HIV and vaccine development, mechanism of HIV entry into CD4 and CD4- cells, anti-HIV therapeutics and viral resistance, search for the causative agent of HIV-negative cases of immunodeficiency, cellular immune responses to HIV-1 in the pathogenesis of AIDS, cellular immune responses to HIV-1 in vaccine development, development of the scid mouse model for HIV studies, receptors for human retroviruses (HIV and HTLV), assembly of HIV virion, function of accessory genes of HIV, interaction of HIV envelope with the cellular receptor, mechanism of viral entry, and mapping of the functional determinants of HIV envelope glycoprotein. *Type:* Research center.

AIDS Reference Guide
Atlantic Information Services, Inc.
1100 17th St. NW, No. 300 Ph: (202)775-9008
Washington, DC 20036 Free: 800-521-4323
  Fax: (202)331-9542
Contact: Steve Goodwin, Editor.
Desc: Acts as an information clearinghouse for planning services and managing the epidemic in workplaces, hospitals, clinics, classrooms and communities. *Type:* Newsletter.

AIDS Research Consortium of Atlanta, Inc.
131 Ponce De Leon Ave. NE, Ph: (404)876-2317
Ste. 130 Fax: (404)872-1701
Atlanta, GA 30308-1962
E-mail: arca@avana.net
URL: http://www.arca.home.mindspring.com
Contact: Melanie Thompson, MD, Prin. Investigator.
Desc: HIV clinical trials and epidemiology. *Type:* Research center.

AIDS Resource Center of Wisconsin
820 N. Plankinton Ave. Ph: (414)273-1991
Milwaukee, WI 53203 Free: 800-359-9272
  Fax: (414)273-2357
URL: http://www.arcw.org
Contact: Doug Nelson, Exec.Dir.
Desc: Provides health and social services for people affected by HIV; aggressive AIDS prevention programs; advocacy for responsive public policy on AIDS; and clinical-based treatment research. *Type:* Association.

AIDS/STD News Report
CD Publications
8204 Fenton St. Ph: (301)588-6380
Silver Spring, MD 20910 Free: 800-666-6380
  Fax: (301)588-6385
E-mail: cdpubs@clark.net
Contact: Sharon Samber, Editor.
Desc: Provides information on funding and pertinent legislative activity. *Type:* Newsletter.

AIDS Weekly
AIDS Weekly/Cancer Weekly
206 Rogers St., N.E., Suite 126 Ph: (770)507-7777
PO Box 5528
Atlanta, GA 30307
URL: http://www.newsfile.com
Desc: Contains the complete text of AIDS Weekly, a newsletter on the prevention, detection, and treatment of Acquired Immune Deficiency Syndrome (AIDS) worldwide.

Covers AIDS-related developments in health care organizations and agencies, patient care and support, clinical drug trials, and announcements of grants for research and education. *Available:* CDC AIDS Weekly Infoline. *Type:* Database.

AIDSDRUGS
AIDS Clinical Trials Information Service (ACTIS)
P.O. Box 6421
Rockville, MD 20849-6421
E-mail: actis@actis.org
URL: http://www.actis.org
Desc: Contains information on more than 80 drugs being tested for use against human immunodeficiency virus (HIV) infection, Acquired Immune Deficiency Syndrome (AIDS), and related opportunistic diseases. Drugs are indexed by Medical Subject Headings (MeSH) and include agent name and synonyms, including trade names and generic name; Chemical Abstracts Service (CAS) Registry Number; adverse reactions and contraindications; pharmacology (i.e., synergistic, antagonistic, or other interaction of the drug with other agents); physical and chemical properties; and manufacturer. *Available:* AIDS Clinical Trials Information Service (ACTIS). *Type:* Database.

AIDServe Indiana
3951 N. Meridian St., Ste. 101 Ph: (317)920-7755
Indianapolis, IN 46208-4011 Free: 800-848-2437
  Fax: (317)926-7823
E-mail: aidserve@aidserve.org
URL: http://www.icaan.org
Contact: Thomas Bartenbach, Pres.
Desc: Prevents the transmission of HIV and improves the quality of life of those infected and those affected by creating access to education and services for all communities in Indiana. Acts as advocates for an effective and compassionate response to HIV. *Type:* Association.

AIDSLINE
U.S. National Library of Medicine (NLM)
MEDLARS Management Section
8600 Rockville Pike Ph: (301)496-3147
Bethesda, MD 20894
URL: http://www.sis.nlm.nih.gov/dirline
Desc: Contains more than 48,000 citations, with some abstracts, to the worldwide literature on Acquired Immune Deficiency Syndrome (AIDS) from the MEDLINE and Health Planning and Administration databases. Covers biomedical, epidemiological, social, behavioral, clinical, and research aspects of the disease as well as health policy issues. *Available:* Ovid Technologies, Inc.; The Dialog Corporation, DataStar; DIMDI (Deutsches Institut fuer Medizinische Dokumentation und Information); The Dialog Corporation, DIALOG; CompuServe Information Service, Knowledge Index; U.S. National Library of Medicine (NLM), TOXNET; PaperChase; STN International; Aries Systems Corporation; EBSCOhost. *Type:* Database.

AIDSTRIALS
AIDS Clinical Trials Information Service (ACTIS)
P.O. Box 6421
Rockville, MD 20849-6421
E-mail: actis@actis.org
URL: http://www.actis.org
Desc: Contains information on more than 750 clinical trials of agents being evaluated for use against human immodeficiency virus (HIV) infection, Acquired Immune Deficiency Syndrome (AIDS), and related opportunistic diseases. Covers open trials as well as closed or completed trials. *Type:* Database.

Alive and Kicking
We the People Living with AIDS/HIV of the Delaware Valley
425 S. Broad St. Ph: (215)545-6868
Philadelphia, PA 19147 Fax: (215)545-8437
E-mail: wtp@critpath.org
Desc: Covers organizational news, schedules, opinions and advocacy. Also reports on medical and treatment news about AIDS/HIV. *Type:* Newsletter.

American Association of AIDS Executives
1525 Santa Barbara St., Ste. 1 Ph: (805)568-1400
Santa Barbara, CA 93101 Fax: (805)564-4381
E-mail: ragnews@aol.com
Contact: James B. Zender, Exec.Dir.
Desc: Coordinates and connects management personnel at HIV/AIDS agencies. *Type:* Association.

American Foundation for AIDS Research
120 Wall Street, 13th floor Ph: (212)806-1600
New York, NY 10005 Free: 800-39-AMFAR
  Fax: (212)806-1601
E-mail: donors@amfar.org
URL: http://www.amfar.org
Contact: Arthur J. Ammann, M.D., Contact.
Desc: Raises funds to support research on HIV/AIDS. *Type:* Association.

The AmfAR Newsletter
American Foundation for AIDS Research
120 Wall St., 13th Fl. Ph: (212)806-1600
New York, NY 10005 Free: 800-392-6327
  Fax: (212)806-1601
URL: http://www.amfar.org.
Contact: Catherine Lemp, Managing Editor, (212)806-1616, cathy.lemp@amfar.org.
Desc: Covers news of the foundation, which is concerned with "ending the continuing HIV/AIDS epidemic." Contains articles on issues such as AIDS education, public poliy, and research. Recurring features include fundraising activities and a public policy update. *Type:* Newsletter.

BETA
San Francisco AIDS Foundation
PO Box 426182 Ph: (415)864-5855
San Francisco, CA 94142-6182 Free: 800-959-1059
E-mail: beta@thecity.sfsu.edu.
URL: http://www.out.org; http://www.hivnet.org/magazines/beta; http://www.sfaf.org/beta.htm1.
Contact: Ronald A. Baker, Editor; Mark Bowers, Managing Editor.
Desc: Reports on current research and clinical trials of treatment for HIV/AIDS. Recurring features include interviews, news of research, and reports of meetings. *Type:* Newsletter.

Body Positive
Body Positive
19 Fulton St., Rm. 308-B Ph: (212)566-7333
New York, NY 10038-2100 Free: 800-566-6599
  Fax: (212)566-4539
E-mail: bodypos@aol.com
Contact: Richard Brigand, Editor.
Desc: Provides information for people who are HIV positive or who have AIDS. Remarks: Also available in Spanish as El Cuerpo Positivo. *Type:* Newsletter.

California AIDS Clearinghouse
Los Angeles Gay and Lesbian Center
1625 N. Schrader Blvd. Ph: (213)845-4180
Los Angeles, CA 90028
URL: http://www.HIVINFO.org

Contact: Phaedra A. Torres, Information Specialist, (213)845-4180, fax: (213)845-4193, lacain@delphi.com. *Desc:* Provides access to HIV Education and Health Education information. Contains more than 100 HIV/AIDS client materials titles. *Available:* Los Angeles Gay and Lesbian Center. *Type:* Database.

CDC National AIDS Clearinghouse
Centers for Disease Control and Prevention
1600 Clifton Rd. NE   Ph: (404)639-3311
Atlanta, GA 30333
E-mail: netinfo@cdc.gov
URL: http://www.cdcnac.org/
Contact: info@cdcnpin.org.

Desc: From the nation's prestigious Centers for Disease Control and Prevention comes this encyclopedic collection of resources and information about AIDS and sexually transmitted diseases. The site also features a good deal of information about tuberculosis, a disease once thought to be virtually eliminated that has now reappeared, often in strains resistant to drug therapy. *Type:* Database.

City of Hope National Medical Center
Strategic Program for Innovative Research in AIDS Therapy
Virology & Infectious Diseases/   Ph: (626)359-2495
   Dept. of Pediatrics   Fax: (626)301-8458
1500 E. Duarte Rd.
Duarte, CA 91010
E-mail: jzaia@cityofhope.org
URL: http://www.cityofhope.org
Contact: Dr. John A. Zaia, Prin.Invest.

Desc: Developmental gene therapy in the treatment of AIDS, including development and delivery of antiviral DNA and RNA; and pathogenesis and treatment of cytomegalovirus infection; and development of gene therapy for cancer and AIDS. *Type:* Research center.

Comprehensive AIDS Center
Northwestern University   Ph: (312)908-7866
   Medical School   Fax: (312)908-5820
680 N. Lake Shore Dr., Ste.
   1106
Chicago, IL 60611
E-mail: s-perez@nwu.edu
Contact: Dr. John P. Phair, Dir.

Desc: Acquired immune deficiency syndrome in adults, molecular virology of human immunodeficiency virus (HIV), and experimental therapy of HIV. *Type:* Research center.

Design Industries Foundation Fighting AIDS
150 W. 26th St., Ste. 602   Ph: (212)727-3100
New York, NY 10001   Fax: (212)727-2574
Contact: David Sheppard, Exec.Dir.

Desc: Serves as a foundation bestowing grants to organizations providing direct patient care and services; preventive, post-diagnostic, and community education; housing, meals, emergency assistance, and legal advocacy; treatment and community-based research. Seeks to educate firms, associations, and individuals through print materials, presentations, and referrals. *Type:* Association.

Executive Office of the President
Office of Policy Development
Domestic Policy Council
Director of National AIDS Policy
Old Executive Office Bldg., Rm.   Ph: (202)456-2216
   216
Washington, DC 20502
Contact: Sandra Thurman, Director.
Type: Government agency, office, or program.

Gay Men's Health Crisis
119 W. 24th St.   Ph: (212)807-6664
New York, NY 10011-1913   Fax: (212)367-7386
Contact: Joshua Lipsman, Dir.
Desc: Social service agency for the clinical treatment of AIDS. Provides support and therapy groups for persons with AIDS and their families. Offers Patient Recreation Services. *Type:* Association.

God's Love We Deliver
166 Avenue of the Americas   Ph: (212)294-8100
New York, NY 10013-1207   Fax: (212)294-8101
Contact: Kathy Spahn, Exec.Dir.
Desc: Nonsectarian volunteer organization. Strives to address the issues of malnutrition and hunger among people living with HIV. *Type:* Association.

Harvard University
Center for Biostatistics in AIDS Research
Harvard School of Public Health   Ph: (617)432-2829
FXB Bldg.   Fax: (617)432-3163
655 Huntington Ave.
Boston, MA 02115
Contact: Stephen W. Lagakos, Dir.
Desc: Treatments for persons infected with HIV. *Type:* Research center.

Indiana University Bloomington
Rural Center for the Study and Promotion of AIDS/STD Prevention
801 E. 7th St.   Ph: (812)855-1718
Bloomington, IN 47405-3085   Free: 800-566-8644
    Fax: (812)855-3717
E-mail: aids@indiana.edu
URL: http://www.indiana.edu/~aids/
Contact: William L. Yarber, Dir.
Desc: AIDS, HIV, and STD prevention in rural areas. *Type:* Research center.

Indiana University-Purdue University at Indianapolis
Indiana AIDS Clinical Trials Unit
550 N. University Blvd., No.   Ph: (317)274-8456
   5550   Free: 800-421-3316
Indianapolis, IN 46202   Fax: (317)274-1876
URL: http://www.iupui.edu/it/indyactu/index.html
Contact: Joseph Wheat, Dir.
Desc: AIDS treatment, including an antiretroviral approach; treatment and prevention of AIDS complications, including pneumocystis, pneumonia, cryptococcal meningitis, histoplasmosis, cytomegalovirus infection, Kaposi's sarcoma, and dementia. *Type:* Research center.

Kansas City AIDS Research Consortium
4050 Pennsylvania, Ste. 230   Ph: (816)756-5116
Kansas City, MO 64111   Fax: (816)756-5121
E-mail: gjohnson@kcarc.org
URL: http://www.kcarc.org
Contact: Gary R. Johnson, Exec.Dir.
Desc: HIV and AIDS clinical trials, opportunistic infections, anti-retrovirals, and HIV wasting treatment. *Type:* Research center.

McGill University
McGill AIDS Centre
3755, Chemin de la Cote-   Ph: (514)340-7536
   Sainte-Catherine   Fax: (514)340-7537
Institut Lady Davis, Bureau 318
Montreal, PQ, Canada H3T
   1E2
URL: http://www.mcgill.ca/jgh/aids/
Contact: Dr. Mark A. Wainberg, Dir.

Desc: Promotes research on all aspects of HIV/AIDS, the development of new drugs, treatments, and vaccines for HIV/AIDS, as well as the development of comprehensive cost-effective models of care and treatment for HIV infection and AIDS. Sponsors basic, clinical, epidemiological, preventive, and psychosocial studies of HIV/AIDS. *Type:* Research center.

Names Project Foundation
310 Townsend St., Ste. 310   Ph: (415)882-5500
San Francisco, CA 94107   Fax: (415)882-6200
E-mail: info@aidsquilt.org
URL: http://www.aidsquilt.org
Contact: Andy Ilves, Exec.Dir.
Desc: Promotes creation of AIDS Memorial Quilt as an "appropriate, compassionate response" to the AIDS epidemic. Goals of the project are to provide a creative means of remembrance and healing; to illustrate the enormity of the AIDS epidemic; to increase public awareness of AIDS; to assist with HIV prevention education; and to raise funds for community-based AIDS service organizations. The 25 acre quilt currently contains 43,000 panels from each of the 50 states and 39 foreign countries bearing the names of persons who have died as a result of AIDS. *Type:* Association.

National AIDS Fund
1400 I St. NW, Ste. 1220   Ph: (202)408-4848
Washington, DC 20005-2208   Fax: (202)408-1818
E-mail: info@aidsfund.org
URL: http://www.aidsfund.org
Contact: Mary Wilson-Byrom, CEO.
Desc: Promotes leadership and generates resources for effective community responses to HIV/AIDS. *Type:* Association.

National AIDS Network
2033 M St. NW, Ste. 800   Ph: (202)293-2437
Washington, DC 20036   Fax: (202)293-2587
Contact: James L. Holm, Exec.Dir.
Desc: Community-based groups providing AIDS education or direct services to individuals with AIDS. Serves as a resource center and networking agency for members; provides information on AIDS service organizations. Makes available financial aid to organizations that provide AIDS education or services; coordinates fundraising activities. *Type:* Association.

The National Directory of AIDS Care
Morgan-Rand Publishing/Volt Directory Marketing
1800 Byberry Rd., Bldg. 8   Ph: (215)938-5511
Huntingdon Valley, PA 19006   Free: 800-677-3839
    Fax: (215)938-5549
Contact: Shawn D. Phillips, Editor.
Desc: Over 6,000 AIDS and HIV resources, including hotlines, health departments, research institutes, testing sites, hospice programs, home health care services, federal government agencies with services related to HIV/AIDS, state and local programs, and education programs and projects offered by the American Red Cross. *Type:* Directory.

National Minority AIDS Council
1931 13th St. NW   Ph: (202)483-6622
Washington, DC 20009-4432   Free: 800-544-0586
    Fax: (202)483-1127
URL: http://www.nmac.org
Contact: Paul A. Kawata, Exec.Dir.
Desc: Public health departments and AIDS service organizations. Serves as a clearinghouse of information on AIDS as it affects minority communities in the U.S. Facilitates discussion among national minority organizations about AIDS. *Type:* Association.

NIA
Association of Black Psychologists
PO Box 55999   Ph: (202)722-0800
Washington, DC 20040   Fax: (202)722-5941
Contact: Djuna S. Craig, Editor.
Desc: Provides information on selected topics related to HIV/AIDS and sexually transmitted diseases (STDs). Offers "technical assistance to CEOs on education and care to persons affected and infected by HIV." Recurring features include a calendar of events and notices of publications available. *Type:* Newsletter.

Northwest AIDS Foundation
127 Broadway Ave. E., Ste. 200   Ph: (206)329-6923
Seattle, WA 98102-5711   Fax: (206)325-2689
Contact: Terry Stone, Exec.Dir.
Desc: Provides services and grants to people with AIDS and funding grants to other AIDS organizations; promotes public education to prevent the spread of the disease. *Type:* Association.

Pediatric AIDS Foundation
2950 31st St. 125th Fl.   Ph: (310)395-9051
Santa Monica, CA 90405-3037   Fax: (310)395-5149
Contact: Susan De Laurentis, CEO.
Desc: Confronts medical problems unique to children infected with HIV/AIDS, and focuses on finding medical answers that will bring hope. *Type:* Association.

Positive News
San Francisco AIDS Foundation
PO Box 426182   Ph: (415)864-5855
San Francisco, CA 94142-6182   Free: 800-959-1059
E-mail: beta@thecity.sfsu.edu.
Contact: Christopher Gortner, Coord.; Ronald Baker, Editor.
Desc: Addresses topics of importance in an easy-to-understand manner to HIV-infected individuals. Highlights resources available in the San Francisco area. *Type:* Newsletter.

Positively Aware
Test Positive Aware Network
1258 W. Belmont   Ph: (773)472-6397
Chicago, IL 60657   Fax: (773)472-7505
Contact: Brett Grodeck, Editor.
Desc: Contains articles on HIV- and-AIDS related issues. Covers medical research treatment and psycho-social issues. *Type:* Newsletter.

Project Inform
205 13th St., No. 2001   Ph: (415)558-8669
San Francisco, CA 94103   Free: 800-822-7422
                                 Fax: (415)558-0684
E-mail: web@projinf.org
URL: http://www.projinf.org
Contact: David Evans, Prog.Dir.
Desc: Information clearinghouse and hot line providing updated information on drug treatments for persons with AIDS or the Human Immunodeficiency Virus. Also provides information on organizations through which the drug treatments can be obtained. Works to speed up research process and focus on promising new treatments. *Type:* Association.

Rutgers University
AIDS Research Group
Institute for Health   Ph: (732)932-8579
30 College Ave.   Fax: (732)932-6872
New Brunswick, NJ 08901-
    1293
E-mail: scrystal@rci.rutgers.edu
Contact: Stephen Crystal, PhD, Dir.

Desc: Social and behavioral research on AIDS, focusing on policy issues and applying social science methodology to the planning and evaluation of programs and policies designed to meet public health objectives. Specific areas of research include HIV health services, long-term care, social networks, mental health programs, the social context of health-related behavior in Hispanic and black subcultures, health cognition and health belief systems, legal aspects of serving endangered and high-risk populations, and cost of care and services utilization studies. *Type:* Research center.

St. Clare's Hospital and Health Center
Spellman Center for HIV-Related Disease
415 W. 51st St.   Ph: (212)459-8409
New York, NY 10019   Fax: (212)459-8489

Contact: Dr. Linda Smith, Med.Dir.

Desc: Clinical drug trials, including immune modulators, anti-retrovirals, prophylactic therapies for infections, DDI, and granulocyte-macrophage colony-stimulating activity factors. *Type:* Research center.

San Francisco AIDS Foundation
995 Market St. 200   Ph: (415)487-3000
San Francisco, CA 94103   Free: 800-367-AIDS
                                 Fax: (415)487-3009
URL: http://www.sfaf.org

Contact: Pat Christen, Exec.Dir.

Desc: Regional organization whose goals are to educate the public on the prevention of AIDS and to make various social service programs accessible to people with AIDS. Provides community forums; develops and distributes educational materials. Provides assistance to people with AIDS in obtaining emergency housing, social security and veterans' benefits, medical and insurance benefits, and legal referral services. *Type:* Association.

Stanford University
Center for AIDS Research
Div. of Infectious Diseases   Ph: (650)723-6231
Rm. S-156   Fax: (650)725-2395
Stanford, CA 94305-5107
E-mail: merigan@leland.stanford.edu
URL: http://www-leland.stanford.edu/group/aids/index.html

Contact: Dr. Thomas Merigan, Dir.

Desc: Antiviral drug studies, including inhibitors of HIV, HBV, and herpes replication using in vitro and in vivo antiviral models. *Type:* Research center.

State University of New York Health Science Center at Stony Brook
SUNY Stony Brook AIDS Treatment and Development Center
Sch. of Med.   Ph: (516)444-1660
Div. of Infect. Diseases   Fax: (516)444-7518
T-15, 080, Rm. 080
Stony Brook, NY 11794-8153
E-mail: rsteigb@mail.som.sunysb.edu
URL: http://www.uhmc.sunysb.edu/internalmed/AIDSHIV/HIVhome.html

Contact: Dr. Roy T. Steigbigel, Dir.

Desc: Human immunodeficiency virus (HIV) research, focusing on pathogenesis, mechanism of replication, and development of inhibitors. *Type:* Research center.

U.S. Department of Health and Human Services
National Center for Infectious Diseases
Division of AIDS, STDS, Tuberculosis Laboratories
Immunology Branch
1600 Clifton Rd., N.E., Rm.   Ph: (404)639-3434
    1202 (MSA-25)   Fax: (404)639-2108
Atlanta, GA 30333
Contact: Dr. J. Steven McDougal, Chf.
Desc: Immunology and Acquired Immunodeficiency Syndrome (AIDS). *Type:* Research center.

U.S. Department of Health and Human Services
National Center for Infectious Diseases
Division of AIDS, STDS and Tuberculosis Laboratories
Retrovirus Diseases Branch
1600 Clifton Rd. NE, G19   Ph: (404)639-1024
Atlanta, GA 30333   Fax: (404)639-1174
Contact: Thomas M. Folks, PhD, Chf.
Desc: Retrovirus diseases and retroviral etiologies of chronic diseases. *Type:* Research center.

U.S. Department of Health and Human Services
National Center for Infectious Diseases
Division of HIV / AIDS
1600 Clifton Rd., N.E.   Ph: (404)639-2076
Mail Stop E-49   Fax: (404)639-2007
Atlanta, GA 30333
URL: http://www.cdc.gov/nchstp/hiv_aids/dhap.htm
Contact: Harold Jaffe, Dir.
Desc: Epidemiologic and laboratory investigations, surveillance, and studies to determine risk factors, transmission patterns, prevalence/incidence of HIV/AIDS, and case reporting for acquired immunodeficiency syndrome. Program also develops and evaluates laboratory methods and procedures for the isolation and characterization of human immunodeficiency virus (HIV) and serodiagnosis and understanding of viral pathogenesis. *Type:* Research center.

U.S. Department of Health and Human Services
National Institute of Allergy and Infectious Diseases
Division of Acquired Immuniodeficiency Syndrome (AIDS)
Basic Science Program
Solar Bldg., Rm. 2C-07   Ph: (301)402-0135
6003 Executive Blvd.   Fax: (301)402-3211
Bethesda, MD 20892
Contact: L. Schrager, MD, Chf.
Desc: Coordinates population-based research that will advance the understanding of the biology and clinical course of HIV infection. Serves as a foundation for advancing treatment and prevention. *Type:* Research center.

U.S. Department of Health and Human Services
National Institute of Allergy and Infectious Diseases
Division of Acquired Immunodeficiency Syndrome (AIDS)
6003 Executive Blvd.   Ph: (301)496-8000
Rockville, MD 20852   Fax: (301)402-1505
E-mail: jk31e@nihigov
URL: http://www.niaid.nih.gov
Contact: Dr. John Killen, MD, Dir.
Desc: Basic knowledge of the pathogenesis, natural history, and transmission of HIV. Promotes progress in the detection, treatment, and prevention of HIV. *Type:* Research center.

U.S. Department of Health and Human Services

National Institute of Allergy and Infectious Diseases

Division of Acquired Immunodeficiency Syndrome (AIDS)

Basic Science Program

Solar Bldg., Rm. 2C-06   Ph: (301)496-8378
6003 Executive Blvd.   Fax: (301)402-3211
Rockville, MD 20852
E-mail: gm16s@nih.gov
URL: http://www.niaid.nih.gov
Contact: Gregory Milman, PhD, Chf.
Desc: Molecular and cellular biology, virology, and immunology of: virus host interactions of HIV and related lentiviruses; mechanisms of disease; and HIV transmission. *Type:* Research center.

U.S. Department of Health and Human Services

National Institute of Allergy and Infectious Diseases

Division of Acquired Immunodeficiency Syndrome (AIDS)

Basic Science Program

Solar Bldg., Rm. 2C-01   Ph: (301)496-8197
6003 Executive Blvd.   Fax: (301)402-3211
Bethesda, MD 20892
Contact: N. Sarver, Actg.Chf.
Desc: Discovery of effective vaccines and therapies for the prevention and treatment of HIV infection and disease. *Type:* Research center.

U.S. Department of Health and Human Services

National Institute of Allergy and Infectious Diseases

Division of Acquired Immunodeficiency Syndrome (AIDS)

Basic Science Program

Solar Bldg. 2C-07   Ph: (301)496-0637
6003 Executive Blvd.   Fax: (301)402-3211
Bethesda, MD 20892-7620
Contact: C. Dieffenbach, PhD, Assoc.Dir.
Desc: Pathogenesis, basic virology, immunobiology, pathobiology, the discovery of novel therapeutic approaches, and epidemiology. *Type:* Research center.

U.S. Department of Health and Human Services

National Institute of Allergy and Infectious Diseases

Division of Acquired Immunodeficiency Syndrome (AIDS)

Biostatistics Research Branch

Solar Bldg., Rm. 2A-22   Ph: (301)496-0694
6003 Executive Blvd.   Fax: (301)480-5703
Rockville, MD 20852
Desc: Methodologic and biostatistical oversight and assistance. *Type:* Research center.

U.S. Department of Health and Human Services

National Institute of Allergy and Infectious Diseases

Division of Acquired Immunodeficiency Syndrome (AIDS)

Epidemiology Project Team

Solar Bldg., Rm. 2C-10   Ph: (301)402-0135
6003 Executive Blvd.   Fax: (301)480-3211
Rockville, MD 20852
Contact: L. Schrager, MD, Chf.
Desc: Epidemiology of HIV. *Type:* Research center.

U.S. Department of Health and Human Services

National Institute of Allergy and Infectious Diseases

Division of Acquired Immunodeficiency Syndrome (AIDS)

Office of Program Operations and Scientific Information

Solar Bldg., Rm. 2A-20   Ph: (301)496-0545
6003 Executive Blvd.   Fax: (301)402-1505
Rockville, MD 20852
E-mail: dK3of@nih.gov
URL: http://www.niaid.nih.gov
Contact: D. Katz, RN, Dir.
Desc: Collects and maintains scientific data and composes reports for the Division of Acquired Immunodeficiency Syndrome. *Type:* Research center.

U.S. Department of Health and Human Services

National Institute of Allergy and Infectious Diseases

Division of Acquired Immunodeficiency Syndrome (AIDS)

Pediatric Project Team

Solar Bldg., Rm. 2C-24   Ph: (301)402-2300
6003 Executive Blvd.   Fax: (301)402-3171
Rockville, MD 20852
Contact: J. McNamara, MD, Chf.
Desc: HIV disease in relation to infants, children, and adolescents. *Type:* Research center.

U.S. Department of Health and Human Services

National Institute of Allergy and Infectious Diseases

Division of Acquired Immunodeficiency Syndrome (AIDS)

Pharmaceutical and Regulatory Affairs Branch

Solar Bldg., Rm. 2B-0A   Ph: (301)496-8213
6003 Executive Blvd.   Fax: (301)480-5703
Rockville, MD 20852
E-mail: jm78k@nih.gov
Contact: Anna Martinez, PhD, Chf.
Desc: Assures that all clinical trials sponsored by DAIDS are conducted in accordance with FDA and Federal regulations. *Type:* Research center.

U.S. Department of Health and Human Services

National Institute of Allergy and Infectious Diseases

Division of Acquired Immunodeficiency Syndrome (AIDS)

Scientific Assessment and Resource Branch

6003 Executive Blvd.   Ph: (301)402-0755
Rockville, MD 20852   Fax: (301)480-5703
Contact: P. Sager, PhD, Chf.
Desc: Conducts reviews to ensure that the Division's activities effectively address the stated scientific goals and priorities. *Type:* Research center.

U.S. Department of Health and Human Services

National Institute of Allergy and Infectious Diseases

Division of Acquired Immunodeficiency Syndrome (AIDS)

Therapeutics Research Program

Solar Bldg., Rm. 2C-26   Ph: (301)402-2304
6003 Executive Blvd.   Fax: (301)402-3171
Bethesda, MD 20892
E-mail: bl17u@nih.gov
URL: http://www.niaid.nih.gov

Contact: B. Laughon, PhD, Chf.
Desc: Improved therapies for the treatment and prophylaxis of OIs associated with HIV disease. *Type:* Research center.

U.S. Department of Health and Human Services

National Institute of Allergy and Infectious Diseases

Division of Acquired Immunodeficiency Syndrome (AIDS)

Therapeutics Research Program

Bldg. 31, Rm. 7A50   Ph: (301)496-5717
31 Center Dr.   Fax: (301)402-0120
Bethesda, MD 20892-2520
Contact: Leslie Fink, Dir.
Desc: Therapeutic strategies directed at: the clinical conditions associated with HIV infection in children and adolescents; and intervention to reduce the risk of transmission of HIV from infected mothers to the infant or fetus. *Type:* Research center.

U.S. Department of Health and Human Services

National Institute of Allergy and Infectious Diseases

Division of Acquired Immunodeficiency Syndrome (AIDS)

Therapeutics Research Program

Solar Bldg., Rm. 2C-22   Ph: (301)496-8210
6003 Executive Blvd.   Fax: (301)402-3171
Rockville, MD 20852
Desc: Facilitates preclinical development of experimental therapies through evaluation in appropriate in vitro and in vivo systems; coordinates research in immunology, virology, and pharmacology as related to the design and conduct of clinical trials; and develops and oversees quality assurance programs for immunology, virology, and pharmacology laboratories engaged in DAIDS-supported research. Maintains a computerized data base of potential HIV and OI therapies. *Type:* Research center.

U.S. Department of Health and Human Services

National Institute of Allergy and Infectious Diseases

Division of Acquired Immunodeficiency Syndrome (AIDS)

Therapeutics Research Program

Solar Bldg.   Ph: (301)496-0700
6003 Executive Blvd.   Fax: (301)402-3171
Rockville, MD 20852
Contact: L. Deyton, MD, Chf.
Desc: Preclinical and clinical research on: therapeutic strategies directed at the treatment of adult primary HIV infection; the augmentation of specific HIV immune responses and general host immunity in HIV-infected individuals; and the neurological complications of HIV infection. *Type:* Research center.

U.S. Department of Health and Human Services

National Institute of Allergy and Infectious Diseases

Division of Acquired Immunodeficiency Syndrome (AIDS)

Therapeutics Research Program

Solar Bldg., Rm. 2B-27   Ph: (301)402-0143
6003 Executive Blvd.   Fax: (301)480-4582
Rockville, MD 20852
E-mail: fbloc@nih.gov
Contact: F. Batzold, PhD, Contact.
Desc: Oversees the technical and administrative management of a program of research grants and contracts sup-

porting clinical research sites carrying out DAIDS-supported clinical trials. These programs include: the Adult and Pediatric AIDS Clinical Trials Group (ACTG); the Terry Beirn Community Programs for Clinical Research on AIDS (CPCRA); the National Hemophilia Foundation (NHF); and the Acute Infection and Early Disease Research Program (AIEDRP). *Type:* Research center.

U.S. Department of Health and Human Services

National Institute of Allergy and Infectious Diseases

Division of Acquired Immunodeficiency Syndrome (AIDS)

Therapeutics Research Program

Solar Bldg., Rm. 3A-06   Ph: (301)496-7728
6003 Executive Blvd.   Fax: (301)402-2508
Bethesda, MD 20892-7630

Contact: D.M. Dixon, PhD, Chf.

Desc: Oversees the technical and administrative management of a program of research grants and contracts that provide coordinating support for the clinical trials organization supported by the TRP. This includes data management, biostatistical analysis, information processing, laboratory specimen tracking, coordinating, monitoring, and operations support. *Type:* Research center.

U.S. Department of Health and Human Services

National Institute of Allergy and Infectious Diseases

Division of Acquired Immunodeficiency Syndrome (AIDS)

Therapeutics Research Program

Solar Bldg., Rm. 2C-19   Ph: (301)496-8210
6003 Executive Blvd.   Fax: (301)402-3171
Rockville, MD 20852

Contact: W. Duncan, Assoc.Dir.

Desc: Therapies against HIV disease, including associated opportunistic infections (OIs) and cancer in adults, infants, children, and adolescents. *Type:* Research center.

U.S. Department of Health and Human Services

National Institute of Allergy and Infectious Diseases

Division of Acquired Immunodeficiency Syndrome (AIDS)

Vaccine and Prevention Research Program

Solar Bldg., Rm. 2A-04   Ph: (301)402-0121
6003 Executive Blvd.   Fax: (301)402-3684
Rockville, MD 20852

Contact: A. Schultz, PhD, Chf.

Desc: Preclinical development and evaluation of safe and effective AIDS vaccines and adjuvants for the prevention of AIDS. *Type:* Research center.

U.S. Department of Health and Human Services

National Institute of Allergy and Infectious Diseases

Division of Acquired Immunodeficiency Syndrome (AIDS)

Vaccine and Prevention Research Program

Solar Bldg., Rm. 2A-03   Ph: (301)402-0121
6003 Executive Blvd.   Fax: (301)402-1506
Rockville, MD 20852

Contact: P. Fast, Actg.Chf.

Desc: Coordinates Phase I and II clinical trials of potential AIDS vaccines. *Type:* Research center.

U.S. Department of Health and Human Services

National Institute of Allergy and Infectious Diseases

Division of Acquired Immunodeficiency Syndrome (AIDS)

Vaccine and Prevention Research Program

Solar Bldg., Rm. 2A-12   Ph: (301)496-6177
6003 Executive Blvd.   Fax: (301)402-3684
Bethesda, MD 20892

Contact: R. Hoff, Chf.

Desc: Large-scale and domestic and international clinical trials of HIV vaccines and other biomedical and behavioral interventions. *Type:* Research center.

U.S. Department of Health and Human Services

National Institutes of Health

Office of AIDS Research

Bldg. 31, Rm. 4CO2   Ph: (301)496-0357
9000 Rockville Pike   Fax: (301)496-2119
Bethesda, MD 20892

Contact: Neal Nathanson, Dir.

Desc: Advises the Director, NIH, and senior staff on the development of NIH-wide policy related to AIDS research, and coordinates NIH intramural and extramural AIDS research activities; Represents the Director, NIH, on all outside AIDS-related committees requiring NIH participation; Provides staff support to the NIH AIDS Advisory Committee; Recommends Intramural/Extramural AIDS research priorities to the Director, NIH; Develops an NIH annual plan and budget for AIDS research; Develops and maintains an information database on Intramural/Extramural AIDS activities and prepares special or recurring reports as needed; Develops information strategies to assure the public is informed of NIH AIDS research activities; Recommends solutions to ethical/legal issues arising from AIDS research; Facilitates cooperation in AIDS research between government, industry, and universities; and Fosters and develops plans for NIH involvement in international AIDS research activities. *Type:* Research center.

University of California, Davis

AIDS Virus Diagnostic Laboratory

One Shields Ave.   Ph: (530)752-8242
Davis, CA 95616-8542   Fax: (530)752-4816

Contact: James R. Carlson, PhD, Dir.

Desc: Human immunodeficiency virus (HIV) serology, HIV production and purification, bioassays of HIV inactivation, comparative retrovirology, and vaccine development. *Type:* Research center.

University of California, Los Angeles

UCLA Center for Clinical AIDS Research and Education

AIDS Clinical Trials Unit

10833 Le Conte Ave., Rm. BH-   Ph: (310)206-6414
412 CHS   Fax: (310)206-3311
Los Angeles, CA 90095-1793
E-mail: rmitsuya@med1.medsch.ucla.edu
URL: http://www.med.ucla.edu/carectr/carehome.htm

Contact: Ronald T. Mitsuyasu, MD, Dir.

Desc: Coordinates clinical research trials on AIDS and HIV-related disease. *Type:* Research center.

University of California, San Diego

Center for AIDS Research

9500 Gilman Dr. 0616   Ph: (619)534-5545
La Jolla, CA 92093-0616   Fax: (619)822-1934
E-mail: csussman@ucsd.edu
URL: http://hsrd.ucsd.edu/cfar

Contact: Flossie Wong-Staal, PhD, Dir.

Desc: Development of improved vaccines and therapies for HIV infection and associated diseases through the study of molecular pathogenesis and immunopathogenesis of HIV infection and clinical trials of therapies and vaccines. *Type:* Research center.

University of California, San Francisco

AIDS Clinical Research Center

Department of Stomatology   Ph: (415)476-8857
Rm. S-612, Box 0422   Fax: (415)476-8919
San Francisco, CA 94143
E-mail: stom%suzi@ccmail.ucsf.edu

Contact: John S. Greenspan, Dir.

Desc: AIDS and Kaposi's sarcoma, including epidemiological studies and tissue and serum virological and immunological investigations. The Clinical Center integrates five support programs: Clinical Trials Coordinating Unit, which manages protocol development, data collection and analysis, and statistical consultation; Laboratory Support for specific trials that require specimen storage, immunological monitoring, or special viral diagnostic procedures; Community Consortium, a network of Bay Area physicians who treat AIDS patients and who enter patients in controlled clinical studies; Clinical Specialties that treat AIDS patients (Pediatrics, Neurology, Oral Medicine, Dermatology, Infectious Disease, Pulmonary, Gastroenterology, Oncology, and Behavioral Medicine); and Administration, which governs the Center, plans and projects budgets, manages project review and awards, and conducts educational programs. *Type:* Research center.

University of California, San Francisco

Center for AIDS Prevention Studies

Prevention Science Group   Ph: (415)597-9106
74 New Montgomery St., Ste.   Fax: (415)597-9213
600
San Francisco, CA 94105
E-mail: tcoates@psg.ucsf.edu
URL: http://www.caps.ucsf.edu/capsweb

Contact: Thomas J. Coates, PhD, Dir.

Desc: Methods to change AIDS high risk behavior. Activities include developing and testing AIDS prevention strategies for at-risk populations, promoting multidisciplinary research on the prevention of HIV disease, funding pilot studies on minority issues in AIDS, and operating the CAPS International Visiting Scholars Program, which brings scholars from Africa, Asia, Eastern Europe, and Latin America to work with CAPS scientists in developing AIDS prevention research protocols. *Type:* Research center.

University of Hawaii

Hawaii AIDS Clinical Research Program

Leahi Hospital   Ph: (808)737-2751
3675 Kilauea Ave.   Fax: (808)735-8529
Young Bldg., 6th Fl.
Honolulu, HI 96816
E-mail: shikuma@hawaii.edu

Contact: Cecilia M. Shikuma, MD, Dir.

Desc: AIDS, HIV, and complications of HIV. *Type:* Research center.

University of South Florida

Center for HIV Education and Research

13301 Bruce B. Downs Blvd.   Ph: (813)974-4430
Tampa, FL 33612-3899   Fax: (813)974-6469
E-mail: hivcntr@fmhi.usf.edu
URL: http://www.fmhi.usf.edu/hiv

Contact: Prof. Michael D. Knox, PhD, Dir.

Desc: Treatment of persons infected with HIV, study of HIV risk factors, and AIDS prevention. Provides current AIDS and HIV information to physicians, psychologists, dentists, nurses, and other health care providers. *Type:* Research center.

Virology & AIDS Abstracts
Cambridge Scientific Abstracts (CSA)
7200 Wisconsin Ave., Ste. 601   Ph: (301)961-6700
Bethesda, MD 20814-4823
E-mail: sales@csa.com
URL: http://www.csa.com
Desc: Contains more than 125,000 citations, with abstracts, to the worldwide literature on human, animal, and plant virology, ranging from replication cycle to oncology, and Acquired Immune Deficiency Syndrome (AIDS). Sources include journals, books, conference proceedings, and reports. *Type:* Database.

Alcoholic Beverages

Alcoholic Beverage Control
Wakeman/Walworth, Inc.
300 N. Washington St.   Ph: (703)549-8606
Alexandria, VA 22314   Free: 800-876-2545
URL: http://statecapitals.com.
Contact: Keyes Walworth, Editor.
Desc: Covers state endeavors affecting the production, marketing, sale, consumption, and taxation of alcoholic beverages. *Type:* Newsletter.

Alcoholic Beverage Executive Newsletter
Alcoholic Beverage Executive Newsletter Inc.
PO Box 3188   Ph: (402)397-5514
Omaha, NE 68103-0188   Fax: (402)397-3843
Contact: Patricia T. Kennedy, Editor and Publisher.
Desc: Provides information about the alcoholic beverage industry. *Type:* Newsletter.

ASBC Newsletter
American Society of Brewing Chemists (ASBC)
3340 Pilot Knob Rd.   Ph: (612)454-7250
St. Paul, MN 55121   Fax: (612)454-0766
E-mail: asbc@scisoc.org
Contact: Karen J. Devries, Editor.
Desc: Provides news items and technical reports on brewing and related matters. Recurring features include news items, abstracts of technical papers, convention news, book reviews, and membership listings and changes. *Type:* Newsletter.

Association of Brewers
PO Box 1679   Ph: (303)447-0816
Boulder, CO 80306-1679   Fax: (303)447-2825
E-mail: service@aob.org
URL: http://www.beertown.org
Contact: Charles N. Papazian, Pres.
Desc: Individuals interested in the homebrewing of beer; beer retailers, consumers, wholesalers, and manufacturers. Disseminates information for homebrewers and those interested in the art of homebrewing and commercial brewing on a small scale ("microbreweries" and "brewpubs"). Offers specialized education; compiles statistics. *Type:* Association.

Beer Institute
122 C St., NW, No. 750   Ph: (202)737-2337
Washington, DC 20001-2109   Free: 800-379-BREW
    Fax: (202)737-7004
E-mail: beer@mnsinc.com
URL: http://www.beerinst.org
Contact: Raymond J. McGrath, Pres.
Desc: Brewers and suppliers to the industry. Protects the market environment allowing for brewers to sell beer profitably, free from what the group views as unfair burdens imposed by government bodies; communicates positions on industry issues to members, related industries, the public, the media, and government officials. Represents members' interests before Congress. *Type:* Association.

Beer Statistics News
Beer Marketer's Insights, Inc.
PO Box 264   Ph: (914)624-2337
West Nyack, NY 10994   Fax: (914)624-2340
Contact: Eric Shepard, Editor; Jim Sullivan, Executive Editor.
Desc: Supplies "all the available data for major brewers' shipments in 39 reporting states." Includes maps, charts, and graphs of market share and shipments data by region and brewer. *Type:* Newsletter.

Beverage Alcohol Market Report
Peregrine Communications
952 Lakeview Dr.   Ph: (212)371-5237
Parkersburg, WV 26104-1618   Free: 800-628-1430
Contact: Perry Luntz, Editor, perrylunt@aol.com.
Desc: Covers international beer, wine, and liquor production, importation, marketing, wholesale distribution, and retailing. Recurring features include reports on legislation affecting the industry, news of market research, calendar of events, job changes, and statistics. *Type:* Newsletter.

Impact International
M. Shanken Communications, Inc.
387 Park Ave. S., 8th Fl.   Ph: (212)684-4224
New York, NY 10016   Free: 800-866-0775
    Fax: (212)684-5424
E-mail: dfleming@mshanken.com
Contact: Marvin R. Shanken, Editor.
Desc: Provides information on the alcohol consumption market of the European Community, Latin America, and the Far East, tax legislation, standards, and licensing. Lists top-selling brands of distilled alcoholic beverages. *Type:* Newsletter.

Import Statistics
National Association of Beverage Importers, Inc.
1025 Vermont Ave. NW, Ste.   Ph: (202)638-1617
    1066   Fax: (202)638-3122
Washington, DC 20005
E-mail: nabi-inc@msn.com
Contact: C. Jean Fellner, Editor.
Desc: Contains Bureau of Census statistics of beverage imports compiled monthly with cumulative comparisons with the same period of the previous year. Presents statistics by the tariff schedules of beer, wines, and spirits categories. *Type:* Newsletter.

Industry World
World Association of the Alcohol Beverage Industries, Inc.
1250 Eye St. NW, Ste. 900   Ph: (202)628-3544
Washington, DC 20005
Contact: Duncan H. Cameron, Editor.
Desc: Provides updates on programs and activities of the Association, an organization of women and men concerned about the alcohol beverage industry as well as community service and their own career and personal growth. Covers industry developments, programs to combat alcohol abuse, and chapter news. *Type:* Newsletter.

National Alcohol Beverage Control Association
4216 King St. W   Ph: (703)578-4200
Alexandria, VA 22302   Fax: (703)820-3551
Contact: James M. Sgueo, Exec.Dir.
Desc: State agencies controlling the purchase, distribution, and sale of alcoholic beverages under the control system; distillery firms and trade associations are associate members. *Type:* Association.

National Association of Bar and Tavern Owners
PO Box 11578   Ph: (954)776-7017
Fort Lauderdale, FL 33339
E-mail: nabto@aol.com
Contact: Richard S. Jett, Pres.
Desc: Individual bar and tavern owners. *Type:* Association.

National Association of Beverage Retailers
5101 River Rd., Ste. 108   Ph: (301)656-1494
Bethesda, MD 20816   Fax: (301)656-7539
E-mail: burcham@nabronline.org
URL: http://www.nabronline.org
Contact: John B. Burcham, Jr., Exec.Dir.
Desc: Federation of associations of alcohol beverage retailers. *Type:* Association.

National Beer Wholesalers' Association
1100 S. Washington   Ph: (703)683-4300
Alexandria, VA 22314   Free: 800-300-6417
    Fax: (703)683-8965
URL: http://www.nbwa.org
Contact: Ronald A. Sarasin, Pres.
Desc: Independent wholesalers of malt beverages and affiliates of the malt beverage industry. *Type:* Association.

National Licensed Beverage Association
4214 King St. W.   Ph: (703)751-9730
Alexandria, VA 22302   Free: 800-441-9894
    Fax: (703)751-9748
E-mail: nlba@msn.com
URL: http://www.nlba.org
Contact: Debra A. Leach, Exec.Dir.
Desc: Bars, taverns, restaurants, cocktail lounges, hotels, and liquor and convenience stores selling alcohol beverages for on-premise consumption or off-premise sales. *Type:* Association.

Wine and Spirits Wholesalers of America
805 15th St. NW, Ste. 430   Ph: (202)371-9792
Washington, DC 20005   Fax: (202)789-2405
E-mail: juanita.duggan@wswa.org
URL: http://www.wswa.org
Contact: Juanita Duggan, CEO.
Desc: Wholesale distributors of domestic and imported wine and distilled spirits. *Type:* Association.

Allergy

Allergy/Immunology Service
Rush Med. College   Ph: (312)942-6296
1725 W. Harrison, Ste. 207   Fax: (312)563-2201
Chicago, IL 60612
E-mail: hgewurz@rpslmc.edu
URL: http://www.rush.edu/med/allergy
Contact: Anita Gewurz, Contact.
Desc: Allergy, basic immunology, and product testing, including therapeutic agent evaluation, allergenic extract developments, laboratory assay development, adverse food reaction pathogensis, Samter Syndrome etiology and pathogenesis, urticaria/angiodema etiology, and hypogammaglobulinemia treatment. *Type:* Research center.

Allergy Research Foundation
11620 Wilshire Blvd., 210   Ph: (310)312-5050
Los Angeles, CA 90025-1767   Fax: (310)575-9292
E-mail: joncorren@hotmail.com
Contact: Jonathan Corren, MD, Dir.
Desc: Issues related to allergies. *Type:* Research center.

American Academy of Allergy, Asthma and Immunology

611 E. Wells St. Ph: (414)272-6071
Milwaukee, WI 53202 Fax: (414)272-6070
E-mail: info@aaaai.org
URL: http://www.aaaai.org

Contact: Rick Iber, Exec.VP.

Desc: Professional society of physicians specializing in allergy and allergic diseases. *Type:* Association.

American College of Allergy, Asthma and Immunology

85 W. Algonquin Rd., Ste. 550 Ph: (847)427-1200
Arlington Heights, IL 60005 Fax: (847)427-1294
E-mail: mail@acaai.org
URL: http://www.allergy.mcg.edu

Contact: James R. Slawny, Exec.Dir.

Desc: Practicing allergists, educators, researchers, and clinical immunologists united to: encourage the study, improve the practice, and advance the cause of clinical immunology and allergy; promote association of and highest possible standards among medical scientists and physicians specializing in clinical immunology and in research, teaching, and treatment of allergy; promote dissemination of information regarding clinical immunology and allergy. Maintains a special program for allergy assistants such as nurses, technologists, and clinic aides of lectures, conferences, seminars, participatory workshops, peer-group discussions, poster programs, and technical and scientific exhibits. *Type:* Association.

Asthma and Allergy Foundation of America

1125 15th St. NW, Ste. 502 Ph: (202)466-7643
Washington, DC 20005 Free: 800-7-ASTHMA
  Fax: (202)466-8940
E-mail: info@aafa.org
URL: http://www.aafa.org

Contact: Mary Worstell, Exec.Dir.

Desc: Dedicated to finding a cure for and controlling asthma and allergic diseases. AAFA serves the estimated 50 million Americans with asthma and allergic diseases through the support of research, patient and public education programs, public and governmental advocacy, and a nationwide network of chapters and education/support groups. *Type:* Association.

Dana-Farber Cancer Institute

Department of Cancer Immunology and AIDS

44 Binney St. Ph: (617)632-3348
Boston, MA 02115 Fax: (617)632-4630
E-mail: hic@dfci.harvard.edu

Contact: Harvey Cantor, Ch.

Desc: T-cell development and function. *Type:* Research center.

Gladstone Institute of Virology and Immunology

San Francisco General Hospital Ph: (415)826-7500
PO Box 419100 Fax: (415)826-1514
San Francisco, CA 94141
E-mail: wgreene@gladstone.ucsf.edu
URL: http://gladstone.ucsf.edu

Contact: Dr. Warner C. Greene, Dir.

Desc: Characteristics of RNA viruses, including HIV, virus cell replication, and viral disease in humans. Also studies the structure of select HIV proteins and their host partners, their interactions with RNA and DNA, and the mechanisms by which they trigger viral growth and pathogenic outcomes. *Type:* Research center.

Harvard University

Laboratory of Immunology

Harvard Medical School Ph: (617)432-1978
200 Longwood, 5th Fl., D-530 Fax: (617)432-2789
Boston, MA 02115
E-mail: dorf@hms.harvard.edu
URL: http://www.med.harvard.edu/dms/immunology/indes.html

Contact: Dr. Martin Dorf, Dir.

Desc: Indentification of chemokines and their receptors. Applications to autoimmunity. *Type:* Research center.

Histamine Research Society of North America

University of Texas SW Medical Ph: (214)648-3004
  Center
Department of Internal
  Medicine and Allergy
Dallas, TX 75235-8859

Contact: Rebecca Gruchalla, MD,PhD, Contact.

Desc: Histamine problems, (histamine is a chemical compound normally involved in physiological regulation of certain body functions, but which in excessive amounts may cause damage, as in allergic reactions). *Type:* Research center.

Hospital for Special Surgery

Research Division

Immunology and Inflammation Section

535 E. 70th St.
New York, NY 10021
URL: http://hss.hss.edu/research/immunology.htm

Contact: K. Elkon, Sect.Hd.

Desc: Basic immune system mechanisms as they impact tissue injury and repair manifested in inflammation and autoimmunity. Studies include exploration of intracellular signaling mechanisms and the different mechanisms engaged by different receptors, analysis of cell receptor polymorphisms and their structure-function relationships, definition of critical cell-cell interactions amongst cells of the immune system, and investigation of apoptosis and its role in shaping immune system function. *Type:* Research center.

Institute for Advanced Studies in Medicine

102 46th St.
Holmes Beach, FL 34217-1814
E-mail: iasm@mindspring.com
URL: http://www.iasm.net

Contact: Kenneth Alonso, MD, Exec.Dir.

Desc: Cancer and AIDS, focusing on biological response modifiers in patients with cancer, AIDS, multiple sclerosis, and other immune disorders; whole body hyperthermia in cancer and AIDS patients, radioisotope use in cancer therapy, and bone marrow purging with human-human monoclonal antibodies against tumor surface antigens for cancer therapy. *Type:* Research center.

International Association of Allergology and Clinical Immunology

611 E. Wells St. Ph: (414)276-6445
Milwaukee, WI 53202 Fax: (414)272-6070
E-mail: info@iaaci.org

Contact: Rick Iber, Exec.Sec.

Desc: Medical practitioners in allergology (the study of allergies and their treatment) and immunology, from 49 national allergology societies in 45 countries. Conducts research; increases awareness of completed and in-progress research programs; develops world standardization of categorization of allergies; establishes criteria for and monitors training of allergists; assesses world environmental conditions. *Type:* Association.

John P. Robarts Research Institute

Immunology Group

100 Perth Dr. Ph: (519)663-5777
PO Box 5015 Fax: (519)663-3789
London, ON, Canada N6A 5K8

Contact: Dr. Calvin Stiller, Dir.

Desc: Molecular biology of immune system, with emphasis on genetic factors of abnormal autoimmune response and control mechanisms of normal immune system. Studies focus on juvenile diabetes, transplant rejection, multiple sclerosis, rheumatoid arthritis, and AIDS. *Type:* Research center.

John P. Robarts Research Institute

London Clinical Trials Research Group

100 Perth Dr. Ph: (519)663-3400
PO Box 5015 Fax: (519)663-3807
London, ON, Canada N6A 5K8
E-mail: lctrg@lctrg.com
URL: http://www.lctrg.com

Contact: Dr. Feagan, Contact.

Desc: Evaluates new medications and treatments in a variety of medical fields. Provides biostatistics and data coordination for national and international trials. *Type:* Research center.

Johns Hopkins University

Asthma and Allergy Center

5501 Hopkins Bayview Cir. Ph: (410)550-2101
Baltimore, MD 21224 Fax: (410)550-1733
URL: http://www.med.jhu.edu/allergy/

Contact: Dr. Lawrence M. Lichtenstein, Dir.

Desc: Allergic diseases and individuals with allergic diseases, pulmonary diseases and individuals with pulmonary diseases, and diseases involving inflammation and immunological processes. *Type:* Research center.

Johns Hopkins University

Center for Immunization Research

Johns Hopkins Univ. Sch. of Ph: (410)955-4376
  Hygiene & Public Health Fax: (410)502-6898
Hampton House, 117
624 N. Broadway
Baltimore, MD 21205
E-mail: dburke@jhsph.edu

Contact: Dr. Donald Burke, MD, Dir.

Desc: Influenza, parainfluenza, respiratory syncytial virus, AIDS, and rotavirus vaccines, hepatitis B, immunoglobulins, and antiviral drug efficacy studies. Uses volunteers 18 years of age or older for vaccine studies and children from the ages of 1 month to 48 months for pediatric vaccine studies. *Type:* Research center.

Johns Hopkins University

Immunologic Disease Cooperative Research Center

Asthma & Allergy Ctr. Ph: (410)550-2101
5501 Hopkins Bayview Circle Fax: (410)550-1733
Baltimore, MD 21224
E-mail: ggreenwo@jhmi.edu

Contact: Dr. Laurence M. Lichtenstein, Dir.

Desc: Causes, prevention, and treatment of immunologically mediated diseases. Studies focus on the release of mediators in asthma, allergic rhinitis, and urticaria; mechanisms of immunotherapy in persons with allergic rhinitis and asthma; the natural history of latex and drug allergy; immunology of anaphylactic reaction in lungs and other organs; and control of asthma in adolescents. *Type:* Research center.

Mayo Clinic and Foundation

Allergic Diseases Research Laboratory

200 1st St. SW   Ph: (507)284-2789
Rochester, MN 55905   Fax: (507)284-5045
E-mail: gleich@mayo.edu
URL: http://www.mayo.edu

Contact: Gerald J. Gleich, MD, Dir.

Desc: Provides a focus for research into the causes, prevention, and management of allergic diseases such as asthma, allergies, contact hypersensitivity, immune deficiencies and infection, and autoimmune disorders plus related studies of fundamental immune mechanisms involving immune cells, antibodies, genetic factors, and immune regulatory systems. Projects focus on functions of the eosinophilic leukocyte, immunotherapy of patients with pollen allergies, and clinical studies of passive immunotherapy in patients allergic to honeybee stings who fail to respond to venom immunotherapy and who are members of beekeeping families. *Type:* Research center.

McGill University

McGill Centre for Clinical Immunobiology and Transplantation

687 av. des Pins ouest   Ph: (514)842-1231
Montreal, PQ, Canada H3A   Fax: (514)843-1683
  1A1
E-mail: rdg@zoo.net

Contact: Dr. Ronald D. Guttmann, Dir.

Desc: Performs joint clinical trials in organ transplantation, conducts autoimmunity and other immunobiology/immunogenetics studies, formulates public policy objectives regarding organ grafting, examines the ethical and legal aspects of transplantation and allocation of scarce resources, and evaluates the cost-effectiveness of transplantation programs. Develops computer expert systms for medical diagnosis and medical education. *Type:* Research center.

MCP Hahnemann University of the Health Sciences

Center for Immunobiology

2900 Queen Ln.   Ph: (215)991-8357
Philadelphia, PA 19129
E-mail: murasko@auhs.edu
URL: http://www.auhs.edu/medschool/centers/
ctrimmun.html

Contact: Donna M. Murasko, PhD, Dir.

Desc: Cellular and molecular immunology, including autoimmunity, transplantation, immune response to cancer and infectious pathogens, development of vaccines and changes in immune response with age. *Type:* Research center.

National Jewish Medical and Research Center

1400 Jackson St.   Ph: (303)388-4461
Denver, CO 80206   Free: 800-222-5864
     Fax: (303)270-2165
E-mail: taussigl@njc.org
URL: http://www.njrc.org

Contact: Lynn M. Taussig, MD, Pres./CEO.

Desc: Basic and clinical research in etiology, progression, manifestation, treatment, rehabilitation, and prevention of pulmonary, allergic, and immunologic diseases. Studies encompass cellular and molecular biology. *Type:* Research center.

Northwestern University

Ernest S. Bazley Asthma and Allergic Disease Center

Northwestern Medical Center

303 E. Chicago Ave.   Ph: (312)908-8172
Chicago, IL 60611   Fax: (312)908-0205
E-mail: rpatterson@nwu.edu
URL: http://www.nwu.edu

Contact: Roy Patterson, MD, Hd.

Desc: Etiology, mechanisms, diagnosis, and treatment of allergic diseases. Studies focus on idiopathic anaphylaxis, potentially fatal asthma, IgE mediated disease, drug allergy, hypersensitivity pneumonitis, allergic bronchopulmonary aspergillosis, anaphylaxis, occupational immunologic lung disease, polymerized allergens for treatment of IgE mediated disease, and animal models of allergic disease. *Type:* Research center.

Ohio State University

Pulmonary Laboratories

Means Hall, N325   Ph: (614)293-4925
1654 Upham Dr.   Fax: (614)293-4799
Columbus, OH 43210
URL: http://www.intmed.med.ohio-state.edu/pulmo/
pulmonary_homepage.htm

Contact: Mark D. Wewers, MD, Dir.

Desc: Mechanisms of allergic, immunologic, and inflammatory diseases, including ventilatory control and respiratory failure, inflammatory mechanisms in adult respiratory distress syndrome, cystic fibrosis, emphysema, staging and therapy of pulmonary neoplasms, respiratory distress in HIV, and occupational lung diseases. Collaborates with the departments of physiology and exercise physiology and with the cardiopulmonary unit of the School of Veterinary Medicine at the University. *Type:* Research center.

Ohio State University

Therapeutic Immunology Laboratories

355 Means Hall   Ph: (614)293-3212
1654 Upham Dr.   Fax: (614)293-4541
Columbus, OH 43210
E-mail: orosz-1@medctr.osu.edu

Contact: Dr. Charles Orosz, Dir.

Desc: Transplantation related immunobiology, inflammation, clinical histocompatibility testing and post-transplant immunologic monitoring, and clinical and experimental immunosuppression. *Type:* Research center.

Oregon Health Sciences University

Transplant and Immunogenetics Laboratory

2611 SW 3rd, Ste. 360   Ph: (503)494-8394
Portland, OR 97201   Fax: (503)494-7695

Contact: Douglas Norman, MD, Dir.

Desc: Human immunobiology of organ transplantation. *Type:* Research center.

Rockefeller University

Laboratory of Bacteriology, Pathogenesis and Immunology

1230 York Ave. DWB 800   Ph: (212)327-8157
New York, NY 10021-6399   Fax: (212)327-8960

Contact: Emil C. Gotschlich, MD, Contact.

Desc: Investigates the parastic mechanisms used by pathogenic bacteria, especially streptococci and neisseria. Also studies the derangements of the human immune system which lead to chronic diseases such as rheumatic fever and glomerulonephritis as a result of infection with streptococci. *Type:* Research center.

Rockefeller University

Laboratory of Cellular Physiology and Immunology

1230 York Ave.   Ph: (212)327-8000
New York, NY 10021-6399   Fax: (212)327-8875
E-mail: stima@rockvax.rockefeller.edu

Contact: Ralph Stiman, Hd.

Desc: Functional properties of eukaryotic cells and their role in physiologic and pathologic events. Using the tools of immunology, cell biology, and biochemistry, the Lab studies problems of inflammation, the immune response, and host defense against parasites and tumor cells. *Type:* Research center.

Rockefeller University

Laboratory of Clinical Microbiology and Immunology

1230 York Ave.   Ph: (212)327-8155
New York, NY 10021   Fax: (212)327-7579
E-mail: zabrisk@rockvax.rockefeller.edu

Contact: Dr. John B. Zabriskie, Dir.

Desc: Microbe-induced autoimmunity and human genetics, including molecular biology emphasizing eukaryotic systems, protein chemistry, and immunology. *Type:* Research center.

Scripps Research Institute

Autoimmune Disease Center

10666 N. Torrey Pines Rd.   Ph: (619)554-8686
La Jolla, CA 92037   Fax: (619)554-6805

Contact: Eng Tan, MD, Dir.

Desc: Immunologic studies on the development of allergic disorders, especially aspirin and related drug sensitivities, bisulfite-sensitivity in asthma, and hereditary angioedema. Investigates the role of leukotrienes in the development of allergic disorders and conducts studies on drug-induced lupus reactions and the role specific autoantibodies may play in the development of the disease. *Type:* Research center.

Sherbrooke University

Immunobiology Research Unit

Faculte de medecine   Ph: (819)346-1110
3001, 12e Ave. Nord   Fax: (819)564-5215
Sherbrooke, PQ, Canada J1H
  5N4
E-mail: mrolaple@courrier.usherb.ca
URL: http://www.crc-cuse.usherb.ca/crccuse/immuno.
html

Contact: Dr. Marek Rola-Pleszczynski, Dir.

Desc: Immunoglobulin gene expression and control, lymphocyte activation pathways and second messengers, stem cell biology, cytokine receptor physiology, structure-function studies of lipid mediator receptors, natural cytotoxicity against tumor cells, ultraviolet-irradiation and immune functions, and immune interactions in atherosclerosis. *Type:* Research center.

State University of New York at Buffalo

Ernest Witebsky Center for Immunology

School of Medicine &   Ph: (716)829-2848
  Biomedical Science   Fax: (716)829-3534
233 Sherman Hall
Buffalo, NY 14214
E-mail: rcunning@ubmed.buffalo.edu

Contact: Dr. Roger K. Cunningham, Dir.

Desc: Provides a basis for collaboration among immunologists working in various departments of the University and local University-affiliated hospitals. *Type:* Research center.

State University of New York Health Science Center at Stony Brook

Asthma and Allergic Diseases Center

Division of Allergy & Clinical Immunology
HSC Level T16-040
Suny at Stony Brook
Stony Brook, NY 11794-8161

Ph: (516)444-8364
Fax: (516)444-3475

Contact: Asst.Prof. Allen P. Kaplan, Contact.

Desc: One of a network of NIAID centers studying the cause, pathogenesis, diagnosis, prevention, and treatment of both naturally occurring and acquired allergic diseases. Examines the biochemical and immunologic mechanisms by which inflammation occurs in allergic diseases, including urticaria (hives), angioedema, asthma, vasculitis, Lyme disease, arthritis, and other rheumatic diseases. *Type:* Research center.

Trudeau Institute, Inc.

PO Box 59
Saranac Lake, NY 12983
E-mail: scooper@trudeauinstitute.org
URL: http://trudeauinstitute.org

Ph: (518)891-3080
Fax: (518)891-5126

Contact: Susan L. Swain, PhD, Dir.

Desc: Cellular immunology, emphasizing lymphocyte physiology and the effector mechanisms of cell-mediated immunity and antimicrobial and antitumor immunity. *Type:* Research center.

Tufts University

Asthma and Allergic Diseases Cooperative Research Center

School of Medicine
750 Washington
Boston, MA 02111

Ph: (617)636-5333
Fax: (617)636-4843

Contact: Dr. John Ohman, Dir.

Desc: Studies of the release of histamine (a body chemical best known for its ability to cause itching, nasal symptoms, hives, or asthma during an allergy attack) to determine whether patients with various allergic disorders either are more sensitive to the effects of histamine or release larger quantities than normal; studies of endothelial cells, which line blood vessels in the human body, and possible interaction of this type of cell with immune system cells and the role of this interaction in an inflammatory disease of blood vessels known as vasculitis; and studies of a type of blood cell known as the eosinophil frequently found in and around the site of an allergic reaction and the interaction of this cell with other immune system functional cells known as lymphocytes. *Type:* Research center.

Tulane University

School of Medicine

Clinical Immunology Section

1700 Perdido St., 3rd Fl.
New Orleans, LA 70112
E-mail: malopez@mailhost.tcs.tulane.edu

Ph: (504)588-5578
Fax: (504)584-3686

Contact: Prof. Manuel Lopez, MD, Dir.

Desc: Provides a focus for research into the causes, prevention, and management of diseases such as asthma, allergies, immune deficiencies and infections, and autoimmune disorders, plus related studies of fundamental immune mechanisms involving immune cells, antibodies, genetic factors, and immune regulatory systems, especially as they relate to the lung. Investigates tobacco smoke products as possible allergens, mechanisms of AIDS, and immunologic mechanisms of occupational and environmental lung disease. *Type:* Research center.

U.S. Department of Defense

Army Medical Research and Materiel Command

Walter Reed Army Institute of Research

Communicable Diseases and Immunology Division

Bldg. 40, Rm. 2129
Washington, DC 20307-5100

Ph: (202)782-3561
Fax: (202)782-0748

Contact: Col. Charles H. Hoke, Jr., Dir.

Desc: Ecology, etiology, pathogenesis, diagnosis, prevention, and therapy of selected diseases of military importance and develop, validate, and apply methods of disease control through the use of immunizing agents (including studies of modification induced in the host by exposure to disease agents); develop methods of production (including actual emergency manufacture) and methods of assaying the biologicals required by the Armed Forces; and provide reference and consultative services on the diagnosis, epidemiology, control, and chemotherapy of infectious diseases of military importance. Divisional components include departments of Bacterial Diseases, Biologics Research, Enteric Infections, Entomology, Immunology, and Virus Disea ses. *Type:* Research center.

U.S. Department of Health and Human Services

Centers for Disease Control and Prevention

Antinuclear Antibody Reference Laboratory

1600 Clifton Rd. NE, Rm. 1202
Mailstop A-25
Atlanta, GA 30333
E-mail: mgbl@cdc.gov

Ph: (404)639-2727
Fax: (404)639-2108

Contact: Dr. J. Steven McDougal, Chf.

Desc: Collaborating scientists from the Arthritis Foundation and CDC have prepared for distribution ten antisera to nuclear components useful in the diagnosis and classification of certain autoimmune diseases. These reference antisera have been used in approximately 1900 laboratories and can be obtained by writing to the ANA Reference Laboratory at the above address. *Type:* Research center.

U.S. Department of Health and Human Services

Centers for Disease Control and Prevention

National Centers for Prevention Services

National Immunization Program

Mail Stop E-05
CDC NIP 1600 Clifton Rd, NE
Atlanta, GA 30333
E-mail: WAO1@NIP.CDC.GOV

Ph: (404)639-8200
Fax: (404)639-8626

Contact: Dr. Walter A. Orenstein, Dir.

Desc: Vaccine-preventable disease control. *Type:* Research center.

U.S. Department of Health and Human Services

Food and Drug Administration

Center for Biologics Evaluation and Research

Division of Allergenic Products and Parasitology

1401 Rockville Pike, Bldg. 29, Rm 129
HFM 410
Rockville, MD 20852
E-mail: tebull@gandalf.cber.nih.gov

Ph: (301)496-2893
Fax: (301)496-4684

Contact: Thomas Bull, Dep.Dir.

Desc: Allergy parasitology, biochemistry, biophysics, immunology, and molecular biology. Comprised of the following Laboratories: Parasitic Biology and Biochemistry, Biophysics, Immunobiochemistry, and Immunoregulation. *Type:* Research center.

U.S. Department of Health and Human Services

Food and Drug Administration

Center for Biologics Evaluation and Research

Division of Viral Products

1401 Rockville Pike
Rockville, MD 20852

Ph: (301)496-3144
Fax: (301)496-1810

Contact: Dr. Dennis W. Trent, Dir.

Desc: Virology, immunology, and cell biology. Research on viral diseases include human and primate retroviruses, herpesviruses, influenza and other respiratory viruses, hepatitis, polioviruses, and pediatric exanthem. *Type:* Research center.

U.S. Department of Health and Human Services

Food and Drug Administration

Center for Biologics Evaluation and Research

Laboratory of Immuno-Chemistry

5510 Nicholson Ln.
Kensington, MD 20895

Ph: (301)594-6733

Contact: Walter Kuff, Contact.

Desc: Chemical research involving the identification, structural elucidation, and quantitation of chemical constituents and impurities of vaccines and other biological products regulated by the Center. Laboratory is responsible for regulatory review of chemical aspects of biological products and for the testing of biological products to determine quantitatively the amounts of various preservatives, metals, stabilizers, adjuvants, chemical inactivators, nitrogen, and residual moisture present. *Type:* Research center.

U.S. Department of Health and Human Services

Food and Drug Administration

Center for Biologics Evaluation and Research

Laboratory of Immunobiochemistry

8800 Rockville Pike
Bethesda, MD 20892

Ph: (301)496-4357

Contact: Yuan L. Devries, PhD, Actg.Chf.

Desc: Characterization of allergenic extracts and the evaluation of the diagnostic and therapeutic safety and efficacy of allergenic extracts. Research program includes biochemical, biophysical, immunological, and molecular biology approaches to the characterization and human immune response to various allergens. *Type:* Research center.

U.S. Department of Health and Human Services

Food and Drug Administration

Center for Biologics Evaluation and Research

Laboratory of Immunology

8800 Rockville Pike
Bethesda, MD 20892

Ph: (301)496-0455
Fax: (301)480-3256

Contact: Giovanna Tosato, MD, Actg.Dir.

Desc: Hematopoietic growth factors, immune response, molecular biology of cytokines and immunoglobulin genes, and regulation of the HIV-1 expression. *Type:* Research center.

U.S. Department of Health and Human Services

Food and Drug Administration

Center for Biologics Evaluation and Research

Laboratory of Immunoregulation

8800 Rockville Pike
Bethesda, MD 20892
E-mail: berkower@al.CBER.FDA.gov

Ph: (301)496-1870
Fax: (301)496-4684

Contact: Ira J. Berkower, MD,PhD, Chf.

Desc: Safety, efficacy, and potency of vaccines for human use including fundamental research into the immunogenecity of viral protein antigen. This includes antigen processing and presentation, as well as antigen specific T cells; the mapping of a new neutralizing site that is shared across a broad spectrum of HIV-1 isolates so that antibodies to this site can potentially neutralize HIV-1 despite antigenic diversity; and how to prepare constructs with increased immunogenecity, while preserving this important site. *Type:* Research center.

U.S. Department of Health and Human Services

National Center for Prevention Services

National Immunization Program

Epidemiology and Surveillance Division

1600 Clifton Rd. NE, No. E-61   Ph: (404)639-3311
Atlanta, GA 30333   Fax: (404)639-8616

Contact: Stephen C. Hadler, Chf.

Desc: Incidence of diseases preventable by vaccination; and conducts studies on the safety and efficacy of new or existing vaccines. *Type:* Research center.

U.S. Department of Health and Human Services

National Institute of Allergy and Infectious Diseases

Asthma and Allergic Diseases Cooperative Research Center

NIH, Bldg. 10, Rm. 11C205   Ph: (301)496-2165
10 Center Dr. MSC1881   Fax: (301)480-8384
Bethesda, MD 20892-1881
E-mail: dean_metcalfe@nih.gov

Contact: Dr. Dean Metcalfe, Dir.

Desc: Studies of the mast cell and its role in causing various allergic diseases, including asthma; and study of mast cell disorders including mastocytosis. *Type:* Research center.

U.S. Department of Health and Human Services

National Institute of Allergy and Infectious Diseases

Division of Allergy, Immunology, and Transplantation

Solar Bldg., Rm. 4A16   Ph: (301)496-1886
9000 Rockville Pike   Fax: (301)402-2571
Bethesda, MD 20892
E-mail: lp13r@nih.gov
URL: http://www.nih.niaid.gov

Contact: Dr. Lawrence Prograis, Dep.Dir.

Desc: Immune system as it functions in the maintenance of health and as it malfunctions in the production of disease. The Division provides leadership in the identification, design, and implementation of basic and clinical research initiatives encompassing a wide range of disorders including: autoimmune diseases such as childhood diabetes, rheumatoid arthritis and multiple sclerosis, allergic diseases such as asthma and occupational and environmental disorders and organ transplant rejection. *Type:* Research center.

U.S. Department of Health and Human Services

National Institute of Allergy and Infectious Diseases

Division of Allergy, Immunology, and Transplantation

Asthma, Allergy and Inflamation Branch

Solar Bldg., Rm. 4A24   Ph: (301)496-8973
Bethesda, MD 20892   Fax: (301)402-2571
E-mail: DR17G@NIH.GOV

Contact: Daniel Rotrosen, Chf.

Desc: Branch supports (through grants, cooperative agreements, career development awards, fellowships, and other mechanisms) basic and clinical research on the etiology, pathogenesis, diagnosis, prevention and treatment of allergic diseases and asthma; it also supports research on mucosal immunity, phagocyte biology and complement. Basic investigations include a study of the regulation of IgE antibody synthesis and IgE interactions with IgE receptors and other IgE binding molecules; studies of the epitopes of allergens and T cells that mediate allergic reations; assessment of the role of cytokines and adhesion molecules in regulating IgE synthesis and allergic inflammation in vitro and in vivo; and molecular and biochemical characterization of molecules expressed on, and in, mast cells, basophils and eosinophils . *Type:* Research center.

U.S. Department of Health and Human Services

National Institute of Allergy and Infectious Diseases

Division of Allergy, Immunology, and Transplantation

Basic Immunology Branch

Solar Bldg., Rm. 4A22   Ph: (301)496-7551
9000 Rockville Pike   Fax: (301)402-2571
Bethesda, MD 20892

Contact: Dr. Helen Quill, Chf.

Desc: Biology and chemistry of the immune system and its products. Immunobiologic studies include: the origin, maturation, localization, and interactions of immunocyte (lymphocyte, plasmocyte, macrophage) populations and subpopulations; the cellular and biochemical mechanisms responsible for antigen processing, tolerance, and enhancement; research in the mechanisms responsible for induction and regulation of the immune response; and studies on lymphokines and other substances produced by immunocytes and other cells that regulate the immune system. *Type:* Research center.

U.S. Department of Health and Human Services

National Institute of Allergy and Infectious Diseases

Division of Allergy, Immunology, and Transplantation

Clinical Immunology Branch

Solar Bldg. 4A19   Ph: (301)496-7104
9000 Rockville Pike   Fax: (301)402-2571
Bethesda, MD 20892

Contact: Howard Dickler, Chf.

Desc: Underlying cellular and molecular mechanisms responsible for the pathogenesis of immunologic diseases, as well as the application of basic knowledge to the etiology, prevention, and management of immunologic disorders, including autoimmune, immune complex, and immunodeficiency diseases and immunoregulatory dysfunctions. A special feature of this program is the support of Asthma, Allergic and Immunologic Disease Cooperative Research Centers (AAIDCRCs). *Type:* Research center.

U.S. Department of Health and Human Services

National Institute of Allergy and Infectious Diseases

Division of Allergy, Immunology and Transplantation

Genetics and Transplantation Branch

Solar Bldg., Rm. 4A14   Ph: (301)496-5598
Bethesda, MD 20892   Fax: (301)402-2571
E-mail: sr8j@nih.gov
URL: http://www.niaid.nih.gov

Contact: Dr. Stephen Rose, Chf.

Desc: Genetic and immunologic mechanisms that are involved in responses to foreign substances such as infecting microorganisms and engrafted tissues. These mechanisms determine susceptibility or resistance to various diseases and the success or failure of organ or tissue grafts. *Type:* Research center.

U.S. Department of Health and Human Services

National Institute of Allergy and Infectious Diseases

Division of Extramural Activities

Solar Bldg., Rm. 3C20   Ph: (301)496-7291
6003 Executive Blvd.   Fax: (301)402-0369
Bethesda, MD 20892

Contact: Lawrence Deyton, Dir.

Desc: Coordinates and provides administrative support for all NIAID program activities in the extramural area. The DEA staff work closely with scientific program staff, grantees, and potential grantees in providing management information, advice, and consultation as needed to fulfill the broad objectives of the NIAID research grants and contracts programs. *Type:* Research center.

U.S. Department of Health and Human Services

National Institute of Allergy and Infectious Diseases

Division of Extramural Activities

Contract Management Branch

Rm. 3C07 Solar Bldg.   Ph: (301)496-0612
6003 Executive Blvd.   Fax: (301)402-0972
Bethesda, MD 20892
E-mail: lp14q@nihi.gov
URL: http://www.niaid.nih.gov/contracts

Contact: Lewis S. Pollack, Chf.

Desc: Contract management. *Type:* Research center.

U.S. Department of Health and Human Services

National Institute of Allergy and Infectious Diseases

Division of Extramural Activities

Grants Management Branch

National Inst. of Health   Ph: (301)402-6400
Solar Bldg., Rm. 4B22-GMB   Fax: (301)480-3780
6003 Executive Blvd.
Bethesda, MD 20892

Contact: Mary Kirker, Chf.

Desc: Supports research activities through grant management. *Type:* Research center.

U.S. Department of Health and Human Services

National Institute of Allergy and Infectious Diseases

Division of Intramural Research

NIH Bldg. 10, Rm. 4A-31   Ph: (301)496-3006
10 Center Dr., MSC 1356   Fax: (301)480-9324
Bethesda, MD 20892-1356
E-mail: tk9c@nih.gov
URL: http://www.niaid.nih.gov

Contact: Dr. Thomas Kindt, Dir.

Desc: Causes of allergic, immunologic, and infectious diseases; research that has developed to the point of clinical application is pursued through clinical trials, performed at the Clinical Center of NIH or in collaboration with university centers. The NIAID Intramural Program has diverse components covering medical research relevant to the Institute's mission and includes laboratories for: Biological Resources; Cellular and Molecular Immunology; Clinical Investigation; Host Defense; Immunogenetics; Immunology; Immunopathology; Immunoregulation; Infectious Diseases; Microbial Immunity; Molecular Microbiology; Parasitic Diseases; Viral Diseases; Microbial Structure and Function Laboratory; and Persistant Viral Diseases. *Type:* Research center.

U.S. Department of Health and Human Services

National Institute of Allergy and Infectious Diseases

Division of Intramural Research

Animal Care Branch

NIH Bldg. 14B-S., Rm. 228   Ph: (301)496-6395
9000 Rockville Pike   Fax: (301)402-0351
Bethesda, MD 20892-5530
E-mail: abarnes@atlas.niaid.nih.gov

Contact: Andrea Barnes, Chf.

Desc: Provides care and support services to NIAID scientists using animals in research. *Type:* Research center.

U.S. Department of Health and Human Services
National Institute of Allergy and Infectious Diseases
Division of Microbiology and Infectious Diseases
Bacteriology and Mycology Branch
6003 Executive Blvd., Rm. 3A06   Ph: (301)496-7728
Rockville, MD 20852   Fax: (301)402-2508
E-mail: RQAI@NIH.GOV
Contact: Dr. Robert L. Quackenbush, Chf.
Desc: Diseases of man caused by bacteria and fungi, including: investigations on the biology and physiology of bacteria and fungi, their morphology, antigenic structure and composition, and toxins and endotoxins; and studies on pathogenesis, immunopathology, host defense mechanisms, diagnostic procedures, therapeutic measures, animal models, and the epidemiology of disease. Specific disease program areas include: medical mycology, tuberculosis, and leprosy; hospital-associated infections; and streptococcal diseases and sequelae; and vector-borne bacterial diseases including Lyme disease. *Type:* Research center.

U.S. Department of Health and Human Services
National Institute of Allergy and Infectious Diseases
Division of Microbiology and Infectious Diseases
Enteric Diseases Branch
Solar Bldg., Rm 3A22   Ph: (301)496-7051
Bethesda, MD 20892   Fax: (301)402-1456
Contact: Dr. Leslye Johnson, Chf.
Desc: Bacterial and viral enteric diseases, viral hepatitis, hepatitis antiviral drug development, hepatitis C, helicobacter pylori, and mucosal immunity. *Type:* Research center.

U.S. Department of Health and Human Services
National Institute of Allergy and Infectious Diseases
Division of Microbiology and Infectious Diseases
Parasitology and International Programs Branch
Solar Bldg., 3A10   Ph: (301)496-2544
Bethesda, MD 20892   Fax: (301)402-0659
E-mail: pipb@exec.niaid.pc.niaid.nih.gov
URL: http://www.niaid.nih.gov
Contact: Dr. Stephanie James, Chf.
Desc: Host/parasite and vector relationships, with the ultimate goal of controlling parasitic diseases through such procedures as chemoprophylaxis, immunoprophylaxis, chemotherapy, and vector control. Research projects involve parasitology and medical entomology and use a broad spectrum of multidisciplinary approaches, including immunology, molecular biology, and biochemistry. *Type:* Research center.

U.S. Department of Health and Human Services
National Institute of Allergy and Infectious Diseases
Division of Microbiology and Infectious Diseases
Respiratory Diseases Branch
Solar Bldg., Rm. 3B06   Ph: (301)496-5305
6003 Executive Blvd.   Fax: (301)496-8030
Bethesda, MD 20892
E-mail: pm23v@nih.gov
Contact: Dr. Pamela McInnes, Chf.
Desc: Acute respiratory disease. Maintains programs in influenza, bacterial and viral respiratory disease, bacterial and viral vaccines, tuberculosis, pertussis, and pneumonia. *Type:* Research center.

U.S. Department of Health and Human Services
National Institute of Allergy and Infectious Diseases
Laboratory of Cellular and Molecular Immunology
NIH Bldg. 4, Rm. 111   Ph: (301)496-1257
9000 Rockville Pike   Fax: (301)496-0877
Bethesda, MD 20892-0420
E-mail: rs34r@nih.gov
Contact: Ronald H. Schwartz, Chf.
Desc: Cellular and molecular immunology. *Type:* Research center.

U.S. Department of Health and Human Services
National Institute of Allergy and Infectious Diseases
Laboratory of Clinical Investigation
NIH Bldg. 10, Rm. 11N228   Ph: (301)496-5807
10 Center Dr., MSC 1888   Fax: (301)496-7383
Bethesda, MD 20892-1888
Contact: Dr. Stephen E. Straus, Chf.
Desc: Allergic, immunologic, and infectious diseases. Specific areas of research interest are: the molecular biology, pathogenesis, prevention and antiviral treatment of herpes virus infections in humans; the role of host defense mechanisms in prevention of infections; the pathogenesis, treatment, and prevention of cryptococcal and candida infections; the molecular basis of macrophage responses to infection; identification of genes that contribute to virulence in E. *Type:* Research center.

U.S. Department of Health and Human Services
National Institute of Allergy and Infectious Diseases
Laboratory of Immunogenetics
NIAID Twinbrook Facility   Ph: (301)496-9589
12441 Parklawn Dr.   Fax: (301)402-0259
Rockville, MD 20852
E-mail: TK9C@NIH.GOV
URL: http://www.niaid.gov/nxsxanlh/labs/iig.htm
Contact: Thomas J. Kindt, PhD, Chf.
Desc: Multigene families that are involved in the control of immune function. Research emphasizes the structure and function of the genes and their products as well as mechanisms for gene regulation. *Type:* Research center.

U.S. Department of Health and Human Services
National Institute of Allergy and Infectious Diseases
Laboratory of Immunology
NIH Bldg. 10, Rm. 11N311   Ph: (301)496-5046
10 Center Dr. MSC 1892   Fax: (301)496-0222
Bethesda, MD 20892
Contact: William Paul, MD, Chf.
Desc: Various aspects of cellular, molecular, and developmental biology of lymphocytes; the regulation of immune responses; immunogenetics; and immunochemistry. Emphasis is on developing an understanding of how the various elements of the immune system function normally and of the role of immune mechanisms in the prevention and pathogenesis of diseases. *Type:* Research center.

U.S. Department of Health and Human Services
National Institute of Allergy and Infectious Diseases
Laboratory of Immunoregulation
NIH Bldg. 10, Rm. 11B13   Ph: (301)496-1124
9000 Rockville Pike   Fax: (301)402-0070
Bethesda, MD 20892
Contact: Dr. Anthony S. Fauci, Chf.
Desc: Mechanisms of activation and immunoregulation of human immune responses in normal individuals and in a variety of disease states characterized by abnormalities of immune function. Recent areas of research interest have included: acquired immunodeficiency syndrome (AIDS); immunoregulation of human lymphocyte function in normal and disease states; immunopathogenic features of immune-mediated diseases; clinical, immunopathogenic, and therapeutic studies in the spectrum of vasculitis; molecular biologic approach to the immune system; and immunopathogenesis of itChlamydia trachomatis/it infection. *Type:* Research center.

U.S. Department of Health and Human Services
National Institute of Allergy and Infectious Diseases
Laboratory of Molecular Structure
Twinbrook II   Ph: (301)496-3213
12441 Parklawn Dr., Dr, 103   Fax: (301)402-0284
Rockville, MD 20852
E-mail: jcoligan@niaid.nih.gov
Contact: John E. Coligan, PhD, Chf.
Desc: Molecular basis of the immune response. Also studies structural biology of immunologically relevant molecules. *Type:* Research center.

U.S. Department of Health and Human Services
National Institute of Allergy and Infectious Diseases
Office of Administrative Management
Extramural Administrative Management Branch
6003 Executive Blvd., Ste. 3B34   Ph: (301)496-7151
Rockville, MD 20852   Fax: (301)402-0520
E-mail: re11d@nih.gov
Contact: Regina A. Ewig, Chf.
Desc: Extramural administrative management. *Type:* Research center.

U.S. Department of Health and Human Services
National Institute of Allergy and Infectious Diseases
Office of Administrative Management
Information Technology and Evaluation Branch
NIH Bldg. 31, Rm. 7A32   Ph: (301)496-6490
9000 Rockville Pike   Fax: (301)402-0120
Bethesda, MD 20892
Contact: Dr. C. David Wise, Chf.
Desc: Supports Institute research through information technology and evaluation activities. *Type:* Research center.

U.S. Department of Health and Human Services
National Institute of Allergy and Infectious Diseases
Office of Communications
NIH Bldg. 31, Rm. 7A50   Ph: (301)496-5717
31 Center Dr., MSC2520   Fax: (301)402-0120
Bethesda, MD 20892-2520
URL: http://www.niaid.nih.gov
Desc: Supports the communication of research activities in the areas of AIDS, allergy, immunology, and infectious diseases. *Type:* Research center.

U.S. Department of Health and Human Services
National Institute of Allergy and Infectious Diseases
Office of Policy Analysis
NIH Bldg. 31, Rm. 7A52   Ph: (301)496-6752
9000 Rockville Pike   Fax: (301)402-0492
Bethesda, MD 20892
E-mail: sc112c@nih.gov
URL: http://www.niaid.nih.gov

Contact: Jane Kinsel, Ph.D., Dir.

Desc: Allergies and infectious diseases. *Type:* Research center.

U.S. Department of Health and Human Services

National Institute of Allergy and Infectious Diseases

Office of Research on Minority and Women's Health

Solar Bldg.
Ph: (301)496-8697
6003 Executive Blvd.
Fax: (301)496-8729
Rockville, MD 20852
E-mail: gc23a@nih.gov

Contact: George W. Counts, Dir.

Desc: Responsible for providing the director of NIAID and his staff with advice and guidance on matters relating to research on minority and women's health and enhanced minority and women's participation in research. Informs scientific and medical communities and other government agencies of NIAID minority and women's health activities and works to involve them in efforts to expand and encourage minority and women's health research and training programs. *Type:* Research center.

U.S. Department of Health and Human Services

National Institute of Allergy and Infectious Diseases

Rocky Mountain Laboratories

Administrative and Facilities Management Section

903 S. 4th St.
Ph: (406)363-9324
Hamilton, MT 59840
Fax: (406)363-9218
E-mail: pat_stewart@nih.gov
URL: http://www.niaid.nih.gov/

Contact: Patricia A. Stewart, Chf.

Desc: Components include the Microbial Structure and Function Laboratory; Microscopy Branch; the Persistent Viral Diseases Laboratory; and Intracellular Parasites Laboratory. *Type:* Research center.

U.S. Department of Health and Human Services

National Institutes of Health

National Institute of Allergy and Infectious Diseases

NIH Bldg. 31, Rm. 7A50
Ph: (301)496-5717
31 Center Dr., MSC2520
Fax: (301)402-0120
Bethesda, MD 20892-2520
URL: http://www.niaid.nih.gov

Contact: Anthony S. Fauci, MD, Dir.

Desc: Causes of allergic, immunologic, and infectious diseases and to the development of better means of preventing, diagnosing, and treating illnesses. Its mission involves studies on: genetic control, maturation, characteristics, and manipulation of the immune system; disorders of the immune system, including asthma and other allergies, immunodeficiency states, and autoimmunity; the role of the immune system in the pathogenesis of chronic diseases such as arthritis, the etiology, epidemiology, and pathogenesis of all types of infections (including those caused by viruses, mycoplasma, bacteria, fungi, and parasites) involving a variety of organ systems; the diagnosis, treatment, and prevention of all types of infections (including research on antimicrobial, antifungal, and antiviral therapy, and vaccines); and the role and mechanism of nucleic acid recombination in microbial agents. *Type:* Research center.

University of Alabama at Birmingham

Asthma, Allergic and Immunologic Diseases Cooperative Research Center

378 Wallace Tumor Inst.
Ph: (205)934-3370
Birmingham, AL 35294-3300
Fax: (205)934-1875
Contact: Max D. Cooper, MD, Dir.

Desc: Humoral immune responses, antibody gene organization, development of idiotypes, and studies of cell clones; and clinical studies of asthma, allergic diseases, and autoimmune diseases, including systemic lupus erythematosus and rheumatoid arthritis. In addition, Center conducts outreach and demonstration programs concerned with asthma and rheumatologic diseases. *Type:* Research center.

University of Alabama at Birmingham

Division of Clinical Immunology and Rheumatology

Tinsley Harrison Tower, 429A
Ph: (205)934-5306
Birmingham, AL 35294-0006
Fax: (205)934-1564
E-mail: robert.kimberly@ccc.uab.edu
URL: http://www.uab.edu
Contact: Dr. Robert P. Kimberly, Dir.

Desc: Rheumatic diseases and clinical immunology, including clinical studies on antibody receptor structure and function, glycopeptide chemistry, chemistry and physiology of complement, biochemical and biophysical properties of immunoglobulins, molecular biology of genetic risk factors, and pathophysiology of bone calcification. Conducts laboratory investigations in macromolecular physical chemistry, protein structure, polysaccharide chemistry, and immunology. *Type:* Research center.

University of Calgary

Health Science Centre

Immunology Research Group

3330 Hospital Dr. NW
Ph: (403)220-8558
Calgary, AB, Canada T2N 4N1
Fax: (403)283-1267
E-mail: pkubes@acs.ucalgary.ca
URL: http://www.csi.ucalgary.ca/irg.nsf
Contact: Dr. Paul Kubes, Chm.

Desc: Characteristics and modulation of immune and inflammatory responses in normal and disease states. *Type:* Research center.

University of California, Davis

Allergy-Clinical Immunology Program

Sch. of Med.
Ph: (916)752-2884
TB 192
Fax: (916)754-6047
Davis, CA 95616
E-mail: ssteuber@ucdavis.edu
Contact: Dr. Suzanne S. Teuber, MD, Dir.

Desc: Cellular immunology and immunochemistry. Explores the immunopathogenesis of systemic rheumatic diseases and autoimmune disorders. *Type:* Research center.

University of California, Los Angeles

Harbor-UCLA Medical Center

Center for Vaccine Research

1124 W. Carson St., Bldg. E6
Ph: (310)222-2346
Torrance, CA 90502
Fax: (310)782-8776
E-mail: joelward@ucla.edu
Contact: Dr. Joel Ward, Dir.

Desc: Clinical, epidemiologic and laboratory studies of vaccines, and vaccine preventable dieases (all age groups, normal and high risk populations). Also studies the mechanisms of immune responses to vaccines and conducts investigational studies on viral and bacterial vaccines. *Type:* Research center.

University of Colorado

Immunology Center

Div. of Allergy & Clinical
Ph: (303)315-7601
Immunology
Fax: (303)315-7642
4200 E. 9th Ave., B164
Denver, CO 80262
Contact: Dr. Brian L. Kotzin, Dir.

Desc: Provides a focus for research into the causes, prevention, and management of diseases such as asthma, allergies, systemic lupus erythematosus, rheumatoid arthritis, immune deficiencies and infection, plus related studies of fundamental immune mechanisms involving immune cells, antibodies, genetic factors, and immune regulatory systems. Ongoing studies include investigations of the genetic bais of autoimmunity, T cell activation in immuno-mediated diseases, mast cell activation in allergic and infectious diseases, the effects of benzopyrenes (from tobacco smoke) on T cell function, mechanisms underlying recurrent miscarriages, the role of soluble T cell receptors in contact hypersensitivity, and xenotransplantation of pancreatic islets. *Type:* Research center.

University of Georgia

Computational Center for Molecular Structure and Design

Department of Chemistry
Ph: (706)542-2043
Athens, GA 30602-2526
Fax: (706)542-2673
E-mail: allinger@sunchem.chem.uga.edu
Contact: Dr. Norman L. Allinger, Dir.

Desc: Molecular conformations and interactions and new computational procedures in the area of molecular mechanics and molecular modeling methods. *Type:* Research center.

University of Illinois at Chicago

Institute for Tuberculosis Research

940 South Hasted
Ph: (312)996-3906
M/C 964 (2014 SEL)
Fax: (312)996-4689
Chicago, IL 60607
E-mail: groves@uic.edu
Contact: Michael J. Groves, PhD, Dir.

Desc: Cellular immunology, including tuberculosis immunity with special reference to use of Bacillus Calmette-Guerin (BCG) vaccine. Active in evaluating BCG vaccine as nonspecific stimulant for immune system in prevention and treatment of cancer in animals and man. *Type:* Research center.

University of Kansas

Allergy and Immunology Clinic

3901 Rainbow Blvd.
Ph: (913)588-6008
Kansas City, KS 66160-7317
Fax: (913)588-3987
E-mail: dstechsc@kmuc.edu
Contact: Dr. Daniel J. Stechschulte, Dir.

Desc: Studies of the normal mechanism that attract and inhibit the accumulation of WBG (type of defense cells) in the lungs and synovial membranes, clinical trials to evaluate the effectiveness of less toxic drugs in the treatment of systemic lupus erythematosus and rheumatoid arthritis, and studies on the role of mediators in the disease course of asthma. *Type:* Research center.

University of Minnesota

Bone Marrow Transplant Program

Box 803
Ph: (612)626-2800
420 Delaware SE
Fax: (612)625-2919
Minneapolis, MN 55455
URL: http://bmt@tc.umn.edu
Contact: Philip B. McGlave, MD, Dir.
Desc: Bone marrow transplantation. *Type:* Research center.

University of Montreal

Immunobiology Research Group

2900 Blvd. Edouard-Montpetit   Ph: (514)343-6376
C.P. 6128, Succursale Centre-   Fax: (514)343-5701
   ville
Montreal, PQ, Canada H3C 3J7

Contact: Dr. Jean Joly, Dir.

Desc: Role of major histocompatibility complex (MHC) and innate resistance genes in the regulation of immune responses and in resistance to infectious agents, development of new vaccine and monoclonal antibody reagents, field testing of immunization protocols, clinical immunodiagnosis and immunopathology, thymic microenvironment, graft rejection, and molecular biology of lymphoid cells. *Type:* Research center.

University of North Carolina at Chapel Hill

Histocompatibility Laboratory

Department of Immunology   Ph: (919)966-4057
1011 Anderson Pavillion   Fax: (919)966-0486
101 Manning Dr.
Chapel Hill, NC 27514
E-mail: jhcmicro.dhl1@mail.unch.unc.edu

Contact: Dr. John Schmitz, Dir.

Desc: Diseases associated with histocompatibility antigens. *Type:* Research center.

University of Quebec

National Institute for Scientific Research

Armand-Frappier Institute

Immunology Research Centre

531, blvd. des Prairies   Ph: (514)686-5332
Laval, PQ, Canada H7N 4Z3   Fax: (514)686-5501
E-mail: suzanne_lemieux@iaf.uquebec.ca

Contact: Suzanne Lemieux, Dir.

Desc: Nutritional and environmental factors of cancer and genetics; cancer epidemiology and anti-tumor immunity; cellular and molecular analysis of immunological effectors, their regulations and mechanisms, and characterization of cellular and molecular interactions; immunomodulation; and therapeutic tools. *Type:* Research center.

University of Southern California

Division of Rheumatology and Immunology

2011 Zonal Ave., HMR 711   Ph: (323)442-1946
Los Angeles, CA 90033   Fax: (323)442-2874
E-mail: dhorwitz@hsc.usc.edu

Contact: David A. Horwitz, MD, Dir.

Desc: Pathogensis of human autoimmune diseases emphasizing systemic lupus erythematosus. Regulation of antibody production, T lymphocyte function, genes involved in susceptibility and resistance. *Type:* Research center.

University of Virginia

Beirne Carter Center for Immunology Research

Health Science Center   Ph: (804)924-9233
Box MR-4-4012   Fax: (804)924-1221
Charlottesville, VA 22908
E-mail: ehh2e@galen.med.virginia.edu
URL: http://www.med.virginia.edu/inter-dis/BBCC/bbcchome.html

Contact: Dr. Thomas J. Braciale, PhD, Dir.

Desc: Basic and clinical immunology, infectious diseases, cancer, autoimmune diseases, and cell signaling in the immune system. *Type:* Research center.

University of Wisconsin

Allergy/Asthma Clinical Research Unit

Medical School   Ph: (608)262-2804
600 Highland Ave.   Fax: (608)265-9890
H6/367 CSC
Madison, WI 53792
E-mail: mjb@medicine.wisc.edu
URL: http://www.medicine.wisc.edu/sections/allergy

Contact: Dr. William Busse, Dir.

Desc: Relationship between viruses and asthma using correlative studies derived from animal models and human experiments. In particular, the effect of virus infections on beta-adrenergic receptor structure, airway mechanics, mediator release from pulmonary alveolar cells, and the late phase reaction are studied. *Type:* Research center.

Washington University in St. Louis

Asthma, Allergic, and Immunological Diseases Cooperative Research Center

660 S. Euclid Ave., Box 8122   Ph: (314)362-9071
St. Louis, MO 63110   Fax: (314)454-0486
E-mail: chaplin@im.wustl.edu

Contact: Dr. David D. Chaplin, Dir.

Desc: Innate immunity and systemic responses cytokines, contact hypersensitivity, epithelial barriers, natural killer cells, T lymphocyte development and subsets, macrophage biology, airway hyperreactivity, and inner city asthma. *Type:* Research center.

Wayne State University

Hybridoma Center

Wayne State Medical Sch.   Ph: (313)577-1592
Department of Immunology &   Fax: (313)577-1155
   Microbiology
540 E. Canfield
Detroit, MI 48201
E-mail: pmontgo@med.wayne.edu

Contact: Dr. Paul C. Montgomery, Dir.

Desc: Preparation of monoclonal antibodies. *Type:* Research center.

West Haven Veterans Hospital

Surgical Immunology Research Laboratory

950 Camel Ave.   Ph: (203)932-5711
West Haven, CT 06516   Fax: (203)937-3878

Contact: Dr. Marvin A. McMillen, Dir.

Desc: Immunology, including lymphocyte signal transduction, neuroenteric mediators of immune functions, and the effects of immunosuppressives on second messengers and activation events. *Type:* Research center.

Alumni

Alumni Association, Framingham State College

42 Adams Rd.   Ph: (508)872-9770
Framingham, MA 01702-2456   Fax: (508)872-9770
E-mail: framalum@ma.ultranet.com

Contact: Marilyn Foley, Exec.Sec.

Desc: Graduates of the Framingham State College (FSC). Promotes ongoing communication and good fellowship among members. *Type:* Association.

Alumni Association of Regents College

7 Columbia Circle   Ph: (518)464-8500
Albany, NY 12203-5159   Free: 888-647-2388
   Fax: (518)464-8777
E-mail: alumni@regents.edu
URL: http://www.regents.edu

Contact: Mark F. Guntrum, Dir.

Desc: Graduates and former students of Regents College. Seeks to advance Regents College and its programs; facilitates ongoing communication and good fellowship among members. *Type:* Association.

Alumni Association of the University of Louisville

Louisville, KY 40292   Ph: (502)852-6184
   Free: 800-813-8635
   Fax: (502)852-6920
E-mail: tssing01@gwise.louisville.edu
URL: http://www.louisville.edu/alumni/

Contact: Tara S. Singer, Exec.V.Pres.

Desc: Graduates and former students of the University of Louisville. Seeks to advance the University and its programs; encourages ongoing communication and good fellowship among members. *Type:* Association.

Brandeis University Alumni Association

Waltham, MA 02454-9110   Ph: (781)736-4100
   Free: 800-333-1948
   Fax: (781)736-4101
E-mail: efinkelstein@brandeis.edu
URL: http://www.brandeis.edu/alumni

Contact: Paul S. Rosenstein, Exec.Dir.

Desc: Graduates of Brandeis University. Seeks to advance the University and its programs; facilitates ongoing communication and good fellowship among members. *Type:* Association.

Brooklyn College of the City University of New York Alumni Association

Brooklyn, NY 11210-2889   Ph: (718)951-5595
   Fax: (718)951-5962

Contact: Samuel Rabinoff, Pres.

Desc: Graduates and former students of Brooklyn College. Seeks to strengthen "the lifelong connection between Brooklyn College and its alumni." *Type:* Association.

California College of Arts and Crafts Alumni Association

1111 8th St.   Ph: (415)703-9500
San Francisco, CA 94107   Fax: (415)703-9537
URL: http://www.ccac-art.edu

Contact: Lorne Buchman, Pres.

Desc: Graduates and former students of the California College of Arts and Crafts. Seeks to advance members' artistic pursuits; provides support and assistance to the California College of Arts and Crafts and its programs. *Type:* Association.

Centenary College of Louisiana Alumni Association

Shreveport, LA 71134-1188   Ph: (318)869-5151
   Free: 800-259-6447
   Fax: (318)869-5026
E-mail: dhening@centenary.edu
URL: http://www.centenary.edu/alumni

Contact: David T. Henington, Dir.

Desc: Graduates and former students of Centenary College. Seeks to advance the College and its programs; facilitates ongoing communication and good fellowship among members. *Type:* Association.

Coastal Carolina Alumni Association

PO Box 261954   Ph: (843)349-2007
Conway, SC 29528-2007   Fax: (843)349-2995
E-mail: mona@coastal.edu

Contact: Mona B. Dukes, Dir.

Desc: Graduates and former students of Coastal Carolina University. Seeks to advance the University and its programs; facilitates ongoing communication and good fellowship among members. *Type:* Association.

College of St. Scholastica Alumni Association

Duluth, MN 55811   Ph: (218)723-6658
E-mail: alumni@css.edu

Desc: Graduates of the College of St. Scholastica. Promotes the advancement of the College of St. *Type:* Association.

D'Youville College Alumni Association
631 Niagara St.　　　　Ph: (716)878-2719
Buffalo, NY 14201-1084　Fax: (716)878-2715
Contact: Marguerite Collesano, Contact.
Desc: Graduates of D'Youville College. Promotes communication and good fellowship among members; seeks to advance D'Youville College and its programs. *Type:* Association.

Emerson College Alumni Association
100 Beacon St.　　　　Ph: (617)824-8535
Boston, MA 02116-1596　Free: 800-255-4259
　　　　　　　　　　　Fax: (617)824-7807
E-mail: alumni@emerson.edu
Desc: Graduates and former students of Emerson College. Seeks to "foster and maintain the spirit and devotion of the alumni in an effort to promote growth and the reputation of the College as a leader in communications and the performing arts." *Type:* Association.

Erskine Alumni Association
2 Washington St.　　　　Ph: (864)379-8881
PO Box 608　　　　　　Fax: (864)379-3164
Due West, SC 29639
E-mail: knight@erskine.edu
URL: http://www.erskine.edu
Contact: D. Aldon Knight, Dir.
Desc: Graduates of Erskine College and Seminary. Seeks to perpetuate friendships among members; promotes the welfare of Erskine College and Seminary. *Type:* Association.

Indiana State University Alumni Association
Terre Haute, IN 47809-1401　Ph: (812)237-3778
　　　　　　　　　　　　　Fax: (812)237-8157
E-mail: devnewt@amberindstate.edu.com
Contact: John P. Newton, Exec.Dir.
Desc: Graduates of the Indiana State University. Promotes communication and good fellowship among members. *Type:* Association.

Jackson State University National Alumni Association
PO Box 17820　　　　　Ph: (601)968-2281
Jackson, MS 39217-0502　Free: 800-578-6622
　　　　　　　　　　　Fax: (601)973-3701
E-mail: jsunaamain@aol.com
Contact: Curtis Johnson, Exec.Dir.
Desc: Graduates and former students of Jackson State University. Seeks to advance the University and its programs; facilitates ongoing communication among members. *Type:* Association.

Lawrence Technological University Alumni Association
21000 W 10 Mile Rd.　　Ph: (248)204-2200
Southfield, MI 48075-1058
Contact: Bruce Annett, Dir.
Desc: Graduates and former students of Lawrence Technological University and the former Detroit Institute of Technology. Seeks to advance the University and its programs. *Type:* Association.

Lincoln University Alumni Association
Office of Alumni Affairs　Ph: (573)681-5570
Lincoln University　　　Fax: (573)681-5892
818 Chestnut St.
Jefferson City, MO 65102
E-mail: nelson@lincoln.edu
URL: http://www.lincolnu.edu
Contact: Sam Duncan, Pres.
Desc: Graduates of Lincoln University. Seeks to advance the University and its programs. *Type:* Association.

Marquette University Alumni Association
Milwaukee, WI 53201-1881　Ph: (414)288-7441
　　　　　　　　　　　　　Free: 800-344-7544
　　　　　　　　　　　　　Fax: (414)288-3956
Contact: Dan J. Mueller, Dir.
Desc: Graduates of Marquette University. Seeks to "help Marquette University, as an urban Catholic, Jesuit institution, become one of the nation's distinguished universities." *Type:* Association.

Northwest Nazarene College Alumni Association
623 Holly St.　　　　　Ph: (208)467-8841
Nampa, ID 83686　　　　Free: 800-654-2411
　　　　　　　　　　　Fax: (208)467-8838
E-mail: alumni@exodus.nnc.edu
Contact: Janice L. McIntyre, Exec.Dir.
Desc: Graduates of the Northwest Nazarene College. Seeks to develop "Christian character within the philosophy and framework of genuine scholarship." *Type:* Association.

Oklahoma Baptists University Alumni Association
Shawnee, OK 74804　　　Ph: (405)878-2706
　　　　　　　　　　　Fax: (405)878-2710
E-mail: alumni@mail.okbu.edu
Contact: Martin L. O'Gwynn, Exec.Dir.
Desc: Graduates of the Oklahoma Baptist University. Seeks to provide opportunities for "graduates and former students to continue and expand relationships between each other and university personnel." *Type:* Association.

Oklahoma City University Alumni Office
2501 N Blackwelder　　　Ph: (405)521-5117
Oklahoma City, OK 73106　Free: 800-872-8984
　　　　　　　　　　　　Fax: (405)521-5191
E-mail: alumni@frodo.okcu.edu
URL: http://www.okcu.edu
Contact: Jennifer R. Poole, Dir.
Desc: Graduates and former students of Oklahoma City University. Promotes ongoing communication among members and between members and current faculty, administration, and students. *Type:* Association.

Ouachita Baptist University Alumni Association
Arkadelphia, AR 71998-0001　Ph: (870)245-5506
　　　　　　　　　　　　　　Free: 800-342-5628
　　　　　　　　　　　　　　Fax: (870)245-5500
E-mail: alumni@alpha.obu.edu
URL: http://www.obu.edu
Contact: Randy Garner, Dir.
Desc: Graduates and former students of Ouachita Baptist University. Promotes ongoing communication and good fellowship among members; seeks to advance the University and its programs. *Type:* Association.

St. Mary's College of California Alumni Association
PO Box 3400　　　　　　Ph: (925)631-4200
Moraga, CA 94575-3400　Free: 800-800-2586
　　　　　　　　　　　Fax: (925)631-4382
E-mail: ggmiller@stmarys-ca.edu
URL: http://www.stmarys-ca.edu
Contact: Giles G. Miller, Dir.
Desc: Graduates and former students of St. Mary's College of California. Seeks to advance the College and its programs; facilitates ongoing communication and good fellowship among members. *Type:* Association.

Southern Connecticut State University Alumni Association
New Haven, CT 06515　　Ph: (203)392-6500
　　　　　　　　　　　Fax: (203)392-6508
E-mail: alumniinfo@scsu.ctstateu.edu
Contact: Jean Figueroa, Pres.
Desc: Graduates and former students of Southern Connecticut State University (SCSU). Seeks to advance SCSU and its programs; facilitates ongoing communication and good fellowship among members. *Type:* Association.

Texas A&M University - Commerce Alumni Association
Commerce, TX 75429-3011　Ph: (903)886-5765
E-mail: alumni_office@tamu-commerce.edu
Contact: Kayla Price, Exec.Dir.
Desc: Graduates of Texas A&M University. Promotes continuing communication and good fellowship among members. *Type:* Association.

Tufts University Alumni Association
95 Talbot Ave.　　　　Ph: (617)627-3526
Medford, MA 02155　　　Free: 800-THE-
　　　　　　　　　　　　　　　　ALUM
　　　　　　　　　　　Fax: (617)627-3938
E-mail: sciolfi@infonet.tufts.edu
Contact: Elliott Lerman, Pres.
Desc: Graduates of Tufts University and former students who completed at least one year of study at the University. Seeks to advance Tufts University and its programs; encourages ongoing communication and good fellowship among members. *Type:* Association.

University of Iowa Alumni Association
100 Levitt Center　　　Ph: (319)335-3294
Iowa City, IA 52242-1797　Free: 800-469-2586
　　　　　　　　　　　　Fax: (319)335-1079
E-mail: kathryn-sayre@uiowa.edu
Contact: Vince Nelson, Exec.Dir.
Desc: Graduates of the University of Iowa. Seeks to advance the University of Iowa and its programs; promotes communication and good fellowship among members. *Type:* Association.

University of Oklahoma Association
900 Asp Ave., Ste. 327　Ph: (405)325-1710
Norman, OK 73019-4051　Fax: (405)325-1709
E-mail: oualumniassoc@ou.edu
Contact: Paul D. Massad, Assoc.V.Pres.
Desc: Graduates and friends of the University of Oklahoma. Seeks to advance the University and its programs; facilitates ongoing communication and good fellowship among members. *Type:* Association.

University of South Dakota Alumni Association
414 E Clark St.　　　　Ph: (605)677-6734
Vermillion, SD 57069-2390　Fax: (605)677-6717
E-mail: alumni@usd.edu
Contact: Dr. Nancy McCahren, Dir.
Desc: Graduates and former students of the University of South Dakota. Seeks to "unite the alumni in a close bond of fellowship; to advance the purposes of the University; to foster and stimulate the loyalty of the alumni; and to promote united and constructive action by the alumni in behalf of the University." *Type:* Association.

University of Wisconsin - Eau Claire Alumni Association
Eau Claire, WI 54702-4004　Ph: (715)836-5189
　　　　　　　　　　　　　Fax: (715)836-4375
E-mail: alumni@uwec.edu
Contact: Vicky Petermann, Dir.
Desc: Graduates of the University of Wisconsin - Eau Claire. Seeks to advance the University and its programs; facilitates student development. *Type:* Association.

Wofford College National Alumni Association
Spartanburg, SC 29303-3663
Ph: (864)597-4185
Fax: (864)597-4219
E-mail: graych@wofford.edu
Contact: Charles H. Gray, Jr., Contact.
Desc: Graduates of Wofford College. Seeks to "unite the alumni and friends of Wofford College in good fellowship and cooperative enterprise with the students, faculty, officers, and trustees of Wofford College." *Type:* Association.

Americas

Americas Society
680 Park Ave.
Ph: (212)249-8950
New York, NY 10021
Fax: (212)249-5868
URL: http://www.americas-society.org
Contact: Ambassador Thomas E. McNamara, Pres.
Desc: Works to educate U.S. citizens about the other nations of the Americas. Fosters mutual understanding of the economic, political, and cultural issues facing Latin America, the Caribbean, and Canada today. *Type:* Association.

Kappa Omicron Nu
4990 Northwind Dr., Ste. 140
Ph: (517)351-8335
East Lansing, MI 48823-5031
Fax: (517)351-8336
E-mail: dmitstifer@kon.org
URL: http://www.kon.org
Contact: Dorothy I. Mitstifer, Exec.Dir.
Desc: Honor society for men and women in family and consumer sciences. Conducts research and educational programs. *Type:* Association.

Organization of American States
17th St. & Constitution Ave.
Ph: (202)458-3000
NW
Fax: (202)458-6421
Washington, DC 20006
URL: http://www.oas.org
Contact: Cesar Gaviria Trujillo, Sec.Gen.
Desc: International organization created to achieve an order of peace and justice among the American nations, to promote their solidarity, to strengthen their collaboration, and to defend their sovereignty, territorial integrity, and independence. Operates through agencies and institutions throughout the hemisphere. Maintains museum of modern Latin American art. *Type:* Association.

Pacifica Foundation
3729 Cahuenga Blvd. W.
Ph: (818)985-8800
North Hollywood, CA 91604
E-mail: srosas@aol.com
Contact: Patricia Scott, Acting Exec.Dir.
Desc: Nonprofit educational corporation owned and operated by the Pacifica National Board of Directors and chartered by the state of California. Operates six noncommercial, listener-supported FM radio stations in five metropolitan areas (KPFA and KPFB, Berkeley, CA; KPFK, Los Angeles, CA; WBAI, New York City; KPFT, Houston, TX; WPFW, Washington, DC). Stations present wide range of music, public affairs, drama, and literature programs, featuring many viewpoints consistent with the goals of the foundation. *Type:* Association.

Pan American Development Foundation
2600 16th St., NW
Ph: (202)458-3969
Washington, DC 20009-4202
Fax: (202)458-6316
Contact: Sarah Horsey-Barr, Exec.Dir.
Desc: Utilizes grants from the public and private sectors to improve the quality of life in Latin America and the Caribbean. *Type:* Association.

Partners of the Americas
1424 K St. NW, Ste. 700
Ph: (202)628-3300
Washington, DC 20005
Fax: (202)628-3306
E-mail: info@partners.poa.com
URL: http://www.partners.net
Contact: Norman Brown, Pres.
Desc: Volunteer private citizens organized in 60 partnerships linking U.S. states with Latin American and Caribbean countries. Goals are to encourage innovative, community-based projects and joint planning among local partnerships; to provide a stimulus to local partnerships in generating additional resources for their technical and cultural exchange projects; to assist in the implementation of effective and ongoing development projects in the Latin American, Mexican, and Caribbean partner areas. *Type:* Association.

Animal Welfare

Alley Cat Allies
PO Box 397
Ph: (202)667-3630
Mount Rainier, MD 20712
Fax: (202)667-3640
URL: http://www.alleycat.org
Contact: Louise Holton, Dir.
Desc: Individuals with an interest in controlling domestic and feral cat populations in the U.S. Promotes humane feral cat population control through trapping and sterilization programs. *Type:* Association.

American Anti-Vivisection Society
801 Old York Rd., Ste.204
Ph: (215)887-0816
Jenkintown, PA 19046
Free: 800-SAY-AAVS
Fax: (215)887-2088
E-mail: aavsonline@aol.com
URL: http://www.aavs.org
Contact: Tina Nelson, Exec. Dir.
Desc: Dedicated to ending experiments on animals in education, research and testing. *Type:* Association.

American Pet Society
406 S. 1st Ave.
Ph: (626)447-2222
Arcadia, CA 91006
Fax: (626)447-8350
E-mail: info@wwpsa.com
Contact: Doug Poindexter, Mgr.
Desc: Promotes responsible pet ownership. Sponsors charitable and educational programs; offers children's services. Produces America's Family Pet Expo. *Type:* Association.

American Society for the Prevention of Cruelty to Animals
424 E. 92nd St.
Ph: (212)876-7700
New York, NY 10128
Fax: (212)876-9571
URL: http://www.aspca.org
Contact: Roger A. Caras, Pres.
Desc: Seeks to: provide effective means for the prevention of cruelty to animals; enforce all laws for the protection of animals; promote appreciation for and humane treatment of animals; maintain shelters for lost, stray, or unwanted animals; operate a veterinary hospital and a major low-cost spay/neuter clinic. *Type:* Association.

Animal Medical Center
510 E. 62nd St.
Ph: (212)838-8100
New York, NY 10021-8383
Fax: (212)832-9630
E-mail: amc1@metgate.metro.org
Contact: Guy L. Pidgeon, Pres. & CEO.
Desc: Provides quality medical and surgical care for small pets; conducts educational programs for veterinarians, students, and technicians; conducts clinical investigations in veterinary and comparative medicine. Sponsors charitable outreach programs including bereavement counseling, pet therapy, and subsidized care for indigent elderly pet owners and guide dog owners; maintains library. *Type:* Association.

Animal Protection Institute of America
2831 Fruitridge Rd.
Ph: (916)731-5521
Sacramento, CA 95820
Free: 800-348-7387
Fax: (916)731-4467
E-mail: onlineAPI@aol.com
URL: http://www.api4animals.org
Contact: Alan H. Berger, Exec.Dir.
Desc: The Animal Protection Institute is a national animal advocacy nonprofit organization formed in 1968 dedicated to protecting animals against abuse through enforcement/legislative actions, investigations, advocacy campaigns, crisis intervention, public awareness, and education. Specific areas of concern are wildlife protection/habitat conservation, companion animals, marine mammals, domestic/farm animals, animals used in research, and humane education. *Type:* Association.

Animals Magazine
Massachusetts Society for the Prevention of Cruelty to Animals and the American Human Education Society
350 S. Huntington Ave.
Ph: (617)541-5065
Boston, MA 02130
Free: 800-998-0797
Fax: (617)522-4885
E-mail: animals@americast.com.
Contact: Joni Praded, Directory/Editor, (617)541-5067, jpraded@mspca.org; Joseph E. Kaknes, Advertising Mgr., (617)541-5090, jkaknes@mspca.org.
Desc: Magazine on wildlife, pets, animal welfare, and environmental issues. *Type:* Periodical.

Anti-Cruelty Society
157 W. Grand Ave.
Ph: (312)644-8338
Chicago, IL 60610
Fax: (312)644-3878
URL: http://www.anticruelty.org
Contact: Jane Stern, Exec.Dir.
Desc: Strives to eliminate cruelty to animals, to educate children on responsibilities of pet ownership, and to provide refuge for abandoned or abused animals. *Type:* Association.

ASPCA Animal Watch Magazine
American Society for the Prevention of Cruelty to Animals (ASPCA)
424 E. 92nd St.
Ph: (212)876-7700
New York, NY 10128
Fax: (212)348-3031
URL: http://www.aspca.org.
Contact: Cindy A. Adams, Editor.
Desc: Concerned with subjects related to "animal welfare, humane education, prevention of cruelty to animals, and over population." Recurring features include editorials, news of research, book, video, and computer program reviews. *Type:* Newsletter.

Associated Humane Societies
124 Evergreen Ave.
Ph: (973)824-7080
Newark, NJ 07114
Fax: (201)824-2720
Contact: Lee Bernstein, Exec.Dir.
Desc: Humane societies seeking to assist wild and domestic animals. Works toward legislation supporting animal welfare. Maintains shelters for injured and abandoned animals; operates Popcorn Park Zoo. *Type:* Association.

Bide-A-Wee Home Association
410 E. 38th St.
Ph: (212)532-6395
New York, NY 10016
Fax: (212)532-4210
URL: http://www.bideawee.org
Contact: Reynaldo C. Samala, Exec.Dir.
Desc: Humane society for the adoption and care of dogs, cats, puppies, and kittens. Shelters unwanted pets. Provides pet adoption services, veterinary clinic services, and burial/cremation services at pet memorial parks. *Type:* Association.

Citizens to End Animal Suffering and Exploitation

PO Box 440456
Somerville, MA 02144
Ph: (617)628-9030
Fax: (617)628-9034
Contact: William Dekok, Admin.Dir.
Desc: Individuals interested in animal rights. Seeks to raise public awareness of animal issues through outreach, legislation, protest, and education. *Type:* Association.

Committee for Humane Legislation

2000 P St. NW, No. 415
Washington, DC 20036
Ph: (202)296-2172
Fax: (202)296-2190
Contact: Priscilla Feral, Exec.Dir.
Desc: Individuals supporting animal legislation at federal and state levels. Seeks to protect animals by: working toward eliminating sport hunting and recreational trapping of wildlife; discouraging the use of animals in experimental research and product testing; providing increased protection for marine mammals. Sponsors educational arm, Friends of Animals. *Type:* Association.

Compassion for Animals Campaign

PO Box 52457
Philadelphia, PA 19115
Ph: (215)396-2587
Fax: (215)396-2516
E-mail: entertainment@juno.com
Contact: Maria Liberati, Spokesperson.
Desc: Promotes public awareness of animal testing performed in the cosmetic and pharmaceutical industries. Encourages support for those companies that do not employ animal testing. Provides strategies to encourage companies to abandon animal testing; offers consulting services for manufacturers seeking alternative testing methods. *Type:* Association.

Dedication and Everlasting Love To Animals

PO Box 9
Glendale, CA 91209-0009
Ph: (818)241-6282
Fax: (805)269-5049
Contact: Leo Grillo, Founder/Pres.
Desc: Humane organization rescuing animals abondoned in the wilderness. *Type:* Association.

Earth Island Institute/International Marine Mammal Project

300 Broadway, Ste. 28
San Francisco, CA 94133
Ph: (415)788-3666
Fax: (415)788-7324
URL: http://www.earthisland.org/ei/
Contact: David Phillips, Exec.Dir.
Desc: Works to make the oceans safe for marine mammals. Works to eliminate dolphin mortality as a by-product of commercial tuna fishing; opposes use of drift and purse-seine nets; works to uphold current international ban on whaling. *Type:* Association.

Farm Animal Reform Movement

PO Box 30654
Bethesda, MD 20824
Ph: (301)530-1737
Free: 800-632-8688
Fax: (301)530-5747
E-mail: farm@farmusa.org
URL: http://www.farmusa.org
Contact: Alex Hershaft, Ph.D., Pres.
Desc: Promotes a plant-based diet eliminates abuse of farm animals and other adverse impacts of animal agriculture. Holds demonstrations and print, radio, and television interviews. Promotes observance of the Great American Meatout on Mar. *Type:* Association.

Farm Sanctuary-East

PO Box 150
Watkins Glen, NY 14891
Ph: (607)583-2225
Fax: (607)583-2041
E-mail: farmsanc@servtech.com
URL: http://www.farmsanctuary.org
Contact: Lorri Bauston, Pres.
Desc: Representatives working to end factory farm animal abuses. Works to: eliminate what the organization terms abusive animal agricultural practices; educate the public on factory farming; promote alternatives to factory farm products. *Type:* Association.

Four Paws Animal Foundation

Arleen Braun
94 Third Ct.
Bartlett, IL 60103-9509
Ph: (630)497-2078
Contact: Arleen Braun, Dir.
Type: Association.

Friends of Animals

777 Post Rd., Ste. 205
Darien, CT 06820
Ph: (203)656-1522
Fax: (203)656-0267
E-mail: foa@igc.org
URL: http://www.friendsofanimals.org
Contact: Priscilla Feral, Pres.
Type: Association.

Friends of Animals

777 Post Rd., Ste. 205
Darien, CT 06820
Ph: (203)866-5223
Fax: (203)656-0267
E-mail: foa@igc.apc.org
URL: http://www.friendsofanimals.org
Contact: Priscilla Feral, Pres.
Desc: Works to reduce and eliminate animal suffering and abuse. *Type:* Association.

Friends of Animals Actionline

Friends of Animals, Inc.
777 Post Rd., Ste. 205
Darien, CT 06820-4721
Ph: (203)656-1522
Fax: (203)656-0267
E-mail: foa@igc.apc.org
URL: http://www.friendsofanimals.org.
Desc: Trade magazine covering animal issues for Friends of Animals, Inc. *Type:* Periodical.

Fund for Animals

200 W. 57th St.
New York, NY 10019
Ph: (212)246-2096
Fax: (212)246-2633
Contact: Marian Probst, Pres.
Desc: Works to protect wildlife and fight cruelty to animals, both domestic and wild, by means of legal action, direct activism, public education, and lobbying. Motto is "We Speak for Those Who Can't"; bumper stickers and buttons reflect theme, "Animals Have Rights, Too." Publicizes and influences public opinion on environmental and animal issues through books, press releases, articles, meetings, and special events. Has exposed, over network television, the cruelty of bullfighting, the clubbing of baby seals, use of the leghold trap, and sport hunting. *Type:* Association.

Humane Farming Association

1550 California St., Ste. 6
San Francisco, CA 94109
Ph: (415)771-2253
Fax: (415)485-0106
URL: http://www.hfa.org
Contact: Bradley S. Miller, Natl.Dir.
Desc: To protect farm animals from cruelty and abuse. *Type:* Association.

Humane News

Associated Humane Societies
124 Evergreen Ave.
Newark, NJ 07114
Ph: (973)824-7080
Fax: (973)824-2720
Contact: Roseann Trezza, Editor.
Desc: Reports on news of the programs and activities of humane societies seeking to assist wild and domestic animals. Provides legislative updates on bills supporting animal welfare. *Type:* Newsletter.

Humane Society of the United States

2100 L St. NW
Washington, DC 20037
Ph: (202)452-1100
Fax: (202)778-6132
E-mail: hsusceo@ix.netcom.com
URL: http://www.hsus.org/

Contact: Paul G. Irwin, Pres.
Desc: Promotes public education to foster respect, understanding, and compassion for all creatures. Programs include: reducing the overbreeding of cats and dogs and promoting responsible pet ownership; eliminating cruelty in hunting and trapping; exposing and eliminating painful uses of animals in research and testing; eliminating the abuse of animals in movies, television productions, circuses, and competitive events such as dogfights, racing, pulling contests, and shows; correcting inhumane conditions for animals in zoos, menageries, pet shops, puppy mills, and kennels; stopping cruelty in the raising, handling, and transporting of animals used for food; addressing critical environmental issues in terms of their impact on animals and humans; protecting endangered wildlife and marine mammals; making national wildlife refuges and parks into true sanctuaries for wildlife; halting the cruelty and destruction of the international trade in wildlife, especially exotic birds and elephant ivory; campaigns to create public awareness and rejection of harvested or farm-raised fur-bearing animals. Campaigns for or against legislation affecting animal protection and monitors enforcement of existing animal protection statutes; works with animal control agencies and local humane societies to establish effective and humane programs. *Type:* Association.

Humane Society of the United States, New England Regional Office

PO Box 619
Jacksonville, VT 05342
Ph: (802)368-2790
Fax: (802)368-2756
Contact: Arnold F. Baer, Dir.
Desc: Individuals dedicated to preventing cruelty to animals. Promotes humane education. *Type:* Association.

In Defense of Animals

131 Camino Alto, Ste. E
Mill Valley, CA 94941
Ph: (415)388-9641
Fax: (415)388-0388
Contact: Dr. Elliot M. Katz, Pres.
Desc: Individuals interested in taking direct action to protect animals from cruel treatment. Attempts to come to the aid of animals experiencing "cruel treatment in the name of science." *Type:* Association.

International Primate Protection League

PO Box 766
Summerville, SC 29484
Ph: (843)871-2280
Fax: (843)871-7988
E-mail: ippl@awod.com
URL: http://www.ippl.org
Contact: Dr. Shirley McGreal, Chwm.
Desc: Zoologists, primate field workers, anthropologists, and other interested individuals; humane societies and animal welfare organizations. Fosters the conservation and protection of nonhuman primates. *Type:* Association.

International Society for Animal Rights

965 Griffin Pond Rd.
Clarks Summit, PA 18411-9214
Free: 800-543-ISAR
E-mail: isar@aol.com
Contact: Susan Altieri, Pres.
Desc: Promotes animal rights through educational programs and legislation. *Type:* Association.

Latham Foundation

Latham Plaza Bldg.
Clement & Schiller Sts.
Alameda, CA 94501
Ph: (510)521-0920
Fax: (510)521-9861
E-mail: lath@aol.com
URL: http://www.Latham.org
Contact: Hugh H. Tebault, III, Pres.
Desc: Promotes the ideas of: interdependence of all living things; justice, kindness, and compassion for all life. *Type:* Association.

Marine Conservation News
Center for Marine Conservation
1725 Desales St. NW, No. 500 Ph: (202)429-5609
Washington, DC 20036
Contact: Roy Krisha, Editor.
Desc: Concerned with the conservation of marine animals and their habitat. Covers events on the national and international levels, including articles and news briefs on commercial and aboriginal whaling, endangered marine species, research, funding, relevant proposals and legislation, and the Center's projects and programs. *Type:* Newsletter.

Michigan Humane Society
7401 Chrysler Dr.
Detroit, MI 48211 Ph: (313)872-3400
E-mail: mail@mihumane.org Fax: (313)872-6698
Contact: Gary Tiscornia, Exec.Dir.
Desc: Works to prevent and eliminate animal cruelty by elevating the moral and legal status of animals. Promotes enforcement, education, legislation, and the provision of veterinary care. *Type:* Association.

Morris Animal Foundation
45 Inverness Dr. E
Englewood, CO 80112 Ph: (303)790-2345
Free: 800-243-2345
Fax: (303)790-4066
URL: http://www.morrisanimalfoundation.org
Contact: Robert Hilsenroth, D.V.M., Exec.Dir.
Desc: Seeks to improve the health and well-being of companion animals and wildlife by funding humane health studies and disseminating information about these studies. *Type:* Association.

National Anti-Vivisection Society
53 W. Jackson, Ste. 1552
Chicago, IL 60604 Ph: (312)427-6065
Free: 800-888-NAVS
Fax: (312)427-6524
E-mail: navs@navs.org
URL: http://www.navs.org
Contact: Mary Margaret Cunniff, Exec.Dir.
Desc: Conducts educational programs and distributes information to acquaint the public with the problems associated with vivisection of animals. *Type:* Association.

National Dog Registry
Box 116
Woodstock, NY 12498-9017 Ph: (914)679-2355
Free: 800-NDR-DOGS
Fax: (914)340-1318
E-mail: info@natldogregistry.com
URL: http://www.natldogregistry.com
Contact: Bette A. Rapoport, Pres.
Desc: Seeks to reduce the traffic in stolen pets and expedite the identification of lost, strayed, injured, or dead animals. *Type:* Association.

National Humane Education Society
521-A E. Market St.
Leesburg, VA 20175 Ph: (703)777-8319
E-mail: natlhumane@aol.com Fax: (703)771-4048
Contact: William J. Kropp.
Desc: Works for animal welfare. *Type:* Association.

No-Kill Directory
Doing Things for Animals, Inc.
c/o Lynda J. Foro
P.O. Box 2165 Ph: (602)977-5793
Sun City, AZ 85372-2165 Fax: (602)977-5838
Contact: Lynda J. Foro, Editor, forodtfa@interacs.com.
Desc: No-kill animal shelters, animal rescue programs, and wildlife rehabilitation centers in the U.S. *Type:* Directory.

Peninsula Humane Society
12 Airport Blvd.
San Mateo, CA 94401 Ph: (650)340-8200
Fax: (650)348-7891
Contact: Penny Cistero, Dir. of Operations.
Type: Association.

Pennsylvania Society for the Prevention of Cruelty to Animals
350 E. Erie Ave. Ph: (215)426-6300
Philadelphia, PA 19134 Fax: (215)426-5848
Contact: Erik Hendricks, Exec.Dir.
Desc: Individuals seeking to improve the condition of animals and strengthen the link between animals and humans. Provides adoption, animal control, cremation, lost and found, and veterinary services. *Type:* Association.

People for the Ethical Treatment of Animals
501 Front St. Ph: (757)622-PETA
Norfolk, VA 23510 Fax: (757)622-0457
E-mail: peta@norfolk.infi.net
URL: http://www.peta-online.org
Contact: Ingrid E. Newkirk, Pres.
Desc: Educational and activist group that opposes all forms of animal exploitation. *Type:* Association.

Performing Animal Welfare Society
PO Box 849 Ph: (209)745-7297
Galt, CA 95632 Fax: (209)745-1809
E-mail: paws@capaccess.org
URL: http://www.envirolink.org/arrs/paws/
Contact: Pat Derby, Founder.
Desc: Works to assist performing animals that are victims of abuse. Rescues animals through intervention, legislation, and purchase; maintains 20-acre sanctuary for rescued animals that cannot be placed in humane facilities. Conducts public education campaigns; lobbies on behalf of exotic and performing animals. *Type:* Association.

Pet Pride
PO Box 1055 Ph: (310)836-5427
Pacific Palisades, CA 90272
Contact: Ruth C. Argust, Pres.
Desc: National humane society for cats. Conducts non-profit shelter and clinic; offers public education programs on proper cat care. Maintains placement service, hall of fame, and speakers' bureau. *Type:* Association.

PETA Animal Times
People for the Ethical Treatment of Animals (PETA)
501 Front St. Ph: (757)622-7382
Norfolk, VA 23510 Fax: (757)628-0783
E-mail: peta@norfolk.infi.net
Contact: Ingrid Newkirk, Editor; Muriel Ducloy, Editorial Coordinator.
Desc: Educates policy-makers and the public about issues involving the unjustifiable abuse of animals and promotes "the inherent rights of sentient animals to be treated with respect and decency." Recurring features include case studies, editorials, cartoons, and a column titled Updates and Actions. *Type:* Newsletter.

Poultry Press
United Poultry Concerns
PO Box 59367 Ph: (301)948-2406
Potomac, MD 20859 Fax: (301)948-2406
URL: http://www.envirolink.org/arrs/upc.
Contact: Karen Davis, Ph.D., Editor.
Desc: Provides information about the treatment of domestic fowl. Aims to improve conditions for poultry, and encourages a vegan diet. *Type:* Newsletter.

Primarily Primates, Inc.
PO Box 15306 Ph: (830)755-4616
San Antonio, TX 78212-8506 Fax: (830)755-2435
URL: http://www.primarilyprimates.org
Contact: Wallace W. Swett, Pres.
Desc: Provides sanctuary, rehabilitation, lifetime care, and shelter to abused or unwanted, non-native species of primates, birds, mammals, and reptiles. Serves as a clearinghouse for the exchange of information on animal care, endangered species husbandry, animal welfare issues, and cruelty cases. Works with the International Union for the Conservation of Nature and Natural Resources to return sheltered animals to their native habitats. *Type:* Association.

Project Breed Rescue Efforts and Education
PO Box 15888 Ph: (202)244-0065
Chevy Chase, MD 20825-5888 Fax: (202)244-0065
Contact: Lori Levin, Pres.
Desc: Breed-specific and species-specific animal rescue volunteers. Serves as a national clearinghouse and reference source for animal rescue, rehabilitation, adoption, and humane education on animal protection efforts. *Type:* Association.

Sea World/Busch Gardens Animal Information Database
Busch Gardens Williamsburg
One Busch Gardens Blvd Ph: (757)253-3350
Point West Commons Fax: (540)231-2139
840 University City Blvd., Ste. 7
1700 Pratt Dr.
Williamsburg, VA 23187-8785
E-mail: bev.info@bev.net
URL: http://www.seaworld.org
Desc: The Sea World/Busch Gardens Animal Information Database is a resource designed to not only instill an appreciation for science but foster a respect for all living creatures and natural environments, conserve valuable natural resources by increasing awareness of the interrelationships of humans and the environment, increase students' basic competencies in science and other disciplines, and provide an educational resource for the entire community. The database contains information on many animals in the Animal Bytes section of the database. *Type:* Database.

United Animal Nations U.S.A.
PO Box 188890 Ph: (916)429-2457
Sacramento, CA 95818-9959 Fax: (916)429-2456
E-mail: info@uan.org
URL: http://www.uan.org
Contact: Deanna Soares, Exec.Dir.
Desc: Promotes kindness to animals; works to prevent animal suffering. *Type:* Association.

United Humanitarians
PO Box 14587 Ph: (215)750-0171
Philadelphia, PA 19115
Contact: Adele P. Hudson, Exec.VP.
Desc: Persons concerned with the welfare of animals. Establishes humane animal control through mass spaying and neutering of pets and the replacement of the present licensing system with a permit system placing complete responsibility on owners, who would be cited for violations rather than impounding and killing pets found at large. Maintains charitable program and speakers' bureau. *Type:* Association.

World Society for the Protection of Animals
29 Perkins St. Ph: (617)522-7000
PO Box 190 Fax: (617)522-7077
Boston, MA 02130
E-mail: wspa@world.std.com

URL: http://www.wspa.org.uk
Contact: Andrew Dickson, Chief Exec.
Desc: Seeks to end the suffering and exploitation of animals worldwide. *Type:* Association.

Anthropology

Wenner-Gren Foundation for Anthropological Research
220 5th Ave., 16th Fl.   Ph: (212)683-5000
New York, NY 10001   Fax: (212)683-9151
Contact: Dr. Sydel Silverman, Pres.
Desc: Supports research in all branches of anthropology including cultural/social, biological/physical, ethnological, archaeological, and anthropological linguistics, and in closely related disciplines concerned with human origins, development, and variation. *Type:* Association.

Antiques

Antique Review—Calendar of Exhibits, Lectures, and Seminars Section
Regional Antique Publications
150 Brambleton Ave.
Norfolk, VA 23510
Contact: Charles R. Muller, Editor.
Desc: List of upcoming shows, auctions, and exhibits dealing with antiques. Principal content of publication is a look at trends in collecting. *Type:* Directory.

Antique Week
Mayhill Publications
27 N. Jefferson St.   Ph: (317)345-5133
PO Box 90   Free: 800-876-5133
Knightstown, IN 46148   Fax: 800-695-8153
Contact: Tom Hoepf, Editor; Connie Swaim, Editor.
Desc: In each issue, 100-150 antiques auctions and antique shows, occurring during the week or two after publication. Each issue also contains separate calendar of about 200-300 antique shows, flea markets, and auctions occurring during the months after publication; separate Central edition (Illinois, Indiana, Iowa, Kentucky, Michigan, Minnesota, Missouri, Ohio, western Pennsylvania, Tennessee, and Wisconsin), and Eastern edition (Connecticut, Delaware, District of Columbia, Maryland, New Jersey, New York, North Carolina, Pennsylvania, Rhode Island, South Carolina, Virginia, and West Virginia). *Type:* Directory.

Collectors Mart Magazine Resource Guide
Krause Publications, Inc.
700 E. State St.   Ph: (715)445-2214
Iola, WI 54990   Free: 800-258-0929
      Fax: (715)445-4087
E-mail: info@krause.com; krause@krause.com
URL: http://www.krause.com; http://www.krause.com.
Contact: Mary Sieber, Editor, sieberm@krause.com.
Desc: List of artists, manufacturers, suppliers, and selected price index of limited edition collectibles, with a focus on secondary markets, including plates, dolls, prints, ornaments, figurines, etc. *Type:* Directory.

Apparel

Apparel Center Directory
Show Communications
32 Soldier Song Ln.   Ph: (610)565-6264
Media, PA 19063   Fax: (610)565-7782
Contact: Jennifer Woolford, Editor.
Desc: About 4,000 clothing manufacturers and brands for men, women, and children in all lines represented by tenants in the Apparel Center and exhibitors at Expocenter, Chicago. *Type:* Directory.

Body Fashions/Intimate Apparel Buyer's Guide
Advanstar Communications
7500 Old Oak Blvd.   Ph: (440)243-8100
Cleveland, OH 44130-3369   Free: 800-225-4569
      Fax: (440)891-2733
E-mail: directories@advanstar.com
URL: http://www.advanstar.com.
Contact: Katie Kretschmer, Editor.
Desc: List of suppliers to the hosiery and underwear industry. *Type:* Directory.

Body Fashions/Intimate Apparel—Directory Issue
Advanstar Communications
7500 Old Oak Blvd.   Ph: (440)243-8100
Cleveland, OH 44130-3369   Free: 800-225-4569
      Fax: (440)891-2733
E-mail: directories@advanstar.com
URL: http://www.advanstar.com.
Contact: Michele Rogers, Publisher, mrogers@advanstar.com.
Desc: Sections listing manufacturers of women's intimate apparel and bodywear along with their suppliers; trade associations; industry clubs; schools of design; New York buying offices. *Type:* Directory.

Hat Life Directory
Hat Life Directory
66 York St.   Ph: (201)434-8322
Jersey City, NJ 07302   Fax: (201)434-8277
E-mail: cfuller@dmcreative.com.
Contact: Peter Annunziata, Publisher.
Desc: About 1,000 hat manufacturers, wholesalers, renovators, and importers of men's headwear, plus trade suppliers listed (SIC 2253, 2352, 5036); includes about 120 Canadian manufacturers. *Type:* Directory.

Hosiery and Bodywear—Buyer's Guide to Support and Control Top Pantyhose Issue
Advanstar Communications
270 Madison Ave.   Ph: (212)951-6708
New York, NY 10016-0695   Fax: (212)686-4841
Contact: Jill Gerson-Price, Editor.
Desc: List of about 50 hosiery manufacturers. *Type:* Directory.

Appraisers

American Society of Appraisers
PO Box 17265   Ph: (703)478-2228
Washington, DC 20041-0265   Free: 800-ASA-VALU
      Fax: (703)742-8471
E-mail: asainfo@apo.com
URL: http://www.appraisers.org
Contact: Edwin W. Baker, Exec.Dir.
Desc: Professional appraisal teaching, testing, and accrediting society concerned with all property. Seeks to "maintain recognition that members are qualified, objective, unbiased appraisers and advisors of property values; establish members' status as expert witnesses before courts, administrative tribunals, agencies, and other governmental and municipal authorities; attain recognition of the profession of value determination in property economics by educational and governmental institutions and bodies." *Type:* Association.

American Society of Farm Managers and Rural Appraisers
950 S. Cherry St., Ste. 508   Ph: (303)758-3513
Denver, CO 80246-2664   Fax: (303)758-0190
E-mail: asfmra@agri-associations.org
URL: http://www.agri-associations.org

Contact: Thomas Lipetzky, Contact.
Desc: Professional farm managers, appraisers, lenders, and researchers in farm and ranch management and/or rural appraisal. Bestows registered ARA (Accredited Rural Appraiser), Accredited Agricultural Consultant (ACC), AFM (Accredited Farm Manager) and RPRA (Real Property Review Appraiser) designations. Operates management and appraisal schools, internet course offerings, seminars, and conferences. *Type:* Association.

Appraisal Institute
875 N. Michigan Ave., Ste.   Ph: (312)335-4100
2400   Fax: (312)335-4400
Chicago, IL 60611-1980
E-mail: joan-groff@ai.ccmail.compuserve.com
URL: http://www.appraisalinstitute.org
Contact: Bert Thornton, Pres.
Desc: General appraisers who hold the MAI or SRPA designations, and residential members who hold the SRA designation. Enforces Code of Professional Ethics and Standards of Professional Appraisal Practice. *Type:* Association.

Appraisers Standards
NEAA
5 Gill Terrace   Ph: (802)228-7444
Ludlow, VT 05149-1003   Fax: (802)228-7444
Contact: Linda L. Tucker, Editor, llt44@ludl.tds.net.
Desc: Features information for appraisers of antiques, fine art and other forms of personal property. Recurring features include book reviews, news of educational opportunities, and a calendar of events. *Type:* Newsletter.

National Association of Independent Fee Appraisers
7501 Murdoch Ave.   Ph: (314)781-6688
St. Louis, MO 63119   Fax: (314)781-2872
Contact: Robert Sneed, Exec. VP.
Desc: Appraisers for real estate groups, savings and loan associations, title insurance groups, governmental agencies, and related industries. Purpose is to raise the standards of the appraisal profession. *Type:* Association.

National Association of Real Estate Appraisers
1224 N. Nokomis NE   Ph: (320)763-7626
Alexandria, MN 56308-5072   Fax: (320)763-9290
E-mail: narea@iami.org
URL: http://www.iami.org/narea.html
Contact: Joan T. Powell, Mng.Dir.
Desc: Real estate appraisers. "To make available the services of the most highly qualified real estate appraisers." *Type:* Association.

Archaeology

Archaeological Conservancy
5301 Central Ave. NE, Ste.   Ph: (505)266-1540
1218
Albuquerque, NM 87108
Contact: Mark Michel, Pres.
Desc: People interested in preserving prehistoric and historic sites for interpretive or research purposes (most members are not professional archaeologists). Seeks to acquire for permanent preservation, through donation or purchase, the ruins of past American cultures, primarily those of American Indians. *Type:* Association.

Archaeological Institute of America
656 Beacon St., 4th Fl.   Ph: (617)353-9361
Boston, MA 02215-2006   Fax: (617)353-6550
E-mail: aia@bu.edu
URL: http://www.archaeological.org
Contact: Mark Meister, Exec.Dir.

Desc: Educational and scientific society of archaeologists and others interested in archaeological study and research. *Type:* Association.

Archaeological Institute of America, Boston
656 Beacon St.   Ph: (617)353-9361
Boston, MA 02215   Fax: (617)353-6550
E-mail: aia@bu.edu
URL: http://www.archaeological.org
Contact: Mark J. Meister, Exec.Dir.
Desc: Professional archeologists and other interested individuals. *Type:* Association.

Archaeology
Archaeological Institute of America
135 William St.   Ph: (212)732-5154
New York, NY 10038   Fax: (212)732-5707
E-mail: archaeol@pipeline.com.
Contact: Peter A. Young, Editor; Charlene Sugihara, Advertising Dir.; Phyllis Pollak Katz, Publisher; Amy Lubelski, Production Mgr.
Desc: Archaeological magazine of worldwide discovery, excavations and ancient cult uses. *Type:* Periodical.

Mercury Project
University of Southern California
Los Angeles, CA 90089   Ph: (213)740-2311
E-mail: mascha@usc.edu
URL: http://www.usc.edu/dept/raiders
Contact: Ken Goldberg, Assistant Professor, goldberg@usc.edu.
Desc: This site represents record of The Mercury Project. It originally conceived as a WWW site which allowed users to tele-operate a robot arm moving over a terrain filled with buried artifacts. *Type:* Database.

Architecture

American Architectural Foundation
1735 New York Ave. NW   Ph: (202)626-7500
Washington, DC 20006   Fax: (202)626-7420
URL: http://www.aia.foundation.com
Contact: William Chaplin, Pres.
Desc: Receives funds for architectural exhibitions, publications, architectural history, and educational programs. *Type:* Association.

American Institute of Architects
1735 New York Ave. NW   Ph: (202)626-7300
Washington, DC 20006   Fax: (202)626-7421
Contact: Terrence M. McDerment, CEO.
Desc: Professional society of architects: regular members are professional, licensed architects; associate members are graduate architects, not yet licensed; emeritus members are retired architects. Fosters professionalism and accountability among members through continuing education and training; promotes design excellence by influencing change in the industry. Sponsors educational programs with schools of architecture, graduate students, and elementary and secondary schools; conducts professional development programs. *Type:* Association.

American Institute of Building Design
991 Post Rd. E   Ph: (203)227-3640
Westport, CT 06880   Free: 800-366-AIBD
   Fax: (203)227-8624
E-mail: aibdnat@aol.com
URL: http://www.aibd.org
Contact: Bobbi Currie, Exec.Dir.
Desc: Professional building designers engaged in the professional practice of designing residential and light commercial buildings. Other membership categories include draftspersons, educators, and students. Corporate members are residential and light commercial building manufacturers. *Type:* Association.

American Society of Landscape Architects
636 Eye St. NW   Ph: (202)898-2444
Washington, DC 20001-3736   Fax: (202)898-1185
URL: http://www.asla.org/asla/
Contact: James G. Dalton, Exec.V.Pres.
Desc: Professional society of landscape architects. Purpose is to promote the advancement of education and skill in the art of landscape architecture as an instrument in service to the public welfare. As the official accrediting agency, seeks to strengthen existing and proposed university programs in landscape architecture. *Type:* Association.

Architectural Digest
Conde Nast Publications, Inc.
140 E. 45th St., 39th Fl.   Ph: (212)880-8800
New York, NY 10017   Free: 800-223-0780
   Fax: (212)880-8248
E-mail: letters@brides.com
Contact: Thomas P. Losee, Jr., Publisher.
Desc: Magazine on interior design, art, and antiques. *Alt. Contact:* 6300 Wilshire Blvd., Los Angeles, CA 90048; telephone: (213)965-3700; fax: (213)937-1458. *Type:* Periodical.

Architectural Record
McGraw-Hill, Inc.
2 Penn Plaza   Ph: (212)904-2000
New York, NY 10121   Free: 800-223-6180
   Fax: (212)904-6068
URL: http://www.mcgraw-hill.com; http://www.mcgraw-hill.com.
Desc: Magazine focusing on architecture. *Type:* Periodical.

Association of Collegiate Schools of Architecture
1735 New York Ave. NW   Ph: (202)785-2324
Washington, DC 20006   Fax: (202)628-0448
E-mail: acsanatl@aol.com
URL: http://www.acsa-arch.org
Contact: John K. Edwards, Exec.Dir.
Desc: Full members are architectural schools; affiliate members are foreign schools or schools without professional architectural programs; participating members are individuals. *Type:* Association.

Avery Architecture Index
Columbia University
Avery Architectural and Fine Arts Library
1172 Amsterdam Ave., MC0301   Ph: (212)854-8407
New York, NY 10027
E-mail: GIRAL@COLUMBIA.EDU
Desc: Contains more than 220,000 articles from more than 700 architecture and related periodicals, emphasizing the fields of architectural design and history. Sources include more than 1000 periodical titles in all Western languages, including all major architectural magazines published in the United States, Great Britain, and the British Commonwealth, as well as most South American, European, and Japanese periodicals with English summaries. *Available:* Research Libraries Group, Inc. (RLG), Research Libraries Information Network (RLIN); Research Libraries Group, Inc. (RLG), CitaDel™ Service. *Type:* Database.

Better Homes and Gardens Building Ideas
Meredith Corp.
1716 Locust St.   Ph: (515)284-3000
Des Moines, IA 50309-3023   Free: 800-678-2674
   Fax: (515)284-3697
Contact: Linda Kast, Editor, (515)284-2892, fax: (515)284-3697, lkast@mdp.com; Jerry Ward, Publisher, (515)284-2532, fax: (515)284-3264; Pat Tomlinson, Advertising Mgr., (212)551-7043, fax: (212)551-7192.

Desc: Magazine offering ideas for designing and building single-family custom homes. *Type:* Periodical.

Builder
Hanley-Wood, Inc.
1 Thomas Circle, Ste. 600   Ph: (202)452-0800
Washington, DC 20005   Fax: (202)785-1974
URL: http://www.builderonline.com.
Contact: Mike Tucker, Executive V.P., Group Publisher, mtucker@hanley-wood.com; Warren Nesbitt, Publisher, wnesbitt@hanley-wood.com; Boyce Thompson, Editor-in-Chief, bthompso@hanley-wood.com.
Desc: Magazine covering housing and construction industry. *Type:* Periodical.

Contemporary Architects
St. James Press, Inc.
27500 Drake Rd.   Ph: (248)699-4253
Farmington Hills, MI 48331-3535   Free: 800-877-4253
   Fax: (248)699-8069
E-mail: galeord@gale.com
Contact: Muriel Emanuel, Editor.
Desc: About 585 architects; international coverage. *Type:* Directory.

Country Home
Meredith Corp.
1716 Locust St.   Ph: (515)284-3000
Des Moines, IA 50309-3023   Free: 800-678-2674
   Fax: (515)284-3697
E-mail: countryh@asm.mdp.com.
Contact: Carol Sheehan, Editor, (515)284-2015, fax: (515)284-2552; Joe Lagani, Publisher, (212)551-7117, fax: (212)551-6918.
Desc: Magazine furnishing information on American interior design, architecture, antiques and collectibles, gardening, art, and culinary endeavor. *Alt. Contact:* Meredith Corp 1716 Locust St., Des Moines, IA 50309-3023; telephone: (515)284-2015, (515)284-2705; fax: (515)284-2552. *Type:* Periodical.

Early American Homes
Primedia Enthusiast Publications
6405 Flank Dr.   Ph: (717)657-9555
Harrisburg, PA 17112-2753   Fax: (717)657-9552
E-mail: eah@cowles.com.
URL: http://www.thehistorynet.com/earlyamericanhomes.
Contact: Mimi Handler, Editor; Diane Meyers, Advertising Dir.
Desc: Magazine devoted to 18th and 19th century arts, crafts, furniture, collectibles, and history. *Type:* Periodical.

ENR Directory of Design Firms
McGraw-Hill, Inc.
2 Penn Plaza   Ph: (212)904-2000
New York, NY 10121   Free: 800-223-6180
   Fax: (212)904-6068
URL: http://www.mcgraw-hill.com
Contact: Paul Herrmannsfeldt, Editor.
Desc: Profiles of 88 architects, architectural engineers, consultants, and other design firms; limited to advertisers. Mini-listings for about 3,950 U.S. firms and 600 foreign firms or foreign offices of U.S. firms. Also includes lists of top 500 design firms in the United States, top 200 international design firms. *Type:* Directory.

ENR—Top 500 Design Firms Issue
McGraw-Hill, Inc.
2 Penn Plaza   Ph: (212)904-2000
New York, NY 10121   Free: 800-223-6180
   Fax: (212)904-6068
URL: http://www.mcgraw-hill.com

Contact: Howard B. Stussman, Editor.

Desc: List of 500 leading architectural, engineering, and specialty design firms selected on basis of annual billings. *Type:* Directory.

ENR—Top International Design Firms Issue

McGraw-Hill, Inc.
2 Penn Plaza   Ph: (212)904-2000
New York, NY 10121   Free: 800-223-6180
     Fax: (212)904-6068
URL: http://www.mcgraw-hill.com

Contact: Howard B. Stussman, Editor.

Desc: List of 200 design firms (including United States firms) competing outside their own national borders who received largest dollar volume of foreign contracts in preceding calendar year. *Type:* Directory.

Fine Homebuilding

Taunton Press
63 S. Main St., Box 5506   Free: 800-926-8776
Newtown, CT 06470-5506   Fax: (203)270-6751
E-mail: jchilds@taunton.com; fh.taunton.com.
URL: http://www.taunton.com

Contact: Kevin Ireton, Editor; Sam Vincent, Advertising; Jon Miller, Publisher, jmiller@taunton.com.

Desc: Magazine for builders, architects, designers, and owner-builders. *Type:* Periodical.

Form & Function

USG Corp.
125 S Franklin St.   Ph: (312)606-4181
Chicago, IL 60606-4678   Fax: (312)606-5566

Contact: William D. Leavitt, Editor, bleavitt@usg.com; Carolyn Hughes, Art Dir.

Desc: Professional magazine covering architectural construction. *Type:* Periodical.

Garlinghouse Home Plans Guide

L. F. Garlinghouse Co., Inc.
282 Main St.   Ph: (203)343-5977
Middletown, CT 06457   Fax: (203)632-0712

Contact: Whitney Garlinghouse, Editor and Publisher.

Desc: Magazine featuring home plans for consumers. *Type:* Periodical.

International Institute of Rural Reconstruction, U.S. Chapter

475 Riverside Dr., Rm. 1035   Ph: (212)870-2992
New York, NY 10115   Fax: (212)870-2981

Contact: Eric Blitz, Dir.

Desc: A private, international training and research institution, based in the Philippines, to foster rural reconstruction and human development through continuing action research on the basic needs of peasant people in developing countries and evolving new and better approaches to meet those needs. Provides high-level leadership training in rural reconstruction techniques, an international extension of its work to stimulate national leaders to implement private rural reconstruction programs in their respective countries. Supports autonomous affiliated programs in the Philippines, India, Thailand, Guatemala, Colombia, and Ghana. *Type:* Association.

Log Homes Illustrated

Goodman Media Group, Inc.
1700 Broadway, 34th Fl.   Ph: (212)541-7100
New York, NY 10019   Fax: (212)245-1241

Contact: Roland Sweet, Editor, (703)765-1902, fax: (703)765-1937; Stacy Durr, Managing Editor; Louisa D. Kearney, Advertising Dir.; Jim Sokolowski, Circulation Dir.

Desc: Consumer magazine covering log home design, building and living. *Type:* Periodical.

National Association of Cuban Architects (in Exile)

Carlos Vertot
71 Totlochee Dr.   Ph: (305)885-8734
Hialeah, FL 33010

Contact: Carlos Vertot, Pres.

Desc: Members of the Colegio de Arquitectos de Cuba, new architects, and students of architecture. Seeks the restoration of a democratic regime in Cuba based on the principles set forth by the Cuban Constitution of 1940. Encourages members to maintain the highest professional skills while in the U.S. *Type:* Association.

National Building Museum

401 F St. NW   Ph: (202)272-2448
Washington, DC 20001   Fax: (202)272-2564
URL: http://www.nbm.org

Contact: Susan Henshaw Jones, Pres. & Dir.

Desc: An organization comprising architectural, engineering, and building trades groups and interested individuals. Collects and disseminates information on building arts, also known as the built environment. Conducts tours of the Pension Building and other buildings in Washington, DC. *Type:* Association.

National Council of Architectural Registration Boards

1735 New York Ave. NW, Ste.   Ph: (202)783-6500
  700   Fax: (202)783-0290
Washington, DC 20006
E-mail: customerservice@ncarb.org
URL: http://www.ncarb.org

Contact: Lenore Lucy, Exec.VP.

Desc: Federation of state boards for the registration of architects in the United States, District of Columbia, Puerto Rico, Virgin Islands, Guam, and the Northern Mariana Islands. *Type:* Association.

Preservation

National Trust for Historic Preservation
1785 Massachusetts Ave. NW   Ph: (202)588-6296
Washington, DC 20036-2117   Free: 800-944-6847
     Fax: (202)588-6223

Contact: Arnold Berke, Editor; Bob Barron, Advertising Mgr.

Desc: Newspaper featuring historic preservation and architecture. *Type:* Periodical.

Tau Sigma Delta

c/o Keith Allen
University of Tennessee
School of Architecture
1715 Volunteer Blvd.
Knoxville, TN 37996-2400

Contact: Keith Allen, Pres.

Desc: Honor society - men and women, architecture, landscape architecture, and allied arts. Presents annual Gold Medal for distinction in design, leadership, and education. *Type:* Association.

Armed Forces

Armed Forces Benefit Association

909 N. Washington St.   Ph: (703)549-4455
Alexandria, VA 22314   Fax: (703)706-5961

Contact: Charles C. Blanton, Ret., Pres.

Desc: Term and permanent insurance association for commissioned and warrant officers and noncommissioned officers in grades E-1 through E-9 of the U.S. Army, Navy, Air Force, Marine Corps, Coast Guard, Public Health Service, National Oceanic and Atmospheric Administration, cadets and midshipmen at the U.S. service academies, and other candidates in U.S. military officer programs, either on active duty or in the National Guard or Ready Reserve. *Type:* Association.

Army and Air Force Mutual Aid Association

102 Sheridan Ave.   Ph: (703)522-3060
Fort Myer, VA 22211-1110   Free: 800-336-4538
     Fax: (703)522-1336
E-mail: info@aafmaa.com
URL: http://www.aafmaa.com

Contact: Bradley J. Snyder, Pres.

Desc: A mutual aid organization providing aid to families of deceased career Army and Air Force officers and non-commissioned officers by immediate payment of a fixed life insurance benefit, assistance with government claims, and lifetime survivor support. *Type:* Association.

Confederate Air Force

PO Box 62000   Ph: (915)563-1000
Midland, TX 79711   Fax: (915)563-8046
URL: http://www.avdigest.com/caf/caf.html

Contact: Robert R. Rice, Exec.Dir.

Desc: Persons interested in preserving, in flying condition, military aircraft that played important roles in World War II; and perpetuating in the minds and hearts of all Americans the spirit and memory of the accomplishments of those planes and the people who built, maintained, and flew them. The organization has acquired a fleet of 134 aircraft that includes 60 different types of planes flown during the war; members participated in over 300 events per year in the U.S. to demonstrate the planes. *Type:* Association.

National Officers Association

PO Box 4975   Ph: (703)438-3060
Reston, VA 20195   Free: 800-248-9632
     Fax: (703)438-3072
E-mail: noa@megascorp.com

Contact: Meghan Monaghan, Dir.

Desc: Commissioned and warrant officers of the uniformed services of the U.S. including active, regular, retired, and reserve officers; surviving and former spouses of uniformed services officers. Promotes the economic well-being of members and their families through benefit plans such as discount buying, Tricare health supplement, travel, automobile warranty extensions, life insurance, and prepaid legal programs. *Type:* Association.

Navy Mutual Aid Association

Henderson Hall   Ph: (703)614-1638
29 Carpenter Rd.   Free: 800-628-6011
Arlington, VA 22212   Fax: (703)695-4635
E-mail: info@navymutual.org
URL: http://www.navymutual.org

Contact: Rear Adm. Philip J. Coady, Pres.

Desc: Veterans' benefits organization providing life insurance and services to Navy, Marine Corps, Coast Guard, National Oceanic and Atmospheric Administration, and Public Health Service personnel. *Type:* Association.

101st Airborne Division Association

PO Box 101   Ph: (937)549-4326
St. Rte. 41   Fax: (513)549-2018
Bentonville, OH 45105-9999
E-mail: 101assn@bright.net
URL: http://www.screamingeagle.org

Contact: Bill Carrington, Exec.Sec.-Treas.

Desc: Individuals who served in the 101st Airborne Division, their families, and history enthusiasts. Preserves the comradeship established in the service and disseminates information. Conducts charitable activities and offers scholarships to members' dependents. *Type:* Association.

37th Division Veterans Association

65 S. Front St., Rm. 432   Ph: (614)228-3788
Columbus, OH 43215

Contact: Gene Collins, Sec.

Desc: Veterans of the 37th Infantry Division (formerly known as the Buckeye Division, representing the state of Ohio) who served in World War I, World War II, or the Korean Conflict. Aims to promote patriotism and fellowship and to assist members in veterans' affairs. Makes available memorabilia. *Type:* Association.

Women's Army Corps Veterans Association

1340 Bayonne Ave.   Ph: (732)350-8176
Whiting, NJ 08759
Contact: Martha A. LaMort, Immediate Past Pres.
Desc: Veterans of the United States Women's Army Corps and Women's Army Auxiliary Corps, women soldiers and officers of the line who are on a tour of active duty with, or have been honorably discharged from, the United States Army, and women who have served honorably or are serving in the United States Reserve or Army National Guard. Seeks "to be of service to all veterans and the communities in which we live and promote justice, tolerance, peace and goodwill." Conducts hospital and community service programs. Supports the Women's Army Corps Museum at Ft. *Type:* Association.

Art

American Art Directory

R. R. Bowker
A Unit of Cahners Business Information
121 Chanlon Rd.   Ph: (908)464-6800
New Providence, NJ 07974   Free: 888-269-5372
    Fax: (908)771-7704
E-mail: info@bowker.com
Contact: Beverly McDonough, Managing Editor.
Desc: Over 7,000 museums, art libraries, and art organizations, and 1,700 art schools; also includes lists of state directors and supervisors of art education in schools, traveling exhibition booking agencies, corporations having art holdings for public viewing, newspapers that carry art notes, art scholarships and fellowships; and 190 national, regional, and state open art exhibitions. *Type:* Directory.

American Artist

BPI Communications, Inc.
1515 Broadway, 11th Fl.   Ph: (212)536-5141
New York, NY 10036   Fax: (212)536-5357
Contact: M. Stephen Doherty, Editor; Don Frost, Publisher.
Desc: Art and educational journal. *Type:* Periodical.

American Society of Artists

PO Box 1326   Ph: (312)751-2500
Palatine, IL 60078
Contact: Nancy J. Fregin, Pres.
Desc: Professional artists and craftspeople. Maintains art referral service and information exchange service. Sponsors art and craft festivals and a Lecture and Demonstration Service. *Type:* Association.

Americans for the Arts

Americans for the Arts
1000 Vermont Ave. NW   Ph: (202)371-2830
Washington, DC 20005   Fax: (202)371-0424
E-mail: webmaster@artsusa.org
URL: http://www.artsusa.org
Desc: Dedicated to the promotion of the arts - especially through education - Americans for the Arts skillfully uses its Web site to lay out its goals for increasing appreciation of the arts in this country. Visitors will learn how to join the organization, either as individuals or as part of larger groups, and also what the organization is doing to achieve its goals. *Type:* Database.

Art in America—Annual Guide to Galleries, Museums, and Artists

Brant Publications Inc.
575 Broadway   Ph: (212)941-2800
New York, NY 10012-3230   Free: 800-925-8059
    Fax: (212)941-2885
E-mail: brantpubs@aol.com
Contact: Cathy Lebowitz, Editor; Steven Anzovin, Editor.
Desc: List of over 3,800 museums, galleries, and other display areas. *Type:* Directory.

Art & Antiques

Trans World Publishing, Inc.
2100 Powers Ferry Rd.   Ph: (770)955-5656
Atlanta, GA 30339   Free: 800-827-0818
    Fax: (770)952-0669
E-mail: artantqmag@aol.com.
Contact: Douglas C. Billian, Publisher; Barbara S. Tapp, Editor-in-Chief; Patti Verbanas, Managing Editor.
Desc: Consumer magazine for those interested in the fine and decorative arts and their settings. *Type:* Periodical.

Art Dealers Association of America—The ADAA Report

Art Dealers Association of America, Inc. (ADAA)
575 Madison Ave.   Ph: (212)940-8590
New York, NY 10022   Fax: (212)940-7013
E-mail: artdeal@rosenman.com
URL: http://www.artdealers.org.
Contact: Robert Fishko, Editor.
Desc: Reflects the aims of the Association, which works to improve the standing of the art gallery business in the U.S. Carries profiles of members and their professional activities. *Type:* Newsletter.

Art Index

H.W. Wilson Company
950 University Ave.   Ph: (718)588-8400
Bronx, NY 10452
E-mail: custserv@hwwilson.com
URL: http://www.hwwilson.com
Contact: Technical Support Department.
Desc: Contains citations to articles, reproductions and book reviews in approximately 313 periodicals, yearbooks, and museum bulletins published worldwide. Covers archaeology, architecture, art history, city planning, crafts, landscape architecture, film, fine arts, folk art, graphic arts, industrial design, interior design, and photography. *Available:* Ovid Technologies, Inc.; OCLC Online Computer Library Center, Inc., OCLC EPIC; OCLC Online Computer Library Center, Inc., OCLC FirstSearch Catalog; SilverPlatter Information, Inc.; The Dialog Corporation, DIALOG; Bell & Howell Information and Learning; H.W. Wilson Company, WilsonWeb. *Type:* Database.

The Art Institute of Chicago WWW Site

Art Institute of Chicago
37 S. Wabash Ave.   Ph: (312)899-5100
Chicago, IL 60603
E-mail: webmaster@artic.edu
URL: http://www.artic.edu
Desc: Prospective and current students of the School of the Art Institute of Chicago (SAIC for short) will be happy to learn about this site. It contains information on the world famous Chicago art museum as well as its affiliated art school. *Type:* Database.

Art Literature International

BHA - Clark Art Institute
225 South St   Ph: (413)458-8260
Williamstown, MA 01267
Contact: Marshall Lapidus, Associate Editor, (413)458-8260, fax: (413)458-8503.

Desc: Contains more than 133,000 citations, with abstracts, to publications on the history of art in Europe since the 4th Century A.D. and in post-Columbian America. *Available:* The Dialog Corporation, DIALOG; Research Libraries Group, Inc. (RLG), Research Libraries Information Network (RLIN). *Type:* Database.

Art & Man

Scholastic, Inc.
555 Broadway   Ph: (212)343-6100
New York, NY 10012   Free: 800-724-6527
    Fax: (212)343-4535
E-mail: custserv@scholastic.com
URL: http://www.scholastic.com
Contact: Margaret Howlett, Editor; Richard Robinson, Publisher.
Desc: Magazine presenting art history for high school students. *Type:* Periodical.

ART PAPERS

Atlanta Art Papers, Inc.
PO Box 5748   Ph: (404)588-1837
Atlanta, GA 31107   Fax: (404)588-1836
Contact: Larisa Gray, Exec. Dir.; Michele Slater, Asst. Dir., mslater@pd.org; Michael Piltari, Editor.
Desc: Journal featuring articles on contemporary art and artists, reviews, newsbriefs, letters, and a classified listing section. *Type:* Periodical.

ARTbibliographies Modern

ABC-CLIO
130 Cremona Dr.   Ph: (805)968-1911
PO Box 1911
Santa Barbara, CA 93116-1911
E-mail: library@abc-clio.com
URL: http://www.abc-clio.com
Contact: Judith L. Burstein, Online Services Coordinator.
Desc: Contains citations, with abstracts, to books, dissertations, exhibition catalogs, and articles from approximately 350 journals in the areas of modern art and design. Covers 20th century art history, artistic media (e.g., sculpture, architecture, painting, photography, and ceramics), and artists. *Available:* CompuServe Information Service, Knowledge Index; ABC-CLIO. *Type:* Database.

The Artist's Magazine

F & W Publications, Inc.
1507 Dana Ave.   Ph: (513)531-2222
Cincinnati, OH 45207   Fax: (513)531-2902
E-mail: tamedit@fwpubs.com.
Contact: Sandra Carpenter, Editor, (513)531-2690; Jeffry Lapin, Publisher; David Lee, Circulation Director.
Desc: Magazine by artists for artists. Covers artwork, working methods, tools, and materials. *Type:* Periodical.

Artists and Writers Syndicate

PO Box 60688   Ph: (202)882-8882
Washington, DC 20039-0688   Fax: (202)829-9283
Contact: Philip Steitz, Pres. Exec. Ed.; Marjorie Steitz, Managing Editor.
Desc: Distributes "These Two Wheels" features to daily newspapers in the US and Canada. *Alt. Contact:* PO Box 60688, Washington, DC 20039-0688; telephone: (202)882-8882; fax: (202)829-9283. *Type:* Periodical.

The ARTnewsletter

ARTnews
48 W. 38th St.   Ph: (212)398-1690
New York, NY 10018   Fax: (212)819-0394
E-mail: goartnews@aol.com
Contact: Kelly Devine Thomas, Editor.
Desc: Presents reviews of forthcoming auctions, analyses of prices, attribution controversies, ownership squabbles,

and case histories of thievery, forgery, and fraud. Discusses the impact of museum exhibitions on the art market, the latest IRS rulings, import and export regulations, legislative hearings, debates and acts, print tax shelters, art insurance, and appraisals. *Type:* Newsletter.

California Arts Council

1300 I St., Ste. 930   Ph: (916)322-6555
Sacramento, CA 95814   Free: 800-201-6201
   Fax: (916)322-6575
E-mail: cac@cwo.com
URL: http://www.cac.ca.gov
Contact: Barbara Pieper, Dir.
Desc: Promotes artistic awareness and participation in California. Works to support, promote, and encourage the arts in this cultural diverse and geographically disparate state. *Type:* Association.

Collector Editions

Collector Communications Corp.
170 5th Ave.   Ph: (212)989-8700
New York, NY 10010   Fax: (212)645-8976
Contact: Joan Muyskens Pursley, Editor; Diane Kane, Publisher, dgkane@juno.com.
Desc: Magazine devoted to collectibles. *Type:* Periodical.

Collectors Mart

Krause Publications, Inc.
700 E. State St.   Ph: (715)445-2214
Iola, WI 54990   Free: 800-258-0929
   Fax: (715)445-4087
E-mail: info@krause.com; krause@krause.com
URL: http://www.krause.com
Contact: Greg Smith, Publisher/Advertising Mgr.; Mary Sieber, Editor; Greg Smith, Advertising Manager.
Desc: Magazine on limited edition art and collectibles. *Type:* Periodical.

College Art Association

275 7th Ave.   Ph: (212)691-1051
New York, NY 10001   Fax: (212)627-2381
E-mail: nyoffice@collegeart.org
URL: http://www.collegeart.org
Contact: Susan Ball, Exec.Dir.
Desc: Professional organization of artists, art historians and fine art educators, museum directors, and curators. Seeks to raise the standards of scholarship and of the teaching of art and art history throughout the country. *Type:* Association.

Dealer Trends

National Art Materials Trade Association (NAMTA)
178 Lakeview Ave.
Clifton, NJ 07011
Contact: John R. Luciano, Editor.
Desc: Reports on art materials dealer surveys. *Type:* Newsletter.

Decorative Artist's Workbook

F & W Publications, Inc.
1507 Dana Ave.   Ph: (513)531-2222
Cincinnati, OH 45207   Fax: (513)531-2902
Contact: Anne Hevener, Editor, dawedit@aol.com; Jeffry Lapin, Publisher; Stephanie Curtis, Advertising Dir., (513)745-0964; David Lee, Circulation Mgr.; Amy Leibrock, Managing Editor.
Desc: Magazine of step-by-step projects for decorative painters. *Type:* Periodical.

Foundation for the Community of Artists

Desc: Service organization for artists and art workers from all disciplines. Provides advocacy for artists' rights. Offers group health and hospitalization program and credit union. *Type:* Association.

GEN ART

145 W 28th St., Ste. 1101   Ph: (212)290-0312
New York, NY 10001   Fax: (212)290-0254
E-mail: info@genart.org
URL: http://www.genart.org
Contact: Adam Walden, Managing Dir.
Desc: Supports and showcases young emerging talent in film, fashion, and the visual arts. *Type:* Association.

Glass Art—Directory to Industry Supplies Issue

Travin, Inc.
Glass Art Magazine   Ph: (303)791-8998
PO Box 260377   Fax: (303)791-7739
Highlands Ranch, CO 80163
E-mail: glassartm@aol.com
Contact: Shawn Waggoner, Editor.
Desc: List of approximately 300 suppliers of stained glass equipment and supplies. *Type:* Directory.

The High Museum of Art

Pegasus Internet
333 Seventh Ave.   Ph: (212)695-5800
New York, NY 10001   Fax: (212)695-9744
E-mail: info@pegasusnet.com
URL: http://www.high.org/
Desc: Offering a variety of links to the arts in Atlanta, the High Museum of Art features information about the museum, exhibitions and films, education, membership, and a link to the museum shop. The site also contains links to the Atlanta College of Art, Woodruff Arts Center; Alliance Theater; and Atlanta Symphony Orchestra. *Type:* Database.

International Artists Network

PO Box 182   Ph: (207)666-8453
Bowdoinham, ME 04008-0182
Contact: Carlo Pittore, Liaison.
Desc: Poets, performance artists, graphic artists, painters, photographers, musicians, and artists whose work has been reproduced in book or magazine form. Promotes communication among artists. *Type:* Association.

John F. Kennedy Center for the Performing Arts National Advisory Committee - Region 5

The Fine Arts Museums of San   Ph: (415)750-7640
   Francisco   Fax: (415)750-7692
M.H. de Young Memorial
San Francisco, CA 94118
E-mail: vprabhu@famsf.org
URL: http://www.thinker.org
Contact: Prabhu Vas, Dir. of Education.
Type: Association.

The Metropolitan Museum of Art Bulletin

Metropolitan Museum of Art
1000 5th Ave.   Ph: (212)879-5500
New York, NY 10028-0198   Fax: (212)472-8725
URL: http://www.netmuseum.org
Contact: Joan Holt, Editor-in-Chief; Tonia L. Payne, Associate Editor.
Desc: Scholarly publication providing information on the Metropolitan Museum of Art's collections. *Type:* Periodical.

Michigan Council for Arts and Cultural Affairs

1200 6th St., Ste. 1180   Ph: (313)256-3735
Detroit, MI 48226   Fax: (313)256-3781
Contact: Betty Boone, Exec.Dir.
Desc: Aims to stimulate, encourage, and expand the arts. Provides financial assistance to individuals and arts organizations. *Type:* Association.

Muse

University of Missouri at Columbia
Museum of Art and Archaeology
1 Pickard Hall   Ph: (573)882-3591
Columbia, MO 65211   Fax: (573)884-4039
Contact: Scherrie Goettsch, Editor, goettsch@museum.missouri.edu; Beth Ann Cobb, Subscription and Exchange Librarian.
Desc: Scholarly journal covering University of Missouri, Museum of Art and Archaeology news. *Type:* Periodical.

National Academy of Design

1083 5th Ave.   Ph: (212)369-4880
New York, NY 10128   Fax: (212)360-6795
URL: http://www.nationalacademyofdesign.org
Contact: Annette Blaugrund, Ph.D., Dir.
Desc: Fine arts museum and society of painters, sculptors, graphic artists, architects, and watercolorists interested in cultivation of the fine arts, education of art students, and presentation of annual exhibitions of work by living artists. Sponsors school of fine arts offering studio classes in painting, drawing, sculpture, printmaking, and architectural drafting. Organizes exhibitions from permanent collections, loan exhibitions, and exhibitions of contemporary art. *Type:* Association.

Ohio Arts Council

727 E. Main St.   Ph: (614)466-2613
Columbus, OH 43205   Fax: (614)466-4494
E-mail: webmaster@mail.oac.ohio.gov
URL: http://www.oac.ohio.gov
Contact: Wayne P. Lawson, Exec.Dir.
Desc: Established as a state agency in 1965, the Ohio Arts Council encourages, supports and promotes the arts in Ohio. With funds from the Ohio legislative and national endowment for the arts, the council provides support to artists and arts organizations. *Type:* Association.

Organizing Artists—A Document and Directory of the National Association of Artists' Organizations

National Association of Artists' Organizations
918 F St. NW, Ste. 611   Ph: (202)347-6350
Washington, DC 20004   Fax: (202)347-7376
E-mail: naaoz@tmn.com; naao@artswire.org
Contact: Roberto Bedoya, Editor.
Desc: Organizations, programs and agencies concerned with the arts, including 300 artist-run organizations, 75 service and advocacy groups, organizations dedicated to health and fundraising, artist colonies, media art centers, government agencies, and foundations. *Type:* Directory.

Pastel Society of America

15 Gramercy Park S   Ph: (212)533-6931
New York, NY 10003   Fax: (212)353-8140
Contact: Christina Debarry, Pres.
Desc: Goal is to unite pastel artists in the U.S. and abroad and to encourage young artists by offering scholarships. Focuses attention on the renaissance of pastel and educates the public on its permanence and strength as an art form. *Type:* Association.

Professional Picture Framers Association

4305 Sarellen Rd.   Ph: (804)226-0430
Richmond, VA 23231   Free: 800-556-6228
   Fax: (804)222-2175
E-mail: ppfa@ppfa.com
URL: http://www.ppfa.com
Contact: Rex P. Boynton, Exec.Dir./CEO.
Desc: Individuals, firms, or corporations engaged in the picture framing and fine art businesses (art dealers, manufacturers, wholesalers, importers, and publishers). To provide guidance and service in developing quality craftsmanship in the art of picture framing. *Type:* Association.

St. James Guide to Black Artists

St. James Press, Inc.
27500 Drake Rd.   Ph: (248)699-4253
Farmington Hills, MI 48331- Free: 800-877-4253
3535   Fax: (248)699-8069
E-mail: galeord@gale.com
Contact: Thomas Riggs, Editor.
Desc: 400 black artists worldwide, including sculptors, painters, printmakers, photographers, illustrators, ceramists, performance artists, filmmakers, quilt makers, wood-carvers, and fiber artists. *Type:* Directory.

Society of Illustrators—Annual of American Illustration

Society of Illustrators
128 E. 63rd St.   Ph: (212)838-2560
New York, NY 10021   Fax: (212)838-2561
E-mail: society@societyillustrators.org
Contact: Jill Bossert, Editor.
Desc: 800 illustrators and art directors. *Type:* Directory.

Society for the Promotion of Japanese Animation

7336 Santa Monica Blvd., Ste.
640
Los Angeles, CA 90046
E-mail: info@anime-expo.org
Contact: Mike Tatsugawa, Pres./CEO.
Desc: Seeks to promote the art of Japanese animation. *Type:* Association.

The Telephone Pioneer

Telephone Pioneers of America
P.O. Box 13888   Ph: (303)571-9274
Denver, CO 80201-3888   Free: 800-872-5995
                            Fax: (303)572-0520
E-mail: rjt@alex.attmail.com.
URL: http://www.telephone-pioneers.arg.
Contact: Bill Maroney, Editor; Bob Earl, Advertising Mgr.
Desc: Membership newspaper. *Type:* Periodical.

Trade Journal Recap

Al Gottlieb
12 Hedden Place   Ph: (908)464-1158
New Providence, NJ 07974
Contact: Al Gottlieb, Editor.
Desc: Lists and describes cartoons printed in trade journals and house organs for the previous months. "Enables cartoonists and gagwriters to slant their material to what magazines are buying, to check on the originality of gags, and to get humorous bases for new cartoons." Provides magazine titles, frequency, and address, issue date, cartoon editor and cartoonist's names, and price paid for cartoons. *Type:* Newsletter.

Traveling Exhibition Information Service Newsletter

The Humanities Exchange
Box 1608   Ph: (813)581-7328
Largo, FL 33779   Fax: (813)585-6398
E-mail: the-iaa@ix.netcom.com
Contact: S. R. Howarth, Editor.
Desc: About 60-70 traveling exhibitions in the arts, sciences, and history prepared by museums, libraries, historical societies, and other nonprofit organizations in the United States, Canada, and Europe. *Type:* Directory.

Umbrella

Umbrella Associates
PO Box 3640   Ph: (310)399-1146
Santa Monica, CA 90408   Fax: (310)399-5070
E-mail: umbrella@ix.netcom.com

URL: http://colophon.com/journal.
Contact: Judith A. Hoffberg, Editor.
Desc: Focuses on "news of artists who publish books and magazines, postcards, and ephemera." Contains news concerning artists' publications, profiles of distribution points, publishers, and alternative media (copy art, computer graphics, video, and performance/mail art). Includes notices of publications available such as books and catalogs, as well as book reviews. *Type:* Newsletter.

Whole Arts Directory

Midmarch Arts
300 Riverside Dr., No. 8A   Ph: (212)666-6990
New York, NY 10025
Contact: Cynthia Navaretta, Editor.
Desc: Organizations, performance groups, archives, registries, festivals, funding resources, etc., with a special interest in the work of women and minorities in visual arts, performance, media, crafts, film, and video. *Type:* Directory.

Who's Who in American Art

Marquis Who's Who
Reed Elsevier
121 Chanlon Rd.   Ph: (908)464-6800
New Providence, NJ 07974   Free: 800-521-8110
                          Fax: (908)771-8645
E-mail: info@marquiswhoswho.com
Contact: Elizabeth Onaran, Managing Editor.
Desc: About 11,800 people active in visual arts, including sculptors, painters, illustrators, printmakers, collectors, curators, writers, educators, dealers, critics, patrons, and museum executives. Also includes cumulative necrology from 1953. *Type:* Directory.

Who's Who in Picture Framing & Fine Art

Professional Picture Framers Association
4305 Sarellen Rd.   Ph: (804)226-0430
Richmond, VA 23231-4311   Fax: (804)222-2175
E-mail: ppfa@ppfa.com
Desc: Over 7,500 galleries, picture framing firms, and suppliers; international coverage. *Type:* Directory.

Arts and Sciences

Affiliate Artists

37 W 65th St.   Ph: (212)580-2000
New York, NY 10023
Contact: Richard C. Clark, Pres.
Desc: Professional singers, dancers, actors, instrumentalists, mimes, and conductors; corporate sponsors. To promote the career development of professional performing artists; to encourage greater business and community involvement in the arts. Produces programs of varying duration where artists perform in concert halls and informal settings such as schools, churches, and factories. *Type:* Association.

American Federation of Arts

41 E. 65th St.   Ph: (212)988-7700
New York, NY 10021   Free: 800-232-0270
                          Fax: (212)861-2487
E-mail: pubinfo@afaweb.org
Desc: Nonprofit art museum service organization. Provides traveling art exhibitions and educational, professional, and technical programs. Seeks to strengthen the ability of museums to "enrich the public's understanding and experience of art". *Type:* Association.

Americans for the Arts

1000 Vermont Ave., NW, 12th   Ph: (202)371-2830
Fl.   Fax: (202)371-0424
Washington, DC 20005
URL: http://www.artsusa.org
Contact: Robert Lynch, Pres. & CEO.
Desc: Groups and individuals dedicated to advancing the arts and culture in communities across the country. Works with cultural organizations, arts and business leaders and patrons to provide leadership, advocacy, visibility, professional development and research and information that will advance support for the arts and culture in our nation's communities. *Type:* Association.

Arts and Business Council

121 W 27th St., Ste. 702   Ph: (212)727-7146
New York, NY 10001   Fax: (212)727-3873
E-mail: arts&business@internetmci.com
URL: http://www.artsandbusiness.org
Contact: Gary P. Steuer, Pres.
Desc: Businesses and nonprofit arts organizations. Promotes the mutuality of arts and business partnerships, strenthening the two sectors through programs that serve the fullest diversity of individuals, organizations, and communites. Programs bring expertise, resources, and leadership talent from business to the arts and promote the arts to business. *Type:* Association.

Arts Management

Radius Group, Inc.
110 Riverside Dr., No. 4E   Ph: (212)579-2039
New York, NY 10024
Contact: Alvin H. Reiss, Editor.
Desc: Covers arts, management, funding, promotion, legislation, grants, personnel, and government and business activity in the arts. Contains news of developments and trends in the arts and items on how specific institutions have solved management, funding, or promotional problems. *Type:* Newsletter.

Dance Theater Workshop

219 W. 19th St.   Ph: (212)691-6500
New York, NY 10011   Fax: (212)633-1974
E-mail: dtw@dtw.org
URL: http://www.dtw.org
Contact: David R. White, Exec.Dir.
Desc: Choreographers, artistic directors, and performing arts companies in related fields. Seeks to create and facilitate performance opportunities for choreographers, composers, and theatre artists and to stimulate the development of new and wider public audiences for the individual artist. Activities include production and sponsorship of 75 artists and companies at the Bessie Schonberg Theater in New York City; preproduction counseling on publicity, promotion, and overall budgetary concerns as well as technical production problems; assistance with specific dance and performance-related administrative questions. *Type:* Association.

Instituto de Arte y Cultura

3501 S. Chicago Ave.   Ph: (612)824-0708
Minneapolis, MN 55407   Fax: (612)825-8971
Contact: Irene Gomez-Bethke, Exec. Dir.
Desc: Sponsors multicultural programs in the state area. Operates clearinghouse for artists; makes available services. *Type:* Association.

Inter-American Council for Education, Science and Culture

Organization of American States
1889 F St. NW, 2nd FL.   Ph: (202)458-3783
Washington, DC 20006   Fax: (202)458-3526
Contact: L. Zuniga, Exec.Sec.

Desc: Representatives of member countries of the Organization of American States ; affiliated members are representative from 22 countries with permanent observer status. Fosters the development of education, science, technology, and culture through its Regional Program of Educational Development, Regional Program of Scientific and Technological Development, Regional Program of Cultural Development, and Fellowship and Training Program. *Type:* Association.

Interlochen Center for the Arts
PO Box 199   Ph: (616)276-7200
Interlochen, MI 49643-0199   Fax: (616)276-6321
URL: http://www.interlochen.k12.mi.us
Contact: Richard F. Odell, Pres.
Desc: Educational center offering two separate programs: the Interlochen Arts Camp and the Interlochen Arts Academy. The Interlochen Arts Camp (staff: 1000; students: 2700) conducts annual summer educational and camping program for 1800 students who enroll in four and eight-week sessions and 900 students from Michigan who attend special two-week, All-State sessions. Conducts programs in music, visual art, dance, theatre and creative writing. *Type:* Association.

Lincoln Center for the Performing Arts
70 Lincoln Center Plz.   Ph: (212)875-5000
New York, NY 10023   Fax: (212)875-5414
Contact: Nathan Leventhal, Pres.
Desc: Acts as the umbrella organization for the Lincoln Center complex and Lincoln Center Productions. Presents and produces over 300 performances each year through such series as *Mostly Mozart, Serious Fun, Jazz at Lincoln Center, Lincoln Center Out of Doors, Midsummer Night Swing,* and *Great Performers.* Operates the Lincoln Center Institute to provide educational programs for schoolchildren, and presents telecasts through "Live from Lincoln Center." *Type:* Association.

National Art Education Association
1916 Association Dr.   Ph: (703)860-8000
Reston, VA 20191   Fax: (703)860-2960
E-mail: naea@dgs.dgsys.com
URL: http://www.naea-reston.org
Contact: Thomas A. Hatfield, Exec.Dir.
Desc: Teachers of art at elementary, middle, secondary, and college levels; colleges, libraries, museums, and other educational institutions. Studies problems of teaching art; encourages research and experimentation. *Type:* Association.

National Arts Stabilization Fund
Nancy Sasser
36 S. Charles St., No. 1515   Ph: (212)490-1400
Baltimore, MD 21201-3020   Fax: (212)557-5016
Contact: Donald J. Kirk, Chm.
Desc: Works to strengthen and stabilize organizations to enable the arts to flourish. *Type:* Association.

National Foundation for Advancement in the Arts
800 Brickell Ave., Ste. 500   Ph: (305)377-1140
Miami, FL 33131   Free: 800-970-ARTS
   Fax: (305)377-1149
E-mail: nfaa@nfaa.org
URL: http://www.nfaa.org
Contact: Bill Banchs, Pres.
Desc: Purpose is to recognize and support aspiring artists during their formative years in art forms including dance, music, music jazz, music voice, theatre, visual arts, photography and writing. Conducts Arts Recognition and Talent Search (ARTS) which identifies promising teenage artists and provides them with financial awards. Operates fellowships in the visual arts program, which provides visual artists with time and space in which to work, and facilitates contact between participants and established professionals in the field. *Type:* Association.

National League of American Pen Women
1300 17th St. NW   Ph: (202)785-1997
Washington, DC 20036   Fax: (202)452-6868
E-mail: ncaw2.@juno.com
Contact: Judith LaFourest, Pres.
Desc: Writers, composers, artists, and professional women in the creative arts. Promotes the professional development of members. *Type:* Association.

Phi Beta Kappa
1785 Massachusetts Ave., NW   Ph: (202)265-3808
Washington, DC 20036   Fax: (202)986-1601
URL: http://www.pbk.org
Contact: Douglas W. Foard, Sec.
Desc: Scholarly honor society for men and women in the liberal arts and sciences. Recognizes scholarly achievement and academic excellence through national programs such as the Phi Beta Kappa book awards, Romanell Professorship in Philosophy, Visiting Scholar and Lectureship programs, and through programs of university chapters and alumni associations, including secondary school teachers workshops, scholarships and awards. *Type:* Association.

Phi Sigma Pi
2119 Ambassador Cir.   Ph: (717)299-4710
Lancaster, PA 17603-2391   Fax: (717)390-3054
E-mail: pspoffice@aol.com
URL: http://www.phisigmapi.org
Contact: Christine M. Blanck, Exec.Dir.
Desc: National honor fraternity. Dedicated to the advancement of scholarship, leadership, and fellowship. *Type:* Association.

Young Audiences
115 E. 92nd St.   Ph: (212)831-8110
New York, NY 10128   Fax: (212)289-1202
URL: http://www.youngaudiences.com
Contact: Richard Bell, Exec.Dir.
Desc: Seeks to have professional ensembles present live educational programs in music, dance, and theatre to children (grades K-12) during school hours. Works to increase the creative and imaginative capacities of children through listening and participating in live performing arts experiences; to help build future audiences for the performing arts; to develop the performing arts resources of communities by training ensembles in educational techniques. Trains musicians, dancers, and actors to present performances, demonstrations, workshops, and residencies in each of the art forms. *Type:* Association.

Astrology
American Astrology
Starlog Group, Inc.
475 Park Ave. S.   Ph: (212)689-2830
New York, NY 10016   Fax: (212)889-7933
Contact: Kenneth Irving, Editor; Lee Chapman, Advertising Mgr.; Norman Jacobs, Publisher; Rita Eisenstein, Editor.
Desc: Astrological magazine. *Type:* Periodical.

The Astro Investor
Mull Publishing
PO Box 11133   Ph: (317)357-6855
Indianapolis, IN 46201-0133   Fax: (317)353-6246
Contact: Carol S. Mull, Editor.
Desc: Forecasts the Dow Jones Industrial Average and comments on stock. *Type:* Newsletter.

Astro*Talk
Matrix Software Inc.
315 Marion Ave.   Ph: (616)796-2483
Big Rapids, MI 49307   Free: 800-PLA-NETS
   Fax: (616)796-3060
E-mail: voices@thenewage.com
URL: http://thenewage.com; http://www.astrologysoftware.com.
Contact: Michael Erlewine, Editor, frank@thenewage.com.
Desc: Follows news and new computer software for astrologers. Recurring features include interviews, news of research, a calendar of events, reports of meetings, news of educational opportunities, and job listings. *Type:* Newsletter.

Dell Horoscope Magazine
Dell Magazines
475 Park Ave. S, 11th Fl.   Ph: (212)686-7188
New York, NY 10016   Fax: (212)686-7414
Contact: Ronnie Grishman, Editor-in-Chief, (212)984-7137; Peter Kanter, Publisher, (212)984-7191.
Desc: Consumer astrology magazine. *Type:* Periodical.

Embassy of Estonia
Embassy of Estonia
2131 Massachusetts Ave. NW   Ph: (202)588-0101
Washington, DC 20008   Fax: (202)588-0108
E-mail: info@estemb.org
URL: http://www.estemb.org/
Desc: This homepage of the Estonian Embassy in Washington, DC, features information about the embassy itself as well as information about the history and culture of the country, travel, and tourism in Estonia, and a list of active Estonian groups in the U.S. *Type:* Database.

NASA/IPAC Extragalactic Database
Caltech
NED   Ph: (626)397-9594
IPAC, M/S 100-22
Pasadena, CA 91125
E-mail: ned@ipac.caltech.edu
URL: http://nedwww.ipac.caltech.edu/
Desc: The NASA/IPAC Extragalactic Database (NED) is an electronic research tool for professional astronomers that provides access to published extragalactic data. It consists of a computer database and a user interface that allows retrieval of information such as positions, names, and basic data for extragalactic objects, as well as bibliographic references and notes from catalogs and other publications. *Type:* Database.

SETI League
433 Liberty St.   Ph: (201)641-1770
PO Box 555   Free: 800-TAU-SETI
Little Ferry, NJ 07643   Fax: (201)641-1771
E-mail: info@setileague.org
URL: http://www.setileague.org/
Contact: Dr. H. Paul Shuch, Exec.Dir.
Desc: Astronomers and other individuals with an interest in the search for extra-terrestrial intelligence (SETI). Seeks to continue the program of the original National Aeronautics and Space Administration SETI program, which was cancelled in 1993. *Type:* Association.

Astronomy
American Astronomical Society
2000 Florida Ave. NW, Ste. 400   Ph: (202)328-2010
Washington, DC 20009   Fax: (202)234-2560
E-mail: aas@aas.org
URL: http://www.aas.org

Contact: Dr. Robert W. Milkey, Exec. Officer.

Desc: Astronomers, physicists, and scientists in related fields. Conducts Visiting Professor in Astronomy Program. Maintains placement service. *Type:* Association.

Astronomical League

Janet A. Stevens
2112 Kingfisher Ln. E   Ph: (847)398-0562
Rolling Meadows, IL 60008
URL: http://astroleague.org/
Contact: Janet Stevens, Exec.Sec.

Desc: Members of 220 astronomical societies and other interested individuals. Promotes the science of astronomy; encourages and coordinates activities of amateur astronomical societies; fosters observational and computational work and craftsmanship in various fields of astronomy; correlates amateur activities with professional research. Sponsors educational programs. *Type:* Association.

Astronomical Society of the Pacific

390 Ashton Ave.   Ph: (415)337-1100
San Francisco, CA 94112   Free: 800-335-2624
          Fax: (415)337-5205
E-mail: membership@stars.sfsu.edu
URL: http://www.aspsky.org
Contact: Robert Havlen, Exec.Dir.

Desc: Professional and amateur astronomers, educators, and laypeople. Goal is to increase public understanding and appreciation of astronomy and to disseminate astronomical information. *Type:* Association.

Astronomy

Kalmbach Publishing Co.
21027 Crossroads Circle   Ph: (414)796-8776
PO Box 1612   Free: 800-446-5489
Waukesha, WI 53187-1612   Fax: (414)796-1615
E-mail: mrmag@mrmag.com
URL: http://kalmbach.com; http://www.kalmbach.com.
Contact: Robert Burnham, Editor; Robert Maas, Publisher; Dan Lance, Advertising Dir.

Desc: Magazine for amateur astronomers. *Type:* Periodical.

Astronomy Magazine

Kalmbach Publishing Co.
21027 Crossroads Circle   Ph: (414)796-8776
PO Box 1612   Free: 800-446-5489
Waukesha, WI 53187-1612   Fax: (414)796-1615
E-mail: mrmag@mrmag.com
URL: http://kalmbach.com; http://www.kalmbach.com.
Contact: Bonnie Gordon, Editor, bgordon@astronomy.com; Dan Koehler, Advertising Mgr.; Debbi Simon, Advertising Representative.

Desc: Magazine for the general public interested in astronomy. *Type:* Periodical.

Hubble Space Telescope Science Archive

Canadian Astronomy Data Centre
5071 W. Saanich Rd.   Ph: (250)363-0052
Victoria, BC, Canada V8X 4M6
E-mail: cadc@dao.nrc.ca
URL: http://cadcwww.dao.nrc.ca/hst.html
Desc: The Hubble Space Telescope Science Archive contains subsets of data from the satellite, especially useful for research astronomers. Images from the telescope are included, and users may search various online catalogs to aid in their research. *Type:* Database.

Sky & Telescope

Sky Publishing Corp.
49 Bay State Rd.   Ph: (617)864-7360
Cambridge, MA 02138   Free: 800-253-0245
          Fax: (617)864-6117
E-mail: skytel@skypub.com.

URL: http://www.skypub.com; http://www.skypub.com.
Contact: Leif J. Robinson, Editor, lrobinson@skypub.com; Kimberly Bennett, Advertising Sales Dir, kbennett@skypub.com; Susan Lit, Assoc. Pub, sblit@skypub.com.

Desc: Magazine on astronomy and space science. *Type:* Periodical.

Welcome to the Planets

Planetary Data System
4800 Oak Grove Dr.   Ph: (626)795-4928
Pasadena, CA 91109   Fax: (626)795-7697
E-mail: pds_operator@jp l.nasa.gov
URL: http://pds.jpl.nasa.gov/planets/
Contact: Jason LaPointe, Web Curator, jason.lapointe@.jpl.nasa.gov.

Desc: The Welcome to the Planets database provides a collection of the best images from NASA's planetary exploration program. The database includes a profile for each Solar System planet and some small bodies, providing information about the size, mass, orbit, surface temperature, highest point, atmosphere components, and surface materials. *Type:* Database.

Atheist

American Atheist Women

PO Box 5733   Ph: (512)458-1244
Parsippany, NJ 07054-6733   Fax: (512)467-9525
E-mail: info@atheists.org
URL: http://www.atheists.org
Contact: Ellen Johnson, Pres.

Desc: Female atheists. united for the enrichment and beautification of life and to emphasize the need for quality living. *Type:* Association.

American Atheists

PO Box 5733   Ph: (908)276-7300
Parsippany, NJ 07054   Fax: (908)276-7402
E-mail: info@theists.org
URL: http://www.atheists.org
Contact: Ellen Johnson, Pres.

Desc: Families supporting the aims of the society, which are: atheism, separation of state and church, and taxation of the church on real estate, income, business, and other profits. Sponsors American Atheist Forum TV series nationwide. Compiles statistics; maintains speakers' bureau. *Type:* Association.

Attorneys

Chicago Bar Association

321 S. Plymouth Ct.   Ph: (312)554-2000
Chicago, IL 60604   Fax: (312)554-2005
Contact: Terrence M. Murphy, Exec.Dir.

Desc: Attorneys and judges working to improve the administration of justice, promote the public good, increase the usefulness of the legal profession, establish and maintain its honor and dignity, and promote the general welfare of its members. Disseminates information; monitors legislation. *Type:* Association.

Florida Bar

Florida Bar Center   Ph: (850)561-5600
650 Apalachee Pkwy.   Free: 800-342-8060
Tallahassee, FL 32399-2300   Fax: (850)561-5826
E-mail: flabarwm@flabar.org
URL: http://www.flabar.org
Contact: John F. Harkness, Jr., Exec.Dir.

Desc: Attorneys in good standing. Seeks to improve the administration of civil and criminal justice, and the availability of legal services to the public. *Type:* Association.

Oregon State Bar

5200 S.W. Meadows Rd.   Ph: (503)620-0222
PO Box 1689   Free: 800-452-8260
Lake Oswego, OR 97035-0889   Fax: (503)684-1366
E-mail: kgarst@osbar.org
URL: http://www.usbar.org
Contact: Karen Garst, Exec.Dir.

Desc: Promotes the administration of justice for all. Promotes high standards of honor, integrity and professional conduct. *Type:* Association.

State Bar of Arizona

111 W. Monroe, Ste. 1800   Ph: (602)252-4804
Phoenix, AZ 85003-1742   Fax: (602)271-4930
E-mail: azbar@staff.azbar.org
URL: http://www.azbar.org
Contact: Stuart Forsyth, Exec.Dir.

Desc: Attorneys in good standing. Seeks to improve the administration of civil and criminal justice, and the availability of legal services to the public. *Type:* Association.

Authors

Author Biographies Master Index

Gale Group Inc.
27500 Drake Rd.   Ph: (248)699-4253
Farmington Hills, MI 48331-   Free: 800-877-GALE
3535   Fax: (248)699-8070
E-mail: galeord@galegroup.com
URL: http://www.galegroup.com.
Contact: Geri Speace, Editor.

Desc: ABMI is a consolidated index of more than 1,140,000 references to biographical sketches on some 400,000 authors of all eras and nations whose listings appear in more than 1,700 editions and volumes of almost 400 English-language biographical dictionaries. Both historical and contemporary works are indexed, including Allibone's "Critical Dictionary of English Literature," Kunitz's "British Authors before 1800," "Twentieth Century Authors," etc., the various Oxford Companions to literatures; and Gale's "Contemporary Authors" and "Something About the Author." Many works devoted to specialized areas of writing—poetry, women writers, etc.—are also indexed. *Type:* Directory.

Authors and Artists for Young Adults

Gale Group Inc.
27500 Drake Rd.   Ph: (248)699-4253
Farmington Hills, MI 48331-   Free: 800-877-GALE
3535   Fax: (248)699-8070
E-mail: galeord@galegroup.com
URL: http://www.galegroup.com.
Contact: Thomas McMahon, Editor.

Desc: Authors and artists who create books, movies, television programs, plays, cartoons, and animated features that are of interest to young adults. Similar in format to "Contemporary Authors" (described separately), each volume covers approximately 20-25 authors and artists. Twenty-nine volumes are now in print. *Type:* Directory.

Authors League of America

330 W. 42nd St., 29th Fl.   Ph: (212)564-8350
New York, NY 10036   Fax: (212)564-8363
E-mail: staff@authorguild.org
URL: http://www.authorguild.org
Contact: Paul Aiken, Exec.Dir.

Desc: Professional organization of authors of books, magazine material, and plays. *Type:* Association.

Children's Authors and Illustrators: An Index to Biographical Dictionaries
Gale Group Inc.

27500 Drake Rd.   Ph: (248)699-4253
Farmington Hills, MI 48331-   Free: 800-877-GALE
   3535   Fax: (248)699-8070
E-mail: galeord@galegroup.com
URL: http://www.galegroup.com.
Contact: Joyce Nakamura, Editor.
Desc: Over 200,000 citations of biographical sketches on some 30,000 authors and illustrators for children listed in 650 reference sources. *Type:* Directory.

Contemporary Authors
Gale Group Inc.

27500 Drake Rd.   Ph: (248)699-4253
Farmington Hills, MI 48331-   Free: 800-877-GALE
   3535   Fax: (248)699-8070
E-mail: galeord@galegroup.com
URL: http://www.galegroup.com.; http://www.gale.com.
Contact: Scot Peacock, Editor.
Desc: First published in the fall of 1962, "Contemporary Authors" is a bio-bibliographical series now covering over 100,000 authors (as of volume 150) who are currently active or who have lived since 1900. Providing detailed commentary about writers' lives and literary achievements, CA entries also offer both a historical and a contemporary review of the authors' critical reputations. *Type:* Directory.

Contemporary Canadian Authors
Gale Group Inc.

27500 Drake Rd.   Ph: (248)699-4253
Farmington Hills, MI 48331-   Free: 800-877-GALE
   3535   Fax: (248)699-8070
E-mail: galeord@galegroup.com
URL: http://www.galegroup.com.
Contact: Robert Lang, Editor.
Desc: Over 200 Canadian contemporary novelists, playwrights, journalists, and scriptwriters. *Type:* Directory.

Contemporary Women Poets
St. James Press, Inc.

27500 Drake Rd.   Ph: (248)699-4253
Farmington Hills, MI 48331-   Free: 800-877-4253
   3535   Fax: (248)699-8069
E-mail: galeord@gale.com
Contact: Pamela L. Shelton, Editor.
Desc: Nearly 250 prominent women poets writing and publishing in the English language and including some foreign-language authors. *Type:* Directory.

Discovering Authors Modules
Gale Group Inc.

27500 Drake Rd.   Ph: (248)699-4253
Farmington Hills, MI 48331-   Free: 800-877-GALE
   3535   Fax: (248)699-8070
E-mail: galeord@galegroup.com
URL: http://www.galegroup.com.; http://www.gale.com.
Contact: James Draper, Editor.
Desc: 1,260 authors divided into six different categories: most-studied authors, multicultural authors, dramatists, novelists, poets, and popular fiction & genre authors. *Type:* Directory.

Exploring Poetry
Gale Group Inc.

27500 Drake Rd.   Ph: (248)699-4253
Farmington Hills, MI 48331-   Free: 800-877-GALE
   3535   Fax: (248)699-8070
E-mail: galeord@galegroup.com
URL: http://www.galegroup.com.; http://www.gale.com.
Type: Directory.

Friends of George Sand
David Powell

Romance, Lang. & Lit.   Ph: (516)463-5485
107 Hofstra University   Fax: (516)463-2310
Hempstead, NY 11549
E-mail: hofcultr@hotsfra.edu
Contact: David A. Powell, Co-Editor-in-Chief.
Desc: Scholars, writers, libraries, organizations, students, and other individuals interested in the life and times of French writer George Sand, pseudonym of Amandine Aurore Lucile Dupin Dudevant (1804-76). Purposes are to coordinate research and scholarship; to serve as clearinghouse for information; to publicize and encourage events that would interest scholars and potential scholars; to facilitate English translations of Sand's works; to examine aspects of her life that augment an appreciation of her work and her time. Conducts educational programs; maintains speakers' bureau. *Type:* Association.

Gale's Literature Resource Center
Gale Group Inc.

27500 Drake Rd.   Ph: (248)699-4253
Farmington Hills, MI 48331-   Free: 800-877-GALE
   3535   Fax: (248)699-8070
E-mail: galeord@galegroup.com
URL: http://www.galegroup.com.; http://www.gale.com.
Desc: More than 90,000 authors and their works. *Type:* Directory.

The Gaylactic Gayzette
Noel Welch

PO Box 675
Lanham, MD 20703-0675
Contact: Noel Welch, Editor.
Desc: Promotes "science fiction, fantasy, and horror among gays, lesbians, bisexuals, and their friends." Contains network and chapter news. Recurring features include a calendar of events. *Type:* Newsletter.

Jane Austen Society of North America

200 East 57th St., No. 15-B   Ph: (212)308-7137
New York, NY 10022   Free: 800-836-3911
   Fax: (212)308-1885
URL: http://www.jasna.org
Contact: Elsa Solender, Pres.
Desc: Writers, scholars, educators, and other individuals interested in the life and works of Jane Austen (1775-1817), English novelist. Encourages interest in Austen and publishes and distributes materials pertaining to her life and works. *Type:* Association.

Junior Discovering Authors
Gale Group Inc.

27500 Drake Rd.   Ph: (248)699-4253
Farmington Hills, MI 48331-   Free: 800-877-GALE
   3535   Fax: (248)699-8070
E-mail: galeord@galegroup.com
URL: http://www.galegroup.com
Contact: Elizabeth Des Chenes, Editor, elizabeth.deschenes@gale.com.
Desc: Over 450 contemporary writers for children and young adults. *Type:* Directory.

The Keep
Midwest Center for Literary Arts, Inc.
The Writers Place

3607 Pennsylvania   Ph: (816)753-1090
Kansas City, MO 64111   Fax: (816)753-1016
E-mail: twpkcmo@aol.com
Contact: Robert Stewart, Editor; Phil Miller, Editor; Susan Whitmore, Editor.
Desc: Provides news of interest to writers in the Kansas City, MO area. *Type:* Newsletter.

Major Authors and Illustrators for Children and Young Adults
Gale Group Inc.

27500 Drake Rd.   Ph: (248)699-4253
Farmington Hills, MI 48331-   Free: 800-877-GALE
   3535   Fax: (248)699-8070
E-mail: galeord@galegroup.com
URL: http://www.galegroup.com.; http://www.gale.com.
Contact: Alan Hedblad, Editor, alan.hedblad@gale.com.
Desc: Nearly 800 of the most-popular and widely read authors and illustrators for children and young adults are covered in the original six-volume set; the supplement provides more than 150 new entries and updates selected others. *Type:* Directory.

Major Twentieth-Century Writers
Gale Group Inc.

27500 Drake Rd.   Ph: (248)699-4253
Farmington Hills, MI 48331-   Free: 800-877-GALE
   3535   Fax: (248)699-8070
E-mail: galeord@galegroup.com
URL: http://www.galegroup.com.; http://www.gale.com.
Desc: Approximately 1,000 widely-known and currently active writers, worldwide. *Type:* Directory.

Ohio Writer
Poets' League of Greater Cleveland
c/o Ron Antonucci   Ph: (216)932-8444
PO Box 91801
Cleveland, OH 44101
Contact: Ron Antonucci, Editor.
Desc: Contains book reviews, announcements, calendars, interviews, and articles of interest to writers living in Ohio. *Type:* Newsletter.

Romance Writers Report
Romance Writers of America, Inc.

3707 F.M. 1960, Ste. 555   Ph: (281)440-6885
Houston, TX 77068   Fax: (281)440-7510
E-mail: info@rwanational.com
URL: http://www.rwanational.com.
Contact: Patricia B. Walker, Editor.
Desc: Provides romance writers with information, assistance, knowledge, and support by publishing agents' special reports, author profiles, and how-to articles. Recurring features include editorials, news of members' activities, letters to the editor, interviews, reports of meetings, book reviews, and a calendar of events. *Type:* Newsletter.

St. James Guide to Crime and Mystery Writers
St. James Press, Inc.

27500 Drake Rd.   Ph: (248)699-4253
Farmington Hills, MI 48331-   Free: 800-877-4253
   3535   Fax: (248)699-8069
E-mail: galeord@gale.com
Contact: Jay P. Pederson, Editor, (320)597-4668, fax: (320)597-4668, jaypederson@compuserve.com.
Desc: Approximately 650 English-language mystery and crime writers. *Type:* Directory.

St. James Guide to Fantasy Writers
St. James Press, Inc.

27500 Drake Rd.   Ph: (248)699-4253
Farmington Hills, MI 48331-   Free: 800-877-4253
   3535   Fax: (248)699-8069
E-mail: galeord@gale.com; interzone@cix.compulink.co.uk.
Contact: David Pringle, Editor.
Desc: More than 400 authors of heroic fantasy, sword and sorcery, humorous fantasy, adult fairy tales and fables. *Type:* Directory.

St. James Guide to Horror, Ghost & Gothic Writers

St. James Press, Inc.
27500 Drake Rd.   Ph: (248)699-4253
Farmington Hills, MI 48331-   Free: 800-877-4253
3535   Fax: (248)699-8069
E-mail: galeord@gale.com
Contact: David Pringle, Editor.
Desc: More than 400 writers in English and 25 foreign-language writers, writing in the genres of horror, Gothic, supernatural tales and more. *Type:* Directory.

St. James Guide to Science Fiction Writers

St. James Press, Inc.
27500 Drake Rd.   Ph: (248)699-4253
Farmington Hills, MI 48331-   Free: 800-877-4253
3535   Fax: (248)699-8069
E-mail: galeord@gale.com
Contact: Jay P. Pederson, Editor, (320)597-4668, fax: (320)597-4668, jaypederson@compuserve.com.
Desc: More than 600 of the world's most prominent writers of science fiction; emphasis is on living writers, with entries included for deceased writers who influenced modern writing. *Type:* Directory.

Scavenger's Newsletter

Janet Fox
519 Ellinwood   Ph: (913)528-3538
Osage City, KS 66523
E-mail: foxscav1@jc.net
URL: http://www.cza.com/scav/index.html.
Contact: Janet Fox, Editor, foxscav1@jc.net.
Desc: Provides information for fantasy, horror, science fiction and mystery writers and artists. Lists markets for these materials. *Type:* Newsletter.

Science Fiction, Fantasy, and Horror Writers

Gale Group Inc.
27500 Drake Rd.   Ph: (248)699-4253
Farmington Hills, MI 48331-   Free: 800-877-GALE
3535   Fax: (248)699-8070
E-mail: galeord@galegroup.com
URL: http://www.galegroup.com.
Desc: 80 writers of the children's and young adults science fiction, fantasy and horror genres, past and current. *Type:* Directory.

Society of Children's Book Writers and Illustrators

345 N. Maple Dr., Ste. 296   Ph: (310)859-9887
Beverly Hills, CA 90210-3869   Fax: (310)859-4877
E-mail: scbwi@juno.com
URL: http://www.scbwi.org
Contact: Stephen Mooser, Pres.
Desc: Individuals with an active interest in children's literature. Acts as a network for the exchange of information among children's writers, editors, publishers, illustrators, and agents. *Type:* Association.

Something about the Author

Gale Group Inc.
27500 Drake Rd.   Ph: (248)699-4253
Farmington Hills, MI 48331-   Free: 800-877-GALE
3535   Fax: (248)699-8070
E-mail: galeord@galegroup.com
URL: http://www.galegroup.com.
Contact: Alan Hedblad, Editor, alan.hedblad@gale.com.
Desc: About 75 authors and illustrators of children's books in each volume. Series (over 100 volumes) includes approximately 10,000 authors who are now living or have died since 1960, and from Volume 15 on, also includes lengthy sketches of authors and illustrators who died before 1960. *Type:* Directory.

Speechwriter's Newsletter

Lawrence Ragan Communications, Inc.
212 W. Superior St., Ste. 200   Ph: (312)335-0037
Chicago, IL 60610   Free: 800-878-5331
    Fax: (312)573-3730
Contact: John Cowan, Editor.
Desc: Offers practical information on speech writing and delivery, written "from the hard-headed point of view of the PR practitioner." Presents excerpts from and commentary on major speeches delivered by corporate, government, and association leaders. Recurring features include letters to the editor, interviews, news of research and educational opportunities, and a calendar of events. *Type:* Newsletter.

The Talisman

The Talisman
719 Swift St.   Ph: (408)425-7847
Santa Cruz, CA 95060-5853
Contact: Blythe Ayne, Editor.
Desc: Covers the romance genre along with its sub-genres, including suspense, occult, futuristic, time travel, and fantasy. Spotlights authors and market news. *Type:* Newsletter.

Twentieth-Century Children's Writers

St. James Press, Inc.
27500 Drake Rd.   Ph: (248)699-4253
Farmington Hills, MI 48331-   Free: 800-877-4253
3535   Fax: (248)699-8069
E-mail: galeord@gale.com
Desc: 700 English-language writers of fiction, poetry, and drama for children. *Type:* Directory.

Twentieth-Century Romance and Historical Writers

St. James Press, Inc.
27500 Drake Rd.   Ph: (248)699-4253
Farmington Hills, MI 48331-   Free: 800-877-4253
3535   Fax: (248)699-8069
E-mail: galeord@gale.com
Contact: A. Vasudevan, Editor.
Desc: Over 500 authors of romantic and historical novels; primarily American and British coverage. *Type:* Directory.

Twentieth-Century Western Writers

Gale Group Inc.
27500 Drake Rd.   Ph: (248)699-4253
Farmington Hills, MI 48331-   Free: 800-877-GALE
3535   Fax: (248)699-8070
E-mail: galeord@galegroup.com
URL: http://www.galegroup.com.
Contact: Geoff Sadler, Editor.
Desc: 489 writers in the American western genre, including novelists, journalists, poets, short story writers, juvenile writers, dramatists. *Type:* Directory.

Twentieth-Century Young Adult Writers

St. James Press, Inc.
27500 Drake Rd.   Ph: (248)699-4253
Farmington Hills, MI 48331-   Free: 800-877-4253
3535   Fax: (248)699-8069
E-mail: galeord@gale.com
Desc: Approximately 400 authors of literature for young adults. *Type:* Directory.

Writer's Digest

F & W Publications, Inc.
1507 Dana Ave.   Ph: (513)531-2222
Cincinnati, OH 45207   Fax: (513)531-2902
E-mail: writersdig@fwpubs.com.
Contact: Melanie Rigney, Editor, (513)531-2690, melanier@fwpubs.com; Jeffry M. Lapin, Publisher; Leslie Winters, Advertising Mgr., (203)661-0515, fax: (203)661-0519, leslie203@juno.com; David Lee, Circulation Director.

Desc: Professional magazine for writers. *Type:* Periodical.

Writers Directory

St. James Press, Inc.
27500 Drake Rd.   Ph: (248)699-4253
Farmington Hills, MI 48331-   Free: 800-877-4253
3535   Fax: (248)699-8069
E-mail: galeord@gale.com
Contact: Miranda H. Ferrara, Editor.
Desc: Over 17,500 living writers world wide published in English who have written at least one work. *Type:* Directory.

Writers Guild of America, East

555 W. 57th St.   Ph: (212)767-7800
New York, NY 10019   Fax: (212)582-1909
E-mail: info@wgaeast.org
URL: http://www.wgaeast.org
Contact: Mona Mangan, Exec.Dir.
Desc: Labor union for professional waiters in motion pictures, television and radio. *Type:* Association.

Writing World

Fern Reiss
44 Tarleton Rd.
Newton Center, MA 02159
Contact: Fern Reiss, Publisher.
Desc: Gives "the juiciest tidbits of interest to writers," such as free publications and products, and offers basic information on finding an agent, book proposals, and query letters. Profiles other writing organizations and each issues spotlights a special genre. *Type:* Newsletter.

Automobiles

ACRA Report

American Car Rental Association (ACRA)
1225 I St., NW No. 500   Ph: (202)682-4761
Washington, DC 20005-3814   Fax: (202)789-4512
Contact: Tam M. Armstrong, Editor; Melanie J. Penoyar, Editor.
Desc: Discusses state and federal legislation affecting the car rental industry. Informs members of action taken by the Board of Directors and ACRA services available to members. *Type:* Newsletter.

All Chevy

McMullen Argus Publishing, Inc.
774 S. Placentia Ave.   Ph: (714)939-2400
Placentia, CA 92870   Fax: (714)572-1864
Contact: Jerry Dexter, Publisher; Dan Sanchez, Editor.
Desc: Auto magazine for Chevrolet car enthusiasts. *Type:* Periodical.

American Automobile Association

1000 AAA Dr.   Ph: (407)444-4240
Heathrow, FL 32746   Fax: (407)444-7380
URL: http://www.aaa.com
Contact: Robert Darbelnet, Pres.
Desc: Federation of automobile clubs (1000 offices) providing domestic and foreign travel services, emergency road services, and insurance. Sponsors public services for traffic safety, better highways, more efficient and safer cars, energy conservation, and improvement of motoring and travel conditions. *Type:* Association.

American Hot Rod Association

N. 111 Hayford Rd.   Ph: (509)244-2372
Spokane, WA 99204   Fax: (509)244-2472
URL: http://www.spokaneracewaypark.com
Contact: Orville Moe, Exec.VP.
Desc: Professional and amateur drag racers from the U.S. and Canada. Goal is to sponsor a series of national drag racing championships. *Type:* Association.

American Motors Owners Association

Darryl A. Salisbury
6756 Cornell St.   Ph: (616)323-0369
Portage, MI 49024-3412   Fax: (616)387-4806
Contact: Darryl A. Salisbury, Pres.
Desc: Owners and enthusiasts of AMC vehicles built from 1958 - 1988. To aid and encourage ownership, use, and enjoyment of AMC vehicles; to encourage preservation and restoration of these vehicles; and to increase communications and fellowship among owners. *Type:* Association.

American Racing 'Zine

Creative Communications Group
3000 Town Ctr., Ste. 1385   Ph: (248)356-5699
Southfield, MI 48075   Fax: (248)356-0377
E-mail: info@c2group.com
URL: http://www.racecar.com
Desc: American Racing 'Zine is for websurfers in search of current race results, standings of racing teams and drivers, the NASCAR schedule, and all topics of interest to the avid racing enthusiast. Chat with fans online via email or in real time. *Type:* Database.

Antique Automobile Club of America

501 W. Governor Rd.   Ph: (717)534-1910
Hershey, PA 17033   Fax: (717)534-9101
Contact: William H. Smith, Exec.Dir.
Desc: Collectors, hobbyists, and others interested in the preservation, maintenance, and restoration of automobiles and in automotive history. Encourages historical research. Sponsors Glidden Tour. *Type:* Association.

Austin-Healey Club of America

PO Box 3220   Free: 877-5HEALEY
Monroe, NC 28111-3220
E-mail: secyahca@aol.com
URL: http://www.serve.com/ahca/
Contact: Edie Anderson, VP/Membership.
Desc: Owners or aficionados of Austin-Healey or Austin-Healey Sprite automobiles. To preserve the Austin-Healey and to maintain the highest standards of the marque by sharing technical and mechanical information within the club and with other Austin-Healey clubs worldwide. Functions as a social group for Austin-Healey owners; promotes courtesy and safety on the roads. Conducts programs on restoration and maintenance of the marque; sponsors a judging school. Holds technical sessions, driving events, and competitions. Compiles list of car serial numbers. *Type:* Association.

Auto & Truck International—Buyer's Guide Issue

Adams Business Media
2101 S. Arlington Heights Rd.,   Ph: (847)427-9512
  Ste. 150   Fax: (847)427-2006
Arlington Heights, IL 60005
E-mail: autonet@mail.aip.com.
Contact: Eric Schroder, Editor.
Desc: List of manufacturers of automotive products; international coverage. *Type:* Directory.

Automobile Magazine

Primedia Publishing
717 5th Ave., 10th Fl.   Ph: (212)745-0500
New York, NY 10022   Fax: (212)745-0599
E-mail: autoletters@primediamags.com.
URL: http://www.automobilemag.com.
Contact: David E. Davis, Jr., Editor/Publication Dir.
Desc: Automotive magazine. *Alt. Contact:* 120 E. Liberty St., Ann Arbor, MI 48104-4193; telephone: (734)994-3500; fax: (734)994-1153; 575 Lexington Ave., 24th Fl., New York, NY 10022. *Type:* Periodical.

Automotive Fleet and Leasing Association— Forum

Automotive Fleet and Leasing Association
21061 S. Western Ave.   Ph: (310)533-2520
Torrance, CA 90501   Fax: (310)533-2506
Contact: Rose Finch, Editor, rose@bobit.com.
Desc: Seeks to keep automotive fleet dealers and leasing agencies updated on important events, membership news, new legislation, and government programs. Recurring features include editorials and letters to the editor. *Type:* Newsletter.

AutoWeek

Crain Communications, Inc.
1400 Woodbridge Ave.   Ph: (313)446-6000
Detroit, MI 48207-3187   Free: 800-678-9595
                  Fax: (313)446-0383
E-mail: letters@autoweek.com; adsales@autoweek.com.
URL: htttp://www.autoweek.com.
Contact: Dutch Mandel, Editor, (313)446-0318, fax: (313)446-1027, dmandel@crain.com; Leon Mandel, Publisher, (313)446-6040, lmandel@crain.com; Jeff Nellett, Advertising Dir., (313)446-0355, jnellett@crain.com.
Desc: Magazine for car enthusiasts includes news coverage and features on vehicles, personalities, and events. Provides coverage of Formula One, CART, NASCAR, and IMSA races. *Type:* Periodical.

Avenues

Automobile of S. California
3333 Fairview Rd., A327   Ph: (714)885-2376
Costa Mesa, CA 92626   Fax: (714)885-2335
Contact: Gail Harrington, Editor-in-Chief; Marc Titel, Publisher; Bob Bradley, Dir. of Advertising; Mike Bonk, Circulation Mgr., (213)741-3472, fax: (213)741-3303.
Desc: Magazine for members of the Automobile Club of Southern California. *Type:* Periodical.

The Blue Seal

National Institute for Automotive Service Excellence
13505 Dulles Technology Dr.   Ph: (703)713-3800
Herndon, VA 22071   Fax: (703)713-0727
Contact: Martin Lawson, Editor.
Desc: Covers news of the Institute's efforts to certify auto, medium/heavy truck, engine machinists, collision repair technicians, and parts specialists. Discusses industry trends, vehicle repair tips, and training information, and highlights activities of ASE-certified technicians. *Type:* Newsletter.

BMW Car Club of America

2130 Massachuetts Ave., No. IA Ph: (617)492-2500
Cambridge, MA 02140   Free: 800-878-9292
                  Fax: (617)876-3424
E-mail: bmwcclub@aol.com
URL: http://www.bmwcca.org
Contact: Mark L. Luckman, Exec.Dir.
Desc: Owners of BMW (Bavarian Motor Works) automobiles and other interested persons. Promotes interest in BMW automobiles through technical, social, and driving events; encourages the exchange of information among members. Club is independent of any commercial interests. *Type:* Association.

Cadillac-LaSalle Club

Jay Ann Edmunds
PO Box 359   Ph: (610)688-7747
Devon, PA 19333   Fax: (610)688-0482
Contact: Jay Ann Edmunds, Membership Sec.
Desc: Persons interested in Cadillac or LaSalle automobiles. Seeks to preserve, restore, and enjoy Cadillac and LaSalle cars of all models. *Type:* Association.

Car Craft

Petersen Publishing Co., L.L.C.
6420 Wilshire Blvd.   Ph: (323)782-2350
Los Angeles, CA 90048-5515 Fax: (323)782-2704
Contact: Jim McGowan, Editor; Bruce Bakke, Publisher; Peter Clancey, Senior Vice President.
Desc: Magazine covering performance cars and drag racing. *Type:* Periodical.

Car Dealer Insider Newsletter

United Communications Group
11300 Rockville Pike, Ste. 1100 Ph: (301)287-2700
Rockville, MD 20852-3030   Free: 800-929-4824
                  Fax: (301)287-2049
E-mail: customer@ucg.com
Contact: Dennis Sullivan, Editor.
Desc: Features marketing tips, advertising ideas, management trends, news on dealer-factory relations, and automotive industry news. *Type:* Newsletter.

Car and Driver

Hachette Filipacchi Magazines, Inc.
1633 Broadway, 41st Fl.   Ph: (212)767-6000
New York, NY 10019   Fax: (212)989-4561
Contact: W. Jeanes, Editor-in-Chief; Csaba Cserve, Editor; Stephen Spence, Managing Editor; D.M. Hufford, Publisher.
Desc: Magazine for automotive enthusiasts. *Type:* Periodical.

Car & Parts Magazine

Car & Parts Magazine
911 Vandemark Rd.   Ph: (937)498-0803
Sidney, OH 45365   Free: 800-448-3611
                  Fax: (937)498-0808
URL: http://www.carsandparts.com.
Contact: Robert Jay Stevens, Editor; Walter Reed, Publisher.
Desc: Magazine for automobile enthusiasts. Includes articles on collector cars, restoration, and automotive history; show and auction reports. *Alt. Contact:* PO Box 482, Sidney, OH 45365; telephone: (937)498-0803; fax: (937)498-0808; toll-free: 800-448-3611. *Type:* Periodical.

Car Rental "Insider"

United Communications Group
11300 Rockville Pike, Ste. 1100 Ph: (301)287-2700
Rockville, MD 20852-3030   Free: 800-929-4824
                  Fax: (301)287-2049
E-mail: customer@ucg.com
Contact: John Kirk, Editor.
Desc: Covers trends, changes, and developments in the automobiles leasing and renting industry. Reports on legislation, consumer purchasing trends, insurance updates, operations management, and franchise developments. *Type:* Newsletter.

Car Talk

Newmarket Network
201 South St.   Ph: (617)423-4499
Boston, MA 02111-2706   Fax: (617)423-4498
E-mail: frontdest@newmarket.net
URL: http://cartalk.cars.com/
Desc: This is the site hosted by Tom and Ray Magliozzi, otherwise known as Click and Clack, of the popular "Car Talk" show on National Public Radio. In additional to all the printed columns dating back to 1992, the site enables users to search for a particular make, model, and year of car offered for sale by dealers in their area (Java is required for this); determine a fair price for a particular used car by specifying options; listen to audio segments from the Car Talk radio show; read comments by others who have a vehicle like theirs (or add their own comments); and learn the specific cost of repairs for a particular vehicle and problem. *Type:* Database.

Carguide Magazine (Le Magazine Carguide)

Formula Publications

447 Speers Rd., Ste. 4
Oakville, ON, Canada L6K 3S7
Ph: (905)842-6591
Fax: (905)842-6843
Contact: Graeme Fletcher, Editor; Tim Lindsay, Managing Editor; J. Scott Robinson, Publisher; Grant Wells, Nat'l. Sales Mgr.; Deadra Worth, Circulation Mgr.
Desc: Magazine on cars. *Type:* Periodical.

Classic Car Club of America

Desc: Hobbyists who collect and restore luxury automobiles built between 1925 and 1948. Annually presents 9 trophies. Maintains library on automotive history; operates museum. *Type:* Association.

Classic Chevy Club International

PO Box 607188
Orlando, FL 32860-7188
Ph: (407)299-1957
Free: 800-456-1957
Fax: (407)299-3341
Contact: James Bruce, Exec. Officer.
Desc: Promotes the preservation and restoration of 1955, 1956, and 1957 Chevrolets. Compiles statistics. Supplies variety of reproduction parts for restoration. *Type:* Association.

Collectible Automobile

Publications International, Ltd.

7373 N. Cicero
Lincolnwood, IL 60646
Ph: (847)676-3470
Fax: (847)676-3671
Contact: John Biel, Editor; Frank Peiler, Publisher.
Desc: Magazine on collectible automobiles. *Type:* Periodical.

Corvette Quarterly

C. E. Publishing

30400 Van Dyke
Warren, MI 48093-2368
Ph: (810)574-9100
Fax: (810)575-9328
Contact: Marla Burdock, Editor, (810)558-7276, fax: (810)558-5897, mburdock@cecom.com; Rick Lafave, Publisher, (810)558-4164, rlafave@cecom.com.
Desc: Magazine for Corvette enthusiasts. *Type:* Periodical.

Dealers Edge

WD & S Publishing

20 Highland Ave.
Metuchen, NJ 08840
Ph: (732)548-4440
Free: 800-321-5312
Fax: (732)603-0690
Contact: Mike Bowers, Editor, mbowers@dealersedge.com.
Desc: Offers management ideas from business-to-business for automobile dealers. *Type:* Newsletter.

Dune Buggies & Hot VWs

Dune Buggies & Hot VWs

2950 Airway, Ste. A7
PO Box 2260
Costa Mesa, CA 92626
Ph: (714)979-2560
Fax: (714)979-3998
Contact: Judy Wright, Publisher; Bruce Simurda, Editor; Linda Dill, Advertising Mgr.
Desc: Magazine offering VW automotive news for the consumer. *Type:* Periodical.

The duPont Registry: A Buyer's Gallery of Fine Automobiles

duPont Publishing, Inc.

3051 Tech Dr.
St. Petersburg, FL 33716
Ph: (727)573-9339
Free: 800-233-1731
Fax: (727)572-5523
E-mail: dupreg@aol.com; mobordo@earthlink.net.
URL: www.dupontregistry.com.
Contact: Ron Barreto, General Mgr., ron@dupontregistry.com; Thomas L. duPont, Publisher, (727)572-4946, tldupont@dupontregistry.com; Steven B. Chapman, President, steve@dupontregistry.com; Jerry A. Britt, COO, (727)561-0505, jerry@dupontregistry.com; John Chapman, National Sales Mgr., johnc@dupontregistry.com; Chris Castelitz, Public Relations Dir., chriscc@dupontregistry.com.

Desc: Glossy, full-color magazine featuring the finest classic, luxury, and exotic cars in the world for sale. *Type:* Periodical.

Early Ford V-8 Club of America

Box 2122
San Leandro, CA 94577
Ph: (925)606-1925
E-mail: fordv8club@aol.com
Contact: Linda McDonald, Exec.Sec.
Desc: Persons interested in restoration of the early Ford V-8 automobile. *Type:* Association.

Fixed Coverage

WD & S Publishing

20 Highland Ave.
Metuchen, NJ 08840
Ph: (732)548-4440
Free: 800-321-5312
Fax: (732)603-0690
Contact: Mike Bowers, Managing Editor, mbowers@dealersedge.com; Loriann Fell, Editor.
Desc: Offers management ideas for auto dealership service managers. *Type:* Newsletter.

Fleet Safety Newsletter

National Safety Council

1121 Spring Lake Dr.
Itasca, IL 60143-3201
Ph: (630)285-1121
Free: 800-539-7468
Fax: (630)285-1315
URL: http://www.nsc.org; http://www.nsc.org.
Contact: Laura Coyne, Editor, (630)775-2276, fax: (630)775-2285.
Desc: Promotes motor fleet safety for commercial vehicles, motorized public transportation, and school buses. *Type:* Newsletter.

Four Wheeler Magazine

General Media Automotive Group

3330 Ocean Park Blvd.
Santa Monica, CA 90405-3211
Ph: (310)392-2998
Fax: (310)392-1171
Contact: John Stewart, Editor; Chris Ballard, Advertising Mgr.
Desc: Magazine on four-wheel-drive vehicles. *Type:* Periodical.

Hemmings Motor News

Watering, Inc.

Rte. 9 West Rd.
Box 256
Bennington, VT 05201-0256
Ph: (802)442-3101
Free: 800-227-4373
Fax: (802)447-1561
E-mail: hmnmail@hemmings.com.
Contact: Keith Haugland, Publisher, (504)564-4510, fax: (505)564-4630; Bill Long, Editor, (504)564-4624, fax: (504)564-4630; Emmett Mckinley, Advertising Dir., (504)564-4570, fax: (504)564-4580; Ernest Asmus, Business Mgr., (504)564-4515, fax: (504)564-4580; Mel Chivers, Circulation Dir., (504)564-4530, fax: (505)564-4580.
Alt. Contact: PO Box 256, Bennington, VT 05201; telephone: (802)442-3101; fax: (802)447-1561; toll-free: 800-227-4373. *Type:* Periodical.

Home & Away Magazine

AAA World

8030 Excelsior Dr.
Madison, WI 53717
Ph: (608)828-2487
Fax: (608)828-2443
Contact: Ernest Stetenfeld, Editor.
Desc: Magazine for American Automobile Association membership. *Type:* Periodical.

Horseless Carriage Club of America

3311 Fairhauer Dr.
Bakersfield, CA 93308
Ph: (661)326-1023
Fax: (661)326-1260
E-mail: john@horseless.com
URL: http://www.horseless.com

Contact: Paul Anthony, Exec.Dir.
Desc: Hobbyists who are interested in the preservation, accessories, archives, and romantic lore of old cars. *Type:* Association.

Hot Rod Magazine

Petersen Publishing Co., L.L.C.

6420 Wilshire Blvd.
Los Angeles, CA 90048-5515
Ph: (323)782-2350
Fax: (323)782-2704
Contact: Harry Hibler, Publisher; Ralph V. Panico, Publisher; Peter F. Clancey, Corporate Marketing and Sales.
Desc: Automotive magazine. *Type:* Periodical.

International Hot Rod Association

PO Box 708
Norwalk, OH 44857
Ph: (419)663-6666
Fax: (419)663-4472
Contact: Bill Bader, Contact.
Desc: Promotes safety and encourages sportsman participation in drag racing. Through the sanctioning of numerous drag strips throughout the country, strives to be the most responsive organization of its kind for both promoters and competitors. Conducts IHRA World Championship Series for professional and sportsman drag racers. *Type:* Association.

International Motor Contest Association

Kathy Root

1800 W. D St.
Box 921
Vinton, IA 52349
Ph: (319)472-2201
Fax: (319)472-2218
E-mail: raceimca@aol.com
URL: http://www.imca.com
Contact: Kathy Root, Pres.
Desc: Auto race drivers, auto race car owners, and mechanics. Auto racing sanctioning body to establish rules, regulations, and specifications. Sanctions competitions for late models, sprint cars, modifieds, and stock cars. *Type:* Association.

International Parking Institute

701 Kenmore Ave., Ste.200
PO Box 7167
Fredericksburg, VA 22404-7167
Ph: (540)371-7535
Fax: (540)371-8022
E-mail: ipi@parking.org
URL: http://www.parking.org
Contact: David L. Ivey, Pres.
Desc: Parking, transit, transportation, public works, and security departments of cities, airports, civic centers, port authorities, colleges, universities, and hospitals; individuals within these departments; engineers, architects, planners, and suppliers to the parking industry. Provides information on developments in the parking field in the areas of management, construction, planning, and technical advancements. Conducts regional seminars on such topics as hospital parking, residential permit parking programs, enforcement, airport parking, garage deterioration, computers, and security. *Type:* Association.

Jaguar Clubs of North America

c/o Jaguar Cars Inc.
555 MacArthur Blvd.
Mahwah, NJ 07430
Ph: (201)818-8144
Fax: (201)818-0281
URL: http://www.jcna.com
Contact: James Morton, Pres.
Desc: Jaguar clubs in U.S., Canada, and Mexico representing a combined membership of 5500. Works to: foster and encourage a spirit of mutual interest and assistance for Jaguar automobile enthusiasts; promote public interest in motoring and motor sports; develop road safety; encourage an improved understanding of traffic laws; promote social and motoring events. *Type:* Association.

Kit Car Illustrated

McMullen Argus Publishing, Inc.
774 S. Placentia Ave.　Ph: (714)939-2400
Placentia, CA 92870　Fax: (714)572-1864
Contact: Mike Blake, Editor, (714)939-2550, mikeb@
mcmullenargus.com; Pat Lester, Advertising Mgr.,
(714)939-2529.
Desc: Magazine for kit car enthusiasts. *Type:* Periodical.

Kustom Kemps of America

RR 1, Box 1714　Ph: (417)847-2940
Bill Hailey Dr.　Fax: (417)847-3647
Cassville, MO 65625-9724
Contact: Jerry E. Titus, Pres.
Desc: Enthusiasts of custom cars and trucks from 1935 to
1964. (Kemp is slang from the late 1950s indicating a cus-
tomized car or truck.) Seeks to restore and manufacture
custom cars of the hot-rodding industry. Operates Late
Model Smoothie Division for nonstock cars and trucks
produced from 1965 to the present. *Type:* Association.

Late Great Chevrolet Association

PO Box 607824　Ph: 800-683-1961
Orlando, FL 32860　Fax: (407)886-7571
URL: http://www.ao.net/chevy55-72
Contact: Robert Snowden, Editor.
Desc: Seeks to preserve and restore 1958-1964 Chevrolets.
Type: Association.

Lincoln and Continental Owners Club

PO Box 28788　Ph: (972)709-6185
Dallas, TX 75228-0788　Free: 800-527-3452
　Fax: (972)296-7920
URL: http://www.lcoc.org
Desc: Persons interested in preserving and restoring Lin-
colns and Continentals. Provides information on location
and exchange of replacement parts and restoration service.
Type: Association.

Low Rider Magazine

Park Avenue Publishing, Inc.
PO Box 648　Ph: (909)598-2300
Walnut, CA 91788-0648　Fax: (909)444-0162
Contact: Alberto Lopez, Publisher; Maria Brown, Adver-
tising Dir.; David M. Cohen, Advertising Dir.
Desc: Hispanic automotive magazine. *Type:* Periodical.

Mercedes-Benz Club of America

1907 Lelaray St.　Ph: (719)633-6427
Colorado Springs, CO 80909　Free: 800-637-2360
　Fax: (719)633-9283
E-mail: info@mbca.org
URL: http://www.mbca.org
Contact: Ron Farrar, Exec.Dir.
Desc: Owners and others interested in Mercedes-Benz cars.
Type: Association.

Metropolitan Owners Club of North America

5009 Barton Rd.　Ph: (608)271-0457
Madison, WI 53711　Fax: (608)274-9494
Contact: Goldie Hurley, Treas.
Desc: Seeks to preserve the Metropolitan automobile pro-
duced by Austin Motor Co., Ltd. *Type:* Association.

MiniTruckin'

McMullen Argus Publishing, Inc.
774 S. Placentia Ave.　Ph: (714)939-2400
Placentia, CA 92870　Fax: (714)572-1864
Contact: Steve Stillwell, Editor; Thomas M. McMullen,
Publisher.
Desc: Magazine for mini-truck enthusiasts. *Type:* Periodi-
cal.

Model A Ford Club of America

250 S. Cypress　Ph: (562)697-2712
La Habra, CA 90631　Fax: (562)690-7452
Contact: Emma Celmer, Exec.Sec.
Desc: Persons interested in restoring and preserving Model
A Ford cars (1928-31). *Type:* Association.

Model "A" Restorers Club

24800 Michigan Ave.　Ph: (313)278-1455
Dearborn, MI 48124　Fax: (313)278-2624
URL: http://www.modelaford.org
Contact: Marian Hierholzer, Sec.
Desc: Automotive enthusiasts. interested in preserving
Model A Ford cars and trucks and related literature and
accessories. *Type:* Association.

Morris Minor Registry

318 Hampton Park　Ph: (614)899-2394
Westerville, OH 43081-5723　Fax: (614)899-2493
E-mail: morrisminr@aol.com
Contact: Tony Burgess, Exec. Officer.
Desc: Owners of Morris Minor automobiles and interested
individuals united for mutual assistance in finding parts
for and repairing the cars. *Type:* Association.

Motor Service

Adams Business Media
2101 S. Arlington Heights Rd.,　Ph: (847)427-9512
　Ste. 150　Fax: (847)427-2006
Arlington Heights, IL 60005
E-mail: autonet@mail.aip.com.
URL: http://www.autotruck.net.
Contact: Eric Schroder, Editor-in-Chief, (847)427-2089,
fax: (847)427-2006, eschroder@mail.aip.com; James Gillespie, Publisher, (847)427-2098, fax: (847)427-2006,
jgillespie@mail.aip.com; Gillian Babicz, Managing Editor,
(847)427-2046, fax: (847)427-2006, gbabicz@mail.aip.
com.
Desc: Magazine for auto repair shops. *Type:* Periodical.

Motor Trend

Petersen Publishing Co., L.L.C.
6420 Wilshire Blvd.　Ph: (323)782-2350
Los Angeles, CA 90048-5515　Fax: (323)782-2704
E-mail: mtletters@aol.com.
URL: http://www.motortrend.com.
Contact: Doug Hamlin, Publisher; C. Van Tune, Editor;
Lee Kelley, President.
Desc: Consumer automotive publication. *Type:* Periodical.

Motor World

Publishing and Business Consultants
4427 W. Slauson Ave.
Los Angeles, CA 90043-2717
Contact: Atia Napoleon, Editor and Publisher.
Desc: Magazine covering personal car maintenance with
information on trends. *Type:* Periodical.

Mustang & Fords

Petersen Publishing Co., L.L.C.
6420 Wilshire Blvd.　Ph: (323)782-2350
Los Angeles, CA 90048-5515　Fax: (323)782-2704
Contact: John Dianna, Publisher; Peter Clancey, Senior
V.P.; Jim Smart, Editor; Chris Horn, Assoc. Publisher.
Desc: Magazine featuring a variety of Mustang events and
other car-related activities across the country. *Alt. Contact:*
6420 Wilshire Blvd., Los Angeles, CA 90048; telephone:
(213)782-2323; fax: (213)782-2263. *Type:* Periodical.

Mustang Illustrated

McMullen Argus Publishing, Inc.
774 S. Placentia Ave.　Ph: (714)939-2400
Placentia, CA 92870　Fax: (714)572-1864
Contact: Bob McClurg, Editor; Jerry Dexter, Publisher;
Arlan Pfohl, Advertising Mgr.
Desc: Magazine for Mustang and high performance Ford
car enthusiasts. *Type:* Periodical.

NARSA National Newsletter

*National Automotive Radiator Service Association
(NARSA)*
PO Box 97　Ph: (215)541-4500
East Greenville, PA 18041　Fax: (215)679-4977
E-mail: narsa@aol.com
Contact: Wayne Juchno, Editor.
Desc: Covers issues of interest to radiator service station
operators and others in the auto repair industry. Recurring
features include news of conferences and a calendar of
events. *Type:* Newsletter.

National Association for Stock Car Auto Racing

PO Box 2875　Ph: (904)253-0611
1801 W Intl. Speedway Blvd.　Fax: (904)258-7646
Daytona Beach, FL 32114
URL: http://www.nascar.com
Contact: Bill France, Pres.
Desc: To sanction and supervise stock car races. Compiles
statistics. *Type:* Association.

National Corvette Owners Association

PO Box 16050　Ph: (703)533-7222
Falls Church, VA 22040-9907　Fax: (703)533-1153
E-mail: ncoassoc@aol.com
URL: http://www.ncoa-vettes.com
Contact: Paul Young, Membership Dir.
Desc: Corvette owners and enthusiasts united to encourage
and increase the enjoyment and popularity of Corvette au-
tomobiles. Provides members with benefits such as insur-
ance, interior discounts, and auto supply discounts.
Maintains reference book collection. *Type:* Association.

National Corvette Restorers Society

6291 Day Rd.　Ph: (513)385-8526
Cincinnati, OH 45252　Fax: (513)385-8554
E-mail: info@ncrs.org
URL: http://www.ncrs.org
Contact: Gary Mortimer, Pres.
Desc: Purposes are the preservation, restoration, and enjoy-
ment of Corvettes produced from 1953 thru 1982 and of
all related material. Encourages and publishes studies and
research pertaining to their development and history.
Conducts research projects and technical sessions. *Type:*
Association.

National Council of Corvette Clubs

6 13th St., Ste. 204　Free: 800-245-VETT
Charlestown, MA 02129
URL: http://www.corvettesnccc.org
Desc: Federation of clubs of owners of Corvette automo-
biles. *Type:* Association.

National Hot Rod Association

2035 Financial Way　Ph: (626)914-4761
Glendora, CA 91740　Free: 800-308-NHRA
　Fax: (626)914-8963
URL: http://www.nhraonline.com/
Contact: Dallas J. Gardner, Pres.
Desc: Persons interested in automobiles modified and designed for performance and acceleration. Sets competition
rules and construction guidelines; sponsors regional and
national drag races; conducts world championship points
tournament and certifies official records. Conducts design
and safety research; provides automotive data. *Type:* Association.

National Street Rod Association

4030 Park Ave.   Ph: (901)452-4030
Memphis, TN 38111   Fax: (901)432-6772

Contact: Gilbert L. Bugg, Jr., VP.

Desc: Street rod builders and enthusiasts. Conducts automotive events; attempts to influence state and federal legislation that is auto-oriented. (Street rods are modified antique cars using new automotive parts). *Type:* Association.

National Tractor Pullers Association

6969 Worthington-Galena Rd.,   Ph: (614)436-1761
Ste. L-1000   Fax: (614)436-0964
Worthington, OH 43085

Contact: David P. Schreier, Pres.

Desc: A divison of World Pulling International. Competitors and associates. Promotes the sport of tractor and truck pulling (a competition in which contestants try to pull a weighted sled with a tractor or truck farther than their opponents before its weight overcomes the power of their machines). *Type:* Association.

North American MGA Register

Desc: Individuals interested in the preservation and enjoyment of MG auto series "A", manufactured from 1955 to 1962. Sponsors technical seminars. *Type:* Association.

NSU Club of America

717 N. 68th St.   Ph: (206)784-5084
Seattle, WA 98103   Fax: (206)784-5084

Contact: Jim Sykes, Contact.

Desc: Owners and enthusiasts of NSU automobiles. (NSU is an acronym for Neckarsulm, the German city where the cars were manufactured.). *Type:* Association.

Office of Defects Investigation Recall Database

Department of Transportation
National Highway Traffic Safety   Free: 888-3274236
    Administration
400 7th St. SW
Washington, DC 20590
E-mail: webmaster@nhtsa.dot.gov
URL: http://www.nhtsa.dot.gov/cars/problems/recalls/recmmy1.cfm

Desc: If it feels like that new vehicle is more of a lemon than a luxury, then steer into this database and see if what you're driving has a history of manufacturing defects or recalls. The NHTSA recall database contains thorough and comprehensive information on vehicle models, manufacturing defects, and recalls to 1900 (although year-to-year coverage in the database doesn't begin until 1949). *Type:* Database.

Ohio Motorist

AAA Ohio Motorists Association
5700 Brecksville Rd.   Ph: (216)606-6700
Independence, OH 44131   Fax: (216)606-6710

Contact: William G. Johnson, Editor and Publisher, (216)606-6701; Philip T. Hartman, Managing Editor, (216)606-6703.

Desc: Automotive and travel news magazine (tabloid). *Type:* Periodical.

Old Cars—Car Club Special Issue

Krause Publications, Inc.
700 E. State St.   Ph: (715)445-2214
Iola, WI 54990   Free: 800-258-0929
    Fax: (715)445-4087
E-mail: info@krause.com; krause@krause.com
URL: http://www.krause.com; http://www.krause.com.

Contact: Brad Bowling, Editor.

Desc: About 1,500 car collector and fancier clubs; coverage includes Canada and United Kingdom. *Type:* Directory.

Packard Automobile Classics

84 Hoy Ave.   Ph: (732)738-7859
Fords, NJ 08863   Fax: (732)738-7625
E-mail: packard40@aol.com

Contact: Stuart Blond, Editor.

Desc: Individuals interested in preserving and restoring Packard automobiles, which were produced between 1899 and 1958. *Type:* Association.

Petersen's Circle Track

Petersen Publishing Co., L.L.C.
6420 Wilshire Blvd.   Ph: (323)782-2350
Los Angeles, CA 90048-5515   Fax: (323)782-2704
E-mail: ctrack@petersenpub.com.

Contact: Ralph V. Panico, Publisher; C.J. Baker, Publisher; Steve Zepezauer, Editor.

Desc: Magazine for racing enthusiasts. *Type:* Periodical.

Petersen's Custom Classic Trucks

Petersen Publishing Co., L.L.C.
6420 Wilshire Blvd.   Ph: (323)782-2350
Los Angeles, CA 90048-5515   Fax: (323)782-2704

Contact: Bob Carpenter, Editor, (213)782-2295, carpentr@petersenpub.com; De Ette Crow, Publisher, (213)782-2712, crowd@petersenpub.com; Andrea DeVuono, Ad Sales, (213)782-2757, fax: (213)782-2746, devuonoa@petersenpub.com; Sheri Arnett, Ad Sales, (213)782-2545, fax: (213)782-2746, arnetts@petersenpub.com.

Desc: Consumer publication covering vintage pickups, panels, and sedan deliveries. *Type:* Periodical.

PML

PML Consulting
PO Box 6010   Ph: (760)940-9170
Oceanside, CA 92058   Free: 888-928-9111
    Fax: (760)940-9170
E-mail: pmletter@aol.com.

Contact: Phil Van Buskirk, Editor and Publisher.

Desc: Includes Porsche-related articles, advertisements, and classified ads. Recurring features include a calendar of events, interviews, news of research, news of educational opportunities, book reviews, and notices of publications available. *Type:* Newsletter.

Pontiac-Oakland Club International

PO Box 9569   Ph: (941)750-9234
Bradenton, FL 34206   Fax: (941)747-1341
E-mail: smokesignalsmagazine@usa.net

Contact: Larry E. Kummer, Exec.Sec.

Desc: Persons interested in the history, restoration, and preservation of Pontiac and Oakland automobiles. Assists owners of Pontiac and Oakland automobiles with the restoration of their vehicles. Maintains staff of volunteer technical advisers. *Type:* Association.

Porsche Club of America

PO Box 30100   Ph: (703)922-9300
Alexandria, VA 22310   Fax: (703)922-9617
URL: http://www.pca.org

Contact: Ruth R. Harte, Exec.Sec.

Desc: Persons owning Porsche automobiles. *Type:* Association.

Recreation Vehicle Dealers Association of America

3930 University Dr., No. 100   Ph: (703)591-7130
Fairfax, VA 22030-2515   Fax: (703)591-0734
E-mail: info@rvda.com

Contact: Michael A. Molino, CAE.

Desc: Firms that have as their principal business the retail sale of recreation vehicles (commonly known as travel trailers, camping trailers, truck campers, and motor homes) and who maintain a permanent business establishment open for business and service on what they sell year-round. Provides information and liaison on government regulation of safety, trade, warranty, and franchising; fosters improved dealer-manufacturer relations; encourages communications among dealers and state and local RV associations. Offers education programs and training, and advertising, sales, and service information. *Type:* Association.

Recreation Vehicle Industry Association

1896 Preston White Dr.   Ph: (703)620-6003
PO Box 2999   Fax: (703)620-5071
Reston, VA 20195
E-mail: dhomefrost@rvia.org
URL: http://www.rvia.com

Contact: David J. Humphreys, Pres.

Desc: Recreation vehicle manufacturers, manufacturers' representatives, and suppliers of accessories and equipment used by manufacturers. Seeks to provide a unified recreation vehicle organization for manufacturers and component parts suppliers of motor homes, travel trailers, truck campers, folding camping trailers, and conversion vehicles. Promotes and represents the growth and concerns of the industry to federal and state government departments, the media, and the public. *Type:* Association.

Road & Track

Hachette Filipacchi Magazines, Inc.
1633 Broadway, 41st Fl.   Ph: (212)767-6000
New York, NY 10019   Fax: (212)989-4561
URL: http://www.roadandtrack.com.

Contact: Thos L. Bryant, Editor; Brian J. McMahon, Sr. VP and Group Publisher.

Desc: Automotive magazine. *Alt. Contact:* 1499 Monrovia Ave., Newport Beach, CA 92663; telephone: (949)720-5300; fax: (949)631-2757. *Type:* Periodical.

Rod & Custom Magazine

Rod & Custom
6420 Wilshire Blvd.   Ph: (323)782-2712
Los Angeles, CA 90048   Fax: (323)782-2223
E-mail: crowd@petersenpub.com.

Contact: Marie Crow DeEtte, Publisher, crowd@petersenpub.com.

Desc: Contemporary street rodding magazine. *Type:* Periodical.

Rolls-Royce Owners' Club

191 Hempt Rd.   Ph: (717)697-4671
Mechanicsburg, PA 17055
E-mail: rroc.hq@rroc.org
URL: http://www.rroc.org

Contact: Timothy E. Younes, Exec.Dir.

Desc: Persons interested in preserving and restoring automobiles produced by Rolls-Royce Ltd., Rolls-Royce Motors, Ltd., Rolls-Royce of America, and Bentley Motors (1931) Ltd. To exchange technical, historical, and general information. *Type:* Association.

RX-7 Club of America

Desc: Mazda RX-7 owners and rotary engine enthusiasts. Provides information on RX-7 cars, including maintenance, tuning, products, and accessories; shares knowledge and experience related to RX-7s and other rotary engines. Keeps members abreast of activities related to RX-7s and obtains discounts on automobile products and services for members. *Type:* Association.

Shelby American Automobile Club
PO Box 480   Ph: (508)696-8685
Chilmark, MA 02535   Fax: (508)696-8687
E-mail: saac@li.com

Contact: Kenneth Eber, Dir.

Desc: Owners and enthusiasts of Shelby G.T. 350 and
G.T. 500, Cobra, Tiger, and Ford G.T. automobiles.
Dedicated to the history, preservation, care, and enjoyment of the sports cars manufactured between 1962 and
1970 by Shelby American, Inc. *Type:* Association.

SHOPtalk
Automotive Engine Rebuilders Association
330 Lexington Dr.   Ph: (847)541-6550
Buffalo Grove, IL 60089-6998   Fax: (847)541-5808

Contact: William Gentes, Editor.

Desc: Recurring features include interviews, news of research, a calendar of events, reports of meetings, news of
educational opportunities, and notices of publications
available. *Type:* Newsletter.

Sport Truck
Petersen Publishing Co., L.L.C.
6420 Wilshire Blvd.   Ph: (323)782-2350
Los Angeles, CA 90048-5515   Fax: (323)782-2704

Contact: Joe Sebergandle, Publisher; Ralph V. Panico,
Publisher; Peter Clancey, Vice President; Peter MacGil-
livray, Editor.

Desc: Magazine covering a range of light-duty trucks, two-
and four-wheel drive; with an emphasis on performance.
Type: Periodical.

Sports Car Club of America
9033 E. Easter Pl.   Ph: (303)694-7222
Englewood, CO 80112   Fax: (303)694-7391
E-mail: admin@scca.org
URL: http://www.scca.org

Contact: Nicholas W. Craw, Pres.

Desc: Competition sports car owners and enthusiasts.
Sanctions professional FIA international events and amateur national and regional races. Sanctions World Challenge and Trans-Am Tour series; also conducts race driver
schools, rallies (professional European-style and precision
driving tests over a given route at an exact speed), gymkha-
nas (intricate driving maneuvers in a cleared area), and
concours d'elegance (rating cars by a correlation of age,
condition, and equipment of the vehicle). *Type:* Association.

Sports Car International
Ross Periodicals
42 Digital Dr., No. 5   Ph: (415)382-0580
Novato, CA 94949-5704   Fax: (415)382-0587

Contact: D. Randy Riggs, Editor, (415)382-2865; Tom
Toldrian, Publisher.

Desc: Magazine featuring articles and graphics for car enthusiasts. *Alt. Contact:* SCI PO Box 1529, Ross, CA
94957; telephone: (415)382-0580, (415)382-0587. *Type:*
Periodical.

Stock Car Racing
General Media
11 Penn Plaza, 12th Fl.   Ph: (212)702-6000
New York, NY 10001   Fax: (212)702-6262

Contact: Dick Berggren, Editor; Doug Gore, Technical
Editor.

Desc: Magazine covering stock car racing. *Alt. Contact:* 65
Parker St., Ste. 2, Newburyport, MA 01950; telephone:
(978)463-3787; fax: (978)463-3250. *Type:* Periodical.

Studebaker Driver's Club
PO Box 1040   Ph: 800-527-3452
Oswego, IL 60543
E-mail: studepubs@aol.com
URL: http://www.studebakerclubs.com/sdc/index.htm

Contact: Laurence Swanson, Publications Dir.

Desc: Owners of Studebaker automobiles and trucks. Attempts to aid in the restoration of, procure parts for, and
reproduce old instruction manuals of the Studebaker car.
Supports Studebaker Vehicle Museum in South Bend, IN.
Type: Association.

TRALA News Bulletin
Truck Renting and Leasing Association (TRALA)
1725 Duke St., Ste. 600   Ph: (703)299-9120
Alexandria, VA 22314-3457   Fax: (703)299-9115
URL: http://www.trala.org; http://www.trala.org.

Contact: Mary S. Payne, Editor, mpayne@trala.org.

Desc: Publishes news and activities of TRALA members
and suppliers. Addresses federal and state legislation and
regulatory issues affecting the industry. *Type:* Newsletter.

Truckin' Magazine
McMullen Argus Publishing, Inc.
774 S. Placentia Ave.   Ph: (714)939-2400
Placentia, CA 92870   Fax: (714)572-1864

Contact: Steve Stillwell, Editor; Thomas M. McMullen,
Publisher; John Nething, Advertising Mgr.

Desc: Magazine about custom vans, mini trucks, and pickups. *Type:* Periodical.

United Four-Wheel Drive Associations
4505 W. 700 S   Ph: (317)729-5862
Shelbyville, IN 46176-9678   Free: 800-448-3932
   Fax: (317)729-5930
E-mail: officemgr@ufwda.org
URL: http://www.ufwda.org

Contact: Dennis Noes, Pres.

Desc: Purpose is to work with land problems and establish
better communication between four-wheelers and the government. *Type:* Association.

United States Camaro Club
PO Box 608167   Ph: (407)880-1967
Orlando, FL 32860   Free: 800-CAM-
   AROS
   Fax: (407)880-1972

Contact: Ken Moorhead, Contact.

Desc: Owners and enthusiasts interested in Camaro automobiles built between 1967 and 1994. Works with technicians and car dealers on writing educational and technical
information concerning the Camaro. *Type:* Association.

Vintage Chevrolet Club of America
PO Box 5387   Ph: (714)633-1310
Orange, CA 92863-5387

Contact: Shirley Whitesell, Sec.

Desc: Persons interested in restoration and preservation of
vintage Chevrolet automobiles. Currently recognizes all
Chevrolet-built vehicles at least 15 years old. Sponsors
meets and car shows. *Type:* Association.

Vintage Triumph Register
8972 Deborah Ct. E.
Livonia, MI 48150
E-mail: vtr@autox.team.net
URL: http://www.vtr.org

Contact: Andy Mace, Pres.

Desc: Persons interested in preserving and enjoying Triumph automobiles. Purposes are to: provide advice and assistance for the maintenance, restoration, and preservation
of the marque; investigate parts and literature sources and
make them available to members; conduct research into
the history of the marque. *Type:* Association.

Westworld Saskatchewan
*Canada Wide Magazines & Communications
Ltd.*
4180 Lougheed Hwy., 4th Fl.   Ph: (604)299-7311
Burnaby, BC, Canada V5C 6A7   Fax: (604)299-9188
E-mail: circulation@canadawide.com

Contact: Peter Negge, Publisher; Rick McMorran, Sales
Mgr.; Pat Price, Editor.

Desc: The west coast's leading magazine serving the members of the CAA. *Type:* Periodical.

WPC Club
PO Box 3504   Ph: (616)375-5535
Kalamazoo, MI 49003-3504   Fax: (616)375-5535
E-mail: wpc@pacific.coast.net
URL: http://www.pacificcoast.net/~wpc/

Contact: Richard Bowman, Pres.

Desc: Individuals dedicated to the preservation, restoration, and enjoyment of Chrysler product cars. Conducts
social activities; houses library. *Type:* Association.

Automotive

Aftermarket Distribution

*Automotive Warehouse Distributors Association
(AWDA)*
9140 Ward Pkwy.   Ph: (816)444-3500
Kansas City, MO 64114   Fax: (816)444-0330
URL: http://www.awda.org.

Contact: Lisa Sorenson, Editor.

Desc: Provides Association members with news of developments affecting the warehouse distribution of automotive
parts and supplies. Supplies operations tips and articles on
marketing and sales techniques. *Type:* Newsletter.

AIADA News
*American International Automobile Dealers
Association (AIADA)*
99 Canal Center Plaza, Ste. 500   Ph: (703)519-7800
Alexandria, VA 22314-1538   Fax: (703)519-7810
E-mail: goaiada@aiada.org
URL: http://www.aiada.org.

Contact: Lori L. Barnes, Editor.

Desc: Offers international auto dealers current news on the
issues impacting the business. *Type:* Newsletter.

**American Automobile Manufacturers
Association**
1401 H St. NW, Ste. 900   Ph: (202)326-5500
Washington, DC 20005   Fax: (202)326-5567

Contact: Andrew H. Card, Jr., Pres. & CEO.

Desc: Trade association whose members are Chrysler Corporation, Ford Motor Company and General Motors. Reviews economic, social and public policies for their impact
on the motor vehicle industry and its customers. *Type:* Association.

**American International Automobile Dealers
Association**
99 Canal Center Plz., Ste. 500   Ph: (703)519-7800
Alexandria, VA 22314   Free: 800-GOA-IADA
   Fax: (703)519-7810
E-mail: goaiada@aiada.org
URL: http://www.aiada.org

Contact: Walter E. Huizenga, Pres.

Desc: Trade association for America's international name-
plate automobile dealerships and their employees who sell
and service automobiles manufactured in the U.S. and
abroad. Works to preserve a free market for international
automobiles in the U.S. *Type:* Association.

ARA Newsletter

Automotive Recyclers Association
3975 Fair Ridge Dr., Ste. 20   Ph: (703)385-1001
Terrace Level North   Free: 888-385-1005
Fairfax, VA 22033-2924   Fax: (703)385-1494
URL: http://www.autorecyc.org
Contact: Gail M. Schell, Editor, gail@autorecyc.org.
Desc: Reports on the activities and interests of the Association and its regional membership. Contains news of governmental affairs concerning the industry, scrap metal and used parts markets. *Type:* Newsletter.

Association of Automotive Aftermarket Distributors

5050 Poplar Ave., Ste. 2020   Ph: (901)682-9090
Memphis, TN 38157-2001   Free: 800-727-8112
   Fax: (901)682-9098
Contact: Michael Lambert, Pres.
Desc: Not-for-profit corporation owned by members who are independent automotive warehouse distributors. *Type:* Association.

Association of International Automobile Manufacturers

1001 19th St. N., Ste. 1200   Ph: (703)525-7788
Arlington, VA 22209   Fax: (703)525-8817
URL: http://www.aiam.org
Contact: Philip A. Hutchinson, Jr., Pres. & CEO.
Desc: Companies that manufacture automobiles or automotive equipment and that import into, or export to, the U.S. Purposes are: to act as a clearinghouse for information, especially with regard to proposed state and federal regulations in the automobile industry as they bear upon imported automobiles; to report proposed regulations by state or federal governments pertaining to equipment standards, licensing, and other matters affecting members. *Type:* Association.

Auto Digest

12377 Paiute Ct.   Ph: (541)923-3936
Powell Butte, OR 97753   Fax: (541)923-3936
E-mail: adigest@aol.com.
Contact: Bill Schaffer, President; Barbara Schaffer, Editor.
Desc: Distributes weekly automotive columns. *Alt. Contact:* 12377 Paiute Ct., Powell Butte, OR 97753; telephone: (541)923-3936; fax: (541)923-3936. *Type:* Periodical.

Auto Financing Update

Warren, Gorham & Lamont R.I.A. Group
90 Fifth Ave., 10th Fl.   Ph: (212)807-2193
New York, NY 10011   Free: 800-950-1216
   Fax: (212)337-4183
Contact: Margaret Murray, Editor.
Desc: Analyzes issues related to automobile financing and leasing, including the effect of new regulations on leasing and loan profitability, innovative marketing tactics, and automation advances. *Type:* Newsletter.

Auto Inc.

Automotive Service Association
PO Box 929   Ph: (817)283-6205
Bedford, TX 76095-0929   Free: 800-272-7467
   Fax: (817)685-0225
E-mail: asainfo@asashop.org; editor@asashop.org.
URL: http://www.asashop.org.
Contact: Ben McNamara, Editor, bmcnamara@asashop.org.
Desc: Carries automotive technical and management material, news of the automotive industry, information on relevant legislation, and news of the Automotive Service Association. *Type:* Newsletter.

Auto News Syndicate

198 Sea Pines Circle   Ph: (904)257-5186
Daytona Beach, FL 32114-1166
Contact: Don O'Reilly, Editor.
Desc: Distributes news on motor sports personalities and motor sports history. *Alt. Contact:* 198 Sea Pines Circle, Daytona Beach, FL 32114-1166; telephone: (904)257-5186. *Type:* Periodical.

Auto Page Syndicate

980 Macungie Ave.   Ph: (610)965-7861
Emmaus, PA 18049   Fax: (610)965-0510
E-mail: jaheilig@aol.com.
Contact: John Heilig, President.
Desc: Distributes Auto Page and other automotive columns. *Alt. Contact:* 980 Macungie Ave., Emmaus, PA 18049; telephone: (610)965-7861; fax: (610)965-0510. *Type:* Periodical.

The Auto Parts Report

Automotive Parts International
PO Box 5950   Ph: (202)857-8454
Bethesda, MD 20824
Desc: Provides news and information on auto parts. *Type:* Newsletter.

Auto Trim and Restyling News—Directory of Product Sources Issue

Bill Communications, Inc.
1115 Northmeadow Pkwy, Ste.   Ph: (404)252-8831
100   Free: 800-241-9034
Roswell, GA 30076   Fax: (404)252-4436
URL: http://www.svi-atl.com; http://www.atrn.com.
Contact: David Doucette, Editor, ddoucette@svi-atl.com.
Desc: Listings of major suppliers, manufacturers, distributors, and importers of interior and exterior trim and accessory products used in customizing cars, trucks, vans, and boats. *Type:* Directory.

Automotive Engine Rebuilders Association

330 Lexington Dr.   Ph: (847)541-6550
Buffalo Grove, IL 60089-6998   Fax: (847)541-5808
E-mail: info@aera.org
URL: http://www.aera.org
Contact: Barry E. Soltz, Pres.
Desc: Wholesalers of automotive replacement parts and equipment with machine shop operations; associate members are suppliers of parts, equipment, tools, and services to the rebuilder members. *Type:* Association.

Automotive Engineering

Society of Automotive Engineers, Inc. (SAE)
400 Commonwealth Dr.   Ph: (724)776-4841
Warrendale, PA 15096-0001   Fax: (724)776-5760
E-mail: magazines@sae.org.
URL: http://www.sae.org.
Contact: Daniel J. Holt, Editor, (724)772-7109, fax: (724)776-9765, holt@sae.org; Larry C. Schneider, Publisher, (724)772-8591, fax: (724)776-4026, larrys@sae.org.
Desc: Magazine for automotive engineers providing technical and design information. *Type:* Periodical.

Automotive Engineering International

SAE International
400 Commonwealth Dr.   Ph: (724)776-4841
Warrendale, PA 15096-0001   Fax: (724)776-4026
E-mail: sae@sae.org; magazines@sae.org.
Contact: Lawrence C. Schneider, Publisher, larrys@sae.org; Daniel J. Holt, Editor-in-Chief, holt@sae.org.
Desc: Magazine for automotive engineers providing technical and design information. *Type:* Periodical.

Automotive Engineering—SAE Membership Directory Issue

Society of Automotive Engineers, Inc. (SAE)
400 Commonwealth Dr.   Ph: (724)776-4841
Warrendale, PA 15096-0001   Fax: (724)776-5760
URL: http://www.sae.org.
Contact: Daniel J. Holt, Editor.
Desc: List of 65,000 members concerned with self-propelled ground, air, and space vehicles worldwide. *Type:* Directory.

Automotive Industries

Cahners Business Information
201 King of Prussia Rd.   Ph: (610)964-4000
Radnor, PA 19087-5114   Fax: (610)964-2915
E-mail: marketaccess@cahners.com
Contact: John McElroy, Editor, jmcelroy@chilton.net; James E. Henne, Publisher.
Desc: Magazine serving original equipment manufacturers in the automotive industry. *Alt. Contact:* Chilton Co. Automotive Industries 2600 Fisher Bldg., Detroit, MI 48202; telephone: (313)875-2090; fax: (313)875-8148. *Type:* Periodical.

Automotive Industry Action Group

26200 Lahser Rd., Ste. 200   Ph: (248)358-3003
Southfield, MI 48034   Fax: (248)358-3253
URL: http://www.aiag.org
Contact: Darlene Miller, Mng.Dir.
Desc: Corporations seeking to improve productivity in the automotive industry. Fosters cooperation among on-highway and off-highway vehicle manufacturers and suppliers. Disseminates information about current industry developments to members. *Type:* Association.

Automotive Information News Service

Forecast International Inc./DMS
22 Commerce Rd.   Ph: (203)426-0800
Newtown, CT 06470
E-mail: sales@forecast1.com
URL: http://www.forecast1.com
Desc: Contains more than 50,000 citations, with abstracts, to the worldwide periodical literature on the automotive, auto component, and engine industries. Covers new products, components, electronics, materials, labor relations, research and development, sales and marketing, manufacturing technology, finance, imports, exports, safety, noise, fuel consumption, and government policies. *Available:* The Dialog Corporation, DataStar; FIZ Technik (Fachinformationszentrum Technik e.V.). *Type:* Database.

Automotive Investor

Mary Ann Liebert, Inc. Publishers
2 Madison Ave.   Ph: (914)834-3100
Larchmont, NY 10538   Fax: (914)834-3771
E-mail: info@liebertpub.com
Contact: George Gillilard, Editor.
Desc: Contains financial information for vintage automobile traders. *Type:* Newsletter.

Automotive Litigation Reporter

Andrews Publications
175 Strafford Ave., Bldg. 4, Ste.   Ph: (610)225-0510
140   Free: 800-345-1101
Wayne, PA 19087   Fax: (610)225-0501
Contact: Nick Sullivan, Editor.
Desc: Covers significant federal and state lawsuits, including pretrial, trial, and appeal proceedings, settlements, and class action suits. Offers complete texts of key decisions and pleadings. *Type:* Newsletter.

Automotive News

Crain Communications, Inc.
1400 Woodbridge Ave.   Ph: (313)446-6000
Detroit, MI 48207-3187   Free: 800-678-9595
    Fax: (313)446-0383
E-mail: autonews@crain.com.
Contact: Peter Brown, Editor, (313)446-1600, pbrown@crain.com; Keith E. Crain, Publisher; Tony Merpi, Advertising Dir., (313)446-6030, fax: (313)446-8030, tmerpi@crain.com.
Desc: Tabloid reporting on all facets of the automotive and truck industry, as well as related businesses. *Type:* Periodical.

Automotive News

Crain Communications Inc.
740 N. Rush St.   Ph: (312)649-5200
Chicago, IL 60611
URL: http://www.crain.com
Desc: Contains the complete text of Automotive News, a weekly newspaper on the automotive industry. Covers news and analyses of production, dealers and dealerships, personnel, service management, law, sales, marketing, advertising, reviews of relevant books, and announcements and reviews of new models. *Available:* LEXIS-NEXIS, NEXIS; Dow Jones Interactive Publishing; Reuters Information Services Inc.; The Gale Group, InfoTrac Web; The Dialog Corporation, DIALOG; Bell & Howell Information and Learning; The Dialog Corporation, DataStar. *Type:* Database.

Automotive News—Market Data Book Issue

Crain Communications, Inc.
1400 Woodbridge Ave.   Ph: (313)446-6000
Detroit, MI 48207-3187   Free: 800-678-9595
    Fax: (313)446-0383
E-mail: autonews@crain.com.
Contact: Anne E. Wright, Editor.
Desc: Statistical review of auto industry. *Type:* Directory.

Automotive Parts and Accessories Association

4600 East-West Hwy., Ste. 300   Ph: (301)654-6664
Bethesda, MD 20814   Fax: (301)654-3299
Contact: Alfred Gasper, Pres.
Desc: Automotive parts and accessories retailers, distributors, manufacturers, and manufacturers' representatives. *Type:* Association.

Automotive Parts Rebuilders Association

4401 Fair Lakes Ct., Ste. 210   Ph: (703)968-2772
Fairfax, VA 22033-3848   Fax: (703)968-2878
E-mail: mail@apra.org
URL: http://www.apra.org
Contact: William C. Gager, Pres.
Desc: Rebuilders of automotive and truck parts (on exchange basis) and suppliers of component parts. *Type:* Association.

Automotive Plastics Newsletter

Market Search Inc.
2727 Holland Sylvania Rd., Ste.   Ph: (419)535-7899
A
Toledo, OH 43615
Desc: Reports on news of the automotive and plastics industry. Also includes forecasts. *Type:* Newsletter.

Automotive Service Association

1901 Airport Fwy.   Ph: (817)283-6205
PO Box 929   Free: 800-272-7467
Bedford, TX 76095-0929   Fax: (817)685-0225
E-mail: asainfo@asashop.org
URL: http://www.asashop.org
Contact: Walter F. Trapp, Pres.

Desc: Automotive service businesses including body, paint, and trim shops, engine rebuilders, radiator shops, brake and wheel alignment services, transmission shops, tune-up services, and air conditioning services; associate members are manufacturers and wholesalers of automotive parts, and the trade press. Represents independent business owners and managers before private agencies and national and state legislative bodies. *Type:* Association.

Automotive Service Industry Association

25 Northwest Point   Ph: (847)228-1310
Elk Grove Village, IL 60007-   Fax: (847)228-1510
1035
E-mail: asia@aftmktusa.org
URL: http://www.aftmkt.com/asia
Contact: Gene A. Gardner, Pres.
Desc: Professionals representing independent automotive wholesalers, warehouse distributors, heavy-duty vehicle and equipment parts distributors, automotive electrical service and supply wholesalers and distributors, manufacturers' representatives, and manufacturers and remanufacturers of replacement parts, tools, equipment, chemicals, refinishing materials, supplies, and accessories. *Type:* Association.

Automotive Warehouse Distributors Association

9140 Ward Pky.   Ph: (816)444-3500
Kansas City, MO 64114   Fax: (816)444-0330
Contact: Jack Creamer, Pres., Contact.
Desc: Warehouse distributors of automotive parts and supplies (215); manufacturers of automotive parts and suppliers (200); publishers (5). *Type:* Association.

Automotive Week

Automotive Week Publishing Co.
PO Box 3495   Ph: (201)694-7792
Wayne, NJ 07474-3495   Fax: (201)694-2817
E-mail: greensheet@auto-week.com.
URL: http://www.auto-week.com.
Contact: Chuck Laverty, Editor and Publisher.
Desc: Covers general market news of the automotive industry. Recurring features include job listings. *Type:* Newsletter.

AutoVantage OnLine

Cendant
Comp-U-Card Division
40 Oakview Dr.   Ph: (203)365-2000
Trumbull, CT 06611
URL: http://www.cendant.com
Desc: Contains descriptions and pricing information on new and used cars. Enables the user to view new and used car pricing summaries, car evaluations, and nationwide listings of some 15,000 service centers offering AutoVantage member discounts on services and repairs. *Available:* Dow Jones & Company, Inc.; Youvelle Renaissance Group, GEnie; Delphi Internet Services Corporation; America Online, Inc.; CompuServe Information Service; Prodigy Services Company, PRODIGY. *Type:* Database.

Body Language

Automotive Body Parts Association
PO Box 820689   Ph: (281)531-0809
Houston, TX 77282-0689   Free: 800-323-5832
    Fax: (281)531-9411
E-mail: autobpa@infohwy.com
URL: http://www.autobpa.com.
Contact: Stan Rodman, Editor.
Desc: Reports news impacting the aftermarket body parts industry, industry trends, and Association news. Recurring features include meeting reports and a calendar of events. *Type:* Newsletter.

Chek-Chart Service Bulletin

H. M. Gousha Co.
1515 Grandview Parkway   Ph: (414)739-2435
Sturtevant, WI 53177   Free: 800-662-6277
    Fax: (414)884-0760
Contact: Rick DuPuy, Editor.
Desc: Covers the service of domestic and imported cars and light trucks. Contains how-to articles, technical highlights of new vehicles, technical articles on fuels and lubricants, and analysis of new vehicle models. *Type:* Newsletter.

Chilton's Motor Age

Cahners Publishing
201 King of Prussia Rd.   Ph: (610)964-4000
Radnor, PA 19089   Fax: (610)964-4348
E-mail: tmolla@chilton.net.
URL: http://www.motorage.com.
Contact: Sarah Frankson, Publisher; Lisa Brody, Editor; Tony Molla, Advertising Mgr.
Desc: Magazine serving the automotive service industry. *Type:* Periodical.

DRI North American Light Vehicle Service

Standard & Poor's DRI
Global Automotive Group
24 Hartwell Ave.   Ph: (781)863-5100
Lexington, MA 02421-3158
URL: http://www.dri.mcgrawhill.com
Contact: Client Resource Center, (781)860-6527, fax: (781)860-6416.
Desc: Contains approximately 1500 monthly time series on the North American automotive industry including Canada, Mexico, and the United States. Provides information on new registrations by make and model, production by make, model, plant, and sales by make. *Available:* Standard & Poor's DRI, Global Automotive Group. *Type:* Database.

DRI World Car Industry Forecast Report

Standard & Poor's DRI
Global Automotive Group
24 Hartwell Ave.   Ph: (781)863-5100
Lexington, MA 02421-3158
URL: http://www.dri.mcgrawhill.com
Contact: Client Services, (617)860-6527, fax: (617)860-6465.
Desc: Contains more than 1500 annual forecasts on the supply, demand, and trade of passenger cars. Covers 29 manufacturers, 5 price and size segments, and 29 countries that are arranged by the following region: Western Europe--Austria, Belgium, Denmark, Finland, France, Germany, Greece, Ireland, Italy, the Netherlands, Norway, Portugal, Spain, Sweden, Switzerland, the United Kingdom; North America--Canada, the United States; Mexico; Asia Pacific--Australia, India, Japan, Malaysia, New Zealand, South Korea, Taiwan; South Africa; Latin America--Argentina, Brazil, Mexico. *Available:* Standard & Poor's DRI, Data Products Division. *Type:* Database.

DRI World Truck Forecast

Standard & Poor's DRI
Global Automotive Group
24 Hartwell Ave.   Ph: (781)863-5100
Lexington, MA 02421-3158
URL: http://www.dri.mcgrawhill.com
Contact: Client Resource Center, (781)860-6527, fax: (781)860-6465.
Desc: Contains more than 2100 annual forecasts for the commercial vehicle market in the following countries: Argentina, Austria, Belgium, Brazil, Canada, Denmark, France, Germany, Italy, India, Japan, Mexico, the Netherlands, Norway, South Korea, Spain, Sweden, Switzerland,

Turkey, the United Kingdom, and the United States. Subject coverage includes the European commercial vehicle market, such as new registrations by gross vehicle weight (GVW) class and country; new registrations by GVW class, manufacturer, and country; production by GVW class and country; production by GVW class and manufacturer; exports by GVW class and country; exports by GVW class and manufacturer. *Available:* Standard & Poor's DRI, Data Products Division. *Type:* Database.

Equipment and Tool Institute

1806 Johns Dr.
Glenview, IL 60025-1657
E-mail: dproven@aol.com
URL: http://www.etools.org
Contact: Donn R. Proven, Exec.Mgr.
Desc: Manufacturers of automotive service equipment and tools. *Type:* Association.

Ph: (847)729-8550
Fax: (847)729-3670

FDA Newsletter

Ford Dealers Alliance (FDA)
Dealers Alliance, Inc.
401 Hackensack Ave.
Continental Plaza
Hackensack, NJ 07601
Contact: Russell LaDue, Editor.
Desc: Covers factory-dealer relations focusing on factory encroachment on dealer equity in their own franchise. Discusses fleet subsidies, sales agreements, terminations, add points, warranty administration, and product distribution. *Type:* Newsletter.

Ph: (201)342-4542
Fax: (201)342-3997

Fleet Equipment—Management Resource Directory Issue

Maple Communications
134 W. Slade St.
Palatine, IL 60067-5031
E-mail: FEmaple@aol.com.
URL: http://www.truklink.com.
Contact: Tom Gelinas, Editor.
Desc: List of about 300 companies that offer training programs in truck maintenance; 40 software vendors who offer computerized maintenance management systems. *Type:* Directory.

Ph: (847)359-6100
Fax: (847)359-6420

Fleet Maintenance & Safety Report

Stamler Publishing Company
PO Box 3367
Branford, CT 06405-1967
Contact: Noelle Talmon, Managing Editor.
Desc: Provides advice on technology and strategies for effective maintenance of vehicle fleets. *Type:* Newsletter.

Ph: (203)488-9808
Free: 800-422-4121
Fax: (203)488-3129

Franchise Focus

International Midas Dealers Association
2841 Main
Kansas City, MO 64108
Contact: Sheila Curry, Editor, sheilac@robstan.com.
Desc: Informs member Midas franchisees of activities performed on their behalf by the Association. Reports on all negotiations between the Association and Midas International, including updates on Association committees, which meet with Midas officials on a regular basis. *Type:* Newsletter.

Ph: (816)472-6632
Fax: (816)472-7765

Gasoline and Automotive Service Dealers Association—Bulletin

Gasoline and Automotive Service Dealers Association (GASDA)
9520 Seaview Ave.
Brooklyn, NY 11236
E-mail: gasda@compuserve.com

Ph: (718)241-1111
Fax: (718)763-6589

Contact: Stanley M. Schuer, Editor.
Desc: Reports on industry news, laws, and regulations affecting service station operators in New York. Updates Association news and provides general tips on operation. *Type:* Newsletter.

The Good Guys

Automatic Transmission Rebuilders Association
2472 Eastman Ave., No. 23
Ventura, CA 93003
Desc: Contains news of the Association, its chapters, and Association programs. Lists service contract and insurance information, job listings, and personnel changes in the Association. *Type:* Newsletter.

Ph: (805)654-1700
Fax: (805)654-0970

Highway Vehicles Safety Database

Society of Automotive Engineers
Electronic Publishing Division
400 Commonwealth Dr.
Warrendale, PA 15096
E-mail: elecpubs@sae.org
URL: http://www.sae.org
Contact: Deb Tack, Marketing Communications Specialist, (724)772-7144, fax: (724)776-3087, elecpubs@sae.org.
Desc: Contains more than 35,000 document summaries (detailed abstracts and bibliographies) of Technology papers, journal articles, magazine articles, standards and specifications, Technology books, and research reports relating to highway vehicle safety. Includes extensive coverage of publications from the United States, Japan, Germany, Italy, the United Kingdom, France, Korea, Brazil, Canada, and other countries. *Available:* Society of Automotive Engineers, Electronic Publishing Division. *Type:* Database.

Ph: (724)772-7144

Inland Automobile Association

W. 1717 4th Ave.
Spokane, WA 99204
Contact: Stanley E. Miller, Pres. CEO.
Desc: Auto club providing members with travel services, including road maps, cruise and airline bookings, insurance, and emergency road assistance. *Type:* Association.

Ph: (509)358-6900
Fax: (509)358-6901

Inter-Industry Conference on Auto Collision Repair

1919 Maitland Dr.
Saginaw, MI 48609-9595
URL: http://www.i-car.com
Contact: Thomas M. Mack, Exec.VP.
Desc: Automobile manufacturers, collision repair shops, insurance companies, tool, equipment, and supply manufacturers, vocational institutions, and related industrial organizations such as auto dismantlers and recyclers, appraisers, and technical publishers. Works to improve the quality, safety, and efficiency of collision repair, especially on newly manufactured fuel-efficient automobiles, through education in the collision repair and insurance industries. Serves as a forum providing for communication among insurance claims representatives, body shop owners and managers, and interested individuals. *Type:* Association.

Ph: (517)781-6294
Free: 800-422-7872
Fax: (517)781-6296

International/New England Motorsports Syndication

84 Smith Ave.
Stoughton, MA 02072
Contact: Lou Modestino, Author.
Alt. Contact: 84 Smith Ave., Stoughton, MA 02072; telephone: (617)344-2837; fax: (617)344-2837. *Type:* Periodical.

Ph: (617)344-2837
Fax: (617)344-2837

International Union, United Automobile, Aerospace and Agricultural Implement Workers of America

8000 E. Jefferson
Detroit, MI 48214
Contact: Stephen P. Yokich, Pres.
Desc: AFL-CIO. *Type:* Association.

Ph: (313)926-5000
Fax: (313)823-6016

The Leaf

Service Specialists Association
4015 Marks Rd., Ste. 2B
Medina, OH 44256
Contact: Cara R. Giebner, Editor.
Desc: Provides news and information for the members of the Association who operate a "full-line spring service shop." Recurring features include news of research, news of members, letters to the editor, book reviews, and a calendar of events. *Type:* Newsletter.

Ph: (330)725-7160
Fax: (330)722-5638

Motor and Equipment Manufacturers Association

10 Laboratory Dr.
PO Box 13966
Research Triangle Park, NC
  27709-3966
URL: http://www.mema.org
Contact: Robert R. Miller, Pres.
Desc: Manufacturers of automotive and heavy-duty original equipment and aftermarket components, maintenance equipment, chemicals, accessories, refinishing supplies, tools, and service equipment united for research into all aspects of the automotive and heavy-duty markets. Provides manufacturer-oriented services and programs including marketing consultation for the automotive industry; federal and state legal, safety, and legislative representation and consultation; personnel services; manpower development workshops; international information. *Type:* Association.

Ph: (919)549-4800
Fax: (919)549-4824

Motor Magazine

Hearst Business Media Corp./IMN Division
5700 Crooks Rd.
PO Box 7032
Troy, MI 48007-7032
Contact: John Lyden, Editor, jlyden@motor.com; Richard Laimbeer, Publisher.
Desc: Magazine for the automotive aftermarket trade, professional mechanics and shop owners. *Type:* Periodical.

Ph: (313)828-7000
Free: 800-544-0929
Fax: (313)828-7008

Motor Matters

4635 Bailey Dr.
Wilmington, DE 19808
Contact: Bill McCormick, General Mgr.
Desc: Distributes automotive news. *Alt. Contact:* 4635 Bailey Dr., Wilmington, DE 19808; telephone: (302)998-1650. *Type:* Periodical.

Ph: (302)998-1650

National Association of Fleet Administrators

100 Wood Ave. S, Ste. 310
Iselin, NJ 08830
E-mail: info@nafa.org
URL: http://www.nafa.org
Contact: David P. Lefever, Exec.Dir.
Desc: Persons responsible for the administration of a motor vehicle fleet of 25 or more units for a firm not commercially engaged in the sale, rental, or lease of motor vehicles. *Type:* Association.

Ph: (732)494-8100
Fax: (732)494-6789

National Automobile Dealers Association

8400 Westpark Dr.
McLean, VA 22102
E-mail: nada@nada.org
URL: http://www.nada.org

Ph: (703)821-7000
Fax: (703)821-7075

Contact: Frank E. McCarthy, Pres.

Desc: Franchised new car and truck dealers. Provides representation for franchised new car and truck dealers in the areas of government, industry, and public affairs. *Type:* Association.

National Dragster
National Hot Rod Association
2035 Financial Way   Ph: (626)914-4761
Glendora, CA 91740   Fax: (626)335-6651
E-mail: nhra@goracing.com
Contact: Phil Burgess, Editor; Jeff Morton, Advertising Dir., fax: (626)914-9929; Adriane Pierson, Business Mgr., (626)914-9929; Cecily Chittick, Production Mgr.
Desc: Magazine. *Alt. Contact:* 2220 E. Alosta, Ste. 101, Glendora, CA 91740; telephone: (626)963-7695; fax: (626)335-4307. *Type:* Periodical.

National Independent Automobile Dealers Association
2521 Brown Blvd.   Ph: (817)640-3838
Arlington, TX 76006-5203 Fax: (817)649-5866
E-mail: rb@niada.com
URL: http://www.niada.com
Contact: R. B. Grisham, Exec.VP.
Desc: Individuals, companies, or corporations licensed by their states as dealers to buy and sell used motor vehicles; associate members are businesses related to or associated with the buying or selling of motor vehicles. Gathers and disseminates information relative to the used car industry; represents used car dealers before regulatory and legislative bodies; provides educational and other programs to help used car dealers understand their responsibilities; works for the betterment of the automobile industry. *Type:* Association.

National Institute for Automotive Service Excellence
13505 Dulles Technology Dr., Ph: (703)713-3800
    Ste. 2   Fax: (703)713-0727
Herndon, VA 20171-3421
URL: http://www.asecert.org
Contact: Ronald H. Weiner, Pres.
Desc: Governed by a 40-member board of directors selected from all sectors of the automotive service industry and from education, government, and consumer groups. Encourages and promotes the highest standards of automotive service in the public interest. *Type:* Association.

National Truck Equipment Association
37400 Hills Tech Dr.   Ph: (248)489-7090
Farmington Hills, MI 48331- Free: 800-441-NTEA
    3414   Fax: (248)489-8590
E-mail: info@ntea.com
URL: http://www.ntea.com
Contact: James D. Carney, Exec.Dir.
Desc: A trade group for commercial truck, truck body, truck equipment, trailer and accessory manufacturers and distributors. *Type:* Association.

NTDRA Dealer News—Who's Who Directory Issue
National Tire Dealers & Retreaders Association (NTDRA)
1250 I St., NW, Ste. 400 Ph: (202)789-2300
Washington, DC 20005   Free: 800-876-8372
                          Fax: (202)682-3999
Contact: C. D. Hylton, III, Editor.
Desc: About 4,008 tire dealers and retreaders, suppliers of related products and services, private brand groups, and local associations that are members of the National Tire Dealers and Retreaders Association; retread plants that have been rated "A" by the association. *Type:* Directory.

Oregon Motorist
AAA Oregon
600 SW Market   Ph: (503)222-6729
Portland, OR 97201   Fax: (503)222-6756
E-mail: feedback@aaaoregon.com
Contact: Anne O'Ryan, Editor, aoryan@transport.com.
Desc: Covers motoring, travel, and highways legislation. *Type:* Newsletter.

Pacheco Automotive News Service
PO Box 6691   Ph: (510)228-7821
Concord, CA 94524   Fax: (510)228-1410
Contact: Lawrence R. Hagin, Pres./Gen. Mgr.
Desc: Distributes automotive features. *Alt. Contact:* PO Box 6691, Concord, CA 94524; telephone: (510)228-7821; fax: (510)228-1410. *Type:* Periodical.

PAR & PWA Newsletter
Performance Automotive Retailer (PAR)
Performance Warehouse Association (PWA)
21311 Hawthorne Blvd., Ste. Ph: (310)543-1523
    103   Fax: (310)543-9623
Torrance, CA 90503
Contact: John Towle, Editor.
Desc: Provides news for the high performance/aftermarket retailer. Features information on new products, customer service techniques, and upcoming events. *Type:* Newsletter.

Pennsylvania American Automobile Association Federation
600 N. 3rd St.   Ph: (717)238-7192
PO Box 2865   Fax: (717)238-6574
Harrisburg, PA 17105
Contact: Ted Leonard, Gen.Mgr.
Desc: Members of Automobile Association of America clubs in Pennsylvania. Works to inform and educate travelers and motorists. *Type:* Association.

Petersen's 4 Wheel & Off Road
Petersen Publishing Co., L.L.C.
6420 Wilshire Blvd.   Ph: (323)782-2350
Los Angeles, CA 90048-5515 Fax: (323)782-2704
Contact: John Dianna, Executive Publisher; Jim Ryan, Publisher.
Desc: Automotive magazine. *Type:* Periodical.

Professional Tool & Equipment News
Professional Tool & Equipment News, Inc.
25401 Cabot Rd., Ste. 209 Ph: (949)830-7520
Laguna Hills, CA 92653   Fax: (949)830-7523
URL: http://www.pten.com.
Contact: Tom Carruthers, Editor, (708)564-0677, fax: (708)564-2708; Rudy Wolf, Publisher; Robert Swenson, Assoc. Publisher, (847)981-0007, fax: (847)981-0025; Anthony Ross, Managing Editor, anton@pten.com.
Desc: Magazine for automotive shop owners and technicians. Reports on new tools and equipment. *Type:* Periodical.

Radiator Reporter
Skyline Publishing Company
PO Box 599   Ph: (708)485-6015
Brookfield, IL 60513-0599 Free: 800-914-2599
                          Fax: (708)485-4237
E-mail: info@radhotline.com
Contact: Ralph McDarmont, Editor.
Desc: Provides news on automotive and industrial radiator repair industry. Includes repair tips, parts sources, and a commentary. *Type:* Newsletter.

SAE Global Mobility Database®
Society of Automotive Engineers
Electronic Publishing Division
400 Commonwealth Dr.   Ph: (724)772-7144
Warrendale, PA 15096
E-mail: elecpubs@sae.org
URL: http://www.sae.org
Contact: Deb Tack, Marketing Communications Specialist, (724)772-7144, fax: (724)776-3087, elecpubs@sae.org.
Desc: Contains more than 99,000 document summaries (detailed abstracts and bibliographies) of technical papers, journal articles, magazine articles, standards and specifications, Technology books, and research reports from authoritative sources. Provides extensive coverage of publications from the United States, Japan, Germany, Italy, the United Kingdom, France, Korea, Brazil, Canada, and other countries. *Available:* Society of Automotive Engineers, Electronic Publishing Division; Questel • Orbit; The Dialog Corporation, DataStar; STN International; European Information Network Services (EINS). *Type:* Database.

SAE International
400 Commonwealth Dr.   Ph: (412)776-4841
Warrendale, PA 15096-0001 Fax: (412)776-5760
URL: http://www.sae.org
Contact: Max E. Rumbaugh, Jr., Exec.VP.
Desc: Collects and disseminates information on mobility technology. Fosters information exchange among the worldwide automotive and aerospace communities. Conducts educational programs. *Type:* Association.

SEMA News
Specialty Equipment Market Association (SEMA)
PO Box 4910   Ph: (909)396-0289
Diamond Bar, CA 91765-0910 Fax: (909)860-0184
URL: http://www.sema.org;   http://www.sema.org/semanews/.
Contact: William Groak, Editor, billg@sema.org; Nora McElfish, Editor.
Desc: Covers the automotive specialty, performance equipment, and accessory sectors. Recurring features include news of government and legislative actions, new products, international markets, and member and Association activities. *Type:* Newsletter.

SMMA Newsletter
SMMA - Small Motors & Motion Association
PO Box 378   Ph: (508)655-4409
Sherborn, MA 01770   Fax: (508)651-3920
Contact: Elizabeth Bevington-Chambers, Editor.
Desc: Disseminates information on Association projects and meetings, and discusses general industry news. Recurring features include news of members and a calendar of events. *Type:* Newsletter.

Specialty Equipment Market Association
PO Box 4910   Ph: (909)396-0289
Diamond Bar, CA 91765-0910 Fax: (909)860-0184
E-mail: sema@sema.org
URL: http://www.sema.org
Contact: Charles R. Blum, Pres.
Desc: Manufacturers, retailers, sales representatives, distributors, motorsports sanctioning groups, and other firms related to the automotive high performance and custom vehicle industry. Represents the industry to governmental agencies and consumer groups. *Type:* Association.

Specialty Vehicle Institute of America
2 Jenner St., Ste. 150   Ph: (714)727-3727
Irvine, CA 92618   Free: 800-887-2887
   Fax: (714)727-4216
Contact: Tim Buche, Pres.
Desc: Trade association representing U.S. distributors of all-terrain vehicles (ATVs). Fosters and promotes safe and responsible use of specialty vehicles. *Type:* Association.

Stahl Headers Newsletter
Stahl Headers
1515 Mount Rose Ave.   Ph: (717)846-1632
York, PA 17403   Fax: (717)854-9486
Contact: Jere Stahl, Editor, jfs@stahlheaders.com.
Desc: Combines the editor's experience with advice and technical insights from the country's leading engine builders to provide the professional with a sounding board for engine-related information. *Type:* Newsletter.

SuperAutomotive Service
Irving-Cloud Publishing Co.
379 Hollow Hill Dr.   Ph: (847)487-7010
Wauconda, IL 60084   Fax: (847)487-5589
Contact: Martin Schultz, Editor; Taylor L. Kennedy, Jr., Publisher; Charles S. Wilson, IV, Sales and Mktg. Dir.
Desc: Trade magazine covering the technical aspects of normal service station/tire dealership/garage repair and service operations. *Type:* Periodical.

Syndicated Automotive News
131 Norlyn Dr.   Ph: (510)935-0809
Walnut Creek, CA 94596-4257   Fax: (510)935-0809
Contact: Bill Russ, Editor; Carey Russ, Asst. Ed.
Desc: Distributes automotive-related features and new car reviews. *Alt. Contact:* 131 Norlyn Dr., Walnut Creek, CA 94596-4257; telephone: (510)935-0809; fax: (510)935-0809. *Type:* Periodical.

TARA News & Topics
Truck-frame & Axle Repair Association (TARA)
7 F Plaza Trinidad (Villages)   Ph: (908)577-8485
Freehold, NJ 07728
Contact: Mr. Silvie Licitra, Editor.
Desc: Deals with repair and modification of heavy-duty truck, trailer, bus, coach, and off-road equipment. Provides news of the Association and covers topics concerning business management, economics, and fleet and owner-operator organizations. *Type:* Newsletter.

Tel-"U"-Gram
Gasoline and Automotive Service Dealers Association (GASDA)
9520 Seaview Ave.   Ph: (718)241-1111
Brooklyn, NY 11236   Fax: (718)763-6589
E-mail: gasda@compuserve.com
Contact: Stanley M. Schuer, Editor.
Desc: Serves members with industry news, updates on laws and regulations, and notices of Association events. Recurring features include news of research, a calendar of events, reports of meetings, and news of educational opportunities. *Type:* Newsletter.

Turbo & Hi-Tech Performance
Illustrated Graphic Communications
9887 Hamilton Ave.   Ph: (714)962-7795
Huntington Beach, CA 92646-8012   Fax: (714)965-2268
E-mail: turbo@turbomagazine.com.
URL: http://www.turbomagazine.com.
Contact: Kipp E. Kington, Publisher; Debbie Perez, Business Mgr.
Desc: Magazine covering automotive performance and engineering. *Type:* Periodical.

Vibration Institute
6262 S. Kingery Hwy., Ste. 212   Ph: (630)654-2254
Willowbrook, IL 60514   Fax: (630)654-2271
E-mail: vibinst@anet-chi.com
URL: http://www.vibinst.org
Contact: Dr. Ronald L. Eshleman, Dir.
Desc: Technicians and engineers (1400); manufacturers and users of mechanical equipment (140). Promotes the exchange of practical information about vibration technology. Organizes seminars on specific topics that include: balancing, rotor/bearing dynamics, torsional vibrations, turbomachinery blading, and shaft vibrations. *Type:* Association.

Ward's Auto World
Ward's Communications
3000 Town Center, Ste. 2750   Ph: (248)357-0800
Southfield, MI 48075-1212   Fax: (248)357-0810
E-mail: wards@wardsauto.com.
URL: http://www.wardsauto.com; http://www.wardsauto.com.
Contact: David C. Smith, Editor-in-Chief; Roger K. Powers, Publisher; Michael A. Arnholt, Managing Editor.
Desc: Business magazine containing news and analysis for middle and upper management within all disciplines of the automotive OEM. *Type:* Periodical.

Ward's Automotive International
Ward's Communications
3000 Town Center, Ste. 2750   Ph: (248)357-0800
Southfield, MI 48075-1212   Fax: (248)357-0810
URL: http://www.wardsauto.com; http://www.wardsauto.com.
Contact: David E. Zoia, Editor.
Desc: Provides a global view of news, technological developments, and trends in the automotive industry worldwide. Remarks: Subscription includes an eight-page, mid-month update and annual wall chart on interrelationships among car makers. *Type:* Newsletter.

Ward's Automotive Reports
Ward's Communications
3000 Town Center, Ste. 2750   Ph: (248)357-0800
Southfield, MI 48075-1212   Fax: (248)357-0810
URL: http://www.wardsauto.com
Contact: David E. Zoia, Editor.
Desc: Reports "vital statistical information and exclusive news of critical interest" to the automotive industry. Remarks: Subscription includes indexes and Ward's Automotive Yearbook. *Type:* Newsletter.

Ward's Engine and Vehicle Technology Update
Ward's Communications
3000 Town Center, Ste. 2750   Ph: (248)357-0800
Southfield, MI 48075-1212   Fax: (248)357-0810
URL: http://www.wardsauto.com; http://www.wardsauto.com.
Contact: David E. Zoia, Editor.
Desc: Reports on and monitors all engine and transmission and other technological developments relating to cars and trucks worldwide. Also discusses marketing and business strategies. *Type:* Newsletter.

Westworld British Columbia
Canada Wide Magazines & Communications Ltd.
4180 Lougheed Hwy., 4th Fl.   Ph: (604)299-7311
Burnaby, BC, Canada V5C 6A7   Fax: (604)299-9188
E-mail: circulation@canadawide.com
Contact: Peter Legge, Publisher; Neil Soper, Publisher; Pat Price, Editor; Rick McMorran, Sales Mgr.
Desc: Consumer magazine for members of the British Columbia Automobile Assn. *Type:* Periodical.

Aviation
The Air Charter Guide
Boston Aviation Services
PO Box 382387   Ph: (617)547-5811
Cambridge, MA 02238-2387   Fax: (617)868-5335
E-mail: acg@guides.com; editorial@guides.com.
URL: http://www.guides.com/acg.
Contact: Andy Henderson, Editor.
Desc: All worldwide operators of aircraft available for on-demand air charter. *Type:* Directory.

Air & Space Smithsonian
Air & Space Smithsonian
AIAA Bldg.   Ph: (202)287-3733
370 L'Enfant Promenade SW,   Fax: (202)287-3163
10th Fl.
Washington, DC 20024-2518
E-mail: airspacedt@aol.com.
URL: http://www.airspacemag.com/.
Contact: George C. Larson, Editor; Ron Walker, Publisher; Louis Kolenda, Advertising Dir.
Desc: Aviation and aerospace magazine. *Alt. Contact:* 901 D St. SW, 10th Fl., Washington, DC 20024; telephone: (202)287-3733; fax: (202)287-3163. *Type:* Periodical.

Aircraft Owners and Pilots Association
421 Aviation Way   Ph: (301)695-2000
Frederick, MD 21701   Free: 800-USA-AOPA
   Fax: (301)695-2375
E-mail: aopahq@aopa.org
URL: http://www.aopa.org
Contact: Phil Boyer, Pres.
Desc: Represents the interests of general aviation pilots and aircraft owners the segment encompassing 187,000 aircraft and 616000 pilots not engaged in airline and military flying. *Type:* Association.

Airline Financial News
Phillips Business Information, Inc.
1201 Seven Locks Rd., Ste. 300   Ph: (301)340-1520
Potomac, MD 20854   Free: 888-707-5809
   Fax: (301)340-3847
E-mail: clientservices.pbi@phillips.com
URL: http://www.aviationtoday.com.
Contact: David Evans, Managing Editor, devans@phillips.com; Steven Lott, Editor, slott@phillips.com.
Desc: Reports on financial aspects of the world airline industry. Remarks: Also available online and via e-mail. *Type:* Newsletter.

Airline Marketing News
Phillips Business Information, Inc.
1201 Seven Locks Rd., Ste. 300   Ph: (301)340-1520
Potomac, MD 20854   Free: 888-707-5809
   Fax: (301)340-3847
E-mail: clientservices.pbi@phillips.com; ggraham@phillips.com; clientservices.pbi@phillips.com.
URL: http://www.phillips.com.
Contact: Heather Montgomery, Editor; Ellen H. Stuhlmann, Publisher.
Desc: Provides information about airline marketing. Topics include frequent flyer programs, news, advertising, and marketing programs. *Type:* Newsletter.

Air Line Pilots Association
535 Herndon Pkwy.   Ph: (703)689-2270
Herndon, VA 20170   Fax: (703)689-4370
URL: http://www.alpa.org
Contact: Capt. Duane E. Woerth, Pres.
Desc: Collective bargaining agent for air line pilots. *Type:* Association.

Allied Pilots Association

14600 Trinity Blvd. No. 500   Ph: (972)988-3188
Fort Worth, TX 76155-2512   Free: 800-323-1470
                                 Fax: (972)606-5668
Contact: Gregg Overman, Dir. of Communications.
Desc: Independent group originating from the Air Line Pilots Association . Collective bargaining agent for the pilots of American Airlines. *Type:* Association.

AOPA Pilot

AOPA Pilot
421 Aviation Way   Ph: (301)695-2350
Frederick, MD 21701-4756   Fax: (301)695-2180
E-mail: acpahq@aopa.org.
URL: http://www.aopa.org.
Contact: Thomas B. Haines, Editor and Publisher; Denis C. Beran, Advertising Mgr.
Desc: Magazine for general aviation pilots and aircraft owners who are members of the Aircraft Owners and Pilots Assn. Articles are tailored to address the special informational requirements of both recreational and business pilots. *Type:* Periodical.

Association of Flight Attendants

1275 K Street NW, Ste. 500   Ph: (202)712-9799
Washington, DC 20005-4090   Free: 800-424-2401
                                 Fax: (202)712-9798
E-mail: afatalk@afanet.org
URL: http://www.flightattendant-afa.org
Contact: Patricia Friend, Pres.
Desc: Airline flight attendants. united for contract representation, arbitration, communicatiions, government affairs, and membership services. *Type:* Association.

Association of Professional Flight Attendants

1004 W. Euless Rd.   Ph: (817)540-0108
Euless, TX 76040   Free: 800-395-2732
                                 Fax: (817)540-2077
E-mail: apfa@apfa.org
URL: http://www.apfa.org
Contact: Kitty Solder, Sec.
Desc: Flight attendants. Seeks to obtain optimal conditions of employment for members. *Type:* Association.

ATC Market Report

The McGraw-Hill Companies
Aviation Week Group
1200 G St. NW, Ste. 200   Ph: (202)383-2403
Washington, DC 20005-3802   Free: 800-752-4959
                                 Fax: (202)383-7956
E-mail: awgnews@mcgraw-hill.com
URL: http://www.awgnews.com.
Contact: Ed Hazelwood, Editor, edhazelwood@interramp.com; edhazelwood@mindspring.com.
Desc: Provides business intelligence on the worldwide air traffic control market. Recurring features include interviews, news of research, a calendar of events, and reports of meetings. *Type:* Newsletter.

Aviation Enthusiast Corner

City University of New York, Brooklyn College
Brooklyn, NY 11210
E-mail: air-info@brooklyn.cuny.edu
URL: http://aeroweb.brooklyn.cuny.edu/
Desc: The Aviation Enthusiast Corner contains information on aviation-related hobbies, including aircraft specifications organized by type, an aviation museum locator, an index of aircraft manufacturers, air show locations, performer info, and performance dates. Numerous links to other aviation and aerospace resources on the Internet round out this site. *Type:* Database.

Aviation History

Primedia History Group
741 Miller Dr., Ste. D-2   Ph: (703)771-9400
Leesburg, VA 20175   Fax: (703)779-8345
URL: http://www.thehistorynet.com.
Contact: Art Sanfelici, Editor; Taura Varda, Advertising Dir.
Desc: Consumer magazine covering aviation history. *Type:* Periodical.

Aviation Medical Bulletin

Harvey W. Watt & Co., Inc.
PO Box 20787   Ph: (404)767-7501
Atlanta, GA 30320   Free: 800-241-6103
                                 Fax: (404)761-8326
Contact: Bill Maness, Editor.
Desc: Provides the latest medical information for those working in the aviation field. Recurring features include news of research. *Type:* Newsletter.

Aviation Telephone Directory

Aviation Telephone Directory
515 W. Lambert Rd., Ste. D   Ph: (714)990-5115
Brea, CA 92821   Free: 800-252-5115
                                 Fax: (714)990-4385
E-mail: atdpub@aol.com
URL: http://www.avteldir.com.
Contact: Jodi Sacco, President.
Desc: In two regional editions, about 34,000 suppliers of aviation products and services; airports and fixed-base operations (FBO's) or port firms. Eastern & Southwestern edition covers Alabama, Arkansas, Connecticut, Florida, Georgia, Kentucky, Louisiana, Maine, Maryland, Massachusetts, Mississippi, New Mexico, New Hampshire, New Jersey, New York, North Carolina, Oklahoma, Pennsylvania, South Carolina, Tennessee, Texas, Vermont, Virginia, and West Virginia; Western and North Central edition covers Alaska, Arizona, California, Colorado, Hawaii, Idaho, Illinois, Indiana, Iowa, Kansas, Michigan, Minnesota, Missouri, Montana, Nebraska, Nevada, Ohio, Oregon, North Dakota, South Dakota, Utah, Washington, Wisconsin, and Wyoming. *Type:* Directory.

Aviation Week & Space Technology

McGraw-Hill, Inc.
2 Penn Plaza   Ph: (212)904-2000
New York, NY 10121   Free: 800-223-6180
                                 Fax: (212)904-6068
URL: http://www.mcgraw-hill.com; http://www.awgnet.com.
Contact: David North, Editor, (202)383-2300, fax: (202)383-2347; Kenneth E. Gazzola, VP/Publisher, (212)904-3451, fax: (212)904-3797.
Desc: Magazine serving the aviation and aerospace market worldwide. *Type:* Periodical.

AVLINE

U.S. National Library of Medicine (NLM)
MEDLARS Management Section
8600 Rockville Pike   Ph: (301)496-3147
Bethesda, MD 20894
URL: http://www.sis.nlm.nih.gov/dirline
Desc: Contains full bibliographic descriptions of more than 21,000 audiovisual and other non-print teaching materials cataloged by U.S. National Library of Medicine (NLM). *Type:* Database.

Brandeis University

Ashton Graybiel Spatial Orientation Lab

415 South St.   Ph: (781)736-2033
MS033   Fax: (781)736-2031
Waltham, MA 02254-9110
E-mail: lackner@binah.cc.brandeis.edu

URL: http://www.brandeis.edu
Contact: James R. Lackner, Dir.
Desc: Human spatial orientation, effects of gravity on vestibulo-ocular reflex, the role of vestibular and cervical sensory and motor activity in hand movement control, oculomotor stability, and effects of different G levels. Also studies human sensorimotor adaptation to unusual force environments. *Type:* Research center.

Brassey's World Aircraft & Systems Directory

Batsford Brassey, Inc.
4380 MacArthur Blvd., 2nd Fl.   Ph: (202)260-0602
Washington, DC 20007   Free: 800-428-5331
                                 Fax: (202)260-0701
E-mail: comments@batsfordbrassey.com; info@batsford.com
URL: http://www.batsford.com
Contact: Michael Taylor, Editor.
Desc: Technical information for aircrafts, and related subjects, including aircraft engines, missiles, and radar systems. *Type:* Directory.

Business Commercial Aviation Planning & Purchasing Handbook

Aviation Week Group
McGraw-Hill, Inc.
4 International Dr.   Ph: (914)939-0300
Rye Brook, NY 10573   Fax: (914)939-1283
Contact: Richard N. Aarons, Editor.
Desc: Directory of airframe and avionics manufacturers, and suppliers of related products and services. *Type:* Directory.

Civil Air Patrol

Bldg. 714   Ph: (334)953-7593
Maxwell AFB, AL 36112-6332   Fax: (334)953-4245
URL: http://www.cap.af.mil
Contact: Col. Paul Albano, Exec. Dir.
Desc: Civilian volunteer auxiliary of the United States Air Force, with membership divided between senior members (35,000) and business members and cadets ranging from 6th grade through age 21 (25,000). Approximately 8,000 members are FAA licensed pilots, flying four out of every five hours on search and rescue missions directed by the Air Force Rescue Coordination Center. Members participate in rescue work during national disasters and cooperate with state and federal authorities in civil defense planning. *Type:* Association.

Embry-Riddle Aeronautical University

Embry-Riddle Aeronautical University
600 S. Clyde Morris Blvd.   Ph: (904)226-6910
Daytona Beach, FL 32114-3900   Free: 800-222-3728
E-mail: admit@db.erau.edu
URL: http://www.db.erau.edu/
Contact: Mike Hamende, Web Admin., hamendem@cts.db.erau.edu.
Desc: At first glance, it is not apparent that Embry-Riddle Aeronautical University (ERAU) has main and extended campuses in Arizona and Europe. However, browsing the site yields cross-referenced data that clarifies any misconception a visitor might have. *Type:* Database.

Flight Physician

Civil Aviation Medical Association
Box 23864   Ph: (405)840-0199
Oklahoma City, OK 73123-   Fax: (405)848-1053
2864
E-mail: jimlharris@aol.com
URL: http://www.civilavmed.com.
Contact: H. Stacy Vereen, M.D., Contact, stacyv@earthlink.net.
Desc: Provides current information on each medical specialty as it applies to aviation. Recurring features include book reviews, news of members, and a calendar of events. *Type:* Newsletter.

Flying

Hachette Filipacchi Magazines, Inc.
1633 Broadway, 41st Fl.   Ph: (212)767-6000
New York, NY 10019   Fax: (212)989-4561
Contact: J. Mac McClellan, Editor-in-Chief; Richard Koenig, Publisher; Wayne Lincourt.
Desc: General aviation magazine. *Alt. Contact:* 500 West Putnam Ave., Greenwich, CT 06830; telephone: (203)622-2700; fax: (203)622-2725. *Type:* Periodical.

Helicopter Association International

1635 Prince St.   Ph: (703)683-4646
Alexandria, VA 22314-2818   Fax: (703)683-4745
E-mail: webmanager@rotor.com
URL: http://www.ROTOR.com
Contact: Roy D. Resauage, Jr., Pres.
Desc: Owners, operators, helicopter enthusiasts, and affiliated companies in the civil helicopter industry. Receives and disseminates information concerning the use, operation, hiring, contracting, and leasing of helicopters. *Type:* Association.

International Association of Machinists and Aerospace Workers

9000 Machinists Pl.   Ph: (301)967-4500
Upper Marlboro, MD 20772   Fax: (301)967-4595
URL: http://www.iamaw.org/
Contact: R. Thomas Buffenbarger, Contact.
Desc: AFL-CIO. *Type:* Association.

International Flight Attendants Association

P.R. Miller
2314 Old New Windsor Pke.   Ph: (410)635-2025
New Windsor, MD 21776
Contact: P. R. Miller, U.S. Rep.
Desc: Flight attendants and flight attendant associations and unions. Strengthens bonds of solidarity among flight attendants through consultation and industry-related projects. *Type:* Association.

National Air Traffic Controllers Association

1150 17th St. NW, Ste. 701   Ph: (202)223-2900
Washington, DC 20036   Fax: (202)659-3991
E-mail: national@natca.org
URL: http://www.natca.org
Contact: Michael McNally, Pres.
Desc: Independent union. Represents U.S. air traffic controllers within the aviation industry and before the government. *Type:* Association.

PAMA News

Professional Aviation Maintenance Association, Inc. (PAMA)
636 Eye St. NW, Ste. 300   Ph: (202)216-9220
Washington, DC 20001-3736   Fax: (202)216-9224
E-mail: hq@pama.org
URL: http://www.pama.org.
Contact: Anne Culver, Editor, (202)216-2369, annec@pama.org.
Desc: Devoted to raising the professional level of the aircraft maintenance technician. Provides practical articles on aviation service problems, discussions of safety standards and procedures, and reports on developments in regulations. *Type:* Newsletter.

Professional Airways Systems Specialists

1150 17th St. NW, Ste. 702   Ph: (202)293-7277
Washington, DC 20036-4603   Fax: (202)293-7727
Contact: Mike Fanfalone, Pres.
Desc: Systems specialists and aviation safety inspectors employed by the Federal Aviation Administration whose responsibilities include legal certification, systems management, installation and maintenance of the National Airspace System and oversight of general and commercial aviation industries. Works to: promote and improve the profession and working conditions of systems specialists and inspectors; preserve and develop safety standards of the air traffic system within the U.S. and its territories. *Type:* Association.

Professional Aviation Maintenance Association

636 Eye St. NW, Ste. 300   Ph: (202)216-9220
Washington, DC 20001-3736   Fax: (202)216-9224
E-mail: hq@pama.org
URL: http://www.pama.org
Contact: Stan Mackiewicz, Pres.
Desc: Airframe and powerplant (A & P) technicians and aviation industry-related companies. Strives to increase the professionalism of the individual aviation technician through greater technical knowledge and better understanding of safety requirements. *Type:* Association.

Rotorbreeze

Bell Helicopter Textron, Inc.
PO Box 482   Ph: (817)280-3847
Fort Worth, TX 76101   Fax: (817)280-3224
Contact: Susan Green, Editor.
Desc: Features coverage of Bell Helicopter products and parts. Contains information on new models, contract bids, suspected defects and recalls, technical specifications, warranties, available spare parts, training, and related publications and safety documents. *Type:* Newsletter.

Seaplane Pilots Association—Water Landing Directory

Seaplane Pilots Association
421 Aviation Way   Ph: (301)695-2083
Frederick, MD 21701   Fax: (301)695-2375
E-mail: spa@aopa.org
URL: http://www.seaplanes.org.
Contact: Robert Richardson, Editor.
Desc: Over 400 licensed seaplane bases, as well as non-licensed landing and refueling spots; coverage includes Canada. *Type:* Directory.

Sport Aviation

Experimental Aircraft Association, Inc. (EAA)
PO Box 3086   Ph: (920)426-4800
Oshkosh, WI 54903-3086   Free: 800-843-8612
                    Fax: (920)426-4828
E-mail: editorial@eaa.org.
URL: http://www.eaa.org.
Contact: Jack Cox, Editor, jcox@eaa.org; Tom Poberezny, Publisher, tomp@eaa.org; Golda Cox, Managing Editor, gcox@eaa.org.
Desc: Sport and general aviation magazine. *Alt. Contact:* telephone: (920)426-6515. *Type:* Periodical.

U.S. Department of Transportation
Federal Aviation Administration
Associate Administrator for Regulation and Certification
Office of Aviation Medicine

800 Independence Ave. SW   Ph: (202)366-4000
Washington, DC 20591
Desc: The Office is responsible for the medical certification of all airmen. It maintains the Civil Aeromedical Institute at the FAA Aeronautical Center in Oklahoma City. *Type:* Government agency, office, or program.

The Weekly of Business Aviation

The McGraw-Hill Companies
Aviation Week Group
1200 G St. NW, Ste. 200   Ph: (202)383-2403
Washington, DC 20005-3802   Free: 800-752-4959
                    Fax: (202)383-7956
E-mail: awgnews@mcgraw-hill.com
URL: http://www.awgnews.com.
Contact: Dave Collogan, Editor.
Desc: Covers trends in the business/corporate aviation market. Contains news on FAA, DOT, and congressional regulations and legislation. *Type:* Newsletter.

World Aviation Directory

Aviation Week
McGraw-Hill, Inc.
1200 G St. NW, Ste. 900   Ph: (202)383-2484
Washington, DC 20005   Free: 800-551-2015
                    Fax: (202)383-2478
E-mail: wad@mcgraw-hill.com.
URL: http://www.wadaviation.com.
Contact: Kent J. Weimer, Editor.
Desc: Aviation, aerospace, and missile manufacturers, including manufacturers of aircraft, spacecraft, piston and jet engines, and component manufacturers and major subcontractors; support services (fuel companies, repair stations, etc.); airports and heliports; airlines; government agencies and associations; airline caterers; air freight companies; international coverage. *Type:* Directory.

Baking

American Bakers Association

1350 Eye St. NW, Ste. 1290   Ph: (202)789-0300
Washington, DC 20005-3005   Fax: (202)898-1164
E-mail: info@americanbakers.org
Contact: Paul C. Abenante, Pres.
Desc: Manufacturers and wholesale distributors of bread, rolls, and pastry products; suppliers of goods and services to bakers. *Type:* Association.

American Deli-Bakery News

Larry Jenkins Associates
PO Box 4365   Ph: (415)512-7229
Kailua Kona, HI 96745-4365
Contact: Larry E. Jenkins, Editor.
Desc: Provides news and information on current trends in the retail food service industry. Concentrates on new construction, people in the industry, government regulations, new equipment and products, and other topics of interest. *Type:* Newsletter.

American Institute of Baking

1213 Bakers Way   Ph: (785)537-4750
PO Box 3999   Fax: (785)537-1493
Manhattan, KS 66505-3999
E-mail: mailbox@aibonline.org
URL: http://www.aibonline.org
Contact: Virgil Smail, Pres.
Desc: Baking research and educational center. Conducts basic and applied research, educational and hands-on training, and in-plant sanitation and worker safety audits. *Type:* Association.

Bakery, Confectionery and Tobacco Workers International Union

10401 Connecticut Ave., Rm.   Ph: (301)933-8600
  400   Fax: (301)946-8452
Kensington, MD 20895
Contact: Frank Hurt, Pres.
Desc: AFL-CIO. *Type:* Association.

BC&T News

Bakery, Confectionery, and Tobacco Workers
International Union
10401 Connecticut Ave.   Ph: (301)933-8600
Kensington, MD 20895-3961   Fax: (301)946-8452
Type: Periodical.

Contact

Canadian Wheat Board
423 Main St.   Ph: (204)983-3421
PO Box 816, Sta. Main   Fax: (204)983-4678
Winnipeg, MB, Canada R3C
   2P5
Contact: Rhea Yates, Editor.

Desc: Provides information on the grain industry in Latin
America and the Caribbean to members of the Canadian
Wheat Board. *Type:* Newsletter.

Dairy-Deli Bake Digest

International Dairy-Deli-Bakery Association
313 Price Pl., Ste. 202   Ph: (608)238-7908
PO Box 5528   Fax: (608)238-6330
Madison, WI 53705-0528
E-mail: iddba@iddba.org
URL: http://www.iddanet.org.
Contact: Carol L. Christison, Editor, cchristison@iddba.
org.

Desc: Supports the Association, which seeks to increase
dairy-deli-bakery business. Focuses on issues of concern to
manufacturers, retailers, brokers, distributors, businesses,
and organizations involved with the dairy-deli-bakery industry. *Type:* Newsletter.

Home Cooking

House of White Birches
306 E. Parr Rd.   Ph: (219)589-4000
Berne, IN 46711   Fax: (219)589-8093
E-mail: home_cooking@whitebirches.com.
URL: http://www.whitebirches.com
Contact: Carl H. Muselman, Publisher; Arthur K. Musel-
man, Publisher; Shelly Vaughan, Editor.

Desc: Magazine with approximately 100 recipes for home
cooks who wish to make home-style foods with common
ingredients. *Type:* Periodical.

The Independent

Independent Bakers Association
PO Box 3731   Ph: (202)333-8190
Washington, DC 20007   Fax: (202)337-3809
E-mail: independentbaker@mindspring.com
Contact: Robert N. Pyle, Editor.

Desc: Carries Association news and brief articles on commodities, taxes, labor, and other matters affecting the baking industry. Recurring features include reports of
conferences, meetings, and the annual convention; election slates; membership updates; and presidential reports.
Type: Newsletter.

Insight

The Retailer's Bakery Association
14239 Park Center Dr.   Ph: (301)725-2149
Laurel, MD 20707   Free: 800-638-0924
                            Fax: (301)725-2187
E-mail: rba@rbanet.com
URL: http://www.rbanet.com.
Desc: Examines trends and issues in the bakery industry.
Features items on bakery production, marketing, business
management, and other topics of interest. *Type:* Newslet-
ter.

Retailer's Bakery Association

Peggy Hoffman
14239 Park Center Dr.   Ph: (301)725-2149
Laurel, MD 20707   Free: 800-638-0924
                            Fax: (301)725-2187
E-mail: rba@rbanet.com
URL: http://www.rbanet.com
Contact: Peter Houstle, Exec.VP.

Desc: Independent and in-store bakeries, food service, specialty bakeries (2500), suppliers of ingredients, tools &
equipment (780); other (220). *Type:* Association.

Banking

ABA Banking Journal

Simmons-Boardman Publishing Corporation
345 Hudson St.   Ph: (212)620-7200
New York, NY 10014
Desc: Contains the complete text of ABA Banking Journal,
a magazine on commercial bank operation and management. Covers employee relations, recruiting, and training;
installment, mortgage, commercial, and industrial lending; correspondent, foreign, and retail banking; deposit
gathering; bank cards; asset and liability management;
data processing and telecommunications; security; government relations; and legal and regulatory developments.
Available: LEXIS-NEXIS, NEXIS. *Type:* Database.

Alternative Currents

Alternatives Federal Credit Union
301 W. State St.   Ph: (607)273-3582
Ithaca, NY 14850   Fax: (607)277-6391
E-mail: afcu@alternatives.org
URL: http://www.alternatives.org/news_current.html.
Contact: Leni Hochman, Editor, lhochman@alternatives.
org.

Desc: Covers issues related to community development
banking and financial services. *Type:* Newsletter.

American Banker Full Text

American Banker - Bond Buyer
One State Street Plaza, 27th Fl.   Ph: (212)803-8366
New York, NY 10004
URL: http://www.americanbanker.com
Desc: Contains the complete text of the American Banker,
a daily newspaper providing news and analysis of the commercial banking and financial services industries. Includes
tabular data; excludes commentaries and stories derived
from other news services. *Available:* The Dialog Corporation, DataStar; Bell & Howell Information and Learning;
The Dialog Corporation, DIALOG; The Dialog Corporation, DIALOG; LEXIS-NEXIS, LEXIS; LEXIS-NEXIS,
NEXIS; LEXIS-NEXIS, NEXIS; FT PROFILE; Thom-
son Financial Services, Inc., I/PLUS Direct. *Type:* Database.

American Banker News Service

American Banker - Bond Buyer
One State Street Plaza, 27th Fl.   Ph: (212)803-8366
New York, NY 10004
URL: http://www.americanbanker.com
Desc: Provides early morning online access to key news re-
ports and statistics about the banking world each day by
12:01 a.m. EST. *Available:* The Dialog Corporation, DI-
ALOG. *Type:* Database.

American Bankers Association

1120 Connecticut Ave. NW   Ph: (202)663-5000
Washington, DC 20036   Free: 800-338-0626
                            Fax: (202)663-7543
URL: http://www.aba.com
Contact: Donald G. Ogilvie, Exec.VP.

Desc: Members are principally commercial banks and trust
companies; combined assets of members represent approx-

imately 90% of the U.S. banking industry; approximately
94% of members are community banks with less than
$500 million in assets. Seeks to enhance the role of com-
merical bankers as preeminent providers of financial services through communications, research, legal action,
lobbying of federal legislative and regulatory bodies, and
education and training programs. *Type:* Association.

American Financial Services Association

919 18th St. NW   Ph: (202)296-5544
Washington, DC 20006   Fax: (202)223-0321
E-mail: afsa@afsamail.com
URL: http://www.americanfinsvcs.org
Contact: H. Randolph Lively, Pres. & CEO.

Desc: Companies whose business is primarily direct credit
lending to consumers and/or the purchase of sales finance
paper on consumer goods. Some members have insurance
and retail subsidiaries; some are themselves subsidiaries of
highly diversified parent corporations. Encourages the
business of financing individuals and families for necessary
and useful purposes, at reasonable charges, including interest; promotes consumer understanding of basic money
management principles as well as constructive uses of consumer credit. *Type:* Association.

America's Community Bankers

900 19th St. NW, Ste. 400   Ph: (202)857-3100
Washington, DC 20006   Fax: (202)296-8716
URL: http://www.acbankers.org
Contact: Paul Schosberg, Pres.

Desc: Savings and loan associations, savings banks, cooperative banks, and state and local savings and loan association leagues in all U.S. states and territories; associate
members are institutions and firms providing products or
services to the savings business. Serves the savings institution business and the public interest by furthering thrift
and home ownership. *Type:* Association.

America's Community Bankers

900 19th St. NW, Ste. 400   Ph: (202)857-3100
Washington, DC 20006   Fax: (202)296-8716
E-mail: infor@acbankers.org
URL: http://www.acbankers.org
Contact: Paul Shoseberg, CEO/Pres.

Desc: Savings banks and savings and loan associations; international savings and loan systems, leagues, or associations. *Type:* Association.

America's Community Bankers—Washington Perspective

America's Community Bankers
900 19th St. NW, Ste. 400   Ph: (202)857-3100
Washington, DC 20006   Fax: (202)857-5581
E-mail: info@acbankers.org
URL: http://www.acbankers.org.
Contact: James A. Eberle, Editor, (202)857-3145, jeber-
le@acbankers.org.

Desc: Provides information on legislative, regulatory, and
political developments affecting the operations of savings
institutions nationwide. *Type:* Newsletter.

Balance of Payments Statistics

International Monetary Fund (IMF)
Statistics Department
700 19th St., N.W.   Ph: (202)623-6180
Washington, DC 20431
Desc: Contains about 45,000 quarterly and annual time
series compiled by the IMF on the international economic
transactions of about 170 individual countries. Data are
grouped by current account, capital account, and financial
account (reserve assets and other financial transactions).
Available: The WEFA Group; Youvelle Renaissance
Group, GEnie. *Type:* Database.

Bancompare Plus

Cates Consulting Analysts, Inc.

1667 K St., N.W., Suite 640   Ph: (202)659-8300
Washington, DC 20006

Desc: Contains the complete text of Bancompare Plus. Contains analytic reports on every FDIC-insured commercial bank and parent (when applicable) and fully consolidated bank holding company information. *Available:* Cates Consulting Analysts, Inc. *Type:* Database.

Bank Asset/Liability Management

Warren, Gorham & Lamont R.I.A. Group

90 Fifth Ave., 10th Fl.   Ph: (212)807-2193
New York, NY 10011   Free: 800-950-1216
    Fax: (212)337-4183

Contact: Jack Rubinson, Editor.

Desc: Considers all aspects of asset/liability management, including gap management, duration analysis, automation, forecasting, and modeling. Offers new approaches to asset/liability management, reports on research in the field, and offers commentary on emerging issues. *Type:* Newsletter.

Bank Auditing and Accounting Report

Warren, Gorham & Lamont, Inc.
RIA Group

PO Box 6159   Free: 800-950-1216
Carol Stream, IL 60197

Contact: Stephen Collins, Editor.

Desc: Provides practical guidance for resolving issues that confront bank professionals every day. *Type:* Newsletter.

Bank Automation News

Phillips Business Information, Inc.

1201 Seven Locks Rd., Ste. 300   Ph: (301)340-1520
Potomac, MD 20854   Free: 888-707-5809
    Fax: (301)340-3847

E-mail: clientservices.pbi@phillips.com

Contact: Nicole Jackson, Asst. Editor, njackson@phillips.com; Julie Klyce, Senior Editor, jkly@phillips.com.

Desc: Reports on automation developments in the banking industry. Details specific equipment and benefits. *Type:* Newsletter.

Bank Digest

Washington Service Bureau, Inc.

655 15th St. NW   Ph: (202)508-0600
Washington, DC 20005   Free: 800-955-5219
    Fax: (202)508-0694

Contact: Nathalie Auer, Editor.

Desc: Provides information about federal banking activity. Includes news from the Federal Reserve, Federal Deposit Insurance Corporation, and Treasury Department. *Type:* Newsletter.

Bank Directors Briefing

Simmons-Boardman Publishing Corp.

345 Hudson St.   Ph: (212)620-7200
New York, NY 10014   Fax: (212)633-1165
URL: http://www.banking.com; http://www.marinelog.com

Contact: Steven A. Cocheo, Editor.

Desc: Presents information on setting policy and providing oversight to enhance a bank's performance. Recurring features include occasional bank earnings surveys. *Type:* Newsletter.

Bank Fraud

Bank Administration Institute

1 N. Franklin St., Ste. 1000   Free: 800-323-8552
Chicago, IL 60606-3401

E-mail: jlewis@wwa.com; dcrandall@bai.org.

Contact: Richard G. Kemmer, Editor.

Desc: Provides information about bank fraud and protection. *Type:* Newsletter.

Bank Human Resources Report

Warren, Gorham & Lamont, Inc.
RIA Group

PO Box 6159   Free: 800-950-1216
Carol Stream, IL 60197

Contact: Selvin Gootar, Editor.

Desc: Discusses current trends in bank human resources management, including promotion policies, compensation, recruiting, training, employee benefits, employment law updates, EEO, interviewing, and human resource development. *Type:* Newsletter.

Bank and Lender Liability Litigation Reporter

Andrews Publications

175 Strafford Ave., Bldg. 4, Ste.   Ph: (610)225-0510
140   Free: 800-345-1101
Wayne, PA 19087   Fax: (610)225-0501

Contact: Denise Breslin Kachiin, Editor.

Desc: Supplies summaries of significant litigation and monitors key decisions and pleadings from cases around the U.S. Includes FDIC (Federal Deposit Insurance Corporation), FSLIC (Federal Savings and Loan Insurance Corporation)and RTC, complaints and related actions among shareholders, officers, directors, insurers, and institutions. *Type:* Newsletter.

Bank Letter

Institutional Investor, Inc.

488 Madison Ave.   Ph: (212)224-3300
New York, NY 10022   Free: 800-543-4444
    Fax: (212)224-3490

URL: http://www.iinews.com.

Contact: Tom Lamont, Editor.

Desc: Features breaking news on the trends, issues, and events that affect major U.S. commercial banks. *Type:* Newsletter.

Bank Loan Report

IDD Enterprises LP

Harborside Financial Center
600 Plaza II, 4th Fl.
Jersey City, NJ 07311

E-mail: blr@iddis.com.

Contact: Mark Kollar, Editor.

Desc: Discusses banking loans and transactions made by large corporations. Recurring features include a column titled Term Sheets. *Type:* Newsletter.

Bank Marketing—Annual Buyer's Guide

Bank Marketing Association

1120 Connecticut Ave., NW   Ph: (202)663-5378
Washington, DC 20036-3902   Free: 800-433-9013
    Fax: (202)828-4540

URL: http://www.bmanet.org

Contact: Kevin Sheridan, Editor.

Desc: List of about 300 advertising agencies and other advertising service suppliers, suppliers of bank equipment and systems, check printers, stationers, computer software consultants, publishers, research services, financial planning services, premium and incentive programs, telemarketing and communications firms, training and education programs, and other suppliers of services and materials to the bank marketing industry. *Type:* Directory.

Bank MergerFax

SNL Securities

321 E. Main St.   Ph: (804)977-1600
PO Box 2124   Fax: (804)977-4466
Charlottesville, VA 22902

E-mail: subscriptions@snl.com

URL: http://www.snlnet.com.

Contact: Christine Atkinson, Editor.

Desc: Summarizes news and statistics of bank mergers and acquisitions, including information on Resolution Trust Corporation (RTC) transactions, Federal Deposit Insurance Corporation (FDIC) transactions, branch sales, merger conversions, other asset sales, and bank/thrift acquisitions via fax. Recurring features include news of research. *Type:* Newsletter.

Bank Mergers & Acquisitions Yearbook

SNL Securities

321 E. Main St.   Ph: (804)977-1600
PO Box 2124   Fax: (804)977-4466
Charlottesville, VA 22902

E-mail: subscriptions@snl.com
URL: http://www.snlnet.com.

Contact: Mark Outlaw, Editor; Holly Gillerlain, Editor.

Desc: Covers all bank and thrift merger activity from the previous year. Includes state-by-state reviews of all private sector whole-bank and whole-thrift transactions, branch sales, merger conversions, and government-assisted transactions announced in that year. *Type:* Newsletter.

Bank Mutual Fund Report

American Banker/Bond Buyer Inc.
International Thomson Publishing Corp.

1 State St. Plaza   Ph: (212)803-8200
New York, NY 10004   Free: 800-362-3807
    Fax: (212)843-9612

Contact: John Jedlicka, Editor; David P. Schutt, Publisher; Hans Winberg, Advertising Mng.

Desc: Covers the bank mutual funds market, including which banks are entering the markets, bank mergers and acquisitions, technological innovations, and market leader's strategies. Provides analysis of legal issues, legal rulings, and litigation affecting all investment management practices of depository institutions. *Type:* Newsletter.

Bank Network News

Faulkner & Gray, Inc.

11 Penn Plaza, 11th Fl.   Ph: (212)967-7000
New York, NY 10001

Desc: Provides analyses of developments in the electronic banking industry. Includes articles on automated teller machines, debit and credit cards, electronic payment at the point of sale, and home banking. *Type:* Database.

Bank Network News

Faulkner & Gray, Inc.

300 S. Wacker Dr., 18th Fl.
Chicago, IL 60606

URL: http://www.faulknergray.com.

Contact: Donald Davis, Editor, don_davis@faulknergray.com; Andrea McKenna Findlay, Assoc. Editor.

Desc: Analyzes developments in the electronic banking industry. Includes articles on automated teller machines, debit and credit cards, electronic payment at the point of sale, home banking and electronic commerce via the Internet. *Type:* Newsletter.

Bank Operations Report

Warren, Gorham & Lamont, Inc.
RIA Group

PO Box 6159   Free: 800-950-1216
Carol Stream, IL 60197

Contact: Nancy Hitchner, Editor.

Desc: Focuses on electronic data processing control, check processing, record keeping, cost control, federal regulation, credit and debit cards, electronic funds transfer system, physical security, and office automation, computer, and systems applications. *Type:* Newsletter.

Bank Rate Monitor

Bank Rate Monitor
11811 U.S. Hwy. 1   Ph: (561)627-7330
North Palm Beach, FL 33408   Fax: (561)627-7335
E-mail: webmastermainel.bankrate.com
URL: http://www.bankrate.com/brm/default.asp
Desc: Need to know the latest rate for a 30-year fixed rate mortgage? Or perhaps you'd like to know what's the best you can do rate-wise on a four-year auto loan? If these and other similar questions are on your mind, there's no place on the Web where you can get quicker and more timely answers than at Bank Rate Monitor. Updated constantly, the site offers the very latest in rate information, including the current rates being paid by financial institutions on savings accounts and certificates of deposit. *Type:* Database.

Bank Safety Directory

Weiss Ratings, Inc.
4176 Burns Rd.   Ph: (561)627-3300
Palm Beach Gardens, FL 33410   Free: 800-289-9222
                                  Fax: (561)625-6685
E-mail: wr@weissinc.com
Desc: Approximately 11,000 commercial and financial institutions in the United States. *Type:* Directory.

Bank Securities Monthly

SNL Securities
321 E. Main St.   Ph: (804)977-1600
PO Box 2124   Fax: (804)977-4466
Charlottesville, VA 22902
E-mail: subscriptions@snl.com
URL: http://www.snl.com.
Contact: Wendy Cholbi, Editor; Steve Tomasi, Editor; John Racine, Editor.
Desc: Provides current financial, market and merger information on policy traded banks. Also includes highlights of the past month and comprehensive industry articles addressing topics such as bank investment opportunities, capital structure, and earnings prospects. *Type:* Newsletter.

Bank Teller's Report

RIA Group
395 Hudson St.   Ph: (212)367-6300
New York, NY 10014   Fax: (212)367-6314
Contact: Joan German, Editor.
Desc: Designed to help bank tellers (and also their supervisors) "sharpen their job skills with tips on endorsements, forgeries, kiters, automation, settling, finding errors in computations and various time- and work-savers." Contains articles and briefs that address tellers' concerns and provides them with news, information, and guidance on bank services and customer service. Recurring features include columns titled One of Those Days (where tellers share frustrating or surprising incidents), Tips From Tellers, and Extraordinary Service (in which tellers share instances of service "beyond the call of duty"). *Type:* Newsletter.

Bankcard Barometer

Card Management Information Services
PO Box 1700   Ph: (301)695-4897
Frederick, MD 21702   Fax: (301)695-5979
URL: http://www.cardweb.com.
Contact: Robert B. McKinley, Editor.
Desc: Provides proprietary statistical data on specific U.S. credit card issuers, including gross receivables, gross accounts, delinquency rate (30/60 day), attrition rate (voluntary/involuntary), charge-offs, recoveries, acquisitions, average balance for staccctive accounts, interest income, number of business cards, non-interest income, card/merchant processor, bankruptcy losses, fraud losses, average portfolio A.P.R., securitized debt, average gold account A.P.R., securitized interest rate, total cards, average standard account annual fee, and historical numbers. *Type:* Newsletter.

Bankcard Update

Card Management Information Services
PO Box 1700   Ph: (301)695-4897
Frederick, MD 21702   Fax: (301)695-5979
E-mail: staff@ramresearch.com.
URL: http://www.ramresearch.com.
Contact: Robert B. McKinley, Editor.
Desc: Focuses on the pricing and marketing of bank credit cards. Covers standard, gold, secured, and business bank credit cards from more than 1,000 issuers (500 monitored on a monthly basis) and provides national and regional breakouts. *Type:* Newsletter.

Bankers Digest

Bonnie Blackman
7515 Greenville Ave., Ste. 901   Ph: (214)373-4544
Dallas, TX 75231-3890   Fax: (214)373-4545
Contact: Bonnie J. Blackman, Editor and Publisher.
Desc: Provides information about the financial industry, focusing on the Southwest United States. *Type:* Newsletter.

The Bankers Letter of the Law

Warren, Gorham & Lamont R.I.A. Group
90 Fifth Ave., 10th Fl.   Ph: (212)807-2193
New York, NY 10011   Free: 800-950-1216
                           Fax: (212)337-4183
Contact: Robert Volk, Editor.
Desc: Reviews important court decisions and changes in state and federal laws and regulations. Reports on such areas of current interest as equal credit opportunity, fair credit billing, truth-in-lending, credit insurance commissions, bankruptcy, loan security, and bank collection practices. *Type:* Newsletter.

Bankers News

American Bankers Association
Products Group
1120 Connecticut Ave. NW   Ph: (202)663-5374
Washington, DC 20036   Free: 800-338-0626
                            Fax: (202)828-4540
Contact: Teresa Dean, Managing Editor, (202)663-5446, fax: (202)663-7578, tdean@aba.com; Edward F. Smith, Publisher, (202)663-5443, fax: (202)663-7578, esmith@aba.com.
Desc: Provides information about the banking and financial industry. *Type:* Newsletter.

Bankers Research

Bankers Research, Inc.
PO Box 431   Ph: (203)227-1237
Westport, CT 06881
Contact: Theodore Volckhausen, Publisher; Ted Volckhausen, Jr., Editor.
Desc: Describes trends and developments in lending. Covers methods of building retail business, commercial real estate and small business lending, credit and debit cards, electronic banking of all types, EDI, and related Internet developments. *Type:* Newsletter.

Banking Information Source

Bell & Howell Information and Learning
300 N. Zeeb Rd.   Ph: (734)761-4700
PO Box 1346
Ann Arbor, MI 48106-1346
E-mail: info@umi.com
URL: http://www.umi.com
Desc: Contains approximately 350,000 citations, and full text articles, to articles and other published materials dealing with the management and marketing of financial services by banks, credit unions, insurance companies, investment and real estate firms, thrift institutions, and

government agencies. Covers advertising, pricing, sales, marketing, pricing, personnel development and compensation, facilities planning, and product innovations. *Available:* The Dialog Corporation, DIALOG; The Dialog Corporation, DIALOG; LEXIS-NEXIS, LEXIS. *Type:* Database.

Banking Policy Report

Law & Business, Inc.
Prentice-Hall, Inc.
1185 Avenue of the Americas,   Ph: (212)597-0200
   No. 37
New York, NY 10036-2601
Contact: Phillip Meyer, Editor.
Desc: Discusses new strategies, techniques, and developments in the financial services industry. *Type:* Newsletter.

Bankstat

Thomson BankWatch, Inc.
61 Broadway - 3rd floor   Ph: (212)845-0300
New York, NY 10006
E-mail: usdin@tfn.com
URL: http://www.bankwatch.com
Desc: Contains annual time series comprising financial details on more than 10,000 banks in more than 190 countries worldwide. Provides a maximum of five years of annual data and, where available, five periods of interim data. *Available:* Data Downlink Corporation. *Type:* Database.

Benefax

SNL Securities
321 E. Main St.   Ph: (804)977-1600
PO Box 2124   Fax: (804)977-4466
Charlottesville, VA 22902
E-mail: subscriptions@snl.com
Contact: Keith Davis, Editor; Reid Nagle, Publisher; Pat LaBue, Subscription Mgr.
Desc: Allows recipients to request more information on particular topics of interest such as executive compensation. Contains summaries of available information. *Type:* Newsletter.

Bloomberg Magazine

Bloomberg L.P.
100 Business Park Dr.   Ph: (609)279-3000
PO Box 888   Free: 800-388-2749
Princeton, NJ 08542-0888   Fax: (609)683-7523
E-mail: magazine@bloomberg.net.
Contact: Michael Bloomberg, Founder/CEO, (212)318-2005, fax: (212)940-1943, mbloomberg@bloomberg.com; David Wachtel, Publisher, (212)893-3895, fax: (212)893-4183; Matthew Winkler, Editor-in-Chief, (212)318-2305, fax: (212)893-5999, mwinkler@bloomberg.com; William Inman, Editor, (609)279-4602, fax: (917)369-8092, binman@bloomberg.com; Darrell Delamaide, Managing Editor, (609)279-7050, fax: (917)369-7085; Paula Plantier, Copy Chief, (609)279-4638, fax: (917)369-7785, pplantier
Desc: Magazine for high-end financial players who subscribe to Bloomberg on-line services. *Type:* Periodical.

BNA Banking Daily

The Bureau of National Affairs, Inc. (BNA)
1231 25th St. NW   Ph: (202)452-4200
Washington, DC 20037
E-mail: bnaplus@bna.com
URL: http://bna.com/mkt/hrl/hrlwdec.htm
Desc: Contains information on judicial, legislative, and regulatory activities affecting financial institutions. Includes analyses of congressional actions, regulatory proposals and changes, and federal and state court decisions. *Available:* LEXIS-NEXIS, LEXIS; West Group, WESTLAW; LEXIS-NEXIS, NEXIS. *Type:* Database.

BNA's Banking Report

The Bureau of National Affairs, Inc. (BNA)
1231 25th St. NW   Ph: (202)452-4200
Washington, DC 20037
E-mail: bnaplus@bna.com
URL: http://bna.com/mkt/hrl/hrlwdec.htm
Contact: BNA PLUS, (202)452-4323, fax: (202)822-8092, bnaplus@bna.com.
Desc: Contains the complete text of BNA'S Banking Report, a newsletter covering federal regulation of the financial services industry. Includes reports and analyses of the administrative and regulatory activities of the Federal Reserve Board, Federal Deposit Insurance Corporation (FDIC), Federal Home Loan Bank Board (FHLBB), National Credit Union Administration (NCUA), and Office of Thrift Supervision. *Available:* LEXIS-NEXIS, LEXIS; West Group, WESTLAW. *Type:* Database.

BNA's Banking Report

Bureau of National Affairs, Inc. (BNA)
1231 25th St. NW   Ph: (202)452-4323
Washington, DC 20037   Free: 800-372-1033
                          Fax: (202)452-7773
E-mail: bnaplus@bna.com
URL: http://www.bna.com/newsstand.
Contact: Pamela Atkins, Managing Editor.
Desc: Reports significant federal regulatory and supervisory developments affecting financial institutions. Covers actions of federal regulatory agencies, Congress, House and Senate committees, and the courts. *Type:* Newsletter.

Bridge MoneyCenter®

Bridge Information Systems, Inc.
Knight-Ridder Financial Information Group
3 World Financial Center   Ph: (212)372-7100
New York, NY 10281
URL: http://www.bridge.com
Desc: Contains real-time and delayed quotes for cash and exchange-market securities as well as news and analyses of U.S. and international financial markets. *Available:* Track Data Corporation; Bridge Information Systems, Inc., Knight-Ridder Financial Information Group. *Type:* Database.

Broadcast Banker/Broker

Paul Kagan Associates, Inc.
126 Clock Tower Pl.   Ph: (831)624-1536
Carmel, CA 93923   Fax: (831)625-3225
E-mail: info@kagan.com
Contact: George Niesen, Editor.
Desc: Acts as a "newsletter on equity and debt financing for radio and television," providing analyses of interest rates and cash flow. Discusses actions taken by successful broadcast station owners to increase assets. *Type:* Newsletter.

California Savings Institutions Directory

R. L. Polk & Co.
2001 Elm Hill Pike   Ph: (615)889-3350
PO Box 305100   Fax: (615)885-3081
Nashville, TN 37230-5100
Desc: Main offices and branches of savings institutions in California. *Type:* Directory.

Callahan's Credit Union Report

Callahan & Associates, Inc.
1001 Connecticut Ave. NW,   Ph: (202)223-3920
  Ste. 1001   Free: 800-446-7453
Washington, DC 20036   Fax: (202)223-1311
E-mail: callahan@creditunions.com
URL: http://www.callahan.com/publications/calreport.htm.
Contact: Brooke Stoddard, Editor.

Desc: Devoted to issues facing the credit union movement. Provides data, policy analysis, and lending case studies. *Type:* Newsletter.

CBA Reports

Consumer Bankers Association (CBA)
1000 Wilson Blvd., Ste. 3012   Ph: (703)276-1750
Arlington, VA 22209   Fax: (703)528-1290
E-mail: cba@cbanet.org
URL: http://www.cbanet.org.
Contact: Fritz Elmendorf, Editor; Ken Reed, Managing Editor.
Desc: Addresses developments of concern to the retail banking industry, as well as covering Association initiatives, lobbying, and educational activities. Recurring features include interviews, news of research and of educational opportunities, a calendar of events, meeting reports, and book reviews. *Type:* Newsletter.

CDCU Report

National Federation of Community Development Credit Unions
120 Wall St., 10th Fl.   Ph: (212)809-1850
New York, NY 10005-3902   Fax: (212)809-3274
E-mail: nfcdcu@nyc.pipeline.com
Contact: Clifford N. Rosenthal, Editor.
Desc: Features news of community reinvestment and development affecting low-income communities and information on financial service delivery for low-income consumers sponsored by the Federation. *Type:* Newsletter.

Centura Highway: Home of the Money Managers

Centura Banks, Inc.
134 North Church St.   Ph: (919)977-4400
PO Box 1220   Fax: (919)977-4800
Rocky Mount, NC 27802
E-mail: email@centura.com
URL: http://www.centura.com
Desc: Provides information about Centura Banks products and services and also corporate information. Also contains tools on how it can help you take charge of your money, like financial calculators that you can use to estimate payments for car loans, mortgages, and personal loans, an on-line money management program that works in conjunction with Quicken or Microsoft Money, a glossary of financial services and jargon, and ideas on how to make your money do more. *Type:* Database.

The CEO Report

United Communications Group
11300 Rockville Pike, Ste. 1100   Ph: (301)287-2700
Rockville, MD 20852-3030   Free: 800-929-4824
                                  Fax: (301)287-2049
E-mail: customer@ucg.com; iapfel@ucg.com.
Desc: Contains information for managers of credit unions. *Type:* Newsletter.

CFO Alert

American Banker/Bond Buyer Inc.
International Thomson Publishing Corp.
1 State St. Plaza   Ph: (212)803-8200
New York, NY 10004   Free: 800-362-3807
                              Fax: (212)843-9612
Contact: David G. Schutt, Publisher; John Hintze, Editor.
Desc: Covers regulatory and accounting changes, capital markets, bank funding news and strategies, asset and liability, automation techniques, and new banking products. Recurring features include interviews with chief financial officers. *Type:* Newsletter.

Chalktalk

Education Credit Union Council
PO Box 7558   Ph: (334)626-3399
Spanish Fort, AL 36577
Contact: Lorraine B. Webster, Editor.
Desc: Supports the Council's goal of providing an opportunity for credit unions to exchange ideas and information. Educates credit union managers and their "official families" and encourages the organization of local and regional independent education credit union groups. *Type:* Newsletter.

Checks and Checking

Faulkner & Gray, Inc.
11 Penn Plaza, 17th Fl.   Ph: (212)967-7000
New York, NY 10001-2006   Free: 800-535-8403
                              Fax: (212)967-7180
E-mail: order@faulknergray.com
Contact: Patricia A. Murphy, Editor; Kurt T. Peters, Publisher.
Desc: Provides information about the checking business. Includes news, analysis, and regulations regarding check payments. *Type:* Newsletter.

Commercial Finance Association

225 W. 34th St.   Ph: (212)594-3490
Ste. 1815   Fax: (212)564-6053
New York, NY 10122
E-mail: lmachlis@csassn.com
URL: http://www.csfa.com
Contact: Leonard Machlis, Exec.Dir.
Desc: Organizations engaged in asset-based financial services including commercial financing and factoring and lending money on a secured basis to small- and medium-sized business firms. Acts as a forum for information and consideration about ideas, opportunities, and legislation concerning asset-based financial services. *Type:* Association.

Commercial Lending Litigation News

LRP Publications
747 Dresher Rd.   Ph: (215)784-0941
PO Box 980   Free: 800-341-7874
Horsham, PA 19044-0980   Fax: (215)784-0870
E-mail: custserve@lrp.com
Contact: Jennifer Drago, Editor.
Desc: Covers liability claims and their policies and procedures, case strategies, court decisions, and jury verdicts. *Type:* Newsletter.

The Community Bank President

Siefer Consultants, Inc.
PO Box 1384   Ph: (712)732-7340
Storm Lake, IA 50588   Free: 800-747-7342
E-mail: siefer@ncn.net
Contact: Joe Sheller, Editor.
Desc: Presents an interchange of ideas and profit-making suggestions for bank presidents. Offers successful techniques used in the areas of business development, cost control, marketing, and personnel. *Type:* Newsletter.

Compliance Action

Compliance Action
PO Box 2841   Free: 800-660-0080
Bala Cynwyd, PA 19004
Contact: George B. Milner, Jr., Publisher; Lucy Griffen, Editor.
Desc: Covers issues pertaining to regulatory compliance in financial institutions. *Type:* Newsletter.

ComplianceFax

SNL Capitol Research
514 10th St. NW, 8th Fl.   Ph: (202)347-5277
Washington, DC 20004   Free: 800-969-4121
           Fax: (202)347-5278
Contact: Damien Josefiak, Product Mgr.
Desc: Provides by fax abstracts of regulatory releases and news stories from federal agencies. Also gives legal briefs on banking-related issues from law firms. *Type:* Newsletter.

Conference of State Bank Supervisors

1015 18th St. NW, Ste. 1100   Ph: (202)296-2840
Washington, DC 20036-5275   Free: 800-886-2727
           Fax: (202)296-1928
URL: http://www.csbsdc.org/index.html
Contact: Neil Millner, Pres.
Desc: State officials (including those from District of Columbia, Guam, Puerto Rico, and the Virgin Islands) responsible for supervision of 8,000 state-chartered banking institutions. Seeks to maintain a strong, decentralized dual banking system that assures flexibility and diversification in state banking and state bank regulation by upgrading state banking laws and improving the efficiency and effectiveness of state banking departments. Conducts schools for state banking department personnel. *Type:* Association.

Consumer Bankers Association

1000 Wilson Blvd., Ste. 3012   Ph: (703)276-1750
Arlington, VA 22209-3908   Fax: (703)528-1290
Contact: Joe Belew, Pres.
Desc: Federally insured deposit-taking institutions. Sponsors Graduate School of Retail Bank Management at the University of Virginia. *Type:* Association.

Consumer Lending News

Siefer Consultants, Inc.
PO Box 1384   Ph: (712)732-7340
Storm Lake, IA 50588   Free: 800-747-7342
E-mail: siefer@ncn.net
Contact: Joe Sheller, Editor.
Desc: Focuses on "what financial institutions are doing to increase their loan portfolios and reduce delinquencies and chargeoffs." Other topics include home equity loans, student loans, credit cards, direct and in-direct auto loans, collections, promotions, credit insurance, credit screening and processing. *Type:* Newsletter.

Cost Control Strategies for Financial Institutions

Siefer Consultants, Inc.
PO Box 1384   Ph: (712)732-7340
Storm Lake, IA 50588   Free: 800-747-7342
E-mail: siefer@ncn.net
Contact: Steve Herron, Editor.
Desc: Features case studies of strategies to reduce operating and interest expense. Includes payroll and benefit costs, interest expense, facility and equipment costs, utility costs, postage and phone expenses, marketing costs, insurance, and data processing. *Type:* Newsletter.

Credit & Collection Managers Letter

Bureau of Business Practice
24 Rope Ferry Rd.   Ph: (860)442-4365
Waterford, CT 06386   Free: 800-243-0876
           Fax: (860)437-3555
URL: http://www.bbpnews.com
Contact: Wayne Muller, Editor, wayne_muller@prenhall.com.
Desc: Addresses the legal issues of credit management, bankruptcy, debt negotiations, and collecting. Recurring features include interviews and book reviews. *Type:* Newsletter.

The Credit Union Accountant

American Banker/Bond Buyer Inc.
International Thomson Publishing Corp.
1 State St. Plaza   Ph: (212)803-8200
New York, NY 10004   Free: 800-362-3807
           Fax: (212)843-9612
Contact: Melanie Waddell, Editor.
Desc: Reports on accounting changes ordered by the NCUA and the Financial Accounting Standards Board. Discusses changes that affect a credit union's internal operations. *Type:* Newsletter.

Credit Union Attorneys Legal Directory

Legal Directory, Inc.
110 S. McDonough   Ph: (334)265-5365
PO Box 1967   Free: 800-448-0461
Montgomery, AL 36102-1967   Fax: (334)261-3489
Desc: Lawyers who represent credit unions or are willing to do so. Listings are paid. *Type:* Directory.

Credit Union Digest

California Credit Union League
PO Box 2322   Ph: (909)628-6044
Pomona, CA 91766-2322   Free: 800-472-1702
           Fax: (909)628-5167
URL: http://www.ccul.org.
Contact: Carol Payne, Editor; Dan Niebrugge, Publisher.
Desc: Provides news and information for credit unions. *Type:* Newsletter.

Credit Union Directors Newsletter

Credit Union National Association, Inc. (CUNA)
Publications and Web Services   Ph: (608)231-4082
  Dept.   Free: 800-356-9655
5710 Mineral Point Rd.   Fax: (608)231-4370
PO Box 431
Madison, WI 53701
URL: http://www.cuna.org.
Contact: Steve Rodgers, Editor, srodgers@cuna.com; Judy Weidman, Managing Editor.
Desc: Supplies current information of interest to board members of credit unions. Covers news, issues, and policies in consumer credit. *Type:* Newsletter.

Credit Union Executive Newsletter

Credit Union National Association, Inc. (CUNA)
Publications and Web Services   Ph: (608)231-4082
  Dept.   Free: 800-356-9655
5710 Mineral Point Rd.   Fax: (608)231-4370
PO Box 431
Madison, WI 53701
Contact: Leigh Gregg, Editor; Kathy Kuehn, Managing Editor, kkuehn@cuna.com.
Desc: Covers trends and perspectives and provides advice on operations for professional credit union managers. Touches upon finance, personnel, marketing, quality-control concerns of credit unions and their competitors, and related topics. *Type:* Newsletter.

Credit Union Executives Society

6410 Enterprise Ln., Ste. 300   Ph: (608)271-2664
Madison, WI 53719-1143   Free: 800-252-2664
           Fax: (608)271-2303
E-mail: cues@cues.org
URL: http://www.cues.org
Contact: Fred Johnson, Pres. & CEO.
Desc: Advances the professional development of credit union CEOs senior management and directors. *Type:* Association.

Credit Union National Association

PO Box 431   Ph: (608)231-4000
Madison, WI 53701   Free: 800-356-9655
URL: http://www.cuna.org
Contact: Daniel A. Mica, Contact.
Desc: Trade association serving more than 90% of local credit unions in the U.S. through their respective state leagues with a total membership of more than 65 million persons. (A credit union is a member-owned, nonprofit institution formed to encourage saving and to offer low interest loans to members, usually people working for the same employer, belonging to the same association, or living in the same community.) Promotes credit union membership, use of services, and organization of new credit unions. *Type:* Association.

Credit Union Newswatch

Credit Union National Association, Inc. (CUNA)
Publications and Web Services   Ph: (608)231-4082
  Dept.   Free: 800-356-9655
5710 Mineral Point Rd.   Fax: (608)231-4370
PO Box 431
Madison, WI 53701
Contact: Steve Bosack, Editor, (202)682-4467, fax: (202)682-9054, stbosack@cuna.com.
Desc: Provides credit unions and the movement's leaders with news and information on legislation, regulation, and governmental affairs; public policy issues; credit union philosophy; actions of other financial service providers and other special interest groups that significantly affect credit unions and the credit union system; and activities of the Association's affiliates' programs and services. Recurring features include a calendar of events, reports of meetings, news of educational opportunities, and notices of publications available. *Type:* Newsletter.

Cross Sales Report

Siefer Consultants, Inc.
PO Box 1384   Ph: (712)732-7340
Storm Lake, IA 50588   Free: 800-747-7342
E-mail: siefer@ncn.net
Contact: Joe Sheller, Editor.
Desc: Provides ideas on how to increase sales to new customers and cross sales to existing customers in financial institutions. Topics discussed are loan and deposit promotions, sales managment, and marketing ideas. *Type:* Newsletter.

CSBS Examiner

Conference of State Bank Supervisors (CSBS)
1015 18th St. NW, Ste. 1100   Ph: (202)296-2840
Washington, DC 20036   Free: 800-886-2727
           Fax: (202)296-1928
URL: http://www.csbs.org.
Contact: Ellen C. Lamb, Editor, (202)728-5728, elamb@csbsdc.org.
Desc: Reports on news affecting the state bank system. Incorporates the former The Supervisor. *Type:* Newsletter.

CUES FYI

Credit Union Executives Society (CUES)
6410 Enterprise Ln., Ste. 300   Ph: (608)271-2664
Madison, WI 53719-1143   Free: 800-252-2664
           Fax: (608)271-2303
E-mail: cues@cues.org
Contact: Sara Landolt, Editor.
Desc: Informs members of the organization's activities and benefits. Includes news about member job changes and awards. *Type:* Newsletter.

D & O Liability Litigation News

Litigation Reporting Service
PO Box 248 Ph: (215)822-9158
Chalfont, PA 18914 Fax: (215)822-9158
Contact: William T. Keough, Editor, billkeo@erols.com.
Desc: Reports on shareholder suits under the Private Securities Litigation Reform Act, D&O insurance disputes, "poison pills" enacted to thwart corporate takeovers, efforts to pierce the "corporate veil" and ongoing litigation over the government's breach of goodwill contracts with failed banks and thrifts. *Type:* Newsletter.

Dealing with Technology

Waters Information Services, Inc.
PO Box 2248 Ph: (607)770-9242
Binghamton, NY 13902-2248 Free: 800-947-7947
E-mail: kmiller@watersinfo.com.
Contact: Peter Harris, Editorial Director.
Desc: Covers workstations, software, data processing and communications technology, marketplace automation, market quotation services, data and news feeds, and other technology issues affecting financial trading markets. Remarks: Alternate fax number: (607) 770-9435. *Type:* Newsletter.

Debit Card News

Faulkner & Gray, Inc.
300 S. Wacker Dr., 18th Fl. Ph: (312)913-1334
Chicago, IL 60606 Fax: (312)913-1365
E-mail: order@faulknergray.com
URL: http://www.faulknergray.com.
Contact: Jeffrey Green, Editor, (312)983-6129, jeff_green@faulknergray.com.
Desc: Offers news and analysis of the debit card industry and electronic payment programs at the point of sale (POS) that involve the use of debit and cards. Specifies banks and retailers participating in retail Electronic Funds Transfer (EFT) programs and describes their systems, equipment, marketing methods, customer acceptance, pricing, and competitive strategies. *Type:* Newsletter.

DEF Digest

Credit Union Executives Society (CUES)
6410 Enterprise Ln., Ste. 300 Ph: (608)271-2664
Madison, WI 53719-1143 Free: 800-252-2664
Fax: (608)271-2303
E-mail: cues@cues.org
Contact: Sara Cox Landolr, Editor, sara@cues.org.
Desc: Contains information on the credit union industry, governance and leadership development opportunities. Recurring features include interviews, reports of meetings, Q & A, news of educational opportunities, and notices of publications available. *Type:* Newsletter.

Defense Credit Union Council—Alert

Defense Credit Union Council
805 15th St. NW, Ste. 300 Ph: (202)682-5993
Washington, DC 20005-2207 Fax: (202)682-9054
E-mail: dcuc@meteor.org
URL: http://www.dcuc.org
Contact: Stacey Carter, Editor, (202)218-9776, scarter@cuna.com.
Desc: Offers news that affects credit unions serving defense establishments. Focuses on information regarding laws and regulations from the Department of Defense. *Type:* Newsletter.

Deposit Growth Strategies

Siefer Consultants, Inc.
PO Box 1384 Ph: (712)732-7340
Storm Lake, IA 50588 Free: 800-747-7342
E-mail: siefer@ncn.net
Contact: Joe Sheller, Editor.

Desc: Cover methods to increase deposits at financial institutions, as well as marketing strategies for deposit growth. Both personal accounts and commercial accounts are covered. *Type:* Newsletter.

Direction of Trade Statistics

International Monetary Fund (IMF)
Statistics Department
700 19th St., N.W. Ph: (202)623-6180
Washington, DC 20431
Desc: Contains more than 58,000 monthly, quarterly, and annual time series of import and export statistics for about 197 countries and their trading partners. The annual series cover 1948 to date; quarterly series cover 1973 to date; monthly series cover 1963 to date. *Available:* Standard & Poor's DRI, Data Products Division; The WEFA Group. *Type:* Database.

Directors & Trustees Digest

America's Community Bankers
900 19th St. NW, Ste. 400 Ph: (202)857-3100
Washington, DC 20006 Fax: (202)857-5581
E-mail: info@acbankers.org
Contact: William T. Marshall, Editor.
Desc: Reports on economic, legislative, and regulatory developments affecting trustees and directors of community banks. *Type:* Newsletter.

DRI Financial and Credit Statistics

Standard & Poor's DRI
Data Products Division
24 Hartwell Ave. Ph: (781)863-5100
Lexington, MA 02421
E-mail: client_services@dri.mcgraw-hill.com
URL: http://www.dri.mcgraw-hill.com
Contact: Client Services, (617)860-6527, fax: (617)860-6416.
Desc: Contains more than 22,000 financial time series, including releases of the Federal Reserve and the U.S. Department of the Treasury. *Available:* Standard & Poor's DRI, Data Products Division. *Type:* Database.

DRI U.S. Central

Standard & Poor's DRI
Data Products Division
24 Hartwell Ave. Ph: (781)863-5100
Lexington, MA 02421
E-mail: client_services@dri.mcgraw-hill.com
URL: http://www.dri.mcgraw-hill.com
Contact: Client Services, (617)860-6527, fax: (617)860-6416.
Desc: Contains more than 18,7000 financial, economic, and demographic time series dealing with the U.S. as an aggregate. *Available:* Standard & Poor's DRI, Data Products Division. *Type:* Database.

Economic Outlook

America's Community Bankers
900 19th St. NW, Ste. 400 Ph: (202)857-3100
Washington, DC 20006-5002 Fax: (202)296-8716
E-mail: info@acbankers.org
Contact: Bob Davis, Editor.
Desc: Analyzes current economic trends that affect community bankers. *Type:* Newsletter.

EFT Report

Phillips Business Information, Inc.
1201 Seven Locks Rd., Ste. 300 Ph: (301)340-1520
Potomac, MD 20854 Free: 888-707-5809
Fax: (301)340-3847
E-mail: clientservices.pbi@phillips.com
URL: http://www.phillips.com; http://www.phillips.com/cgi/catalog/info?EFT.

Contact: Joshua Zecher, Editor.
Desc: Supplies current information on electronic funds transfer, home banking, and automated teller machines. Names financial institutions and their activities in these developments. *Type:* Newsletter.

Endpoint Express

United Communications Group
11300 Rockville Pike, Ste. 1100 Ph: (301)287-2700
Rockville, MD 20852-3030 Free: 800-929-4824
Fax: (301)287-2049
E-mail: customer@ucg.com
Contact: Cathy Glassman, Editor.
Desc: Concerned with comprehensive coverage of bank payment systems, such as check processing and electronic funds transfer. Contains case studies, news, trends, and reports of developments within the industry. *Type:* Newsletter.

Farm Credit Council

50 F St. NW, Ste. 900 Ph: (202)626-8710
Washington, DC 20001 Free: 800-525-2345
Fax: (202)626-8718
URL: http://www.fccouncil.com
Contact: William R. Weber, Pres.
Desc: Represents the Farm Credit System, a nationwide system of cooperative financial institutions that lends to agriculture and rural America. Makes loans to agricultural producers, rural homebuyers, farmer cooperatives, and rural utilities. *Type:* Association.

Federal Reserve Bank of Atlanta—Financial Update

Federal Reserve Bank of Atlanta
104 Marietta St. Ph: (404)521-8269
Atlanta, GA 30303-2713 Fax: (404)521-8050
URL: http://www.frbatlanta.org.
Contact: Pierce Nelson.
Desc: Provides articles on developments in the payments system and discusses issues pertaining to bank supervision, financial instruments, services, publications, and regulation. *Type:* Newsletter.

Federal Reserve Bank of New York—Current Issues in Economics and Finance

Federal Reserve Bank of New York
Public Information Department Ph: (212)720-6134
33 Liberty St. Fax: (212)720-6628
New York, NY 10045
E-mail: PIPUBS@ny.frb.org.
URL: http://www.ny.frb.org.
Desc: Focuses on current trends in banking, investment, and capital markets. *Type:* Newsletter.

Fee Income Growth Strategies

Siefer Consultants, Inc.
PO Box 1384 Ph: (712)732-7340
Storm Lake, IA 50588 Free: 800-747-7342
E-mail: siefer@ncn.net
Contact: Steve Herron, Editor.
Desc: Discusses the role of fees and service charges for money orders, cashier's checks, nonsufficient funds, loans, automatic teller machine cards, and other ancillary services in the profitability of financial institutions. *Type:* Newsletter.

Fee Income Report

Siefer Consultants, Inc.
PO Box 1384 Ph: (712)732-7340
Storm Lake, IA 50588 Free: 800-747-7342
E-mail: siefer@ncn.net
Contact: Steve Herron, Editor.
Desc: Discusses opportunities for financial institutions to increase service charge income and generate commission

income. Methods include personal and commercial checking accounts, overdrafts, safe deposit boxes, savings accounts, transaction cards, consumer loans, commercial loans, and other ancillary services. *Type:* Newsletter.

Finance Company Weekly

SNL Securities
321 E. Main St.   Ph: (804)977-1600
PO Box 2124   Fax: (804)977-4466
Charlottesville, VA 22902
E-mail: subscriptions@snl.com

Contact: David Meadors, Editor; John Racine, Editor; Reig Nagle, Publisher; Pat LaBua, Subscription Mgr.

Desc: Contains news on publicly and privately traded finance companies. Includes consumer, commercial, credit card companies, pawn shops, and leasing companies. *Type:* Newsletter.

FINANCIAL

The WEFA Group
1110 Vermont Ave., NW   Ph: (202)775-0610
Washington, DC 20005
URL: http://www.fdic.gov

Desc: Contains more than 4000 weekly, monthly, quarterly, and annual financial time series on all key financial indicators for the U.S. market. *Available:* The WEFA Group. *Type:* Database.

Financial Industry Issues

Federal Reserve Bank of Dallas
PO Box 655906   Ph: (214)651-5254
Dallas, TX 75265-5906   Free: 800-333-4460

Contact: Jeffery W. Gunther, Editor; Thomas F. Siems, Editor.

Desc: Devoted to scholarly research into the forces that shape banking and finance. Provides in-depth articles. *Type:* Newsletter.

Financial Observer

CCH Canadian Ltd.
90 Sheppard Ave., Ste. 300   Ph: (416)441-0086
North York, ON, Canada M2N   Free: 800-268-4522
6X1   Fax: 800-461-4131
URL: http://www.ca.cch.com

Contact: Brad Morrison, Editor; Michael Dyet, Advertising Dir.; Rick Humphrey, Marketing Director.

Desc: Reports on the Canadian financial industry and developments abroad. *Type:* Newsletter.

The Financial 1,000

Monitor Publishing Co.
104 5th Ave., 2nd Fl.   Ph: (212)627-4140
New York, NY 10011   Fax: (212)645-0931

Desc: 30,000 executives of the top 1,000 banks, Wall Street firms, thrifts, and insurance companies. *Type:* Directory.

Financial Services M&A Insider

SNL Securities
321 E. Main St.   Ph: (804)977-1600
PO Box 2124   Fax: (804)977-4466
Charlottesville, VA 22902
E-mail: subscriptions@snl.com

Contact: John Racine, Editor; L. Todd Vencil, Editor; Reid Nagle, Publisher; Pat LaBua, Subscription Mgr.

Desc: Features articles and information on financial services. Covers mortgage banks, finance companies, investment advisors, and broker/dealers. *Type:* Newsletter.

Financial Technology Insight

Elsevier Science Inc.
655 Avenue of the Americas   Ph: (212)989-5800
New York, NY 10010   Fax: (212)633-3990
E-mail: usinfo@elsevier.com
URL: http://www.elsevier.com

Desc: Reports on computer and communications technology applications in banks and other financial Industry. *Type:* Newsletter.

First Friday

ASCU
PO Box 5488   Ph: (608)238-2646
Madison, WI 53705   Fax: (608)238-2646

Contact: Walter Polner, Editor.

Desc: Provides economics research and money market information of value to credit unions in immediate and long range planning. Focuses on financial institutions, savings trends, consumer lending trends, and new administrative rulings. *Type:* Newsletter.

Fitzroy Dearborn Directory of the World's Banks

Fitzroy Dearborn Publishers
919 N. Michigan Ave.   Ph: (312)587-0131
Chicago, IL 60611   Free: 800-850-8102
     Fax: (312)587-1049
E-mail: fitzroyd@aol.com
URL: http://www.fitzroydearborn.com

Desc: More than 10,000 national, commercial, investment, and development banks, worldwide. *Type:* Directory.

Florida Banker

Florida Bankers Association
1001 Thomasville Rd., No. 201   Ph: (850)224-2265
PO Box 1360   Fax: (850)224-2423
Tallahassee, FL 32302-1360

Contact: Wendy A. Barager, Editor.

Desc: Presents banking industry news and information from a Florida perspective. *Type:* Newsletter.

Foreign Exchange

The WEFA Group
1110 Vermont Ave., NW   Ph: (202)775-0610
Washington, DC 20005
URL: http://www.fdic.gov

Desc: Provides daily, weekly, and monthly historical data on foreign exchange rates on the U.S. dollar for 185 countries. *Available:* The WEFA Group. *Type:* Database.

FWANY Newsletter

Financial Women's Association of New York (FWANY)
215 Park Ave. S., Ste. 1713   Ph: (212)533-2141
New York, NY 10003   Fax: (212)982-3008
E-mail: info@fwa.org

Contact: Keren Solomon, Editor.

Desc: Provides information on the Association's programs and members. Recurring features include a calendar of events. *Type:* Newsletter.

F.Y.I Newsletter

Credit Union Executives Society (CUES)
6410 Enterprise Ln., Ste. 300   Ph: (608)271-2664
Madison, WI 53719-1143   Free: 800-252-2664
     Fax: (608)271-2303
E-mail: cues@cues.org
URL: http://www.cues.org/fyi.htm

Contact: Sara Landott, Editor, sara@cues.org.

Desc: Reports on subjects of interest to operations officers of financial institutions, particularly those employed in credit unions. Carries notes from the Association's advisory committee, member updates, and news items reflecting the Association's dedication to the professional growth and development of its members. *Type:* Newsletter.

Golembe Reports

CHG Consulting, Inc.
PO Box 1119   Ph: (561)243-1205
Delray Beach, FL 33447-1119   Fax: (561)243-0635

Contact: Carter H. Golembe, Editor.

Desc: Analyzes major public policy issues affecting financial institutions. Examines the long-term implication of developments in the financial industry. *Type:* Newsletter.

Hotline

Western League of Savings Institutions
9841 Airport Blvd., Ste. 418   Ph: (310)414-8300
Los Angeles, CA 90045-5416

Contact: Kathleen Wedeking, Editor.

Desc: Covers news developments within the industry, including reports of industry trends, mergers, and government/industry appointments. Discusses legislative and regulatory activities that affect the industry with emphasis on those issues distinctly applicable to savings institutions. *Type:* Newsletter.

Illinois Banknews

Illinois Bankers Association (IBA)
111 W. Jackson, Ste. 910   Ph: (312)347-3400
Chicago, IL 60604   Free: 800-878-2265
     Fax: (312)453-8956
E-mail: illbankers@aol.com

Contact: Christina M. Tornaso, Editor-in-Chief.

Desc: Published to provide bank directors, officers, chief executive officers, and other bankers' associations with Association and general banking industry news. Monitors legislative and regulatory developments at the state and federal levels. *Type:* Newsletter.

Independent Bankers Association of America

1 Thomas Cir. NW, Ste. 400   Ph: (202)659-8111
Washington, DC 20005   Free: 800-422-8439
     Fax: (202)659-1413
E-mail: info@ibaa.org
URL: http://www.ibaa.org

Contact: Kenneth A. Guenther, Exec.VP.

Desc: Provides legislative and regulatory information and representation for community or "Main Street" financial institutions and opposes "concentration of banking and commercial powers." *Type:* Association.

Inside B&C Lending

Inside Mortgage Finance Publications
PO Box 42518   Ph: (301)951-1240
Washington, DC 20015   Fax: (301)656-1709

Contact: Andrew Analore, Editor.

Desc: Covers the market of mortgage lending to borrowers whose credit is less than perfect. Provides information on such topics as loan grading, regulatory developments, and various B&C originators. *Type:* Newsletter.

Inside Commercial Mortgage Finance

Inside Mortgage Finance Publications, Inc.
PO Box 42387   Ph: (301)951-1240
Washington, DC 20015-0987   Fax: (301)656-1709

Desc: Focuses on commercial mortgage lending. Includes topics such as conduit activity, portfolio and correspondent lending, and servicing activity. *Type:* Newsletter.

Inside MBS & ABS

Inside Mortgage Finance Publications, Inc.
7910 Woodmont Ave., Ste. 906   Ph: (301)951-1240
Bethesda, MD 20814   Fax: (301)656-1709
URL: http://www.imfpubs.com.

Contact: John Bancroft, Managing Editor.

Desc: Covers the mortgage-related securities market and secondary mortgage market, including regulatory and market developments for derivative products. Also covers ABS and CMBS markets. *Type:* Newsletter.

Inside Mortgage Compliance

Inside Mortgage Finance Publications, Inc.
PO Box 42387   Ph: (301)951-1240
Washington, DC 20015-0987   Fax: (301)656-1709
URL: http://www.imfpubs.com.

Contact: George Brooks, Editor.

Desc: A Monthly Report On Community Reinvestment And Mortgage Disclosure For The 1990s. Covers issues pertaining to mortgage lending as affected by the Community Reinvestment Act (CRA) and Home Mortgage Disclosure Act (HMDA). *Type:* Newsletter.

Inside Mortgage Finance

Inside Mortgage Finance Publications, Inc.
7910 Woodmont Ave., Ste. 906   Ph: (301)951-1240
Bethesda, MD 20814   Fax: (301)656-1709
URL: http://www.imfpubs.com.

Contact: John Bancroft, Managing Editor.

Desc: Contains coverage and analysis of market trends and developments affecting the residential (primary) mortgage market. Includes extensive data on mortgage originations and servicing as well as secondary market activity. *Type:* Newsletter.

Inside Mortgage Technology

Inside Mortgage Finance Publications
PO Box 42518   Ph: (301)951-1240
Washington, DC 20015   Fax: (301)656-1709
URL: http://www.imfpubs.com.

Contact: John Bancroft, Managing Editor; Charlyne H. McWilliams, Assoc. Editor.

Desc: Provides information on developments in the use of technology as it relates to the mortgage industry. *Type:* Newsletter.

Institute of International Bankers

299 Park Ave., 17th Fl.
New York, NY 10171

Contact: Lawrence R. Uhlick, Exec.Dir.

Desc: Individuals representing 235 non-U.S. banks with offices in the United States. Seeks to foster and develop knowledge of international banking and credit. *Type:* Association.

Institutional Investor

Institutional Investor, Inc.
477 Madison Ave.   Ph: (212)224-3800
New York, NY 10022
URL: http://www.iinews.com

Desc: Contains the complete text of Institutional Investor magazine. Covers mergers and acquisitions, money management, corporate finances, investor relations, pension funds, global capital markets, and insurance. *Available:* LEXIS-NEXIS, LEXIS; LEXIS-NEXIS, NEXIS. *Type:* Database.

Insurance Daily

SNL Securities
321 E. Main St.   Ph: (804)977-1600
PO Box 2124   Fax: (804)977-4466
Charlottesville, VA 22902
E-mail: subscriptions@snl.com

Contact: Mike Deane, Editor; Reid Nagle, Publisher; Pat LaBua, Subscription Mgr.

Desc: Provides information on the insurance industry. Features news releases, filings, and news on top-performing stocks, insider trades, ownership filings, and legislative issues. *Type:* Newsletter.

The Insurance M&A Newsletter

SNL Securities
321 E. Main St.   Ph: (804)977-1600
PO Box 2124   Fax: (804)977-4466
Charlottesville, VA 22902
E-mail: subscriptions@snl.com

Contact: John Racine, Editor; L. Todd Vencil, Editor; Mark Kilduff, Editor; Reig Nagle, Publisher; Pat LaBua, Subscription Mgr.

Desc: Features articles and financial information on insurance mergers and acquisitions activity. Covers insurance companies, insurance brokers and agencies, managed care companies, and hospital administrators. *Type:* Newsletter.

Insurance Weekly

SNL Securities
321 E. Main St.   Ph: (804)977-1600
PO Box 2124   Fax: (804)977-4466
Charlottesville, VA 22902
E-mail: subscriptions@snl.com

Contact: Pat LaBua, Subscription Mgr.; Mike Deane, Editor; Reid Nagle, Publisher.

Desc: Summarizes events, market activity, and regulatory filings affecting insurance companies and insurance brokers. *Type:* Newsletter.

International Banking Regulator

American Banker/Bond Buyer Inc.
International Thomson Publishing Corp.
1 State St. Plaza   Ph: (212)803-8200
New York, NY 10004   Free: 800-362-3807
                                Fax: (212)843-9612

Contact: William Acworth, Editor.

Desc: Devoted to the interests and concerns of foreign banks operating in the U.S., such as the Foreign Bank Supervision Enhancement Act, trade finance, offshore tax havens, loan syndications, and state banking regulations. Recurring features include interviews, reports of meetings, a calendar of events. *Type:* Newsletter.

International Financial Services Association

Dan Taylor
1 World Trade Ctr., Ste. 2269   Ph: (212)466-3352
New York, NY 10048   Fax: (212)432-0544
URL: http://www.intlbanking.org

Contact: Dan Taylor, Pres.

Desc: Banks involved in international banking operations. Provides a forum to solve operational problems currently facing the global financial service community. Conducts research; sponsors educational programs. *Type:* Association.

International Financial Statistics

International Monetary Fund (IMF)
Statistics Department
700 19th St., N.W.   Ph: (202)623-6180
Washington, DC 20431

Desc: Contains more than 28,000 annual, quarterly, and monthly time series of economic and financial statistics on more than 200 countries, supplemented by world and area aggregates for key time series. Annual series cover 1948 to date; quarterly and monthly series cover 1957 to date; some monthly series cover 1985 to date. *Available:* FAME Information Services, Inc.; Standard & Poor's DRI, Data Products Division; GE Information Services (GEIS); MG, L'Architecte de l'Information Strategique, GSI-ECO; The WEFA Group. *Type:* Database.

ITA:/finserv

Association for Interactive Media
1301 Connecticut Ave. NW,   Ph: (202)408-0008
   5th Fl.   Fax: (202)408-0111
Washington, DC 20036
E-mail: info@interactivehq.org

Contact: Steven Pastorkovich, Editor.

Desc: Provides news and information on online banking, research studies, new banking technologies, interactive product offerings, and joint ventures. *Type:* Newsletter.

Item Processing Report

Phillips Business Information, Inc.
1201 Seven Locks Rd., Ste. 300 Ph: (301)340-1520
Potomac, MD 20854   Free: 888-707-5809
                                Fax: (301)340-3847
E-mail: clientservices.pbi@phillips.com
URL: http://www.phillips.com; http://www.phillips.com/cgi/catalog/info?IPR.

Contact: Mark Brousseau, Editor.

Desc: Monitors developments in the processing of remittances and checks, including image processing, optical character recognition, check truncation, hardware, and software. Remarks: Absorbed The Powell Report, 1992. *Type:* Newsletter.

Kansas City Fed Letter

Federal Reserve Bank of Kansas City
925 Grand Blvd.   Ph: (816)881-2683
Kansas City, MO 64198-0001   Fax: (816)881-2569
URL: http://www.kc.frb.org; http://www.kc.frb.org.

Contact: Lori Hand, Editor.

Desc: Contains news on the Federal Reserve System and the Kansas City Federal Reserve. Reports economic and financial developments. *Type:* Newsletter.

Knight-Ridder/Tribune Business News

Knight-Ridder/Tribune Information Services
790 National Press Bldg.   Ph: (202)383-6134
Washington, DC 20045
URL: http://www.knight-ridder.com

Contact: Robert Harris, Director.

Desc: Provides coverage of business and finance news, corporate developments, and stock, bond, and commodity markets. Contains the complete text of all business and related news produced by more than 80 newspapers and magazines, including all 28 Knight-Ridder general circulation daily newspapers, 4 Tribune Co. *Available:* The Dialog Corporation, DIALOG; The Dialog Corporation, DIALOG; Infomart Online; Infomart Online; Infomart Assistant, Infomart Online; Infomart Dialog Limited. *Type:* Database.

Letter of Credit Update

Government Information Services
1725 K St. NW, Ste. 700   Ph: (202)872-4000
Washington, DC 20006   Free: 800-677-3789
                                Fax: (202)739-9657
URL: http://www.thompson.com/tpg/paca.

Contact: Elizabeth Judd, Editor, (202)739-9547.

Desc: Covers legislative and judicial developments concerning letter of credit (L/C) practices. Features articles on L/C basics and the innovative use of L/Cs, drafting tips, and behind-the-scenes coverage of banking and trade organizations. *Type:* Newsletter.

LEXIS® Banking Library

LEXIS-NEXIS
9443 Springboro Pike   Ph: (937)865-6800
PO Box 933
Dayton, OH 45401-0933
URL: http://www.lex-nexis.com

Desc: Contains information on the federal regulations of banks, bank holding companies, thrifts, and credit unions.

Also contains selected case law pertaining to federal banking issues, and full-text sources providing news and insight on the banking industry. *Available:* LEXIS-NEXIS, LEXIS. *Type:* Database.

LEXIS® Financial Information Service

LEXIS-NEXIS
9443 Springboro Pike   Ph: (937)865-6800
PO Box 933
Dayton, OH 45401-0933
URL: http://www.lex-nexis.com
Desc: Provides business and financial information through a comprehensive company library containing the following files: • Earnings Projections (Zacks Earnings Estimator). • Securities and Exchange Commission Filings--includes 10-Q, 10-K,annual reports, and proxy statements; DISCLOSURE Database; and the SEC News Digest. *Available:* LEXIS-NEXIS, LEXIS. *Type:* Database.

Louisiana Banker

Louisiana Bankers Association
666 North St.   Ph: (225)387-3282
PO Box 2871   Fax: (225)343-3159
Baton Rouge, LA 70821
Contact: Jayme Foster, Editor, foster@lba.org.
Type: Newsletter.

Mark Bernkopf's Central Banking Resource Center

Mark Bernkopf's Central Banking Resource Center
4001 N. 9th St., Ste. 1110   Ph: (703)516-9265
Arlington, VA 22203-1964   Fax: (703)243-2103
URL: http://patriot.net/~bernkopf/
Contact: Mark Bernkopf, markb@erols.com.
Desc: Mark Bernkopf's Central Banking Resource Center provides an impressive array of central banking information and links, making this an outstanding resource for anyone seeking information on central banks as well as on ministries of finance and economics. The site contains links to many major ministries of finance, financial research seminars and conferences, financial news, bankers' associations, and a host of other related sites. *Type:* Database.

Merger Strategy Report

SNL Securities
321 E. Main St.   Ph: (804)977-1600
PO Box 2124   Fax: (804)977-4466
Charlottesville, VA 22902
E-mail: subscriptions@snl.com
Contact: Erik Withrow, Editor; John Minor, Editor; Reid Nagle, Publisher; Pat LaBua, Subscription Mgr.
Desc: Contains information on regional mergers and acquisitions. Includes lists of deals and ranking of advisors and lawyers. *Type:* Newsletter.

Microbanker's High-Tech Banking Strategies

Microbanker, Inc.
PO Box 708   Ph: (518)745-7071
Lake George, NY 12845-0708   Fax: (518)745-7009
E-mail: webmaster@microbanker.com
Contact: Roy Urrico, Editor, royurrico@microbanker.com.
Desc: Discusses the merits of software programs, management information systems, and other technologies having applications to the automation of banking functions within financial institutions. Examines systems and programs currently being implemented by various institutions and provides names and telephone numbers of people to contact for further information. *Type:* Newsletter.

Money Watch Bulletin

IWS Inc.
24 Canterbury Rd.   Ph: (516)766-5850
Rockville Centre, NY 11570   Free: 800-323-0548
                            Fax: (516)766-5919
Contact: Tyler G. Hicks, Editor.
Desc: Covers lenders and other sources of business and real estate loans and grants. Supplies a minimum of 100 lending sources per issue, including lender name, address, telephone number, and major lending interests. *Type:* Newsletter.

Mortgage Bankers Association of America

Janice Stango
1125 15th St. NW   Ph: (202)861-6500
Washington, DC 20005   Fax: (202)785-2967
Contact: Poul Beid, Exec.VP.
Desc: Principal lending and investor interests in the mortgage finance field, including mortgage banking firms, commercial banks, life insurance companies, title companies, and savings and loan associations. Seeks to improve methods of originating, servicing, and marketing loans of residential and income-producing properties through industry education and cooperation with federal agencies and the Congress. *Type:* Association.

Mortgage Banking Sourcebook

Real Estate Finance Press
1125 15th St. NW   Ph: (202)861-6989
Washington, DC 20005   Free: 800-793-MBAA
                            Fax: (202)861-0736
Desc: Federal, state, and private agencies and associations involved in the real estate finance industry. *Type:* Directory.

Mortgage Finance Review

Mortgage Bankers Association of America
1125 15th St. NW   Free: 800-793-MBAA
Washington, DC 20005
Contact: David Lereah, Editor, david_lereah@mbaa.org.
Desc: Brings information on mortgage banking industry developments, issues and data as it affects the real estate finance industry. Reports on industry trends, including housing starts, origination volume and market share, trends in delinquencies and foreclosures, and movement of refinancing activity. *Type:* Newsletter.

Mortgage Market Trends

Canada Mortgage and Housing Corp. (CMHC)
700 Montreal Rd.   Ph: (613)748-2000
Ottawa, ON, Canada K1A 0P7 Fax: (613)748-2098
URL: http://www.cmhc-schl.qc.ca; http://www.chmos-sd-mloc.ceds.com.
Contact: A. Manouchehri, Managing Editor, (613)748-2506, fax: (613)748-2156, amanouch@cmhc-schol.gc.ca.
Desc: Features articles and information about Canada's mortgage industry, including products, trends, and companies. Recurring features include interviews and comparison charts. *Type:* Newsletter.

Mortgage Marketplace

American Banker/Bond Buyer Inc.
International Thomson Publishing Corp.
1 State St. Plaza   Ph: (212)803-8200
New York, NY 10004   Free: 800-362-3807
                            Fax: (212)843-9612
Contact: Richard Bays, Editor.
Desc: Monitors factors affecting the mortgage securities market, including legislation, political developments, regulations, and accounting issues. *Type:* Newsletter.

The Mortgage Report

American Consolidated Capital Inc.
Box 2681   Ph: (561)744-3394
Jupiter, FL 33468
Contact: Howard Cook, Editor.
Desc: Provides information on purchasing secured mortgages. *Type:* Newsletter.

NABCA Bulletin

National Association for Bank Cost and Management Accounting (NABCA)
7950 E. La Junta Rd.
Scottsdale, AZ 85255-2798
E-mail: nabca@concentric.net
Desc: Monitors NABCA events and profiles NABCA members and committees. Recurring features include reports of meetings and workshops and a calendar of events. *Type:* Newsletter.

NASCUS Stateline

National Association of State Credit Union Supervisors (NASCUS)
1901 N. Moore St., No. 203   Ph: (703)528-8351
Arlington, VA 22209   Fax: (703)528-3248
E-mail: offices@nascus.org
URL: http://www.NASCUS.org.
Contact: Ronda Combs, Editor, (703)528-0669.
Desc: Publishes news of Association activities and legislative developments affecting credit unions. *Type:* Newsletter.

National Association of Federal Credit Unions—Update

National Association of Federal Credit Unions (NAFCU)
PO Box 3769   Ph: (703)522-4770
Washington, DC 20007   Free: 800-344-5580
                            Fax: (703)524-1082
E-mail: nafcu@nafcunet.org; update@nafcunet.org.
URL: http://www.nafcunet.org.
Contact: Patrick M. Keefe, Editor; Susan M. Broaddus, Managing Editor.
Desc: Provides news of legislative, regulatory, and market events that are relevant to the operations of federally chartered credit unions. Reports NAFCU's positions on these issues. *Type:* Newsletter.

National Association of Mortgage Brokers

8201 Greensboro Dr., Ste. 300   Ph: (703)610-9009
Mc Lean, VA 22102   Fax: (703)610-9005
URL: http://www.namb.com
Contact: Brian J. Kinsella, Exec.VP.
Desc: Mortgage brokers who seek to increase professionalism and to foster business relationships among members. Offers three levels of professional certification. Compiles statistics. *Type:* Association.

National Automated Clearing House Association

13665 Dulles Technology Dr.,   Ph: (703)561-1100
  Suite 300   Free: 800-487-9180
Herndon, VA 20171   Fax: (703)787-0996
URL: http://www.nacha.org
Contact: Elliott McEntee, CEO & Pres.
Desc: Automated Clearing House (ACH) association. Provides an interregional exchange for electronic debits and credits among ACHs and to establish and administer nationwide standards and operating rules for ACHs. *Type:* Association.

The NCUA Watch

American Banker/Bond Buyer Inc.
International Thomson Publishing Corp.
1 State St. Plaza   Ph: (212)803-8200
New York, NY 10004   Free: 800-362-3807
                            Fax: (212)843-9612

Contact: Melanie Waddell, Editor.

Desc: Analyzes legislative and regulatory issues affecting credit unions and the National Credit Union Administration (NCUA). Includes comments on regulatory initiatives, coverage of NCUA legal activities, and lists of credit union mergers and membership changes. *Type:* Newsletter.

New Jersey League News

New Jersey League - Community & Savings Bankers
411 North Ave. E.   Ph: (908)272-8500
Cranford, NJ 07016-2444   Fax: (908)272-6626
URL: http://www.njleague.com.

Contact: Samuel J. Damiano, Editor; James M. Meredith, Assoc. Editor.

Desc: Focuses on the savings institution industry. *Type:* Newsletter.

The New York Banker

New York Bankers Association
99 Park Ave., 4th Fl.   Ph: (212)297-1600
New York, NY 10016   Fax: (212)949-1183
URL: http://www.nyba.com.

Contact: Janice L. Linhares, Editor.

Desc: Presents articles of interest to the New York State commercial banking industry. Reports on pertinent legislative issues and on Association-sponsored schools and seminars. *Type:* Newsletter.

NIBESA News

National Independent Bank Equipment & Systems Association (NIBESA)
1411 Peterson, Ste. 101   Ph: (847)825-8419
Park Ridge, IL 60068   Free: 800-843-6082
                            Fax: (847)825-8445
E-mail: nibesa@nibesa.com

Contact: Ann Walk, Editor.

Desc: Informs members of developments and trends in the bank equipment industry. Recurring features include editorials and news of the Association and its members. *Type:* Newsletter.

Operations Alert

America's Community Bankers
900 19th St. NW, Ste. 400   Ph: (202)857-3100
Washington, DC 20006   Fax: (202)857-5581
E-mail: info@acbankers.org

Contact: Brian Nixon, Editor; Jeffrey Noe, Editor.

Desc: Reviews recent regulatory and product developments that affect community bank operations. *Type:* Newsletter.

Payments System Report

National Automated Clearing House Association
13665 Dulles Technology Dr.,   Ph: (703)561-1100
Ste. 300   Free: 800-487-9180
Herndon, VA 20171   Fax: (703)742-8713
E-mail: info@nacha.org; psr@nacha.org.

Contact: Michael Herd, Editor.

Desc: Provides information about ACH Network and the payments industry. Includes industry news and analysis. *Type:* Newsletter.

Perspectives

Federal Reserve Bank of Dallas
PO Box 655906   Ph: (214)651-5254
Dallas, TX 75265-5906   Free: 800-333-4460

Contact: Jennifer Afflerbach, Editor; Monica Reeves, Editor.

Desc: Discusses various banking and community topics. *Type:* Newsletter.

Polk Financial Institutions Directory

Thomson Financial Publishing, Inc.
1321 Murfreesboro Rd., Ste.   Ph: (615)889-3350
731   Free: 800-827-2265
PO Box 305100   Fax: (615)885-3081
Nashville, TN 37230-5100

Desc: 15,000 banks and their branches; over 2,000 head offices, and 15,500 branches of savings and loan associations; over 5,500 credit unions with assets over $5 million; Federal Reserve System and other U.S. government and state government banking agencies; bank holding, commercial finance, and leasing companies; ocverage includes the United States, Canada, Mexico, and Central America. *Type:* Directory.

Pratt's Letter

A.S. Pratt & Sons
1911 Fort Myer Dr., Ste. 308   Ph: (703)528-0145
Arlington, VA 22209   Free: 800-572-2797

Contact: Alan B. Rice, Editor.

Desc: Alerts banks on Washington, D.C. developments. *Type:* Newsletter.

Problem Asset Reporter

Dorset Group, Inc.
11 Penn Plaza   Fax: (212)695-8172
New York, NY 10001

Contact: Stan Strachan, Editor; Mark Fogarty, Editor; Brian Collins, Editor.

Desc: Reports on the activities of the Resolution Trust Corporation and the FDIC Division of Resolution, and the U.S. governments. *Type:* Newsletter.

Quality Customer Service

Siefer Consultants, Inc.
PO Box 1384   Ph: (712)732-7340
Storm Lake, IA 50588   Free: 800-747-7342
E-mail: siefer@ncn.net

Contact: Steve Herron, Editor.

Desc: "Designed to help financial institutions develop an effective service culture to maximize customer retention and attract new customers." Customer service ideas include programs to monitor service, employee training, dealing with unhappy customers, telephone answering techniques, customer appreciation events, plus marketing strategies. *Type:* Newsletter.

Regional Economic Digest

Federal Reserve Bank of Kansas City
925 Grand Blvd.   Ph: (816)881-2683
Kansas City, MO 64198-0001   Fax: (816)881-2569
URL: http://www.kc.frb.org; http://www.kc.frb.org.

Contact: Lowell Jones, Editor.

Desc: Focuses on regional developments for Federal Reserve Bank of Kansas City. Reports on agricultural credit conditions and farm real estate values, and provides information on the total loans, investments, and deposits of member financial institutions. *Type:* Newsletter.

Regulatory Checklist

Western League of Savings Institutions
9841 Airport Blvd., Ste. 418   Ph: (310)414-8300
Los Angeles, CA 90045-5416

Contact: Cathy Moran, Editor.

Desc: Covers federal regulations, emphasizing those developments of interest to the savings industry. Lists regulatory actions and provides a short synopsis, concentrating on the implications relating to savings institutions. *Type:* Newsletter.

Regulatory Compliance Watch

American Banker/Bond Buyer Inc.
International Thomson Publishing Corp.
1 State St. Plaza   Ph: (212)803-8200
New York, NY 10004   Free: 800-362-3807
                            Fax: (212)843-9612

Desc: Reports on federal legislative and regulatory developments affecting banks, savings and loan, associations, and credit unions. Lists and analyzes current regulatory changes. *Type:* Newsletter.

Regulatory Risk Monitor

United Communications Group
11300 Rockville Pike, Ste. 1100   Ph: (301)287-2700
Rockville, MD 20852-3030   Free: 800-929-4824
                            Fax: (301)287-2049
E-mail: customer@ucg.com

Contact: Chris McCarter, Editor, (310)287-2425, fax: (310)816-8945, cmccarter@ucg.com; Dennis Sullivan, Publisher.

Desc: Provides information on financial institutions' enforcement and regulations. *Type:* Newsletter.

REIT Daily Fax

SNL Securities
321 E. Main St.   Ph: (804)977-1600
PO Box 2124   Fax: (804)977-4466
Charlottesville, VA 22902
E-mail: subscriptions@snl.com

Contact: Glenn Doggett, Editor; Chandler Spears, Editor; Reig Nagle, Publisher; Pat LaBua, Subscription Mgr.

Desc: Features industry events, condensed news stories, recent capital offerings, and market information of interest to REIT industry professionals and investors. *Type:* Newsletter.

Research

Research Magazine, Inc.
2201 3rd St.   Ph: (415)621-0220
San Francisco, CA 94107-0905   Fax: (415)621-0735
E-mail: webmaster@researchmag.com.

Contact: Gil Weinreich, Managing Editor; Robert Tyndall, Publisher, (415)437-4205, rtyndall@researchmag.com.

Desc: Magazine for stockbrokers including corporate profiles, financial data, articles on investment products, finance selling techniques and tools. *Type:* Periodical.

The Review of Banking & Financial Services

Standard & Poor's
25 Broadway   Ph: (212)208-8000
New York, NY 10004-1064   Free: 800-221-5277
                            Fax: (212)208-0040
URL: http://www.stockinfo.standardpoor.com; http://www.standardandpoors.com/ratings.

Contact: Michael Finkelstein, Editor.

Type: Newsletter.

Robert Morris Associates/Association of Lending and Credit Risk Professionals

1 Liberty Pl.   Ph: (215)446-4000
1650 Market St., Ste. 2300   Fax: (215)446-4101
Philadelphia, PA 19103-7398

Contact: Allen W. Sanborn Reed, Pres./CEO.

Desc: Commercial and savings banks, and savings and loan, and other financial services companies. *Type:* Association.

The Safe Deposit Bulletin
New York State Safe Deposit Association
Box 5074, Rockefeller Center Ph: (212)484-2260
Sta. Fax: (516)883-8429
New York, NY 10185
Contact: Paul J. Sanchez, Editor.
Desc: Discusses topics on safe and sound business practice for safe deposit organizations. Recurring features include news of research, notices of publications available, a calendar of events, news of educational opportunities, Association news, current legal and regulatory changes, current practices and procedures and Q&A section. *Type:* Newsletter.

Secured Transactions Monthly
Warren, Gorham & Lamont R.I.A. Group
90 Fifth Ave., 10th Fl. Ph: (212)807-2193
New York, NY 10011 Free: 800-950-1216
  Fax: (212)337-4183
Contact: Barkley Clark, Editor; Barbara Brewer Clark, Editor.
Desc: Provides information on ways that lenders, lending institutions, and their lawyers can make secure loans and protect those loans that are less secure. *Type:* Newsletter.

Seller/Servicer Update
Inside Mortgage Finance Publications, Inc.
7910 Woodmont Ave., Ste. 906 Ph: (301)951-1240
Bethesda, MD 20814 Fax: (301)656-1709
URL: http://www.imfpubs.com.
Contact: George Brooks, Editor.
Desc: Covers issues in the mortgage companies and servicing industry, including activities of mortgage associations and government agencies, regulations, and mortgage market trends and developments. *Type:* Newsletter.

SNL Daily BankFax
SNL Securities
321 E. Main St. Ph: (804)977-1600
PO Box 2124 Fax: (804)977-4466
Charlottesville, VA 22902
E-mail: subscriptions@snl.com
URL: http://www.snl.com.
Contact: Virginia Needham, Editor; John Racine, Editor; Mark Saunders, Editor.
Desc: A daily fax of the most up-to-date information available on the banking industry featuring the latest news releases, merger activity, stock highlights, and all of the previous day's regulatory filings and important events. *Type:* Newsletter.

SNL Daily ThriftWatch
SNL Securities
321 E. Main St. Ph: (804)977-1600
PO Box 2124 Fax: (804)977-4466
Charlottesville, VA 22902
E-mail: subscriptions@snl.com
URL: http://www.snl.com.
Contact: Virginia Needham, Editor; John Racine, Editor.
Desc: Imparts news by fax on mergers, dividend and earning announcements, stock highlights, interest rates, and the latest updates in the thrift industry. *Type:* Newsletter.

SNL Mortgage Bank Weekly
SNL Securities
321 E. Main St. Ph: (804)977-1600
PO Box 2124 Fax: (804)977-4466
Charlottesville, VA 22902
E-mail: subscriptions@snl.com
URL: http://www.snl.com.
Contact: David Meadors, Editor; John Racine, Editor.
Desc: Reports by fax a concise and thorough summary of the previous week's news and market information affecting mortgage banks, Freddic Mac, Fannie Mae and the secondary mortgage markets. *Type:* Newsletter.

SNL Weekly Bankfax
SNL Securities
321 E. Main St. Ph: (804)977-1600
PO Box 2124 Fax: (804)977-4466
Charlottesville, VA 22902
E-mail: subscriptions@snl.com
Contact: Steve Tomasi, Editor; Eric Croson, Editor; Reid Nagle, Publisher; John Racine, Editor-in-Chief; Pat LaBue, Subscription Mgr.
Desc: Summary of events, market activity, and regulatory filings for the Northeastern, Southern, Midwestern, and Western regions. *Type:* Newsletter.

SNL Weekly ComplianceFax
SNL Securities
321 E. Main St. Ph: (804)977-1600
PO Box 2124 Fax: (804)977-4466
Charlottesville, VA 22902
E-mail: subscriptions@snl.com
Contact: Todd L. Davenport, Editor; Reid Nagle, Publisher; Pat LaBua, Subscription Mgr.
Desc: Synopsis of regulatory issues affecting banks and thrifts with excerpts from government agencies, Congress, and industry sources. Includes an index of regulatory documents that provides a quick reference for agency releases, court documents, and congressional bills and testimony. *Type:* Newsletter.

The State Advisor
American Council of State Savings Supervisors
PO Box 34175 Ph: (703)922-5153
Washington, DC 20043-4175 Fax: (703)922-6237
Contact: Diane Homiak, Editor.
Desc: Reports on financial institutions legislation as it affects state-chartered savings associations and their regulators. *Type:* Newsletter.

TASDA Educational Bulletin
American Safe Deposit Association
PO Box 519 Ph: (317)738-4432
Franklin, IN 46131 Fax: (317)738-5267
Contact: Joyce A. McLin, Editor.
Desc: Provides articles and information on safe deposit and related topics. Remarks: Bulletin is a supplement to AC-CESS, a quarterly magazine. *Type:* Newsletter.

Teikoku Databank Kaisha Nenkan
Teikoku Databank America, Inc.
747 Third Ave., 25th Fl. Ph: (212)421-9805
New York, NY 10017 Fax: (212)421-9806
E-mail: koshi@teikoku.com
Desc: In two volumes, approximately 150,000 banks and companies in Japan. *Type:* Directory.

Teller Sense
Bureau of Business Practice
24 Rope Ferry Rd. Ph: (860)442-4365
Waterford, CT 06386 Free: 800-243-0876
  Fax: (860)437-3555
URL: http://www.bbpnews.com; http://www.bbpnews.com.
Contact: Jeanne Morton, Editor, jeanne_morton@prenhall.com.
Desc: Highlights a single topic per issue to assist tellers in performing their job effectively. Covers such subjects as customer service, cross-selling, self improvement, crime detection, and human relations skills. *Type:* Newsletter.

Teller Vision
Bureau of Business Practice
24 Rope Ferry Rd. Ph: (860)442-4365
Waterford, CT 06386 Free: 800-243-0876
  Fax: (860)437-3555
URL: http://www.bbpnews.com; http://www.bbpnews.com.
Contact: Jeanne Moorton, Editor, jeanne_moorton@prenhall.com.
Desc: Helps bank/credit union customer-contact employees keep abreast of changes and trends in the banking industry. Covers customer relations, cross-selling techniques, teller training methods, and security issues. *Type:* Newsletter.

The Texas Financial Institutions Directory & Fact Book
R. L. Polk & Co.
2001 Elm Hill Pike Ph: (615)889-3350
PO Box 305100 Fax: (615)885-3081
Nashville, TN 37230-5100
Desc: Main offices and branches of banks, savings and loans, and credit unions in the state of Texas. *Type:* Directory.

Thomson Bank Directory
Thomson Financial Publishing
4709 Golf Rd., 6th Fl. Ph: (847)676-9600
Skokie, IL 60076-1253 Free: 800-321-3373
  Fax: (847)933-8101
URL: http://www.tfp.com; http://www.bankinfo.com
Contact: Elizabeth F. Swann, Vice President.
Desc: In three volumes, about 11,000 banks and 50,000 branches of United States banks, and 60,000 foreign banks and branches engaged in foreign banking; Federal Reserve system and other United States government and state government banking agencies; 500 largest North American and International commercial banks; paper and automated clearinghouses. Volumes 1 and 2 contain North American listings; volumes 3 and 4, international listings (also cited as " Thomson International Bank Directory"); volume 5, Worldwide Correspondents Guide containing key correspondent data to facilitate funds transfer. *Type:* Directory.

Thomson Credit Union Directory
Thomson Financial Publishing
4709 Golf Rd., 6th Fl. Ph: (847)676-9600
Skokie, IL 60076-1253 Free: 800-321-3373
  Fax: (847)933-8101
URL: http://www.tfp.com; http://www.bankinfo.com
Contact: Peggy Hayner, Editor.
Desc: Approximately 12,000 credit unions and head offices and over 6,000 branches. *Type:* Directory.

Thomson Regulation CC Directory
Thomson Financial Publishing
4709 Golf Rd., 6th Fl. Ph: (847)676-9600
Skokie, IL 60076-1253 Free: 800-321-3373
  Fax: (847)933-8101
URL: http://www.tfp.com; http://www.bankinfo.com
Contact: Marie King, Editor.
Desc: About 30,000 financial institutions. *Type:* Directory.

Thomson Savings Directory
Thomson Financial Publishing
4709 Golf Rd., 6th Fl. Ph: (847)676-9600
Skokie, IL 60076-1253 Free: 800-321-3373
  Fax: (847)933-8101
URL: http://www.tfp.com; http://www.bankinfo.com
Contact: Peggy Hayner, Editor.
Desc: Nearly 2,000 savings institutions and their 13,000 branch offices. *Type:* Directory.

Thomson's International Banking Regulator

American Banker/Bond Buyer Inc.
International Thomson Publishing Corp.
1 State St. Plaza   Ph: (212)803-8200
New York, NY 10004   Free: 800-362-3807
                           Fax: (212)843-9612
Contact: Craig Webb, Editor.
Desc: Tracks legislative, regulatory, and other changes in the banking and securities markets worldwide. Focuses on European Community developments. *Type:* Newsletter.

The Uniform Commercial Code Law Letter

Warren, Gorham & Lamont R.I.A. Group
90 Fifth Ave., 10th Fl.   Ph: (212)807-2193
New York, NY 10011   Free: 800-950-1216
                           Fax: (212)337-4183
Contact: Thomas M. Quinn, Editor.
Desc: Analyzes federal and state court decisions under the Uniform Commercial Code (UCC). "Offers compliance ideas and techniques developed by leading corporations and banks for use under the Code." Contains case histories, a column titled On the Shelf (reviews of recent publications), and a section titled Consumer Credit Report (incorporating the Truth-in-Lending Review), which tracks developments in current credit topics in courts and legislatures. *Type:* Newsletter.

Walker's Manual of Community Bank Stocks

Walker's Manual, LLC
3650 Mt. Diablo Blvd., Ste. 240   Ph: (510)283-9993
Lafayette, CA 94549   Free: 800-932-2922
                                  Fax: (510)283-9513
E-mail: info@walkersotc.com
Desc: 502 community banks in the United States—community banks are financed with less than $10 million and usually serve a limited geographic area. *Type:* Directory.

Washington Weekly Report

Independent Bankers Association of America
1 Thomas Circle NW, Ste. 950   Ph: (202)659-8111
Washington, DC 20005
Contact: Kenneth Guenther, Editor.
Desc: Follows federal banking legislation and policy making. *Type:* Newsletter.

WESTLAW® Finance & Banking Library

West Group
620 Opperman Dr.   Ph: (651)687-7000
St. Paul, MN 55164-0526
URL: http://www.westgroup.com
Desc: Contains the complete text of U.S. federal and state court decisions, statutes and regulations, administrative law publications, specialized files, and texts and periodicals dealing with the financial services industry. *Available:* West Group, WESTLAW. *Type:* Database.

World Bank News

World Bank
1818 H St., NW   Ph: (202)473-1010
Rm. F4K-256   Fax: (202)522-2125
Washington, DC 20433
E-mail: books@worldbank.org
URL: http://www.worldbank.org/html/extdr/extcs/news.html
Contact: Joelle Dehasse, Editor.
Desc: Provides news concerning the World Bank. Spotlights development projects, loan approvals, and research results. *Type:* Newsletter.

World Bank Watch

Bernan Associates
4611-F Assembly Dr.   Ph: (301)459-2255
Lanham, MD 20706-4391   Free: 800-274-4447
                           Fax: (301)459-0056
E-mail: query@bernan.com
URL: http://www.bernan.com
Desc: Examines the projects and policies of development banks worldwide. Covers government-supported investments and financing for Third World nations. *Type:* Newsletter.

World Council of Credit Unions—Perspectives

World Council of Credit Unions
PO Box 2982   Ph: (608)231-7130
Madison, WI 53701   Fax: (608)238-8020
URL: http://www.woccu.org.
Contact: Christopher Baker, CEO.
Desc: Focuses on World Council's projects and activities. *Type:* Newsletter.

Baptist

ABW Ministries

PO Box 851   Ph: (610)768-2288
Valley Forge, PA 19482-0851   Free: 800-ABC-3USA
                           Fax: (610)768-2275
E-mail: danielweiss@abc-usa.org
URL: http://www.abc-usa.org
Contact: Carol F. Sutton, Exec.Dir.
Desc: Women who belong to an American Baptist church. Seeks to undergird the total program of the American Baptist Churches of the U.S.A., through support of missions and church service projects. Conducts studies and acts in matters involving Christian social concern, including local, national, and international affairs; sponsors programs to meet the specific needs of women as well as to integrate them into the life of the church. *Type:* Association.

All-Ukrainian Evangelical Baptist Fellowship

6751 Riverside Dr.   Ph: (708)788-0999
Berwyn, IL 60402   Fax: (708)788-0999
Contact: Rev. Vladimir Domashovetz, Pres.
Desc: Associations, churches, and church members. Purpose is to coordinate the worldwide ministries of associations of Ukrainian Baptist churches and other church-related organizations and institutions located in countries of the free world. *Type:* Association.

Baptist Bible Fellowship International

PO Box 191   Ph: (417)862-5001
Springfield, MO 65801   Fax: (417)865-0794
E-mail: 76043.2702@compuserve.com
URL: http://www.bbfi.org/
Contact: Bob Baird, Mission Dir.
Desc: Missionaries and churches in 90 countries. Promotes missionary activities. Operates Baptist Bible College and Baptist Bible School of Theology, both in Springfield, Missouri and Baptist Bible College East in Boston, Massachusetts. *Type:* Association.

Baptist Mid-Missions

7749 Webster Rd.   Ph: (440)826-3930
PO Box 308011   Fax: (440)826-4457
Cleveland, OH 44130
E-mail: info@bmm.org
Contact: Dr. Gary L. Anderson, Pres.
Desc: Serves as a medium through which orthodox Baptist churches may cooperate in Baptist missionary activities, direct their missionary funds and refer their young people who are called to missionary service. Supports 558 foreign and 274 active home missionaries. Provides children services. *Type:* Association.

Baptist Mission of North America

137 Winckles St.   Ph: (216)365-7308
PO Box 1078
Elyria, OH 44036
Contact: Dr. Harold Garland, Pres.
Desc: Missionaries and ministers. Seeks to establish Baptist churches across the North American continent. Works closely with the local church on home mission activities. *Type:* Association.

Baptist World Alliance

6733 Curran St.   Ph: (703)790-8980
Mc Lean, VA 22101-6005   Fax: (703)893-5160
E-mail: bwa@bwanet.org
URL: http://www.bwanet.org
Contact: Denton Lotz, Gen.Sec.-Treas.
Desc: International Baptist bodies representing more than 42,000,000 individuals. "To exist as an expression of the essential oneness of Baptist people in the Lord Jesus Christ; to impart inspiration to the fellowship; and to provide channels for sharing concerns and skills in witness and ministry." Focuses major activities in the areas of: communications; evangelism and education; world aid; study and research; promotion and development. Conducts relief programs, such as sending aid to distressed peoples and assisting in the rehabilitation of refugees from political and other oppressions. *Type:* Association.

Board of Home Missions of the National Association of Free Will Baptists

PO Box 5002   Ph: (615)731-6812
Antioch, TN 37011   Fax: (615)731-7655
Contact: Trymon Messer, Gen.Dir.
Desc: Free Will Baptist ministers. Promotes evangelistic and church growth activities and the establishment of Free Will Baptist churches in North America. Endorses chaplains for the armed forces. *Type:* Association.

Board of International Ministries

American Baptist Churches in the U.S.A.
PO Box 851   Ph: (610)768-2000
Valley Forge, PA 19482-0851   Free: 800-222-3872
                           Fax: (610)768-2088
E-mail: 102262.713@compuserve.com
URL: http://www.abc-USA.org
Contact: Dr. John A. Sundquist, Exec.Dir.
Desc: A board of the American Baptist Churches in the U.S.A. Conducts educational, evangelistic, development and medical mission projects in Africa, Asia, the Caribbean, Central America, South America, and Europe. Administers the Boville-Murray Vacation Bible School Fund. *Type:* Association.

Brotherhood Commission

4200 N Point Pkwy   Free: 800-727-6466
Alpharetta, GA 30022-4174
Contact: Dr. James D. Williams, Pres.
Desc: An agency of the Southern Baptist Convention. Men and boys who are members of Southern Baptist churches and who have an interest in Christian missions. Attempts to help churches involve men and boys in missions. *Type:* Association.

CBInternational

PO Box 5   Ph: (630)260-3800
Wheaton, IL 60189   Fax: (630)665-1418
E-mail: cbi@cb.usa.com
URL: http://www.cbi.org
Contact: Dr. Hans W. Finzel, Exec.Dir.
Desc: Independent Baptist mission society with 750 evangelical missionaries in 60 countries. *Type:* Association.

Conservative Baptist Association of America

PO Box 66
Wheaton, IL 60189
Ph: (630)260-3800
Fax: (630)653-5387
E-mail: cbamerica@aol.com
URL: http://www.cbamerica.org
Contact: Rev. Ed Mitchell, Exec.Admin.
Desc: Provides leadership, fellowship, counseling services, and specialized support ministries to 1,200 member churches in an effort "to advance the cause of Christ through worship, evangelism, instruction, and service throughout the world." Conducts charitable program; offers placement service, chaplaincy endorsement. *Type:* Association.

Continental Baptist Mission

5900 Alpine NW
Comstock Park, MI 49321
Ph: (616)784-7190
Fax: (616)784-3330
E-mail: cbm@cbmoffice.org
URL: http://www.ourworld.compuserve.com/homepages/cbm
Contact: Gerald K. Webber, D.D., Pres.
Desc: Missionaries. Purpose is to establish Baptist churches in the U.S. and Canada. *Type:* Association.

Ethics and Religious Liberty Commission of the Southern Baptist Convention

901 Commerce St., Ste. 550
Nashville, TN 37203
Ph: (615)244-2495
Fax: (615)242-0065
URL: http://www.erlc.com
Contact: Richard D. Land, Pres.
Desc: An agency of the Southern Baptist Convention representing 38,000 churches and 15,000,000 individuals. Provides a program of moral education, leadership, and action based on biblical principles and contemporary social analysis relating to family life, human relations, economics, daily work, citizenship, war and peace, religious liberty, and other issues. Offers suggestions to churches; works to affect legislation regarding moral and social issues. *Type:* Association.

General Association of General Baptists

100 Stinson Dr.
Poplar Bluff, MO 63901
Ph: (573)785-7746
Contact: Ron Black, Exec.Dir.
Desc: Individuals interested in encouraging fellowship through cooperative means. (General Baptists encourage acceptance of other denominations in cooperative mission work.) Conducts overseas mission work. *Type:* Association.

General Association of Regular Baptist Churches

1300 N. Meacham Rd.
Schaumburg, IL 60173-4806
Ph: (847)843-1600
Fax: (847)843-3757
E-mail: garbc@garbc.org
URL: http://www.garbc.org
Contact: Rev. John Greening, Nat.Rep.
Desc: Baptist church members from 1415 churches. Perpetuates historic faith and fellowship as delineated in the Bible. Works to advance member churches. *Type:* Association.

National Baptist Convention, U.S.A.

1700 Baptist World Center Dr.
Nashville, TN 37207
Ph: (615)228-6292
Fax: (615)226-8757
URL: http://www.nbcusa.org
Contact: Dr. Henry J. Lyons, Pres.
Desc: Seeks to: promote home and foreign missions; encourage and support Christian education; publish and distribute Sunday School and other religious literature. Operates youth camps, student centers, and the American Baptist Theological Seminary. *Type:* Association.

National Baptist Deacons Convention of America

9500 Reams Rd.
Richmond, VA 23236
Ph: (804)330-3057
Contact: James H. Taylor, Jr., Pres.
Desc: Aims to: increase the knowledge of the work of Missionary Baptist Deacons; support their work in domestic and foreign missions. Works in 22 states. Conducts Bible study and leadership training conferences. *Type:* Association.

Woman's Missionary Union

100 Missionary Ridge
PO Box 830711
Birmingham, AL 35283-0010
Ph: (205)991-8100
Free: 800-968-7301
Fax: (205)995-4846
E-mail: email@wmu.org
URL: http://www.wmu.com
Contact: Dellanna W. O'Brien, Exec.Dir.
Desc: Female members of churches that are part of the Southern Baptist Convention. Works to teach, support, and promote individual involvement in missions. *Type:* Association.

Baseball

American Legion Baseball

PO Box 1055
Indianapolis, IN 46206
Ph: (317)630-1213
Fax: (317)630-1369
E-mail: tal@legion.org
URL: http://www.legion.org
Contact: James R. Quinlan, Coord.
Desc: Teams of teenagers playing supervised summer baseball under leadership provided by volunteer adult managers and coaches. Teams are locally financed by individuals, service clubs, and commercial business firms. Purposes are to: stimulate greater baseball activity in local communities; help preserve and improve recreational facilities; aid in the development and improvement of the physical fitness of America's youth; combat juvenile delinquency through positive methods. *Type:* Association.

Babe Ruth Baseball/Softball

PO Box 5000
1770 Brunswick Pike
Trenton, NJ 08638
Ph: (609)695-1434
Fax: (609)695-2505
URL: http://www.baberuthleague.org
Contact: Ronald Tellefsen, CEO & Pres.
Desc: Supervises baseball and softball activity for youths five through 18 years of age. Conducts eight World Series annually. Sponsors workshops. *Type:* Association.

Ballard Strikes Softball Magazine

ASA/USA Softball
2801 NE 50th St.
Oklahoma City, OK 73111
Ph: (405)424-5266
Fax: (405)424-4734
E-mail: info@softball.org.
Contact: Ron Babb, Editor, (405)425-3434, rabb@softball.org.
Desc: Official magazine of ASA/USA Softball. *Type:* Periodical.

Baseball Digest

Century Publishing Co.
990 Grove St.
Evanston, IL 60201-4370
Ph: (847)491-6440
Fax: (847)491-0459
E-mail: century@wwa.com
Contact: John Kuenster, Editor; Norman Jacobs, President/Publisher.
Desc: Magazine featuring major league baseball. *Type:* Periodical.

George Khoury Association of Baseball Leagues

5400 Meramec Bottom Rd.
St. Louis, MO 63128
Ph: (314)849-8900
Fax: (314)849-8901
Contact: George G. Khoury, Exec.Dir.
Desc: Boys and girls seven years of age and older who play baseball or softball in 60,000 leagues organized by local fraternal, church, service or community organizations, or by individuals. Believes good citizens can be built on baseball diamonds much better than in back alleys. *Type:* Association.

Little League Baseball

PO Box 3485
Williamsport, PA 17701
Ph: (570)326-1921
E-mail: communications@littleleague.org
URL: http://www.littleleague.org/
Contact: Lance Van Avken, Dir. of Media Relations.
Desc: Children 5 to 18 years of age. Organizes baseball and softball programs (more than 22,000) in every state, 90 countries, and U.S. territorial possessions (largest youth sports program in the world). *Type:* Association.

National Amateur Baseball Federation

PO Box 705
Bowie, MD 20718
Ph: (301)262-5005
Fax: (301)262-5005
Contact: Charles M. Blackburn, Exec.Dir.
Desc: Amateur baseball associations. Promotes noncommercialized baseball in the U.S. Sponsors tournaments in 8 age groups: 12 years and under; 14 years and under; 16 years and under; high school division, 18 years and under; college division, 22 years and under; major division; and/ 10 & under rookie division. *Type:* Association.

Pony Baseball and Softball

PO Box 225
Washington, PA 15301
Ph: (724)225-1060
Fax: (724)225-9852
E-mail: pony@pulsenet.com
URL: http://www.pony.org
Contact: Abraham Key, Pres./CEO.
Type: Association.

Society for American Baseball Research

812 Huron Rd. E, No. 719
Cleveland, OH 44115
Ph: (216)575-0500
Fax: (216)575-0502
E-mail: info@sabr.org
URL: http://www.sabr.org
Contact: Morris Eckhouse, Exec.Dir.
Desc: Anyone with a genuine interest in baseball statistics and history. Works to establish an accurate historical and statistical account of baseball from its origin; coordinate and facilitate the dissemination of baseball research information; foster the study of baseball as a significant American social and athletic institution. Conducts individual research or as part of committee project. *Type:* Association.

Society for American Baseball Research—Membership Directory

Society for American Baseball Research
812 Huron Rd. E., No. 719
Cleveland, OH 44115
Ph: (216)575-0500
Fax: (216)575-0502
E-mail: info@sabr.org
URL: http://www.sabr.org
Contact: Morris Eckhouse, Editor.
Desc: More than 6,600 persons with a special interest in baseball research, statistics, and history. *Type:* Directory.

USA TODAY Baseball Weekly

USA TODAY
1000 Wilson Blvd.
Arlington, VA 22229
Ph: (703)276-3400
Free: 800-872-0001
Fax: (703)558-8004
E-mail: bbweekly@usat.com.

Contact: Paul White, Editor, (703)276-3756, fax: (703)558-4678; Keith Cutler, Publisher, (703)276-4565, fax: (703)558-4646; TBD, National Ad Account Mgr., (212)715-2198, fax: (212)935-6396; A. Lynn Busby, Classified Ad Mgr., (703)276-5471, fax: (703)558-8004, lbusby@usatoday.com; Tom Kelly, VP, Circulation, (703)276-6314, fax: (703)247-3185, tlkelly@usatoday.com; Lee Ivory, Executive Editor, (703)558-4646; Steven Larson, Account Executive, (312)321-7724, fax: (312)670-9962, spl
Desc: Newsprint baseball magazine. *Type:* Periodical.

The Write Direction
John Skipper
707 6th St. SE
Mason City, IA 50401-4155   Ph: (515)423-2283
Contact: John Skipper, Editor.
Desc: Offers writing tips and techniques; identifies problem areas and possible solutions. Covers both fictional and nonfictional writing. *Type:* Newsletter.

Basketball

Basketball Digest
Century Publishing Co.
990 Grove St.   Ph: (847)491-6440
Evanston, IL 60201-4370   Fax: (847)491-0459
E-mail: century@wwa.com
Contact: Norman Jacobs, Publisher; Dale Jacobs, Production Dir.
Desc: Magazine covering pro basketball action. *Type:* Periodical.

Fastball
Cox Interactive Media, Inc.
530 Means St., NW   Ph: (404)572-1800
Atlanta, GA 30318   Fax: (404)572-1801
E-mail: webmaster@cimedia.com
URL: http://www.fastball.com/
Contact: Tom Amon, General Manager, tamon@cimedia.com.
Desc: The site provides in-depth news coverage for all the teams of the American and the National baseball leagues, along with information such as scores, statistics, injuries, standings, and much more. Other features include a chat room, sports collectibles news and information, fantasy baseball leagues, video game reviews, and more. *Type:* Database.

International Association of Approved Basketball Officials
12321 Middlebrook Rd.   Ph: (301)601-8013
Germantown, MD 20874   Fax: (301)601-8018
E-mail: info@iaabo.org
URL: http://www.iaabo.org
Contact: Paul Francis, Jr., Exec.Dir.
Desc: Basketball officials in 13 countries. Purpose is to recruit and continually educate basketball officials and clinicians. *Type:* Association.

Women's Basketball Coaches Association
4646 B Lawrenceville Hwy.   Ph: (770)279-8027
Lilburn, GA 30047   Fax: (770)279-8473
URL: http://www.wbca.org
Contact: Betty Jaynes, CEO.
Desc: Head basketball coaches, assistants, athletic directors, officials, media personnel, organizations lending financial support to the association, and others interested in women's basketball. Purposes are to foster amateur sports competitions at both national and international levels, and to promote a reputable image of women's basketball by developing the game. Works to refine rules, regulations, and procedures that will enhance athletic leadership, sportsmanship, and women's participation in basketball. *Type:* Association.

Beverages

Ale Street News
Tuscarora Inc.
Box 1125   Ph: (201)368-9100
Maywood, NJ 07607   Free: 800-351-ALES
          Fax: (201)368-9101
URL: http://www.alestreetnews.com.
Contact: Tony Forder, Editor and Publisher, tony@alestreet.news.com; Jack Babin, Publisher.
Desc: Newspaper for beer ienthusiasts, home brewers and the craft brewing industry. *Type:* Periodical.

Bartender Magazine
Foley Publishing
PO Box 158   Ph: (908)766-6006
Liberty Corner, NJ 07938   Fax: (908)766-6607
E-mail: barmag@aol.com.
URL: http://www.bartender.com.
Contact: Jaclyn W. Foley, Editor; Raymond P. Foley, Publisher; Loretta J. Natiello, Assistant Editor.
Desc: Trade magazine. *Type:* Periodical.

Beverage Digest
John Sicher
PO Box 621   Ph: (914)244-0700
Bedford Hills, NY 10507   Fax: (914)244-0774
E-mail: beverage-digest@aol.com.
Contact: John Sicher, Editor and Publisher.
Desc: Focuses primarily on soft drinks. Reports on industry news in relation to pricing, marketing, competition, mergers and acquisitions, and new products. *Type:* Newsletter.

Beverage Industry—Annual Manual Issue
Stagnito Publishing Co., an MWC Company
1935 Shermer Rd., Ste. 100   Ph: (847)205-5660
Northbrook, IL 60062   Fax: (847)205-5680
Contact: Joan Holleran, Editor; Sarah Theodore, Assoc. Ed.
Desc: List of over 1,700 companies supplying equipment and materials to the soft drink, beer, wine, bottled water, and juice industries; industry associations; bottling and supply franchise companies; beer importers distributors; manufacturers' representatives; soft drink distributors. *Type:* Directory.

Beverage World Periscope
Bill Communications, Inc.
226 W. 26th St., 10th Fl.   Ph: (212)822-5930
New York, NY 10001-6700   Fax: (212)822-5931
E-mail: periworld@aol.com.
Contact: Greg Prince, Editor.
Desc: Contains information of interest to individuals in the beverage industry. *Type:* Newsletter.

Brewery and Soft Drink Workers Conference - U.S.A. and Canada
25 Louisiana Ave. NW   Ph: (202)624-6922
Washington, DC 20001   Fax: (202)624-6925
Contact: David W. Laughton, Dir.
Desc: Promotes the interests of brewery and soft drink workers in the United States and Canada. *Type:* Association.

BSR on Tap
Bay Sports Review
PO Box 4520   Ph: (925)934-7647
Berkeley, CA 94704   Fax: (925)934-7650
Contact: Christopher Weills, Publisher; Paul Matson, Editor; Pat Cline, Contributor.
Desc: Provides people in the sports bar, restaurant, and beverage industry a vehicle to communicate their message to decision makers with authority to purchase products for their business. Recurring features include interviews, news of research, a calendar of events, reports of meetings, and news of educational opportunities. *Type:* Newsletter.

Coffee at Work
National Coffee Service Association
8201 Greensboro Dr., Ste. 300   Ph: (703)715-1181
McLean, VA 22102-3814   Fax: (703)715-1194
Desc: Provides companies involved in the office coffee service industry with reports on trends and developments in the industry. Covers technological advances, government regulations, sales and advertising, business management, and other topics of interest. *Type:* Newsletter.

Directory and Buyers' Guide of the Vineyard Industry of North America
Wines & Vines
1800 Lincoln Ave.   Ph: (415)453-9700
San Rafael, CA 94901   Fax: (415)453-2517
Desc: Over 1,000 wineries in the U.S., Canada, and Mexico. *Type:* Directory.

International Bottled Water Association
1700 Diagonal Rd., Ste. 650   Ph: (703)683-5213
Alexandria, VA 22314   Fax: (703)683-4074
URL: http://www.bottledwater.org
Contact: Sylvia E. Swanson, Pres.
Desc: Bottled water plants; distributors; manufacturers of bottled water supplies; international bottlers, distributors and suppliers. *Type:* Association.

Kane's Beverage Week
Whitaker Newsletters, Inc.
313 South Ave.   Ph: (908)889-6336
PO Box 340   Free: 800-359-6049
Fanwood, NJ 07023-0340   Fax: (908)889-6339
E-mail: BevNews@aol.com
Contact: Joel Whitaker, Editor.
Desc: Presents news items pertaining to the marketing, advertising, and distribution of alcoholic and other types of beverages. Also reports on social, health, and legal issues affecting the beverage industry. *Type:* Newsletter.

Mixin'
American Bartenders' Association
PO Box D   Free: 800-935-3232
Plant City, FL 33564   Fax: (813)752-2768
Contact: Linda Harrell, Editor.
Desc: Supports the Association's dedication to strengthening the position of professional bartenders, bar managers, and bar owners throughout the industry and in the legislature. Includes news of interest to those in the beverage business such as announcements of new products and services, changing prices, alterations in government regulations, and profit-making suggestions. *Type:* Newsletter.

National Association of Beverage Importers—Member Letter
National Association of Beverage Importers, Inc.
1025 Vermont Ave. NW, Ste.   Ph: (202)638-1617
1066   Fax: (202)638-3122
Washington, DC 20005
E-mail: nabi-inc@msn.com
Contact: Bob Maxwell, Editor.
Desc: Highlights government legislation and other actions affecting the import of alcoholic beverages. Discusses international trade policy, regulations, and trends. *Type:* Newsletter.

National Soft Drink Association
1101 16th St., NW   Ph: (202)463-6732
Washington, DC 20036   Fax: (202)463-8178
E-mail: info@nsda.org
URL: http://www.nsda.org
Contact: William L. Ball, III, Pres.
Desc: Active members are bottlers and distributors of soft drinks and franchise companies; associate members are suppliers of materials and services. Objectives include government affairs activities on the national and state levels; discussion of industry problems; general improvement of operating procedures. *Type:* Association.

NBPA's Voice

National Beverage Packaging Association (NBPA)

200 Daingerfield Rd.	Ph: (703)684-1080
Alexandria, VA 22314	Free: 800-331-8816
	Fax: (703)548-6563

Contact: Wesley J. Trochlil, Editor.

Desc: Covers activities of chapters of the Association in the U.S. Recurring features include update from national president. *Type:* Newsletter.

Soft Drink Letter

Whitaker Newsletters, Inc.

313 South Ave.	Ph: (908)889-6336
PO Box 340	Free: 800-359-6049
Fanwood, NJ 07023-0340	Fax: (908)889-6339
E-mail: BevNews@aol.com	

Contact: Fred T. Rossi, Editor.

Desc: Covers news pertaining to the beverage industry with emphasis on soft drinks, mixers, and bottled water. Includes reports on new products and federal/state regulations, interviews with leading industry executives, marketing trends, and advertising and marketing research. *Type:* Newsletter.

Soft Drink Lines

National Soft Drink Association

1101 16th St. NW	Ph: (202)463-6732
Washington, DC 20036	Fax: (202)463-8178

Contact: Leslie Schreiber, Editor.

Desc: Highlights legislative and regulatory developments affecting the soft drink industry. Reviews news of the Association. *Type:* Newsletter.

Specialty Coffee Association of America

1 World Trade Center, No.	Ph: (562)624-4100
1200	Fax: (562)624-4101
Long Beach, CA 90831-0800	
URL: http://www.scaa.org	

Contact: Ted R. Lingle, Exec.Dir.

Desc: Coffee roasters, green coffee brokers, retailers, distributors, and others involved in the gourmet coffee industry. Objectives are to: provide business, professional, promotional, and educational assistance in the areas of cultivation, processing, preparation, and marketing of specialty coffee; increase consumer awareness, understanding, and consumption of specialty coffee. Provides a forum for discussion of the purpose and unified character of the industry and represents members in national and regional coffee concerns. *Type:* Association.

Specialty Coffee Retailer—Buyers Guide Issue

Adams Business Media

2101 S. Arlington Heights Rd.,	Ph: (847)427-9512
Ste. 150	Fax: (847)427-2006
Arlington Heights, IL 60005	

Contact: Sue Gillerlain, Editor.

Desc: Manufacturers and distributors serving coffee shops, bars, and carts with equipment, food, food serving supplies, coffee, and coffee accessories. *Type:* Directory.

Tea Talk

R & R Publications

PO Box 860	Ph: (415)331-1557
Sausalito, CA 94966	Fax: (415)331-1557
E-mail: teatalk@aol.com.	

Contact: Diana Rosen, Editor.

Desc: Provides information about tea and global tea ceremonies. *Type:* Newsletter.

Bible

American Bible Society

1865 Broadway	Ph: (212)408-1200
New York, NY 10023-7505	Free: 800-32-BIBLE
	Fax: (212)408-1456
E-mail: pwaller@americanbible.org	
URL: http://www.americanbible.org	

Contact: Dr. Michael A. Maus, Dir. of Communications.

Desc: Dedicated to making the Bible readily available to people in the U.S. and around the world. Its sole purpose is the translation, publication and distribution of the Holy Scriptures. *Type:* Association.

American Bible Society Record

American Bible Society

1865 Broadway	Ph: (212)408-1200
New York, NY 10023	Free: 800-322-4253
	Fax: (212)408-1512
E-mail: absrecord@americanbible.org.	
URL: http://www.americanbible.org; http://www.americanbible.org.	

Contact: Peter Fruerherd, Editor, pfruerherd@americanbible.org.

Desc: Magazine presenting articles about the work and missions of the American Bible Society. *Alt. Contact:* 1865 Broadway, New York, NY 10023; telephone: (212)408-1344; fax: (212)408-1456. *Type:* Periodical.

BCM International

237 Fairfield Ave.	Ph: (610)352-7177
Upper Darby, PA 19082	Fax: (610)352-5561
E-mail: 103046.613@compuserve.com	

Contact: Rev. Robert T. Evans, Pres.

Desc: Evangelical and fundamentalist missionaries whose purpose is to lead children, teens, and adults, in the U.S. and abroad, to a deeper faith in Jesus Christ. Seeks to: establish individuals in Christian life and service; encourage church attendance; establish self-governing, self-supporting, and self-propagating evangelical churches. *Type:* Association.

Bible (King James Version)

Thomas Nelson Publishers

Nelson Pl. at Elm Hill Pike	Ph: (615)889-9000
PO Box 141000	
Nashville, TN 37214-1000	

Contact: Maudine West, (615)889-9000, fax: (615)391-5225.

Desc: Contains the complete text of the Old and New Testaments of the 1769 edition of The Holy Bible published by Thomas Nelson Publishers. Typical data elements include book name, citation, chapter number, chapter text, verse number, verse, and text. *Available:* The Dialog Corporation, DIALOG; CompuServe Information Service, Knowledge Index. *Type:* Database.

Bible League

16801 Van Dam Rd.	Ph: (708)331-2094
South Holland, IL 60473	Free: 800-334-7017
	Fax: (708)331-7172
URL: http://www.bibleleague.org	

Contact: Rev. Dennis M. Mulder, Pres.

Desc: Distributes Scriptures in the U.S. and in foreign countries in cooperation with local organizations and churches. Conducts charitable and educational programs; provides children's services; maintains speakers' bureau. *Type:* Association.

In Other Words

Wycliffe Bible Translators

PO Box 2727	Free: 800-922-5433
Huntington Beach, CA 92647	
E-mail: info_usa@wycliffe.org	

Contact: Susan Van Wynen, Editor; Pixie Christensen, Editor.

Desc: Contains news of the organization, which seeks to provide translations of the Bible in all languages of the world that do not have it. Reports on the progress of such translations and other activities of the organization. *Type:* Newsletter.

International Bible Society

1820 Jet Stream Dr.	Ph: (719)488-9200
Colorado Springs, CO 80921-	Free: 800-524-1588
3696	Fax: (719)488-3840
E-mail: ibs@gospelcom.net	
URL: http://www.gospelcom.net/ibs	

Contact: Lars B. Dunberg, Intl.Pres.

Desc: A nondenominational mission organization engaged in the translation, publication, and worldwide distribution of Scriptures. Makes available Scriptures translated by Wycliffe Bible Translators and its own translation staff; provides selections of Scriptures complimentary or at low cost for use in evangelism programs by individuals, churches, and organizations. *Type:* Association.

Lutheran Bible Translators

303 N. Lake St.	Ph: (630)897-0660
Box 2050	Free: 800-53-BIBLE
Aurora, IL 60507-2050	Fax: (630)897-3567
E-mail: lbt@xc.org	
URL: http://www.LBT.org	

Contact: Rev. Robert Rogner, Exec.Dir.

Desc: Independent Lutheran missionary organization working in over 20 countries around the globe. Strives to bring God's Word to people for the first time in their own language. This entails Bible translation and literacy work as well as the production of vernacular media materials for use by indigenous people and groups. *Type:* Association.

Our Bible Matters

Canadian Bible Society

10 Carnforth Rd.	Ph: (416)757-4171
Toronto, ON, Canada M4A	Free: 800-465-2425
2S4	Fax: (416)757-3376
URL: http://www.canbible.ca; http://www.canbible.ca.	

Contact: Connie Stamp, Editor.

Desc: Publishes information on Bible Society news and events from around the world, including translation, publication, and distribution of the Scriptures. Recurring features include interviews, news of research, a calendar of events, reports of meetings, notices of publications available, and columns titled a word from the National Director. *Type:* Newsletter.

Pocket Testament League

11 Toll Gate Rd.	Ph: (717)626-1919
PO Box 800	Free: 800-636-8785
Lititz, PA 17543-7026	Fax: (717)626-5553
E-mail: tptl@ptd.net	
URL: http://www.tptl.org	

Contact: John Kubinec, Assoc.Dir.

Desc: Worldwide evangelistic ministry with missionaries, associates, and nationals active in evangelism with an emphasis on Scripture distribution, including the U.S.A.; proclaiming the gospel of salvation through our Lord Jesus Christ, encouraging Christian growth in established churches, and newly formed assemblies of believers. Provides speakers for churches and Christian organizations. *Type:* Association.

Society of Biblical Literature

1201 Clairmont Ave., Ste. 300	Ph: (404)636-4744
Decatur, GA 30030	Fax: (404)248-0815
E-mail: sblexec@emory.edu	
URL: http://www.sbl-site.org	

Contact: Kent Harold Richards, Exec.Dir.

Desc: Professors and persons interested in religious studies, especially as related to the study of the Bible. Seeks to "stimulate the critical investigation of classical biblical literature, together with other related literature, by the exchange of scholarly research both in published form and in public forum." Endeavors to support those disciplines and subdisciplines pertinent to the illumination of the literatures and religions of the ancient Near Eastern and Mediterranean regions, including the study of ancient languages, textual criticism, history, and archaeology. *Type:* Association.

Weekly Bible Reader
Standard Publishing

8121 Hamilton Ave.	Ph: (513)931-4050
Cincinnati, OH 45231	Fax: (513)931-0950

Contact: Marcy Levering, Editor; Mark A. Taylor, Publisher, (513)931-4050.

Desc: Religious magazine for children in the first and second grades. *Type:* Periodical.

Biographies

Abridged Biography and Genealogy Master Index
Gale Group Inc.

27500 Drake Rd.	Ph: (248)699-4253
Farmington Hills, MI 48331-3535	Free: 800-877-GALE
	Fax: (248)699-8070

E-mail: galeord@galegroup.com
URL: http://www.galegroup.com.

Contact: Barbara McNeil, Editor.

Desc: This publication indexes 2,150,000 citations to individuals in more than 260 biographical dictionaries and "who's who" publications that are most often found or used in libraries. An abridged version of "Biography and Genealogy Master Index", published in 1980, and its annual updates through 1995. *Type:* Directory.

The African American Almanac
Gale Group Inc.

27500 Drake Rd.	Ph: (248)699-4253
Farmington Hills, MI 48331-3535	Free: 800-877-GALE
	Fax: (248)699-8070

E-mail: galeord@galegroup.com
URL: http://www.galegroup.com.

Contact: L. Mpho Mabunda, Editor.

Desc: African American firsts, significant documents, Africa and the black diaspora, slavery, civil rights, law, politics, business, family, education, religion, literature, entertainment, the arts, science and technology, sports, the military, and award winners. Principal content of publication is an all-in-one resource to significant dates, movements, legislation, and people in African American history and culture in the United States. *Type:* Directory.

African Americans Information Directory
Gale Group Inc.

27500 Drake Rd.	Ph: (248)699-4253
Farmington Hills, MI 48331-3535	Free: 800-877-GALE
	Fax: (248)699-8070

E-mail: galeord@galegroup.com
URL: http://www.galegroup.com.

Desc: Approximately 5,300 sources of information on a variety of aspects of African American life and culture, including national, state, and local organizations; publishers of newspapers, periodicals, newsletters, and other publications and videos; television and radio stations; traditionally black colleges and universities; library collections; museums and other cultural institutions; black studies programs and research centers; federal and state government agencies; black religious organizations; awards, honors, and prizes; educational scholarships, fellowships, and loans; and the leading 100 Black-owned businesses in terms of revenue. *Type:* Directory.

Almanac of Famous People
Gale Group Inc.

27500 Drake Rd.	Ph: (248)699-4253
Farmington Hills, MI 48331-3535	Free: 800-877-GALE
	Fax: (248)699-8070

E-mail: galeord@galegroup.com
URL: http://www.galegroup.com.; http://www.gale.com.

Contact: Frank V. Castronova, Editor.

Desc: Published in two volumes, this is a combination quick reference to biographical facts and index to sources of information on over 30,000 newsworthy persons, past and present; includes figures from sports, entertainment, government, business, religion, science, history, etc. *Type:* Directory.

Asian Americans Information Directory
Gale Group Inc.

27500 Drake Rd.	Ph: (248)699-4253
Farmington Hills, MI 48331-3535	Free: 800-877-GALE
	Fax: (248)699-8070

E-mail: galeord@galegroup.com
URL: http://www.galegroup.com.

Contact: Charles Montney, Editor.

Desc: 5,200 sources of information on Asian and Pacific American life and culture in the U.S. and Canada, including national, state, provincial, and local organizations; newspapers, newsletters, journals, directories, publishers, and videos; television and radio stations; research and study centers, university area studies programs; library and museum collections; federal and state government agencies; embassies and consulates from Asian/Pacific countries; and educational scholarships, fellowships, and loans. *Type:* Directory.

Bio-Base: A Master Index on Microfiche to Biographical Sketches Found in Current and Retrospective Biographical Dictionaries
Gale Group Inc.

27500 Drake Rd.	Ph: (248)699-4253
Farmington Hills, MI 48331-3535	Free: 800-877-GALE
	Fax: (248)699-8070

E-mail: galeord@galegroup.com
URL: http://www.galegroup.com.; http://www.gale.com.

Contact: Geri Speace, Editor.

Desc: Microfiche. More than 11.5 million citations for sketches found in some 2,700 volumes and editions of more than 1,000 biographical dictionaries and who's whos; includes all citations in Gale's "Biography and Genealogy Master Index" and its annual updates. *Type:* Directory.

Black Resource Guide
Black Resource Guide, Inc.

501 Oneida Pl. NW	Ph: (202)291-4373
Washington, DC 20011	Fax: (202)291-4373

Contact: R. Benjamin Johnson, Publisher; Jacqueline L. Johnson, Publisher.

Desc: Over 4,500 organizations and individuals especially relevant to or comprised primarily of Black Americans, including adoption agencies, business and bar associations, colleges, public administrators, book publishers, church denominations, financial institutions, sports agents, Urban League directors, hospitals, museums, embassies and consulates, and others; also included are Blacks in federal elected and appointed positions; individuals are chosen for their prominence in Black America. *Type:* Directory.

The Complete Marquis Who's Who on CD-ROM
Marquis Who's Who
Reed Elsevier

121 Chanlon Rd.	Ph: (908)464-6800
New Providence, NJ 07974	Free: 800-521-8110
	Fax: (908)771-8645

E-mail: info@marquiswhoswho.com

Desc: More than 700,000 biographies from Who's Who in America, the four regional Who's Whos, Who's Who of American Women, volumes 9 and 10 of Who's Who in America, Who's Who in the World, and Who's Who for nine professions. *Type:* Directory.

Contemporary Black Biography
Gale Group Inc.

27500 Drake Rd.	Ph: (248)699-4253
Farmington Hills, MI 48331-3535	Free: 800-877-GALE
	Fax: (248)699-8070

E-mail: galeord@galegroup.com
URL: http://www.galegroup.com.; http://www.gale.com.
Contact: Shirelle Phelps, Editor.

Desc: In each volume, approximately 65 notable Black persons of the 20th Century. *Type:* Directory.

Countries of the World and Their Leaders Yearbook
Gale Group Inc.

27500 Drake Rd.	Ph: (248)699-4253
Farmington Hills, MI 48331-3535	Free: 800-877-GALE
	Fax: (248)699-8070

E-mail: galeord@galegroup.com
URL: http://www.galegroup.com.
Contact: Brian Rajewski, Editor.

Desc: Lists of United States embassies, consulates, and foreign service posts in over 190 countries worldwide. Principal content of publication is "Background Notes on Countries of the World," by the U.S. State Department. *Type:* Directory.

Discovering Multicultural America
Gale Group Inc.

27500 Drake Rd.	Ph: (248)699-4253
Farmington Hills, MI 48331-3535	Free: 800-877-GALE
	Fax: (248)699-8070

E-mail: galeord@galegroup.com
URL: http://www.galegroup.com.; http://www.gale.com.

Desc: America's largest ethnic groups: African Americans, Asian Americans, Hispanic Americans, and Native North Americans. Information includes 2,000 biographical profiles, 2,500 historical and topical essays, 500 overviews of ethnic landmarks, 350 significant documents, 3,100 timeline events, 5,000 contact organizations, 500 full-text articles. *Type:* Directory.

Encyclopedia of World Biography
Gale Group Inc.

27500 Drake Rd.	Ph: (248)699-4253
Farmington Hills, MI 48331-3535	Free: 800-877-GALE
	Fax: (248)699-8070

E-mail: galeord@galegroup.com
URL: http://www.galegroup.com.
Contact: Paula K. Byers, Editor; Suzanne M. Bourgoin, Editor.

Desc: Biographical coverage of more than 7,000 living and deceased individuals from a variety of backgrounds. *Type:* Directory.

Gale Encyclopedia of Multicultural America
Gale Group Inc.

27500 Drake Rd.	Ph: (248)699-4253
Farmington Hills, MI 48331-3535	Free: 800-877-GALE
	Fax: (248)699-8070

E-mail: galeord@galegroup.com

URL: http://www.galegroup.com.
Desc: Listings of organizations and research centers. *Type:* Directory.

Global Who's Who of the World

Baron's Who's Who
412 N. Coast Hwy., Ste. B110   Ph: (949)497-8615
Laguna Beach, CA 92651   Fax: (949)786-8918
E-mail: info@baronswhoswho.com
URL: http://www.baronswhoswho.com;   http://
baronswhoswho.com/global/gwwdet.htm.
Contact: John L. Pellam, Editor.
Desc: Prominent and influential personalities throughout the world. *Type:* Directory.

Newsmakers

Gale Group Inc.
27500 Drake Rd.   Ph: (248)699-4253
Farmington Hills, MI 48331-   Free: 800-877-GALE
    3535   Fax: (248)699-8070
E-mail: galeord@galegroup.com
URL: http://www.galegroup.com.; http://www.gale.com.
Contact: Terrie Rooney, Editor, terrie_rooney@gale.com.
Desc: "Newsmakers" is a series of biographies of "individuals who are quite well known and about whom information is widely available in newspapers and magazines but not in reference books, and people who are less well known but who, because of the importance or interesting nature of their activities, are currently in the news and are deserving of wide coverage." Each quarterly paperbound issue covers approximately 50 newsmakers with emphasis on topical issues. The annual hardbound cumulation includes all of the biographies from the first three issues and adds approximately 50 more entries, for a total of 200 biographies. *Type:* Directory.

Profiles of Worldwide Government Leaders

Keesing's Worldwide, LLC
PO Box 5590   Ph: (301)718-8770
Washington, DC 20016-1190   Free: 800-332-3535
    Fax: (301)718-8494
E-mail: info@keesings.com
Contact: Alan J. Day, Editor, ar@keesings.com.
Desc: World leaders and top government officials from 195 countries. *Type:* Directory.

Who's Who in America

Marquis Who's Who
Reed Elsevier
121 Chanlon Rd.   Ph: (908)464-6800
New Providence, NJ 07974   Free: 800-521-8110
    Fax: (908)771-8645
E-mail: info@marquiswhoswho.com
Contact: Paul Canning, Marketing Director.
Desc: Three volume set with more than 90,000 persons, primarily in the United States, considered to be of current national reference interest because of achievement or position. *Type:* Directory.

Who's Who Among African Americans

Gale Group Inc.
27500 Drake Rd.   Ph: (248)699-4253
Farmington Hills, MI 48331-   Free: 800-877-GALE
    3535   Fax: (248)699-8070
E-mail: galeord@galegroup.com
URL: http://www.galegroup.com.; http://www.gale.com.
Contact: Shirelle Phelps, Editor.
Desc: Over 20,000 African American leaders in government, business, education, religion, communications, civic affairs, the arts, law, medicine, science, sports, and entertainment. *Type:* Directory.

Who's Who in the East

Marquis Who's Who
Reed Elsevier
121 Chanlon Rd.   Ph: (908)464-6800
New Providence, NJ 07974   Free: 800-521-8110
    Fax: (908)771-8645
E-mail: info@marquiswhoswho.com
Contact: Samuel J. Dempsey, Managing Editor.
Desc: About 26,000 persons living in Connecticut, Delaware, District of Columbia, Maine, Maryland, Massachusetts, New Hampshire, New Jersey, New York, Pennsylvania, Rhode Island, and Vermont, plus the Canadian provinces of New Brunswick, Newfoundland, Nova Scotia, Prince Edward Island, Quebec, and the eastern half of Ontario. *Type:* Directory.

Who's Who in the Midwest

Marquis Who's Who
Reed Elsevier
121 Chanlon Rd.   Ph: (908)464-6800
New Providence, NJ 07974   Free: 800-521-8110
    Fax: (908)771-8645
E-mail: info@marquiswhoswho.com
Contact: Paul Canning, Marketing Director; Samuel J. Dempsey, Managing Editor.
Desc: More than 23,100 persons of regional interest living in Illinois, Indiana, Iowa, Kansas, Michigan, Minnesota, Missouri, Nebraska, North Dakota, Ohio, South Dakota, and Wisconsin, Manitoba and western Ontario, Canada. *Type:* Directory.

Who's Who of Nobel Prize Winners, 1901-1995

Oryx Press
4041 N. Central Ave., Ste. 700   Ph: (602)265-2651
Phoenix, AZ 85012-3397   Free: 800-279-6799
    Fax: 800-279-4663
E-mail: info@oryxpress.com
URL: http://www.oryxpress.com
Contact: Bernard S. Schlessinger, Editor; June H. Schlessinger, Editor.
Desc: 658 Nobel Prize winners. *Type:* Directory.

Who's Who in Technology

Gale Group Inc.
27500 Drake Rd.   Ph: (248)699-4253
Farmington Hills, MI 48331-   Free: 800-877-GALE
    3535   Fax: (248)699-8070
E-mail: galeord@galegroup.com
URL: http://www.galegroup.com.; http://www.gale.com.
Contact: Kimberley A. McGrath, Editor, kimberley.mcgrath@gale.com.
Desc: 25,000 North American men and women working in more than 1,000 scientific and technological fields. *Type:* Directory.

Who's Who in Television

Packard Publishing Co.
PO Box 2187   Ph: (626)791-5367
Beverly Hills, CA 90213
E-mail: filmbiz200@aol.com
Contact: Rodman W. Gregg, co-editor; James Hanson, co-editor.
Desc: Approximately 2,000 studios, production companies, networks, writers, directors, and other professionals involved in cable and network television. *Type:* Directory.

Who's Who in the West

Marquis Who's Who
Reed Elsevier
121 Chanlon Rd.   Ph: (908)464-6800
New Providence, NJ 07974   Free: 800-521-8110
    Fax: (908)771-8645
E-mail: info@marquiswhoswho.com

Contact: Lisa Weissbard, Managing Editor.
Desc: Approximately 23,500 persons living in Alaska, Arizona, California, Colorado, Hawaii, Idaho, Montana, Nevada, New Mexico, Oregon, Utah, Washington, and Wyoming, plus the Canadian provinces of Alberta, British Columbia, and Saskatchewan. *Type:* Directory.

Who's Who in the World

Marquis Who's Who
Reed Elsevier
121 Chanlon Rd.   Ph: (908)464-6800
New Providence, NJ 07974   Free: 800-521-8110
    Fax: (908)771-8645
E-mail: info@marquiswhoswho.com
Contact: Samuel J. Dempsey, Managing Editor.
Desc: Over 35,000 persons considered to be of current international reference interest because of achievement or position. *Type:* Directory.

Biology

American Institute of Biological Sciences

1444 I St. NW, Ste. 200   Ph: (202)628-1500
Washington, DC 20005-2210   Fax: (202)628-1509
E-mail: jkolder@aibs.org
URL: http://www.aibs.org
Contact: Dr. Ricard T. O'Grady, Exec.Dir.
Desc: Professional biological associations and laboratories whose members have an interest in the life sciences. Promotes unity and effectiveness of effort among persons engaged in biological research, education, and application of biological sciences, including agriculture, environment, and medicine. *Type:* Association.

American Society for Biochemistry and Molecular Biology

9650 Rockville Pike   Ph: (301)530-7145
Bethesda, MD 20814   Fax: (301)571-1824
E-mail: asbmb@asbmb.faseb.org
URL: http://www.faseb.org/asbmb
Contact: Charles C. Hancock, Exec. Officer.
Desc: Biochemists and molecular biologists who have conducted and published original investigations in biological chemistry and/or molecular biology. *Type:* Association.

American Society for Cell Biology

9650 Rockville Pike   Ph: (301)530-7153
Bethesda, MD 20814   Fax: (301)530-7139
E-mail: ascbinfo@ascb.org
URL: http://www.ascb.org/ascb
Contact: Elizabeth Marincola, Exec.Dir.
Desc: Scientists with educational or research experience in cell biology or an allied field. Offers placement service. *Type:* Association.

American Society for Microbiology

1325 Massachusetts Ave. NW   Ph: (202)737-3600
Washington, DC 20005-4171   Fax: (202)942-8341
Contact: Michael I. Goldberg, Ph.D., Exec.Dir.
Desc: Scientific society of microbiologists. Promotes the advancement of scientific knowledge in order to improve education in microbiology. Encourages the highest professional and ethical standards, and the adoption of sound legislative and regulatory policies affecting the discipline of microbiology at all levels. *Type:* Association.

American Type Culture Collection

10801 University Blvd.   Ph: (703)365-2700
Manassas, VA 20110-2209   Free: 800-638-6597
URL: http://www.atcc.org
Contact: Raymond H. Cypess, Pres. & CEO.
Desc: A private organization seeking to collect, propagate, preserve, and distribute authentic cultures of microorga-

nisms and genetic materials for reference purposes for use in educational, research, and other scientific and industrial activities. Conducts research in cryobiology, microbial systematics, and karyology. Maintains depository for cultures involved in patent applications and for confidential safe-keeping of proprietary cultures. *Type:* Association.

Arthritis Centre Biomechanics Laboratory

Toronto Hospital, Toronto Western Div.
399 Bathurst St., Fp b-104
Toronto, ON, Canada M5T 2S8
Ph: (416)603-5921
Fax: (416)368-3437

Contact: Dr. Ogelvey Harris, Actg.Dir.

Desc: In vitro and mechanical testing of human, animal, and synthetic specimens, design and development of new implants and measurement devices, strain-gaging, FSRs, Fuji prescale film, and custom wear and fatigue testing of materials incorporating custom wear test machines. Holds a patent for an artificial spinal disc. *Type:* Research center.

ASFA Marine Biotechnology Abstracts

Cambridge Scientific Abstracts (CSA)
7200 Wisconsin Ave., Ste. 601
Bethesda, MD 20814-4823
Ph: (301)961-6700
E-mail: sales@csa.com
URL: http://www.csa.com

Desc: Contains more than 6000 citations, with abstracts, to worldwide literature on molecular biology and molecular genetics applied specifically to marine and aquatic organisms. Includes coverage of relevant U.S., U.K., and Japanese patents. *Type:* Database.

Association for the Advancement of Medical Instrumentation

3330 Washington Blvd., Ste. 400
Arlington, VA 22201
Ph: (703)525-4890
Free: 800-332-2264
Fax: (703)276-0793

Contact: Michael J. Miller, Pres.

Desc: Clinical engineers, biomedical equipment technicians, physicians, hospital administrators, consultants, engineers, manufacturers of medical devices, nurses researchers and others interested in medical instrumentation. Purpose is to improve the quality of medical care through the application, development, and management of technology. Maintains placement service. *Type:* Association.

Augusta Biomedical Research Corporation

PO Box 3134
Augusta, GA 30914-3134
Ph: (706)823-2238
Fax: (706)823-3949

Contact: Nancy M. Parks, Exec.Dir.

Desc: Alzheimer's disease, strokes, cardiology, infectious diseases, gastroenterology, surgery, schizophrenia, neurology, mental health, substance abuse, and Parkinson's Disease. *Type:* Research center.

Baylor University

Baylor Research Institute

3409 Worth St.
Dallas, TX 75242
Ph: (214)820-2687
Fax: (214)820-4952

Contact: John Fordtran, MD, Pres.

Desc: Biomedicine, including digestive diseases, oncology, photobiology, organ transplants, muscle physiology, and metabolic diseases. *Type:* Research center.

Beta Beta Beta

PO Box 428
Ocean Grove, NJ 07756-0428

Contact: Dawn B. Rohrs, Natl. Sec.-Treas.

Desc: Honorary and professional society - men and women, biology. Seeks to improve the understanding and appreciation of biological study and extend the boundaries of human knowledge through scientific research. *Type:* Association.

BioBusiness®

BIOSIS
Two Commerce Square
2001 Market St., Ste. 700
Philadelphia, PA 19103-7095
Ph: (215)587-4800
E-mail: info@mail.biosis.org
URL: http://www.biosis.org

Desc: Contains over 900,000 citations, many with abstracts, to the worldwide periodical literature on business applications of biological and biomedical research. Covers agriculture and forestry, cosmetics, environment, food technology, genetic engineering, occupational health, pharmaceutical products, and other industries affected by biotechnological developments. *Available:* The Dialog Corporation, DataStar; The Dialog Corporation, DIALOG; STN International. *Type:* Database.

Biological Abstracts®

BIOSIS
Two Commerce Square
2001 Market St., Ste. 700
Philadelphia, PA 19103-7095
Ph: (215)587-4800
E-mail: info@mail.biosis.org
URL: http://www.biosis.org

Contact: Sharon F. Suer, Senior Marketing Specialist, (215)587-2036, sfsver@mail.biosis.org.

Desc: Contains more than 5 million records and citations with abstracts, to the world's biological and biomedical literature dealing with research in the life sciences. Covers articles from nearly 5500 international periodicals and journals. *Available:* SilverPlatter Information, Inc.; Ovid Technologies, Inc. *Type:* Database.

Biology Digest

Plexus Publishing, Inc.
143 Old Marlton Pike
Medford, NJ 08055
Ph: (609)654-6500
E-mail: info@plexuspub.com
URL: http://www.infotoday.com

Contact: Thomas H. Hogan, President, fax: (609)654-4309.

Desc: Contains citations, with detailed abstracts, to the worldwide life sciences literature. Abstracts are written for use in secondary and undergraduate life sciences courses. *Available:* OCLC Online Computer Library Center, Inc., OCLC EPIC; Cambridge Scientific Abstracts (CSA); NewsBank, Inc. *Type:* Database.

Biomedical Engineering Society

1901 Pennsylvania Ave., NW, Ste. 401
Washington, DC 20006
Ph: (202)496-9663
Fax: (202)466-8489
E-mail: bmes@netcom.com
URL: http://www.bmes.com

Contact: Patricia I. Horner, Exec.Dir.

Desc: Biomedical, chemical, electrical, and mechanical engineers, physicians, managers, and university professors representing all fields of biomedical engineering; students and corporations. Encourages the development, dissemination, integration, and utilization of knowledge in biomedical engineering. *Type:* Association.

Biophysical Society

Rosalba Kampman
9650 Rockville Pike, Rm. 0512
Bethesda, MD 20814
Ph: (301)530-7114
Fax: (301)530-7133
E-mail: society@biophysics.faseb.org
URL: http://www.biophysics.org/biophys/

Contact: Rosalba Kampman, Exec.Dir.

Desc: Biophysicists, physical biochemists, and physical and biological scientists interested in the application of physical laws and techniques to the analysis of biological or living phenomena. Maintains placement service. *Type:* Association.

BIOSIS Evolution

BioSciences Information Service (BIOSIS)
2100 Arch St.
Philadelphia, PA 19103-1399
Ph: (215)587-4847
Free: 800-523-4806
Fax: (215)587-2016
E-mail: info@mail.biosis.org
URL: http://www.biosis.org/htmls/evol_top.html.

Contact: Sharon F. Suer, Editor, sfsuer@mail.biosis.org.

Desc: Serves subscribers to BIOSIS, "the world's largest English language abstracting and indexing service for biological and biomedical research." Reports on new BIOSIS product developments, pricing and distribution of current products and services, and educational programs. Provides descriptions on training courses for BIOSIS online services, vendor news affecting BIOSIS databases, information on the availability of the databases, and tips on searching the databases. *Type:* Newsletter.

BIOSIS Previews®

BIOSIS
Two Commerce Square
2001 Market St., Ste. 700
Philadelphia, PA 19103-7095
Ph: (215)587-4800
E-mail: info@mail.biosis.org
URL: http://www.biosis.org

Contact: fax: (215)587-2016 U.S./Can., info@mail.biosis.org.

Desc: Contains more than 12 million citations, with abstracts (for approximately 50 percent of the records), to worldwide literature on research in the life sciences: microbiology; plant and animal science; experimental medicine; agriculture; pharmacology; ecology; biochemistry; biotechnology; and neurology. Covers original research reports, reviews of original research, history and philosophy of biology and biomedicine, and documentation and retrieval of biological information. *Available:* Ovid Technologies, Inc.; The Dialog Corporation, DataStar; The Dialog Corporation, DIALOG; STN International; OCLC Online Computer Library Center, Inc., OCLC EPIC; NIFTY Corporation, NIFTY-SERVE; European Information Network Services (EINS); Canada Institute for Scientific and Technical Information (CISTI); DIMDI (Deutsches Institut fuer Medizinische Dokumentation und Information); NERAC, Inc.; The Royal Society of Chemistry (RSC), Information Services. *Type:* Database.

Biotechnology Industry Organization

1625 K St. NW, Ste. 1100
Washington, DC 20006
Ph: (202)857-0244
Free: 800-255-3304
Fax: (202)857-0237

Contact: Carl Feldbaum, Pres.

Desc: Provides information on biotechnology issues pertaining to U.S. and international regulations, patents, finance, and other problems confronting members. Organizes workshops and seminars; maintains educational dialogue with Congress, non-U.S. governmental bodies, regulatory agencies, and the public. Represents over 740 biotechnology companies, academic institutions and state biotechnology centers in 46 state and 25 nations. Members are involved in the research and development of health care, agricultural and environmental biotechnology products. *Type:* Association.

Brigham and Women's Hospital

Diagnostic Molecular Biology Laboratory

75 Francis St.
Boston, MA 02115
Ph: (617)732-7442
Fax: (617)277-9019

Contact: Dr. Jeffrey Sklar, Dir.

Desc: Molecular biology, human genetics, and molecular oncology, including nucleic acid analysis for the diagnosis of cancer, inherited conditions, and infectious disorders. *Type:* Research center.

Cancer Biotherapy Research Group

PO Box 680757   Ph: (615)791-6393
Franklin, TN 37068-0757   Fax: (615)791-4719
E-mail: cbrg_cancer@compuserve.com
URL: http://www.cbrg.org
Contact: Rosalie A. Crispin, Exec.Dir.
Desc: Clinical cancer research, focusing on the treatment of solid cancer tumors in adults and the use of biologicals and biological response modifiers alone or in combination with other treatment modalities. *Type:* Research center.

Carnegie Mellon University

Center for Light Microscope Imaging and Biotechnology

Sci. & Tech. Ctr.   Ph: (412)268-3461
4400 5th Ave.   Fax: (412)268-6571
Pittsburgh, PA 15213-2683
E-mail: taylor@cmu.edu
URL: http://www.stc.cmu.edu
Contact: Dr. D. Lansing Taylor, PhD, Dir.
Desc: Develops instruments and reagents for the investigation of high-resolution cell and tissue structure and function, utilizing multiple paramater fluorescence microscope systems and computer-based image analysis in two and three dimensions. *Type:* Research center.

Case Western Reserve University

Developmental Biology Center

2109 Adelbert Rd.   Ph: (216)368-2428
Cleveland, OH 44106-4901   Fax: (216)368-3182
Contact: Dr. Urs Rutishauser, Dir.
Desc: Developmental biology, genetics, neuroscience, molecular biology, regeneration, regulation of normal and neoplastic growth, biophysics, and biochemistry. *Type:* Research center.

Catholic University of America

Center for Advanced Training in Cell and Molecular Biology

103 McCort-Ward Bldg.   Ph: (202)319-6161
Cardinal Station   Fax: (202)319-4467
Washington, DC 20064
E-mail: cua-catcmb@cua.edu
URL: http://www.cua.edu/www/catc
Contact: Venigalla B. Rao, PhD, Dir.
Desc: Focuses on new and established biomedically related concepts and technologies for research, industrial applications, and diagnostic laboratory techniques. Established as a national center providing training for scientists and technicians. *Type:* Research center.

Center for Advanced Biotechnology and Medicine

679 Hoes Ln.   Ph: (732)235-5300
Piscataway, NJ 08854-5638   Fax: (732)235-4850
E-mail: cabm@mbcl.rutgers.edu
URL: http://www.cabm.rutgers.edu
Contact: Dr. Aaron J. Shatkin, Dir.
Desc: Cell and developmental biology, molecular pharmacology, molecular genetics, and structural biology. Collaborates with biopharmaceutical firms in New Jersey on technology transfer and research and development. *Type:* Research center.

Center for Biomedical Research

Population Council   Ph: (212)327-8717
1230 York Ave.   Fax: (212)327-7678
New York, NY 10021
E-mail: e-johansson@popcbr.rockefeller.edu
Contact: Dr. Elof Johansson, VP.
Desc: Physiology of human reproduction, especially the male reproductive system, including studies on gameto-genesis, sperm ultrastructure, steroid receptors, hormone action, and testicular function. Contraceptive development includes studies on subdermal implants, the contraceptive ring, the levonorgestrel-releasing intrauterine device, an LHRH analog for ovulation inhibition in women and for spermatogenic inhibition in men, and pregnancy vaccines. *Type:* Research center.

Center for Crystallographic Research

Roswell Park Cancer Institute   Ph: (716)845-3135
Elem & Carlton Sts.   Fax: (716)845-8899
Buffalo, NY 14263
E-mail: roswhui@acsu.buffalo.edu
Contact: Dr. Sek Wen Hui, PhD, Dir.
Desc: Conformational studies of nucleotides, peptides, and carbohydrates to determine interatomic arrangements in biological substances using nuclear magnetic resonance and electron spin resonance. Research is oriented to the field of cancer. *Type:* Research center.

Center for Intelligent Biomedical Devices and Musculoskeletal Systems

Colorado School of Mines   Ph: (303)384-2033
Brown Bldg., Rm. 3301
700 Illinois
Golden, CO 80401
URL: http://www.mines.edu/research/ibdms/html/mission_statement.html
Contact: Dr. Rahmat Shoureshi, Dir.
Desc: Advances in biomedical devices and musculoskeletal systems to enhance the quality of life for citizens with disabilities and reduce health care costs. Areas of interest include smart implants for hips and knees, enhanced mobility, and musculoskeletal systems stimulus. *Type:* Research center.

City College of City University of New York

Center for the Study of the Cellular and Molecular Basis of Development

Science Bldg., Rm. 501   Ph: (212)650-8300
138th St. & Convent Ave.   Fax: (212)650-7989
New York, NY 10031
E-mail: jerry@scisun.sci.ccny.cuny.edu
Contact: Dr. Guyden, Dir.
Desc: Molecular biology, including biomolecular structure and function, gene expression and regulation, cellular and organismal function, and neurobiology. *Type:* Research center.

City of Hope Beckman Research Institute

Division of Biology

1500 E. Duarte Rd.   Ph: (626)357-2571
Duarte, CA 91010   Fax: (626)930-5486
URL: http://www.cityofhope.org
Contact: Charles M. Balch, MD, Pres./CEO.
Desc: Molecular mechanisms of living systems. Research activities are carried out in Departments of Biology, Molecular Biochemistry, Molecular Genetics, and Theoretical Biology. *Type:* Research center.

Cleveland FES Center

11000 Cedar Ave., Ste. 230   Ph: (216)231-3257
Cleveland, OH 44106-3052   Free: 800-666-2353
    Fax: (216)231-3258
E-mail: cleve_fes@po.cwru.edu
URL: http://feswww.fes.cwru.edu
Contact: P. Hunter Peckham, PhD, Dir.
Desc: Functional electrical stimulation (FES) in the restoration of muscle control or sensory function, particularly in the areas of lower and upper extremity deficits, scoliosis, spasticity, respiratory insufficiency, and bladder function. Studies focus on computer-controlled and implanted FES systems for paraplegic and quadraplegic users, persons with hemiplegia due to cerebral trauma or stroke, and persons with spinal cord injuries. *Type:* Research center.

Columbia University

Artificial Organs Research Laboratory

Department of Chemical   Ph: (212)854-4448
   Engineering   Fax: (212)854-8725
814 Mudd
New York, NY 10027
E-mail: leonard@columbia.edu
URL: http://www.columbia.edu/~leonard
Contact: Prof. Edward F. Leonard, Dir.
Desc: Engineering and technical solutions for problems associated with extracorporeal circulation, cardiovascular implants, and artificial organs. Also studies blood-biomaterial interactions, extracorporeal immunotherapies, and photochemical reactions to transform cells and inactivate viruses. *Type:* Research center.

Columbia University

Biochemistry and Molecular Biophysics Laboratory

630 W. 168th St.   Ph: (212)305-3881
New York, NY 10032   Fax: (212)305-7932
E-mail: dhirsh@columbia.edu
Contact: Dr. David Hirsh, Chr.
Desc: Biochemistry, molecular biology, biophysics, and biochemical genetics, including X-ray diffraction studies of biological macromolecules, structure and function of membrane receptors and transport proteins, computer studies of protein and nucleic acid structure and function, NMR spectroscopy, neutron and electron diffraction, enzymology, regulation of transcription and translation in prokaryotic and eukaryotic cells, molecular virology, genomic and cDNA cloning in prokaryotes and eukaryotes, recombinant DNA technology, gene transfer and somatic-cell genetics, DNA sequencing, in vitro site-specific mutagenesis of cloned DNA, the role of oncogenes in neoplasia, control of gene expression in development, role of growth factors, regulation of oxygen transport by hemoglobin, hormonal regulation of ion transport, immunochemical properties of membrane antigens, structure and composition of synaptic components, metabolism of neurotransmitters, neurotoxic proteins and protein hormones, and chemical carcinogenesis. *Type:* Research center.

CSA Life Sciences Collection

Cambridge Scientific Abstracts (CSA)
7200 Wisconsin Ave., Ste. 601   Ph: (301)961-6700
Bethesda, MD 20814-4823
E-mail: sales@csa.com
URL: http://www.csa.com
Desc: Contains more than 1.6 million citations, with abstracts, to the world's life sciences literature. Corresponds to the following 19 abstracting journals published by CSA: • ASFA Marine Biotechnology Abstracts. *Available:* The Dialog Corporation, DIALOG; The Dialog Corporation, DIALOG; CompuServe Information Service, Knowledge Index; STN International; STN International; EBSCO-host; Ovid Technologies, Inc. *Type:* Database.

CSA Neurosciences Abstracts

Cambridge Scientific Abstracts (CSA)
7200 Wisconsin Ave., Ste. 601   Ph: (301)961-6700
Bethesda, MD 20814-4823
E-mail: sales@csa.com
URL: http://www.csa.com
Desc: Contains more than 160,000 citations, with abstracts, to the worldwide literature relating to both vertebrate and invertebrate neurosciences and endocrinology. Sources include specialist literature such as journals, books, conference proceedings, and reports. *Type:* Database.

Duke University

Center for In Vivo Microscopy

Department of Radiology   Ph: (919)684-7754
PO Box 3302   Fax: (919)684-7122
Duke Univ. Med. Ctr.
Durham, NC 27710
E-mail: gaj@orion.mc.duke.edu
URL: http://www.civm.mc.duke.edu

Contact: G. Allan Johnson, PhD, Dir.

Desc: Magnetic resonance microscopy, imaging of disease models, drug discovery and validation, pulmonary imaging toxicology testing and evaluation in live animals, and in vivo histology and microscopy. *Type:* Research center.

Duke University

Marine Biomedical Center

Nicholas Sch. of the Env.   Ph: (252)504-7508
   Marine Lab   Fax: (252)504-7648
135 Duke Marine Lab Rd.
Beaufort, NC 28516-9721
E-mail: bbw@mail.duke.edu
URL: http://www.env.duke.edu/research-centers/biomed.html

Contact: Dr. Celia Bonaventura, Dir.

Desc: Marine organisms and marine systems as they relate to human health and the health of the environment. Research conducted in the fields of oceanography, chemistry, biochemistry, developmental and behavioral biology, and physiology has led to specific studies on the continental shelf, trace metals in marine and estuarine ecosystems, photosynthetic physiology of marine plants, maritime and pelagic birds, and behavioral toxicology. *Type:* Research center.

Emory-Georgia Tech Biomedical Technology Research Center

Georgia Institute of Technology   Ph: (404)894-2849
Institute for Bioengineering and   Fax: (404)894-2291
   Bioscience
281 Ferst
Atlanta, GA 30332-0363
E-mail: ajit.yoganathan@che.gatech.edu
URL: http://www.gatech.edu

Contact: Prof. Ajit P. Yoganathan, Codir.

Desc: Cardiovascular mechanics, corneal mechanics, medical imaging, biomedical artificial intelligence, biomedical instrumentation, vascular biology, tissue engineering, telemedicine. *Type:* Research center.

Emory University

Yerkes Regional Primate Research Center

Atlanta, GA 30322   Ph: (404)727-7707
   Fax: (404)727-0623
E-mail: insel@rmy.emory.edu
URL: http://www.emory.edu

Contact: Dr. Thomas R. Insel, MD, Dir.

Desc: Primate studies, including neuroscience, psychobiology, microbiology and immunology, molecular medicine, and vision research. Specialty areas within the foregoing fields include drug abuse, aging, neurophysiology, neuroendocrinology, cardiovascular studies related to coronary disease, effects of drugs on behavior, social behavior, language capacities, in vitro fertilization, endocrine studies of reproductive cycles, diseases of nonhuman primates, infectious and degenerative diseases (including AIDS and retroviral immunodeficiency disorders) and vaccine development. *Type:* Research center.

Endocrinology Research Laboratory

Dept. of Veterans Affairs   Ph: (925)372-2076
   Medical Center   Fax: (925)372-2185
Medical Services III
150 Muir Rd.
Martinez, CA 94553

Contact: Arthur Swislocki, Assoc.Chf., Med.Ser.

Desc: Basic and clinical diabetes and hypertension related research. *Type:* Research center.

EPG Research Foundation, Inc.

111 E. Shore Rd.   Ph: (516)365-1288
Manhasset, NY 11030-2922   Fax: (516)365-7522
E-mail: epglabs@igc.apc.org

Contact: Dr. J.L. Logan, Dir.

Desc: Molecular biology. *Type:* Research center.

Federation of American Societies for Experimental Biology

9650 Rockville Pike   Ph: (301)530-7000
Bethesda, MD 20814-3998   Fax: (301)530-7001
E-mail: admin@faseb.org
URL: http://www.faseb.org

Contact: Michael J. Jackson, Ph.D., Exec.Dir.

Desc: Federation of scientific societies with a total of 40,000 members: The American Physiological Society; American Society for Biochemistry and Molecular Biology; American Society for Pharmacology and Experimental Therapeutics; American Society for Investigative Pathology; American Society for Nutritional Sciences; The American Association of Immunologists; The American Society for Cell Biology; Biophysical Society; American Association of Anatomists; The Protein Society . Maintains placement service. *Type:* Association.

Foundation for Hand Research

310 E. 30th St.   Ph: (212)685-3834
New York, NY 10016   Fax: (212)545-1388

Contact: Dr. Robert Beasley, Contact.

Desc: Upper extremity disorders, focusing on hand research and education. Also collaborates with bioengineers in developing prosthetic hand devices, joint replacements, and other technical devices. *Type:* Research center.

GI Research Laboratory

4150 Clement St.   Ph: (415)750-2095
151-M2   Fax: (415)750-6972
San Francisco, CA 94121

Contact: Dr. Young S. Kim, Dir.

Desc: Molecular biology and cell biology, including studies on DNA cloning and sequencing, PCR, vector construction, site-directed mutagenesis, eukaryotic gene transfection, and oncogene and tumor suppressor gene molecular biology. *Type:* Research center.

Helicon Foundation

4622 Santa Fe St.   Ph: (619)272-3884
San Diego, CA 92109   Free: 800-726-8696
   Fax: (619)272-1621
E-mail: cathomas@ix.netcom.com

Contact: Dr. Charles A. Thomas, Jr., Pres.

Desc: Basic biological research in biochemistry, molecular biology, and genetics, including studies on oxidative damage to cellular DNA, structure of chromosomal telomeres, chromatin structure, and role of lipids in radical formation. Seeks to define the biochemical basis of disease prevention through antioxidant diagnostics. *Type:* Research center.

Hospital for Special Surgery

Fannie E. Rippel Flow Cytometry Core Facility

Caspary Research Bldg., Rm. 215
535 E. 70th St.
New York, NY 10021
URL: http://hss.hss.edu/research/flow/index.htm

Contact: Dr. William Telford, Dir.

Desc: Flow cytometric technology. *Type:* Research center.

Hospital for Special Surgery

Research Division

Biomechanics and Biomaterials Section

535 E. 70th St.
New York, NY 10021
URL: http://hss.hss.edu/research/biomechanics.htm

Contact: Timothy Wright, PhD, Sect.Hd.

Desc: Application of principles of mechanics and materials science in order to understand and treat orthopedic problems. *Type:* Research center.

Indiana University-Purdue University at Indianapolis

Biomechanics and Biomaterials Research Center

415 N. Lansing St.   Ph: (317)274-8822
Indianapolis, IN 46202
URL: http://www.indiana.edu/~rugs/ctrdir/bbrc.html

Contact: Dr. George K. Stookey, Dir.

Desc: Biomechanics, biomaterials, musculoskeletal research, polymers with therapeutic potential, and new dental restorative materials. *Type:* Research center.

Indiana University-Purdue University at Indianapolis

Human Performance and Biomechanics Laboratory

901 W. New York St.   Ph: (317)274-0608
Indianapolis, IN 46202   Fax: (317)278-2041
E-mail: amikesky@iupui.edu
URL: http://www.indiana.edu/~rugs/ctrdir/hpmbl.html

Contact: Alan E. Mikesky, Dir.

Desc: Sports medicine and biomechanics. *Type:* Research center.

Iowa State University of Science and Technology

Cell and Hybridoma Facility

1104 Molecular Biology Bldg.   Ph: (515)294-9837
Ames, IA 50011   Fax: (515)294-0453
E-mail: kharkins@iastate.edu
URL: http://biotech.iastate.edu/facilities/cellhyb/homepage.htm

Contact: Dr. Kristi R. Harkins, Mgr.

Desc: Production of monoclonal antibody-secreting hybridomas, including cell fusion, ascites fluid production, and development strategies; production of polyclonal antibodies; and analyses via flow cytometry of cells and organelles. *Type:* Research center.

Johns Hopkins University

Biomechanics Research Laboratory

Department of Orthopaedic   Ph: (410)532-4489
   Surgery   Fax: (410)532-4488
5601 Loch Raven Blvd., 4N
Baltimore, MD 21239
E-mail: eychao@eagle.gsh.jhu.edu
URL: http://www.biomech.jhu.edu/index.html

Contact: Dr. Edmund Y.S. Chao, Contact.

Desc: Orthopedic concerns and the application of engineering principles to the better treatment and care of patients. *Type:* Research center.

Johns Hopkins University

Polymeric Biomaterials Laboratory

School of Medicine	Ph: (410)955-0075
Department of Biomedical	Fax: (410)955-0549
Engineering	
729 Ross Bldg.	
Baltimore, MD 21205	

E-mail: kleong@bme.jhu.edu
URL: http://www.bme.jhu.edu/~apietrom/leonglab/
Contact: Dr. Kam W. Leong, Prin. Investigator.
Desc: Application of synthetic and biological polymers to drug delivery, gene therapy, and tissue engineering, particularly controlled delivery of cytokines and cytokine genes for cancer immunotherapy, particulate HIV vaccine design, combinative gene and drug therapy of cystic fibrosis; and synthesis of new biodegradable poly(phosphoesters) for drug-carrier and tissue scaffold applications. *Type:* Research center.

Joint Program in Biomedical Engineering

University of Texas	Ph: (214)648-2052
Southwestern Medical Center	Fax: (214)648-2979
at Dallas	
5323 Harry Hines Blvd., Rm.	
G8.248	
Dallas, TX 75235-9130	

E-mail: robert.eberhart@email.swmed.edu
URL: http://www.swmed.edu/home_pages/bme/indes.html
Contact: Prof. Robert C. Eberhart, PhD, Contact.
Desc: Biomedical engineering, including studies in magnetic resonance, gamma and ultrasound image analysis, orthopedics, human performance, biocompatible materials, biomechanics, artificial organs, biosensors, soft tissue biomechanics, neurological signal acquisition and analysis, recombinant DNA technology, human genome project and gene therapy. *Type:* Research center.

Kansas State University

University Biochemistry Facility

Department of Biochemistry	Ph: (913)532-6121
104 Willard Hall	Fax: (913)532-7278
Manhattan, KS 66506-3702	

E-mail: bchter@ksuvm.ksu.edu
URL: http://www.ksu.edu:80/bchem/research.html
Contact: Dr. Thomas Roche, Hd.
Desc: Biochemistry research, including protein sequencing, peptide sequencing, and oligonucleotide synthesis. *Type:* Research center.

Laval University

Laboratory of Experimental Tissue Engineering

Hopital du Saint-Sacrement	Ph: (418)682-7663
Research Centre	Fax: (418)682-8000
1050, chemin Sainte-Foy	
Quebec, PQ, Canada G1S 4L8	

E-mail: francois.auger@chg.ulaval.ca
Contact: Francois A. Auger, MD, Dir.
Desc: Clinical and experimental human tissue engineering (blood vessel, skin, musculoskeletal, bronchial, occular), including tissue transplantation and developing applications for living tissue equivalents such as percutaneous absorption, toxicology, and wound healing. *Type:* Research center.

Laval University

Medical Research Centre

Research Centre on the Biology of Reproduction

2705, boulevard Laurier	Ph: (418)656-4141
Ste. Foy, PQ, Canada G1V 4G2	Fax: (418)654-2765

E-mail: mafortier@crchul.ulaval.ca

URL: http://www.crbr.ulaval.ca
Contact: Michel A. Fortier, PhD, Dir.

Desc: Physiological, cellular, and molecular factors leading to the production of viable embryos, male infertility and contraception, sexual differentiation, implantation and the maintenance of pregnancy. Focuses on the development and applications of new reproductive techniques for domestic animals and humans. *Type:* Research center.

Laval University

Molecular Microbiology and Protein Engineering Group

Departement de microbiologie	Ph: (418)656-3070
Faculte de medecine	Fax: (418)656-7176
4142 Pav. Charles Marchand	
Quebec, PQ, Canada G1K 7P4	

E-mail: rclevesq@rsvs.ulaval.ca

Contact: Roger C. Levesque, Dir.

Desc: Structure-function analysis of B-lactamases, dihydrofolate reductase and superoxide dismutase in pathogenic microorganisms. Studies also include molecular genetics, phylogeny, and evolution of multiresistant transposons, and sequencing pseudomonas genome. *Type:* Research center.

Laval University

Quebec Biomaterials Institute Inc.

Research Centre	Ph: (418)525-4485
St. Francois d'Assise Pavillion,	Fax: (418)525-4372
CHUQ	
10, l'Espinay St.	
Quebec, PQ, Canada G1L 3L5	

E-mail: robert.guidoin@crsfa.ulaval.ca

Contact: Robert Guidoin, PhD, Dir.

Desc: Cardiology, including blood conduits, artificial hearts, and heart valves; magnetic resonance, including new surface coils; follow-up of implanted devices; artificial skin and wound healing; drug delivery systems; and breast implants. *Type:* Research center.

Lawrence Berkeley National Laboratory

National Tritium Labelling Facility

75-123	Ph: (510)486-4373
1 Cyclotron Rd.	Fax: (510)486-4877
Berkeley, CA 94720	

E-mail: dewemmer@lbl.gov
URL: http://www.lbl.gov/LBL-Programs/NTLF.html

Contact: David E. Wemmer, PhD, Dir.

Desc: Provides specialty equipment and professional assistance for biomedical researchers to produce very high specific activity tritiated compounds, with high radiochemical purity. Labeling is achieved via one of the major tritiation techniques: hydrogenation, dehalogenation, methylation, hydride reduction, or exchange. *Type:* Research center.

Linus Pauling Institute of Science and Medicine

571 Weniger Hall	Ph: (415)327-4064
Oregon State University	Fax: (415)327-8564
Corvallis, OR 97331-6512	

Contact: Stephen Lawson, CEO.

Desc: Founded by Linus Pauling, renowned scientist, humanitarian, educator, health proponent, and winner of two Nobel Prizes. Conducts experimental research in human health, particularly related to the relation between micronutrients and health and disease. Special fields of interest include cardiovascular disease, nutritional biochemisty, cancer and toxicology. *Type:* Association.

Louisiana State University

Pennington Biomedical Research Center

6400 Perkins Rd.	Ph: (504)763-2500
Baton Rouge, LA 70808-4124	Fax: (504)763-2525

URL: http://www.pbrc.edu
Contact: George A. Bray, MD, Exec.Dir.
Desc: Nutritional physiology and metabolism, molecular and cellular nutrition, nutrition and behavior, nutritional epidemiology, neurobiology, taste physiology, clinical physchology, biostatistics, and metabolic studies. *Type:* Research center.

McGill University Health Centre

Research Institute

1650 Cedar Ave.	Ph: (514)934-8038
Montreal, PQ, Canada H3G	Fax: (514)933-7146
1A4	

E-mail: md88@musica.mcgill.ca
Contact: Dr. Emil Skamere, Dir.
Desc: General biomedical research. *Type:* Research center.

Medical Biology Institute

3550 General Atomics Ct.	Ph: (619)450-3033
San Diego, CA 92121-1122	Fax: (619)554-0614

Contact: Dr. David H. Katz, Pres.
Desc: Immunology, membrane and molecular biology, and developmental biology. Specific diseases being studied include allergy and asthma, rheumatoid arthritis, juvenile-onset diabetes, cancer, lupus, multiple sclerosis, and AIDS. *Type:* Research center.

Medical Research Foundation of Oregon

1121 SW Salmon St., Ste. 200	Ph: (503)228-1730
Portland, OR 97205-2021	Fax: (503)228-9588

Contact: Lori Mueller, Dir.
Desc: Biomedical research. *Type:* Research center.

Medical University of South Carolina

Marine Biomedicine and Environmental Sciences

221 Ft. Johnson Rd.	Ph: (803)762-5530
Charleston, SC 29412	Fax: (803)762-5535

E-mail: lacyer@musc.edu
Contact: Dr. Eric R. Lacy, Dir.
Desc: Marine organisms and their cells as models, particularly in toxicology, immunology, pathology, parasitology, and microbiology studies. *Type:* Research center.

Meharry Medical College

Research Center of Excellence in Cell and Molecular Biology

Microbiology Dept.	Ph: (615)327-6193
Nashville, TN 37208-3599	Fax: (615)327-5621

E-mail: gchill@ccvax.mmc.edu
Contact: Dr. George C. Hill, Prog.Dir.
Desc: Membrane biology, molecular biology, biochemistry, and immunology. Projects include an investigation of DNA replication mechanisms in normal and abnormal cell growth, viral infection, and the process of mutation; and biophysical analysis of enzyme cytochrome b5 activity in fat metabolism. *Type:* Research center.

Milwaukee School of Engineering

Electrical Engineering and Biomedical Science

1025 N. Broadway	Ph: (414)277-7331
Milwaukee, WI 53202-3109	Fax: (414)277-7465

E-mail: canino@kirk.msoe.edu
URL: http://www.msoe.edu
Contact: Dr. Vincent R. Canino, Dir.
Desc: Biomedical instrumentation systems, including the design and evaluation of extra-corporeal perfusion instrumentation. *Type:* Research center.

Mt. Sinai Medical Center

Harry Pearlman Biomedical Research Institute

4300 Alton Rd. Ph: (305)674-2790
Miami Beach, FL 33140 Fax: (305)674-2198

Contact: Dr. William Abraham, Dir.

Desc: Pulmonary medicine, sleep disorders, pharmacology, dermatology, obstetrics and gynecology, infectious diseases, nuclear medicine, arthritis, and tumor biology. *Type:* Research center.

Mount Sinai School of Medicine of City University of New York

Brookdale Center for Molecular Biology

1 Gustave L Levy Plz. Ph: (212)241-4272
Box 1126 Fax: (212)860-9279
New York, NY 10029-6574

E-mail: rlazzar@smtplink.mssm.edu

URL: http://www.mssm.edu

Contact: Dr. Robert Lazzarini, Dir.

Desc: Molecular biology and medicine, including molecular neurobiology; developmental molecular biology; receptor and channel structure, function, and regulation; hormone, oncogene, and growth factor actions; the molecular and genetic basis of disease; cytokine action; and control of gene transcription. *Type:* Research center.

National Academy of Sciences/National Academy of Engineering/Institute of Medicine/National Research Council Publications and Reports

National Academy Press

2101 Constitution Ave. NW Ph: (202)334-2000
Washington, DC 20418-0007 Free: 800-624-6242

E-mail: wwwfdk@nas.edu

URL: http://www.nas.edu/homepage/pubs/pubs.html

Desc: This site was created by the National Academy of Sciences to publish books and reports issued by the National Academy of Sciences, the National Academy of Engineering, the Institute of Medicine, and the National Research Council, all operating under the charter granted to the National Academy of Sciences by the Congress of the United States. *Type:* Database.

National Association for Biomedical Research

818 Connecticut Ave. NW, Ste. Ph: (202)857-0540
303 Fax: (202)659-1902
Washington, DC 20006

E-mail: info@nabr.org

URL: http://www.nabr.org

Contact: Ms. Frankie L. Trull, Pres.

Desc: Biomedical research, education, and testing, focusing on using laboratory animals for such purposes, monitors and attempts to infulence legislation and regulations on behalf of members dependent on laboratory animals for research and testing. *Type:* Research center.

National Biomedical Research Foundation

3900 Reservoir Rd. NW Ph: (202)687-2121
Washington, DC 20007 Fax: (202)687-1662

E-mail: pirmail@nbrf.georgetown.edu

URL: http://www-nbrf.georgetown.edu

Contact: Dr. Robert S. Ledley, Pres.

Desc: Application of computers and electronic technology to medical research, including biomedical picture pattern analysis, biology, biochemistry, origins of life, and computer technology. Specific research projects include studies on automatic chromosome analysis, biomedical instrumentation, computer aid to medical diagnosis, and genetics, evolution, and function of proteins and nucleic acids. *Type:* Research center.

National Science Foundation

Directorate for Biological Sciences

Division of Molecular and Cellular Biosciences

Biomolecular Structure and Function Program

4201 Wilson Blvd. Ph: (703)306-1444
Arlington, VA 22230 Fax: (703)306-0355

E-mail: kshukla@nsf.gov

Contact: Kamal Shukla, Prog.Dir.

Desc: Supports research that uses physical techniques to investigate basic biological phenomena; and research on the physical interactions of macromolecules with other molecules or their environment. The program focuses on major biomolecules (such as proteins, nucleic acids, lipids, and carbohydrates), their complexes, and their structurally and functionally important aggregates (e.g., membranes). *Type:* Research center.

National Science Foundation

Directorate for Biological Sciences

Division of Molecular and Cellular Biosciences

Ecological and Evolutionary Physiology Program

4201 Wilson Blvd. Ph: (703)306-1421
Arlington, VA 22230 Fax: (703)306-0349

E-mail: zeppley@nsf.gov

URL: http://www.nsf.gov

Contact: Zoe A. Eppley, Prog.Dir.

Desc: Physiological processes, including studies on the characteristics and evolution of mechanisms (such as endocrine and neuroendocrine systems) that initiate, integrate, and regulate physiological functions in tissues, organs, and organisms; and physiological adaptation of animals to environmental variables, including conditions of stress. *Type:* Research center.

National Science Foundation

Directorate for Engineering

Division of Bioengineering and Environmental Systems

4201 Wilson Blvd., Rm. 565 Ph: (703)306-1320
Arlington, VA 22230 Fax: (703)306-0312

E-mail: jfouke@nsf.gov

URL: http://www.nsf.gov

Contact: Janie M. Fouke, Dir.

Desc: Critical engineering systems are those that are essential either because they significantly affect the economic viability and security needs of the nation, or because they are required for maintaining the public infrastructure. Major program areas include: bioengineerig and aiding the disabled; and environmental and ocean systems. *Type:* Research center.

National Science Foundation

Directorate for Engineering

Division of Bioengineering and Environmental Systems

Biochemical Engineering Program

4201 Wilson Blvd., Rm. 565 Ph: (703)306-1319
Arlington, VA 22230 Fax: (703)306-0312

E-mail: fheineke@nsf.gov

Contact: Dr. Frederick Heineken, Prog.Dir.

Desc: Design and development of novel bioreactors, bioseparation systems, and the control of biochemical processes, as well as research aimed at improved utilization of biologically based resources. This includes support for programs in biochemical engineering fundamentals, biomass processing, and food process engineering. *Type:* Research center.

Northwestern University

Center for Biotechnology

1801 Maple Ave. Ph: (847)467-1453
Evanston, IL 60201-2125 Fax: (847)467-2180

E-mail: biotech@nwu.edu

URL: http://www.nucb.nwu.edu

Contact: Alicia Loffler, Dir.

Desc: Cooperates with industry on issues of national and international significance. *Type:* Research center.

Oklahoma Medical Research Foundation

825 NE 13th St. Ph: (405)271-7210
Oklahoma City, OK 73104 Free: 800-522-0211
  Fax: (405)271-3980

E-mail: Don-Capra@omrs.ouhsc.edu

Contact: J. Donald Capraan, MD, Pres.

Desc: Cardiovascular disease, cancer, arthritis, and thrombosis/hematology, including fundamental studies carried out in individually organized laboratories in the areas of molecular biology, biomembranes, lipoproteins, protein chemistry, intermediate metabolism, and genetics. *Type:* Research center.

Oklahoma Medical Research Foundation

Protein Studies Program

825 NE 13th St. Ph: (405)271-7291
Oklahoma City, OK 73104 Fax: (405)271-7249

E-mail: jordan-tang@omrf.uokhsc.edu

Contact: Dr. Jordan Tang, Dir.

Desc: Protein structure and function, including cloning, expression and mutagenesis of protease genes, mechanisms of proteases, proteolysis by lysosomal enzymes, and streptokinase interaction with plasminogen fibrinolysis. A major interest is the role of proteins in chemical carcinogenesis, particularly the role of proteins responsible for the intracellular transport of the carcinogen, benzopyrene. *Type:* Research center.

Oklahoma State University

Microbiology and Molecular Genetics

Life Sci. East 316 Ph: (405)744-9950
Stillwater, OK 74078-9947 Fax: (405)744-6790

E-mail: pooky@okway.okstate.edu

Desc: Production and characterization of hybridomas and monoclonal antibodies and production of polyclonal antiserum. *Type:* Research center.

Oregon Health Sciences University

Biomedical Information Communication Center

3181 SW Sam Jackson Park Rd. Ph: (503)494-4809
Portland, OR 97201-3098 Fax: (503)494-4551

URL: http://ohsu.edu/bicc-informatics/

Desc: Health informatics. BICC comprises four divisions: Health Informatics, Information Services, Information Technology, and Educational Communications. *Type:* Research center.

Oregon Health Sciences University

Vollum Institute

3181 SW Sam Jackson Park Ph: (503)494-5042
Rd., L474 Fax: (503)494-4590
Portland, OR 97201-3098

E-mail: goodmanr@ohsu.edu

URL: http://www.ohsu.edu/vollum

Contact: Dr. Richard Goodman, PhD, Dir.

Desc: Molecular biology, protein chemistry, virology, and immunology of the endocrine system and brain and nervous system. Also conducts studies in electrophysiology and pharmacology. *Type:* Research center.

Oregon Institute of Science and Medicine

2251 Dick George Rd.　　　Ph: (541)592-4142
Cave Junction, OR 97523-9622　Fax: (541)592-2597
E-mail: art@oism.org
URL: http://www.oism.org
Contact: Arthur B. Robinson, PhD, Pres.
Desc: Protein chemistry, molecular biology, nutrition and preventive medicine, and medical diagnostic techniques. *Type:* Research center.

Pacific Northwest Research Institute

720 Broadway Ave.　　　Ph: (206)726-1200
Seattle, WA 98122　　　Fax: (206)726-1217
E-mail: rpr@pnrf.org
Contact: R. Paul Robertson, MD, CEO/Sci.Dir.
Desc: Medical sciences, including Type I and II diabetes, pancreas and islet transplantation, environmental biochemistry, membrane biochemistry, biochemical oncology, molecular epidemiology, and cell and molecular biology. *Type:* Research center.

Palo Alto Medical Foundation for Health Care, Research, and Education

400 Channing Ave.　　　Ph: (650)321-4121
Palo Alto, CA 94301-2726　Fax: (650)329-8423
URL: http://www.pamf.org
Contact: Robert W. Janplis, MD, Dir.
Desc: Basic and clinical biomedical research. *Type:* Research center.

Phi Sigma

Dr. John M. Speer
Botany Dept.　　　　Ph: (217)581-6237
207-D Life Science Bldg.　Fax: (217)581-7141
Eastern Illinois University
Charleston, IL 61920
Contact: Dr. John M. Speer, Contact.
Desc: Honor society - pure and applied biological sciences. Chapter programs include lecture series, informal workshops, laboratory visits and demonstrations, field trips, exhibits, and other scientific endeavors and social activities. Presents certificates and awards. *Type:* Association.

Philadelphia Biomedical Research Institute

100 Ross & Royal Rds.　　Ph: (610)962-0615
King of Prussia, PA 19406　Fax: (610)962-0614
E-mail: sttohnishi@aol.com
Contact: S. Tsuyoshi Ohnishi, PhD, Dir.
Desc: Mechanisms, methods of diagnosis, and pharmacological treatment of membrane-linked diseases through investigation of structure-function relationship in normal and abnormal biological membranes. Studies focus on the role of calcium ions in membrane structure and function; development of drugs to prevent ischemia-related membrane damages in the heart, liver, and brain; renal manifestations of ischemia during alcohol ingestation; sickle cell anemia; malignant hyperthermia; development of chemotherapies for malaria, cancer, and AIDS. *Type:* Research center.

Picower Institute for Medical Research

350 Community Dr., 4th Fl.　Ph: (516)365-4200
Manhasset, NY 11030　　Fax: (516)365-5090
E-mail: ejones@picower.edu
URL: http://www.picower.edu
Contact: Dr. Jesse Roth, Pres./CEO.
Desc: Pathogenesis of diseases in order to discover the technology to treat them. Major areas of investigation include metabolic diseases, inflammation, and infectious diseases. *Type:* Research center.

Polytechnical School of Montreal

Research Group in Biomechanics and Biomaterials

Institut de genie biomedical　Ph: (514)340-4378
CP 6079, Succursale Centre-ville　Fax: (514)340-4611
Montreal, PQ, Canada H3C
　3A7
E-mail: yahia@grbb.polymtl.ca
URL: http://www.grbb.polymtl.ca
Contact: L'Hocine Yahia, Dir.
Desc: Biomechanical behavior of the musculoskeletal system, including the following: modelling of the behavior of human joints and biological tissues; graphic representation of biological structures; biomechanics and microstructure of biological tissues and artificial substitutes; computer-aided design and manufacturing of orthopedic and rehabilitation devices; and stress analysis of knee implants. *Type:* Research center.

Protein Engineering Network of Centres of Excellence

Univ. of Alberta　　　Ph: (403)492-8851
750 Heritage Medical Res.　Fax: (403)492-6695
　Centre
Edmonton, AB, Canada T6G
　2S2
E-mail: robert.hodges@ualberta.ca
URL: http://www.pence.ualberta.ca
Contact: Dr. Robert Hodges, Dir.
Desc: Three-dimensional structural, functional, and design studies of selected proteins, including cellular growth factors and their receptors, metalloproteins, proteinases of diseases, enzymes and technologies to synthesize complex carbohydrates, synthetic vaccines and immunological products, and design of proteins. *Type:* Research center.

Regenstrief Institute for Health Care Research

1001 W. 10th St.　　　Ph: (317)630-6221
Indianapolis, IN 46202　　Fax: (317)630-6611
URL: http://www.regenstrief.org
Contact: Dr. Clement McDonald, Dir.
Desc: Health care, including use of computers in health care delivery, and use of engineering and computer techniques to improve medical diagnosis and therapy. *Type:* Research center.

Rice University

Institute of Biosciences and Bioengineering

6100 Main St.　　　　Ph: (713)527-6034
Houston, TX 77005-1892　Fax: (713)285-5154
E-mail: ibb@rice.edu
URL: http://www-bioc.rice.edu/Institute/IBB
Contact: Dr. Larry V. McIntire, Ch.
Desc: Application of engineering skills to problems in biology and medicine, including cellular and tissue engineering, studies on circulation assistance devices, cardiovascular tissue mechanics, blood proteins, effects of physical forces on various components of blood, fluid mechanics and transport processes related to cardiovascular system, hematologic complications with prostheses, rheology, fluid mechanics of blood and blood flow, tissue culture reactor evaluation, biochemical reactor engineering, applications of artificial intelligence in bioreactor control and dynamics, plant cell bioreactors, bioseparation systems, and development of in vitro methods for studying cellular mechanisms of thrombosis and atherogenesis. *Type:* Research center.

Riverside Research Institute

Lawrence H. O'Neil Research Center

330 W. 42nd St.　　　Ph: (212)563-4545
New York, NY 10036-6902　Fax: (212)502-1729
Contact: Dr. Marvin King, Pres.

Desc: Biomedical ultrasound, electromagnetic scattering and interactions, photonic systems, signal processing, image processing, radar, military systems, and computer modeling of physical processes in ultrasound and electromagneticism. *Type:* Research center.

Rockefeller University

National Resource for Mass Spectrometry of Biological Macro-Molecules

1230 York Ave.　　　Ph: (212)327-8849
New York, NY 10021　　Fax: (212)327-7547
E-mail: chait@rockvax.rockefelleredu
Contact: Dr. Brian T. Chait, Dir.
Desc: Application of mass spectrometry to biomedical problems. *Type:* Research center.

Rosenstiel Basic Medical Sciences Research Center

Brandeis University　　Ph: (617)736-2400
415 South St.　　　　Fax: (617)736-2405
Waltham, MA 02254
E-mail: petsko@binah.brandeis.edu
URL: http://www.rose.brandeis.edu/
Contact: Dr. Gregory Petsko, Dir.
Desc: Genetics and molecular biology, biochemistry, structural biology, protein crytallography, microbiology, biophysics, and cellular immunology. *Type:* Research center.

Rutgers University

Bureau of Biological Research

FAS Div. of Life Science. -　Ph: (732)445-3972
　Nelson Biological Labs.　Fax: (732)445-0644
604 Allison Rd.
Piscataway, NJ 08854-8082
E-mail: martin@biology.rutgers.edu
Contact: Charles Martin, Dir.
Desc: Neurobiology and physiology, cell and developmental biology, molecular biology, biomoleculer structure, biochemistry. *Type:* Research center.

Rutgers University

Cell and Cell Products Fermentation Facility

Waksman Institute　　　Ph: (732)445-2925
PO Box 759　　　　Fax: (732)445-5735
Piscataway, NJ 08855-0759
E-mail: callanan@mbcl.rutgers.edu
URL: http://www.waksman.rutgers.edu/~ferment
Contact: Kenneth R. Callanan, Mgr.
Desc: Cell fermentation and production of primary and secondary metabolites such as recombinant proteins, hormones, enzymes, regulatory proteins, and antiviral, antibacterial, and antifungal compounds. *Type:* Research center.

Saint Francis Hospital and Medical Center

Department of Research

114 Woodland St.　　　Ph: (860)714-4068
Hartford, CT 06105　　Fax: (860)714-8053
E-mail: ecanalis@stfranciscare.org
Contact: Dr. Ernesto Canalis, Dir.
Desc: Cell and molecular biology, protein biochemistry. *Type:* Research center.

St. Francis Xavier University

Biomechanics Research Laboratory

Biology Dept.　　　　Ph: (902)867-5116
PO Box 5000　　　　Fax: (902)867-2389
Antigonish, NS, Canada B2G
　2W5
E-mail: edemont@stfx.ca
URL: http://iago.stfx.ca/people/edemont/biomechanics-lab.html

Contact: M. Edwin DeMont, Dir.

Desc: Biological fluid dynamics and biomaterials. *Type:* Research center.

Salk Institute for Biological Studies

PO Box 85800   Ph: (619)453-4100
San Diego, CA 92186-5800   Fax: (619)552-8285
E-mail: pollard@salk.edu
URL: http://www.salk.edu

Contact: Thomas Pollard, Pres.

Desc: Cellular and molecular biology and neuroscience with particular emphasis on immunology, cancer, molecular genetics, tumor virology, reproductive biology, neurobiology, neuroendocrinology, growth control, prebiotic chemistry, and neurotransmitter/neuroreceptor structure and function; research aimed toward the discovery of cause, prevention, control, and cure of disease. *Type:* Research center.

San Francisco State University

Center for Biomedical Laboratory Science

1600 Holloway Ave.   Ph: (415)338-1696
San Francisco, CA 94132   Fax: (415)338-7747
E-mail: wbigler@sfsu.edu
URL: http://www.sfsu.edu/cbls

Contact: Dr. William N. Bigler, Dir.

Desc: Clinical chemistry, immunology, microbiology, hematology, and virology. *Type:* Research center.

Science Tools

Pharmacia Biotech, Inc.

Molecular Biology Reagents Div.   Ph: (414)227-3618
2202 N. Bartlett Ave.   Fax: (414)227-3765
Milwaukee, WI 53202
E-mail: science.tools.@usmil.pharmacia.se.
URL: http://www.biotech.pharmacia.se.

Contact: Kathleen A. Gorski, Managing Editor.

Desc: Dedicated to communicating new applications, product developments and useful technical suggestions for Pharmacia Biotech, Inc. products to researchers in life sciences. *Type:* Newsletter.

Sherbrooke University

Actinomycete Biology Research Group

Department de biologie   Ph: (819)821-8000
Faculte des sciences   Fax: (819)821-8049
Sherbrooke, PQ, Canada J1K
    2R1
E-mail: rbrzezin@courrier.usher.ca

Contact: Ryszard Brzezinski, Contact.

Desc: Molecular biology and genetic engineering of actinomycetes, gene cloning and characterization, development of new cloning vectors. Studies on pathogenesis mechanisms of potato scab. *Type:* Research center.

Sherbrooke University

Fundamental Electrophysiology Research Group

Department de physiologie et de   Ph: (819)564-5302
    biophysique   Fax: (819)564-5399
Faculte de medecine
3001 12th N.
Sherbrooke, PQ, Canada J1H
    5N4
E-mail: dgirardi@courrier.usherb.ca

Contact: Marcel Daniel-Payet, Dir.

Desc: Electrophysiology and neuropharmacology in visual perception, excitation contraction coupling, involvement of ionic channels in the stimulus-secretion process, control of body fluid volumes, maturation of prenatal control of ventilation, antiepileptic effects of adenosine, function and regulation of ionic channels of sarcoplasmic reticulum in skeletal and cardiac muscles, physiopathology of cardiac electrical alterations, electrophysiological basis of normal and pathological automaticity, and ionic channels in airway smooth muscle. *Type:* Research center.

Sierra Biomedical Research Corporation

1000 Locust St.   Ph: (775)328-1487
Reno, NV 89520-0102   Fax: (775)328-1816

Contact: Aaron Smith, PhD, Exec.Dir.

Desc: Biomedical and clinical research. *Type:* Research center.

Southern University and Agricultural and Mechanical College

Health Research Center

Lee Hall, Rm. 128   Ph: (504)771-4240
Southern Branch   Fax: (504)771-3607
PO Box 9921
Baton Rouge, LA 70813
E-mail: fachristian@juno.com

Contact: Dr. Frederick A. Christian, Dir.

Desc: Biomedical research, including projects in immunology, bacteriology, parasitology, organic chemistry, biochemistry, textile chemistry, virology, cell physiology, molecular biology, physical chemistry, mechanical engineering, inorganic chemistry, reproductive physiology, and mycology. *Type:* Research center.

Southwest Biomedical Research Institute

7203 E. Valley View Rd.   Ph: (602)945-4363
Scottsdale, AZ 85250-6447   Free: 800-333-4363
    Fax: (602)423-9116

Desc: Genetic diseases and chromosome disorders, cancer and cancer genetics, transplantation genetics, kidney and other transplants, immunogenetics, recombinant DNA diagnostics and research, birth defects, Jewish genetic diseases, prenatal education, and prenatal diagnosis. *Type:* Research center.

Southwest Foundation for Biomedical Research

PO Box 760549   Ph: (210)674-1410
San Antonio, TX 78245-0549   Fax: (210)670-3301
E-mail: fledford@sfbr.org
URL: http://www.sfbr.org

Contact: Dr. Frank F. Ledford, Jr., Pres.

Desc: Arteriosclerosis, hypertension, cancer, pulmonary disease, aging, genetics, endocrinology, reproductive physiology, virology, neuropharmacology, behavioral science, and organic chemistry. *Type:* Research center.

State University of New York at Buffalo

Center for Positron Emission Tomography

105 Parker Hall   Ph: (716)838-5889
Buffalo, NY 14214   Fax: (716)838-4918
E-mail: bob@nucmed.buffalo.edu
URL: http://www.nucmed.buffalo.edu/cpethm.htm

Contact: Dr. Robert E. Ackerhalt, Dir.

Desc: Neurology, oncology, and cardiology, focusing on the use of Positron Emission Tomography (PET). *Type:* Research center.

Tampa Bay Research Institute

10900 Roosevelt Blvd.   Ph: (813)576-6675
St. Petersburg, FL 33716   Fax: (813)577-9862
E-mail: tbri@intnet.net

Contact: Dr. Akiko Tanaka, Pres.

Desc: Molecular genetics, virology, cellular biochemistry, AIDS, gene therapy, cytokines, and cancer. *Type:* Research center.

Texas A&M University

Alkek Institute of Biosciences and Technology

Texas Med. Ctr.   Ph: (713)677-7700
2121 W. Holcombe Blvd.   Fax: (713)677-7725
Houston, TX 77030-3303
E-mail: fbazer@cum.Tamu.edu
URL: http://keck.tamu.edu/ibt/ibt.htm

Contact: Fuller W. Bazer, PhD, Dir.

Desc: Genome research, mammalian DNA and RNA viruses, eucaryotic gene expression, neurobiology, human nutrition, matrix biology, plant molecular biology, and cancer biology. *Type:* Research center.

Thomas Jefferson University

Daniel Baugh Institute

Jefferson Alumni Hall   Ph: (215)503-7820
1020 Locust St.   Fax: (215)923-3808
Philadelphia, PA 19107

Desc: Developmental biology; reproductive toxicology; biochemical, molecular and genetic mechanisms of birth defects; tissue and embryo culture, molecular biology, and cell biology. *Type:* Research center.

Thomas Jefferson University

Jefferson Institute of Molecular Medicine

450 BLSB   Ph: (215)503-5785
233 S. 10th St.   Fax: (215)503-5788
Philadelphia, PA 19107
E-mail: jouni.uitto@mail.tju.edu

Contact: Dr. Jouni Uitto, Dir.

Desc: Biochemistry and molecular medicine. *Type:* Research center.

Tulane University

Biomaterials Laboratory

Sch. of Med.   Ph: (504)588-2273
1430 Tulane Ave.   Fax: (504)584-2722
S.L. 32
New Orleans, LA 70112-2699

Contact: Stephen D. Cook, PhD, Dir.

Desc: Biomaterials, including study of the properties of porous materials and materials-bone interfaces; surface studies of tissue-implant interactions; and corrosion resistance analysis, especially degradation characteristics of materials in an in vivo environment. Conducts histological and microradiographic evaluations of bone and implant composites. *Type:* Research center.

U.S. Department of Defense

Air Force Materiel Command

Armstrong Laboratory

Division of Biodynamics and Biocommunications

ATTN: AL/CFB   Ph: (513)255-3602
Wright Patterson AFB, OH   Fax: (513)255-2781
    45433-7901

Contact: Dr. Thomas J. Moore, Chf.

Desc: Conducts a multidisciplinary research and development program to protect man against mechanical force environments, provide him with the best protective equipment, and guarantee his full performance capability. The Division's program includes basic research, exploratory development, advanced development, and operational systems support in the areas of: noise, impact, acceleration, vibration, locomotion, microgravity, pilot performance, aircraft operations, communication effectiveness, aircrew protection, and emergency escape. *Type:* Research center.

U.S. Department of Defense

Air Force Materiel Command

Armstrong Laboratory

Division of Human Engineering

2255 H St.   Ph: (513)255-7580
Wright Patterson AFB, OH   Fax: (513)255-7596
    45433-7022
E-mail: KBOFF@AL.WPAFB.AF.MIL

Contact: Dr. Kenneth R. Boff, Chf.

Desc: Seeks to enable and ensure effective integration of humans with technology in U.S. Air Force systems. *Type:* Research center.

U.S. Department of Defense
Army Medical Research and Materiel Command
Walter Reed Army Institute of Research
Biometrics Division
Washington, DC 20307-5100   Ph: (202)782-3151
        Fax: (202)782-6950
E-mail: litrio@wrair-emh1.army.mil
Contact: Lt.Col. John P. Litrio, Dir.
Desc: Provides automation, biomedical engineering, and biostatistics services and support to all elements of the Institute; manages the WRAIR automation program; and advises and provides consultative services on experimental design, data analysis, data processing, systems engineering, and data communications. *Type:* Research center.

U.S. Department of Defense
Army Medical Research and Materiel Command
Walter Reed Army Institute of Research
Department of Membrane Biology
Washington, DC 20307-5100   Ph: (202)782-3248
        Fax: (202)782-0721
E-mail: biochem@wrair-emhl.army.mil
Contact: Bhupendra Doctor, Chf.
Desc: Use of biological products, such as exogenous cholinesterases, and pharmaceutical products, such as huperzine, as pretreatment drugs for organophosphate exposure. Work includes studies designed to elucidate the three-dimensional structure of the cholinesterases, the mechanisms of inhibition by reversible and nonreversible inhibitors, and the reactivation of the cholinesterases by oximes. *Type:* Research center.

U.S. Department of Health and Human Services
Food and Drug Administration
Center for Biologics Evaluation and Research
1401 Rockville Pike   Ph: (301)827-0370
Rockville, MD 20852   Fax: (301)827-0440
E-mail: @AL.CBER.FDA.GOV
Contact: Kathryn C. Zoon, Dir.
Desc: Ensures the safety, efficacy, potency, and purity of biological products intended for use in the treatment, prevention, or cure of human diseases. Reviews the safety and effectiveness of vaccines, blood products, diagnostic products, and other biological and biotechnology-derived human products. *Type:* Research center.

U.S. Department of Health and Human Services
Food and Drug Administration
Center for Biologics Evaluation and Research
Division of Cytokine Biology
1401 Rockville Pike   Ph: (301)827-1735
Rockville, MD 20852   Fax: (301)402-1659
Contact: Dr. David Finbloom, Dir.
Desc: Cytokine and growth factor products. Studies interferons, interleukins, colony stimulating factors; and growth factors. *Type:* Research center.

U.S. Department of Health and Human Services
Food and Drug Administration
Center for Biologics Evaluation and Research
Division of Hematology
1401 Rockville Pike   Ph: (301)496-4833
Rockville, MD 20852   Fax: (301)402-2780
E-mail: weinstein@cber.fda.gov
Contact: Mark J. Weinstein, PhD, Dir.
Desc: Responsible for the safety, potency, purity, and efficacy of blood/plasma-derived/r-DNA biotechnology-derived therapeutic products. These include agents used in the management of clotting and bleeding disorders, immune deficiencies, hematologic malignancies, hypovolemia, anemia and related pathophysiologic states, and transplantation and autoimmune diseases. *Type:* Research center.

U.S. Department of Health and Human Services
Food and Drug Administration
Center for Biologics Evaluation and Research
Division of Monoclonal Antibodies
1401 Rockville Pike   Ph: (301)827-0850
HFM-555, NIH Bldg. 29, B   Fax: (301)827-0852
   Rm. 3NN-16
Rockville, MD 20852
E-mail: stein@cber.fda.gov
URL: http://www.fda.gov
Contact: Kathryn E. Stein, PhD, Dir.
Desc: Monoclonal antibody structure and function; the regulation of antibody synthesis; the functions of radionuclide and toxin coupled monoclonal antibody therapeutics; and basic mechanisms involving the biology and physiology of cells involved in the immune system. *Type:* Research center.

U.S. Department of Health and Human Services
Food and Drug Administration
Center for Biologics Evaluation and Research
Laboratory of Biophysics
8800 Rockville Pike   Ph: (301)435-2035
Bethesda, MD 20892   Fax: (301)496-4680
E-mail: rwpastor@deimos.cber.nih.gov
Contact: Richard W. Pastor, PhD, Chf.
Desc: Development and application of high resolution NMR methods and light scattering for structural studies of biomacromolecules; development and application of computer modelling methods for studies of biomacromolecules; and characterization and development of adjuvants. *Type:* Research center.

U.S. Department of Health and Human Services
Food and Drug Administration
Center for Biologics Evaluation and Research
Laboratory of Cell Biology-Antibodies
8800 Rockville Pike   Ph: (301)496-4538
Bethesda, MD 20892   Fax: (301)402-2780
Contact: Thomas Hoffman, MD, Chf.
Desc: Cell biology of the immune system, including experimental use of monoclonal antibodies in tumor imaging and treatment, studies of the biochemical consequences of stimulation of the T-cell antigen receptor by monoclonal antibodies directed to distinct epitopes on the receptor, and fundamental studies of effector function of immune cells (monocytes and T- & B-cells) and their modulation by lymphokines. Current interests focus on the role of homeotic genes in the immune system. *Type:* Research center.

U.S. Department of Health and Human Services
Food and Drug Administration
Center for Biologics Evaluation and Research
Laboratory of Cell Biology-Cytokine
1401 Rockville Pike   Ph: (301)827-1735
Rockville, MD 20852   Fax: (301)402-1659
Contact: David S. Finbloom, MD, Actg.Chf.
Desc: Characterization of new cytokines and growth factors, structure, functional relationship, and role in human growth. *Type:* Research center.

U.S. Department of Health and Human Services
Food and Drug Administration
Center for Biologics Evaluation and Research
Laboratory of Cell Viral Regulations
FDA-CBER, HFM-541   Ph: (301)827-1806
Bldg. 29-A   Fax: (301)480-3256
Bethesda, MD 20892
E-mail: max@cber.fda.gov
Contact: Dr. Edward E. Max, Chf.
Desc: Regulation of immunoglobulin gene expression by cytokines and cell interactions focusing on the function of several immunoglobulin gene enhancers and the regulation of immunoglobulin isotype switching at the DNA level. Also focuses on the interaction of HIV with cells of the immune system centering on: the structural correlates of targets of neutralizing antibodies; and the activation of T cells by HIV through the T cell receptor and the surface molecules (other than CD4) that mediate viral entry into cells. *Type:* Research center.

U.S. Department of Health and Human Services
Food and Drug Administration
Center for Biologics Evaluation and Research
Laboratory of Chemical Biology
8800 Rockville Pike   Ph: (301)827-1735
Bethesda, MD 20892   Fax: (301)402-1659
Contact: Blair A. Fraser, Chf.
Desc: Biologically active peptides and proteins. Principal research efforts include isolation and structural analysis of novel neuropeptides, identification and isolation of precursor peptides, and identification of metabolic events responsible for post-translational protein processing. *Type:* Research center.

U.S. Department of Health and Human Services
Food and Drug Administration
Center for Biologics Evaluation and Research
Laboratory of Cytokine Research
29 Lincoln Dr.   Ph: (301)827-1720
Bethesda, MD 20892   Fax: (301)402-1659
Contact: David S. Finbloom, MD, Dir.
Desc: Structure and function of interferons and their receptors; identification and characterization of cytokines that modulate the function of monocytes and macrophages; mechanisms of interferon beta regulated gene expression; antitumor activities of cytokine or anticytokine receptor antibody toxin fusion proteins; and AIDS studies. *Type:* Research center.

U.S. Department of Health and Human Services
Food and Drug Administration
Center for Biologics Evaluation and Research
Laboratory of Developement Biology
1401 Rockville Pike, HFM-515   Ph: (301)827-0462
Rockville, MD 20852-1448   Fax: (301)827-0449
Contact: Philip D. Noguchi, MD, Actg.Chf.
Desc: Biology and developmental control of gene expression. Principal research efforts involve: identification of genetic elements that control the temporal and spatial expression of genes in itDrosophila/it; elucidation of the role of homeobox genes in limb and organ development; and characterization of bone morphogenetic factors. *Type:* Research center.

U.S. Department of Health and Human Services

Food and Drug Administration

Center for Biologics Evaluation and Research

Laboratory of DNA Virus Research

1401 Rockville Pike	Ph: (301)827-0650
Rockville, MD 20852	Fax: (301)496-1810

E-mail: lewisa@cb55055530.cber.fda.gov

Contact: Andrew Lewis, Contact.

Desc: Molecular biology of DNA viruses with emphasis on human herpesviruses and poxviruses. Focuses on gene expression, virus vectors, viral latency, viral replication, and immune responses. *Type:* Research center.

U.S. Department of Health and Human Services

Food and Drug Administration

Center for Biologics Evaluation and Research

Laboratory of Hepatitis

1401 Rockville Pike, Ste. 200N	Ph: (301)594-6715
Bethesda, MD 20892	Fax: (301)594-5209

Contact: Robin M. Biswas, MD, Chf.

Desc: Hepatitis B and non-A, non-B hepatitis/hepatitis. Research activities include development of new methods of detecting viral hepatitis markers in serum, plasma, and other tissues. *Type:* Research center.

U.S. Department of Health and Human Services

Food and Drug Administration

Center for Biologics Evaluation and Research

Laboratory of Hepatitis Viruses

8800 Rockville Pike Vivuses	Ph: (301)827-1880
Bethesda, MD 20892	Fax: (301)402-5585

E-mail: LABHR@HELIX.NIH.GOV

Contact: Stephen M. Feinstone, MD, Chf.

Desc: Molecular biology of the hepatitis A virus, emphasizing viral pathogenesis, replication, and antigenic structure. Supports a project on novel methods of producing hepatitis A vaccines. *Type:* Research center.

U.S. Department of Health and Human Services

Food and Drug Administration

Center for Biologics Evaluation and Research

Laboratory of Molecular and Developemental Immunology

8800 Rockville Pike	Ph: (301)827-0717
Bethesda, MD 20892	Fax: (301)827-0852

E-mail: STEIN@A1.CBER.FDA.GOV

Contact: Kathryn E. Stein, PhD, Actg.Chf.

Desc: Delineating the differences in the immune response to thymus-independent and thymus-dependent forms of polysaccharide antigens and the mechanism of signal transduction by thymus-independent antigens. Projects include: molecular analysis of monoclonal antibodies examining the roles of genetics and of the form of the antigen used for immunization. *Type:* Research center.

U.S. Department of Health and Human Services

Food and Drug Administration

Center for Biologics Evaluation and Research

Laboratory of Molecular Immunology

1401 Rockville Pike	Ph: (301)827-0450
Rockville, MD 20852-1448	Fax: (301)827-0449

E-mail: epsteins@al.cber.fda.gov

Contact: Suzanne Epstein, PhD, Chf.

Desc: T- and B-cell immunity. Principal research efforts include: immune responses to viruses; T-cell and B-cell response to vaccine antigens; and B cell development and neoplasia. *Type:* Research center.

U.S. Department of Health and Human Services

Food and Drug Administration

Center for Biologics Evaluation and Research

Laboratory of Molecular Virology

8800 Rockville Pike, Bldg. 29B	Ph: (301)594-6708
Bethesda, MD 20892	

Contact: Indira Hewlett, PhD, Chf.

Desc: Retrovirus detection and inactivation to improve the safety of the nation's blood supply using gene amplification by polymerase chain reaction as an analytical tool. Develops rapid and direct assays for retroviral expression in cell culture and reverse transcriptase; performs research on HIV pathogenesis and antiviral approaches to the control of HIV infection. *Type:* Research center.

U.S. Department of Health and Human Services

Food and Drug Administration

Center for Biologics Evaluation and Research

Laboratory of Mycobacteria

1401 Rockville Pike	Ph: (301)496-9559
Rockville, MD 20852	

E-mail: brennan@helix.nih.gov

Contact: Michael J. Brennan, PhD, Chf.

Desc: Development of novel vaccines for tuberculosis including research on DNA vaccines, immunopathogenesis of intracellular pathogens and bacterial adherene mechanisms. Areas of interest include molecular microbiology, immunology and bacterial pathogenesis. *Type:* Research center.

U.S. Department of Health and Human Services

Food and Drug Administration

Center for Biologics Evaluation and Research

Laboratory of Parasitic Biology and Biochemistry

1401 Rockville Pike, HFM 416	Ph: (301)496-2205
Rockville, MD 20852	Fax: (301)496-4684

E-mail: nakhasi@cber.fda.gov

Contact: Hira Nakhasi, Lab.Chf.

Desc: Structure, function, and biosynthesis of macromolecules. Principal studies on the molecular mechanism of rubella virus pathogenicity and attenuation; and identification and cloning of stage-specific genes and antigens for the malaria parasite, itPlasmodium falciparium/it, and the leishmania parasite, itLeishmania major/it. *Type:* Research center.

U.S. Department of Health and Human Services

Food and Drug Administration

Center for Biologics Evaluation and Research

Laboratory of Pertussis

8800 Rockville Pike	Ph: (301)402-3553
Bethesda, MD 20892	Fax: (301)402-2776

Contact: Drusilla Burns, PhD, Chf.

Desc: Regulation of bacterial vaccines (particularly pertussis vaccine). Initiates, directs, and participates in research on the immunochemistry of itBordetella pertussis/it and host parasite interactions in pertussis prerequisite to the development of improved pertussis vaccines and their control and clinical use. *Type:* Research center.

U.S. Department of Health and Human Services

Food and Drug Administration

Center for Biologics Evaluation and Research

Laboratory of Respiratory Viruses

8800 Rockville Pike	Free: 888-463-6332
Bethesda, MD 20892	

Contact: Roland A. Levandowski, MD, Actg.Chf.

Desc: Human respiratory viral diseases, including influenza viruses, respiratory syncytial viruses, parainfluenza viruses, and rhinoviruses. Techniques employed are intended to permit understanding of the biology of the individual agents through genomic evaluation as well as the biology of the individual agents through in vivo and in vitro studies of cellular and humoral immune parameters. *Type:* Research center.

U.S. Department of Health and Human Services

Food and Drug Administration

Center for Biologics Evaluation and Research

Laboratory of Retroviruses

8800 Rockville Pike	Ph: (301)496-2426
Bethesda, MD 20892	Fax: (301)496-1810

Contact: Hannah Golding, PhD, Chf.

Desc: Human Immunodeficiency Virus (HIV) and other retroviruses. Studies emphasize the immunology and pathogenesis of AIDS as well as other retrovirus infections. *Type:* Research center.

U.S. Department of Health and Human Services

Food and Drug Administration

Center for Biologics Evaluation and Research

Office of Therapeutics Research and Review

1401 Rockville Pike	Ph: (301)827-5098
HM-500	Fax: (301)827-5395
Rockville, MD 20851	

E-mail: siegel@AI.cber.fda.gov

URL: http://www.fda.cber.com

Contact: J. Siegel, Dir.

Desc: Development, manufacture, testing, and activities of therapeutic biological products including those related to AIDS and those prepared by genetic engineering and synthetic procedures. This is done in order to develop and maintain a scientific base for establishing standards designed to ensure the continued safety, purity, potency, and effectiveness of biological therapeutics products. *Type:* Research center.

U.S. Department of Health and Human Services

Food and Drug Administration

Center for Biologics Evaluation and Research

Office of Vaccines Research and Review

8800 Rockville Pike	Ph: (301)948-5079
Bethesda, MD 20892	Fax: (301)490-4091

Contact: M. Carolyn Hardegree, MD, Dir.

Desc: Development, manufacture, testing, and actions of vaccines and related biological products and allergenic products, including those related to AIDS. Seeks to develop and maintain a scientific base for establishing standards designed to ensure the continued safety, purity, potency, and effectiveness of vaccines and related biological products. *Type:* Research center.

U.S. Department of Health and Human Services

Food and Drug Administration

Center for Biologics Evaulation and Research

Laboratory of Enteric and Sexually Transmitted Diseases

8800 Rockville Pike	Ph: (301)496-1893
Bethesda, MD 20892	Fax: (301)402-2776

E-mail: kopecko@a1.cber.fda.gov

URL: http://www.cber.fda.gov

Contact: Dennis Kopecko, PhD, Chf.

Desc: Genetic and molecular bases of disease pathogenesis and the host's immune response to infection. Biochemical, immunological, molecular genetic and cell biology methods (including recombinant DNA, in vitro cell cultures, electron and fluorescent microscopy, video/confocal imaging, and molecular immunological technologies) and animal model systems that are employed to analyze the determinants of bacterial virulence, gene expression control mechanisms, and their functional nature in pathogenesis. *Type:* Research center.

U.S. Department of Health and Human Services

National Cancer Institute

Laboratory of Biochemistry

NIH Bldg. 37, Rm. 4E28   Ph: (301)496-5957
9000 Rockville Pike   Fax: (301)402-3095
Bethesda, MD 20892
E-mail: ckl@helix.nih.gov

Contact: Claude Klee, MD, Chf., Lab. of Biochem.

Desc: Relationship between structure and function in biological systems and on the regulation of cellular processes. The research involves prokaryotes and a range of eukaryote systems selected because of their potential for yielding important information on cellular structure, function, regulation, development, and differentiation. *Type:* Research center.

U.S. Department of Health and Human Services

National Cancer Institute

Laboratory of Biological Chemistry

NIH Bldg. 37   Ph: (301)496-4116
9000 Rockville Pike   Fax: (301)496-5839
Bethesda, MD 20892

Contact: Dr. Richard Cysyk, Chf.

Desc: Cellular reactions that are critical to the control of tumor cell proliferation or differentiation. Recent advances in cell biology are evaluated for possible targets, and agents are designed to interact with these targets and are evaluated for biochemical and antitumor effectiveness. *Type:* Research center.

U.S. Department of Health and Human Services

National Cancer Institute

Laboratory of Biology

NIH Bldg. 37, Rm. 2A19   Ph: (301)496-6441
9000 Rockville Pike   Fax: (301)496-3238
Bethesda, MD 20892
E-mail: zda@cu.nih.gov

Contact: Dr. Joseph A. DiPaolo, Chf.

Desc: Modulation of the transformation process that leads to malignancy. The primary objective is to determine the crucial molecular and physiological changes that occur in cells that have been treated with chemical viruses or physical agents as they transform from the normal to the neoplastic state. *Type:* Research center.

U.S. Department of Health and Human Services

National Cancer Institute

Laboratory of Cellular Carcinogenesis and Tumor Promotion

National Cancer Institute Bldg.   Ph: (301)496-2162
   37 Rm. 3B25   Fax: (301)496-8709
37 Convent Dr. MSC 4255
Bethesda, MD 20892-4255

Contact: Dr. Stuart Yuspa, Chf.

Desc: Molecular and biological changes that occur at the cellular and tissue level during the process of carcinogenesis. Objectives are to: define normal regulatory mechanisms for cellular growth and differentiation; determine the mechanism by which carcinogens alter normal regulation and the biological nature of these alterations; investigate the mechanism by which tumor promoters enhance the expression of carcinogen-induced alterations; identify cellular determinants for enhanced susceptibility or resistance to carcinogens and tumor promoters; and elucidate the mechanism by which certain pharmacologic agents inhibit carcinogenesis. *Type:* Research center.

U.S. Department of Health and Human Services

National Cancer Institute

Laboratory of Cellular and Molecular Biology

NIH Bldg. 37, Rm. 1E24   Ph: (301)496-9683
9000 Rockville Pike   Fax: (301)496-8479
Bethesda, MD 20892
E-mail: piercej@dc37a.nci.nih.gov

Contact: Dr. Jacalyn H. Pierce, Chf.

Desc: Cancer, focusing on cellular and molecular biology. and virus-induced cancers of animals to the search for viral etiology of human tumors; and analyze the effect of environmental agents or specific mechanisms that control and promote transformation in mammalian cells. *Type:* Research center.

U.S. Department of Health and Human Services

National Cancer Institute

Laboratory of Cellular Oncology

NIH Bldg. 36, Rm. 1D32   Ph: (301)496-9513
9000 Rockville Pike   Fax: (301)480-5322
Bethesda, MD 20892

Contact: Dr. Douglas R. Lowy, Chf.

Desc: Genetics and immunology of oncogenesis. Studies seek to identify critical differences between normal and neoplastic cells. *Type:* Research center.

U.S. Department of Health and Human Services

National Cancer Institute

Laboratory of Experimental Carcinogenesis

NIH Bldg. 37, Rm. 3C28   Ph: (301)496-1935
9000 Rockville Pike   Fax: (301)496-0734
Bethesda, MD 20892

Contact: Dr. Snorri S. Thorgeirsson, Chf.

Desc: Elucidate mechanisms of malignant transformation in human and animal cells by chemical carcinogens; determine critical cellular and genetic factors involved in initiation, promotion, and progression of transformed cells; and apply the knowledge obtained from studying animal models toward effective prevention of cancer in man. Principal areas of research interest are the use of transgenic mouse models in cancer research, molecular and cellular aspects of hepatic stem cells; multidrug resistant gene family; chemical carcinogenesis and mutagenesis; molecular biology; and protein chemistry. *Type:* Research center.

U.S. Department of Health and Human Services

National Cancer Institute

Laboratory of Experimental Immunology

NCI-CRDC   Ph: (301)846-1323
Bldg. 560, Rm. 3193 NCI   Fax: (301)846-1673
Frederick, MD 21702-1201

Contact: John Ortaldo, Chf.

Desc: Cellular and humoral components of the immune response that may be involved in resistance to tumor growth; studies growth factors and other biological response modifiers (BRMs) that may be involved in the regulation of tumor growth; studies the mechanism of action of various biologicals at the cellular and molecular level; develops new biologicals and BRMs and investigates the effects of selected BRMs on the host and on tumor growth; and develops protocols for optimal biological response modification and evaluates the therapeutic efficacy of these substances in experimental animal tumor systems and cancer patients. *Type:* Research center.

U.S. Department of Health and Human Services

National Cancer Institute

Laboratory of Human Carcinogenesis

NIH Bldg. 37, Rm. 2C05   Ph: (301)496-2048
37 Convent Dr.   Fax: (301)496-0497
Bethesda, MD 20892-4255

Contact: Curtis Harris, Chf.

Desc: Mechanisms of carcinogenesis in epithelial cells from humans and experimental animals; experimental approaches in biological systems for the extrapolation of carcinogenesis data and mechanisms from experimental animals to the human situation; and host factors that determine differences in carcinogenic susceptibility among individuals. Research is carried out in three areas: molecular and biochemical epidemiology; carcinogen macromolecular interaction; and in vitro carcinogenesis. *Type:* Research center.

U.S. Department of Health and Human Services

National Cancer Institute

Laboratory of Mathematical Biology

Frederick Cancer Research and   Ph: (301)846-5532
   Development Center   Fax: (301)846-5598
Bldg. 469, Rm. 151
Frederick, MD 21702-1201
E-mail: jmaizel@ncifcrf.gov
URL: http://www-lecb.ncifcrf.gov
Contact: Dr. Jacob V. Maizel, Chf.

Desc: Studies nucleic acid sequences, protein sequences, and macromolecular structure (including prediction of molecular structure) using methods of computation; kinetics of metabolic systems using computational and modeling methodology; applications of image analysis to micrographs and two-dimensional gels; theoretical immunology; and membrane biophysics and structure. *Type:* Research center.

U.S. Department of Health and Human Services

National Cancer Institute

Laboratory of Medicinal Chemistry

NIH Bldg. 37, Rm. 5CO2   Ph: (301)496-8065
37 Convent Dr. MSC 4255   Fax: (301)402-2275
Bethesda, MD 20892-4255

Contact: Victor E. Marquez, Chf.

Desc: Rational discovery of antitumor agents; implements basic research on the mechanisms of antitumor drug action and drug toxicity; incorporates knowledge of biochemical/molecular mechanisms into a drug synthesis program aimed at optimizing drug efficacy through enhancement of antitumor activity/selectivity and/or minimization of toxicity; and develops strategies for improving the clinical utility of new or existing anticancer drugs by overcoming tumor resistance and/or by protection of normal tissues against toxicity. Compounds with potential antitumor activity are synthesized and effects of such agents are assessed in experimental tumor systems in vitro and in vivo and on a variety of potential subcellular target sites (e.g., nucleic acids, nuclear proteins, microtubular protein, and enzyme systems). *Type:* Research center.

U.S. Department of Health and Human Services

National Cancer Institute

Laboratory of Molecular Biology

NIH Bldg. 37, Rm. 4E16   Ph: (301)496-4797
37 Convent Dr. MSC-4255   Fax: (301)402-1344
Bethesda, MD 20892-4255
E-mail: pasta@helix.nih.gov
Contact: Dr. Ira H. Pastan, Chf.

Desc: Immunotoxins for treatment of human cancer. To accomplish this, Pseudomonas exotoxin is coupled to monoclonal antibodies that react with specific human cancers. *Type:* Research center.

U.S. Department of Health and Human Services

National Cancer Institute

Laboratory of Molecular Carcinogenesis

NIH Bldg. 37, Rm. 3E24   Ph: (301)496-6849
9000 Rockville Pike   Fax: (301)496-8419
Bethesda, MD 20892

Contact: Harry V. Gelboin, PhD, Chf.

Desc: Cellular and biochemical events and mechanisms involved in carcinogenesis. Activities include: examination of the unusual properties of cells from patients who may be predisposed to cancer because of hereditary disease and investigation of various mechanisms of DNA repair using DNA transfection and sequencing to define the genomic changes observed; investigation of the genetics, multiplicity, and structure of the drug and carcinogen metabolizing enzyme systems; studies using monoclonal antibodies to gain an understanding of individual differences and their relationship to drug and carcinogen sensitivity; investigation of the mutation, recombination, and repair caused by carcinogen treatment using shuttle vectors that replicate in mammalian and bacterial cells; and studies of the relationship between the structure and function in chromatin (using biochemical and immunological methods), including evaluation of the regulatory properties of the non-histone proteins. *Type:* Research center.

U.S. Department of Health and Human Services

National Cancer Institute

Laboratory of Molecular Virology

NIH Bldg. 41, Rm. B602   Ph: (301)496-6202
9000 Rockville Pike   Fax: (301)496-4951
Bethesda, MD 20892

E-mail: hagerg@dce.41.nci.nih.gov

URL: http://ex.nci.nih.gov/RESEARCH/basic/lrbge/

Contact: Dr. Gordon Hager, Chf.

Desc: Normal and abnormal regulation of gene expression. Studies employ methods from molecular biology, immunology, virology, and cell biology in an attempt to determine in specific cases what signals regulate gene expression. *Type:* Research center.

U.S. Department of Health and Human Services

National Cancer Institute

Laboratory of Tumor Cell Biology

NIH Bldg. 37, Rm. 6A11   Ph: (301)496-6007
9000 Rockville Pike   Fax: (301)496-8394
Bethesda, MD 20892

Contact: Dr. Genoveffa Franchini, Chf.

Desc: Cellular proliferation, cell differentiation, and biochemical growth characteristics of normal and malignant mammalian cells both in vivo and in vitro, which will permit the optimal use of antitumor agents in the treatment of cancer and AIDS. Particular attention is given to human leukemias and lymphomas, acquired immunodeficiency syndrome (AIDS), Kaposi's sarcoma, antiviral agents, and vaccine development. *Type:* Research center.

U.S. Department of Health and Human Services

National Cancer Institute

Laboratory of Tumor Immunology and Biology

NIH Bldg. 10, Rm. 8B07   Ph: (301)496-4343
10 Center Dr.   Fax: (301)496-2756
Bethesda, MD 20892

E-mail: js141c@nih.gov

URL: http://www.nci.nih.gov/intra/itib/LTIBPAGE.htm

Contact: Jeffrey Schlom, PhD, Chf.

Desc: Immunologic markers specific for or associated with various human neoplasms, with the ultimate aim of applying these toward the diagnosis, prognosis, and treatment of human cancer. Activities focus on: the generation and characterization of monoclonal antibodies to tumor-associated determinants, with particular emphasis on the study of human carcinomas; conjugation of monoclonal antibodies to isotopes or toxins to aid in the diagnosis, localization, and potential elimination of tumor cells; studies on the association between specific murine and human genetic elements and tumorigenesis using techniques of gene cloning and molecular hybridization; and development of immunoassays to aid in the characterization of human tumor cell populations and in the diagnosis or prognosis of certain human cancers. *Type:* Research center.

U.S. Department of Health and Human Services

National Center for Infectious Diseases

Division of Parasitic Diseases

Biology and Diagnostics Branch

4770 Buford Hwy., MS F13   Ph: (404)488-4419
Atlanta, GA 30341-3724   Fax: (404)488-4253

E-mail: mle1@ciddpd2.em.cdc.gov

Contact: Mark Eberhard, Chf.

Desc: Parasitic infections; develops new methodologies for diagnosis, and implements currently available methodologies for diagnosis, of parasitic infections; provides laboratory support necessary for the diagnosis of etiologic agents in outbreak investigations of parasitic diseases; and performs kit and/or reagent evaluations when necessary to provide appropriate, accurate, standardized, and state-of-the-art diagnosis of parasitic infections. *Type:* Research center.

U.S. Department of Health and Human Services

National Center for Infectious Diseases

Division of Parasitic Diseases

Biology and Diagnostics Branch

4770 Buford Hwy., MS F13   Ph: (404)488-4077
Atlanta, GA 30341-3724   Fax: (404)488-4253

E-mail: wec1@cdc.gov

Contact: William E. Collins, Chf.

Desc: Parasitic diseases to define etiology, transmission dynamics, populations at risk, host-parasite relationships, host immune responses, and effective chemotherapy; provides advice, assistance, and training in the prevention and control of parasitic diseases; sponsors laboratory studies of selected parasites, emphasizing animal models and in vitro systems for parasitic relationship, chemotherapy, and vaccine evaluation studies. *Type:* Research center.

U.S. Department of Health and Human Services

National Center for Research Resource

Biomedical Technology Area

One Rockledge Centre, Ste.   Ph: (301)435-0755
6050   Fax: (301)480-3659
6705 Rockledge Dr.
MSC 7965
Bethesda, MD 20892

E-mail: ospio@ep.ncrr.nih.gov

URL: http://www.ncrr.nih.gov

Desc: High performance computing, molecular and cellular structural biology technologies, biomedical engineering, noninvasive imaging and spectroscopy, and mathematical modeling and computer simulations. *Type:* Research center.

U.S. Department of Health and Human Services

National Center for Research Resources

Biomedical Engineering and Instrumentation Program

NIH Bldg. 13, Rm. 3N17   Ph: (301)496-4741
9000 Rockville Pike   Fax: (301)496-6608
Bethesda, MD 20892

Contact: Dr. Henry Eden, Actg.Dir.

Desc: Supports NIH intramural scientists in applications of engineering, mathematics, physics, and the physical sciences to the solution of problems in biology and medicine through collaborations involving measurement, imaging, mathematical modeling, or design of specialized equipment; and construction, modification, maintenance, repair, or lease of scientific equipment. *Type:* Research center.

U.S. Department of Health and Human Services

National Center for Research Resources

Biomedical Research Technology Program

Biocalorinetry Center

107 Mudd Hall   Ph: (410)516-7917
3400 N. Charles St.   Fax: (410)516-6469
Baltimore, MD 21218-2685

Contact: Dr. Ernesto Freire, Contact.

Desc: Calorimetric measurement of energetics and thermodynamic mechanisms of biological materials. Current research includes: thermodynamics of protein folding and protein interacting; structural thermodynamic analysis of protein folding and protein binding reactions; structure based prediction of protein stability and binding affinities; protein conformational changes induced by ligand binding, pH or solvent conditions; and protein-membrane, protein-DNA and other ligand binding phenomena. *Type:* Research center.

U.S. Department of Health and Human Services

National Center for Research Resources

Biomedical Research Technology Program

Biomedical Magnetic Resonance Research and Technology Center

2100 S. Goodwin Ave.   Ph: (217)244-0600
Urbana, IL 61801   Fax: (217)244-1330

E-mail: bmrl@bmrl.med.uiuc.edu

URL: http://bmrl.med.uiuc.edu:8080/

Contact: Paul C. Lauterbur, PhD, Dir.

Desc: Microscopic nuclear magnetic resonance imaging; relaxation dispersion curves; and spectra of small specimens. Current research includes: microscopy, image processing and visualization, perfusion and diffusion measurements, new techniques for spectral localization, contrast agent development and characterization, microdomain techniques, retinal metabolism, muscle function, cold adaptation, thermotolerance, obstetrical/gyncecological biopsy studies, labeling and tracking of neural cells, developmental effects on brain metabolism, real-time instrument operation over the World Wide Web, MRI contrast agent synthesis, characterization and testing, targeted contrast agents. *Type:* Research center.

U.S. Department of Health and Human Services

National Center for Research Resources

Biomedical Technology Program

1 Rockledge Centre, Rm. 6030   Ph: (301)435-0772
6705 Rockledge Rd., MSC 7965   Fax: (301)480-3775
Bethesda, MD 20892-7965

Contact: Dov Jaron, Dir.

Desc: Physical sciences, mathematics, engineering, and computer sciences; biology; and medicine. Its purpose is to support and develop biomedically relevant technologies to be utilized by health scientists in solving biomedical and clinical research problems. *Type:* Research center.

U.S. Department of Health and Human Services

National Heart, Lung, and Blood Institute

Laboratory of Biochemical Genetics

NIH Bldg. 36, Rm. 1C-06   Ph: (301)496-2401
9000 Rockville Pike   Fax: (301)402-0270
Bethesda, MD 20892

Contact: Marshall Nirenberg, PhD, Chf.

Desc: Molecular Biology and Macromolecules. The Molecular Biology Section studies basic problems in molecular biology and biochemistry, particularly those that pertain to the development of the nervous system. *Type:* Research center.

U.S. Department of Health and Human Services

National Heart, Lung, and Blood Institute

Laboratory of Biochemistry

NIH Bldg. 3, Rm. 222   Ph: (301)496-4096
9000 Rockville Pike   Fax: (301)496-0599
Bethesda, MD 20892

Contact: Dr. P. Boon Chock, Chf.

Desc: Biochemistry, primarily as related to control of metabolic processes; amino acid metabolism; vitamin B-12 metabolism; selenium biochemistry; and aging (specifically, the role of post-translational modifications of enzymes in protein turnover and aging). *Type:* Research center.

U.S. Department of Health and Human Services

National Institute on Aging

Biology of Aging Program

7201 Wisconsin Ave., Ste. 2C-   Ph: (301)496-4996
   231   Fax: (301)402-0010
Bethesda, MD 20892
E-mail: sprottr@gw.nia.nih.gov
URL: http://www.nih.gov
Contact: Dr. Richard L. Sprott, Assoc.Dir.

Desc: Basic mechanisms involved in aging processes and age-related disease. It funds research and training in ten main areas: biochemistry; genetics; endocrinology; immunology; nutrition and metabolism; molecular biology; pathobiology; cell biology, physiology; and biomarkers of aging. *Type:* Research center.

U.S. Department of Health and Human Services

National Institute on Aging

Laboratory of Cellular and Molecular Biology

Gerontology Research Center   Ph: (410)558-8172
5600 Nathan Shock Dr.   Fax: (410)558-8323
Box 11
Baltimore, MD 21224
E-mail: lindsayc@grc.nia.nih.gov
URL: http://www.grc.nia.nih.gov/branches/lcmb/lcmb.htm
Contact: Carol Lindsay, Lab.Sec.

Desc: Basic biological and biochemical mechanisms of aging. Activities include research into the mechanism of stress responses, hormone/neurotransmitter, signal transduction, neurodegeneration/protection, behavior, erythrocyte oxyradical production and aging, and NMR methodology and applications. *Type:* Research center.

U.S. Department of Health and Human Services

National Institute on Aging

Laboratory of Molecular Genetics

5600 Nathan Shock Dr.   Ph: (410)558-8162
Baltimore, MD 21224-6823   Fax: (410)558-8157
E-mail: vbohr@nih.gov
Contact: Dr. Vilhelm A. Bohr, Chf.

Desc: Fundamental nature of aging at the molecular level, including studies on changes in gene structure and function with aging. Researchers utilize the techniques of molecular genetics to examine age-related alterations in cellular function and the DNA repair processes. *Type:* Research center.

U.S. Department of Health and Human Services

National Institute of Arthritis and Musculoskeletal and Skin Diseases

Intramural Research Program

Laboratory of Skin Biology

N.I.H. Bldg. 6, Rm. 425   Ph: (301)496-1578
9000 Rockville Pike   Fax: (301)402-2886
Bethesda, MD 20892
Contact: Peter Steinert, Chf.

Desc: Structural, molecular, and cellular biology and genetics of skin proteins. *Type:* Research center.

U.S. Department of Health and Human Services

National Institute of Dental Research

Laboratory of Developmental Biology

NIH Bldg. 30, Rm. 421   Ph: (301)496-5974
30 Convent Dr. MSC 4370   Fax: (301)402-0897
Bethesda, MD 20892-4370

Contact: Kenneth M. Yamada, Chf.

Desc: Structure, function, and regulation of extracellular matrix molecules, their receptors, and other cell interaction systems. Research focuses on examining the functions and regulation of these systems in normal and abnormal development of craniofacial and other tissues; connective tissue remodeling; tumor metastasis and invasion; and other diseases and disorders involving extracellular molecules. *Type:* Research center.

U.S. Department of Health and Human Services

National Institute of Diabetes and Digestive and Kidney Diseases

Laboratory of Analytical Chemistry

NIH Bldg. 8, Rm. B2A-17   Ph: (301)496-5304
9000 Rockville Pike   Fax: (301)402-1967
Bethesda, MD 20892

Contact: Edwin Becker, Actg.Chf.

Desc: Provides consultation and technical assistance to Institute scientists in the area of instrumental and chemical analysis, particularly related to experimental design and interpretation of spectra. *Type:* Research center.

U.S. Department of Health and Human Services

National Institute of Diabetes and Digestive and Kidney Diseases

Laboratory of Biochemistry and Metabolism

NIH Bldg. 10, Rm. 9N119   Ph: (301)496-4391
10 Center Dr. MSC-1812   Fax: (301)496-0839
Bethesda, MD 20892-1812
E-mail: wbjakoby@helix.nih.gov

Contact: William B. Jakoby, Chf.

Desc: Understanding of the basic biochemical mechanisms involved in both normal and abnormal biological processes. Principal fields of interest include enzymology, molecular biology, cell biology, and toxicological aspects of cell activities. *Type:* Research center.

U.S. Department of Health and Human Services

National Institute of Diabetes and Digestive and Kidney Diseases

Laboratory of Cell Biology and Genetics

NIH Bldg. 8, Rm. 403   Ph: (301)496-3435
9000 Rockville Pike   Fax: (301)402-3298
Bethesda, MD 20892

Contact: Dr. Harvey B. Pollard, Chf.

Desc: Mechanisms regulating secretion of hormones and transmitters from endocrine nerve and endothelial cells. Other work includes analysis of endocytosis and phagocytosis by macrophages and macrophage cell lines and studies on the structure of nerve and other cell types by both light and electron microscopy; immunology and cytogenetics of autoimmunity; and the molecular biology of viral genomes. *Type:* Research center.

U.S. Department of Health and Human Services

National Institute of Diabetes and Digestive and Kidney Diseases

Laboratory of Cellular and Developmental Biology

NIH Bldg. 6, Rm. B1-26   Ph: (301)496-6125
6 Center Dr. MSC-2715   Fax: (301)496-5239
Bethesda, MD 20892-2715

Contact: Jurrien Dean, MD, Chf.

Desc: Endocrinology, including research on hormonal regulation of enzymes involved in chylomicron uptake and metabolism in adipose and mammary tissues, the influence of hormones on cellular development and metabolism, and the disposition of fat and metabolites in the cell as viewed from ultrastructural studies; nutritional biochemistry, including studies on the structural and functional aspects of dihydrofolic reductase and other enzymes involved in folic acid metabolism and the intermediary metabolism of lipids, carbohydrates, and amino acids in the small intestine; membrane regulation, including studies on the mechanism of action of hormones on adenylate cyclase and other membrane regulatory processes; and developmental biochemistry, including studies on the structure and function of chromatin and the regulation of gene function during development. *Type:* Research center.

U.S. Department of Health and Human Services

National Institute of Diabetes and Digestive and Kidney Diseases

Laboratory of Chemical Physics

NIH Bldg. 5   Ph: (301)496-1024
15 Center Dr. MSC-0520   Fax: (301)435-2413
Bethesda, MD 20892-0520

Contact: William A. Eaton, Chf.

Desc: Application of modern physical techniques to the study of a wide range of biological problems. Much of the research involves the use of a variety of spectroscopic methods (e.g., nuclear and electron magnetic resonance, laser-Raman and resonance Raman spectroscopy), electric-field-induced dichroism, ultraviolet and visible microspectrophotometry, and time-resolved absorption spectroscopy with nanosecond lasers. *Type:* Research center.

U.S. Department of Health and Human Services

National Institute of Diabetes and Digestive and Kidney Diseases

Laboratory of Molecular and Cellular Biology

NIH Bldg. 8, Rm. 309   Ph: (301)496-1490
9000 Rockville Pike   Fax: (301)402-0053
Bethesda, MD 20892

Contact: Dr. Nancy G. Nossal, Chf.

Desc: Molecular and cellular biology. Principal areas of research interest include: replication and gene regulation; development of adenoassociated virus vectors for genetic engineering and gene therapy; endocrine regulation of mammary gland development and tumors; growth factors; and glucocorticoid hormones. *Type:* Research center.

U.S. Department of Health and Human Services

National Institute of Diabetes and Digestive and Kidney Diseases

Laboratory of Structural Biology

NIH Bldg. 8, Rm. 111   Ph: (301)496-3093
9000 Rockville Pike
Bethesda, MD 20892

Contact: Dr. Foulds, Dir.

Desc: Structural biology. *Type:* Research center.

U.S. Department of Health and Human Services

National Institute of Environmental Health Sciences

Division of Intramural Research

Laboratory of Molecular Biophysics

PO Box 12233   Ph: (919)541-4575
Research Triangle Park, NC   Fax: (919)541-5750
    27709
E-mail: CHIGNELL@NIEHS.NIH.GOV

Contact: Dr. Colin F. Chignell, Chf.

Desc: Spectroscopic methods to monitor the molecular interactions that occur between environmental agents and biological systems; develop, improve, and utilize analytical methodology for specified chemical agents; and conduct biochemical, physical, organic, and bio-organic studies of environmental agents and their conversion products, with emphasis on biomechanism elucidation. *Type:* Research center.

U.S. Department of Health and Human Services

National Institute of General Medical Sciences

Biophysics and Physiological Sciences Program

5333 Westbard Ave., Rm. 909   Fax: (301)594-7700
Bethesda, MD 20892
E-mail: CZJ@CU.NIH.GOV

Contact: James Cassatt, Actg.Dir.

Desc: Three major objectives: to apply the physical, chemical, physiological, and engineering sciences to solve significant biomedical problems; to develop new and improved instruments and techniques for research at the molecular, cellular, and organismic levels; and to broaden and strengthen the scientific base in those areas of clinical and physiological research for which the Institute is responsible. Supported research ranges from studies on the structure of proteins to clinical investigations and includes certain aspects of the behavioral sciences. *Type:* Research center.

U.S. Department of Health and Human Services

National Institute of General Medical Sciences

Cell Biology and Biophysics Division

Natcher Bldg.   Ph: (301)594-0828
45 Center Dr.   Fax: (301)480-2004
Bethesda, MD 20892-6200
E-mail: czj@gm1.nigms.nih.gov
URL: http://www.nih.gov

Contact: James Cassatt, Dir.

Desc: Study of molecular structure. *Type:* Research center.

U.S. Department of Health and Human Services

National Institute of General Medical Sciences

Cellular and Molecular Basis of Disease Program

903 Westwood Bldg.   Ph: (301)496-7021
5333 Westbard Ave.   Fax: (301)402-0019
Bethesda, MD 20892

Contact: Charles A. Miller, PhD, Dir.

Desc: Biophysical and biochemical description and analysis of molecular events in normal and diseased cells and with the structure and function of cell organelles and membranes at molecular and subcellular levels as well as the cellular level. The Program's goal is to develop better understanding of the structure and function of human cells and cells of other species, with the basic premise that many forms of human disease occur ultimately as the direct result of disturbed or abnormal function of cells. *Type:* Research center.

U.S. Department of Health and Human Services

National Institute of General Medical Sciences

Division of Cell Biology and Biophysics

Biophysics Branch

45 Center Dr., MSC 6200   Ph: (301)594-0828
Bethesda, MD 20892-6200   Fax: (301)480-2004

Contact: Dr. Keith Murry, Contact.

Desc: Biophysics and bioengineering. Areas of emphasis in biophysical research include: the determination of the structures of proteins and nucleic acids; studies of the structural features that determine macromolecular conformation; the structural analysis of macromolecular interactions and of ligand-macro molecular interactions; the development of physical methodology for the analysis of molecular structure; and the development and use of theoretical methods to investigate biological systems. *Type:* Research center.

U.S. Department of Health and Human Services

National Institute of General Medical Sciences

Division of Cell Biology and Biophysics

Cell Biology Branch

45 Center Dr., MSC 6200   Ph: (301)594-0828
Bethesda, MD 20892-6200   Fax: (301)480-2004

Desc: Molecular and biochemical activities of cells and subcellular components, as well as on the role of cellular dysfunction in disease. Emphasis is placed on research with applications to more than one cell type, model system, or disease state, as well as research that does not fall within the disease-oriented mission of another of the National Institutes of Health. *Type:* Research center.

U.S. Department of Health and Human Services

National Institute of Mental Health

Intramural Research Programs Division (Basic Research)

Cell Biology Laboratory

NIH Bldg. 36, Rm. 2A-11   Ph: (301)496-9444
9000 Rockville Pike   Fax: (301)402-1748
Bethesda, MD 20892

Contact: Michael J. Brownstein, Chf.

Desc: Light and electron microscope-level neuroanatomy, chronobiology, developmental neurobiology, biosynthesis of biologically active molecules, isolation of novel peptide hormones, and regulation of intracellular processes by chemical messenger. Laboratory has a section on biochemical pharmacology. *Type:* Research center.

U.S. Department of Health and Human Services

National Institute of Mental Health

Intramural Research Programs Division (Basic Research)

General and Comparative Biochemistry Laboratory

NIH Bldg. 36, Rm. 3D28   Ph: (301)496-3241
36 Convent Dr., MSC 4094   Fax: (301)402-4747
Bethesda, MD 20892-4094

Contact: Giulio L. Cantoni, MD, Chf.

Desc: Mechanisms and pathways of biological methylation, alkaloid biosynthesis, peptides, cellular differentiation, and gene expression in eukaryotes. Focus is on the enzymatic mechanisms in methyl transfer reactions, mechanism of drug addiction, muscle differentiation in cell culture, and genetic engineering. *Type:* Research center.

U.S. Department of Health and Human Services

National Institute of Mental Health

Intramural Research Programs Division (Basic Research)

Molecular Biology Laboratory

NIH Bldg. 36, Rm. 1B-08   Ph: (301)496-6945
9000 Rockville Pike   Fax: (301)402-0245
Bethesda, MD 20892
E-mail: davidn@helix.nih.gov

Contact: David Neville, MD, Chf.

Desc: Comprises sections on biophysical chemistry, molecular genetics, and regulatory proteins. *Type:* Research center.

U.S. Department of Health and Human Services

National Institute for Occupational Safety and Health

Biomedical and Behavioral Science Division

Applied Biology Branch

Robert A. Taft Laboratories   Ph: (513)533-8433
4676 Columbia Pkwy.   Fax: (513)533-8494
Cincinnati, OH 45226-1998

Contact: Lloyd Stettler, PhD, Chf.

Desc: Biological monitoring and immunochemistry/immunotoxicology studies, inhalation toxicology, animal husbandry, and pathology. *Type:* Research center.

U.S. Department of Health and Human Services

National Institute for Occupational Safety and Health

Physical Sciences and Engineering Division

Engineering Control Technology Branch

Robert A. Taft Laboratories   Ph: (513)841-4221
Mail Stop R-5   Fax: (513)841-4506
4676 Columbia Pkwy.
Cincinnati, OH 45226-1998

Contact: Robert Hughes, Actg.Chf.

Desc: Planning and conducting worksite and laboratory research to identify and evaluate engineering control technology that will prevent worker exposure to toxic substances and harmful physical agents; promoting the transfer and widespread application of effective preventive engineering control measures for safeguarding worker health; providing engineering expertise in formulating effective and credible workplace standards; and providing technical consultation to other elements of the National Institute for Occupational Safety and Health and the Department of Labor in the application of new and improved techniques for hazard prevention and engineering controls. Branch comprises sections for chemical industry, minerals, materials processing, and general industry. *Type:* Research center.

U.S. Department of Health and Human Services

National Institute for Occupational Safety and Health

Physical Sciences and Engineering Division

Measurements Research Support Branch

Robert A. Taft Laboratories   Ph: (513)841-4263
4676 Columbia Pkwy.   Fax: (513)841-4500
Cincinnati, OH 45226-1998

Contact: Robert Larkin, Chf.

Desc: Sampling and analytical chemistry measurements for industrial hygiene field investigations and other National Institute for Occupational Safety and Health activities; and provides field industrial hygiene measurement support, including research, to develop new sampling and analysis techniques. Branch comprised of sections for measurement, development, and support. *Type:* Research center.

U.S. Department of Health and Human Services

National Institutes of Health

National Center for Biotechnology Information

Bldg. 38A   Ph: (301)496-2475
8600 Rockville Pike   Fax: (301)480-9241
Bethesda, MD 20894
Contact: David J. Lipman, MD, Dir.
Desc: Supports and develops biotechnology databases. Operates GenInfo Backbone Database. *Type:* Research center.

U.S. Department of Health and Human Services

National Institutes of Health

National Center for Research Resources

NIH Bldg. 31, Rm. 3B11   Ph: (301)496-5793
31 Center Dr.   Fax: (301)402-0006
Bethesda, MD 20892-2618
E-mail: ospio@ncrr.nih.gov
URL: http://www.ncrr.nih.gov
Contact: Dr. Judith L. Vaitukaitis, Dir.
Desc: The National Center for Research Resources? (NCRR) mission is to be a ?catalyst for discovery? for NIH-supported investigations throughout the Nation by providing a broad range of technologies, research models and resources that contribute to major scientific breakthroughs. The NCRR supports primary research to create and develop these critical resources, models and technologies, promotes resource sharing and collaborations within and across scientific disciplines, enhances research competitiveness through institutional development, increases student and public understanding of the health sciences, and provides career development for biomedical investigators to address new and emerging research needs. *Type:* Research center.

U.S. Department of Health and Human Services

TAFT Laboratory

Biomedical and Behavioral Science Division

4676 Columbia Pkwy.   Ph: (513)533-8462
MS-C22   Fax: (513)533-8510
Cincinnati, OH 45226
E-mail: ded2@cdc.gov
Contact: Derek E. Dunn, Contact.
Desc: Occupational stress, ergonomics, toxicology, and physical agents to determine safety and health consequences of occupational exposures. It also investigates health and safety problems resulting from new industrial technologies and develops biological monitoring and diagnostic procedures to improve health, safety performance, functional capacity, and life expectancy of workers. *Type:* Research center.

U.S. Department of Transportation

Federal Aviation Administration

Office of Aviation Medicine

Biomedical and Behavioral Sciences Branch

800 Independence Ave., S.W.   Ph: (202)366-6910
Washington, DC 20591   Fax: (202)366-7105
Contact: Dr. William T. Shepherd, Mgr.
Desc: Develops research programs related to the requirements of other FAA organizations, including the Office of Flight Standards and the Office of Airworthiness. Research is typically conducted in-house by the Biomedical and Behavioral Sciences Branch or at the FAA's Civil Aeromedical Institute in Oklahoma City. *Type:* Research center.

University of Akron

Institute for Biomedical Engineering Research

Olson Engineering Research   Ph: (330)972-6651
   Center   Fax: (330)374-8834
Akron, OH 44325-0302
E-mail: iber@guts.biomed.uakron.edu

URL: http://www.biomed.uakron.edu
Contact: Dr. Stanley E. Rittgers, Dir.
Desc: Biomedical engineering, using and coordinating expertise and resources of biological, medical, engineering, and other scientific disciplines in greater Akron area for conducting research and promoting educational programs at the University, area hospitals, and the College of Medicine. *Type:* Research center.

University of Alberta

Alberta Peptide Institute

728 Heritage Med. Res. Ctr.   Ph: (403)492-2522
Edmonton, AB, Canada T6G   Fax: (403)492-1473
   2S2
E-mail: bob.parker@ualberta.ca
URL: http://www.biochem.ualberta.ca/Biochem
Contact: J.M. Robert Parker, Mgr.
Desc: Peptide synthesis, analysis, and purification, amino acid analysis, sequencing, and mass spectrometry. *Type:* Research center.

University of Arkansas at Little Rock

Biomedical Research Center

College of Pharmacy, Slot 522-3   Ph: (501)686-6493
4301 W. Markham   Fax: (501)686-6057
Little Rock, AR 72205
E-mail: compadrecesarm@exchange.wams.edu
URL: http://www.amanda.uams.edu
Desc: Molecular modeling, including protein structure function relationships, toxicity modeling, and pharmacokinetic modeling; anatomical visualization, 3-D animation, and educational development. *Type:* Research center.

University of Arkansas at Little Rock

Particle Accelerator Lab

Physics Dept.   Ph: (501)569-3275
2801 S. Univ. Ave.   Fax: (501)569-3314
Little Rock, AR 72204
E-mail: aarollefson@uarl.edu
Contact: Dr. Andre Rollefson, Contact.
Desc: Fast-neutron radiobiology with cultured cells. *Type:* Research center.

University of British Columbia

Biotechnology Laboratory

Wesbrook Bldg., Rm. 237   Ph: (604)822-4838
6174 University Blvd.   Fax: (604)822-2114
Vancouver, BC, Canada V6T
   1Z3
E-mail: kilburn@unixg.ubc.ca
URL: http://www.biotech.ubc.ca
Contact: Dr. Douglas G. Kilburn, Dir.
Desc: Molecular genetics as related to forest, plant, and animal biology and medicine. Interests include process engineering and fermentation studies. *Type:* Research center.

University of Calgary

Molecular and Developmental Biology Research Group

Faculty of Medicine   Ph: (403)220-4476
3330 Hospital Dr. NW   Fax: (403)270-0737
Calgary, AB, Canada T2N 4N1
E-mail: jmcghee@acs.ucalgary.ca
Contact: James D. McGhee, PhD, Ch.
Desc: Molecular approaches to problems of cellular differentiation, differential gene expression during early development, gametogenesis and embryogenesis, and molecular genetics. Activities focus on molecular biology with extensive use of recombinant DNA technology applied to problems of developmental biology, as well as on many aspects of genetics, from classical mouse genetics to embryo transformation with manipulated genes. *Type:* Research center.

University of California, Irvine

Hitachi Chemical Research Center

1003 Health Science Rd. W.   Ph: (714)725-2721
Irvine, CA 92697   Fax: (714)725-2727
E-mail: j2jacobs@uci.edu
Contact: Dr. Jack Jacobs, Dir.
Desc: Molecular biology and biotechnology, focusing on cancer therapeutics, and cell and developmental biology. *Type:* Research center.

University of California, Los Angeles

Department of Molecular and Medical Pharmacology

Crump Institute for Biological Imaging

23-138 CHS   Ph: (310)825-6539
UCLA Sch. of Med.   Fax: (310)825-6267
PO Box 951735 Ave.
Los Angeles, CA 90095-1735
E-mail: mphelps@mednet.ucla.edu
URL: http://www.nuc.ucla.edu
Contact: Prof. Norton Simon, Chm.
Desc: Biological imaging technologies, including positron emmision tomography; autoradiographic images for in viro and in vitro assays of biochemical and biological process in tissue preparations; fluorescent microscopy to provide images of changing chemical environments in tissue and isolated cell preparations; and image based communication and educational systems using game strategies, expert systems, knowledge navigators, and personal computers. *Type:* Research center.

University of California, San Diego

Institute for Biomedical Engineering

9500 Gilman Dr.   Ph: (619)822-2290
Mail Code 0427   Fax: (619)822-1160
La Jolla, CA 92093-0427
E-mail: schien@ucsd.edu
URL: http://www.bioeng.ucsd.edu
Contact: Dr. Shu Chien, Dir.
Desc: Biomedical engineering, emphasizing structure-function relationships in normal and pathological tissues and the development of biological substitutes to restore, maintain, or improve tissue functions. Tissue studies focus on the heart, blood, lung, kidney, liver, pancreas, muscle, bone, cartilage, tendon, ligament, skin, nerve, brain, retina, and cochlea. *Type:* Research center.

University of California, San Francisco

Computer Graphics Laboratory

Sch. of Pharmacy   Ph: (415)476-2299
Department of Pharmaceutical   Fax: (415)502-1755
   Chemistry
San Francisco, CA 94143-0446
E-mail: tef@cgl.ucsf.edu
URL: http://www.cgl.ucsf.edu/
Contact: Thomas Ferrin, PhD, Dir.
Desc: Computational approaches to the structure and function of large biological molecules using three-dimensional computer graphics as the principal mode of interaction. Activities include development of real-time algorithms and numerical analysis techniques for interactive visualization and manipulation of nucleic acids, proteins, and protein-ligand complexes. *Type:* Research center.

University of California, San Francisco

Mass Spectrometry Facility

Department of Pharmaceutical   Ph: (415)476-5641
   Chemistry   Fax: (415)502-1655
San Francisco, CA 94143
E-mail: alb@itsa.ucsf.edu
URL: http://donatello/ucsf.edu
Contact: Prof. A.L. Burlingame, Dir.

Desc: Molecular identification problems in human health and disease and biological chemistry, including studies in chemical and biochemical structure and mechanism. Conducts investigations of the structure of covalently modified informational biopolymers, drug metabolism, chemical carcinogenesis, signal transduction, proteins in cancer biology, irreversible inhibitors of cytochrome P-450, various genetic diseases, and membrane-bound glycoproteins, such as acetylcholine receptor and esterase, and scrapie glycoprotein. *Type:* Research center.

University of California, San Francisco
Nuclear Magnetic Resonance Laboratory
Department of Pharmaceutical   Ph: (415)476-1916
   Chemistry   Fax: (415)476-0688
Medical Sciences Bldg. S-926
PO Box 0446
San Francisco, CA 94143-0446
E-mail: james@picasso.ucsf.edu
URL: http://picasso.ucsf.edu/

Contact: Prof. T.L. James, Contact.

Desc: Theory and practice of nuclear magnetic resonance and computer modeling studies of proteins and nucleic acids. Performs quantitative determinations of molecular structure in noncrystalline environments using nuclear Overhauser effects and complete relaxation matrix calculations. *Type:* Research center.

University of Chicago
EM Core Facility for Biological Research
920 E. 58th St.   Ph: (773)702-1650
Chicago, IL 60637   Fax: (773)702-3172
E-mail: am29@midway.uchicago.edu
URL: http://gingi.uchicago.edu

Contact: Dr. Anthony P. Mahowald, Co-Dir.

Desc: Biomedical research, including cell biology and molecular imaging. *Type:* Research center.

University of Chicago
Lipoprotein Study Unit
5841 Maryland   Ph: (773)702-1775
MC 5041   Fax: (773)702-4534
Chicago, IL 60637
E-mail: ascanu@medicine.bsd.uchicago.edu

Contact: Dr. Angelo M. Scanu, Dir.

Desc: Atherosclerotic cardiovascular disease, genetics of lipoprotein disorders, and structure and function of lipoproteins. *Type:* Research center.

University of Colorado
Clinical Mass Spectrometry Research Resource
4200 E. 9th Ave.   Ph: (303)315-7286
Denver, CO 80262   Fax: (303)315-7097
E-mail: paul.fennessey@uchsc.edu
URL: http://www.uchsc.edu

Contact: Dr. P.V. Fennessey, Co-Dir.

Desc: Clinical applications of mass spectrometry, including gas chromatograph mass spectrometry, high resolution mass spectrometry, bioactive substances, and application of fast atom bombardment mass spectrometry to biomolecules. Emphasizes methods for synthesis of internal standards for the quantitative analysis of bioactive molecules found in physiological fluids, identification of steroid profiles in patients with biochemical and pathological irregularities, and stable isotope studies for measuring the utilization of important metabolic intermediates in humans. *Type:* Research center.

University of Connecticut Health Center
Biomolecular Structure Analysis Center
263 Farmington Ave.   Ph: (860)679-2545
Farmington, CT 06030-2017   Fax: (860)679-1989
E-mail: herbette@bsac.uchc.edu

Contact: Dr. Leo G. Herbette, Dir.

Desc: Drug-membrane interaction, drug-receptor interaction, membrane drug design, pulmonary surfactant research, and collagen structure research as it relates to cardiology, alcoholism, Alzheimer's disease, CNS disorders, skeletal and smooth muscle disorders, and atherosclerosis. *Type:* Research center.

University of Florida
Bioglass Research Center
JHMHC, J-413   Ph: (352)462-0805
Gainesville, FL 32610   Fax: (352)462-0806

Contact: Dr. Larry L. Hench, Dir.

Desc: Development and clinical trials of devices made from Bioglass materials in medical and dental applications and basic investigations into the mechanisms of tissue response to bioactive materials. *Type:* Research center.

University of Florida
Interdisciplinary Center for Biotechnology Research
Box 110580   Ph: (352)392-8408
Gainesville, FL 32611   Fax: (352)392-8598
E-mail: schuster@biotech.ufl.edu
URL: http://www.biotech.ufl.edu/

Contact: Dr. Sheldon M. Schuster, Dir.

Desc: Biotechnology, including flow cytometric analysis, DNA sequencing and synthesis, hybridoma technologies, protein microisolation, peptide synthesis, electron microscopy, biological computing, and genetics and reproductive analyses. Research activities include biotechnologies for ecological, evolutionary, and conservation sciences. *Type:* Research center.

University of Hawaii at Manoa
Pacific Biomedical Research Center
1993 East-West Rd.   Ph: (808)956-7401
Honolulu, HI 96822   Fax: (808)956-4768
E-mail: fgreenwd@pbrc.hawaii.edu
URL: http://www.pbrc.hawaii.edu

Contact: Dr. Fredrick C. Greenwood, Dir.

Desc: Cell biology, neuro-behavioral biology, molecular biology, matrix pathobiology, biotechnology, Hawaiian evolutionary and conservation biology, molecular endocrinology, retrovirology (HIV and HTLV-1), infectious diseases, and native Hawaiian health research. *Type:* Research center.

University of Illinois at Chicago
Laboratory for Molecular Biology
Department of Biological Sci.,   Ph: (312)996-9239
   MC 067   Fax: (312)413-2691
900 S. Ashland
Chicago, IL 60607-7020
URL: http://www.uic.edu/depts/bios/lmb.html

Contact: Don Morrison, Coord.

Desc: Regulatory mechanisms involving signal transduction pathways and eukaryotic developmental systems. *Type:* Research center.

University of Illinois at Chicago
Research Resources Center
835 S. Wolcott Ave., Rm. E102   Ph: (312)996-7600
Chicago, IL 60612-7341   Fax: (312)996-0539
E-mail: charlieb@uic.edu
URL: http://www.rrc.uic.edu/

Contact: Dr. C.E. Brown, Dir.,RRC-East.

Desc: Electronic and mechanical instrumentation, environmental stress, biostatistics, micro and mini computer programming and databases, atomic force/tunneling microscopy, electron microscopy, atomic absorption spectrometry, nuclear magnetic resonance spectrometry, mass spectrometry, flow cytometry, and protein sequencing/peptide synthesizing. *Type:* Research center.

University of Illinois at Urbana-Champaign
Electron Paramagnetic Resonance Research Center
College of Medicine   Ph: (217)244-1186
190 Medical Sciences Bldg.   Fax: (217)333-8868
506 S. Mathews Ave.
Urbana, IL 61801
E-mail: IERC@uiuc.edu
URL: http://IERC.scs.uiuc.edu

Contact: R. Linn Belford, PhD, Dir.

Desc: Free radicals and metal ion centers, especially in biological systems; characterization of metalloproteins; development and evaluation of S-band (2-4 GHz) ESE, high-frequency (e.g. 94GHz) EPR, and low-frequency DNP spectrometry; EPR study of paramagnetic contrast agents for magnetic resonance imaging (MRI); research in EPR and ENDOR theory; dynamics in biomolecules; protein folding and unfolding. *Type:* Research center.

University of Iowa
Flow Cytometry Facility
College of Med.   Ph: (319)335-8103
48 EMRB   Fax: (319)335-8049
Iowa City, IA 52242

Contact: Justin Fishbaugh, Tech.Dir.

Desc: Cytometry research in the biomedical sciences, including cell biology, cancer biology, immunology, neurology, hepatology, pathology, tumor biology, and genetics. *Type:* Research center.

University of Iowa
Hybridoma Facility
College of Med.   Ph: (319)335-8004
238 Eckstein Medical Research   Fax: (319)335-6718
   Bldg.
EMRB
Iowa City, IA 52242-1101

Contact: Dr. Charles Lovig, Contact.

Desc: Provides monoclonal antibodies, tissue cultures, and reagents for cell cultures to individual investigators for their research. *Type:* Research center.

University of Iowa
Molecular Analysis Facility
355 EMRB   Ph: (319)353-5489
Iowa City, IA 52242   Fax: (319)335-7925
E-mail: kamel_harrata@uiowa.edu

Contact: Kamel Harrata, Dir.

Desc: Proteins and peptides, focusing on amino acid composition and sequence, peptide synthesis, HPLC separations, and equilibrium and kinetic solution spectroscopy. *Type:* Research center.

University of Kansas
Biochemical Research Service Laboratory
Department of Chemistry   Ph: (913)864-4166
Lawrence, KS 66045   Fax: (913)864-5396
E-mail: alterman@kuhub.cc.ukans.edu
URL: http://www.idl.ukans.edu/awalresc/brsl/brsl.html

Contact: Mike Alterman, Dir.

Desc: Although primarily a service facility, the Laboratory cultures large quantities of microorganisms, purifies and characterizes enzymes and other biological materials, immobilizes proteins, studies enzyme kinetics, and performs amino acid analyses, protein sequence analyses, peptide synthesis, and automated DNA sequencing, and peptide synthesis. *Type:* Research center.

University of Kansas
Higuchi Biosciences Center
Center for Biomedical Research
Smissman Res. Laboratories   Ph: (785)864-5140
2099 Constant Ave.   Fax: (785)864-3578
Lawrence, KS 66047
E-mail: ekm@smissman.hbc.ukas.edu
URL: http://www.hbc.ukans.edu
Contact: Dr. Elias K. Michaelis, Dir.

Desc: Integration of various aspects of drug design currently directed at several specific diseases such as epilepsy, cancer, heart and lung disease, and various mental disorders. Conducts biomedical and chemical projects in neurotransmitter receptors, ion transport mechanisms, phase transport kinetics, metabolism as a barrier to drug delivery, and development of highly sensitive bioanalytical techniques. *Type:* Research center.

University of Manitoba
Manitoba Institute of Cell Biology
100 Olivia St.   Ph: (204)787-2112
Winnipeg, MB, Canada R3E   Fax: (204)787-2190
0V9
E-mail: agreenb@cc.umanitoba.ca
URL: http://www.umanitoba.ca/institutes/manitoba_institute_cell_biology/
Contact: Dr. Arnold Greenberg, Dir.

Desc: Molecular mechanisms of cancer and other diseases, through cell biology, molecular biology, biochemistry, experimental chemotherapy, tumor immunology, and somatic cell genetics. *Type:* Research center.

University of Maryland
Graduate Program in Molecular and Cell Biology
Microbiology Bldg.   Ph: (301)405-6991
College Park, MD 20742   Fax: (301)314-9921
E-mail: mocbgrad@deans.umd.edu
URL: http://www.life.umd.edu/grad/mocb/index.html
Contact: Dr. Ibrahim Z. Ades, Prog.Dir.

Desc: Molecular genetics, cell biology, regulation of gene expression, molecular virology and immunology, membrane biochemistry, photoregulation, cell mobility, signal transduction, host-parasite interactions, transport channels, protein and enzyme and function, and neural processes. *Type:* Research center.

University of Maryland
Medical Biotechnology Center
618 W. Lombard St.   Ph: (410)706-8181
Baltimore, MD 21201   Fax: (410)706-8184
E-mail: tramont@umvi.umd.edu
URL: http://www.umvi.umd.edu
Contact: Dr. Edmund C. Tramont, Dir.

Desc: Vaccinology, AIDS, immunology, bioimaging, biosensing, bioanalysis, molecular neurobiology, and molecular genetics and gene therapy. *Type:* Research center.

University of Michigan
Biology Laboratory
2310 Sch. of Dentistry   Ph: (734)763-0017
1101 N. University Ave.
Ann Arbor, MI 48109
Contact: Donald B. Clewell, Dir.

Desc: Gene expression in bacteria, focusing on antibiotic resistance, pathogenicity, gene translocation between DNA molecules and bacterial cells, and mobile genetic elements including plasmids and transposons. *Type:* Research center.

University of Minnesota
Biomedical Engineering Center
Box 609 Mayo   Ph: (612)624-7116
7-121 Basic Sci. & Biomedical   Fax: (612)624-1121
Engg. Bldg.
Minneapolis, MN 55455
E-mail: hoffm003@maroon.tc.umn.edu
URL: http://www.med.umn.edu/bmec
Contact: William Hoffman, Asst.

Desc: The application of engineering principles to advance human health and well-being. *Type:* Research center.

University of Minnesota
Hormel Institute
801 16th Ave. NE   Ph: (507)433-8804
Austin, MN 55912   Fax: (507)437-9606
E-mail: schmi081@maroon.tc.umn.edu
URL: http://www.smig.net/hi
Contact: Dr. Harald H.O. Schmid, Exec.Dir.

Desc: Biochemistry, bio-organic chemistry, biophysics, cell biology, and molecular biology relating to biological membranes and cellular signal transduction. Topics include membrane assembly and packing properties, regulation of lipolytic enzymes, and the role of membrane lipids in heart disease and cancer. *Type:* Research center.

University of Minnesota
Minnesota Molecular and Cellular Therapeutics Program
1900 Fitch Ave.   Ph: (612)624-8700
St. Paul, MN 55108   Fax: (612)624-1777
URL: http://www.med.umn.edu/mmct/mmct.html
Contact: John S. Coleman, Dir.

Desc: Gene therapy, cell therapy (which involves the purification, expansion and genetic modification of blood and bone marrow cells), biotherapeutics, and educational issues. *Type:* Research center.

University of Mississippi
Molecular Modeling Laboratory
Sch. of Pharmacy   Ph: (601)232-7101
417 Faser Hall   Fax: (601)232-5638
University, MS 38677
E-mail: mrcds@cotton.vislab.olemiss.edu
Contact: Robert D. Sindelar, PhD, Dir.

Desc: Molecular research, including graphics-assisted structure activity relationships, small molecule/large molecule interactions, and computer-aided drug design. *Type:* Research center.

University of Montreal
Biomedical Modeling Research Group
Institut de genie biomedical   Ph: (514)343-7515
C.P. 6128, succursale Centre-   Fax: (514)343-6112
Ville
Montreal, PQ, Canada H3C 3J7
E-mail: roberge@igb.umontreal.ca
URL: http://www.igb.umontreal.ca/grmb/
Contact: Fernand A. Roberge, Dir.

Desc: Computer simulation and mathematical modeling in cardiac electrophysiology, biomechanics of joints, and characterization of biological tissues by imaging. *Type:* Research center.

University of Montreal
Institute of Biomedical Engineering
Faculte de medicine   Ph: (514)343-6357
C.P. 6128 Centreville   Fax: (514)343-6112
Montreal, PQ, Canada H3C 3J7
E-mail: leblanc@igb.umontreal.ca
URL: http://www.igb.umontreal.ca

Contact: Prof. A. Robert LeBlanc, Dir.
Desc: Cardiac electrophysiology, biomechanics, electrocardiology, biomedical modelling, neuromuscular physiology, and clinical engineering. *Type:* Research center.

University of Montreal
Membrane Transport Research Group
PO Box 6128, Downtown Sta.   Ph: (514)343-7924
Montreal, PQ, Canada H3C 3J7   Fax: (514)343-7146
E-mail: grtm@ere.umontreal.ca
Contact: Remy Sauve, PhD, Dir.

Desc: Transport of ions, sugars, and amino acids in renal, intestinal and endothelial cells, including ionic permeability of cellular membranes of epithelia, molecular biology of transporters, computer simulation of atomic models, transport energetics, cell ultrastructure and transport, and cell primary cultures. *Type:* Research center.

University of New Brunswick
Institute of Biomedical Engineering
PO Box 4400   Ph: (506)453-4966
Fredericton, NB, Canada E3B   Fax: (506)453-4827
5A3
E-mail: biden@unb.ca
URL: http://www.unb.ca
Contact: Edmund N. Biden, Dir.

Desc: Interaction of man and modern technology, particularly in health care. Research focuses on developing electronic control systems for artificial limbs, bioelectric signal processing, modeling of human operators and muscle function, applications of electronic instrumentation in orthopedics, medical imaging, ergonomics, exercise physiology, and biomechanics. *Type:* Research center.

University of North Dakota
Ireland Research Laboratory
Department of Biochemistry,   Ph: (701)777-3937
School of Medicine and Health   Fax: (701)777-2382
Science
PO Box 9037
Grand Forks, ND 58202
E-mail: biochem@mail.med.und.nodak.edu
URL: http://www.med.und.nodak.edu/depts/biochem/home.htm
Contact: Dr. Robert Nordlie, Chm.

Desc: Medical sciences, including studies on intermediary metabolism of amino acids, carbohydrates, bacterial and mammalian enzymology, mechanism of hormone action, transport mechanisms, biological energetics, natural products, and experimental leukemia. Also studies circulation, tissue culture, molecular biology of transformed cells, and impact of tumors on hepatic glucose-6-phosphatose. *Type:* Research center.

University of Notre Dame
Lobund Laboratory
Notre Dame, IN 46556   Ph: (219)631-7564
   Fax: (219)631-8583
URL: http://www.nd.edu
Contact: Dr. Morris Pollard, Dir.

Desc: Research on prostate cancer including the development and use of model systems to study nutrition and endocrine manipulations for prevention and treatment of the disease; metastasis and angiogenesis. *Type:* Research center.

University of Pennsylvania
William Pepper Laboratory
Hospital of Univ. of   Ph: (215)662-3435
Pennsylvania   Fax: (215)349-5090
Philadelphia, PA 19104
E-mail: donald_young@pathla.med.upenn.edu

URL: http://www.med.upenn.edu/path/

Contact: Donald S. Young, MD, Dir.

Desc: Microbiology, immunology, clinical chemistry, hematology, toxicology, therapeutic drug monitoring characterization and specificity of blood group, characterization and specificity of blood group antibodies, clinical correlation of disturbances of endocrine metabolism, coagulation disorders, and clinical enzymology. Conducts complete histocompatability evaluations, blood component therapy, therapeutic plasma exchange, therapeutic red cell exchange procedures, tumor receptor-site studies, as well as basic research in cancer biology, endocrine biochemistry, and membrane biology. *Type:* Research center.

University of Quebec at Trois-Rivieres
Research Group in Membrane Biotechnology
CP 500   Ph: (819)376-5052
Trois-Rivieres, PQ, Canada G9A   Fax: (819)376-5084
    5H7
E-mail: claude_gicquaud@uqtr.uquebec.ca

Contact: Claude Gicquaud, Dir.

Desc: Fundamental research on the use of artificial membrane systems applied to biophysical and medical problems. Research includes the study of cytoskeleton-membrane interactions, pharmacological use of liposomes, and physiochemical basis of membrane interactions with physiologically active substances. *Type:* Research center.

University of Tennessee
Medical Center at Knoxville
Grad. Sch. of Med.   Ph: (423)544-9290
1924 Alcoa Hwy.   Fax: (423)544-6819
Knoxville, TN 37920
E-mail: mcaudle@utk.edu

Contact: Dr. Michael R. Caudle, Dean.

Desc: Hematology, oncology, and the molecular processes of disease, including cellular and humoral immunity, colon cancer and colitis, cytogenetics, experimental and comparative pathology, platelet function, immunobiology, and membrane transport. *Type:* Research center.

University of Tennessee
Molecular Resource Center
801 Molecular Sci. Bldg.   Ph: (901)448-6175
858 Madison Ave.   Fax: (901)448-8462
Memphis, TN 38163
E-mail: tcooper@utmeml.utmem.edu

Contact: Dr. Terrance G. Cooper, Contact.

Desc: Function and regulation of genes. Conducts experiments with gene replication and with isolation and manipulation of genetic components, with applications to cancer. *Type:* Research center.

University of Texas at Arlington
Center for Medicinal Chemistry Research
Department of Chemistry   Ph: (817)273-3171
PO Box 19065   Fax: (817)272-3808
Arlington, TX 76019
E-mail: ternay@uta.edu
URL: http://www.utachem.uta.edu

Contact: Dr. A.L. Ternay, Jr., Dir.

Desc: Studies antimicrobial/viral agents, medicaments used in the field of mental health, and substances to protect individuals from exposure to hazardous chemicals. Encourages students interested in careers in medicine to conduct research in the basic sciences, especially chemistry and biochemistry. *Type:* Research center.

University of Texas at Austin
Biochemical Institute
Welch 5.266   Ph: (512)471-1105
Austin, TX 78712   Fax: (512)471-8696
E-mail: m.hackert@mail.utexas.edu

Contact: Dr. Marvin L. Hackert, Dir.

Desc: Drug metabolism, mechanism and regulation of protein synthesis, structure, function, and regulation of enzymes and other proteins, nutritional aspects of human disease, and cloning, sequencing, and site specific mutagenesis of genes, their regulation, and repair. *Type:* Research center.

University of Texas at Austin
Biomedical Engineering Graduate Program
Engineering Science Bldg. 610   Ph: (512)471-4679
Austin, TX 78712-1084   Fax: (512)471-0616
E-mail: kdiller@mail.utexas.edu
URL: http://www.ece.utexas.edu/bme

Contact: Dr. Kenneth R. Diller, Dir.

Desc: Application of scientific and engineering knowledge to the solution of medical problems. Projects deal with molecular bioengineering, antibiotic synthesis, spectroscopic detection of early cancers, diagnostic applications of tissue fluorescence, image analysis by computer, cryopreservation of organs and tissues, quantitative thermographic imaging, electrosurgical safety, thrombosis on injured vessel and atherosclerotic surfaces and on polymeric biomaterials, pulsatile-flow cardiopulmonary bypass, chromatographic features of polar and nonpolar cardiac glycosides, hyperthermia in cancer therapy, effects of coenzyme Q-10 on cardiac function, biodegradable polymer implants for use in surgery, computer graphics analysis of sport biomechanics, rheology of synovial fluids, robotic surgical lasers, laser-tissue interaction, structure and function of hybrid proteins, and microvascular analysis of burn wounds. *Type:* Research center.

University of Texas at Austin
Center for Biotechnology
Rm. WEL 4.260C   Ph: (512)471-3279
Austin, TX 78712-1159   Fax: (512)471-8696
E-mail: bkitto@mail.utexas.edu

Contact: Barrie Kitto, PhD, Dir.

Desc: Biotechnology. *Type:* Research center.

University of Texas at Dallas
Molecular and Cell Biology Program
Mail Stop FO3.1   Ph: (214)883-2500
PO Box 830688   Fax: (214)883-2409
Richardson, TX 75083-0688
URL: http://www.utdallas.edu/

Contact: Dr. Ron Yasbin, Prog.Hd.

Desc: Biochemistry, macromolecular physical chemistry, microbial and molecular genetics, and cell biology. *Type:* Research center.

University of Texas Health Science Center at San Antonio
Center for the Enhancement of the Biology/Biomaterials Interface
7703 Floyd Curl Dr.   Ph: (210)567-2023
San Antonio, TX 78284-7823   Fax: (210)567-2052
E-mail: boyanb@uthscsa.edu
URL: http://www.uthscsa.edu

Contact: Dr. Barbara D. Boyan, PhD, Dir.

Desc: Cell function regulation, including studies on immunologic regulation, microbial pathogenesis, skeletal tissues, cell biology, and mediators. Fields of application include biomedicine, biology/biomaterial interfaces, wear debris, and nutrition. *Type:* Research center.

University of Texas Health Science Center at San Antonio
Institute for Biotechnology
15355 Lambda   Ph: (210)567-7000
San Antonio, TX 78245-3207   Fax: (210)567-7277
E-mail: hottle@uthscsa.edu

Contact: Dr. Wen-Hwa Lee, Dir.

Desc: Biotechnology and molecular medicine. *Type:* Research center.

University of Texas--Houston Health Science Center
Analytical Chemistry Center
PO Box 20708   Ph: (713)500-6280
Houston, TX 77225   Fax: (713)500-0651
E-mail: bseifert@bmb.med.uth.tmc.edu
URL: http://www-bmb.med.uth.tmc.edu

Contact: Dr. William E. Seifert, Jr., Asst.Dir., Tech. Srvcs.

Desc: Seeks to meet the needs of the biomedical research community by offering access to analytical instrumentation and methodology. Specialties include structural analysis and molecular weight determination of peptides and other organic compounds by mass spectrometry, protein sequencing, peptide synthesis, chromatographic separations and quantitative measurements, and stable isotope applications. *Type:* Research center.

University of Texas Medical Branch at Galveston
Marine Biomedical Institute
301 University Blvd.   Ph: (409)772-2103
Galveston, TX 77555-1069   Fax: (409)772-4687
E-mail: wdwillis@utmb.edu
URL: http://snapper.utmb.edu/mbi

Contact: Dr. William D. Willis, Jr., Dir.

Desc: Studies on problems in comparative neurobiology, marine medicine and biology, and biophysics. *Type:* Research center.

University of Texas Medical Branch at Galveston
Sealy Center for Molecular Science
5.104 Medical Research Bldg.,   Ph: (409)772-3367
   Rte. 1068   Fax: (409)772-6334
301 University Blvd.
Galveston, TX 77555-1068
E-mail: pipper@scms.utmb.edu
URL: http://www.utmb.edu

Contact: Dr. E. Brad Thompson, Interim Dir.

Desc: Molecular biology and biochemistry. Specialized research includes eukaryotic DNA repair, HIV molecular biology, molecular toxicology and oncology, transcription regulation, signal transduction steroids and apoptosis. *Type:* Research center.

University of Utah
Center for Engineering Design
3176 Merrill Engineering   Ph: (801)581-6499
   Building   Fax: (801)581-5304
Salt Lake City, UT 84112

Contact: Dr. Stephen C. Jacobsen, Dir.

Desc: Robotic design and control, including teleporated and entertainment robots; actuator technology; touch sensors; micro-electromechanical systems; biomechanics; bioengineering; rehabilitation research, including projects in artificial limb design; and micro pumps and fluid delivery systems. *Type:* Research center.

University of Utah

Institute for Biomedical Engineering

803 N., 300 W.   Ph: (801)581-6991
Salt Lake City, UT 84103   Fax: (801)581-4044
E-mail: don.b.olsen@m.cc.utah.edu
Contact: Dr. Don B. Olsen, Dir.
Desc: Design, development, and fabrication of cardiac as-sist devices, cardiac replacement devices with animal im-plantation and complete follow-up studies, basic physiologic and psychophysical studies of the effects of electrical stimulation in the scala tympani of deaf human volunteers, testing of new artificial kidneys, peritoneal ac-cess devices for peritoneal dialysis, drug metabolism in pa-tients with end state renal disease, dialysis with high flux dialysers, research with chemical effect field transistors, re-search into the efficacy of insulin administered by in-traperitoneal route, new access routers for peritoneal dialysis and peritoneal access routes for diabetes, artificial hearing and arms, implantation of a totally artificial heart in a human patient, and biomaterials research. Cooperates with Department of Biomedical Design for design and manufacture of compact hemodialysis machines and peri-toneal access devices. *Type:* Research center.

University of Virginia

Center for Cell Signaling

Health Science Center, 577   Ph: (804)924-1235
Charlottesville, VA 22908   Fax: (804)924-1236
E-mail: signals@virginia.edu
URL: http://www.med.virgnia. edu/inter-dis/signaling/celsig00.html
Contact: Dr. David L. Brautigan, PhD, Dir.
Desc: Molecular biology of cellular signaling processes, in-cluding membranes, receptors, transduction, genome-level signals, and molecular structure. *Type:* Research center.

University of Washington

Department of Bioengineering

Simulation Resource in Circulatory Mass Transport and Exchange Center

Box 357962   Ph: (206)685-2005
Seattle, WA 98195   Fax: (206)685-2651
E-mail: jbb@nsr.bioeng.washington.edu
URL: http://nsr.bioeng.washington.edu
Contact: James B. Bassingthwaighte, Dir.
Desc: Logical structures for experiment design and analy-sis, including automating and fitting models to data, as-sessing the goodness-of-fit, choosing numerical approximations and, in some situations, the form of the model. Studies include estimates of conductances of capil-lary and cell membranes, volumes of distribution, and re-gional flows in organs; identification of receptor affinities and metabolic rates in intact organs via various tracer tech-niques; and development of an interactive simulation sys-tem that permits formulation of models without programming. *Type:* Research center.

University of Washington

Engineering Research Center for Engineered Biomaterials

College of Engineering

Box 351720   Ph: (206)616-8646
Seattle, WA 98195-1720   Fax: (206)616-9763
E-mail: ratner@uweb.engr.washington.edu
URL: http://www.uweb.engr.washington.edu
Contact: Dr. Buddy D. Ratner, Dir.
Desc: Exploitation of specific biological recognition mech-anisms in order to develop a new generation of biomateri-als for medical implants that will heal in the body in a facile, physiologically normal manner. *Type:* Research cen-ter.

University of Washington

National ESCA and Surface Analysis Center for Biomedical Problems

Depts. of Bioengineering &   Ph: (206)685-1229
     Chem. Engg.   Fax: (206)543-3778
Box 351750
Seattle, WA 98195-1750
E-mail: castner@nb.engr.washington.edu
URL: http://www.esca.cheme.washington.edu/nb/
Contact: David G. Castner, PhD, Dir.
Desc: Surface analysis of biomaterial, polymer, and biolog-ical surfaces. Research directed toward integrating electron spectroscopy for chemical analysis (ESCA), secondary ion mass spectrometry (SIMS), other surface analysis methods into standard analytical tools for biomedical sciences. *Type:* Research center.

University of Waterloo

Biotechnology Research Centre

200 University Ave. W.   Ph: (519)888-4567
Waterloo, ON, Canada N2L   Fax: (519)746-0614
     3G1
E-mail: glick@sciborg.uwaterloo.ca
Contact: Dr. B.R. Glick, Exec.Dir.
Desc: Fundamental and applied R&D, including research in molecular biology, genetics, cell culture, biochemistry, bioorganic and natural products chemistry, enyzmology, molecular modeling, bioreactor and bioprocess develop-ment, bioseparations engineering and environmental bio-technology. *Type:* Research center.

W. Alton Jones Cell Science Center, Inc.

10 Old Barn Rd.   Ph: (518)523-1250
Lake Placid, NY 12946-1009   Fax: (518)523-1849
E-mail: jstevens@northnet.org
URL: http://www.cell-science.org
Contact: James L. Stevens, Dir.
Desc: Molecular and cellular regulation of growth and de-velopment, including cancer. Specific interests include in-tracellular and intercellular signalling pathwaysand growth factors; protein chemistry and visual cycle proteins; role of protein kinases in cell signalling; adipocyte, thymocyte, and endothelial cell and molecular biology; molecular reg-ulation of wound repair; and regulation of molecular stress responses. *Type:* Research center.

Wake Forest University

Lipid Analytic Laboratory

Sch. of Med.   Ph: (910)716-2672
Gray Bldg., Rm. 2063   Fax: (910)716-6279
Medical Center Blvd.
Winston Salem, NC 27157-1072
E-mail: rstclair@wfubmc.edu
URL: http://wfubmc.edu/ord/cores/core12.html
Contact: Richard W. St. Clair, PhD, Lab.Dir.
Desc: Provision of standardized plasma lipid and lipopro-tein analyses for clinical and research pruposes. *Type:* Re-search center.

Wake Forest University

MICROMED

Wake Forest University School   Ph: (336)716-2675
     of Medicine   Fax: (336)716-6174
300 Medical Center Blvd.
Winston Salem, NC 27157-1092
E-mail: jjerome@bgsm.edu
Contact: Dr. W. Gray Jerome, Dir.
Desc: Biomedicine with emphasis on atherosclerosis, mi-crobiology, immunology, pathology, and biochemistry.

Ongoing projects include cytochemical and immuno-chemical studies of lysosomes in arterial cells and macro-phages, ultrastructural correlates of lipid metabolism, binding and cytoplasmic translocation of plasma lipopro-teins, structural correlation of biochemical events in thrombosis and thrombolysis, spatial organization of proteoglycans, collagen, other extracellular matrix proteins during progression of cardiovascular disease, and 3-D computer imaging and quantitation of cells and organ-elles. *Type:* Research center.

Washington University in St. Louis

Biomedical Research Program

Sch. of Med.   Ph: (314)362-5300
Department of Internal Med.,   Fax: (314)362-5306
     Box 8212
660 S. Euclid
St. Louis, MO 63110
Contact: David Kipnis, M.D., Dir.
Desc: Allocates funds for exploratory and basic research and product development on the proteins, peptides, and other molecules regulating cellular communication and function. Facilitates the exchange of information between individual investigators in the Medical School and Mon-santo's scientists. *Type:* Research center.

Wayne State University

Bioengineering Center

Gurdjian-Lissner Biomechanics Laboratory

818 W. Hancock St.   Ph: (313)577-1344
Detroit, MI 48202   Fax: (313)577-8333
E-mail: king@rrb.eng.wayne.edu
URL: http://www.ttb.eng.wayne.edu
Contact: Dr. Albert I. King, Dir.
Desc: Bioengineering sciences, including studies on head/neck injury mechanisms and prevention of such injuries. *Type:* Research center.

Webb-Waring Antioxidant Research Institute

4200 E. 9th Ave.   Ph: (303)315-8231
Box C-321   Fax: (303)315-8541
Denver, CO 80262
E-mail: jmarecki@uchse.edu
URL: http://www.uchsc.edu/sm/wuring/webages
Contact: John E. Repine, MD, Pres./Dir.
Desc: Role of oxygen radicals in health and diseases, oxi-dants and antioxidants, air pollution, basic immunology, biochemistry, genetics, cell biology, pathology, and physi-ology. *Type:* Research center.

Whitehead Institute for Biomedical Research

9 Cambridge Ctr.   Ph: (617)258-5000
Cambridge, MA 02142   Fax: (617)258-9872
E-mail: info@wi.mit.edu
URL: http://www.wi.mit.edu/home.html
Contact: Dr. Gerald Fink, Dir.
Desc: Molecular processes underlying biological develop-ment as related to developmental and molecular biology, cancer, membranes, virology, AIDS, vaccine development, plant biology, and yeast. *Type:* Research center.

Wistar Institute

3601 Spruce St.   Ph: (215)898-3926
Philadelphia, PA 19104   Fax: (215)573-2097
E-mail: rovera@wistar.upenn.edu
URL: http://www.wistar.upenn.edu
Contact: Giovanni Rovera, MD, Dir./CEO.
Desc: Virology and immunology using a molecular-based approach primarily to cancer as well as virus-induced dis-eases, degenerative diseases such as Alzheimer's and au-toimmune diseases including multiple sclerosis,

rheumatoid arthritis, lupus, scleroderma, and phemphigo. Specific areas of research include structural biology emphasizing the structure of viruses and the interaction of a variety of ligands to cell surface receptors; tumor biology emphasizing early embryonic development, including the development of the immune and cardiovascular systems; molecular genetics, focusing on suppressor genes and oncogenes in leukemias, lymphomas, childhood cancers, melanomas, breast carcinomas, bladder carcinomas, and tumors of the gastrointestinal tract; and tumor immunology, particularly emphasizing on gene therapy and immune therapy. *Type:* Research center.

W.M. Keck Center for Computational Biology

6100 S. Main St., Mail Stop 141   Ph: (713)527-4752
Houston, TX 77005   Fax: (713)527-4659
E-mail: keckcenter@bioc.rice.edu
URL: http://www.bioc.rice.edu/keck
Contact: George N. Phillips, Co-Dir.
Desc: Biological research, including chemistry and molecular biology of DNA binding, molecular genetics of inborn errors of metabolism, electron crystallography and tomography of macromolecular assemblies, DNA sequence information and human disease, computational neuroscience, parallel computation and language, high resolution NMR spectroscopy of macromolecular structure and dynamics, computation in molecular genetics, computation in image reconstruction and biofluid mechanics, structure and metabolism of lipoproteins, rapid kinetics of hemeprotein-ligand reactions, structure and function of electron transport proteins, nicotonic synaptic transmission in the central nervous system, X-ray crystallography, molecular dynamics of proteins and nucleic acids, a tomic structures and functions of proteins, artificial intelligence, and design and analysis of algorithms. *Type:* Research center.

Worcester Foundation of Biomedical Research

222 Maple Ave.   Ph: (508)842-8921
Shrewsbury, MA 01545-2795   Fax: (508)842-7762
E-mail: worcesterfoundation@sci.wfbr.edu
URL: http://www.sci.wfbr.edu
Contact: Thoru Pederson, PhD, Assoc. Vice Chancellor.
Desc: Molecular and cellular aspects of growth and development as related to cancer biology, endocrine and reproductive biology, and neurobiology. *Type:* Research center.

Worcester Polytechnic Institute
Biomedical Engineering Department

100 Institute Rd.   Ph: (508)831-5447
Worcester, MA 01609   Fax: (508)831-5541
E-mail: rapeura@wpi.edu
URL: http://www.wpi.edu/academic/depts/biomedeng/
Contact: Dr. Robert Peura, Dir.
Desc: Biomedical engineering, human and animal medicine, biological science, biochemistry, and biotechnology, focusing on improving the practice of medicine and health care, promoting disease prevention, developing new diagnostic and therapeutic modalities, and addressing the economies of biotechnology, pharmaceutical, and medical devices. Specific areas of research include noninvasive diagnosis, biosensors, bioprocess, innovation management, cell and molecular biology, and evaluation of development studies. *Type:* Research center.

Yeshiva University
Analytical Imaging Facility

Albert Einstein Coll. of Med.   Ph: (718)430-3547
Resnick Campus
1300 Morris Park Ave.
Bronx, NY 10461
URL: http://www.ca.aecom.yu.edu

Contact: Dr. John Condeelis, Sci.Dir.
Desc: Analytical imaging for medical studies. *Type:* Research center.

Boating

American Boat Builders & Repairers Association—Bulletin

American Boat Builders & Repairers Association
425 E. 79th St., Apt.1006   Ph: (212)396-4246
New York, NY 10021-1006   Fax: (212)396-4243
E-mail: abbra2@aol.com
Contact: Suzanne B. Sloan, CMM, Editor.
Desc: Covers matters of interest and concern to boatbuilders, boatyards, and marinas. *Type:* Newsletter.

American Canoe Association

7432 Alban Station Rd., Ste. B-232   Ph: (703)451-0141
Springfield, VA 22150   Fax: (703)451-2245
E-mail: acadirect@aol.com
URL: http://www.ACA-Paddler.org
Contact: William T. Spitzer, Pres.
Desc: Dedicated to the sport of canoeing and kayaking and to the preservation of streams and rivers. *Type:* Association.

American Power Boat Association

PO Box 377   Ph: (810)773-9700
17640 E. 9 Mile Rd.   Fax: (810)773-6490
Eastpointe, MI 48021
E-mail: apbahq@aol.com
URL: http://www.apba.org/index.html
Contact: Gloria J. Urbin, Exec.Admin.
Desc: Governing body for the promotion of power boat racing in the United States and national authority for world records as compiled by the Union of International Motorboating. *Type:* Association.

American Sailing Association

13922 Marquesas Way   Ph: (310)822-7171
Marina del Rey, CA 90292   Fax: (310)822-4741
E-mail: info@american0sailing.com
Contact: Leonard Shabes, Exec.Dir.
Desc: Sailing instructors (2500), sailing schools (180), and students (40,000). Objectives are to promote sailing safety and internationally recognized standards for sail education. Provides accreditation to sailing schools and instructors nationwide. *Type:* Association.

American Sailing Association Foundation

American Sailing Association
13922 Marquesas Way   Ph: (310)822-7171
Marina del Rey, CA 90292   Fax: (310)822-4741
E-mail: info@american-sailing.com
URL: http://www.american-sailing.com
Contact: Harry Munns, Pres.
Desc: Sailing enthusiasts. Promotes amateur water sports and fosters sailing education and boating safety. Sponsors Council of Disabled Sailors, a project designed to provide opportunities for handicapped sailors to sail within their physical limitations. *Type:* Association.

Antique and Classic Boat Society

422 James St.   Ph: (315)686-2628
Clayton, NY 13624   Fax: (315)686-2680
E-mail: hqs@acbs.org
URL: http://www.acbs.org
Contact: Debi Florek, Admin.
Desc: Individuals interested in antique and classic boating. Serves as an information clearinghouse and fosters the exchange of information and ideas. Works to establish and monitor protocol as it relates to antique and classic boating. *Type:* Association.

Boat Owners Association of the United States

880 S. Pickett St.   Ph: (703)823-9550
Alexandria, VA 22304   Free: 800-937-9307
   Fax: (703)461-2847
URL: http://www.boatus.com
Contact: Richard Schwartz, Pres.
Desc: Owners or prospective owners of recreational boats. Independent, consumer service organization offering representation, benefits, and programs for boat owners. Services include: legislative and regulatory representation on issues affecting boaters' interests; marine insurance; navigation chart service; boating equipment and accessories; long-term boat financing; boating regulations and forms service; charter and group travel services; sale and chartering exchange; marine surveyor and admiralty lawyer reference service; assistance with individual boating problems and towing reimbursement; association flag. *Type:* Association.

BOAT/U.S. Magazine

Boat Owners Association of the United States
880 S. Pickett St.   Ph: (703)823-9550
Alexandria, VA 22304   Fax: (703)461-2855
Contact: Michael Sciulla, Editor.
Desc: Consumer publication covering legislative, regulatory, and consumer issues of interest to recreational boat owners. *Type:* Periodical.

Boating Magazine

Hachette Filipacchi Magazines, Inc.
1633 Broadway, 41st Fl.   Ph: (212)767-6000
New York, NY 10019   Fax: (212)989-4561
E-mail: btngmag@aol.com.
Contact: Richard Amann, Vice President/Publisher, (212)767-5571, fax: (212)767-5618; Jonathan Stone, Advertising Dir., (212)767-5577, fax: (212)767-5618.
Desc: Magazine reporting on boat tests, new gear, electronics, and sport fishing for pleasure power boaters. *Type:* Periodical.

Boating World

Trans World Publishing, Inc.
2100 Powers Ferry Rd.   Ph: (770)955-5656
Atlanta, GA 30339   Free: 800-827-0818
   Fax: (770)952-0669
Contact: Joe Skorupa, Editor; Douglas Billian, Publisher; Jay Perkins, Publisher.
Desc: Magazine directed to active-lifestyle boaters in the up-to-35 ft. powerboat market. Provides articles and features on all aspects of the boating industry for the novice to the experienced boater. *Type:* Periodical.

Cruising World Magazine

Cruising World Publications, Inc.
5520 Park Ave.   Ph: (203)373-2102
Trumbull, CT 06611-0395
Contact: Bernadette Bernon, Editor; Gordon Medenica, Pres./Publisher; Sally Helme, Marine Ad. Sales Dir., (401)847-1588, fax: (401)848-5048.
Desc: Boating magazine for those who enjoy cruising under sail. *Type:* Periodical.

Inland Lake Yachting Association

PO Box 311   Ph: (414)275-6921
Fontana, WI 53125   Fax: (414)275-6921
E-mail: scowslants@aol.com
URL: http://www.ilya.org
Contact: James A. Smith, Exec.Sec.
Desc: Sailing enthusiasts. Sponsors regattas; approves class specifications. Provides sailing instruction. *Type:* Association.

Inter/Port

National Marine Manufacturers Association
200 E. Randolph St., No. 5100   Ph: (312)946-6262
Chicago, IL 60601-6528   Fax: (312)946-0401
Contact: Nancy Fehr, Editor.
Desc: Provides information on boating legislation, market research, marine engineering, and other subjects of significance to pleasure-boating equipment manufacturers. Recurring features include financial news of industry firms, items on personnel. *Type:* Newsletter.

Inter-Lake Yachting Association

7758 Lucerne Dr., Apt. 25
Cleveland, OH 44130-8509
Contact: J.E. Crain, Exec.Sec.
Desc: Yacht and boat clubs in Michigan, Pennsylvania, Indiana, New York, Ohio, and Ontario, Canada. *Type:* Association.

International Hobie Class Association

4935 N Calle Esquina   Ph: (520)299-0609
Tucson, AZ 85718   Fax: (520)577-8486
E-mail: ihca@aol.com
URL: http://www.sailing.org/hobie
Contact: Ron Palmer, Ex.Dir.
Desc: Groups of Hobie One-Design Class sailboat owners who sail together in fleets. Promotes sailing and racing of Hobie Cat sailboats. *Type:* Association.

International Lightning Class Association

PO Box 658   Ph: (614)885-0475
Worthington, OH 43085   Fax: (614)885-4219
E-mail: ilcahq@netset.com
URL: http://www.sailing.org/lightning/
Contact: Karen Johnson, Exec.Sec.
Desc: Owners and crew of Lightning Class sailing yachts. Promotes Lightning Class yacht racing without geographical limitation, under uniform rules, and between boats of identical design. *Type:* Association.

Motor Boating & Sailing

Hearst Magazines
959 8th Ave.   Ph: (212)649-2000
New York, NY 10019-5905
Contact: Peter A. Janssen, Editor and Publisher, (212)649-4099, fax: (212)489-9258; Mark Magnani, Advertising Mgr., (212)649-4092, fax: (212)489-9258.
Desc: Magazine focusing on boats, engines, and accessories. *Alt. Contact:* 250 W. 55th St., 4th Fl., New York, NY 10019; telephone: (212)649-4112; fax: (212)489-9258. *Type:* Periodical.

National Marine Representatives Association Newsletter

National Marine Representatives Association
PO Box 360   Ph: (847)662-3167
Gurnee, IL 60031   Fax: (847)336-7126
Contact: David McCloskey, Editor.
Desc: Covers Association business, membership activities, and regional news. *Type:* Newsletter.

NMMA Boat Show News

National Marine Manufacturers Association (NMMA)
600 3rd Ave., 23 Fl.   Ph: (212)922-1212
New York, NY 10016   Fax: (212)922-9607
Contact: Henry Brehm, Editor.
Desc: Reviews boat shows. Reports industry trends. *Type:* Newsletter.

Power and Motoryacht

Primedia
249 West 17th St.   Ph: (212)462-3600
New York, NY 10011   Fax: (212)367-8330
URL: http://www.yachtworld.com.
Contact: Richard Thiel, Editor; John Bean, Publisher.
Desc: Magazine for owners of large powerboats. *Type:* Periodical.

Sailboat Buyers Guide

Primedia, Inc.
84 State St., Ste. 9C   Ph: (617)720-8600
Boston, MA 02109   Fax: (617)723-0911
E-mail: sail@channel1.com
URL: http://.www.sailbuyersguide.com.
Contact: Sarah Day, Manager.
Desc: Over 2,000 sailboat and equipment manufacturers. *Type:* Directory.

San Juan 21 Class Association

211 Gloria   Ph: (919)355-6974
Greenville, NC 27858
Contact: Ken Gurganus, Sec.-Treas.
Desc: Owners and skippers of San Juan 21 sailing sloops. Promotes San Juan 21 sailing and one-design racing. Sponsors national, regional, and local regattas and cruising activities. *Type:* Association.

Seaworthy

Boat Owners Association of the United States
880 S. Pickett St.   Ph: (703)823-9550
Alexandria, VA 22304   Fax: (703)461-2855
E-mail: seaworthy@boatus.com.
URL: http://www.boatus.com.
Contact: Robert Adriance, Jr., Editor, badriance@boatus.com.
Desc: Seeks to help boaters avoid accidents. Studies actual claims and suggests how they could have been avoided. *Type:* Newsletter.

Trailer Boats Magazine

Poole Publications, Inc.
20700 Belshaw Ave.   Ph: (310)537-6322
PO Box 5427   Fax: (310)537-8735
Carson, CA 90749-5427
E-mail: tbmeditors@aol.com.
Contact: Ralph Poole, President; Wiley Poole, Publisher.
Desc: Magazine for owners and prospective buyers of trailerable boats under 30 feet. *Type:* Periodical.

United States Power Squadrons

1504 Blue Ridge Rd.   Ph: (919)821-0281
PO Box 30423   Free: 888-367-8777
Raleigh, NC 27607   Fax: (919)836-0813
E-mail: uspsquadrons@mindspring.com
URL: http://www.usps.org
Contact: Art Farr, Chief Commander.
Desc: Pleasure boat owners and others interested in studying navigation and acquiring boating skills. Offers free instruction in safe boating to the public; conducts courses for members in seamanship, advanced piloting, celestial navigation, marine electronics, engine maintenance, sailing, cruise planning, and meteorology. *Type:* Association.

U.S. Sailing Association

PO Box 1260   Ph: (401)849-5200
Portsmouth, RI 02871-0924   Free: 800-US-SAIL1
    Fax: (401)849-5208
Contact: Terry Harper, Exec.Dir.
Desc: Coordinating and governing body of sailboat racing in U.S. Membership includes yacht clubs, associations, and individuals. Sponsors 23 US Sailing championships. *Type:* Association.

WoodenBoat

WoodenBoat Publications, Inc.
Naskeag Rd.   Ph: (207)359-4651
PO Box 78   Free: 800-273-SHIP
Brooklin, ME 04616   Fax: (207)359-8920
E-mail: wbstore@woodenboat.
URL: http://www.woodenboat.com
Contact: Matthew Murphy, Editor; Carl Cramer, Publisher.
Desc: Magazine covering the design, building, care, preservation, and use of wooden boats, including commercial and pleasure, old and new, sail and power. *Type:* Periodical.

Yachting Club of America

Box 1040   Ph: (941)642-4448
Marco Island, FL 34146   Fax: (941)642-5284
URL: http://www.ycaol.com
Contact: David J. Martindell, Pres.
Desc: Yachtsmen. Seeks to advance yachting, its facilities, and the relationship between yachting organizations through a viable fraternity of yachtsmen. *Type:* Association.

Yachting Magazine

Times Mirror Magazines, Inc.
2 Park Ave.   Ph: (212)779-5000
New York, NY 10016-5601   Fax: (212)779-5522
E-mail: editor@yachtingnet.com.
URL: http://www.yachtingnet.com.
Contact: Charles Barthold, Editor-in-Chief, cbarthold@yachtingnet.com; Peter Bechenbach, Publisher, (212)779-5085, fax: (212)725-1035, pbechenbach@yachtingnet.com.
Desc: Yachting magazine for affluent, experienced sail and power yachtsmen. *Alt. Contact:* 20 E. Elm St., Greenwich, CT 06830; telephone: (203)625-4480; fax: (203)625-4481. *Type:* Periodical.

Books

The Abbey Newsletter

Abbey Publications, Inc.
7105 Geneva Dr.   Ph: (512)929-3992
Austin, TX 78723-1510   Fax: (512)929-3995
E-mail: abbeypub@flash.net
URL: http://www.palimpsest.stanford.edu/byorg/abbey/; http://www.palimpsest.stanford.edu/byorg/abbey.
Contact: Ellen R. McCrady, Editor.
Desc: Encourages the development of library and archival conservation, particularly technical advances and cross-disciplinary research in the field. Covers book repair and the conservation of books, papers, photographs, and non-paper materials. *Type:* Newsletter.

American Book Trade Directory

R. R. Bowker
A Unit of Cahners Business Information
121 Chanlon Rd.   Ph: (908)464-6800
New Providence, NJ 07974   Free: 888-269-5372
    Fax: (908)771-7704
E-mail: info@bowker.com
Contact: Karen Hallard, Managing Editor.
Desc: More than 30,350 bookstores and other book outlets in the United States and Canada; 1,500 United States and Canadian book wholesalers and paperback distributors. Also included are sections of auctioneers of literary property, exporters/importers, booktrade associations, foreign language book dealers, book and literary appraisers, and rental library chains. *Type:* Directory.

The APHA Newsletter

American Printing History Association
PO Box 4922, Grand Central   Ph: (212)930-9220
Sta.   Fax: (212)302-4815
New York, NY 10163
Contact: Lissa Dodington, Editor.
Desc: Contains a two-page essay on some aspect of printing history and brief news items concerning the history of printing, the book arts, letterpress printing, papermaking, and related subjects. Covers the activities of the Association and small presses utilizing traditional printing techniques. *Type:* Newsletter.

Bern Porter International

Unique Publishing Co.
18 Benner Rd.   Ph: (610)948-5343
Royersford, PA 19468
Contact: Sheila Holtz, Editor; Natasha Bernstein, Editor.
Desc: Covers the literary scence, including plays and critical essays of international interest. Recurring features include book reviews. *Type:* Newsletter.

Binders Bulletin

Binding Industries of America
70 E. Lake St.   Ph: 312)372-7606
Chicago, IL 60601   Fax: (312)704-5025
Contact: James R. Niesen, Editor.
Desc: Contains management tips and industry news for this association of trade binders and loose leaf manufacturers. Recurring features include a calendar of events, news of members, and listings of equipment wanted or for sale. *Type:* Newsletter.

Binders' Guild Newsletter

Binders' Guild
154 Wedgewood Cir.   Ph: (732)544-8319
Eatontown, NJ 07724
Contact: Susan Lunas, Editor, slunas@iname.com.
Desc: Focuses on hand bookbinding. Conveys news of the craft and of persons prominent in the field; describes techniques; and reprints relevant pieces from other publications. *Type:* Newsletter.

Book Marketing and Publicity

Infocom Group
5900 Hollis St., Ste. R2   Ph: (510)596-9300
Emeryville, CA 94608   Free: 800-959-1059
                            Fax: (510)596-9331
Contact: Aimee Grove, Editorial Dir.; Judy Hirni, Editor.
Desc: Provides information on strategies and techniques that may increase book sales. *Type:* Newsletter.

Book Promotion Hotline

Ad-Lib Publications
51 1/2 W. Adams   Ph: (515)472-6617
Fairfield, IA 52556   Free: 800-669-0773
                            Fax: (515)472-3186
E-mail: adlib100@aol.com
Contact: Marie Kiefer, Editor.
Desc: Lists 75 to 100 media and book marketing contacts per issue. Verifies the information the same week the newsletter is published. *Type:* Newsletter.

Book Review Digest

H.W. Wilson Company
950 University Ave.   Ph: (718)588-8400
Bronx, NY 10452
E-mail: custserv@hwwilson.com
URL: http://www.hwwilson.com
Contact: Technical Support Department., techmail@info. hwwilson.com.
Desc: Contains citations, each with excerpts of reviews, to current reviews of English-language books. Covers popu-

lar and scholarly works of fiction and non-fiction, as well as juvenile literature. *Available:* CompuServe Information Service; OCLC Online Computer Library Center, Inc., OCLC EPIC; OCLC Online Computer Library Center, Inc., OCLC FirstSearch Catalog; SilverPlatter Information, Inc.; The Dialog Corporation, DIALOG; Bell & Howell Information and Learning; H.W. Wilson Company, WilsonWeb. *Type:* Database.

Book Review Index

The Gale Group
27500 Drake Rd.   Ph: (248)699-4253
Farmington Hills, MI 48331-
3535
URL: http://www.galegroup.com
Contact: Customer Service. Toll-free: 800-877-GALE.
Desc: Contains citations to reviews of books, books-on-tape, and new periodicals appearing in some 600 periodicals, journals, and book review publications, representing a wide range of popular, academic, and professional interests. Coverage is oriented toward the humanities and social sciences, including literature, fine arts, history, education, and library science. *Available:* The Dialog Corporation, DIALOG. *Type:* Database.

Book Reviews Data Base

Cineman Syndicate
PO Box 4433   Ph: (914)692-4572
Middletown, NY 10941-4433
E-mail: MCI Mail: 213-9111
URL: http://www.minireviews.com
Contact: Jay A. Brown, Publisher., (914)692-8311, fax: (914)692-8311.
Desc: Provides brief critiques of new and forthcoming fiction and nonfiction books. Includes the Wall Street Journal top ten bestseller lists for fiction and nonfiction hardcover and trade and mass market paperbacks. *Available:* Bloomberg Financial Markets; Dow Jones Interactive Publishing. *Type:* Database.

Book Talk

New Mexico Book League
8632 Horacio Pl. NE   Ph: (505)299-8940
Albuquerque, NM 87111   Fax: (505)294-8032
Contact: Carol A. Myers, Editor.
Desc: Contains articles on the book field in the southwestern United States. Recurring features include book reviews on Southwestern titles and interviews. *Type:* Newsletter.

Bookman's Price Index

Gale Group Inc.
27500 Drake Rd.   Ph: (248)699-4253
Farmington Hills, MI 48331- Free: 800-877-GALE
3535   Fax: (248)699-8070
E-mail: galeord@galegroup.com
URL: http://www.galegroup.com.
Contact: Anne F. McGrath, Editor.
Desc: Rare and collectible books offered for sale by nearly 150 bookdealers in the United States, Canada, and the United Kingdom. *Type:* Directory.

Books in Print Online

R.R. Bowker
121 Chanlon Rd.   Ph: (908)464-6800
New Providence, NJ 07974
URL: http://www.bowker.com
Contact: Yvette Berthel, Tape/Online, (908)665-2854, fax: (908)771-7756, yvette.berthel@bowker.com.
Desc: Contains bibliographic descriptions and ordering information for more than 1.9 million books currently in print or declared out of print (from July 1979 to date), and soon-to-be-published titles from some 50,000 pub-

lishers. *Available:* Ovid Technologies, Inc.; The Dialog Corporation, DIALOG; Ameritech Library Services, Vista; OCLC Online Computer Library Center, Inc., OCLC EPIC; OCLC Online Computer Library Center, Inc., OCLC FirstSearch Catalog; LEXIS-NEXIS, NEXIS; EBSCO Publishing; The Gale Group, InfoTrac Web; SilverPlatter Information, Inc. *Type:* Database.

Bookseller

Bookseller
14026 N. Ridgelawn Rd.   Ph: (217)382-4502
Martinsville, IL 62442   Fax: (217)382-4502
E-mail: bookdc@ccipost.net
Contact: Dwight Connelly, Editor.
Desc: Contains editorials of interest to the out-of-print book trade. Provides a search service for books with listings of books wanted and books for sale. *Type:* Newsletter.

Bookselling This Week

American Booksellers Association (ABA)
828 S. Broadway   Ph: (914)591-2665
Tarrytown, NY 10591   Free: 800-637-0037
                            Fax: (914)631-8391
E-mail: info@bookweb.org; editorial@bookweb.org.
Contact: Dan Cullen, Editor, dcullen@bookweb.org; Robert Keymer, Assoc. Publisher, rkeymer@bookweb.org.
Desc: Contains information on book selling. *Type:* Newsletter.

Children's Book News

Canadian Children's Book Centre
35 Spadina Rd.   Ph: (416)975-0010
Toronto, ON, Canada M5R   Fax: (416)975-1839
2S9
E-mail: ccbc@lglobal.com
Contact: Gillian O'Reilly, Editor.
Desc: Contains news, reviews, and information on Canadian children's literature. Recurring features include letters to the editor, interviews, a calendar of events, reports of meetings, notices of publications available, and ideas for book related activities for kids. *Type:* Newsletter.

Computer Book Review

Computer Book Review
PO Box 61067
Honolulu, HI 96839
URL: http://www.bookwire.com/cbr/
Contact: cbr@bookwire.com.
Desc: This site contains reviews of computer publications. The site is divided into several reviewing categories which include Apple, Business Software, DBMS, General, General Software, Graphics & DTP, Hardware, Internet, Multimedia, Networking, Programming, Technology Management, Unix, Windows, and World Wide Web. *Type:* Database.

Cumulative Book Index

H.W. Wilson Company
950 University Ave.   Ph: (718)588-8400
Bronx, NY 10452
E-mail: custserv@hwwilson.com
URL: http://www.hwwilson.com
Contact: Technical Support Department., techmail@info. hwwilson.com.
Desc: Contains more than 750,000 citations to English-language books published worldwide. Also covers books that are partially in English, including dictionaries, phrase books, and other aids to language learning. *Available:* Bell & Howell Information and Learning; Ovid Technologies, Inc.; OCLC Online Computer Library Center, Inc., OCLC EPIC; OCLC Online Computer Library Center, Inc., OCLC FirstSearch Catalog; SilverPlatter Information, Inc.; The Dialog Corporation, DIALOG; H.W. Wilson Company, WilsonWeb. *Type:* Database.

Great Books Foundation

35 E. Wacker Dr., Ste. 2300   Ph: (312)332-5870
Chicago, IL 60601-2298   Free: 800-222-5870
                                Fax: (312)407-0334
E-mail: agb@gbf.mhs.compuserve.com
URL: http://www.greatbooks.org
Contact: Alice Owen Letvin, Pres.
Desc: Provides people of all ages with the opportunity to read, discuss, and learn from outstanding works of literature. Publishes the Junior Great Books Curriculum, a daily program of interpretive reading, writing, and discussion with the goal of bringing higher literacy within reach of all students, K-12. The curriculum includes the Junior Great Books Read-Aloud program for grades K-1, Junior Great Books for grades 2-9, and Introduction to Great Books for grades 10-12. *Type:* Association.

Guild of Book Workers—Membership List

Guild of Book Workers, Inc.
521 5th Ave.   Ph: (212)292-4444
New York, NY 10175
Contact: Bernadette Callery, Editor.
Desc: About 800 amateur and professional workers in the hand book crafts of bookbinding, calligraphy, illuminating, and decorative papermaking. *Type:* Directory.

Guild of Book Workers Newsletter

Guild of Book Workers, Inc.
521 5th Ave.   Ph: (212)292-4444
New York, NY 10175
Contact: Margaret Johnson, Editor.
Desc: Covers issues in book arts, binding, book conservation, calligraphy, and printing. Recurring features include letters to the editor, interviews, news of research, a calendar of events, reports of meetings, news of educational opportunities, job listings, book reviews, and notices of publications available. *Type:* Newsletter.

Heartland Critiques

Julie Meisinger
125 E. Linden   Ph: (816)252-6656
Independence, MO 64050-4407
Contact: Julie Meisinger, Editor.
Desc: Critiques romance novels, including historicals, contemporaries, and series. Furnishes book rankings and offers cover quotes. *Type:* Newsletter.

Inner Journeys

Gateways Books and Tapes
PO Box 370   Ph: (530)272-0180
Nevada City, CA 95959   Free: 800-869-0658
                                Fax: (530)272-0184
E-mail: gateways@oro.net; brdotwn@oro.net; ij@gatewaysbooksandtapes.com.
URL: http://www.gatewaysbooksandtapes.com; http://www.gatewaysbooksandtapes.com/innerjourneys.
Contact: Iven Lourie, Editor, ilourieassistantoro.net.
Desc: Specializes in small press publications on consciousness, metaphysics, psychology, health, science fiction, and fine art. Recurring features include book reviews and notices of publications available. *Type:* Newsletter.

Kirkus Reviews

Kirkus Associates, LP
200 Park Ave. S.   Ph: (212)777-4554
New York, NY 10003   Fax: (212)979-1352
Contact: Anne Larsen, Executive Editor, larsenx13@aol.com.
Desc: Publishes book reviews on current titles of both fiction and nonfiction for adults and children. Also provides author, publisher, price, and page count. *Type:* Newsletter.

Magazine and Bookseller

North American Publishing Co.
401 N. Broad St.   Ph: (215)238-5300
Philadelphia, PA 19108   Free: 800-777-8074
                                Fax: (215)238-5270
URL: http://www.napco.com
Contact: Patricia H. McCarthy, Editor; Michael Tierno, Publisher.
Desc: Merchandising and marketing magazine for retailers and wholesalers of paperback books, magazines, comic books, and trading cards. Serves the single copy (newsstand) market. *Alt. Contact:* 322 8th, 3rd Fl., New York, NY 10001; telephone: (212)620-7330; fax: (212)620-7335. *Type:* Periodical.

Mail Order Book Sellers Newsletter

Mitchell Enterprises
7019 Linden St.   Ph: (713)923-6765
Houston, TX 77087   Fax: (713)923-1655
E-mail: mitchell-ent@juno.com
Contact: Billy Mitchell, Editor, mitchell-ent@juno.com.
Desc: Informs on "how to sit back and rake in a bundle selling books by mail." Offers and tips and advice from printing to marketing. Features information on books, reports, software, and Dropship/wholesale. *Type:* Newsletter.

MCBA Newsletter

Minnesota Center for Book Arts (MCBA)
24 N. 3rd St.   Ph: (612)338-3634
Minneapolis, MN 55401   Fax: (612)338-1562
E-mail: mcba@mnbookarts.org
Contact: Ruth Wikoff-Jones, Editor.
Desc: Focuses on the field of book arts, including letterpress printing, bookbinding, and papermaking. Reviews current and future Center exhibitions and announces classes available at the Center. *Type:* Newsletter.

NOBS Newsletter

Northern Ohio Bibliophilic Society (NOBS)
5887 Roc Marie Ave.   Ph: (330)678-0371
Kent, OH 44240
Contact: Dean Keller, Editor.
Desc: Devoted to the recognition, dissemination and preservation of fine and antiquarian books. *Type:* Newsletter.

The Reader's Review

The Book Sellers Network
2966 Diamond St.   Ph: (415)585-2639
San Francisco, CA 94131   Fax: (415)337-2064
Contact: Peter Phillips, Review Editor.
Desc: Provides marketing analysis of new titles for booksellers and librarians, suggesting which title are sellable and have abiding value. Places an emphasis on arts and crafts, nonfiction and literary fiction for adults and children, religion, philosophy, metaphysics, and cultural studies. *Type:* Newsletter.

Steve Brock Book Reviews on the Internet

2323 Mapleton   Ph: (303)786-7375
Boulder, CO 80304
E-mail: sbrock@ucsub.colorado.edu.
URL: http://ucsub.colorado.edu-brock.
Contact: Steve Brock, Book Reviewer.
Alt. Contact: 2323 Mapleton, Boulder, CO 80304; telephone: (303)786-7375. *Type:* Periodical.

The Usual Suspects/Mystery Fiction Lineup

Box 3308 Merchandise Mart   Ph: (847)559-8108
Chicago, IL 60654-0308   Fax: (847)559-8158
Desc: Distributes author interviews and book reviews. *Alt. Contact:* Box 3308 Merchandise Mart, Chicago, IL 60654-0308; telephone: (847)559-8108; fax: (847)559-8158. *Type:* Periodical.

Botany

American Botanical Council

PO Box 144345   Ph: (512)926-4900
Austin, TX 78723   Free: 800-373-7105
                                Fax: (512)926-2345
E-mail: abc@herbalgram.org
URL: http://www.herbalgram.org
Contact: Mark Blumenthal, Exec.Dir.
Desc: Seeks to gather and disseminate information on herbs, medicinal plants, and herbal research; increase public awareness and professional knowledge of the historical role and current potential of plants in medicine; promote understanding regarding the importance of preserving native plant populations in temperate and tropical zones. Conducts educational and public outreach programs. Operates speakers' bureau. *Type:* Association.

American Orchid Society

6000 S. Olive Ave.   Ph: (561)585-8666
West Palm Beach, FL 33405   Fax: (561)585-0654
E-mail: theaos@compuserve.com
URL: http://www.orchidweb.org
Contact: Lee S. Cooke, Exec.Dir.
Desc: Professional growers, botanists, hobbyists, and others interested in extending the knowledge, production, use, and appreciation of orchids. Conducts competitions. Operates speakers' bureau. *Type:* Association.

American Phytopathological Society

3340 Pilot Knob Rd.   Ph: (651)454-7250
St. Paul, MN 55121-2097   Fax: (651)454-0766
E-mail: aps@scisoc.org
URL: http://www.scisoc.org
Contact: Steven C. Nelson, Exec.VP.
Desc: Professional educators, researchers, and others interested in the study and control of plant diseases. Maintains 46 committees. *Type:* Association.

American Society of Plant Physiologists

15501 Monona Dr.   Ph: (301)251-0560
Rockville, MD 20855-2768   Fax: (301)279-2996
E-mail: aspp@aspp.org
URL: http://www.aspp.org
Contact: John Lisack, Jr., Exec.Dir.
Desc: Professional society of plant physiologists, plant biochemists, and other plant scientists engaged in research and teaching. *Type:* Association.

Arboretum Leaves

Holden Arboretum
9500 Sperry Rd.   Ph: (440)946-4400
Kirtland, OH 44094-5172   Fax: (440)256-1655
E-mail: holden@pop.holdenarb.org
Contact: Florence Mustric, Editor, (216)321-1393.
Desc: Covers Arboretum events and people and topics in horticulture, botany, and natural history. Recurring features include a calendar of events and book reviews. *Type:* Newsletter.

Clippings

Atlanta Botanical Garden
Box 77246   Ph: (404)876-5859
Atlanta, GA 30357   Fax: (404)876-7472
Contact: Julie Herron, Editor; Geri Lzufer, Managing Editor.
Desc: Contains gardening tips, updates on plant conservation, the status of plant collections, and coverage of Garden events. Recurring features include a calendar of events, news of educational opportunities, and columns titled Director's Report, Garden Troubleshooter, Garden Update, Fuqua Conservatory Update, Plant of the Moment, and Hotline Help. *Type:* Newsletter.

Connecticut Greenhouse Newsletter
Cooperative Extension System
College of Agriculture and Natural Resources
University of Connecticut
1376 Storrs Rd., U-67   Ph: (860)486-0627
Storrs Mansfield, CT 06269-   Fax: (860)486-0682
   4067
E-mail: store@canr1.ca5.ulonn.edu
Contact: Richard J. McAvoy, Editor, rmacavoy@canr1.
cag.uconn.edu.
Desc: Deals with the culture of greenhouse crops and plant
care, with brief articles by experts in the field. Also features
articles on marketing of horticultural crops and green-
house engineering. *Type:* Newsletter.

CSPP/SCPV Bulletin
Canadian Society of Plant Physiologists (CSPP)
Institut de Recherche Enbiologie   Ph: (514)872-8491
   Vegetale   Fax: (514)872-9406
Universite de Montreal
Montreal, PQ, Canada H1X
   2B2
Contact: Dr. H.S. Saini, Editor, SainiH@ere.UMontreal.
Ca.
Desc: Contains information, news, and job advertisements
of interest to plant physiologists in Canada. Remarks:
Publisher also known as La Societe Canadienne de Phy-
siologie Vegetale (SCPV). *Type:* Newsletter.

Desert Botanical Garden
1201 N. Galvin Pky.   Ph: (602)941-1225
Phoenix, AZ 85008   Fax: (602)754-8124
URL: http://www.dbg.org
Contact: Carolyn O'Malley, Exec.Dir.
Desc: Museum dedicated to the study, propagation, and
display of the flora of arid lands. *Type:* Association.

Epiphyllum Society of America—Bulletin
Epiphyllum Society of America
PO Box 1395   Ph: (310)670-8148
Monrovia, CA 91017
Contact: Raymon Eden, Editor.
Desc: Reflects the aims of the Society, which are to collect,
study and grow the Epiphyllums—the true species, the hy-
brids, and the closely related species of cacti; to provide
the opportunity and place to exhibit plants, flowers, and
arrangements; and to promote interest in these plants
among other persons. Recurring features include correspondence from readers and announcements of meetings,
shows, plant sales, and garden tours. *Type:* Newsletter.

Flora of North America Newsletter
Flora of North America Association (FNA)
Missouri Botanical Garden
PO Box 299   Ph: (314)577-9515
St. Louis, MO 63166   Fax: (314)577-9558
URL: http://www.mobot.org; http://www.fna.org.
Contact: Nancy R. Morin, Editor; Judith M. Unger, Edi-
tor, unger@fna.org.
Desc: Communicates news of FNA projects and other top-
ics of interest to floristic researchers. Recurring features in-
clude news of research, reports of meetings, job listings,
and notices of publications available. *Type:* Newsletter.

The Garden Newsletter
Friends of the State Botanical Garden of
Georgia, Inc.
University of Georgia   Ph: (706)542-1244
2450 S. Milledge Ave.   Fax: (706)542-3091
Athens, GA 30605-1624
E-mail: cherokee@negia.net
Contact: Misty Herrin, Editor.
Desc: Publicizes events, exhibitions, programs, and re-
search occurring at the Garden and its Visitor Center/
Conservatory Complex. Contains news of the Friends and
University staff involved with the Botanical Garden. *Type:*
Newsletter.

Gesneriad Research Foundation
1873 Oak St.
Sarasota, FL 34236
Contact: Dr. Hans Wiehler, Res.Dir.
Desc: Individuals and groups interested in the welfare and
preservation of the plant family Gesneriaceae, which includes gloxinias, saintpaulia, and columneas. Conducts
biosystematic research. Sponsors graduate student projects
and expeditions to tropical rain forests. *Type:* Association.

Herbarium News
Missouri Botanical Garden
PO Box 299   Ph: (314)577-5123
St. Louis, MO 63166   Fax: (314)577-9598
Contact: James C. Solomon, Editor.
Desc: Covers current events in the institutional and univer-
sity herbarium community. Recurring features include
news from institutions, listings of publications, resources
and positions available, news of research, book reviews,
and announcements of events. *Type:* Newsletter.

Herbarium Pacificum News
Bishop Museum Press
1525 Bernice St.   Ph: (808)847-3511
Honolulu, HI 96817-2704   Fax: (808)847-8252
E-mail: museum@bishopmuseum.org
Desc: Provides users and other botanical institutions with
news of the activities and events of the Herbarium Pacificum. Follows the activites of staff members in the department. *Type:* Newsletter.

Lady Bird Johnson Wildflower Center
4801 La Crosse Ave.   Ph: (512)292-4200
Austin, TX 78739   Fax: (512)292-4627
E-mail: wildflower@wildflower.org
URL: http://www.wildflower.org
Contact: Dr. Robert Breunig, Exec.Dir.
Desc: Educates the public about the enviornmental neces-
sity, economic value, and natural beauty of native plants.
Type: Association.

Nematological Abstracts
CAB International
CABI Publishing
10 E. 40th St., Ste. 3203   Ph: (212)481-7018
New York, NY 10016
E-mail: cabi-nao@cabi.org
URL: http://www.cabi.org
Desc: Contains citations, with abstracts, to current periodi-
cal and other published literature relating to plant nema-
tology and allied topics. Corresponds to Nematological
Abstracts and in part to the online CAB ABSTRACTS
and CAB PLANT PROTECTION databases and the
CAB ABSTRACTS on CD-ROM and CABPESTCD
products. *Type:* Database.

Norfolk Botanical Garden Society Newsletter
Norfolk Botanical Garden
Azalea Garden Rd.   Ph: (757)441-5830
Norfolk, VA 23518   Fax: (757)853-8294
Contact: Jill Doczi, Editor.
Desc: Offers current information from the Society's Horticulture, Education, Development, Membership, and Marketing Departments. Features collections information,
general horticultural information, an education program
calendar, a Garden events calendar, a children's educational activity page, tips for gardeners, promotionals from the
Garden Gift Shop, and membership and development information. *Type:* Newsletter.

North Carolina Botanical Garden Newsletter
Botanical Garden Foundation
Totten Center, CB 3375   Ph: (919)962-0522
The University of North   Fax: (919)962-3531
   Carolina at Chapel Hill
Chapel Hill, NC 27599-3375
URL: http://www.unc.edu/depts/ncbg.
Contact: Sandra Brooks-Mathers, Editor, bksmthrs@
email.unc.edu.
Desc: Reports North Carolina Botanical Garden activities
and events and updates readers on Master Plan progress.
Features articles on native plant cultivation, propagation
and conservation. *Type:* Newsletter.

Plant Breeding Abstracts
CAB International
CABI Publishing
10 E. 40th St., Ste. 3203   Ph: (212)481-7018
New York, NY 10016
E-mail: cabi-nao@cabi.org
URL: http://www.cabi.org
Desc: Contains citations, with abstracts, to current periodi-
cal and other published literature relating to crop breeding
and genetics. Corresponds to Plant Breeding Abstracts and
in part to the online CAB ABSTRACTS database and the
CAB ABSTRACTS on CD-ROM product. *Type:* Data-
base.

Queens Botanical Garden News
Queens Botanical Garden Society, Inc.
43-50 Main St.   Ph: (718)886-3800
Flushing, NY 11355   Fax: (718)463-0263
Contact: Betty Scott, Education/Public Programs Coord.
Desc: Contains gardening information and news of Society
events. Recurring features include a calendar of events,
news of educational opportunities, and lists of volunteer
positions available. *Type:* Newsletter.

The Sonoran Quarterly
Desert Botanical Garden
1201 N. Galvin Pkwy.   Ph: (602)941-1225
Phoenix, AZ 85008   Fax: (602)754-8124
URL: http://www.dbg.org
Desc: Contains brief articles on desert plants and animals
and reports on the research programs and other activities
of the Garden, including book reviews and information
on the Garden's botanical collection, and library collections. *Type:* Newsletter.

Virginia Native Plant Society Bulletin
Virginia Native Plant Society
Box 844
Annandale, VA 22003
Contact: Nancy Sorrells, Editor, (540)377-6390, fax:
(540)332-9989, nsorrell@leo.vala.edu.
Desc: Examines the native plants of Virginia and provides
information on botany. *Type:* Newsletter.

Bowling

American Bowling Congress
5301 S. 76th St.   Ph: (414)421-9000
Bowling Headquarters   Fax: (414)421-1194
Greendale, WI 53129-1127
URL: http://www.bowl.org
Contact: Roger Dalkin, Exec.Dir.
Desc: Includes organized tenpin bowlers in the United
States, Puerto Rico, Canada, and U.S. military installa-
tions worldwide. Sponsors a variety of annual tournament
competition and annual writing contest which formally
recognizes outstanding bowling journalism. *Type:* Associa-
tion.

Bowling Digest

Century Publishing Co.
990 Grove St.
Evanston, IL 60201-4370   Ph: (847)491-6440
    Fax: (847)491-0459
E-mail: century@wwa.com
Contact: Norman Jacobs, Publisher; Dale Jacobs, Director; James O'Connor, Managing Editor.
Desc: Magazine featuring tips and information for bowlers and fans. *Type:* Periodical.

Bowling Magazine

American Bowling Congress
5301 S. 76th St.   Ph: (414)423-3232
Greendale, WI 53129   Fax: (414)421-7977
Contact: Bill Vint, Editor, bvint@execpc.com; John Dill, Advertising Mgr., (612)856-2465, fax: (612)856-3479.
Desc: Magazine covering bowling news. *Alt. Contact:* telephone: (414)641-2003; fax: (414)641-2005. *Type:* Periodical.

Ladies Professional Bowlers Tour

7171 Cherryvale Blvd.   Ph: (815)332-5756
Rockford, IL 61112   Fax: (815)332-9636
Contact: John F. Falzone, Pres.
Desc: Professional women bowlers. *Type:* Association.

Michigan State Bowling Association

4853 W. M-61 Hwy.   Ph: (517)426-8403
Gladwin, MI 48624   Fax: (517)426-1896
Contact: Frank Peters, Exec.Dir.
Desc: Bowlers and bowling organizations. Conducts state championship bowling tournament. *Type:* Association.

Michigan Women's Bowling Association

PO Box 1705   Ph: (517)631-7260
Midland, MI 48641-1705   Fax: (517)631-8087
Contact: Shirley Thomas, Exec.Sec.
Desc: Women bowlers and women's bowling organizations. Conducts state bowling tournament. *Type:* Association.

National Bowling Association

377 Park Ave. S., 7th Fl.   Ph: (212)689-8308
New York, NY 10016   Fax: (212)725-5063
Contact: Margaret S. Lee, Exec.Sec.-Treas.
Desc: Seeks to: foster good sportsmanship, fellowship, and friendship; increase the interests, talents, and skills of adult and youth bowlers; create national awareness and interest in civic and community programs. Participates in and promotes bowling tournaments and other activities. Sponsors fundraising programs for sickle cell anemia and the United Negro College Fund. *Type:* Association.

National Duckpin Bowling Congress

4991 Fairview Ave.   Ph: (410)636-2695
Linthicum Heights, MD 21090   Free: 800-221-3564
    Fax: (410)636-3256
URL: http://www.duckpins.net
Contact: Charles B. Lavin, Jr., Exec.Dir.
Desc: Rulemaking and governing body for duckpin bowling. *Type:* Association.

Women's International Bowling Congress

5301 S. 76th St.   Ph: (414)421-9000
Greendale, WI 53129   Fax: (414)421-4420
Contact: Roseann Kuhn, Exec.Dir.
Desc: Women bowlers of American tenpins. Sanctions bowling for women and associations in 20 countries. Provides uniform qualifications, rules, and regulations to govern WIBC sanctioned teams, leagues, leadership opportunities, and tournaments. *Type:* Association.

Young American Bowling Alliance

5301 S. 76th St.   Ph: (414)421-4700
Greendale, WI 53129   Fax: (414)421-1301
Contact: Jim Zebehazy, Exec.Dir.
Desc: Youths, 21 years of age and under, who bowl in sanctioned tenpin leagues that do not offer money or merchandise prizes; administers separate Pee Wee Club for bowlers ages three to seven. Issues League Sanction Certificates; gives emblems, plaques, certificates, jackets, and rings for qualifying high games, high series, and special feats; provides league awards kits to recognized leagues; trains adults as instructors and coaches; conducts bowling management and leadership seminars; promotes tournaments through local administrative associations. Holds National Junior Bowling Championships and National Intercollegiate Program Bowling Championships. *Type:* Association.

Boxing

International Veteran Boxers Association

35 Brady Ave.   Ph: (914)235-6820
New Rochelle, NY 10805   Fax: (914)654-9785
Contact: Scoop Gallello, Pres.
Desc: Former professional and amateur boxers, referees, boxing judges, and other interested individuals united to raise funds for former boxers in need. Maintains museum and hall of fame. Operates charitable program; compiles statistics. *Type:* Association.

The Ring

The Ring Magazine, Inc.
7002 W. Butler Pike   Ph: (215)643-3571
PO Box 910   Fax: (215)628-3571
Ambler, PA 19002
Contact: Steve Farhood, Editor; Jeff Ryan, Managing Editor; Stanley Weston, Publisher; Stuart M. Saks, Publisher.
Desc: Magazine covering international professional boxing. *Type:* Periodical.

United States of America Boxing

One Olympic Plz.   Ph: (719)578-4506
Colorado Springs, CO 80909   Fax: (719)632-3426
E-mail: usaboxing@aol.com
URL: http://www.usaboxing.org
Contact: Paul Montville, Exec. Dir.
Desc: Amateur boxers; boxing referees, judges, timers, administrators, officials, and coaches. Objectives are to promote and develop Olympic-style boxing in the U.S. Compiles statistics. *Type:* Association.

Broadcasting

African Time Broadcasting, Inc.

421 7th Ave.   Ph: (212)244-2760
Ste. 1012   Fax: (212)244-2761
New York, NY 10001
Contact: Dame Babou, Contact.
Desc: Talk radio and news format. *Alt. Contact:* 421 7th Ave., Ste. 1012, New York, NY 10001; telephone: (212)244-2760; fax: (212)244-2761. *Type:* Periodical.

American Federation of Television and Radio Artists

260 Madison Ave.   Ph: (212)532-0800
New York, NY 10016   Fax: (212)532-2242
Contact: Bruce A. York, Exec.Dir.
Desc: AFL-CIO. *Type:* Association.

ASCRT/AERTC Bulletin

Association for the Study of Canadian Radio and Television (ASCRT)
Centre for Broadcasting Studies,   Ph: (514)848-7719
  Rm. S-LB-227   Fax: (514)848-4501
1455 de Maisonneuve Blvd., W.
Montreal, PQ, Canada H3G
  1M8
Contact: James Turner, Editor.
Desc: Presents news, reviews, and issues regarding broadcasting and research. Recurring features include interviews, news of research, a calendar of events, reports of meetings, and book reviews. *Type:* Newsletter.

ASIAcom

Baskerville Communications Corp.
PO Box 6589   Ph: (818)461-9667
Torrance, CA 90504-9960   Free: 800-533-5909
    Fax: (818)461-9661
Contact: Mr. Newman, Contact.
Desc: A business newsletter on Asia Pacific television, cable, satellite, and telecommunications. Includes news and analysis on media and telecommunications business developments and opportunities in the Asia Pacific region. *Type:* Newsletter.

Association of America's Public Television Stations

1350 Connecticut Ave. NW,   Ph: (202)887-1700
  Ste. 200   Fax: (202)293-2422
Washington, DC 20036
E-mail: info@apts.org
URL: http://www.apts.org
Contact: David Brugger, Pres.
Desc: Public television licensees whose goal is to organize efforts of public television stations in areas of planning and research, and in representation before the government. Maintains current information on the public television system including such areas as licensee characteristics, financing, and industry trends; makes projections on system growth and income. Monitors social, economic, and demographic trends that have an impact on public television services. *Type:* Association.

B. Stats

Paul Kagan Associates, Inc.
126 Clock Tower Pl.   Ph: (831)624-1536
Carmel, CA 93923   Fax: (831)625-3225
E-mail: info@kagan.com
Contact: Paul Kagan, Editor.
Desc: Discusses the sale of broadcast stations in the U.S., covering both AM and FM radio and television stations. Provides financial data on station transfers and contains five-year projections of revenues for all broadcast markets. *Type:* Newsletter.

Baskerville's EuroCom

Baskerville Communications Corp.
PO Box 6589   Ph: (818)461-9667
Torrance, CA 90504-9960   Free: 800-533-5909
    Fax: (818)461-9661
Contact: Mr. Newman, Contact.
Desc: Provides news on European telecommunications, cable, and satellites. Explores the European markets, including cable systems, fiber optics, broadband, satellite, Intranets, and mobile and fixed telephony. *Type:* Newsletter.

Broadcast Investor

Paul Kagan Associates, Inc.
126 Clock Tower Pl.   Ph: (831)624-1536
Carmel, CA 93923   Fax: (831)625-3225
E-mail: info@kagan.com

Contact: George Niesen, Editor.

Desc: Evaluates the values of radio and television stations and publicly-held broadcast companies. *Type:* Newsletter.

Broadcast News Ltd.

36 King St. E.   Ph: (416)364-3172
Toronto, ON, Canada M5C   Fax: (416)364-8896
2L9
Contact: Wayne Waldroff, General Mgr.; Phil Adler, Business Mgr.

Desc: News wire format. *Alt. Contact:* 36 King St. E., Toronto, ON, Canada M5C 2L9; telephone: (416)364-3172; fax: (416)364-8896. *Type:* Periodical.

Broadcasters Letter

Video, Teleconference & Radio Center
U.S. Department of Agriculture (USDA)
Office of Communications   Ph: (202)720-6072
Washington, DC 20250-1360   Fax: (202)720-5773
URL: http://www.usda.gov/news/pubs/bdcaster/dos.
Contact: Larry A. Quinn, Editor, larry.quinn@usda.gov.

Desc: Highlights recent developments of U.S. Department of Agriculture (USDA) and in agriculture. *Type:* Newsletter.

Broadcasting and Cable's TV International

Baskerville Communications Corp.
PO Box 6589   Ph: (818)461-9667
Torrance, CA 90504-9960   Free: 800-533-5909
    Fax: (818)461-9661
Contact: Mr. Newman, Contact.

Desc: Contains information on the worldwide television, cable, and satellite markets. Includes news and strategic analysis on international broadcast, cable, satellite, digital, pay and pay-per-view, program ratings, and in-depth market and company profiles. *Type:* Newsletter.

Canadian Broadcasting Corporation CBC/ Societe Radio Canada SRC

250 Lanark Ave.   Ph: (613)724-1200
PO Box 3220
Sta. C
Ottawa, ON, Canada K1Y 1E4
Contact: Perrin Beatty, President; Guylaine Saucier, Chw.; Louise Tremblay, Sr. VP Resources; Michael McEwen, Sr. Advisor; Robert Hertzog, VP Internal Audit; Gerald Flaherty, VP Gen. Counsel/Corp. Sec.; George C.B. Smith, VP Human Resources; Robert O'Reilly, Acting Sr. Dir. Corp. Comm. and Public A.

Desc: News and information format. *Alt. Contact:* 250 Lanark Ave., PO Box 3220, Sta. C, Ottawa, ON, Canada K1Y 1E4; telephone: (613)724-1200; Box 500, Sta. A, Toronto, ON, Canada M5W 1E6; telephone: (416)205-3311; Box 6000, Montreal, PQ, Canada H3C 3A8; telephone: (514)597-5970. *Type:* Periodical.

Chancellor Broadcasting Network

Union Plaza Hotel   Ph: (702)798-1798
1 Main St.   Fax: (702)798-2922
Las Vegas, NV 89101
Contact: David Papandrea, CEO/Pres.; Art Bell, Affiliate Relations Mgr.

Desc: Talk radio format. *Alt. Contact:* Union Plaza Hotel, 1 Main St., Las Vegas, NV 89101; telephone: (702)798-1798; fax: (702)798-2922. *Type:* Periodical.

Corporation for Public Broadcasting

901 E St. NW   Ph: (202)879-9600
Washington, DC 20004-2037   Fax: (202)783-1019
Contact: Robert I. Coonrod, Pres.

Desc: A private, nonprofit corporation authorized under Public Broadcasting Act of 1967. Funded by U.S. government. *Type:* Association.

CTAM, The Marketing Society for the Cable and Telecommunications Industry

201 N. Union, Ste. 440   Ph: (703)549-4200
Alexandria, VA 22314   Fax: (703)684-1167
E-mail: ctam@ctam.com
URL: http://www.ctam.com
Contact: Char Beales, Pres./CEO.

Desc: Network of cable and telecommunications professionals dedicated to the pursuit of marketing excellence. Provides its members with competitive marketing resources including education, research, networking and leadership opportunities. *Type:* Association.

Educational Broadcasting Corporation

356 W. 58th St.   Ph: (212)560-2000
New York, NY 10019   Fax: (212)582-3297
Contact: William F. Baker, Pres.

Desc: Owner and licensee of WNET/Channel 13, the principal public television station in New York City. Produces programs distributed by the Public Broadcasting Service to 350 noncommercial television stations in the U.S., Hawaii, Guam, and Puerto Rico. Conducts educational and cultural broadcasts; operates outreach programs to schools and community groups. *Type:* Association.

Family Stations Inc.

290 Hegenberger Rd.   Ph: (510)568-6200
Oakland, CA 94621   Fax: (510)633-7983
Contact: Harold E. Camping, Pres./Gen. Mgr.; Scott Smith, Vice President.

Alt. Contact: 290 Hegenberger Rd., Oakland, CA 94621; telephone: (510)568-6200; fax: (510)633-7983. *Type:* Periodical.

Flix

1633 Broadway   Ph: (212)708-1600
37th Fl.   Fax: (212)208-1212
New York, NY 10019
Alt. Contact: 1633 Broadway, 37th Fl., New York, NY 10019; telephone: (212)708-1600; fax: (212)208-1212. *Type:* Periodical.

FMedia!

FM Atlas Publishing
PO Box 336   Ph: (218)879-7676
Esko, MN 55733-0336   Free: 800-605-2219
    Fax: (218)879-8333
E-mail: fmatlas@aol.com
URL: http://members.aol.com/fmatlas/home.html
Contact: Bruce F. Elving, Ph.D., Editor.

Desc: Lists information on the facilities and formats of FM radio, including new station grants and applications. Also provides official and unofficial news and comments, as well as FM Dxing and FM reception concerns. *Type:* Newsletter.

GBI Gear Broadcasting International, Inc.

Weybosset St.   Ph: (401)331-6072
Box 23172   Free: 800-468-8424
Providence, RI 02903
Contact: Edward R. Robalisky, Chm./Pres.; Jack G. Thayer, Exec. VP; G.A. Rainone, Finance VP; Noel Howard, Engineering VP; James Raposa, Broadcast Development Services.

Desc: Cable news format. *Alt. Contact:* Weybosset St., Box 23172, Providence, RI 02903; telephone: (401)331-6072; toll-free: 800-468-8424. *Type:* Periodical.

Georgia Network

1819 Peachtree St. NE
Ste. 700
Atlanta, GA 30309-1849
Alt. Contact: 1819 Peachtree St. NE, Ste. 700, Atlanta, GA 30309-1849. *Type:* Periodical.

Global Mobile

Baskerville Communications Corp.
PO Box 6589   Ph: (818)461-9667
Torrance, CA 90504-9960   Free: 800-533-5909
    Fax: (818)461-9661
Contact: Mr. Newman, Contact.

Desc: Consists of mobile communications markets. Includes news and analysis from various mobile sectors worldwide such as cellular PCS, satellites, license opportunities, street prices, subscriber growth, and forecasts. *Type:* Newsletter.

Global Mobile Daily

Baskerville Communications Corp.
PO Box 6589   Ph: (818)461-9667
Torrance, CA 90504-9960   Free: 800-533-5909
    Fax: (818)461-9661
Contact: Mr. Newman, Contact.

Desc: Provides analysis of worldwide mobile developments including third generation and fixed-mobile convergence, financial valuation of deals, and new license opportunities. Remarks: Available via fax and e-mail. *Type:* Newsletter.

Global Satellite Network

14958 Ventura Blvd.   Ph: (818)906-1888
Sherman Oaks, CA 91403   Fax: (818)906-9736
Contact: Howard Gillman, President; Mare Jeffries, General Mgr.; Maria Musaitef, Sr. Dir. Affiliate Relations.

Desc: Syndicated shows format. *Alt. Contact:* 14958 Ventura Blvd., Sherman Oaks, CA 91403; telephone: (818)906-1888; fax: (818)906-9736. *Type:* Periodical.

Hope Reports—Briefing

Hope Reports, Inc.
58 Carverdale Dr.   Ph: (716)442-1310
Rochester, NY 14618-4004   Fax: (716)442-1725
E-mail: hopereport@aol.com
Contact: Thomas W. Hope, Editor.

Desc: Publishes the findings of Hope Reports, Inc., a research and consulting firm for the audiovisual communications industries. Reports significant industry developments, research highlights, sales indexes, projected sales, and market trends. *Type:* Newsletter.

Independent Broadcasters Network

2 Corporate Dr.   Ph: (813)573-4402
Ste. 530   Fax: (813)573-3501
Clearwater, FL 34622
Contact: Steve Wiegner, President; Doug Stephan, Vice President.

Desc: Two-way talk radio format. *Alt. Contact:* 2 Corporate Dr., Ste. 530, Clearwater, FL 34622; telephone: (813)573-4402; fax: (813)573-3501. *Type:* Periodical.

Insiders Sportsletter

American Sportscasters Association, Inc.
5 Beekman St., No. 814   Ph: (212)227-8080
New York, NY 10038   Fax: (212)571-0556
Contact: Louis O. Schwartz, Editor.

Desc: Highlights Association programs promoting excellence and recognition in the field of sportscasting. Carries profiles of award winners and interviews with sportscasting professionals. *Type:* Newsletter.

LatinCom

Baskerville Communications Corp.
PO Box 6589   Ph: (818)461-9667
Torrance, CA 90504-9960   Free: 800-533-5909
    Fax: (818)461-9661
Contact: Mr. Newman, Contact.

Desc: Provides information on the Latin American telecommunications, cable, and satellite industries. Includes news on cable systems, fiber optics, broadband, satellite, Intranets, and mobile and fixed telephony. *Type:* Newsletter.

Lode Star

1102 N. Springbrook   Ph: (503)223-6146
Newberg, OR 97132   Fax: (503)538-9382

Contact: Fred W. Hudson, President; Mike Beard, MAN.

Alt. Contact: 1102 N. Springbrook, Newburg, OR 97132; telephone: (503)223-6146; fax: (503)538-9382. *Type:* Periodical.

Media Law Reporter

Bureau of National Affairs, Inc. (BNA)
1231 25th St. NW   Ph: (202)452-4323
Washington, DC 20037   Free: 800-372-1033
    Fax: (202)452-7773
E-mail: bnaplus@bna.com

Contact: Mary Anne Pazanowski, Managing Editor.

Desc: Covers federal and state court decisions and selected agency rulings affecting the communications media. *Type:* Newsletter.

Moody Broadcasting Network

820 N. LaSalle Dr.   Ph: (312)329-4433
Chicago, IL 60610   Free: 800-621-7031
    Fax: (312)329-4339

Contact: Bob Norris, Broadcast Development Mgr.; Bob West, Network Development Dir.

Alt. Contact: 820 N. LaSalle Dr., Chicago, IL 60610; telephone: (312)329-4433; fax: (312)329-4339; toll-free: 800-621-7031. *Type:* Periodical.

Mutual Broadcasting System, Inc.

1755 S. Jefferson Davis Hwy.   Ph: (703)413-8300
Arlington, VA 22202   Fax: (703)413-8445

Contact: Jack B. Clements, President; George Barber, Station Relations VP; Margaret M. Solomon, Operations VP; Barton J. Tessler, News VP.

Desc: Talk radio and news format. *Alt. Contact:* 1755 S. Jefferson Davis Hwy., Arlington, VA 22202; telephone: (703)413-8300; fax: (703)413-8445; Westwood One Inc. *Type:* Periodical.

NAB World

National Association of Broadcasters
1771 N St. NW   Ph: (202)429-5477
Washington, DC 20036-2891   Free: 800-368-5644
    Fax: (202)775-3515
E-mail: nabpubs@nab.org

Contact: Tom Butts, Editor.

Desc: Tracks the domestic and international broadcasting industry (radio and television) with emphasis on management, sales, promotions, and engineering/technology issues. Features pertinent industry news and information on NAB conferences, products, and services. *Type:* Newsletter.

National Academy of Television Arts and Sciences

111 W. 57th St., Ste. 1020   Ph: (212)586-8424
New York, NY 10019   Fax: (212)246-8129

Contact: John Cannon, Pres.

Desc: Persons engaged in television performing, art directing, cinematography, directing, taping, tape editing, choreography, engineering, film editing, music, production, and writing. Advances the arts and sciences of television and fosters creative leadership in the television industry for artistic, cultural, educational, and technological progress; recognizes outstanding achievements in the television industry by conferring annual awards for excellence (Emmy Awards). *Type:* Association.

National Association Broadcast Employees and Technicians - Communications Workers of America

501 3rd St. NW, 8th Fl.   Ph: (202)434-1254
Washington, DC 20001   Fax: (202)434-1426
E-mail: nabetcwa@aol.com

Contact: John S. Clark, Pres.

Desc: AFL-CIO. *Type:* Association.

National Association of Broadcasters

1771 N. St. NW   Ph: (202)429-5300
Washington, DC 20036   Fax: (202)429-5343

Contact: Edward O. Fritts, CEO & Pres.

Desc: Representatives of radio and television stations and networks; associate members include producers of equipment and programs. Seeks to ensure the viability, strength, and success of free, over-the-air broadcasters; serves as an information resource to the industry. Monitors and reports on events regarding radio and television broadcasting. *Type:* Association.

National Broadcasting Society - Alpha Epsilon Rho

Prof. Janie M. Byrne
Millersville University   Ph: (717)872-3996
Dept of Communications &   Fax: (717)872-3700
    Theatre
Millersville, PA 17551
E-mail: jbyrne@mu2.millersv.edu

Contact: Jamie M. Byrne, Pres.

Desc: Professional society - men and women, radio-television. *Type:* Association.

National Public Radio

635 Massachusetts Ave. NW   Ph: (202)414-2000
Washington, DC 20001   Fax: (202)414-3329
URL: http://www.npr.org

Contact: Kevin Klose, Pres.

Desc: Funded principally by its member stations, with additional support from foundations and corporations. NPR is the only nationwide interconnected public radio system in the U.S. Originates and disseminates news, cultural, and programming information through live satellite distribution. *Type:* Association.

National Religious Broadcasters

7839 Ashton Ave.   Ph: (703)330-7000
Manassas, VA 20109   Fax: (703)330-7100
URL: http://www.nrb.org

Contact: Dr. Brandt Gustavson, Pres.

Desc: Religious radio and television program producers; religious radio and television station owners and operators within the U.S. and Canada; foreign broadcasters interested in religious broadcasting throughout the world. Seeks to support those providing programming for radio and television and those engaging in the operation of religious radio and television stations. *Type:* Association.

News Media Update

Reporters Committee for Freedom of the Press
1101 Wilson Blvd., Ste. 1910   Ph: (703)807-2100
Arlington, VA 22209   Fax: (703)807-2109
E-mail: rcfp@rcfp.org

Desc: Provides news briefs on events and court cases affecting the print and broadcast news media and publishers. Organized under the headings First Amendment & FOI; Postal & Business; and Postal, Business & Telecommunications. *Type:* Newsletter.

North Carolina News Network

Box 12900   Ph: (919)890-6030
Raleigh, NC 27605   Fax: (919)890-6024

Contact: George Habel, General Mgr.; Clayton Henkel, News Mgr.

Alt. Contact: Box 12900, Raleigh, NC 27605; telephone: (919)890-6030; fax: (919)890-6024; News office; telephone: (919)890-6024; fax: (919)890-6192. *Type:* Periodical.

Olympia Broadcasting Networks

7745 Carondelet Ave.   Ph: (314)727-8900
St. Louis, MO 63105   Fax: (314)727-4115

Contact: Stephen Bunyard, President; Jay Goldman, Vice President; Bill Latz, Vice President; John McElfresh, Vice President.

Desc: Format comprises aports, comedy, and country music. *Alt. Contact:* 7745 Carondelet Ave., St. Louis, MO 63105; telephone: (314)727-8900; fax: (314)727-4115. *Type:* Periodical.

Pacifica Network News

2390 Champlain St. NW   Ph: (202)588-0999
2nd Fl.   Fax: (202)588-0987
Washington, DC 20009-2620

Contact: Julie Drizin, Bureau Chief; Patricia Guadalupe, News Dir.; Verna Avery Brown, Anchor Pacifica Network News; Amy Goodman, Anchor Democracy Now!.

Desc: News format. *Alt. Contact:* 2390 Champlain St. NW, 2nd Fl., Washington, DC 20009-2620; telephone: (202)588-0999; fax: (202)588-0987. *Type:* Periodical.

PROMAX International

2029 Century Park East, Ste.   Ph: (310)788-7600
    555   Fax: (310)788-7616
Los Angeles, CA 90067-3283
URL: http://www.promax.org

Contact: Tina Gaines, Pres. & CEO.

Desc: Advertising, public relations, and promotion managers of cable, radio, and television stations, systems and networks; syndicators. Seeks to: advance the role and increase the effectiveness of promotion and marketing within the industry, related industries, and educational communities. *Type:* Association.

Public Broadcasting Report

Warren Publishing, Inc.
2115 Ward Ct. NW   Ph: (202)872-9200
Washington, DC 20037   Fax: (202)296-4397
E-mail: warrenpub@mindspring.com
URL: http://www.telecommunications.com

Contact: Sasha Samberg-Champion, Managing Editor.

Desc: Covers funding, programming, and regulations involving public television and radio. Monitors activities at National Public Radio (NPR), the Public Broadcasting System (PBS), the Federal Communications Commission (FCC), the National Telecommunications and Information Administration (NTIA), and the Corporation for Public Broadcasting (CPB). *Type:* Newsletter.

Public Broadcasting Service

1320 Braddock Pl.   Ph: (703)739-5000
Alexandria, VA 22314   Fax: (703)739-0775

Contact: Ervin S. Duggan, Pres. & CEO.

Desc: Private, nonprofit membership corporation providing quality programming and related services to 345 noncommercial, educational television stations throughout the United States, Puerto Rico, the Virgin Islands, Guam and American Samoa. PBS is the leader in quality children's, cultural, educational, nature, news, public affairs, science and skills programming.. Among the noteworthy programs distributed by PBS are Sesame Street, Mr. *Type:* Association.

Radio-Television News Directors Association

1000 Connecticut Ave. NW,   Ph: (202)659-6510
Ste. 615   Free: 800-80-RTNDA
Washington, DC 20036-5302   Fax: (202)223-4007
E-mail: rtnda@rtnda.org

URL: http://www.rtnda.org/rtnda/

Desc: Professional society of heads of news departments for broadcast and cable stations and networks; associate members are journalists engaged in the preparation and presentation of broadcast news and teachers of electronic journalism; other members represent industry services, public relations departments of business firms, public relations firms, and networks. Works to improve standards of electronic journalism; defends rights of journalists to access news; promotes journalism training to meet specific needs of the industry. Operates placement service and speakers' bureau. *Type:* Association.

Satellite International

Baskerville Communications Corp.
PO Box 6589   Ph: (818)461-9667
Torrance, CA 90504-9960   Free: 800-533-5909
                                    Fax: (818)461-9661
Contact: Mr. Newman, Contact.

Desc: Contains analytical reports on the satellite industry and satellite services, including TV and video, fixed and mobile telecoms, and distribution of broadband multimedia service. Remarks: Available in print and PDF formats. *Type:* Newsletter.

Standard Broadcast News

2 St. Claire Ave. W   Ph: (416)323-6824
Toronto, ON, Canada M4V   Fax: (416)323-6825
  1L6
Desc: News wire format. *Alt. Contact:* 2 St. Claire Ave. W, Toronto, ON, Canada M4V 1L6; telephone: (416)323-6824; fax: (416)323-6825. *Type:* Periodical.

$wap $hop

National Association of Broadcasters
1771 N St. NW   Ph: (202)429-5477
Washington, DC 20036-2891   Free: 800-368-5644
                                    Fax: (202)775-3515
E-mail: nabpubs@nab.org
Contact: Tom Butts, Managing Editor; David Young, Editor.

Desc: Provides money-making and money-saving ideas for the National Association of Broadcasters small market radio members. *Type:* Newsletter.

Talk Radio/Talk TV

Professional Press
PO Box 3581   Ph: (919)942-8020
Chapel Hill, NC 27515   Free: 800-277-8960
                                    Fax: (919)942-3094
Contact: Austin Kemp, Editor.

Desc: Profiles authors, athletes, entertainers, politicians, and other famous personalities who desire radio and/or television interviews. Explores aspects of their lives that may be of interest to talk show hosts, producers, and program directors. *Type:* Newsletter.

TV International Daily

Baskerville Communications Corp.
PO Box 6589   Ph: (818)461-9667
Torrance, CA 90504-9960   Free: 800-533-5909
                                    Fax: (818)461-9661
Contact: Mr. Newman, Contact.

Desc: Provides news on international television, cable, satellite, digital, and pay and pay-per-view. Remarks: Available via fax or e-mail. *Type:* Newsletter.

Women in Cable and Telecommunications

230 W. Monroe St., Ste. 730   Ph: (312)634-2330
Chicago, IL 60606-4702   Fax: (312)634-2345
E-mail: information@wict.org
URL: http://www.wict.org
Contact: Pamela V. Williams, Exec.Dir.

Desc: Empowers and educate women to achieve their professional goals by providing opportunities for leadership, networking and advocacy. *Type:* Association.

Building Industries

American Fence Association

5300 Memorial Dr., Ste. 116   Ph: (404)299-5413
Stone Mountain, GA 30083   Free: 800-822-4342
                                    Fax: (404)299-8927
E-mail: afa@mindspring.com
URL: http://www.americanfenceassoc.org
Contact: Terry Dempsey, Jr., CAE, Exec.VP.

Desc: Fence contractors, manufacturers, and wholesalers; associate members are general contractors, architects, and insurance companies. Promotes the fence industry in 17 countries. Sponsors field training school and certification program. *Type:* Association.

Association of the Wall and Ceiling Industries - International

803 West Broad St., Ste. 600   Ph: (703)534-8300
Falls Church, VA 22046-3108   Fax: (703)534-8307
E-mail: info@awci.org
URL: http://www.AWCI.ORG
Contact: Steven A. Etkin, Exec.VP.

Desc: Acoustical tile, drywall, demountable partitions, lathing and plastering, fireproofing, light-gauge steel framing, stacco and exterior insulation finish systems. *Type:* Association.

Brick Industry Association

11490 Commerce Park Dr.   Ph: (703)620-0010
Reston, VA 20191   Fax: (703)620-3928
E-mail: brickinfo@bia.org
URL: http://www.bia.org
Contact: Nelson J. Cooney, Pres.

Desc: Manufacturers of clay brick. *Type:* Association.

Building Officials and Code Administrators International

4051 W. Flossmoor Rd.   Ph: (708)799-2300
Country Club Hills, IL 60478-   Fax: (708)799-4981
  5795
E-mail: member@bocai.org
URL: http://www.bocai.org
Contact: Paul K. Heilstedt, P.E., CEO.

Desc: Governmental officials and agencies and other interests concerned with administering or formulating building, fire, mechanical, plumbing, zoning, housing regulations. Promulgates the BOCA National Codes and the ICC Internatinal Codes suitable for adoption by reference by governmental entities. *Type:* Association.

Design-Build Institute of America

Jeffrey L. Beard
1010 Massachusetts Ave. NW,   Ph: (202)682-0110
  Ste. 350   Fax: (202)682-5877
Washington, DC 20001
E-mail: dbia@dbia.org
URL: http://www.dbia.org
Contact: Jeffrey L. Beard, Exec.Off.

Desc: Companies and individuals concerned with integrated architecture, engineering, and construction services; related companies and service providers including financial institutions, real estate agencies, and building operators. Promotes DesignBuild project delivery, through which professional design and construction of buildings is arranged for under a single source responsibility contract. *Type:* Association.

EIFS Industry Members Association

3000 Corporate Center Dr. Ste   Ph: (770)968-7945
  270   Free: 800-294-3462
Morrow, GA 30260   Fax: (770)968-5818
URL: http://www.eifsfacts.com
Contact: Steve Klamke, Exec.Dir.

Desc: Those in the exterior insulation and finish systems industry. Dedicated to improving the exterior insulation industry and widening the use of its products through collective action. Conducts educational and research programs. *Type:* Association.

International Association of Plumbing and Mechanical Officials

20001 Walnut Dr. S   Ph: (909)595-8449
Walnut, CA 91789-2825   Fax: (909)594-3690
E-mail: iapmo@earthlink.net
URL: http://www.iapmo.org
Contact: Donald Laughlin, Chief Admin. Officer.

Desc: Government agencies, administrative officials, sales representatives, manufacturers, associations, and members of associations related to the plumbing field. Sponsors and writes Uniform Plumbing Codes; also sponsors Uniform Mechanical Code. Sponsors speakers' bureau. *Type:* Association.

International Conference of Building Officials

5360 Workman Mill Rd.   Ph: (562)699-0541
Whittier, CA 90601-2298   Free: 800-284-4406
                                    Fax: (562)695-4694
URL: http://www.icbo.org
Contact: Jon Traw, Pres.

Desc: Representatives of local, regional, and state governments. Seeks to publish, maintain, and promote the Uniform Building Code and related documents; investigate and research principles underlying safety to life and property in the construction, use, and location of buildings and related structures; develop and promulgate uniformity in regulations pertaining to building construction; educate the building official; formulate guidelines for the administration of building inspection departments. Conducts training programs, courses, and certification programs for code enforcement inspectors. *Type:* Association.

National Aggregates Association

1110 Bonifant St., Ste 400   Ph: (301)562-1940
Silver Spring, MD 20910   Free: 800-NAA-1020
                                    Fax: (301)587-9419
E-mail: bdivver@nationalaggregates.org
URL: http://www.nationalaggregates.org
Contact: Barbara Divver, Dir. of Membership.

Desc: Provides information to the construction industry and represents producers of sand, gravel, crushed and broken stone before legislative, regulatory, and technical organizations. *Type:* Association.

National Asphalt Pavement Association

NAPA Bldg.   Ph: (301)731-4748
5100 Forbes Blvd.   Free: 888-468-6499
Lanham, MD 20706-4413   Fax: (301)731-4621
E-mail: napa@hotmix.org
URL: http://www.hotmix.org
Contact: Mike Acott, Pres.

Desc: Manufacturers and producers of scientifically proportioned hot mix asphalt for use in all paving, including highways, airfields, and environmental usages. Membership includes hot mix producers, paving contractors, equipment manufacturers, engineering consultants, and others. Supports research and publishes in formation on: producing, stockpiling, and feeding of the aggregate to the manufacturing facility; drying; methods of screening, storing, and proportioning in the manufacturing facility; production of the hot mix asphalt; transporting mix to paver; laydown procedure and rolling; general workmanship; and related construction practices and materials. *Type:* Association.

National Board of Boiler and Pressure Vessel Inspectors

1055 Crupper Ave. Ph: (614)888-8320
Columbus, OH 43229 Fax: (614)888-0750
E-mail: ajustin@nationalboard.org
URL: http://www.nationalboard.org
Contact: Albert J. Justin, Exec.Dir.

Desc: Represents North American government agencies empowered to assure adherence to code construction and repair of boilers and pressure vessels. Promotes greater safety through maintaining uniformity in the construction, installation, repair, maintenance and inspection of boilers and pressure vessels. *Type:* Association.

National Conference of States on Building Codes and Standards

505 Huntmar Park Dr., Ste. Ph: (703)467-2045
210 Free: 800-DOC-
Herndon, VA 20170 CODE
 Fax: (703)481-3596
E-mail: jweisel@ncbcs.org
URL: http://www.ncsbcs.org
Contact: Robert C. Wible, Exec.Dir.

Desc: States (including District of Columbia, Puerto Rico, and the Virgin Islands), building code officials, building-related manufacturers, associations, educators, and consumer groups seeking a cooperative solution to the multiple problems in the entire building regulatory system. Seeks to: provide a forum for discussion of problems related to the administration of building programs by state regulatory officers; provide a mechanism for developing solutions to problems identified by the conference; assist in the development of programs leading to the adoption and administration of uniform comprehensive building codes and standards where such uniformity is deemed necessary for interstate purposes; encourage acceptance of modular and indus trialized building and pre-assembled building components; develop an effective voice for state officials before the American National Standards Institute and the committees of nationally recognized standards-generating organizations; develop standards and code practices that will encourage the introduction and uniform recognition of innovations in building materials; establish standards for building accessibility by disabled individuals; support the evolution of comprehensive training and educational programs at recognized educational institutions for personnel connected with the enforcement of building regulations; foster cooperation among government officials concerned with building regulations.

National Sash and Door Jobbers Association

10225 Robert Trent Jones Ph: (727)372-3665
 Pkwy. Free: 800-786-SASH
New Port Richey, FL 34655- Fax: (727)372-2879
 4649
E-mail: info@nsdja.com
URL: http://www.nsdja.com
Contact: Robert T. O'Keefe, Pres. & CEO.

Desc: Wholesale distributors of windows, door, millwork, and related products. Conducts research and statistical studies. Offers millwork home study course and audiovisual program dealing with product knowledge; furnishes group insurance. *Type:* Association.

National Stone Association

1415 Elliot Pl. NW Ph: (202)342-1100
Washington, DC 20007 Free: 800-342-1415
 Fax: (202)342-0702
URL: http://www.aggregates.org
Contact: J. Joy Wilson, Pres.

Desc: Producers and processors of crushed stone aggregates used for all construction purposes, concrete asphalt aggregates, railroad ballast, and chemical, metallurgical, and ag-

ricultural processes; manufacturers of machinery, equipment, and supplies used in production of crushed stone; firms providing technical, assistance on environmental, safety and health matters, engineering, and/or scientific services. Activities include research, assistance in environmental, safety, and health matters, engineering consultation and testing, management training programs, product promotion, public relations, and representation in Washington, DC. Conducts educational programs. *Type:* Association.

National Wood Flooring Association

16388 Westwoods Business Pk. Free: 800-422-4556
Ellisville, MO 63021 Fax: (314)391-6137
E-mail: natlwood@aol.com
URL: http://www.woodfloors.org
Contact: Edward S. Korczak, CAE, Exec.Dir.

Desc: Individuals, firms, and corporations engaged in the manufacture, distribution, installation, or sale of wood flooring and allied products. Purposes are to: unite all segments of the wood flooring industry; coordinate marketing and advertising programs of members; educate professionals and consumers about the benefits of wood flooring; increase the market share of the wood flooring industry. Works to develop product standards and a code of professional ethics within the industry. *Type:* Association.

North American Insulation Manufacturers Association

44 Canal Center Plz., Ste. 310 Ph: (703)684-0084
Alexandria, VA 22314 Fax: (703)684-0427
E-mail: insulation@naima.org
URL: http://www.naima.org
Contact: Kenneth D. Mentzer, Exec.VP.

Desc: Manufacturers of fiber glass, rock wool, and slag wool insulation products. Promotes energy efficiency and environmental preservation through the use of fiber glass, rock wool, and slag wool insulation products. Encourages safe production and use of insulation products. *Type:* Association.

People & Profits

People & Profits

PO Box 16711 Ph: (864)232-5264
Greenville, SC 29606 Free: 800-277-7888
 Fax: (864)467-0595
Contact: Bill Lee, Editor.

Desc: Provides information on building supply dealers. *Type:* Newsletter.

Scaffold Industry Association

20335 Ventura Blvd., No. 310 Ph: (818)610-0320
Woodland Hills, CA 91364 Fax: (818)610-0323
Contact: Gary Larson, Exec.VP.

Desc: Firms or individuals that manufacture, sell, or contract for the erection and/or rental of scaffolding, aerial platforms, and shoring or for any device used in the support of workers, material, or equipment. Activities include meetings, educational seminars, research, accident prevention insurance programs for members. Provides safety training aids such as videos, slides, warning signs and a scaffolder training program. *Type:* Association.

Southern Building Code Congress, International

900 Montclair Rd. Ph: (205)591-1853
Birmingham, AL 35213 Fax: (205)592-7001
URL: http://www.sbcci.org
Contact: William J. Tangye, CEO.

Desc: Active members are state, county, municipal, or other government subdivisions (2400); associate members are trade associations, architects, engineers, contractors, and related groups or persons (5100). Seeks to develop, maintain, and promote the adoption of the Standard Building, Gas, Plumbing, Mechanical, Fire Prevention, and Housing Codes. *Type:* Association.

Thermal Insulation Manufacturers Association

29 Bank St. Ph: (203)324-7533
Stamford, CT 06901 Fax: (203)324-5132
Contact: Frank J. Rauscher, Jr., P, Exec.Dir.

Desc: Manufacturers of thermal insulation products. Fosters energy conservation through insulation; develops application and performance standards; disseminates information. Conducts experiments, research programs, and testing regarding the health effects of manmade vitreous fibers. *Type:* Association.

Building Trades

ABG Division United Steel Worker

3362 Hollenberg Dr. Ph: (314)739-6142
Bridgeton, MO 63044 Fax: (314)739-1216
Contact: John Murphy, Dir.

Desc: AFL-CIO; Canadian Labour Congress. *Type:* Association.

American Architectural Manufacturers Association

1827 Walden Office Sq., Ste. Ph: (847)303-5664
 104 Fax: (847)303-5774
Schaumburg, IL 60173-4268
E-mail: webmaster@aamanet.org
URL: http://www.aamanet.org
Contact: Steve Sullivan, Exec. VP.

Desc: Manufacturers of architectural products including: prime and combination storm windows; sliding glass and combination storm doors; window and curtain-walls; store fronts and entrances; siding; soffits, fascia, gutters, downspouts, skylights, space enclosures, and mobile home components. *Type:* Association.

American Society of Home Inspectors

PO Box 95588 Free: 800-743-2744
Palatine, IL 60095 Fax: (847)290-1920
E-mail: hq@ashi.com
URL: http://www.ashi.com
Contact: Robert J. Paterkiewicz, CAE, Contact.

Desc: Professional home inspectors whose goals are to: establish home inspector qualifications; set standards of practice for home inspections; adhere to a code of ethics; keep the concept of "objective third party" intact; inform members of the most advanced methods and techniques. Conducts seminars through regional chapters. *Type:* Association.

Architectural Woodwork Institute

1952 Isaac Newton Sq. Ph: (703)733-0600
Reston, VA 20190 Fax: (703)733-0584
E-mail: jdurham@awinet.org
URL: http://www.awinet.org
Contact: Judith B. Durham, Exec.VP.

Desc: Manufacturers of architectural woodwork products (casework, fixtures, and panelings) and associated suppliers of equipment and materials. Works to: raise industry standards; research new and improved materials and methods; publish technical data helpful in the design and use of architectural woodwork. *Type:* Association.

Asphalt Institute

Research Park Dr. Ph: (606)288-4960
PO Box 14052 Fax: (606)288-4999
Lexington, KY 40512-4052
URL: http://www.asphaltinstitute.org
Contact: Edward L. Miller, Pres.

Desc: Refiners of asphalt products from crude petroleum and related asphalt businesses. Conducts extensive program of education, research, and engineering service related to asphalt products. Sponsors workshops and seminars. *Type:* Association.

Building and Construction Trades Department - AFL-CIO

1155 15th St. NW, 4th Fl.   Ph: (202)347-1461
Washington, DC 20005   Fax: (202)628-0724

URL: http://www.buildingtrades.org/

Contact: Robert A. Georgine, Contact.

Desc: Federation of labor unions in the construction industry including asbestos workers, bricklayers, masons, plasterers, carpenters, electrical workers, elevator constructors, operating engineers, granite cutters, hod carriers, common laborers, iron workers, carpet, tile and stone workers, painters, decorators, paper hangers, plumbers, steam fitters, roofers, boilermakers, lathers, sheet metal workers, and other related trades. Maintains liaison with Center to Protect Workers Rights, which provides independent research and support. *Type:* Association.

Door and Access Systems

Door and Access Systems Manufacturers Association (DASMA)

1300 Sumner   Ph: (216)241-7333
Cleveland, OH 44115-2851   Fax: (216)241-0105

E-mail: dasma@taol.com

Contact: William Wendling, Editor, (216)241-7407, fax: (216)622-1559, wwwendl@aol.com.

Desc: Contains "current industry news for manufacturers of garage doors and garage door components." Recurring features include news of research, news of members, notices of publications available, reports of meetings, and a calendar of events. *Type:* Newsletter.

International Brotherhood of Painters and Allied Trades

United Unions Bldg.   Ph: (202)637-0720
1750 New York Ave. NW   Fax: (202)637-0771
Washington, DC 20006

Contact: A. L. Monroe, Gen.Pres.

Desc: AFL-CIO. *Type:* Association.

International Union of Bricklayers and Allied Craftsmen

815 15th St. NW   Ph: (202)783-3788
Washington, DC 20005   Fax: (202)393-0219

Contact: John T. Joyce, Pres.

Desc: AFL-CIO. *Type:* Association.

International Union of Operating Engineers

1125 17th St. NW   Ph: (202)429-9100
Washington, DC 20036   Fax: (202)429-0316

Contact: Frank Hanley, Pres.

Desc: AFL-CIO. *Type:* Association.

Journal of the International Union of Bricklayers & Allied Craftworkers

Journal of the International Union of Bricklayers & Allied Craftworkers

815 15th St. NW   Ph: (202)383-3136
Washington, DC 20005   Fax: (202)737-2708

URL: http://www.bacweb.org.

Contact: Craig Weir, Editor.

Desc: Tabloid for trade union members. *Type:* Periodical.

Laborers' International Union of North America

905 16th St. NW   Ph: (202)737-8320
Washington, DC 20006   Fax: (202)737-2754

URL: http://www.liuna.org

Contact: Arthur A. Coia, Gen.Pres.

Desc: AFL-CIO. *Type:* Association.

Managing Housing Letter

CD Publications

8204 Fenton St.   Ph: (301)588-6380
Silver Spring, MD 20910   Free: 800-666-6380
     Fax: (301)588-6385

E-mail: cdpubs@clark.net

Contact: Philip Porado, Editor.

Desc: Provides news and advice for owners and managers of rental housing—public, private, and subsidized—including news from Washington and practical management tips. Recurring features include news of research. *Type:* Newsletter.

Operative Plasterers and Cement Masons International Association of U.S. and Canada

14405 Laurel Place, Ste. 300   Ph: (301)470-4200
Laurel, MD 20707   Fax: (301)470-2502

E-mail: opcmiaintl@opcnia.org

URL: http://www.opcmia.org

Contact: John J. Dougherty, Gen.Pres.

Desc: AFL-CIO. *Type:* Association.

The Renovator's Supply

The Renovator's Supply

Renovator's Old Mill   Ph: (413)659-3773
Millers Falls, MA 01349   Fax: (413)659-3796

Contact: Clau de Jeanloz, Editor and Publisher.

Desc: Home service magazine. *Type:* Periodical.

Skylines

Building Owners & Managers Association International

1201 New York Ave. SW, Ste.   Ph: (202)408-2662
300   Fax: (202)371-0181
Washington, DC 20005

URL: http://www.boma.org; http://www.boma.org.

Contact: Stephanie J. Oppenheimer, Editor, (202)326-6315, soppen@boma.org; Lisa Prats, (212)326-6351.

Desc: Covers news affecting the commercial real estate industry. *Type:* Newsletter.

Southern Building Code Congress International

900 Montclair Rd.   Ph: (205)591-1853
Birmingham, AL 35213   Fax: (205)599-9893

E-mail: info@sbcci.org

URL: http://www.sbcci.org

Contact: William J. Tangye, CEO.

Desc: Provides standardized set of building codes. Holds annual hearings. *Type:* Association.

United Brotherhood of Carpenters and Joiners of America

101 Constitution Ave. NW   Ph: (202)546-6206
Washington, DC 20001   Fax: (202)546-5724

Contact: Douglas J. McCarron, Gen.Pres.

Desc: AFL-CIO. *Type:* Association.

United Union of Roofers, Waterproofers and Allied Workers

1660 L St. NW, Ste. 800   Ph: (202)463-7663
Washington, DC 20036   Fax: (202)463-6906

Contact: Earl Kruse, Pres.

Desc: AFL-CIO. *Type:* Association.

Business

Ability and Enterprise

Canadian Council on Rehabilitation and Work (CCRW)

500 University Ave., Ste. 302   Ph: (416)260-3060
Toronto, ON, Canada M5G   Fax: (416)260-3093
1V7

E-mail: info@ccrw.org

URL: http://www.workink.com.

Contact: Gary Annable, Editor.

Desc: Contains information about the employment of people with disabilities. *Type:* Newsletter.

The ABQ Correspondent

ABQ Communications Corporation

PO Box 1432   Ph: (505)897-0822
Corrales, NM 87048   Fax: (505)898-6525

E-mail: correspo@swcp.com.

URL: http://www.swcp.com/correspo.

Contact: Nelson Winkless, Editor.

Desc: Offers entertaining reports on phenomena, insights, products, and people of potential value to the reader. *Type:* Newsletter.

The Accidental Entrepreneur

Dixie Darr

3421 Alcott St.   Ph: (303)433-0345
Denver, CO 80211

E-mail: sknkwrks@ix.netcom.com.

Contact: Dixie Darr, Editor and Publisher.

Desc: Provides help and information about entrepreneurship and component careers. *Type:* Newsletter.

ACTION

Senior Executives Association (SEA)

PO Box 44808   Ph: (202)927-7000
Washington, DC 20026   Fax: (202)927-5192

E-mail: seniorexec@aol.com

URL: http://www.seniorexecs.com.

Contact: Valerie Norton, Editor.

Desc: Informs members of news of the administration, and relevant judicial and legislative issues. Recurring features include a calendar of events, reports of meetings, news of educational opportunities, and a column titled Legislative Update. *Type:* Newsletter.

Action Report for Business Leaders

Delaware County Chamber of Commerce

602 E. Baltimore Pike   Ph: (610)565-3677
Media, PA 19063   Fax: (610)565-1606

Contact: Madeline Pfaff, Editor.

Desc: Provides business and legislative news to businesses and Chamber members. Recurring features include a calendar of events and columns titled Welcome New Members, Legislative Digest, By the Way, Guest Column, and Featured Member of the Month. *Type:* Newsletter.

Advocacy Institute

1707 L Street NW, Ste. 400   Ph: (202)659-8475
Washington, DC 20036   Fax: (202)659-8484

URL: http://www.advocacy.org

Contact: David Cohen, Co.-Director.

Desc: Strengthen the capacity of social and economic justice advocates to influence and change public policy. Provides training and counseling to environmental, consumer, health, and other nonprofit public interest organizations on how to deal effectively with public policy issues. *Type:* Association.

Alabama Business Directory

infoUSA

5711 S. 86th Circle   Ph: (402)593-4600
PO Box 27347   Free: 800-555-6124
Omaha, NE 68127   Fax: (402)331-5481
E-mail: internet@infousa.com
URL: http://www.abii.com.
Contact: Peter J. Wilmarth, Publisher.
Desc: 157,000 businesses in Alabama. *Type:* Directory.

Alameda County Commerce & Industry Directory

Database Publishing Co.

1590 S. Lewis St.   Ph: (714)778-6400
PO Box 70024   Free: 800-888-8434
Anaheim, CA 92825-0024   Fax: (714)778-6811
E-mail: sales@databasepublishing.com
URL: http://www.databasepublishing.com; http://www.databasepublishing.com.
Desc: Some 4,100 manufacturers, wholesalers, and service companies, plus 9,500 key executives in Alameda County, California. *Type:* Directory.

Alaska Business Directory

infoUSA

5711 S. 86th Circle   Ph: (402)593-4600
PO Box 27347   Free: 800-555-6124
Omaha, NE 68127   Fax: (402)331-5481
E-mail: internet@infousa.com
URL: http://www.abii.com.
Contact: Peter J. Wilmarth, Publisher.
Desc: 35,000 businesses in Alaska. *Type:* Directory.

Alberta Egg Producers Board Newsletter

Alberta Egg Producers Board

1915 - 32nd Ave. NE, Ste. 15   Ph: (403)250-1197
Calgary, AB, Canada T2E 7C8   Fax: (403)250-9216
Desc: Provides news and information of interest to the egg producers in Alberta. *Type:* Newsletter.

The Alliance Analyst

Michael S. Robinson

415 S. Van Pelt St., Ste. B3   Ph: (215)546-2441
Philadelphia, PA 19146   Fax: (215)546-3292
Contact: Michael S. Robinson, Publisher.
Desc: Provides information about corporate alliances. Recurring features include legal, investment, and management advice, case studies, and columns titled Industry Focus, Indicators, International, Legal Watch, and Monitor. *Type:* Newsletter.

Alpha Beta Gamma International

75 Grasslands Rd.   Ph: (914)785-6877
Valhalla, NY 10595   Fax: (914)785-6481
E-mail: ceo@abg.org
Contact: Dr. John D. Christesen, CEO.
Desc: Honor Society - Business. Students enrolled at accredited two-year community, technical, and junior colleges; also initiates distinguished International business persons and academics as honorary members. *Type:* Association.

Alpha Iota Delta

Georgia State University   Ph: (404)651-4000
Decision Sciences Dept.   Fax: (404)651-3498
Atlanta, GA 30303
E-mail: dscbsg@gsu.edu
URL: http://www.dsi.gsu.edu/
Contact: Bikramjit S. Garcha, Exec.Dir.
Desc: Honorary fraternity - men and women, decision sciences. *Type:* Association.

Alpha Kappa Psi

9595 Angola Ct.   Ph: (317)872-1553
Indianapolis, IN 46268-1119   Fax: (317)872-1567
E-mail: gary@akpsi.com
Contact: Gary L. Epperson, CAE, Exec.Dir.
Desc: Professional fraternity - business administration. *Type:* Association.

America International Business Directory

ChinoWorld International Publishing

8210 Gorman Ave., Apt. 360
Laurel, MD 20707-3559
Contact: Alex Wang, Editor; Xin Chen, Editor; Faye Chen, Editor.
Desc: Approximately 2,000 companies in the U.S. interested in doing business with Chinese companies. *Type:* Directory.

American Association of Minority Businesses

Charles L. Kelly

537 W. Sugar Creek Rd., Ste.   Ph: (704)921-2262
104   Fax: (704)921-2910
Charlotte, NC 28213
Contact: Charles L. Kelly, CEO & Pres.
Desc: Businesses in the United States that are owned or operated by individuals belonging to a racial or ethnic minority. Promotes effective, ethical, and profitable operation of minority-owned businesses. *Type:* Association.

American Big Businesses Directory

infoUSA

5711 S. 86th Circle   Ph: (402)593-4600
PO Box 27347   Free: 800-555-6124
Omaha, NE 68127   Fax: (402)331-5481
E-mail: internet@infousa.com
URL: http://www.abii.com.
Desc: 184,108 U.S. businesses with more than 100 employees, and 347,000 key executives and directors. CD-ROM version contains 160,000 top firms and 431,000 key executives. *Type:* Directory.

American Business

American Business

80 Central Park West, Ste. 16B   Ph: (212)581-2000
New York, NY 10023
Contact: Ralph Ginzburg, Editor and Publisher; Richard K. Greene, Editor.
Desc: Business and finance magazine. *Type:* Periodical.

American Business in China

Caravel, Inc.

23545 Crenshaw Blvd., 101E   Ph: (310)325-0100
Torrance, CA 90505   Fax: (310)325-2583
Contact: Davisson K. Chang, Editor.
Desc: More than 1,000 U.S. firms with offices in China and Hong Kong, including Beijing, Shanghai, and Guangzhou. *Type:* Directory.

American Business Directories Series

infoUSA

5711 S. 86th Circle   Ph: (402)593-4600
PO Box 27347   Free: 800-555-6124
Omaha, NE 68127   Fax: (402)331-5481
E-mail: internet@infousa.com
URL: http://www.abii.com.
Desc: A series of over 1,600 lists of businesses or organizations compiled from the "Yellow Pages" of 5,000 telephone books nationwide. Titles for the directories are derived from the subject headings of the "Yellow Pages." DIP users should look in the subject index first to locate a title from this series. *Type:* Directory.

American Business Directory

infoUSA

5711 S. 86th Circle   Ph: (402)593-4595
P.O. Box 27347
Omaha, NE 68127
E-mail: internet@infousa.com
URL: http://www.infousa.com
Desc: Contains telephone directory listings for more than 10 million businesses in all ZIP Code areas of the United States. For each company, provides name, address, ZIP Code, telephone number, Standard Industrial Classification (SIC) codes, contact name, yellow page categories, size of yellow page advertisement, and year in which the business was first listed in the given category. *Available:* The Dialog Corporation, DIALOG. *Type:* Database.

American Business Locations Directory

Gale Group Inc.

27500 Drake Rd.   Ph: (248)699-4253
Farmington Hills, MI 48331-   Free: 800-877-GALE
3535   Fax: (248)699-8070
E-mail: galeord@galegroup.com
URL: http://www.galegroup.com.
Desc: Over 150,000 U.S. locations of the largest 1,000 industrial and service companies. *Type:* Directory.

American Business Women's Association

9100 Ward Pky.   Ph: (816)361-6621
PO Box 8728   Free: 800-214-6222
Kansas City, MO 64114-0728   Fax: (816)361-4991
E-mail: info@abwahq.org
URL: http://www.abwahq.org
Contact: Carolyn B. Elman, Exec.Dir.
Desc: Women in business, including women owning or operating their own businesses, women in professions, and women employed in any level of government, education, or retailing, manufacturing, and service companies. Provides opportunities for businesswomen to help themselves and others grow personally and professionally through leadership, education, networking support, and national recognition. Offers leadership training, business skills training and business education; special membership options for retired businesswomen and the Company Connection for business owners, a resume service, credit card and programs, various travel and insurance benefits. *Type:* Association.

American Businessmen's Club

4001 Summitview, Bldg. 4-179   Ph: (509)248-2801
Yakima, WA 98908-2945   Fax: (509)248-2801
Contact: C. Wynn Schaub, International Dir.
Desc: Businesspeople in the United States. *Type:* Association.

American Export Register

Thomas Publishing Co.
International Division

5 Penn Plaza   Ph: (212)629-1177
New York, NY 10001   Fax: (212)629-1140
Contact: Kathleen Cooper, Editor; Eric Fusco, Research Editor.
Desc: Over 45,000 companies in the United States exporting products and services, United States and foreign government services to exporters and importers, chambers of commerce abroad, embassies and consulates in the U.S., and financial and transportation services such as airlines, steamship lines, freight forwarders, customs brokers, and banks, international cargo carriers and carriers, world trade centers. *Type:* Directory.

An American Guide to Doing Business in Australia

PacRim Publishing
150 S. Glenoaks Blvd., Ste.　Ph: (818)848-2376
　8054　Free: 800-220-8346
Burbank, CA 91502　Fax: (818)848-7021
Contact: John Boal, Editor.
Desc: Individuals in the U.S. involved in trade with Australia; sources of related exporting, importing, investing and business information, including trade shows, publications, chambers of commerce, consulates general, Australian Trade Commission offices, and U.S. government trade programs. *Type:* Directory.

The American Heritage 40

Forbes American Heritage Magazine
60 5th Ave.　Ph: (212)206-5500
New York, NY 10011
E-mail: mail@americanheritage.com
URL: http://www.americanheritage.com/98/oct/40index.htm
Desc: This fascinating biographical listing profiles the 40 wealthiest Americans of all time, of which only three are still alive. Provided by Forbes American Heritage magazine, the list contains some of those you'd expect - Bill Gates, John D. *Type:* Database.

American Society of Association Executives

1575 I St. NW　Ph: (202)626-2723
Washington, DC 20005-1168　Fax: (202)371-8825
E-mail: asae@asaenet.org
URL: http://www.asaenet.org
Contact: Michael S. Olson, CAE, Pres.
Desc: Professional society of paid executives of international, national, state, and local trade, professional, and philanthropic associations. Seeks to educate association executives on effective management, including: the proper objectives, functions, and activities of associations; the basic principles of association management; the legal aspects of association activity; policies relating to association management; efficient methods, procedures, and techniques of association management; the responsibilities and professional standards of association executives. *Type:* Association.

American Wholesalers and Distributors Directory

Gale Group Inc.
27500 Drake Rd.　Ph: (248)699-4253
Farmington Hills, MI 48331-　Free: 800-877-GALE
　3535　Fax: (248)699-8070
E-mail: galeord@galegroup.com
URL: http://www.galegroup.com.; http://www.gale.com.
Contact: Rebecca Marlowe-Ferguson, Editor, rebecca.marlowe@gale.com.
Desc: More than 26,500 wholesalers and distributors of consumer products in the U.S. *Type:* Directory.

America's Corporate Families

Dun & Bradstreet
3 Sylvan Way　Ph: (973)605-6442
Parsippany, NJ 07054-3896　Free: 800-526-0651
　Fax: (973)605-6911
E-mail: dnbmdd@dnb.com
Desc: Approximately 11,000 U.S. corporations and their 76,000 subsidiaries, divisions, and branches. Ultimate companies must meet all of the following criteria for inclusion: two or more business locations, 250 or more employees at that location or in excess of $25 million in sales volume or a tangible net worth greater than $500,000, and controlling interest in one or more subsidiary company. *Type:* Directory.

Andean Weekly Fax Bulletin

Orbis Publications, LLC
3201 New Mexico Ave. NW,　Ph: (202)237-0155
　Ste. 249　Fax: (202)237-0596
Washington, DC 20016
E-mail: orbis@orbispub.com
URL: http://www.orbispub.com.
Contact: Richard W. Foster, Editor.
Desc: Reports on political, economic and business events in Chile, Colombia, Peru and Venezuela via fax. *Type:* Newsletter.

Antitrust Policy: An On-line Resource Linking Economic Research, Policy, and Cases

Vanderbilt University - The Owen Graduate School of Management
Nashville, TN 37203　Ph: (615)343-6009
E-mail: Luke.M.Froebe@vanderbuilt.edu
URL: http://www.antitrust.org/
Contact: Chad Bockius, webmaster@antitrust.org.
Desc: The Antitrust Policy WWW page provides information about merger and antitrust policy. The site contains a lot of information from economic fields and merger model concepts such as simulating the effects of mergers using linear demand curves as well as detailed information on price fixing, merger, and vertical restraints. *Type:* Database.

APICS-The Performance Advantage

Lionheart Publishing Inc.
2555 Cumberland Pkwy., Ste.　Ph: (404)431-0867
　299　Free: 800-392-7294
Atlanta, GA 30339　Fax: (404)432-6969
E-mail: info@lionhrtpub.com; lpi@lionhrtpub.com.
URL: http://www.lionheartpub.com
Contact: David Greenfield, Editor.
Desc: Manufacturing sector publication. *Type:* Periodical.

Argentina Weekly Fax Bulletin

Orbis Publications, LLC
3201 New Mexico Ave. NW,　Ph: (202)237-0155
　Ste. 249　Fax: (202)237-0596
Washington, DC 20016
E-mail: orbis@orbispub.com
URL: http://www.orbispub.com.
Contact: Richard W. Foster, Editor.
Desc: Reports on political, economic and business events in Argentina via fax. *Type:* Newsletter.

Arizona Business Directory

infoUSA
5711 S. 86th Circle　Ph: (402)593-4600
PO Box 27347　Free: 800-555-6124
Omaha, NE 68127　Fax: (402)331-5481
E-mail: internet@infousa.com
URL: http://www.abii.com.
Contact: Peter J. Wilmarth, Publisher.
Desc: 162,000 businesses in Arizona. *Type:* Directory.

Arizona Business Gazette

Phoenix Newspapers, Inc. - Library, LI-18
PO Box 100　Ph: (602)444-8114
Phoenix, AZ 85001
URL: http://www.azcentral.com
Desc: Contains the complete text of news items and feature articles from the Arizona Business Gazette, a weekly newspaper covering commercial, industrial, and agricultural developments in Arizona. Regional coverage emphasizes high-technology industries, resort and real estate financing and development, and water rights in the southwest United States. *Available:* Bell & Howell Information and Learning; LEXIS-NEXIS, NEXIS. *Type:* Database.

Arizona Republic/Phoenix Gazette/Arizona Business Gazette

Phoenix Newspapers, Inc. - Library, LI-18
PO Box 100　Ph: (602)444-8114
Phoenix, AZ 85001
URL: http://www.azcentral.com
Desc: Contains the complete text of news items and feature articles from the Arizona Republic and Phoenix Gazette daily newspapers as well as the weekly Arizona Business Gazette. Regional coverage emphasizes the aerospace industry, high technology, tourism, real estate development, military contracts, and Native American issues. *Available:* The Dialog Corporation, DIALOG; The Dialog Corporation, DIALOG; CompuServe Information Service, Knowledge Index; Phoenix Newspapers, Inc. - Library, LI-18; Dow Jones Interactive Publishing. *Type:* Database.

Arizona's Economy

University of Arizona
1502 N. Highland Ave.　Ph: (602)621-2484
Tucson, AZ 85721-0001　Fax: (602)626-2155
Contact: Diana Hunter, Editor.
Desc: Reports on economic and business topics pertaining to Arizona. Provides statistical data. *Type:* Newsletter.

ARK On-Demand Online

Thomson Financial Securities Data (TFSD)
Two Gateway Center　Ph: (973)622-3100
Newark, NJ 07102
URL: http://www.securitiesdata.com
Contact: I/Plus Direct Client Services.
Desc: Contains citations to annual reports, interim statements, and year-end results issued by more than 25,000 public companies in Europe, Asia, Africa, Canada, Latin America, and the Pacific Rim. *Available:* Thomson Financial Services, Inc., I/PLUS Direct. *Type:* Database.

Arkansas Business Bulletin

University of Arkansas
College of Engineering
Engineering Center　Ph: (501)575-4151
Fayetteville, AR 72701
Desc: Covers economic information, including statistics, reports, and articles, relating to Arkansas. *Type:* Newsletter.

Arkansas Business Directory

infoUSA
5711 S. 86th Circle　Ph: (402)593-4600
PO Box 27347　Free: 800-555-6124
Omaha, NE 68127　Fax: (402)331-5481
E-mail: internet@infousa.com
URL: http://www.abii.com.
Contact: Peter J. Wilmarth, Publisher.
Desc: 104,000 businesses in Arkansas. *Type:* Directory.

AR100 Award Show

Black Book Marketing Group
10 Aston Pl., 6th Fl.　Ph: (212)539-9800
New York, NY 10003　Free: 800-841-1246
　Fax: (212)539-9801
Contact: Laura Branchini, President & COO.
Desc: Lists of winners at the AR100 Award Show, which recognizes excellence in the field of annual reports; includes photographers, design firms, illustrators, printers, and paper companies; includes listings and ads. *Type:* Directory.

The Ashland Source

Ashland, Inc.
Box 391
Ashland, KY 41114
Contact: Doug Sheils, Editor.

Desc: Provides information for employees and retirees of Ashland Inc. *Type:* Newsletter.

ASIA-PACIFIC
Aristarchus Knowledge Industries Inc.
P.O. Box 45610
Seattle, WA 98105
E-mail: APAC (DIALMAIL)
Desc: Contains more than 226,000 citations, with some abstracts, to literature on business, economics, and industry in the Pacific Rim nations, including East Asia, Southeast Asia, the Indian subcontinent, the Middle East, Australia, and the Pacific Island nations. *Available:* The Dialog Corporation, DIALOG. *Type:* Database.

Assets Protection
Assets Protection Publishing
PO Box 5323   Ph: (608)231-6730
Madison, WI 53705-0323   Fax: (608)231-6730
Contact: Paul Shaw, Editor and Publisher.
Desc: Provides management with ideas and tools to create and maintain a practical, cost-effective company-specific compliance program which will help assess and mitigate legal risks as well as enhance controls required to carry out management's objective of protecting the enterprise's assets and earning power. *Type:* Newsletter.

Association for Corporate Growth
1926 Waukegan Rd., Ste. 1   Ph: (847)699-1331
Glenview, IL 60025-1770   Free: 800-699-1331
                                     Fax: (847)657-6819
E-mail: acghq@tcag.com
URL: http://www.acg.org
Contact: Carl A. Wangman, CAE, Exec.Dir.
Desc: Representatives of firms that manufacture a wide range of consumer and industrial products; supply services closely related to the planning and growth activities of such companies. *Type:* Association.

Atlanta Professional Women's Directory
Atlanta Professional Women's Directory, Inc.
PO Box 490
Dacula, GA 30019-0490
Contact: Joy L. Murray, Publisher.
Desc: Nearly 800 companies in over 90 professional and business categories in Atlanta, Georgia, which are owned or represented by women; women's organizations; other sources of information. *Type:* Directory.

Atlantic City Convention and Visitors Authority
2314 Pacific Ave.   Ph: (609)348-7100
Atlantic City, NJ 08401   Fax: (609)345-3685
URL: http://www.atlanticcitynj.com
Contact: Marshall E. Murdaugh, Exec.Dir.
Desc: Promotes convention business and tourism in Atlantic City, NJ. *Type:* Association.

Atlantic Report
Atlantic Provinces Economic Council
5121 Sackville St., Ste. 500   Ph: (902)422-6516
Halifax, NS, Canada B3J 1K1   Fax: (902)429-6803
E-mail: apec@fox.nstn.ns.ca
Desc: Covers developments affecting economic conditions in Canada's Atlantic provinces, including activities in industry, agriculture, health care, consumer behavior, and government programs and legislation. *Type:* Newsletter.

Australian Key Business Directory
Dun & Bradstreet
3 Sylvan Way   Ph: (973)605-6442
Parsippany, NJ 07054-3896   Free: 800-526-0651
                                     Fax: (973)605-6911
E-mail: dnbmdd@dnb.com

Desc: Leading companies in Australia whose annual sales are $10 million and who have 500 or more employees. *Type:* Directory.

AZB/Arizona Business
Center for Business Research
Arizona State University
College of Business
Box 874406   Ph: (602)965-3961
Tempe, AZ 85287-4406   Fax: (602)965-5458
E-mail: asucbr@asuvm.inne.asu.edu
Contact: Colleen Crosby, Editor.
Desc: Reports on current research conducted by the Center on the Arizona economy. Includes a Metropolitan Phoenix Consumer Price Index (CPI), Arizona Leading Index, demographics, and other economic indicators. *Type:* Newsletter.

Bankruptcy File
Infomart Dialog Limited
1450 Don Mills Rd.   Ph: (416)442-2198
Don Mills, ON, Canada M3B
2X7
E-mail: helpdesk@infomart.ca
URL: http://www.infomart.com/
Contact: Client Service Consultants, (416)442-2198, fax: (416)442-2126, helpdesk@infomart.ca.
Desc: Contains summary data on approximately 280,000 bankruptcy filings in Canada, as well as data on approximately 900 trustees (i.e., parties who administer bankruptcies). For each bankruptcy, includes name and address of the bankrupt, estate code, estate type (e.g., non-business), 4-digit Canadian Standard Industrial Classification code, Official Receiver's regional office location, type of discharge (e.g., absolute, conditional), estate opening date, discharge date, estate trustee code, declared value of estate assets, and total value of gross dividends paid to creditors. *Available:* Infomart Dialog Limited. *Type:* Database.

Barron's National Business & Financial Weekly
Dow Jones & Company, Inc.
P.O. Box 300   Ph: (609)520-4000
Princeton, NJ 08543-0300
URL: http://www.dj.com
Desc: Provides the complete text of articles, including tables, covering the U.S. national business and financial scene. *Available:* Dow Jones Interactive Publishing. *Type:* Database.

Basic Guide to Exporting
Todd Publications
PO Box 635   Ph: (914)358-6213
Nyack, NY 10960   Free: 800-747-1056
                                     Fax: (914)358-1059
E-mail: toddpub@aol.com
URL: http://www.toddpublications.com
Desc: Sources for aid in understanding foreign business practices, government regulations, taxes, and currency. *Type:* Directory.

BC Politics. . .The Month
Provincial Newsletters Div.
Monday Publications
1609 Blanshard St.   Ph: (604)382-6188
Victoria, BC, Canada V8W 2J5   Free: 800-661-6335
                                     Fax: (604)382-9172
Contact: Janis Robertson, Editor.
Desc: Provides a summary of articles from the previous issues of BC Politics. . .The Week, plus additional analysis and a special month-end view by noted columnist Hubert Beyer. Includes new British Columbia legislation, government, members' bills and order-in-council. *Type:* Newsletter.

BC Politics. . .The Week
Provincial Newsletters Div.
Monday Publications
1609 Blanshard St.   Ph: (604)382-6188
Victoria, BC, Canada V8W 2J5   Free: 800-661-6335
                                     Fax: (604)382-9172
Contact: Janis Robertson, Managing Editor.
Desc: Reports on and analyzes political-economic news events in the British Columbia legislature. Recurring features include overview of House business, Question Period and Legislative Committees, a summary of news releases and other public documents, highlights from Orders-in-Council, including official cabinet decisions. *Type:* Newsletter.

Benchmarking Network Association
4606 FM 1960 W, Ste. 300   Ph: (281)440-5044
Houston, TX 77069   Fax: (281)440-6677
E-mail: benchmar@well.com
URL: http://www.benchmarkingnetwork.com
Contact: Mark T. Czarnecki, Pres.
Desc: Works to promote benchmarking among members. *Type:* Association.

Beta Gamma Sigma
11701 Borman Dr., Ste. 320   Ph: (314)432-5650
St. Louis, MO 63146   Fax: (314)432-7083
E-mail: bgshonors@betagammasigma.org
URL: http://www.betagammasigma.org
Contact: James A. Viehland, Exec.Dir.
Desc: National honor society. *Type:* Association.

BLACK CAREERS
Project Magazine, Inc.
PO Box 8214   Ph: (215)387-1600
Philadelphia, PA 19101-8214
Contact: Emory W. Washington, Editor and Publisher; Herbert Bass, Editor; D. Gooden, Circulation Mgr.
Desc: Business news magazine for minority college graduates and working professionals in business, industry, and government. Provides job search information and career guidance and development. *Type:* Periodical.

Black Enterprise
Earl Graves Publishing Co.
130 5th Ave.   Ph: (212)242-8000
New York, NY 10011   Free: 800-727-7777
                                     Fax: (212)886-9610
E-mail: benyc_ads@blackenterprise.com; besubscribe@blackenterprise.com.
Contact: Earl G. Graves, Editor and Publisher; Earl G. Graves, Jr., Pres./CEO.
Desc: Black-oriented business magazine. *Type:* Periodical.

Black Enterprise—Top Black Businesses Issue
Earl Graves Publishing Co.
130 5th Ave.   Ph: (212)242-8000
New York, NY 10011   Free: 800-727-7777
                                     Fax: (212)886-9610
E-mail: benyc_ads@blackenterprise.com
URL: http://www.blackenterprise.com.
Contact: Earl G. Graves, Editor.
Desc: Lists of 100 Black-owned industrial/service companies with sales of $18 million or above; 25 banks with total assets of $3.6 billion or more; 10 insurance companies with total assets of about $689 million or more; and 100 auto dealers with sales of $17 million or above; 20 advertising agencies with total billings of $795 million or more; 15 investment banks with issues totalling $123 billion. *Type:* Directory.

Bloomberg Business News
499 Park Ave.   Ph: (212)318-2300
15th Fl.   Free: 800-448-5678
New York, NY 10022   Fax: (212)980-2480

Contact: Matthew Winkler, Editor-in-Chief.

Alt. Contact: 499 Park Ave., 15th Fl., New York, NY 10022; telephone: (212)318-2300; fax: (212)980-2480; toll-free: 800-448-5678. *Type:* Periodical.

BNA International Business and Finance Daily
The Bureau of National Affairs, Inc. (BNA)
1231 25th St. NW   Ph: (202)452-4200
Washington, DC 20037
E-mail: bnaplus@bna.com
URL: http://bna.com/mkt/hrl/hrlwdec.htm

Contact: BNA PLUS, (202)452-4323, fax: (202)822-8092, bnaplus@bna.com.

Desc: Contains information for international business and financial developments. Business reporting includes international mergers and acquisitions, tax treaties and laws, economic and labor developments, and intellectual property issues. *Available:* LEXIS-NEXIS, LEXIS; The Dialog Corporation, DIALOG; West Group, WESTLAW. *Type:* Database.

BONAT's Diversified
255 N. El Cielo   Ph: (619)324-1503
Ste. 688   Fax: (714)660-8551
Palm Springs, CA 92262

Contact: Natalie Carlton, President; Teresa Carlton, VP/Sec.; Sylvia Resnick, Beauty; Sheila Cluff, Fitness; Frances Sheridan Goulard, Health and Diet.

Desc: Distributes feature articles concerning women, including beauty, health, exercise, hair and make-up, puzzles, and cartoons. *Alt. Contact:* 255 N. El Cielo, Ste. 688, Palm Springs, CA 92262; telephone: (619)324-1503; fax: (714)660-8551. *Type:* Periodical.

The Book of Lists
Orange County Business Journal
2600 Michelson Blvd., Ste. 170   Ph: (949)833-8373
Irvine, CA 92612   Fax: (949)833-8751

Contact: Roger Bloom, Editor; Rick Reiff, Editor.

Desc: Leading employers and private companies located in Orange County, California. *Type:* Directory.

Book of Lists
Orlando Business Journal
315 E. Robinson St., No. 250   Ph: (407)649-8470
Orlando, FL 32801   Fax: (407)649-8469
E-mail: orlando@amcity.com

Contact: Kent Hoover, Editor.

Desc: Contains "Top 25 Lists" for over 40 types of businesses in central Florida, including public and private companies, office buildings, industrial parks, meeting facilities, convention hotels, construction companies, placement agencies, service companies, and others. *Type:* Directory.

Boston Business Journal—Book of Lists
P & L Publications, Inc.
200 High St.   Ph: (617)330-1000
Boston, MA 02110   Fax: (617)330-1016

Contact: Jay Fitzgerald, Editor.

Desc: "Top 25" financial institutions, computer companies, law firms, insurance companies, advertising firms, architectural firms, and other companies and organizations in the Boston, Massachusetts area. *Type:* Directory.

Bradco High Desert Report
The Bradco Companies
PO Box 2710   Ph: (760)951-5111
Victorville, CA 92393-2710   Fax: (760)951-5113

Contact: Joseph W. Brady, Publisher; Lowell Draper, Editor; Lee Blocker, Editor; Jill Hanson, Editor.

Desc: Focuses on development opportunities and economic overview in the Victor Valley and North San Bernadino County, described as "one of Southern California's fastest growing areas." *Type:* Newsletter.

Brands and Their Companies
Gale Group Inc.
27500 Drake Rd.   Ph: (248)699-4253
Farmington Hills, MI 48331-   Free: 800-877-GALE
3535   Fax: (248)699-8070
E-mail: galeord@galegroup.com; usbus@gale.com.
URL: http://www.galegroup.com.; http://www.gale.com.

Contact: Christine A. Kesler, Editor.

Desc: Approximately 360,000 trade names, trademarks, and brand names of consumer-oriented products and their 84,000 manufacturers, importers, marketers, or distributors. *Type:* Directory.

Brands and Their Companies
The Gale Group
27500 Drake Rd.   Ph: (248)699-4253
Farmington Hills, MI 48331-3535
URL: http://www.galegroup.com

Desc: Contains listings of more than 340,000 trade names, trademarks, and brand names of consumer goods available from more than 73,000 owners and distributors. *Available:* The Dialog Corporation, DIALOG; The Gale Group, GaleNet; LEXIS-NEXIS, NEXIS. *Type:* Database.

Brazil Company Handbook
Hoover's, Inc.
1033 La Posada Dr., Ste. 250   Ph: (512)374-4500
Austin, TX 78752   Fax: (512)374-4501
E-mail: orders@hoovers.com
URL: http://www.hoovers.com

Desc: About 85 of Brazil's largest public companies; 56 money managers and investment advisors. *Type:* Directory.

Brazil Dez Mil
Dun & Bradstreet
3 Sylvan Way   Ph: (973)605-6442
Parsippany, NJ 07054-3896   Free: 800-526-0651
    Fax: (973)605-6911
E-mail: dnbmdd@dnb.com

Desc: 10,000 of the largest companies in Brazil. *Type:* Directory.

Brazil Key Business Directory
Dun & Bradstreet
3 Sylvan Way   Ph: (973)605-6442
Parsippany, NJ 07054-3896   Free: 800-526-0651
    Fax: (973)605-6911
E-mail: dnbmdd@dnb.com

Desc: Leading companies in Brazil whose annual sales are $10 million and who have 500 or more employees. *Type:* Directory.

Brazil—Rio de Janeiro Annual Directory and Mercosul Business Guide
U.S. Chamber of Commerce
International Division Publications
1615 H St. NW   Ph: (202)463-5460
Washington, DC 20062-2000   Fax: (202)463-3114

Desc: Brazilian executives, branch offices, corporate headquarters abroad, representatives abroad, and capital. *Type:* Directory.

Brazil—Sao Paulo Yearbook
U.S. Chamber of Commerce
International Division Publications
1615 H St. NW   Ph: (202)463-5460
Washington, DC 20062-2000   Fax: (202)463-3114

Desc: 1,000 local and multinational companies in Brazil. *Type:* Directory.

Brazil Watch Fax Bulletin
Orbis Publications, LLC
3201 New Mexico Ave. NW,   Ph: (202)237-0155
Ste. 249   Fax: (202)237-0596
Washington, DC 20016
E-mail: orbis@orbispub.com
URL: http://www.orbispub.com.

Contact: Richard Foster, Editor.

Desc: Reports on political, economic and business events in Brazil via fax. *Type:* Newsletter.

Brazilian-American Business Review/Directory
Brazilian-American Chamber of Commerce, Inc.
509 Madison Ave., Ste. 304   Ph: (212)751-4691
New York, NY 10022   Fax: (212)751-7692
E-mail: info@brazilcham.com; pubs@brazilcham.com.
URL: http://www.brazilcham.com

Contact: Sueli Bonaparte, Editor.

Desc: Brazilian and American businesses interested in developing trade and investment between the two countries. *Type:* Directory.

Brazilian-American Who's Who
Brazilian-American Chamber of Commerce, Inc.
509 Madison Ave., Ste. 304   Ph: (212)751-4691
New York, NY 10022   Fax: (212)751-7692
E-mail: info@brazilcham.com; pubs@brazilcham.com.
URL: http://www.brazilcham.com

Contact: Christopher Buettner, chris@brazilcham.com.

Desc: More than 1,300 firms, subsidiaries, and affiliates operating and/or having interests in both the United States and Brazil. *Type:* Directory.

Briefing on Office Technologies
National Institute of Business Management
1750 Old Meadow Rd., Ste.   Ph: (703)905-8000
302   Free: 800-543-2049
Mc Lean, VA 22102   Fax: (703)905-8042

Contact: Pat DiDomenico, Editor.

Desc: Covers news, trends, and strategies pertaining to office technology. *Type:* Newsletter.

Bruce Bortz's Maryland Report
Bancroft Information Group, Inc.
PO Box 65360   Ph: (410)358-0658
Baltimore, MD 21209
E-mail: lharris@bancroftpress.com.

Contact: Bruce Bortz, President.

Desc: Monitors Maryland's $4 billion a year contract activity. *Type:* Newsletter.

Buckmaster's Annual Stockholder Reports
Buckmaster Publishing
6196 Jefferson Hwy.   Ph: (540)894-5777
Mineral, VA 23117   Free: 800-282-5628
    Fax: (540)894-9141
E-mail: info@buck.com
URL: http://www.buck.com; http://buck.com/libmain.html.

Desc: Annual reports of Fortune 500 corporations. *Type:* Directory.

Buffalo Niagara Partnership Membership Directory

Buffalo Niagara Partnership
Chamber of Commerce for Western New York
300 Main Place Tower   Ph: (716)852-7100
Buffalo, NY 14202-3797   Fax: (716)852-2761
URL: http://www.thepartnership.org.

Contact: Julie R. Hazzan, Editor.

Desc: About 3,800 manufacturers, service organizations, and minority- and women-owned businesses. *Type:* Directory.

Business & Acquisition Newsletter

Newsletters International, Inc.
2600 S. Gessner Rd.   Ph: (713)783-0100
Houston, TX 77063

Contact: Len Fox, Editor.

Desc: Contains highly confidential information about companies that want to buy or sell companies, divisions, subsidiaries, product lines, and patents. Includes information on sources of capital to finance purchases of such operations and suggestions on how to structure, negotiate, and complete such deals. *Type:* Newsletter.

The Business Advocate

U.S. Chamber of Commerce
International Division Publications
1615 H St. NW   Ph: (202)463-5460
Washington, DC 20062-2000   Fax: (202)463-3114

Contact: Mary McElveen, Editor; Bob Gotshall, Advertising Dir.

Desc: Magazine reporting economic and business trends affecting the national business community and the economy. Supplement to Nation's Business. *Type:* Periodical.

Business Concepts

Publishing and Business Consultants
4427 W. Slauson Ave.
Los Angeles, CA 90043-2717

Contact: Atia Napoleon, Editor and Publisher.

Desc: Magazine featuring money-making ideas and new business opportunities. *Type:* Periodical.

Business Council of New York State—The Wire

Business Council of New York State, Inc.
152 Washington Ave.   Ph: (518)465-7511
Albany, NY 12210   Fax: (518)465-4389

Contact: Melissa Bower, Editor.

Desc: Covers Council activities and legislation pertinent employers. Contains news of meetings. *Type:* Newsletter.

Business Dateline®

Bell & Howell Information and Learning
300 N. Zeeb Rd.   Ph: (734)761-4700
PO Box 1346
Ann Arbor, MI 48106-1346
E-mail: info@umi.com
URL: http://www.umi.com

Contact: UMI Help Line. Toll-free: 800-626-2823.

Desc: Contains the complete text of more than 550,000 articles from over 450 U.S. and Canadian hard-to-find local and regional business publications. *Available:* The Dialog Corporation, DIALOG; Dow Jones Interactive Publishing; OCLC Online Computer Library Center, Inc., OCLC EPIC; LEXIS-NEXIS, NEXIS; CompuServe Information Service. *Type:* Database.

Business Directory of the New Independent States

Market Knowledge
Triumph Books
644 S. Clark St.   Ph: (312)939-3300
Chicago, IL 60605   Fax: (312)663-3557
Contact: David Escarraz, Editor.

Desc: About 4,000 Commonwealth of Independent States businesses licensed for import/export. *Type:* Directory.

Business Ethics Resource

Business Ethics Foundation
150 Buckminster Rd.   Ph: (617)232-6565
Brookline, MA 02445-5806   Fax: (617)232-2775
Contact: William H.P. Smith, Editor; Verne E. Henderson, President, vhender@aol.com.

Desc: Monitors and provides information on ethics in business. Recurring features include book reviews, letters to the editor, interviews, news of research, corporate stories, cartoons, and editorials. *Type:* Newsletter.

Business Features Syndicate

PO Box A   Ph: (603)922-8338
North Stratford, NH 03590   Fax: (603)922-8339
E-mail: fjwx43b@prodigy.com.
Contact: Dana K. Cassell, Editor.

Desc: Distributes business management, how-to, sales, marketing, home-business, and retailing features. *Alt. Contact:* PO Box A, North Stratford, NH 03590; telephone: (603)922-8338; fax: (603)922-8339. *Type:* Periodical.

Business Ideas & Shortcuts

Editorial Board
IBIS
PO Box 4082   Ph: (714)552-8494
Irvine, CA 92710-4082
Contact: Peter Joseph, Editor.

Desc: Contains special reports, practical ideas, tips, and guidelines on current business opportunities and shortcuts to profits. Covers specific topics, such as how to be a manufacturer without investing; how to get free national advertising; how to protect your business; and how to tap overlooked sources of financing. *Type:* Newsletter.

Business Index™

The Gale Group
27500 Drake Rd.   Ph: (248)699-4253
Farmington Hills, MI 48331-
3535
URL: http://www.galegroup.com
Contact: Jim Knight, (650)378-5000, fax: (800)676-2345.
Desc: Contains more than 3 million citations, with some abstracts, to articles in more than 800 specialized business, management, and trade journals, some 80 regional and local journals and newspapers, and business-related articles published in approximately 3000 additional newspapers, magazines, and serial publications. Each citation includes a reference to the complete text of the item, available for more than 400 publications, in the Business Collection on microfilm. *Available:* CARL Corporation. *Type:* Database.

Business & Industry Journal

Greater Dallas Chamber
1201 Elm St., Ste. 2000   Ph: (214)746-6704
Dallas, TX 75270   Fax: (214)746-6799
E-mail: mchapman@dallaschamber.org.
Contact: Laura Brumley, Editor; Charlotte Fowler, Editor; John Christian, Editor.
Desc: Listings of the top 200 Dallas area employers and the top 20 employers within nearly 40 industries. *Type:* Directory.

Business Information Alert

Alert Publications, Inc.
401 W. Fullerton Pkwy.   Ph: (773)525-7594
Chicago, IL 60614-2810   Fax: (773)525-7015
E-mail: alertpub@compuserve.com
URL: http://www.alertpub.com.
Contact: Donna Tuke Heroy, Editor.

Desc: Provides news and information on the U.S. business information industry. *Type:* Newsletter.

The Business Information Report

Dun & Bradstreet Business Credit Services
One Diamond Hill Rd.   Ph: (908)665-5000
PO Box 27
Murray Hill, NJ 07974-0027
URL: http://www.dnb.com
Desc: Provides comprehensive information for more than 10 million public and private U.S. company locations. *Available:* West Group, WESTLAW. *Type:* Database.

The Business Information Report

Dun & Bradstreet
1 Diamond Hill Rd.   Ph: (908)665-5732
Murray Hill, NJ 07974   Free: 800-526-0651
                             Fax: (908)665-5722
E-mail: dnbmdd@mail.dnb.com
URL: http://www.dnb.com/
Desc: More than 9 million public and private U.S. companies. *Type:* Directory.

The Business Initiative Newsletter

Ecomedia
315 E. 65th St.   Ph: (212)794-8902
New York, NY 10021
Contact: Betsy Combier, Editor; John Aigner, Publisher.
Desc: Focuses on ethics in the workplace. *Type:* Newsletter.

Business Journal's Directory of Business & Government

Business Journal of New Jersey, Inc.
50 Highway 9   Ph: (908)972-1170
Morganville, NJ 07751   Free: 800-678-2565
                             Fax: (908)972-7965
Desc: 26,000 businesses and government agencies in New Jersey. *Type:* Directory.

Business Journal's High Tech Directory

Business Journal of New Jersey, Inc.
50 Highway 9   Ph: (908)972-1170
Morganville, NJ 07751   Free: 800-678-2565
                             Fax: (908)972-7965
Desc: 4,500 high tech companies located in New Jersey. *Type:* Directory.

Business Latin America

Treasury & Risk Management
111 W. 57th St., 11th Fl.   Ph: (212)459-3004
New York, NY 10019-2211   Fax: (212)459-3007
E-mail: newyork@eiu.com; bla@engny.mhs.compuserve.com.
Contact: Anna Szterenfeld, Consulting Editor.
Desc: Concentrates on business and investment in Latin American and the Caribbean. *Type:* Newsletter.

Business Life Magazine

Business Life Magazine
PO Box 2065   Ph: (818)240-7088
Glendale, CA 91209
E-mail: marketing@businesslife.com
URL: http://www.businesslife.com/
Desc: This publication covers the Southern California business community. It includes information on conferences, real estate, business trends, and lifestyles. *Type:* Database.

Business in Nebraska

Bureau of Business Research
University of Nebraska-Lincoln   Ph: (402)472-2334
114 CBA   Fax: (402)472-3878
Lincoln, NE 68588-0406
URL: http://www.cba.unl.edu/bbr/bbr.html.
Contact: F. Charles Lamphear, Editor, clamphear@unl.edu.
Desc: Covers business in Nebraska. Recurring features include columns titled County of the Month. *Type:* Newsletter.

Business Newsfeatures

20630 Harper Ste. 103   Ph: (313)886-2331
Harper Woods, MI 48225
Contact: Robert H. Meyering, Operations/Mktg.; Carl Meyering, Editor.
Desc: Distributes financial news. *Alt. Contact:* 20630 Harper Ste. 103, Harper Woods, MI 48225; telephone: (313)886-2331. *Type:* Periodical.

Business Organizations, Agencies, and Publications Directory

The Gale Group
27500 Drake Rd.   Ph: (248)699-4253
Farmington Hills, MI 48331-
3535
URL: http://www.galegroup.com
Contact: Customer Service. Toll-free: 800-877-GALE.
Desc: Provides descriptions of more than 34,000 new and established organizations, agencies, and publications that are sources of current information on U.S. and international business and industry. *Available:* OCLC Online Computer Library Center, Inc., OCLC EPIC; OCLC Online Computer Library Center, Inc., OCLC FirstSearch Catalog. *Type:* Database.

Business Organizations, Agencies, and Publications Directory

Gale Group Inc.
27500 Drake Rd.   Ph: (248)699-4253
Farmington Hills, MI 48331-   Free: 800-877-GALE
3535   Fax: (248)699-8070
E-mail: galeord@galegroup.com
URL: http://www.galegroup.com.; http://www.gale.com.
Contact: Sonya Hill, Editor.
Desc: Approximately 37,000 organizations and publications of all kinds that are helpful in business, including trade, business, commercial, and labor associations; government agencies and advisory organizations; commodity and stock exchanges; United States and foreign diplomatic offices; regional planning and development agencies; convention, fair, and trade organizations; franchise companies; information centers; computerized information services; research centers; graduate schools of business; special libraries; periodicals, directories; national, state and local chambers of commerce. *Type:* Directory.

Business Periodicals Index

H.W. Wilson Company
950 University Ave.   Ph: (718)588-8400
Bronx, NY 10452
E-mail: custserv@hwwilson.com
URL: http://www.hwwilson.com
Contact: Technical Support Department., techmail@info.hwwilson.com.
Desc: Contains citations to articles and book reviews in some 400 business periodicals covering 25 business specialties. Includes feature articles, interviews, biographical sketches of business leaders, book reviews, research developments, new product reviews, and reports of associations, societies, and conferences. *Available:* Bell & Howell Information and Learning; Ovid Technologies, Inc.; OCLC Online Computer Library Center, Inc., OCLC EPIC; OCLC Online Computer Library Center, Inc., OCLC FirstSearch Catalog; SilverPlatter Information, Inc.; The Dialog Corporation, DIALOG; H.W. Wilson Company, WilsonWeb. *Type:* Database.

Business Phone Book USA

Omnigraphics Inc.
2500 Penobscot Bldg.   Ph: (313)961-1340
Detroit, MI 48226   Free: 800-234-1340
                                  Fax: (313)961-1383
E-mail: info@omnigraphics.com
URL: http://www.omnigraphics.com
Contact: Darren L. Smith, Editor.
Desc: Approximately 132,500 U.S. businesses, federal, state, and local government offices, banks, colleges and universities, associations, labor unions, political organizations, newspapers, magazines, TV and radio stations, foundations, postal and shipping services, hospitals, office equipment suppliers, airlines, hotels and motels, profiles of top cities, accountants, law firms, computer firms, foreign corporations, overseas trade contacts, and other professional services. Also covers internet access providers; internet mailing lists, publications, and sources; freenets. Personal names now included. *Type:* Directory.

Business Planning Advisory

WPI Communications, Inc.
55 Morris Ave.   Ph: (201)467-8700
Springfield, NJ 07081   Fax: (201)467-0368
Contact: Ken Berry, Editor.
Desc: Offers advice on business planning. *Type:* Newsletter.

Business Plans Handbook

Gale Group Inc.
27500 Drake Rd.   Ph: (248)699-4253
Farmington Hills, MI 48331-   Free: 800-877-GALE
3535   Fax: (248)699-8070
E-mail: galeord@galegroup.com
URL: http://www.galegroup.com.
Contact: William Harmer, Editor; Terrance W. Peck, Editor.
Desc: A collection of 24 actual business plans, including executive summaries, market profiles and analyses, product and production information, and management, personnel, and financial data. Appendix includes sample business plan template; two fictional plans; listings of small business associations, consultants, venture capital/finance companies; SBA and SBDC offices; SCORE offices; small business term glossary; and a bibliography containing citations for articles and publications relating to small business. *Type:* Directory.

Business and the Press

Phillips Business Information, Inc.
1201 Seven Locks Rd., Ste. 300   Ph: (301)340-1520
Potomac, MD 20854   Free: 888-707-5809
                                  Fax: (301)340-3847
E-mail: clientservices.pbi@phillips.com
Desc: Focuses on the relationship between business and the press. *Type:* Newsletter.

Business Publication Advertising Source

SRDS
1700 Higgins Rd.   Ph: (847)375-5000
Des Plaines, IL 60018-5605   Free: 800-851-7737
                                  Fax: (847)375-5001
E-mail: contact@srds.com
URL: http://www.srds.com.
Contact: Peter Spina, Editor.
Desc: More than 7,500 U.S. and international business, trade, and technical publications; over 600 card deck listings. *Type:* Directory.

Business Rankings Annual

Gale Group Inc.
27500 Drake Rd.   Ph: (248)699-4253
Farmington Hills, MI 48331-   Free: 800-877-GALE
3535   Fax: (248)699-8070
E-mail: galeord@galegroup.com
URL: http://www.galegroup.com.; http://www.gale.com.
Contact: Sheila Dow, Editor, sheila.dow@gale.com.
Desc: "Business Rankings Annual" is a collection of about 4,800 citations of ranked lists of companies or other entities, together with the top 10 (or so) entries from each list. The citations are selected from the files of the Business Library of the Brooklyn Public Library, which has collected 10,000 ranked lists from periodicals, directories, and other publications. Entries cover domestic, international, and foreign rankings. *Type:* Directory.

A Business Researcher's Interests

Brint Research Institute
PO Box 15635   Ph: (954)916-1585
Ft. Lauderdale, FL 33318   Fax: (954)916-1585
E-mail: inquiry@brint.com
URL: http://www.brint.com/
Desc: An enormous archive of articles, reports, links, and analyses related to business, management, and associated technology issues, BRINT offers a wide range of material on practically any business issue that might arise. This site houses dozens of reports and articles on such topics as "out of the box" thinking, business and technology, and knowledge management. *Type:* Database.

Business Start-Ups

Entrepreneur's Media Inc.
2392 Morse Ave.   Ph: (949)261-2325
Irvine, CA 92614   Fax: (714)755-4211
E-mail: entmag@entrepreneurmag.com; bsumag@entrepreneurmag.com
URL: http://www.entrepreneurmag.com.
Contact: Karen Axelton, Managing Editor; Lee Jones, Publisher, (212)563-8080, fax: (212)563-3852.
Desc: Magazine for Generation X entrepreneurs (age 35 and under). Articles cover hot businesses to start; ideas for running and growing a business; cutting-edge technology; management; motivation and more. *Type:* Periodical.

Business Strategies Bulletin

CCH Inc.
2700 Lake Cook Rd.   Ph: (847)267-7000
Riverwoods, IL 60015   Free: 800-449-8114
                                  Fax: (847)224-8299
URL: http://www.cch.com; http://www.cch.com.
Contact: Kathleen A. Larrison, Editor; Thomas Werst, Editor.
Desc: Reports tax and business planning information for all sizes of business, with emphasis on small to mid-sized business advisors. *Type:* Newsletter.

Business Today (Princeton)

Foundation for Student Communication, Inc.
305 Aaron Burr Hall   Ph: (609)258-1111
Princeton University   Fax: (609)258-1222
Princeton, NJ 08540
E-mail: fscint@princeton.edu
Contact: Roger Ahn, Publisher.
Desc: Student business publication. *Type:* Periodical.

Business Trends

Economics Department
Bank of Hawaii
PO Box 2900   Ph: (808)537-8307
Honolulu, HI 96846   Fax: (808)536-9433
URL: http://www.boh.com/econ/.
Contact: Paul Brewbaker, Editor-in-Chief; Susan Atwell, Managing Editor.

Desc: Reports on economic conditions and economic issues in Hawaii and the Pacific Islands' economics. *Type:* Newsletter.

Business Trends Report

Business Research
537 Newport Center Dr., Ste. 355   Ph: (714)854-2550
Newport Beach, CA 92660-   Fax: (714)854-2550
6937

Contact: Thomas Thompson, Editor and Publisher.

Desc: Summarizes top U.S. business, investment, and travel newsletters. *Type:* Newsletter.

Business Week

McGraw-Hill, Inc.
1221 Avenue of the Americas   Ph: (212)512-6410
New York, NY 10020

Desc: Contains the complete text of Business Week, a business and industry news magazine. Covers finance, labor and production, corporate news and investment policies, and the effects of legislative and regulatory developments on commerce. *Available:* LEXIS-NEXIS, NEXIS; FT PROFILE; Dow Jones Interactive Publishing; The Dialog Corporation, DIALOG; Bell & Howell Information and Learning. *Type:* Database.

Business Week

McGraw-Hill, Inc.
2 Penn Plaza   Ph: (212)904-2000
New York, NY 10121   Free: 800-223-6180
  Fax: (212)904-6068

URL: http://www.mcgraw-hill.com; http://www.mcgraw-hill.com; http://www.businessweek.com.

Contact: Stephen B. Shepard, Editor, (212)512-6893; David G. Ferm, Publisher; William P. Kupper, Jr., Sr. VP Associate Publisher.

Desc: Magazine providing business news and intelligence for executives. *Type:* Periodical.

Business Week—Corporate Scoreboard Issue

McGraw-Hill, Inc.
2 Penn Plaza   Ph: (212)904-2000
New York, NY 10121   Free: 800-223-6180
  Fax: (212)904-6068

URL: http://www.mcgraw-hill.com

Contact: Fred Jespersen, Editor.

Desc: List of sales and profits for 900 major U.S. companies in all business, industrial, and financial categories, with extensive analytical text. *Type:* Directory.

Business Week—1,000 Issue

McGraw-Hill, Inc.
2 Penn Plaza   Ph: (212)904-2000
New York, NY 10121   Free: 800-223-6180
  Fax: (212)904-6068

URL: http://www.mcgraw-hill.com

Desc: List of 1,000 U.S. corporations by market value in all business, industrial, and financial categories, with financial results for preceding year and extensive analytical text. *Type:* Directory.

Business Week—Survey of Executive Compensation Issue

McGraw-Hill, Inc.
2 Penn Plaza   Ph: (212)904-2000
New York, NY 10121   Free: 800-223-6180
  Fax: (212)904-6068

URL: http://www.mcgraw-hill.com

Desc: Executives in major industries of the United States and their compensation in salary, bonuses, stock options, stock appreciation rights. *Type:* Directory.

BUSINESS WIRE

Business Wire
44 Montgomery St., 39th Floor   Ph: (415)986-4422
San Francisco, CA 94104

E-mail: sandy@bizwire.com

Contact: Sandy Malloy, Sr. Information Specialist, (415)986-4422, fax: (415)956-0450, sandy@bizwire.com.

Desc: Contains the complete text of more than 242,000 press releases from more than 17,000 companies and other organizations (e.g., hospitals, universities). Covers new products, legal actions, financial information, personnel changes, and company announcements of general interest. *Available:* Bridge Information Systems, Inc., Knight-Ridder Financial Information Group; Delphi Internet Services Corporation; The Dialog Corporation, DIALOG; Dow Jones Interactive Publishing; LEXIS-NEXIS, NEXIS; AT&T EasyLink Services; America Online, Inc.; BT North America, Inc.; CompuServe Information Service, Knowledge Index; CompuServe Information Service; Bloomberg Financial Markets; Prodigy Services Company, PRODIGY. *Type:* Database.

Business Wire

44 Montgomery St.   Ph: (415)986-4422
39th Fl.   Fax: (415)788-5335
San Francisco, CA 94104

Contact: Lorry I. Lokey, President; Cathy Baron Tamraz, Sr. VP; Terry Vitorelo, VP Ops.; Michael Lissauer, VP Mktg. & Creative Svcs.

Desc: Distributes press releases. *Alt. Contact:* 44 Montgomery St., 39th Fl., San Francisco, CA 94104; telephone: (415)986-4422; fax: (415)788-5335. *Type:* Periodical.

Businessmen's Expectations

Dun & Bradstreet
1 World Trade Ctr., 14th Fl.   Ph: (212)593-6800
New York, NY 10048

Desc: Provides business information. *Type:* Newsletter.

BusinessTech

Tribeca Research Inc.
90 Hudson St.   Ph: (212)431-8700
New York, NY 10013-2831   Fax: (212)431-8777

E-mail: btech@businesstech.com.

URL: http://businesstech.com.

Contact: Neal M. Goldsmith, Editor and Publisher; Edward Rosenfeld, Editor and Publisher.

Desc: Provides information and analysis about corporate technology strategy and the Internet. *Type:* Newsletter.

Buyerism Newsletter

WWWWW/Information Services, Inc.
PO Box 10046   Ph: (716)461-1888
Rochester, NY 14610-0046

Contact: Robert A. Fowler, Editor and Publisher.

Desc: Deals with starting a business and other related topics. *Type:* Newsletter.

Buyouts

Securities Data Publishing Inc.
1290 Avenue of the Americas   Ph: (212)765-5311
New York, NY 10104   Free: 800-455-5844
  Fax: (212)937-0420

E-mail: sdp@tfn.com; reedj@tfn.com.

Contact: Robert B. Dunn, Managing Editor, (212)830-9664, robert.dunn@trf.com.

Desc: Examines activities in the management buyout and leveraged acquisition industries. Covers leveraged buyout (LBO) investment organizations and transactions, new equity partnerships, and emerging trends. *Type:* Newsletter.

CableFAX Daily

Phillips Business Information, Inc.
1201 Seven Locks Rd., Ste. 300   Ph: (301)340-1520
Potomac, MD 20854   Free: 888-707-5809
  Fax: (301)340-3847

E-mail: clientservices.pbi@phillips.com

Contact: Seth Arenstein, Editor, sarenstein@phillips.com.

Desc: Covers business, government, and finance. Recurring features include columns titled Paul Maxwell, Techfax, International Notebook, Broadband Bulletin, and Programmers Page. *Type:* Newsletter.

California Business—California's 100 Fastest Growing Companies Issue

MZ Media Group, Inc.
221 Main St., Ste. 700   Ph: (415)543-4600
San Francisco, CA 94105   Free: 800-927-1200
  Fax: (415)543-8232

Desc: List of 100 fastest growing firms, based on earnings per share for two-year period. *Type:* Directory.

California Business Directory

infoUSA
5711 S. 86th Circle   Ph: (402)593-4600
PO Box 27347   Free: 800-555-6124
Omaha, NE 68127   Fax: (402)331-5481

E-mail: internet@infousa.com

URL: http://www.abii.com.

Contact: Peter J. Wilmarth, Publisher.

Desc: In two volumes (Northern and Southern), 1,263,000 businesses in California. *Type:* Directory.

California Business Register

Database Publishing Co.
1590 S. Lewis St.   Ph: (714)778-6400
PO Box 70024   Free: 800-888-8434
Anaheim, CA 92825-0024   Fax: (714)778-6811

E-mail: sales@databasepublishing.com

URL: http://www.databasepublishing.com; http://www.databasepublishing.com.

Desc: 60,000 of California's top manufacturers, wholesalers, service and high tech companies, as well as 150,000 top California business executives. *Type:* Directory.

California International Trade Register

Database Publishing Co.
1590 S. Lewis St.   Ph: (714)778-6400
PO Box 70024   Free: 800-888-8434
Anaheim, CA 92825-0024   Fax: (714)778-6811

E-mail: sales@databasepublishing.com

URL: http://www.databasepublishing.com; http://www.databasepublishing.com.

Desc: Some 8,000 manufacturers, wholesalers, trading companies, and other firms exporting or importing goods and services in California. Includes 25,560 key executives. *Type:* Directory.

Canada NewsWire

Canada NEWSWire Ltd.
WaterPark Place, Ste. 914   Ph: (416)863-9350
10 Bay St.
Toronto, ON, Canada M5J 2R8

E-mail: cnw@newswire.ca

URL: http://www.newswire.ca

Contact: Alison Fraser, National Marketing Manager, (416)863-2136, alisonf@newswire.ca.

Desc: Contains the complete text of news releases issued by approximately 5000 organizations and transmitted to the press by Canada NewsWire. Source organizations include private companies, associations, political parties, unions, sports and entertainment organizations, educational and scientific institutions, and municipal, provincial, and federal government agencies. *Available:* Globe Information Services, Info Globe Online; Infomart Online; QL Systems Limited, QUICKLAW; Dow Jones Interactive Publishing; LEXIS-NEXIS, NEXIS; LEXIS-NEXIS, LEXIS; The Dialog Corporation, DIALOG; Bell & Howell Information and Learning; Infomart Assistant, Infomart Online; Infomart Dialog Limited. *Type:* Database.

The Canada-U.S. Free Trade Agreement

External Affairs Canada
International Trade Commissions Group
125 Sussex Dr.　　Ph: (613)996-9134
Ottawa, ON, Canada K1A 0G2
E-mail: ski.extott@extott09.x400.gc.ca

Desc: Contains the complete text of the 1987 Canada-U.S. Free Trade Agreement, including notes and tariff schedules. *Available:* QL Systems Limited, QUICKLAW. *Type:* Database.

Canada West Foundation

Canada West Foundation
630 3rd Ave. SW, No. 550
Calgary, AB, Canada T2P 4L4　Ph: (403)264-9535
　　　　Fax: (403)269-4776
E-mail: cwf@freenet.calgary.ab.ca
URL: http://www.cwf.ca/

Desc: This site offers a brief history of the Foundation, its aims and objectives, schedule of upcoming vents, an online library of publications which can be ordered in print format, economic bulletins and other statistics about western Canada. You will also find CWFax, a periodic comment on current research activities. *Type:* Database.

Canadian Business

CB Media Ltd.
777 Bay St., 5th Fl.　　Ph: (416)596-5999
Toronto, ON, Canada M5W　Fax: (416)596-5111
1A7

Contact: Arthur Johnson, Editor; Paul Jones, Publisher.

Desc: A management magazine with a strategic focus and a global outlook. *Type:* Periodical.

Canadian Company Histories

St. James Press, Inc.
27500 Drake Rd.　　Ph: (248)699-4253
Farmington Hills, MI 48331-　Free: 800-877-4253
3535　　　　Fax: (248)699-8069
E-mail: galeord@gale.com

Contact: Tina Grant, Editor.

Desc: 80 of Canada's most significant companies. *Type:* Directory.

Canadian Corporate Names

Infomart Dialog Limited
1450 Don Mills Rd.　　Ph: (416)442-2198
Don Mills, ON, Canada M3B
2X7
E-mail: helpdesk@infomart.ca
URL: http://www.infomart.com/

Contact: Client Service Consultants, (416)442-2198, fax: (416)442-2126, helpdesk@infomart.ca.

Desc: Contains descriptive information on more than 3 million Canadian federal and provincial incorporated businesses. Includes corporation name, incorporation date, whether federally or provincially incorporated, province of incorporation, current legal status (e.g., bankrupt, dissolved), and status date. *Available:* Infomart Online; Infomart Dialog Limited. *Type:* Database.

Canadian Employment Law Today

MPL Communications Inc.
133 Richmond St., Ste. 700　Ph: (416)869-1177
Toronto, ON, Canada M5H　Fax: (416)869-0616
3M8

Desc: Contains "topical coverage and analysis of critical legal issues affecting business in Canada." *Type:* Newsletter.

Canadian Enhanced Dun's Market Identifiers™

Dun & Bradstreet Canada
5770 Hurontario St.　　Ph: (905)568-6000
PO Box 6200, Station A
Mississauga, ON, Canada L5R
3G5
URL: http://www.dnb.ca

Desc: Contains identifying, descriptive, and sales information on more than 900,000 Canadian companies, including branch offices and subsidiaries with 5 or more employees. *Available:* The Dialog Corporation, DIALOG; The Dialog Corporation, DIALOG; NIFTY Corporation, NIFTY-SERVE; The Dialog Corporation, DataStar; West Group, WESTLAW; CompuServe Information Service; AT&T EasyLink Services. *Type:* Database.

Canadian Press Information Network

The Canadian Press (CP)
36 King St. E.　　Ph: (416)364-0321
Toronto, ON, Canada M5C
2L9
E-mail: pn@cp.org
URL: http://www.cp.org

Desc: Contains daily business news reports supplied by Canadian Press, Associated Press, Reuters, and the Canadian Parliament and provincial legislatures. Covers agriculture, automotive industry, banking, communications, economy, energy, environment, forestry, government, labor, mining, publishing, and trade. *Available:* The Canadian Press (CP); QL Systems Limited, QUICKLAW. *Type:* Database.

CanCorp Plus Canadian Financial Database

Micromedia Ltd.
20 Victoria St.　　Ph: (416)362-5211
Toronto, ON, Canada M5C
2N8
E-mail: info@micromedia.on.ca
URL: http://www.micromedia.on.ca

Contact: Lynn Fraser, Manager, Corporate & Directory Information Databases.

Desc: Contains descriptive and financial data for more than 11,000 public, private, and Canadian government-owned (crown) corporations. *Available:* The Dialog Corporation, DIALOG; Infomart Online; The Dialog Corporation, DataStar; LEXIS-NEXIS, LEXIS; Infomart Dialog Limited. *Type:* Database.

CBI Online

Equifax Inc.
1600 Peachtree St. NW　Ph: (404)885-8158
Atlanta, GA 30309

Contact: Barbara Wilkes, Editor.

Desc: Covers CBI's services, legislative, and industry news. *Type:* Newsletter.

CD/Corporate: U.K. Private Companies

OneSource Information Services
150 CambridgePark Dr.　Ph: (617)441-7000
Cambridge, MA 02140
E-mail: tamar_shay@onesource.com
URL: http://www.onesource.com

Desc: Contains descriptive and financial data on more than 129,000 public and private U.K. registered companies in approximately 250 industries. *Type:* Database.

CD/Corporate: U.K. Public Companies

OneSource Information Services
150 CambridgePark Dr.　Ph: (617)441-7000
Cambridge, MA 02140
E-mail: tamar_shay@onesource.com
URL: http://www.onesource.com

Desc: Contains descriptive and financial data and news for some 5000 U.K listed, Unlisted Securities Market (USM), and Third Market companies. Corporate profiles include basic company information, subsidiaries, number of employees, officers, U.K. *Type:* Database.

CD/Corporate: U.S. Private

OneSource Information Services Inc.
150 Cambridge Park Dr.　Ph: (617)441-7000
Cambridge, MA 02140　Free: 800-554-5501
　　　　Fax: (617)441-7058

Desc: CD-Rom. 115,000 private and public parent companies, subsidiaries, and major divisions, with an emphasis on private companies. Includes more detailed information on the 6,000 largest private firms. Based on data from "Ward's Business Directory," "Macmillan's Directory of Leading Private Companies", and "PTS PROMT" database. *Type:* Directory.

Center for International Private Enterprise

1155 15th St. NW, Ste. 700　Ph: (202)721-9200
Washington, DC 20005　Fax: (202)721-9250
E-mail: cipe@cipe.org
URL: http://www.cipe.org/

Contact: John D. Sullivan, Exec. Dir.

Desc: Encourages the growth of voluntary business organizations and private enterprise systems abroad, such as chambers of commerce, trade associations, employers' organizations, and business-oriented research groups, particularly in developing countries. Helps business communities abroad strengthen their organizational capabilities; creates exchanges among business leaders and institutions to strengthen the international private enterprise system; encourages development of active business participation in the political process. Activities include: developing leadership training for association executives and their voluntary leadership to strengthen business institutions; developing communications programs and educational materials for youth, employees, women's groups, academic institutions, government officials, political leaders, and other audiences to encourage entrepreneurship. *Type:* Association.

Centerlines

International Association of Conference Centers
243 N. Lindbergh Blvd.　Ph: (314)993-8575
St. Louis, MO 63141　Fax: (314)993-8919
E-mail: info@iacconline.com; clincs@iacconline.com.
URL: http://www.iacconline.com/

Contact: Steve Smith, Editor.

Desc: Provides news and information about the conference center industry, and about the proceedings of the International Association of Conference Centers. Recurring features include a calendar of events and reports of meetings, and columns titled Committee Spotlight. *Type:* Newsletter.

The CEO Club Newsletter

Chief Executive Officers Clubs (CEO Clubs)
Center for Entrepreneurial Management, Inc.
180 Varick St., Penthouse　Ph: (212)633-0060
New York, NY 10014-4606　Fax: (212)633-0063
E-mail: ceoclubs@bway.net
URL: http://www.ceo-clubs.org.

Contact: Joseph Mancuso, Editor.

Desc: Serves as an information exchange among members from different chapters of the Club. Contains bulletins of products and services offered or needed by members. *Type:* Newsletter.

Chamber South Business Directory

Image Factory
6410 SW 80th St.　　　　　　Ph: (305)661-1621
Miami, FL 33143
Desc: About 4,400 member businesses, organizations, and other community resources in South Dade County, Florida. *Type:* Directory.

Chicago Creative Directory

Chicago Creative Directory
333 N. Michigan, Ste. 810　　Ph: (312)236-7337
Chicago, IL 60601　　　　　　Fax: (312)236-6078
E-mail: info@creativedir.com
URL:　http://www.creativedir.com/;　http://www.creativedir.com.
Contact: Beaver Hansen, Publisher.
Desc: Over 6,000 advertising agencies, photographers, sound studios, talent agencies, audiovisual services, and others offering creative and production services. *Type:* Directory.

Chicago Regional Purchasing Council—Affiliate Member Directory

Chicago Regional Purchasing Council
11 S. La Salle St.　　　　　　Ph: (312)263-0105
Chicago, IL 60603　　　　　　Fax: (312)263-0280
Desc: About 400 minority-owned firms in Illinois and northern Indiana offering professional, commercial, and industrial products and services. *Type:* Directory.

China Business Directory

China Business Information Center
175 Linmore Dr.　　　　　　Ph: (510)252-9888
Fremont, CA 94539　　　　　　Fax: (510)623-6955
Contact: Dr. Wayne Y. Chao, Editor; Wang Ji Qing, Editor.
Desc: More than 25,000 companies in the People's Republic of China, excluding Taiwan and Hong Kong, with assets over $1.5 million. *Type:* Directory.

China Weekly Fax Bulletin

Orbis Publications, LLC
3201 New Mexico Ave. NW,　Ph: (202)237-0155
　Ste. 249　　　　　　　　　Fax: (202)237-0596
Washington, DC 20016
E-mail: orbis@orbispub.com
Contact: Richard Foster, Editor.
Desc: Reports on political, economic and business events in China via fax. *Type:* Newsletter.

China's Enterprises & Companies Database

AsiaInfo Services, Inc.
5201 Great American Pkwy.,　Ph: (408)970-9788
　Ste. 226　　　　　　　　　Fax: (408)970-9366
Santa Clara, CA 95054
E-mail: products@asiainfo.com; cecdb@asiainfo.com.
Desc: Over 100,000 public and private companies in China, including commercial, manufacturing, and service industries. *Type:* Directory.

Chinese Business in America

Caravel, Inc.
23545 Crenshaw Blvd., 101E　Ph: (310)325-0100
Torrance, CA 90505　　　　　Fax: (310)325-2583
Contact: Davisson K. Chang, Editor.
Desc: Approximately 3,000 ethnic Chinese importers/exporters in the U.S. *Type:* Directory.

Christian Aid Mission

3045 Ivy Rd.　　　　　　　　Ph: (804)977-5650
Charlottesville, VA 22903　　Fax: (804)295-6814
Contact: Richard E. Brown, Pres.

Desc: Christian fundamentalist organization that seeks to "establish witness for the Lord Jesus Christ throughout the world." *Type:* Association.

CIO Magazine

International Data Group
5 Speen St.　　　　　　　　Ph: (508)879-0700
PO Box 9171　　　　　　　　Free: 800-343-4935
Framingham, MA 01701　　　Fax: (508)875-8931
URL: http://www.cio.com.
Contact: Lew McCreary, Editorial Dirctor, (508)935-4618, mccreary@cio.com; Joe Levy, Publisher, (508)935-4274, fax: (508)872-3759, jlevy@cio.com; Cathy O'Leary Hayes, Mktg. Vice Pres., (508)935-4521, fax: (508)877-0618, chayes@cio.com; Abbie Lundberg, Editor, (508)935-4731, lundberg@cid.com.
Desc: Publication for Chief Information Officers (CIOs) and other senior executives. *Alt. Contact:* 492 Old Connecticut Path, PO Box 9208, Framingham, MA 01701-9208; telephone: (508)872-0080; fax: (508)879-7784; toll-free: 800-942-4672. *Type:* Periodical.

City of Clinton Economic Development Office

Dick Helton
118 W Washington　　　　　Ph: (217)935-6552
PO Box 378　　　　　　　　Fax: (217)935-4136
Clinton, IL 61727
Contact: Thomas R. Edmunds, Mayor.
Type: Association.

City of St. Croix Falls

710 Hwy 35 S　　　　　　　Ph: (715)483-3929
Saint Croix Falls, WI 54024-　Fax: (715)483-1618
　9240
Contact: Gregory S. Withers, City Adm.
Type: Association.

CIX® Association

Commercial Internet eXchange Association
1024 Sterling Rd., Ste. 104A　Ph: (703)709-8200
Herndon, VA 20170
URL: http://www.cix.org/
Contact: Lou Scanlan, helpdesk@cix.org.
Desc: The Commercial Internet Exchange (CIX) web site provides information about the commercialization of the Internet. Hot topics such as SPAM and phone line technology are prominent here, along with other data concerning regulations and CIX membership information. *Type:* Database.

Classified Directory of Products & Services

SMC Business Councils
1400 S. Braddock Ave.　　　Ph: (412)371-1500
Pittsburgh, PA 15218　　　　Free: 800-588-3260
　　　　　　　　　　　　　Fax: (412)371-0460
E-mail: info@smc.org
URL: http://www.smc.org.
Contact: Lee Taddonio, Editor, lee@smc.org.
Desc: Over 5,000 small business concerns in central and western Pennsylvania. *Type:* Directory.

Colorado Business Directory

infoUSA
5711 S. 86th Circle　　　　　Ph: (402)593-4600
PO Box 27347　　　　　　　Free: 800-555-6124
Omaha, NE 68127　　　　　　Fax: (402)331-5481
E-mail: internet@infousa.com
URL: http://www.abii.com.
Contact: Peter J. Wilmarth, Publisher.
Desc: 192,000 businesses in Colorado. *Type:* Directory.

CommerceNet

CommerceNet, Inc.
4005 Miranda Ave., Ste. 175　Ph: (415)858-1930
Palo Alto, CA 94304　　　　Fax: (415)858-1936
E-mail: feedback@commerce.net
URL: http://www.commerce.net/
Desc: CommerceNet's goal is to help people and business increase business electronically, while increasing their trust in somewhat new industry of electronic commerce. Resources consist of news, current CommerceNet project data, Internet demographics, and other points of interest not only to businesses interested in electronic commerce, but to consumers as well. *Type:* Database.

Communication News

American Society of Association Executives
1575 I St. NW　　　　　　　Ph: (202)626-2723
Washington, DC 20005　　　Fax: (202)408-8825
E-mail: asae@asaenet.org
URL: http://www.asaenet.org/sections/communications.
Contact: LaRonda Famodu, Editor, lfamodu@asaenet.org.
Desc: Focuses on public relations, writing and editing, publications management, postal rates and regulations, advertising sales, censorship, and printing and typography. Advises readers on how to improve their publications and alerts them to pertinent legal and legislative action and upcoming conventions and courses. *Type:* Newsletter.

Communication Solutions

Progressive Business Publications
370 Technology Dr.　　　　　Ph: (610)695-8600
Malvern, PA 19355　　　　　Free: 800-220-5000
　　　　　　　　　　　　　Fax: (610)651-2981
URL: http://www.pbp.com.
Contact: Ken Dooley, Editor.
Desc: Spotlights the latest highlights on the art of communicaiton. *Type:* Newsletter.

Communicator's Notebook

Pacific Dialogue
33 Ferry Ct.　　　　　　　　Ph: (212)979-7395
Stratford, CT 06497-6064
Contact: Robert J. Miko, Editor.
Desc: Provides notes and "how-to" guidance for institutional communicators and discusses relevant software. Recurring features include news of research, a calendar of events, reports of meetings, news of educational opportunities, book reviews, and notices of publications available. *Type:* Newsletter.

Companies International

Gale Group Inc.
27500 Drake Rd.　　　　　　Ph: (248)699-4253
Farmington Hills, MI 48331-　Free: 800-877-GALE
　3535　　　　　　　　　　Fax: (248)699-8070
E-mail: galeord@galegroup.com
URL: http://www.galegroup.com.; http://www.gale.com.
Contact: Kim Forster, Editor.
Desc: CD-ROM. Approximately 300,000 businesses worldwide; includes 101,000 U.S. firms from "Ward's Business Directory of Private and Public Companies" and more than 200,000 companies in 180 countries around the world from "World Business Directory". *Type:* Directory.

Companies and Their Brands

Gale Group Inc.
27500 Drake Rd.　　　　　　Ph: (248)699-4253
Farmington Hills, MI 48331-　Free: 800-877-GALE
　3535　　　　　　　　　　Fax: (248)699-8070
E-mail: galeord@galegroup.com
URL: http://www.galegroup.com.; http://www.gale.com.
Contact: Christine A. Kesler, Editor.

Desc: Over 84,000 companies that manufacture, distribute, import, or otherwise market their 365,000 consumer-oriented products. *Type:* Directory.

Company Credit Reports
Teikoku Databank America, Inc.
747 Third Ave., 25th Fl.   Ph: (212)421-9805
New York, NY 10017
E-mail: koshi@teikoku.com
URL: http://www.teikoku.com/
Desc: Contains company profiles and credit information for more than 300,000 Japanese companies. For each company, provides name, address, telephone number, year founded, principal activities, number of employees, location of branches, directors, principal shareholders and respective holdings, principal suppliers and customers, and company history. *Available:* Teikoku Databank, Ltd., COSMOSNET. *Type:* Database.

Company Intelligence
Information Access Co.
362 Lakeside Dr.   Ph: (650)378-5000
Foster City, CA 94404   Free: 800-227-8431
                    Fax: (650)358-4759
E-mail: cemarketing@iacnet.com
URL: http://www.iacnet.com; http://www.iachet.com.
Desc: Over 160,000 private and public U.S. companies, and 30,000 international companies. *Type:* Directory.

Company Intelligence®
The Gale Group
27500 Drake Rd.   Ph: (248)699-4253
Farmington Hills, MI 48331-
3535
URL: http://www.galegroup.com
Contact: (650)378-5000, fax: (800)676-2345.
Desc: Contains information on more than 120,000 public and private U.S. companies and 30,000 international companies. *Available:* The Dialog Corporation, DIALOG; LEXIS-NEXIS, NEXIS; The Dialog Corporation, DataStar. *Type:* Database.

Company ProFile™
The Gale Group
27500 Drake Rd.   Ph: (248)699-4253
Farmington Hills, MI 48331-
3535
URL: http://www.galegroup.com
Contact: (650)378-5000, fax: (800)676-2345.
Desc: Contains descriptive and financial information on more than 100,000 public and private U.S. companies. *Available:* CARL Corporation; Ameritech Library Services, Vista; The Gale Group, InfoTrac Web. *Type:* Database.

Competitive Concepts
EMS Network International
858 Longview Rd.   Ph: (415)342-5259
Burlingame, CA 94010-6974   Fax: (415)344-5005
Contact: Nancy Shays, Publisher; E. Michael Shays, Editor.
Desc: Provides business ideas and concepts. *Type:* Newsletter.

COMPUSTAT (Global) Data
Standard & Poor's Compustat
7400 S. Alton Court   Ph: (303)771-6510
Englewood, CO 80112
URL: http://compustat.com
Desc: Provides corporate financial data covering more than 11,000 publicly traded industrial and financial companies in 70 countries. Covers companies that comprise the FTS&P and Morgan Stanley Capital International Indexes, as well as those used for local market indexes. *Available:* Interactive Data Corporation; IDD Enterprises LP, IDD Plus. *Type:* Database.

COMTEX Top Headlines
COMTEX Scientific Corporation
4900 Seminary Rd., Ste. 800   Ph: (703)820-2000
Alexandria, VA 22311
E-mail: info@comtexnews.com
URL: http://www.comtexnews.com
Desc: Lists the ten most significant news stories of the day in ten different news categories. The categories include business, community, entertainment, environment, finance, government, healthcare, high tech, international, and sports. *Available:* COMTEX Scientific Corporation; Youvelle Renaissance Group, GEnie. *Type:* Database.

Connecticut Business Directory
infoUSA
5711 S. 86th Circle   Ph: (402)593-4600
PO Box 27347   Free: 800-555-6124
Omaha, NE 68127   Fax: (402)331-5481
E-mail: internet@infousa.com
URL: http://www.abii.com.
Contact: Peter J. Wilmarth, Publisher.
Desc: 145,000 businesses in Connecticut. *Type:* Directory.

Connecticut Society of Association Executives Newsletter
Connecticut Society of Association Executives
49 East Ave.   Ph: (203)845-9015
Norwalk, CT 06851   Fax: (203)847-1304
E-mail: ctsae@snet.net
Contact: Penny Daziel, Editor.
Desc: Addresses issues of association management. Promotes the mission of the Society, which seeks to enhance the professionalism of association executives, to improve their performance, and to assist these executives and their organizations in dealing effectively with public policy. *Type:* Newsletter.

Consultants and Consulting Organizations Directory
Gale Group Inc.
27500 Drake Rd.   Ph: (248)699-4253
Farmington Hills, MI 48331-   Free: 800-877-GALE
3535   Fax: (248)699-8070
E-mail: galeord@galegroup.com
URL: http://www.galegroup.com.; http://www.gale.com.
Contact: Julie Mitchell, Editor, julie.mitchell@gale.com.
Desc: Over 22,000 firms, individuals, and and organizations active in consulting. *Type:* Directory.

Consultants and Consulting Organizations Directory
The Gale Group
27500 Drake Rd.   Ph: (248)699-4253
Farmington Hills, MI 48331-
3535
URL: http://www.galegroup.com
Contact: Customer Service. Toll-free: 800-877-GALE.
Desc: Contains information on more than 23,000 organizations and individuals available as consultants to business, industry, and government. Covers agriculture, architecture, art, business and finance, computers and data processing, education, engineering, science and technology, environment, health and medicine, human resources management, manufacturing, marketing and sales, and social issues. *Available:* The Gale Group, GaleNet. *Type:* Database.

Consultants News
Kennedy Information
One Kennedy Pl., Rte. 12 S.   Ph: (603)585-6544
Fitzwilliam, NH 03447   Free: 800-531-0007
                    Fax: (603)585-9555
E-mail: bookstore@kennedy.info.com;   co-editor@kennedyinfo.com.

URL: http://www.kennedyinfo.com/cn.html.
Contact: Marshall Cooper, Exec. Ed., cn-editor@kennedyinfo.com.
Desc: The authoritative voice of the consulting industry, covering news, analysis, practice advice, proprietary data and opinion. *Type:* Newsletter.

Consulting Opportunities Journal
Consultants National Resource Center
PO Box 430   Ph: (301)791-9332
Clear Spring, MD 21722
Contact: Stephen Lanning, Editor.
Desc: Covers professional services market. *Type:* Newsletter.

Continental Franchise Review
Sparks Publishing & Reporting Corp.
7009 S. Potomac, No. 109   Ph: (303)799-1112
Englewood, CO 80112   Free: 800-938-1044
                    Fax: (303)799-1115
E-mail: efrnews@sni.net.
Contact: Nancy Weingartner, Editor.
Desc: Provides analysis and information on franchising, including trends and legal and financial aspects. Recurring features include domestic and international franchising news, questions and answers, and an editorial column. *Type:* Newsletter.

Contra Costa County Commerce & Industry Directory
Database Publishing Co.
1590 S. Lewis St.   Ph: (714)778-6400
PO Box 70024   Free: 800-888-8434
Anaheim, CA 92825-0024   Fax: (714)778-6811
E-mail: sales@databasepublishing.com
URL: http://www.databasepublishing.com; http://www.databasepublishing.com.
Desc: 3,650 manufacturers, wholesalers, and service firms, plus 5,300 key executives in Contra Costa County, California. *Type:* Directory.

Corporate Affiliations Online
National Register Publishing Co.
121 Chanlon Rd.   Ph: (908)464-6800
New Providence, NJ 07974   Free: 800-521-8110
                    Fax: (908)508-7671
E-mail: info@renp.com
URL: http://www.reedref.com
Desc: Business profiles and corporate linkage for 114,000 companies worldwide. *Type:* Directory.

Corporate Affiliations Online
National Register Publishing (NRP)
121 Chanlon Rd.   Ph: (908)464-6800
New Providence, NJ 07974
Desc: Contains descriptive and financial information on some 15,000 major domestic and foreign corporations and their more than 100,000 subsidiaries, divisions, and affiliates worldwide. Covers all companies (and their affiliates) listed on the New York and American Stock Exchanges, all companies with affiliates that are traded over-the-counter, and major privately held companies and their affiliates. *Available:* The Dialog Corporation, DIALOG; The Dialog Corporation, DIALOG; CompuServe Information Service. *Type:* Database.

Corporate Affiliations Plus
National Register Publishing Co.
121 Chanlon Rd.   Ph: (908)464-6800
New Providence, NJ 07974   Free: 800-521-8110
                    Fax: (908)508-7671
E-mail: info@renp.com
URL: http://www.reedref.com

Contact: Patricia Flinsch-Rodriguez, Editor.

Desc: CD-ROM. Covers corporate statistics and current financial information on over 15,000 domestic and foreign companies and their 99,000 subsidiaries, as well as 286,000 key executives. *Type:* Directory.

Corporate Directions

CCH Inc.

2700 Lake Cook Rd. Ph: (847)267-7000
Riverwoods, IL 60015 Free: 800-449-8114
  Fax: (847)224-8299

URL: http://www.cch.com

Contact: Charles W. Edwards, Editor.

Desc: Discusses coverage of SEC news and regulations affecting publicly-traded companies and their officers and directors. Follows trends in corporate goverance and investor relations. *Type:* Newsletter.

The Corporate Directory of U.S. Public Companies

Walker's Western Research

1650 Borel Pl., No. 130 Ph: (415)341-1110
San Mateo, CA 94402 Free: 800-258-5737
  Fax: (415)341-2351

E-mail: walkersres@aol.com

URL: http://www.walkersresearch.com.

Contact: Elizabeth Walsh, Editor.

Desc: More than 10,000 publicly held corporations traded on the New York or American exchanges, NASDAQ, or other over-the-counter markets. Includes foreign companies filing American Depositary Receipts. *Type:* Directory.

Corporate Ethics Monitor

EthicScan Canada Limited

PO Box 54034 Ph: (416)783-6776
Toronto, ON, Canada M6A Fax: (416)783-7386
3B7

E-mail: ethic@concentric.net

Contact: Len Brooks, Editor; David Nitkin, Publisher.

Desc: Provides information about corporate ethics and social responsibility. *Type:* Newsletter.

The Corporate Examiner

Interfaith Center on Corporate Responsibility (ICCR)

475 Riverside Dr., Rm. 550 Ph: (212)870-2295
New York, NY 10115-0050 Fax: (212)870-2023

Contact: Diane Bratcher, Editor.

Desc: Examines "policies and practices of major U.S. corporations with regard to South Africa, labor, environment, equal employment, minorities, women, military production, government, and foreign investment." Recurring features include editorials, news of research, news of members, news of corporate activities, reviews of resource materials, and a supplement titled ICCR Brief. *Type:* Newsletter.

Corporate Growth Report

Quality Services Co.

5290 Overpass Rd. Ph: (805)964-7841
Santa Barbara, CA 93111 Free: 800-266-3888
  Fax: (805)964-1073

E-mail: comedy@silcom.com

Contact: Nancy Rothlein, Editor.

Desc: Reports merger, acquisition, and divestiture activity, including in-depth analysis of major transactions. Publishes statistics on seller's and buyer's sales, profits, net worth, book value and earnings per share, and multiples of earnings, sales, and net worth compared with purchase price. *Type:* Newsletter.

Corporate Growth Report Weekly

Quality Services Co.

5290 Overpass Rd. Ph: (805)964-7841
Santa Barbara, CA 93111 Free: 800-266-3888
  Fax: (805)964-1073

E-mail: comedy@silcom.com

Contact: Walter Jurek, Editor.

Desc: Current acquisition and merger transactions. *Type:* Directory.

Corporate Officers and Directors Liability Litigation Reporter

Andrews Publications

175 Strafford Ave., Bldg. 4, Ste. Ph: (610)225-0510
140 Free: 800-345-1101
Wayne, PA 19087 Fax: (610)225-0501

Contact: Frank Reynolds, Editor.

Desc: Covers major developments and lawsuits in the field of corporate fiduciary responsibility litigation. Reports on pretrial, trial, and appeal proceedings, as well as settlements and class action lawsuits. *Type:* Newsletter.

Corporate 1000—A Directory of Who Runs the Top 1000 Corporations

Monitor Publishing Co.

104 5th Ave., 2nd Fl. Ph: (212)627-4140
New York, NY 10011 Fax: (212)645-0931

Desc: The top 1,000 corporations in the U.S., including manufacturing, service, financial, transportation, and utilities companies. *Type:* Directory.

Corporate Report Fact Book

Corporate Report Minnesota

105 S. 5th St., Ste. 100 Ph: (612)338-4288
Minneapolis, MN 55402 Fax: (612)373-0195

URL: http://www.corpreport.com.

Contact: Tom Smith, Editor, (612)373-0165, tsmith@amcity.com.

Desc: About 320 public corporations in the Ninth Federal Reserve District (Minnesota, North and South Dakota, Montana, upper Michigan, and northwestern Wisconsin) having stock actively traded; 1,550 privately owned companies with over 50 employees; 650 regional operations with over 50 employees, 115 non-profit corporations; 600 top executives in businesses of the upper Midwest. *Type:* Directory.

Corporate Restructuring

MLR Enterprises

229 S. 18th St., 3rd Fl. Ph: (215)790-7000
Philadelphia, PA 19103-6144 Free: 800-637-4464

Contact: Robert Rock, Publisher; Martin Sikora, Editor; Roxanne Christensen, Circulation Mgr.

Desc: Publishes reports on current restructuring techniques with an emphasis on the legal and financial aspects. Also lists 100 corporate restructures monthly. *Type:* Newsletter.

Corporate Social Issues Reporter

Investor Responsibility Research Center, Inc. (IRRC)

1350 Connecticut Ave., NW, Ph: (202)833-0700
Ste. 700 Fax: (202)833-3555
Washington, DC 20036

E-mail: mktg@irrc.org.

URL: http://www.irrc.org; http://www.irrc.org.

Contact: Meg Voorhes, Editor.

Desc: Monitors the status of specific corporations' social responsibility shareholder resolutions. Reports on public policies and regulations that affect investor responsibility and on Securities and Exchange Commission rulings concerning shareholders' access to proxy statements. *Type:* Newsletter.

Corporate Yellow Book

Leadership Directories, Inc.

104 5th Ave. Ph: (212)627-4140
New York, NY 10011 Fax: (212)645-0931

E-mail: info@leadershipdirectories.com; corporate@leadershipdirectories.com.

URL: http://www.leadershipdirectories.com; http://www.leadershipdirectories.com.

Contact: Catherine Shih, Editor.

Desc: Over 51,000 key executives from the leading public and private U.S. manufacturing, service, and utility companies, and more than 10,000 board members and their outside affiliations. *Type:* Directory.

CorpTech Directory of Technology Companies

Corporate Technology Information Services, Inc. (CorpTech)

12 Alfred St., Ste. 200 Ph: (781)932-3100
Woburn, MA 01801-1915 Free: 800-333-8036
  Fax: (781)932-6335

E-mail: sales@corptech.com

URL: http://www.corptech.com; http://www.corptech.com.

Contact: Steven Parker, Editor.

Desc: Over 45,000 manufacturers and developers in the United States of high-tech products. Technologies covered include factory automation, robotics, biotechnology, chemicals, computers, defense, energy, environmental, manufacturing equipment, advanced materials, medical, pharmaceuticals, photonics, software, subassemblies and components, test and measurement, telecommunications, and transportation. *Type:* Directory.

The Cose Update

Greater Cleveland Growth Association

200 Tower City Center Ph: (216)621-3300
50 Public Sq.
Cleveland, OH 44113

Contact: Lorilynn Valderrama, Editor.

Desc: Covers economic development, legislative issues, and general business news in the Cleveland area. *Type:* Newsletter.

The Costco Connection

BPA International

270 Madison Ave. Ph: (212)779-3200
New York, NY 10016-0699 Fax: (212)725-1721

E-mail: pricos@halcyon.com.

URL: http://www.costco.com.

Contact: Bob Craves, Publisher; David W. Fuller, Editor, (206)313-8510; Anita Thompson, Managing Editor, (206)313-6442; Ron Damiani, Assoc. Editor, Eastern Canada, (514)686-5793; Lorelle Gilpin, Assoc. Editor, Western Canada, (604)444-9304; Jane Klein Shucklin, Advertising Mgr., (206)313-8277; Loretta Lawrence, Mktg./Advertising Coord., Western Canada, (604)444-9309; Nathalie Richard, Advertising Sup., Eastern Canada, (514)686-4467; Delmy Azmitia, Advertising Coord., Eastern Canada,

Desc: Magazine serving small businesses who are members of Costco Wholesale. *Type:* Periodical.

Council of Asian American Business Associations of California—Directory

Council of Asian American Business Associations of California

1670 Pine St. Ph: (415)921-5910
San Francisco, CA 94109 Fax: (415)921-0182

E-mail: info@asianinc.org

Contact: Darlene Mar, Editor, fax: (510)337-9173, darlenemar@worldnet.att.net.

Desc: Over 2,000 Asian-American professional, commercial, and industrial firms; 10 plus trade associations. *Type:* Directory.

Council for Economic Opportunities in Greater Cleveland

1228 Euclid Ave., Ste. 700   Ph: (216)696-9077
Cleveland, OH 44115-1831   Fax: (216)696-0770

URL: http://www.cwru.edu/affil/ceogc/ceogc.htm

Contact: J. Middelton, Exec. Dir.

Desc: Helps families attain economic self-sufficiency. Engaged in anti-poverty programs and initiatives aimed at helping families and individuals attain economic self-sufficiency. *Type:* Association.

Council on Economic Priorities—Research Report

Council on Economic Priorities
30 Irving Pl.   Ph: (212)420-1133
New York, NY 10003   Free: 800-729-4237
    Fax: (212)420-0988

E-mail: info@cepnyc.org

URL: http://www.cepnyc.org; http://www.accesspt.com.

Contact: Alice Tepper Marlin, Editor, atmarlin@cepnyc.org.

Desc: Focuses on the practices of U.S. corporations in the areas of corporate social responsibility, defense spending, and environmental issues. *Type:* Newsletter.

County Business Structures

The WEFA Group
1110 Vermont Ave., NW   Ph: (202)775-0610
Washington, DC 20005

URL: http://www.fdic.gov

Desc: Contains more than 1 million records of employment and business establishment data at the county level, including number of employees for the mid-March pay period, number of business establishments, and number of establishments by 12 employee-size classes for all 3140 U.S. counties. *Available:* The WEFA Group. *Type:* Database.

Cracking Latin America: A Country-by-Country Guide to Doing Business in the World's Newest Emerging Markets

Probus Publishing Co.
1333 Burr Ridge Pkwy.
Burr Ridge, IL 60521-6489

Contact: Allyn Enderlyn, Editor; Oliver C. Dziggel, Editor.

Desc: Lists of companies, agencies, and organizations in Central and South America valuable to foreign firms seeking to do business there. Principal content of publication is information on markets, demographics, the economy, and business policies and etiquette in Central and South American Countries. *Type:* Directory.

Cracking the Pacific Rim: A Country-by-Country Guide to Doing Business in the World's Newest Emerging Markets

Probus Publishing Co.
1333 Burr Ridge Pkwy.
Burr Ridge, IL 60521-6489

Contact: Allyn Enderlyn, Editor; Oliver C. Dziggel, Editor.

Desc: Lists of companies, agencies, and organizations in Hong Kong, Indonesia, Japan, Korea, Malaysia, the Philippines, Singapore, Taiwan, and Thailand valuable to foreign firms seeking to do business there. Principal content of publication is information on markets, demographics, the economy, and business policies and etiquette in Pacific Rim countries. *Type:* Directory.

Crain's Chicago Business

Crain Communications Inc.
740 N. Rush St.   Ph: (312)649-5200
Chicago, IL 60611

URL: http://www.crain.com

Desc: Contains the complete text of Crain's Chicago Business, a newspaper covering developments in business, industry, and finance in the Chicago, Illinois area. Includes local wage and salary surveys. *Available:* LEXIS-NEXIS, NEXIS; Dow Jones Interactive Publishing; Reuters Information Services Inc.; The Gale Group, InfoTrac Web; Profound Inc., The Dialog Corporation. *Type:* Database.

Crain's Cleveland Business

Crain Communications Inc.
740 N. Rush St.   Ph: (312)649-5200
Chicago, IL 60611

URL: http://www.crain.com

Desc: Contains the complete text of Crain's Cleveland Business, a newspaper covering developments in business, finance, and industry in the Cleveland, Ohio metropolitan area. Includes feature articles on local firms and business people. *Available:* LEXIS-NEXIS, NEXIS; Dow Jones Interactive Publishing; Profound Inc., The Dialog Corporation; Reuters Information Services Inc.; The Gale Group, InfoTrac Web. *Type:* Database.

Crain's Detroit Business

Crain Communications Inc.
740 N. Rush St.   Ph: (312)649-5200
Chicago, IL 60611

URL: http://www.crain.com

Desc: Contains the complete text of Crain's Detroit Business, a weekly publication reporting news relating to the Detroit non-automotive business community. Includes profiles of companies and their executives. *Available:* LEXIS-NEXIS, NEXIS; Dow Jones Interactive Publishing; Profound Inc., The Dialog Corporation; Reuters Information Services Inc.; The Gale Group, InfoTrac Web. *Type:* Database.

Crain's New York Business

Crain Communications Inc.
740 N. Rush St.   Ph: (312)649-5200
Chicago, IL 60611

URL: http://www.crain.com

Desc: Contains the complete text of Crain's New York Business, a newspaper covering developments in business, finance, and industry in the New York City metropolitan area. Includes feature articles on top accounting firms and privately held companies. *Available:* LEXIS-NEXIS, NEXIS; Dow Jones Interactive Publishing; Profound Inc., The Dialog Corporation; Reuters Information Services Inc.; The Gale Group, InfoTrac Web. *Type:* Database.

Credit & Finance

Publishing and Business Consultants
4427 W. Slauson Ave.
Los Angeles, CA 90043-2717

Contact: Atia Napoleon, Editor and Publisher.

Desc: Magazine covering personal credit with emphasis on finance. *Type:* Periodical.

Credit Reference Directory

infoUSA
5711 S. 86th Circle   Ph: (402)593-4600
PO Box 27347   Free: 800-555-6124
Omaha, NE 68127   Fax: (402)331-5481

E-mail: internet@infousa.com; credit@abii.com.

URL: http://www.businessinfo.abii.com.

Desc: 10,000,000 businesses in the U.S. *Type:* Directory.

Crescenta Valley Business Directory

Crescenta Valley Chamber of Commerce
3131 Foothill Blvd., Ste. M   Ph: (818)248-4957
La Crescenta, CA 91214   Fax: (818)248-9387

Contact: Jean Maluccio, President; Sharon Beauchamp, Editor; Liz Church, Editor.

Desc: Member companies and organizations in La Crescenta, La Canada, Montrose, Sunland, and Tujunga, California. *Type:* Directory.

Customer Satisfaction Technology

The Customer Service Group
215 Park Ave. S., Ste. 1301   Ph: (212)228-0246
New York, NY 10003   Fax: (212)228-0376

Desc: Provides techniques on improving customer satisfaction, increasing productivity, and cutting costs with technology. Includes information on companies and business and technology such as Internet-based systems, fax capabilities, databases, and phone systems. *Type:* Newsletter.

CyberHound's Guide to Companies on the Internet

Gale Group Inc.
27500 Drake Rd.   Ph: (248)699-4253
Farmington Hills, MI 48331-   Free: 800-877-GALE
3535   Fax: (248)699-8070

E-mail: galeord@galegroup.com

URL: http://www.galegroup.com.;   http://www.cyberhound.com/.

Desc: Over 2,000 corporate sites, including top companies and information industry companies. *Type:* Directory.

D & B Business Rankings

Dun & Bradstreet
3 Sylvan Way   Ph: (973)605-6442
Parsippany, NJ 07054-3896   Free: 800-526-0651
    Fax: (973)605-6911

E-mail: dnbmdd@dnb.com

Desc: Over 25,000 leading U.S. public and private businesses. *Type:* Directory.

D & B Consultants Directory

Dun & Bradstreet
3 Sylvan Way   Ph: (973)605-6442
Parsippany, NJ 07054-3896   Free: 800-526-0651
    Fax: (973)605-6911

E-mail: dnbmdd@dnb.com

Desc: Top 30,000 U.S. consulting firms in more than 200 areas of specialization. *Type:* Directory.

D & B Directory of Service Companies

Dun & Bradstreet
3 Sylvan Way   Ph: (973)605-6442
Parsippany, NJ 07054-3896   Free: 800-526-0651
    Fax: (973)605-6911

E-mail: dnbmdd@dnb.com

Desc: 50,000 U.S. businesses in the service sector, private and public, including accounting, auditing and bookkeeping, advertising and public relations, architecture and engineering, consumer services, executive search, health, hospitality, management consulting, motion pictures, repair, research, social services, and law. *Type:* Directory.

D & B Europa Directory

Dun & Bradstreet
3 Sylvan Way   Ph: (973)605-6442
Parsippany, NJ 07054-3896   Free: 800-526-0651
    Fax: (973)605-6911

E-mail: dnbmdd@dnb.com

Desc: More than 62,000 leading manufacturers, distributors, finance, and service companies in 20 European countries. *Type:* Directory.

D & B Million Dollar Directory

Dun & Bradstreet
3 Sylvan Way   Ph: (973)605-6442
Parsippany, NJ 07054-3896   Free: 800-526-0651
   Fax: (973)605-6911
E-mail: dnbmdd@dnb.com
URL: http://www.dnbmdd.com.

Desc: 160,000 public and private businesses with either a net worth of $500,000 or more, 250 or more employees at that location, or $25,000,000 or more in sales volume; includes industrial corporations, utilities, transportation companies, bank and trust companies, stock brokers, mutual and stock insurance companies, wholesalers, retailers, and domestic subsidiaries of foreign corporations. *Type:* Directory.

D & B Million Dollar Directory—Top 50,000 Companies

Dun & Bradstreet
3 Sylvan Way   Ph: (973)605-6442
Parsippany, NJ 07054-3896   Free: 800-526-0651
   Fax: (973)605-6911
E-mail: dnbmdd@dnb.com
URL: http://www.dnbmdd.com.

Desc: 50,000 top corporations, utilities, transportation companies, bank and trust companies, stock brokers, mutual and stock insurance companies, wholesalers, retailers, and domestic subsidiaries of foreign corporations; business must have 250 or more employees at main location, or have at least $25 million in sales volume. *Type:* Directory.

D & B Principal International Businesses: The World Marketing Directory

Dun & Bradstreet
3 Sylvan Way   Ph: (973)605-6442
Parsippany, NJ 07054-3896   Free: 800-526-0651
   Fax: (973)605-6911
E-mail: dnbmdd@dnb.com

Desc: Approximately 50,000 leading businesses in all lines, outside of the U.S., in 140 countries. *Type:* Directory.

Daily News Section, Standard Corporation Records

Standard & Poor's
25 Broadway   Ph: (212)208-8000
New York, NY 10004-1064   Free: 800-221-5277
   Fax: (212)208-0040
URL: http://www.stockinfo.standardpoor.com; http://www.stockinfo.standardpoor.com.

Contact: John J. Daly, Editor.

Desc: Reports factual items on earnings, registrations and offerings, mergers and acquisitions, ratings, bankruptcies, dividend changes, and management changes. *Type:* Newsletter.

Daily Report for Executives

The Bureau of National Affairs, Inc. (BNA)
1231 25th St. NW   Ph: (202)452-4200
Washington, DC 20037
E-mail: bnaplus@bna.com
URL: http://bna.com/mkt/hrl/hrlwdec.htm

Desc: Contains comprehensive information on significant government legal, regulatory, economic, and tax developments of interest to businesspersons. Comprises the following 14 files: • Today's Summaries--contains a brief overview and summary of the day's most important stories. *Available:* West Group, WESTLAW; LEXIS-NEXIS, LEXIS; LEXIS-NEXIS, NEXIS. *Type:* Database.

Daily Report for Executives

Bureau of National Affairs, Inc. (BNA)
1231 25th St. NW   Ph: (202)452-4323
Washington, DC 20037   Free: 800-372-1033
   Fax: (202)452-7773
E-mail: bnaplus@bna.com

Contact: Toby McIntosh, Managing Editor.

Desc: A daily notification service covering legislative, regulatory, legal, and economic developments which affect both national and international businesses. Available via lotus notes and the world wide web. *Type:* Newsletter.

D&B Dun's Electronic Business Directory

Dun & Bradstreet
3 Sylvan Way   Ph: (973)605-6000
Parsippany, NJ 07054
E-mail: dnbmdd@mail.dnb.com
URL: http://www.dnb.com

Desc: Contains directory information on more than 9.7 million businesses and professionals in the U.S. Provides data for both public and private companies, including name, address, telephone number, business type, SIC code, number of employees, D-U-N-S Number, industry and city population. *Available:* CompuServe Information Service; AT&T EasyLink Services; West Group, WESTLAW; The Dialog Corporation, DIALOG. *Type:* Database.

D&B Dun's Financial Records Plus™

Dun & Bradstreet
3 Sylvan Way   Ph: (973)605-6000
Parsippany, NJ 07054
E-mail: dnbmdd@mail.dnb.com
URL: http://www.dnb.com

Desc: Contains information on approximately 2.7 million United States companies. Provides complete spreadsheet analysis, industry comparisons, and company history and operations data on 700,000 organizations, as well as history and operations information only for an additional 1.5 million companies. *Available:* The Dialog Corporation, DIALOG; Dow Jones Interactive Publishing; Information America (IA); CompuServe Information Service. *Type:* Database.

D&B Dun's Market Identifiers

Dun & Bradstreet
3 Sylvan Way   Ph: (973)605-6000
Parsippany, NJ 07054
E-mail: dnbmdd@mail.dnb.com
URL: http://www.dnb.com

Desc: Contains current information on approximately 11 million public and private U.S. companies. *Available:* The Dialog Corporation, DataStar; Dow Jones Interactive Publishing; CompuServe Information Service; AT&T EasyLink Services; Youvelle Renaissance Group, GEnie; Information America (IA); West Group, WESTLAW. *Type:* Database.

D&B European Dun's Market Identifiers™

Dun & Bradstreet
3 Sylvan Way   Ph: (973)605-6000
Parsippany, NJ 07054
E-mail: dnbmdd@mail.dnb.com
URL: http://www.dnb.com

Desc: Contains mailing, descriptive, and financial information on approximately 4 million companies in 56 European countries. *Available:* The Dialog Corporation, DIALOG; The Dialog Corporation, DIALOG; NIFTY Corporation, NIFTY-SERVE; West Group, WESTLAW; CompuServe Information Service; AT&T EasyLink Services; European Information Network Services (EINS). *Type:* Database.

Datalog

Business Intelligence Program
SRI International
333 Ravenswood Ave.   Ph: (650)859-4600
Menlo Park, CA 94025   Fax: (650)859-4544

Contact: Leslie Ashmore, Editor.

Desc: Serves the aims of the program "to provide decision makers with leading edge information about significant changes in the business environment and new developments in corporate policy and management." Catalogs recent B-I-P and SRI research for business planning. *Type:* Newsletter.

DealBase II: An Electronic Database of Acquisition Opportunities

Business Publications, Inc.
5060 Shoreham Pl., Ste. 200   Ph: (619)457-7577
San Diego, CA 92122-5904   Fax: (619)453-1091

Contact: Carl W. Bayne, Editor.

Desc: Over 675 of middle market companies, currently available for acquisition, with annual revenues between 3 and 75 million dollars. *Type:* Directory.

Delaware Business Directory

infoUSA
5711 S. 86th Circle   Ph: (402)593-4600
PO Box 27347   Free: 800-555-6124
Omaha, NE 68127   Fax: (402)331-5481
E-mail: internet@infousa.com
URL: http://www.abii.com.

Contact: Peter J. Wilmarth, Publisher.

Desc: 29,000 businesses in Delaware. *Type:* Directory.

Delaware Corporate Litigation Reporter

Andrews Publications
175 Strafford Ave., Bldg. 4, Ste.   Ph: (610)225-0510
140   Free: 800-345-1101
Wayne, PA 19087   Fax: (610)225-0501

Contact: Frank Reynolds, Editor.

Desc: "Offers in-depth coverage of lawsuits involving business judgment as well as shareholder and derivative actions." Reproduces full texts of key court opinions, briefs, responses, and complaints. *Type:* Newsletter.

Delaware Today Aware

Delaware Today, Inc.
PO Box 2087
Wilmington, DE 19899-2087

Contact: Len Quinn, Publisher; Peter Mucha, Editor.

Desc: Spotlights businesses in Delaware. *Type:* Newsletter.

Delta Mu Delta

Central Office   Ph: (314)432-8785
PO Box 46935   Fax: (314)432-7083
St. Louis, MO 63146-6935
E-mail: deltamudelta@deltamudelta.org
URL: http://www.deltamudelta.org

Contact: James A. Viehland, Dir. of Office Services.

Desc: Honor society - business administration. *Type:* Association.

Delta Sigma Pi

330 S. Campus Ave.   Ph: (513)523-1907
PO Box 230   Fax: (513)523-7292
Oxford, OH 45056
E-mail: centraloffice@dspnet.org
URL: http://www.dspnet.org

Contact: William C. Schilling, Exec.Dir.

Desc: Professional fraternity - commerce and business administration. Operates Delta Sigma Pi Leadership Foundation. Maintains museum; sponsors competitions; offers computerized services; compiles statistics. *Type:* Association.

Denver Business Journal—Top Twenty-Five Book of Lists Issue

Denver Business Journal
1700 Broadway, Ste. 515   Ph: (303)837-3500
Denver, CO 80290   Fax: (303)837-3535
Contact: Henry Dubroff, Editor.
Desc: Lists of the 25 (in most cases) largest or most profitable entities in 72 categories comprising service companies, associations, hospitals, retailers, ski resorts, colleges and universities, and other organizations in the Denver, Colorado area. *Type:* Directory.

Dept of Economic Development

Mr. Andis Udris
805 Central Ave. No. 710   Ph: (513)352-3950
Cincinnati, OH 45202   Fax: (513)352-6257
E-mail: andi.udris@cinecon.rec.org
URL: http://www.cincinnatigov.com
Contact: Andi Udris, Dir.
Type: Association.

Dial-A-Fax Business Directory

Dial-A-Fax Directories Corp.
930 Fox Pavilion   Ph: (215)887-5700
Jenkintown, PA 19046   Fax: (215)887-7076
E-mail: berylwolk@aol.com
Desc: Approximately 209,000 companies in the United States. *Type:* Directory.

DIALOG Company Name Finder™

The Dialog Corporation
DIALOG
11000 Regency Pkwy., Ste. 400   Ph: (919)462-8600
Cary, NC 27511
URL: http://www.dialog.com
Contact: Marketing.
Desc: Designed as a search aid to locate company information in DIALOG databases. Contains more than 30 million citations to company names from more than 100 databases shown in the form in which they appear in the original database index, including abbreviations, punctuation, and spelling variations. *Available:* The Dialog Corporation, DIALOG. *Type:* Database.

Directorio Profesional Hispano

Blanca Balbi
PO Box 408   Ph: (718)762-1432
Flushing, NY 11352
Contact: George E. Balbi, Editor.
Desc: Over 5,000 Hispanic doctors, optometrists, dentists, lawyers, architects, and accountants, with offices in the eastern United States. *Type:* Directory.

Director's Monthly

National Association of Corporate Directors
1707 L St. NW, Ste. 560   Ph: (202)775-0509
Washington, DC 20036   Fax: (202)775-4857
Contact: Alexandra Lajovx, Editor.
Desc: Reports current issues and events of interest to corporate directors. Covers such topics as outside versus inside directors, audit, compensation, nominating committees, disclosure requirements, antitrust violations, and conflicts of interest. *Type:* Newsletter.

Directory of American Agribusiness

Agricultural Resources & Communications, Inc.
4210 Wam-Teau Dr.   Ph: (785)456-9705
Wamego, KS 66547-9377   Free: 800-404-7940
                                 Fax: (913)456-9705
E-mail: agrescom@mail.midusa.net
Contact: Chris Wilson, Editor.
Desc: Over 7,200 leading companies in agricultural chemicals, implements, seed, grain, feed, food processing, animal health and services, including public relations and consulting in 27 different types of agribusinesses in the U.S. *Type:* Directory.

Directory of American Firms Operating in Foreign Countries

Uniworld Business Publications Inc.
257 Central Park West, Ste.   Ph: (212)496-2448
10A   Fax: (212)769-0413
New York, NY 10024-4110
E-mail: uniworldbp@aol.com
URL: http://www.uniworldbp.com.
Contact: Barbara D. Fiorito, Editor.
Desc: About 2,450 American corporations with 29,500 subsidiaries or affiliates outside the United States. *Type:* Directory.

Directory of Arizona Exporters

International Trade Division
Arizona Department of Commerce
3800 N. Central, Ste. 1500   Ph: (602)280-1371
Phoenix, AZ 85012   Fax: (602)280-1378
E-mail: intl@ep.state.az.us
Desc: 1,000 Arizona enterprises currently involved in international trade. *Type:* Directory.

Directory of Blue Chip Companies

infoUSA
5711 S. 86th Circle   Ph: (402)593-4600
PO Box 27347   Free: 800-555-6124
Omaha, NE 68127   Fax: (402)331-5481
E-mail: internet@infousa.com
URL: http://www.abii.com.
Type: Directory.

The Directory of Business Information Resources

Grey House Publishing
Pocket Knife Square   Ph: (860)435-0868
Lakeville, CT 06039   Free: 800-562-2139
                                 Fax: (860)435-0867
E-mail: books@li.com
URL: http://www.greyhouse.com
Contact: Leslie Mackenzie, Editor.
Desc: 3,320 associations, 2,770 trade shows, 3,002 magazines, 2,130 newsletters, and over 3,000 directories and databases serving 93 business professions or specialties. *Type:* Directory.

Directory of Companies Offering Dividend Reinvestment Plans

Evergreen Enterprises
PO Box 763   Ph: (301)549-3939
Laurel, MD 20725-0763
Contact: Sumie Kinoshita, Editor.
Desc: Approximately 880 companies that offer dividend reinvestment and optional cash purchase plans. *Type:* Directory.

Directory of Corporate Affiliations

National Register Publishing (NRP)
121 Chanlon Rd.   Ph: (908)464-6800
New Providence, NJ 07974
Contact: John Sonta, fax: (908)508-7671, jsonta@renp.com.
Desc: Provides information on more than 120,000 U.S. parent companies, divisions, subsidiaries, joint ventures, and affiliates worldwide. *Available:* LEXIS-NEXIS, NEXIS; The Dialog Corporation, DIALOG; LEXIS-NEXIS; OneSource Information Services. *Type:* Database.

Directory of Corporate Affiliations International

National Register Publishing (NRP)
121 Chanlon Rd.   Ph: (908)464-6800
New Providence, NJ 07974
Desc: Provides information on approximately 2300 foreign parent companies with revenues of more than $50 million

annually, in some 80 countries and their 42,000 U.S. and foreign divisions, subsidiaries, and affiliates as well as more than 54,000 key executives. *Available:* LEXIS-NEXIS, NEXIS; The Dialog Corporation, DIALOG; The Dialog Corporation, DIALOG. *Type:* Database.

Directory of Corporate Affiliations Library

National Register Publishing Co.
121 Chanlon Rd.   Ph: (908)464-6800
New Providence, NJ 07974   Free: 800-521-8110
                                 Fax: (908)508-7671
E-mail: info@renp.com
URL: http://www.reedref.com
Contact: Patricia Flinsch-Rodriguez, Editor.
Desc: A 5-volume set listing public and private companies worldwide. Comprises the following: Master Index (volumes 1 and 2); U.S. Public Companies (volume 3), listing 4,100 parent companies and 42,000 subsidiaries, affiliates, and divisions worldwide; U.S. Private Companies (volume 4), listing 8,800 privately held companies and 12,150 U.S. and international subsidiaries; and International Public and Private Companies (volume 5), listing 2,450 parent companies and 52,000 subsidiaries worldwide. *Type:* Directory.

Directory of Corporate Affiliations/U.S. Private

National Register Publishing Co.
121 Chanlon Rd.   Ph: (908)464-6800
New Providence, NJ 07974   Free: 800-521-8110
                                 Fax: (908)508-7671
E-mail: info@renp.com
URL: http://www.reedref.com
Desc: Business and financial information on over 8,900 top privately held U.S. parent companies—with more than $10,000,000 in revenue—and their 12,200 subsidiaries, divisions, and affiliates worldwide, as well as 77,00 key executives. *Type:* Directory.

Directory of Corporate Affiliations/U.S. Public

National Register Publishing Co.
121 Chanlon Rd.   Ph: (908)464-6800
New Providence, NJ 07974   Free: 800-521-8110
                                 Fax: (908)508-7671
E-mail: info@renp.com
URL: http://www.reedref.com
Contact: Tom Bachmann, Editor, tbachmann@renp.com.
Desc: Business and financial information on approximately 3,800 U.S. parent companies and 44,500 subsidiaries, divisions, and affiliates worldwide, as well as 140,000 key executives. *Type:* Directory.

Directory of Foreign Firms Operating in the United States

Uniworld Business Publications Inc.
257 Central Park West, Ste.   Ph: (212)496-2448
10A   Fax: (212)769-0413
New York, NY 10024-4110
E-mail: uniworldbp@aol.com
URL: http://www.uniworldbp.com.
Contact: Barbara D. Fiorito, Editor.
Desc: Approximately 2,350 firms in 71 countries that own or have substantial investments in about 5,200 U.S. companies. *Type:* Directory.

Directory of Indian Owned Businesses

All Indian Pueblo Council, Inc.
New Mexico Native American Business Development Center (NMNABDC)
3939 San Pedro NE, Ste. D   Ph: (505)889-9092
PO Box 3256
Albuquerque, NM 87190
Desc: About 200 firms offering professional, commercial, and industrial products and services in New Mexico. *Type:* Directory.

Directory of Japanese-Affiliated Companies in USA & Canada

Database SL
c/o Taylor & Francis, Inc.   Ph: (215)785-5800
1900 Frost Rd., Ste. 101   Free: 800-821-8312
Bristol, PA 19007   Fax: (215)785-5515
E-mail: bkorders@tandfpa.com.

Desc: Approximately 8,200 Japanese-affiliated companies operating in North America. *Type:* Directory.

Directory of Major Corporations: Central Puget Sound Region

Greater Seattle Chamber of Commerce
1301 5th Ave., Ste. 2400   Ph: (206)389-7200
Seattle, WA 98101-2603   Fax: (206)389-7288
URL: http://www.seattlechamber.com

Contact: Gina Morales, Editor.

Desc: About 1,000 corporations, medical and educational institutions, and government and social agencies in the central Puget Sound region with 100 or more employees. *Type:* Directory.

Directory of Minority Suppliers

Indiana Regional Minority Supplier Development Council
PO Box 44801   Ph: (317)923-2110
Indianapolis, IN 46244-0801   Fax: (317)923-2204

Contact: Jeffery L. Donald, Editor.

Desc: About 450 firms offering professional, commercial, and industrial products and services. *Type:* Directory.

Directory of Minority and Women Owned Businesses

Louisiana Office of Minority and Women's Business Enterprise
Department of Economic Development
Box 94185   Ph: (504)342-5373
Baton Rouge, LA 70804-9185

Desc: Minority- and women-owned firms offering professional, commercial, and industrial products and services. *Type:* Directory.

Directory of Multinationals

Stockton Press
345 Park Ave. S.   Ph: (212)689-9200
New York, NY 10010   Free: 800-221-2123
          Fax: (212)689-9711
E-mail: grove@grovestocktn.com.

Contact: John Stopford, Editor.

Desc: Approximately 450 multinational corporations with sales of $1 billion during 1996 and significant foreign investments. *Type:* Directory.

Directory of U.S. Importers/Directory of U.S. Exporters

The Journal of Commerce
454 Marshall St.   Ph: (908)859-1300
Phillipsburg, NJ 08865   Free: 800-222-0356
          Fax: (908)454-6507
URL: http://www.pierspub.com.

Contact: Alice Shields, Operations Mgr.

Desc: Approximately 55,000 U.S. firms with import and export interests; export and import managers, agents, and merchants in the United States; world ports; consulates and embassies. *Type:* Directory.

Directory of Washington, DC Chief Executive Officers

Labor Market Information and Research Division
District of Columbia Department of Employment Services
500 C St. NW   Ph: (202)724-7213
Washington, DC 20001   Fax: (202)724-7216
Contact: Richard F. Groner, Editor.

Desc: 200 large nongovernmental companies in the District of Columbia, selected on the basis of number of employees. *Type:* Directory.

Disclosure SEC Database

Disclosure Inc.
5161 River Rd.   Ph: (301)951-1753
Bethesda, MD 20816
E-mail: info@disclosure.com
URL: http://www.disclosure.com

Desc: Contains corporate and financial information on more than 11,000 publicly owned companies that file reports with the U.S. Securities and Exchange Commission (SEC). *Available:* ADP Financial Information Services (ADP/FIS); CompuServe Information Service; The Dialog Corporation, DIALOG; The Dialog Corporation, DIALOG; Dow Jones & Company, Inc.; LEXIS-NEXIS, LEXIS; Quotron Systems, Inc.; The Dialog Corporation, DataStar; NlightN. *Type:* Database.

Doing Business in the U.S.

Matthew Bender & Company
Two Park Ave.   Ph: (212)448-2118
New York, NY 10016   Free: 800-252-9257
          Fax: (212)448-2749

Contact: J. O'Brien, Editor.

Desc: Functions as a guide to U.S. business operations in accounting, banking, law, and other areas. *Type:* Newsletter.

Dow Jones International News

Dow Jones & Company, Inc.
P.O. Box 300   Ph: (609)520-4000
Princeton, NJ 08543-0300
URL: http://www.dj.com

Desc: Contains the complete text of business, financial, and economic news as well as analyses, commentaries, and statistics on international events that affect business. Also includes news about more than 6000 companies worldwide and developments in international stock, bond, currency, precious metals, and petroleum markets. *Available:* Dow Jones & Company, Inc. *Type:* Database.

Dow Jones News

Dow Jones & Company, Inc.
P.O. Box 300   Ph: (609)520-4000
Princeton, NJ 08543-0300
URL: http://www.dj.com

Desc: Reports up-to-the-minute news concerning business and finance worldwide for companies, industries, the stock market, and the general economy. Provides coverage as current as 30 seconds and as far back as 90 days as transmitted through the Dow Jones News Service, the Broadtape service. *Available:* Dow Jones & Company, Inc.; FT PROFILE; European Information Network Services (EINS). *Type:* Database.

Dow Jones News/Retrieval

Dow Jones & Company, Inc.
P.O. Box 300   Ph: (609)520-4000
Princeton, NJ 08543-0300
URL: http://www.dj.com

Desc: Covers topics of interest to U.S. business markets. *Available:* Dow Jones & Company, Inc. *Type:* Database.

Dow Jones Text Library

Dow Jones & Company, Inc.
P.O. Box 300   Ph: (609)520-4000
Princeton, NJ 08543-0300
URL: http://www.dj.com

Desc: Contains more than 3400 national, regional, and local publications plus business and trade publications, including exclusive information from Dow Jones. Searchable by company name and personal names, corporate stock symbol, industry and government codes, complex Boolean terms, and miscellaneous codes (e.g., for ticker news, current-day earnings, economic news, foreign news). *Available:* Dow Jones & Company, Inc. *Type:* Database.

The Dream Merchant Newsletter

John K. Moreland
2309 Torrance Blvd., Ste. 201   Ph: (310)328-1925
Torrance, CA 90501   Fax: (310)328-1844
Contact: Mike Foley, Editor; John K. Moreland, Publisher.

Desc: Covers creation and marketing of new products and services. *Type:* Newsletter.

DRI U.S. Prices

Standard & Poor's DRI
Data Products Division
24 Hartwell Ave.   Ph: (781)863-5100
Lexington, MA 02421
E-mail: client_services@dri.mcgraw-hill.com
URL: http://www.dri.mcgraw-hill.com
Contact: Client Services, (617)860-6527, fax: (617)860-6416.

Desc: Contains approximately 30,000 monthly, semiannual, and annual time series on consumer, producer, and industry sector price indexes. *Available:* Standard & Poor's DRI, Data Products Division. *Type:* Database.

Dun & Bradstreet Business Locator

Dun & Bradstreet
3 Sylvan Way   Ph: (973)605-6442
Parsippany, NJ 07054-3896   Free: 800-526-0651
          Fax: (973)605-6911
E-mail: dnbmdd@dnb.com
Desc: Locations of more than 12,000,000 businesses in the U.S. *Type:* Directory.

Dun & Bradstreet Canadian Key Business Directory

Dun & Bradstreet
3 Sylvan Way   Ph: (973)605-6442
Parsippany, NJ 07054-3896   Free: 800-526-0651
          Fax: (973)605-6911
E-mail: dnbmdd@dnb.com
Desc: Top 20,000 public and private businesses in Canada. *Type:* Directory.

Dun & Bradstreet Dunserve II

Dun & Bradstreet Canada
5770 Hurontario St.   Ph: (905)568-6000
PO Box 6200, Station A
Mississauga, ON, Canada L5R 3G5
URL: http://www.dnb.ca
Desc: Contains information on more than 650,000 Canadian business establishments. For each establishment, includes company name; address; telephone number; chief executive officer; type of business; D-U-N-S number; company status; subsidiary; manufacturing activity; language preference; geographic codes (province, county, city, SMSA); U.S. and Canadian Standard Industrial Classification codes (primary and secondary); year that current control of company was established; last date record was updated; number of employees at the listed location; total number of employees at all company locations; and total sales volume for listed location. *Available:* Infomart Online. *Type:* Database.

Dun & Bradstreet Guide to Hong Kong Businesses

Dun & Bradstreet
3 Sylvan Way   Ph: (973)605-6442
Parsippany, NJ 07054-3896   Free: 800-526-0651
   Fax: (973)605-6911

E-mail: dnbmdd@dnb.com
Desc: 20,000 companies in Hong Kong, including foreign-owned companies operating in Hong Kong. *Type:* Directory.

Dun & Bradstreet Million Dollar Disc Plus

Dun & Bradstreet
3 Sylvan Way   Ph: (973)605-6442
Parsippany, NJ 07054-3896   Free: 800-526-0651
   Fax: (973)605-6911

E-mail: dnbmdd@dnb.com
URL: http://www.dnbmdd.com.
Desc: 400,000 public and private companies in the U.S. *Type:* Directory.

Dun & Bradstreet Reference Book of American Businesses

Dun & Bradstreet
3 Sylvan Way   Ph: (973)605-6442
Parsippany, NJ 07054-3896   Free: 800-526-0651
   Fax: (973)605-6911

E-mail: dnbmdd@dnb.com
Desc: More than 3 million large and small, public and private U.S. companies. *Type:* Directory.

Dun & Bradstreet Regional Business Directories

Dun & Bradstreet
3 Sylvan Way   Ph: (973)605-6442
Parsippany, NJ 07054-3896   Free: 800-526-0651
   Fax: (973)605-6911

E-mail: dnbmdd@dnb.com
Desc: Top 20,000 businesses in one of 54 metropolitan areas in the U.S. *Type:* Directory.

Dun & Bradstreet State Sales Guide

Dun & Bradstreet
3 Sylvan Way   Ph: (973)605-6442
Parsippany, NJ 07054-3896   Free: 800-526-0651
   Fax: (973)605-6911

E-mail: dnbmdd@dnb.com
Desc: All businesses in each state that are included in Dun & Bradstreet's national "Reference Book of American Business." A separate "State Sales Guide" is published for each state and the District of Columbia. *Type:* Directory.

Dun & Bradstreet 25,000 Series Directory

Dun & Bradstreet
3 Sylvan Way   Ph: (973)605-6442
Parsippany, NJ 07054-3896   Free: 800-526-0651
   Fax: (973)605-6911

E-mail: dnbmdd@dnb.com
Desc: In three separate volumes, top 25,000 businesses, based on number of employees, for the Asia Pacific, Latin America, and Western Europe. *Type:* Directory.

Dun's Asia Pacific Key Business Enterprises

Dun & Bradstreet
3 Sylvan Way   Ph: (973)605-6442
Parsippany, NJ 07054-3896   Free: 800-526-0651
   Fax: (973)605-6911

E-mail: dnbmdd@dnb.com
Desc: 30,000 leading companies in 14 Pacific Rim countries whose annual sales are $10 million and who have 500 or more employees. *Type:* Directory.

Dun's Family Tree Report

Dun & Bradstreet Business Credit Services
One Diamond Hill Rd.   Ph: (908)665-5000
PO Box 27
Murray Hill, NJ 07974-0027
URL: http://www.dnb.com
Desc: Contains "trees" for approximately 200,000 corporations and their subsidiaries or branch companies. For each corporate tree (average is 4 members per family), includes company names, addresses, telephone numbers, corporate relationships (e.g., holding company, headquarters, branch), Standard Industrial Classification (SIC) codes, names of key personnel, sales volumes, net worths, and D&B rating. *Available:* West Group, WESTLAW; West Group, WESTLAW. *Type:* Database.

Dun's 15,000 Largest Companies—Belgium

Dun & Bradstreet
3 Sylvan Way   Ph: (973)605-6442
Parsippany, NJ 07054-3896   Free: 800-526-0651
   Fax: (973)605-6911

E-mail: dnbmdd@dnb.com
Desc: 15,000 industrial, trading, banking, insurance, and service companies in Belgium. *Type:* Directory.

Dun's 15,000 Largest Companies—Portugal

Dun & Bradstreet
3 Sylvan Way   Ph: (973)605-6442
Parsippany, NJ 07054-3896   Free: 800-526-0651
   Fax: (973)605-6911

E-mail: dnbmdd@dnb.com
Desc: 15,000 industrial, trading, banking, insurance, and service companies in Portugal. *Type:* Directory.

Dun's 15,000 Largest Companies—Spain

Dun & Bradstreet
3 Sylvan Way   Ph: (973)605-6442
Parsippany, NJ 07054-3896   Free: 800-526-0651
   Fax: (973)605-6911

E-mail: dnbmdd@dnb.com
Desc: 15,000 industrial, trading, banking, insurance, and service companies in Spain. *Type:* Directory.

Dun's Key Decision-Makers in Hong Kong Business

Dun & Bradstreet
3 Sylvan Way   Ph: (973)605-6442
Parsippany, NJ 07054-3896   Free: 800-526-0651
   Fax: (973)605-6911

E-mail: dnbmdd@dnb.com
Desc: 8,000 directors and senior executives from leading businesses in Hong Kong. *Type:* Directory.

Dun's Middle Market Disc

Dun & Bradstreet
3 Sylvan Way   Ph: (973)605-6442
Parsippany, NJ 07054-3896   Free: 800-526-0651
   Fax: (973)605-6911

E-mail: dnbmdd@dnb.com
URL: http://www.dnbmdd.com.
Desc: CD-ROM. Approximately 150,000 mid-sized U.S. companies (those with between $4 million and $25 million in sales or with 100 to 250 employees). *Type:* Directory.

Dun's Regional Business Directory

Dun & Bradstreet
3 Sylvan Way   Ph: (973)605-6442
Parsippany, NJ 07054-3896   Free: 800-526-0651
   Fax: (973)605-6911

E-mail: dnbmdd@dnb.com
Desc: In regional three-volume sets, approximately 20,000 companies employing 10 or more persons in each of 52 metropolitan areas. *Type:* Directory.

Dun's 20,000 Netherlands

Dun & Bradstreet
3 Sylvan Way   Ph: (973)605-6442
Parsippany, NJ 07054-3896   Free: 800-526-0651
   Fax: (973)605-6911

E-mail: dnbmdd@dnb.com
Desc: 20,000 industrial, trading, banking, insurance, and service companies in the Netherlands. *Type:* Directory.

East Asian Executive Reports

International Executive Reports, Ltd.
717 D St., N.W., Room 300   Ph: (202)628-6900
Washington, DC 20004-2807
Desc: Contains the complete text of East Asian Executive Reports, a journal covering the financial, legal, and practical aspects of conducting business in 15 East Asian countries. Covers the local requirements for agents and sponsors, branch offices, joint ventures, importing, contracting, government tendering, licensing, sourcing and technology transfer, labor, product liability, dispute resolution, intellectual property, forex, investment project financing, taxation, repatriation of profits, marketing and advertising. *Available:* LEXIS-NEXIS, NEXIS; LEXIS-NEXIS, LEXIS; West Group, WESTLAW. *Type:* Database.

The East-West Business Directory

Transnational Corporations and Management Division
Department of Economic and Social Development
United Nations
New York, NY 10017
Desc: Approximately 863 companies that have central and eastern European capital participation, located in over 20 European and North American countries, Australia, and Japan. *Type:* Directory.

The Eastern Europe Business Database CD-ROM

American Directory Corp.
PO Box 7426   Ph: (718)797-4311
New York, NY 10116   Fax: (718)596-4852
URL: http://www.didik.com/eecd.htm
Desc: 60,000 companies and other businesses in Eastern Europe and the former Soviet Union. *Type:* Directory.

Eastern European Business Directory

Gale Group Inc.
27500 Drake Rd.   Ph: (248)699-4253
Farmington Hills, MI 48331-   Free: 800-877-GALE
3535   Fax: (248)699-8070
E-mail: galeord@galegroup.com
URL: http://www.galegroup.com.
Contact: Frank X. Didik, Editor.
Desc: Over 7,000 companies and organizations in Bulgaria, former Czechoslovakia, Hungary, Poland, Romania, former East Germany, and the western part of the former Soviet Union. *Type:* Directory.

Eastern New England Regional Industrial Buying Guide

Thomas Regional Directory Co., Inc.
5 Penn Plaza   Ph: (212)629-2100
New York, NY 10001   Fax: (212)290-7335
E-mail: info@trdnet.com
URL: http://www.thomasregional.com.
Contact: Marie McGurk, Editorial Dir.; Adrienne Toth, Managing Editor; Nancy Bromberg, Contracts Administration Mgr.
Desc: Nearly 20,000 listings of manufacturers of industrial products; related industrial services, such as trucking and maintenance services; distributors and manufacturers' representatives in Maine, New Hampshire, Rhode Island and eastern Massachusetts. *Type:* Directory.

Economic Development Corp. of Los Angeles

Lee Harrington

515 S Flower St. No. 32FL Ph: (213)622-4300
Los Angeles, CA 90071-2201 Fax: (213)622-7100
E-mail: laedc-info@laedc.org
URL: http://www.laedc.org

Contact: Lee Harrington, Pres.

Type: Association.

The Economist

Treasury & Risk Management

111 W. 57th St., 11th Fl. Ph: (212)459-3004
New York, NY 10019-2211 Fax: (212)459-3007
E-mail: newyork@eiu.com

Contact: Bill Emmott, Editor; Marjorie Scardino, Chief Executive Officer; Willy Morgan, Publisher North America; Elizabeth Maher, Chief Operating Officer,NA; Richard O'Rorke, Chief Financial Officer,NA.

Desc: International magazine reporting on news, world affairs, business, and finance. *Type:* Periodical.

Editor's Workshop

Lawrence Ragan Communications, Inc.

212 W. Superior St., Ste. 200 Ph: (312)335-0037
Chicago, IL 60610 Free: 800-878-5331
Fax: (312)573-3730

Contact: Kate Vitale, Editor.

Desc: Furnishes how-to advice on writing, editing, design, photography, and business writing. *Type:* Newsletter.

Effective Business Writing

Economics Press, Inc.

12 Daniel Rd. Ph: (973)227-1224
Fairfield, NJ 07004-2565 Free: 800-526-2554
Fax: (973)526-2554
E-mail: info@epinc.com; order@epinc.com
URL: http://www.epinc.com

Contact: Linda Bullock, Editor.

Desc: Offers tips on business writing improvement. *Type:* Newsletter.

The Electronic Commerce Guide

Mecklermedia Corp.

20 Ketchum St. Ph: (203)226-6967
Westport, CT 06880 Fax: (203)454-5840
E-mail: eisenberg@mecklermedia.com
URL: http://e-comm.internet.com/

Contact: lrush@internet.com.

Desc: No form of business is growing at quite so astounding a rate as electronic commerce. Fueled by the advent of the Internet, this rapidly growing means of doing business has become a key part of everyday life. *Type:* Database.

Electronic Commerce News

Phillips Business Information, Inc.

1201 Seven Locks Rd., Ste. 300 Ph: (301)340-1520
Potomac, MD 20854 Free: 888-707-5809
Fax: (301)340-3847
E-mail: clientservices.pbi@phillips.com
URL: http://www.ectoday.com; http://www.ectoday.com.

Contact: John Scheinman, Senior Editor, jscheinman@ phillips.com; Angela Duff, Publisher.

Desc: Publishes "news and analysis on the business of integrating information technologies to support electronic commerce." *Type:* Newsletter.

Elevator World—Source Issue

Elevator World, Inc.

356 Morgan Ave. Ph: (334)479-4514
Mobile, AL 36606 Free: 800-730-5093
Fax: (334)479-7043
E-mail: sales@elevator-world.com
URL: http://www.elevator-world.com; http://www. elevator-world.com.

Contact: Robert S. Caporale, Editor, editorial@ elevatorworld.com.

Desc: Lists of about 450 elevator manufacturers and suppliers to the industry; consultants and 109 trade associations; international coverage. *Type:* Directory.

Elliot Gold's TeleSpan

TeleSpan Publishing Corporation

50 W. Palm St. Ph: (818)797-5482
Altadena, CA 91001-4337 Fax: (818)797-2035
E-mail: telespanpb@aol.com

Contact: Elliot Gold, Editor.

Desc: Tracks activities of companies and personnel in the teleconferencing field. Offers opinions in addition to facts. *Type:* Newsletter.

Emerging Market Debt Report

American Banker/Bond Buyer Inc.
International Thomson Publishing Corp.

1 State St. Plaza Ph: (212)803-8200
New York, NY 10004 Free: 800-362-3807
Fax: (212)843-9612

Contact: Mary D'Ambrosio, Editor.

Desc: Provides information about debt and political stability in emerging countries. *Type:* Newsletter.

Empire State Developments

New York State Department of Economic Development

1 Commerce Plaza Ph: (518)474-4116
Albany, NY 12245 Free: 800-CALL-NYS
Fax: (518)486-6416

Contact: Jan Conray, Editor.

Desc: Publicizes the activities and functions of the Department, which promotes the growth of business and industry in New York. *Type:* Newsletter.

Employment Equity Update

Canadian Training Communications

44 Laird Dr., Ste. 300 Ph: (416)696-9299
Toronto, ON, Canada M4G Fax: (416)696-8409
3T2

Contact: Shelley Boyes, Editor; Susan Baka, Publisher.

Desc: Covers Canadian employment equity. Includes news and legislation information. *Type:* Newsletter.

Employment Practices Update

WestGroup

375 Hudson St. Ph: (212)929-7500
New York, NY 10014 Free: 800-422-2101
Fax: (212)807-6209

Contact: Andrew J. Ruzicho, Editor; Louis A. Jacobs, Editor.

Desc: Discusses such topics as employment decisions, willful violations, reduction-in-force terminations, age discrimination, and erroneous credibility determinations. *Type:* Newsletter.

Encyclopedia of Associations

The Gale Group

27500 Drake Rd. Ph: (248)699-4253
Farmington Hills, MI 48331-
3535
URL: http://www.galegroup.com

Contact: Customer Service. Toll-free: 800-877-GALE.

Desc: Provides detailed descriptions of more than 160,000 international and U.S. national, regional, state, and local membership organizations in all fields. *Available:* The Dialog Corporation, DIALOG; LEXIS-NEXIS, NEXIS; Ameritech Library Services, Vista. *Type:* Database.

Encyclopedia of Business Information Sources

Gale Group Inc.

27500 Drake Rd. Ph: (248)699-4253
Farmington Hills, MI 48331- Free: 800-877-GALE
3535 Fax: (248)699-8070
E-mail: galeord@galegroup.com
URL: http://www.galegroup.com.; http://www.gale.com.

Contact: James Woy, Editor.

Desc: Over 28,000 sources of industry- and business-related information, such as periodicals, trade associations, directories, handbooks, bibliographies, and online, internet, and CD-ROM databases. *Type:* Directory.

Encyclopedia of Business Information Sources: Europe

Gale Group Inc.

27500 Drake Rd. Ph: (248)699-4253
Farmington Hills, MI 48331- Free: 800-877-GALE
3535 Fax: (248)699-8070
E-mail: galeord@galegroup.com
URL: http://www.galegroup.com.; http://www.gale.com.

Contact: M. Balachandran, Editor.

Desc: Over 11,000 sources of information on over 450 European business-related topics; includes almanacs and yearbooks, directories, handbooks and manuals, online databases, periodicals, newsletters, research centers, statistics sources, and trade associations. *Type:* Directory.

Encyclopedia of Emerging Industries

Gale Group Inc.

27500 Drake Rd. Ph: (248)699-4253
Farmington Hills, MI 48331- Free: 800-877-GALE
3535 Fax: (248)699-8070
E-mail: galeord@galegroup.com
URL: http://www.galegroup.com.

Contact: Jane A. Malonis, Editor; Holly M. Selden, Editor.

Desc: 88 emerging business fields. *Type:* Directory.

Entrepreneur Magazine

Entrepreneur's Media Inc.

2392 Morse Ave. Ph: (949)261-2325
Irvine, CA 92614 Fax: (714)755-4211
E-mail: entmag@entrepreneurmag.com; entmag@ entrepreneurmag.com.
URL: http://www.entrepreneurmag.com.

Contact: Rieva Lesonsky, Editorial Dir.

Desc: Magazine covering small business management and operation. *Type:* Periodical.

Entrepreneur Magazine—Franchise 500 Survey Issue

Entrepreneur's Media Inc.

2392 Morse Ave. Ph: (949)261-2325
Irvine, CA 92614 Fax: (714)755-4211
E-mail: entmag@entrepreneurmag.com
URL: http://www.entrepreneurmag.com.

Contact: Maria Anton, Editor; Rieva Lesonsky, Editor.

Desc: Listing and ranking of over 1,000 franchisors in the United States and Canada. *Type:* Directory.

Entrepreneur's Alert
Entrepreneur's Guild
142 Morris Ave.   Ph: (201)263-2988
Mountain Lakes, NJ 07046-
   1127
Contact: Berkeley Fleming, Publisher; Richard Samson, Editor.
Desc: Offers advice for persons who want to start a business. *Type:* Newsletter.

EOA Entrepreneurs of America
Enterprise Publishing, Inc.
520 N. Dearborn St.   Fax: (312)654-0277
Chicago, IL 60610
Contact: Janice Yohai, Editor.
Desc: Spotlights entrepreneurship in the U.S. *Type:* Newsletter.

ERISA Top 25,000 Companies
Dun & Bradstreet
3 Sylvan Way   Ph: (973)605-6442
Parsippany, NJ 07054-3896   Free: 800-526-0651
   Fax: (973)605-6911
E-mail: dnbmdd@dnb.com
Desc: 25,000 companies with the largest combined sum of the assets in their pension plans. *Type:* Directory.

Euromedia Acquisitions
Paul Kagan Associates, Inc.
126 Clock Tower Pl.   Ph: (831)624-1536
Carmel, CA 93923-8734   Fax: (831)625-3225
E-mail: info@kagan.com
Contact: Paul Kagan, Publisher; Johanne Hardy, Editor; Judy Pinney, Circulation Mgr.
Desc: Tracks corporate sales, acquistions, mergers, and buyouts. *Type:* Newsletter.

European Business Services Directory
Gale Group Inc.
27500 Drake Rd.   Ph: (248)699-4253
Farmington Hills, MI 48331-   Free: 800-877-GALE
   3535   Fax: (248)699-8070
E-mail: galeord@galegroup.com
URL: http://www.galegroup.com.
Contact: Michael B. Huellmantel, Editor.
Desc: 20,000 European companies providing business-related services, such as executive recruiters, banks, law and accounting firms, and advertising agencies. *Type:* Directory.

European Consultants Directory
Gale Group Inc.
27500 Drake Rd.   Ph: (248)699-4253
Farmington Hills, MI 48331-   Free: 800-877-GALE
   3535   Fax: (248)699-8070
E-mail: galeord@galegroup.com
URL: http://www.galegroup.com.; http://www.gale.com.
Contact: Karin E. Koek, Editor.
Desc: About 5,000 consultants and consulting firms in Europe. *Type:* Directory.

European Venture Capital Journal
Venture Economics, Inc.
40 W. 57th St., 11th Fl.   Ph: (212)765-5311
New York, NY 10019   Free: 800-455-5844
   Fax: (212)765-6123
Contact: Kathleen Devlin, Editor-in-Chief, devlin@tfn.com; Jennifer Jury, Editor.
Desc: Reports on developments in the venture capital industry in Europe. Contains news, analysis, and data on Europe's venture capital/buyout industries. *Type:* Newsletter.

European Wholesalers and Distributors Directory
Gale Group Inc.
27500 Drake Rd.   Ph: (248)699-4253
Farmington Hills, MI 48331-   Free: 800-877-GALE
   3535   Fax: (248)699-8070
E-mail: galeord@galegroup.com
URL: http://www.galegroup.com.
Contact: Linda Irvin, Editor.
Desc: Over 5,500 wholesalers and distributors of consumer goods and industrial products in Europe. *Type:* Directory.

Executive Intelligence Review News Services
PO Box 17390   Ph: (703)777-9451
Washington, DC 20041   Fax: (703)771-9492
Alt. Contact: PO Box 17390, Washington, DC 20041; telephone: (703)777-9451; fax: (703)771-9492. *Type:* Periodical.

Executive Speeches
Executive Speaker
PO Box 292437   Ph: (937)294-8493
Dayton, OH 45429   Fax: (937)294-6044
E-mail: mail@executive-speaker.com
URL: http://www.executive-speaker.com
Contact: Robert O. Skovgard, Editor.
Desc: Provides information on full texts of speeches by executives. Remarks: Also available on microfilm. *Type:* Newsletter.

Executive Strategies
National Institute of Business Management
1750 Old Meadow Rd., Ste.   Ph: (703)905-8000
   302   Free: 800-543-2049
Mc Lean, VA 22102   Fax: (703)905-8042
Contact: Morey Stettner, Editor.
Desc: Contains strategies to help readers develop and advance their management careers. Recurring features include interviews, reports of meetings, and book reviews. *Type:* Newsletter.

Executive's Digest
Dartnell Marketing Publications
286 Congress St., 6th Fl.   Free: 800-468-3038
Boston, MA 02210   Fax: (617)451-8149
Contact: Christopher Ackley, Sales Representative.
Desc: Publishes business articles. *Type:* Newsletter.

Exhibit Mexico
Proteus Publishing
306 S. Main St., Ste. 1C-162   Ph: (734)668-2743
Ann Arbor, MI 48104   Fax: (734)668-8535
E-mail: 102130.3646@compuserve.com
Contact: Dell Deaton, Editor and Publisher.
Type: Newsletter.

Exhibiting Results!
Proteus Publishing
306 S. Main St., Ste. 1C-162   Ph: (734)668-2743
Ann Arbor, MI 48104   Fax: (734)668-8535
E-mail: 102130.3646@compuserve.com
Contact: Dell Deaton.
Desc: Provides information about trade shows. Includes industry trends and advice for maximizing the value of trade shows. *Type:* Newsletter.

The Expert Marketplace
Dun & Bradstreet
1 Diamond Hill Rd.   Ph: (908)665-5732
Murray Hill, NJ 07974   Free: 800-526-0651
   Fax: (908)665-5722
E-mail: dnbmdd@mail.dnb.com

URL: http://www.dnb.com/; http://expert-market.com/index-excite.html.
Desc: More than 200,000 business consulting firms, business case studies and business improvement articles. *Type:* Directory.

The Export Yellow Pages
US West Dex, Inc.
198 Inverness Dr. West   Ph: (303)784-2319
Englewood, CO 80112   Free: 800-288-2582
URL: http://export.uswest.com.
Contact: Mike Brady, Editor.
Desc: Approximately 16,000 U.S. suppliers distributed worldwide through U.S. Commerce Department channels. *Type:* Directory.

Exporters Directory
infoUSA
5711 S. 86th Circle   Ph: (402)593-4600
PO Box 27347   Free: 800-555-6124
Omaha, NE 68127   Fax: (402)331-5481
E-mail: internet@infousa.com
URL: http://www.abii.com.
Type: Directory.

Extra Equity for Homebuyers
Extra Equity for Homebuyers
216 Greens Farms Sta.   Ph: (203)254-1690
Greens Farms, CT 06436   Fax: (203)255-3707
Contact: William A. O'Brien, Publisher; Bob Griswold, Advertising Dir.
Desc: Magazine for people who are about to move to a new home. *Type:* Periodical.

F & S Indexes
The Gale Group
27500 Drake Rd.   Ph: (248)699-4253
Farmington Hills, MI 48331-
   3535
URL: http://www.galegroup.com
Contact: (650)378-5000, fax: (800)676-2345.
Desc: Contains approximately 3.9 million citations to worldwide literature on companies, products, and industries. Covers acquisitions and mergers, new products, technology, socio-political and economic factors affecting industries, analyses of companies by securities firms, and forecasts of sales and profits. *Available:* The Dialog Corporation, DataStar; The Dialog Corporation, DIALOG; The Gale Group, InfoTrac Web. *Type:* Database.

The Facilitator
Nurre Ink
PO Box 670705   Ph: (972)243-1356
Dallas, TX 75367-0705   Fax: (972)243-1357
Contact: Susan M. Nurre, Editor and Publisher, snurre@thefacilitator.com.
Desc: Provides articles written by facilitators that are designed to link facilitators from around the world in a forum of sharing, networking, and communicating. Includes updates on training, automated meeting tools, and resources. *Type:* Newsletter.

Family Tree
Dun & Bradstreet
1 Diamond Hill Rd.   Ph: (908)665-5732
Murray Hill, NJ 07974   Free: 800-526-0651
   Fax: (908)665-5722
E-mail: dnbmdd@mail.dnb.com
URL: http://www.dnb.com/
Desc: About 200,000 corporations and their subsidiaries and branch companies. *Type:* Directory.

Fast Company

Fast Company
1290 Avenue of the Americas   Ph: (212)830-1500
New York, NY 10104   Fax: (212)830-1640
E-mail: advertising@fastcompany.com;   loop@
fastcompany.com.
URL: http://www.fastcompany.com.
Contact: Thomas R. Evans, President; Alan M. Webber,
Editor; William C. Taylor, Editor.
Desc: Business magazine covering the changes underway
in how business competes, and the practices that shape
how work gets done. Also profiles the people, teams, products, and ideas that define the emerging world of business.
Alt. Contact: 77 N Washington St., Boston, MA 02114;
telephone: (617)973-0300; fax: (617)973-0373. *Type:* Periodical.

Faulkner & Gray's European Business Directory

Faulkner & Gray, Inc.
11 Penn Plaza, 17th Fl.   Ph: (212)967-7000
New York, NY 10001-2006   Free: 800-535-8403
                                 Fax: (212)967-7180
E-mail: order@faulknergray.com
Desc: Over 2,000 attorneys, accountants, consultants,
search firms, translators, shippers, commercial and investment banks, and industry leaders in Europe and the U.S.
interested in or presently doing business in Europe. *Type:*
Directory.

Federal Filings Business Newswire

Federal Filings, Inc.
1250 H St. NW, 11th Fl.   Ph: (202)393-7400
Washington, DC 20005
URL: http://www.fedfil.com/index.htm
Contact: John Curren, Product Manager.
Desc: A real-time newswire providing proprietary news, fi-
nancial data, and investment research from the U.S. Secur-
ities and Exchange Commission (SEC), other U.S.
Securities and Exchange Commission (SEC), other U.S.
federal government agencies, Capitol Hill, and bankrupt-
cy courts. *Available:* Dow Jones & Company, Inc. *Type:*
Database.

Federal Reserve Bulletin

Board of Governors of the Federal Reserve System
20th & Constitution Ave. NW   Ph: (202)452-3244
Washington, DC 20551   Fax: (202)728-5886
Desc: Discusses current business conditions, focusing on
financial statistics, both domestically and internationally.
Type: Newsletter.

Federation of German Industries

Representative of German Industry and Trade
1627 Eye St. NW   Ph: (202)659-4777
Washington, DC 20006   Fax: (202)659-4779
Contact: Jakob Esser, Pres.
Desc: Organizations representing 95% of private industry
in Germany. *Type:* Association.

Finance, Insurance & Real Estate USA: Industry Analyses, Statistics, and Leading Organizations

Gale Group Inc.
27500 Drake Rd.   Ph: (248)699-4253
Farmington Hills, MI 48331-   Free: 800-877-GALE
3535   Fax: (248)699-8070
E-mail: galeord@galegroup.com; ecdi@statrom.com.
URL: http://www.galegroup.com.; http://www.gale.com.
Contact: Arsen J. Darnay, Editor, (248)356-6990, fax:
(248)356-6426.
Desc: Lists of up to 100 leading companies in banking, finance, insurance, real estate, and related sectors, selected
on the basis of annual revenue. *Type:* Directory.

Financial World—200 Hottest Growth Companies

Financial World Partners
1328 Broadway, 3rd Fl.   Ph: (212)594-5030
New York, NY 10001   Free: 800-829-5916
                                 Fax: (212)629-0026
Contact: Geoffrey N. Smith, Editor.
Desc: List of companies selected on the basis of earnings
per share growth rate over a 10-year period ending with
current year; minimum growth rate used is 5 percent.
Type: Directory.

500 Contractors Receiving the Largest Dollar Volume of Prime Contract Awards for RDT&E

U.S. Department of Defense
The Pentagon   Ph: (703)545-6700
Washington, DC 20301
Desc: 500 largest contractors (including business, nonprofit organizations, foreign contractors, and government
agencies) that received the largest dollar volume of prime
contract awards over $25,000 for military research, devel-
opment, test, and evaluation projects. *Type:* Directory.

Florida Business Directory

infoUSA
5711 S. 86th Circle   Ph: (402)593-4600
PO Box 27347   Free: 800-555-6124
Omaha, NE 68127   Fax: (402)331-5481
E-mail: internet@infousa.com
URL: http://www.abii.com.
Contact: Peter J. Wilmarth, Publisher.
Desc: 616,000 businesses in Florida. *Type:* Directory.

Florida Creative Sourcebook

Graphis Publishing Group
Art 1 Graphic Expeditors, Inc.   Ph: (407)660-9505
PO Box 547992
Orlando, FL 32854-7992
Contact: M. Wesley Pusey, Editor.
Desc: More than 3,000 illustrators, photographers, audio-
visual services, and various creative marketing talent. *Type:*
Directory.

Florida Trend

Trend Magazines, Inc.
P.O. Box 611   Ph: (813)821-5800
St. Petersburg, FL 33731-0611
URL: http://www.fltrend.com
Contact: Janice Sharp, (813)821-5800.
Desc: Provides the complete text of Florida Trend, a
monthly publication covering Florida business, econom-
ics, finance, and real estate. Includes profiles of Florida
corporations and executives, analysis of economic trends,
and columns covering state and federal government, pub-
lic policy, fine dining, and real estate. *Available:* Bell &
Howell Information and Learning; LEXIS-NEXIS,
NEXIS. *Type:* Database.

The Florida Update

Mentor Communications
PO Box 290   Ph: (516)741-8887
Manhasset, NY 11030   Fax: (516)741-3131
Contact: Hank Boerner, Editor.
Desc: Supplies business executives with information and
analysis on Florida commerce. Provides news of specific
industries and companies and monitors general business
trends. *Type:* Newsletter.

Folio (Oklahoma City)

Department of Commerce
Box 26980   Ph: (405)815-5256
Oklahoma City, OK 73126-   Fax: (405)815-5281
0980
URL: http://www.odoc.state.ok.us.
Contact: Tracy Alford, Editor, Tracy_Alford@odoc.state.
ok.us.
Desc: Provides information on business and commerce in
Oklahoma City. *Type:* Newsletter.

Forbes

Forbes Investors Advisory Institute
60 5th Ave.   Ph: (212)620-2210
New York, NY 10011   Fax: (212)206-5174
E-mail: letters@forbesdigital.com
URL: http://www.forbes.com.
Contact: Malcolm S. Forbes, Jr., Editor-in-Chief; Caspar
W. Weinberger, Publisher; Jeffrey M. Cunningham, Pub-
lisher.
Desc: Magazine reporting on industry, business and fi-
nance management. *Type:* Periodical.

Forbes—Chief Executive Compensation Survey Issue

Forbes Magazine
60 5th Ave.   Ph: (212)620-2200
New York, NY 10011   Fax: (212)206-5174
E-mail: letters@forbesdigital.com
Contact: James W. Michaels, Editor.
Desc: List of 800 firms. *Type:* Directory.

Forbes—Forbes Four Hundred Issue

Forbes Magazine
60 5th Ave.   Ph: (212)620-2200
New York, NY 10011   Fax: (212)206-5174
E-mail: letters@forbesdigital.com
Contact: Peter Newcomb, Editor.
Desc: List of 400 Americans judged by "Forbes" to be the
wealthiest persons in the country, with personal fortunes
over $300 million dollars. *Type:* Directory.

Forbes—Platinum 400-America's Best Big Companies

Forbes Magazine
60 5th Ave.   Ph: (212)620-2200
New York, NY 10011   Fax: (212)206-5174
E-mail: letters@forbesdigital.com
URL: http://www.forbes.com.
Contact: William Baldwin, Editor.
Desc: List of 400 leading publicly owned corporations.
Type: Directory.

Forbes—The Forbes International 500 Issue

Forbes
60 5th Ave.   Ph: (212)620-2370
New York, NY 10011
URL: http://www.forbes.com.
Contact: James W. Michaels, Editor.
Desc: Lists of 100 largest foreign investments in the United
States, 100 largest United States multinationals, and 500
largest foreign corporations. *Type:* Directory.

Forbes—Up-and-Comers 200: Best Small Companies in America Issue

Forbes Magazine
60 5th Ave.   Ph: (212)620-2200
New York, NY 10011   Fax: (212)206-5174
E-mail: letters@forbesdigital.com
URL: http://www.forbes.com.
Contact: Steve Kichen, Editor of tabular material, ski-
chen@forbes.com.

Desc: List of 200 small companies judged to be high quality and fast-growing on the basis of 5-year return on equity and other qualitative measurements. Also includes a list of the 100 best small companies outside the U.S. Note: Issue does not carry address or CEO information for the foreign companies. *Type:* Directory.

Foreign Representatives in the U.S. Yellow Book

Leadership Directories, Inc.
104 5th Ave.   Ph: (212)627-4140
New York, NY 10011   Fax: (212)645-0931
E-mail: info@leadershipdirectories.com;
foreignrepresentatives@leadershipdirectories.com.
URL: http://www.leadershipdirectories.com; http://www.leadershipdirectories.com.
Contact: Seth Zupnik, Editor.
Desc: More than 1,300 foreign corporations and over 340 foreign financial institutions with U.S. operations, embassies, and consulates for more than 175 countries; 51 law firms; 375 foreign press outlets, 18 intergovernmental organizations. *Type:* Directory.

Foreign Subsidiaries in Michigan

Global Business Development
Michigan Economic Development Corporation
PO Box 30105   Ph: (517)335-5884
Lansing, MI 48909   Fax: (517)335-2521
Contact: Kathy O'Neill, Editor.
Desc: Over 930 Michigan subsidiaries of companies from outside the U.S. *Type:* Directory.

Foreign Trade Association of Southern California—Roster & Directory: Who's Who in Foreign Trade

Foreign Trade Association of Southern California
900 Wilshire Blvd., Ste. 1434   Ph: (213)627-0634
Los Angeles, CA 90017   Fax: (213)627-0398
E-mail: foreigntrade@earthlink.net
URL: http://www.ftasc.org/foreigntrade.
Contact: Anita Harja, Editor.
Desc: About 400 corporate members, and foreign trade delegates and consular officers; 140 U.S. foreign service representatives. Lists U.S. government services, international organizations and consulates. Also contains a classified section. *Type:* Directory.

Fortune

Time Inc.
Time-Life Bldg.   Ph: (212)522-1212
New York, NY 10020
URL: http://www.pathfinder.com/time
Desc: Contains the complete text of Fortune, a magazine covering trends and developments in the business community. Includes articles on corporate successes, failures, mergers, and marketing plans; political actions affecting business; analyses and forecasts of national and regional economic trends; and recommendations on personal investing. *Available:* LEXIS-NEXIS, NEXIS; The Dialog Corporation, DIALOG. *Type:* Database.

Fortune

Time Inc.
Time-Life Bldg., Rockefeller   Ph: (212)522-1212
Center   Fax: (212)522-0315
1271 Avenue of the Americas
New York, NY 10020
URL: http://www.fortune.com.
Contact: John Huey, Managing Editor; Geoffrey Colvin, Editorial Dir.; Michael Pepe, Group Publisher; Jolene Sykes, Publisher; Bob Maund, Associate Publisher; Terry McDevitt, Contact.
Desc: Business and industry magazine printed in regional and demographic editions. *Type:* Periodical.

Foundation Center

79 5th Ave.   Ph: (212)620-4230
New York, NY 10003   Free: 800-424-9836
      Fax: (212)691-1828
E-mail: feedback@fdncenter.org
URL: http://www.fdncenter.org
Contact: Sara Engelhardt, Pres.
Desc: Not an association. Established as an educational organization to: acquire, organize, and disseminate information about foundations and the grants they award; collect and make available published information about the foundation field and about its relationships to government and society, including historical records and supporting references in related fields. Conducts a fee based Associates Program that provides special services, including answers to fundraising questions, photocopies by mail and custom computer searches. *Type:* Association.

Fourth Corner Economic Development Group

Fred Sexton
1203 Cornwall Ave.   Ph: (360)676-4255
PO Box 2803   Fax: (360)647-9413
Bellingham, WA 98227
E-mail: bwedc@bwedc.org
URL: http://www.bwedc.org/edc/
Contact: Fred Sexton, Pres.
Type: Association.

Franchise Handbook

Enterprise Magazines, Inc.
1020 N. Broadway, Ste. 111   Ph: (414)272-9977
Milwaukee, WI 53202   Free: 800-272-0246
      Fax: (414)272-9973
E-mail: info@franchise1.com
URL: http://www.franchise1.com.
Contact: Michael McDermott, Editor; Maria Lahm, Managing Editor.
Desc: Firms offering franchises. *Type:* Directory.

Franchise World

International Franchise Association
1350 New York Ave. NW, Ste.   Ph: (202)628-8000
900   Free: 800-543-1038
Washington, DC 20005-4709   Fax: (202)628-0812
E-mail: ifa@franchise.org
URL: http://www.franchise.org
Contact: D. Kendall Edwards, Editor; Matthew Shay, Editor.
Desc: Reviews domestic and international legal and legislative developments related to franchising. Discusses the implications of these developments for franchisors and franchisees. *Type:* Newsletter.

Fraser Forum

Fraser Institute
9th Fl., 1770 Burrard St.   Ph: (604)688-0221
Vancouver, BC, Canada V0J   Free: 800-665-3558
3G7   Fax: (604)688-8539
E-mail: info@fraserinstitute.ca
URL: http://www.fraserinstitute.ca;   http://www.fraserinstitute.ca.
Contact: Kristin McCahon, Editor.
Desc: Carries articles that promote the Institute's objective of the redirection of public attention to the role of competitive markets in providing for the well-being of Canadians. Recurring features include interviews, news of research, news of educational opportunities, notices of publications available, and a column titled Editor's Notes. *Type:* Newsletter.

The Fraser Opinion Letter

Fraser Management Associates, Inc.
309 S. Willard St.   Ph: (802)658-0322
PO Box 494   Fax: (802)658-0260
Burlington, VT 05402
E-mail: info@fraser.com; newsletters@fraser.com.
Contact: James L. Fraser, Editor, jim@fraser.com.
Desc: Discusses current economic events and trends in business, finance, and public thinking from a "human and essentially fundamental approach." *Type:* Newsletter.

Frost & Sullivan Market Research Reports

Frost & Sullivan
2525 Charleston Rd.   Ph: (650)961-9000
Mountain View, CA 94043
E-mail: rpecoraro@frost.com
URL: http://www.frost.com
Contact: Elaine Higgins, (415)961-9000, fax: (415)961-5042.
Desc: Contains summaries of some 1500 Frost & Sullivan market research reports, providing analyses and forecasts of market size and share by product and company. Industries analyzed include chemicals, communications, consumer products, data processing, defense, electronics, food, health, instrumentation, machinery, and transportation. *Available:* The Dialog Corporation, DataStar. *Type:* Database.

Future Business Leaders of America - Phi Beta Lambda

1912 Association Dr.   Ph: (703)860-3334
Reston, VA 20191-1591   Free: 800-325-2946
      Fax: (703)758-0749
E-mail: general@fbla.org
URL: http://www.fbla-pbl.org.
Contact: Ms. Jean M. Buckley, Pres. & CEO.
Desc: Maintains 4 divisions: Future Business Leaders of America for high school students preparing for business and office careers; Phi Beta Lambda for post-secondary and college men and women enrolled in business, office, or teacher education programs; professional division for business persons; middle level for students in junior high schools. *Type:* Association.

Gale Business Resources

Gale Group Inc.
27500 Drake Rd.   Ph: (248)699-4253
Farmington Hills, MI 48331-   Free: 800-877-GALE
3535   Fax: (248)699-8070
E-mail: galeord@galegroup.com
URL: http://www.galegroup.com.; http://galenet.gale.com; http://www.gale.com.
Contact: Theresa McFarlane, Editor, theresa.macfarlan@gale.com; Virgil Burton, III, Editor, virgil.burton@gale.com.
Desc: Vital information on more than 450,000 businesses and 1,000 industries worldwide. *Type:* Directory.

The Georgeson Report

Georgeson & Company, Inc.
88 Pine St.   Ph: (212)440-9800
Wall St. Plaza   Fax: (212)440-9010
New York, NY 10005
E-mail: admin@georgeson.com
URL: http://www.georgeson.com.
Contact: David Drake, Editor, (212)440-9861, fax: (212)440-9009, ddrake@georgeson.com.
Desc: Concerns management of publicly-owned companies. Contains articles, surveys, and commentary on various aspects of management/investor relations: stockholder communications, advertising, tender offers, developments in the Securities and Exchange Commission, and legal considerations. *Type:* Newsletter.

Georgia Business Directory

infoUSA

5711 S. 86th Circle
PO Box 27347
Omaha, NE 68127

Ph: (402)593-4600
Free: 800-555-6124
Fax: (402)331-5481

E-mail: internet@infousa.com
URL: http://www.abii.com.

Contact: Peter J. Wilmarth, Publisher.

Desc: 281,000 businesses in Georgia. *Type:* Directory.

Georgia Business and Economic Conditions

Selig Center for Economic Growth

University of Georgia
Terry College of Business
Athens, GA 30602

Ph: (706)542-4085
Fax: (706)542-3858

E-mail: selig@cbacc.cba.uga.edu

Contact: Lorena M. Akioka, Editor.

Desc: Carries articles concerning the business and economic climate in Georgia. Discusses conditions in Georgia in relation to the Southeast. *Type:* Newsletter.

Georgia Trend

Grimes Publications of Georgia, Inc.

624 S. Milledge Ave.
Athens, GA 30605-5804

Ph: (706)354-0463

E-mail: gtrend@aol.com

Desc: Provides the complete text of Georgia Trend, a monthly publication covering Georgia business, economics, finance, and real estate. Includes profiles of Georgia corporations and executives, analysis of economic trends, and columns covering state and federal government, public policy, fine dining, state history, and the media. *Available:* Bell & Howell Information and Learning; LEXIS-NEXIS, NEXIS. *Type:* Database.

Global Report

Citicorp

153 E. 53rd St.
New York, NY 10043

Ph: (212)559-4822

Desc: Contains information on worldwide business and finance. Comprises the following 6 files: • Foreign Exchange--contains real-time spot and cross rates for 100 currencies, spot and forward rates for all major currencies, historical rates for 26 countries, and a summary of central bank activity. *Available:* FAME Information Services, Inc.; Globe Information Services, Info Globe Online; CompuServe Information Service. *Type:* Database.

Globalbase™

The Gale Group

27500 Drake Rd.
Farmington Hills, MI 48331-3535

Ph: (248)699-4253

URL: http://www.galegroup.com

Contact: (650)378-5000, fax: (800)676-2345.

Desc: Contains approximately 1.5 million summaries of business news reports from more than 1000 publications worldwide. Includes marketing, advertising, and retail sales; new products, services, and technologies; recent legislation; corporate acquisitions and mergers; and business trends and economic forecasts, covering a variety of business sectors: leisure, food, and beverages; automobile industry and automotive services; transportation; science and technology, including electronics and engineering; chemicals, energy resources, and forest products and packaging; construction; health care and pharmaceuticals; financial services; and information technology and telecommunications. *Available:* The Dialog Corporation, DataStar; The Dialog Corporation, DIALOG; Gesellschaft fur Betriebswirtschaftliche Information mbH (GBI); FT PROFILE; Bell & Howell Information and Learning. *Type:* Database.

Globe and Mail Report on Business

Globe and Mail Publishing

444 Front St. W.
Toronto, ON, Canada M5V 2S9

Ph: (416)585-5250
Fax: (416)585-5249

Contact: I. Carman, Editor.

Desc: Provides business information. *Type:* Newsletter.

The Globe and Mail Report on Business Magazine

The Globe & Mail

444 Front St. W.
Toronto, ON, Canada M5V 2S9

Ph: (416)585-5000
Fax: (416)585-5705

URL: http://www.globeandmail.com.

Contact: Cheri Natale, Editor.

Desc: Business report magazine. *Type:* Periodical.

Going Places

Florida Movers and Warehousemen's Association, Inc.

335 Beard St.
Tallahassee, FL 32303

Ph: (850)222-6000
Fax: (850)681-2890

Contact: Susan Trainor, Editor; Michelle Cyr, Advertising Mgr., michelle@assocofc.attmail.com.

Desc: Directed toward moving and storage companies. *Type:* Newsletter.

Government Prime Contractors Directory

Government Data Publications, Inc.

1661 MacDonald Ave.
Brooklyn, NY 11230

Ph: (718)627-0819
Fax: (718)998-5960

Contact: Siegfried Lobel, Editor.

Desc: Organizations that received government prime contracts during the previous two years. *Type:* Directory.

The Grandich Report

Grandich Publications

PO Box 354
Perrineville, NJ 08535-0354

Ph: (732)905-3822

Contact: Peter Grandich, Editor.

Desc: Covers Canadian stocks. Analyzes banking and finance, bonds, currencies, energy, economics, metals, new issues, oil, gas, mining, options, penny stocks, precious metals, natural resources, securities, technology, and stock exchanges as they pertain to U.S. trade relations and Canadian markets. *Type:* Newsletter.

Grantee's Action Alert Bulletin

Master Guide Publishers

PO Box 27203
Salt Lake City, UT 84127-0203

Ph: (801)561-1556
Fax: (801)561-8495

Contact: Vince Harding, Editor.

Desc: Publishes business information. *Type:* Newsletter.

Greater Allegheny Regional Industrial Buying Guide

Thomas Regional Directory Co., Inc.

5 Penn Plaza
New York, NY 10001

Ph: (212)629-2100
Fax: (212)290-7335

E-mail: info@trdnet.com
URL: http://www.thomasregional.com.

Contact: Marie McGurk, Editorial Dir.; Adrienne Toth, Managing Editor; Nancy Bromberg, Contracts Administration Mgr.

Desc: Over 15,000 listings of manufacturers of industrial products; related industrial services, such as trucking and maintenance services; distributors; and manufacturers' representatives in western Pennsylvania, eastern Ohio and West Virginia. *Type:* Directory.

Greater Boise Employer Directory

Career Center
Boise State University

Boise, ID 83725

Ph: (208)385-1747
Free: 800-824-7017
Fax: (208)385-3437

E-mail: career@bsu.idbsu.edu

Contact: Richard P. Rapp, Editor, rappr@boisestate.edu.

Desc: Over 1,100 companies and organizations in the greater Boise, Idaho area. *Type:* Directory.

Greater Carolinas Regional Industrial Buying Guide

Thomas Regional Directory Co., Inc.

5 Penn Plaza
New York, NY 10001

Ph: (212)629-2100
Fax: (212)290-7335

E-mail: info@trdnet.com
URL: http://www.thomasregional.com.

Contact: Marie McGurk, Editorial Dir.; Adrienne Toth, Managing Editor; Nancy Bromberg, Contracts Administration Mgr.

Desc: Nearly 30,000 listings of manufacturers of industrial products; related industrial services, such as trucking and maintenance services; distributors; and manufacturers' representatives in North Carolina, South Carolina, and Eastern Georgia. *Type:* Directory.

Greater Cincinnati Chamber of Commerce—Business Connections Directory

Greater Cincinnati Chamber of Commerce

300 Carew Tower
441 Vine St.
Cincinnati, OH 45202-2812

Ph: (513)579-3100
Fax: (513)579-3101

E-mail: hmilss@gccc.com.
URL: http://www.gccc.com.

Contact: Keith Stichtenoth, Manager, keithstichtenoth@gccc.com.

Desc: Approximately 6,000 member and nonmember firms in the Greater Cincinnati area (Hamilton, Clermont, Butler, Brown, and Warren counties in Ohio; Boone, Campbell, Grant, Gallatin, Pendleton, and Kenton counties in Kentucky; Dearborn and Ohio counties in Indiana). *Type:* Directory.

Greater Cincinnati Convention and Visitors Bureau

Michael Wilson

300 W 6th St.
Cincinnati, OH 45202

Ph: (513)621-2142
Fax: (513)621-5020

Contact: Michael J. Wilson, Pres.

Desc: Strives to impact the greater Cincinnati area economy through conventions, trade shows, and visitor expenditures. *Type:* Association.

Greater Cincinnati International Trade Directory

Greater Cincinnati Chamber of Commerce

300 Carew Tower
441 Vine St.
Cincinnati, OH 45202-2812

Ph: (513)579-3100
Fax: (513)579-3101

URL: http://www.gccc.com.

Contact: Rene Thomas, Editor, rthomas@gccc.com.

Desc: Over 950 importers and exporters; related service firms and organizations such as state government trade offices, attorneys, financial institutions, certified public accountants, freight forwarders, custom brokers, and language and export marketing services. *Type:* Directory.

Greater Delaware Valley Regional Industrial Buying Guide

Thomas Regional Directory Co., Inc.

5 Penn Plaza
New York, NY 10001

Ph: (212)629-2100
Fax: (212)290-7335

E-mail: info@trdnet.com

URL: http://www.thomasregional.com.

Contact: Marie McGurk, Editorial Dir.; Adrienne Toth, Managing Editor; Nancy Bromberg, Contracts Administration Mgr.

Desc: Nearly 25,000 listings of manufacturers of industrial products; related industrial services, such as trucking and maintenance services; distributors; and manufacturers' representatives in eastern Pennsylvania and the adjacent counties of Delaware and New Jersey. *Type:* Directory.

Greater Kansas City Convention and Visitors Bureau

1100 Main St., Ste. 2550	Ph: (816)221-5242
Kansas City, MO 64105	Free: 800-767-7700
	Fax: (816)691-3805

E-mail: modell@visitkc.com
URL: http://kansascity.com
Contact: Wayne Chapell, Pres.
Desc: To promote Kansas City, MO as a convention and tourist destination. *Type:* Association.

Greater O'Hare Association—Interaction

Greater O'Hare Association
PO Box 1516   Ph: (708)350-2944
Elk Grove Village, IL 60009
Contact: Lisa Zeigler, Editor.
Desc: Lists news of the Association, which promotes business in the Greater O'Hare area. Features information about Association programs and groups, legislation, and news affecting business. *Type:* Newsletter.

The Greater Washington Board of Trade—Membership Directory

Greater Washington Board of Trade
1129 20th St. NW, Ste. 200   Ph: (202)857-5900
Washington, DC 20036   Fax: (202)223-2648
Contact: Leslie L. Mejia, Editor, lesliemejia@bot.org.
Desc: Over 1,000 member firms in the greater Washington, DC, metropolitan area. *Type:* Directory.

Guide to the Port of New York-New Jersey

Port Authority of New York and New Jersey
One World Trade Center   Ph: (212)466-7000
No. 64E   Fax: (212)435-2999
New York, NY 10048
Contact: Catherine Durds, Editor.
Desc: Commercial shipping facilities at the port areas of New York and New Jersey: about 20 freight terminals; Port Authority offices and U.S. government departments; 80 international trade, maritime, and transportation associations; 385 companies providing trucking and freight hauling services; 90 warehouse facilities; 500 international freight forwarders, custom house brokers, and firms that combine the services of forwarder and broker; 55 airlines providing freight services from John F. Kennedy International Airport, LaGuardia Airport, and Newark International Airport; 75 steamship lines, steamship line agents, terminal operators and steve dores; 1,230 companies providing maritime services, e.g. international banking, marine insurance, contracting, brokering, and engineering; 180 suppliers of marine equipment; and 85 inland (i.e. interstate) freight services. *Type:* Directory.

Harrison County Development Commission

c/o Michael Olivier, Exec.Dir.   Ph: (228)863-3807
2510 14th St. No. 1105   Fax: (228)863-4555
PO Box 1870
Gulfport, MS 39502
E-mail: hcdc@datasync.com
URL: http://www.gulfcoast.org
Contact: Michael Olivier, Contact.
Desc: County economic development agency representing local government entities. *Type:* Association.

Harvard Business Review

Harvard Business School Publishing Corp.
60 Harvard Way   Ph: (617)495-6800
Boston, MA 02163   Fax: (617)495-9933
E-mail: hbr_editorial@hbsp.harvard.edu
URL: http://www.hosp.harvard.edu.
Contact: Stephen Sykes, Assoc. Publisher, (617)496-8166; Peter Van Leight, Advertising Dir., (212)872-9280, fax: (212)838-6535.
Desc: Magazine for business executives. *Type:* Periodical.

Harvard Business Review Online

Harvard Business School Publishing
60 Harvard Way   Ph: (617)495-6700
Boston, MA 02163-1098
E-mail: custserv@hbsp.edu
URL: http://www.hbsp.harvard.edu
Contact: Betsy Bellar Production Technology Specialist, (617)496-2484, fax: (617)496-8066, bbellar@cchbspub.har.
Desc: Contains more than 3300 citations, with abstracts (from 1967) and the complete text (from 1976), to articles appearing in the Harvard Business Review. Also includes citations, with abstracts, to approximately 700 classic articles published between 1925 and 1970. *Available:* Ovid Technologies, Inc.; The Dialog Corporation, DataStar; The Dialog Corporation, DIALOG; CompuServe Information Service, Knowledge Index; LEXIS-NEXIS, NEXIS. *Type:* Database.

Hawaii Business Directory

Hawaii Business Directory, Inc.
1164 Bishop St., Ste. 1502   Ph: (808)526-2287
Honolulu, HI 96813   Fax: (808)526-2289
Contact: John L. Witwer, Editor.
Desc: About 37,000 manufacturers, wholesalers, retailers, and service firms. *Type:* Directory.

Hawaii Business Directory

infoUSA
5711 S. 86th Circle   Ph: (402)593-4600
PO Box 27347   Free: 800-555-6124
Omaha, NE 68127   Fax: (402)331-5481
E-mail: internet@infousa.com
URL: http://www.abii.com.
Contact: Peter J. Wilmarth, Publisher.
Desc: 52,000 businesses in Hawaii. *Type:* Directory.

Headquarters, San Diego County

Greater San Diego Chamber of Commerce
402 W. Broadway, Ste. 1000   Ph: (619)544-1300
San Diego, CA 92101-3585   Fax: (619)234-0571
E-mail: info@sdchamber.org
URL: http://www.sdchamber.org
Contact: Gale Sonora, Editor.
Desc: About 400 firms maintaining their primary corporate offices in San Diego County. *Type:* Directory.

Hinsdale Community Directory

Hinsdale Chamber of Commerce (HCC)
22 E. 1st St.   Ph: (630)323-3952
Hinsdale, IL 60521   Fax: (630)323-3953
Contact: Harriet Vina, Editor.
Desc: Member businesses, clubs and organizations, public and private schools, public officials and community services in Hinsdale, Illinois. *Type:* Directory.

Hispanic Business

Hispanic Business
425 Pine Ave.   Ph: (805)964-4554
Santa Barbara, CA 93117-3709   Fax: (805)964-5539
E-mail: info@hbinc.com

URL: http://www.hispanstar.com.
Contact: Jesus Chavarria, Publisher, jchavarria@mail.hbinc.com; Vaughn Hagerty, Managing Editor, vhagerty@mail.hbinc.com; Jeff D. Vitucci, Dir. of Research Services, jvitucci@mail.hbinc.com.
Desc: English-language business magazine catering to Hispanic professionals, executives, and entrepreneurs. *Type:* Periodical.

Hollywood Agents and Managers Directory

Hollywood Creative Directory
3000 W. Olympic Blvd., Ste.   Ph: (310)315-4815
2525   Free: 800-815-0503
Santa Monica, CA 90404   Fax: (310)315-4816
E-mail: hcd@hcdonline.com
URL: http://www.hcdonline.com.
Contact: Barbara Dugan, Editor, bdugan@hcdonline.com.
Desc: Over 1,200 Talent & Literary Agencies & Mgrs. in LA, NY & over 4,000 names. IN Agency name, address, phone, fax, names and titles of key personnel, product or service. *Type:* Directory.

Home Business Made Easy

Todd Publications
PO Box 635   Ph: (914)358-6213
Nyack, NY 10960   Free: 800-747-1056
                        Fax: (914)358-1059
E-mail: toddpub@aol.com
URL: http://www.toddpublications.com
Desc: 153 different business that can be run from home full or part time based on interest, lifestyle, and finances. *Type:* Directory.

Hoover's Company Capsules on CD-ROM

Hoover's, Inc.
1033 La Posada Dr., Ste. 250   Ph: (512)374-4500
Austin, TX 78752   Fax: (512)374-4501
E-mail: orders@hoovers.com
URL: http://www.hoovers.com; http://www.hoovers.com.
Desc: CD-ROM contains information on approximately 11,000 U.S. companies and over 30,000 CEOs and CFOs. *Type:* Directory.

Hoover's Handbook of American Business

Hoover's, Inc.
1033 La Posada Dr., Ste. 250   Ph: (512)374-4500
Austin, TX 78752   Fax: (512)374-4501
E-mail: orders@hoovers.com
URL: http://www.hoovers.com; http://www.hoovers.com.
Contact: James R. Talbot, Editor.
Desc: Approximately 750 U.S. companies. *Type:* Directory.

Hoover's Handbook of Emerging Companies

Hoover's, Inc.
1033 La Posada Dr., Ste. 250   Ph: (512)374-4500
Austin, TX 78752   Fax: (512)374-4501
E-mail: orders@hoovers.com
URL: http://www.hoovers.com; http://www.hoovers.com.
Desc: 300 rapidly growing companies. *Type:* Directory.

Hoover's Handbook of Private Companies

Hoover's, Inc.
1033 La Posada Dr., Ste. 250   Ph: (512)374-4500
Austin, TX 78752   Fax: (512)374-4501
E-mail: orders@hoovers.com
URL: http://www.hoovers.com; http://www.hoovers.com.
Desc: 800 privately held companies and other enterprises; 250 firms are covered in detail. *Type:* Directory.

Hoover's Handbook of World Business

Hoover's, Inc.
1033 La Posada Dr., Ste. 250   Ph: (512)374-4500
Austin, TX 78752   Fax: (512)374-4501
E-mail: orders@hoovers.com
URL: http://www.hoovers.com; http://www.hoovers.com.

Contact: Patrick J. Spain, Editor.

Desc: Approximately 300 companies headquartered outside the U.S., including many with substantial activity in the U.S.; global enterprises, businesses that dominate their respective industries, and representative companies from all major industries. *Type:* Directory.

Hoover's MasterList of Major U.S. Companies

Hoover's, Inc.
1033 La Posada Dr., Ste. 250   Ph: (512)374-4500
Austin, TX 78752   Fax: (512)374-4501
E-mail: orders@hoovers.com
URL: http://www.hoovers.com; http://www.hoovers.com.

Desc: Approximately 5,100 of the largest public and private companies in the U.S. *Type:* Directory.

Hoover's Online

Hoover's, Inc.
1033 La Posada Dr., Ste. 250   Ph: (512)374-4500
Austin, TX 78752   Fax: (512)374-4501
E-mail: info@hoovers.com
URL: http://www.hoovers.com

Desc: Hoover's Online offers business and company information via in-depth news reports, industry data (such as stock reports), and industry analysis. *Type:* Database.

Houston Business

Federal Reserve Bank of Dallas
Houston Branch
PO Box 2578
Houston, TX 77252
URL: http://www.dallasfed.org.

Contact: Bill Gilmer, (713)652-1546, bill.gilmer@dal.frb.org.

Desc: Provides a perspective on the Houston, Texas economy. *Type:* Newsletter.

IB (Independent Business)

Group IV Communications, Inc.
125 Auburn Court, Ste. 100   Ph: (805)496-6156
Thousand Oaks, CA 91362-   Fax: (805)496-5469
   3617
E-mail: gosmallbiz@aol.com.

Contact: Daniel Kehrer, Editor; Mike Carpenter, Publisher; Maryann Hammers, Managing Editor.

Desc: Magazine for small business owners. *Type:* Periodical.

IBA News

Institute of Business Appraisers
PO Box 1447   Ph: (561)732-3202
Boynton Beach, FL 33425   Free: 800-299-4130
   Fax: (561)732-4304
E-mail: ibahq@aol.com
Contact: Raymond C. Miles, Editor.

Desc: Directed toward business appraising and supplies news of the Institute. Recurring features include news of research, a calendar of events, reports of meetings, book reviews, and notices of publications available. *Type:* Newsletter.

IC2 Update

IC2 Institute
University of Texas at Austin
2815 San Gabriel   Ph: (512)475-8900
Austin, TX 78705   Free: 800-215-6782
   Fax: (512)475-8901
E-mail: mail@icc.utexas.edu
Contact: Nancy Richey, Editor.

Desc: Focuses on the study and analysis of information on the enterprise system. Includes news of research, conferences, notices of publications available, and news on other activities. *Type:* Newsletter.

Idaho Business Directory

infoUSA
5711 S. 86th Circle   Ph: (402)593-4600
PO Box 27347   Free: 800-555-6124
Omaha, NE 68127   Fax: (402)331-5481
E-mail: internet@infousa.com
URL: http://www.abii.com.
Contact: Peter J. Wilmarth, Publisher.
Desc: 57,000 businesses in Idaho. *Type:* Directory.

Illinois Business Directory

infoUSA
5711 S. 86th Circle   Ph: (402)593-4600
PO Box 27347   Free: 800-555-6124
Omaha, NE 68127   Fax: (402)331-5481
E-mail: internet@infousa.com
URL: http://www.abii.com.
Contact: Peter J. Wilmarth, Publisher.
Desc: 483,000 businesses in Illinois. *Type:* Directory.

Import/Export USA

Gale Group Inc.
27500 Drake Rd.   Ph: (248)699-4253
Farmington Hills, MI 48331-   Free: 800-877-GALE
   3535   Fax: (248)699-8070
E-mail: galeord@galegroup.com
URL: http://www.galegroup.com.
Contact: Mike Weaver, Editor, mike.weaver@gale.com.
Desc: U.S. import and export data on more than 20,000 commodities and 85,000 international importing and exporting companies. *Type:* Directory.

Importers Directory

infoUSA
5711 S. 86th Circle   Ph: (402)593-4600
PO Box 27347   Free: 800-555-6124
Omaha, NE 68127   Fax: (402)331-5481
E-mail: internet@infousa.com
URL: http://www.abii.com.
Type: Directory.

In Touch

The City Centre Business Association of Windsor
375 Oullette Ave., Ste. 202   Ph: (519)252-5723
Windsor, ON, Canada N9A 4J1   Fax: (519)252-6817
Contact: Fran Funaro, Managing Editor.
Desc: Acts as the publication of The City Centre Business Association of Windsor. Recurring features include news of members and a calendar of events. *Type:* Newsletter.

Income Opportunities

IO Publications, Inc.
1500 Broadway   Ph: (212)642-0600
New York, NY 10036-4015   Free: 800-289-7852
   Fax: (212)768-3769
E-mail: incomeed@aol.com; income@aol.com.
Contact: Linda Molnar, Editor; Don Mazzella, Publisher.
Desc: Magazine focusing on money making opportunities. *Type:* Periodical.

Inc. Magazine

The Goldhirsh Group
38 Commercial Wharf   Ph: (617)248-8000
Boston, MA 02110   Free: 800-842-1343
   Fax: (617)248-8090
E-mail: editors@inc.com.
URL: http://www.inc.com.

Contact: George Gendron, Editor; Riley McDonaugh, Publisher; Gary Mirkin, Advertising Dir.

Desc: Business and finance magazine for business owners and managers. *Type:* Periodical.

Incorporated News

Incorporated News, Inc.
2533 N. Carson St.   Ph: (702)885-9748
Carson City, NV 89701   Fax: (702)883-4874
Contact: Jack Heller, Editor.

Desc: Covers taxation developments, business and incorporation strategies for asset protection, and tax minimization, with emphasis on the advantages of incorporating in "tax-free" Nevada. *Type:* Newsletter.

Inc. Technology

The Goldhirsh Group
38 Commercial Wharf   Ph: (617)248-8000
Boston, MA 02110   Free: 800-842-1343
   Fax: (617)248-8090
E-mail: tech@inc.com.
URL: http://www.inc.com; http://www.inc.com.

Contact: Emily Esterson, Assoc. Ed.; Thea Singer, Articles Editor.

Desc: Magazine covering technological issues for small to mid-size companies. *Type:* Periodical.

Inc.—The Inc. 500 Issue

Inc. Publishing Corp.
38 Commercial Wharf   Ph: (617)248-8000
Boston, MA 02110   Fax: (617)248-8090
E-mail: editors@inc.com
URL: http://www.inc.com.

Contact: Joshua Hyatt, Editor.

Desc: List of 500 fastest-growing privately held companies based on percentage increase in sales over the five year period prior to compilation of current year's list. *Type:* Directory.

India Weekly Fax Bulletin

Orbis Publications, LLC
3201 New Mexico Ave. NW,   Ph: (202)237-0155
   Ste. 249   Fax: (202)237-0596
Washington, DC 20016
E-mail: orbis@orbispub.com
URL: http://www.orbispub.com.

Contact: Richard W. Foster, Editor.

Desc: Reports on political, economic and business events in India via fax. *Type:* Newsletter.

Indiana Business Directory

infoUSA
5711 S. 86th Circle   Ph: (402)593-4600
PO Box 27347   Free: 800-555-6124
Omaha, NE 68127   Fax: (402)331-5481
E-mail: internet@infousa.com
URL: http://www.abii.com.

Contact: Peter J. Wilmarth, Publisher.

Desc: 219,000 businesses in Indiana. *Type:* Directory.

Indiana Directory of International Business Services

International Trade Division Indiana Department of Commerce

1 N. Capitol, Ste. 700　　　Ph: (317)233-3762
Indianapolis, IN 46204-2288　Fax: (317)232-4146

Contact: Luana Leonard, Editor.

Desc: Over 350 consultants, translators, banks, freight forwarders, and service providers located in Indiana and servicing the international trade industry. *Type:* Directory.

Indianapolis Convention and Visitors Association

1 RCA Dome, Ste. 100　　Ph: (317)639-4282
Indianapolis, IN 46225　　Free: 800-323-INDY
　　　　　　　　　　　　Fax: (317)639-5273

URL: http://www.indy.org

Contact: Wm.K. McGowan, Jr., Pres./CEO.

Desc: Promotes business and tourism in the Indianapolis, IN area. *Type:* Association.

Indonesia Weekly Fax Bulletin

Orbis Publications, LLC

3201 New Mexico Ave. NW,　Ph: (202)237-0155
　Ste. 249　　　　　　　　Fax: (202)237-0596
Washington, DC 20016
E-mail: orbis@orbispub.com
URL: http://www.orbispub.com.

Contact: Richard Foster, Editor.

Desc: Reports on political, economic and business events in Indonesia via fax. *Type:* Newsletter.

Industrial Maintenance and Plant Operation

Cahners Business Information

201 King of Prussia Rd.　　Ph: (610)964-4000
Radnor, PA 19087-5114　　Fax: (610)964-2915
E-mail: marketaccess@cahners.com
URL: http://www.impomag.com.

Contact: Dave Johnson, Editor, (610)964-4057, fax: (610)964-4947; George Hutter, Publisher, (610)964-4659, fax: (610)964-4947, ghutter@chilton.net; Hank Pendrak, Marketing Mgr., (610)964-4041, fax: (610)964-4947, hpendrak@chilton.net.

Desc: Product news magazine (tabloid) serving the plant engineering, maintenance, replacement, and operations markets. *Type:* Periodical.

Industrial Product Bulletin

Cahners Business Information

New Product Information Division

301 Gibraltar Dr.　　　　Ph: (973)292-5100
Morris Plains, NJ 07950　Fax: (973)539-3476

Contact: Anita LaFond, Editor; Dave Esola, Publisher; Todd Baker, Assoc. Publisher.

Desc: Magazine reporting new product information on manufacturing equipment, maintenance supplies, and high technology developments. *Type:* Periodical.

Industrial Reps of Overseas Countries & Overseas Buying Reps

Todd Publications

PO Box 635　　　　　　Ph: (914)358-6213
Nyack, NY 10960　　　　Free: 800-747-1056
　　　　　　　　　　　Fax: (914)358-1059

E-mail: toddpub@aol.com
URL: http://www.toddpublications.com

Desc: 400 agencies, trade missions, consulate generals and firms in the U.S. representing 110 foreign countries to help in exporting products. *Type:* Directory.

Industries in Transition

Business Communications Co., Inc.

25 Van Zant St.　　　　Ph: (203)853-4266
Norwalk, CT 06855-1781　Fax: (203)853-0348
E-mail: buscom2@aol.com
URL: http://www.buscom.com; http://www.buscom.com/.

Contact: Malika Rajan, Editor.

Desc: Covers the news sources and distills the important developments in America's changing industries. Provides information on the economy, identifies the markets primary and radial changes place, analyzes the causes and the effects, and gives details relevant to industry decision makers. *Type:* Newsletter.

Industry Focus

Association of Business Support Services International, Inc.

22875 Savi Ranch Pkwy., Ste.　Ph: (714)282-9398
　H　　　　　　　　　　　Free: 800-237-1462
Yorba Linda, CA 92887-4619　Fax: (714)282-8630
E-mail: abssi4you@aol.com
URL: http://www.abssi.org.

Contact: Lynette M. Smith, CPS, Editor.

Desc: Deals with every facet of business support service operations: pricing, successful new sales techniques for adding clients, dealing with clients and employees, work scheduling, forms and contracts, financial management, equipment and technology. Contains input from ABSSI members. *Type:* Newsletter.

Industry Trends & Analysis

Decision Resources, Inc.

1100 Winter St.　　　　Ph: (781)487-3707
Waltham, MA 02451-1238
E-mail: wolosins@dresources.com
URL: http://www.dresources.com

Contact: Thea C. Wolosinski, Director of Database Services.

Desc: Contains premier research and analysis from a global network of industry and academia experts. Covers areas such as biotechnology, pharmaceuticals, health care delivery, diagnostics, drug discovery, disease management, therapy markets, information systems, performance materials, as well as the chemical, food, and telecommunications industries. *Available:* The Dialog Corporation, DIALOG. *Type:* Database.

Industry Week

Penton Publishing Company

1100 Superior Ave.　　　Ph: (216)696-7000
Cleveland, OH 44114
URL: http://www.industryweek.com

Contact: Anita Schlott, Administrative Assistant, (216)696-7000, fax: (216)696-7670.

Desc: Contains the complete text of Industry Week magazine, focusing on three broad management areas: the ongoing development of people and organizations; technological developments that create new products and services; and political, economic, and social issues that impact industry management. Reports economic indicators (including gross national product, industrial production, retail sales, housing starts, unemployment, personal income, capital spending, and consumer and producer prices) and provides analyses of current economic trends, with commentary by econometrician Michael K. *Available:* LEXIS-NEXIS, NEXIS. *Type:* Database.

Info Franchise Newsletter

Info Press Inc.

728 Center St.　　　　Ph: (716)754-4669
Box 550　　　　　　　Free: 888-806-2665
Lewiston, NY 14092　　Fax: (905)688-7728
E-mail: infopress@infonews.com
URL: http://infonews.com/franchise; http://infonews.com/franchise.

Contact: Edward L. Dixon, Jr., Editor; Jo-Anne Rittenhouse, Asst. Editor.

Desc: Covers business format franchising in the U.S., Canada, and overseas; reports on trends, legislation and litigation, and on developments in the franchising business scene. Recurring features include lists of new franchisors, including descriptions, contact addresses and telephone numbers for each; and address changes of franchisor headquarters. *Type:* Newsletter.

INFOCUS

Business Forms Management Association, Inc.

319 SW Washington, Ste. 710　Ph: (503)227-3393
Portland, OR 97204　　　　　Fax: (503)274-7667
E-mail: infocus@bfmu.org; bfma@bfma.org; infocus@bfmu.org.

Contact: Christie Holmgren, Editor.

Desc: Focuses on products, services, and trends in the forms-systems environment. Recurring features include a calendar of events, reports of meetings, news of educational opportunities, book reviews, and notices of publications available, new product reviews, and a feature article on a trend in forms management. *Type:* Newsletter.

The Information Catalog

Kalorama Information, LLC

641 6th Ave.　　　　　Ph: (212)807-2716
New York, NY 10011　　Free: 800-298-5699
　　　　　　　　　　　Fax: (212)807-2716
E-mail: info@findexonline.com
URL: http://www.findexonline.com.

Contact: Michael Latshaw, Editor.

Desc: Lists reports, surveys, reference books, and studies of over 35 industries in regard to market sizes, new products, performance forecasts, competitor profiles, and technological advances. *Type:* Newsletter.

informationLINK

Nonprofit Resource Center of Texas

PO Box 15070　　　　Ph: (210)227-4333
San Antonio, TX 78212-8270　Fax: (210)227-0310
E-mail: fic@fic.org

Contact: Carol Petri, Publications Mgr.

Desc: Provides information and resources for non-profit organizations in Texas. Recurring features include notices of publications available and a calendar of events. *Type:* Newsletter.

Inside U.S. Trade

Inside Washington Publishers

PO Box 7167　　　　　Ph: (703)416-8500
Ben Franklin Sta.　　　Free: 800-424-9068
Washington, DC 20044-7167
E-mail: iwp@iwpnews.com

Contact: Jutta Hennig, Editor.

Desc: Reports on government and industry trade. Recurring features include interviews. *Type:* Newsletter.

Insiders Money-Making Report

Publishers Media

PO Box 1295　　　　　Ph: (619)282-5822
El Cajon, CA 92022-1295　Fax: (619)588-9103
E-mail: onlinemedia@accessl.com

Contact: Russ von Hoelscher, Editor.

Desc: Provides information on, and evaluation of, businesses, home businesses, and mail order opportunities. *Type:* Newsletter.

Inter-Corporate Ownership

Infomart Dialog Limited
1450 Don Mills Rd.   Ph: (416)442-2198
Don Mills, ON, Canada M3B
   2X7
E-mail: helpdesk@infomart.ca
URL: http://www.infomart.com/
Contact: Client Services Consultants, (416)442-2198, fax:
(416)442-2126, helpdesk@infomart.ca.
Desc: Contains corporate names of 45,000 Canadian and
non-Canadian holding and held companies doing business
in Canada. Users can display names in hierarchical levels
of ownership with percentage of ownership for each company's holdings in other companies. *Available:* Infomart
Online; Infomart Dialog Limited. *Type:* Database.

International Affiliates

Dun & Bradstreet
3 Sylvan Way   Ph: (973)605-6442
Parsippany, NJ 07054-3896   Free: 800-526-0651
                                      Fax: (973)605-6911
E-mail: dnbmdd@dnb.com
Desc: Approximately 3,000 foreign ultimate parent companies and their 11,000 U.S. subsidiaries and nearly 3,000
U.S. ultimate parent corporations and their 18,000 foreign subsidiaries. Listings limited to multinational corporate families having at least one U.S. family member and
at least one foreign family member. Any ultimate company with only one subsidiary must have a minimym of 250
total employees (including the subsidiary company's) in
order to qualify. Corporations operating wholly and exclusively within the U.S. or within countries outside the U.S.
are not covered. *Type:* Directory.

The International Alliance, An Association of Executive and Professional Women

PO Box 1119   Ph: (410)472-4221
Sparks-Glencoe   Fax: (410)472-2920
Baltimore, MD 21152
E-mail: MAXX28b@prodigy.com
URL: http://www.t-i-a.com
Contact: Rosemary McAvoy, Exec.Dir.
Desc: Local networks (32) comprising 10,000 professional
and executive women in 12 countries; individual busines-
swomen without a network affiliation (225) are alliance as-
sociates. Seeks to:. promote recognition of the
achievements of women in business; encourage placement
of women in senior executive positions; maintain high
standards of professional competence among members.
Type: Association.

International Association of African and American Black Business People

18900 Schoolcraft
Detroit, MI 48223
Contact: William Bert Johnson, Pres.
Desc: African and African-American businesspersons. Establishes, operates, and fosters business education and related activities among African-American and African
members of the business community worldwide. *Type:* Association.

International Association of Assembly Managers

4425 W. Airport Fwy., Ste. 590   Ph: (972)255-8020
Irving, TX 75062   Fax: (972)255-9582
E-mail: iaam.info@iaam.org
URL: http://www.iaam.org
Contact: Jack Zimmer, CAE, Exec.Dir.
Desc: Auditorium, arena, stadium, convention center, the-
atre, amphitheatre, and exhibit hall managers. Conducts
seminars in auditorium, arena, and performing arts facility
management. Maintains databank of documents pertain-
ing to the industry. *Type:* Association.

International Association of Convention and Visitor Bureaus

2000 L St. NW, Ste. 702   Ph: (202)296-7888
Washington, DC 20036-4990   Fax: (202)296-7889
URL: http://www.iacvb.org
Contact: Edward L. Nielsen, MHS, Pres. & CEO.
Desc: Trade association founded to promote sound profes-
sional practices in the solicitation and servicing of meet-
ings and conventions. *Type:* Association.

International Brands and Their Companies

Gale Group Inc.
27500 Drake Rd.   Ph: (248)699-4253
Farmington Hills, MI 48331-   Free: 800-877-GALE
   3535   Fax: (248)699-8070
E-mail: galeord@galegroup.com
URL: http://www.galegroup.com.
Contact: Linda Irvin, Editor.
Desc: About 84,000 trademarks, trade names, and brands
of consumer products from 28,000 international manu-
facturers, importers, and distributors. *Type:* Directory.

International Business Information Services

PO Box 4082   Ph: (714)552-8494
Irvine, CA 92710-4082   Fax: (714)552-8494
Contact: B.N. Zelenka, Mng. Dir.; Andrew Raymond,
Mktg. and Service Mgr.
Desc: Distributes business, international business, and en-
trepreneurial columns. *Alt. Contact:* PO Box 4082, Irvine,
CA 92716-4082; telephone: (714)552-8494; fax:
(714)552-8494. *Type:* Periodical.

International Business Quick Reference Guide

U.S. Chamber of Commerce
International Division Publications
1615 H St. NW   Ph: (202)463-5460
Washington, DC 20062-2000   Fax: (202)463-3114
Desc: American Chambers of Commerce abroad, foreign
chambers of commerce in the U.S., embassies, overseas assistance, Commerce Departments and contacts. Chamber,
department or embassy name, address, phone, contact
name, title. *Type:* Directory.

International Business in South Africa

Investor Responsibility Research Center, Inc.
(IRRC)
1350 Connecticut Ave., NW,   Ph: (202)833-0700
   Ste. 700   Fax: (202)833-3555
Washington, DC 20036
URL: http://www.irrc.org
Contact: Meg Voorhes, Editor.
Desc: About 600 non-U.S. companies with business links
to South Africa. *Type:* Directory.

International Business and Trade Directories

Grey House Publishing
Pocket Knife Square   Ph: (860)435-0868
Lakeville, CT 06039   Free: 800-562-2139
                                     Fax: (860)435-0867
E-mail: books@li.com
URL: http://www.greyhouse.com
Contact: Richard Gottlieb, Editor.
Desc: Approximately 8,000 directories concerned with in-
ternational business and trade. *Type:* Directory.

International BusinessMan News Bureau

535 5th Ave.   Ph: (212)476-0802
33rd Fl.   Fax: (212)663-1663
PO Box 5595
New York, NY 10185
E-mail: 3418747@mcimail.com.
Contact: J.J. Edwards, Chairman/CEO/Ed.-in-Chief;
Ellen M. Vahidi, President; E.J. Edwards, VP/Bureau
Chief; C.P. Hennessy, VP/Food Ed. Test Kitchen.

Desc: Distributes media consultation information. *Alt.
Contact:* 535 5th Ave., 33rd Fl., PO Box 5595, New York,
NY 10185; telephone: (212)476-0802; fax: (212)663-
1663. *Type:* Periodical.

International BusinessMan News Report

International BusinessMan News Bureau
535 5th Ave., 33rd Fl.   Ph: (212)503-0802
New York, NY 10017   Fax: (212)253-4285
Desc: Provides contact information on and direct tele-
phone numbers to international financers and banks.
Type: Newsletter.

International Companies and Their Brands

Gale Group Inc.
27500 Drake Rd.   Ph: (248)699-4253
Farmington Hills, MI 48331-   Free: 800-877-GALE
   3535   Fax: (248)699-8070
E-mail: galeord@galegroup.com
URL: http://www.galegroup.com.
Contact: Linda Irvin, Editor.
Desc: Approximately 28,000 companies that manufacture,
distribute, import, or otherwise market consumer products in countries other than the United States. *Type:* Directory.

International Dallas

Greater Dallas Chamber
1201 Elm St., Ste. 2000   Ph: (214)746-6704
Dallas, TX 75270   Fax: (214)746-6799
E-mail: mchapman@dallaschamber.org.
Contact: Laura Brumley, Editor; Charlotte Fowler, Editor;
John Christian, Editor.
Desc: Listings of over 1,500 international businesses in the
Dallas/Ft. Worth area, including importers, exporters, for-
eign-owned companies, plus trade statistics and a guide to
exporting. *Type:* Directory.

International Directory of Company Histories

St. James Press, Inc.
27500 Drake Rd.   Ph: (248)699-4253
Farmington Hills, MI 48331-   Free: 800-877-4253
   3535   Fax: (248)699-8069
E-mail: galeord@gale.com
Contact: Tina Grant, Editor; Jay Pederson, Editor.
Desc: In 28 volumes, over 3,800 leading companies world-
wide. *Type:* Directory.

International Directory of Corporate Affiliations

National Register Publishing Co.
121 Chanlon Rd.   Ph: (908)464-6800
New Providence, NJ 07974   Free: 800-521-8110
                                     Fax: (908)508-7671
E-mail: info@renp.com
URL: http://www.reedref.com
Desc: Approximately 1,500 U.S. and approximately 1,600
non-U.S. parent companies and their approximately
30,000 subsidiaries. *Type:* Directory.

International Dun's Market Identifiers™

Dun & Bradstreet
3 Sylvan Way   Ph: (973)605-6000
Parsippany, NJ 07054
E-mail: dnbmdd@mail.dnb.com
URL: http://www.dnb.com
Desc: Contains financial, marketing, and ownership data
on more than 10 million publicly and privately owned
companies in more than 200 countries around the world.
Provides directory listings, sales volume and marketing
data, and references to parent companies. *Available:* The
Dialog Corporation, DIALOG; NIFTY Corporation,
NIFTY-SERVE; Dow Jones Interactive Publishing; West
Group, WESTLAW; CompuServe Information Service;
AT&T EasyLink Services; Bell & Howell Information and
Learning; Information America (IA). *Type:* Database.

International Executive Service Corps

333 Ludlow St.   Ph: (203)967-6000
Stamford, CT 06902   Free: 800-243-2531
         Fax: (203)324-2531
E-mail: btarr@mail.iesc.org
URL: http://www.iesc.org

Contact: Hobart C. Gardiner, Pres.

Desc: Provides technical and managerial assistance to enterprises, organizations and government bodies in transitional economies and developing countries. IESC's primary resource is the knowledge, skill and experience of its 13,000 industry experts. IESC's network of experts includes high-level professionals drawn from nearly every area of private enterprise, government and nongovernmental organizations. *Type:* Association.

International Houston Directory

R. L. Polk & Co.
2001 Elm Hill Pike   Ph: (615)889-3350
PO Box 305100   Fax: (615)885-3081
Nashville, TN 37230-5100

Desc: 2,380 foreign and domestic firms and organizations involved in international business in Houston. *Type:* Directory.

International Information Directory

Congressional Quarterly
1414 22nd St. NW   Ph: (202)887-8500
Washington, DC 20037   Free: 800-638-1710
         Fax: 800-380-3810
URL: http://books.cq.com

Desc: Over 4,000 organizations (in four basic categories: U.S. government agencies, international intergovernmental agencies, domestic nonprofit agencies, and international nonprofit agencies) in different fields including education, government and politics, health, transportation, etc. *Type:* Directory.

International Quality

Underwriters Laboratories, Inc.
333 Pfingsten Rd.   Ph: (847)272-8800
Northbrook, IL 60062-2096   Fax: (847)272-0472
E-mail: northbrook@ul.com

Contact: Holly J. Schubert, Editor.

Desc: Focuses on high tech product testing. *Type:* Newsletter.

International Trade Directory of Contacts/Sources/Services

Hilary House Publishers, Inc.
4001 N. Ocean Blvd., No. 1101   Ph: (561)750-7822
Boca Raton, FL 33431

Contact: Edward Stern, Editor.

Desc: More than 14,800 U.S. organizations and key executives in 26 international business categories. *Type:* Directory.

International Wealth Success

IWS Inc.
24 Canterbury Rd.   Ph: (516)766-5850
Rockville Centre, NY 11570   Free: 800-323-0548
         Fax: (516)766-5919

Contact: Tyler G. Hicks, Editor.

Desc: Covers methods of making money in a successful business, including sources of business capital, real estate income methods, mail order, import/export, franchising, and licensing of products. Recurring features include news of export/import opportunities and a column on capital sources. *Type:* Newsletter.

Invest to Compete Alliance

1010 Pennsylvania Ave. SE   Ph: (202)546-4995
Washington, DC 20003   Fax: (202)544-7926
Contact: Garland Miller, Exec.Dir.

Desc: Individuals and corporations in the manufacturing and service industries. Works to address the impact of tax legislation, especially the loss of investment tax credit, upon the business community. *Type:* Association.

Investext®

Thomson Financial Securities Data (TFSD)
Two Gateway Center   Ph: (973)622-3100
Newark, NJ 07102
URL: http://www.securitiesdata.com

Desc: Contains the full-image text of international company and industry reports from approximately 250 of the world's leading investment banks, brokerage houses, and consulting firms. Each report provides in-depth analysis of companies, industries, products, and regions, providing insight on industry trends, market share, business strategies, emerging technologies, and other areas of interest. *Available:* Thomson Financial Services, Inc., I/PLUS Direct; CompuServe Information Service; The Dialog Corporation, DataStar; The Dialog Corporation, DIALOG; Dow Jones Interactive Publishing; STN International; Bell & Howell Information and Learning; FT PROFILE; Sandpoint Company, Sandpoint Hoover™; FIZ Technik (Fachinformationszentrum Technik e.V.); European Information Network Services (EINS); Data Downlink Corporation. *Type:* Database.

Investext: International Company and Industry Reports

Thomson Financial Securities Data
Thomson Financial Services
22 Thomson Pl.   Ph: (617)856-2704
Boston, MA 02210   Free: 800-662-7878
         Fax: (617)330-1986
E-mail: john.webber@tfn.com
URL: http://www.tfsd.com.

Contact: David Irving, Editor.

Desc: More than 2,000,000 reports on over 50,000 public and private companies in every industry worldwide. *Type:* Directory.

Iowa Business Directory

infoUSA
5711 S. 86th Circle   Ph: (402)593-4600
PO Box 27347   Free: 800-555-6124
Omaha, NE 68127   Fax: (402)331-5481
E-mail: internet@infousa.com
URL: http://www.abii.com.

Contact: Peter J. Wilmarth, Publisher.

Desc: 130,000 businesses in Iowa. *Type:* Directory.

IPI Parking Buyers Guide

International Parking Institute (IPI)
PO Box 7167   Ph: (540)371-7535
Fredericksburg, VA 22404   Fax: (540)371-8022
E-mail: ipi@parking.org
URL: http://www.parking.org.

Contact: David L. Ivey, Editor.

Desc: More than 160 suppliers of parking equipment and services, including access control systems, fee computers, coin handling and collection equipment, printing services, data processing equipment, etc. *Type:* Directory.

It's Your Business!

Saskatoon Public Library
311 23rd St. E.   Ph: (306)975-7530
Saskatoon, SK, Canada S7K 0J6   Fax: (306)975-7766

Desc: Educates the reader about business resources and services at the library. *Type:* Newsletter.

IT'$ YOUR MONEY - The National Unclaimed Property Database

Knowledge in Motion, Inc.
1825 Ponce de Leon Blvd., Ste.   Ph: (305)441-0610
   239
Coral Gables, FL 33134-4418
E-mail: info@unclaimed-property.com
URL: http://www.unclaimed-property.com/index.htm

Desc: If you think there might be an uncashed check, an unknown inheritance, or an unclaimed fortune out there with your name on it, take a look at this site first to see if anything turns up. Part of a nationwide database of unclaimed property, this site lets you search among billions of dollars worth of orphaned goods and funds that might actually belong to you or someone you know. *Type:* Database.

Jamieson and Associates—Trends

Jamieson and Associates
4133 W. 45th St.   Ph: (612)920-3770
Minneapolis, MN 55424-1040   Fax: (612)920-6454
Contact: Rich Jamieson, Editor.

Desc: Reports on current trends in the communication industry. Describes trends through current developments in communication facility design, media production, and communication consulting done by Jamieson and Associates. *Type:* Newsletter.

Japan 250,000 CD-ROM

Dun & Bradstreet
3 Sylvan Way   Ph: (973)605-6442
Parsippany, NJ 07054-3896   Free: 800-526-0651
         Fax: (973)605-6911
E-mail: dnbmdd@dnb.com

Desc: Top 250,000 businesses in Japan. *Type:* Directory.

Japan-U.S. Trade and Technology

Japan Information Access Project
2000 P St. NW, Ste. 620   Ph: (202)822-6040
Washington, DC 20036-5915   Fax: (202)822-6044
E-mail: access@hmjc.org

Desc: Information sources related to trading with Japan, including U.S. government agencies, international organizations, lobbyists and Japanese governmental agencies. *Type:* Directory.

Japanese-Affiliated Companies in U.S.A. and Canada

Japan External Trade Organization (JETRO)
1221 Avenue of the Americas   Ph: (212)997-0400
New York, NY 10020   Fax: (212)997-0464
URL: http://www.jetro.org

Contact: Shigeo Kawamoto, Editor.

Desc: 9,870 Japanese firms, restaurants, and various information sources. *Type:* Directory.

Joint Venture Directory of the New Independent States

Market Knowledge
Triumph Books
644 S. Clark St.   Ph: (312)939-3300
Chicago, IL 60605   Fax: (312)663-3557
Contact: David Escarraz, Editor.

Desc: About 2,650 firms in the Commonwealth of Independent States that are joint ventures between CIS companies and foreign firms. *Type:* Directory.

The Journal of Corporate Renewal

Turnaround Management Association
230 N. Michigan Ave., Ste.   Ph: (312)857-7734
   1310   Fax: (312)857-7739
Chicago, IL 60601
Contact: Deborah L. Fletcher, Editor.

Desc: Provides news and information about corporate renewal. *Type:* Newsletter.

Kansas Business Directory

infoUSA

5711 S. 86th Circle	Ph: (402)593-4600
PO Box 27347	Free: 800-555-6124
Omaha, NE 68127	Fax: (402)331-5481

E-mail: internet@infousa.com

URL: http://www.abii.com.

Contact: Peter J. Wilmarth, Publisher.

Desc: 123,000 businesses in Kansas. *Type:* Directory.

Kentucky Business Directory

infoUSA

5711 S. 86th Circle	Ph: (402)593-4600
PO Box 27347	Free: 800-555-6124
Omaha, NE 68127	Fax: (402)331-5481

E-mail: internet@infousa.com

URL: http://www.abii.com.

Contact: Peter J. Wilmarth, Publisher.

Desc: 133,000 businesses in Kentucky. *Type:* Directory.

Kentucky State Handbook

The Bar List Publishing Co.

PO Box 948	Ph: (847)498-0100
Northbrook, IL 60065	Free: 800-726-1007
	Fax: (847)498-6695

E-mail: info@barlist.com

Contact: Leslie Rodgers, Editor.

Desc: Licensed property, liability, and life insurance companies and agencies, adjusters, and appraisers (SIC 094) in Kentucky. *Type:* Directory.

Key Business Directory—Latin America

Dun & Bradstreet

3 Sylvan Way	Ph: (973)605-6442
Parsippany, NJ 07054-3896	Free: 800-526-0651
	Fax: (973)605-6911

E-mail: dnbmdd@dnb.com

Desc: Leading companies in Latin America whose annual sales are $10 million and who have 500 or more employees. *Type:* Directory.

KIOSK: CBCA

Micromedia Ltd.

20 Victoria St.	Ph: (416)362-5211
Toronto, ON, Canada M5C 2N8	

E-mail: info@micromedia.on.ca

URL: http://www.micromedia.on.ca

Desc: Contains more than 1.65 million citations to articles in more than 200 English-language business periodicals, 300 popular periodicals, and 10 daily newspapers published in Canada. Articles cover product, company, and industry information; national, provincial, and local news; editorials and selected letters to the editor; government activities; labor news; crime; sports; obituaries; biographies; reviews; art; children's literature; cooking; education; health; history; hobbies; music; nature; recreation; science; social issues; and travel. *Available:* The Dialog Corporation, DIALOG. *Type:* Database.

The Kiplinger California Letter

Kiplinger Washington Editors, Inc.

1729 H St. NW	Ph: (202)887-6491
Washington, DC 20006	Free: 800-544-0155
	Fax: (202)887-6542

Contact: John Fogarty, Editor.

Desc: Publishes "information and guidance for anyone with a business, investment, real estate, or residence interest in California." Covers Washington developments that affect California, areas of growth, politics and legislation, defense spending, construction, highways, tourism, and finance. *Type:* Newsletter.

Kocham Business Directory

Korean Chamber of Commerce & Industry in USA, Inc.

460 Park Ave., Ste. 410	Ph: (212)644-0140
New York, NY 10022	Fax: (212)644-9106

E-mail: shinnn@kocham.org.

Contact: Kwangrip Byun, Editor.

Desc: About 700 offices of leading Korean companies operated by Korean nationals located throughout the United States. Other Korean service firms (banks, trade organizations, etc.) are also listed. *Type:* Directory.

Korean Business Directory

Korea Times NY

42-22 27th St.	Ph: (718)482-1111
Long Island City, NY 11101	Free: 800-482-1199
	Fax: (718)784-9131

Desc: Approximately 4,000 business operated by Koreans residing in the U.S. *Type:* Directory.

Kyodo News

Kyodo News International, Inc.

50 Rockefeller Plaza, Ste. 803	Ph: (212)397-3723
New York, NY 10020	Free: 800-536-3510

Desc: Carries major news developments in business, industries, and government from Japan and other Asian countries. Includes major market data. *Type:* Newsletter.

LA/C Business Bulletin

Latin America/Caribbean Business Development Center

U.S. Department of Commerce

1401 Constitution Ave. NW, Rm. H-3025	Ph: (202)482-0703
	Fax: (202)482-4726
Washington, DC 20230	

Contact: Walter Schaffer, Editor.

Desc: Networks trade professionals. Reports news on Latin America and Caribbean economic conditions and developments. *Type:* Newsletter.

Latin American Product Guide

Todd Publications

PO Box 635	Ph: (914)358-6213
Nyack, NY 10960	Free: 800-747-1056
	Fax: (914)358-1059

E-mail: toddpub@aol.com

URL: http://www.toddpublications.com

Contact: Carlos DePaula, Editor.

Desc: Over 10,000 exporters from 18 Latin American countries. *Type:* Directory.

Law Department Management Adviser

Business Laws Inc.

11630 Chillicothe Rd.	Ph: (440)729-7996
Chesterland, OH 44026	Free: 800-759-0929
	Fax: (440)729-0645

E-mail: hancock@counsel.com

URL: http://www.Businesslaws.com

Contact: William A. Hancock, Editor.

Desc: Covers litigation management and law department management. *Type:* Newsletter.

Leadership Library on CD-ROM

Leadership Directories, Inc.

104 5th Ave.	Ph: (212)627-4140
New York, NY 10011	Fax: (212)645-0931

E-mail: info@leadershipdirectories.com

URL: http://www.leadershipdirectories.com; http://www.leadershipdirectories.com.

Contact: Rob Zangara, Editor.

Desc: Over 400,000 leaders in business, government and professional organizations in the United States. *Type:* Directory.

Legacies

Center for Entrepreneurship

Box 98011	Ph: (817)755-2265
Baylor University	Fax: (817)755-2271
Waco, TX 76798-8011	

Contact: Nancy Upton, Editor.

Desc: Discusses family businesses. *Type:* Newsletter.

LEXIS® Corporate Law Library

LEXIS-NEXIS

9443 Springboro Pike	Ph: (937)865-6800
PO Box 933	
Dayton, OH 45401-0933	

URL: http://www.lex-nexis.com

Desc: Contains information on state case law involving private, municipal, and non-profit corporations, as well as Delaware Federal and state case law and topical Business publications. Designed to meet the needs of those who handle corporate matters. *Available:* LEXIS-NEXIS, LEXIS. *Type:* Database.

LEXIS® State Corporation Information Library

LEXIS-NEXIS

9443 Springboro Pike	Ph: (937)865-6800
PO Box 933	
Dayton, OH 45401-0933	

URL: http://www.lex-nexis.com

Desc: Contains descriptive information on companies doing business in California, Colorado, Connecticut, Delaware, Georgia, Illinois, Indiana, Maryland, Massachusetts, Michigan, Missouri, Nevada, New York, Pennsylvania, Texas, and Wisconsin. For each company, records include name and address, form and date of incorporation, type of business, number of employees, and names and titles of principal officers. *Available:* LEXIS-NEXIS, LEXIS. *Type:* Database.

List of Minority Firms in North & South Carolina

Carolinas Minority Supplier Development Councils

Hatteras Bldg., Ste. 10640	Ph: (704)536-2884
5624 Executive Center Dr., Ste. 106	Fax: (704)536-8856
Charlotte, NC 28212	

Contact: Terry Fullard, Editor.

Desc: About 430 minority-owned firms offering professional, commercial, and industrial products and services. *Type:* Directory.

London Business School: A SourceGuide to European Company Information

Gale Group Inc.

27500 Drake Rd.	Ph: (248)699-4253
Farmington Hills, MI 48331-3535	Free: 800-877-GALE
	Fax: (248)699-8070

E-mail: galeord@galegroup.com

URL: http://www.galegroup.com.

Desc: Over 1,000 business information resources in 18 European countries, including trade councils, government agencies, directories, databases, newspapers, newsletters, and other media. *Type:* Directory.

Louisiana Business Directory

infoUSA

5711 S. 86th Circle	Ph: (402)593-4600
PO Box 27347	Free: 800-555-6124
Omaha, NE 68127	Fax: (402)331-5481

E-mail: internet@infousa.com

URL: http://www.abii.com.

Contact: Peter J. Wilmarth, Publisher.

Desc: 171,000 businesses in Louisiana. *Type:* Directory.

Louisiana Business Survey

University of New Orleans
Division of Business & Economic Research
New Orleans, LA 70148-0001
Contact: Patricia Connor, Editor.
Desc: Surveys Louisiana business and economic research.
Type: Newsletter.

Louisiana-Mississippi State Handbook

The Bar List Publishing Co.
PO Box 948   Ph: (847)498-0100
Northbrook, IL 60065   Free: 800-726-1007
                              Fax: (847)498-6695
E-mail: info@barlist.com
Contact: Leslie Rodgers, Editor; Bruce Rodgers, Publisher.
Desc: Liability, and life insurance companies and agencies, adjusters, and appraisers (SIC 094) in Louisiana and Mississippi. *Type:* Directory.

M & A Filings

Charles E. Simon & Co.
1090 Vermont Ave., N.W., Ste.   Ph: (202)408-3129
420
Washington, DC 20005
Contact: Patrick McEvoy, Jr., Manager, SEC Services.
Desc: Contains citations, with abstracts, to more than 127,000 corporate merger and acquisition documents filed with the U.S. Securities and Exchange Commission (SEC). *Available:* The Dialog Corporation, DIALOG; The Dialog Corporation, DIALOG. *Type:* Database.

MacRae's Blue Book

MacRae's Blue Book
MacRae's OEM Mart, Inc.
65 Bleecker St.   Ph: (212)673-4700
New York, NY 10012-2420   Free: 800-622-7237
                              Fax: (212)475-1790
URL: http://d-net.com/macraes.
Contact: Mary O'Hara Smith, Editor, marys@nytri.com.
Desc: About 50,000 manufacturing firms. *Type:* Directory.

Maine Business Directory

infoUSA
5711 S. 86th Circle   Ph: (402)593-4600
PO Box 27347   Free: 800-555-6124
Omaha, NE 68127   Fax: (402)331-5481
E-mail: internet@infousa.com
URL: http://www.abii.com.
Contact: Peter J. Wilmarth, Publisher.
Desc: 61,000 businesses in Maine. *Type:* Directory.

Marconi's International Register

Telegraphic Cable & Radio Registrations, Inc.
PO Box 14   Ph: (914)632-8171
Larchmont, NY 10538-0014   Fax: (914)632-8171
E-mail: marconis99@aol.com; marconis99@aol.com.
Contact: Joanne Clark, Editor.
Desc: 45,000 firms worldwide which do business internationally. *Type:* Directory.

Marcus Report

Bedford House
1800 Ironstone Mnr. Pickering   Ph: (905)831-3000
Toronto, ON, Canada L1W   Fax: (416)340-9809
3T9
Contact: Bruce Marcus, Editor.
Desc: Publishes business news and information. *Type:* Newsletter.

Market Guide

Market Guide, Inc.
2001 Marcus Ave., Ste. S. 200   Ph: (516)327-2400
Lake Success, NY 11042-1011   Fax: (516)327-2425
URL: http://www.marketguide.com.
Desc: Over 8,000 public companies, U.S. and foreign, trading on the New York, American, Nasdaq and OTC (Over the counter) exchanges. *Type:* Directory.

Market Guide Select Over-the-Counter Stock Edition

Market Guide, Inc.
2001 Marcus Ave., Ste. S. 200   Ph: (516)327-2400
Lake Success, NY 11042-1011   Fax: (516)327-2425
Contact: Jeffrey Geisenheimer, Editor.
Desc: 800 NASDAQ OTC companies. *Type:* Directory.

Market Share

Source Strategies, Inc.
PO Box 120055   Ph: (210)734-3434
San Antonio, TX 78212   Fax: (210)735-7970
Contact: Bruce Walker, Editor.
Desc: Tracks the performance of major hotel chains, using Texas census comptroller files. *Type:* Newsletter.

Market Share and Business Rankings Annual

Gale Group Inc.
27500 Drake Rd.   Ph: (248)699-4253
Farmington Hills, MI 48331-   Free: 800-877-GALE
3535   Fax: (248)699-8070
E-mail: galeord@galegroup.com
URL: http://www.galegroup.com.
Contact: Donna Wood, Editor.
Desc: Over 40,000 market shares and business rankings and coverage of 960 SICs. *Type:* Directory.

Market Share Reporter

The Gale Group
27500 Drake Rd.   Ph: (248)699-4253
Farmington Hills, MI 48331-
3535
URL: http://www.galegroup.com
Desc: Provides market share data on companies, institutions, brand names, products, commodities, and services. Covers more than 16,000 reports. *Available:* LEXIS-NEXIS, NEXIS; Data Downlink Corporation; Infonautics Corporation. *Type:* Database.

Marketplace

Institute for the Study of Business Markets (ISBM)
Pennsylvania State University
402 Business Administration   Ph: (814)863-2782
Bldg.   Fax: (814)863-0413
University Park, PA 16802-3004
E-mail: gwh3@psu.edu.
Contact: Dr. Ralph A. Oliva, Exec. Director; Bob Donath, Editor.
Desc: Supplies information on business marketing topics and Institute meetings and seminars. *Type:* Newsletter.

Martin Brower's Orange County Report

Martin Brower
180 Newport Center Dr., No.   Ph: (949)720-8414
180
Newport Beach, CA 92660
Contact: Martin Brower, Editor.
Desc: Presented in the form of a "confidential letter" to business, professional, governmental, and institutional leaders having an interest in Orange County, California. Monitors economic and business trends and forecasts change in the area. *Type:* Newsletter.

Maryland Business Directory

infoUSA
5711 S. 86th Circle   Ph: (402)593-4600
PO Box 27347   Free: 800-555-6124
Omaha, NE 68127   Fax: (402)331-5481
E-mail: internet@infousa.com
URL: http://www.abii.com.
Contact: Peter J. Wilmarth, Publisher.
Desc: 193,000 businesses in Maryland. *Type:* Directory.

Massachusetts Business Directory

infoUSA
5711 S. 86th Circle   Ph: (402)593-4600
PO Box 27347   Free: 800-555-6124
Omaha, NE 68127   Fax: (402)331-5481
E-mail: internet@infousa.com
URL: http://www.abii.com.
Contact: Peter J. Wilmarth, Publisher.
Desc: 282,000 businesses in Massachusetts. *Type:* Directory.

Material Handling Product News

Cahners Business Information
New Product Information Division
301 Gibraltar Dr.   Ph: (973)292-5100
Morris Plains, NJ 07950   Fax: (973)539-3476
URL: http://www.mhpn.com.
Contact: Barry Strobel, Publisher, bstrobel@gordon.cahners.com; Joseph Pagnotta, Editor, jpagnotta@gordon.cahners.com.
Desc: Magazine serving material handling and packaging personnel in manufacturing and non-manufacturing industries, including the warehousing and storage industries. *Type:* Periodical.

The McGraw-Hill Companies Publications Online

McGraw-Hill Companies, Inc.
148 Princeton-Hightstown Rd.   Ph: (609)426-5000
Hightstown, NJ 08520
E-mail: 13957 (DIALMAIL)
Desc: Contains the complete text of 13 business magazines and 34 newsletters published by McGraw-Hill as follows: • Aerospace Daily (since 1989). • Aerospace Propulsion (since 1991) (no longer updated). *Available:* The Dialog Corporation, DIALOG; Dow Jones Interactive Publishing; LEXIS-NEXIS; Bell & Howell Information and Learning. *Type:* Database.

Meeting Professionals International

4455 LBJ Freeway, Ste. 1200   Ph: (972)702-3000
Dallas, TX 75244-5903   Fax: (972)702-3070
URL: http://www.mpiweb.org
Contact: Edwin Griffin, Jr., CAE, Pres./CEO.
Desc: Meeting planners, full meeting consultants, and suppliers of goods and services. Works to: improve meeting method education; create an "open platform" for research and experimentation. *Type:* Association.

Meetings & Conventions

Reed Travel Group
500 Plaza Dr.   Ph: (201)902-1600
Secaucus, NJ 07094-3626   Free: 800-334-2811
                              Fax: (201)319-1628
Contact: Morton L. Silverman, Publisher; Paul Zanowski, Associate Publisher.
Desc: Magazine focusing on meetings, conferences and trade show. *Type:* Periodical.

Memphis Economy

Bureau of Business & Economic Research
University of Memphis
Campus Box 526482   Ph: (901)678-2281
Memphis, TN 38152-6482   Fax: (901)678-4086
Contact: Stephen Smith, Editor, scsmith@cc.memphis.edu.
Desc: Provides a monthly review of the Memphis economy. *Type:* Newsletter.

Memphis Regional Purchasing Council—Minority Business Directory

Memphis Regional Purchasing Council
22 N. Front St., Ste. 200
Memphis, TN 38101
Desc: About 70 firms offering professional, commercial, industrial, and consumer products and services. *Type:* Directory.

Merger Management Report

Securities Data Publishing Inc.
1290 Avenue of the Americas   Ph: (212)765-5311
New York, NY 10104   Free: 800-455-5844
                                Fax: (212)937-0420
E-mail: sdp@tfn.com
Contact: Ted Weissberg, Editor; Patricia Pierro, Circulation Mgr.
Desc: Publishes interviews with top merger executives on mergers, acquisitions, opportunities, and successes. *Type:* Newsletter.

Mergers & Acquisitions Magazine—Rosters

Securities Data Publishing
Circulation Dept.   Ph: (212)432-0045
40 W. 57th St., 11th Fl.
New York, NY 10019
E-mail: subscribe@iddis.com.
Contact: Martin Sikora, Editor.
Desc: Each issue includes a roster in three sections: "Mergers & Acquisitions," covering major deals concluded between American firms; "Foreign Investment in the U.S.," covering foreign firms which acquired companies in the United States; and "U.S. Investment Abroad," covering acquisitions by United States firms in other countries. *Type:* Directory.

Mergers and Acquisitions Report

Securities Data Publishing Inc.
1290 Avenue of the Americas   Ph: (212)765-5311
New York, NY 10104   Free: 800-455-5844
                                Fax: (212)937-0420
E-mail: sdp@tfn.com
Contact: Judith Radler Cohen, Editor.
Desc: Reports on mergers, acquisitions, and diversification strategies being employed by leading U.S. corporations, and some foreign firms; contains bankruptcy and restructuring news. *Type:* Newsletter.

Metro Orlando International Business Directory

Greater Orlando Chamber of Commerce
75 S. Ivanhoe Blvd.   Ph: (407)418-4490
PO Box 1234   Fax: (407)839-5020
Orlando, FL 32802-1234
Contact: Frank Billingsley, Editor.
Desc: About 400 central Florida, manufacturers, distributors, services, and support organizations involved in world trade. *Type:* Directory.

Metroplex Business Directory—Dallas Area

Business Marketing Source
2501 Ave. J, No. 120   Ph: (817)530-2500
Arlington, TX 76006   Fax: (817)530-2525
Desc: Over 88,000 businesses in the Dallas, Texas area. *Type:* Directory.

Metroplex Business Directory—Tarrant Area

Business Marketing Source
2501 Ave. J, No. 120   Ph: (817)530-2500
Arlington, TX 76006   Fax: (817)530-2525
Desc: Approximately 47,500 businesses in Tarrant Area, Texas. *Type:* Directory.

Metropolitan Detroit Convention and Visitors Bureau

100 Renaissance Center, Ste.   Ph: (313)259-4333
   1900   Free: 800-DET-ROIT
Detroit, MI 48243   Fax: (313)259-7583
URL: http://www.visitdetroit.com
Contact: William McLaughlin, Contact.
Desc: Promotes convention business and tourism in area. *Type:* Association.

Mexican Product Guide

Todd Publications
PO Box 635   Ph: (914)358-6213
Nyack, NY 10960   Free: 800-747-1056
                               Fax: (914)358-1059
E-mail: toddpub@aol.com
URL: http://www.toddpublications.com
Contact: Carlos DePaula, Editor.
Desc: Over 3,000 Mexican importers and exporters. *Type:* Directory.

Mexico Business Monthly

Kal Wagenheim
52 Maple Ave.   Ph: (973)762-1565
Maplewood, NJ 07040   Free: 800-647-9990
                               Fax: (973)762-9585
E-mail: mexcarib@compuserve.com
Contact: Kal Wagenheim, Editor.
Desc: Contains news of business and economic developments in Mexico. Recurring features include news of research, book reviews, and a calendar of events. *Type:* Newsletter.

Mexico Company Handbook

Hoover's, Inc.
1033 La Posada Dr., Ste. 250   Ph: (512)374-4500
Austin, TX 78752   Fax: (512)374-4501
E-mail: orders@hoovers.com
URL: http://www.hoovers.com
Desc: About 70 of Mexico's largest public companies and 8 mutual funds and investment advisors. *Type:* Directory.

Mexico Watch

Orbis Publications, LLC
3201 New Mexico Ave. NW,   Ph: (202)237-0155
   Ste. 249   Fax: (202)237-0596
Washington, DC 20016
E-mail: orbis@orbispub.com
URL: http://www.orbispub.com.
Contact: Richard Foster, Editor.
Desc: Reports on political, economic and business events in Mexico. *Type:* Newsletter.

Mexico Weekly Fax Bulletin

Orbis Publications, LLC
3201 New Mexico Ave. NW,   Ph: (202)237-0155
   Ste. 249   Fax: (202)237-0596
Washington, DC 20016
E-mail: orbis@orbispub.com
URL: http://www.orbispub.com.
Contact: Richard Foster.
Desc: Reports on political, economic and business events in Mexico via fax. *Type:* Newsletter.

Michigan Business Directory

infoUSA
5711 S. 86th Circle   Ph: (402)593-4600
PO Box 27347   Free: 800-555-6124
Omaha, NE 68127   Fax: (402)331-5481
E-mail: internet@infousa.com
URL: http://www.abii.com.
Contact: Peter J. Wilmarth, Publisher.
Desc: 380,000 businesses in Michigan. *Type:* Directory.

Michigan Distributors Directory

Pick Publications, Inc.
24293 Telegraph Rd., No. 140   Ph: (810)827-7111
Southfield, MI 48034   Free: 800-247-1558
                               Fax: (810)827-7119
E-mail: pickincl@aol.com
Contact: Paul Pickell, President.
Desc: About 27,000 distributors, wholesalers, and manufacturers' representatives in Michigan. *Type:* Directory.

Mid-Atlantic/Capital Cities Regional Industrial Buying Guide

Thomas Regional Directory Co., Inc.
5 Penn Plaza   Ph: (212)629-2100
New York, NY 10001   Fax: (212)290-7335
E-mail: info@trdnet.com
URL: http://www.thomasregional.com.
Contact: Marie McGurk, Editorial Dir.; Adrienne Toth, Managing Editor; Nancy Bromberg, Contracts Administration Mgr.
Desc: 16,500 manufacturers of industrial products; related industrial services, such as trucking and maintenance services; distributors; and manufacturers' representatives in Delaware, the District of Columbia, Maryland, Virginia and West Virginia. *Type:* Directory.

Middle East Business Intelligence

NVST.COM
717 D St. NW, No. 300   Ph: (202)628-7767
Washington, DC 20004-2807   Free: 800-809-0666
                               Fax: (202)628-6618
Contact: William C. Hearn, Editor; Mimi Mann, Editor.
Desc: Contains new contracting and sales leads in Middle Eastern countries, with description and contact names, addresses and phone and fax numbers. Features latest government tender offers and alerts readers to future business opportunities. *Type:* Newsletter.

Middle East Executive Reports

International Executive Reports, Ltd.
717 D St., N.W., Room 300   Ph: (202)628-6900
Washington, DC 20004-2807
Desc: Contains the complete text of Middle East Executive Reports, a journal covering the practical, legal, and financial aspects of conducting business in 19 Middle Eastern countries. It provides in-depth information on export/import, contracting and tendering rules, agents, registrations, taxation, labor rules, local content requirements, licensing and technology transfer, joint venturing, investment requirements, intellectual property, marketing and advertising, forex and repatriation of profits, and other topics. *Available:* LEXIS-NEXIS, NEXIS; LEXIS-NEXIS, LEXIS; West Group, WESTLAW. *Type:* Database.

Mind Play

Innovation Network
451 E 58th Ave., No. 4625   Ph: (303)308-1088
Box 468   Fax: (303)295-6108
Denver, CO 80216
E-mail: staff@thinksmart.com
Contact: Cynthia Carlisle, Editor and Publisher, (512)302-4123, inspace1@aol.com.
Desc: Provides information about creativity and innovation in business. Recurring features include book reviews, software reviews, and advice. *Type:* Newsletter.

Minnesota Business Directory

infoUSA

5711 S. 86th Circle
PO Box 27347
Omaha, NE 68127
E-mail: internet@infousa.com
URL: http://www.abii.com.

Ph: (402)593-4600
Free: 800-555-6124
Fax: (402)331-5481

Contact: Peter J. Wilmarth, Publisher.
Desc: 197,000 businesses in Minnesota. *Type:* Directory.

Minority Business Information Center

*National Minority Supplier Development
Council (NMSDC)*

1040 Avenue of the Americas,
  2nd Fl.
New York, NY 10018
E-mail: nmsdc1@aol.com

Ph: (212)944-2430
Fax: (212)719-9611

Contact: Terri Myers, Editor.
Desc: Approximately 15,000 companies that are certified by the NMSDC as minority owned. *Type:* Directory.

Minority Supplier Directory

New England Minority Purchasing Council

4 Copley Pl.
Box 145
Boston, MA 02116-6504
E-mail: webmaster@nempc.org.

Ph: (617)578-8900
Fax: (617)578-8902

Contact: May Ling Tong, Editor.
Desc: Over 400 firms offering professional, commercial, and industrial products and services in Maine, Massachusetts, New Hampshire, Rhode Island, and Vermont. *Type:* Directory.

Mississippi Business Directory

infoUSA

5711 S. 86th Circle
PO Box 27347
Omaha, NE 68127
E-mail: internet@infousa.com
URL: http://www.abii.com.

Ph: (402)593-4600
Free: 800-555-6124
Fax: (402)331-5481

Contact: Peter J. Wilmarth, Publisher.
Desc: 98,000 businesses in Mississippi. *Type:* Directory.

Mississippi Gulf Coast Convention and Visitors Bureau

Stephen B. Richer

135 Ct. House Rd.
PO Box 6128
Gulfport, MS 39506-6128
E-mail: expc@gulfcoast.org
URL: http://www.gulfcoast.org

Ph: (601)896-6699
Fax: (601)896-6796

Contact: Stephen B. Richer, Exec.Dir.
Desc: Marketing the Mississippi Gulf Coast as a tourism destination. *Type:* Association.

Missouri Business Directory

infoUSA

5711 S. 86th Circle
PO Box 27347
Omaha, NE 68127
E-mail: internet@infousa.com
URL: http://www.abii.com.

Ph: (402)593-4600
Free: 800-555-6124
Fax: (402)331-5481

Contact: Peter J. Wilmarth, Publisher.
Desc: 229,000 businesses in Missouri. *Type:* Directory.

Modern Materials Handling

Cahners Publishing Company

275 Washington St.
Newton, MA 02458

Ph: (617)558-2119
Fax: (617)558-4700

Contact: Ray Kulwiec, Editor; William G. Sbordon, Publisher.
Desc: Publication featuring materials handling. *Type:* Periodical.

Money Making Opportunities

Success Publishing International

11071 Ventura Blvd.
Studio City, CA 91604-3548
URL: http://www.moneymakingopps.com.

Ph: (818)980-9166
Fax: (818)980-7829

Contact: Donald H. Perry, Publisher; Roger C. Perry, Account Exec.
Desc: Magazine Source for small business opportunity seekers. *Type:* Periodical.

Montana Business Directory

infoUSA

5711 S. 86th Circle
PO Box 27347
Omaha, NE 68127
E-mail: internet@infousa.com
URL: http://www.abii.com.

Ph: (402)593-4600
Free: 800-555-6124
Fax: (402)331-5481

Contact: Peter J. Wilmarth, Publisher.
Desc: 50,000 businesses in Montana. *Type:* Directory.

Moody's Company Data

*Moody's Financial Information Services
Dun & Bradstreet Corp.*

99 Church St.
New York, NY 10007

Ph: (212)553-0300
Free: 800-342-5647
Fax: (212)553-4700

E-mail: fis@moodys.com
URL: http://www.moodys.com/fisonline.
Contact: Dan Zottoli, Editor.
Desc: CD-ROM. Over 10,000 public companies. *Type:* Directory.

Moody's Corporate Profiles

Moody's Financial Information Services

99 Church St.
New York, NY 10007
URL: http://www.moodys.com/fis

Ph: (212)553-0546

Desc: Contains descriptive and financial information on more than 5000 publicly held U.S. companies. *Type:* Database.

Moody's Handbook of NASDAQ Stocks

Financial Information Services (FIS)

60 Madison Ave., 6th Fl.
New York, NY 10010

Ph: (212)413-7601
Free: 800-342-5647
Fax: (212)413-7777

E-mail: fis@fisonline.com
URL: http://www.fisonline.com.
Contact: Sean Pollard, Editor; Samuel A. Young, Editor.
Desc: Over 600 corporations whose stocks are among the most actively traded in dollar volume on the Nasdaq market. *Type:* Directory.

Moody's Industrial Manual

Financial Information Services (FIS)

60 Madison Ave., 6th Fl.
New York, NY 10010

Ph: (212)413-7601
Free: 800-342-5647
Fax: (212)413-7777

E-mail: fis@fisonline.com
URL: http://www.fisonline.com.
Contact: John Ieraci, Editor.
Desc: Nearly 2,000 companies listed on the New York, American, or regional stock exchanges. *Type:* Directory.

Moody's International Manual

Financial Information Services (FIS)

60 Madison Ave., 6th Fl.
New York, NY 10010

Ph: (212)413-7601
Free: 800-342-5647
Fax: (212)413-7777

E-mail: fis@fisonline.com
URL: http://www.fisonline.com.
Contact: John Ieraci, Editor.

Desc: Approximately 11,000 multinational companies incorporated outside the United States and active in the banking, finance, insurance, industrial, utility, and transportation industries. *Type:* Directory.

Moody's OTC Industrial Manual

*Moody's Financial Information Services
Dun & Bradstreet Corp.*

99 Church St.
New York, NY 10007

Ph: (212)553-0300
Free: 800-342-5647
Fax: (212)553-4700

E-mail: fis@moodys.com
URL: http://www.moodys.com/fis.
Contact: John Ieraci, Editor-in-Chief.
Desc: Nearly 3,000 companies whose stock is traded over the counter. *Type:* Directory.

Mutual Funds Magazine

Mutual Funds Magazine

2200 SW 10th St.
Deerfield Beach, FL 33442-8799

Ph: (954)421-1000
Free: 800-818-8973
Fax: (954)570-8200

E-mail: gkp@mfmag.com.
URL: http://www.mfmag.com.
Contact: Norman Fosback, Editor-in-Chief; Edward C. Frey, Publisher.
Desc: Magazine providing information on choosing mutual funds. *Type:* Periodical.

Nasco Products Co.

23600 Cloverlawn
Oak Park, MI 48237

Ph: (248)547-7056

Contact: Norma Schonwetter, President.
Desc: Distributes microwave column. *Alt. Contact:* 23600 Cloverlawn, Oak Park, MI 48237; telephone: (248)547-7056. *Type:* Periodical.

Nasdaq Fact Book & Company Directory

*Corporate Communications
National Association of Securities Dealers, Inc.*

1735 K St. NW
Washington, DC 20006-1500

Ph: (202)728-6900
Fax: (202)728-8882

Desc: More than 5,000 companies whose securities are actively traded on the Nasdaq Stock Market. *Type:* Directory.

Nashville Business Directory

Nashville Business Directory

PO Box 23229
Nashville, TN 37202-3229

Ph: (615)248-2222
Fax: (615)248-6246

Desc: 14,100 businesses in Nashville, Tennessee. *Type:* Directory.

National American Indian Business Directory

*National Center for American Indian Enterprise
Development*

953 E. Juanita Ave.
Mesa, AZ 85204

Ph: (602)545-1298
Free: 800-462-2433
Fax: (602)545-4208

E-mail: ncaiedlah@aol.com
URL: http://www.ncaied.org.
Contact: Linda Alexius Hagerty, Editor.
Desc: Firms offering professional, commercial, and industrial products and services. *Type:* Directory.

National Association of Business Consultants

9438 U.S. Highway 19 N.
Ste. 101
Port Richey, FL 34668
E-mail: doctorjhl@aol.com
URL: http://www.nabc-inc.com
Contact: Angela Bradley, Exec.Dir.

Ph: (727)862-1016
Free: 800-390-8024
Fax: (727)862-2276

Desc: Financial planners, accountants, bankers, lawyers, sales, and marketing staff, educators, engineers, social workers. Seeks to maintain the highest standard of ethics within the business consulting industry. *Type:* Association.

National Association for Female Executives

135 W. 50th St., 16th Fl.   Ph: (212)445-6235
New York, NY 10020   Free: 800-634-NAFE
   Fax: (212)445-6228
E-mail: nafe@nafe.com
URL: http://www.nafe.com
Contact: Kim Calero, Pres.
Desc: Career women in all phases of business. Purpose is to make women aware of the need to plan for career and financial success and to create tools to support these goals. *Type:* Association.

National Association of the Professions

350 Fairway Dr., Ste. 200   Ph: (954)571-1877
Hillsboro Executive Center   Free: 800-221-2168
North   Fax: (954)571-8582
Deerfield Beach, FL 33441-1084
E-mail: ppsone@msn.com
URL: http://www.nap-assn.com
Contact: Joseph P. Santoli, Jr., Manager, Membership Services.
Desc: Individuals active in professions requiring an advanced education. Offers a wide range of economic and financial services to professionals, including group buying discounts, group insurance, and accounts receivable collections and electronic credit services. *Type:* Association.

National Association of Women Business Owners

1100 Wayne Ave., Ste. 830   Ph: (301)608-2590
Silver Spring, MD 20910   Free: 800-55N-
   AWBO
   Fax: (301)608-2596
E-mail: national@nawbo.org
URL: http://www.nawbo.org
Contact: Debra Hickerson, COO.
Desc: Women who own and operate their own businesses. Purposes are: to identify and bring together women business owners in mutual support; to communicate and share experience and talents with others; to use collective influence to broaden opportunities for women in business. *Type:* Association.

National Black MBA Association Newsletter

National Black MBA Association
180 N. Michigan, Ste. 1400   Ph: (312)236-2622
Chicago, IL 60601   Fax: (312)236-4131
Contact: Tamara M. Brown, Editor.
Desc: Serves as a communication network for members who hold masters degrees in business administration and organization constituent bases. Reports on chapter activities, other national MBA programs, and on the efforts of the Association to further the skills of the minority manager through continuing business education. *Type:* Newsletter.

National Business League

107 Harbor Circle
New Orleans, LA 70126-1101
Contact: Sherman Copilin, Pres.
Desc: Organizational vehicle for minority businesspeople. Promotes the economic development of minorities. Encourages minority ownership and management of small businesses and supports full minority participation within the free enterprise system. *Type:* Association.

National Business Woman

Business and Professional Women's Foundation
2012 Massachusetts Ave. NW   Ph: (202)293-1200
Washington, DC 20036   Fax: (202)861-0298
Contact: A. Antoanela Barcutian, Senior Editor, (202)293-1100, abarcutain@bpwusa.org.
Desc: Magazine for working women that promotes workplace equity issues. *Type:* Periodical.

National Center for Minority Business Research and Development

PO Box 36068   Ph: (410)323-0162
Towson, MD 21286-6068   Free: 800-466-2627
   Fax: (410)323-0163
Contact: Duncan V. Idokogi, Pres./CEO.
Desc: Works to provide minority and women entrepreneurs with resources to succeed in the marketplace. *Type:* Association.

National Center for Nonprofit Boards

1828 L St. NW, Ste. 900   Ph: (202)452-6262
Washington, DC 20036   Free: 800-883-6262
   Fax: (202)452-6299
E-mail: ncnb@ncnb.org
URL: http://www.ncnb.org
Contact: Judith O'Conner, Pres.
Desc: Seeks to improve the effectiveness of nonprofit organizations in fields such as arts and culture, conservation, religion, youth development, public policy, health and medicine, and social welfare by strengthening their governing boards. Operates free information center. Assists nonprofit organizations in designing and organizing training programs, workshops, and conferences for board members and chief executives. *Type:* Association.

National Directory of Minority-Owned Business Firms

Business Research Services, Inc.
4201 Connecticut Ave. NW,   Ph: (202)364-6473
Ste. 610   Free: 800-845-8420
Washington, DC 20008   Fax: (202)686-3228
E-mail: brspubs@sba8a.com
URL: http://www.sba8a.com
Contact: Thomas D. Johnson, President.
Desc: Over 20,000 minority-owned businesses. *Type:* Directory.

National Directory of Minority-Owned Business Firms

Todd Publications
PO Box 635   Ph: (914)358-6213
Nyack, NY 10960   Free: 800-747-1056
   Fax: (914)358-1059
E-mail: toddpub@aol.com
URL: http://www.toddpublications.com
Desc: Over 40,000 minority-owned businesses in the U.S. *Type:* Directory.

National Directory of State Business Licensing and Regulation

Gale Group Inc.
27500 Drake Rd.   Ph: (248)699-4253
Farmington Hills, MI 48331-   Free: 800-877-GALE
3535   Fax: (248)699-8070
E-mail: galeord@galegroup.com
URL: http://www.galegroup.com.
Desc: Business licenses and regulations from more than 1,000 state and federal agencies and boards. *Type:* Directory.

National Directory of Woman-Owned Business Firms

Business Research Services, Inc.
4201 Connecticut Ave. NW,   Ph: (202)364-6473
Ste. 610   Free: 800-845-8420
Washington, DC 20008   Fax: (202)686-3228
E-mail: brspubs@sba8a.com
URL: http://www.sba8a.com
Contact: Thomas D. Johnson, President.
Desc: Over 10,000 woman-owned businesses. *Type:* Directory.

National Executive Service Corps

120 Wall St. 16th Fl.   Ph: (212)269-1234
New York, NY 10005   Fax: (212)269-0959
E-mail: natles@aol.com
Contact: Richard M. Clarke, Chm.
Desc: Provides consulting services to nonprofit educational, health care, social services, cultural, and religious organizations. Services are supplied through experienced, senior-level businesspeople who act as volunteer management consultants. Key management issues addressed by NESC in the past year include: fund-raising strategies, information systems, marketing, strategic planning, organizational review, human resources and board effectiveness. *Type:* Association.

National Minority Supplier Development Council

1040 6th Ave., 2nd Fl.   Ph: (212)944-2430
New York, NY 10018   Fax: (212)719-9611
URL: http://www.nmsdcus.org
Contact: Harriet Michel, Pres.
Desc: Provides a direct link between its 3,500 corporate members and minority-owned businesses (Black, Hispanic, Asian and Native American) and increased procurement and business opportunities for minority businesses of all sizes. *Type:* Association.

National Review of Corporate Acquisitions

Acquisition Resource Corporation
55 Main St.   Ph: (415)435-2175
Tiburon, CA 94920   Fax: (415)435-6310
Contact: Frederick H. Potts, Editor.
Desc: Summaries of trends and analysis of transactions in corporate mergers and acquisitions. Recurring features include interviews, reports of meetings, book reviews, and companies listed for sale. *Type:* Newsletter.

National Service Directory

Dun & Bradstreet
3 Sylvan Way   Ph: (973)605-6442
Parsippany, NJ 07054-3896   Free: 800-526-0651
   Fax: (973)605-6911
E-mail: dnbmdd@dnb.com
Desc: Approximately 17,000 service companies in Canada. *Type:* Directory.

Nation's Business

U.S. Chamber of Commerce
International Division Publications
1615 H St. NW   Ph: (202)463-5460
Washington, DC 20062-2000   Fax: (202)463-3114
Contact: Mary McElveen, Editor; David A. Roe, Publisher; Pete McCutchen, Advertising Dir.
Desc: Business magazine for small businesses. *Type:* Periodical.

The Navigator

Chart Your Course International

2814 Hwy. 212 SW   Ph: (770)860-9464
Conyers, GA 30094   Free: 800-821-2487
     Fax: (770)760-0581

URL: http://www.chartcourse.com.

Contact: Gregory P. Smith, President, greg@chartcourse.com.

Desc: Publishes advice, how-to tips, and trends in business, including management, TQM, leadership, customer service. Recurring features include news of research, a calendar of events, and a column titled Improving Productivity. *Type:* Newsletter.

Nebraska Business Directory

infoUSA

5711 S. 86th Circle   Ph: (402)593-4600
PO Box 27347   Free: 800-555-6124
Omaha, NE 68127   Fax: (402)331-5481

E-mail: internet@infousa.com
URL: http://www.abii.com.

Contact: Peter J. Wilmarth, Publisher.

Desc: 80,000 businesses in Nebraska. *Type:* Directory.

Nebraska Statutes on Selected Business Topics

Nebraska Economic Development Department

301 Centennial Mall, S.   Ph: (402)471-3111
PO Box 94666   Free: 800-426-6505
Lincoln, NE 68509-4666   Fax: (402)471-3778

URL: http://assist.ded.state.ne.us/statutes.html

Contact: Steve Williams, stevew@ded2.ded.state.ne.us.

Desc: The Nebraska Economic Development Department provides business and community information produced by the Internet Community, with particular emphasis on Nebraska people and resources. Topics range from details concerning the Nebraska Business Corporation Act to data on the Environmental Lead Hazard Control Act. *Type:* Database.

Nest Egg

Securities Data Publishing

Circulation Dept.   Ph: (212)432-0045
40 W. 57th St., 11th Fl.
New York, NY 10019

Contact: Brad L. White, Associate Publisher; Rick Norris, Publisher; T.P. Donahue, Jr., Manager.

Desc: Personal Finance Tabloid. *Type:* Periodical.

Netherlands Convention Bureau

355 Lexington Ave., 21st Fl.   Ph: (212)370-7360
New York, NY 10017   Fax: (212)370-9507

E-mail: hbowwmeester@goholland.com
URL: http://www.nlcongress.nl

Contact: Ms. Hanneke Bouwmeester.

Desc: Provides services to organizations in the U.S. wishing to hold conventions in the Netherlands. *Type:* Association.

The Network Connection

Resources for Women, Inc.

5210 E. Pima, Ste. 130   Ph: (520)881-4506
Tucson, AZ 85712   Fax: (520)881-1955

Contact: Donna M. Reed, Editor.

Desc: Focuses on professional and personal networking while providing information about member businesses. Recurring features include interviews, a calendar of events, reports of meetings, job listings, and book reviews. *Type:* Newsletter.

Network of Small Businesses—Membership Directory

Network of Small Businesses (NSB)

5420 Mayfield Rd., Ste. 205   Ph: (216)442-5600
Lyndhurst, OH 44124   Fax: (216)449-3227

Contact: Irwin Friedman, Editor.

Desc: Owners and others involved in small businesses (defined as 250 employees or less), including investors, venture funders, and business owners. *Type:* Directory.

Networking-Newsletter

United States Hispanic Chamber of Commerce

1019 19th St. NW, Ste. 200   Ph: (202)842-1212
Washington, DC 20036

Contact: Maxine Weber, Editor.

Desc: Acts as a business information network. *Type:* Newsletter.

Nevada Business Directory

infoUSA

5711 S. 86th Circle   Ph: (402)593-4600
PO Box 27347   Free: 800-555-6124
Omaha, NE 68127   Fax: (402)331-5481

E-mail: internet@infousa.com
URL: http://www.abii.com.

Contact: Peter J. Wilmarth, Publisher.

Desc: 62,000 businesses in Nevada. *Type:* Directory.

New Age Networking Magazine

Destiny Productions for Print, Radio & Cable Promotions

3395 S. Jones Blvd., No. 217   Ph: (702)648-3898
Las Vegas, NV 89102   Free: 800-457-0654
     Fax: (702)648-3898

E-mail: DestinyMag@aol.com
URL: http://www.members.aol.com/destinymag/mw1.

Contact: Jody Williams, Contact.

Desc: Professional magazine covering business for proprietors and others. *Type:* Periodical.

New Hampshire Business Directory

infoUSA

5711 S. 86th Circle   Ph: (402)593-4600
PO Box 27347   Free: 800-555-6124
Omaha, NE 68127   Fax: (402)331-5481

E-mail: internet@infousa.com
URL: http://www.abii.com.

Contact: Peter J. Wilmarth, Publisher.

Desc: 60,000 businesses in New Hampshire. *Type:* Directory.

New Hampshire Department of Resources and Economic Development—Agenda

New Hampshire Division of Economic Development

PO Box 1856   Ph: (603)271-2341
Concord, NH 03302-1856   Fax: (603)271-6784

E-mail: dedinfo@dred.state.nh.us

Contact: Margaret M. Joyce, Editor.

Desc: Presents news on business and industrial development, international commerce and travel and tourism. *Type:* Newsletter.

New Jersey Business Directory

infoUSA

5711 S. 86th Circle   Ph: (402)593-4600
PO Box 27347   Free: 800-555-6124
Omaha, NE 68127   Fax: (402)331-5481

E-mail: internet@infousa.com
URL: http://www.abii.com.

Contact: Peter J. Wilmarth, Publisher.

Desc: 318,000 businesses in New Jersey. *Type:* Directory.

New Jersey Business and Industry Association

102 W. State St.   Ph: (609)393-7707
Trenton, NJ 08608-1102   Fax: (609)695-0442

Contact: Joseph E. Gonzalez, Jr., Pres.

Desc: Businesses. Works to improve business climate through lobbying. *Type:* Association.

New Jersey Business—Top 100 Employers Issue

New Jersey Business Magazine

310 Passaic Ave.   Ph: (201)882-5004
Fairfield, NJ 07004   Fax: (201)882-4648

E-mail: njbmag@intac.com

Contact: James T. Prior, Editor-in-Chief.

Type: Directory.

New Jersey State Handbook

The Bar List Publishing Co.

PO Box 948   Ph: (847)498-0100
Northbrook, IL 60065   Free: 800-726-1007
     Fax: (847)498-6695

E-mail: info@barlist.com

Contact: Leslie Rodgers, Editor.

Desc: Licensed property, liability, and life insurance companies and agencies, adjusters, and appraisers (SIC 094) in New Jersey. *Type:* Directory.

New Mexico Business Directory

infoUSA

5711 S. 86th Circle   Ph: (402)593-4600
PO Box 27347   Free: 800-555-6124
Omaha, NE 68127   Fax: (402)331-5481

E-mail: internet@infousa.com
URL: http://www.abii.com.

Contact: Peter J. Wilmarth, Publisher.

Desc: 70,000 businesses in New Mexico. *Type:* Directory.

New Plant Report

Conway Data, Inc.

35 Technology Pkwy., Ste. 150   Ph: (770)446-6996
Norcross, GA 30092   Fax: (770)263-8825

E-mail: info.mgr@conway.com
URL: http://www.sitenet

Contact: Doris Alexander, Editor, doris.alexander@conway.com.

Desc: Covers significant new or expanding office and industrial facilities, hotels, and commercial properties. Listings meet at least one of the following criteria: investment of $1 million, 20,000 square feet, or 50 or more employees. *Type:* Directory.

New Product Announcements/Plus

The Gale Group

27500 Drake Rd.   Ph: (248)699-4253
Farmington Hills, MI 48331-3535

URL: http://www.galegroup.com

Desc: Contains the complete text of approximately 200,000 press releases from more than 15,000 companies on new products and technologies and corporate activities. Covers announcements of new products and services, product modifications, and new technologies and processes from manufacturers, distributors, and service companies in nearly 60 industries (e.g., communications, medical and health services, textiles). *Available:* The Dialog Corporation, DataStar; The Dialog Corporation, DIALOG; NIFTY Corporation, NIFTY-SERVE. *Type:* Database.

New York Business Directory

infoUSA

5711 S. 86th Circle

PO Box 27347   Ph: (402)593-4600

Omaha, NE 68127   Free: 800-555-6124

E-mail: internet@infousa.com Fax: (402)331-5481

URL: http://www.abii.com.

Contact: Peter J. Wilmarth, Publisher.

Desc: In two volumes (Metro and Upstate), 736,000 businesses in New York state. *Type:* Directory.

News/Retrieval Symbols Directory

Dow Jones & Company, Inc.

P.O. Box 300   Ph: (609)520-4000

Princeton, NJ 08543-0300

URL: http://www.dj.com

Desc: Contains more than 20,000 ticker symbols and other market symbols (e.g., CUSIP numbers, Standard Industrial Classification (SIC) codes) used in business databases available through Dow Jones News/Retrieval. Provides equivalent full corporate name or similar identifier for stocks, corporate bonds, Treasury issues, mutual funds, stock options, and foreign bonds. *Available:* Dow Jones & Company, Inc. *Type:* Database.

News & Views

Business Forms Management Association, Inc.

319 SW Washington, Ste. 710 Ph: (503)227-3393

Portland, OR 97204   Fax: (503)274-7667

E-mail: infocus@bfmu.org; bfma@bfma.org

Contact: Christie Holmgren, Editor.

Desc: Provides information about business forms management. Recurring features include interviews, a calendar of events, news of educational opportunities, and job listings. *Type:* Newsletter.

Newswire ASAP™

The Gale Group

27500 Drake Rd.   Ph: (248)699-4253

Farmington Hills, MI 48331-

  3535

URL: http://www.galegroup.com

Contact: (650)378-5000, fax: (800)676-2345.

Desc: Provides citations and the complete text of more than 1 million news releases and wire stories from the following twelve international news wire services: • Agencia EFE (1991 to date). • BusinessWire. *Available:* The Dialog Corporation, DIALOG. *Type:* Database.

The NonProfit Times On-Line

The NonProfit Times

240 Cedar Knolls Rd., Ste. 318 Ph: (973)734-1700

Cedar Knolls, NJ 07927

URL: http://www.nptimes.com/

Desc: The leading business publication for nonprofit management serving organizations in the United States and beyond. Each issue contains a special support, news, columns, and departments which include letters to the editor, calendar of events, news makers, reader service, and classified ads. *Type:* Database.

Nordic Stock Guide

Delphi Economics AB

Hans Nilsson   Ph: (201)867-4303

8 Bonn Place   Fax: (201)867-4666

Weehawken, NJ 07087

Desc: Nearly 250 public companies in Denmark, Finland, Norway, and Sweden. *Type:* Directory.

The North American Export Pages

US West Dex, Inc.

198 Inverness Dr. West   Ph: (303)784-2319

Englewood, CO 80112   Free: 800-288-2582

URL: http://export.uswest.com.

Contact: Mike Brady, Editor.

Desc: Approximately 50,000 suppliers from the United States, Canada, and Mexico wishing to export products worldwide. *Type:* Directory.

North American Fireworks Trade Directory

American Fireworks News

HC67-Box 30   Ph: (570)828-8417

Dingmans Ferry, PA 18328 Fax: (570)828-8695

E-mail: afn@98.net

URL: http://www.98.net/afn

Contact: John M. Drewes, Editor.

Desc: Over 600 fireworks manufacturers, importers, distributors, wholesalers, in U.S., Canada & Mexico; special effects specialists, suppliers, insurance brokers, trade associations, consultants, laboratories, and producers. *Type:* Directory.

North American Free Trade and Investment Report

WorldTrade Executive, Inc.

2250 Main St., Ste. 100   Ph: (978)287-0301

PO Box 761   Fax: (978)287-0302

Concord, MA 01742

E-mail: info@wtexec.com

Contact: Gary A. Brown, Editor.

Desc: Covers NAFTA implementation and related issues and other trade, investment, and regulatory developments in Mexico, Canada, and the U.S. *Type:* Newsletter.

North of Boston Convention and Visitors Bureau

Michelle Meehan

248 Cabot St.   Ph: (508)921-4990

PO Box 642   Free: 800-742-5306

Beverly, MA 01915   Fax: (508)921-4956

URL: http://www.northofboston.org

Desc: Works to promote the north of Boston region as a travel destination. Members include those involved in lodging, dining, attractions, chambers of commerce & other travel related businesses. *Type:* Association.

North Carolina Business Directory

infoUSA

5711 S. 86th Circle   Ph: (402)593-4600

PO Box 27347   Free: 800-555-6124

Omaha, NE 68127   Fax: (402)331-5481

E-mail: internet@infousa.com

URL: http://www.abii.com.

Contact: Peter J. Wilmarth, Publisher.

Desc: 292,000 businesses in North Carolina. *Type:* Directory.

North Dakota Business Directory

infoUSA

5711 S. 86th Circle   Ph: (402)593-4600

PO Box 27347   Free: 800-555-6124

Omaha, NE 68127   Fax: (402)331-5481

E-mail: internet@infousa.com

URL: http://www.abii.com.

Contact: Peter J. Wilmarth, Publisher.

Desc: 36,000 businesses in North Dakota. *Type:* Directory.

North and South Carolina State Handbook

The Bar List Publishing Co.

PO Box 948   Ph: (847)498-0100

Northbrook, IL 60065   Free: 800-726-1007

               Fax: (847)498-6695

E-mail: info@barlist.com

Contact: Bruce Rodgers, Publisher; Leslie Rodgers, Editor.

Desc: Licensed property, liability, and life insurance companies and agencies, adjusters, and appraisers (SIC 094) in North Carolina and South Carolina. *Type:* Directory.

North Texas/Oklahoma Regional Industrial Buying Guide

Thomas Regional Directory Co., Inc.

5 Penn Plaza   Ph: (212)629-2100

New York, NY 10001   Fax: (212)290-7335

E-mail: info@trdnet.com

URL: http://www.thomasregional.com.

Contact: Marie McGurk, Editorial Dir.; Adrienne Toth, Managing Editor; Nancy Bromberg, Contract Administration Mgr.

Desc: More than 26,000 listings of manufacturers of industrial products; related industrial services, such as trucking and maintenance services; distributors; and manufacturers' representatives in Oklahoma, northern Texas, Wichita, KS, Shreveport, Louisiana, and Joplin, Missouri. *Type:* Directory.

Northern Kentucky

Northern Kentucky Chamber of Commerce

300 Buttermilk Pike, Ste. 330 Ph: (606)578-8800

Ft. Mitchell, KY 41017   Fax: (606)578-8802

Desc: Approximately 1,800 member businesses of the Northern Kentucky Chamber of Commerce, comprising Boone, Campbell, and Kenton Counties. *Type:* Directory.

NPI Techno View Times

Nosh Productions, Inc.

2013 16th St.   Ph: (415)896-6674

San Francisco, CA 94103-4818 Fax: (415)896-6675

URL: http://www.nosh.com.

Contact: NaNoshka Johnson, CEO, nanoshka@nosh.com.

Desc: Aims to keep abreast of the latest computer technology and, with that technology, develop new and better business solutions. *Type:* Newsletter.

Office Hours

Economics Press, Inc.

12 Daniel Rd.   Ph: (973)227-1224

Fairfield, NJ 07004-2565   Free: 800-526-2554

               Fax: (973)526-2554

E-mail: info@epinc.com; order@epinc.com

URL: http://www.epinc.com

Contact: Linda Bullock, Editor.

Desc: Discusses proper attitudes, businesslike dress, behavior and responsibility, and other "work ethic" topics and offers tips for office staff on improving interoffice relationships. Emphasizes the personal benefits of improving habits, job satisfaction, career advancement, and job security. *Type:* Newsletter.

The Office Professional

Professional Training Associates, Inc.

210 Commerce Blvd.   Ph: (512)255-6006

Round Rock, TX 78664-2189 Free: 800-424-2112

E-mail: demwit@protrain.com; toped@aol.com.

Contact: Marilyn Johnson, Editor.

Desc: Provides information on new developments and ideas in office systems and procedures. Covers topics such as successful communication techniques, professional human relation skills, career development, secretarial methods, management thinking, and office technology. *Type:* Newsletter.

Ohio Business Directory
infoUSA
5711 S. 86th Circle   Ph: (402)593-4600
PO Box 27347   Free: 800-555-6124
Omaha, NE 68127   Fax: (402)331-5481
E-mail: internet@infousa.com
URL: http://www.abii.com.
Contact: Peter J. Wilmarth, Publisher.
Desc: 446,000 businesses in Ohio. *Type:* Directory.

Ohio Valley Regional Industrial Buying Guide
Thomas Regional Directory Co., Inc.
5 Penn Plaza   Ph: (212)629-2100
New York, NY 10001   Fax: (212)290-7335
E-mail: info@trdnet.com
URL: http://www.thomasregional.com.
Contact: Marie McGurk, Editorial Dir.; Adrienne Toth, Managing Editor; Nancy Bromberg, Contracts Administration Mgr.
Desc: Nearly 29,000 listings of manufacturers of industrial products; related industrial services, such as trucking and maintenance services; distributors; and manufacturers' representatives in Kentucky and in parts of Indiana, Ohio and West Virginia. *Type:* Directory.

Oklahoma Business Directory
infoUSA
5711 S. 86th Circle   Ph: (402)593-4600
PO Box 27347   Free: 800-555-6124
Omaha, NE 68127   Fax: (402)331-5481
E-mail: internet@infousa.com
URL: http://www.abii.com.
Contact: Peter J. Wilmarth, Publisher.
Desc: 151,000 businesses in Oklahoma. *Type:* Directory.

On Buying or Selling a Business
F.W. Robbins and Co.
1416 W. Fletcher   Ph: (773)327-9393
Chicago, IL 60657   Fax: (773)327-6055
URL: http://www.mcs.net/~frobbins.
Contact: Frank Robbins, Editor.
Desc: Covers aspects and steps of buying and selling a business, including valuation, negotiation, and current deals available. This newsletter is faxed. *Type:* Newsletter.

On Center
Center for Creative Leadership
One Leadership Pl.   Ph: (336)286-4480
PO Box 26300   Fax: (336)282-3284
Greensboro, NC 27438-6300
E-mail: info@leaders.ccl.org
URL: http://www.ccl.org; http:www.ccl.org.
Contact: Rebecca Garau, Editor, (336)286-4038, fax: (336)286-4285, garaur@leaders.ccl.org.
Desc: Provides information on the activities of the Center for Creative Leadership. Recurring features include notices of publications available, news of members, and news of upcoming conferences. *Type:* Newsletter.

On the Mark
Corporate Communications
333 Pfingsten Rd.   Ph: (847)272-8800
Northbrook, IL 60062   Fax: (847)509-6235
E-mail: northbrook@ul.com; poilockr@ul.com.
URL: http://www.ul.com.
Contact: Carole Feil, Editor, feilc@ul.com; Michael Nissen, Editor, nissenm@ul.com.
Desc: Trade magazine covering business issues. *Type:* Periodical.

100 Best Stocks To Own in America
Dearborn Financial Publishing, Inc.
155 N. Wacker Dr.   Ph: (312)836-4400
Chicago, IL 60606   Free: 800-621-9621
                          Fax: (312)836-1021
E-mail: poole@dearborn.com.
URL: http://www.dearborn-financial.com
Contact: Gene Walden, Author.
Desc: 100 U.S. companies whose stocks are rated highly as investment options by the author. *Type:* Directory.

100 Companies Receiving the Largest Dollar Volume of Prime Contract Awards
U.S. Department of Defense
The Pentagon   Ph: (703)545-6700
Washington, DC 20301
Desc: 100 companies (with their subsidiaries) that received the largest dollar volume of military prime contract awards over $25,000 during the fiscal year covered. *Type:* Directory.

Opportunity Evaluation Newsletter
G.C. Associates
PO Box 28521   Ph: (360)671-6799
Bellingham, WA 98228
Contact: George Czerlinski, Editor.
Desc: Gives evaluation of business and financial opportunities and rates them on a scale from one to 10 (10 being the highest). Also covers new and previously reviewed opportunities biannually. *Type:* Newsletter.

Opportunity Hot-Line
Opportunity Hot-Line
c/o Business Network   Ph: (440)442-5600
5420 Mayfield Rd., No. 205 Fax: (440)449-3227
Cleveland, OH 44124
Contact: Irwin Friedman, Editor.
Desc: Provides information on partner search, grant writing, and venture funding. *Type:* Newsletter.

Oregon Business Directory
infoUSA
5711 S. 86th Circle   Ph: (402)593-4600
PO Box 27347   Free: 800-555-6124
Omaha, NE 68127   Fax: (402)331-5481
E-mail: internet@infousa.com
URL: http://www.abii.com.
Contact: Peter J. Wilmarth, Publisher.
Desc: 150,000 businesses in Oregon. *Type:* Directory.

Organization Development Network
76 S. Orange Ave., Ste. 101 Ph: (973)763-7337
South Orange, NJ 07079-1923 Fax: (973)763-7488
URL: http://www.odnet.org
Contact: Richard A. Ungerer, Exec.Dir.
Desc: Practitioners, academics, managers, and students employed or interested in organization development. Works to enhance and provide opportunities for colleagueship and professional development. *Type:* Association.

Overseas Business Reports
University of Missouri, St. Louis
Thomas Jefferson Library   Ph: (314)516-5059
St. Louis, MO 63121
URL: http://www.umsl.edu/services/govdocs/obr/index.html
Contact: Raleigh Muns, Reference Librarian, srcmuns@umslvma.umsl.edu.
Desc: The Overseas Business Reports database is a collection of overseas business reports from various countries, with an emphasis on information useful for potential U.S. sellers and investors. *Type:* Database.

Pacific Dialogue
Pacific Dialogue
33 Ferry Ct.   Ph: (212)979-7395
Stratford, CT 06497-6064
Contact: Robert J. Miko, Editor.
Desc: Deals with United States and Pacific corporate communications, including marketing, advertising, public affairs, telecommunications, personal communication, and software and personal computers (PCs) for business managers. Recurring features include news of research, a calendar of events, reports of meetings, news of educational opportunities, book reviews, and notices of publications available. *Type:* Newsletter.

Paginas Amarillas en Espanol del Sur de Texas
APS Communication
121 Interpark Blvd., Ste. 200 Ph: (210)402-0200
San Antonio, TX 78216-1844   Fax: (210)495-7925
URL: http://www.spanishyellowpages.com.
Contact: Chris Schuchart, Editor.
Desc: Businesses in seven southern Texas cities and 10 major cities in Mexico. *Type:* Directory.

Panama Annual Directory
U.S. Chamber of Commerce
International Division Publications
1615 H St. NW   Ph: (202)463-5460
Washington, DC 20062-2000 Fax: (202)463-3114
Desc: 300 companies in Panama. *Type:* Directory.

Partnership Tax Planning & Practice
CCH Inc.
2700 Lake Cook Rd.   Ph: (847)267-7000
Riverwoods, IL 60015   Free: 800-449-8114
                          Fax: (847)224-8299
URL: http://www.cch.com; http://www.cch.com; http://business.cch.com.
Contact: James Rooney, Editor.
Desc: Explanatory comments on partnership, taxation, full text of pertinent code and acquisition provisions, post 1954 revenue rulings, revenue procedures. *Type:* Newsletter.

PATCA Newsletter
Professional and Technical Consultants Association
849-B Independence Ave.   Ph: (650)903-8305
Mountain View, CA 94043   Free: 800-747-2822
                          Fax: (650)967-0995
E-mail: office@patca.org; info@patca.org
URL: http://www.patca.org; http://www.patca.org.
Contact: Stan Turnbull, Editor.
Desc: Acts as a forum for the exchange of information on consulting and consulting practices. Provides professional support for member independent consultants active in business, industry, and government. *Type:* Newsletter.

Pennsylvania Business Directory
infoUSA
5711 S. 86th Circle   Ph: (402)593-4600
PO Box 27347   Free: 800-555-6124
Omaha, NE 68127   Fax: (402)331-5481
E-mail: internet@infousa.com
URL: http://www.abii.com.
Contact: Peter J. Wilmarth, Publisher.
Desc: 478,000 businesses in Pennsylvania. *Type:* Directory.

PersiaNet
Emory University
Atlanta, GA 30322   Ph: (404)727-6216
E-mail: ccarlsn@emory.edu
URL: http://userwww.service.emory.edu/~sebrahi/PersiaNet.html

Contact: Steven Ebrahimi, sebrahi@emory.edu.

Desc: PersiaNet takes you on a virtual tour of 4000 years of Iranian culture. The site includes a large amount of demographic, economic, political and cultural information. *Type:* Database.

Personal Success—The Newsletter

Du Vall Press Financial Publications
Box 14   Fax: (517)655-5208
Williamston, MI 48895
E-mail: daxforpersonalsuccess@juno.com.
Contact: Dean F.V. DuVall, Sr., Editor; SuEllen M. Headley, Communications Director.
Desc: Deals with business, economic, investment, and health issues that impact personal success. Recurring features include letters to the editor, interviews, news of research, news of educational opportunities, book reviews, and notices of publications available. *Type:* Newsletter.

Perspectives

International Sign Association (ISA)
707 N. St. Asaph St.   Ph: (703)836-4012
Alexandria, VA 22314   Fax: (703)836-8353
Contact: Shane M. Artim, Editor.
Desc: Provides information about government affairs issues that affect the sign industry. Recurring features include notices of publications available and columns titled View from the Hill and Capitol Hill Roundup. *Type:* Newsletter.

Phi Chi Theta

1704 Hanks St.   Ph: (409)764-6690
Lufkin, TX 75904   Fax: (409)637-0966
E-mail: phichi@icc.net
URL: http://www.phichitheta.org
Contact: Leslie A. Trout, Exec.Dir.
Desc: Co-ed professional fraternity - business and economics. Maintains hall of fame; sponsors educational programs. *Type:* Association.

Phi Gamma Nu

6745 Cheryl Ann Dr.   Ph: (216)524-0934
Seven Hills, OH 44131
E-mail: exdir@ameritech.net
Contact: Lorraine A. Scott, Exec.Dir.
Desc: Professional fraternity - business administration and economics. *Type:* Association.

Phi Theta Pi

2103 Cortez Rd.   Ph: (904)641-9006
Jacksonville, FL 32246   Free: 888-608-9841
                                 Fax: (904)641-9006
E-mail: ptpfrat@aol.com
URL: http://www.phithetapi.org
Contact: Richard B. Glover, Grand Sec.-Treas.
Desc: Honorary fraternity of businessmen and women (includes faculty members). *Type:* Association.

Philadelphia Business Journal—Book of Business Lists Issue

Philadelphia Business Journal
400 Market St., Ste. 300   Ph: (215)238-1450
Philadelphia, PA 19106   Fax: (215)238-1466
Contact: Jack Roberts, Editor.
Desc: About 60 ranked lists (about 25 names per list) of major public and private businesses and organizations, including banks, brokers, construction companies, hospitals, schools, child-care centers, law firms, hotels, apartment complexes, office parks, architects, ad agencies, and employers in the Philadelphia area. *Type:* Directory.

Pierce County Department of Community Services

8815 S. Tacoma Way, Ste. 202   Ph: (253)798-7205
Tacoma, WA 98499   Free: 800-992-2456
                                 Fax: (253)798-6604
URL: http://www.co.pierce.wa.us
Contact: Linda Hurley Ishem, Dir.
Type: Association.

Pittsburgh High Technology Council Directory

Pittsburgh High Technology Council
2000 Technology, Ste. 500   Ph: (412)687-2700
Pittsburgh, PA 15219   Free: 800-388-8820
                                 Fax: (412)687-0200
E-mail: info@phtc.org.
URL: http://www.tc-p.com.
Contact: Kevin O'Neil, Editor.
Desc: Over 1,500 advanced technology manufacturers, suppliers, venture capital companies, professional service firms, research facilities, economic development organizations, and academic and civic organizations fostering the increase of high technology in western Pennsylvania. *Type:* Directory.

Point of View

Roldo Bartimole
PO Box 14328   Ph: (216)321-2757
Cleveland, OH 44114-0328
Contact: Roldo Bartimole, Editor.
Desc: Contributes "fact and opinion, based on research, experience, feelings and interaction with others," on activities of private business, city politics, news media, and civic and charitable organizations in and around Cleveland, Ohio. *Type:* Newsletter.

Points West Chronicle

Center for the New West
600 World Trade Center   Ph: (303)572-5400
1625 Broadway   Fax: (303)572-5499
Denver, CO 80202
E-mail: cfnwinfo@newwest.org
URL: http://www.newwest.org.
Contact: Robert C. Wurmstedt, Editor.
Desc: Explores the recent economic transformations of American society. Focuses on business formation, entrepreneurship, technological innovation, changes in demography, family life, and the workplace. *Type:* Newsletter.

Ports of Discovery

Prairie du Chien Area Chamber of Commerce
PO Box 326   Ph: (608)326-8555
Prairie du Chien, WI 53821   Free: 800-PDC-1673
                                 Fax: (608)326-7744
E-mail: pdcoc@mhtc.net
Contact: Michelle Quick, Executive Director; Kaye Morel, Executive Secretary.
Desc: Approximately 150 businesses in Prairie du Chien, Wisconsin and Marquette and McGregor, Iowa. *Type:* Directory.

Portuguese Trade Commission

590 5th Ave.   Ph: (212)354-4610
New York, NY 10036   Fax: (212)575-4737
Contact: Elia Rodrigues, Dir.
Desc: Promotes exports from Portugal to the U.S. and helps American importers and businesses find sources in Portugal. *Type:* Association.

PR Newswire

PR Newswire, Inc.
810 Seventh Ave., 35th Fl.
New York, NY 10019
Desc: Contains the complete text of more than 1.6 million news releases issued by a variety of organizations and trans-

mitted to the press by PR Newswire. Covers primarily business and financial news as well as sports, labor, entertainment, medicine, science, and general interest news. *Available:* BT North America, Inc.; The Dialog Corporation, DIALOG; The Dialog Corporation, DIALOG; Dow Jones & Company, Inc.; LEXIS-NEXIS, NEXIS; LEXIS-NEXIS, NEXIS; Track Data Corporation; Bloomberg Financial Markets; NewsEdge Corporation; Delphi Internet Services Corporation; CompuServe Information Service, Knowledge Index. *Type:* Database.

Privacy and American Business

Center for Social and Legal Research
2 University Plz., Ste. 414   Ph: (201)996-1154
Hackensack, NJ 07601   Fax: (201)996-1883
E-mail: ctrslr@aol.com
URL: http://www.pandab.org.
Contact: Lorrie Sherwood, Exec. Editor; Alan F. Westin, Editor and Publisher; Robert R. Belair, Senior Editor.
Desc: Provides information about the use of personal information in business. Topics include privacy issues in employment, consumer, financial industries, telecommunications, and uses direct marketing and interna tional data protection. *Type:* Newsletter.

Procurement Automated Source System (PASS)

Office of Procurement Assistance
U.S. Small Business Administration
409 3rd St. SW   Ph: (202)205-6469
Washington, DC 20416
Desc: Online database. More than 180,000 small businesses (including some 29,000 minority-owned, 44,000 woman-owned, and 51,000 veteran-owned businesses) seeking government procurement contracts. *Type:* Directory.

PRODUCTSCAN

Marketing Intelligence Service, Ltd.
6473-D State Rte. 64   Ph: (716)374-6326
Naples, NY 14512-9726   Free: 800-836-5710
                                 Fax: (716)374-5217
E-mail: mi@productscan.com
URL: http://www.productscan.com.
Contact: Daniel Smith, Editor.
Desc: Approximately 200,000 new consumer goods launched in U.S. and Canadian retail markets as well as in 18 countries outside North America. Compiled from the newsletters " Product Alert" and " International Product Alert." *Type:* Directory.

Professional Convention Management Association

100 Vestavia Pkwy., Ste. 220   Ph: (205)823-7262
Birmingham, AL 35216   Fax: (205)822-3891
URL: http://www.pcma.org
Contact: Roy B. Evans, CAE, CEO/Exec.VP.
Desc: Convention, meeting, and exhibition planners, managers, and CEOs of non-profit organizations. Works to increase the effectiveness of meetings, conventions, and exhibitions through education and promotion of the value of the meetings industry to the general public. *Type:* Association.

Professional Regulation News

National Organization for Competency Assurance
1200 19th St. NW, Ste. 300   Ph: (202)857-1165
Washington, DC 20036-2422   Fax: (202)223-4579
E-mail: info@noca.org
URL: http://www.noca.org.
Contact: Bonnie M. Aubin, Editor and Publisher.
Desc: Provides information about professional licensing and certification. Topics include state and federal regulations. *Type:* Newsletter.

Profile

Greater Omaha Chamber of Commerce
1301 Harney St.   Ph: (402)346-5000
Omaha, NE 68102   Fax: (402)346-7050
E-mail: gocc@accessomaha.com
Contact: Jason Bash, Editor, jbash@accessomaha.com;
Tess Fogarty, Assistant Editor.
Desc: Covers events and information relating to Omaha
businesses. *Type:* Newsletter.

Profit

CB Media Ltd.
777 Bay St., 5th Fl.   Ph: (416)596-5999
Toronto, ON, Canada M5W   Fax: (416)596-5111
1A7
E-mail: profit@cbmedia.ca.
Contact: Rick Spence, Editor; Paul Jones, Publisher; Jennifer Myers, Associate Editor.
Desc: A management magazine for owner/presidents of independent companies. *Type:* Periodical.

PROMT™

The Gale Group
27500 Drake Rd.   Ph: (248)699-4253
Farmington Hills, MI 48331-3535
URL: http://www.galegroup.com
Contact: (650)378-5000, fax: (800)676-2345.
Desc: Contains more than 100,000 citations, with abstracts and selected full texts, to the worldwide business literature on companies, markets, products, and technologies for major international, national, and regional manufacturing and service industries. Covers new products and technologies, mergers and acquisitions, capital expenditures, market data, product sales, marketing strategies, foreign trade, and regulations. *Available:* The Dialog Corporation, DataStar; The Dialog Corporation, DIALOG; NIFTY Corporation, NIFTY-SERVE; Thomson Financial Services, Inc., I/PLUS Direct; Questel • Orbit; FT PROFILE; Handelsblatt GmbH, GENIOS Wirtschaftsdatenbanken; STN International; Bell & Howell Information and Learning; The Gale Group, InfoTrac Web. *Type:* Database.

PSI Research Memo

PSI Research/Oasis Press
PO Box 3727   Ph: (541)479-9464
Central Point, OR 97502   Fax: (541)476-1479
E-mail: info@psi-research.com
URL: http://www.psi-research.com
Desc: Focuses on business issues. *Type:* Newsletter.

Public Affairs Council

2033 K St., Ste. 700   Ph: (202)872-1790
Washington, DC 20036   Fax: (202)835-8343
URL: http://www.pac.org
Contact: Douglas Pinkham, Pres.
Desc: Corporate public affairs executives representing member corporations and trade associations. Encourages members of the business community to be active and informed participants in political affairs and to provide thoughtful leadership in the fields of corporate citizenship and social responsibility. *Type:* Association.

Public Companies

infoUSA
5711 S. 86th Circle   Ph: (402)593-4600
PO Box 27347   Free: 800-555-6124
Omaha, NE 68127   Fax: (402)331-5481
E-mail: internet@infousa.com
URL: http://www.abii.com.
Type: Directory.

Puerto Rico Business Review

Government Development Bank for Puerto Rico
PO Box 42001   Ph: (787)728-9200
San Juan, PR 00940-2001   Fax: (787)268-5496
Contact: Amarilys Ortiz Medina, Editor.
Desc: Covers business and finance related to Puerto Rico. Carries research articles from government and business leaders and government agencies on the Puerto Rican economy. *Type:* Newsletter.

Puerto Rico Report from Washington

EPIN Publishing
7400 Lakeview Dr., No. 402   Ph: (301)365-3621
Bethesda, MD 20817   Fax: (301)365-2782
Contact: James McDonough, Editor.
Desc: Reports on events in Washington, DC, that affect business in Puerto Rico. *Type:* Newsletter.

Quality Management

Bureau of Business Practice
24 Rope Ferry Rd.   Ph: (860)442-4365
Waterford, CT 06386   Free: 800-243-0876
     Fax: (860)437-3555
URL: http://www.bbpnews.com
Contact: Peter Hawkins, Editor, peter_hawkins@prenhall.com; Elaine Stattler, Managing Editor.
Desc: Covers best practices in product companies. Helps quality managers improve performance in their organizations. *Type:* Newsletter.

Quarterly Business Failures Report

Dun & Bradstreet
1 World Trade Ctr., 14th Fl.   Ph: (212)593-6800
New York, NY 10048
Contact: A.M. Dowden, Publisher; F.R. Brown, Editor; Nova Culver, Circulation Mgr.
Desc: Covers recent business failures. *Type:* Newsletter.

Queensborough

Queens Chamber of Commerce
75-20 Astoria Blvd., Ste. 140   Ph: (718)898-8500
Jackson Heights, NY 11370   Fax: (718)898-8599
E-mail: queenschamber@worldnet.att.net
Contact: Eric Robinson, Editor.
Desc: Focuses on business trends in Queens County, New York. *Type:* Newsletter.

Quincy Business News

John R. Graham, Inc.
40 Oval Rd.   Ph: (617)328-0069
Quincy, MA 02170   Fax: (617)471-1504
Contact: Rob Keane, Editor; Rob Keane, Editor.
Desc: Provides information on Quincy businesses. Includes one feature business per issue. *Type:* Newsletter.

R & D Magazine

Cahners Publishing Company
275 Washington St.   Ph: (617)558-2119
Newton, MA 02458   Fax: (617)558-4700
Contact: Rob Cassidy, Editor.
Desc: Magazine covering the field of applied research and development. *Type:* Periodical.

Ragan's Annual Report Review

Lawrence Ragan Communications, Inc.
316 N. Michigan Ave., Ste. 300   Ph: (312)960-4100
Chicago, IL 60601   Free: 800-878-5331
     Fax: (312)960-4105
E-mail: cservice@ragan.com
Contact: Mark Ragan, Publisher; Robert Long, Managing Editor.
Desc: Provides business trends, tips, and tactics. *Type:* Newsletter.

The Real Entrepreneur

Bo-Mar Enterprises
PO Box I   Ph: (706)694-8441
Varnell, GA 30756-1009
Contact: Bob Riemke, Editor/Publisher.
Desc: Presents business and investment opportunities, new products, services, and materials to entrepreneurs. Recurring features include news of research, news of educational opportunities, book reviews, notices of publications available, and classified Real Opportunities section. *Type:* Newsletter.

Recession-Recovery Watch

Center for International Business Cycle Research
c/o Fiber Inc.
122 E. 42nd St., Rm. 1512   Ph: (212)688-2222
New York, NY 10168-1599
Contact: Dr. Victor Zarnowitz, Editor.
Desc: Designed to assist in the evaluation of current business conditions. Examines inflation and employment in the U.S., analyzing data in the light of previous recession-recovery patterns. *Type:* Newsletter.

Reference Book of Corporate Managements

Dun & Bradstreet
3 Sylvan Way   Ph: (973)605-6442
Parsippany, NJ 07054-3896   Free: 800-526-0651
     Fax: (973)605-6911
E-mail: dnbmdd@dnb.com
Desc: Management executives at over 12,000 leading U.S. companies. *Type:* Directory.

Reference Book for World Traders

Croner Publications, Inc.
10951 Sorrento Valley Rd., Ste.   Ph: (619)546-1894
1-D   Free: 800-441-4033
San Diego, CA 92121   Fax: (619)546-1955
E-mail: paul@croner.com
URL: http://www.sdic.net/croner
Contact: Ruth Jordan, Editor.
Desc: In three volumes, information for the export trade industry. Volume 1 contains a list of International Trade Commission district offices, Small Business Administration district offices, trade organizations, data banks and mailing lists, sources for statistics, marketing and financing information, and other sources of trade information. Volumes 2 and 3 contain information on 185 foreign countries, including consulates and embassies, hotels, ports, trade associations, etc. *Type:* Directory.

Regional Directory of Minority & Woman-Owned Business Firms

Business Research Services, Inc.
4201 Connecticut Ave. NW,   Ph: (202)364-6473
Ste. 610   Free: 800-845-8420
Washington, DC 20008   Fax: (202)686-3228
E-mail: brspubs@sba8a.com
URL: http://www.sba8a.com
Contact: Thomas D. Johnson, President.
Desc: Published in 3 regional volumes: Eastern, Central, and Western. Based on "National Directory of Minority-Owned Business Firms" and "National Directory of Woman-Owned Business Firms". *Type:* Directory.

Regional Update

Federal Reserve Bank of Atlanta
104 Marietta St.   Ph: (404)521-8269
Atlanta, GA 30303-2713   Fax: (404)521-8050
URL: http://www.frAtlanta.org.
Contact: Ellen Arth, Circulation Mgr.; Carole Starkey, Art Director.
Desc: Publishes financial news for Atlanta and surrounding areas. *Type:* Newsletter.

Registered Representative

Intertec Publishing
18818 Teller Ave., Ste. 280   Ph: (949)851-2220
Irvine, CA 92612   Free: 800-621-0720
   Fax: (949)851-1636
URL: http://www.rrmag.com.
Contact: Dan Jamieson, Editor; Rich Santos, Publisher, rich_santos@intertec.com; Tammy Candella, Production Dir.
Desc: Magazine providing comprehensive coverage of securities industry trends directly affecting the job performance and productivity of retail stockbrokers. *Type:* Periodical.

Relocatable Business

Relocatable Business Inc.
PO Box 220214   Free: 800-927-1310
Great Neck, NY 11020   Fax: (516)466-8672
E-mail: business@relocatable.com.
URL: http://www.relocatable.com.
Contact: Nancy Henigson, Editor.
Desc: Publishes listings of going businesses that can be purchased, moved, and operated without loss of customers. *Type:* Newsletter.

Report on Business Magazine

The Globe & Mail
444 Front St. W.   Ph: (416)585-5000
Toronto, ON, Canada M5V   Fax: (416)585-5705
2S9
URL: http://www.robmagazine.com.
Contact: David Olive, Editor, (416)585-5316, fax: (416)585-5705; Stephen Petherbridge, Publisher, (416)585-5554, fax: (416)585-5641; Cheri Natale, Advertising Mgr., (416)585-5410, cnatale@globeandmail.ca.
Desc: Business magazine supplement to the Globe and Mail. *Type:* Periodical.

Report on IBM

DataTrends Publications Inc.
PO Box 4460   Ph: (703)779-0574
Leesburg, VA 20177   Free: 800-766-8130
   Fax: (703)779-2267
E-mail: dtrends@ix.netcom.com
URL: http://www.newsstand.lotus.com.
Contact: Jeff Caruso, Managing Editor.
Desc: Involved with International Business Machines Corporation (IBM) activities and lines of business, with emphasis on information systems in businesses, factories and homes. Contains news and articles on new IBM introductions, new markets and market strategies, and industry trends. *Type:* Newsletter.

Resource Guide Oregon High Technology

The Greater Hillsboro Chamber of Commerce
334 SE 5th Ave.   Ph: (503)693-1104
Hillsboro, OR 97123   Fax: (503)693-6716
E-mail: sueleblanc@hilchamber.org.
Contact: Howard Rice, Editor.
Desc: Over 3,000 electronic, computer, and other high-technology manufacturers, support companies and service organizations in Oregon and southwestern Washington. *Type:* Directory.

Reuter Business Report

Reuters Information Services Inc.
1700 Broadway   Ph: (212)603-3300
New York, NY 10019
Desc: Contains news and information on U.S. business trends, including market reports for stocks, the dollar, credit and bond prices, commodities, and futures. *Available:* LEXIS-NEXIS, NEXIS; LEXIS-NEXIS, NEXIS; LEXIS-NEXIS, LEXIS. *Type:* Database.

Review for CFOs & Investment Bankers

Brumberg Publications
124 Harvard St.   Ph: (617)734-1979
Brookline, MA 02146   Fax: (617)734-1989
E-mail: brumberg@compuserve.com
Contact: Bruce Brumberg, Editor.
Desc: Strategies and trends in capital raising and financial restructuring. *Type:* Newsletter.

Rhode Island Business Directory

infoUSA
5711 S. 86th Circle   Ph: (402)593-4600
PO Box 27347   Free: 800-555-6124
Omaha, NE 68127   Fax: (402)331-5481
E-mail: internet@infousa.com
URL: http://www.abii.com.
Contact: Peter J. Wilmarth, Publisher.
Desc: 44,000 businesses in Rhode Island. *Type:* Directory.

Roanoke Regional Chamber of Commerce Focus on Business

Roanoke Regional Chamber of Commerce
212 S. Jefferson St.   Ph: (540)983-0700
Roanoke, VA 24019   Fax: (540)983-0723
E-mail: business@roanokechamber.org
Contact: Kathleen H. Kinsey, Editor.
Desc: Contains information of interest to Roanoke area businesses. Recurring features include interviews, editorial and articles on legislative issues written from the business perspective, calendar of events, reports of meetings, news of educational opportunities, and news of members. *Type:* Newsletter.

Rocky Mountain High Technology Directory

Leading Edge Communications Inc.
1121 Old Hwy. 99 S.   Ph: (541)482-4990
Ashland, OR 97520   Fax: (541)482-4993
Contact: Philip W. Boesche, Editor; Kimberley L. Boesche, Editor.
Desc: Over 5,100 manufacturers and research and development firms in Arizona, Colorado, Montana, Nevada, New Mexico, Utah, and Wyoming engaged in high technology activities, including work with aerospace equipment and systems, biotechnology devices and materials, communications, computers, electronics, genetics, instruments, material handling systems, medical diagnostics, medical electronics, microelectronics, office automation, pharmaceuticals, robotics, video equipment, and other categories. *Type:* Directory.

The Rose Sheet

FDC Reports, Inc.
5550 Friendship Blvd., Suite 1   Ph: (301)657-9830
Chevy Chase, MD 20815
E-mail: fdcr@clark.net
URL: http://www.fdcreports.com
Desc: Monitors regulatory and legal developments for the cosmetics, toiletries, fragrances, and skin care industries, as well as scientific developments and testing methodologies. Also reports on cosmetics industry news, covering mergers and acquisitions, Europe 1992 developments, marketing strategies, new product introductions, and promotions and advertising at retail. *Available:* LEXIS-NEXIS, LEXIS; The Dialog Corporation, DIALOG; The Dialog Corporation, DIALOG; Ovid Technologies, Inc.; Ovid Technologies, Inc. *Type:* Database.

Russia and Commonwealth Business Law Report

LRP Publications
747 Dresher Rd.   Ph: (215)784-0941
PO Box 980   Free: 800-341-7874
Horsham, PA 19044-0980   Fax: (215)784-0870
E-mail: custserve@lrp.com
Contact: Al Celmer, Editor.
Desc: Contains text and analysis of legal and regulatory developments from the former Soviet republics for Western lawyers and business persons whose companies and clients transact, or wish to transact, business in Russia and the Commonwealth of Independent States. *Type:* Newsletter.

S Corporations Guide

CCH Inc.
2700 Lake Cook Rd.   Ph: (847)267-7000
Riverwoods, IL 60015   Free: 800-449-8114
   Fax: (847)224-8299
URL: http://www.cch.com
Contact: James Rooney, Editor; Joan Goode, Advertising Dir.
Desc: Publishes the rules for attaining and keeping an S Corporation status. *Type:* Newsletter.

S & P MarketScope

Standard & Poor's
25 Broadway   Ph: (212)208-8000
New York, NY 10004-1064   Free: 800-221-5277
   Fax: (212)208-0040
URL: http://www.stockinfo.standardpoor.com
Contact: Shauna Morrison, Managing Editor.
Desc: Over 7,000 companies in the "Reference Section" of Standard and Poors database, including all NYSE and ASE listed companies and 3,500 NASDAQ listed companies. *Type:* Directory.

S & P Online

Standard & Poor's
25 Broadway   Ph: (212)208-8363
New York, NY 10004-1064
URL: http://www.standardandpoors.com/ratings
Contact: Mary Maher, Marketing Manager, Electronic Services., (212)208-8429, fax: (212)412-0459.
Desc: Contains descriptive information on approximately 5600 publicly and privately held U.S. and non-U.S. corporations. For each company, provides name, address, telephone number, description of products and services, earnings outlook, historical earnings and dividends, and product line summaries. *Available:* CompuServe Information Service. *Type:* Database.

Saint John Business Today

Saint John Board of Trade
40 King St.   Ph: (506)634-8111
PO Box 6037   Fax: (506)632-2008
Saint John, NB, Canada E2L
4R5
Contact: Darryl Goyetche, Editor.
Desc: Discusses business, economics, and domestic commerce. Recurring features include interviews, news of research, reports of meetings, and columns titled the President's Column, Around the Board, the Committee File, Member Profile, the Bottomline, Business Barometer, and Welcome Aboard. *Type:* Newsletter.

St. Louis Market Record

Merchants Exchange of St. Louis
230 S. Bemiston, Ste. 1450   Ph: (314)725-5222
St. Louis, MO 63105   Fax: (314)725-4632
Contact: Gayle Moser, Editor.
Desc: Provides St. Louis market statistics in such fields as futures, membership trades, call sessions, seasonal range, nominal cash grain, cash feed, grain stocks, and barge freight rates. *Type:* Newsletter.

Sales Prospector

Westgate Publishing Co., Inc.

PO Box 185   Ph: (847)899-1271
Lake Bluff, IL 60044-0185   Free: 800-752-4050
    Fax: (847)899-2546

Desc: List of 80 to 100 industrial, commercial, and institutional construction, expansion, renovation, modernization, and relocation projects in new or existing buildings; reports on 100-150 firms in each newsletter. *Type:* Directory.

San Francisco Business Times—Book of Lists

San Francisco Business Times

Embarcadero Center West   Ph: (415)989-2522
275 Battery St., Ste. 940   Fax: (415)398-2494
San Francisco, CA 94111
E-mail: sanfrancisco@amcity.com
Contact: Steve Symanovich, Editor.
Desc: Compilation of lists of the top 25 companies in various industries in the Bay Area. *Type:* Directory.

San Mateo County Commerce & Industry Directory

Database Publishing Co.

1590 S. Lewis St.   Ph: (714)778-6400
PO Box 70024   Free: 800-888-8434
Anaheim, CA 92825-0024   Fax: (714)778-6811
E-mail: sales@databasepublishing.com
URL: http://www.databasepublishing.com; http://www.databasepublishing.com.
Desc: Some 2,800 manufacturers, wholesalers, and service companies, plus 6,150 executives, in San Mateo County, California. *Type:* Directory.

Santa Clara County Commerce & Industry Directory

Database Publishing Co.

1590 S. Lewis St.   Ph: (714)778-6400
PO Box 70024   Free: 800-888-8434
Anaheim, CA 92825-0024   Fax: (714)778-6811
E-mail: sales@databasepublishing.com
URL: http://www.databasepublishing.com; http://www.databasepublishing.com.
Desc: Some 5,000 manufacturers, wholesalers, and service companies—with an emphasis on high tech—in Santa Clara County, California. Includes 13,000 key executives. *Type:* Directory.

Santa Clarita Valley IndustryGuide

PDC Information Resources

1464 Madera Rd., Ste. N181   Ph: (805)584-0844
Simi Valley, CA 93065
Contact: Stephen Marinoff, Editor.
Desc: About 500 manufacturers and service companies with five or more employees located in the Santa Clarita Valley, California area. *Type:* Directory.

SEC & Business News

Worldwide Videotex-Telcom

PO Box 3273   Ph: (561)738-2276
Boynton Beach, FL 33424
E-mail: markedit@juno.com
Contact: Mark Wright, Publisher.
Desc: Contains the complete text of SEC Case Monitor, a monthly newsletter covering administrative, civil, and criminal case decisions from the U.S. Securities and Exchange Commission (SEC). *Type:* Database.

SEC Online

Disclosure Inc.

5161 River Rd.   Ph: (301)951-1753
Bethesda, MD 20816
E-mail: info@disclosure.com

URL: http://www.disclosure.com
Desc: Contains reports filed by public corporations with the U.S. Securities and Exchange Commission (SEC). *Available:* Thomson Financial Services, Inc., I/PLUS Direct; The Dialog Corporation, DIALOG; The Dialog Corporation, DIALOG; LEXIS-NEXIS, LEXIS; West Group, WESTLAW; Information America (IA); Dow Jones & Company, Inc.; Disclosure Inc.; Bridge Information Systems, Inc., Knight-Ridder Financial Information Group; Telescan, Inc.; Track Data Corporation; Bloomberg Financial Markets. *Type:* Database.

Self-Employed America

National Association for the Self-Employed

2121 Precinct Line Rd.   Ph: (817)428-4243
Hurst, TX 76054   Fax: (817)428-4210
URL: http://www.nase.org.
Contact: Heidi M. Williams, Managing Editor.
Desc: Magazine deseminating information on topics of interest to small-business owners, such as marketing, management, and pertinent legislative developments. Also presents success stories concerning Association members and describes Association activities. *Alt. Contact:* 2121 Precinct Line Rd., Hurst, TX 76054. *Type:* Periodical.

Senior Law Report

CD Publications

8204 Fenton St.   Ph: (301)588-6380
Silver Spring, MD 20910   Free: 800-666-6380
    Fax: (301)588-6385

E-mail: cdpubs@clark.net
Contact: William Gatesman, J.D., Editor.
Desc: Covers analysis of court rulings affecting age discrimination, social security, Medicare and seniors issues. *Type:* Newsletter.

Service Industries USA: Industry Analyses, Statistics, and Leading Organizations

Gale Group Inc.

27500 Drake Rd.   Ph: (248)699-4253
Farmington Hills, MI 48331-   Free: 800-877-GALE
3535   Fax: (248)699-8070
E-mail: galeord@galegroup.com; ecdi@statrom.com.
URL: http://www.galegroup.com.; http://www.gale.com.
Contact: Arsen J. Darnay, Editor, (248)356-6990, fax: (248)356-6426.
Desc: Lists of up to 75 leading companies and nonprofit organizations in service-related industries in the U.S., based on annual revenue. *Type:* Directory.

Service Reporter—Buyers Guide Issue

Technical Reporting Corp.

Palmer Publishing Co.

PO Box 3938   Ph: (907)373-9756
Palmer, AK 99645-3938   Fax: (907)745-6292
Contact: Ed Schwenn, Editor.
Desc: List of wholesalers, manufacturers, and exporters of air conditioning, heating, ventilating, and refrigerating equipment; trade associations. *Type:* Directory.

Set-Aside Alert

Washington Business Information, Inc.

1117 N. 19th St., No. 200   Ph: (703)247-3434
Arlington, VA 22209-1798   Fax: (703)247-3421
Contact: Margaret Ryan, Editor.
Desc: Addresses issues of interest to 8(a) SDB minority- and women-owned businesses that have federal government clientele. Covers networking and contact opportunities. *Type:* Newsletter.

Shoko Newsletter

Honolulu Japanese Chamber of Commerce

2454 S. Beretania St.   Ph: (808)949-5531
Honolulu, HI 96826   Fax: (808)949-3020
E-mail: hjcc@hula.net
Contact: John M. Tamura, Editor.
Desc: Provides articles concerning business and commerce in Hawaii. Recurring features include a calendar of events and columns titled President's Message and Duffer's Bulletin. *Type:* Newsletter.

Sibbald Guide to Every Public and the Top 150 Private Companies in Oklahoma, Louisiana, and Arkansas

Acorn Press, Inc.

14 Springhill   Ph: (201)895-7299
Randolph, NJ 07869
Contact: D. Evans, Publisher.
Desc: 285 public and privately-held corporations and financial institutions in Oklahoma, Louisiana, and Arkansas. *Type:* Directory.

Sibbald Guide to the Top 250 Public Companies and Top 250 Private Companies in Georgia, Florida, and the Carolinas

Acorn Press, Inc.

14 Springhill   Ph: (201)895-7299
Randolph, NJ 07869
Contact: D. Evans, Publisher.
Desc: 500 public and privately-held corporations and financial institutions in Georgia, Florida, and North and South Carolina. *Type:* Directory.

Sid Cato's Newsletter on Annual Reports

Cato Communications, Inc.

PO Box 19850   Ph: (616)344-2286
Kalamazoo, MI 49019-0850   Fax: (616)344-4145
E-mail: sidcato@sidcato.com
URL: http://www.sidcato.com.
Contact: Sid Cato, Editor, sidcato@sidcato.com.
Desc: Provides comment and criticism of the corporate annual report to shareholders. Discusses trends and reviews annual reports. *Type:* Newsletter.

Small Business Sourcebook

Gale Group Inc.

27500 Drake Rd.   Ph: (248)699-4253
Farmington Hills, MI 48331-   Free: 800-877-GALE
3535   Fax: (248)699-8070
E-mail: galeord@galegroup.com
URL: http://www.galegroup.com.; http://www.gale.com.
Contact: Theresa J. MacFarlane, Editor, theresa.macfarlane@gale.com; Amy R. Suchowski, Editor, amy.suchowski@gale.com.
Desc: Contains profiles for 336 specific types of small business. Each profile contains sources of start-up information, associations, educational programs, reference works, sources of supplies, statistical sources, trade periodicals, videos, trade shows and conventions, consultants, franchises, databases, business systems and software, libraries, research centers, and Internet databases. *Type:* Directory.

Smaller Business Association of New England—Membership Directory

Smaller Business Association of New England (SBANE)

204 2nd Ave.   Ph: (781)890-9070
Waltham, MA 02451   Free: 800-366-6803
    Fax: (781)890-4567

E-mail: info@sbane.org
URL: http://www.pbane.org
Contact: Julie M. Scofield, Editor.
Type: Directory.

Smoke Signals: Business Directory of Indian Country U.S.A.

Arrowstar Publishing
PO Box 100134   Ph: (303)715-9292
Colorado, CO 80250-0134   Fax: (303)936-7374
Contact: Dr. Gregory W. Frazier, Editor.
Desc: Approximately 3,500 American Indian and Alaska Native owned and operated businesses. *Type:* Directory.

Sorkins Directory of Business & Government— Chicago Edition

Sorkins Directories, Inc.
1001 Craig Rd., Ste. 260   Ph: (314)872-2101
St. Louis, MO 63146-6212   Free: 800-758-3228
                 Fax: (314)872-2102
E-mail: sorkins@sorkins.com
URL: http://www.sorkinsonline.com.
Contact: Pam Sorkin, Editor; Murray Sorkin, Editor.
Desc: Approximately 80,000 public and private companies, government agencies, and 400,000 executives in Illinois. Also includes areas of Wisconsin, Michigan, and Indiana. *Type:* Directory.

South Carolina Business Directory

infoUSA
5711 S. 86th Circle   Ph: (402)593-4600
PO Box 27347   Free: 800-555-6124
Omaha, NE 68127   Fax: (402)331-5481
E-mail: internet@infousa.com
URL: http://www.abii.com.
Contact: Peter J. Wilmarth, Publisher.
Desc: 144,000 businesses in South Carolina. *Type:* Directory.

South Dakota Business Directory

infoUSA
5711 S. 86th Circle   Ph: (402)593-4600
PO Box 27347   Free: 800-555-6124
Omaha, NE 68127   Fax: (402)331-5481
E-mail: internet@infousa.com
URL: http://www.abii.com.
Contact: Peter J. Wilmarth, Publisher.
Desc: 37,000 businesses in South Dakota. *Type:* Directory.

South Dakota Business Review

Business Research Bureau
University of South Dakota
School of Business   Ph: (605)677-5287
414 E. Clark   Fax: (605)677-5427
Vermillion, SD 57069-2390
Contact: Stephen Tracy, Editor.
Desc: Discusses business series. *Type:* Newsletter.

South Georgia Business Journal

South Georgia Business Journal, Inc.
PO Box 2036   Ph: (912)228-1299
Thomasville, GA 31799   Fax: (912)228-7033
E-mail: sgcoc@surfsouth.com
Contact: Lloyd Eckberg, Editor, Publisher & Editor.
Desc: Provides news and economic information on southern Georgia's (61 counties) businesses. Features issues on legislation, financial and business developments, and strategies. *Type:* Newsletter.

Southern California Business Directory and Buyers Guide

Database Publishing Co.
1590 S. Lewis St.   Ph: (714)778-6400
PO Box 70024   Free: 800-888-8434
Anaheim, CA 92825-0024   Fax: (714)778-6811
E-mail: sales@databasepublishing.com
URL: http://www.databasepublishing.com; http://www.databasepublishing.com.

Desc: Over 30,000 manufacturers, distributors, and service firms in 13 southern California counties. *Type:* Directory.

Southern Mississippi Plan and Development District

2015 15th St A   Ph: (228)868-2311
Gulfport, MS 39501-2021   Fax: (228)868-7094
E-mail: lesn@earthlink.net
URL: http://www.smpdd.com
Contact: Leslie Newcomb, Exec.Dir.
Desc: Promotes economic development in South Mississippi. *Type:* Association.

Southwest Economy

Federal Reserve Bank of Dallas
PO Box 655906   Ph: (214)651-5254
Dallas, TX 75265-5906   Free: 800-333-4460
Contact: W. Michael Cox, Editor; Mine K. Yucel, Editor.
Desc: Supplies articles that discuss the various aspects of the Southwest economy. *Type:* Newsletter.

Spain's 30,000 Top Companies

Dun & Bradstreet
3 Sylvan Way   Ph: (973)605-6442
Parsippany, NJ 07054-3896   Free: 800-526-0651
                 Fax: (973)605-6911
E-mail: dnbmdd@dnb.com
Desc: 15,000 companies in Spain with annual sales of at least $500,000. *Type:* Directory.

Standard Directory of Advertisers

National Register Publishing (NRP)
121 Chanlon Rd.   Ph: (908)464-6800
New Providence, NJ 07974
Desc: Contains information on more than 25,000 companies that place national and/or regional advertising of more than $200,000 annually. *Available:* LEXIS-NEXIS, NEXIS; The Dialog Corporation, DIALOG. *Type:* Database.

Standard & Poor's Corporate Descriptions plus NEWS

Standard & Poor's
25 Broadway   Ph: (212)208-8363
New York, NY 10004-1064
URL: http://www.standardandpoors.com/ratings
Contact: Michael A. Antinoro, Director, (212)208-8364, fax: (212)412-0459.
Desc: Provides strategic and financial information on approximately 12,000 publicly held U.S. and non-U.S. corporations that trade securities on the New York Stock Exchange, American Stock Exchange, regional stock exchanges, the NASDAQ system, Over-the-Counter in the United States, and selected Canadian and international stock exchanges. *Available:* The Dialog Corporation, DIALOG; FactSet Data Systems, Inc.; LEXIS-NEXIS. *Type:* Database.

Standard & Poor's Corporation Records

Standard & Poor's
25 Broadway   Ph: (212)208-8000
New York, NY 10004-1064   Free: 800-221-5277
                 Fax: (212)208-0040
URL: http://www.stockinfo.standardpoor.com
Contact: Carol Puricelli, Editor.
Desc: Over 12,000 publicly-owned companies. *Type:* Directory.

Standard & Poor's Daily News

Standard & Poor's
25 Broadway   Ph: (212)208-8363
New York, NY 10004-1064
URL: http://www.standardandpoors.com/ratings

Contact: Mary Maher, Marketing Manager, Electronic Services., (212)208-8429, fax: (212)412-0459.
Desc: Contains the complete text of more than 800,000 financial news stories related to any of some 12,000 leading public corporations. Covers these topics: financial statements, including annual reports, preliminary annual earnings, current position, interim earnings, and proforma reports; changes in dividend payments; sale of securities, with details of issues; Standard & Poor's Bond ratings; company estimates of sales, earnings, and capital and research expenditures; acquisition and merger activities; contract awards, new products and price increases; plants and additions; lease arrangements; joint ventures; changes to lines of business; changes in officers and directors; and all other corporate news of public interest. *Available:* The Dialog Corporation, DIALOG; CompuServe Information Service, Knowledge Index; LEXIS-NEXIS, LEXIS; LEXIS-NEXIS, NEXIS. *Type:* Database.

Standard & Poor's 500 Directory

Index Products & Services
Standard & Poor's Corp.
25 Broadway   Ph: (212)208-8705
New York, NY 10004   Free: 800-233-2310
                 Fax: (212)412-0586
Contact: Cindy Cizazio, Editor.
Desc: The 500 companies included in the Standard & Poor's 500 Stock Index. *Type:* Directory.

Standard & Poor's MarketScope

Standard & Poor's
MarketScope Services
25 Broadway, 18th Fl.   Ph: (212)208-8600
New York, NY 10004-1064
URL: http://www.standardandpoors.com/ratings
Desc: A financial information service that contains descriptive and financial data on more than 7500 companies, reports and analysis of the stock and bond markets, and financial investment news. Comprised of the following 2 section: • Reference Section--contains descriptive information for each company, including background information, commentaries on future prospects, earnings and dividend projections (for 1100 major companies), and sales and earnings data by lines of business. *Available:* CompuServe Information Service; Dow Jones Interactive Publishing; Quotron Systems, Inc.; Track Data Corporation; ADP Network Services, Inc.; Telerate Systems Inc.; Telescan, Inc.; Beta Systems; Bunker Ramo; Shark Information Systems; Bloomberg Financial Markets. *Type:* Database.

Standard & Poor's MidCap 400 Directory

Index Products & Services
Standard & Poor's Corp.
25 Broadway   Ph: (212)208-8705
New York, NY 10004   Free: 800-233-2310
                 Fax: (212)412-0586
Contact: Cindy Azazio, Editor.
Desc: The 400 companies included in the Standard & Poor's MidCap 400 Index. *Type:* Directory.

Standard & Poor's Register - Biographical

Standard & Poor's
25 Broadway   Ph: (212)208-8363
New York, NY 10004-1064
URL: http://www.standardandpoors.com/ratings
Contact: Mary Maher, Marketing Manager, Electronic Services., (212)208-8429, fax: (212)412-0459.
Desc: Contains biographical profiles of more than 71,000 prominent business executives and directors of publicly and privately held U.S. and non-U.S. corporations. *Available:* The Dialog Corporation, DIALOG; The Dialog Corporation, DIALOG; CompuServe Information Service, Knowledge Index; LEXIS-NEXIS, LEXIS. *Type:* Database.

Standard & Poor's Register - Corporate

Standard & Poor's
25 Broadway   Ph: (212)208-8363
New York, NY 10004-1064
URL: http://www.standardandpoors.com/ratings

Contact: Mary Maher, Marketing Manager, Electronic Services., (212)208-8429, fax: (212)412-0459.

Desc: Contains descriptive information on more than 56,000 publicly and privately held U.S. and non-U.S. corporations. *Available:* The Dialog Corporation, DIALOG; The Dialog Corporation, DIALOG; CompuServe Information Service, Knowledge Index; LEXIS-NEXIS, LEXIS; LEXIS-NEXIS, NEXIS. *Type:* Database.

Standard & Poor's Register of Corporations, Directors and Executives

Standard & Poor's
25 Broadway   Ph: (212)208-8000
New York, NY 10004-1064   Free: 800-221-5277
                               Fax: (212)208-0040
URL: http://www.stockinfo.standardpoor.com

Contact: Thomas A. Lupo, Publisher.

Desc: Over 55,000 public and privately held corporations in the United States, including names and titles of over 400,000 officials (Volume 1); 70,000 biographies of directors and executives (Volume 2). *Type:* Directory.

STAT-SCAN

Wright Investors' Service (WIS)
1000 Lafayette Blvd.   Ph: (203)330-5000
Bridgeport, CT 06604
E-mail: fundswisconsini.com
URL: http://www.wisi.com

Contact: Harivadan K. Kapadia, Sr. V.P., (203)330-5090.

Desc: Contains company profile and fundamental analysis and price performance data for more than 3000 companies listed on the New York Stock Exchange (excluding closed-end investment companies, real estate investment trusts, and securities brokerage firms) and selected other publicly owned companies. Includes Worldscope-assigned quality ratings and percentile rankings based on quality, investment acceptance, financial strength, profitability and stability, growth, current value, and timing as well as projected earnings and dividends for the next 2 years and a 5-year projected growth rate for earnings and dividends compared with the last 5 years, when available. *Available:* Quotron Systems, Inc. *Type:* Database.

State Journal

State Journal Corporation
PO Box 28   Ph: (304)344-1630
Charleston, WV 25321   Fax: (304)345-2721

Contact: Jack Bailey.

Desc: Covers business issues in West Virginia; contains profiles and opinions. Recurring features include letters to the editor, interviews, and new business listings. *Type:* Newsletter.

State Sources of Company Intelligence

Washington Researchers
416 Hungerford Dr., Ste. 315   Ph: (301)251-9550
Rockville, MD 20850   Fax: (301)251-9526
E-mail: research@researchers.com

Contact: Michele Newman.

Desc: State sources of company intelligence in the U.S., including information about plants, expansions, equipment, processes, finances, strategies, executives, as well as associations, organizations, and publications that focus on state-related issues. *Type:* Directory.

Stockholders & Creditors News Service

Andrews Publications
175 Strafford Ave., Bldg. 4, Ste.   Ph: (610)225-0510
140   Free: 800-345-1101
Wayne, PA 19087   Fax: (610)225-0501

Contact: Bob Sullivan, Editor.

Desc: Reports on proceedings under Chapter II of the Bankruptcy Reform Act concerning the LTV Corporation. *Type:* Newsletter.

Strategic Direction Newsletter

Strategic Direction Publishers
5352 Ashley Rd.   Ph: (703)830-5507
Fairfax, VA 22030   Fax: (703)830-5506

Desc: Offers strategic direction for businesses. *Type:* Newsletter.

Subsidiaries & Affiliates of U.S. Companies in Brazil

U.S. Chamber of Commerce
International Division Publications
1615 H St. NW   Ph: (202)463-5460
Washington, DC 20062-2000   Fax: (202)463-3114

Desc: U.S. subsidiary and affiliate companies in Brazil. *Type:* Directory.

Subsidiaries of German Firms in the U.S.

German American Chamber of Commerce
40 W. 57th St.   Ph: (212)974-8830
New York, NY 10019-4092   Fax: (212)974-8867
E-mail: gaccny@compuserve.com

Contact: Sven C. Oehme, Editor.

Desc: Over 1,700 German firms and subsidiaries in the U.S. *Type:* Directory.

Success Magazine

Success Magazine
733 3rd Ave., 10th Fl.   Ph: (212)883-7100
New York, NY 10017   Fax: (212)949-7002
E-mail: letters@successmagazine.com.
URL: http://www.successmagazine.com.

Contact: Jon Spoelstra, Publisher; Joanna Smith Bears, Editor, jbsers@successmagazine.com.

Desc: Entrepreneurial business magazine. *Type:* Periodical.

Success Orientation

Success Publications, Inc.
PO Drawer 487   Ph: (770)992-6060
Roswell, GA 30077-0487   Free: 800-672-8677

Contact: Dr. DuPree Jordan, Jr., Editor and Publisher.

Desc: Contains ideas and articles which focus on personal and professional development. *Type:* Newsletter.

Successful Meetings

Successful Meetings
355 Park Ave. S.   Ph: (212)592-6403
New York, NY 10010   Fax: (212)592-6600
E-mail: 72262.427@compuserve.com.
URL: http://www.sucessmtgs.com.

Contact: Stan Itzkowitz, Advertising Mgr., (212)592-6437, fax: (212)592-6409, sitzkowitz@billcom.com; Julie Barker, Editor-in-Chief, (212)592-6420, jbarker@successmtgs.com; Richard O'Connor, Publisher, (212)592-6416, roconnor@successmtgs.com.

Desc: Magazine focusing on conventions, meetings, exhibits, training, and incentive travel. Includes annual directory issue. *Type:* Periodical.

The Supervisor's Guide to Cost Control

Clement Communications, Inc.
Concord Industrial Park   Ph: (610)459-1700
10 LaCrue Ave.   Free: 800-345-8101
Concordville, PA 19331   Fax: (610)459-0936
E-mail: editor@clement.com.

Contact: Linda Brandon, Managing Editor; Mike Johnson, Sr.Ed.; George Clement, Publisher.

Desc: Provides supervisors and managers with information and techniques on cutting costs within a business. Includes articles on banking, increasing productivity, and employee recognition. *Type:* Newsletter.

The Supervisor's Guide to Improved Customer Service & Retention

Clement Communications, Inc.
Concord Industrial Park   Ph: (610)459-1700
10 LaCrue Ave.   Free: 800-345-8101
Concordville, PA 19331   Fax: (610)459-0936
E-mail: editor@clement.com.

Contact: Mike Johnson, Sr. Editor; Robi Miller, Managing Editor; Maureen Solon, Exec. Editor; George Clement, Publisher.

Desc: Provides managers and supervisors with techniques and strategies to improve customer service and employee satisfaction. Includes information on recruiting higher quality employees. *Type:* Newsletter.

Swap Meet Magazine

Forum Publishing Co.
383 E. Main St.   Ph: (516)574-5000
Centerport, NY 11721   Fax: (516)754-0630
E-mail: forum123@juno.com
URL: http://www.forum123.com

Desc: Manufacturers and importers of jewelry, electronics, clothing, cosmetics, watches, novelties, and other items that are sold to merchandise retailers and flee market vendors at wholesale prices. *Type:* Directory.

Sweden in America

Swedish-American Chamber of Commerce
599 Lexington Ave., 12th Fl.   Ph: (212)838-5530
New York, NY 10022   Free: (212)838-5530
                               Fax: (212)755-7953

Contact: Margaretha S. Murphy, Editor.

Desc: Companies in the U.S. with ties to Sweden. *Type:* Directory.

Sweden Online

Swedish Trade Council, North America
150 N. Michigan Ave., Ste.   Ph: (312)781-6222
1200   Free: 888-ASK-
Chicago, IL 60601-7594   SWED
                               Fax: (312)346-0683
E-mail: info@arsswedentrade.com
URL: http://www.swedentrade.com/

Desc: The Swedish Trade council Provides information for North Americans considering business in, traveling to or just plain curious about Sweden. Includes yellow pages of Swedish-American companies. *Type:* Database.

Swedish Related Companies in the U.S.A.

Swedish-American Chamber of Commerce
599 Lexington Ave., 12th Fl.   Ph: (212)838-5530
New York, NY 10022   Free: (212)838-5530
                               Fax: (212)755-7953

Contact: Margaretha S. Murphy, Editor.

Desc: Swedish-related companies in the U.S. and their parent companies; chambers of commerce, trade offices, embassies and consulates, information offices, and tourist offices. *Type:* Directory.

Taiwan Product Guide

Todd Publications
PO Box 635 Ph: (914)358-6213
Nyack, NY 10960 Free: 800-747-1056
Fax: (914)358-1059

E-mail: toddpub@aol.com
URL: http://www.toddpublications.com
Contact: Carlos DePaula, Editor.
Desc: More than 6,000 Taiwan exporters. *Type:* Directory.

Taiwan's Leading Corporations

Dun & Bradstreet
3 Sylvan Way Ph: (973)605-6442
Parsippany, NJ 07054-3896 Free: 800-526-0651
Fax: (973)605-6911

E-mail: dnbmdd@dnb.com
Desc: 8,000 leading public and private companies in Taiwan. *Type:* Directory.

Taking Stocks

The Business Journal
PO Box 14490 Ph: (503)274-8733
Portland, OR 97293 Fax: (503)227-2650
E-mail: pdxbj@teleport.com.
Contact: Nancy Nilles, Editor.
Desc: About 75 public firms that are either based in Portland, Oregon, or have a strong presence there. *Type:* Directory.

Tampa Bay Business Guild

1222 S. Dale Mabry, Ste. 656 Ph: (813)237-3751
Tampa, FL 33629-5009
E-mail: tbbg@aol.com
Contact: Bob Gunter, Pres.
Desc: Business owners, consumers, and professionals united to improve business and cultural opportunities in the gay and lesbian community. *Type:* Association.

Target Atlanta

The Atlanta Journal and Constitution
72 Marietta St. NW Ph: (404)526-5151
PO Box 4689 Free: 800-846-6672
Atlanta, GA 30302-4689 Fax: (404)526-5746
Contact: Tamara Witt, Editor.
Desc: Provides information to businesses aiming to "target" the city of Atlanta, Georgia. Carries market trends, retailing innovations and areas of potential, and advertising and merchandising suggestions for all industries. *Type:* Newsletter.

TD Quarterly Economic Report

TD Economics
Toronto Dominion Bank Ph: (416)982-8065
PO Box 1, TD Centre Fax: (416)944-5536
Toronto, ON, Canada M5K 1A2
E-mail: economic@tdbank.ca.
URL: http://www.tdbank.ca.
Contact: Ruth Getter, Editor.
Desc: Presents current economic conditions in Canada, the U.S., and overseas. Includes forecasts of economic activity, inflation, interest rates, and exchange rates. *Type:* Newsletter.

Technology Dallas

Greater Dallas Chamber
1201 Elm St., Ste. 2000 Ph: (214)746-6704
Dallas, TX 75270 Fax: (214)746-6799
E-mail: mchapman@dallaschamber.org.
Contact: Laura Brumley, Editor; Charlotte Fowler, Editor; John Christian, Editor.
Desc: High technology and related companies in the greater Dallas area. *Type:* Directory.

Technology Directory—San Diego County Edition

Alexander Publishing
PO Box 840 Ph: (619)454-6420
La Jolla, CA 92038-0840 Free: 800-605-6150
Fax: (619)454-6315

E-mail: meyer@alexandercap.com
Contact: Jennifer Jackson, Editor, jennifer@alexandercap.com.
Desc: Over 840 high-technology firms producing or marketing products in San Diego County. *Type:* Directory.

Teikoku Databank: Japanese Companies

TecSpec
5849 Lost Mountain Rd.
Roanoke, VA 24018-8017

Desc: Approximately 220,000 Japanese corporations; all have designated official English-language company names or most of them are taking place in "Kaisha Neukan." *Type:* Directory.

Tennessee Business Directory

infoUSA
5711 S. 86th Circle Ph: (402)593-4600
PO Box 27347 Free: 800-555-6124
Omaha, NE 68127 Fax: (402)331-5481
E-mail: internet@infousa.com
URL: http://www.abii.com.

Contact: Peter J. Wilmarth, Publisher.

Desc: 202,000 businesses in Tennessee. *Type:* Directory.

Tennessee State Handbook

The Bar List Publishing Co.
PO Box 948 Ph: (847)498-0100
Northbrook, IL 60065 Free: 800-726-1007
Fax: (847)498-6695

E-mail: info@barlist.com

Contact: Leslie Rodgers, Editor.

Desc: Licensed property, liability, and life insurance companies and agencies, adjusters, and appraisers (SIC 094) in Tennessee. *Type:* Directory.

Texas Business Directory

infoUSA
5711 S. 86th Circle Ph: (402)593-4600
PO Box 27347 Free: 800-555-6124
Omaha, NE 68127 Fax: (402)331-5481
E-mail: internet@infousa.com
URL: http://www.abii.com.

Contact: Peter J. Wilmarth, Publisher.

Desc: 757,000 businesses in Texas. *Type:* Directory.

Texas Business Review

Bureau of Business Research
Graduate School of Business
University of Texas at Austin
PO Box 7459 Ph: (512)471-1616
Austin, TX 78713 Free: 888-212-4386
Fax: (512)471-1063
E-mail: bbr@uts.cc.utexas.edu; danhardy@mail.utexas.edu.
URL: http://www.utexas.edu/depts/bbr.

Contact: Lois G. Shrout, Editor, (512)475-7809, fax: (512)475-7809, sallyf@mail.utexas.edu.

Desc: Comments on the current economic climate in Texas and the Southwest. *Type:* Newsletter.

Texas/Louisiana Gulf Coast Regional Industrial Buying Guide

Thomas Regional Directory Co., Inc.
5 Penn Plaza Ph: (212)629-2100
New York, NY 10001 Fax: (212)290-7335
E-mail: info@trdnet.com
URL: http://www.thomasregional.com.
Contact: Marie McGurk, Editorial Dir.; Adrienne Toth, Managing Editor; Nancy Bromberg, Contracts Administration Mgr.
Desc: More than 25,000 manufacturers of industrial products; related industrial services, such as trucking and maintenance services; distributors; and manufacturers' representatives in the southern portions of Texas and Louisiana. *Type:* Directory.

Thailand Product Guide

Todd Publications
PO Box 635 Ph: (914)358-6213
Nyack, NY 10960 Free: 800-747-1056
Fax: (914)358-1059

E-mail: toddpub@aol.com
URL: http://www.toddpublications.com
Contact: Carlos DePaula, Editor.
Desc: Over 1,500 Thailand exporters. *Type:* Directory.

Town of Hempstead Economic Development

c/o Robert Francis, Ph: (516)538-7100
Commissioner Fax: (516)538-4264
200 N Franklin St.
Hempstead, NY 11550
Contact: Robert Francis, Commissioner.
Type: Association.

Trade & Industry ASAP™

The Gale Group
27500 Drake Rd. Ph: (248)699-4253
Farmington Hills, MI 48331-3535
URL: http://www.galegroup.com
Contact: (650)378-5000, fax: (800)676-2345.
Desc: Contains the complete text, citations, and abstracts (since 1992) for more than 1.58 million selected articles appearing in more than 200 chosen from the 500-plus business and trade periodicals indexed in Trade and Industry Index (described in a separate entry). Includes the complete text of press releases from BusinessWire, PR Newswire, and Kyodo News International, Inc. *Available:* The Dialog Corporation, DataStar; Bell & Howell Information and Learning. *Type:* Database.

TRADEMARKSCAN—U.S. State

Thomson & Thomson
500 Victory Rd. Ph: (617)479-1600
North Quincy, MA 02171-3145 Free: 888-477-3447
Fax: (617)786-8381

URL: http://www.thomson-thomson.com.
Desc: Over 970,000 trademarks registered with the secretaries of state in the U.S. and Puerto Rico. *Type:* Directory.

Trade Show Exhibitors Association

5501 Backlick Rd., Ste. 105 Ph: (703)941-3725
Springfield, VA 22151 Fax: (703)941-8275
E-mail: tsea@tsea.org
Contact: Michael Bandy, Pres.
Desc: Exhibitors working to improve the effectiveness of trade shows as a marketing tool. Purposes are to promote the progress and development of trade show exhibiting; to collect and disseminate trade show information; conduct studies, surveys, and stated projects designed to improve trade shows; to foster good relations and communications

with organizations representing others in the industry; to undertake other activities necessary to promote the welfare of member companies. Sponsors Exhibit Industry Education Foundation and professional exhibiting seminars; the forum series of educational programs on key issues affecting the industry. *Type:* Association.

Trendwatch

Mentor Communications
PO Box 290   Ph: (516)741-8887
Manhasset, NY 11030   Fax: (516)741-3131
Contact: Hank Boerner, Editor.

Desc: "Designed to be informative, provocative, entertaining, and above all enlightening," presenting personal observations concerning trends and developments that affect the American business community. Monitors local, regional, national, and international developments and trends, with an emphasis on tracking the "American Spirit" and its function in commerce and government. *Type:* Newsletter.

Troubled Company Prospector

Beard Group, Inc.
PO Box 9867   Ph: (301)951-6400
Washington, DC 20016   Fax: (301)951-3621
E-mail: chris@beard.com
Contact: Annamarie Martin, Editor.

Desc: Focuses on companies in transition. *Type:* Newsletter.

TRW Trade Payment Guide

TRW Business Credit Services
505 City Pkwy. W., 10th Fl. Ph: (714)385-7700
Orange, CA 92868   Free: 800-344-0603
                             Fax: (714)938-2586
Desc: About 2,500,000 credit active business locations. *Type:* Directory.

Try Us: National Minority Business Directory

Try Us Resources, Inc.
2105 Central Ave. NE   Ph: (612)781-6819
Minneapolis, MN 55418   Fax: (612)781-0109
E-mail: tryusdir@mr.net
URL: http://www.tryusdir.com
Contact: Leslie Bonds, Editor.

Desc: Over 7,000 minority-owned companies capable of supplying their goods and services on national or regional levels. *Type:* Directory.

Tulsa Business Chronicle

World Publishing Co.
315 S. Boulder Ave.   Ph: (918)581-8583
P.O. Box 1770
Tulsa, OK 74102
E-mail: worldlib@ionet.net
Contact: Austin Farley, Library Director, (918)581-8583, fax: (918)581-8425, worldlib@ionet.net.

Desc: Contains the complete text of the Tulsa Business Chronicle, a weekly publication providing coverage of business news of interest to Tulsa-area business professionals. Covers such areas of local industry as energy, aerospace, computer, and health care/medical services, as well as such large Tulsa-based corporations as American Airlines, McDonnell-Douglas, Rockwell International, and Sun-Oil. *Available:* LEXIS-NEXIS, NEXIS. *Type:* Database.

The UK/USA Investment Directory & Business Resource

British-American Chamber of Commerce
52 Vanderbilt, 20th Fl.   Ph: (212)661-4060
New York, NY 10017   Fax: (212)661-4074
URL: http://www.bacc.org; http://www.uk-usadirectory.com.

Desc: Over 6,000 British and American companies and their approximately 4,000 subsidiaries in the United Kingdom and the United States. *Type:* Directory.

U.S. - ASEAN Business Council

Executive Director
1400 L St. NW, Ste. 375   Ph: (202)289-1911
Washington, DC 20005-3509   Fax: (202)289-0519
E-mail: jehayes@usasean.org
URL: http://www.us-asean.org
Contact: Joseph Hayes, Exec.Dir.

Desc: Promotes increased trade between the United States and the countries comprising the Association of South East Asian Nations. *Type:* Association.

U.S. Business Reporter

The Dialog Corporation
DIALOG
11000 Regency Pkwy., Ste. 400 Ph: (919)462-8600
Cary, NC 27511
URL: http://www.dialog.com
Contact: Marketing.

Desc: Contains the complete text of the Business News sections from selected U.S. newspapers and newswires. *Available:* The Dialog Corporation, DIALOG. *Type:* Database.

U.S. Business in South Africa

Investor Responsibility Research Center, Inc. (IRRC)
1350 Connecticut Ave., NW,   Ph: (202)833-0700
  Ste. 700   Fax: (202)833-3555
Washington, DC 20036
URL: http://www.irrc.org
Contact: Meg Voorhes, Editor.

Desc: Over 550 U.S. companies with business links to South Africa. *Type:* Directory.

United States Council for International Business

1212 Ave. of the Americas, 21st Ph: (212)354-4480
  Fl.   Fax: (212)575-0327
New York, NY 10036
E-mail: info@uscib.org
URL: http://www.uscib.org
Contact: Abraham Katz, Pres.

Desc: Serves as the U.S. National Committee of the International Chamber of Commerce. Enables multinational enterprises to operate effectively by representing their interests to intergovernmental and governmental bodies and by keeping enterprises advised of international developments having a major impact on their operations. *Type:* Association.

U.S. Firms in Germany

German American Chamber of Commerce
40 W. 57th St.   Ph: (212)974-8830
New York, NY 10019-4092   Fax: (212)974-8867
E-mail: gaccny@compuserve.com
Desc: Over 700 U.S. companies located in Germany. *Type:* Directory.

U.S. National Center for Nonprofit Boards

U.S. National Center for Nonprofit Boards
PO Box 92294   Ph: (202)452-6262
Washington, DC 20090-2294   Free: 800-883-6262
                             Fax: (202)452-6299
E-mail: ncbn@ncnb.org
URL: http://www.ncnb.org/html/home.html
Desc: The National Center for Nonprofit Boards (NCNB) provides information to improve the effectiveness of nonprofit organizations by strengthening their boards of directors through working together. It includes information on key issues in nonprofit governance, articles on responsibilities of the board chairperson, creating successful advisory committees, nonprofit bylaws, and a sample job description for a chief executive. *Type:* Database.

U.S. News & World Report

U.S. News and World Report, Inc.
2400 N St., N.W.   Ph: (202)955-2000
Washington, DC 20037
URL: http://www.usnews.com
Desc: Contains the complete text of U.S. News & World Report magazine, covering national and international political, economic, and business news. *Available:* Bell & Howell Information and Learning. *Type:* Database.

UPI News

United Press International (UPI)
1510 H St. NW   Ph: (202)898-8000
Washington, DC 20005
URL: http://www.upi.com
Desc: Contains the complete text of news items transmitted over the United Press International newswire. Includes national and international news, current events, the political scene at the federal and state government levels, business and financial sports news, columns and commentaries, and standing features. *Available:* The Dialog Corporation, DIALOG; The Dialog Corporation, DIALOG; CompuServe Information Service, Knowledge Index; AT&T EasyLink Services. *Type:* Database.

UPSIDE

UPSIDE Media Inc.
2015 Pioneer Ct.   Ph: (650)377-0950
San Mateo, CA 94403-1736   Fax: (650)377-1961
E-mail: subs@upside.com; edit@upside.com.
Contact: Richard Brandt, Editor; Jody Stathakis, Advertising Dir.; Frank Ha, Circulation Mgr.

Desc: Consumer magazine covering business and technology. *Type:* Periodical.

USA/France Business and Culture Update

Integrated Information Technologies
3 Church Circle, Ste. 211   Ph: (410)280-1616
Annapolis, MD 21401   Free: 800-FRANCE95
                             Fax: (410)280-1617
Contact: Karen S. Burns, Editor.

Desc: List of organizations or sources providing information to businesses wishing to enter markets in France. *Type:* Directory.

USMTR/NAFTA Information Center Databases

Texas A&M International University
5201 University Blvd.   Ph: (956)326-2001
Laredo, TX 78041-1900
URL: http://e3-5b.tamiu.edu/search.htm
Contact: nafta@tamiu.edu.

Desc: This full-text database contains information, articles, and other material on NAFTA (the North American Free Trade Agreement) and its effects. Search by keywords to find NAFTA-related information on commerce, trade, and economics in the United States, Mexico, and Central and South America. *Type:* Database.

USSR Business

Stamm Publishing, Ltd.
389-810 W. Broadway   Fax: (604)873-4347
Vancouver, BC, Canada V5Z
  4C9
Contact: R. Stamm, Editor.

Desc: Reports on business activity and news in the former Soviet Union. *Type:* Newsletter.

Utah Business Directory

infoUSA
5711 S. 86th Circle   Ph: (402)593-4600
PO Box 27347   Free: 800-555-6124
Omaha, NE 68127   Fax: (402)331-5481
E-mail: internet@infousa.com

URL: http://www.abii.com.

Contact: Peter J. Wilmarth, Publisher.

Desc: 75,000 businesses in Utah. *Type:* Directory.

Utah Economic and Business Review

Bureau of Economic & Business Research
1645 E. Campus Center Dr., Ph: (801)581-6333
  Rm. 401 Fax: (801)581-3354
Salt Lake City, UT 84112-9302
E-mail: bureau@business.utah.edu
URL: http://www.business.utah.edu/BEBR/

Desc: Reviews businesses and economics in Utah. Recurring features include a column titled Utah Business Statistics. *Type:* Newsletter.

VARBUSINESS

CMP Media Inc.
600 Community Dr. Ph: (516)562-5000
Manhasset, NY 11030 Fax: (516)562-7830
URL: http://www.cmp.net

Contact: Tom Farre, Executive Editor; Claire DiMarco, Publisher.

Desc: A management-related publication featuring trends and profiles of people in the VAR market. *Type:* Periodical.

Venezuela Yearbook

U.S. Chamber of Commerce
International Division Publications
1615 H St. NW Ph: (202)463-5460
Washington, DC 20062-2000 Fax: (202)463-3114

Desc: Businesses and business contacts in Venezuela and Venezuelan contacts in the U.S. *Type:* Directory.

Ventura County IndustryGuide

PDC Information Resources
1464 Madera Rd., Ste. N181 Ph: (805)584-0844
Simi Valley, CA 93065

Contact: Stephen Marinoff, Editor.

Desc: Approximately 2,000 manufacturers and service companies in the Ventura County, California area. *Type:* Directory.

Vermont Business Directory

infoUSA
5711 S. 86th Circle Ph: (402)593-4600
PO Box 27347 Free: 800-555-6124
Omaha, NE 68127 Fax: (402)331-5481
E-mail: internet@infousa.com
URL: http://www.abii.com.

Contact: Peter J. Wilmarth, Publisher.

Desc: 31,000 businesses in Vermont. *Type:* Directory.

Virginia Business Directory

infoUSA
5711 S. 86th Circle Ph: (402)593-4600
PO Box 27347 Free: 800-555-6124
Omaha, NE 68127 Fax: (402)331-5481
E-mail: internet@infousa.com
URL: http://www.abii.com.

Contact: Peter J. Wilmarth, Publisher.

Desc: 253,000 businesses in Virginia. *Type:* Directory.

Virginia State Handbook

The Bar List Publishing Co.
PO Box 948 Ph: (847)498-0100
Northbrook, IL 60065 Free: 800-726-1007
  Fax: (847)498-6695
E-mail: info@barlist.com

Contact: Leslie Rodgers, Editor; Bruce Rodgers, Editor.

Desc: Licensed property, liability, and life insurance companies and agencies, adjusters, and appraisers (SIC 094) in Virginia. *Type:* Directory.

Virginia Vendor Listing of Minority Businesses

Virginia State Office of Minority Business Enterprise
200-202 9th St. Office Bldg. Ph: (804)786-5560
Richmond, VA 23219

Contact: Daisy Williams, Editor.

Desc: Nearly 3,000 firms offering professional, commercial, industrial, and consumer products and services. *Type:* Directory.

The Wall Street Journal

Dow Jones & Company, Inc.
P.O. Box 300 Ph: (609)520-4000
Princeton, NJ 08543-0300
URL: http://www.dj.com

Desc: Contains the complete text of The Wall Street Journal, a daily newspaper reporting news and developments affecting national and international business, finance, and economics. Covers all news stories and features. *Available:* Dow Jones & Company, Inc.; Dow Jones & Company, Inc.; LEXIS-NEXIS, NEXIS; Bell & Howell Information and Learning, UMI Ondisc. *Type:* Database.

Wall Street Journal

Dow Jones & Co., Inc.
200 Liberty St. Ph: (212)416-3675
New York, NY 10281 Free: 800-622-ASIA
  Fax: (212)416-2676

Contact: Robert Bartley, Editor; Peter R. Kann, Publisher; Paul Atkinson, V.P. Advertising.

Desc: Newspaper reporting on national business and finance. *Type:* Periodical.

The Wall Street Journal (Midwest Edition)

Dow Jones & Co., Inc.
1 S. Wacker Dr., Ste. 2100 Ph: (312)750-4000
Chicago, IL 60606 Fax: (312)750-4153

Contact: Joe Gurgone, Midwest Administration.

Desc: National business and finance newspaper. *Type:* Periodical.

Wall Street Journal (Western Edition)

Dow Jones & Co., Inc.
201 California St., Ste. 1350 Ph: (415)986-6886
San Francisco, CA 94111 Fax: (415)956-0797

Contact: Paul Atkinson, Advertising Mgr.

Desc: National business and finance newspaper. *Type:* Periodical.

Ward's Business Directory of U.S. Private and Public Companies

Gale Group Inc.
27500 Drake Rd. Ph: (248)699-4253
Farmington Hills, MI 48331- Free: 800-877-GALE
  3535 Fax: (248)699-8070
E-mail: galeord@galegroup.com
URL: http://www.galegroup.com.; http://www.gale.com.

Contact: Andrea deJong, Editor, andreadejong@galegroup.com.

Desc: Approximately 90,000 companies, 90% of which are privately owned, representing all industries. *Type:* Directory.

Ward's Private Company Profiles

Gale Group Inc.
27500 Drake Rd. Ph: (248)699-4253
Farmington Hills, MI 48331- Free: 800-877-GALE
  3535 Fax: (248)699-8070
E-mail: galeord@galegroup.com
URL: http://www.galegroup.com.; http://www.gale.com.

Contact: Jennifer Mast, Editor.

Desc: In each volume, 150 leading privately held companies in the U.S. *Type:* Directory.

Washington Business

Association of Washington Business
1414 S. Cherry St. Ph: (206)943-1600
PO Box 658
Olympia, WA 98501-2341

Contact: Bill Carter, Editor.

Desc: Tracks Association activities and discusses issues related to business management, such as human resources, fiscal policy, and work environment. Recurring features include letters to the editor, interviews, news of research, a calendar of events, reports of meetings, and news of educational opportunities. *Type:* Newsletter.

Washington Business Directory

infoUSA
5711 S. 86th Circle Ph: (402)593-4600
PO Box 27347 Free: 800-555-6124
Omaha, NE 68127 Fax: (402)331-5481
E-mail: internet@infousa.com
URL: http://www.abii.com.

Contact: Peter J. Wilmarth, Publisher.

Desc: 239,000 businesses in Washington state. *Type:* Directory.

Washington DC Business Directory

infoUSA
5711 S. 86th Circle Ph: (402)593-4600
PO Box 27347 Free: 800-555-6124
Omaha, NE 68127 Fax: (402)331-5481
E-mail: internet@infousa.com
URL: http://www.abii.com.

Contact: Peter J. Wilmarth, Publisher.

Desc: 155,000 businesses in Washington, D.C. *Type:* Directory.

Washington/Puerto Rico Newsline

Atlantic Communications
PO Box 247 Ph: (540)298-2003
Elkton, VA 22827 Fax: (540)298-2347

Contact: Ed Konstant, Editor.

Desc: Directed toward those with business interests in Puerto Rico. Provides current information on legislative and political developments in Washington affecting the Puerto Rican economy. *Type:* Newsletter.

Washington State Migrant Council

301 N First St. No. 1 Ph: (509)837-8909
Sunnyside, WA 98944 Free: 800-223-8515
  Fax: (509)839-5220

Contact: Carlos M. Diaz, Exec.Dir.
Type: Association.

West Virginia Business Directory

infoUSA
5711 S. 86th Circle Ph: (402)593-4600
PO Box 27347 Free: 800-555-6124
Omaha, NE 68127 Fax: (402)331-5481
E-mail: internet@infousa.com
URL: http://www.abii.com.

Contact: Peter J. Wilmarth, Publisher.

Desc: 67,000 businesses in West Virginia. *Type:* Directory.

Western Association News—Resource Directory Section

Schneider Publishing Co.
13274 Fiji Way, 4th Fl. Ph: (310)577-3700
Marina del Rey, CA 90292 Fax: (310)577-3715
E-mail: info@schneiderpublishing.com; sandi@schneiderpublishing.com; jennifer@schneiderpublishing.com; ann@schneiderpublishing.com.

Contact: Timothy Schneider, Editor.

Desc: Directory sections covering a segment of the convention and meeting industry in the western U.S. and Canada. Topics include: hotel/meeting facilities; suppliers and service providers; convention and visitors bureaus; speakers and speakers bureaus; and convention centers. All listings are paid. *Type:* Directory.

Western New England Regional Industrial Buying Guide

Thomas Regional Directory Co., Inc.
5 Penn Plaza
New York, NY 10001   Ph: (212)629-2100
   Fax: (212)290-7335
E-mail: info@trdnet.com
URL: http://www.thomasregional.com.

Contact: Marie McGurk, Editorial Dir.; Adrienne Toth, Managing Editor; Nancy Bromberg, Contracts Administration Mgr.

Desc: Over 18,000 listings of manufacturers; related industrial services, such as trucking and maintenance services; distributors; and manufacturers' representatives in Connecticut, Vermont, norhtern New York and western Massachusetts. *Type:* Directory.

Western States Exporters and Importers Database

Database Publishing Co.
1590 S. Lewis St.   Ph: (714)778-6400
PO Box 70024   Free: 800-888-8434
Anaheim, CA 92825-0024   Fax: (714)778-6811
E-mail: sales@databasepublishing.com
URL: http://www.databasepublishing.com; http://www.databasepublishing.com/.

Desc: 11,500 exporting and 5,000 importing companies in Alaska, Arizona, California, Colorado, Hawaii, Idaho, Montana, New Mexico, Nevada, Oregon, Utah, Washington, and Wyoming. *Type:* Directory.

Western States Technology Companies Database

Database Publishing Co.
1590 S. Lewis St.   Ph: (714)778-6400
PO Box 70024   Free: 800-888-8434
Anaheim, CA 92825-0024   Fax: (714)778-6811
E-mail: sales@databasepublishing.com
URL: http://www.databasepublishing.com; http://www.databasepublishing.com/.

Desc: Over 20,000 technology-based manufacturers, software developers, and other high tech companies in Alaska, Arizona, California, Colorado, Hawaii, Idaho, Montana, New Mexico, Nevada, Oregon, Utah, Washington, Wyoming; over 40,000 owners, CEOs, and key executives. *Type:* Directory.

WESTLAW® Antitrust and Trade Regulation

West Group
620 Opperman Dr.   Ph: (651)687-7000
St. Paul, MN 55164-0526
URL: http://www.westgroup.com

Desc: Contains the complete text of U.S. federal court decisions, statutes and regulations, administrative law publications, specialized files, and texts and periodicals dealing with antitrust law, business regulations, and consumer protection, as well as consumer product safety, mergers and takeovers, trade regulation, and unfair competition. *Available:* West Group, WESTLAW. *Type:* Database.

Who Knows Who: Networking through Corporate Boards

Who Knows Who Publishers
PO Box 13062   Ph: (510)601-1556
Berkeley, CA 94702   Fax: (510)655-1123

Contact: Jeannette E. Glynn, Editor.

Desc: List of over 1,000 companies noted by either Fortune magazine or Forbes magazine, or both; over 120 major foundations. *Type:* Directory.

Who Owns Whom

Dun & Bradstreet
3 Sylvan Way   Ph: (973)605-6442
Parsippany, NJ 07054-3896   Free: 800-526-0651
   Fax: (973)605-6911
E-mail: dnbmdd@dnb.com

Desc: In four regional volumes, approximately 320,000 company affiliates and subsidiaries of more than 23,000 companies in Australia and the Far East, North America, the United Kingdom and Ireland, and Continental Europe. *Type:* Directory.

Who's on Top?

Hoover's, Inc.
1033 La Posada Dr., Ste. 250   Ph: (512)374-4500
Austin, TX 78752   Fax: (512)374-4501
E-mail: info@hoovers.com
URL: http://www.hoovers.com/features/whosontop/lists.html

Desc: The Hoover's List of Lists site has compiled links to external surveys that rank companies and people in numerous ways including sales figures, company size, and reputation. *Type:* Database.

Who's Who of European Business and Industry

Triumph Books
1436 W. Randolph St.   Ph: (312)939-0959
Chicago, IL 60607   Free: 800-626-4330
   Fax: (312)733-3017

Desc: Over 9,500 European business executives (volume 1) and over 1,400 companies (volume 2). *Type:* Directory.

Wichita Business Journal—Book of Lists

Wichita Business Journal
110 S. Main St., Ste. 200   Ph: (316)267-6406
Wichita, KS 67202-3745   Fax: (316)267-6406
Contact: Tim Travis, Editor.

Desc: About 1,500 manufacturers, industries, service organizations, and other businesses rated as the 25 largest in their fields in the Wichita, Kansas area, including Butler, Harvey, Reno, and Sedgwick counties. *Type:* Directory.

Williams Report

Joe Williams Communications
300 SE 4th St.   Ph: (918)336-2267
PO Box 924   Free: 800-833-5946
Bartlesville, OK 74005   Fax: (918)336-2733
E-mail: joewmscomm@aol.com
Contact: Joe Williams, Editor.

Desc: Seeks to improve employee communications through innovative communication ideas and strategies. Offers ideas in a variety of areas, including publications, video, photography, bulletin board programs, and communication sessions. *Type:* Newsletter.

Wilson Business Abstracts

H.W. Wilson Company
950 University Ave.   Ph: (718)588-8400
Bronx, NY 10452
E-mail: custserv@hwwilson.com
URL: http://www.hwwilson.com
Contact: Technical Support Department., techmail@info.hwwilson.com.

Desc: Contains citations, with abstracts (from June 1990 to date), to all articles cited in the Business Periodicals Index. Covers such general topics as accounting, advertising, economics, finance, management, marketing, and occupational health and safety, as well as such specific industries as banking, the chemical industry, and real estate. *Available:* H.W. Wilson Company, WilsonWeb; H.W. Wilson Company, WilsonWeb; Bell & Howell Information and Learning; Bell & Howell Information and

Learning; OCLC Online Computer Library Center, Inc., OCLC EPIC; OCLC Online Computer Library Center, Inc., OCLC FirstSearch Catalog; OCLC Online Computer Library Center, Inc., OCLC FirstSearch Catalog; Ovid Technologies, Inc.; Ovid Technologies, Inc.; SilverPlatter Information, Inc.; The Dialog Corporation, DIALOG; The Dialog Corporation, DIALOG. *Type:* Database.

Wire Journal International Reference Guide

Wire Journal, Inc.
Wire Association International
1570 Boston Post Rd.   Ph: (203)453-2777
PO Box 578   Fax: (203)453-8384
Guilford, CT 06437-0578
URL: http://www.wirenet.org.
Contact: Janice E. Swindells, Editor, jswindells@wirenet.org.

Desc: Manufacturers and suppliers of steel and nonferrous rods, strip, wire, wire products, electrical wire and cable, fiber optics, and machinery and equipment to the industry (SIC 33). *Type:* Directory.

Wisconsin Business Directory

infoUSA
5711 S. 86th Circle   Ph: (402)593-4600
PO Box 27347   Free: 800-555-6124
Omaha, NE 68127   Fax: (402)331-5481
E-mail: internet@infousa.com
URL: http://www.abii.com.
Contact: Peter J. Wilmarth, Publisher.

Desc: 223,000 businesses in Wisconsin. *Type:* Directory.

Wisconsin Exports!

WMC Foundation
501 E. Washington Ave.   Ph: (608)258-3400
PO Box 352   Free: 800-328-2567
Madison, WI 53701-0352   Fax: (608)258-3413
E-mail: wmc@wmc.org; dbm@wmc.org.
Contact: J. Mandt, Editor.

Desc: Approximately 300 manufacturers and wholesalers in the state of Wisconsin that export their products in the international market. *Type:* Directory.

Wisconsin Minority-Owned Business Directory

Wisconsin Department of Commerce
PO Box 7970   Ph: (608)267-9550
Madison, WI 53707   Free: 800-HELP-BUS
   Fax: (608)267-2829

Contact: Erick Flint, Editor.

Desc: About 650 non-retail minority firms. *Type:* Directory.

WNC Business Journal

Nason & Associates
PO Box 8204   Ph: (828)298-1322
Asheville, NC 28814-8204   Fax: (828)298-1312

Contact: Steve Nason, Editor; Marilyn Nason, Editor and Publisher; Michelle Ramsey, Advertising Dir.

Desc: Discusses business topics for 28 western counties in North Carolina. *Type:* Newsletter.

Working Solo

John Wiley & Sons, Inc.
605 3rd Ave.   Ph: (212)850-6000
New York, NY 10158   Free: 800-255-5945
   Fax: (212)850-6088
E-mail: info@qm.jwiley.com; permreq@wiley.com; office@workingsolo.com.
URL: http://www.wiley.com
Desc: More than 1,000 solo business opportunities, as well as a resource section on publications, organizations, and other essential contacts for solo professionals. *Type:* Directory.

Working Solo Sourcebook
John Wiley & Sons, Inc.

605 3rd Ave. Ph: (212)850-6000
New York, NY 10158 Free: 800-255-5945
  Fax: (212)850-6088
E-mail: info@qm.jwiley.com; permreq@wiley.com; office@workingsolo.com.
URL: http://www.wiley.com

Desc: More than 1,200 important business resources for entrepreneurs of all levels of experience and all types of businesses, including books, tapes, videos, training programs, associations, outlets, government agencies and programs. *Type:* Directory.

World Business Directory
Gale Group Inc.

27500 Drake Rd. Ph: (248)699-4253
Farmington Hills, MI 48331- Free: 800-877-GALE
3535 Fax: (248)699-8070
E-mail: galeord@galegroup.com
URL: http://www.galegroup.com.; http://www.gale.com.
Contact: Kim Ellen Forster, Editor; Jacqueline K. Mueckenheim, Editor.

Desc: Nearly 140,000 companies in over 180 countries involved in international trade. *Type:* Directory.

World Databases in Business
National Register Publishing Co.

121 Chanlon Rd. Ph: (908)464-6800
New Providence, NJ 07974 Free: 800-521-8110
  Fax: (908)508-7671
E-mail: info@renp.com
URL: http://www.reedref.com
Contact: C.J. Armstrong, Editor.

Desc: Business information on databases, including CD-ROM, magnetic tape, diskette, online, fax, or databroadcast worldwide. *Type:* Directory.

World Presidents Organization

11 Canal Ctr., Ste. 105 Ph: (703)684-4900
Alexandria, VA 22314 Fax: (703)684-4955
E-mail: sheryl_check@wpo.org
URL: http://www.wpo.org
Contact: Robert Strade, Exec.VP.

Desc: Corporate executives, all of whom are former members of the Young Presidents' Organization. Purpose is to function as a graduate school for former members of YPO. *Type:* Association.

World Trade Centers Association

1 World Trade Center, Ste. Ph: (212)435-7168
7701 Fax: (212)435-2810
New York, NY 10048
URL: http://www.wtca.org
Contact: Guy F. Tozzoli, Pres.

Desc: Regular members are organizations substantially involved in the development or operation of a World Trade Center. Affiliate members are chambers of commerce and organizations sponsoring Executive Business clubs, libraries, exhibit facilities, and other trade center-related activities. Seeks to encourage expansion of world trade, promote international business relationships, and increase Third World participation in world trade. *Type:* Association.

Worldprofit Online Magazine
Worldprofit, Inc.

PO Box 38-2767 Ph: (617)547-6372
Cambridge, MA 02238 Fax: (617)547-0061
URL: http://www.worldprofit.com.
Contact: Dr. Jeffrey Lant, Contact, drjlant@worldprofit.com.

Desc: Business development magazine of particular interest to small businesses. Available online only. *Type:* Periodical.

Worldscope
Primark Financial Information Division

5161 River Rd. Ph: (301)951-1300
Bethesda, MD 20816 Free: 800-228-3220
  Fax: (301)951-1753
E-mail: info@diclosure.com; jwolf@wisi.com; menheneott@wisi.com.

Desc: Profiles, company financial statement data, ratios, and stock performance of approximately 20,000 companies listed on leading stock exchanges worldwide. *Type:* Directory.

Worldwide Riches Opportunities
IWS Inc.

24 Canterbury Rd. Ph: (516)766-5850
Rockville Centre, NY 11570 Free: 800-323-0548
  Fax: (516)766-5919
Desc: Approximately 5,000 overseas firms seeking products to import from the United States. *Type:* Directory.

Wyoming Business Directory
infoUSA

5711 S. 86th Circle Ph: (402)593-4600
PO Box 27347 Free: 800-555-6124
Omaha, NE 68127 Fax: (402)331-5481
E-mail: internet@infousa.com
URL: http://www.abii.com.
Contact: Peter J. Wilmarth, Publisher.
Desc: 28,000 businesses in Wyoming. *Type:* Directory.

Young Entrepreneurs' Organization

1321 Duke St., Ste. 300 Ph: (703)519-6700
Alexandria, VA 22314 Fax: (703)519-1864
URL: http://www.yeo.org
Contact: Brien Biondi, Exec.Dir.

Desc: Entrepreneurs under the age of 40 who have either founded, or own a firm with annual gross revenues exceeding $1,000,000. Serves as a focal point for communication among members; provides educational programs; facilitates small group meetings with leading entrepreneurs. *Type:* Association.

Your Chamber In Action
Spokane Area Chamber of Commerce

801 W. Riverside, 4th Fl. Ph: (509)624-1393
Spokane, WA 99210 Fax: (509)747-0077
URL: http://www.chamberspokane.org.
Contact: Libby Barnes, Editor, (509)459-4109, lbarnes@chamber.spokane.net.

Desc: Covers Chamber issues and events pertinent to Spokane area businesses. Recurring features include news of meetings and columns titled Kudos, Congratulations, and Good News. *Type:* Newsletter.

Business Education

AACSB-The International Association for Management Education

600 Emerson Rd., Ste. 300 Ph: (314)872-8481
St. Louis, MO 63141-6762 Fax: (314)872-8495
URL: http://www.aacsb.edu
Contact: William K. Laidlaw, Jr., Exec.VP.

Desc: Institutions offering accredited programs of instruction in business administration and accounting at the college level; nonaccredited schools; business firms; governmental and professional organizations; educational institutions and organizations outside the U.S. Provides accreditation for bachelor's, master's, and doctoral degree programs in business administration and accounting. Serves as a professional association for management education. *Type:* Association.

AIESEC - United States

135 W. 50th St., 17th Fl. Ph: (212)757-3774
New York, NY 10020 Fax: (212)757-4062
E-mail: aiesec@us.aiesec.org
Contact: Melissa Swenson, Exchange Dev. Coor.

Desc: Students of economics or business and related fields presently studying at affiliated universities worldwide. Objective is the development of internationally educated managers. *Type:* Association.

American Society for Training and Development

Box 1443 Ph: (703)683-8100
1640 King St. Fax: (703)683-8103
Alexandria, VA 22313
Contact: Laura Liswood, Pres.

Desc: Professional association for persons engaged in the training and development of business, industry, education, and government employees. Undertakes special research projects and acts as clearinghouse. Operates 3000 volume information center on human resource development. *Type:* Association.

CDS International, Inc.

871 United Nations Plz., 15th Ph: (212)497-3500
Fl. Fax: (212)497-3535
New York, NY 10017-1814
E-mail: info@cdsintl.org
URL: http://www.cdsintl.org
Contact: Wolfgang Linz, Exec.Dir.

Desc: Purpose is to improve international business through service to individuals, corporations, and educational institutions. *Type:* Association.

Decision Line
Decision Sciences Institute

University Plaza Ph: (404)651-4000
Atlanta, GA 30303 Fax: (404)651-2804
E-mail: dsi@gsu.edu; hjacobs@gsu.edu.
URL: http://www.jso.edu/~dsiadm.
Contact: Barbara B. Flynn, Editor.

Desc: Informs business executives and faculty of research and developments in the area of decision sciences. Promotes further education in the processes of decision-making for business students. *Type:* Newsletter.

Delta Pi Epsilon

PO Box 4340 Ph: (501)562-1233
Little Rock, AR 72214 Fax: (501)562-1293
E-mail: dpe@ipa.net
URL: http://www.dpe.org
Contact: Robert B. Mitchell, Exec.Dir.

Desc: Professional society - men and women, business education. *Type:* Association.

Foundation for Student Communication

305 Aaron Burr Hall, Rm. 305 Ph: (609)258-1111
Princeton, NJ 08544-1011 Fax: (609)258-1222
Contact: Andrew O'Brien, Senior Editor.

Desc: Student subscribers and conference participants who desire to promote communication among students and businesspersons. Sponsors student/business forums. *Type:* Association.

Junior Achievement

One Education Way Ph: (719)540-8000
Colorado Springs, CO 80906 Fax: (719)540-9150
URL: http://www.ja.org
Contact: James B. Hayes, Pres. & CEO.

Desc: Educates and inspires young people to value free enterprise, business and economics to improve the quality of their lives. *Type:* Association.

Junior Achievement of Southern California

Garry Hickman

6250 Forest Lawn Dr. Ph: (213)957-1818
Los Angeles, CA 90068 Fax: (213)957-0585
E-mail: losangca@worldnet.att.net
Contact: Gary Hickman, Pres.
Desc: Volunteers from the teaching profession and the business industry providing students with economic education and opportunities to learn how the American business system operates. *Type:* Association.

National Association for the Exchange of Industrial Resources

560 McClure St. Ph: (309)343-0704
PO Box 8076 Free: 800-562-0955
Galesburg, IL 61401 Fax: (309)343-0862
E-mail: member.naeir@misslink.net
URL: http://www.misslink.net/naeir/naeir.htm
Contact: Gary C. Smith, Pres. & CEO.
Desc: Seeks to match donated industrial supplies and equipment with schools and nonprofit organizations. Sponsors National Gifts in Kind program. *Type:* Association.

National Black MBA Association

180 N. Michigan Ave., Ste. Ph: (312)236-2622
1400 Fax: (312)236-4131
Chicago, IL 60601
URL: http://www.nbmbaa.org
Contact: Antoinette Malveaux, Exec.Dir.
Desc: Business professionals, lawyers, accountants, and engineers concerned with the role of blacks who hold advanced management degrees. Works to create economic and intellectual wealth for the black community. Encourages blacks to pursue continuing business education; assists students preparing to enter the business world. *Type:* Association.

National Business Education Association

1914 Association Dr. Ph: (703)860-8300
Reston, VA 20191-1596 Fax: (703)620-4483
E-mail: nbea@nbea.org
URL: http://www.nbea.org/nbea.html
Contact: Dr. Janet M. Treichel, Exec.Dir.
Desc: Teachers of business subjects in secondary and postsecondary schools and colleges; administrators and research workers in business education; businesspersons interested in business education; teachers in educational institutions training business teachers. High school and college students preparing for careers in business. *Type:* Association.

Pi Omega Pi

Dr. Lynn Wasson

Southwest Missouri State Ph: (417)836-6355
University Fax: (417)836-6337
Department of Management
Springfield, MO 65804-0094
E-mail: lew537f@wpgate.smsu.edu
Contact: Dr. Lynn Wasson, Sponsor.
Desc: Honor society - men and women, business education. *Type:* Association.

Cancer

AICR Newsletter

American Institute for Cancer Research (AICR)

1759 R St. NW Ph: (202)328-7744
Washington, DC 20009-2552 Free: 800-843-8114
 Fax: (202)328-7226
URL: http://www.aicr.org/aicr.
Contact: Christine Murray, Editor; Marilyn Gentry, Exec. Editor; Catherine Macpherson, MS, RD, Asst. Editor.

Desc: Examines the relationship between diet and cancer, recommending diet changes which may reduce cancer risks. Recurring features include health and nutrition information, news of research, and editorials. *Type:* Newsletter.

Albany Medical College

Center for Cancer and Blood Disorders

MC-52 47 New Scotland. Ave. Ph: (518)262-5297
Albany, NY 12208 Fax: (518)262-5975
Contact: Peter Burkart, MD, Hd.
Desc: Cancer and blood disorders, focusing on medical oncology, hematology, radiotherapy, pathology, surgery, and bone marrow transplantation. *Type:* Research center.

Albert Einstein Comprehensive Cancer Center

Albert Einstein College of Ph: (718)430-2302
 Medicine Fax: (718)430-8550
Chanin Bldg., Rm. 209
1300 Morris Park Ave.
Bronx, NY 10461
E-mail: igoldman@aecom.yu.edu
URL: http://www.ca.aecom.yu.edu
Contact: I. David Goldman, MD, Dir.
Desc: Cancer, including studies on carcinogenesis and chemotherapeutic agents, regulation of growth and function in normal and cancer cells, cell structure and metabolism in normal and cancer cells, immuno-oncology, viral oncology, genetics, membrane synthesis, nucleic acid synthesis, gene expression in malignant cells, and cell function and regulation. Conducts clinical cancer studies. *Type:* Research center.

Allegheny University Hospital

Barry Ashbee Research Laboratories

230 N. Broad & Vine Sts. Ph: (215)762-7026
Philadelphia, PA 19102 Fax: (215)762-8857
Contact: Dr. Isadore Brodsky, Dir.
Desc: Leukemia research. *Type:* Research center.

AMC Cancer Research Center

1600 Pierce St. Ph: (303)233-6501
Lakewood, CO 80214 Fax: (303)239-3340
E-mail: tormeyd@amc.org
Contact: Douglass C. Tormey, PhD, Dir.
Desc: Cancer prevention and control, focusing on early diagnosis, nutrition, chemoprevention, metabolic epidemiology, and intervention trials in human populations, particularly women and underserved populations. Promotes the application of knowledge to reduce cancer incidence and mortality rates. *Type:* Research center.

American Association for Cancer Research

Public Ledger Bldg., Ste. 826 Ph: (215)440-9300
150 S. Independence Mall W. Fax: (215)440-9313
Philadelphia, PA 19106-3483
E-mail: foti@aacr.org
URL: http://www.aacr.org
Contact: Margaret Foti, Contact.
Desc: Cancer, focusing on observation, problems, and new significant research. *Type:* Research center.

American Association for Cancer Research

Public Ledger Bldg., Ste. 826 Ph: (215)440-9300
150 S. Independence Mall W. Fax: (215)440-9313
Philadelphia, PA 19106-3483
E-mail: aacr@aacr.org
URL: http://www.aacr.org
Contact: Margaret Foti, Ph.D, Exec.Dir.
Desc: Works to facilitate communication and dissemination of information among scientists and others dedicated to cancer research; seeks to advance understanding of cancer etiology, prevention, diagnosis and treatment throughout the world. *Type:* Association.

American Cancer Society

1599 Clifton Rd. NE Ph: (404)320-3333
Atlanta, GA 30329 Free: 800-ACS-2345
 Fax: (404)329-7530
URL: http://www.cancer.org
Contact: John R. Seffrin, Ph.D., CEO.
Desc: Provides special services to cancer patients. *Type:* Association.

American Cancer Society - Commonwealth Division

Garry L. Pincock

Rte. 422 and Sipe Ave. Ph: (717)533-6144
PO Box 897 Free: 800-227-2345
Hershey, PA 17033-0897 Fax: (717)534-1075
URL: http://www.cancer.org
Contact: Frank P. McGrady, Chief Operations Officer.
Desc: A nationwide community-based voluntary health organization dedicated to eliminating cancer as a major health problem through prevention and diminishing suffering from cancer through education, research, advocacy, and service. *Type:* Association.

American Cancer Society, Jefferson City Chapter

1100 Pennsylvania Ave. Ph: (314)893-4800
Kansas City, MO 64105-1346 Fax: (314)893-2017
Contact: Gerald G. Quick, Contact.
Desc: Volunteers supporting education and research in cancer prevention, diagnosis, detection, and treatment. *Type:* Association.

American Cancer Society - New York State Division

PO Box 7 Ph: (315)437-7025
East Syracuse, NY 13057 Fax: (315)437-0540
Contact: Donald Distasio, Exec.V.Pres.
Desc: Medical and lay persons from New York's upstate counties. Dedicated to the elimination and prevention of cancer as a major health problem through research and education. *Type:* Association.

American Institute for Cancer Research

1759 R St. NW Ph: (202)328-7744
Washington, DC 20009 Free: 800-843-8114
 Fax: (202)328-7226
E-mail: research@aicr.org
URL: http://www.aicr.org
Contact: Marilyn Gentry, Exec.Dir.
Desc: Provides grants to universities and nonprofit institutions on the role of diet and nutrition in the prevention and adjuvant treatment of cancer. *Type:* Research center.

American Italian Cancer Foundation

872 Madison Ave. Ste. 2b Ph: (212)628-9090
New York, NY 10021-4121 Fax: (212)516-6089
Contact: Gilda Zane, Exec.Dir.
Desc: Breast and prostate cancer. *Type:* Research center.

American Society of Clinical Oncology

225 Reinekers Ln., Ste. 650 Ph: (703)299-0150
Alexandria, VA 22314 Fax: (703)299 1044
E-mail: asco@asco.org
URL: http://www.asco.org
Contact: John R. Durant, Exec.VP.
Desc: Physicians who treat people with cancer. Sets the standard for patient care worldwide, and leads the fight for more effective cancer threatments, increased funding for clinical and translational research. *Type:* Association.

Aplastic Anemia Foundation of America

PO Box 613   Ph: 800-747-2820
Annapolis, MD 21404-0613   Fax: (410)867-0240
E-mail: aafacenter@aol.com
URL: http://www.aplastic.org
Contact: Marilyn Baker, Exec.Dir.
Desc: Serves as an information source for persons with aplastic anemia and myelodysplastic syndromes. *Type:* Association.

Arizona State University

Cancer Research Institute

Tempe, AZ 85287-1604   Ph: (602)965-3351
   Fax: (602)965-8558
Contact: Dr. George R. Pettit, Dir.
Desc: Discovery of new cancer chemotherapeutic drugs for human treatment employing organic chemistry, biochemistry, and biology, including a unique program concerned with isolation, structural identification, and syntheses of naturally occurring anticancer agents from marine animals, plants, and microorganisms. *Type:* Research center.

Association of American Cancer Institutes

666 Elm St.   Ph: (716)845-3028
Buffalo, NY 14263-0001   Fax: (716)845-8178
Contact: Dr. Max Wicha, Pres.
Desc: Causes, nature, prevention, treatment, and rehabilitation of cancer. *Type:* Research center.

Association for Research of Childhood Cancer

PO Box 251   Ph: (716)681-4433
Buffalo, NY 14225-0251
Contact: Ann O'Donnell, Pres.
Desc: Pediatric cancer, focusing on funding, expanding, and continuing of research centers. Also provides seed money for pilot projects in cancer research. *Type:* Research center.

Barbara Ann Karmanos Cancer Institute

110 E. Warren   Ph: (313)833-0710
Detroit, MI 48201   Free: 800-KARMANOS
   Fax: (313)993-7165
E-mail: web@karmanos.org
URL: http://www.kci.wayne.edu
Contact: William P. Peters, MD,PHD, Pres.
Desc: Conducts cancer research; educates public and professional community; provides care and services to cancer patients and their families. Provides community outreach services. *Type:* Association.

Barbara Ann Karmanos Cancer Institute

4100 John R   Free: 800-KAR-
Detroit, MI 48201   MANOS
   Fax: (313)993-7165
E-mail: petersw@karmanos.org
URL: http://www.karmanos.org
Contact: Dr. William P. Peters, Dir.
Desc: Treatment, diagnosis, and prevention of cancer. *Type:* Research center.

Bay Area Tumor Institute

400 30th St., Ste. 301   Ph: (510)465-8570
Oakland, CA 94609-3305   Fax: (510)465-8588
E-mail: bsiegel@batinst.org
URL: http://www.batinst.org
Contact: Barry B. Siegel, Pres.
Desc: Phase 2 and phase 3 clinical drug trials for cancer therapy. *Type:* Research center.

Baylor University Medical Center

Blood and Bone Marrow Transplantation Services

3535 Worth St., Ste. 5 Collins   Ph: (214)820-2610
Dallas, TX 75246   Fax: (214)818-9681
E-mail: jw.fay@baylordallas.edu
URL: http://www.bhcs.com/bits/bonemarrow/bonemarrow.html
Contact: Joseph W. Fay, MD, Dir.
Desc: Bone marrow transplantation research in leukemia/lymphoma studies, including graft-vs-host disease, evaluation of immune recovery post transplant, evaluation of growth factors in transplantation, and applications of molecular biology/gene rearrangement in marrow transplantation, and dendritic cell transplantation. *Type:* Research center.

Baystate Medical Center

Wesson Women's Unit

3300 Main Street   Ph: (413)794-7045
Springfield, MA 01107   Fax: (413)784-3613
Contact: Dr. Ronald Burkman, MD, Dir.
Desc: Hematology/oncology, including protocol studies in the treatment of cancers of the breast, gastrointestinal tract, lung, bladder, renal system, cervix and ovaries, and head and neck. Also studies treatment for Hodgkin's disease, leukemia, lymphomas, melanomas, and sarcomas. *Type:* Research center.

Beth Israel Deaconess Medical Center

Laboratory of Cancer Biology

West Campus   Ph: (617)632-0622
Department of Surgery   Fax: (617)632-0625
21-27 Burlington Ave., Rm. 553
One Deaconess Rd.
Boston, MA 02115
E-mail: thomasp@warren.med.harvard.edu
Contact: Peter Thomas, PhD, Res.Dir.
Desc: Human and animal cancer, including studies on biochemistry, cell and membrane biology, immunology, molecular biology, and virology of solid tumors. Develops and conducts clinical human studies on new diagnostic and therapeutic regimes for solid tumors. *Type:* Research center.

Biotechnology Newswatch

McGraw-Hill, Inc.
2 Penn Plaza   Ph: (212)904-2000
New York, NY 10121   Free: 800-223-6180
   Fax: (212)904-6068
URL: http://www.mcgraw-hill.com
Contact: Mara Bovsun, Chief Editor.
Desc: Provides an overview of the biotechnology industry through capsule summaries of significant news items and a compilation of research and business stories. Recurring features include interviews, news of research, a calendar of events, reports of meetings, and columns titled Business Briefs and Japan Watch. *Type:* Newsletter.

The Blood Center

PO Box 2178   Ph: (414)937-6355
Milwaukee, WI 53201-2178   Fax: (414)937-6284
E-mail: chris_m@bcsew.edu
URL: http://www.bloodctrwise.org
Contact: John W. Adamson, MD, Exec.V.Pres./Dir.
Desc: Blood-related research in the areas of platelets, hemostasis/thrombosis, immunogenetics, vascular biology, and transfusion medicine. Major activities include the collection and distribution of blood and blood products, basic research, clinical laboratory testing, and bone marrow donor recruitment. *Type:* Research center.

Blood and Marrow Transplant Laboratory

Children's Hospital of Orange   Ph: (714)289-4060
County   Fax: (714)516-4277
455 S. Main St.
Orange, CA 92868
E-mail: vslone@choc.org
Contact: Dr. Leonard Sender, Dir.
Desc: Bone marrow immunology experiments, including tumor purging using chemotherapy and monoclonal antibodies, molecular detection of minimal residual disease, purification of hematopoietic stem cells, and purging and cultivation of bone marrow. Also studies umbilical cord blood harvesting, storage, and expansion; and T-cell depletion for unrelated bone marrow transplantation. *Type:* Research center.

Boston Sickle Cell Center

Boston City Hospital   Ph: (617)534-5727
1 Boston Medical Centre Pl.   Fax: (617)534-5739
Boston, MA 02118
E-mail: lillian.mcmahon@bmc.org
Contact: Dr. Lillian E.C. McMahon, Dir.
Desc: Sickle cell trait and sickle cell anemia/disease, including molecular, cellular, tissue, and organ studies. Investigates glucose 6-phosphate dehydrogenase deficiency, coagulation and carbomylation of hemoglobin S, antisickling compounds, red cell membrane alterations, fetal jeopardy, fetal hemoglobin synthesis, cardiac manifestations, lung function, and infection. *Type:* Research center.

Boston University

Cancer Research Center

80 E. Concord St.   Ph: (617)638-4173
Boston, MA 02118   Fax: (617)638-4176
E-mail: dfaller@bu.edu
Contact: Douglas V. Faller, Dir.
Desc: Cancer, including cellular and molecular biology, receptors, carcinogenesis, immunology, toxicology, molecular genetics, nucleic acid damage and repair, mechanism of action of chemotherapeutic agents, and new approaches to cancer treatment. Affiliated hospitals provide a wide variety of specialized approaches to clinical management of cancer, including surgery, radiation therapy, chemotherapy, and immunotherapy. *Type:* Research center.

Breast Cancer Information Clearinghouse

New York State Education and Research Network
200 Elwood Davis Rd.   Ph: (315)453-2912
Syracuse, NY 13212-4311   Fax: (315)453-3052
E-mail: : webmaster@nysernet.org
URL: http://nysernet.org/bcic/
Contact: Jim Brennan, Actg.Exec. Officer, Dir. of Govt. Prog., jbrennan@nysernet.org.
Desc: The Breast Cancer Information Clearinghouse database provides information for breast cancer patients and their families and includes patient education materials, statistical information, lists of ACR accredited mammography facilities in New York State, listings of support groups around the country, articles from the National Alliance of Breast Cancer Organizations's newsletter, and relevant state and federal legislation relating to breast cancer. *Type:* Database.

Breast Cancer Survivor

Breast Cancer Survivor Network
221 SE 34th Ave.   Ph: (561)364-4182
Boynton Beach, FL 33435   Free: 888-422-4630
   Fax: (561)364-1162
E-mail: bcsnetwork@aol.com
Contact: Mindy Parsons, Editor.
Desc: Provides information and support for women and men touched by breast cancer. Recurring features include book reviews and columns titled Oncologist, Oncology Pharmacist, and Personal Journey. *Type:* Newsletter.

Brigham Young University
Cancer Research Center
S125 ESC   Ph: (801)378-3913
Provo, UT 84602   Fax: (801)378-5474
E-mail: cancer_research@byu.edu
URL: http://cpms.byu.edu/cancerresearch
Contact: Daniel L. Simmons, PhD, Dir.

Desc: Chemistry and biochemistry of nucleic acids and their derivatives as potential medicinal agents, including synthesis of antiviral and antitumor agents, detection of carcinogenic materials in the environment, isolation and study of antitumor agents from natural products, and study of the biochemical mechanism of action of various antitumor agents. *Type:* Research center.

British Columbia Cancer Agency
British Columbia Cancer Research Centre
601 W. 10th Ave.   Ph: (604)877-6010
Vancouver, BC, Canada V5Z   Fax: (604)877-6150
   1L3
E-mail: vling@bccancer.bc.ca
URL: http://www.bccancer.bc.ca
Contact: Dr. Victor Ling, V.Pres., Res.

Desc: Maintains six departments for cancer research: Medical biophysics, studying biological effects of ionizing radiation and improvements in radiotherapy; medical oncology advanced therapeutics developing new methods of diagnosis and advances in the administration of chemotherapy; cancer endocrinology, investigating application of hormonal therapy to various cancer sites; Terry Fox Laboratory, evaluating diagnosis and treatment of cancers of the blood and lymphatic system; cancer imaging, performing computerized screening of cancer cells; and cancer control research, studying geographic mappings of cancer in British Columbia, epidemiology of cancer in British Columbia, risk factors. *Type:* Research center.

British Columbia Cancer Agency
British Columbia Cancer Research Centre
Department of Cancer Endocrinology
601 W. 10th Ave.   Ph: (604)877-6015
Vancouver, BC, Canada V5Z   Fax: (604)877-6011
   4E6
E-mail: bruchovs@unixg.ubc.ca
URL: http://www.bccancer.bc.ca
Contact: Dr. N. Bruchovsky, Hd.

Desc: Development of new modes of endocrine therapy for the management of cancers of the breast, endometrium, and prostate. Emphasis is on mechanism of action of testosterone, control of neoplastic growth by androgens and other hormones, markers of androgen action in human prostate, stromal-epithelial interactions in the pathogenesis of benign prostatic hyperplasia, the role of hormones of the anterior pituitary in the growth of breast carcinoma and malignant lymphoma, the biological and biochemical changes in malignant lymphoma during progression from dependent to autonomous growth, and the development of anti-receptor antibodies specifically for malignant melanoma. *Type:* Research center.

British Columbia Cancer Agency
British Columbia Cancer Research Centre
Medical Biophysics Department
601 W. 10th Ave.   Ph: (604)877-6010
Vancouver, BC, Canada V5Z   Fax: (604)877-6002
   1L3
E-mail: rdurand@bccancer.bc.ca
URL: http://www.bccancer.bc.ca/research/mb/mbd.htm
Contact: Dr. R.E. Durand, Hd.

Desc: Laboratory and clinical studies on control of cancer, particularly radiation therapy and adjuncts to radiation therapy, including radiosensitizers and chemotherapy. Also conducts basic studies of mutagenesis and radiation damage mechanisms. *Type:* Research center.

British Columbia Cancer Agency
British Columbia Cancer Research Centre
Terry Fox Laboratory for Hematology/Oncology
601 W. 10th Ave.   Ph: (604)877-6070
Vancouver, BC, Canada V5Z   Fax: (604)877-0712
   1L3
E-mail: allen@terryfox.ubc.ca
URL: http://www.terryfox.ubc.ca
Contact: Dr. Allen C. Eaves, Dir.

Desc: Hematology and oncology, particularly the regulation of growth and differentiation in normal and malignant hemopoiesis and lymphopoiesis. Research activities focus on studies of hemopoietic progenitors, bone marrow transplantation, gene therapy, cell adhesion, metastasis, growth factors and receptors, and signal transduction mechanisms. *Type:* Research center.

British Columbia Cancer Agency
British Columbia Cancer Research Centre
Vancouver Cancer Centre
601 W. 10th Ave.   Ph: (604)877-6000
Vancouver, BC, Canada V5Z   Free: 800-663-3333
   1L3   Fax: (604)877-0585
E-mail: soreilly@bc.cancer.bc.ca
Contact: Dr. Susan O'Reilly, Hd.

Desc: Development of new therapeutic and diagnostic procedures for cancer patients, use of biological agents such as interferon and IL-2, new methods of delivery of anticancer drugs, including use of liposomes, mechanisms of mutations to resistance within tumors, and development of genetically engineered tumor cell vaccines. *Type:* Research center.

British Columbia Children's Hospital
BC Research Institute for Child and Family
Health-Cytogenetics
4480 Oak St.   Ph: (604)875-2304
Vancouver, BC, Canada V6H   Fax: (604)875-3601
   3V4
E-mail: dkalousek@wpog.childhosp.bc.ca
Contact: Prof. Dagmar K. Kalousek, Dir.

Desc: Chromosomal mosaicism and its effect on human intrauterine development, specifically the correlation between chromosomal complement of placenta and intrauterine development of the fetus. *Type:* Research center.

Burnham Institute
10901 N. Torrey Pines Rd.   Ph: (619)455-6480
La Jolla, CA 92037   Fax: (619)646-3199
E-mail: ruoslahti@burnham-inst.org
URL: http://www.burnhaminstitute.org/
Contact: Erkki Ruoslahti, MD, Pres./CEO.

Desc: Oncodevelopmental biology, cell-matrix interactions, gene cloning, tumor markers, differentiation of teratocarcinoma, lymphocyte differentiation and neoplasia, basement membrane proteins, and oncotrophoblast gene expression. *Type:* Research center.

Burzynski Research Institute
12000 Richmond Ave., Ste. 260 Ph: (713)597-0111
Houston, TX 77082-2431   Fax: (713)597-1166
E-mail: jpaszkowia@aol.com
URL: http://www.cancermed.com
Contact: Dr. Stanislaw R. Burzynski, Founder.

Desc: Antineoplastons A 10 and AS21 in the treatment of cancer. Antineoplastons are peptides and amino acid derivatives that are apoptosis inducers, working at the level of p53 tumor suppressor genes and ras oncogenes. *Type:* Research center.

Canadian Reference Centre for Cancer
Pathology
Ottawa Civic Hospital   Ph: (613)728-1723
60 Ruskin Ave.   Fax: (613)728-0811
Ottawa, ON, Canada K1Y 4M9
Contact: Dr. Jane Thomas, Dir.

Desc: Tumor pathology, including the biology of borderline malignant ovarian tumors and pathology of mesothelial tumors. *Type:* Research center.

Cancer Biotechnology Weekly
AIDS Weekly/Cancer Weekly
206 Rogers St., N.E., Suite 126 Ph: (770)507-7777
PO Box 5528
Atlanta, GA 30307
URL: http://www.newsfile.com

Desc: Contains the complete text of Cancer Biotechnology Weekly, a newsletter on developments in detection, treatment, and prevention of cancer worldwide. Covers news from health care agencies and organizations, development and testing of therapeutic drugs and medical procedures, and announcements of research grants and educational programs. *Available:* NCI Cancer Weekly Infoline. *Type:* Database.

Cancer Care
1180 Ave. of the Americas   Ph: (212)221-3300
New York, NY 10036   Fax: (212)719-0263
Contact: Harvey I. Newman, Exec.Dir.

Desc: Voluntary social service agency that functions as the service arm of the National Cancer Care Foundation. Provides professional social work counseling and guidance to help patients and families cope with the emotional, psychological, and financial consequences of cancer. In conjunction with professional counseling and where appropriate to the individual casework plan, supplementary financial aid may be given to self-supporting families to share the cost of home care services such as nursing care, home health aides, housekeepers, child care, and transportation. *Type:* Association.

Cancer Care of New Jersey
241 Millburn Ave., Ste. 241-C Ph: (973)379-7500
Millburn, NJ 07041   Free: 800-813-4673
                               Fax: (973)379-1082
E-mail: cancarenj@aol.com
URL: http://www.cancercare.org
Contact: David Lyons, Exec.Dir.

Desc: Provides professional counseling to cancer patients and their families; information and referral to homemaking services and hospices; supplementary financial assistance for homecare, childcare, transportation to treatments, and pain medication costs; Information and education on cancer and cancer prevention and coping. *Type:* Association.

Cancer Care Ontario
620 University Ave.   Ph: (416)971-9800
Toronto, ON, Canada M5G   Fax: (416)971-6888
   2L7
E-mail: chollenb@cancercarr.on.ca
URL: http://www.cancercare.on.ca
Contact: Dr. C.H. Hollenberg, Pres./CEO.

Desc: Cancer prevention, early detection, diagnosis, treatment, and supportive care. Supports basic and clinical scientists at eight Regional Cancer Centers throughout Ontario and in the Division of Epidemiology and Statistics. *Type:* Research center.

Cancer Communication

*Patient Advocates for Advanced Cancer
Treatment, Inc.*

1143 Parmelee NW   Ph: (616)453-1477
Grand Rapids, MI 49504   Fax: (616)453-1846
E-mail: pca@pcapaactinc.com

Desc: Provides updated information regarding the detection, diagnosis, evaluation, and treatment of prostate cancer. Recurring features include letters to the editor, news of research, reports of meetings and conferences, reviews of journal publications, listing of support groups, and acknowledgement of contributions. *Type:* Newsletter.

Cancer and Leukemia Group B

208 S. LaSalle, Ste. 2000   Ph: (773)702-9171
Chicago, IL 60604-1104   Fax: (773)345-0117
E-mail: ksartell@midway.uchicago.edu
URL: http://www.calgb.uchicago.edu

Contact: Richard L. Schilsky, MD, Gp.Chm.

Desc: Cooperative group conducting therapeutic multimodal, multi-institutional, randomized cancer clinical trials primarily in seven disease areas: leukemia, lymphoma, breast, gastrointestinal, prostate, respiratory and melanoma. Aims to increase the number of cases brought under complete remission from cancer by increasing knowledge of the disease process and appropriate treatments. *Type:* Research center.

Cancer Research Center

3501 Berrywood Dr.   Ph: (573)875-2255
Columbia, MO 65201   Fax: (573)443-1202
E-mail: abe@biosci.mbp.missouri.edu
URL: http://www.columbiainfo.com/cancrlab/

Contact: Dr. Abraham Eisenstark, Dir.

Desc: Basic oncology and studies in immunology, microbiology, protein biochemistry, bioengineering, carcinogenesis, and cancer detection. Specific studies include biochemical markers for early detection of cancer cells, environmental carcinogenesis, and oxidative cellular damage. *Type:* Research center.

Cancer Research Foundation

135 S. LaSalle St., Ste. 2348   Ph: (312)630-0055
Chicago, IL 60603-4115   Fax: (312)630-0075

Contact: Merle Goldblatt Cohen, Pres.

Desc: Funds laboratory and clinical cancer research at Chicago universities and medical schools. *Type:* Research center.

Cancer Research Fund of the Damon Runyon-Walter Winchell Foundation

675 3rd Ave., 25th Fl.   Ph: (212)697-9100
New York, NY 10017   Free: 800-445-2494
    Fax: (212)697-4050
E-mail: crfinfo@cancerresearchfund.org
URL: http://www.cancerresearchfund.org

Contact: Rebecca R. Kry, Exec.Dir.

Desc: Cancer research funding, focusing on supporting postdoctoral and physician scientists through fellowship grants and independent investigators in their first faculty position. Activities include selling tickets through its own Theater Ticket Service. *Type:* Research center.

Cancer Research Institute, Inc.

681 5th Ave.   Ph: (212)688-7515
New York, NY 10022   Free: 800-99-
    CANCER
    Fax: (212)832-9376
E-mail: canceres@aol.com
URL: http://www.cancerresearch.org

Contact: Carlos A. Ferrer, Chm.

Desc: Supports research projects in fundamental immunology and cancer immunology that seek to develop cancer therapies based on the immune system. *Type:* Research center.

Cancer Research Laboratory

Children's Hospital of Orange   Ph: (714)532-8548
  County   Fax: (714)516-4277
455 S. Main St.
Orange, CA 92868
E-mail: vslone@choc.org

Contact: Dr. Leonard Sender, Dir.

Desc: Experimental hematopoiesis, tumor vaccines. *Type:* Research center.

Cancer Resource Center

4600 Valley Rd., Ste. 336   Ph: (402)483-2827
Lincoln, NE 68510   Free: 800-487-8786
    Fax: (402)483-2882
E-mail: doneel@lmef.org
URL: http://www.lmef.org

Contact: Barb Morton, Dir.

Desc: Oncology, especially pathology and radiotherapy, and drug studies for pharmaceutical companies. *Type:* Research center.

CANCERLIT®

U.S. National Cancer Institute

Bethesda, MD 20892   Ph: (301)496-6644
E-mail: hardingb@otd.nci.nih.gov
URL: http://www.cancernet.nci.nih.gov

Desc: Contains more than 1.4 million citations, with abstracts, to the worldwide literature on oncological epidemiology, pathology, treatment, and research. Covers diagnostic procedures, molecular and cell biology, cancer virology and immunology, carcinogens and carcinogenesis, and anti-cancer drug development. *Available:* Ovid Technologies, Inc.; Ovid Technologies, Inc.; The Dialog Corporation, DataStar; The Dialog Corporation, DIALOG; The Dialog Corporation, DIALOG; DIMDI (Deutsches Institut fuer Medizinische Dokumentation und Information); DIMDI (Deutsches Institut fuer Medizinische Dokumentation und Information); Karolinska Institute Library and Information Center/ Karolinska Institutets Bibliotek och Informationscentral (KIBIC), Medical Information Center (MIC); U.S. National Library of Medicine (NLM), TOXNET; University of Tsukuba, Science Information Processing Center; STN International; STN International; Aries Systems Corporation; EBSCOhost. *Type:* Database.

Candlelighters Childhood Cancer Foundation

7910 Woodmont Ave., Ste. 460   Ph: (301)657-8401
Bethesda, MD 20814-3015   Free: 800-366-2223
    Fax: (301)718-2686
E-mail: info@candlelighters.org
URL: http://www.candlelighters.org

Contact: Carolyn Corry, Exec.Dir.

Desc: Educates, supports, serves and advocates for children and adolescents with cancer, their family members, survivors of childhood cancer, and professionals who work with them. Coordinates a network of more than 400 peer support groups and contacts for parents of children/adolescents with cancer. *Type:* Association.

The Carcinogenic Potency Project

Carcinogenic Potency Database

Mail Stop: Barker
1 Cyclotron Rd.
Lawrence Berkeley Laboratory
Berkeley, CA 94720
E-mail: cpdb@potency.berkeley.edu
URL: http://potency.berkeley.edu/cpdb.html

Contact: Lois Swirsky Gold.

Desc: A technical and scientific research database, the Carcinogenic Potency Database provides standardized and easily accessible information on the results of chronic,

long-term animal cancer tests. The database contains qualitative and quantitative information, including details on the test subjects and features of the experiments, that can be used as the basis for further research and investigation into carcinogenesis and cancer-causing agents. *Type:* Database.

Carcinoid Cancer Foundation, Inc.

1751 York Ave.   Ph: (212)722-3132
New York, NY 10128   Fax: (212)831-3031
E-mail: warner_md@carcinoid.org
URL: http://www.carcinoid.org

Contact: David H. Polinger, Pres.

Desc: Carcinoid tumors, carcinoid syndrome, and other related neuroendocrine tumors. *Type:* Research center.

Carson-Newman College
Cancer Research Project

Jefferson City, TN 37760   Ph: (423)475-9061

Contact: Dr. Carl T. Bahner, Dir.

Desc: Provides compounds for testing against tumors in animals and the AIDS virus; and tuberculosis; and drug delivery targeting. *Type:* Research center.

CC Newsletter

*Patient Advocates for Advanced Cancer
Treatment, Inc.*

1143 Parmelee NW   Ph: (616)453-1477
Grand Rapids, MI 49504   Fax: (616)453-1846
E-mail: pca@pcapaactinc.com

Contact: Janet E. Ney, Editor.

Desc: Contains reviews of current publications of prostate cancer research. Recurring features include reports of meetings and lists of affiliated prostate cancer research physicians. *Type:* Newsletter.

Center for Blood Research

800 Huntington Ave.   Ph: (617)731-6470
Boston, MA 02115   Fax: (617)278-3493

Contact: Richard L. Korn, Exec.V.Pres.

Desc: Human blood, including multidisciplinary studies on heart disease, diabetes, cancer, AIDS, hemophilia, sickle cell anemia, mental illness, hepatitis, Rh factor in pregnancy, serum proteins, blood collection methods, preservation of formed elements, methods of plasma fractionation, and characterization of plasma components. *Type:* Research center.

Center for Molecular Medicine and Immunology

520 Belleville Ave.   Ph: (973)844-7000
Belleville, NJ 07109   Fax: (973)844-7020
E-mail: gscancer@worldnet.att.net

Contact: Dr. David M. Goldenberg, Pres.

Desc: Molecular immunology, nuclear medicine, immunobiology, and molecular genetics. Seeks to advance cancer detection techniques and translate them into methods of treatment and control. *Type:* Research center.

Center for Radiation Therapy

5758 S. Maryland Ave.   Ph: (773)702-0817
MC 9006   Fax: (773)834-7233
Chicago, IL 60637
E-mail: rrw@rover.uchicago.edu

Contact: Ralph Weichselbaum, MD, Dir.

Desc: Cancer and treatment, including studies in radiation oncology, radiation biology, chemotherapy, and oncology information systems. *Type:* Research center.

Center for Research in Thrombolysis

Brigham & Women's Hospital   Ph: (617)732-5771
10 Vinings St.   Fax: (617)732-5753
Boston, MA 02115

Contact: Jack O'Connor, Contact.

Desc: Biochemistry and molecular biology of the mammalian fibrinolytic system. Projects include isolating and cloning membrane receptors and constructing and characterizing mutant forms of fibrinolytic inhibitors. *Type:* Research center.

Charity Hospital of New Orleans

Oncology Treatment Unit

Med.Ctr. of Louisiana   Ph: (504)568-3214
1532 Tulane Ave.   Fax: (504)568-3653
New Orleans, LA 70112

Contact: James Wm. C. Holmes, Dir.

Desc: Cancer, including clinical studies in chemotherapy, immunotherapy, surgery, and hyperthermia. *Type:* Research center.

Chemical Carcinogenesis Research Information System

U.S. National Library of Medicine (NLM)
Specialized Information Services Division
8600 Rockville Pike   Ph: (301)496-6531
Bethesda, MD 20894

E-mail: toxmail@toxnetmail.nlm.nih.gov
URL: http://toxnet.nlm.nih.gov

Contact: CCRIS Representative, (301)496-6531, fax: (301)480-3537, toxmail@tox.alm.nih.gov.

Desc: Contains citations, with data extracted, to the worldwide literature on test conditions and results of the carcinogenicity, co-carcinogenicity, mutagenicity, and tumor promotion and inhibition of over 5700 chemical substances. Both positive and negative results are reported. *Available:* Oxford Molecular Group, Chemical Information Systems; DIMDI (Deutsches Institut fuer Medizinische Dokumentation und Information); U.S. National Library of Medicine (NLM), TOXNET. *Type:* Database.

Chicago Medical School

H.M. Bligh Cancer Research Laboratories

3333 Green Bay Rd.   Ph: (847)578-3435
North Chicago, IL 60064   Fax: (847)578-3432
E-mail: springeg@mis.finchcms.edu

Contact: Prof. Georg F. Springer, MD, Contact.

Desc: Human cancer research, especially breast and lung cancer. Research activities include early immunodetection of carcinomas, and active use of T/Tn antigen vaccine to prevent recurrence of advanced breast carcinoma. *Type:* Research center.

Children's Center for Cancer and Blood Disorders

University of South Carolina   Ph: (803)434-3533
    School of Medicine   Fax: (803)434-3094
Richland Memorial Hospital
7 Richland Medical Park, Ste. 203
Columbia, SC 29203
E-mail: ronnie.neuberg@rmh.edu

Contact: Dr. Ronnie W. Neuberg, Dir.

Desc: Causes, treatments, and prevention of childhood cancer. Current research includes retinoids as cancer differentiating agents and as chemopreventitives. *Type:* Research center.

Children's Leukemia Research Association

585 Stewart Ave., Ste. 536   Ph: (516)222-1944
Garden City, NY 11530   Fax: (516)222-0457

Contact: Allan D. Weinberg, Exec.Dir.

Desc: Leukemia research and public awareness of the disease. *Type:* Research center.

Colorado Cancer Research Program

3955 E. Exposition, No. 104   Ph: (303)777-2663
Denver, CO 80209   Free: 888-785-6789
    Fax: (303)777-2642

E-mail: nmccrp@aol.com
URL: http://members.aol.com/ccrphp

Contact: Peter C. Raich, MD, Prin. Investigator.

Desc: Cancer and oncology. *Type:* Research center.

Columbia University

Herbert Irving Comprehensive Cancer Center

701 W. 168th St., Ste. PH 18-   Ph: (212)305-8610
    200   Fax: (212)305-6889
New York, NY 10032

E-mail: corinne@cuccfa.ccc.columbia.edu
URL: http://www.ccc.columbia.edu/

Contact: Karen Antman, MD, Dir.

Desc: The Center is organized into divisions: basic research; clinical research; cancer causation and prevention. Research areas include molecular tumor virology, oncogenes and molecular genetics, biophysics, cell biology, basic mechanisms of carcinogenesis, molecular epidemiology, biochemistry, endocrinology, and developmental biology. *Type:* Research center.

Columbia University

Herbert Irving Comprehensive Cancer Center

Institute of Cancer Research

630 W. 168th St.   Ph: (212)305-9327
PH 18-200   Fax: (212)305-7846
New York, NY 10032
E-mail: kha4@columbia.edu

Contact: Karen Antman, MD, Dir.

Desc: Cancer research. *Type:* Research center.

Community Cancer Programs in the U.S.

Association of Community Cancer Centers
11600 Nebel St., Ste. 201   Ph: (301)984-9496
Rockville, MD 20852   Fax: (301)770-1949

Contact: Lee E. Mortenson, Editor.

Desc: Approximately 560 freestanding and hospital-based cancer programs and therapies. *Type:* Directory.

Comprehensive Sickle Cell Center

Children's Hospital Med. Ctr.   Ph: (513)636-4541
3333 Burnet Ave.   Free: 800-344-2462
Cincinnati, OH 45229   Fax: (513)636-5562
E-mail: clint.joiner@CHMCC.org

Contact: Dr. Clinton Joiner, Dir.

Desc: Sickle cell disease, including molecular, cellular, tissue, and organ studies. Conducts clinical trials and seeks to translate research to improved health care. *Type:* Research center.

Comprehensive Sickle Cell Center

Harlem Hospital   Ph: (212)939-1700
Sickle Cell Dept., Rm. 6146   Fax: (212)939-1692
506 Lenox Ave.
New York, NY 10037

Contact: Dr. Jeanne A. Smith, Dir.

Desc: Sickle cell disease, including studies of pathophysiological aspects, intellectual growth and development of children with sickle cell and a llied diseases, biochemical factors involved in the clinical severity of the disease. *Type:* Research center.

Cross Cancer Institute

11560 University Ave.   Ph: (403)432-8771
Edmonton, AB, Canada T6G   Fax: (403)432-8411
    1Z2
E-mail: carolcas@cancerboard.ab.ca

Contact: Dr. A.L.A. Fields, Dir.

Desc: Molecular oncology, medical physics and biophysics, radiation and solid tumor biology, tumor immunobiology, and experimental radiotherapy and chemotherapy. The Institute is linked to the Provincial Cancer Registry. *Type:* Research center.

CTRC Research Foundation

14960 Omicron Dr.   Ph: (210)677-3800
San Antonio, TX 78245   Fax: (210)677-0058
URL: http://www.ctrc.saci.org

Contact: Daniel D. Von Hoff, MD, Pres.

Desc: Causes and treatment of cancer, emphasizing the development of new anticancer agents. Maintains the Institute for Drug Development, a division that studies and tests drugs awaiting Food and Drug Administration approval. *Type:* Research center.

Dana-Farber Cancer Institute

44 Binney St.   Ph: (617)632-2155
Boston, MA 02115   Fax: (617)632-2161

Contact: Dr. David Nathan, Pres.

Desc: Medical oncology, cancer pharmacology, pediatric oncology, cell growth and regulation, cancer genetics, human retrovirology, tumor immunology and virology, immunogenetics, lymphocyte biology, biostatistics and epidemiology, molecular carcinogenesis, biochemical pharmacology, neoplastic disease mechanisms, structural molecular biology, membrane immunochemistry, cancer control, tumor virus genetics, immunopathology, gene regulation, eukaryotic transcription, molecular biology, molecular genetics, molecular immunology, molecular immunobiology, medicine, gynecologic oncology, oncodiagnostic radiology and nuclear medicine, radiotherapy, and surgical oncology. *Type:* Research center.

Dana-Farber Cancer Institute

Department of Biostatistical Science

44 Binney St.   Ph: (617)632-3012
Boston, MA 02115   Fax: (617)632-2444
E-mail: dph@jimmy.harvard.edu

Contact: Dr. David P. Harrington, Ch.

Desc: Organized into the laboratories of biostatistics and computing, which carry on a multifaceted program combining independent research, collaboration, and consulting in quantitative methods as they apply to cancer research. Project areas include methodological research in statistics, mathematical models in chronic disease epidemiology, statistical computing, and applied probability and database research. *Type:* Research center.

Drew/Meharry/Morehouse Consortium Cancer Center

1005 D.B. Todd Blvd.   Ph: (615)327-6927
Nashville, TN 37208   Fax: (615)327-5838

Contact: Margaret Hargreaves, MD, Dir.

Desc: Cancer prevention and control, including epidemiological and behavioral research planning and implementation, and therapeutic clinical cancer trials. *Type:* Research center.

Duke University

Comprehensive Sickle Cell Center

Med. Ctr.   Ph: (919)684-6464
Box 3939   Fax: (919)681-6174
Durham, NC 27710
E-mail: telen002@mc.duke.edu

Contact: Marilyn J. Telen, M.D., Dir.

Desc: Sickle cell disease, including molecular, cellular, tissue, and organ studies. Conducts clinical trials. *Type:* Research center.

Duke University

Duke Comprehensive Cancer Center

DUMC, Box 3843   Ph: (919)684-3377
Durham, NC 27710   Fax: (919)684-5653
URL: http://www.canctr.mc.duke.edu
Contact: Dr. O. Michael Colvin, Dir.

Desc: Prevention, detection, diagnosis, and treatment of cancer, including multidisciplinary studies in cellular and molecular biology, chemical and environmental carcinogenesis, ultrastructure, cell genetics, virology, tumor immunology, epidemiology, and biostatistics. Conducts clinical investigations. *Type:* Research center.

Duke University

Southeastern Regional Trophoblastic Disease Center

Med. Ctr.   Ph: (252)684-3008
PO Box 3244   Fax: (252)684-6161
Durham, NC 27710
Contact: Dr. Charles B. Hammond, Co-Dir.

Desc: Research related to assay techniques for human chorionic gonadotropin as a tumor marker, the natural history of trophoblastic tumors, and effective therapy for trophoblastic disease. *Type:* Research center.

Eastern Cooperative Oncology Group

303 Boylston St.   Ph: (617)632-3610
Brookline, MA 02146-7648   Fax: (617)632-2990
E-mail: pbates@pgh.auhs.edu
URL: http://ecog.dfci.harvard.edu
Contact: Dr. Robert Comis, Chm.

Desc: Multidisciplinary cancer trials, including treatment, biologic and basic research, and cancer control and prevention. *Type:* Research center.

Emory University

Georgia Center for Cancer Statistics

1462 Clifton Rd. NE   Ph: (404)727-8700
Atlanta, GA 30322   Fax: (404)727-7261
E-mail: jliff@sph.emory.edu
Contact: Jonathan M. Liff, PhD, Dir.

Desc: Serves as a cancer registry for five counties of metropolitan Atlanta and ten rural counties in central Georgia. Seeks to monitor the incidence of cancer in a geographically defined population, identify groups with unusual risks of cancer, monitor oncologic practices within the community, assess the survival experience of cancer patients, and provide a resource for epidemiological and biostatistical studies and training. *Type:* Research center.

Emory University

Winship Cancer Center

1365 Clifton, Bldg. B, Ste. 4100   Ph: (404)778-5177
Atlanta, GA 30322   Fax: (404)778-5048
Contact: Dr. William Wood, Actg.Dir.

Desc: A university-based cancer center coordinating multidisciplinary basic and clinical cancer research, improving methods of treatment, diagnosis, and prevention, training health professionals, and transferring cancer knowledge to surrounding communities. *Type:* Research center.

The Extra Mile

1501 W. Lynn St.   Ph: (717)682-9081
Shamokin, PA 17872   Fax: (717)682-8734
Contact: Greg Zyla, Author.

Desc: Distributes automotive columns and features. *Alt. Contact:* 1501 W. Lynn St., Shamokin, PA 17872; telephone: (717)682-9081; fax: (717)682-8734. *Type:* Periodical.

Fitzpatrick Oncology Center

Champlain Valley Physicians   Ph: (518)561-2000
  Hospital   Fax: (518)562-7531
75 Beekman St.
Plattsburgh, NY 12901
URL: http://www.cvph.org/welcome.html
Contact: Debbie Donahue, Mgr.

Desc: Oncological clinical research. *Type:* Research center.

Foundation for Advanced Cancer Studies, Inc.

PO Box M
Frederick, MD 21702-1211
URL: http://www.facsi.org
Contact: Dr. G. Vande Woude, Pres.

Desc: Basic cancer research, focusing on the rapid dissemination of new research information to scientists, clinicians, and the public. *Type:* Research center.

Foundation for Blood Research

PO Box 190   Ph: (207)883-4131
Scarborough, ME 04070-0190   Free: 800-639-8605
                                  Fax: (207)883-1527
URL: http://www.sbr.org
Contact: Robert F. Ritchie, MD, Pres.

Desc: Health science education, epidemiology, genetics, immunology, oncology, perinatology, rheumatology, prenatal diagnosis, and cancer. Immunochemical analysis of human blood and other body fluids is performed and coupled with epidemiological data both for research on and for use in computer applications in disease diagnosis. *Type:* Research center.

Foundation for Research and Treatment of Cancer

4800 Fillmore Ave., No. 1359   Ph: (703)575-8987
Alexandria, VA 22311
Contact: Dr. Nour Safi, Dir.

Desc: Studies in mice of monoclonal antibodies as a diagnostic tool and treatment for cancer. *Type:* Research center.

Fox Chase Cancer Center

7701 Burholme Ave.   Ph: (215)728-6900
Philadelphia, PA 19111   Fax: (215)728-2571
E-mail: rc_young@fccc.edu
URL: http://www.fccc.edu
Contact: Robert C. Young, MD, Pres.

Desc: Cancer, including oncogenes, tumor-suppressing genes, chemical carcinogens, immunology, virology, membrane biology, and molecular structure (basic science division); immunotherapy and other investigational therapies including interferons and specific monoclonal antibodies, tumor-cell resistance to therapeutic drugs and radiation, diagnostic imaging, and NMR spectroscopy (medical science division); identification of high cancer risk individuals, risk reduction and early detection, and impact of environmental and genetic factors (population science division). *Type:* Research center.

Fred Hutchinson Cancer Research Center

1100 Fairview Ave. N.   Ph: (206)667-5000
PO Box 19024   Free: 800-4CA-NCER
Seattle, WA 98109-1024   Fax: (206)667-5268
E-mail: lhartwel@fhcrc.org
URL: http://www.fhcrc.org
Contact: Dr. Leland Hartwell, Dir.

Desc: Cancer, including basic, clinical, and public health sciences. Research programs include basic science, molecular medicine, human immunogenetics, marrow transplantation, organ systems, pain and toxicity, pediatric oncology, transplantation biology, biostatistics, cancer biology, cancer prevention research, and epidemiology. *Type:* Research center.

Front Line

Susan G. Komen Breast Cancer Foundation
Occidental Tower   Ph: (972)855-1600
5005 LBJ Freeway, Ste. 370   Free: 800-462-9273
Dallas, TX 75244   Fax: (972)855-1605
URL: http://www.komen.org;   http://www.
breastcancerinfo.com.
Contact: Emily Downward, Editor, edownward@komen.
org.

Desc: Provides information about breast cancer. Recurring features include news of research, a calendar of events, awards, and organization news. *Type:* Newsletter.

Garden State Cancer Center

John P. Caufield Technology Extension Center for Investigational Cancer Treatment

520 Belleville Ave.   Ph: (973)844-7000
Belleville, NJ 07109   Fax: (973)844-7020
E-mail: gscancer@worldnet.att.net
Contact: Dr. David M. Goldenberg, Dir.

Desc: Develops and provides new and more effective technologies for the early detection, diagnosis, and treatment of cancer; facilitates the transfer of investigational, diagnostic and treatment methods to New Jersey practitioners and hospitals; provides minority populations with access to state-of-the-art cancer protocols and treatment within their own community. *Type:* Research center.

Georgetown University

Vincent T. Lombardi Cancer Center

Research Bldg., E501   Ph: (202)687-2110
3970 Reservoir Rd. NW   Fax: (202)687-6402
Washington, DC 20007
URL: http://lombardi.georgetown.edu
Contact: Marc Lippman, MD, Dir.

Desc: Prevention, detection, diagnosis, and treatment of cancer, including clinical and basic science activities in all oncologic specialties (surgery, medicine, gynecology, pediatrics, radiology, pathology, urology, and immunology) and basic science studies in pharmacology, biochemistry, radiation biology, virology, molecular genetics, analytic chemistry, flow cytometry, and electron microscopy. *Type:* Research center.

Geraldine Brush Cancer Research Institute

California Pacific Med. Ctr.   Ph: (415)561-1728
Sterm Bldg.   Fax: (415)561-1390
2330 Clay St.
San Francisco, CA 94115
E-mail: helene@cooper.cpmc.org
Contact: Dr. Nancy M. Lee, Co-Dir.

Desc: Advanced molecular and cellular biology studies of human cancer. Special emphasis on breast cancer. *Type:* Research center.

Goodwin Institute for Cancer Research

1850 NW 69th Ave.   Ph: (954)587-9020
Plantation, FL 33313   Fax: (954)587-6378
E-mail: goddwin@gate.net
URL: http://www.gicr.com
Contact: Michael J. Dauphinee, PhD, Dir.

Desc: Fundamental investigations in biological sciences using specific pathogen-free animals to develop human tumor xenograft models and to determine association between viruses and cancer and to improve cancer therapy by drug synergism, immunotherapy and improved delivery of treatment modalities. Studies cover hybridoma technology and application, tumor therapy, immunohistochemistry, herpes simplex virus (mechanisms of latency and vaccine development), hemopoietic and tumor stem cell growth (promotion and inhibition), potentiation of chemotherapeutic responses by hyperthermia and DMSO, and tumor behavior in immunosuppressed animals. *Type:* Research center.

H. Lee Moffitt Cancer Center and Research Institute
12902 Magnolia Dr. Ph: (813)972-4673
Tampa, FL 33612 Fax: (813)972-3919
E-mail: ruckdeschel@moffitt.usf.edu
URL: http://www.moffitt.usf.edu
Contact: John C. Ruckdeschel, MD, Dir./CEO.
Desc: Basic, clinical, and cancer control programs in immunology, molecular oncology, experimental therapeutics, genetic immunotherapy, behavioral oncology, cancer prevention, tobacco intervention, digital medical imaging. Conducts clinical programs in all disease sites, including breast; thoracic oncology, cutaneous, and bone marrow transplantation, etc. *Type:* Research center.

Hamilton Regional Cancer Center
699 Concession St. Ph: (905)387-9495
Hamilton, ON, Canada L8V Fax: (905)575-6326
5C2
E-mail: mlevine@cancercare.uh.ca
Contact: Dr. Mark Levine, CEO.
Desc: Basic research focusing on tumor cell signalling and experimental therapeutics and clinical trials and supportive care research in cancer. Translational research focusing on new therapeutics from basic to clinical is highly encouraged. *Type:* Research center.

Harvard Medical School
Laboratory of Viral Pathogenesis
Dana-Farber Cancer Institute Ph: (617)632-3719
44 Binney St. Fax: (617)632-3112
Boston, MA 02115
E-mail: ruth_ruprecht@dfci.harvard.edu
Contact: Dr. Ruth M. Ruprecht, Ch.
Desc: Molecular biology and immunology, focusing on the interaction of retroviruses with cells and host organisms. *Type:* Research center.

Harvard University
Harvard Cyclotron Laboratory
44 Oxford St. Ph: (617)495-2885
Cambridge, MA 02138 Fax: (617)495-8054
E-mail: wagner@huhepl
URL: http://neurosurgery.mgh.harvard.edu/hcl/
Contact: Miles S. Wagner, Dir.
Desc: Proton beam technology for medical applications in both experimental and routine treatment of benign and cancerous tumors, including associated technical developments and clinical trials of proton radiation therapy and radiobiology. Other interests include proton activation analysis and other uses of proton beams, accelerator design study, and occasional radiation damage studies for commercial uses from aerospace and similar industries. *Type:* Research center.

Harvard University
Laboratory for Cell and Molecular Biology
New England Deaconess Ph: (617)632-9982
Hospital, Department of Fax: (617)632-9992
Med.
Burl Bldg., 5th Fl.
185 Pilgrim Rd.
Boston, MA 02215
Contact: Dr. Arthur J. Sytkowski, Dir.
Desc: Biology of blood cell production, control mechanisms involved in normal cell growth and development, and identification of factors responsible for malignant transformation and neoplastic or cancerous growth. Ongoing studies include identifying the structural and functional properties of the erythropoietin molecule and the mechanisms of interaction with its receptor on the cell surface, identifying the role of cellular oncogenes in blood cell growth and differentiation, characterizing erythropoietin early response genes, and investigating gene therapy and erythroid burst promoting activity. *Type:* Research center.

Head and Neck Center
2157 Main St. Ph: (716)862-1830
Buffalo, NY 14214 Fax: (716)862-1839
Contact: Dr. John M. Lore, Jr., Dir.
Desc: Basic and clinical studies on head and neck cancer, especially in the areas of wound healing, bone regeneration, and biomaterials. *Type:* Research center.

Hereditary Cancer Institute
Creighton Univ. Ph: (402)280-2942
Sch. of Med. Fax: (402)280-1734
2500 California Plz.
Omaha, NE 68178
E-mail: htlynch@creighton.edu
Contact: Henry T. Lynch, MD, Pres.
Desc: Hereditary cancer, including studies of its incidence and patterns. Disseminates current genetic, diagnostic, and therapeutic information to patients. *Type:* Research center.

Hipple Cancer Research Center
4100 S. Kettering Blvd. Ph: (937)293-8508
Dayton, OH 45439-2092 Fax: (937)293-7652
E-mail: hipple@hipple.org
Contact: Dr. Martin J. Murphy, Jr., Pres./CEO.
Desc: Cancer, primarily studies on hematopoietic growth factors, interferon mechanism of action, developing cloning technology, and the biology of metastasis. *Type:* Research center.

H.L. Snyder Memorial Research Foundation
1407 Wheat Rd. Ph: (316)221-4080
Winfield, KS 67156 Fax: (316)221-6825
E-mail: snyderrf@horizon.hit.net
Contact: Larry D. Smith, Dir.
Desc: Biochemical and molecular biological studies of diseases, especially cancer. Develops clinical assays for early cancer detection. *Type:* Research center.

Howard University
Cancer Center
2041 Georgia Ave. NW Ph: (202)806-7697
Washington, DC 20060 Fax: (202)667-1686
URL: http://www.howard.edu
Contact: Dr. Lucille Adams-Campbell, Actg.Dir.
Desc: Multidisciplinary genomic research of African-Americans. Basic research includes molecular biology of cancer, mechanisms of metastases, tumor immunology, pharmacology of antineoplastic drugs, clinical chemotherapeutic research, pilot studies for the treatment of various neoplasms, and radiotherapeutic research, including intraoperative radiation therapy, hyperthermia, and combined modality therapy. *Type:* Research center.

Howard University
Center for Sickle Cell Disease
2121 Georgia Ave. NW Ph: (202)806-7930
Washington, DC 20059 Fax: (202)806-4517
Contact: Dr. Oswaldo Castro, Dir.
Desc: Sickle cell disease, including basic and clinical investigations of its nature, causes, effects, and potential control. Develops and implements high quality total care for victims of the disease. *Type:* Research center.

IAL News
International Association of Laryngectomees (IAL)
7440 N. Shadeland Ave., Ste. Ph: (317)570-4568
100 Fax: (317)570-4570
Indianapolis, IN 46250
Contact: Jane S. Del Vecchio, Editor; Wayne Baker, Co-editor.
Desc: Provides information on rehabilitation of laryngectomy patients. Recurring features include reports of meetings. *Type:* Newsletter.

Illinois Oncology Research Association
900 Main St., Ste. 780 Ph: (309)671-5180
Peoria, IL 61602 Fax: (309)672-4138
E-mail: info@ohaci.com
URL: http://www.ohaci.com
Desc: Cancer treatment and control, including chemotherapy, immunotherapy, hormonal therapy, and radiation therapy. *Type:* Research center.

Indiana University
Herman B. Wells Center for Pediatric Research
Sch. of Med. Ph: (317)274-8900
702 Barnhill Dr., Rm. 2600 Fax: (317)274-5378
Indianapolis, IN 46202
E-mail: dwilliam@indyvax.iupui.edu
URL: http://www.iupui.edu/~wellsctr/
Contact: Dr. David Williams, Dir.
Desc: Hematology and oncology, cell biology of polarized cells (including the blood-brain barrier), protein sorting in eukaryotic cells, bone marrow transplantation, clinical oncology research, pediatric oncology, developmental biology of neuroblastoma, gene transfer into stem cells, tumor immunology, clinical aspects of childhood acute myelogenous leukemia, the role of protein phosphorylation in control of cell proliferation and differentiation, clinical aspects and molecular biology of neutrophil disorders, neurooncology, late effects of CNS therapy, clinical aspects of suportive care of oncology patients, therapy for neuroblastoma, clinical use of hemotopoietic growth factors, secondary leukemias, clinical aspects of hemostasis, molecular biology of myeloid-specific gene expression, cancer biogenesis using neuroblastoma as a model, and molecular biology of nuclear retinoic acid receptors in myeloid leukemia, neuroblastoma cells, endocrinology, neonatology, and pulmonary. *Type:* Research center.

Indiana University-Purdue University at Indianapolis
Center for Nursing Research
1111 Middle Dr., Rm. 338 Ph: (317)274-7627
Indianapolis, IN 46202
E-mail: iyjk100@indyvax.iupui.edu
URL: http://www.iupui.edu/~nursing/cnresrc.html
Contact: Dr. Victoria L. Champion, Dir.
Desc: Breast and prostate cancer. *Type:* Research center.

Indiana University-Purdue University at Indianapolis
Laboratory for Experimental Oncology
Sch. of Med. Ph: (317)274-7921
699 West St. Fax: (317)274-3939
Indianapolis, IN 46202-5119
E-mail: qw1@indy.bax.iupui.edu
Contact: Prof. George Weber, MD, Dir.
Desc: Biochemical pharmacology and chemotherapy of experimental and clinical cancer. *Type:* Research center.

Institute for Cancer and Blood Diseases
Alleheny Univ. Ph: (215)762-7026
Broad & Vine Sts. Fax: (215)762-8857
HU-MS412
Philadelphia, PA 19102
Contact: Dr. Isadore Brodsky, Dir.
Desc: Basic research program with possible clinical trials in the following areas: interferon, oncogenesis, differentiation, molecular biology, viral oncogenesis, immunology, cell biology, and cytogenesis. *Type:* Research center.

Institute for Cancer and Blood Research
150 N. Robertson Blvd., Ste. Ph: (310)657-4706
316 Fax: (310)657-2185
Beverly Hills, CA 90211
E-mail: labscience@worldnet.att.net

Contact: Dr. Howard R. Bierman, Sci.Dir.

Desc: Biochemical regulation of cell growth and control of leukocyte maturation in leukemias, including clinical studies to isolate and purify substances that stimulate cell division and maintain normal maturation of neoplastic cells; ultrastructural immunolocalization of novel protein products in myeloid leukemias; prediagnostic detection of cancer, oncogenes, and products for antioncogenes; detailed computer analysis of predictive-oriented data acquired from healthy subjects and patients with neoplastic disease; investigation of tumor diathesis, including preclinical diagnosis of multiple primary neoplasms and studies of families to define increased susceptibility to develop neoplasms; and continuing studies of dermatoglyphics, predictive profiles, and other genetic markers as they relate to neoplasia. *Type:* Research center.

Institute for Cancer Research

Fox Chase Cancer Ctr.   Ph: (215)728-2490
7701 Burholme Ave.   Fax: (215)728-2778
Philadelphia, PA 19111
E-mail: am_skalka@fccc.edu
URL: http://www.fccc.edu
Contact: Dr. Anna Marie Skalka, Dir.

Desc: Causes, nature, diagnosis, and treatment of cancer, including studies in cellular, molecular, and developmental biology, immunology, molecular oncology, structural biology, and virology. *Type:* Research center.

Intercenter Cancer Research Group, Inc.

1180 N. Indian Canyon Dr.,   Ph: (760)416-4730
Ste. E-320   Fax: (760)416-4735
Palm Springs, CA 92262
Desc: Oncology in the areas of breast, prostate, lung, and colon cancers, focusing on clinical trials involving hormonal treatments, chemotherapy, monoclonal antibodies, cytokines, as well as prevention trials. *Type:* Research center.

International Association for Comparative Research on Leukemia and Related Diseases

Harvard Sch. of Public Health   Ph: (617)432-1023
FXB, Room 405   Fax: (617)739-8348
651 Huntington Ave.
Boston, MA 02215
Contact: Dr. Myron Essex, Sec.Gen.

Desc: Leukemia and related diseases, focusing on the comparative aspects of different disciplines in order to develop new hypotheses and introduce comparable working methods. *Type:* Research center.

Iowa Oncology Research Association

1223 Center St., Ste. 19   Ph: (515)244-7586
Des Moines, IA 50309-1014   Fax: (515)244-3037
Contact: Roscoe F. Morton, MD, Prin.Invest.

Desc: Clinical cancer studies, including new chemotherapy agents and radiation therapy techniques. *Type:* Research center.

Jerome H. Holland Laboratory

American Red Cross   Ph: (301)738-0623
15601 Crabbs Branch Way   Fax: (301)738-0553
Rockville, MD 20855
E-mail: hoyer@usa.redcross.org
URL: http://biomed.redcross.org/research
Contact: Leon W. Hoyer, MD, Dir.

Desc: Blood cells, blood proteins, cytokines, receptors, blood services technology, tissue biology, epidemiology of transfusion-transmitted diseases, plasma derivatives, adhesion factors, angiogenesis, inflammation. Conducts basic and applied research and development for the Biomedical Services Division of the American Red Cross. *Type:* Research center.

J.L. and Helen Kellogg Cancer Care Center

Evanston Hospital   Ph: (847)570-2110
2650 Ridge Ave.   Fax: (847)570-2918
Evanston, IL 60201
E-mail: J.Kmandeicar@nwu.edu
Contact: Dr. J.D. Khandekar, Dir.

Desc: Treatment and diagnosis of cancer, including phase 1 and 2 studies, evaluation of new drug protocols, role of hyperthermia in the treatment of tumors, and brain tumor studies. Basic and clinical research also includes studies of breast, head and neck, lung, bladder, and pancreatic cancers, blood clotting and fibrinolytic mechanisms in tumor patients, thromboembolic problems in cancer patients, pituitary tumor surgery, immunology/virology, microbiology, hematology, clinical biochemistry, pharmacology, diagnosis by fine needle aspiration techniques, oncogens, medical oncology, and psychiatry. *Type:* Research center.

Johns Hopkins University

Oncology Center

600 N. Wolfe St., Rm. 157   Ph: (410)955-8822
Baltimore, MD 21287-8943   Fax: (410)955-6787
E-mail: mabeloff@welchlink.welch.jhu.edu
URL: http://www.med.jhu.edu/cancerctr/
Contact: Martin D. Abeloff, MD, Dir.

Desc: Cancer and related disorders, with bone marrow transplantation, cancer biology, medical oncology, pediatric oncology, pharmacology and experimental therapeutics, and radiological sciences. Activities emphasize the application of new knowledge to management of patients with cancer and prevention of neoplastic diseases and their complications, with major aim of the several complementary research programs of the Center being an increased understanding of human neoplasia and more effective clinical management. *Type:* Research center.

Johns Hopkins University

Physiological Mechanics and Transport Laboratory

School of Medicine   Ph: (410)614-5929
Department of Biomedical   Fax: (410)614-8796
  Engineering
Baltimore, MD 21205
E-mail: medwards@bme.jhu.edu
URL: http://www.bme.jhu.edu/~apopel/PMTL.html
Contact: Prof. Aleksander S. Popel, PhD, Contact.

Desc: Mechanics and regulation of blood flow, oxygen transport to tissue, blood flow and molecular transport in the cerebral circulation, and the mechanics and electromotility of the cochlear outer hair cell. *Type:* Research center.

Kansas City Clinical Oncology Program

6601 Rockhill Rd.   Ph: (816)276-7834
Kansas City, MO 64131-9000   Fax: (816)926-2292
E-mail: kccop@kccop.org
URL: http://www.kccop.org
Contact: Leslie Herst, Dir.

Desc: Oncological clinical trials. *Type:* Research center.

Kansas State University

Center for Basic Cancer Research

1500 Hayes Dr., Ste. B   Ph: (913)532-6705
Manhattan, KS 66502-5014   Fax: (913)776-5273
E-mail: terryj@ksu.edu
URL: http://www.ksu.edu/cancer.center
Contact: Dr. Terry C. Johnson, Dir.

Desc: Cancer autonomy and metastasis; tumor initiation, promotion, and progression; chemotherapeutic compounds; growth regulation, the immune system, and other cellular interactions; and oncogene expression. *Type:* Research center.

Kentucky Cancer Program

University of Kentucky/Markey   Ph: (606)323-6541
  Cancer Center   Fax: (606)323-6990
206 Davis Mills Bldg.
800 Rose St.
Lexington, KY 40536-0098
E-mail: lhl@delos.kcr.uky.edu
URL: http://www.kcr.uky.edu/home.html
Contact: Linda H. Linville, PhD, Div.Dir.

Desc: Cancer control. Collects and disseminates information leading to improved prevention, diagnosis, and treatment of cancer. *Type:* Research center.

Laboratory of Signal Transduction

Memorial Sloan-Kettering   Ph: (212)639-8573
  Cancer Ctr.   Fax: (212)639-2767
1275 York Ave.
Box 254
New York, NY 10021
Contact: Dr. Richard Kolesnick, Prin.Invest.

Desc: Signal transduction for cytokines and hormones, including tumor necrosis factor-alpha, interleukin-1, and activin. *Type:* Research center.

Laboratory of Tumor Antigen Immunochemistry

Memorial Sloan-Kettering   Ph: (212)639-2257
  Cancer Ctr.   Fax: (212)717-3379
1275 York Ave.
New York, NY 10021
E-mail: klloyd@ski.mskcc.org
URL: http://www.mskcc.,edu
Contact: Dr. Kenneth O. Lloyd, Contact.

Desc: Monoclonal antibodies and carbohydrate antigens. *Type:* Research center.

Laval University

Cancer Research Centre

Hotel-Dieu de Quebec   Ph: (418)691-5281
9 McMahon   Fax: (418)691-5439
Quebec, PQ, Canada G1R 2J6
E-mail: Luc.Belanger@crhdq.ulaval.ca
URL: http://www.crhdq.ulaval.ca
Contact: Dr. Luc Belanger, Sci.Dir.

Desc: Cellular and molecular mechanisms relating differentiation and cancer, including genomic organization and molecular regulation of fetoprotein, histones, metallothionein, oncogenes, cytochromes P-450 and developmental tyrosine kinase genes, developmental genes in embryonic stem cell mice, structure of active versus inactive chromatin, nature of neoplastic liver cell progenitors, role of growth factor-cell interactions in tissue growth, differentiation and neoplasia, cell surface markers of bladder cancer, hormone receptors, mechanisms of ribosomal transcription, action of DNA intercalating drugs, carcinogen activation, and mutagenesis. Also conducts research and development activities in clinical oncology, cancer epidemiology and psycho-oncology. *Type:* Research center.

Laval University

Medical Research Centre

Molecular Endocrinology Research Group

2705, boulevard Laurier   Ph: (418)654-2296
Ste. Foy, PQ, Canada G1V 4G2   Fax: (418)654-2761
E-mail: fernand.labrie@crchul.ulaval.ca
URL: http://www.crchul.ulaval.ca
Contact: Dr. Fernand Labrie, Dir.

Desc: Prostate and other hormone-sensitive cancers, strategies for early screening for prostate cancer, mechanisms regulating C-19 steroid formation by adrenal glands, characterization of effects of steroid sex hormones, adrenal hormone effects on brain dopaminergic systems, molecular mechanisms responsible for the expression of genes in specific tissues and their extinction in others, cloning and characterization of enzymes implicated in steroidogenesis, hormonal control of growth factors, polyamine biosynthesis in human breast cancer, and regulation of the expression of enzymes involved in steroidogenesis in placenta and adrenal glands. *Type:* Research center.

Leukemia Society of America

600 3rd Ave.
New York, NY 10016

Ph: (212)573-8484
Free: 800-955-4LSA
Fax: (212)856-9686

E-mail: infocenter@leukemia.org
URL: http://www.leukemia.org
Contact: Dwayne Howell, Pres. & CEO.
Desc: Raises funds to combat leukemia, lymphoma, Hodgkin's Disease and myeloma through research, patient service, and public and professional education and advocacy. Sponsors medical symposia; conducts research; provides financial aid for patients and free information; sponsors support groups. *Type:* Association.

Loma Linda University
Cancer Institute

11360 Mountain View Ave.,
Ste. E
PO Box 2000
Loma Linda, CA 92354

Ph: (909)799-6003
Fax: (909)799-6020

E-mail: RIS@lluci.llu.edu
URL: http://www.llu.edu/llu/ci/
Contact: Dr. James M. Slater, Dir.
Desc: Cancer prevention and treatment, specifically molecular genetics, neurosciences, and cancer cell and molecular biology and their relationships to cancer; and translating basic science findings into clinical applications. *Type:* Research center.

London Regional Cancer Centre

790 Commissioners Rd. E.
London, ON, Canada N6A 4L6

Ph: (519)685-8640
Fax: (519)685-8614

E-mail: llevin@lrcc.on.ca
URL: http://www.lrcc.on.ca/
Contact: Dr. Leslie Levin, CEO.
Desc: Molecular biology of cancer, with emphasis on tumor metastasis and progression and on drug resistance studies; molecular endocrinology, with emphasis on intracellular transportation of steroid hormones; and steroid receptors in breast cancer. Studies include physics and radiation oncology, including 3-D imaging, brachytherapy, portal imaging, and clinical trials. *Type:* Research center.

Manitoba Cancer Treatment and Research Foundation

100 Olivia St.
Winnipeg, MB, Canada R3E 0V9

Ph: (204)787-2241
Fax: (204)787-1184

E-mail: brent.schacter@mctrf.mb.ca
URL: http://mctrf.mb.ca
Contact: Dr. Brent A. Schacter, Pres./CEO.
Desc: Cancer treatment and research, including radiation oncology, surgical oncology, hematology, medical oncology, pediatric oncology, gynecologic oncology, medical physics, epidemiology, biostatistics, molecular biology, biochemical pharmacology, and immunology. Clinical trial research in association with NSABP, NCIC, CCSG, RTOG. *Type:* Research center.

Mary Bird Perkins Cancer Center

4950 Essen Ln.
Baton Rouge, LA 70809

Ph: (504)767-0847
Fax: (504)766-0218

Contact: Michael H. Martin, Pres./CEO.
Desc: Radiation and medical oncology treatment, including participation in national clinical trials of the Radiation Therapy Oncology Group and the Southwest Oncology Group, as well as pharmaceutical and in-house studies. *Type:* Research center.

Massachusetts General Hospital
Cancer Center

149 13th St., Bldg. 149
Charlestown, MA 02129

Ph: (617)726-5610
Fax: (617)726-5637

E-mail: isselbacher@helix.mgh.harvard.edu
Contact: Kurt Isselbacher, MD, Dir.
Desc: Cell cycle regulation and cancer genetics, including breast, colon, and melanoma, and metastasis. *Type:* Research center.

Massachusetts Institute of Technology
Center for Cancer Research

77 Massachusetts Ave.
E17-110
Cambridge, MA 02139-4307

Ph: (617)253-6400
Fax: (617)252-1891

E-mail: rohynes@mit.edu
URL: http://www.web.mit.edu/ccrhq/www/
Contact: Dr. Richard O. Hynes, Dir.
Desc: Cancer biology, emphasizing molecular biology, genetics, cell biology, developmental biology, and immunology. Specific areas of research include split genes and RNA splicing, cloning oncogenes and tumor suppressor genes from human tumors, T-cell receptors, integrin receptors and cell adhesion, mechanisms, used by tumor cells to evade chemotherapy, gene identification for myotonic dystrophy, Huntington's disease, and Wilm's tumor, the generation of various strains of mutant mice, biochemical mechanisms controlling RNA transcription and splicing, HIV gene studies, cytotoxic and helper T lymphocytes, lymphocyte antigen-specific receptors, molecular mechanisms of antigen presentation, cell surface proteins and cellular adhesion and migration, and cytoskeletal proteins and cell motility and shape. *Type:* Research center.

Mayo Cancer Center

200 1st St. SW
Rochester, MN 55905

Ph: (507)284-9589
Fax: (507)284-9349

E-mail: prendergast@mayo.edu
URL: http://www.mayo.edu
Contact: Dr. Franklyn G. Prendergast, Dir.
Desc: Broad-based cancer research program ranging from basic and clinical science to clinical studies on prevention, detection, diagnosis, and treatment of cancer. Participates as a comprehensive cancer center for conducting research, improving methods of treatment, diagnosis, and prevention, training health professionals, and transferring cancer knowledge to surrounding communities in National Cancer Institute's nationwide coordination program, established under National Cancer Act of 1971. *Type:* Research center.

McGill University
McGill Cancer Centre

McIntyre Med. Sci. Bldg.
3655 Drummond St.
Montreal, PQ, Canada H3G 1Y6

Ph: (514)398-3535
Fax: (514)398-6769

E-mail: stanners@medcor.mcgill.ca
Contact: Dr. Clifford Stanners, Dir.
Desc: Cancer, including molecular biology of human and murine carcinoembryonic antigen, family nature and regulation of mammalian origins of DNA replication, molecular biology of dominant and recessive oncogenes, cancer related cellular surface sugar-containing molecules, and molecular basis of spatial differentiation in mice and its aberration in tumors. *Type:* Research center.

McMaster University
Cancer Research Group

Department of Pathology
Hamilton, ON, Canada L8S 4K1

Ph: (905)525-9140
Fax: (905)546-9940

E-mail: smiley@fhs.mcmaster.ca

URL: http://www.mcmaster.ca
Contact: Frank Graham, Coord.
Desc: DNA tumor viruses, including the molecular biology of the adenoviruses and herpesviruses. *Type:* Research center.

MCP Hahnemann University of the Health Sciences
Center for Neurovirology and Neurooncology
Laboratory of Molecular Oncology

Broad & Vine, Mail Stop 406
Philadelphia, PA 19102-1192

Ph: (215)762-3221

URL: http://www.auhs.edu/medschool/centers/ctrnvnonc.html
Contact: Ron Gartenhaus, MD, Dir.
Desc: Molecular pathogenesis of leukemias/lymphomas, the role of microsatellite instability and allelic loss in oncogenesis, and functional inactivation of tumor supressor genes in HTLV-1 transformed lymphocytes. *Type:* Research center.

Medical College of Georgia
Sickle Cell Center

AC 1004
Augusta, GA 30912-3128

Ph: (706)721-9640
Fax: (706)721-9637

E-mail: akutlar@mail.mcg.edu
Contact: Dr. Abdullah Kutlar, Dir.
Desc: Hemoglobinopathy detection, identification, and characterization, including studies of factors determining severity of sickle cell anemia in adults and the young child, cardiac evaluation of children with sickle cell anemia, thalassemia in association with sickle cell syndromes, biochemical studies in sickle cell anemia and related disorders with special emphasis on heterogeneity of Hb F, immunological identification, DNA gene mapping of hemoglobin variants, nucleotide sequence, and thalassemia genes, and characterization of hemoglobin variants. *Type:* Research center.

Medical College of Ohio
Cancer Research Division

Department of Pathology, HE 202
3055 Arlington Ave.
Toledo, OH 43614-5806

Ph: (419)383-4918
Fax: (419)383-3089

E-mail: hschut@.mco.edu
Contact: Dr. Herman A.J. Schut, Contact.
Desc: Cancer, including chemical carcinogenesis, chemoprevention, molecular biology, toxicology, and tissue culture. Specific research includes oncogene activation and suppressor gene inactivation in cancer, inhibition of cancer by dietary components, and regulation of tumor promotion. *Type:* Research center.

Medical College of Wisconsin
Cancer Center

8701 Watertown Plank Rd.
Milwaukee, WI 53226

Ph: (414)805-4455
Fax: (414)805-4354

E-mail: mkircher@post.its.mcw.edu
Contact: J. Frank Wilson, MD, Dir.
Desc: Experimental Therapy program focuses on developing new agents and strategies for the treatment of cancer, including photodynamic therapy; understanding cell resistance, focusing on glutathione, iron metabolism and nitric oxide; and limiting the toxicity and side effects of cancer treatment, focusing on gastrointestinal effects and chronic renal damage caused by radiation therapy; Cancer Biologyand Molecular Genetics Program studies regulatory mechanisms at the structural, cellular and molecular levels in the following areas: regulation of cell growth and orcogenesis, development, virology and viral transformation,

and molecular diagnostics; Cancer Prevention and Control Program conducts several multi-year studies in behavioral interventions are on-going in the areas of environmental hazards (pesticides and cancer risk), smoking cessation interventions, skin cancer prevention education, early screening education and nutrition education; research interest in quality of life issues in the areas of pediatric, breast and head/neck cancers; and studies in chemotherapeutic agents in cancer prevention; Bone Marrow Transplantation/Immunology Program conducts ongoing studies in T-cell depletion, cytokines, graft-vs-host disease; autologous, allogenic, and unrelated donor therapies; lymphocyte infusion; International Bone Marrow Transplant Registry. *Type:* Research center.

Meharry Medical College

Comprehensive Sickle Cell Center

1005 D.B. Todd Blvd.   Ph: (615)327-6763
Nashville, TN 37208   Fax: (615)327-6008
E-mail: sickle90@ccvax.mmc.edu
Contact: Dr. Ernest A. Turner, MD, Dir.
Desc: Basic, clinical, and psychosocial research in sickle cell disease and variants of the disease in the fields of biochemistry, biology, molecular biology, medicine, pediatric medicine, social science, and psychiatry. *Type:* Research center.

Memorial Sloan-Kettering Cancer Center

1275 York Ave.   Ph: (212)639-2000
New York, NY 10021   Fax: (212)639-5850
URL: http://www.mskcc.org
Contact: Dr. Paul A. Marks, Pres.
Desc: Molecular biology, cell biology and genetics, cellular biochemistry and biophysics, immunology, and molecular pharmacology and therapeutics. Aims to advance the understanding of the nature and fundamental causes of cancer and improve the means available for its prevention, diagnosis, and treatment. *Type:* Research center.

Memorial Sloan-Kettering Cancer Center

Cooperative Core Laboratories and Clinical Nutrition Research Unit

Box 140   Ph: (212)639-8352
1275 York Ave.   Fax: (212)639-5115
New York, NY 10021
E-mail: rivlinr@mskcc.org
Contact: Dr. Richard S. Rivlin, Prin.Investor.
Desc: Promotes nutrition activities to advance multidisciplinary research, upgrade teaching of nutrition for medical students, physicians, and other health professionals, and improve the clinical care of patients at participating medical centers and in the general population. *Type:* Research center.

Memorial Sloan-Kettering Cancer Center

Laboratory of GI Tumor Biology

1275 York Ave.   Ph: (212)639-8379
Box 244   Fax: (212)717-3053
New York, NY 10021
Contact: Dr. Eileen A. Friedman, Dir.
Desc: Signal transduction initiated by DAGs and FGF's through a common cellular tyrosine kinase substrate, focusing on pathway characterization and alteration during both enterocytic and goblet cell differentiation. *Type:* Research center.

Mercy Cancer Institute

Cancer Research Laboratory

Mercy Regional Oncology Ctr. Ph: (412)232-5754
1400 Locust St.   Fax: (412)232-5753
Pittsburgh, PA 15219
E-mail: ssingh@mercy.pmhs.org
Contact: Shivendra V. Singh, Dir.
Desc: Molecular biology studies in the areas of akylating and multi-drug resistance and the characterization of po-

tentially new lung cancer genes. Studies to determine mechanism of cancer prevention by garlic organosulfides, investigate toxicological relevance of human glutathione S-transferase Pl-l polymorphism in relation to suceptibility to cancer induced by environmental pollutants such as polycyclic aromatic hydrocarbons. *Type:* Research center.

Michigan State University

Carcinogenesis Laboratory

341 Food Safety & Toxicology   Ph: (517)353-7785
  Bldg.   Fax: (517)353-9004
East Lansing, MI 48824
E-mail: maher@com.msu.edu
URL: http://www.com.msu.edu/carcino/
Contact: Veronica M. Maher, PhD, Univ. Distinguished Prof.
Desc: Carcinogenesis, including research in cellular and molecular biology, mutagenesis, mammalian cell DNA repair, and homologous recombination. *Type:* Research center.

Montreal Cancer Institute

1560 Sherbrooke St. E.   Ph: (514)281-6055
Montreal, PQ, Canada H2L   Fax: (514)896-4689
  4M1
E-mail: info@icm.qc.ca
URL: http://www.icm.qc.ca
Contact: Dr. Pierre Chartrand, Dir.
Desc: Viral carcinogenesis, molecular biology, genetic engineering, biochemical changes associated with neoplastic transformation, epidemiology of cancer, and clinical pharmacology. *Type:* Research center.

Mountain States Tumor Institute, Inc.

100 E. Idaho   Ph: (208)381-3132
Boise, ID 83712-6241   Fax: (208)381-2974
Contact: Sharon Frelleson, RN, Clin.Res.Coord.
Desc: Adult and pediatric oncology clinical trials. *Type:* Research center.

National Alliance of Breast Cancer Organizations

9 E. 37th St., 10th Fl.   Ph: (212)719-0154
New York, NY 10016   Free: 800-719-9154
                           Fax: (212)689-1213
E-mail: NABCOinfo@aol.com
URL: http://www.nabco.org
Contact: Amy Langer, Exec.Dir.
Desc: Breast centers; hospitals; government health offices; and support and research organizations providing information about breast cancer and breast diseases from early detection through continuing care. Serves as a resource for: organizations requiring information about breast cancer programs and organizations and medical advances; individuals seeking information about research, developments, and treatment options for breast cancer. Seeks to influence public and private health policy on issues pertaining to breast cancer, such as insurance reimbursement, health care legislation, and research funding priorities. *Type:* Association.

National Black Leadership Initiative on Cancer

Charles Drew Univ. of Med. &   Ph: (323)294-8211
  Sci.   Fax: (323)294-8917
3762 Santa Rosalia
Los Angeles, CA 90008
URL: http://cdrewu.edu/com.servs/nblic.intro.html
Contact: Pha Patrick, Dir.
Desc: Cancer prevention and mortality in the black community. *Type:* Research center.

National Breast Cancer Coalition

1707 L St. NW, Ste. 1060   Ph: (202)296-7477
Washington, DC 20036   Free: 800-622-2838
                            Fax: (202)265-6854
URL: http://www.natlbcc.org
Contact: Fran Visco, Pres.
Desc: Breast cancer survivors and their family members; other individuals with an interest in breast cancer and its prevention, diagnosis, and treatment. Seeks to "eradicate breast cancer by focusing the public and scientific community, Congress and the Administration on the disease and by educating and activating women who have been diagnosed with breast cancer and all women and men concerned about the issue". *Type:* Association.

National Cancer Institute of Canada

Clinical Trials Group

82 Barrie St.   Ph: (613)545-6430
Kingston, ON, Canada K7L Fax: (613)545-2941
  3N6
E-mail: paterj@ncic.ctg.queensu.ca
URL: http://www.ctg.queensu.ca/public_site/mission.htm
Contact: Dr. J.L. Pater, Dir.
Desc: Cancer, cancer therapy, and supportive care. *Type:* Research center.

National Foundation for Cancer Research

4600 East West Hwy., Ste. 525   Ph: (301)654-1250
Bethesda, MD 20814   Free: 800-321-CURE
                               Fax: (301)654-5824
E-mail: fcsjr@nfcr.org
URL: http://www.nfcr.org
Contact: Franklin Salisbury, Jr., Pres.
Desc: Contracts with major universities for basic science cancer research in the fields of biophysics, theoretical physics and chemistry, biochemistry, chemistry, and biological sciences. *Type:* Research center.

National Foundation for Cancer Research

4600 W. West Hwy., Ste. 525   Ph: (301)654-1250
Bethesda, MD 20814   Free: 800-321-2873
                               Fax: (301)654-5824
E-mail: fcsj@snfcr.org
URL: http://www.nfcr.org
Contact: Franklin C. Salisbury, Jr., Pres.
Desc: Purpose is to conduct basic scientific research and scientific investigation of the structure and function of normal and abnormal cells. *Type:* Association.

National Surgical Adjuvant Breast and Bowel Project

East Commons Professional   Ph: (412)330-4600
  Bldg.   Fax: (412)330-4661
4 Allegheny Center, 5th Fl.
Pittsburgh, PA 15212-5234
URL: http://www.nsabp.pitt.edu
Contact: Dr. Norman Wolmark, Chm.
Desc: Breast and bowel cancer treatments and breast cancer prevention. Operates in cooperation with over 300 member institutions throughout the U.S., Canada, Puerto Rico, and Australia. *Type:* Research center.

New England Medical Center Hospitals, Inc.

Gynecologic Oncology Group

750 Washington St.   Ph: (617)636-6058
Box 232   Fax: (617)636-3258
Boston, MA 02111
E-mail: evelyn.nunez@es.nemc.org
URL: http://www.nemc.org
Contact: Evelyn R. Nunez, MD, Dir.
Desc: Treatment of gynecologic cancer. Evaluates surgical techniques, radiation therapy, and new chemotherapeutic agents. *Type:* Research center.

New York Medical College

Institute of Breast Diseases

Munger Pavilion, Rm. G-13   Ph: (914)493-8770
Valhalla, NY 10595   Fax: (914)493-1651
E-mail: zachrau@nymc.edu
Contact: Reinhard E. Zachrau, MD, Contact.
Desc: Breast diseases, including skin window reactivity and second primary breast cancer. *Type:* Research center.

New York University

Kaplan Comprehensive Cancer Center

550 1st Ave.   Ph: (212)263-5349
New York, NY 10016   Fax: (212)263-8211
E-mail: ira.goodman@atmccmsf.med.nyu.edu
URL: http://www.med.nyu.edu/kccc/homepage.html
Contact: Franco Muggia, MD, Dir.
Desc: Cancer research is carried out in designated program units of cancer epidemiology and prevention, cell interactions, clinical oncology, environmental carcinogenesis, genetic and molecular toxicology, growth regulation, molecular and tumor immunology, and molecular and viral oncology. *Type:* Research center.

Norris Cotton Cancer Center

Dartmouth-Hitchcock Med. Ctr.   Ph: (603)650-6300
Lebanon, NH 03756   Free: 800-639-6918
   Fax: (603)650-6333
E-mail: norris.cotton.cancer.center@dartmouth.edu
URL: http://nccc.hitchcock.org/
Contact: E. Robert Greenberg, MD, Contact.
Desc: Clinical treatment trials, including bone marrow transplantation, chemotherapy trials, intraoperative radiation therapy, and monoclonal antibody treatment. Studies are conducted in the areas of tumor immunology, radiobiology, chemical carcinogenesis, cancer epidemiology, cancer control, cytogenetics, tumor endocrinology, molecular genetics, cancer risk, and palliative care. *Type:* Research center.

North Central Cancer Treatment Group

Operations Office   Ph: (507)284-9682
200 1st St. SW   Fax: (507)284-1902
Rochester, MN 55905
E-mail: kuhlmann.marilyn@mayo.edu
URL: http://ncctg.mayo.edu
Contact: Dr. Michael J. O'Connell, Chm.
Desc: Cancer research and therapy, including surgery, medical oncology, therapeutic radiology, pathology, and cancer control. Seeks to transfer nationwide cancer research and therapy to patients at the community level. *Type:* Research center.

Northeast Louisiana University

Cancer Research Center

700 University Ave.   Ph: (318)342-1819
Monroe, LA 71209   Free: 800-423-8192
   Fax: (318)342-1824
Desc: Cancer research, including epidemiology and causes of bladder, breast, prostate, myelo-proliferative, and lympho-proliferative cancers. *Type:* Research center.

Northern California Cancer Center

32960 Alvarado-Niles Rd., Ste.   Ph: (510)429-2500
600   Fax: (510)429-2550
Union City, CA 94587
E-mail: dwest@nccc.org
URL: http://www.nccc.org
Contact: Dee W. West, PhD, Exec.Dir.
Desc: Conducts multidisciplinary studies in epidemiology and related fields. Also conducts cancer research and demonstration activities (detection, psychosocial, prevention, nutrition) with communities in the Center's service area, focusing on the minority populations and the underserved. *Type:* Research center.

Northwestern University

John I. Brewer Trophoblastic Disease Center

Prentice Women's Hospital   Ph: (312)908-7365
333 E. Superior, Ste. 420   Fax: (312)908-2188
Chicago, IL 60611
E-mail: jlurain@nmh.org
Contact: John R. Lurain, MD, Dir.
Desc: Pathology, epidemiology, and experimental chemotherapy in patients with trophoblastic diseases; experimental protocols and new chemotherapeutic agents and combinations of agents; pathologic studies of choriocarcinoma and hydatidiform mole; and the effect of oral contraceptive use on the development of gestational trophoblastic diseases. *Type:* Research center.

Northwestern University

Robert H. Lurie Cancer Center

Olson Pavilion 8250   Ph: (312)908-5250
303 E. Chicago Ave.   Fax: (312)908-1372
Chicago, IL 60611-3008
E-mail: s-rosen@nwu.edu
URL: http://www.nums.nwu.edu/lurie/
Contact: Steven T. Rosen, MD, Dir.
Desc: The Center has six established programs. Basic science programs include adhesion, motility, and angiogenesis; differentiation and development; hormone action and signal transduction; and molecular oncogenesis. *Type:* Research center.

Noujaim Institute for Pharmaceutical Oncology Research

University of Alberta   Ph: (403)492-5905
3118 Dentistry/Pharmacy Bldg.
Edmonton, AB, Canada T6G
2N8
URL: http://www.ualberta.ca/~noujaim
Contact: Prof. Leonard I. Wiebe, PhD, Dir.
Desc: Drug-based cancer diagnosis and therapy. *Type:* Research center.

Ohio Cancer Research Associates

50 W. Broad St., Ste. 1132   Ph: (614)224-1127
Columbus, OH 43215-3388   Fax: (614)224-0654
E-mail: ocra@ohiocancer.org
URL: http://www.ohiocancer.org
Contact: Dennis Zack, Dir.
Desc: Cancer "seed money" research projects. *Type:* Research center.

Ohio State University

Comprehensive Cancer Center

300 W. 10th Ave., Ste. 519   Ph: (614)293-3304
Columbus, OH 43210   Free: 800-293-5066
   Fax: (614)293-3132
URL: http://www-cancer.med.ohio-state.edu
Contact: Clara D. Bloomfield, MD, Dir.
Desc: Carcinogenesis, cancer chemoprevention, cancer control, immunology, developmental therapeutics, hormones and cancer, molecular biology, RNA oncogenic virus, neuro-oncology, head and neck oncology, urologic oncology, and pediatric oncology. Investigations also cover bone marrow transplantation, biochemistry and genetics, breast cancer, clinical trials, and pharmacology and toxicology. *Type:* Research center.

Ohio State University

Division of Hematology and Oncology

320 W. 10th Ave.   Ph: (614)293-8619
A437 Starling-Loving Hall   Fax: (614)293-3112
Columbus, OH 43210
E-mail: bloomfield-1@medctr.osu.edu
URL: http://www.medohio-state.edu

Contact: Clara D. Bloomfield, MD, Dir.
Desc: Research, patient service, and training through a fellowship program on various aspects of hematology and oncology, including cancer immunology, human cancer genetics, lymphocyte signaling, importance of complement in host defense against malignancy, the role of oxygen radicals in mononuclear effector cells and tumor cell targets, and clinical research in the development, implementation, and assessment of protocols in the treatment of leukemia, lymphoma, bone marrow transplantation, and solid tumors. The training program is designed to provide postdoctoral fellowship experience in the development and performance of clinical and laboratory research projects related to hematology and medical oncology. *Type:* Research center.

Oklahoma Medical Research Foundation

Immunobiology and Cancer Research Program

825 NE 13th St.   Ph: (405)271-7905
Oklahoma City, OK 73104   Fax: (405)271-8568
Contact: Paul W. Kincade, PhD, Hd.
Desc: Mechanisms for regulation of B lymphocyte production in lymphopoietic tissues, including cytokines, hormones, and cell adhesion molecules. *Type:* Research center.

Oncogenes & Growth Factors Abstracts

Cambridge Scientific Abstracts (CSA)
7200 Wisconsin Ave., Ste. 601   Ph: (301)961-6700
Bethesda, MD 20814-4823
E-mail: sales@csa.com
URL: http://www.csa.com
Desc: Contains 13,000 citations, with abstracts, to the worldwide literature on cancer research and the molecular basis of malignant transformations. Sources include specialist literature such as journals, books, conference proceedings, and reports. *Type:* Database.

Ontario Cancer Institute/Princess Margaret Hospital

610 University Ave.   Ph: (416)340-3300
Toronto, ON, Canada M5G   Fax: (416)340-3179
2M9
Contact: Dr. Alan Hudson, CEO.
Desc: Cancer research, including studies on mechanisms regulating cellular growth and differentiation (with emphasis on the hemopoietic system), cellular and molecular immunology (particularly mechanisms involved in immune-recognition), molecular structure (including physical and molecular biological approaches to macromolecular structure and interactions), experimental therapy (including radiobiology and chemotherapy), clinical physics and epidemiology (including research in preventative oncology, quality of life, and clinical trials methodology). Participates in local, national, and international trials, including studies of all sites and types of malignancies, imaging techniques, and therapeutic trials. *Type:* Research center.

Oregon Health Sciences University

Clinical Immunology and Hormone Receptor Laboratory

Pathology - L471   Ph: (503)494-4107
3181 SW Sam Jackson Park Rd.   Fax: (503)494-0731
Portland, OR 97201-3098
E-mail: bakkea@ohsu.edu
URL: http://www.ohsu.edu
Contact: Dr. Antony Bakke, Dir.
Desc: Breast cancer, including tissue analyses to establish whether certain hormone receptor molecules are present in breast cancer cells and whether tumor cells are likely to depend on hormones for growth, and DNA content and surface marker studies by flow cytometry. *Type:* Research center.

Palo Alto Institute of Molecular Medicine

2462 Wyandotte St.   Ph: (650)694-1420
Mountain View, CA 94043   Fax: (650)694-7717
E-mail: paimm@aol.com
URL: http://www.pano.com/paimm
Contact: Dr. James W. Larrick, Dir.
Desc: Cellular and molecular biology, cancer, and immunoinflammatory diseases. *Type:* Research center.

Patient Advocates for Advanced Cancer Treatment

1143 Parmelee NW   Ph: (616)453-1477
Grand Rapids, MI 49504-3844   Fax: (616)453-1846
E-mail: paact@compuserve.com
URL: http://www.osz.com/paact
Contact: Lloyd J. Ney, Sr., Exec. Officer.
Desc: Prostate cancer patients and physicians. Engages in advocacy activities. Provides educational materials to those with prostate cancer. *Type:* Association.

Physician Data Query Cancer Information File

U.S. National Cancer Institute
Bethesda, MD 20892   Ph: (301)496-6644
E-mail: hardingb@otd.nci.nih.gov
URL: http://www.cancernet.nci.nih.gov
Desc: Contains treatment, supportive care, screening and prevention information, and investigational drug information of interest to cancer patients. Comprises the following files: • Treatment Information: includes the complete text of prognosis and treatment information for the major types of cancer in children and adults, including AIDS-related malignancies. *Available:* Ovid Technologies, Inc.; U.S. National Library of Medicine (NLM), TOXNET. *Type:* Database.

Physician Data Query Directory File

U.S. National Cancer Institute
Bethesda, MD 20892   Ph: (301)496-6644
E-mail: hardingb@otd.nci.nih.gov
URL: http://www.cancernet.nci.nih.gov
Desc: Contains the names, addresses, and telephone numbers for more than 21,000 names, addresses, and telephone numbers of physicians involved extensively in the treatment of cancer patients. Includes names from the membership directories of major oncologic societies, and names of clinical investigators. *Available:* Ovid Technologies, Inc.; Ovid Technologies, Inc.; U.S. National Library of Medicine (NLM), TOXNET. *Type:* Database.

Physician Data Query Protocol File

U.S. National Cancer Institute
Bethesda, MD 20892   Ph: (301)496-6644
E-mail: hardingb@otd.nci.nih.gov
URL: http://www.cancernet.nci.nih.gov
Desc: Contains information on more than 1500 summaries of clinical trials that are open for patient accrual or have been approved for patient accrual. Also contains protocols for cancer treatment, supportive care, early detection and prevention, as well as 8000 summaries of protocols that have been completed or are no longer accepting patients. *Available:* Ovid Technologies, Inc.; Ovid Technologies, Inc.; U.S. National Library of Medicine (NLM), TOXNET. *Type:* Database.

Pohl Cancer Research Laboratory, Inc.

Georgia College C BX 082   Ph: (912)453-4565
Department of Chemistry &   Fax: (912)453-5271
  Physics
Milledgeville, GA 31061
E-mail: dpohl@mail.gcsu.edu
Contact: Prof. Douglas G. Pohl, Dir.
Desc: Cancer research, including electroactive polymers, dielectrophoresis, biophysics, electric properties of cells, cellular response to electric fields, and cell growth and control. Applications of research include instrumentation, diagnostics, and cell fusion apparatus. *Type:* Research center.

Purdue University

Cancer Center

Life Sci. Res. Bldg.   Ph: (765)494-9129
1524 Hansen   Fax: (765)494-9193
West Lafayette, IN 47907-1524
Contact: Richard F. Borch, MD, Dir.
Desc: Experimental therapeutics and diagnostics, structural biology, cell growth and differentiation. *Type:* Research center.

Revici Foundation for Lipid Research

200 West 57th St.   Ph: (212)246-5122
New York, NY 10019   Fax: (212)246-1535
Contact: Anita Whiteburg, MD, Dir.
Desc: Develops lipid therapy for various physiopathological conditions. Conducts studies on experimental theories in oncology, particulary the use of lipid therapy in physiopathological conditions. *Type:* Research center.

Rockefeller University

Laboratory of Molecular Oncology

1230 York Ave.   Ph: (212)327-8803
New York, NY 10021-6399   Fax: (212)327-7943
E-mail: saburo@rockvax.rockefeller.edu
Contact: Prof. Hidesaburo Hanafusa, Hd.
Desc: Mechanisms of carcinogenesis in virus-induced cancers. *Type:* Research center.

Roger Williams General Hospital

Roger Williams Cancer Center

Roger Williams Medical Center   Ph: (401)456-2082
825 Chalkstone Ave.   Fax: (401)456-2658
Providence, RI 02908
Contact: Robin Davies, Contact.
Desc: Cancer research program with drug development, cancer biology, radiation biology, neurology, and clinical studies components. *Type:* Research center.

Roswell Park Cancer Institute

Elm & Carlton Sts.   Ph: (716)845-2300
Buffalo, NY 14263   Free: 800-685-6825
    Fax: (716)845-3545
URL: http://www.roswellpark.org
Contact: Dr. David C. Hohn, Pres.
Desc: Molecular biology, biophysics, genetics, immunology, experimental therapeutics,and epidemiology of cancer, including the clinical application of recent findings in cancer research and the effectiveness of surgery, chemotherapy, and radiation in cancer therapy. Research program includes work in drug development, pharmacokinetics, crystallography, photodynamic therapy, and biological response modifiers. *Type:* Research center.

Roswell Park Cancer Institute

Laboratory of Flow Cytometry

Elm and Carlton Sts.   Ph: (716)845-8471
Buffalo, NY 14263   Fax: (716)845-8806
E-mail: stewart@sc3101.med.buffalo.edu
URL: http://rcpi.med.buffalo.edu/
Contact: Dr. Carleton Stewart, Dir.
Desc: Licensed reference laboratory for the classification by immunophenotyping of leukemias and lymphomas, monitoring of transplant patients, and evaluation of DNA in solid tumors. Also uses multiparameter flow cytometry to study normal myeloid cell differentiation and the development of molecular phenotyping. *Type:* Research center.

Roswell Park Cancer Institute

Transgenic Facility

Molecular & Cellular Biology   Ph: (716)845-4572
  Dept.
273 Cell & Virus Annex
Elm & Carlton Sts.
Buffalo, NY 14263
E-mail: gross@mcbio.med.buffalo.edu
URL: http://rpci.med.buffalo.edu/scientific.report/
transgen.html
Contact: Kenneth W. Gross, PhD, Dir.
Desc: Transgenics, including genome modification. *Type:* Research center.

Roswellness

Roswell Park Cancer Institute
Elm and Carlton St.s   Ph: (716)845-4565
Buffalo, NY 14263   Fax: (716)845-3575
Contact: Colleen Karuza, Editor.
Desc: Reports on news and events of the Roswell Park Cancer Institute in New York. Recurring features include news of research and columns titled Life After Cancer, Volunteer Spotlight, Endowment Funds, Donor Honor Roll, and Special People. *Type:* Newsletter.

Rush University

Bone Marrow Transplant Center

Rush-Presbyterian-St. Luke's   Ph: (312)942-6173
  Med. Ctr.   Fax: (312)733-1590
1653 W. Congress Pky.
Chicago, IL 60612
E-mail: hklingem@rush.edu
Contact: Dr. Hans Klingemann, Dir.
Desc: Bone marrow transplantation in the treatment of leukemia, malignant lymphoma, myeloma, breast cancer, and graft-versus host disease in allogenic bone marrow transplantation. *Type:* Research center.

Rush University

Rush Cancer Institute

Rush-Presbyterian-St. Luke's   Ph: (312)563-2190
  Med. Ctr.   Fax: (312)455-9635
1725 W. Harrison St.
Professional Bldg. I
Chicago, IL 60612
URL: http://www.rpslmc.edu
Contact: Harvey D. Preisler, MD, Dir.
Desc: Cancer, including biochemistry, immunology surveillance, virology, lymphoid leukemia, and psychosocial studies. Participates in the National Cancer Institute's nationwide program for coordinating multidisciplinary basic and clincial cancer research, improving methods of treatment, diagnosis, and prevention, training health professionals, and transferring cancer knowledge to surrounding communities. *Type:* Research center.

Rutgers University

Laboratory for Cancer Research

Department of Chemical   Ph: (732)445-4940
  Biology   Fax: (732)445-0687
College of Pharmacy
160 Frelinghuysen Rd.
Piscataway, NJ 08854-8022
URL: http://www.eohsi.rutgers.edu/lcr
Contact: Prof. Allan H. Conney, Dir.
Desc: Mechanisms of chemical carcinogenesis and mutagenesis; mechanisms of inhibition of carcinogenesis; factors influencing the metabolism and action of drugs, carcinogens, environmental chemicals and steroid hormones; regulation and biological significance of multiple cytochromes P-450; drug interactions; induced synthesis of microsomal enzymes. *Type:* Research center.

Saint Albert's Cancer AIDS Research Foundation
2659 Commercial SE, Ste. 248   Ph: (503)399-8030
Salem, OR 97302

Contact: Donald A. Breck, Founder.

Desc: Individuals who support research on cancer and on AIDS. Promotes charitable, educational, and research programs. *Type:* Association.

St. Francis Hospital (Tulsa, OK)

Natalie Warren Bryant Cancer Center
Warren Cancer Research   Ph: (918)491-5878
    Foundation   Fax: (918)494-1527
6151 S. Yale, Ste. B103
Tulsa, OK 74136
E-mail: keller@Jimmy.harvard.edu

Contact: Dr. Alan M. Keller, Co-Prin. Investigator.

Desc: Bone marrow transplants, medical oncology, radiotherapy, pathology, and surgery. Conducts clinical trials. *Type:* Research center.

St. Louis University

Institute for Molecular Virology
3681 Park Ave.   Ph: (314)577-8403
St. Louis, MO 63110   Fax: (314)577-8406

Contact: Dr. Maurice Green, Chm.

Desc: Molecular biology, virology, cell biologiy, oncology, and AIDS, including structure and function of human viruses and mechanism of virus replication and cell transformation by ribonucleic and deoxyribose acid tumor viruses. *Type:* Research center.

Salk Institute for Biological Studies

Cancer Center
PO Box 85800   Ph: (619)453-4100
San Diego, CA 92186-5800   Fax: (619)457-4765
E-mail: eckhart@salk.edu
URL: http://www.salk.edu

Contact: Dr. Walter Eckhart, Dir.

Desc: Participates as one of a group of selected nonclinical cancer centers in National Cancer Institute's nationwide program for coordinating multidisciplinary basic and clinical cancer research, improving methods of treatment, diagnosis, and prevention, training health professionals, and transferring cancer knowledge to surrounding communities, established under National Cancer Act of 1971. Areas of research include molecular biology, virology, cell biology, and developmental biology. *Type:* Research center.

Santa Barbara Breast Cancer Institute
1230-M Coast Village Circle   Ph: (805)565-2244
Santa Barbara, CA 93108   Fax: (805)565-2246

Contact: Jenny Millan, Exec.Dir.

Desc: Breast cancer, including methods of detection and treatment. *Type:* Research center.

Saskatoon Cancer Centre

Cancer Research Unit
20 Campus Dr.   Ph: (306)655-2778
Saskatoon, SK, Canada S7N   Fax: (306)655-2639
    4H4
E-mail: scarlsen@scf.sk.ca

Contact: Dr. S.A. Carlsen, Dir.

Desc: Basic cancer research, including elucidation of the properties of signal transduction, oncogene expression, tumor metastasis, drug sensitivity, and genetic engineering of novel biological reagents for tumor diagnosis and therapy. *Type:* Research center.

Share

SHARE
1501 Broadway   Ph: (212)719-0364
New York, NY 10036   Fax: (212)869-3431

Desc: Acts as a forum for information, meetings, resources, and support groups for women with breast or ovarian cancer. *Type:* Newsletter.

Sherbrooke University

Quebec Network of Genetic Screening
3001, 12e Ave. Nord   Ph: (819)564-5393
Sherbrooke, PQ, Canada J1H   Fax: (819)564-5217
    5N4
E-mail: sgenetiq@courrier.usherb.ca

Contact: Bernard Lemieux, Dir.

Desc: Clinical and biological aspects of screening infants for neuroblastoma in order to determine the effectiveness of screening and to better understand neuroblastoma biology. *Type:* Research center.

Sickle Cell Association of the Texas Gulf Coast
2626 S. Loop W., Ste. 245   Ph: (713)666-0300
Houston, TX 77054   Fax: (713)666-0217
E-mail: scatgc@sicklecell-texas.org

Contact: Rebecca Jasso, Exec.Dir.

Desc: Performs laboratory tests to identify persons with sickle cell disease. *Type:* Research center.

Skin Cancer Foundation
245 5th Ave., Ste. 1403   Ph: (212)725-5176
New York, NY 10016   Free: 800-SKIN-490
    Fax: (212)725-5751
E-mail: info@skincancer.org
URL: http://www.skincancer.org

Contact: Perry Robins, Pres.

Desc: Sponsors medical symposia and public education programs on the prevention and early recognition of skin cancer. Grants its Seal of Recommendation to sunscreen products that meet the criteria and standards established by the SCF as effective aids in the prevention of sun-induced damage to the skin. *Type:* Association.

Society for the Study of Blood
VA Medical   Ph: (718)836-6600
800 Poly Pl.   Fax: (718)630-2822
Brooklyn, NY 11209

Contact: Dr. Carol Luhrs, Contact.

Desc: Hematology, blood groupings, transfusion, physiology, and pathology of blood. *Type:* Research center.

Stanford University

Cancer Biology Research Laboratory
School of Medicine, Rm.   Ph: (650)723-5881
    GK103   Fax: (650)723-7382
Stanford, CA 94305-5468
E-mail: mbrown@leland.stanford.edu
URL: http://www.stanford.edu

Contact: Dr. J. Martin Brown, Dir.

Desc: Molecular aspects of DNA repair, the consequences of the hypoxic environment of solid tumors and means of overcoming the resistance of solid tumors to cancer therapy. Human and murine cancer studies, including virologic, biologic, and immunologic characterization of several cell lines of human malignant lymphomas. *Type:* Research center.

Stanford University

Oncology Day Care Center/Comprehensive Cancer Clinic
Stanford Med. Ctr., Rm. H0274   Ph: (650)723-7621
300 Pasteur Dr.   Fax: (650)725-9113
Stanford, CA 94305-5216
URL: http://www-med.stanford.edu/school/oncology/index.html

Contact: Charlotte Jacobs, MD, Chf. of Clinic.

Desc: Lymphoma, Hodgkin's disease, breast cancer, genitourinary cancers, lung cancer, gastrointestinal cancers, brain tumors, gynecological cancers, head and neck cancer and new drug development. *Type:* Research center.

Stehlin Foundation for Cancer Research
1315 St. Joseph Pkwy., Ste.   Ph: (713)659-1336
    1818   Fax: (713)659-1503
Houston, TX 77002
URL: http://www.stehlin.org

Contact: Robert Anderson, Exec.Dir.

Desc: Tissue culture of human cancers, transplantation of human cancers into athymic mice, experimental chemotherapy of human cancers growing in tissue culture or nude mice, investigation and development of new anti-cancer drugs, immunology of human cancers, effects of heat on human cancers, development and treatment of breast cancer, relationships between virus and human cancer, rapid screening of anticancer drugs and clinical trials for potential anti-cancer drugs. *Type:* Research center.

Strang Cancer Prevention Center
428 E. 72nd St.   Ph: (212)794-4900
New York, NY 10021   Fax: (212)794-0749
E-mail: mosborne@strang.org
URL: http://www.strang.org

Contact: Dr. Michael P. Osborne, Pres./CEO.

Desc: Prevention and cure of cancer through early detection. Conducts genetics research, epidemiology risk modelling, and cancer prevention trials. *Type:* Research center.

Swedish Tumor Institute
1221-1225 Madison St.   Ph: (206)386-2323
Seattle, WA 98104   Fax: (206)386-2393
URL: http://www.dtesh.seanet.com

Contact: Donald W. Tesh, MD, Dir.

Desc: Cancer, including research, treatment, prevention, pain management, early detection, genetics, and related psychosocial issues. Center also conducts on Phase I-III clinical trials in treatment, prevention, control, and epidemiology of cancer, and investigates methods of instruction in cancer pain management. *Type:* Research center.

Syracuse Cancer Research Institute
600 E. Genesee St.   Ph: (315)472-6616
Syracuse, NY 13202-3111
URL: http://www.ngen.com/hs-cancer

Contact: Joseph Gold, MD, Dir.

Desc: Cachexia, or weight loss and debilitation as a result of cancer. Specifically studies the drug hydrazine sulfate, a chemical that acts to block the body's chemical machinery which converts lactic acid, amino acids, and other carbon 2-5 molecules to glucose and thus depletes the normal body energy pools; and experimental combinations of chemotherapy with hydrazine sulfate and cytotoxic chemotherapeutic agents, hormones, and recombinant DNA products. *Type:* Research center.

Temple University

Fels Institute for Cancer Research and Molecular Biology

Sch. of Med. Ph: (215)707-4300
3307 N. Broad St., Rm. 150 Fax: (215)707-4588
Philadelphia, PA 19140
URL: http://www.temple.edu/departments/fels/

Contact: E. Premkumar Reddy, Dir.

Desc: Basic sciences, with emphasis on biochemical, molecular, and genetic aspects of cancer, including molecular biology, cell biology, and biochemistry. *Type:* Research center.

Texas Cancer Data Center

1515 Holcombe Blvd. Ph: (713)792-2277
Box 223 Fax: (713)794-1951
Houston, TX 77030
URL: http://www.txcander.org

Contact: Lewis E. Foxhill, MD, Contact.

Desc: Reduction of human suffering and economic impact of cancer on Texans by the collection of computerized information on cancer resources, services, and statistics. *Type:* Research center.

Thomas Jefferson University

Cardeza Foundation for Hematologic Research

1015 Walnut St. Ph: (215)955-7786
Philadelphia, PA 19107 Fax: (215)955-2366
E-mail: sandor.shapiro@mail.tju.edu
URL: http://jeffline.tju.edu/CWIS/DEPT/Medicine/Cardeza

Contact: Sandor S. Shapiro, MD, Dir.

Desc: Hematologic research. Maintains a blood bank, hemophilia and sickle cell centers, and a photographic unit. *Type:* Research center.

Thomas Jefferson University

Jefferson Cancer Institute

233 S. 10th St., Rm. 1050 Ph: (215)503-4645
Philadelphia, PA 19107-6799 Fax: (215)923-3528
E-mail: c-croce@lac.jci.tju.edu

Contact: Carlo M. Croce, MS, Contact.

Desc: Genetics, including molecular genetic analysis of the normal human genome, cytogenetics of aneuploidy syndromes, genetics of the immune system, genetics of collagen and extracellular matrix genes, and molecular genetics of human hematopoietic neoplasias and solid tumors; immunology, including antigen presentation, autoimmunity, B-cell development, cancer immunology, cell growth regulation and differentiation, cellular immunology, cell activation and signal transduction, cytokines, developmental immunology, and immunochemistry; and microbiology and molecular virology, including chemical and antigenic structure of virus particles, viral replication, antiviral agents, regulation of viral gene expression, viral oncogenes, virus-cell interactions, latent virus infections, neurovirology, microbial immunology, microbial pathogenesis, antiparasite vaccine development, cell biology of malaria, and immunobiology of river blindness. *Type:* Research center.

Thompson Cancer Survival Center

1915 White Ave. Ph: (423)541-1350
Knoxville, TN 37916 Fax: (423)541-1162
URL: http://www.thompsoncancer.com

Contact: Timothy J. Panella, MD, Dir.

Desc: Oncology, including phase I, II, and III trials of drug, radiation, or biology therapies and laser treatments. Center comprises the following research departments: Clinical Trials; Laser Photodynamic Therapy; and Bone Marrow Transplant Laboratory. *Type:* Research center.

Tom Baker Cancer Centre

1331 29th St. NW Ph: (403)670-1711
Calgary, AB, Canada T2N 4N2 Fax: (403)283-1651
E-mail: gstuart@acs.ucalgary.ca

Contact: Dr. Gavin C.E. Stuart, Dir.

Desc: Cancer, concentrating on interleukins, cell and molecular biology, metastasis, oncogenes, immunology of melanoma, and neuroblastoma and small cell lung cancer. Clinical trials focus on cancer therapy, biotherapy, epidemiology, and prevention. *Type:* Research center.

Tulane University

Cancer Center

1430 Tulane Ave., Box SL-68 Ph: (504)585-6060
New Orleans, LA 70122-2699 Fax: (504)585-6077
E-mail: rweiner@mailhost.tcs.tulane.edu
URL: http://www.tmc.tulane.edu/cancer

Contact: Dr. Roy S. Weiner, Dir.

Desc: Cancer, including AIDS-related cancers, biochemistry, bone marrow transplant, breast cnacer, chemotherapy, diet and nutrition, endocrine, environmental carcinogens, epidemiology, eye, ear, nose, and throat, gastro-intestinal cancer, general cancer research, genetics, genito-urinary, gynecological and obstetric, head and neck cancer, hepatocellular cancer, Hodgkin's disease, Kidney cancer, leukemia, lung and esophageal cancer, lymphoma, melanoma, myeloma, occupational carcinogens, opthamology, otolaryngology, ovarian and cervical cancers, pain and anesthesia, pediatric oncology, prevention of cancer, prostate cancer, psych-oncology, racial and ethnic factors, radiation and radiotherapy, skin cancer, surgical oncology, and Wilms' tumor. *Type:* Research center.

United Cancer Council

8009 Fishback Rd.
Indianapolis, IN 46298-1047

Contact: Randall B. Grove, Pres.

Desc: Federation of independent cancer agencies who receive their support from the United Way of America . Promotes programs of direct service to cancer patients and their families and encourages public and professional education regarding the cause and cure of cancer. Awards research grants. *Type:* Association.

U.S. Department of Health and Human Services
Food and Drug Administration
Center for Bilogics Evaluation and Research
Laboratory of Hemostasis

1401 Rockville Pike Ph: (301)496-4833
Rockville, MD 20852 Fax: (301)402-2780
E-mail: weinstein@a1.cber.fda.gov

Contact: Mark Weinstein, PhD, Actg.Chf.

Desc: Characterization of proteins involved in hemostasis and thrombosis. Biochemical research includes receptor and binding studies, and analysis of protein structure and function. *Type:* Research center.

U.S. Department of Health and Human Services
Food and Drug Administration
Center for Biologics Evaluation and Research
Bone Marrow Growth Factors Staff

9000 Rockville Pike Ph: (301)496-6968
Bldg. 37, Rm. 5C25 Fax: (301)480-3256
Bethesda, MD 20892

Contact: Dov H. Pluznik, PhD, Actg.Chf.

Desc: Cellular and molecular mechanisms involved in the production of hematopoietic growth factors and the differentiation of hematopoietic cells. *Type:* Research center.

U.S. Department of Health and Human Services
Food and Drug Administration
Center for Biologics Evaluation and Research
Division of Hematology

1401 Rockville Pike Ph: (301)402-4634
Rockville, MD 20852 Fax: (301)402-2780

Contact: Donald L. Tankersley, Chf.

Desc: Plasma volume expanders, immunoglobulins, and hepatitis B. Investigates thermally-induced albumin denaturation and thermal stabilization of albumin by saturated fatty acid anions; studies IgG dimer by electron microscopy and affinity chromatography; and conducts experiments to determine if the neutralization of hepatitis B virus infectivity could be achieved by formation of immune complexes with anti-HBs, which include antisera produced against a synthetic peptide of S region of the hepatitis B surface and antigen. *Type:* Research center.

U.S. Department of Health and Human Services
Food and Drug Administration
Center for Biologics Evaluation and Research
Division of Transfusion Transmitted Diseases

1401 Rockville Pike, HFM-310 Ph: (301)827-3008
Rockville, MD 20852 Fax: (301)480-7928
E-mail: mied@cber.fda.gov

Contact: Paul A. Mied, PhD, Dep.Dir.

Desc: To enhance our understanding of the natural history of retroviral diseases and assays to detect them and to develop methods to improve those assays; to understand the pathogenesis of the hepatitis viruses (HBV, HCV, HGV) and the development and use of assays to detect them; and to examine the extent, and significance, of transmission of pathogenic bacteria by blood and blood components. All three programs are directed at enhancing the safety of blood and blood derivatives. *Type:* Research center.

U.S. Department of Health and Human Services
Food and Drug Administration
Center for Biologics Evaluation and Research
Laboratory of Cellular Hematology

1401 Rockville Pike, HFM-335 Ph: (301)496-2577
Rockville, MD 20852 Fax: (301)402-2780

Contact: Liana Harvath, PhD, Chf.

Desc: Leukocytes, platelets, and signal transduction. Operates a hemoglobin and blood substitutes program. *Type:* Research center.

U.S. Department of Health and Human Services
Food and Drug Administration
Center for Biologics Evaluation and Research
Molecular Tumor Biology Staff

1401 Rockville Pike Ph: (301)827-0471
Rockville, MD 20852 Fax: (301)827-0449
E-mail: puri@cber.fda.gov

Contact: Raj Puri, MD,PhD, Chf.

Desc: Biology of receptors on human tumor cells; mechanisms of lentivirus infection and expression; MRNA editing. *Type:* Research center.

U.S. Department of Health and Human Services
National Cancer Institute

NIH Bldg. 31, Rm. 10A24 Ph: (301)496-5583
9000 Rockville Pike Fax: (301)402-2594
Bethesda, MD 20892

Contact: Dr. Samuel Broder, Dir.

Desc: The Institute has developed a National Cancer Program to expand existing scientific knowledge on cancer cause and prevention as well as on the diagnosis, treatment, and rehabilitation of cancer patients. This program is carried out at NCI laboratories in Bethesda, MD; at the Frederick Cancer Research and Development Center in Frederick, MD; and through NCI support for programs conducted throughout the nation. *Type:* Research center.

**U.S. Department of Health and Human Services
National Cancer Institute
Basic Sciences Division
Basic Research Laboratory**

NIH Bldg. 4l, Rm. C111   Ph: (301)496-7608
9000 Rockville Pike   Fax: (301)402-0055
Bethesda, MD 20892
Contact: Dr. Douglas Lowy, Chf.
Desc: Mechanisms of carcinogenesis and malignant transformation in human and animal cells, particularly in instances where there is an association with tumor viruses; and conducts research to determine critical cellular and molecular factors involved in virus-associated transformation and carcinogenesis. Studies are designed to: identify and characterize exogenous viruses associated with the initiation or progression of neoplasia in humans or animals as models for human neoplasia; elucidate the mechanisms by which viruses associated with naturally occurring carcinomas may induce or initiate neoplasia; characterize and define the biology and molecular biology of viruses associated with naturally occurring carcinomas; identify and characterize factors involved in viral and cellular gene regulation pertinent to carcinogenesis; and elucidate and define the cellular and molecular basis of transformation and carcinogenic progression. *Type:* Research center.

**U.S. Department of Health and Human Services
National Cancer Institute
Basic Sciences Division
Basic Research Laboratory**

Frederick Cancer Research and   Ph: (301)846-1318
   Development Center   Fax: (301)846-6164
Bldg. 469, Rm. 104 FCRDC
Frederick, MD 21702
E-mail: kcannon@mail.ncifcrf.gov
Contact: Karen Cannon, Sec.
Desc: Plans and conducts research on the cellular, molecular, genetic, biochemical and immunological mechanism affecting the progression, diagnosis and treatment of cancer; and collaborates with scientists from other research programs within the National Cancer Institute and the National Institutes of Health. *Type:* Research center.

**U.S. Department of Health and Human Services
National Cancer Institute
Division of Basic Sciences
Intramural Research Program**

NIH Bldg. 31, Ste. 3A11   Ph: (301)496-4345
9000 Rockville Pike   Fax: (301)496-0775
Bethesda, MD 20892
Contact: Dr. Douglas R. Lowy, Dep.Dir.
Desc: Program comprises branches for Immunology and laboratories for studies in biochemistry, cell biology, cellular oncology, genetics, immunobiology, mathematical biology, molecular biology, tumor immunology and biology. *Type:* Research center.

**U.S. Department of Health and Human Services
National Cancer Institute
Division of Cancer Biology**

6130 Executive Blvd.   Ph: (301)496-8636
EPN Bldg., Ste. 500   Fax: (301)496-8656
Rockville, MD 20852
E-mail: fa5n@nih.gov
URL: http://www.nci.nih.gov/dcb/dcbhom.htm
Contact: Faye C. Austin, PhD, Dir.
Desc: Extramural and basic and applied research on cancer cell biology and immunology, including the biological and health effects of exposures to ionizing and non-ionizing radiation, and the role of chemical, physical and biological agents, acting separately or together, in the development of cancer. Principal components include the Cancer Biology Branch, Cancer Immunology Branch, Cancer Genetics Branch Biological Carcinogenesis Branch, Chemical and Physical Carcinogenesis Branch, and Radiation Effects Branch. *Type:* Research center.

**U.S. Department of Health and Human Services
National Cancer Institute
Division of Cancer Biology
Cancer Biology Branch**

6130 Executive Blvd., Rm. 505   Ph: (301)496-7028
Rockville, MD 20852   Fax: (301)402-1037
E-mail: cf33a@nih.gov
URL: http://www.nci.nih.gov/dcb/cbbhom.htm
Contact: Colette S. Freeman, PhD, Chf.
Desc: Facilitates and supports basic biological research aimed at defin ing elements of the phenotype of the malignant cell through interdisciplinary approaches. Areas of emphasis include both positive and negative regulation of cell growth and differentiation, mechanisms involved in the process of metastasis and of angiogenesis, the influence of the extracellular environment on the tumor cell, and the molecular biology of cancer cells. *Type:* Research center.

**U.S. Department of Health and Human Services
National Cancer Institute
Division of Cancer Biology
Cancer Genetics Branch**

6130 Executive Blvd., EPN 700   Ph: (301)496-1591
Rockville, MD 20852   Fax: (301)402-7819
Contact: Dr. Sheila E. Taube, Chf.
Desc: Early detection, diagnosis (including staging, grading, and prognosis), and monitoring of changes during therapy or progression of disease. Projects in these areas are frequently concerned with improvement of existing techniques as well as the development of new tests and procedures. *Type:* Research center.

**U.S. Department of Health and Human Services
National Cancer Institute
Division of Cancer Biology
Cancer Immunology Branch**

Executive Plaza N., Rm. 501   Ph: (301)496-7815
6130 Executive Blvd.   Fax: (301)496-8656
Rockville, MD 20852-7381
E-mail: js150x@nih.gov
URL: http://www.nci.nih.gov
Contact: John A. Sogn, PhD, Chf.
Desc: Molecular immunology and cellular immunology, with special emphasis on understanding the role of the i mmune system in the development, growth, and spread of tumors as it relates to the problems of cause, prevention, treatment, and diagnosis of malignant diseases. *Type:* Research center.

**U.S. Department of Health and Human Services
National Cancer Institute
Division of Cancer Biology
Chemical and Physical Carcinogenesis Program**

6006 Executive Blvd., Ste. 220   Ph: (301)496-5471
MSC 7055   Fax: (301)496-1040
Bethesda, MD 20892-7055
E-mail: dl58s@nih.gov
URL: http://nci.nih.gov/DCB/DCBhom.htm
Contact: Dr. David Longfellow, Chf.
Desc: Occurrence and inhibition of cancer caused or promoted by chemical or physical agents, acting separately or together, or in combination with biological agents; and provides a broad spectrum of information, advice, and consultation to individual scientists and institutional science management officials relative to NIH and NCI funding and scientific review policies and procedures, preparation of grant applications, and choice of funding instruments. The Branch also: provides NCI management with recommendations as to funding needs, priorities, and

strategies for the support of relevant research areas consistent with the current state of development of individual research activities and the promise of new initiatives; plans, develops, and manages research resources necessary for the conduct of the coordinated research program; and plans, organizes, and conducts meetings and workshops to further program objectives and maintains contact with the relevant scientific community to identify and evaluate new research trends relating to its program responsibilities. *Type:* Research center.

**U.S. Department of Health and Human Services
National Cancer Institute
Division of Cancer Biology
Radiation Effects Branch**

6130 Executive Blvd.   Ph: (301)496-9326
Rockville, MD 20852-7391   Fax: (301)496-1224
E-mail: bw36@nih.gov
URL: http://www.nih.gov
Contact: Bruce Wachholz, Chf.
Desc: Mechanisms of radiation-induced mutagenesis and carcinogenesis including supportive studies in radiation chemistry, radiation physics, molecular biology, cytogenetics and cell transformation; studies of cancer among selected populations exposed to radionuclides intentionally or accidentally released into the environment. *Type:* Research center.

**U.S. Department of Health and Human Services
National Cancer Institute
Division of Cancer Control and Population Sciences
Extramural Epidemiology and Genetics Program**

6130 Executive Blvd., Rm. 535   Ph: (301)496-9600
Bethesda, MD 20892-7395   Fax: (301)402-4279
URL: http://dccps.nci.nih.gov/egp/
Contact: Dr. G. Iris Obrams, Dir.
Desc: Plans, develops, directs and manages a national extramural program of basic and applied research in biometry, epidemiology, and related multidisciplinary activities; establishes program priorities and evaluates program effectiveness; provides a broad spectrum of information, advice, and consultation to individual scientists and institutional sciences management officials concerning National Institutes of Health and National Cancer Institute (NCI) funding and scientific review policies and procedures, preparation of grant applications, and choice of funding instruments; provides (NCI) management with recommendations as to funding needs, priorities and strategies for the support of relevant research areas consistent with the current state of development of individual research activities and the promise of new initiatives; plans, develops, and manages research resources necessary for the conduct of the coordinated research program; and plans, organizes, and conducts meetings and workshops to further program objectives. *Type:* Research center.

**U.S. Department of Health and Human Services
National Cancer Institute
Division of Cancer Epidemiology and Genetics**

6130 Executive Blvd., Rm. 543   Ph: (301)496-1611
Rockville, MD 20852   Fax: (301)496-1297
Contact: Dr. Jerry M. Rice, Actg.Dir.
Desc: Cause and natural history of cancer and means for preventing ca ncer, through direct in-house research and through research contracts; evaluates mechanisms of cancer induction by viruses and by environmental carcinogenic hazards; serves as the focal point for the federal government on the synthesis of clinical, epidemiological, and experimental data relating to the causes of cancer; and advises the Institute Director on basic research activities as they relate to cancer cause and prevention. Division is organized under programs for Biological Carcinogenesis, Chemical and Physical Carcinogenesis, and Epidemiology and Biostatistics. *Type:* Research center.

U.S. Department of Health and Human Services

National Cancer Institute

Division of Cancer Epidemiology and Genetics

Biological Carcinogenesis Program

NIH Bldg. 41, Rm. A100   Ph: (301)496-4241
6130 Executive Blvd.
Bethesda, MD 20892

Contact: Edward Tabor, MD, Assoc.Dir.

Desc: Includes six intramural laboratories and one extramural branch devot ed to the study of viral causes of cancer and the role of oncogenes in carcinogenesis. Research includes studies of human immunodeficiency virus (HIV); simian immunodeficiency virus (SIV); human T-cell lymphotropic virus type I (HTLV-I); papillomaviruses; and oncogenes. *Type:* Research center.

U.S. Department of Health and Human Services

National Cancer Institute

Division of Cancer Epidemiology and Genetics

Epidemiology and Biostatistics Program

EPS - 7018   Ph: (301)496-5785
Bethesda, MD 20892-7236   Fax: (301)496-1854
E-mail: hoover@epndce.nci.nih.gov

Contact: Dr. Peggy Tucker, Chf.

Desc: Activities of the Clinical Epidemiology Branch include: status and future prospects for research in specific areas of clinical observations of cancer patients and from clinical studies of families epistimology. and occupational groups and correlation of these results with laboratory findings; studies of the late effects of childhood cancer and the therapy of childhood cancer; operation of a clinic dealing with the genetics of human cancer to evaluate factors affecting risks of specific types of cancer such as neurofibromatosis; and preparation of analytical reviews to define current status and future prospects for research in specific areas of clinical epidemiology. *Type:* Research center.

U.S. Department of Health and Human Services

National Cancer Institute

Division of Cancer Prevention and Control

NIH Bldg. 31, Rm. 10A49   Ph: (301)496-9569
31 Center Dr.   Fax: (301)496-9931
Bethesda, MD 20892-2580
E-mail: bk76@nci.gov
URL: http://www.dcpc.nci.nih.gov

Contact: Dr. Barnett S. Kramer, Dep.Dir.

Desc: Planning and directing extramural programs of cancer prevention research; planning a program of laboratory, clinical and biometric research on cancer prevention; applying ststistical, analytical, and other quantitative methods to monitor, evaluate, and report on trends in, and the impact of cancer; developing and supporting research training and career development in cancer prevention and control; and coordinating program activities with other organizations. DCP is comprised of two major program areas: the Prevention Program and the Early Detection and Community Oncology Program. *Type:* Research center.

U.S. Department of Health and Human Services

National Cancer Institute

Division of Cancer Prevention and Control

Cancer Control Research Program

6130 Executive Blvd., Rm. 241   Ph: (301)496-8585
Rockville, MD 20852   Fax: (301)496-8675

Contact: Mark Manley, Chf.

Desc: Responsible for the development, implementation, and evaluation of an extramural research program aimed at reducing risk factors for cancer and increasing early detection of cancer. *Type:* Research center.

U.S. Department of Health and Human Services

National Cancer Institute

Division of Cancer Prevention and Control

Cancer Control Research Program

6130 Executive Blvd, Rm. 232   Ph: (301)496-8594
Rockville, MD 20852   Fax: (301)480-6637

Contact: Thomas J. Glynn, PhD, Chf.

Desc: Widespread use of proven health promotion and other cancer prevention and management techniques by health professionals, patients and their families, populations at elevated risk, and the general public; monitor basic and clinical research activities in order to identify new interventions that will reduce cancer rates in populations and to facilitate research on their application; provide training opportunities for research and/or application of cancer prevention and management interventions; establish program priorities, allocate resources, and integrate the projects of the various participating branches; and provide programmatic and consultative support to other divisional, institute, governmental, and private sector organizations that facilitate the application of proven cancer control interventions in populations. Program comprises branches for Cancer Control Applications, Health Promotion Science, and Special Population Studies. *Type:* Research center.

U.S. Department of Health and Human Services

National Cancer Institute

Division of Cancer Prevention and Control

Cancer Prevention Program

Executive Plaza N., Rm. 201   Ph: (301)496-8563
Bethesda, MD 20892   Fax: (301)402-0553
E-mail: kelloffg@dcpcepn.nci.nih.gov

Contact: Gary J. Kelloff, MD, Chf.

Desc: Chemoprevention involves the study and development of selected micronutrients or other small molecular weight substances for the purposes of reducing cancer incidence. Research has focused on identifying or demonstrating (in animal models, epidemiological studies, and human clinical trials) natural or synthetic agents that can lower cancer incidence. *Type:* Research center.

U.S. Department of Health and Human Services

National Cancer Institute

Division of Cancer Prevention and Control

Early Detection and Community Oncology Program

310 Center Dr., Rm. 10A 409   Ph: (301)496-9569
Bethesda, MD 20892   Fax: (301)496-9931
E-mail: kramerb@dcpc31.nci.nih.gov

Contact: Dr. Barnett S. Kramer, Dep.Dir., DCPC.

Desc: Cancer centers and scientific investigations to improve cancer treatment, rehabilitation, and continuing care. EDCOP encourages collaboration and transfer of technology and information among cancer centers, community hospitals, physicians, and other health professionals; seeks ways to enhance the efforts of centers and community resources to advance cancer control; and stimulates integrated research, both basic and clinical, for specific cancers (breast, large bowel, pancreas, prostate, and urinary bladder). *Type:* Research center.

U.S. Department of Health and Human Services

National Cancer Institute

Division of Cancer Prevention and Population Sciences

Cancer Surveillance Research Program

Executive Plaza North, Rm. 343   Ph: (301)496-8506
6130 Executive Blvd., MSC   Fax: (301)496-9949
7350
Rockville, MD 20852-7350
E-mail: edwardsb@dcpcenp.nci.nih.gov

Contact: Dr. Brenda K. Edwards, Assoc.Dir.

Desc: Impact of cancer and monitor the effects of cancer prevention and control activities in research, prevention, screening, treatment, and rehabilitation. Program also provides application research support for a broad range of activities in the Cancer Prevention and Control Division. *Type:* Research center.

U.S. Department of Health and Human Services

National Cancer Institute

Division of Cancer Treatment and Diagnosis

Developmental Therapeutics Program

Frederick Cancer Research and   Ph: (301)846-5387
Development Center   Fax: (301)846-6178
Fairview Center, Ste. 206
PO Box B 2-1201
Frederick, MD 21702-1201
E-mail: cragg@dtpax2.ncifcrf.gov
URL: http://epnws1.ncifcrf.gov:2345/dis3d/dtp.html

Contact: Dr. Gordon Cragg, Chf.

Desc: Acquisition of novel natural products for testing for anticancer anti-HIV activity via fermentation programs; and plant and marine organism collection and extraction projects. *Type:* Research center.

U.S. Department of Health and Human Services

National Cancer Institute

Division of Cancer Treatment, Diagnosis and Centers

NIH Bldg. 31, 3A44   Ph: (301)496-4291
31 Center Dr., MSC 2440   Fax: (301)496-0826
Bethesda, MD 20892-2440

Contact: Dr. Robert Wittes, Dir.

Desc: Cancer treatment activities with the objective of curing or controlling cancer in man by utilizing combination modalities (including chemical, surgical, radiological, and certain immunological techniques); administers a total drug development program; and serves as the national focal point for information and data on cancer treatment studies. Division components are: Cancer Therapy Evaluation Program; Developmental Therapeutics Program; Radiation Research Program; Diagnostic Imaging Program; Cancer Diagnosis Program. *Type:* Research center.

U.S. Department of Health and Human Services

National Cancer Institute

Division of Cancer Treatment, Diagnosis and Centers

Biological Response Modifiers Program

Frederick Cancer Research and   Ph: (301)846-1098
Development Center, Bldg.   Fax: (301)846-5429
1052
Frederick, MD 21702-1201

Contact: Dr. Stephen Creckmore, Chf.

Desc: Preclinical and clinical biological response modifiers re search in the biomedical community. The Branch monitors Phase I and early Phase II clinical studies that assess biological effects of biological response modifiers in cancer patients and correlate changes in the biological modifications with antitumor activity. *Type:* Research center.

U.S. Department of Health and Human Services

National Cancer Institute

Division of Cancer Treatment, Diagnosis, and Centers

Cancer Centers Branch

6130 Executive Blvd., Rm. 502   Ph: (301)496-8531
MSC7383   Fax: (301)402-0181
Bethesda, MD 20892-7383
E-mail: holmesm@dcbdcep1.nci.nih.gov
URL: http://www.nci.nih.gov/cancer centers/
Contact: Margaret E. Holmes, PhD, Chf.

Desc: Multidisciplinary cancer research efforts in the areas of basic, clinical and cancer prevention, control and population sciences. The Cancer Center Support Grant (CCSG) is intended to provide infrastructure for academic and research institutions for establishing and sustaining an interdisciplinary research focus on cancer. *Type:* Research center.

U.S. Department of Health and Human Services

National Cancer Institute

Division of Cancer Treatment, Diagnosis and Centers

Clinical Oncology Program

NCI-NNMC   Ph: (301)496-0901
8901 Wisconsin   Fax: (301)496-0047
Bethesda, MD 20889-5105
E-mail: allegrac@cnavmed.nci.nih.gov
Contact: Dr. Carmen Allegra, Chf.

Desc: New modes of detection, staging, and treatment of human cancers by integrat ing clinical and laboratory research with an emphasis on understanding the fundamental biology of human tumor cells and applying these lessons to the clinic. By combining the most recent techniques of cellular and molecular biology with innovative clinical treatment studies, entering patients into other NCI protocols, and providing clinical care to Department of Defense patients for the Naval Hospital, the Branch represents a unique resource to both the National Cancer Institute and the Naval Hospital. *Type:* Research center.

U.S. Department of Health and Human Services

National Cancer Institute

Division of Cancer Treatment, Diagnosis and Centers

Developmental Therapeutics Program

Executive Plaza N. Rm. 843   Ph: (301)496-8720
Rockville, MD 20852-7458   Fax: (301)402-0831
E-mail: sausville@dtpax2.ncifcrf.gov
URL: http://dtp.nci.nih.gov/
Contact: Dr. Edward A. Sausville, Assoc.Dir.

Desc: Preclinical discovery and development of anticancer and anti-HIV agents for the Division of Cancer Treatment and Diagnosis, focusing on chemotherapy and comprising both extramural and intramural elements. The extramural component includes nine branches: Antiviral Evaluation Branch; Biological Resources Branch; Biological Testing Branch; Drug Synthesis and Chemistry Branch; Grants and Contracts Operations Branch; Information Technology Branch; Natural Products Branch; Pharmaceutical Resources Branch; Pharmacology and Toxicology Branch. *Type:* Research center.

U.S. Department of Health and Human Services

National Cancer Institute

Division of Cancer Treatment, Diagnosis and Centers

Developmental Therapeutics Program

Executive Plaza D, Ste. 837   Ph: (301)496-3246
Bethesda, MD 20892   Fax: (301)402-3394
URL: http://epnws1.ncifcrf.gov:2345/dis3d/aeb/aeb.html

Contact: Dr. Robert H. Shoemaker, Chf.
Desc: Manages the AIDS drug discovery program. *Type:* Research center.

U.S. Department of Health and Human Services

National Cancer Institute

Division of Clinical Sciences

NIH Bldg. 10, Rm. 12N214   Ph: (301)496-4251
10 Center Dr. MSC 1904   Fax: (301)496-9962
Bethesda, MD 20892-1904
E-mail: gc45e@nih.gov
Contact: Dr. Gregory A. Curt, Clin.Dir.

Desc: Intramural treatment-research arm of the e National Cancer Institute. It comprises branches for: Clinical Pharmacology, Medicine, NCI-Navy Medical Oncology, Pediatrics, Radiation Oncology, and Surgery. *Type:* Research center.

U.S. Department of Health and Human Services

National Cancer Institute

Division of Clinical Sciences

Cancer Prevention Studies Branch

Executive Plaza N., Rm. 211,   Ph: (301)496-8559
MS 7326   Fax: (301)435-8644
9000 Rockville Pike
Bethesda, MD 20892-7326
URL: http://www.dcpc.nci.nih.gov/cpsb
Contact: Philip R. Taylor, Chf.

Desc: Cancer control. It conducts intramural research in the areas of die t, nutrition, and cancer; genetics and cancer; cancer chemoprevention; and other cancer prevention strategies aimed at lowering human cancer risk. *Type:* Research center.

U.S. Department of Health and Human Services

National Cancer Institute

Division of Clinical Sciences

Cancer Therapy Evaluation Program

Executive Plaza N., Rm. 739   Ph: (301)496-4836
Bethesda, MD 20892   Fax: (301)402-0560
E-mail: RICH@BRB.NCI.NIH.GOV
URL: http://ctep.info.nih.gov/BRB
Contact: Dr. Richard Simon, Chf.

Desc: Integral unit of Cancer Treatment and Diagnosis Division. It develops and evaluates clinical and biological data relating to cancer treatment. *Type:* Research center.

U.S. Department of Health and Human Services

National Cancer Institute

Division of Clinical Sciences

Cancer Therapy Evaluation Program

Executive Plaza N., Rm. 741   Ph: (301)496-6056
Bethesda, MD 20892   Fax: (301)402-0557
Contact: Dr. Richard Ungerleider, Chf.

Desc: Scientific administration of the national cooperative clinical trials groups, and portfolios of investigator-initiated (traditional and program project) grants in the medical oncology, pediatric oncology, and surgical oncology programs. *Type:* Research center.

U.S. Department of Health and Human Services

National Cancer Institute

Division of Clinical Sciences

Cancer Therapy Evaluation Program

742 Executive Plaza N.   Ph: (301)496-6138
Bethesda, MD 20892   Fax: (301)402-0084
Contact: Michaele Christian, Assoc.Dir.

Desc: Responsible for the administration and coordination of the majority of the extramural clinical trials suppor ted by the Cancer Treatment Division. These programs include the activities of the clinical cooperative groups, the Phase I and Phase II drug development contractors, and the holders of investigator-initiated grants relating to cancer treatment. *Type:* Research center.

U.S. Department of Health and Human Services

National Cancer Institute

Division of Clinical Sciences

Intramural Research Program

NIH Bldg. 10, Rm. 4N115   Ph: (301)496-6653
10 Center Dr. MSC1374   Fax: (301)496-9956
Bethesda, MD 20892-1374
E-mail: tawald@helix.nih.gov
Contact: Dr. Thomas A. Waldmann, Chf.

Desc: Clinical and laboratory investigations focusing on performing molecular analyses of lymphocyte development and function, including purification of transactivating factors and the genes that encode them; developing antigen processing and the presentation to T lymphocytes with applications to vaccine design for AIDS and cancer; characterizing the multisubunit IL-2 and IL-15 receptors and developing their use as a target for immunotherapy using humanized monoclonal antibodies armed with toxins and alpha and beta emitting radionuclides; studying the arrangement of immunoglobulin and T-cell antigen receptor genes in normal and neoplastic cells; and evaluating biochemical events that accompany cell growth and the hormonal control of this growth as they relate to the study of malignancies. *Type:* Research center.

U.S. Department of Health and Human Services

National Cancer Institute

Division of Clinical Sciences

Medicine Branch

NIH Bldg. 10, Rm. 12N226   Ph: (301)496-4916
9000 Rockville Pike   Fax: (301)402-0172
Bethesda, MD 20892
Contact: Dr. Carmen Allegra, Actg.Ch.

Desc: Adult medical oncology unit with clinical programs emphasizing the broad area of internal medicine as related to cancer. Clinical emphasis is given to the diagnosis, staging, and treatment of Hodgkin's disease, malignant lymphomas, breast cancer, ovarian carcinoma, sarcomas, melanoma, AIDS/Kaposi's Sarcoma, chronic leukemias, and testicular carcinoma. *Type:* Research center.

U.S. Department of Health and Human Services

National Cancer Institute

Division of Extramural Activities

6130 Executive Blvd. Ste. 600   Ph: (301)496-5147
Bethesda, MD 20892   Fax: (301)402-0956
E-mail: kaltm@dea.nci.nih.gov
URL: http://www.nci.nih.gov
Contact: Marvin R. Kalt, PhD, Dir.

Desc: Administers and directs the National Cancer Institute's grant and contract review and processing activities; provides initial technical and scientific merit review of grants and contracts for the Institute; represents NCI on overall NIH extramural and collaborative program policy committees, coordinates such policy within NCI, and develops and recommends NCI policies and procedures as related to the review of grants and contracts; coordinates the Institute's review of research grant and training programs with the National Cancer Advisory Board; coordinates the implementation of committee management policies within NCI and provides the Institute's staff support for the National Cancer Advisory Board; coordinates program planning and evaluation in the extramural area; and provides scientific reports and analyses to the Institute's grant and contract programs. Principal components are the Grants Review Branch, Special Review Referral and Resources Branch, Office of Advisory Activities, and the Research Analysis and Evaluation Branch, which analyzes and indexes the scientific content of all grants awarded by NCI as well as NCI contracts and extramural programs. *Type:* Research center.

U.S. Department of Health and Human Services

National Cancer Institute

Division of Extramural Activities

Special Review and Resources

6130 Executive Blvd. EPN Rm.   Ph: (301)496-7903
605   Fax: (301)402-0742

Bethesda, MD 20892

Contact: Wilna A. Woods, PhD, Ch.

Desc: Branch reviews the technical merit of all research and development, scientific resource, and scientific support contract proposals submitted to NCI in response to Requests for Proposals (RFPs). *Type:* Research center.

U.S. Department of Health and Human Services

National Cancer Institute

Frederick Cancer Research and Development Center

PO Box B   Ph: (301)846-1108

Frederick, MD 21702-1201   Fax: (301)846-1494

Desc: Cancer causes, biology, diagnosis, and treatment, and AIDS studies. The basic research program (operated by the biomedical research firm Advanced BioScience Laboratories, Inc.) and the NCI intramural research programs involve studies in macromolecular structure and function; mechanisms for inducing cancer using carcinogens; activation and expression of oncogenes; mechanisms, evolution, and control of transformation; in vitro and in vivo screening for cancer and AIDS therapeutic agents; regulation of host defense mechanisms; therapeutic use of immune effector mechanisms; phase I and II clinical trials of biological and chemotherapeutic agents; identification and regulation of AIDS virus genes and proteins; and genetics of cell differentiation and development. *Type:* Research center.

U.S. Department of Health and Human Services

National Cancer Institute

International Cancer Information Center

Bldg. 82, Rm. 113   Ph: (301)496-9096

9030 Old Georgetown Rd.   Fax: (301)480-8105

Bethesda, MD 20892

Contact: Gisele Sarosy, MD, Chf.

Desc: Purpose of ICRDB is to collect, analyze, and disseminate all data useful in prevention, diagnosis, treatment and supportive care of cancer and, as feasible, to disseminate results of cancer research undertaken in any country for the use of anyone conducting cancer research in any country. *Type:* Research center.

U.S. Department of Health and Human Services

National Cancer Institute

Laboratory of Cell Biology

NIH Bldg. 37, Rm. A09   Ph: (301)496-1530

37 Convent Dr. MSC 4255   Fax: (301)402-0450

Bethesda, MD 20892-4255

E-mail: mgottesman@nih.gov

Contact: Michael M. Gottesman, MD, Chf., Lab. of Cel Biology.

Desc: Basic cell biology in relation to cancer immunology. Major emphasis is on characterization of tumor antigens biochemically and immunologically and the immune responses they evoke. *Type:* Research center.

U.S. Department of Health and Human Services

National Cancer Institute

Laboratory of Chemoprevention

NIH Bldg. 41, Rm. C629   Ph: (301)496-5391

9000 Rockville Pike   Fax: (301)496-8395

Bethesda, MD 20892

E-mail: Robertsa@dce41.nci.nih.gov

URL: http://rex.nci.nih.gov/RESEARCH/basic/lc/lcpage.htm

Contact: Dr. Anita Roberts, Chf.

Desc: Cell regulation by transfering growth factor-B; carcinogenesis. *Type:* Research center.

U.S. Department of Health and Human Services

National Cancer Institute

Laboratory of Comparative Carcinogenesis

Frederick Cancer Research and   Ph: (301)846-1241

Development Center   Fax: (301)846-5946

Frederick, MD 21702-1201

Contact: Dr. Larry Keefer, PhD, Chf.

Desc: Effects of chemical carcinogens in rodents and non-human primates in order to identify differences between species that are important for interspecies extrapolations of the effects of chemical agents, including extrapolations to man, and that afford experimental approaches to the elucidation of mechanisms in chemical carcinogenesis. Research is oriented toward identification of susceptibility and resistance to chemical carcinogenesis and toward identification, description, and investigation of mechanisms for interspecies differences and for cell and organ specificity in chemical carcinogenesis. *Type:* Research center.

U.S. Department of Health and Human Services

National Cancer Institute

Laboratory of Experimental Pathology

Federal Bldg., Rm. 618D   Ph: (301)496-2818

7500 Wisconsin   Fax: (301)402-1829

Bethesda, MD 20892-9123

Contact: Dr. Umberto Saffiotti, Chf.

Desc: Neoplastic transformation and its underlying mechanisms, with particular emphasis on epithelial target cells. It plans, develops, and implements research on the experimental pathology of carcinogenesis, and is especially concerned with the induction of neoplasia by chemical and physical factors in epithelial tissues. *Type:* Research center.

U.S. Department of Health and Human Services

National Cancer Institute

Laboratory of Immunobiology

Frederick Cancer Research and   Ph: (301)846-1557

Development Center   Fax: (301)846-6145

Ft. Detrick

Immunobiology Bldg. 560, Rm. 12-71

Frederick, MD 21702-1201

Contact: Dr. Berton Zbar, Chf.

Desc: Mechanisms of the effector arm of the immune system and cancer genetics. Its program comprises three interacting areas: the Office of the Chief, the Immunopathology Section, and the Cellular Immunity Section. *Type:* Research center.

U.S. Department of Health and Human Services

National Cancer Institute

Laboratory of Molecular Immunoregulation

Frederick Cancer Research and   Ph: (301)846-1551

Development Center   Fax: (301)846-7042

Bldg. 560 Rm. 21-89A

Frederick, MD 21702-1201

E-mail: oppenhei@ncifcrf.gov

URL: http://rex.nci.nih.gov/RESEARCH/basic/lmi

Contact: Dr. Joost Oppenheim, Chf.

Desc: Biochemical and molecular effects of biological response modifiers on host resistance to cancer. It investigates at a molecular level the inter- and intracellular processes that regulate host defense mechanisms, including isolation of proteins, RNA, and DNA that regulate production and activities of lymphokines, cytokines, and their receptors. *Type:* Research center.

U.S. Department of Health and Human Services

National Cancer Institute

Laboratory of Viral Carcinogenesis

Frederick Cancer Research and   Ph: (301)846-1296

Development Center   Fax: (301)846-1686

Bldg. 560, Rm. 21-105

Frederick, MD 21702-1201

E-mail: obrien@nciferf.gov

Contact: Stephen O'Brien, PhD, Chf.

Desc: Genetic and cellular mechanism of neoplastic transformation in man and mammalian model systems. Studies are conducted on the specific cellular genes that participate in transformation from several distinct approaches. *Type:* Research center.

U.S. Department of Health and Human Services

National Cancer Institute

Memorial Sloan-Kettering Cancer Center

Institute for Cancer Research

1275 York Ave.   Ph: (212)639-8352

New York, NY 10021   Fax: (212)639-5115

Contact: Dr. Richard S. Rivlin, Prog.Dir.

Desc: Nutrition and cancer prevention; bone and mineral metabolism; energy intake expenditure; immunology and infection; lipid metabolism; cellular growth; vitamins and trace elements; DNA repair and gene expression; hormonal regulation. *Type:* Research center.

U.S. Department of Health and Human Services

National Cancer Institute

Office of the Deputy Directory for Extramural Sciences

Comprehensive Minority Biomedical Section

Executive Plaza N.   Ph: (301)496-7344

6130 Executive Blvd., Rm. 620   Fax: (301)402-4551

Bethesda, MD 20892

E-mail: ss16i@nih.gov

Contact: Dr. Sanya A. Springfield, PhD, Dir.

Desc: Program reflects a broad-based approach to every aspect of the minority cancer problem, with particular focus on the cancer incidence mortality disparity between the black community and the general population. Emphasis is on increased funding for research by minority scientists, concerted enrollment of minority physicians and patients in clinical trials programs, cancer prevention and awareness heightening, and training and manpower development. *Type:* Research center.

U.S. Department of Health and Human Services

National Cancer Institute

Office of the Director

Office of Special Populations Research

Executive Plaza N., Rm. 240   Ph: (301)496-8589

6130 Executive Blvd., MSC   Fax: (301)496-8675
6120

Bethesda, MD 20892-6120

E-mail: ga17s@nih.gov

Contact: Dr. George A. Alexander, Chf.

Desc: Cancer prevention and control in special populations. *Type:* Research center.

U.S. Department of Health and Human Services

National Cancer Institute

Office of International Affairs

6130 Executive Blvd. Ste 100   Ph: (301)496-4761

Bethesda, MD 20892-7301   Fax: (301)496-3954

E-mail: nc6@cu.nih.gov

URL: http://www.icic.nci.nih.gov/oia/master.html

Contact: Dr. Federico Welsch, Assoc.Dir.

Desc: Promotes cooperative research through exchange programs with institutes in foreign countries; provides cancer research information worldwide, directly and through other institutions; and maintains liaison with international organizations and agencies involved in cancer research. *Type:* Research center.

U.S. Department of Health and Human Services
National Cancer Institute
Office of Technology Development
Executive Plaza South, Rm. 450   Ph: (301)496-0477
6120 Executive Blvd.   Fax: (301)402-2117
Rockville, MD 20852
E-mail: mayst@otd.nci.nih.gov
Contact: Dr. Thomas Mays, Dir.
Desc: Responsible for administering cooperative research and development agreements with industry and universities; and providing patent management and licensing support. *Type:* Research center.

U.S. Department of Health and Human Services
National Heart, Lung, and Blood Institute
Division of Blood Diseases and Resources
2 Rockledge Center   Ph: (301)480-8080
6701 Rockledge Dr., MSC 7590   Fax: (301)480-0867
Bethesda, MD 20892-7590
E-mail: reidc@govgate.nhlbi.nih.gov
Contact: Dr. Clarice A. Reid, Dir.
Desc: Division plans and directs NHLBI's research grant, contract, and training programs to improve the diagnosis, prevention, and treatment of blood diseases and related disorders and to assure the efficient and safe use of an adequate supply of high-quality blood and blood products. Programs include fundamental and clinical research; professional development and training; and education, prevention, and control activities to assure orderly application of knowledge gained from research. *Type:* Research center.

U.S. Department of Health and Human Services
National Heart, Lung, and Blood Institute
Sickle Cell Disease Scientific Research Group
2 Rockledge Centre   Ph: (301)435-0055
6701 Rockledge Dr. MSC 7950   Fax: (301)480-0868
Bethesda, MD 20892-7950
Desc: Provides a bridge for rapid translation and transfer of basic and clinical research on sickle cell disease to health care at the community level. The centers combine fundamental and clinical research, clinical trials, training and community service in an appproach designed to concentrate resources, facilities, and personnel in a focused approach to the problems posed by sickle cell disease. *Type:* Research center.

U.S. Department of Health and Human Services
National Heart, Lung, and Blood Institute
Specialized Centers of Research in Transfusion
Medicine
Federal Bldg., Rm. 504   Ph: (301)496-1537
7550 Wisconsin Ave.
Bethesda, MD 20892
Contact: Dr. Luiz Barbosa, Contact.
Desc: Availability, efficacy, safety, and quality of blood and blood products for therapeutic uses. Specific research areas includes molecular biology, immunology, transfusion-transmitted viruses, leukemia, bone marrow transplantation, and renal transplantation. *Type:* Research center.

U.S. Department of Health and Human Services
National Institute of Dental Research
Oral and Pharyngeal Cancer Branch
NIH Bldg. 30 Rm. 211   Ph: (301)496-3695
30 Convent Dr. MSC 4340   Fax: (301)402-0823
Bethesda, MD 20892-4340
Contact: J. Silvio Gutkind, PhD, Chf.
Desc: Normal and aberrant functions of tissues, cells, and molecules as they relate to oral disease and other disease states, placing a special emphasis on the etiology, diagnosis, treatment, and prevention of oral tumors. Fields of study include cell biology, molecular biology, developmental biology, enzymology, immunochemistry, and protein chemistry. *Type:* Research center.

U.S. Department of Health and Human Services
National Institute of Diabetes and Digestive
and Kidney Diseases
Division of Intramural Research
Clinical Hematology Branch
NIH Bldg. 10, Rm. 4D51   Ph: (301)496-4787
9000 Rockville Pike   Fax: (301)402-4978
Bethesda, MD 20892
Contact: Dr. N. Raphael Shulman, Chf.
Desc: Problems in the fields of immunohematology, platelet physiology and metabolism, and blood coagulation. Current interests include mechanisms of immune cellular injury involving drug-, allo-, and auto-antibodies, correlation of platelet metabolism and membrane reactions with function, and interrelationships between cellular and humoral factors in hemostasis. *Type:* Research center.

U.S. Department of Health and Human Services
National Institute of Diabetes and Digestive
and Kidney Diseases
Division of Kidney, Urologic, and Hematologic
Diseases
Hematology Program
DKUHD   Ph: (301)594-7717
Natcher Bldg   Fax: (301)480-3510
45 Center Dr. MSC 6600
Bethesda, MD 20892-6600
E-mail: badmand@ep.niddk.nih.gov
URL: http://www.niddk.nih.gov
Contact: David G. Badman, PhD, Prog.Dir.
Desc: Blood, including: hemoglobin structure and genetics; anemias of chronic diseases such as chronic renal failure; molecular and cellular role of erythropoietin; iron metabolism, transport, and storage; iron overload and deficiency; white blood cell metabolism and function; development of new iron chelating compounds for clinical use and testing the toxicity of these compounds; and hematologic aspects of AIDS, including bone marrow suppression; hematopoiesis, including stem cell biology; and gene therapy research. *Type:* Research center.

U.S. Department of Health and Human Services
National Institutes of Health
National Cancer Institute
9000 Rockville Pike   Ph: (301)496-5585
Bethesda, MD 20892   Free: 800-422-6237
URL: http://www.nci.nih.gov/
Contact: Richard Klausner, MD, Director.
Desc: NCI has developed a National Cancer Program to expand existing scientific knowledge on cancer cause and prevention, as well as on the diagnosis, treatment, and rehabilitation of cancer patients. Research activities, conducted in the Institute's laboratories or supported through grants or contracts, include many investigative approaches to cancer, including chemistry, biochemistry, biology, molecular biology, immunology, radiation, physics, experimental chemotherapy, epidemiology, biometry, radiotherapy, and pharmacology. *Type:* Government agency, office, or program.

University of Alabama at Birmingham
Comprehensive Cancer Center
1824 6th Ave. S., Rm. 237   Ph: (205)934-5077
Birmingham, AL 35294   Fax: (205)975-7428
E-mail: al.lobuglio@ccc.uab.edu
URL: http://www.ccc.uab.edu/
Contact: Dr. Albert F. LoBuglio, Dir.
Desc: Oncology, involving medicine, dentistry, surgery, bone marrow transplantation, basic science, pathology, radiation oncology, obstetrics and gynecology, virology, bio-

physics, molecular biology, epidemiology, and pediatrics. Programs concentrate on the molecular biology and molecular genetics of malignant tranformation, (including oncogene and retroviral mechanisms), nature of the transformed membrane, structure of its antigens and their biologic function, and role and interaction of T and B cells in protection against cancer. *Type:* Research center.

University of Alberta
Cancer Research Group in Molecular
Mechanisms of Growth Control
Department of Biochemistry   Ph: (403)492-7976
Edmonton, AB, Canada T6G   Fax: (403)492-9556
2H7
E-mail: jim.stone@ualberta.ca
Contact: Dr. James C. Stone, Dir.
Desc: Cancer, including eukaryotic growth control, polypeptide growth factors, intracellular signaling methods, and oncogenes. *Type:* Research center.

University of Arizona
Arizona Cancer Center
PO Box 245024   Ph: (520)626-6044
Tucson, AZ 85724   Fax: (520)626-2284
E-mail: webmaster@azcc.arizona.edu
URL: http://www.azcc.arizona.edu
Contact: Dr. Sydney E. Salmon, Dir.
Desc: Clinical and laboratory cancer studies, including microarray technology, tumor cell kinetics, clinical pharmacology and pharmacokinetics, new drug development, drug resistance mechanisms, human tumor cloning, markers of cellular activity in malignant tumors, cell and molecular biology, immunology, carcinogenesis, medical imaging, cancer prevention and control, cytogenetics, pain management, stereotactic radiosurgery, bone marrow transplantation, gene therapy, epidemiology, and biostatistics. Clinical studies focus on histological tumor types, staging of disease, tumor kinetics, measurement of tumor burden, and new approaches to chemotherapy. *Type:* Research center.

University of Arkansas for Medical Sciences
Arkansas Cancer Research Center
Slot 623 UAMS   Ph: (501)686-6000
4301 W. Markham   Fax: (501)686-8165
Little Rock, AR 72205
E-mail: westbrookkentc@exchange.uams.edu
URL: http://www.acrc.uams.edu
Contact: Kent C. Westbrook, MD, Med.Dir.
Desc: Molecular, cellular, and genetic mechanisms of cancer therapies, including studies in immunology, mechanisms of metastases, radiation enteropathy, cell surface proteases, growth factors and cytokines, angiogenesis, cell genesis and differentiation. A multidisciplinary approach ensures that results are quickly translatable to the clinic and bedside. *Type:* Research center.

University of Calgary
Cancer Biology Research Group
Health Sci. Centre   Ph: (403)220-8695
3330 Hospital Dr. NW   Fax: (403)283-8727
Calgary, AB, Canada T2N 4N1
E-mail: kriabowo@alberta.ucalgary.ca
URL: http://www.ucalgary.ca/~young/cbrg.html
Contact: Dr. K.T. Riabowol, Chm.
Desc: Cell and molecular biology and their importance in the development and treatment of human cancers, including growth regulation, cell adhesion and metastasis, tumor differentiation, gene expression, cell surface markers, experimental cancer therapy, and relationship of cancer and aging. *Type:* Research center.

University of California at Berkeley

Cancer Research Laboratory

447 Life Sci. Addition   Ph: (510)642-4711
Berkeley, CA 94720-2751   Fax: (510)642-5741
E-mail: jallison@uclink4.berkeley.edu
URL: http://www.crl.lsa/
Contact: Dr. James P. Allison, Dir.

Desc: Biology of epithelial neoplasia, with special emphasis on mammary and hepatic cancers; molecular pathogenesis of leukemia; factors involved in transformation of normal cells to neoplastic cells; and mechanism of neoplasia. Also studies production of monoclonal antibodies to cell surface structures altered during neoplastic transformation. *Type:* Research center.

University of California, Irvine

Cancer Research Institute

Biology Science II, Rm. 3221   Ph: (949)824-5886
Irvine, CA 92697-3905   Fax: (949)824-4023
E-mail: hyfan@uci.edu
Contact: Dr. Hung Fan, Dir.

Desc: Focuses on immunology, virology, and growth factors, emphasizing basic research in various aspects of cancer. Also conducts studies in other areas central to understanding regulation in eukaryotic cells. *Type:* Research center.

University of California, Los Angeles

Marrow and Stem Cell Transplantation Program

Center for Health Science.   Ph: (310)206-5755
Los Angeles, CA 90095-1678   Fax: (310)206-5511
E-mail: mterrito@med1.medsch.ucla.edu
Contact: Mary Territo, MD, Dir.

Desc: Treatment of leukemia, lymphoma, myeloma, breast cancer, solid tumors, and aplastic anemia. Evaluates the use of bone marrow, cord blood, and stem cell transplantation as treatment for a number of hematologic and malignant diseases. *Type:* Research center.

University of California, Los Angeles

UCLA Jonsson Comprehensive Cancer Center

Box 951781   Ph: (310)825-5268
Los Angeles, CA 90095-1781   Fax: (310)206-5553
E-mail: kirwin@jccc.medsch.ucla.edu
URL: http://www.cancer.mednet.ucla.edu
Contact: Dr. Judith C. Gasson, PhD, Dir.

Desc: Cancer, including both basic science research in molecular, cellular, and developmental biology, signal transduction, tumor immunology, and viral and chemical carcinogenesis and clinical/translational research in breast and women's reproductive cancers, hematopoietic malignancies and bone marrow transplantation, prostate oncology, and solid tumor oncology in the following fields: central nervous system, thoracic, gastrointestinal, musculoskeletal, melanoma, and head and neck. Also conducts cancer prevention and control demonstration and research projects under the headings of patients and survivors, and healthy and at-risk populations. *Type:* Research center.

University of California, San Diego

Cancer Center

9500 Gilman Dr.   Ph: (619)822-1222
Mail Code 0658   Fax: (619)822-0207
La Jolla, CA 92093
E-mail: dedavis@ucsd.edu
URL: http://cancer.ucsd.edu
Contact: Dr. David Tarin, Dir.

Desc: Cancer, including clinical trials, education and treatment, and studies in the areas of cancer genetics, cancer prevention and control, cancer biology, cancer pharmacology, translational oncology, pallative care oncology, and molecular virology. *Type:* Research center.

University of California, San Francisco

Brain Tumor Research Center

Box 0520   Ph: (415)476-2905
San Francisco, CA 94143-0520   Fax: (415)502-0613
E-mail: ddeen@ucsfvm.ucsf.edu
URL: http://marlin.ucsf.edu/neuro
Contact: Mitchel S. Berger, MD, Dir.

Desc: Cytotoxic therapies, radiation therapy, and chemotherapy; elucidates the difference between normal brain cells and brain tumor cells; molecular biology of brain tumors. *Type:* Research center.

University of California, San Francisco

Cancer Center and Cancer Research Institute

Box 1297   Ph: (415)476-2201
San Francisco, CA 94143-1297   Fax: (415)502-4199
E-mail: tlee@cc.ucsf.edu
URL: http://cc.ucsf.edu/
Contact: Frank McCormick, Dir.

Desc: Cancer and hematology, endocrinology, fundamental properties of cell membranes, role of interferon and cell-cell interactions in immune response to cancer, surface markers on leukemic cells, role of viruses in cancer, management of breast cancer, factors involved in control of cell proliferation and differentiation, use of liposomes to deliver drug and macromolecules into cells, mechanism of membrane fusion, molecular pharmacology of antineoplastic drugs, and interaction between the coagulation and fibrinolytic systems and cancer cells. *Type:* Research center.

University of California, San Francisco

Northern California Comprehensive Sickle Cell Center

San Francisco General Hospital   Ph: (415)206-5169
1001 Potrero Ave., Rm. 331,   Fax: (415)206-3071
     Bldg. 100
San Francisco, CA 94110
E-mail: wmentzer@sfghpeds.ucsf.edu
Contact: William C. Mentzer, MD, Dir.

Desc: Sickle cell disease, including molecular, cellular, tissue, and organ studies. Conducts clinical trials. *Type:* Research center.

University of Chicago

Ben May Institute for Cancer Research

5841 S. Maryland Ave.   Ph: (773)702-6993
MC 6027   Fax: (773)702-4476
Chicago, IL 60637
E-mail: admin@ben-may.bsd.uchicago.edu
URL: http://ben-may.bsd.uchicago.edu
Contact: Dr. Jeffrey Bluestone, Dir.

Desc: Cancer and hormone-dependent tumors, including cancer of breast and prostate through studies in immunobiology, biochemistry, clinical medicine, experimental pathology, organic chemistry, and physiology on morphology and function of cells. *Type:* Research center.

University of Chicago

Cancer Research Center

5841 S. Maryland Ave.   Ph: (773)702-6180
Box MC1140   Fax: (773)702-9311
Chicago, IL 60637
E-mail: rlschils@mcis.bsd.uchicago.edu
URL: http://www-uccrc.uchicago.edu
Contact: Richard L. Schilsky, MD, Dir.

Desc: Causes, prevention, and treatment of cancer, including investigations of gynecologic cancers, lung cancer, head and neck cancer, pediatric cancers, gastro-intestinal cancers, breast cancer, lymphoma, leukemia, autologous bone marrow transplantation. Conducts research in cancer biology, molecular genetics, tumor immunology, developmental therapeutics, clinical research, diagnostics using radiology and radionuclide imaging, radiotherapy, radiation physics, radiation biology, developmental biology, and biochemistry. *Type:* Research center.

University of Cincinnati

Barrett Cancer Center

234 Goodman St.   Ph: (513)558-3200
Cincinnati, OH 45267-4281   Fax: (513)558-5680
URL: http://barrett.med.uc.edu
Contact: John C. Winkelmann, MD, Assoc. Dir., Clinical Services.

Desc: Cancer, in conjunction with the National Surgical Adjuvant Breast Project, Southwest Oncology Group, Gynecologic Oncology Group, and Radiation Therapy Oncology Group. Also studies gynecologic oncology, surgical oncology, neurologic oncology, and radiation therapy and radiation oncology. *Type:* Research center.

University of Florida

Division of Medical Hematology/Oncology

Box 100277 JHMHC   Ph: (352)392-3000
Gainesville, FL 32610   Fax: (352)392-8530
URL: http://www.ufl.edu
Contact: Dr. Richard Lottenberg, Ch.

Desc: Oncology, including medicine, radiotherapy, pathology, and surgery. Focuses on growth regulation of normal and malignant cells. *Type:* Research center.

University of Florida

Radiation Oncology Clinic

Shands Cancer Ctr.   Ph: (352)395-0287
PO Box 100385   Fax: (352)395-0546
Gainesville, FL 32610-0385
E-mail: mendenan.radonc@Shands.ufl.edu
Contact: Dr. Nancy Mendenhall, Dept.Ch.

Desc: Cancer and radiation therapy and treatment. *Type:* Research center.

University of Hawaii

Cancer Research Center of Hawaii

1236 Lauhala St.   Ph: (808)586-3013
Honolulu, HI 96813   Fax: (808)586-3009
E-mail: brian@crch.hawaii.edu
URL: http://www2.hawaii.edu./crch
Contact: Brian F. Issell, MD, Dir.

Desc: Cancer, with major emphasis in cancer epidemiology, focused on multidisciplinary cancer etiology studies that utilize Hawaii's unique ethnic population distribution for basic and demographic research; basic science, including environmental carcinogenesis, experimental therapeutics, and cell transformation and differentiation; and prevention and control; research, including clinical treatment trials, chemoprevention and other cancer control interventions. *Type:* Research center.

University of Illinois at Chicago

Surgical Oncology

College of Med.   Ph: (312)996-6666
Clinical Sci. Bldg.   Fax: (312)996-9365
MC 820
840 S. Wood St.
Chicago, IL 60612
Contact: Dr. Tapas K. Das Gupta, Dir.

Desc: Tumor biology, including molecular biology and molecular genetics, drug development, chemoprevention, drug resistance, genetic rearrangement, gene regulation, signal transduction, epidemiology prevention, and clinical research. Center specializes in the study of cancers of the head and neck region, breast, esophagus, stomach, small and large bowel, colon and rectum, liver and pancreas, skin, and soft body tissue. *Type:* Research center.

University of Iowa
Cancer Center
5970Z JPP Ph: (319)353-8620
Iowa City, IA 52242 Free: 800-237-1225
Fax: (319)353-8988
E-mail: George-Weiner@uiowa.edu
URL: http://www.vh.org
Contact: George J. Weiner, MD, Interim Dir.
Desc: Clinical cancer programs involving breast cancer; bone marrow transplantation and brain and spinal cord tumors; cancers of the eye; digestive system cancers; female reproductive tumors; head and neck tumors; leukemia and lymphoma; melanoma and sarcoma; supportive care and pain management; thoracic cancer; and urologic tumors, interdisciplinary diagnostic and therapeutic strategies, and modalities. Center oncologists participate in seven national cooperative study groups and engage in shared management programs with physicians referring patients to the University of Iowa Hospitals and Clinics. *Type:* Research center.

University of Kansas
Kansas Cancer Institute
Med. Ctr. Ph: (913)588-4700
3901 Rainbow Blvd. Fax: (913)588-4701
Kansas City, KS 66160-7312
URL: http://www.2.kumc.edu/kcl/
Contact: Dr. William Jewell, MD, Dir.
Desc: Cancer, including interdisciplinary studies on its prevention, detection, and diagnosis. Programs focus on hormonally regulated cancers, chemotherapy, radiation therapy, immunotherapy, surgical therapy, psychosocial rehabilitation of pediatric patients and families, drug development, cellular and molecular biology, chemical and environmental carcinogenesis, tumor immunology, epidemiology, and biostatistics. *Type:* Research center.

University of Kentucky
Children's Cancer Study Group
College of Med. Ph: (606)323-5694
Lexington, KY 40536 Fax: (606)257-6048
E-mail: jtdunc0@pop.uky.edu
Contact: M.F. Greenwood, MD, Dir.
Desc: Pediatric oncology, including clinical trials and bone marrow transplantation. *Type:* Research center.

University of Kentucky
Lucille Parker Markey Cancer Center
800 Rose St. Ph: (606)257-4500
Lexington, KY 40536-0093 Fax: (606)323-2074
E-mail: kaf@delos.kcr.uky.edu
URL: http://www.kcr.uky.edu/markey.html
Contact: Kenneth A. Foon, MD, Dir.
Desc: Cancer research, including tumor immunology, molecular genetics, signal transduction, mechanisms of carcinogenesis, experimental therapeutics, and clinical trials. Core facilities include macromolecular structure, flow cytometry, tissue procurement, clinical research office, NMR spectroscopy, and transgenic cell construction. *Type:* Research center.

University of Louisville
Henry Vogt Cancer Research Institute
James Graham Brown Cancer Ph: (502)852-6905
Ctr. Fax: (502)852-8026
529 S. Jackson St.
Louisville, KY 40202
URL: http://bcc.louisville.edu
Contact: Kay Lloyd, MD, Actg.Dir.
Desc: Molecular hematology/oncology, marrow transplantation, hormone receptors, anticancer drug development, molecular carcinogenesis, methods of drug delivery, laser therapy, growth factors, and drug disposition (clinical pharmacy). *Type:* Research center.

University of Manitoba
RH Laboratory
Health Sci. Ctr. Ph: (204)787-2755
735 Notre Dame Ave., 5th Fl. Fax: (204)787-2628
Winnipeg, MB, Canada R3E
0L8
E-mail: zelinsk@ccm.umanitoba.ca
Contact: Dr. Marlis Schroder, Sci.Dir.
Desc: Incidence and inheritance of red cell antigens, genetic linkage analyses of these and other genetic markers with application in chromosome mapping, modes of immunization, and prevention thereof, and prediction of severity and treatment of hemolytic disease of the newborn. Serves as a reference laboratory for identification of antigens and antibody specificity and as a referral center for intrauterine transfusions. *Type:* Research center.

University of Maryland at Baltimore
University of Maryland Greenbaum Cancer Center
22 S. Greene St. Ph: (410)328-5506
Baltimore, MD 21201 Fax: (410)328-2578
E-mail: pharris@umcc01.umcc.ab.umd.edu
URL: http://www.umn.edu/cancer
Contact: Stanford Stass, MD, Dir.
Desc: Pharmacology, clinical pharmacology, infectious diseases, molecular biology, pathology, cytogenetics, immunology, electron microscopy, and drug and combined modality treatment of cancer patients, with emphasis on acute leukemia, breast cancer, sarcomas, lymphomas, lung cancer, and other solid tumors. Maintains programs in the following areas: the chemotherapeutic approach to cancer therapy and the development of experimental protocols; infectious disease relationship to cancer; cell component therapy and cellular replacement; critical care of cancer patients; pharmacology and the use of cancer chemotherapeutic agents; anti-cancer drug development; combined modalities treatments, biological treatment; cellular and molecular biology of cancer; supportive care; and pharmacokinetics and pharmacodynamics of antineoplastic agents. *Type:* Research center.

University of Medicine and Dentistry of New Jersey
The Cancer Institute of New Jersey
195 Little Albany St. Ph: (732)235-2465
New Brunswick, NJ 08901 Fax: (732)235-6949
URL: http://www-cinj.umdnj.edu
Contact: William N. Hait, PhD, Dir.
Desc: Basic, clinical and translational cancer. *Type:* Research center.

University of Miami
Sylvester Comprehensive Cancer Center
Sch. of Med. Ph: (305)548-4918
1475 NW 12 Ave. Fax: (305)243-4901
Miami, FL 33136
E-mail: asauerte@mednet.med.miami.edu
Contact: Dr. Goodwin, Dir.
Desc: Cancer, including clinical investigation related to treatment of cancer, especially solid tumors of adults; molecular and cell biology as related to causation and pathogenesis of cancer; epidemiological research as related to environmental etiology of cancer in Florida and its prevention; and cellular differentiation, cell population kinetics, epidemiology of cancer, viral oncology, and immunology. Participates as one of 28 comprehensive cancer centers for conducting multidisciplinary research, improving methods of treatment, diagnosis, and prevention, training health professionals, and transferring cancer knowledge to surrounding communities in National Cancer Institute's nationwide coordination program for development of means to reduce incidence, morbidity, an d mortality of cancer as established under National Cancer Act of 1971. *Type:* Research center.

University of Michigan
Comprehensive Cancer Center
Cancer Res. Committee Ph: (734)936-9603
6303 Cancer Center Fax: (734)936-9582
Ann Arbor, MI 48109-0942
E-mail: maryrex@cancer.med.umich.edu
URL: http://www.cancer.med.umich.edu/
Contact: Dr. Eric Fearon, Chm.
Desc: Responsible for stimulating interest in cancer and clinical research in cell biology among faculty and students of the University and procurement of funds for support of their research. Funds dispensed on basis of formal applications submitted to the Committee. *Type:* Research center.

University of Michigan
Division of Hematology/Oncology
7216 CCGC, Box 0948 Ph: (734)764-8100
1500 E. Medical Center Dr. Fax: (734)936-7376
Ann Arbor, MI 48109-0948
E-mail: robtodd@uvi.im.med.umich.edu
URL: http://www.med.umich.edu/intmed/
Contact: Dr. Robert F. Todd, III, Div.Ch.
Desc: Hematology, solid tumor, and neoplasia, including anemias, leukemia-lymphomas, immunohematologic disorders, coagulation defects and lipid-protein-coagulation interrelationships, and tumor cell growth and control. Biochemical, molecular biological, cytologic, immunologic, tissue culture, and isotopic techniques are employed to investigate factors concerned with regulation of cell growth and proliferation and variables that influence response to therapy. *Type:* Research center.

University of Minnesota
Hematology, Oncology and Transplantation Division
420 Delaware St. SE, Box 480 Ph: (612)624-7915
Minneapolis, MN 55455 Free: 800-888-8642
Fax: (612)626-1441
E-mail: mcgla001@tc.umn.edu
URL: http://www.umn.edu
Contact: Philip B. McGlave, MD, Dir.
Desc: Pediatric, surgical, medical, and radiation oncology in the areas of breast cancer, acute leukemia, lung cancer, lymphomas, testicular cancer, ovarian cancer, melanoma, and autologous marrow transplantation. Participates in cooperative group research, investigates local protocol, performs clinical analyses of malignancies. *Type:* Research center.

University of Nebraska Medical Center
Eppley Institute for Research in Cancer and Allied Diseases
600 S. 42nd St. Ph: (402)559-4238
Omaha, NE 68198-6805 Fax: (402)559-4651
E-mail: bgold@unmc.edu
URL: http://www.unmc.edu/eppley
Contact: Dr. Barry Gold, Interim Dir.
Desc: Mechanisms, causes, prevention, early diagnosis, and treatment of cancer, including programs in molecular, cellular and structural biology, and developmental therapeutics. *Type:* Research center.

University of Nevada, Reno
Allie M. Lee Cancer Research Laboratory
Department of Biochemistry, Ph: (702)784-4107
Mailstop 330 Fax: (702)784-1419
Reno, NV 89557
E-mail: pardini@fs.scs.unr.edu
URL: http://biochem.med.unr.edu/ronpar/rcancer.html
Contact: Dr. Ronald S. Pardini, Dir.
Desc: Pharmacological investigations on effects of inhibition of mitochondrial electron and energy transfer path-

ways on tumor metabolism, including natural plant products, especially quinones and phenolic derivatives. Emphasizes oxidative stress and anti-oxidant enzymes. *Type:* Research center.

University of Nevada, Reno

Natural Products Lab

Department of Biochemistry   Ph: (702)784-6031
MS 330   Fax: (702)784-1419
Reno, NV 89557
E-mail: pardini@fs.cs.unr.edu
URL: http://biochem.med.unr.edu/ronpar/rcancer.html
Contact: Dr. Ronald S. Pardini, Dir.

Desc: Cancer, biochemical pharmacology, and oxidative stress, including investigations of biochemical mechanisms of antitumor drugs and evaluations of the role of oxidative stress in the anticancer activity of drugs. *Type:* Research center.

University of New Mexico

Cancer Research and Treatment Center

900 Camino de Salud NE   Ph: (505)272-2151
Albuquerque, NM 87131-5636   Fax: (505)272-2841
E-mail: lkvols@salud.unm.edu
URL: http://www.hsc.unm.edu/clinical.html
Contact: Dr. Larry K. Kvols, Dir. & CEO.

Desc: Clinical investigations in growth-factor-supplemented high dose chemotherapy, hyperthermia, and various national cooperative group trials; tumor immunology; non-invasive diagnostic technology and development of magnetic resonance imaging; cell surface marker studies in hematopoetic and solid tumors; HPV/cervical cancer; hepatitis virus replication; HTLV-I and II; and cancer in Hispanics and Native Americans. Studies also include biology of natural killer cells and molecular mechanisms of immunosuppression, gene expression, signal transduction, oncogenes, and immune regulation. *Type:* Research center.

University of New Mexico

Clinical and Magnetic Resonance Research Center

1201 Yale Blvd. NE   Ph: (505)272-0760
Albuquerque, NM 87131   Fax: (505)272-4056
E-mail: cford@salud.unm.edu
URL: http://cmrrc.unm.edu
Contact: Dr. Corey C. Ford, Contact.

Desc: Magnetic resonance imaging and spectroscopy, neurology, multiple sclerosis, stroke, traumatic brain surgery, lupus, and schizophrenia. *Type:* Research center.

University of New Mexico

New Mexico Tumor Registry

900 Camino de Salud NE   Ph: (505)272-5541
Albuquerque, NM 87131   Fax: (505)272-8572
E-mail: ckey@nmtr.unm.edu
Contact: Dr. Charles R. Key, Co-Dir.

Desc: Cancer epidemiology, with emphasis on Hispanics and American Indians. Participates in the NCI's SEER (Surveillance Epidemiology and End Results) Program. *Type:* Research center.

University of North Carolina at Chapel Hill

Center for Thrombosis and Hemostasis

UNC-CH School of Medicine   Ph: (919)966-3704
Campus Box 7015   Fax: (919)966-6012
Chapel Hill, NC 27599-7015
URL: http://www.med.unc.edu/thromb/
Contact: Gilbert C. White, II, MD, Dir.

Desc: Thrombosis and hemostasis; the genetics and molecular biology of blood coagulation, including recombinant

factors VIII and VIIA and the rationale for treatment or prophylaxis of thrombosis and hemorrhage, including research on peptide growth factors, platelets, lipoprotein metabolism, von Willebrand factor, factor VIII, fibrinogen and fibrin assembly, fibronectin, protease inhibitors, heparin and antithrombins, endothelial cell culture, thrombin and prothrombin, and factor IX and its variants, factor X, acute phase reactants, actin filament system, and gene replacement therapy. *Type:* Research center.

University of North Carolina at Chapel Hill

UNC Lineberger Comprehensive Cancer Center

Lineberger   Ph: (919)966-3036
CB 7295   Fax: (919)966-3015
Chapel Hill, NC 27599-7295
E-mail: dgs@med.unc.edu
URL: http://cancer.med.unc.edu

Contact: Dr. H. Shelton Earp, III, Dir.

Desc: Virology, cancer cell biology, immunology, molecular carcinogenesis, molecular therapeutics, epidemiology, clinical research, breast cancer, radiobiology and imaging, bone marrow transplantation, and cancer prevention and control including interdisciplinary studies. *Type:* Research center.

University of Oklahoma

Thrombosis & Coagulation Laboratory

Oklahoma University Hospital,   Ph: (405)271-7715
Rm. EB 400   Fax: (405)271-3620
PO Box 26307
Oklahoma City, OK 73126

Contact: William Kern, Dir.

Desc: Thrombosis, fibrinolysis, and anticoagulation. Develops clinical assays for protein C and protein S. *Type:* Research center.

University of Pennsylvania

Cancer Center

6 Penn Tower   Ph: (215)662-6334
3400 Spruce St.   Fax: (215)349-5326
Philadelphia, PA 19104-4283
E-mail: glickjh@mail.med.upenn.edu

Contact: John H. Glick, MD, Dir.

Desc: Cancer biology, diagnosis, cause, prevention, treatment, control, and rehabilitation, including programs in immunobiology, tumor cell biology, gene structure and regulation, virology, clinical investigations, pediatric oncology, tumor metabolism, epidemiology, statistics, melanoma, psychosocial oncology, and cancer control. *Type:* Research center.

University of Pennsylvania

Comparative Leukemia Unit

New Bolton Center   Ph: (610)444-5800
382 W. St. Rd.   Fax: (610)444-4724
Kennett Square, PA 19348
URL: http://www.upenn.edu

Contact: Jorge Ferrer, MD, Dir.

Desc: Cancer research focusing primarily on the etiology and pathogenesis of bovine leukemia for the development of a new relevant animal model system for studies on the etiology, pathogenesis, and immunoprophylaxis of viral-induced leukemia in humans. Studies include bovine leukemia virus (BLV) and its relationship to other retroviruses, particularly human T-cell lymphotropic virus type one (HTLV-I) and acquired immune deficiency syndrome (AIDS) virus. *Type:* Research center.

University of Pittsburgh

Health Sciences

3471 5th Ave., Ste. 201   Ph: (412)692-4670
Pittsburgh, PA 15213   Free: 800-237-4724
   Fax: (412)692-4665
E-mail: herbermanrb@msx.upmc.edu
URL: http://www.upci.upmc.edu
Contact: Dr. Ronald Herberman, Dir.

Desc: Develops interactive programs in basic and clinical cancer research; prevention, early detection, and treatment of cancer; and public and professional education. Basic research focuses on cellular, molecular, and biochemical interactions in cancer development. *Type:* Research center.

University of Puerto Rico

Puerto Rico Cancer Center

GPO Box 305067   Ph: (787)763-2443
San Juan, PR 00936   Fax: (787)751-6242
Contact: Dr. Reynold Lopez-Enriquez, Dir.

Desc: Cancer biology and carcinogenesis, solid-state carcinogenesis, bioactivation of precarcinogens, asbestos carcinogenesis, synthesis of antineoplastic agents, synthesis of radiosensitizers, tumor immunology, dietary factors in carcinogenesis, and radiation. Seeks cancer control through the Center's Cancer Tumor Registry, Detection Program, and public education. *Type:* Research center.

University of Rochester

Cancer Center

601 Elmwood Ave., Box 704   Ph: (716)275-4911
Rochester, NY 14642   Fax: (716)273-1042
E-mail: emessing@urmc.rochester.edu
URL: http://www.rochester.edu
Contact: Edw. M. Messing, MD, Interim Dir.

Desc: Diagnosis and therapy of cancer, with particular emphasis on experimental therapeutics. Conducts laboratory research in biochemical genetics, radiation biology, immunology, endocrine biochemistry, and cancer pharmacology, utilizing animal tumor research, biomathematics/statistics, cell culture, nucleic acid sequencing, and ultrastructure facilities. *Type:* Research center.

University of Southern California

Comprehensive Sickle Cell Center

2025 Zonal Ave., Rm. 304   Ph: (213)342-1259
Los Angeles, CA 90033   Fax: (213)342-1255
E-mail: cagejohn@hsc.usc.edu
Contact: Dr. Cage S. Johnson, Dir.

Desc: Sickle cell disease, including studies on molecular biology of red cells, fetal hemoglobin identification, and renal, cardiovascular, and endocrine functions. *Type:* Research center.

University of Southern California

Hematology, Hematologic Malignancy and Retrovial Research Program

Hematology Res. Faculty   Ph: (323)865-3913
1441 Eastlake Ave.   Fax: (323)865-0060
M/S 34 Division of Hematology
Los Angeles, CA 90033
E-mail: hornor@hsc.usc.edu
URL: http://ccnt.hsc.usc.edu/hamatology/index.html
Contact: Alexandra Levine, MD, Hd.

Desc: Hematologic malignancies, including non-Hodgkin's lymphoma, Hodgkin's disease, leukemia and multiple myeloma; bone marrow transplantation program, including state-of-the-art gene therapy and marking program; HIV, and AIDS-related cancers, including lymphoma, Kaposi's sarcoma, and cervical cancer; and immune-based therapy for malignant disease. Other areas include hemostasis, including studies on blood coagulation, platelets, etiology of thrombosis, chemical separation and characterization of blood clotting factors and antibody to blood clotting factors; sickle cell disease and other hemoglobinopathies. *Type:* Research center.

University of Southern California
Hematopathology Unit
1200 N. State St., Rm 2422   Ph: (213)226-7064
Los Angeles, CA 90033   Fax: (213)226-7119
E-mail: nathwani@hsc.usc.edu
Contact: Dr. Bharat N. Nathwani, Ch.
Desc: Investigates neoplasms of hematopoietic system, molecular biology, and polymerase chain reactions. *Type:* Research center.

University of Southern California
Medical Oncology Research Program
1441 Eastlake Ave.   Ph: (213)764-3963
Los Angeles, CA 90033   Fax: (213)754-0116
E-mail: dmoody@hsc.usc.edu
Contact: Derek Raghavan, MD, Dir.
Desc: Medical oncology, chemotherapy, and immunotherapy of cancer. Conducts laboratory and clinical investigations into the biology and treatment of cancer, including studies on innovative treatments, new drugs and biological agents, locoregional therapy such as hyperthermia, and preclinical and clinical pharmacology. *Type:* Research center.

University of Southern California
Norris Comprehensive Cancer Center
1441 Eastlake Ave.   Ph: (323)865-3000
Los Angeles, CA 90033-0800   Fax: (323)865-0102
E-mail: jones_p@froggy.hsc.usc.edu
URL: http://ccnt.hsc.usc.edu/
Contact: Peter A. Jones, PhD, Dir.
Desc: Multidisciplinary basic, clinical, epidemiological and translational studies in the following program areas: molecular genetics, cell biology, developmental therapeutics and clinical trials, cancer epidemeology, cancer control research, gemitourinary cancer, gastrointestinal cancer, breast cancer, and hematologic malignancies/retroviral disease. *Type:* Research center.

University of Tennessee
Memphis Cancer Center
N327 Van Vleet Bldg.   Ph: (901)448-5150
3 N. Dunlap St.   Fax: (901)448-5033
Memphis, TN 38163
E-mail: hniell@utmem1.utmem.edu
Contact: Harvey B. Niell, MD, Dir.
Desc: Detection, evaluation, and treatment of cancer, specifically, clinical therapeutic research, cancer drug development, cell growth and regulation, and gene regulation and expression. *Type:* Research center.

University of Tennessee, Knoxville
Experimental Oncology Laboratory
PO Box 1071   Ph: (423)974-5875
Knoxville, TN 37901-1071   Fax: (423)974-5616
Contact: Dr. H.M. Schuller, Dir.
Desc: Oncology research, focusing on role of receptor mediated signal transduction pathways and their role in chemical carcinogenesis mechanisms. *Type:* Research center.

University of Tennessee, Knoxville
Human Immunology and Cancer Program
1924 Alcoa Hwy.   Ph: (423)544-9165
Knoxville, TN 37920   Fax: (423)544-6865
E-mail: asolomon@wizard.hosp.utmck.edu
URL: http://www.mcutk.edu/docs/hicp/htcp/htcp/htm
Contact: Alan Solomon, MD, Dir.
Desc: Multiple myeloma, AL amyloidosis, and monoclonal B cell-related neoplasms. Conducts basic and clinical investigations related to the pathogenesis, diagnosis, and treatment of patients with B cell immunoproliferative diseases. *Type:* Research center.

University of Texas
M.D. Anderson Cancer Center
Texas Med. Ctr.   Ph: (713)792-7500
1515 Holcombe Blvd.   Fax: (713)790-9492
Houston, TX 77030
URL: http://www.mdanderson.org
Contact: Frederick F. Becker, MD, V.Pres., Res.
Desc: Chemotherapy, laser surgery, biologic response modifiers, imaging techniques, blood component utilization, fast neutron therapy, pharmacology, radiation physics, radiobiology, cell biology, molecular pathology, veterinary medicine, tumor biology, virology, human genetics, molecular genetics, immunology, biochemistry, molecular biology, invasion and metastasis, biomathematics and biostatistics, chemical carcinogenesis, epidemiology, behavioral science, and cancer prevention. Operates a diversified program of clinical and basic science research related to cancer designed to improve early detection, diagnostic techniques, therapy, rehabilitation, and cancer prevention. *Type:* Research center.

University of Texas
M.D. Anderson Cancer Center
Levit Radiologic-Pathologic Institute
1515 Holcombe Blvd., Mail   Ph: (713)792-6214
    Stop 208   Fax: (713)792-0812
Houston, TX 77030
E-mail: jgrossman@mdanderson.org
URL: http://mdacc.tmc.edu
Contact: John E. Grossman, Dir.
Desc: Treatment of cancer patients and the diagnosis and prevention of cancer. Also involved in imaging support for multi-disciplinary treatment conferences, electronic publishing, and simplified communication of patient records between referring consulting physicians. *Type:* Research center.

University of Texas Medical Branch at Galveston
Sealy Center for Oncology and Hematology/ Educational Cancer Center
Galveston, TX 77550-0630   Ph: (409)747-1935
    Fax: (409)747-1938
E-mail: smay@utmb.edu
URL: http://www2.utmb.edu/scoh/
Contact: W. Stratford May, MD, Dir.
Desc: Stem cell biology, signal transduction, cancer biology, molecular immunology, molecular virology, cancer gene discovery and regulation, cancer education, cancer prevention and control, and radiation, surgical, and medical oncology. Participates as one of a group of clinical and basic science centers for cancer research in nationwide program for development of means to reduce incidence, morbidity, and mortality of cancer established under National Cancer Act of 1971. *Type:* Research center.

University of Texas Southwestern Medical Center at Dallas
Sickle Cell Case Management Program
5323 Harry Hines Blvd.   Ph: (214)648-8594
Dallas, TX 75235-9063   Fax: (214)648-3122
E-mail: gbuch2@mednet.swmed.edu
Contact: Dr. George Buchanan, Dir.
Desc: Researches morbidity and mortality of pediatric sickle cell patients. *Type:* Research center.

University of Utah
Rocky Mountain Cancer Data System
420 Chipeta Way, Rm. 120   Ph: (801)581-4307
Salt Lake City, UT 84108   Fax: (801)581-5704
E-mail: LRD@RMCDS1.MED.UTAH.EDU
Contact: Lawrence Derrick, Asst.Dir.

Desc: Cancer. Provides data to participating hospitals and state registries. *Type:* Research center.

University of Vermont
Vermont Cancer Center
Medial Alumni Bldg.   Ph: (802)656-4414
Burlington, VT 05405-0068   Fax: (802)656-8788
E-mail: vcc@uvm.edu
URL: http://www.vtmednet.org/vcc/index.html
Contact: Dr. David W. Yandell, Dir.
Desc: Cancer, including multidisciplinary programs in drug development, cancer genetics, clinical research, cancer control research, DNA repair, and signaling. Conducts clinical studies in cancer chemotherapy, surgical oncology, radiotherapy and pediatric hematology-oncology. *Type:* Research center.

University of Wisconsin
Comprehensive Cancer Center
600 Highland Ave.   Ph: (608)263-8600
Madison, WI 53792   Fax: (608)263-8613
URL: http://www.biostat.wisc.edu/cancer/cancer.html
Contact: John E. Niederhuber, MD, Dir.
Desc: Biology of cancer, focused on human-oriented problems in cause, prevention, tumor localization and treatment. Conducts studies in eye, breast, prostate, and bladder cancers, medical oncology, hyperthermia, immunobiology, radiobiology, experimental chemotherapy, hematologic oncology, pediatric oncology, radiation oncology, biostatistics, and medical physics. *Type:* Research center.

University of Wisconsin--Madison
Hematology Research Laboratory
Medical Science Center, Rm.   Ph: (608)262-1576
    4459   Fax: (608)263-4969
1300 University Ave.
Madison, WI 53706
E-mail: dfmosher@facstaff.wisc.edu
Contact: Dr. Deane Mosher, Dir.
Desc: Biology and biochemistry. Conducts studies on cell cultures, particularly the plasma proteins, fibronectin, vitronectin, and the platelet protein thrombospondin. *Type:* Research center.

University of Wisconsin--Madison
McArdle Laboratory for Cancer Research
1400 University Ave.   Ph: (608)262-2177
Madison, WI 53706   Fax: (608)262-2824
URL: http://www.mcardle.wisc.edu
Contact: Dr. Norman Drinkwater, Dir.
Desc: Cellular, developmental, molecular, animal cell, and viral biology; and genetics, biochemistry, and immunology. Emphasizes mechanisms and controls of transcription, translation, and replication in cells and viruses; mechanisms of environmental, chemical, and viral carcinogenesis; and chemistry and metabolism of nucleic acids and proteins. *Type:* Research center.

Virginia Commonwealth University
Massey Cancer Center
Box 980037   Ph: (804)828-0450
401 College St.   Fax: (804)828-8453
Richmond, VA 23298-0037
URL: http://www.views.vcu.edu/mcc/
Contact: Dr. Gordon D. Ginder, MD, Dir.
Desc: Molecular biology, immunobiology, developmental therapeutics, neurooncology, carcinogenesis, hematopoiesis, bone marrow transplantation, cancer prevention, and structural biology. Clinical studies include translational research and participation in national cooperative groups. *Type:* Research center.

Wake Forest University

Comprehensive Cancer Center

Medical Center Blvd.   Ph: (336)716-7971
Winston Salem, NC 27157-   Fax: (336)716-0293
   1082
E-mail: ftorti@wfubmc.edu
URL: http://www.wfubmc.edu/cancer/
Contact: Dr. Frank M. Torti, Dir.

Desc: Cause and therapy of cancer, in a multidisciplinary effort to determine cause of cancer and to develop more effective means of treating malignant disease. *Type:* Research center.

Walt Disney Memorial Cancer Institute

Cancer Research Division

12722 Research Pkwy.   Ph: (407)380-9977
Orlando, FL 32826   Fax: (407)380-9978
E-mail: barry@sneezy.fhis.net
Contact: Barry Schweitzer, PhD, Contact.

Desc: Cancer, including cell biology and cell regulation, molecular biology, structural biology and drug design, and hemostasis and thrombosis. *Type:* Research center.

Walt Disney Memorial Cancer Institute

Hemostasis and Thrombosis Research Unit

2501 N. Orange Ave., Ste. 786   Ph: (407)303-2440
Orlando, FL 32804   Fax: (407)303-2441
E-mail: john_francis@mail.fhmis.net
Contact: John L. Francis, PhD, Dir.

Desc: Cell biology, cancer, thrombosis and clinical trials. *Type:* Research center.

Walther Cancer Institute, Inc.

3202 N. Meridian St.   Ph: (317)921-2040
Indianapolis, IN 46208   Fax: (317)924-4688
URL: http://www.walther.org
Contact: Joseph E. Walther, MD, Pres./CEO.

Desc: Treatment, prevention, and cure of cancer and studies on the care of cancer patients and families. *Type:* Research center.

Walther Cancer Institute, Inc.

Mary Margaret Walther Program for Cancer Care Research

Indiana Univ.   Ph: (317)274-9970
Sch. of Nursing   Fax: (317)278-2021
1111 Middle Dr., Rm. 340J
Indianapolis, IN 46202
E-mail: iyjk100@iupui.edu
URL: http://www.walther.org/care/start.html
Contact: Dr. Victoria L. Champion, Dir.

Desc: Behavioral research related to cancer survivorship, cancer prevention/control, and cancer care delivery, focusing on developing an interdisciplinary effort to conduct behavioral research improving the quality of life for cancer patients and their families through intervention research that addresses the psychological, economic, sociological and spiritual needs of those going through the cancer experience; increasing early detection of cancer and decrease the occurrence of cancer through individual, family, and community behaviors; and improving the delivery of cost-effective cancer care by health professionals to cancer patients and their families. *Type:* Research center.

Walther Cancer Institute, Inc.

Walther Oncology Center

Indiana University School of   Ph: (317)274-7510
   Medicine   Fax: (317)274-7592
1044 W. Walnut St., Rm. 302
Indianapolis, IN 46202-5121
E-mail: hbroxmey@iupui.edu
URL: http://www.iupui.edu/~woc/

Contact: Hal E. Broxmeyer, PhD, Sci.Dir.

Desc: Blood cell and solid tumor studies, including regulation of the production of normal and cancer cells and umbilical cord blood transplantation, growth factors, suppressor molecules, receptors, gene regulation, oncogenes, differentiation, signal transduction, phosphorylation, cell division cycle genes, and protein tyrosine phosphatases. *Type:* Research center.

West Virginia University

Mary Babb Randolph Cancer Center

Health Sci. Ctr.   Ph: (304)293-3528
PO Box 9300   Fax: (304)293-4667
Morgantown, WV 26506
E-mail: fbutcher@wvumbrccl.hsc.wvu.edu
URL: http://www.hsc.wvu.edu/mbrcc/
Contact: Dr. Fred Butcher, Dir.

Desc: Clinical and scientific cancer research concentrating on residents of West Virginia. *Type:* Research center.

Yale University

Center for Molecular Medicine

School of Medicine   Ph: (203)737-2263
295 Congress Ave.   Fax: (203)737-2267
New Haven, CT 06519
E-mail: vincent.machesi@yale.edu
URL: http://www.info.med.yale.edu/bcmm/
Contact: Dr. Vincent Machesi, Dir.

Desc: Molecular oncology and medicine, focusing on multicellular oncology and organisms. *Type:* Research center.

Yale University

Yale Cancer Center

333 Cedar St.   Ph: (203)785-4371
PO Box 208028   Fax: (203)785-4116
New Haven, CT 06520-8028
E-mail: vincent.devita@yale.edu
URL: http://www.med.yale.edu/ycc
Contact: Dr. Vincent T. DeVita, Jr., Dir.

Desc: Cell biology, developmental therapeutics, immunology, molecular oncology and development, molecular virology, as well as cancer prevention and control, and cancer genetics. Clinical research programs include therapeutic radiology, pediatric oncology, gynecologic oncology, stem cell biology and transplantation, genetic therapymedical oncology and hematology, breast cancer, and lymphoma. *Type:* Research center.

Cardiology

American College of Cardiology

9111 Old Georgetown Rd.   Ph: (301)897-5400
Bethesda, MD 20814-1699   Free: 800-253-4636
                                   Fax: (301)897-9745
E-mail: exec@acc.org
URL: http://www.acc.org
Contact: Christine W. McEntee, Exec.VP.

Desc: Professional society of physicians, surgeons, and scientists specializing in cardiology (heart) and cardiovascular (circulatory) diseases. *Type:* Association.

American College of Chest Physicians

3300 Dundee Rd.   Ph: (847)498-1400
Northbrook, IL 60062   Free: 800-343-ACCP
                                   Fax: (847)498-5460
E-mail: accp@chestnet.org
URL: http://www.chestnet.org
Contact: Alvin Lever, Exec.VP/CEO.

Desc: Professional society of physicians and surgeons specializing in diseases of the chest (heart and lungs). Promotes undergraduate and postgraduate medical education and research in the field. Sponsors forums. *Type:* Association.

American Heart Association

7272 Greenville Ave.   Ph: (214)373-6300
Dallas, TX 75231-4596   Free: 800-242-1793
                                   Fax: (214)987-4334
URL: http://www.americanheart.org
Contact: M. Cass Wheeler, CEO.

Desc: Physicians, scientists, and laypersons. Supports research, education, and community service programs with the objective of reducing premature death and disability from cardiovascular diseases and stroke; coordinates the efforts of physicians, nurses, health professionals, and others engaged in the fight against heart and circulatory disease. Financed entirely by voluntary contributions of the public, principally during the Heart Campaign held in February. *Type:* Association.

American Heart Association Desert/Mountain Affiliate

2929 S. 48th St.   Ph: (602)414-5353
Tempe, AZ 85282-3145   Free: 800-AHA-USA1
                                   Fax: (602)414-5355
URL: http://www.amhrt.org
Contact: Rick Brennan, Exec. VP.

Desc: To support research, education, and community service programs with the objective of reducing premature death and disability from cardiovascular disease and stroke. *Type:* Association.

American Society of Echocardiography

4101 Lake Boone Trl., Ste. 201   Ph: (919)787-5181
Raleigh, NC 27607   Fax: (919)787-4916
E-mail: ase@mercury.interpath.com
URL: http://www.asecho.org
Contact: Sharon Perry, Exec.Dir.

Desc: Physicians and sonographers specializing in ultrasound heart imaging and diagnosis. Promotes excellence in the ultrasonic examination of the heart and assists in establishing standards for education of physicians and cardiac-sonographers in echocardiography. Sponsors educational activities including distribution of self-testing materials, continuing education calendar, and annual scientific sessions. *Type:* Association.

American Society of Nuclear Cardiology

9111 Old Georgetown Rd.   Ph: (301)493-2360
Bethesda, MD 20814   Fax: (301)493-2376
E-mail: admin@asnc.org
URL: http://www.asnc.org
Contact: William D. Nelligan, Exec.Dir.

Desc: Physicians, scientists, technologist, biomedical engineers and health care workers. Seeks to foster optimal delivery of nuclear cardiology services and promote research. *Type:* Association.

Arizona Heart Institute

2632 N. 20th St.   Ph: (602)266-2200
Phoenix, AZ 85006   Fax: (602)240-5862
URL: http://www.azheart.com
Contact: Robert K. Strumpf, MD, Dir. of Interventional Cardiology.

Desc: Ambulatory cardiovascular drugs, including medications for hypertension, angina pectoris, cholesterol reduction, congestive heart failure, and peripheral vascular occlusive disease. Also investigates cardiovascular diagnostic testing procedures and nonpharmacological interventions. *Type:* Research center.

Association of Black Cardiologists

225 Peachtree St., Ste. 1420   Ph: (404)582-8777
Atlanta, GA 30303   Free: 800-753-9222
                                   Fax: (404)582-8778
URL: http://www.abcardio.org
Contact: B. Waine Kong, PhD,JD, CEO.

Desc: Physicians and other health professionals interested in lowering mortality and morbidity resulting from cardiovascular diseases. Seeks to improve prevention and treatment of cardiovascular diseases. Conducts educational and research programs; maintains speakers' bureau. *Type:* Association.

Baylor College of Medicine
DeBakey Heart Center
Texas Med. Ctr.   Ph: (713)798-8600
One Baylor Plz.   Fax: (713)793-1192
Houston, TX 77030
Contact: Dr. Michael E. DeBakey, Dir.
Desc: Atherosclerosis with an emphasis on lipoprotein structure and function and cholesterol metabolism; cardiovascular studies on calcium metabolism, fatty acid metabolism, and cellular ultrastructure; cardiology and cardiovascular surgery, including therapeutic intervention in heart failure, ischemic cardiomyopathy, and role of complement in myocardial infarction; transplantation; and hypertension studies that focus on aldosteronerenin ratio antihypertensive agents. Community outreach studies include control of blood pressure, diabetes, and diet modification. *Type:* Research center.

Bockus Research Institute
Grad. Hospital   Ph: (215)893-2000
415 S. 19th St.   Fax: (215)893-4178
Philadelphia, PA 19146
Contact: Dr. Robert H. Cox, Dir.
Desc: Cardiovascular physiology with specific emphasis on excitation-contraction coupling in smooth and cardiac muscle. Activities include signal transduction mechanisims involving inositol lipids; regulation of contraction in intact and skinned preparations; laser photolysis of caged compounds; whole cell and patch clamp electrophysiological studies of ion channels in cardiac and vascular muscle; and studies of regulation of cytoplasmic calcium using ratiometric fluorescence probes. *Type:* Research center.

Boston University
Whitaker Cardiovascular Institute
700 Albany St.   Ph: (617)638-4890
Boston, MA 02118   Fax: (617)638-4066
E-mail: jloscalz@acs.bu.edu
Contact: Dr. Joseph Loscalzo, Dir.
Desc: Basic and clinical research relating to cardiovascular diseases, including studies on hypertension, atherosclerosis, lipoprotein metabolism, thrombosis, ischemic heart disease, vascular biology, cardiac surgery, and cardiovascular epidemiology. *Type:* Research center.

Cardiothoracic Research and Education Foundation
PO Box 23220   Ph: (619)541-1444
San Diego, CA 92193   Fax: (619)541-1447
E-mail: cref@amainc.com
URL: http://www.ama.inc.com
Contact: Karen Morgan, Contact.
Desc: Cardiothoracic surgery. *Type:* Research center.

Cardiovascular Credentialing International
4456 Corporation Ln., Ste. 120   Ph: (804)497-3380
Virginia Beach, VA 23462   Free: 800-326-0268
    Fax: (804)497-3491
E-mail: ccircvt@nettek.net
Contact: Julia Dow, Exec.Dir.
Desc: Cardiovascular technologists involved in the allied health professions. Conducts testing of allied health professionals throughout the U.S. *Type:* Association.

Charles R. Drew University of Medicine and Science
Hypertension Research Center
1621 E. 120th St., MP 11   Ph: (213)563-5927
Los Angeles, CA 90059   Fax: (213)563-4924
Contact: Harry Ward, MD, Dir.
Desc: Epidemiology, causes, and treatment of high blood pressure in blacks. Analyzes twin studies to assess genetic and environmental factors in blood pressure variations. *Type:* Research center.

Children's HeartLink
5075 Arcadia Ave.   Ph: (612)928-4860
Minneapolis, MN 55436-2306   Fax: (612)928-4859
E-mail: chl@mtn.org
URL: http://www.childrensheartlink.org
Contact: Claudia Liebrecht, Pres.
Desc: Medical charity and service agency. Advocates the prevention and treatment of heart disease in needy children throughout the world; helps selected developing countries expand and improve their cardiac services for children. *Type:* Association.

Cornell University
Division of Hypertension
New York Hospital-Cornell   Ph: (212)746-2189
   Med. Ctr.   Fax: (212)746-8277
520 E. 70th St.
New York, NY 10021
E-mail: paugust@mail.med.cornell.edu
Contact: Phyllis August, MD, Ch.
Desc: Research into causation, diagnosis, and treatment of hypertension and related disorders of the heart, kidneys, and adrenal glands. Research also includes pathogenesis and treatment of heart attacks, congestive heart failure, renal failure, and stroke. *Type:* Research center.

Creighton University
Cardiac Center
3006 Webster St.   Ph: (402)280-4566
Omaha, NE 68131   Fax: (402)280-4938
E-mail: smm@cardiac.creighton.edu
Contact: Dr. Mohiuddin, Med.Dir.
Desc: Cardiology, including drug research, medical care, valvular diseases, invasive and noninvasive treatment techniques, electrocardiogram tests, pacemakers, implants, and ventricular assist devices. *Type:* Research center.

Creighton University
Midwest Hypertension Research Clinic
601 N. 30th St., Ste. 6730   Ph: (402)280-4336
Omaha, NE 68131   Fax: (402)280-4101
Contact: Dr. William Pettinger, Dir.
Desc: Causes and treatment of hypertension and related medical problems. Current research focuses on the molecular genetics of hypertension. *Type:* Research center.

Duke University
Engineering Research Center for Emerging Cardiovascular Technologies
B237 Levine Sci. Res. Ctr.   Ph: (919)660-5137
Box 90295   Fax: (919)684-8886
Durham, NC 27708-0295
URL: http://cect.egr.duke.edu
Contact: Olaf T. von Ramm, PhD, Dir.
Desc: Cardiovascular devices and technologies, including biosensors, implantable defibrillators, real-time 3-D ultrasound imaging equipment, custom integrated electronics, and systems design and simulation. Facilitates technology transfer and promotes interaction between engineering students and industrial investigators. *Type:* Research center.

Duke University
Specialized Center of Research in Congestive Heart Failure
Dept. of Med.   Ph: (252)684-3962
Division of Cardiology   Fax: (252)681-5392
Box 3845
Durham, NC 27710
E-mail: hcs@galactose.mc.duke.edu
Contact: Harold C. Strauss, MD, Admin.
Desc: Congestive heart failure disease. *Type:* Research center.

Emory University
Cardiac Catheterization Laboratory
1364 Clifton Rd. NE   Ph: (404)712-4677
Atlanta, GA 30322   Fax: (404)712-5622
E-mail: Nicolas_Chronos@emory.org
URL: http://www.emory.edu
Contact: Dr. Nicolas A. F. Chronos, Dir.Res.
Desc: Cardiovascular hemodynamics and coronary circulation. *Type:* Research center.

Falor Center for Vascular Studies
Summa Health System/Akron   Ph: (330)375-3693
   City Hospital   Fax: (330)375-4648
525 E. Market St.
Akron, OH 44309
E-mail: schmidts@summa-health.org
Contact: Dr. Steven Schmidt, Dir.
Desc: Vascular cells, focusing on cell and molecular biology, hyperplasia, and wound healing. *Type:* Research center.

Framingham Heart Study
5 Thurber St.   Ph: (508)935-3400
Framingham, MA 01702   Fax: (508)626-1262
Contact: Daniel Levy, MD, Dir.
Desc: Constitutional and conditioning factors in atherosclerotic, hypertensive, and cardiovascular diseases based on a long-term study of a section of the population of Framingham, Massachusetts. There were 5209 men and women who originally participated in the study, begun in 1948, and subsequent studies have focused on 5124 descendents and spouses of descendents in the second generation. *Type:* Research center.

George Washington University
Lipid Research Clinic
908 New Hampshire Ave. NW,   Ph: (202)676-5150
   Ste. 500   Fax: (202)659-8627
Washington, DC 20037
Contact: Judith Hsia, Dir.
Desc: Clinical trials of cholesterol and prevention of heart disease, including cholesterol lowering food and fibers, products, and medication. Also studies cholesterol lowering in senior citizens and trials of postmenopausal hormone replacement and heart disease risk factors in women. *Type:* Research center.

Gladstone Institute of Cardiovascular Disease
San Francisco General Hospital   Ph: (415)826-7500
PO Box 419100   Fax: (415)285-5632
San Francisco, CA 94141-9100
URL: http://www.gladstone.ucsf.edu
Contact: Robert W. Mahley, MD, Dir.
Desc: Lipoprotein metabolism and biochemistry, cell biology and arterial wall metabolism, molecular biology, and clinical nutrition and metabolism, including studies of the molecular structures of various liproteins and their function in transporting blood cholesterol, the relationship of diet to cholesterol levels, and the role of platelets and white blood cells in thrombosis and atherosclerosis. *Type:* Research center.

Good Samaritan Hospital

Heart Institute

1225 Wilshire Blvd.   Ph: (213)977-4040
Los Angeles, CA 90017-2395   Fax: (213)977-4107
E-mail: rkloner@goodsam.org
Contact: Dr. Robert A. Kloner, PhD, Dir.

Desc: Myocardial biochemistry, myocardial infarction, effects of toxins on the heart, clinical hypertension trials, and lipid trials. *Type:* Research center.

Harvard Medical School

Physicians' Health Study Research Group

Brigham and Women's Hospital   Ph: (617)732-4969
900 Commonwealth Ave.   Fax: (617)734-1437
Boston, MA 02215
Contact: Dr. Charles Hennekens, Dir.

Desc: Investigates the effect of aspirin on reducing heart attack risk and the effect of beta-carotene on reducing cancer risk and risk of cardiovascular disease. *Type:* Research center.

Harvard Thorndike Laboratory

330 Brookline Ave.   Ph: (617)667-3020
Boston, MA 02215   Fax: (617)667-1615
E-mail: jmorgan@bidmc.harvard.edu
Contact: Dr. James P. Morgan, Dir.

Desc: Effects of drugs and disease on cardiac hypertrophy and failure; cardiovascular effects of drug abuse. Specific areas of research include cardiac and vasculary pharmacology, physiology, and biochemistry. *Type:* Research center.

Heart Disease Research Foundation

50 Court St.   Ph: (718)649-6210
Brooklyn, NY 11201
Contact: Dr. Yoshiaki Omura, ScD, Dir. of Med.Res.

Desc: Early diagnosis, prevention, and treatment of cardiovascular diseases and related medical and social problems. Studies include the effects of acupuncture and electrotherapeutics on blood chemistry and the cardiovascular system and clinical approaches of these methods directed toward the treatment of abnormal brain circulation and blood pressure and lower extremity circulatory disturbances. *Type:* Research center.

Heart Institute of Spokane

122 W. 7th Ave., Ste. 230   Ph: (509)625-3020
Spokane, WA 99204   Fax: (509)625-3007
E-mail: ktuttle@this.org
URL: http://www.this.org
Contact: Katherine R. Tuttle, MD, Dir.

Desc: Cardiovascular disease. *Type:* Research center.

Heart Research Foundation of Sacramento

3900 J St.   Ph: (916)456-3365
Sacramento, CA 95819   Fax: (916)452-7579
Contact: Patti Gantenbein, Exec.Dir.

Desc: Clinical and pathological studies of atherosclerosis, experimental cardiovascular pharmaceutical testing, and coronary, myocardial, and conduction system morphology. *Type:* Research center.

Heart and Stroke Foundation of British Columbia and Yukon

1212 W. Broadway   Ph: (604)736-4404
Vancouver, BC, Canada V6H   Fax: (604)736-8732
  3V2
E-mail: mnyst@heartstroke.istar.ca
URL: http://www.hst.ca
Contact: Brian O'Connor, Pres.

Desc: Provides research support in the form of personnel awards and grants-in-aid for studies on heart disease and stroke. Fellowships provide salary support for young scientists just beginning a career in research. *Type:* Research center.

Heart and Stroke Foundation of Canada

222 Queen St., Ste. 1402   Ph: (613)569-4361
Ottawa, ON, Canada K1P 5V9   Fax: (613)569-3278
E-mail: mctaylor.nsfc@sypatico.ca
URL: http://www.hsf.ca/research
Contact: Audrey Vandewater, Pres.

Desc: Provides grants for research in cardiovascular and cerebrovascular diseases, particularly the elucidation of fundamental laws and the development of materials, devices, systems, or methods useful in treating stroke, heart attack, hypertension, and effects of smoking. *Type:* Research center.

Heart and Stroke Foundation of Newfoundland and Labrador

169-173 Water St.   Ph: (709)753-8521
PO Box 5819   Fax: (709)753-3117
St. John's, NF, Canada A1C
  5X3
E-mail: heartstroke.nfldlab@nf.sympatico.ca
Contact: Stephen Browne, Exec.Dir.

Desc: Causes of and cures for cardiovascular and cerebrovascular disease. *Type:* Research center.

Heart and Stroke Foundation of Nova Scotia

5523 Spring Garden Rd., Ste.   Ph: (902)423-7530
  204   Fax: (902)492-1464
Halifax, NS, Canada B3J 3T1
URL: http://www.hwc.ca:8080/.hsfc/
Contact: J.E. Fraser, Exec.Dir.

Desc: Cardiovascular and cerebrovascular basic and clinical research, including educational and behavioral science approaches to cardiovascular health. *Type:* Research center.

Heart and Stroke Foundation of Saskatchewan Inc.

279 3rd Ave. N.   Ph: (306)244-2124
Saskatoon, SK, Canada S7K   Free: 800-HSF-INFO
  2H8   Fax: (306)664-4016
Contact: Diane Waterer, Exec.Dir.

Desc: Supports grants-in-aid and fellowship research devoted to the study, prevention, and reduction of disability and death from heart disease and stroke. *Type:* Research center.

Heineman Medical Research

PO Box 35457   Ph: (828)374-0505
Charlotte, NC 28235   Fax: (828)342-5763
Contact: Francis Robicsek, MD, Pres.

Desc: Diseases of heart, lungs, and great vessels, with special interest in organ preservation, electrophysiology, and laser applications to arrhythmias and vascular diseases. *Type:* Research center.

Henry Ford Hospital

Hypertension and Vascular Research Division

7123 E&R Bldg.   Ph: (313)876-2103
2799 W. Grand Blvd.   Fax: (313)876-1479
Detroit, MI 48202
Contact: Dr. Oscar A. Carretero, Div.Hd.

Desc: Etiology and pathogenesis of hypertension, vasoactive hormones, and vascular disease. *Type:* Research center.

Hope Heart Institute

528 18th Ave.   Ph: (206)320-2001
Seattle, WA 98122   Fax: (206)323-2300
Contact: William P. Hammond, MD, Medical Dir./Pres.

Desc: Heart and blood vessel research. Develops new grafts to replace diseased artery tissue. *Type:* Research center.

Indiana University-Purdue University at Indianapolis

Hypertension Research Center

541 Clinical Dr., Rm. 423   Ph: (317)274-8153
Indianapolis, IN 46202-5111   Fax: (317)274-7700
E-mail: mweinbe@indyvax.iupui.edu
Contact: Dr. Myron H. Weinberger, Dir.

Desc: Hypertension, including a broad-based, multidisciplinary research program of clinical studies involving genetics of hypertension, pathophysiology of hypertension with plasma renin suppression, role of renin and aldosterone in toxemia of pregnancy, causes of childhood hypertension, and role of renin and aldosterone in heart failure. Also studies myocardial metabolism and cyclic AMP system in spontaneously hypertensive rats, role of sympathetic nervous system in human experimental forms of hypertension, control of renin release in vitro and of renal sodium handling, role of sodium in blood pressure, sodium restriction in the treatment of hypertension, and role of calcium and potassium in blood pressure. *Type:* Research center.

Institute for Clinical Research, Inc.

PO Box 29545   Ph: (202)462-6820
Washington, DC 20017-0745
Contact: Richard F. Levine, Chm.

Desc: Hypertension, cardiology, infectious diseases, and oncology. *Type:* Research center.

John P. Robarts Research Institute

Heart and Circulation Group

100 Perth Dr.   Ph: (519)663-5777
PO Box 5015   Fax: (519)663-3789
London, ON, Canada N6A 5K8
Contact: Dr. William Kostuk, Dir.

Desc: Causes and treatment of heart rhythm disorders, including research in heart mapping, cryosurgery, and implantable defibrillators for arrhythmia. Also studies new methods of tissue preservation and mechanical circulatory support, development of prosthetic valves, microcirculation, and heart failure and cardiac transplantation. *Type:* Research center.

Johns Hopkins University

Cardiac Bioelectric Systems Laboratory

School of Medicine   Ph: (410)955-9603
Department of Biomedical   Fax: (410)955-0549
  Engineering
Traylor Research Bldg., 7th Fl.
720 Rutland Ave.
Baltimore, MD 21205
E-mail: ltung@bme.jhu.edu
URL: http://www.bme.jhu.edu/~ltung/CBS_Lab/cbsl.html
Contact: Leslie Tung, PhD, Dir.

Desc: Electrical properties of the heart, in particular as they relate at the cellular and multicellular levels to defibrillation and arrhythmia. *Type:* Research center.

Johns Hopkins University

Computational Modeling Group

School of Medicine   Ph: (410)955-3131
Department of Biomedical   Fax: (410)955-0549
  Engineering
720 Rutland Ave.
Baltimore, MD 21205
E-mail: rwinslow@bme.jhu.edu
URL: http://www.bme.jhu.edu/~rwinslow/
Contact: Prof. Raimond L. Winslow, Contact.

Desc: Understanding the origins of cardiac arrhythmias through the use of biophysically detailed computer models. *Type:* Research center.

Johns Hopkins University

Ischemic Heart Disease Specialized Center of Research

Johns Hopkins Hospital   Ph: (410)955-5997
600 N. Wolfe St.   Fax: (410)955-0852
Baltimore, MD 21287
E-mail: lbecker@welchlink.welch.jhu.edu

Contact: Lewis C. Becker, MD, Dir.

Desc: Reperfusion injury and other aspects of ischemic heart disease, including cellular, physiological, engineering, and patient studies. Conducts a cardiology fellows program. *Type:* Research center.

Johns Hopkins University

Lipid Research Atherosclerosis Unit

CMSC, Rm. 604   Ph: (410)955-3197
600 N. Wolfe St.   Fax: (410)955-1276
Baltimore, MD 21287-3654
E-mail: pokwit@welchlink.welch.jhu.edu

Contact: Dr. Peter Kwiterovich, Contact.

Desc: Lipids, lipoproteins, apolipoproteins, atherosclerosis, genetics, coronary artery diseases, and basic serum proteins. *Type:* Research center.

Johns Hopkins University

Vascular Bioengineering Laboratory

School of Medicine   Ph: (410)955-3131
Department of Biomedical   Fax: (410)955-0549
   Engineering
720 Rutland Ave.
Baltimore, MD 21205
E-mail: ralevria@bme.jhu.edu
URL: http://www.bme.jhu.edu/~thuang/lab/lab.html

Contact: B. Rita Alevriadou, PhD, Prin. Investigator.

Desc: Effects of flow-induced mechanical forces on molecular mechanisms of blood cell adhesion and metabolism, protein synthesis and genetic expression of vascular endothelial cells to identify better treatments for cardiovascular diseases. *Type:* Research center.

Krannert Institute of Cardiology

1111 W. 10th St.   Ph: (317)630-7261
Indianapolis, IN 46202-4800   Fax: (317)274-9697
E-mail: dzipes@iupui.edu

Contact: Janet Hutcheson, Contact.

Desc: Electrophysiology, cardiac membrane biology, echocardiography, vascular biology, exercise physiology, and cardiovascular transgenics. *Type:* Research center.

Laval University

Cardiopulmonary Institute

2725, chemin Ste-Foy   Ph: (418)656-4760
Ste. Foy, PQ, Canada G1V 4G5   Fax: (418)656-4509
E-mail: yvon.cormier@med.ulaval.ca

Contact: Yvon Cormier, MD, Dir.

Desc: All major fields of cardiopulmonary diseases. *Type:* Research center.

Laval University

Medical Research Centre

Hypertension Research Group

2705, boulevard Laurier S120-A   Ph: (418)654-2107
Ste. Foy, PQ, Canada G1V 4G2   Fax: (418)654-2759
E-mail: e.lacourciere@crchul.ulaval.ca

Contact: Yves Lacourciere, Dir.

Desc: Cause and prevention of cardiovascular disease, including physical exercise, arterial hypertension, the relationship between type II diabetes and hypertension, the anatomy and physiology of neurotransmisison circuits of stress and hypertension, the efficacy of new drugs, and the effects of exercise and weight loss on controlling hypertension in obese patients. *Type:* Research center.

Laval University

Medical Research Centre

Lipid Research Centre

2705, boulevard Laurier, TR-93   Ph: (418)654-2133
Ste. Foy, PQ, Canada G1V 4G2   Fax: (418)654-2145
E-mail: jean-pierre.despres@crchul.ulaval.ca

Contact: Jean-Pierre Despres, PhD, Dir.

Desc: Pharmacological studies on hypolipidemic agents, lipoproteins, apoproteins, LDL receptors, lipoprotein lipase and hepatic lipase activity, abdominal and visceral obesity, metabolism and genetic polymorphism, nutritional studies on polysaturated and omega fatty acids, and epidemiology of ischemic heart disease in the region of Quebec City. *Type:* Research center.

Loyola University Chicago

Heart Transplant and Heart Failure Program

2160 S. 1st Ave.   Ph: (708)216-4810
Maywood, IL 60153   Fax: (708)327-2770
E-mail: mmullen@luc.edu

Contact: Dr. G. Martin Mullen, Dir.

Desc: Cardiac transplantation and immunology, including allograft rejection, vascular diseases, and transplant tolerance. *Type:* Research center.

Masonic Medical Research Laboratory

2150 Bleecker St.   Ph: (315)735-2217
Utica, NY 13501   Fax: (315)735-5648
E-mail: ca@mmrl.edu
URL: http://www.mmrl.edu

Contact: Dr. Charles Antzelevitch, Exec.Dir.

Desc: Ischemic heart disease, cardiac arrhythmias, forms of sudden cardiac death known as idiopathic ventricular fibrillation or the Brugada Syndrome death as well as the cellular basis for the different waves found in the electrocardiogram. Other fields of study include molecular biology and understanding the role of the immune system in the development of autoimmune diseases, such as, hypertension, vasculitis and lupus erythematosus. *Type:* Research center.

MCP Hahnemann University of the Health Sciences

Cardiothoracic Surgery Department

Broad & Vine Sts.   Ph: (215)762-7803
Philadelphia, PA 19102   Fax: (215)762-1858
E-mail: wechsla@wpo.auhs.edu

Contact: Andrew Wechsler, Chm.

Desc: Diseases of the heart and great vessels, including studies in myocardial metabolism, physioloy, electrophysiology, cardiac surgery, echocardiography, pharmacology, and nuclear cardiology. Initiates research in causes, diagnosis, and treatment of cardiac and pulmonary disease. *Type:* Research center.

MCP Hahnemann University of the Health Sciences

Center for the Study of Atherosclerosis

2900 Queen Ln.   Ph: (215)991-8300
Philadelphia, PA 19129   Fax: (215)843-8849
E-mail: phillim@wpo.auhs
URL: http://www.auhs.edu

Contact: Dr. Michael Phillips, Dir.

Desc: Etiology, maintenance, and reduction of lipoproteins in atherosclerosis. *Type:* Research center.

MCP Hahnemann University of the Health Sciences

Institute for Cardiovascular Research

Allegheny General Hospital   Ph: (412)359-8255
320 E. North Ave.
Pittsburgh, PA 15212
URL: http://www.mcphu.edu/institutes/instcardio.html

Contact: Stephen F. Vatner, MD, Dir.

Desc: Cardiovascular disease. *Type:* Research center.

Medical University of South Carolina

Confocal Microscopy and Computer Image Analysis Center

Department of Cell Biology &   Ph: (843)792-3779
   Anatomy   Fax: (843)792-0664
171 Ashley Ave.
Charleston, SC 29425-2204
E-mail: litkell@musc.edu
URL: http://www.musc.edu/mmi

Contact: Dr. Larry L. Litke, Dir.

Desc: Cell biology and cellular and molecular influences on cardiovascular development. *Type:* Research center.

Mended Hearts

7272 Greenville Ave.   Ph: (214)706-1442
Dallas, TX 75231-4596   Fax: (214)706-5231

Contact: Darla Bonham, Exec.Dir.

Desc: Persons who have heart disease; their families and friends. Works to: provide advice, encouragement, and services to heart disease patients and to their families; establish programs of assistance to surgeons, physicians, and hospitals. Conducts and assists in research programs designed to benefit heart patients. *Type:* Association.

Miami Heart Research Institute

801 Arthur Godfrey Rd., 5th Fl.   Ph: (305)674-3020
Miami Beach, FL 33140   Fax: (305)535-3642
E-mail: mhri@miamiheart.com
URL: http://www.miamiheartresearch.org

Contact: Kathleen DuCasse, CEO, Contact.

Desc: Cardiovascular disease, including tracking genetic cardiovascular abnormalities, sudden cardiac death, emergency response resuscitation techniques, stress reduction techniques as well as hypertension and cholesterol studies. *Type:* Research center.

Midwest Heart Research Foundation

2340 Highland Ave., Ste. 310   Ph: (630)932-2165
Lombard, IL 60148   Fax: (630)268-9609

Contact: John F. Moran, MD, Med.Dir.

Desc: Cardiovascular medicine clinical research. *Type:* Research center.

Minneapolis Vascular Institute

6545 France Ave. S., Ste. 485   Ph: (612)929-6994
Edina, MN 55435   Fax: (612)924-1540

Contact: Ruth K. Edwards, RN, Exec.Dir.

Desc: Peripheral vascular disease and diabetic revasculization. *Type:* Research center.

Minnesota Heart Institute Foundation

920 E. 28th St., Ste. 100   Ph: (612)863-3833
Minneapolis, MN 55407-1139   Fax: (612)863-3801
URL: http://www.mplsheartfoundation.org

Contact: Ford Watson Bell, DVM, Dir.

Desc: Clinical cardiovascular studies with emphasis on cardiac death in the young. *Type:* Research center.

New England Medical Center Hospitals, Inc.
Center for Cardiovascular Health Services
Research
New England Med. Ctr., Box
63
750 Washington St.
Boston, MA 02111
E-mail: hpselker@es.nemc.org
Contact: Harry P. Selker, MD, Ch.
Ph: (617)636-5009
Fax: (617)636-8023
Desc: Cardiovascular health services, particularly in the development and testing of predictive instruments for acute cardiac ischemia, thrombolytic therapy, and the use of cardiac care units in hospitals. *Type:* Research center.

New York Institute for Vascular Studies, Inc.
438 Jill Ct.
Yorktown Heights, NY 10598-
2006
E-mail: maxsml@msn.com
Contact: Steven Levine, Dir.
Ph: (914)962-0030
Fax: (914)962-0030
Desc: Vascular disease and surgery. *Type:* Research center.

North American Society of Pacing and
Electrophysiology
2 Vision Dr.
Natick, MA 01760-2059
E-mail: info@naspe.org
URL: http://www.naspe.org
Contact: Carol J. McGlinchey, Exec.Dir.
Ph: (508)647-0100
Fax: (508)647-0124
Desc: Physicians, scientists, and allied professionals throughout the world dedicated to the study and management or cardiac arrhythmias; to improve the care of patients by promoting research, education and training, and providing leadership towards optimal health care policies and standards. *Type:* Association.

Northern Illinois Heart Institute, Inc.
87 N. Airliet St., Ste. G16
Elgin, IL 60120-2104
Contact: Dr. Cavallo, Dir.
Ph: (847)695-5333
Fax: (847)695-5398
Desc: Cardiovascular health. *Type:* Research center.

Oklahoma Medical Research Foundation
Cardiovascular Biology Research Program
825 NE 13th St.
Oklahoma City, OK 73104
Ph: (405)271-6673
Free: 800-522-0211
Fax: (405)271-3137
E-mail: Jdonald-capra@omrf.ouhsc.edu
URL: http://www.omrf.ouhsc.edu/OMRF/Research/15/
Welcome.html
Contact: J. Donald Capra, MD, Pres.
Desc: Cardiovascular disease, especially blood clotting and inflammatory aspects of vascular diseases; structure determination of blood coagulation enzymes and design of inhibitors; regulation of inflammation by the coagulation system and the impact of inflammation on coagulation; mechanisms by which autoimmune diseases modulate blood coagulation and vascular function; septic shock; and the mechanisms of leukocyte binding to vascular endothelium. Gene deletion and transgenic approaches are designed to identify targets for therapeutic intervention. *Type:* Research center.

Oklahoma Medical Research Foundation
Lipid and Lipoprotein Laboratory
825 NE 13th St.
Oklahoma City, OK 73104
E-mail: hamptonk@omrf.oukhsc.edu
Contact: Dr. Petar Alaupovic, PhD, Contact.
Ph: (405)271-7703
Fax: (405)271-8575
Desc: Chemistry and metabolism of plasma lipid transport, pathophysiology and treatment of dyslipoproteinemias, and model systems of atherosclerosis, including studies on the chemistry and interaction of lipoprotein particles, formation and lipolytic degradation of lipoprotein particles, dietary and drug treatment of dyslipoproteinemias, and determination of apolipoprotein profiles in dyslipoproteinemias. *Type:* Research center.

Oregon Health Sciences University
Congenital Heart Research Center
3181 SW Sam Jackson Park
Rd., L-464
Portland, OR 97201-3098
E-mail: rhumanl@ohsu.edu
URL: http://www.ohsu.edu/chrc
Contact: Kent L. Thornburg, PhD, Exec.Dir.
Ph: (503)494-2382
Fax: (503)494-4352
Desc: The role of fetal heart development in congenital heart defects and the link between fetal heart development and adult heart disease. *Type:* Research center.

Oregon Health Sciences University
Institute for Nutrition and Cardiovascular
Research
Div. of Nephrology &
Hypertension
3314 SW U.S. Veterans
Hospital Rd., PP 262
Portland, OR 97201
Contact: David A. McCarron, MD, Hd.
Ph: (503)494-8490
Fax: (503)494-5330
Desc: Nutritional and metabolic factors that contribute to blood pressure regulation, particularly in the areas of calcium metabolism, cellular mechanisms, and the role of nutrition in cardiovascular physiology. *Type:* Research center.

Ottawa Heart Institute Research Corp.
40 Ruskin St.
Ottawa, ON, Canada K1Y 4W7
E-mail: dbeanlands@heartinst.on.ca
Contact: Dr. Donald S. Beanlands, Pres./Chm.
Ph: (613)761-4721
Fax: (613)761-4214
Desc: Cardiac diseases, emphasizing arteriosclerosis research and dyslipidemia, hypertension, cell and molecular biology of the heart, vascular biology, pharmacology, medical devices, artificial hearts, clinical trials and prevention and rehabilitation. *Type:* Research center.

Pacific Vascular Research Foundation
601 Montgomery St., Ste. 900
San Francisco, CA 94111-2603
Contact: Sharon C. Collins, Dir.
Ph: (415)291-7201
Fax: (415)291-7214
Desc: Issues related to vascular health. *Type:* Research center.

Pennsylvania State University
Artificial Heart Research Project
Milton S. Hershey Medical
Center
500 University Dr.
Hershey, PA 17033
E-mail: grosenberg@psu.edu
URL: http://www.collmed.psu.edu/attorg
Contact: Gerson Rosenberg, PhD, Dir.
Ph: (717)531-4494
Fax: (717)531-4464
Desc: Development of an implantable, long-term, motor-driven left ventricular assist pump, an implantable, pneumatically-driven total artificial heart, and an implantable, motor-driven electric artificial heart, including all aspects of design of implantable blood pumps, implantable energy convertors, bench testing and evaluation, and animal implantation studies. *Type:* Research center.

Pennsylvania State University
Henry Hood Research Program
Danville, PA 17822-2601
Ph: (717)271-6659
(717)271-5886
Contact: David J. Carey, MD, Asst.Dir.
Desc: Cardiovascular disease and developmental biology at the cellular and molecular biology level; clinical research in areas of cancer and cardiovascular disease; and investigational drug studies. *Type:* Research center.

Rees-Stealy Research Foundation
2001 4th Ave.
San Diego, CA 92101
E-mail: mdios@aol.com
Contact: Dr. H.D. Peabody, Jr., Dir.
Ph: (619)235-8744
Fax: (619)235-8745
Desc: Basic cardiac research involving cardio myocyte contractility studies. Research includes the analysis of recording heart cell function, utilizing the video camera technique of living motion using electronic devices for computer transfer, heart cell preparation, and cell culture. *Type:* Research center.

Rocky Mountain Clinical Research, Inc.
29 Rogers Ct.
Golden, CO 80401-6515
Contact: Gail Danhour, Exec.Dir.
Ph: (303)279-1550
Fax: (303)278-2602
Desc: Medical research, clinical drug trials, and the development of new diagnostic techniques. *Type:* Research center.

Rush University
Rush Heart Institute
Rush-Presbyterian-St. Luke's
Med. Ctr.
1653 W. Congress Pky.
Chicago, IL 60612
URL: http://www.rush.edu/med/heart
Contact: Dr. Joseph E. Parillo, Med.Dir.
Ph: (312)563-2129
Free: 800-942-4144
Fax: (312)942-4039
Desc: Medical cardiovascular research, including cardiac and vascular physiology and cardiovascular surgery, including open heart procedures and major aortic replacement surgery. *Type:* Research center.

St. Francis Hospital (Brookville, NY)
DeMatteis Center for Education and Research
Northern Blvd.
Glen Head, NY 11545
Contact: Sean Callahan, Admin.Dir.
Ph: (516)629-2038
Desc: Heart studies, focusing on drugs and diet in reversing coronary heart disease. *Type:* Research center.

San Francisco Heart Institute
1900 Sullivan Ave.
Daly City, CA 94015
E-mail: rshaw@chw.edu
URL: http://www.sfhi.com
Contact: Richard E. Shaw, PhD, Dir.Res. & Oper.
Ph: (650)991-6712
Fax: (650)755-7315
Desc: Analysis of success, complications, and long-term outcome of coronary angioplasty and cardiac surgery; technological advances applied to angioplasty, including new dilatation balloons, lasers, and coronary stents; transdermal therapies in treatment of hypertension; and atherectomy (rotational and directional) research. *Type:* Research center.

Spokane Heart Research Foundation
801 W. 5th Ave., Ste. 317
Spokane, WA 99204-2823
Ph: (509)624-6000
Free: 888-644-5844
Fax: (509)624-5844
Contact: Marc A. DeWood, MD, Dir.
Desc: Cardiac and heart issues, focusing on heart failure, hypertension, and arrhythmia. *Type:* Research center.

Temple University
Sol Sherry Thrombosis Research Center
Old Med. School
3400 N. Broad St., Rm. 300
Philadelphia, PA 19140
E-mail: colmanr@vm.temple.edu
URL: http://www.temple.edu/SSTRC/
Contact: Robert W. Colman, MD, Dir.
Ph: (215)707-4665
Fax: (215)707-2783
Desc: Thrombotic hemorrhage disorders, biochemistry and molecular biology of blood coagulation, platelet structure and function, and vascular biology and angiogeneses. Clinical studies are conducted. *Type:* Research center.

Texas A&M University

Microcirculation Research Institute

College of Medicine   Ph: (409)845-7816
College Station, TX 77843-1114   Fax: (409)847-8635
E-mail: granger@tamu.edu
URL: http://www.mphywww.tamu.edu/mri.html
Contact: Dr. Harris J. Granger, Dir.

Desc: Applies high technology to analysis of normal and diseased microscopic blood vessels, including studies on bloodflow in both normal and diseased states, basic control and exchange processes in microcirculation, role of microcirculation in hypertension, edema, stroke, and diabetes, computer analysis of microscopic images, cellular and molecular bases of endothelial and vascular smooth muscle functions, and pathobiology of inflammation and ischemic injury. *Type:* Research center.

Texas Heart Institute

PO Box 20345   Ph: (713)791-4011
Houston, TX 77225-0345   Fax: (713)791-3089
URL: http://www.tmc.edu/thi/
Contact: Denton A. Cooley, MD, Pres./CEO.

Desc: Diseases of the heart and cardiovascular system. Specific areas of study include cardiovascular surgery, including coronary artery bypass surgery, valve replacement, transplantation, and mechanical circulatory support and replacement/assist devices; invasive and non-invasive cardiology, including molecular biochemistry; cardiovascular anesthesiology and pathology; and biostatistics and epidemiology. *Type:* Research center.

Thomas Jefferson University

Ischemia-Shock Research Center

Department of Physiology   Ph: (215)503-7760
1020 Locust St.   Fax: (215)503-2073
Philadelphia, PA 19107-6799
E-mail: lefer1@jeflin.tju.edu
URL: http://147.140.131.44/physhome/ph.html1
Contact: Dr. Allan M. Lefer, Dir.

Desc: Myocardial, splanchnic, and cerebral ischemia and circulatory shock, particularly pathophysiology and therapeutics. Promotes collaborative research among members, facilitates basic science and joint research efforts, and provides research opportunities to fellows. *Type:* Research center.

Tulane University

Tulane Center for Cardiovascular Health

1430 Tulane Ave., SL 29   Ph: (504)585-7197
New Orleans, LA 70112   Fax: (504)585-7194
E-mail: berenson@mailhost.tcs.tulane.edu
URL: http://www1.omi.tulane.edu/cardiohealth/
Contact: Gerald S. Berenson, MD, Dir.

Desc: Cardiovascular disease risk factors in children and young adults, including a descriptive epidemiology study (Bogalusa Heart Study), laboratory investigations on the mechanisms of arteriosclerosis, structural studies of proteoglycans, and health education and promotion in elementary school children (Health Ahead/Heart Smart). *Type:* Research center.

United Calvinist Youth

1333 Alger SE   Ph: (616)241-5616
PO Box 7259   Fax: (616)241-5558
Grand Rapids, MI 49510
Contact: Gordon Dornbush, Office Mgr.

Desc: Federation of youth (ages 8 and up), primarily of the Christian Reformed denomination. Promotes the interests and growth of youth organizations in the Christian Reformed and similar Calvinistic churches by providing suitable study and reading material and conducting volunteer service programs, leaders training courses, and rallies. *Type:* Association.

U.S. Department of Health and Human Services

National Heart, Lung, and Blood Institute

NIH Bldg. 31, Rm. 5A52   Ph: (301)496-5166
31 Center Dr. MSC 2486   Fax: (301)402-0818
Bethesda, MD 20892-2486
E-mail: lenfantc@gwgate.nhlbi.nih.gov
URL: http://www.nhlbi.nih.gov/nhlbi/nhlbi.htm
Contact: Claude Lenfant, Dir.

Desc: Responsible for a national program of research leading to the prevention and treatment of heart, lung, and blood diseases. The scope of the Institute's effort encompasses all forms of heart and vascular disease (except the consequences of cerebrovascular disease), most forms of pulmonary disease (except cancers), sleep disorders, many blood diseases (including sickle cell disease), and the utilization of blood resources. *Type:* Research center.

U.S. Department of Health and Human Services

National Heart, Lung, and Blood Institute

Division of Epidemiology and Clinical Applications

2 Rockledge Centre   Ph: (301)439-0422
6701 Rockledge Dr. MSC 7938   Fax: (301)480-1864
Bethesda, MD 20892-7938
Contact: Lawrence Friedman, MD, Dir.

Desc: Epidemiological studies, clinical trials, basic and applied behavioral research, demonstration and education research, and projects for disease prevention and health promotion in heart, vascular, pulmonary, and blood diseases and blood resources. It maintains surveillance over developments in its program area and assesses the national need for research on the prevention, diagnosis, and treatment of these diseases by maintaining the necessary scientific management capability to foster and guide an effective attack upon them. *Type:* Research center.

U.S. Department of Health and Human Services

National Heart, Lung, and Blood Institute

Division of Epidemiology and Clinical Applications

Clinical Applications and Prevention Program

2 Rockledge Centre   Ph: (301)435-0414
6701 Rockledge Dr. MSC 7936   Fax: (301)480-1669
Bethesda, MD 20892-7936
Contact: Dr. Jeffrey Cutler, Dir., CAPP, DECA.

Desc: Supports clinical trials, demonstration and educational research, basic and applied behavioral research, and projects for the prevention of cardiovascular, lung, and blood diseases as well as therapeutic measures. Principal areas of research are preventive medicine, nutrition, behavioral medicine, cardiology, and community demonstration and education projects. *Type:* Research center.

U.S. Department of Health and Human Services

National Heart, Lung, and Blood Institute

Division of Epidemiology and Clinical Applications

Epidemiology and Biometry Program

2 Rockledge Centre   Ph: (301)435-0707
6701 Rockledge Dr., MSC 7934   Fax: (301)480-1667
Bethesda, MD 20892-7934
E-mail: manolio@nih.gov
Contact: Dr. Teri Manolio, Dir. Epidemiology and Biometry Program.

Desc: Risk factors (e.g., elevated cholesterol and blood pressure, smoking, diabetes, type A personality, lack of physical activity) for coronary heart disease, hypertension, stroke, and peripheral vascular disease as well as for lung and blood diseases. Research interests include causes and predictors associated with the onset and course of heart disease, hypertension, stroke, peripheral vascular disease, and lung and blood diseases. *Type:* Research center.

U.S. Department of Health and Human Services

National Heart, Lung, and Blood Institute

Division of Extramual Affairs

6701 Rockledge Dr. MSC 7924,   Ph: (301)435-0260
Ste. 7100   Fax: (301)435-0831
Bethesda, MD 20892-7924
Contact: Dr. Ronald G. Geller, Dir.

Desc: Responsible for advising the Director of the Institute on research contract, grant, and research training program policies. It represents the Institute on overall NIH committees on extramural program policy, oversees compliance with such policy within NHLBI, and coordinates the Institute's research grant and research training and development programs with the National Heart, Lung, and Blood Advisory Council. *Type:* Research center.

U.S. Department of Health and Human Services

National Heart, Lung, and Blood Institute

Division of Heart and Vascular Diseases

Two Rockledge Centre, Ste.   Ph: (301)435-0466
9044   Fax: (301)480-1336
6701 Rockledge Dr. MSC 7940
Bethesda, MD 20892-7940
Contact: Dr. Stephen Mockrin, Actg.Dir.

Desc: Control of heart and vascular diseases. Major areas of investigat ion include arrythmias, congenital and infectious diseases, heart failure, ischemic heart disease, interventional cardiology, bioengineering, atherosclerosis, hypertension, vascular biology, vascular medicine, cardiovascular homeostasis and bionutrition, and molecular genetics and medicine. *Type:* Research center.

U.S. Department of Health and Human Services

National Heart, Lung, and Blood Institute

Division of Heart and Vascular Diseases

Heart Research Program

2 Rockledge Ctr., Ste. 9192   Ph: (301)435-0504
6701 Rocklegge Dr., MSC 7940   Fax: (301)480-1454
Bethesda, MD 20892-7940
E-mail: ps48j@nih.gov
URL: http://www.nhlbi.nih.gov/personal/laura/nhlbi/extlocal.html
Contact: Peter M. Spooner, PhD, Contact.

Desc: Administers research grants and implements new research programs in the basic medical sciences as related to cardiology, physiology, anatomy, pharmacology, biochemistry, and bioengineering. *Type:* Research center.

U.S. Department of Health and Human Services

National Heart, Lung, and Blood Institute

Division of Heart and Vascular Diseases

Heart Research Program

Two Rockledge Centre   Ph: (301)435-0494
6701 Rockledge Dr., MSC 7940   Fax: (301)480-7971
Bethesda, MD 20892-7940
E-mail: desvignp@gwgate.nhlbi.nih.gov
Contact: Patrice Desvigne-Nickens, MD, Dir., Heart Research Prog.

Desc: Heart function; normal and abnormal mechanisms of heart action; advanced diagnostic methods; and therapies for cardiac and vascular disorders. Research includes studies on myocardial infarction (MI); angina pectoris; arrhythmias; cardiac resuscitation; quantification of infarct size; heart muscle changes during ischemia; effectiveness of thrombolytic therapy in patients with acute MI; effects of coronary bypass grafts on morbidity and mortality in chronic coronary heart disease patients with stable angina pectoris; the effects of PTCA in patients with coronary disease; prototype cardiovascular devices for partial or total replacement of heart function; and development of devices and techniques for noninvasive detection and measurement of arteriosclerotic plaques within the carotid, coronary, and larger arteries of the limbs. *Type:* Research center.

U.S. Department of Health and Human Services

National Heart, Lung, and Blood Institute

Division of Heart and Vascular Diseases

Heart Research Program

Two Rockledge Center   Ph: (301)435-0513

6701 Rockledge Drive, Rm.   Fax: (301)480-1336
9178

Bethesda, MD 20892-7940

E-mail: jw53F@nih.gov

Contact: Dr. John T. Watson, PhD, Chf.

Desc: Mechanical circulatory support, biomaterials (blood-material interactions), and diagnostic and therapeutic devices, as well as technolgy transfer through Small Business Innovation Research Grants. *Type:* Research center.

U.S. Department of Health and Human Services

National Heart, Lung, and Blood Institute

Division of Heart and Vascular Diseases

Heart Research Training and Development Group

2 Rockledge Ctr., Ste. 9044   Ph: (301)435-0535

6701 Rockledge Dr., MSC 7940   Fax: (301)480-1454

Bethesda, MD 20892-7940

E-mail: mc63a@nih.gov

Contact: Dr. Michael A. Commarato, Chf.

Desc: Administers training grants, fellowships, and career program awards to individuals and academic institutions for research training relating to cardiovascular disease. *Type:* Research center.

U.S. Department of Health and Human Services

National Heart, Lung, and Blood Institute

Division of Heart and Vascular Diseases

Specialized Centers of Research in Coronary and Peripheral Vascular Disease, Heart Failure, and Congenital Heart

2 Rockledge Ctr.   Ph: (301)435-0466

6701 Rockledge Dr.   Fax: (301)480-7971

Bethesda, MD 20892

Desc: Supports cardiac and vascular disease research through grants. *Type:* Research center.

U.S. Department of Health and Human Services

National Heart, Lung, and Blood Institute

Division of Heart and Vascular Diseases

Vascular Research Program

Two Rockledge Center, Ste.   Ph: (301)496-1613
10193   Fax: (301)480-2849

6701 Rockledge Drive, MSC
7956

Bethesda, MD 20892-7956

E-mail: drw@cu.nih.gov

URL: http://www.nhlbi.nih.gov/personal/laura/nhlbi/extlocal.html

Contact: David M. Robinson, PhD, Dir.

Desc: Arteriosclerosis, lipid metabolism, hypertension, vascular biology and medicine, and molecular genetics and medicine. This includes support for: research grants; Specialized Centers of Research (SCORs) in arteriosclerosis and hypertension; and nonhuman primate resources to facilitate study of disease states. *Type:* Research center.

U.S. Department of Health and Human Services

National Heart, Lung, and Blood Institute

Division of Intramural Research

NIH Bldg. 10, Rm. 7N214   Ph: (301)496-2116

9000 Rockville Pike   Fax: (301)402-0013

Bethesda, MD 20892

Contact: Dr. Edward Korn, Dir.

Desc: Basic laboratory and clinical research in heart, blood vessel, and lung diseases and certain blood diseases (such as sickle cell anemia and hemophilia); and development of technology related to cardiovascular, pulmonary, and hematologic disorders. Division maintains communication with other programs of the Institute to facilitate early practical application of basic research findings. *Type:* Research center.

U.S. Department of Health and Human Services

National Heart, Lung, and Blood Institute

Division of Intramural Research

Cardiology Branch

NIH Bldg. 10, Rm 7B-14   Ph: (301)496-5817

10 Center Dr. MSC 1650   Fax: (301)402-0888

Bethesda, MD 20892

Contact: Dr. Richard O. Cannon, III, Actg.Chf.

Desc: Clinical and basic research efforts, including: studies into the genetic causes and pathophysiologic mechanisms responsible for hypertrophic cardiomyopathy; development of approaches to revascularize the ischemic heart, including the promotion of angiogenesis; studies into pathogenesis and treatment of coronary artery disease and of myocardial iscemia secondary to microvascular disease; elucidation of the mechanisms responsible for Syndrome X (chest pain in the presence of normal coronary arteries); elucidation of the molecular mechanisms responsible for restenosis; development of gene therapy for the treatment of restenosis and atherosclerosis; studies of vascular effects of estrogen and anti-estrogen therapies; and the development of techniques to detect stunned and hibernating myocardium and the elucidation of responsible mechanisms. *Type:* Research center.

U.S. Department of Health and Human Services

National Heart, Lung, and Blood Institute

Division of Intramural Research

Hematology Branch

NIH Bldg. 10, Rm. 7C103   Ph: (301)496-5093

10 Center Dr. MSC 1652   Fax: (301)496-8396

Bethesda, MD 20892-1652

E-mail: youngn@gwgate.nhlbi.nih.gov

Contact: Dr. Neal S. Young, Chf.

Desc: Normal and abnormal hematopoiesis. Clinical research is conducted on patients with bone marrow failure syndromes, especially aplastic anemia, Fancon's anemia, and myelodysplasia; inherited anemias, including sickle cell anemia and thalassemia; and hematologic malignancies, including chronic myelogenous leukemia and multiple myeloma. *Type:* Research center.

U.S. Department of Health and Human Services

National Heart, Lung, and Blood Institute

Division of Intramural Research

Hypertension-Endocrine Branch

NIH Bldg. 10, Rm. 8C103   Ph: (301)496-1518

10 Center Dr. MSC 1754   Fax: (301)402-1679

Bethesda, MD 20892-1754

Desc: Causes of hypertension and the development of better forms of therapy. Activities are carried out in two main areas: a wide spectrum of research, ranging from basic biochemistry, physiology, and pharmacology to the study of chemical factors in disease and clinical response to drugs, with major emphasis on hypertension; and a broad research program on the molecular mechanism of neuronal function (studies relate primarily to the properties and regulation of enzymes responsible for the biosynthesis of neurohumoral amines). *Type:* Research center.

U.S. Department of Health and Human Services

National Heart, Lung, and Blood Institute

Division of Intramural Research

Molecular Disease Branch

NIH Bldg. 10, Rm. 7N115   Ph: (301)496-5095

10 Center Dr., MSC 1666   Fax: (301)402-0190

Bethesda, MD 20892-1666

Contact: Dr. H. Bryan Brewer, Chf.

Desc: Elucidation of the molecular mechanisms involved in lipid transport and metabolism in normal individuals and patients with disorders of lipid metabolism and atherosclerosis. Biochemical studies involve protein chemistry, immunology, tissue culture, molecular biology, and enzymology. *Type:* Research center.

U.S. Department of Health and Human Services

National Heart, Lung, and Blood Institute

Laboratory of Biophysical Chemistry

NIH Bldg. 10, Rm. 7N318   Ph: (301)496-2135

9000 Rockville Pike   Fax: (301)402-3404

Bethesda, MD 20892-1676

E-mail: hmfales@helix.nih.gov

Contact: Dr. Henry M. Fales, Chf.

Desc: Physical and chemical properties of molecules with a view to elucidating their biochemical functions. Specialties are nuclear magnetic resonance, mass spectrometry, computational chemistry, chromatography, and laboratory computer techniques. *Type:* Research center.

U.S. Department of Health and Human Services

National Heart, Lung, and Blood Institute

Laboratory of Cardiac Energetics

NIH Bldg. 10, Rm. B1D 416   Ph: (301)496-3658

10 Center Dr. MSC 1061   Fax: (301)402-2389

Bethesda, MD 20892

E-mail: RSB@ZEUS.NHLBI.NIH.GOV

Contact: Dr. Robert Balaban, Chf.

Desc: Cardiology, nuclear magnetic resonance imaging/spectrography, cardiac energetics, and optical spectroscopy. *Type:* Research center.

U.S. Department of Health and Human Services

National Heart, Lung, and Blood Institute

Laboratory of Cell Biology

NIH Bldg. 3, Rm. B1-22   Ph: (301)496-1616

3 Center Dr. MSC 0301   Fax: (301)402-1519

Bethesda, MD 20892-0301

E-mail: edk@nih.gov

Contact: Edward Korn, PhD, Chf.

Desc: Regulation of the polymerization and enzymatic activity of actin and myosin, the two major cytoskeletal proteins of the membrane-cytoskeleton complex of non-muscle cells. Activities involve studying the ways in which ATP hydrolysis regulates actin polymerization and how myosin phosphorylation regulates myosin polymerization, actomyosin ATP-ase activity, and contractile activity. *Type:* Research center.

U.S. Department of Health and Human Services

National Heart, Lung, and Blood Institute

Laboratory of Cell Signaling

NIH Bldg. 3   Ph: (301)496-9646

9000 Rockville Pike   Fax: (301)480-0357

Bethesda, MD 20892

Contact: Dr. Sue Rhee, Chf.

Desc: Cell signaling in relation to the human heart, lung, and blood interaction. *Type:* Research center.

U.S. Department of Health and Human Services

National Heart, Lung, and Blood Institute

Laboratory of Molecular Cardiology

NIH Bldg. 10, Rm. 8N-202   Ph: (301)496-1865
110 Center Dr. MSC 1762   Fax: (301)402-1542
Bethesda, MD 20892
E-mail: ra19t@nih.gov

Contact: Dr. Robert S. Adelstein, Chf.

Desc: Regulation function and expression of the contractile proteins in muscle and nonmuscle cells. The role of calcium, calmodulin, and phosphorylation in regulating actinmyosin interaction is of particular interest. *Type:* Research center.

U.S. Department of Health and Human Services

National Heart, Lung, and Blood Institute

Specialized Centers of Research on Arteriosclerosis

National Heart, Lung, and   Ph: (301)435-0550
   Blood Inst.   Fax: (301)480-2858
Two Rockledge Center, Ste.
   10193, MSC 79516
6701 Rockledge Dr.
Bethesda, MD 20892-7956

Contact: Dr. David M. Robinson, Dir.

Desc: Hyperlipidemia and vascular diseases, including animal and tissue studies and other basic laboratory investigations. The research goal is to expidite development and application of new knowledge essential to improved diagnosis, treatment, and prevention of these disorders. *Type:* Research center.

U.S. Department of Health and Human Services

National Heart, Lung, and Blood Institute

Specialized Centers of Research on Ischemic Heart Disease

National Heart, Lung, and   Ph: (301)435-0505
   Blood Inst.   Fax: (301)480-1454
6701 Rockledge Dr., MSC 7940
Bethesda, MD 20892
E-mail: jf46f@nih.gov

Contact: Dr. John Fakunding, Contact.

Desc: Myocardial infarction, angina pectoris, heart rhythum disturbances, heart failure, and emergency and rehabilitation techniques and procedures. The research goal is to expedite development and application of new knowledge essential for improved diagnosis, treatment, and prevention of these disorders. *Type:* Research center.

U.S. Department of Health and Human Services

National Institute on Aging

Laboratory of Cardiovascular Science

Gerontology Research Center,   Ph: (410)558-8210
   Rm. 3B03   Fax: (410)558-8150
5600 Nathan Shock Dr.
Baltimore, MD 21224
E-mail: anders.d@grc.nia.nih.gov

Contact: Dr. Edward G. Lakatta, Chf., Behavioral Hypertension.

Desc: Basic mechanisms that control myocardial and vascular function. Studies are extended to describe the influence of age and age-related chronic pathologic conditions in studies conducted in human and animal models. *Type:* Research center.

U.S. Department of Health and Human Services

National Institute on Aging

Laboratory of Cardiovascular Science

Membrane Biology Section

Gerontology Research Center,   Ph: (410)558-8202
   Rm. 1B04   Fax: (410)558-8150
5600 Nathan Shock Dr.
Baltimore, MD 21224
Contact: Dr. Jeffrey Froehlich, Chf.

Desc: Ion and metabolite transport across biological membranes; studies how the translocation mechanisms are regulated by hormones, pharmacological agents, diet, and other pathophysiological effectors; and explores the mechanisms by which these systems are modified during the aging process and in age-associated disease. Also studies angiogenesis and smooth muscle function with special emphasis on intracellular ion metabolism. *Type:* Research center.

U.S. Department of Health and Human Services

National Institutes of Health

National Heart, Lung, and Blood Institute

9000 Rockville Pike   Ph: (301)496-2411
Bethesda, MD 20892   Fax: (301)402-0818
URL: http://www.nhlbi.nih.gov/nhlbi/nhlbi.htm/
Contact: Claude J.M. Lenfant, MD, Director.

Desc: NHLBI provides leadership for a national program in diseases of the heart, blood vessels, blood, lungs, and in the use of blood and the management of blood resources. It plans, conducts, fosters, and supports an integrated and coordinated program of research, investigations, clinical trials, and demonstrations relating to the causes, prevention, methods of diagnosis and treatment of heart, blood vessel, lung, and blood diseases through research performed in its own laboratories and through contracts and grants to scientific institutions and to individual scientists. *Type:* Government agency, office, or program.

University of Alabama at Birmingham

Alabama Congenital Heart Disease Diagnosis and Treatment Center

1900 University Blvd., Ste. 760   Ph: (205)934-2344
Birmingham, AL 35294-0016   Fax: (205)934-7514
E-mail: albert.pacifico@ccc.uab.edu
Contact: Dr. Albert D. Pacifico, Dir.
Desc: Seeks to improve the results of surgery on patients with congenital heart disease. Performs heart catheterizations and other operations to correct congenital heart defects. *Type:* Research center.

University of Alabama at Birmingham

Cardiovascular Research and Training Center

1900 Univ. Blvd., Rm. 311   Ph: (205)934-3624
   THT   Fax: (205)975-5150
Birmingham, AL 35294-0006
E-mail: bbourge@uab.edu
Contact: Robert Bourge, MD, Dir.
Desc: Heart and blood vessels, including interdisciplinary and crossdisciplinary studies of basic function of cardiovascular system in normal and abnormal states. Studies include nuclear magnetic resonance imaging and spectroscopy of myocardial damage, radionuclide assessment of myocardial perfusion and left ventricular function, molecular biology of the myocardial contractile proteins, mechanism of cardiac homograft rejection, and basic and clinical investigations of hypertension, including vascular smooth muscle, neural factors, renal function abnormalities and post-renal-transplantation, and essential hypertension. *Type:* Research center.

University of Arizona

University Heart Center

Arizona Health Sci. Ctr.   Ph: (520)626-6221
1501 N. Campbell Ave.   Fax: (520)626-0967
Tucson, AZ 85724-5037
E-mail: gaewy@aol.com

Contact: Dr. Gordon A. Ewy, Dir.

Desc: Multidisciplinary studies of the heart, including basic, preclinical and clinical research. Basic research focuses on cell growth and development, including genetics, biochemistry, and molecular biology; preclinical research focuses on the microvascular, pharmacologic, and physiologic aspects of heart disease; and clinical research focuses on new drugs, techniques, devices, and interventions. *Type:* Research center.

University of British Columbia

Atherosclerosis Specialty Laboratory

St. Paul's Hospital   Ph: (604)631-5616
1081 Burrard St., Rm. 180   Fax: (604)631-5590
Vancouver, BC, Canada V6Z
   1Y6
E-mail: jshill@interchange.ubc.ca
URL: http://www.healthyheart.org

Contact: Dr. John S. Hill, Contact.

Desc: Lipids and lipoproteins, lipoprotein metabolism, inherited disorders of lipoprotein metabolism, the enzymes lecithin, cholesterol acyltransferase (LCAT), heatic lipase (HL), and lipoprotein lipase (LPL). Conducts clinical research trials. *Type:* Research center.

University of British Columbia

McDonald Research Wing

St. Paul's Hospital   Ph: (604)682-2344
1081 Burrard   Fax: (604)631-5568
Vancouver, BC, Canada V6Z
   1Y6
E-mail: glim@prl.pulmonary.ubc.ca
URL: http://www.pulmonary.ubc.ca

Contact: Dr. J.C. Hogg, MD, Dir.

Desc: Pulmonary, cardiovascular and critical care research, including studies of asthma, chronic obstructive pulmonary disease, and acute lung injury. Areas of study include latent viral infections in the heart, pathology, biochemistry, molecular biology, physiology, immunology, structure and ultrastructure, and toxicology. *Type:* Research center.

University of Calgary

Cardiovascular Research Group

Faculty of Med.   Ph: (403)220-4525
Health Sci. Ctr.   Fax: (403)270-0313
3330 Hospital Dr. NW
Calgary, AB, Canada T2N 4N1
E-mail: henk@cvr.ucalgary
URL: http://www.cvr.ucalgary.ca

Contact: Dr. Henk J. ter Keurs, Contact.

Desc: Clinical and basic cardiac electrophysiology, cardiac mechanics, and heart failure. Research thrusts include: ion channels, electrophysiology, and arrhythmias, focusing on cardiovascular electrophysiology of cardiac and smooth muscle under physiological and pathophysiological conditions; electrical-mechanical coupling, cardiovascular mechanics, and congestive heart failure, emphasizing electrical-mechanical coupling and cardiovascular mechanics under physiological and pathophysiological conditions; and ischemia and interventional cardiology, focusing on coronary ischemia and reperfusion. *Type:* Research center.

University of California at Berkeley

Cholesterol, Genetics and Heart Disease Institute

1875 S. Grant St., Ste. 700 Ph: (650)367-1960
San Mateo, CA 94402 Free: 800-HEA-RT89
 Fax: (650)365-1948

E-mail: superko@best.com
URL: http://www.heartdisease.org

Contact: Dr. Robert Superko, Dir.

Desc: Atherosclerosis and lipidology. *Type:* Research center.

University of California, Los Angeles

Cardiovascular Research Laboratory

675 Charles E. Young Dr. S. Ph: (310)825-6713
MRLB, Rm. 3645 Fax: (310)206-5777
Los Angeles, CA 90095-1760
E-mail: jweiss@mednet.ucla.edu
URL: http://www.heartlab.mednet.ucla.edu

Contact: Dr. James Weiss, Dir.

Desc: Cellular and subcellular mechanisms of cardiac contraction, including ultrastructure, ion exchange and compartmentation, and studies in electrophysiology, mechanics, and biochemistry. *Type:* Research center.

University of California, San Diego

Specialized Center of Research in Heart Failure

9500 Gilman Rd. Ph: (619)534-3347
Department of Med., 0613B Fax: (619)534-1626
La Jolla, CA 92093-0613
E-mail: jross@ucsd.edu

Contact: Dr. John Ross, Jr., Dir.

Desc: Application of mouse genetics to identify the signaling pathways which mediate cardiac dysfunction; identification and cloning of candidate genes for hypertrophy and heart failure using the development of novel genetic-based animal models of ventricular hypertrophy and failure utilizing promoters that can target expression of a given transgene in to the cardiac ventricles; in vivo phenotypic characterization of transgenic murine models harboring candidate genes using newly developed quantitative echocardiographic and hemodynamic methods; studies on the effects of growth factors in heart failure; studies on the genetic bases for familial dilated cardiomyopathy in well-defined kindreds using linkage analysis; the alignment of physiologic biochemical and molecular techniques to study the bases for maladaptive effects of adrenergic stimulation at the receptor and post-receptor levels in animal models and human tissue; physiologic studies on the cardiac effects of abnormal force-frequency relations in experimental models and in patients with heart failure and of the recently-discovered key role of adrenergic control of force-frequency relations. heart muscle after ischemia, including specific proteins, mRNAs, and sodium channel genes; and conducts clinical studies on coronary reactivity after cholesterol lowering. *Type:* Research center.

University of California, San Diego

Specialized Center of Research in Molecular Medical and Atherosclerosis

Department of Med., 0682 Ph: (619)534-0569
9500 Gilman Dr. Fax: (619)534-2005
La Jolla, CA 92093-0682
E-mail: dsteinberg@ucsd.edu

Contact: Dr. Daniel Steinberg, Co-Dir.

Desc: Arteriosclerosis and atherogenesis, including studies of lipoprotein metabolism, oxidation of low density lipoprotein molecules, and molecular basis of arteriosclerosis. *Type:* Research center.

University of California, San Francisco

Cardiovascular Research Institute

Intravascular Ultrasound Laboratory

UCSF Moffitt-Long Hospitals Ph: (415)476-6285
505 Parnassus Ave., M 1347 Fax: (415)476-1020
San Francisco, CA 94143-0130
E-mail: chou@cardio.ucsf.edu
URL: http://wwwcardio.his.ucsf.edu/cardhomepage/labs/ivus.html

Contact: Tony Chou, MD, Dir.

Desc: Use of catheter-based ultrasound devices to examine coronary physiology. *Type:* Research center.

University of California, San Francisco

Vascular Research Laboratory

Cardiology Div., 134 Free: 800-827-3478
San Francisco, CA 94143
E-mail: chou@medicine.ucsf.edu
URL: http://wwwcardio.his.ucsf.edu/cardhomepage/labs/international.html

Contact: Tony Chou, MD, Contact.

Desc: Determinants of vascular tone and its role in the genesis of atherosclerotic disease, specifically the effects of sex steroid hormones on the conductance and resistance arterial vasculature in coronary, pulmonary, and systemic circulation. *Type:* Research center.

University of Cincinnati

Cardio-Vascular Laboratory

Univ. Hospital Ph: (513)558-5148
234 Goodman Ave. Fax: (513)558-3515
Cincinnati, OH 45267-0756

Contact: David Eppert, Mgr.

Desc: Computerized vascular research, including ultrasound, instrumentation, and pharmaceutical research. *Type:* Research center.

University of Cincinnati

Cardiovascular Research Center

231 Bethesda Ave. Ph: (513)558-4721
Cincinnati, OH 45267-0542 Fax: (513)558-3131
E-mail: walshra@ucbeh.san.uc.edu
URL: http://www.med.uc.edu/cardiology

Contact: Dr. Richard A. Walsh, Dir.

Desc: Cardiology and drug device clinical trials. *Type:* Research center.

University of Florida

Hypertension Center

Department of Physiology Ph: (352)392-3791
College of Med. Fax: (352)846-0270
PO Box 100274
Gainesville, FL 32610-0274
E-mail: mip@phys.med.ufl.edu
URL: http://www.med.ufl.edu/phys

Contact: Dr. M. Ian Phillips, DSc, Chm.

Desc: Hypertension, including renal mechanisms of hypertension and brain control of blood pressure, epidemiological studies in African Americans, models of hypertension in animals, and cellular and molecular studies in vitro. Focuses particularly on the study of the renin-angiotensin system and antisense oligodeoxynucleotides and viral vectors in an effort to develop gene therapy for cardiovascular disease. *Type:* Research center.

University of Houston

Institute for Cardiovascular Studies

SR2, Rm. 460 Ph: (713)743-1218
4800 Calhoun Blvd. Fax: (713)743-1232
Houston, TX 77204-5515
E-mail: jandhyala@uh.edu

Contact: Dr. B.S. Jandhyala, Dir.

Desc: Cardiovascular research, including central and peripheral control of the cardiovascular system and renal functions, central mechanisms of endogenous opiates and other polypeptides, antihypertensive compounds, pharmacology of compounds affecting cardiovascular function, microcirculation and physiology of exercise, biomedical pharmacology, ischemia-reperfusion injury, oxygen free radicals, anti-oxidants, and organ protection. *Type:* Research center.

University of Iowa

Iowa Cardiovascular Center

College of Med. Ph: (319)335-8588
616 MRC Fax: (319)335-6969
Iowa City, IA 52242-1182

Contact: Prof. Francois M. Abboud, Dir.

Desc: Coronary and vascular disease, hypertension, lipid arteriosclerosis, the regulation of circulation in pathological states, neurovascular control, clinical management of lipid disorders, lipoproteins, cerebral blood vessels, occupational and immunologic lung disease, cystic fibrosis, and cardiovascular research training program. *Type:* Research center.

University of Iowa

Lipid Research Clinic

Department of Internal Ph: (319)335-8201
 Medicine/Preventive Free: 800-887-6917
 Medicine Fax: (319)335-6671
Westlawn 2188
Iowa City, IA 52242
E-mail: helmut-schrott@uiowa.edu

Contact: Helmut G. Schrott, MD, Dir.

Desc: Lipids, including the relationship of cholesterol and other blood lipids to heart disease. Conducts studies on cholesterol reducing effects of lipid lowering drugs. *Type:* Research center.

University of Kentucky

Sanders-Brown Center on Aging

Stroke Program

101 Sanders-Brown Bldg. Ph: (606)257-5560
800 S. Limestone St. Fax: (606)257-8990
Lexington, KY 40536-0230
E-mail: swillia@pop.uky.edu
URL: http://www.mc.uky.edu/stroke

Contact: Dr. L. Creed Pettigrew, Dir.

Desc: Clinical studies of warfarin versus aspirin in recurrent stroke treatment, vitamins in stroke prevention, proteolysis in cerebral ischemia, neural substrates of emotion after stroke, deep white matter changes after vascular dementia, apolipoprotein E in neuronal cell death. *Type:* Research center.

University of Louisville

Center for Applied Microcirculatory Research

Department of Med. Ph: (502)852-7562
Health Sci. Ctr., Rm. 1115 Fax: (502)852-7215
Louisville, KY 40292
E-mail: fnmill01@ulkyvm.louisville.edu
URL: http://www.louisville.edu/medschool/camr

Contact: Frederick N. Miller, PhD, Dir.

Desc: Measurements of small blood vessel behavior in humans and animals during various clinical situations and human feasibility studies for application of microcirculatory science in clinical surgery and medicine. Also involved with computer hardware and software engineering development and animal studies. *Type:* Research center.

University of Michigan
Division of Cardiology

1500 E. Medical Center Dr.   Ph: (734)936-5255
Ann Arbor, MI 48109-0366   Fax: (734)936-5256
Contact: Elizabeth Nabel, Dir.

Desc: Diagnosis, treatment, and prevention of cardiovascular disease, including new therapeutic approaches to patients with heart failure and development of digital coronary and left ventricular angiography and digital echocardiography, myocardial reperfusion with thrombolytic agents and acute PTCA, and electrophysiology with emphasis on catheter ablation techniques. Also studies molecular biology of myocardial proteins and vascular adhesion molecules as well as new approaches to gene transfer into specific vascular beds. *Type:* Research center.

University of Michigan
Division of Hypertension

3918 Taubman Ctr.   Ph: (734)936-4790
Ann Arbor, MI 48109-0356   Fax: (734)936-8898
Contact: Dr. S. Julius, Ch.

Desc: Hypertension and hyperlipidemia, including pathophysiology of various forms of human hypertension, epidemiology, mechanism of action of drugs, and improvement of health care delivery. *Type:* Research center.

University of Minnesota
Experimental Surgical Research Laboratories

UMHC, Box 220   Ph: (612)625-5914
420 Delaware St. SE   Fax: (612)626-6949
Minneapolis, MN 55455
E-mail: bianc001@tc.umn.edu
URL: http://www.med.umn.edu/bmec/bmec_csrl.html
Contact: Richard Bianco, Dir.

Desc: Cardiovascular surgery. *Type:* Research center.

University of Missouri--Columbia
Division of Cardiothoracic Surgery

Sch. of Med.   Ph: (573)882-6954
Med. Sci. Bldg., MA 312   Fax: (573)884-0437
1 Hospital Dr.
Columbia, MO 65212
E-mail: curtisj@health.missouri.edu
URL: http://www.surgery.missouri.edu
Contact: Dr. Jack Curtis, Hd.

Desc: Cardiac physiology and cardiothoracic surgery. *Type:* Research center.

University of Missouri--Columbia
John M. Dalton Cardiovascular Research Center

Research Park   Ph: (573)882-7586
Columbia, MO 65211   Fax: (573)884-4232
URL: http://www.missouri.edu/~dalton/
Contact: Edward H. Blaine, PhD, Dir.

Desc: Multidisciplinary research in health science and related areas, emphasizing cardiovascular studies. *Type:* Research center.

University of Montreal
Montreal Heart Institute
Research Centre

5000 Belanger St.   Ph: (514)376-3330
Montreal, PQ, Canada H1T   Fax: (514)376-1355
    1C8
E-mail: nattel@icm.umontreal.ca
URL: http://icm-mhi.org
Contact: Dr. Stanley Nattel, MD, Dir.

Desc: Cardiovascular physiology, pharmacology, molecular biology, and electrophysiology. Develops visualization techniques such as quantitative angiography, numerical angiography, and videodensitometry in echocardiography and nuclear medicine. *Type:* Research center.

University of Montreal
Multidisciplinary Research Group on Hypertension

Clinical Research Institute of   Ph: (514)987-5528
    Montreal   Fax: (514)987-5602
110 Pine Ave. W.
Montreal, PQ, Canada H2W
    1R7
E-mail: schiffe@ircm.umontreal.ca
URL: http://www.ircm.umontreal.ca/
Contact: Dr. Ernesto L. Schiffrin, Dir.

Desc: Biochemistry; molecular biology; cellular physiology; pharmacology and clinical and experimental pathophysiology of hypertension, with an emphasis on the renin-angiotensin system, the neurobiology of hypertension, and the biology of blood vessels; the role of vasoactive peptides, particularly angiotensin, endothelin, and the role of endothelium; the effects of antihypertensive treatment on blood vessels of hypertensive patients; and the biochemical, molecular, and genetic determinants of elevated blood pressure. *Type:* Research center.

University of Southern California
Cardiovascular Care Research

1200 N. State St., Rm. 8350   Ph: (323)226-7116
Box 305   Fax: (323)226-2195
Los Angeles, CA 90033
Contact: Dr. L. Julian Haywood, Dir.

Desc: Clinical pathophysiology and management of myocardial infarction and other cardiovascular disorders, rhythm disturbances of the heart, computer-based monitoring techniques, vectorcardiography, and related investigations of electrophysiology, with emphasis on noninvasive methods, the use of radioisotopes in nuclear cardiology, and other radiological techniques. *Type:* Research center.

University of Tennessee
Division of Cardiovascular Diseases

951 Court Ave.   Ph: (901)448-5759
Memphis, TN 38163   Fax: (901)448-8084
Contact: Dr. Jay M. Sullivan, Ch.

Desc: Cardiovascular system in health and disease, including investigations of hypertension, hemodynamics, echocardiographs, estrogen replacement, and cardiovascular pharmacology. *Type:* Research center.

University of Texas Medical Branch at Galveston
Cardiovascular/Thoracic Surgery

301 University Blvd.   Ph: (409)772-1203
6.120 John Scaly Annex   Fax: (409)772-1421
Galveston, TX 77555-0528
E-mail: vconti@utmb.edu
Contact: Dr. Vincent R. Conti, Dir.

Desc: Myocardial metabolism with ischemia using the isolated working rat heart and isolated cardiac mitochondria. Also conducts laboratory and clinical studies of the physiologic effects of cardiopulmonary bypass. *Type:* Research center.

University of Texas Southwestern Medical Center at Dallas
Cardiology Division

5323 Harry Hines Blvd., Rm.   Ph: (214)648-1400
    NB11.200   Fax: (214)648-1450
Dallas, TX 75235-8573
E-mail: williams@ryburn.swmed.edu
URL: http://www.swmed.edu/home_pages/cardiology/index.html
Contact: R. Sanders Williams, MD, Chf.

Desc: Cardiology, including molecular biology of the cardiovascular system, clinical and basic studies of heart disease, and clinical and basic studies of congestive heart failure. *Type:* Research center.

University of Toronto
Centre for Cardiovascular Research

The Toronto Hospital   Ph: (416)340-4790
Eaton Wing 13 N., Ste. 208   Fax: (416)340-5985
200 Elizabeth St.
Toronto, ON, Canada M5G
    2C4
E-mail: msole@torhosp.toronto.on.ca
Contact: Michael J. Sole, MD, Dir.

Desc: Atherosclerotic cardiovascular disease, myocardial hypertrophy and failure, and arrhythmias and sudden death. *Type:* Research center.

University of Utah
Artificial Heart Research Laboratory

803 North 300 West, Ste. 180   Ph: (801)581-6991
Salt Lake City, UT 84103-1414   Fax: (801)581-4044
E-mail: don.b.olsen@m.cc.utah.edu
Contact: Dr. Don B. Olsen, Dir.

Desc: Cardiac replacement, cardiac assist devices, and artificial organs, including investigations into acute and chronic ventricular assist and total replacement, cardiac valves, total artificial hearts (pneumatic, electrohydraulic, and electromechanical), and associated pathophysiology. Experiments concern the introduction of such devices in sheep and calves. *Type:* Research center.

University of Utah
Cardiovascular Genetic Research Clinic

410 Chipeta Way, Rm. 161   Ph: (801)581-3888
Salt Lake City, UT 84108   Fax: (801)581-6862
Desc: Cardiovascular genetics, focusing on the correlations between environment, genetics, and the incidence of early heart disease. *Type:* Research center.

University of Utah
CVRTI

95 S 2000 E Back   Ph: (801)581-8183
Salt Lake City, UT 84112-5000   Fax: (801)581-3128
E-mail: robert_lux@gatormail.cvrti.utah.edu
Contact: Dr. Robert L. Lux, Dir.

Desc: Cardiac electrophysiology, electrocardiography, pharmacology, and biochemistry, including animal experimentation, observations on patients, and computer modeling. *Type:* Research center.

University of Virginia
Cardiovascular Research Center

Health Sci. Ctr., Box 56   Ph: (804)924-0109
MR-4 Bldg., 6th Fl.   Fax: (804)924-2828
Charlottesville, VA 22908
E-mail: cimcon@virginia.edu
URL: http://hsc.virginia.edu/medicine/inter-dis/cvrc
Contact: Brian R. Duling, PhD, Dir.

Desc: Cardiovascular disease. *Type:* Research center.

University of Virginia
Vascular Medicine and Preventive Cardiology Unit

Medical Center   Ph: (804)924-2765
Box 146   Free: 800-251-3627
Charlottesville, VA 22908   Fax: (804)924-9604
E-mail: cayers@virginia.edu
URL: http://www.virginia.edu/
Contact: Dr. Carlos R. Ayers, Dir.

Desc: Cardiovascular problems, including hypertension, hyperlipidemia, renal blood flow, xenon washout technique, renin-angiotensin-aldosterone metabolism, catecholamine metabolism, plethysmography, peripheral vascular physiology and disease, and cardiovascular risk reduction. *Type:* Research center.

University of Wisconsin--Madison

Biodynamics Laboratory

2000 Observatory Dr., Rm. 1149
Madison, WI 53706-1189

Ph: (608)263-6308
Fax: (608)262-1656

Contact: Dr. Greg Cartee, Co-Dir.

Desc: Mechanisms associated with the response and adaptation of humans and animals to exercise and environmental stress, focusing on cardiorespiratory and musculoskeletal systems. *Type:* Research center.

Vanderbilt University

Autonomic Dysfunction Center

AA-3228 Medical Center N.
Nashville, TN 37232-2195
E-mail: david.robertson@mcmail.vanderbilt.edu
URL: http://www.mc.vanderbilt.edu/gcrc/space/index.html

Ph: (615)343-6499
Fax: (615)343-8649

Contact: Dr. David Robertson, Dir.

Desc: Pathophysiology of autonomic disorders and orthostatic hypotension, including dopamine-B-hydroxylase deficiency, a syndrome characterized by congenital absence of norepinephrine and epinephrine. Other areas of research focus on therapeutic modalities for the management of orthostatic intolerance and tachycardia, Shy-Drager syndrome, multiple system atrophy, and baroreflex failure in human subjects. *Type:* Research center.

Victoria Heart Institute Foundation

315-1900 Richmond Ave.
Victoria, BC, Canada V8R 4R2
E-mail: vhif@vhif.org
URL: http://www.vhif.org/html/about_vhif.htm

Ph: (250)595-1884
Fax: (250)595-5367

Contact: Prof. John Jackson, Chm.

Desc: Cardiovascular disease. *Type:* Research center.

Wake Forest University

Hypertension and Vascular Disease Center

School of Medicine
Medical Center Blvd.
Winston Salem, NC 27157-1032
E-mail: cferrari@wfubme.edu
URL: http://www.is.wfu.edu/bgsm/surg-sci/hyp.html

Ph: (910)716-5819
Free: 800-277-8839
Fax: (910)716-6644

Contact: Dr. Carlos Ferrario, Dir.

Desc: Hypertension and cardiovascular disease. Activities include a clinical hypertension drug trial to treat high blood pressure on individuals 70 years or older and two clinical hypertension drug trials to treat high blood pressure on individuals 21 years or older. *Type:* Research center.

Washington University in St. Louis

Atherosclerosis, Nutrition, and Lipid Research Division

660 S. Euclid Ave.
Box 8046
St. Louis, MO 63110
E-mail: semenkov@im.wustl.edu
URL: http://internalmed.wustl.edu

Ph: (314)362-7038
Fax: (314)362-3513

Contact: Clay F. Semenkovich, MD, Assoc.Dir.

Desc: Atherosclerosis and lipid disorders, including research on genetic lipid disorders, atherogenesis and the roles of growth factors, cytokines, and chemically modified oxidized lipoproteins. Uses chemical, molecular, biologic, immunologic and cell culture techniques for studies of lipogenesis, lipoprotein structure and function. *Type:* Research center.

Catholic

Agape: Gospel of Life Disciples

PO Box 192
Franklin, LA 70538

Ph: (318)828-2375
Fax: (318)828-4039

Contact: Bernard Bergeron Broussard, Dir.

Desc: Catholics loyal to the teaching of the Church and in agreement with Pope John Paul. Works to put an end to all violence against life, including abortion, artificial contraception, capital punishment, euthanasia, racism, ethnic cleansing, biological engineering, pornography, addictive drugs, child and spousal abuse and war. *Type:* Association.

Anglican Fellowship of Prayer

PO Box 31
Orlando, FL 32802
E-mail: mary@afp.org
URL: http://www.afp.org

Ph: (407)438-3166
Fax: (407)856-1578

Contact: Mary C. Hilton, Exec. Sec.

Desc: Conducts educational programs. *Type:* Association.

Apostleship of Prayer

3 Stephan Ave.
New Hyde Park, NY 11040
E-mail: aposprayer@aol.com
URL: http://www.cin.org/ap/

Ph: (516)328-9777
Fax: (516)328-6039

Contact: Rev. John H. Rainaldo, SJ, Dir.

Desc: Catholics throughout the world who promise to say daily, and live according to the spirit of, the Daily Offering. Promotes a "spirit of prayer, in union with the Risen Christ, in order to cooperate in the salvation of souls under the leadership of the Pope as the Vicar of Christ and the Catholic hierarchy." Distributes letters to all Catholic pastors in the U.S. and to selected members of AP annually. *Type:* Association.

Apostolate for Family Consecrations

Catholic Familyland
3375 County R., No. 36
Bloomingdale, OH 43910-7903

Ph: (740)765-4301
Free: 800-FOR-MARY
Fax: (740)765-5561

E-mail: info@familyland.org
URL: http://www.familyland.org

Contact: Jerome F. Coniker, Pres.

Desc: Individuals interested in bringing the family closer to God. Seeks to transform neighborhoods into God-centered communities. Produces weekly and daily television and radio programs as well as other videotaped and broadcast programs including Be Not Afraid Family Hours, First Saturday, and Sacred Heart Enthronement. *Type:* Association.

Association of Marian Helpers

Eden Hill
Stockbridge, MA 01263

Ph: (413)298-3691
Free: 800-462-7426
Fax: (413)298-3583

E-mail: fr.joseph@marian.org
URL: http://www.marian.org

Contact: Fr. Joseph, MIC, Dir.

Desc: Promotes "the message of Divine Mercy and devotion to the Immaculate Virgin Mary." Seeks to advance the mission and works of Marian priests and brothers worldwide. *Type:* Association.

Assumption Guild

PO Box 35190
Brighton, MA 02135

Ph: (617)783-0495
Fax: (617)783-8030

Contact: Rev. Stephen Goquen, Dir.

Desc: Fundraising organization that financially aids young men who want to become Assumptionist priests. Membership in the guild is by contribution. Sponsors the Catholic Mass Association. *Type:* Association.

Blue Army of Our Lady of Fatima, U.S.A.

Mountain View Rd.
PO Box 976
Washington, NJ 07882
E-mail: bluearmy@ix.netcom.com
URL: http://www.bluearmy.com

Ph: (908)689-1701
Fax: (908)689-6279

Contact: Most Rev. James S. Sullivan, Pres.

Desc: Roman Catholics and others in the U.S. who "acknowledge the spiritual Maternity of Mary over mankind and recognize her as the Mother of God." *Type:* Association.

Capuchin-Franciscans (Province of St. Joseph)

1760 Mt. Elliott
Detroit, MI 48207

Ph: (313)579-2100
Fax: (313)579-0461

Contact: Daniel Fox, Provincial Minister.

Desc: Franciscan fraternity of Catholic priests and brothers dedicated to working among the poor, homeless, elderly, and others who are "suffering from injustices of society." Objective is to "empower the powerless" through work in parishes, retreat houses, hospitals, nursing homes, meal programs, high school seminaries, overseas missions, and prisons. *Type:* Association.

Catholic Aid Association

3499 Lexington Ave. N.
St. Paul, MN 55126
E-mail: caa@catholicaid.com
URL: http://www.catholicaid.qpg.com

Ph: (612)490-0170
Fax: (612)490-0746

Contact: Michael F. McGovern, Pres.

Desc: Fraternal benefit insurance association. Individuals affiliated with 160 church societies. Provides grants to Catholic schools and religious education programs. *Type:* Association.

Catholic Association of Foresters

347 Commonwealth Ave.
Boston, MA 02115-1999

Ph: (617)536-8221
Free: 800-282-CAOF
Fax: (617)536-2819

Contact: Joseph A. McVeigh, High Sec.-Treas.

Desc: Fraternal benefit life insurance organization of Catholics. *Type:* Association.

Catholic Church Extension Society of the U.S.A.

150 S Wacker Dr., 20th Floor
Chicago, IL 60606-4200

Ph: (312)236-7240
Free: 800-842-7804
Fax: (312)236-5276

Contact: Rev. Monsignor Kenneth Velo, Pres.

Desc: Individuals interested in supporting and spreading the Roman Catholic faith across the U.S. and its territories, especially home mission areas. Purposes are to raise funds to support priests and religious and lay ministers; build chapel and catechetical centers; provide disaster relief; subsidize various religious education, campus ministry, and evangelization programs in home missions. *Type:* Association.

Catholic Daughters of the Americas

10 W. 71st St.
New York, NY 10023
E-mail: cddfnatl@aol.com

Ph: (212)877-3041
Fax: (212)724-5923

Contact: Margaret O'Brien, Exec. Dir.

Desc: Catholic women involved in religious, charitable, and educational projects. *Type:* Association.

Catholic Family Life Insurance

PO Box 11563
Milwaukee, WI 53211

Ph: (414)961-0500
Fax: (414)961-0103

Contact: Bill Eimers, Pres.

Desc: Fraternal benefit life insurance society for persons of the Catholic faith. *Type:* Association.

Catholic Golden Age

430 Penn Ave. Ph: (717)342-3294
Scranton, PA 18503 Free: 800-836-5699
  Fax: (717)963-0149
Contact: Rev. Gerald N. Dino, Pres.
Desc: Catholics 50 years of age and over. To study and discuss the meaning of a longer life and gerontology, emphasizing religion and spirituality; to provide older persons with motivation to lead self-fulfilling lives; and to emphasize the role of religious faith in the endeavors and activities of older people. Assists the aged in their social, physical, economic, intellectual, and spiritual needs. *Type:* Association.

Catholic Knights of America

3525 Hampton Ave. Ph: (314)351-1029
St. Louis, MO 63139 Fax: (314)351-9937
E-mail: cka.agency@juno.com
URL: http://www.ckoa.com/
Contact: John F. Kenawell, Natl. Pres.
Desc: Fraternal benefit life, annuity, and health insurance society. Supports Pro-Life activities, offers matching gift program for church and community projects. Maintains museum. *Type:* Association.

Catholic Knights Insurance Society

1100 W. Wells St. Ph: (414)273-6266
Milwaukee, WI 53233 Free: 800-927-2547
  Fax: (414)223-3201
Contact: Daniel J. Steininger, Pres.
Desc: Fraternal benefit life insurance society for Catholics. Local branches carry out educational and social programs and support various Catholic Action activities. Offers fraternal programs, including financial planning seminars, group travel programs, mortgage loans, newborn infant benefits, and access to film library resource. *Type:* Association.

Catholic League for Religious and Civil Rights

1011 1st Ave. Ph: (212)371-3191
New York, NY 10022 Fax: (212)371-3394
E-mail: cl@catholicleague.org
URL: http://www.catholicleague.org
Contact: William A. Donohue, Pres.
Desc: Catholics defending their civil rights. Works to establish the right of Catholic lay and clergy to participate in American society without defamation or discrimination. *Type:* Association.

Catholic Life Insurance Union

1635 NE Loop 410, Ste. 300 Ph: (210)828-9921
San Antonio, TX 78209 Fax: (210)828-4629
Contact: J. Michael Belz, Pres.
Desc: Fraternal benefit life insurance society. Sponsors competitions. *Type:* Association.

Catholic Order of Foresters

355 Shuman Blvd. Ph: (630)983-4900
PO Box 3012 Fax: (630)983-4057
Naperville, IL 60566-7012
Contact: Robert Ciesla, High Chief Ranger.
Desc: Fraternal benefit legal reserve life insurance society, promoting "friendship, unity and true Christian charity among its members." *Type:* Association.

Catholic Workman

PO Box 47 Ph: (612)758-2229
New Prague, MN 56071 Fax: (612)758-6221
Contact: Steve Bisek, CEO.
Desc: Fraternal benefit life insurance organization of practicing Catholics and their families. *Type:* Association.

Catholics Speak Out

PO Box 5206 Ph: (301)699-0042
Hyattsville, MD 20782 Fax: (301)864-2182
E-mail: cso@quixote.org
URL: http://www.quixote.org/cso
Contact: Maureen Fiedler, S.L., Contact.
Desc: Catholics, clergy, and other interested individuals. A project of the Quixote Center. Serves as a network of Catholics seeking to implement change within the Roman Catholic church. *Type:* Association.

Catholics United for the Faith

827 N. 4th St. Ph: (614)283-2484
Steubenville, OH 43952 Free: 800-693-2484
  Fax: (614)283-4011
E-mail: camartini@aol.com
URL: http://www.cuf.org
Contact: Curtis A. Martin, Pres.
Desc: Roman Catholics advocating the support, defense, and advancement of the efforts of the teaching church. Seeks to further among Catholic laity the renewal of the faith called for by Second Vatican Council. Works toward cooperation among bishops, priests, and laymen. *Type:* Association.

Central Association of the Miraculous Medal

1811 W. St. Joseph St. Ph: (573)547-2508
Perryville, MO 63775-1598
E-mail: wobrien@enter.net
URL: http://www.amm.org
Contact: Rev. William J. O'Brien, C.M., Dir.
Desc: Religious organization promoting devotion to the Blessed Virgin Mary through the Miraculous Medal. (In an apparition in France in 1830, Mary appeared before Catherine Laboure and commissioned her to make the medal of the Immaculate Conception, now known as the Miraculous Medal.) Helps support Vincentian seminarians and infirm priests; assists the poor and needy. *Type:* Association.

The Christophers

12 E. 48th St. Ph: (212)759-4050
New York, NY 10017 Free: 888-298-4050
  Fax: (212)838-5073
E-mail: tci@idt.net
Contact: Stephanie Ratta, Editor-in-Chief.
Desc: Encourages positive action based on Judao-Christian principles, particularly in education, government, business, and communications. Activities emphasize two basic ideas: "there's nobody like you" and "you can make a difference." Produces the annual, Three Minutes a Day book and pamphlets in English and Spanish. Conducts Christopher leadership training courses. *Type:* Association.

Columbian Squires

1 Columbus Plz. Ph: (203)772-2130
New Haven, CT 06510-3326 Fax: (203)772-1923
URL: http://www.kofc-supreme-council.org
Contact: Ronald J. Tracz, VP.
Desc: International fraternity of young Catholic men (12-18 years old) throughout the United States, Canada, Mexico, the Philippines, Puerto Rico, the Bahamas, the Virgin Islands and Guam. Promotes leadership building activities for youth. Sponsored by Knights of Columbus. *Type:* Association.

First Catholic Slovak Ladies Association

24950 Chagrin Blvd. Ph: (216)464-8015
Beachwood, OH 44122 Fax: (216)464-8717
Contact: Maryann Johanek, Pres.
Desc: Fraternal benefit life insurance society. *Type:* Association.

Focolare Movement

200 Cardinal Rd. Ph: (914)229-0230
Hyde Park, NY 12538 Fax: (914)229-1770
E-mail: ssilvi@att.net
URL: http://www.focolare.org
Contact: Sharry Silvi, Women's Dir.
Desc: International lay movement of more than four million persons whose aim is "to work for the realization of Christ's final prayer for unity" and to spread the Gospel in the world through their own lives. *Type:* Association.

Holy Childhood Association

1720 Massachusetts Ave. NW Ph: (202)775-8637
Washington, DC 20036-1968 Fax: (202)429-2987
Contact: Rev. Francis W. Wright, Dir.
Desc: Children in Catholic schools and religious education programs. Serves as the official children's mission society of the Catholic church. Provides assistance to children in more than 100 countries. *Type:* Association.

International Catholic Deaf Association - United States Section

8002 S. Sawyer Rd. Ph: (630)887-9472
Darien, IL 60561-5227 Fax: (630)887-8850
E-mail: kgkush@aol.com
Contact: Kathleen Kush, Home Off.Mgr.
Desc: Deaf persons of the Catholic faith, priests, other religious and laypeople interested in work with the deaf, and parents of deaf children. Maintains special fund for support of missionary priests in their work with the deaf; compiles statistics on adult Catholic deaf and Catholic pupils in state, provincial, and city day schools and classes for the deaf; encourages local groups to arrange monthly communion and Sunday masses with sermons in sign language; promotes sports for the deaf. Works for the passage of legislation beneficial to the deaf. *Type:* Association.

Knights of Columbus

1 Columbus Plz. Ph: (203)772-2130
New Haven, CT 06510-3326 Fax: (203)773-3000
URL: http://www.kofc-supreme-council.org
Contact: Virgil C. Dechant, Supreme Knight.
Desc: Fraternal society of Catholic men, 18 years of age or over. Classes of membership include associate and insurance. Maintains museum. *Type:* Association.

Knights of the Immaculata Movement

1600 W. Park Ave. Ph: (847)367-7800
Libertyville, IL 60048 Fax: (847)367-7831
E-mail: mail@marytown.org
URL: http://www.marytown.org
Contact: Fr. Patrick Greenough, Dir.
Desc: Men, women, and young people of all ages and backgrounds who are practicing Catholics in good standing and who have committed themselves to the ideal of the movement by a "spiritual interior act of total oblation." Objectives are evangelization and "universal understanding, acceptance, and implementation of the role of Mary, the Immaculate Conception, in evangelization." *Type:* Association.

Knights of Peter Claver

1825 Orleans Ave. Ph: (504)821-4225
New Orleans, LA 70116 Fax: (504)821-4253
Contact: W. Charles Keyes, Jr., Exec.Sec.
Desc: Fraternal society of Roman Catholic men. Objectives are to: support local pastors, parishes, and the bishop of the diocese; participate in community activities and civic improvements; encourage Apostolic and Catholic action by laypersons; foster recreational assemblies and facilities; provide social and intellectual fellowship for members, as well as guidance and participation in the ever-changing texture of social and economic life; encourages youth participation. Sponsors workshops, fundraising projects, and educational and recreational activities. *Type:* Association.

Lay Carmelite Order of the Blessed Virgin Mary of Mount Carmel

Aylesford Carmelite Center   Ph: (630)969-5050
8501 Bailey Rd.   Fax: (630)969-5536
Darien, IL 60561-8417
Contact: Rev. Patrick McMahon, Dir.
Desc: Secular branch of the Carmelite Order consisting of Catholic men and women, 17 years of age and older, living the Carmelite Rule according to their state in life: married, single, or widowed. Seeks to serve the needs of the church by living the evangelical life according to Carmelite spirituality. Structure consists of separate communities that determine the needs of members. *Type:* Association.

Lithuanian Roman Catholic Federation of America

4545 W. 63rd St.   Ph: (773)585-9500
Chicago, IL 60629   Fax: (773)346-5640
Contact: Saulius V. Kuprys, Pres.
Desc: Lithuanian-American Catholic organizations, parishes, religious orders, and publications; agencies and institutions; individuals. Seeks to unite Lithuanian-American Catholics; promotes Catholic action; upholds Lithuanian culture. Operates a camp and retreat center in Michigan; collects archival material about immigration history; is establishing audio- and videocassette library in Lithuanian and English on educational and religious topics. *Type:* Association.

Marian Movement of Priests

PO Box 8   Ph: (207)398-3375
St. Francis, ME 04774   Fax: (207)398-3352
Contact: Fr. Albert G. Roux, Dir.
Desc: International group of priests and others whose objective is personal consecration to the Immaculate Heart of Mary and fidelity to the Catholic church and Pope. Provides lectures and a spiritual program of renewal. *Type:* Association.

National Catholic Society of Foresters

320 S. School St.
Mount Prospect, IL 60056-3334
Contact: Sue Koleczek, Pres.
Desc: Fraternal benefit insurance society that insures members of the Roman Catholic church of all ages and spouses of Catholics. Sponsors essay and membership contests annually. *Type:* Association.

National Christian Life Community of the United States of America

3601 Lindell Blvd. No. 421   Ph: (314)977-7370
St. Louis, MO 63108-3393   Fax: (314)977-7371
Contact: Dolores Celentano, Pres.
Desc: Roman Catholic adults, parish and interparish groups, and high school and college students. Aim is to develop and sustain individuals who commit themselves to service the church and the world in every area of life. Goals are: to develop interior spiritual freedom in individuals through the spiritual exercises of St. *Type:* Association.

National Conference of Catholic Bishops

3211 4th St. NE   Ph: (202)541-3000
Washington, DC 20017-1194   Fax: (202)541-3322
URL: http://www.nccbuscc.org
Contact: Msgr. Dennis M. Schnurr, Gen.Sec.
Desc: Canonical body through which the Catholic bishops of the U.S., in the words of the Second Vatican Council decree calling for such an organization, "jointly exercise their pastoral office." The bishops collaborate with other members of the church through the United States Catholic Conference. Maintains 23 standing committees. *Type:* Association.

National Cursillo Movement

PO Box 210226   Ph: (214)339-6321
Dallas, TX 75211   Fax: (214)339-6322
Contact: Thomas E. Sarg, Exec.Dir.
Desc: Catholic church movement aimed at seeking lay Christian leaders in all walks of life and committing them to work toward changing their environments according to the Gospel. *Type:* Association.

National Office for Black Catholics

3025 4th St. NE   Ph: (202)635-1778
Washington, DC 20017
Contact: Walter Hubbard, Dir.
Desc: Black priests, sisters, brothers, and laypersons of the Catholic church. Participating organizations: National Black Sisters' Conference; National Black Catholic Clergy Caucus. Serves as a "foundation for the renewal of the credibility of the church in the black community." Works to coordinate actions designed "to liberate black people and to serve as a unifying strength." Plans to: have specialists and technicians working within the black community to coordinate community organization and development; provide leadership training for youth; attack problems of poverty and deprivation; sensitize blacks to their heritage through historical, cultural, and liturgical experience. *Type:* Association.

Night Adoration in the Home

National Enthronement Center
PO Box 111   Ph: (508)999-2680
Fairhaven, MA 02719-0111
Contact: Rev. Columban Crotty, SSCC, Dir.
Desc: Spiritual organization of Catholics who spend at least one hour each month (between the hours of 9 p.m. and 6 a.m.) in a spirit of reparation for sins and offenses against God. *Type:* Association.

Nocturnal Adoration Society

184 E. 76 St.   Ph: (212)288-5082
New York, NY 10021   Fax: (212)861-1076
URL: http://www.blessedsacrament.com.
Contact: Bernard J. Camire, Dir.
Desc: Catholic prayer organization whose members gather in church during the nighttime hours once a month. *Type:* Association.

Official Catholic Directory

P. J. Kenedy & Sons
121 Chanlon Rd.   Ph: (908)464-6800
New Providence, NJ 07974   Free: 800-521-8110
                             Fax: (908)665-2894
E-mail: info@renp.com
Contact: Jeanne Hanline, Editor, jhanline@renp.com.
Desc: Over 60,000 clerical and lay leaders of the institutions, organizations, and possessions of the Catholic Church in the U.S. and the Vatican. *Type:* Directory.

Opus Dei

99 Overlook Cir.   Ph: (914)235-1201
New Rochelle, NY 10804
E-mail: newyork@opusdei.org
URL: http://www.opusdei.org
Contact: Msgr. James Kelly, Contact.
Desc: "A personal prelature of the Catholic church founded by the Spanish priest, Josemaria Escriva, with the aim of spreading throughout society a profound awareness of the universal call of holiness and apostolate through one's professional work carried out with freedom and personal responsibility." Is established worldwide, with members of more than 90 nationalities. The organization includes a number of secular priests. Principal activity is to counsel the individual members and others in their efforts to practice Christian virtues. *Type:* Association.

Order of Alhambra

4200 Leeds Ave.   Ph: (410)242-0660
Baltimore, MD 21229   Fax: (410)536-5729
URL: http://www.orderalhambra.org
Contact: Angelo Miere, Supreme Cmdr.
Type: Association.

Paulist Memorial Society

Paulist Fathers   Ph: (201)825-8959
997 Macarthur Blvd.   Fax: (201)825-1286
Mahwah, NJ 07430
Contact: Rosine J. Reynolds, Exec.Dir.
Desc: Catholic organization to promote missionary activity in evangelism, reconciliation, and ecumenism throughout North America. *Type:* Association.

Paulist National Catholic Evangelization Association

3031 4th St. NE   Ph: (202)832-5022
Washington, DC 20017-1102   Free: 800-237-5515
                             Fax: (202)269-0209
E-mail: pncea@pncea.org
URL: http://www.paulist.org/pncea
Contact: Rev. Kenneth Boyack, CSP, Dir.
Desc: Individuals interested in Catholic evangelization in America. Purpose is to heighten awareness among active American Catholics regarding nonpracticing Catholics and those with no church affiliation. Seeks to develop programs and materials aimed at inviting the inactive back into the church and encouraging those with no church to sample the Catholic way of life. *Type:* Association.

Pious Union of Prayer

c/o Sisters of St. Joseph of Peace   Ph: (201)798-4141
541 Pavonia Ave.
PO Box 288
Jersey City, NJ 07303
Contact: Sr. Mary Kuiken, CSJP, Editor.
Desc: Catholic spiritual organization under the Sisters of St. Joseph of Peace. "For united prayer and a sharing of the fruits of the apostolate." *Type:* Association.

Reparation Society of the Immaculate Heart of Mary

8006 Caliburn Ct.   Ph: (410)360-1817
Pasadena, MD 21122
Contact: Rev. Casimir M. Peterson, Pres.
Desc: "Catholics freely promising fulfillment of the Blessed Virgin's request given at Fatima, Portugal, in 1917." Members recite the Rosary daily and practice Christian penance along with special devotions on the First Saturday. Conducts public holy hours on the First Saturday and sponsors daily radio Rosary program. *Type:* Association.

Sacred Heart League

PO Box 300   Ph: (601)781-1360
Walls, MS 38680   Fax: (601)781-3340
URL: http://www.sacredheartleague.org
Contact: Rev. Robert Hess, Pres.
Desc: Roman Catholics who have special devotion to the Sacred Heart of Jesus. Program services include the Sacred Heart Auto League that promotes prayerful and careful driving and the Apostolate of the Printed Word that publishes, propagates, and distributes devotional literature. Contributions are used for education of candidates to the priesthood; support of the Sacred Heart Southern Missions (including establishment of missions and churches; educational programs for children, especially for the underprivileged; social services for the poor, the sick, and the aged). *Type:* Association.

Serra International
65 E. Wacker Pl., No. 1210 Ph: (312)782-2163
Chicago, IL 60601-7203 Fax: (312)782-2358
E-mail: serraus@aol.com
URL: http://www.serra-center.org
Contact: Robert J. Raccuglia, Exec.Dir.

Desc: Catholic men's and women's clubs in 31 countries. Seeks to "foster vocations to the Catholic priesthood and religious life, develop appreciation of the ministerial priesthood and of all religious vocations in the Catholic church, and to further Catholicism by encouraging its members to fulfill their Christian vocation to service." Conducts surveys and research projects. Holds seminars and leadership training meetings. *Type:* Association.

Sisters of Charity of Saint Vincent de Paul
Mount St. Vincent Mother Ph: (902)457-3500
  House Fax: (902)457-3506
150 Bedford Hwy.
Halifax, NS, Canada B3M 3J5
Contact: Sr. Mary Louise Brink, Gen. Superior.
Desc: Catholic sisters involved in teaching and other works of charity. *Type:* Association.

Society of the Little Flower
1313 Frontage Rd. Ph: (708)968-9400
Darien, IL 60561 Free: 800-621-2806
 Fax: (708)968-9542
Contact: Father Robert E. Colaresi, Dir.
Desc: To aid boys studying for the priesthood in Carmelite Seminaries. *Type:* Association.

Society for the Propagation of the Faith
366 5th Ave. Ph: (212)563-8700
New York, NY 10001 Free: 800-431-2222
 Fax: (212)563-8725
URL: http://www.propfaith.org
Contact: Bishop William J. McCormack, Natl.Dir.
Desc: Objectives are: to assist the Pope and the bishops of the Catholic church in animating a universal missionary spirit and in awakening an interest in worldwide mission of the Church among the whole People of God; to educate Catholics about the missionary nature and activity of the Church. *Type:* Association.

Supreme Commandery Knights of Saint John
Maj. Gen. Joseph Hauser, Jr.
89 S. Pine Ave. Ph: (518)453-5675
Albany, NY 12208 Fax: (518)453-5675
Contact: Maj.Gen. Joseph Hauser, Jr., Supreme Sec.
Desc: Catholic fraternal organization under patronage of St. John the Baptist. Provides honor guards for church activities; assists charitable organizations. *Type:* Association.

Supreme Ladies Auxiliary Knights of St. John
2330 Kirby Dr. Ph: (202)526-5322
Temple Hills, MD 20748-3265
Contact: Ann H. Johnson, Supreme Sec.
Desc: Fraternal society of Catholic women. *Type:* Association.

Tekakwitha Conference National Center
PO Box 6768 Ph: (406)727-0147
Great Falls, MT 59406-6768 Fax: (406)452-9845
Contact: Kateri Mitchell, Exec.Dir.
Desc: Catholic missionaries among American Indians; Eskimo and American Indian deacons and laypersons involved in ministry. Develops Catholic evangelization in the areas of Native American ministry, catechesis, liturgy, family life, evangelical liberation, ecumenical cooperation, and urban ministry, spirituality, and theology. Provides a forum for the exchange of ideas among Catholic Native Americans, Eskimos, and missionaries. *Type:* Association.

United States Catholic Conference
3211 4th St. NE Ph: (202)541-3000
Washington, DC 20017-1194 Fax: (202)541-3322
URL: http://www.nccbuscc.org
Contact: Msgr. Dennis M. Schaurr, Gen.Sec.
Desc: Civil entity of the American Catholic Bishops "assisting them in their service to the Church in this country by uniting the people of God where voluntary, collective action on a broad diocesan level is needed." Provides an organizational structure and the resources needed to insure coordination, cooperation, and assistance in the public, educational, and social concerns of the Church at the national, regional, state, interdiocesan and, as appropriate, diocesan levels. Makes available standing order service for sources concerned with the Catholic Church. *Type:* Association.

Vietnamese Catholic Federation in the U.S.A.
PO Box 1419 Ph: (504)392-1630
Gretna, LA 70053-1419 Fax: (504)391-9793
Contact: Vietchau Duc Ngyen, Pres.
Desc: Catholic communities united to encourage the participation of Vietnamese people in the Catholic church and to promote spiritual welfare and unity among them. Informs and instructs Vietnamese on being responsible members of the Catholic church. Fosters preservation of Vietnamese culture and heritage and works toward peaceful solutions to the problems in Vietnam. *Type:* Association.

Western Catholic Union
510 Maine St. Ph: (217)223-9721
Quincy, IL 62301 Free: 800-223-4928
 Fax: (217)223-9726
Contact: Mark A. Wiewel, Pres.
Desc: Fraternal benefit life insurance society. *Type:* Association.

Women's Ordination Conference
PO Box 2693 Ph: (703)352-1006
Fairfax, VA 22031 Fax: (703)352-5181
E-mail: wo696@aol.com
Contact: Andrea M. Johnson.
Desc: Roman Catholic women and men, lay and ordained, who believe that women have the right to participate fully in church life, including the priestly ministry. Plans to continue prayer, support, networking, and lobbying until sexism is removed from the process of priestly ordination and from the structures and understandings of the Roman Catholic church. *Type:* Association.

Cats

Cat Fanciers' Association
1805 Atlantic Ave. Ph: (732)528-9797
PO Box 1005 Fax: (732)528-7391
Manasquan, NJ 08736-0805
URL: http://www.cfainc.org/cfa/
Contact: Thomas H. Dent, Exec.Dir.
Desc: Federation of all-breed and specialty cat clubs. Promotes the welfare of cats, register pedigrees, and license shows held under association rules. *Type:* Association.

Cat Fanciers' Association—Yearbook
Cat Fanciers' Association, Inc.
1805 Atlantic Ph: (732)528-9797
PO Box 1005 Fax: (732)528-7391
Manasquan, NJ 08736-0805
E-mail: cak@cfainc.org
Contact: Marna Fogarty, Editor.
Desc: List of cat clubs, cat breeders. *Type:* Directory.

Catnip
Tufts University
School of Veterinary Medicine
200 Westboro Rd.
North Grafton, MA 01536-
 1895
Contact: Gloria Parkinson, Editor.
Desc: Addresses health care issues for cats, including such topics as diet, nutrition, preventive care, and diseases. *Type:* Newsletter.

CATS
CATS
PO Box 1790 Ph: (309)682-6626
Peoria, IL 61656 Fax: (309)679-5454
E-mail: info@catsmag.com; pjspubs15@aol.com.
URL: http://www.catsmag.com.
Contact: Annette Gentry Bailey, Editor; Marty Gale, Publisher, (312)609-4302, fax: (312)236-2413.
Desc: Magazine for the cat enthusiast. *Type:* Periodical.

Cattle

Alberta Hereford Association Newsletter
Alberta Hereford Association
3411 52nd Ave. Ph: (403)227-5246
Innisfail, AB, Canada T4G 1E2 Fax: (403)227-5264
Contact: Sharon Yeast, Editor.
Desc: Contains educational information on the Alberta Hereford industry and agriculture in general. *Type:* Newsletter.

American Angus Association
3201 Frederick Blvd. Ph: (816)383-5100
St. Joseph, MO 64506 Fax: (816)233-9703
E-mail: angus@angus.org
URL: http://www.angus.org
Contact: Richard L. Spader, Exec.VP.
Desc: Breeders and owners of purebred Angus cattle. Maintains registry for purebred Angus cattle. Collects, verifies, and publishes performance information, pedigrees, and transfers of ownership; offers premiums for the public exhibition of cattle. *Type:* Association.

American Dexter Cattle Association Bulletin
American Dexter Cattle Association
26804 Ebenezer Ph: (660)463-7704
Concordia, MO 64020 Fax: (660)463-7704
Desc: Provides information on the Dexter cattle breed. *Type:* Newsletter.

American Hereford Association
1501 Wyandotte Ph: (816)842-3757
Kansas City, MO 64108
E-mail: records@hereford.org
URL: http://www.hereford.org
Contact: Craig Husshines, Exec.VP.
Desc: Breeders of purebred Hereford cattle. Maintains registry, pedigree, and performance records; provides fieldman assistance and guidance; operates speakers' bureau; conducts research programs; maintains hall of fame and museum; sponsors competitions; compiles statistics. *Type:* Association.

American Jersey Cattle Association
6486 E. Main St. Ph: (614)861-3636
Reynoldsburg, OH 43068-2362 Fax: (614)861-8040
E-mail: usjersey@iwaynet.net
URL: http://www.usjersey.com
Contact: Calvin Covington, Exec.Sec.
Desc: Owners and breeders of Jersey cattle. Promotes sale and use of Jersey milk through National All-Jersey Inc., an affiliate. *Type:* Association.

American Polled Hereford Association

PO Box 14059
Kansas City, MO 64101-0059
Contact: Larry J. Heidebrecht, Pres.
Desc: Breeders and owners of registered purebred Polled Hereford beef cattle. *Type:* Association.

American Simmental Association

c/o Jerry Lipsey   Ph: (406)587-4531
1 Simmental Way   Fax: (406)587-9301
Bozeman, MT 59715
E-mail: simmental@simngene.com
Contact: Jerry Lipsey, Exec. V.P.
Desc: Promotes registration and improvement of the breeds of Simmental and Simbrah cattle in the U.S. *Type:* Association.

The Bagpipe

American Highland Cattle Association
200 Livestock Exchange Bldg.   Ph: (303)292-9102
4701 Marion St.   Fax: (303)292-9171
Denver, CO 80216
E-mail: ahca@envisionet.net
Contact: Chris Davidson, Editor and Publisher.
Desc: Provides news and information about the Association, members, and their breed. Contains articles to help breeders improve the quality of their cattle; stories; management; announcements and reports of meetings and conventions. *Type:* Newsletter.

Beef Promotion and Research Board

PO Box 3316   Ph: (303)220-9890
Englewood, CO 80155   Free: 800-388-2333
    Fax: (303)220-9280
Contact: Monte Reese, Chief Operating Officer.
Desc: Beef producers. Coordinates public relations, marketing, and dissemination of information for the beef industry. Conducts promotional, consumer information, and industry information campaigns; fosters communication among beef producers; sponsors research. *Type:* Association.

Braford News

United Braford Breeders
422 E. Main, Ste. 218   Ph: (409)569-8200
Nacogdoches, TX 75961   Fax: (409)569-9556
E-mail: ubb@brafords.org
Contact: Rodney L. Roberson, Editor.
Desc: Contains articles on breeding, raising, and selling Braford cattle. *Type:* Newsletter.

CowTown America

National Cattlemen's Beef Association
PO Box 3469   Ph: (303)694-0305
Englewood, CO 80155   Fax: (303)694-2851
E-mail: cows@beff.org
URL: http://www.cowtown.org
Desc: The NCBA site provides a vast array of information about beef, including recipes, industry data, a kid's section (Burger Town), audio/video clips and images, information on nutrition, health, and other issues of interest. *Type:* Database.

Holstein Association USA

1 Holstein Pl.   Ph: (802)254-4551
Brattleboro, VT 05302-0808   Free: 800-952-5200
    Fax: (802)254-8251
URL: http://www.holstein.com
Contact: Steven Kerr, Exec. Officer.
Desc: Breeders of Holstein cattle. *Type:* Association.

Holstein Junior Program

c/o Holstein Association USA,   Ph: (802)254-4551
Inc.   Free: 800-952-5200
1 Holstein Pl.   Fax: (802)254-8251
Brattleboro, VT 05302-0808
URL: http://www.holsteinusa.com
Contact: Richard Keene, Pres.
Desc: Young people interested in farming. Encourages interest in animals, especially Holstein cattle. Sponsors youth-operated programs. *Type:* Association.

National Cattlemen's Beef Association

PO Box 3469   Ph: (303)694-0305
Englewood, CO 80155   Fax: (303)694-2851
E-mail: cattle@ncanet.org
URL: http://www.beef.org
Contact: Charles P. Schroeder, CEO.
Desc: Corporation of 46 state and 29 beef breed registry associations representing 230,000 farmers, ranchers, breeders, and feeders of beef cattle. Functions as central agency for national public information, legislative, and industry liaison for the beef cattle business. *Type:* Association.

North American Limousin Foundation

7383 S Alton Way, Ste. 100   Ph: (303)220-1693
Englewood, CO 80112   Fax: (303)220-1884
E-mail: jedwards@nalf.org
URL: http://www.nalf.org
Contact: John Edwards, Exec.VP.
Desc: Individuals who own and raise Limousin cattle. Purposes are to: promote the Limousin breed; record performance of the cattle; issue registrations and keep the herd book. Sponsors BEEF performance program. *Type:* Association.

The Park Post

White Park Cattle Association of America
419 N. Water St.   Ph: (515)795-2013
Madrid, IA 50156
Contact: Joyce Fisher, Editor.
Desc: Serves owners and those interested in White Park cattle by publishing pedigrees, promoting the purity of the breed, and seeking to enhance its recognition. Includes news items of interest to members. *Type:* Newsletter.

Red Angus Association of America

Box 4201, I-35, N.   Ph: (817)387-3502
Denton, TX 76207   Fax: (817)383-4036
URL: http://www.redangus.org
Contact: Dr. Robert Hough, Exec.Sec.
Desc: Breeders of purebred Red Angus cattle. Seeks to improve the breed through application of scientific methods of selection. *Type:* Association.

Red Brangus Bull-Pen

American Red Brangus Association
3995 E. Highway 290   Ph: (512)858-7285
Dripping Springs, TX 78620-   Fax: (512)858-7084
4205
E-mail: arba@texas.net
Contact: Caren Cowen Bremer, Editor.
Desc: Focuses on the Red Brangus breed of cattle, specifically the pure-breed, and the activities that surround them. Covers breeders field days, shows, awards, and Association news. *Type:* Newsletter.

Texas Longhorn Breeders Association of America

2315 N. Main St., Ste. 402   Ph: (817)625-6241
Fort Worth, TX 76106   Fax: (817)625-1388
E-mail: tblaa@tlbaa.com
Contact: Don L. King, Exec.Dir.

Desc: Individuals, firms, and organizations interested in the Texas Longhorn breed of cattle. Promotes public awareness of the Texas Longhorn, its link with history, and its role in modern beef production. Encourages practices to preserve purity of the breed and recognizes Texas Longhorn cattle breeders. *Type:* Association.

Watusi

Ankole Watusi International Registry (AWIR)
PO Box 5306   Ph: (913)592-4050
Pueblo, CO 81002
E-mail: watusi@aol.com.
Contact: Elizabeth Lundgren, Editor.
Desc: Provides information on Ankole-Watusi cattle. *Type:* Newsletter.

Ceramics

American Ceramic Society

PO Box 6136   Ph: (614)890-4700
Westerville, OH 43086-6136   Fax: (614)899-6109
E-mail: customersrvc@acers.org
URL: http://www.acers.org
Contact: W. Paul Holbrook, Exec.Dir.
Desc: Professional society of scientists, engineers, educators, plant operators, and others interested in the glass, cements, refractories, nuclear ceramics, whitewares, electronics, engineering, and structural clay products industries. Disseminates scientific and technical information through its publications and technical meetings. Conducts continuing education courses and training such as the Precollege Education Program. *Type:* Association.

Belleek Collectors' International Society

9893 Georgetown Pike, Ste. 525   Ph: (703)847-6207
Great Falls, VA 22066   Free: 800-235-5335
    Fax: (703)847-6201
E-mail: angelamoore@belleek.com
URL: http://www.belleek.ie
Contact: Angela H. Moore, Contact.
Desc: Collectors and persons interested in purchasing limited editions of pottery produced by Belleek Ireland, Inc. *Type:* Association.

Ceramic Abstracts

Cambridge Scientific Abstracts (CSA)
7200 Wisconsin Ave., Ste. 601   Ph: (301)961-6700
Bethesda, MD 20814-4823
E-mail: sales@csa.com
URL: http://www.csa.com
Desc: Contains more than 206,000 citations, with abstracts, to approximately 350 worldwide sources of literature on ceramic materials. Covers abrasives, art and archaeology, cements and plasters, limes, ceramic-metal systems, chemistry, design, dielectrics, electronic ceramics, engineering materials, glass, glass processing and properties, instruments and testing, kilns, dryers, furnaces, and fuels, magnetic materials, oxide and nonoxide materials, nuclear materials, physics, piezoelectrics and ferroelectrics, production processes and equipment, raw materials, refractories, semiconductors, structural clay, superconductors, and whitewares. *Available:* The Dialog Corporation, DIALOG; STN International. *Type:* Database.

M. I. Hummel Club

Goebel Plz.   Ph: (609)737-8777
PO Box 11   Free: 800-666-2582
Pennington, NJ 08534   Fax: (609)737-1545
Contact: Kenneth LeFevre, Pres.
Desc: Collectors of M.I. Hummel figurines. *Type:* Association.

M. I. Hummel Club—Insights

M.I. Hummel Club
PO Box 11
Pennington, NJ 08534

Ph: (609)737-8777
Free: 800-666-CLUB
Fax: (609)737-1545

Desc: Features news of interest to collectors of the M.I. Hummel figurines. *Type:* Newsletter.

NISTCERAM (NIST Structural Ceramic Databases)

U.S. National Institute of Standards and Technology (NIST)
Ceramics Division
Bldg. 223, Mailstop A256
Gaithersburg, MD 20899
E-mail: ronald.munro@nist.gov

Ph: (301)975-6127

Contact: Ronald Munro, Physicist, ronald.munroe@nist.gov.

Desc: Contains thermal and mechanical property data for structural ceramics. Covers such properties as flexural yield strength, density, fracture toughness, elastic modulus, and thermal expansion coefficient. *Available:* U.S. National Institute of Standards and Technology (NIST), Ceramics Division. *Type:* Database.

Western Tile Directory

CTIOA Publications, Inc.
12061 W. Jefferson Blvd.
Culver City, CA 90230

Ph: (310)574-7800
Fax: (818)889-8145

Desc: About 550 member manufacturers of ceramic tile in the western United States; distributors, contractors, trade unions, and related associations are also included. *Type:* Directory.

Chambers of Commerce

ACCRA Research in Review

American Chamber of Commerce Researchers Association (ACCRA)
4232 King St.
Alexandria, VA 22302-1507
E-mail: accra@acce.org

Contact: Christian D. Faulkner, Editor.

Desc: Carries information on research methodology specific to the study of community economic development. *Type:* Newsletter.

American Chamber of Commerce Executives

4232 King St.
Alexandria, VA 22302

Ph: (703)998-0072
Free: 800-394-2223
Fax: (703)931-5624

Contact: Paul J. Greeley, Jr., C, Pres.

Desc: Professional society of chamber of commerce executives and staff members. *Type:* Association.

American Chambers of Commerce Abroad

U.S. Chamber of Commerce
International Division Publications
1615 H St. NW
Washington, DC 20062-2000
URL: http://www.uschamber.org.

Ph: (202)463-5460
Fax: (202)463-3114

Desc: 78 American chambers of commerce in 68 countries. *Type:* Directory.

Bismarck-Mandan Area Chamber of Commerce—Membership Directory

Bismarck-Mandan Area Chamber of Commerce (BMACC)
PO Box 1675
Bismarck, ND 58502-1675
E-mail: office@chmbr.org

Ph: (701)223-5660
Fax: (701)255-6125

Desc: 1025 member businesses in Bismarck and Mandan, North Dakota. *Type:* Directory.

BizVoice Quickline

Indiana Chamber of Commerce
115 W. Washington St., Ste. 850S
Indianapolis, IN 46204
E-mail: baustin@in.net.
URL: http://www.indianachamber.com/icc/.

Ph: (317)264-6854
Free: 800-804-6854
Fax: (317)264-6855

Contact: Tom Schuman, Editor, tschuman@indianachamber.com.

Desc: Details the current business climate for the 5,500 member businesses of the Indiana Chamber of Commerce. Recurring features include news, conference and semina r opportunities. *Type:* Newsletter.

Bolivia—American Chamber of Commerce—Membership Directory

U.S. Chamber of Commerce
International Division Publications
1615 H St. NW
Washington, DC 20062-2000

Ph: (202)463-5460
Fax: (202)463-3114

Desc: American and Bolivian companies and individuals interested in the development of trade within and between the two countries. *Type:* Directory.

Brazilian-American Chamber of Commerce

509 Madison Ave., Ste. 304
New York, NY 10022
E-mail: info@brazilcham.com

Ph: (212)751-4691
Fax: (212)751-7692

Contact: Sueli Bonaparte, Exec.Dir.

Desc: Corporations, partnerships, financial institutions, and individuals either in the U.S. or Brazil interested in fostering two-way trade and investment between the countries. Compiles statistics and provides special mailings, press releases, information, and business contacts. *Type:* Association.

Business Bulletin

Kentucky Chamber of Commerce
PO Box 187
Frankfort, KY 40601

Ph: (502)695-4700
Fax: (502)695-6824

Contact: Debbie Gibson, Editor.

Desc: Supports the Chamber of Commerce, a "broad based business organization of business people who are willing to work together to make Kentucky the place in which to live and make a living." Seeks to inform members of recent developments on a state and national level that affect business interests in Kentucky. Reports on small business issues, legislative and regulatory actions affecting business in general, and projects and events sponsored by the Chamber of Commerce. *Type:* Newsletter.

Business Perspectives

Waterloo Chamber of Commerce
215 E. 4th St.
PO Box 1587
Waterloo, IA 50704

Ph: (319)233-8431
Fax: (319)233-4580

Desc: Carries news of the Chamber; reports on seminars, conventions, and the city's educational concerns. Recurring features include a calendar of events and columns titled Chamber Events, Membership Services, Convention & Visitors Bureau, Community/Governmental Affairs, and Business Development. *Type:* Newsletter.

California Chamber of Commerce—Alert

California Chamber of Commerce
1201 K St., 12th Fl.
PO Box 1736
Sacramento, CA 95812-1736
E-mail: alert@calchambet.com.

Ph: (916)444-6670
Fax: (916)444-6685

Contact: Ann Amioka, Editor.

Desc: Focuses on legislative, regulatory, and policy issues of concern to California businesses of all sizes. *Remarks:* Includes supplement, Small Business Advocate, 10/yr. *Type:* Newsletter.

Carson City Area Chamber of Commerce—Membership Business Directory

Carson City Area Chamber of Commerce
1900 S. Carson St., Ste. 100
Carson City, NV 89701
E-mail: ccchamber@semp.net

Ph: (702)882-1565
Fax: (702)882-4179

Desc: Approximately 850 community profile and business listing member businesses in the greater Carson City, Nevada area. *Type:* Directory.

Chamber of Commerce of Hawaii—Member Referral Directory

Chamber of Commerce of Hawaii
1132 Bishop St., Ste. 402
Honolulu, HI 96813
E-mail: info@cochawaii.org

Ph: (808)545-4300
Fax: (808)545-4309

Contact: Sam Powell, Editor.

Desc: About 1,800 member firms in Hawaii; about 18 associate chambers of commerce and affiliate organizations. *Type:* Directory.

Chamber of Commerce On-Line

The Greater New York Chamber of Commerce
350 Fifth Ave., Ste. 3304
New York, NY 10118
E-mail: info@chamber.com
URL: http://www.chamber.com/

Ph: (212)244-0003

Desc: Here you'll find information on businesses in New York City, what is arguably the largest and most active concentration of commercial and business enterprises in the country, if not the world. Search this database by keyword (including name, location, or other information), or browse an alphabetical list of NYC Chamber members, arranged by business category such as advertising agencies, book shops, and transportation providers. *Type:* Database.

Chamber of Commerce of the United States—Association Agenda

Chamber of Commerce of the United States
1615 H St. NW
Washington, DC 20062
URL: http://www.uschamber.org.

Ph: (202)463-5560
Fax: (202)822-2468

Contact: J.P. Moery, Editor, jmorey@uschamber.com.

Desc: Contains news of interest to member associations of the Chamber of Commerce. *Type:* Newsletter.

Chamber of Commerce of the United States - U.S. Chamber

1615 H St. NW
Washington, DC 20062

Ph: (202)659-6000
Fax: (202)463-5836

Contact: Thomas J. Donohue, Pres. & CEO.

Desc: National federation of business organizations and companies. Membership includes chambers of commerce, trade and professional associations, and companies. Determines and makes known to the government the recommendations of the business community on national issues and problems affecting the economy and the future of the country. *Type:* Association.

Chamber Currents

Greater Richmond Chamber of Commerce
201 E. Franklin St.
Richmond, VA 23219

Ph: (804)648-1234
Fax: (804)780-0344

Contact: Heidi F. Chadwick, Editor, (804)783-9348.

Desc: Covers the activities of and issues pertinent to business in Richmond, Virginia. Recurring features include a calendar of events and reports of meetings. *Type:* Newsletter.

Chamber Executive

American Chamber of Commerce Executives
4232 King St.   Ph: (703)998-0072
Alexandria, VA 22302-9950   Fax: (703)931-5624
E-mail: admin@acce.org; chamberexecutive@acce.org.
URL: http://www.acce.org.

Contact: Marlus Mulckhuyse, ACCE, Managing Editor, (703)998-3525, mmulckhuyse@acce.org.

Desc: Covers Chamber management issues, including economic development, international trade, membership development and retention, government relations, small business, and tourism development. *Type:* Newsletter.

The Chamber Executive Network

Hakes Publications
PO Box 603   Ph: (712)732-7718
Storm Lake, IA 50588
E-mail: dick@hakespublications.com

Contact: Dick Hakes, Editor.

Desc: Emphasizes Chamber fundraisers, membership recruitment, and promotions. Recurring features include interviews, news of research, book reviews, and notices of publications available. *Type:* Newsletter.

Chamber Membership Directory/Consumer Guide

Greater Phoenix Chamber of Commerce
201 N. Central, Ste. 2700   Ph: (602)254-5521
Phoenix, AZ 85073   Fax: (602)495-8913
E-mail: info@phoenixchamber.com

Desc: More than 2,300 member firms of the Phoenix Chamber of Commerce. *Type:* Directory.

The Chamber News

Grand Rapids Area Chamber of Commerce
111 Pearl St. NW   Ph: (616)771-0338
Grand Rapids, MI 49503-2831   Fax: (616)771-0318

Contact: Karen Gentry, Editor.

Desc: Provides information on monthly chamber events and local business issues. Recurring features include calendar of events. *Type:* Newsletter.

Chamber News (Hartsville)

Greater Hartsville Chamber of Commerce
PO Box 578   Ph: (803)332-6401
Hartsville, SC 29551   Fax: (803)332-8017

Contact: Nancy Truesdale, Editor.

Desc: Reports on chamber meetings and business developments. Recurring features include a calendar of events and news of educational opportunities. *Type:* Newsletter.

Chamber Progress Report

Greater Providence Chamber of Commerce
30 Exchange Ter.   Ph: (401)521-5000
Providence, RI 02903-1793   Fax: (401)751-2434
URL: http://www.provchamber.com.

Contact: Pam Sefrino, Managing Editor, psefrino@provchambers.com.

Desc: Covers Chamber priorities, activities, and initiatives. Recurring features include business news, a calendar of events, reports of programs, and columns titled Chamber Chatter, New Members, Marketplace, and small business snapshots. *Type:* Newsletter.

Chamber Report

Greater Manchester Chamber of Commerce
889 Elm St., 3rd Fl.   Ph: (603)666-6600
Manchester, NH 03101-2000   Fax: (603)626-0910
E-mail: info@manchester-chamber.org
URL: http://www.manchester-chamber.org.

Contact: Patricia M. Drelick, Editor, pattid@manchester-chamber.org.

Desc: Supplies business news, economic data, and seminar information. Recurring features include a calendar of events, reports of meetings, and news of educational opportunities. *Type:* Newsletter.

Chamber Update

Tacoma-Pierce County Chamber of Commerce
PO Box 1933   Ph: (253)627-2175
Tacoma, WA 98401-1933   Fax: (253)597-7305

Contact: Denise Erdahl Ploof, Editor.

Desc: Reports on the activities of the Tacoma-Pierce County Chamber of Commerce. *Type:* Newsletter.

Chambers of Commerce

Greater San Diego Chamber of Commerce
402 W. Broadway, Ste. 1000   Ph: (619)544-1300
San Diego, CA 92101-3585   Fax: (619)234-0571
E-mail: info@sdchamber.org
URL: http://www.sdchamber.org

Contact: Chris McCoy, Editor.

Desc: Approximately 30 chambers of commerce in San Diego County. *Type:* Directory.

Chambers of Commerce Directory

infoUSA
5711 S. 86th Circle   Ph: (402)593-4600
PO Box 27347   Free: 800-555-6124
Omaha, NE 68127   Fax: (402)331-5481
E-mail: internet@infousa.com
URL: http://www.abii.com.

Type: Directory.

Communications Executive

ACCE Communications Council
American Chamber of Commerce Executives (ACCE)
4232 King St.   Ph: (703)998-0072
Alexandria, VA 22302-9950   Fax: (703)931-5624

Contact: Will Harvie, Editor, wharvie@acce.org.

Desc: Covers Council conferences and projects; includes tips on effective chamber communications practices. *Type:* Newsletter.

Connecticut Market Data

Connecticut Department of Economic and Community Development
505 Hudson St.   Ph: (860)270-8000
Hartford, CT 06106   Free: 888-860-GOCT
                                 Fax: (860)270-8100
E-mail: decd@po.state.ct.us
URL: http://www.state.ct.us/ecd; http://www.state.ct.us/ecd/research.

Desc: Lists of Connecticut chambers of commerce, largest employers, regional planning agencies, and business support programs. Principal content is a detailed statistical survey compiling information on population and economic characteristics of Connecticut. *Type:* Directory.

Costa Rican-American Chamber of Commerce—Membership Directory

U.S. Chamber of Commerce
International Division Publications
1615 H St. NW   Ph: (202)463-5460
Washington, DC 20062-2000   Fax: (202)463-3114

Desc: Over 300 American and Costa Rican firms interested in the development of trade within and between the two countries. *Type:* Directory.

Cronical

Swedish-American Chamber of Commerce
599 Lexington Ave., 12th Fl.   Ph: (212)838-5530
New York, NY 10022   Free: (212)838-5530
                                 Fax: (212)755-7953

Contact: Margaretha S. Murphy, Editor.

Desc: Concerned with developments in the Swedish and U.S. business communities: unemployment rates, industry plans and investments, exports, government measures to stimulate the economy, and similar subjects. *Type:* Newsletter.

District of Columbia Chamber of Commerce

District of Columbia Chamber of Commerce
1301 Pennsylvania Ave., Ste.   Ph: (202)347-7201
  309   Fax: (202)347-3538
Washington, DC 20004
E-mail: mail@dcchamber.org
URL: http://www.dcchamber.org/

Desc: This site offers a welcome message from Dana B. Stebbins, President of the Chamber for 1996, membership info, calendar of events and list of member web pages. *Type:* Database.

Dominican Republic—American Chamber of Commerce—Membership Directory

U.S. Chamber of Commerce
International Division Publications
1615 H St. NW   Ph: (202)463-5460
Washington, DC 20062-2000   Fax: (202)463-3114

Desc: American and Dominican Republic companies and individuals interested in the development of trade within and between the two countries. *Type:* Directory.

El Salvador—American Chamber of Commerce—Membership Directory

U.S. Chamber of Commerce
International Division Publications
1615 H St. NW   Ph: (202)463-5460
Washington, DC 20062-2000   Fax: (202)463-3114

Desc: Companies in the U.S. and El Salvador and individuals interested in the development of trade within and between the two countries. *Type:* Directory.

Exec Report

Illinois State Chamber of Commerce
215 E. Adams   Ph: (217)522-5512
Springfield, IL 62701-1199   Fax: (217)522-5518

Contact: Julie Brennan, Editor.

Desc: Provides news of interest to Illinois businesses, with particular focus on state laws, regulations, and human resources issues. Recurring features include a calendar of events. *Type:* Newsletter.

German American Chamber of Commerce—Membership Directory

German American Chamber of Commerce
40 W. 57th St.   Ph: (212)974-8830
New York, NY 10019-4092   Fax: (212)974-8867
E-mail: gaccny@compuserve.com

Contact: Michael L. Mohr, Editor.

Desc: Approximately 2,000 chamber members in the United States and Germany. *Type:* Directory.

German American Trade Magazine

German American Chamber of Commerce
40 W. 57th St.   Ph: (212)974-8830
New York, NY 10019-4092   Fax: (212)974-8867
E-mail: gaccny@compuserve.com

Contact: Inge Orth, Editor-in-Chief, (212)9748850, fax: (212)315-2183, ingeo@yahoo.com.

Desc: Deals with micro and macroeconomic issues in the German economy as well as bilateral business/economic relationships between the U.S. and Germany. *Type:* Newsletter.

Greater Columbia Chamber of Commerce—Focal Points

Greater Columbia Chamber of Commerce
PO Box 1360
Columbia, SC 29202
E-mail: info@gcbn.com
Ph: (803)733-1110
Fax: (803)733-1149
Contact: Erin A. Galloway, Editor.
Desc: Provides articles on Chamber-related topics. Recurring features include a calendar of events, reports of meetings, and notices of publications available. *Type:* Newsletter.

Greater Detroit Chamber of Commerce

600 W. Lafayette Blvd.
Detroit, MI 48226
Ph: (313)964-4000
Fax: (313)964-0038
Contact: Richard E. Blouse, Jr., Pres.
Desc: Business and professional community; nonprofit organizations; concerned individuals. Promotes business and community development in the southeastern Michigan counties of Lapeer, Livingston, Macomb, Monroe, Oakland, St. *Type:* Association.

The Greater Hartford Chamber of Commerce Directory

Greater Hartford Chamber of Commerce
250 Constitution Plaza
Hartford, CT 06103
Ph: (203)525-4451
Fax: (203)527-9696
URL: http://www.metrohartford.com.
Contact: Gary Flynn, Editor.
Desc: Approximately 2,500 businesses and chambers of commerce within the 33 towns that comprise the Greater Hartford, Connecticut area. *Type:* Directory.

Greater Omaha Chamber of Commerce—Profile

Greater Omaha Chamber of Commerce
1301 Harney St.
Omaha, NE 68102
Ph: (402)346-5000
Fax: (402)346-7050
E-mail: gocc@accessomaha.com
URL: www.accessomaha.com.
Contact: Vicki Krecek, Editor.
Desc: Presents information on the business climate of the Greater Omaha area. Recurring features include economic trends, news of members, and a calendar of events. *Type:* Newsletter.

Greater Orlando Chamber of Commerce—Membership Directory

Greater Orlando Chamber of Commerce
75 S. Ivanhoe Blvd.
PO Box 1234
Orlando, FL 32802-1234
Ph: (407)418-4490
Fax: (407)839-5020
Desc: Nearly 5,000 companies in the metropolitan Orlando area. *Type:* Directory.

Greater Pittsburgh Chamber of Commerce—Membership Directory and Economic Profile

Greater Pittsburgh Chamber of Commerce
425 6th Ave.
Pittsburgh, PA 15219-1811
Ph: (412)392-4500
Fax: (412)392-4520
URL: http://www.chamber.pgh.com; http://www.pittsburghchamber.com.
Contact: Barbara McNees, Editor.
Desc: Approximately 2,300 members of the Greater Pittsburgh Chamber of Commerce. *Type:* Directory.

Greater Port Huron Area Chamber of Commerce Newsletter

Greater Port Huron-Area Chamber of Commerce
920 Pine Grove Ave.
Port Huron, MI 48060
Ph: (810)985-7101
Fax: (810)985-7311
Desc: Tracks activities and positions of the Chamber. *Type:* Newsletter.

The Insider

Toledo Area Chamber of Commerce
300 Madison Ave., Executive Ste. 200
Toledo, OH 43604-1575
Ph: (419)243-8191
Fax: (419)241-8302
URL: http://toledo.chamber.com.
Contact: Matt Schroder, Editor.
Desc: Reports on Chamber of Commerce activities and Toledo businesses. *Type:* Newsletter.

Jacksonville Chamber of Commerce

3 Independence Dr.
Jacksonville, FL 32202
Ph: (904)366-6660
Fax: (904)632-0617
Contact: Walter Lee, Pres.
Desc: Promotes business and community development in Jacksonville, FL. Conducts seminars and other programs. *Type:* Association.

Just Between Friends

Greater North Highlands Chamber of Commerce
3720 Madison Ave.
PO Box 20
North Highlands, CA 95660-0020
Ph: (916)334-2214
Contact: Sonja Reyes, Editor.
Desc: Provides news and coverage of activities of the Commerce. Recurring features include a calendar of events and columns titled Did You Know, Message from the President, Events, and Thank You. *Type:* Newsletter.

Land O' Lakes Chamber of Commerce

PO Box 599
6484 Hwy. 45 N.
Land O' Lakes, WI 54540
Ph: (715)547-3432
Free: 800-236-3432
Contact: Bob Klager, Pres.
Desc: Promotes business and community development in Land O'Lakes, WI. Holds annual Headwaters Classic Dogsled Races, Family Fun Day, Colorama, Winter Festival, and Art Impressions art show. *Type:* Association.

Maywood Chamber of Commerce—Community Guide

Maywood Chamber of Commerce
411 Madison
Maywood, IL 60153
Ph: (708)345-1100
Fax: (708)345-9701
Desc: Businesses, churches, schools, and civic and social organizations in Maywood, Illinois. *Type:* Directory.

MetroJackson Commerce

MetroJackson Chamber of Commerce
201 S. President St.
PO Box 22548
Jackson, MS 39225-2548
Ph: (601)948-7575
Fax: (601)352-5539
Contact: Duane A. O'Neill, Pres. & Publisher; Kay M. Maghan, Editor.
Desc: Features news of the MetroJackson Chamber of Commerce and corporate participation in Jackson's community. *Type:* Newsletter.

Moberly Area Chamber of Commerce

211 W. Reed
PO Box 602
Moberly, MO 65270
Ph: (816)263-6070
Fax: (816)263-9443
Contact: J.W. Vallinger, III, VP.
Desc: Promotes business and community development in Moberly and the Randolph County, MO area. Sponsors and or co-sponsors Fairs, and Christmas parade. *Type:* Association.

National Association of African American Chambers of Commerce

750 St. Paul Place, Ste. 1920
Dallas, TX 75201
Ph: (214)871-3060
Fax: (214)871-3020
E-mail: naaacc@aol.com
Contact: Tom Houston, CEO & Pres.
Desc: Black chambers of commerce organized to create a strategy for members of local chambers to share in the collective buying power of black minority communities. Primary focus is on the tourism industry, because, according to the association, blacks spend approximately $25 billion in the tourism market each year, but black-owned businesses net very little from this industry. Conducts training sessions to acquaint black businesspeople with the tourism market and marketing strategies. *Type:* Association.

National Membership Directory of the French-American Chamber of Commerce

French-American Chamber of Commerce in the United States, Inc.
1350 Avenue of the Americas, 6th Fl.
New York, NY 10019
Ph: (212)765-4460
Fax: (212)765-4650
Contact: Serge Bellanger, Editor; Lenir Drake, Editor.
Desc: About 3,500 member companies and individuals in the U.S. and 400 members in France involved in business between the two countries; lists include members of the seventeen regional chapters in the U.S., the national officers and directors, the Paris office, diplomatic and consular offices of both countries, American and French-American organizations, and official French services. *Type:* Directory.

Netherlands Chamber of Commerce in the United States

1 Rockefeller Plz., 14th Fl.
New York, NY 10020
Ph: (212)265-6460
Fax: (212)265-6402
E-mail: ncocny@compuserve.com
Contact: Kersen J. de Jong, Mng.Dir.
Desc: Chamber of commerce. *Type:* Association.

New York-London Briefing

British-American Chamber of Commerce
52 Vanderbilt, 20th Fl.
New York, NY 10017
Ph: (212)661-4060
Fax: (212)661-4074
Contact: Johanna Walker, Editor, jwalker@bacc.org.
Desc: Coverage of activities of the BACC and its members. *Type:* Newsletter.

North Penn Chamber of Commerce—Membership Directory

North Penn Chamber of Commerce
1515 N. Broad St.
Lansdale, PA 19446-1111
Ph: (215)362-9200
Fax: (215)362-0393
Desc: More than 900 member businesses and industries in Montgomery, Bucks, and Chester counties in Pennsylvania. *Type:* Directory.

Outlook/Indonesia

American-Indonesian Chamber of Commerce
711 3rd Ave., 17th Fl.
New York, NY 10017-4046
Ph: (212)370-1440
Fax: (212)867-9882
Contact: Wayne Forrest, Editor.
Desc: Reports on current American-Indonesia economic and political trends. Recurring features include news of research, a calendar of events, reports of meetings, a summary of Chamber activities, and columns titled New Members, Key Economic Indicators, Economic Trends and Development, and Corporate News. *Type:* Newsletter.

**Rancho Mirage Chamber of Commerce—
Membership Directory & Buyers Guide**
Rancho Mirage Chamber of Commerce
42-464 Rancho Mirage Ln.   Ph: (619)568-9351
Rancho Mirage, CA 92270   Fax: (619)779-9684
Contact: Stuart Ackley, Jr., Editor.
Desc: Approximately 350 member businesses in Rancho
Mirage, California. *Type:* Directory.

Ruskin Chamber of Commerce—Area Guide
Ruskin Chamber of Commerce
315 S. Tamiami Trail   Ph: (813)645-3808
Ruskin, FL 33570   Fax: (813)645-2099
E-mail: ruskinchamber@integracom.net
Contact: Sarah Lind, Exec. VP.
Desc: Over 300 businesses and organizations in greater
Ruskin, Florida, in southern Hillsborough County. *Type:*
Directory.

**St. Paul Area Chamber of Commerce—
Membership Directory and Buyer's Guide**
St. Paul Area Chamber of Commerce
332 Minnasota St., Ste. N-205   Ph: (612)223-5000
St. Paul, MN 55101   Fax: (612)223-5119
Desc: 1,700 members of the St. Paul Area Chamber of
Commerce. *Type:* Directory.

Spectrum Quarterly
Greater Columbia Chamber of Commerce
PO Box 1360   Ph: (803)733-1110
Columbia, SC 29202   Fax: (803)733-1149
E-mail: info@gcbn.com
URL: http://www.gcbn.com.
Contact: Lisa Brindel, Editor, (803)733-1117, lbrindel@
gcbn.com.
Desc: Features Chamber and community events. Recur-
ring features include a calendar of events and a column ti-
tled New Members. *Type:* Newsletter.

Stethoscope
*National Association of Residents and Interns
(NARI)*
Hillsboro Executive Center   Ph: (954)571-1877
  North   Fax: (954)571-8582
350 Fairway Dr., Ste. 200
Deerfield Beach, FL 33441-1834
Contact: B. Lydia Young, Editor, youngpps@aol.com.
Desc: Provides current information on the financial and
practice management aspects of medical and dental prac-
tices. "Focuses on the economic, tax, investment, and ca-
reer concerns of the young doctor." Recurring features
include Association news and news of research. *Type:*
Newsletter.

Sullivan Chamber of Commerce Newsletter
Sullivan Chamber of Commerce
2 W. Springfield   Ph: (573)468-3314
PO Box 536   Fax: (573)860-2313
Sullivan, MO 63080
E-mail: chamber@fidnet.com
Contact: Sandi Stother, Editor.
Desc: Provides news of Chamber-sponsored events and
projects. Includes a calendar of events and reports of meet-
ings. *Type:* Newsletter.

**Swedish-American Chamber of Commerce of
the United States—Directory**
Swedish-American Chamber of Commerce
599 Lexington Ave., 12th Fl.   Ph: (212)838-5530
New York, NY 10022   Free: (212)838-5530
          Fax: (212)755-7953
Contact: Margaretha Murphy, Editor.
Desc: About 1,800 United States and 200 Swedish members of the chamber, concerned with promoting commercial relations between the two countries. *Type:* Directory.

Tarzana Topics
Tarzana Chamber of Commerce
PO Box 570414   Ph: (818)343-3687
Tarzana, CA 91357   Fax: (818)343-1134
URL: http://www.tarzana.org.
Desc: Provides news of Chamber of Commerce projects
and activities. Discusses school schedules and their affect
on the business community, news of members of the po-
lice force, local cleanup projects, legislative issues, and ex-
ecutive board news. *Type:* Newsletter.

**Trinidad & Tobago—American Chamber of
Commerce—Membership Directory**
U.S. Chamber of Commerce
International Division Publications
1615 H St. NW   Ph: (202)463-5460
Washington, DC 20062-2000   Fax: (202)463-3114
Desc: Companies in the U.S. and Trinidad and Tobago
and individuals interested in the development of trade
within and between the two countries. *Type:* Directory.

U.S. Hispanic Chamber of Commerce
1019 19th St. NW, Ste. 200   Ph: (202)842-1212
Washington, DC 20036   Fax: (202)842-3221
Contact: George Herrera, Pres. & CEO.
Desc: Hispanic and other business firms interested in. the
development of Hispanic business and promotion of business leadership and economic interests in the Hispanic
community. *Type:* Association.

U.S. Junior Chamber of Commerce
PO Box 7   Ph: (918)584-2481
4 W. 21st St.   Fax: (918)584-4422
Tulsa, OK 74114-1116
E-mail: usjaycees@earthlink.net
URL: http://www.usjaycees.org
Contact: John Shiroma, Exec.VP.
Desc: Civic service organization of young people, aged 21-
39, dedicated to providing leadership training for its mem-
bers through active participation in local community ser-
vice programs. Annually selects nation's Ten Outstanding
Young Americans, Four Outstanding Young Farmers, and
Ten Healthy American Fitness Leaders; administers Inter-
national BB Gun Match and shooting education program,
anti-youth smoking program, national leadership academy, and Social Security reform Town Hall meeting.
Maintains Hall of Fame exhibit hall and museum. *Type:*
Association.

**West St. Louis County Chamber of Commerce—
Membership Directory**
West St. Louis County Chamber of Commerce
16419 Village Plaza View Dr.   Ph: (314)458-6200
Wildwood, MO 63011-4913   Fax: (314)458-6710
E-mail: wslccc@swbell.net
Contact: Cheryl Dohrmann, Editor.
Desc: About 380 member companies in West St. Louis
County, Missouri. *Type:* Directory.

**Westchester/LAX Chamber of Commerce—
Membership Directory & Buyers Guide**
Westchester/LAX Chamber of Commerce
9800 S. Sepulveda Blvd., Ste.   Ph: (310)645-5151
  214   Fax: (310)645-0130
Westchester, CA 90045
Contact: Richard S. Musella, Editor.
Desc: Approximately 500 member businesses; local government officials, schools, churches, and organizations in
the Westchester, California area, including Playa del Rey
and the Los Angeles International Airport area. *Type:* Directory.

Chemicals

ACSESS
Membership Division
American Chemical Society (ACS)
1155 16th St. NW   Ph: (202)452-2120
Washington, DC 20036   Free: 800-227-5558
          Fax: (202)872-6337
E-mail: acsess@acs.org.
URL: http://www.acs.org.
Contact: Allison Edmondson, Editor.
Desc: Discusses products, services, activities, and events of
the Society. *Type:* Newsletter.

Adhesive Trends
Adhesives Manufacturers Association
401 N. Michigan Ave.   Ph: (312)644-6610
Chicago, IL 60611-4267   Fax: (312)527-6783
E-mail: ama@sba.com
Contact: Sue Zeiler, Editor.
Desc: Informs members of developments within the Asso-
ciation and the adhesives industry, as well as monitoring
relevant legislation, tax information, and economic trends.
Recurring features include news of research, reports of
meetings, notices of publications available, information on
raw material availability, and a calendar of events. *Type:*
Newsletter.

American Crop Protection Association
1156 15th St. NW, Ste. 400   Ph: (202)296-1585
Washington, DC 20005   Fax: (202)463-0474
URL: http://www.acpa.org
Contact: Jay J. Vroom, Pres.
Desc: Firms engaged the formulation, manufacture and
distribution of agricultural crop protection and pest con-
trol products ACPA. Members produce, sell, and distrib-
ute the active ingredients used in agricultural products.
Type: Association.

**American Electroplaters and Surface Finishers
Society**
12644 Research Pky.   Ph: (407)281-6441
Orlando, FL 32826   Fax: (407)281-6446
E-mail: aesf@aesf.org
URL: http://www.aesf.org
Contact: Ted Witt, Exec.Dir.
Desc: International professional society of scientists, tech-
nicians, job shop operators, and others interested in re-
search in electroplating, surface finishing, and allied arts.
Offers classroom training courses, home study courses, co-
operative programs, and voluntary certification program.
Type: Association.

BAKER
Mallinckrodt Baker Inc.
222 Red School Lane   Ph: (908)859-2151
Phillipsburg, NJ 08865
URL: http://www.jbaker.com
Desc: Contains the complete text of more than 1800 Material Safety Data Sheets (MSDS), which provide product
identification and safety information for chemical substances. Typical data elements include product name; formula; formula weight; CAS Registry Number; NIOSH/
RTECS Number; common synonyms; product codes;
hazard rating for health; flammability; reactivity; contact;
boiling point; melting point; specific gravity; solubility;
appearance and odor; vapor pressure; vapor density; evaporation rate; flashpoint; NFPA 704M rating; flammable
limit; fire extinguishing media; special fire-fighting procedures; unusual fire and explosion hazards; toxic gases produced; threshold limit value; permissible exposure limit;
carcinogenicity; effects of overexposure; target organs;
medical conditions aggravated by exposure; routes of

entry; emergency and first aid procedures; stability; hazardous polymerization; incompatibles; decomposition products; spill, discharge, and disposal procedures; protective equipment; storage color code and special precautions; and domestic and international transportation data. *Available:* Oxford Molecular Group, Chemical Information Systems. *Type:* Database.

BNA Chemical Regulation Reporter

The Bureau of National Affairs, Inc. (BNA)
1231 25th St. NW   Ph: (202)452-4200
Washington, DC 20037
E-mail: bnaplus@bna.com
URL: http://bna.com/mkt/hrl/hrlwdec.htm
Contact: BNA PLUS, (202)452-4323, fax: (202)822-8092, bnaplus@bna.com.
Desc: Contains the complete text of the current developments section of Chemical Regulation Reporter, covering legislative and regulatory developments affecting production and use of pesticides, new and existing chemical regulations, and biotechnology, including control of chemicals in the air, water, land, workplace, and during transport. Covers proposed legislation and regulations, research and testing reports, enforcement activities, reporting requirements, and policy statements. *Available:* LEXIS-NEXIS, LEXIS; West Group, WESTLAW. *Type:* Database.

CAOLD

Chemical Abstracts Service (CAS)
2540 Olentangy River Rd.   Ph: (614)447-3731
P.O. Box 3012
Columbus, OH 43210-0012
E-mail: help@cas.org
URL: http://www.cas.org/
Contact: STN Help Desk: 800-848-6533., help@cas.org.
Desc: Contains CA reference numbers citations, CAS Registry Numbers, document type, author names, abstract titles, and patent asignees for patents and documents abstracted in Chemical Abstracts from 1907 to 1967 that cite substances registered in the CAS Registry System, more than 3 million documents and 800,000 patents. *Available:* STN International. *Type:* Database.

Center for Chemical Process Safety

American Institute of Chemical Engineers
3 Park Ave. Lbby. 2   Free: 800-AIC-HEME
New York, NY 10016-5902
Contact: Jack Weaver, Dir.
Desc: Chemical and hydrocarbon manufacturers; engineering firms. Purpose is to study process safety issues in the chemical and hydrocarbon industries and publish and disseminate the results. *Type:* Association.

ChemEcology

Chemical Manufacturers Association
1300 Wilson Blvd.   Ph: (703)741-5804
Arlington, VA 22209   Fax: (703)741-6804
Desc: Covers environmental and health and safety issues of concern to both the chemical industry and the public. Summarizes federal and state regulatory actions, research, industry developments, emerging technologies, and advances in pollution control. *Type:* Newsletter.

Chemical Engineering Buyers Guide

McGraw-Hill, Inc.
2 Penn Plaza   Ph: (212)904-2000
New York, NY 10121   Free: 800-223-6180
                                 Fax: (212)904-6068
URL: http://www.mcgraw-hill.com; http://www.che.com.
Contact: Christopher Sloboda, Editor.
Desc: List of over 4,000 firms supplying equipment, materials, and services to the chemical process industries. *Type:* Directory.

Chemical Hazards Response Information System

U.S. Coast Guard
Data Management
AMSCB-ACL   Ph: (410)436-3391
Aberdeen Proving Ground, MD
  21010-5424
URL: http://www.uscg.mil/
Contact: D.M. Smith, LCDR, USLG.
Desc: Contains information for use in responding to emergencies that arise during the transport of hazardous chemicals. Covers more than 1200 chemical substances, including chemical names and synonyms, molecular formula, chemical reactivity, biological and fire hazard potential, and chemical and physical properties. *Available:* Oxford Molecular Group, Chemical Information Systems. *Type:* Database.

Chemical Manufacturers Association

1300 Wilson Blvd.   Ph: (703)741-5000
Arlington, VA 22209   Fax: (703)741-6000
URL: http://www.cmahq.com
Contact: Frederick L. Webber, Pres.&CEO.
Desc: Manufacturers of chemicals. Conducts advocacy and administers research in areas of broad import to chemical manufacturing, such as pollution prevention and other special research programs. Conducts committee studies. *Type:* Association.

Chemical Week—Financial Survey of the 300 Largest Companies in the U.S. Chemical Process Industries Issue

Chemical Week Associates
888 7th Ave., 26th Fl.   Ph: (212)621-4900
New York, NY 10106   Fax: (212)621-4949
Contact: Emily Plishner, Editor.
Desc: 300 chemical process companies in the U.S. *Type:* Directory.

CHEMLIST (Regulated Chemicals Listing)

Chemical Abstracts Service (CAS)
2540 Olentangy River Rd.   Ph: (614)447-3731
P.O. Box 3012
Columbus, OH 43210-0012
E-mail: help@cas.org
URL: http://www.cas.org/
Desc: Contains information on more than 206,000 substances that are regulated or on advisory list for anyone who uses, manufactures, processes, stores, or transports chemical substances. *Available:* STN International. *Type:* Database.

CHEMSEARCH

The Dialog Corporation
DIALOG
11000 Regency Pkwy., Ste. 400   Ph: (919)462-8600
Cary, NC 27511
URL: http://www.dialog.com
Contact: Marketing.
Desc: Contains more than 14 million records covering chemical substances registered since 1957. Includes substances that have been cited one or more times in Chemical Abstracts since 1967. *Available:* The Dialog Corporation, DIALOG; Questel • Orbit. *Type:* Database.

Chlorine Institute

2001 L St. NW, No. 506   Ph: (202)775-2790
Washington, DC 20036   Fax: (202)223-7225
Contact: Dr. Robert G. Smerko, Pres.
Desc: Manufacturers of chlorine and caustic soda; other members are packagers of chlorine and manufacturers of equipment for chlorine production and handling. Promotes safe production and handling of chlorine, caustic soda, caustic potash sodium hypochlorite and hydrogen chloride. Caustic soda and caustic potash are co-products of chlorine. *Type:* Association.

CLAIMS™ Compound Registry

IFI/Plenum Data Corporation
3202 Kirkwood Highway Ste.   Ph: (302)998-0478
  203
Wilmington, DE 19808
E-mail: ifiplenum@aol.com
Contact: Jim Brown, Customer Service, (302)998-0478, fax: (302)998-0733.
Desc: Contains a listing of more than 16,000 chemical compounds used in conjunction with the CLAIMS/ UNITERM and CLAIMS/COMPREHENSIVE databases. Each record includes the IFI compound term number, main compound name, available synonyms, molecular formula, element count, fragment codes, and fragment terms. *Available:* The Dialog Corporation, DIALOG; Questel • Orbit; STN International; ChemWeb, Inc. *Type:* Database.

Coatings

National Paint & Coatings Association
1500 Rhode Island Ave. NW   Ph: (202)462-6272
Washington, DC 20005-5503   Fax: (202)462-8549
E-mail: npca@paint.org
Contact: Lisa Warren, Editor, lwarren@paint.org.
Desc: Covers legislative, regulatory, and judicial issues affecting the paint and coatings industry. Recurring features include news of research, a calendar of events, notices of publications available, reports of meetings, and editorials. *Type:* Newsletter.

Coil Lines

National Coil Coaters Association
401 N. Michigan Ave., Ste.   Ph: (312)321-6894
  2200   Fax: (312)527-6640
Chicago, IL 60611-4267
E-mail: ncca@sba.com
Contact: Dan Consiglio, Editor.
Desc: Provides news of issues related to the coil coating industry, including marketing, market trends, government legislation and regulatory activity affecting the industry, and metal supplies and markets. Recurring features include reports of meetings, news of educational opportunities, notices of publications available, a section featuring technical information, and a calendar of events. *Type:* Newsletter.

CSCHEM

Chemical Sources International Inc.
PO Box 1824   Ph: (864)646-7840
Clemson, SC 29633-1824
URL: http://www.chemsources.com
Contact: Mike Desing.
Desc: Contains information on more than 190,000 chemical products supplied by companies indexed in CSCORP. For each product, provides chemical or trade name; applications of trade-named products (e.g., algaecides, antimicrobial agents, fungistats); and supplier name. *Available:* STN International; The Dialog Corporation, DataStar. *Type:* Database.

DIPPR Data Compilation of Pure Compound Properties

American Institute of Chemical Engineers (AIChE)
3 Park Ave.   Ph: (212)591-7338
New York, NY 10016-5901
URL: http://www.aiche.org/
Contact: Technical Database Services (TDS), (212)245-0384, fax: (212)247-0587.
Desc: Contains physical, thermodynamic, and transport property data for 1700 commercially important chemicals. Includes chemical name, Chemical Abstracts Service

(CAS) Registry Number, molecular formula, compound family name, 26 single-value property constants (e.g., dipole moment, flash point), 13 temperature-dependent properties (e.g., ideal gas heat capacity, liquid density), regression equations and coefficients for calculating temperature-dependent values, data quality codes, and references to data sources. *Available:* STN International. *Type:* Database.

Federation of Societies for Coatings Technology

492 Norristown Rd.
Blue Bell, PA 19422

Contact: Robert F. Ziegler, Exec.VP.

Desc: Chemists, chemical engineers, technologists, and supervisory production personnel in the decorative and protective coatings industry and allied industries. Works to gather and disseminate practical and technical facts, data, and standards fundamental to the manufacturing and use of paints, varnishes, lacquers, related protective coatings, and printing inks. *Type:* Association.

The Finishing Line

Association for Finishing Processes
Society of Manufacturing Engineers
PO Box 930   Ph: (313)271-1500
1 SME Dr.   Free: 800-733-4SME
Dearborn, MI 48121-0930
URL: http://www.sme.org.

Contact: Thomas C. Akas, Editor, akastom@sme.org.

Desc: Concerned with topics related to industrial finishes, such as powder coating, radiation curing, waterborne, high solids, coating and finishing of plastics, and surface preparation. Provides information on government regulations, new products and technology, and educational opportunities in the field of finishing. *Type:* Newsletter.

Handbook of Industrial Surfactants

Ashgate Publishing Co.
Old Post Rd.   Ph: (802)276-3162
Brookfield, VT 05036   Fax: (802)276-3837
E-mail: info@ashgatechem.com

Contact: Michael Ash, Editor; Irene Ash, Editor.

Desc: Manufacturers of 16,000 trade-named surface-active agents for industrial applications. *Type:* Directory.

Hazardous Chemicals Information and Disposal Data Base

University of Alberta
Department of Chemistry
Rm. W3-35 Chemistry Bldg.   Ph: (403)492-4969
Edmonton, AB, Canada T6G
2G2

Contact: Dr. Margaret-Ann Armour, margaret-ann. armour@ualberta.ca.

Desc: Contains data on the handling and disposal of more than 220 hazardous chemical substances. Includes chemical name and molecular formula, physical and chemical properties, biological and fire hazard potential, hazardous reactions, and detailed instructions for waste disposal and spillage handling. *Available:* Oxford Molecular Group, Chemical Information Systems. *Type:* Database.

Industrial Chemical Research Association

2547 Monroe St.   Ph: (313)669-0360
Dearborn, MI 48124

Contact: Harold Castor, Pres.

Desc: Manufacturers, marketers, researchers, formulators, salesmen, and suppliers of industrial chemical products. Goal is to promote research, safe practices, improved selling efficiency, and fellowship among members. Maintains speakers' bureau; provides educational and research programs. *Type:* Association.

International Chemical Workers Union

1655 W. Market St.   Ph: (330)867-2444
Akron, OH 44313   Fax: (330)867-0544

Contact: Frank D. Martino, Pres.

Desc: AFL-CIO. *Type:* Association.

Iota Sigma Pi

Dr. Barbara Sawrey
Chemistry Department   Ph: (619)534-2263
UC San Diego   Fax: (619)534-7687
La Jolla, CA 92093-0303

Desc: Professional honor sorority - chemistry. *Type:* Association.

NAOSMM Newsline

National Association of Scientific Materials Managers (NAOSMM)
c/o Barbara Neff   Ph: (610)660-1790
St. Joseph's University
Chemisty Department
5600 City Ave.
Philadelphia, PA 19131

Contact: Barbara Neff, Editor, bneff@sjuphil.sju.edu; Janet Chrisman, Editor.

Desc: Discusses the issues of acquisition, storage and distribution of scientific materials. Recurring features include Association news, book reviews, and federal legislation updates. *Type:* Newsletter.

National Paint and Coatings Association

1500 Rhode Island Ave. NW   Ph: (202)462-6272
Washington, DC 20005-5597   Fax: (202)462-8549
E-mail: npca@paint.org
URL: http://www.paint.org

Contact: James A. Doyle, Pres.

Desc: Manufacturers of paints and chemical coatings; suppliers of raw materials and equipment. *Type:* Association.

National Pest Control Association

8100 Oak St.   Ph: (703)573-8330
Dunn Loring, VA 22027   Free: 800-678-NPCA
                              Fax: (703)573-4116

Contact: Robert F. Lederer, Exec.VP.

Desc: Firms engaged in control of insects, rodents, birds, and other pests, in or around structures, through use of insecticides, rodenticides, miticides, fumigants, and nonchemical methods. Provides advisory services on control procedures, new products, and safety and business administration practices. Promotes June as National Pest Control Month. *Type:* Association.

NUMERIGUIDE

Chemical Abstracts Service (CAS)
2540 Olentangy River Rd.   Ph: (614)447-3731
P.O. Box 3012
Columbus, OH 43210-0012
E-mail: help@cas.org
URL: http://www.cas.org/

Contact: STN International, fax: (614)447-3751, help@cas.org.

Desc: Contains information on the more than 1910 numeric properties included in the numeric databases available through STN International. For each property, provides preferred property name, definition, synonyms, default units for the property, search and display qualifiers, notes regarding the use of the property in individual STN databases, and property hierarchy. *Available:* STN International. *Type:* Database.

OHS MSDS On-Line

MDL Information Systems, Inc.
14600 Catalina St.   Ph: (510)895-1313
San Leandro, CA 94577
E-mail: ohs@mdli.com
URL: http://www.mdli.com

Desc: Contains Material Safety Data Sheets (MSDSs) for more than 19,000 unique chemicals, primarily raw ingredients plus more than 3,000 common chemical mixtures. OHS MSDSs are independently researched, resulting in thorough and unbiased information. *Available:* MDL Information Systems, Inc.; STN International. *Type:* Database.

Oil, Chemical and Atomic Workers International Union

255 Union Blvd.   Ph: (303)987-2229
Lakewood, CO 80228-8200   Free: 800-824-7300
                              Fax: (303)987-1967
E-mail: ocawiure@aol.com
URL: http://www.ocaw.org

Contact: Robert E. Wages, Pres.

Desc: AFL-CIO. *Type:* Association.

Purchasing/CPI Edition—Chemicals Yellow Pages

Cahners Publishing Co.
275 Washington St.   Ph: (617)964-3030
Newton, MA 02158   Fax: (617)558-4700

Contact: Kevin R. Fitzgerald, Editor.

Desc: Manufacturers and distributors of 10,000 chemicals and raw materials; manufacturers and distributors of containers and packaging; transportation services and storage facilities; environmental services companies. *Type:* Directory.

Registry of Toxic Effects of Chemical Substances

U.S. National Institute for Occupational Safety and Health (NIOSH)
Education and Information Division
Information Resources Branch
4676 Columbia Pkwy.   Ph: (513)533-8359
Cincinnati, OH 45226

Contact: Jeanne Goshorn, RTECS Representative.

Desc: Contains data on the toxic effects of more than 113,000 chemicals. Each entry contains the Chemical Abstracts Service (CAS) name and Registry Number, synonyms, molecular formula, and one or more measures of toxicity, including acute and chronic in vivo data, in vitro mutagenesis data, skin and eye irritation data, and reproductive and tumorigenic effects data. *Available:* The Dialog Corporation, DIALOG; DIMDI (Deutsches Institut fuer Medizinische Dokumentation und Information); U.S. National Library of Medicine (NLM), TOXNET; The Dialog Corporation, DataStar; STN International. *Type:* Database.

Silicones Environmental Health and Safety Council

1767 Business Center Dr., Ste.   Ph: (703)438-3943
302   Fax: (703)438-3113
Reston, VA 20190-5332
E-mail: sehsc1@aol.com

Contact: William H. Smock, Exec.Dir.

Desc: Organosilicones manufacturers. Coordinates programs dealing with health, environmental, and safety issues of interest to the industry. *Type:* Association.

Specialty Chemicals Source Book

Synapse Information Resources
1247 Taft Ave.   Ph: (607)748-4145
Endicott, NY 13760   Free: 888-SYN-CHEM
   Fax: (607)786-3966
E-mail: salesinfo@synapseinfo.com
Contact: Irene Ash, Editor, iash@synapseinfo.com.
Desc: Chemicals and approximately 4,000 chemical manufacturers worldwide that supply chemicals. *Type:* Directory.

SSPC: The Society for Protective Coatings

40 24th St., 6th Fl.   Ph: (412)281-2331
Pittsburgh, PA 15222-4656   Free: 877-281-7772
   Fax: (412)281-9992
URL: http://www.sspc.org
Contact: Dr. Bernard R. Appleman, Exec.Dir.
Desc: Seeks to advance the technology and promote the use of protective coatings to preserve industrial, marine and commercial structures, components and substrates. *Type:* Association.

Sulphur Institute

1140 Connecticut Ave. NW,   Ph: (202)331-9660
Ste. 612   Fax: (202)293-2940
Washington, DC 20036
E-mail: sulphur@sulphurinstitute.org
Contact: Robert J. Morris, Pres.
Desc: The Sulphur Institute is an international organization representing the sulphur industry. TSI's purpose is to promote and expand the use of sulphur in all forms worldwide. *Type:* Association.

Synthetic Organic Chemical Manufacturers Association

1850 M St. NW, Ste. 700   Ph: (202)721-4100
Washington, DC 20036   Fax: (202)296-8120
URL: http://www.socma.com
Contact: Graydon R. Powers, Pres.
Desc: Manufacturers of synthetic organic chemicals, which are products manufactured from coal, natural gas, crude petroleum, and certain natural substances such as vegetable oils, fats, proteins, carbohydrates, rosin, grains, and their derivatives. *Type:* Association.

Tank Talk

Steel Tank Institute
570 Oakwood Rd.   Ph: (847)438-8265
Lake Zurich, IL 60047   Fax: (847)438-4509
Contact: Jon Schwerman, Editor.
Desc: Monitors technological developments and general trends in the underground and above-ground storage tank industry. Reports on local, state, and federal legislative and regulatory actions affecting the steel tank industry. *Type:* Newsletter.

TOXLINE™

U.S. National Library of Medicine (NLM)
Specialized Information Services Division
8600 Rockville Pike   Ph: (301)496-6531
Bethesda, MD 20894
E-mail: toxmail@toxnetmail.nlm.nih.gov
URL: http://toxnet.nlm.nih.gov
Desc: Contains citations, with abstracts, to the worldwide literature in all areas of toxicology, including chemicals and pharmaceuticals, pesticides, environmental pollutants, and mutagens and teratogens. Comprises these discrete files corresponding to the online TOXLINE database: • Aneuploidy (ANEUPL)--contains approximately 3600 citations to literature on research in aneuploidy (numeric chromosome abnormalities) in human and experimental

systems. *Available:* The Dialog Corporation, DataStar; The Dialog Corporation, DIALOG; U.S. National Library of Medicine (NLM), TOXNET; STN International; STN International; DIMDI (Deutsches Institut fuer Medizinische Dokumentation und Information); DIMDI (Deutsches Institut fuer Medizinische Dokumentation und Information); STN International; DIMDI (Deutsches Institut fuer Medizinische Dokumentation und Information). *Type:* Database.

VCH Book News

VCH Publishers, Inc.
605 3rd Ave.   Ph: (212)850-6000
New York, NY 10158   Free: 800-367-8249
   Fax: (212)850-6088
Contact: Pete Jansic, Editor.
Desc: Features new VCH publications, monographs, and reference sets in the fields of chemistry, chemical engineering, food science, physics, and life sciences. *Type:* Newsletter.

Vendors to the Trade

Chemical Specialties Manufacturers Association (CSMA)
1913 Eye St. NW   Ph: (202)872-8110
Washington, DC 20006   Fax: (202)872-8114
Contact: Lynne R. Harris, Editor.
Desc: About 110 suppliers to the chemically formulated consumer products industry. *Type:* Directory.

Chemistry

Alpha Chi Sigma

2141 N. Franklin Rd.   Ph: (317)357-5944
Indianapolis, IN 46219
Contact: Paul R. Jones, Sec.-Treas.
Desc: Professional fraternity - chemistry. Offers a leadership program. *Type:* Association.

American Association for Clinical Chemistry

2101 L St. NW, Ste. 202   Ph: (202)857-0717
Washington, DC 20037-1526   Free: 800-892-1400
   Fax: (202)887-5093
E-mail: info@aacc.org
URL: http://www.aacc.org
Contact: Richard Flaherty, Exec.VP.
Desc: Clinical laboratory scientists and others engaged in the practice of clinical chemistry in independent laboratories, hospitals, and allied institutions. Maintains Endowment Fund for Research in Clinical Chemistry. *Type:* Association.

American Chemical Society

1155 16th St. NW   Ph: (202)872-4600
Washington, DC 20036   Free: 800-227-5558
   Fax: (202)872-4615
E-mail: meminfo@acs.org
URL: http://www.acs.org
Contact: John K. Crum, Exec.Dir.
Desc: Scientific and educational society of chemists and chemical engineers. *Type:* Association.

American Chemical Society News Service

1155 16th St. NW   Ph: (202)872-4450
Washington, DC 20036   Fax: (202)872-4370
E-mail: mdc93@acs.org.
Desc: Distributes news on chemical-related research. *Alt. Contact:* 1155 16th St. NW, Washington, DC 20036; telephone: (202)872-4450; fax: (202)872-4370. *Type:* Periodical.

American Institute of Chemical Engineers

3 Park Avenue   Ph: (212)591-7338
New York, NY 10016-5901   Free: 800-242-4363
   Fax: (212)752-3294
URL: http://www.aiche.org
Contact: Mr. Glenn Taylor, Exec.Dir.
Desc: Professional society of chemical engineers. Establishes standards for chemical engineering curricula; offers employment services. Presents technical conferences, petrochemical and refining exposition, and continuing education programs. *Type:* Association.

AOAC International

481 N. Frederick Ave., No. 500   Ph: (301)924-7077
Gaithersburg, MD 20877-2504   Fax: (301)924-7089
E-mail: aoac@aoac.org
URL: http://www.aoac.org
Contact: Raymond Matulis, Exec.Dir.
Desc: Government, academic, and industry analytical scientists who develop, test, and collaboratively study methods for analyzing fertilizers, foods, feeds, pesticides, drugs, cosmetics, and other products related to agriculture and public health. Offers short courses for analytical laboratory personnel in chemical and microbiological quality assurance, lab waste management, statistics, giving expert testimony, and technical writing. *Type:* Association.

CA File

Chemical Abstracts Service (CAS)
2540 Olentangy River Rd.   Ph: (614)447-3731
P.O. Box 3012
Columbus, OH 43210-0012
E-mail: help@cas.org
URL: http://www.cas.org/
Contact: STN Help Desk: 800-848-6533.
Desc: Contains more than 11 million citations, with abstracts, to the worldwide literature in the field of chemistry. Covers organic, analytical, physical, applied, macromolecular, and biochemical chemistry, as well as chemical engineering. *Available:* STN International. *Type:* Database.

CA Search

Chemical Abstracts Service (CAS)
2540 Olentangy River Rd.   Ph: (614)447-3731
P.O. Box 3012
Columbus, OH 43210-0012
E-mail: help@cas.org
URL: http://www.cas.org/
Desc: Contains more than 12 million citations to the worldwide literature in the field of chemistry. Covers organic, analytical, physical, applied, macromolecular, and biochemical chemistry, as well as chemical engineering. *Available:* Ovid Technologies, Inc.; The Dialog Corporation, DataStar; The Dialog Corporation, DIALOG; Questel • Orbit; NIFTY Corporation, NIFTY-SERVE; European Information Network Services (EINS). *Type:* Database.

CAS Registry File

Chemical Abstracts Service (CAS)
2540 Olentangy River Rd.   Ph: (614)447-3731
P.O. Box 3012
Columbus, OH 43210-0012
E-mail: help@cas.org
URL: http://www.cas.org/
Desc: Contains structure, name, and formula information for more than 16 million substances identified by Chemical Abstracts Service in journals and patents. Covers more than 23,000,000 substance names. *Available:* The Dialog Corporation, DataStar; STN International; The Dialog Corporation, DIALOG; Questel • Orbit. *Type:* Database.

CASREACT

Chemical Abstracts Service (CAS)
2540 Olentangy River Rd.   Ph: (614)447-3731
P.O. Box 3012
Columbus, OH 43210-0012
E-mail: help@cas.org
URL: http://www.cas.org/
Contact: STN Help Desk: 800-848-6533.
Desc: Contains citations, with abstracts, to the worldwide literature on chemical reactions. Covers more than 1.2 million single-step reactions and more than 1.7 million multistep reactions from more than 124,000 documents. *Available:* STN International. *Type:* Database.

CEH Online

SRI Consulting
Chemical Business Research Division
Specialty Chemicals Update Program
333 Ravenswood Ave.   Ph: (650)859-5037
Menlo Park, CA 94025-3493
E-mail: stakahashi@sric.sri.com
Contact: Santha Takahashi, Coordinator Online Services, stakahashi@sric.sri.com.
Desc: Contains economic data for more than 13,000 major commodity and specialty chemical products (e.g., basic petrochemicals, organic chemicals, intermediates, polymers, inorganic chemicals, agricultural chemicals) and families of chemical products (e.g., medicinals, surfactants). *Available:* The Dialog Corporation, DIALOG. *Type:* Database.

Center for Process Analytical Chemistry

Box 351700   Ph: (206)685-2326
Seattle, WA 98195-1700   Fax: (206)543-6506
E-mail: cpac@cpac.washington.edu
URL: http://www.cpac.washington.edu
Contact: Dr. Mel Koch, Exec.Dir.
Desc: Companies involved in analytical chemistry. *Type:* Association.

Chapman and Hall Chemical Database

Chapman and Hall Inc.
Electronic Publishing Team
c/o Kluwer Publishing   Ph: (781)871-6600
101 Philip Dr.
Norwell, MA 02061
URL: http://www.kap.nl
Contact: Dr. Stephen Jeffery, Projects Manager, ( )44 1718650066, fax: ( )44 1715520101, stephen.jeffery@chall.co.uk.
Desc: Contains physical and chemical properties data on more than 440,000 important substances selected by a panel of experts. Includes molecular weight and formula; melting, freezing, and boiling point; solubility; relative density; optical rotation; dissociation constants; uses; reactions; and Chemical Abstracts Service (CAS) Registry Number, derivative names, synonyms, and variant compounds. *Available:* The Dialog Corporation, DIALOG; The Dialog Corporation, DIALOG; CompuServe Information Service, Knowledge Index. *Type:* Database.

Chemical Abstracts Service Source Index

Chemical Abstracts Service (CAS)
2540 Olentangy River Rd.   Ph: (614)447-3731
P.O. Box 3012
Columbus, OH 43210-0012
E-mail: help@cas.org
URL: http://www.cas.org/
Contact: Charlie Hatfield, (614)447-3867, chatfield@cas.org.
Desc: Contains bibliographic information on more than 70,000 serial and non-serial publications held by more

than 350 libraries worldwide. For each title, provides National Union Catalog (NUC) codes to indicate libraries that have copies of the publication and codes for document suppliers from whom individual papers are available. *Available:* Questel • Orbit. *Type:* Database.

Chemical Abstracts Service Student Edition

Chemical Abstracts Service (CAS)
2540 Olentangy River Rd.   Ph: (614)447-3731
P.O. Box 3012
Columbus, OH 43210-0012
E-mail: help@cas.org
URL: http://www.cas.org/
Contact: Nita Dean, (614)761-5002, fax: (614)764-6096, nita_dean@oclc.org.
Desc: Provides indexing and abtracts of approximately 1.5 million items meant to meet the needs and interests of undergraduate students. *Type:* Database.

Chemical Engineering

McGraw-Hill, Inc.
1221 Avenue of the Americas   Ph: (212)512-6410
New York, NY 10020
Desc: Contains the complete text of Chemical Engineering magazine, covering the chemical processing industries. Includes technical reports, indexes of equipment and machinery costs and wholesale chemical prices, reports of new products and processes, book reviews, descriptions of new computer hardware and software for chemical engineering, and feature articles on industry issues (e.g., toxic waste control). *Available:* LEXIS-NEXIS, NEXIS; ChemWeb, Inc.; The Dialog Corporation, DIALOG; Dow Jones Interactive Publishing. *Type:* Database.

Chemical Equipment

Cahners Business Information
New Product Information Division
301 Gibraltar Dr.   Ph: (973)292-5100
Morris Plains, NJ 07950   Fax: (973)539-3476
Contact: Geoff Bridgman, Editor; Frank Ramsey, Publisher.
Desc: Tabloid on the chemical process industry. *Type:* Periodical.

Chemical Industry Notes

Chemical Abstracts Service (CAS)
2540 Olentangy River Rd.   Ph: (614)447-3731
P.O. Box 3012
Columbus, OH 43210-0012
E-mail: help@cas.org
URL: http://www.cas.org/
Contact: Help desk.
Desc: Contains more than 1 million records, with abstracts, to the worldwide business literature on the chemical industry. Topics covered include production, pricing, sales, facilities, products, processes, corporate and government activities, and people. *Available:* The Dialog Corporation, DIALOG; Questel • Orbit; The Dialog Corporation, DataStar. *Type:* Database.

Chemical Journal of AOAC International

AOAC International
481 N. Fredrick Ave., Ste. 500   Ph: (301)924-7077
Gaithersburg, MD 20877-2417
E-mail: aoac@aoac.org
URL: http://www.aoac.org
Desc: Contains the complete text of approximately 3000 research articles (including captions, references, and footnotes, but excluding illustrations) from the Journal of AOAC International. *Available:* STN International. *Type:* Database.

Chemical Journals of the American Chemical Society

American Chemical Society (ACS)
1155 16th St., NW   Ph: (202)293-9704
Washington, DC 20036
E-mail: service@acs.org
URL: http://pubs.acs.org
Desc: Contains the complete text and page images of 25 primary journals published by the American Chemical Society (including captions, references, and footnotes for all articles; illustrations from articles dating 1992 to date have been scanned from the original pages and are included). Covers • Accounts of Chemical Research. *Available:* American Chemical Society (ACS). *Type:* Database.

Chemical Processing

Putman Publishing Co.
555 W. Pierce Rd., Ste. 301   Ph: (630)467-1300
Itasca, IL 60143   Fax: (630)467-1109
Contact: Bob Strack, Editor; Larry Potter, Publisher; John Cappelletti, Advertising Mgr.
Desc: Magazine for the chemical process industry. *Type:* Periodical.

CSCORP

Chemical Sources International Inc.
PO Box 1824   Ph: (864)646-7840
Clemson, SC 29633-1824
URL: http://www.chemsources.com
Desc: Contains information on more than 7400 suppliers of some 180,000 chemical products indexed in CS-CHEM. For each supplier, provides company name, main and branch office addresses and functions (e.g., sales, shipping), contact numbers, and applications of chemicals (e.g., bleaching agents, corrosion inhibitors) supplied by the companies. *Available:* STN International; The Dialog Corporation, DataStar. *Type:* Database.

Dictionary of Natural Products on CD-ROM

Chapman and Hall Inc.
Electronic Publishing Team
c/o Kluwer Publishing   Ph: (781)871-6600
101 Philip Dr.
Norwell, MA 02061
URL: http://www.kap.nl
Contact: Eleanor Gordon, eleanor.gordon@chall.co.uk.
Desc: Contains physical and chemical properties data on more than 110,000 natural products. For each product, provides name; molecular weight and formula; melting, freezing, and boiling point; solubility; relative density; optical rotation; dissociation constants; uses; reactions; and Chemical Abstracts Service (CAS) Registry Number; derivative names; synonyms; and variant compounds. *Available:* ChemWeb, Inc. *Type:* Database.

Dictionary of Organic Compounds on CD-ROM

Chapman and Hall Inc.
Electronic Publishing Team
c/o Kluwer Publishing   Ph: (781)871-6600
101 Philip Dr.
Norwell, MA 02061
URL: http://www.kap.nl
Contact: Eleanor Gordon, eleanor.gordon@chall.co.uk.
Desc: Contains physical and chemical properties data on more than 170,000 organic compounds. For each compound, provides name; molecular weight and formula; melting, freezing, and boiling point; solubility; relative density; optical rotation; dissociation constants; uses; reactions; and Chemical Abstracts Service (CAS) Registry Number; derivative names; synonyms; and variant compounds. *Available:* ChemWeb, Inc. *Type:* Database.

Encyclopedia of Polymer Science and Engineering Online

John Wiley & Sons, Inc.
605 Third Ave.   Ph: (212)850-6194
New York, NY 10158-0012
URL: http://www.wiley.com
Desc: Contains the complete text of the Encyclopedia of Polymer Science and Engineering, 2nd Edition. Includes text and cited references. *Available:* The Dialog Corporation, DIALOG. *Type:* Database.

Environmental Mutagen Information Center Data Base

Oak Ridge National Laboratory
Toxicology and Risk Analysis
Environmental Mutagen Information Center (EMIC)
1060 Commerce Park   Ph: (423)574-7871
Oak Ridge, TN 37831-6480
E-mail: tug@ornl.gov
Contact: Elizabeth T. Owens, EMIC Coordinator.
Desc: Contains more than 88,000 citations to the worldwide literature on chemical, biological, and physical agents that have been tested for mutagenic activity. Records include Chemical Abstracts Service (CAS) Registry Numbers. *Available:* U.S. National Library of Medicine (NLM), TOXNET. *Type:* Database.

High-Tech Materials Alert

Technical Insights
John Wiley and Sons, Inc.
32 N. Dean St.   Ph: (201)568-4744
Englewood, NJ 07631
E-mail: TIInf@wiley.com
URL: http://www.wiley.comm/technicalinsights
Contact: Kristine Swain, Director, Computer Operations, htmainfo@insights.com.
Desc: Contains the complete text of High-Tech Materials Alert, a monthly newsletter on commercial opportunities for advanced materials, including ceramics, polymers, metals, reinforcing fibers, composites, optical materials, intermetallics, biomaterials, superconductors, films and coatings, conductive polymers, quasi-crystals, and materials for surface modification. Covers research and development, market studies, and licensing and joint venture opportunities. *Available:* CompuServe Information Service. *Type:* Database.

NISTFLUIDS

U.S. National Institute of Standards and Technology (NIST)
Office of Standard Reference Data
820/113   Ph: (301)975-2208
Gaithersburg, MD 20899
URL: http://www.nist.gov/srd
Contact: Joan Sauerwein, (301)975-2208, fax: (301)925-0416, sidata@nist.gov.
Desc: Contains programs for calculating thermophysical and transport properties of cryogenic fluids, including argon, butane, ethane, ethylene, helium, para-hydrogen, isobutane, methane, nitrogen, nitrogen trifluoride, oxygen, and propane, more than a wide range of temperatures and pressures. Users can calculate values for pressure, temperature, internal energy, enthalpy, entropy, specific heat capacities, speed of sound, dynamic viscosity, thermal conductivity, and dielectric constants. *Type:* Database.

Nucleic Acids Abstracts

Cambridge Scientific Abstracts (CSA)
7200 Wisconsin Ave., Ste. 601   Ph: (301)961-6700
Bethesda, MD 20814-4823
E-mail: sales@csa.com
URL: http://www.csa.com

Desc: Contains more than 168,000 citations and abstracts of International periodical and other literature covering all aspects of nucleic acids. Sources include such specialist literature sources as journals, books, conference proceedings, and reports. *Type:* Database.

Phi Lambda Upsilon

Dr. James E. George
Depauw University   Ph: (317)658-4600
Chemistry Department
Greencastle, IN 46135
Contact: Dr. James E. George, Nat.Sec.
Desc: Honor society for students in chemistry, biochemistry, and chemical engineering. *Type:* Association.

PHYTOTOX

University of Oklahoma
Department of Botany and Microbiology
601 Elm Ave., Room 1100   Ph: (405)325-4321
Norman, OK 73019
Desc: Contains records relating to the biological effects of the application of organic chemicals to terrestrial plants. Both natural and synthetic organic compounds administered to native, crop, or weed plant species have been included. *Available:* Oxford Molecular Group, Chemical Information Systems; Technical Database Services, Inc. (TDS), TDS Numerica. *Type:* Database.

Processing

Putman Publishing Co.
555 W. Pierce Rd., Ste. 301   Ph: (630)467-1300
Itasca, IL 60143   Fax: (630)467-1109
Contact: Joan Leeney, Editor, jleeney@aol.com; Michael Wasson, Publisher, mlwasson@aol.com.
Desc: Equipment selection guide *Type:* Periodical.

Registry of Mass Spectral Data

John Wiley & Sons, Inc.
605 Third Ave.   Ph: (212)850-6194
New York, NY 10158-0012
URL: http://www.wiley.com
Desc: Contains approximately 140,000 mass spectra of more than 118,144 different chemical substances. The spectra are from the Registry of Mass Spectral Data (5th edition) published by John Wiley & Sons. *Available:* Oxford Molecular Group, Chemical Information Systems. *Type:* Database.

Ribosomal Database Project

Michigan State University
East Lansing, MI 48824-1325   Ph: (517)353-9021
                                  Fax: (517)353-2917
E-mail: urbance@psssun.pss.msu.edu
URL: http://rdp.life.uiuc.edu/index2.html
Contact: Dr. Chuck Parker, rdp@vitro.cme.msu.edu.
Desc: The Ribosomal Database Project (RDP) provides ribosome related data services to the scientific community, including online data analysis, rRNA derived phylogenetic trees, and aligned and annotated rRNA sequences. The database has been established to help scientists and others utilize the large and rapidly growing collection of ribosomal sequence data; at present the project is limited to small and large sub-unit ribosomal RNA sequences. *Type:* Database.

Toxicology Abstracts

Cambridge Scientific Abstracts (CSA)
7200 Wisconsin Ave., Ste. 601   Ph: (301)961-6700
Bethesda, MD 20814-4823
E-mail: sales@csa.com
URL: http://www.csa.com
Contact: Anthea Gotto, Manager of Electronic Services, (301)961-6795, fax: (301)961-6720, anthea@csa.com.

Desc: Contains more than 137,000 citations, with abstracts, to the worldwide literature on toxicology. Covers clinical toxicology, including acute or chronic poisoning from drugs, medicines, and chemicals; toxic risks in the workplace; and environmental toxicology. *Type:* Database.

Child Health

ALSAC - St. Jude Children's Research Hospital

501 St. Jude Pl.   Ph: (901)522-9733
Memphis, TN 38105   Free: 800-USS-JUDE
                                  Fax: (901)523-6658
URL: http://www.stjude.org
Contact: Richard C. Shadyac, Exec.Dir.
Desc: Fundraising organization maintaining St. Jude Children's Research Hospital and laboratories in Memphis, TN. Conducts research and children's services and provides patient care in children's catastrophic diseases. *Type:* Association.

American Academy of Pediatrics

Division of Health Policy Research

141 NW Point Blvd.   Ph: (847)228-5005
PO Box 927   Fax: (847)228-9651
Elk Grove Village, IL 60009-0927
E-mail: byudkowsky@aap.org
URL: http://www.aap.org
Contact: Beth K. Yudkowsky, Dir.
Desc: Organization, financing, and delivery of child health care, including studies on third-party payment programs, health care for low-income and high-risk children, office practices, the distribution of pediatricians, evaluations of pediatric programs, functional outcomes, and health workforce. *Type:* Research center.

American Sudden Infant Death Syndrome Institute

2480 Windy Hill Rd., Ste. 380   Ph: (770)612-1030
Marietta, GA 30067   Free: 800-232-SIDS
                                  Fax: (770)612-8277
E-mail: prevent@sids.org
URL: http://www.sids.org
Contact: Alfred Steinschneider, MD PhD, Pres.
Desc: Sudden Infant Death Syndrome (SIDS), commonly known as crib death, including the search for abnormalities in SIDS victims, study of normal and abnormal infant control mechanisms, pregnancy-related factors, identification of infants at risk, effectiveness of preventive measures, effect of SIDS on families, and effect of preventive measures on families. *Type:* Research center.

Association of Maternal and Child Health Programs

1220 19th St. NW Ste 801   Ph: (202)775-0436
Washington, DC 20036   Fax: (202)775-0061
E-mail: chess@amchp.org
URL: http://www.amchp1.org
Contact: Catherine Hess, Exec.Dir.
Desc: Individuals responsible for or involved in the administration of state and territorial maternal and child health programs and programs for children with special health care needs. Seeks to: inform public and private sector decision makers of the health care needs of mothers and children; develop and recommend maternal and child health policies and programs; develop coalitions with other interested organizations. Promotes exchange of ideas and experiences among members; studies and reports on the health of and services for mothers and children; develops models and standards for and provides technical assistance to maternal and child health programs. *Type:* Association.

Ball State University

Public Health Entomology Laboratory

2000 University Ave.   Ph: (765)285-1504
Muncie, IN 47306   Fax: (765)285-2351
E-mail: rpinger@bsu.edu
URL: http://www.bsu.edu/chs/phs/phel.html

Contact: Dr. Robert R. Pinger, Dir.

Desc: Ticks and tick-borne diseases in Indiana, and other insects affecting human and animal health. Projects include a Rocky Mountain spotted fever and lyme disease tick testing program funded by the Indiana State Department of Health. *Type:* Research center.

Baylor College of Medicine

General Clinical Research Center

Texas Children's and the   Ph: (713)798-7038
  Methodist Hospital   Fax: (713)798-7098
1 Baylor Plaza, MC 1-3420
Houston, TX 77030
E-mail: dbier@bcn.tmc.edu

Contact: Dr. Dennis M. Bier, Prog.Dir.

Desc: Cardiology, endocrinology, gastroenterology, genetics, infectious diseases, pulmonary system, pharmacology, immunology, hematology, rheumatology, and renal disease, including studies on ventricular dysrhythmias, hypopituitarism, bile acid metabolism, argininemia, HIV, and renal tubular acidosis. *Type:* Research center.

Baylor College of Medicine

Meyer Center for Developmental Pediatrics

Texas Children's Hospital Feigin Ph: (713)770-3400
  Center   Fax: (713)770-3399
6621 Fannin St., Mail Code 3-
2335
Houston, TX 77030

Desc: Developmentally disabled, developmental pediatrics, learning disabilities, low-birth-weight infants, maternal medications, cytomegalo inclusion virus, congenital rubella syndrome, neonatal intracranial hemorrhage, outcome prematurity, and attention deficit/hyperactivity disorder. *Type:* Research center.

Baylor University

Child Health Research Center

College of Med.   Ph: (713)798-6776
Department of Pediatrics   Fax: (713)798-7119
One Baylor Plaza
Houston, TX 77030
E-mail: mhaymond@bcm.tmc.edu
URL: http://www.kornade.ere.umontreal.ca/~jezequej

Contact: Morey Haymond, MD, Prog.Dir.

Desc: Pediatrics, focusing on the areas of molecular genetics, cell biology, and developmental biology. *Type:* Research center.

Brooklyn College of City University of New York

Infant Study Center

Dept. of Psychology   Ph: (718)951-5033
Brooklyn, NY 11210   Fax: (718)951-4825
E-mail: louiseh@brooklyn.cuny.edu

Contact: Dr. Louise Hainline, Hd.

Desc: Visual development in infancy, including studies of acuity, pattern perception, color vision, eye movement control, and perception of complex events. Assessment procedures utilize photo-refraction methods, visual-evoked response techniques, and electrophysiological studies of dyslexia. *Type:* Research center.

Canadian Institute of Child Health

885 Meadowlands Dr. E., Ste. Ph: (613)224-4144
  512   Fax: (613)224-4145
Ottawa, ON, Canada K2C 3N2
E-mail: cich@igs.net
URL: http://www.cich.ca

Contact: Dawn Walker, Exec.Dir.

Desc: Improving the health and well-being of children and youth in Canada. The objectives to accomplish this vision include monitoring the health and well-being of children and youth; improving the health and well-being of mothers and infants; creating safe, supportive, nurturing environments for children; and encouraging cooperation between consumers, professionals, industry and government agencies to ensure a better life for Canadian children. *Type:* Research center.

Center for Human Nutrition, Inc.

502 S. 44th St., Rm. 3007   Ph: (402)559-5500
Omaha, NE 68105   Fax: (402)559-7302
E-mail: agrandje@unmc.edu

Contact: Ann C. Grandjean, EdD, Dir.

Desc: Basic and clinical nutrition studies, clinical trials, intervention studies, and post marketing studies. *Type:* Research center.

Child Health Research Center

Children's Hospital   Ph: (617)355-6366
Newborn Med.   Fax: (617)355-7677
300 Longwood Ave.
Boston, MA 02115
E-mail: bernfield@a1.tch.harvard.edu

Contact: Dr. Merton Bernfield, Dir.

Desc: Child health, particularly developmental biology. *Type:* Research center.

Child Health Talk

National Black Child Development Institute
1023 15th St. NW, Ste. 600 Ph: (202)387-1281
Washington, DC 20005   Fax: (202)234-1738

Contact: Kim Sanwogou, Editor.

Desc: Provides information and guidance to parents on health issues facing African American children. *Type:* Newsletter.

Child Nutrition Today

Child Nutrition-Program Administration
State Education Dept.
Education Bldg., Rm. 548   Ph: (518)474-3956
Albany, NY 12234-0001   Fax: (518)473-0018

Contact: Diane Colton, Editor.

Desc: Relates school lunch and breakfast programs and their operation to New York school personnel and the community. Also includes regulations, training updates, and best practices. *Type:* Newsletter.

Children's Health Fund

317 E. 64th St.   Ph: (212)535-9400
New York, NY 10021   Fax: (212)535-7488

Contact: Irwin Redlener, M.D., Pres.

Desc: Supports pediatric programs for chldren who are homeless, poor, or have no other access to medical care. Maintains Children's Health Projects in urban and rural areas throughout the United States. Provides mobile medical units in order to bring health care to deserving children. *Type:* Association.

Children's Heart and Health Institute of Texas

PO Box 3966   Ph: (512)887-4505
Corpus Christi, TX 78463   Fax: (512)887-0539

Contact: Laura Berlanga, CEO.

Desc: Pediatric cardiology. Projects include investigations of the prevalence of developmental disabilities and heart disease risk factors in various counties, coronary disease among Hispanic children, arterial sclerotic heart disease, hypertension, and prevention. *Type:* Research center.

Children's Hospice International Newsletter

Ann A. Dailey
2202 Mt. Vernon Ave., Ste. 3C Ph: (703)684-0330
Alexandria, VA 22301   Free: 800-242-4453
                Fax: (703)684-0226

Desc: Examines issues and resources on children's hospice care. Recurring features include a calendar of events, book reviews, and notices of publications available. *Type:* Newsletter.

Children's Hospital of Alabama

S.E. Child Safety Institute

1600 7th Ave. S.   Ph: (205)939-9720
Birmingham, AL 35233   Fax: (205)939-9245

Contact: Dr. Bill King, Dir.

Desc: Poisonings, including studies on prescription drug ingestions in preschool age children, research on adolescent parasuicides, and epidemiology of childhood trauma. Provides statewide poison control. *Type:* Research center.

Children's Hospital Oakland Research Institute

747 52nd St.   Ph: (510)428-3502
Oakland, CA 94609   Fax: (510)428-3608
E-mail: blubin@mail.cho.org
URL: http://www.kidsfirst.org

Contact: Dr. Bertram Lubin, Dir. of Med.Res.

Desc: Biomedical research, including cellular immunology and the development of antigenicity, lipid metabolism, and the structure and function of cellular and model membranes, with emphasis on signal transduction, the molecular components involved in metabolic pathways, hypertension, vascular disease, hematology, platelet aggregation, gene therapy, cystic fibrosis, experimental surgery, and nutrition as these are related to pediatric problems. Special areas of research include in sickle cell disease, bioiron metabolism, cystic fibrosis, cancer gene markers, storage diseases, and pulmonary function in neonates. *Type:* Research center.

Children's Hospital Research Center

3020 Children's Way, MC 5074 Ph: (619)576-5934
San Diego, CA 92123   Fax: (619)495-8589
E-mail: CRS5074@aol.com

Contact: Carl R. Schneiderman, Exec.Dir.

Desc: Causes and prevention of childhood diseases, including studies in diagnostic techniques and methods, neurosciences, autism, language development, sudden infant death syndrome, and industrial technology. *Type:* Research center.

Children's Hospital Research Foundation

3333 Burnet Ave.   Ph: (513)636-4588
Cincinnati, OH 45229-3039 Fax: (513)636-8453
E-mail: thomas.boat@chmcc.org
URL: http://www.chmcc.org/chrf.html

Contact: Thomas F. Boat, MD, Dir.

Desc: Molecular and cell biology, biochemistry, physiology, microbiology, pathology, and clinical investigations of infancy and childhood, and animal models of childhood illnesses. Research activities are carried out in the divisions of adolescent medicine, allergy/immunology, general pediatrics, development biology, cardiology, molecular cardiovascular biology, clinical pharmacology, critical care medicine, emergency medicine, endocrinology, gastroenterology, hematology-oncology, human genetics, infectious disease, developmental disabilities, inflammatory mechanisms, molecular cardiovascular biology, neonatology, nephrology, neurology, pathology, child psychology, child psychiatry, pulmonary biology, pulmonary medicine, radiology, rheumatology, and surgery. *Type:* Research center.

Children's Hospital Research Foundation

Clinical Research Center

3333 Burnet Ave. Ph: (513)636-4412
Cincinnati, OH 45229-3039 Fax: (513)636-4695
E-mail: james.heubi@chmcc.org
URL: http://www.chmcc.org/crc.html
Contact: Dr. James Heubi, Dir.

Desc: Pediatrics, including studies of congenital and acquired diseases of the gastrointestinal tract, pancreas, and
liver, cholestatic liver disease, hepatic storage diseases, and
cystic fibrosis. Endocrinology program studies growth, diabetes mellitus, hypertension, child and adult bone disease
(including rickets and osteoporosis), and insulin sensitivity. *Type:* Research center.

Children's Research Institute

700 Children's Dr. Ph: (614)722-2700
Columbus, OH 43205 Fax: (614)722-2716
E-mail: pjohnson@chi.osu.edu
URL: http://www.childrenscolumbus.org
Contact: Phil Johnson, Contact.

Desc: Neonatology, pediatrics, children's cancer chemotherapy, cancer immunology, molecular retrovirology, gastroenterology, genetics, gene transfer infectious diseases,
nutrition, pathology, surgery, virology, metabolic disorders, cystic fibrosis, pulmonology, pharmacology/
toxicology, cardiology, and clinical problems of infancy
and childhood. *Type:* Research center.

Children's Research Institute

111 Michigan Ave., NW Ph: (202)884-4007
Washington, DC 20010 Fax: (202)884-5988
E-mail: cfinney@cnmc.org
URL: http://www.cnmc.org
Contact: Gordon Avery, MD, COO.

Desc: Pediatric research on the prevention, management,
and treatment of childhood diseases. Studies focus on
tumor cell biology, brain research, molecular virology and
genetics, AIDS and other infectious diseases, cardiovasular
disease, and pharmacy. *Type:* Research center.

Children's Services Report

Manisses Communications Group, Inc.
208 Governor St. Ph: (401)831-6020
Providence, RI 02906-3246 Free: 800-333-7771
  Fax: (401)861-6370
E-mail: manissescs@manisses.com

Desc: Provides news and analysis on children's programs
in mental health, addiction, juvenile justice, and social services. Covers information on the impact of managed care,
public policy, field developments, and case studies. *Type:*
Newsletter.

Conte Institute for Environmental Health

The Berkshire Common Ph: (413)443-1740
2 South St., Ste. 370 Fax: (413)443-1740
Pittsfield, MA 01201
Contact: Arthur D. Bloom, MD, Pres.

Desc: Environmental health, biological aspects of remediation, genetic studies of differences in individual variation
in response to environmental agents, and environmental
factors in neurodegenerative disorders. Operates the International Scientific Program in Environmental Health to
set research priorities in Central and Eastern Europe. *Type:*
Research center.

Cornell University

Children's Clinical Research Center

New York Hospital--Cornell Ph: (212)746-3484
  Med. Ctr. Fax: (212)746-8821
525 E. 68th St., Rm. M425
New York, NY 10021
Contact: Maria I. New, MD, Prog.Dir.

Desc: Steroidogenesis, hypertension, growth disorders,
bone mineral metabolism, thalassemia, psychosocial fail-
ure-to-thrive, renal disorders, and pediatric AIDS. The
Center's eight beds, specialized equipment, and staff provide a multidisciplinary, controlled research environment
separate from facilities serving the Medical College. *Type:*
Research center.

Cornell University

Laboratory of Pediatric Critical Care

525 68th St. Ph: (212)746-3056
New York, NY 10021 Fax: (212)746-8332
E-mail: hmushay@mail.ed.cornell.edu
Contact: Dr. H. Michael Ushay, Dir.

Desc: Adrenergic receptor pharmacology, including recep-
tor-related events at the cellular and molecular levels, and
molecular biology of acute lung injury. *Type:* Research
center.

Daycare Health

Mathanna Publications
PO Box 5351 Ph: (206)671-4350
Bellingham, WA 98227-9970
Contact: Paula B. Kobos, Editor.

Desc: Shares multidisciplinary health information with
child care and health care professionals, educators, and
regulatory agencies. *Type:* Newsletter.

Duke University

Division of Pediatric Hematology Oncology

Box 2916 Ph: (919)684-3401
Durham, NC 27710 Fax: (919)681-7950
E-mail: rosof001@mc.duke.edu
URL: http://www.canctr.mc.duke.edu/PHO_OLD/pho
Contact: Dr. Philip Rosoff, MD, Div.Ch.

Desc: Clinical trials of new cancer therapies for children.
Special interests include neuro-oncology and bone marrow
transplantation. *Type:* Research center.

Duke University

Pediatric Cardiac Catheterization Laboratory

Pediatric Cardiology Ph: (919)684-3574
Duke Univ. Med. Ctr. Fax: (919)681-8927
PO Box 3090, Rm. 7607 DHN
Durham, NC 27710
E-mail: olaugoo1@mc.duke.edu
Contact: Dr. Martin P. O'Laughlin, MD, Dir.

Desc: Pediatric cardiology, including development of cath-
eter-delivered devices to treat congenital heart disease.
Type: Research center.

Florida State University

Center for Prevention and Early Intervention

1339 E. Lafayette St. Ph: (904)644-6166
Tallahassee, FL 32301-4770 Fax: (904)644-0492
E-mail: mgraham@mailer.fsu.edu
URL: http://www.ispa.fsu.edu/cpeip/
Contact: Dr. Mimi A. Graham, Dir.

Desc: Child growth and development, particularly the first
five years; maternal and child health and early intervention
issues on a state and national basis. Seeks to build families,
prevent disabilities and other handicapping conditions,
and minimize environmental and biological risks to young
children. *Type:* Research center.

**General Clinical Research Center at Children's
Hospital of Philadelphia**

Abramson Res. Ctr. Ph: (215)590-2017
34th & Civic Center Blvd., Rm. Fax: (215)590-2025
  1202
Philadelphia, PA 19104
E-mail: starr@email.chop.edu

URL: http://www.chop.edu/research/programs/gcrc/gcrc.
htm
Contact: Stuart E. Starr, MD, Prog.Dir.

Desc: Biomedicine, allergy and immunology, cardiology,
diabetes endocrinology, gastroenterology, gene therapy,
genetics, hematology, infectious disease, metabolism,
neonatology, neurology, nutrition, and oncology. *Type:*
Research center.

**General Clinical Research Center at Children's
Hospital of Pittsburgh**

3705 5th Ave. Ph: (412)692-5573
Pittsburgh, PA 15213 Fax: (412)692-6783
Contact: Dr. Peter A. Lee, Dir.

Desc: Biomedicine, allergy and immunology, endocrinology, hematology and oncology, infectious disease, metabolism, nutrition, otolaryngology, pulmonology,
pharmacology, transplantation surgery, gastroenterology,
and diabetes mellitus. *Type:* Research center.

Howard University

Child Development Center

Dept. of Pediatrics and Child Ph: (202)806-6973
  Health Fax: (202)806-7940
College of Medicine
525 Bryant St., NW Ste.100
Box 19
Washington, DC 20059
Contact: Sheila J. Moseend, Dir.

Desc: Child development and handicapping conditions of
childhood, including interdisciplinary studies in pediatrics, neurology, genetics, psychology, speech pathology,
and infant development. *Type:* Research center.

**Indiana University-Purdue University at
Indianapolis**

Riley Child and Adolescent Psychiatry Clinic

702 Barnhill Dr., Rm. 3701 Ph: (317)274-8162
Indianapolis, IN 46202-5200 Fax: (317)278-0609
E-mail: cmcdougl@iupui.edu
Contact: Christopher J. McDougle, MD, Dir.

Desc: Clinical phenomenology, neurobiology and psychopharmacology of autistic and related pervasive developmental disorders, obsessive-compulsive and chronic tic
disorders, attention-deficit and other disruptive behavior
disorders, and mood disorders. *Type:* Research center.

Institute for Health and Disability

University of Minnesota, Box Ph: (612)624-3939
  721 Fax: (612)626-2134
420 Delaware St. SE
Minneapolis, MN 55455
E-mail: instihd@tc.umn.edu
URL: http://www.peds.umn.edu./centers/ind
Contact: Marty Smith, Exec.Dir.

Desc: Psychological and social development of children
with chronic illness and disability. Activities include child
and family assessments, longitudinal research, developing
data focused on children with disabilities, and managed
care. *Type:* Research center.

Jewish Child Care Association of New York

575 Lexington Ave. Ph: (212)371-1313
New York, NY 10022 Fax: (212)371-1275
Contact: Paul Gitelson, DSW, Exec.V.Pres.

Desc: Provides services, including day care, mental health
and preventive programs, adoption assistance, tutoring,
group homes, foster home care, and extended residential
care to children. *Type:* Association.

Johns Hopkins University

Center for Adolescent Health Promotion and Disease Prevention

School of Hygiene and Public Health   Ph: (410)614-3953
Fax: (410)614-3956
2007 E. Monument St.
Baltimore, MD 21205
E-mail: calexand@jhsph.edu
URL: http://www.jhsph.edu/hao/cah/ceninfo.htm

Contact: Dr. Cheryl Alexander, Dir.

Desc: Health needs of adolescents, including developmental transitions which serve as opportunities for community-based health promotion interventions; interventions to modify risk-taking behaviors; interventions which involve the family, school, and community settings; academic-community partnerships to enhance the delivery of health services to adolescents; and dissemination of adolescent health information to practitioners and policy makers. *Type:* Research center.

Johns Hopkins University

Child Health Research Center

600 N. Wolfe St., CMSC 2-116   Ph: (410)955-5976
Baltimore, MD 21287   Fax: (410)955-9850
E-mail: gdover@welchlink.welch.jhu.edu

Contact: Dr. George Dover, Dir.

Desc: Applies molecular biology techniques to the diagnosis, treatment, and prevention of genetic and acquired hematologic disorders in children. Activities focus on developing techniques to analyze genes and gene products, especially those required for normal development. *Type:* Research center.

Legacy Clinical Research and Technology Center

1225 NE 2nd Ave. .   Ph: (503)413-2191
Portland, OR 97208-3950   Fax: (503)413-4942
E-mail: lkiesow@lhs.org
URL: http://www.centerwatch.com

Contact: Dr. Lutz A. Kiesow, Ch. of Res.

Desc: Cardiology, pediatrics, neonatalogy, trauma, burns, infectious diseases, pediatric/adult endocrinology, pediatric/adult diabetes, ophthalmology, neurology. *Type:* Research center.

Massachusetts General Hospital

Pediatric Pulmonary Unit

VBKBA 015, 55 Fruit St.   Ph: (617)726-5576
Boston, MA 02114   Fax: (617)726-1036
E-mail: shannon.daniel@mgh.harvard.edu
URL: http://www.mgh.harvard.edu

Contact: Daniel Shannon, MD, Ch., Pediatriac Pulmonary Unit.

Desc: Sudden infant death, the role of mast cells and eosinophils in asthma and the regulation of lung development. *Type:* Research center.

McGill University

Cytogenetic Laboratory

Montreal Children's Hosp., Rm. A-808   Ph: (514)934-4432
Fax: (514)934-4385
2300 Tupper St.
Montreal, PQ, Canada H3H 1P3
E-mail: aduncyt@mchnurse.mchis.mcg

Contact: Dr. Alessandra Duncan, Dir.

Desc: Cytogenetics, molecular genetics, reproductive genetics, and teratology. *Type:* Research center.

McGill University

Montreal Children's Hospital Research Institute

2300 Tupper St.   Fax: (514)934-4331
Montreal, PQ, Canada H3Z 2Z3
E-mail: MBDJ@musica.mcgill.ca

Contact: Roy Gravel, Dir.

Desc: Basic, clinical, and epidemiologic research into various disorders affecting infants and children, including diabetes, prematurity cystic fibrosis, abnormal growth, learning disabilities, hyperactivity, and genetic diseases. *Type:* Research center.

Medical University of South Carolina

Department of Pediatrics

Division of Genetics and Child Development

The Vince Moseley Center

171 Ashley Ave.   Ph: (803)792-3190
Charleston, SC 29425   Fax: (803)792-6799
E-mail: pais@musc.edu
URL: http://www.musc.edu

Contact: Dr. Michelle Macias, Med.Dir.

Desc: Genetic disorders and diseases; learning problems and communication disorders research, including attention deficit disorder, cognitive strengths and weaknesses, physical therapy, speech/language pathology, family dynamics, and self-esteem. *Type:* Research center.

Miami Children's Hospital Research Institute

3100 SW 62nd St.   Ph: (305)663-8522
Miami, FL 33155   Fax: (305)663-2461
E-mail: richard.warren@mch.com

Contact: Dr. Richard J. Warren, Admin.Dir.

Desc: Genetic vectoring, nutrition, hematology/oncology, immunology, forensic DNA identity, cardiac surgery, critical care physiology, nephrology. *Type:* Research center.

National Cancer Institute

Pediatric Oncology Group

Statistical Office

104 N. Main St., Ste. 600   Ph: (352)392-5198
Gainesville, FL 32601   Fax: (352)392-8162
E-mail: jon@pog.ufl.edu
URL: http://www.pog.ufl.edu

Contact: Dr. Jonathan Shuster, Gp. Stat.

Desc: Pathobiology of childhood cancers, focusing on control measures and improving treatment outcomes. *Type:* Research center.

New England Medical Center Hospitals, Inc.

National Pediatric Trauma Registry

Department of PM & R   Ph: (617)636-5037
750 Washington St.   Fax: (617)636-5513
Box 75 K-R
Boston, MA 02111
E-mail: cdiscala_tra@opal.tufts.edu
URL: http://www.nemc.org/rehab

Contact: Dr. Carla DiScala, Dir.

Desc: Information registry supporting research on childhood trauma, including causes of pediatric injury, morbidity and mortality consequences, treatment efficacies, and pediatric rehabilitation services. *Type:* Research center.

Pediatric Clinical Trials International

700 Children's Dr.   Ph: (614)722-2551
Columbus, OH 43205-2696   Fax: (614)722-2662
E-mail: PinyerdB@PedCTI.com
URL: http://www.centerwatch.com

Contact: Belinda Pinyerd, PhD, Dir.,Oper.

Desc: Childhood illnesses, pharmacology, metabolic and infectious diseases, drug metabolism in children, and endocrine disorders of children. *Type:* Research center.

Pediatric Oncology Group

Operations Office   Ph: (312)482-9944
645 N. Michigan Ave., Ste. 910   Fax: (312)482-9460
Chicago, IL 60611

Contact: Mary Klonowski, Admin.

Desc: Investigations of childhood cancers. Provides a national cooperative mechanism to promote new treatment methods through comparison of patients who receive different treatments. *Type:* Research center.

Pediatric Research Institute

Cardinal Glennon Children's Hospital   Ph: (314)577-5623
Fax: (314)577-5398
3662 Park Ave.
St. Louis, MO 63110
E-mail: raycg@slu.edu

Contact: C. George Ray, MD, Dir.

Desc: Surfactant production in lung development, intrauterine growth retardation, regulation of gene expression in liver and muscle cells, oncogene expression, the role of the osteoblast in bone homeostasis, and microbial genetics. *Type:* Research center.

Pediatric Rheumatoid Clinic

Duke Med. Ctr.   Ph: (252)684-6575
Box 3212   Fax: (252)684-6616
Durham, NC 27710

Contact: Dr. Deborah Kredich, Contact.

Desc: Clinical and laboratory pediatric rheumatology and immunology. *Type:* Research center.

Research Institute of The Hospital for Sick Children

555 University Ave.   Ph: (416)813-5724
Toronto, ON, Canada M5G 1X8   Fax: (416)813-5085
URL: http://www.sickkids.on.ca

Contact: Dr. Manuel Buchwald, Dir. and Ch. of Res.

Desc: Basic and clinical research focused on improving, understanding, preventing, treating and curing children's diseases. Six disciplinary research programs: genetics and genomic biology; structural biology and biochemistry; cell biology; developmental biology; integrative biology; population health sciences. *Type:* Research center.

RTC for Children's Mental Health—Update

Research and Training Center for Children's Mental Health
University of South Florida   Ph: (813)974-4661
Florida Mental Health Institute
13301 Bruce B. Downs Blvd.
Tampa, FL 33612

Desc: Focuses on "improving services for children with emotional disabilities." Recurring features include news of research. *Type:* Newsletter.

Rush University

Pediatric Critical Care Research Center

Rush-Presbyterian-St. Luke's Medical Center   Ph: (312)942-6194
Fax: (312)942-4370
1653 W. Congress Pkwy.
Chicago, IL 60612
E-mail: sbarnes2@rpslsnc.edu

Contact: Dr. Steven Barnes, Res.Dir.

Desc: Pediatric patients, analgesia (for pain relief), sedation, bronchilitis, neonatal tetenis in Nigeria. *Type:* Research center.

St. Jude Children's Research Hospital

332 N. Lauderdale   Ph: (901)495-3301
Memphis, TN 38105-2794   Fax: (901)525-2720
E-mail: info@stjude.org
URL: http://www.stjude.org

Contact: Arthur W. Nienhuis, MD, Dir.

Desc: Pediatric studies in hematology, oncology, infectious diseases, neurology, cardiopulmonary diseases, diagnostic imaging, pharmacokinetics, psychology, and pathology; biomedical studies in biochemistry, immunology, pharmacology, virology and molecular biology, tumor cell biology, experimental oncology, genetics, biostatistics, structural biology, surgery and developmental neurobiology. *Type:* Research center.

Shriners Hospital for Children (St. Louis, MO)
Metabolic Research Unit
2001 S. Lindbergh Blvd.
St. Louis, MO 63131-3597
Ph: (314)432-3600
Fax: (314)432-2930
Contact: Michael P. Whyte, MD, Med.Dir.
Desc: Metabolic bone diseases and skeletal dysplasias in children, including evaluation of potential medical therapies and analysis of inheritance factors. *Type:* Research center.

Sleep Disorders Center for Children
Children's Med. Ctr. of Dallas
1935 Motor St.
Dallas, TX 75235
Ph: (214)640-2793
Fax: (214)640-7671
Contact: Dr. John Herman, Dir.
Desc: Studies infants with respiratory problems, children with obstructive sleep apnea, and excessive daytime sleepiness (narcolepsy). Conducts studies of vigilance and related visual evoked potentials. *Type:* Research center.

Society for Pediatric Research
3400 Research Forest Dr., Ste. B7
The Woodlands, TX 77381
Ph: (281)419-0052
Fax: (281)419-0082
E-mail: info@aps-spr.org
URL: http://www.aps-spr.org
Contact: Debbie Anagnostelis, Contact.
Desc: Infancy and childhood diseases. *Type:* Research center.

Southwest SIDS Research Institute, Inc.
100 Medical Dr.
Lake Jackson, TX 77566-5674
Ph: (409)299-2814
Free: 800-245-SIDS
Fax: (409)297-6682
E-mail: swsids@sat.net
URL: http://www.swsids.hicd.com
Contact: Judith A. Henslee, Exec.Dir.
Desc: Sudden Infant Death Sydrome (SIDS). *Type:* Research center.

State University of New York Health Science Center at Brooklyn
Child Psychiatry Research Program
451 Clarkson Ave., Box 32
J Bldg.
Brooklyn, NY 11203
Ph: (718)270-1430
Fax: (718)778-5397
Contact: Dr. Katz, Dir.
Desc: Behavioral and physiological investigation of development and pathology. Projects include observations of mother-child interaction during infancy and later stages, the objective study of children with behavior disorders, autism, minimal brain damage, and mental retardation. *Type:* Research center.

State University of New York Health Science Center at Brooklyn
Infant and Child Behavior Laboratory
450 Clarkson Ave., Box 1203
Brooklyn, NY 11203
Ph: (718)270-2598
Fax: (718)270-3910
Contact: Dr. Joan Hittelman, Dir.
Desc: Infant development, including evaluation of various methods of eye protection in jaundiced newborn infants undergoing phototherapy with respect to behavioral, physiological, and biochemical parameters; studies of the contribution of the neonate's sex to the parent-child interaction, particularly with respect to neonatal eye contact and maternal attitudes toward the baby; and follow-up of high risk infants (infants born weighing less than 1000 grams and infants exposed to the HIV virus). *Type:* Research center.

Temple University
Motor Development Laboratory
Pearson Hall
Philadelphia, PA 19122
Ph: (215)204-1960
Fax: (215)204-4662
Contact: Dr. Marcella V. Ridenour, Dir.
Desc: Motor development of infants and young children, including studies on safety of toys, juvenile furniture, cribs, strollers, walkers, high chairs, tricycles and wheeled toys, and playgrounds. Performs biomechanics analysis of infants and young children and evaluations of toys and play equipment through the use of motion pictures. *Type:* Research center.

Texas Scottish Rite Hospital for Children
Research Department
2222 Welborn St.
Dallas, TX 75219
Ph: (214)559-7877
Fax: (214)559-7872
Contact: Richard H. Browne, PhD, Admin.Dir. of Res.
Desc: Treatment of children with orthopedic and neuromuscular disorders. Primary areas of focus are bioengineering and orthopedic biomechanics, including Ilizarov fixators, spine mechanics, spinal implants design and evaluation, and physical properties of bone; and neurophysiology, including gait analysis and muscle strength assessment. *Type:* Research center.

United Nations Children's Fund
United Nations Children's Fund
333 E. 38th St.
New York, NY 10016
Ph: (212)326-7344
Fax: (212)326-7768
E-mail: netmaster@unicef.org
URL: http://www.unicef.org/
Desc: The United Nations Children's Fund database contains information on the work of UNICEF, including its major programs in child survival and development, its advocacy of the rights of the child and its long-term human development efforts, as well as its emergency humanitarian role. Publications information, catalogs, statistics, and other details are available on this site as well. *Type:* Database.

U.S. Department of Health and Human Services
Administration for Children and Families
National Center on Child Abuse and Neglect
330 C St., S.W.
Washington, DC 20447
Ph: (202)385-7565
Free: 800--FYI-3366
Fax: (202)385-3206
E-mail: nccanch@calib.com
URL: http://www.calib.com/nccanch
Contact: Candy Hughes, Proj.Dir.
Desc: Conducts research; collects, analyzes, and disseminates information; provides assistance to states and communities in developing programs and activities related to the prevention, identification, and treatment of child abuse and neglect; and coordinates Federal efforts to combat child maltreatment. *Type:* Research center.

U.S. Department of Health and Human Services
Food and Drug Administration
Center for Biologics Evaluation and Research
Laboratory of Pediatric Diseases
1401 Rockville Pike, HFM 460
Rockville, MD 20852
Ph: (301)496-5041
Fax: (301)496-1810
Contact: Ronald E. Lundquist, PhD, Actg.Chf.
Desc: Pathogenesis and molecular biology of childhood infections (such as polio and measles), and their epidemiology and prevention. Emphasizes attenuated, recombinant (vaccinia, adenovirus), or genetically engineered vaccines. *Type:* Research center.

U.S. Department of Health and Human Services
National Cancer Institute
Division of Clinical Sciences
Pediatric Oncology Branch
10 Center Dr. MSC-1928
NIH Bldg. 10, Rm. 13N240
9000 Rockville Pike
Bethesda, MD 20892-1928
Ph: (301)496-4256
Fax: (301)402-0575
URL: http://www.nih.gov
Contact: Lee J. Helman, MD, Chf.
Desc: Acute leukemias, non-Hodgkin's malignant lymphomas (especially Burkitt's lymphoma), soft-tis sue sarcomas, osteogenic sarcoma, Ewing's sarcoma, neuroblastoma, and children with HIV infection. Children and adolescents are accepted for treatment. *Type:* Research center.

U.S. Department of Health and Human Services
National Center for Infectious Diseases
Division of Bacterial and Mycotic Diseases
Childhood and Respirtory Diseases Branch
Mail Stop C23
1600 Clifton Rd., N.E.
Atlanta, GA 30333
Ph: (404)639-2215
Fax: (404)639-3970
Contact: Tiffany Neal, Contact.
Desc: Laboratory and epidemiologic investigations of organisms except enteric and sexually transmitted diseases. Principal subjects of study are influenzae, type b; meningitidis; Group A streptococcus; Group B streptococcus; Brazilian purpuric fever, sipneumoniae, legionella infections, chlamydia and mycoplasma infections, and otitis media. *Type:* Research center.

U.S. Department of Health and Human Services
National Institute of Mental Health
Intramural Research Programs Division (Clinical Research)
Child Psychiatry Branch
NIH Bldg. 10, Rm. 3N-202
10 Center Dr., MSC 1600
Bethesda, MD 20892-1600
Ph: (301)496-6080
Fax: (301)402-0296
E-mail: rapoport@helix.nih.gov
Contact: Judith L. Rapoport, MD, Chf.
Desc: Biological aspects of child psychiatry, including childhood schizophrenia, obsessive compulsive disorder, and hyperactivity. Areas of interest include pediatric psychopharmacology and brain imaging in child psychiatry. *Type:* Research center.

U.S. Department of Health and Human Services
National Institutes of Health
National Institute of Child Health and Human Development
9000 Rockville Pike
Bethesda, MD 20892
Ph: (301)496-5133
Fax: (301)402-1104
URL: http://www.nih.gov/nichd/
Contact: Duane F. Alexander, MD, Director.
Desc: The Institute conducts and supports biomedical and behavioral research on child health and maternal health;

on problems of human development, with special reference to mental retardation; and on family structure, the dynamics of human population, and the reproductive process. Information related to these research findings is disseminated to other researchers, medical practitioners, and the general public to improve the health of children and their families. *Type:* Government agency, office, or program.

University of Alabama at Birmingham

Civitan International Research Center/Alabama UAP

1719 6th Ave. S. Ph: (205)934-8900
Birmingham, AL 35294-0021 Fax: (205)975-6330
E-mail: cramey@civmail.circ.uab.edu
URL: http://www.circ.uab.edu

Contact: Dr. Sharon Ramey, Co-Dir.

Desc: Stress in families with a handicapped child, parents' perception of temperament of handicapped and non-handicapped infants, and developmentally disabled individuals and their families. Projects include studies of the memory function of children who are mentally retarded, the relationship between cognitive development and increasing auditory impairment of people with Down's syndrome, Head Start Program research, a Patient Outcomes Research Team, and the effects of therapeutic positioning on functional activities. *Type:* Research center.

University of California, San Francisco

Pediatric Clinical Research Center

Department of Pediatrics Ph: (415)476-2171
Moffit Hospital, Rm. 679 Fax: (415)476-3466
San Francisco, CA 94143
E-mail: wara@itsa.ucsf.edu

Contact: Diane W. Wara, MD, Dir.

Desc: Behavioral sciences, biochemistry, endocrinology, gastroenterology, genetics, hematology, immunology, nephrology, oncology, nutrition, pharmacology, and radiation therapy, and HIV. *Type:* Research center.

University of California, Santa Barbara

Autism Research Center

Res. Off., Graduate Sch. of Ph: (805)893-2416
 Educ.
Phelps Hall, Rm. 2206
Santa Barbara, CA
URL: http://education.ucsb.edu/~doniel/autism.html

Contact: Merith Cosden, Ph.D., Dir.

Desc: Autism, especially education for autistic children; the effect of treatment programs on the child, the child's family and the integration of the child in the school setting and the community; and the development and use of non-aversive treatment for severe problems such as self-injury and aggression, as often seen in autistic children. *Type:* Research center.

University of Chicago

La Rabida Research and Policy Center for the Study of Children and Families with Special Health Care Needs

E. 65th St. & Lake Michigan Ph: (773)363-6700
Chicago, IL 60649 Fax: (773)363-7160
E-mail: edenekwo@midway.uchicago.edu

Contact: Dr. Edem Ekwo, PhD, Exec.Dir.

Desc: Economic, psychological, sociological, educational, cultural, and medical effects of childhood chronic illness and disability on families and society. Areas of research include pediatric HIV/AIDS, cross-cultural themes, patterns of health care financing, effective foster care for medically complex children, community-based service systems, and the nature of family constellations, including the tracking of child development in varying family and institutional contexts, and intervention studies. *Type:* Research center.

University of Cincinnati

Shriners Hospitals for Children--Cincinnati

3229 Burnet Ave. Ph: (513)872-6000
Cincinnati, OH 45229-3095 Fax: (513)872-6999

Contact: Glenn D. Warden, MD, Dir.

Desc: Burns, including nutrition, infection, coverage (autografts/allografts), conversion (topical antimicrobials), pain, scar formation, and care and treatment of children who have suffered from thermal injuries and resulting problems. *Type:* Research center.

University of Colorado

General Clinical Research Center--Pediatric

Health Sci. Ctr. Ph: (303)837-2957
4200 E. 9th Ave. Fax: (303)764-8407
Box C225
Denver, CO 80262

Contact: K. Michael Hambidge, MD, Prog.Dir.

Desc: Developmental behavior, diabetes mellitus, gastroenterology, genetics, hematology, immunology, infectious disease, metabolism, neonatology, neurology, nephrology, nutrition, and pulmonary physiology. *Type:* Research center.

University of Florida

Institute for Child Health Policy

5700 SW 34th St., Ste. 323 Ph: (352)392-5904
Gainesville, FL 32608 Fax: (352)392-8822
E-mail: info@ichp.edu
URL: http://www.ichp.edu

Contact: Steve A. Freedman, PhD, Dir.

Desc: Child health policy and family and child health care delivery issues, including development of an equitable and comprehensive child health policy model for states; development of case management programs for children with special health care needs; development of health care financing strategies, including school enrollment-based health insurance; and comprehensive program development and health services research and evaluation. *Type:* Research center.

University of Iowa

Child Health Research Center

Department of Pediatrics Ph: (319)356-0469
Iowa City, IA 52242 Fax: (319)356-4855
E-mail: frank-morriss@uiowa.edu

Contact: Dr. Frank H. Morriss, Jr., Dir.

Desc: Pediatrics, particularly developmental molecular biology. Activities emphasize the identification and localization of genes on the human genome, investigations of the mechanisms used by specific genes to regulate the synthesis and timing of gene products, and a study on the effects of gene products on the structure and function of developing tissues. *Type:* Research center.

University of Kansas

Child and Family Research Center

4001 Dole Ph: (913)864-0528
Lawrence, KS 66045 Fax: (913)864-5202
E-mail: cckansas@kuhub.cc.ukans.edu
URL: http://www.ukans.edu/hdfl/public-html

Contact: Marion O'Brien, Dir.

Desc: Processes of social-emotional development and learning in children, early receptive and expressive language development, early intervention, and parent-infant interaction in normal and high-risk infants. *Type:* Research center.

University of Maryland

Sudden Infant Death Syndrome Institute

22 S. Greene St., Rm. N5W67 Ph: (410)328-3363
Baltimore, MD 21201 Fax: (410)328-0645
E-mail: narmeny@umabnet.abumd.edu

Contact: Robert Meny, Contact.

Desc: Sudden Infant Death Syndrome (SIDS), including efforts to detect abnormalities present before or at death, correlation of data from clinical evaluation of infants at risk (especially those suffering from apnea or cyanosis), development of animal models to test hypotheses about the etiology of SIDS, examination of tissues from infants who have died from SIDS and other illnesses, animal studies to determine the relationship of specific tissue abnormalities to cause of death, and the psychological effect of infant death on family members. *Type:* Research center.

University of Miami

Mailman Center for Child Development

D-820 Ph: (305)243-6801
PO Box 016820 Fax: (305)243-5978
Miami, FL 33101
E-mail: turbano@peds.med.miami.edu
URL: http://pediatrics.med.miami.edu

Contact: Mary Theresa Urbano, PhD, Actg.Dir.

Desc: Developmental disabilities, genetic disorders, sensory disorders, and child behavior and development, including prevention and intervention strategies. *Type:* Research center.

University of Nebraska Medical Center

Munroe-Meyer Institute

985450 Nebraska Medical Ph: (402)559-6400
 Center Free: 800-65M-EYER
Omaha, NE 68198-5450 Fax: (402)559-5737
E-mail: mleibowi@unmc.edu
URL: http://www.unmc.edu/mrimedia/meyertes.html

Contact: Dr. Bruce Buehler, Dir.

Desc: Problems and needs of children and adults (medical, genetic, or behavioral), including interdisciplinary studies on congenital disorders, dentistry, infant development, language and cognitive disorders, behavioral disorders, and sensory/motor development. Subject populations include families receiving service at the Institute, infants, preschoolers, adolescents, and adults with developmental disabilities. *Type:* Research center.

University of South Florida

Research and Training Center for Children's Mental Health

Florida Mental Health Institute Ph: (813)974-4661
13301 Bruce B. Downs Blvd. Fax: (813)974-6257
Tampa, FL 33612-3899
E-mail: friedman@hal.fmhi.usf.edu
URL: http://www.lumpy.fmhi.usf.edu

Contact: Robert M. Friedman, PhD, Exec.Dir.

Desc: Children and adolescents with emotional disturbances, focusing on characteristics and development; factors associated with successful transition to adulthood; the relationship between functional abilities and successful employment, residential, educational, and social outcomes; identification and evaluation of model programs to assist transition from school to work; efficacy and cost-effectiveness of alternatives to residential treatment; and financing options, incentives, and disincentives for community and home-treatment. *Type:* Research center.

University of Tennessee

Center of Excellence in Pediatric Pharmacokinetics and Therapeutics

Pharmacokinetics
St. Jude Children's Res. Hosp.
332 N. Lauderdale
Memphis, TN 38105
Ph: (901)495-3663
Fax: (901)525-6869

E-mail: william.evans@stjude.org

Contact: Dr. William E. Evans, Co-Dir.

Desc: Drug therapy research in children. Seeks to promote and protect children's well-being by minimizing or eliminating pharmaceutical risks. *Type:* Research center.

University of Texas Medical Branch at Galveston

Child Health Research Center

Department of Pediatrics
301 University Blvd.
Galveston, TX 77555-0351
Ph: (409)772-1596
Fax: (409)747-4995

E-mail: pogra@utmb.edu
URL: http://www.utmb.edu/pedi/

Contact: Dr. P.L. Ogra, Chm.

Desc: Pediatrics, focusing on applying research in developmental immunology, improving health, and combatting childhhod diseases. *Type:* Research center.

University of Wisconsin--Madison

Children's Cancer Group

Department of Pediatrics
Div. of Hematology/Oncology, K4/438
600 Highland Ave.
Madison, WI 53792
Ph: (608)263-6200
Fax: (608)263-4226

E-mail: psqaynon@facstaff.wisc.edu
URL: http://www2.medsch.wisc.edu/

Contact: Dr. Paul Gaynon, Prin.Invest.

Desc: Pediatric oncology, including trials of new treatment regimens. *Type:* Research center.

University of Wisconsin--Madison

Pediatric Pulmonary Center

Clinical Science Center
Univeristy Hospitals
Madison, WI 53792-4108
Ph: (608)263-8555
Fax: (608)263-0510

E-mail: cggreen@facstaff.wisc.edu
URL: http://www2.medsch.wisc.edu/childrenshops/ppc/ppchome.html

Contact: Dr. Christopher G. Green, MD, Dir.

Desc: Cystic fibrosis and other respiratory diseases of children. *Type:* Research center.

USDA Agricultural Research Service

Children's Nutrition Research Center

Baylor College of Med.
1100 Bates St.
Houston, TX 77030
Ph: (713)798-7000
Fax: (713)798-7098

E-mail: dbier@bcm.tmc.edu
URL: http://www.bcm.tmc.edu/cnrc

Contact: Dr. Dennis M. Bier, Dir.

Desc: Nutrition for infants, children, adolescents, and women during lactation and pregnancy. Conducts studies to determine dietary standards and measure nutritional status in children from conception through adolescence and in pregnant and lactating women, develops methods to investigate specific nutrient needs of infants, examines the relationship between nutrient, growth, and development, defines nutrient needs for optimal growth and development, and establishes normal biochemical standards for use in nutritional assessments. *Type:* Research center.

Washington University in St. Louis

William Greenleaf Eliot Division of Child Psychiatry

4940 Children's Place
St. Louis, MO 63110
Ph: (314)454-2724
Fax: (314)454-2330

E-mail: rtodd@genpsy.wustl.edu

Contact: Dr. Richard D. Todd, Dir.

Desc: Pharmacotherapy and genetics of childhood depression and bipolar disorder, children of alcoholics, prevention of conduct disorders, neuroimaging of childhood affective disorders, epidemiology of childhood psychiatric disorders, infant and preschool psychiatric disorders, childhood bipolar disorder, twin and genotyping studies of attention deficit/hyperactivity disorder. *Type:* Research center.

W.M. Krogman Center for Research in Child Growth and Development

University of Pennsylvania
4019 St. Irving
Philadelphia, PA 19104-6003
Ph: (215)898-1470
Fax: (215)573-7369

E-mail: growth@wal6000e.udc.upenn.edu
URL: http://www.upenn.edu/krogman

Contact: Dr. Solomon H. Katz, Dir.

Desc: Obesity, nutrition, and other health and mental disorders, epidemiology of high blood pressure in adolescents, neuropsychological development, developmental disorders, hypertension, and subclinical lead intoxication and other trace element studies in children. Also establishes norms of physical growth and development of Philadelphia and international children from birth to 17 years of age, including norms for head, face, and jaws (cephalometric and roentgenographic cephalometric), body (height, weight, somatometric size, and proportion of trunk and limbs), and maturation levels (via X-ray films and hand and knee), applied to clinical problems in medicine and dentistry. *Type:* Research center.

Yale University

Child Health Research Center

Department of Pediatrics
PO Box 208081
New Haven, CT 06520
Ph: (203)737-5970
Fax: (203)737-5972

E-mail: joseph.warshaw@yale.edu

Contact: Dr. Joseph Warshaw, Chm.

Desc: Cellular and molecular biological studies of normal development and the ability of the fetus and child to adapt to environmental or genetic influences. *Type:* Research center.

Yale University

Children's Clinical Research Center

Sch. of Med.
Department of Pediatrics
PO Box 208064
New Haven, CT 06520-8064
Ph: (203)785-4648
Fax: (203)737-1998

URL: http://www.med.yale.edu

Contact: Dr. William V. Tamborlane, Jr., Prog.Dir.

Desc: Pediatric problems, including metabolic, hematologic, neurologic, cardiovascular disease, and social and psychological aspects of patient care. *Type:* Research center.

Yale University

Pediatric Cystic Fibrosis Research Center

Sch. of Med.
333 Cedar St.
PO Box 208064
New Haven, CT 06520-8064
Ph: (203)785-2480
Fax: (203)785-6337

E-mail: regina.palazoo@yale.edu

Contact: Dr. Regina M. Palazzo, Jr., Dir.

Desc: Cystic fibrosis and related respiratory diseases of children, with special emphasis on control of respiration. *Type:* Research center.

Yeshiva University

Preventive Intervention Research Center for Child Health

1300 Morris Park Ave.
Bronx, NY 10461
Ph: (718)918-4390
Fax: (718)918-4388

E-mail: rstein@aecom.yu.edu

Contact: Ruth E.K. Stein, MD, Dir.

Desc: Children with serious ongoing health problems (infancy through adolescence) and their families and the effect of parental illness on children. Activities include preventive interventions for children with asthma and HIV/AIDS, secondary analyses of large scale data sets on childhood disability, measurement development on chronic conditions, functional status and social support. *Type:* Research center.

Your Child's Wellness Newsletter

H/K Communications Inc.
244 Madison Ave.
New York, NY 10016
Ph: (212)983-6880
Free: 800-938-1915
Fax: (212)983-1220

E-mail: hkcomm@pipeline.com

Contact: Reuben Reiman, Editor.

Desc: Promotes children's health. Recurring features include Product safety alerts, recipes, and columns titled Ask the Doctor, Short Takes, Nutrition News, Taste Bites, Thinking About Health, Medicine Update, and Parting Shots. *Type:* Newsletter.

ZERO TO THREE/National Center for Infants, Toddlers and Families

734 15th St. NW, Ste. 1000
Washington, DC 20005
Ph: (202)638-1144
Fax: (202)638-0851

E-mail: m.melmed@zerotothree.org
URL: http://www.zerotothree.org

Contact: Matthew E. Melmed, Exec.Dir.

Desc: Parent informational needs (conducted through survey and focus groups) and development of a diagnostic classification system for mental health and development disorders of infants and young children. *Type:* Research center.

Child Welfare

American Humane Association Children's Division

63 Inverness Dr. E
Englewood, CO 80112-5117
Ph: (303)792-9900
Free: 800-227-4645
Fax: (303)792-3333

E-mail: children@americanhumane.org
URL: http://www.amerhumane.org

Contact: Karen Farestad, Ph.D., Dir.

Desc: Individuals and agencies who seek to protect children from neglect and abuse. Works to insure effective and responsive community child protective services. *Type:* Association.

Care Development

PO Box 2356
Bangor, ME 04402-2356
Ph: (207)945-4240
Free: 800-236-2273
Fax: (207)990-3660

E-mail: info@caredev.org

Contact: James Souza, Pres.

Desc: Social service, mental health agency serving children and families. *Type:* Association.

Catholic Guardian Society

1011 1st Ave.
New York, NY 10022
Ph: (212)371-1000
Fax: (212)371-1512

Contact: John J. Frein, Exec.Dir.

Desc: Cares for dependent, neglected, abused, and delinquent children. *Type:* Association.

Child Welfare Institute

1349 W. Peachtree NE, Ste. 900
Atlanta, GA 30309
Ph: (404)876-1934
Fax: (404)876-7949
E-mail: tmorton@gocwi.org
URL: http://www.gocwi.org
Contact: Thomas D. Morton, Pres.
Desc: Individuals interested in child welfare issues. Supports programs promoting foster parenting, adoption, reunification of foster children with their birthparents, child abuse and neglect, and other issues. Disseminates information to the public; provides organizational development and training consultation services. *Type:* Association.

Child Welfare League of America

440 1st St. NW, 3rd Fl.
Washington, DC 20001
Ph: (202)638-2952
Fax: (202)638-4004
URL: http://www.cwla.org
Contact: David S. Liederman, Exec.Dir.
Desc: Works to improve care and services for abused, dependent, or neglected children, youth, and their families. *Type:* Association.

Children of the Night

14530 Sylvan St.
Van Nuys, CA 91411
Ph: (818)908-4474
Free: 800-551-1300
Fax: (818)908-1468
E-mail: cotnll@aol.com
URL: http://www.childrenofthenight.org
Contact: Dr. Lois Lee, Pres.
Desc: To provide protection and support for street children, usually runaways, ages 11-17 who are involved in pornography or prostitution. Provides shelter, a 24 hour hotline, and a street outreach program. Places street children with drug programs, counselors, and in independent living situations. *Type:* Association.

Children Now

1212 Broadway 5th Fl.
Oakland, CA 94612
Ph: (510)763-2444
Free: 800-CHILD-44
Fax: (510)763-1974
E-mail: children@childrennow.org
URL: http://www.childrennow.org
Contact: Lois Salisbury, Pres.
Desc: Children Now is a nonpartisan, independent voice for America's children. Through innovative research and communications strategies, it promotes pioneering solutions to improve the lives of America's children. Our programs reach parents, lawmakers, concerned citizens, business, media and community leaders, building partnerships to affect positive change. *Type:* Association.

Committee for Children

2203 Airport Way S, Ste. 500
Seattle, WA 98134-2027
Ph: (206)343-1223
Free: 800-634-4449
Fax: (206)343-1445
E-mail: webmatron@cfchildren.org
URL: http://www.cfchildren.org
Contact: Michael Arch, Exec.Dir.
Desc: Develops curricula for preschool, elementary, and junior high school students nationwide. *Type:* Association.

International Child Resource Institute

1581 Le Roy Ave.
Berkeley, CA 94708-1941
E-mail: icrichild@aol.com
Contact: Ken Jaffe, Exec.Dir.
Desc: Individuals interested in issues regarding day care for children, including maternal and child health, child abuse prevention, neglect, and other children's issues. Organizations and companies that furnish or are engaged in child care. Implements model projects to gather information on techniques and practices involved in innovative forms of child care and child health. *Type:* Association.

Juvenile Welfare Board of Pinellas County

6698 68th Ave. N, Ste. A
Pinellas Park, FL 33781-5060
Ph: (727)547-5600
Fax: (727)547-5610
Contact: James E. Mills, ACSW, Exec.Dir.
Desc: Independent special taxing district in Pinellas County, FL dedicated to providing preventive and early interventive children's services. Plans, coordinates, and funds services for children and families; researches, reviews, and recommends legislative and public policies. *Type:* Association.

Kempe Children's Center Neglect

Donald C. Bross
1825 Marion St.
Denver, CO 80218
Ph: (303)864-5252
E-mail: brass.donald@tchden.org
URL: http://www.kempecenter.org
Contact: Robertq Clyman, M.D., Dir.
Type: Association.

Massachusetts Society for the Prevention of Cruelty to Children

43 Mt. Vernon St.
Boston, MA 02108
Ph: (617)227-2280
Free: 800-392-6046
Contact: Loretta W. Kowal, Exec.Dir.
Desc: Individuals dedicated to protecting and promoting the rights and well-being of children. Provides educational programs to prevent and treat child abuse, family counseling, advocacy, and emergency services. *Type:* Association.

National Center for Missing and Exploited Children

2101 Wilson Blvd., Ste. 550
Arlington, VA 22201
Ph: (703)235-3900
Free: 800-843-5678
Fax: (703)235-4067
Contact: Ernest E. Allen, Pres.
Desc: To aid parents and law enforcement agencies in preventing child exploitation and in locating missing children. *Type:* Association.

National Center for Prosecution of Child Abuse

99 Canal Center Plaza, Ste. 510
Alexandria, VA 22314
Ph: (703)739-0321
Fax: (703)549-6259
Contact: Daniel Armagh, Dir.
Desc: Program of the American Prosecutors Research Institute . Provides technical assistance and training to prosecutors and child abuse professionals. Conducts workshops and symposia and publishes guides and a free newsletter. *Type:* Association.

National Coalition for the Protection of Children and Families

800 Compton Rd., Ste. 9224
Cincinnati, OH 45231
Ph: (513)521-6227
Fax: (513)521-6337
E-mail: ncpcf@eos.net
URL: http://www.nationalcoalition.org
Contact: Rick Schatz, Pres.
Desc: Works to unite, train, and assist religious, civic and legal groups and individuals who seek to eliminate obscenity, child pornography, and material harmful to minors. *Type:* Association.

National Committee to Prevent Child Abuse

21 Tamal Vista Blvd., Ste. 209
Corte Madera, CA 94925
Free: 800-626-9671
Fax: (415)924-1379
E-mail: ncpca@childabuse.org
URL: http://www.childabuse.org
Contact: A. Sidney Johnson, III, Exec.Dir.
Desc: Seeks to stimulate greater public awareness of the incidence, origins, nature, and effects of child abuse. *Type:* Association.

National Resource Center for Youth Services

Elizabeth Richards
202 W. 8th St.
Tulsa, OK 74119-1419
Ph: (918)585-2986
Fax: (918)592-1841
E-mail: hlock@ou.edu
URL: http://www.nrcys.ou.edu
Contact: James Walker, Dir.
Desc: Works to improve the quality of life for at-risk youth and their families by improving the effectiveness of human services. *Type:* Association.

National Safe Kids Campaign

1301 Pennsylvania Ave. NW, No. 1000
Washington, DC 20004
Ph: (202)662-0600
Fax: (202)393-2072
E-mail: info@safekids.org
URL: http://www.safekids.org
Contact: Heather Paul.
Desc: Grass roots coalitions of medical and safety organizations, government leaders, teachers, parents, and interested others working to create safer homes and communities for children. Seeks to raise public awareness of injury prevention through the media. *Type:* Association.

Neighborhood House Association/Head Start Program of San Diego County

5660 Copley Dr.
San Diego, CA 92111-7902
Ph: (619)715-2642
Fax: (619)715-2672
E-mail: nhals@erlss.com
Contact: Barbara Y. Fielding, Dir.
Desc: Provides child care for children aged three to five from low-income families in San Diego, CA. *Type:* Association.

Pearl S. Buck International

PO Box 181
Green Hills Farm
Perkasie, PA 18944-0181
Ph: (215)249-0100
Free: 800-220-BUCK
Fax: (215)249-9657
Contact: Mr. Long Ngryen, Chief Financial Officer.
Desc: Established by author Pearl Buck (1892-1973) to raise funds for the education, medical assistance, and support of displaced children, especially Amerasians (children born of Asian mothers and American fathers). Currently sponsors over 6000 children in India, Korea, Japan, the Philippines, Taiwan, Thailand, and Vietnam. *Type:* Association.

Roberta Jo Society

414 Tiffin Tower
Chillicothe, OH 45601-3242
Ph: (740)772-5527
Contact: Mr. Andrew Steely, Exec.Dir.
Desc: Missing children agency named after Roberta Jo Steely, a three-year-old child who disappeared on June 26, 1980. The society, which was founded by her father, serves as a research and information clearinghouse for parents of missing children. Seeks to alter attitudes toward parents of lost children. *Type:* Association.

United Nations Children's Fund

3 United Nations Plz.
New York, NY 10017
Ph: (212)326-7000
Fax: (212)888-7465
E-mail: netmaster@unicef.org
Contact: Carol Bellamy, Exec.Dir.
Desc: Semi-autonomous U.N. agency working for sustainable human development to ensure the survival, protection, and development of children. *Type:* Association.

Variety Clubs International

350 5th Ave., Ste. 1119
New York, NY 10118
Ph: (212)695-3818
Fax: (212)695-3857
Contact: Mrs. Rosalie Sochinski, Exec.Dir.
Desc: Entertainment and leisure-related industries. Sponsors programs to raise funds for children's facilities such as hospitals, special treatment centers, camps, and day nurseries. *Type:* Association.

Village of Childhelp
PO Box 247 Ph: (909)845-3155
14700 Manzanita Park Rd. Fax: (909)845-8412
Beaumont, CA 92223
Contact: Thomas N. Alexander, Admin.
Desc: A project of Childhelp U.S.A. Residential program designed exclusively for abused children and their families. *Type:* Association.

Children

American Baby
Primedia Publishing
249 W. 17th St., 3rd Fl. Ph: (212)462-3300
New York, NY 10011-5300 Fax: (212)367-8332
Contact: Judith Nolte, Editor; Darcy Miller, Publisher; Bob Davidowitz, Advertising Dir.
Desc: Magazine. *Type:* Periodical.

Angelcare
PO Box 600370 Ph: (619)562-0631
San Diego, CA 92160-0370 Free: 888-264-5227
Fax: (619)258-8671
E-mail: childrensa@aol.com
URL: http://www.angelcare.org
Contact: Dr. T. J. Grosser, CEO & Pres.
Desc: Nondenominational charitable program that provides nutritional, medical, and educational assistance to needy children in Southeast Asia, Africa, Latin America, Eastern Europe, and U.S. Provides resources to meet health needs, including nutrition supplements ("Nutri-Paks"), medicine, and the services of physicians, nurses, nutritionists, and paramedics. Operates primary health care clinics in Nairobi, Kenya, and Malaysia. *Type:* Association.

Association for Children for Enforcement of Support
2260 Upton Ave. Ph: (419)472-6609
Toledo, OH 43606 Free: 800-537-7072
Fax: (419)472-6295
E-mail: natces@earthlink.net
URL: http://www.childsupport-aces.org
Contact: Geraldine Jensen, Pres.
Desc: Custodial parents seeking legal enforcement of child support. Provides educational information about the legal rights involved in child support enforcement. Advocates improved child support enforcement services from the government. *Type:* Association.

Baby Talk
Time-Warner, Inc.
25 W. 43rd St. Ph: (212)840-4200
New York, NY 10036 Fax: (212)827-0019
Contact: Trisna Thompson, Editor-in-Chief; John Hartig, President; Fred Levine, Editor-in-Chief; Lori Frumm, Publisher; Lori Nash, Publisher.
Desc: Magazine for new and expectant parents. *Type:* Periodical.

Better Boys Foundation
3333 W. Arthington St., Ste. Ph: (312)595-9903
139 Fax: (312)595-9909
Chicago, IL 60624-4146
Contact: Gary Mayberry, Exec.Dir.
Desc: Local organization formed to help youngsters become better students and citizens by providing academic support, cultural enrichment, counseling, and recreational activities. Maintains Nana's House, a 15-bed, temporary living facility for homeless youth. The National Football League Players Association has designated the foundation as its official charity. *Type:* Association.

Big Brothers Big Sisters of America
230 N. 13th St. Ph: (215)567-7000
Philadelphia, PA 19107 Fax: (215)567-0394
E-mail: bbbsa@aol.com
Contact: Thomas M. McKenna, Exec.Dir.
Desc: Federation of professionally staffed local agencies administered by volunteer boards of directors. Operates One-To-One program which matches a child from a single parent home with an adult volunteer who serves as a mentor and role model. The match is made with assistance of a professionally trained caseworker who also supervises and supports the One-To-One relationship. *Type:* Association.

Bowker's Directory of Audiocassettes for Children
R. R. Bowker
121 Chanlon Rd. Ph: (908)464-6800
New Providence, NJ 07974 Free: 800-521-8110
Fax: (908)665-6688
E-mail: techsupport@bowker.com
URL: http://www.bowker.com
Desc: More than 10,000 fiction and nonfiction audiocassette titles for children from pre-school through 8th grade. *Type:* Directory.

Campus Life
Christianity Today, Inc.
465 Gundersen Dr. Ph: (630)260-6200
Carol Stream, IL 60188 Fax: (630)260-0114
URL: http://www.christianity.net/campuslife.
Contact: Chris Lutes, Editor; Harold Smith, Exec. Editor, cledit@aol.com.
Desc: Magazine for high school and early college students espousing Christian-centered values and faith. *Type:* Periodical.

Child Abuse and Neglect Clearinghouse: Online Databases and Directories
National Clearinghouse on Child Abuse and Neglect Information
330 C St. SW Free: 800-394-3366
Washington, DC 20447 Fax: (703)385-3206
E-mail: nccanch@calib.com
URL: http://www.calib.com/nccanch/database/index.htm
Contact: webmaster@calib.com.
Desc: A service of the National Clearinghouse on Child Abuse and Neglect Information, this online database can be searched for information and documents related to the abuse, neglect, and mistreatment of children. Search the database by hundreds of different topics and keywords. *Type:* Database.

Child Care Action Campaign
330 7th Ave., 17th Fl. Ph: (212)239-0138
New York, NY 10001 Fax: (212)268-6515
E-mail: ccacgen@aol.com
Contact: Faith Wohl, Pres.
Desc: Individuals and organizations interested and active in child care; corporations and financial institutions; labor organizations; editors of leading women's magazines; leaders in government and representatives of civic organizations. Purposes are to alert the country to the problems of and need for child care services; prepare and disseminate information responsive to inquiries resulting from publicity; analyze existing services and identify gaps; work directly with communities to stimulate the development of local task forces and long-range plans for improved and coordinated services. Brings pressing legislative action or inaction to public attention. *Type:* Association.

Child Labor Monitor
National Consumers League
1701 K St. NW, Ste. 1200 Ph: (202)835-3323
Washington, DC 20006 Fax: (202)835-0747
E-mail: nclncl@aol.com
URL: http://www.nclnet.org
Contact: Darlene S. Adkins, Editor, dsadkins@avalonis.com.
Desc: Presents information on state, national, and international efforts to end child labor exploitation. Recurring features include news of research and initiatives and columns titled Federal Update, State Action, International Watch, Resources and Announcements, and Activist Alert. *Type:* Newsletter.

Childhelp U.S.A.
1345 N El Centro Ave. Ph: (323)465-4016
Hollywood, CA 90028
E-mail: info@childhelpusa.org
URL: http://www.childhelpusa.org
Contact: Sara O'Meara, Bd.Chm.
Desc: Works toward research, prevention, and treatment of child abuse. Has established the Village of Childhelp, a residential center devoted to the care and treatment of abused and neglected children. Maintains an aftercare program utilizing professional counseling services and therapeutic foster homes. *Type:* Association.

Childreach, United States Member of Plan International
155 Plan Way Ph: (401)738-5600
Warwick, RI 02886 Free: 800-556-7918
Fax: (401)738-5608
URL: http://www.childreach.org
Contact: Samuel A. Worthington, Pres. & Natl.Exec.Dir.
Desc: U.S. member of Plan International. U.S. sponsors assisting 100,000 needy children in 40 countries of Africa, Asia, Central America, the Caribbean, and South America. *Type:* Association.

Children, Inc.
PO Box 5381 Ph: (804)359-4562
1000 Westover Rd. Free: 800-538-5381
Richmond, VA 23220 Fax: (804)353-7541
E-mail: cirichmond@aol.com
Contact: Jeanne Clarke Wood, Pres. & Intl.Dir.
Desc: International organization assisting children of all races and creeds, administering to their physical, mental, and spiritual needs. Works in 20 countries, assisting 12,000 children in more than 199 projects. Provides food, clothing, school supplies, medical needs, and other personal necessities. *Type:* Association.

Children Now
Children Now
1212 Broadway, 5th Fl. Ph: (510)763-2444
c/o Lorena Hernandez Free: 800-CHILD-44
Oakland, CA 94612 Fax: (510)763-1974
E-mail: children@childrennow.org
URL: http://www.dnai.com/~children/
Desc: Children Now is a nonpartisan policy and advocacy organization for children. This site is a complete resource on children's issues. *Type:* Database.

Children's Art Foundation
PO Box 83 Ph: (831)426-5557
Santa Cruz, CA 95063 Free: 800-447-4569
Fax: (831)426-1161
E-mail: editor@stonesoup.com
URL: http://www.stonesoup.com
Contact: Gerry Mandel, Co-Dir.
Desc: The Children's Art Foundation publishes Stone Soup, maintains a collection of children's art from around

the world, and has a Web site. Stone Soup is the international bi-monthly magazine of stories, poems, and art by young people through age 13. The Web site includes exemplary writing and art by young people, as well as supplementary materials for teachers, parents and children. *Type:* Association.

Children's Committee 10

PO Box 16133   Ph: (209)439-0821
Fresno, CA 93755
Contact: Vincent J. Lavery, Chm.
Desc: Volunteer civic group members, businesses, and individuals interested in bringing children of Northern Ireland, Lebanon, and South Africa to the United States each year for a seven-week summer vacation away from the stressful conditions of their homeland. Goal is to secure private homes for these children's summer visits and to raise funds for their transportation and insurance. *Type:* Association.

Children's Defense Fund

25 E St. NW   Ph: (202)628-8787
Washington, DC 20001   Fax: (202)662-3510
Contact: Marian Wright Edelman, Pres.
Desc: Provides systematic, long-range advocacy on behalf of the nation's children and teenagers. *Type:* Association.

Children's Digest

Children's Better Health Institute
1100 Waterway Blvd.   Ph: (317)636-8881
PO Box 567   Free: 800-558-2376
Indianapolis, IN 46202-2156   Fax: (317)684-8094
E-mail: cbhiseif@tcon.net
Contact: Danny Lee, Editor.
Desc: Magazine on children's health, exercise, nutrition, and safety for ages 9-12. *Alt. Contact:* PO Box 567, Indianapolis, IN 46206. *Type:* Periodical.

Children's Express

1440 New York Ave. NW   Ph: (202)737-7377
Ste. 510   Fax: (202)737-0193
Washington, DC 20005
URL: http://www.ce.org.
Contact: Lee Wood, Acting Exec. Dir./VP Mktg. & Comm., lwood@dc.ce.org; Judith Fiske Moak, VP Dev.; Monette Austin, Editor.
Desc: Distributes news service. *Alt. Contact:* 1440 New York Ave. NW, Ste. 510, Washington, DC 20005; telephone: (202)737-7377; fax: (202)737-0193. *Type:* Periodical.

Children's Playmate Magazine

Children's Better Health Institute
1100 Waterway Blvd.   Ph: (317)636-8881
PO Box 567   Free: 800-558-2376
Indianapolis, IN 46202-2156   Fax: (317)684-8094
E-mail: cbhiseif@tcon.net
Contact: Terry Harshman, Editor.
Desc: Magazine on children's health, exercise, nutrition, and safety for ages 6-8. *Type:* Periodical.

Children's Television Workshop

1 Lincoln Plz.   Ph: (212)595-3456
New York, NY 10023   Fax: (212)875-6111
Contact: David V. B. Britt, Pres.
Desc: Research and development laboratory that explores new uses of television and related communications media for educational and informational purposes, both in the U.S. and elsewhere in the world. Created and produced educational television series, including "Sesame Street," "The Electric Company," "3-2-1 Contact," and "Square One TV." Maintains library. *Type:* Association.

Children's Wish Foundation International

8615 Roswell Rd.   Ph: (770)393-9474
Atlanta, GA 30350   Free: 800-323-WISH
     Fax: (770)393-0683
E-mail: childrenswish@mindspring.com
URL: http://www.childrenswish.org
Desc: Seeks to fulfill the wishes of terminally ill children under 18 years old. Maintains speakers' bureau; compiles statistics. Provides children's services throughout North America, Europe, and Asia. *Type:* Association.

Christian Children's Fund

2821 Emerywood Pky.   Ph: (804)756-2700
Box 26484   Free: 800-776-6767
Richmond, VA 23261-5066   Fax: (804)756-2718
URL: http://www.christianchildrensfund.org
Contact: Dr. Margaret C. McCullough, Pres.
Desc: International, nonsectarian child development organization providing food, clothing, medical care and educational opportunities to children of all races and creeds. Works through the donations of sponsors who maintain personal contact with the child they help support. Provides assistance to needy children and their families in 32 countries including the U.S.A. *Type:* Association.

Compassion International

3955 Cragwood Dr.   Ph: (719)594-9900
PO Box 7000   Free: 800-336-7676
Colorado Springs, CO 80997   Fax: (719)594-6271
E-mail: ciinfo@us.ci.org
URL: http://www.as.ci.org
Contact: Wesley K. Stafford, Pres.
Desc: Offers ministry to children in underdeveloped and developing countries; provides for educational, physical, material, and spiritual needs. Programs include: schools (financial support sent to schools); family helper plans (care within family unit); children's homes (financial support); hostels (financial support sent to hostels); special care centers (physical and mental health care facilities); meal sponsorship (hot lunch five days/week for school children); scholarship (enables children to attend schools away from their homes and villages); student centers (assists children with their studies); commodities (provides pharmaceuticals and other materials to medical facilities around the world); domestic (assists needy American children in inner cities and Indian reservations). Maintains speakers' bureau. *Type:* Association.

Comprehensive Day Care Programs

Stevens Adm. Center   Ph: (215)351-7200
Spring Garden at 13th St.   Fax: (215)351-7165
Philadelphia, PA 19123
Contact: Ernestine Redd, Exec. Officer.
Desc: Day care centers serving 3900 children of low-income families. Aims to help each child fulfill his or her own potential in intellectual, social, emotional, and physical development. Provides opportunities in self-development to parents; seeks to emphasize the parental role and responsibility in the development of the child. *Type:* Association.

Day Care USA Newsletter

United Communications Group
11300 Rockville Pike, Ste. 1100   Ph: (301)287-2700
Rockville, MD 20852-3030   Free: 800-929-4824
     Fax: (301)287-2049
E-mail: customer@ucg.com
Contact: Charles Pekow, Editor, (301)493-6926, cpekow@capaccess.org.
Desc: Discusses news of funding and legislative news pertaining to early childhood opportunities. *Type:* Newsletter.

Dolphin Log

The Cousteau Society
870 Greenbrier Cir., Ste. 402   Ph: (757)523-9335
Chesapeake, VA 23320   Free: 800-441-4395
     Fax: (757)523-2747
E-mail: cousteau@infi.net; cousteauny@aol.com.
URL: http://www.cousteau.org.
Contact: Elizabeth Foley, Editor.
Desc: Magazine for readers, ages 7-13, covering subjects related to the global water system. *Alt. Contact:* Dolphin Log Magazine, 777 United Nations Plaza, New York, NY 10017; telephone: (212)949-6290; fax: (212)949-6296. *Type:* Periodical.

Dream Factory

1218 S. 3rd St.   Ph: (502)637-8700
Louisville, KY 40203-2906   Free: 800-456-7556
     Fax: (502)637-8744
E-mail: dfhq@aol.com
URL: http://www.dreamfactoryinc.com
Contact: Denis P. Heavrin, Nat.Exec.Dir.
Desc: Volunteers devoted to granting the dreams of chronically or critically ill children. Seeks to: bring smiles to the faces of seriously ill children; promote a better family atmosphere during a prolonged illness; involve the community in granting wishes to children; raise funds necessary to provide dreams. Has honored requests for photographs of celebrities, trips to Disney World, a visit to Buckingham Palace, and for the building of a home. *Type:* Association.

Foster Grandparent Program

c/o Corporation For National   Ph: (202)606-5000
Service   Free: 800-424-8867
1201 New York Ave. NW   Fax: (202)565-2743
Washington, DC 20525
URL: http://www.cns.gov
Contact: Thomas E. Endres, Dir.
Desc: A program administered by the Corporation for National Service, part of the federal government. Volunteers are low-income persons (age 60 and over) who provide person-to-person assistance to children with special or exceptional needs. Provides services to abused and neglected children, children with learning disabilities, children with AIDS, teen parents, and juvenile delinquents. *Type:* Association.

Futures for Children

9600 Tennyson St. NE   Ph: (505)821-2828
Albuquerque, NM 87122-2282   Free: 800-545-6843
     Fax: (505)821-4141
E-mail: futuresfc@aol.com
URL: http://www.futurechild.org
Contact: Jim West, Pres.
Desc: Community development organization working to encourage and motivate people in underdeveloped areas to improve their communities through self-help programs. Is currently working with 22 American Indian tribes in the southwestern United States. *Type:* Association.

Highlights for Children

Boysville Publishing
803 Church St.   Ph: (717)253-1080
Honesdale, PA 18431   Fax: (717)253-0179
E-mail: highlights@ezaccess.net.
Contact: Kent L. Brown Jr., Editor; Tom White, Advertising Mgr.; Jack Myers, Ph.D.; Rich Wallace, Editor; Rosanne S. Guararra, Advertising Mgr.
Desc: Magazine for children ages 2-12 years. *Type:* Periodical.

Holt International Children's Services

PO Box 2880   Ph: (541)687-2202
Eugene, OR 97402   Fax: (541)683-6175
E-mail: info@holtintl.org
URL: http://www.holtintl.org
Contact: John L. Williams, Exec.Dir.

Desc: To deinstitutionalize children in developing countries by rehabilitating biological families, encouraging adoption within the developing country, and arranging inter-country adoption when in the best interest of the child. Offers assistance to children in Korea, India, the Philippines, Thailand, Vietnam, Hong Kong, China, Romania, and Latin America, as well as the U.S. Provides funds for food, clothing, housing, and medical care until an adoptive home can be found. *Type:* Association.

Humpty Dumpty's Magazine

Children's Better Health Institute
1100 Waterway Blvd.   Ph: (317)636-8881
PO Box 567   Free: 800-558-2376
Indianapolis, IN 46202-2156   Fax: (317)684-8094
E-mail: cbhiseif@tcon.net
Contact: Nancy S. Axelrad, Editor.

Desc: Health, exercise, nutrition, and safety magazine for children ages four to six. *Alt. Contact:* PO Box 567, Indianapolis, IN 46206; telephone: (317)636-8881; fax: (317)684-8094. *Type:* Periodical.

Institutes for the Achievement of Human Potential

8801 Stenton Ave.   Ph: (215)233-2050
Philadelphia, PA 19138   Fax: (215)233-9312
E-mail: chipm@earthlink.net
Contact: Janet Doman, Dir.

Desc: Promotes the achievement of full potential for all individuals. *Type:* Association.

International Lactation Consultant Association

4101 Lk. Boone Trl., Ste. 201   Ph: (919)787-5181
Raleigh, NC 27607   Fax: (919)787-4916
E-mail: ilca@erols.com
URL: http://www.ilca.org
Contact: Amy Spangler, Pres.

Desc: Lactation consultants, institutions, and health professionals from 20 countries interested in breastfeeding and lactation. Works to: establish and maintain quality educational and practice standards and ethical principles for lactation consultants; initiate and conduct continuing education and research in the field; promote work concerning lactation/breastfeeding issues; increase public and health care worker awareness of lactation and breastfeeding. Facilitates communication among members. *Type:* Association.

Jack And Jill

Children's Better Health Institute
1100 Waterway Blvd.   Ph: (317)636-8881
PO Box 567   Free: 800-558-2376
Indianapolis, IN 46202-2156   Fax: (317)684-8094
E-mail: cbhiseif@tcon.net
Contact: Daniel Lee, Editor.

Desc: General magazine for children ages 7-10. *Type:* Periodical.

Jack and Jill of America

2802 Gulfstream Ct.   Ph: (407)843-6132
Orlando, FL 32805-5811   Fax: (407)422-7071
Contact: Barbara B. Newton, Exec.Sec.

Desc: Parents interested in "PEP" (parenting, education, and political involvement). Objectives are to create a medium of contact among children to stimulate growth and development and to provide them with a constructive cultural, civic, recreational, and social program. *Type:* Association.

Kid City

Children's Television Workshop Magazine Group
1 Lincoln Plaza   Ph: (212)595-3456
New York, NY 10023   Free: 800-678-0613
   Fax: (212)875-6101

Contact: Maureen Hunter-Bone, Editor-in-Chief; Nina Link, Publisher; Jeffrey Haley, Advertising V.P.

Desc: Magazine encouraging children to read, write, and learn about the world. *Type:* Periodical.

KidSmart

PO Box 333   Ph: (908)534-1793
Whitehouse Station, NJ 08889   Fax: (908)534-9881
E-mail: mblamarca@aol.com.

Contact: Maureen B. LaMarca, Author.

Alt. Contact: PO Box 333, Whitehouse St., NJ 08889; telephone: (908)534-1793; fax: (908)534-9881. *Type:* Periodical.

KIND News

National Association for Humane and Environmental Education (NAHEE)
PO Box 362   Ph: (860)434-8666
East Haddam, CT 06423   Fax: (860)434-9579
E-mail: nahee@nahee.org; kindnews@nahee.org.
URL: http://www.nahee.org; http://www.kindnews.org.

Contact: Bill DeRosa, Dir. of Publications, derosa@nahee.org; Dorothy Weller, Dir. of Outreach, fax: (860)434-6282, weller@nahee.org.

Desc: In-classroom newspaper for children. *Type:* Periodical.

La Leche League International

1400 Meacham   Ph: (847)519-7730
Schaumburg, IL 60173   Free: 800-LA-LECHE
   Fax: (847)519-7730
URL: http://www.lalecheleague.org
Contact: Paulina de Smith, Exec.Dir.

Desc: Helps mothers worldwide to breastfeed through mother-to-mother support, encouragement, information, and education and promotes a better understanding of breastfeeding as an important element in the healthy development of the baby and mother. Provides support through informal discussions and individualized phone counseling. Group maintains that breastfeeding infants will encourage closer family relationships. *Type:* Association.

Ladybug

The Cricket Magazine Group
315 5th St.   Ph: (815)224-6656
Peru, IL 61354   Free: 800-588-8585
   Fax: (815)224-6615
Contact: Marianne Carus, Editor-in-Chief; Bob Harper, Publisher; John Toraason, General Mgr.

Desc: Magazine of ideas, adventures, and activities for children ages 2 to 6. *Type:* Periodical.

Make-A-Wish Foundation of America

100 W. Clarendon Ave., Ste.   Ph: (602)279-9474
2200   Free: 800-722-WISH
Phoenix, AZ 85013-3518   Fax: (602)275-0855
E-mail: mawfa@wish.org
URL: http://www.wish.org
Contact: Herbert J. Paine, Pres./CEO.

Desc: Grants wishes to children with terminal or life-threatening illnesses, thereby providing these children and their families with special memories and a welcome respite from the daily stress of their situation. *Type:* Association.

Make-A-Wish Foundation of South Florida

PO Box 17377   Ph: (954)967-9474
Ft. Lauderdale, FL 33318   Free: 888-773-9474
   Fax: (954)987-7159
E-mail: sfla@wish.org
Contact: Nancy Strom, Pres.CEO.

Desc: Seeks to grant the wishes of children under the age of 18 who suffer from life-threatening illnesses. *Type:* Association.

Metrokids Magazine

Metrokids
1080 N. Delaware Ave., Ste.   Ph: (215)291-5560
702   Fax: (215)291-5563
Philadelphia, PA 19125
E-mail: metrokids@family.com
Contact: Nancy Lisagor, Editor; Amanda Hathaway, Executive Ed.

Desc: Regional magazine for families. *Type:* Periodical.

National Association of Child Care Resource and Referral Agencies

1319 F St. NW, Ste. 606   Ph: (202)393-5501
Washington, DC 20004   Fax: (202)393-1109
E-mail: hn5018@handsnet.org
URL: http://www.childcarerr.org
Contact: Yasmina Vinci, Contact.

Desc: Community-based child care resource and referral programs that promote a diverse, high quality child care system with parental choice that is accessible to all families. Exercises national leadership to build such a system promotes growth and development of quality resource and referral services. *Type:* Association.

National Black Child Development Institute

1023 15th St. NW, Ste. 600   Ph: (202)387-1281
Washington, DC 20005   Fax: (202)234-1738
Contact: Evelyn K. Moore, Pres.

Desc: Individuals dedicated to improving the quality of life for African American children and youth. Conducts direct services and advocacy campaigns aimed at both national and local public policies focusing on issues of health, child welfare, education, and child care. Organizes and trains network of members in a volunteer grassroots affiliate system to voice concerns regarding policies that affect black children and their families. *Type:* Association.

National Data Archive on Child Abuse and Neglect

Cornell University - Family Life Development Center
Ithaca, NY 14853-4401   Ph: (607)255-7794
E-mail: DataCAN@cornell.edu
URL: http://www.ndacan.cornell.edu
Contact: John Eckenrode, Ph.D., Principal Investigator, jje1@cornell.edu.

Desc: The National Data Archive on Child Abuse and Neglect acquires, preserves, and disseminates datasets relevant to the study of child abuse and neglect. This data is utilized in secondary analysis and is distributed in ready-to-use formats for microcomputers and mainframes. *Type:* Database.

Peanut Butter

Scholastic, Inc.
555 Broadway   Ph: (212)343-6100
New York, NY 10012   Free: 800-724-6527
   Fax: (212)343-4535
E-mail: custserv@scholastic.com
URL: http://www.scholastic.com
Contact: Nancy Krulik, Editor; Grace Maccarone, Advertising Mgr.

Desc: Magazine for children in kindergarten and first grade. *Type:* Periodical.

Pockets Magazine

The Upper Room
1908 Grand Ave.   Ph: (615)340-7333
Nashville, TN 37202   Free: 800-925-6847
                            Fax: (615)340-7006
E-mail: pockets@upperroom.org.
URL: http://www.upperroom.org
Contact: Janet R. Knight, Editor, (615)340-7238, jknight@upperroom.org; Stephen D. Bryant, Publisher.
Desc: Religious magazine for children 6 to 12 years old. *Type:* Periodical.

Ranger Rick

National Wildlife Magazine
8925 Leesburg Pike   Ph: (703)790-4524
Vienna, VA 22184   Fax: (703)790-4544
E-mail: info@nwf.org
URL: http://www.nwf.org
Contact: E. Gerald Bishop, Editor, bishop@nwf.org.
Desc: Nature magazine for children ages 7 to 12. *Type:* Periodical.

Save the Children Federation

54 Wilton Rd.   Ph: (203)221-4000
Westport, CT 06880   Fax: (203)454-3914
Contact: Charles F. MacCormack, Pres.
Desc: Voluntary, nonsectarian agency that assists children, families, and communities in the U.S. and abroad to achieve social and economic stability through community development and family selfhelp projects such as health, education and economic opportunities; offers aid to victims of disaster. Programs are designed to "contribute to the growth, dignity, independence and self-reliance of the individual." Conducts programs in Afghanistan, Angola, Armenia, Azerbaijan, Bangladesh, Bhutan, Bolivia, Burkina Faso, Cambodia, Cameroon, Colombia, Costa Rica, Croatia/Bosnian Refugees, Dominican Republic, Egypt, El Salvador, Ethiopia, Gambia, Gaza/West Bank, Georgia, Greece, Haiti, Honduras, Indonesia, Jordan, Korea, Laos, Lebanon, Malawi, Mali, Mexico, Mozambique, Nepal, Nicaragua, Pakistan, Philippines, Somalia, Sudan, Thailand, Tunisia, Vietnam, and Zimbabwe. *Type:* Association.

Sesame Street Magazine and Parent's Guide

Children's Television Workshop Magazine Group
1 Lincoln Plaza   Ph: (212)595-3456
New York, NY 10023   Free: 800-678-0613
                            Fax: (212)875-6101
Contact: Ira Wolfman, Editor; Nina B. Link, Publisher; Gail Delott, Advertising Dir.
Desc: Magazine for pre-schoolers with accompanying magazine for parents. *Type:* Periodical.

Shriners Hospitals for Children

2900 Rocky Point Dr.   Ph: (813)281-0300
Tampa, FL 33607   Free: 800-237-5055
URL: http://www.hq.org
Contact: Lewis K. Molnar, Exec.VP.
Desc: SHC operated orthopaedic hospitals (19) and burn hospitals (3) founded by and affiliated with the Imperial Council of the Ancient Arabic Order of the Nobles of the Mystic Shrine for North America. Provides no-cost orthopedic and burn care to children under 18 years of age. Maintains the Shriners Hospitals for Children Endowment Fund. *Type:* Association.

Society for Research in Child Development

University of Michigan   Ph: (313)998-6578
300 N. Ingalls, 10th Level   Fax: (313)998-6569
Ann Arbor, MI 48109-0406
E-mail: srcd@umich.edu
Contact: John W. Hagen, Exec. Officer.

Desc: Professional interdisciplinary society composed of anthropologists, educators, nutritionists, pediatricians, physiologists, psychiatrists, psychologists, sociologists, and statisticians. Works to further research in the area of child development. *Type:* Association.

Southern Early Childhood Association

PO Box 55930   Ph: (501)663-0353
Little Rock, AR 72215-5930   Free: 800-305-7322
                            Fax: (501)663-2114
E-mail: seca@aristotle.net
URL: http://www.seca50.net
Contact: Glenda Bean, Interim Exec.Dir.
Desc: Early childhood educators, day care providers, program administrators, researchers, teacher trainers, and parents from the U.S. and abroad who share a common concern for the well-being of young children. Provides a unified voice on vital local, state, and federal issues affecting young children. *Type:* Association.

Spider

Carus Publishing
315 5th St.   Ph: (815)224-6656
Peru, IL 61354   Free: 800-588-8585
                            Fax: (815)224-6615
Contact: Marianne Carus, Editor-in-Chief; Bob Harper, Publisher; Laura Tillotson, Editor.
Desc: Magazine of stories, games, and projects for children ages 6 to 9. *Type:* Periodical.

Sports Illustrated for Kids

Time Inc.
Time-Life Bldg., Rockefeller   Ph: (212)522-1212
   Center   Fax: (212)522-0315
1271 Avenue of the Americas
New York, NY 10020
Contact: Craig Neff, Managing Editor.
Desc: Sports magazine for children. *Type:* Periodical.

Starlight Children's Foundation

12424 Wilshire Blvd., Ste. 1050   Ph: (310)207-5558
Los Angeles, CA 90025-1044   Free: 800-274-7827
                                 Fax: (310)207-2554
URL: http://www.starlight.org
Contact: Katherine Culpepper, Exec.Dir.
Desc: Individuals who work to help fulfill the wishes of critically, chronically, and terminally ill children. Attempts to arrange and finance children's wishes such as special trips, presents, or meeting a favorite celebrity. Provides entertainment programs in pediatric hospitals in the form of parties, celebrity visits, and fun centers. *Type:* Association.

Surprises

The Publishing Group, Inc.
1200 N. 7th St.   Ph: (612)881-3183
Minneapolis, MN 55411-4400 Fax: (612)881-2172
URL: http://www.surprises.com.
Contact: Tim Drake, Editor.
Desc: Interactive magazine for children ages 5-12 years. *Type:* Periodical.

Toy Tips

Toy Tips
749 N 17th St.   Ph: (414)288-3124
Milwaukee, WI 53233
E-mail: manannea@toytips.com; toytips@toytips.com.
URL: http://www.toytips.com.
Contact: Marianne Szymanski, (414)288-3124, fax: (310)553-8848, mananne@toytips.com.
Desc: Consumer magazine covering research on toys. *Type:* Periodical.

Toyfare, The Toy Magazine

Wizard Entertainment
151 Wells Ave.   Ph: (914)268-2000
Congers, NY 10920   Fax: (914)268-6357
URL: http://www.wizardworld.com.
Contact: Scott Beatty, Editor, scotbeatty@aol.com; Ken Scrudato, Advertising Dir.; Paul Rolnick, Circ. & Dist. Director.
Desc: Consumer magazine covering toys, action figures and related collectibles. *Type:* Periodical.

Turtle Magazine for Preschool Kids

Children's Better Health Institute
1100 Waterway Blvd.   Ph: (317)636-8881
PO Box 567   Free: 800-558-2376
Indianapolis, IN 46202-2156 Fax: (317)684-8094
E-mail: cbhiseif@tcon.net; cbhiseif@trader.com.
Contact: Terry Harshman, Editor; Bart Rivers, Art Director; Cory SerVaas, M.D., Editorial Director; Greg Joray, Executive Publisher.
Desc: Magazine for children (ages 2-5 years) with an emphasis on health, fitness and exercise. *Type:* Periodical.

U.S. Committee for the United Nations Children's Fund

333 E. 38th St.   Ph: (212)686-5522
New York, NY 10016   Free: 800-FOR-KIDS
                            Fax: (212)779-1679
E-mail: webmaster@unicefusa.org
URL: http://www.unicefusa.org
Contact: Charles J. Lyons, Pres.
Desc: Fundraisers, educates and advocates on behalf of children worldwide. Strives to inform the people of the U.S. on programs of the United Nations Children's Fund and to provide opportunities for American citizens and groups to support its activities and appeals. *Type:* Association.

U.S. Kids

Children's Better Health Institute
1100 Waterway Blvd.   Ph: (317)636-8881
PO Box 567   Free: 800-558-2376
Indianapolis, IN 46202-2156 Fax: (317)684-8094
E-mail: cbhiseif@tcon.net
Contact: Nancy Axelrad, Editor.
Desc: Magazine featuring stories and activities geared for children. *Type:* Periodical.

Wizard

Wizard Entertainment
151 Wells Ave.   Ph: (914)268-2000
Congers, NY 10920   Fax: (914)268-6357
URL: http://www.wizardworld.com.
Contact: Brian Cunningham, Editor; Ken Scrudato, Advertising Mgr.; Paul Rolnick, Circulation Mgr.
Desc: Consumer magazine covering comics, video games, toys, and related topics. *Type:* Periodical.

Your Big Backyard

National Wildlife Federation (NWF)
8925 Leesburg Pike   Ph: (703)790-4000
Vienna, VA 22184-0001   Free: 800-822-9919
                            Fax: (703)442-7332
Contact: Donna Johnson, Editor; Tammy Tylenda, Art Dir.
Desc: Consumer magazine covering nature for pre-school aged children. *Type:* Periodical.

Zillions

Consumers Union of U.S., Inc.

101 Truman Ave.   Ph: (914)378-2000

Yonkers, NY 10703-1057   Free: 800-234-2188

                                            Fax: (914)378-2904

Contact: C. Baecher, Editor, (914)378-2550, fax: (914)378-2916; Karen McNulty, Managing Editor, (914)378-2553, fax: (914)378-2916.

Desc: Children's educational magazine. *Type:* Periodical.

China

China Agribusiness Report

The Asia Letter Group

PO Box 92619

Los Angeles, CA 90009

Type: Newsletter.

China Business & Trade

Welsh Pony and Cob Society of America

PO Box 2977   Ph: (703)667-6195

Winchester, VA 22601

Contact: Justin Ford, Editor.

Desc: Covers recent commercial and economic developments in the People's Republic of China and their effect on trade. Focuses on recent commercial contracts and negotiations between China and international market economies. *Type:* Newsletter.

China Institute in America

125 E. 65th St.   Ph: (212)744-8181

New York, NY 10021   Fax: (212)628-4159

Contact: Torrey Whitman, Pres.

Desc: Promotes the understanding of Chinese civilization, culture, heritage and current affairs through classroom teaching and seminars, art exhibitions, public programs, teacher education, lectures and symposia. *Type:* Association.

China News Digest

China News Digest International, Inc.

CND/HXWZ

PO Box 10111

Gaithersburg, MD 20898-0111

E-mail: banners@cnd.org

URL: http://www.cnd.org/

Contact: CND Manager, webmaster@cnd.org.

Desc: The volunteer run China News Digest provides access to current and past issues of CND publications and other information packages. Information available includes full text of Asian news articles, newswire reports, photos, and more. *Type:* Database.

China Telecom

Information Gatekeepers Inc.

214 Harvard Ave.   Ph: (617)232-3111

Boston, MA 02134   Free: 800-323-1088

                                          Fax: (617)734-8562

E-mail: info@igigroup.com

URL: http://wwwigigroup.com; http://www.igigroup.com.

Contact: Hui Pan, Editor.

Desc: Reports on current events in telecommunications developments occuring in China. Recurring features include a calendar of events. *Type:* Newsletter.

China Watch

Orbis Publications, LLC

3201 New Mexico Ave. NW,   Ph: (202)237-0155

Ste. 249   Fax: (202)237-0596

Washington, DC 20016

E-mail: orbis@orbispub.com

Desc: Reports on political, economic, and business events in China. *Type:* Newsletter.

Chinese Alliance for Democracy

PO Box 15273   Ph: (202)797-2722

Washington, DC 20003   Fax: (202)797-2803

Contact: Mr. Daihai Yu, Chm.

Desc: Individuals of Chinese descent united to promote human rights, freedom, democracy, and rule by law in the People's Republic of China. Works with universities to communicate its concerns to students and faculty. Maintains speakers' bureau. *Type:* Association.

Chinese Daily News

Chinese Daily News, Inc.

1588 Corporate Center Dr.   Ph: (213)268-4982

Monterey Park, CA 91754   Fax: (213)265-3476

Contact: Shih-yaw Chen, Editor, (213)268-2600, fax: (213)263-9860.

Desc: General newspaper (Chinese). *Type:* Periodical.

Focus on China

Ward's Communications

3000 Town Center, Ste. 2750   Ph: (248)357-0800

Southfield, MI 48075-1212   Fax: (248)357-0810

URL: http://www.wardsauto.com

Contact: David E. Zoia, Editor.

Desc: Details events in China's automotive industry. Features statistics. *Type:* Newsletter.

Free the Fathers

845 Oak St.   Ph: (423)756-9660

Chattanooga, TN 37403   Fax: (423)756-7298

Contact: John Davies, Pres.

Desc: Concerned individuals who work to secure freedom for imprisoned Catholic priests, nuns, and laity in communist and other totalitarian countries, particulary the People's Republic of China. According to the organization, Catholic priests are being tortured and imprisoned in China because they are "devout Christians in a nation where atheism still rules with an iron hand." Conducts news media interviews to alert people to the issue. *Type:* Association.

Independent Federation of Chinese Students and Scholars

733 15th St. NW, Ste. 440   Ph: (202)347-0017

Washington, DC 20005   Fax: (202)347-0018

E-mail: hq@ifcss.org

Contact: Jinghong Li, Chm. & CEO.

Desc: Organizations representing the interests of over 50,000 Chinese students and scholars in the U.S.A. Promotes democracy and human rights in China. *Type:* Association.

National Committee on United States-China Relations

71 W. 23rd St., Ste. 1901   Ph: (212)645-9677

New York, NY 10010-4102   Fax: (212)645-1695

E-mail: info@ncuscr.org

URL: http://www.ncuscr.org

Contact: Douglas P. Murray, Pres.

Desc: Nonpartisan educational organization that encourages understanding of the People's Republic of China and the United States among citizens of both countries. Membership includes Americans who share the belief that increased public knowledge of China and of the relations between the U.S. and China enhances international understanding, contributes to the effective conduct of foreign policy, and strengthens the U.S.-China relationship. *Type:* Association.

Organization of Chinese Americans

1001 Connecticut Ave. NW,   Ph: (202)223-5500

Ste. 707   Fax: (202)296-0540

Washington, DC 20036

E-mail: oca@ocanatl.org

URL: http://www.ocanatl.org

Contact: Daphne Kwok, Exec.Dir.

Desc: U.S. citizens and permanent residents over age 18, most of whom are Chinese/Americans. Strives to advance the cause and foster public awareness of the needs and concerns of Chinese/ Americans in the U.S., to promote participation through advancement of equal rights, responsibilities, and opportunities, and to promote cultural awareness. *Type:* Association.

Society on Economics and Management in China

School of Business

Rutgers University

Piscataway, NJ 08854-8054   Ph: (732)445-3582

Contact: Dr. Cheng-few Lee, Editor; Dr. Bikki Jaggi, Editor.

Desc: Covers events in economics, management, accounting, and marketing in China. Also provides limited news of other Asian countries. *Type:* Newsletter.

Ward's Focus on China

Ward's Communications

3000 Town Center, Ste. 2750   Ph: (248)357-0800

Southfield, MI 48075-1212   Fax: (248)357-0810

URL: http://www.wardsauto.com

Contact: David Zoia, Editor.

Desc: Contains data, news, and analysis of the automobile industry in China. *Type:* Newsletter.

Chiropractic

American Chiropractic Association

1701 Clarendon Blvd.   Ph: (703)276-8800

Arlington, VA 22209   Free: 800-986-4636

                                          Fax: (703)243-2593

URL: http://www.amerchiro.org

Contact: Garrett F. Cuneo, HCD, Exec.VP.

Desc: Enhances the philosophy, science, and art of chiropractic, and the professional welfare of individuals in the field. Promotes legislation defining chiropractic health care and improves the public's awareness and utilization of chiropractic. Conducts chiropractic survey and statistical study; maintains library. *Type:* Association.

American Spinal Research Foundation

90 E. Tasman Dr.   Ph: (408)944-6066

San Jose, CA 95134-1617   Free: 800-256-3792

                                          Fax: (408)944-6118

E-mail: asrf98@usa.net

URL: http://www.asrf.org

Contact: Patricia C. Brennan, PhD, Pres.

Desc: Back pain, headache and other spine related problems. *Type:* Research center.

Chiropractors' Association of Saskatchewan— The Bulletin

Chiropractors' Association of Saskatchewan

3420A Hill Ave.   Ph: (306)585-1411

Regina, SK, Canada S4S 0W9   Fax: (306)585-0685

E-mail: cas@netfx.com

Contact: Dr. J.E. Brandt, Editor.

Desc: Features letters to the editor, interviews, news of research, a calendar of events, reports of meetings, news of educational opportunities, job listings, and notices of publications available. *Type:* Newsletter.

Foundation for Chiropractic Education and Research

1330 Beacon St., Ste. 315
Brookline, MA 02446-3202

Ph: (617)734-3397
Free: 888-690-1378
Fax: (617)734-0989

E-mail: rosnerfcer@aol.com
URL: http://www.fcer.org

Contact: Anthony Rosner, PhD, Dir. of Res. & Edu.

Desc: Stimulates and supports scientific research to enhance the knowledge and practice of chiropractic medicine. Research areas include biomechanical studies of the spine and related soft tissue structures; the relationship between spine and body functions; the effects of manipulation upon various body functions; clinical traits of spinal manipulation; the effectiveness of manipulation for various conditions; reliability of various chiropractic analytical and diagnostic procedures; the various instrumentations used in chiropractic; and surveys of utilization of chiropractic treatment and epidemiological and sociological studies. *Type:* Research center.

Foundation for Chiropractic Education and Research

PO Box 4689
Des Moines, IA 50306-4689

Contact: DeAnna L. Beck, Dir.Admin.

Desc: Chiropractors and laymen. Provides funding for scientific research and research training that will "enhance the knowledge and practice of chiropractic as a conservative approach to health care restoration, maintenance, and disease prevention." *Type:* Association.

Northwestern College of Chiropractic

Center for Clinical Studies

2501 W. 84th St.
Bloomington, MN 55431

Ph: (612)885-5444
Fax: (612)888-1957

E-mail: csawyer@nwchiro-edu

Contact: Charles E. Sawyer, DC, VP.

Desc: Chiropractic clinical research, including ambulatory health care. *Type:* Research center.

Parker Chiropractic Resource Foundation

PO Box 40444
Fort Worth, TX 76140-0444

Ph: (817)293-6444
Free: 800-950-8044
Fax: (817)293-0776

Contact: Chance Parker, Pres.

Desc: Doctors of chiropractic. Seeks to keep the chiropractic profession abreast of new developments, practices, and procedures concerning the administration of health care. *Type:* Association.

Precision Chiropractic Research Society

3462 Windsor Ct.
Costa Mesa, CA 92626

Ph: (714)641-4700

Contact: Mr. A.C. Fulkerson, Pres.

Desc: Spinal problems and treatment, including an investigation of the relationship between the cure for headaches and spinal adjustment. Also studies Duchennne muscular dystrophy. *Type:* Research center.

Sacro Occipital Research Society International

PO Box 8245
Prairie Village, KS 66208

Ph: (913)384-2748

Contact: Dr. Cameron DeCamp, Contact.

Desc: Chiropractic studies, focusing on the sacro occipital area of the brain. *Type:* Research center.

Christianity

ACDA Bulletin

Association of Catholic Diocesan Archivists (ACDA)

711 W. Monroe St.
Chicago, IL 60661-3515

Ph: (773)736-5150

Contact: Christine Taylor, Editor, taylorcm@aol.com.

Desc: Recurring features include reports of meetings, news of educational opportunities, job listings, book reviews, and notices of publications available. *Type:* Newsletter.

Advent Christian General Conference of America

PO Box 23152
Charlotte, NC 28227

Ph: (704)545-6161
Fax: (704)573-0712

E-mail: acpub@adventchristian.org

Contact: David E. Ross, Exec.Dir.

Desc: An evangelical organization comprising 306 Advent Christian churches in The U.S. and Canada. Seeks to share the Christian faith around the world by encouraging reliance on the Scriptures. *Type:* Association.

Aid to the Church in Need

PO Box 576
Deer Park, NY 11729-0576

Ph: (516)242-8321
Free: 800-628-NEED
Fax: (516)243-1922

URL: http://www.churchinneed.org

Contact: Sarkis Boghjalian, Dir.

Desc: Catholic organization approved by the Holy See (but open to all Christians). Works through pastoral and social aid to support the Catholic Church wherever persecuted or threatened. *Type:* Association.

Alban Institute

7315 Wisconsin Ave., Ste. 1250 W.
Bethesda, MD 20814-3211

Ph: (301)718-4407
Free: 800-486-1318
Fax: (301)718-1958

E-mail: lnist@alban.com
URL: http://www.alban.org

Contact: James P. Wind, Pres.

Desc: Laity, clergy, executives, and seminary and agency personnel primarily interested in building better congregations. Works to encourage congregations to be vigorous and faithful so that they may equip the people of God to minister within their faith communities and in the world. Assists those who lead or care for congregations; gathers, generates, and shares practical knowledge across denominational lines through action research, consulting and training services, publications, and continuing education. *Type:* Association.

American Council of Christian Churches

PO Box 5455
Bethlehem, PA 18015

Ph: (610)865-3009
Fax: (610)865-3033

E-mail: accc@juno.com
URL: http://www.amcouncilcc.org/

Contact: Dr. Ralph Colas, Exec.Dir.

Desc: Comprised of major religious denominations including Bible Presbyterian Churches, Evangelical Methodist Churches, Fellowship of Fundamental Bible Churches, Free Presbyterian Churches of North America, Fundamental Methodist Churches, General Association of Regular Baptist Churches, Independent Baptist Fellowship of North America, Independent Churches Affiliated, and hundreds of independent churches. ("Each denomination retains its identity and full autonomy, but cannot be associated with the World or National Councils of Churches or the National Association of Evangelicals."). Promotes fellowship and cooperation among "Bible-believing" churches. *Type:* Association.

American TFP

PO Box 1868
York, PA 17405

Ph: (717)225-7197
Fax: (717)225-7479

E-mail: tfp@tfp.org
URL: http://www.tfp.org

Contact: Raymond E. Drake, Pres.

Desc: Works to enlighten public opinion on the values of the religious and cultural heritage of Christian civilization. Stresses the importance of youth programs and other programs dealing with the family and related sociological issues. Promotes research and the cultural and intellectual development of individuals and institutions through grants and scholarships. *Type:* Association.

Amici

American Friends of the Vatican Library

157 Lakeshore Rd.
Grosse Pointe Farms, MI 48236

Ph: (313)885-8855

Contact: Joy Blouin, Editor.

Desc: Reports the progress of the Friends' efforts toward the preservation and addition to the collection of the Vatican Library. Carries articles about the Library's history, holdings, and personnel. *Type:* Newsletter.

Association of Christian Schools International

731 Chapel Hills Dr.
Colorado Springs, CO 80920

Ph: (719)528-6906
Fax: (719)531-0631

URL: http://www.acsi.org

Contact: Dr. Ken Smitherman, Pres.

Desc: Seeks to enable Christian educators and schools worldwide to effectively prepare students for life. *Type:* Association.

The Association of Marian Helpers Bulletin

Marian Helpers Center

Eden Hill
Stockbridge, MA 01263

Ph: (413)298-3691
Free: 800-462-7426
Fax: (413)298-3583

E-mail: dmintl@aol.com.
URL: http://www.marian.org; http://www.carian.org.

Contact: Fr. Joseph Joseph, M.I.C., Director and Publisher; Vinny Flinn, Exec. Editor.

Desc: Official magazine of the Association of Marian Helpers. *Type:* Periodical.

Awake!

Watchtower Bible and Tract Society of New York, Inc.

25 Columbia Heights
Brooklyn, NY 11201

Ph: (718)560-5600
Fax: (914)560-5619

Contact: James N. Pellechia, Contact, (718)560-5600, fax: (718)560-5619, ghawkins@wtbts.org.

Desc: Nonpolitical journal that reports the news, tells about people in many countries, and examines religion and science. Available in 83 languages. *Type:* Periodical.

The Baptist Courier

Baptist Courier, Inc.

PO Drawer 2168
Greenville, SC 29602

Ph: (864)232-8736
Fax: (803)232-8488

Contact: Dr. John E. Roberts, Editor.

Desc: Religious newsmagazine. *Type:* Periodical.

Baptist Messenger

Baptist General Convention of Oklahoma

PO Box 12130
Oklahoma City, OK 73157-2130

Ph: (405)942-3800
Fax: (405)942-3075

E-mail: baptistmessenger@bgco.org; slane@bgco.org.

Contact: John Yeats, Editor, jyeats@bgco.org.

Desc: Newspaper containing religious news and commentary for Southern Baptists. *Type:* Periodical.

The Baptist Record

Mississippi Baptist Convention
PO Box 530   Ph: (601)968-3800
Jackson, MS 39205
E-mail: 70420.37@compuserve.com

Contact: William H. Perkins, Editor; Carl White, Assoc. Editor; Florence Larrimore, Editorial Assoc.; Debbie Sills, Adv. Coord.; Joylin Davis, Layout/Design; Renee Walley, Circulation Mgr.; Betty Anne Bailey, Bookkeeper.

Desc: Baptist magazine (tabloid). *Alt. Contact:* POB 530, Jackson, MS 39205. *Type:* Periodical.

Breaking Bread

Capuchin Soup Kitchen
1760 Mt. Elliot Ave.   Ph: (313)579-2100
Detroit, MI 48207-3496   Fax: (313)579-0461

Contact: Gerald F. Brisson, Development Dir.

Desc: Communicates news and functions of the Soup Kitchen. Spotlights volunteers and donations. *Type:* Newsletter.

Catalyst

Catholic League for Religious and Civil Rights
1011 1st Ave.   Ph: (212)371-3191
New York, NY 10022   Fax: (212)371-3394
E-mail: cl@catholicleague.org.
URL: http://www.catholicleague.org.

Contact: William Donohue, Publisher; Rick Hinshaw, Editor.

Desc: Journal discussing Catholic perspectives on social, moral, and ethical issues. *Type:* Periodical.

Catholic Digest

Catholic Digest
2115 Summit Ave.   Ph: (651)962-6725
St. Paul, MN 55105-1081   Fax: (651)962-6755
E-mail: CDigest@stthomas.edu.
URL: http://www.catholicdigest.org.

Contact: Richard Reece, Editor, (651)962-6741; L. Thomas Kelly, Publisher, (651)962-6730; Dianne Talmage, Production Mgr., (651)962-6743; Deborah Frey, Circ. Dir., (212)870-2552; Thomas Rickert, Advertising Dir., (651)962-6734.

Desc: General interest magazine for Catholics. *Type:* Periodical.

Catholic Forester Magazine

Catholic Order of Foresters
355 Shuman Blvd.   Ph: (630)983-3380
PO Box 3012   Free: 800-552-0145
Naperville, IL 60566-7012   Fax: (630)983-3384

Contact: Dorothy Deer, Editor.

Desc: Fraternal and general interest magazine. *Type:* Periodical.

Catholic Near East

Catholic Near East Welfare Association
1011 1st Ave.   Ph: (212)826-1480
New York, NY 10022   Free: 800-44-CNEWA
   Fax: (212)826-8979

E-mail: cnewa@cnewa.org

Contact: Michael J.L. La Civita, Executive Editor.

Desc: Magazine featuring articles on the people and churches of the Middle East, Northeast Africa, India, and Eastern Europe. Includes descriptions of the humanitarian and pastoral work of the association. *Type:* Periodical.

Catholic New York

Ecclesiastical Communications Corp.
1011 1st Ave.   Ph: (212)688-2399
PO Box 5133   Fax: (212)688-2642
New York, NY 10150-5133
E-mail: cny@cny.org.
URL: http://www.cny.org.

Contact: Anne M. Buckley, Editor; Arthur L. McKenna, General Mgr.

Desc: Religious tabloid. *Type:* Periodical.

Catholic News Service

3211 4th St. NE   Ph: (202)541-3250
Washington, DC 20017-1100   Fax: (202)541-3255
E-mail: cnsinfo@aol.com.

Contact: Thomas N. Lorsung, Dir./Ed.-in-Chief; James M. Lackey, Gen. News Ed.; David Gibson, Features Ed.; Julie L. Asher, Natl. Ed.

Desc: Distributes general news concerning Catholics. *Alt. Contact:* 3211 4th St. NE, Washington, DC 20017-1100; telephone: (202)541-3250; fax: (202)541-3255. *Type:* Periodical.

Catholic Relief Services (U.S. Catholic Conference)

209 W. Fayette St.   Ph: (410)625-2220
Baltimore, MD 21201   Fax: (410)685-1635

Contact: Kenneth Hackett, Exec.Dir.

Desc: Nonpolitical, nonevangelical, official overseas relief and selfhelp development agency of the American Catholic community. Conducts programs of disaster response, refugee relief and rehabilitation, social welfare services, and socio-economic development in 67 countries. Distributes food, clothing, and medicine. *Type:* Association.

The Catholic Spirit

Catholic Bulletin Publishing Co.
244 Dayton Ave.   Ph: (612)291-4444
St. Paul, MN 55102-1892   Fax: (612)291-4460
E-mail: cathspirit@aol.com.

Contact: Dennis W. Heaney, Assoc. Publisher.

Desc: Catholic publication. *Type:* Periodical.

The Catholic Sun

Roman Catholic Diocese of Phoenix
400 E. Monroe   Ph: (602)257-5565
PO Box 13549   Fax: (602)258-6404
Phoenix, AZ 85002-3549
E-mail: cdcasserly@aol.com; a2cathsun@aol.com.
URL: http://www.catholicsun.org.

Contact: Christopher Gunty, Assoc. Publisher, (602)257-5564, cguntysun@aol.com; Bishop Thomas J. O'Brien, Publisher, (602)257-5567; Lynn R. Wurth, Advertising Mgr., (602)257-5567, lwurth@cathdioc.org.

Desc: Religious newspaper providing news, information, and commentary about the Catholic church and the Catholic Diocese of Phoenix, Arizona. *Type:* Periodical.

Catholic Worker

Catholic Worker
36 E. 1st St.   Ph: (212)677-8627
New York, NY 10003

Contact: Sabra McKenzie Hamilton, Managing Editor.

Desc: Catholic periodical for those who advocate and practice non-violence, voluntary poverty, and gospel works of mercy. *Type:* Periodical.

CGA World

Catholic Golden Age
430 Penn Ave.   Ph: (717)342-3294
PO Box 3658   Free: 800-836-5699
Scranton, PA 18505-0658   Fax: (717)963-0149

Contact: Barbara Pegula, Editor.

Desc: Magazine for Catholics aged 50 and over. *Type:* Periodical.

CHAC Info

Catholic Health Association of Canada (CHAC)
1247 Kilborn Pl.   Ph: (613)731-7148
Ottawa, ON, Canada K1H 6K9   Fax: (613)731-7797
E-mail: chac@web.net

Contact: Maryse Blouin, Editor.

Desc: Tracks the activities of the Association. Recurring features include a calendar of events, reports of meetings, news of educational opportunities and awards, and job listings. *Type:* Newsletter.

Christian Business Men's Committee of U.S.A.

1800 McCallie Ave.   Ph: (423)698-4444
Chattanooga, TN 37404   Free: 800-575-2262
   Fax: (615)629-4434

E-mail: membership@abmc.com
URL: http://www.cbmc.com

Contact: Phil Downer, Pres.

Desc: Committees of businessmen of various religious denominations and from different metropolitan areas of the country working together "to present Jesus Christ as Savior and Lord to business and professional men and to develop Christian business and professional men to carry out the great commission." Members and guests meet together for meals, in workplace settings, in homes and in informal gatherings to discuss the realities and principles of biblical truth in the contemporary business world. *Type:* Association.

The Christian Chronicle

Oklahoma Christian University of Science and Arts
Box 11000   Ph: (405)425-5070
Oklahoma City, OK 73136-1100   Fax: (405)425-5076
E-mail: chronicle@oc.edu.

Contact: Dr. Bailey McBride, Editor; Glover Shipp, Managing Editor; Lindy Adams, Assist. Managing Editor; Heather Wolken, Graphic Designer; Dale Jones, Advertising Mgr.; Dr. Lynn McMillon, General Mgr.; Dr. Gwen Atwire, Office Mgr.

Desc: Religious tabloid containing church news, human interest stories, book reviews, features about social issues, and international mission updates. *Type:* Periodical.

Christian Crusade

PO Box 977   Ph: (918)438-4234
Tulsa, OK 74102   Fax: (918)438-4235

Contact: Dr. Billy James Hargis, Pres.

Desc: Christian educational ministry whose purposes are "to safeguard and preserve the conservative Christian ideals upon which America was founded; to protect our cherished freedoms, the heritage of every American"; to oppose persons or organizations who endorse socialist or communist philosophies and to expose publicly the infiltration of such influences into American life; as well as to defend the gospel of Jesus Christ. Opposes U.S. participation in the UN, "federal interference in schools, housing and other matters constitutionally belonging to the states," and government competition with private business. *Type:* Association.

Christian Defense League

PO Box 449   Ph: (504)279-5940
Arabi, LA 70032   Fax: (504)277-5626

Contact: James K. Warner, Exec. Officer.

Desc: Promotes preservation of traditional Christian values and the development of Christian public leaders in the U.S.; Conducts educational and research programs. Operates speakers' bureau. *Type:* Association.

Christian Endeavor International

PO Box 2106
Columbus, OH 43216-2106
Contact: Rev. Keith Miller, Acting Exec.Dir.
Desc: Christ-centered, youth oriented ministry which assists local churches in reaching young people with the Gospel of Jesus Christ, discipling them in their Christian faith, equipping them for Christian ministry, and service in their local churches, community and world. It reaches across denominational, cultural, racial and geographic boundaries. *Type:* Association.

Christian Family Renewal

Box 73   Ph: (209)297-7818
Clovis, CA 93613
Contact: Michael Norris, Pres.
Desc: Christians concerned with problems of the modern family. Promotes Christian solutions to problems in business, and education counseling. Sponsors home study programs in Christian counseling and nutrition. *Type:* Association.

Christian Herald Association

132 Madison Ave.   Ph: (212)684-2800
New York, NY 10016   Fax: (212)684-3740
Contact: Edward H. Morgan, Pres.
Desc: Christian organization committed to "preaching the good news of Jesus Christ and obeying Christ's call to help those in need." *Type:* Association.

Christian Management Report

Christian Management Report
PO Box 4638   Ph: (909)861-8861
Diamond Bar, CA 91765   Fax: (909)860-8247
E-mail: 74407.233@compuserve.com.
Contact: DeWayne Herbroudson, Executive Editor.
Desc: Informs and reports on current issues affecting management in Christian ministries. Provides tax and legal information. *Type:* Newsletter.

Christian Reader

Christianity Today, Inc.
465 Gundersen Dr.   Ph: (630)260-6200
Carol Stream, IL 60188   Fax: (630)260-0114
URL: http://www.christianreader.net.
Contact: Bonne Steffen, Editor, creditoria@aol.com; Marshall Shelley, Exec. Editor.
Desc: A digest magazine of the best in Christian reading. *Type:* Periodical.

Christian Research Institute International

Box 7000   Ph: (949)858-6100
Rancho Santa Margarita, CA   Free: 888-700-0CRI
  92688-7000   Fax: (949)858-6111
E-mail: p-young@ix.netcom.com
URL: http://www.equip.org
Contact: Hank Hanegraaff, Pres.
Desc: Interdenominational, evangelical, Christian apologetics organization that disseminates information on the cults, the occult, religious movements, ethics, and doctrinal controversies in light of historic, orthodox Christianity. Broadcasts daily, live, call-in radio program, the "Bible Answer Man" which is heard in the U.S. and Canada. *Type:* Association.

Christian Research Report

Christian Research Institute (CRI)
PO Box 7000   Ph: (949)858-6111
Rancho Santa Margarita, CA   Fax: (949)858-6100
  92688
URL: http://www.equip.org.
Contact: Hank Hanegraaff.
Desc: Keeps readers current on the world of the cults, the occult, world religions, and aberrant Christian groups. Lists free materials available and activities of Institute staff. *Type:* Newsletter.

Christian Times

KompuKeen Publishing Inc.
PO Box 2606   Ph: (619)660-5500
El Cajon, CA 92021   Fax: (619)660-5505
E-mail: chtimes@cts.com.
Contact: Theresa L. Keener, Editor; Lamar H. Keener, Publisher.
Desc: Publication featuring local, state, and national news from a christian perspective. *Type:* Periodical.

Christianity Today

Christianity Today, Inc.
465 Gundersen Dr.   Ph: (630)260-6200
Carol Stream, IL 60188   Fax: (630)260-0114
URL: http://www.christianity.net/ct.
Contact: David Neff, Exec. Editor, ctedit@aol.com; Michael G. Maudlin, Managing Editor; Linda Schambach, Exec. Dir., Advertising.
Desc: Religious magazine. *Type:* Periodical.

Church News

Deseret Book Co.
40 E. South Temple   Ph: (801)534-1515
PO Box 30178   Free: 800-453-3876
Salt Lake City, UT 84130   Fax: (801)578-3338
URL: http://www.deseretnews.com/cn-home.htm.
Contact: Dell Van Orden, Editor; Gerry Avant, Contact; Steve Hondy, Contact.
Desc: Newspaper reporting church activities. *Type:* Periodical.

Columban Mission

Society of St. Columban
St. Columbans, NE 68056   Ph: (402)291-1920
                                (402)291-4984
E-mail: cioffero@omnilinx.net; cgmo@aol.com.
Contact: Rev. Richard Steinhilber, Editor; Rev. Brendan O'Sullivan, Publisher.
Desc: Magazine about Catholic missions outside the U.S., informing readers of the work of Columban Fathers. *Type:* Periodical.

Company

American Jesuits
3441 N. Ashland Ave.   Ph: (312)281-1534
Chicago, IL 60657   Free: 800-955-5538
                                Fax: (312)281-2667
E-mail: editor@companysj.com.
URL: http://www.companysj.com.
Contact: Martin McHugh, Editor.
Desc: Religious magazine for the American Society of Jesus (Jesuits) and those who work with them. *Type:* Periodical.

Concerned Women for America

1015 15th NW, Ste. 1100   Ph: (202)488-7000
Washington, DC 20005   Free: 800-458-8797
                                Fax: (202)488-0806
URL: http://www.cwfa.org
Contact: Beverly LaHaye, Chm.
Desc: Works to protect and promote Biblical values among all citizens - first through prayer, then education, and finally by influencing society. Goal is "for women and like-minded men, from all walks of life, to come together and restore the family to its traditional purpose and thereby allow each member of the family to realize their God-given potential and be more responsible citizens." *Type:* Association.

Cowboys for Christ

PO Box 7557   Ph: (817)236-0023
Fort Worth, TX 76111   Fax: (817)236-0004
E-mail: cowboysforchrist@juno.com

Contact: Ted K. Pressley, Pres.
Desc: Works in conjunction with local churches to provide evangelistic outreach services. *Type:* Association.

Decision

The Billy Graham Evangelistic Association
PO Box 779   Ph: (612)338-0500
Minneapolis, MN 55440   Fax: (612)335-1299
Contact: Roger Palms, Editor.
Desc: Religious magazine. (Also available in a braille edition.) *Type:* Periodical.

Discipleship Journal

NavPress
7899 Lexington Dr.   Ph: (719)531-3528
Colorado Springs, CO 80920   Fax: (719)598-7128
URL: http://www.navigators.org/djhome.html.
Contact: Peter Mayberry, Assoc. Publisher, (719)531-3528; Susan Maycinik, Editor, (719)531-3529, smaycini@navigato.mhs.compuserve.com; Adam Holz, Assoc. Editor; Sue Kline, Managing Editor, (719)531-3514; Anne Meskey Elhajoui, Art Dir., (719)531-3527; Marcy Shultz, Asst. Dir., (719)531-3526; Dave Wilson, Advertising/Marketing Dir., (719)531-3579; Bob Yates, Advertising Account Manager, (719)531-3558; June Whitely, Fulfillment Dir., (719)531-3501; Jon Killingsworth, Circulation Mgr.
Desc: Evangelical Christian magazine presenting biblical perspectives on Christian growth and ministry with an emphasis on putting principles into practice. *Alt. Contact:* PO Box 35004, Colorado Springs, CO 80935; telephone: (719)548-9222; fax: (719)598-7128. *Type:* Periodical.

Divine Word Missionaries

Divine Word Missionaries
PO Box 6099   Ph: (847)272-7600
Techny, IL 60082-6099   Fax: (847)272-8572
Contact: Rev. Thomas A. Krosnicki, S.V.D., Editor.
Desc: Magazine reporting on the Society's missionary activities. *Type:* Periodical.

The Ensign of the Church of Jesus Christ of the Latter-day Saints

Church of Jesus Christ of Latter-day Saints
50 E. North Temple St.   Ph: (801)240-2210
Salt Lake City, UT 84150-3226 Fax: (801)240-5997
E-mail: jonesme@ldschurch.org.
Contact: Jay M. Todd, Managing Editor.
Desc: Magazine for adult members and friends of the church. *Type:* Periodical.

Episcopal Life

The Episcopal Church in the United States
815 2nd Ave.   Ph: (212)867-8400
New York, NY 10017   Fax: (212)867-0395
E-mail: episcopal.life@ecunet.org.
Contact: Jerrold F. Hames, Editor, (800)334-7626; Ed Stannard, News Editor; Nan Cobbey, Features Editor; Dorothy Kelso, Advertising Director, (800)330-0757.
Desc: Independently edited national newspaper of the Episcopal Church. *Type:* Periodical.

Extension

Catholic Church Extension Society
150 S. Wacker Dr., No. 20th   Ph: (312)236-7240
Chicago, IL 60606-4103   Fax: (312)236-5276
Contact: Brad Collins, Editor; Mr. Richard A. Ritter, Publisher.
Desc: Magazine reporting on activities and issues of the American home missions. *Type:* Periodical.

Fairfield County Catholic
Fairfield County Catholic
238 Jewett Ave.   Ph: (203)372-4301
Bridgeport, CT 06606   Fax: (203)374-2044
E-mail: fccatholic@snet.net.
Contact: Dr. Joseph McAleer, Editor; Ralph Lazzaro, Advertising Mgr.
Desc: Official newspaper of the Roman Catholic Diocese of Bridgeport, (Fairfield county), CT. *Type:* Periodical.

The Family Digest
The Family Digest
PO Box 26126   Ph: (612)929-6765
Minneapolis, MN 55426   Free: 800-722-0985
Contact: Corine B. Erlandson, Editor; Clancy Mylan, President.
Desc: Catholic family and parish magazine. *Alt. Contact:* PO Box 40137, Fort Wayne, IN 46804. *Type:* Periodical.

The Fatima Crusader
National Committee for National Pilgrim Virgin of Canada
PO Box 602   Ph: (905)871-7607
Fort Erie, ON, Canada L2A   Free: 800-263-8160
5X3   Fax: (905)871-3646
E-mail: fatima@vaxxine.com; info@fatima.org.
URL: http://www.fatima.org.
Contact: Coralie Graham, Editor.
Desc: Magazine promoting devotion to Our Lady and knowledge of Her message at Fatima. *Type:* Periodical.

Federation of Protestant Welfare Agencies
281 Park Ave. S.   Ph: (212)777-4800
New York, NY 10010   Fax: (212)673-4085
E-mail: info@fpwa.org
Contact: Megan E. McLaughlin, D.S.W., Exec.Dir.
Desc: Umbrella organization of approximately 260 affiliated voluntary human service agencies serving over 1.5 million people in the New York metropolitan area. Provides consultative services, educational programs, referral services, and recruitment and screening of volunteers for member agencies and selfhelp community groups. Provides information and conducts advocacy program on proposed and needed legislation and regulations dealing with social welfare. *Type:* Association.

The Florida Catholic
The Florida Catholic
PO Box 609512   Ph: (407)423-3438
Orlando, FL 32860-9512   Free: 800-377-3438
   Fax: (407)660-2977
URL: http://www.flcath.org.
Contact: Henry Libersat, Editor/General Mgr., (407)660-9141, sdemontrichard@flcath.org; Steve Paradis, Managing Editor, sparadis@flcath.org.
Desc: Official newspaper (tabloid) of the Diocese of Orlando. *Type:* Periodical.

FMA Focus
Franciscan Misson Associates (FMA)
274-280 W. Lincoln Ave.   Ph: (914)664-5604
PO Box 598   Fax: (914)664-3017
Mt. Vernon, NY 10551-0598
Contact: Fr. Robert Campagna, Editor.
Desc: Emphasizes missionary commitment to the Catholic church. *Type:* Newsletter.

Focus on the Family Clubhouse
Focus on the Family
8605 Explorer Dr.   Ph: (719)531-3400
Colorado Springs, CO 80920-   Free: 800-232-6459
1051   Fax: (719)548-5860
E-mail: tifeditor@fotf.org

Contact: Jesse Florea, Editor; Annette Bourland, Asst. Editor.
Desc: Consumer Christian magazine for children ages 8-12 years. *Type:* Periodical.

Forward Day by Day
Forward Movement Publications
412 Sycamore St.   Ph: (513)721-6659
Cincinnati, OH 45202   Free: 800-543-1813
   Fax: (513)721-0729
E-mail: forwardmovement@msn.com
URL: http://www.forwardmovement.org
Contact: Rev. Edward S. Gleason, Editor & Director, egleason@eos.net.
Desc: Daily devotional guide. *Type:* Periodical.

Foundation for American Christian Education
4225 Portsmouth Blvd., Ste. B   Ph: (757)488-6601
Chesapeake, VA 23321-9588   Free: 800-352-FACE
   Fax: (757)488-5593
URL: http://www.face.net
Contact: Rosalie J. Slater, Contact.
Desc: Works to research, document, publish and teach the Christian heritage of education and government in the United States. *Type:* Association.

The Friend of Brother Andre
Oratoire St. Joseph Du-Mont-Royal
3800, Chemin Queen Mary   Ph: (514)733-8211
Montreal, PQ, Canada H3V   Fax: (514)733-9735
1H6
E-mail: pereweb@saint-joseph.org.
Contact: Charles E. Smith.
Desc: Contains news of events at the Montreal Shrine and feature articles on Brother Andre. *Type:* Newsletter.

Frontline Report
Society of African Missions
23 Bliss Ave.   Ph: (201)567-0450
Tenafly, NJ 07670   Fax: (201)567-7156
URL: http://www.smafathers.org.
Contact: Linda Telesco, Editor, smausa-m@smafathers.org.
Desc: Highlights the activities of Roman Catholic missionaries. Promotes the establishment of native clergy. *Type:* Newsletter.

Full Gospel Business Men's Fellowship International
PO Box 19714   Ph: (949)260-0700
Irvine, CA 92623-9714   Fax: (949)260-0718
E-mail: fgbmfi@ix.netcom.com
URL: http://www.fgbmfi.org
Contact: Richard Shakarian, Pres.
Desc: Association of local chapters of men "who profess belief in fundamental Christian doctrine, especially the baptism with the Holy Spirit as recorded in Acts 2:4 ('And they were filled with the Holy Ghost and began to speak with other tongues, as the Spirit gave them utterance')." Originally formed by members of Pentecostal churches, FGBMFI has come to include increasing numbers of persons from the historic Protestant churches such as Episcopalians, Presbyterians, Baptists, Methodists, and from the Roman Catholic church. Its members practice speaking in tongues, the phenomenon known as glossolalia. Attempts to make tongue speaking an added dimension of the Christian experience in mainstream churches, rather than splitting off to form new groups. *Type:* Association.

Glenmary Challenge
Glenmary Home Missioners
PO Box 465618   Ph: (513)874-8900
Cincinnati, OH 45246   Free: 800-935-0975
   Fax: (513)874-1690
Contact: Karen Hurley, Editor; Betty Freedman, Production Mgr.
Desc: Magazine reporting Catholic missionary activities in 70 areas of the US. *Type:* Periodical.

IFCA International
3520 Fairlanes Ave.   Ph: (616)531-1840
PO Box 810   Free: 800-347-1840
Grandville, MI 49468   Fax: (616)531-1814
Contact: Dr. Richard I. Gregory, Exec.Dir.
Desc: Ministers, missionaries, youth leaders, musicians, and ministerial students (1248); churches and organizations (712). Seeks to offer independent fundamentalist churches the benefits of unity, while allowing them to keep their autonomy. *Type:* Association.

Intercessors for America
17 Royal St. SW   Ph: (703)777-0003
PO Box 4477   Fax: (703)777-2324
Leesburg, VA 20175
E-mail: usapray@aol.com
URL: http://www.ifa-usapray.org
Contact: Gary Bergel, Pres.
Desc: Christian ministry. Encourages "effective prayer and fasting for the church, the nation, and their leaders." *Type:* Association.

International Order of the King's Daughters and Sons
34 Vincent Ave.   Ph: (716)357-4951
PO Box 1017
Chautauqua, NY 14722
Contact: Marilyn C. Furman, Office Mgr.
Desc: International, interdenominational, interracial organization for development of spiritual life and stimulation of Christian activities. Local groups operate camps, day care centers, homes for the aged, hospitals, and other service institutions. Sponsors specialized education programs. *Type:* Association.

Jews for Jesus Newsletter
Jews for Jesus
60 Haight St.   Ph: (415)864-2600
San Francisco, CA 94102-5895   Fax: (415)552-8325
E-mail: jf@jews-for-jesus.org, purplepome@aol.com
Contact: Ruth Rosen, Editor.
Desc: Carries stories on Jewish holidays, history, and culture as they relate to Christianity. Publishes inspirational articles on the Christian faith and also news of the organization. *Type:* Newsletter.

Jubilee
Prison Fellowship
PO Box 17500   Ph: (703)834-3675
Washington, DC 20041-0500   Fax: (703)318-0235
Contact: David Carlson, Editor; Becky Beane, Editor; Evelyn Bence, Editor.
Desc: To tell the story of Prison Fellowship's ministry to prisoners, ex-prisoners, and their families, and to challenge the church to radical discipleship and active commitment to Christ. *Type:* Newsletter.

Leaves
Mariannhill Mission Society
PO Box 87   Ph: (313)561-2330
Dearborn, MI 48121-0087
Contact: Rev. Thomas Heier, C.M.M., Editor-in-Chief.
Desc: Magazine providing religious and spiritual encouragement for families. *Type:* Periodical.

Living with Christ

Novalis

49 Front St. E., 2nd Fl. Ph: (416)363-3303
Toronto, ON, Canada M5E Free: 800-387-7164
1B3 Fax: (416)363-9409
E-mail: novalis@interlog.com; pambrunl@ustpaul.
uottawa.ca.

Contact: Louise Pambrun, Editor.

Desc: Roman Catholic missalette, including the complete daily Mass readings. *Alt. Contact:* Saint Paul University, 223 Main St., Ottawa, ON, Canada K1S 1C4; telephone: (613)751-4012; fax: (613)782-3004. *Type:* Periodical.

Living Faith

Creative Communications for the Parish

1564 Fencorp Dr. Free: 800-325-9414
Fenton, MO 63026
E-mail: ccp@creativecomm.com

Contact: James E. Adams, Editor; Mark Neilsen, Assoc. Editor.

Desc: Devotional magazine. *Type:* Periodical.

The Long Island Catholic

The Long Island Catholic

99 N. Village Ave. Ph: (516)594-1000
PO Box 9009 Free: 800-532-8542
Rockville Centre, NY 11571 Fax: (516)594-1092
E-mail: tlic@ix.netcom.com.

Contact: Elizabeth O'Connor, Editor; Most Rev. John R. McGann, Publisher; Marion DeMott, Advertising Mgr.

Desc: Official newspaper of the Diocese of Rockville Centre, on Long Island. *Type:* Periodical.

Lutheran Journal

Macalester Park Publishing Company

7317 Cahill Rd., Ste. 201 Ph: (612)561-1234
Minneapolis, MN 55439 Free: 800-407-9078
  Fax: (612)941-3010
Contact: Rev. Armin U. Deye, Editor; Michael L. Beard, Publisher.

Desc: Religious magazine. *Type:* Periodical.

The Lutheran Layman

International Lutheran Laymen's League

2185 Hampton Ave. Ph: (314)951-4100
St. Louis, MO 63139 Fax: (314)951-4295
Contact: Gerald Perschbacher, Editor.

Desc: International Lutheran Layman's League membership magazine with news about Lutheran Hour Ministries. *Type:* Periodical.

Lutheran Witness

Board for Communication Services/The Lutheran Church--Missouri Synod

1333 S. Kirkwood Rd., Ph: (314)965-9000
St. Louis, MO 63122-7295 Fax: (314)965-3396
Contact: Rev. David Mahsman, Editor, (314)965-9000, fax: (314)965-3396, david.mahsman@lcms.org; Karen Andersen, Advertising Mgr., (314)268-1101, karena@cphnet.org.

Desc: Lutheran magazine. *Type:* Periodical.

Lutheran Woman Today

Augsburg Fortress, Publishers

100 S. Fifth St., Ste. 700 Ph: (612)330-3300
PO Box 1209 Free: 800-426-0115
Minneapolis, MN 55440-1209 Fax: (612)330-3455
Contact: Nancy Stelling, Editor.

Desc: Women of the Evangelical Lutheran Church bible study magazine. *Type:* Periodical.

Message

Review and Herald Publishing Association

55 W. Oak Ridge Dr. Ph: (301)393-3000
Hagerstown, MD 21740 Free: 800-765-6955
  Fax: (301)393-3292
E-mail: message@rhpa.org

Contact: Rhoda K. Johnson, Editorial Secretary; Dr. Ron Smith, Editor.

Desc: Religious magazine for African-Americans. *Type:* Periodical.

The Miraculous Medal

Central Association of the Miraculous Medal

475 E. Chelten Ave. Ph: (215)848-1010
Philadelphia, PA 19144-5785
Contact: William J. O'Brien, C.M, Editor and Publisher.

Desc: Catholic magazine. *Type:* Periodical.

Mission Magazine

Society for the Propagation of the Faith

366 5th Ave., 12th Fl. Ph: (212)563-8700
New York, NY 10001 Free: 800-431-2222
  Fax: (212)563-8725
E-mail: zamcat@aol.com

Contact: Mary Regis McLoughlin, Editor, (212)563-8726; Monica Yehle, Managing Editor, (212)563-8706; Patricia Macias, Comm. Coordinator, (212)563-8729.

Desc: Magazine seeking to foster a missionary spirit among Catholics. *Type:* Periodical.

Missionhurst

Missionhurst

4651 N. 25th St. Ph: (703)528-3804
Arlington, VA 22207 Fax: (703)522-7864
Contact: Rev. Bill Wyndaele, Editor; Donna Lynne Rolls, Asst. editor.

Desc: Magazine promoting missionary awareness and informing benefactors of missionary activities. *Type:* Periodical.

Mountain Movers

General Council of the Assemblies of God Gospel Publishing House

1445 Boonville Ave. Ph: (417)862-2781
Springfield, MO 65802-1894 Fax: (417)862-0416
Contact: John T. Maempa, Editor; Charles Hungerford, Managing Editor.

Desc: Magazine about Assemblies of God foreign missions. *Type:* Periodical.

Narramore Christian Foundation

250 W. Colorado Blvd., Ste. Ph: (626)821-8400
200 Fax: (626)821-8409
PO Box 661900
Arcadia, CA 91066-1900
E-mail: 102132.3065@compuserve.com

Contact: Dr. Clyde M. Narramore, Pres.

Desc: To help prevent and solve human problems through the application of scriptural and psychological principles and insights. *Type:* Association.

National Catholic Educational Association

1077 30th St. NW, Ste. 100 Ph: (202)337-6232
Washington, DC 20007 Fax: (202)333-6706
URL: http://www.nca.org

Contact: Leonard DeFiore, CSJ, Pres.

Desc: Catholic schools and religious education centers from kindergarten through graduate school levels; individuals. *Type:* Association.

National Catholic Women's Union

3835 Westminster Pl. Ph: (314)371-1653
St. Louis, MO 63108-3492

Contact: Rev. John H. Miller, CSC, Dir.

Desc: Individual Catholic women and affiliated societies interested in Catholic social action. Sponsors religious activities, works of charity, mission activities, and maternity guilds. Promotes vocations to the priesthood and the religious life. *Type:* Association.

National Collegiate Association for Research of Principles

4 W. 43rd St. Ph: (212)382-2402
New York, NY 10036 Fax: (212)382-2005
E-mail: worldcarp@aol.com
URL: http://www.worldcarp.org

Contact: Michael Balcomb.

Desc: College students interested in reviving religious spirit, especially Christianity, on campus. Revives moral educational values. *Type:* Association.

National Woman's Christian Temperance Union

1730 Chicago Ave. Ph: (847)864-1396
Evanston, IL 60201-4585 Fax: (708)864-9497
E-mail: sarah@wctu.org
URL: http://www.wctu.org

Contact: Sarah F. Ward, Pres.

Desc: Nonpartisan, interdenominational Christian women dedicated to educating America's youth about the harmful effects of alcohol, narcotic drugs, and tobacco on the human body and American society. Seeks to build sentiment for total abstinence through teaching the relation of alcohol to the mental, moral, social, spiritual and physical well-being of the individual and the nation. Promotes essay, poster, picture coloring, and speech medal contests as well as intercollegiate oratorical contests on alcohol and related problems; produces literature on temperance for use in schools and churches; sponsors total abstinence training camps for children and youth; makes available research materials to professionals and students; conducts philanthropic activities. *Type:* Association.

The Navigators

PO Box 6000 Ph: (719)598-1212
Colorado Springs, CO 80934 Fax: (719)260-0479
E-mail: navs@gospelcom.net
URL: http://www.navigators.org

Contact: Alan Andrews, Dir.

Desc: Christian service organization to "evangelize, establish, and equip laymen and women and to train workers for Christ." Staff of individuals representing 59 nationalities serve in 103 countries. Maintains year-round conference center and summer youth camps. *Type:* Association.

Officers' Christian Fellowship of the U.S.A.

3784 South Inca Free: 800-424-1984
Englewood, CO 80110
E-mail: ocf@compuserve.com
URL: http://www.ocfusa.org

Contact: Arthur J. Athens, Exec.Dir.

Desc: Officers from all branches of the U.S. Armed Forces whose commitment to Jesus Christ includes both concern for and expression within the military. Objectives are: to strengthen members to maturity in their spiritual and secular lives; to help members lead men and women in the military to commit their lives to Jesus Christ and to grow to spiritual maturity; to encourage members in spirit-led prayer, Bible study, and Christian witness. *Type:* Association.

Our Sunday Visitor

Our Sunday Visitor Publishing
200 Noll Plaza
Huntington, IN 46750
Ph: (219)356-8400
Free: 800-348-2440
Fax: (219)356-8472

E-mail: osvinc@osv.com; oursunvis@osv.com.

Contact: Greg Erlandson, Editor-in-Chief; Robert P. Lockwood, Publisher; Peter Schownir, Advertising Dir.

Desc: Roman Catholic weekly newspaper. *Type:* Periodical.

Peale Center for Christian Living

66 E. Main St.
Pawling, NY 12564-1409
Ph: (914)855-5000
Fax: (914)855-1462

Contact: John Temple, CEO.

Desc: Prints and distributes messages books, pamphlets, and magazines. Provides Dial-A-Prayer and radio programming. Conducts School of Practical Christianity for Ministers. *Type:* Association.

Pentecostal Assemblies of the World, Inc.

3939 Meadows Dr.
Indianapolis, IN 46205
Ph: (317)547-9541
Fax: (317)543-0512

E-mail: pawinc@indy.net

Contact: John E. Hampton, Admin.

Desc: Pastors, evangelists, and missionaries united to spread the Gospel throughout the world. Seeks to unify religious doctrine and establish new churches. *Type:* Association.

Petro Process Directory

Atlantic Communications
1635 W. Alabama
Houston, TX 77006-4196
Ph: (713)529-1616
Free: 800-654-1480
Fax: (713)523-7804

E-mail: ac@oilonline.com

URL: http://www.oilonline.com/atcom.html.

Contact: James W. Self, Editor; Joey Villaireal, Editor; Sheila Renfro, Editor.

Desc: 9,000 companies in the United States engaged in petrochemical and refining industries; suppliers of products and services to the industry. *Type:* Directory.

Pittsburgh Catholic

Pittsburgh Catholic Publishing Associates, Inc.
135 1st Ave., No. 200
Pittsburgh, PA 15222-1506
Ph: (412)471-1252
Fax: (412)471-4228

Contact: William Fodiak, Editor; Jack Lee, Advertising Mgr.; Carmella Weismantle, Editor.

Desc: General religious interest magazine. *Type:* Periodical.

Plymouth Rock Foundation

Fisk Mill
PO Box 577
Marlborough, NH 03455
Ph: (603)876-4685
Free: 800-210-1620
Fax: (603)876-4128

E-mail: plymrock@top.monad.net

URL: http://www.plymrock.org

Contact: Rus Walton, Exec.Dir.

Desc: Purposes are: "to advance God's Biblical principles of self and civil government as the only real basis for a society of free people; to help restore the foundation of the American Christian Republic; to be a vital part of the total ministry commissioned by our Lord and Savior." Believes that "an American reformation, if it is to be, must begin with Christians, and that it must be done on an individual basis." Sponsors Christian Freedom Institutes. Maintains Christian Committees of Correspondence as local action/service units. Conducts workshops and seminars for pastors and Christian educators in biblical principles of government and education and America's Christian history. *Type:* Association.

Portals of Prayer

Concordia Publishing House
3558 S. Jefferson Ave.
St. Louis, MO 63118
Ph: (314)268-1000
Free: 800-325-3040
Fax: (314)268-1329

Desc: Religion and theology magazine (English, German and large print). *Type:* Periodical.

The Presbyterian

The Presbyterian
920 S. I-35 E.
Denton, TX 76205-7898
Ph: (817)382-9656
Fax: (817)383-8253

Contact: Carolyn J. Frazier, Managing Editor; Richard A. Thompson, Exec. Editor.

Desc: Regional Presbyterian newspaper. *Type:* Periodical.

Presbyterian Lay Committee

PO Box 2210
Lenoir, NC 28645-2210
Ph: (828)758-8716
Fax: (828)758-0920

E-mail: laymanletters@layman.org

URL: http://www.layman.org

Contact: Parker T. Williamson, Exec.Ed.

Desc: Encourages Presbyterian laymen to emphasize the church's mission of spiritual leadership and the teachings of the Bible as the authoritative Word of God. *Type:* Association.

The Presbyterian Layman

The Presbyterian Lay Committee, Inc.
PO Box 2210
Lenoir, NC 28645
Ph: (828)758-8716

URL: http://www.layman.org.

Contact: Parker T. Williamson, Editor.

Desc: Newspaper for Presbyterian Church (U.S.A.). *Alt. Contact:* 136 Tremont Park Drive, PO Box 2210, Lenoir, NC 28645; telephone: (828)758-8716; fax: (828)758-0920. *Type:* Periodical.

Presbyterian Men

100 Witherspoon
Louisville, KY 40202
Ph: (502)569-5485
Fax: (502)569-8263

Contact: Rev. Lloyd Duravant, Exec.Sec.

Desc: Laymen's organization of the Presbyterian Church (U.S.A.). *Type:* Association.

Presbyterian Women

100 Witherspoon St.
Louisville, KY 40202
Ph: (502)569-5365
Free: 800-872-3283
Fax: (502)569-8026

Contact: Gladys Strachan, Exec.Dir.

Desc: Purposes are to promote the Presbyterian church and its teachings and to provide a forum for Presbyterian women. Administers to the needs of individuals through missions worldwide; defends the rights of those who are economically and politically powerless; makes political and social commitments to issues involving justice, peace, freedom, and world hunger; examines topics such as apartheid, child abandonment, rape, divorce, and displaced women. Participates in Presbyterian educational ministry and the training of church leaders. *Type:* Association.

Presbyterians for Renewal

8134 New LaGrange Rd., Ste. 227
Louisville, KY 40222
Ph: (502)425-4630
Fax: (502)423-8324

Contact: Betty Moore, Exec.Dir.

Desc: Supporters are individuals, congregations, and foundations. Trains church officers. Conducts renewal weekends, officer retreats, and marriage enrichment programs. *Type:* Association.

Pulpit Helps

AMG Publishers
6815 Shallowford Rd.
Chattanooga, TN 37421
Ph: (423)894-6060
Free: 800-251-7206
Fax: (423)510-8074

E-mail: amgpublisher@aol.com

URL: http://www.amginternational.org

Contact: Spiros Zodhiates, Editor; Bob Dasal, editor@pulpithelps.com.

Desc: Religious newspaper (tabloid) containing sermon outlines, articles, and advice. *Alt. Contact:* Carlton Dunn & Associates 332 N. Broadway, Pitman, NJ 08071; telephone: (609)582-0690; fax: (609)582-1206. *Type:* Periodical.

Religion News Service

1101 Connecticut Ave. NW
Ste. 350
Washington, DC 20036
Ph: (202)463-8777
Fax: (202)463-0033

URL: http://www.nj.com/rns.

Contact: Dale Hanson, Publisher; David Anderson, Editor.

Desc: Distributes religious news service. *Alt. Contact:* 1101 Connecticut Ave. NW, Ste. 350, Washington, DC 20036; telephone: (202)463-8777; fax: (202)463-0033. *Type:* Periodical.

Religious Drawings Inc.

6624 Golf Hill Dr.
Dallas, TX 75232
Ph: (214)371-3986

Contact: Jack Hamm, Artist/Dir.; D.A. Alexander, Sec.

Alt. Contact: 6624 Golf Hill Dr., Dallas, TX 75232; telephone: (214)371-3986. *Type:* Periodical.

St. Anthony Messenger

Franciscan Friars of St. John Baptist Province
1615 Republic St.
Cincinnati, OH 45210
Ph: (513)241-5615
Free: 800-488-0488
Fax: (513)241-0399

E-mail: stanthony@americancatholic.org.

URL: http://www.americancatholic.org.

Contact: Rev. Norman Perry, Editor; Rev. Jeremy Harrington, Publisher; Barbara K. Baker, Advertising Mgr.; Thomas Shumate, Business Mgr.

Desc: Family-Oriented National Catholic magazine. *Type:* Periodical.

St. Louis Review

St. Louis Review
462 N. Taylor Ave.
St. Louis, MO 63108
Ph: (314)531-9700
Fax: (314)531-2269

E-mail: slreview@i1.net.

Contact: Rev. Dennis M. Delaney, Editor; Paul Pennick, Managing Editor; Archbishop Justin Rigali, Publisher; Thomas L. Courtaway, Comptroller.

Desc: Catholic newspaper. *Type:* Periodical.

Salesian

Salesian Missions
2 Lefevre Ln.
PO Box 30
New Rochelle, NY 10802
Ph: (914)633-8344
Fax: (914)633-7404

E-mail: missionsug@aol.com.

Contact: Rev. James Marra, Director; Rev. Donald Delaney, Editor.

Desc: Magazine describing work done by Salesians in the missions. *Type:* Periodical.

SCRIBE

Scribe Media
5606 Medical Circle   Ph: (608)271-1025
Madison, WI 53719   Free: 800-373-9692
    Fax: (608)271-1150
E-mail: scribe@xc.org
Contact: Gordon Govier, Editor.
Desc: Concerned about informational programming in religious broadcasting and broadcast journalism. Recurring features include letters to the editor, interviews, news of research, a collection, reports of meetings, news of educational opportunities, job listings, and book reviews. *Type:* Newsletter.

The Secret Place

American Baptist Churches, USA
PO Box 851   Ph: (610)768-2000
Valley Forge, PA 19482-0851   Free: 800-ABC-3USA
    Fax: (610)768-2320
Contact: Kathleen Hayes, Sr. Ed.
Desc: Devotional magazine (large print edition is available). *Type:* Periodical.

Sojourners

2401 15th St. NW   Ph: (202)328-8842
Washington, DC 20009   Free: 800-714-7474
    Fax: (202)328-8757
E-mail: sojourners@sojourners.com
URL: http://www.sojourners.com
Contact: James E. Wallis, Pres.
Desc: Seeks to raise critical issues confronting Christians in America today. *Type:* Association.

The Texas Catholic Herald

The Texas Catholic Herald
1700 San Jacinto St.   Ph: (713)659-5461
Houston, TX 77002   Fax: (713)659-3444
E-mail: veretas@aol.com; tcl1122@aol.com.
Contact: Jacqueline Srouji, Exec. Ed.; Most Rev. Joseph A. Fiorenza, Publisher.
Desc: Official newspaper (tabloid) of the Catholic Diocese of Galveston-Houston. *Type:* Periodical.

Today's Christian Woman

Christianity Today, Inc.
465 Gundersen Dr.   Ph: (630)260-6200
Carol Stream, IL 60188   Fax: (630)260-0114
E-mail: tcwedit@aol.com.
URL: http://www.christianity.net/tcw.
Contact: Ramona Cramer Tucker, Editor, tcwedit@aol.com; Jane J. Struckbrink, Sr. Ed.; Harold L. Myra, Publisher.
Desc: Religious magazine for contemporary Christian women. *Type:* Periodical.

United Church Board for World Ministries

700 Prospect Ave. E., 6th Fl.   Ph: (216)736-3200
Cleveland, OH 44115   Fax: (216)736-3259
URL: http://www.ucc.org.globalministries
Contact: David Hirano, Exec.VP.
Desc: Clergy and laypersons of the United Church of Christ. Purposes are to: work with Christians worldwide to bring people into "fellowship with Jesus Christ"; proclaim the gospel and be a witness to God's love in the world; support individuals working to strengthen their churches, improve their lives, and be witnesses in their communities; raise public conciousness of the effects that U.S. social, political, and economic policies have on other countries; encourage globally responsible actions by individuals and bureaucracies. *Type:* Association.

United States Catholic Conference/Migration and Refugee Services

3211 4th St. NE   Ph: (202)541-3352
Washington, DC 20017-1194   Fax: (202)722-8755
E-mail: mrs@nccbuscc.org
URL: http://www.nccbuscc.org/mrs
Contact: Mark Franken, Contact.
Desc: Public policy and social action office of the U.S. Catholic Conference, on matters of migration, refugee, and immigration. Provides program support ad regional coordination for a network of 110 diocesan refugee resettlement offices. *Type:* Association.

Unity Magazine

Unity School of Christianity
1901 NW Blue Pkwy.   Ph: (816)524-3550
Unity Village, MO 64065-0001
E-mail: umag@unityworldhq.org.
Contact: Philip White, Editor; Janet McNamara, Managing Editor.
Desc: Religious magazine printing metaphysical and inspirational articles and poems. A spiritual resouce for daily living. Presenting practical ideas for a living a more spiritual life. Emphasizing the unity of all people-with each other and with God. *Type:* Periodical.

Virtue

Christianity Today, Inc.
465 Gundersen Dr.   Ph: (630)260-6200
Carol Stream, IL 60188   Fax: (630)260-0114
E-mail: virtuemag@aol.com.
Contact: Harold Smith, Publisher; Linda Schambach, VP, Sales/Advertising.
Desc: Christian magazine for women. *Type:* Periodical.

Waifs' Messenger

Mission of Our Lady of Mercy Inc.
1140 W. Jackson   Ph: (312)738-7560
Chicago, IL 60607   Fax: (312)738-9250
Contact: John Riss, Editor, (312)738-7565.
Desc: Magazine reporting on activities of the young men and women of Mercy Home for Boys & Girls and seeking to inspire support. *Type:* Periodical.

The Windsor Star

The Windsor Star
167 Ferry St.   Ph: (519)255-5711
Windsor, ON, Canada N9A   Fax: (519)255-5778
4M5
Contact: Andre Prefontaine, Publisher; James Bruce, Editor; Robert Becker, Advertising Dir.; Glen Ross, Director; Mike Dunnell, Managing Editor; Bill Hickey, Metro Editor; Rob Van Nie, Sports Editor; Harry Van Vugt, Entertainment Editor; Lisa Monforton, Lifestyles Editor; Doug Williamson, Business.
Desc: Newspaper. *Type:* Periodical.

Women of the Church of God

1303 E. 5th St.   Ph: (765)642-0256
Anderson, IN 46012   Fax: (317)642-5652
Contact: Linda Mason, Natl. Coord.
Desc: Women affiliated with the Church of God (Anderson, IN). Seeks to creatively and effectively extend the gospel of Jesus Christ, promote spiritual and personal growth, build friendship and interdependence, widen mental horizons and enlarge vision, and encourage the stewardship of all of life. *Type:* Association.

The Wooden Bell

Catholic Relief Services
209 W. Fayette St.   Ph: (410)625-2220
Baltimore, MD 21201-3443   Free: 800-736-3467
    Fax: (410)234-2983
E-mail: webmaster@catholicrelief.org.
URL: http://www.catholicrelief.org.
Contact: Margaret Guellich, CFRE, Editor.
Desc: Disseminates current news on the assistance provided to the needy in 75 countries by the Service, which is a non-political, non-evangelical, official overseas relief and self-help development agency of the American Catholic community. Publishes feature articles on on-going projects and disaster relief aid. *Type:* Newsletter.

The Word Among Us

The Word Among Us Press
9639 Dr. Perry Rd., No. 126   Ph: (301)831-1262
Ijamsville, MD 21754   Free: 800-775-
    WORD
    Fax: (301)831-1188
Contact: Jeff Smith, Publisher; Leo Zanchettin, Editor.
Desc: Magazine containing articles to help Catholics read, understand, and act on the teachings of scripture and live the Christian life. *Type:* Periodical.

World's Christian Endeavor Union

PO Box 2106   Ph: (614)258-3947
Columbus, OH 43216-2106
Contact: David G. Jackson, Exec.Dir. & Gen.Sec.
Desc: Christian Endeavor societies and unions (interdenominational groups of Christian laymen) in over 75 countries and island groups. Fosters fellowship and unity among members and promotes and reinforces the interests of the Christian Endeavor movement worldwide. Encourages contact with Christians outside of the societies. *Type:* Association.

Your Church

Christianity Today, Inc.
465 Gundersen Dr.   Ph: (630)260-6200
Carol Stream, IL 60188   Fax: (630)260-0114
E-mail: yceditor@aol.com.
Contact: Phyllis Ten Elshof, Editor, yceditor@aol.com.
Desc: Magazine about church business administration. *Type:* Periodical.

Civil Rights and Liberties

American-Arab Relations Committee

Box 416   Ph: (516)889-0005
New York, NY 10017   Fax: (516)889-0005
Desc: Persons concerned about the goal of improving American-Arab relations and the establishment of a peaceful and democratic Palestine. Does not take stands on problems of the Arab world and inter-Arab relations or on domestic issues within the U.S. Opposes fascism, anti-Semitism, and Zionism. *Type:* Association.

American Civil Liberties Union

125 Broad St. 18 Fl.   Ph: (212)549-2500
New York, NY 10004-2400   Fax: (212)549-2646
E-mail: aclu@aclu.org
URL: http://www.aclu.org/
Contact: Ira Glasser, Exec.Dir.
Desc: Champions the rights set forth in the Bill of Rights of the U.S. Constitution: freedom of speech, press, assembly, and religion; due process of law and fair trial; equality before the law regardless of race, color, sexual orientation, national origin, political opinion, or religious belief. Activities include litigation, advocacy, and public education. *Type:* Association.

Anti-Defamation League

823 United Nations Plz.　　Ph: (212)490-2525
New York, NY 10017　　Fax: (212)867-0779
Contact: Abraham H. Foxman, Dir.
Desc: Seeks to stop the defamation of Jewish people and to secure justice and fair treatment to all citizens alike. *Type:* Association.

Center for Constitutional Rights

666 Broadway, 7th Fl.　　Ph: (212)614-6464
New York, NY 10012　　Fax: (212)614-6499
E-mail: ccr@igc.apc.org
Contact: Ron D. Daniels, Exec.Dir.
Desc: Legal and edeucational organization dedicated to advancing and protecting "the rights guaranteed by the United States Constitution and the Universal Declaration of Human Rights." Committed to the "creative use of law" as a positive force for social change. Sponsors the Ella Baker Student Program. *Type:* Association.

Citizens Committee for the Right to Keep and Bear Arms

Liberty Park　　Ph: (425)454-4911
12500 NE 10th Pl.　　Fax: (206)451-3959
Bellevue, WA 98005
Contact: Ken Jacobson, Exec.Dir.
Desc: Citizens interested in defending the Second Amendment; more than 150 members of Congress serve on the advisory board. Conducts educational and political activities, and in-depth studies on gun legislation. Conducts lobbying activities. *Type:* Association.

Constitutional Rights Foundation

601 S. Kingsley Dr.　　Ph: (213)487-5590
Los Angeles, CA 90005　　Free: 800-488-4CRF
　　Fax: (213)386-0459
E-mail: crf@crf-usa.org
URL: http://www.crf_usa.org
Contact: Todd Clark, Exec.Dir.
Desc: Helps young people to better understand the workings of the democratic system and encourage them to undertake a positive role in American society. CRF is striving to empower a new generation of engaged citizens, urging them to familiarize themselves with the substance of our Constitution and civil institutions. Mentoring programs, professional internships, leadership development, community problem solving, teacher training and educational materials highlight some of the way in which CRF is working to lead young Americans towards a future based on democratic values and responsible action. *Type:* Association.

Detroit Urban League

208 Mack Ave.　　Ph: (313)832-4600
Detroit, MI 48201　　Fax: (313)832-3222
Contact: N. Charles Anderson, Pres./CEO.
Desc: Works to enable African-Americans, and other minorities, to reach their full potential. Programs and services focus on the areas of employment, health and substance abuse, male and female responsibility, nutritional education, senior citizen development, and education. *Type:* Association.

Drug Policy Foundation

4455 Connecticut Ave. NW,　　Ph: (202)537-5005
　　Ste. B-500　　Fax: (202)537-3007
Washington, DC 20008-2328
E-mail: dpf@dpf.org
URL: http://www.dpf.org
Contact: Robert A. Stewart, Communications Dir.
Desc: Promotes alternative methods such as legalization, decriminalization, and medicalization of currently illegal substances including marijuana and heroin, to curb drug abuse while protecting the rights of the individual. Believes that legal drugs, clean needles, and effective drug treatment would vastly improve the health of addicts, slow the spread of AIDS, and decrease crime. Strongly opposes the use of urine tests in employment. *Type:* Association.

Individual Freedom Federation

6558 Claremore Ct.　　Ph: (517)738-7496
West Bloomfield, MI 48322
Contact: Edward M. Mielock, Pres.
Desc: Individuals united to aid what the federation regards as victims of "destructive" cults and to provide support to victims' friends and families. (According to IFF, a cult is destructive when it uses mind control and psychological coercion to gain and hold converts.) Conducts educational campaign stressing the nature and dangers of "destructive" cults; teaches ways to prevent conversion of susceptible individuals. Operates speakers' bureau. *Type:* Association.

International Society for Individual Liberty

836-B Southampton Rd., No.　　Ph: (707)746-8796
　　299　　Fax: (707)746-8797
Benicia, CA 94510
E-mail: isil@isil.org
URL: http://www.isil.org
Contact: Vincent H. Miller, Pres. & Editor.
Desc: Individuals and organizations who seek to establish a free and peaceful world through libertarian doctrine. Advocates free market economics and individual liberty; exchanges ideas and strategies with fellow members. *Type:* Association.

Judge David L. Bazelon Center for Mental Health Law

1101 15th St. NW, Ste. 1212　　Ph: (202)467-5730
Washington, DC 20005-5002　　Fax: (202)223-0409
E-mail: bazelon@nicom.com
URL: http://www.bazelon.org
Contact: Robert E. Bernstein, Ph.D., Exec.Dir.
Desc: Purpose is to clarify, establish, and enforce the legal rights of people with mental and developmental disabilities. Provides technical assistance and training to lawyers, consumer groups, providers of mental health and supported housing services, and policymakers at federal, state, and local levels. Staff attorneys have represented individual plaintiffs and leading national consumer and professional associations in landmark lawsuits that have established many rights of people with mental and developmental disabilities including the rights to: appropriate education, compensation for institution-maintaining labor, and fair consideration for access to federal assistance. *Type:* Association.

National Association for the Advancement of Colored People

4805 Mt. Hope Dr.　　Ph: (410)358-8900
Baltimore, MD 21215　　Fax: (410)358-3818
URL: http://www.naacp.org/
Contact: Kwasie Mfume, Pres.
Desc: Persons "of all races and religions" who believe in the objectives and methods of the NAACP. To achieve equal rights through the democratic process and eliminate racial prejudice by removing racial discrimination in housing, employment, voting, schools, the courts, transportation, recreation, prisons, and business enterprises. Offers referral services, tutorials, job referrals, and day care. *Type:* Association.

National Association for the Advancement of Colored People Legal Defense and Educational Fund

99 Hudson St., 16th Fl.　　Ph: (212)219-1900
New York, NY 10013　　Fax: (212)226-7592
Contact: Elaine R. Jones, Dir.-Counsel.
Desc: Legal arm of the civil rights movement, functioning independently from and no longer part of the National Association for the Advancement of Colored People since the mid-1950s. Works to provide and support litigation in behalf of blacks, other racial minorities, and women defend-

ing their legal and constitutional rights against discrimination in employment, education, housing, and other areas. Represents civil rights groups as well as individual citizens who have bona fide civil rights claims. *Type:* Association.

National Association to Protect Individual Rights

Karen Morison
5015 Gadsen　　Ph: (703)425-5347
Fairfax, VA 22032-3411
Contact: Karen Morison, Pres.
Type: Association.

National Coalition Against Censorship

275 7th Ave., 20th Fl.　　Ph: (212)807-6222
New York, NY 10001　　Fax: (212)807-6245
E-mail: Ncac@netcom.com
URL: http://www.ncac.org/
Contact: Joan E. Bertin, Exec.Dir.
Desc: Participants are 48 national nonprofit organizations united to preserve and advance freedom of thought, inquiry, and expression. Holds that "freedom of communication is the indispensable condition of a healthy democracy," and that "censorship constitutes an unacceptable dictatorship over our minds, and a dangerous opening to religious, political, artistic, and intellectual repression." Helps participating organizations to educate their own members about the dangers of censorship and how to oppose it. Helps organize state and local anti-censorship groups. *Type:* Association.

National Organization for the Reform of Marijuana Laws

1001 Connecticut Ave. NW,　　Ph: (202)483-5500
　　Ste. 710　　Fax: (202)483-0057
Washington, DC 20036
E-mail: norml@norml.org
URL: http://www.norml.org
Contact: R. Keith Stroup, Esq., Exec.Dir.
Desc: Public education organization working for change in U.S. policy regarding marijuana. Seeks a more reasonable treatment of marjuana consumers in federal, state, and local laws and policies. *Type:* Association.

National Urban League

120 Wall St.　　Ph: (212)558-5300
New York, NY 10005　　Fax: (212)344-5332
Contact: Hugh Price, CEO & Pres.
Desc: Voluntary nonpartisan community service agency of civic, professional, business, labor, and religious leaders with a staff of trained social workers and other professionals. Aims to eliminate racial segregation and discrimination in the United States and to achieve parity for blacks and other minorities in every phase of American life. Works to eliminate institutional racism and to provide direct service to minorities in the areas of employment, housing, education, social welfare, health, family planning, mental retardation, law and consumer affairs, youth and student affairs, labor affairs, veterans' affairs, and community and minority business development. *Type:* Association.

People for the American Way

2000 M St. NW, Ste. 400　　Ph: (202)467-4999
Washington, DC 20036　　Fax: (202)293-2672
E-mail: pfaw@pfaw.org
URL: http://www.pfaw.org
Contact: Carole Shields, Pres.
Desc: Nonpartisan constitutional liberties organization. Religious, business, media, and labor figures committed to reaffirming the traditional American values of pluralism, diversity, and freedom of expression and religion. PFAW was developed out of concern that an antidemocratic and divisive climate was being created by groups that sought to use religion and religious symbols for political purposes. *Type:* Association.

Radio Association Defending Airwave Rights
4949 S. 25A
Tipp City, OH 45371
Ph: (937)667-5472
Fax: (937)667-3178
URL: http://www.radar.org
Contact: Janice Lee, Pres.
Desc: Manufacturers, dealers, and distributors of radar detectors; individual motorists with an interest in laws governing use of automotive radar. Works to maintain the legality of the operation and sale of radar detectors; promotes the common interests of the radar detection industry. *Type:* Association.

Second Amendment Foundation
12500 NE 10th Pl.
Bellevue, WA 98005
Ph: (206)454-7012
Free: 800-426-4302
Fax: (206)451-3959
URL: http://www.saf.org
Contact: Joseph P. Tartaro, Pres.
Desc: Individuals dedicated to promoting a better understanding of "your constitutional right to privately own and possess firearms." *Type:* Association.

Southern Poverty Law Center
PO Box 2087
Montgomery, AL 36102
Ph: (334)264-0286
Fax: (334)264-0629
URL: http://www.splcenter.org
Contact: Joseph J. Levin, Jr., Pres.
Desc: Seeks to protect and advance the legal and civil rights of poor people, regardless of race, through education and litigation. The center is currently involved in several lawsuits representing individuals injured or threatened by activities of white supremacy groups. Attempts to develop techniques and strategies that can be used by private attorneys. *Type:* Association.

SPLC Report
Southern Poverty Law Center
PO Box 548
Montgomery, AL 36101-0548
Ph: (334)264-0286
Fax: (334)264-8891
Contact: Penny Weaver, Editor.
Desc: Reviews advances in the legal rights of the poor and monitors and reports Ku Klux Klan and other militant hate group activities nationwide. Apprises readers of progress of Teaching Tolerence education project. *Type:* Newsletter.

WESTLAW® Civil Rights Databases
West Group
620 Opperman Dr.
St. Paul, MN 55164-0526
Ph: (651)687-7000
URL: http://www.westgroup.com
Contact: WEST Reference Attorneys. Toll-Free No.: (800) REF-ATTY.
Desc: Contains the complete text of U.S. federal court decisions, statutes and regulations, administrative law publications, and texts and periodicals dealing with civil rights. *Available:* West Group, WESTLAW. *Type:* Database.

Clubs

Club Managers Association of America
1733 King St.
Alexandria, VA 22314
Ph: (703)739-9500
Fax: (703)739-0124
E-mail: cmaa@cmaa.org
URL: http://www.cmaa.org
Contact: James B. Singerling, Exec.VP.
Desc: Professional managers and assistant managers of private golf, yacht, athletic, city, country, luncheon, university, and military clubs. Encourages education and advancement of members and promotes efficient and successful club operations. *Type:* Association.

Goldmine—Fan Club Directory
Krause Publications, Inc.
700 E. State St.
Iola, WI 54990
Ph: (715)445-2214
Free: 800-258-0929
Fax: (715)445-4087
E-mail: info@krause.com; krause@krause.com
URL: http://www.krause.com; http://www.krause.com.
Contact: Greg Loescher, Editor.
Desc: List of more than 400 fan clubs for musical recording artists. Featured inside the Roots of Rock Digest. *Type:* Directory.

Jaycees Magazine
The U.S. Junior Chamber of Commerce
PO Box 7
Tulsa, OK 74102-0007
Ph: (918)584-2481
Fax: (918)584-4422
E-mail: usjaycees@earthlink.com.
Contact: Rebecca Currington, Editor.
Desc: Official publication of the U.S. Junior Chamber of Commerce. *Type:* Periodical.

Marquette Magazine
Marquette Magazine
Marquette University
PO Box 1881
Milwaukee, WI 53201-1881
Ph: (414)288-7448
Fax: (414)288-7197
E-mail: mumagazine@marquette.edu.
Desc: University magazine. *Type:* Periodical.

National Conference of State Societies
Longworth House Office Bldg.
PO Box 180
Washington, DC 20515
Ph: (202)686-6292
Free: 800-200-0090
Fax: (703)455-1643
E-mail: ncss@ziplink.net
URL: http://www.ziplink.net/~ncss
Contact: John Pannullo, Pres.
Desc: Constituent societies with a total membership of 25,000 delegates from the 50 states and U.S. territories of Guam, American Samoa, and the U.S. Virgin Islands, Commonwealth of Puerto Rico, and the District of Columbia. *Type:* Association.

National Forum (Auburn)
Honor Society of Phi Kappa Phi
129 Quad Center
Mell St.
Auburn, AL 36849-5306
Ph: (334)844-5200
Fax: (334)844-5994
Contact: James P. Kaetz, Editor, kaetzjp@mail.auburn.edu; Mary Wood Littleton, Assoc. Editor; Stephanie Johns Bond, Assoc. Editor.
Desc: Journal of the Honor Society of Phi Kappa Phi covering education. *Type:* Periodical.

The Optimist Magazine
Optimist International
4494 Lindell Blvd.
St. Louis, MO 63108
Ph: (314)371-6000
Free: 800-678-8389
Fax: (314)371-6006
E-mail: headquarters@optimist.org; magazine@optimist.org.
Contact: Dena Hull, Editor.
Desc: Official publication of Optimist International. *Type:* Periodical.

Private Clubs
Associate Clubs Publications, Inc.
3030 LBJ Freeway, Ste. 350
Dallas, TX 75234-7395
Ph: (972)888-7547
Free: 800-433-5079
Fax: (972)888-7338
E-mail: privateclubs@clubcorp.com.
Contact: Louis Marroquin, Sr. Ed., (972)888-7314, louis.marroquin@clubcorp.com; Patricia Baldwin, Editor-in-Chief, (912)888-7472; Dana Fay, Advertising Dir., (912)888-7374, dana.fay@clubcorp.com.

Desc: Magazine for members of city clubs, country clubs, and resorts. *Type:* Periodical.

75 Club News
Association for Union Democracy, Inc.
500 State St.
Brooklyn, NY 11217-1803
Ph: (718)855-6650
Fax: (718)855-6799
E-mail: aud@igc.apc.org
Contact: Carl Biers, Editor.
Desc: Reports developments in union democracy. Recurring features include letters to the editor, reports of meetings, book reviews, and notices of publications available. *Type:* Newsletter.

United Federation of Doll Clubs
10920 N. Ambassador Dr., Ste. 130
Kansas City, MO 64153
Ph: (904)221-3106
Fax: (904)221-2044
E-mail: ufdc@aol.com
URL: http://www.ufdc.org
Contact: Priscilla Chansky, Central Office Mgr.
Desc: Doll collectors, museums, libraries. Promotes educational and charitable work. *Type:* Association.

Vocational Industrial Clubs of America
PO Box 3000
Leesburg, VA 20177-0300
Ph: (703)777-8810
Free: 800-321-VICA
Fax: (703)777-8999
E-mail: anyinfo@vica.org
URL: http://www.vica.org
Contact: Stephen Denby, Exec.Dir.
Desc: Federation of state associations and local chapters of people in trade, industrial, technical and health occupations programs in high schools, area vocational schools, and community colleges in the U.S., the Virgin Islands, and Puerto Rico. Organized by a representative group of state club sponsors and the National Association of State Supervisors of Trade and Industrial Education. Promotes high standards of workmanship, scholarship, and trade ethics; develops students' leadership abilities and sense of civic responsibility; promotes industrial safety; encourages cooperation of students, teachers, community leaders, labor, and business. *Type:* Association.

Coaching

National Alliance for Youth Sports
2050 Vista Pkwy.
West Palm Beach, FL 33411-2718
Ph: (561)684-1141
Free: 800-729-2057
Fax: (561)684-2546
E-mail: nays@nays.org
URL: http://www.nays.org
Contact: Fred C. Engh, Pres.
Desc: Seeks to improve youth league sports programming in order to make sports a positive, fun experience for all youths. Has developed National Standards for Youth Sports and operated Say Yes to Better Sports for Kids program. Conducts research and educational programs. *Type:* Association.

National Federation Interscholastic Coaches Association
PO Box 20626
11724 NW Plaza Cir.
Kansas City, MO 64195
Ph: (816)464-5400
Fax: (816)464-5571
Contact: Don Sparks, Dir.
Desc: High school athletic coaches. Promotes professional growth and image of interscholastic sports coaches; provides a forum for coaches to make suggestions on rules and procedures in high school sports in the U.S. Cooperates with state high school athletic associations and uses extensive committee structure to ensure grass roots involvement and input from the local, state, and national levels. *Type:* Association.

National High School Athletic Coaches Association
PO Box 2569
Gig Harbor, WA 98335-4569
Contact: Brett Trotter, Exec.Dir.
Desc: High school coaches and athletic directors; athletic directors for school systems; executive secretaries of state high school coaches; state high school coaches associations. Public members are college coaches, former high school coaches, adult athletic trainers, principals, officials, and sporting goods salesmen. Formed to give greater national prestige and professional status to high school coaching and to promote cooperation among coaches, school administrators, the press, game officials, and the public. *Type:* Association.

Collecting

American Bell Association International
12250 Birdhaven Ln.   Ph: (314)843-2214
St. Louis, MO 63128
Contact: Eleanor Evans, Editor.
Desc: Bell collectors, enthusiasts, ringers, antique dealers, and bell dealers. Maintains historical files; makes available scholarships in bell studies. *Type:* Association.

American Numismatic Association
818 N. Cascade Ave.   Ph: (719)632-2646
Colorado Springs, CO 80903-   Fax: (719)634-4085
   3279
E-mail: ana@money.org
URL: http://www.csd.net/users/anaweb
Contact: Peggy A. Hofmann, Exec.Dir.
Desc: Collectors of coins, medals, tokens, and paper money. Promotes the study, research, and publication of articles on coins, coinage, and history of money. Sponsors correspondence courses; conducts research. *Type:* Association.

American Philatelic Society
100 Oakwood Ave.   Ph: (814)237-3803
PO Box 8000   Fax: (814)237-6128
State College, PA 16803-8000
E-mail: flsente@stamps.org
URL: http://www.west.net/~stamps1/aps.html
Contact: Robert E. Lamb, Exec.Dir.
Desc: Collectors of postage and revenue stamps, first day covers, postal history, and related philatelic items. Helps members buy and sell stamps; operates expertizing service; offers stamp insurance program; circulates slide programs. Maintains hall of fame; offers correspondence courses; accredits judges for philatelic competitions. *Type:* Association.

Antique Detective Syndicate
4794 NE 17th Ave.   Ph: (305)491-5368
Ft. Lauderdale, FL 33334-5610   Fax: (305)491-8481
Contact: Anne Gilbert, Pres./Writer.
Alt. Contact: 4794 NE 17th Ave., Ft. Lauderdale, FL 33334-5610; telephone: (305)491-5368; fax: (305)491-8481. *Type:* Periodical.

Auctions Today
Auction Marketing Institute
8880 Ballentine   Ph: (913)541-8115
Overland Park, KS 66214   Fax: (913)894-5281
E-mail: aucmktinst@aol.com
Contact: Ann Wood, Editor.
Desc: Promotes the educational activities of the Institute. Carries miscellaneous items of interest to member auctioneers and for candidates for membership. *Type:* Newsletter.

Bill Nelson Newsletter
Bill Nelson
PO Box 41630   Ph: (520)629-0868
Tucson, AZ 85717   Free: 800-368-8434
          Fax: (520)629-0387
E-mail: sales@pinsbymail.com;   sales@
billnelsonnewsletter.com.
Contact: Bill Nelson, Editor.
Desc: Features news, advertisements, and information relating to all aspects of collecting lapel and hat pins and buttons. Also provides information for obtaining free pins. *Type:* Newsletter.

Case Collectors Club
PO Box 4000   Ph: (814)368-4123
Bradford, PA 16701   Free: 800-523-6350
          Fax: (814)368-1736
Contact: Cindy Keane, Contact.
Desc: Knife collectors. Provides members with information about Case knives. Offers special edition knives annually. *Type:* Association.

The Coin Dealer Newsletter
Ron Downing
PO Box 7939   Ph: (310)515-7369
Torrance, CA 90504   Fax: (310)515-7534
E-mail: cdn@greysheet.com.
Contact: Dennis R. Baker, Editor.
Desc: Provides information on U.S. coinage, 1793 to present. *Type:* Newsletter.

Coin Prices
Krause Publications, Inc.
700 E. State St.   Ph: (715)445-2214
Iola, WI 54990   Free: 800-258-0929
          Fax: (715)445-4087
E-mail: info@krause.com; krause@krause.com
URL: http://www.krause.com
Contact: Robert E. Wilhite, Editor, wilhiter@krause.com; Rick Groth, Publisher, grothr@krause.com; Joel Edler, Advertising Mgr., elderj@krause.com.
Desc: Price guide for United States coins. *Type:* Periodical.

Coin World
Amos Press, Inc.
911 Vandemark Rd.   Ph: (937)498-0800
PO Box 150   Free: 800-673-8311
Sidney, OH 45365-0150   Fax: (937)498-0812
URL: http://www.coinworld.
Contact: Beth Deisher, Editor, cweditor@amospress.com; Ann Marie Aldrich, Publisher, aaldrich@coinworld.com.
Desc: Coin collecting newspaper. *Alt. Contact:* PO Box 150, Sidney, OH 45365-0150; telephone: (937)498-0800; fax: (937)498-0812; toll-free: 800-673-8311. *Type:* Periodical.

The COINfidential Report
Bale Publications
5121 St. Charles Ave.   Ph: (504)895-5750
New Orleans, LA 70115
Contact: Don Bale, Jr., Editor.
Desc: Features coin, stock and bullion market forecasts and analyses, plus inside information and best coin and stock bets. Recurring features include interviews, book reviews, and notices of publications available. *Type:* Newsletter.

Collectibles, Flea Market Finds
Goodman Media Group, Inc.
1700 Broadway, 34th Fl.   Ph: (212)541-7100
New York, NY 10019   Fax: (212)245-1241
Contact: Cathy Cook, Editor.
Desc: Consumer magazine covering 20th century collectibles of all kinds. *Type:* Periodical.

Cover Collectors Circuit Club
Allan J. Bagnall
RD 1, Box 1025   Ph: (717)235-2542
New Freedom, PA 17349   Fax: (717)235-4360
E-mail: stampclub@aol.com
Contact: Allan J. Bagnall, Exec. Officer.
Desc: Stamp and philatelic cover collectors. Facilitates exchange of information through correspondence and contact among collectors throughout the world. *Type:* Association.

The Currency Dealer Newsletter
Ron Downing
PO Box 7939   Ph: (310)515-7369
Torrance, CA 90504   Fax: (310)515-7534
E-mail: CDN@greysheet.com.
Contact: Dennis R. Baker, Editor.
Desc: Concerned with U.S. currency, 1861 to present. *Type:* Newsletter.

Doll World—Doll Show Calendar Section
House of White Birches
306 E. Parr Rd.   Ph: (219)589-4000
Berne, IN 46711   Fax: (219)589-8093
E-mail: doll_world@whitebirches.com.
URL: http://www.whitebirches.com
Contact: Vicki Steensma, Editor.
Desc: List of doll shows and other doll events scheduled to take place in the United States and Canada within the following two months. *Type:* Directory.

Hello Again
Jay Hickerson
PO Box 4321   Ph: (203)248-2887
Hamden, CT 06514   Fax: (203)281-1322
Contact: Jay Hickerson, Editor, jayhick@aol.com.
Desc: Concerned primarily with trading and collecting vintage radio programs. Offers information on new shows in circulation. *Type:* Newsletter.

Hummel Collectors Club
1261 University Dr.   Free: 888-548-6635
Yardley, PA 19067-2857   Fax: (215)321-7367
E-mail: hummels@bellatlantic.net
URL: http://www.hummels.com
Contact: Dorothy Dous, Exec. Officer.
Desc: Dealers and collectors interested in Hummel figurines, plates, bells, lamps, music boxes, and other items based on the drawings by a German nun, Sister Maria Innocentia Hummel. Seeks to familiarize collectors with trademarks, mold variations, and rare pieces, and to discover and document one-of-a-kind rarities. *Type:* Association.

International Association of Jim Beam Bottle and Specialties Clubs
2015 Burlington Ave.   Ph: (309)853-3370
Kewanee, IL 61443-8348   Fax: (309)852-8517
URL: http://www.beam_wade.org
Contact: Shirley Sumbles, Exec.Sec.
Desc: Individuals interested in studying, stimulating, and encouraging interest in Jim Beam bottle collecting; individual affiliates must be affiliated through their local club with IAJBBSC. To further the hobby of Jim Beam bottle collecting. Beam china bottles are manufactured by the Regal China Co. *Type:* Association.

International Blade Collectors
Krause Publications
700 E. State St.   Ph: (715)445-2214
Iola, WI 54990   Fax: (715)445-4087
Contact: Tom Paar, Publisher.

Desc: Individuals who collect, buy, sell, manufacture, or study cutlery, particularly knives and swords. Objectives are to promote knife appreciation and advance the knife industry. *Type:* Association.

Kovels on Antiques and Collectibles

Antiques, Inc.

22000 Shaker Blvd.	Ph: (216)752-2252
Shaker Heights, OH 44122	Fax: (216)752-3115

Contact: Ralph Kovel, Editor; Terry Kovel, Editor.

Desc: Provides information about antiques and collectibles. Highlights different antiques and collectibles each month, and includes tips for buying and selling. *Type:* Newsletter.

Krystonia Collectors Club

Precious Art/Panton

125 W. Ellsworth Rd.	Ph: (734)663-1885
Ann Arbor, MI 48108	Fax: (734)663-2343

Contact: Elena Largen, Club Dir.

Desc: Individuals interested in collecting Krystonia role-playing game figurines, a fantasy line consisting of dragons and wizards made of porcelain. *Type:* Association.

Massey Collectors News—Wild Harvest

Keith Oltrogge

Box 529	Ph: (319)984-5292
Denver, IA 50622	

Contact: Keith Oltrogge, Editor, fax: (319)984-6408, keitho@sbt.net.

Desc: Provides information for collectors of tractors and farm equipment. *Type:* Newsletter.

Memories of Yesterday Collectors Society

225 Windsor Dr.	Ph: (630)875-5600
PO Box 499	Fax: (630)875-5348
Itasca, IL 60143-0499	

URL: http://www.little-elegance.com/memories/memories.htm

Contact: Barbara Schrage, Marketing Mgr.

Desc: Producer of porcelain bisque figurines. *Type:* Association.

Midwest Old Settlers and Threshers Association

405 E. Threshers Rd.	Ph: (319)385-8937
Mount Pleasant, IA 52641	Fax: (319)385-0563

Contact: Lennis Moore, Admin.Dir.

Desc: Persons interested in old steam equipment, threshers, gas engines, farm tractors, antique automobiles, narrow gauge railroad, trolley lines, and other artifacts of early agriculture and pioneer days. *Type:* Association.

National Association of Miniature Enthusiasts

130 N. Rangeline Rd.	Ph: (317)571-8094
PO Box 69	Fax: (317)571-8105
Carmel, IN 46032	

URL: http://www.miniatures.org

Contact: John Purcell, Exec.Dir.

Desc: Works to stimulate and enhance interest in the construction and collection of miniatures as historical and creative art forms. *Type:* Association.

National Association of Watch and Clock Collectors

514 Poplar St.	Ph: (717)684-8261
Columbia, PA 17512-2130	Fax: (717)684-0878

URL: http://www.nawcc.org

Contact: Thomas J. Bartels, Exec.Dir.

Desc: Collectors, historians, craftsmen, dealers, and others interested in timekeeping devices and horology. Seeks to preserve horological data, to prepare information about the mechanics of timepieces and their repair, and to aid members in buying or selling watches, clocks, and related items. NAWCC School of Horology offers a clock repair program and a watch repair program. *Type:* Association.

Pin and Button Newsletter

Bill Nelson

PO Box 41630	Ph: (520)629-0868
Tucson, AZ 85717	Free: 800-368-8434
	Fax: (520)629-0387

E-mail: sales@pinsbymail.com

Contact: Bill Nelson, Editor.

Desc: Contains news, advertisements, and tips for beginner pin/button collectors, and information on where to write for free pins and buttons. *Type:* Newsletter.

The Questers

210 S. Quince St.	Ph: (215)923-5183
Philadelphia, PA 19107	

Contact: Lois Newton, Pres.

Desc: Promotes the study and appreciation of antiques and objects of art and their historical backgrounds; aids in the restoration and preservation of historical places. Has donated several antique pieces to the White House and has contributed financially to historic houses, villages, and foundations. Sponsors annual scholarship at Columbia University for graduate studies in the field of architectural restoration. *Type:* Association.

Space Philatelists International Society

c/o Martin J. Michaelson
PO Box 771
West Nyack, NY 10994

Contact: Martin J. Michaelson, Exec.Dir.

Desc: Collectors of space stamps and commemorative covers in 20 countries. Advises members of pictorial cancels, special covers, future satellite launches, astronaut visits, and other space-related events. Maintains 200 volume library. *Type:* Association.

Stein Collectors International

281 Shore Dr.
Burr Ridge, IL 60521

Contact: Paticia Jahn, Exec.Dir.

Desc: Collectors and individuals in 10 countries interested in steins and other drinking vessels. (Steins are covered drinking mugs, usually used for beer. Most steins originate in Germany, where they have been made for nearly 5 centuries. Materials used have included copper, glass, ivory, pewter, porcelain, pottery, silver, and stoneware.). Fosters the collection and study of antique and modern beer steins. *Type:* Association.

Thimble Collectors International

564 Linden St.	Ph: (716)271-8816
Rochester, NY 14620-2421	Fax: (716)244-2673

Contact: Mary Innes Wagner, Publicity Chm.

Desc: Collectors in 16 countries interested in learning about thimbles. Promotes research and study; standardizes names of thimble types and designs. Educates members in collecting, storage, cataloging, and display of thimbles. *Type:* Association.

Train Collectors Association

PO Box 248	Ph: (717)687-8623
Strasburg, PA 17579-0248	Fax: (717)687-0742

E-mail: toytrain@traincollectors.org
URL: http://www.traincollectors.org

Contact: John V. Luppino, Operations Mgr.

Desc: Collectors of tin-plate toy trains (mass produced models rather than hand-crafted trains). Operates public museum; maintains library; conducts research and educational programs; compiles statistics. *Type:* Association.

Colleges and Universities

Albion College Home Page

Albion College

611 East Porter St.	Ph: (517)629-1000
Albion, MI 49224	

E-mail: lduff@albion.edu
URL: http://www.albion.edu/

Desc: For a relatively small college, Albion has put together an extremely sophisticated Web site, easy to navigate and pleasing to the eye. Whatever you're looking for, you should be able to locate it quickly on the Albion site. *Type:* Database.

Allentown College of Saint Francis de Sales

Allentown College of Saint Francis de Sales

2755 Station Ave.	Ph: (610)282-1100
Center Valley, PA 18034	

E-mail: www@ds1.allencol.edu
URL: http://ds1.allencol.edu/

Desc: The Allentown College web site reflects this institution's feelings toward its students. Amid the standard college fare (admissions, athletics, and so on) you can find links to career resources, job lines, and other employment services. *Type:* Database.

Alumnus

Southern Illinois University at Carbondale

Communications Bldg.	Ph: (618)536-3311
PO Box 6887	Fax: (618)453-3248
Carbondale, IL 62901	

Contact: Laraine J. Wright, Editor.

Desc: University alumni magazine. *Type:* Periodical.

American Association of Colleges for Teacher Education

1307 New York Ave.	Ph: (202)293-2450
N.W., Ste. 300	Fax: (202)457-8095
Washington, DC 20005	

Contact: David G. Imig, CEO.

Desc: Colleges and universities concerned with the preparation and development of professionals in education and human resources. Seeks to improve the quality of institutional programs of the education profession. *Type:* Association.

American Association of Collegiate Registrars and Admissions Officers

1 Dupont Cir. NW, Ste. 520	Ph: (202)293-9161
Washington, DC 20036	Fax: (202)872-8857

E-mail: info@aacrao.com
URL: http://www.aacrao.com

Contact: Wayne E. Becraft, Exec.Dir.

Desc: Degree-granting postsecondary institutions (2400), government agencies, and higher education coordinating boards, private educational organizations, and education-oriented businesses. Promotes higher education and furthers the professional development of members working in admissions, enrollment management, institutional research, records, and registration. *Type:* Association.

American Association of Collegiate Registrars and Admissions Officers—Member Guide

American Association of Collegiate Registrars and Admissions Officers

1 Dupont Circle NW, Ste. 520	Ph: (202)293-9161
Washington, DC 20036-1135	Fax: (202)872-8857

E-mail: info@aacrao.com
URL: http://www.aacrao.com

Contact: Saira Burki, Editor, burkis@aacrao.nche.edu.

Desc: More than 2,400 member institutions and about 9,200 college and university registrars, financial aid officers, admissions officers, and officials of international education and institutional research organizations. *Type:* Directory.

American Association of Community Colleges

National Center for Higher   Ph: (202)728-0200
   Educ.   Fax: (202)833-2467
1 Dupont Cir. NW, Ste. 410
Washington, DC 20036-1176
E-mail: mlatif@aacc.nche.edu
Contact: David Pierce, Pres. & CEO.
Desc: Community colleges; individual associates interested in community college development; corporate, educational, foundation, and international associate members. Office of Federal Relations monitors federal educational programming and legislation. *Type:* Association.

American Association of University Professors

1012 14th St. NW, 5th Fl.   Ph: (202)737-5900
Washington, DC 20005   Free: 800-424-2973
   Fax: (202)737-5526
Contact: Mary Burgan, Gen.Sec.
Desc: College and university teachers, research scholars, and academic librarians. Purposes are to facilitate cooperation among teachers and research scholars in universities, colleges, and professional schools, for the promotion of higher education and research, and to increase the usefulness and advance the standards, ideals, and welfare of the profession. Compiles statistics. *Type:* Association.

American Community Colleges

Oryx Press
4041 N. Central Ave., Ste. 700   Ph: (602)265-2651
Phoenix, AZ 85012-3397   Free: 800-279-6799
   Fax: 800-279-4663
E-mail: info@oryxpress.com
URL: http://www.oryxpress.com
Desc: Nearly 1,200 accredited schools offering associate degree programs. *Type:* Directory.

American Friends of Cambridge University

Stephen C. Price
708 3rd Ave., 14th Fl.   Ph: (212)880-2840
New York, NY 10017   Fax: (212)880-2850
E-mail: cambrdgusa@aol.com
Contact: Stephen C. Price, Pres.
Desc: Philanthropic foundation working to raise funds in support of Cambridge University and its constituent colleges. Provides and supports Cambridge Alumni network in America. *Type:* Association.

American School & University—Who's Who Directory and Buyers' Guide

Intertec Publishing Corp.
9800 Metcalf Ave.   Ph: (913)341-1300
Overland Park, KS 66212   Free: 800-400-5945
   Fax: (913)967-1328
E-mail: asu@intertec.com.
Contact: Joe Agron, Editor.
Desc: List of companies supplying products and services for physical plants and business offices of schools, colleges, and universities. *Type:* Directory.

Antioch New England Graduate School Home Page

Antioch University
40 Avon St.   Ph: (603)357-3122
Keene, NH 03431-3516
URL: http://sparc.antiochne.edu/
Contact: webmaster@antiochne.edu.
Desc: Pleasant images and an embossed background take the Antioch New England Home Page to a visual level rarely seen on college sites. Enrollment, financial aid, course information; it's all here. *Type:* Database.

APPA: The Association of Higher Education Facilities Officers

1643 Prince St.   Ph: (703)684-1446
Alexandria, VA 22314-2818   Fax: (703)549-2772
E-mail: info@appa.org
URL: http://www.appa.org
Contact: E. Lander Medlin, Exec.VP.
Desc: Promotes excellence in the administration, care, operation, planning, and development of facilities (buildings, grounds, and power plants) used by colleges and universities. Conducts research programs; compiles statistics. *Type:* Association.

Arizona State University

Arizona State University
University Dr. and Mill Ave.   Ph: (602)965-9011
Tempe, AZ 85287
E-mail: email-q@asu.edu
URL: http://www.asu.edu/
Desc: This page permits readers to select whether to explore the Arizona State University website in graphics/audio mode or text-only. The graphic version takes only slightly longer to load than the text based version and is well worth the extra few seconds it takes to access. *Type:* Database.

Association of American Universities

1200 New York Ave., Ste. 550   Ph: (202)408-7500
Washington, DC 20005   Fax: (202)408-8184
URL: http://www.tulane.edu/~aau/
Contact: Cornelius J. Pings, Pres.
Desc: Executive heads of universities. Membership is determined by appraisal of breadth and quality of a university's research and education efforts. Conducts activities to encourage cooperative consideration of major issues concerning research universities, and to enable members to communicate effectively with the federal government. *Type:* Association.

Association of Community College Trustees

1740 N St. NW   Ph: (202)775-4667
Washington, DC 20036   Fax: (202)223-1297
Contact: Ray Taylor, Pres.
Desc: Community college or technical college boards or boards of other accredited postsecondary educational institutions that offer courses that lead to degrees or objectives less than a baccalaureate degree; boards of educational institutions of other nations that are considered as being postsecondary, but not baccalaureate, by that nation. Objectives are: to provide education to trustees in order to improve the governance of the institutions; to unify trustees in order to give direction to the community college movement through the development of resolutions and policies; to promote the philosophical concept of the community college and technical college. Develops liaisons with other national and international organizations concerned with the community college movement; sponsors Chief Executive Search Service, assisting boards of trustees in selection of a chief executive; maintains Board Retreat Service, providing advice through expert trustees. *Type:* Association.

Association of Governing Boards of Universities and Colleges

1 Dupont Cir. NW, Ste. 400   Ph: (202)296-8400
Washington, DC 20036   Free: 800-356-6317
   Fax: (202)223-7053
URL: http://www.agb.org
Contact: Richard T. Ingram, Pres.
Desc: Members are governing boards of public and private 2- and 4-year colleges and universities; constituents include regents, trustees, presidents, and other high-level administrators of colleges and universities. Addresses the

problems and responsibilities of trusteeship in all sectors of higher education and the relationships of trustees and regents to the president, the faculty, and the student body. Operates Zwingle Resource Center; conducts the National Conference on Trusteeship. *Type:* Association.

At BG (Bowling Green)

Bowling Green State University
Office of Public Relations   Ph: (419)372-2616
Bowling Green, OH 43403   Fax: (419)372-2617
Contact: Clifton Boutelle, Editor, cboutel@bgnet.bgsu.edu; Dennis Bova, Managing Editor.
Desc: Alumni magazine. *Type:* Periodical.

Atlantic Community College Home Page

Atlantic Community College
5100 Black Horse Pike   Ph: (609)343-4900
Mays Landing, NJ 08330-2699
E-mail: accweb@nsvm.atlantic.edu
URL: http://www.atlantic.edu/
Contact: Douglas Hedges, Webmaster.
Desc: This straightforward page supplies substantial information about Atlantic Community College and the surrounding area. Information concerning enrollment, financial aid, faculty, and everything else expected at a college site can be found quickly and easily by simply clicking on the desired category. *Type:* Database.

Auburn University Home Page

Auburn University
Auburn, AL 36849   Ph: (334)844-4000
E-mail: webmaster@mail.auburn.edu
URL: http://www.auburn.edu/
Desc: The Auburn University web page offers readers a choice of several links to specific sites such as admissions, departments, research, organizations, technology, campus events, and athletics information. Certainly one of the most in-depth university sites on the net, however, library links cater almost exclusively to faculty and students - non-registered users may only browse to locate holdings within the library. *Type:* Database.

Augustana College

Augustana College
639 38th St.   Ph: (309)794-7000
Rock Island, IL 61201-2296   Free: 800-798-8100
E-mail: webmaster@augustana.edu
URL: http://www.augustana.edu/
Desc: If you're a graduating high school senior and you've been going through all the thousands of possible colleges and university sites on the Web, then you know it can take a frustrating hour or two just to search through a handful of sites. The Augustana College site is clear and uncluttered, with a refreshing absence of extraneous information. *Type:* Database.

Austin College

Austin College
900 N. Grand Ave.   Ph: (903)813-2000
Sherman, TX 75090-4440   Free: 800-442-5363
   Fax: (903)813-3199
E-mail: info@austinc.edu
URL: http://www.austinc.edu
Contact: webmaster@austinc.edu.
Desc: Supplying a wide array of information concerning itself and the community surrounding it, the Austin College web site is quite complete. Thorough data concerning enrollment, financial aid, and academics can be found quite easily--even though a search engine is not supplied. *Type:* Database.

Barron's Best Buys in College Education

Barron's Educational Series, Inc.

250 Wireless Blvd. Ph: (516)434-3311
Hauppauge, NY 11788 Free: 800-645-3476
  Fax: (516)434-3723
E-mail: info@barronseduc.com; barrons269@aol.com.
URL: http://www.barronseduc.com; http://www.barronseduc.com.
Contact: Max Reed, Editor.
Desc: Approximately 300 colleges in the United States offering quality education at a reasonable price. *Type:* Directory.

Barron's Profiles of American Colleges

Barron's Educational Series, Inc.

250 Wireless Blvd. Ph: (516)434-3311
Hauppauge, NY 11788 Free: 800-645-3476
  Fax: (516)434-3723
E-mail: info@barronseduc.com; barrons269@aol.com.
URL: http://www.barronseduc.com
Contact: Max Reed, Editor.
Desc: More than 1,650 colleges and universities in North America and abroad. *Type:* Directory.

Barry University

Barry University

11300 NE Second Ave. Ph: (305)899-3000
Miami Shores, FL 33161-6695 Free: 800-756-6000
URL: http://martin.barry.edu/
Contact: webmaster@barry.edu.
Desc: Founded nearly 60 years ago by the Dominican Order of the Catholic Church, Barry University is a private, co-educational school in South Florida. The university serves an undergraduate student body of nearly 2,000 and is proud of its 13:1 ratio of students to faculty. *Type:* Database.

Bates College Online

Bates College

Lewiston, ME 04240 Ph: (207)786-6255
E-mail: www@bates.edu
URL: http://www.bates.edu/
Contact: Ronald Meldrum, rmeldrum@bates.edu.
Desc: Bates College's Web site is well organized and attractively packaged and should be a useful tool for current students and faculty as well as high school students who may be considering applying for admission. For those who are not too familiar with this liberal arts college in Lewiston, Maine, your first stop at the Web site should be the About Bates page, which offers a brief description and history of the college as well as a virtual tour of its campus. *Type:* Database.

Beaver College

Beaver College - Computer Services

450 S. Easton Rd.
Glenside, PA 19038
E-mail: skarren@www.beaver.edu
URL: http://www.beaver.edu/
Desc: Beaver College serves up the standard college fare of admissions, administration, financial aid, and event information with pleasant images combined with interesting text. Be sure to check out the Center for Education Abroad section to learn how you can pursue a degree in one of six countries, including Great Britain and Greece. *Type:* Database.

Belmont University

Belmont University

1900 Belmont Blvd. Ph: (615)460-6000
Nashville, TN 37212-3757
URL: http://www.belmont.edu/
Contact: Michael Davis, davism@mail.belmont.edu.

Desc: Straightforward yet pleasing to the eye, the web site offered by Belmont University is quite a feat. Thorough organization of topics ranging from academics and research to enrollment and student affairs makes navigation simple, and a search routine makes this site even better. *Type:* Database.

Berea College

Berea College

Berea, KY 40404
E-mail: webmaster@popmail.berea.edu
URL: http://www.berea.edu/
Contact: Ed Ford, Ed_Ford@Berea.edu.
Desc: Berea College, located in eastern Kentucky, bills itself as "a different kind of a place." Visitors to the college's very attractively designed Web site will learn just how very different. In an era of astronomical tuition fees at colleges across the country, Berea charges no tuition at all. *Type:* Database.

Bethel College

Bethel College

300 East 27 St. Ph: (316)283-2500
North Newton, KS 67117 Fax: (316)284-5286
E-mail: webmaster@bethelks.edu
URL: http://www.bethelks.edu/
Desc: Founded more than a century ago by the Mennonite Church, Bethel College is a small liberal arts college in North Newton, Kansas, that serves a co-educational student body of more than 600 students. Its Web site, though not as elaborate as those of some larger colleges, does help to acquaint the visitor with what the college has to offer and also serves as a useful resource for its students and faculty members. *Type:* Database.

Bethune-Cookman College National Alumni Association

640 Mary McLeod Bethune Ph: (904)255-1401
  Blvd. Fax: (904)257-3025
Daytona Beach, FL 32114
Contact: Pinkie Oliver, V. Pres.
Desc: Perpetuates the history, ideas, and philosophy of Bethune-Cookman College by conducting educational studies. *Type:* Association.

Black American Colleges and Universities

Gale Group Inc.

27500 Drake Rd. Ph: (248)699-4253
Farmington Hills, MI 48331- Free: 800-877-GALE
  3535 Fax: (248)699-8070
E-mail: galeord@galegroup.com
URL: http://www.galegroup.com.
Contact: Levirn Hill, Editor.
Desc: Over 100 historically Black colleges and universities in the U.S. *Type:* Directory.

The Black Collegian

Black Collegiate Services, Inc.

140 Carondelet St. Ph: (504)523-0154
New Orleans, LA 70130-2526 Fax: (504)523-0271
E-mail: leon@black-collegiate.com
URL: http://www.black.collegian.com.
Contact: Preston J. Edwards, Publisher, preston@black-collegiate.com; Melba L. Nevills, Contact.
Desc: Career opportunity magazine featuring job searching, role models, interviews, entertainment, art, and African-American history. *Type:* Periodical.

Boise State University

Boise State University

1910 University Dr.
Boise, ID 83725
E-mail: elknox@bsu.idbsu.edu

URL: http://www.idbsu.edu/
Desc: The Boise State University (BSU) website not only gives users access to information concerning BSU, but also the community of Boise. Links include information geared for visitors (both on the net and on-campus) events, activities, administration, and alumni. *Type:* Database.

BOSTONIA

Boston University

10 Lenox St.
Brookline, MA 02146
Contact: Jerrold Hickey, Editor.
Desc: Boston University alumni magazine. *Type:* Periodical.

Bowdoin College

Bowdoin College

Brunswick, ME 04011 Ph: (207)725-3000
E-mail: webcoordinator@polar.bowdoin.edu
URL: http://www.bowdoin.edu/
Desc: An excellent resource for current and prospective students alike, the Bowdoin Web site offers a wealth of general information about the college. For current students, the site serves as an electronic guide to the vast array of services the college offers. *Type:* Database.

Bowling Green State University

Bowling Green State University

Bowling Green, OH 43403
E-mail: webmaster@bgnet.bgsu.edu
URL: http://www.bgsu.edu/
Desc: Information concerning academics, admissions, financial aid, and much more is yours for the taking on the Bowling Green State University web site. A virtual tour is available to new students, as well as event information and searchable e-mail and phone number directories. *Type:* Database.

Bradley University

Bradley University

1501 W. Bradley Ave. Ph: (309)676-7611
Peoria, IL 61625
E-mail: webmaster@www.bradley.edu
URL: http://www.bradley.edu/
Desc: The Bradley University Web site offers easy access to important information needed by prospective students as well as those already enrolled at the university. Also thoughtfully provided is a link to the Web site of Peoria, Illinois, the university's hometown. *Type:* Database.

Bridgewater College

Bridgewater College

402 E. College St. Ph: (540)828-8000
Bridgewater, VA 22812
E-mail: www@bridgewater.edu
URL: http://www.bridgewater.edu
Desc: The Bridgewater College web site contains all of the general college facts can be found here, including athletics, academic departmental information, a campus tour, and more. An online admissions application is provided if you just can't wait for snail-mail. *Type:* Database.

Brigham Young Magazine

Brigham Young University

403 CB Ph: (801)378-6691
Provo, UT 84602 Fax: (801)378-5386
E-mail: bymag@byu.edu.
URL: http://www.byu.edu/bym.
Contact: Jeff McClellan, Editor, (801)378-8762, jeff_mcclellan@byu.edu; Norm Darais, Exec. Editor.
Desc: Alumni magazine. *Type:* Periodical.

Brigham Young University

Brigham Young University
Provo, UT 84602   Ph: (801)378-INFO
E-mail: web-team@byu.edu
URL: http://www.byu.edu

Desc: Easy to navigate, nice on the eye and loaded with data-- this describes the Brigham Young University web site perfectly. All of the required information is here, from admissions (with an online application) to continuing education programs. *Type:* Database.

Broward Community College

Broward Community College
225 E. Las Olas Blvd.   Ph: (954)761-7464
Fort Lauderdale, FL 33301
E-mail: info@email.broward.cc.fl.us
URL: http://www.broward.cc.fl.us/

Desc: The Broward Community College home page gives the user an option of five links: Information Technology, Threads, College Info, What's New, Search, Site Info, and Legal. The information provided is everything you might need to know about the college and the surrounding area. *Type:* Database.

Brown Alumni Magazine

Brown University
PO Box 1854
Providence, RI 02912-3613   Ph: (401)863-2873
                                    Fax: (401)863-9599
E-mail: bam@brownvm.brown.edu.
URL: http://www.brown.edu/adminstration/brown_alumni_magazine.

Contact: Norman Boucher, Editor, anne_diffily@brown.edu.

Desc: Collegiate alumni magazine. *Type:* Periodical.

Brown University

Brown University
Providence, RI 02912   Ph: (401)863-1000
E-mail: webmaster@brown.edu
URL: http://www.brown.edu/

Desc: The Brown University site manages to convey some detailed information concerning athletics, academics, library resources, and administration. While enrollment information is a bit scarce, you can obtain an application via e-mail. *Type:* Database.

Bucknell University

Bucknell University
Lewisburg, PA 17837   Ph: (717)523-1271
E-mail: webmaster@bucknell.edu
URL: http://www.bucknell.edu/

Desc: Offering information about the university and the community, the Bucknell web site is quite thorough. All of the expected data is available, including enrollment, financial aid, student organizations, and more. *Type:* Database.

California Monthly

California Alumni Association
Alumni House   Ph: (510)642-5781
Berkeley, CA 94720-7520   Free: 800-225-2586
                                   Fax: (510)642-6252
URL: http://www.alumni.berkeley.edu.

Contact: Russell Schoch, Editor, (510)642-5782, russ@alumni.berkeley.edu; William Rodarmor, Managing Editor, (510)642-0760, rodarmor@alumni.berkeley.edu; Lora Dinga, Advertising Mgr., (415)898-6400.

Desc: University alumni magazine. *Type:* Periodical.

Cedarville College

Cedarville College
PO Box 601
Cedarville, OH 45314
E-mail: webmaster@cedarville.edu
URL: http://ivy.cedarville.edu/

Desc: Cedarville College, a Baptist college of arts, sciences, and professional programs, provides a web site that includes all of the information one would expect. Information concerning enrollment, sports, student organizations, and the like is here. *Type:* Database.

Centre College Home Page

Centre College
600 W. Walnut St.   Ph: (606)238-2500
Danville, KY 40422-1394   Free: 800-423-6236
E-mail: campbelj@centre.edu
URL: http://www.centre.edu/

Desc: Founded in 1819 by Presbyterians, Centre College is a small liberal arts college serving a student body of about 1,000. Its Web site is filled with information valuable to both current and prospective students. *Type:* Database.

Christian Brothers University

Christian Brothers University
650 East Pkwy. S.   Ph: (901)321-3000
Memphis, TN 38104
E-mail: webmaster@cbu.edu
URL: http://odin.cbu.edu/

Desc: The web site provided by Christian Brothers University contains much information about admissions, academics, and much more. Also included are an online catalog and a link to CBU Webcast. *Type:* Database.

Clarkson University

Clarkson University
Potsdam, NY 13699-5760   Ph: (315)268-6484
E-mail: cullenpa@craft.camp.clarkson.edu
URL: http://www.clarkson.edu/

Desc: A flashy neon sign graphic opens this well designed site, allowing various types of navigation for the reader. All of the standard college information can be found here, from admissions to alumni associations. *Type:* Database.

Cleveland State University

Cleveland State University
1983 E. 24th St.
Cleveland, OH 44115
E-mail: webmaster@csuohio.edu
URL: http://www.csuohio.edu/

Desc: This friendly web site posted by Cleveland State University covers almost every aspect of college life, from academics to student organizations. Prospective students will find most of their needs met in the Student Admission Guide, which contains an entire application package, a campus map, and more. *Type:* Database.

Collective Bargaining Newsletter

American Association of University Professors
1012 14th St. NW, Ste. 500   Ph: (202)737-5900
Washington, DC 20005   Free: 800-424-2973
                                   Fax: (202)737-5526
E-mail: aaup@aaup.org
Contact: Cindy Long, Editor.
Desc: Provides news and views relating to salary, contracts, academic positions, advancement of educational standards, collective bargaining and the general welfare of the profession. Recurring features include news of members, news of research, and notices of Association events and activities. *Type:* Newsletter.

College Blue Book

Macmillan Publishing Co.
Macmillan Library Reference Group
PO Box 159   Free: 800-257-5157
Thorndike, ME 04986
Contact: Thomas M. Wright, Editor.
Desc: Consists of five numbered volumes covering 3,000 two- and four-year colleges and universities, professional schools in medicine, law, etc.; over 7,500 trade, technical, and business schools, and community colleges; over 2,000 public and private sources of financial aid; coverage includes Canada. *Type:* Directory.

The College of Charleston Home Page

The College of Charleston
66 George St.
Charleston, SC 29424-0001
E-mail: webster@cofc.edu
URL: http://www.cofc.edu./

Desc: A beautiful title graphic leads the way into this extremely thorough site. Everything that you would expect from a college resource is here for the taking. *Type:* Database.

College Media Directory

Oxbridge Communications Inc.
150 5th Ave., Ste. 302   Ph: (212)741-0231
New York, NY 10011   Free: 800-955-0231
                                   Fax: (212)633-2938
E-mail: info@mediafinder.com
URL: http://www.mediafinder.com.
Contact: Joy Goldstein, Editor; Savita Ali, Editor.
Desc: 6,000 student-run newspapers, magazines, and yearbooks on 3,500 college campuses. *Type:* Directory.

College of Medicine at the University of Cincinnati

University of Cincinnati
Cincinnati, OH 45221-0038
URL: http://www.med.uc.edu/htdocs/medicine/uccom.htm
Contact: lieberma@ucbeh.san.uc.edu.
Desc: The University of Cincinnati College of Medicine web site supplies admissions information, class and clinical schedules, residency programs, and much more. A liberal dose of links to medical sites on the WWW is also provided. *Type:* Database.

College Store Executive—College Store Associations Directory Issue

Executive Business Media, Inc.
825 Old Country Rd.   Ph: (516)334-3030
PO Box 1500   Fax: (516)334-3059
Westbury, NY 11590-0812
E-mail: ebmpubs@ix.netcom.com
Contact: Robert Moran, Managing Editor.
Desc: List of state and regional associations of college stores. *Type:* Directory.

College Store Executive—Directory of Leased Store Operators Issue

Executive Business Media, Inc.
825 Old Country Rd.   Ph: (516)334-3030
PO Box 1500   Fax: (516)334-3059
Westbury, NY 11590-0812
E-mail: ebmpubs@ix.netcom.com
Contact: Steve Hajdu, Editor.
Desc: List of over 300 college book stores operated by lessees. *Type:* Directory.

College Transfer Guide

School Guide Publications
210 North Ave.   Ph: (914)632-7771
New Rochelle, NY 10801 Free: 800-433-7771
                        Fax: (914)632-3412
E-mail: info@schoolguides.com
URL: http://www.schoolguides.com.
Contact: Jeanne Marie Healy, Editor.
Desc: About 500 four-year colleges in the Northeast and Midwest that accept transfer students. *Type:* Directory.

College and University Home Pages

Massachusetts Institute of Technology
77 Massachusetts Ave.   Ph: (617)253-1000
Cambridge, MA 02139-4307
E-mail: web-request@mit.edu
URL: http://www.mit.edu:8001/people/cdemello/univ.html
Contact: Christina DeMello, cdemello@mit.edu.
Desc: A listing of more than 3000 college and university home pages from around the world can be found in this site. An alphabetical listing of the schools is provided, as well as a geographical listing. *Type:* Database.

College of Wooster

College of Wooster
Wooster, OH 44691
E-mail: webmaster@wooster.edu
URL: http://www.wooster.edu/
Desc: The Wooster College web site delivers nothing but solid information. Among some pleasant images you will find all of the usual college information, including academic programs, news, a virtual tour of the college, and even regional information. *Type:* Database.

Colorado State University

Colorado State University
Fort Collins, CO 80523   Ph: (970)491-1101
E-mail: webmaster@colostate.edu
URL: http://www.colostate.edu
Contact: webmaster@colostate.edu.
Desc: The Colorado State University web site provides readers an easy to use platform to navigate this website. Information is discreetly divided according to target reader-prospective students, current students, parents and family, alumni, visitors and friends, and faculty and staff. *Type:* Database.

Cornell College Home Page

Cornell College
600 First St. W.   Ph: (319)895-4000
Mount Vernon, IA 52314-1098
E-mail: communications@cornell-iowa.edu
URL: http://www.cornell-iowa.edu/
Desc: Eastern Iowa's Cornell College is a small United Methodist-affiliated school which uses a teaching method called One-Course-At-A-Time (OCAAT). According to information posted on the college's Web site, students study one subject all term. *Type:* Database.

Creighton University

Creighton University
2500 California Plz.   Ph: (402)280-2700
Omaha, NE 68178
E-mail: webmaster@creighton.edu
URL: http://www.creighton.edu/
Desc: The designers of Creighton University's Web site have accomplished a rare feat: they've somehow managed to infuse the school's Web presence with a distinct personality. The site literally radiates school spirit. *Type:* Database.

CUPA News

College and University Personnel Association (CUPA)
1233 20th St. NW, Ste. 301   Ph: (202)429-0311
Washington, DC 20036   Fax: (202)429-0149
URL: http://www.cupa.org; http://www.cupa.org.
Contact: Melissa Edeburn, Editor, edeburn@cupainet.upa.org.
Desc: Reports on the special research projects, surveys, publications, and consulting activities of the Association, which is interested in the improvement of campus personnel administration. Disseminates information to members regarding federal rules and regulations affecting higher education institutions. *Type:* Newsletter.

CWRU

Case Western Reserve University
10900 Euclid Ave.   Ph: (216)368-3068
Cleveland, OH 44106   Fax: (216)368-4835
Contact: Ken Kesegich, Editor.
Desc: College magazine. *Type:* Periodical.

Dallas Baptist University

Dallas Baptist University
3000 Mountain Creek Pkwy.   Ph: (214)333-7100
Dallas, TX 75211-9299
E-mail: info@dbu.edu
URL: http://www.dbu.edu
Desc: The Dallas Baptist University site has a main menu through which it is easy to find information concerning admissions, adult programs, financial aid, and more. There is plenty of information offered here to answer many of the questions a potential or currently attending student may have. *Type:* Database.

Dartmouth College

Dartmouth College
Hanover, NH 03755   Ph: (603)646-1110
E-mail: webmaster@dartmouth.edu
URL: http://www.dartmouth.edu/
Desc: This is the opening page for Dartmouth, which sports an extensive index of topics. Following one of these links, you will find more topics. *Type:* Database.

Davis and Elkins College

Davis and Elkins College
100 Campus Dr.   Free: 800-624-3157
Elkins, WV 26241
URL: http://www.dne.wvnet.edu/
Contact: webmaster@euclid.dne.wvnet.edu.
Desc: Chock full of historical photographs, the Davis and Elkins College web site includes community information as well as college data. Everything from academics (including special programs) to golf can be found just by following the links. *Type:* Database.

DePaul University

DePaul University
1 E. Jackson Blvd.   Ph: (312)362-8000
Chicago, IL 60604-2287
E-mail: kgallagh@wppost.depaul.edu
URL: http://www.depaul.edu/
Desc: The DePaul University home page is cordoned off so that specific data is not cross-linked but organized and geared to visitors, students, faculty and staff, alumni, and visitors. (A majority of this site will appeal to prospective students.) Since the server will only respond to user requests from the .depaul.edu network, most library and institution-specific databases are inaccessible to visitors who are not affiliated with DePaul University. *Type:* Database.

Directory of College Cooperative Education Programs

Oryx Press
4041 N. Central Ave., Ste. 700   Ph: (602)265-2651
Phoenix, AZ 85012-3397   Free: 800-279-6799
                                 Fax: 800-279-4663
E-mail: info@oryxpress.com
URL: http://www.oryxpress.com
Desc: Approximately 1,000 cooperative education programs offered at colleges and universities throughout the U.S. *Type:* Directory.

Dixie College

Dixie College
225 S. 700 E.   Ph: (435)652-7575
St. George, UT 84770   Fax: (435)656-4087
E-mail: admissions@cc.dixie.edu
URL: http://www.dixie.edu
Contact: webmaster@cc.dixie.edu.
Desc: Graphics fill the title page of the Dixie College home page, telling you exactly where everything is. If you want admissions information, simply click on the Enrollment and Costs graphic. *Type:* Database.

Drake University

Drake University
2507 University Ave.   Ph: (515)271-3181
Des Moines, IA 50311-4505   Free: 800-44-DRAKE
E-mail: dw3751s@acad.drake.edu
URL: http://www.drake.edu/
Desc: Drake University's Web site is a valuable resource for both current and prospective students. For those already attending the university, the site offers a convenient electronic directory of key campus addresses and phone numbers as well as an online guide to campus organizations, the student code of conduct, the college's peer mentor program, and other aspects of campus life. *Type:* Database.

Drew University

Drew University
Madison, NJ 07940   Ph: (973)408-3000
E-mail: webmaster@drew.edu
URL: http://www.drew.edu/
Desc: Take a walk through "The Forest" on this well designed university web site. With beautiful imagery and an easy to navigate design, the Drew University site is quite a pleasure. *Type:* Database.

Duquesne University

Duquesne University
600 Forbes Ave.   Ph: (412)396-6000
Pittsburgh, PA 15282
E-mail: webmaster@www.duq.edu
URL: http://www.duq.edu
Desc: Admissions information, student life, and a map of the campus are just part of what the Duquesne University web site has to offer. Providing a pull down menu of shortcuts and a search engine, this site attempts to ease the burden of extensive research. *Type:* Database.

East Carolina University

East Carolina University
Greenville, NC 27858-4353   Ph: (919)328-6131
E-mail: webmastr@ecuvm.cis.ecu.edu
URL: http://www.ecu.edu/
Desc: Admissions, financial aid, athletics, events, and more can be found at this comprehensive site maintained by East Carolina University. The layout-specific categories listed under sub-headings makes for a quick study as to what's available-and a search engine is provided to make finding topics even easier. *Type:* Database.

Eastern Mennonite University

Eastern Mennonite University
1200 Park Rd.   Ph: (540)432-4000
Harrisonburg, VA 22802-2462   Fax: (540)432-4444
E-mail: info@emu.edu
URL: http://www.emu.edu

Desc: The Eastern Mennonite University title page is neatly organized to make browsing a snap. The full range of university information can be accessed here, from a campus map and events to undergraduate, graduate, and seminary programs. *Type:* Database.

Eastern New Mexico University Home Page

Eastern New Mexico University
Portales, NM 88130
E-mail: webmaster@www.enmu.edu
URL: http://oasis.enmu.edu/

Desc: Easy to navigate and extremely attractive, the Eastern New Mexico University Home Page not only delivers all of the information required of a university site, but also manages to look good. From enrollment to dining to academics to athletics, it's all here. *Type:* Database.

Emory Magazine

Emory University
1655 N. Decatur Rd.   Ph: (404)727-7872
Atlanta, GA 30322   Fax: (404)727-0169
E-mail: emorymag@emory.edu.
URL: http://www.emory.edu/emory_magazine.

Contact: Andrew W.M. Beierle, Editor.

Desc: Magazine for university alumni. *Type:* Periodical.

Ferris State University

Ferris State University
901 S. State St.   Ph: (616)592-2000
Big Rapids, MI 49307
URL: http://www.ferris.edu/

Contact: Dale Hobart, web@ferris.edu.

Desc: Ferris State's Web site features a really spectacular welcome page, filled with eye-catching graphics and push-button links to the key sections of the university's site. The obvious drawback to such a graphics-rich page, of course, is the time it takes to load into your computer unless you're linked to the Internet by cable. *Type:* Database.

Financing Graduate School

Peterson's
202 Carnegie Center   Ph: (609)243-9111
PO Box 2123   Free: 800-338-3282
Princeton, NJ 08543-2123   Fax: (609)243-9150
URL: http://www.peterson.com; http://www.petersons.com.

Desc: List of directories, database programs, and other reference material relevant to graduate students seeking financial aid. Principal content of publication is information on graduate school financial aid. *Type:* Directory.

Florida Atlantic University Home Page

Florida Atlantic University
777 Glades Rd.   Ph: (407)367-3000
PO Box 3091
Boca Raton, FL 33431-0991
E-mail: barton@fau.edu
URL: http://www.fau.edu/

Desc: This is the home site for Florida Atlantic University. Both text and graphics versions are available to browsers. *Type:* Database.

Franklin & Marshall College

Franklin & Marshall College
PO Box 3003   Ph: (717)291-3951
Lancaster, PA 17604-3003   Fax: (717)291-4389
E-mail: admission@FandM.edu
URL: http://www.fandm.edu/

Desc: Navigation is made simple on the F&M web site. This site offers lots of information from enrollment and campus maps to news and alumni affiliations. *Type:* Database.

Fund Your Way through College: Uncovering 1,700 Great Opportunities in Undergraduate Financial Aid.

Gale Group Inc.
27500 Drake Rd.   Ph: (248)699-4253
Farmington Hills, MI 48331-   Free: 800-877-GALE
3535   Fax: (248)699-8070
E-mail: galeord@galegroup.com
URL: http://www.galegroup.com.

Contact: Donna Batten, Editor; Deb Kirby.

Desc: 1,700 scholarships, grants, loans, awards, internships, and prizes for undergraduate students. *Type:* Directory.

The Gaelic College of Celtic Arts & Crafts

The Gaelic College of Celtic Arts & Crafts
PO Box 9   Ph: (902)295-3411
Baddeck, NS, Canada B0E 1B0   Fax: (902)295-2912
E-mail: gaelcoll@atcon.com
URL: http://www.compu-clone.ns.ca/~jdaisley/

Desc: Have you been looking for a place where you can learn piping, Gaelic language and song, Scottish small pipes, Cape Breton fiddle, weaving, Scottish country dance, Highland dance, Celtic harp, or the accordion? This site is full of everything Celtic. This site is devoted to carrying on the valued traditions of the Scottish Highlands. *Type:* Database.

George Mason University

George Mason University
4400 University Dr.   Ph: (703)993-1000
Fairfax, VA 22030-4444
E-mail: webmaster@gmu.edu
URL: http://www.gmu.edu

Desc: The web site maintained by George Mason University sports an easy to navigate design with nice backgrounds, a list all of the topics available, and a link to a search routine, making it is quite easy to find information here. The Admissions section offers several different online applications, ranging from freshmen to graduate enrollment. *Type:* Database.

Georgetown Magazine

Georgetown University
Office of Alumni & University   Ph: (202)687-4317
  Relations   Fax: (202)687-2311
2115 Wisconsin Ave., Ste. 500
Washington, DC 20057
E-mail: gumag@gunet.georgetown.edu.

Contact: Nancy Freiberg-Robertson, Editor.

Desc: Magazine for alumni, parents, faculty, and staff of Georgetown University. *Type:* Periodical.

Georgetown University

Georgetown University
Washington, DC 20057-1002   Ph: (202)687-3600
                                     Fax: (202)687-5084
URL: http://www.georgetown.edu/

Desc: The Georgetown University home page is a nicely tailored graphics driven page that offers readers in-depth information on the university and the surrounding area. Links include information on academic programs, both undergraduate and graduate admissions, the law center, the medical center, alumni, and library access. *Type:* Database.

Goshen College

Goshen College
1700 S. Main St.   Ph: (219)535-7000
Goshen, IN 46526   Free: 800-348-7422
                                     Fax: (219)535-7660
E-mail: arachnid@goshen.edu
URL: http://physix.goshen.edu/

Desc: A four-year, liberal arts college located about 120 miles east of Chicago in Indiana, Goshen College was founded and is operated as a ministry by the Mennonite Church. Drawing on its strong Christian heritage, the college puts particular emphasis upon service as part of its curriculum. *Type:* Database.

Grand Valley State University

Grand Valley State University
Allendale, MI 49401-9403   Ph: (616)895-6611
                                     Free: 800-748-0246
URL: http://www.gvsu.edu/

Desc: Grand Valley State University's Web site provides an excellent introduction to the school for those unfamiliar with it as well as a handy tool for current students and faculty members. One quick way to get a feel for the university is to take the virtual tour of its campus. *Type:* Database.

Great Basin College

University of Nevada - Computing Center - System Computing Services, North
Mail Stop 270   Ph: (702)784-6557
Reno, NV 89557-0023   Fax: (702)784-1108
E-mail: webmaster@scs.unr.edu
URL: http://www.scs.unr.edu/gbc/
Contact: gba@scs.unr.edu.

Desc: This attractively designed Web site is loaded with helpful information about Nevada's Great Basin College for both current and prospective students, as well as faculty members and alumni. The site's incredibly detailed admissions section takes most of the guesswork out of this tedious procedure. *Type:* Database.

Hampden-Sydney College

Hampden-Sydney College
Hampden Sydney, VA 23943   Ph: (804)223-6000
E-mail: webmaster@hsc.edu
URL: http://www.hsc.edu

Desc: The Hampden-Sydney College, a private four year men's liberal arts college, resides amid beautiful trees in Hampden-Sydney, Virginia, and serves up a fact-filled web site. Want to enroll? Simply fill out the online applications form. *Type:* Database.

Hanover College

Hanover College
PO Box 108   Ph: (812)866-7000
Hanover, IN 47243   Free: 800-213-2178
E-mail: admission@hanover.edu
URL: http://www.hanover.edu/
Contact: Heather Spinner, spinner@hanover.edu.

Desc: Founded in 1827, Hanover College is a small liberal arts college affiliated with the Presbyterian Church (U.S.A.). Visitors to the school's Web site, which is well-designed and easy to navigate, will find a wealth of information about Hanover and the community in which it operates. *Type:* Database.

Hartwick College Home Page

Hartwick College
West St.
Oneonta, NY 13820
E-mail: webmaster@hartwick.edu
URL: http://www.hartwick.edu/

Desc: Founded in 1797, this liberal arts institution maintains a detailed web site that is quite easy to navigate. Offering everything from admissions information to school publications, this site is extremely thorough. *Type:* Database.

Harvard Magazine

Harvard Magazine
7 Ware St. Ph: (617)495-5746
Cambridge, MA 02138 Free: 800-648-4499
Fax: (617)495-0324
URL: www.harvard_magazine.com.
Contact: John S. Rosenberg, Editor, (617)496-6707, john_rosenberg@harvard.edu; Ed Antos, Advertising Dir., (617)496-6658, ed_antos@harvard.edu; Bob Fitta, Advertising Account Mgr., (617)496-6631, bob_fitta@harvard.edu; Eriko Ogawa, Dir. of Marketing, (617)496-6687, eriko_ogawa@harvard.edu; Karline Kosdrosky, NE Regional Advertising Mgr., (617)496-4032, karline_kosdrosky@harvard.edu; Felecia Carter, Dir. of Circulation, (617)496-6694, felecia_carter@harvard.edu.
Desc: Alumni magazine. *Type:* Periodical.

Hesston College Home Page

Hesston College
Box 3000 Ph: (316)327-4221
Hesston, KS 67062-2093 Fax: (316)327-8300
E-mail: davidg@hesston.edu
URL: http://www.hesston.edu
Desc: Another of the "simple is as simple does"-style Web sites. Links listed on the front page are accurately named. *Type:* Database.

Hillsdale College Home Page

Hillsdale College
33 East College St. Ph: (517)437-7341
Hillsdale, MI 49242 Fax: (517)437-3923
E-mail: webmaster@ac.hillsdale.edu
URL: http://www.hillsdale.edu/
Desc: Founded in 1844, Hillsdale College is an independent co-educational school in southern Michigan located midway between Chicago and Cleveland. Information on its Web site, which features a search engine, is logically organized and attractively displayed. *Type:* Database.

Hobart and William Smith Colleges

Hobart and William Smith Colleges
Geneva, NY 14456
E-mail: cooke@hws.edu
URL: http://www.hws.edu//
Contact: webmaster@hws.edu.
Desc: This site is maintained by two small colleges, one for men and the other for women. The directions to these institutes of higher education are both very detailed. *Type:* Database.

Hollins College Home Page

Hollins College
7916 Williamson Rd. Ph: (540)362-6000
Roanoke, VA 24020
URL: http://www.hollins.edu
Contact: webmaster@hollins.edu.
Desc: The Hollins College Home Page features a lovely panoramic view of the Front Quad, along with links to all the information about this college that you may need, including information about admissions, athletics, the administration, and more. *Type:* Database.

Howard University Home Page

Howard University
2400 Sixth St. Ph: (202)806-6100
Washington, DC 20059
E-mail: webmaster@howard.edu
URL: http://www.howard.edu/
Desc: The Howard University (HU) web page, announces itself as the largest community of African-American scholars in the world, is one of the most elaborate university web-sites on the net. The site supports a link to a photo gallery maintained by the university for those who wish to see more of the campus. *Type:* Database.

Illinois Alumni

University of Illinois Alumni Association
227 Illini Union Ph: (217)333-1471
1401 W Green St. Fax: (217)333-7803
Urbana, IL 61801
E-mail: alumni@uiuc.edu; illinoisalumni@uiuc.edu.
Contact: Vanessa Faurie, Editor.
Desc: Alumni association magazine. *Type:* Periodical.

Illinois Institute of Technology

Illinois Institute of Technology
3300 South Federal St. Ph: (312)567-3000
Chicago, IL 60616-3793
E-mail: webmaster@www.iit.edu
URL: http://www.iit.edu/
Desc: The Illinois Institute of Technology's home page contains detailed information on admissions, research, events, student services, libraries, and much more. A search engine is provided to help users locate material. *Type:* Database.

Illinois State University Alumni Today

Illinois State University
University Communications Ph: (309)438-8404
Campus Box 3420 Fax: (309)438-8411
Normal, IL 61790
Contact: David Mathis, Editor, drmathis@ilstu.edu.
Desc: College alumni tabloid. *Type:* Periodical.

Indiana Alumni Magazine

Indiana University Alumni Association
1000 E. 17th St. Ph: (812)855-4822
Bloomington, IN 47408-1521 Free: 800-824-3044
Fax: (812)855-4228
E-mail: iualumni@indiana.edu
Contact: Judith Schroeder, Editor, (812)855-5785, jschroed@indiana.edu; Andrea Crawford, Advertising Mgr., (812)855-5785, acrawfor@indiana.edu; Lauren Bryant, Managing Editor, (812)855-5785, labryant@indiana.edu.
Desc: Magazine for college alumni. *Type:* Periodical.

Indiana State University

Indiana State University
210 North Seventh St. Free: 800-742-0891
Terre Haute, IN 47809
E-mail: webmaster@indstate.edu
URL: http://www.indstate.edu/
Desc: Indiana State University, with a student body of about 11,000, prides itself on its central Midwest location, within a three-hour drive of Chicago, Cincinnati, Indianapolis, Louisville, and St. Louis. *Type:* Database.

Insider Magazine

Michiana Ventures, Inc.
4124 Oakton St. Ph: (847)673-3703
Skokie, IL 60076 Fax: (847)329-0358
URL: http://www.insideread.com/
Contact: Mark Jansen, Publisher; Rita Cook, Editorial Dir.; Maxine Milks, Assoc. Publisher.
Desc: Magazine focusing on entertainment, careers, and issues concerning 18-34 year olds. *Type:* Periodical.

Institute for American Universities

PO Box 592 Ph: (847)864-6876
Evanston, IL 60204 Free: 800-221-2051
Fax: (847)864-6897
E-mail: iauusa@univ-aix.fr
URL: http://www.univ-aix.fr/iau/iau.html
Contact: Dr. David Wilsford, Pres.
Desc: Provides a program of study abroad for American undergraduates from more than 700 United States universities. Courses of study include French, European Studies, French Civilization, European Business, Economics, Studio Arts, Archaeology and Ancient History, and International Relations. *Type:* Association.

The Iowa Stater

Iowa State University
105 Communications Bldg. Ph: (515)294-3129
Ames, IA 50011-0001 Fax: (515)294-9748
E-mail: stater@iastate.edu.
URL: http://www.iastate.edu/lastater/tisindex.html.
Contact: Linda Charles, Managing Editor, lacharl@iastate.edu.
Desc: Magazine for university alumni. *Type:* Periodical.

Joliet Junior College

Joliet Junior College
1215 Houbolt Rd. Ph: (815)729-9020
Joliet, IL 60431-8938
E-mail: webmaster@www2.jjc.cc.il.us
URL: http://www.jjc.cc.il.us
Contact: Scott Olsen, Supervisor of Academic Computing.
Desc: The oldest public community college in the United States, Joliet Junior College today serves more than 10,000 students enrolled in credit courses and another 21,000 in noncredit sessions. The college's Web site is a valuable tool for current students or those who are planning to apply for admission. *Type:* Database.

Jones College

Jones College
5353 Arlington Expy. Ph: (904)743-1122
Jacksonville, FL 32211
URL: http://unix.jones.edu/
Contact: Ken Jones, webmaster@jones.edu.
Desc: Jacksonville's Jones College (JC) has three off-campus programs which are linked to the main web site. In addition to virtual tours of each campus, online catalogues, seminars, and library resources make this closer to realizing a virtual internet academic institution than a majority of college/university sites. *Type:* Database.

Kalamazoo College Home Page

Kalamazoo College
1200 Academy St. Ph: (616)337-7166
Kalamazoo, MI 49006-3295
E-mail: web@kzoo.edu
URL: http://www.kzoo.edu/
Desc: A private liberal arts college midway between Detroit and Chicago, Kalamazoo College boasts that is graduates leave the school with not just a diploma but with a resume as well. The college's program of career-development internships is well documented in its very attractively designed Web site. *Type:* Database.

Kean College of New Jersey Home Page

Kean College
Union, NJ 07083
E-mail: webmaster@turbo.kean.edu
URL: http://turbo.kean.edu/
Desc: The Kean College of New Jersey Home Page has just about everything, including admissions information, academic program breakdowns, and sports information. Weather, government agencies, and health and fitness information augment this comprehensive look at not only the college, but also New Jersey. *Type:* Database.

Keene State College Home Page

Keene State College
229 Main St. Ph: (603)358-1909
Keene, NH 03435 Free: 800-572-1909
E-mail: WebMaster@Keene.edu.
URL: http://www.keene.edu/
Desc: Filled to bursting with information, the Keene State College Home Page is a pleasure to read. Not only does it provide all of the information necessary (admission information, course schedules, and the like), but it also offers links concerned with the state of New Hampshire--including weather and residential information. *Type:* Database.

Kirtland Community College

Kirtland Community College
10775 N. Saint Helen Rd.   Ph: (517)275-5121
Roscommon, MI 48653
E-mail: web@kirtland.cc.mi.us
URL: http://www.kirtland.cc.mi.us/
Contact: Lori Loveland, lovelanl@kirtland.cc.mi.us.
Desc: Kirtland is a two-year community college serving more than 2,500 students in a largely rural area of Michigan about 170 miles from Detroit. Its Web site is filled with information helpful to current students and those who are considering studying there. *Type:* Database.

Kutztown University of Pennsylvania

Kutztown University of Pennsylvania
Kutztown, PA 19530   Ph: (610)683-4000
E-mail: morrison@kutztown.edu
URL: http://www.kutztown.edu/
Desc: Providing all of the general information necessary, Kutztown University's web site will come in handy for prospective and currently enrolled students. The admissions information is detailed (and an online admissions form is provided if you just can't wait). *Type:* Database.

Lafayette College

Lafayette College
Office of Public Information   Ph: (610)250-5120
17 Watson Hall
Easton, PA 18042
URL: http://www.lafayette.edu/
Contact: Patricia Facciponti, faccipop@lafayette.edu.
Desc: Providing details concerning admissions, athletics, course schedules, alumni services, and more, the Lafayette College web site is packed with information. The Internet Resources section provides links to a diverse selection of topics, from anthropology to finance A searchable campus directory is also provided. *Type:* Database.

Langston University Research & Extension

Langston University
Langston, OK 73050
URL: http://www.luresext.edu/
Contact: tmack@luresext.edu.
Desc: This site labels itself as the Nation's Leader In Research And Extension For Goats. This site, despite the rather bizarre material involved, takes itself very seriously. *Type:* Database.

LASPAU: Academic and Professional Programs for the Americas

25 Mt. Auburn St.   Ph: (617)495-5255
Cambridge, MA 02138-6095   Fax: (617)495-8990
E-mail: laspau@harvard.edu
URL: http://www.laspau.harvard.edu
Contact: Ned D. Strong, Exec.Dir.
Desc: Designs, develops, and implements academic exchange programs on behalf of individuals and institutions in the United States, Canada, Latin America, and the Caribbean. *Type:* Association.

Lehigh University

Lehigh University
27 Memorial Dr. W.   Ph: (610)758-3000
Bethlehem, PA 18015
URL: http://www.lehigh.edu/
Contact: www@lehigh.edu.
Desc: Lehigh University's contribution to the WWW provides not only an extensive look at the institution, but also grants students the ability to design their own web sites. All of the general university topics are available here, from course schedules and departmental information to financial aid and job placement. *Type:* Database.

Les Diplomes

Les Diplomes de l'Universite de Montreal
3750 rue Jean-Brillant, Ste. 410   Ph: (514)343-6230
Montreal, PQ, Canada H3T   Fax: (514)343-5798
  1P1
Contact: Michel Saint-Laurent, Editor.
Desc: Alumni magazine. *Type:* Periodical.

Louisiana State University

Louisiana State University
Baton Rouge, LA 70803   Ph: (504)388-1175
E-mail: webmaster@lsu.edu
URL: http://www.lsu.edu/
Desc: Louisiana State University in Baton Rouge is larger than many small cities in this country, serving a community of more than 30,000 students, faculty members, and support staff. Its Web site, despite the unfortunate absence of a search engine, is an excellent resource for members of that community as well as others who would like to learn a little bit more about Louisiana's premier state-supported school. *Type:* Database.

Louisiana Tech University

Louisiana Tech University
PO Box 3178   Ph: (318)257-3036
Ruston, LA 71272   Free: 800-528-3241
E-mail: milstead@cab.latech.edu
URL: http://www.latech.edu/
Desc: Attractively designed and easy to navigate, Louisiana Tech University's Web site offers a wealth of information that should be useful to members of its student body and faculty as well as prospective students. The topics covered at the site rang from admissions policy and financial aid to the school's athletics program and student life. *Type:* Database.

Loyola Magazine

Loyola University of Chicago
820 N. Michigan Ave., Lewis   Ph: (312)915-6407
  Towers, Ste. 1500   Free: 800-424-1513
Chicago, IL 60611   Fax: (312)915-6450
Contact: Bill Noblitt, Editor-in-Chief.
Desc: Collegiate magazine. *Type:* Periodical.

Loyola University, Chicago

Loyola University, Chicago
6526 N. Sheridan Rd. (Lake   Ph: (773)274-3000
  Shore Campus)
Chicago, IL 60626
E-mail: webmaster@luc.edu
URL: http://www.luc.edu/
Desc: Even though Chicago is packed full of universities, colleges, and institutes, there's always room for one more. In fact, Loyola University is one of the city's oldest institutions of higher learning. *Type:* Database.

Maine Maritime Academy

Maine Maritime Academy
Castine, ME 04420   Ph: 800-464-6565
   Free: 800-227-8465
URL: http://www.mainemaritime.edu/
Desc: According to this site, more than 95% of the students who earn a degree at the Maine Maritime Academy land jobs in their respective fields. That's an impressive figure. *Type:* Database.

Manhattan College Home Page

Manhattan College
Manhattan College Pkwy.   Free: 800-622-9355
Riverdale, NY 10471
E-mail: cduggan@manhattan.edu
URL: http://www.mancol.edu/
Desc: The contents of this site, maintained by Manhattan College, are quite evident on the title page. Simply point and click and you will be at the information you wished to find. *Type:* Database.

Marlboro College

Marlboro College
Marlboro, VT 05344   Ph: (802)257-4333
E-mail: web@marlboro.edu
URL: http://akbar.marlboro.edu
Desc: The Marlboro College Home Page serves up a good deal of information, including the standard college fare from admissions to alumni. Numerous campus photos, a map, and a link to information concerning the beautiful state of Vermont are available. *Type:* Database.

Marymount Manhattan College

Marymount Manhattan College
221 E. 71st St.   Ph: (212)517-0555
New York, NY 10021
URL: http://marymount.mmm.edu/home.htm
Desc: This pleasant site, hosted by Marymount Manhattan College, offers all of the standard college fare in a fairly simple format. Excellent images and backgrounds accompany the plethora of data available here; there is plenty of information for the current or potential student. *Type:* Database.

Mayville State University Home Page

Mayville State University
Mayville, ND 58257   Ph: (701)858-3000
E-mail: jay_henrick@mail.masu.nodak.edu
URL: http://www.masu.nodak.edu/
Desc: The design of this site, provided by Mayville State University in North Dakota, fluctuates from sparse to cluttered. This makes navigation a bit tedious at times. *Type:* Database.

McMurry University

McMurry University - Office of Admissions
McMurry Station Box 278   Ph: (915)691-6226
Abilene, TX 79697   Free: 800-460-2392
E-mail: webmaster@ww.mcm.edu
URL: http://www.mcm.acu.edu/
Desc: Fast and easy to use, the McMurry University web site is a must see for prospective and current students alike. All of the broad topics, including admissions, academics, and computer guides can be found on the title page. *Type:* Database.

Meredith College

Interpath WebPress
711 Hillsborough St.
Raleigh, NC 27605
E-mail: info@interpath.net
URL: http://www.meredith.edu/
Desc: This college, dedicated to the education of women, has created a web site that addresses any question a potential student may have on the title page. Here you will find a succinct list of all that this site has to offer, including academics, financial aid, and admissions. *Type:* Database.

The Metropolitan Community Colleges

The Metropolitan Community Colleges
3200 Broadway   Ph: (816)759-1166
Kansas City, MO 64111
URL: http://www.kcmetro.cc.mo.us/
Desc: A well designed, beautiful interface highlights this rather small site. Don't let size fool you, however. *Type:* Database.

Michigan Alumnus

University of Michigan
200 Fletcher St.   Ph: (734)764-0384
Ann Arbor, MI 48109-1007   Free: 800-847-4764
   Fax: (734)764-4506
Contact: Noreen Ferris Wolcott, Editor; Marie L. Frost, Advertising Coord., (734)763-9706, frostm@umich.edu.

Desc: Collegiate magazine. *Type:* Periodical.

Michigan State University

Michigan State University
East Lansing, MI 48824-1318
E-mail: webmaster@msu.edu
URL: http://www.msu.edu/

Desc: Michigan State University's Web site provides visitors with a wealth of information about the university. For prospective students, there is an extensive Admissions section offering details about financial aid, campus visits, and academic programs. *Type:* Database.

Middle Tennessee State University

Middle Tennessee State University
1301 Main St.   Ph: (615)898-2111
Murfreesboro, TN 37132-0001   Free: 800-433-MTSU
                                 Fax: (615)898-5478
E-mail: admissions@MTSU.edu
URL: http://frank.mtsu.edu/

Desc: Admissions, academics, community information, course calendars, a campus map, and much more can all be had with a simple click of the mouse. Online keyword searching is available, as well as course catalogs and numerous links to relevant pages. *Type:* Database.

Midwestern State University

Midwestern State University
Office of School Relations   Ph: (940)397-4334
3410 Taft Blvd.   Free: 800-842-1922
Wichita Falls, TX 76308-2099
E-mail: school.relations@nexus.mwsu.edu
URL: http://www.mwsu.edu

Contact: Jim Hall, Webmaster, jim.hall@nexus.mwsu.edu.
Desc: At the Midwestern State University site, the area for prospective students is clearly designated and supplies all of the information necessary to begin the enrollment process. Other areas range from alumni relations to tools for use on the Internet. *Type:* Database.

Milligan College

Milligan College
PO Box 500   Free: 800-262-8337
Milligan College, TN 37682
URL: http://www.milligan.edu
Contact: teeah@naxs.com.
Desc: This informative site, offered by Milligan College, provides all of the standard fare expected of a site of this type. Course schedules and descriptions, departmental data, admissions information, and much more can be accessed here. *Type:* Database.

The Minot State University Home Page

Minot State University
Minot, ND 58707   Ph: (701)858-3000
URL: http://www.misu.nodak.edu/
Contact: strube@misu.nodak.edu.
Desc: This dry, no-nonsense site divides its space between supplying information about Minot State University and linking up to the information superhighway. Here readers will find campus employment opportunities, local weather links, student directories, and other information pertaining to the university. *Type:* Database.

MIZZOU Magazine

Alumni Association of the University of Missouri
407 Donald W. Reynolds   Ph: (573)882-7357
  Alumni and Visitor Center   Fax: (573)882-7290
Columbia, MO 65211
E-mail: mizzou@muccmail.missouri.edu.
Contact: Karen Worley, Editor, karen_s_worley@ muccmail.missouri.edu; Tanya Stitt, Advertising Dir.
Desc: University alumni magazine. *Type:* Periodical.

Montana State University-Bozeman

Montana State University
Bozeman, MT 59717
URL: http://www.montana.edu/
Contact: www@montana.edu.
Desc: This beautifully designed Web site not only provides a wealth of information about Montana State University (from admission to graduation) but also gives enough detail on the surrounding area to make any reader want to visit Bozeman. The description and images on display at the MSU site are beautiful. *Type:* Database.

Montclair State University

Montclair State University
1 Normal Avenue   Ph: (973)655-4000
Upper Montclair, NJ 07043
URL: http://www.montclair.edu/
Desc: From admissions to Internet resources, readers will find just about any information they're looking for on this easily navigated site maintained by Montclair State University's Office of Academic Computing and Technology. While visually lacking some much-needed graphics, it is possible to quickly gather data here--just jump in and follow the instructions. *Type:* Database.

NACS College Store—Buyers' Guide Issue

National Association of College Stores
500 E. Lorain St.   Ph: (440)775-7777
Oberlin, OH 44074-1294   Free: 800-622-7498
                                 Fax: (440)775-4769
E-mail: info@nacs.org; thecollegestore@nacs.org.
URL: http://www.nacs.org.
Contact: Cynthia D'Angelo, Editor, cdangelo@nacs.org.
Desc: About 1,200 firms that supply general products and services to college bookstores. *Type:* Directory.

National Association for Campus Activities

13 Harbison Way   Ph: (803)732-6222
Columbia, SC 29212   Free: 800-845-2338
                                 Fax: (803)749-1047
URL: http://www.naca.org
Contact: Alan Davis, Exec.Dir.
Desc: Institutions of higher education (1200); associate members (550) are firms whose services or products are related to campus activities, events, and programs; professional members (380). Assists in the educational development of programmers (both student and staff) at member institutions in all areas of extracurricular activities including entertainment, recreation, and the arts; disseminates educational information to members via publications. Maintains hall of fame; compiles statistics; operates placement service. *Type:* Association.

National Association for College Admission Counseling

1631 Prince St.   Ph: (703)836-2222
Alexandria, VA 22314-2818   Fax: (703)836-8015
URL: http://www.nacac.com
Contact: Joyce E. Smith, Exec.Dir.
Desc: Public, parochial, and independent secondary schools; school systems; public and private two-year colleges, four-year colleges, and universities; independent counselors and educational organizations concerned with secondary school guidance, college admission, and financial aid. Seeks to establish and maintain high professional standards in college admission guidance; develop useful and efficient college guidance programs and materials; foster and expand the relationships between and among secondary schools and colleges. Conducts state and regional conferences, seminars and workshops, and research projects. *Type:* Association.

National Association for College Admission Counseling Membership Directory

National Association for College Admission Counseling
1631 Prince St.   Ph: (703)836-2222
Alexandria, VA 22314-2818   Free: 800-822-6285
                                 Fax: (703)836-8015
URL: http://www.nacac.com; http://www.nacac.com.
Contact: Marody Faulkner, Editor.
Desc: 6,500 member high schools, school districts, colleges and universities, professional associations, independent counselors, and individuals. *Type:* Directory.

National Association of College and University Food Services

Joseph H. Spina
Michigan State University   Ph: (517)332-2494
Manly Miles Bldg.   Fax: (517)332-8144
1405 S. Harrison, Ste. 305
East Lansing, MI 48824
URL: http://www.nacufs.org/nacufs
Contact: Joseph H. Spina, Ph.D., Exec.Dir., CAE.
Desc: Food services in operation at colleges or universities; residence centers; student centers. Advances and promotes the highest standards of food preparation and service on college and university campuses. *Type:* Association.

National Association of Colleges and Employers

62 Highland Ave.   Ph: (610)868-1421
Bethlehem, PA 18017   Free: 800-544-5272
                                 Fax: (610)868-0208
URL: http://www.jobweb.org
Contact: Marilyn Mackes, Contact.
Desc: Provides information services to career planning and placement directors at two- and four-year colleges and universities, as well as to human resources professionals who hire college graduates. *Type:* Association.

National Association for Equal Opportunity in Higher Education

8701 Georgia Ave., Ste. 200   Ph: (301)650-2440
Silver Spring, MD 20910   Fax: (301)495-3306
Contact: Dr. Henry Ponder, CEO/Pres.
Desc: Provides a unified framework representing historically and predominantly black universities and colleges and similarly situated institutions in their attempt to continue as viable forces in American society. Seeks to build a case for securing increased support from federal agencies, philanthropic foundations, and other sources, and to increase black leadership of educational organizations and membership on federal boards and commissions relating to education. Offers placement service. *Type:* Association.

National Association of Independent Colleges and Universities

1025 Connecticut Ave, Ste. 700   Ph: (202)785-8866
Washington, DC 20036
URL: http://www.naicu.edu
Contact: David L. Warren, Pres.
Desc: Independent colleges and universities throughout the United States; 23 national and 42 state associations of such colleges. Serves as a unified voice for independent higher education, by initiating and influencing public policies that will foster the optimum opportunities for higher education to serve the education needs of society; to promote public policies that will assure all students the widest range of choices of institutions and programs that best meet their educational needs; to defend institutional integrity, freedom, and diversity, and work to minimize governmental intrusion into higher education; to support fiscal and tax policies that provide maximum encouragement for charitable giving to independent colleges and universities;

to increase public awareness and understanding of the contributions made by independent higher education in meeting public needs through teaching, research, and community service; to coordinate efforts with member institutions and state associations to promote positive actions toward independent higher education at the state and local levels of government; to gather data and provide analysis of public policy issues that concern the independent sector. *Type:* Association.

National Faculty Directory

Gale Group Inc.
27500 Drake Rd.　　　　　Ph: (248)699-4253
Farmington Hills, MI 48331-　Free: 800-877-GALE
3535　　　　　　　　　　Fax: (248)699-8070
E-mail: galeord@galegroup.com
URL: http://www.galegroup.com.

Desc: More than 650,000 (40,000 more in supplement) teaching faculty members at over 3,840 junior colleges, colleges, and universities in the United States and those in Canada that give instruction in English. *Type:* Directory.

NEA Higher Education Advocate

National Education Association of the United States
1201 16th St. NW　　　　　Ph: (202)822-7214
Washington, DC 20036　　　Fax: (202)822-7206
URL: http://www.nea.org/he.
Contact: Con Lehane, Editor, clehane@nea.org.

Desc: Concentrates on news and issues affecting higher education. Recurring features include news of higher education, collective bargaining, and teaching and learning in higher education. *Type:* Newsletter.

New Jersey Institute of Technology

New Jersey Institute of Technology
University Heights　　　　Ph: (201)596-3000
Newark, NJ 07102
E-mail: webmaster@njit.edu
URL: http://www.njit.edu/

Desc: The NJIT web site is quite an eye-opener. Not only does it offer an extremely comprehensive look at the college and its surrounding area, but it does so with many well-placed graphics. *Type:* Database.

New Mexico Institute of Mining and Technology

New Mexico Tech - Public Information Office
801 Leroy Pl.　　　　　　Free: 800-428-8324
Socorro, NM 87801
E-mail: pio@nmt.edu
URL: http://www.nmt.edu/

Desc: If you are looking for a web site loaded with beautiful images, the New Mexico Tech home page will satisfy your needs. Buffer this with loads of important information for prospective and current students and you have a site that is a must see! All of the information one would expect on a college site (from admissions to graduation) is provided along with weather reports, community information, and a tour through the campus utilizing dazzling graphics and well-written text. *Type:* Database.

New Mexico Tech

New Mexico Tech
Socorro, NM 87801　　　　Free: 800-428-8324
E-mail: info@tesc.edu
URL: http://www.nmt.edu/

Desc: All of the information one would expect on a college site (from admissions to graduation) is provided along with weather reports, community information, and a tour through the campus utilizing dazzling graphics and well-written text. *Type:* Database.

Nicholls State University

Nicholls State University
Thibodaux, LA 70310
E-mail: nichweb@www.nich.edu
URL: http://server.nich.edu/~nsu/

Desc: Nicholls State University, which celebrated its fiftieth birthday in 1998, is a mid-sized state-supported school in the heart of South Louisiana's Cajun country. Its Web site offers pretty much what one would expect from a school of this size. *Type:* Database.

North Carolina Community College System

North Carolina Community College System
200 W. Jones St.　　　　　Ph: (919)733-7051
Raleigh, NC 27603　　　　Fax: (919)733-0680
E-mail: webmastr@ncccs.cc.nc.us
URL: http://bull.ncdcc.cc.nc.us/

Desc: For a no frills overview of North Carolina community college prospects, this is the site to check out. Here you will find links to colleges, employment, various administrative projects, and more. *Type:* Database.

North Dakota State College of Science

North Dakota State College of Science
Wahpeton, ND 58076　　　Free: 800-342-4325
E-mail: webmaster@www.ndscs.nodak.edu
URL: http://www.ndscs.nodak.edu/

Desc: The NDSCS web site allows for clear, crisp navigation. All of the information is here for the taking, provided you are ready to get your hands a little dirty while digging. *Type:* Database.

North Dakota State University

North Dakota State University
1301 North University
Fargo, ND 58105
E-mail: webmaster@www.ndsu.nodak.edu
URL: http://www.ndsu.nodak.edu/

Desc: North Dakota University provides an easy-to-follow, colorful interface on its cover page. Contents include admissions and registration data, a campus map, academic program details, and more. *Type:* Database.

Northern Kentucky University

Northern Kentucky University
Nunn Drive　　　　　　　Ph: (606)572-5220
Highland Heights, KY 41099　Free: 800-637-9948
E-mail: webmaster@nku.edu
URL: http://www.nku.edu/

Desc: Based in northern Kentucky, not far from Cincinnati, Ohio, Northern Kentucky University serves a student body of nearly 12,000. Its Web site offers a fairly straightforward introduction to the university and its history. *Type:* Database.

Northwest Nazarene College

Northwest Nazarene College
623 Holly St.　　　　　　Ph: (208)467-8011
Nampa, ID 83686　　　　　Free: 800-NNC-4YOU
URL: http://www.nnc.edu/

Contact: John Neil, Information Resources Analyst, jrneil@nnc.edu.

Desc: Northwest Nazarene College calls itself a distinctly Christian liberal arts college. Its Web site offers access to information about the school's campus, athletic programs, alumni, and much more. *Type:* Database.

Northwestern University

Northwestern University
Department of University　　Ph: (847)491-4885
　Relations
555 Clark St.
Evanston, IL 60208-1230
E-mail: jmwright@nwu.edu
URL: http://www.nwu.edu/

Desc: The Northwestern University Web site is vast but is designed in such a fashion that if offers visitors a quick and easy way to locate information about admissions, courses, faculty, and administration. With an extensive online help file, search engine, index, and electronic directory, the information is never more than a few keystrokes away. *Type:* Database.

Norwich University

Norwich University
65 S. Main St.　　　　　　Ph: (802)485-2000
Northfield, VT 05663　　　Fax: (802)485-2032
E-mail: webmaster@norwich.edu
URL: http://www.norwich.edu

Desc: From the opening page, you know you're on a military site. A concise menu leaves you with no question of where to proceed on the site provided by Norwich University. *Type:* Database.

Notre Dame Magazine

University of Notre Dame
415 Administration Bldg.　　Ph: (219)631-5000
Notre Dame, IN 46556　　　Fax: (219)239-6947
URL: http://www.nd.ndu.
Contact: Walton R. Collins, Editor.

Desc: Magazine for university alumni and friends. *Type:* Periodical.

Ohio State Alumni Magazine

The Ohio State University Alumni Association, Inc.
2400 Olentangy River Rd.　Ph: (614)292-3811
Columbus, OH 43210-1061　Fax: (614)292-7697
Contact: Linda S. Crossley, Editor-in-Chief, crossley.6@osu.edu; Dan L. Heinlen, Publisher, (614)292-6881, heinlen.4@osu.edu; Deborah S. Sawyer, Advertising Sales Rep., (614)846-2084.

Desc: University alumni magazine. *Type:* Periodical.

Old Dominion University

Old Dominion University
Norfolk, VA 23529　　　　Ph: (757)683-3000
E-mail: web@maui.cc.odu.edu
URL: http://web.odu.edu/

Desc: The Old Dominion University contains an abundance of information for prospective students, current students, parents--or even passers-by. If you've never been to this site before, it's a good idea to go directly to the search engine near the bottom of the title page. *Type:* Database.

ON WISCONSIN

Wisconsin Alumni Association
650 N. Lake St.　　　　　Ph: (608)262-2551
Madison, WI 53706　　　　Free: 888-947-2586
　　　　　　　　　　　　Fax: (608)262-3332
E-mail: waa@badger.alumni.wisc.edu
URL: http://www.wisc.edu/waa
Contact: Susan Pigorsch, Editor, (608)262-9639, susanpigorsch@badger.alumni.wisc.edu.

Desc: Magazine for alumni of University of Wisconsin. *Type:* Periodical.

Oral Roberts University

Oral Roberts University
7777 S. Lewis Ave.
Tulsa, OK 74171
E-mail: webmaster@oru.edu
URL: http://www.oru.edu/

Desc: The Oral Roberts University web site feels more like a brochure to Disney World than a site dedicated to an institute of higher learning. Advertising for various religious publications and other such subjects reside here. *Type:* Database.

Oregon Quarterly

University of Oregon
5228 University of Oregon   Ph: (541)346-5047
Eugene, OR 97403-5228   Fax: (541)346-5571
E-mail: quarterly@oregon.uoregon.edu.

Contact: Guy Maynard, Editor, (541)346-5048, fax: (541)346-5571, gmaynard@oregon.voregon.edu.

Desc: Collegiate magazine for alumni and faculty of the University of Oregon. *Type:* Periodical.

Oregon State University

Oregon State University
Corvallis, OR 97331-4501   Ph: (541)737-1000
                               Free: 800-291-4192
E-mail: libraryi@ccmail.orst.edu
URL: http://www.orst.edu/

Desc: This extremely comprehensive site offers an online admission form as well as all of the facts that you need to know to begin life at a major university. Campus maps, athletic information, even a section devoted to Corvallis and Oregon, can be found here with little effort. *Type:* Database.

The Penn Stater

Penn State Alumni Association
University House   Ph: (814)865-6516
University Park, PA 16802   Free: 800-546-5466
                              Fax: (814)865-3325
E-mail: pennstater@psu.edu.

Contact: Tina Hay, Editor, tinahay@psu.edu; Giovanna Genard, Advertising Mgr., (814)865-9973; Vicki Glembocki, Assoc. Editor, (814)863-3253, vxg5@psu.edu.

Desc: Alumni magazine. *Alt. Contact:* 141 W. Beaver Ave., Ste. 15, University Park, PA 16802; telephone: (814)863-1275; fax: (814)863-5690; toll-free: 800-546-5466. *Type:* Periodical.

Peterson's College Database

Peterson's
202 Carnegie Center   Ph: (609)243-9111
PO Box 2123
Princeton, NJ 08540
E-mail: peters.custsvc@pgi.petersons.com
URL: http://www.petersons.com

Desc: Contains current information on approximately 3300 colleges and universities in the U.S. and Canada. *Available:* CompuServe Information Service, Knowledge Index; Dow Jones Interactive Publishing; The Gale Group, InfoTrac Web. *Type:* Database.

Peterson's Guide to Four-Year Colleges

Peterson's
202 Carnegie Center   Ph: (609)243-9111
PO Box 2123   Free: 800-338-3282
Princeton, NJ 08543-2123   Fax: (609)243-9150
URL: http://www.peterson.com
Contact: Susan Dilts, Editor.

Desc: Nearly 2,000 four-year undergraduate institutions that grant baccalaureate degrees in the United States and Canada. *Type:* Directory.

Peterson's Guide to Graduate & Professional Programs in Engineering and Applied Sciences

Peterson's
202 Carnegie Center   Ph: (609)243-9111
PO Box 2123   Free: 800-338-3282
Princeton, NJ 08543-2123   Fax: (609)243-9150
URL: http://www.peterson.com

Desc: Colleges offering master's, doctoral, and professional programs in engineering and applied sciences. *Type:* Directory.

Peterson's Guide to Graduate & Professional Programs in the Humanities, Arts, and Social Sciences

Peterson's
202 Carnegie Center   Ph: (609)243-9111
PO Box 2123   Free: 800-338-3282
Princeton, NJ 08543-2123   Fax: (609)243-9150
URL: http://www.peterson.com

Desc: Colleges offering master's, doctoral, and professional programs in humanities, arts, and social sciences. *Type:* Directory.

Peterson's Professional Degree Programs in the Visual and Performing Arts

Peterson's
202 Carnegie Center   Ph: (609)243-9111
PO Box 2123   Free: 800-338-3282
Princeton, NJ 08543-2123   Fax: (609)243-9150
URL: http://www.peterson.com; http://www.petersons.com.

Contact: Ellen Beal, Editor.

Desc: Professional degree programs in studio art, music, dance, and theater. *Type:* Directory.

Pitt Magazine

University of Pittsburgh
400 Craig Hall   Ph: (412)624-4147
Pittsburgh, PA 15260   Fax: (412)624-1021
E-mail: pitt.mag@pitt.edu.

Contact: Sally Ann Flecker, Editor.

Desc: University magazine. *Type:* Periodical.

Plymouth State College Home Page

Plymouth State College
17 High St.   Ph: (603)535-5000
Plymouth, NH 03264-1595
E-mail: ted@oz.plymouth.edu
URL: http://www.plymouth.edu/

Desc: The Plymouth State college site provides all of the normal college fare (admissions, academic, and related information) in a pleasant, easy to navigate format. Though the opening graphic is a bit of a memory clog, the rest of the site moves at a reasonable pace. *Type:* Database.

Profiles

York University
Department of Communications
4700 Keele St., Ste. 280   Ph: (416)736-5476
York Lanes   Fax: (416)736-5681
Toronto, ON, Canada M3J 1P3
E-mail: yorkalum@yorku.ca.
URL: http://www.yorku.ca/profiles.

Contact: Jessie-May Rowntree, Publisher, (416)736-5476; Michael Todd, Managing Editor, (416)736-2100x22090, mtodd@yorku.ca; Maggie McGregor, Adv. Coor., (416)736-2100, mcgregor@yorku.ca.

Desc: Alumni magazine. *Type:* Periodical.

The Quad

West Chester State University
253 Sykes Union Bldg.   Ph: (610)436-2793
West Chester, PA 19383-0001   Fax: (215)436-2287
E-mail: quad@wcupa.edu.

Contact: Kristyn Martin, Contact.

Desc: Collegiate newspaper. *Type:* Periodical.

Queen's Alumni Review

Queen's University
Dept. of Alumni Affairs   Ph: (613)533-2060
Summerhill Bldg.   Free: 800-267-7837
Kingston, ON, Canada K7L   Fax: (613)533-6777
  3N6
E-mail: review@post.queensu.ca.
URL: http://info-queensv.ca/alumni/al/rev.htm.

Contact: Kenneth Cuthbertson, Editor, cuthberk@post.queensu.ca; Daphne Tao, Advertising Mgr., taod@post.queensu.ca.

Desc: Alumni magazine. *Type:* Periodical.

Quilter's Newsletter Magazine

Leman Publications, Inc.
6700 W. 44th Ave.   Ph: (303)420-4272
Wheat Ridge, CO 80034   Fax: (303)420-7358

Contact: Bonnie Leman, Editor and Publisher; Tina L. Battock, Advertising Mgr.; Robert Kaslik, President.

Desc: Magazine featuring quilting techniques, patterns, and designs; events, exhibitions, trade news, and suppliers' information. *Type:* Periodical.

Quincy University World Wide Web Home Page

Quincy University
1800 College Ave.   Ph: (217)222-8020
Quincy, IL 62301-2699   Free: 800-688-4295
E-mail: webmaster@quincy.edu
URL: http://shamino.quincy.edu/

Desc: Founded in 1860 by Franciscans, Quincy University is a liberal arts college located on the Mississippi River in west central Illinois. Its Web site offers details about the university and the community in which it is located, including campus life, admissions information, library catalogs, curricula offerings, financial aid, and athletics. *Type:* Database.

Radford University

Radford University
E. Norwood St.   Ph: (540)831-5000
Radford, VA 24142
E-mail: ruadmiss@runet.edu
URL: http://www.runet.edu/

Contact: Rick Rogers, rrodgers@runet.edu.

Desc: The Radford University web site is quite thorough, with plenty of information available to digest. An online admissions form is available, as well as all of the standard university information (academic programs, athletics, and the like). *Type:* Database.

Reed College

Reed College
3202 SE Woodstock Blvd.   Ph: (503)771-1112
Portland, OR 97202-8199
E-mail: www@reed.edu
URL: http://www.reed.edu/

Desc: Reed College offers an informative look at itself and the Portland area in its little corner of the WWW. Everything necessary for a college site is here, from student life to academics. *Type:* Database.

Rensselaer Polytechnic Institute

Rensselaer Polytechnic Institute
110 8th St.   Ph: (518)276-6000
Troy, NY 12180
E-mail: rpinfo-support@rpi.edu
URL: http://www.rpi.edu/

Desc: Easy to navigate with a touch of way-cool (and fast loading) graphics, the RPI web site is quite a find. All of the requirements for a site of this type are here--from admissions to publications. *Type:* Database.

Rice University

Rice University
6100 Main St.   Ph: (713)527-8101
PO Box 1892
Houston, TX 77251-1892
E-mail: riceinfo@rice.edu
URL: http://riceinfo.rice.edu/

Desc: As with many university sites, Rice offers a title page with each topic listed as a sub-category of a larger section. This type of menu allows for ease of navigation, as well as the ability to quick scan the page to find specific information--thus alleviating the need for a search engine. *Type:* Database.

Rider University

Rider University
2083 Lawrenceville Rd.   Ph: (609)896-5000
Lawrenceville, NJ 08648-3099
E-mail: question@rider.edu
URL: http://www.rider.edu/

Desc: Though lacking information concerning the area surrounding the university, Rider's web site is quite impressive. The layout is very striking and easy to navigate, providing a wealth of information with a simple click of the mouse button. *Type:* Database.

Roanoke College Home Page

Roanoke College
221 College Lane   Ph: (540)375-2500
Salem, VA 24153-3794
E-mail: webadmin@roanoke.edu
URL: http://sundae.roanoke.edu/index.html

Desc: Roanoke College dishes up a web site that its students should be proud of. The usual college fare can be found here, with an index to help speed you on your way. *Type:* Database.

Rockefeller University

Rockefeller University
1230 York Ave.   Ph: (212)327-8000
New York, NY 10021
URL: http://www.rockefeller.edu/

Desc: Rockefeller University offers a pleasing cover page with a colorful, easy to understand interface. Users will find all of the standard college information, including admissions and financial aid information. *Type:* Database.

Rockhurst College

Rockhurst College
1100 Rockhurst Rd.   Ph: (816)501-4000
Kansas City, MO 64110-2561   Free: 800-842-6776
URL: http://www.rockhurst.edu/
Contact: mccoy@vax2.rockhurst.edu.

Desc: Based in Kansas City, Missouri, Rockhurst College is a Jesuit liberal arts college serving a student body of nearly 3,000. Its attractive Web site is easy to navigate, providing an important resource for both prospective and existing students. *Type:* Database.

Rocky Mountain College

Rocky Mountain College
1511 Poly Dr.   Ph: (406)657-1000
Billings, MT 59102-1796   Free: 800-877-6259
                                Fax: (406)259-9751
E-mail: rmc@rocky.edu
URL: http://www.rocky.edu/

Desc: This site, maintained by Rocky Mountain College of Billings, Montana, is easy to navigate and uncluttered and boats a very colorful and attractive cover page. There's no mystery to this site: simply point and click. *Type:* Database.

Rowan College of New Jersey Home Page

Rowan College of New Jersey
201 Mullica Hill Rd.   Ph: (609)256-4000
Glassboro, NJ 08028-1701
E-mail: webmaster@rowan.edu
URL: http://www.rowan.edu/

Desc: With a minimum of graphics and a pleasing background, the web site of Rowan College of New Jersey loads quite quickly. It supplies all of the general information necessary to provide an overview of the college, including enrollment and financial aid data. *Type:* Database.

Rutgers Magazine

Rutgers Magazine
Alexander Johnston Hall   Ph: (908)932-7315
New Brunswick, NJ 08903   Fax: (908)932-8412
Contact: Lori Chambers, Editor, lchambe@ communications.rutgers.edu; Diana Baroni, Advertising Mgr.; Bill Glovin, Sr. Editor.

Desc: University alumni magazine. *Type:* Periodical.

Saint Joseph's College

Saint Joseph's College
Highway 231   Ph: (219)866-6000
Rensselaer, IN 47978
E-mail: webmaster@saintjoe.edu
URL: http://munchkin.saintjoe.edu/

Desc: Located in northwestern Indiana, Saint Joseph's College may be small but in some ways, it is blazing new trails for institutions many times its size. Saint Joseph's is one of the few U.S. institutions that can boast a fully fiber-optic networked campus. *Type:* Database.

St. Joseph's University

St. Joseph's University
5600 City Ave.   Ph: (610)660-1000
Philadelphia, PA 19131
URL: http://www.sju.edu/

Desc: At the Joseph's University WWW site you can find a wealth of information about this institution of higher learning. In-depth sections cover everything from admissions and athletics to library and research resources. *Type:* Database.

Sam Houston State University

Sam Houston State University
Huntsville, TX 77341   Ph: (409)294-1111
E-mail: helpdesk@shsu.edu
URL: http://www.shsu.edu

Desc: Sam Houston, Texas' greatest hero, would be very proud of the university named in his honor. SHSU offers a web site that is extremely thorough. *Type:* Database.

Seton Hall University

Seton Hall University
400 South Orange Avenue   Ph: (973)761-9000
South Orange, NJ 07079
E-mail: Webmaster@pirate.shu.edu
URL: http://pirate.shu.edu/

Desc: Easy to navigate and very eye-catching, the Seton Hall university web site provides a wealth of information

in a concise format. Be ready to use the search engine (one of the most thorough presented on a university site) because there is enough data here to keep you locked on your computer for hours. *Type:* Database.

Sewanee: The University of the South

Sewanee University
735 University Ave.
Sewanee, TN 37383-1000
E-mail: webmaster@sewanee.edu
URL: http://www.sewanee.edu/

Desc: Some of the text at the Sewanee web site is extremely small-and therefore quite difficult to read. This aside, there is plenty of information here to satisfy anyone interested in attending this institution. *Type:* Database.

Society for College and University Planning

4251 Plymouth Rd., Ste. D   Ph: (734)998-7832
Ann Arbor, MI 48105-2785   Fax: (734)998-6532
E-mail: scup@umich.edu
URL: http://www.scup.org
Contact: Jolene Knapp, Exec.Dir.

Desc: University and college presidents, vice presidents, directors, deans, and faculty interested in higher education planning; government agencies; corporations; private consultants. Provides bibliographic information. Undertakes studies and research projects in higher education planning. *Type:* Association.

Southampton College Home Page

Long Island University - Southampton College
239 Montauk Hwy.
Southampton, NY 11968-4198
E-mail: Info@southampton.liunet.edu
URL: http://www.southampton.liunet.edu/
Contact: Arvind Borde, borde@aurora.liunet.edu.

Desc: Though this site's title page is quite colorful, the text is placed in vertical columns, making initial navigation a bit clumsy. Once past this, however, Southampton College's site is smooth sailing. *Type:* Database.

Southern Methodist University Home Page

Southern Methodist University
PO Box 750174   Ph: (214)768-2000
Dallas, TX 75275   Fax: (214)768-3449
E-mail: help@smu.edu
URL: http://www.smu.edu
Contact: Janine McKay, webmaster@smu.edu.

Desc: The SMU web site provides everything a prospective student would need in order to start the applications process rolling. It also provides comprehensive information for the currently attending student, with everything from athletics to campus news. *Type:* Database.

Southwest Texas State University

Southwest Texas State University
601 University Dr.   Ph: (512)245-2111
San Marcos, TX 78666-4604
E-mail: webmaster@swt.edu
URL: http://www.swt.edu

Desc: The Southwest Texas State University web site provides a handy index which allows you to leap right to any particular item without the wait. This site is a veritable treasure-trove of information, offering anything from student organization and administration information to on-line publications. *Type:* Database.

Southwestern Adventist University

Southwestern Adventist University
100 Hillcrest Dr.   Ph: (817)556-4731
Keene, TX 76059
E-mail: webmaster@swau.edu
URL: http://www.swac.edu/

Desc: Southwestern Adventist University home page has a user friendly design: simply click on the topic and follow the path to whatever specifics you need. It is the standard university fare that is offered here, with details on the admissions procedure, academics, financial aid, and so on. *Type:* Database.

Stanford Magazine

Stanford Alumni Association
Stanford University   Ph: (415)723-2021
Bowman Alumni House   Fax: (415)723-8597
Stanford, CA 94305
URL: http://www.stanfordmag.org.
Contact: Ellen Williams, Business Mgr., (650)723-0863, ellenwi@leland.stanford.edu; Bob Cohn, Editor, (650)725-5109; Bambi Nicklen, Art Dir., (650)725-1085.
Desc: Alumni magazine. *Alt. Contact:* Bowman Alumni House, Stanford, CA 94305-4005; telephone: (650)725-0672; fax: (650)725-8676. *Type:* Periodical.

State University of New York, Binghamton

State University of New York, Binghamton University
PO Box 6000   Ph: (607)777-2000
Binghamton, NY 13902-6000
URL: http://www.binghamton.edu/
Desc: Binghamton University, founded in 1946, offers up a web site that is straightforward and easy to use. Readers can navigate to various locations in the site via a bitmap or an extended list of topics. *Type:* Database.

State University of New York, Cortland

State University of New York, Cortland
PO Box 2000   Ph: (607)753-2011
Cortland, NY 13045-0900
URL: http://www.cortland.edu/
Contact: webmaster@www.cortland.edu.
Desc: The Cortland branch of the State University of New York offers a fine site that is rich in all of the information one would expect. Admissions, events, athletics, and the like can all be found here with little effort. *Type:* Database.

State University of New York, Oswego

State University of New York, Oswego
Rt. 104   Ph: (315)341-2500
Oswego, NY 13126
E-mail: webwiz@oswego.edu
URL: http://www.oswego.edu/
Desc: With a layout that manages to be straightforward and confused at the same time, the SUNY Oswego web site still manages to provide all of the information that an interested reader could ask for. All of the characteristic topics are here, from admissions to graduate studies. *Type:* Database.

Stephen F. Austin State University

Stephen F. Austin State University
Nacogdoches, TX 75962   Ph: (409)468-2011
URL: http://www.sfasu.edu/
Contact: J. Pyle, webmaster, webmaster@sfasu.edu.
Desc: An inspiring purple and gold menu/title graphic blazes across the top of the Stephen F. Austin State University home page. *Type:* Database.

Stevens Institute of Technology

Stevens Institute of Technology
Castle Point on the Hudson   Ph: (201)216-5105
Hoboken, NJ 07030
E-mail: webmaster@stevens-tech.edu
URL: http://www.stevens-tech.edu/
Desc: The Stevens Institute of Technology web site tends to focus on function over form. It does its job quite well, containing almost all of the information a prospective student could ask for. *Type:* Database.

Sweet Briar College

Sweet Briar College
Sweet Briar, VA 24595   Ph: (804)381-6262
URL: http://www.sbc.edu
Contact: Dave Blount, dblount@sbc.edu.
Desc: The Sweet Briar College web site is geared toward its clientele: women, offering not only the general information expected from a site of this type (admissions, academic programs, and so on), but also links to various Internet resources. In order to assist prospective international students, this site is also available in Spanish and French. *Type:* Database.

Syracuse University

Syracuse University
Syracuse, NY 13244
E-mail: webmaster@www.syr.edu
URL: http://www.syr.edu/
Desc: A treasure-trove of information is what you will find at the Syracuse University home page. All of the elements one would hope to find on a university site, from academic life and events to employment and sports information, can be found here with the click of a mouse button. *Type:* Database.

Tech Topics

Georgia Tech Alumni Association
190 North Ave. NW   Ph: (404)894-2391
Atlanta, GA 30313   Fax: (404)894-5113
E-mail: editor@alumni.gatech.edu.
Contact: John C. Dunn, Editor; Hoyt Coffee, Assoc. Editor; Robb Stanek, Marketing & Advertising Dir.
Desc: Alumni newspaper. *Type:* Periodical.

Technology Teacher—Directory of Colleges and Universities Offering Degrees in Technology Education Issue

International Technology Education Association
1914 Association Dr., Ste. 201   Ph: (703)860-2100
Reston, VA 20190   Fax: (703)860-0353
E-mail: itea@iris.org
URL: http://www.iteawww.org
Contact: Kathleen Sheehan, Editor-in-Chief.
Desc: About 80 colleges and universities that offer undergraduate and graduate degrees in technology education; includes Canada. *Type:* Directory.

Temple Review

Temple University
University Services Bldg., Rm.   Ph: (215)204-6445
   601   Fax: (215)204-4704
Philadelphia, PA 19122
E-mail: treview@blue.temple.edu.
Contact: Ruth Schultz, Editor, (215)204-6446.
Desc: University alumni magazine. *Type:* Periodical.

Tennessee Technological University

Tennessee Tech
Cookeville, TN 38505   Ph: (931)372-3888
E-mail: webmaster@tntech.edu
URL: http://www.tntech.edu
Desc: Welcome to Tennessee Technological University. This web site is organized quite clearly, with topics subdivided beneath titled links. *Type:* Database.

Texas A&M University

Computing and Information Services at Texas A&M
Teague Bldg.   Ph: (409)845-3211
College Station, TX 77843
E-mail: webmaster@net.tamu.edu
URL: http://www.tamu.edu/index.html

Desc: The Texas A&M University web site is quite a formidable presence on the WWW. All of the broad topics concerning the university are listed on the title page--and below is a search routine that uses the concept of a meta search. *Type:* Database.

Texas Christian University

Texas Christian University
2800 S. University Dr.   Ph: (817)257-7000
Fort Worth, TX 76129
E-mail: frogmail@tcu.edu (admissions)
URL: http://www.tcu.edu
Contact: webmaster@tcu.edu.
Desc: The TCU Home Page makes it fairly easy to find general information. The categories are all on the title page, from admissions to student life, and there is a search engine to help you locate specific information. *Type:* Database.

Traditions

University of Connecticut
1266 Storrs Rd.   Ph: (860)486-2377
Storrs, CT 06269-5144   Fax: (860)486-2063
Contact: Gary E. Frank, Editor.
Desc: Alumni magazine. *Type:* Periodical.

Trinity University

Trinity University
715 Stadium Dr.   Ph: (210)736-7011
San Antonio, TX 78212-7200
E-mail: admissions@trinity.edu
URL: http://www.trinity.edu
Contact: sjones@trinity.edu.
Desc: The Trinity University's web site you will find all of the information necessary to get the enrollment process rolling, well as academic program listings, a calendar, a campus tour, and information about San Antonio, the community around the university. *Type:* Database.

Truckee Meadows Community College Homepage

Truckee Meadows Community College
7000 Dandini Blvd.   Ph: (702)673-7042
Reno, NV 89512-3999
E-mail: webmaster@tmcc.edu
URL: http://www.tmcc.edu/
Contact: Cathy Catania, catania@scs.unr.edu.
Desc: Truckee Meadows Community College, which serves more than 10,000 students in and around Reno, Nevada, has put together a very effective Web site that should be helpful to both current and prospective students. Here, one will find a wealth of information about TMCC's student and faculty services, admissions requirements, class schedules, and employment opportunities. *Type:* Database.

Tulanian

Tulane Publications
3439 Prytania St., Ste. 400   Ph: (504)865-5714
New Orleans, LA 70115   Fax: (504)865-5621
E-mail: tulanian@mailhost.tcs.tulane.edu.
Contact: Suzanne Johnson, Editor.
Desc: Magazine for college alumni. *Type:* Periodical.

UBC Alumni Chronicle

University of British Columbia Alumni Association
6251 Cecil Green Park Rd.   Ph: (604)822-8913
Vancouver, BC, Canada V6T   Free: 800-882-3088
   1Z1   Fax: (604)822-8928
E-mail: alumni@alumni.vbc.ca.
URL: http://www.alumni.ubc.ca.
Contact: Chris Petty, Editor.

Desc: University alumni magazine. *Alt. Contact:* 6251 Cecil Green Pk. Rd., Vancouver, BC, Canada V6T 1Z1; telephone: (604)822-8914. *Type:* Periodical.

UCLA Magazine

University of California, Los Angeles
10920 Wilshire Blvd., Ste. 1500   Ph: (310)794-6880
Los Angeles, CA 90024-6517   Fax: (310)794-6883
E-mail: magazine@support.ucla.edu.
URL: http://www.urelations.ucla.edu/ucomm/pubs/UCLAMag/.
Contact: David Greenwald, Editor, (310)794-6852, fax: (310)794-6883, davidg@support.ucla.edu.
Desc: General interest magazine with articles based on the research and expertise of the UCLA faculty. *Type:* Periodical.

UMASS Magazine

University of Massachusetts
Munson Hall   Ph: (413)545-2991
Amherst, MA 01003   Fax: (413)545-3824
E-mail: umassmag@umassp.edu
URL: http://www.umass.edu/umassmag/.
Contact: Patricia Wright, Editor, pwright@urd.umass.edu.
Desc: Magazine containing collegiate and alumni news. *Type:* Periodical.

Union College

Union College
Schenectady, NY 12308-3107
E-mail: wwwstaff@union.edu
URL: http://www.union.edu/
Desc: The Union College is rich in information and is quite easy to navigate. Enrollment, financial aid, student life, and much more can be found here. *Type:* Database.

The Union Institute

440 E. McMillan St.   Ph: (513)861-6400
Cincinnati, OH 45206-1947   Free: 800-486-3116
   Fax: (513)861-0779
Contact: Robert T. Conley, Pres.
Desc: Undergraduate studies centers. Has developed innovative alternative models for baccalaureate and doctoral degree programs. Operates the College of Undergraduate Studies, which offers undergraduate programs. *Type:* Association.

United Negro College Fund

8260 Willow Oak Corp. Dr.   Ph: (703)205-3432
Fairfax, VA 22031   Free: 800-331-2244
   Fax: (703)205-3575
Contact: William H. Gray, III, CEO & Pres.
Desc: Comprehensive educational assistance organization providing fundraising, educational programs, and technical assistance primarily to its 41 historically black private colleges and universities and graduate and professional schools, all of which are private and fully accredited. *Type:* Association.

University of Alabama

University of Alabama
Tuscaloosa, AL 35487   Ph: (205)348-6010
E-mail: jpduvall@ur.ua.edu
URL: http://www.ua.edu/
Contact: Jan Pruitt Duvall, Director of Publications, jpduvall@sa.ua.edu.
Desc: This university site is great destination for visitors who want to explore the possibility of pursuing studies at the University of Alabama. Information is well-organized, divided in directories which give an overview of student life at University of Alabama. *Type:* Database.

University of Arkansas

University of Arkansas
Fayetteville, AR 72701   Free: (501)575-2000
E-mail: webmast@www.uark.edu
URL: http://www.uark.edu/
Desc: The University of Arkansas (UA) website provides information of interest to prospective students, enrolled students and faculty. Links to specific public sites will serve visitors well--admissions, departments, research, organizations, technology, campus events, and athletics information. *Type:* Database.

University of British Columbia Home Page

University of British Columbia
2329 West Mall
Vancouver, BC, Canada V6T 1Z4
URL: http://www.ubc.ca/
Desc: A brightly colored collage of pictures greets you as you enter the world of the University of British Columbia. This home page appears at first glance to be simplistic, but when you delve into the ante regions you will be pleasantly surprised. *Type:* Database.

University of Central Florida

University of Central Florida
PO Box 160000   Ph: (407)823-2000
Orlando, FL 32816
URL: http://www.ucf.edu/
Contact: Tad Simmons, simmons@pegasus.cc.ucf.edu.
Desc: The University of Central Florida (UCF) presents an informative graphics linked presentation page complete with a search engine to help navigate the university site. Unlike some university websites which seem to strictly cater to prospective students, this site intends to provide a cyber/virtual campus which students and faculty access to enhance the academic experience at UCF. *Type:* Database.

University of Chicago

University of Chicago
5801 S. Ellis Ave.   Ph: (773)702-1234
Chicago, IL 60637
URL: http://www.uchicago.edu/
Desc: One of the premier U.S. institutions of higher education, the University of Chicago has created a Web site that is packed with information yet easy to navigate. *Type:* Database.

University of Chicago Magazine

University of Chicago Magazine
1313 E. 60th St., Rm. 224   Ph: (773)702-2163
Chicago, IL 60637   Fax: (773)702-2166
E-mail: uchicago-magazine@uchicago.edu.
URL: http://www2.uchicago.edu/alumni/alumni.mag.
Contact: Mary Ruth Yoe, Editor, (773)702-2164, ddog@midway.uchicago.edu.
Desc: University alumni magazine. *Type:* Periodical.

University of Cincinnati

University of Cincinnati
Cincinnati, OH 45221-0038
E-mail: webmaster@uc.edu
URL: http://www.uc.edu/
Desc: This somewhat plain site delivers information concerning admissions, financial aid, academics, and more for the University of Cincinnati. The rather convoluted style of this site may have you digging for specifics, so be prepared to spend some time here; no search engine is provided. *Type:* Database.

University of Cincinnati - College of Pharmacy

University of Cincinnati
Cincinnati, OH 45267-0004
URL: http://inpharmatics.uc.edu/
Contact: Dr. William K. Fant, bill.fant@uc.edu.
Desc: What does it take to become a pharmacist? Here at the University of Cincinnati's College of Pharmacy web site you can get the answer to that question and more. All of the standard college fare, from admissions and course information to student organizations and graduate program information can be found here. *Type:* Database.

University of Dallas

University of Dallas
1845 E. Northgate Dr.   Ph: (972)721-5000
Irving, TX 75062
URL: http://www.udallas.edu
Contact: C.W. Eaker, eaker@acad.udallas.edu.
Desc: The University of Dallas Home Page contains all of the information needed by prospective students as well are information on the college site in Rome and graduate programs. Look under the link for Constantin College of Liberal Arts for undergraduate admissions information, as well as under the UD Web Pages section. *Type:* Database.

University of Dayton

University of Dayton
Dayton, OH 45469-1679
URL: http://www.udayton.edu/
Contact: webinfo@udayton.edu.
Desc: A virtual tour, programs of study, and information concerning admissions and academics can be found on the University of Dayton web site. While finding specific information is something of a chore, it is all offered here. *Type:* Database.

University of Dayton Quarterly

University of Dayton
300 College Park   Ph: (937)229-3241
Dayton, OH 45469-1659   Fax: (937)229-3063
E-mail: quarterly@udayton.edu.
Contact: Thomas M. Columbus, Editor.
Desc: Collegiate magazine. *Type:* Periodical.

University of Delaware

University of Delaware
Newark, DE 19716
E-mail: www@udel.edu
URL: http://www.udel.edu
Desc: The University of Delaware's web page provides readers fast access to their campus brochure and more. Everything you want to know about learning and research, campus life, offices and services is on your screen. *Type:* Database.

University of Denver Home Page

University of Denver
2199 South University Blvd.   Ph: (303)871-2000
Denver, CO 80208
URL: http://www.du.edu/
Desc: Information on the University of Denver (UD). Unlike some universities which use their home page as a jumpstation for academic department and affiliate/attendant divisions, the UD site is nominally in support of students and prospective students. *Type:* Database.

University of Florida

University of Florida
Gainesville, FL 32611   Ph: (352)392-3261
E-mail: www@www.ufl.edu
URL: http://www.ufl.edu/
Desc: The University of Florida web-site includes educational links, a search engine, sports, and admissions information. However, since the university is rather large, a hotlink directory lists independently operated servers and websites for tenant departments, institutes, schools, and organizations. *Type:* Database.

University of Houston

University of Houston
4800 Calhoun St.   Ph: (713)743-1000
Houston, TX 77204
E-mail: www@uh.edu
URL: http://www.uh.edu

Desc: The University of Houston's information packed web site contains pertinent data from enrollment and academics to campus maps and libraries. A boolean search is provided to help make everything offered accessible in the fastest possible manner. *Type:* Database.

University of Idaho Home Page

University of Idaho
Moscow, ID 83844-3133   Free: 888-884-3246
E-mail: webhelp@uidaho.edu
URL: http://www.uidaho.edu/

Desc: The University of Idaho home page includes information on academics, alumni, events, and services-all of the subjects one would expect to find on an university web page. But this site provides more than a source information database which appeals only to prospective students. *Type:* Database.

University of Iowa

University of Iowa
Iowa City, IA 52242   Ph: (319)335-3500
E-mail: webmaster@www.uiowa.edu
URL: http://lime.weeg.uiowa.edu/

Desc: The University of Iowa's home page is a fine addition to the World Wide Web. Visitors to the site are greeted with a glossy, magazine-like front page that offers a choice between a full-graphics or text-only display. *Type:* Database.

University of Kansas

University of Kansas
Lawrence, KS 66045   Ph: (785)864-3506
E-mail: kufacts@ukans.edu
URL: http://www.ukans.edu/

Desc: The University of Kansas is a sprawling state-supported school with facilities in several parts of Kansas. Fittingly, the front page of the university's Web site gives the visitor the choice of which of those facilities he or she would like to access. *Type:* Database.

University of Kentucky

University of Kentucky
Lexington, KY 40506-0054   Ph: (606)257-9000
URL: http://www.uky.edu/

Desc: The University of Kentucky's Web site is a study in the creation of sub-menus. Users are presented with a battery of button-style links, quickly giving rise to the question of "where to begin?" It's a good question. *Type:* Database.

University of Louisville

University of Louisville
Louisville, KY 40292   Ph: (502)852-5555
                              Free: 800-334-8635
E-mail: webmaster@homer.louisville.edu
URL: http://www.louisville.edu/

Desc: The University of Louisville, a state-supported school in Kentucky's largest metropolitan area, traces its history back to the founding of the Jefferson Seminary in 1798. A private university until it joined the state system of higher education in 1970, Louisville has put together a nicely organized Web site that should prove valuable to the school's more than 20,000 students as well as others planning to attend. *Type:* Database.

University of Maine

University of Maine
Orono, ME 04469
E-mail: umweb@maine.edu
URL: http://www.umaine.edu/

Desc: One of the country's first universities to launch its own Web site, the University of Maine is still a mighty presence on the World Wide Web. An extremely attractive site with loads of campus images, the school's presence on the Internet is made all the easier to navigate by the specialized menus its offers for specific groups of visitors. *Type:* Database.

University of Memphis Home Page

University of Memphis, Webservices
Administration Bldg. Rm. 303   Ph: (901)678-2606
Memphis, TN 38152   Fax: (901)678-3607
E-mail: www@cc.memphis.edu
URL: http://oolong.memphis.edu/

Contact: K. Welch, Pagemaster, kwelch@memphis.edu.

Desc: The University of Memphis Home Page is efficient and nice to look at, and contains information on topics from enrollment and academics to alumni and athletics. *Type:* Database.

University of Michigan

University of Michigan
Ann Arbor, MI 48109   Ph: (734)764-1817
E-mail: um-gateway@umich.edu
URL: http://www.umich.edu/

Desc: The University of Michigan Web site serves up an awesome collection of information that should be helpful to both current and prospective students, as well as faculty members, alumni, and researchers. There are customized directories for those specific groups and a couple of others. *Type:* Database.

University of Missouri, Columbia - College of Education

University of Missouri, Columbia
College of Education   Ph: (573)882-8311
118 Hill Hall   Fax: (573)884-5785
Columbia, MO 65211
URL: http://tiger.coe.missouri.edu/

Contact: Richard Andrews, dean@coe.missouri.edu.

Desc: The College of Education at the University of Missouri's main campus in Columbia is well represented at this Web site, which offers detailed information about the school's administration and its academic programs. A helpful tool for students and faculty as well as prospective students, the site is well designed and easy to navigate. *Type:* Database.

University of Missouri, Rolla

University of Missouri, Rolla
1870 Miner Circle   Ph: (573)341-4111
Rolla, MO 65409-1060
E-mail: webmaster@umr.edu
URL: http://www.umr.edu/

Desc: This site, maintained by the Rolla campus of the University of Missouri, provides extensive information concerning the college, its academic and athletic programs, and faculty. The simplicity of the UMR site's cover page design gives the visitor an early glimpse into the ease with which the site can be navigated. *Type:* Database.

University of Montana-Missoula

University of Montana
Missoula, MT 59812   Ph: (406)243-0211
E-mail: webdev@selway.umt.edu
URL: http://www.umt.edu/

Desc: The words "quick," "easy," and "pleasant" describe this site perfectly. A bitmapped title page menu acts as a launching pad to other pages at this site. *Type:* Database.

University of Nebraska, Omaha

University of Nebraska, Omaha
60th and Dodge Sts.   Ph: (402)554-2800
Omaha, NE 68182
E-mail: www@unomaha.edu
URL: http://www.unomaha.edu/

Desc: The University of Nebraska at Omaha home page is well designed and easy to navigate. All of the standard university information is covered, from admissions and financial aid to graduate studies and events. *Type:* Database.

University of Nevada, Las Vegas

University of Nevada, Las Vegas
4505 Maryland Pkwy.   Ph: (702)895-3011
Las Vegas, NV 89154   Fax: (702)895-3850
URL: http://www.unlv.edu/

Contact: unlvwebmaster@ccmail.nevada.edu.

Desc: This site, designed much like a university press kit, has almost everything that a prospective (or current) student could ask for. From downloadable application forms and admissions information to the latest from UNLV's alumni association, this site is loaded with helpful information about the university. *Type:* Database.

University of Nevada, Reno

University of Nevada, Reno
Reno, NV 89557   Ph: (702)784-1110
E-mail: webmaster@unr.edu
URL: http://www.unr.edu/

Contact: carson@unr.edu.

Desc: The Web site of the University of Nevada at Reno does double duty, operating both as a clearinghouse for standard university information and a dynamic online newsletter with the latest news developments from the UNR campus. Another feature particularly attractive for current students and faculty members is the weekly calendar, highlighting events of interest scheduled during the current week. *Type:* Database.

University of North Carolina, Asheville

University of North Carolina, Asheville
Asheville, NC 28804-3299
E-mail: webmaster@unca.edu
URL: http://www.unca.edu/

Desc: With a pleasant layout and easy navigation, the web site of the University of North Carolina at Asheville is quite a nice stop on the information superhighway. The standard university information can be found here, from admissions and financial aid to athletics and student life. *Type:* Database.

University of North Carolina, Chapel Hill

University of North Carolina, Chapel Hill
Chapel Hill, NC 27599   Ph: (919)962-2211
URL: http://www.unc.edu/

Desc: From the unique title page layout you know that you're in for a little something special at the UNC Chapel Hill web site. Indeed, not only does this site offer all of the information expected (admissions, financial aid information, academics, and the like) but it also displays an amount of pride rarely encountered on the WWW. *Type:* Database.

University of North Carolina, Greensboro

University of North Carolina, Greensboro
Greensboro, NC 27412-5001
URL: http://www.uncg.edu/

Desc: This easy to navigate site provides a plethora of useful information to anyone interested in attending the Greensboro branch of the University of North Carolina. Admissions, academic programs, athletics, continuing education, and much more can be found here. *Type:* Database.

University of North Dakota Alumni Review

University of North Dakota Alumni Association & Foundation
PO Box 8157
Grand Forks, ND 58202-8157
Ph: (701)777-2611
Free: 800-543-8764
Fax: (701)777-4054
URL: undinfound.nodak.edu; http://www.nodak.edu/org/alumni.

Contact: Larry Stammen, Pub. Info. Dir., lstammen@prairie.nodak.edu; Earl S. Strinden, Publisher.

Desc: University alumni tabloid. *Type:* Periodical.

University of North Texas

University of North Texas
PO Box 13797
Denton, TX 76203
Ph: (940)565-2000
E-mail: www@unt.edu
URL: http://www.unt.edu

Desc: This quick loading site, served up by the University of North Texas, manages to retain a nice balance between graphics and text. You can easily find what you're looking for with the new search engine. *Type:* Database.

University of Notre Dame

University of Notre Dame
Notre Dame, IN 46556
Ph: (219)631-5000
E-mail: www@www.nd.edu
URL: http://www.nd.edu/

Desc: The University of Notre Dame is far more than the Fighting Irish, the school's justly famous football team. Much more. *Type:* Database.

University of Ottawa

University of Ottawa
550 Cumberland
Ottawa, ON, Canada K1N 6N5
Ph: (613)562-5700
E-mail: webmaster@uottawa.ca
URL: http://www.uottawa.ca/

Desc: All of the standard university information is available at this University of Ottawa's site, including admissions information, departmental data, library resources and more, such as links to information on the nation's capital region. The information is immediately presented in both French and English. *Type:* Database.

University of Puget Sound

University of Puget Sound
1500 N. Warner
Tacoma, WA 98416
Ph: (253)756-3100
Fax: (253)756-3500
E-mail: cwis@mail.ups.edu
URL: http://www.ups.edu

Contact: Jean Huskamp, webmaster@mail.ups.edu.

Desc: Quite thorough in scope, this site really delivers the information. General information concerning the university includes several images, a campus map, and more. *Type:* Database.

University of Richmond

University of Richmond
Richmond, VA 23173
Ph: (804)289-8000
E-mail: webmaster@richmond.edu
URL: http://www.urich.edu/

Desc: Some beautiful images are available in the campus photo album of the University of Richmond. Everything from admissions to campus publications can be found here with just a little bit of digging. *Type:* Database.

University of Southwestern Louisiana

University of Southwestern Louisiana
PO Box 41008
Ph: (318)482-1000
104 University Cir.
Lafayette, LA 70504-2651
E-mail: webmaster@usl.edu
URL: http://www.usl.edu/

Desc: Looks are deceiving on the University of Southwestern Louisiana's Web page. At first glance it looks fairly plain and unexciting. *Type:* Database.

University of Tennessee, Knoxville

University of Tennessee, Knoxville
Knoxville, TN 37996
Ph: (423)974-1000
E-mail: webmaster@utk.edu
URL: http://www.utk.edu/

Desc: An interesting interface and some lovely graphics greet you on the UTK web site. All of the information (from admissions to alumni) that prospective and currently attending students could need can be found here with little effort. *Type:* Database.

University of Tennessee, Martin

University of Tennessee, Martin, - Office of Admissions
Martin, TN 38238
Ph: (901)587-7000
Free: 800-829-UTM1
E-mail: webmaster@utm.edu
URL: http://www.utm.edu

Desc: The University of Tennessee at Martin web site contains all of the academic and administrative information that you have come to expect from a university site (admissions, financial aid, course schedules, and the like), but it also includes a live camera image that is updated every sixty seconds. *Type:* Database.

University of Texas, Austin

UT TeamWeb
Austin, TX 78712
Ph: (512)475-7348
URL: http://www.utexas.edu
Contact: www@www.utexas.edu.

Desc: The University of Texas at Austin's web site contains lots of information on UT academics, research, events, and much more. The overall layout makes navigation a breeze and a search option is provided. *Type:* Database.

University of Toledo

University of Toledo
Toledo, OH 43606
E-mail: gopher@gopher.utoledo.edu
URL: http://www.utoledo.edu/

Desc: There are several criteria that raise a university site above many others; the University of Toledo web page has them all. Here you will find all of the standard information provided by all institutes of higher learning: admissions, academics, athletics, student organizations, and the like. *Type:* Database.

University of Tulsa

University of Tulsa
600 S. College Ave.
Ph: (918)631-2000
Tulsa, OK 74104-3189
E-mail: webmaster@utulsa.edu
URL: http://www.utulsa.edu/

Desc: Overall, The University of Tulsa offers a complete web site. Information ranges from enrollment and tuition to graduate school and employment. *Type:* Database.

University of Utah

University of Utah - Admissions Office
201 S. 1460 E. Rm. 250S
Ph: (801)581-7200
Salt Lake City, UT 84112
E-mail: webmaster@unicomm.utah.edu
URL: http://www.utah.edu

Desc: A pleasant background graces the University of Utah's home page. Along with this nice presentation comes loads of information. *Type:* Database.

University of Vermont

University of Vermont
360 Waterman Bldg.
Ph: (802)656-2045
Burlington, VT 05405
Fax: (802)656-8230
E-mail: helpline@uvm.edu
URL: http://www.uvm.edu
Contact: webmaster@uvm.edu.

Desc: Once you look around the University of Vermont's web site for a bit you will discover a wealth of information. Athletics, events, and alumni share the page with links to the many departments and schools that this university has to offer. *Type:* Database.

University of Virginia

University of Virginia
Charlottesville, VA 22903
Ph: (804)924-0311
E-mail: webmaster@virginia.edu
URL: http://www.virginia.edu

Desc: This no-nonsense site provided by the University of Virginia offers facts not only about the university, but also about the community in which it serves. Admissions, academics, community information, and much more can be found in no time. *Type:* Database.

University of Windsor

University of Windsor
401 Sunset
Windsor, ON, Canada N9B 3P4
URL: http://www.uwindsor.ca/index.html

Desc: The University of Windsor's site offer information presented in a concise manner with a search engine available for hunting down specifics. The campus maps are broken down into some interesting categories. *Type:* Database.

University of Wisconsin, Eau Claire

University of Wisconsin, Eau Claire
PO Box 4004
Ph: (715)836-2637
Eau Claire, WI 54702
Fax: (715)836-2380
E-mail: web@www.uwec.edu
URL: http://www.uwec.edu/

Desc: The Eau Claire chapter of the University of Wisconsin posts this informative web site. The admissions section offers details on topics ranging from enrollment requirements to dining. *Type:* Database.

University of Wisconsin, Milwaukee

University of Wisconsin, Milwaukee
PO Box 413
Ph: (414)229-1122
Milwaukee, WI 53201
E-mail: www@uwm.edu
URL: http://www.uwm.edu/

Desc: The University of Wisconsin-Milwaukee Home Page offers some valuable information for prospective and currently attending students. The interface is a little vague, but after searching around a bit you will find everything from admissions information to course descriptions. *Type:* Database.

University of Wisconsin, Platteville

University of Wisconsin, Platteville
1 University Plaza
Ph: (608)342-1125
Platteville, WI 53818
E-mail: wwwmgr@uwplatt.edu
URL: http://www.uwplatt.edu/

Desc: Clearly labeled and quite informative, the University of Wisconsin's Platteville campus offers a fine web site. Everything is offered up front here; you can either follow the appropriate links through various pages to their destination or use the handy search routine. *Type:* Database.

University of Wisconsin, River Falls

University of Wisconsin, River Falls
410 S. Third St.   Ph: (715)425-3911
River Falls, WI 54022
E-mail: webmaster@uwrf.edu
URL: http://www.uwrf.edu

Desc: Containing information about the state, the community, and the university, the UWRF web site is extremely detailed. The topics are very precise, ranging from information for prospective students (who have their own little corner here) to administration and technology. *Type:* Database.

University of Wisconsin, Stevens Point

University of Wisconsin, Stevens Point
Stevens Point, WI 54481   Ph: (715)346-0123
URL: http://www.uwsp.edu/
Contact: webmaster@uwsp.edu.

Desc: With loads of data, a rapid download time, and pleasant backgrounds, the UWSP web site has much to offer. Detailed admissions instructions are provided, as well as links to academic advisement, news and events, student organizations, library resources, and much more. *Type:* Database.

University of Wisconsin, Stout

University of Wisconsin, Stout
Menomonie, WI 54751   Ph: (715)232-1122
                                 Fax: (715)232-1667
E-mail: webmaster@uwstout.edu
URL: http://www.uwstout.edu/

Desc: This web site supplies a wealth of information about the University of Wisconsin-Stout. Here you will find academics, services for the faculty and staff, news, and links to various Internet resources. *Type:* Database.

University of Wisconsin, Superior

University of Wisconsin, Superior
Belknap & Catlin   Ph: (715)394-8101
PO Box 2000
Superior, WI 54880
E-mail: webteam@uwsuper.edu
URL: http://www.uwsuper.edu/

Desc: The University of Wisconsin-Superior web site provides the general about the university, from academic data and course schedules to alumni and student organizations. While an online applications form is not supplied, an e-mail address is given so that you can order the document itself. *Type:* Database.

University of Wisconsin, Whitewater

University of Wisconsin, Whitewater
800 W. Main St.
Whitewater, WI 53190
E-mail: webmaster@uwwvax.uww.edu.
URL: http://www.uww.edu/

Desc: This site focuses on the University of Wisconsin's Whitewater campus. Detailed information can be found here concerning all elements of the university, from admissions to alumni. *Type:* Database.

University of Wyoming

University of Wyoming
Laramie, WY 82071   Ph: (307)766-5160
                                 Free: 800-342-5996
URL: http://www.uwyo.edu/
Contact: webmaster.sis@uwyo.edu.

Desc: The site offered by the University of Wyoming is nothing but an information juggernaut. A detailed academics section is supplied, comprised of course descriptions, multidisciplinary and mentoring programs, and much more. *Type:* Database.

USC Trojan Family

University of Southern California
Office of Public   Ph: (213)740-2684
Communications   Fax: (213)740-1746
University Park (KAP 246)
Los Angeles, CA 90089-2537
Contact: Susan Heitman, Editor.

Desc: Alumni magazine. Includes reviews of faculty publications. *Type:* Periodical.

Utah State University

Utah State University, Editorial
1500 University Blvd.   Ph: (435)797-1000
Logan, UT 84322-0500
E-mail: webmaster@www.usu.edu
URL: http://www.usu.edu

Desc: A beautiful title graphic eases you into this fact-filled site offered by Utah State University. While navigation is quite simple, this site is so loaded with information that you'll need to use the provided search engine. *Type:* Database.

Utah Valley State University

Utah Valley State College, Information
800 W. 1200 S.   Ph: (801)222-8000
Orem, UT 84058
E-mail: asayli@uvsc.edu
URL: http://www.uvsc.edu
Contact: Timothy Loveridge, loveriti@uvsc.edu.

Desc: The Utah Valley State College web site is packed with useful information for both current as well as prospective students. A downloadable application for admissions is available, as well as all of the general information usually found on a site of this type (athletics, financial aid, a campus map, and so on). *Type:* Database.

Vanderbilt University - Blair School of Music

Vanderbilt University
2300 West End Ave.
Nashville, TN 37203
E-mail: www@vanderbilt.edu
URL: http://www.vanderbilt.edu/Blair/htdocs/
Blairhome.html
Contact: Blair-web@vanderbilt.edu.

Desc: The Vanderbilt University's Blair School of Music web site includes information for music as well as non-music majors and ranges from enrollment topics to alumni organizations. Many of the images provided on this site are quite attractive and augment the simplistic design quite well. *Type:* Database.

Virginia Commonwealth University

Virginia Commonwealth University
821 W. Franklin St.   Ph: (804)828-0100
Richmond, VA 23284
E-mail: webmaster@www.vcu.edu
URL: http://www.vcu.edu

Desc: The Virginia Commonwealth University site provides detailed information from enrollment (a veritable encyclopedia of admissions information is provided) to athletics (including ticket information and links to other sports sites). *Type:* Database.

Washington State University Hilltopics

Washington State University
Pullman, WA 99164-1040   Ph: (509)335-3581
                                 Fax: (509)335-0932
URL: http://cougnet.wsu.edu/hilltopicssnew/.
Contact: Patrick Caraher, Editor, (209)3351247, fax: (509)3350932, caraher@wsu.edu.

Desc: University relations newspaper (tabloid) for alumni, parents, friends, and benefactors. *Alt. Contact:* Washington State University PO Box 641040, Pullman, WA 99164-1040; telephone: (509)335-1247; fax: (509)335-0932. *Type:* Periodical.

Washington University in St. Louis

Washington University, St. Louis
One Brookings Dr.   Ph: (314)935-6000
St. Louis, MO 63130
E-mail: webmaster@wustl.edu
URL: http://www.wustl.edu/

Desc: The designers of this attractive site for Washington University of St. Louis have obviously taken great pains to ensure that the information available here can be readily located and accessed by users. *Type:* Database.

Weber State University

Weber State University
3750 Harrison Blvd.   Ph: (801)626-6000
Ogden, UT 84408
E-mail: webmaster@weber.edu
URL: http://www.weber.edu

Contact: jyeaman@weber.edu.

Desc: The Weber State University web site is rather extensive but well organized. Besides the usual information for current students, prospective students, faculty, and staff, there is a new link to information on student accident and health insurance, and information on on-line courses. *Type:* Database.

West Virginia University

West Virginia University
PO Box 6009   Free: 800-344-9884
Morgantown, WV 26506-6009
URL: http://www.wvu.edu/

Contact: webmaster@www.arc.wvu.edu.

Desc: The West Virginia University web site has all of the information you would expect from a university, including course schedules, athletics, alumni affiliations. Do you want to know how to be a WVU Mountaineer? If so, check out the admissions area. *Type:* Database.

West Virginia University Alumni Magazine

West Virginia University
PO Box 6690   Ph: (304)293-6368
Morgantown, WV 26506-6690   Fax: (304)293-4762
E-mail: wvumag@wvu.edu.
URL: http://www.wvu.edu.

Contact: Tony Cook, Editor, tcook7@wvu.edu; Laura Spitznagle, Editors Asst., lspitzno@wvu.edu; Lisa Ammons, Advertising Rep., (304)293-2821, fax: (304)293-4105, lammons@wvu.edu.

Desc: College alumni magazine. *Type:* Periodical.

Western Carolina University

Western Carolina University
Cullowhee, NC 28723   Ph: (704)227-7211
URL: http://www.wcu.edu/

Desc: Western Carolina University serves up information ranging from enrollment and graduate studies to athletics and campus publications. The title page says it all; simply look for the sub-heading of whatever topic you are interested in, click on it, and you're there. *Type:* Database.

Western Kentucky University

Western Kentucky University
Bowling Green, KY 42101
E-mail: wwwmaint@wkuweb1.wku.edu
URL: http://www.msc.wku.edu/

Desc: Bowling Green is home to this Kentucky university. And if the images on the home page of this Web site are any indication, it is a very pretty place indeed. *Type:* Database.

Western Washington University

Western Washington University
516 High St.   Ph: (360)650-3000
Bellingham, WA 98225   Fax: (360)650-7369
E-mail: webmaster@cc.wwu.edu
URL: http://www.wwu.edu

Desc: The WWU features ClassFinder, which enables students to plan the following semester via the Web. It is searchable by department, GUR category, number of credits, day the class meets, and time class begins. *Type:* Database.

Westminster College

Westminster College
504 Westminster Ave.   Ph: (573)642-3361
Fulton, MO 65251
E-mail: bennete@micro.wcmo.edu
URL: http://www.westminster-mo.edu/

Desc: A prestigious liberal arts school in Fulton, Missouri, Westminster College will long be remembered as the forum for Winston Churchill's famous 1946 speech warning of an "Iron Curtain" descending across Europe. Its Web site is well designed, attractive, and loaded with all the information current or prospective students could possibly want. *Type:* Database.

Wichita State University

Wichita State University
1845 N. Fairmount   Ph: (316)978-3045
Wichita, KS 67260-0062   Fax: (316)978-3776
URL: http://www.twsu.edu/

Desc: If the graphic version of Wichita State University's Web site is any indication of the quality of the education it offers, it's hard to imagine a need for any other school. Navigation is made simple through a graphical text, a site index, and a search engine. *Type:* Database.

Widener University

Widener University
Chester, PA 19013
URL: http://www.widener.edu/widener.html

Contact: Larry Withers, Larry.K.Withers@Widener.Edu.

Desc: While the design leaves a bit to be desired (due to graphics and tiny text that make it difficult to read), this functional site provided by Widener University does its job quite well. Admissions, academics, career placement information, and more can be found here with the click of a mouse button. *Type:* Database.

Wittenberg University

Wittenberg University
Springfield, OH 45501-0720   Free: 800-677-7558
E-mail: webmaster@wittenberg.edu
URL: http://www.wittenberg.edu/

Desc: It is enough that a university site has a layout that is easy to navigate. It is a benefit when it has a search engine to cut down on the red tape. *Type:* Database.

WMU, The Magazine

Western Michigan University
1201 Oliver St.   Ph: (616)387-8400
Kalamazoo, MI 49008-3899   Fax: (616)387-8422
URL: http://www.wmich.edu.

Contact: David H. Smith, Contact, (616)387-8431, david.h.smith@wmich.edu; Jeanne Baron, Contact, (616)387-8433, jeanne.baron@wmich.edu.

Desc: Alumni magazine. *Type:* Periodical.

Commodities

American Soybean Association

12125 Woodcrest Executive Dr., Ph: (314)576-1770
    Ste. 100   Free: 800-688-7692
St. Louis, MO 63141   Fax: (314)576-2786
URL: http://www.oilseeds.org
Contact: Steve Censky, CEO.

Desc: National, non-profit, grassroots membership organization that develops and implements policies to increase the profitability of its members and the entire soybean industry. *Type:* Association.

ASE & VSE Advisor

Lombardi Publishing Co.
51 Toro Rd.   Ph: (416)633-1600
North York, ON, Canada M3J   Fax: (416)633-6188
    2A4

Contact: Mitchell Clark, Editor.

Desc: Provides recommendations on speculative stocks traded on the Alberta and Vancouver stock exchanges. *Type:* Newsletter.

Board of Trade of the City of Chicago

141 W. Jackson Blvd., 6th Fl.   Ph: (312)435-3500
Chicago, IL 60604-2994   Fax: (312)341-3392
Contact: Thomas R. Donovan, CEO & Pres.

Desc: Futures exchange - contracts based on agricultural products, financial instruments, precious metals, and options on futures. Is responsible for the development and economic justification of existing and new contracts. Sponsors seminars, conferences, and classes for industry and other user or user-oriented groups and the public. *Type:* Association.

Brock Report

Brock & Associates
2050 W. Good Hope Rd.   Ph: (414)251-5500
Milwaukee, WI 53209   Free: 800-558-3431
                                Fax: (414)251-3140
E-mail: breport@agmarketing.com.
URL: http://www.agmarketing.com.
Contact: Douglas Hansen, Editor; Richard Brock, Publisher.

Desc: Focuses on agricultural commodities. Provides fundamental and technical analysis, and advice. *Type:* Newsletter.

Bruce Gould on Commodities

Bruce Gould Publications
PO Box 16   Fax: (509)422-5109
Seattle, WA 98111
Contact: Bruce Gould, Editor.

Desc: Discusses investment opportunities and trading techniques for the commodity futures market from the viewpoint of investors and potential investors. *Type:* Newsletter.

Canadian Gold Stock Advisory

Lombardi Publishing Co.
51 Toro Rd.   Ph: (416)633-1600
North York, ON, Canada M3J   Fax: (416)633-6188
    2A4

Desc: Offers advice on all major TSE gold stocks. Recommends a core holding portfolio. *Type:* Newsletter.

Chartcraft Weekly Futures Service

Chartcraft, Inc.
30 Church St.   Ph: (914)632-0422
PO Box 2046
New Rochelle, NY 10801
Contact: John E. Gray, Editor.

Desc: Provides information on the Dow Jones Future, Dow Jones and C.R.B. Spot Indexes. *Type:* Newsletter.

Chicago Mercantile Exchange

30 S. Wacker Dr.   Ph: (312)930-1000
Chicago, IL 60606   Fax: (312)648-3625
E-mail: news@cme.com
URL: http://www.cme.com
Contact: William J. Brodsky, CEO & Pres.

Desc: Commodity futures exchange for live hogs, feeder cattle, live beef cattle, frozen pork bellies (bacon), lumber, gold, foreign currencies, government securities, bank debt, and equity financial instruments; also deals with options on equity futures, interest rates, foreign currencies, and livestock. Maintains speakers' bureau; conducts research programs to help develop new contracts and update existing contracts; compiles statistics. Operates library of 3000 books on various aspects of futures trading. *Type:* Association.

Coffee, Sugar and Cocoa Exchange

4 World Trade Center   Ph: (212)742-6000
New York, NY 10048   Free: 800-HEDGE-IT
                                Fax: (212)748-4321
E-mail: webmaster@csce.com
URL: http://www.csce.com
Contact: James J. Bowe, Pres.

Desc: Commodity exchange. (Producers, exporters, importers, refiners, roasters, and processors of coffee, sugar, or cocoa; commission and brokerage houses) members of exchange. *Type:* Association.

Commodex System

Equidex, Inc.
7000 Blvd. E   Ph: (201)868-2600
Guttenberg, NJ 07093
E-mail: futures01@aol.com.
URL: http://www.commodex.com.
Contact: Philip Gotthelf, Editor.

Desc: Functions as a daily commodity trading system, following up to 40 commodities. Bases formula upon correlations of price, volume, and open interest. *Type:* Newsletter.

Commodities Litigation Reporter

Andrews Publications
175 Strafford Ave., Bldg. 4, Ste.   Ph: (610)225-0510
    140   Free: 800-345-1101
Wayne, PA 19087   Fax: (610)225-0501
Contact: Barbara Pizzirani, Editor.

Desc: Reports on the rights and responsibilities of customers and futures commission merchants under Commodity Exchange Act and Commission rules. Monitors commodities market related litigation at the pretrial, trial, and appellate levels and reprints texts of key decisions and pleadings. *Type:* Newsletter.

Commodity Exchange

4 World Trade Center   Ph: (212)938-2900
New York, NY 10048   Fax: (212)432-1154
Contact: Patrick Thompson, Pres.

Desc: Maintains speakers' bureau. *Type:* Association.

Commodity Futures Forecast

Equidex, Inc.
7000 Blvd. E   Ph: (201)868-2600
Guttenberg, NJ 07093
Contact: Philip Gotthelf, Editor.

Desc: Provides analysis and recommendations for active commodity futures markets. Gives specific instructions on purchases, sales, spreads, stop protection, and profit taking. *Type:* Newsletter.

Commodity News Services Inc.

2020 W. 89th St.   Ph: (913)642-7373
PO Box 6053
Leawood, KS 66206

Contact: Dr. Paul Tucker, President; Paul Cooper, Mng. Dir. of the Americas; Kimberly Wilson, VP HR.

Desc: Distributes financial news. *Alt. Contact:* 2020 W. 89th St., PO Box 6053, Leawood, KS 66206; telephone: (913)642-7373. *Type:* Periodical.

Commodity Price Charts

Futures Communications Co., Inc.

250 S. Wacker, Ste. 1150   Ph: (312)977-0999
Chicago, IL 60606   Free: 800-635-3931
                Fax: (312)977-1042

Contact: Tim Roche, Publisher.

Desc: Publishes bar charts of commodity futures contracts, charting volume, open interest, relative strength index, stochastics, ADX, % R, and moving averages. Provides brief commentary on graphed data, pointing out trends, formations, and objectives. *Type:* Newsletter.

Commodity Quotations Inc.

600 Merinock Ave.   Ph: (914)381-7000
Harrison, NY 10528

Contact: Grace Gassney, President; Russ Schiff, Vice President.

Desc: Distributes real time financial information. *Alt. Contact:* 600 Merinock Ave., Harrison, NY 10528; telephone: (914)381-7000. *Type:* Periodical.

Commodity Traders Club News

Commodity Traders Club

34522 N. Scottsdale Rd. No.   Ph: (602)595-1777
  477   Fax: (602)595-1717
Scottsdale, AZ 85262
E-mail: ctcn@webtrading.com
URL: htp://www.webtrading.com.

Contact: Dave Green, Editor and Publisher, dave@webtrading.com.

Desc: Acts as an information forum written by and for traders. Topics include profitable trading, how to save money, and various trading systems, products, and services. *Type:* Newsletter.

Commodity Traders Consumer Reports

Courtney Smith

67 E. 11th St., Apt. 514   Ph: (212)736-2368
New York, NY 10003-4616 Free: 800-832-6065
                Fax: (212)736-2367
E-mail: babcock@spider.lloyd.com; ctcr@ctcr.investors.net.

Contact: Courtney Smith, Editor.

Desc: Follows recommendations of commodity trading advisors and publishes summaries of their closed trades. Also contains educational articles aimed to improve skills of commodity futures traders. *Type:* Newsletter.

Commodity Trend Service

Commodity Trend Service

1201 U.S. Highway 1, Ste. 350 Ph: (407)622-7623
North Palm Beach, FL 33408

Contact: Dennis Dunn, Editor.

Desc: Supplies daily commodity charts with high/low/close data; multiple charts (volume and open interest, point and figure, and weekly continuation charts) are included for some commodities. Offers market predictions and trading information for the following week arranged by commodity. *Type:* Newsletter.

Consensus, National Futures & Financial Weekly

Consensus, Inc.

1737 McGee, Ste. 401   Ph: (816)471-3862
Kansas City, MO 64108   Free: 800-383-1441
                Fax: (816)221-2045

E-mail: editor@consensus-inc.com
URL: http://www.consensus-inc.com.

Contact: Robert E. Salva, Editor, rsalva@aol.com.

Desc: Presents market letters, special reports, and buy/sell advice from over 100 sources. Covers all stock and financial markets, metals, agricultural markets, livestock, grains, and oilseeds. *Type:* Newsletter.

Cotton Trade Report

New York Cotton Exchange

4 World Trade Center   Ph: (212)748-1000
New York, NY 10048
Contact: Tim Barry, Editor.

Desc: Contains analyses of conditions, trends, and prospects in the cotton trade; domestic cotton crop progress during the growing season; U.S. Government activities in the cotton trade; and economic conditions affecting the cotton trade and market. *Type:* Newsletter.

CRB Commodity Index Report

Bridge Information Systems

30 S. Wacker Dr., No. 1810 Ph: (312)454-1801
Chicago, IL 60606-7404   Free: 800-621-5271
                Fax: (312)454-0239

E-mail: crbinfo@bridge.com

Desc: "A comprehensive weekly report on commodity indices and cash prices." Carries the CRB Futures Price Index and the CRB Spot Market Index. Provides statistics for the last five business days and for the previous week, month, and year. *Type:* Newsletter.

CRB Futures Market Service

Commodity Research Bureau Inc.

30 S. Wacker Dr., Ste. 1810 Ph: (312)454-1801
Chicago, IL 60606-7404   Free: 800-621-5271
                Fax: (312)454-0239

E-mail: crbinfo@bridge.com
URL: http://www.crbindex.com.

Contact: Robert Hafer, Editor, bhafer@bridge.com.

Desc: "Discusses developments that will affect the future status of supply, demand, and price movements for the different commodities traded on the futures markets." *Type:* Newsletter.

CSC Clearing Corporation

4 World Trade Center, Ste. Ph: (212)775-0090
  7300 A   Fax: (212)488-9041
New York, NY 10048
Contact: Sid Branson, Pres.

Desc: Commodity importers, manufacturers, and investment brokerage organizations. Clears cocoa, coffee, and sugar contracts made on the Coffee, Sugar and Cocoa Exchange and guarantees the integrity of such contracts. *Type:* Association.

Daily Market Report

Coffee, Sugar & Cocoa Exchange, Inc.

4 World Trade Center, Ste. Ph: (212)938-2800
  52-9E
New York, NY 10048
Desc: Provides trading prices, open interest, and volume for coffee, sugar, and cocoa, including spot prices for sugar, warehouse stocks for coffee and cocoa, and opening and closing prices for London coffee and sugar and Paris cocoa. *Type:* Newsletter.

Doane's Agricultural Report

Doane Agricultural Services

11701 Borman Dr., Ste. 100 Ph: (314)569-2700
St. Louis, MO 63146-4199 Fax: (314)569-1083
Contact: Allen Dever, Editor.

Desc: Covers the marketing of commodities (such as cattle, hogs, corn, wheat, and soybeans), as well as providing agricultural, economic, management, and production information. Discusses such topics as profit management, prices, outlook, machinery, buildings, equipment, taxes, social security, law, and government. *Type:* Newsletter.

DRI Commodities

Standard & Poor's DRI
Data Products Division

24 Hartwell Ave.   Ph: (781)863-5100
Lexington, MA 02421
E-mail: client_services@dri.mcgraw-hill.com
URL: http://www.dri.mcgraw-hill.com

Contact: Client Services, (617)860-6527, fax: (617)860-6416.

Desc: Contains more than 273,000 daily time series of price and trading data for major commodities traded on markets in the U.S., Canada, Europe, and Singapore. *Available:* Standard & Poor's DRI, Data Products Division; Standard & Poor's DRI, Data Products Division. *Type:* Database.

Friedberg's Commodity & Currency Comments

Friedberg Commodity Management Inc.

181 Bay St., Ste. 250   Ph: (416)364-1171
Toronto, ON, Canada M5J 2T3 Fax: (416)364-0572
Contact: Albert Friedberg, Editor.

Desc: Contains information on commodities, international currency bond values, and futures and options trading. *Type:* Newsletter.

Futures International Law Letter

Commodities Law Press Associates

40 Broad St., 20th Fl.   Fax: (212)371-1084
New York, NY 10004
Contact: Richard A. Miller, Editor.

Desc: Monitors legal and regulatory developments affecting commodities and securities industries, including information on litigation, legislation, taxation, pensions, and banking. Analyzes the impact of specific cases and decisions. *Type:* Newsletter.

Futures and Options Factors: The Futures Portfolio Advisor

Wasendorf and Associates, Inc.

1304 W. 1st St.   Ph: (319)268-0441
PO Box 849   Free: 800-553-1711
Cedar Falls, IA 50613   Fax: (319)277-0880
Contact: Russell R. Wasendorf, Editor.

Desc: Analyzes actively traded commodity futures markets in the U.S. based on commodity index analysis in various market groupings, including grains, meats, metals, food/fiber, and financial/currencies. *Type:* Newsletter.

Gold News

Gold Institute

1112 16th St. NW, Ste. 240 Ph: (202)835-0185
Washington, DC 20036   Fax: (202)835-0155
E-mail: goldnews@goldinstitute.org
Contact: Larry Kahaner, Editor.

Desc: Reports on trends affecting gold and the gold markets. Recurring features include reports of meetings, news of research, and chart of gold prices within the year. *Type:* Newsletter.

HALCO Trading Strategies

HALCO Commodity Research
PO Box 795429   Ph: (214)373-2766
Dallas, TX 75379   Free: 800-527-6826
Contact: James H. Jones, Editor.
Desc: Utilizes the HAL method of cyclical analysis. Provides daily, monthly, and weekly continuation charts on the futures market, with indication of dominant cycles; accompanied by bull and bear analysis and trading strategies for 16 markets. *Type:* Newsletter.

Hjort Associates, Inc.—Viewpoint

Hjort Associates, Inc.
105 S. 6th St.   Ph: (515)993-5933
Adel, IA 50003   Fax: (515)993-5932
Contact: Douglas C. Hjort, Editor.
Desc: Addresses marketing problems faced by U.S. agricultural producers. *Type:* Newsletter.

Livestock, Meat, and Wool Market News

Livestock and Seed Division
Agricultural Marketing Service
U.S. Department of Agriculture (USDA)
South Bldg., Rm. 2613   Ph: (202)720-6231
PO Box 96456   Fax: (202)690-3732
Washington, DC 20090-6456
URL: http://www.usda.gov.
Contact: Kim Harmon, Editor, kim.harmon@usda.gov.
Desc: Publishes weekly livestock, meat, and wool marketing statistics. Includes narrative summaries of the week's livestock, meat, and wool marketing situation in the United States. *Type:* Newsletter.

Managed Account Reports

Managed Account Reports, Inc.
220 5th Ave., 19th Fl.   Ph: (212)213-6202
New York, NY 10001   Free: 800-638-2525
    Fax: (212)213-1870
E-mail: subs@marhedge.com
Contact: Morton S. Baratz, Editor.
Desc: Designed to help investors select the appropriate money manager. Presents in-depth reports on commodity trading advisors by identifing individual companies and discussing their principals, types of accounts handled, amount of money under management, fees and commissions charged, and past performances. *Type:* Newsletter.

Market Vane's Bullish Consensus

Market Vane Corporation
PO Box 90490   Ph: (818)441-3457
Pasadena, CA 91109-0490
Contact: Richard Ishida, Editor.
Desc: Features a poll of trader sentiment in over 30 of the most actively-traded markets, which is intended to signify market trends and turns. Provides a track record of recommended positions, fundamental and open interest analysis of each market, and current recommendations with commentary. *Type:* Newsletter.

Myers on Futures

Steven R. Myers
PO Box 777
Summerfield, FL 34492-0777
Contact: Steven R. Myers, Editor.
Desc: Provides technical analysis of commodity futures. *Type:* Newsletter.

National Association of Wheat Growers

415 2nd St. NE, Ste. 300   Ph: (202)547-7800
Washington, DC 20002   Fax: (202)546-2638
E-mail: wheatworld@wheatworld.org
URL: http://www.wheatworld.org

Contact: Margie Williams, Interim CEO.
Desc: Federation of 23 state wheat growers associations. Represents wheat grower interest in educational, legislative, and regulatory projects and issues for wheat farmers in Washington, DC. *Type:* Association.

National Sunflower Association

4023 State St.   Ph: (701)328-5100
Bismarck, ND 58501   Free: 888-718-7033
    Fax: (701)328-5101
URL: http://www.sunflowernsa.com
Contact: Larry Kleingartner, Exec.Dir.
Desc: Growers, firms, and organizations associated with the sunflower and its products, including growers' councils, seed companies, processors, exporters, researchers, chemical firms, and merchandisers. Promotes the development of the sunflower industry. Seeks to improve sunflower production through research and education and to expand markets for sunflower products in the U.S. *Type:* Association.

New York Mercantile Exchange

1 North End Ave.   Ph: (212)299-2000
World Financial Ctr.   Fax: (212)301-4700
New York, NY 10282-1101
URL: http://www.nymex.com
Contact: Daniel Rappaport, Chm.
Desc: Brokerage houses, businesses with commercial interests in commodities, and professional traders. Provides a mechanism for trading futures and options. Compiles trading statistics for public distribution. *Type:* Association.

Newsline

Association of Sales & Marketing Companies
2100 Reston Pkwy., Ste. 400   Ph: (703)758-7790
Reston, VA 20191   Fax: (703)758-7787
E-mail: info@asmc.org
Contact: Karen Connell, Editor, connell@asmc.org.
Desc: Informs members about NFBA events and services and brings members in contact with manufacturers seeking broker representation. Recurring features include news of members and a calendar of events. *Type:* Newsletter.

NGI's Daily Gas Price Index

Intelligence Press
PO Box 70587   Ph: (703)318-8848
Washington, DC 20024   Free: 800-427-5747
    Fax: (703)318-0597
URL: http://www.intelligencepress.com.
Contact: Ellen Beswick, Editor, ellen@ngigpi.com.
Desc: Presents cash and futures market prices, market volatility and options valuation tables, state and federal tax and oversight, and corporate actions across the continent. Remarks: Available via fax. *Type:* Newsletter.

Oil & Gas Advisory

Lombardi Publishing Co.
51 Toro Rd.   Ph: (416)633-1600
North York, ON, Canada M3J   Fax: (416)633-6188
2A4
Contact: Mitchell Clark, Editor.
Desc: Provides recommendations on TSE 300 oil and gas stocks, details the movement of large gas retailers, top exploration, and junior oil companies. Recurring features include the top five stock picks, the top five speculative stocks, and the quote of the month. *Type:* Newsletter.

Opportunities in Options

Opportunities in Options
300 Esplanade Dr., No. 200   Ph: (805)278-4350
Oxnard, CA 93030   Free: 800-456-9699
    Fax: (805)278-4364
E-mail: oio@mail.westnet

URL: http://www.oio.com.
Contact: David L. Caplan, Editor.
Desc: Reports on commodities options. *Type:* Newsletter.

Ostaro's Market Newsletter

Svarg Syndicate Inc.
303 5th Ave., Ste. 1909   Ph: (212)686-4121
New York, NY 10016
Contact: D. Ostaro, Editor.
Desc: Focuses on gold, silver, interest rates, currencies, the Dow Jones Industrial Average, and the world situation as it affects world markets. Analyzes and charts the DJIA and Gold (major sentimental shifts) for one month. *Type:* Newsletter.

Plains Cotton Growers

4510 Englewood Ave.   Ph: (806)792-4904
Lubbock, TX 79414   Fax: (806)792-4906
E-mail: mail@plainscotton.org
URL: http://www.plainscotton.org
Contact: Steve Verett, Exec.VP.
Desc: Cotton producers, ginners, oil mills, warehouses, and allied businesses; membership concentrated in west Texas. Furthers the use of high plains cotton through research, promotion, advertising, legislative activities, and technical assistance to cotton mills. Provides statistics on cotton production, acreage, quality, varieties, and spinning performance. *Type:* Association.

Pocket Charts

Wasendorf and Associates, Inc.
1304 W. 1st St.   Ph: (319)268-0441
PO Box 849   Free: 800-553-1711
Cedar Falls, IA 50613   Fax: (319)277-0880
Contact: Russell R. Wasendorf, Editor.
Desc: Supplies over seventy daily bar charts, including volume and open interest, for near term futures. Contains agricultural, energy, metals, currencies, financials, and index futures. *Type:* Newsletter.

Quarterly Performance Report

Managed Account Reports, Inc.
220 5th Ave., 19th Fl.   Ph: (212)213-6202
New York, NY 10001   Free: 800-638-2525
    Fax: (212)213-1870
E-mail: subs@marhedge.com
Contact: Morton S. Baratz, Editor.
Desc: Contains statistical information on commodity trading advisors and commodity pool operators mentioned in Managed Accounts Reports (see separate listing). Each individual trading advisor is rated by performance and operating statistics in the areas of Net Asset Value (NAV) per unit, MAR performance index, rate of return, profits/losses, largest drawdown, and number of individual accounts, limited partnerships, and total dollars managed. *Type:* Newsletter.

Real News Letter

Investors' Update
525 W. Manchester Blvd.   Ph: (213)674-3330
Inglewood, CA 90301
Contact: Richard J. Schwary, Editor.
Desc: Provides investment information for rare coins and the precious metals market, as well as commodity futures markets. Carries economic statistics and news of world events affecting investors. *Type:* Newsletter.

Standard & Poor's Review of Securities & Commodities Regulation

Standard & Poor's
25 Broadway   Ph: (212)208-8000
New York, NY 10004-1064   Free: 800-221-5277
                               Fax: (212)208-0040
URL: http://www.stockinfo.standardpoor.com
Contact: Michael O. Finkelstein, Editor.
Desc: Carries signed technical legal articles on various aspects of the securities and commodities markets. Recent topics have included plea bargaining in securities cases and advertising of securities products in the U.S. and Europe. *Type:* Newsletter.

The Superinvestor Hotsheet

The Hume Group
2839 Pace Verry Rd., St.e 1170   Fax: (770)432-0567
Atlanta, GA 30339-5770
Contact: Eric Kirzner, Editor; Larry Spears, Editor.
Desc: Tracks futures trades based on "The Superinvestor Files," a series of 29 strategies for reducing risk and increasing profit in futures trading. Remarks: Toll-free telephone number in Canada is 800-733-4863. *Type:* Newsletter.

System: Futures & Commodities

Lombardi Publishing Co.
51 Toro Rd.   Ph: (416)633-1600
North York, ON, Canada M3J   Fax: (416)633-6188
2A4
Contact: George Leong, Editor.
Desc: Provides trading advice on up to 20 futures and commodities. Includes market analysis, and technical analysis. *Type:* Newsletter.

Tomorrow's Commodities

Techno-Fundamental Investments, Inc.
PO Box 14111   Ph: (602)996-2908
Scottsdale, AZ 85267
Contact: Bob Jubb, Editor.
Desc: Gives investment information and recommendations for commodities. *Type:* Newsletter.

Trends in Futures

Futures Communications Co., Inc.
250 S. Wacker, Ste. 1150   Ph: (312)977-0999
Chicago, IL 60606   Free: 800-635-3931
                               Fax: (312)977-1042
Contact: Steve Briese, Editor.
Desc: Analyzes futures markets for speculators. *Type:* Newsletter.

U.S. Wheat Associates

1620 I St. NW, Ste. 801   Ph: (202)463-0999
Washington, DC 20006   Fax: (202)785-1052
URL: http://www.uswheat.org
Contact: Alan T. Tracy, Pres.
Desc: Federation of state wheat commissions and grower organizations. *Type:* Association.

U.S.A. Rice Council

PO Box 740123   Ph: (713)270-6699
Houston, TX 77274   Free: 800-888-7423
                               Fax: (713)270-9021
E-mail: ellen@za.usarice.com
URL: http://www.usarice.com
Contact: Ellen Terpstra, Pres.
Desc: Rice producers, millers, dryers, packagers, and others in the rice industry in Arkansas, California, Louisiana, Mississippi, Missouri, and Texas. Provides worldwide advertising and promotion services to the rice industry. *Type:* Association.

Weekly Report of the Market

Coffee, Sugar & Cocoa Exchange, Inc.
4 World Trade Center, Ste.   Ph: (212)938-2800
52-9E
New York, NY 10048
Desc: Reports weekly trading statistics, market highlights and summaries, and other pertinent information concerning coffee, sugar, and cocoa. *Type:* Newsletter.

World Commodity Perspective

Elliott Wave International, Inc.
PO Box 1618   Ph: (770)536-0309
Gainesville, GA 30503   Free: 800-336-1618
                               Fax: (770)536-2514
E-mail: customerservice@elliottwave.com
URL: http://www.elliottwave.com
Contact: Jim Martens, Currency Specialist.
Desc: Provides market analysis for investors and fund managers. Recurring features include news of research. *Type:* Newsletter.

Communications

A & A

PO Box 330008   Ph: (817)292-1855
Fort Worth, TX 76163-0008   Fax: (817)292-1855
Contact: Elaine Sandra Abramson, President; Stan Abramson, Sr. VP; Mitchell Lee, VP Mktg. & Sales; Deborah Abramson, VP Spec. Proj.
Desc: Distributes columns related to the arts and appraising fine and decorative arts. *Alt. Contact:* PO Box 330008, Fort Worth, TX 76163-0008; telephone: (817)292-1855; fax: (817)292-1855. *Type:* Periodical.

Accuracy in Media

4455 Connecticut Ave. NW,   Ph: (202)364-4401
Ste. 330   Free: 800-787-0044
Washington, DC 20008   Fax: (202)364-4098
E-mail: ar@aim.org
URL: http://www.aim.org
Contact: Donald K. Irvine, Exec.Sec.
Desc: Nonpartisan, news media watchdog organization. Receives complaints from the public on factual errors made by the news media. *Type:* Association.

ACUTA: The Association for Telecommunication Professionals in Higher Education

152 W Zandale Dr., Ste. 200   Ph: (606)278-3338
Lexington, KY 40503   Fax: (606)278-3268
E-mail: jsemer@acuta.org
URL: http://www.acuta.org
Contact: Jeri A. Semer, Exec.Dir.
Desc: University and college administrators of telecommunications services; persons involved in the educational telecommunications industry. Works to improve the professional competence of college and university telecommunications administrators. *Type:* Association.

A.D. Kahn Inc.

24901 Northwestern Hwy.   Ph: (248)355-4100
Ste. 316-B   Fax: (248)356-4344
Southfield, MI 48075-2207
Contact: A. David Kahn, Editor.
Alt. Contact: 24901 Northwestern Hwy., Ste. 316-B, Southfield, MI 48075-2207; telephone: (248)355-4100; fax: (248)356-4344. *Type:* Periodical.

The Advisor Group

18530 Mack Ave.   Ph: (313)822-7712
No. 229   Fax: (313)822-7712
Grosse Pointe Farms, MI 48236
Contact: Bruce Hubbard, Author; Holly A. Olmstead Hubbard, Author.

Desc: Distributes automotive travel car and truck features; photographs. *Alt. Contact:* 18530 Mack Ave., No. 229, Grosse Pointe Farms, MI 48236; telephone: (313)822-7712; fax: (313)822-7712. *Type:* Periodical.

Agencia Efe/Efe News Service

1252 National Press Bldg.   Ph: (202)745-7692
Washington, DC 20045   Fax: (202)393-4119
Contact: Fernando Pajares, Bureau Chief.
Alt. Contact: 1252 National Press Bldg., Washington, DC 20045; telephone: (202)745-7692; fax: (202)393-4119. *Type:* Periodical.

The Agency

PO Box 139   Ph: (516)544-0703
Kings Park, NY 11754
Contact: Joel Cook, Ed./Author; Loretta Cook, Ed./Admin.; Denise Tellier, Ed./Admin.
Desc: Distributes magazine articles and newspaper columns. *Alt. Contact:* PO Box 139, Kings Park, NY 11754; telephone: (516)544-0703. *Type:* Periodical.

Agency for Instructional Technology

Box A   Ph: (812)339-2203
Bloomington, IN 47402-0120   Free: 800-457-4509
                               Fax: (812)333-4278
E-mail: ait@ait.net
URL: http://www.ait.net
Contact: Michael F. Sullivan, Exec.Dir.
Desc: Aims to strengthen education by providing leadership and service to the education community through cooperative development, acquisition, and distribution of technology-based instructional materials. Makes available over 2500 instructional programs in such areas as early childhood, health and safety, art, vocational education, career guidance, science, math, social studies, and staff development, for use as learning resources. *Type:* Association.

AIM Accuracy in Media Report

4455 Connecticut Ave. NW   Ph: (202)364-4401
Ste. 330   Fax: (202)364-4098
Washington, DC 20008
E-mail: ar@take.aim.org.
URL: http://take.aim.org.
Contact: Reed Irvine, Chm.; Joseph Goulden, Dir. Media Anl.; Donald K. Irvine, Exec. Sec.; Deborah Lambert, Pub. Aff. Dir.; Bernard Yoh, Dir. of Communications.
Desc: Distributes newsletters and newspapers. *Alt. Contact:* 4455 Connecticut Ave. NW, Ste. 330, Washington, DC 20008; telephone: (202)364-4401; fax: (202)364-4098. *Type:* Periodical.

The Alburn Bureau

Box 2345   Ph: (520)325-9501
Tucson, AZ 85702
Contact: Leo Sonderegger, Director.
Alt. Contact: Box 2345, Tucson, AZ 85702; telephone: (520)325-9501. *Type:* Periodical.

Allied Feature Syndicate/Electronic Manufacturing News

Rte. 1 Box 43C   Ph: (417)673-2860
Webb City, MO 64870
Contact: Robert Blanset, Editor.
Desc: Distributes electronic manufacturing news and features. *Alt. Contact:* Rte. 1 Box 43C, Webb City, MO 64870; telephone: (417)673-2860. *Type:* Periodical.

Amanda y Rocinante

36 Crest St.   Ph: (203)933-8118
West Haven, CT 06516
Contact: Dorothy Torres, Artist; Resurreccion Espinosa, Writer.

Alt. Contact: 36 Crest St., West Haven, CT 06516; telephone: (203)933-8118. *Type:* Periodical.

American International Syndicate

1324 N. 3rd St. Ph: (816)279-9315
St. Joseph, MO 64501

Contact: Gerald Bennett, Pres./Cartoon Ed.; Linda Bennett, Exec. VP; Wes Clark, VP/Art Dir.; Robert Brown, VP Mktg.; Joyce Clark, Mktg. Dir.; Jose E. Isonore, Mng. Dir. Far East Asia.

Desc: Distributes automotive; children's editorial; home decorating and nature features; comic strips; puzzles. *Alt. Contact:* 1324 N. 3rd St., St. Joseph, MO 64501; telephone: (816)279-9315. *Type:* Periodical.

The American News Service

RR 1 Black Fox Rd. Ph: (802)254-6167
Brattleboro, VT 05301 Fax: (802)254-1227
E-mail: ans@.sover.net.
URL: http://www.americannews.com.

Contact: Paul Martin DuBois, Publisher; Frances Moore Lappe, Editor; Richard Meyer, Managing Editor; Gwen Barrett, Assoc. Features Ed.; William Bole, Assoc. Ed.

Desc: Distributes American Bookshelf, a weekly book review; Time Out America, an entertainment review; In Brief legal review; American Health Watch; consumer product reports; travel and vacation features. *Alt. Contact:* RR 1 Black Fox Rd., Brattleboro, VT 05301; telephone: (802)254-6167; fax: (802)254-1227. *Type:* Periodical.

American Women in Radio and Television— News and Views

American Women in Radio and Television
1650 Tysons Blvd., Ste. 200 Ph: (703)506-3290
Mc Lean, VA 22102 Fax: (703)506-3266
Contact: Christine Murphy, Editor.

Desc: Provides news of the radio and television industry, focusing on women who are active in the field. Carries organization news and program ideas. *Type:* Newsletter.

America's Network Directory/Telecom Sourcebook

Advanstar Communications
7500 Old Oak Blvd. Ph: (440)243-8100
Cleveland, OH 44130-3369 Free: 800-225-4569
  Fax: (440)891-2733

E-mail: directories@advanstar.com.
URL: http://www.advanstar.com.
Contact: Karen Eagle, Editor, keagle@advanstar.com.

Desc: Over 5,000 companies involved in all facets of the telecommunications industry in the U.S. and international marketplace, including local telephone providers, long distance providers, holding companies, cellular providers and manufacturers/suppliers of equipment and services. *Type:* Directory.

Ampersand Communications

2311 S. Bayshore Dr. Ph: (305)285-2200
Miami, FL 33133

Contact: Rosalie Leposky, Marketing; George Leposky, Editor, gleposky@juno.com.

Desc: Distributes EnviroScan HealthScan; Golden Years Business Insights; Business Travel; and Travel Adventures. *Alt. Contact:* 2311 S. Bayshore Dr., Miami, FL 33133; telephone: (305)285-2200. *Type:* Periodical.

Another Way

1251 Virginia Ave. Ph: (540)434-6701
Harrisonburg, VA 22801-2497 Free: 800-999-3534
E-mail: melodie@mennomedia.org.
Contact: Melodie M. Davis, Self-Syndicator.

Desc: Distributes column on family career and social issues. *Alt. Contact:* 1251 Virginia Ave., Harrisonburg, VA 22801-2497; telephone: (540)434-6701; toll-free: 800-999-3534. *Type:* Periodical.

AP Network News

1825 K St. NW Ph: (202)736-1100
Ste. 710 Fax: (202)736-1199
Washington, DC 20006
Contact: Brad Kalbfeld, Deputy Dir./Mng. Editor.
Alt. Contact: 1825 K St. NW, Ste. 710, Washington, DC 20006; telephone: (202)736-1100; fax: (202)736-1199; Associated Press Broadcast Services. *Type:* Periodical.

Aquino International

PO Box 125 Ph: (802)767-9341
Rochester, VT 05767 Fax: (802)767-4526
E-mail: aquinoint@aol.com.
URL: http://www.aaquino.com.
Contact: Andres Aquino, Owner.

Desc: Distributes photography. *Alt. Contact:* PO Box 125, Rochester, VT 05767; telephone: (802)767-9341; fax: (802)767-4526. *Type:* Periodical.

The Asia-Pacific Satellite Directory

Phillips Publishing International, Inc.
7811 Montrose Rd. Ph: (301)340-2100
Potomac, MD 20854 Fax: (301)424-0245

Desc: Asian-Pacific satellite companies and contacts. Includes industry trends and projections, satellite system details, and country profiles. *Type:* Directory.

Association for Educational Communications and Technology

1025 Vermont Ave. NW, Ste. Ph: (202)347-7834
  820 Fax: (202)347-7839
Washington, DC 20005
E-mail: aect@aect.org
URL: http://www.aect.org
Contact: Stan Zenor, Exec.Dir.

Desc: Instructional technology professionals. Provides leadership in educational com munications and technology by lnking professionals holding a common interest in the use of educational technology and its application of the learning process. *Type:* Association.

ATM Tactics

Phillips Infotech
1111 Marlkress Rd, Ste. 101 Ph: (609)424-1100
Cherry Hill, NJ 08003 Free: 800-678-4642
  Fax: (609)424-1999

E-mail: cborn@phillips.com
Contact: Bob Olson, Editor.

Desc: Contains detailed specifications on ATM switching systems, multiplexes, bridge/routes, CSS/EUE, and network management products. Remarks: Only available on diskette, tape or CD-Rom. *Type:* Newsletter.

AV Video & Multimedia Producer

Knowledge Industry Publications, Inc.
701 Westchester Ave. Ph: (914)328-9157
White Plains, NY 10604 Free: 800-800-5474
  Fax: (914)328-9093

E-mail: kipimktg@kipi.com; avvmmp@kipi.com.
URL: http://www.kipinet.com; http://www.kipinet.com.
Contact: Nick Dager, Editor; Steven Klapow, Managing Editor; Ollie Bieniemy, Publisher; Jeff Hartford, Circulation Director.

Desc: Magazine covering audio-visual, video and multimedia production, presentation, people, technology and techniques. *Type:* Periodical.

Barringer Huff and Stuart

310 5th St. Ph: (804)528-2356
Lynchburg, VA 24504
Contact: Paul Barringer, Author/Owner.

Desc: Distributes financial planning articles. *Alt. Contact:* 310 5th St., Lynchburg, VA 24504; telephone: (804)528-2356. *Type:* Periodical.

Blah, Blah, Blah

The Kamber Group
1920 L St. NW, No. 700 Ph: (202)223-8700
Washington, DC 20036 Fax: (202)659-5559
URL: http://www.kamber.com/blahmain/html.
Contact: Gavin McDonald, Editor; Heather McNamara, Editor.

Desc: Reports on company's recent achievements, activities, and awards. *Type:* Newsletter.

Blockbuster

Blockbuster Entertainment Corp.
1 Blockbuster Plaza Ph: (954)832-3000
Fort Lauderdale, FL 33301 Fax: (954)832-4525
Contact: J.P. Faber, Editor; Ron Castell, Publisher.
Type: Periodical.

Business Wire Newsletter

Business Wire
44 Montgomery St., No. 3900 Ph: (415)986-4422
San Francisco, CA 94104 Fax: (415)788-5335
Contact: Lorry I. Lokey, Editor.

Desc: Covers news and trends in public relations, journalism, and related communications endeavors. *Type:* Newsletter.

Cable World

Intertec Publishing
5680 Greenwood Plaza Blvd., Ph: (303)741-2901
  Ste. 100 Fax: (720)489-3225
Englewood, CO 80111
URL: http://www.intertec.com.
Contact: Paul Kagan, Editor.

Desc: Discusses methods of marketing and selling new media such as cable and pay television and provides information on the results of recent advertising campaigns. Recurring features include case studies of selected companies. *Type:* Newsletter.

Canadian Communications Reports

Evert Communications Ltd.
1296 Carling Ave. Ph: (613)728-4621
Ottawa, ON, Canada K1Z 7K8 Fax: (613)728-0385
E-mail: newsdesk@evert.com; services@evert.com
URL: http://www.evert.com.
Contact: Debbie Lawes, Editor.

Desc: Details developments in the provision of communications services in the Canadian market. Covers policy and regulatory matters, technical and service standards, sources of funding, marketing strategies, new technology and activities. *Type:* Newsletter.

CAP Communications—Contacts

CAP Communications
35-20 Broadway Ph: (718)721-0508
Astoria, NY 11106 Fax: (718)274-3387
E-mail: contactspr@aol.com.
Contact: Madeleine Gillis, Editor.

Desc: Provides information on specific editorial needs of newspapers, magazines, wire feature services, and radio and television program directors. Carries media description, area of interest, and addresses and phone numbers of contact persons. *Type:* Newsletter.

CAVE Newsletter

Catholic Audio-Visual Educators Association (CAVE)
PO Box 9257
Pittsburgh, PA 15224
Contact: John Manear, Editor.

Desc: Focuses on the various mediums of communication, their use, and effect on society. Publishes information in layman's terms on the technical advances and the social impact of those advances in films, slides, filmstrips, video and audio cassettes, television, and cable television. *Type:* Newsletter.

CEMAgram

CEMA
C/O Anne Weimann
25 Elmwood Ave.
Trumbull, CT 06611

Ph: (203)372-2260
Fax: (203)579-4413

Contact: Hedy Seigel, Editor; Carole Braunschweig, Editor.

Desc: Publishes current information regarding media activities and legislation in Connecticut and the rest of the nation. Recurring features include interviews, news of research, a collection, reports of meetings, news of educational opportunities, and notices of publications available. *Type:* Newsletter.

Center for Investigative Reporting

500 Howard St., 2nd Fl.
San Francisco, CA 94105-3008

Ph: (415)543-1200
Free: 800-733-0015
Fax: (415)543-8311

E-mail: cir@igc.org
Contact: Dan Noyes, Exec.Dir.
Desc: Investigative journalists engaged in the in-depth reporting of economic, environmental, energy, social justice, public policy, and constitutional government issues. Produces investigative television documentaries, newspaper and magazine articles, books, and reports; provides investigative and editorial consulting services to television news, publications, and nonprofit organizations. Conducts internship program, and classes for journalism students and others on techniques of investigative reporting. *Type:* Association.

Charles Woodson

PO Box 11883
Berkeley, CA 94712-2883

Ph: (510)643-6614
Fax: (510)642-3555

E-mail: woodson@soe.berkeley.edu.
Contact: Charles Woodson, Author.
Alt. Contact: PO Box 11883, Berkeley, CA 94712-2883; telephone: (510)643-6614; fax: (510)642-3555. *Type:* Periodical.

Collins Communications

381 Broadway
Westwood, NJ 07675

Ph: (201)358-2929
Fax: (201)358-2824

Contact: Chaunce Hayden, Editor.
Alt. Contact: 381 Broadway, Westwood, NJ 07675; telephone: (201)358-2929; fax: (201)358-2824. *Type:* Periodical.

Coming Attractions

Star Video Entertainment LP
550 Grand St.
Jersey City, NJ 07302-4115

Ph: (201)333-4600
Fax: (201)333-1609

Contact: Anne Sherber, Managing Editor; Richard W. Goffman, Publisher.
Desc: Consumer magazine listing new releases on videocassette by in-store date. Distributed through retail outlets. *Type:* Periodical.

Committee to Protect Journalists

330 7th Ave., 12th Fl.
New York, NY 10001

Ph: (212)465-1004
Fax: (212)465-9568

E-mail: info@cpj.org
URL: http://www.cpj.org
Contact: Ann K. Cooper, Exec.Dir.
Desc: Media organizations, human rights groups, and journalists. Supports journalists around the world who have been subjected to human rights violations. Is concerned about efforts by governments to limit the ability of foreign correspondents and local journalists to practice their profession. *Type:* Association.

Communication

National Technical Information Service (NTIS)
U.S. Department of Commerce
5285 Port Royal Rd.
Springfield, VA 22161-0001

Ph: (703)605-6000
Free: 800-553-NTIS
Fax: (703)605-6900

E-mail: orders@ntis.fedworld.gov
Desc: Publishes abstracts with full bibliographic citations in the areas of common carrier and satellite communication and information theory; graphics, policies, regulations, and studies; radio and television equipment; and sociopolitical and verbal communication. Alerts readers to related published material available from NTIS and other sources. *Type:* Newsletter.

Communications Daily

Warren Publishing, Inc.
2115 Ward Ct. NW
Washington, DC 20037

Ph: (202)872-9200
Fax: (202)296-4397

E-mail: warrenpub@mindspring.com
URL: http://www.telecommunications.com
Contact: Albert Warren, Editor.
Desc: Covers telephone and data communications, broadcasting, cable TV, teleconferencing, satellite communications, electronic publishing, and emerging technologies. Recurring features include personnel updates, obituaries, statistics, trade show news, and news of research. *Type:* Newsletter.

Communications Library (CLCD)

Phillips Infotech
1111 Marlkress Rd, Ste. 101
Cherry Hill, NJ 08003

Ph: (609)424-1100
Free: 800-678-4642
Fax: (609)424-1999

E-mail: cborn@phillips.com
Contact: Don Stuart, Editor.
Desc: Describes and evaluates communications products and services available in the domestic marketplace. Focuses on the wired and wireless voice and data communications marketplace, providing product/service price data and evaluation based upon comparison and user comments. *Type:* Newsletter.

Computing & Communications Law & Protection

Assets Protection Publishing
PO Box 5323
Madison, WI 53705-0323

Ph: (608)231-6730
Fax: (608)231-6730

URL: http://www.townnews.con/mt/acantha.
Contact: Paul Shaw, Editor and Publisher.
Desc: Devoted to computer and communications security, audit, and law. *Type:* Newsletter.

Cowles/Simba Report on Database Marketing

SIMBA Information Inc.
11 Riverbend Dr. S.
PO Box 4234
Stamford, CT 06907-0234

Ph: (203)358-4100
Free: 800-307-2529
Fax: (203)358-5824

E-mail: info@simbanet.com
URL: http://www.simbanet.com
Contact: Lynn Dougherty, Editor.
Desc: Reports on technology, database marketing applications in package goods, publishing finance, and customer relations. Covers all issues related to database marketing. *Type:* Newsletter.

Curt Schleier Reviews

646 Jones Rd.
River Vale, NJ 07675

Ph: (201)391-7135
Fax: (201)391-7135

E-mail: curt_s@compuserve.com.
Contact: Curt Schleier, President.
Desc: Distributes book and television reviews, author/celebrity interviews, and industry news. *Alt. Contact:* 646 Jones Rd., River Vale, NJ 07675; telephone: (201)391-7135; fax: (201)391-7135. *Type:* Periodical.

David V. Tilton

PO Box 3516
North Ft. Myers, FL 33918

Ph: (941)656-0225
Fax: (941)656-5177

E-mail: stamps@yaxcorp.com.
Contact: David V. Tilton, Self-Syndicator/Owner/Writer.
Desc: Distributes weekly newspaper column--Stamps. *Alt. Contact:* PO Box 3516, North Ft. Myers, FL 33918; telephone: (941)656-0225; fax: (941)656-5177. *Type:* Periodical.

The DBS Report

Paul Kagan Associates, Inc.
126 Clock Tower Pl.
Carmel, CA 93923

Ph: (831)624-1536
Fax: (831)625-3225

E-mail: info@kagan.com
Contact: George Niesen, Editor.
Desc: Provides analysis of direct-to-home satellite ventures and projections of future trends, costs, and values. *Type:* Newsletter.

Dots and Dashes

Morse Telegraph Club
415 S. Rife St.
Dillon, MT 59725

Ph: (406)683-2331

Contact: John M. Barrows, Editor.
Desc: Perpetuates the tradition of the telegraph profession through articles and anecdotes about the use of Morse and International codes and operators, manufacturers, and users of telegraphs. Recurring features include member and chapter news, letters to the editor, and reports of meetings. *Type:* Newsletter.

EDUCAUSE

1112 16th St. NW, Ste. 600
Washington, DC 20036

Ph: (202)872-4200
Fax: (202)872-4318

Contact: Robert C. Heterick, Jr., Pres.
Desc: Colleges, universities, and nonprofit educational service organizations. Promotes resource sharing among colleges and universities in the application of computing, communications, and information technology in higher education. *Type:* Association.

Eleven

WTTW/Chicago
5400 N. St. Louis Ave.
Chicago, IL 60625-4623

Ph: (773)583-5000
Fax: (773)509-5305

E-mail: 70550.143@compuserve.com; hpp@wwnet.com.
URL: http://www.wttw.com.
Contact: Carol Lezak, Editor, (847)205-3165, fax: (847)564-8197; Denise Kowalski, Managing Editor, (773)509-5442, fax: (773)509-5305; Shaunese Teamer, Advertising Mgr., (773)509-5441, fax: (773)509-5305.
Desc: Magazine for WTTW, Chicago's public television station. *Type:* Periodical.

Epsilon Pi Tau

Bowling Green State University
Technology Bldg.
Bowling Green, OH 43403

Ph: (419)372-2425
Fax: (419)372-2800

E-mail: mswanso@bgnet.bgsu.edu
Contact: Dr. Jerry Streichler, Exec.Dir.
Desc: International honorary for professions in technology. Supports research. *Type:* Association.

European Media Business & Finance

Phillips Business Information, Inc.
1201 Seven Locks Rd., Ste. 300
Potomac, MD 20854

Ph: (301)340-1520
Free: 888-707-5809
Fax: (301)340-3847

E-mail: clientservices.pbi@phillips.com; ijumpstart.com.
Contact: John P. Ourand, Senior Editor, jourand@ phillips.com.
Desc: Reports on news and analysis for investment acquisition, distribution, licensing, and business development strategies. Also covers venture capital, distribution and acquisition news, stock review charts, and new media bulletins. *Type:* Newsletter.

Exclamation Point

Robinson Kurtin Communications
201 E. 42nd St.   Ph: (212)983-5757
New York, NY 10017   Fax: (212)983-5751
E-mail: robinsonk@aol.com
Contact: Sondra Kurtin, Publisher; James Schulman, Editor.
Desc: Features articles on communication topics. *Type:* Newsletter.

The Exclusive Communicator

The WOMEN IN COMMUNICATIONS Foundation
6900 Newman Rd.   Ph: (703)803-3728
Clifton, VA 20124-1613   Fax: (703)803-3729
E-mail: vangardfin@aol.com; vangardfdn@aol.com.
Contact: Colleen Phelan, Editor.
Desc: Covers communications issues, trends and news for senior level communicators. *Type:* Newsletter.

Fairness and Accuracy in Reporting

130 W. 25th St.   Ph: (212)633-6700
New York, NY 10001   Fax: (212)727-7668
E-mail: fair@fair.org
URL: http://www.fair.org/fair
Contact: Janine Jackson, Program Dir.
Desc: Promotes the rights of U.S. citizens to a free press and free speech; encourages pluralism in media. Brings public attention to the performance of the media in specific areas. *Type:* Association.

Feature

Feature Publishing Ltd.
2100 St. Catherine St. W., 10th   Ph: (514)939-5036
Fl.   Fax: (514)939-1515
Montreal, PQ, Canada H3H
2T3
E-mail: editor@feature.ca
Contact: Marvin Boisvert, Publisher, (939)5024, fax: (939)1515; David Sherman, Managing Editor; Heidy Kavalenko, Production Mgr.; Nathalie Abitbol, Distribution Supervisor.
Desc: Consumer magazine published for English Pay Television subscribers in eastern Canada. *Type:* Periodical.

Fiber Optics and Communications Newsletter

Information Gatekeepers Inc.
214 Harvard Ave.   Ph: (617)232-3111
Boston, MA 02134   Free: 800-323-1088
    Fax: (617)734-8562
E-mail: info@igigroup.com
URL: http://wwwigigroup.com
Contact: Paul Polishuk, Editor.
Desc: Focuses on news of developments in the fiber optics industry, especially the uses of fiber optics in telecommunications. Includes information on contracts awarded, market intelligence, applications, upcoming events, and new technology. *Type:* Newsletter.

Fiberoptic Marketing Intelligence (FMI)

KMI Corp.
America's Cup Ave. at 31 Bridge   Ph: (401)849-6771
St.   Free: 800-343-4035
Newport, RI 02840   Fax: (401)847-5866
E-mail: info@kmicorp.com
URL: http://www.kmicorp.com
Contact: Kurt Ruderman, Editor.
Desc: Features news of international companies that are implementing the use of fiber optics and the emerging market for fiber optics. *Type:* Newsletter.

From the Ground Up

4621 Congress Dr.   Ph: (517)631-2333
Midland, MI 48642   Fax: (517)631-2359
E-mail: echutchi@aol.com.
Contact: Edward Hutchison, Author/Owner.
Desc: Distributes weekly and seasonal lawn and garden features. *Alt. Contact:* 4621 Congress Dr., Midland, MI 48642; telephone: (517)631-2333; fax: (517)631-2359. *Type:* Periodical.

Gary Stevens Associates

235 W. 56th St.   Ph: (212)265-8054
Ste. 11-B   Fax: (212)582-3152
New York, NY 10019
Contact: Gary Stevens, President; Jacqueline Gonzalez, Vice President.
Alt. Contact: 235 W. 56th St., Ste. 11-B, New York, NY 10019; telephone: (212)265-8054; fax: (212)582-3152. *Type:* Periodical.

General Mobile Radio Service National Repeater Guide

Personal Radio Steering Group
PO Box 2851   Ph: (734)662-4533
Ann Arbor, MI 48106
E-mail: prsg@provide.net
Contact: Corwin D. Moore, Jr., Editor.
Desc: About 4,000 repeaters. *Type:* Directory.

Glenmoor Enterprise Media Group

383 S. Main St.   Fax: (707)459-6027
Ste. 203
Willits, CA 91602
Contact: Ron C. Moorhead, General Mgr.
Desc: Distributes automotive, travel, and lifestyle news. *Alt. Contact:* 383 S. Main St., Ste. 203, Willits, CA 91602, (707)459-6027; fax: (707)459-6027. *Type:* Periodical.

Goddess Communications

847 A. Ave.   Ph: (212)631-3520
Ste. 171
New York, NY 10017
Contact: Laurie Sue Brockway, Editor.
Desc: Distributes articles on women, features for women, sex information column. *Alt. Contact:* 847 A. Ave., Ste. 171, New York, NY 10017; telephone: (212)631-3520. *Type:* Periodical.

Grammar Gremlins

PO Box 2121   Ph: (423)688-3400
Knoxville, TN 37901
Contact: Don K. Ferguson, Author.
Desc: Distributes grammar columns. *Alt. Contact:* PO Box 2121, Knoxville, TN 37901; telephone: (423)688-3400. *Type:* Periodical.

Groene & Groene

206 Lake Mamie Rd.   Ph: (904)736-0313
DeLand, FL 32724
Contact: Janet Groene, Writer.
Desc: Distributes columns on travel, food, automotive, and outdoors. *Alt. Contact:* 206 Lake Mamie Rd., DeLand, FL 32724; telephone: (904)736-0313. *Type:* Periodical.

Gulbranson Communications Group

5317 Spy Glass Dr.   Ph: (804)366-5224
Norfolk, VA 23518   Fax: (804)366-0661
E-mail: karen5@ix.netcom.com.
Contact: Karen Gulbranson, Principal.
Desc: Distributes humor/lifestyle column. *Alt. Contact:* 5317 Spy Glass Dr., Norfolk, VA 23518; telephone: (804)366-5224; fax: (804)366-0661. *Type:* Periodical.

Harvard Communications Update

Harvard Business School Press
Harvard Business School Publishing
60 Harvard Way   Ph: (617)495-6700
Boston, MA 02163   Free: 800-545-7685
    Fax: (617)496-8066
E-mail: custserv@hbsp.harvard.edu
URL: http://www.hbsp.harvard.edu; http://www.hbsp.harvard.edu.
Contact: Nick Morgan, Editor.
Desc: Provides information and techniques for managers on effective communication. *Type:* Newsletter.

Health Sciences Consortium

201 Silver Cedar Ct.   Ph: (919)942-8731
Chapel Hill, NC 27514   Fax: (919)942-3689
E-mail: jadcoxhsc@aol.com
Contact: Frank B. Penta, Ed.D., Exec.Dir.
Desc: Cooperative of health science institutions dedicated to publishing effective instructional materials at a low cost. Distributes audiovisual and computer-based instructional programs. *Type:* Association.

ICA Newsletter

International Communication Association (ICA)
PO Box 9589   Ph: (512)454-8299
Austin, TX 78766-9589   Fax: (512)451-6270
E-mail: icahdq@uts.cc.utexas.edu
Contact: Barbara C. Stooksberry, Editor, barbacs@aol.com.
Desc: Covers programs and people in communication studies worldwide. Recurring features include news of the Association and its members and a calendar of events. *Type:* Newsletter.

IDB Communications Group Inc.

10525 W. Washington Blvd.   Ph: (213)870-9000
Culver City, CA 90232   Fax: (213)240-3901
Contact: Jeffrey P. Sudkoff, Chmn. & CEO; Edward R. Cheramy, President; Peter F. Hartz, Sr. VP Marketing; Dave Anderson, VP Operations.
Alt. Contact: 10525 W. Washington Blvd., Culver City, CA 90232; telephone: (213)870-9000; fax: (213)240-3901. *Type:* Periodical.

ILA Listening Post

International Listening Association (ILA)
c/o Diana Corley Schnapp,   Ph: (913)685-9228
Exec. Dir.   Free: 800-452-4505
PO Box 25324   Fax: (913)685-9235
Shawnee Mission, KS 66225-
5324
E-mail: ilistening@aol.com
URL: http://www.listen.org.
Desc: Functions as the official newsletter of the Association, which promotes listening as an important communication tool. Furnishes pertinent information to professionals interested in listening development and research. *Type:* Newsletter.

In a Nutshell

119 Washington Ave.   Ph: (718)698-6979
Staten Island, NY 10314   Fax: (718)698-3535
E-mail: nutshell@h2net.net.
URL: http://www.h2net.net/p/nutshell.
Contact: Barbara Naness, Author/Owner.
Desc: Distributes humor column. *Alt. Contact:* 119 Washington Ave., Staten Island, NY 10314; telephone: (718)698-6979; fax: (718)698-3535. *Type:* Periodical.

The Information Advisor
Find/SVP
625 6th Ave.
New York, NY 10011
Ph: (212)645-4500
Free: 800-FIN-DSVP
Fax: (212)645-7681
E-mail: infoadvisor@findsvp.com
URL: http://www.findsvp.com/.
Contact: Robert I. Berkman, Editor, rberkman@javanet.com.
Desc: Supplies business data users information on comparing and evaluating competing information sources. Provides comparison charts, reviews, advice on data reliability, and quality for both online and print business information produced in the U.S., Europe, Asia, and Latin America. *Type:* Newsletter.

InfoTips on Ideas to Paper
Word Processing, Etc.
PO Box 47196
Oak Park, MI 48237
Ph: (810)548-5207
Contact: Barbara D. Malone, Editor.
Desc: Provides information for those who have ideas which need to be put to paper. Topics include word processing, writing, proofreading, and designing. *Type:* Newsletter.

Institute for the Transfer of Technology to Education
c/o National School Boards
Association
1680 Duke St.
Alexandria, VA 22314
Ph: (703)838-6722
Fax: (703)683-7590
E-mail: itte@nsba.org
URL: http://www.nsba.org/itte
Contact: Anne Bryant, Exec. Dir.
Desc: A program of the National School Boards Association . Seeks to educate policymakers, administrators, educators, manufacturers, and the public about the current status and future potential of technology in schools with the goal of creating a more effective education system. Established the Technology Leadership Network, which helps school districts and education service centers share experiences and aggregate their influence in dealing with technology developers. *Type:* Association.

Interactive Daily
Phillips Business Information, Inc.
1201 Seven Locks Rd., Ste. 300
Potomac, MD 20854
Ph: (301)340-1520
Free: 888-707-5809
Fax: (301)340-3847
E-mail: clientservices.pbi@phillips.com
Contact: Chris McCarter, Editor.
Desc: Discusses emerging technologies, electronic content, mergers/acqusitions, and partnerships. Also publishes a weekly report on platforms and technologies. *Type:* Newsletter.

Interactive Video News
Phillips Business Information, Inc.
1201 Seven Locks Rd., Ste. 300
Potomac, MD 20854
Ph: (301)340-1520
Free: 888-707-5809
Fax: (301)340-3847
E-mail: clientservices.pbi@phillips.com
Contact: Marvin V. Greene, Editor.
Desc: Reports on and analyzes new residential information and entertainment media and related business opportunities. *Type:* Newsletter.

Interconnect
Smiths Industries Aerospace
4141 Eastern Ave. SE
Grand Rapids, MI 49508-3469
Ph: (616)241-7000
Fax: (616)241-7858
Contact: Jennifer Villarreal, Editor.
Desc: Covers Smiths Industries news and events. *Type:* Newsletter.

International Association of Business Communicators
1 Hallidie Plz., Ste. 600
San Francisco, CA 94102
Ph: (415)433-3400
Fax: (415)362-8762
E-mail: leader_centre@iabc.com
URL: http://www.iabc.com
Contact: Elizabeth Allan, ABC, CAE Pres.,CEO.
Desc: Communication managers, public relations directors, writers, editors, audiovisual specialists, and others in the public relations and organizational communication field who use a variety of media to communicate with internal audiences (employees, management, association members, and leaders) and external audiences (media, customers, dealers, investors, and government). Conducts research in the communication field and encourages establishment of college-level programs in organizational communication. Offers accreditation program; conducts surveys on employee communication effectiveness and media trends. *Type:* Association.

International Communication Bulletin
College of Communication
University of Alabama
PO Box 870172
414-C Reese Phifer Hall
Tuscaloosa, AL 35487-0217
Ph: (205)348-7158
Fax: (205)348-2401
Contact: Yorgo Pasadeos, Editor.
Desc: "Devoted to news and research about international mass media systems and the theory and methodology of cross-cultural communication." Contains news of the communication division of the Association. Recurring features include lists conferences and seminars, recent publications, research centers, fellowships, grants, and bibliographies. *Type:* Newsletter.

Internet Week
CMP Media Inc.
600 Community Dr.
Manhasset, NY 11030
Ph: (516)562-5000
Fax: (516)562-7830
URL: http://www.cmp.net; http://www.internetwk.com.
Contact: Tom A. Smith, Exec. Dir., (516)562-7122, tasmith@cmp.com.
Desc: A networking newspaper. *Alt. Contact:* telephone: (516)562-5530; fax: (516)562-5055. *Type:* Periodical.

James Raia
2301 J St.
Ste. 205
Sacramento, CA 95816
Ph: (916)448-5122
Fax: (916)448-0205
E-mail: raiaruns@aol.com.
Contact: James Raia, Self-Syndicator.
Desc: Distributes running health and fitness column. *Alt. Contact:* 2301 J St., Ste. 205, Sacramento, CA 96816; telephone: (916)448-5122; fax: (916)448-0205. *Type:* Periodical.

Jan & Bill Moeller
4912 Hickory St.
Omaha, NE 68106
Ph: (402)553-3654
Contact: Jan Moeller, Author; Bill Moeller, Author.
Desc: Distributes travel, historical, and RVing columns. *Alt. Contact:* 4912 Hickory St., Omaha, NE 68106; telephone: (402)553-3654. *Type:* Periodical.

Janice Hubbard
400 North
500 West 7-8
Moab, UT 84532
Ph: (801)259-9139
E-mail: jahn@sisna.com.
Contact: Janice Hubbard, Self-Syndicator.
Desc: Distributes humor column, general interest features, articles, and essays. *Alt. Contact:* 400 North, 500 West 7-8, Moab, UT 84532; telephone: (801)259-9139. *Type:* Periodical.

Jerry D. Mead Enterprises
PO Box 1598
Carson City, NV 89702
Ph: (702)884-2648
Fax: (702)884-2484
E-mail: winetrader@aol.com.
URL: http://www.wines.com/ winetrader/.
Contact: Jerry D. Mead ED.
Desc: Distributes wine, food, and travel. *Alt. Contact:* PO Box 1598, Carson City, NV 89702; telephone: (702)884-2648; fax: (702)884-2484. *Type:* Periodical.

Joe Sharpnack
PO Box 3325
Iowa City, IA 52244
Ph: (319)644-2398
Alt. Contact: PO Box 3325, Iowa City, IA 52244; telephone: (319)644-2398. *Type:* Periodical.

Joseph Peter Simini
PO Box 31420
San Francisco, CA 94131-0420
Ph: (415)282-1950
Contact: Joseph Peter Simini, Self-Syndicator.
Desc: Distributes column on business and personal finance. *Alt. Contact:* PO Box 31420, San Francisco, CA 94131-0420; telephone: (415)282-1950. *Type:* Periodical.

Kagan Media Index
Paul Kagan Associates, Inc.
126 Clock Tower Pl.
Carmel, CA 93923
Ph: (831)624-1536
Fax: (831)625-3225
E-mail: info@kagan.com
Contact: George Niesen, Editor.
Desc: Analyzes the entertainment and electronic media, providing a comprehensive compilation of industry statistics for use in strategy and planning, investment decisions, marketing and advertising, and other related needs. Aims to publish "all the key financial market data you need to correlate historic and future media growth with the national and world economies." Recurring features include news briefs, stock market indexes, and industrial trade data. *Type:* Newsletter.

KCTS/Nine Magazine
KCTS Television
401 Mercer
Seattle, WA 98109
Ph: (206)728-6463
Fax: (206)443-6691
E-mail: mcing@kcts.org.
Contact: Paul Heppner, Advertising Dir., (206)443-0445.
Desc: Public television program guide. *Type:* Periodical.

Krebbs Cycle Productions
3940 Hilyard St.
Eugene, OR 97405
Ph: (503)344-3416
Fax: (503)344-3057
E-mail: pysamer@aol.com.
Contact: Yuri Samer, Author/Owner.
Alt. Contact: 3940 Hilyard St., Eugene, OR 97405; telephone: (503)344-3416; fax: (503)344-3057. *Type:* Periodical.

Landmark Designs Inc.
33127 Saginaw Rd. E
Cottage Grove, OR 97424
Ph: (541)767-0660
Free: 800-562-1041
Fax: (541)562-1041
E-mail: jamar@landmarkdesigns.com.
Contact: J.E. McAlexander, President; W.S. McAlexander, Vice President; M.J. McAlexander, Treas.
Desc: Distributes weekly home design column. *Alt. Contact:* 33127 Saginaw Rd. E, Cottage Grove, OR 97424; telephone: (541)767-0660; fax: (541)562-1041; toll-free: 800-562-1041. *Type:* Periodical.

Levin Represents
PO Box 5575
Santa Monica, CA 90409
Ph: (310)392-5146
Fax: (310)392-3856
Contact: Deborah Levin, President.

Desc: Distributes weekly single column cartoon. *Alt. Contact:* PO Box 5575, Santa Monica, CA 90409; telephone: (310)392-5146; fax: (310)392-3856. *Type:* Periodical.

LEXIS® Federal Communications Library
LEXIS-NEXIS
9443 Springboro Pike   Ph: (937)865-6800
PO Box 933
Dayton, OH 45401-0933
URL: http://www.lex-nexis.com
Desc: Contains Federal Communications Commission (FCC) materials including decisions, Reports, the FCC Daily Digest, Federal case law relevant to communications regulations, Title 47 of the U.S. Code Service and the Code of Federal Regulations, selected materials from the Federal Register, pending Federal legislation, communications Industry publications, Reports on the activities of Federal regulatory agencies and the Federal News Service. *Available:* LEXIS-NEXIS, LEXIS. *Type:* Database.

Listening Inc.
8716 Pine Ave.   Ph: (219)938-6962
Gary, IN 46403
E-mail: addup@crown.net.
Desc: Distributes parenting and family features including The Add Attention Deficit Disorder, Family Today, The Second Time Around, and The Divorced Family. *Alt. Contact:* 8716 Pine Ave., Gary, IN 46403; telephone: (219)938-6962. *Type:* Periodical.

Lister Hill National Center for Biomedical Communications
Natl. Library of Medicine   Ph: (301)496-4441
8600 Rockville Pike
Bethesda, MD 20894
Contact: Daniel Masys, M.D., Dir.
Desc: With the National Library of Medicine, conducts research and development programs in three categories: computer and information science used for the problems of medical libraries, biomedical research, and health care delivery; biomedical image engineering, including image acquisition, processing, storage, retrieval, and communications; and use of new technologies for health professions education. *Type:* Association.

Lona O'Connor
10887 Old Bridgeport Ln.   Ph: (561)487-5104
Boca Raton, FL 33498
E-mail: lona13@aol.com.
Contact: Lona O'Connor, Author.
Desc: Distributes workplace advice column. *Alt. Contact:* 10887 Old Bridgeport Ln., Boca Raton, FL 33498; telephone: (561)487-5104. *Type:* Periodical.

Mark-Morgan Inc.
14 E. Washington St.   Ph: (770)253-5355
Newnan, GA 30263
Contact: Robert David Boyd, President; Rosalyn M. Boyd, Sec./Treas.
Desc: Distributes political cartoons. *Alt. Contact:* 14 E. Washington St., Newnan, GA 30263; telephone: (770)253-5355. *Type:* Periodical.

The MarketPlace Project
566 Fairfield Rd.   Ph: (609)443-4012
East Windsor, NJ 08520   Fax: (609)443-9841
Contact: Lawrence H. Zisman, Author; Anabel Kligerman, Author.
Alt. Contact: 566 Fairfield Rd., East Windsor, NJ 08520; telephone: (609)443-4012; fax: (609)443-9841. *Type:* Periodical.

Marks & Frederick Associates Inc.
PO Box 267   Ph: (860)927-3948
Kent, CT 06757   Fax: (860)927-3959
E-mail: teetah@aol.com.
Contact: Ted Marks, President.
Desc: Distributes general news, international news, and financial information. *Alt. Contact:* PO Box 267, Kent, CT 06757; telephone: (860)927-3948; fax: (860)927-3959. *Type:* Periodical.

Masterfile
175 Bloor St. E.   Free: 800-387-9010
South Tower   Fax: (416)929-2104
2nd Fl.
Toronto, ON, Canada M4W 3R8
URL: http://www.masterfile.com.
Contact: Steve Pigeon, Pres./Gen. Mgr.
Alt. Contact: 175 Bloor St. E., South Tower, 2nd Fl., Toronto, ON, Canada M4W 3R8; fax: (416)929-2104; toll-free: 800-387-9010. *Type:* Periodical.

Media General News Service Inc.
1214 National Press Bldg.   Ph: (202)662-7660
Washington, DC 20045
Contact: John Hall, Bureau Chief.
Desc: Distributes general news. *Alt. Contact:* 1214 National Press Bldg., Washington, DC 20045; telephone: (202)662-7660. *Type:* Periodical.

Media Inc's Master Lists
Media Index Publishing Inc.
PO Box 24365   Ph: (206)382-9220
Seattle, WA 98124-0365   Fax: (206)382-9437
E-mail: media@media-inc.com
URL: http://www.media-inc.com
Contact: Richard K. Woltjer, Editor.
Desc: The Pacific Northwest's top media, marketing, and creative services companies and ranks the top ad agencies, film/video production companies, audio recording studios, and radio/TV stations in Oregon, and Washington. *Type:* Directory.

Media Industry Newsletter
Phillips Business Information, Inc.
1201 Seven Locks Rd., Ste. 300   Ph: (301)340-1520
Potomac, MD 20854   Free: 888-707-5809
   Fax: (301)340-3847
E-mail: clientservices.pbi@phillips.com
URL: http://www.phillipsbusinessinfo
Contact: Steven Cohn, Editor.
Desc: Covers the media industry, including advertising, marketing, publishing, radio, and television. Recurring features include weekly box scores of advertising pages in major magazines, salaries of top executives, earnings reports, and news of people in the industry. *Type:* Newsletter.

Media & the Law
SIMBA Information Inc.
11 River Bend Dr. S   Ph: (203)358-4100
PO Box 4234   Free: 800-307-2529
Stamford, CT 06907-0234   Fax: (203)358-5824
E-mail: simbainfo@simbanet.com
Desc: Provides legal information for those in the media. Includes news of pending and ongoing lawsuits, advice to reduce risk, and insight from experts. *Type:* Newsletter.

Media Matters
Media Dynamics, Inc.
18 E 41st St., No. 1806   Ph: (212)683-7895
New York, NY 10017-6222   Fax: (212)683-7684
E-mail: info@mediadynamicsinc.com

URL: http://www.mediadynamicsinc.com.
Contact: Edward Papazian, Editor.
Desc: Focuses on the media's role as opinion shapers and advertising vehicles. Relevant developments are monitored, and supported by analytical reports, trend data, forecasts, and suggestions for new directions. *Type:* Newsletter.

The Media Maven
3793 Plume Fern Ct.   Ph: (770)947-0117
Douglasville, GA 30135-2784
Contact: Howard Hopwood, Self-Syndicator.
Desc: Distributes column on entertainment, movies, and media. *Alt. Contact:* 3793 Plume Fern Ct., Douglasville, GA 30135-2784; telephone: (770)947-0117. *Type:* Periodical.

Media Mergers & Acquisitions
Paul Kagan Associates, Inc.
126 Clock Tower Pl.   Ph: (831)624-1536
Carmel, CA 93923   Fax: (831)625-3225
E-mail: info@kagan.com
Contact: George Niesen, Editor.
Desc: Evaluates merger and acquisition activity in the communications industry. Covers publishing, advertising, television, radio, and motion picture industries. *Type:* Newsletter.

Media Report to Women
Communication Research Associates, Inc.
10606 Mantz Rd.   Ph: (301)445-3231
Silver Spring, MD 20903-1228
Contact: Sheila Gibbons, Editor, sheilagib@aol.com.
Desc: Discusses Women's concerns about media. Carries documents and reports on women's actions worldwide in areas such as the employment of women in the media and the portrayal of women in the media. *Type:* Newsletter.

Megalo Media Inc.
PO Box 678   Ph: (212)535-6811
Syosset, NY 11791
Contact: J. Baxter Newgate, President; Sandy Applegreen, Ed./VP; Paul Merebloom, Assoc. Ed.
Alt. Contact: PO Box 678, Syosset, NY 11791; telephone: (212)535-6811. *Type:* Periodical.

Micrographics and Hybrid Imaging Systems Newsletter
Microfilm Publishing, Inc.
PO Box 950   Ph: (914)834-3044
Larchmont, NY 10538   Fax: (914)834-3993
E-mail: MNgreensht@aol.com; mngreensht@aol.com.
Contact: Mitchell M. Badler, Editor; Dorothy Miceli, Asst. Publisher-Editor.
Desc: Provides information about events, companies, and people in fields related to micrographics and hybrid imaging systems services, equipment, and business applications. Reports applications, new products, developments in technology, and government actions affecting micrographics and hybrid imaging. *Type:* Newsletter.

Mobile Phone News
Phillips Business Information, Inc.
1201 Seven Locks Rd., Ste. 300   Ph: (301)340-1520
Potomac, MD 20854   Free: 888-707-5809
   Fax: (301)340-3847
E-mail: clientservices.pbi@phillips.com
Contact: Aaryn Hypio-Slafky, Editor, ahypio@phillips.com; Joelle Martin, Publisher & Vice President.
Desc: Covers the marketing strategies, financial successes and failures, and regulation of cellular mobile telephone. *Type:* Newsletter.

Morality in Media

475 Riverside Dr., Rm. 239   Ph: (212)870-3222
New York, NY 10115   Fax: (212)870-2765
E-mail: mimnyc@ix.netcom.com
URL: http://www.netcom.com/~mimnyc
Contact: Robert W. Peters, Pres.
Desc: Works to "stop the illegal traffic in hardcore pornography constitutionally through vigorous enforcement of state and federal obscenity laws," and to uphold standards of decency in the media. Operates the National Obscenity Law Center, a clearinghouse of legal information on obscenity cases and materials for prosecutors and other interested attorneys. Holds annual White Ribbon Against Pornography (WRAP) Campaign and annual Turn Off TV Day. *Type:* Association.

Mountain Media

PO Box 4422   Ph: (702)870-3515
Las Vegas, NV 89127-4422
E-mail: vin@intermind.net.
URL: http://www.nguworld.com/ vindex/.
Contact: Vin Suprynowicz, President.
Desc: Distributes semiweekly political column. *Alt. Contact:* PO Box 4422, Las Vegas, NV 89127-4422; telephone: (702)870-3515. *Type:* Periodical.

Mullich Communications

908 W. Marshall St.   Ph: (610)279-5473
Norristown, PA 19401   Fax: (610)239-0843
E-mail: 74777.1235@compuserve.com.
Contact: Joe Mullich, Owner/Writer; John Breckenridge, Business Mgr.
Alt. Contact: 908 W. Marshall St., Norristown, PA 19401; telephone: (610)279-5473; fax: (610)239-0843. *Type:* Periodical.

Multicultural Link

Who's What & Where, Inc.
PO Box 4935
Huntsville, AL 35815-4935
Contact: Mary Bullard-Johnson, Editor.
Desc: Critiques and monitors the media. *Type:* Newsletter.

Multimedia Wire

Phillips Business Information, Inc.
1201 Seven Locks Rd., Ste. 300   Ph: (301)340-1520
Potomac, MD 20854   Free: 888-707-5809
    Fax: (301)340-3847
E-mail: clientservices.pbi@phillips.com
URL: http://www.mmwire.com.
Contact: Seth Arenstein, Managing Editor; Scott Nance, Reporter, snance@phillips.com.
Desc: Keeps abreast of the current news of the online multimedia interactive entertainment industries. Provides a weekly report on multimedia stocks. *Type:* Newsletter.

The Name Game Co. Inc.

401 SW 54th Ave.   Ph: (954)321-0032
Plantation, FL 33317   Free: 800-583-6056
    Fax: (954)321-8617
Contact: Melodye Hecht Icart, President; Mitchell J. Free, VP Sales & Dev.; Gary Zehner, Exec. Dir.
Desc: Distributes circulation and ad promotions contests. *Alt. Contact:* 401 SW 54th Ave., Plantation, FL 33317; telephone: (954)321-0032; fax: (954)321-8617; toll-free: 800-583-6056. *Type:* Periodical.

National Hispanic Media Coalition

3550 Wilshire Blvd., Ste. 670   Ph: (213)385-8574
Los Angeles, CA 90010   Fax: (213)384-1505
E-mail: anogales@earthlink.net
URL: http://www.nhmc.com
Contact: Alex Nogales, Chair.

Desc: Promotes the employment and image of Hispanic Americans in radio, television, and film. *Type:* Association.

North America

Syndicate 216 E. 45th St.   Ph: (212)455-4000
New York, NY 10017   Free: 800-526-5464
Contact: Joseph F. D'Angelo, President; Jay Kennedy, Comics Ed.; Lawrence T. Olsen, Exec. VP & Gen. Mgr.; Ted Hannah, Dir. Adv. & PR; Paul G. Eberhart, Dir. Ops.; Maria Carmicino, Managing Editor; Richard P. Heimlich, Asst. Sales Mgr.; John Killian, Asst. Sales Mgr./Midwest Sales; Dick Lafave, Southwest Sales; John Perry, Southeast Sales; George Haeberlein, Sales Mgr.; James F. Nolan, Color Comics Mgr.; Jack Walsh, Dir. Print Sales; Richard Wilson, Weekly Serv. Natl. Sales Dir.; Dian
Desc: Distributes automotive, business, and personal finance commentary; entertainment, humor, lifestyle, advice, mental and physical fitness, and sports features; comic strips, graphic services, games, and puzzles. Part of King Features Syndicate Inc. *Alt. Contact:* Syndicate 216 E. 45th St., New York, NY 10017; telephone: (212)455-4000; toll-free: 800-526-5464. *Type:* Periodical.

ONSAT

Triple D Publishing, Inc.
1300 S. Dekalb St.   Ph: (704)482-9673
PO Box 2347   Free: 800-234-0021
Shelby, NC 28152   Fax: (704)484-6976
E-mail: onsat@tripled.com.
URL: http://tripled.com.
Contact: Jim H. Cothran, Editor, jcothran@tripled.com; Douglas G. Brown, Publisher, (704)484-7301, bway@tripled.com; David Melton, Editor, (704)482-9673, dmelton@tripled.com; Nelli Williams, Advertising Mgr., (704)484-7307, fax: (704)484-7335, nwilliams@tripled.
Desc: Weekly programming guide. *Alt. Contact:* PO Box 167, Shelby, NC 28151; telephone: (704)484-7305; fax: (704)484-8558. *Type:* Periodical.

Plexers Inc.

3827 Los Santos Dr.   Ph: (916)677-3632
Cameron Park, CA 95682-8601
Contact: Joe Scales, President; Thomas J. Lester, V; David Hammond, Treas.
Desc: Distributes word puzzles. *Alt. Contact:* 3827 Los Santos Dr., Cameron Park, CA 95682-8601; telephone: (916)677-3632. *Type:* Periodical.

PrimeTime

PrimeTime Publishing Inc.
5308 Calgary Trl.   Ph: (403)434-7424
Edmonton, AB, Canada T6H   Fax: (403)437-0123
4J8
Contact: Karen Paulgaard, Editor, (403)434-7424, fax: (403)437-0123; Harold Roozen, Publisher.
Desc: Magazine for Western Canadian pay TV subscribers. *Type:* Periodical.

Primeurs

Feature Publishing Ltd.
2100 St. Catherine St. W., 10th   Ph: (514)939-5036
Fl.   Fax: (514)939-1515
Montreal, PQ, Canada H3H
2T3
E-mail: editor@feature.ca
Contact: Mireille Du Hamel, Director; Marvin Boisvert, Pres./Publisher; Nathalie Abitbol, Distribution Supervisor.
Desc: Magazine of specialty channel programming for cable TV subscribers (French). *Type:* Periodical.

Print Marketing Concepts

10590 Westoffice Dr.   Ph: (713)780-7055
Ste. 250   Fax: (713)780-9731
Houston, TX 77042
Contact: Charles Dye, President; Robin L. Good, VP-Natl. Sales; Nancy Kissman, Controller.
Alt. Contact: 10590 Westoffice Dr., Ste. 250, Houston, TX 77042; telephone: (713)780-7055; fax: (713)780-9731. *Type:* Periodical.

PTR

Pacific Telecommunications Council
2454 S. Beretania St., Ste. 302   Ph: (808)941-3789
Honolulu, HI 96826-1596   Fax: (808)944-4874
E-mail: info@ptc.org
URL: http://www.ptc.org; http://www.ptc.org.
Contact: Richard Nickelson, Editor, richard@ptc.org.
Desc: Provides analytical articles on telecommunications broadcasting and informatics in or affecting the Asia-Pacific region. Covers international policy issues, industry trends, and telecommunication and convergence industry technology. *Type:* Newsletter.

QST

American Radio Relay League, Inc.
225 Main St.   Ph: (860)594-0200
Newington, CT 06111   Fax: (860)594-0259
E-mail: qst@arrl.org; hqcarrl.org.
Contact: Mark Wilson, Editor; Hanan Suleiman, Advertising Mgr.
Desc: Amateur radio magazine. *Type:* Periodical.

REACT Team Contact Directory

Radio Emergency Associated Communications Teams (REACT) International, Inc.
5210 Auth Rd., Ste. 403
Suitland, MD 20746
Contact: Deanne Earwood, Editor.
Desc: Approximately 650 teams that monitor citizen's band radio Channel 9 for local emergencies. *Type:* Directory.

Rich Markgraf

1830 Ave. del Mundo   Ph: (619)435-2514
No. 1107
Coronado, CA 92118
Contact: Richard Markgraf, Self-Syndicator.
Desc: Distributes weekly humor columns. *Alt. Contact:* 1830 Ave. del Mundo, No. 1107, Coronado, CA 92118; telephone: (619)435-2514. *Type:* Periodical.

Richard Kolkman

PO Box 68256   Ph: (317)858-0630
Indianapolis, IN 46268
E-mail: bigflatcit@aol.com.
Contact: Richard Kolkman, Cartoonist.
Desc: Distributes weekly comic strip. *Alt. Contact:* PO Box 68256, Indianapolis, IN 46268; telephone: (317)858-0630. *Type:* Periodical.

Richard Lynn Enterprises

3741 N. 400 E   Ph: (219)782-2345
Lagro, IN 46941
Contact: R.J. Lynn, President.
Desc: Distributes educational daily cartoon strip. *Alt. Contact:* 3741 N. 400 E, Lagro, IN 46941; telephone: (219)782-2345. *Type:* Periodical.

Sam Mantics Enterprise

PO Box 7727   Ph: (415)854-3132
Menlo Park, CA 94026   Fax: (415)854-9698
URL: http://syndicate.com.

Contact: Carey Orr Cook, Pres./Cartoon Ed., corrcook@ syndicate.com; Kylie Cook, Internet/WWW Ed.; Rich Encounter, Graphic Artist.

Alt. Contact: PO Box 7727, Menlo Park, CA 94026; telephone: (415)854-3132; fax: (415)854-9698. *Type:* Periodical.

Satellite News

Phillips Business Information, Inc.
1201 Seven Locks Rd., Ste. 300   Ph: (301)340-1520
Potomac, MD 20854   Free: 888-707-5809
      Fax: (301)340-3847
E-mail: clientservices.pbi@phillips.com
URL: http://www.phillips.com.
Contact: Paul Dykewicz, Editor, fax: (301)424-2709, pdykewicz@phillips.com; David Bross, Publisher.

Desc: Provides business insights and analysis into the commercial satellite industry including new satellite applications, developing technologies, and unfolding partnerships. Recurring features include columns titled Satellite Spotlight, DBS News, Satellite News, Newsmaker Interiews, Satellite Circuit, and Satellite News Financial Ticker. *Type:* Newsletter.

Satellite Orbit

Commtek Communications Corp.
8330 Boone Blvd., Ste. 600   Ph: (703)827-0511
Vienna, VA 22182-2624   Fax: (703)356-6179
E-mail: satorbit@aol.com.
Contact: Phillip Swann, Publisher; David G. Wolford, Chairman of the Board; John Misrasi, President.

Desc: Magazine devoted to entertainment and home satellite television listings. *Type:* Periodical.

Satellite Week

Warren Publishing, Inc.
2115 Ward Ct. NW   Ph: (202)872-9200
Washington, DC 20037   Fax: (202)296-4397
E-mail: warrenpub@mindspring.com
URL: http://www.telecommunications.com
Contact: Terry Banks, Managing Editor.

Desc: Presents the latest developments in satellite broadcasting, telecommunications, earth observation, and space industrialization. Reports new technology and regulation of the industry. *Type:* Newsletter.

Science Communications

5318 Stirling Ct.
Newark, CA 94650-1352
Contact: Pat Kite, Writer/Ed.

Desc: Distributes gardening column. *Alt. Contact:* 5318 Stirling Ct., Newark, CA 94650-1352. *Type:* Periodical.

Screening Room

PO Box 2236   Ph: (413)442-1256
Pittsfield, MA 01202-2236   Fax: (413)443-2445
Contact: Jonathan Levine, Self-Syndicator.

Alt. Contact: PO Box 2236, Pittsfield, MA 01202-2236; telephone: (413)442-1256; fax: (413)443-2445. *Type:* Periodical.

Shetland Productions

4679 Goodland Park Rd.   Ph: (608)222-5522
Madison, WI 53711
URL: http://www.msn.fullfeed.com/muskrat.
Contact: Eleanor Williams, Editor; Alexander Schiller, Office Mgr.; Robert Kovalic, Business Mgr.; Becky Weiner, Associate Ed.

Alt. Contact: 4679 Goodland Park Rd., Madison, WI 53711; telephone: (608)222-5522. *Type:* Periodical.

Singer Media Corp.

Seaview Business Park   Ph: (714)498-7227
1030 Calle Cordillera No. 106   Fax: (714)498-2162
San Clemente, CA 92673
E-mail: singer@deltanet.com.
Contact: Helen J. Lee, Vice President; Mayra Gomez, Licensing Dir. West; Lynnette In, Licensing Dir. East.

Desc: Distributes features on celebrities, health, fitness, business, and women's issues. *Alt. Contact:* Seaview Business Park, 1030 Calle Cordillera No. 106, San Clemente, CA 92673; telephone: (714)498-7227; fax: (714)498-2162. *Type:* Periodical.

Small Talk

45 Commonwealth Ave.   Ph: (617)267-1396
Boston, MA 02116
Contact: Alan H. Kelly, Jr., Creative Dir.; Frances Kelly, Talent.

Desc: Distributes comic single panel. *Alt. Contact:* 45 Commonwealth Ave., Boston, MA 02116; telephone: (617)267-1396. *Type:* Periodical.

Society for Technical Communication

901 N. Stuart St., Ste. 904   Ph: (703)522-4114
Arlington, VA 22203-1854   Fax: (703)522-2075
E-mail: stc@stc-va.org
URL: http://www.stc-va.org
Contact: William C. Stolgitis, Exec.Dir./Counsel.

Desc: Writers, editors, educators, scientists, engineers, artists, publishers, and others professionally engaged in or interested in some phase of the field of technical communication; companies, corporations, organizations, and agencies interested in the aims of the society. Seeks to advance the theory and practice of technical communication in all media. *Type:* Association.

Southern California Focus

1720 Oak St.   Ph: (213)452-3918
Santa Monica, CA 90405
E-mail: tdelias@aol.com.
Contact: Thomas Elias, Author.

Desc: Distributes general news, politics, and sports columns. *Alt. Contact:* 1720 Oak St., Santa Monica, CA 90405; telephone: (213)452-3918. *Type:* Periodical.

Southern Educational Communications Association

PO Box 50008   Ph: (803)799-5517
Columbia, SC 29250   Fax: (803)771-4831
Contact: Skip Hinton, President.

Alt. Contact: PO Box 50008, Columbia, SC 29250; telephone: (803)799-5517; fax: (803)771-4831. *Type:* Periodical.

Speaker's Idea File

Lawrence Ragan Communications, Inc.
212 W. Superior St., Ste. 200   Ph: (312)335-0037
Chicago, IL 60610   Free: 800-878-5331
      Fax: (312)573-3730
Contact: Lawrence Ragan, Editor.

Desc: Provides quotes, tips, and secrets for presentations and speeches. Supplies how-to articles, trends, forecasts, stories, anecdotes, and statistics. *Type:* Newsletter.

Speaking of Soaps Inc.

331 Boyle Ave.   Ph: (201)790-1582
Totowa, NJ 07512   Fax: (201)790-1936
Alt. Contact: 331 Boyle Ave., Totowa, NJ 07512; telephone: (201)790-1582; fax: (201)790-1936. *Type:* Periodical.

Spectrum Multilanguage Communications— Spectrum Newsletter

Spectrum Multilanguage Communications
225 W. 39th St.   Ph: (212)391-3940
New York, NY 10018   Fax: (212)921-5246
E-mail: 76046.2123@compuserve.com
Contact: Richard N. Weltz, Editor.

Desc: Includes articles and information relevant to multinational and multilanguage advertising, marketing, and graphics. Emphasizes the uses of foreign language typography and discusses languages and communications in general. *Type:* Newsletter.

Stamping Grounds

25 E. Penn St.   Ph: (516)431-6697
PO Box 632
Long Beach, NY 11561
Contact: Joseph Zollman, Owner/Author.

Desc: Distributes educational information for stamp collectors and columns concerning stamp history. *Alt. Contact:* 25 E. Penn St., PO Box 632, Long Beach, NY 11561; telephone: (516)431-6697. *Type:* Periodical.

Starweek Magazine

Toronto Star Newspapers Ltd.
1 Yonge St., 5th Fl.   Ph: (416)367-2000
Toronto, ON, Canada M5E
1E6
Contact: Julie Lefebure, Director; Marc Ouimet, Editor-in-Chief; Leonie Marin, Publicity; Kim Zarrazin Gjerstad, Technincal Director; Guillame Marcille, Editor; Jonathan Lauallee, Editor; Marie-Andree Girard, Editor; Alec Castonguay, Editor; Guillame Forest, Photographer; Anne-Marie Pelletier, Correcter.

Desc: TV magazine. *Type:* Periodical.

The Strategist

1300 3rd St. S   Ph: (941)434-5555
Ste. 203E   Fax: (941)434-5604
Naples, FL 34102
URL: http://www.thestrategist.com.
Contact: Alan Legatz, Proprietor, alanlegatz@olsusa.com; Janet Long, Asst.; Angela Krape, Asst.

Alt. Contact: 1300 3rd St. S, Ste. 203E, Naples, FL 34102; telephone: (941)434-5555; fax: (941)434-5604. *Type:* Periodical.

Sylvia Di Pietro

55 W. 14th St.   Ph: (212)255-4059
Ste. 4-H   Fax: (212)255-4059
New York, NY 10011
E-mail: qbly@prodigy.com.
Contact: Sylvia Di Pietro, Self-Syndicator.

Desc: Distributes column on children, romance, career, and finance. *Alt. Contact:* 55 W. 14th St., Ste. 4-H, New York, NY 10011; telephone: (212)255-4059; fax: (212)255-4059. *Type:* Periodical.

Taming the Workplace

3003 14th Ave. W   Ph: (206)284-9566
Ste. 201   Fax: (206)282-5183
Seattle, WA 98119
E-mail: mrscribe@aol.com.
Contact: Eric L. Zoeckler, Columnist.

Desc: Distributes weekly column on workplace issues. *Alt. Contact:* 3003 14th Ave. W, Ste. 201, Seattle, WA 98119; telephone: (206)284-9566; fax: (206)282-5183. *Type:* Periodical.

Ted Larsen Media

96 Columbus Ave.   Ph: (508)741-3916
Salem, MA 01970   Fax: (508)741-3916
E-mail: tlmedia@aol.com.

Contact: Ted Larsen, Editor and Publisher.

Desc: Distributes weekly column on seasonal food, travel, and wine recipes. *Alt. Contact:* 96 Columbus Ave., Salem, MA 01970; telephone: (508)741-3916; fax: (508)741-3916. *Type:* Periodical.

TimesFax: A Unique Digest of The New York Times

New York Times Information Services Group
122 E. 42nd St., 14th Fl.   Fax: (212)499-3436
New York, NY 10168
URL: http://www.nytimesfax.com
Contact: Erik Adler, Web Master, webmaster@nytimesfax.com.

Desc: TimesFax is a service offered by the New York Times, providing an eight-page synopsis of this paper via fax. This site allows users to subscribe to this service and also provides specific delivery information, a sample copy, and staff data. *Type:* Database.

Trade Service Corp.

10996 Torreyana Rd.   Ph: (619)457-5920
San Diego, CA 92121   Fax: (619)457-4923
Contact: J. A. Simpson, President; A.M. Dubreville, Exec. VP/CFO; D.T. Fleming, Exec. VP.
Alt. Contact: 10996 Torreyana Rd., San Diego, CA 92121; telephone: (619)457-5920; fax: (619)457-4923. *Type:* Periodical.

Video Event

Connell Communications Inc.
86 Elm St.   Ph: (603)924-7271
Peterborough, NH 03458-1052   Fax: (603)924-7013
Contact: Melissa Stephenson, Editor, mstephenson@ceiweb.com; T. James Connell, Publisher; Matt Redd, Advertising Mgr.

Desc: Magazine serving the video retail and consumer marketplace. *Type:* Periodical.

Western Association News—Speakers and Speakers Bureau Directory Issue

Schneider Publishing Co.
13274 Fiji Way, 4th Fl.   Ph: (310)577-3700
Marina del Rey, CA 90292   Fax: (310)577-3715
E-mail: info@schneiderpublishing.com; ann@schneiderpublishing.com; sandi@schneiderpublishing.com; jennifer@schneiderpublishing.com.
Contact: Timothy Schneider, Editor.

Desc: List of speakers and speakers' bureaus available for association meetings in the western United States, including Hawaii, Texas, Alaska, and Canada. *Type:* Directory.

WETA Magazine

WETA Publishing
Box 2626   Ph: (703)845-8085
Washington, DC 20013-2626   Fax: (703)998-3412
Contact: Pat Good, Editor, (703)845-8084, pgood@weta.com; Ingrid Bond, Advertising Mgr.

Desc: Member magazine of public television channel 26 and radio station WETA/FM 91 in the metropolitan Washington, DC area. *Type:* Periodical.

What's Brewing

160 Dexter Ave.   Ph: (203)235-1758
Meriden, CT 06450   Fax: (203)639-0210
Contact: Jim Zebora, Self-Syndicator, jimzbrewer@aol.com.

Desc: Distributes information on beer and brewing. *Alt. Contact:* 160 Dexter Ave., Meriden, CT 06450; telephone: (203)235-1758; fax: (203)639-0210. *Type:* Periodical.

What's Up Information Services

1200 Ashwood Pkwy.   Ph: (404)671-0200
No. 575   Fax: (404)671-0110
Atlanta, GA 30338
Contact: Richard Warner, President; Steven Kelman, VP Sales; Lynn Lebreton, VP Tech.; Malenka Warner, Vice President; Adam Brown, Dir. Internet Mktg.

Desc: Distributes press releases. *Alt. Contact:* 1200 Ashwood Pkwy., No. 575, Atlanta, GA 30338; telephone: (404)671-0200; fax: (404)671-0110. *Type:* Periodical.

White Castle Communications

PO Box 295   Ph: (860)567-5336
Morris, CT 06763   Fax: (860)567-5336
Contact: William Clifford, Owner/Ed.

Desc: Distributes column on wine food and travel. *Alt. Contact:* PO Box 295, Morris, CT 06763; telephone: (860)567-5336; fax: (860)567-5336. *Type:* Periodical.

Who's Who in the Media and Communications

Marquis Who's Who
Reed Elsevier
121 Chanlon Rd.   Ph: (908)464-6800
New Providence, NJ 07974   Free: 800-521-8110
    Fax: (908)771-8645
E-mail: info@marquiswhoswho.com

Desc: More than 18,500 professionals in print journalism, broadcasting, publishing, television, public relations, advertising, radio, telecommunications, interactive multimedia, and education. *Type:* Directory.

William A. Alan

26 McKelvey Ave.   Ph: (412)242-2332
Pittsburgh, PA 15218
Contact: William A. Alan, Columnist.

Desc: Distributes business/industry economic news, especially automotive data. *Alt. Contact:* 26 McKelvey Ave., Pittsburgh, PA 15218; telephone: (412)242-2332. *Type:* Periodical.

Wireless Market Stats

Paul Kagan Associates, Inc.
126 Clock Tower Pl.   Ph: (831)624-1536
Carmel, CA 93923   Fax: (831)625-3225
E-mail: info@kagan.com
Contact: George Niesen, Editor.

Desc: Covers metropolitan and rural cellular telephone market efficiency, plus operating statistics, economic and demographic data for cellular, PCs, ESMP, and paging. *Type:* Newsletter.

Working Communicator

Lawrence Ragan Communications, Inc.
212 W. Superior St., Ste. 200   Ph: (312)335-0037
Chicago, IL 60610   Free: 800-878-5331
    Fax: (312)573-3730
Contact: John Cowan, Editor.

Desc: Offers news and information intended to improve the communication skills of individuals within organizations. Covers writing, editing, designing, photography, speech writing, lecturing, letter and report writing, direct mail, advertising, and sales promotion techniques. *Type:* Newsletter.

Worldwide Videotex Update

Worldwide Videotex
PO Box 3273   Ph: (561)738-2276
Boynton Beach, FL 33424-3273
URL: http://www.wvpubs.com

Desc: Reports on electronic mail, online services, satellite communication, videotex, teleconferencing, teletext, and other television related technologies. Focuses on information of interest to marketers. *Type:* Newsletter.

Writers Guild of America, East Newsletter

Writers Guild of America, East
555 W. 57th St.   Ph: (212)767-7800
New York, NY 10019   Fax: (212)582-1909
URL: http://www.wgaeast.org.
Contact: Alex Goldstein, Editor.

Desc: Contains news of importance to members of the Writers Guild, East, a union representing writers in the motion picture, television, and radio industries. Provides articles on union activities, contract negotiations, union benefits, industry developments, and personal items. *Type:* Newsletter.

Community Development

ACCION International

120 Beacon St.   Ph: (617)492-4930
Somerville, MA 02143   Fax: (617)876-9509
E-mail: info@accion.org
URL: http://www.accion.org
Contact: Robin Ratcliffe, VP & Dept. Mgr.

Desc: Provides financial services to the self-employed poor in 15 Latin American countries and 9 U.S. cities. Works to reduce poverty and unemployment by providing loans and business support to microentrepreneurs in low-income communities through a network of affiliated institutions. *Type:* Association.

Big Lakes Regional Council

200 Southwind Pl., Ste. 202   Ph: (785)776-4859
Manhattan, KS 66503-3186   Fax: (785)776-1646
Contact: J. Everett Mitchell, Exec. Dir.

Desc: Regional planning and community development agency. Conducts economic, housing, and environmental programs. *Type:* Association.

Capital Area Planning Council

2512 Interstate Hwy. 35 S., Ste.   Ph: (512)443-7653
220   Fax: (512)443-7658
Austin, TX 78704
E-mail: betty.voights@mail.capnet.state.tx.us
Contact: Betty Voights, Exec.Dir.
Type: Association.

Center for Community Action of B'Nai Birth International

1640 Rhode Island Ave. NW   Ph: (202)857-6582
Washington, DC 20036   Fax: (202)857-1099
E-mail: cca@bnaibrith.org
URL: http://www.bnaibrith.org/
Contact: Rhonda Love, Exec.Dir.

Desc: A department of B'nai B'rith International . Works to resolve social problems such as hunger and poverty through community service; encourages and trains members to become community volunteers. Sponsors food drives, voter registration campaigns, and nursing home visitation services. *Type:* Association.

Center for Neighborhood Technology

2125 W. North Ave.   Ph: (773)278-4800
Chicago, IL 60647   Fax: (773)278-3840
E-mail: info@cnt.org
URL: http://www.cnt.org
Contact: Scott Bernstein, Pres.

Desc: Formulates public policy recommendations on community development and the environment and carries out demonstration projects that foster sustainable communities. *Type:* Association.

Central Savannah River Area Planning and Development Commission
2123 Wrightsboro Rd.   Ph: (706)737-1823
PO Box 2800   Fax: (706)737-1459
Augusta, GA 30914-2800
URL: http://www.csrardc.org
Contact: Timothy F. Maund, Exec. Dir.
Type: Association.

City Hostess International
Desc: Owners of independent local welcoming services. Such organizations call on newcomers, acquaint them with facts about the city, and give them gifts and gift certificates for free services or products supplied by sponsoring merchants. Each service sponsors a club for newcomers. *Type:* Association.

Community Associations Institute
1630 Duke St.   Ph: (703)548-8600
Alexandria, VA 22314   Fax: (703)684-1581
URL: http://www.caionline.org
Contact: Barbara Byrd-Keenan, CAE, Pres.
Desc: Condominium and homeowner associations, cooperatives, and association-governed planned communities of all sizes and architectural types; community or property managers and management firms; individual homeowners; community association managers and management firms; public officials; and lawyers, accountants, engineers, reserve specialists, builder/developers and other providers of professional services and products for CAs. Seeks to educate and represent America's 205,000 residential condominium, cooperative and homeowner associations and related professionals and service providers. *Type:* Association.

Delaware Valley Regional Planning Commission
Bourse Bldg., 8th Fl.   Ph: (215)592-1800
111 S. Independence Mall E. Fax: (215)592-9125
Philadelphia, PA 19106
URL: http://www.dvrpc.org/
Contact: John J. Coscia, Exec. Dir.
Desc: Members and alternates; state and local officials, State DOT's (NJ and PA) Governor's Office, Office of Community Affairs, city officials, non-voting members; FHWA, HUD, transit authorities, port authority, FTA, USEPA, citizens committee. *Type:* Association.

East Alabama Regional Planning and Development Commission
PO Box 2186   Ph: (205)237-6741
Anniston, AL 36202   Fax: (205)237-6763
E-mail: earpdc@earpdc.org
Contact: James W. Curtis, Exec. Dir.
Type: Association.

Independence Plan for Neighborhood Councils
201 W. Maple   Ph: (816)833-4225
Independence, MO 64050   Fax: (816)833-4251
Contact: Bob Bruch, Pres.
Desc: Objectives are to act as a model group for communities worldwide and promote community leadership by pooling human resources for neighborhood and community development. *Type:* Association.

Institute for Community Economics
57 School St.   Ph: (413)746-8660
Springfield, MA 01105   Fax: (413)746-8862
E-mail: iceonomic@aol.com
Contact: Carol Lewis, Dir. of Admin. & Personnel.
Desc: Provides technical and organizational assistance and low cost financing to community-based groups such as community land trusts (CLTs), community loan funds (CLFs), and limited-equity housing cooperatives; these groups in turn help rural and urban low-income communities gain access to land, housing, and capital and other resources. Operates Revolving Loan Fund to aid community-based nonprofit organizations such as CLTs and other non-profit housing organizations. *Type:* Association.

Institute for Sustainable Communities
56 College St.   Ph: (802)229-2900
Montpelier, VT 05602   Fax: (802)228-2919
E-mail: iso@iscvt.org
Contact: George Hamilton, Exec.Dir.
Desc: Environmental protection and community development organizations. Promotes sustainable economic development that responds to local needs and is supportable by local infrastructure and administrative capabilities. *Type:* Association.

Nashua Regional Planning Commission
115 Main St.   Ph: (603)883-0366
PO Box 847   Fax: (603)883-6572
Nashua, NH 03061
E-mail: staff@nashuarpc.com
URL: http://www.nashuarpc.org
Contact: Andrew Singelakis, Exec.Dir.
Desc: Organization the provides planning services to member communities. Addresses inter and intra regional issues. *Type:* Association.

National Association for the Southern Poor
712A 3rd St. SW   Ph: (202)554-3265
Washington, DC 20024-3104   Fax: (202)488-0735
E-mail: naspoor@aol.com
Contact: Donald Anderson, Exec.Dir.
Desc: Black, low-income individuals in Virginia, North Carolina, South Carolina, and Georgia, Mississippi, Illinois, Ohio, Washington, D.C., Chicago, and Cleveland. Seeks to create local organizations, known as Assemblies, through which low-income people can become involved in local decision-making regarding community services and opportunities. *Type:* Association.

National Black Media Coalition
PO Box 10310   Ph: (301)593-3600
Silver Spring, MD 20914-0310 Fax: (301)593-3604
Contact: Carmen Marshall, Exec.Dir.
Desc: Black media advocacy group seeking to maximize media access for blacks and other minorities in the communications industry through employment, ownership, and programming. Has been recognized by the FCC, Congress, and trade organizations concerned with blacks and other minorities in the media. Past activities include participating in FCC rulemaking proceedings, speaking before university and professional audiences, conducting classes, and negotiating affirmative action plans with large media corporations. *Type:* Association.

National Center for Neighborhood Enterprise
1424 16th St. NW, Ste. 300   Ph: (202)518-6500
Washington, DC 20036   Fax: (202)588-0314
E-mail: info@ncne.com
URL: http://www.ncne.com
Contact: Robert L. Woodson, Sr., Pres.
Desc: Empowers neighborhood leaders to promote solutions that reduce crime and violence, restore families, revitalize low-income communities and create economic enterprise. Provides training, technical assistance, public policy initiatives, and linkages to sources of support. *Type:* Association.

National Congress for Community Economic Development
1030 15th St., Ste. 325   Ph: (202)289-9020
Washington, DC 20005   Fax: (202)289-7051
URL: http://www.ncced.org
Contact: Roy Priest, Pres. & CEO.
Desc: Community development corporations, community action agencies, and rural co-ops involved in community economic development. Provides a national program of promotion, partnership, and assistance for organizations in community-based economic development; monitors legislative issues. *Type:* Association.

Northern Virginia Planning District Commission
7535 Little River Tpke., Ste. Ph: (703)642-0700
  100   Fax: (703)642-5077
Annandale, VA 22003
E-mail: info@NVPDC.state.va.us
URL: http://www.NVPDC.state.va.us
Contact: G. Mark Gibb, Exec. Dir.
Desc: The Northern Virginia Planning District Commission is an organization of local governments in Northern Virginia, created in 1969 to promote the physical, social and economic development of the region in an orderly and efficient manner. Member jurisdictions are Arlington, Fairfax, Loudoun, and Prince William Counties; the cities of Alexandria, Falls Church, Manassas, and Manassas Park; and the Towns of Dumfries, Herndon, Leesburg and Vienna. *Type:* Association.

South Alabama Regional Planning Commission
651 Church St.   Ph: (334)433-6541
PO Box 1665   Fax: (334)433-6009
Mobile, AL 36602
E-mail: russwimberly@sarpe.org
URL: http://www.sarpc.org
Contact: Russell J. Wimberly, Exec. Dir.
Desc: /County Governments and municipalities therein. *Type:* Association.

Computer Science

Adrenalin Labs
CalWeb Internet Services
1111 Howe Ave., Ste. 300   Ph: (916)641-9320
Sacramento, CA 95825   Free: 800-509-9322
                             Fax: (916)641-9329
E-mail: info@calweb.com
URL: http://www.calweb.com/~dstoflet/index.html
Contact: Darryl Stoflet, dstoflet@calweb.com.
Desc: This virtual laboratory has some pretty nifty net experiments for you to enjoy, and even play with yourself. Most of the examples, requiring newer versions of either Netscape or MSIE browsers, show some innovative ways to manipulate the way you present your web pages in several different web-based languages. *Type:* Database.

American Computer Scientists Association
Daniel Louis Grossman, Esq.
11 Commerce Dr., 3rd Fl.   Ph: (908)272-0016
Cranford, NJ 07016-3531   Fax: (908)272-6297
URL: http://www.acsa2000.net/1996b2.html
Contact: Daniel Louis Grossman, Esq.
Desc: Works for computer scientists. *Type:* Association.

American Programmer
Cutter Information Corporation
37 Broadway, Ste. 1   Ph: (781)648-8702
Arlington, MA 02174-5552   Free: 800-325-3717
                             Fax: (781)648-1950
E-mail: klovering@cutter.com
Contact: Ed Yourdon, Editor; Ann Farbman, Marketing Mgr.

Desc: Technical journal focusing on various IT topics. Recurring features include articles written by field experts. *Type:* Newsletter.

APL Quote Quad

Association for Computing Machinery
1515 Broadway   Ph: (212)869-7440
New York, NY 10036   Free: 800-342-6626
E-mail: acmhelp@acm.org

Contact: Jon McGrew, Editor.

Desc: Facilitates the exchange of information on APL programming language among its users and developers. Recurring features include news of research, Group reports, news of members, and a calendar of events. *Type:* Newsletter.

Association for Computing Machinery

Association for Computing Machinery
1515 Broadway   Ph: (212)869-7440
One Astor Plaza   Fax: (212)944-1318
New York, NY 10036-5701
E-mail: acmhelp@acm.org
URL: http://www.acm.org/

Desc: This well-built site offers membership info, a large list of online publications, Chapter activities and contests for programmers, career enhancement and employment opportunities, as well as a calendar of conferences and events and several links devoted to serving the community through the technical outreach program. *Type:* Database.

Asterisk Journal of Documentation

Association for Computing Machinery
1515 Broadway   Ph: (212)869-7440
New York, NY 10036   Free: 800-342-6626
E-mail: acmhelp@acm.org

Contact: T.R. Girill, Editor.

Desc: Contains announcements and reports about international conferences on systems documentation. Examines documents produced by systems analysts, programmers, and project managers in their work to investigate, design, and develop new systems. *Type:* Newsletter.

BYTE

McGraw-Hill, Inc.
1221 Avenue of the Americas   Ph: (212)512-6410
New York, NY 10020

Desc: Contains the complete text of BYTE, a magazine covering news and information on microcomputer products and their applications. *Available:* LEXIS-NEXIS, NEXIS. *Type:* Database.

BYTE Information Exchange

Delphi Internet Services Corporation
BYTE Information Exchange (BIX)
1030 Massachusetts Ave.   Ph: (617)491-3342
Cambridge, MA 02138
E-mail: service@delphi.com
URL: http://www.delphi.com

Desc: An online electronic conferencing system offering a forum for the discussion and exchange of information on a variety of topics of interest to personal computer users. Covers personal computers (including specific brands), operating systems, computer applications, semiconductors and microprocessor chips, new technologies, microcomputing, telecommunications, artificial intelligence, and computer languages. *Available:* Delphi Internet Services Corporation, BYTE Information Exchange (BIX). *Type:* Database.

Computer Law & Tax Report

Roditti Reports Corp.
PO Box 2066   Ph: (212)879-3325
New York, NY 10021-0052   Fax: (212)879-4496
Contact: Esther C. Roditti, Editor.
Desc: Reports on recent laws, including cases and legislation, affecting computer users and industry. Provides a highlight, historical and other context, such as analysis and editorial comments. *Type:* Newsletter.

Computer Measurement Group

151 Fries Mill Rd., Ste. 104
Turnersville, NJ 08012-2016
Contact: Judith Keel, Exec.Dir.
Desc: Computer professionals. Acts as an information clearinghouse and provides educational programs for those involved in evaluating computer performance. *Type:* Association.

The Computer Museum

The Computer Museum Network
300 Congress St.   Ph: (617)426-2800
Boston, MA 02210
E-mail: heath@tcm.org
URL: http://www.tcm.org/
Contact: Gail Jennes, jennes@tcm.org.
Desc: This website supports and provides information about exhibitions and educational programs offered by The Computer Museum in Boston, Massachusetts (USA). Exhibits and programs change periodically. *Type:* Database.

The Computer Paper

The Computer Paper
Carrall St., Ste. 503-425   Ph: (604)688-2120
Vancouver, BC, Canada V6B   Fax: (604)688-4680
6E3
E-mail: editors@tcp.ca
URL: http://tcp.ca
Desc: The Computer Paper covers a wide range of computer-related subjects, including industry news, product reviews, regular features on Internet, Mac, and PC topics, how-to articles, and more. The current issue and back issues are available. *Type:* Database.

Computer Virus Myths

Barn Owl Software
PO Box 1115   Ph: (618)632-7345
O Fallon, IL 62269   Fax: (618)632-2339
E-mail: us@kumite.com
URL: http://kumite.com/myths/home.htm
Contact: Rob Rosenberger, us@kumite.com.
Desc: No single word in the English language has such a chilling effect on computer enthusiasts everywhere as "VIRUS." However, are computer viruses as widespread as the media and some of your well-meaning friends would have you believe? Apparently not, according to Rob Rosenberger, an internationally-known expert on computer virus myths and hoaxes. Find out what really happened during the Michaelangelo scare of 1992 or the more recent Hare virus scare that swept the nation. *Type:* Database.

Computers, Control & Information Theory

National Technical Information Service (NTIS)
U.S. Department of Commerce
5285 Port Royal Rd.   Ph: (703)605-6000
Springfield, VA 22161-0001   Free: 800-553-NTIS
   Fax: (703)605-6900
E-mail: orders@ntis.fedworld.gov
Desc: Publishes abstracts with full bibliographic citations in the areas of computer hardware and software; control systems and control theory; information processing standards; information theory; and pattern recognition and image processing. Alerts readers to related published materials available from NTIS and other sources. *Type:* Newsletter.

Computing Research Association

Computing Research Association
1100 Seventeenth St. NW, Ste.   Ph: (202)234-2111
507   Fax: (202)667-1066
Washington, DC 20036-4632
E-mail: info@cra.org
URL: http://cra.org/
Contact: webmaster@cra.org.
Desc: The CRA uses its web site to keep members and the public abreast of professional news and information related to public policy, as well as promoting information about the association's programs. For professionals in the field, there's a listing of job openings. *Type:* Database.

Cool Tool of the Day

Carton Donofrio Interactive
120 West Fayette St.   Ph: (410)576-9000
Baltimore, MD 21201   Fax: (410)576-5090
URL: http://www.cooltool.com/
Contact: Sean Carton, seancarton@earthlink.net.
Desc: Every day, this Web site highlights and reviews a "cool" Internet tool for the software-addicted masses. If the tool of the day intrigues you and it's something you'd like to add to your software collection, just follow the link to a site from which you may download it. *Type:* Database.

Corporation for Open Systems International

PO Box 3346   Ph: (703)205-2700
Merrifield, VA 22116-3346   Fax: (703)846-8590
Contact: William Biagi, Pres.
Desc: Computer vendors and users. Accelerates the implementation, deployment, and usage of standards-based, interoperable, open systems networking products and services. *Type:* Association.

CyberScape Daily

Faulkner Information Services
114 Cooper Center   Ph: (609)662-2070
7905 Browning Rd.   Free: 800-843-0460
Pennsauken, NJ 08109   Fax: (609)662-3380
E-mail: systems@faulkner.com
URL: http://www.faulkner.com/cyberscape/
Desc: CyberScape Daily covers news, reviews, and articles on converging technologies. The company profiles, product reviews, articles, and news updates are supplemented by links to related companies or information. *Type:* Database.

The Icon Analyst

The Icon Project
Department of Computer   Ph: (520)621-6613
Science   Fax: (520)621-4246
University of Arizona
Tucson, AZ 85721
E-mail: icon-orders@cs.arizona.edu; icon-orders@cs.arizona.edu.
URL: http://www.cs.arizona.edu.
Contact: Madge T. Griswold, Editor; Ralph E. Griswold, Editor, ralph@cs.arizona.edu.
Desc: Presents technical information on icon programming language. Recurring features include news of research and columns titled Programming Tips and From the Wizards. *Type:* Newsletter.

The Icon Newsletter

The Icon Project
Department of Computer   Ph: (520)621-6613
Science   Fax: (520)621-4246
University of Arizona
Tucson, AZ 85721
E-mail: icon-orders@cs.arizona.edu
URL: http://www.cs.arizona.edu/icon/.
Contact: Ralph E. Griswold, Editor, ralph@cs.arizona.edu; Madge T. Griswold, Editor.

Desc: Disseminates data related to the computer programming language Icon. Contains information on implementation, programming techniques, research in progress, and references to the current literature on Icon. *Type:* Newsletter.

IEEE Computer Society

1730 Massachusetts Ave. NW Ph: (202)371-0101
Washington, DC 20036 Fax: (202)728-9614
E-mail: csinfo@computer.org
URL: http://www.computer.org
Contact: T. Michael Elliott, Exec.Dir.

Desc: Computer professionals. Promotes the development of computer and information sciences and fosters communication within the information processing community. Sponsors conferences, symposia, workshops, tutorials, technical meetings, and seminars. *Type:* Association.

The International Association of Hewlett-Packard Computing Professionals

The International Association of Hewlett-Packard Computing Professionals
1192 Borregas Ave. Ph: (408)747-0227
Sunnyvale, CA 94089 Free: 800-468-3739
 Fax: (408)747-0947
E-mail: info@interex.org
URL: http://www.interex.org/
Contact: webmaster@interex.org.

Desc: This site provides up-to-date information and solutions for HP hardware, software, and operating issues. Current events, membership info, publications, and many electronic resources are provided to browsers. *Type:* Database.

International Computer Science Institute

International Computer Science Institute
1947 Center St., Ste. 6000 Ph: (510)643-9153
Berkeley, CA 94704-1198
URL: http://www.icsi.berkeley.edu/
Contact: web@icsi.berkeley.edu.

Desc: The ICSI uses its web site to provide both organizational news and information--including news of upcoming seminars--and a vast amount of technical information on ICSI research and projects. *Type:* Database.

International Society for Technology in Education

1787 Agate St. Ph: (541)346-4414
Eugene, OR 97403-1923 Free: 800-336-5191
 Fax: (541)346-5890
E-mail: iste@oregon.uoregon.edu
URL: http://www.iste.org
Contact: Maia S. Howes, Exec.Sec.

Desc: Teachers, administrators, computer and curriculum coordinators, and others interested in improving the quality of education through the innovative use of technology. Facilitates exchange of information and resources between international policy makers and professional organizations; encourages research and evaluation relating to the use of technology in education. Maintains the Private Sector Council to promote cooperation among private sector organizations to identify needs and establish standards for hardware, software, and other technology-based educational systems, products, and services. *Type:* Association.

Lognet

Loglan Institute, Inc.
3009 Peters Way Ph: (619)270-1691
San Diego, CA 92117
E-mail: loglan@compuserve.com
URL: http://www.halcyon.com/loglan/welcome.html/.
Contact: Terry Smithwick, Editor.

Desc: Offers computer programmers, logicians, anthropologists, and others interested in logical language news and research findings relating to the development of Loglan, a concise, man-machine interface language. *Type:* Newsletter.

National Computer Security Association

1200 Walnut Bottom Rd. Ph: (717)258-1816
Carlisle, PA 17013 Free: 800-488-4595
 Fax: (717)243-8642
E-mail: office@ncsa.com
URL: http://www.icsa.net

Contact: Peter Tippett, Pres.

Desc: Works to improve security and confidence in global computing through awareness and the continuous education of products, systems, and people. *Type:* Association.

Online Newsletter

Information Intelligence, Inc.
PO Box 31098 Ph: (602)996-2283
Phoenix, AZ 85046
E-mail: rhuleatt@infointelligence.com
URL: http://www.infointelligence.com/www/iii-info; http://www.infointelligence.com/www/iii-info.

Contact: Richard S. Huleatt, Editor, rhuleatt@ infointelligence.com.

Desc: Tracks developments in the fields of CD-ROM and online services. Contains news of online/CD-ROM developments and events, mergers and acquisitions, personnel movements, telecommunications and networks, new equipment and developments, microcomputer hardware and software, new and forthcoming databases, forthcoming meetings, and publications and user aids. *Type:* Newsletter.

PC Computing Online

Ziff-Davis Inc.
650 Townsend St. Ph: (415)551-4500
San Francisco, CA 94103
URL: http://www.zdnet.com/pccomp/

Contact: pcc_webmaster@zd.com.

Desc: This publication covers many facets of home and business computing for mid-advanced level PC users. The information is timely and authoritative, from the editors of PC Computing Magazine. *Type:* Database.

PC Magazine Online

Ziff-Davis Inc.
650 Townsend St. Ph: (415)551-4500
San Francisco, CA 94103
URL: http://www.pcmag.com/

Desc: This publication covers the computer industry, and home and business use of PC hardware and software. The publication is up to date and detailed, with particularly good sections on the Internet and in-depth hardware reviews. *Type:* Database.

SIGMETRICS Performance Evaluation Review

Special Interest Group on Programming Languages (SIGPLAN)
Association for Computing Machinery
1515 Broadway Ph: (212)869-7440
New York, NY 10036 Free: 800-342-6626
 Fax: (212)302-5826
E-mail: acmhelp@acm.org

Contact: Blaine Gaither, Editor.

Desc: Provides articles on computer system performance for individuals "whose interests include advancing the state of the art as well as applying existing tools, and for whom the driving force is the performance of computer systems rather than the mathematics of system modeling." Serves as a vehicle for the distribution of annual SIGMETRICS conference proceedings. *Type:* Newsletter.

SIGPLAN FORTRAN Forum

Special Interest Group on Programming Languages (SIGPLAN)
Association for Computing Machinery
1515 Broadway Ph: (212)869-7440
New York, NY 10036 Free: 800-342-6626
 Fax: (212)302-5826
E-mail: acmhelp@acm.org
Contact: Loren Meissner.

Desc: "Encompasses the FORTRAN language, its usage, portability, standardization, and further evolution as well as the implementation of FORTRAN processors." Remarks: The toll-free telephone number in New Jersey is 800-932-0878. *Type:* Newsletter.

SIGPLAN Notices

Special Interest Group on Programming Languages (SIGPLAN)
Association for Computing Machinery
1515 Broadway Ph: (212)869-7440
New York, NY 10036 Free: 800-342-6626
 Fax: (212)302-5826
E-mail: acmhelp@acm.org
URL: http://www.elvis.rowan.edu/sigplan.
Contact: Michael Berman, Editor.

Desc: Examines all aspects of programming languages and programming languages processors. Utilizes practical and theoretical approaches to such areas as programming methodology; language definition and design; principles and techniques of computer implementation; general purpose and application-oriented languages; and teaching of programming languages. *Type:* Newsletter.

Software Economics Letter

Computer Economics, Inc.
5841 Edison Pl. Ph: (619)438-8100
Carlsbad, CA 92008 Free: (619)431-1126
E-mail: custserv@compecon.com
URL: http://www.computereconomics.com.
Contact: Mark McManus, Managing Editor.

Desc: Covers the management and control of software investments. Provides the corporate user and information systems (IS) communities with analysis of software issues. *Type:* Newsletter.

Software Engineering Technical Committee Newsletter

Software Engineering Technical Committee
IEEE Computer Society
Institute of Electrical & Electronics Engineers, Inc. (IEEE)
1730 Massachusetts Ave. NW
Washington, DC 20036-1992
Contact: Sam Redwine, Editor.

Desc: Contains proceedings and information on organizations and databases of interest to Society members. Recurring features include a calendar of events, meeting minutes, calls for papers, notices of publications available from the Society, and the column Letter From the Chair. *Type:* Newsletter.

UNIX Update

Worldwide Videotex
PO Box 3273 Ph: (561)738-2276
Boynton Beach, FL 33424-3273
URL: http://www.wvpubs.com.

Desc: Compiles information on UNIX hardware and software products, enhancements, research, and developments. Emphasizes marketing strategies of UNIX vendors. *Type:* Newsletter.

Windows 95 FAQ

Glen Cove Computing
Vallejo, CA 94591   Ph: (707)647-2405
URL: http://www.glencove.com/win95faq.htm
Contact: Hans Klarenbeek, Author, hansie@wantree.com.au.

Desc: Having trouble with Windows 95? This is a list of Frequently Asked Questions (FAQ), including information on shortcuts, adding sound effects, augmenting the look of your desktop, customizing your DOS Mode, and much more. *Type:* Database.

Computer Users

ACM Ada Letters

Special Interest Group on Ada
Association for Computing Machinery
1515 Broadway   Ph: (212)869-7440
New York, NY 10036   Free: 800-342-6626
     Fax: (212)944-1318
Contact: K. M. George, Editor.

Desc: Disseminates information about Ada computer language, including its usage, environment, standardization, and implementation. Updates members on the activities of the association, which functions as a special interest group of the Association for Computing Machinery. *Type:* Newsletter.

Association for Computing Machinery

1515 Broadway, 17th Fl.   Ph: (212)626-0500
New York, NY 10036   Fax: (212)944-1318
E-mail: acmhelp@acm.org
Contact: Cynthia Ryan, Mgr.

Desc: A special interest group of the Association for Computing Machinery. Biological, medical, behavioral, and computer scientists; hospital administrators; programmers and others interested in application of computer methods to biological, behavioral, and medical problems. Stimulates understanding of the use and potential of computers in the biosciences; encourages presentation of papers at medical and computer conferences and conventions. *Type:* Association.

The Association for Work Process Improvement

185 Devonshire St., Ste. 770   Ph: (617)426-1167
Boston, MA 02110-9555   Free: 800-99T-AWPI
     Fax: (617)521-8675
E-mail: info@tawpi.org
URL: http://www.tawpi.org
Contact: Kerry C. Stackpole, CAE, Pres.

Desc: Companies using recognition technologies equipment and vendors of that equipment. Purposes are: to advance the application of such technologies as a means of automating remittance and document processing; to promote better understanding and improvement of the capabilities of the equipment; to encourage use of recognition technology equipment among vendors and users. *Type:* Association.

Berkeley Macintosh Users Group

2055 Center St.   Ph: (510)549-2684
Berkeley, CA 94704   Fax: (510)849-9026
E-mail: info@bmug.org
URL: http://www.bmug.org
Contact: Hal Gibson, Exec.Dir.

Desc: Represents the interests of Macintosh and other graphical interface computer users. Maintains library of Freeware and shareware software. Offers technical assistance for members including: emergency data recovery; hardware/RAM installation; a technical helpline. *Type:* Association.

Common

230 W. Monroe
Ste. 220
Chicago, IL 60606
E-mail: common@common.org
URL: http://www.common.org
Contact: Cynthia Dajka, Exec.Dir.

Desc: Individuals and organizations united to advance the effective use of equipment among users of IBM computers and data processing machines. Promotes the free interchange of information about the machines and their installation and usage. Maintains liaison with IBM in an effort to improve customer services and hardware and software operation. *Type:* Association.

Computing News

Computing Center
University of Oregon   Ph: (541)346-1724
Eugene, OR 97403   Fax: (541)346-4397
URL: http://cc.uoregon.edu/cnews/; http://www.cc.uoregon.edu/cnews/.
Contact: Joyce Winslow, Editor, jwins@oregon.uoregon.edu.

Desc: Describes changes and updates in the University Computing Center's hardware and software. *Type:* Newsletter.

DANUG Newsletter

Detroit Area Network User Group (DANUG)
Box 69015   Ph: (810)788-6619
Pleasant Ridge, MI 48069
E-mail: jstanesa@mich.com.
URL: http://www.danug.org.
Contact: Joel Stanesa, Editor.

Desc: Chronicles software and hardware release and attempts to shed a "user's view" on network products. Also provides news of the Group. *Type:* Newsletter.

Dial Up! Gale's Bulletin Board Locator

Gale Group Inc.
27500 Drake Rd.   Ph: (248)699-4253
Farmington Hills, MI 48331-   Free: 800-877-GALE
     3535   Fax: (248)699-8070
E-mail: galeord@galegroup.com
URL: http://www.galegroup.com.
Desc: Approximately 10,000 U.S. bulletin boards available via dialup access (with a modem and computer). *Type:* Directory.

Digital Equipment Computer Users Society

2 Results Way   Ph: (508)467-9150
MR02-1/C16   Free: 800-DEC-US55
Marlboro, MA 01752   Fax: (508)467-9153
E-mail: webmaster@decus.org
URL: http://www.decus.org
Contact: Jack Novia, V.Pres.

Desc: Information Technology professionals interested in the products, services, and technologies of Digital Equipment Corporation and related vendors. Promotes the unimpeded exhange of information, with the goal of helping its members and their organizations to be more successful. *Type:* Association.

Enterprise Networking Association

290 Turnpike Rd., Ste. 324   Ph: (312)644-6610
Westboro, MA 01581   Free: 800-730-ABUI
     Fax: (312)321-5133
URL: http://www.enanet.org
Contact: Bob Whelan, Pres.

Desc: Provides a vehicle for communicating information about managing and implementing evolving enterprise network technologies. *Type:* Association.

EnVision

National Partnership for Advanced
Computational Infrastruction (NPACI)
UCSD MC 0505   Ph: (619)534-5000
9500 Gilman Dr.   Fax: (619)534-8380
La Jolla, CA 92093-0505
E-mail: info@npaci.edu
URL: http://www.npaci.edu/enVision.
Contact: David Hart, Editor, (619)534-8314, fax: (619)534-8380, dhart@sdsc.edu; Ann Redelfs, Managing Editor, (619)534-5032, fax: (619)534-5113, rdelfs@dsc.edu.

Desc: Reports research conducted at the Center. *Type:* Newsletter.

Federation of Computer Users in the Medical Sciences

Desc: Medical professionals interested in utilizing computers in their practices. Seeks to educate medical professionals about computer systems; offers assistance and advice in choosing a system geared toward the needs of the medical professional. Organizes Consultant Certification Program, which trains and certifies computer consultants who work in the medical field. *Type:* Association.

GUIDE International Corporation

401 N. Michigan Ave.   Ph: (312)644-6610
Chicago, IL 60611-4267   Fax: (312)321-5116
Contact: Ron Higgin, Pres.

Desc: Information system professionals. Offers business and enterprise programming solutions on a range of processing platforms. *Type:* Association.

INTEREXPRESS

INTEREX, The International Association of
Hewlett-Packard Computer Users
1192 Borregas Ave.   Ph: (408)747-0227
PO Box 3439   Free: 800-INT-EREX
Sunnyvale, CA 94088-3439   Fax: (408)747-0947
E-mail: obillo@interex.org
Contact: Dick Kranz, Editor.

Desc: Provides industry, technical, and Association news for users of Hewlett-Packard 3000/1000/9000 and personal computers. Lists names and addresses of Hewlett-Packard user group contacts worldwide. *Type:* Newsletter.

International Tandem Users' Group

401 N. Michigan   Ph: (312)321-6851
Chicago, IL 60611-4267   Free: 800-845-ITUG
     Fax: (312)321-5158
E-mail: itug@ue.itug.org
URL: http://www.itug.org
Contact: Neil Clark, Exec.Dir.

Desc: Tandem computer owners and operators. Fosters communication between user groups, Tandem Computers, Inc., and international organizations. *Type:* Association.

NASPA

7044 S. 13th St.   Ph: (414)768-8000
Milwaukee, WI 53154   Fax: (414)768-8001
E-mail: sherer@naspa.net
URL: http://www.naspa.net
Contact: M. Zizis, VP-CFO.

Desc: Technicians and technical management personnel in 80 countries who work in corporate data processing. Dedicated to enhancing the level of technical education among members through publications, public domain software, electronic information sharing, job and career assistance, and scholarships and grants. Conducts charitable and educational programs; maintains speakers' bureau and placement service; compiles statistics. *Type:* Association.

National AppleWorks Users Group

PO Box 87453   Ph: (313)454-1115
Canton, MI 48187   Fax: (313)454-1965
Contact: Cathleen Merritt, Dir.

Desc: Interested individuals. Acts as technical support group for users of AppleWorks software, an interactive spreadsheet, word processor, and database. Conducts seminars. *Type:* Association.

National Association of Desktop Publishers

462 Old Boston St.   Ph: (978)887-7900
Topsfield, MA 01983   Free: 800-874-4113
     Fax: (978)887-6117

E-mail: nadtp@aol.com
Contact: Barry Harrigan, Pres.

Desc: Professional and nonprofessional desktop publishers. *Type:* Association.

National PC Users Group

Box 1076   Ph: (814)237-5511
Lemont, PA 16851-1076
E-mail: npug@gnn.com
Contact: Richard Shoemaker, Founder.

Desc: Users of personal computers and printers and MS-DOS computer systems. Provides support and technical information to users. Offers co-op program allowing members to purchase items and supplies below retail costs and provides disk format conversion services (for a fee). *Type:* Association.

North Texas PC News

North Texas PC Users Group, Inc.
2025 Rockereek Dr.   Ph: (817)275-4109
Arlington, TX 76010
Contact: Reagan Andrews, Editor.

Desc: Publishes articles on IBM and IBM-compatible personal computers, peripherals, software, and operating systems. Provides a forum for the exchange of information of interest among members and with user groups in other areas. *Type:* Newsletter.

Online Reporter

G2 Computer Intelligence, Inc.
3 Maple Pl.   Ph: (516)759-7025
Glen Head, NY 11545-9864   Fax: (516)759-7028
E-mail: paperboy@g2news.com; news@92news.com.
URL: http://www.92news.com.
Contact: Maureen O'Gara, Editor.

Desc: Reports news on Java, e-business, and security. *Type:* Newsletter.

Scroll

Wordstar Processing Users' Group, Inc. (W/PUG)
PO Box 16-1443   Ph: (305)274-0099
Miami, FL 33116-1443
E-mail: cbabbage@ix.netcom.com.
URL: http://www.cuenet.com/cbabbage/wordstar.
Contact: Dr. David M. Rafky, Editor.

Desc: Provides news regarding various aspects of word processing with WordStar software, includes reviews of word processing software, computer tips, a glossary of terms used in each issue, and information for writers. Recurring features include letters to the editor, news of research, and book reviews. *Type:* Newsletter.

SIGIR Forum

Special Interest Group on Programming Languages (SIGPLAN)
Association for Computing Machinery
1515 Broadway   Ph: (212)869-7440
New York, NY 10036   Free: 800-342-6626
     Fax: (212)302-5826

E-mail: acmhelp@acm.org

URL: http://www.acm.org/sigir/.
Contact: Fazli Can, Editor; Bill Hersh, Editor.

Desc: Concerned with how machines may be used in the storage, retrieval, and dissemination of information, including news and information relating to retrieval theory, programming, file preparation, searching strategy, output schemes, systems evaluation, and development of equipment best suited for these tasks. Also contains proceedings of annual international SIGIR conferences. *Type:* Newsletter.

Uniforum Association

10440 Shaker Dr., Ste. 203   Free: 800-255-5620
Columbia, MD 21046-1292
E-mail: membership@uniforum.org
Contact: Richard H. Jaross, Exec.Dir.

Desc: Vendor-independent association for computer developers, vendors, and end users. Promotes the exchange of information about Open Systems and related hardware, software, applications, and standards. *Type:* Association.

USENIX Association

2560 9th St., Ste. 215   Ph: (510)528-8649
Berkeley, CA 94710   Fax: (510)548-5738
E-mail: office@usenix.org
URL: http://www.usenix.org
Contact: Ellie Young, Exec.Dir.

Desc: Individuals (6500) with an interest in Advanced Computing Systems in a professional or technical capacity; and (commercial computer firms) institutions, colleges and universities, and research institutes (1700). Promotes innovation in advanced computing systems; fosters the development of research and technological information pertaining to advanced computer systems; encourages and assists in the establishment of regional UNIX users' groups. *Type:* Association.

Ventura Publisher User's Group

719 Locust St.   Ph: (408)227-5030
San Jose, CA 95110-2905
Contact: Robert Moody, Exec. Officer.

Desc: Users of Ventura computer software system. Works to heighten knowledge and understanding of Ventura software. Provides information exchange and technical support to members. *Type:* Association.

Computers

A-E-C Automation Newsletter

Technology Automation Services
PO Box 3593   Ph: (303)770-1728
Englewood, CO 80155-3593   Free: 800-328-3211
     Fax: (303)770-3660

URL: http://www.aecnews.com.
Contact: David Weisberg, Editor and Publisher.

Desc: Provides information on computer hardware and software, networks, and business practices for the architecture, engineering, and construction industries and for users of automated mapping/facility management and GIS systems. Includes articles on vendors and new technology. *Type:* Newsletter.

Adobe Magazine

Adobe Systems, Inc.
411 1st Ave. S.   Ph: (206)470-7000
Seattle, WA 98104-2871   Free: 800-866-8006
     Fax: (206)470-7106

E-mail: magazine.editor@adobe.com.
Contact: Christine Yarrow, Editor-in-Chief; Jeff Lalier, Adv. Coord.; Leslie Nakagawa, Production/Bus. Mgr.; Retsu Takahashi, Production/Circulation Asst.; Kimberly Chilcutt, Circulation/Adv. Asst.; Tamis Nordling, Editor; Jenna Ashley, Art Dir.

Desc: Software magazine including design tips, descriptions of compatible products, and new product information. *Type:* Periodical.

AIM Post

Association for Interactive Media
1301 Connecticut Ave. NW,   Ph: (202)408-0008
   5th Fl.   Fax: (202)408-0111
Washington, DC 20036
E-mail: info@interactivehq.org; editor@interactivehq.org.

Desc: Summarizes major developments in the Internet industry. Provides insight into product offerings and activities of companies and personnel in this industry. *Type:* Newsletter.

Alpha Forum

Alpha Forum, Inc.
276 Fair St.
Kingston, NY 12401-3848
E-mail: smartin@capecod.net.
Contact: Tom Marcellus, Editor.

Desc: Contains tips, techniques, and application articles for Alpha Software's Alpha Four. *Type:* Newsletter.

Amateur Computerist

Amateur Computerist
PO Box 250101
New York, NY 10025-1531
URL: http://www.cc.columbia.edu/~hauben.acn/.
Contact: Ronda Hauben, Editor.

Desc: Provides advice and instruction for the novice computer user. Covers hardware, software, and information technology. *Type:* Newsletter.

American Society for Technion-Israel Institute of Technology

810 7th Ave., 24th Fl.   Ph: (212)262-6200
New York, NY 10019   Fax: (212)262-6155
URL: http://www.ats.org
Contact: Melvyn H. Bloom, Exec.VP.

Desc: Support organization in the United States for the Technion-Israel Institute of Technology. Leading American organization supporting higher education in Israel. Provides financial and technical support to the Institute, maintains speakers' bureau; bestows awards; operates charitable program. *Type:* Association.

Amy D. Wohl's Opinions

Wohl Associates
915 Montgomery Ave., Ste. 309   Ph: (610)667-4842
Narberth, PA 19072   Fax: (610)667-3081
E-mail: opinions@wohl.com.
Contact: Amy D. Wohl, Editor, amy@wohl.com.

Desc: Concentrates on the latest developments in computer technology and software and their effects on the end-user. Covers personal computers, computer companies, and industry trends. *Type:* Newsletter.

The Anderson Report on Computer Graphics

Altus Marketing, Inc.
c/o Susan H. Mow
558 Rock Springs Rd. NE
Atlanta, GA 30324-5104
Contact: Marcia Brooks, Editor.

Desc: Covers CAD/CAM (Computer-Aided Design/Computer-Aided Manufacturing), CAE (Computer-Aided Engineering), and computer graphics. Features information on new hardware and software products, industry activities, trends, and emerging technology. *Type:* Newsletter.

Andrew Seybold's Outlook on Communications and Computing

Pinecrest Press, Inc.
PO Box 2460   Ph: (408)338-7701
Boulder Creek, CA 95006-2460
Contact: Andrew M. Seybold, Editor-in-Chief; Linda Seybold, Editor.
Desc: Offers news, views, analysis, and informed perspective on issues in the computing and communications industry. Recurring features include new product reviews, news of research, and trends. *Type:* Newsletter.

Apple Library Users Group Newsletter

Apple Computer, Inc.
1 Infinite Loop   Ph: (408)996-1010
Mail F. 304-2A   Fax: (408)725-8502
Cupertino, CA 95014
URL: http://www.alug.apple.com/.
Contact: Monica Ertel, Editor.
Desc: Serves as an exchange for information concerning the use of Apple and Macintosh computers in libraries and information centers of all sizes. Recurring features include news of research, book reviews, news from members, answers to readers' questions, a calendar of events, and columns titled News From/About Apple, Software Reviews, and Information From Our Vendors. *Type:* Newsletter.

ARC News

Environmental Systems Research Institute
380 New York St.   Ph: (909)793-2853
Redlands, CA 92373-8100   Fax: (909)793-5953
Desc: Magazine covering geography, maps and mapping, and computers. *Type:* Periodical.

Archtek! Home Of The SmartLink Modems

Archtek America Corp.
18549 E. Gale Ave.   Ph: (626)912-9800
City of Industry, CA 91748   Fax: (626)912-9700
E-mail: sales@archtek.com
URL: http://www.archtek.com/
Desc: Find out all about modems at this web site. Archtek America Corp. *Type:* Database.

Association for Computing Machinery

Special Interest Group on Data Communication
1515 Broadway, 17th Fl.
New York, NY 10036
URL: http://www.acm.org/sigcomm.
Contact: Martha Steenstrup, Editor.
Desc: Serves as a forum for computing professionals in the data communications field. Focuses on network architecture, including the Internet, network protocols, and distributed systems. *Type:* Newsletter.

Automatic I.D. News

Advanstar Communications
Raritan Plaza III   Ph: (732)225-9500
101 Fieldcrest Ave.   Fax: (732)225-0211
Edison, NJ 08837
E-mail: adcnewswire@superfill.com; autoid@advanstar.com.
URL: http://www.autoidnews.com.
Contact: Robin Klombers, Publisher, rklombers@advanstar.com; John Burnell, Editor, (440)891-2788, jburnelle@advanstar.com; Jeanne Johnson, Production Mgr., (218)723-9200, fax: (218)723-9576, jjohnson@advanstar.com.
Desc: Trade magazine. *Alt. Contact:* 7500 Old Oak Blvd., Cleveland, OH 44130-3369; telephone: (440)243-8100; fax: (440)891-2675. *Type:* Periodical.

BackOffice Magazine

BackOffice Magazine
10 Tara Blvd., 5th Fl.   Ph: (603)891-9281
Nashua, NH 03062-2801   Free: 800-225-0555
     Fax: (603)891-9297
E-mail: marketing@backoffice.com; chrisa@pennwell.com.
URL: http://www.backofficemag.com.
Contact: David Anderson, (603)891-9481, davea@pennwell.com; Barrie Sosinsky, (603)891-9344, barnes@pennwell.com.
Desc: Magazine for information technology professionals building and implementing client/server applications in a Windows NT server environment. *Type:* Periodical.

Barry95--Windows 95 Software, Support, & Silliness

Interport Communications
1133 Broadway   Ph: (212)989-1128
New York, NY 10010
E-mail: webmaster@interport.net
URL: http://www.users.interport.net/~barry/
Contact: Barry Louis, barry@interport.net.
Desc: The author has put together quite a few links to various useful Windows95 utilities and software; his most popular section remains, "The Newest on the Net." Be wary of 'Silliness' in the title, there's not much fun here but lots of useful utilities which are downloadable. *Type:* Database.

A Bit More. . .

Northern Virginia Osborne Users Group
7007 Brocton Ct.   Ph: (703)569-2213
Springfield, VA 22150
Contact: William E. Kost, Editor.
Desc: Aims to support and educate personal computer users by providing articles, news, reviews, and software documentation. Emphasizes CP/M, MS-DOS and Windows. *Type:* Newsletter.

Bits & Bytes Review

Bits & Bytes Computer Resources
623 N. Iowa Ave.   Ph: (406)862-7280
Whitefish, MT 59937   Fax: (406)862-0876
E-mail: info@bitsbytescomputer.com
Contact: John J. Hughes, Editor, jhughes@cyberport.net.
Desc: Keeps academic computer users abreast of current news and information within the world of microcomputers. Uses clear, technical explanations to review new products and contains news of grants, fellowships, data bases, hardware, software, CD-ROM, newsletters, journals, software catalogs, and utilities. *Type:* Newsletter.

Black Box On-line Catalog

Black Box Corp.
1000 Park Dr.   Ph: (724)746-5500
Lawrence, PA 15055-1018   Fax: (724)746-0746
E-mail: info@blackbox.com
URL: http://www.blackbox.com
Desc: Black Box is a vendor of online connectivity products such as modems, CSU/DSUs. switches, cabling and racks. *Type:* Database.

A Brief History Of Silicon Valley

Silicon Valley Online
PO Box 103   Ph: (408)364-1500
New Almaden, CA 95042   Fax: (408)364-1470
E-mail: jill@silvalonline.com
URL: http://www.silvalonline.com/silhist.html
Desc: A brief text history of Silicon Valley, including a short bibliography. *Type:* Database.

Broadband Networking News

Phillips Business Information, Inc.
1201 Seven Locks Rd., Ste. 300   Ph: (301)340-1520
Potomac, MD 20854   Free: 888-707-5809
     Fax: (301)340-3847
E-mail: clientservices.pbi@phillips.com
URL: http://www.Phillips-com/TelecomWeb.
Contact: Jon Spofford, Editor, jspofford@phillips.com.
Desc: Provides news and analysis of high-speed data transfer strategies, in-depth case studies, comparison charts on new broadband products and services, and ideas to help boost data transfer efficiencies and cut costs. Covers such technologies as ATM (asynchronous transfer mode) and SMDS (switched multimegabit data service), and frame relay. *Type:* Newsletter.

Business Computer Report

Guidera Publishing Corporation
39 Sheridan Park Cir. No. 6-7   Ph: (803)681-3399
Bluffton, SC 29910-6025
Contact: Lawrence Oakly, Editor.
Desc: Reviews business applications software and hardware for IBM and compatible computers. *Type:* Newsletter.

BYTE

The McGraw-Hill Companies, Inc.
29 Hartwell Ave.   Ph: (617)860-6336
Lexington, MA 02173-3154   Fax: (617)860-6179
URL: http://www.byte.com.
Contact: Kevin McPherson, Publisher, (781)860-6020, fax: (781)860-6179, kmcphers@mcgraw-hill.com; Mark Schlack, Editor-in-Chief, (781)860-6827, fax: (781)860-6572, mschlack@mcgraw-hill.com.
Desc: Tracks and analyzes emerging technologies and products for multi-platform environments with editorial focus on building networked applications, Internet/Intranet/Extranet strategies, managing data, and network integration. *Type:* Periodical.

CAD/CAM Update

Worldwide Videotex
PO Box 3273   Ph: (561)738-2276
Boynton Beach, FL 33424-3273
URL: http://www.wvpubs.com.
Desc: Covers computer-aided design and manufacturing (CAD/CAM) and their industries. *Type:* Newsletter.

Camcorder & Computer Video

Miller Magazines, Inc.
4880 Market St.   Ph: (805)644-3824
Ventura, CA 93003   Fax: (805)644-3875
E-mail: camcoromg@aol.com.
Contact: Bob Wolenik, Editor; James Miller, Publisher; Bonnie Jane Mason, Assoc. Editor/New Products Editor.
Desc: Magazine on home video and desktop video technology for consumers and prosumers. *Alt. Contact:* 4800 Market St., Ventura, CA 93003-7783; telephone: (805)644-3824; fax: (805)644-3875. *Type:* Periodical.

CD Computing News

Worldwide Videotex
PO Box 3273   Ph: (561)738-2276
Boynton Beach, FL 33424-3273
URL: http://www.wvpubs.com.
Contact: Mark Wright, Editor, markedit@juno.com.
Desc: Provides coverage of "the projects, products, and developments of the commercial applications of CD-ROM, CD-I, and all the other optical storage devices used in computing." Concentrates on information relating to successful marketing strategies. *Type:* Newsletter.

CD-ROM Databases

Worldwide Videotex
PO Box 3273   Ph: (561)738-2276
Boynton Beach, FL 33424-3273
E-mail: markedit@juno.com.
URL: http://www.wvpubs.com.
Contact: Mark Wright, Editor, markedit@juno.com.
Desc: Lists CD-ROM titles currently being marketed, including information on prices, vendors, and categories.
Type: Newsletter.

Chef's Choice Touch Screen Point of Sale

Chef's Choice
9865 Leopard St.   Ph: (512)241-6164
Corpus Christi, TX 78410   Fax: (512)241-6972
E-mail: chefschoice@earthlink.net
URL: http://home.earthlink.net/~chefschoice/
Desc: Restauranteurs considering automating their restaurants should benefit from this web site. Chef's Choice provides valuable information on its touch-screen software modules that allow restaurant owners to use the capabilities they presently require and upgrade these capabilities as needed. *Type:* Database.

Cipher Newsletter

Technical Committee on Security & Privacy
IEEE Computer Society
1730 Massachusetts Ave. NW
Washington, DC 20036-1992
Contact: Avi Rubin, Editor; Paul Syverson, Editor.
Desc: Concerned with computer privacy and security issues. Contains project summaries, descriptions of research projects, and technical and nontechnical papers. *Type:* Newsletter.

CIRT Newsletter

Computer and Information Resources and Technology (CIRT)
University of New Mexico
2701 Campus Blvd. NE   Ph: (505)277-8123
Albuquerque, NM 87131-6064   Fax: (505)277-8101
URL: http://techedit.unm.edu/newsletter_html/
newsletter.html.
Contact: Catherine Luther, Editor.
Desc: Presents information on CIRT's computer services and general computer topics. *Type:* Newsletter.

Client/Server Computing

Sentry Technology Group
One Research Dr.   Ph: (508)366-2031
Suite 400-B   Free: 800-225-9218
Westborough, MA 01581-3907   Fax: (508)836-4732
E-mail: clientserver@mcimail.com.
URL: http://www.sentrytech.com.
Contact: John Kerr, Editor-in-Chief; Bill Orth, National Sales Manager; Mary-Ann Gajewski, Production Mgr.; Kathleen Kenny, Circulation Mgr.
Desc: Magazine providing information to client/server decision makers in large organizations. *Type:* Periodical.

Client Server News

G2 Computer Intelligence, Inc.
3 Maple Pl.   Ph: (516)759-7025
Glen Head, NY 11545-9864   Fax: (516)759-7028
E-mail: paperboy@g2news.com; news@g2news.com.
URL: http://www.g2news.com.
Desc: Provides news on Windows NT and Microsoft.
Type: Newsletter.

CMC News

Computers and the Media Center (CMC)
515 Oak St., N.   Ph: (507)263-3711
Cannon Falls, MN 55009
Contact: Jim Deacon, Editor, jbdeacon@rconnect.com.
Desc: Acts as a forum where library/media specialists can share information on computer use. Contains reviews of library utility programs on the microcomputer and articles on the management of microcomputers in library/media centers. *Type:* Newsletter.

COM-AND

Management Advisory Publications
PO Box 81151   Ph: (781)235-2895
Wellesley Hills, MA 02181   Fax: (781)235-5757
E-mail: jaykmasp@aol.com.
Contact: Javier F. Kuong, Editor.
Desc: Focuses on trends and developments in the information systems and data communications fields, as well as providing practical guidelines, standards, and ideas on information technologies as they affect audit and control matters. Presents tutorials on a topic of current interest in the field of I/S audit and internal controls. *Type:* Newsletter.

COM-SAC

Management Advisory Publications
PO Box 81151   Ph: (781)235-2895
Wellesley Hills, MA 02181   Fax: (781)235-5757
E-mail: jaykmasp@aol.com.
Contact: Javier F. Kuong, Editor.
Desc: Presents a comprehensive digest of literature on computer security, auditing, and controls compiled from reviews of over 100 journals. Contains professionally critiqued and analyzed entries describing computer literature, in-depth tutorials on current topics, and suggestions for problem-solving in security and control situations. *Type:* Newsletter.

Communications of the ACM

Association for Computing Machinery
1515 Broadway   Ph: (212)869-7440
New York, NY 10036   Free: 800-843-6626
                                Fax: (212)869-0581
Contact: Walter Andrzejewski, Advertising Dir.; Diane Crawford, Executive Editor.
Desc: Computing news magazine. *Type:* Periodical.

CommunicationsWeek

CMP Media Inc.
600 Community Dr.   Ph: (516)562-5000
Manhasset, NY 11030
URL: http://www.cmp.com
Desc: Contains the complete text of CommunicationsWeek, a weekly newspaper covering developments in computer networking, private (wide area) networking, and public telecommunications network. *Available:* LEXIS-NEXIS, NEXIS; LEXIS-NEXIS, NEXIS. *Type:* Database.

Compaq Compass

Compaq Computer Corp.
PO Box 692000, MS 580304   Ph: (281)927-8877
Houston, TX 77269-2000   Fax: (281)514-2611
URL: http://www.compaq.com/compass.
Contact: Julie Bradshaw, Editor.
Desc: Customer newsletter customized by industry, company size, and job title. *Type:* Newsletter.

Computer Architecture News

Special Interest Group on Computer Architecture (SIGARCH)
Association for Computing Machinery
1515 Broadway   Ph: (212)869-7440
New York, NY 10036   Free: 800-342-6626
E-mail: acmhelp@acm.org.
URL: http://www.acm.org.
Contact: Doug DeGroot, Editor.
Desc: "SIGARCH serves a unique community of computer professionals working on the forefront of computer design in both industry and academia. It is ACM's primary forum for interchange of ideas about tomorrow's hardware." Includes the ISCA and ASPLOS proceedings. *Type:* Newsletter.

Computer ASAP™

The Gale Group
27500 Drake Rd.   Ph: (248)699-4253
Farmington Hills, MI 48331-
    3535
URL: http://www.galegroup.com
Contact: (650)378-5000, fax: (800)676-2345.
Desc: Contains citations to and the complete text of more than 212,000 articles published in the computer industry's leading publications and indexed in the Computer Database. Covers approximately 70 percent of the articles in the following publications: • AI Expert. *Available:* CompuServe Information Service; The Gale Group, InfoTrac Web. *Type:* Database.

Computer Conference Analysis Newsletter

GIGA Information Group
1 Longwater Circle   Ph: (781)982-9500
Norwell, MA 02061-1620   Free: 800-847-9980
                                Fax: (781)982-1724
E-mail: smartin@gigasd.com
Contact: Don Felice, Editor.
Desc: Reports on and critiques selected computer conferences, seminars and symposia. *Type:* Newsletter.

Computer Currents

Computer Currents Publishing, Inc.
1250 Ninth St.   Ph: (510)527-0333
Berkeley, CA 94710   Free: 800-365-7773
                                Fax: (510)527-4106
E-mail: cceditorial@compcurr.com; ccgenmail@
compcurr.com; mail@compcurr.com.
URL: http://www.currents.net.
Contact: Robert Luhn, Editor-in-Chief; Stan Politi, Publisher.
Desc: Magazine for business microcomputer users. *Type:* Periodical.

Computer Database™

The Gale Group
27500 Drake Rd.   Ph: (248)699-4253
Farmington Hills, MI 48331-
    3535
URL: http://www.galegroup.com
Contact: (650)378-5000, fax: (800)676-2345.
Desc: Contains more than 265,000 citations, with abstracts, to literature from some 150 trade journals, industry newsletters, and platform-specific publications covering computers, the computer industry, and related fields, including telecommunications and electronics. Covers business and industry applications; computer graphics; consumer information; database management systems; hardware and software design, development, and reviews; peripherals; home computers; new products; performance evaluations; programming languages; operating systems; phototypesetting; and word processing. *Available:* CompuServe Information Service, Knowledge Index; The Dialog Corporation, DataStar; The Dialog Corporation, DIALOG; CARL Corporation. *Type:* Database.

Computer Economics Networking Strategies Report

Computer Economics, Inc.
5841 Edison Pl.
Carlsbad, CA 92008-6519
Ph: (760)438-8100
Free: 800-326-8100
Fax: (760)431-1126
E-mail: info@compecan.com
URL: http://www.computereconomics.com; http://www.computereconomics.com.
Contact: Anne Zalatan, Editor-in-Chief.
Desc: Provides an executive overview for Management Information Systems (MIS) and network professionals who are involved in network strategic planning and implementation. Covers such topics as comparative analyses of hardware and software systems, costs of ownership studies, analyses of emerging protocols and standards, and cost-saving opportunities. *Type:* Newsletter.

Computer Economics Report

Computer Economics, Inc.
5841 Edison Pl.
Carlsbad, CA 92008-6519
Ph: (760)438-8100
Free: 800-326-8100
Fax: (760)431-1126
E-mail: info@compecan.com
URL: http://www.computereconomics.com; http://www.computereconomics.com.
Contact: Anne Zalatan, Editor-in-Chief.
Desc: Provides analyses of new IBM technologies and acquisition and financial management strategies from an end-user perspective. Recurring features include cost comparisons, price/performance analyses, new product forecasts, and evaluations of acquisition techniques for medium and large computer systems. *Type:* Newsletter.

Computer Fraud & Security Bulletin

Elsevier Science Inc.
655 Avenue of the Americas
New York, NY 10010
Ph: (212)989-5800
Fax: (212)633-3990
E-mail: usinfo@elsevier.com
URL: http://www.elsevier.com
Contact: Tina Monk, Editor.
Desc: Describes computer-based systems security risks and provides appropriate counter measures. *Type:* Newsletter.

Computer and Information Systems Abstracts

Cambridge Scientific Abstracts (CSA)
7200 Wisconsin Ave., Ste. 601
Bethesda, MD 20814-4823
Ph: (301)961-6700
E-mail: sales@csa.com
URL: http://www.csa.com
Desc: Contains more than 280,000 citations, with abstracts, to the worldwide literature on theoretical and applied computer science. Sources include books, journals, conference proceedings, and government reports. *Available:* STN International; STN International. *Type:* Database.

Computer Life

Ziff-Davis Inc.
28 E. 28th St.
New York, NY 10016
Ph: (212)503-3500
Fax: (212)503-5799
URL: http://www.ziff-davis.com.
Desc: Magazine for adults who use computers for non-business purposes. *Type:* Periodical.

Computer News Full Text

International Data Group (IDG)
IDG Communications
5 Speen St.
Framingham, MA 01701
Ph: (508)875-5000
URL: http://www.nwfusion.com
Desc: Contains the complete text of more than 18,300 articles from the Computerworld and NetworkWorld, weekly journals providing news on developing computer and networking technologies and products. Covers companies involved in the computer and networking industries as well. *Available:* The Dialog Corporation, DIALOG; CompuServe Information Service, Knowledge Index. *Type:* Database.

The Computer Paper

Canada Computer Paper Inc.
99 Atlantic Ave., Ste. 408
Toronto, ON, Canada M6K 3J8
Ph: (416)588-1580
Fax: (416)588-8574
E-mail: letters@tcp.ca.
URL: http://www.tcp.ca.
Desc: Periodical serving the computer user in business, education, and at home. *Type:* Periodical.

The Computer Phonebook

No Starch Press
555 De Haro St., Ste. 250
San Francisco, CA 94107
Ph: (415)863-9900
Free: 800-420-7240
Fax: (415)863-9950
E-mail: info@nostarch.com
URL: http://www.nostarch.com
Desc: More than 14,000 computer hardware and software manufacturing companies in the U.S. and Canada. *Type:* Directory.

Computer Price Guide

Computer Economics, Inc.
5841 Edison Pl.
Carlsbad, CA 92008-6519
Ph: (760)438-8100
Free: 800-326-8100
Fax: (760)431-1126
E-mail: info@compecan.com
URL: http://www.computereconomics.com; http://www.computereconomics.com.
Contact: Anne Zalatan, Editor-in-Chief.
Desc: Provides price and market information for used IMB Computers. *Type:* Newsletter.

Computer Professionals for Social Responsibility

Computer Professionals for Social Responsibility
PO Box 717
Palo Alto, CA 94302
Ph: (415)322-3778
Fax: (415)322-4748
E-mail: webmaster@cpsr.org
URL: http://www.cpsr.org/dox/home.html
Desc: The Computer Professionals for Social Responsibility provides information about CPSR along with numerous publications regarding topics of concern. Included are such topics as domain names for the Internet, the Year 2000 dilemma, Star Wars, conferences, caching, and the ever-present email nightmare-SPAM. *Type:* Database.

Computer Protocols

Worldwide Videotex
PO Box 3273
Boynton Beach, FL 33424-3273
Ph: (561)738-2276
URL: http://www.wvpubs.com.
Contact: Mark Wright, Editor, markedit@juno.com.
Desc: Provides details on OSI protocol products and marketing plans. Recurring features include news of research, a calendar of events, and book reviews. *Type:* Newsletter.

Computer Quick 45,000 Products

Computer Quick
165 8th St., Ste. 309
San Francisco, CA 94103
Ph: (415)861-8330
Fax: (415)861-8380
E-mail: Service@cqk.com
URL: http://www.cqk.com/
Desc: The Computer Quick Web site consists of about 6 screens which are designed to make selection and ordering of products as easy as possible. The site is designed primarily for a customer who already has a product in mind, and is looking for a good price and fast delivery. *Type:* Database.

Computer Reseller News

CMP Media Inc.
600 Community Dr.
Manhasset, NY 11030
Ph: (516)562-5000
URL: http://www.cmp.com
Desc: Contains the complete text of Computer Reseller News, a weekly newspaper for dealers and distributors of microcomputer hardware, software, and peripherals. Covers new products, industry statistics and trends, and marketing strategies. *Available:* LEXIS-NEXIS, NEXIS; LEXIS-NEXIS, NEXIS. *Type:* Database.

Computer Security

Computer Security Institute
600 Harrison St.
San Francisco, CA 94107
Ph: (415)905-2626
Free: 800-227-4675
Fax: (415)905-2218
E-mail: csi@mfi.com
Contact: Patrice Rapalus, Editor.
Desc: Deals with data access controls, microcomputers, communications, and personnel security. Also discusses risk analysis, fire protection, disaster recovery, and fraud and computer crime. *Type:* Newsletter.

Computer Shopper

Ziff-Davis Inc.
28 E. 28th St.
New York, NY 10016
Ph: (212)503-3500
Fax: (212)503-5799
URL: http://www.ziff-davis.com.
Contact: John Blackford, Editor-in-Chief; Al DeGuido, Publisher; Scott J. Seltz, National Sales Mgr., (212)503-3760; Pamela Feldman, Asst. Sales Mgr., (212)503-3923.
Desc: Computer magazine. *Alt. Contact:* One Park Ave., New York, NY 10016; telephone: (212)503-3900; fax: (212)503-3999. *Type:* Periodical.

Computer Shopper Online

Ziff-Davis Inc.
650 Townsend St.
San Francisco, CA 94103
Ph: (415)551-4500
URL: http://www.zdnet.com/cshopper/
Desc: This publication covers computer hardware/software purchasing from the consumer perspective, especially dealing with mail-order vendors. It is chock full of price and performance reviews of all types of hardware, and some software. *Type:* Database.

Computer Survival Journal

Enterprise Publications
400 E 59th St., No. 9-F
New York, NY 10022
Ph: (212)755-4363
Contact: Tom Weston, Editor.
Desc: Consumer magazine covering computers. *Type:* Periodical.

Computer VARs & Systems Integrators

Chain Store Guide Information Services
3922 Coconut Palm Dr.
Tampa, FL 33619
Ph: (813)627-6800
Free: 800-927-9292
Fax: (813)627-6882
E-mail: info@csgis.com
Contact: Ashley Valdes, Editor; Shelley Alsalser, Editor.
Desc: Profiles of more than 5,200 value added resellers and systems integrators, and 19,000 key executives and buying personnel. *Type:* Directory.

Computer Virus Help Desk

IndyWeb
6508 E. Washington St.
Indianapolis, IN 46219
E-mail: webmaster@indyweb.net
URL: http://www.indyweb.net/~cvhd/index.html
Desc: This site, sponsored by IndyWeb, provides the reader with numerous documents concerning viruses and antivirus software. Lists of various wild computer viruses and their properties are offered to allow a possible infection to be identified. *Type:* Database.

Computer Workstation

Worldwide Videotex
PO Box 3273   Ph: (561)738-2276
Boynton Beach, FL 33424-3273
URL: http://www.wvpubs.com.
Contact: Mark Wright, Editor, markedit@juno.com.
Desc: Provides news and information on computer work-stations used in network applications, computer-aided design, computer-aided engineering, and other business and industrial applications to improve productivity. Recurring features include news of research and book reviews. *Type:* Newsletter.

Computerized Processes

Worldwide Videotex
PO Box 3273   Ph: (561)738-2276
Boynton Beach, FL 33424-3273
URL: http://www.wvpubs.com.
Desc: Discusses emerging computer and electronic technologies for increasing efficiency and productivity of manufacturing. *Type:* Newsletter.

ComputerLetter

ComputerLetter
120 Wooster St., 6th Fl. North   Ph: (212)343-1900
New York, NY 10012-5200   Fax: (212)343-1915
E-mail: infotechnologyhnologicp.com;   events@
technological.com.
Contact: Richard A. Shaffer, Editor.
Desc: Covers business issues in the technological venues and technology issues in the world of business. *Type:* Newsletter.

Computers and Society

Special Interest Group on Programming Languages (SIGPLAN)
Association for Computing Machinery
1515 Broadway   Ph: (212)869-7440
New York, NY 10036   Free: 800-342-6626
                                     Fax: (212)302-5826
E-mail: acmhelp@acm.org
Contact: Tom Jewett, Editor.
Desc: Offers computer and physical scientists, professionals, and other interested individuals current news and information concerning the application and impact of computers in society. *Type:* Newsletter.

ComputerSelect

The Gale Group
27500 Drake Rd.   Ph: (248)699-4253
Farmington Hills, MI 48331-
  3535
URL: http://www.galegroup.com
Contact: (650)378-5000, fax: (800)676-2345.
Desc: Contains the complete text of 5134 issues of the leading 120 computer publications. Includes specifications for 70,000 products along with contact and profile information for 13,000 VARs, vendors, and manufacturers. *Available:* The Gale Group, InfoTrac Web. *Type:* Database.

ComputerTown, United States of America!

c/o People's Computer Co.
2682 Bishop Dr., Ste. 107
San Ramon, CA 94583
Contact: Jane Nissen Laidley, Exec.Dir.
Desc: A computer literacy project which promotes the exposure of computers to people of all ages. Objectives are: to provide the general public with access to microcomputers in a variety of non-formal educational settings nationwide and to distribute an implementation package that explains how to start ComputerTown projects in local communities. Sponsors a series of on-going classes and community workshops at local libraries, schools, and museums. *Type:* Association.

ComputerUser

220 S. 6th St.   Ph: (612)339-7571
Ste. 500
Minneapolis, MN 55402-4507
E-mail: cueditor@usinternet.com.
Contact: Steve Deyo, Editor; Rachel Hanlein, Managing Editor.
Alt. Contact: 220 S. 6th St., Ste. 500, Minneapolis, MN 55402-4507; telephone: (612)339-7571. *Type:* Periodical.

Computerworld

International Data Group
5 Speen St.   Ph: (508)879-0700
PO Box 9171   Free: 800-343-4935
Framingham, MA 01701   Fax: (508)875-8931
URL: http://www.computerworld.com.
Contact: Paul Gillin, Editor; Mike Rogers, Publisher.
Desc: Newspaper for information systems executives. *Alt. Contact:* 500 Old Connecticut Path, Framingham, MA 01701; telephone: (508)879-0700; fax: (508)875-8931. *Type:* Periodical.

Computerworld

International Data Group (IDG)
IDG Communications
5 Speen St.   Ph: (508)875-5000
Framingham, MA 01701
URL: http://www.nwfusion.com
Contact: (508)879-0700.
Desc: Contains the complete text of Computerworld, a newspaper on the computer industry. Includes more than 26,000 articles and nearly 750 accompanying graphics. *Available:* LEXIS-NEXIS, NEXIS. *Type:* Database.

Computerworld

Computerworld
500 Old Connecticut Path   Ph: (508)879-0700
Framingham, MA 01701   Fax: (508)875-6310
E-mail: help@cw.com
URL: http://www.computerworld.com/
Desc: Anyone seeking computer-related information will benefit from this highly informative, material-rich web site. Based on the print Computerworld magazine, the Computerworld site provides extensive information on latest trends, news, developments, and events in the computer industry, all in a streamlined and highly navigable format. *Type:* Database.

ComputerWorld Campus Edition

ComputerWorld Inc.
500 Old Connecticut Path   Ph: (508)879-0700
Framingham, MA 01701-4649   Free: 800-343-6474
                                     Fax: (508)875-3202
URL: http://careers.computerworld.com.
Contact: Paul Gillin, Editor-in-Chief; John Corrigan, Vice President; Derek Hulitzky, derek_hulitzky@cw.com.
Desc: Magazine containing computer career information for graduating college and university students. *Type:* Periodical.

Computing Technology Industry Association—Membership Directory

Computing Technology Industry Association
450 E. 22nd St., Ste. 230   Ph: (630)268-1818
Lombard, IL 60148-6158   Fax: (630)268-1384
E-mail: info@comptia.org
URL: http://www.comptia.org.
Contact: Kelle Meza, Editor.
Desc: 7,500 member computer hardware and software manufacturers, distributors, associate members, and resellers. *Type:* Directory.

Computists' Weekly

Computists International
4064 Sutherland Dr.   Ph: (650)493-4176
Palo Alto, CA 94303   Free: 888-625-5385
E-mail: editor@computists.com.
URL: http://www.computists.com.
Contact: Dr. Kenneth I. Laws, Editor, laws@computists.com.
Desc: Features news and opportunities in artificial intelligence, information science, and computer science. Remarks: Available online only. *Type:* Newsletter.

ComputorEdge

The Byte Buyer, Inc.
3655 Ruffin Rd., No. 100   Ph: (619)573-0315
San Diego, CA 92123-1833   Free: 800-573-3247
                                     Fax: (619)573-0205
URL: http://www.computoredge.com.
Contact: John San Filippo, Editor, editor@computoredge.com; Elvira Phipps, Advertising Mgr.
Desc: ComputorEdge is the nation's largest regional computer weekly, with editions in Southern California and Colorado. The magazine provides non-technical, entertaining articles on all aspects of computer hardware and software, including productivity, advice, personal experience and an occasional piece of computer-related fiction. While focusing on novice and intermediate computer users and shoppers, our well-educated readers also include experts. *Type:* Periodical.

Configured Systems Home Page

Configured Systems, Inc.
180 Tices Ln.   Ph: (732)249-3559
East Brunswick, NJ 08816   Fax: (732)220-9406
URL: http://www.config-sys.com/
Contact: mike@config-sys.com.
Desc: This site should appeal to CAD users, because it showcases the AutoDesk CAD family of products. There is considerable information about Configured Systems, Inc. *Type:* Database.

Connecting Atari Computers to the Internet

Primenet
1224 E. Washington St.
Phoenix, AZ 85034
E-mail: info@primenet.com
URL: http://www.primenet.com/~whittam/atarinet.html
Contact: whittam@primenet.com.
Desc: This is a site that is dedicated to the Atari computer lover. On this page there are instructions and links that will give Atari users access to the Internet. *Type:* Database.

Contingency Planning & Recovery Journal (CPR-J)

Management Advisory Publications
PO Box 81151   Ph: (781)235-2895
Wellesley Hills, MA 02181   Fax: (781)235-5757
E-mail: jaykmasp@aol.com.
Contact: J.F. Kuong, Editor; C. Winters, Editor.
Desc: Devoted solely to issues, developments, problems, and solutions related to the field of EDP (electronic data processing) contingency planning and recovery. Relates current news items in and outside the field to business continuity and recovery. *Type:* Newsletter.

Control Engineering

Cahners Business Information
1350 E. Touhy Ave.   Ph: (847)635-8800
Des Plaines, IL 60018   Free: 800-446-6551
                                     Fax: (847)635-6856
E-mail: bkinross@cahners.com
Contact: Michael Babb, Editor; Thomas H. Barry, Publisher; Susan Johnson, Production Mgr.

Desc: Magazine covering control and instrumentation systems. *Type:* Periodical.

CPU Info Center

University of California, Berkeley
211-12 Cory Hall No. 1772   Ph: (510)642-9350
EECS Department   Fax: (510)642-2739
Berkeley, CA 94720-1772
URL: http://infopad.eecs.berkeley.edu/CIC/

Contact: Tom Burd, Site Manager, burd@eecs.berkeley.edu.

Desc: The CPU Information Center provides information about the central processing unit of computer hardware. The information includes the latest news in development as well as historical data, publications information, technical documents, and more. *Type:* Database.

Cryptosystems Journal

Tony S. Patti
485 Middle Holland Rd.   Ph: (215)579-9888
Holland, PA 18966
E-mail: Crypto@compuserve.com
URL: http://ourworld.compuserve.com/homepages/crypto.

Contact: Tony S. Patti, Editor.

Desc: Focuses on the implementation of cryptographic systems (encryption and decryption) on IBM personal computers for the education and research in computer science, mathematics, and engineering. Remarks: Diskettes or CD-ROM accompany each issue. *Type:* Newsletter.

The Culpepper Letter

Culpepper and Associates, Inc.
1000 Mansell Exchange West,   Ph: (770)641-5440
Ste. 210   Fax: (770)641-5401
Alpharetta, GA 30022
E-mail: sales@culpepper.com

Contact: Mimi Anderson, Editor, mimi@culpepper.com.

Desc: Carries "practical how-to articles on proven methods to increase sales and marketing productivity," along with current data on industry sales and marketing practices. Ranges over such topics as direct mail, telemarketing, sales quotas and compensation, pricing, and public relations. *Type:* Newsletter.

Current ACITS

Academic Computing and Instructional Technology Services
University of Texas at Austin   Ph: (512)475-9267
Austin, TX 78712   Fax: (512)475-9282
E-mail: newsletter@cc.utexas.edu.
URL: http://www.utexas.edu/cc/newsletter/.

Contact: Dr. Barney C. McCartney, Editor, b.mccartney@cc.utexas.edu.

Desc: Contains news from the academic computing center. *Type:* Newsletter.

Current Cites

Information Systems and Instruction and Support
University of California at Berkeley
Berkeley, CA 94720-6000

Contact: Teri Andrews-Rinne, Editor.

Desc: Abstracts articles from journals in librarianship and computer technology covering optical disc technologies, computer networks and information transfer, electronic publishing, hypermedia, and multimedia. Includes brief annotations with most citations. *Type:* Newsletter.

Cutter IT Journal

Cutter Information Corporation
37 Broadway, Ste. 1   Ph: (781)648-8702
Arlington, MA 02174-5552   Free: 800-325-3717
   Fax: (781)648-1950

E-mail: klovering@cutter.com
Contact: Ed Yourdon, Editor.
Desc: Provides details of software development. *Type:* Newsletter.

Cyberian Outpost Home Page

Cyberian Outpost
27 N. Main St.   Ph: (860)927-2050
PO Box 636   Free: 800-856-9800
Kent, CT 06757   Fax: (860)927-8375
E-mail: sales@outpost.com
URL: http://www.cybout.com/

Desc: The Cyberian Outpost Home Page is a one-stop computer shop containing purchasing information on PCS, Macs, notebooks, powerbooks, modems, monitors, printers, scanners, drives, and networks. You can find almost 120,000 individual software titles among its many offerings. *Type:* Database.

Data Management Strategies

Cutter Information Corporation
37 Broadway, Ste. 1   Ph: (781)648-8702
Arlington, MA 02174-5552   Free: 800-325-3717
   Fax: (781)648-1950

E-mail: klovering@cutter.com
URL: http://www.cutter.com.
Contact: Curt Hall, Editor.

Desc: Contains product reviews and critiques, techology assessments, and industry forecasts and trends. Recurring features include include a calendar of events and notices of publications available. *Type:* Newsletter.

Database

Online, Inc.
213 Danbury Rd.   Ph: (203)761-1466
Wilton, CT 06897-4007   Free: 800-248-8466
   Fax: (203)761-1444
E-mail: info@onlineinc.com; dbmag@onlineinc.com.
URL: http://www.onlineinc.com; http://www.onlineinc.com/database.
Contact: Marydee Ojala, Editor.

Desc: Provides "how-to" articles and information on online and CD-ROM databases. Recurring features include letters to the editor, interviews, reports of meetings, and book reviews. *Type:* Newsletter.

Datamation

Cahners Publishing Company
275 Washington St.   Ph: (617)558-2119
Newton, MA 02458   Fax: (617)558-4700
E-mail: bsemich@cahners.com.
URL: http://www.datamation.com.
Contact: Carole Sacino, Publisher; Regina Twiss, Marketing Manager; J. William Semich, Editor-in-Chief; Ellen Romanow, Editor.

Desc: Magazine on computers and information processing. *Type:* Periodical.

The DataTrends Report on DEC

DataTrends Publications Inc.
PO Box 4460   Ph: (703)779-0574
Leesburg, VA 20177   Free: 800-766-8130
   Fax: (703)779-2267
E-mail: dtrends@ix.netcom.com
Contact: Jeff Caruso, Editor.
Desc: Reports on DEC marketing, networking, network management, software, systems service, and other user issues. *Type:* Newsletter.

DIALINDEX®

The Dialog Corporation
DIALOG
11000 Regency Pkwy., Ste. 400   Ph: (919)462-8600
Cary, NC 27511
URL: http://www.dialog.com
Contact: Marketing.

Desc: Database locator for existing files on Knight-Ridder Information Inc., excluding menu-driven files. Provides the number of postings for each search statement in each of the specified databases. *Available:* The Dialog Corporation, DIALOG. *Type:* Database.

Dick Oliver's Nonlinear Nonsense

Cedar Software
R.R. 1, Box 4495   Ph: (802)888-5275
Wolcott, VT 05680   Fax: (802)888-3009
E-mail: nn@netletter.com.
URL: http://netletter.com.
Contact: Dick Oliver, Editor.
Desc: Provides information on books and computer software pertaining to fractal modeling, chaos science, and creative graphics. *Type:* Newsletter.

DIGEX

DIGEX Incorporated
One DIGEX Plz.   Ph: (301)847-5000
Beltsville, MD 20705   Free: 800-969-9090
   Fax: (301)847-5215
E-mail: webmaster@digex.net
URL: http://www.digex.net
Desc: DIGEX is an Internet service provider and much, much more. DIGEX offers an extensive array of high-speed connectivity options to network your business, from their T1 DIGEX Leased Line to their state-of-the-art fiber optic DIGEX FNS and DIGEX SMDS. *Type:* Database.

Digit

Information Technology Services
University of Colorado
Campus Box 455   Ph: (303)492-8172
Boulder, CO 80309-0455   Fax: (303)492-4198
E-mail: itsfeedback@colorado.edu; digit@colorado.edu.
URL: http://www.colorado.EDU/ITS/Digit; http://www.colorado.edu/cns/digit.
Contact: Wendy DuBow, Editor, (303)492-3878, wendy.dubow@colorado.edu.

Desc: Carries items on the use of University computer, network and telecommunication resources, including review articles, articles on computing on campus, and announcements of pertinent events and activities. Recurring features include news of educational opportunities and how-to documents. *Type:* Newsletter.

The Digital Alumni

The Digital Alumni, Inc.
PO Box 789   Ph: (603)673-6248
Amherst, NH 03031   Fax: (603)673-9492
E-mail: info@decalumni.com
URL: http://www.decalumni.com (for members).
Contact: Jan Bunker, Editor and Publisher, (603)673-6248, jbunker@decalumni.com.

Desc: Acts as a forum for communication among former Digital Equipment Corporation employees. *Type:* Newsletter.

Digital News & Review

Cahners Publishing Company
275 Washington St.   Ph: (617)558-2119
Newton, MA 02458   Fax: (617)558-4700
Contact: Paul Nesdore, Editor; Steve Twombly, Publisher; Wayne Howe, Advertising Dir.; Gwen Brady, Contact; Jennifer London, Sales Coord.

Type: Periodical.

Digital Technical Journal

Digital Equipment Corp.
Compaq Computer Corp.   Free: 800-344-4825
550 King Street, LKG1-2/W7
Littleton, MA 01460-1289
E-mail: dtj@digital.com
URL: http://www.digital.com/info/DTJ/home.html
Desc: The Digital Technical Journal is a refereed journal published quarterly by Digital Equipment Corporation. Articles focus on system engineering, software design, and other technical issues related to computers and computer systems. *Type:* Database.

Distributed Computing Monitor

Patricia Seybold Group
85 Devonshire St., 5th Fl.   Ph: (617)742-5200
Boston, MA 02109-3504   Free: 800-826-2424
                                Fax: (617)742-1028
URL: http://www.psgroup.com.
Contact: Anne Thomas, Editor, athomas@psgroup.com.
Desc: Covers trends and applications within distributed network computing. *Type:* Newsletter.

Do It With Lotus 1-2-3 for Windows

IDG Newsletter Corporation
PO Box 35160
Louisville, KY 40232-5160
Desc: Provides information about Lotus 1-2-3 spreadsheet program for Windows. Includes tips, techniques, and guidance. *Type:* Newsletter.

Do It With Lotus SmartSuite for Windows

IDG Newsletter Corporation
PO Box 35160
Louisville, KY 40232-5160
Desc: Provides information about Lotus SmartSuite. Includes tips and advice about Lotus 1-2-3, Word Pro, Freelance Graphics, Lotus Approach, and Lotus Organizer. *Type:* Newsletter.

Do It With Macintosh System 7.5

IDG Newsletter Corporation
PO Box 35160
Louisville, KY 40232-5160
Desc: Provides information about the Macintosh Operating System 7.5. Includes tips and advice about system software, applications, networks, multimedia, and the Internet. *Type:* Newsletter.

Do It With Microsoft Office for Windows

IDG Newsletter Corporation
PO Box 35160
Louisville, KY 40232-5160
Desc: Provides information about Microsoft Office software. Includes tips and advice about Microsoft Word, Excel, PowerPoint, and Access. *Type:* Newsletter.

Do It With Microsoft Publisher for Windows

IDG Newsletter Corporation
PO Box 35160
Louisville, KY 40232-5160
Desc: Provides information about Microsoft Publisher. Includes design advice, tips, and projects. *Type:* Newsletter.

Do It With Windows 95

IDG Newsletter Corporation
PO Box 35160
Louisville, KY 40232-5160
Desc: Provides information about Microsoft Windows 95. Topics include tips and advice, and the Internet. *Type:* Newsletter.

Dr. Dobb's Journal

Miller Freeman, Inc.—Entertainment Technology Group
411 Borel Ave., Ste. 100   Ph: (650)358-9500
San Mateo, CA 94402   Fax: (650)358-9966
URL: http://www.ddj.com.
Contact: Jonathan Erickson, Editor, (785)842-4818, fax: (785)842-4524, jerickson@mfi.com; Peter Westerman, Publisher, (415)655-4231, pwesterman@mfi.com.
Desc: Magazine. *Type:* Periodical.

Dr. Solomon's Online

S&S Software International Inc.
1 New England Executive Pk.   Free: 800-701-9648
Burlington, MA 01803   Fax: (781)273-7474
E-mail: techhelp@us.drsolomon.com
URL: http://www.drsolomon.com/home/home.cfm
Desc: Dr Solomon's Software is a developer of computer virus detection, identification and disinfection tools for all major operating systems, Groupware applications and e-mail. Dr Solomon's also develops solutions for software and hardware auditing, network management and system administration and a helpdesk management system for support environments. *Type:* Database.

DoIT Now

Division of Information Technology
University of Wisconsin-Madison
1210 W. Dayton St.   Ph: (608)263-4800
Madison, WI 53706   Fax: (608)262-4679
E-mail: doit_now@doit.wisc.edu.
URL: http://www.wisc.edu/doit/.
Contact: Diane Stojanovich Books, Managing Editor.
Desc: Furnishes news on information technology at UW-Madison. *Type:* Newsletter.

Dot.Com

Business Communications Co., Inc.
25 Van Zant St.   Ph: (203)853-4266
Norwalk, CT 06855-1781   Fax: (203)853-0348
E-mail: buscom2@aol.com
URL: http://www.buscom.com; http://www.buscom.com/.
Contact: Betsy Fisher, Editor.
Desc: Covers software and hardware, advertising and marketing, graphic interfaces, and interconnectability on the Internet. Remarks:: Available online only. *Type:* Newsletter.

DSSCourse

Data Storage Systems Center (DSSC)
Carnegie Mellon University   Ph: (412)268-6600
Pittsburgh, PA 15213   Fax: (412)268-3497
Contact: Meg A. Papa, Editor.
Desc: Reports on research conducted at the Center as well as the activities of faculty and students. Recurring features include notices of publications available and news of seminars and workshops. *Type:* Newsletter.

EarthBank Association of North America

Desc: Individuals and organizations feeling an ecological, social, and personal responsibility in their economic and financial activities. Purpose is to facilitate the emergence of a bioregional, self-reliant, and democratic economic system. Promotes an economy that is "sustainable" and therefore includes: individual, community, and regional self-reliance; cooperative enterprises and businesses serving human needs; equal distribution of surplus resources; ecological sustainability; humane and socially responsive values; personal ethics. *Type:* Association.

EDI Bi-Monthly Report

Congressional Information Bureau, Inc.
3030 Clarendon Blvd. No. 202   Ph: (703)516-4801
Arlington, VA 22201-2845   Fax: (703)516-4804
E-mail: info@cibpubs.com
Contact: Robert Cazalas, Editor.
Desc: Serves as a clearinghouse on uses of and developments in electronic data interchange (EDI). Recurring features include interviews, news of research, a calendar of events, reports of meetings, news of educational opportunities, book reviews, and notices of publications available. *Type:* Newsletter.

EDI News

Phillips Business Information, Inc.
1201 Seven Locks Rd., Ste. 300   Ph: (301)340-1520
Potomac, MD 20854   Free: 888-707-5809
                                Fax: (301)340-3847
E-mail: clientservices.pbi@phillips.com
URL: http://www.phillips.com.
Contact: Rika Tadjer, Editor.
Desc: Contains inside news coverage of the implementation of electronic data interchange (EDI) technology by end-users, conversion strategies, developments in the marketplace, growth projections, status reports on industry initiatives, and changes in industry standards. Remarks: Incorporates the former Electronic Trade & Transport News and Quick Response News, merged July 1992. *Type:* Newsletter.

EDP Weekly

Millin Publishing Group, Inc.
714 Church St.   Ph: (703)739-8500
Alexandria, VA 22314   Fax: (703)739-8505
Contact: Charles Bailey, Editor; Mike Cotter, Editor.
Desc: Reports news concerning all aspects of the computer industry. Covers standards, licensing agreements, patents issued, industry growth statistics, new technology, and pertinent legislation. *Type:* Newsletter.

EDPACS

Auerbach Publications
535 Fifth Ave., Ste. 806   Ph: (212)286-1010
New York, NY 10017   Free: 800-272-7737
                                Fax: (212)297-9176
E-mail: orders@cvcpress.com
Contact: Belden Mendus, Editor.
Desc: Provides news for information audit and security professionals. Recurring features include case studies and articles by "expert practitioners" in the field, abstracts of relevant articles in other publications, book reviews, announcements, and commentaries. *Type:* Newsletter.

EECS/ERL News

EECS/ERL News
Department of Electrical Engineering & Computer Sciences (EECS)
University of California, Berkeley
203 Cory Hall, 1770   Ph: (510)643-6685
Berkeley, CA 94720-1770   Fax: (510)643-6694
E-mail: ilp@eecs.berkeley.edu
Contact: Janie Ellison, Editor, janie@eecs.berkeley.edu.
Desc: Covers faculty appointments and activities. Contains news of research, awards, and notices of publications available. *Type:* Newsletter.

Electronic Public Information Newsletter

EPIN Publishing
PO Box 21001   Ph: (301)365-3621
Washington, DC 20009
E-mail: epin@access.digest.net
Contact: James McDonough, Editor.
Desc: Reports on policy and technical issues on the transformation of public information to electronic form. Discusses issues such as public access, public dissemination of electronic information generated and/or controlled by the federal government, and privatization. *Type:* Newsletter.

Enterprise Systems Journal

Boucher Communications Inc.

1300 Virginia Dr., Ste. 400   Ph: (215)643-8000
Fort Washington, PA 19034-   Fax: (215)643-8099
3221
URL: http://www.boucher1.com; http://www.esj.com.

Contact: Calvin Carr, Publisher, carrcb@esj.com; Charlie Simpson, Editor-in-Chief, simpsoncm@esj.com.

Desc: Journal providing authoritative, in-depth information for all IS professionals in IBM host-based enterprises. *Type:* Periodical.

The ESKAY Update

ESKAY Corporation

5245 Yeager Rd.   Ph: (801)295-5315
Salt Lake City, UT 84116-2877   Free: 800-253-1003
E-mail: info@eskay.com
URL: http://www.eskay.com.

Contact: Gary Dulude, Editor.

Desc: Promotes the widespread acceptance and use of quality, affordable, and innovative modular Automted Storage and Retrieval Systems (AS/RS) in small to large companies in a variety of industries with diverse material handling applications. Recurring features include interviews, news of research, reports of meetings, news of educational opportunities, application features, case studies, product announcements, new literature, trends in the marketplace, and columns titled Letter from the President and New Contracts. *Type:* Newsletter.

The Evans Report

Evans Research Corporation

1 Eva Rd., Ste. 309   Ph: (416)621-8814
Etobieoke, ON, Canada M9E   Fax: (416)621-8031
4Z3

Contact: Bill Fournier, Director of Research.

Desc: Provides statistics on and makes forecasts concerning revenues and trends in the Canadian information technology industry. Derives information from market research data. *Type:* Newsletter.

Family PC

Ziff-Davis Inc.

28 E. 28th St.   Ph: (212)503-3500
New York, NY 10016   Fax: (212)503-5799

Contact: Robin Raskin, (512)503-4345, fax: (212)503-4399, robin_raskin@zd.com; Todd Anderman, Assoc. Pub., (212)503-4330, todd_anderman@zd.com.

Desc: Magazine aimed at families with computers. *Type:* Periodical.

Family PC On The Web

Ziff-Davis Inc.

650 Townsend St.   Ph: (415)551-4500
San Francisco, CA 94103
URL: http://www.zdnet.com/familypc/

Desc: This colorful publication focuses on the computing needs of families and children. It includes reviews of software and web sites appropriate for families, as well as detailed hardware reviews and the latest computer news. *Type:* Database.

Federal Computer Week

International Data Group

5 Speen St.   Ph: (508)879-0700
PO Box 9171   Free: 800-343-4935
Framingham, MA 01701   Fax: (508)875-8931

Contact: Anne Armstrong, Editor-in-Chief; Steve Vito, Publisher; Brad Bass, Editor.

Desc: Computer newspaper (tabloid) for government systems decision-makers. *Alt. Contact:* 3141 Fairview Park Dr., Ste. 777, Falls Church, VA 22042; telephone: (703)876-5100; fax: (703)876-5126. *Type:* Periodical.

Foxtalk

Pinnacle Publishing, Inc.

PO Box 72255   Ph: (770)565-1763
Marietta, GA 30007-2255   Free: 800-788-1900
   Fax: (770)565-8232
E-mail: foxtalk@pinpub.com.
URL: http://www.pinpub.com.

Contact: Whil Hentzen, Editor.

Desc: Features tips, product reviews, and shortcuts for Microsoft Corporation's FoxPRO. *Type:* Newsletter.

FT Systems Newsletter

ITOM International Company

PO Box 1450   Ph: (650)948-4516
Los Altos, CA 94023

Contact: Omri Serlin, Editor, omris@cup.portal.com; omri@juno.com.

Desc: Analyzes important market, company, and product developments in Fault-Tolerant (FT) computers and On-Line Transaction Processing (OLTP) systems. Recurring features include news of research, reports of meetings, and a calendar of events. *Type:* Newsletter.

Geospatial Information and Technology Association

14456 E. Evans Ave.   Ph: (303)337-0513
Aurora, CO 80014   Fax: (303)337-1001
E-mail: staff@gita.org
URL: http://www.gita.org

Contact: Robert M. Samborski, Exec.Dir.

Desc: Representatives from utilities, municipalities, and the telecommunications industry; vendors, service companies, and consultants. Focuses on "excellence in geospatial information techniques". Promotes education and the exchange of information in the AM/FM/GIS industry. *Type:* Association.

GNU's Bulletin

Free Software Foundation

59 Temple Pl., Ste. 330   Ph: (617)542-5942
Boston, MA 02111-1307   Fax: (617)542-2652
E-mail: gnu@prep.ai.mit.edu.

Desc: Reports on the activities of the Association, which is "dedicated to eliminating restrictions on copying, redistribution, understanding, and modification of computer programs." Remarks: Sample issue available in hard copy for a stamped self-addressed envelope, but a subscription list is not maintained text is available on-line as well. *Type:* Newsletter.

Government Computer News

Cahners Publishing Company

1350 E. Touhy Ave.   Ph: (847)635-8800
Des Plaines, IL 60018
URL: http://www.cahners.com

Desc: Contains the complete text of Government Computer News, a semimonthy publication covering minicomputers, microcomputers, mainframes, information resource management, and new products and applications used in federal and state government. *Available:* LEXIS-NEXIS, NEXIS. *Type:* Database.

Government Computer News

Cahners Publishing Company

275 Washington St.   Ph: (617)558-2119
Newton, MA 02458   Fax: (617)558-4700
URL: http://www.gcn.com.

Contact: Thomas R. Temin, Editor; Gary R. Squires, Publisher; Franke Pass, Jr., Production Dir.; Elaine Ross, Business Mgr.; Linda Carpenter, Editorial Asst.

Desc: Magazine for government technical and management executives responsible for managing and buying information technology products and services. Covers computer/communications news, trends, applications, and products impacting government operations. *Alt. Contact:* 8601 Georgia Ave., Ste. 300, Silver Spring, MD 20910; telephone: (301)650-2000; fax: (301)650-2111. *Type:* Periodical.

Gratefully Yours

National Library of Medicine
National Institutes of Health
U.S. Department of Health and Human Services

8600 Rockville Pike, Bldg. 38   Ph: (301)496-7771
Bethesda, MD 20894   Free: 800-272-4787
   Fax: (301)496-7831

Contact: Mel F. Brdlik, Editor.

Desc: Serves "as a forum for exchanging information between the National Library of Medicine and members of the NLM online network." Recurring features include news of research and a collection. *Type:* Newsletter.

The Gray Sheet: IDC's Forecast of IT Opportunity

International Data Corporation (IDC)

5 Speen St.   Free: 800-217-9828
Framingham, MA 01701
E-mail: graysheet@idcresearch.com.
URL: http://www.idc.com.

Contact: Molly Upton, Editor, (508)935-4661, fax: (508)935-4397, mupton@idc.com.

Desc: Provides news of original research and explains important trends in the worldwide information technology industry. Analyzes, segments, and sizes worldwide computer markets. *Type:* Newsletter.

GUI Program News

Worldwide Videotex

PO Box 3273   Ph: (561)738-2276
Boynton Beach, FL 33424-3273
URL: http://www.wvpubs.com.

Desc: Covers applications of graphical user interfaces (GUI) for personal computers and workstations, including Windows, 3.0, OS/2 Presentation Manager, OPEN LOOK, MOTIF, and NextStep. Emphasizes vendor marketing techniques. *Type:* Newsletter.

gw2k.com

Gateway

610 Gateway Dr.   Ph: (605)232-2000
PO Box 2000   Free: 800-846-4208
North Sioux City, SD 57049-   Fax: (605)232-2023
2000
URL: http://www.gw2k.com

Desc: Features detailed product descriptions and ordering information for consumers, businesses, institutions, and organizations. Notably, you can order your Gateway computer on-line. *Type:* Database.

Hands On!

TERC

2067 Massachusetts Ave.   Ph: (617)547-0430
Cambridge, MA 02140   Fax: (617)349-3535
E-mail: communications@terc.edu
URL: http://www.terc.edu.

Contact: Peggy Kapisovsky, Editor.

Desc: Focuses on innovative education programs and activities in science, mathematics, and technology. *Type:* Newsletter.

Hewlett-Packard Homepage

Hewlett-Packard

3000 Hanover St.   Ph: (415)857-1501
Palo Alto, CA 94304   Fax: (415)857-7299
URL: http://www.hp.com

Desc: Provides in depth information on HP products and services, including printers, tape drives, PCs, and networking equipment. Also includes detailed technical support information, along with industry news. *Type:* Database.

Home-Office Computing
Scholastic, Inc.
555 Broadway   Ph: (212)343-6100
New York, NY 10012   Free: 800-724-6527
   Fax: (212)343-4535
E-mail: custserv@scholastic.com
URL: http://www.scholastic.com
Contact: Cathy Grayson Brower, Executive Editor; Hugh Roome, Publisher; Bernadette Grey, Editor-in-Chief.
Desc: Magazine focusing on computers and related technology for working at home. *Type:* Periodical.

Home PC
CMP Media Inc.
600 Community Dr.   Ph: (516)562-5000
Manhasset, NY 11030   Fax: (516)562-7830
URL: http://www.cmp.net
Contact: Ellen Pearlman, Editor-in-Chief, (516)562-5000, fax: (516)562-7007; Amy Lipton, Executive Editor.
Desc: Magazine aimed at families with computers. *Type:* Periodical.

The HP Palmtop Paper
Thaddeus Computing, Inc.
110 North Court   Ph: (515)472-6330
PO Box 869   Free: 800-373-6114
Fairfield, IA 52556   Fax: (515)472-1879
E-mail: orders@thaddeus.com
URL: http://www.thaddeus.com.
Contact: Hal Goldstein, Editor; Richard Hall, Editor.
Desc: Support publication for Hewlett-Packard Palmtop and Windows CE users. *Type:* Newsletter.

I Mall Inc.
I Mall Inc.
4400 Coldwater Blvd., Ste. 200   Ph: (818)509-3600
Studio City, CA 91604   Fax: (818)509-3641
URL: http://www.imall.com
Desc: The bane of the traditional Internet user, Internet shopping malls have come a long way since they first opened for business way back in 1994 and 1995. Among these, I Mall stands out for the extensive variety of "shops" it hosts. *Type:* Database.

I/S Analyzer
The 400 Group
990 Washington St., Ste. 308   Ph: (617)320-8909
Dedham, MA 02026   Free: 800-477-7359
   Fax: (617)320-9466
E-mail: customer@the400group.com
Contact: Rob Shapiro, Publisher, robs@the400group.com; Joanne Cummings, Editor.
Desc: Focuses on management issues of concern to information systems and data processing executives. Focuses in-depth on one topic per issue, with commentary, relevant case studies, and a concluding summary. *Type:* Newsletter.

IEEE Computer Society
IEEE Computer Society
10662 Los Vaqueros Cir.   Ph: (714)821-8380
PO Box 3014   Free: 800-272-6657
Los Alamitos, CA 90720-1264   Fax: (714)821-4010
E-mail: webmaster@computer.org
URL: http://www.computer.org/
Desc: The IEEE Computer Society provides information on the Society's conferences and tutorials, applications, research-oriented journals, local and student branch chapters, technical committees, and standards working groups. Directories are available, as well as a calendar of events, educational information, and an interesting section detailing the history of computing. *Type:* Database.

III Newsletters
Information Intelligence, Inc. (III)
P.O. Box 31098   Ph: (602)996-2283
Phoenix, AZ 85046
E-mail: rhuleatt@infointelligence.com
URL: http://www.infointelligence.com/www/iii-info
Contact: Richard S. Huleatt, (602)996-2283, info@infointelligence.com.
Desc: Contains the full-text corresponding to the online and print editions of three newsletters (1980-1989): • Online Newsletter; • Online Libraries and Microcomputers; • Online Hotline. *Available:* Colorado Alliance of Research Libraries. *Type:* Database.

Imaging Magazine
Telecom Library, Inc.
12 W. 21st St.   Ph: (212)691-8215
New York, NY 10011   Free: 800-999-0345
   Fax: (212)691-1191
Contact: Mark Young, Editor, markyoung@imagingmagazine.com; Muriel Fullam, Business Mgr., muriel@nyoffice.mhs.com.
Desc: Magazine for information professionals. Topics include desktop publishing, magnetic and optical imaging, and computer imaging accessories. *Type:* Periodical.

In Command
Economics Press, Inc.
12 Daniel Rd.   Ph: (973)227-1224
Fairfield, NJ 07004-2565   Free: 800-526-2554
   Fax: (973)526-2554
E-mail: info@epinc.com; order@epinc.com
URL: http://www.epinc.com
Contact: Phil Hall, Editor.
Desc: Reviews word processing skills and training. Remarks: Closed series of 45 issues offered in bulk or over 45 weeks. *Type:* Newsletter.

The Independent
Independent Computer Consultants Association
PO Box 27412   Ph: (314)892-1675
443 N. New Ballas, No. 249   Free: 800-774-4222
St. Louis, MO 63141   Fax: (314)487-1345
E-mail: 70007.1407@compuserve.com
URL: http://www.icca.org.
Desc: Supports the Association by seeking to promote professionalism among member computer consultants, to increase awareness of products and services available, and to disseminate news and information about Association activities and benefits. Reports legislative and regulatory developments as well as information on marketing and business materials available. *Type:* Newsletter.

InfoAdvantage Internet Guide
InfoAdvantage
500 108th Ave. NE, Ste. 800   Ph: (425)869-2157
Bellevue, WA 98004   Fax: (425)869-6551
E-mail: info@businesscity.com
URL: http://www.businesscity.com
Contact: Eva Chiu, Publisher, echiu@infoadvantage.com.
Desc: Tracks current business information resources, references, and methods to create a competitive advantage on the Internet. Reviews business content websites. *Type:* Newsletter.

INFOMINE
University of California, Riverside
Riverside, CA 92521
URL: http://lib-www.ucr.edu/
Contact: Steve Mitchell, Sciences Ref. Libn., smitch@ucrac1.ucr.edu.
Desc: INFOMINE is a virtual library of indexed and annotated links to over 10000 Internet resources, including databases, Internet guides, electronic books and journals, conference proceedings, listservs, library catalogs, bulletin boards, articles, and directories, among others. One of the first Web-based, academic virtual libraries, INFOMINE allows users to browse by date, or table of contents, and browse or search by title, subject, or keyword. *Type:* Database.

Infoperspectives
Technology News of America, Inc.
110 Greene St., No. 1101   Ph: (212)334-9750
New York, NY 10012-3824
Contact: Hest Wiener, Editor.
Desc: Looks at IBM and compatible companies. Focuses on mainframe computers. *Type:* Newsletter.

The Information Freeway Report
Washington Researchers
416 Hungerford Dr., Ste. 315   Ph: (301)251-9550
Rockville, MD 20850   Fax: (301)251-9526
E-mail: research@researchers.com
URL: http://www.researchers.com/pub/businint/sample.html.
Contact: Leila K. Kight, President and Publisher.
Desc: Monitors the Internet and provides business and government information that is available by modem, free of charge, and not available on commercial databases. *Type:* Newsletter.

Information Industry Directory
Gale Group Inc.
27500 Drake Rd.   Ph: (248)699-4253
Farmington Hills, MI 48331-3535   Free: 800-877-GALE
   Fax: (248)699-8070
E-mail: galeord@galegroup.com
URL: http://www.galegroup.com.; http://www.gale.com.
Contact: Joe Tardiff, Editor, joe_tardiff@gale.com.
Desc: Approximately 8,800 organizations, systems, and services involved in the production and distribution of information in electronic form: database producers and their products, online host services, internet services, bulletin board systems, CD-ROM publishers and service companies, videotex/teletext information services, transactional services, library and information networks, bibliographic utilities, library management systems, information retrieval software, mailing list services, fee-based information on demand services, document delivery sources, data collection and analysis centers and firms, and related consultants, service companies, professional and trade associations, publishers, and research activities. *Type:* Directory.

Information Superhighways
Information Gatekeepers Inc.
214 Harvard Ave.   Ph: (617)232-3111
Boston, MA 02134   Free: 800-323-1088
   Fax: (617)734-8562
E-mail: info@igigroup.com
URL: http://wwwigigroup.com
Contact: Nomi Burstein, Managing Editor.
Desc: Covers major policy, regulation, technical, marketing, and user aspects of information technology/superhighways. *Type:* Newsletter.

Information Technology Association of America
c/o ITAA
1616 N. Fort Meyer Dr., Ste. 1300   Ph: (703)522-5055
   Fax: (703)525-2279
Arlington, VA 22209-9998
Contact: Harris Miller, Pres.
Desc: A division of the Information Technology Association of America . Software companies involved in the development or marketing of software for personal, midrange, and mainframe computers. Promotes the software industry and addresses specific problems of the industry. *Type:* Association.

Computers

Information Technology Association of America—Membership Directory

Information Technology Association of America (ITAA)
1616 N. Fort Myer Dr., Ste. 1300   Ph: (703)522-5055
Arlington, VA 22209   Fax: (703)525-2279

Contact: Paul Green, Editor.

Desc: About 350 member information technology organizations primarily in the U.S.; limited international coverage. *Type:* Directory.

Information Technology Digest

University of Michigan
535 W. William   Ph: (313)763-8980
Ann Arbor, MI 48103   Fax: (313)763-8937
E-mail: digest.team@umich.edu.
URL: http://www.itd.umich.edu/ITdigest/.

Contact: Janet Eaton, Editor.

Desc: Covers computing at the University. *Type:* Newsletter.

Information Technology Industry Council

1250 Eye St. NW, Ste. 200   Ph: (202)737-8888
Washington, DC 20005   Fax: (202)638-4922
E-mail: webmaster@itic.org
URL: http://www.itic.org

Contact: Rhett B. Dawson, Pres.

Desc: Represents manufacturers of information technology products. Serves as secretariat and technology for ANSI-accredited standards committee x3 information technology group. *Type:* Association.

Information WEEK

CMP Media Inc.
600 Community Dr.   Ph: (516)562-5000
Manhasset, NY 11030   Fax: (516)562-7830
URL: http://www.cmp.net; http://www.techweb.cmp.com.

Contact: E. Drake Lundell, Jr., Publisher; Jim Richardson, Publisher; Charles L. Martin, Jr., Publisher; Laurie Schnepf, Editor; Dawn Williams, Advertising Mgr.

Desc: Magazine focusing on data and information processing news and strategies. *Type:* Periodical.

Information Week

CMP Media Inc.
600 Community Dr.   Ph: (516)562-5000
Manhasset, NY 11030
URL: http://www.cmp.com

Desc: Contains the complete text of Information Week, a weekly newspaper covering companies, individuals, products, and events in the computer and communications industries. *Available:* LEXIS-NEXIS, NEXIS. *Type:* Database.

InfoTech Report

International City/County Management Association
777 N. Capitol St. NE, Ste. 500   Ph: (202)289-4262
Washington, DC 20002-4201   Free: 800-745-8780
    Fax: (202)962-3500
URL: http://www.icma.org

Contact: Christine Ulrich, Editor.

Desc: Provides information on information technology and telecommunications applications in local government and public agencies. Covers recent innovations regarding software and microcomputers. *Type:* Newsletter.

InfoWorld

InfoWorld
155 Bovet Rd.   Free: 800-227-8365
San Mateo, CA 94402   Fax: (415)312-0580

Contact: Jim Martin, Publisher; Stewart Alsop, President; Michael Lowe, Editor-in-Chief; Patrick Crotty, Sr. VP Circulation/Research; Joel Deceuster, Vice President; Joel Deceuster, Assoc. Publisher.

Desc: Weekly IS publication. *Alt. Contact:* 155 Bovet Rd., Ste. 800, San Mateo, CA 94402-3115; telephone: (415)572-7341; fax: (415)358-1269. *Type:* Periodical.

InfoWorld Direct

International Data Group
5 Speen St.   Ph: (508)879-0700
PO Box 9171   Free: 800-343-4935
Framingham, MA 01701   Fax: (508)875-8931

Desc: Magazine focusing on purchasing software and hardware products. *Type:* Periodical.

Inlet Web News and Notes

Inlet Web News & Notes
818 Dows Rd. SE   Ph: (319)369-0096
Cedar Rapids, IA 52403   Free: 800-823-0096
    Fax: (319)369-3089
E-mail: inlet@inlet.com

Contact: Lisa Slattery, Editor.

Desc: Contains information on topics relating to publishing data on the Internet. Recurring features include news of research. *Type:* Newsletter.

Inside ILE

The 400 Group
990 Washington St., Ste. 308   Ph: (617)320-8909
Dedham, MA 02026   Free: 800-477-7359
    Fax: (617)320-9466
E-mail: customer@the400group.com

Contact: Ron Turull, Editor, ront@the400group.com.

Desc: Provides suggestions and recommendations on how to best utilize ILE to increase productivity. *Type:* Newsletter.

Inside Microsoft Word 6

The Cobb Group
500 Canal View Blvd.   Free: 800-223-8720
Rochester, NY 14623-2800

Contact: Jody Gilbert, Editor.

Desc: Offers articles on applications, time-saving routines, and problem-solving relating to Microsoft's Word 6 computer software. *Type:* Newsletter.

Inside the New Computer Industry

Andrew Allison, Publisher
25420 Via Cicindela   Ph: (408)626-4361
Carmel, CA 93923-8412   Fax: (408)626-4362
URL: http://www.aallison.com.

Contact: Andrew Allison, Editor and Publisher, aallison@mbay.net.

Desc: Analyses strategic issues and trends in the computer industry. *Type:* Newsletter.

Inside Version 3

The 400 Group
990 Washington St., Ste. 308   Ph: (617)320-8909
Dedham, MA 02026   Free: 800-477-7359
    Fax: (617)320-9466
E-mail: customer@the400group.com

Contact: Ron Turull, ED, rturull@the400group.com.

Desc: Assists computer users in strategies and methods to successful use OS/400. *Type:* Newsletter.

Inside Wordperfect for Windows

The Cobb Group
500 Canal View Blvd.   Free: 800-223-8720
Rochester, NY 14623-2800

Contact: Duane Spurlock, Editor.

Desc: Offers tips and techniques for WordPerfect for Windows users who have either beginning, intermediate, or advanced levels of experience with the wordprocessing software. Recurring features include letters to the editor. *Type:* Newsletter.

Insider Weekly for AS/400 Managers

The 400 Group
990 Washington St., Ste. 308   Ph: (617)320-8909
Dedham, MA 02026   Free: 800-477-7359
    Fax: (617)320-9466
E-mail: customer@the400group.com
URL: http://www.the400group.com.

Contact: Rizal Ahmed, Editor, rizala@the400group.com.

Desc: Reports on IBM's AS/400 system. Includes IBM's strategic AS/400 plans. *Type:* Newsletter.

INSPEC™

Institute of Electrical and Electronics Engineers (IEEE)
445 Hoes Ln.   Ph: (732)562-5390
Piscataway, NJ 08855
E-mail: iel@ieee.org
URL: http://www.ieee.org

Desc: Contains more than 6 million citations, with abstracts, to the worldwide literature in physics, electronics and electrical engineering, computers and control, and information technology. Primary coverage is of journal articles and papers presented at conferences, although significant books, technical reports, and dissertations are also included. *Available:* Ovid Technologies, Inc.; Ovid Technologies, Inc.; France Ministry of Defense, Delegation Generale pour l'Armement, Centre de Documentation de l'Armement (CEDOCAR); The Dialog Corporation, DataStar; The Dialog Corporation, DIALOG; The Dialog Corporation, DIALOG; CompuServe Information Service, Knowledge Index; FIZ Technik (Fachinformationszentrum Technik e.V.); Questel • Orbit; Questel • Orbit; STN International; STN International; National Science Council, Science and Technology Information Center Network (STICNET); OCLC Online Computer Library Center, Inc., OCLC EPIC; OCLC Online Computer Library Center, Inc., OCLC FirstSearch Catalog; NIFTY Corporation, NIFTY-SERVE; European Information Network Services (EINS). *Type:* Database.

Institute for Certification of Computing Professionals

2200 E. Devon Ave., Ste. 247   Ph: (847)299-4227
Des Plaines, IL 60018   Free: 800-U-GET-CCP
    Fax: (847)299-4280
E-mail: 74040.3722@compuserve.com
URL: http://www.iccp.org

Contact: Cynthia A. Blaese, Contact.

Desc: Professional societies united to. promote the development of computer examinations which are of high quality, directed toward information technology professionals, and designed to encourage competence and professionalism. *Type:* Association.

Intel Corp.

Intel Corp.
2200 Mission College Blvd.   Ph: (408)765-8080
Santa Clara, CA 95052-8119   Free: 800-628-8686
    Fax: (408)765-1402
E-mail: support@cs.intel.com
URL: http://www.intel.com

Desc: Logically laid-out and attractively designed, this site makes it easy to find what you're looking for. Special sections for developers, customer support, and resellers are provided right on the homepage, along with areas to click on for detailed product and company information, technology tips, cool software, Intel forums, press releases, and a custom news option. *Type:* Database.

Intelligent Software Strategies

Cutter Information Corporation
37 Broadway, Ste. 1   Ph: (781)648-8702
Arlington, MA 02174-5552   Free: 800-325-3717
                                 Fax: (781)648-1950
E-mail: klovering@cutter.com
URL: http://www.cutter.com.
Contact: Curt Hall, Editor.
Desc: Contains product reviews and critiques, technology assessments, and industry forecasts and trends. Recurring features include a calendar of events and notices of publications available. *Type:* Newsletter.

Intelligent Systems Report

AIWeek Inc.
2555 Cumberland Pkwy., Ste.   Ph: (770)431-0867
  299   Free: 800-392-7294
Atlanta, GA 30339   Fax: (770)432-6969
E-mail: info@lionhrtpub.com
URL: http://lionhrtpub.com.
Contact: David Blanchard, Editor, blanchard@lionhrtpub.com.
Desc: Provides news concerning the development of intelligent computing systems. Spotlights such topics as AI, expert systems, neural networks, fuzzy logic, voice recognition, multimedia, and virtual reality. *Type:* Newsletter.

Inter@ctive Week

ZDNet Publishing
650 Townsend St.   Ph: (415)551-4500
San Francisco, CA 94103
E-mail: webmaster@zd.com
URL: http://www.zdnet.com/intweek/
Contact: dkamil@zd.com.
Desc: This site is a combination of online-only content and articles from the print version of the magazine. It covers all aspects of computer networks and interactivity, including news about telecommunications, cable, wireless, the Internet, commercial online services, Web sites du jour, business, and technology stocks. *Type:* Database.

INTEREX

1192 Borregas Ave.   Ph: 800-468-3739
Sunnyvale, CA 94089   Free: 800-INT-EREX
                                 Fax: (408)747-0947
E-mail: info@interex.org
URL: http://www.interex.org
Contact: Chuck Piercey, Exec.Dir.
Desc: Users of Hewlett-Packard (HP) computers and related equipment. Promotes the exchange of information between HP computer users and HP. Provides members with the opportunity to constructively influence the design and development of these systems, including HP-UX, MPE, RTE, and workstations. *Type:* Association.

International Disk Drive Equipment and Materials Association

3255 Scott Blvd., Ste. 2-102   Ph: (408)330-8100
Santa Clara, CA 95054-3013   Fax: (408)492-1425
E-mail: idema@idema.org
URL: http://www.idema.org
Contact: Debbie Lee, Program Mgr.
Desc: Corporations (720), individuals (100), and universities (12) with an interest in data storage technologies. Promotes the technological, manufacturing, marketing, and business progress of the data storage industry. *Type:* Association.

International Software Report

RM Publishing Corporation
29327 Stonecrest Rd.   Ph: (310)544-5539
Rolling Hills Estates, CA 90275-
  5707
Contact: Martha Newton, Editor.
Desc: Discusses software end-users, vendors, and products. Tracks trends in alliances, support, and government regulation. *Type:* Newsletter.

Internet Business Report

Jupiter Communications
627 Broadway, 2nd Fl.   Ph: (212)780-6060
New York, NY 10012-2612   Free: 800-488-4345
                                 Fax: (212)780-6075
URL: http://www.jup.com.
Contact: Ross Scott Rubin, Group Dir., Consumer Internet Tech.
Desc: Delivers an insider's perspective on the events that impact business on the Internet. Examines the tools and technologies that are making a difference to consumer-focused businesses and keeps abreast of the top players that are transforming the way consumers receive information and entertainment. *Type:* Newsletter.

The Internet Connection

Bernan Associates
4611-F Assembly Dr.   Ph: (301)459-2255
Lanham, MD 20706-4391   Free: 800-274-4447
                                 Fax: (301)459-0056
E-mail: query@bernan.com
URL: http://www.bernan.com
Desc: Devoted to "finding free or low-cost information available from the U.S. government on the Internet." *Type:* Newsletter.

Internet Help Desk

OneNet Communications, Inc.
9944 Reading Rd.   Ph: (513)554-1638
Cincinnati, OH 45241   Free: 800-315-1411
E-mail: webmaster@one.net
URL: http://w3.one.net/~alward/
Contact: Amy Ward, alward@one.net.
Desc: The Internet Help Desk provides expert tools combined with advice on troubleshooting software and connection problems for Internet users. There is a troubleshooting section for sending and receiving email, connecting to a telnet, FTP, or Web site, Windows 3.1 GPFs and system crashes, and more. *Type:* Database.

Internet Integrator

Corry Publishing, Inc.
2840 W. 21st St.   Ph: (814)838-0025
Erie, PA 16506-9945   Free: 800-368-9597
                                 Fax: (814)836-9605
Contact: Rich Peterman, Editor.
Desc: Provides advice and information for third-party web developers, out-of-house web consultants, and subcontract web site builders and marketers working on web development for a profit. Recurring features include interviews. *Type:* Newsletter.

The Internet Newsroom

Editors Service
PO Box 737   Ph: (301)365-8065
Glen Echo, MD 20812   Fax: (301)365-0639
E-mail: editors@editors-service.com
Contact: T.K. Maloy, Editor.
Desc: Serves as users guide to the Internet. Recurring features include news of research. *Type:* Newsletter.

Internet Society

12020 Sunrise Valley Dr., Ste.   Ph: (703)648-9888
  210   Fax: (703)648-9887
Reston, VA 20191-3429
E-mail: membership@isoc.org
URL: http://www.isoc.org
Contact: Donald M. Heath, Pres.
Desc: Technologists, developers, educators, researchers, government representatives, and business people. Seeks to ensure global cooperation and coordination for the Internet and related internetworking technologies and applications. *Type:* Association.

Internet Week

Phillips Business Information, Inc.
1201 Seven Locks Rd., Ste. 300   Ph: (301)340-1520
Potomac, MD 20854   Free: 888-707-5809
                                 Fax: (301)340-3847
E-mail: clientservices.pbi@phillips.com
URL: http://www.phillips.com/iw.
Contact: Kerry O'Rourke, Editor, korouke@phillips.com.
Desc: Provides information about business opportunities on the Internet. Includes market news and analysis. *Type:* Newsletter.

Internet.com

Mecklermedia Corporation
20 Ketchum St.   Ph: (203)226-6967
Westport, CT 06880   Fax: (203)454-5840
E-mail: info@mecklermedia.com
URL: http://www.internet.com/
Contact: feedback@internet.com.
Desc: This comprehensive site keeps users up to date on Internet news and resources. The Electronic Commerce Guide features links to sites related to the electronic commerce industry. *Type:* Database.

INTRAnet News

Publications Resource Group (PRG)
PO Box 765   Ph: (413)664-6185
North Adams, MA 01247   Fax: (413)664-9343
Contact: Lawrence Gasman, Editor.
Desc: Focuses on developments in the Intranet mearketplace. Includes information on applications, products, and services, and what companies are implementing Intranets. *Type:* Newsletter.

Intranet Professional

Information Today, Inc.
143 Old Marlton Pike   Ph: (609)654-6266
Medford, NJ 08055   Free: 800-300-9868
                                 Fax: (609)654-4309
E-mail: custserv@infotoday.com
URL: http://www.infotoday.com
Contact: Howard McQueen, Editor.
Desc: Provides information on the development of library Intranets, including search engines, document management systems, collaboration systems, and access to databases. Also includes advice and tips from systems librarians, web designers and engineers on how to implement Intranet technologies. *Type:* Newsletter.

ISDN User

Information Gatekeepers Inc.
214 Harvard Ave.   Ph: (617)232-3111
Boston, MA 02134   Free: 800-323-1088
                                 Fax: (617)734-8562
E-mail: info@igigroup.com
URL: http://www.igigroup.com
Contact: Paul Polishuk, Editor.
Desc: Provides news ISDN (Integrated Services Digital Network) applications, tariffs, user groups, technology, equipment, and software. *Type:* Newsletter.

IT Consulting

Corry Publishing, Inc.
2840 W. 21st St.
Erie, PA 16506-9945

Ph: (814)838-0025
Free: 800-368-9597
Fax: (814)836-9605

Contact: Rob Bernath, Editor.

Desc: Assists computer professionals in advancing their careers and businesses. Recurring features include news of educational opportunities, job listings, and billing rate surveys. *Type:* Newsletter.

Japan Computer Industry Scan

Kyodo News International, Inc.
50 Rockefeller Plaza, Rm. 803
New York, NY 10020

Ph: (212)397-3723

URL: http://www.kyodonews.com

Desc: Contains news of developments in the Japanese computer industry and markets. Covers such topics as research and development, market shares and production quotas, licensing agreements with non-Japanese manufacturers, and the Japanese market for U.S. computer products. *Type:* Database.

The Jeffries Letter

Jeffries Research
2263 Callender Rd.
Arroyo Grande, CA 93420

Ph: (805)343-5444
Fax: (805)343-2118

E-mail: info@jeffriesletter.com.

Contact: Ron Jeffries, Editor.

Desc: Provides analysis and commentary of advanced networking industry. *Type:* Newsletter.

Journal of Computing and Information

Trent University
Petersborough, ON, Canada
K9J 7B8

E-mail: jci@trentu.ca

URL: http://phoenix.trentu.ca/jci/

Desc: The Journal of Computing and Information is an archive of papers from seven different conferences and the contributions of hundreds of researchers. The presentations cover a wide variety of topics. *Type:* Database.

Kermit News

Kermit Distribution and Development
Academic Information Systems
612 W. 115th St.
New York, NY 10025

Ph: (212)854-3703
Fax: (212)663-8202

URL: http://www.columbia.edu/kermit/.

Contact: Christine M. Gianone, Editor.

Desc: Focuses on Kermit communications software program, including new releases, technical articles and applications. *Type:* Newsletter.

The KERNEL

Waters Computing Center
Rose-Hulman Institute of Technology
5500 Wabash Ave.
Terre Haute, IN 47803

Ph: (812)877-1511
Fax: (812)877-8121

Contact: Nancy J. Bauer, Editor.

Desc: Provides news and information on computing and data communications. *Type:* Newsletter.

Keystone Center

The Keystone Center
1628 St. John Rd.
Keystone, CO 80435-7707

Ph: (970)468-5822
Fax: (970)262-0152

Contact: Robert W. Craig, Pres.

Desc: Center for environmental dispute resolution and education. Conducts national policy dialogues on environmental, energy, natural resources, health and science/technology issues. *Type:* Association.

Keywords

SPSS Inc.
444 N. Michigan Ave.
Chicago, IL 60611

Ph: (312)329-2400
Fax: (312)329-3668

Contact: David Pittman, Editor.

Desc: Intended for users of SPSS, Inc. computer software. *Type:* Newsletter.

Kids Web World

Computer Dynamics
PO Box 523
Mason, OH 45040

Ph: (513)398-5934
Free: 888-932-4543
Fax: (513)398-5931

E-mail: 100550.563@compuserve.com

Contact: Sonja Leonard, Editor.

Desc: Contains information for parents about kids and the Internet and kids and computers. Recurring features include interviews, news of research, notices of publications available, and columns titled Virtual Internet Field Trip, Computers in the Classroom, and Online Service Review. *Type:* Newsletter.

KM World

Knowledge Asset Media, Inc.
18 Bayview St.
Camden, ME 04843

Ph: (207)236-8524
Fax: (207)236-6452

E-mail: editor@kmworld.com.

URL: http://www.kmworld.com.

Contact: Andy Moore, Ed. in Chief/Co-Publisher, andy_moore@kmworld.com; Dan Bolita, Executive Ed., dan_bolita@kmworld.com; Jennifer McIntosh, Managing Ed., jennifer_mcintosh@kmworld.com; Bruce Taylor, President/CEO, bruck_taylor@kmworld.com.

Desc: Journal focusing on the applications of knowledge management solutions as they apply to business and corporations. *Type:* Periodical.

LAN Product News

Worldwide Videotex
PO Box 3273
Boynton Beach, FL 33424-3273

Ph: (561)738-2276

E-mail: markedit@juno.com.

URL: http://www.wvpubs.com.

Desc: Discusses developments on the local area network (LAN) industry. Highlights application hardware and software, market planning, news of research, and industry standardization. *Type:* Newsletter.

LAN Times

McGraw-Hill, Inc.
221 Main St., 8th Fl.
San Francisco, CA 94105-1921

Ph: (415)495-4200

Contact: Michela O'Connor Abrams, Publisher; Mariann Layne, Editor; Mark Rose, Director; Kurt Johnson, Editor.

Desc: Journal on technical concepts, analysis, and developments regarding local area networks. *Alt. Contact:* PO Box 652, Hightstown, NJ 08520-0652; fax: (609)426-5592. *Type:* Periodical.

Link-Up

Information Today, Inc.
143 Old Marlton Pike
Medford, NJ 08055-9936

Ph: (609)654-6266

E-mail: custserv@infotoday.com.

Desc: Contains the complete text of Link-Up, a newspaper covering electronic information products and services for consumers, educators, and businesses. Covers online databases and services, bulletin boards, electronic mail systems, and computer hardware, software, and peripherals. *Available:* Information Today, Inc. *Type:* Database.

Local Area Networks Newsletter

Information Gatekeepers Inc.
214 Harvard Ave.
Boston, MA 02134

Ph: (617)232-3111
Free: 800-323-1088
Fax: (617)734-8562

E-mail: info@igigroup.com

URL: http://wwwigigroup.com

Contact: Paul Polishuk, Editor.

Desc: Provides information on new developments and products in the LAN (Local Area Networks) industry. Discusses both foreign and domestic markets, including new LAN purchases and installations, and management changes. *Type:* Newsletter.

Macintosh Tips & Tricks

Giles Road Press
PO Box 20337
Wickenburg, AZ 85358

Ph: (520)684-1011
Fax: (520)684-3965

E-mail: gilesrdprs@aol.com

URL: http://www.intac.com/~gilesrd/; http://www.gilesrd.com.

Contact: Maria L. Langer, Editor.

Desc: Features product news, how-to articles, and shortcuts or "Quick Tips" for Macintosh computer users. Recurring features include editor's and "freebies" column. *Type:* Newsletter.

MacUser

Ziff-Davis Publishing Company
50 Beale St. 13th Floor
San Francisco, CA 94105-1813

Ph: (415)547-8000

URL: http://www.cdnet.com

Desc: Contains the complete text of MacUser, a monthly publication providing product information for Apple Macintosh personal computer users. *Available:* LEXIS-NEXIS, NEXIS; LEXIS-NEXIS, NEXIS. *Type:* Database.

MacUser

Ziff-Davis Publishing Co.
950 Tower Ln.
Foster City, CA 94404

Ph: (415)378-5520
Fax: (415)341-7242

Contact: Jon Zilber, Editor; Janet Ryan Publisher; Jonathan Layne, Publisher.

Desc: Magazine for Macintosh computer users. Editorial provides product reviews and analysis. *Type:* Periodical.

MacWeek

Ziff-Davis Publishing Co.
50 Beale St., 14th Fl.
San Francisco, CA 94105

Ph: (415)243-3500
Fax: (415)243-3535

E-mail: macweek@zd.com.

URL: http://www.macweek.com.

Contact: Rick LePage, Publisher/Editor-in-Chief; David Morgenstern, Editor.

Desc: Trade magazine (tabloid) for business users of Macintosh computers and other work stations. *Type:* Periodical.

MacWeek

MacWeek, Inc.
301 Howard St., 15th Fl.
San Francisco, CA 94105

Ph: (415)243-3500

URL: http://www.zd.net.com

Desc: Contains the complete text of MacWeek, a magazine covering all aspects of the Apple Macintosh personal computer and other workstations. Includes product news and reviews, applications, feature articles, and opinion columns. *Available:* LEXIS-NEXIS, NEXIS; LEXIS-NEXIS, LEXIS. *Type:* Database.

Macworld

International Data Group

5 Speen St.   Ph: (508)879-0700
PO Box 9171   Free: 800-343-4935
Framingham, MA 01701   Fax: (508)875-8931
E-mail: macworld@macworld.com.

Contact: Colin Crawford, (415)267-1757, fax: (415)974-7464, colin_crawford@macworld.com; Matt Sweeney, Publisher, (415)978-3271, fax: (415)974-7464, matt_sweeney@macworld.com; Steve Plevin, Advertising Mgr., (415)978-3738, fax: (415)924-7464, steve_plevin@macworld.com; Adrian Mello, Editor-in-Chief, (415)978-3246, adrian_mellow@macworld.com.

Desc: Magazine serving users of the Apple Macintosh personal computer, associated peripheral equipment, and software. *Alt. Contact:* 501 2nd St., Ste. 500, San Francisco, CA 94107-1431; telephone: (415)243-0505; fax: (415)442-0766. *Type:* Periodical.

Mag ZINE

Mag Innovision, Inc.

2801 S. Yale St.   Ph: (714)751-2008
Santa Ana, CA 92704   Fax: (714)751-5522
E-mail: dzimmer@maginnovision.com
URL: http://www.maginnovision.com/

Contact: webmaster@maginnovision.com.

Desc: Mag Innovision is one of the world's leading manufacturers of 14 to 21-inch computer display monitors and the company's web site is a good place to find out about the products they have to offer. Probably the most valuable resource here is the glossary which explains all those terms that are constantly being thrown at you in ads and brochures. *Type:* Database.

Mainframe Computing

Worldwide Videotex

PO Box 3273   Ph: (561)738-2276
Boynton Beach, FL 33424-3273
E-mail: markedit@juno.com.
URL: http://www.wvpubs.com.

Desc: Reports on developments in application software and hardware, operating and network systems, and peripherals involving mainframe systems and supercomputers. Includes information on strategies planning and the market. *Type:* Newsletter.

Managing LAN Costs

Institute of Management & Administration, Inc.

29 W. 35th St., 5th Fl.   Ph: (212)244-0360
New York, NY 10001-2299   Fax: (212)564-0465
E-mail: subserve@ioma.com
URL: http://www.ioma.com

Contact: Marc Coroz, Editor; Perry Patterson, Publisher.

Desc: Provides information on managing computer network costs. *Type:* Newsletter.

Mass Storage News

Corry Publishing, Inc.

2840 W. 21st St.   Ph: (814)838-0025
Erie, PA 16506-9945   Free: 800-368-9597
    Fax: (814)836-9605

Contact: Mike Downing, Editor.

Desc: Provides information for vendors, end users, and the distribution channel for mass storage hardware and software on data storage and retrieval. *Type:* Newsletter.

Media Computing

Dreamscape Productions

510 Woodhaven   Ph: (408)685-8818
Aptos, CA 95003-5522
URL: www.dreamscapenet.com.

Contact: Sheridan Tatsuno, Editor, statsuno@aol.com.

Desc: Supplies analysis of multimedia, internet, intranet, and web computing issues. Recurring features include interviews and reports of meetings. *Type:* Newsletter.

Media Depot: One Stop Multimedia Resource Center

Media Depot, Inc.

209 Erie St.   Ph: (909)629-2597
Pomona, CA 91768   Fax: (909)629-7084
E-mail: mediadpt@mediadpt.com
URL: http://www.mediadpt.com/

Desc: For information on multimedia hardware, stop by this site. Media Depot provides information on its speakers, headphones, pointing devices, and other related accessories here. *Type:* Database.

The Memory Place

McDonald and Associates

2544 S. 156th Cir.   Ph: (402)691-8248
Omaha, NE 68130-2510   Free: 800-306-8901
    Fax: (402)691-8548
E-mail: info@memoryplace.com
URL: http://www.buymemory.com

Desc: If you are considering upgrading your computer's memory, then this web site is definitely worth visiting. McDonald and Associates offers a variety of memory grades and options for PCs and Macs. *Type:* Database.

The Merck Index Online

Merck & Co. Inc.

PO Box 2000   Ph: (732)594-4000
Rahway, NJ 07065
URL: http://www.merck.com

Contact: Sandra S. McKeluey, Senior Technology Associate, (908)594-4890.

Desc: Contains the complete text of more than 10,430 monographs describing approximately 30,000 chemicals, drugs, biologicals, and veterinary and agricultural products. Includes Merck Index monograph number, monograph title, CAS Registry Number, molecular formula, molecular weight, molecular composition, molecular element, CA chemical name, synonyms, trademark and company name, bibliographic citations, patent number, derivative substance name, derivative molecular formula, and physical property information including melting point, melting point text, optical rotation text, optical rotation, reference keys present, and datakeys present. *Available:* Oxford Molecular Group, Chemical Information Systems; The Dialog Corporation, DIALOG; The Dialog Corporation, DIALOG; CompuServe Information Service, Knowledge Index; STN International; STN International. *Type:* Database.

MichNet News

Merit Network, Inc.

c/o Mariella Wells   Ph: (313)764-9430
4251 Plymouth Rd., Ste. C   Fax: (313)647-3185
Ann Arbor, MI 48105-2785
URL: http://www.merit.edu/michnet/michnet.news/.

Contact: Mariella Wells, Editor.

Desc: Contains information on MichNet (Michigan's regional computer network) and about the hosts and services that can be reached through MichNet. Remarks: Available in hard copy and electronic formats. *Type:* Newsletter.

Microcomputer Abstracts

Information Today, Inc.

143 Old Marlton Pike   Ph: (609)654-6266
Medford, NJ 08055-9936
E-mail: custserv@infotoday.com

Contact: Daniel R. Franzen, Editor.

Desc: Contains more than 192,500 citations, with abstracts, to reviews and commentaries on the use and applications of microcomputers and software packages. Covers more than 100 traditional and cutting-edge publications on microcomputing in business, industry, education, libraries, and in the home. *Available:* The Dialog Corporation, DIALOG; CompuServe Information Service, Knowledge Index; OCLC Online Computer Library Center, Inc., OCLC EPIC; OCLC Online Computer Library Center, Inc., OCLC FirstSearch Catalog; Cambridge Scientific Abstracts (CSA); EBSCOhost; Information Today, Inc. *Type:* Database.

Microcomputer Software Guide Online

R.R. Bowker

121 Chanlon Rd.   Ph: (908)464-6800
New Providence, NJ 07974
URL: http://www.bowker.com

Contact: Marin Mixon, Marketing Mgr., Info@bowker.com.

Desc: Contains fully annotated listings for more than 23,000 new and established software programs available in the United States from more than 4000 publishers. For each program, provides program status; program title; release date; compatible hardware; operating systems required; programming languages; memory requirements; price information; manual availability; warranty information; description; publisher name, address, telephone number; ISBN; ordering information; and distributor name, address, and Standard Address Number. *Available:* The Dialog Corporation, DIALOG; CompuServe Information Service, Knowledge Index. *Type:* Database.

Microcomputer Trainer

Microcomputer Trainer

696 9th St.   Ph: (201)330-8923
PO Box 2487   Fax: (201)330-0163
Secaucus, NJ 07096-2487

Contact: Loretta Weiss-Morris, Editor, loretta@panix.com.

Desc: Reports on instructional techniques for enhancing motivation, increasing retention, boosting profiency, and building the confidence of end users of microcomputers in a corporate setting. Reviews training products and services. *Type:* Newsletter.

MicroLeads Vendor Directory on Disk

Chromatic Communications Enterprises, Inc.

PO Box 30127   Ph: (510)945-1602
Walnut Creek, CA 94598   Free: 800-782-DISK
    Fax: (707)746-0542

Contact: Michael Shipp, Editor.

Desc: Diskette. Covers about 12,000 firms supplying products and services to the microcomputer market; includes manufacturers of software, hardware, peripherals, and accessories, distributors, software and hardware support services, publishers of books and periodicals, and franchised and company-owned chains of microcomputing equipment and accessories retailers. *Type:* Directory.

Microprocessor Report

MicroDesign Resources

298 S. Sunnyvale Ave.   Ph: (408)328-3900
Sunnyvale, CA 94086-6245   Fax: (408)737-2242
E-mail: cs@mdr.zd.com
URL: www.mdronline.com.

Contact: Keith Diefendorf, Editor-in-Chief.

Desc: "The leading technical publication for the microprocessor industry." Dedicated to providing unbiased, in-depth, critical analysis of new high-performance microprocessor developments. This newsletter is exclusively subscriber-supported. *Type:* Newsletter.

Microsearch

Information, Inc.
7700 Old Georgetown Rd.   Ph: (301)215-4688
7th Fl.
Bethesda, MD 20814
E-mail: news@infoinc.com
URL: http://www.webplus.net/assoc_fr.html
Desc: Contains more than 50,000 citations, with abstracts, to reviews of more than 12,000 microcomputer products from approximately 200 publications, including Byte, InfoWorld, Macworld, and Personal Computing. Covers hardware, software, peripherals, and accessories. *Available:* Questel • Orbit. *Type:* Database.

Microsoft SQL Server Professional

Pinnacle Publishing, Inc.
1503 Johnson Ferry Rd., Ste.   Ph: (770)565-1763
   100   Free: 800-788-1900
Marietta, GA 30062   Fax: (770)565-8232
URL: http://www.pinpub.com.
Contact: Karen Watterson, Editor.
Desc: Publishes technical articles on optimizing performance, using shared procedures, and integrating SQL server into workgroup and enterprise applications. Also covers the Internet. *Type:* Newsletter.

Mini'app'les

Minnesota Apple Computer Users' Group, Inc.
PO Box 796   Ph: (612)229-6952
Hopkins, MN 55343
Contact: Hugh Johnson, Editor.
Desc: Features articles on new products and techniques for Apple Computer users. Carries hardware and software reviews and listings of meetings and other events of interest. *Type:* Newsletter.

Min's New Media Report

Min's New Media Report
1201 Seven Locks Rd., No. 300   Ph: (301)340-7788
Potomac, MD 20854-2958   Fax: (301)424-8602
Contact: Rob Runett, Editor, rrunett@phillips.com; Angela Duff, Publisher; Nancy Corey, Marketing Mgr.
Desc: Provides news on business relations and strategies and tactics to increase online publishing and new media business. *Type:* Newsletter.

Mobile Computing and Communications

Curtco Freedom Group
29160 Heathercliff Rd., No.
   200
Malibu, CA 90265-6105
URL: http://www.mobilecomputing.com.
Contact: Colette Kronick, Publisher; Brian Nadel, Editor-in-Chief.
Desc: Magazine for people interested in mobile communications and mobile computing. *Alt. Contact:* 156 W 56th St., New York, NY 10019; telephone: (212)547-6300; fax: (212)333-5560. *Type:* Periodical.

Modem User News

Worldwide Videotex
PO Box 3273   Ph: (561)738-2276
Boynton Beach, FL 33424-3273
E-mail: markedit@gnn.com; markedit@juno.com.
URL: http://www.wvpubs.com.
Desc: Covers developments and innovations in modem services. Provides news of user applications, product technologies, and supplies for computers and facsimile machines. *Type:* Newsletter.

Multimedia Week

Phillips Business Information, Inc.
1201 Seven Locks Rd., Ste. 300   Ph: (301)340-1520
Potomac, MD 20854   Free: 888-707-5809
    Fax: (301)340-3847
E-mail: clientservices.pbi@phillips.com
Contact: Judith Abrams, Editor.
Desc: Provides news, market analysis, application issues, competitive close-ups, company profiles, announcements, and industry trends in the area of multimedia. Covers hardware and software. *Type:* Newsletter.

Multimedia World

International Data Group
5 Speen St.   Ph: (508)879-0700
PO Box 9171   Free: 800-343-4935
Framingham, MA 01701   Fax: (508)875-8931
E-mail: multimedia@pcworld.com.
URL: http://www.mmworld.com.
Contact: Greg Mason, Publisher; Russell Glitman, Executive Editor; Mark Taussig, Associate Publisher.
Desc: Magazine covering computer multimedia hardware and software. *Alt. Contact:* 501 2nd St., San Francisco, CA 94107; telephone: (415)281-8650; fax: (415)281-3915. *Type:* Periodical.

NACOMEX Insider

NACOMEX USA, Inc.
48 Broadway   Ph: (914)757-2626
Box 394   Free: 800-NAC-
Tivoli, NY 12583   OMEX
    Fax: (914)757-4144
E-mail: zises@nacomex.com; publications@macomex.com.
Contact: Robert Zises, Editor, zises@nacomex.com.
Desc: Provides information on historical values, current tactics, and residual value forecasting for ad valorem tax, bankruptcy, loss compensation, and related purposes. Recurring features include news of research and a column titled Industry Round-up. *Type:* Newsletter.

National Association of Computer Consultant Businesses

PO Box 4266   Ph: (336)273-8878
Greensboro, NC 27404-4266   Fax: (336)273-2878
E-mail: naccb@naccb.org
URL: http://www.naccb.org
Contact: Peggy Noell Smith, Exec. Dir.
Desc: Firms that provide the services of highly technical professionals, such as computer programmers, systems analysts, engineers, to clients in need of temporary technical support. Promotes legal and economic environment favorable to the technical services industry, including protection of a firm's freedom to choose either employees or independent contractors when supplying services to clients. Encourages professional standards in the industry; serves as a support mechanism for members. *Type:* Association.

The National Report on Computers & Health

United Communications Group
11300 Rockville Pike, Suite   Ph: (301)816-8950
   1100
Rockville, MD 20852
E-mail: joshcohen@ucg.com
URL: http://www.ucg.com
Contact: Phillip Kemelor.
Desc: Contains the complete text of The National Report on Computers and Health, a newsletter covering computer and communications hardware and software for the health care industry. Includes data security strategies, Medicare regulations affecting hospital data processing, and new product announcements. *Available:* The Gale Group. *Type:* Database.

The National Report on Computers & Health

United Communications Group
11300 Rockville Pike, Ste. 1100   Ph: (301)287-2700
Rockville, MD 20852-3030   Free: 800-929-4824
    Fax: (301)287-2049
E-mail: customer@ucg.com
Contact: Jonathan Stern, Publisher, jstern@ucg.com.
Desc: Reports on data processing and clinical hospital information systems. *Type:* Newsletter.

Neoware

Neoware
400 Feheley Dr.   Ph: (610)277-8300
King of Prussia, PA 19406   Free: 800-636-9273
    Fax: (610)275-5739
E-mail: info@neoware.com
URL: http://www.neoware.com
Desc: HDS Network systems is now called Neoware. A good place to learn about "thin clients" and the network computer (NC). *Type:* Database.

The Netly News

TIME.com
Time & Life Bldg.
1271 Sixth Ave., 5th Fl.
New York, NY 10020
URL: http://cgi.pathfinder.com/@@
5iCtogUAHCtX9C@z/netly/
Contact: thenetlynews@pathfinder.com.
Desc: "If it happened online, it's Netly News." This site offers articles and details about the latest happenings in the online world. In addition to providing text and images, it also uses video and audio, bulletin boards, and humor to tell the story. *Type:* Database.

Network Computing

CMP Media Inc.
600 Community Dr.   Ph: (516)562-5000
Manhasset, NY 11030   Fax: (516)562-7830
URL: http://www.cmp.net;   http://www.techweb.cmp.com.
Contact: Patricia Schmidt, Editor-in-Chief; Deborah Gisonni, Publisher.
Desc: A new publication with a strong focus on PC lan to mainframe network applications targeting a technical and managerial audience. *Type:* Periodical.

Network Magazine

Miller Freeman, Inc.
600 Harrison St.   Ph: (650)905-2200
San Francisco, CA 94107   Free: 800-227-4675
    Fax: (650)908-6604
E-mail: techlearning_editors@mfi.com
URL: http://www.millerfreeman.com;   http://www.networkmagazine.com.
Contact: Steve Steinke, Editor-in-Chief, (415)905-2358, fax: (415)905-2587; Elizabeth Clark, Executive Editor, (770)933-0116, fax: (770)933-0666; Peter May, Publisher, (415)905-2345, fax: (415)908-6602, jtoping@mfi.com; Liam Passmore, Marketing Mgr., (415)905-2516, fax: (415)905-2587, lpassmore@mfi.com.
Desc: Trade journal. *Type:* Periodical.

Network Monitor

Elsevier Science Inc.
655 Avenue of the Americas   Ph: (212)989-5800
New York, NY 10010   Fax: (212)633-3990
E-mail: usinfo@elsevier.com
URL: http://www.elsevier.com
Desc: Contains information pertaining to networking and open systems. Emphasizes European market news. *Type:* Newsletter.

Network World

International Data Group

5 Speen St.   Ph: (508)879-0700
PO Box 9171   Free: 800-343-4935
Framingham, MA 01701   Fax: (508)875-8931
URL: http://www.nwtusion.com.

Contact: John Gallant, Editor; Colin Ungaro, CEO; Ann Finn, Production Mgr.; Evilec Thibeault, Publisher.

Desc: The newsweekly of enterprise network computing. *Alt. Contact:* 161 Worcester Rd., PO Box 9172, Framingham, MA 01701-9172; telephone: (508)875-6400; fax: (508)820-3467; toll-free: 800-622-1108. *Type:* Periodical.

Network World

International Data Group (IDG)

IDG Communications

5 Speen St.   Ph: (508)875-5000
Framingham, MA 01701
URL: http://www.nwfusion.com

Desc: Contains the complete text of Network World, a newspaper covering technical and commercial developments in voice and data telecommunications networking. Covers local and international networking, including trend analyses, corporate news, and descriptions, with vendor contact information, of new communications software. *Available:* LEXIS-NEXIS, NEXIS. *Type:* Database.

NOMINE

LEXIS-NEXIS

9443 Springboro Pike   Ph: (937)865-6800
PO Box 933
Dayton, OH 45401-0933
URL: http://www.lex-nexis.com

Desc: Provides information on President Bush's nomination of Judge Clarence Thomas to the U.S. Supreme Court. *Type:* Database.

North Coast Commodore Users Group—Link

North Coast Commodore Users Group

PO Box 515   Ph: (814)734-4589
Erie, PA 16512-0515

Contact: Calvin McAdoo, Editor; Ted Gocal, Editor.

Desc: Offers programming tips, software program descriptions and reviews, and articles examining aspects of computing for users of Commodore personal computers. Defines computer terms and deals with such topics as computer maintenance, performing back-ups, and program applications. *Type:* Newsletter.

The Notes Report

IDG Newsletter Corporation

PO Box 35160
Louisville, KY 40232-5160

Desc: Provides information about Lotus Notes. Includes tips and product information. *Type:* Newsletter.

NSF Network News

InterNIC Information Services

General Atomics

PO Box 85608
San Diego, CA 92186-9784
E-mail: info@is.internic.net

Desc: Communicates current information to midlevel and campus NICs and end-users. Features articles that discuss tools, training, and new items on the InterNIC. *Type:* Newsletter.

Object-Oriented Strategies

Paul Harman

2040 Polk St.   Ph: (415)669-1860
Box 334
San Francisco, CA 94109-2520

Contact: Paul Harmon, Editor.

Desc: Contains product reviews, industry news and trends, and market forecasts. Recurring features include a calendar of events, reports of meetings, and notices of publications available. *Type:* Newsletter.

Ocean Information Systems, Inc.

Ocean Information Systems, Inc.

688 Arrow Grand Cir.   Ph: (818)339-8888
Covina, CA 91722   Fax: (818)859-7668
E-mail: sales@ocean-usa.com
URL: http://www.ocean-usa.com/ocean/

Desc: A handsome, informative site for this designer and manufacturer of computer components and peripherals. Product information includes Committee specs and large photos. *Type:* Database.

Office Systems 96

Office Systems

PO Box 908   Ph: (215)628-7716
Spring House, PA 19477   Fax: (215)540-8041

Contact: Scott Cullen, Editor, sculos@aol.com; Rich Kunkel, Publisher.

Desc: Magazine containing information for key decision makers responsible for purchasing business equipment, office supplies, and computer and telecommunications systems. *Alt. Contact:* 1111 Bethlehem Pike, Spring House, PA 19477; telephone: (215)628-7792; fax: (215)540-8041. *Type:* Periodical.

OHIONETWORK

OHIONET

1500 W. Lane Ave.   Ph: (614)486-2966
Columbus, OH 43221-3975

Contact: Sue Henderson, Editor.

Desc: Provides technical, administrative, and general information of use to member libraries. Focuses on the services and products of OCLC (Online Computer Library Center). *Type:* Newsletter.

Online Libraries and Microcomputers

Information Intelligence, Inc.

PO Box 31098   Ph: (602)996-2283
Phoenix, AZ 85046
E-mail: rhuleatt@infointelligence.com
URL: http://www.infointelligence.com/www/iii-info; http://www.infointelligence.com/www/iii-info.

Contact: George S. Machovec, Editor; Richard S. Huleatt, Editor, rhuleatt@infointelligence.com.

Desc: Covers new library online and automation applications, library-oriented software and hardware for online and CD-ROM use, library networks, new online and CD-ROM databases, and people in the online/CD-ROM fields. Recurring features include editorials and notices of forthcoming meetings and new publications. *Type:* Newsletter.

Online Marketplace

Jupiter Communications

627 Broadway, 2nd Fl.   Ph: (212)780-6060
New York, NY 10012-2612   Free: 800-488-4345
     Fax: (212)780-6075

Contact: Nicole Vanderbilt, Analyst.

Desc: Keeps abreast of the fast-emerging developments in the digital marketplace and emerging interactive technologies. Reports on players and devices to provide the "inside scoop" on this marketplace. *Type:* Newsletter.

Online Newsletter

Information Intelligence, Inc. (III)

P.O. Box 31098   Ph: (602)996-2283
Phoenix, AZ 85046
E-mail: rhuleatt@infointelligence.com
URL: http://www.infointelligence.com/www/iii-info

Desc: Contains the complete text of Online Newsletter, providing news and information about online and CD-ROM trends and developments in the international information industry. Features new online/CD-ROM developments and events, mergers and acquisitions, product development editorials, people in the news, telecommunications and networks (including the Internet), microcomputer hardware and software, new and forthcoming databases (online, CD-ROM, and diskette), meetings, publications, and user aids. *Available:* The Dialog Corporation, DIALOG; The Dialog Corporation, DataStar; STN International; Bell & Howell Information and Learning; LEXIS-NEXIS; Dow Jones Interactive Publishing. *Type:* Database.

Oracle Magazine

Oracle Corp.

500 Oracle Parkway, Mailstop   Ph: (650)506-7000
  5OP10   Fax: (650)633-2424
Redwood City, CA 94065
URL: http://www.oramag.com.

Contact: Stuart Gold, Advertising Mgr., (650)506-6652, stgold@us.oracle.com; Julie Gibbs, Editor, jgibbs@us.oracle.com.

Desc: Covers database, development, and technology issues of importance to IT professionals. *Type:* Periodical.

The OSINetter Newsletter

Architecture Technology Corp.

9971 Valley View Rd.   Ph: (612)829-5864
Eden Prairie, MN 55344   Fax: (612)829-5871
E-mail: atcorp@atcorp.com
URL: http://www.atcorp.com

Contact: Dr. Kenneth J. Thurber, Editor; Gordon A. Palzer, Editor.

Desc: Covers product and company activity in the area of Open Systems Interconnection (OSI). Contains U.S. and international news, product announcements, reports on standards developments, and finance and personnel news. *Type:* Newsletter.

PACS & Networking News

Miller Freeman, Inc.

600 Harrison St., 4th Fl.   Ph: (415)905-2202
San Francisco, CA 94107   Free: 800-444-4881
     Fax: (415)905-2235
URL: http://www.pacnews.com.

Contact: Erik Ridley, Editor, eridley@mfi.com.

Desc: Covers topics regarding the development and implementation of picture archiving and communications systems, teleradiology, and telemedicine. Recurring features include news of research, a calendar of events, reports of meetings, letters to the editor, company profiles, hospital profiles, and recent purchases. *Type:* Newsletter.

PC Business Products

Worldwide Videotex

PO Box 3273   Ph: (561)738-2276
Boynton Beach, FL 33424-3273
E-mail: markedit@gnn.com; markedit@juno.com.
URL: http://www.wvpubs.com.

Desc: Covers developments in software and hardware products and services. Includes list of performance ratings and prices. *Type:* Newsletter.

PC Computing

Ziff-Davis Inc.

28 E. 28th St.   Ph: (212)503-3500
New York, NY 10016   Fax: (212)503-5799

Contact: Janet Ryan, Publisher.

Desc: Magazine on personal computers. *Type:* Periodical.

PC Friendly Internet Page

University of Oregon
Eugene, OR 97403   Ph: (541)346-3111
E-mail: www-feedback@lists.uoregon.edu
URL: http://darkwing.uoregon.edu/~wharmon/
Contact: wharmon@oregon.uoregon.edu.

Desc: If you need to know anything about the Internet, this site can probably point you in the right direction. An excellent gateway to information about the Net, the PC Friendly Internet Page divides its links into the following categories: HTML, Hardware, Hardware Prices, Magazines, Software, Subjects, and Links, the last of which offers links to sites offering information that doesn't fall into any of the previous categories. *Type:* Database.

PC Magazine

Ziff-Davis Inc.
28 E. 28th St.   Ph: (212)503-3500
New York, NY 10016   Fax: (212)503-5799
Contact: Michael Miller, Editor-in-Chief; Jake Kirchner, Editor.

Desc: Consumer magazine focusing on the personal computer industry. *Type:* Periodical.

PC Magazine

Ziff-Davis Publishing Company
50 Beale St. 13th Floor   Ph: (415)547-8000
San Francisco, CA 94105-1813
URL: http://www.cdnet.com

Desc: Contains the complete text of PC Magazine, which covers IBM/MS-DOS standard personal computers and products. Corresponds to the online PC Magazine database. *Available:* CompuServe Information Service; LEXIS-NEXIS, NEXIS; Ziff-Davis Publishing, ZiffNet; America Online, Inc. *Type:* Database.

PC Novice

Sandhills Publishing
120 W. Harvest Dr.   Ph: (402)479-2181
PO Box 85310   Free: 800-331-4890
Lincoln, NE 68501-5310   Fax: (402)479-2195
Contact: Ronald D. Kobler, Managing Editor.

Desc: Magazine for personal computer users. *Type:* Periodical.

PC Street Price Index

John Murphy
Metro Computing   Ph: (609)784-8866
10 Foster Ave., Ste. E-1
Gibbsboro, NJ 08026
Contact: John Murphy, Editor.

Desc: Concentrates on the latest developments in computer technology and their effects on the corporate end-user. Covers software, personal computers, computer companies, and industry trends. *Type:* Newsletter.

PC Today Online

Sandhills Publishing
PO Box 85310   Ph: (402)458-4520
Lincoln, NE 68501-5310   Free: 800-544-1296
     Fax: (402)479-2120
E-mail: feedback@pctoday.com
URL: http://www.pctoday.com/
Contact: webmaster@pctoday.com.

Desc: Like most computer publications, PC Today offers buyers the wide variety of product information found in catalogs combined with the helpful, professional insight of a national computer magazine. Whether you want to research pricing, locate a vendor, or purchase hardware or software, PC Today Online is a tool you won't want to do without. *Type:* Database.

PC Week

Ziff-Davis Publishing Co.
10 Presidents Landing   Ph: (617)393-3700
Medford, MA 02155-5146   Free: 800-451-1032
URL: http://www.pcweek.com.
Contact: Eric Lindquist, Editor, elindquist@pcweek.ziff.com; Donald J. Byrnes, Publisher.

Desc: Tabloid featuring microcomputer products and developments. *Type:* Periodical.

PC WORLD

International Data Group
5 Speen St.   Ph: (508)879-0700
PO Box 9171   Free: 800-343-4935
Framingham, MA 01701   Fax: (508)875-8931
URL: http://www.pcworld.com.
Contact: Phil Lemmons, Editorial Dir.; Jeff Edman, Publisher; Richard Marino, President/CEO; Cathryn Baskin, Editor-in-Chief.
Alt. Contact: 501 2nd St., Ste. 600, San Francisco, CA 94107-1437; telephone: (415)243-0500; fax: (415)442-1891; toll-free: 800-PC-WORLD. *Type:* Periodical.

PCNetter Newsletter

Architecture Technology Corp.
9971 Valley View Rd.   Ph: (612)829-5864
Eden Prairie, MN 55344   Fax: (612)829-5871
E-mail: atcorp@atcorp.com
URL: http://www.atcorp.com
Contact: Dr. Kenneth J. Thurber, Editor; Gordon A. Palzer, Editor.

Desc: Provides an overview of news in the personal computer industry as well as new product introductions in key areas of communications (local area networks and microhost), hardware (system and peripherals), software, and workstations/servers. Recurring features include three special reports on important new companies, products, and trends; and financial and personnel news. *Type:* Newsletter.

pcOrder

pcOrder
5000 Plaza on the Lake   Ph: (512)684-1100
Austin, TX 78746   Fax: (512)684-1200
E-mail: stephanie_derrick@pcorder.com
URL: http://www.pcOrder.com/
Desc: With the support of major computer manufacturers, distributors and resellers, pcOrder has developed and deployed an independent, Internet-based electronic commerce system that provides resellers and corporate end-users with the ability to automatically configure systems, to compare pricing and availability, validate compatibility and electronically place orders. At the same time, it provides manufacturers and distributors with improved market data and a new interactive forum for marketing. *Type:* Database.

PC's Mean Business

CD Kloek & Associates
843 E. Main St., Suite 100   Fax: (503)776-3429
Medford, OR 97504-7137
Contact: Chris Kloek, Publisher.

Desc: Explores the use of personal computers for home and small business applications. *Type:* Newsletter.

PenWare MobiNetix Home Page

PenWare
500 Oakmead Pkwy.   Ph: (408)524-4200
Sunnyvale, CA 94086-4056   Free: (408)524-4299
     Fax: (408)524-4298
E-mail: penware@penware.com
URL: http://www.penware.com/
Desc: PenWare helps "conduct and conclude electronic transactions" by developing computer hardware and soft-

ware to meet the transaction needs of retail, hospitality, financial, and security businesses. Their transaction applications range from capturing payment data and electronic signatures to secure storage of business data and reproducing sales receipts. *Type:* Database.

Performance Computing

Miller Freeman, Inc.
600 Harrison St.   Ph: (650)905-2200
San Francisco, CA 94107   Free: 800-227-4675
     Fax: (650)908-6604
E-mail: techlearning_editors@mfi.com
URL: http://www.millerfreeman.com; http://www.performance-computing.com.
Contact: Mark Hall, Editor, (650)655-4233, mhall@mfi.com; John Keough, Publisher, (650)655-4229, jkeough@mfi.com.

Desc: Magazine for professional users of UNIX and UNIX-like systems, and Windows NT. *Alt. Contact:* telephone: (650)655-4224. *Type:* Periodical.

Planet Drum Foundation

PO Box 31251   Ph: (415)285-6556
Shasta Bioregion   Fax: (415)285-6563
San Francisco, CA 94131
E-mail: planetdrum@igc.org
URL: http://www.planetdrum.org
Contact: Peter Berg, Dir.

Desc: The Planet Drum Foundation defines a bioregion as a "whole life-place, a distinct area with coherent and interconnected plant and animal communities, often defined by a watershed." *Type:* Association.

PlugIn Datamation: Profit and Value from Information Technology

Datamation
8773 S. Ridgeline Blvd.   Ph: (303)470-4466
Highlands Ranch, CO 80126-   Fax: (303)470-4691
2329
E-mail: cahners.subs@denver.cahners.com
URL: http://www.datamation.com

Desc: The WWW edition of this integrated systems journal is chock full of tantalizing bonuses like a software library, job links, daily computer news updates, and corporate links. While the articles tend to be targeted towards educated users and professionals, the writing is good enough and simple enough that anyone can understand it. *Type:* Database.

Point Line Poly - Host

Stover Publishing
19 South St.   Ph: (802)459-6358
Proctor, VT 05765-1224
Contact: Daniel Stover, President.

Desc: Provides users of ARC/INFO software with tips, tricks, macros, tutorials, and other useful information to help them better utilize the software. Recurring features include letters to the editor, a collection, reports of meeting, job listings, book reviews, and columns titled User Submitted Macro and Off the Wire. *Type:* Newsletter.

Productivity Software

Worldwide Videotex
PO Box 3273   Ph: (561)738-2276
Boynton Beach, FL 33424-3273
E-mail: markedit@juno.com

Desc: Provides information on computer software. *Type:* Newsletter.

Provantage

Provantage
7249 Whipple Ave. NW   Ph: (330)494-8715
North Canton, OH 44720-7143   Free: 800-336-1166
                              Fax: (330)494-5260
E-mail: sales@provantage.com
URL: http://www.provantage.com/

Desc: This independent online computer superstore and mail order business boasts an attractive, innovative Internet site that's updated daily and contains every product the company carries. Lots of detailed descriptions, images, cross references, hotlinks, easy-to-use searches, and specials like Weekly Features combine to provide you with useful information on a wide variety of products. *Type:* Database.

PSC News

Pittsburgh Supercomputing Center (PSC)
4400 5th Ave., MI Bldg.   Ph: (412)268-4960
Pittsburgh, PA 15213   Fax: (412)268-5832
URL: http://www.psc.edu/publications.

Contact: Vivian M. Benton, Editor, benton@psc.edu.

Desc: Keeps the scientific community informed of center activities and acquisition of major hardware and software. Recurring features include news of research, a calendar of events, reports of meetings, and notices of publications available. *Type:* Newsletter.

Public-Access Computer Systems News

University of Houston Libraries
4800 Calhoun   Ph: (713)749-4242
Houston, TX 77204-2091   Fax: (713)743-9748
E-mail: libpacs@uhupvm1.uh.edu
URL: http://info.lib.uh.edu/pacsnews.html.

Contact: Linda Thompson, Editor; Ann Thornton, Editor.

Desc: Contains brief items on end-user computer systems in libraries. Remarks: Available electronically only. *Type:* Newsletter.

Publish

International Data Group
5 Speen St.   Ph: (508)879-0700
PO Box 9171   Free: 800-343-4935
Framingham, MA 01701   Fax: (508)875-8931
URL: http://www.publish.com.

Contact: Jake Widman, Editor, editor@publish.com; Gene Gable, Publisher/President; Nathalie Valletter, Art Director; Batel Libes, Operations Mgr.; Rick Reynolds, Director; Ed Chittenden, Director; Mark Naman, Managing Editor; Peter Guastella, Circulation Director; Neil Versen, Assoc. Publisher/VP of Sales & Marketing.

Desc: Magazine about the new technological tools of graphic design including information about how they are used and how they are evolving in the Design and Computer Age. *Alt. Contact:* 501 2nd St., Ste. 310, San Francisco, CA 94107; telephone: (415)243-0600; fax: (415)975-2613. *Type:* Periodical.

Puget Sound Computer User

KFH Publications
3530 Bagley Ave. N.   Ph: (206)547-4950
Seattle, WA 98103   Free: 800-897-8230
                              Fax: (206)545-6591
URL: http://www.pfcu.com.

Contact: Sharon Baerng, Editor, editor@pscu.com; Ray Kehl, Publisher, raykehl@pscu.com; Lora Holloway, Advertising Sales.

Desc: Magazine providing advice on purchasing and using hardware and software. *Type:* Periodical.

QA Quest

Quality Assurance Institute
9222 Bay Point Dr.   Ph: (407)363-1111
Orlando, FL 32819   Fax: (407)363-1112
URL: http://www.qaiusa.com.
Contact: Kathy West, Editor.
Desc: Publishes interpretations of articles relating to quality assurance in the field of information services. Recurring features include book reviews, interviews with key personnel, and an article on quality benchmarking. *Type:* Newsletter.

Quality Progress—Quality Assurance and Quality Control Software Directory Issue

American Society for Quality
611 E. Wisconsin Ave.   Ph: (414)272-8575
Milwaukee, WI 53204   Free: 800-248-1946
                              Fax: (414)272-1734
URL: http://www.asq.org.
Contact: Miles Maguire, Editor, mmaguire@asq.org.
Desc: List of companies that offer computer software packages for quality assurance and quality control. Entries includes: company name, address, phone, fax, software title, price, format, program description, hardware requirements, and matrix. *Type:* Directory.

Quantum PC Report for CPAs

Quantum Professional Publishing
700 Larkspur Landing, Ste. 199   Ph: (415)789-8800
Larkspur, CA 94939   Free: 800-325-8858
E-mail: info@quantum.org
Contact: Jack C. McClure, Editor.
Desc: Provides information on personal computer hardware and software for the accounting industry. Recurring features include columns titled Product Review, Short Takes, Lotus Power, and Abstracts. *Type:* Newsletter.

Rainbow-Pcar Reviews On-Line

Falsoft Ink, Inc.
9509 U.S. Hwy. 42   Ph: (502)228-4492
PO Box 385   Fax: (502)228-5121
Prospect, KY 40059-0385
E-mail: lonnie@rainbowpcur.com; editor@rainbowpcur.com.
Contact: Maggie Bunevitch, Managing Editor; Lawrence C. Falk, Publisher; Graycee Claster, Western Sales Dir.; Kim Lewis, Eastern Sales Dir.
Desc: Complete & comprehensive reviews of PC computer hardware & software. *Type:* Periodical.

Rapid Prototyping Report

CAD/CAM Publishing
1010 Turquoise St., Ste. 320   Ph: (619)488-0533
San Diego, CA 92109   Fax: (619)488-6052
E-mail: cadcentral@cadcamnet.com
URL: http://www.cadcamnet.com
Contact: Pat Wright, Contact.
Desc: Contains trends on the rapid prototyping and stereolithography industry. *Type:* Newsletter.

The Records and Information Management Report

GP Subscription Publications
88 Post Rd. W.   Ph: (203)226-3571
PO Box 5007   Free: 800-225-5800
Westport, CT 06881   Fax: (203)226-6009
Contact: Ann Balough, Editor; Gerry Katz, Managing Editor, gkatz@greenwood.com.
Desc: Covers retrieval, storage, destruction, forms management, indexing, and inventorying of computer documentation. *Type:* Newsletter.

Recreational & Educational Computing

Dr. Michael Ecker
909 Violet Terr.   Ph: (570)586-2784
Clarks Summit, PA 18411-9206
E-mail: mwe1@psu.edu.
Contact: Dr. M. Ecker, Editor.
Desc: Devoted to computer recreations, math applications, teasers, challenges, graphics, programming, and reviews. *Type:* Newsletter.

Reseller Management

Post-Newsweek Business Information
8500 Leesburg Pkwy., Ste. 7500
Vienna, VA 22182
URL: http://www.resellermgmt.com.
Contact: G. Hale, Editor-in-Chief, ghale@resellermgmt.com; S. Biolous, Associate Publisher, sbiolous@ix.netcom.com; W. Bryan Wadworth, Executive Editor, bwadworth@resellermgmt.com; Kate Zwald, Managing Editor, kzwald@resellermgmt.com.
Desc: Computer trade magazine for computer dealers and value added resellers, emphasizing reseller management issues. *Alt. Contact:* 800 South St., Ste. 305, Waltham, MA 02154; telephone: (781)692-1055; fax: (781)692-1077. *Type:* Periodical.

Residential Micro Systems

Syndication Div.   Ph: (704)588-2453
9124-E York Rd.
Charlotte, NC 28273
Contact: David A. Butler, President.
Desc: Distributes home automation column. *Alt. Contact:* Syndication Div., 9124-E York Rd., Charlotte, NC 28273; telephone: (704)588-2453. *Type:* Periodical.

Responsible Computing

National Center for Computer Crime Data
1222-B 17th Ave.   Ph: (408)475-4457
Santa Cruz, CA 95062   Fax: (408)475-5336
Contact: Jay Bloombecker, Editor.
Desc: Concerned with computer crime law, computer crimes, computer security, industrial security implications of computer use, cumulative trauma disorder, and computer/communications policy. Recurring features include letters to the editor, interviews, news of research, news of educational opportunities, book reviews, notices of publications available, and legal case summaries. *Type:* Newsletter.

Roger Pence's Microsoft and the AS/400 Letter

The 400 Group
990 Washington St., Ste. 308   Ph: (617)320-8909
Dedham, MA 02026   Free: 800-477-7359
                                Fax: (617)320-9466
E-mail: customer@the400group.com
URL: http://www.the400group.com.
Contact: Roger Pence, Editor.
Desc: Provides strategies and advice to help computer users integrated AS/400 software with Windows servers and desktops. Includes software installation and configuration tips. *Type:* Newsletter.

RUCS Newsletter

Rutgers University Computing Services (RUCS)
Hill Center, Busch Campus   Ph: (908)445-2425
PO Box 879   Fax: (908)445-2021
Piscataway, NJ 08854
E-mail: newsletter@nbcs.rutgers.edu.
URL: http://www.nbcs.rutgers.edu/nbcs/newsletter/.
Contact: Beverly B. Madron, Editor; Susan R. Hagan, Editor.
Desc: Contains articles on computing for Rutgers audience. Provides changes to RUCS computing policies, procedures equipment, software, and computing facilities. *Type:* Newsletter.

SAGE - The System Administrator's Guild

USENIX Association

2560 Ninth St., Ste. 215   Ph: (510)528-8649
Berkeley, CA 94710   Fax: (510)548-5738
E-mail: office@usenix.org
URL: http://www.usenix.org/sage/
Contact: Peter Collinson, webster@usenix.org.
Desc: The System Administrators Guild (SAGE) is a Special Technical Group of the USENIX Association. It is organized to advance the status of computer system administration as a profession. *Type:* Database.

SARC Virus Encyclopedia

Symantec Corporation

175 W. Broadway   Ph: (541)994-6054
Eugene, OR 97401   Free: 800-441-7234
    Fax: (541)984-8020
URL: http://www.symantec.com/avcenter/vinfodb.html
Desc: Software manufacturer Symantec makes available this excellent encyclopedia of information on thousands of computer viruses and their many variants. Click on an alphabetical range in the index and you'll be presented with a huge list of viruses to choose from. *Type:* Database.

Scan/The Data Capture Report

Corry Publishing Inc.

2840 W. 21st St.   Ph: (814)838-0025
Erie, PA 16506   Free: 800-368-9597
    Fax: (814)835-1764
E-mail: corrypub@corrypub.com
Contact: Jon Rick Morgan, Editor, rickm@corrypub.com.
Desc: Provides information about automatic data capture including bar coding, radio frequency, magnetic strip, voice recognition, optical character recognition, smart cards, biometrics, application software, and memory tags. Recurring features include interviews, news of research, reports of meetings, news of educational opportunities, product reviews, and financial information. *Type:* Newsletter.

Scan Newsletter

Scan Newsletters

11 Middle Neck Rd.
Great Neck, NY 11021
Contact: George Goldberg, Editor.
Desc: Provides news and information at the managerial level for all industries involved with bar-code scanning and related technologies. Contains articles on technological developments, historical perspectives, reports of conferences, and activities of individual companies. *Type:* Newsletter.

Scout Business Software Directory

Melange Media Corp.

11757 W. Ken Caryl Ave.,   Ph: (303)972-7236
F-329   Free: 800-873-7157
Littleton, CO 80127-3719   Fax: (303)727-7376
E-mail: vendor@scoutdirectory.com.
Contact: Dave Derby, Editor, dederby@melangemedia.com.
Desc: Vendors of 14,000 IBM System AS/400, S/36, client/server, PC/LAN, and RS/6000 computer software packages worldwide; software consultants. *Type:* Directory.

Screen Saver Connection

CRL Network Services

One Kearny St.   Ph: (415)837-5300
San Francisco, CA 94108   Fax: (415)392-9000
E-mail: webmaster@crl.com
URL: http://www.crl.com/~colocomp/ss.htm
Desc: Once you get past all of the annoying web-ads, you will most probably find something of interest here. Even though there is no longer a safety need for screen savers, there still exists that bit of playfulness in us all that just requires them. *Type:* Database.

Sensors Buyers Guide

Helmers Publishing, Inc.

174 Concord St.   Ph: (603)924-9631
PO Box 874   Fax: (603)924-7408
Peterborough, NH 03458
E-mail: seneditors@helmers.com.
URL: http://www.sensorsmag.com.

Contact: Barbara G. Goode, Editor, bgoode@helmers.com.

Desc: Magazine listing manufacturers of sensors and related products. *Type:* Periodical.

Sensors - The Journal of Applied Sensor Technology

Helmers Publishing, Inc.

174 Concord St.   Ph: (603)924-9631
PO Box 874   Fax: (603)924-7408
Peterborough, NH 03458
E-mail: seneditors@helmers.com.
URL: http://www.sensorsmag.com.

Contact: Barbara G. Goode, Editor, bgoode@helmers.com; Steve Robbins, Publisher, srobbins@helmers.com.

Desc: Technical magazine covering the development and application of sensors. *Type:* Periodical.

The Serlin Report on Parallel Processing

ITOM International Company

PO Box 1450   Ph: (650)948-4516
Los Altos, CA 94023

Contact: Omri Serlin, Editor, omris@cup.portal.com; omri@juno.com.

Desc: Analyzes important market, company, and product developments in supercomputers and parallel systems. Recurring features include news of research, reports of meetings, and a calendar of events. *Type:* Newsletter.

SIGART Newsletter

Special Interest Group on Artificial Intelligence (SIGART)

Association for Computing Machinery

1515 Broadway, 17th Fl.   Ph: (212)626-0500
New York, NY 10036-5701   Free: 800-342-6626
    Fax: (212)944-1318
E-mail: acmhelp@acm.org.
URL: http://www.acm.org.

Contact: Keith Price, Editor.

Desc: Publishes reviewed papers, announcements, correspondence, reviews, conference reports, bibliographies and other information of interest to the artificial intelligence community. *Type:* Newsletter.

SIGCAPH Newsletter

Special Interest Group on Programming Languages (SIGPLAN)

Association for Computing Machinery

1515 Broadway   Ph: (212)869-7440
New York, NY 10036   Free: 800-342-6626
    Fax: (212)302-5826
E-mail: acmhelp@acm.org

Desc: Supports the Group's concern to promote professional interests of computing personnel with the physically handicapped; promotes the "application of computing and information technology toward solutions of disability problems and to perform a public education function in support of computing careers for suitably trained blind, deaf, or motor impaired persons." Remarks: Toll-free number in New Jersey is 800-932-0878. *Type:* Newsletter.

SIGCOMM Computer Communication Review

Special Interest Group on Programming Languages (SIGPLAN)

Association for Computing Machinery

1515 Broadway   Ph: (212)869-7440
New York, NY 10036   Free: 800-342-6626
    Fax: (212)302-5826

E-mail: acmhelp@acm.org
URL: http://www.acm.org/sigcomm.
Contact: Martha Steenstrup, Editor.
Desc: Deals with topics relating to computer communications, distributed systems, file systems, memory management, and networks. Includes proceedings of the biennial Data Communications Symposium, of which SIGCOMM is a sponsor. *Type:* Newsletter.

SIGCSE Bulletin

Special Interest Group on Programming Languages (SIGPLAN)

Association for Computing Machinery

1515 Broadway   Ph: (212)869-7440
New York, NY 10036   Free: 800-342-6626
    Fax: (212)302-5826

E-mail: acmhelp@acm.org
Contact: James Miller, Editor.
Desc: Intended for college educators who are attempting to develop, implement, or evaluate computer science programs and courses. Provides a forum for the solution of common problems and the discussion of related issues. *Type:* Newsletter.

SIGCUE Outlook

Special Interest Group on Programming Languages (SIGPLAN)

Association for Computing Machinery

1515 Broadway   Ph: (212)869-7440
New York, NY 10036   Free: 800-342-6626
    Fax: (212)302-5826

E-mail: acmhelp@acm.org
Contact: Ruth Anne Ross, Editor; Paul L. Ross, Editor.
Desc: Informs educators at all levels who are interested in using the computer and related technology to aid the educational process. Focus is on the discussion of concepts, methods, and policies that relate to the central issues of instructional computing. *Type:* Newsletter.

SIGDA Newsletter

Special Interest Group on Design Automation (SIGDA)

Association for Computing Machinery

1515 Broadway   Ph: (212)869-7440
New York, NY 10036   Free: 800-342-6626
E-mail: acmhelp@acm.org
URL: http://www.acm.org.
Contact: Patrick M. Hefferan, Editor.
Desc: Focuses on current research in design automation, computer programs for Computer-Aided Design/Computer-Aided Manufacturing (CAD/CAM), and testing of electronic and mechanical equipment. Also concerned with optimization and heuristic methods for automating, aiding, documenting, and controlling the design process. *Type:* Newsletter.

SIGOPS Operating Systems Review

Special Interest Group on Programming Languages (SIGPLAN)

Association for Computing Machinery

1515 Broadway   Ph: (212)869-7440
New York, NY 10036   Free: 800-342-6626
    Fax: (212)302-5826

E-mail: acmhelp@acm.org
Contact: William Waite, Editor.
Desc: Reports on significant advances in operating systems, covering topics in distributed systems, file systems, perfor-

mance, process management, and protection. Focuses on architecture for multiprogramming, multiprocessing, and time-sharing; resource management, evaluation and simulation; reliability and security of data; and communications among computing processes. *Type:* Newsletter.

SIGSAC Review
Special Interest Group on Programming
Languages (SIGPLAN)
Association for Computing Machinery
1515 Broadway   Ph: (212)869-7440
New York, NY 10036   Free: 800-342-6626
                                        Fax: (212)302-5826
E-mail: acmhelp@acm.org
URL: http://www.acm.org/sig_hp/sigsac.html.
Contact: Catherine Meadows, Editor.
Desc: Examines issues relating to technology and practice in the fields of computer security, audit, and control. Examines such topics as control of access to resources, identity verification, risk analysis and certification of programs, and architectural foundations for security systems. *Type:* Newsletter.

SIGSOFT Software Engineering Notes
Association for Computing Machinery
1515 Broadway   Ph: (212)869-7440
New York, NY 10036   Free: 800-342-6626
E-mail: acmhelp@acm.org
Contact: Will Tracz, Editor, will.tracz@lmco.com.
Desc: Tracks developments in programming and software maintenance processes, as well as the use of computers to provide and maintain timely, higher quality, cost-effective, and durable software. Contains proceedings of software engineering workshops and symposia. *Type:* Newsletter.

SIGUCCS Newsletter
Special Interest Group on Programming
Languages (SIGPLAN)
Association for Computing Machinery
1515 Broadway   Ph: (212)869-7440
New York, NY 10036   Free: 800-342-6626
                                        Fax: (212)302-5826
E-mail: acmhelp@acm.org
Contact: Rita Seplowitz, Editor.
Desc: Concerned with the improvement of all types of computer center services in small and large colleges and universities. Examines topics in the areas of minicomputers, networks, computer center management, user services, and mutual problems. *Type:* Newsletter.

Simulation
Society for Computer Simulation
4838 Ronson Ct., Ste. L   Ph: (619)277-3888
San Diego, CA 92111   Fax: (619)277-3930
E-mail: scs@scs.org
URL: http://www.scs.org
Contact: Charles Shub, Editor-in-Chief; Lorrie Mowat, Managing Editor.
Desc: Reviews technical articles on new developments and applications in computer simulation. Includes editorials, a calendar of events, reports of meetings, and a price list of simulated software. *Type:* Newsletter.

Smart Access
Pinnacle Publishing, Inc.
PO Box 72255   Ph: (770)565-1763
Marietta, GA 30007-2255   Free: 800-788-1900
                                        Fax: (770)565-8232
E-mail: smartacc@pinpub.com.
URL: http://www.pinpub.com.
Contact: Paul Litwin, Editor.
Desc: Contains tips, techniques, and application articles for Microsoft Corporation's Microsoft Access. Also includes an accompanying source code disk. *Type:* Newsletter.

Smart Media Business
Knowledge Industry Publications, Inc.
701 Westchester Ave.   Ph: (914)328-9157
White Plains, NY 10604   Free: 800-800-5474
                                        Fax: (914)328-9093
E-mail: kipimktg@kipi.com
URL: http://www.kipinet.com
Contact: Cliff Roth, Editor.
Desc: Contains information on multimedia and interactive television. *Type:* Newsletter.

SNA Perspective
The Saratoga Group
12980 Saratoga Ave., Ste. E   Ph: (408)446-9115
Saratoga, CA 95070   Free: 800-638-3266
                                        Fax: (408)446-9134
Contact: Don Czubek, Editor.
Desc: Monitors new IBM products and discusses related applications and implications for IBM Systems Network Architecture (SNA) users. Recurring features include news of announcements made by IBM concerning various programs and networks and columns titled CSI Seminars and Technical Publications. *Type:* Newsletter.

SnapShots
Patricia Seybold Group
85 Devonshire St., 5th Fl.   Ph: (617)742-5200
Boston, MA 02109-3504   Free: 800-826-2424
                                        Fax: (617)742-1028
Contact: Ronni T. Marshak, Editor-in-Chief.
Desc: Provides descriptions of new software products and vendor strategies with analysis and business benefits. Focuses on products and trends and analyzes their success rate, the appropriate target audience, expected product directions, and projected impact on the industry. *Type:* Newsletter.

Society for Information Display
31 E Julian St.   Ph: (408)977-1013
San Jose, CA 95112-4006   Fax: (408)977-1531
E-mail: office@sid.org
URL: http://www.sid.org
Contact: Dee Dumont, Exec.Dir.
Desc: Scientists, engineers, students, others, and business firms dealing with information display problems. Encourages scientific, literary, and educational advancement of information display and its allied arts and sciences, including the disciplines of display theory, display device and systems development, and the psychological and physiological effects of display systems on the human senses. Plans to establish central repository for information and to develop definitions and standards in the field. *Type:* Association.

SoftBase: Reviews, Companies, and Products
Information Sources, Inc.
1173 Colusa Ave.   Ph: (510)525-6220
PO Box 8120
Berkeley, CA 94707
E-mail: rkoolish@ad.com
Contact: Ruth Koolish, President, (510)525-6220, fax: (510)525-1568.
Desc: Contains information on the Information Technology industry. Includes company information, including personnel names, addresses, telephone numbers, URLs, e-mails, and a description of the company. *Available:* The Dialog Corporation, DataStar; The Dialog Corporation, DIALOG; CompuServe Information Service, Knowledge Index; Cambridge Scientific Abstracts (CSA); National Information Services Corporation (NISC), NISC DISCover. *Type:* Database.

Softletter
Jeffrey Tarter
17 Main St.   Ph: (617)924-3944
Watertown, MA 02472   Fax: (617)924-7288
E-mail: info@softletter.com.
URL: http://www.softletter.com.
Contact: Jeffrey Tarter, Editor.
Desc: Analyzes market trends and company strategies in microcomputer software publishing and development. Recurring features include industry statistics and case studies. *Type:* Newsletter.

Software and CD-ROM Reviews on File
Facts On File News Services
Division of PRIMEDIA Reference Corporation
11 Penn Plaza, 15th Fl.   Ph: (212)290-8090
New York, NY 10001-2006   Free: 800-363-7976
                                        Fax: (212)967-9051
E-mail: info@facts.com
Contact: Jonathan Rabinovitz, Managing Editor, rabinovitz@facts.com.
Desc: Abstracts software and CD-ROM reviews taken from more than 100 magazines each month, covering more than 70 software programs. Includes product descriptions and data on system requirements. *Type:* Newsletter.

Software Development Manager
International Management Services, Inc.
363 E. Central St.   Ph: (508)520-1555
Franklin, MA 02038-1300   Fax: (508)520-1558
E-mail: info@intmgmtsvcs.com
URL: http://www.intmgmtsvcs.com
Contact: Raymond Wenig, Editor.
Desc: Contains articles of interest to firms and individuals who are designing and developing computer software. Recurring features include news of software methodologies, task management techniques, leading technical teams, and professional development concepts. *Type:* Newsletter.

The Software Encyclopedia
R. R. Bowker
A Unit of Cahners Business Information
121 Chanlon Rd.   Ph: (908)464-6800
New Providence, NJ 07974   Free: 888-269-5372
                                        Fax: (908)771-7704
E-mail: info@bowker.com
URL: http://www.bowker.com.
Contact: Barbara Holton, Editor; D. Gravesande, Editor.
Desc: Over 23,000 software programs from over 4,000 publishers of software programs. *Type:* Directory.

Software Futures
Art Data Services Inc.
928 Broadway   Ph: (212)677-0409
New York, NY 10010   Fax: (212)677-0463
URL: http://www.computerwire.com.
Contact: Gary Flood, Editor.
Desc: Explores software development. Recurring features include news of research. *Type:* Newsletter.

The Software History Center
The Software History Center
c/o Burton Grad Associates, Inc.   Fax: (203)222-8728
101 Post Road E.
Westport, CT 06880
URL: http://www.softwarehistory.org/
Contact: luannej@sprynet.com.
Desc: A project which seeks to detail the history of software, including the people who created it, and the companies that marketed it starting from its beginnings in the 1950s. Focuses primarily on the non-PC world, and instead on business application and system software written for IBM mainframe and midrange computers. *Type:* Database.

Software Industry Report

Computer Age
Millin Publishing Group, Inc.
714 Church St.   Ph: (703)739-8500
Alexandria, VA 22314-4202   Fax: (703)739-8505

Contact: Charles Bailey, Editor; Mike Cotter, Editor.

Desc: Monitors issues relating to all aspects of the software industry, including market analysis and trends, legislative and legal activity affecting the industry, new technologies and products, and new applications for software. Recurring features include industry analysis and forecasting for industry management level personnel; news of corporate activity, including mergers and contracts. *Type:* Newsletter.

Software Magazine

Sentry Technology Group
One Research Dr.   Ph: (508)366-2031
Suite 400-B   Free: 800-225-9218
Westborough, MA 01581-3907   Fax: (508)836-4732
E-mail: softwaremagazine@mcimail.com.
URL: http://www.sentrytech.com.

Contact: Don Fagan, Publisher; Patrick Porter, Editor; Kym Gilhooly, Managing Editor; Deborah Radcliff, West Coast Editor; Dave Brousell, Editorial Dir.; Daniela Cimino, Assoc. Editor; Susan Mael, New Products Editor; Kathleen Kenny, Circulation Mgr.; Julekha Dash, Staff Writer; Julie D'Errico, Design Asst.; Mary-Ann Gajewski, Production Mgr.; Dave Swanson, Design Director.

Desc: Computer magazine. *Alt. Contact:* One Research Dr., Ste. 400B, Westborough, MA 01581; telephone: (508)366-2031; fax: (508)366-8104. *Type:* Periodical.

The Software Quality Advisor

Rice Consulting Services
PO Box 891284   Ph: (405)692-7331
Oklahoma City, OK 73189   Fax: (405)692-7570
E-mail: rcs@telepath.com

Contact: Randy Rice, Editor.

Desc: Advises on building and maintaining quality software. Features articles on software quality assurance and software testing. *Type:* Newsletter.

Software Spectrum Inc.

Software Spectrum Inc.
2140 Merritt Dr.   Ph: (214)864-5100
Garland, TX 75041   Free: 800-624-0503
                             Fax: (214)864-7878
E-mail: Interl@SWSpectrum.com
URL: http://www.swspectrum.com

Desc: With its recent acquisition of Egghead Software, Software Spectrum is far and away the world's largest reseller of packaged software. If you want to find out more about this software reselling giant, you can browse through corporate background information and press releases. *Type:* Database.

Software Success

The 400 Group
990 Washington St., Ste. 308   Ph: (617)320-8909
Dedham, MA 02026   Free: 800-477-7359
                                Fax: (617)320-9466
E-mail: customer@the400group.com

Contact: Rob Shapiro, Publisher, robs@softwaresuccess. com; Suzanne Hildreth, Editor.

Desc: Provides "strategic approaches to marketing, distribution, pricing, lead generation, product support, funding, legal issues, and technology trends" in the computer software industry. *Type:* Newsletter.

Software Tech News

Data & Analysis Center for Software (DACS)
PO Box 1400   Ph: (315)334-4905
Rome, NY 13442-1400   Free: 800-214-7921
                              Fax: (315)334-4965
E-mail: dacs@dacs.dtic.mil; cust-liasn@dacs.dtic.mil
URL: http://www.utica.kaman.com; http://www.dacs.com.

Contact: Lon R. Dean, Editor.

Desc: Disseminates information and news about software technology and engineering, especially as required by the U.S. Department of Defense. *Type:* Newsletter.

Special Interest Group on Software Engineering

Association for Computing Machinery
1515 Broadway   Ph: (212)869-7440
New York, NY 10036   Fax: (212)302-5826

Contact: Dick Taylor, Chm.

Desc: A special interest group of the Association for Computing Machinery. Computer professionals interested in the technology of software creation and evolution. Promotes exchange of ideas and information. *Type:* Association.

Sun Microsystems, Inc.

Sun Microsystems, Inc.
2550 Garcia Ave.   Ph: (415)786-7737
Mountain View, CA 94043
URL: http://www.sun.com

Contact: webmaster@sun.com.

Desc: Sun Microsystems is a Fortune 500 leader in enterprise network computing. Their site offers extensive product and technology information, as well as news about the latest developments in Java and Solaris. *Type:* Database.

Talk2000

Humber College
205 Humber College Blvd.   Ph: (416)675-6622
Toronto, ON, Canada M9W   Fax: (416)675-2427
  5L7
URL: http://humnet.humberc.on.ca/talk2000.htm
Contact: Jay Gary, talk2000@rmii.com.

Desc: This site aims to be resource for anyone seeking comprehensive information on all things related to the year 2000. Although a large portion of the site is devoted to current and back issues of the *Let's Talk 2000* magazine, you will also find a FAQ page, an exhaustive introduction to a range of issues surrounding the new millenium, a list of millenial resources, and an online store. *Type:* Database.

Tandy Corp.

Tandy Corp.
1800 One Tandy Ctr.   Ph: (817)390-3011
Ft. Worth, TX 76102
E-mail: info@tandy.com
URL: http://www.tandy.com

Desc: Tandy Corporation is a retailer consumer electronics and computers, best known for the approximately 7,000 RadioShack stores and dealers across the nation. In addition to links to RadioShack and TechAmerica home pages (which offer a wealth of information on their products), this site offers detailed corporate information. *Type:* Database.

Technical Computing Report

CAD/CAM Publishing
1010 Turquoise St., Ste. 320   Ph: (619)488-0533
San Diego, CA 92109   Fax: (619)488-6052
E-mail: cadcentral@cadcamnet.com
URL: http://www.cadcamnet.com
Contact: Pat Wright, Contact.

Desc: Provides information on the hardware side of CAD/CAM. *Type:* Newsletter.

Technology Trends

Enterprise Technology Corporation
305 Madison Ave.   Ph: (212)972-1860
New York, NY 10165   Fax: (212)687-6126

Contact: Kevin J. Merz, Editor.

Desc: Discusses news on computer software technology and its perceived value to the business community. *Type:* Newsletter.

Telecom Tactics-Business Systems

Phillips Infotech
1111 Marlkress Rd, Ste. 101   Ph: (609)424-1100
Cherry Hill, NJ 08003   Free: 800-678-4642
                               Fax: (609)424-1999
E-mail: cborn@phillips.com

Contact: Don Stuart, Editor.

Desc: Contains detailed specifications on key sets, PBX, ACD, voice mail, video conferencing, and call accounting prducts. Includes search program. *Type:* Newsletter.

TeleVideo, Inc.

TeleVideo, Inc.
2345 Harris Way   Ph: (408)954-8333
San Jose, CA 95131   Fax: (408)954-0931
E-mail: webmaster@televideoinc
URL: http://www.televideoinc.com/

Desc: TeleVideo develops and markets video display devices, such as terminals, PC & Apple Macintosh-compatible monitors, and multimedia products. If you seek information on these kinds of products, then the Product Information page should help you find it. *Type:* Database.

Token Perspectives Newsletter

Architecture Technology Corp.
9971 Valley View Rd.   Ph: (612)829-5864
Eden Prairie, MN 55344   Fax: (612)829-5871
E-mail: atcorp@atcorp.com
URL: http://www.atcorp.com
Contact: Dr. Kenneth J. Thurber, Editor; Gordon A. Palzer, Editor.

Desc: Monitors and analyzes major developments involving IBM local-area networks, focusing on the IBM Token Ring LAN, FDDI, ATM, and Frame-Relay Networking. Discusses performance and standards issues, IBM management strategy, and product development. *Type:* Newsletter.

Toronto Computes!

Canada Computer Paper Inc.
99 Atlantic Ave., Ste. 408   Ph: (416)588-1580
Toronto, ON, Canada M6K 3J8   Fax: (416)588-8574
Contact: Mara Gulens, Editor.

Desc: Magazine for the microcomputer user. *Alt. Contact:* 3661 W. 4th Ave., Ste. 8, Vancouver, BC, Canada V6R 1P2. *Type:* Periodical.

Traveling Software

Traveling Software
18702 North Creek Pkwy.   Ph: (206)483-8088
Bothell, WA 98011   Free: 800-343-8080
                             Fax: (206)487-5440
E-mail: info@travsoft.com
URL: http://www.travsoft.com
Contact: webmaster@travsoft.com.

Desc: Back in the dark ages of computing--around 1986--Traveling Software introduced LapLink, one of the first PC-to-PC file transfer programs. Allowing data transfer between the then new 3.5-inch disk drives and the standard 5.25-inch drives, LapLink soon became the best-selling file transfer product on the market, garnering numerous industry awards. *Type:* Database.

The Tufnut Works - Computer Theft Protection Systems

Tufnut Computer Theft Protection Systems
PO Box 39   Ph: (505)424-1954
Tesuque, NM 87574   Free: 800-227-0949
                             Fax: (505)424-1956
E-mail: tufnut@tufnut.com
URL: http://www.tufnut.com/

Desc: To find out about Tufnut theft-prevention devices, come to this Web site. Not only does Tufnut develop security cables for computer hardware but also for other electronic wares such as VCRs and stereos. *Type:* Database.

2000A.D.

2000A.D.
PO Box 538   Ph: (718)871-4202
Brooklyn, NY 11202-0538   Free: 800-643-TICK
E-mail: tick@tickticktick.com
URL: http://www.tickticktick.com/

Desc: Tick, Tick, Tick. . *Type:* Database.

Underground Computers, Inc.

Underground Computers, Inc.
1739 28th St. SW   Ph: (616)249-3007
Wyoming, MI 49509   Fax: (616)249-3555
E-mail: undcom@undcom.com
URL: http://www.undcom.com/

Desc: If you're looking for new, used, or refurbished computers, then you may want to visit Underground Computers' web site. UC specializes in both desktop and laptop models and offers Technology support as well. *Type:* Database.

UniForum WWW Server Home Page

UniForum Association
10440 Shaker Dr., Ste. 203   Ph: (410)715-9500
Columbia, MD 21046   Free: 800-333-8649
                             Fax: (301)596-8803
URL: http://www.uniforum.org/

Contact: Mark Neal, markn@uniforum.org.

Desc: Non-profit UniForum makes this site available to help all sorts of open systems users, including software developers, end users, retailers, systems analysts, Technology executives, and systems vendors. The site provides a variety of resources to enable these open-systems professionals to stay on top of the industry and its developments. *Type:* Database.

Unigram X

G2 Computer Intelligence, Inc.
3 Maple Pl.   Ph: (516)759-7025
Glen Head, NY 11545-9864   Fax: (516)759-7028
E-mail: paperboy@g2news.com; news@92news.com.
URL: http://www.92news.com.

Contact: Maureen O'Gara, Editor, ogara@g2news.com.

Desc: Reports recent news on UNIX software. *Type:* Newsletter.

Unisys World

Publications and Communications, Inc.
579 N. Valley Mills, Ste. 3 Ph: (254)399-6860
Waco, TX 76710   Fax: (254)399-6651
E-mail: uw@pcinews.com.
URL: http://www.pcinews.com.

Contact: Christy Raines, Editor.

Desc: Provides information on Unisys Network Computing Group systems and mainframes. *Type:* Newsletter.

Used Computer Mall

Used Computer Mall
PO Box 710362   Ph: (619)449-9041
San Diego, CA 92171   Fax: (619)449-7929
E-mail: mall@usedcomputer.com
URL: http://www.usedcomputer.com/

Desc: A good site for those who want to buy or sell used computer equipment. The micropricer gives you a good range of asking prices for used equipment. *Type:* Database.

Video Software Dealers Association

16530 Ventura Blvd., Ste. 400   Ph: (818)385-1500
Encino, CA 91436   Fax: (818)385-0567
URL: http://www.vsda.org
Contact: Jeffery Eves, Pres.

Desc: Retailers and distributors of videocassettes and videodiscs; associate members are major studios or independent companies that produce video programming and manufacturers of video games, accessories, and other goods and services for the video software industry. Represents and acts as spokesperson for the video software merchandising industry. Conducts statistical survey of video retailing; offers legal counsel representing members' interests in Washington, DC. *Type:* Association.

Virtual Computer History Museum

Virginia Polytechnic Institute and State University
Blacksburg, VA 24061-0202
E-mail: museum@ei.cs.vt.edu
URL: http://video.cs.vt.edu:90/history/

Desc: From the dawn of time there has been a continuing quest for an ever quicker and more efficient way to make calculations. Prehistoric man no doubt sought a better way to keep track of the number of mammoths he had killed than cutting another mark on the wall of his cave. *Type:* Database.

Visual C Developer

Pinnacle Publishing, Inc.
PO Box 72255   Ph: (770)565-1763
Marietta, GA 30007-2255   Free: 800-788-1900
                             Fax: (770)565-8232
URL: http://www.pinpub.com.
Contact: Roland Winkler, Senior Editor.

Desc: Provides programming advice and tips for programmers. *Type:* Newsletter.

We Compute

We Compute, Inc.
1560 Bayview Ave., No. 302   Ph: (416)481-1955
Toronto, ON, Canada M4G   Free: 888-328-5488
  3B8   Fax: (416)481-2819
E-mail: editors@we-compute.com; ads@we-compute.com.
URL: http://www.we-compute.com.
Contact: Eric McMillan, Editor and Publisher; Matt Walsh, Advertising Mgr.

Desc: Consumer magazine covering computers for home and small businesses. *Type:* Periodical.

Web Marketing for IT Companies

Corry Publishing, Inc.
2840 W. 21st St.   Ph: (814)838-0025
Erie, PA 16506-9945   Free: 800-368-9597
                             Fax: (814)836-9605
Contact: Rich Peterman, Editor.

Desc: Provides information for marketing management executives in the information technology industry. Offers advice on how to create a successful web site and develop profitable web marketing strategies. *Type:* Newsletter.

WebTrack

Jupiter Communications
627 Broadway, 2nd Fl.   Ph: (212)780-6060
New York, NY 10012-2612   Free: 800-488-4345
                             Fax: (212)780-6075
Contact: Peter Storck, Group Dir., Advertising.

Desc: Focuses exclusively on the online advertising market. Provides analysis on buyers and sellers of online advertising, as well as the trends in the marketplace. *Type:* Newsletter.

Window Sources

Ziff-Davis Inc.
28 E. 28th St.   Ph: (212)503-3500
New York, NY 10016   Fax: (212)503-5799
URL: http://www.ziff-davis.com.
Contact: Gus Venditto, Editor; Karla Spormann, Publisher.

Desc: Publication for the users of Windows based PC's. *Type:* Periodical.

Windows Magazine

CMP Media Inc.
600 Community Dr.   Ph: (516)562-5000
Manhasset, NY 11030   Fax: (516)562-7830
URL: http://www.cmp.net; techweb.cmp.com.
Contact: Mark Holdrieth, Publisher; Mike Elgan, Editor.

Desc: Magazine on Windows software. *Type:* Periodical.

Windows 95 Journal Online

IDG Newsletter Corporation
PO Box 35160
Louisville, KY 40232-5160
Contact: Jim Welp, Executive Editor.

Desc: Carries onlines how-to articles and tips about Windows 95 software through the world wide web. Recurring features include letters to the editor, news of research, and columns titled Product Reviews and Bug Reports. *Type:* Newsletter.

Windows '95 Letter

Mendham Technology Group
144 Talmadge Rd.   Ph: (201)543-2273
Mendham, NJ 07945   Fax: (201)543-6033
Contact: Carole Patton, Editor.

Desc: Covers news of the computer industry, specifically the Microsoft Windows 95 environment. Includes special reports on computer megatrends. *Type:* Newsletter.

WINSURFER

IDG Newsletter Corporation
PO Box 35160
Louisville, KY 40232-5160
URL: http://www.idgnews.com/win95.
Contact: Jim Welp, Executive Editor.

Desc: Online newsletter that provides tips and techniques for Windows 95 and Windows NT. *Type:* Newsletter.

Wired

Wired USA
520 3rd St., 4th Fl.   Ph: (415)276-5000
San Francisco, CA 94107-1815 Free: 800-769-4733
                             Fax: (415)276-5100
E-mail: info@wired.com.
Contact: Katrina Heron, Editor-in-Chief; Kevin Kelly, Editor; Dana Lyon, Publisher, dana@wired.com.

Desc: Consumer magazine focusing on the digital revolution's impact on business, culture, and society. *Type:* Periodical.

Workgroup Computing Report

Patricia Seybold Group
85 Devonshire St., 5th Fl.   Ph: (617)742-5200
Boston, MA 02109-3504   Free: 800-826-2424
   Fax: (617)742-1028
Contact: Ronni T. Marshak, Editor.
Desc: Covers trends in workgroup computing, including groupware, client-server environments, and enterprise-wide solutions. Tracks key issues, new products, and evolving technologies in the corporate computing environment. *Type:* Newsletter.

Working Smarter with Microsoft Excel

OneOnOne Computer Training
2055 Army Trail Rd., Dept.   Ph: (630)628-0500
  GR, Ste. 100   Free: 800-424-8668
Addison, IL 60101-1493   Fax: (630)628-0550
E-mail: oneoneone@pincom.com
URL: http://www.oootraining.com
Contact: B. Alan August, Editor.
Desc: Designed to improve office productivity. Focuses on continuous training, reinforcing skills, and exploring the full capabilities of the software, Microsoft Excel. *Type:* Newsletter.

Working Smarter with Microsoft Word

OneOnOne Computer Training
2055 Army Trail Rd., Dept.   Ph: (630)628-0500
  GR, Ste. 100   Free: 800-424-8668
Addison, IL 60101-1493   Fax: (630)628-0550
E-mail: oneoneone@pincom.com
URL: http://www.oootraining.com
Contact: Sally Hargrave, Editor.
Desc: Designed to improve office productivity. Focuses on continuous training, reinforcing skills, and exploring the full capabilities of the software. *Type:* Newsletter.

Working Smarter with WordPerfect

OneOnOne Computer Training
2055 Army Trail Rd., Dept.   Ph: (630)628-0500
  GR, Ste. 100   Free: 800-424-8668
Addison, IL 60101-1493   Fax: (630)628-0550
E-mail: oneoneone@pincom.com
URL: http://www.oootraining.com
Contact: Sally Hargrave, Editor.
Desc: Aims to improve office productivity by exploring the full capabilities of the software. Provides quick tips, self-tests, tutorials, plus questions and answers. *Type:* Newsletter.

The World of Lotus

Lotus Development Corporation
55 Cambridge Pkwy.   Ph: (617)693-3585
Cambridge, MA 02142
URL: http://www.lotus.com
Desc: Contains information on Lotus-related products, company news, and other developments. Features software libraries and interactive forums, each geared to a different LOTUS software product. *Available:* CompuServe Information Service. *Type:* Database.

Worldclass

Mike Kuiack & Associates
406 - 1616 Pendrell St.   Ph: (604)689-7107
Vancouver, BC, Canada V6G   Fax: (604)689-7611
  1S8
E-mail: mkuiack@direct.ca
URL: http://web.idirect.com/~tiger/
Desc: Worldclass is a daily updated guide to the Web's best global business sites. It features Instant free access and step-by-step commentary for 500 top business sites in 70 countries, chosen based on usefulness to world commerce, timeliness, ease of use, and presentation. *Type:* Database.

Worldwide Databases

Worldwide Videotex
PO Box 3273   Ph: (561)738-2276
Boynton Beach, FL 33424-3273
E-mail: markedit@gnn.com; markedit@juno.com.
URL: http://www.wvpubs.com.
Desc: Provides news of activity on computer databases. Includes information on product development, improvements, distribution rights, and user applications. *Type:* Newsletter.

Xpedite Systems, Inc.

Xpedite Systems, Inc.
446 Highway 35   Ph: (908)544-9595
Eatontown, NJ 07724   Free: 800-546-1541
   Fax: (908)542-9436
E-mail: webmaster@xpedite.com
URL: http://www.xpedite.com
Desc: Xpedite Systems describes itself by saying that Xpedite Service means fast, easy, and convenient information distribution, and the best customer service in the industry. They will save you time and money when you need to quickly distribute information to multiple locations. *Type:* Database.

Yahoo! Internet Life

Ziff-Davis Inc.
28 E. 28th St.   Ph: (212)503-3500
New York, NY 10016   Fax: (212)503-5799
URL: http://www.yil.com.
Contact: Jim Spanfeller, Publisher; Barry Golson, Editor-in-Chief; Derek A. Baker, Managing Editor; Karen Lee, Advertising Coord.; Paul J. Turcotte, Assoc. Publisher.
Desc: Magazine reporting on all aspects of the Internet including the latest Internet software tools, changes in the industry, and reviews of sites, chats, and newsgroups. *Type:* Periodical.

The Year 2000 Practitioner

Auerbach Publications
535 Fifth Ave., Ste. 806   Ph: (212)286-1010
New York, NY 10017   Free: 800-272-7737
   Fax: (212)297-9176
E-mail: orders@cvcpress.com
Contact: John Wyzalek, Editor.
Desc: Contains the latest possible solutions for the year 2000 computing problems. Inlcuda a "road map" for information systems organizations to follow to strive to ensure their systems and companies do not crash due to the millennium date problem. *Type:* Newsletter.

Y2K™

U.S. Small Business Administration
409 3rd St. SW   Free: 800-827-5722
Washington, DC 20416
URL: http://www.sba.gov/y2k/
Contact: y2k@sba.gov.
Desc: Sponsored by the SBA, this site is the ultimate authority for small business owners looking to conquer the year 2000 problem. After outlining the specifics of the problem, the site goes on to explain how businesses can best prepare for the millenium. *Type:* Database.

Concrete

Aberdeen's Concrete Construction—Buyers' Guide Issue

The Aberdeen Group
426 S. Westgate St.   Ph: (630)543-0870
Addison, IL 60101-4546   Free: 800-837-0870
   Fax: (630)543-3112
E-mail: aberdeen@wocnet.com; cceditor@wocnet.com.

URL: http://www.worldofconcrete.com.
Contact: Ward Malisch, Editor, wmalisch@wocnet.com.
Desc: List of suppliers of concrete-related products and services. Includes list of trade, technical, and standards organizations in the field. *Type:* Directory.

American Portland Cement Alliance

1225 Eye St., NW, Ste. 300   Ph: (202)408-9494
Washington, DC 20005   Fax: (202)408-0877
Contact: Richard C. Creighton, Pres.
Desc: Manufacturers of Portland cement. Conducts governmental affairs activities. Compiles statistics. *Type:* Association.

Cement, Lime, Gypsum, and Allied Workers Division

New Brotherhood Bldg., Ste.   Ph: (913)371-2640
  570   Fax: (913)281-8106
753 State Ave.
Kansas City, KS 66101
Contact: C.W. Jones, Pres.
Desc: AFL-CIO. A division of the International Brotherhood of Boilermakers, Iron Shipbuilders, Blacksmiths, Forgers and Helpers. *Type:* Association.

Cement, Quarry and Mineral Aggregates Newsletter

National Safety Council
1121 Spring Lake Dr.   Ph: (630)285-1121
Itasca, IL 60143-3201   Free: 800-539-7468
   Fax: (630)285-1315
URL: http://www.nsc.org
Contact: Kathy Henderson, Editor.
Desc: Concerned with industrial and occupational safety for people working in cement, quarries, and mineral aggregates. Carries accident prevention information, news of research on safety factors, and case histories. *Type:* Newsletter.

CM News

National Concrete Masonry Association
2302 Horse Pen Rd.   Ph: (703)713-1900
Herndon, VA 20171   Fax: (703)713-1910
E-mail: ncma@ncma.org
URL: http://www.ncma.org.
Contact: Ms. Randi Hertzberg, Editor, (443)394-0401, fax: (443)394-0130, hertzberg@worldnet.att.net.
Desc: Focuses on the manufacturing and marketing of concrete masonry products and the managment of production plants. Covers legislative and regulatory developments, production and marketing developments, and new products and services of interest to the industry. *Type:* Newsletter.

National Concrete Masonry Association

2302 Horse Pen Rd.   Ph: (703)713-1900
Herndon, VA 20171-3499   Fax: (703)713-1910
E-mail: ncma@ncma.org
URL: http://www.ncma.org
Contact: Chris Stinebert, Pres.
Desc: Manufacturers of concrete masonry units (concrete blocks) segmental retaining wall units and paving block; associate members are machinery, cement, and aggregate manufacturers. Conducts testing and research on masonry units and masonry assemblies. Compiles statistics. *Type:* Association.

National Precast Concrete Association

10333 N. Meridian St., Ste. 272   Ph: (317)571-9500
Indianapolis, IN 46290-1081   Free: 800-366-7731
   Fax: (317)571-0041
E-mail: npca@precast.org
Contact: Ty Gable, CAE, Pres.

Desc: Producers of precast concrete products in all categories (small stock, agricultural, architectural, utility, and sewage disposal systems); suppliers to the industry; those interested in the technical and educational aspects of precast concrete. Promotes the use of precast concrete; advocates improvement of techniques for the purpose of developing high standards of quality. Encourages cooperation between concrete products producers and architects, engineers, real estate developers, contractors, and government officials. *Type:* Association.

National Ready Mixed Concrete Association

900 Spring St.   Ph: (301)587-1400
Silver Spring, MD 20910   Free: 888-84-
                    NRMCA
                    Fax: (301)585-4219

E-mail: bgarbini@nrmca.org
URL: http://www.nrmca.org
Contact: Robert Garbini, Pres.
Desc: Producers of ready mixed concrete and suppliers of services, equipment and materials to ready mixed concrete industry. *Type:* Association.

Portland Cement Association

5420 Old Orchard Rd.   Ph: (847)966-6200
Skokie, IL 60077-1083   Fax: (847)966-8389
URL: http://www.portcement.org
Contact: John P. Gleason, Jr., Pres.
Desc: Manufacturers and marketers of portland cement in the U.S. and Canada. Seeks to improve and extend the uses of portland cement and concrete through market promotion, research and development, educational programs, and representation with governmental entities. *Type:* Association.

Conservation

Adirondack Council

Box D-2   Ph: (518)873-2240
Church St.   Free: 800-842-PARK
Elizabethtown, NY 12932 Fax: (518)873-6675
URL: http://www.crisny.org/not-for-profit/adkcncl
Contact: Timothy Burke, Exec.Dir.
Desc: Individuals and organizations concerned with preserving the Adirondack Park in northern New York. Fosters awareness of the values and resources of the Adirondack Park and promotes its preservation along with enhancement of its wild and scenic qualities. Seeks management of public lands in the park in a manner compatible with the park's needs and qualities. *Type:* Association.

AMC Outdoors

Appalachian Mountain Club
5 Joy St.   Ph: (617)523-0636
Boston, MA 02108   Fax: (617)523-0722
E-mail: amcoutdoors@amcinfo.org.
Contact: Jane Roy Brown, jroybrown@amcinfo.org wow; Madeline Eno, Publisher, meno@amcinfo.org.
Desc: Outdoor recreation and conservation magazine. *Type:* Periodical.

American Forests

910 17th St. NW, No. 600 Ph: (202)955-4500
Washington, DC 20006   Free: 800-368-5748
                  Fax: (202)955-4588
E-mail: member@amfor.org
URL: http://www.amfor.org
Contact: Deborah Gangloff, Exec.Dir.
Desc: A citizens' conservation organization working to advance the intelligent management and use of forests, soil, water, wildlife, and all other natural resources. Promotes public appreciation of natural resources and the part they play in the social, recreational, and economic life of the U.S. *Type:* Association.

American Oceans Campaign

725 Arizona Ave., Ste. 102 Ph: (310)576-6162
Santa Monica, CA 90401   Free: 800-8-
                  OCEAN-0
                  Fax: (310)576-6170
E-mail: aoc@earthlink.net
URL: http://www.americanoceans.org
Contact: David Younkman, Exec.Dir.
Desc: Safeguards the vitality of the oceans and coastal waters. Committed to scientific information in advocating for sound public policy; developing partnerships with all entities interested in protecting the environment. Seeks to ensure healthy sources of food and coastal recreation as well as to protect the ocean's grandeur for future generations. *Type:* Association.

American Recycling Market Directories

Recycling Data Management Corp.
PO Box 577   Ph: (613)448-2383
Ogdensburg, NY 13669   Free: 800-267-0707
                  Fax: 877-471-3258
E-mail: info@recyclingdata.com
URL: http://www.recyclingdata.com.
Contact: Robert Boulanger, Editor.
Desc: Approximately 17,000 recycling markets throughout the U.S. and Canada, including dealers, processors, brokers, mills, foundries, and equipment and special service companies. *Type:* Directory.

American Rivers

1025 Vermont Ave. NW, Ste. Ph: (202)347-7550
720   Free: 800-296-6900
Washington, DC 20005   Fax: (202)347-9240
E-mail: amrivers@amrivers.org
URL: http://www.amrivers.org
Contact: Rebecca R. Wodder, Pres.
Desc: A public interest group working to preserve and restore America's river systems; fosters a river stewardship ethic. *Type:* Association.

The Amicus Journal

Natural Resources Defense Council
40 W. 20 St.   Ph: (212)727-2700
New York, NY 10011   Fax: (212)727-1773
Contact: Kathrin Day Lassila, Editor; Dana Nadel Foley, Managing Editor; Peggy Alevrontas, Editorial Assistant; Brian Swann, Poetry Editor.
Desc: Magazine covering regional, national and international environmental affairs. *Type:* Periodical.

Audubon Naturalist Society of the Central Atlantic States

8940 Jones Mill Rd.   Ph: (301)652-9188
Chevy Chase, MD 20815 Fax: (301)951-7179
E-mail: jomoyers@aol.com
Contact: Mike Nelson, Exec.Dir.
Desc: Persons interested in environmental education and protection. Seeks to further sound conservation practices, and to protect birds and other wildlife and the environment on which they depend. *Type:* Association.

Center for Marine Conservation

1725 DeSales St. NW, Ste. 600 Ph: (202)429-5609
Washington, DC 20036   Fax: (202)872-0619
E-mail: cmc@dccmc.org
URL: http://www.cmc-ocean.org
Contact: Roger E. McManus, Pres.
Desc: Dedicated to the conservation and protection of the marine wildlife and their habitats. *Type:* Association.

Center for Plant Conservation

Missouri Botanical Garden Ph: (314)577-9450
PO Box 299   Fax: (314)577-9465
St. Louis, MO 63166
E-mail: cpc@mobot.org
URL: http://www.mobot.org/cpc
Contact: Dr. Brien A. Meilleur, Pres. and Exec. Dir.
Desc: Individuals and organizations interested in rare plant conservation at botanical gardens and arboreta. Gathers and disseminates information regarding rare and endangered plants indigenous to the U.S. *Type:* Association.

Coastal Conservation Association

4801 Woodway, Ste. 220 W. Ph: (713)626-4234
Houston, TX 77056   Fax: (713)626-5852
Contact: David G. Cummins, Sec.Treas.
Desc: Organizations, corporations, and individuals interested in conserving the natural resources of U.S. saltwater coastal areas. Seeks to advance the protection and conservation of all marine life. *Type:* Association.

Conservation Foundation

1250 24th St. NW, Ste. 400 Ph: (202)293-4800
Washington, DC 20037
Contact: Kathryn Fuller, Pres.
Desc: Encourages wise management of the earth's resources through research and communication. Conducts programs in land use (rural resources, urban conservation, public lands), water resources, environmental dispute resolution, environmental institutions and trends, and pollution and toxic substances control. Sponsors interdisciplinary research, education, and information programs to develop knowledge, improve techniques, and stimulate public and private awareness and action to improve the quality of the environment. *Type:* Association.

Conservation International

2501 M St., NW Ste. 200 Ph: (202)429-5660
Washington, DC 20037   Fax: (202)887-5188
E-mail: pseligmann@conservation.org
URL: http://www.conservation.org
Contact: Peter Seligmann, Pres.
Desc: Corporations and individuals in 15 countries interested in environmental protection and conservation. Cooperates with governments and other organizations to help all nations develop the ability to sustain biological diversity and the ecosystems that support life on earth while addressing basic economic and social needs. Has sponsored an agreement whereby a portion of Bolivia's debt to United States banks was forgiven in exchange for Bolivia's promise to protect a part of the Amazon rainforest; other project sites include Costa Rica and Mexico. *Type:* Association.

ConservatioNews

Arizona State University Libraries
Department of Archives and Manuscripts
Box 871006   Ph: (602)965-3145
Tempe, AZ 85287-1006 Fax: (602)965-9169
E-mail: iacrps@asuvm.inre.asu.edu.
Contact: Robert P. Spinder, Editor; Heather McIntyre, Editor.
Desc: Concerned with the preservation of paper documents, magnetic media, published materials, photographs, and film. Carries articles on the theory and practice of conservation, questions and answers to specific problems, and product news. *Type:* Newsletter.

DEFENDERS Magazine

Defenders of Wildlife
1101 14th St. NW, Ste. 1400 Ph: (202)682-9400
Washington, DC 20005   Fax: (202)682-1331
E-mail: info@defenders.com

Contact: James G. Deane, Editor.

Desc: Wildlife conservation magazine. *Type:* Periodical.

Eco

Financial World Partners

1328 Broadway, 3rd Fl. Ph: (212)594-5030

New York, NY 10001 Free: 800-829-5916

Fax: (212)629-0026

Desc: Magazine covering issues that affect both business and the environment. *Type:* Periodical.

Eco-Notes

Gelder's Global Gig

800 Grand Ave., Ste. AG8135 Ph: (619)994-9976

Carlsbad, CA 92008 Fax: (619)632-0220

Contact: P.J. Grimes, Editor; Jeff Gelder, Editor, gelderhead@aol.com.

Desc: Committed to "spreading environmental and social messages through music." Offers practical advice on conservation, recycling, and environmental protection. Recurring features include a calendar of events, book reviews, and notices of publications available. *Type:* Newsletter.

Environmental News Network

Environmental News Network

Box 1996 Ph: (208)726-3649

Sun Valley, ID 83353 Fax: (208)726-2476

E-mail: news@enn.com

URL: http://www.enn.com.

Contact: Steven Schowengerdt, Editor-in-Chief; Hillary Mayell, Managing Editor; Tom Iselin, Business Development.

Desc: Online magazine covering environmental and science topics. *Type:* Periodical.

Federation of Western Outdoor Clubs

512 E. Boylston Ave., No. 106 Ph: (206)522-6475

Seattle, WA 98102

E-mail: patmarty@srv.net

Contact: Martin Huebner, Contact.

Desc: Outdoor clubs in the western U.S. with combined membership of 500,000. Promotes conservation of forests, wildlife, and natural features. *Type:* Association.

Friends of the Earth

1025 Vermont Ave NW, Ste. Ph: (202)783-7400

300 Fax: (202)783-0444

Washington, DC 20005

E-mail: foe@foe.org

Contact: Brent Blackwelder, Pres.

Desc: Dedicated to protecting the planet from environmental disaster; preserving biological and ethnic diversity; empowers citizens to have an effective voice in environmental decision; promotes use of tax dollars to protect the environment; other interests include groundwater and ozone protection, toxic waste cleanup, and reforming the World Bank and sustainable development which addressed the need to reduce over-consumption in the U.S. *Type:* Association.

Global Change Master Directory

NASA Goddard Flight Center

Code 902 Ph: (301)441-4202

Greenbelt, MD 20771 Fax: (301)441-9486

E-mail: gcmduso@gcmd.gsfc.nasa.gov

URL: http://gcmd.gsfc.nasa.gov/.

Contact: Lola Olsen, Editor, (301)614-5361, olsen@gcmd.gsfc.nasa.gov.

Desc: Availability and location of satellite-based observations of Earth's environment for the scientific community. *Type:* Directory.

Great Lakes Fishery Commission

2100 Commonwealth Blvd., Ste. Ph: (734)662-3209

209 Fax: (734)741-2010

Ann Arbor, MI 48105

URL: http://www.glfc.org

Contact: C.I. Goddard, Exec.Sec.

Desc: Representatives of the governments of Canada and the United States Develops coordinated research programs in the Great Lakes and recommends measures permitting the maximum sustained productivity of the lakes. Runs a sea lamprey control program and facilities implementation of the joint strategic olan for management of Great Lakes Fisheries. *Type:* Association.

Great Lakes United

Cassety Hall Ph: (716)886-0142

1300 Elmwood Ave. Fax: (716)886-0303

Buffalo, NY 14222

URL: http://www.glu.org

Contact: Margaret Wooster, Exec.Dir.

Desc: International conservation coalition formed by representatives of environmental, sports, union, community, and business groups (200) that promote the conservation and enhancement of the Great Lakes ecosystem; interested individuals (650). Serves as an advisory organization and source of information exchange. Target issues include: hazardous and toxic substances; biodiversity and habitat protection; pollution protection in areas of concern; sustainable use of water resources. *Type:* Association.

Greater Yellowstone Coalition

13 S. Willson Ph: (406)586-1593

PO Box 1874 Fax: (406)586-0851

Bozeman, MT 59771

E-mail: gyc@gyc.desktop.org

URL: http://www.desktop.org/gyc

Contact: Mike Clark, Exec.Dir.

Desc: Individuals and groups concerned with conservation, wildlife, and the environment. Purpose is to conserve and protect the Greater Yellowstone Ecosystem, the 18 million acre area including and surrounding Yellowstone National Park, WY, and Grand Teton National Park, WY, and the full range of its life. *Type:* Association.

The Green Pages

US West Dex, Inc.

198 Inverness Dr. West Ph: (303)784-2319

Englewood, CO 80112 Free: 800-288-2582

URL: http://export.uswest.com.

Contact: Mike Brady, Editor.

Desc: Approximately 300 U.S. suppliers to the environmental industry distributed worldwide through U.S. Commerce Department channels. *Type:* Directory.

Greenpeace Magazine

Greenpeace USA

1436 U St. NW Ph: (202)462-1177

Washington, DC 20009 Free: 800-326-0959

Fax: (202)483-8683

E-mail: gp@sharewest.com.

URL: http://www.greenpeaceusa.org.

Contact: David Barre, Editor-in-Chief, (202)319-2486, davidbarre@wdc.greenpeace.org; Naomi Perian s, Writer/Assoc. Editor, (202)319-2422, naomi.perian@wdc.greenpeace.org; Rob King, Production Coord., (202)319-2460, rob.king@wdc.greepeace.org; Jay Townsend, Editor-in-Chief.

Desc: Magazine covering environmental issues and the activities of Greenpeace. *Type:* Periodical.

International Association of Fish and Wildlife Agencies Newsletter

International Association of Fish and Wildlife Agencies (IAFWA)

444 N. Capitol St. NW, Ste. Ph: (202)624-7890

544 Fax: (202)624-7891

Washington, DC 20001

Contact: Francine Gillus, Editor.

Desc: Promotes the economic importance of conserving natural resources and managing wildlife property as sources of recreation and food supply. Provides information on conservation legislation, administration, and enforcement. *Type:* Newsletter.

Izaak Walton League of America

IWLA Conservation Center Ph: (301)548-0150

707 Conservation Ln. Free: 800-IKE-LINE

Gaithersburg, MD 20878 Fax: (301)548-0146

E-mail: general@iwla.org

URL: http://www.iwla.org

Contact: Paul Hansen, Exec.Dir.

Desc: Works to educate the public to conserve, maintain, protect, and restore the soil, forest, water, and other natural resources of the U.S.; promotes the enjoyment and wholesome utilization of these resources. *Type:* Association.

Izaak Walton League of America Endowment

PO Box 824 Ph: (319)351-7073

Iowa City, IA 52244

Contact: Robert C. Russell, Exec.Sec.

Desc: Individuals, families, students, corporations, and members of Izaak Walton League of America working towards saving America's natural resources. Dedicated to conservation goals through education, science, and the acquisition of endangered lands. Is instrumental in quickly purchasing strategic parcels of land without the burden of red tape and time-consuming decisions of government agencies. *Type:* Association.

John Birch Society

PO Box 8040 Ph: (920)749-3780

Appleton, WI 54913 Fax: (920)749-5062

E-mail: jbs@jbs.org

URL: http://www.jbs.org

Contact: John F. McManus, Pres.

Desc: Individuals who believe that the American system of government (Constitutional Republic) is the "finest yet developed by man." Believes in the traditional moral values of a Judeo-Christian heritage, and that it is the cornerstone to western civilization. Provides action programs, professional leadership training, educational information, youth program, and book and video production. *Type:* Association.

Land Trust Alliance

1319 F St. NW, Ste. 501 Ph: (202)638-4725

Washington, DC 20004-1106 Fax: (202)638-4730

URL: http://www.lta.org

Contact: Jean Hocker, Pres.

Desc: Local, regional, and national land conservation organizations, organized as land trusts; interested individuals. Works to advance the land trust movement; makes available resources and training services to land trusts. Fosters supportive public policies and seeks to increase public awareness of land trusts and their goals. *Type:* Association.

Left Green Perspectives

Left Green Perspectives

Box 111

Burlington, VT 05402

URL: http://ise.rootmedia.org/lgp

Contact: Janet Biehl, Editor, jbiehl@together.net; Murray Bookchin, Editor.

Desc: Provides theoretical analyses, news, and information on social ecology. *Type:* Newsletter.

Massachusetts Audubon Society

208 S. Great Rd. Ph: (781)259-9500
Lincoln, MA 01773 Free: 800-AUD-
  UBON
  Fax: (781)259-8899
URL: http://www.massaudubon.org

Contact: Dr. Gerard A. Bertrand, Pres.

Type: Association.

The Millennium Institute

The Millennium Institute
1117 N. 19th St., Ste. 900 Ph: (703)841-0048
Arlington, VA 22209-1708 Fax: (703)841-0050
E-mail: millennium-info@igc.apc.org
URL: http://www.igc.apc.org/millennium/

Contact: Gerald Barney, President, millennium@igc.apc.org.

Desc: The Millennium Institute aims to provide the impetus for a *redirection of human civilization toward a peaceful, just, and sustainable future.* This is an extensive collection of scholarly resources on the millennium and related topics that provides the very useful items. *Type:* Database.

Minnesota Valley Action Council

Nichols Office Ctr.-410 Jackson Ph: (507)345-6822
St. Free: 800-767-7139
Mankato, MN 56001 Fax: (507)345-2414
URL: http://www.ic.mankato.mn.us/reg9/mvac/mvac.html

Contact: John Woodwick, Exec.Dir.

Type: Association.

National Association of Conservation Districts

509 Capitol Ct. NE Ph: (202)547-6223
Washington, DC 20002 Fax: (202)547-6450
E-mail: eshea@nacdnet.org
URL: http://www.nacdnet.org

Contact: Ernest C. Shea, CEO.

Desc: Soil and water conservation districts organized by the citizens of watersheds, counties, or communities under provisions of state laws. Directs and coordinates, through local self-government efforts, the conservation and development of soil, water, and related natural resources. Districts include over 90% of the nation's privately owned land. *Type:* Association.

National Audubon Society

PO Box 52529 Ph: (212)979-3000
Boulder, CO 80322-2529 Fax: (212)353-0377
E-mail: webmaster@list.audubon.org
URL: http://www.audubon.org

Contact: John Flicker, Pres.

Desc: Works to conserve and restore natural exosystems, focusing on birds and other wildlife for the benefit of humanity and the earth's biological diversity. *Type:* Association.

National Audubon Society, Northeast Region

200 Trallium Ln. Ph: (518)869-9731
Albany, NY 12203-3818 Fax: (518)869-0737

Contact: David J. Miller, V.Pres.

Desc: Individuals in New York and New England interested in the conservation of wildlife, the environment, and natural resources. *Type:* Association.

National Parks

National Parks & Conservation Association
1776 Massachusetts Ave. NW, Ph: (202)223-6722
Ste. 200 Fax: (202)659-0650
Washington, DC 20036

Contact: Leslie Happ, Editor-in-Chief.

Desc: Magazine on issues affecting our National Parks. *Alt. Contact:* 1776 Massachusetts Ave. N.W., Washington, DC 20036; telephone: (202)223-6722, (202)659-0650. *Type:* Periodical.

National Wildlife Federation

8925 Leesburg Pike Ph: (703)790-4000
Vienna, VA 22184
URL: http://www.nwf.org

Contact: Mark Van Putten, Pres.

Desc: Nation's largest member-supported conservation group, with over four million members and supporters. Federation of state and territorial affiliates, associate members and individual conservationist-contributors. Seeks to educate, inspire and assist individuals and organizations of diverse cultures to conserve wildlife and other natural resources and to protect the earth's environment in order to achieve a peaceful, equitable and sustainable future. *Type:* Association.

Natural History Magazine

American Museum of Natural History
79th St. & Central Park W. Ph: (212)769-5000
New York, NY 10024 Fax: (212)769-5511
E-mail: nhmag@amnh.org

Contact: Mark Furlong, Publisher, fax: (212)769-5055, mfurlong@amnh.org; Bruce Stutz, Editor, bstutz@aminh.org; Gale Page, Dir. of Marketing, gpage@amnh.org.

Desc: Magazine covering natural science, anthropology, archeology, and zoology. *Type:* Periodical.

Natural Resources Defense Council

40 W. 20th St. Ph: (212)727-2700
New York, NY 10011 Fax: (212)727-1773
E-mail: nrdcinfo@nrdc.org
URL: http://www.nrdc.org

Contact: John H. Adams, Exec.Dir.

Desc: Lawyers, scientists, public health specialists, and transportation, energy, land use, and economic planners. Dedicated to the wise management of natural resources through research, public education, and the development of public policies. Concerns include land use, coastal protection, air and water pollution, nuclear safety and energy production, toxic substances, and protection of wilderness and wildlife. *Type:* Association.

Nature Conservancy

4245 Fairfax Dr., Ste. 100 Ph: (703)841-5300
Arlington, VA 22203-1606 Free: 800-628-6860
  Fax: (703)841-1283
URL: http://www.tnc.org

Contact: John C. Sawhill, Pres.

Desc: Dedicated to the preservation of biological diversity through land and water protection of natural areas. Identifies ecologically significant lands and protects them through gift, purchase, or cooperative management agreements with government or private agencies, voluntary arrangements with private landowners, and cost-saving methods of protection. Provides long-term stewardship for 1600 conservancy-owned preserves and makes most conservancy lands available for nondestructive use on request by educational and scientific organizations. *Type:* Association.

Nature Conservancy

The Nature Conservancy
1815 N. Lynn St. Ph: (703)841-5300
Arlington, VA 22209-2003 Free: 800-628-6860
  Fax: (703)841-9692
URL: http://www.tnc.org.

Contact: Ron Geatz, Editor.

Desc: Magazine reporting on the global preservation of natural diversity. *Type:* Periodical.

New York State Conservation Council

8 E. Main St. Ph: (315)894-3302
Ilion, NY 13357 Fax: (315)894-2893

Contact: Howard O. Cushing, Pres.

Desc: Sportsmen and conservationists interested in the intelligent use and management of natural resources. *Type:* Association.

New York State Conservationist

New York State Dept. of Environmental Conservation
50 Wolf Rd., Rm. 548 Ph: (518)457-5547
Albany, NY 12233-4502 Free: 800-678-6399
  Fax: (518)457-0858

Contact: R.W. Groneman, Editor, rwgronem@gw.dec.state.ny.us.

Desc: Consumer magazine. *Alt. Contact:* 50 Wolf Rd., Rm. 548, Albany, NY 12233-4502; telephone: (518)457-5547; fax: (518)457-0858. *Type:* Periodical.

Official Recycled Products Guide

Recycling Data Management Corp.
PO Box 577 Ph: (613)448-2383
Ogdensburg, NY 13669 Free: 800-267-0707
  Fax: 877-471-3258
E-mail: info@recyclingdata.com
URL: http://www.recyclingdata.com.

Contact: Jackie Boulanger, Editor.

Desc: Nearly 650 manufacturers, distributors, and converters of recycled products in North America. *Type:* Directory.

Pennsylvania Game News

Pennsylvania Game Commission
2001 Elmerton Ave. Ph: (717)787-3745
Harrisburg, PA 17110-9797 Free: 888-888-1019
  Fax: (717)772-0542
E-mail: info@pgc.state.pa.us

Contact: Bob Mitchell, Editor.

Desc: Hunting and wildlife conservation magazine. *Type:* Periodical.

Pollution Equipment News

Rimbach Publishing, Inc.
8650 Babcock Blvd. Ph: (412)364-5366
Pittsburgh, PA 15237 Free: 800-245-3182
  Fax: (412)369-9720
E-mail: rimbach@sgi.net

Contact: David C. Lavender, Editor; Norberta Rimbach, Publisher.

Desc: Pollution control equipment and products magazine (tabloid). *Type:* Periodical.

Rainforest Action Network

221 Pine St., Ste. 500 Free: 800-989-RAIN
San Francisco, CA 94104
E-mail: rainforest@igc.apc.org
URL: http://www.ran.org

Contact: Kelly Quirke, Exec. Dir.

Desc: Seeks to preserve the world's rainforests through activism on issues including the logging and importation of tropical timber, cattle ranching in rainforests, the activities of international development banks, and the rights of indigenous rainforest peoples. Sponsors letter writing campaigns, boycotts, and demonstrations; conducts grass roots organizing in the U.S., builds coalitions, and collaborates with other environmental, scientific, and grass roots groups; facilitates communication among U.S. and Third World organizers. *Type:* Association.

Rainforest Alliance

65 Bleecker St. Ph: (212)677-1900
New York, NY 10012 Free: 888-MY-
EARTH
Fax: (212)677-2187
E-mail: canopy@ra.org
URL: http://www.rainforest-alliance.org
Contact: Daniel Katz, Exec. Dir.
Desc: Works for the conservation of tropical forests for the benefit of the global community. Develops and promotes economically viable and socially desirable alternatives to the destruction of tropical forests, an endangered, biologically diverse natural resource. Educates and researches the social and natural sciences; develops cooperative partnerships with businesses, governments and local peoples. *Type:* Association.

Recycling Sourcebook

Gale Group Inc.
27500 Drake Rd. Ph: (248)699-4253
Farmington Hills, MI 48331- Free: 800-877-GALE
3535 Fax: (248)699-8070
E-mail: galeord@galegroup.com
URL: http://www.galegroup.com.
Desc: Organizations concerned with policies, programs, and implications of recycling in the U.S.; companies performing recycling services. An appendix lists products made with recycled or recyclable materials and their manufacturers. *Type:* Directory.

Save the Redwoods League

114 Sansome St., Rm. 605 Ph: (415)362-2352
San Francisco, CA 94104-3814 Fax: (415)362-7017
E-mail: saveredwoods@igc.org
URL: http://www.savetheredwoods.org
Contact: Mary A. Angle, Exec.Dir.
Desc: Persons interested in preserving representative stands of Coast Redwoods and Giant Sequoias, as well as other trees, principally in California. Works with California State Parks Commission and the National Park Service to establish Redwood Parks. *Type:* Association.

The Seedhead News

Native Seeds/SEARCH
526 N. 4th Ave. Ph: (520)622-5561
Tucson, AZ 85705 Fax: (520)622-5591
E-mail: nss@azstarnet.com
URL: http://www.azstarnet.com/~nss/.
Contact: Brooke Gebow, Editor; Laura Alexander, Editor.
Desc: Concerned with the conservation of traditional crops and their wild relatives in the Southwestern United States. Discusses seed searching and the seedstocks available through this education and research organization. *Type:* Newsletter.

Soil and Water Conservation Society

7515 NE Ankeny Rd. Ph: (515)289-2331
Ankeny, IA 50021 Fax: (515)289-1227
E-mail: swcs@swcs.org
URL: http://www.swcs.org
Contact: Douglas M. Kleine, CAE, Exec.VP.
Desc: Soil and water conservationists and others in fields related to the use, conservation, and management of natural resources. Objective is to advance the science and art of good land and water use. Offers unpaid internships to qualified students. *Type:* Association.

Student Conservation Association

PO Box 550 Ph: (603)543-1700
689 River Rd. Fax: (603)543-1828
Charlestown, NH 03603-0550
URL: http://www.sca-inc.org
Contact: Dale Penny, Pres.
Desc: Individuals, foundations, corporations, and groups who support the association's programs. *Type:* Association.

Treelines

Saskatchewan Forestry Association
PO Box 400 Ph: (306)763-2189
Prince Albert, SK, Canada S6V Fax: (306)764-7463
5R7
Contact: Marie Grono, Editor.
Desc: Covers forest resources and forestry issues in Saskatchewan. Recurring features include news of association activities, news of members, and a calendar of events. *Type:* Newsletter.

TreePeople

12601 Mulholland Dr. Ph: (818)753-4600
Beverly Hills, CA 90210 Fax: (818)753-4625
E-mail: treepeople@treepeople.org
URL: http://www.treepeople.org
Contact: Andy Lipkis, Pres. & Founder.
Desc: Environmental problem solving organization, operating primarily in southern California, promoting community action, global awareness, environmental education, and an active role in the planting and care of trees. Conducts education and training seminars. Volunteers plant trees throughout Los Angeles, CA and its surrounding mountain area. *Type:* Association.

Trust for Public Land

116 New Montgomery St., 4th Ph: (415)495-4014
Fl. Free: 800-714-LAND
San Francisco, CA 94105 Fax: (415)495-4103
E-mail: mail@tpl.org
URL: http://www.tpl.org
Contact: Martin J. Rosen, Pres.
Desc: Dedicated to acquiring and preserving land in urban and rural areas for public use. Provides urban and community groups with training and technical assistance in land acquisition. Acquires recreational, historic, and scenic lands for conveyance to local, state, and federal agencies and nonprofit organizations for open space protection and public use. *Type:* Association.

United States Tourist Council

Drawer 1875 Ph: (301)565-5155
Washington, DC 20013-1875
Contact: Dr. Stanford West, Exec.Dir.
Desc: Conservation-concerned individuals who travel; institutions and industries that supply goods and services to the traveler. Objectives are to achieve: historic and scenic preservation; wilderness and roadside development; ecology through sound planning and education; support of scientific studies of natural wilderness areas. *Type:* Association.

Waterfowl U.S.A.

Box 50 Ph: (803)637-5767
Waterfowl Bldg. Fax: (803)637-6983
Edgefield, SC 29824
Contact: Roger White, Pres.
Desc: Hunters, conservationists, and others dedicated to raising money for developing, preserving, restoring, and maintaining waterfowl habitats in the U.S. Seeks to: publicize the needs of waterfowl; develop state and local wetland projects; improve waterfowl resting areas, wood duck nest boxes, and planting areas that feed migrating and resident waterfowl; establish public shooting areas. *Type:* Association.

West Virginia State Soil Conservation Agency

1900 Kanawha Blvd. E Ph: (304)558-2204
Charleston, WV 25305-0193 Fax: (304)340-4839
E-mail: jedowdy@wvsca.org
URL: http://www.wvsca.org
Contact: Lance Tabor, Exec.Dir.
Type: Association.

Whalewatch

Whale Adoption Project
International Wildlife Coalition
70 E. Falmouth Hwy. Ph: (508)548-8328
East Falmouth, MA 02536-5954 Fax: (508)548-8542
Contact: Donna Hart, Editor.
Desc: Informs members as to the progress of the Coalition's Whale Adoption Project, issues concerning marine mammals and the actions individuals can take to protect wildlife and the environment. *Type:* Newsletter.

The Wilderness Society

900 17th St. NW Ph: (202)833-2300
Washington, DC 20006-2596 Free: 800-843-9453
Fax: (202)429-3958
URL: http://www.wilderness.org/
Contact: William H. Meadows, III, Pres.
Desc: Purposes include the establishment of the land ethic as a basic element of American culture and philosophy, and the education of a broader and more committed wilderness preservation and land protection constituency. Focuses on federal, legislative, and administrative actions affecting public lands, including national forests, parks, and wildlife refuges, and Bureau of Land Management lands. Encourages Congress to designate appropriate public lands as wilderness areas. *Type:* Association.

Wildlife Conservation Society

2300 Southern Blvd. Ph: (718)220-5100
Bronx, NY 10460 Fax: (212)220-7114
E-mail: join@wcs.org
URL: http://www.wcs.org
Contact: William Conway, Pres.
Desc: Supporters of international species survival strategies and habitat/ecosystem conservation projects. Operates Bronx Zoo, Aquarium for Wildlife Conservation, and three other wildlife centers in New York. Publishes and disseminates environmental education curricula to nationwide school audience, including extensive teacher training programs. *Type:* Association.

Wildlife Habitat Council

1010 Wayne Ave., Ste. 920 Ph: (301)588-8994
Silver Spring, MD 20910 Fax: (301)588-4629
E-mail: whc@wildlifehc.org
URL: http://www.wildlifehc.org
Contact: William W. Howard, Pres.
Desc: A joint effort between the conservation and corporate communities designed to help corporations develop their lands for wildlife. Provides technical assistance in establishing and maintaining responsible corporate wildlife management practices, habitat certification, information sharing, employee involvement, and community outreach. *Type:* Association.

Wisconsin Natural Resources

Department of Natural Resources
Box 7921 Ph: (608)266-1510
Madison, WI 53707 Fax: (608)264-6293
E-mail: sperld@dnr.state.wi.us
Contact: David L. Sperling, Editor; Maureen Merozzi, Asst. Editor; Kathryn Kahler, Circulation; Pam Hujanen, Promotions.
Desc: Consumer magazine covering the local environment, natural resources, conservation, and the outdoors. *Type:* Periodical.

Wolf Haven International
3111 Offut Lake Rd.　Ph: (360)264-4695
Tenino, WA 98589　Free: 800-448-9653
　Fax: (360)264-4639
E-mail: information@wolfhaven.org
URL: http://www.wolfhaven.org
Contact: Julie Palmquist, Info. Coord.

Desc: Individuals interested in the conservation and understanding of wolves and wolf populations. Seeks to educate the public and increase awareness of the need for conservation. Provides presentations to school, civic, and professional groups. *Type:* Association.

World Environment Center
419 Park Ave. S., Ste. 1800　Ph: (212)683-4700
New York, NY 10016　Fax: (212)683-5053
E-mail: webmaster@wec.org
URL: http://www.wec.org
Contact: Antony Marcil, Pres. & CEO.

Desc: Works to strengthen industrial and urban environmental, health, and safety policies by establishing and promoting partnerships among industry, government, and nongovernmental organizations. *Type:* Association.

World Resources Institute
1709 New York Ave. NW, Ste.　Ph: (202)638-6300
　700　Fax: (202)638-0036
Washington, DC 20006
E-mail: wri@igc.apc.org
Contact: Deanna Madvin Wolfire, Contact.

Desc: Scientists and other academics with an interest in the environment and development. Promotes environmentally sustainable economic and community development globally; seeks to identify and introduce alternative and renewable energy sources. *Type:* Association.

World Watch Institute
1776 Massachusetts Ave. NW　Fax: (202)296-7365
Washington, DC 20036-1904
Contact: Hilary French, Contact.

Desc: Environmental and development researchers. Seeks to raise public understanding of global environmental issues. *Type:* Association.

World Wildlife Fund
1250 24th St. NW　Ph: (202)293-4800
Washington, DC 20037　Free: 800-225-5993
　Fax: (202)293-9211
URL: http://www.wwf.org
Contact: Kathryn Fuller, Pres.

Desc: Supported by contributions from individuals, funds, corporations, and foundations. Seeks to protect the biological resources upon which human well-being depends. Emphasizes preservation of endangered and threatened species of wildlife and plants as well as habitats and natural areas anywhere in the world. *Type:* Association.

World Wildlife Fund—Focus
Anne Hummer
1250 24th St. NW　Ph: (202)293-4800
Washington, DC 20037
Contact: David Slater, Editor.

Desc: Addresses the concerns of the World Wildlife Fund-U.S., which is "dedicated to saving endangered wildlife and habitats around the world and to protecting the biological resources upon which human well-being depends." Discusses issues such as migratory birds, development of national parks, and illegal trade in wildlife. Act. *Type:* Newsletter.

Conservative

American Conservative Union
1007 Cameron St.　Ph: (703)836-8602
Alexandria, VA 22314-2426　Free: 800-ACU-7345
　Fax: (703)836-8606
E-mail: acu@conservative.org
URL: http://www.conservative.org
Contact: Jeff Hollingsworth, Exec.Dir.

Desc: Lobbying organization seeking to mobilize resources of responsible conservative activists across the country and further the general cause of conservatism. Lobbies and educates in subject areas, such as political activity, foreign and military policy, domestic economic policy, legal policy, social issues, etc. Rates members of Congress on important legislation. *Type:* Association.

American Society for the Defense of Tradition, Family and Property
PO Box 1868　Ph: (717)225-7147
York, PA 17405　Fax: (717)225-7479
Contact: Raymond E. Drake, Pres.

Desc: Volunteers and supporters united to defend the ideals of tradition, family, and property, and to peacefully and legally oppose what the society believes are socialist and Marxist views of life. Although the group is a civic organization, it draws its inspiration from the traditional doctrine of the Catholic church. The organization originated from a growing concern over what it felt were the "tragic consequences" stemming from the moral, religious, political, and economic crises affecting the West. *Type:* Association.

Christian-Patriots Defense League/Citizen's Emergency Defense System
PO Box 565　Ph: (618)665-3937
Flora, IL 62839
Contact: John Harrell, Founder.

Desc: Conservative Christians and patriots. Believes several nations of the world will invade and plunder the U.S. in the near future. *Type:* Association.

Conservative Alliance
2900 Eisenhower Ave., No.　Fax: (703)329-2411
　200-C
Alexandria, VA 22314
Contact: J. Barry Bitzer, Exec.Dir.

Desc: Individuals and corporations interested in strong national defense, private enterprise, and less government intervention, regulation, and spending. Educates and activates the public on governmental affairs affecting national defense, economy, and human rights. Activities include lobbying, radio talk shows, speakers' bureau, and informational service. *Type:* Association.

The Conservative Caucus
450 Maple Ave. E　Ph: (703)938-9626
Vienna, VA 22180　Fax: (703)281-4108
E-mail: corndorf@cais.com
URL: http://www.conservativeusa.org
Contact: Howard Phillips, Chrm.

Desc: Seeks to build a grass roots "new majority" lobbying coalition in every congressional district, through which conservatives can achieve the strategic capacity to set the agenda for public debate, define issues on their own terms, and develop effective leadership. *Type:* Association.

The Conservative Caucus Research, Analysis and Education Foundation
450 Maple Ave. E., Ste. 309　Ph: (703)281-6782
Vienna, VA 22180　Fax: (703)281-4108
Contact: Howard Phillips, Pres.

Desc: Conservative individuals interested in staying informed of the activities of the federal government. Disseminates information concerning the actions and expenditures of the federal government. *Type:* Association.

Conservative Majority for Citizen's Rights
302 Briarwood Cir. NW　Ph: (904)862-6211
Fort Walton Beach, FL 32548-　Fax: (904)862-6211
　3904
Contact: James Stanley Harkins, Sr., Pres.

Desc: International and national conservative organizations; individuals promoting a conservative government. Provides on-call citizen aid through political advocacy. *Type:* Association.

Council of Conservative Citizens
PO Box 221683　Ph: (314)291-8474
St. Louis, MO 63122　Fax: (314)344-1096
E-mail: info@cofcc.org
URL: http://www.cofcc.org
Contact: Gordon Lee Baum, CEO.

Desc: Members of state and local councils who are dedicated to "the principles of states' rights." Provides a network of groups and individuals that support the conservative majority. Rejects Affirmative Action programs. Compiles statistics; maintains speakers' bureau; conducts educational and research programs. *Type:* Association.

Criminal Politics
Patterson Publishing
PO Box 37432　Ph: (513)475-0100
Cincinnati, OH 45222　Free: 800-543-0486
　Fax: (513)475-6014
E-mail: crimpol@eos.net.
URL: http://www.criminalpolitics.com.
Contact: L.T. Patterson, Editor.

Desc: Contains articles on politics, economics, investments; pending, proposed, and current legislation and how this affects the public; Swiss banking; and general money management. Recurring features include statistics, book reviews, and news of research. *Type:* Newsletter.

Ducks Unlimited
Ducks Unlimited
1 Waterfowl Way　Ph: (901)758-3825
Memphis, TN 38120　Free: 800-453-8257
　Fax: (901)758-3850
URL: http://www.ducks.org.
Contact: Tom Fulgham, Editor-in-Chief, (901)758-3777, fax: (901)758-3909; Beth Bryan, Advertising Dir., (901)758-3779, fax: (901)758-3909, bbryan@ducks.org.
Desc: Magazine on waterfowl, wildlife conservation. *Type:* Periodical.

Eagle Forum
Box 618　Ph: (618)462-5415
Alton, IL 62002　Fax: (618)462-8909
E-mail: eagle@eagleforum.org
URL: http://www.eagleforum.org
Contact: Phyllis Schlafly, Pres.

Desc: Men and women advocating issues involving family, education, literacy and national defense through local, state, and federal government. *Type:* Association.

Freedom House/National Forum Foundation
1319 18th St. NW　Ph: (202)296-5101
Washington, DC 20036　Fax: (202)296-5256
E-mail: nff@nff.org
URL: http://www.nff.org
Contact: James S. Denton, Pres.

Desc: The National Forum Foundation is a non-partisan, 501(c)(3) educational and research organization dedicated to promoting political and economic freedom. The NFF has been active in the emerging democracies of the former East Bloc since 1989. *Type:* Association.

Fund for a Conservative Majority

PO Box 6829   Ph: (703)820-3830
Arlington, VA 22206   Fax: (703)820-4081

Contact: Robert C. Heckman, Chm.

Desc: Seeks to create a conservative majority in Congress. Trains young campaign workers and provides financial assistance to conservative candidates. *Type:* Association.

Intercollegiate Studies Institute

PO Box 4431   Ph: (302)652-4600
Wilmington, DE 19807-0431   Free: 800-526-7022
                               Fax: (302)652-1760

Contact: T. Kenneth Cribb, Jr., Pres.

Desc: Nonpartisan, educational organization directed primarily at the college campus. Seeks to develop among college students and professors an understanding of "the conservative philosophy of individual liberty, limited government, free-market economics, the right of private property, and the spiritual and moral underpinnings of this philosophy." Promotes sound scholarship within the disciplines of economics, sociology, literature, political science, history, and philosophy. Arranges lecture tours; provides a forum for students to meet with prominent scholars. *Type:* Association.

Liberty Lobby

300 Independence Ave. SE   Ph: (202)546-5611
Washington, DC 20003
E-mail: libertylob@aol.com
URL: http://www.spotlight.org

Contact: Vincent J. Ryan, Policy Bd.Chm.

Desc: "Nationalists and populists interested in political action in behalf of 110 issues which are pro-individual liberty and pro-patriotic." Supports free gold market, lower taxes, fewer farm controls, less government spending, protective immigration laws, repeal of the Sixteenth and Twenty-Fifth Amendments, separation of church and state, the right to keep and bear arms, states' rights, an end to forced busing, and withdrawal from the United Nations . *Type:* Association.

The Limbaugh Letter

Radio-Active Media, Inc.
366 Madison Ave., 7th Fl.   Ph: (212)661-7500
New York, NY 10017-3122   Fax: (212)563-9166

Contact: Rush Limbaugh, Editor; Diana Schneider, Editor.

Desc: Serves as a vehicle for disseminating the viewpoints of conservative radio talk show personality and author, Rush Limbaugh, on a variety of political topics. Recurring features include letters to the editor, interviews with political leaders, conservative thinkers, and other "prominent people," and columns titled Equal Time, Stupid Quotes, and According to Me. *Type:* Newsletter.

National Conservative Political Action Committee

618 S. Alfred St.   Ph: (703)684-1800
Alexandria, VA 22314-4002

Contact: Maiselle Dolan Shortley, Chm.

Desc: Political conservatives seeking to replace liberal politicians with conservatives in office. Unaffiliated with either the Democratic or Republican parties, the committee offers candidates such services as: polling, research, campaign management training, advice on media, public opinion trends, press relations, and fundraising in lieu of monetary contributions. Believes that well-planned services are more valuable than cash contributions in that a well-defined campaign is more advantageous than one that is simply well-funded. *Type:* Association.

Notes from FEE

Foundation for Economic Education, Inc.
30 S. Broadway   Ph: (914)591-7230
Irvington on Hudson, NY   Free: 800-452-3518
10533   Fax: (914)591-8910
E-mail: freeman@westnet.com

Contact: Beth A. Hoffman, Editor; Hans Sennholz, Publisher.

Desc: Discusses alternatives to state intervention in human affairs: the free market, private property, limited government concepts, and philosophical antecedents. Recurring features include a calendar of events, a list of newly published books, a short essay by Hans Sennholz, and reprints from other publications. *Type:* Newsletter.

Religious Roundtable

PO Box 11467   Ph: (901)458-3795
Memphis, TN 38111   Fax: (901)324-0265

Contact: Edward E. McAteer, Pres.

Desc: Coalition of "dedicated national leaders who have one concern - the moral rebirth of America," which they believe is an "absolute necessity if Western civilization and the Judeo-Christian ethics upon which it has been based are to survive." Focuses on public policy concerning issues such as the American family, decent television, freedom of worship, Israel, and opposition to abortion, child abuse, homosexuality, and pornography. Sponsors prayer meetings, and receives briefings from national leaders. Lobbying arm, Roundtable Issues and Answers, sponsors Christians for a Strong America to encourage the maintenance of a strong national defense program. *Type:* Association.

Young America's Foundation

110 Elden St.   Ph: (703)318-9608
Herndon, VA 20170   Free: 800-292-9231
                               Fax: (703)318-9122
E-mail: yaf@yaf.org
URL: http://www.yaf.org

Contact: Ron Robinson, Pres.

Desc: Works to acquaint American youth with the principles of American government in order that they may have a fuller understanding of contemporary public policy questions. *Type:* Association.

Construction

American Concrete Institute

PO Box 9094   Ph: (248)848-3700
Farmington Hills, MI 48333-   Fax: (248)848-3701
9094
E-mail: techinq@aci-ini.org
URL: http://www.aci-int.org

Contact: James G. Toscas, Exec.VP.

Desc: Technical society of engineers, architects, contractors, educators, and others interested in improving techniques of design construction and maintenance of concrete products and structures. Operates speakers' bureau; offers specialized education seminars. Maintains 112 technical committees. *Type:* Association.

American Contract Bridge League

2990 Airways Blvd.   Ph: (901)332-5586
Memphis, TN 38116-3847   Free: 800-467-1623
                               Fax: (901)398-7754
E-mail: acbl@acbl.org
URL: http://www.acbl.org

Contact: David O. Silber, CEO.

Desc: Contract bridge players (in Canada, U.S., Mexico, Bermuda, and Puerto Rico) who take part in club, local, regional, and North American tournaments. Establishes, interprets, and enforces rules and regulations governing the game of contract bridge. Maintains record of masterpoints awarded to individuals at tournaments and club games. *Type:* Association.

American Contract Bridge League, Inc.—The Bridge Bulletin

American Contract Bridge League, Inc.
2990 Airways Blvd.   Ph: (901)332-5586
Memphis, TN 38116-3847   Free: 800-467-1623
                               Fax: (901)398-7754
E-mail: acbl@acbl.org

Contact: Brent Manley, Executive Editor, editor@acbl.org.

Desc: Contains contract bridge information, tournaments, features, instructive articles. *Type:* Newsletter.

American Institute of Steel Construction

1 E. Wacker Dr., Ste. 3100   Ph: (312)670-2400
Chicago, IL 60601-2001   Fax: (312)670-5403
URL: http://www.aisc.org

Contact: Lou Gurthet, Pres.

Desc: Fabricators who erect structural steel for buildings and bridges. Sponsors research cooperatively with other industry groups and independently at engineering colleges. Program includes studies on welded and bolted connections, composite design, allowable stress and load factor design in steel, buckling problems, and techniques of painting structural steel. *Type:* Association.

Asphalt Roofing Manufacturers Association Newsletter

Asphalt Roofing Manufacturers Association (ARMA)
4041 Powder Mill Rd., Ste. 404 Ph: (301)348-2002
Beltsville, MD 20705   Fax: (301)348-2020

Contact: Joe Hobson, Editor/Dir. of Communications.

Desc: Reports news and information of interest to professionals in the asphalt roofing industry. Highlights Association activities and discusses developments in the industry, including occupational safety and health measures, changes in industry codes and standards, environmental issues, and legislative and regulatory actions. *Type:* Newsletter.

Associated Equipment Distributors—Contact

Associated Equipment Distributors
615 W. 22nd St.   Ph: (630)574-0650
Oak Brook, IL 60523   Free: 800-388-0650
                               Fax: (630)574-0132
E-mail: info@aednet.org
URL: http://www.aednet.org; http://www.aednet.org.

Contact: Katharine Abbott Zowaski, Editor.

Desc: Features news of the construction equipment distribution industry and Association's programs. Recurring features include news of research, a calendar of events, reports of meetings, and news of educational opportunities. *Type:* Newsletter.

Association of Construction Inspectors

1224 N. Nokomis N.E.   Ph: (320)763-7525
Alexandria, MN 56308   Fax: (320)763-9290
E-mail: aci@iami.org
URL: http://www.iami.org/aci.iam

Contact: Joan T. Powell, Managing Dir.

Desc: Works to provide education, training, standards and professional recognition to construction inspectors and project managers. *Type:* Association.

Building Design & Construction

Cahners Business Information
1350 E. Touhy Ave.   Ph: (847)635-8800
Des Plaines, IL 60018   Free: 800-446-6551
                               Fax: (847)635-6856
E-mail: bkinross@cahners.com
URL: http://www.bdcmag.com.

Contact: Bill Kinross, Publisher, (847)390-2650, bkinross@cahners.com; John Gregerson, Editor-in-Chief, jgregerson@cahners.com.

Desc: Magazine on business and technology for the design and construction of commercial, institutional, and industrial buildings. *Alt. Contact:* PO Box 5080, Des Plaines, IL 60017-5080; telephone: (847)635-8800; fax: (847)390-2152. *Type:* Periodical.

The Carpenter

United Brotherhood of Carpenters and Joiners of America, AFL-CIO
101 Constitution Ave. NW   Ph: (202)546-6206
Washington, DC 20001   Fax: (202)547-8979

Contact: Andris Silins, Editor; David Patterson, Advertising Mgr., dpatter867@aol.com; Monte Byers, Communication Dir.; Dave Ransom, Managing Editor.

Desc: Official magazine of the Carpenters' Union. *Type:* Periodical.

Cedar Shake and Shingle Bureau—Membership Directory and Buyer's Guide

Cedar Shake and Shingle Bureau
PO Box 1178   Ph: (604)462-8961
Sumas, WA 98295   Fax: (604)462-9386
E-mail: info@cedarbureau.com
URL: http://www.cedarbureau.org.

Contact: Darlene Jacuk, Editor; Lynne Christensen, Editor.

Desc: About 270 member manufacturing mills in the Pacific Northwest and British Columbia, Canada; approximately 200 affiliated roofing applicators, builders, architects, remodelers, and suppliers of related products and services. *Type:* Directory.

CEE News

Intertec Publishing Corp.
9800 Metcalf Ave.   Ph: (913)341-1300
Overland Park, KS 66212   Free: 800-400-5945
    Fax: (913)967-1328

Contact: Stuart M. Lewis, Editor; Richard A. Hathaway, Publisher; Bob MacArthur, Assoc. Publisher.

Desc: Electrical construction industry magazine. *Type:* Periodical.

Ceilings & Interior Systems Construction Association—Directory

Ceilings and Interior Systems Construction Association
1500 Lincoln Hwy., No. 202   Ph: (630)584-1919
St. Charles, IL 60174   Fax: (630)584-2003
E-mail: cisca@juno.com
URL: http://www.cisca.org

Contact: John Sanger, Editor.

Desc: Member contractors, distributors, and independent agents, and manufacturers and suppliers of interior construction products and services. *Type:* Directory.

CM Advisor

Construction Management Association of America, Inc.
7918 Jones Branch Dr., Ste. 540   Ph: (703)356-2622
Mc Lean, VA 22102-3307   Fax: (703)356-6388
E-mail: cmaa@iandigex.net

Contact: Bruce D'Agostino, Editor.

Desc: Provides information on construction management and its technical, legal, and legislative issues. Recurring features include letters to the editor, news of research, a calendar of events, reports of meetings, news of educational opportunities, book reviews, notices of publications available, and columns titled Legal Digest and Washington Viewpoint. *Type:* Newsletter.

Cockshaw's Construction Labor News & Opinion

Communications Counselors, Inc.
PO Box 427   Ph: (610)353-0123
Newtown Square, PA 19073   Fax: (610)353-0111
Contact: Peter A. Cockshaw, Editor.

Desc: Reports on and analyzes construction labor-management problems. Explores such topics as union versus nonunion market share, wage-price trends, work practices, productivity, and collective bargaining. *Type:* Newsletter.

The Complete Sourcebook

Microtronics
PO Box 200   Ph: (516)783-5793
Massapequa Park, NY 11762-   Fax: (516)221-3245
0200
E-mail: rita@digitalsky.net.
URL: http://www.complete-sourcebook.com.
Contact: Jay Fruin, Editor, jay@digitalsky.net.

Desc: 4,800 companies worldwide that supply products for builders and decorators ranging from curtains to tile. *Type:* Directory.

Construction—Directory & Buyer's Guide Issue

HES, Inc.
26 Long Hill Rd.
PO Box 362
Guilford, CT 06437-0362
E-mail: en@hes.com.
Contact: Amy Hubber, Editor.

Desc: Directory of about 3,000 construction equipment distributors in Maryland, the District of Columbia, Virginia, West Virginia, and North Carolina; government agencies, suppliers, and trade associations. *Type:* Directory.

Construction Division Newsletter

National Safety Council
1121 Spring Lake Dr.   Ph: (630)285-1121
Itasca, IL 60143-3201   Free: 800-539-7468
    Fax: (630)285-1315
URL: http://www.nsc.org; http://www.nsc.org.
Contact: Laura Coyne, Editor, (630)775-2276, fax: (630)775-2285.

Desc: Focuses on industrial and occupational safety in the construction industry. Carries items on such topics as safe work practices and products; accident prevention; and successful industrial safety programs and policies. *Type:* Newsletter.

Construction Equipment

Cahners Business Information
1350 E. Touhy Ave.   Ph: (847)635-8800
Des Plaines, IL 60018   Free: 800-446-6551
    Fax: (847)635-6856
E-mail: bkinross@cahners.com
Contact: Kirk Landers, Editor, (847)390-2173, landers@cahners.com; Daniel Pels, pels@cahners.com.

Desc: Magazine with information and ideas for managers of construction equipment and trucks. *Type:* Periodical.

Construction Equipment—Buyers Guide Issue

Cahners Business Information
1350 E. Touhy Ave.   Ph: (847)635-8800
Des Plaines, IL 60018   Free: 800-446-6551
    Fax: (847)635-6856
E-mail: bkinross@cahners.com
URL: http://www.coneQ.com/.
Contact: Kirk Landers, Editor; Kirk Landers, Editor.

Desc: List of over 900 products, 1,800 manufacturers of construction equipment, 5,500 distributors, and brief listings of financing, bonding, and management services, and trade associations. Plus, complete comparitive specifications on more than 2,500 models. *Type:* Directory.

Construction Equipment—Construction Giants Issue

Cahners Business Information
1350 E. Touhy Ave.   Ph: (847)635-8800
Des Plaines, IL 60018   Free: 800-446-6551
    Fax: (847)635-6856
E-mail: bkinross@cahners.com
Contact: Kirk Landers, Editor.

Desc: Listing of approximately 250 of the largest equipment-owning heavy construction contractors, engaged in earthmoving, paving, building, and materials production owning over $10 million in equipment. *Type:* Directory.

Construction Innovation

Publications
Institute for Research in   Ph: (613)993-2463
Construction   Fax: (613)952-7673
Building M-20
Ottawa, ON, Canada K1A 0R6
E-mail: irc.client.services@nrc.ca
URL: http://www.nrc.ca/irc/newsletter/toc.html.
Contact: Jane Swartz, Editor, jane.swartz@nrc.ca.

Desc: Trade magazine covering research, product evaluations, and code developments in the construction industry. *Type:* Periodical.

Construction Labor Report

Bureau of National Affairs, Inc. (BNA)
1231 25th St. NW   Ph: (202)452-4323
Washington, DC 20037   Free: 800-372-1033
    Fax: (202)452-7773
E-mail: bnaplus@bna.com
Contact: Jerome Ashton, Managing Editor.

Desc: Covers union-management relations in the construction industry. Reports on significant legislative, judicial, economic, management, and union developments. *Type:* Newsletter.

Construction News—Directory & Buyer's Guide Issue

Construction News
10825 Financial Centre Pkwy.,   Ph: (501)227-8551
Ste. 131   Free: 800-766-2611
Little Rock, AR 72211-3555   Fax: (501)227-6856
Contact: Danny Straessle, Editor.

Desc: Directory of suppliers, manufacturers, and distributors of construction machinery in Oklahoma, Arkansas, western Tennessee, Louisiana, and Mississippi, and manufacturers with representation in the area. *Type:* Directory.

Construction Products

Cahners Business Information
1350 E. Touhy Ave.   Ph: (847)635-8800
Des Plaines, IL 60018   Free: 800-446-6551
    Fax: (847)635-6856
E-mail: bkinross@cahners.com
Contact: Michael J. Porcaro, Publisher; Tom Klemens, Editor.

Desc: Trade magazine for machinery, materials, and management tools. *Type:* Periodical.

Contact

Associated Equipment Distributors
615 W. 22nd St.   Ph: (630)574-0650
Oak Brook, IL 60523   Free: 800-388-0650
    Fax: (630)574-0132
E-mail: info@aednet.org
URL: http://www.aednet.org; http://www.aednet.org.
Contact: Katharine Abbott Zowaski, Editor.

Desc: Covers developments and trends in the construction equipment manufacturing and distribution industry. Recurring features include news of members and research, news of educational opportunities, coverage of meetings, a calendar of events, and industry developments. *Type:* Newsletter.

County Building Permits

The WEFA Group
1110 Vermont Ave., NW   Ph: (202)775-0610
Washington, DC 20005
URL: http://www.fdic.gov

Desc: Contains approximately 136,000 monthly and annual time series covering numbers of building permits issued and construction valuations for 5 types of residential structures. Also covers construction values for 6 types of non-residential structures. *Available:* The WEFA Group. *Type:* Database.

Directory of Building Codes & Regulations

National Conference of States on Building Codes and Standards
505 Huntmar Park Dr., Ste.   Ph: (703)437-0100
    210   Free: 800-362-2633
Herndon, VA 20170   Fax: (703)481-3596
E-mail: membership@ncsbcs.org
URL: http://www.ncsbcs.org; http://www.ncsbcs.org.
Contact: Jill Moreschi, Editor, jmoreschi@ncsbcs.org.

Desc: Directory of state and city government officials responsible for enforcing and administering building codes and regulations. *Type:* Directory.

Dixie Contractor—Directory Issue

Dixie Contractor
209-A Swanton Way   Ph: (404)377-2683
Decatur, GA 30030   Fax: (404)371-1509
Contact: Steve Hudson, Editor.

Desc: List of construction equipment distributors serving Alabama, Florida, Georgia, South Carolina, and middle and east Tennessee; construction equipment manufacturers nationwide. *Type:* Directory.

Dodge DataLine2

McGraw-Hill, Inc.
Construction Information Group
F.W. Dodge Division
1221 Avenue of the Americas   Ph: (212)512-4291
New York, NY 10020
URL: http://www.fwdodge.com
Contact: Eric J. Kalkbrenner, Director Electronic Media.

Desc: Contains information on more than 500,000 current construction projects in various stages of development. Includes project cost, square footage, structural descriptions, and name and contact information for owners, architects, engineers, and contractors. *Available:* McGraw-Hill, Inc., Construction Information Group, F.W. Dodge Division. *Type:* Database.

ENR—Top 400 Construction Contractors Issue

McGraw-Hill, Inc.
2 Penn Plaza   Ph: (212)904-2000
New York, NY 10121   Free: 800-223-6180
    Fax: (212)904-6068
URL: http://www.mcgraw-hill.com
Contact: Howard B. Stussman, Editor.

Desc: List of 400 United States contractors receiving largest dollar volumes of contracts in preceding calendar year. Separate lists of 50 largest design/construct management firms; 50 largest program and construction managers; 25 building contractors; 25 heavy contractors. *Type:* Directory.

ENR—Top 100 Construction Management Firms Issue

McGraw-Hill, Inc.
2 Penn Plaza   Ph: (212)904-2000
New York, NY 10121   Free: 800-223-6180
    Fax: (212)904-6068
URL: http://www.mcgraw-hill.com
Contact: Howard B. Stussman, Editor.

Desc: List of the top 100 leading construction and program management firms with the largest dollar volume in new construction management contracts on a for-fee only basis and an at-risk basis in the previous year. *Type:* Directory.

ENR—Top Owners Issue

McGraw-Hill, Inc.
2 Penn Plaza   Ph: (212)904-2000
New York, NY 10121   Free: 800-223-6180
    Fax: (212)904-6068
URL: http://www.mcgraw-hill.com
Contact: Howard B. Stussman, Editor.

Desc: List of 700 companies that had the largest expenditures for building construction and building acquisition in the previous year. *Type:* Directory.

ENR—Top 600 Specialty Contractors Issue

McGraw-Hill, Inc.
2 Penn Plaza   Ph: (212)904-2000
New York, NY 10121   Free: 800-223-6180
    Fax: (212)904-6068
URL: http://www.mcgraw-hill.com
Contact: Howard B. Stussman, Editor.

Desc: Lists of the 600 largest U.S. specialty subcontractors with sub-lists of top firms in mechanical contracting (50 firms), electrical (50), excavation-foundation (20), steel erection (20), roofing (20), sheet metal (20), demolition-wrecking (20), glazing curtain wall (20), masonry (20), concrete (20), utilities (20), painting (20), wall/ceiling (20), and asbestos abatement (20). *Type:* Directory.

Equipment Today

Cygnus Publishing Inc.
1233 Janesville Ave.   Ph: (920)563-6388
Fort Atkinson, WI 53538   Free: 800-547-7377
    Fax: (920)563-1699

Contact: Kate Miller, Editor, (920)563-1677, kmiller@equipmenttoday.com; Bruce Rabe, Publisher, (920)563-1636.

Desc: Heavy construction equipment trade tabloid. *Alt. Contact:* telephone: (920)563-1677; fax: (920)563-1702. *Type:* Periodical.

Equipment World

Randall Publishing Co.
Box 2029   Ph: (205)349-2990
Tuscaloosa, AL 35403   Free: 800-633-5953
    Fax: (205)349-4174
URL: http://www.equipmentworld.com.

Contact: Marcia Gruver, Editor, mgruverm@randallpub.com; Jim Longton, Assoc. Publisher, jlongton@randallpub.com.

Desc: Magazine providing construction equipment information including application, purchase, maintenance, and replacement. *Type:* Periodical.

First Line Supervisor

The Dartnell Corp.
360 Hiatt Dr.   Free: 800-621-5463
Palm Beach Gardens, FL 33418   Fax: (561)622-2423
E-mail: dartnell@dartnellcorp.com; firstline@dartnellcorp.com.
URL: http://www.dartnellcorp.com

Desc: Training newsletter designed to improve performance through how-to articles on all aspects of first-line supervision in a manufacturing environment. *Type:* Newsletter.

FM Data Monthly

Tradeline, Inc.
115 Orinda Way   Ph: (925)254-1744
PO Box 1568   Fax: (925)254-1093
Orinda, CA 94563
E-mail: fmdm@fmdata.com.
URL: http://www.fmdata.com/fmdm.

Contact: Steven Westfall, Executive Editor.

Desc: Provides current field data on the planning, design, construction, and renovation of a variety of corporate and institutional projects. Analyzes management strategies and budgetary priorities. *Type:* Newsletter.

Focus on Construction and Engineering

Focus on Construction and Engineering
4350 Wickiow Ct.   Ph: (770)886-6820
Suwanee, GA 30024   Fax: (770)844-6361
E-mail: focus@cris.com

Contact: Kevin C. Morris, Editor.

Desc: Provides job information to members of the construction industry in United States and overseas. Recurring features include columns titled Jobs Update, Management Changes, and New Projects. *Type:* Newsletter.

Government Product News—December Buyers Guide Issue

Penton Media Inc.
1100 Superior Ave.   Ph: (216)696-7000
Cleveland, OH 44114-2543   Fax: (216)931-9524
E-mail: corpcomm@penton.com

Contact: Leslie Drahos, Editor.

Desc: List of over 2,100 manufacturers of construction products and equipment. *Type:* Directory.

MSA Building Permits

The WEFA Group
1110 Vermont Ave., NW   Ph: (202)775-0610
Washington, DC 20005
URL: http://www.fdic.gov

Desc: Contains more than 11,000 monthly and annual time series covering numbers of building permits issued and construction values for 5 types of residential structures. Also covers construction values for 6 types of non-residential structures. *Available:* The WEFA Group. *Type:* Database.

MSA and State Housing and Construction

The WEFA Group
1110 Vermont Ave., NW   Ph: (202)775-0610
Washington, DC 20005
URL: http://www.fdic.gov

Desc: Contains approximately 36,900 weekly, monthly, quarterly, and annual time series for the United States as a whole, the fifty U.S. states, and selected U.S. regional areas as well as approximately 11,900 weekly, monthly, quarterly, and annual time series for most of the 320 Metropolitan Statistical Areas (MSAs). *Available:* The WEFA Group. *Type:* Database.

Nation's Building News

Nations Building News
1201 15th St. NW   Ph: (202)822-0525
Washington, DC 20005-2800   Fax: (202)861-2131
Contact: Tim Ahern, Editor; John M. Hemsworth, Publishing Dir.

Desc: Trade magazine (tabloid) covering home building and all related industries. *Type:* Periodical.

Old-House Journal

DoveTale Publishers

2 Main St. Ph: (508)283-3200
Gloucester, MA 01930 Fax: (508)283-4629

Contact: Patricia Poore, Editor; Bill O'Donnell, Publisher.

Desc: Magazine containing practical articles about the restoration, decoration, and maintenance of houses built before 1940. *Type:* Periodical.

Professional Builder

Cahners Business Information

1350 E. Touhy Ave. Ph: (847)635-8800
Des Plaines, IL 60018 Free: 800-446-6551
Fax: (847)635-6856

E-mail: bkinross@cahners.com

URL: http://www.probuilder.com.

Contact: Jay McKenzie, Publisher, (847)390-2155, jmckenzie@cahners.com; Jim Carper, Editor, (847)390-2112. *Alt. Contact:* 1350 E. Touhy Ave., Des Plaines, IL 60018. *Type:* Periodical.

Public Works Manual

Public Works Journal Corp.

200 S. Broad St. Ph: (201)445-5800
Ridgewood, NJ 07451 Free: 800-524-2364
Fax: (201)445-5170

URL: http://www.pwmag.com.

Contact: James Kircher, Editor, jkircher@pwmag.com; Judy Flanigan, Editor, jflanigan@pwmag.com; Paul Kobelt, Editor, pkobelt@pwmag.com.

Desc: List of about 3,500 manufacturers and distributors of equipment, materials, services, computers, and software used in the design, construction, maintenance, and operation of streets and highways, water systems, wastewater and solid wastes processing, and recreation areas. *Type:* Directory.

The Punch List

American Arbitration Association

140 W. 51st St. Ph: (212)484-4000
New York, NY 10020-1203 Fax: (212)541-4041

URL: http://www.adr.org

Contact: Susan C. Zuckerman, Editor.

Desc: Covers news of alternative dispute resolution developments in the construction industry. *Type:* Newsletter.

Qualified Remodeler Magazine

Cygnus Publishing Inc.

1233 Janesville Ave. Ph: (920)563-6388
Fort Atkinson, WI 53538 Free: 800-547-7377
Fax: (920)563-1699

Contact: Kirk Laughlin, Editor.

Desc: Magazine for remodeling contractor/distributors. *Type:* Periodical.

Remodeling

Hanley-Wood, Inc.

1 Thomas Circle, Ste. 600 Ph: (202)452-0800
Washington, DC 20005 Fax: (202)785-1974

URL: http://www.remodeling.hw.net.

Contact: Paul Deffenbaugh, Editor-in-Chief, (202)736-3359; Jack Brannigan, Publisher, (847)267-1080, fax: (847)267-1088.

Desc: Trade magazine for the professional remodeling industry. *Type:* Periodical.

Remodeling—Product Guide

Hanley-Wood, Inc.

1 Thomas Circle, Ste. 600 Ph: (202)452-0800
Washington, DC 20005 Fax: (202)785-1974

Contact: Peter Vandevanter, Editor; Cheryl Weber, Mng. Editor, cweber@hanley-wood.com.

Desc: List of more than 2,000 manufacturers and suppliers serving the remodeling contracting industry; list of industry-related associations. *Type:* Directory.

Rocky Mountain Construction—Buyer's Guide and Directory Issue

Rocky Mountain Construction Magazine, Inc.

2403 Champa St. Ph: (303)295-0630
Denver, CO 80205 Fax: (303)295-2159

Contact: F. Hol Wagner, Jr., Editor.

Desc: Guide to construction equipment manufacturers, their distributors, and other construction industry suppliers in Arizona, Colorado, Idaho, Nevada, New Mexico, Utah, Wyoming, and the El Paso, Texas trade area. *Type:* Directory.

Roofing/Siding/Insulation—Trade Directory Issue (RSI)

Advanstar Communications

7500 Old Oak Blvd. Ph: (440)243-8100
Cleveland, OH 44130-3369 Free: 800-225-4569
Fax: (440)891-2733

E-mail: directories@advanstar.com

URL: http://www.advanstar.com.

Contact: Michael Russo, Editor, mrusso@advanstar.com.

Desc: Manufacturers, wholesalers, representatives, and distributors of products and equipment for the roofing, siding, insulation, and solar industries; trade associations are also included. *Type:* Directory.

Texas Contractor—Buyer's Guide and Directory Issue

Construction Market Data

1111 Stemmons Hwy. Ph: (972)484-4267
Dallas, TX 75229

Contact: Trey Randal, Editor.

Desc: List of manufacturers and distributors of supplies and equipment for the heavy construction industry in Texas. Also includes national associations, auctioneers, financing and leasing institutes, and special services. *Type:* Directory.

Timber Frame Homes

Home Buyer Publications, Inc.

4200-T Lafayette Center Dr. Ph: (703)222-9411
PO Box 220039 Free: 800-826-3893
Chantilly, VA 20151 Fax: (703)222-3209

Contact: Janice Brewster, Editor.

Desc: About 300 builders of timber frame homes, and 100 suppliers of products related to the timber frame industry. *Type:* Directory.

Consumers

The AD-PAK (Raleigh Edition)

AD-PAK of North Carolina

525 Pylon Dr. Ph: (919)832-9496
Raleigh, NC 27606 Fax: (919)832-7281

Contact: Roger A. Stephenson, Publisher, rstephen@nando.com; Candi Griffin, Sales Manager.

Desc: Shopper. *Type:* Periodical.

Adam Magazine

Players International Publications

8060 Melrose Ave. Ph: (213)653-8060
Los Angeles, CA 90046 Fax: (213)682-2932

Contact: Jared Rutter, Editor; Tim Connelly, Advertising Mgr.

Desc: Magazine for adult males. *Type:* Periodical.

Ads Express

Milwaukee Express News

10001 W. Lisbon Ave. Ph: (414)466-3933
Milwaukee, WI 53222 Fax: (414)466-2040

Contact: Ken Ubert, Publisher; John McLtone, Editor.

Desc: Community newspaper. *Type:* Periodical.

The Advertiser

Lakes Area Advertiser, Inc.

236 Rte. 173 Ph: (847)395-4444
Antioch, IL 60002 Fax: (847)395-8480

Contact: Carol Anderson, Publisher; James D. Hyerdall, Advertising Mgr.; William Pringle, Circulation Mgr.; Mark Mehaffey, Operations.

Desc: Shopper. *Type:* Periodical.

The Advertiser

Sun Coast Media

200 E. Venice Ave. Ph: (813)484-2611
Venice, FL 34285 Fax: (813)485-3036

Contact: Don Moore, Editor; Derek Dunn-Rankin, Publisher; Lang Capasso, Advertising Mgr.

Desc: Shopper. *Type:* Periodical.

American Consumer Alliance

John D. Reeves

770 W Granada Blvd., Ste. 250 Ph: (904)676-9966
Ormond Beach, FL 32174-5180 Free: 800-324-1858
Fax: (904)676-9994

Contact: John D. Reeves, Pres.

Desc: Consumers. Works to expand members' purchasing power and options in selected areas of products and services. *Type:* Association.

Area Shopper

Conneautville Courier

PO Box C Ph: (814)587-2033
Conneautville, PA 16406 Fax: (814)587-3720

Contact: Jesse Haas, Editor; Herbert O. Haas, Publisher.

Desc: Shopper. *Type:* Periodical.

Arizona Pennysaver

Arizona Pennysaver, L.L.C.

250 W. 1st St. Ph: (602)968-5700
Tempe, AZ 85282 Fax: (602)968-8694

E-mail: psaver@aol.com.

Contact: Steve Ferber, Publisher, successm@aol.com; Ed Marks, Publisher.

Desc: Shopper, published in 32 zoned editions. *Type:* Periodical.

Bakersfield's Shopper

Hamilton Diversified Services, Inc.

3611 Stockdale Hwy., Ste. H
Bakersfield, CA 93309

Desc: Newspaper. *Alt. Contact:* 5725 Canberra Ave., Bakersfield, CA 93307-6611. *Type:* Periodical.

Bankcard Holders of America

9729 Days Farm Dr.
Vienna, VA 22182-7304

Contact: Ruth Susswein, Exec.Dir.

Desc: Bank and credit card holders. Educates the American public about the wise and careful use of credit. *Type:* Association.

BNA Product Liability Daily

The Bureau of National Affairs, Inc. (BNA)

1231 25th St. NW Ph: (202)452-4200
Washington, DC 20037

E-mail: bnaplus@bna.com

URL: http://bna.com/mkt/hrl/hrlwdec.htm

Desc: Contains the complete text of news articles and analyses covering judicial, administrative, legislative, and industry developments relating to product safety and liability. *Available:* LEXIS-NEXIS, LEXIS; West Group, WESTLAW. *Type:* Database.

Brooklyn Marketeer

Larry Ross Advertising
2625 E. 14th St.   Ph: (718)934-7676
Brooklyn, NY 11235   Fax: (718)934-7885
Contact: Michelle Ross, Editor; Barry Manning, Advertising Mgr.; Larry Ross, Publisher; Steve Fine, Editor; Terry Mallach, Advertising Mgr.
Desc: Shopping guide (tabloid). *Type:* Periodical.

Carrier Pigeon

ADD, Inc.
150 James Way   Ph: (215)322-6920
Southampton, PA 18966-3857   Fax: (215)322-5492
Contact: David Tomasini, General Mgr.; Rick Morrison, Operations.
Desc: Shopper with entertainment and community news. *Type:* Periodical.

Center for Science in the Public Interest

1875 Connecticut Ave. NW,   Ph: (202)332-9110
    No. 300   Fax: (202)265-4954
Washington, DC 20009-5728
E-mail: cspi@cspinet.org
URL: http://www.cspinet.org
Contact: Michael Jacobson, Ph.D., Exec.Dir.
Desc: Scientists, nutrition educators, and lawyers concerned with the effects of science and technology on society. Past work has centered primarily on food safety and nutrition problems at the national level. Monitors current research and federal agencies that oversee food safety, trade, and nutrition. *Type:* Association.

Citizens Action Coalition

2015 Western Ave.   Ph: (219)232-7905
South Bend, IN 46629   Fax: (219)232-7945
E-mail: cac.sbend@cwixmail.com
URL: http://www.citact.org
Contact: Christopher Williams, Exec.Dir.
Desc: Consumer, environmental, and labor organizations; interested individuals. Represents residents of Indiana in utility, home care, farm, environmental, and other issues. *Type:* Association.

Closeout News Magazine

Closeout News, Inc.
331 S. State College Blvd.   Ph: (714)870-0313
Fullerton, CA 92831   Free: 800-600-7040
                                    Fax: (714)870-1552
E-mail: pilot616@aol.com.
URL: http://www.closeoutnews.com.
Contact: Benadette Archuleta, General Mgr.; Chirstel Chang, Operations Supervisor.
Desc: Tabloid focusing on surplus and closeout merchandise. *Type:* Periodical.

Columbia/Wrightsville Merchandiser

Engle Publishing Co.
PO Box 500   Ph: (717)653-4300
Mount Joy, PA 17552-0500   Free: 800-800-1833
                                    Fax: (717)653-1833
Contact: C. A. Engle, Publisher; Patrick Lee, Advertising Mgr.; J. R. Rutt, Circulation Mgr.
Desc: Shopper. *Type:* Periodical.

Committee for a Constructive Tomorrow

PO Box 65722   Ph: (202)429-2737
Washington, DC 20035   Fax: (301)858-0944
E-mail: info@cfact.org
URL: http://www.cfact.org
Contact: David Rothbard, Pres.
Desc: Works to "balance the public debate of consumer and environmental issues". Produces a daily radio commentary. Conducts education programs. *Type:* Association.

Conestoga Valley/Pequea Valley Penny Saver

Engle Publishing Co.
PO Box 500   Ph: (717)653-4300
Mount Joy, PA 17552-0500   Free: 800-800-1833
                                    Fax: (717)653-1833
Contact: C. A. Engle, Publisher; Patrick Lee, Advertising Mgr.; J. R. Rutt, Circulation Mgr.
Desc: Shopper. *Type:* Periodical.

Consumer Confidence Survey

The Conference Board, Inc.
845 3rd Ave.   Ph: (212)759-0900
New York, NY 10022-6679   Fax: (212)980-7014
E-mail: info@conference-board.org
URL: http://www.conference-board.org; http://www.crc-conquest.org.
Contact: Lynn Franco, Editor.
Desc: Publishes results of a special ongoing consumer attitude survey. Carries information on appraisal of business conditions and employment; plans to buy major durable goods such as homes, cars, and appliances; and intended vacations and chosen means of travel. *Type:* Newsletter.

Consumer Credit and Truth-in-Lending Compliance Report

RIA Group
395 Hudson St.   Ph: (212)367-6300
New York, NY 10014   Free: 800-431-9025
                                    Fax: (212)367-6314
Contact: Earl Phillips, Editor.
Desc: Reports on recent changes in the consumer credit field. Acts as a compliance guide on the Equal Credit Opportunity Act, Truth-in-Lending, debt collection practices, credit cards, service contracts, insurance, and related areas. *Type:* Newsletter.

Consumer Education Research Center

350 Scotland Rd.   Ph: (973)676-6663
Orange, NJ 07050   Free: 800-872-0121
                                    Fax: (973)676-3241
Contact: Robert L. Berko, Exec.Dir.
Desc: International consumer protection organization which researches and publishes consumer education materials for use by consumers, schools, and libraries. *Type:* Association.

Consumer Federation of America

1424 16th St. NW, Ste. 604   Ph: (202)387-6121
Washington, DC 20036
Contact: Stephen J. Brobeck, Exec.Dir.
Desc: National, regional, state, and local consumer groups; consumer cooperatives; public utilities and labor organizations; state and local protection agencies. Objectives are to: support activities of members; gather and disseminate information on consumer issues; serve as an advocate of pro-consumer policies before Congress, regulatory agencies, and the courts. *Type:* Association.

Consumer Information Center

18th and F St. NW, Rm. G-142 Free: 888-8-PUEBLO
Washington, DC 20405   Fax: (202)501-4281
E-mail: cic.info@pueblo.gsa.gov

URL: http://www.pueblo.gsa.gov
Contact: Teresa Nasif, Dir.
Desc: A department of the General Services Administration. Established by Presidential Order in 1970 to assist federal agencies to develop, promote, and distribute information of interest to consumers and to increase public awareness of this information. *Type:* Association.

Consumer Protection

Federal Trade Commission
Bureau of Consumer Protection   Ph: (202)FTC-HELP
CRC-240
Washington, DC 20580
URL: http://www.ftc.gov/ftc/consumer.htm
Contact: Gregory E. Hales, Webmaster, webmaster@ftc.gov.
Desc: This database maintained by the Federal Trade Commission covers such issues as consumer fraud, misleading advertising, credit card information and scams, other consumer protection matters, and antitrust or competition issues in many different areas. Also covered are proposed rules and regulations and recall notices. *Type:* Database.

Consumer Reports

Consumers Union of U.S., Inc.
101 Truman Ave.   Ph: (914)378-2000
Yonkers, NY 10703-1057   Free: 800-234-2188
                                   Fax: (914)378-2904
URL: http://www.consumers.org.
Contact: Eileen Denver, Editor; David Heim, Advertising Mgr.; David Helm, Managing Editor.
Desc: Magazine featuring analyses and investigative reporting of products. *Type:* Periodical.

Consumer Reports

Consumers Union of United States, Inc.
101 Truman Ave.   Ph: (914)378-2000
Yonkers, NY 10703-1057
URL: http://www.consumerreport.org
Desc: Contains the complete text of Consumer Reports, a monthly consumer advisory magazine containing results of product tests and purchasing recommendations. Covers products and services of significant cost as well as lower-priced products that are typically bought frequently or in large quantities, including such products as appliances, automobiles, electronic goods (e.g., television sets, compact disc players), prepared foods (e.g., breakfast cereals), home products (e.g., lawn mowers, air-conditioners), and personal care products (e.g., blow dryers, toothpaste). *Available:* CompuServe Information Service; LEXIS-NEXIS, NEXIS; Prodigy Services Company, PRODIGY; America Online, Inc.; The Dialog Corporation, DIALOG; The Dialog Corporation, DIALOG. *Type:* Database.

Consumer Sourcebook

Gale Group Inc.
27500 Drake Rd.   Ph: (248)699-4253
Farmington Hills, MI 48331-   Free: 800-877-GALE
    3535   Fax: (248)699-8070
E-mail: galeord@galegroup.com
URL: http://www.galegroup.com.; http://www.gale.com.
Contact: Sonya Hill, Editor, sonya.hill@gale.com.
Desc: Over 17,000 federal, state, and local government agencies and offices; national, regional, and grass roots associations and organizations; and information centers, clearing houses, publications, multimedia resources, media contacts, and corporate consumer affairs and customer services offices that provide aid and information to the consumer in such areas as health, environmental concerns, government performance, product safety, automotive concerns, credit and personal finance, education, employment, food and durgs, insurance, legal affairs, mass communications, real estate, transportation and travel, and utilities. *Type:* Directory.

CONSUMERS DIGEST

Consumers Digest Inc.

8001 N. Lincoln Ave.   Ph: (847)763-9200

Skokie, IL 60077-3657   Free: 800-727-4438

Fax: (847)763-0200

Contact: John Manos, Editor; Randy Weber, Publisher; Howard Plissner, VP/Dir. of Advertising, (212)685-9489, fax: (212)685-9528; J. Raymond Quinn, Marketing Research Dir., (212)685-9489, fax: (212)685-9528.

Desc: Magazine featuring product and service evaluation, information, and advice. *Type:* Periodical.

Consumers Union of United States

101 Truman Ave.   Ph: (914)378-2000

Yonkers, NY 10703   Fax: (914)378-2900

Contact: Rhoda H. Karpatkin, Pres.

Desc: Testing, rating, and reporting organization providing information on competing brands of appliances, automobiles, food products, and household equipment. "To provide consumers with information and advice on consumer goods and services; to give information and assistance on all financial matters affecting consumers; to initiate and to cooperate with individual and group efforts seeking to create, maintain, and enhance the quality of life for consumers." Regional offices represent consumer interests in the legislature, courts, and administrative agencies. Derives income from sale of its publication, *Consumer Reports*, and other publications. *Type:* Association.

Council of Better Business Bureaus

4200 Wilson Blvd., Ste. 800   Ph: (703)276-0100

Arlington, VA 22203-1804   Fax: (703)525-8277

E-mail: bbb@bbb.org

URL: http://www.bbb.org

Contact: James L. Bast, Pres. & CEO.

Desc: Supported by 325 companies and 132 local Better Business Bureaus operated autonomously in the United States and Puerto Rico, which are in turn supported by 270,000 local business members. Seeks to promote and foster the highest ethical relationship between businesses and the public through voluntary self-regulation, consumer and business education, and service excellence. *Type:* Association.

Country Peddler

Country Peddler

PO Box 492   Ph: (502)842-3314

Bowling Green, KY 42102   Fax: (502)842-4220

URL: http://bowlinggreen.ky.net/countrypeddler.

Contact: Kyda West, Publisher; Belinda Saltzman, Publisher.

Desc: Shopper (tabloid). *Type:* Periodical.

Dallas Greensheet

Greensheet Inc.

2601 Main St., 3rd Fl.   Ph: (713)371-3500

Houston, TX 77002   Free: 800-793-6543

Fax: (713)371-3702

Contact: Floyd Mills, General Mgr., (214)905-8248, fax: (214)905-8251.

Desc: Shopper. *Alt. Contact:* 7929 Brookriver Dr. No. 700, Dallas, TX 75247-4900; telephone: (214)905-8200; fax: (214)905-8239. *Type:* Periodical.

Dillsburg Shopper

Engle Publishing Co.

PO Box 500   Ph: (717)653-4300

Mount Joy, PA 17552-0500   Free: 800-800-1833

Fax: (717)653-1833

Contact: C. A. Engle, Publisher; Patrick Lee, Advertising Mgr.; J. R. Rutt, Circulation Mgr.

Desc: Shopper. *Type:* Periodical.

East Shore Shopper

Engle Publishing Co.

PO Box 500   Ph: (717)653-4300

Mount Joy, PA 17552-0500   Free: 800-800-1833

Fax: (717)653-1833

Contact: C. A. Engle, Publisher; Patrick Lee, Advertising Mgr.

Desc: Shopping guide. *Type:* Periodical.

Federal Trade Commission Consumer Brochures

Web Communications

2880 Soquel Ave., Ste. 8   Fax: (831)464-1631

Santa Cruz, CA 95062

E-mail: info@webcom.com

URL: http://www.webcom.com/lewrose/brochures.html

Contact: Lewis Rose, lewrose@netcom.com.

Desc: The Federal Trade Commission Consumer Brochures database provides the full text of over 100 consumer brochures issued by the Federal Trade Commissioner's Office of Consumer & Business Education. Such brochures as Art Fraud, Car Financing Scams, Gemstone Investing, and Truth in Leasing can be found here. *Type:* Database.

Flashes Kalamazoo Shopper

Stauffer Communications, Inc.

595 Jenner Dr.   Ph: (616)673-2141

Allegan, MI 49010-1567   Free: 800-968-4415

Fax: (616)673-4761

E-mail: fpi595@aol.com

Contact: Dave Moored, General Mgr., dmoored@flashespublishers.com; Allen Louks, Sales Mgr., acmnlouks@aol.com; Tony Fales, Team Leader, fax: (616)262-9288.

Desc: Shopper/weekly newspaper. *Alt. Contact:* 7837 Sprinkle Rd., Kalamazoo, MI 49002; telephone: (616)324-1000; fax: (616)324-1005; toll-free: 800-968-2527. *Type:* Periodical.

The Flyer

The Flyer

201 Kelsey Ln.   Ph: (813)626-9430

Tampa, FL 33619   Fax: (813)626-8923

Contact: Jim Kendall, Publisher, (813)626-4812.

Desc: Shopper. *Type:* Periodical.

Food Extra

Greenville News

PO Box 1688   Ph: (864)298-4100

Greenville, SC 29602   Free: 800-274-7879

Fax: (864)298-4395

Desc: Shopping guide. *Type:* Periodical.

Franklin/Hales Corners Enterprise

This Week Publications

2325 Park Lawn Dr. Ste. R.   Ph: (414)798-1234

Waukesha, WI 53186   Fax: (414)798-1222

Desc: Community newspaper. *Type:* Periodical.

Freebies

Freebies Publishing Co.

1135 Eugenia Pl.   Ph: (805)566-1225

PO Box 5025   Fax: (805)566-0305

Carpinteria, CA 93014-5025

E-mail: freebies@aol.com; freebies@earthlink.net.

Contact: Abel Magana, Editor; Harry Short, Publisher.

Desc: Consumer publication containing information on free product samples. *Alt. Contact:* 1135 Eugenia Pl, Carpinteria, CA 93014 5025; telephone: (805)566-1225; fax: (805)566-1407. *Type:* Periodical.

Gap/Oxford Community Courier

Engle Publishing Co.

PO Box 500   Ph: (717)653-4300

Mount Joy, PA 17552-0500   Free: 800-800-1833

Fax: (717)653-1833

Contact: C. A. Engle, Publisher; Patrick Lee, Advertising Mgr.; J. R. Rutt, Circulation Mgr.

Desc: Shopper. *Type:* Periodical.

General Reference Center

The Gale Group

27500 Drake Rd.   Ph: (248)699-4253

Farmington Hills, MI 48331-3535

URL: http://www.galegroup.com

Contact: (650)378-5000, fax: (800)676-2345.

Desc: General Reference Center provide access to an integrated set of full text general interest sources: magazines, newpaper articles, children's magazines, almanacs, encyclopedias, dictionaries, reference books, and more. It covers feature articles, news reports, editorials, product evaluations, biographical pieces, and reviews of books, movies, plays, recordings, concerts, and restaurants. *Available:* CompuServe Information Service; The Dialog Corporation, DataStar; CARL Corporation; Ameritech Library Services, Vista; The Gale Group, InfoTrac Web. *Type:* Database.

Genesee Valley

Genesee Valley Publications Inc.

1471 W. Henrietta Rd.   Ph: (716)226-8111

Avon, NY 14414   Fax: (716)226-3390

E-mail: penny4@frontiernet.net.

Contact: Steve Harrison, Publisher/Owner; Kimberly Dougherty, VP/Owner.

Desc: Shopping guide published in six editions serving Monroe, Livingston, Ontario, and Genesee counties in New York State. *Type:* Periodical.

Greater Reading Area Merchandiser

Kapp Advertising Service, Inc.

PO Box 840   Ph: (717)273-8127

Lebanon, PA 17042   Fax: (717)273-0420

E-mail: kapp@nbn.net; sales@themerchandiser.com.

Contact: Robert S. Kapp, Publisher, kapp@nbn.net; Joseph J. McDonald, General Mgr.; Valerie A. Stokes, Sales Mgr./Contact.

Desc: Shopper serving metropolitan Reading, Pennsylvania. *Type:* Periodical.

Greater Rochester Advertiser

Greater Rochester Advertiser

201 Main St.   Ph: (716)385-1974

East Rochester, NY 14445   Free: 800-388-1514

Fax: (716)385-3507

Contact: Peter J. Stahlbrodt, Editor and Publisher; Bridgette Yaxley-Korlou, Features Editor.

Desc: Shopping guide. *Type:* Periodical.

Greenfield/Greendale Enterprise

This Week Publications

2325 Park Lawn Dr. Ste. R.   Ph: (414)798-1234

Waukesha, WI 53186   Fax: (414)798-1222

Contact: Barb Falk, Managing Editor.

Desc: Weekly community newspaper. *Type:* Periodical.

The Guide News

Fry Communications, Inc.

800 W. Church St.   Ph: (717)766-0211

Mechanicsburg, PA 17055   Fax: (717)691-5796

Contact: Ted Shope, Publisher.

Desc: Shopper circulating in four counties. *Type:* Periodical.

Hempfield/Mountville Merchandiser

Engle Publishing Co.
PO Box 500
Mount Joy, PA 17552-0500   Ph: (717)653-4300
   Free: 800-800-1833
   Fax: (717)653-1833
Contact: C. A. Engle, Publisher; Patrick Lee, Advertising Mgr.; J. R. Rutt, Circulation Mgr.
Desc: Shopper. *Type:* Periodical.

Hershey/Palmyra Community Courier

Engle Publishing Co.
PO Box 500
Mount Joy, PA 17552-0500   Ph: (717)653-4300
   Free: 800-800-1833
   Fax: (717)653-1833
Contact: C. A. Engle, Publisher; Patrick Lee, Advertising Mgr.; J. R. Rutt, Circulation Mgr.
Desc: Shopper. *Type:* Periodical.

Home Automation News

Home Automation Association
1444 I St. NW, No. 700
Washington, DC 20005-2210   Ph: (202)712-9050
   Fax: (202)216-9646
E-mail: HAA@bostromdc.com
Contact: Mark Wright, Editor.
Desc: Carries Association news and articles on international trends in the integrated home control industry. Recurring features include new product announcements, product reviews, and news of members. *Type:* Newsletter.

Home Mechanix

Times Mirror Magazines, Inc.
2 Park Ave.
New York, NY 10016-5601   Ph: (212)779-5000
   Fax: (212)779-5522
URL: http://www.homeideas.com.
Contact: Michael Chotiner, Editor; John B. Crawley, Publisher; John Young, Advertising Mgr.
Desc: Magazine for homeowners and automobile owners. *Type:* Periodical.

Houston Greensheet

Greensheet Inc.
2601 Main St., 3rd Fl.
Houston, TX 77002   Ph: (713)371-3500
   Free: 800-793-6543
   Fax: (713)371-3702
Contact: Kathleen Douglass, Publisher; Darlene Hajduk, Assistant Publisher.
Desc: Shopper. *Type:* Periodical.

ICSA News

International Customer Service Association (ICSA)
401 N. Michigan Ave.
Chicago, IL 60611-4267   Ph: (312)321-6800
   Fax: (312)321-6869
E-mail: icsa@sba.com
URL: http://www.icsa.com.
Contact: Barbara Wolf, Editor.
Desc: Publishes news of the Association, whose mission is "to develop the theory and understanding of the total quality service process, advance the art and science of managing that process, and encourage professional dialogue in the achievement of customer satisfaction." Recurring features include columns titled From the Executive Board, Chapter News, Industry Articles, Management Tips, Introducing ICSA, and International Service Issues. *Type:* Newsletter.

Interactive Home

Jupiter Communications
627 Broadway, 2nd Fl.
New York, NY 10012-2612   Ph: (212)780-6060
   Free: 800-488-4345
   Fax: (212)780-6075
E-mail: jupiter@jup.com.

URL: http://www.jup.com.
Contact: Wen Liao, Senior Analyst.
Desc: Provides market intelligence on the ever-evolving consumer technology market. Publishes news and analysis on: personal computers, interactive television, handheld devices, cable modems, broadband technology, home ISDN, the CD-ROM evolution, home automation, interactive standards—everything you need to help formulate a profitable strategy while staying one step ahead of your competition. *Type:* Newsletter.

Jacksonville Shopping Guide

CAN Media Jacksonville, Inc.
3801 University Blvd. W.   Ph: (904)737-7320
Jacksonville, FL 32217   Fax: (904)737-2274
Contact: Terry Mitton, General Mgr.; Joyce Lydon, Publisher.
Desc: Shopper (tabloid). *Type:* Periodical.

Kitchener-Waterloo Pennysaver

Kitchner-Waterloo Pennysaver
685 Wabanaki   Ph: (519)894-1400
Kitchener, ON, Canada N2C   Fax: (519)894-5401
2G3
Contact: Martin McNaulty, Sales Mgr.
Desc: Shopper with news. *Type:* Periodical.

Lake County Market Journal

Market Journal
PO Box 410   Ph: (847)223-3200
Grayslake, IL 60030-0410   Fax: (847)223-9390
Desc: Shopping guide (tabloid). *Type:* Periodical.

Lee County Shopper

Breeze Publishing Co.
PO Box 151306   Ph: (941)574-1110
Cape Coral, FL 33915-1306   Fax: (941)574-3403
Contact: Joel Jenkins, General Mgr.; Jack Glarrow, Advertising Mgr.
Desc: Shopper. *Type:* Periodical.

Little Nickel Classifieds

Little Nickel Classifieds
3701-148th St. SW   Ph: (425)742-7244
Lynnwood, WA 98037   Fax: (425)742-8740
URL: http://www.littlenickel.com.
Contact: Mario van Dongen, General Mgr., mariov@aa.net.
Desc: Shopping guide. *Type:* Periodical.

London Pennysaver

London Pennysaver
244 Adelaide St. S.   Ph: (519)685-2020
London, ON, Canada N5Z 3L1   Fax: (519)649-0908
Contact: M. Bastow, General Mgr.
Desc: Shopper. *Type:* Periodical.

Magazine Index™

The Gale Group
27500 Drake Rd.   Ph: (248)699-4253
Farmington Hills, MI 48331-3535
URL: http://www.galegroup.com
Contact: (650)378-5000, fax: (800)676-2345.
Desc: Contains more than 3.1 million citations, with abstracts (since 1973) of articles published in more than 400 general-interest and consumer magazines published in the United States and Canada as well as The New York Times. Covers feature articles, news reports, editorials, product evaluations, biographical pieces, short stories, poetry, recipes, reviews, and other features. *Available:* The Dialog Corporation, DataStar; The Dialog Corporation, DIALOG; CompuServe Information Service, Knowledge Index; CARL Corporation. *Type:* Database.

Mailbox Values Shopper

Mailbox Values Shopper
10737 Gateway W., Ste. 250   Ph: (915)541-3400
El Paso, TX 79935-4906
Contact: Jose A. Vina, Publisher.
Desc: Shopper. *Alt. Contact:* 10737 Gateway W., Ste. 250, El Paso, TX 79935-4906; telephone: (915)594-3910. *Type:* Periodical.

The Marketeer Islander

Larry Ross Advertising
2625 E. 14th St.   Ph: (718)934-7676
Brooklyn, NY 11235   Fax: (718)934-7885
Contact: Lenora Brown, Publisher; Alan Brown, Publisher; Harry Kashuck, Editor; Barbara Conner, Editor.
Desc: Shopper. *Type:* Periodical.

Maryland Pennysaver

Maryland Pennysaver
1342 Charwood Rd   Ph: (410)684-2700
Hanover, MD 21076   Free: 800-736-6972
   Fax: (410)684-2065
URL: http://www.mdpennysaver.com.
Contact: Denny Guastaferro, Pub./Chief Operating Officer, (410)684-2600, fax: (410)865-4545.
Desc: Shopper. *Type:* Periodical.

The Middletown Shopper

Engle Publishing Co.
PO Box 500
Mount Joy, PA 17552-0500   Ph: (717)653-4300
   Free: 800-800-1833
   Fax: (717)653-1833
Contact: C. A. Engle, Publisher; Patrick Lee, Advertising Mgr.
Desc: Shopping guide. *Type:* Periodical.

Millersville Advertiser

Engle Publishing Co.
PO Box 500
Mount Joy, PA 17552-0500   Ph: (717)653-4300
   Free: 800-800-1833
   Fax: (717)653-1833
Contact: C. A. Engle, Publisher; Patrick Lee, Advertising Mgr.; J. R. Rutt, Circulation Mgr.
Desc: Shopper. *Type:* Periodical.

Morgantown/Honeybrook Community Courier

Engle Publishing Co.
PO Box 500
Mount Joy, PA 17552-0500   Ph: (717)653-4300
   Free: 800-800-1833
   Fax: (717)653-1833
Contact: C. A. Engle, Publisher; Patrick Lee, Advertising Mgr.; J. R. Rutt, Circulation Mgr.
Desc: Shopper. *Type:* Periodical.

National Alliance of Supermarket Shoppers

c/o Martin Sloane
300 SE 5th Ave. Apt. 2120
Boca Raton, FL 33432-5059
Contact: Martin Sloane, Exec. Officer.
Desc: Supermarket shoppers and consumers. Monitors activities of government protection agencies, such as the Federal Trade Commission; takes part in legislative activities concerning consumer issues; conducts negotiations with retailers and manufacturers on consumer complaints and provides shoppers with guidance in resolving individual problems. Furnishes national media with Action Alerts to mobilize support on supermarket consumer issues; sends Action Letter complaints to supermarkets and manufacturers. *Type:* Association.

National Consumer Law Center
18 Tremont St., Ste. 400   Ph: (617)523-8010
Boston, MA 02108   Fax: (617)523-7398
URL: http://www.consumerlaw.org
Contact: Willard Ogburn, Exec.Dir.
Desc: A specialized resource in consumer and energy law funded by federal, state, and foundation grants. Lawyers provide research, technical consulting, and in-depth assistance to Legal Services Program lawyers and state agencies throughout the nation. Defines recurring patterns in the problems of low-income consumers and develops a series of alternative solutions utilizing litigation, legislation, lawyer training, and development of new service delivery systems. *Type:* Association.

National Consumers League
1701 K St. NW, No. 1200   Ph: (202)835-3323
Washington, DC 20006   Fax: (202)835-0747
E-mail: nclncl@aol.com
URL: http://www.fraud.org/
Contact: Linda Golodner, Pres.
Desc: Encourages citizen participation in governmental and business decision making. Conducts research, educational, and advocacy programs on such consumer and worker issues as insurance, credit, health, privacy, minimum wage, telecommunications, labor standards, telemarketing and internet fraud, and food and drug safety. Coordinates the Alliance Against Fraud in Telemarketing, For a Safer America Coalition, and the Child Labor Coalition. *Type:* Association.

NCLC REPORTS Newsletter
National Consumer Law Center Inc.
18 Tremont St. Ste. 400   Ph: (617)523-8010
Boston, MA 02108   Fax: (617)523-7398
Contact: Kathleen Keest, Editor.
Desc: Profiles the latest consumer law ideas and developments. *Type:* Newsletter.

New Berlin Enterprise
This Week Publications
2325 Park Lawn Dr. Ste. R.   Ph: (414)798-1234
Waukesha, WI 53186   Fax: (414)798-1222
Desc: Weekly community newspaper. *Type:* Periodical.

New Consumer Institute
PO Box 51   Ph: (847)526-0552
Wauconda, IL 60084   Fax: (847)487-0010
E-mail: johnw1@aol.com
Contact: John Wasik, Envir. Bus. & Tech. Columnist.
Desc: Distributes business and environment features. *Alt. Contact:* PO Box 51, Wauconda, IL 60084; telephone: (847)526-0552; fax: (847)487-0010. *Type:* Periodical.

North Shore Today
The Sale Line, Inc.
6851 Jericho Tpke.   Ph: (516)496-4300
Syosset, NY 11791   Fax: (516)496-9898
Contact: Mark Schlau, Editor and Publisher; Shannon Holtz, Marketing Dir.
Desc: Shopper. *Type:* Periodical.

The Original Pennysaver
The Pennysaver
2830 Orbiter St.   Ph: (714)996-8900
Brea, CA 92822   Fax: (714)993-4711
URL: http://www.thepennysaver.com.
Contact: Harry Buckel, Editor and Publisher; Peter Gorman, Exec. V.P.; R. Steve Morris, V.P. Sales and Mktg.; Ken Fricka, Contact.
Desc: Shopper. *Type:* Periodical.

Ottawa Pennysaver
Ottawa Pennysaver
48 Colonnade Rd.   Ph: (613)723-1707
Nepean, ON, Canada K2E 7J6   Fax: (613)723-7186
Contact: Dino Cefaloni, Editor.
Desc: Shopper. *Type:* Periodical.

Pasco Shopper
Sunpress Publications, Inc.
13032 U.S. Hwy. 301   Ph: (352)567-5639
PO Box 187   Fax: (352)567-5640
Dade City, FL 33525
Contact: J.W. Owens, Publisher.
Desc: Shopper. *Type:* Periodical.

Penny Saver
Publications, Inc.
621 4th Ave. SE   Ph: (319)399-5900
Cedar Rapids, IA 52401   Fax: (319)399-5918
Contact: Steven H. Hunter, Publisher; Lisa Fisher, Admin. Asst./Adv. Services.
Desc: Shopping guide. *Type:* Periodical.

The Penny Saver
Penny Saver Publications, Inc.
6901 W. 159th St.   Ph: (708)633-6890
Tinley Park, IL 60477   Fax: (708)633-4919
Contact: Norman Rosinski, Editor and Publisher.
Desc: Shopping guide (tabloid) printed in 22 zoned editions. *Type:* Periodical.

Pennypower Shopping News
Pennypower Shopping News, Inc.
1636 S. Glenstone   Ph: (417)887-9000
Springfield, MO 65804   Fax: (417)887-9006
Contact: Dan Davis, General Mgr.
Desc: Shopper. *Type:* Periodical.

Pennysaver
Eastern Sierra Publishing, Inc.
PO Box 2500   Ph: (702)883-4322
Carson City, NV 89702   Fax: (702)883-4311
Contact: Jim Alldis, Publisher; Carol Dyer, Editor.
Desc: Shopper. *Type:* Periodical.

Pennysaver
Guinan Publishing Corp.
1538 Old Country Rd.   Ph: (516)249-0750
Plainview, NY 11803   Fax: (516)249-0789
URL: http://www.news12.com.
Contact: Robert Costine, Jr., Publisher; Rose Costine, Editor.
Desc: Shopper. *Type:* Periodical.

PennySaver
PennySaver
1300 Specialty Dr.   Ph: (760)599-1400
Vista, CA 92083   Free: 800-925-8118
   Fax: (760)598-1117
URL: http://www.thepennysaver.com.
Contact: William Carman, President; David E. Clark, Dir. of Marketing.
Desc: Shopper. *Alt. Contact:* 1300 Specialty Dr., Vista, CA 92083; telephone: (619)599-1400; fax: (619)598-1113. *Type:* Periodical.

Pennysaver
Hart-Hanks Communications
1261 E. Dyer Rd., Ste. 100   Ph: (714)996-8900
Santa Ana, CA 92705-5605   Fax: (714)241-1049
URL: http://www.thepennysaver.com.
Contact: H. C. Van Ausdeln, Publisher.

Desc: Shopper. *Type:* Periodical.

The Pennysaver
The New Pennysaver Group, Inc.
101 Executive Blvd.   Ph: (914)592-5222
Elmsford, NY 10523   Fax: (914)592-4816
Contact: Herbert Solomon, Contact; Sid Sutter, Contact; Ed Levitt, Contact; David Miller, Contact.
Desc: Shopper. *Type:* Periodical.

PennySaver/San Diego South
PennySaver/San Diego South
5575 Ruffin Rd.   Ph: (619)576-6130
San Diego, CA 92123   Free: 888-736-6972
   Fax: (619)576-6040
URL: http://www.pennysaverusa.com.
Contact: Tim Sherman, General Manager, (619)576-6040.
Desc: Shopper. *Type:* Periodical.

Phoenixville Community Courier
Engle Publishing Co.
PO Box 500   Ph: (717)653-4300
Mount Joy, PA 17552-0500   Free: 800-800-1833
   Fax: (717)653-1833
Contact: C. A. Engle, Publisher; Patrick Lee, Advertising Mgr.; J. R. Rutt, Circulation Mgr.
Desc: Shopper. *Type:* Periodical.

POS News
Faulkner & Gray, Inc.
11 Penn Plaza, 11th Fl.   Ph: (212)967-7000
New York, NY 10001
Desc: Contains information on the use of debit cards and credit cards for electronic payment at the retail point of sale. Covers strategic marketing, technology, and financial issues as they affect the use of cards at retail locations. *Available:* The Gale Group, InfoTrac Web. *Type:* Database.

Potpourri
Potpourri Shoppers, Inc.
1350 Duane Ave.   Ph: (408)562-9482
Santa Clara, CA 95054   Free: 800-479-4795
   Fax: (408)986-5350
E-mail: info@potpourri.com
URL: http://www.potpourri.com.
Contact: Loren G. Dalton, President, (408)562-9480, fax: (408)562-9474; Doug Thompsonn, CFO, (408)562-9446; John Frahm, Dir. of Ops., (408)562-9484; Howard Young, Dir. of Sales, (408)562-9486, fax: (408)562-9487; Paul Corsaro, Dir. of Major Accts., (408)362-9487.
Desc: Shopper distributed in three San Francisco Bay area counties. *Type:* Periodical.

Prime Time
Richner Communications
379 Central Ave.   Ph: (516)569-4000
Lawrence, NY 11559-1616   Fax: (516)569-4942
E-mail: teamherald@aol.com.
Contact: Clifford Richner, Publisher.
Desc: Shopper with television and cable listings. *Type:* Periodical.

Product ReviewNet
The Rain Corporation
121 Barry Rd. Ext.   Ph: (508)791-1171
Worcester, MA 01609
URL: http://www.productreviewnet.com/home.html
Contact: info@productreviewnet.com.
Desc: This exceptional source of consumer information brings you product review abstracts on thousands of products, tools, appliances, doodads, and gadgets. Search by keyword or menu for condensed, to-the-point information on cellular phones, computers and computer software, guns, electronics, home appliances, and dozens more categories of items we all need and want. *Type:* Database.

Public Citizen

1600 20th St., NW   Ph: (202)588-1000
Washington, DC 20009   Fax: (202)588-7798
E-mail: pcmail@citizen.org
URL: http://www.citizen.org
Contact: Joan Claybrook, Pres.
Desc: Formed by Ralph Nader to support the work of citizen advocates. Areas of focus include: consumer rights in the marketplace, safe products, a healthful environment and workplace, clean and safe energy sources, corporate and government accountability, group buying to enhance marketplace clients, and citizen empowerment. Methods for change include lobbying, litigation, monitoring government agencies, research, and public education including special reports, periodicals, expert testimony, and news media coverage. *Type:* Association.

Public Citizen's Congress Watch

215 Pennsylvania Ave. SE   Ph: (202)546-4996
Washington, DC 20003   Fax: (202)547-7392
E-mail: jamie@citizen.org
URL: http://www.citizen.org/congress
Contact: Frank Clemente, Dir.
Desc: Congressional lobby representing consumer interests, specifically citizens' access to government decision-making, campaign finance reform, product safety, product liability health care, and medical malpractice issues and reducing corporate subsidies. *Type:* Association.

Public Eye Certified Safe Shopping Sites

WMS
24307 Magic Mountain Pkwy.   Free: 800-409-6476
Valencia, CA 91355
E-mail: wms@thepubliceye.com
URL: http://www.thepubliceye.com/
Desc: With the stated goal of "testing, certifying, and monitoring Internet businesses for reliability," the Public Eye serves as an online consumer protection group. Their research involves finding out which companies are reliable and safe to do business with, and which ones aren't. *Type:* Database.

Readers' Guide Abstracts

H.W. Wilson Company
950 University Ave.   Ph: (718)588-8400
Bronx, NY 10452
E-mail: custserv@hwwilson.com
URL: http://www.hwwilson.com
Contact: Technical Support Department., techmail@info.hwwilson.com.
Desc: Contains more than one million citations, with abstracts, to all articles from 304 publications cited in the Readers' Guide to Periodical Literature, except for book reviews and works of creative literature. Covers the arts, business, computers, crafts, current events, education, fashion, food and cooking, health, history, home improvement, news, photography, politics, science, and sports. *Available:* H.W. Wilson Company, WilsonWeb; H.W. Wilson Company, WilsonWeb; Ovid Technologies, Inc.; Ovid Technologies, Inc.; OCLC Online Computer Library Center, Inc., OCLC EPIC; OCLC Online Computer Library Center, Inc., OCLC FirstSearch Catalog; OCLC Online Computer Library Center, Inc., OCLC FirstSearch Catalog; Ameritech Library Services, Vista; SilverPlatter Information, Inc.; SilverPlatter Information, Inc. *Type:* Database.

Rental Guide

Rental Guide Magazine
1600 Capital Circle SW   Ph: (904)574-2111
Tallahassee, FL 32310-9246   Free: 800-277-7800
     Fax: (904)574-2525
URL: http://www.homes.com.
Contact: Tom Scardino, Vice Pres./Publishing.

Desc: Rental guide magazine for the Seattle/Puget Sound Area. *Type:* Periodical.

Results Media Shopper's Guide

Newport Media
250 Miller Pl.   Ph: (516)393-9277
Hicksville, NY 11801   Fax: (516)393-9304
Contact: Stu Carroll, Circulation Coord.
Desc: Shopping guide. *Type:* Periodical.

Ron Bernthal

PO Drawer 259   Ph: (919)434-1529
Hurleyville, NY 12747   Fax: (914)434-4806
Desc: Distributes commentary on travel books food and wine. *Alt. Contact:* PO Drawer 259, Hurleyville, NY 12747; telephone: (919)434-1529; fax: (914)434-4806. *Type:* Periodical.

Savannah Pennysaver

Morris Newspaper Corp.
PO Box 8167   Ph: (912)233-1281
Savannah, GA 31412   Fax: (912)232-4639
URL: http://www.savpennysaver.com.
Contact: Steve Hartley, General Mgr.
Desc: Shopper (tabloid), issued in three editions. *Alt. Contact:* PO Box 5100, Savannah, GA 31414-5100; telephone: (912)238-2040; fax: (912)238-2141; toll-free: 800-643-1468. *Type:* Periodical.

Scientists' Institute for Public Information

355 Lexington Ave., 16th Fl.   Ph: (212)661-9110
New York, NY 10017   Free: 800-223-1730
     Fax: (212)599-6432
Contact: Alan McGowan, Pres.
Desc: Fosters the dissemination of objective scientific data on current social issues linked to science and technology. Maintains the Media Resource Service. *Type:* Association.

Self-Help Reporter Newsletter

National Self-Help Clearinghouse
25 W. 43rd St., Ste. 620   Ph: (212)354-8525
New York, NY 10036-7406   Fax: (212)642-1956
Contact: Audrey Gartner, Editor.
Desc: Provides information on self-help mutual aid group activities, theory and practice of self-help, news on the self-help movement and where it is heading, and research findings. Recurring features include news of research, reports of meetings, and book reviews. *Type:* Newsletter.

Shopper Stopper

Shopper Stopper
327 Palisade   Ph: (608)493-2291
Merrimac, WI 53561   Free: 800-444-0446
     Fax: (608)493-2074
E-mail: sales@shopperstopper.com.
Contact: Kirk Olson, Publisher, kirk@shopperstopper.com; Shellie Benish, Sales Mgr., shellie@shopperstopper.com.
Desc: Shopper. *Type:* Periodical.

Shoppers Advantage/Comp-u-store Online

Cendant
Comp-U-Card Division
40 Oakview Dr.   Ph: (203)365-2000
Trumbull, CT 06611
URL: http://www.cendant.com
Contact: Lew Bednarczuk, Product Manager, Interactive Services.
Desc: Provides descriptions and prices for more than 250,000 brand name consumer products, including televisions, personal computers and software, appliances, luggage, jewelry, cameras, furniture, musical instruments, and

stereo equipment. Current bargains are also available. *Available:* CompuServe Information Service; Dow Jones & Company, Inc.; Youvelle Renaissance Group, GEnie; Delphi Internet Services Corporation; America Online, Inc.; Cendant, Comp-U-Card Division; Prodigy Services Company, PRODIGY; Worldplay ImagiNation. *Type:* Database.

The Shopping News

The Shopping News
4808 S. Buckner Blvd.   Ph: (214)388-3431
Dallas, TX 75227   Fax: (214)388-1194
Contact: Robert A. Harty Jr., Publisher.
Desc: Shopper. *Alt. Contact:* 4808 S. Buckner Blvd., Dallas, TX 75227; telephone: (214)388-3431; fax: (214)388-1194. *Type:* Periodical.

Sioux Falls Shopping News

Sioux Falls Shopping News, Inc.
4005 S. Western Ave.   Ph: (605)339-3633
PO Box 5184   Free: 800-843-6805
Sioux Falls, SD 57117-5148   Fax: (605)335-6873
Contact: K. A. Lesnar, Editor and Publisher.
Desc: Shopper. *Type:* Periodical.

South Jersey Shoppers Guide

South Jersey Shoppers Guide
8 Ranoldo Terrace   Ph: (609)616-4900
Cherry Hill, NJ 08034-2132   Free: 800-229-8775
     Fax: (609)616-0299
Contact: Gerry Haggerty, Publisher, ghaggerty@newportmed.com; Michael Lawless, Advertising Dir.
Desc: Shopper newspaper (tabloid). *Type:* Periodical.

Staten Island Pennysaver

Staten Island Register
2100 Clove Rd.   Ph: (718)447-4700
Staten Island, NY 10305   Fax: (718)816-7719
Contact: Joanne Lent, Publisher.
Desc: Shopper. *Type:* Periodical.

Survey-Net™

Inter Commerce Corporation
PO Box 7638   Ph: (504)831-9717
Metairie, LA 70010-7638   Free: 800-628-1131
     Fax: (504)834-2160
E-mail: webmaster@survey.net
URL: http://www.survey.net/
Desc: Survey-Net is the source for user demographics on the Internet. They provide users with up-to-date information, demographics and opinions from the WWW community. *Type:* Database.

This Week

This Week Publications
600 W. John St.   Ph: (516)536-6201
Hicksville, NY 11735   Fax: (516)753-9067
Contact: James F. Ruppel, Managing Editor; Stan Henry, Publisher; Thomas Rohr, General Mgr.
Desc: Suburban shopper serving Long Island with 73 local editions. *Type:* Periodical.

This Week Publications

This Week Publications
2325 Park Lawn Dr. Ste. R.   Ph: (414)798-1234
Waukesha, WI 53186   Fax: (414)798-1222
E-mail: wapa1class@aol.com.
Contact: John Pfeifer, Pub./Sales Mgr.
Desc: Weekly shopper. *Type:* Periodical.

Thrifty Nickel

Thrifty Nickel
PO Box 7423   Ph: (703)536-5700
Falls Church, VA 22040   Fax: (703)536-2907

Contact: Frances K. Manning, Editor.

Desc: Want ads newspaper (tabloid). *Alt. Contact:* 127 S. Washington St., Falls Church, VA 22046. *Type:* Periodical.

Tippers Anonymous

77 Leland Farm Rd.   Ph: (508)881-8052
Ashland, MA 01721-2340

Contact: Robert S. Farrington, Pres.

Desc: Individuals who dine out with some regularity and who are dedicated to "improving service and restoring its reward, tipping, to its rightful status." (TIP stands for: To Insure Promptness.). The group does not oppose tipping but does feel that its meaning has been lost in the hectic pace of modern times. *Type:* Association.

Tippers International

PO Box 2351   Ph: (920)231-5852
Oshkosh, WI 54903   Fax: (920)232-3663
E-mail: dragon@osh.earthreach.com
URL: http://www.atiainc.com/tippers.htm

Contact: John E. Schein, Pres.

Desc: Individuals, organizations, and corporations united to help create better communication between customer and service and management people and to restore tipping to its original concept. The word "tip" for services rendered is an acronym meaning "to insure promptness." Seeks to combat high prices and inferior products. Members receive cards and identifying symbols that can be left with service people (waiters, taxi drivers, housekeepers) and indicate members' satisfaction or dissatisfaction with services received. If service is good, members leave a card with a gratuity, indicating why the gratuity is given. If service is poor, members leave a card explaining why no gratuity is being given. *Type:* Association.

Tirekicking Today

Consumer Survival
5320 W. Foster   Ph: (773)545-4084
Chicago, IL 60630   Fax: (773)545-4084
E-mail: tiretody@ix.netcom.com
URL: http://www.tirekick.com.

Contact: James M. Flammang, Editor and Publisher; Marianne E. Flammang, Associate Editor.

Desc: Reports news of the auto industry of interest to consumers. Recurring features include new car reviews, purchasing advice, analysis of trends and technology, and information on the latest safety issues. *Type:* Newsletter.

Town Crier

Towndan Enterprises, Inc.
PO Box 576   Ph: (219)362-8519
La Porte, IN 46352   Fax: (219)325-0677

Contact: Gregory L. Jones, President.

Desc: Shopper. *Type:* Periodical.

Tucson Shopper

Shopper's Guide, Inc.
250 W. 1st St.   Ph: (602)968-5700
Tempe, AZ 85281   Fax: (602)968-8694
E-mail: shopperads@aol.com.

Desc: Shopping guide zoned in 26 community editions. *Alt. Contact:* 1861 W. Grant Rd., Tucson, AZ 85745; telephone: (602)622-0101; fax: (602)622-9651. *Type:* Periodical.

West Shore Shopper (Camp Hill Edition)

Engle Publishing Co.
PO Box 500   Ph: (717)653-4300
Mount Joy, PA 17552-0500   Free: 800-800-1833
   Fax: (717)653-1833

Contact: Patrick S. Lee, Editor.

Desc: Shopper. *Type:* Periodical.

WESTLAW® Products Liability Library

West Group
620 Opperman Dr.   Ph: (651)687-7000
St. Paul, MN 55164-0526
URL: http://www.westgroup.com

Desc: Contains the complete text of U.S. federal and state court decisions, specialized files, and texts and periodicals dealing with product liability. *Available:* West Group, WESTLAW. *Type:* Database.

Willow Street Advertiser

Engle Publishing Co.
PO Box 500   Ph: (717)653-4300
Mount Joy, PA 17552-0500   Free: 800-800-1833
   Fax: (717)653-1833

Contact: C. A. Engle, Publisher; Patrick Lee, Advertising Mgr.; J. R. Rutt, Circulation Mgr.

Desc: Shopper. *Type:* Periodical.

Windsor Pennysaver

Netmar, Inc.
369 York St.
PO Box 5020
London, ON, Canada N6A 4L6
E-mail: wpenysvr@mnsinet.

Contact: Bill Reason, General Mgr.

Desc: Shopper. *Alt. Contact:* 2610 Pillette Rd., Windsor, ON, Canada N8T 1R1; telephone: (519)944-7070; fax: (519)944-4088. *Type:* Periodical.

The Yankee Trader

Osprey Publications, Inc.
1 Glenmere Ln.   Ph: (516)331-3300
Coram, NY 11727   Fax: (516)331-3481
E-mail: yankeetrad@aol.com.

Contact: John W. Sutter, Editor and Publisher.

Desc: Shopping guide. *Type:* Periodical.

Contests

Lottery Player's Magazine

Regal Communications Corp.
321 New Albany Rd.   Ph: (609)778-8900
Moorestown, NJ 08057-1120

Contact: Denise Strub, Editor; Samuel W. Valenza, Jr., Publisher; Ted Corbin, Advertising Mgr.

Desc: Lottery and gaming magazine. *Type:* Periodical.

Winning!

NewsLinc
PO Box 5300   Ph: (918)491-6100
Jenks, OK 74037-5300   Fax: (918)491-9410
E-mail: staff@jwcom.com.

Contact: Steven M. Brown, Managing Editor, sbrown@natcom.publications.com.

Desc: Covers contests, sweepstakes, gambling, lotteries, and bingo. *Type:* Newsletter.

Contractors

Associated Builders and Contractors

1300 N. 17th St.   Ph: (703)812-2000
Arlington, VA 22209   Fax: (703)812-8200
E-mail: bakum@abc.org
URL: http://www.abc.org
Contact: Charles E. Hawkins, III, Exec.VP.

Desc: Construction contractors, subcontractors, suppliers, and associates. Aim is to foster and perpetuate the principles of rewarding construction workers and management on the basis of merit. Sponsors management education programs and craft training; also sponsors apprenticeship and skill training programs. *Type:* Association.

Associated General Contractors of America

1957 E St. NW   Ph: (202)393-2040
Washington, DC 20006   Fax: (202)347-4004
E-mail: info@agc.org
URL: http://www.agc.org
Contact: Stephen E. Sondherr, Exec.VP & CEO.

Desc: General construction contractors; subcontractors; industry suppliers; service firms. Provides market services through its divisions. Conducts special conferences and seminars designed specifically for construction firms. *Type:* Association.

Building Service Contractors Association International

10201 Lee Hwy., Ste. 225   Ph: (703)359-7090
Fairfax, VA 22030   Free: 800-368-3414
   Fax: (703)352-0493
URL: http://www.bscai.org
Contact: Carol A. Dean, Exec.VP.

Desc: Firms and corporations in 40 countries engaged in contracting building maintenance services including the provision of labor, purchasing materials, and janitorial cleaning and maintenance of a building or its surroundings; associate members are manufacturers of cleaning supplies and equipment. Seeks to provide a unified voice for building service contractors and to promote increased recognition by government, property owners, and the general business and professional public. Conducts continuing study and action, through committees and special task groups on areas such as public affairs, costs and ratios, uniform accounting, industrial relations and personnel, marketing and sales, contract improvement, research and planning, materials and supplies sources, group insurance, management training, statistics collection, safety, and insurance costs. *Type:* Association.

Construction Financial Management Association

29 Emmons Dr., ste. F-50   Ph: (609)452-8000
Princeton, NJ 08540-1413   Fax: (609)452-0474
E-mail: info@cfma.org
URL: http://www.cfma.org
Contact: William M. Schwab, Exec.Dir.

Desc: Contractors, subcontractors, architects, real estate developers, and engineers; associate members are equipment and material suppliers, accountants, lawyers, bankers, and others involved with the financial management of the construction industry. Provides a forum for the exchange of ideas; coordinates educational programs dedicated to improving the professional standards of financial management in the construction industry. Offers expanded national programs, technical assistance, and industry representation. *Type:* Association.

Construction Specifications Institute

601 Madison St.   Ph: (703)684-0300
Alexandria, VA 22314-1791   Free: 800-689-2900
   Fax: (703)684-0465
E-mail: csimail@csinet.org

URL: http://www.csinet.org

Contact: Gregory Balestrero, Exec.Dir.

Desc: Individuals concerned with the specifications and documents used for construction projects. Membership includes architects, professional engineers, specifiers, contractors, product manufacturers, teachers and research workers in architectural and engineering fields, and building maintenance engineers. Dedicated to advancing construction technology through communication, service, education, and research. *Type:* Association.

Consultants' & Contractors' Newsletter
FVI & Wendy Vandamme
105 N. Main St.   Ph: (201)299-1535
Boonton, NJ 07005   Free: 800-836-0667
                                 Fax: (201)335-4866
Contact: Wendy Vandame, Editor.

Desc: Covers the data processing consulting industry. Contains articles on tax law changes and the IRS, the Department of Labor, marketing, recruiting, and trade shows and other events. *Type:* Newsletter.

Contractor's Directory
Government Data Publications, Inc.
1661 MacDonald Ave.   Ph: (718)627-0819
Brooklyn, NY 11230   Fax: (718)998-5960
Contact: Siegfried Lobel, Publisher.

Desc: Contractors who have received government contracts under Public Law 95-507, which requires preferential treatment of small business for subcontracts. *Type:* Directory.

Contractors Register
Contractors Register, Inc.
PO Box 500   Ph: (914)245-0200
Jefferson Valley, NY 10535-   Free: 800-431-2584
0500   Fax: (914)245-0288
E-mail: info@thebluebook.com

Desc: General contractors, subcontractors, architects, engineers, material and equipment dealers and manufacturers in the U.S. *Type:* Directory.

CRA Review
Charles River Associates
200 Clarendon St., T-33   Ph: (617)425-3000
Boston, MA 02116-5092   Fax: (617)425-3132
Desc: Highlights "significant research results of our consulting work for clients." Recurring features include news of research. *Type:* Newsletter.

Independent Electrical Contractors
2010 A Eisenhower Ave.   Ph: (703)549-7351
Alexandria, VA 22314   Free: 800-456-4324
                                 Fax: (703)549-7448
E-mail: ieccasey@aol.com
URL: http://www.ieci.org
Contact: Dwight L. Casey, Exec.VP.

Desc: Independent electrical contractors, small and large, primarily open shop. Promotes the interests of members; works to eliminate "unwise and unfair business practices" and to protect its members against "unfair or unjust taxes and legislative enactments." *Type:* Association.

International Interior Design Association
341 Merchandise Mart   Ph: (312)467-1950
Chicago, IL 60654-1104   Free: 888-799-IIDA
                                Fax: (312)467-0779
E-mail: iidahq@iida.org
URL: http://www.iida.com
Contact: Elisabeth Houston, Exec.VP/CEO.

Desc: Professional interior designers, including designers of commerical, healthcare, hospitality, government, retail, residential facilities; educators; researchers; representatives of allied manufacturing sources. *Type:* Association.

Log House Builder's Association of North America
22203 S.R. 203   Ph: (360)794-4469
Monroe, WA 98272
E-mail: loghouse@premier1.net
URL: http://www.premierl.net/~loghouse
Contact: Skip Ellsworth, Pres.

Desc: Log house builders (professional and nonprofessional); interested individuals. Sponsors an intensive three-month apprenticeship program to train and certify journeymen log house builders. Maintains speakers' bureau and library including a collection of log house photographs and building plans that have been approved by building code officials. *Type:* Association.

Mechanical Contractors Association of America
1385 Piccard Dr.   Ph: (301)869-5800
Rockville, MD 20850-4329   Free: 800-556-3653
                                 Fax: (301)990-9690
E-mail: john@mcaa.org
URL: http://www.mcaa.org
Contact: John Gentille, Exec.VP/CEO.

Desc: Contractors who furnish, install, and service piping systems and related equipment for heating, cooling, refrigeration, ventilating, and air conditioning systems. Works to standardize materials and methods used in the industry. *Type:* Association.

National Association of Home Builders of the U.S.
1201 15th St. NW   Ph: (202)822-0200
Washington, DC 20005   Fax: (202)822-0559
URL: http://www.nahb.com
Contact: Kent W. Colton, Exec.VP.

Desc: Single and multifamily home builders, commercial builders, and others associated with the building industry. Lobbies on behalf of the housing industry and conducts public affairs activities to increase public understanding of housing and the economy. Collects and disseminates data on current developments in home building and home builders' plans through its Economics Department and nationwide Metropolitan Housing Forecast. *Type:* Association.

National Association of Plumbing-Heating-Cooling Contractors
180 S. Washington St.   Ph: (703)237-8100
PO Box 6808   Free: 800-533-7694
Falls Church, VA 22040   Fax: (703)237-7442
E-mail: naphcc@naphcc.org
URL: http://www.naphcc.org
Contact: Allen Inlow, CEO.

Desc: Federation of state and local associations of plumbing, heating, and cooling contractors. Seeks to advance sanitation, encourage sanitary laws, and generally improve the plumbing, heating, ventilating, and air conditioning industries. *Type:* Association.

National Electrical Contractors Association
3 Bethesda Metro Ctr., Ste.   Ph: (301)657-3110
1100   Fax: (301)215-4500
Bethesda, MD 20814
E-mail: neca@necanet.org
URL: http://www.necanet.org
Contact: John M. Grau, Exec. VP.

Desc: Contractors erecting, installing, repairing, servicing, and maintaining electric wiring, equipment, and appliances. *Type:* Association.

National Insulation Association
99 Canal Center Plz., Ste. 222   Ph: (703)683-6422
Alexandria, VA 22314   Fax: (703)549-4838
E-mail: niainfo@insulation.org

URL: http://www.insulation.org
Contact: William W. Pitkin, Exec.VP.

Desc: Insulation and asbestos abatement contractors, distributors, and manufacturers. *Type:* Association.

National Roofing Contractors Association
10255 W. Higgins Rd., Ste. 600   Ph: (847)299-9070
Rosemont, IL 60018-5607   Free: 800-323-9545
                                 Fax: (847)299-1183
E-mail: nrca@nrca.net
URL: http://www.nrca.net
Contact: William A. Good, CAE, Exec.VP.

Desc: Roofing, roof deck, and waterproofing contractors and industry-related associate members. Assists members to successfully satisfy their customers through technical support, testing and research, education, marketing, government relations, and consultation. *Type:* Association.

National Roofing Contractors Association—Membership Directory
National Roofing Contractors Association
10255 W. Higgins Rd., Ste. 600   Ph: (847)299-9070
Rosemont, IL 60018-5607   Free: 800-323-9545
                                 Fax: (847)299-1183
E-mail: nrca@nrca.net
URL: http://www.roofonline.org.
Contact: Alison LaValley, Editor.

Desc: 3,000 contractors applying all types of commercial and residential roofing; 600 associate member manufacturers, suppliers, and distributors; 300 foreign members; and 100 institutions and related industries. *Type:* Directory.

National Utility Contractors' Association
4301 N. Fairfax Dr., Ste. 360   Ph: (703)358-9300
Arlington, VA 22203-1627   Fax: (703)358-9307
Contact: William G. Harley, Exec.VP.

Desc: Utility contractors engaged in construction of utility lines (pipes for storm and sanitary sewers and drainage, water lines, cables, ducts, conduits, and other utility work) and related projects such as sanitation, sewage disposal, and irrigation; suppliers to the industry. Represents interest of contractors in legislative and public hearings on the local, state, and national levels, with regard to promulgation of state and local codes and federal programs relating to needs of communities for proper utilities, water pollution programs, urban renewal, area redevelopment, and public works that may affect utility contractors. Fosters safety education. *Type:* Association.

NCAC Newsletter
National Council of Acoustical Consultants (NCAC)
66 Morris Ave., Ste. 1A   Ph: (201)564-5859
Springfield, NJ 07081-1409   Fax: (201)564-7480
Contact: Peter Allen, Editor.

Desc: Provides news for the acoustical consulting community. *Type:* Newsletter.

Cooking

American Institute of Wine and Food
1550 Bryant St., Ste. 700   Ph: (415)255-3000
San Francisco, CA 94103   Free: 800-274-AIWF
                                 Fax: (415)255-2874
E-mail: aiwfmember@aol.com
Contact: Sandra McCanley, Interim Exec.Dir.

Desc: Chefs, restaurateurs, winemakers, journalists, and others interested in the art of wine and fine cuisine. Promotes a broad exchange of information and ideas to benefit all who care about wine and food. Seeks to advance the understanding, appreciation and quality of food and drink. *Type:* Association.

The Asian Foodbookery
The Asian Foodbookery
PO Box 15947   Ph: (206)523-3575
Seattle, WA 98115
Contact: R.W. Lucky, Editor and Publisher, lucky8rice@aol.com.
Desc: "Explores the authentic, the ethnic and the emergent fusions." Provides recipes, essays, travel accounts, interviews, and Asian cookbook reviews. *Type:* Newsletter.

Better Homes and Gardens Special Interest Publications Low Calorie/Low Fat Recipes
Meredith Corp.
1716 Locust St.   Ph: (515)284-3000
Des Moines, IA 50309-3023   Free: 800-678-2674
                         Fax: (515)284-3697
E-mail: acolvill@mdp.com.
Contact: Steve Levinson, Publisher, slevinson@nyc.mdp.com; Patrick Tomlinson, Advertising Dir.; Peggy Leib, Advertising Service Mgr.
Desc: Consumer magazine covering healthy recipes. *Type:* Periodical.

Bon Appetit
Conde Nast Publications, Inc.
140 E. 45th St., 39th Fl.   Ph: (212)880-8800
New York, NY 10017   Free: 800-223-0780
                         Fax: (212)880-8248
E-mail: letters@brides.com
URL: http://www.epicurious.com/b-ba/b00-home/ba.html.
Contact: William J. Garry, Editor-in-Chief; Lynn W. Heiler, Publisher; Daniel Lagani, Associate Publisher; Carol Campbell, Advertising Mgr.
Desc: Lifestyle magazine covering food, travel, and entertaining. *Alt. Contact:* 6300 Wilshire Blvd., Los Angeles, CA 90048; telephone: (213)965-3600; fax: (213)937-1206. *Type:* Periodical.

Bread Pudding Recipe Exchange
Prosperity & Profits Unlimited, Distribution Services
PO Box 416   Ph: (303)575-5676
Denver, CO 80201-0416
Contact: A. Doyle, Editor.
Desc: Presents recipe possibilities for bread pudding, sample greetings, and more. *Type:* Newsletter.

Cinnamon Hearts
Ken Helton
PO Box 578340   Ph: (209)572-0769
Modesto, CA 95357   Fax: (209)572-0769
Contact: Marilyn Helton, Editor; Ken Helton, Publisher.
Desc: Blends art, writing, and cooking by way of feature articles, recipes, and nostalgic drawings. Recurring features include book reviews. *Type:* Newsletter.

Classic Cookbooks
Pillsbury Co.
200 6th St., M.S. 28M7   Ph: (612)330-4475
Minneapolis, MN 55402   Fax: (612)330-4875
Contact: Sally Peters, Publisher; William Monn, Manager.
Desc: Magazine containing new recipes. *Type:* Periodical.

Convivium
CeeVee Publications
PO Box 835   Ph: (330)386-1123
East Liverpool, OH 43920-5835   Fax: (330)FUN-NJOY
E-mail: conviv@raex.com.
Contact: Catherine S. Vodrey, Editor.
Desc: A Decidedly Unstuffy Food and Cooking Letter. Contains easy recipes, reviews of cookbooks and food catalogs, and humorous essays on cooking and entertaining. *Type:* Newsletter.

Cooking on the Edge
Jill Cornfield
25 E. 86th St., Ste. 6G   Ph: (212)296-4485
New York, NY 10028
Contact: Jill Cornfield, Editor and Publisher.
Desc: Features personal stories about life and the kitchen with simple recipes. Recurring features include book reviews. *Type:* Newsletter.

Cuisine Concepts
1406 Thomas Pl.   Ph: (817)732-4758
Fort Worth, TX 76107
Contact: Renie Steves, Writer, reniesteves@msn.com; Sterling Steves, Writer.
Desc: Distributes tax and finance information. *Alt. Contact:* 1406 Thomas Pl., Fort Worth, TX 76107; telephone: (817)732-4758. *Type:* Periodical.

The Culinary Sleuth
Nora Fraser
1238 E. 85th St.
Brooklyn, NY 11236
E-mail: norkitchen@aol.com
Desc: Provides news on food history, folklore, nutrition, cookbook reviews, and food information resources. Includes free recipe offers. *Type:* Newsletter.

Eating Well Magazine
Eating Well, Inc.
823A Ferry Rd.   Ph: (802)425-3961
Charlotte, VT 05445   Free: 800-344-3350
                         Fax: (802)425-3675
URL: EatingWell.com.
Contact: Marcelle Langon DiFalco, Editor-in-Chief, fax: (802)425-4666, ewelledit@aol.com; Elizabeth Normand Hiser, M.S., Nutrition Editor; Missy Chase, Publisher, (212)767-5161, fax: (212)767-5160; E. Michelle Amlong, Advertising Dir., (212)767-5166, fax: (212)767-5160; Patsy Jamieson, Food Editor, (802)425-3961, fax: (802)425-7675, ewelledit@aol.com.
Desc: Food magazine with emphasis on delicious low-fat cooking and sensible nutrition. *Alt. Contact:* Hachette Filipacchi Magazines, Inc. 1633 Broadway, New York, NY 10019; telephone: (212)767-6000. *Type:* Periodical.

ESSENCE
Canadian Federation of Chefs & Cooks
582 Somerset St. W   Ph: (613)563-2433
Ottawa, ON, Canada K1R 5K2   Fax: (613)237-9900
Contact: Julius Pokomandy, Editor.
Desc: Promotes national culinary events, information from chefs, skills upgrading, and product information. Recurring features include letters to the editor, interviews, news of research, a calendar of events, reports of meetings, and news of educational opportunities. *Type:* Newsletter.

Favorite Brand Name Recipes Magazine
Publications International, Ltd.
7373 N. Cicero   Ph: (847)676-3470
Lincolnwood, IL 60646   Fax: (847)676-3671
Contact: Ivy Lester, Publisher.
Desc: Recipe magazine. *Alt. Contact:* 3681 Carver Hall, Ames, IA 50011. *Type:* Periodical.

Fine Cooking Magazine
Taunton Press
63 S. Main St., Box 5506   Free: 800-926-8776
Newtown, CT 06470-5506   Fax: (203)270-6751
E-mail: jchilds@taunton.com; finecook@taunton.com.
URL: http://www.taunton.com
Contact: Christine Arrington, Publisher; Martha Holmberg, Editor.
Desc: Magazine focusing on food preparation. *Type:* Periodical.

Food & Drink
Liquor Control Board of Ontario
55 Lakeshore Blvd. E   Ph: (416)365-5906
Toronto, ON, Canada M5E   Fax: (416)365-5935
1A4
Contact: Michelle Oosterman, Editor.
Desc: Consumer magazine covering home entertainment. *Type:* Periodical.

Food & Wine
American Express Publishing Corp.
1120 Avenue of the Americas   Ph: (212)382-5600
New York, NY 10036   Free: 800-333-6569
                         Fax: (212)382-5877
URL: http://www.food&wine.com.
Contact: Ila Stanger, Editor; Nicholas Niles, Publisher.
Desc: Magazine devoted to food and wine. *Type:* Periodical.

Gourmet-The Magazine of Good Living
Conde Nast Publications, Inc.
140 E. 45th St., 39th Fl.   Ph: (212)880-8800
New York, NY 10017   Free: 800-223-0780
                         Fax: (212)880-8248
E-mail: letters@brides.com
URL: http://www.epicurious.com.
Contact: Gail Zweigenthal, Editor; Peter King Hunsinger, Publisher.
Desc: Consumer magazine focusing on quality travel, dining, cooking, and entertaining. *Type:* Periodical.

Growing Gourmet
Cinnabarr/Bear Paw Press
2245 Lariat Trail   Ph: (972)294-4609
Frisco, TX 75034   Fax: (972)294-4609
Contact: Sharon Flanagain, Editor, sharon@foodnotes.com.
Desc: Introduces children to cooking techniques, kitchen equipment, kitchen vocabulary manners and recipes with the aim of teaching them patience, reading skills, following directions, hand-eye coordination, and cultural appreciation. *Type:* Newsletter.

No Salt Week-The Newsletter
Prosperity & Profits Unlimited, Distribution Services
PO Box 416   Ph: (303)575-5676
Denver, CO 80201-0416
Contact: A. Doyle, Editor.
Desc: Presents possibilities for herb and spice blends that contain no added salt. Also contains ideas for cooking and much more. *Type:* Newsletter.

Pillsbury Fast & Healthy Magazine
Pillsbury Co.
200 6th St., M.S. 28M7   Ph: (612)330-4475
Minneapolis, MN 55402   Fax: (612)330-4875
Contact: Betsy Wray, Editor; Sally Peters, Publisher; Diane B. Anderson, Manager; Karen Goodsell, Circulation Mgr.
Desc: Food magazine featuring healthy 30-minute recipes for active people. *Type:* Periodical.

Shenandoah Seasons
Julie B. Gochenour
989 Black Bear Rd.   Ph: (540)436-3117
Maurertown, VA 22644-2839   Free: 800-233-3836
                         Fax: (540)436-8115
URL: http://www.creative-homeliving.com/world_Kitchen/shenandoah.
Contact: Julie B. Gochenour, Editor, (540)459-3209, fax: (540)459-2401, snowbird@shentel.net; Elizabeth H. Cottrell, Editor, elizcot@shentel.net.

Desc: Presents regional recipes, reflections on changing seasons, Valley history and lore, and special Valley places. Recurring features include letters to the editor, a collection, and columns titled The Light Touch, What's in Season, and Out & About. *Type:* Newsletter.

Simply Seafood
Waterfront Press Co.
5305 Shilshole Ave. NW, Ste.   Ph: (206)789-6506
200   Fax: (206)789-9193
Seattle, WA 98107
E-mail: wfpress@wolfenet.com; simplyeditor@wfpress.com.
Contact: Peter Redmayne, Editor; Laurie Munnis, Advertising Dir.; Tally Armand, Circulation Mgr.
Desc: Magazine focusing on seafood. Includes recipes and articles on how to purchase seafood. *Type:* Periodical.

Taste of Home
Reiman Publications, LLC
5400 S. 60th St.   Ph: (414)423-0100
Greendale, WI 53129-1404   Free: 800-682-9019
                           Fax: (414)423-8463
Contact: Kathy Pohl, Exec. Editor; Coleen Martin, Food Editor; Vicky Moseley, Art Dir.; John Lebrun, Sr. Vice-President, Circulation, fax: (414)423-1143.
Desc: Consumer magazine covering food and cooking. *Type:* Periodical.

Copyright/Trademarks/Patents

TRADEMARKSCAN—Austria
Thomson & Thomson
500 Victory Rd.   Ph: (617)479-1600
North Quincy, MA 02171-3145   Free: 888-477-3447
                           Fax: (617)786-8381
URL: http://www.thomson-thomson.com.
Desc: Information on over 395,000 active registered trademarks on file at Oesterreichisches Patentamt. Also included are International Register trademark registrations filed through the World Intellectual Property Organization from January 1, 1989 forward, requesting protection in Austria. *Type:* Directory.

TRADEMARKSCAN—Benelux
Thomson & Thomson
500 Victory Rd.   Ph: (617)479-1600
North Quincy, MA 02171-3145   Free: 888-477-3447
                           Fax: (617)786-8381
URL: http://www.thomson-thomson.com.
Desc: Information on over 675,000 active registered trademarks and applications on file at Benelux-Merkenbureau. Also included are International Register trademark registrations filed through the World Intellectual Property Organization from January 1, 1989 forward, requesting protection in Benelux. *Type:* Directory.

TRADEMARKSCAN—Canada
Thomson & Thomson
500 Victory Rd.   Ph: (617)479-1600
North Quincy, MA 02171-3145   Free: 888-477-3447
                           Fax: (617)786-8381
URL: http://www.thomson-thomson.com.
Desc: Over 627,000 trademark registrations and applications filed with Canadian Intellectual Property Office. *Type:* Directory.

TRADEMARKSCAN—Denmark
Thomson & Thomson
500 Victory Rd.   Ph: (617)479-1600
North Quincy, MA 02171-3145   Free: 888-477-3447
                           Fax: (617)786-8381
URL: http://www.thomson-thomson.com.

Desc: Over 200,000 active registered trademarks and applications on file at Patentdirektoratet. Also included are inactive records from January 1, 1992 forward. *Type:* Directory.

TRADEMARKSCAN—European Community
Thomson & Thomson
500 Victory Rd.   Ph: (617)479-1600
North Quincy, MA 02171-3145   Free: 888-477-3447
                           Fax: (617)786-8381
URL: http://www.thomson-thomson.com.
Desc: Over 78,000 trademark registrations and applications filed with the trademark registry of the Office of Harmonization in the Internal Market (OHIM). *Type:* Directory.

TRADEMARKSCAN—France
Thomson & Thomson
500 Victory Rd.   Ph: (617)479-1600
North Quincy, MA 02171-3145   Free: 888-477-3447
                           Fax: (617)786-8381
URL: http://www.thomson-thomson.com.
Desc: Over 1,100,000 active registered trademarks and applications on file at Institut National de la Propriete Industrielle. Also included are International Register trademark registrations filed through the World Intellectual Property Organization from January 1, 1989 forward, requesting protection in France. *Type:* Directory.

TRADEMARKSCAN—Germany
Thomson & Thomson
500 Victory Rd.   Ph: (617)479-1600
North Quincy, MA 02171-3145   Free: 888-477-3447
                           Fax: (617)786-8381
URL: http://www.thomson-thomson.com.
Desc: Over 960,000 active registered trademarks and applications on file at Deutsches Patentamt. Also included are International Register trademark registrations filed through the World Intellectual Property Organization from January 1, 1989 forward, requesting protection in Germany. *Type:* Directory.

TRADEMARKSCAN—International Register
Thomson & Thomson
500 Victory Rd.   Ph: (617)479-1600
North Quincy, MA 02171-3145   Free: 888-477-3447
                           Fax: (617)786-8381
URL: http://www.thomson-thomson.com.
Desc: Over 400,000 active registered trademarks on file at the World Intellectual Property Organization. Also included are inactive records from January 1, 1989 forward. *Type:* Directory.

TRADEMARKSCAN—Italy
Thomson & Thomson
500 Victory Rd.   Ph: (617)479-1600
North Quincy, MA 02171-3145   Free: 888-477-3447
                           Fax: (617)786-8381
URL: http://www.thomson-thomson.com.
Desc: Over 870,000 active registered trademarks and applications on file at Ufficio Italiano Brevetti e marchi. Also included are International Register trademark registrations filed through the World Intellectual Property Organization from January 1, 1989 forward, requesting protection in Italy. *Type:* Directory.

TRADEMARKSCAN—Liechtenstein
Thomson & Thomson
500 Victory Rd.   Ph: (617)479-1600
North Quincy, MA 02171-3145   Free: 888-477-3447
                           Fax: (617)786-8381
URL: http://www.thomson-thomson.com.
Desc: Over 170,000 active registered trademarks on file at Amt fur Volkswirtschaft Geistiges Eigentum. Also includ-

ed are International Register trademark registrations filed through the World Intellectual Property Organization from January 1, 1989 forward, requesting protection in Liechtenstein. *Type:* Directory.

TRADEMARKSCAN—Monaco
Thomson & Thomson
500 Victory Rd.   Ph: (617)479-1600
North Quincy, MA 02171-3145   Free: 888-477-3447
                           Fax: (617)786-8381
URL: http://www.thomson-thomson.com.
Desc: Over 150,000 active registered trademarks on file at Propriete Industrielle Litteraire et Artistique. Also included are International Register trademark registrations filed through the World Intellectual Property Organization from January 1, 1989 forward, requesting protection in Monaco. *Type:* Directory.

TRADEMARKSCAN—Spain
Thomson & Thomson
500 Victory Rd.   Ph: (617)479-1600
North Quincy, MA 02171-3145   Free: 888-477-3447
                           Fax: (617)786-8381
URL: http://www.thomson-thomson.com.
Desc: 1.2 million active registered trademarks on file at the Oficina Espanol de Patentes Y Marcas; International Register trademark registrations filed through the World Intellectual Property Organization. *Type:* Directory.

TRADEMARKSCAN—Switzerland
Thomson & Thomson
500 Victory Rd.   Ph: (617)479-1600
North Quincy, MA 02171-3145   Free: 888-477-3447
                           Fax: (617)786-8381
URL: http://www.thomson-thomson.com.
Desc: Over 500,000 active registered trademarks and applications on file at Bundesamt fur geistiges Eigentum. Also included are International Register trademark registrations filed through the World Intellectual Property Organization from January 1, 1989 forward, requesting protection in Switzerland. *Type:* Directory.

TRADEMARKSCAN—U.K.
Thomson & Thomson
500 Victory Rd.   Ph: (617)479-1600
North Quincy, MA 02171-3145   Free: 888-477-3447
                           Fax: (617)786-8381
URL: http://www.thomson-thomson.com.
Desc: Information on over 690,000 trademark registrations and applications filed with the Trade Marks Branch of the Patent Office of the United Kingdom (UKPO). Includes active trademarks applications and registration from 1876, lapsed applications from July 1988, and lapsed registration from July 1983. *Type:* Directory.

Cosmetics/Hair

American Salon's Green Book
Advanstar Communications
7500 Old Oak Blvd.   Ph: (440)243-8100
Cleveland, OH 44130-3369   Free: 800-225-4569
                           Fax: (440)891-2733
E-mail: directories@advanstar.com
URL: http://www.advanstar.com.
Contact: Amanda Hathaway, Editor, ahathaway@advanstar.com.
Desc: About 1,300 manufacturers of supplies and equipment for barbers and cosmetologists; 130 manufacturers' representatives; 3,200 distributors; employment agencies, show management companies, and related trade organizations. *Type:* Directory.

Crafts

ACCI Newsletter

Association of Crafts & Creative Industries (ACCI)

1100-H Brandywine Blvd.   Ph: (740)452-4541
PO Box 3388   Free: 888-360-2224
Zanesville, OH 43702-3388   Fax: (740)452-2552

Contact: Julie Fox, Editor.

Desc: Seeks to promote ways to improve methods of retailing crafts and creative merchandise. Supplies retailing techniques, news of upcoming shows and events, and news of members and membership benefits. *Type:* Newsletter.

American Association of Woodturners— Directory

American Association of Woodturners

3200 Lexington Ave.   Ph: (651)484-9094
Shoreview, MN 55126   Fax: (651)484-1724
E-mail: aaw@citilink.com

Contact: Mary Lacer, Editor.

Desc: More than 7,100 artisans, collectors, manufacturers and suppliers of woodcrafts who demonstrate, lecture about, or exhibit woodcrafts produced on a lathe. *Type:* Directory.

American Craft Council

72 Spring St.-6th Fl.   Ph: (212)274-0630
New York, NY 10012-4019   Fax: (212)274-0650
E-mail: council@craftcouncil.org

Contact: Jeffrey Larris, Exec.Dir.

Desc: Craftspeople; art professionals, consumers, and organizations. Works to increase public awareness and appreciation of American crafts (including clay, fiber, glass, metal, wood, and mixed media). *Type:* Association.

American Patchwork and Quilting

Mennonite Central Committee

21 S. 12th St.   Ph: (717)859-1151
PO Box 500   Fax: (717)859-2171
Akron, PA 17501
E-mail: mailbox@mcc.org

Contact: William Reed, Publisher; Bev Rivers, Editor-in-Chief.

Desc: Magazine which instructs and inspires quilters in all aspects of the art of quilt-making. *Alt. Contact:* 1912 Grand Ave., Des Moines, IA 50309-3379; telephone: (515)284-2681; fax: (515)284-3884. *Type:* Periodical.

American Quilter's Society

PO Box 3290   Ph: (502)898-7903
Paducah, KY 42001   Fax: (502)898-8890
E-mail: aqsquilt@apex.net

Contact: Meredith Schroeder, Publisher & Pres.

Desc: Quilters, quilt shops, and quilt guilds. Promotes quilters and quilting; encourages improvement in quilting skills. *Type:* Association.

American Sewing Guild

9140 Ward Pkwy., Ste. 200   Ph: (816)444-3500
Kansas City, MO 64114   Free: 877-ICANSEW
   Fax: (816)444-0330
E-mail: info@asg.org
URL: http://www.asg.org

Contact: Marcia Willman, Exec.Dir.

Desc: Home sewers and people interested in sewing. Provides current sewing information and advice through lectures, demonstrations, classes, seminars, and fashion shows. *Type:* Association.

And Sew On

PO Box 71   Ph: (908)722-5676
Martinsville, NJ 08836

Contact: Alida Macor, Pres./Author.

Desc: Distributes sewing/needlecraft column. *Alt. Contact:* PO Box 71, Martinsville, NJ 08836; telephone: (908)722-5676. *Type:* Periodical.

Annie's Quick & Easy Pattern Club Newsletter

Annie's Attic

1 Annie Ln.   Ph: (903)636-4303
Big Sandy, TX 75755-9400

Contact: Annie Potter, Editor; Andy Ashley, Editor.

Desc: Carries crochet and sewing patterns for a wide variety of useful and novelty items, with complete instructions and full color illustration. Recurring features include an information exchange and announcements of award-winning items. *Type:* Newsletter.

The Blade

Krause Publications, Inc.

700 E. State St.   Ph: (715)445-2214
Iola, WI 54990   Free: 800-258-0929
   Fax: (715)445-4087
E-mail: info@krause.com; krause@krause.com
URL: http://www.krause.com

Contact: Tom Paar, Publisher; Steve Shackleford, Editor; Steve McCowen, Advertising Dir.

Desc: Magazine providing information about knives. *Type:* Periodical.

Christmas Helps & Holiday Baking

The Family Circle, Inc.

110 5th Ave.   Ph: (212)463-1673
New York, NY 10011   Fax: (212)463-1906
E-mail: fclp@familycircle.com.

Contact: Eric Simon, Advertising Mgr.

Desc: Consumer magazine covering crafts and recipes for Christmas. *Alt. Contact:* 375 Lexington Ave., New York, NY 10017; telephone: (212)499-2000; fax: (212)499-1987. *Type:* Periodical.

Country Sampler

Sampler Publications, Inc.

707 Kautz Rd.   Ph: (630)377-8000
St. Charles, IL 60174   Fax: (630)377-8914
URL: http://www.sampler.com.

Contact: Mark A. Nickel, CEO; Margaret Kernan, President; Robert Sexton, Circulation Mgr.

Desc: Country arts, crafts, and interior design magazine. *Type:* Periodical.

Crafting Traditions

Reiman Publications, LLC

5400 S. 60th St.   Ph: (414)423-0100
Greendale, WI 53129-1404   Free: 800-682-9019
   Fax: (414)423-8463

Contact: Kathleen Anderson, Editor.

Desc: How-to guide for country arts and crafts. *Type:* Periodical.

The Crafts Fair Guide

Consumer Awareness Learning Laboratory

PO Box 386   Ph: (609)935-6264
Penns Grove, NJ 08069-0386

Contact: Lee Spiegel, Editor; Dianne Spiegel, Editor.

Desc: Participant evaluations of about 1,000 recurring arts and crafts shows per year. *Type:* Directory.

Crafts Magazine

Primedia Special Interest Publication

2 News Plaza   Ph: (309)682-6626
PO Box 1790   Free: 800-521-2885
Peoria, IL 61656-1790   Fax: (309)682-7394
E-mail: crafts@primediasi.com.

Contact: Miriam Olson, Editor; Steve Elzy, President; Mike Irish, Associate Publisher; Harry Sailer, VP/General Mgr.

Desc: Crafts is a how-to magazine which offers attractive projects in a variety in crafting techniques, such as painting, cross stitch, papercrafts, plastic canvas, polymer clay, fabric crafts, florals, dollmaking, crochet and others. Crafts provides full-size patterns, complete instructions and clear photos that show the projects' details. *Type:* Periodical.

Crafts 'N Things

Clapper Publishing Co., Inc.

2400 Devon, Ste. 375   Ph: (847)635-5800
Des Plaines, IL 60018-4618   Fax: (847)635-6311
E-mail: clappercom@compuserve.com; 72567.1066@compuserve.com.
URL: http://www.craftnet.org/crafts-n-things.

Contact: Nona Piorkowski, Editor, npiorkowski@clapper.com; Stuart Hochwert, Vice President, shochwert@clapper.com; Toni Ballentine, Circulation Mgr., tballentine@clapper.com; Marie Clapper, Publisher & President, mclapper@clapper.com.

Desc: Craft magazine. *Type:* Periodical.

Creative Machine Newsletter

Open Chain Publishing

PO Box 2634   Ph: (650)366-4440
Menlo Park, CA 94026-2634   Fax: (650)366-4455

Contact: Robbie Fanning, Editor and Publisher.

Desc: Contains information on sewing. Includes information on new products, trade shows, and software. *Type:* Newsletter.

Creative Woodworks and Crafts

All American Crafts, Inc.

243 Newton-Sparta Rd.   Ph: (973)383-8080
Newton, NJ 07860   Free: 800-877-5527
   Fax: (973)383-8133
E-mail: craftpub@aol.com; cwwandc@aol.com.

Contact: George Ahlers, Editor; Robert Becker, Advertising Mgr.; Marie-Claire MacDonald, Circulation Mgr.

Desc: Consumer magazine covering crafts and woodworking. *Alt. Contact:* telephone: (973)383-8080; fax: (973)383-8133. *Type:* Periodical.

Crochet Association International

PO Box 131   Ph: (770)445-7137
Dallas, GA 30132

Contact: William E. Elmore, Exec.Dir.

Desc: Crocheters, craft store owners and distributors, yarn and cord dealers and manufacturers, and craft magazine and book publishers. Goals are to gather, distribute, and promote creation of useful heirlooms and to assist those interested in the art of crocheting. Provides educational opportunities through workshops, fairs, and seminars. *Type:* Association.

The Cross Stitcher

Clapper Publishing Co., Inc.

2400 Devon, Ste. 375   Ph: (847)635-5800
Des Plaines, IL 60018-4618   Fax: (847)635-6311
E-mail: clappercom@compuserve.com; 72567.1066@compuserve.com.
URL: http://www.craftnet.org/cross-stitcher.

Contact: B.J. McDonald, Editor, (512)251-3306, fax: (521)251-3306, bjmcdonald@clapper.com; Stuart Hochwert, VP of Marketing & Sales, shochwert@clapper.com; Toni Ballentine, Circulation Mgr., tballentine@clapper.com; Marie Clapper, Publisher & President, mclapper@clapper.com.

Desc: Publication featuring cross stitch charts and designs. *Type:* Periodical.

Decorative Woodcrafts

Meredith Corp.
1716 Locust St.   Ph: (515)284-3000
Des Moines, IA 50309-3023   Free: 800-678-2674
                                Fax: (515)284-3697
Contact: William Reed, Publisher; Jon Book, National Sales Mgr.; Beverly Rivers, Editor-in-Chief; Mary Bendgen, Art Dir.; Maureen Ruth, Marketing and Ancillary Sales Dir.; Marjon Schaefer, Managing Editor; Maureen Miller, Assoc. Art Dir.; Susan Sidler, Circulation Mgr.; Rick Pallister, Marketing Mgr.
Desc: Instructional magazine for decorative painters and woodcraft enthusiasts. *Alt. Contact:* 1912 Grand Ave., Des Moines, IA 50304-3379; telephone: (515)284-2509, (515)284-3343; fax: (515)284-3884. *Type:* Periodical.

Doll Artisan Guild

35 Main St.   Ph: (607)432-4977
PO Box 1113   Fax: (607)432-2042
Oneonta, NY 13820-5113
Contact: Rolf E. Ericson, Exec.Dir.
Desc: For individuals interested in authentic reproductions of antique porcelain dolls, modern dolls, and creation of original porcelain dolls. Educates members about the art of dollmaking; conducts seminars on the reproduction of dolls. Offers manufacturers' discounts on supplies. *Type:* Association.

Doll Crafter

Scott Publications
30595 8 Mile Rd.   Ph: (248)477-6650
Livonia, MI 48152-1798   Free: 800-458-8237
                                Fax: (248)477-6795
E-mail: 104137.1254@compuserve.com
Contact: Barbara Campbell, Editor; Robert H. Keessen, Publisher; Shannon Colby, Advertising Mgr.; Jeanette Foxe, Distributor Mgr.
Desc: Dollcrafting magazine focusing on porcelain dollmaking with emphasis on reproductions. *Type:* Periodical.

DOLLS

Collector Communications Corp.
170 5th Ave.   Ph: (212)989-8700
New York, NY 10010   Fax: (212)645-8976
Contact: Stephanie Finnegan, Editor; Robert Rowe, Publisher; India Thybulle, Advertising Dir.
Desc: Magazine reporting on antique and contemporary dolls, collecting, and hobbies. *Type:* Periodical.

Embroiderers' Guild of America

335 W. Broadway, Ste. 100   Ph: (502)589-6956
Louisville, KY 40202   Fax: (502)584-7900
E-mail: egahq@aol.com
URL: http://www.ega.usa.org
Contact: Bonnie Key, Office Mgr.
Desc: People interested in the art of needlework. Purpose is to set and maintain high standards of design, color, and workmanship in all kinds of embroidery. Sponsors exhibitions; offers examinations for teaching certification; serves as an information source for needlework in the U.S. *Type:* Association.

FineScale Modeler

Kalmbach Publishing Co.
21027 Crossroads Circle   Ph: (414)796-8776
PO Box 1612   Free: 800-446-5489
Waukesha, WI 53187-1612   Fax: (414)796-1615
E-mail: mrmag@mrmag.com
URL: http://kalmbach.com; http://www.finescale.com.
Contact: Bob Hayden, Editor, rhayden@finescale.com; Walter J. Mundschau, Publisher.

Desc: Magazine on modeling techniques. *Type:* Periodical.

Handcraft Illustrated

Handcraft Illustrated
17 Station St.   Ph: (617)232-1000
Brookline, MA 02146   Fax: (617)232-1572
E-mail: handcraftillustrated@bcpress.com.
Contact: Carol Sterbenz, Editor.
Desc: Magazine covering step-by-step, do-it-yourself craft projects. *Type:* Periodical.

Hobby Industry Association of America

319 E. 54th St.   Ph: (201)794-1133
Elmwood Park, NJ 07407   Fax: (201)797-0657
E-mail: hia@ix.netcom.com
Contact: Patricia Koziol, Exec.Dir.
Desc: Manufacturers, wholesalers, retailers, publishers, and allied firms in the craft and hobby industry. To promote the interest of all persons engaged in the buying, selling, or manufacturing of hobby and craft merchandise; to conceive, develop, and implement programs for members to achieve greater individual growth. Conducts seminars and educational workshops; sponsors national trade show. *Type:* Association.

Home Sewing Association

1350 Broadway, Ste. 1601   Ph: (212)714-1633
New York, NY 10018   Fax: (212)714-1655
E-mail: ahsca@aol.com
URL: http://www.sewing.org
Contact: Joan Campbell, CAE, Exec.VP.
Desc: Manufacturers (300) and retailers (600) of home sewing merchandise, including fabrics, patterns, sewing machines, sewing notions, needlework, and crafts. *Type:* Association.

Hooked on Crochet

The Needlecraft Shop, LLC.
23 Old Pecan Rd.   Ph: (903)636-4011
Big Sandy, TX 75755   Free: 800-259-4000
                                Fax: (903)636-4088
E-mail: customer_service@needlecraftshop.com.
Contact: Jennifer McClain, Senior Editor, fax: (903)636-4099, jennifer_mcclain@needlecraftshop.com.
Desc: Magazine featuring basic crochet designs and easy to make patterns. *Type:* Periodical.

International Doll Makers Association

Lucille Garrard
2127 Past Park   Ph: (504)888-4701
Metairie, LA 70001   Fax: (504)454-8782
E-mail: josiemull@aol.com
Contact: Josie Mull, Pres.
Desc: Dollmakers. Works as an educational organization in the area of dollmaking. *Type:* Association.

The Knitting Guild of America

PO Box 1606   Ph: (423)524-2401
Knoxville, TN 37901   Free: 800-274-6034
                                Fax: (423)524-8677
E-mail: tkga@tkga.com
URL: http://www.tkga.com
Contact: Carol S. Wigginton, Founder.
Desc: Shop owners and individuals interested in knitting. Provides education and a means of communication to those wishing to improve the quality of workmanship and creativity of their knitting projects. *Type:* Association.

Lionel Railroader Club

PO Box 748   Ph: (810)949-4100
New Baltimore, MI 48047-0748   Fax: (810)949-3340
URL: http://www.lionel.com

Contact: Brenda Schlutow, Coord.
Desc: Children and adults who are enthusiasts of Lionel electric trains. Purposes are to provide information on Lionel trains, train layouts, new products, and games and to act as supply resource through the club's newsletter. *Type:* Association.

MIAA Industry News

Miniatures Industry Association of America
1100-H Brandywine Blvd.   Ph: (614)452-4541
PO Box 3388   Fax: (614)452-2552
Zanesville, OH 43702-3388
E-mail: miaa.info@offinger.com
Contact: Debby Johnston, Editor.
Desc: Seeks to inform businesses involved in the dollhouse and miniatures industry. Provides retail tips, association news, and a listing of upcoming trade shows and events. *Type:* Newsletter.

Model Airplane News

Air Age Publishing, Inc.
100 East Ridge   Ph: (203)431-9000
Ridgefield, CT 06877   Fax: (203)431-3000
Contact: Tom Atwood, Editor; Louis De Francesco, Publisher.
Desc: Magazine on radio-controlled model airplanes and helicopters. *Type:* Periodical.

Model Railroader

Kalmbach Publishing Co.
21027 Crossroads Circle   Ph: (414)796-8776
PO Box 1612   Free: 800-446-5489
Waukesha, WI 53187-1612   Fax: (414)796-1615
E-mail: mrmag@mrmag.com
URL: http://kalmbach.com
Contact: Russ Larson, Publisher, (414)798-6520, rlarson@kalmbach.com; Andy Sperando, Editor, (414)798-6461, asperandeo@mrmag.com; Erik Bergstrom, Ad Sales Mgr., ebergstrom@kalmbach.com.
Desc: Model railroad hobby magazine. *Type:* Periodical.

National Model Railroad Association

4121 Cromwell Rd.   Ph: (423)892-2846
Chattanooga, TN 37421   Fax: (423)899-4869
URL: http://www.nmra.org
Contact: Connie Rudder, Exec.Dir.
Desc: Amateur model railroad hobbyists, railroad dealers, manufacturers, and others interested in scale model railroads and equipment. *Type:* Association.

National Quilting Association

PO Box 393   Ph: (410)461-5733
Ellicott City, MD 21041-0393   Fax: (410)461-3693
E-mail: nqa@erols.com
URL: http://www.his.com/queenb/nqa
Contact: Gayle Sternheim, Exec. Asst.
Desc: Persons interested in quilts or quilting. Works to further understanding of quilts or quilting and to compile information about quilts, past and present. *Type:* Association.

National Society of Tole and Decorative Painters

393 N. McLean Blvd.   Ph: (316)269-9300
Wichita, KS 67203-9300   Fax: (316)269-9191
Contact: Kay Blair, Exec.Dir.
Desc: Individuals interested in tole and decorative painting; decorative painting supplies retailers, distributors, and wholesalers. Goals are to: further interest in the field; increase the quality of teaching and painting; promote an awareness of quality in the field. *Type:* Association.

National Woodcarvers Association

7424 Miami Ave. Ph: (513)561-0627
Cincinnati, OH 45243
E-mail: nwca@chipchats.org
URL: http://www.chipchats.org
Contact: Edward F. Gallenstein, Pres.
Desc: Amateur and professional woodcarvers and whittlers; suppliers of tools and products for the hobby; writers and publishers of books and magazines about carving. *Type:* Association.

Origami USA

15 W. 77th St. Ph: (212)769-5635
New York, NY 10024-5192 Fax: (212)769-5668
URL: http://www.origami-usa.org
Contact: Toby Schwartz, Pres.
Desc: Individuals interested in promoting origami. (Origami is an art of paperfolding that originated in ancient China and was introduced and popularized in the U.S. by Lillian Oppenheimer, author of several children's books.). *Type:* Association.

Pack-O-Fun

Clapper Publishing Co., Inc.
2400 Devon, Ste. 375 Ph: (847)635-5800
Des Plaines, IL 60018-4618 Fax: (847)635-6311
E-mail: clappercom@compuserve.com; 72567.1066@ compuserve.com.
URL: http://www.craftnet.org/pack-o-fun.
Contact: Marie Clapper, President & Publisher, mclappercom@clapper.com; Billie Ciancio, Editor, bciancio@ clapper.com; Stuart Hockwert, VP of Marketing & Sales, shockwert@clapper.com; Toni Ballentine, Circulation Mgr., tballentine@clapper.com.
Desc: Magazine devoted to family and group crafts and activities. *Type:* Periodical.

Plastercrafter

National Plastercraft Association
0465 N 300 E Ph: (317)529-9575
Albion, IN 46701
Desc: Disseminates information to retailers, manufacturers, and distributors of plastercraft products for the hobby industry. Relates news of the Association's promotional activities, undertaken to enhance the industry's image. *Type:* Newsletter.

Plastic Canvas! Magazine

The Needlecraft Shop, LLC.
23 Old Pecan Rd. Ph: (903)636-4011
Big Sandy, TX 75755 Free: 800-259-4000
 Fax: (903)636-4088
Contact: Janet Perrin, Editor, fax: (903)636-4099, janet-perrin@needlecraftshop.com.
Desc: Craft magazine offering patterns (plastic canvas). *Type:* Periodical.

Quick & Easy Crafts

House of White Birches
306 E. Parr Rd. Ph: (219)589-4000
Berne, IN 46711 Fax: (219)589-8093
Contact: Beth Schwartz Wheeler, Editor; John Robinson, CEO; Vivian Rothe, Editorial Director; Scott Moss, Marketing Director; George Hague, Ad Manager.
Desc: Magazine covering sewing, patchwork, knitting, embroidery, crochet, and cross-stitch. *Type:* Periodical.

Quick & Easy Plastic Canvas

The Needlecraft Shop, LLC.
23 Old Pecan Rd. Ph: (903)636-4011
Big Sandy, TX 75755 Free: 800-259-4000
 Fax: (903)636-4088
Contact: Janet Perrin.

Desc: Craft magazine offering plastic canvas patterns. *Type:* Periodical.

Quilt World—Quilt Show Directory Section

House of White Birches
306 E. Parr Rd. Ph: (219)589-4000
Berne, IN 46711 Fax: (219)589-8093
E-mail: quilt_world@whitebirches.com.
URL: http://www.whitebirches.com
Contact: Sandra Hatch, Editor.
Desc: Lists of quilt shows, seminars, sales, and other quilting events in the United States and Canada to be held within the following two months. *Type:* Directory.

R/C Modeler

R/C Modeler Corp.
144 W. Sierra Madre Blvd. Ph: (626)355-1476
PO Box 487 Fax: (626)355-6415
Sierra Madre, CA 91024-2435
Contact: Patricia E. Crews, Editor; Kathy Acton, Advertising Mgr.
Desc: Magazine covering radio controlled model airplanes, boats, cars and helicopters. *Type:* Periodical.

Railroad Model Craftsman

Carstens Publications Inc.
PO Box 700 Ph: (973)383-3355
Newton, NJ 07860-0700 Fax: (973)383-4064
E-mail: carstens@nac.net
Contact: William Schaumburg, Editor; Harold H. Carstens, Publisher; John Earley, Advertising Dir.
Desc: Model railroading (building, operating, and collecting) magazine. *Type:* Periodical.

Sew Beautiful

Martha Pullen Co., Inc.
518 Madison St. Ph: (256)533-9586
Huntsville, AL 35801-4205 Fax: (256)533-9630
Contact: Kathy Brower, Editorial Dir.; Martha Pullen, Publisher; Leighann Simmons, Art and Production Dir.
Desc: Magazine of heirloom and heirloom related sewing featuring techniques, articles, designs, and pictorials. *Type:* Periodical.

Sew News

Primedia Special Interest Publication
2 News Plaza Ph: (309)682-6626
PO Box 1790 Free: 800-521-2885
Peoria, IL 61656-1790 Fax: (309)682-7394
E-mail: sewnews@aol.com.
URL: http://www.sewnews.com.
Contact: Linda Griepentrog, Editor, snlindag@aol.com; Tina Battock, Publisher, tbattock@primediasi.com.
Desc: Magazine on fashion sewing news, products, and patterns. Includes interviews with designers. *Alt. Contact:* 741 Corporate Circle, Golden, CO 80401; telephone: (303)278-1010; fax: (303)277-0370; toll-free: 800-881-6634. *Type:* Periodical.

Shuttle Spindle and Dyepot

Handweavers Guild of America, Inc.
3327 Duluth Hwy., Ste. 201 Ph: (770)495-7702
Duluth, GA 30096-3339 Fax: (770)495-7703
E-mail: 73744.202@compuserve.com
URL: http://www.weavespindye.org.
Contact: Sandra Bowles, Editor.
Desc: List of weaving exhibits, arts and crafts fairs. *Type:* Directory.

Sports Cards Magazine & Price Guide

Krause Publications, Inc.
700 E. State St. Ph: (715)445-2214
Iola, WI 54990 Free: 800-258-0929
 Fax: (715)445-4087
E-mail: info@krause.com; krause@krause.com
URL: http://www.krause.com
Contact: Hugh McAloon, Publisher; Greg Ambrosins, Editor; Mark Williams, Advertising Mgr.
Desc: Magazine for collectors of sports cards. Features profiles of current and former stars, investment tips, and card price guide. *Type:* Periodical.

Threads

Taunton Press
63 S. Main St., Box 5506 Free: 800-926-8776
Newtown, CT 06470-5506 Fax: (203)270-6751
E-mail: jchilds@taunton.com
URL: http://www.taunton.com
Contact: Betsy Levine, Publisher; Amy Yanagi, Editor; Jan Wahlin, Publisher; Michelle Brown, Advertising Mgr.
Desc: Magazine for sewers, knitters, and fabric and fiber craftspeople. Focus is on garment design, materials, and techniques. *Type:* Periodical.

Tole World

EGW Publishing Co.
1041 Shary Cir. Ph: (925)671-9852
Concord, CA 94518 Fax: (925)671-0692
Contact: Judy Swager, Editor, jswager@egw.com; D'Ann Giordano, Advertising Mgr., rwilson@egw.com.
Desc: Magazine for tole and decorative painting hobbyists. *Type:* Periodical.

Toy Train Operating Society

25 W. Walnut St., Ste. 308 Ph: (626)578-0673
Pasadena, CA 91103 Fax: (626)578-0750
E-mail: ttos@ttos.org
URL: http://www.ttos.org
Contact: Jerry Price, Pres.
Desc: Collectors and operators of toy trains united to share expertise and mutual enjoyment. Conducts charitable program and children's services; sponsors competitions; compiles statistics. Maintains speakers' bureau, and museum. *Type:* Association.

Trains Magazine

Kalmbach Publishing Co.
21027 Crossroads Circle Ph: (414)796-8776
PO Box 1612 Free: 800-446-5489
Waukesha, WI 53187-1612 Fax: (414)796-1615
E-mail: mrmag@mrmag.com; editor@trains.com.
URL: http://kalmbach.com
Contact: Kevin Keefe, Contact, kkeefe@trains.com; Harold L. Miller, Jr., Contact, hmiller@trains.com.
Desc: Magazine covering steam, diesel, passenger, and freight operations. *Type:* Periodical.

Vogue Knitting Magazine

Butterick Co., Inc.
161 6th Ave. Ph: (212)620-2500
New York, NY 10013 Fax: (212)620-2736
Contact: Art Joinnides, Publisher; Gay Bryant, Editor; Michelle Brown, Advertising Dir.
Desc: Fashion magazine for knitters. *Alt. Contact:* 161 6th Ave, New York, NY 10013. *Type:* Periodical.

Vogue Patterns Magazine

Butterick Co., Inc.
161 6th Ave. Ph: (212)620-2500
New York, NY 10013 Fax: (212)620-2736
Contact: Cindy Rose, Editor; Art Joinnides, Publisher; Michelle Brown, Advertising Dir.

Desc: Magazine devoted to fashions and home sewing. *Type:* Periodical.

WOOD
Meredith Corp.
1716 Locust St. Ph: (515)284-3000
Des Moines, IA 50309-3023 Free: 800-678-2674
 Fax: (515)284-3697
URL: http://woodmagazine.com.
Contact: William Reed, Publisher; Larry Clayton, Editor; Rick Pallister, Marketing Mgr/Media Contact.
Desc: Magazine for people who enjoy woodworking. *Alt. Contact:* 1912 Grand Ave., Des Moines, IA 50309-3379; telephone: (515)284-2235; fax: (515)284-3343. *Type:* Periodical.

Wood Strokes & Woodcrafts
EGW Publishing Co.
1041 Shary Cir. Ph: (925)671-9852
Concord, CA 94518 Fax: (925)671-0692
URL: http://www.woodstrokes.com.
Contact: Sandra Wagner, Editor.
Desc: Consumer magazine covering wood crafts. *Type:* Periodical.

Workbench
August Home Publishing
2200 Grand Ave. Ph: (515)282-7000
Des Moines, IA 50312 Free: 800-311-3991
 Fax: (515)283-0447
E-mail: workbench@workbenchmag.com.
URL: http://www.augusthome.com.
Contact: Christopher A. Inman, Editor; Donald B. Peschke, Publisher; John Macarthy, VP Finance/Circulation; George Clark, Advertising Sales Mgr., fax: (515)283-2003; George Chmielarz, Production Dir.
Desc: Home improvement, woodworking, and remodeling magazine. *Type:* Periodical.

Criminal Justice

Alston Wilkes Society
2215 Devine St. Ph: (803)799-2490
Columbia, SC 29205 Fax: (803)540-7223
E-mail: aws1@bellsouth.net
URL: http://www.brickandivy.com/awvh/
Contact: S. Anne Walker, Exec.Dir.
Desc: Operates in South Carolina to assist inmates, homeless veterans, individuals and those being families who are at-risk. These services are provided in order to help them become responsible and productive citizens. Services include: employment and housing assistance, information and referral, crisis intervention, pre-release and parole counseling, individual and group counseling, life skills instruction, and innovative, supportive, and therapeutic prevention projects. *Type:* Association.

American Correctional Association
4380 Forbes Blvd. Ph: (301)918-1800
Lanham, MD 20706-4322 Free: 800-222-5646
 Fax: (301)918-1900
URL: http://www.corrections.com/aca
Contact: James A. Gondles, Jr., Exec.Dir.
Desc: Correctional administrators, wardens, superintendents, members of prison and parole boards, probation officers, psychologists, educators, sociologists, and other individuals; institutions and associations involved in the correctional field. Promotes improved correctional standards, including selection of personnel, care, supervision, education, training, employment, treatment, and post-release adjustment of inmates. Studies causes of crime and juvenile delinquency and methods of crime control and prevention through grants and contracts. *Type:* Association.

Center for Alternative Sentencing and Employment Services
346 Broadway Ph: (212)732-0076
New York, NY 10013
Contact: Joel Copperman, Exec.Dir.
Desc: Seeks to provide alternatives to incarceration services in the Supreme and Criminal Courts. Operates two programs: the Court Employment Project, providing counseling, education, employment, and vocational training to young felony offenders, and the Community Service Sentencing Project, providing social services to misdemeanor offenders and requiring them to perform 70 hours of community service. *Type:* Association.

Center for Intelligence Studies
3826 Milan Dr., S. 1 Ph: (703)836-5044
Alexandria, VA 22305
Contact: Pamela Simpkins, Exec.Dir.
Desc: Participants contribute to CIS activities in support of the Federal Bureau of Investigation, the National Security Agency, the Defense Intelligence Agency, and the Central Intelligence Agency. Disseminates information and offers congressional advice on policies, legislation, and activities that affect the capabilities of the FBI, NSA, DIA, or CIA. Maintains extensive files on intelligence group operations and press-related stories. *Type:* Association.

Citizen's Crime Watch of Dade County
1515 N.W. 79th Ave. Ph: (305)470-1670
Miami, FL 33126 Fax: (305)470-1676
Contact: Merle Hall, Exec.Dir.
Desc: Seeks to educate the public on crime prevention. Sponsors Police Appreciation Week, which honors citizens who aid in criminal arrest. *Type:* Association.

Crime-Free America
57 U St. NW Ph: (202)319-2991
Washington, DC 20001-1010
E-mail: cfa@crime-free.org
URL: http://www.crime-free.org
Contact: Kevin Hein, Pres.
Desc: Works to reverse the threefold rise in crime rates of the last 40 years in America. *Type:* Association.

Crime Free America
Crime Free America
57 U St. NW
Washington, DC 20001-1010
E-mail: cfa@crime-free.org
URL: http://announce.com/cfa/cfa.htm
Desc: The site provides a good amount of authoritative information about crime including information taken directly from the FBI Crime Report. Visitors to the site can navigate easily among "Crime Watch," "Crime Data," and "Crime Forum," to review information including crime stories, statistics, and discussion. *Type:* Database.

Criminal Justice Periodical Index
Bell & Howell Information and Learning
300 N. Zeeb Rd. Ph: (734)761-4700
PO Box 1346
Ann Arbor, MI 48106-1346
E-mail: info@umi.com
URL: http://www.umi.com
Desc: Contains more than 287,000 citations to articles in 120 magazines, journals, newsletters, and law reporting publications on the administration of justice and law enforcement. Corresponds to Criminal Justice Periodical Index. *Available:* The Dialog Corporation, DIALOG; The Dialog Corporation, DIALOG. *Type:* Database.

Dallas Police Homepage
Internet America
One Dallas Ctr.
350 N. St. Paul, Ste. 200
Dallas, TX 75201
E-mail: tallen@ci.dallas.tx.us
URL: http://www.airmail.net/dpd/
Desc: The Dallas Police Homepage offers a wealth of crime prevention information as well as Dallas crime data, brochures, employment information, and resources such as maps, an image bank of vehicles and people, and patrol station statistics. *Type:* Database.

Families Against Mandatory Minimums Foundation
1621 K St. NW, Ste. 1400 Ph: (202)822-6700
Washington, DC 20006 Fax: (202)822-6704
E-mail: famm@famm.org
URL: http://www.famm.org
Contact: Julie Stewart, Pres.
Desc: Citizens interested in the reform of statutory mandatory minimum sentences. Opposes mandatory sentencing laws passed by Congress in 1986 as well as state mandatory minimum sentences. Offers information and analysis of mandatory minimum sentences to federal and state legislators, the public, and the media. *Type:* Association.

Federal Bureau of Investigation
Federal Bureau of Investigation
935 Pennsylvania Ave. NW
Washington, DC 20535
URL: http://www.fbi.gov
Desc: Visitors to this site may choose topics of interest as diverse as "Your FBI" and "Kids and Teens Educational Page." This website provides visitors with access to information about recent reports, investigations, and current topics. There are statistics from the Uniform Crime Reports, and fact sheets. *Type:* Database.

Friends Outside
551 Stockton Ave. Ph: (408)295-6133
San Jose, CA 95126
Contact: Judy Evans, Exec.Dir.
Desc: Staff and volunteers seeking to stop the perpetuation of poverty and crime. Assists prison inmates in assuming responsibility for their own successful reintegration into society. *Type:* Association.

International Association of Correctional Officers
PO Box 81826 Ph: (312)996-5401
Lincoln, NE 68501-1826 Free: 800-255-2382
 Fax: (312)413-0458
URL: http://www.acsp.uic.edu/iaco/about.htm
Desc: Correctional facility officers on the national, state, and local levels; sheriffs; other employees in the corrections field or related fields interested in the study and practice of good corrections principles. Promotes the development of innovative services, evaluation, and inter-professional cooperation in order to increase the effectiveness of correctional facilities. *Type:* Association.

International Narcotic Enforcement Officers Association
112 State St., Ste. 1200 Ph: (518)463-6232
Albany, NY 12207 Fax: (518)432-3378
URL: http://www.ineoa.org
Contact: John J. Bellizzi, Exec.Dir.
Desc: Narcotic enforcement officers, government employees, and others from 60 countries concerned with narcotics control. Seeks ways to improve: laws relative to narcotics, depressants, stimulants, and hallucinogens and enforcement of such laws; police methods; administration of justice. *Type:* Association.

Justice Fellowship

PO Box 16069   Ph: (703)904-7312
Washington, DC 20041-6069   Free: 800-217-2743
      Fax: (703)478-9679
E-mail: jf@pfm.org
Contact: Pat Nolan, Pres.
Desc: Equips concerned citizens to promote reforms that hold offenders responsible for their acts, protect the public, and help restore victims' losses. *Type:* Association.

Justice Research and Statistics Association

777 N. Capitol St. NE, Ste. 801   Ph: (202)842-9330
Washington, DC 20002   Fax: (202)842-9329
E-mail: cjinfo@jrsa.org
URL: http://www.jrsainfo.org
Contact: Joan C. Weiss, Exec.Dir.
Desc: Heads of state statistical units in criminal justice are voting members; others are associate members. Seeks to further the collection, analysis, dissemination, and use of data concerning crime and criminal justice at the federal and state levels; assist in the identification and transfer of techniques for analyzing criminal justice data. *Type:* Association.

Milton S. Eisenhower Foundation

1660 L St. NW, Ste. 200   Ph: (202)429-0440
Washington, DC 20036   Fax: (202)452-0169
Contact: Dr. Lynn A. Curtis, Pres.
Desc: Dedicated to youth investment and economic development in the inner-city by reducing the school dropout rate, crime, welfare dependency, drug abuse, unemployment, and family instability. Works as a "mediating institution" to finance, technically assist, and evaluate minority nonprofit organizations. Assists more than 30 local programs based on the themes of: organizing neighborhoods; early intervention for at-risk youth; creating extended families; facilitating employment and remedial education. *Type:* Association.

National Center on Institutions and Alternatives

3125 Mount Vernon Ave.   Ph: (703)684-0373
Alexandria, VA 22305-2640   Fax: (703)684-6037
E-mail: info@ncianet.org
URL: http://www.ncianet.org/ncia
Contact: Jerome G. Miller, Pres.
Desc: Serves as clearinghouse primarily on decarceration and aids in developing and promoting strategies and actions to reduce the number of people involuntarily institutionalized. Goals include: finding alternatives to mental hospitals; developing, promoting, and supervising enduring alternatives to prison programs; eliminating unnecessary lockup in massive, impersonal prisons, and juvenile training schools. Sponsors the Client Specific Planning Program to provide a systematized development of comprehensive, highly structured, alternative-to-prison, sentencing plans for presentation to the courts. *Type:* Association.

National Center on Institutions and Alternatives: Innovation in Justice

National Center on Institutions and Alternatives
3125 Mt. Vernon Ave.   Ph: (703)684-0373
Alexandria, VA 22305   Fax: (703)684-6037
URL: http://www.ncianet.org/ncia/
Contact: Mary Cate Rush, ncia@igc.apc.org.
Desc: The site contains information about the commission and its findings, including loads of statistical data, reports on state safety, and plenty of detailed, in-depth publications. *Type:* Database.

National Center for Juvenile Justice

710 5th Ave., Ste. 300   Ph: (412)227-6950
Pittsburgh, PA 15219-3000   Fax: (412)227-6955
E-mail: ncjj@ncianet.org

URL: http://www.ncjj.org
Contact: Hunter Hurst, Dir.
Desc: Research division of the National Council of Juvenile and Family Court Judges. Encourages progressive administration of juvenile justice and all its components through research and dissemination of pertinent data. Assumes the responsibility for collecting juvenile court statistics nationally since 1975, and has undertaken to improve both the quality and quantity of the statistics. *Type:* Association.

National Center for Victims of Crime

2111 Wilson Blvd., Ste. 300   Ph: (703)276-2880
Arlington, VA 22201   Free: 800-FYI-CALL
    Fax: (703)276-2889
E-mail: ncvc@ncvc.org
URL: http://www.ncvc.org
Contact: Susan Herman, Exec.Dir.
Desc: Goal is to function as a national resource center to seek redress for injustices done to crime victims. *Type:* Association.

National Criminal Justice Association

444 N. Capitol St. NW, Ste.   Ph: (202)624-1440
   618   Fax: (202)508-3859
Washington, DC 20001
E-mail: ncja@sso.org
URL: http://www.sso.org/ncja/ncja.htm
Contact: Cabell C. Cropper, Exec.VP.
Desc: State and local criminal justice planners, police chiefs, judges, prosecutors, defenders, corrections officials, educators, researchers, and elected officials. Promotes innovation in the criminal justice system through the focused coordination of law enforcement, the courts, corrections, and juvenile justice. Seeks to: focus attention on national issues and developments related to the control of crime; determine and effectively express the states' collective views on pending legislative and administrative action encompassing criminal and juvenile justice; improve the states' administration of their criminal and juvenile justice responsibilities through the development and dissemination of information to and among states. *Type:* Association.

NCJRS (National Criminal Justice Reference Service)

U.S. National Institute of Justice (NIJ)
National Criminal Justice Reference Service (NCJRS)
PO Box 6000   Ph: (301)251-5500
Rockville, MD 20849-6000
E-mail: askncjrs@aspensys.com
Desc: Contains more than 155,000 citations, with abstracts on all aspects of law enforcement, crime prevention and security, criminal justice, and juvenile justice. Topics covered range from arson to victimization, and source materials covered range from preliminary research to detailed descriptions of successful programs. *Available:* The Dialog Corporation, DIALOG; The Dialog Corporation, DIALOG. *Type:* Database.

Offender Aid and Restoration U.S.A.

One North Third St., Ste. 200   Ph: (804)643-2746
Richmond, VA 23219   Fax: (804)643-1187
Contact: Barbara A. Slayden, Exec.Dir.
Desc: Operates 9 Offender Aid and Restoration (OAR) programs in 5 states. Mission of OAR is to promote, develop, and operate community-based alternatives to incarceration in order to make the criminal justice system more just and effective. Brings citizen volunteers into jails, diverts offenders from jails and prisons, and helps restore them to the community. *Type:* Association.

Prison-Ashram Project

Rte. 1, Box 201-N   Ph: (919)304-2220
Durham, NC 27705   Fax: (919)304-3220
URL: http://www.humankindness.org
Contact: Bo Lozoff, Dir.
Desc: Prisoners and their families, prison staff and volunteers, handicapped shut-ins, and interested individuals. Provides encouragement and advice to prisoners and other shut-ins who want to use their time in spiritual training. Believes "if one is tired enough of being a prison inmate, then he or she can live instead as a prison monk or nun, using the cloistered lifestyle, the regular hours, the inaccessibility of friends, distractions, or entertainment, to one's advantage just as in an ashram." (An ashram is an institution similar to a monastery, except that most residents stay for a brief period of time.) Sponsors book projects to help subscribers find specific titles or books on general areas of spiritual study. *Type:* Association.

Prison Fellowship International

PO Box 17500   Ph: (703)481-0000
Washington, DC 20041   Fax: (703)481-0003
E-mail: info@pfi.org
URL: http://www.pfi.org
Contact: Ronald W. Nikkel, Pres./CEO.
Desc: National Prison Fellowship organizations devoted to holistic Christian ministry in prisons and welfare communities for prisoners, ex-prisoners, victims, and their families. Promotes restorative justice in the criminal justice system and assists in implementing effective alternatives to incarceration. Offers consultation and assistance in developing additional Prison Fellowship movements. *Type:* Association.

Prison Fellowship Ministries

PO Box 17500   Ph: (703)478-0100
Washington, DC 20041   Fax: (703)318-0235
URL: http://www.pfm.org
Contact: Charles Colson, Chmn.
Desc: Encourages Christians to work in prisons and to assist communities in ministering to prisoners, ex-offenders, victims, and their families. Works towards a fair and effective criminal justice system. Trains volunteers for in-prison ministries. *Type:* Association.

Prison Fellowship Ministries of Northern New England

PO Box 1079   Ph: (603)672-2033
Amherst, NH 03031   Fax: (603)672-2033
Contact: Charles W. Colson, Chm.
Desc: Individuals committed to sharing the gospel with prisoners, ex-prisoners, their families and crime victims. Assists churches in ministry to prisoners and promotes biblical standards of justice in criminal justice system. *Type:* Association.

Prisoners' Rights Union

Executive Director
PO Box 1019   Ph: (916)441-4214
Sacramento, CA 95812-1019   Fax: (916)441-4297
Contact: Mark Meyers, Dir.
Desc: Dedicated to educating prisoners, parolees, their families, friends, advocates and society that prisoners are people and what rights prisoners do have, where to find them and how to enforce them. *Type:* Association.

Rehabilitation Research Foundation

Box 1425   Ph: (573)874-8791
Columbia, MO 65205-1425   Fax: (314)874-0814
Contact: Dr. Earl-Clayton Grandstaff, Sr., Exec. Officer.
Desc: Plans, funds, and evaluates innovative programs in the areas of prison reform, offender re-socialization, and mental health. Acts as consultant to governments (national, state, local, and foreign) and private agencies and societies. Holds retreats. *Type:* Association.

USCCCN National Clearinghouse on Satanic Crime in America

PO Box 1092   Ph: (732)226-8767
South Orange, NJ 07079   Fax: (732)226-8767
E-mail: ncscia@aol.com
URL: http://www.bigfoot.com/~AmericanFocus
Contact: Dr. Alan Peterson, Exec.Dir.
Desc: Educates the public on satanic and occult-related crimes and criminal activities being perpetrated against humans and animals. Disseminates information and intelligence to law enforcement, criminal justice, corrections, clergy, educators, citizens and others through publications, audiobooks, videos, computer software, seminars, workshops, conventions, training programs, and radio, television, and internet programming. Sponsors speakers' bureau; operates referral service. *Type:* Association.

Weekly Criminal Bulletin

Canada Law Book Inc.
240 Edward St.   Ph: (905)841-6472
Aurora, ON, Canada L4G 3S9
URL: http://www.canadalawbook.com
Desc: Contains more than 35,900 summaries of judgments in criminal cases tried in the federal and provincial courts in Canada. Includes cases tried under the Criminal Code, Combines Investigation Act, Competition Act, Narcotics Control Act, and the Young Offenders Act. *Available:* QL Systems Limited, QUICKLAW; LEXIS-NEXIS. *Type:* Database.

WESTLAW® Criminal Justice

West Group
620 Opperman Dr.   Ph: (651)687-7000
St. Paul, MN 55164-0526
URL: http://www.westgroup.com
Desc: Contains the complete text of U.S. federal court decisions, statutes and regulations, state court decisions, specialized sources, and texts and periodicals dealing with criminal law, including the nature, investigation, prosecution, and punishment of crimes. *Available:* West Group, WESTLAW. *Type:* Database.

Women's Prison Association

110 2nd Ave.   Ph: (212)674-1163
New York, NY 10003   Fax: (212)677-1981
Contact: Ann L. Jacobs, Exec.Dir.
Desc: Service agency that aids women involved in the criminal justice system and their families. *Type:* Association.

Cycling

Adventure Cycling Association

150 E. Pine   Ph: (406)721-1776
PO Box 8308   Free: 800-755-2453
Missoula, MT 59807   Fax: (406)721-8754
E-mail: acabike@adv-cycling.org
URL: http://www.adv-cycling.org
Contact: Gary MacFadden, Exec.Dir.
Desc: Present focus is on the research, maintenance, and mapping of over 20,000 miles of bicycle touring and mountain biking routes. *Type:* Association.

American Bicycle Association

PO Box 718   Ph: (602)961-1903
Chandler, AZ 85244   Free: 800-878-7453
     Fax: (602)961-1842
Contact: Clayton John, Pres.
Desc: Bicycle Motocross (BMX) racing enthusiasts. Sanctions thousands of local races across the U.S.; administers 20 national competitions each year. Maintains library; bestows award. *Type:* Association.

Bicycling

Rodale Books
400 S. 10th St.   Ph: (610)967-5171
Emmaus, PA 18098-0099   Fax: (610)967-7722
E-mail: ddonche1@rodalepress.com; bicmaydm@aol.com.
URL: http://www.rodalepress.com
Contact: Ed Pavelka, Executive Editor; Mike Greehan, Publisher; Bill Strickland, Managing Editor; Geoff Drake, Editor; Pat Ritter, Advertising Mgr.; Jim Delash, Circulation Mgr.; Debbie Welch, Office Mgr.
Desc: World's largest magazine about bicycle riding and equipment. *Type:* Periodical.

International Mountain Bicycling Association

PO Box 7578   Ph: (303)545-9011
Boulder, CO 80306   Fax: (303)545-9026
E-mail: imba@aol.com
URL: http://www.imba.com
Contact: Tim Blumenthal, Exec.Dir.
Desc: Seeks to provide a positive image for all mountain bikers. Works to keep existing trails open and helps to create new trail riding opportunities. *Type:* Association.

International Randonneurs

Old Engine House No. 2   Ph: (315)471-2101
727 N. Salina St.   Fax: (315)471-5994
Syracuse, NY 13208
E-mail: konengr@worldnet.att.net
Contact: James L. Konski, Exec. Officer.
Desc: Amateur long-distance bicyclists. Promotes bicycling and challenges members to achieve higher speeds and greater distances. *Type:* Association.

League of American Bicyclists

1612 K St. NW, Ste 401   Ph: (202)822-1333
Washington, DC 20006   Free: 800-288-BIKE
Contact: Jody Newman, Pres.
Desc: Bicyclists and bicycle clubs. Promotes bicycling for recreation and transportation as well as bicyclists' rights to the roads; exchanges information, adventures, enthusiasm, and news about events, equipment, and leading personalities in the world of bicycling. Sponsors the Effective Cycling Program, in which volunteer instructors teach others to bicycle competently on the roads. *Type:* Association.

Mountain Bike

Rodale Books
400 S. 10th St.   Ph: (610)967-5171
Emmaus, PA 18098-0099   Fax: (610)967-7722
E-mail: ddonche1@rodalepress.com
URL: http://www.rodalepress.com; mtnbikedm@aol.com.
Contact: Nelson Pena, Publisher.
Desc: Riding techniques and product information for the mountain bike enthusiast. *Type:* Periodical.

Mountain Bike Action

Daisy/Hi-Torque Publishing Co., Inc.
25233 Anca Dr.   Ph: (805)295-1910
Valencia, CA 91355   Free: 800-767-0345
     Fax: (805)295-1278
Contact: Jody Weisel, Editor; R.S. Hinz, Publisher; Scott Wallenberg, Advertising Mgr.
Desc: Magazine on off-road bicycling. *Type:* Periodical.

National Bicycle League

3958 Brown Park Dr., Ste. D   Ph: (614)777-1625
Hilliard, OH 43026   Fax: (614)777-1680
E-mail: nbl@iwaynet.net
URL: http://www.nbl.org
Contact: Bob Tedesco, CEO.

Desc: BMX racers. (BMX stands for bicycle motocross, a race of unmotorized bicycles on a tight course of 600 to 1000 ft. over natural terrain that includes steep hills, sharp turns, and jumps.) Objective is to establish rules and regulations for BMX races. *Type:* Association.

Outspokin'

National Bicycle Dealers
2240 University Dr. No. 130   Ph: (714)722-6909
Newport Beach, CA 92660-3319
Contact: Fred Clements, Editor.
Desc: Offers bicycle retailing and management tips, and provides consumer survey results. Recurring features include Association and industry news. *Type:* Newsletter.

Tandem Club of America

Jack and Susan Goertz
2220 Vanessa Dr.   Ph: (205)991-7766
Birmingham, AL 35242   Fax: (205)991-7766
E-mail: tca_of_a@mindspring.com
Contact: Bruce and Judi Bachelder, Treas.
Desc: Tandem bicycling teams. Seeks to form network of tandem bicyclists and promote information exchange on tandems, exercise, appreciation of the environment, and companionship. *Type:* Association.

United States Cycling Federation

USOC
1 Olympic Plz.   Ph: (719)578-4581
Colorado Springs, CO 80909   Fax: (719)578-4596
Contact: Lisa Voight, Exec.Dir.
Desc: Governing body of amateur cycling in the United States. Supervises and controls all amateur bicycle competitions; promotes safety education of bicyclists. Sponsors national championships. *Type:* Association.

VeloNews Race Coverage

Great Outdoors.com
611 S. Congress Ave., Ste. 350   Ph: (512)416-5043
Austin, TX 78704
E-mail: info@greatoutdoors.com
URL: http://www.greatoutdoors.com/velonews/race/
Desc: This site provides data concerning races of all types from around the world. The coverage includes a calendar of events, maps, routes, profiles on the riders and drivers, and lore from past races. *Type:* Database.

Dairy

ADGA News & Events

American Dairy Goat Association
PO Box 865   Ph: (828)286-3801
Spindale, NC 28160   Fax: (828)287-0476
E-mail: adgajdw2@aol.com
URL: http://www.adga.org.
Contact: Shirley C. McKenzie, Communications Coordinator, adgascm@aol.com.
Desc: Covers news, events, and issues of the Association. Recurring features include a calendar of events and reports of meetings. *Type:* Newsletter.

American Dairy Association

O'Hare International Ctr.   Ph: (847)803-2000
10255 W. Higgins Rd., Ste. 900   Fax: (847)803-2077
Rosemont, IL 60018-5616
Contact: Gordon McDonald, Group Exec.
Desc: Federation of 17 regional and state dairy farmers' associations. *Type:* Association.

Cheese Importers Association of America— Bulletin

Cheese Importers Association of America, Inc.
460 Park Ave.   Ph: (212)753-7500
New York, NY 10022-1906

Desc: Provides information and statistics pertaining to the cheese importing business. *Type:* Newsletter.

Cheesemakers' Journal

Cheesemakers' Journal
PO Box 216   Fax: (413)587-0402
Northampton, MA 01061
E-mail: cheese@javanet.com
URL: http://www.cheesewizard.com.
Contact: Robert L. Carroll, Editor and Publisher.
Desc: Contains information on cheese, cheesemaking, and cheesemakers. Provides stories from around the world and resources for free information on cheese and dairy foods. *Type:* Newsletter.

Dairy Council Digest

National Dairy Council
10255 W. Higgins Rd., No.   Ph: (847)803-2000
  900   Free: 800-426-8271
Rosemont, IL 60018
URL: http://www.nationaldairycouncil.org.
Contact: Lois McBean, Editor.
Desc: Reviews and interprets recent nutrition research. Recurring features include single-topic research articles, with bibliographies, and abstracts of scientific articles. *Type:* Newsletter.

Dairy and Food Industries Supply Association— Regulatory Update

Dairy and Food Industries Supply Association, Inc. (DFISA)
1451 Dolley Madison Blvd.   Ph: (703)761-2600
Mc Lean, VA 22101-3850   Fax: (703)761-4334
E-mail: info@dfisa.org
Desc: Reports on regulatory activities of the Federal Government that affect the dairy and food processing industries. Recurring features include reports of meetings. *Type:* Newsletter.

Dairy Industry Statistics

California Agricultural Statistics Service
U.S. Department of Agriculture (USDA)
PO Box 1258   Ph: (916)654-0895
Sacramento, CA 95812
Desc: Features information on California's manufactured dairy products, milk production, utilization, and prices. *Type:* Newsletter.

Dairy Information Bulletin

California Agricultural Statistics Service
U.S. Department of Agriculture (USDA)
PO Box 1258   Ph: (916)654-0895
Sacramento, CA 95812
Desc: Reports on California's dairy industry. Features news on the commercial production, utilization, and sales of milk. *Type:* Newsletter.

Dairy Report

Dairy Report
Queens Park   Ph: (416)326-3221
Legislative Bldg.   Fax: (416)326-9892
Toronto, ON, Canada M7A
  1B6
Contact: Cyril Fernandes, Editor.
Desc: Provides news of the dairy industry in Ontario. Includes information on milk use, production of dairy products, prices, and milk shipments. *Type:* Newsletter.

Dairy Today

Farm Journal, Inc.
Centre Square W.   Ph: (215)557-8900
1500 Market St., 28th Fl.   Free: 800-523-1538
Philadelphia, PA 19102-2148   Fax: (215)568-4238
E-mail: dairytoday@aol.com
URL: http://www.dairytoday.com.
Contact: Jim Dickrell, Editor; Roger D. Randall, President, (215)557-8932, rrandall@farmjournal.com; Jerry Gunderson, Publisher, (215)557-5769, jgunderson@farmjournal.com.
Desc: Agricultural magazine for dairy managers and producers. *Alt. Contact:* PO Box 1167, 261 East Broadway, Monticello, MN 55362; telephone: (612)271-3363; fax: (612)271-3360. *Type:* Periodical.

Hoard's Dairyman

W.D. Hoard & Sons Co.
28 West Milwaukee Ave.   Ph: (920)563-5551
Fort Atkinson, WI 53538   Fax: (920)563-7298
E-mail: hoards@hoards.com; hoards@intaccess.com.
Contact: William D. Knox, Editor and Publisher; Gary L. Vorpahl, Advertising Mgr.
Desc: Tabloid. *Type:* Periodical.

IAFIS Reporter

International Association of Food Industry Suppliers
1451 Dolley Madison Blvd.   Ph: (703)761-2600
Mc Lean, VA 22101-3850   Fax: (703)761-4334
E-mail: info@iafis.org
URL: http://www.iafis.org.
Contact: Mary G. O'Dea, Editor, modea@iafis.org.
Desc: Concerned with dairy and food industry suppliers. Recurring features include reports on meetings of the Association, news of members, and business columns on growth and development. *Type:* Newsletter.

Ice Cream Reporter

Find/SVP
625 6th Ave.   Ph: (212)645-4500
New York, NY 10011   Free: 800-FIN-DSVP
                                Fax: (212)645-7681
E-mail: infoadvisor@findsvp.com
URL: http://www.findsvp.com/.
Contact: Howard Waxman, Editor.
Desc: Covers ice cream and related product industries, including information on new products, mergers and acquisitions, legislation, sales, marketing, research and development, distribution, and packaging. Recurring features include a column titled Last Licks. *Type:* Newsletter.

International Association of Food Industry Suppliers

1451 Dolley Madison Blvd.   Ph: (703)761-2600
Mc Lean, VA 22101-3850   Fax: (703)761-4334
E-mail: info@iafis.org
URL: http://www.iafis.org
Contact: Charlie Bray, CAE, Pres.
Desc: Manufacturers and distributors of dairy and food processing and packaging equipment, machinery, ingredients, and supplies. *Type:* Association.

Michigan Milk Messenger

Michigan Milk Producers Association (MMPA)
PO Box 8002   Ph: (810)474-6672
Novi, MI 48376-8002   Fax: (810)474-0924
Contact: Laura Moser, Editor.
Desc: Reports on developments of the Association in marketing and the dairy farming industry. *Type:* Newsletter.

National Dairy Shrine

Maurice E. Core
1224 Alton Darby Creek Rd.   Ph: (614)878-5333
Columbus, OH 43228-9792   Fax: (614)870-2622
E-mail: cobass@aol.com
URL: http://www.dairyshrine.org
Contact: Maurice E. Core, Exec.Dir.
Desc: Persons interested in the dairy industry, including cattle breeders and educators. Maintains portrait gallery and museum in Ft. Atkinson, WI "to honor great dairymen of the past, recognize great dairymen of the present, and inspire dairy leaders of the future." *Type:* Association.

National Milk Producers Federation

2101 Wilson Blvd., Suite 400   Ph: (703)243-6111
Arlington, VA 22201   Fax: (703)841-9328
E-mail: nmpf@aol.com
URL: http://www.nmpf.org
Contact: Jerry Kozak, CEO.
Desc: Federation of 30 dairy cooperatives representing the major portion of all milk marketed by farmers. *Type:* Association.

News for Dairy Co-Ops

National Milk Producers Federation
2101 Wilson Blvd., 4th Fl.   Ph: (703)243-6111
Arlington, VA 22201   Fax: (703)841-9328
E-mail: nmpf@aol.com
Contact: Christopher Galen, Editor, CGalen@nmpf.org.
Desc: Highlights dairy issues and Federation activities. *Type:* Newsletter.

Tech News Quarterly

American Dairy Products Institute
300 W. Washington St., Ste.   Ph: (312)782-4888
  400   Fax: (312)782-5299
Chicago, IL 60606-1756
E-mail: adpi@flash.net
Desc: Provides abstracts of articles of current research in the dairy science field. *Type:* Newsletter.

3-A Progress Report

International Association of Food Industry Suppliers
1451 Dolley Madison Blvd.   Ph: (703)761-2600
Mc Lean, VA 22101-3850   Fax: (703)761-4334
E-mail: info@iafis.org; pshort@iafis.org.
Contact: Thomas M. Gilmore, Editor, tgilmore@iafis.org.
Desc: Follows the activities of the 3-A Sanitary Standards Committees. *Type:* Newsletter.

United States National Dairy Database

The University of Maryland
College Park, MD 20742   Ph: (301)405-1000
E-mail: inforM-editor@umail.umd.edu
URL: http://www.inform.umd.edu/EdRes/Topic/AgrEnv/ndd/dcow.html
Contact: Mark Varner, Extension Dairy Scientist, varner@umd5.umd.edu.
Desc: This no-frills database is a wealth of information for the dairy farmer, cattle rancher, extension agent, or agriculturalist. You can find full-text reports, fact sheets, and technical details on a wide range of subjects critical to a dairy operation, including cattle care and well-being, animal health and nutrition, business management, marketing, new technologies, and other subjects. *Type:* Database.

Weekly Insiders Dairy & Egg Letter
Urner Barry Publications, Inc.
Box 389   Ph: (732)240-5330
Toms River, NJ 08754   Free: 800-932-0617
                                          Fax: (732)341-0891
E-mail: mail@urnerbarry.com
Contact: Richard A. Brown, Editor.
Desc: Provides market information and statistics on egg and dairy products. *Type:* Newsletter.

Dance

American Ballet Competition
2000 Hamilton, Ste. C200   Ph: (215)636-9000
Philadelphia, PA 19130   Free: 800-523-0961
                                          Fax: (215)829-0508
E-mail: rswartz001@aol.com
Contact: F. Randolph Swartz, Exec.Dir.
Desc: Committee established to select and prepare the U.S. team for participation in the annual International Ballet Competition (the "Olympics of Dance"). *Type:* Association.

American Dance Festival
Box 90772   Ph: (919)684-6402
Durham, NC 27708-0772   Fax: (919)684-5459
E-mail: adfnc@acpub.duke.edu
Contact: Allison Savicz, Pres.
Desc: A modern dance producing and service organization for modern dancers and modern dance choreographers. Seeks to create greater public awareness of the field of modern dance and its particular needs. Sponsors American and foreign artists performing in the U.S. *Type:* Association.

Ballet Theatre Foundation
890 Broadway   Ph: (212)477-3030
New York, NY 10003-1278   Fax: (212)254-5938
URL: http://www.abt.org
Contact: Michael Kaiser, Exec. Dir.
Desc: Parent organization of American Ballet Theatre. Offers special events, open rehearsals, priority ticket buying, and telephone reservations for members. ABT consists of 75 dancers, conducts an annual national tour, has toured overseas, and maintains a repertoire of more than 100 classic, contemporary, humorous, serious, story, and abstract ballets. *Type:* Association.

Country Dance and Song Society
132 Main St.   Ph: (413)268-7426
P.O. Box 338   Fax: (413)268-7471
Haydenville, MA 01039-0338
E-mail: office@cdss.org
URL: http://www.cdss.org
Contact: Bradley R. Foster, Dir.
Desc: Amateur and professional musicians; dance historians. Promotes modern use of English and Angelo-American folk dances, songs, and music. *Type:* Association.

Dance Educators of America
PO Box 607   Ph: (914)636-3200
Pelham, NY 10803-0607   Free: 800-229-3868
                                          Fax: (914)636-5895
E-mail: dancedea@aol.com
URL: http://www.deadance.com
Contact: Vickie Sheer, Exec.Dir.
Desc: Qualified dance teachers who pass an examination and subscribe to a code of ethics and advertising rules and regulations. Works to further and promote the education of teachers in the performing arts and stage arts and of dance in all its forms. *Type:* Association.

Dance Masters of America
PO Box 610533   Ph: (718)225-4013
Bayside, NY 11361-0533   Fax: (718)225-4293
Contact: Robert Mann, Sec.
Desc: Dance teachers. Seeks to further the art of teaching dance. Sponsors: Performing Arts Competition Scholarship Auditions, Miss Dance of America Pageant, and Mr. *Type:* Association.

International Tap Association
PO Box 356   Ph: (303)443-7989
Boulder, CO 80306   Fax: (303)449-7732
E-mail: intertap@concentric.net
URL: http://www.tapdance.org/
Contact: Jacqueline K. Szablewski, Program Dir.
Desc: Tap dancers, choreographers, teachers, scholars, students, and interested individuals. Promotes the understanding, preservation, and development of tap dance as an art form. *Type:* Association.

National Dance Association
1900 Association Dr.   Ph: (703)476-3436
Reston, VA 20191-1599   Fax: (703)476-9527
E-mail: nda@aahpend.org
Contact: Dr. Jane Bonbright, Exec. Dir.
Desc: Dance educators, choreographers, schools and dance/arts administrators, researchers, performers, dance medicine/science specialists, technologists, therapists and others associated with dance/arts education. Works with 140 federal and state agencie, arts and education associations, foundations, and businesses and corporations to ensure that: (1) quality dance/arts education is available to all Americans regardless of age, sex, ability, interest, or culture; and (2) quality dance/arts education becomes a part of U.S. education for all children. *Type:* Association.

National Dance Institute
594 Broadway, Rm. 805   Ph: (212)226-0083
New York, NY 10012   Fax: (212)226-0761
Contact: Ellen Wrinstein, Artistic Dir.
Desc: Participants are students in 18 public and private schools in New York City and northern New Jersey. Seeks to introduce dance as a catalyst for all the arts as part of the school curriculum to promote individual development and build self-esteem. Teaches weekly dance classes to young children to enable them to experience the challenge and joy of the arts. *Type:* Association.

National Square Dance Convention
2936 Bella Vista   Ph: (405)732-6796
Midwest City, OK 73110
Contact: Howard B. Thornton, Dir. of Info.
Desc: Liaison organization of square dance clubs and dancers. Principal activity is sponsorship of the convention which includes: square and round dancing; folk dancing; contra and old-time dancing. *Type:* Association.

Sacred Dance Guild
201 Hewitt   Ph: (618)457-8603
Carbondale, IL 62901
Contact: Joan Flanigan, Pres.
Desc: Students, directors, dancers, choreographers, sponsors and others interested in dance. Works to stimulate interest in dance as a religious art form and to provide a means of communication and training for dance choirs. Supports and encourages workshops. *Type:* Association.

United Square Dancers of America
Jim Weber
1316 Middlebrook Dr.
Liberty, MO 64068   Ph: (816)781-3598
E-mail: usda@usda.org
Contact: Jim Weber, Information & Publications.

Desc: Square dancers united to provide a forum for integration between dancers and leaders. Represents dancer's views to callers, instructors, commercial enterprises, national and international organizations, and other dancers. *Type:* Association.

United States Amateur Ballroom Dancers Association
PO Box 128   Ph: (717)235-6656
New Freedom, PA 17349   Free: 800-447-9047
                                          Fax: (717)235-4183
E-mail: usabdacent@aol.com
URL: http://www.usabda.org
Contact: Mary Schaufert, Central Office Mgr.
Desc: Individuals interested in participating in or observing amateur ballroom dancing. Promotes ballroom dancing as an amateur social recreational activity and competitive sport at local and national levels. *Type:* Association.

World Congress of Teachers of Dancing
United States National Institute of Dance
38 S. Arlington Ave.   Ph: (201)673-9225
PO Box 245
East Orange, NJ 07019
Contact: Trevor Cox, Dir.
Desc: A division of the United States National Institute of Dance . Colleges, universities, professional dance schools, and teachers of dancing. Seeks to maintain global standards of excellence in dance. *Type:* Association.

Darts

American Darts Organization
PO Box 2203   Ph: (714)827-2472
Anaheim, CA 92814
E-mail: darts@infohwy.com
URL: http://www.cyberdarts.com/ado/index.html
Contact: Katie Harris, Sec.
Desc: Dart players, manufacturers, and suppliers. Purpose is to promote the sport of darts. *Type:* Association.

AMOA National Dart Association
Leslie Murphy
5613 W. 74th St.   Free: 800-808-9884
Indianapolis, IN 46278-1753   Fax: (317)387-0999
URL: http://www.nda.org
Contact: Leslie Murphy, Exec.Dir.
Desc: Sport associations; manufacturers and vendors. Acts as sanctioning body for the sport of electronic darting. *Type:* Association.

U.S. Darting Association
282 N. Henry St.   Ph: (718)389-7755
Brooklyn, NY 11222   Fax: (718)389-8445
Contact: Robert T. McLeod, Pres.
Desc: Dedicated to the advancement of serious darting. Activities include tournaments and league coordination. Compiles statistics. *Type:* Association.

Defense

Alliance Defense Fund
PO Box 54370   Ph: (602)953-1200
Phoenix, AZ 85028   Free: 800-835-5233
                                          Fax: (602)953-5630
E-mail: aesaaf@azlink.com
Contact: Alan E. Sears, Pres.
Desc: Works to promote religious civil liberties, sanctity of life and family values. *Type:* Association.

American Defense Institute

1055 N. Fairfax St., 2nd Fl. Ph: (703)519-7000
Alexandria, VA 22314 Fax: (703)519-6392
E-mail: ebml@americandefinst.org
Contact: Robert D. Thompson, Dir. of Programs.
Desc: Non-partisan public policy foundation promoting a strong national defense. *Type:* Association.

Atlantic Trade Report & Global Defense Industry

Bergerac International, Ltd.
4431 Broad Run Church Rd. Ph: (540)349-2922
Warrenton, VA 20187 Fax: (540)349-9161
Contact: Jean-Loup R. Combemale, Editor.
Desc: Deals with trade and the global defense industry. Recurring features include interviews, news of research, calendar of events, reports of meetings, and notices of publications available. *Type:* Newsletter.

Carroll's Defense Industry Charts

Carroll Publishing
4701 Sangamore Rd., No. S155 Ph: (301)263-9800
Bethesda, MD 20816 Free: 800-336-4240
 Fax: (301)263-9801
E-mail: custsvc@carrollpub.com
URL: http://www.carrolpub.com; http://www.carrollpub.com.
Contact: Mary Maloof, Editor.
Desc: In organizational chart form (175 charts), more than 100 companies and 9,000 of their executives responsible for nearly 85% of total Department of Defense (DoD) contract awards. *Type:* Directory.

Council for Inter-American Security Foundation

L. Francis Bouchey
1700 K St. NW, Ste. 650 Ph: (202)296-3712
Washington, DC 20006 Fax: (202)296-3786
Contact: L. Francis Bouchey, Pres.
Desc: Persons interested in defense and foreign policy issues pertaining to the Western Hemisphere. Purpose is to broaden cross-cultural understanding and cooperation among non-Marxist, political, academic, and private sector leaders throughout the Americas; to promote U.S. policies conducive to freedom and security of the Western Hemisphere. *Type:* Association.

Daily Defense News Capsules

United Communications Group
11300 Rockville Pike, Suite Ph: (301)816-8950
1100
Rockville, MD 20852
E-mail: joshcohen@ucg.com
URL: http://www.ucg.com
Desc: Contains the complete text of Periscope--Daily Defense News Capsules, providing abstracts of international press coverage of military and defense news. Sources include newswires and major news publications worldwide. *Available:* United Communications Group, PERISCOPE. *Type:* Database.

Defense & Aerospace Electronics

Pasha Publications, Inc.
1600 Wilson Blvd., Ste. 600 Ph: (703)528-1244
Arlington, VA 22209
E-mail: superfnd@psha.com
URL: http://www.207.197.196.194
Desc: Contains the complete text of Defense & Aerospace Electronics, a biweekly newsletter on technical, budgetary, and commercial developments in the design and procurement of military command control and communications systems. *Available:* LEXIS-NEXIS, NEXIS; LEXIS-NEXIS, NEXIS. *Type:* Database.

DMS/FI Market Intelligence Reports

Forecast International Inc./DMS
22 Commerce Rd. Ph: (203)426-0800
Newtown, CT 06470
E-mail: sales@forecast1.com
URL: http://www.forecast1.com
Contact: Monty Nebinger, Data Products Manager.
Desc: Contains the complete text of more than 11,000 reports published in the Annual Marketing Services series published by Forecast International Inc./DMS. Covers activities within the aerospace and defense industries worldwide. *Available:* The Dialog Corporation, DIALOG. *Type:* Database.

Inter-American Defense Board

2600 16th St. NW Ph: (202)939-6600
Washington, DC 20441 Fax: (202)939-6620
Contact: Maj.Gen. John Thompson, Chm.
Desc: Government-appointed military officers and advisers of North, Central, and South America. Studies and recommends measures concerning the collective self-defense of the American continent and the standardization of military organizations and operations. Promotes close military collaboration among governments of the Western Hemisphere. *Type:* Association.

International Defense Review

Jane's Information Group
1340 Braddock Pl., Ste. 300 Ph: (703)683-3700
Alexandria, VA 22314-1657
E-mail: info@janes.com
URL: http://www.janes.com
Contact: Rahul Belani, Information Technology Manager, (703)683-3700, fax: (800)836-0297, info@janes.com.
Desc: Contains the complete text of International Defense Review, a monthly magazine covering technical and strategic developments in air, land, and naval defense systems. Includes announcements of international contract awards and requests for proposals, and reviews of major defense programs by status and country. *Available:* Bell & Howell Information and Learning; The Dialog Corporation, DIALOG; Dow Jones Interactive Publishing; NewsEdge Corporation; LEXIS-NEXIS; Profound Inc., The Dialog Corporation. *Type:* Database.

Jane's All the World's Aircraft

Jane's Information Group
1340 Braddock Pl., Ste. 300 Ph: (703)683-3700
Alexandria, VA 22314-1657
E-mail: info@janes.com
URL: http://www.janes.com
Desc: Contains the complete text, including images, of Jane's All the World's Aircraft, covering all aspects of commercial and military aircraft in production or under development. Covers aircraft, aero engines, sport aircraft, microlights, sailplanes, hang gliders, airships, balloons, first flights, and official records for commercial, private, and military organizations in 49 countries. *Available:* Jane's Information Group. *Type:* Database.

Jane's Armory & Artillery Upgrades

Jane's Information Group
1340 Braddock Pl., Ste. 300 Ph: (703)683-3700
Alexandria, VA 22314-1657
E-mail: info@janes.com
URL: http://www.janes.com
Contact: Rahul Belani, info@Janes.com.
Desc: Contains the complete text of Jane's Armour & Artillery Upgrades, covering all aspects of modernizing subsystems and upgrades for land-based armored vehicles and machinery in production or under development. Covers co-axial machine guns, vehicle mounted anti-tank guided

weapons, automatic loaders, ammunition, armor systems, smoke dischargers, grenades and decoys, laser detectors, fire detection and suppression, engines, transmissions, powerpacks, mobility, tracks, suspensions, turrets and cupolas, weapon control and stabilization systems, fire control systems, land navigation systems, laser rangefinders, and sighting systems. *Available:* Jane's Information Group. *Type:* Database.

Jane's Armour and Artillery

Jane's Information Group
1340 Braddock Pl., Ste. 300 Ph: (703)683-3700
Alexandria, VA 22314-1657
E-mail: info@janes.com
URL: http://www.janes.com
Contact: Rahul Belani, (703)683-3700, fax: (800)836-0297, info@Janes.com.
Desc: Contains the complete text of Jane's Armour & Artillery, covering all aspects of land-based weapons and defense systems in production or under development. Covers self-propelled and towed field artillery systems, multiple rocket systems, coastal defense weapons, guns, missiles, private venture vehicles, and inventories of systems by country. *Available:* Jane's Information Group. *Type:* Database.

Jane's Avionics

Jane's Information Group
1340 Braddock Pl., Ste. 300 Ph: (703)683-3700
Alexandria, VA 22314-1657
E-mail: info@janes.com
URL: http://www.janes.com
Desc: Contains the complete text of Jane's Avionics, covering all aspects of electronic equipment and systems installed in civilian and military aircraft, in production, or under development. Covers more than 2700 products, including cockpit instruments and multi-mode radars. *Available:* Jane's Information Group. *Type:* Database.

Jane's C4I Systems

Jane's Information Group
1340 Braddock Pl., Ste. 300 Ph: (703)683-3700
Alexandria, VA 22314-1657
E-mail: info@janes.com
URL: http://www.janes.com
Desc: Contains the complete text of Jane's C4I Systems, covering all aspects of command, control, communications, and intelligence equipment and systems (more than 1000) in production or under development. Covers multiservice national, bilateral, multinational, and single-service programs, command information systems, communications networks, and intelligence gathering systems. *Available:* Jane's Information Group. *Type:* Database.

Jane's Electro-Optics Systems

Jane's Information Group
1340 Braddock Pl., Ste. 300 Ph: (703)683-3700
Alexandria, VA 22314-1657
E-mail: info@janes.com
URL: http://www.janes.com
Desc: Contains the complete text of Jane's Electro-Optics Systems, covering all aspects of more than 500 airborne, land-based, and naval surveillance equipment and systems in production or under development from more than 200 developers. Covers electro-optical surveillance, optical surveillance, target tracking and marking, land-based remotely placed systems, surveillance and reconnaisance radar, acoustic systems, fixed-wing target location and marking systems, helicopter sighting, observation and marking systems, image processing and interpretation, and aircraft launchers and control systems. *Available:* Jane's Information Group. *Type:* Database.

Jane's Fighting Ships
Jane's Information Group
1340 Braddock Pl., Ste. 300   Ph: (703)683-3700
Alexandria, VA 22314-1657
E-mail: info@janes.com
URL: http://www.janes.com
Desc: Contains the complete text and images of Jane's Fighting Ships, covering all aspects of military ships in production or under development. Covers more than 8000 major warships by number and class name, building program, hull, weapon systems, aircraft, modernization, structure, operational details, and sales. *Available:* Jane's Information Group. *Type:* Database.

Jane's Infantry Weapons
Jane's Information Group
1340 Braddock Pl., Ste. 300   Ph: (703)683-3700
Alexandria, VA 22314-1657
E-mail: info@janes.com
URL: http://www.janes.com
Desc: Contains the complete text of Jane's Infantry Weapons, covering all aspects of land-based weaponry in production or under development. Covers more than 1700 weapons accessories from 252 manufacturers in 69 manufacturing countries; includes pistols, submachine guns, rifles, small arms ammunition, light support weapons, body armor, grenades, mortars, and anti-tank weapons. *Available:* Jane's Information Group. *Type:* Database.

Jane's Land-Based Air Defence
Jane's Information Group
1340 Braddock Pl., Ste. 300   Ph: (703)683-3700
Alexandria, VA 22314-1657
E-mail: info@janes.com
URL: http://www.janes.com
Desc: Contains the complete text of Jane's Land-Based Air Defence, covering all aspects of stationary and mobile military defense systems in production or under development in more than 126 countries worldwide. Covers surface-to-air missiles, anti-aircraft systems, sights for installation on towed anti-aircraft guns, and inventories of systems by country. *Available:* Jane's Information Group. *Type:* Database.

Jane's Military Communications
Jane's Information Group
1340 Braddock Pl., Ste. 300   Ph: (703)683-3700
Alexandria, VA 22314-1657
E-mail: info@janes.com
URL: http://www.janes.com
Desc: Contains the complete text of Jane's Military Communications, covering all aspects of communications equipment and systems in production or under development. Covers more than 4000 items of equipment from nearly 200 manufacturers in 30 countries; includes radio communications, including satellite systems and equipment, air force and navy systems and equipment, terrestrial microwave and tropospheric scatter equipment, and ground-based and tactical ground systems, as well as line communications and message switching; data transmission and reception, modems, and terminals; encryption and security; electronic warfare surveillance and signal analysis, direction finding, and jamming; FAX; audio ancillaries; antennas and masts antenna tables; test and measurement; and laser and optical equipment. *Available:* Jane's Information Group. *Type:* Database.

Jane's Military Vehicles and Logistics
Jane's Information Group
1340 Braddock Pl., Ste. 300   Ph: (703)683-3700
Alexandria, VA 22314-1657
E-mail: info@janes.com
URL: http://www.janes.com
Desc: Contains the complete text of Jane's Military Vehicles and Logistics, covering maintenance, movement, and procurement of military equipment, personnel, and supplies. Covers more than 2000 items of logistical equipment, including recovery vehicles and equipment, bridging systems, transportation systems, mines, mine laying and mine detection systems, portable roadways and railways, and shelters. *Available:* Jane's Information Group. *Type:* Database.

Jane's Radar and Electronic Warfare Systems
Jane's Information Group
1340 Braddock Pl., Ste. 300   Ph: (703)683-3700
Alexandria, VA 22314-1657
E-mail: info@janes.com
URL: http://www.janes.com
Desc: Contains the complete text of Jane's Radar & Electronic Warfare Systems, covering all aspects of land-, air-, and sea-based defense radar and electronic warfare systems in production or under development. Radar systems include international air defense systems, land-based air defense radars, battlefield and ground surveillance radars, naval surveillance and navigation radars, naval fire control radars, airborne fire control radars, IFF, ATC, instrumentation and ranging radars, spaceborne radars, passive IR detection, and simulation systems. *Available:* Jane's Information Group. *Type:* Database.

Jane's Simulation and Training Systems
Jane's Information Group
1340 Braddock Pl., Ste. 300   Ph: (703)683-3700
Alexandria, VA 22314-1657
E-mail: info@janes.com
URL: http://www.janes.com
Desc: Contains the complete text of Jane's Simulation and Training Systems, covering all aspects of military training systems in production or under development. Covers aircraft procedure trainers, air-to-air combat trainers, flight simulators, EW training systems, weapon and attack simulators, ship handling simulators, operations/command trainers, submarine steering and depth control simulators, naval target systems, damage control trainers, small arms range equipment, full caliber gunnery ranges, small arms marksmanship systems, weapon fire and effect simulators, anti-tank missile trainers, tank simulators, and crew trainers. *Available:* Jane's Information Group. *Type:* Database.

Jane's Underwater Warfare Systems
Jane's Information Group
1340 Braddock Pl., Ste. 300   Ph: (703)683-3700
Alexandria, VA 22314-1657
E-mail: info@janes.com
URL: http://www.janes.com
Desc: Contains the complete text of Jane's Underwater Warfare Systems, covering all aspects of underwater equipment and systems installed in aircraft, ships, or submarines, in production, or under development. Covers more than 700 shipborne, submarine-borne, and airborne systems for underwater warfare from 168 international manufacturers; includes mines and mine countermeasures, sonar, sonobuoys, processing and display equipment, underwater communications, ranges and targets, hydrographic systems, acoustic and electromagnetic countermeasures, oceanography, degaussing systems, and submarine electro-optics. *Available:* Jane's Information Group. *Type:* Database.

Jewish Institute for National Security Affairs
1717 K St. NW, Ste. 800   Ph: (202)543-4100
Washington, DC 20006   Fax: (202)296-6452
E-mail: clw@clw.org
URL: http://www.jinsa.org
Contact: Thomas Neumann, Exec.Dir.
Desc: Objectives are to inform the American Jewish community of "the vital necessity for an adequate American defense program"; inform the defense and national security community of the value of strategic cooperation between the U.S. and Israel. *Type:* Association.

Leonard Peltier Defense Committee
PO Box 583   Ph: (913)842-5774
Lawrence, KS 66044   Fax: (913)842-5796
E-mail: lpdc@idir.net
Contact: Lisa Faruolo, Office Mgr.
Desc: Seeks to gain justice for Leonard Peltier through promotion, education, and public speaking. *Type:* Association.

Democratic Party

College Democrats of America
Democratic National Committee
430 S. Capitol St. SE   Ph: (202)479-5189
Washington, DC 20003   Fax: (202)488-5075
E-mail: cda@democrats.org
URL: http://www.democrats.org/college_democrats
Contact: Jeff Shulman, Exec.Dir.
Desc: National chapters on college campuses comprising students, both undergraduate and graduate. Seeks to stimulate in young people an active interest in government affairs; to encourage involvement in the political process; to promote the principles of the Democratic Party; and to elect Democrats to all levels of office. *Type:* Association.

Committee for a Democratic Majority
426 C St. NE, Rear Bldg.   Ph: (202)544-4889
Washington, DC 20002
Contact: Jill Gimmel, Dir.
Desc: National political action committee formed to assist Democratic candidates in upcoming U.S. House and Senate races. *Type:* Association.

National Federation of Democratic Women
5422 2nd St. NW   Ph: (202)723-8182
Washington, DC 20011   Fax: (202)723-8182
Contact: Annette C. Jones, Pres.
Desc: Democratic women's organizations; state, local, and regional clubs; individuals. Organized to develop leadership among women locally and nationally, both as party workers and elected public officials. Goal is to unite the women of the party and to encourage full participation of women on every level of the party structure by promoting the exchange of ideas and communication. *Type:* Association.

National Rainbow Coalition
1002 Wisconsin Ave. NW   Ph: (202)333-5270
Washington, DC 20007   Fax: (202)728-1192
Contact: Rev. Jesse L. Jackson, Sr., Pres.
Desc: Promotes the creation of a better nation and world by lifting the hope of all Americans and assuring economic justice, peace, human rights, and dignity for all. Works to build a consensus in the areas of civil rights, government, politics, labor, education, religion, business, academia, the environment, health care, and other issues; provides a platform for debate at the national, state, and local levels. Encourages the development of a new political leadership committed to progressive domestic and international policies and programs, leading to a more humane society. *Type:* Association.

Young Democrats of America
Democratic National Committee
430 S. Capitol St. SE
Washington, DC 20003
URL: http://www.democrats.org/yda
Contact: Kim Kiely, Pres.
Desc: A division of the Democratic National Committee. Official youth (35 and under) organization of the Democratic party. Seeks to encourage young men and women to take an active part in politics and to become members of the Democratic party. *Type:* Association.

Dentistry

Academy of General Dentistry
211 E. Chicago Ave., Ste. 1200 Ph: (312)440-4300
Chicago, IL 60611 Fax: (312)440-0559
E-mail: agddented@agd.org
URL: http://www.agd.org
Contact: Harold E. Donnell, Jr., Exec.Dir.
Desc: Dentists dedicated to promoting the continuing education and professional development of general practitioners. *Type:* Association.

Academy of Osseointegration
401 N. Michigan Ave. Ph: (312)321-5169
Chicago, IL 60611-4267 Free: 800-656-7736
E-mail: academy@osseo.org
URL: http://www.osseo.org
Contact: Thomas Stautzenbach, Exec.Dir.
Desc: Works for the advancement of osseointegration among dentists, physicians and related professionals. *Type:* Association.

ADA News
ADA Publishing Co., Inc.
211 E. Chicago Ave. Ph: (312)440-2791
Chicago, IL 60611 Free: 800-621-8099
  Fax: (312)440-3538
E-mail: adapco@ada.org; adanews@ada.org.
Contact: Judy Jakush, Editor; Duane Billek, Advertising Sales Mgr.
Desc: Dental newspaper (tabloid). *Type:* Periodical.

Alliance of the American Dental Association
211 E. Chicago Ave., No. 918 Ph: (312)440-2865
Chicago, IL 60611 Fax: (312)440-2587
E-mail: aadaco@saol.com
URL: http://www.aadaco.com
Contact: Kathleen Cooper, Exec.Dir.
Desc: Spouses of dentists. Promotes public dental health and creates public awareness of dentistry. *Type:* Association.

Alpha Omega International Dental Fraternity
1314 Bedford Ave., Ste. 206 Ph: (410)602-3300
Baltimore, MD 21208 Free: 800-677-8468
  Fax: (410)602-3394
Contact: Stephanie Block, Exec.Dir.
Desc: Professional fraternity - dentistry. Encourages fraternalism and monitors discrimination in dental schools. Maintains the Alpha Omega Foundation, which sends funds to dental schools in Israel and the U.S. *Type:* Association.

American Academy of Pediatric Dentistry
211 E. Chicago Ave., Ste. 700 Ph: (312)337-2169
Chicago, IL 60611 Fax: (312)337-6329
URL: http://www.aapd.org
Contact: Dr. John A. Bogert, Exec.Dir.
Desc: Professional society of dentists whose practice is limited to children; teachers and researchers in pediatric dentistry. Seeks to advance the specialty of pediatric dentistry through practice, education, and research. Sponsors graduate student pediatric dentistry award program. *Type:* Association.

American Academy of Periodontology
737 N. Michigan Ave., Ste. 800 Ph: (312)787-5518
Chicago, IL 60611-2615 Fax: (312)787-3670
E-mail: dawn@perio.org
URL: http://www.perio.org
Contact: Alice DeForest, Exec.Dir.
Desc: Professional society of dentists specializing in treatment of supporting and surrounding tissues of the teeth and their diseases. *Type:* Association.

American Association for Dental Research
1619 Duke St. Ph: (703)548-0066
Alexandria, VA 22314 Fax: (703)548-1883
E-mail: research@iadv.com
URL: http://www.iadr.com
Contact: Eli Schwartz, DDS, Exec.Dir.
Desc: Dentists, researchers, dental schools, and dental products manufacturing companies. Seeks to promote better dental health and research activities. *Type:* Association.

American Association for Dental Research
1619 Duke St. Ph: (703)548-0066
Alexandria, VA 22314 Fax: (703)548-1883
E-mail: research@iadr.com
URL: http://www.iadr.com
Contact: Dr. Eli Schwarz, Exec.Dir.
Desc: Promotes the advancement of multidisciplinary research of the oral cavity, the adjacent structures, and their relation to the body as a whole. American Association for Dental Research (AADR) supports research fellows and trainees. *Type:* Research center.

American Association of Dental Schools
1625 Massachusetts Ave. NW, Ph: (202)667-9433
  Ste. 600 Fax: (202)667-0642
Washington, DC 20036
E-mail: aads@aads.jhu.edu
URL: http://www.aads.jhu.edu
Contact: Richard Valachovic, Exec.Dir.
Desc: Individuals interested in dental education; schools of dentistry, graduate dentistry, and dental auxiliary education in the U.S., Canada, and Puerto Rico; affiliated institutions of the federal government. To promote better teaching and education in dentistry and dental research and to facilitate exchange of ideas among dental educators. Sponsors meetings, conferences, and workshops; conducts surveys, studies, and special projects and publishes their results. *Type:* Association.

American Association of Dental Victims
3318 E. 7th St. Ph: (562)433-9009
Long Beach, CA 90804
Contact: Faye L. Willard, Founder.
Desc: Consumer-oriented movement composed of individuals who feel they have received improper, often harmful, treatment from dentists. Works to encourage the media to inform the public of issues that the association believes are not being addressed and to apply pressure on dentists and their supporters to improve conditions and the means of redress for injured dental patients. *Type:* Association.

American Association of Endodontists
211 E. Chicago Ave., Ste. 1100 Ph: (312)266-7255
Chicago, IL 60611 Fax: (312)266-9867
E-mail: webmaster@aae.org
URL: http://www.aae.org
Contact: Irma S. Kudo, Exec.Dir.
Desc: Endodontic specialists and other interested professionals. (Endodontics is a branch of dentistry that deals with the soft tissues inside the tooth.). Seeks to promote the exchange of ideas, to stimulate research, and to encourage the highest standard of quality care in the practice of endodontics. *Type:* Association.

American Association of Orthodontists
401 N. Lindbergh Blvd. Ph: (314)993-1700
St. Louis, MO 63141-7816 Fax: (314)997-1745
URL: http://www.aaortho.org
Contact: Ronald S. Moen, Exec.Dir.
Desc: Professional society of orthodontists. To advance the art and science of orthodontics through continuing education, encouragement of research and cooperation with other health groups. Maintains museum. *Type:* Association.

American College of Prosthodontists
211 E Chicago Ave., Ste. 1000 Ph: (312)573-1260
Chicago, IL 60611-2616 Free: 800-378-1260
  Fax: (312)573-1257
E-mail: acp@prosthodontics.org
URL: http://www.prosthodontics.org
Contact: Steve Hines, Exec.Dir.
Desc: Dentists specializing in prosthetics who are either board certified, board eligible, or under training in approved graduate or residency programs. Seeks to improve prosthodontic treatment for patients by encouraging educational activities designed to bring new ideas, techniques, and research into clinical practice. Sponsors annual prosthodontic research competition. *Type:* Association.

American Dental Assistants Association
203 N. LaSalle St., Ste. 1320 Ph: (312)541-1550
Chicago, IL 60601-1225 Free: 800-SEE-ADAA
  Fax: (312)541-1496
E-mail: adaa1@aol.com
URL: http://www.members.aol.com/adaa1/index.html
Contact: Lawrence H. Sepin, Exec.Dir.
Desc: Individuals employed as dental assistants in dental offices, clinics, hospitals, or institutions; instructors of dental assistants; dental students. Sponsors workshops and seminars; maintains governmental liaison. Offers group insurance; maintains scholarship trust fund. *Type:* Association.

American Dental Association
211 E. Chicago Ave. Ph: (312)440-2500
Chicago, IL 60611 Fax: (312)440-2800
E-mail: publicinfo@ada.org
URL: http://www.ada.org
Contact: John S. Zapp, D.D.S., Exec.Dir.
Desc: Professional society of dentists. Encourages the improvement of the health of the public and promotes the art and science of dentistry in matters of legislation and regulations. Inspects and accredits dental schools and schools for dental hygienists, assistants, and laboratory technicians. *Type:* Association.

American Dental Hygienists' Association
444 N. Michigan Ave., Ste. Ph: (312)440-8900
  3400 Free: 800-243-ADHA
Chicago, IL 60611 Fax: (312)440-6780
E-mail: mail@adha.net
URL: http://www.adha.org
Contact: Stanley B. Peck, Exec.Dir.
Desc: Professional organization of licensed dental hygienists possessing a degree or certificate in dental hygiene granted by an accredited school of dental hygiene. Administers Dental Hygiene Candidate Aptitude Testing Program and makes available scholarships, research grants, and continuing education programs. Maintains accrediting service through the American Dental Association's Commission on Dental Accreditation. *Type:* Association.

American Endodontic Society
1440 N. Harbor Blvd., Ste. 719 Ph: (714)870-5590
Fullerton, CA 92835
Contact: Dr. Ramon Werts, Exec.Dir.
Desc: Dentists united to. promote and provide educational and scientific information on simplified root canal therapy for the general practitioner. *Type:* Association.

American Society for the Advancement of Anesthesia in Dentistry
6 E. Union Ave. Ph: (732)469-9050
Bound Brook, NJ 08805 Fax: (732)271-1985
Contact: Dr. David Crystal, Exec.Sec.
Desc: Anesthesia in dentistry, including the study of sedation and its relation to physiologic sleep and the use of sedatives in dentistry. *Type:* Research center.

American Society for the Study of Orthodontics

5012 204th St.
Flushing, NY 11364-1041
Contact: Daisy N. Buchalter, Exec.Sec.
Desc: Theoretical, didactic, and applied orthodontics.
Type: Research center.

American Student Dental Association

211 E. Chicago Ave., Ste. 1160   Ph: (312)440-2795
Chicago, IL 60611   Fax: (312)440-2820
Contact: Karen S. Cervenka, CAE, Exec. Dir.
Desc: Predoctoral and postdoctoral dental students organized to improve the quality of dental education and to promote the accessibility of oral health care. Additional membership categories include predental, postdoctoral, international and associate. Represents dental students before legislative bodies, organizations, and associations that affect dental students. *Type:* Association.

Case Western Reserve University

Bolton-Brush Growth Study Center

Bolton Dental Bldg., 3rd Fl.   Ph: (216)368-6715
10900 Euclid Ave.   Fax: (216)368-3204
Cleveland, OH 44106-4905
E-mail: mgh4@po.cwru.edu
URL: http://scourge.cwru.edu
Contact: Dr. B. Holly Broadbent, Jr., Dir.
Desc: Investigations into the growth and development of dentition, face and cranium, and roentgenographic studies of the epiphyses of the human body. Conducts an ongoing study of longitudinal cephalometric radiographs and dental casts. *Type:* Research center.

Clinical Research Foundation

212 Church Ave., Ste. A   Ph: (619)420-8696
Chula Vista, CA 91910-2703   Free: 800-900-0489
   Fax: (619)420-6915
Contact: Naomi Tanaka, Exec.Dir.
Desc: Head, neck and temporomandibular joint (TMJ) diagnosis, treatment and management; anatomy, radiography, and other therapies; restorative dentistry. *Type:* Research center.

The Compendium of Continuing Education in Dentistry

Dental Learning Systems Co., Inc.
Div. of Medical World   Ph: (732)656-1143
  Communications, Inc.   Free: 800-926-7636
241 Forsgate Dr.
PO Box 505
Jamesburg, NJ 08831-0505
E-mail: kathleenp@dentallearning.com;   helenc@
dentallearning.com.
URL: http://www.dentallearning.com.
Contact: Dr. D. Walter Cohen, Editor; Daniel W. Perkins, Publisher.
Desc: Dentistry journal publishing examinations qualified for continuing education credits. *Type:* Periodical.

Craniofacial Center

1847 Old York Rd.   Ph: (215)657-7788
Abington, PA 19001   Fax: (215)657-5483
Contact: Dr. Neil Gottehrer, Dir.
Desc: Clinical research on dental implants, including type of implant, longevity, and coatings used on implants. *Type:* Research center.

Delta Sigma Delta

W323 S3380 Hwy. E   Ph: (414)968-2030
Dousman, WI 53118   Free: 800-335-8744
   Fax: (414)968-5850
Contact: Dr. John H. Prey, Supreme Scribe.
Desc: Professional fraternity - dentistry. *Type:* Association.

Dental Computer Newsletter

Andent, Inc.
1000 North Ave.   Ph: (847)223-5077
Waukegan, IL 60085   Fax: (847)223-5077
E-mail: 102254.525@compuserve.com
Contact: Ellis J. Neiburger, DDS, Editor.
Desc: Emphasizes "practical use of all brands of computers for the professional office." Provides news of the computer industry as well as computer-use tips, information on computer gadgets and systems, and system recommendations. Recurring features include editorials, news of research, letters to the editor, news of members, book reviews, and columns titled Education, Hardware, Software, Specials, and Report on Hardware/Software. *Type:* Newsletter.

Dental Economics

PennWell Publishing Co.
1421 S. Sheridan Rd.   Ph: (918)835-3161
Tulsa, OK 74112   Free: 800-331-4463
   Fax: (918)831-9834
URL: http://www.pennwell.com;   http://www.
dentaleconomics.com.
Contact: Penny Anderson, Sr. Editor; Ron Combs, Assoc. Editor; Melba Koch, Asst. Editor; Lyle Hoyt, Publisher; Jim Pfister, Exec. VP; Dick Coleman, VP of Marketing; Joan Roof, Circulation Mgr.; Dr. Joseph A. Blaes, Editor, joeb@pennwell.com; Mike Reeder, Art Dir.; Vicki Cheeseman, Business Operations Analyst; Mark Hartley, Group Editorial Dir.; Margaret Pagel, National Sales Mgr.
Desc: Magazine featuring business-related articles for dentists. *Alt. Contact:* 1421 S. Sheridan Rd., Tulsa, OK 74112. *Type:* Periodical.

Dental Products Report

MEDEC Dental Communications
2 Northfield Plaza No. 300   Ph: (847)441-3700
Northfield, IL 60093   Free: 800-323-3337
   Fax: (847)441-3702
E-mail: dpr@medec.com.
URL: http://www.medec.com/dpr/.
Contact: Gail Weisman, Editor, (847)441-3722, gail.weisman@medec.com; Roger Colahan, Publisher, (847)441-3707, roger.calahan@medec.com.
Desc: Professional tabloid for dentists. Covering new products, new literature, conferences, technical exhibits, esthetic dentistry techniques, and infection-control procedures. *Type:* Periodical.

Dentaletter

MPL Communications Inc.
133 Richmond St., Ste. 700   Ph: (416)869-1177
Toronto, ON, Canada M5H   Fax: (416)869-0616
  3M8
Contact: Dr. Brian Waters, Editor; John Hobez, Managing Editor.
Desc: Publishes news of dental research. Also covers related web sites. *Type:* Newsletter.

Dentistry Today

Dentistry Today
26 Park St.   Ph: (973)783-3935
Montclair, NJ 07042   Fax: (973)783-7112
Contact: Paul F. Radcliffe, Publisher; W. Ted Fetner, Editor, (973)783-3190; James F. Radcliffe, Advertising Mgr.
Desc: Dental magazine (tabloid). *Type:* Periodical.

The Dentist's Patient Newsletter

Newsletters Ink
1866 Colonial Village Ln.   Ph: (717)393-1010
PO Box 11177   Free: 800-822-1858
Lancaster, PA 17605-1177
URL: http://www.ns.wentworth.com:80/tt/.

Contact: Gregory A. Gilson, General Mgr.
Desc: Offers customized patient newsletters geared toward the dental patient. Discusses a variety of dental-related topics. *Type:* Newsletter.

Forsyth Dental Center

140 Fenway   Ph: (617)262-5200
Boston, MA 02115-3799   Fax: (617)437-6250
E-mail: dpdepaola@forsyth.org
URL: http://www.forsyth.org
Contact: Dr. Dominick P. DePaola, Pres.
Desc: Physical, biomedical, and clinical sciences pertinent to field of oral biology. Seeks to obtain a better understanding of normal and diseased structures of the oral cavity and its related parts, including bioadhesion, molecular genetics, immunology, biomineralization, clinical trials, cytokine biology, periodontology, electron microscopy, nutrition, and craniofacial growth and development. *Type:* Research center.

Indiana University-Purdue University at Indianapolis

Oral Health Research Institute

415 Lansing St.   Ph: (317)274-7868
Indianapolis, IN 46202-2876   Fax: (317)278-1071
E-mail: gstookey@iusd.iupui.edu
URL: http://www.iusd.iupui.edu/~ww/research/industry
Contact: Dr. George K. Stookey, Dir.
Desc: Studies of the etiology and prevention of dental caries and periodontal disease, and biocompatibility of dental materials. Investigates preventive measures concentrated on fluorides and antimicrobial agents, including a wide variety of in vitro test procedures, research on a number of animal models for determining safety and therapeutic potential, and human clinical investigations of safety and efficacy. *Type:* Research center.

International Association for Dental Research

1619 Duke St.   Ph: (703)548-0066
Alexandria, VA 22314   Fax: (703)548-1883
E-mail: research@iadr.com
URL: http://www.iadr.com
Contact: Eli Schwarz, DDS, MPH, PHD, Exec.Dir.
Desc: Individuals engaged or interested in advancing research in the various aspects of dental and related sciences. *Type:* Association.

International Association for Dental Research

Craniofacial Biology Group

Baylor College of Dentistry   Ph: (214)828-8277
Department of Biomedical   Fax: (214)828-8951
  Sciences
PO Box 660677
Dallas, TX 75266-0677
E-mail: pdechow@ont.com
Contact: Dr. Paul C. Dechow, Contact.
Desc: Craniofacial biology, including anthropology, teratology, pharmacology, orthodontics, pedodontics, genetics, cellular biology, anatomy, pediatrics, and neurology. *Type:* Research center.

International Congress of Oral Implantologists

248 Lorraine Ave., 3rd Fl.   Ph: (973)783-6300
Upper Montclair, NJ 07043   Fax: (973)783-1175
E-mail: icoi@dentalimplants.com
Contact: R. Craig Johnson, Exec.Dir.
Desc: Dentists and oral surgeons dedicated to the teaching of and research in oral implantology (branch of dentistry dealing with dental implants placed into or on top of the jaw bone). Offers fellowship and course certification programs. Compiles statistics and maintains registry of current research in the field. *Type:* Association.

Journal of the American Dental Association

ADA Publishing Co., Inc.
211 E. Chicago Ave.   Ph: (312)440-2791
Chicago, IL 60611   Free: 800-621-8099
                            Fax: (312)440-3538
E-mail: adapco@ada.org
URL: http://www.ada.org.
Contact: Dr. Lawrence Meskin, Editor, (312)440-7475, fax: (312)440-3538, meskinl@ada.org; Laura Kosden, CEO/Publisher, (312)440-2790, kosdenl@ada.org; James Berry, Associate Publisher, Editorial, (312)440-2786, berryj@ada.org; Gabriela Radulescu, Assoc. Publisher, Marketing & Operations, (312)440-2519, radulescug@ada.org.
Desc: Trade journal for the dental profession. *Type:* Periodical.

Laval University

Research Group of Oral Ecology

Pavillon de medecine dentair   Ph: (418)656-5985
Quebec, PQ, Canada G1K 7P4   Fax: (418)656-2861
E-mail: greb@greb.ulaval.ca
URL: http://www.fsg.ulaval.ca/greb/index.html
Contact: Denis Mayrand, Dir.
Desc: Studies the biological equilibrium between host and microorganism, including prevention of microbial diseases of the mouth, early identification of high-risk subjects, and outcome predictions of elaborate and frequently expensive curative treatments. *Type:* Research center.

Managed Dental Care

Business Information Services, Inc.
12811 North Point Ln.   Ph: (301)604-4001
Laurel, MD 20708   Free: 800-559-8550
                               Fax: (301)604-5126
E-mail: businfosvc@aol.com
Contact: James Gutman, Publisher; Sheila Moldover, Editor, (301)279-0762, fax: (301)294-6412, skmoldover@aol.com.
Desc: Devoted exclusively to business news, analysis, and advice from experts in all aspects of the managed dental care field. *Type:* Newsletter.

Medical Professionals Financial Digest

American Professional Practice Association (APPA)
Hillsboro Executive Center   Ph: (954)571-1877
  North   Fax: (954)571-8582
350 Fairway Dr., Ste. 200
Deerfield Beach, FL 33441-1834
E-mail: ppsone@msn.com
Contact: B. Lydia Young, Editor, youngpp@aol.com.
Desc: Focuses on the business aspects of medical and dental practice. Covers topics such as tax and estate planning, personal money management, investing, office management, staff training, and benefits and services. *Type:* Newsletter.

Medical Research Council of Canada

Periodontal Physiology Group

Univ. of Toronto   Ph: (416)978-8728
1 King's College Cir.   Fax: (416)978-5956
Med. Sci. Bldg., Rm. 4384
Toronto, ON, Canada M5S
  1A8
E-mail: jarosodek@utoronto.ca
URL: http://www.civ.utoronto.ca
Contact: J. Sodek, Dir.
Desc: Structure and function of periodontal tissues (tooth supporting apparatus), regulation of cell activity, and relationships to periodontal disease and tooth implants. *Type:* Research center.

National Association of Dental Laboratories

8201 Greensboro Dr., Ste. 300   Ph: (703)610-9035
Mc Lean, VA 22102   Free: 800-950-1150
                                 Fax: (703)610-9005
E-mail: cbeeton@nadl.org
URL: http://www.nadl.org
Contact: Terry L. Peters, Exec.Dir.
Desc: Develops criteria for ethical dental laboratories. *Type:* Association.

National Board for Certification in Dental Technology

National Association of Dental Laboratories
8201 Greensboro Dr., Ste. 300   Ph: (703)610-9036
Mc Lean, VA 22102   Free: 800-684-5310
                                 Fax: (703)610-9005
E-mail: nadl@nadl.org
URL: http://www.nadl.org
Contact: Sandra Stewart Ludes, Program Dir.
Desc: Certifies dental technicians with formal education in dental technology and a minimum of three years' experience who have passed written and practical exams administered by the NBC. Provides continuing education to certificants and recognizes competent dental technicians. Also certifies dental laboratories that meet published standards for personnel, facility and infection control practice. *Type:* Association.

National Foundation of Dentistry for the Handicapped

1800 15th St., Unit 100   Ph: (303)534-5360
Denver, CO 80202   Fax: (303)534-5290
Contact: Larry Coffee, D.D.S., Exec.Dir.
Desc: Promotes preventive dentistry for handicapped individuals in order to reduce dental disease. Sponsors Campaign of Concern which enlists the cooperation of members of the dental profession, special education personnel, disabled individuals and their parents, counselors, and civic organizations in helping developmentally disabled people enjoy good dental health. The campaign currently serves 35,000 people in seven states. *Type:* Association.

New York University

David B. Kriser Dental Center

345 E. 24th St.   Ph: (212)998-9794
New York, NY 10010   Fax: (212)995-3529
E-mail: afesv@library.med.nyu.edu
Contact: Dr. Van B. Afes, Dir.
Desc: Dentistry, dental history, and allied health sciences. *Type:* Research center.

Ohio State University

George C. Paffenbarger Dental Research Laboratory

College of Dentistry   Ph: (614)292-0880
Postle Hall   Fax: (614)292-9422
305 W. 12th Ave.
Columbus, OH 43210
E-mail: rosenstiel.1@osu.edu
URL: http://www.osu.edu/units/dentistry
Contact: Dr. S.F. Rosenstiel, Dir.
Desc: Dental bio-materials engineering. Currently studying dental polymers, maxillo-facial polymer synthesis, and optical properties of esthetic biomaterials. *Type:* Research center.

Omicron Kappa Upsilon

Coll. of Dentistry   Ph: (402)472-1339
University of Nebraska   Fax: (402)472-5290
40th & Hodrege
Lincoln, NE 68583-0740
Contact: Jan John, Sec.

Desc: Honorary society of men and women in the field of dentistry. *Type:* Association.

Oral Health America

410 N. Michigan Ave., Ste. 352   Ph: (312)836-9900
Chicago, IL 60611-4211   Free: 800-523-3438
                                 Fax: (312)836-9986
URL: http://www.oralhealthamerica.org
Contact: Robert J. Klaus, Pres. & CEO.
Desc: Funds dental education, research, and service programs. Operates speakers' bureau. *Type:* Association.

Oral and Maxillofacial Surgery Foundation

9700 W. Bryn Mawr Ave.   Ph: (847)678-6200
Rosemont, IL 60018-5701   Free: 800-822-6637
                                 Fax: (847)678-6286
E-mail: dhanson@aaoms.org
URL: http://www.aaoms.org
Contact: Dr. Robert Rinaldi, Exec.Dir.
Desc: Oral and maxillofacial surgery focusing on providing fellowships and grants to both residents and investigators and financial support of other special projects and activities. *Type:* Research center.

Orthodontic Education and Research Foundation

3320 Rutger   Ph: (314)577-8189
St. Louis, MO 63104   Fax: (314)268-5191
Contact: Becky Moscal, Contact.
Desc: Orthodontics, focusing on research and education. *Type:* Research center.

Psi Omega

1040 Savannah Hwy.   Ph: (803)556-0573
Charleston, SC 29407   Fax: (803)556-6311
E-mail: psio@ibm.net
Contact: Dr. B. Thomas Kays, Co-Exec.Dir.
Desc: Professional fraternity - dentistry. *Type:* Association.

Society for Occlusal Studies

1010 Carondelet Dr., No. 410   Ph: (816)941-0509
Kansas City, MO 64114   Fax: (816)941-4832
Contact: Dr. Bernard Williams, Contact.
Desc: Occlusion (bringing opposing surfaces of the teeth of the two jaws into contact) and effective occlusion treatments. *Type:* Research center.

State University of New York at Buffalo

Center for Dental Studies

School of Dental Medicine   Ph: (716)829-3848
250 Squire Hall   Fax: (716)837-7623
Buffalo, NY 14214
E-mail: Seb_Ciancio@sdm.buffalo.edu
URL: http://www.sdm.buffalo.edu/research/ccds/clinic.html
Contact: Dr. Sebastian G. Ciancio, Dir.
Desc: Dental research, including new product evaluation. *Type:* Research center.

State University of New York at Buffalo

Comprehensive Oral Health Research Center of Discovery

Foster Hall   Ph: (716)829-2854
Buffalo, NY 14214   Fax: (716)829-2387
E-mail: rjgenco@acsu.buffalo.edu
URL: http://research.sdm.buffalo.edu
Contact: Dr. Robert J. Genco, Chm./Dir.
Desc: Laboratory, clinical, and epidemiological investigations of periodontal disease, particularly the etiology, risk factors pathogenesis, and management of this and other chronic bacterial infections; Specific areas of study include microbiology, host response mechanisms, clinical analysis, risk factors, and the development of genetic probes, novel antibiotics, and growth factors as they apply to periodontal diseases. Periodontal disease as a factor in poor diabetic control, cardiovascular disease, respiratory disease and other systemic conditions is also under investigation. *Type:* Research center.

Supertooth News
Delta Dental Plan of California
PO Box 7736   Ph: (415)977-7903
San Francisco, CA 94120   Fax: (415)543-6326
URL: http://www.deltadentalca.org.
Contact: Karen Rathmell, Editor, krathmell@delta.org.
Desc: Covers Delta news, policies and new clients. Provides suggestions to expedite and simplify claims processing and notices of processing seminars. *Type:* Newsletter.

Telecommunications for the Deaf, Inc.
8630 Fenton St., Ste. 604   Ph: (301)589-3006
Silver Spring, MD 20910-3803   Fax: (301)589-3797
E-mail: tdiexdir@aol.com
URL: http://www.tdi-online.org
Contact: Claude Stout, Exec.Dir.
Desc: Hearing impaired individuals and their families, and organizations participating in telecommunications over regular telephone lines through special equipment. Strives to constantly improve technology and accessibility for all who rely on visual telecommunications. *Type:* Association.

U.S. Department of Health and Human Services
National Institute of Dental Research
NIH Bldg. 31, Rm. 5B49   Ph: (301)496-4261
31 Center Dr., MSC 2190   Fax: (301)496-9988
Bethesda, MD 20892-2190
Contact: Dr. Harold Slavkin, Dir.
Desc: Normal development, maintenance, and aging of the oral and facial tissues, and the cause, prevention, and methods of diagnosis and treatment of oral diseases and conditions. Principal areas of research include dental caries; periodontal disease; congenital and acquired craniofacial malformations; orofacial pain and sensory-motor dysfunction; oral soft tissue diseases; AIDS; salivary glands and secretions; mineralized tissues and fluoride studies; pulp biology; nutrition research; behavioral studies; implants, replants, and transplants; and restorative dental materials. *Type:* Research center.

U.S. Department of Health and Human Services
National Institute of Dental Research
Division of Epidemiology and Oral Disease Prevention
45 Center Dr., MSC 6401, RM.   Ph: (301)594-7651
   4A5-13D   Fax: (301)480-8322
5333 Westbard Ave., Rm. 528
Bethesda, MD 20892-6401
Contact: Dr. L. Jackson Brown, Dir.
Desc: Descriptive and analytical epidemiologic studies of the etiology, distribution, and trends in dental caries, periodontal diseases, and other oral diseases and disorders. Program's Disease Prevention and Health Promotion Branch manages activities involving health promotion research and application. *Type:* Research center.

U.S. Department of Health and Human Services
National Institute of Dental Research
Division of Epidemiology and Oral Disease Prevention
Analytical Studies and Health Assessment Branch
Natcher Bldg.   Ph: (301)594-5589
45 Center Dr., MSC 6401   Fax: (301)480-8326
Bethesda, MD 20892-6401
URL: http://www.nidr.nih.gov
Contact: Dr. Deborah Winn, PhD, Chf.
Desc: Epidemiology and oral disease prevention focusing on analytical studies and health assessment. *Type:* Research center.

U.S. Department of Health and Human Services
National Institute of Dental Research
Division of Epidemiology and Oral Disease Prevention
Molecular Epidemiology and Disease Indicators Branch
Natcher Bldg., Rm. 4AS-49   Ph: (301)594-4830
45 Center Dr., MSC 6401   Fax: (301)480-8327
Bethesda, MD 20892-6401
Contact: Dr. Scott Diehl, Chf.
Desc: Descriptive and epidemiological studies of the etiology, distribution, and trends in dental caries, periodontal disease, and other oral diseases and disorders. *Type:* Research center.

U.S. Department of Health and Human Services
National Institute of Dental Research
Division of Epidemiology and Oral Disease Prevention
Oral Health Promotion, Risk Factors, Molecular Epidemiology Branch
Natcher Bldg., Rm. 3AN-44D   Ph: (301)594-5579
45 Center Dr., MSC 6401   Fax: (301)480-8254
Bethesda, MD 20892
Desc: Clinical trials and epidemiological studies related to the prevention of dental caries. *Type:* Research center.

U.S. Department of Health and Human Services
National Institute of Dental Research
Division of Extramural Research
Natcher Bldg.   Ph: (301)594-7711
45 Center Dr. MSC-6402   Fax: (301)480-8318
Bethesda, MD 20892-6402
E-mail: ricardo.martinez@nih.gov
URL: http://www.nidcr.nih.gov
Contact: J. Ricardo Martinez, Dir.
Desc: Administers grant and contract funds for research and training research manpower. Support is provided for investigations ranging from basic laboratory studies on the causes of oral disorders to clinical trials of new therapies or means of disease prevention. *Type:* Research center.

U.S. Department of Health and Human Services
National Institute of Dental Research
Division of Extramural Research
Behavior Pain, Oral Motor and Oral Sensory, and Epidemiology Branch
NIH 4S   Ph: (301)594-2095
9000 Rockville Pike
Bethesda, MD 20892
Contact: Patricia S. Bryant, Dir.
Desc: Dental research focusing on behavior, pain, oral motor and sensory, and epidemiology. *Type:* Research center.

U.S. Department of Health and Human Services
National Institute of Dental Research
Division of Extramural Research
Chronic Disabling Diseases Program
Natcher Building   Ph: (301)594-4836
45 Center Dr. MSC 6402   Fax: (301)480-8318
Bethesda, MD 20892-6402
E-mail: kenneth_gruber@nih.gov
URL: http://www.nih.gov
Contact: Dr. Kenneth A. Gruber, Contact.
Desc: Normal and abnormal craniofacial growth, development, and function, with emphasis on research pertaining to etiology and treatment. *Type:* Research center.

U.S. Department of Health and Human Services
National Institute of Dental Research
Division of Extramural Research
Grants Management Section
45 Center Dr., Rm. 4AS-55   Ph: (301)594-4800
Bethesda, MD 20892   Fax: (301)480-8301
Desc: Supports extramural research through grant and contract awards. *Type:* Research center.

U.S. Department of Health and Human Services
National Institute of Dental Research
Division of Extramural Research
Oral Soft Tissue Diseases and AIDS Program
45 Center Dr., MSC 6402   Ph: (301)594-5500
Bethesda, MD 20892   Fax: (301)480-8318
Desc: Etiology, diagnosis, treatment, and prevention of oral soft tissue diseases and disorders and AIDS as related to oral health. *Type:* Research center.

U.S. Department of Health and Human Services
National Institute of Dental Research
Division of Extramural Research
Periodontal Disease Program
Bldg. 45, Rm. 4AN-32R   Ph: (301)594-2421
Bethesda, MD 20892-6402   Fax: (301)480-8318
Contact: Dennis Mangan, Chf.
Desc: Cause, nature, diagnosis, treatment, and prevention of periodontal diseases. In studies of periodontal diseases, special attention is given to the identification and characterization of microorganisms that cause these diseases and to the host responses they evoke. *Type:* Research center.

U.S. Department of Health and Human Services
National Institute of Dental Research
Division of Extramural Research
Salivary Glands and Oral Biology Program
NIH 4S   Ph: (301)594-5500
45 Center Dr.
Bethesda, MD 20892
Contact: Gerassimos Roussos, Dir.
Desc: Development, structure, function, and diseases of the salivary glands in an attempt to determine the influence of salivary constituents on oral health. *Type:* Research center.

U.S. Department of Health and Human Services
National Institute of Dental Research
Division of Intramural Research
30 Convent Dr. MSC 4326   Ph: (301)496-1483
Bldg. 30, Rm. 132   Fax: (301)402-1512
Bethesda, MD 20892-4326
Contact: Dr. Henning Birkedal-Hansen, Dir.
Desc: Oral diseases, including periodontal disease and related disorders, by using the latest techniques in molecular biology, immunology, and cell biology. Areas of interest include the biochemistry, structure, function, and development of bone, teeth, salivary glands, and connective tissues; the role of bacteria and viruses in oral disease; genetic disorders and tumors of the oral cavity; studies on the cause and treatment of acute and chronic pain; and the development of new and improved diagnostic methods. *Type:* Research center.

U.S. Department of Health and Human Services
National Institute of Dental Research
Division of Intramural Research
Bone Research Branch
NIH Bldg. 30, Rm. 106   Ph: (301)496-6255
9000 Rockville Pike   Fax: (301)402-0824
Bethesda, MD 20892
E-mail: probey@yoda.nidr.nih.gov
Contact: Pamela Gehron Robey, Chf.
Desc: Structure, development, biosynthesis, and regulation of bones, teeth, and cartilaginous tissues. Emphasis is on studies of acquired and heritable disorders of the skeleton. *Type:* Research center.

U.S. Department of Health and Human Services
National Institute of Dental Research
Division of Intramural Research
Neurobiology and Anesthesiology Branch
NIH Bldg. 49, Rm. IA-04   Ph: (301)496-6804
9000 Rockville Pike   Fax: (301)402-0667
Bethesda, MD 20892
Desc: Oral-facial sensation, emphasizing mechanisms of pain and the development of new methods for controlling pain in humans. Branch sections utilize anatomical, physiological, behavioral, pharmacological, and psychophysical techniques to study neural function as it relates to the processing of sensory signals about the threat of tissue-damaging stimulation. *Type:* Research center.

U.S. Department of Health and Human Services
National Institute of Dental Research
Division of Intramural Research
Pain and Neurosensory Mechanism Branch
Bldg. 10, Rm. 3C403   Ph: (301)496-5483
9000 Rockville Pike   Fax: (301)402-0667
Bethesda, MD 20892
Contact: Dr. Ronald Dubner, Chf.
Desc: Collaborates with other units of the National Institutes of Health to conduct research on chronic pain problems of the face and oral cavity as well as reflex sympathetic dystrophy, cancer pain, diabetic neuropathy, and shingles. Multidisciplinary efforts involve studies in basic science, neurology, oncology, dentistry, pharmacology, and psychology to generate new understanding of pain mechanisms and pain control. *Type:* Research center.

U.S. Department of Health and Human Services
National Institute of Dental Research
Infectious Diseases and Non-AIDS Program
Bldg. 45, Rm. 4AN-32F   Ph: (301)594-5500
Bethesda, MD 20892-6402
E-mail: dennis.mangan@nih.gov
URL: http://www.nidcr.nih.gov
Contact: Dr. Dennis Mangan, Dir.
Desc: Application of basic research findings in the areas of microbiology, immunology, and pharmacology in clinical investigations of patients with oral infectious disease. Program supports studies to establish the causative organisms in oral diseases; determine the host response to these causative organisms; improve therapeutic techniques and regimens; and develop preventive measures. *Type:* Research center.

U.S. Department of Health and Human Services
National Institute of Dental Research
Laboratory of Immunology
NIH Bldg. 30   Ph: (301)496-4178
30 Covent Dr.   Fax: (301)402-1064
Bethesda, MD 20892
Contact: Dr. Stephan E. Mergenhagen, Chf.

Desc: Cellular and molecular basis of acute and chronic inflammatory diseases. More specifically, research is focused on the contributions of mononuclear leukocytes and cytokines to the regulation of connective tissue catabolism, tissue repair and inflammation, and to the development of chronic inflammatory diseases which include AIDS, rheumatoid arthritis, and chronic periodontitis. *Type:* Research center.

U.S. Department of Health and Human Services
National Institute of Dental Research
Laboratory of Microbial Ecology
NIH Bldg. 30, Rm. 316   Ph: (301)496-2232
9000 Rockville Pike   Fax: (301)402-0396
Bethesda, MD 20892
Desc: Microbial ecology. *Type:* Research center.

U.S. Department of Health and Human Services
National Institute of Dental Research
Office of Extramural Program Review
Basic Sciences Review Branch
Parklawn Bldg., Rm. 10-42   Ph: (301)443-2620
Rockville, MD 20857   Fax: (301)443-0538
Contact: Kursheed Asghar, Chf.
Desc: Coordinates initial scientific review of applications for center research grants, small research grants, conference grants, institutional training grants, short-term grants, and fellowship grants. *Type:* Research center.

U.S. Department of Health and Human Services
National Institute of Dental Research
Office of Planning, Evaluation, and Data Systems
NIH Westwood Bldg., Rm. 503   Ph: (301)496-7723
Bethesda, MD 20892   Fax: (301)496-4180
Desc: Supports dental research for the Institute. *Type:* Research center.

U.S. Department of Health and Human Services
National Institute of Dental Research
Specialized Research Centers
5333 Westbard Ave.   Ph: (301)594-7638
Westwood Bldg., Rm. 503   Fax: (301)594-7616
Bethesda, MD 20892
Contact: Dr. Lois K. Cohen, Dir.
Desc: Centers attract outstanding scientists from different fields to universities to work as multidisciplinary teams on a wide variety of basic and clinical dental research problems. The program has developed collaborative research efforts with investigators within and outside the field of dental research. *Type:* Research center.

U.S. Department of Health and Human Services
National Institutes of Health
National Institute of Dental Research
9000 Rockville Pike   Ph: (301)496-6621
Bethesda, MD 20892
URL: http://www.nidr.nih.gov/
Contact: Harold C. Slavkin, Director.
Desc: The Institute supports and conducts clinical and laboratory research into the causes, prevention, diagnosis, and treatment of oral diseases and conditions. *Type:* Government agency, office, or program.

University of Alabama at Birmingham
Regional Maxillofacial Prosthetics Treatment and Training Center
1813 6th Ave. S., B-50   Ph: (205)934-3356
Birmingham, AL 35294   Fax: (205)975-6519
Contact: Dr. Kirk Gardner, Dir.

Desc: Methods and materials for maxillofacial prostheses, also clinical aspects of fabrication techniques and basic industrial and laboratory research and testing of new and improved materials in polymers, silicones, and rubbers to be used as skin substitutes. *Type:* Research center.

University of Alabama at Birmingham
Research Center in Oral Biology
845 S. 19th St.   Ph: (205)934-3470
BBRB 258/5   Fax: (205)934-1426
Birmingham, AL 35294-2170
E-mail: suemich@uab.edu
URL: http://www.uab.edu
Contact: Dr. Suzanne M. Michalek, Dir.
Desc: Oral biology, mucosal immunology, and connective tissue biochemistry. *Type:* Research center.

University of California, Los Angeles
Dental Research Institute
Ctr. for Health Sci.   Ph: (310)206-8045
Box 951668   Fax: (310)825-0921
Los Angeles, CA 90095-1668
E-mail: npark@dent.ucla.edu
URL: http://www.dent.ucla.edu/
Contact: Dr. No-Hee Park, PhD, Dir.
Desc: Oral cancer, molecular oncology, viral oncology, molecular mechanisms of periodontal diseases, ultrastructure and cell biology, dental implantology, TMJ disorders and orofacial pain, neuroimmunology, molecular immunology, AIDS/HIV immunology, pain control/pharmacology, biomaterials, and wound repair/keloid tissue formation mechanisms. Also conducts clinical dental science studies. *Type:* Research center.

University of Florida
Claude D. Pepper Center for Research on Oral Health in Aging
Box 100416, JHMHSC   Ph: (352)392-6796
Gainesville, FL 32610   Fax: (352)846-0588
E-mail: mheft@dental.ufl.edu
Contact: Dr. Marc Heft, Dir.
Desc: Health services research and basic oral-health functions of the elderly, including the development of periodontal disease, the effects of medications on saliva production, and the effects of aging on the senses. *Type:* Research center.

University of Florida
Periodontal Disease Research Center
JHMHC, Box 100442   Ph: (352)392-4377
Gainesville, FL 32610   Fax: (352)392-2361
E-mail: jbraddy@dental.ufl.edu
URL: http://www.dental.ufl.edu/
Contact: Dr. William P. McArthur, Dir.
Desc: Microbial etiology of destructive periodontal diseases, antibiotic therapy in the treatment of periodontal diseases, mechanisms of bacterial attachment to teeth, bacterial virulence factors in periodontal diseases, and immune response to bacterial antigens. Evaluates risk factors for periodontal disease. *Type:* Research center.

University of Illinois at Chicago
Center for Molecular Biology of Oral Diseases
801 S. Paulina   Ph: (312)996-6118
M/C 860   Fax: (312)413-1604
Chicago, IL 60612
URL: http://www.uic.edu/depts/cmbod/center.html
Contact: Dr. Donald A. Chambers, Dir.
Desc: Molecular biological approaches to pathobiology, including the molecular biology of cell proliferation and differentiation, the molecular basis of hematology, immunobiology and the inflammatory response, and mechanisms of host-microbial interaction. *Type:* Research center.

University of Iowa

Center for Clinical Studies

College of Dentistry   Ph: (319)335-7414
Iowa City, IA 52242   Fax: (319)335-8895
E-mail: nellie-kremenak@uiowa.edu
URL: http://indy.radiology.uiowa.edu/Beyond/Dentistry/dows.html
Contact: Dr. James S. Wefel, Dir.
Desc: Oral health, including disease processes (caries, periodontal disease, and oral lesions), restorative materials, and preventive techniques and agents. *Type:* Research center.

University of Iowa

Dows Institute for Dental Research

Dental Sci. Bldg.   Ph: (319)335-7388
Iowa City, IA 52242   Fax: (319)335-8895
E-mail: chris-white@uiowa.edu
URL: http://indy.radiology.uiowa.edu/Beyond/Dentistry/dows.html
Contact: Dr. Christopher A. Squier, Assoc. Dean, Res.
Desc: Normal and pathological development and ultrastructure of oral soft tissues, cariology, oral microbiology, implant biomaterials and bone. Center for Clinical Studies performs research and testing of new oral health materials, products, and treatment modalities in normal and special populations. *Type:* Research center.

University of Maryland

Center for the Study of Human Performance in Dentistry

Baltimore College of Dental   Ph: (410)706-7342
  Surgery   Fax: (410)706-3028
666 W. Baltimore St.
Dental School
Baltimore, MD 21201-1586
E-mail: mmb001@dental.umaryland.edu
Contact: Michael M. Belenky, Dir.
Desc: Physical posture and ergonomic process for practicing dentistry, human-centered ergonomics for preclinical psychomotor education, and psychomotor skill applications to patient dental care. Studies optimal proprioceptive posture for peak performance, patient support, aseptic performance process, facility design, performance logic, performance simulation, psychomotor education, and the reduction/elimination of back, neck, and shoulder pain. *Type:* Research center.

University of Medicine and Dentistry of New Jersey

Dental Research Center

NJ Dental Sch.   Ph: (973)972-3728
University Heights   Fax: (973)972-0045
110 Bergen St.
Newark, NJ 07103-2400
E-mail: finedh@umdnj.edu
Contact: Dr. Daniel H. Fine, Dir.
Desc: Host-bacterial interactions in infectious diseases, such as periodontal diseases, mucositis, colitis, cloning of virulence genes that enable attachment and penetration of noxious substances; mucus-drug interaction; synthesis, cotranslational, and posttranslational processing of mucus glycoproteins; sulfation; proteoglycans; and intergrins. *Type:* Research center.

University of Michigan

Bacteriology Laboratory

3209 School of Dentistry   Ph: (734)764-8386
1101 N. University Ave.   Fax: (734)764-7406
Ann Arbor, MI 48109
E-mail: wloesche@umich.edu
Contact: Walter J. Loesche, PhD, Dir.

Desc: Oral bacteria and its role in human tooth decay and periodontal disease. Current studies focus on the development of diagnostic indicators of anaerobic infections in periodontal disease, the treatment of anaerobic infections, and the connection between good dental health, xerostomia, swallowing, cardiovascular disease, and aspiration pneumonia in senior citizens. *Type:* Research center.

University of Michigan

Biomaterials Research Center

Sch. of Dentistry   Ph: (734)763-9339
Department of Biologic &   Fax: (734)647-5293
  Materials Sci.
1011 N. University Ave.
Ann Arbor, MI 48109-1078
E-mail: wjobrien@umich.edu
URL: http://www.umich.edu
Contact: Dr. William J. O'Brien, Dir.
Desc: Develops elastomers for dental prostheses and denture liners, polymerceramic composites for dental restorations, and advanced ceramics for crowns and bridges. Also establishes biocompatibility of dental materials. *Type:* Research center.

University of Michigan

Clinical Research Laboratories

1390 School of Dentistry   Ph: (734)763-3325
1011 N. University Ave.   Fax: (734)936-0374
Ann Arbor, MI 48109
E-mail: homlay@umich.edu
Contact: Dr. Hom-Lay Wang, Dir.
Desc: Etiology of periodontal diseases, focusing on preventive and surgical methods; determining risk factors to predict and treat periodontal disease; assessment of the effectiveness of specific factors and materials in the regeneration of tissues lost through disease; and assessment of implant materials for optimal osseous integration. *Type:* Research center.

University of Michigan

Electrodiagnostic and Electromyographic Laboratory

1011 N. University St.   Ph: (734)763-3346
Ann Arbor, MI 48109   Fax: (734)663-7133
E-mail: sew@umich.edu
Contact: Dr. Sven E. Widmalm, Dir.
Desc: Etiology and treatment of functional disturbances of the masticatory system, including disturbances of the muscles and joints of mastication. *Type:* Research center.

University of Michigan

Experimental Pathology Laboratory

5223 School of Dentistry   Ph: (734)647-4326
1101 N. University Ave.   Fax: (734)764-2469
Ann Arbor, MI 48109
E-mail: thanks@umich.edu
Contact: Dr. Carl T. Hanks, Contact.
Desc: Biocompatibility of materials meant for use in the human body. Current studies include diffusion of molecules in various biological environments, cellular chemotaxis and adhesion to synthetic substrates, cytotoxicity to eukaryotic cells by materials, differentiation of various cell types on synthetic and natural substrates, and macrophage-assisted lymphocytic transformation. *Type:* Research center.

University of Michigan

Immunology Laboratory

4208 School of Dentistry   Ph: (734)647-3912
1011 N. University Ave.   Fax: (734)764-2425
Ann Arbor, MI 48109
E-mail: lopatin@umich.edu

URL: http://www.umich.edu
Contact: Dennis E. Lopatin, Dir.
Desc: Aspects of the interactions between the oral microbial flora and the immune system. Studies address humoral immunity to specific oral microorganisms; cellular networks involved in the responses to different classes of antigens; oral factors that create risk for the development of a variety of diseases and negative health consequences such as caries, periodontal disease, aspiration pneumonia, cardiovascular disease, and immunochemical reagents for the identification of specific microorganisms in dental plaque. *Type:* Research center.

University of Michigan

Prosthodontic Research Laboratory

1011 N. University, Rm. 1064   Ph: (734)763-5280
Ann Arbor, MI 48109-1078   Fax: (734)763-3453
E-mail: brl@umich.edu
URL: http://www.umich.edu
Contact: Prof. Brien R. Lang, Dir.
Desc: Measures wear of prosthodontic devices and conducts serial and longitudinal biopsies of bone. *Type:* Research center.

University of Minnesota

Dental Research Institute

18-104 Moos Tower   Ph: (612)626-3349
515 Delaware St. SE   Fax: (612)626-7017
Minneapolis, MN 55455
E-mail: dri@tc.umn.edu
URL: http://www.umn.edu/dri/
Contact: Prof. Charles F. Schachtele, PhD, Dir.
Desc: Coordinates research and training proposals, pilot projects funding, space and equipment maintenance, and research faculty recruitment and development. *Type:* Research center.

University of Minnesota

Dental Research Institute

Dental Research Center

18-104 Moos Tower   Ph: (612)626-5722
515 Delaware St. SE   Fax: (612)626-2651
Minneapolis, MN 55455
E-mail: bpihls@maroon.tc.umn.edu
URL: http://www.maroon.tc.umn.edu
Contact: Dr. Bruce L. Pihlstrom, Dir.
Desc: Neurobiology, including microdialysis for evaluations of biochemical responses to inflammation and pharmacologic modulation; biochemical techniques for studying pain and tenderness at trigger points and the effects of transcutaneous electrical nerve stimulation; laser doppler probes to measure gingival blood flows as a potential diagnostic aid for periodontal disease; biotelemetry; CAD/CAM technology for manufacturing appliances and restorations for the repair of lost or damaged teeth; dental implants; drug studies; dental plaque; saliva analysis; and anaerobic microbiology. *Type:* Research center.

University of Minnesota

Minnesota Dental Research Center for Biomaterials and Biomechanics

16-212 Moos Tower   Ph: (612)625-9636
515 Delaware St., SE   Fax: (612)626-1484
Sch. of Dentistry
Minneapolis, MN 55455
E-mail: dougl1001@maroon.tc.umn.edu
URL: http://web.dent.umn.edu
Contact: Dr. William Douglas, Dir.
Desc: Conducts research on the density dependent growth of dental and other bacterial plaques; neural pathways and electronic anaesthesia; and the development of simulated

dental wear, including lubrication and friction of dental wear structures, toothbrush biomechanics, and the fracture toughness of dental hard tissues. Program missions include investigation of new evaluative technologies in biomechanics, service evaluation of biomaterials, and the clinical measurement of anatomic change in oral structures. *Type:* Research center.

University of Minnesota

Minnesota Oral Health Clinical Research Center

School of Dentistry	Ph: (612)626-5722
17-116 Moos Health Sciences	Fax: (612)626-2651
Tower	
Minneapolis, MN 55455	

E-mail: bpihls@maroon.tc.umn.edu
URL: http://www.edu/1.umn.edu/dri/rescenters/mohcrc.html

Contact: Dr. Bruce L. Pihlstrom, Contact.

Desc: Dentistry, including materials and restorative sciences, oral facial pain and neuroscience, and caries and periodontal disease. *Type:* Research center.

University of Missouri--Kansas City

Dental Research Program

650 E. 25th St.	Ph: (816)235-2021
Kansas City, MO 64108	Free: 800-887-4447
	Fax: (816)235-2157

URL: http://www.umkc.edu/dentistry/resear.html

Contact: Karen B. Williams, Coord., Grants Admin.

Desc: Biochemistry, dental biomaterials, radiology, analgesics, and pathology, related to dentistry. Clinical programs include study of anomalies of oral region, hard and soft tissues, prosthodontics, occlusion, durapatite particles, prostaglandins and analgesic inflammation, orthodontics, pedodontics, oral diagnosis, periodontics, bone physiology, dental caries, and related pathoses. *Type:* Research center.

University of North Carolina at Chapel Hill

Dental Research Center

Rm. 101, CB 7455	Ph: (919)966-1538
Chapel Hill, NC 27599-7455	Fax: (919)966-3683

E-mail: pat_flood@dentistry.unc.edu
URL: http://www.unc.edu

Contact: Dr. Patrick Flood, PhD, Dir.

Desc: Oral health problems organized into several primary areas: biomaterials research, growth mechanisms, hemostasis research, mechanisms of mineralization, neural mechanisms, biology of extracellular matrices, viral properties and host-pathogen interaction in oral biology, involving both basic and clinical research. Studies problems in oral health related to growth, development, and function of craniofacial region. *Type:* Research center.

University of Pennsylvania

Research Center in Oral Biology

4010 Locust St.	Ph: (215)898-8994
Philadelphia, PA 19104-6002	Fax: (215)573-2324

E-mail: jrosen@biochem.dental.upenn.edu

Contact: Dr. Joel Rosenbloom, Dir.

Desc: Oral health, including team studies on biochemistry of connective and hard tissues, analyses of structural and functional constituents of oral microbes, and immunobiology of oral tissues and investigation of plaque formation and effect on periodontal tissues. *Type:* Research center.

University of Rochester

Eastman Dental Center

625 Elmwood Ave.	Ph: (716)275-5001
Rochester, NY 14620	Fax: (716)244-8772

URL: http://www.urmc.rochester.edu/edc

Contact: Ronald J. Billings, DDS, Dir.

Desc: Clinical and basic scientific research on all aspects of oral disease, including dental caries, periodontal disease, craniofacial disorders, oral pain and health behavior. *Type:* Research center.

University of Rochester

Rochester Institute for Biomedical Sciences

Center for Oral Biology

601 Elmwood Ave., Medical	Ph: (716)275-3441
Center Box 611	Fax: (716)473-2679
Rochester, NY 14642-8611	

E-mail: lawrence_tabak@urmc.rochester.edu
URL: http://www.urmc.rochester.edu/ribs/oralbio/welcome.html

Contact: Dr. Lawrence Tabak, Dir.

Desc: Saliva glucosyltransferase interactions on surfaces, polysaccharide metabolism by oral bacteria, base production in dental plaque, molecular biology of periodontal pathogens, regulation of mucous cell secretion, basic and applied microbial physiology, interaction of infectious eukaryotic microorganisms with host defense systems, mechanisms and regulation of fluid and electrolyte secretion, genetic engineering of bacteria and regulation of bacterial gene expression, and biosynthesis, structure, function of mucin-glycoproteins, craniofacial development, and role of D-glycosylation in oro-pharyngeal development. *Type:* Research center.

University of Southern California

Center for Craniofacial Molecular Biology

Sch. of Dentistry	Ph: (323)442-3170
2250 Alcazar St.	Fax: (323)442-2981
CSA 103	
Los Angeles, CA 90033	

E-mail: shuler@zygote.hsc.usc.edu
URL: http://www.usc.edu/hsc/dental/ccmb/index.html

Contact: Dr. Charles F. Shuler, Dir.

Desc: Craniofacial molecular biology, including cleft palate, congenital malformations, myogenesis, and taste and biotechnologies. *Type:* Research center.

University of Southern California

Laboratory for Developmental Genetics

Department of Basic Sci.	Ph: (213)740-1400
Sch. of Dentistry	Fax: (213)740-7650
Univ. Park	
Los Angeles, CA 90089-0641	

E-mail: tjaskoll@hsc.usc.edu

Contact: Dr. T. Jaskoll, Co-Dir.

Desc: Cellular, molecular, and developmental biology issues associated with craniofacial, and salivary gland, and lung morphogenesis, including studies of secondary palate, and craniofacial genetics. *Type:* Research center.

University of Toronto

Office of Associate Dean of Research

Faculty of Dentistry	Ph: (416)979-4921
124 Edward St.	Fax: (416)979-4936
Toronto, ON, Canada M5G	
1G6	

E-mail: jheersche@dental.utoronto.ca

Contact: Prof. Johan N.M. Heersche, Assoc. Dean.

Desc: Coordinates all research activities within the Faculty of Dentistry in the fields of biometrics, biochemistry, epidemiology, cell biology, molecular biology, bacteriology, neurophysiology, electron microscopy, and histology, including studies on metabolism of oral tissues in health and disease states, organic and inorganic constituents of teeth, protein composition of saliva, cellular elements, tooth development, biomaterials, neural mechanisms of oral/facial function, regulation of bone cell differentiation and bone cell metabolism, (including bone formation and resorption), clinical studies related to many of these basic science areas, including craniofacial growth and development, implantology, restorative materials, periodontal disease, healthcare systems, feeding disorders, pain, gerontology, and oral cancer. *Type:* Research center.

University of Washington

Research Center in Oral Biology

Box 357480	Ph: (206)543-5599
Seattle, WA 98195	Fax: (206)685-8024

E-mail: bdale@u.washington.edu

Contact: Dr. Beverly Dale-Crunk, Dir.

Desc: Wound healing and tissue regeneration at the molecular and genetic levels and genetic regulation of cell growth and synthetic activities. *Type:* Research center.

Virginia Commonwealth University

Clinical Research Center for Periodontal Diseases

521 N. 11th St.	Ph: (804)828-9185
PO Box 980566	Fax: (804)828-5787
Richmond, VA 23298-0566	

Contact: Dr. Harvey A. Schenkein, Dir.

Desc: Periodontal diseases, including bacteriology, immunology, and genetics, to determine causative bacteria and the mechanism and role of host response in pathogenesis in order to devise improved preventive and therapeutic methods. *Type:* Research center.

Word of Mouth

Delta Dental Plan of California

PO Box 7736	Ph: (415)972-8487
San Francisco, CA 94120	Fax: (415)972-8466

Contact: Natashae Curry, Editor, (415)977-7923, fax: (415)563-6326, ncurry@delta.org.

Desc: Reports on new dental benefits programs and services provided by the company and lists clients joining the plan. Recurring features include a column titled Supertooth Dental Health Tips, providing information on dental care and disease. *Type:* Newsletter.

Xi Psi Phi

c/o Dr. Keith W. Dickey	Ph: (618)463-1889
1623 Washington Ave., No. 300	
Alton, IL 62002	

E-mail: xipsiphi@hotmail.com

Contact: Dr. Keith W. Dickey, Sec.-Treas.

Desc: Professional dental fraternity - dentistry. Maintains Hall of Fame. Conducts educational programs. *Type:* Association.

Dermatology

American Academy of Dermatology

930 N. Meacham Rd.	Ph: (847)330-0230
Schaumburg, IL 60173	Free: 888-462-3376
	Fax: (847)330-0050

URL: http://www.aad.org

Contact: Bradford W. Claxton, Exec.Dir.

Desc: Professional society of medical doctors specializing in skin diseases. Conducts educational programs. Provides placement service; compiles statistics. *Type:* Association.

Baylor University

Baylor Hair Research and Treatment Center

3600 Gaston Ave., Ste. 1058   Ph: (214)820-4247
Dallas, TX 75246   Fax: (214)824-1900
Contact: David A. Whiting, MD, Dir.
Desc: Hair-related problems, including hair loss, abnormal hair texture, scalp disease, hair overgrowth, and nail disorders. Activities include studies of methods to stimulate hair growth, studies of hair transplantation, and evaluation of transverse sections of the scalp. *Type:* Research center.

Dystrophic Epidermolysis Bullosa Research Association of America

40 Rector St.   Ph: (212)513-4090
New York, NY 10006   Fax: (212)513-4099
E-mail: debraorg@erols.com
URL: http://www.debra.org
Contact: Miriam Feder, Contact.
Desc: Epidermolysis Bullosa patients and their families. (Epidermolysis Bullosa represents a group of inherited disorders of the skin characterized by formation of blisters resulting from the most minimal trauma.). *Type:* Research center.

Fulton Skin Institute

1617 Westcliff Dr., Ste. 100   Ph: (714)631-3376
Newport Beach, CA 92660   Fax: (714)631-1284
Contact: Dr. James E. Fulton, Jr., Contact.
Desc: Cosmetic surgery, aggravating factors, and pathogenesis and treatment of acne. *Type:* Research center.

Indiana University-Purdue University at Indianapolis

Hackney Dermatopathology Research Laboratory

975 W. Walnut St., Rm. 349   Ph: (317)274-7115
Indianapolis, IN 46202
URL: http://www.indiana.edu/~rugs/ctrdir/hdrl.html
Contact: Dan F. Spandau, Dir.
Desc: Skin diseases, including skin cancer and psoriasis and the genetic changes that occur with these conditions. Wound healing and the aging of skin are also studied. *Type:* Research center.

Massachusetts General Hospital

Harvard Cutaneous Biology Research Center

MGH-East, Bldg. 149   Ph: (617)726-4425
Charlestown, MA 02129   Fax: (617)726-4027
E-mail: jparrish.@brc.mgh.hr.edu
Contact: Dr. John Parrish, Dir.
Desc: Dermatology, including photobiology of skin, including photoimmunology, photoaging, free radical biology and photoprotection; pigment cell biology; growth and differentiation of epidermis, hair and nails, and keratin biochemistry; immunology, allergy, inflammation, and modifiers of host response; physical properties of skin, including water content, percutaneous transport of chemicals, and optical properties; physiology and pharmacology of the skin; and biology of dermis and dermal-epidermal junction and their constituents. *Type:* Research center.

National Psoriasis Foundation

6600 SW 92nd, Ste. 300   Ph: (503)244-7404
Portland, OR 97223   Fax: (503)245-0626
E-mail: getinfo@npfusa.org
URL: http://www.psoriasis.org
Contact: Gail M. Zimmerman, Exec.Dir.
Desc: Psoriasis, including investigations into causes, treatment, and cure of this dermatological disease. Provides funds to researchers. *Type:* Research center.

National Psoriasis Foundation

6600 SW 92nd, Ste. 300   Ph: (503)244-7404
Portland, OR 97223-7195   Free: 800-723-9166
    Fax: (503)245-0626
E-mail: getinfo@npfusa.org
URL: http://www.psoriasis.org
Contact: Gail M. Zimmerman, Exec.Dir.
Desc: Individuals suffering from psoriasis, or psoriatic arthritis, their families and friends; physicians, nurses, and representatives of pharmaceutical companies. Supports research at various university research centers. Facilitates communication through pen pal programs, group sessions, and other activities. *Type:* Association.

National Vitiligo Foundation

PO Box 6337   Ph: (903)531-0074
Tyler, TX 75703   Fax: (903)531-9767
E-mail: 73071.33@compuserve.com
URL: http://www.nvfi.org
Contact: Jerri Bossley, Exec.Dir.
Desc: Doctors and patients; contributors and supporters. Provides information and counseling to vitiligo patients and their families. *Type:* Association.

Psoriasis Research Association

107 Vista del Grande   Ph: (650)593-1394
San Carlos, CA 94070
Contact: Diane Bradley Mullins, Exec.Sec. & Founder.
Desc: Psoriasis, a chronic skin disease characterized by red patches covered with white scales, focusing on the causes and cure of the disease. *Type:* Research center.

Psoriasis Research Institute

600 Town & Country Village   Ph: (415)326-1848
Palo Alto, CA 94301   Fax: (415)326-1262
E-mail: emfpri@aol.com
URL: http://www.best.com/psorhelp
Contact: Eugene M. Farber, MD, Pres.
Desc: Biochemistry, virology, epidemiology, pharmacology, and pathology, with the goal of finding the cause of and a cure for psoriasis. *Type:* Research center.

Rockefeller University

Laboratory for Investigative Dermatology

1230 York Ave.   Ph: (212)327-8091
New York, NY 10021-6399   Fax: (212)327-8232
E-mail: kruegej@rockvax.rockfeller.edu
Contact: James G. Krueger, MD, Hd.
Desc: A variety of skin conditions, including the biology of epithelial cells and the study of psoriasis. *Type:* Research center.

U.S. Department of Health and Human Services National Cancer Institute Division of Clinical Sciences Intramural Research Program

NIH Bldg. 10, Rm. 12N238   Ph: (301)496-2481
9000 Rockville Pike   Fax: (301)496-5370
Bethesda, MD 20892
Contact: Dr. Stephen Katz, Chf.
Desc: Growth and differentiation of epithelium and lymphoreticu lar tissues in normal, hyperplastic, neoplastic, and inflammatory states; protein synthesis by epithelium, especially of tonofilaments, keratohaylin, and actin; immunologic determinants of tissue behavior in normal and neoplastic states; immunologic abnormalities in blistering diseases of the skin; physiology of lymphoreticular cells and lymphokine formation; and the biological activity of oncogenic viruses. Also studied are experimental allergic contact dermatitis; genodermatoses; biochemistry and keratinization; xeroderma pigmentosum, an inherited disease of sun sensitivity, and multiple cutaneous cancer with abnormal DNA repair; clinical, chemical, and ultrastructural effects of vitamin A on skin; the oncogenic potential of tumor viruses; and the development of therapy of epithelial cancers, skin lymphomas, and keratinizing diseases of the skin. *Type:* Research center.

U.S. Department of Health and Human Services National Institute of Arthritis and Musculoskeletal and Skin Diseases Extramural Activities Program Skin Diseases Branch

Bldg. 45, Rm. 5AS25L   Ph: (301)594-5017
45 Center Dr.   Fax: (301)480-4543
Bethesda, MD 20892-6500
E-mail: moshella@ep.niams.nih.gov
Contact: Alan N. Moshell, MD, Dir.
Desc: Structure, function, and physiology of skin as well as on the causes and improved treatment of a wide variety of skin diseases, including psoriasis, lupus, eczema, vitiligo, bullous skin diseases, acne, and ichthyosis. *Type:* Research center.

U.S. Department of Health and Human Services National Institutes of Health National Institute of Arthritis and Musculoskeletal and Skin Diseases

9000 Rockville Pike   Ph: (301)496-4353
Bethesda, MD 20892
URL: http://www.nih.gov/niams/
Contact: Steven I. Katz, MD, Director.
Desc: The Institute conducts and supports fundamental research in the major disease categories of arthritis and musculoskeletal and skin diseases through research performed in its own laboratories and clinics, epidemiologic studies, research contracts and grants, and cooperative agreements to scientific institutions and to individuals. It also supports training of manpower in fundamental sciences and clinical disciplines and conducts educational activities, including the collection and dissemination of health educational materials on these diseases. *Type:* Government agency, office, or program.

University of California, San Francisco

Dermatology Drug Research Unit

515 Spruce   Ph: (415)476-4701
Box 1212   Fax: (415)502-4126
San Francisco, CA 94143
Contact: John Koo, MD, Dir.
Desc: Conducts clinical testing of new or existing pharmacologic agents used in the treatment of skin disorders and develops protocols for drug testing. Areas of interest include phototherapy, psoriasis, and psychodermatology. *Type:* Research center.

Diabetes

American Association of Diabetes Educators

100 W. Monroe, 4th Fl.   Ph: (312)424-2426
Chicago, IL 60603-1901   Free: 800-338-DMED
    Fax: (312)424-2427
URL: http://www.aadenet.org
Contact: James J. Balija, Exec.Dir.
Desc: Nurses, dietitians, social workers, physicians, pharmacists, podiatrists, and others involved in teaching diabetes self-management to diabetics. Purposes are: to provide educational opportunities for the professional growth and development of members; to promote the development of quality diabetes education for the diabetic consumer; to foster communication and cooperation among individuals and organizations involved in diabetes patient education. Offers continuing education programs for diabetes educators. *Type:* Association.

American Diabetes Association

1660 Duke St.   Ph: (703)549-1500
Alexandria, VA 22314   Free: 800-DIABETES
    Fax: (703)836-7439
E-mail: customerservice@diabetes.org

URL: http://www.diabetes.org

Contact: John H. Graham, IV, CEO.

Desc: Physicians, laypersons, and health professionals interested in diabetes mellitus. Promotes research, information and advocacy to find a prevention and cure for diabetes and to improve the lives of all people with diabetes. *Type:* Association.

Joslin Diabetes Center

1 Joslin Pl.   Ph: (617)732-2400
Boston, MA 02136   Fax: (617)732-2562
URL: http://www.joslin.harvard.edu

Contact: Dr. Kenneth E. Quickel, Pres.

Desc: Supported by persons interested in advancing knowledge and improving treatment of diabetes with the eventual goal of discovering a means of prevention and cure. *Type:* Association.

Disabilities

Ability Building Center

1911 14th St. NW   Ph: (507)281-6262
Rochester, MN 55901   Fax: (507)281-6270

Contact: Wally Bigelow, Exec.Dir.

Desc: Provides training and employment for disabled individuals. *Type:* Association.

Ability Magazine

Ability Magazine
1001 W. 17th St.   Ph: (714)854-8700
Costa Mesa, CA 92627   Fax: (714)548-5966
E-mail: ability@pacbell.net.
URL: http://www.abilitymagazine.com.

Contact: Fred Bailey, Editor; Chet Cooper, Advertising Mgr.

Desc: Lifestyle magazine featuring celebrity interviews about health and diabetes, new technologies, and general human interest. *Type:* Periodical.

Accommodating Disabilities

CCH Inc.
2700 Lake Cook Rd.   Ph: (847)267-7000
Riverwoods, IL 60015   Free: 800-449-8114
    Fax: (847)224-8299
URL: http://www.cch.com

Contact: Gretta J. Sancho, JD, Editor.

Desc: Provides information on developments in disability discrimination law, and offers practical advice on compliance. Recurring features include letters to the editor, interviews, news of research, a calendar of events, reports of meetings, and book reviews. *Type:* Newsletter.

Add-Up

Listening, Inc.
8716 Pine Ave.   Ph: (219)938-6962
Gary, IN 46403
E-mail: addup@crown.net

Contact: Richard Bennett, Editor.

Desc: Provides information about treating and reversing attention deficit disorder. Recurring features include letters to the editor, interviews, news of research, a calendar of events, and book reviews. *Type:* Newsletter.

American Association on Mental Retardation

444 North Capitol St., N.W.   Ph: (202)387-1968
    Ste. 846   Free: 800-424-3688
Washington, DC 20001-1512   Fax: (202)387-2193
E-mail: aamr@access.digex.net
URL: http://www.aamr.org

Contact: M. Doreen Croser, Exec.Dir.

Desc: Mental retardation, including studies on programmatic aspects of service to persons with mental retardation in residential facilities and community-based settings. Prevention, behavioral, family support, employment, education and health are other areas of research and programmatic concern. *Type:* Research center.

American Council of the Blind

1155 15th St. NW, Ste. 720   Ph: (202)467-5081
Washington, DC 20005   Free: 800-424-8666
    Fax: (202)467-5085
E-mail: info@acb.org
URL: http://www.acb.org

Contact: Charles Crawford, Exec. Dir.

Desc: Blind and visually impaired persons. Serves as a national information clearinghouse on blindness for individuals, organizations, and institutions. Provides information and advisory service on federal legislation, administrative action, and rule-making on the national and state levels. *Type:* Association.

American Council of the Blind Enterprises and Services

120 S. 6th St., Ste. 1005   Ph: (612)332-3242
Minneapolis, MN 55402-1839   Free: 800-866-3242
    Fax: (612)332-7850
E-mail: acbesall@ix.netcom.com

Contact: James R. Olsen, Exec.Dir.

Desc: Board of directors of the American Council of the Blind. Owns and operates 11 ACB thrift stores, owned and operated by blind persons, which help finance ACB and its programs and aid the blind and visually impaired in leading productive and independent lives. *Type:* Association.

American Disability Association

2201 Sixth Ave. South   Ph: (205)323-3030
Birmingham, AL 35233   Fax: (205)251-7417
E-mail: wjf@bellsouth.net
URL: http://www.adanet.org

Contact: William J. Freeman, Pres.

Desc: Serves as a support group for individuals with disabilities. Provides exchange of information on disability issues. Makes available children's services, educational and research programs, and charitable services. *Type:* Association.

American Foundation for the Blind

11 Penn Plz., Ste. 300   Ph: (212)502-7600
New York, NY 10001   Free: 800-AFB-LINE
    Fax: (212)502-7777
E-mail: afbinfo@afb.org
URL: http://www.afb.org

Contact: Carl R. Augusto, Pres.

Desc: Dedicated to helping those who cannot see live like those who do. *Type:* Association.

American Printing House for the Blind

1839 Frankfort Ave.   Ph: (502)895-2405
PO Box 6085   Free: 800-223-1839
Louisville, KY 40206-0085   Fax: (502)899-2274
E-mail: info@aph.org
URL: http://www.aph.org

Contact: Dr. Tuck Tinsley, III, Pres.

Desc: Produces literature in all media (braille, large type, recorded, computer disc) for the blind. Manufactures educational aids for special use by visually impaired students, such as preschool and vocational materials and talking educational software. *Type:* Association.

Americans With Disabilities Act Manual

The Bureau of National Affairs, Inc. (BNA)
1231 25th St. NW   Ph: (202)452-4200
Washington, DC 20037
E-mail: bnaplus@bna.com
URL: http://bna.com/mkt/hrl/hrlwdec.htm

Desc: Contains the complete text of the Americans With Disabilities Act (ADA). Covers all five titles including Title I, Employment; Title II, Public Service and Transportation; Title III, Public Accommodations and Commercial Facilities; Title IV, Telecommunications; and Title V, Miscellaneous Provisions. *Type:* Database.

The ARC

500 E. Border St., Ste. 300   Ph: (817)261-6003
Arlington, TX 76010   Fax: (817)277-3491
E-mail: thearc@metronet.com
URL: http://www.TheArc.org

Contact: Alan Abeson, Ed.D., Exec.Dir.

Desc: Parents, professional workers, and others interested in individuals with mental retardation. Works on local, state, and national levels to promote services, research, public understanding, and legislation for people with mental retardation and their families. *Type:* Association.

Architectural and Transportation Barriers Compliance Board

1331 F St. NW, Ste. 1000   Ph: (202)272-5434
Washington, DC 20004-1111

Desc: The Board was established to investigate and examine alternative approaches to the architectural, transportation, and attitudinal barriers confronting disabled persons; determine what measures are being taken by federal, state, and local governments and by other public and private agencies to eliminate those barriers; and promote the use of the International Accessibility Symbol in all public facilities that meet the standards prescribed by the Administrator of the General Services Administration Board. *Type:* Government agency, office, or program.

Arkansas Easter Seal Society

3920 Woodland Heights Rd.   Ph: (501)227-3600
Little Rock, AR 72212-2495   Free: 800-527-2033
    Fax: (501)227-3601
E-mail: aess@cei.net
URL: http://www.arkeasterseals.org

Contact: Sharon Moone-Jochums, CEO.

Desc: Establishes and conducts programs that serve people with disabilities. Services provided include therapy, nursing care, job training, and residential rehabilitative care. *Type:* Association.

Associated Services for the Blind

919 Walnut St.   Ph: (215)627-0600
Philadelphia, PA 19107   Fax: (215)922-0692
E-mail: asbinfo@libertynet.org

Contact: Patricia C. Johnson, Chief Exec. Officer.

Desc: Multiservice agency that provides services to blind and visually impaired people. Objective is to help blind and visually impaired people live independently. Activities include: operating a braille printing house that transcribes print materials into braille; radio reading service that reads newspapers and magazines over closed-circuit radio. *Type:* Association.

Association for Advancement of Blind and Retarded

1508 College Point Blvd.   Ph: (718)523-2222
PO Box 560247   Fax: (718)321-8688
College Point, NY 11356

Contact: Christopher Weldon, Exec.Dir.

Desc: Community groups and individuals interested in multihandicapped blind and severely retarded adults. Operates: 12 group residences providing intermediate care facilities for blind and retarded adults; two- to six-day treatment centers for blind, multihandicapped, and severely retarded adults; summer camp for blind and multihandicapped people. Provides information and referral services. *Type:* Association.

Association of Birth Defect Children

930 Woodcock Rd., Ste. 225   Ph: (407)245-7035
Orlando, FL 32803   Free: 800-313-ABDC
    Fax: (407)895-0824
E-mail: abdc@marketweb.com
URL: http://www.birthdefects.org

Contact: Betty Mekdeci, Exec.Dir.

Desc: Parents, health professionals, educators, members of Congress, hospitals, libraries, organizations and services for the handicapped, and individuals united to prevent birth defects, especially those associated with drugs, chemicals, radiation, and other environmental substances. Provides parents, educators, and professionals in medical- and health-related fields with information on birth defects and research in prosthetics. *Type:* Association.

Association for Children with Retarded Mental Development

345 Hudson St.   Ph: (212)741-0100
New York, NY 10014   Fax: (212)627-8318
E-mail: acrmd@mail.idt.net
URL: http://www.acrmd.com

Contact: Arthur Roza, Exec.Dir.

Desc: Professionals, parents, siblings, and others interested in mentally retarded and developmentally disabled adults. Membership centered in New York City area. Offers professionally supervised programs for mentally retarded and developmentally disabled adults, including vocational rehabilitation, dual diagnosis programs, job placement, rehabilitation workshops, activities for daily living, day treatment, day training, supported work, and family support programs. *Type:* Association.

Autism Services Center

Prichard Bldg.   Ph: (304)525-8014
605 9th St., PO Box 507   Fax: (304)525-8026
Huntington, WV 25710-0507

Contact: Ruth C. Sullivan, Ph.D., Dir.

Desc: Works to improve the processes by which appropriate and professional training, consulting, advocacy, and information are provided to individuals responsible for the welfare and care of autistic individuals and others with developmental disabilities. Maintains roster of autism professionals, researchers, therapists, and educators. *Type:* Association.

Autism Services Center

605 9th St.   Ph: (304)525-8014
PO Box 507   Fax: (304)525-8026
Huntington, WV 25710-0507

Contact: Ruth C. Sullivan, Ph.D., Exec.Dir.

Desc: Service agency for individuals with autism and other developmental disabilities, and their families. (Autism is a disorder of communication and behavior which often manifests itself in social isolation, severe language deficiency, and compulsive insistence on routine and ritual in daily activities.) Assists families and agencies attempting to meet the unique needs of individuals with autism and other developmental disabilities; makes available technical assistance in designing programs. Provides supervised apartments, group homes, respite services, independent living services, and job-coached employment. *Type:* Association.

Autism Society of America

7910 Woodmont Ave., Ste. 300   Ph: (301)657-0881
Bethesda, MD 20814   Free: 800-3AU-TISM
     Fax: (301)657-0869
URL: http://www.autism-society.org/

Contact: Audrey Horne, Pres.

Desc: Parents, teachers, psychologists, speech therapists, pediatricians, neurologists, and others interested in the welfare of children with severe disorders of communication and behavior. Informs the public of the symptoms and problems of children and adults with autism; promotes better understanding of the condition in general; aids physicians in making earlier and more accurate diagnoses. *Type:* Association.

Baylor College of Medicine
Mental Retardation Research Center

1 Baylor Plaza - T807   Ph: (713)798-6523
Houston, TX 77030   Fax: (713)798-8728
E-mail: hzognbi@bcm.tmc.edu

Contact: Huda Y. Zoghbi, MD, Dir.

Desc: Supports interdisciplinary research in mental retardation and its prevention. Topics include: Rett syndrome, epilepsy, Angelman and Prader-Willi syndrome, gene therapy, human X chromosome, cytomegalovirus infection, group b streptococci, chondrodysplasia punctata, and spinocerebellar ataxia, Fragile X Syndrome, Aicardi Syndrome, HIV infection, metabolic disorders, Incontinentia Pigmenti, Williams Syndrome. *Type:* Research center.

Bethphage Messenger

Bethphage
Lind Center, Ste. A   Ph: (402)896-3884
4980 S. 118th St.   Free: 800-279-1234
Omaha, NE 68137-2221   Fax: (402)896-1511

Contact: Linda Harvey, Editor.

Desc: Provides news and information on developmental disabilities and Bethphage programs. *Type:* Newsletter.

Blinded Veterans Association

477 H St. NW   Ph: (202)371-8880
Washington, DC 20001   Free: 800-669-7079
     Fax: (202)371-8258

Contact: Thomas H. Miller, Ph.D., Exec.Dir.

Desc: Veterans who lost their sight as a result of military service in the armed forces of the U.S.; associate members are veterans whose loss of sight was not connected with military service. Assists blinded veterans in attaining benefits and employment and with reestablishing themselves as adjusted, active, and productive citizens in their communities. Offers placement service; supports research programs; compiles statistics. *Type:* Association.

Boston University
Human Bioenergetics Laboratory

635 Commonwealth Ave., 4th   Ph: (617)353-2719
Fl.   Fax: (617)353-7567
Boston, MA 02215

Contact: Dr. Roger Fielding, Dir.

Desc: Exercise physiology and fitness for disabled and non-disabled populations. *Type:* Research center.

Braille Institute

741 N. Vermont Ave.   Ph: (213)663-1111
Los Angeles, CA 90029

Contact: Russell W. Kirbey, Exec.Dir.

Desc: Provides education, counseling, job placement, rehabilitation, and other services for the blind. Maintains free library of over 600,000 volumes in braille, on cassettes, and on "talking book" recordings. Maintains 15 community centers in southern California. *Type:* Association.

Braille Institute of America

741 N Vermont Ave.   Ph: (213)663-1111
Los Angeles, CA 90029   Free: 800-BRA-ILLE
     Fax: (213)663-0867
URL: http://www.brailleinstitute.org

Contact: Leslie E. Stocker, Pres.

Desc: Provides educational training and services to blind and visually impaired persons in the Southern California area. Operates speakers' bureau and local community and outreach programs. *Type:* Association.

Canine Companions for Independence

PO Box 446   Ph: (707)577-1700
Santa Rosa, CA 95402-0446   Free: 800-572-2275
     Fax: (707)577-1711
E-mail: info@caninecompanions.org
URL: http://www.caninecompanions.org/

Contact: Mr. Corey Hudson, Exec.Dir.

Desc: Provides to people with disabilities, specially-bred and trained dogs enabling them to lead more personally fulfilling and socially productive lives. Believes that human attendance care is reduced with the aid these dogs provide. Provides four types of Canine Companions: Hearing Dogs trained to alert the hearing-impaired to sounds such as the doorbell, smoke alarm, or a baby's cry; Assisted Service dogs used for children with disabilities, people with developmental disabilities, or anywhere the supervision of a third party is required; Service Dogs trained to provide physical assistance, such as retrieving dropped objects, operating elevator buttons and light switches, and pulling wheelchairs and Facility dogs placed with professionals in facilities where interaction with a dog will be beneficial to the mental or physical health of those in their care. *Type:* Association.

CANUC:H

National Library of Canada
Acquisitions and Bibliographic Services Branch
Union Catalogue Division
395 Wellington St.   Ph: (613)997-7990
Ottawa, ON, Canada K1A 0N4
E-mail: union.catalogue@nlc-bnc.ca

Contact: Ellen Katic, (819)997-1422, fax: (819)953-0291, unioncatalogue@ncl-bnc.ca.

Desc: Contains bibliographic descriptions of approximately 122,000 alternate format materials (braille, large print, talking books, described videos, closed and open-captioned videos, and computer files) held in Canadian libraries and other institutions available for interlibrary loan. Includes a companion registry, Canadian Works in Progress (CANWIP), which lists prepublication titles produced by Canadian nonprofit institutions serving visually-impaired persons. *Available:* Ovid Technologies, Inc. *Type:* Database.

Carroll Center for the Blind

770 Centre St.   Ph: (617)969-6200
Newton, MA 02458   Free: 800-852-3131
     Fax: (617)969-6204
E-mail: rrosenbaum@carroll.org
URL: http://www.tiac.net/uuers/carrollb

Contact: Rachel Ethier Rosenbaum, Pres.

Desc: Provides programs for resident and commuter clients. *Type:* Association.

Center for Family Support

333 7th Ave., 9th Fl.   Ph: (212)629-7939
New York, NY 10001   Fax: (212)239-2211
URL: http://www.cfsny.org

Contact: Steven Vernikoff, Exec.Dir.

Desc: Service agency devoted to the physical well-being and development of the retarded child and the sound mental health of the parents. Helps families with retarded children with all aspects of home care including counseling, referrals, home aide service, and consultation. Offers intervention for parents at the birth of a retarded child with in-home support, guidance, and infant stimulation. *Type:* Association.

Center on Promoting Employment

Institute for Community Ph: (617)355-4668
 Inclusion
Children's Hospital
300 Longwood Ave.
Boston, MA 02115
E-mail: kiernanw@a1.tch.harvard.edu
URL: http://www.childrenshospital.org/ici/programs/
research/rrtc/
Contact: William E. Kiernan, PhD, Proj.Dir.
Desc: Promotion of successful employment outcomes for
individuals with disabilities through the study of best practices in the job search for individuals with disabilities, employer practices, assistive technology and job
accommodation practices, and a survey of state vocational
rehabilitation practices. *Type:* Research center.

Challenged Conquistadors

Shaun Best
SAU Box 750 Ph: (501)235-4539
Magnolia, AR 71753 Free: 800-501-0139
 Fax: (501)235-4800
E-mail: swbest@mail.sausag.edu
Contact: Shaun Best, Pres.
Desc: Works to increase self preservation, reduce dependency, and eradicate negative stereotypes, myths, and stigmas. *Type:* Association.

Christian Record Services

4444 S. 52nd St. Ph: (402)488-0981
Lincoln, NE 68516-1302 Fax: (402)488-7582
E-mail: 74617.236@compuserve.com
URL: http://www.tagnet.org/crs
Contact: Lawrence J. Pitcher, Contact.
Desc: Assists blind, visually impaired, and hearing impaired individuals. Sponsors Bible correspondence
courses. Representatives visit about 40,000 blind people
annually. *Type:* Association.

Complete Directory for People with Disabilities

Grey House Publishing
Pocket Knife Square Ph: (860)435-0868
Lakeville, CT 06039 Free: 800-562-2139
 Fax: (860)435-0867
E-mail: books@li.com
URL: http://www.greyhouse.com
Desc: Over 8,000 products, services, organizations and facilities available for the disabled, including assistive devices, publications, camps, educational programs, housing,
recreation, rehabilitation services, associations, travel and
transportation services, and conferences and shows. *Type:*
Directory.

Council on Quality Leadership in support for People with Disabilities

100 West Rd., Ste. 406 Ph: (410)583-0060
Towson, MD 21204 Fax: (410)583-0063
E-mail: info@thecouncil.org
URL: http://www.thecouncil.org
Contact: James F. Gardner, Ph.D., Pres./CEO.
Desc: Devoted to improving the quality of services available to people with disabilities. *Type:* Association.

Directory of Facilities and Services for the Learning Disabled

Academic Therapy Publications
High Noon Books/Ann Arbor Pub.
20 Commercial Blvd. Ph: (415)883-3314
Novato, CA 94949-6191 Free: 800-422-7249
 Fax: (415)883-3720
E-mail: atpub@aol.com
Contact: Betty Lou Kratoville, Editor.
Desc: About 300 facilities which help children and adults
with diagnosed learning disabilities; publishers and pro-

ducers of books and other materials; organizations and
agencies; educational journals; special education clearing
houses; educational software networks and distributors.
Type: Directory.

Disability Funding News

CD Publications
8204 Fenton St. Ph: (301)588-6380
Silver Spring, MD 20910 Free: 800-666-6380
 Fax: (301)588-6385
E-mail: cdpubs@clark.net
Contact: Leonard Curry, Editorial Dir.; William P. Hoar,
Managing Editor.
Desc: Provides "in-depth coverage of all the latest federal
funding available to support your programs, with detailed
grant listings." Also covers national issues which affect the
disabled. *Type:* Newsletter.

Disability Leave & Absence Reporter

Bureau of Business Practice
24 Rope Ferry Rd. Ph: (860)442-4365
Waterford, CT 06386 Free: 800-243-0876
 Fax: (860)437-3555
URL: http://www.bbpnews.com
Contact: Mary-Lou Devine, Editor, mary_lou-devine@
prenhall.com.
Desc: Provides information and tips for complying with
workers' compensation laws, the ADA, and the FMLA. Includes news, court rulings, expert advice, and sample policies. *Type:* Newsletter.

Disability Resources Monthly

Disability Resources
4 Glatter Ln. Ph: (516)585-0290
Centereach, NY 11720-1032 Fax: (516)585-0290
E-mail: info@disabilityresources.org
Contact: Julie Klauber, Editor, jklauber@
disabilityresources.org.
Desc: Features short topical articles, reviews, and news
items about disability-related books, pamphlets, periodicals, videotapes, organizations, and computer resources.
Type: Newsletter.

Disabled Sports USA

451 Hungerford Dr., Ste. 100 Ph: (301)217-0960
Rockville, MD 20850 Fax: (301)217-0968
Contact: Kirk M. Bauer, Exec.Dir.
Desc: Promotes sports and recreation opportunities for individuals with physical disabilities. Provides direct services
to people with mobility impairments, including amputations, paraplegia, quadriplegia, spinal cord injuries, stroke,
head injuries, cerebral palsy, polio, muscular dystrophy,
multiple sclerosis, arthrogryposis, birth defects, neuromuscular disabilities, and visual impairments. Offers and sanctions recreational winter and summer programs, including
learn-to-ski, learn-to-sail, and learn-to-race clinics, competitive alpine and nordic skiing, archery, basketball, cycling, lawnbowling, shooting, swimming, table tennis,
track and field, volleyball, sailing, and weighlifting. *Type:*
Association.

Dyslexia Research Institute

4745 Centerville Rd. Ph: (850)893-2216
Tallahassee, FL 32308-2899 Fax: (850)893-2440
E-mail: dri@dyslexia-add.org
URL: http://www.Dylexia-add.org
Contact: Dr. Patricia K. Hardman, Dir.
Desc: Dyslexia and attention deficit disorders, including
educational techniques, teacher training, diagnostic procedures, biochemistry, allergies, and links alcoholism and
eye movement. *Type:* Research center.

Easter Seal Society of Rhode Island

667 Waterman Ave. Ph: (401)438-9500
East Providence, RI 02914 Fax: (401)438-3760
E-mail: ccmsc@brainiac.com
URL: http://www.brainiac.com/meetingstreet
Contact: Dean E. Martins.
Desc: Conducts programs to assist people with disabilities.
Performs support and information services. *Type:* Association.

Easter Seal Society of Southern California

1801 E. Edinger Ave., Ste. 190 Ph: (714)834-1111
Santa Ana, CA 92705-4749 Fax: (714)834-1128
URL: http://www.essc.org
Contact: Mark Whitley, Pres.
Desc: Conducts programs to assist people with disabilities.
Performs support and information services. *Type:* Association.

Easter Seals Delaware & Maryland's Eastern Shore

New Castle Corporate Ph: (302)324-4444
 Commons Free: 800-677-3800
61 Commons Blvd. Fax: (302)324-4441
New Castle, DE 19720
URL: http://www.ravenet.com/easterseals/index.hmtl
Contact: Sandra J. Tuttle, CEO/Pres.
Desc: Conducts programs to assist people with disabilities.
Performs support and information services. *Type:* Association.

Fidelco Guide Dog Foundation

PO Box 142 Ph: (860)243-5200
Bloomfield, CT 06002 Fax: (860)243-7215
E-mail: pr@fidelco.org
URL: http://www.fidelco.org
Contact: George J. Salpietro, Sr.VP.
Desc: Purpose is to breed, train, and place Fidelco German
shepherd guide dogs with blind persons (the Fidelco shepherd is a special breed ideally suited for guide work because
of its intelligence, strength, health, and stability). Provides
"In-Community" training services to blind persons; reviews performance of the guide dog teams (dog and blind
individual) to see that satisfactory level of achievement is
maintained; utilizes genetic processes and clinical methods
to improve and refine the breed; maintains an ongoing
program for development and improvement of training
methods. Fidelco puppies are raised in a volunteer family
for the first 12-14 months, then trained by FGDF staff for
six months before final introduction to and training in the
workplace and home environment of the blind recipient
with a trainer's help. *Type:* Association.

Florida Easter Seal Society

1040 Woodcock RD STE 215
Orlando, FL 32803-3510
Contact: Robert J. Griggs, Pres.
Desc: Seeks to provide assistance to individuals in any way
disabled. *Type:* Association.

Foundation Fighting Blindness

Executive Plaza 1, Ste. 800 Ph: (410)785-1414
11350 McCormick Rd. Free: 888-394-3937
Hunt Valley, MD 21031-1014 Fax: (410)771-9470
URL: http://www.blindness.org
Contact: Robert Gray, CEO.
Desc: Works to fund research on causes, cures and prevention of retinitis pigmentosa (RP), Usher Syndrome, macular degeneration and related retinal degenerations. *Type:*
Association.

Goodwill Industries/Easter Seal Society of Minnesota
2543 Como Ave.   Ph: (612)646-2591
St. Paul, MN 55108-1298   Free: 800-669-6719
                               Fax: (612)649-0302
Contact: Michael Wirth-Davis, Pres/CEO.
Desc: Provides education, job training, and employment services for people with disabilities or disadvantages. *Type:* Association.

Goodwill Industries International
9200 Rockville Pike   Ph: (301)530-6500
Bethesda, MD 20814   Free: 800-664-6577
                               Fax: (301)530-1516
E-mail: cbragale@Goodwill.org
URL: http://www.goodwill.org
Contact: Fred Grandy, Pres. & CEO.
Desc: Federation of Goodwill Industries organizations across North America and the world are concerned primarily with providing employment, training, evaluation, counseling, placement, job training, and other vocational rehabilitation services and opportunities for individual growth for people with disabilities and other special needs. Member Goodwill Industries organizations collect donated goods and sell them in Goodwill retail stores as a means of providing employment and generating income. Conducts seminars and training programs; compiles statistics. *Type:* Association.

The Guardian
Pennsylvania Association for the Blind
2843 N. Front St.   Ph: (717)234-3261
Harrisburg, PA 17110-1284
Contact: William C. Range, Editor.
Desc: Educates children on eye health and safety and blindness. Publishes news of Sergeant Seymour's Eye Safety Program and provides information on related subjects. *Type:* Newsletter.

Guide Dog Foundation for the Blind
371 E. Jericho Tpke.   Ph: (516)265-2121
Smithtown, NY 11787   Free: 800-548-4337
                               Fax: (516)361-5192
E-mail: wjones@guidedog.org
URL: http://www.guidedog.org
Contact: Wells B. Jones, CAE, Exec.Dir.
Desc: Works to provide independence and mobility for qualified blind applicants by presenting them with trained guide dogs, free of charge. Dogs are raised in volunteer homes for the first year, then trained for four to six months. Conducts 25-day residential training program for blind persons and guide dogs at Smithtown, NY. *Type:* Association.

Guide Dogs for the Blind
PO Box 151200   Ph: (415)499-4000
San Rafael, CA 94915-1200   Free: 800-295-4050
                               Fax: (415)499-4035
E-mail: iadministration@guidedogs.com
URL: http://www.guidedogs.com
Contact: Richard A. Bobb, Pres. & CEO.
Desc: Supported by individuals, firms, foundations, clubs, and bequests. Provides guide dogs and in-residence training on their use to qualified blind persons, free of charge. *Type:* Association.

Guiding Eyes for the Blind
611 Granite Springs Rd.   Ph: (914)245-4024
Yorktown Heights, NY 10598   Free: 800-942-0149
E-mail: info@guiding-eyes.org
URL: http://www.guiding-eyes.org
Contact: William D. Badger, Pres. CEO.
Desc: Provides fully trained guide dogs and instruction in their use to visually impaired and blind individuals including special needs students with additional challenges. Conducts 3-year course for instructors and 4-week training programs for blind persons in proper use and care of guide dogs at Yorktown Heights, NY. Provides in-service education for staff and seminars for orientation and mobility instructors and other rehabilitation professionals. *Type:* Association.

Hagerstown Goodwill Industries
223 N. Prospect St.   Ph: (301)733-7330
Hagerstown, MD 21740   Fax: (301)739-7144
Contact: Craig M. Maclean, Exec.Dir.
Desc: To provide vocational training and placement services to the disabled and disadvantaged. *Type:* Association.

Handicapped Scuba Association
1104 El. Prado   Ph: (949)498-6128
San Clemente, CA 92672   Fax: (949)498-6128
E-mail: hsahdq@compuserve.com
URL: http://www.ourworld.compuserve.com/
homepages/hsahdq
Contact: Jim Gatacre, Program Dir.
Desc: Individuals with handicaps and interested others. Purpose is to advance and promote scuba diving among the handicapped. *Type:* Association.

Headlines
The Migraine Association of Canada
1912-365 Bloor St. E.   Ph: (416)920-4916
Toronto, ON, Canada M4W   Free: 800-663-3557
    3L4   Fax: (416)920-3677
Contact: Shaaron McDonald, Editor.
Desc: Supports migraine headache sufferers. Provides educational information. *Type:* Newsletter.

Helen Keller International
90 Washington St., 15th Fl.   Ph: (212)943-0890
New York, NY 10006   Fax: (212)943-1220
E-mail: info@hki.org
URL: http://www.hki.org
Contact: John M. Palmer, Pres.
Desc: Assists governments and voluntary agencies throughout Asia, Africa, and the Americas (including the United States) to establish and integrate, into their national health and welfare systems, services to prevent or cure eye diseases and blindness and to rehabilitate and educate visually disabled persons. Focuses on programs in the prevention and treatment of blindness caused by malnutrition, trachoma, onchocerciasis and cataracts. Trains health workers at all levels in the use of specially developed materials to diagnose and treat eye problems and to refer patients to hospitals. *Type:* Association.

IMPACT
Recording for the Blind & Dyslexic
20 Roszel Rd.   Ph: (609)520-8044
Princeton, NJ 08540   Fax: (609)520-7996
Contact: Diane Blaszka, Editor.
Desc: Reports news of the programs of Recording of the Blind and Dyslexic, "a national, nonprofit organization that provides educational resources for those who cannot read standard print because of a visual, perceptual, or other physical disability." Carries articles, features, and news about the 80,000 volume Master Tape Library, the accomplishments and achievements of those who use RFB&D recorded textbooks and disks, and the volunteers who read, monitor, and prepare the tapes and disks. *Type:* Newsletter.

In Touch
Talking Book Program (TBP)
Texas State Library
PO Box 12927   Ph: (512)463-5458
Austin, TX 78711-2927   Free: 800-252-9605
                               Fax: (512)463-5436
E-mail: tbp.services@tsl.state.tx.us
URL: http://www.link.tsl.state.tx.us/.dir/tbp_intouch.
dir/.
Desc: Reports on new services and publications available for blind, visually-impaired, learning disabled, and physically handicapped Texans. Contains stories on topics of interest to persons with reading-related disabilities. *Type:* Newsletter.

In Touch Networks
15 W. 65th St.   Ph: (212)769-6270
New York, NY 10023   Fax: (212)769-4148
Contact: Pete Williamson, Gen.Mgr.
Desc: Volunteer service that allows blind or physically impaired people to listen to readings of articles from more than 100 newspapers and magazines via closed-circuit radio. *Type:* Association.

Inclusion Times
National Professional Resources, Inc.
25 S. Regent St.   Ph: (914)937-8879
Port Chester, NY 10573   Free: 800-453-7461
                               Fax: (914)937-9327
Contact: Robert M. Hanson, Ed.D., Editor.
Desc: Presents information and ideas about "what people are calling inclusion" for children and youths with disabilities. Discusses topics such as physical education, personnel development, behavioral disorders, and court updates. *Type:* Newsletter.

Inside MS
National Multiple Sclerosis Society
733 3rd Ave.   Ph: (212)986-3240
New York, NY 10017   Free: 800-FIGHT-MS
                               Fax: (212)986-7981
E-mail: info@nmss.org
URL: http://www.nmss.org.
Contact: Martha King, Editor, editor@nmss.org.
Desc: Presents articles on topics of interest to persons with multiple sclerosis (MS) and their families. Recurring features include news of research, symptom management, letters, and columns titled According to the Law, Resource Roundup, You & Me, and Book and Video Reviews. *Type:* Newsletter.

Institute for Community Inclusion
Children's Hospital   Ph: (617)355-6956
300 Longwood Ave.   Fax: (617)355-7940
Boston, MA 02115
E-mail: kiernanw@a1.harvard.tch.edu
URL: http://www.childrenshospital.org/ici
Contact: William E. Kiernan, PhD, Dir.
Desc: Etiology of mental retardation, the impact of AIDS in adult populations, the development of employment opportunities for people with disabilities using natural supports, the development of supports for infants at risk, development of a managed care design for children with complex medical needs served in community settings, and clinical investigation of issues of autism and related behavior in community settings. *Type:* Research center.

International Center for the Disabled
340 E. 24th St.   Ph: (212)679-0100
New York, NY 10010   Fax: (212)585-6161
E-mail: ccgodfrey@aol.com
Contact: Herbert H. Krauss, PhD, Dir. of Rehabilitation Res.

Desc: Promising techniques designed to prevent, reduce, and control disabilities arising from persistent physical disorders. Studies focus on the control of deterioration and disability associated with recurring ear infections in children, symptom magnification in those with disabling conditions, and factors associated with gainful employment. *Type:* Research center.

International Society of Refractive Surgery

1175 Springs Centre South   Ph: (407)786-7446
   Blvd., Ste. 152   Free: 888-813-ISRS
Altamonte Springs, FL 32714   Fax: (407)786-7447
E-mail: isrs@isrs.org
URL: http://www.isrs.org

Contact: Elizabeth Best, Exec.Dir.

Desc: Eye care professionals. Provides scientific research, knowledge, and information to all individuals who are interested in refractive surgery. *Type:* Association.

Jewish Braille Institute of America

110 E. 30th St.   Ph: (212)889-2525
New York, NY 10016   Free: 800-433-1531
   Fax: (212)689-3692
E-mail: admin@jewishbraille.org
URL: http://www.jewishbraille.org

Contact: Gerald M. Kass, Exec.VP.

Desc: Serves the religious, cultural, educational, and communal needs of the Jewish blind, visually impaired, and reading disabled, and provides information on Judaism to the blind in general. Distributes materials in braille, audio cassette, and large print Provides services in over 40 countries, including the U.S., Isreal, and the former Soviet Union. Is accredited as a non-governmental organization of the United Nations. *Type:* Association.

Jewish Guild for the Blind

15 W. 65th St.   Ph: (212)769-6200
New York, NY 10023   Fax: (212)595-4907
URL: http://www.jgb.org

Contact: Alan R. Morse, Pres. & CEO.

Desc: Service agency for blind, visually handicapped, and multihandicapped people of all ages, races, and creeds. Provides social work, counseling, and AIDS case management; job development, placement, and training; support group services; rehabilitation, including vocational, high school equivalency training in orientation and mobility, activities of daily living, and transcription typing; adapted physical education; communication skills; medical services; adult day healthcare program, GuildCare, in New York City, Yonkers, Bronx, Buffalo, Niagara Falls, and Albany, New York. Operates Early Intervention Program for infants and preschoolers (up to age 5); school for multihandicapped children; state licensed psychiatric clinic for emotionally disturbed blind persons and their families; day treatment programs for multihandicapped blind adults; Joselow House, an intermediate care facility for blind developmentally disabled adults; and other services. *Type:* Association.

Keren-Or, Inc.

350 7th Ave., Rm. 200   Ph: (212)279-4070
New York, NY 10001   Fax: (212)279-4043

Contact: Sheila E. Stein, Exec.Dir.

Desc: Maintains the Keren-Or Center for Multi-Handicapped Blind Children in Jerusalem for rehabilitation and training which houses more than 70 children and young adults. Funds acquired through public contributions (70%) and Israeli government funding. *Type:* Association.

Leader Dogs for the Blind

1039 S. Rochester Rd.   Ph: (248)651-9011
Rochester, MI 48307   Free: 888-777-5332
   Fax: (248)651-5812
E-mail: ldftb@ix.netcom.com
URL: http://www.leaderdog.org

Contact: William C. Hansen, Pres.

Desc: Trains dogs to serve as guides for blind persons and conducts a supervised course of training to coordinate blind persons and their Leader Dogs as operating units; there is no charge for the service. *Type:* Association.

Learning Disabilities Association of America

4156 Library Rd.   Ph: (412)341-1515
Pittsburgh, PA 15234   Free: 888-300-6710
   Fax: (412)344-0224
E-mail: ldanatl@usaor.net
URL: http://www.ldanatl.org

Contact: Jean Petersen, Exec.Dir.

Desc: Parents of children with learning disabilities; interested professionals. Works to "advance the education and general well-being of children with adequate intelligence who have learning disabilities arising from perceptual, conceptual, or subtle coordinative problems, sometimes accompanied by behavior difficulties." *Type:* Association.

Little City Foundation

1760 W. Algonquin Rd.   Ph: (847)358-5510
Palatine, IL 60067   Fax: (847)358-3291
URL: http://www.LittleCity.org

Contact: Alan J. Dachman, Exec.Dir.

Desc: Provides state-of-the-art community based services and service coordination to help children and adults with mental retardation or other developmental, emotional, and behavioral challenges to lead meaningful, productive, and dignified lives. Services include housing, employment, recreation, foster care, adoption, home-based support, service coordination, media and studio arts, advocacy, and public education. *Type:* Association.

Louisiana State University Human Development Center

Sch. of Allied Health Professions   Ph: (504)942-8200
1100 Florida Ave., Bldg. 138   Fax: (504)942-8305
New Orleans, LA 70119-2799

Contact: Robert E. Crow, PhD, Dir.

Desc: Developmental disabilities, including educational technology, curriculum research, and integrated basic and applied behavioral interventions. Operates as a University Affiliated Program for interdisciplinary training, research, and dissemination. *Type:* Research center.

Lutheran Braille Workers

Box 5000   Ph: (909)795-8977
Yucaipa, CA 92399   Fax: (909)795-8970
E-mail: lbwbraille@aol.com
URL: http://members.aol.com/lbwbraille/lbw.htm

Contact: Loyd Coppenger, Exec.Dir.

Desc: Volunteers staffing 201 work centers worldwide, through which they seek to bring the Bible to the blind and visually impaired. Teaches sighted volunteers to transcribe printed material into braille and large print. Produces and distributes free biblical and devotional material in braille and large print in 40 languages. *Type:* Association.

Mental Retardation Research and Human Development Center

300 Longwood Ave.   Ph: (617)355-7046
Boston, MA 02115   Fax: (617)738-1542
E-mail: volpe_j@a1.tch.harvard.edu

Contact: Joseph Volpe, MD, Prog.Dir.

Desc: Causes of mental retardation, including multidisciplinary studies in genetics, neuroscience, behavioral science, and clinical application of results of such studies. *Type:* Research center.

Miami Jewish Home and Hospital for the Aged Stein Gerontological Institute, Inc.

5200 NE 2nd Ave.   Ph: (305)762-1465
Miami, FL 33137-2706   Free: 800-322-7881
   Fax: (305)762-1445
URL: http://www.douglasgardens.com

Contact: Dr. Seth B. Goldsmith, Dir.

Desc: Promotes greater independence for the disabled through technology. *Type:* Research center.

National Association of Protection and Advocacy Systems

900 2nd St. NE, Ste. 211   Ph: (202)408-9514
Washington, DC 20002   Fax: (202)408-9520

Contact: Curtis L. Decker, Exec.Dir.

Desc: Executive directors and designees of state or territorial Developmental Disability, Mentally Ill Protection and Advocacy Systems, and Client Assistance Programs. Furthers the human, civil, and legal rights of persons with disabilities; advances the interests of protection and advocacy systems; facilitates coordination and mutual support among such systems and enhance their capacity to provide optimal services. Offers professional training; collects data. *Type:* Association.

National Association of State Directors of Special Education

1800 Diagonal Rd., Ste. 320   Ph: (703)519-3800
Alexandria, VA 22314   Fax: (703)519-3808

Contact: Martha J. Fields, Exec.Dir.

Desc: Professional society of state directors; consultants, supervisors, and administrators who have statewide responsibilities for administering special education programs. Provides services to state agencies to facilitate their efforts to maximize educational outcomes for individuals with disabilities. *Type:* Association.

National Braille Press Release

National Braille Press, Inc.
88 St. Stephen St.   Ph: (617)266-6160
Boston, MA 02115   Free: 800-548-7323
   Fax: (617)437-0456
E-mail: orders@nbp.org

Contact: Sarah Ellis, Editor.

Desc: Covers the activities of the National Braille Press. *Type:* Newsletter.

National Center for Disability Services

201 I.U. Willets Rd.   Ph: (516)747-5400
Albertson, NY 11507   Fax: (516)746-3298

Contact: Dr. Edmund Cortez, Pres.

Desc: Serves as a center providing educational, vocational, rehabilitation, and research opportunities for persons with disabilities. Work is conducted through the following: Abilities Health and Rehabilitation Services, a New York state licensed diagnostic and treatment center which offers comprehensive outpatient programs in physical therapy, occupational therapy, speech therapy, and psychological services; Career and Employment Institute, which evaluates, trains, and counsels more than 600 adults with disabilities each year, with the goal of productive competitive employment; Henry Viscardi School, which conducts early childhood, elementary, and secondary programs, as well as adult and continuing education programs; Research and Training Institute, which conducts research on the education, employment, and career development of persons with disabilities, and holds seminars and workshops for rehabilitation services professionals. Maintains library and speakers' bureau; compiles statistics; offers placement service; conducts research and educational programs. *Type:* Association.

National Center for Learning Disabilities

381 Park Ave. S., Ste. 1401　　Ph: (212)545-7510
New York, NY 10016　　Free: 888-575-7373
　　Fax: (212)545-9665
URL: http://www.ncld.org
Contact: James Wendorf, Exec.Dir.
Desc: Dedicated to improving the lives of the millions of Americans affected by learning disabilities. Services include national information and referral; educational programs; public outreach and communications; and legislative advocacy. *Type:* Association.

National Council on Disability

1331 F St. NW, Ste. 1050　　Ph: (202)272-2004
Washington, DC 20004
Desc: The Council reviews all laws, programs, and policies of the federal government that affect individuals with disabilities. The Council then makes recommendations to the President, Congress, and federal agencies on these issues. *Type:* Government agency, office, or program.

National Down Syndrome Congress

7000 Peachtree Dunwoody Rd.,　Free: 800-232-NDSC
　Bldg. 5, Ste. 100
Atlanta, GA 30328
E-mail: ndsccenter@aol.com
URL: http://members.carol.net/ndsc
Contact: Frank Murphy, Exec.Dir.
Desc: Families of individuals with Down Syndrome; educators, health professionals, and other interested individuals. Works to promote the welfare of persons with Down Syndrome (DS), a chromosomal disorder which occurs in approximately one in every 800 to 1100 births and usually causes delays in physical and intellectual development; its exact cause is unknown. *Type:* Association.

National Down Syndrome Society

666 Broadway　　Ph: (212)460-9330
New York, NY 10012　　Free: 800-221-4602
　　Fax: (212)979-2873
E-mail: ndss@info.org
URL: http://www.ndss.org
Contact: Myra Madnick, Exec.Dir.
Desc: Devoted to funding research into the causes and treatment of Down Syndrome. *Type:* Association.

National Federation of the Blind

1800 Johnson St.　　Ph: (410)659-9314
Baltimore, MD 21230　　Free: 800-638-7518
　　Fax: (410)685-5653
URL: http://www.nfb.org
Contact: Marc Maurer, Pres.
Desc: Federation of state (50 plus Washington, DC and Puerto Rico) and local (600) organizations representing 50,000 blind people. Seeks the complete equality and integration of the blind into society. *Type:* Association.

National Industries for the Blind

1901 N. Beauregard St., Ste.　　Ph: (703)998-0770
　200　　Fax: (703)998-8268
Alexandria, VA 22311-1727
E-mail: info@nib.org
URL: http://www.nib.org
Contact: James D. Gibbons, Pres./CEO.
Desc: Association of agencies employing blind persons who undertake the production of certain goods and services for the federal government under the Javits-Wagner-O'Day Act. Offers gainful employment in these industries, located in 38 states, Puerto Rico, and the District of Columbia for those blind or multidisabled blind persons who are able and willing to work. Researches and recommends new products, prices, and price revisions to the Committee for Purchase From People Who Are Blind or Severely Disabled; allocates federal work orders among these agencies. *Type:* Association.

National Institute for Rehabilitation Engineering

PO Box T　　Ph: (973)853-6585
Hewitt, NJ 07421　　Free: 800-736-2216
　　Fax: (914)986-6511
E-mail: dons@warwick.net
URL: http://www.theoffice.net/nire
Contact: Donald Selwyn, Exec.VP.
Desc: Multidisciplinary research, training, and service organization providing custom-designed and custom-made tools and devices, along with intensive personal task-performance and driver training, to aid the handicapped person in becoming more self-sufficient and independent. Often an organization of "last resort" for permanently, severely, or multihandicapped persons, the NIRE is staffed by electronics engineers, physicists, psychologists, optometrists, and other volunteers who work as a team with the handicapped person. These specialists review the handicapped person's abilities, disabilities, and task-performance goals and are thus able to help advise, plan, and implement programs to increase the person's abilities to perform desired tasks, using a combination of methods involving different practitioners and disciplines. Staff members also adapt, modify, and construct equipment specially suited to the individual client's need. No handicapped person is denied the institute's services due to an inability to pay, and fees for others are based on each person's income and means. *Type:* Association.

National Network for the Disabled

Linda Walls
PO Box 3574　　Ph: (310)638-5717
Gardena, CA 90247-7274　　Fax: (310)638-5986
Contact: Linda Walls, Founder-Pres.
Desc: Provides support, companionship, and networking opportunities for elderly individuals and parents of disabled children. *Type:* Association.

National Odd Shoe Exchange

3200 N. Delaware St.
Chandler, AZ 85225-1100
Contact: Jeanne L. Sallman, Dir.
Desc: Service organization to bring together persons with mutual shoe problems (foot amputees and persons having feet which differ physically due to disease, injury, or accident). The exchange supplies names of persons of similar ages and tastes in shoe styles who have extra shoes or who are seeking someone with whom to exchange mismated footwear. These persons then make their own arrangements for the disposal of shoes they now have and for purchase of future pairs. *Type:* Association.

National Science Foundation

Directorate of Engineering

Division of Bioengineering and Environmental Systems

Bioengineering and Aiding Persons with Disabilities Program

4201 Wilson Blvd., Rm. 565　　Ph: (703)306-1319
Arlington, VA 22230　　Fax: (703)306-0312
E-mail: jfourke@nsf.gov
URL: http://www.eng.nsf.gov.bes/bes.htm
Contact: Janie Fouke, Div.Dir.
Desc: Provides funding for fundamental and applied academic engineering research relevant to medical needs. To qualify for support, investigations should be directed toward engineering research associated with the characterization, restoration, or substitution of human structure, function, or control. *Type:* Research center.

NCRTM News

National Clearinghouse of Rehabilitation Training Materials (NCHRTM)
5202 N. Richmond Hill Dr.　　Ph: (405)624-7650
Oklahoma State University　　Free: 800-223-5219
Stillwater, OK 74078-4080　　Fax: (405)624-0695
URL: http://nchrtm.okstate.edu.
Contact: David J. Brooks, Editor, brookdj@okstate.edu.
Desc: Announces new acquisitions of mixed media materials of the National Clearing House and provides brief descriptions. Provides annotations of noteworthy products offered from other sources and notices of additional products/services relating to the rehabilitation of persons with disabilities. *Type:* Newsletter.

New York State Institute for Basic Research in Developmental Disabilities

1050 Forest Hill Rd.　　Ph: (718)494-0600
Staten Island, NY 10314-6399　　Fax: (718)698-3803
E-mail: Roger.McClanahan@omr.state.ny.us
URL: http://www.omr.state.ny.us/ibr.htm
Contact: Dr. Henry M. Wisniewski, Dir.
Desc: Molecular biology and developmental biochemistry of human development, developmental disabilities, and clinical, behavioral, and developmental psychology of mental retardation, including neuroimmunology, membrane biochemistry, lipid biochemistry, neurotransmitter physiology and pathology, inborn errors of metabolism, blood-brain barrier, and persistent, latent, and unconventional viruses. Focuses on the causes and prevention of developmental disabilities, aging and Alzheimer's disease, Down's syndrome, fragile X syndrome, autism, fetal alcohol syndrome, neurodegenerative diseases, pediatric AIDS and neuroinfectious diseases, environmental neurotoxicology (including alcohol, lead, aluminum, and cocaine), prevention (including vaccines, diagnostic tests, and early intervention), and treatment (including drug evaluation). *Type:* Research center.

NISH

2235 Cedar Ln.　　Ph: (703)560-6800
Vienna, VA 22182-5200　　Fax: (703)849-8916
Contact: Daniel W. McKinnon, Jr., Pres.
Desc: Provides employment opportunities for people with severe disabilities under the Javits-Wagner O'Day Act. Promotes their placement into competitive industry. Conducts research and development to identify to the government commodities and services which are feasible for production and/or performance by work centers. *Type:* Association.

Northern Rocky Mountain Easter Seal Society/ Goodwill Industries

4400 Central Ave.　　Ph: (406)761-3680
Great Falls, MT 59405　　Free: 800-627-7889
　　Fax: (406)761-5110
URL: http://www.goodwill.org/greatfalls
Contact: Sally Cerny, Pres.
Desc: Conducts programs to assist people with disabilities. Performs support and information services. *Type:* Association.

Northwest Woodhaven Center Inc.

2900 Southampton Rd.　　Ph: (215)671-5001
Philadelphia, PA 19154　　Fax: (215)671-7522
Contact: Michael Barton, MD, V.Pres.
Desc: Treatment effectiveness, program evaluation, clinical treatment research (medications and behavior modification), and policy research in mental retardation at Woodhaven Center, a University-operated residential program for mentally retarded persons. *Type:* Research center.

Ohio State University

Nisonger Center for Mental Retardation and Developmental Disabilities

1581 Dodd Dr.   Ph: (614)292-8365
Columbus, OH 43210-1296   Fax: (614)292-3727
E-mail: reiss.7@osu.edu
URL: http://www.osu.edu
Contact: Steven Reiss, PhD, Dir.

Desc: Developmental disabilities, psychometric assessment, rehabilitation engineering, psychopathology, psychopharmacology, adults and aging, and family studies. Special attention given to applied research related to mental retardation and development and implementation of training programs to prepare professional personnel to work with the developmentally disabled. *Type:* Research center.

Ozad Institute for Developmental Disabilities

Windsor Regional Hospital   Ph: (519)257-5219
3901 Connaught Ave.   Fax: (519)257-5212
Windsor, ON, Canada
E-mail: ozad@mnsi.net
Contact: John Strang, PhD, Dir.

Desc: Developmental disabilities in children, focusing on applied neuropsychological research, autism and related disorders, and developmental handicap research. *Type:* Research center.

People with Special Needs/Down's Syndrome Report

People with Special Needs/Down's Syndrome Report
1409 N. 1st St.
Aberdeen, SD 57401
E-mail: robjohns@sendi.sendit.nodak.edu.
Desc: Covers current Down's syndrome information and issues. *Type:* Newsletter.

Pilot Dogs

625 W. Town St.   Ph: (614)221-6367
Columbus, OH 43215   Fax: (614)221-1577
Contact: J. Jay Gray, Exec.Dir.

Desc: Provides guide dogs and training for the blind. *Type:* Association.

President's Committee on Employment of People With Disabilities

1331 F St. NW, Ste. 300   Ph: (202)376-6200
Washington, DC 20004-1107   Fax: (202)376-6219
Desc: Seeks to identify and eliminate barriers standing in the way of full social and vocational opportunities for physically handicapped, mentally retarded, and mentally restored persons; promotes employment opportunities for the physically and mentally handicapped. *Type:* Government agency, office, or program.

Prevent Blindness America

500 E. Remington Rd.   Ph: (847)843-2020
Schaumburg, IL 60173   Free: 800-331-2020
                        Fax: (847)843-8458

E-mail: info@preventblindness.org
URL: http://www.preventblindness.org
Contact: Richard Hellner, Pres. and CEO.

Desc: Professionals and laypersons interested in preventing blindness and preserving sight through nationwide comprehensive programs of public and professional education, research, industrial, and community services. Services include promotion and support of local glaucoma screening programs, preschool vision testing, industrial eye safety, and collection of statistical and other data on nature and extent of causes of blindness and defective vision. Operates a toll-free information center dealing with eye health and safety topics. *Type:* Association.

Prosthetics Research Study

675 S. Lane St., Ste. 100   Ph: (206)903-8136
Seattle, WA 98104-2942   Fax: (206)903-8141
E-mail: info@prs-research.org
URL: http://www.prs-research.org
Contact: David A. Boone, Dir.

Desc: Wound healing and limb viability, prosthesis research and development, mobility aids and artificial limbs, functional electrical physiological response, pain control, neuromuscular assist devices, electrical osteogenesis, mechanical engineering and automated fabrication of prosthetic components and mobility aids, and amputation surgery and post-surgical management. *Type:* Research center.

Protestant Guild for Human Services

411 Waverley Oaks Rd., Ste.   Ph: (781)893-6000
  104   Fax: (781)893-1171
Waltham, MA 02452
Contact: Edmund T. Hagerty, Exec.Dir.

Desc: Individuals who wish to contribute to the welfare of persons who are blind or visually handicapped, deaf or hearing impaired, mentally impaired, or multihandicapped. Sponsors a chaplaincy program that provides support and advocacy to blind and visually handicapped persons. Provides information and referral by acting as liaison between blind individuals and appropriate community service organizations. *Type:* Association.

Quest

Muscular Dystrophy Association, Inc.
3300 E. Sunrise Dr.   Ph: (520)529-2000
Tucson, AZ 85718   Free: 800-572-1717
                       Fax: (520)529-5300

E-mail: publications@mdausa.org
URL: http://www.mdausa.org.
Desc: Magazine focusing on issues important to people who have muscular dystrophy and other neuromuscular diseases. *Type:* Periodical.

Recording for the Blind

20 Roszel Rd.   Ph: (609)452-0606
Princeton, NJ 08540   Free: 800-803-7201
                      Fax: (609)987-8116

E-mail: info@rfbd.org
URL: http://www.rfbd.org
Contact: Ritchie L. Geisel, Pres.

Desc: Provides library services, computerized books, books on audiotape, and other educational materials free of charge to individuals who are unable to read standard print because of a visual, physical, or perceptual disability. Materials are produced by 4800 volunteers at 31 recording studios throughout the U.S. Titles recorded supplement, but do not duplicate, those of the Library of Congress Talking Book program. *Type:* Association.

Rehabilitation Gazette

Gazette International Networking Institute (GINI)
4207 Lindell Blvd., Rm. 110   Ph: (314)534-0475
St. Louis, MO 63108-2915   Fax: (314)534-5070
E-mail: gini_intl@msn.com
URL: www.post-polio.org.
Contact: Joan Headley, Editor.

Desc: Covers issues of interest to individuals with disabilities. Recurring features include articles about independent living, a calendar of events, and disability related resources. *Type:* Newsletter.

Research and Development Institute

PO Box 351   Ph: (815)895-3078
Sycamore, IL 60178-2738   Fax: (815)895-2448
E-mail: gkapper@niu.edu

Contact: Dr. Gaylen G. Kapperman, Dir.

Desc: Rehabilitation and education for disabled persons, with emphasis on blindness and visual impairment. *Type:* Research center.

Research to Prevent Blindness

645 Madison Ave.   Ph: (212)752-4333
New York, NY 10022-1010   Free: 800-621-0026
                          Fax: (212)688-6231

E-mail: info@rpbusa.org
Contact: Diane S. Swift, Pres.

Desc: National voluntary health foundation supported by foundations, corporations, and voluntary gifts and bequests from individuals. Established to stimulate basic and applied research into the causes, prevention, and treatment of blinding eye diseases. *Type:* Association.

Research and Training Center on Managed Care and Disability

102 Irving St. NW   Ph: (202)466-1900
Washington, DC 20010
URL: http://www.nrhrc.org/wintnews.htm1mcdis
Contact: Gerben DeJong, PhD, Dir.

Desc: Delivery of quality health care to people with disabilities, particularly the impact of alternative managed care arrangements on the provision of acute care services for working-age people with disabilities. *Type:* Research center.

Retinitis Pigmentosa International

Helen Harris
PO Box 900   Ph: (818)992-0500
Woodland Hills, CA 91365   Free: 800-FIGHT-RP
                           Fax: (818)992-3265

E-mail: rpint@pacbell.net
URL: http://www.rpinternational.org
Contact: Helen Harris, Pres.

Desc: Seeks to raise funds to support research and provide human service programs to assist the visually impaired. *Type:* Association.

Scene

Braille Institute Press
741 N. Vermont Ave.   Ph: (323)663-1111
Los Angeles, CA 90029   Free: 800-BRA-ILLE
                        Fax: (323)663-0867

E-mail: info@brailleinstitute.org
URL: http://www.brailleinstitute.org
Contact: Joe Shaw, Editor.

Desc: Seeks to enhance public awareness about the abilities of people who are blind or visually impaired to enjoy full, productive and independent lives as a result of the Institute's assistance. Promotes the Institute's educational training programs, recreational and counseling services, library and braille press services and special events. *Type:* Newsletter.

Sharing Solutions

Lighthouse International
111 E. 59th St.   Ph: (212)821-1202
New York, NY 10022-1202   Free: 800-829-0500
E-mail: sharingsolutions@lighthouse.org.
URL: http://www.lighthouse.org; http://www.lighthouse.org.

Contact: Carol Sussman-Skalka, Editor-in-Chief, (212)821-9481, csussman@lighthouse.org.

Desc: Concerned with vision impairment of the elderly. *Type:* Newsletter.

Special Olympics Florida

8 Broadway, Ste. D   Ph: (407)870-2292
Kissimmee, FL 34741-5712   Free: 800-322-4376
    Fax: (407)870-9810
URL: http://www.specolyfl.com
Contact: Monty Castevens, Pres./CEO.
Desc: Provides sports training and athletic competition to over 19,000 mentally handicapped adults and children throughout Florida. *Type:* Association.

Special Olympics International

1325 G St., NW, Ste. 500   Ph: (202)628-3630
Washington, DC 20005   Fax: (202)824-0200
URL: http://www.specialolympics.org/
Contact: Timothy R. Shriver, Chief Executive Officer.
Desc: Created by the Joseph P. Kennedy, Jr. Foundation to promote physical fitness, sports training, and athletic competition for children and adults with mental retardation. *Type:* Association.

Special Olympics Southern California

6071 Bristol Pky, Ste. 100   Ph: (310)215-8380
Culver City, CA 90230-6601   Fax: (310)215-8388
E-mail: scso@scso.org
Contact: Richard L. Van Kirk, Pres/CEO.
Type: Association.

Support Dogs

10755 Indianhead Industrial   Ph: (314)423-1988
  Blvd.   Fax: (314)423-5564
St. Louis, MO 63132
E-mail: supportdogs@msn.com
Contact: Joan Pace, Exec.Dir.
Desc: Helps people with special needs achieve greater independence and improve the quality of their lives by providing them with professionally trained dogs. *Type:* Association.

Surgical Eye Expeditions International

27 C-2 E. De La Guerra St.   Ph: (805)963-3303
Santa Barbara, CA 93101   Free: 800-20T-0SEE
    Fax: (805)965-3564
E-mail: seeintl@west.net
Contact: Baillie R. Brown, Pres.
Desc: Provides free sight-restoring surgery to indigent and disadvantaged blind individuals in the United States and throughout the developing world. *Type:* Association.

Talking Book Topics

National Library Service for the Blind and Physically Handicapped
Library of Congress
1291 Taylor St., NW   Ph: (202)707-5100
Washington, DC 20542   Free: 800-424-8567
    Fax: (202)707-0712
E-mail: nls@loc.gov
URL: http://www.loc.gov/nls.
Contact: George Thuronyi, Editor, (202)707-9281, fax: (202)707-0712, gthu@loc.gov.
Desc: Catalog of books available to the visually and physically handicapped. Also produces a recorded edition and a large print edition. *Alt. Contact:* Publications & Media Section NLS/BPH, Washington, DC 20542; telephone: (202)707-9281; fax: (202)707-0712. *Type:* Periodical.

TD Access and Safety Report

Serif Press, Inc.
1331 H St. NW   Ph: (202)737-4650
Washington, DC 20005   Free: 800-221-4272
    Fax: (202)783-1931
E-mail: serifpress@aol.com
Contact: Roseann Schwaderer, Editor.
Desc: Addresses issues concerning the transportation of disabled persons in the U.S., including transit, paratransit,

lawsuits, liability, and contracts. Recurring features include letters to the editor, interviews, news of research, a calendar of events, and a column titled Working in ADA Compliance. *Type:* Newsletter.

U.S. Department of Education

Office of Special Education and Rehabilitative Services

c/o Department of Education   Ph: (202)708-5366
600 Independence Ave. SW   Free: 800-USA-
Washington, DC 20202   LEARN
URL: http://www.ed.gov/
Contact: Judith E. Heumann, Assistant Secretary.
Desc: The Office of Special Education and Rehabilitative Services provides leadership to ensure that people with disabilities have services, resources, and equal opportunities to learn, work, and live as fully-integrated, contributing members of society. OSERS supports programs that serve millions of disabled children, youth, and adults and that impact on the lives of the nation's 49 million citizens with disabilities. *Type:* Government agency, office, or program.

U.S. Department of Health and Human Services

Administration for Children and Families

Administration on Developmental Disabilities

370 L'Enfant Promenade SW   Ph: (202)690-6590
Washington, DC 20447
Desc: The Administration on Developmental Disabilities (ADD) assists states in increasing the provision of quality services to persons with developmental disabilities through the development and implementation of a comprehensive state plan which makes optimal use of all existing resources for the provision of treatment, services and habilitation in least restrictive environments, and protection of the rights of individuals with developmental disabilities. ADD administers formula grants program to address these goals and oversees project grants which provide administrative and operations support to interdisciplinary training programs for specialized personnel, clinical services, and research program services for the developmentally disabled; and administers grants for projects aimed at removing physical, mental, social, and environmental barriers encountered by developmentally disabled persons. *Type:* Government agency, office, or program.

U.S. Department of Health and Human Services

Center for Community Inclusion

University of Maine   Ph: (207)581-1084
5717 Corbett Hall   Fax: (207)581-1231
Orono, ME 04469-5717
E-mail: susan-russell@umit.maine.edu
URL: http://www.llume.maine.edu/~cci
Contact: Susan Russell, Contact.
Desc: Development disabilities, focusing on improving the quality of life for persons with development disabilities and their families and policy development and analyses in Maine. *Type:* Research center.

U.S. Department of Health and Human Services

National Center for Health Statistics

Office of Vital and Health Statistics Systems

Health Interview Statistics Division

6525 Belcrest Rd.   Ph: (301)436-7089
Hyattsville, MD 20782   Fax: (301)436-3484
E-mail: amh1@cdc.sov
URL: http://www.cdc.gov
Contact: Dr. Ann M. Hardy, Actg.Dir.
Desc: Responsible for maintaining, analyzing, and preparing reports from National Health Interview Survey data. Areas of interest include estimates on illness and disability, use of health care services, and other health-related topics. *Type:* Research center.

U.S. Department of Health and Human Services

National Institutes of Health

National Institute on Deafness and Other Communication Disorders

9000 Rockville Pike   Ph: (301)496-7243
Bethesda, MD 20892
URL: http://www.nih.gov/nidcd/
Contact: James F. Battey, Jr., Director.
Desc: NIDCD conducts and supports research and training with respect to disorders of hearing and other communication processes, including diseases affecting hearing, balance, voice, speech, language, touch, taste, and smell through research performed in its own laboratories; a program of research grants, individual and institutional research training awards, career development awards, center grants, and contracts to public and private research institutions and organizations. *Type:* Government agency, office, or program.

U.S. Department of Health and Human Services

Office of Family, Community and Long-Term Care Policy

Division of Disability, Aging and Long-Term Care Policy

200 Independence Ave. SW,   Ph: (202)690-7000
  Rm. 424E   Fax: (202)690-7203
Washington, DC 20201
Contact: Mary Harahan, Dir.
Desc: Financing, organization, and delivery of services to chronically impaired populations; informs the Department's policy development process. Recent work has centered on the needs of the impaired elderly and mentally disabled. *Type:* Research center.

U.S. Department of Health and Human Services

Research and Training Center on Rural Disabilities

Univ. of Montana   Ph: (406)243-5467
52 Corbin Hall   Fax: (406)243-2349
Missoula, MT 59812
Contact: Dr. Tom Seekins, Dir.
Desc: Employment and vocational rehabilitation service needs of people with disabilities in rural areas; intervention development to improve employment outcomes; self-employment and economic development models; rural independent living; improvement of transportation, health care, housing, and accessibility; rural models for prevention of secondary disabilities; disability legislation and American Indian Tribes; and alternative models of delivery of rural rehabilitation services. *Type:* Research center.

U.S. Department of Veterans Affairs

Veterans Benefits Administration

Vocational Rehabilitation Service

810 Vermont Ave. NW   Ph: (202)273-4900
Washington, DC 20420
URL: http://www.va.gov/
Contact: Jeffrey T. Goetz, Director.
Desc: The Vocational Rehabilitation Service administers programs for vocational rehabilitation of disabled veterans, readjustment educational benefits for veterans of post-Korean conflict service, and education assistance for spouses, surviving spouses, and children of veterans who are permanently and totally disabled or die from disability incurred or aggravated in active service in the Armed Forces, or are prisoners of war, or are missing in action. Special restorative training is also available to eligible children. *Type:* Government agency, office, or program.

U.S. Library of Congress

National Library Service for the Blind and Physically Handicapped

1291 Taylor St. NW   Ph: (202)707-5100
Washington, DC 20542-4960

Desc: Talking and braille books and magazines are distributed through 150 regional and subregional libraries to blind and physically handicapped residents of the U.S. and its territories. *Type:* Government agency, office, or program.

Universal Design Newsletter

Universal Designers and Consultants, Inc.

6 Grant Ave.   Ph: (301)270-2470
Takoma Park, MD 20912   Free: 888-631-7192
    Fax: (301)270-8199

E-mail: udandc@erols.com

Contact: Monique Silverio, Editor, (703)620-6611, fax: (703)715-0568, silverio@erols.com.

Desc: Focuses on universal design of buildings, products, and systems for the physically disabled. Also provides news of the organization. *Type:* Newsletter.

University Affiliated Cincinnati Center for Developmental Disorders

Pavilion Bldg.   Ph: (513)636-4626
3333 Burnet Ave.   Fax: (513)636-7361
Cincinnati, OH 45229-3039
URL: http://www.chmcc.org

Contact: Dr. Sonya Oppenheimer, Dir.

Desc: Prevention, early detection, and improved methods of therapy and management of developmental disabilities. Also studies genetics, learning disabilities, and birth defects. *Type:* Research center.

University of California, Los Angeles

Mental Retardation Research Center

760 Westwood Plz.   Ph: (310)825-5542
Los Angeles, CA 90024-1759   Fax: (310)206-5060
E-mail: jdevellis@mednet.ucla.edu
URL: http://www.mrrc.npi.ucla.edu/

Contact: Dr. Jean de Vellis, PhD, Dir.

Desc: Mental retardation and related aspects of human development, including interdisciplinary basic and clinical studies on problems in developmental biology, human genetics, neurobiochemistry, neurophysiology, and sociobehavioral categories. Collaborates with other institutes, schools, and departments at the University. *Type:* Research center.

University of California, San Francisco

Disability Statistics Center

Institute for Health and Aging   Ph: (415)502-5210
3333 California St., Ste. 340
San Francisco, CA 94118
E-mail: Information_Specialist@quickmail.ucsf.edu
URL: http://dsc.ucsf.edu/

Contact: Mitchell P. LaPlante, PhD, Dir.

Desc: Production and dissemination of statistical information on disability and the status of people with disabilities in society and the establishment and monitoring of indicators on how conditions are changing to meet their health, housing, economic and social needs. *Type:* Research center.

University of Chicago

Joseph P. Kennedy, Jr., Mental Retardation Research Center

Wyler Children's Hospital   Ph: (773)702-6428
5841 S. Maryland Ave., MC   Fax: (773)702-9234
    5058
Chicago, IL 60637
E-mail: n-schwartz@uchicago.edu
URL: http://peds-www.bsd.uchicago.edu/sections/Kennedy/index.html

Contact: Dr. Nancy B. Schwartz, Dir.

Desc: Mental retardation, emphasizing membrane glycococonjugate structure and synthesis, lysosomes (inborn errors of metabolism), regulation of enzymatic action, protein chemistry, chemistry and metabolism of sphingolipids and other lipids and lipoprotein complexes, carbohydrate chemistry, biology of biochemistry of the extracellular matrix (normal development and inborn errors), collagen gene structure and expression, DNA sequence studies, DNA methylation and chromatin structure, recombinant DNA technology, cell-free translation and transcription in differentiating eukaryotic cells, regulation of gene expression and mRNA regulation during embryonic development, regulation of catecholamine neurotransmitter biosynthesis and secretion, signal transduction pathways in neuronal systems, opioid actions during embryogenesis and opioid signal transduction, muscarinic receptor signal transduction pathways in differentiating neurons, proteoglycan participation in CNS histomorphogenesis, glia phenotypes and the role of protein kinases, electron microscope visualization of specific gene products in differentiating nervous system and cartilage (use of monoclonal antibodies), neurotransmitter receptor structure and function, mechanisms of synapse formation, neurobiology and neuropathology of dopaminergic pathways, regulation of myelination (oligodendrocyte neurobiology), isolation and tissue culture of specialized cells.

University of Connecticut

Division of Child and Family Studies

Dowling North MC6222   Ph: (860)679-4632
263 Farmington Ave.   Fax: (860)679-1368
Farmington, CT 06030-6222
E-mail: bruder@nso1.uchc.edu

Contact: Mary Beth Bruder, PhD, Dir.

Desc: Developmental disabilities, psychosocial developmental needs mainly for children who are disabled. Establishes research and training programs in early intervention for children with disabilities and their families, trains early intervention researchers and personnel, and develops comprehensive and integrated service delivery systems that are family and community centered. *Type:* Research center.

University of Georgia

Georgia University Affiliated Program

850 College Station Rd.   Ph: (706)542-3457
Athens, GA 30602   Fax: (706)542-4815
E-mail: 20@uga.edu

Contact: Dr. Zolinda Stoneman, Dir.

Desc: Research, teaching, training, and public service in the field of developmentally disabled persons, especially pertaining to family relations and community services. *Type:* Research center.

University of Illinois at Chicago

Center for Handicapped Children

840 S. Wood St.   Ph: (312)996-7202
Chicago, IL 60612   Fax: (312)413-3445

Contact: Janie Gawrys, Coord. of Clin. Svcs.

Desc: Neurologically handicapped children and those with inborn metabolic or endocrine disorders, including inter-

departmental studies on growth and development, and maternal phenylketonuria (PKU). Clinical activities include developmental/medical diagnostic assessments of children with developmental disabilities and operation of a genetic/metabolic clinic with a state PKU center. *Type:* Research center.

University of Kansas

Kansas Center for Mental Retardation and Human Development

Institute for Life Span Studies

Parsons Research Center

PO Box 738   Ph: (316)421-6550
Parsons, KS 67357   Fax: (316)421-0954
E-mail: ksaunders@parsons.lsi.ukans.edu

Contact: Dr. Kathryn Saunders, Dir.

Desc: Experimental analysis of cognitive functions, including discrimination, classification, and representation skills among retarded persons; language and communication behavior, including social, and symbolic behaviors of severely retarded persons; and analysis and treatment of chronic aberrant behavior, behavioral pharmacology, and reading. *Type:* Research center.

University of Kansas

Mental Retardation and Human Development Research Center

University of Kansas Medical   Ph: (913)588-5970
Center   Fax: (913)588-5677
3901 Rainbow Blvd.
Kansas City, KS 66160-7336
E-mail: pcheney@kumc.edu
URL: http://www2.kumc.edu/mrrc

Contact: Dr. Paul D. Cheney, Dir.

Desc: Fundamental problems of mental retardation and developmental disabilties, including molecular biology and physiology of pregnancy, neuroendocrinology, fetal development, impaired fetal and infant development, infant language, cognitive development, prenatal and postnatal risk factors, developmental neurobiology and neuroplasticity. Conducts animal models studies concerning pregnancy, early developmental processes, and neurobiological mechanisms involved in motor and sensory functions of the brain and neuropathology of AIDS. *Type:* Research center.

University of Louisville

Child Evaluation Center

571 S. Floyd, Ste. 100   Ph: (502)852-5331
Louisville, KY 40202-3828   Fax: (502)852-0955

Contact: Bernard Weisskopf, MD, Dir.

Desc: Developmentally disabled and handicapped children in Kentucky. Clinical research is conducted in support of the following clinical, evaluative, and consultative service programs: diagnosis and evaluation, learning disorders, genetics and dysmorphology, genetics testing, education and counseling, genetics laboratory, community clinics and outreach, hyperactive child treatment, infant therapy, behavior modification, diagnostic teaching, pastoral counseling, and cytogenetics laboratory. *Type:* Research center.

University of Michigan

Center for Human Growth and Development

300 N. Ingalls Bldg., 10th Level   Ph: (734)764-2443
Ann Arbor, MI 48109-0406   Fax: (734)936-9288
E-mail: blozoff@umich.edu
URL: http://www.umich.edu/~chgdwww/

Contact: Dr. Betsy Lozoff, Dir.

Desc: Human growth and development through childhood and adolescence, including interdisciplinary studies on normal and abnormal behavioral, physical, and mental development, focusing especially on the challenges to children who grow up in adverse conditions. *Type:* Research center.

University of Mississippi

Research and Training Center for the Handicapped

School Ed. Bldg. 207   Ph: (601)232-5806
University, MS 38677   Fax: (601)232-5376
Contact: Dr. James W. Mann, Dir.
Desc: Physical and mental handicaps, including blindness, deafness, muteness, mental disease, and developmental disabilities. Conducts statewide surveys. *Type:* Research center.

University of Montana

University Affiliated Rural Institute on Disabilities

52 N. Corbin Hall   Ph: (406)243-5467
Missoula, MT 59812   Free: 800-732-0323
   Fax: (406)243-4730
E-mail: rtvogels@selway.umt.edu
URL: http://www.ruralinstitute.umt.edu
Contact: R. Timm Vogelsberg, Dir.
Desc: Human resources and technical services for rural Americans with disabilities. Studies encompass the areas of employment, housing, transportation, health promotion, secondary conditions, special education, social work, guidance and counseling, physical medicine and rehabilitation, mechanical and rehabilitation engineering, business management, sociology, and interpersonal communication. *Type:* Research center.

University of Washington

Center on Human Development and Disability

Box 357920   Ph: (206)543-2832
Seattle, WA 98195-7920   Fax: (206)543-3417
E-mail: chdd@u.washington.edu
URL: http://www.weber.u.washington.edu/~chddwww
Contact: Michael J. Guralnick, PhD, Dir.
Desc: Biomedical and behavioral research of human development, including studies in developmental biology, perinatal biology, neurological sciences, psychology, psychiatry, speech and hearing sciences, social work, nursing, and special education. *Type:* Research center.

University of Wisconsin--Stout

Research and Training Center on Community Rehabilitation Programs to Improve Employment Outcomes

College of Education and   Ph: (715)232-1389
   Human Development
Stout Vocational Rehabilitation
   Institute
Menomonie, WI 54751
E-mail: mcaleesd@uwstout.edu
URL: http://www.chd.uwstout.edu/svri/rtc.html
Contact: Dr. Daniel C. McAlees, Dir.
Desc: Improvement of community-based rehabilitation through vocational transition of people with disabilities from community-based rehabilitation programs into competitive employment. *Type:* Research center.

Utah State University

Center for Persons with Disabilities

6800 Old Main Hill   Ph: (435)797-1981
Logan, UT 84322-6800   Fax: (435)797-3944
E-mail: marv@cpd2.usu.edu
URL: http://www.cpd.usu.edu
Contact: Dr. Marvin G. Fifield, Dir.
Desc: Developmental disabilities including biomedical research, the use of incidental teaching to promote social skills, and assistive technologies, including videodiscs. *Type:* Research center.

Vanderbilt University

John F. Kennedy Center for Research on Human Development

Peabody College, Box 40   Ph: (615)322-8240
Nashville, TN 37203   Fax: (615)322-8236
E-mail: jan.rosemergy@vanderbilt.edu
URL: http://www.vanderbilt.edu/kennedy
Contact: Travis Thompson, PhD, Dir.
Desc: Behavioral, biomedical, and educational aspects of mental retardation and other disabilities and child development, including cognitive strategies, social and communicative processes, neural development, neural plasticity. Investigates cognitive modifiability, computer applications to facilitate thinking and learning, normal and abnormal nervous system maturation, perceptual and locomotor behavior, self-injurious behavior, language and social development, development of aggressive behavior, early education of mentally retarded and economically disadvantaged children. *Type:* Research center.

Vendorscope

Randolph-Sheppard Vendors of America
1527 Royal Rd.   Ph: (605)229-4129
Aberdeen, SD 57401
Contact: Dean Flewwellin, Editor.
Desc: Reports on issues pertinent to the Business Enterprise Program for Blind Vendors. Recurring features include letters to the editor, interviews, news of research, a calendar of events, reports of meetings, news of educational opportunities, job listings, book reviews, notices of publications available, news of conventions and legislative action, and a column titled Mini-Mumbles from "Mean Dean." Remarks: Also available on audiocassette. *Type:* Newsletter.

Virginia Commonwealth University

Rehabilitation Research and Training Center on Supported Employment

PO Box 980568   Ph: (804)828-1851
Richmond, VA 23284-0568   Fax: (804)828-2193
E-mail: pwehman@atlas.vcu.edu
URL: http://www.vcu.edu/rrtcweb
Contact: Paul Wehman, PhD, Prin. Investigator.
Desc: Supported employment for persons with disabilities, including policy analysis, consumer satisfaction, vocational integration, school-to-work transition, and benefit cost analysis. *Type:* Research center.

Vision Community Services Resource Update

Vision Community Services
818 Mt. Auburn St.   Ph: (617)926-4232
Watertown, MA 02472   Free: 800-852-3029
   Fax: (617)926-1412
Contact: Fran Weisse, Editor.
Desc: Remarks: Available in large print or on cassette. *Type:* Newsletter.

Waisman Center

Univ. of Wisconsin--Madison   Ph: (608)263-5940
1500 Highland Ave.   Fax: (608)263-0529
Madison, WI 53705
E-mail: dolan@waisman.wisc.edu
URL: http://www.waisman.wisc.edu
Contact: Terrence R. Dolan, PhD, Dir.
Desc: Individuals with developmental disabilities, including noncompromised infants, children, and adults, as well as nonhuman subjects. Studies focus on genetics, molecular biology, neurochemistry, sensory and perceptual processes, neurophysiology, communication processes, development intervention processes, and biological, behavioral, and social processes across the lifespan. *Type:* Research center.

Western Michigan University

Enabling Technology Center

3509 Sangren   Ph: (616)387-4382
Kalamazoo, MI 49008-5194   Fax: (616)387-5703
E-mail: etc@wmich.edu
Contact: Christine M. Bahr, PhD, Dir.
Desc: Research and development of enabling technology for individuals with disabilities. *Type:* Research center.

Word From Washington

United Cerebral Palsy Associations, Inc. (UCPA)
1600 L St. NW, Ste. 700   Ph: (202)776-0406
Washington, DC 20036-5602   Free: 800-USA-5UCP
   Fax: (202)776-0414
Contact: Jenifer Simpson, Editor.
Desc: Covers federal legislation, programs, and policy and regulatory actions affecting persons with disabilities. Discusses Medicaid, child health, appropriations, special education, transportation, ADA, vocational rehabilitation, housing, Social Security, assistive technology, social services, and activities of concerned groups. *Type:* Newsletter.

Worksight

Rehabilitation Research and Training Center on Blindness and Low Vision
Mississippi State University
PO Box 6189   Ph: (601)325-2001
Mississippi State, MS 39762   Free: 800-675-7782
   Fax: (601)325-8989
E-mail: rrtc@ra.msstate.edu
Contact: Kelly S. Schaefer, Editor, (601)325-1363, schaefer@ra.msstate.edu.
Desc: Discusses news, activities, research, and training programs of the Rehabilitation Research and Training Center on Blindness and Low Vision. *Type:* Newsletter.

World Institute on Disability

510 16th St., Ste. 100   Ph: (510)763-4100
Oakland, CA 94612-1500   Fax: (510)763-4109
E-mail: wid@wid.org
URL: http://www.wid.org
Contact: Deborah Kaplan, Exec.Dir.
Desc: International public policy center that conducts research on disability issues and overcoming obstacles to independent living for all people with disabilities. *Type:* Association.

Xavier Society for the Blind

154 E. 23rd St.   Ph: (212)473-7800
New York, NY 10010   Free: 800-637-9193
   Fax: (212)473-7801
Contact: Alfred Caruana, Dir.
Desc: A center for publications, primarily Catholic, for the blind and visually handicapped, supported by charitable contributions. Transcribes numerous titles, including religious textbooks. Maintains a circulating library of books and other materials in braille, large type, and on tape. *Type:* Association.

Yeshiva University

Rose F. Kennedy Center for Research in Mental Retardation and Developmental Disabilities

Albert Einstein College of Med.   Ph: (718)430-2468
1410 Pelham Pkwy. S.   Fax: (718)881-2281
Bronx, NY 10461
E-mail: arezzo@aecom.yu.edu
Contact: Dr. Joseph C. Arezzo, Interim Dir.
Desc: Mental retardation and other forms of aberrant human development, including biomedical, behavioral, educational, and social studies. *Type:* Research center.

Young Adult Institute and Workshop

460 W. 34th St.   Ph: (212)563-7474
New York, NY 10001   Fax: (212)268-1083
URL: http://www.yai.org
Contact: Joel M. Levy, Exec.Dir.
Desc: Provides comprehensive programs that enable people with development disabilities, mental retardation, learning disabilities, emotional disturbance, or brain damage to progress from a state of isolation and dependency to a more productive, self-sufficient, and integrated role in society. Offering an alternative to institutionalization and focussing on the development of a series of supportive community services to maintain individuals' independence, individuality, inclusion and productivity within the community; seeking to prevent instututalization by providing services in local communities to assist parents through family supports or waiver programs to help prevent out of home placement, supporting families in the community thorough primary helathcare for children and adults, certified home health care, specialty therapy services. *Type:* Association.

Diseases

American Lung Association of Louisiana

333 St. Charles Ave., Ste. 500   Ph: (504)523-5864
New Orleans, LA 70130   Free: 800-486-4872
    Fax: (504)523-5867
Contact: Ben Fontaine, Exec.Dir. & CEO.
Desc: Promotes educational programs and research to prevent and control lung disease. Provides child health, clean air, and non-smokers rights advocacy. *Type:* Association.

American Lung Association of Ohio

1950 Arlingate Lane   Ph: (614)279-1700
Columbus, OH 43228   Fax: (614)279-4940
E-mail: lunginfo@ohio.lungusa.org
URL: http://www/wpcoil.com/business/ala
Desc: Works to prevent and control lung disease. *Type:* Association.

Centers for Disease Control and Prevention
Division of Vector-Borne Infectious Diseases

PO Box 2087   Ph: (970)221-6400
Fort Collins, CO 80522-2087   Fax: (970)221-6476
E-mail: djg2@cdc.gov
URL: http://www.cdc.gov
Contact: Dr. Duane J. Gubler, Dir.
Desc: Arthropod-borne viruses, Lyme disease, tularemia, relapsing fever, bubonic plague, and vector biology and control, including field research on disease ecology, epidemiology, pathogen-vector relationships, pathogenesis, molecular biology, and genetically engineered vaccines. *Type:* Research center.

Cystic Fibrosis Foundation

6931 Arlington Rd.,Ste. 200   Ph: (301)951-4422
Bethesda, MD 20814-5200   Free: 800-FIG-HTCF
    Fax: (301)951-6378
E-mail: info@cff.org
URL: http://www.cff.org
Desc: Conducts charitable activities. The CFF supports medical and scientific programs to find the means to cure CF through research, education, and patient programs. *Type:* Association.

Cystic Fibrosis Foundation Lone Star Chapter

8620 N New Braunfels Ave., Ste   Ph: (210)829-7267
110   Fax: (210)829-4204
San Antonio, TX 78217-6361
URL: http://www.cff.org
Contact: Marti Alpard, Exec.Dir.
Desc: Raises funds to benefit cystic fibrosis research. The Cystic Fibrosis Foundation was established in 1955 to raise money for researchj to find a cure for cystic fibrosis and to improve the quality of life for 30,000 children and young adults with the disease. *Type:* Association.

U.S. Department of Health and Human Services
National Heart, Lung, and Blood Institute
Division of Intramural Research
Molecular Disease Branch

NIH Bldg. 10, Rm. 5N113   Ph: (301)496-4826
10 Center Dr., MSC 1422   Fax: (301)402-4359
Bethesda, MD 20892-1422
Contact: Howard S. Kruth, MD, Chf.
Desc: Atherosclerosis. *Type:* Research center.

Dogs

Afghan Hound Club of America

Barb Bornstein
6018 E Osborn Rd.   Ph: (602)994-0150
Scottsdale, AZ 85257   Fax: (602)423-3457
E-mail: barb@trims.com
URL: http://www.akc.org/clubs/ahca
Contact: Barb Bornstein, Corr.Sec.
Desc: Breeders and owners of purebred Afghan hounds. *Type:* Association.

AKC Gazette—List of Clubs Issues

American Kennel Club
51 Madison Ave.   Ph: (212)696-8200
New York, NY 10010   Fax: (212)696-8299
E-mail: info@akc.org
URL: http://www.akg.org/akc.
Contact: Diane Vasey, Editor-in-Chief.
Desc: List of over 4,500 American Kennel Club member clubs is published in April; list of most popular dog breeds, based on AKC registration statistics is also included. *Type:* Directory.

American Brittany Club

10370 Fleming Rd.   Ph: (618)985-2336
Carterville, IL 62918-3350   Fax: (618)985-5103
E-mail: trimnatchbritts@midamer.net
URL: http://www.akc.org/clubs/brit
Contact: Mary Jo Trimble, Sec.
Desc: Owners, breeders, and exhibitors of purebred Brittany dogs united to discourage the breed from becoming split into groups of "field dogs" and "bench dogs" and to strive to keep it forever a "dual dog." Maintains hall of fame. *Type:* Association.

American Kennel Club

5580 Centerview Dr., Ste. 200   Ph: (919)233-9767
Raleigh, NC 27606   Fax: (919)233-3740
E-mail: info@akc.org
URL: http://www.akc.org
Contact: Alfred L. Cheaure, CEO.
Desc: All-breed, specialty breed, obedience, and field trial dog clubs. *Type:* Association.

American Pomeranian Club

3910 Concord Pl.   Ph: (903)832-7742
Texarkana, TX 75501   Fax: (903)838-1707
E-mail: brenda.turner@gor.state.ar.us
Contact: Brenda Turner, Corres.Secy.
Desc: Breeders and owners of purebred Pomeranians. Compiles statistics; offers children's services; participates in charitable program. Conducts educational programs. *Type:* Association.

American Shetland and Sheepdog Association

Lyn Krivanek
3010 Sentinel Hts. Rd.   Ph: (315)677-9296
Lafayette, NY 13084-9628
E-mail: dundee3@aol.com
URL: http://www.assa.org

Contact: Lyn Krivanek, Corres.Sec.
Desc: Experienced Sheltie fanciers devoted to the betterment of the Shetland Sheepdog breed. Establishes breeding standards. *Type:* Association.

Australian Shepherd Club of America

6091 E. State Hwy. 21   Free: 800-892-2722
Bryan, TX 77808-9652   Fax: (409)778-1898
E-mail: asca@mail.myriad.net
URL: http://www.asca.org
Contact: Sandy Tubbs, Pres.
Desc: Promotes the breeding of purebred Australian shepherds. Provides education on ethical breeding practices and encourages quality competitions. Maintains breed standards. *Type:* Association.

Chinese Shar-Pei Club of America

210 White Chapel Ct.   Ph: (817)329-5856
Southlake, TX 76092   Fax: (817)251-2513
E-mail: cathi@cspca.com
URL: http://www.cspca.com
Contact: Georgette Schaefer, Sec.
Desc: Individuals interested in the preservation and improvement of the Chinese Shar-Pei dog. Seeks to educate the public on the characteristics and appearances of the Chinese Shar-Pei breed. Establishes standards for the breed. *Type:* Association.

Dalmatian Club of America

Sharon Boyd
2316 McCrary Rd.   Ph: (281)342-8407
Richmond, TX 77469   Fax: (281)342-9716
E-mail: cgrc32A@prodigy.com
Contact: Sharon Boyd, Sec.
Desc: Owners, breeders, and exhibitors of purebred dalmatians. Conducts specialized education and research programs; compiles statistics. Maintains biographical archives. *Type:* Association.

Doberman Pinscher Club of America

Mrs. Tommie F. Jones
RR 001 Box 142-A   Ph: (850)668-1735
Monticello, FL 32344-9721   Fax: (850)668-1735
Contact: Mrs. Tommie F. Jones, Corr.Sec.
Desc: Breeders and owners of purebred Doberman Pinschers. Objectives are to: preserve and protect the breed; urge members to accept the standard of the breed as approved by the American Kennel Club; encourage sportsmanlike competition. *Type:* Association.

German Shepherd Dog Club of America

17 W. Ivy Ln.   Ph: (201)568-5806
Englewood, NJ 07631
Contact: Ellie Goede, Corr.Sec.
Desc: Individuals with an interest in German Shepherds. *Type:* Association.

Hunting Retriever Club

United Kennel Club
100 E. Kilgore Rd.   Ph: (616)343-9020
Kalamazoo, MI 49002   Fax: (616)343-7037
URL: http://www.ukcdogs.com
Contact: Michelle O'Malley-Morgan, Ed. Adv.
Desc: Duck and bird hunters and upland game hunters interested in retrievers. Established to train and test hunting retrievers; to maintain the inherent working qualities of hunting dogs in their natural environment; and to use humane, thoughtful, and proven dog training techniques. Offers children's services and educational programs. *Type:* Association.

Newfoundland Club of America

c/o Tracy Warneke
PO Box 151
Bourne, MA 02532

Contact: Tracy Warneke, Contact.

Desc: Owners and breeders of purebred Newfoundland dogs. Conducts regional specialties and water trials. Operates national and regional rescue service for displaced Newfoundland dogs. *Type:* Association.

Poodle Club of America

Charles R. Thomasson II
503 Martineau Dr.　　　　Ph: (804)530-1605
Chester, VA 23831

Contact: Charles Thomasson, Corr.Sec.

Desc: Owners, breeders, exhibitors, and judges of purebred poodles. Works to: encourage and promote owning, breeding, and training of purebred poodles and formation of local poodle specialty clubs; urge acceptance of American Kennel Club standards as sole criteria; protect and advance interests of the breed; conduct sanctioned and licensed specialty shows and obedience trials under regulations of the AKC. *Type:* Association.

Siberian Husky Club of America

Fain Zimmerman
210 Madera Dr.　　　　Ph: (512)576-5531
Victoria, TX 77905-0611　　Fax: (512)576-5531

Contact: Fain Zimmerman, Corr.Sec.

Desc: Exhibitors, owners and breeders of Siberian husky dogs, a medium-sized working dog with body proportions and form reflecting a balance of power, speed, and endurance, with well furred body, ears, and brush tail curved over the back; the breed is probably best known as a sled dog and is often used in competitive racing. Compiles breed records, responsible for writing the breed standard, ethical breeding codes, public information, National Speciality shows. Gives funds to research laboratories. *Type:* Association.

Vizsla Club of America

Florence Duggan
451 Longfellow Ave.　　　Ph: (908)789-9774
Westfield, NJ 07090　　　Fax: (410)643-4871

Contact: Sandy Parady, Pres.

Desc: Owners of Vizsla pointer-retriever dogs, which are native to Hungary. Encourages high standards in breeding for hunting ability and conformation; promotes interest in training the Vizsla for field trials, as gundogs, in obedience, for bench shows, and as companions; supports research and education to reduce or eliminate undesirable or detrimental congenital traits in the breed; sponsors trial and specialty show. *Type:* Association.

Worldwide Kennel Club

342 Pelham Rd.　　　　Ph: (914)654-8574
New Rochelle, NY 10805　Fax: (914)654-0364
E-mail: wwkclcom@aol.com
URL: http://www.worldwidekennel.8p9.com/

Contact: Roseanne Nuzzolo, Contact & Pres.

Desc: People interested in exhibiting, running, registering, purchasing, or selling purebred dogs. Dedicated to the protection and advancement of these dogs. Works to adopt and enforce uniform rules and regulations and encourage breed improvement and adherence to breed standards. *Type:* Association.

Your Dog

Tufts University
School of Veterinary Medicine
200 Westboro Rd.
North Grafton, MA 01536-
　1895

Contact: Linda Ross, D.V.M., Editor-in-Chief; Gloria Parkinson, Editor.

Desc: Publishes medical and behavioral advice and tips on dogs by veterinarians. Recurring features include columns titled My Dog and Chewing It Over. *Type:* Newsletter.

Donors

Eye-Bank for Sight Restoration

120 Wall St., 3rd Fl.　　　Ph: (212)742-9000
New York, NY 10005-3902　Fax: (212)269-3139
Contact: Mary Jane O'Neill, Exec.Dir.

Desc: Collects and distributes healthy corneal tissue obtained from individuals who have arranged to donate their eyes, or whose relatives have authorized such donation, at the time of death. *Type:* Association.

The Living Bank

PO Box 6725　　　　　Ph: (713)961-9431
Houston, TX 77265-6725　Free: 800-528-2971
　　　　　　　　　　　Fax: (713)961-0979

E-mail: info@livingbank.org
URL: http://www.livingbank.org
Contact: Clella Atkins, Admin. Asst.

Desc: National registry created to help those persons who, upon their deaths, wish to donate a part or parts of their bodies for the purposes of transplantation, therapy, or medical research. *Type:* Association.

National Marrow Donor Program

Steve Beseke
3433 Broadway NE, Ste. 500　Ph: (612)627-5800
Minneapolis, MN 55413-1762　Free: 800-MAR-
　　　　　　　　　　　　　　　ROW2
　　　　　　　　　　　　　Fax: (612)627-5895

E-mail: chowe@NMDP.org
URL: http://www.marrow.org
Contact: Craig W.S. Howe, MD,PhD, CEO.

Desc: Donor and bone marrow transplant centers. Acts as a central registry of U.S. bone marrow donors; works to develop a large pool of potential donors and facilitate searches and matching of donors and recipients; tests the effectiveness of unrelated donor transplants. *Type:* Association.

National Temporal Bone, Hearing and Balance Pathology Registry

Massachusetts Eye and Ear　　Ph: (617)573-3711
　Infirmary　　　　　　　　　Free: 800-822-1327
243 Charles St.　　　　　　　Fax: (617)573-3838
Boston, MA 02114-3096
E-mail: tbregsitry@meei.harvard.edu
URL: http://www.tbregistry.org
Contact: Dr. Joseph B. Nadol, Jr., Contact.

Desc: Promotes research of hearing and balance disorders through the study of the temporal bone and related brain structures. *Type:* Association.

Ecology

A Basin-wide Information On-Line Service

George Mason University - Biology Department - BIOS Project
4400 University Dr.　　　Ph: (703)993-1000
Fairfax, VA 22030-4444　Free: 800-662-2747
E-mail: bios@envirolink.org

URL: http://web.gmu.edu/bios/

Desc: The BIOS database provides reviews and updates on the Chesapeake Bay region's physical and biological resources, and current information on regional environmental activities and organizations. Individual watersheds are included on a voluntary basis by various groups. *Type:* Database.

EarthSave International

600 Distillery Commons, Ste.
　200
Louisville, KY 40206-1922
E-mail: earthsave@aol.com
URL: http://www.earthsave.org

Contact: Patricia Carney, Exec.Dir.

Desc: EarthSave promotes food choices that are haelthy for the planet. We educate, inspire and empower people to take positive action for all life on Earth. *Type:* Association.

Ecological Society of America

2010 Massachusetts Ave. NW,　Ph: (202)833-8773
　Ste. 400　　　　　　　　　　Fax: (202)833-8775
Washington, DC 20036
E-mail: esahq@esa.org
URL: http://www.sdsc.edu/~ESA/

Contact: Brian Keller, Exec.Dir.

Desc: Educators, professional ecologists, and scientists interested in the study of plants, animals, and man in relation to their environment. Seeks to develop better understanding of biological processes and their contribution to agriculture, forestry, wildlife and range management, fisheries, industry, public health, and conservation. *Type:* Association.

Ecology Abstracts

Cambridge Scientific Abstracts (CSA)
7200 Wisconsin Ave., Ste. 601　Ph: (301)961-6700
Bethesda, MD 20814-4823
E-mail: sales@csa.com
URL: http://www.csa.com

Desc: Contains 216,000 citations, with abstracts, to the worldwide literature on ecology and the environment. Focus is on how microbes, plants, and animals interact with each other and with the environment. *Available:* National Information Services Corporation (NISC), BiblioLine. *Type:* Database.

Ecology Center

2530 San Pablo Ave.　　　Ph: (510)548-2220
Berkeley, CA 94702

Contact: Robert Huang, Exec. Officer.

Desc: Dedicated to informing the public about environmental problems and ecologically sound alternatives. Conducts educational and informational programs and recycling program for newspapers, glass, and metal containers. Sponsors farmer's markets and gardening classes. *Type:* Association.

Environmental and Energy Study Institute

122 C St. NW, Ste. 722　　Ph: (202)628-6500
Washington, DC 20001　　Fax: (202)737-5299
URL: http://www.eenews.net

Contact: Carol Werner, Exec.Dir.

Desc: Promotes environmentally sustainable societies by working to educate policy makers and the general public on related issues including groundwater protection, water efficiency, and global climate change. Cooperates with NGOs governmental organizations and private sector. Conducts educational programs. *Type:* Association.

Environmental Opportunities
Environmental Opportunities
PO Box 1253   Ph: (508)627-7418
Edgartown, MA 02539   Fax: (508)627-7418
E-mail: msandsl@tidepool.com.
Contact: Sanford Berry, Editor.
Desc: Lists and describes environmental job openings throughout the U.S. in areas such as administration, consulting, media/publishing, nature centers, organizations, preservation, research, teaching, and seasonal positions/internships. *Type:* Newsletter.

Point Foundation
1408 Mission Ave.   Ph: (415)256-2800
San Rafael, CA 94901   Fax: (415)256-2808
E-mail: wer@well.com
Contact: Alexander Gault, Publisher.
Desc: Sponsors educational and ecological publications. *Type:* Association.

Sierra Club
85 2nd St. 2nd Fl.   Ph: (415)977-5500
San Francisco, CA 94105-3459   Fax: (415)977-5799
E-mail: information@sierraclub.org
URL: http://www.sierraclub.org
Contact: Carl Pope, Exec.Dir.
Desc: Individuals concerned with nature and its interrelationship to human beings. Promotes protection and conservation of the natural resources of the U.S. *Type:* Association.

Sierra Student Coalition
PO Box 2402   Ph: (401)861-6012
Providence, RI 02906   Free: 888-JOIN-SSC
    Fax: (401)861-6241
E-mail: ssc-info@ssc.org
URL: http://www.ssc.org
Desc: Students interested in ecology and environmental protection. Activist program of the Sierra Club . *Type:* Association.

Economics

Alabama Business and Economic Indicators
Center for Business and Economic Research
University of Alabama
Box 870221   Ph: (205)348-6191
Tuscaloosa, AL 35487   Fax: (205)348-2951
E-mail: uacber@cba.ua.edu; dhamilto@cba.ua.edu.
URL: http://www.cba.ua.edu/~cber.
Contact: Annette Watters, Editor.
Desc: Deals with business and the economy in Alabama and the Southeast. Supplies statistical tables. *Type:* Newsletter.

American Council for Capital Formation
1750 K St. NW, Ste. 400   Ph: (202)293-5811
Washington, DC 20006   Fax: (202)785-8165
E-mail: info@accf.org
URL: http://www.accf.org
Contact: Mark Bloomfield, Pres.
Desc: Supported by individuals, businesses, foundations, and associations. Purposes are: to communicate the capital formation issue to the public, national opinion leaders, and members of Congress; "to actively encourage saving and investment, which are essential for a strong economy, by advocating sound tax, regulatory, environmental policies that do not hinder economic growth and capital formation." Prepares and submits testimony before congressional committees; prepares articles, books, and reports on issues of importance to capital formation. *Type:* Association.

American Economic Association
2014 Broadway, Ste. 305   Ph: (615)322-2595
Nashville, TN 37203-2418   Fax: (615)343-7590
URL: http://www.vanderbilt.edu/AEA
Contact: John J. Siegfried, Sec.
Desc: Educators, business executives, government administrators, journalists, lawyers, and others interested in economics and its application to present-day problems. Encourages historical and statistical research into actual conditions of industrial life and provides a nonpartisan forum for economic discussion. *Type:* Association.

American Institute for Economic Research—Research Reports
American Institute for Economic Research
Division St.   Ph: (413)528-1216
PO Box 1000   Fax: (413)528-0103
Great Barrington, MA 01230
E-mail: aier@world.std.com
URL: http://world.std.com/~aier/; http://world.std.com/~aier/.
Contact: Larry Pratt, Editor.
Desc: Presents the results of the institute's research, including analyses of significant economic developments and their implications, especially the statistical indications of business-cycle changes. *Type:* Newsletter.

Asia Forecast
The WEFA Group
1110 Vermont Ave., NW   Ph: (202)775-0610
Washington, DC 20005
URL: http://www.fdic.gov
Desc: Contains detailed macroeconomic forecasts for Asian countries, covering national accounts, exports, imports, balance of payments, prices, debt, debt servicing, exchange rates, industrial production, labor, and population. Corresponds to the online Asia Forecast database. *Available:* The WEFA Group. *Type:* Database.

Asian Economic News
Kyodo News International, Inc.
50 Rockefeller Plaza, Rm. 803   Ph: (212)397-3723
New York, NY 10020
URL: http://www.kyodonews.com
Desc: Contains the complete text of articles covering economic news in the Far East, excluding Japan. Covers World Bank and International Monetary Fund (IMF) loans to newly industrializing economies (NIEs), overseas relief aid, labor and trade conditions, and weather catastrophes. *Type:* Database.

Bank One Arizona Blue Chip Economic Forecast
Bank One Economic Outlook Center
Arizona State University   Ph: (602)965-5543
College of Business   Free: 800-448-0432
Tempe, AZ 85287-4406   Fax: (602)965-5458
Contact: Robert J. Eggert, Sr., Editor; Tracy Clark, Editor; Elliott Pollack, Editor.
Desc: Provides consensus forecasts of various indicators for the state of Arizona for the current year and the next. Includes a Special Question column with a changing topic each month. *Type:* Newsletter.

Barren River Area Development District
PO Box 90005   Ph: (502)781-2381
Bowling Green, KY 42102   Fax: (502)842-0768
E-mail: braddjack@aol.com
URL: http://www.bradd.org
Contact: Jack Eversole, Exec. Dir.
Desc: Elected officers and community leaders from a 10-county area serving as a council of governments for regional planning, economic development, and program administration services. *Type:* Association.

Baxter
Baxter Brothers, Inc.
1030 E. Putnam   Ph: (203)637-4559
Greenwich, CT 06830
Contact: William Baxter, Editor.
Desc: Examines the U.S. economy in order to anticipate price trends and business movements for investment purposes. *Type:* Newsletter.

Beyond the Bottom Line
Economics Press, Inc.
12 Daniel Rd.   Ph: (973)227-1224
Fairfield, NJ 07004-2565   Free: 800-526-2554
    Fax: (973)526-2554
E-mail: info@epinc.com; order@epinc.com
URL: http://www.epinc.com
Contact: Robert Guder, Editor; Ann Lanahan, Circulation Mgr.
Desc: Publishes business and economic information. *Type:* Newsletter.

Blue Chip Economic Indicators
Capitol Publications, Inc.
1101 King St., Ste. 444   Ph: (703)683-4100
Alexandria, VA 22314   Free: 800-655-5597
    Fax: (703)739-6517
Contact: Margie Weiner, Publisher; Randell Moore, Editor; Liz Soper, Circulation Mgr.
Desc: Provides economic forecasts for 14 key economic indicators. *Type:* Newsletter.

Blue Chip Job Growth Update
Bank One Economics Outlook Center
Arizona State University   Ph: (602)965-5543
College of Business   Free: 800-448-0432
Tempe, AZ 85287-4406   Fax: (602)965-5458
URL: http://www.cob.asu.edu/seid/eoc.
Contact: Robert J. Eggert, Sr., Exec. Editor; Yolanda Strozier, Editor, yolanda.strozier@asu.edu.
Desc: Provides monthly and annual data on non-agricultural job growth for all 50 states and the top 50 Metropolitan Statistical Areas. *Type:* Newsletter.

The Boot Cove Economic Forecast
Voight Industries, Inc.
PO Box 200   Ph: (207)733-5593
Lubec, ME 04652
Contact: R.O. Voight, Editor.
Desc: Covers major economic and political events, assessing their impact on the economy. Tracks major economic statistics with forecast trend lines, specializing in Federal Reserve, oil, the dollar, and the Dow Jones Industrial. *Type:* Newsletter.

Brazos Valley Council of Governments
1706 E. 29th St.   Ph: (409)775-4244
PO Drawer 4128   Fax: (409)775-3466
Bryan, TX 77805-4128
E-mail: info@bvcog.org
URL: http://www.bvcog.org
Contact: Tom Wilkinson, Jr., Exec.Dir.
Desc: Representatives of county governments of Brazos, Burleson, Grimes, Leon, Madison, Robertson, and Washington counties, TX. Assists members in formulating strategies for economic growth and development. *Type:* Association.

Building Communities through Manufacturing
Technology and Economic Development
301 Tarrow, Ste. 119   Ph: (409)845-2907
College Station, TX 77843-8000   Free: 800-625-4876
    Fax: (409)845-3559
E-mail: ecwhite@teexnet.tamu.edu.

Contact: Leslie Hill, Editor; Rodney Rather, Editor.

Desc: Discusses community development and economic growth. Deals with dangers and successes of development trends. *Type:* Newsletter.

Business and Economics

National Technical Information Service (NTIS)
U.S. Department of Commerce
5285 Port Royal Rd.   Ph: (703)605-6000
Springfield, VA 22161-0001   Free: 800-553-NTIS
                             Fax: (703)605-6900
E-mail: orders@ntis.fedworld.gov

Desc: Publishes abstracts of business and economic information available from the National Technical Information Service. *Type:* Newsletter.

Business Executives' Expectations

The Conference Board, Inc.
845 3rd Ave.   Ph: (212)759-0900
New York, NY 10022-6679   Fax: (212)980-7014
E-mail: info@conference-board.org
URL: http://www.conference-board.org
Contact: Lynn Franco, Editor.

Desc: Provides narrative and tabular material describing business executives' appraisal of the current economy and their expectations for the succeeding six months. Carries evaluations for separate industries and for the economy in general. *Type:* Newsletter.

Caribbean Update

Kal Wagenheim
52 Maple Ave.   Ph: (973)762-1565
Maplewood, NJ 07040   Free: 800-647-9990
                             Fax: (973)762-9585
E-mail: mexcarib@compuserve.com; mexcarib@tiac.net.
Contact: Kal Wagenheim, Editor.

Desc: Contains news of business and economic developments in the Caribbean and Central America. Provides country-by-country coverage, as well as regional items. *Type:* Newsletter.

Cato Policy Report

Cato Institute
1000 Massachusetts Ave. NW   Ph: (202)842-0200
Washington, DC 20001-5403   Free: 800-767-1241
                             Fax: (202)842-3490
E-mail: catl@cato.org
URL: http://www.individualrights.org; http://www.cato.org.
Contact: David D. Boaz, Editor.

Desc: "Provides in-depth evaluations of public policies and discusses appropriate solutions." Covers monetary policy, taxation, inflation, labor issues, energy, foreign policy, and the regulatory process. Takes a critical stance against excessive government controls. *Type:* Newsletter.

CEPR Perspectives

Center for Economic Policy Research
Stanford University, MC:6015
Landau Economic Center   Ph: (415)725-1872
Stanford, CA 94305   Fax: (415)723-8611
Contact: Michelle Mosman, Editor.

Desc: Updates information on conferences, events, and publications. *Type:* Newsletter.

Charting the Economy

Robert G. Williams
PO Box 829   Ph: (860)667-9909
New Haven, CT 06504
Contact: Robert G. Williams, Editor and Publisher.

Desc: Provides information about economic matters. Covers the stock market, interest rates, and business cycles. *Type:* Newsletter.

Chicago Fed Letter

Federal Reserve Bank of Chicago
Public Affairs Department   Ph: (312)322-5111
230 S. LaSalle   Fax: (312)322-5515
Chicago, IL 60604
E-mail: shortlin@nr.infi.net.
URL: http://www.frbchi.org.
Contact: Helen O. Koshy, Editor.

Desc: Essays on contemporary economic and financial developments. *Type:* Newsletter.

CHILE

Embassy of Chile
Economic Dept.
1736 Massachusetts Ave. NW   Ph: (202)785-1746
Washington, DC 20036   Fax: (202)659-3220

Desc: Publishes news of the economic state of Chile. Topics include foreign investment, trade, the economy, commerce, and industry. *Type:* Newsletter.

Chronicle of Latin American Economic Affairs

University of New Mexico
Latin American Institute
Latin America Data Base (LADB)
801 Yale, NE   Ph: (505)277-6839
Albuquerque, NM 87131-1016
E-mail: info@ladb.unm.edu
URL: http://ladb.unm.edu
Contact: Roma Arellano.

Desc: Contains the complete text of Chronicle of Latin American Economic Affairs, a weekly newsletter reporting news and analyses of economic developments in Latin American and Caribbean countries. Covers regional economic integration, trade, agriculture, debt, investment, and balance of payments. *Available:* LEXIS-NEXIS, NEXIS; Latin America Data Base; LEXIS-NEXIS. *Type:* Database.

Committee for Economic Development

2000 L St. NW, Ste. 700   Ph: (202)296-5860
Washington, DC 20036   Fax: (202)223-0776
E-mail: ckolb@ced.org
URL: http://www.ced.org
Contact: Charles Kolb, Pres.

Desc: Trustees are heads of major corporations or university presidents. Working with expert advisers, the committee conducts research and formulates policy recommendations on national and international economic issues, including education, trade policy, U.S.-Japan economic relations, and problems of the inner city. Through its studies and reports, seeks to: contribute to full employment, higher living standards, and increased opportunities for all; promote economic growth and stability; strengthen the concepts and institutions essential to progress in a free society. *Type:* Association.

Concord Coalition

Paula Price
1019 19th St. NW, Ste. 810
Washington, DC 20036
Contact: Paula Price, Contact.

Desc: Individuals and organizations. Promotes development of "a sound economy for future generations." *Type:* Association.

The Conference Board

845 3rd Ave.   Ph: (212)759-0900
New York, NY 10022   Fax: (212)980-7014
E-mail: info@conference-board.org
URL: http://www.conference-board.org
Contact: Richard E. Cavanagh, Pres. & CEO.

Desc: Corporations, government agencies, libraries, colleges, and universities. Fact-finding institution that conducts research and publishes studies on business economics and management experience. *Type:* Association.

DCCA News

Illinois Department of Commerce and
Community Affairs
620 E. Adams St.   Ph: (217)785-6092
Springfield, IL 62701-1615   Fax: (217)524-3701
URL: http://www.commerce.state.il.us.
Contact: Lynn Morford, Editor, lmorford@commercestate.il.us.

Desc: Monitors Illinois economic development, particularly DCCA-related programs and activities. *Type:* Newsletter.

DRI Asian Forecast

Standard & Poor's DRI
Data Products Division
24 Hartwell Ave.   Ph: (781)863-5100
Lexington, MA 02421
E-mail: client_services@dri.mcgraw-hill.com
URL: http://www.dri.mcgraw-hill.com
Contact: Client Services, (617)860-6527, fax: (617)860-6416.

Desc: Contains annual historical and forecast time series on the individual economies of 11 Asian countries (Australia, Hong Kong, India, Indonesia, Korea, Malaysia, the People's Republic of China, the Philippines, Singapore, Taiwan, and Thailand) and the regional economy of all 11 nations, members of the Association of South East Asian Nations (ASEAN), and Newly Industrializing Countries (Hong Kong, Korea, Singapore, and Taiwan). Covers gross domestic product (GDP) by type of expenditure, inflation rates, income, population, trade, balance of payments, industrial production, foreign debt, money supply, and currency exchange rates. *Available:* Standard & Poor's DRI, Data Products Division. *Type:* Database.

DRI Canadian Model History

Standard & Poor's DRI
Data Products Division
24 Hartwell Ave.   Ph: (781)863-5100
Lexington, MA 02421
E-mail: client_services@dri.mcgraw-hill.com
URL: http://www.dri.mcgraw-hill.com
Contact: Client Resource Center, (781)860-6527, fax: (781)860-6416.

Desc: Provides information on the state of the Canadian economy at the national level. Includes time series on potential GDP, total factor productivity, and the user cost of capital for sectors. *Available:* Standard & Poor's DRI, Data Products Division. *Type:* Database.

DRI Canadian Quarterly Model Forecast

Standard & Poor's DRI
Data Products Division
24 Hartwell Ave.   Ph: (781)863-5100
Lexington, MA 02421
E-mail: client_services@dri.mcgraw-hill.com
URL: http://www.dri.mcgraw-hill.com
Contact: Client Resource Center, (781)860-6527, fax: (781)860-6416.

Desc: Provides the DRI outlook for the Canadian economy at the national level. Includes short-term forecasts for nine to twelve quarters, long-term forecasts for twelve to 15 years, and extended long-term forecasts for 25 years. *Available:* Standard & Poor's DRI, Data Products Division. *Type:* Database.

DRI Canadian Regional Forecast

Standard & Poor's DRI
Data Products Division
24 Hartwell Ave.   Ph: (781)863-5100
Lexington, MA 02421
E-mail: client_services@dri.mcgraw-hill.com
URL: http://www.dri.mcgraw-hill.com

Contact: Client Resource Center, (781)860-6527, fax: (781)860-6416.

Desc: Contains more than 300 historical and forecast annual time series covering economic and demographic conditions in Alberta, British Columbia, Manitoba, Ontario, Quebec, Saskatchewan, and the Atlantic provinces. Covers the following categories: regional forecasts for the Canadian economy, covering industry production, including total (nominal and real), and real industrial production by two-digit SIC (Standard Industrial Classification) code; investment, including residential construction and nonresidential construction; population and labor market, including total population, population 15 years and older, births and deaths and net migration, employment, unemployment rates, labor force 15 years and older, and participation rates 15 years and older; income and prices, including wages, salaries, and other personal income, personal and disposable income, direct personal taxes, and Consumer Price Index; housing starts and stocks (single, multiple, and total); and retail sales. *Available:* Standard & Poor's DRI, Data Products Division. *Type:* Database.

DRI Cost Information Service Forecast

Standard & Poor's DRI
Data Products Division
24 Hartwell Ave.   Ph: (781)863-5100
Lexington, MA 02421
E-mail: client_services@dri.mcgraw-hill.com
URL: http://www.dri.mcgraw-hill.com

Contact: Client Resource Center, (781)860-6527, fax: (781)860-6416.

Desc: Contains indexed data for producer and consumer prices, hourly earnings, employment costs, international prices and wages, building and plant costs, and metals and steel. Sources are varied and include the Bureau of Labor Statistics, international government statistical agencies and trade publications. *Available:* Standard & Poor's DRI, Data Products Division. *Type:* Database.

DRI County Forecast

Standard & Poor's DRI
Data Products Division
24 Hartwell Ave.   Ph: (781)863-5100
Lexington, MA 02421
E-mail: client_services@dri.mcgraw-hill.com
URL: http://www.dri.mcgraw-hill.com

Contact: Client Services, (617)860-6527, fax: (617)860-6416.

Desc: Provides annual projections of key economic and demographic dimensions for all 3134 U.S. counties. *Available:* Standard & Poor's DRI, Data Products Division. *Type:* Database.

DRI European Sectoral

Standard & Poor's DRI
Data Products Division
24 Hartwell Ave.   Ph: (781)863-5100
Lexington, MA 02421
E-mail: client_services@dri.mcgraw-hill.com
URL: http://www.dri.mcgraw-hill.com

Contact: Client Services, (617)860-6527, fax: (617)860-6416.

Desc: Contains 3000 monthly, quarterly, and annual time series on various economic sectors, including agriculture, energy, construction, industry, and services. Covers consumption and consumer prices, employment and wages, imports and exports in real and nominal terms, investment, prices by industry, value added, and output. *Available:* Standard & Poor's DRI, Data Products Division. *Type:* Database.

DRI European Sectoral Model Forecast

Standard & Poor's DRI
Data Products Division
24 Hartwell Ave.   Ph: (781)863-5100
Lexington, MA 02421
E-mail: client_services@dri.mcgraw-hill.com
URL: http://www.dri.mcgraw-hill.com

Contact: Client Services, (617)860-6527, fax: (617)860-6416.

Desc: Contains more than 4000 monthly, quarterly, and annual forecasts on European industrial production and consumption. Covers production at a 50-sector level; and production, value added, exports and imports, prices, employment, wages and salaries per employee, input costs, and domestic demand at a 20-sector level. *Type:* Database.

DRI International Cost Forecasting

Standard & Poor's DRI
Data Products Division
24 Hartwell Ave.   Ph: (781)863-5100
Lexington, MA 02421
E-mail: client_services@dri.mcgraw-hill.com
URL: http://www.dri.mcgraw-hill.com

Contact: Client Resource Center, (781)860-6527, fax: (781)860-6416.

Desc: Contains approximately 1800 quarterly and monthly time series for producer and wholesale price indexes, construction costs, and wages and earnings for the Federal Republic of Germany, France, Italy, Japan, and the United Kingdom. Includes construction cost and earnings data for 46 industrial and construction sectors, and wholesale and producer price indexes for more than 700 commodities. *Available:* Standard & Poor's DRI, Data Products Division. *Type:* Database.

DRI Long-Term Industry Forecast

Standard & Poor's DRI
Data Products Division
24 Hartwell Ave.   Ph: (781)863-5100
Lexington, MA 02421
E-mail: client_services@dri.mcgraw-hill.com
URL: http://www.dri.mcgraw-hill.com

Contact: Client Services, (617)860-6527, fax: (617)860-6416.

Desc: Contains more than 4000 annual forecasts on output, employment, productivity, price indices imports, and exports for 242 industries at a 4-digit Standard Industrial Classification (SIC) code level. Also provides and gross margins for 48 industries at a 2-digit SIC code level, Forecasts reflect interindustry relationships. *Available:* Standard & Poor's DRI, Data Products Division. *Type:* Database.

DRI Metropolitan Area Forecast

Standard & Poor's DRI
Data Products Division
24 Hartwell Ave.   Ph: (781)863-5100
Lexington, MA 02421
E-mail: client_services@dri.mcgraw-hill.com
URL: http://www.dri.mcgraw-hill.com

Contact: Client Resource Center, (781)860-6527, fax: (781)860-6416.

Desc: Provides more than 7650 quarterly and annual economic and demographic forecasts for the top 100 Metropolitan Statistical Areas (MSAs) and annual forecasts for 213 MSAs. Covers industry employment for durable, nondurable, and total manufacturing, and nonmanufacturing at one-digit Standard Industrial Classification (SIC) code level; total, wage and salary, and nonwage income and per capita personal income; total resident population; housing permits for top 100 MSAs for total, single-family, and multi-family; labor market indicators for top 100 MSAs for total and participation rate of labor force, employment by place of residence, and unemployment rate. *Available:* Standard & Poor's DRI, Data Products Division. *Type:* Database.

DRI Middle East and African Forecast

Standard & Poor's DRI
Data Products Division
24 Hartwell Ave.   Ph: (781)863-5100
Lexington, MA 02421
E-mail: client_services@dri.mcgraw-hill.com
URL: http://www.dri.mcgraw-hill.com

Desc: Contains more than 500 annual historical and forecast time series for 10 Middle Eastern and African economies. Covers gross domestic product (GDP) by type of expenditure, trade and balance of payments accounts, oil production, foreign debt positions, money supply, exchange rates, income, inflation, and population. *Type:* Database.

DRI Regional Industry Forecast

Standard & Poor's DRI
Data Products Division
24 Hartwell Ave.   Ph: (781)863-5100
Lexington, MA 02421
E-mail: client_services@dri.mcgraw-hill.com
URL: http://www.dri.mcgraw-hill.com

Contact: Client Services, (617)860-6527, fax: (617)860-6416.

Desc: Contains approximately 61,000 annual forecasts on industrial activity for all U.S. states, Washington, D.C., and 9 regions. *Available:* Standard & Poor's DRI, Data Products Division. *Type:* Database.

DRI U.S. Macro Model Forecast

Standard & Poor's DRI
Data Products Division
24 Hartwell Ave.   Ph: (781)863-5100
Lexington, MA 02421
E-mail: client_services@dri.mcgraw-hill.com
URL: http://www.dri.mcgraw-hill.com

Contact: Client Services, (617)860-6527, fax: (617)860-6416.

Desc: Provides detailed projections of U.S. economic activity and financial conditions. *Available:* Standard & Poor's DRI, Data Products Division. *Type:* Database.

DRI U.S. Macro Model History

Standard & Poor's DRI
Data Products Division
24 Hartwell Ave.   Ph: (781)863-5100
Lexington, MA 02421
E-mail: client_services@dri.mcgraw-hill.com
URL: http://www.dri.mcgraw-hill.com

Contact: Client Services, (617)860-6527, fax: (617)860-6416.

Desc: Provides history on 1200 key indicators of the state of the U.S. economy with series available from 1947. *Available:* Standard & Poor's DRI, Data Products Division. *Type:* Database.

DRI U.S. Regional Model History

Standard & Poor's DRI
Data Products Division
24 Hartwell Ave.   Ph: (781)863-5100
Lexington, MA 02421
E-mail: client_services@dri.mcgraw-hill.com
URL: http://www.dri.mcgraw-hill.com

Contact: Client Services, (617)860-6527, fax: (617)860-6416.

Desc: Contains approximately 6000 time series at the regional and state level, including industry employment and production, income, prices and wages, and housing and demographic information. Data are drawn from DRI's proprietary regional databank. *Available:* Standard & Poor's DRI, Data Products Division. *Type:* Database.

DRI World Forecast

Standard & Poor's DRI
Data Products Division
24 Hartwell Ave.   Ph: (781)863-5100
Lexington, MA 02421
E-mail: client_services@dri.mcgraw-hill.com
URL: http://www.dri.mcgraw-hill.com
Contact: Client Resource Center, (781)860-6527, fax: (781)860-6416.
Desc: Contains more than 7000 historical and forecast economic time series for 46 countries and five world regions. For each country, provides approximately 100 indicators adjusted to accommodate cross-country comparisons. *Available:* Standard & Poor's DRI, Data Products Division. *Type:* Database.

Early Warning Forecast

Cahners Publishing Company
275 Washington St.   Ph: (617)558-2119
Newton, MA 02458   Fax: (617)558-4700
Contact: Bill Wood, Editor.
Desc: Provides analysis and presents up-to-date forecasts for business and industry, including the industrial production, housing, the gross national product (GNP), consumer spending, corporate profits, electronics, construction, metals, and the "Cahners Early Warning Indicator." Recurring features include an economic outlook and an insert devoted to business forecasting assistance. *Type:* Newsletter.

EcoCentral

University of New Mexico
Latin American Institute
Latin America Data Base (LADB)
801 Yale, NE   Ph: (505)277-6839
Albuquerque, NM 87131-1016
E-mail: info@ladb.unm.edu
URL: http://ladb.unm.edu
Contact: Rebecca Reynolds Bannister, Director, (505)277-6839, fax: (505)277-6837, info@ladb.unm.edu.
Desc: Contains the complete text of EcoCentral, a weekly newsletter reporting news on political, economic, and social developments in Central America and the Caribbean, including Cuba. Covers military and civilian actions in regional conflicts and sustainable development issues. *Available:* Latin America Data Base; LEXIS-NEXIS. *Type:* Database.

ECONBASE: Time Series & Forecasts

The WEFA Group
1110 Vermont Ave., NW   Ph: (202)775-0610
Washington, DC 20005
URL: http://www.fdic.gov
Desc: Contains approximately 13,000 monthly, quarterly, and annual economic time series. Includes national, state, Metropolitan Statistical Area (MSA), and Consolidated Metropolitan Statistical Area (CMSA) data for the U.S., and national aggregate data for more than 30 other countries. *Available:* The Dialog Corporation, DIALOG. *Type:* Database.

EconLit

American Economic Association
4615 Fifth Ave.   Ph: (412)268-3869
Pittsburgh, PA 15213-3661
E-mail: info@econlit.org
URL: http://www.econlit.org
Contact: Drucilla Ekwurzel, Associate Editor.
Desc: Contains more than 370,000 citations, with abstracts, to articles from more than 525 economics journals. Includes selected abstracts from 1987 to 1989 and abstracts for all articles since 1989. *Available:* OCLC Online Computer Library Center, Inc., OCLC EPIC; EBSCOhost; Ovid Technologies, Inc.; SilverPlatter Information, Inc. *Type:* Database.

Economic Development

Wakeman/Walworth, Inc.
300 N. Washington St.   Ph: (703)549-8606
Alexandria, VA 22314   Free: 800-876-2545
URL: http://statecapitals.com.
Contact: Keyes Walworth, Editor.
Desc: Covers state efforts to attract new industry, jobs, commerce, and tourism, including such factors as environmental requirements, mass transportation policies, highway construction plans, utility rates, changes in labor laws, tax policies, and enterprise zones. Provides information on urban development programs as affected by growth control legislation, state construction programs, and building codes. *Type:* Newsletter.

Economic Development Research Focus

Economic Development Institute
Georgia Tech
Georgia Institute of Technology
O'Keefe Bldg., Rm. 205   Ph: (404)894-3475
Atlanta, GA 30332   Fax: (404)894-0069
URL: http://www.ceds.gatech.edu/focus/focus.html.
Contact: Lincoln S. Bates, Editor.
Desc: Reports on the progress and results of studies undertaken by the Economic Development Research Program. Covers relevant topics, legislation and resources; and presents success stories. *Type:* Newsletter.

Economic History Services

Miami University - Cliometric Society
Oxford, OH 45056
E-mail: manager@eh.net
URL: http://cs.muohio.edu/
Contact: Samuel H. Williamson, Executive Director, swilliamson@cs.muohio.edu.
Desc: Educators looking for teaching resources about economics should visit the Economic History Services. The site houses book reviews of economics texts, course syllabi in a number of courses, both European and American, archives of Listservs, and directories to the following professional organizations: The Business History Conference, The Cliometric Society, and The Economic History Association Directory. *Type:* Database.

Economic Indicators

First Hawaiian Bank
Research Dept.
Box 3200   Ph: (808)525-6151
Honolulu, HI 96847   Fax: (808)525-6204
Contact: Dr. Leroy O. Laney, Editor.
Desc: Monitors business, finance, and economic conditions of Hawaii. *Type:* Newsletter.

Economic Issues

Lawrence J. McQuillan
179 E. Franklin St.   Fax: (919)489-3024
PO Box 989
Chapel Hill, NC 27514-0989
E-mail: ljmcq@aol.com
Contact: Lawrence J. McQuillan, Ph.D., Editor.
Desc: Reviews economic journal articles that are relevant to current public-policy discussions. Topics include monetary and fiscal policy and government regulation. *Type:* Newsletter.

Economic News from Austria

Austrian Press and Information Service
3524 International Ct. NW   Ph: (202)895-6775
Washington, DC 20008-3027   Fax: (202)895-6772
E-mail: austroinfo@aol.com; austroinfo@austria.org
URL: http://www.austria.org; http://www.austria.org.
Contact: Ulf Pacher, Managing Editor; Martin Eichtinger, Editor-in-Chief.

Desc: Publishes articles about the Austrian economy. Recurring features include columns titled Economic News Briefs, Introducing, and Austria in the Media. *Type:* Newsletter.

Economic Week

Citibank - GFNA
399 Park Ave.   Fax: (212)793-4968
New York, NY 10043
Contact: Richard Schultz, Contact.
Desc: Reports on financial analysis relating to worldwide economic conditions and developments. *Type:* Newsletter.

EconWPA

Washington University - Economics Department
Campus Box 1208
One Brookings Dr.
St. Louis, MO 63130
URL: http://econwpa.wustl.edu/wpawelcome.html
Contact: Bob Parks, bparks@wuecona.wustl.edu.
Desc: The Economics Working Paper Archive is an electronic archive of working papers, data, and computer programs. The archive provides an automated system for the archiving and distribution of working papers in all areas of economics. *Type:* Database.

Employment & the Economy

New Jersey Department of Labor
Labor Planning & Analysis
5th Fl., CN 057   Ph: (609)292-7376
Trenton, NJ 08625-0057   Fax: (609)633-9240
URL: http://www.wnjpin.state.nj.us.
Contact: Jan J. DeJong, Editor.
Desc: Provides statistics and articles on the economy and employment trends in four counties in the Atlantic Coastal Region. Recurring features include listings of job opportunities and construction project updates. *Type:* Newsletter.

Employment & the Economy: Northern Region

New Jersey Department of Labor
Labor Planning & Analysis
5th Fl., CN 057   Ph: (609)292-7376
Trenton, NJ 08625-0057   Fax: (609)633-9240
URL: http://www.wnjpin.state.nj.us.
Contact: Jan J. DeJong, Editor.
Desc: Covers economic trends and developments in 11 northern New Jersey counties, including employment conditions and construction project updates. Recurring features include list of job opportunities. *Type:* Newsletter.

Employment & the Economy: Southern Region

New Jersey Department of Labor
Labor Planning & Analysis
5th Fl., CN 057   Ph: (609)292-7376
Trenton, NJ 08625-0057   Fax: (609)633-9240
URL: http://www.wnjpin.state.nj.us.
Contact: Jan J. DeJong, Editor.
Desc: Covers economic developments in six counties in southern New Jersey, including employment conditions and construction project updates. Recurring features include a list of job opportunities. *Type:* Newsletter.

Employment Opportunities for Business Economists

National Association for Business Economics
1233 20th St., Ste. 505   Ph: (202)463-6223
Washington, DC 20036   Fax: (202)463-6239
E-mail: nabe@nabe.com
URL: http://www.nabe.com
Contact: Anne Picker, Editor.
Desc: Features listings of job openings for business economists and analysts. *Type:* Newsletter.

Evans Economics Analysis and Commentary

Evans Investment Advisors, Inc.
720 Ingleside PL
Evanston, IL 60201-1710

Desc: Reports changes in economic activity to all major financial markets. Comprises more than 20 files that provide forecasts and reports on the effect of economic variables on debt and equity markets. *Available:* Telerate Systems Inc.; Quotron Systems, Inc.; Bloomberg Financial Markets; Bridge Information Systems, Inc., Knight-Ridder Financial Information Group. *Type:* Database.

Evans Electronic News Service

Evans Investment Advisors, Inc.
720 Ingleside PL
Evanston, IL 60201-1710

Desc: Contains commentary and analyses, with statistics, of U.S. economic and financial forecasts. *Available:* LEXIS-NEXIS, LEXIS; LEXIS-NEXIS, NEXIS; Telerate Systems Inc.; Evans Investment Advisors, Inc. *Type:* Database.

Federal Reserve Bank of Chicago

Federal Reserve Bank of Chicago
230 S. LaSalle St.   Ph: (312)322-5111
PO Box 834   Fax: (312)322-5515
Chicago, IL 60690-0834
E-mail: information.chi@chi.frb.org
URL: http://www.frbchi.org/

Desc: The Federal Reserve Bank of Chicago database contains information about the economy and economic policy, and includes information on financial markets, monetary policy, Fed locations, Federal Reserve Publications (full text and bibliographic citations), and more. Information is to provide help to academics, bankers, consumers, community groups, educators and media in economic issues. *Type:* Database.

Federal Reserve Bank of Cleveland—Economic Commentary

Federal Reserve Bank of Cleveland
1455 E. 6th   Ph: (216)579-2000
Cleveland, OH 44114   Fax: (216)579-3050
URL: http://www.clev.frb.org.

Contact: Robin Ratliff, Editor; Tess Ferg, Editor.

Desc: Features articles on regional, national, and international issues in economics. *Type:* Newsletter.

Financial Forecast

The WEFA Group
1110 Vermont Ave., NW   Ph: (202)775-0610
Washington, DC 20005
URL: http://www.fdic.gov

Contact: Arvinder Singh, Financial Analyst, (215)660-6473.

Desc: Contains approximately 250 monthly time series of historical and forecast data on key financial market indicators for the U.S. Sources include government agencies and central banks. *Available:* The WEFA Group. *Type:* Database.

Forecasts & Strategies

Phillips Business Information, Inc.
1201 Seven Locks Rd., Ste. 300   Ph: (301)340-1520
Potomac, MD 20854   Free: 888-707-5809
      Fax: (301)340-3847
E-mail: clientservices.pbi@phillips.com
URL: http://www.phillips.com; http://www.forecasts-strategies.com/.

Contact: Mark Skousen, Editor.

Desc: Analyzes financial matters from a conservative, libertarian point of view. Reports on inflation, taxes, government controls, investment strategies, foreign investing, insurance and annuities, financial privacy, and banking and credit cards. *Type:* Newsletter.

FRBSF Economic Letter

Economic Research Department
Federal Reserve Bank of San Francisco (FRBSF)
PO Box 7702   Ph: (415)974-2246
San Francisco, CA 94120   Fax: (415)974-2168
E-mail: frbsfres.publications@sf.frb.org.
URL: http://www.frbsf.org.

Contact: Judith Goff, Editor.

Desc: Contains one article per issue analyzing current economic and regulatory developments on the regional or national level. *Type:* Newsletter.

Future Economic Trends

Conservative Publishing Corp.
4309 Hatch   Ph: (702)390-3391
North Las Vegas, NV 89030

Contact: C.J. Jones, Editor; Jerry Green, Editor.

Desc: Covers economic and political science in an historical perspective. *Type:* Newsletter.

German Macroeconomic

The WEFA Group
1110 Vermont Ave., NW   Ph: (202)775-0610
Washington, DC 20005
URL: http://www.fdic.gov

Desc: Contains more than 23,000 time series of Germany macroeconomic data, covering national accounts, banking, securities, balance of payments, currencies, production, wages, prices, employment, new orders, and seasonally adjusted data. Also includes industry-specific data. *Available:* The WEFA Group. *Type:* Database.

Global Economic Outlook

Economics Department
The Bank of Nova Scotia
44 King St. W.   Ph: (416)866-6253
Toronto, ON, Canada M5H   Fax: (416)866-2829
1H1

Desc: Outlines economic trends in the G7 countries. Provides outlook of Canadian economic activity on a provincial industrial and financial level. *Type:* Newsletter.

Gold Newsletter

Jefferson Financial, Inc.
2400 Jefferson Hwy., Ste. 600   Ph: (504)837-3033
Jefferson, LA 70121   Free: 800-877-8847
      Fax: (504)837-4885
E-mail: gnlmail@jeffinc.com.

Contact: James U. Blanchard, III, Editor; Brien Lundin, Editor.

Desc: Reports on the relationship between gold and the economic system. Covers news of the "world gold markets, monetary reform, international economics, inflation, deflation, future of gold prices," and related economic and political matters. *Type:* Newsletter.

Greater Phoenix Blue Chip Economic Forecast

Bank One Economic Outlook Center
Arizona State University   Ph: (602)965-5543
College of Business   Free: 800-448-0432
Tempe, AZ 85287-4406   Fax: (602)965-5458

Contact: Patti Carras, Editor; Tracy Clark, Editor; Elliott Pollack, Editor.

Desc: Provides consensus forecasts for the current year and the next for the economy and real estate markets for the metropolitan Phoenix area. Remarks: Sponsor the Phoenix Chamber of Commerce. *Type:* Newsletter.

Growth Strategies

Growth Strategies
2118 Wilshire Blvd., Ste. 826   Ph: (310)451-2990
Santa Monica, CA 90403   Fax: (310)828-0427

Contact: Dr. Roger Selbert, Editor.

Desc: Provides identification and analysis of economic, social, demographic, technological, lifestyle, consumer, business, management, and marketing trends. *Type:* Newsletter.

Holland Bulletin

Netherlands Foreign Trade Agency
c/o Netherlands Consulate   Ph: (212)246-1429
General   Fax: (212)333-3603
1 Rockefeller Plaza, 11th Fl.
New York, NY 10020-2094
E-mail: nlgovnyc@internetmci.com

Desc: Focuses on news, products, and economics from the Netherlands. Recurring features include news of research and calendar of events. *Type:* Newsletter.

Human Economy Newsletter

Human Economy Center
Mankato State University
PO Box 28
West Swanzey, NH 03469-0028

Contact: John Applegath, Editor.

Desc: Disseminates information concerning the Center, which was created "to provide encouragement, exchange of information, and new developments for those of us who see the necessity for a new kind of economics if humanity is to survive." Discusses economic problems and issues. *Type:* Newsletter.

IDBAmerica

Inter-American Development Bank (IDB)
1300 New York Ave. NW   Ph: (202)623-1374
Washington, DC 20577   Fax: (202)789-2835
E-mail: editor@idab.org; idb-books@iadb.org.
URL: http://www.iadb.org.

Contact: Roger Hamilton, Editor, rogerh@iadb.org.

Desc: Reports on economics and social development trends in Latin America and the Caribbean and on the activities of the Bank. Recurring features include notices of publications available, and columns titled Focus, The Bank, The Region, Bank in Action, New Projects, Gazette, and Newsmakers. *Type:* Newsletter.

Ideas Into Action

Mercatus Center
George Mason University
4084 University Dr., Ste. 208   Ph: (703)934-6970
Fairfax, VA 22030-6815   Fax: (703)934-1578
E-mail: mercatus@gmu.edu

Contact: Colleen Morretta, Editor, (730)934-6580, cmorrett@gmu.edu.

Desc: Reports on the programs, activities, and personalities of the Center. *Type:* Newsletter.

IMF Survey

International Monetary Fund
700 19th St. NW   Ph: (202)623-7430
Washington, DC 20431   Fax: (202)623-7201
E-mail: jlavin@imf.org; imfsurvey@imf.org.
URL: http://www.imf.org; http://www.lmf.org.

Contact: Ian S. McDonald, Editor-in-Chief, (202)623-7530, fax: (202)623-6149, imcdonald@imf.org.

Desc: Timely news on topics of general interest in the fields of international finance, country economics, trade, and commodities. Contains information on the IMF's activities, including press releases, major management speeches, and lending activity data rates. *Type:* Newsletter.

The Insiders

Institute for Econometric Research
2200 SW 10th St.   Ph: (954)421-1000
Deerfield Beach, FL 33442   Free: 800-442-9000
                                   Fax: 800-338-4528

Contact: Norman G. Fosback, Editor.

Desc: Provides information on "what corporate insiders, America's most knowledgeable investors, are doing with their company stocks." Remarks: Maintains a telephone hotline. *Type:* Newsletter.

Inter-American Development Bank

1300 New York Ave. NW   Ph: (202)623-1000
Washington, DC 20577   Fax: (202)623-3096
E-mail: webmaster@iadb.org
URL: http://www.iadb.org

Contact: Enrique V. Iglesias, Pres.

Desc: Western Hemisphere countries (28); other interested countries (18). Seeks to help accelerate the economic and social development of members in Latin America and the Caribbean. Works to: promote the investment of public and private capital in the region; use its own capital, as well as funds raised in financial markets and other available resources, for financing high-priority projects; supplement private investment when capital is not available on reasonable terms and conditions; encourage members to direct their policies toward better use of their natural resources while fostering growth of their foreign trade and development of complementary economies in Latin America; provide technical cooperation for the preparation, financing, and execution of development plans and projects, including the study of priorities and formulation of specific project proposals; contribute to the strengthening of the institutional base of lesser-developed member countries. *Type:* Association.

International Finance Corporation

2121 Pennsylvania Ave., NW   Ph: (202)477-1234
Washington, DC 20433   Fax: (202)947-4384
E-mail: webmaster@ifc.org
URL: http://www.ifc.org

Contact: Peter Woicke, Exec.VP.

Desc: Member of the World Bank Group. Works to improve the economies of developing countries by promoting private sector growth. Provides venture capital for enterprises that develop local markets. *Type:* Association.

International Monetary Fund

700 19th St. NW   Ph: (202)623-7000
Washington, DC 20431   Fax: (202)623-4661

Contact: Michel Camdessus, Mng.Dir.

Desc: National governments. Works to: facilitate monetary cooperation through consultation and collaboration among member nations; assist in the balanced expansion of trade and thus contribute to the internal development and prosperity of member nations; maintain stability in monetary exchange arrangements, particularly to avoid exchange depreciations; participate in establishing a multilateral system of payments between member nations and in eliminating exchange restrictions that hamper trade; make available the resources of the fund to provide member nations with a means of assuaging economic difficulties. Maintains the IMF Institute, which conducts training courses and seminars and provides lecturers on subjects such as compilation of statistics and formulation and execution of balance of payment policies. *Type:* Association.

INTLINE

The WEFA Group
1110 Vermont Ave., NW   Ph: (202)775-0610
Washington, DC 20005
URL: http://www.fdic.gov

Desc: Contains approximately 7000 daily, weekly, monthly, quarterly, and annual time series providing coverage of principal macroeconomic data for more than 40 countries worldwide, including Argentina, Australia, Austria, Belgium, Brazil, Canada, Chile, Colombia, Denmark, Finland, France, Germany, Greece, Hong Kong, India, Indonesia, Ireland, Italy, Japan, Korea, Malaysia, Mexico, the Netherlands, New Zealand, Norway, the Philippines, Singapore, South Africa, Spain, Sweden, Switzerland, Taiwan, Thailand, the United Kingdom, and the United States. Corresponds to the online INTLINE database. *Available:* The WEFA Group. *Type:* Database.

Jefferson County Committee for Economic Opportunity

300 8th Ave. W   Ph: (205)327-7500
Birmingham, AL 35204   Fax: (205)327-7549

Contact: Ms. Gayle Cunningham, Exec.Dir.

Type: Association.

The Kiplinger Washington Letter

Kiplinger Washington Editors, Inc.
1729 H St. NW   Ph: (202)887-6491
Washington, DC 20006   Free: 800-544-0155
                                   Fax: (202)887-6542

Contact: Austin H. Kiplinger, Editor.

Desc: Provides information on current events and future outlook in business, economics, legislation, politics, finance, labor, and other topics of interest to business professionals. *Type:* Newsletter.

Lagniappe Letter

Latin American Information Services Inc.
159 W. 53rd St., 28th Fl.   Ph: (212)765-5520
New York, NY 10019-6090   Free: 800-278-7043
                                   Fax: (212)765-2927
E-mail: rwerrett@lais.com.
URL: http://www.lais.com; http://www.lais.com.

Contact: Rosemary H. Werrett, Editor and Publisher, rwerrett@pipeline.com.

Desc: Reports on key economic, political, and financial developments in the large markets of South and Central America, including Argentina, Bolivia, Brazil, Chile, Colombia, Cuba, Mexico, Peru, Venezuela, and Ecuador. Remarks: Subscription price includes Lagniappe Quarterly Monitor. *Type:* Newsletter.

Lagniappe Quarterly Monitor

Latin American Information Services Inc.
159 W. 53rd St., 28th Fl.   Ph: (212)765-5520
New York, NY 10019-6090   Free: 800-278-7043
                                   Fax: (212)765-2927
URL: http://www.lais.com; http://www.lais.com.

Contact: Rosemary H. Werrett, Editor, rwerrett@pipeline.com.

Desc: Tracks financial and production trends in the nine large Latin American markets, including Argentina, Bolivia, Brazil, Chile, Colombia, Mexico, Peru, Venezuela, and Ecuador. Features short-term forecasts and a section titled Company Monitor, which tracks company expansions, acquisitions, and sell-outs. *Type:* Newsletter.

Latin America Forecast

The WEFA Group
1110 Vermont Ave., NW   Ph: (202)775-0610
Washington, DC 20005
URL: http://www.fdic.gov

Desc: Contains more than 1500 time series of economic data and forecasts for nine countries in Latin America. Macroeconomics forecasts available for Argentina, Brazil, Chile, Colombia, Ecuador, Mexico, Peru, Uruguay, and Venezuela. *Available:* The WEFA Group. *Type:* Database.

The Levy Institute Forecast

Forecasting Center
Jerome Levy Economics Institute
69 South Moger Ave.   Free: 888-244-8617
Mt. Kisco, NY 10549   Fax: (914)666-0725

Contact: David A. Levy, Editor.

Desc: Provides analyses and forecasts of U.S. business conditions. *Type:* Newsletter.

The Lyke Report

Lyke Publications, Inc.
PO Box 290   Ph: (847)724-7714
Glenview, IL 60025   Free: 800-725-7714
E-mail: lyke@compuserve.com

Contact: John Lyke, Editor.

Desc: Monitors hard money and financial newsletters for news, commentary, and predictions. *Type:* Newsletter.

Marple's Business Newsletter

Newsletter Publishing Corporation
117 Mercer St., Ste. 200   Ph: (206)281-9609
Seattle, WA 98119-3960   Fax: (206)281-8035
E-mail: marples@compuserve.com; marpes@compuserve.com.

Contact: Michael J. Parks, Editor.

Desc: Reports business and economic conditions in the Pacific Northwest (Washington, Oregon, Idaho, Montana), with some coverage of Alaska. Includes coverage of publicly-held companies of the region, with emphasis on basic industry such as forest products. *Type:* Newsletter.

Mexico Consensus Economic Forecast

Bank One Economic Outlook Center
Arizona State University   Ph: (602)965-5543
College of Business   Free: 800-448-0432
Tempe, AZ 85287-4406   Fax: (602)965-5458
URL: http://www.cob.asu.edu/seid/eoc/eocmex.html.

Contact: Lee R. McPheters, Editor.

Desc: Provides forecasts and an analysis of the Mexico economy. Remarks: Available online or in print format. *Type:* Newsletter.

Missouri Economic Indicators

University of Missouri Columbia
Business and Public Administration Research Center
10 Professional Bldg.   Ph: (573)882-4805
Columbia, MO 65211   Fax: (573)882-5563
E-mail: researchcenter@rc.missouri.edu

Contact: Edward H. Robb, Director.

Desc: Contains state, SMSA, and labor market area economic details and projections. Includes discussions of topics such as personal income, employment, labor force, housing starts and consumer price index data. *Type:* Newsletter.

Monetary & Economic Review

FAMC Inc.
3500 JFK Pkwy.   Ph: (970)223-4962
Fort Collins, CO 80525   Free: 800-336-7000
                                   Fax: (970)223-4996

Contact: Larry Bates, Editor.

Desc: Provides geopolitical-economic review and analysis of various markets from a Biblical perspective. Recurring features include letters to the editor, news of research, reports of meetings, book reviews, and columns titled Inside Washington, Political Insights, Financial Insights, Taxes, and Biblical Insights. *Type:* Newsletter.

Monthly Economic Review

Infometrica Limited
Box 828, Sta. B   Ph: (613)238-4831
Ottawa, ON, Canada K1P 5P9   Fax: (613)203-7698
E-mail: staff@infometrica.com
Desc: Provides economic analysis and forecasts of Canada.
Type: Newsletter.

The Munnings Report

The Munnings Group, Inc.
PO Box 560667   Ph: (305)655-9592
Miami, FL 33256-0667   Fax: (305)254-2980
E-mail: themunnrpt@aol.com.
Contact: Winston D. Munnings, Managing Editor.
Desc: Compiles summary information on the Bahamas, its policies, development, business, and finance. Features viewpoints and perspectives on topics of interest to subscribers and others with a vested interest in the Bahamas. *Type:* Newsletter.

Myers' Finance Review

Soundview Publications Inc.
1350 Center Dr., Ste. 100   Ph: (404)668-0432
Dunwoody, GA 30338   Free: 800-728-2288
Contact: John Myers, Editor.
Desc: Covers the world political and economic situation with emphasis on its effect upon international monetary conditions, gold and silver, the stock market, bonds, and interest rates. *Type:* Newsletter.

NABE News

National Association for Business Economics
1233 20th St., Ste. 505   Ph: (202)463-6223
Washington, DC 20036   Fax: (202)463-6239
E-mail: nabe@nabe.com
URL: http://www.nabe.com
Contact: Anne Picker, Editor.
Desc: Concerned with business economics. Serves this professional Association of persons employed by private, institutional, or government concerns in the area of business-related economic analysis. *Type:* Newsletter.

National Association for Business Economics

1233 20th St. NW, Ste. 505   Ph: (202)463-6223
Washington, DC 20036   Fax: (202)463-6239
E-mail: nabe@nabe.com
URL: http://www.nabe.com
Contact: Susan Doolittle, Exec. Dir.
Desc: Professional society of institutions, businesses, and students with an active interest in business economics and individuals who are employed by academic, private, or governmental concerns in the area of business-related economic issues. Maintains placement service for members; conducts several seminars per year. Maintains speakers' bureau. *Type:* Association.

National Bureau of Economic Research

1050 Massachusetts Ave.   Ph: (617)868-3900
Cambridge, MA 02138   Fax: (617)868-2742
Contact: Martin Feldstein, Pres.
Type: Association.

National Council on Economic Education

1140 Avenue of the Americas   Ph: (212)730-7007
New York, NY 10036   Free: 800-338-1192
                                   Fax: (212)730-1793
E-mail: ncee@eaglobal.org
URL: http://www.nationalcouncil.org
Contact: Robert F. Duvall, Ph.D., Pres. & CEO.
Desc: Economists, educators, and representatives from business, labor, and finance dedicated to improving eco-

nomic education by improving the quality and increasing the quantity of economics being taught in all levels of schools and colleges. Initiates curriculum development and research; experiments with new economics courses and ways to prepare teachers and students; provides updated teacher-pupil materials; coordinates national and local programs in economics education. Provides consulting services to educators; sponsors workshops; tests new methods in practical school situations. *Type:* Association.

National Income and Product Accounts

Haver Analytics
60 E. 42nd St., Ste. 3310   Ph: (212)986-9300
New York, NY 10165
E-mail: data@haver.com
URL: http://www.haver.com
Desc: National Income and Product Accounts data, covering national product and income; personl income and outlays; government receipts and expenditures; foreign transactions; savings and investment; product, income, and employment bu industry; implicit price degltors and price indexes, suppementary tables; not seasonally adjusted estimates, and unpublished tables. *Available:* Haver Analytics; The WEFA Group. *Type:* Database.

The NBER Digest

National Bureau of Economic Research, Inc.
1050 Massachusetts Ave.   Ph: (617)868-3900
Cambridge, MA 02138   Fax: (617)349-3955
URL: http://www.nber.org; http://www.nber.org/digest.
Contact: Donna Zerwitz, Editor, zerwitz@nber.org.
Desc: Summarizes several NBER Working Papers, which are "intended to make preliminary research results available to economists in the hope of encouraging discussion and suggestions for revision." *Type:* Newsletter.

Nebraska Department of Economic Development

Nebraska Department of Economic Development
PO Box 94666   Ph: (402)471-3111
301 Centennial Mall S.   Free: 800-426-6505
Lincoln, NE 68509-4666   Fax: (402)471-3778
URL: http://www.ded.state.ne.us
Contact: Maxine Moul, Director, maxine@dedl.ded.state.ne.us.
Desc: The Nebraska Department of Economic Development site contains Nebraska business and community information, jobs and careers, travel in Nebraska, international trade and investments, economic reports, news, press releases, and much more. *Type:* Database.

Nebraska Development News

Nebraska Department of Economic Development
301 Centennial Mall S.   Ph: (402)471-3111
PO Box 94666   Free: 800-426-6505
Lincoln, NE 68509-4666   Fax: (402)471-3778
E-mail: otis@ded1.ded.state.ne.us.
URL: http://www.pio.state.new.us/index.html.
Contact: Donald G. Wright, Managing Editor, (402)471-3789, fax: (402)471-6683; Susan Sitzmann, Editor, (402)471-3789, sitzmann@ded1.ded.state.ne.us.
Desc: Provides information concerning community and rural development, business assistance, business recruitment, and tourism. *Type:* Newsletter.

The Objective American Newsletter

The Objective American
1574 Coburg Rd., Ste. 242   Ph: (541)935-8716
Eugene, OR 97401   Fax: (541)935-8713
E-mail: editor@ObjectiveAmerican.com
URL: http://www.ObjectiveAmerican.com.
Contact: E.G. Ross, Editor.
Desc: Provides a "monthly analysis of economics, politics, defense, and self-help developments—with an emphasis on the value of independent thinking." *Type:* Newsletter.

Omicron Delta Epsilon

PO Box 1486   Ph: (601)264-3113
Hattiesburg, MS 39403   Fax: (601)264-3669
E-mail: odecf@aol.com
URL: http://www.cba.va.edu/~ode
Contact: Dr. William D. Gunther, Exec.Sec.-Treas.
Desc: Honor society of men and women in economics.
Type: Association.

The Perryman Report

Texas Economic Publishers
510 N. Valley Mills Dr., Ste.   Ph: (254)751-7411
300   Free: 800-749-8705
Waco, TX 76710   Fax: (254)751-7855
E-mail: info@perrymangroup.com
Contact: Dr. M. Ray Perryman, Publisher; Nancy Cunningham, Editor, nancyc@perrymangroup.com.
Desc: Offers forecasts, insights, and commentary on Texas, U.S., and global economic activity. Recurring features include notices of available publications and a column titled Perryman's Commentary, regional Texas Outlook, "Look Back" of economic events during last 20 years in Texas. *Type:* Newsletter.

Philadelphia Fed: Federal Reserve Bank of Philadelphia

LibertyNet
University City Science Center   Ph: (215)387-6440
3624 Market St.
Philadelphia, PA 19104
E-mail: pat.lenar@phil.frb.org
URL: http://www.phil.frb.org
Desc: The Federal Reserve Bank of Philadelphia database contains information on the bank and its activities, including publications, working papers, survey statistics, press releases, and regional data. *Type:* Database.

Political Risk Letter

The PRS Group
6320 Fly Rd., Ste. 102   Ph: (315)431-0511
PO Box 248   Fax: (315)431-0200
East Syracuse, NY 13057-0248
E-mail: custserv@prsgroup.com
URL: http://www.polrisk.com.
Contact: William D. Coplin, Editor; Michael K. O'Leary, Editor.
Desc: Offers concise political and economic forecasts for both 18 month and 5 year time spans. Provides country risk forecasts and analysis on 100 countries around the world and provides indepth coverage on 20 countries. *Type:* Newsletter.

The Positive Economist Bulletin

The Objective American
1574 Coburg Rd., Ste. 242   Ph: (541)935-8716
Eugene, OR 97401   Fax: (541)935-8713
E-mail: editor@ObjectiveAmerican.com
Contact: E.G. Ross, Editor.
Desc: Explores new successes in economic problems to fight "economic hypochondria." Covers new economic and political developments. Recurring features include news of research and book reviews. *Type:* Newsletter.

Prechter's Global Market Perspective

Elliott Wave International
200 Main St., Hunt Tower, Ste.   Ph: (770)536-0309
400   Free: 800-336-1618
Gainesville, GA 30501   Fax: (770)536-2514
E-mail: customerservice@elliottwave.com
Desc: Covers all important stock, currency, and interest rate markets worldwide. Also discusses economic developments, gold, silver, and crude oil. *Type:* Newsletter.

Quarterly Domestic & Global Forecasts of Key Economic Indicators

Graceway Publishing Co.
Box 670159   Ph: (718)463-3914
Flushing, NY 11367   Fax: (718)544-9086
E-mail: forecast@nyio.com; IBF@ibforecast.com.
Contact: Dennis F. Ellis, Editor.
Desc: Forecasts key economic indicators such as GDP, inflation, and balance of payments in 47 countries. Includes industry, interest rate, and foreign exchange forecasts of nine major countries. *Type:* Newsletter.

Rundt's Business Intelligence Briefs

S.J. Rundt & Associates, Inc.
130 E. 63rd St.   Ph: (212)838-0141
New York, NY 10021   Fax: (973)744-3073
E-mail: info@rundtsintelligence.com; rundtintel@rundtintelligence.com.
URL: http://www.rundtsintelligence.com.
Contact: Hans P. Belcsak, Editor.
Desc: Covers international economic and political developments and prospects. Reports on foreign exchange and currency. *Type:* Newsletter.

Scan-a-Bid

United Nations
Development Business/Development Forum
1 United Nations Plaza, Rm.   Ph: (212)963-1515
    DC1-570
G.C.P.O. Box 5850
New York, NY 10163-5850
E-mail: dbusiness@un.org
Contact: S.A. Hunter, (212)963-8459.
Desc: Contains requests for quotations on major construction projects worldwide financed by international organizations. For each project, includes name of project, country, type of project (e.g., dam, highway), building materials required, amount of money allocated for project, and name of person and organization to contact for further information. *Available:* The Dialog Corporation, DataStar; The Dialog Corporation, DataStar; United Nations, Development Business/Development Forum. *Type:* Database.

The Sentinel

Citizens for a Sound Economy (CSE)
1250 H St. NW, Ste. 700   Ph: (202)783-3870
Washington, DC 20005   Free: 888-JOIN-CSE
    Fax: (202)783-4687
Contact: Steve Slattery, Editor.
Desc: Updates activities of Citizens for a Sound Economy (CSE) and CSE Foundation, and on issues of vital importance to a free-market economy. *Type:* Newsletter.

SourceMex: Economic News On Mexico

University of New Mexico
Latin American Institute
Latin America Data Base (LADB)
801 Yale, NE   Ph: (505)277-6839
Albuquerque, NM 87131-1016
E-mail: info@ladb.unm.edu
URL: http://ladb.unm.edu
Contact: Rebecca Reynolds Bannister, Director, (505)277-6839, fax: (505)277-6837, info@ladb.unm.edu.
Desc: Contains the complete text of SourceMex: Economic News and Analysis on Mexico, a weekly newsletter on economic conditions in Mexico. Covers private foreign and domestic investment, public sector finances and planning, foreign trade, foreign debt, the oil industry, agriculture and other extractive industries, macroeconomic indicators and projections, and socioeconomic welfare. *Available:* LEXIS-NEXIS, NEXIS; Latin America Data Base. *Type:* Database.

South Carolina Economic Indicators

University of South Carolina
College of Business Administration
Publications   Ph: (803)777-2510
Columbia, SC 29208-0001
Contact: Douglas P. Woodward, Editor.
Desc: Monitors South Carolina's leading economic indicators as well as coincident indicators and other signs of advance and decline. Organizes data into five tables and three graphs and provides a page of interpretive text. *Type:* Newsletter.

Straight Talk

The Conference Board, Inc.
845 3rd Ave.   Ph: (212)759-0900
New York, NY 10022-6679   Fax: (212)980-7014
E-mail: info@conference-board.org
URL: http://www.conference-board.org
Contact: Gail D. Fosler, Editor.
Desc: Provides information and news for business professionals. Includes economic forecasts. *Type:* Newsletter.

Summary of Proposed Projects

United Nations
Development Business/Development Forum
1 United Nations Plaza, Rm.   Ph: (212)963-1515
    DC1-570
G.C.P.O. Box 5850
New York, NY 10163-5850
E-mail: dbusiness@un.org
Contact: Brent Anderson, (202)458-2397, fax: (202)522-3316.
Desc: Contains the complete text of the updated Monthly Operational Summaries (MOS) of The World Bank and the Inter-American Development Bank as well as the Quarterly Operational Summary (QOS) of the African Development Bank. Includes the entire summary and indicates the country, development bank, MOS or QOS citation, sector code, indication of a new or revised project, and description. *Available:* The Dialog Corporation, DataStar; The Dialog Corporation, DataStar. *Type:* Database.

Tennessee Economic Development Quarterly

Department of Economic and Community Development
Rachel Jackson Bldg., 8th Fl.
Nashville, TN 37243-0405
Contact: Leigh Wieland, Editor.
Desc: Highlights Tennessee's economic growth and business climate. *Type:* Newsletter.

The Trends Journal

Trends Research Institute
PO Box 660   Ph: (914)876-6700
Rhinebeck, NY 12572   Free: 800-25-TREND
    Fax: (914)758-5252
E-mail: joneill@trendsresearch.com
Contact: Gerald Celente, Editor, gcelente@trendsresearch.com.
Desc: Tracks trends "affecting your business, your profession, and your life." Forecasts over 300 trend categories, including consumer, social, economic, political, media, health, family, and education trends. Recurring features include columns titled Trends in the News, Hot Trends to Watch, and Trend Tracking Tips. *Type:* Newsletter.

U.S. General Macroeconomic Indicators

The WEFA Group
1110 Vermont Ave., NW   Ph: (202)775-0610
Washington, DC 20005
URL: http://www.fdic.gov
Desc: Contains approximately 13,500 daily, weekly, ten day, monthly, quarterly, semiannual, and annual time se-

ries on the United States economy. Provides macroeconomic data on the United States economy with primary emphasis on general economic indicators. *Available:* The WEFA Group. *Type:* Database.

URPE Newsletter

Union for Radical Political Economics (U.R. P.E.)
Dept. of Economics   Ph: (909)776-5888
University of California   Fax: (909)787-5685
Riverside, CA 92521
E-mail: urpe@igc.apc.org
Desc: Contains news of Union activities and issues. Recurring features include news of meetings and conferences, calendar of events, news of research, a calendar of events, news of educational opportunities, book reviews, and job listings. *Type:* Newsletter.

Vista

Federal Reserve Bank of Dallas
San Antonio Branch
PO Box 1471
San Antonio, TX 78295-1471
URL: http://www.dallasfed.org.
Contact: Keith Phillips, Editor, (210)978-1409, keith.r.phillips@dal.frb.org; Jennifer Afflerbach, Copy Editor.
Desc: Studies economic issues and trends in South Texas. *Type:* Newsletter.

West Virginia Economic Summary

West Virginia Bureau of Employment Programs
112 California Ave.   Ph: (304)558-2660
Charleston, WV 25305-0112   Fax: (304)558-1343
URL: http://www.state.wv.us/bep.
Contact: David Calvert, Editor; Rita Wiseman, Editor.
Desc: Details economic statistics and information for the state of West Virginia, including employment, unemployment, payroll employment by industry, women workers, average hours and earnings, larbor market trends, seasonally adjusted employment/unemployment, economic indicators, county labor force statistics, payroll employment by county, metropolitan statistical areas, workers compensation, and unemployment insurance. *Type:* Newsletter.

Western Blue Chip Economic Forecast

Bank One Economic Outlook Center
Arizona State University   Ph: (602)965-5543
College of Business   Free: 800-448-0432
Tempe, AZ 85287-4406   Fax: (602)965-5458
URL: http://www.cob.asu.edu/seid/eoc.
Contact: Robert J. Eggert, Sr., Editor; Lee R. McPheters, Editor; Tracy Clark, Editor.
Desc: Provides consensus economic forecasts for the current year and the next for each of the 10 western states: Arizona, California, Colorado, Nevada, New Mexico, Idaho, Oregon, Washington, Utah, and Texas; and for the region as a whole. *Type:* Newsletter.

What Is to Be Read

Cooperative Economics News Service
1736 Columbia Rd. NW, Ste.   Ph: (202)387-1753
    202   Fax: (202)898-3309
Washington, DC 20009
Contact: Henry Leland, Editor, lelaudh@seiu.org.
Desc: Presents summaries on economic books currently published. Includes topics such as work, organization, sociology, politics, women's studies, urban affairs, and race/ethic studies. *Type:* Newsletter.

Ecumenical

Congress of National Black Churches
1225 Eye St. NW, Ste. 750   Ph: (202)371-1091
Washington, DC 20005   Fax: (202)371-0908
URL: http://www.cnbc.org
Contact: Ms. Sullivan Robinson, Exec.Dir.
Desc: Coalition of eight historically black denominations. Purpose: to promote unity, charity, and fellowship among the member denominations; to provide the opportunity for the identification and implementation of program efforts that may be achieved more effectively through collective action than by any single denomination. *Type:* Association.

Ecumenical Celebrations
Church Women United
475 Riverside Dr., Rm. 812   Ph: (212)870-3035
New York, NY 10115   Free: 800-298-5551
   Fax: (212)870-2338
Contact: Rev. Mary Cline Detrick, Dir.
Desc: Project of Church Women United. Participants include Protestant, Roman Catholic, Orthodox, and other Christian women. Plans, produces, and promotes World Day of Prayer (first Friday of March), May Fellowship Day (first Friday of May), and World Community Day (first Friday of November). *Type:* Association.

Faith at Work
106 E. Broad St., Ste. B   Ph: (703)237-3426
Falls Church, VA 22046   Fax: (703)237-0157
E-mail: FthAtWrk@aol.com
Contact: Marjory Bankson, Pres.
Desc: Ecumenical ministry of church professionals and laypeople. *Type:* Association.

The Interchurch Center
475 Riverside Dr., Rm. 253   Ph: (212)870-2931
New York, NY 10115-0099   Fax: (212)870-2440
E-mail: papket@interchurch-center.org
URL: http://www.metro.org/members/icelib.html
Contact: Mary E. McNamara, Pres. & Exec.Dir.
Desc: A center for ecumenical and interfaith cooperation; serves as national headquarters building for a number of religious organizations and their boards and agencies including the National Council of the Churches of Christ in the U.S.A. , American Baptist Church, Presbyterian Church (U.S.A.), Reformed Church in America, United Church of Christ, and United Methodist Church. *Type:* Association.

National Cathedral Association
Massachusetts & Wisconsin   Ph: (202)537-6242
   Aves. NW   Free: 800-NCA-6304
Washington, DC 20016   Fax: (202)537-5639
E-mail: nca@cathedral.org
URL: http://www.cathedral.org
Contact: Dennis L. Fruitt, Dir.
Desc: National group of persons from many denominations who contribute to support and extend the ministry of the Washington Cathedral (the Cathedral Church of St. Peter and St. Paul in Washington, DC, also known as the National Cathedral), which has no congregation of its own. *Type:* Association.

National Conference for Community and Justice
71 5th Ave., Ste. 1100   Ph: (212)206-0006
New York, NY 10003-3095   Fax: (212)255-6177
URL: http://www.nccj.org
Contact: Sanford Cloud, Jr., Pres.
Desc: Individuals from all racial, religious, cultural and ethnic groups who, without compromise of conscience or of their distinctive religious differences, work together for

better human relations. Works to: promote through education, conflict resolution and advocacy, understanding, and cooperation among all religious, ethnic cultural groups and races; analyze, moderate, and finally eliminate intergroup prejudices that disfigure religious, business, social, and political relations, with a view to the establishment of a social order in which the religious ideals of whole communities and justice shall become the standards of human relationships. Organizes programs on topics including adults, youth, community relations and the administration of justice, equal opportunity in the workplace, community, interfaith relations and with youth and emerging leaders. *Type:* Association.

National Council of the Churches of Christ in the U.S.A.
475 Riverside Dr.   Ph: (212)870-2227
New York, NY 10115   Fax: (212)870-2030
E-mail: news@ncccusa.org
URL: http://www.ncccusa.org
Contact: Joan B. Campbell, Gen.Sec.
Desc: To serve as a community of its constituent communions in manifesting oneness in Jesus Christ as Divine Lord and Savior and to do together those things which can better be done united than separated. *Type:* Association.

National Ecumenical Coalition
4300 Old Dominion Dr., Apt.
   710
Arlington, VA 22207-3226
Desc: Religious groups represented by one or more delegates. Acts as clearinghouse for religious, charitable, literary, and educational information. *Type:* Association.

Education

A-V Online
Access Innovations, Inc.
National Information Center for Educational Media
PO Box 8640   Ph: (505)998-0800
Albuquerque, NM 87198-8640
E-mail: nicem@nicem.com
URL: http://www.nicem.com
Contact: Roy Morgan, Executive Director, (505)265-3591, fax: (505)256-1080, nicem@nicem.com.
Desc: Contains more than 430,000 citations, with abstracts, to non-print educational materials for all educational levels, from pre-school through professional or graduate programs. Covers the following media: 16mm films, 35mm filmstrips, overhead transparencies, audio tapes, video tapes, phonograph records, slides, and 8mm motion picture cartridges, software, and CD-ROMs. *Available:* SilverPlatter Information, Inc. *Type:* Database.

Academic Alliances
c/o American Association of   Ph: (202)293-6440
   Higher Educ.
1 Dupont Cir., Ste. 360
Washington, DC 20036
Desc: Teachers from primary to postgraduate levels united in local groups called alliances. Works to improve the quality of teaching in the U.S.; encourages the professional development of teachers. Seeks to ease what the group feels is isolation from school administration felt by many teachers and professors. *Type:* Association.

Academy for Educational Development
1825 Connecticut Ave. NW   Ph: (202)884-8000
Washington, DC 20009-5721   Fax: (202)884-8400
E-mail: admindc@aed.org
URL: http://www.aed.org
Contact: Stephen F. Moseley, Pres. & CEO.

Desc: Seeks to address human resource and economic development needs through education, communication, and the dissemination of information. *Type:* Association.

Accrediting Council for Continuing Education and Training
1722 N. St., NW   Ph: (202)955-1113
Washington, DC 20036-2981   Fax: (202)955-1118
URL: http://www.accet.org
Contact: Roger J. Williams, Exec.Dir.
Desc: Purpose is to raise the quality of continuing education programs through accreditation, consultation, and related means. Institutional membership includes brood cross-section of organizations providing courses/programs for professional and vocational development. *Type:* Association.

ACT—Activity
ACT National Office   Ph: (319)337-1410
2201 N. Dodge St.   Fax: (319)337-1014
PO Box 168
Iowa City, IA 52243-0168
E-mail: corpcomms@delta.org
Contact: Dan Lechay, Editor.
Desc: Discusses college admissions; placement; financial aid; computer-based career guidance; certification and licensure for professions; and educational testing and measurement. Recurring features include editorials, a calendar of events, news of research, news of members, and a column titled Commentary. *Type:* Newsletter.

Administrator
Magna Publications, Inc.
2718 Dryden Dr.   Ph: (608)249-3580
Madison, WI 53704   Free: 800-433-0499
   Fax: (608)246-3597
E-mail: custserv@magnapubs.com; editor@magnapubs. com.
Contact: Paul Steinbach, Editor, paul.steinbach@ magnapubs.com.
Desc: Covers finances, administration, and fundraising. Deals with trustees and management of colleges and universities. *Type:* Newsletter.

Alabama Parent-Teacher Association
470 S. Union St.   Ph: (334)834-2501
Montgomery, AL 36104-4330   Free: 800-328-1897
   Fax: (334)834-2504
E-mail: al_office@pta.org
URL: http://alabamapta.org
Contact: Beth Powell, Exec.Dir.
Desc: Parents, students, and teachers promoting cooperation and quality education. Holds leadership workshops. *Type:* Association.

Alpha Delta Kappa
1615 W. 92nd St.   Ph: (816)363-5525
Kansas City, MO 64114   Free: 800-247-2311
   Fax: (816)363-4010
E-mail: alphadeltakappa@worldnet.att.net
URL: http://www.alphadeltakappa.org
Contact: Janice M. Estell, Exec.Admin.
Desc: Honorary sorority. *Type:* Association.

Alpha Phi Sigma
c/o Dr. John A. Ludrick   Ph: (405)774-3235
Southwestern Oklahoma State
   Univ.
Weatherford, OK 73096
E-mail: ludricj@swosu.edu
Contact: Dr. John A. Ludrick, Pres.
Desc: Scholastic honor society - men and women, open to all disciplines. *Type:* Association.

Alternative Assessments in Practice Database

Center for the Study of Evaluation/Annex
1320 Moore Hall   Ph: (310)206-1532
Mailbox 951522
Los Angeles, CA 90095-1522
E-mail: webmaster@cse.ucla.edu
URL: http://www.cse.ucla.edu/database.htm
Contact: Kim Hurst, kim@cse.ucla.edu.
Desc: For the teacher, school administrator, or assessment developer who is looking for alternative means of student performance evaluation, this database will be a rich source of information on new assessment methods. With listings of more than 300 developers of new assessments to search among, the database offers detailed background and information on assessment type and purpose, subject matter, scoring and availability, and skills measured. *Type:* Database.

American Association of Classified School Employees

1020 Fairfax St., 4th Fl.   Ph: (703)684-3601
Alexandria, VA 22314
Contact: Arnie Schneider, Exec.Dir.
Desc: Persons employed by public school systems in non-teaching positions. Promotes a spirit of cooperation and understanding among employees and their employers; fosters adequate financial improvements for public school employees through collective bargaining, legislative channels, and other legal procedures; promotes improved retirement benefits for public school employees; represents public school employees in their employment relations with their employers. *Type:* Association.

American Association of School Administrators

1801 N. Moore St.   Ph: (703)528-0700
Arlington, VA 22209   Fax: (703)841-1543
URL: http://www.aasa.org
Contact: Paul Houston, Exec.Dir.
Desc: Professional association of administrators and executives of school systems and educational service agencies; school district superintendents; central, building, and service unit administrators; presidents of colleges, deans, and professors of educational administration; placement officers; executive directors and administrators of education associations; heads of private schools. Sponsors numerous professional development seminars annually through its National Academy for School Executives, "dedicated to excellence in educational system leadership." Founded Educational Research Service . Maintains numerous standing and ad hoc committees. *Type:* Association.

American Council on Education

1 Dupont Cir. NW, Ste. 800   Ph: (202)939-9300
Washington, DC 20036   Fax: (202)833-4760
E-mail: web@ace.nche.edu
URL: http://www.acenet.edu
Contact: Stanley O. Ikenberry, Pres.
Desc: A council of colleges and universities, educational organizations, and affiliates. Represents accredited, degree-granting postsecondary institutions directly or through national and regional higher education associations; advocates on their behalf before Congress, the federal government, and federal and state courts. Advances education and educational methods through comprehensive voluntary action on the part of American educational associations, organizations, and institutions. *Type:* Association.

American Educator

American Federation of Teachers
555 New Jersey Ave. NW   Ph: (202)879-4430
Washington, DC 20001-2079   Fax: (202)879-2014
E-mail: afteditor@aol.com
Contact: Liz McPike, Editor.
Desc: Magazine on education. *Type:* Periodical.

American Federation of School Administrators

1729 21st St. NW   Ph: (202)986-4209
Washington, DC 20009   Fax: (202)986-4211
E-mail: afsa@admin.org
Contact: Joe L. Greene, Pres.
Desc: Principals, vice-principals, directors, supervisors, and administrators involved in pedagogical education. Purposes are to: achieve the highest goals in education; maintain and improve standards, benefits, and conditions for personnel without regard to color, race, sex, background, or national origin; obtain job security; protect seniority and merit; cooperate with all responsible organizations in education; promote understanding, participation, and support of the public, communities, and agencies; be alert to resist attacks and campaigns that would create or entrench a spoils system; promote democratic society by supporting full educational opportunities for every child and student in the nation. *Type:* Association.

American Federation of Teachers

555 New Jersey Ave. NW   Ph: (202)879-4400
Washington, DC 20001   Free: 800-238-1133
    Fax: (202)879-4545
E-mail: online@aft.org
URL: http://www.aft.org//index.htm
Contact: Sandra Feldman, Pres.
Desc: AFL-CIO. Works with teachers and other educational employees at the state and local level in organizing, collective bargaining, research, educational issues, and public relations. Conducts research in areas such as educational reform, bilingual education, teacher certification, and evaluation and national assessments and standards. *Type:* Association.

American Foundrymen's Society

505 State St.   Ph: (708)824-0181
Des Plaines, IL 60016-8399   Free: 800-537-4237
    Fax: (708)824-7848
URL: http://www.afsinc.org
Contact: Charles H. Jones, Exec.VP.
Desc: Technical, trade and management association of foundrymen, patternmakers, technologists, and educators. *Type:* Association.

American Institute, Inc.

4301 Fairfax Dr., Ste. 630
Arlington, VA 22203-1627
Contact: Irvine Laidlaw, Owner.
Desc: Serves the advanced educational needs of professionals by providing interdisciplinary programs directed at the information needs engendered by today's rapid rate of technological change. *Type:* Association.

American Mensa

1229 Corporate Dr. West   Ph: (817)607-0060
Arlington, TX 76006   Free: 800-66M-ENSA
    Fax: (817)649-5232
E-mail: americanmensa@compuserve.com
URL: http://www.us.mensa.org
Contact: Pamela Donahoo, Exec.Dir.
Desc: Individuals who have scored in the top two percent of the general population on a standardized intelligence test. Strives to identity and foster human intelligence for the benefit of humanity; to encourage research into intelligence; and to provide a stimulating and social environment for its members. *Type:* Association.

American Montessori Society

281 Park Ave. S., 6th Fl.   Ph: (212)358-1250
New York, NY 10010   Fax: (212)358-1256
E-mail: dssf@juno.coml.com
URL: http://www.amshq.org
Contact: Michael Eanes, Dir.

Desc: School affiliates and teacher training affiliates; heads of schools, teachers, parents, non-Montessori educators, and other interested individuals dedicated to stimulating the use of the Montessori teaching approach and promoting better education for all children. Formed to meet demands of growing interest in the Montessori approach to early learning. Developed in Italy in 1907 by Dr. *Type:* Association.

American School Counselor Association

801 N. Fairfax St., Ste. 310   Ph: (703)683-2722
Alexandria, VA 22314   Free: 800-306-4722
    Fax: (703)683-1619
E-mail: asca@erols.com
URL: http://www.schoolcounselor.org
Contact: Nancy S. Perry, Exec.Dir.
Desc: School counselors; professionals engaged in school counseling or related activities at least 50% of the time; students; other interested individuals. Promotes human rights, children's welfare, healthy learning environments, and positive interpersonal relationships; fosters academic, occupational, personal, and social growth among members. *Type:* Association.

American Teacher

American Federation of Teachers
555 New Jersey Ave. NW   Ph: (202)879-4430
Washington, DC 20001-2079   Fax: (202)879-2014
E-mail: afteditor@aol.com; wleague74@aol.com.
Contact: Trish Gorman, Editor, (202)879-4430, tgorman@aft.org; Mike Rose, Editor, mrose@aft.org.
Desc: Newspaper focusing on issues of education and the labor union. *Type:* Periodical.

Arbitration in the Schools

American Arbitration Association
140 W. 51st St.   Ph: (212)484-4000
New York, NY 10020-1203   Fax: (212)541-4041
URL: http://www.adr.org
Desc: Reports on labor relations in the schools and arbitration cases in educational institutions at all levels. Includes summaries of cases and the decisions reached in settlements. *Type:* Newsletter.

Arizona Education Association

100 W. Clarendon Ste. 1600   Ph: (602)264-1774
Phoenix, AZ 85013-3511   Free: 800-352-5411
    Fax: (602)240-6887
Contact: Betty Saglern, Exec.Dir.
Desc: Labor union for teachers and educational support personnel in Arizona. *Type:* Association.

AskERIC, Education Information with the Personal Touch

Syracuse University - Center for Science & Technology ERIC Clearinghouse on Information and Technology
Syracuse, NY 13244-4100   Ph: (315)443-3640
    Free: 800-464-9107
    Fax: (315)443-5448
E-mail: eric@ericir.syr.edu
URL: http://ericir.syr.edu/
Contact: Pauline Lynch, AskERIC Coordinator, askeric@akeric.org.
Desc: AskERIC is a project of the ERIC Clearinghouse on Information & Technology at Syracuse University. It encompasses the resources of the entire ERIC system and beyond. *Type:* Database.

ASPIRA Association

1444 I St. NW, Ste. 800   Ph: (202)835-3600
Washington, DC 20005-2210   Fax: (202)835-3613
Contact: Ronald Blackburn-Moreno, Natl.Exec.Dir.

Desc: Grass roots organization working to provide leadership development and educational assistance to Latino persons, thus advancing the Hispanic community. (Aspira is the Spanish word for aspire.) Offers educational counseling for high school and college students. Provides a forum for group discussions, workshops, tutoring, and assistance in applying for college admission, scholarships, and loans; establishes high school clubs. *Type:* Association.

Association for Childhood Education International

17904 Georgia Ave., Ste. 215 Ph: (301)570-2111
Olney, MD 20832 Free: 800-423-3563
Fax: (301)570-2212
E-mail: aceihq@aol.com
URL: http://www.udel.edu/bateman/acei
Contact: Gerald Odland, Exec.Dir.
Desc: Teachers, parents, and other caregivers in 31 countries. interested in promoting good educational practices for children from infancy through early adolescence. *Type:* Association.

Association of Independent Schools in New England

Association of Independent Schools in New England
100 Grossman Dr., Ste. 301 Ph: (617)849-3080
Braintree, MA 02184 Fax: (617)849-1618
E-mail: info@aisne.org
URL: http://www.aisne.org
Desc: The AISNE provides a listing of independent schools along with map locations, criteria for qualification, and explanations of various services the association provides, such as marketing assistance, training, and purchasing programs. *Type:* Database.

Association for Supervision and Curriculum Development

Association for Supervision and Curriculum Development
1903 N. Beauregard St. Ph: (703)578-9600
Alexandria, VA 22311-1714 Free: 800-933-2723
Fax: (703)575-5400
E-mail: member@ascd.org
URL: http://www.ascd.org/
Desc: This site provides a wide range of information about the Association's aims and activities, publications and professional development programs. A complete list of services, membership info and a bookstore offering audio and video resources as well as books adds practicality to the site. *Type:* Database.

Association for Supervision and Curriculum Development

1703 N Beauregard St. Ph: (703)549-9110
Alexandria, VA 22311-1717 Free: 800-933-2773
Fax: (703)549-3891
URL: http://www.asod.org
Contact: Gene R. Carter, Exec.Dir.
Desc: Professional organization of supervisors, curriculum coordinators and directors, consultants, professors of education, classroom teachers, principals, superintendents, parents, students, and others interested in school improvement at all levels of education. Provides professional development experiences and training in curriculum and supervision; disseminates information; encourages research, evaluation, and theory development. Provides Research Information Service. *Type:* Association.

Association of Texas Professional Educators

305 E Huntland Dr Ste 300 Ph: (512)467-0071
Austin, TX 78752-3730 Free: 800-777-2873
Fax: (512)467-6150
E-mail: atpe@atpe.org

URL: http://www.atpe.org
Contact: Doug Rogers, Exec.Dir.
Desc: Classroom teachers, administrators, and support personnel. Promotes the general welfare of its members. *Type:* Association.

Athletic Scholarships

Facts On File, Inc.
11 Penn Plz. Ph: (212)967-8800
New York, NY 10001-2006 Free: 800-322-8755
Fax: (212)967-9196
E-mail: lmilberg@factsonfile.com
URL: http://www.factsonfile.com; http://www.factsonfile.com.
Contact: Andy Clark, Editor; Amy Clark, Editor.
Desc: Colleges and universities that award athletic scholarships. *Type:* Directory.

The Atrium Society

The Atrium Society
PO Box 816 Ph: 800-848-6021
Middlebury, VT 05753
E-mail: atrium@sover.net
URL: http://www.atriumsoc.org/index.html
Desc: Featuring details of the Education for Peace Programs, this site site also offers an introduction to the aims and activities of the Society, pages devoted to education through martial arts and an online bookstore with ordering information. *Type:* Database.

A.U. Online

Anderson University
1100 E. Fifth St. Ph: (765)649-9071
Anderson, IN 46012 Free: 800-428-6414
E-mail: webmaster@anderson.edu
URL: http://www.anderson.edu/
Desc: Anderson University, founded and supported by the Church of God, offers prospective and current students access to its Web site, which can be easily navigated using the search engine provided. One may access detailed information about the school's administration, student life, course offerings, and the layout of the campus. *Type:* Database.

Awards, Honors, and Prizes

Gale Group Inc.
27500 Drake Rd. Ph: (248)699-4253
Farmington Hills, MI 48331- Free: 800-877-GALE
3535 Fax: (248)699-8070
E-mail: galeord@galegroup.com
URL: http://www.galegroup.com.; http://www.gale.com.
Contact: Donna Batten, Editor, donna_batten@gale.com.
Desc: Volume 1 covers more than 16,000 awards given by organizations in the U.S. and Canada, in recognition of achievement, and major competitive prizes, some fellowships are also described; Volume 2 contains approximately 8,000 foreign and international awards. *Type:* Directory.

Barron's Guide to Law Schools

Barron's Educational Series, Inc.
250 Wireless Blvd. Ph: (516)434-3311
Hauppauge, NY 11788 Free: 800-645-3476
Fax: (516)434-3723
E-mail: info@barronseduc.com; barrons269@aol.com.
URL: http://www.barronseduc.com
Desc: All American Bar Association (ABA) approved law schools, and selected law schools not approved by the ABA. *Type:* Directory.

Barron's How to Prepare for the Law School Admission Test (LSAT)

Barron's Educational Series, Inc.
250 Wireless Blvd. Ph: (516)434-3311
Hauppauge, NY 11788 Free: 800-645-3476
Fax: (516)434-3723
E-mail: info@barronseduc.com
URL: http://www.barronseduc.com
Contact: Jerry Bobrow, Editor.
Desc: Chart data on over 175 ABA-accredited American law schools. *Type:* Directory.

A Better Chance

419 Boylston St. Ph: (617)421-0950
Boston, MA 02116 Free: 800-562-7865
Fax: (617)421-0965
E-mail: info@abetterchance.org
URL: http://www.abetterchance.org
Contact: Judith B. Griffin, Pres.
Desc: Identifies, recruits, and places academically talented and motivated minority students into leading independent secondary schools and selected public schools. *Type:* Association.

Between Classes

Elderhostel, Inc.
75 Federal St. Ph: (617)426-7788
Boston, MA 02110 Fax: (617)426-8351
Contact: Cady Goldfield, Editor.
Desc: Supplies information on activities of the organization, which is a network of educational institutions offering low-cost, short-term residential academic programs for adults 55 years of age and over. Promotes educational opportunities for the elderly. *Type:* Newsletter.

Black Employment and Education Magazine

Hamdani Communications Inc.
Bldg. 56, Ste. 282 Ph: (404)469-5891
2625 Piedmont Rd.
Atlanta, GA 30324
Contact: S. Barry Hamdani, Editor and Publisher.
Desc: Periodical for black college and trade school students and professors. *Type:* Periodical.

British Schools and Universities Foundation

575 Madison Ave., Ste. 1006 Ph: (212)662-5576
New York, NY 10022-2511 Free: 800-309-4706
E-mail: bsuf@mcimail.com
Contact: A. Scott Bushey, Pres.
Type: Association.

The Buffer

Computing and Information Resources
University of Denver
2020 S. Race St. Ph: (303)871-4506
Denver, CO 80208
E-mail: buffer@du.edu.
URL: http://www.du.edu/~buffer/buffer.html.
Contact: Thea Deley, Editor.
Desc: Describes computing activities at the University of Denver as well as a wide range of other computer-related topics. *Type:* Newsletter.

Cable in the Classroom

CCI/Crosby Publishing
141 Portland St., Ste. 7100 Ph: (617)494-4997
Cambridge, MA 02139 Fax: (617)494-4898
Contact: Stephen P. Crosby, Publisher; Al Race, Editor; Nina Bohn, Sales Dir.; Bill Whalen, Project Mgr.
Desc: Magazine directing teachers to quality educational television programs. *Type:* Periodical.

California Educator

California Teachers Association

1705 Murchison Dr. Ph: (415)697-1400
PO Box 921 Fax: (415)697-0786
Burlingame, CA 94010

Contact: Trudy Willis, Editor, (916)443-3354, fax: (916)443-3055; Greg Smith, Advertising Mgr.

Desc: California Teachers Association tabloid covering political and professional issues. *Type:* Periodical.

California Parents-Teachers Association

PO Box 15015 Ph: (213)620-1100
Los Angeles, CA 90015 Fax: (213)620-1411
E-mail: ptacala@aol.com

Contact: Roberta Boardman, Office Admin.

Desc: Parents and teachers. Represents members' interests; conducts lobbying activities. *Type:* Association.

The California School Employee

California School Employees Association

2045 Lundy Ave. Ph: (408)263-8000
PO Box 640 Fax: (408)954-0948
San Jose, CA 95106

Contact: Douglas Crooks, Public Relations Dir., dcrooks@csea.com.

Desc: Tabloid for school employees. *Alt. Contact:* 2045 Lundy Ave., San Jose, CA 95131; telephone: (408)263-8000; fax: (408)954-0948. *Type:* Periodical.

Career Colleges Association

950 1st St. NE, Ste. 900 Ph: (202)336-6700
Washington, DC 20002

Contact: John G. Pucciano, Pres.

Desc: Independent business schools and junior and senior colleges of business. Sponsors an accrediting commission for postsecondary and collegiate institutions. *Type:* Association.

Career World

Weekly Reader Corp.

200 First Stamford Pl. Ph: (203)705-3500
PO Box 120023 Fax: (203)705-1661
Stamford, CT 06912-0023

Contact: Carole Rubenstein, Editor, (847)205-3000, fax: (847)564-8197, ruben@glcomm.com; Richard LeBrasseur, President and Publisher; Eric Ecker, V.P. of Circulation and Marketing, (203)705-3500, fax: (203)705-1662.

Desc: Magazine serving as a guide to jobs and careers for students in grades 7-12 *Alt. Contact:* 900 Skokie Blvd., Northbrook, IL 60062-4028; telephone: (847)205-3000, (708)564-8197; fax: (847)564-8197. *Type:* Periodical.

Catalyst

Western Center for Microcomputers in Special Education, Inc.

1259 El Camino Real, Ste. 275 Ph: (650)855-8064
Menlo Park, CA 94025 Fax: (650)324-1119
E-mail: thecatalyst@mail.earthlink.net.

Desc: Features information on the use of computers in special education. *Type:* Newsletter.

Center for Adult Learning and Educational Credentials

One Dupont Circle NW, Ste. Ph: (202)939-9475
250 Fax: (202)775-8578
Washington, DC 20036-1193
E-mail: susan_robinson@ace.nche.edu
URL: http://www.acenet.edu

Contact: Susan Porter Robinson, VP & Dir.

Desc: A division of the American Council on Education. Educators representing colleges and universities, postsecondary education associations, and secondary schools. Evaluates learning acquired in noncollegiate settings; monitors educational credit and credentialing policies and practices for postsecondary education; provides guidance to postsecondary education institutions for developing policies and procedures for evaluating extrainstitutional learning and awarding credit for it; operates the ACE Registries, which provide a record of an individual's educational accomplishments for which credit is recommended by ACE. *Type:* Association.

Certification and Accreditation Programs Directory

Gale Group Inc.

27500 Drake Rd. Ph: (248)699-4253
Farmington Hills, MI 48331- Free: 800-877-GALE
3535 Fax: (248)699-8070
E-mail: galeord@galegroup.com
URL: http://www.galegroup.com.; http://www.gale.com.

Contact: Michael Pare, Editor.

Desc: Over 1,700 voluntary certification programs and approximately 300 accreditation programs offered by private organizations (not state-sponsored). *Type:* Directory.

The Chronicle of Higher Education

The Chronicle of Higher Education

1255 23rd St. NW, Ste. 700 Ph: (202)466-1000
Washington, DC 20037-1125 Fax: (202)296-2691
URL: http://chronicle.com.

Contact: Corbin Gwaltney, Editor; Robinette D. Ross, Publisher.

Desc: Higher education magazine (tabloid). *Type:* Periodical.

Chronicle of Higher Education—Events in Academe Section

The Chronicle of Higher Education

1255 23rd St. NW, Ste. 700 Ph: (202)466-1000
Washington, DC 20037-1125 Fax: (202)296-2691
E-mail: editor@chronicle.com.

Contact: Edith Taylor, Editor, edith.taylor@chronicle.com.

Desc: List of organizations which sponsor conferences, seminars, and other events in higher education. *Type:* Directory.

CITS Technical Update

Center for Information Technology Services (CITS)

University of Cincinnati

45 Beecher Hall, Mail Location Ph: (513)556-6383
0088
Cincinnati, OH 45221-0088

Contact: Mary Jane Clark, Editor.

Desc: Deals exclusively with computer-related topics. Details changes in the CITS systems, policies, and services. *Type:* Newsletter.

Classroom Connect

Classroom Connect

431 Madrid Ave. Free: 800-638-1639
Torrance, CA 90501-1430 Fax: 888-801-8299
E-mail: connect@classroom.com
URL: http://www.classroom.net/

Desc: Classroom Connect is a rich resource that will help locate some of the most interesting and useful information that is available to K-12 educators online. This site is a cooperative effort between the staff of Classroom Connect (a print magazine) and educators around the globe. *Type:* Database.

The College Board News

College Entrance Examination Board

45 Columbus Ave. Ph: (212)713-8000
New York, NY 10023-6992 Fax: (212)713-8309
URL: http://www.collegboard.org; http://www.collegeboard.org.

Contact: Nancy M. Viggiano, Editor.

Desc: Provides news of the College Board's activities, services, programs, and concerns to secondary and postsecondary educational institutions and policymakers. *Type:* Newsletter.

College Outlook

Townsend Outlook Publishing Co.

20 E. Gregory Ph: (816)361-0616
Kansas City, MO 64114-1118 Free: 800-274-8867
 Fax: (816)361-6164

E-mail: topstaff@gvi.net

URL: http://www.product.com/top.

Contact: Marty Denzer, Editor; Clayton Allan, VP, Sales/Mktg.

Desc: High school student recruitment magazine. *Type:* Periodical.

Colorado Education and Library Directory

Colorado Department of Education

201 E. Colfax Ave. Ph: (303)866-6937
Denver, CO 80203-1799 Fax: (303)830-0793
URL: http://www.cde.state.co.us.

Contact: Jody Ohmert Nordbye, Editor.

Desc: State department of education offices and personnel; state advisory committees; 176 public school districts and 1,544 individual public schools; boards of cooperative educational services (BOCES); seven library service systems; academic, institutional, public, and special libraries; vocational schools, colleges, and universities; and education groups and professional organizations. *Type:* Directory.

Commonwealth of Learning

Commonwealth of Learning

1285 W. Broadway, Ste. 600 Ph: (604)775-8200
Vancouver, BC, Canada V6H Fax: (604)775-8210
3X8
E-mail: info@col.org
URL: http://www.col.org

Desc: The idea of distance education--using technology to teach individuals in their own homeland, no matter how remote--first arose in the 1950s. Today, the explosion in technology that has resulted in video conferencing, online universities, and the World Wide Web. *Type:* Database.

Communities in Schools

1199 N Fairfax Ph: (703)519-8999
Ste 300 Free: 800-CIS-4KIDS
Alexandria, VA 22314 Fax: (703)519-7213
E-mail: cis@cisnet.org
URL: http://www.cisnet.org

Contact: William E. Milliken, Pres.

Desc: Champions the connection of needed community resources with schools to help young people successfully learn, stay in school and prepare for life. *Type:* Association.

Connecticut State Federation of Teachers

1781 Wilbur Cross Pkwy. Ph: (203)828-1400
Berlin, CT 06037

Desc: Union representing teachers, education support personnel, state employees, health care workers, and higher education faculty. Produces monthly cable television program. *Type:* Association.

Contests for Students: All You Need to Know to Enter and Win 600 Contests

Gale Group Inc.
27500 Drake Rd.
Farmington Hills, MI 48331-3535
Ph: (248)699-4253
Free: 800-877-GALE
Fax: (248)699-8070
E-mail: galeord@galegroup.com
URL: http://www.galegroup.com.

Contact: Mary Ellen Snodgrass, Editor.

Desc: Over 600 contest in 20 subject areas for students. *Type:* Directory.

Council for Advancement and Support of Education

1307 New York Ave. NW,, Ste. 1000
Washington, DC 20005
Ph: (202)328-5900
Fax: (202)387-4973

Contact: Eustace Theodore, Pres.

Desc: Members are colleges, universities, and independent elementary and secondary schools. Individual member representatives serve these institutions as alumni, fundraising, public relations, admissions, government relations, and publications officers. Serves as national clearinghouse for corporate matching gift information. *Type:* Association.

Council for Basic Education

1319 F St. NW, Ste. 900
Washington, DC 20004-1152
Ph: (202)347-4171
Fax: (202)347-5047
E-mail: info@c-b-e.org
URL: http://www.c-b-e.org

Contact: Christopher T. Cross, Pres.

Desc: Educators, parents, policymakers, legislators, and concerned citizens promoting the teaching and learning of the liberal arts including geography, government, English, mathematics, science, history, foreign languages, and the arts. *Type:* Association.

Council of Chief State School Officers

1 Massachusetts Ave. NW, Ste. 700
Washington, DC 20001
Ph: (202)408-5505
Fax: (202)408-8072
E-mail: info@ccsso.org
URL: http://www.ccsso.org

Contact: Gordon M. Ambach, Exec.Dir.

Desc: Public officials who head the departments of elementary and secondary education in the states, the District of Columbia, the Department of Defense Schools and five U.S. extra-state jurisdictions. Expresses members' consensus views on major issues which the Council advocates before the President, federal agencies, the Congress, education organizations, and the public. *Type:* Association.

The Council Chronicle

National Council of Teachers of English (NCTE)
1111 W. Kenyon Rd.
Urbana, IL 61801-1096
Ph: (217)328-3870
Free: 877-369-6283
Fax: (217)328-0977
E-mail: orders@ncte.org; chronicle@ncte.org.
URL: http://www.ncte.org; http://www.ncte.org.

Contact: Felice A. Kaufmann, Editor.

Desc: Presents news of interest to English/language arts teachers at all levels, including articles on education legislation, societal trends, and changes of policy and practice that affect classroom teachers. Published by the National Council of Teachers of English. *Type:* Newsletter.

The Council Chronicle

National Council of Teachers of English (NCTE)
1111 W. Kenyon Rd.
Urbana, IL 61801-1096
Ph: (217)328-3870
Free: 877-369-6283
Fax: (217)328-0977
E-mail: orders@ncte.org
URL: http://www.ncte.org; http://www.ncte.org.

Contact: Felice Kaufman, Editor; Carrie Stewart, Advertising Mgr.

Desc: Newspaper for teachers of English or language arts at all levels. *Type:* Periodical.

Council for Exceptional Children

1920 Association Dr.
Reston, VA 20191-1589
Ph: (703)620-3660
Free: 888-CEC-SPED
Fax: (703)264-9494
E-mail: service@cec.sped.org
URL: http://www.cec.sped.org

Contact: Nancy D. Safer, Contact.

Desc: Administrators, teachers, parents, and others who work with and on behalf of children with disabilities and/or who are gifted. Seeks to improve the educational outcomes for individuals with exceptionalities - children, youth, and young adults with disabilities and/or who are gifted. *Type:* Association.

Counterpoint

LRP Publications
747 Dresher Rd.
PO Box 980
Horsham, PA 19044-0980
Ph: (215)784-0941
Free: 800-341-7874
Fax: (215)784-0870
E-mail: custserve@lrp.com
URL: http://www.lrp.com/ed.

Contact: Lisa Lombardo, Contact, (215)784-0860.

Desc: Newspaper for teachers of students who are gifted or who have disabilities featuring classroom methods and curriculums. *Type:* Periodical.

Creative Classroom

Creative Classroom Publishing, LLC
149 5th Ave., 12th Fl.
New York, NY 10011
Ph: (212)353-3639
Fax: (212)353-8030
URL: http://www.creativeclassroom.com.

Desc: Magazine for elementary school teachers. *Type:* Periodical.

Danforth Foundation

231 S. Bemiston, Ste. 1080
St. Louis, MO 63105
Ph: (314)862-6200
Fax: (314)862-2003

Contact: Dr. Bruce Anderson, Pres.

Desc: Seeks to improve the quality of teaching and learning at the precollegiate level. Provides grants and funds programs in an effort to provide opportunities for professional development of high school administrators and expand the knowledge, skills, vision, and commitment of policymakers in education. Programs include: Danforth School Administrators Fellowship for professional growth and development opportunities for senior high school principals in selected urban school districts; Danforth Seminars for Federal Judges and Educators, which provide workshops for federal judges and educational leaders to examine issues related to education and the courts; Danforth Program for School Board Members, which provides professional growth and development activities for members of selected boards of large cities; Dorthy Danforth Compton Fellowships for minority doctoral candidates to study in preparation for careers in college and university teaching. *Type:* Association.

Directory of Grants in the Humanities

Oryx Press
4041 N. Central Ave., Ste. 700
Phoenix, AZ 85012-3397
Ph: (602)265-2651
Free: 800-279-6799
Fax: 800-279-4663
E-mail: info@oryxpress.com
URL: http://www.oryxpress.com; http://www.higherconnect.com/grantselect.

Contact: Millie Hannum, Editor.

Desc: 200 new grants, 3,800 current funding programs, and more than 750 grants for artists' exhbitions, performances, and video/film production. *Type:* Directory.

Dissertation Abstracts Online

Bell & Howell Information and Learning
300 N. Zeeb Rd.
PO Box 1346
Ann Arbor, MI 48106-1346
Ph: (734)761-4700
E-mail: info@umi.com
URL: http://www.umi.com

Desc: Contains more than 1.1 million citations, with abstracts (since 1980), to dissertations accepted for doctoral degrees by accredited North American educational institutions and more than 200 institutions elsewhere. Corresponds to Dissertation Abstracts International (DAI), American Doctoral Dissertations (ADD), and Comprehensive Dissertation Index (CDI), and to the online Dissertation Abstracts database. *Available:* Ovid Technologies, Inc.; OCLC Online Computer Library Center, Inc., OCLC EPIC; The Dialog Corporation, DIALOG; CompuServe Information Service, Knowledge Index; University of Tsukuba, Science Information Processing Center; The Dialog Corporation, DataStar; STN International; Research Libraries Group, Inc. (RLG), CitaDel™ Service; OCLC Online Computer Library Center, Inc., OCLC FirstSearch Catalog. *Type:* Database.

Dollars for Scholars

7703 Normandale Rd., Ste. 110
Edina, MN 55435-5311
Ph: (612)830-7300
Free: 800-279-2083
Fax: (612)830-1929
E-mail: commcsfa@aol.com
URL: http://www.citizens.scholarship-foundation.org

Contact: William C. Nelsen, Pres.

Desc: National Network of 780 grassroots scholarship foundations in 40 states that raise funds and provide financial and academic support to local students seeking postsecondary education. *Type:* Association.

Earthwatch Institute

680 Mt. Auburn St.
Box 9104
Watertown, MA 02471-9104
Ph: (617)926-8200
Free: 800-776-0188
Fax: (617)926-8532
E-mail: info@earthwatch.org
URL: http://www.earthwatch.org

Contact: Roger Bergen, Pres.

Desc: Research and educational organization that allows individuals who have an avocational interest in science and the humanities to become working members of research teams led by highly qualified scientists. Team members support, physically and financially, ongoing scientific research projects in exchange for being able to work as research assistants for a 1 to 3-week period. Teams consist of 2 to 20 people; projects include field work in most disciplines of the sciences (archaeology, earth, marine and life sciences, zoology, ornithology, astronomy, ecology, and marine science) and in the humanities (anthropology, folklore, and history). *Type:* Association.

Editorial Projects in Education

6935 Arlington Ste. 100
Bethesda, MD 20814
Ph: (301)280-3100
Fax: (301)280-3200
Contact: Virginia Edwards, Pres.
Desc: Board of directors is composed of educators, journalists, and foundation administrators in the U.S. Devoted

to dissemination of information on education via journalistic means. Maintains collection of materials relating to education primarily from newspapers, books and periodicals. *Type:* Association.

Education Commission of the States

707 17th St., Ste. 2700   Ph: (303)299-3600
Denver, CO 80202-3427   Fax: (303)296-8332
E-mail: ecs@ecs.org
URL: http://www.ecs.org
Contact: Frank Newman, Pres.

Desc: 7 representatives from each of the member states, the District of Columbia, American Samoa, Puerto Rico, and the Virgin Islands. Includes the governor of the state, four persons appointed by the governor, and two state legislators. Serves as the operating arm and the governing board of the Interstate Compact for Education, an agreement between the states to join together for the improvement of education by establishing a partnership of political and educational leadership. *Type:* Association.

Education Development Center

55 Chapel St.   Ph: (617)969-7100
Newton, MA 02458   Fax: (617)244-3436
Contact: Janet Whitla, Pres.

Desc: A nonprofit institution financed by contracts and/or grants from U.S. government agencies, private educational foundations, foreign governments, and sales of materials, for the purpose of comprehensive educational improvement. Programs involve teachers, administrators, curriculum specialists, researchers, media specialists, academicians, scientists, technicians, and educationally-minded citizens "who pool their talents and ideas for the common purpose of improving education." *Type:* Association.

Education Index

H.W. Wilson Company
950 University Ave.   Ph: (718)588-8400
Bronx, NY 10452
E-mail: custserv@hwwilson.com
URL: http://www.hwwilson.com
Contact: Technical Support Department., techmail@info.hwwilson.com.

Desc: Contains citations to articles, interviews, selected editorials and letters to the editor, and reviews of books, educational films, and software from approximately 500 English-language periodicals, monographs, and yearbooks in the field of education. Covers school administration; pre-school, elementary, secondary, higher, and adult education; counseling and personnel services; teacher and vocational education; and teaching methods. *Available:* H.W. Wilson Company, WilsonWeb; H.W. Wilson Company, WilsonWeb; Ovid Technologies, Inc.; OCLC Online Computer Library Center, Inc., OCLC EPIC; OCLC Online Computer Library Center, Inc., OCLC FirstSearch Catalog; NlightN. *Type:* Database.

Education-Social Sciences

TradeWave Corp.
3636 Executive Center Dr., Ste. 100
Austin, TX 78731
E-mail: info@tradewave.com
URL: http://www.einet.net/galaxy/Social-Sciences/Education.html
Desc: The Education - Social Sciences database (part of Galaxy, The Professional's Guide to a World of Information) contains a wealth of information and resources concerning academic institutions. Topics include adult education, curriculum and instruction, guidance and counseling, and higher education resources. *Type:* Database.

Education Technology News

Business Publishers, Inc.
8737 Colesville Rd., Ste. 1100   Ph: (301)589-5103
Silver Spring, MD 20910   Free: 800-274-6737
    Fax: (301)587-4530
E-mail: bpinews@bpinews.com
URL: http://www.bpinews.com.
Contact: Brian Love, Editor, (301)587-6300, fax: (301)587-1081, blove@bpinews.com.

Desc: Covers new educational computer and software products for use in teaching and training programs. Provides information on innovative school programs, federal funding, grants, research studies, corporate gifts and much more. *Type:* Newsletter.

Education Today

Family Education Network
20 Park Plaza, Ste. 1215   Ph: (617)542-6500
Boston, MA 02116   Fax: (617)542-6564
Contact: Lynn McBrien, Editor-in-Chief.

Desc: Designed to help parents with the education of their kids. Covers trends in education, what's working, and parent tips. *Type:* Newsletter.

Education Update

Association for Supervision and Curriculum Development
1703 N. Beauregard St.   Ph: (703)578-9600
Alexandria, VA 22311   Free: 800-933-2723
    Fax: (703)578-5400
E-mail: info@ascd.org
Contact: Scott Willis, Editor.

Desc: Provides news of the activities and projects of the Association, which is devoted to "developing leadership for quality in education." Discusses innovative teaching techniques and programs; assesses traditional education standards and testing; and emphasizes the need to teach the skills that students will need to enable them to think critically, reason, and solve problems. Recurring features include reports of meetings and notices of publications available. *Type:* Newsletter.

Education Week on the Web

Education Week
6935 Arlington Rd., Ste. 100   Ph: (301)280-3100
Bethesda, MD 20814-5233   Fax: (301)280-3250
E-mail: webster@epe.org
URL: http://www.edweek.org/
Contact: Jeanne McCann, Online Editor.

Desc: Education Week on the Web offers a wealth of information for those interested in schools and education reform. Various pages such as Current Events and Research comments on topics such as school vouchers, the Internet's education, and California's Proposition 227. *Type:* Database.

Education World

American Fidelity Educational Services
2000 N. Classen Blvd.
Oklahoma City, OK 73106
E-mail: Brian.Mauck@af.group.com
URL: http://www.education-world.com/
Contact: webmaster@education-world.com.

Desc: For teachers at the elementary and secondary level, this site, sponsored by American Fidelity Educational Services, this site is a valuable resource. Attractively designed and easy to navigate, Education World has a wealth of help for educators under the following categories: Lesson Planning; News/Eye on Schools; Curriculum; Books in Education; and Administrators. *Type:* Database.

Educational Directory Online

Dun and Bradstreet Market Data Retrieval (MDR)
One Forest Pkwy.   Ph: (203)926-4800
Shelton, CT 06484-2117
E-mail: mdrinfo@mail.dnb.com

Desc: Contains information on all schools from daycare through college level, plus every public library in the United States and Canada. The database includes extensive demographic and technology information, and more than 4 million educators by name and job title. *Type:* Database.

Educational Leadership

Association for Supervision and Curriculum Development
1703 N. Beauregard St.   Ph: (703)578-9600
Alexandria, VA 22311   Free: 800-933-2723
    Fax: (703)578-5400
E-mail: info@ascd.org; el@ascd.org.
URL: http://www.ascd.org.
Contact: Marge Scherer, Editor; Teola T. Jones, Advertising Mgr.

Desc: Magazine on curriculum, instruction, supervision, and leadership in schools. *Type:* Periodical.

Educational Rankings Annual

Gale Group Inc.
27500 Drake Rd.   Ph: (248)699-4253
Farmington Hills, MI 48331-   Free: 800-877-GALE
3535   Fax: (248)699-8070
E-mail: galeord@galegroup.com
URL: http://www.galegroup.com.
Contact: Lynn C. Hattendorf, Editor.

Desc: "Educational Rankings Annual" is a collection of more than 4,000 lists or rankings on all facets of education, generally citing the top 10 entries from each list. The citations in the annual are selected from newspapers, popular and scholarly periodicals, college guides, government publications, etc. *Type:* Directory.

Educational Technology Markets

Nelson B. Heller & Associates
9933 Lawler Ave., No. 560   Ph: (847)674-6282
Skokie, IL 60077   Fax: (847)674-2882
E-mail: info@hellerreports.com
URL: http://www.hellerreports.com.
Contact: Anne Wujcik, Editor, (703)548-1420, fax: (703)548-1037, anne@hellerreports.com.

Desc: Offers information on developing and marketing computer hardware and software, satellites, videos, and other technologies for education institutions. Recurring features include a calendar of events. *Type:* Newsletter.

El-Hi Textbooks and Serials in Print

R. R. Bowker
A Unit of Cahners Business Information
121 Chanlon Rd.   Ph: (908)464-6800
New Providence, NJ 07974   Free: 888-269-5372
    Fax: (908)771-7704
E-mail: info@bowker.com
URL: http://www.bowker.com.
Contact: Doreen Gravesande, Editor; Barbara Holton, Editor.

Desc: List of more than 1,000 publishers of elementary and secondary level textbooks and related teaching materials. *Type:* Directory.

ELS Language Centers/Oklahoma City

ELS Language Centers
5761 Buckingham Pkwy., Ste.   Ph: (310)342-4100
55   Free: 800-468-8978
Culver City, CA 90230   Fax: (310)342-4104
E-mail: info55@els.com

URL: http://www.els.com/okcity.htm

Desc: This Oklahoma branch of the ELS Language Centers, residing on the Oklahoma City University Campus, offers some specific information concerning its curriculum. Housing options, tuition fees, the standard weather conditions for the area, and more can be found here with little effort. *Type:* Database.

ERIC®

U.S. Department of Education
Office of Educational Research and Improvement (OERI)
ERIC Processing and Reference Facility
1100 West St.   Ph: (301)497-4080
Laurel, MD 20707
E-mail: ERICFAC@INET.ED.GOV

Contact: Ted Brandhorst, Director, (301)497-4080, fax: (301)953-0263, ericfoc@inet.ed.gov.

Desc: Contains more than 954,000 records from both the journal and report literature in the field of education and education-related areas. Journal literature corresponds to Current Index to Journals in Education (CIJE). *Available:* Ovid Technologies, Inc.; The Dialog Corporation, DIALOG; OCLC Online Computer Library Center, Inc., OCLC FirstSearch Catalog; The Dialog Corporation, DataStar; National Information Services Corporation (NISC), BiblioLine; EBSCOhost. *Type:* Database.

ERIC Clearinghouse on Assessment and Evaluation

Catholic University of America - Department of Education
O'Boyle Hall   Ph: (202)319-7449
Washington, DC 20064   Free: 800-464-3742
E-mail: webmaster@ericae.edu.cua.edu
URL: http://ericae.net/main.htm

Contact: Larry Rudner, rudner@cua.edu.

Desc: The ERIC Clearinghouse on Assessment and Evaluation provides information and resources pertaining to educational assessment, evaluation and learning theory. Featured are searches of the ERIC/Educational Testing Service Test File to locate test descriptions, searches of the Buros and Pro-Ed Test Review Locators to identify books containing reviews of specific tests, measurement and evaluation news, full text essays on alternative assessment, and other essays of interest to parents. *Type:* Database.

ERIC Directory of Education-Related Information Centers

ACCESS ERIC
2277 Research Blvd.   Ph: (301)519-5264
Rockville, MD 20850   Free: 800-LET-ERIC
                                Fax: (301)519-6760
E-mail: accesseric@accesseric.org
URL: http://www.aspensys.com/eric; http://www.ed.gov/BASISDB/EROD/direct/SF.

Contact: Michael Heeg, Editor; Carol Boston, Editor.

Desc: More than 450 education-related information centers in the United States. *Type:* Directory.

ERIC (Educational Resources Information Center)

ERIC Processing and Reference Facility
U.S. Office of Educational Research and Improvement
1100 West St., 2nd Fl.   Ph: (301)497-4080
Laurel, MD 20707-3598   Free: 800-799-3742
                                Fax: (301)953-0263
E-mail: ericfac@inet.ed.gov

Desc: In separate files: "Resources in Education" (RIE) file, education-related documents; "Current Index to Journals in Education" (CIJE) file, articles from about 900 periodicals of interest to the education profession. *Type:* Directory.

Eternal Degrees in the Information Age

Oryx Press
4041 N. Central Ave., Ste. 700   Ph: (602)265-2651
Phoenix, AZ 85012-3397   Free: 800-279-6799
                                 Fax: 800-279-4663
E-mail: info@oryxpress.com
URL: http://www.oryxpress.com

Contact: Eugene Sullivan, Editor.

Desc: Over 280 alternative and external degree programs at colleges and universities in the U.S. *Type:* Directory.

ETS Developments

Test Collection
Educational Testing Service
Rosedale Rd.   Ph: (609)734-5682
Princeton, NJ 08541   Fax: (609)734-5410

Contact: Albert Benderson, Editor.

Desc: Features articles on developments in educational research, psychometrics, and testing programs, as well as reporting news of ETS. Carries news of research into educational policy and practice and human learning. *Type:* Newsletter.

Events

Magna Publications, Inc.
2718 Dryden Dr.   Ph: (608)246-3580
Madison, WI 53704-3086   Free: 800-433-0499
                                Fax: (608)246-3597
E-mail: custserv@magnapubs.com; eventsahar@aol.com.
URL: http://www.magnapubs.com

Contact: Paul Steinbach, Editor, paul.steinbach@magnapubs.com.

Desc: Provides information for higher education event planners. *Type:* Newsletter.

Exceptional Child Education Resources

Council for Exceptional Children (CEC)
1920 Association Dr.   Ph: (703)264-9474
Reston, VA 20191
URL: http://www.cec.sped.org

Contact: Information Specialist, fax: (703)620-2521, eri-cec@cec.sped.org.

Desc: Contains more than 100,000 records composed of citations and abstracts of English-language print and non-print materials dealing with the education and development of people with exceptionalities, both those with disabilities and those who are gifted. *Available:* iNet 2000; SilverPlatter Information, Inc. *Type:* Database.

Explorer

Great Lakes Collaborative
33500 Van Born Rd.
PO Box 807
Wayne, MI 48184-2497
E-mail: webmaster@greatlakes.k12.mi.us
URL: http://server2.greatlakes.k12.mi.us/

Contact: webmaster@greatlakes.k12.mi.us.

Desc: Explorer is a collection of mathematics and science educational resources for kindergarten through 12th grade. Included are projects, research materials and lesson plans for teacher and students alike. *Type:* Database.

Fast Times

Fast Times
810 Los Vallecitos Blvd., Ste.   Ph: (760)591-9433
210   Fax: (760)591-9105
San Marcos, CA 92069-1449

Contact: Steven Posner, Editor; Jeff Lederman, Publisher; Elisabeth Cline, Advertising Mgr.

Desc: Magazine for high school students to be used as part of classroom assignments in social studies. *Type:* Periodical.

Florida Institute of Technology

Florida Institute of Technology
150 W. University Blvd.   Ph: (407)674-8000
Melbourne, FL 32901-6975   Free: 800-888-4348
E-mail: www@fit.edu
URL: http://www.fit.edu/

Contact: Leris Hambleton, lhamblet@fit.edu.

Desc: The Florida Institute of Technology (FIT) offers readers pleasing graphics in addition to information designed with prospective/attending students in mind. Visitors interested in finding out more FIT can read, in a brochure style presentation, text concerning aspects of life at FIT, faculty bios and contacts, and brief information concerning research currently being performed at the institution. *Type:* Database.

Florida Student Association

327 Office Plaza Dr., Ste. 202   Ph: (850)877-7500
Tallahassee, FL 32301-2755   Fax: (850)877-6898
E-mail: kevin@fsa1.org
URL: http://www.fsa1.org

Contact: Kevin M. Mayeux, Exec.Dir.

Desc: College and university students. Lobbies at state and federal levels. *Type:* Association.

FREEDOM Magazine

Church of Scientology International
6331 Hollywood Blvd., Ste.   Ph: (213)960-3500
1200   Free: 888-576-FREE
Los Angeles, CA 90028-6329   Fax: (213)960-3508
URL: http://www.freedommag.org.

Contact: Aron Mason, Editor-in-Chief; Tom Whittle, Editor, editor@freedommag.org.

Desc: Magazine emphasizing social reform, national news and human rights. *Type:* Periodical.

Friends of Choice in Urban Schools

1530 16th St. NW, Ste. B1   Ph: (202)387-0405
Washington, DC 20036-1445

Contact: Robert Came, Exec.Dir.

Type: Association.

Future Problem Solving Program

2500 Packard St., Ste. 110   Ph: (734)973-8781
Ann Arbor, MI 48104-6827   Fax: (734)973-1986
E-mail: fpsolve@aol.com
URL: http://www.fpsp.org

Contact: Cory Kiner, Asst.Dir.

Desc: Students and teacher-coaches. Purpose is to motivate and assist students in developing and improving creative thinking, information gathering, and other skills in communication, problem solving, research, and teamwork. Seeks to increase students' interest in the future and encourages them to exercise creative, critical, and analytical thought. *Type:* Association.

Grolier Multimedia Encyclopedia Online

Grolier Educational
90 Sherman Tpke.   Ph: (203)797-3530
Danbury, CT 06816
URL: http://gi.grolier.com

Contact: Maryanne Piazza, Director of Marketing Communications, (203)797-3365, fax: (203)797-3835, mpiazza@grolier.com.

Desc: Provides the complete text of the Academic American Encyclopedia. Contains approximately 35,000 articles, providing current information on a full range of topics and persons in all subject areas. *Available:* Dow Jones Interactive Publishing. *Type:* Database.

Guide to International Education in the United States

Gale Group Inc.

27500 Drake Rd.   Ph: (248)699-4253
Farmington Hills, MI 48331-   Free: 800-877-GALE
3535   Fax: (248)699-8070
E-mail: galeord@galegroup.com
URL: http://www.galegroup.com.

Contact: David S. Hoopes, Editor; Kathleen R. Hoopes, Editor.

Desc: Approximately 3,800 organizations, academic programs, and resources in the U.S. and Canada related to international and intercultural education, international affairs, cultural relations, world issues, world region area studies, area studies by country, peace and conflict resolution, study abroad, foreign language learning, and English as a second language. *Type:* Directory.

High/Scope Educational Research Foundation

600 N. River St.   Ph: (734)485-2000
Ypsilanti, MI 48198-2898   Free: 800-40-PRESS
    Fax: (734)485-0704
E-mail: info@highscope.org
URL: http://www.highscope.org

Contact: David P. Weikart, Pres.

Desc: Goal is to develop practical alternatives to the traditional methods of educating children and training teachers. Engages in curriculum development for children from infancy through the high school years; conducts workshops and seminars for the training of teachers; conducts evaluative research for its own and other educational programs; holds professional conferences; produces multimedia training packages to supplement face-to-face teacher training. Offers programs in preschool education and has developed materials, computer applications, and an in-service training system for early childhood centers that have chosen to implement the High/Scope Preschool Curriculum; has also developed a cognitively oriented elementary curriculum based on educational principles derived from the child development theories of Jean Piaget. *Type:* Association.

Home School Legal Defense Association

PO Box 3000   Ph: (540)338-5600
Purcellville, VA 20134-9000   Fax: (540)338-2733
E-mail: mailroom@hslda.org
URL: http://www.hslda.org

Contact: Charles L. Hurst, Office Mgr.

Desc: Families that educate their children at home rather than enrolling them in a public or private school. Provides legal assistance to families whose attempts to educate their children at home are challenged by state government or the local school board. Monitors legal and legislative developments nationwide pertaining to what the group believes is a family's right to educate its children at home. *Type:* Association.

Hotlist: Kids Did This!

The Franklin Institute Science Museum

222 N. 20th St.   Ph: (215)448-1200
Philadelphia, PA 19103
E-mail: webteam@www.fi.edu
URL: http://sln.fi.edu/tfi/hotlists/kids.html

Contact: baumann@fi.edu.

Desc: Kids Did This! features entirely kid-produced items, with categories broken down into science, art, social studies, mathematics, language arts, school newspapers, and miscellaneous. *Type:* Database.

IBM Kiosk for Higher Education

University of Washington - IBM Kiosk for Education

Mail Stop FC-06   Ph: (206)543-5604
Seattle, WA 98195
E-mail: ike@ike.engr.washington.edu
URL: http://www.hied.ibm.com/

Contact: Gregory Zick, Professor of Electrical Engineering.

Desc: The IBM Kiosk for Higher Education provides links to curriculum resources; associations and conferences; technical sites; software on the net; university and college information; internet information related to higher education; general higher education information. *Type:* Database.

IES, Institute for the International Education of Students

223 W. Ohio St.   Ph: (312)944-1750
Chicago, IL 60610   Free: 800-995-2300
    Fax: (312)944-1448
E-mail: info@iesabroad.org
URL: http://wwwiesabroad.org

Contact: Dr. Mary Dweyer, Pres.

Desc: Affiliated colleges and universities; institutions; students; faculty. Conducts undergraduate study programs with European and Asian universities for U.S. college students; develops and conducts specially designed European study programs for U.S. colleges and universities. *Type:* Association.

Illinois Education Association

100 E. Edwards St.   Ph: (217)544-0706
Springfield, IL 62704-1999   Free: 800-252-8076
    Fax: (217)544-0706

Contact: Clayton Marquardt, Exec.Dir.

Type: Association.

In Motion

General Learning Communications

900 Skokie Blvd., Ste. 200   Ph: (847)205-3000
Northbrook, IL 60062   Fax: (847)564-8197

Contact: Carole Rubenstein, Editor, (847)205-3141, ruben@glcomm.com; Julio Abreu, Publisher, jabreu@lcomm.com.

Desc: Driver education magazine. *Type:* Periodical.

In Touch

Information Technology Services
University of Western Ontario

Natural Sciences Centre   Ph: (519)661-2151
London, ON, Canada N6A 5B7   Fax: (519)661-3486
E-mail: in.touch@julian.uwo.ca
URL: http://www.uwo.ca/its/doc/newsletters/InTouch/.

Contact: Merran Neville, Editor, mneville@julian.uwo.ca.

Desc: Carries articles on computing and related technology relevant to its university subscribers. *Type:* Newsletter.

Independent School Guide for Washington DC and Surrounding Area

Independent School Guide

7315 Brookville Rd.   Ph: (301)986-5370
Chevy Chase, MD 20815   Fax: (301)718-4651
URL: http://www.washingtonschoolguide.com

Contact: Lois Coerper, Editor; Shirley Mersereau, Editor.

Desc: Over 370 independent schools (including parochial schools) in the Washington, DC area, including Maryland and Virginia. *Type:* Directory.

The Independent Study Catalog: A Guide to Continuing Education through Correspondence Courses

Peterson's

202 Carnegie Center   Ph: (609)243-9111
PO Box 2123   Free: 800-338-3282
Princeton, NJ 08543-2123   Fax: (609)243-9150
URL: http://www.peterson.com

Contact: Susan Dilts, Editor.

Desc: Nearly 100 colleges and universities that offer credit and non-credit independent study courses at the undergraduate, graduate, and/or high school levels. *Type:* Directory.

Institute for Educational Leadership

1001 Connecticut Ave. NW,   Ph: (202)822-8405
   Ste. 310   Fax: (202)872-4050
Washington, DC 20036
Contact: Michael Usdan, Pres.

Desc: Coordinates programs at national, state, and local levels that are designed to support and enhance the capabilities of educators and policymakers. Areas of interest include: leadership development and expanding the talents, skills, and vision of those working in education and related fields; informing and linking policymakers within and across sectors; establishing access to policy and analysis expertise and providing for specialized interests through ongoing networks, research, and communication. Works to identify emerging issues and options for policymakers whose decisions about allocations of resources and priorities affect the quality of education in the U.S. *Type:* Association.

Instructor

Scholastic, Inc.

555 Broadway   Ph: (212)343-6100
New York, NY 10012   Free: 800-724-6527
    Fax: (212)343-4535
E-mail: custserv@scholastic.com
URL: http://www.scholastic.com; http://www.scholastic.com/instructor.

Contact: Mickey Revenaugh, Contact.

Desc: Educational magazine. *Type:* Periodical.

Instructor Magazine

Scholastic Corp.

555 Broadway   Ph: (212)343-6100
New York, NY 10012
URL: http://www.scholastic.com/Instructor/
Contact: instructoreditor@scholastic.com.

Desc: A 'zine for primary- and middle-school teachers from Scholastic. Topics covered range far and wide and include strategies for integrating curriculum, professional development opportunities, and help with assessing students. *Type:* Database.

International Christian Education Association

13165 Cloverdale   Ph: (810)399-6500
Oak Park, MI 48237   Fax: (810)399-1662
Contact: D. Gene Williams, Exec.Dir.

Desc: Churches and interested individuals. Promotes Christian education through interdenominational programs. Offers Summer Ministries Training Institute, Evangelism Training Institute, and Sunday School Superintendent Training Institute. *Type:* Association.

International Foundation for Gender Education

PO Box 229   Ph: (781)899-2212
Waltham, MA 02454   Fax: (781)899-5703
E-mail: ifge@ifge.org
URL: http://www.ifge.org
Contact: Nancy Nangeroni, Exec.Dir.

Desc: Serves as an educational resource for the transgender, cross-dressing and transsexual community and those persons affected by or serving that community. *Type:* Association.

International Reading Association
800 Barksdale Rd.   Ph: (302)731-1600
PO Box 8139   Fax: (302)731-1057
Newark, DE 19714-8139
E-mail: pubinfo@reading.org
Contact: Alan Farstrup, Exec.Dir.
Desc: Teachers, reading specialists, consultants, administrators, supervisors, researchers, psychologists, librarians, and parents interested in promoting literacy. Seeks to improve the quality of reading instruction and promote literacy worldwide. Disseminates information pertaining to research on reading, including information on adult literacy, early childhood and literacy development, international education, literature for children and adolescents, and teacher education and professional development. *Type:* Association.

International University Foundation
1301 S. Noland Rd.   Ph: (816)461-3633
Independence, MO 64055
Contact: Dr. John Wayne Johnston, Pres.
Desc: Individuals (60824) and institutions (30) united to advance the free flow of information and personnel between universities worldwide. *Type:* Association.

Junior Classical League
Miami University   Ph: (513)529-7741
Oxford, OH 45056   Fax: (513)529-7742
E-mail: americanclassicalleague@muohio.edu
Contact: Geri Dutra, Adm.Sec.
Desc: High school students studying Latin. Sponsored by the American Classical League to encourage an interest in and appreciation of the civilization, language, literature, and art of ancient Greece and Rome and to provide young people with an understanding of the debt American culture owes to classical antiquity. *Type:* Association.

Junior Scholastic
Scholastic, Inc.
555 Broadway   Ph: (212)343-6100
New York, NY 10012   Free: 800-724-6527
    Fax: (212)343-4535
E-mail: custserv@scholastic.com; jr@scholastic.com.
URL: http://www.scholastic.com
Contact: Lee Baier, Editor; Richard Robinson, Publisher; G. Estabrook Kindred, Advertising Mgr.
Desc: Social studies magazine. *Type:* Periodical.

Kappa Delta Epsilon
Dr. Fran T. Carter
2561 Rocky Ridge Rd.   Ph: (205)822-4106
Birmingham, AL 35243   Fax: (205)822-4106
E-mail: j_fcarter@juno.com
Contact: Dr. Fran T. Carter, Natl.Exec.Dir.
Desc: Honorary professional fraternity - education. Conducts educational programs. *Type:* Association.

Kappa Delta Pi
3707 Woodview Trace   Ph: (317)871-4900
Indianapolis, IN 46268-1158   Free: 800-284-3167
    Fax: (317)704-2323
URL: http://www.kdp.org
Contact: Michael P. Wolfe, Exec.Dir.
Desc: Honor society - men and women, education. Conducts research projects. Recognizes and rewards excellence in education. *Type:* Association.

Kappa Phi Kappa
Judson Jones
820 S. Montez Dr.   Ph: (205)426-6149
Bessemer, AL 35023
Contact: Judson Jones, Contact.
Desc: Professional fraternity, education. Sponsors competitions. *Type:* Association.

Kentucky Congress of Parents and Teachers
PO Box 654   Ph: (502)564-4378
Frankfort, KY 40602-0654   Fax: (502)564-2599
Contact: Vicki Ensor, Office Admin.
Desc: Parents, teachers, students, principals, administrators, and others interested in uniting the forces of home, school, and community in behalf of children and youth enrolled in the state's school districts. *Type:* Association.

Kirk-Othmer Encyclopedia of Chemical Technology
John Wiley & Sons, Inc.
605 Third Ave.   Ph: (212)850-6194
New York, NY 10158-0012
URL: http://www.wiley.com
Desc: Contains the complete text, including citations, tables, and abstracts, of many volumes of the latest edition of the Kirk-Othmer Encyclopedia of Chemical Technology. Covers chemical technology in the areas of energy, health, safety, and new materials: agricultural chemicals; chemical engineering; coatings and inks; composite materials; drugs, cosmetics, and biomaterials; dyes, pigments, and brighteners; ecology and industrial hygiene; energy conversion and technology; fats and waxes; fermentation and enzyme technology; fibers, textiles, and leather; food and animal nutrition; fossil fuels and derivatives; glass, ceramics, and cement; industrial organic and inorganic chemicals; metals, metallurgy, and metal alloys; plastics and elastomers; semiconductors and electronic materials; surfactants, detergents, and emulsion technology; water supply, purification, and reuse; and wood, paper, and industrial carbohydrates. *Available:* The Dialog Corporation, DIALOG; CompuServe Information Service, Knowledge Index. *Type:* Database.

Learning
The Education Center, Inc.
3515 W. Market St.   Ph: (336)854-0309
Greensboro, NC 27403   Free: 800-334-0298
    Fax: (336)547-1586
E-mail: learning@vcoml.com.
URL: http://www.theeducationcenter.com.
Contact: Annie Teich, Publisher, ateich@theeducationcenter.com; Anne Credi, Advertising Director, (336)851-8351, acredi@theeducationcenter.com.
Desc: Definitive guide to products and services for K-6 grade teachers in the classroom. *Type:* Periodical.

Let's Find Out
Scholastic, Inc.
555 Broadway   Ph: (212)343-6100
New York, NY 10012   Free: 800-724-6527
    Fax: (212)343-4535
E-mail: custserv@scholastic.com
URL: http://www.scholastic.com
Contact: Susan Canizares, Editor-in-Chief, fax: (212)343-6619, scanizares@scholastic.com; Linda Koons, Publisher.
Desc: Magazine for kindergarten and pre-school children. *Type:* Periodical.

Marquis Who's Who in American Education
Marquis Who's Who
Reed Elsevier
121 Chanlon Rd.   Ph: (908)464-6800
New Providence, NJ 07974   Free: 800-521-8110
    Fax: (908)771-8645
E-mail: info@marquiswhoswho.com
Contact: Lisa Weissbard, Managing Editor.
Desc: Approximately 27,000 leaders in the field of education. *Type:* Directory.

Maryland Congress of Parents and Teachers
3121 St. Paul St., Ste. 25   Ph: (410)235-7290
Baltimore, MD 21218   Fax: (410)235-0357
URL: http://www.pta.org
Contact: Carmela Veit, Pres.
Desc: Promotes the welfare of children in the home, school, community, and place of worship. *Type:* Association.

The MBA Newsletter
Kwartler Communications Inc.
79 Verbena Ave.   Ph: (516)488-2010
Floral Park, NY 11001   Fax: (516)488-2025
E-mail: 76514.305@compuserve.com
Contact: Richard Kwartler, Editor.
Desc: Provides international coverage of administration, external affairs, admissions, academic programs, development, placement, and new technology concerning MBA and other masters degree programs in business administration. Recurring features include profiles of business schools throughout the globe. *Type:* Newsletter.

MEA Voice
Michigan Education Association
1216 Kendale Blvd.   Ph: (517)332-6551
Box 2573   Free: 800-292-1934
East Lansing, MI 48826-2573   Fax: (517)337-5414
E-mail: drk@mea.org.
URL: http://www.mea.org.
Contact: Dennis Keenon, Editor, dkeenan1@aol.com.
Desc: Educational tabloid for teachers union. *Type:* Periodical.

Middle States Association of Colleges and Schools
3624 Market St.   Ph: (215)662-5600
Philadelphia, PA 19104   Fax: (215)662-5950
E-mail: kevinmsa@aol.com
URL: http://www.middlestate.org
Contact: Kevin Fitzpatrick, Bus.Mgr.
Desc: Nongovernmental, voluntary organization of colleges and universities, secondary schools, and elementary schools in Panama, Delaware, District of Columbia, Maryland, New Jersey, New York, Pennsylvania, Puerto Rico, and the Virgin Islands, that have been accredited by either the Commission on Higher Education, the Commission on Secondary Schools, or the Commission on Elementary Schools. One of six regional accrediting agencies in the U.S. *Type:* Association.

Missouri Department of Elementary and Secondary Education
Missouri Department of Elementary and Secondary Education
PO Box 480   Ph: (573)751-4212
Jefferson City, MO 65102-0480   Fax: (573)751-1179
E-mail: pubinfo@mail.dese.state.mo.us
URL: http://services.dese.state.mo.us
Desc: The Missouri Department of Elementary & Secondary Education database contains material to support Missouri students, teachers, parents, administrators, and others interested in improving educational effectiveness. This site contains information about department's publications, programs and services, as well as links to employment opportunities, Missouri K-12 schools, Missouri School Improvement Program, school finance and laws and more. *Type:* Database.

NAFSA/Association of International Educators
1307 New York Ave. NW, 8th Fl.   Ph: (202)737-3699
    Fax: (202)737-3657
Washington, DC 20005
E-mail: inbox@nafsa.org

URL: http://www.nafsa.org

Contact: Archer Brown, Deputy Exec.Dir.

Desc: Individuals, organizations, and institutions dealing with international educational exchange, including foreign student advisers, overseas educational advisers, credentials and admissions officers, administrators and teachers of English as a second language, community support personnel, study-abroad administrators, and embassy cultural or educational personnel. Promotes self-regulation standards and responsibilities in international educational exchange; offers professional development opportunities primarily through publications, workshops, grants, and regional and national conferences. Advocates for increased awareness and support of international education and exchange on campuses, in government, and in communities. *Type:* Association.

National Academy of Education

New York University   Ph: (212)998-9035
School of Education   Fax: (212)995-4435
726 Broadway, 5th Fl.
New York, NY 10003-9580
URL: http://www.nae.nyu.edu

Desc: Honorary society of leaders in education. Offers advice and assistance to the federal government and national foundations. Administers post-doctoral fellowship program to ensure the future of research in education concerning key educational issues. *Type:* Association.

National Accrediting Commission of Cosmetology Arts and Sciences

901 N. Stuart St., No. 900   Ph: (703)527-7600
Arlington, VA 22203   Fax: (703)527-8811
E-mail: naccas@erols.com
URL: http://www.naccas.org
Contact: Mark Gross, CEO.

Desc: Accrediting body for schools of cosmetology; presently there are 1030 accredited schools. Objectives are to: raise standards of cosmetology schools throughout the country; encourage use of modern educational methods and techniques; stimulate self-improvement by the schools. Sponsors standards and professional team training workshops. *Type:* Association.

National Association of American School Employees and Retirees

Desc: School employees, retirees, and their immediate families. Promotes the education, health, and welfare of members. Offers members free legal services on personal and professional matters; provides information on benefits to retirees and information on jobs and housing to teachers seeking transfers. *Type:* Association.

National Association for the Education of Young Children

1509 16th St. NW   Ph: (202)232-8777
Washington, DC 20036   Free: 800-424-2460
    Fax: (202)328-1846
E-mail: naeyc@naeyc.org
URL: http://www.naeyc.org
Contact: Dr. Mark R. Ginsburg, Exec.Dir./CEO.

Desc: Teachers and directors of preschool and primary schools, kindergartens, child care centers, cooperatives, church schools, and groups having similar programs for young children; early childhood education and child development educators, trainers, and researchers. Open to all individuals interested in serving and acting on behalf of the needs and rights of young children, with primary focus on the provision of educational services and resources. Sponsors a public education campaign entitled "Week of the Young Child." Offers voluntary accreditation for early childhood schools and centers through the National Academy of Early Childhood Programs. *Type:* Association.

National Association of Elementary School Principals

1615 Duke St.   Ph: (703)684-3345
Alexandria, VA 22314   Fax: (703)548-6021
URL: http://www.anaesp.org

Contact: Dr. Samuel G. Sava, Exec.Dir.

Desc: Professional association of principals, assistant or vice principals, and aspiring principals; persons engaged in educational research and in the professional education of elementary and middle school administrators. Sponsors National Distinguished Principals Program, President's Award for Educational Excellence, American Student Council Association, National Fellows Program, and Institute for Reflective Practice. Offers professional development workshops throughout the year. *Type:* Association.

National Association for Family and Community Education

PO Box 835   Ph: (606)586-8333
Burlington, KY 41005-0835   Fax: (606)586-8348
E-mail: nafcehq@juno.com
URL: http://www.nafce.org

Contact: Judy DeWitz, Pres.

Desc: Men and women who are members of state family and community education associations in 43 states, the Virgin Islands, and Puerto Rico. Educational organization assisting individuals and family members in identifying and solving family and community problems, in cooperation with local resources, state land-grant universities, and the United States Department of Agriculture. Educational programs are concerned with children's issues, environmental problems, and literacy. *Type:* Association.

National Association of Graduate-Professional Students

209 Pennsylvania Ave., SE   Free: 888-88N-AGPS
Washington, DC 20003
E-mail: nagps@netcom.com
URL: http://www.nagps.org

Contact: Debbie Davis, Exec.Dir.

Desc: Improves the quality of graduate and professional student life. Promotes the interests and welfare of these students in public and private universities, as well as in the public and private agencies. Acts as a clearinghouse for information on graduate and professional student groups at all stages of development. *Type:* Association.

National Association of Independent Schools

1620 L St. NW, Ste. 1100   Ph: (202)973-9700
Washington, DC 20036-5605   Fax: (202)973-9790

Contact: Peter Relic, Pres.

Desc: Independent elementary and secondary school members; regional associations of independent schools and related associations. Provides curricular and administrative research and services. Conducts educational programs; compiles statistics. *Type:* Association.

National Association of Partners in Education

901 N. Pitt St., Ste. 320   Ph: (703)836-4880
Alexandria, VA 22314   Fax: (703)836-6941
E-mail: napehq@napehq.org
URL: http://www.napehq.org

Contact: Daniel W. Merenda, Pres.

Desc: School superintendents, principals, teachers, school board members, advisory board members, school volunteers, senior citizens, business representatives, and community groups. Provides strategic planning, program development, and communication for the formation and growth of effective partnerships. *Type:* Association.

National Association of Secondary School Principals

1904 Association Dr.   Ph: (703)860-0200
Reston, VA 20191   Free: 800-253-7746
    Fax: (703)476-5432
E-mail: nassp@nassp.org
URL: http://www.nassp.org

Contact: Dr. Gerald N. Tirozzi, Exec.Dir.

Desc: High school and middle head school principals and assistant principals; other persons engaged in secondary school administration and/or supervision; college professors teaching courses in secondary education. Sponsors National Association of Student Councils, National Honor Society, National Association of Student Activity Advisers, Partnerships International and National Junior Honor Society. Conducts competitions. *Type:* Association.

National Association of State Boards of Education

1012 Cameron St.   Ph: (703)684-4000
Alexandria, VA 22314   Fax: (703)836-2313
E-mail: boards@nasbe.org
URL: http://www.nasbe.org

Contact: Brendal Welburn, Exec.Dir.

Desc: Members of state and territorial boards of education. Aims are to: study problems of mutual interest and concern, improving communication and cooperation among the state boards; maintain an effective liaison with educator groups; exchange and disseminate information concerning educational programs and activities; coordinate activities and studies toward a nationwide consensus on education. *Type:* Association.

National Association of Student Activity Advisers

1904 Association Dr.   Ph: (703)860-0200
Reston, VA 20191   Fax: (703)476-5432
E-mail: nassp@nassp.org
URL: http://www.nassp.org

Contact: Rocco Marano, Dir.

Desc: School organization advisers, directors of student activities, deans, assistant principals, and administrators affiliated with student activity programs. Supports student involvement in the educational process and promotes leadership training. Maintains library of information concerning students and youth activity. *Type:* Association.

National Association of Student Councils

1904 Association Dr.   Ph: (703)860-0200
Reston, VA 20191   Fax: (703)476-5432
E-mail: nasc@nassp.org
URL: http://www.nassp.org/dsa

Contact: Rocco Marano, Dir.

Desc: Student councils in secondary schools. To develop student government; to improve student-teacher relationships; to assist in the management of the school; to provide orderly direction of student activities; to charter school clubs and other organizations. *Type:* Association.

National Center for Community Education

1017 Avon St.   Ph: (810)238-0463
Flint, MI 48503   Fax: (810)238-9211
E-mail: ncce@tir.com

Contact: Dan Cady, Exec. Dir.

Desc: To provide short-term training workshops for persons entering and/or working in the field of community education. *Type:* Association.

National Center for Education Statistics
U.S. Department of Education - National Center for Education Statistics
600 Independence Ave. SW   Ph: (202)219-1828
Washington, DC 20202-0498   Free: 800-USA-
                                          LEARN
                                 Fax: (202)401-2000
E-mail: NCESwebmaster@ed.gov
URL: http://nces.ed.gov/
Desc: The National Center for Education Statistics (NCES) is the primary Federal agency responsible for the collection, analysis and the reporting of data related to education in the United States. It was established to collect and report "...statistics and information showing the condition and progress of education in the United States and other nations in order to promote and accelerate the improvement of American education." The site includes a wealth of information on publications, educational statistics, state and national projects, information and linkages to state departments of education, education news, available services, experts by topic, collaborative educational partnerships, and results from a variety of educational surveys. *Type:* Database.

National Conference of Diocesan Directors of Religious Education
3021 4th St. NE   Ph: (202)636-3826
Washington, DC 20017-1102   Fax: (202)832-2712
Contact: Neil Parent, Exec.Dir.
Desc: Diocesan directors of religious education and their staff; publishers, academics, Diocesan religious education, Associations, and individuals interested in religious education. Fosters communication and unity among members. *Type:* Association.

National Council of Educational Opportunity Associations
1025 Vermont Ave. NW, Ste.   Ph: (202)347-7430
  1201   Fax: (202)347-0786
Washington, DC 20005
Contact: Arnold Mitchem, Exec.Dir.
Desc: Regional organizations concerned with increasing educational opportunities for lower income students in higher education. *Type:* Association.

National Education Association
1201 16th St. NW   Ph: (202)833-4000
Washington, DC 20036   Fax: (202)822-7767
URL: http://www.nea.org
Contact: Don Cameron, Exec.Dir.
Desc: Professional organization and union of elementary and secondary school teachers, college and university professors, administrators, principals, counselors, and others concerned with education. *Type:* Association.

National Foundation for the Improvement of Education
1201 16th St. NW   Ph: (202)822-7840
Washington, DC 20036-3207   Fax: (202)822-7779
URL: http://www.nfie.org
Contact: Dr. Judith . Renyi, Exec.Dir.
Desc: Seeks to improve the quality of education in the nation's public schools by ensuring that teachers have access to on-going, high-quality and strategic professional development throughout their careers. *Type:* Association.

National Head Start Association
1651 Prince St.   Ph: (703)739-0875
Alexandria, VA 22314   Fax: (703)739-0878
URL: http://www.nhsa.org
Contact: Sarah M. Greene, CEO.
Desc: Members of National Head Start Parent Association, National Head Start Directors Association, National Head Start Staff Association, National Head Start Friends Association, and others interested in the Head Start Program. Upgrades the quality and quantity of Head Start Program services. *Type:* Association.

National Institute for Applied Behavioral Science
300 N. Lee St., No. 300   Ph: (703)548-8840
Alexandria, VA 22314   Free: 800-277-4685
                                Fax: (703)548-3179
E-mail: info@ntl.org
URL: http://www.ntl.org
Contact: Diane Porter, Pres./CEO.
Desc: Nonprofit corporation offering training, consultation, research, and publication services. *Type:* Association.

National Middle School Association
4151 Executive Parkway, Ste.   Ph: (614)895-4730
  300   Free: 800-528-6672
Westerville, OH 43081   Fax: (614)895-4750
URL: http://www.nmsa.org
Contact: Sue Swaim, Exec.Dir.
Desc: Educators and laypeople interested in middle school education. Promotes the development and growth of the middle school as a distinct and necessary entity in the structure of American education; provides forums for the sharing of ideas and innovations; cooperates with organizations and associations with common interests. *Type:* Association.

National School Boards Association
1680 Duke St.   Ph: (703)838-6722
Alexandria, VA 22314-3493   Fax: (703)683-7590
URL: http://www.nsba.org
Contact: Dr. Anne L. Bryant, Exec.Dir.
Desc: Federation of state school boards associations and the boards of education in the District of Columbia, Guam, Hawaii, the Virgin Islands, and Puerto Rico. Advocates equity for primary and secondary public school children through legal counsel, research studies, programs and services for members, annual conferences, and magazines. *Type:* Association.

NEA Now
National Education Association (NEA)
NEA Professional Library
1201 16th St., NW   Ph: (202)833-4000
Washington, DC 20036   Free: 800-229-4200
                                Fax: (202)822-7974
E-mail: plibz@aol.com
URL: http://www.nea.org
Contact: Steve Lemken, Editor.
Desc: Offers Association news and leadership ideas for professional educators in elementary- through college-level positions. *Type:* Newsletter.

NEA Today
National Education Association (NEA)
NEA Professional Library
1201 16th St., NW   Ph: (202)833-4000
Washington, DC 20036   Free: 800-229-4200
                                Fax: (202)822-7974
E-mail: plibz@aol.com
URL: http://www.nea.org
Contact: Bill Fischer, Editor; Sam Pizzigati, Publisher; Suzanne Wade, Advertising Coord.
Desc: Education magazine. *Type:* Periodical.

Nebraska State Education Association
605 S. 14th St.   Ph: (402)475-7611
Lincoln, NE 68508   Free: 800-742-0047
                                Fax: (402)475-2630
URL: http://www.nsea.org
Contact: James R. Griess, Exec.Dir.
Desc: Represents members' interests; conducts lobbying activities. Holds seminars and workshops. *Type:* Association.

New Jersey Education Association
180 W. State St.   Ph: (609)599-4561
PO Box 1211
Trenton, NJ 08607
Contact: Robert Bonazzi, Exec.Dir.
Desc: Labor union for teachers. Promotes educational interests' of New Jersey; equal educational opportunity for all students; and the interests of employees. *Type:* Association.

New York State Congress of Parents and Teachers
1 Wembley Sq.   Ph: (518)452-8808
Albany, NY 12205-3830   Fax: (518)452-8105
Contact: Carolyn Fiori, Pres.
Desc: Parents and teachers. Promotes the welfare of children. *Type:* Association.

New York State United Teachers
159 Wolf Rd.   Ph: (518)459-5400
Box 15008   Free: 800-342-9810
Albany, NY 12212-5008   Fax: (518)454-6450
Contact: Thomas Y. Hobart, Pres.
Desc: Educators organized to protect and advance industry interests. *Type:* Association.

The New York Teacher
New York State United Teachers
159 Wolf Rd., Box 15-008   Ph: (518)459-5400
Albany, NY 12212-5008   Fax: (518)459-6736
URL: http://www.nysut.org
Contact: Deborah Hormel Ward, Editor; Sheryl M. Allen, Advertising Coordinator.
Desc: Publication focusing on education in the United States. *Type:* Periodical.

News for You
New Readers Press
PO Box 131   Ph: (315)422-9121
Syracuse, NY 13210   Free: 800-448-8878
                                Fax: (315)422-5561
E-mail: nfy@laubach.org.
URL: http://www.newreaderspress.com
Contact: Heidi Stephens, Editor, fax: (315)422-6369, hstephens@laubach.org.
Desc: Adult basic education, high school remedial, and easy English (ESL) newspaper. *Type:* Periodical.

Nigerian Students Union in the Americas
c/o Granville U. Osuji
654 Girard St. NW, Apt. 512
Washington, DC 20001-2936
Contact: Granville U. Osuji, Contact.
Desc: Nigerian students at institutions of higher learning in North and South America and neighboring islands. Disseminates information about Nigeria and Africa; cooperates with other African student unions in the Americas and with Nigerian student unions in Nigeria and other parts of the world. Maintains placement service and speakers' bureau. *Type:* Association.

NJEA Review
New Jersey Education Association
180 W. State St.   Ph: (609)599-4561
Box 1211   Fax: (609)392-6321
Trenton, NJ 08607
Contact: Martha De Blieu, Editor; Eileen Lake, Advertising Mgr.
Desc: Educational journal for public school employees. *Type:* Periodical.

Northwest Regional Educational Laboratory

Northwest Regional Educational Laboratory
101 SW Main St., Ste. 500   Ph: (503)275-9500
Portland, OR 97204
E-mail: webmaster@nwrel.org
URL: http://www.nwrel.org/
Desc: The Northwest Regional Educational Laboratory's (NWREL) site was created to give information about research and development activities in delivering equitable, high-quality educational programs for children, youth, and adults. NWREL provides research and development assistance to education, government, community agencies, business, and labor. *Type:* Database.

Ohio Congress of Parents and Teachers

Barbara Sprague
40 Northwoods Blvd., Ste. A   Ph: (614)781-6344
Columbus, OH 43235-4718   Free: 800-699-6628
    Fax: (614)781-6349
Contact: Barbara Sprague, Exec.Admin.
Desc: Parents and teachers of public school students. Promotes the education, health, and welfare of children. *Type:* Association.

Ohio Education Association

225 E. Broad St.   Ph: (614)228-4526
PO Box 2550   Free: 800-282-1500
Columbus, OH 43216   Fax: (614)228-8771
E-mail: sunderme@oea.columbus.oh.us
URL: http://www.oea.columbus.oh.us
Contact: William Sundermeyer, Exec.Dir.
Type: Association.

Ohio Schools

Ohio Education Association
225 E. Broad St.   Ph: (614)227-3050
Box 2550   Free: 800-282-1500
Columbus, OH 43216   Fax: (614)224-5659
Contact: Julie Newhall, Editor; Maxine Flynn, Advertising Asst., flynnmax@oea.columbus.oh.us.
Desc: Magazine for education professionals in Ohio. *Type:* Periodical.

Ontario Education Resources Information System

Ontario Institute for Studies in Education of the University of Toronto
Ozseiut Library
252 Bloor St. W., 3rd Floor   Ph: (416)923-6641
Toronto, ON, Canada M5S 1V6
URL: http://www.oise.utoronto.ca
Desc: Contains more than 18,000 citations, with abstracts, to educational research reports, curriculum guidelines, learning materials for elementary and secondary schools, policy papers, and related materials prepared or sponsored by the Ministry of Education, the Ministry of Colleges and Universities, school boards, and other educational organizations and agencies in Ontario, Canada. Information provided on each document includes title, material type (e.g., research, textbook), language, author, corporate author, publication information, date, educational level, target population, special features and/or components, funding source, contact person, and availability. *Available:* Ontario Institute for Studies in Education of the University of Toronto, Ozseiut Library. *Type:* Database.

The Oryx Guide to Distance Learning

Oryx Press
4041 N. Central Ave., Ste. 700   Ph: (602)265-2651
Phoenix, AZ 85012-3397   Free: 800-279-6799
    Fax: 800-279-4663
E-mail: info@oryxpress.com

URL: http://www.oryxpress.com
Contact: William Burgess, Editor.
Desc: 115 institutions offering 1,500 courses in independent study, including colleges, universities, umbrella organizations, and official state groups. *Type:* Directory.

OTF (FEO) Interaction

Ontario Teachers' Federation
1260 Bay St., Ste. 700   Ph: (416)966-3424
Toronto, ON, Canada M5R 2B5   Fax: (416)966-5450
Contact: Kathleen Devlin, Editor, kathdevl@enoreo.on.ca.
Desc: Education periodical. *Type:* Periodical.

Parent Cooperative Pre-Schools International

Leta Mach
1401 New York Ave. NW, Ste. 1100   Free: 800-636-6222
Washington, DC 20005-2102
URL: http://www.cooperative.org
Contact: Leta Mach, Liaison.
Desc: Individuals and groups in 6 countries interested in preschool education in nonprofit nursery schools operated by parents on a cooperative basis. Provides information and research services for members; collects manuals and educational materials pertaining to parent cooperative preschools; encourages exchange of ideas and experiences among member schools. *Type:* Association.

Patterson's American Education

Educational Directories Inc.
PO Box 199   Ph: (847)459-0605
Mount Prospect, IL 60056-0199   Free: 800-357-6183
    Fax: (847)459-0608
E-mail: edi@ameritech.net
Contact: Wayne Moody, Editor.
Desc: Over 11,400 school districts in the United States; more than 34,000 public, private, and Catholic high schools, middle schools, and junior high schools; approximately 300 parochial superintendents; 400 territorial schools; 400 state department of education personnel; 400 educational associations. *Type:* Directory.

Pennsylvania Education

Bureau of Press & Communications
Pennsylvania State Department of Education
333 Market St.   Ph: (717)783-9802
Harrisburg, PA 17126-0333   Fax: (717)783-4517
Desc: Provides teachers, administrators, and other educators with information on education in Pennsylvania, kindergarten through college. Carries news of teaching grants and awards, scholarship programs for students, current educational legislation, and new educational methods and projects tried in schools across the state. *Type:* Newsletter.

Pennsylvania State Education Association

400 N. Third St.   Ph: (717)255-7000
Harrisburg, PA 17101   Free: 800-944-7732
    Fax: (717)255-7124
Contact: Carmen J. Matino, Exec.Dir.
Desc: Education Association that provides labor union services, for elementary and high school teachers, social workers, psychologists, hygienists, school employees and health care workers. Conducts lobbying activities; holds seminars; develops education reform proposals. *Type:* Association.

Per Scholas

131 Walnut Ave., 6th Fl.   Ph: (718)292-2300
Bronx, NY 10454   Free: 800-877-4068
    Fax: (718)292-4736
E-mail: info@perscholas.org
URL: http://www.perscholas.org

Contact: Dr. Deborah MacFarlane, Contact.
Desc: Works to provide schools with new computers at the lowest cost. *Type:* Association.

Peterson's GRADLINE

Peterson's
202 Carnegie Center   Ph: (609)243-9111
PO Box 2123
Princeton, NJ 08540
E-mail: peters.custsvc@pgi.petersons.com
URL: http://www.petersons.com
Desc: Contains descriptions of more than 30,000 graduate and professional education programs in more than 300 academic disciplines offered by more than 1440 accredited colleges and universities in the U.S. and Canada. *Available:* CompuServe Information Service, Knowledge Index; SilverPlatter Information, Inc.; The Gale Group, InfoTrac Web. *Type:* Database.

Peterson's Learning Adventures Around the World

Peterson's
202 Carnegie Center   Ph: (609)243-9111
PO Box 2123   Free: 800-338-3282
Princeton, NJ 08543-2123   Fax: (609)243-9150
URL: http://www.peterson.com; http://www.petersons.com.
Contact: Ellen Beal, Editor.
Desc: Approximately 1,800 learning vacations; international coverage. *Type:* Directory.

Peterson's Sports Scholarships

Peterson's
202 Carnegie Center   Ph: (609)243-9111
PO Box 2123   Free: 800-338-3282
Princeton, NJ 08543-2123   Fax: (609)243-9150
URL: http://www.peterson.com; http://www.petersons.com.
Desc: Over 1,400 four-year and 400 two-year colleges in the U.S. that maintain athletic programs that often provide scholarships. *Type:* Directory.

Peterson's Study Abroad

Peterson's
202 Carnegie Center   Ph: (609)243-9111
PO Box 2123   Free: 800-338-3282
Princeton, NJ 08543-2123   Fax: (609)243-9150
URL: http://www.peterson.com; http://www.petersons.com.
Contact: Ellen Beal, Editor.
Desc: Academic year and semester Study Abroad programs. *Type:* Directory.

Peterson's Vocational and Technical Schools and Programs

Peterson's
202 Carnegie Center   Ph: (609)243-9111
PO Box 2123   Free: 800-338-3282
Princeton, NJ 08543-2123   Fax: (609)243-9150
URL: http://www.peterson.com
Contact: Diane Hepburn, Editor.
Desc: Approximately 5,800 accredited vocational and technical schools that offer training programs in over 370 career fields. Available in separate eastern and western U.S. regional editions. *Type:* Directory.

Phi Theta Kappa, International Honor Society

PO Box 13729   Ph: (601)957-2241
Jackson, MS 39236-3729   Free: 800-946-9995
    Fax: (601)957-2625
URL: http://www.ptk.org
Contact: Rod A. Risley, Exec.Dir.
Desc: International honor society - men and women, education (two-year colleges). Administers an alumni association. Sponsors Honors Institute and National Leadership Development Program. *Type:* Association.

Pi Lambda Theta

4101 E. 3rd St.   Ph: (812)339-3411
PO Box 6626   Free: 800-487-3411
Bloomington, IN 47407-6626   Fax: (812)339-3462
E-mail: root@pilambda.org
URL: http://www.pilambda.org
Contact: J. Ogden Hamilton.

Desc: Founded by educators inn 1910, Pi Lambda Theta is the oldest national honor society in the field of education. The association maintains the highest academic admission standards, and also recognizes certification by the National Board for Professional Teaching Standards as a sufficcient criterion for admission, Its Career Services Network consists of searchable job listings, a member resume database, and a network of members who have volunteered to assist in member job searches. The national biennial leadership conference employs facilitator-assisted, participant-focused format. *Type:* Association.

Professional and Occupational Licensing Directory

Gale Group Inc.
27500 Drake Rd.   Ph: (248)699-4253
Farmington Hills, MI 48331-   Free: 800-877-GALE
3535   Fax: (248)699-8070
E-mail: galeord@galegroup.com
URL: http://www.galegroup.com.; http://www.gale.com.
Contact: David Bianco, Editor.

Desc: Approximately 9,400 listings of national and state licensing information for all occupations that require licensing, registration, or certification in the United States. *Type:* Directory.

Project Appleseed: The National Campaign for Public School Improvement

7209 Dorset at Midland Blvd.   Ph: (314)726-0536
St. Louis, MO 63130   Fax: (314)725-2319
E-mail: pledgenow@aol.com
URL: http://www.a-zuc.com/org/apples/index.htm
Contact: Kevin S. Walker, Pres.

Desc: Advocates the improvement in public education by increasing parental involvement in all of the public school districts in the country. *Type:* Association.

Public Education Network

601 13th St., Ste. 290 N   Ph: (202)628-7460
Washington, DC 20005   Fax: (202)628-1893
E-mail: pefnet@petnet.org
URL: http://www.PEFNet.org/PEN
Contact: Wendy D. Puriefoy, Pres.

Desc: Promotes improved public education through the development of local education funds (LEFs). (A local education fund is a community-based, nonprofit organization dedicated to improving public school system by broadening the constituency of support for public education and working toward school improvement.) Provides information and technical assistance on LEFs to interested parties. Services include telephone and on-site consultation, conferences and seminars, data and survey information, and materials on LEFs. *Type:* Association.

Public Schools of North Carolina Infoweb

N.C. Department of Public Instruction
Raleigh, NC 27601-2825
URL: http://www.dpi.state.nc.us/
Contact: pcory@dpi.state.nc.us.

Desc: The Public Schools of North Carolina Infoweb provides information for teachers, parents, and other interested parties. Employment opportunities are also listed. *Type:* Database.

Quest International

PO Box 4850   Ph: (614)522-6400
Newark, OH 43058-4850   Fax: (614)522-6580
E-mail: questnet@alink.com
URL: http://www.quest.edu
Contact: Rick Little, CEO.

Desc: Aids in helping students, parents, and teachers, kindergarten through 12th grade, to learn basic life skills in areas of problem solving, interpersonal communication, increasing self-esteem, prevention of drug and alcohol abuse, and conflict resolution. Sponsors 3-day workshops for teachers, counselors, and other professionals and leadership training for students and parents to assist in continuing the effort at the community level. Offers seminars on parent, student, and community involvement; provides children's services; maintains speakers' bureau; conducts research. *Type:* Association.

Reading Is Fundamental

600 Maryland Ave. SW, Ste.   Ph: (202)287-3220
600   Free: 877-743-7323
Washington, DC 20024   Fax: (202)287-3196
URL: http://www.si.edu/rif
Contact: Dr. William Trueheart, Pres.

Desc: Volunteer groups composed of community leaders, educators, librarians, parents, and service club members who sponsor local grass roots reading motivation programs serving 3,750,000 children nationwide. Purpose is to involve youngsters, preschool to high school age, in reading activities aimed at showing that reading is fun. Provides services to parents to help them encourage reading in the home. *Type:* Association.

Reading Today

International Reading Association
800 Barksdale Rd.   Ph: (302)731-1600
PO Box 8139   Free: 800-336-7323
Newark, DE 19714-8139   Fax: (302)731-1057
E-mail: readingtoday@reading.org.
Contact: John Micklos, Jr., Editor, jmicklos@reading.org; Linda Hunter, Advertising Mgr.

Desc: Professional newspaper of the International Reading Association. *Type:* Periodical.

Renaissance Educational Associates

4817 N. County Rd. 29   Ph: (303)679-4309
Loveland, CO 80538   Fax: (303)679-4233
Contact: Kristy Clark, Pres.

Desc: Education professionals and others who believe that educators should "exemplify the finest, most beautiful and noble examples of the creative process of living." Seeks to provide a "focus of maturity and integrity in education." Offers summer leadership institute. Conducts seminars, workshops, and public talks for educators, parents, and other groups interested in creative and integrative education. Maintains speakers' bureau. *Type:* Association.

Research for Better Schools

Research for Better Schools
444 N. 3rd St.   Fax: (215)574-0133
Philadelphia, PA 19123-4107
E-mail: webmaster@www.rbs.org
URL: http://www.rbs.org/

Desc: The Research for Better Schools database announces seminars, conferences, workshops, publications, and products of interest to K-12 educators. The RBS database contains information of interest to educators including studies in applied research, communications, national networking, publications, needs assessment and evaluation, rural education, state assistance, transitions in early learning, urban education, and a math and science consortium. *Type:* Database.

Rural Education Directory: Organizations and Resources

ERIC Clearinghouse on Rural Education and Small Schools
Appalachia Educational   Ph: (304)347-0400
   Laboratory   Free: 800-624-9120
1031 Quarrier St.   Fax: (304)347-0487
PO Box 1348
Charleston, WV 25325-1348
E-mail: ericrc@ael.org; ericrc@ael.org.
URL: http://www.ael.org.
Contact: Patricia Cahape Hammer, Editor.

Desc: Organizations and resources (nongovernment organizations, federal and state government agencies, and journals) involved in rural education. *Type:* Directory.

Salzburg Seminar

c/o The Marble Works   Ph: (802)388-0007
2 Maple Street   Fax: (802)388-1030
Box 886
Middlebury, VT 05753
E-mail: info@fc.salsem.org
Contact: Olin Robison, Pres.

Desc: Promotes intercultural, interdisciplinary dialogue among conceptual thinkers and policymakers and mid-career professionals of demonstrated performance and potential. Fosters the development of a global community through the widening of personal, intellectual, and cultural horizons. Encourages a deepened respect for the experience and perceptions of others. *Type:* Association.

Scholarships, Fellowships and Loans

Gale Group Inc.
27500 Drake Rd.   Ph: (248)699-4253
Farmington Hills, MI 48331-   Free: 800-877-GALE
3535   Fax: (248)699-8070
E-mail: galeord@galegroup.com
URL: http://www.galegroup.com.; http://www.gale.com.
Contact: Donna Batten, Editor.

Desc: Over 3,700 sources of education related financial aid for students and professionals at all level of study. *Type:* Directory.

Scholastic Action

Scholastic, Inc.
555 Broadway   Ph: (212)343-6100
New York, NY 10012   Free: 800-724-6527
                      Fax: (212)343-4535
E-mail: custserv@scholastic.com
URL: http://www.scholastic.com
Contact: Lara Galen, Editor; Dick Robinson, Publisher.

Desc: Reading magazine for grades 7-9. *Type:* Periodical.

Scholastic News Citizen Edition

Scholastic, Inc.
555 Broadway   Ph: (212)343-6100
New York, NY 10012   Free: 800-724-6527
                      Fax: (212)343-4535
E-mail: custserv@scholastic.com
URL: http://www.scholastic.com
Contact: John Lent, Publisher.

Desc: Magazine for 5th grade school children. *Type:* Periodical.

Scholastic News Explorer Edition

Scholastic, Inc.
555 Broadway   Ph: (212)343-6100
New York, NY 10012   Free: 800-724-6527
                      Fax: (212)343-4535
E-mail: custserv@scholastic.com
URL: http://www.scholastic.com
Contact: John Lent, Publisher.

Desc: Magazine for 4th grade school children. *Type:* Periodical.

Scholastic News Newstime Edition

Scholastic, Inc.
555 Broadway   Ph: (212)343-6100
New York, NY 10012   Free: 800-724-6527
                      Fax: (212)343-4535
E-mail: custserv@scholastic.com
URL: http://www.scholastic.com
Contact: John Lent, Editor and Publisher; Edward Chenetz, Advertising Mgr.
Desc: Magazine for 5th and 6th grade school children.
Type: Periodical.

Scholastic News Pilot Edition

Scholastic, Inc.
555 Broadway   Ph: (212)343-6100
New York, NY 10012   Free: 800-724-6527
                      Fax: (212)343-4535
E-mail: custserv@scholastic.com
URL: http://www.scholastic.com
Contact: John Lent, Publisher.
Desc: Magazine for 1st grade school children. *Type:* Periodical.

Scholastic News Ranger Edition

Scholastic, Inc.
555 Broadway   Ph: (212)343-6100
New York, NY 10012   Free: 800-724-6527
                      Fax: (212)343-4535
E-mail: custserv@scholastic.com
URL: http://www.scholastic.com
Contact: John Lent, Publisher.
Desc: Magazine for 2nd grade school children. *Type:* Periodical.

Scholastic News Trails Edition

Scholastic, Inc.
555 Broadway   Ph: (212)343-6100
New York, NY 10012   Free: 800-724-6527
                      Fax: (212)343-4535
E-mail: custserv@scholastic.com
URL: http://www.scholastic.com
Contact: John Lent, Publisher.
Desc: Magazine for 3rd grade school children. *Type:* Periodical.

Scholastic Scope

Scholastic, Inc.
555 Broadway   Ph: (212)343-6100
New York, NY 10012   Free: 800-724-6527
                      Fax: (212)343-4535
E-mail: custserv@scholastic.com
URL: http://www.scholastic.com
Contact: Denise Rinaldo, Editor; Hugh Roome, Publisher; G. Eastabrook Kindred, Advertising Mgr.
Desc: Language arts magazine for students in grades 6-12.
Type: Periodical.

Scholastic Update

Scholastic, Inc.
555 Broadway   Ph: (212)343-6100
New York, NY 10012   Free: 800-724-6527
                      Fax: (212)343-4535
E-mail: custserv@scholastic.com
URL: http://www.scholastic.com
Contact: Steven Manning, Editor; Hugh Roome, Publisher; G. Brooke Kindred, Advertising Mgr.
Desc: Social studies magazine for grades 8-12 (high school network comprised of: Scholastic Update, Choices, Voice, Scope, and Science World). *Type:* Periodical.

School Marketing Newsletter

School Market Research Institute Inc.
PO Box 10   Ph: (860)345-4018
1721 Saybrook Rd.   Fax: (860)345-3985
Haddam, CT 06438-0010
E-mail: school.market@snet.net
Contact: Lynn Vosburgh, Editor; Robert Stimolo, Publisher.
Desc: Provides information about marketing to schools. Includes statistics, market trends, and expert advice. *Type:* Newsletter.

School Planning and Management—Annual Buyers Guide Issue

Peter Li, Inc.
330 Progress Rd.   Ph: (937)847-5900
Dayton, OH 45449   Free: 800-523-4625
                      Fax: (937)847-5910
Contact: Jane Lieberth, Editor, jlieberth@aol.com.
Desc: Lists of manufacturers and suppliers of products and services to educational facilities and systems. *Type:* Directory.

Schoolhouse Videos and CDs

Schoolhouse Videos & More
400 Morris Ave.   Ph: 888-724-6654
Long Branch, NJ 07740
E-mail: school@nando.net
URL: http://www.schoolroom.com
Desc: This site is a gold mine for homeschoolers, students, and teachers alike. Check out their vast subject matter lists and extensive selection of more than 7,000 educational videos and CDS and then order online. *Type:* Database.

Science Training Program Directory for Teachers & Students

Science Service, Inc.
1719 N St. NW   Ph: (202)785-2255
Washington, DC 20036 Fax: (202)785-1243
E-mail: sciedu@sciserv.org
URL: http://www.sciserv.org.
Contact: Sharon Manley, Editor.
Desc: Institutions of higher education offering nearly 500 programs in science, engineering, and mathematics to high school students; programs cover material and laboratory study not usually available in secondary schools. *Type:* Directory.

SIS Workbook

Seminar Information Service, Inc. (SIS)
17752 Skypark Circle, Ste. 210   Ph: (949)261-9104
Irvine, CA 92614   Fax: (949)261-1963
E-mail: seminfo@aol.com
URL: http://www.seminarinformation.com.
Contact: Catherine Bellizzi, President.
Desc: Over 700 sponsors of more than 100,000 business and technical seminars. *Type:* Directory.

Southern Association of Colleges and Schools

1866 Southern Ln.   Ph: (404)679-4500
Decatur, GA 30033   Fax: (404)679-4533
URL: http://www.sacs.org
Contact: Dr. James T. Rogers, Chief Adm. Off.
Desc: Colleges, universities, secondary schools, and elementary schools in Alabama, Florida, Georgia, Kentucky, Louisiana, Mississippi, North Carolina, South Carolina, Tennessee, Texas, Virginia, and Latin America, accredited by an appropriate commission. *Type:* Association.

State Student Association of Massachusetts

162 Boylston St.   Ph: (617)357-1995
Boston, MA 02116
Contact: Joseph A. Langis, Exec.Dir.

Desc: Undergraduate and graduate students attending public institutions of higher learning. Lobbies for students to the state legislature as well as boards of trustees for public institutions. *Type:* Association.

Student Contact Book

Gale Group Inc.
27500 Drake Rd.   Ph: (248)699-4253
Farmington Hills, MI 48331-   Free: 800-877-GALE
3535   Fax: (248)699-8070
E-mail: galeord@galegroup.com; galenp@mail.msen.com.
URL: http://www.galegroup.com.; http://www.gale.com.
Contact: Annette Novallo, Editor.
Desc: 800 organizations and 300 publications of interest to students from junior high school through community college levels who are preparing papers and speeches on topics of current interest or who are investigating career opportunities; includes associations, clearinghouses, government agencies, and companies that provide information free or for less than $25, as well as biographical sources. *Type:* Directory.

studyabroad.com - Study Abroad Programs Directory

studyabroad.com
265 E. Dutton Mill Rd.   Ph: (610)494-5095
Aston, PA 19014   Fax: (610)497-3812
E-mail: webmaster@studyabroad.com
URL: http://www.studyabroad.com/
Desc: When you're ready to expand your education to an international level, turn to this database to find an extensive listing of study abroad programs for students at all stages in their schooling. Search for programs by country and you'll be presented with lists of dozens of options for education, internships, experience, and training. *Type:* Database.

Teacher Magazine

Editorial Projects in Education, Inc.
6935 Arlington Rd., Ste. 100   Ph: (301)280-3100
Bethesda, MD 20814   Fax: (301)280-3250
E-mail: ads@epe.org; tm@epe.org.
Contact: Ronald A. Wolk, Editor; Carolyn Kaye, Assoc. Publisher; Michael McKennna, Advertising Dir.
Desc: Professional magazine for elementary and secondary teachers. *Type:* Periodical.

Teaching/K-8

Teaching/K-8
40 Richards Ave.   Ph: (203)855-2650
Norwalk, CT 06854-2509   Free: 800-249-9363
                      Fax: (203)855-2656
E-mail: teachingk8@aol.com.
Contact: Patricia Broderick, Editorial Dir., pat@teachingk-8.com; Allen A. Raymond, Publisher, allen@teachingk-8.com.
Desc: Magazine for elementary teachers. *Type:* Periodical.

Technology Student Association

1914 Association Dr. Ph: (703)860-9000
Reston, VA 20191   Fax: (703)758-4852
E-mail: tsa@iris.org
URL: http://www.tsawww.org
Contact: Dr. Rosanne T. White, Exec.Dir.
Desc: Elementary, junior high, and senior high school students who are presently enrolled in or have completed technology education courses. Goals are to assist students in making informed occupational choices through experiences in technology programs and to help prepare them for entry into technology-related careers. Provides opportunities for students to meet and work with leaders from industry to gain career information and to adapt learning experiences from other instructional areas. *Type:* Association.

T.H.E. Journal

T. H. E. Journal
150 El Camino Real, No. 112   Ph: (714)730-4011
Tustin, CA 92780   Fax: (714)730-3739
E-mail: wladuke@thejournal.com
URL: http://www.thejournal.com.

Contact: Bill Willis, Managing Editor, editorial@
thejournal.com; Wendy LaDuke, Publisher, wladuke@
thejournal.com.

Desc: Application of technology journal for educators and
administrators in higher ed ucation, K-12 and industry
training. *Type:* Periodical.

Thought & Action

*National Education Association of the United
States*
1201 16th St. NW   Ph: (202)822-7214
Washington, DC 20036   Fax: (202)822-7206
URL: http://www.nea.org/he.

Contact: Con Lehane, Editor, clehane@nea.org.

Desc: Journal covering higher education. *Type:* Periodical.

Tidings

*National School Supply and Equipment
Association*
8300 Colesville Rd., Ste. 250   Ph: (301)495-0240
Silver Spring, MD 20910-3243   Free: 800-395-5550
                                     Fax: (301)495-3330
E-mail: nssea@nssea.org
URL: http://www.nssea.com.

Contact: Kathy Jentz, Editor.

Desc: Presents general school supply and equipment industry news. Provides articles on the economy and its impact
on education, and items on general management methods.
Type: Newsletter.

The Training Information Source

Training Information Source, Inc.
1424 Clayton St., Ste. 200   Ph: (303)698-8181
Denver, CO 80210   Fax: (303)698-8139
E-mail: info@training-info.com
URL: http://www.training-info.com/

Desc: If you or someone in your company needs training
- in computers, writing, management skills, practically
anything - this site might be a good first place to turn to
locate sources of training in your area. This database can
be searched via keyword or phrase, with searches narrowed
by location, subject matter, trainer name, and type. *Type:*
Database.

TSTA Advocate

Texas State Teachers Association
316 W. 12th St.   Ph: (512)476-5355
Austin, TX 78701   Fax: (512)469-0766
Contact: Debbie Mohondro, Editor.

Desc: Educational journal. *Type:* Periodical.

UniGuide Academic Guide to the Internet

Aldea Communications, Inc.
2380 Camino Vida Roble, Ste.   Ph: (760)929-0580
   A   Fax: (760)929-0580
Carlsbad, CA 92009
E-mail: info@aldea.com; uniguide@aldea.com.
URL: http://ds.internic.net/aldea/.

Desc: Approximately 2,000 web sites in academia, including biological sciences; computer and information sciences; education and human resources; engineering;
geosciences; mathematical and physical sciences; social,
behavioral, and economic sciences; liberal arts. *Type:* Directory.

United Board for Christian Higher Education in Asia

475 Riverside Dr., Rm. 1221   Ph: (212)870-2601
New York, NY 10115   Fax: (212)870-2322
E-mail: staff@ubchea.org
URL: http://www.unitedboard.org

Contact: Dr. David W. Vikner, Pres.

Desc: Works with 80 Christian and state colleges, universities, and associations of universities in China and East and
Southeast Asian countries. *Type:* Association.

University of Toronto Magazine

University of Toronto
Department of Public Affairs
21 King's College Circle   Ph: (416)978-5947
Toronto, ON, Canada M5S 3J3   Fax: (416)978-1632

Contact: Karina Dahlin, Editor; Karen Hanley, Editor.

Desc: Alumni magazine. *Alt. Contact:* telephone:
(416)978-2988; fax: (416)978-7430. *Type:* Periodical.

Up With People

1 International Court   Ph: (303)460-7100
Broomfield, CO 80021   Fax: (303)438-7301
E-mail: misc@upwithpeople.org
URL: http://www.upwithpeople.org

Contact: William H. Lively, Pres. & C.E.O.

Desc: Seeks to develop the potential in people to bring the
world together through friendship and understanding. Offers the Worldsmart program to students 17-25 using the
unique combination of international travel, multicultural
living, performing arts and community service. *Type:* Association.

Utah Congress of Parents and Teachers

1037 E South Temple   Ph: (801)359-3875
Salt Lake City, UT 84102   Free: 800-246-3875
                                     Fax: (801)537-7827
E-mail: utahpta@m.k12.ut.us
URL: http://www.pta.k12.ut.us

Contact: Barbara Willie.

Desc: Parents, teachers, students, principals, administrators, and others interested in uniting the forces of home,
school, and community in behalf of children and youth
enrolled in the state's school districts. *Type:* Association.

Virtual School Distributed Learning Community

Middle of Nowhere Web
9940 Bent Tree Ln.   Ph: (703)361-4751
Manassas, VA 20111-4234   Fax: (703)257-1823
URL: http://www.virtualschool.edu/index.html

Contact: Brad Cox, Ph.D., bcox@gmu.edu.

Desc: This phenomenal collection of articles and links to
articles covers issues of concern to persons using the Internet as a teaching and informational tool. Here you will
find dozens of articles on such topics as digital property,
big brother, cyberporn, economics, social construction,
Web technology, programming languages, and more.
Type: Database.

The VOICE for Education

Pennsylvania State Education Association
400 N. 3rd St.   Ph: (717)255-7134
PO Box 1724   Fax: (717)255-7124
Harrisburg, PA 17105

Contact: William H. Johnson, Jr., Editor, wjohnson@psea.
mail.org.

Desc: Newspaper (tabloid) reporting on current issues in
education for association members. *Type:* Periodical.

Vose Education Resources Page

Beaverton School District
16550 SW Merlo Rd.   Ph: (503)591-8000
Beaverton, OR 97006
E-mail: www@beavton.k12.or.us
URL: http://www.beavton.k12.or.us/vose/resources/
starter.html

Contact: Bill Shearer, Bill_Schearer@beavton.k12.or.us.

Desc: The Vose Education Resources Page provides information to introduce students and teachers to the Internet.
The database includes many links to numerous types of
educational materials in science, math, social studies, humanities, audio resources, and general education. *Type:*
Database.

Weekly Reader (Pre-K edition)

Weekly Reader Corp.
200 First Stamford Pl.   Ph: (203)705-3500
PO Box 120023   Fax: (203)705-1661
Stamford, CT 06912-0023

Contact: Sandra Maccarone, Editor-in-Chief, (203)638-
2452; Richard LeBrausseur, Publisher, (203)638-2667,
fax: (203)346-5994; Thaddeus Kozlowski, Vice President,
(203)638-2425, fax: (203)346-5964.

Desc: Educational newspaper for the pre-kindergarten
classroom. *Type:* Periodical.

WESTLAW® Education Databases

West Group
620 Opperman Dr.   Ph: (651)687-7000
St. Paul, MN 55164-0526
URL: http://www.westgroup.com

Contact: WEST Reference Attorneys. Toll free No. (800)
REF-ATTY.

Desc: Contains the complete text of U.S. federal court decisions, state court decisions from all 50 states and the District of Columbia, statutes and regulations, administrative
law publications, specialized files, and texts and periodicals
dealing with education, including such aspects as contracts, management of educational institutions, and the
rights and liabilities of teachers, administrators, students,
and elected officials. *Available:* West Group, WESTLAW.
Type: Database.

Who's Who among American High School Students

Educational Communications, Inc.
721 N. McKinley Rd.   Ph: (847)295-6650
Lake Forest, IL 60045   Fax: (847)295-3972
Contact: Paul C. Krouse, Editor.

Desc: About 719,000 United States high school students
who have been recommended for inclusion by their
schools or youth organizations on the basis of academic
attainment or leadership in extra-curricular activities, athletics, or community service, and who have maintained at
least a "B" grade point average. *Type:* Directory.

Willamette University

Willamette University
900 State St.   Ph: (503)370-6300
Salem, OR 97301
E-mail: webmaster@willamette.edu
URL: http://www.willamette.edu/

Desc: This site contains specific information about Willamette University in Salem, OR, and its surrounding
community. Includes information on how to apply, campus resources, alumni, and student life. *Type:* Database.

World Education

44 Farnsworth St.   Ph: (617)482-9485
Boston, MA 02210   Fax: (617)482-0617
E-mail: Wei@worlded.org
URL: http://www.worlded.com

Contact: Joel H. Lamstein, Pres.

Desc: Provides professional assistance to help design non-formal adult education programs. *Type:* Association.

YMCA of Greater New York, Vanderbilt Branch
224 E. 47th St.   Ph: (212)756-9600
New York, NY 10017   Fax: (212)755-7579
URL: http://www.ymcanyc.org
Contact: Betsy Jacobs, Exec. Officer.
Desc: Seeks to develop and improve the spiritual, social, mental, and physical well-being of children, young people and adults. Conducts charitable activities; sponsors sports competitions, includes guest rooms. *Type:* Association.

Young Children
National Association for the Education of Young Children
1509 16th St. NW   Ph: (202)232-8777
Washington, DC 20036-1426   Free: 800-424-2460
     Fax: (202)328-1846
E-mail: naeyc@naeyc.org; editorial@naeyc.org.
Contact: Polly Greenberg, Editor.
Desc: Professional journal on the education of young children (up to age 8). *Type:* Periodical.

Electrical

Action Committee for Rural Electrification
4301 Wilson Blvd.   Ph: (703)907-5826
Arlington, VA 22203-1860   Fax: (703)907-5516
E-mail: mike.wellwhan@nreca.org
Contact: Robert M. Dawson, Dir.
Desc: Rural electric cooperative directors, managers, consumers and employees. Advocates support for rural electrification. *Type:* Association.

Country Living (Ohio)
Ohio Rural Electric Cooperatives, Inc.
6677 Busch Blvd.   Ph: (614)846-5757
PO Box 26036   Fax: (614)846-7108
Columbus, OH 43226-0036
Contact: Jeff Brehm, Editor.
Desc: Magazine serving rural electricity cooperatives. *Type:* Periodical.

EGSA Powerline
Electrical Generating Systems Association (EGSA)
1650 S. Dixie Hwy.   Ph: (954)755-2677
Boca Raton, FL 33432-7462
Contact: James S. McMullen, Editor.
Desc: Contains news of the Association and articles on technological and legislative developments, new standards, and unusual applications for generator sets. Recurring features include news of members, news of research, convention and committee reports, and columns titled Industry News, Rep Rap, Distributors Corner, and Technical Advisor. *Type:* Newsletter.

Electric Consumer
Indiana Statewide Rural Electric Cooperative
PO Box 24517   Ph: (317)487-2220
Indianapolis, IN 46224   Free: 800-340-7362
     Fax: (317)247-5220
E-mail: ec@indremcs.org.
Contact: Emily Born Schilling, Editor, (317)487-2241, eschilli@indremcs.org; Richard G. Biever, Senior Editor, (317)487-2242, rbieverf@indremcs.org.
Desc: Rural electric cooperative magazine. *Type:* Periodical.

Electric Utility Benchmarking Association
4606 FM 1960 West, Ste. 300   Ph: (281)440-5044
Houston, TX 77069-9949   Fax: (281)440-6677
E-mail: euba@ebenchmarking.com
URL: http://www.euba.com
Contact: Mark Czarnecki, Exec. Officer.
Desc: Organizations who produce and/or distribute electricity. Works to identify the best business processes to assist members in delivering excellent services to their customers. *Type:* Association.

Electronic Chemical News
Chemical Week Associates
888 7th Ave., 26th Fl.   Ph: (212)621-4900
New York, NY 10106   Fax: (212)621-4949
Contact: David Hunter, Editor.
Desc: Covers market developments concerning electronic chemicals, materials, and processes used in the manufacture of computers and other electronic components. *Type:* Newsletter.

Enchantment
New Mexico Rural Electric Cooperatives
614 Don Gaspar Ave.   Ph: (505)982-4671
Santa Fe, NM 87501   Fax: (505)982-0153
E-mail: enchantment@nmreca.org.
Contact: Don Begley, Editor, dbegley@nmreca.org.
Desc: Magazine for rural electrification consumers. *Type:* Periodical.

Farm Light & Power
Farm Light & Power Publications, Ltd.
2352 Smith St.   Ph: (306)525-3305
Regina, SK, Canada S4P 2P6   Fax: (306)757-1810
Contact: L.T. Bradley, Publisher.
Desc: Farm electrification journal. *Type:* Periodical.

GEORGIA Magazine
Georgia Electric Membership Corp.
PO Box 1707   Ph: (770)270-6950
Tucker, GA 30085   Free: 800-544-4362
     Fax: (770)270-6995
E-mail: magazine@georgiaemc.com.
Contact: Laurel George, Advertising Mgr., laurel.george@georgiaemc.com; Ann Orowski, Editor.
Desc: General interest magazine for and about Georgians *Type:* Periodical.

IEEE Power Engineering Society
IEEE Corporate Office
3 Park Ave., 17th Fl.   Ph: (212)419-7900
New York, NY 10016-5997
Desc: A society of the Institute of Electrical and Electronics Engineers . Promotes the study of: electrical power system engineering; electrical power generating facilities; fundamental technologies used in the control and conversion of electric power; requirements, planning, analysis, reliability, operation, and economics of electrical generating, transmission, and distribution systems for general industrial, commercial, public, and domestic use. *Type:* Association.

Illinois Rural Electric News
Association of Illinois Electric Cooperatives
PO Box 3787   Ph: (217)529-5561
Springfield, IL 62708   Fax: (217)529-5810
Contact: John Lourey, Editor.
Desc: Rural electric magazine. *Type:* Periodical.

International Association of Electrical Inspectors
PO Box 830848   Ph: (972)235-1455
Richardson, TX 75083-0848   Free: 800-786-4234
     Fax: (972)235-3855
E-mail: iaei@compuserve.com
URL: http://www.iaei.com
Contact: Philip H. Cox, Exec.Dir.
Desc: State, federal, county, city, industrial, utility, and insurance electrical inspectors; associate members are electricians, contractors, manufacturers, engineers, architects, and wiremen. Promotes the safe use of electrical wiring and equipment in compliance with the National Electrical Code and other electrical codes. Conducts educational programs. *Type:* Association.

International Sign Association
707 North St. Asaph St.   Ph: (703)836-4012
Alexandria, VA 22314-1911   Fax: (703)836-8353
URL: http://www.signs.org
Contact: Mark Wm. Lappen, JD, Pres. & CEO.
Desc: Industry related businesses and professionals serving the on premise sign & graphics community. Offers communication, educational, legislative, and technical programs. *Type:* Association.

Iowa REC News
Iowa Association of Electric Cooperatives
8525 Douglas, No. 48   Ph: (515)276-5350
Urbandale, IA 50322   Fax: (515)276-7946
Contact: Robert A. Dikelman, Editor.
Desc: Magazine for members of rural electric cooperatives. *Type:* Periodical.

National Association of Electrical Distributors
1100 Corporate Square Dr., Ste.   Ph: (314)991-9000
100   Fax: (314)991-3060
St. Louis, MO 63132
E-mail: info@naed.org
URL: http://www.naed.org
Contact: Joel Hoiland, Pres.
Desc: Wholesale distributors of electrical supplies and apparatus. Maintains numerous committees. *Type:* Association.

National Electrical Manufacturers Association
1300 North 17th St., Ste. 1847   Ph: (703)841-3200
Arlington, VA 22209   Fax: (703)841-5900
Contact: Malcolm E. O'Hagan, Pres.
Desc: Companies that manufacture equipment used for the generation, transmission, distribution, control, and utilization of electric power, such as electrical machinery, motors, industrial automation, construction, utility, medical diagnostic imaging, transportation, communication, and lighting equipment. Objectives are: to maintain and improve quality and reliability of products; to insure safety standards in manufacture and use of products; to organize and act upon members' interests in productivity, competition from overseas suppliers, energy conservation and efficiency, marketing opportunities, economic matters, and product liability. Develops product standards covering such matters as nomenclature, ratings, performance, testing, and dimen s ions; participates in developing National Electrical Code and National Electrical Safety Codes, and advocates their acceptance by state and local authorities; conducts regulatory and legislative analyses on issues of concern to electrical manufacturers; compiles and issues periodic summaries of statistical data on such factors as sales, new orders, unfilled orders, cancellations, production, and inventories. *Type:* Association.

National Electrical Manufacturers Representatives Association
660 White Plains Rd., Ste. 600   Ph: (914)524-8650
Tarrytown, NY 10591   Fax: (914)273-6785
E-mail: nemra@nemra.org
URL: http://www.nemra.org
Contact: Henry P. Bergson, Pres.
Desc: North American trade association dedicated to promoting continuing education, professionalism, and the use of independent manufacturers representatives in the electrical industry. *Type:* Association.

National Rural Electric Cooperative Association
4301 Wilson Blvd.   Ph: (703)907-5500
Arlington, VA 22203-1860
E-mail: nreca@nreca.org
Contact: Glenn English, CEO.
Desc: Rural electric cooperative systems, public power districts, and public utility districts in 46 states. Activities include: legislative representation; energy and regulatory; management institutes; professional conferences; training and consulting services; insurance and safety programs; international program; wage and salary surveys. *Type:* Association.

NETA World—InterNational Electrical Testing Association Membership Directory
InterNational Electrical Testing Association
PO Box 687   Ph: (303)697-8441
Morrison, CO 80465   Fax: (303)697-8431
E-mail: neta@netaworld.org
Contact: Dr. Mary R. Jordan, Editor.
Desc: Directory of about 60 member companies. *Type:* Directory.

North American Electric Reliability Council
North American Electric Reliability Council
Princeton Forrestal Village   Ph: (609)452-8060
116-390 Village Blvd.   Fax: (609)452-9550
Princeton, NJ 08540-5731
E-mail: info@nerc.com
URL: http://www.nerc.com/
Desc: NERC's mission is to help keep the lights on. Formed in the late 1960s following a blackout that affected the northeastern U.S. and Ontario, Canada, NERC promotes the reliability of the North American electricity supply. *Type:* Database.

Penn Lines
Pennsylvania Rural Electric Association
PO Box 1266   Ph: (717)233-5704
212 Locust St.   Fax: (717)234-1309
Harrisburg, PA 17108
URL: http://www.prea.com/Pennlines/plonline.htm.
Contact: Perry Stambaugh, Editor, perry_stambaugh@prea.com; Vonnie Kloss, Advertising Mgr., vonnie_kloss@prea.com.
Desc: Magazine on rural issues, lifestyles and home energy use. *Type:* Periodical.

Rural Missouri
Association of Missouri Electric Cooperatives, Inc.
2722 E. McCarty St.   Ph: (573)635-6857
PO Box 1645   Fax: (573)635-2314
Jefferson City, MO 65102
E-mail: ruralmo@socket.net.
Contact: Jim McCarty, Editor; Jeff Joiner, Managing Editor; Mary Davis, Advertising Mgr.; Frank Stork, Publisher; Bob McEdwen, Field Editor; Heather Berry, Asst. Editor.
Desc: Magazine serving electric cooperative consumers. *Type:* Periodical.

Tennessee Valley Public Power Association
1201 Chestnut St.   Ph: (615)756-6511
Chattanooga, TN 37402
Contact: Jerry Campbell, Exec.Dir.
Desc: Municipal and rural cooperative electric systems that buy power wholesale from the Tennessee Valley Authority. Encourages greater development of the distribution and utilization of electricity in the Tennessee Valley area through the combined efforts and interchange of ideas of members. Represents members in dealings with TVA; maintains representative in Washington, DC, to testify before Congress and keep members informed of legislative activities. *Type:* Association.

TODAY in Mississippi
Electric Power Association of Mississippi, Inc.
2805 Greenway Dr.   Ph: (601)922-2341
PO Box 7897   Free: 800-933-7897
Jackson, MS 39204-3306   Fax: (601)922-9869
E-mail: today@epaofms.com.
Contact: Debbie Stringer, Editor; Joe Fannin, Advertising Mgr., jfannin@tsixroads.com.
Desc: Statewide Newspaper covering political, economic, and legislative rura electrification matters statewide for EPA member-owners. *Type:* Periodical.

Electronics

AIM U.S.A.
634 Alpha Dr.   Ph: (412)963-8588
Pittsburgh, PA 15238-2802   Free: 800-338-0206
    Fax: (412)963-8753
E-mail: adc@aimusa.org
URL: http://www.aimusa.org
Contact: Larry W. Roberts, Pres. & CEO.
Desc: Association of companies committed to providing leadership and focus on Automatic Identification and Data Capture (AIDC). Suppliers of AIDC equipment and systems, such as bar code, magnetic stripe, radio frequency, machine vision, voice technology, optical character recognition, and systems integration technologies. Provides forum for exchange of information on Automatic Data Collection (ADC) technology. *Type:* Association.

American Electronics Association
5201 Great America Pkwy., Ste.   Ph: (408)987-4200
    520   Free: 800-284-4232
Santa Clara, CA 95054   Fax: (408)986-1247
URL: http://www.aeanet.org
Contact: William T. Archey, CEO & Pres.
Desc: Trade association representing the U.S. technology industry. Fosters a healthy business climate; conducts networking programs for industry executives. *Type:* Association.

Association of Old Crows
1000 N. Payne St.   Ph: (703)549-1600
Alexandria, VA 22314   Fax: (703)549-2589
E-mail: crows@aochq.org
URL: http://www.aochq.org
Contact: Vern Luke, Exec.Dir.
Desc: Professional association of scientists, engineers, managers, operators, educators, military personnel, and others engaged in the science of electronic, command, control, and information warfare, and related areas. The term "Old Crows" emerged during World War II when the U.S. and allied bombing raids were first outfitted with radio and radar receivers and transmitters, code named "Ravens." Operators were known as "Raven Operators" and later as "Old Crows." *Type:* Association.

Audio
Hachette Filipacchi Magazines, Inc.
1633 Broadway, 41st Fl.   Ph: (212)767-6000
New York, NY 10019   Fax: (212)989-4561
Contact: Michael Riggs, Editor, (212)767-6066, fax: (212)767-5633, mdriggs@aol.com; Tony Catalano, Group Pub., (212)767-6061, fax: (212)489-4536, tocat16@aol.com; R. Scott Constantine, Publisher, (212)767-6346, fax: (212)489-4536, hfmsc@aol.com.
Desc: Consumer stereo equipment magazine. *Type:* Periodical.

Audio Engineering Society
60 E. 42nd St., Rm. 2520   Ph: (212)661-8528
New York, NY 10017   Fax: (212)682-0477
Contact: Roger Furness, Exec.Dir.
Desc: Engineers, administrators, and technicians who design or operate recording and reproducing equipment for radio, television, motion picture, and recording studios, or who produce, install, and operate disc, magnetic tape, and sound amplifying equipment; educators who use recording in teaching, or who teach acoustics, electronics, and other sciences basic to the recording and reproducing of sound; administrators, sales engineers, and technicians in the sound industry and related fields. Operates educational and research foundation. *Type:* Association.

Car Stereo Review
Car Stereo Review
1633 Broadway, 45th Fl.   Ph: (212)767-6020
New York, NY 10019   Fax: (212)333-2434
E-mail: carsterev@aol.com.
Contact: Mike Mettler, Editor-in-Chief, (212)767-6314; Gerald McCarthy, Managing Editor, (212)767-6697; Chuck Tannert, Senior Editor, (212)767-6073; Doug Newcomb, Executive Editor, (310)455-3500, fax: (310)455-3126, surfrsr@aol.com; William Burton, Technical Director, (909)686-4605, fax: (909)686-1852, wburtoncsr@aol.com.
Desc: Magazine covering car sound systems, with articles, product reviews, and buyer's guides and music reviews. Covers purchase, installation, maintenance, accessories, and security. *Type:* Periodical.

Consumer Electronics Vision
Consumer Electronics Manufacturers Association
2500 Wilson Blvd.   Ph: (703)907-7609
Arlington, VA 22201   Fax: (703)907-7690
Contact: Robert MacMillan, Editor.
Desc: Provides news and information concerning mobile electronics, audio, radar, security, and cellular communications. Examines the manufacture, market trends, and installation of mobile electronics. *Type:* Newsletter.

East European Report
Semiconductor Equipment & Materials International (SEMI)
805 E. Middlefield Rd.   Ph: (650)964-5111
Mountain View, CA 94043   Fax: (650)967-5375
E-mail: semihq@semi.org; newsletters@semi.org.
URL: http://www.semi.org; http://www.semi.org.
Desc: Provides "business bulletins on the developing East European marketplace, research and development, joint ventures/trade agreements with the West, and foreign investment in Eastern Europe." Also covers government and economic issues, industrial developments, market size and data, and companies and market opportunities. Delivered by electronic mail. *Type:* Newsletter.

EDN Products and Careers

Cahners Publishing Company
275 Washington St.   Ph: (617)558-2119
Newton, MA 02458   Fax: (617)558-4700
Contact: Jon Titus, Editorial Dir.; Roy Forsberg, Publisher; Jeffrey Patterson, Sales Mgr.
Desc: Newspaper (tabloid) of technology, products, and careers for engineers and engineering managers. *Type:* Periodical.

EE Evaluation Engineering

Nelson Publishing, Inc.
2500 Tamiami Tr. N.   Ph: (941)966-9521
Nokomis, FL 34275-3482   Fax: (941)966-2590
E-mail: nelpub@ix.netcom.com; ee@nelsonpub.com.
URL: http://www.nelsonpub.com/ee/.
Contact: Paul Milo, Editor, pmilo@nelsonpub.com; Stephen Berlin, Publisher, sberlin@nelsonpub.com.
Desc: Trade magazine covering electronic engineering, evaluation and test. *Type:* Periodical.

Electrical Product News

Business Marketing & Publishing, Inc.
PO Box 7457   Ph: (203)834-9959
Wilton, CT 06897
Contact: George B. Young, Editor.
Desc: Covers electrical products and distributor services. Provides information on new products, product applications, manufacturer programs supporting product sales, features added to existing products, special promotions and incentive programs, and marketing/sales news. *Type:* Newsletter.

Electrical Sales Builder

Business Marketing & Publishing, Inc.
PO Box 7457   Ph: (203)834-9959
Wilton, CT 06897
Contact: George B. Young, Editor.
Desc: Presents condensed editorial coverage of electrical manufacturers' sales aids, product literature, catalogs, distributor sales support services, and product news and information. Focuses on marketing tool advantages. *Type:* Newsletter.

Electronic Advertising & Marketplace Report

SIMBA Information Inc.
11 River Bend Dr. S   Ph: (203)358-4100
PO Box 4234   Free: 800-307-2529
Stamford, CT 06907-0234   Fax: (203)358-5824
E-mail: simbainfo@simbanet.com; simbainfo@simbanet.com.
Contact: Linda Kapp, Managing Editor.
Desc: Provides facts, figures, competitive data, and analysis on how to profitably advertise, markt, or sell products through electronic media. Features exclusive statistics of Web ad revenues and electronic transactions, analysis and opinion on industry developments, electronic commerce technology news, and competitive intelligence. *Type:* Newsletter.

Electronic Buyers' News

CMP Media Inc.
600 Community Dr.   Ph: (516)562-5000
Manhasset, NY 11030
URL: http://www.cmp.com
Desc: Contains the complete text of Electronic Buyers' News, a weekly newsletter about the electronics industry. Covers pricing and discounts, product reviews, and purchasing strategies. *Available:* LEXIS-NEXIS, NEXIS; LEXIS-NEXIS, NEXIS. *Type:* Database.

Electronic Buyers' News—Specialized and Local/Regional Distributors Directory Issue

CMP Media Inc.
600 Community Dr.   Ph: (516)562-5000
Manhasset, NY 11030   Fax: (516)562-7830
URL: http://www.cmp.net
Contact: Susan Scheck, Associate Editor, Products & Listings.
Desc: List of about 325 distributors of electronic products and supplies operating on less than national scale, or offering only one or a few products nationwide. *Type:* Directory.

Electronic Buyers' News—Top 50 Distributors Issue

CMP Media Inc.
600 Community Dr.   Ph: (516)562-5000
Manhasset, NY 11030   Fax: (516)562-7830
URL: http://www.cmp.net
Contact: David Gabel, Editor.
Desc: List of electronics distributors ranked by annual gross sales. *Type:* Directory.

Electronic Design

Penton Media Inc.
611 Rte. 46 W.   Ph: (201)393-6060
Hasbrouck Heights, NJ 07604 Free: 800-526-6052
                           Fax: (201)393-6242
E-mail: info@buyused.com
URL: http://www.penton.com/ed.
Contact: Roger Allan, Exec. Editor, (201)393-6057; John French, Advertising Mgr., (201)393-6255, fax: (201)393-0204; Paul C. Mazzacano, Publisher.
Desc: Professional magazine covering current information in the field of electronic design. *Alt. Contact:* telephone: (201)393-6262; fax: (201)393-6242. *Type:* Periodical.

Electronic Display World

Stanford Resources, Inc.
20 Greatoans Blvd., Ste. 200 Ph: (408)360-8400
San Jose, CA 95119-1309   Fax: (408)360-8410
E-mail: sales@stanfordresources.com
URL: http://www.stanfordresources.com
Contact: Brian T. Fedrow, Editor-in-Chief; Joseph A. Castellano, Publisher.
Desc: Covers the worldwide electronic display industry, including technical developments, market analyses and forecasts, applications, and corporate and professional activities. Recurring features include letters to the editor, a calendar of events, the Component Bulletin Board, the Equipment Maker's Page, and Display Classroom. *Type:* Newsletter.

Electronic Engineering Times

CMP Media Inc.
600 Community Dr.   Ph: (516)562-5000
Manhasset, NY 11030   Fax: (516)562-7830
E-mail: techweb@cmp.com.
URL: http://www.cmp.net
Contact: Girish Mhatre, Publisher; Steve Weitzner, Publisher.
Desc: Weekly Trade Newspaper. *Type:* Periodical.

Electronic Imaging Report

Phillips Business Information, Inc.
1201 Seven Locks Rd., Ste. 300 Ph: (301)340-1520
Potomac, MD 20854   Free: 888-707-5809
                            Fax: (301)340-3847
E-mail: clientservices.pbi@phillips.com
URL: http://www.phillips.com.
Contact: Alex Linder, Editor.
Desc: Provides news and analysis on electronic imaging systems. *Remarks:* Absorbs the former Image Systems, published by Rotchild Consultants. *Type:* Newsletter.

Electronic Industries Association

2500 Wilson Blvd.   Ph: (703)907-7500
Arlington, VA 22201   Fax: (703)907-7501
URL: http://www.eia.org
Contact: Peter F. McCloskey, Pres.
Desc: Committed to the competitiveness of the American producer, EIA represents all companies involved in the design and manufacture of electronic components, parts, systems and equipment for communications, industrial, government and consumer uses. Has represented U.S. electronics manufacturers for more than 73 years. *Type:* Association.

Electronic Industries Foundation

2500 Wilson Blvd., Ste. 210   Ph: (703)907-7400
Arlington, VA 22201-3834   Fax: (703)907-7401
E-mail: angiem@eia.org
URL: http://www.eia.org/eif
Contact: Molly M. Mannon, Pres.
Desc: Purposes are to encourage electronics industry firms to participate in programs that help solve social problems and increase employment opportunities for minority youth and disabled people in the electronics industry. Participates in private and governmental planning and policy-making boards, councils, and advisory groups. Sponsors: the Rehabilitation Engineering Center to improve the technology and marketability of devices to aid disabled people; Project With Industry to help place disabled persons in competitive employment. *Type:* Association.

Electronic Products

Hearst Business Media Corp./IIMN Division
5700 Crooks Rd.   Ph: (313)828-7000
PO Box 7032   Free: 800-544-0929
Troy, MI 48007-7032   Fax: (313)828-7008
E-mail: rpell@hearstelectelectroweb.com.
URL: http://electronicproducts.com.
Contact: Frank Egan, Editor and Publisher.
Desc: Magazine for electronic design engineers and management. *Type:* Periodical.

Electronics Business Buyer—Value-Added Directory

Cahners Publishing Company
275 Washington St.   Ph: (617)558-2119
Newton, MA 02458   Fax: (617)558-4700
Contact: Jim Carbone, Editor.
Desc: List of over 500 value-added distributors of electronics equipment and components in North America. *Type:* Directory.

Electronics and Communications Abstracts

Cambridge Scientific Abstracts (CSA)
7200 Wisconsin Ave., Ste. 601 Ph: (301)961-6700
Bethesda, MD 20814-4823
E-mail: sales@csa.com
URL: http://www.csa.com
Desc: Contains more than 177,000 citations, with abstracts, to the worldwide literature on electronics and communications. Covers theoretical and applied research, as well as business and marketing information, in these areas: electronic systems, electronic physics, electronic circuits and devices, communications, and optical engineering. *Available:* STN International; STN International. *Type:* Database.

Electronics Now

Gernsback Publications Inc.
500 Bicounty Blvd.   Ph: (516)293-3000
Farmingdale, NY 11735   Fax: (516)293-3115
E-mail: eneditor@gernsback.com.
URL: http://www.gernsback.com.
Contact: Carl Laron, Editor, claron@gernsbach.com; Larry Steckler, Publisher; Marie Falcon, Advertising Dir.; Theresa Lombardo, Circulation Dir.; Ruby Yee, Production Dir.

Desc: Magazine focusing on computers, video, audio, technology, and electronics service. *Type:* Periodical.

E.T.G. State News
Electronic Technicians Guild of Massachusetts, Inc.
202 Central St.　　　Ph: (617)923-9926
Winchendon, MA 01475
E-mail: etgnews@aol.com.

Contact: Robert Ayan, Jr., Editor.

Desc: Provides news of interest to persons involved in the electronic service and repair industry in Massachusetts. *Type:* Newsletter.

European Component Source Directory
Europartners Databases, Inc.
3638 Palmetto Ave.　　　Ph: (305)445-3280
Miami, FL 33133　　　Fax: (305)445-3732
E-mail: sales@europartner.com

Desc: More than 8,000 manufacturers, 3,000 distributors, and importers of electronic components in 35 European countries, including producers and distributors of semiconductors, passives, and electromechanical components. *Type:* Directory.

Evaluation Engineering—ATE Buyers' Guide
Nelson Publishing, Inc.
2500 Tamiami Tr. N.　　　Ph: (941)966-9521
Nokomis, FL 34275-3482　　　Fax: (941)966-2590
E-mail: nelpub@ix.netcom.com
URL: http://www.nelsonpub.com/ee/.

Contact: Paul Milo, Editor, pmilo@nelsonpub.com.

Desc: Companies that manufacture or rent/sell Automated Testing Equipment (ATE) products, such as ASIC ATE, bare-board ATE, burn-in systems/products, device testers, ISDN test systems, power supply testers, smart power testers, switching systems, and wafer probing. *Type:* Directory.

Evaluation Engineering—EMC Buyers' Guide
Nelson Publishing, Inc.
2500 Tamiami Tr. N.　　　Ph: (941)966-9521
Nokomis, FL 34275-3482　　　Fax: (941)966-2590
E-mail: nelpub@ix.netcom.com
URL: http://www.nelsonpub.com/ee/.

Contact: Paul Milo, Editor, pmilo@nelsonpub.com.

Desc: Companies involved in the testing or control of Electromagnetic Interference (EMI) and Radio Frequency Interference (RFI), including manufacturers of absorption materials, antennas, connectors, gaskets, shielded enclosures and rooms, surge suppressors, test equipment, filters, chokes, shielding coatings, and Tempest products. *Type:* Directory.

Evaluation Engineering—Environmental Test Buyers' Guide
Nelson Publishing, Inc.
2500 Tamiami Tr. N.　　　Ph: (941)966-9521
Nokomis, FL 34275-3482　　　Fax: (941)966-2590
E-mail: nelpub@ix.netcom.com
URL: http://www.nelsonpub.com/ee/.

Contact: Paul Milo, Editor, pmilo@nelsonpub.com.

Desc: Companies that provide environmental equipment to the electronics industry, such as burn-in chambers and systems, Environmental Stress Screening (ESS) systems, humidity chambers, sockets adapters, thermal shock equipment, and vibrations equipment. *Type:* Directory.

Evaluation Engineering—ESD Annual Buyers' Guide
Nelson Publishing, Inc.
2500 Tamiami Tr. N.　　　Ph: (941)966-9521
Nokomis, FL 34275-3482　　　Fax: (941)966-2590
E-mail: nelpub@ix.netcom.com
URL: http://www.nelsonpub.com/ee/.

Contact: Paul Milo, Editor, pmilo@nelsonpub.com.

Desc: Companies that provide products and services designed to protect sensitive devices, assemblies, and equipment from Electrostatic Discharge (ESD). *Type:* Directory.

Evaluation Engineering—Instrumentation Buyers' Guide
Nelson Publishing, Inc.
2500 Tamiami Tr. N.　　　Ph: (941)966-9521
Nokomis, FL 34275-3482　　　Fax: (941)966-2590
E-mail: nelpub@ix.netcom.com
URL: http://www.nelsonpub.com/ee/.

Contact: Paul Milo, Editor, pmilo@nelsonpub.com.

Desc: Companies that manufacture or rent/sell instrumentation products for the electronics industry, such as continuity testers, data acquisition systems, device testers, function generators, logic analyzers, oscilloscopes, recorders/data loggers, rental/used instruments, spectrum analyzers, VXIbus products, and waveform analyzers. *Type:* Directory.

Evaluation Engineering—Test Labs/Services Buyers' Guide
Nelson Publishing, Inc.
2500 Tamiami Tr. N.　　　Ph: (941)966-9521
Nokomis, FL 34275-3482　　　Fax: (941)966-2590
E-mail: nelpub@ix.netcom.com
URL: http://www.nelsonpub.com/ee/.

Contact: Paul Milo, Editor, pmilo@nelsonpub.com.

Desc: Laboratories and organizations providing testing services for the electronics industry, such as board testing, component qualification, destructive physical analysis, environmental testing, failure analysis, product safety testing, stress screening, surface analysis, and X-ray analysis; organizations providing consulting services, training materials, seminars, and lease/rent test equipment. *Type:* Directory.

Federation of Westinghouse Independent Salaried Unions
1940 James St.　　　Ph: (412)829-1770
Monroeville, PA 15146　　　Fax: (412)829-1851
Contact: Damion Testa, Pres.
Desc: Independent. Electrical production workers united to create strength through unified action and to serve as a coordinating agency for member locals. Reviews new or revised position descriptions and evaluations, including local labor agreements, prior to their acceptance or execution. *Type:* Association.

Henderson Electronic Market Forecast
Henderson Ventures
101 1st St., No. 444　　　Ph: (415)961-2900
Los Altos, CA 94022　　　Fax: (415)961-3090
Contact: Edward Henderson, Editor.
Desc: Forecasts the national and international electronics market. Recurring features include economic/electronic equipment and components analysis. *Type:* Newsletter.

IEEE Circuits and Systems Society
IEEE Corporate Office
3 Park Ave., 17th Fl.　　　Ph: (212)419-7900
New York, NY 10016-5997
Contact: Charles Alexander, Pres.
Desc: A society of the Institute of Electrical and Electronics Engineers . Disseminates information on the design and theory of operations involving circuits used in radio and electronics equipment; such information covers methods, algorithms, and man-machine interfaces for physical and logical design. *Type:* Association.

IEEE Industrial Electronics Society
COF Elect. & Comp. Eng.
Dept.
The Univ. of Tennessee
Knoxville, TN 37996-2100
Contact: James C. Hung, Pres.
Desc: A society of the Institute of Electrical and Electronics Engineers . Studies the application of electronics and electrical sciences to the control of industrial processes. *Type:* Association.

IEEE Lasers and Electro-Optics Society
445 Hoes Ln.　　　Ph: (732)562-3892
PO Box 1331　　　Fax: (732)562-8434
Piscataway, NJ 08855-1331
E-mail: g.walters@ieee.org
URL: http://www.ieee.org/leos
Contact: Edward F. Labuda, Exec.Dir.
Desc: Serves as a forum for discussion of quantum electronics, optoelectronic theory, and techniques and applications, and the design, development, and manufacture of photobic systems and subsystems (such as lasers and fiber optics). *Type:* Association.

Imaging Supplies Monthly
GIGA Information Group
1 Longwater Circle　　　Ph: (781)982-9500
Norwell, MA 02061-1620　　　Free: 800-847-9980
　　　　　　Fax: (781)982-1724
E-mail: smartin@gigasd.com
Contact: David W. Hatch, Dir. of Publications.
Desc: Provides analysis of industry trends, issues, technology, and products. Recurring features include news of research, reports of meetings, notices of publications available, and a column titled Product Notes. *Type:* Newsletter.

insideNESDA
National Electronics Service Dealer's Association, Inc. (NESDA)
2708 W. Berry　　　Ph: (817)921-9061
Fort Worth, TX 76109
Contact: Wallace Harrison, Editor.
Desc: Conveys news and opinion on the Association and its functions. Comprises part of a supplement to Professional Electronics magazine, along with NESDA Update. *Type:* Newsletter.

Institute of Electrical and Electronics Engineers
3 Park Ave., Ste. 17A　　　Ph: (212)419-7900
New York, NY 10016-5902　　　Fax: (212)752-4929
Contact: Daniel Senese, Pres.
Desc: Engineers and scientists in electrical engineering, electronics, and allied fields; membership includes 47,000 students. Conducts lecture courses at the local level on topics of current engineering and scientific interest. Assists student groups. *Type:* Association.

Institute for Interconnecting and Packaging Electronic Circuits
2215 Sanders Rd.　　　Ph: (847)509-9700
Northbrook, IL 60062-6135　　　Fax: (847)509-9798
URL: http://www.ipc.org
Contact: Thomas J. Dammrich, Pres.
Desc: Companies that are producers and users of electronic interconnections for electronic equipment. *Type:* Association.

International Brotherhood of Electrical Workers
1125 15th St. NW　　　Ph: (202)833-7000
Washington, DC 20005　　　Fax: (202)728-6056
URL: http://www.ibew.org/
Contact: J. J. Barry, Pres.

Desc: AFL-CIO. *Type:* Association.

The International Display Report

Semiconductor Equipment & Materials International (SEMI)

805 E. Middlefield Rd.   Ph: (650)964-5111
Mountain View, CA 94043   Fax: (650)967-5375
E-mail: semihq@semi.org; newsletters@semi.org.
URL: http://www.semi.org; http://www.semi.org.
Desc: Offers "analysis of marketing, government, supplier, and technology issues facing the worldwide electronic display industry." Each report focuses on a single, timely issue and provides in-depth coverage. Delivered by electronic mail. *Type:* Newsletter.

International High Technology Report

Amersham Associates

1209 G St. NE   Ph: (202)396-2568
Washington, DC 20002-4423
Contact: Frances Healey, Circulation Mgr.
Desc: Reports high technology news from around the world. *Type:* Newsletter.

International Microelectronic and Packaging Society

1850 Centennial Park Dr., Ste.   Ph: (703)758-1060
  105   Free: 888-464-6277
Reston, VA 20191-1517   Fax: (703)758-1066
E-mail: imaps@imaps.org
URL: http://www.imaps.org
Contact: Richard Breck, Exec.Dir.
Desc: Electronics engineers and specialists in industry, business, and education. Encourages the exchange of information across boundaries of fields of specialization; supports close interactions between the complementary technologies of ceramics, thick and thin films, semiconductor packaging, discrete semiconductor devices, and monolithic circuits. Promotes and assists in the development and expansion of microelectronics instruction in schools and departments of electrical and electronic engineering. *Type:* Association.

International Union of Electronic, Electrical, Salaried, Machine, and Furniture Workers

1126 16th St. NW   Ph: (202)785-7200
Washington, DC 20036   Fax: (202)785-4563
Contact: Ed Fire, Pres.
Desc: AFL-CIO affiliate. Negotiates collective bargaining agreements; maintains apprenticeship programs. *Type:* Association.

International Wafer Fab News

Semiconductor Equipment & Materials International (SEMI)

805 E. Middlefield Rd.   Ph: (650)964-5111
Mountain View, CA 94043   Fax: (650)967-5375
E-mail: semihq@semi.org; newsletters@semi.org.
URL: http://www.semi.org; http://www.semi.org.
Desc: Provides the latest on semiconductor capital spending in the U.S. "Highlights and analyzes individual company capacity utilization rates, capital spending plans, and purchasing strategies." Focuses on plans for new fabs, expansions, and upgrades. *Type:* Newsletter.

Manufacturing Market Insider

JBT Communications

PO Box 782   Ph: (781)444-2154
Needham Heights, MA 02494-   Fax: (781)455-8409
  0006
E-mail: jbt@mfgmkt.com
URL: http://www.mfgmkt.com.
Contact: John Tuck, Editor and Publisher.
Desc: Covers outsourcing and the contract manufacturing of electronics. Includes news of acquisitions, expansions, and contract awards. *Type:* Newsletter.

Market Update

Semiconductor Equipment & Materials International (SEMI)

805 E. Middlefield Rd.   Ph: (650)964-5111
Mountain View, CA 94043   Fax: (650)967-5375
E-mail: semihq@semi.org; newsletters@semi.org.
URL: http://www.semi.org; http://www.semi.org.
Desc: Analyzes "the latest technical and marketing data for equipment, chemicals, processing, and Ics." Also "serves to update past purchasers of multi-client reports from the publisher." Delivered by electronic mail. *Type:* Newsletter.

Microwaves & RF Directory Issue

Penton Media Inc.

611 Rte. 46 W.   Ph: (201)393-6060
Hasbrouck Heights, NJ 07604   Free: 800-526-6052
          Fax: (201)393-6242
E-mail: info@buyused.com
Contact: Jack Browne, Editor.
Desc: About 2,000 manufacturers of high-frequency equipment components, including antennas and accessories, materials and accessories, passive components, semiconductors, solid-state components, systems and subsystems, test instruments and equipment, and tubes and amplifiers; worldwide coverage. *Type:* Directory.

National Electronic Distributors Association—Membership Directory

National Electronic Distributors Association

1111 Alderman Dr., Ste. 400   Ph: (678)393-9990
Alpharetta, GA 30005   Free: 800-347-6332
          Fax: (678)393-9998
E-mail: info@nedassoc.org
Contact: Janet Wood, Editor.
Desc: Approximately 200 member distributors and 200 member manufacturers of electronics products, plus 1,100 branch offices. *Type:* Directory.

NESDA Update

National Electronics Service Dealer's Association, Inc. (NESDA)

2708 W. Berry   Ph: (817)921-9061
Fort Worth, TX 76109
Contact: Wallace Harrison, Editor-in-Chief.
Desc: Supplies information as a supplement to Pro Service Magazine. Features news of the electronics, computer, and appliance industries. *Type:* Newsletter.

Pathfinder Focus

Semiconductor Equipment & Materials International (SEMI)

805 E. Middlefield Rd.   Ph: (650)964-5111
Mountain View, CA 94043   Fax: (650)967-5375
E-mail: semihq@semi.org; newsletters@semi.org.
URL: http://www.semi.org; http://www.semi.org.
Desc: Identifies and analyzes "key strategic issues and emerging market drivers for the semiconductor industry." Delivered by electronic mail. *Type:* Newsletter.

Printout

GIGA Information Group

1 Longwater Circle   Ph: (781)982-9500
Norwell, MA 02061-1620   Free: 800-847-9980
          Fax: (781)982-1724
E-mail: smartin@gigasd.com
Contact: David W. Hatch, Dir. of Publications.
Desc: Provides analysis of industry trends, issues, technology, and products. Recurring features include news of research, reports of meetings, notices of publications available, and a column titled Product Notes. *Type:* Newsletter.

Products and Technology Bulletin

Semiconductor Equipment & Materials International (SEMI)

805 E. Middlefield Rd.   Ph: (650)964-5111
Mountain View, CA 94043   Fax: (650)967-5375
E-mail: semihq@semi.org; newsletters@semi.org.
URL: http://www.semi.org; http://www.semi.org.
Desc: Provides global market trends in the semiconductor and flat panel display equipment and materials industry, along with editorial commentary. Delivered by electronic mail. *Type:* Newsletter.

Semiconductor Equipment and Materials International

805 E. Middlefield Rd.   Ph: (650)964-5111
Mountain View, CA 94043   Fax: (650)967-5375
Contact: Stan Myers, Pres.
Desc: Firms, corporations, and individuals engaged in supplying fabrication equipment, materials, or services to the semiconductor industry. Develops voluntary technical standards for the semiconductor industry. *Type:* Association.

Semiconductor Industry Association

181 Metro Dr.   Ph: (408)436-6646
San Jose, CA 95110-1344   Fax: (408)246-2830
Contact: George Scalise, Pres.
Desc: Companies that produce semiconductor products such as discrete components, integrated circuits, and microprocessors. Compiles industry trade statistics. Affiliate: Semiconductor Research Corporation and SEMATECH. *Type:* Association.

Sensors Buyers Guide

Helmers Publishing, Inc.

174 Concord St.   Ph: (603)924-9631
PO Box 874   Fax: (603)924-7408
Peterborough, NH 03458
E-mail: info@sensormag.com; editors@sensorsmag.com.
URL: http://www.sensorsmag.com.
Contact: Carol Swartz, Editor; Barbara Goode, Editor.
Desc: Lists manufacturers and vendors of sensors and transducers for use in high-technology applications engineering. Also covers related products and services. *Type:* Directory.

Television Digest with Consumer Electronics

Warren Publishing, Inc.

2115 Ward Ct. NW   Ph: (202)872-9200
Washington, DC 20037   Fax: (202)296-4397
E-mail: warrenpub@mindspring.com
URL: http://www.telecommunications.com
Contact: Albert Warren, Editor; Dawson Nail, Editor; Paul Gluckman, Bureau Chief, (212)686-5410, fax: (212)889-5097.
Desc: Monitors trends in the television broadcasting and cable industries and in consumer electronics equipment manufacturing and distribution. Reports on networks, stations, ratings, advertising, federal agencies, programming, technology, foreign developments, finance, and related subjects. *Type:* Newsletter.

Test & Measurement World—Annual Buyer's Guide

Cahners Business Information

275 Washington St.   Ph: (617)964-3030
Newton, MA 02458   Fax: (617)558-4470
E-mail: tmw@cahners.com.
URL: http://www.tmworld.com.
Contact: Jonathan Titus, Editor.
Desc: Manufacturers and distributors of electronics test, measurement, and inspection equipment. *Type:* Directory.

Uniform Code Council
7887 Washington Village Dr., Ph: (937)435-3870
Ste. 300 Fax: (937)435-7317
Dayton, OH 45459-8605
URL: http://www.uc-council.org
Contact: Tom Rittenhouse, Pres.
Desc: Manufacturers-processors and retailers-wholesalers of products sold through high-volume checkstands. To develop a universal product code system for assigning a unique identification number to every product sold in the U.S. *Type:* Association.

United Electrical, Radio and Machine Workers of America
1 Gateway Ctr., Ste. 1400 Ph: (412)471-8919
Pittsburgh, PA 15222-1416 Fax: (412)471-8999
Contact: John Hovis, Pres.
Desc: Independent union representing workers in the electrical manufacturing and electronics industries including General Electric, Westinghouse, Allen Bradley, American Standard, Litton, and Bendix. *Type:* Association.

West European Report
Semiconductor Equipment & Materials International (SEMI)
805 E. Middlefield Rd. Ph: (650)964-5111
Mountain View, CA 94043 Fax: (650)967-5375
E-mail: semihq@semi.org; newsletters@semi.org.
URL: http://www.semi.org; http://www.semi.org.
Desc: Publishes information on "West European business developments within the electronics industry such as company operations, government and economic issues, and business activity." Delivered by electronic mail. *Type:* Newsletter.

The Word
Electronic Service Dealers Association of Illinois
4927 W. Irving Park Rd. Ph: (773)282-9400
Chicago, IL 60641
Contact: George J. Weiss, Editor.
Desc: Discusses aspects of the electronics service industry. Reports on warranty and regulatory information, general business tips, Association news, and general industry news. *Type:* Newsletter.

Elks

Benevolent and Protective Order of Elks
National Headquarters Offices Ph: (773)755-4700
2750 N. Lakeview Ave. Fax: (773)755-4701
Chicago, IL 60614-1889
E-mail: grandlodge@elks.org
URL: http://www.elks.org
Contact: Jack M. Jersen, Grand Sec.
Desc: Fraternal and benevolent society. Administers Elks National Foundation, a private charitable trust fund. *Type:* Association.

The Elks Magazine
The Elks Magazine
425 W. Diversey Pkwy. Ph: (773)528-4500
Chicago, IL 60614-6196
E-mail: elksmag@elks.org.
URL: http://www.elksmag.com.
Contact: Fred D. Oakes, Publisher.
Desc: Fraternal magazine. *Type:* Periodical.

Improved Benevolent Protective Order of Elks of the World
PO Box 159 Ph: (252)358-7661
Winton, NC 27986 Fax: (252)358-7681
Contact: Donald P. Wilson, Grand Exalted Ruler.

Desc: International fraternal organization of primarily black membership. Concerned with civil liberties and equal opportunity. *Type:* Association.

Emergency

National Association for Search and Rescue
4500 Southgate Pl., Ste. 100 Ph: (703)222-6277
Chantilly, VA 20151-1714 Fax: (703)222-6283
E-mail: info@nasar.org
URL: http://www.nasar.org
Contact: Lawrence Jacobson, Exec. VP.
Desc: Directors or coordinators of state and regional emergency rescue services; medical rescue, fire, and emergency personnel; organizations or associations involved in search, rescue, or survival activities; state rescue-related agencies. Promotes and develops search and rescue (SAR) and disaster response capabilities. *Type:* Association.

Emergency Medicine

American College of Emergency Physicians
PO Box 619911 Ph: (972)550-0911
Dallas, TX 75261-9911 Fax: (972)580-2816
URL: http://www.acep.org
Contact: Dr. Colin C. Rorrie, Jr., Exec.Dir.
Desc: Physicians who devote a significant portion of their professional time to emergency medicine. Aim is to provide a unifying direction of purpose in the field, which is a new medical specialty. Encourages training of emergency physicians, with the aim of improving emergency department care in hospitals; conducts continuing education programs for emergency physicians and other healthcare personnel. *Type:* Association.

Community Emergency Care Association
5530 Wisconsin Ave.
PO Box 70153
Washington, DC 20088
Contact: Sean P. MacTire, Exec.Dir.
Desc: Public health/preventive medicine organization primarily focused on prehospital emergency medical/trauma care and emergency services. Fosters advancements and improvements in prehospital emergency and trauma care, emergency medicine and in-hospital trauma care by focusing increased emphasis on the aspects of public health care, preventive medicine and field trauma care, thereby decreasing the mortality and morbidity rates of accident, injury, sudden illness and disease. Promotes and directs research into the epidemiology of trauma and into control via preventive medicine programs and conducts ongoing research for improving fire, rescue, and police capability. *Type:* Association.

Denali Medical Research
1930 S. Broadway Ph: (970)242-4358
Grand Junction, CO 81503 Fax: (970)244-8466
E-mail: phack@ruralhealth.org
Contact: Dr. Peter Hackett, MD, Dir.
Desc: Prevention, diagnosis, and treatment of frostbite, mountain sickness, hypothermia, near drowning, and trauma subsequent to cold conditions. Studies means of rescue and transportation of victims of the above. *Type:* Research center.

Emergency Management Today
Emergency Management Group
1508 E. 86th St., Ste. 315 Ph: (317)475-9572
Indianapolis, IN 46240 Fax: (317)475-9403
E-mail: info@psamerica.com
URL: http://www.emergencypsa.com/disaster/index.html.

Contact: A.J. Strong, Assoc. Editor, astrong@psamerica.com.
Desc: Covers events, trends, developments, and technologies in the management of major emergencies and disasters by cities, states, nations, and industries in North America. Recurring features include interviews, news of research, reports of meetings, job listings, and book reviews. *Type:* Newsletter.

Emergency Medicine Alert
American Health Consultants, Inc.
3525 Piedmont Rd., Bldg. 6, Ph: (404)262-7436
Ste. 400 Free: 800-688-2421
Atlanta, GA 30305 Fax: (404)262-7837
E-mail: 75057.1533@compuserve.com; custserv@ahcpub.com.
URL: http://www.ahcpub.com.
Contact: Richard A. Harrigan, M.D., Editor.
Desc: Provides information on developments and improvements in emergency medicine. *Type:* Newsletter.

Emergency Nurses Association
915 Lee St. Ph: 800-900-9659
Des Plaines, IL 60018 Free: 800-243-8362
Fax: (847)698-9406
E-mail: enainfo@ena.org
URL: http://www.ena.org
Contact: Patricia VanDoren-Blake, CAE.
Desc: Registered nurses, licensed practical nurses, and licensed vocational nurses; emergency medical technicians or nurses and members of allied health fields engaged or interested in emergency patient care. Objectives are: to promote emergency nursing and to establish standards in the field; to work with other health-related organizations toward the improvement of emergency care; to serve as a resource for emergency nursing education and research. Seeks to identify and address emergency nursing issues. *Type:* Association.

EMERGINDEX® System
MICROMEDEX®, Inc.
6200 Syracuse Way South, Ste. Ph: (303)486-6400
300
Englewood, CO 80111-4740
E-mail: info@mdx.com
URL: http://www.micromedex.com
Contact: Customer Support.
Desc: Contains information on emergency, traumatic injury, and acute care medicine, diagnosis, and treatment. Comprises the following 2 files: • Clinical Reviews--contains reviews of emergency and acute care treatment protocols. *Type:* Database.

IAEM Bulletin
International Association of Emergency Managers
111 Park Place Ph: (703)538-1795
Falls Church, VA 22046-4513 Fax: (703)241-5603
E-mail: iaem@aol.com
Contact: Elizabeth B. Armstrong, Executive Director; Shari Coffin, Editor.
Desc: Provides information on resources available, regulatory and legislative initiatives, and current issues on emergency management. Recurring features include news of research, a calendar of events, news of educational opportunities, and notices of publications available. *Type:* Newsletter.

Institute of Critical Care Medicine
1695 N. Sunrise Way Ph: (760)323-6867
Bldg. 3 Fax: (760)323-6167
Palm Springs, CA 92262
E-mail: weilm@aol.com
URL: http://www.members.aol.com/weilm/iccm/iccm.htm

Contact: Dr. Max Harry Weil, Pres.

Desc: Critically ill patients, especially those in coronary care, intensive care, concentrated care, post anaesthesia recovery, and emergency services, suffering from heart attacks, accidents, post-surgical complications, overwhelming infections, blood loss, trauma, central nervous system injury, circulatory shock, burns, and shock from a variety of causes. Interdisciplinary studies focus on critical care medicine, automation of bedside equipment, computer application to bedside medicine, hospital environment, cardiopulmonary resuscitation, physiological instrumentation, and ethical studies of patient care. *Type:* Research center.

Iowa's Center for Agricultural Safety and Health

Institute of Agric. Med.   Fax: (319)335-4225
Univ. of Iowa Oakdale Campus
Iowa City, IA 52242-5000
E-mail: kelly-donham@uiowa.edu

Contact: Kelley J. Donham, DVM, Dir.

Desc: Coordinates state's resources to improve the health and safety of Iowa's farm families, farm workers, and the agricultural community. Priority areas include provision of agricultural health and safety services, prevention of tractor injuries, prevention of injuries and illnesses in farm youth, prevention of illnesses among producers working in livestock confinement operations, and surveillance of farm injuries and illnesses. *Type:* Research center.

Loyola University Chicago

Burn and Shock Trauma Institute

Loyola Univ. Med. Ctr.   Ph: (708)327-2400
Bldg. 110, 4th Fl.   Fax: (708)327-2813
Maywood, IL 60153
E-mail: rgamell@luc.edu
URL: http://www.lumc.edu/burnshock

Contact: Richard L. Gamelli, MD, Dir.

Desc: Body responses to injury and post-injury sequelae of infection, metabolic change, alteration in host defense, and wound healing. Clinical research in care and management of injury victims, injury analysis and prevention, etiology, epidemiology, cost, rehabilitation, and outcome of trauma. *Type:* Research center.

Medic Alert Foundation International

2323 Colorado Ave.   Ph: (209)668-3333
Turlock, CA 95382   Free: 800-432-5378
          Fax: (209)669-2495
E-mail: inquiries@medicalert.org
URL: http://www.medicalert.org

Contact: Tanya J. Glazebrook, Pres./CEO.

Desc: Medical information service open to all. Computerized, confidential medical file, Medic Alert emblem on pendant or bracelet engraved with primary medical condition and can call collect number to access 24-hour Emergency Response Center. Information is uses to speed diagnosis, accurate treatment and save lives. *Type:* Association.

Medic Alert Traveler

Medicalert
2323 Colorado Ave.
Turlock, CA 95382

Contact: Michelle Y. Stevenson, Editor.

Desc: Provides information on the services the Medic Alert organization offers its members. Offers suggestions for safe traveling for those with health conditions. *Type:* Newsletter.

Memorial University of Newfoundland Centre for Offshore and Remote Medicine

Health Sci. Centre   Ph: (709)737-6433
St. John's, NF, Canada A1B   Fax: (709)737-6400
  3V6

Contact: Dr. Henry J. Manson, Dir.

Desc: Petroleum related offshore health and safety, telemedicine and teleconferencing, hypermedic medicine, occupational medicine, and hypothermia, survival, and immersion suits. *Type:* Research center.

Mercy Medical Airlift

PO Box 1940   Ph: (703)361-1191
Manassas, VA 20108   Free: 800-296-1217
          Fax: (703)361-1792
E-mail: mercymed@aol.com
URL: http://www.mercymedical.org
Contact: Kelp Armstrong, V.Pres.
Type: Association.

Miracle Flights for Kids

2756 N. Green Valley Pkwy.,   Ph: (702)261-0494
  No. 115   Free: 800-FLY-1711
Henderson, NV 89014   Fax: (702)261-0497
E-mail: miraclefh@aol.com
Contact: Ann McGee, Pres.
Desc: Provides free commercial air transportation to families who are unable to get to medical treatments far from home. *Type:* Association.

National Registry of Emergency Medical Technicians

PO Box 29233   Ph: (614)888-4484
Columbus, OH 43229   Fax: (614)888-8920
E-mail: nremtwebofc@attmail.com
URL: http://www.nremt.org
Contact: William E. Brown, Jr., Exec.Dir.
Desc: Promotes the improved delivery of emergency medical services by:. *Type:* Association.

On the Scene

Pittsburgh Research Institute
600 Forbes Ave.
Pittsburgh, PA 15282

Desc: Covers injury and trauma information, research, and policy affecting trauma center programs. Recurring features include notices of publications available and columns titled Legislative Update and Trauma Registry Corner. *Type:* Newsletter.

R.A. Cowley Shock Trauma Center

University of Maryland Shock   Ph: (410)328-3774
  Trauma Center   Fax: (410)328-8925
22 S. Greene St.
Baltimore, MD 21201-1595
E-mail: jashworth@trauma.av.umd.edu
URL: http://4103282337
Contact: John W. Ashworth, III, Dir.
Desc: Clinical research on resuscitation and treatment of critically ill and severely injured. Crash injury research studies focus on automotive safety and design based on in-depth engineering analysis of automotive crashes. *Type:* Research center.

Trauma Foundation

San Francisco General Hospital   Ph: (415)821-8209
Bldg. 1, Rm. 300   Fax: (415)282-2563
San Francisco, CA 94110
E-mail: traumafdn@traumafdn.org
URL: http://www.tf.org
Contact: Andrew McGuire, Exec.Dir.
Desc: Injury and violence prevention, public policy, and epidemiology, including epidemiology of traumatic injuries and health policy research on such issues as fire-safe cigarettes, motorcycle helmets, burn injury prevention, violence prevention, handgun control, and alcohol policy. *Type:* Research center.

U.S. Department of Health and Human Services

National Institute of General Medical Sciences

Trauma and Burn Center Program

Westwood Bldg., Rm. 905   Ph: (301)594-7774
45 Center Dr.   Fax: (301)594-7700
Box 6200
Bethesda, MD 20892-6200

Contact: Dr. Lee Van Lenten, Prog.Admin.

Desc: Provides support for multidisciplinary basic laboratory investigations. Studies include energy exchange and metabolism, cellular changes in shock, and sepsis. *Type:* Research center.

University of Calgary

Injury Research Unit

410, 301-14 St. NW   Ph: (403)531-3383
Calgary, AB, Canada T2N 2A1   Fax: (403)283-2805
E-mail: vppanlil@acs.ucalgary.ca

Contact: Vladimir P. Panlilio, Adjunct Asst.Prof.

Desc: Conducts multidisciplinary contract studies of motor vehicle accidents. Specific projects include the study of injuries in accidents involving light trucks, vans, and passenger cars; pedestrian injury; protection of children with handicaps in motor vehicles; effectiveness of child car seats; injury scoring; and air cushion restraint systems. *Type:* Research center.

University of California, San Diego

Division of Pulmonary and Critical Care Medicine

200 W. Arbor Dr.   Ph: (619)543-5970
San Diego, CA 92103-8372   Fax: (619)543-2751
URL: http://www.ucsd.edu

Contact: Andrew L. Ries, MD, Contact.

Desc: Chronic obstructive pulmonary disease, tuberculosis, acute respiratory failure, including its pathogenesis and management. *Type:* Research center.

University of Pittsburgh

Safar Center for Resuscitation Research

3434 5th Ave.   Ph: (412)383-1900
Pittsburgh, PA 15260   Fax: (412)624-0943
E-mail: kochanek@smtp.anes.upmc.edu
URL: http://www.safar.pitt.edu

Contact: Patrick M. Kochanek, MD, Dir.

Desc: Traumatic brain injury and mechanisms of secondary injury, cardiopulmonary arrest and resuscitation, disaster medicine, and suspended animation. *Type:* Research center.

West Virginia University

West Virginia Poison Center

3110 MacCorkle Ave. SE   Ph: (304)347-1212
Charleston, WV 25304   Fax: (304)348-9560

Contact: Elizabeth J. Scharman, Dir.

Desc: Demographics of poison victims and epidemiology of poisoning. Research is conducted in support of the Center's service program in poison prevention and management. *Type:* Research center.

Wilderness Medicine Newsletter

Holly A. Weber
PO Box 3150   Ph: (603)447-6711
Conway, NH 03818-3150   Fax: (603)447-2310
E-mail: solo@stonehearth.com

Contact: Holly Weber, Managing Editor; Buck Tilton, Contributing Editor; Frank Hubbell, DO, Contributing Editor; Bryan Yeaton, Contributing Editor.

Desc: Discusses practices and ideas regarding medical care and treatment in remote environments. Provides information on bacteria and viruses, techniques, medication, and seminars. *Type:* Newsletter.

Employee Benefits

ACA Journal

American Compensation Association (ACA)
14040 N. Northsight Blvd.   Ph: (602)951-9191
Scottsdale, AZ 85260

Contact: Michael A. Bennett, Editor.

Desc: Offers strategic-focused articles dealing with topics such as compensation, benefits, and human resources management. *Type:* Newsletter.

ACA News

American Compensation Association (ACA)
14040 N. Northsight Blvd.   Ph: (602)951-9191
Scottsdale, AZ 85260

Contact: Rodney K. Platt, Editor.

Desc: Concentrates on issues in the fields of compensation and benefits and human resource management. Includes legislative updates, resources, and case studies. *Type:* Newsletter.

American Society of Pension Actuaries

4350 N. Fairfax Dr., Ste. 820   Ph: (703)516-9300
Arlington, VA 22203   Fax: (703)516-9308
E-mail: aspa@pixpc.com
URL: http://www.aspa.org

Contact: Brian H. Graff, Exec. Dir.

Desc: Individuals involved in the consulting, administrative, and design aspects of the employee benefit business. Promotes high standards in the profession; provides nine-part educational program. *Type:* Association.

Association of Private Pension and Welfare Plans

1212 New York Ave. NW, Ste.   Ph: (202)289-6700
1250   Fax: (202)289-4582
Washington, DC 20005-3987
URL: http://www.appwp.org

Contact: James A. Klein, Pres.

Desc: Membership includes large and small industrial, financial, and professional companies. Serves as the business community's lobbying arm on employee benefits policy. *Type:* Association.

Bank Wage-Hour and Personnel Report

A.S. Pratt & Sons
1911 Fort Myer Dr., Ste. 308   Ph: (703)528-0145
Arlington, VA 22209   Free: 800-572-2797

Desc: Provides information about federal employment regulations. Focuses on financial institutions. *Type:* Newsletter.

Benefits Communicator

HR Communication Services
PO Box 671   Ph: (804)751-5003
Richmond, VA 23218-0671

Contact: Ann Black, Editor, ablack8653@aol.com.

Desc: Reports trends and issues in benefits administration and employee communications. Recurring features include news of research, reports of meetings, notices of publications available, and a column titled Quick Tips. *Type:* Newsletter.

BenefitsLink

BenefitsLink, Inc.
1014 E. Robinson St.   Ph: (407)841-3717
Orlando, FL 32801   Fax: (407)841-3054
URL: http://www.benefitslink.com/index.shtml

Contact: Dave Baker, Webmaster, erisa@benefitslink.com.

Desc: Anyone with a question about their benefits will probably be able to find an answer here. In the unlikely event that this site doesn't hold the answer, there are a number of links to other Internet benefit resources. *Type:* Database.

BNA Pension & Benefits Reporter

The Bureau of National Affairs, Inc. (BNA)
1231 25th St. NW   Ph: (202)452-4200
Washington, DC 20037
E-mail: bnaplus@bna.com
URL: http://bna.com/mkt/hrl/hrlwdec.htm

Contact: BNA PLUS, (202)452-4323, fax: (202)822-8092, bnaplus@bna.com.

Desc: Contains the complete text of the current developments section of the BNA Pension Reporter, covering legislative, regulatory, and judicial activities related to pensions and benefits. Includes taxation of benefits, individual retirement accounts, and fringe benefits. *Available:* LEXIS-NEXIS, LEXIS; West Group, WESTLAW; LEXIS-NEXIS, NEXIS. *Type:* Database.

BNA Pension & Benefits Reporter

Bureau of National Affairs, Inc. (BNA)
1231 25th St. NW   Ph: (202)452-4323
Washington, DC 20037   Free: 800-372-1033
    Fax: (202)452-7773
E-mail: bnaplus@bna.com

Contact: David A. Sayre, Editor.

Desc: Covers pension developments stemming from the passage of the Employee Retirement Income Security Act of 1974 (ERISA) and its amendments. Discusses pension and welfare benefit regulations, standards, enforcement actions, court decisions, legislative and administrative actions, agency options, and employee benefit trust fund requirements. *Type:* Newsletter.

BNA Pensions & Benefits Daily

The Bureau of National Affairs, Inc. (BNA)
1231 25th St. NW   Ph: (202)452-4200
Washington, DC 20037
E-mail: bnaplus@bna.com
URL: http://bna.com/mkt/hrl/hrlwdec.htm

Desc: Contains current information on significant judicial, legislative, and regulatory developments affecting employee benefits and pension planning. Covers federal and state court decisions, legislation, and regulations relating to health insurance, tax reform, benefits, and pensions. *Available:* LEXIS-NEXIS, LEXIS; West Group, WESTLAW; LEXIS-NEXIS, NEXIS. *Type:* Database.

BNA's Workers' Compensation Report

Bureau of National Affairs, Inc. (BNA)
1231 25th St. NW   Ph: (202)452-4323
Washington, DC 20037   Free: 800-372-1033
    Fax: (202)452-7773
E-mail: bnaplus@bna.com

Contact: Gail Moorstein, Managing Editor, gmoorstein@bna.com.

Desc: Covers national and state workers' compensation developments. Provides information on legal, legislative, and industry developments, actions, and trends related to workers' compensation. *Type:* Newsletter.

Business Insurance—Directory of Employee Assistance Program Providers and Dependent Care Resource and Referral Services

Crain Communications, Inc.
740 N. Rush St.   Ph: (312)649-5200
Chicago, IL 60611-2590   Fax: (312)649-5360

Contact: Sandra L. Budde, Editor.

Desc: Directory of more than 120 employee assistance providers and approximately 10 dependent care providers. *Type:* Directory.

Business Insurance Directory of 401(K) Plan Administrators

Crain Communications, Inc.
740 N. Rush St.   Ph: (312)649-5200
Chicago, IL 60611-2590   Fax: (312)649-5360

Contact: Sandra L. Budde, Editor.

Desc: List of over 75 companies that administer 401(K) insurance plans. *Type:* Directory.

Business Insurance—Employee Benefit Information Systems Issue

Crain Communications, Inc.
740 N. Rush St.   Ph: (312)649-5200
Chicago, IL 60611-2590   Fax: (312)649-5360

Contact: Sandra L. Budde, Editor.

Desc: Directory of approximately 70 employee benefit information system developers/vendors in the United States. *Type:* Directory.

Canadian Alliance of British Pensioners Newsletter

Canadian Alliance of British Pensioners
605 Royal York Rd., Ste. 202   Ph: (416)253-6402
Toronto, ON, Canada M8Y   Fax: (416)253-6402
4G5

Contact: Douglas T. Ross, President, (416)929-5494, fax: (416)929-1892.

Desc: Follows the Association's lobbying to effect a cost of living increase to be paid to British pensioners residing in Canada, from the viewpoint that the current policy is "manifestly immoral and discriminatory." Supplies an alphabetical list of constituencies and members of Parliament. Recurring features include interviews, news of research, a calendar of events, and reports of meetings. *Type:* Newsletter.

Compensation

Bureau of National Affairs, Inc. (BNA)
1231 25th St. NW   Ph: (202)452-4323
Washington, DC 20037   Free: 800-372-1033
    Fax: (202)452-7773
E-mail: bnaplus@bna.com

Contact: Jeff Day, Managing Editor.

Desc: Offers legal clarification and practical advice on employers' pay and benefit policies. Discusses such topics as health care cost containment, payroll laws and taxes, workers compensation laws, pension law (ERISA), job evaluation, benefit plans, compensation administration, incentive systems, and independent contractors. *Type:* Newsletter.

Compensation and Benefits for Law Offices

Institute of Management & Administration, Inc.
29 W. 35th St., 5th Fl.   Ph: (212)244-0360
New York, NY 10001-2299   Fax: (212)564-0465
E-mail: subserve@ioma.com; ctimmers@ioma.com.
URL: http://www.ioma.com

Contact: Usu Isom-Rodriguez, Editor; Lee Rath, Publisher.

Desc: Provides cost reduction tips for law offices. *Type:* Newsletter.

Compensation Benefits Newsletter

Research Institute of America
PO Box 5159   Free: 800-431-9025
Carol Stream, IL 60197

Desc: Reports on up-to-date federal compliance rules and regulations and related information. *Type:* Newsletter.

Compensation & Benefits Report

Bureau of Business Practice
24 Rope Ferry Rd. Ph: (860)442-4365
Waterford, CT 06386 Free: 800-243-0876
       Fax: (860)437-3555
URL: http://www.bbpnews.com
Contact: Joanne Mitchell-George, Managing Editor, joan-ne_mitchell-george@prenhall.com.
Desc: Provides legislative news concerning benefits and compensation. Reports and explains consequences of recent court cases. *Type:* Newsletter.

Controller's Cost Report

Warren, Gorham & Lamont, Inc.
RIA Group
PO Box 6159 Free: 800-950-1216
Carol Stream, IL 60197
Contact: D. Cummings, Editor.
Desc: Provides practical guidance on how to control costs and improve your company's performance. *Type:* Newsletter.

Corporate Jobs Outlook!

Plunkett Research, Ltd.
PO Drawer 541737 Ph: (713)932-0000
Houston, TX 77254-1737 Fax: (713)932-7080
E-mail: sales@plunkettresearch.com
Contact: Jack W. Plunkett, Editor and Publisher.
Desc: Provides information about corporate employment opportunities. Includes salaries, benefits, and hiring policies. *Type:* Newsletter.

EBRI Issue Brief

Employee Benefit Research Institute
2121 K St. NW, Ste. 600 Ph: (202)659-0670
Washington, DC 20037-1896 Fax: (202)775-6312
E-mail: publications@ebri.org
URL: http://www.ebri.org.
Contact: Dallas Salisbury, Editor.
Desc: Examines, analyzes, and interprets key issues and trends in the employee benefits field. Covers one topic in-depth in each issue. *Type:* Newsletter.

Employee Benefit Notes

Employee Benefit Research Institute
2121 K St. NW, Ste. 600 Ph: (202)659-0670
Washington, DC 20037-1896 Fax: (202)775-6312
E-mail: publications@ebri.org
URL: http://www.ebri.org.
Contact: Dallas Salisbury, Editor.
Desc: "Analyzes and discusses newly released employee benefits data and reviews a wide range of policy issues, research and publications." Recurring features include news of research, legal analysis, legislative updates. *Type:* Newsletter.

Employee Benefit Research Institute

2121 K St. NW, Ste. 600 Ph: (202)659-0670
Washington, DC 20037 Fax: (202)775-6312
E-mail: info@ebri.org
URL: http://www.ebri.org
Contact: Dallas Lincoln Salisbury, Pres. & CEO.
Desc: Corporations, consulting firms, banks, insurance companies, unions, and others with an interest in the future of employee benefit programs. Purpose is to contribute to the development of effective and responsible public policy in the field of employee benefits through research, publications, educational programs, seminars, and direct communication. Sponsors a broad range of studies on retirement income, health, disability, and other benefit programs; disseminates study results. *Type:* Association.

Employee Benefits Alert

Warren, Gorham & Lamont R.I.A. Group
90 Fifth Ave., 10th Fl. Ph: (212)807-2193
New York, NY 10011 Free: 800-950-1216
       Fax: (212)337-4183
Contact: John D. Reynolds, Editor.
Desc: Provides information on the latest ideas and developments in the fields of employee benefits. Offers advice and up-to-date coverage on IRS actions, employment law, benefits planning, social security developments, and related topics. *Type:* Newsletter.

Employee Benefits Basics

International Foundation of Employee Benefit Plans
PO Box 69 Ph: (414)786-6700
Brookfield, WI 53008-0069 Free: 888-334-3327
       Fax: (414)786-8670
E-mail: books@ifebp.org
URL: http://www.ifebp.org
Contact: Mary Jo Brzezinski, Editor.
Desc: Features basic introductory articles on one aspect of employee benefits per issue. Recurring features include notices of publications available. *Type:* Newsletter.

Employee Benefits Cases

Bureau of National Affairs, Inc. (BNA)
1231 25th St. NW Ph: (202)452-4323
Washington, DC 20037 Free: 800-372-1033
       Fax: (202)452-7773
E-mail: bnaplus@bna.com
URL: http://www.bna.com.
Contact: David A. Sayre, Managing Editor.
Desc: Reports full text of federal and state court opinions and selected decisions of arbitrators and the National Labor Relations Board on employee benefits issues. Recurring features include a cumulative index digest, tables of cases, a topical index, and a classification guide. *Type:* Newsletter.

Employee Benefits Digest

International Foundation of Employee Benefit Plans
PO Box 69 Ph: (414)786-6700
Brookfield, WI 53008-0069 Free: 888-334-3327
       Fax: (414)786-8670
E-mail: books@ifebp.org
URL: http://www.ifebp.org
Contact: Mary Jo Brezinski, Editor.
Desc: Covers the field of employee benefits. Recurring features include notices of publications and educational opportunities, news and announcements for members, and a review of current literature. *Type:* Newsletter.

Employee Benefits Management Directions

CCH Inc.
2700 Lake Cook Rd. Ph: (847)267-7000
Riverwoods, IL 60015 Free: 800-449-8114
       Fax: (847)224-8299
URL: http://www.cch.com
Desc: Considers new trends in employee benefits management, including 401k plans, family leave programs, health insurance, retirement plans, and relocation assistance. Provides tax information and news of legislation and court cases. *Type:* Newsletter.

Employee Benefits Review

S. Harman & Associates, Inc.
PO Box 1129 Ph: (410)795-9296
Sykesville, MD 21784 Fax: (410)549-1261
E-mail: sharmaninc@sharmansite.com
Contact: Saundra K. Harman, Editor.
Desc: Covers labor, personnel, and technical issues in the federal personnel area. Lists upcoming conferences, workshops, and training seminars. *Type:* Newsletter.

Employee Compensation

Business & Legal Reports, Inc.
39 Academy St. Ph: (203)318-0000
Madison, CT 06443 Free: 800-727-5257
       Fax: (203)245-2559
E-mail: service@blr.com
Contact: Stephen Fouvnier, J.D., Managing Editor.
Desc: News, comment, and prognostication on employee compension, and benefits. *Type:* Newsletter.

Employee Ownership Report

National Center for Employee Ownership
1201 Martin Luther King Jr. Ph: (510)272-9461
Way Fax: (510)272-9510
Oakland, CA 94612
E-mail: nceo@nceo.org
URL: http://www.nceo.org; http://www.nceo.org.
Desc: Provides information and news regarding employee ownership, employee stock ownership plans, participation, and communication. *Type:* Newsletter.

Employers Association

Richard J. Daniel
8848 -H Red Oak Blvd. Ph: (704)522-8011
Charlotte, NC 28217-5518 Fax: (704)522-8105
URL: http://www.employersassoc.com
Contact: Richard J. Daniel, Pres./CEO.
Desc: Works to promote human resources services. *Type:* Association.

Employers Council on Flexible Compensation

927 15th St. NW, Ste. 1000 Ph: (202)659-4300
Washington, DC 20005 Fax: (202)371-1467
E-mail: infoecfc@ecfc.org
URL: http://www.ecfc.org
Contact: K. E. Feltman, Exec.Dir.
Desc: Employers who have implemented or are interested in flexible compensation plans allowing employees to choose from a variety of benefits packages. Promotes flexible compensation plans including cafeteria plans, cash-or-deferred plans, and other defined contribution plans. *Type:* Association.

ESOP Report

The ESOP Association
1726 M St. NW, Ste. 501 Ph: (202)293-2971
Washington, DC 20036-4507 Fax: (202)293-7568
E-mail: esop@the-esop-emplowner.org.
URL: http://www.the-esop-emplowner.org.
Contact: J. Michael Keeling, President.
Desc: Discusses issues and developments affecting Employee Stock Ownership Plans (ESOPs). Addresses legal, administrative, educational, and communication aspects of managing these employee benefit plans. *Type:* Newsletter.

Executive Compensation Reports

Harcourt Brace & Co.
6277 Sea Harbor Dr. Ph: (407)345-2000
Orlando, FL 32887 Free: 800-346-8648
       Fax: (407)345-8388
E-mail: dppub@acess.digex.net
URL: http://www.access.digex.net/~ppub.
Contact: Carol Bowie, Editor.
Desc: Provides executive compensation information and data. *Type:* Newsletter.

Flexible Benefits

Aspen Law & Business/Panel Publishers
1185 Avenue of the Americas, Ph: (212)597-0200
37th Fl. Free: 800-447-1777
New York, NY 10036 Fax: (212)597-0338
Contact: Gregory E. Matthews, Editor.

Desc: Features news and research of interest to benefit managers and consultants. Focus is on employee benefits that involve choice. *Type:* Newsletter.

Highlights
Foster Higgins
125 Broad St.   Fax: (212)574-9120
New York, NY 10004
URL: http://www.fosterhiggins.com.
Contact: Ann Webre, Editor, webre-a@fosterhiggins.com.
Desc: Publishes news and information on all types of benefits, including health plans, 401(k), and pensions. Also reports on government and IRS legislation. *Type:* Newsletter.

The HR Executive's Purchasing Resource
LRP Publications
747 Dresher Rd.   Ph: (215)784-0941
PO Box 980   Free: 800-341-7874
Horsham, PA 19044-0980   Fax: (215)784-0870
E-mail: custserve@lrp.com
URL: http://workindex.com.
Contact: David Shadovitz, Editor.
Desc: Approximately 100 vendor companies and associations serving all aspects of human resources administration, including benefits, consulting and information services, software, employee assistance programs, health care, meeting and conference facilities, out placement and recruitment services, pension and retirement, recognition awards and incentives, relocation services, safety and security, temporary services, testing and assessment, training and development, and other services. *Type:* Directory.

IBIS Briefing Service
Charles D. Spencer & Associates, Inc.
250 S. Wacker Dr., Ste. 600   Ph: (312)993-7900
Chicago, IL 60606-5834   Free: 800-555-5490
                                  Fax: (312)993-7910
E-mail: spencernet@mindspring.com
Contact: Bruce Spencer, Editor and Publisher; Erin Murphy, Asst. Editor; Cathleen Reidy, Advertising Dir.
Desc: Provides information on employee benefit plans and programs from around the world. *Type:* Newsletter.

International Foundation of Employee Benefit Plans
18700 W. Bluemound Rd.   Ph: (414)786-6700
PO Box 69   Free: 888-334-3327
Brookfield, WI 53008   Fax: (414)786-8670
E-mail: pr@ifebp.org
URL: http://www.ifebp.org
Contact: John A. Altobelli, CEO.
Desc: Jointly trusteed, public, Canadian, and company-sponsored employee benefit plans; administrators, labor organizations, employer associations, benefit consultants, investment counselors, insurance consultants, banks, attorneys, accountants, actuaries, and others who service or are interested in the field of employee benefit plans. Cosponsors the Certified Employee Benefit Specialist Program (CEBS) in the United States and Canada, a ten-course college-level study program leading to a professional designation in the employee benefits field. Conducts research on all aspects of employee benefit plan management; funds graduate and postgraduate studies. *Type:* Association.

International Personnel Management Association—Agency Issues
International Personnel Management Association
1617 Duke St.   Ph: (703)549-7100
Alexandria, VA 22314   Fax: (703)684-0948
E-mail: ipma@ipma-hr.org
URL: http://www.ipma-hr.org.

Contact: Karen D. Smith, Editor.
Desc: Presents news and information on medical, family leave, and educational assistance legislation, illiteracy, military leave, and pensions. *Type:* Newsletter.

IOMA's Report on Defined Contribution Plan Investing
Institute of Management & Administration, Inc.
29 W. 35th St., 5th Fl.   Ph: (212)244-0360
New York, NY 10001-2299   Fax: (212)564-0465
E-mail: subserve@ioma.com
URL: http://www.ioma.com; http://www.ioma.com/.
Contact: Sean G. Hanna, Editor.
Desc: Provides market news and coverage of trends for the defined contribution industry. Includes GIC yields, investment manager performance, DC Plan company stock holdings, and asset allocation trends. *Type:* Newsletter.

Legal-Legislative Reporter
International Foundation of Employee Benefit Plans
PO Box 69   Ph: (414)786-6700
Brookfield, WI 53008-0069   Free: 888-334-3327
                                  Fax: (414)786-8670
E-mail: books@ifebp.org
URL: http://www.ifebp.org
Contact: Jeffrey C. Pepper, Editor.
Desc: Presents news of court and legislative actions pertinent to employee benefit plans. *Type:* Newsletter.

National Committee to Preserve Social Security and Medicare
10 G St. NE, Suite 600   Ph: (202)216-0420
Washington, DC 20002   Free: 800-966-1935
                                  Fax: (202)216-0451
Contact: Martha A. McSteen, CEO/Pres.
Desc: Grassroots senior citizens' advocacy and education association. Seeks to inform its members and the public through forums, presentations, written correspondence, and telephone communication. *Type:* Association.

National Public Employment Reporter
LRP Publications
747 Dresher Rd.   Ph: (215)784-0941
PO Box 980   Free: 800-341-7874
Horsham, PA 19044-0980   Fax: (215)784-0870
E-mail: custserve@lrp.com
Contact: Virginia Kretschman, Managing Editor.
Desc: Provides coverage of the public employment field. Features extensive reporting on state and local public employment. *Type:* Newsletter.

Payroll Legal Alert
Alexander Hamilton Institute
70 Hilltop Rd.   Ph: (201)825-3377
Ramsey, NJ 07446-1119   Free: 800-879-2441
                                  Fax: (201)825-8696
E-mail: custsvc@ahipubs.com
URL: http://www.ahipubs.com
Contact: Alice Gilman, ESQ, Editor.
Desc: Covers aspects of payroll operations, including key tax, employment law, benefits laws, regulations, rulings, and cases. Includes new trends in tax and employment law, ideas on benefits, wage and hour traps, and unemployment issues. *Type:* Newsletter.

Pension Fund Litigation Reporter
Andrews Publications
175 Strafford Ave., Bldg. 4, Ste. Ph: (610)225-0510
140   Free: 800-345-1101
Wayne, PA 19087   Fax: (610)225-0501
URL: http://www.andrewspub.com.
Contact: Robert W. McSherry, Editor, bobmc@andrewspub.com.

Type: Newsletter.

Pension Plan Guide—Summary
CCH Inc.
2700 Lake Cook Rd.   Ph: (847)267-7000
Riverwoods, IL 60015   Free: 800-449-8114
                                  Fax: (847)224-8299
URL: http://www.cch.com
Contact: Theodore Simons, Editor.
Desc: Focuses on pension nondiscrimination rules, benefit trends, court decisions, IRS and ERISA regulation and releases, withdrawal liability, and Supreme Court actions regarding pension plans. *Type:* Newsletter.

Pensions and Deferred Compensation Update
CCH Inc.
2700 Lake Cook Rd.   Ph: (847)267-7000
Riverwoods, IL 60015   Free: 800-449-8114
                                  Fax: (847)224-8299
URL: http://www.cch.com
Contact: Ted Simons, Managing Editor.
Desc: Provides news on pension plans and deferred compensation. Topics include pending legislation, IRS and Labor Department rulings, and court decisions. *Type:* Newsletter.

Retirement Plans Bulletin
Universal Pensions, Inc.
431 Golf Course Rd. N.   Ph: (218)829-4781
PO Box 979   Free: 800-346-3860
Brainerd, MN 56401   Fax: (218)829-2106
Contact: Jennifer Olsen, Editor.
Desc: Covers news and information affecting the administration and regulation of IRAs, Roth IRAs, Education IRAs, MSAs, qualified retirement plans and SIMPLES. *Type:* Newsletter.

Society of Professional Benefit Administrators
Two Wisconsin Cir., Ste. 670   Ph: (301)718-7722
Chevy Chase, MD 20815-7003   Fax: (301)718-9440
Contact: Frederick D. Hunt, Jr., Pres.
Desc: Third Party Administration (TPA), contract employee benefit plan administration firms. Member firms provide out-of-house professional benefit administration and claims services for client employee benefit plans. Deals with employee benefits and such issues as: the Employee Retirement Income Security Act (ERISA); tax; health insurance; self-funding of benefit plans. *Type:* Association.

Tax Management Compensation Planning
Tax Management Inc.
Bureau of National Affairs, Inc.
1250 23rd St. NW   Ph: (202)833-7240
Washington, DC 20037   Free: 800-372-1033
URL: http://taxmanagement.bna.com.
Contact: Glenn B. Davis, Managing Editor.
Desc: Covers tax planning problems involving employee benefits and executive compensation. Recurring features include detailed analyses, working papers, and bibliographies. *Type:* Newsletter.

Work/Life Today
National Institute of Business Management
1750 Old Meadow Rd., Ste.   Ph: (703)905-8000
302   Free: 800-543-2049
Mc Lean, VA 22102   Fax: (703)905-8042
Contact: Michael Levin-Epstein, Editor; March Levin-Epstein, Editor.
Desc: Provides information on "family-friendly" benefit programs. *Type:* Newsletter.

Workers' Comp Advisor - Texas Edition

Genesis Publishing, Inc.

12626 High Bluff Dr., Ste. 325   Ph: (619)453-0858

San Diego, CA 92130-2073

Contact: Donna M. Buys, Editor.

Desc: Contains information on workers' compensation and occupational medicine issues. Recurring features include letters to the editor, interviews, news of research, a calendar of events, reports of meetings, news of educational opportunities, book reviews, notices of publications available, and a column titled Med-Legal Brief. *Type:* Newsletter.

Workers' Compensation Law Bulletin

Quinlan Publishing Company

23 Drydock Ave.   Ph: (617)542-0048

Boston, MA 02210   Free: 800-229-2084

    Fax: (617)345-9646

E-mail: quinlanp@quinlan.com

Contact: Carol Johnson Perkins, Editor.

Desc: Summarizes in layman's terms recent court cases deriving from the worker compensation law, with specific identification of cases and brief explanations of the court decisions. *Type:* Newsletter.

Workers Compensation Outlook

Standard Publishing Corp.

155 Federal St.   Ph: (617)457-0600

Boston, MA 02110-9637   Free: 800-682-5759

    Fax: (617)457-0608

E-mail: stnd@earthlink.net

Contact: Meike Olin, Editor.

Desc: Provides practical solutions to workers' compensation problems. Features information on cutting compensation costs while maintaining coverage in today's market; cost controlling; improving coverage; and staying abreast on program developments. *Type:* Newsletter.

Employment

ACSM's Career Services Bulletin

American College of Sports Medicine

PO Box 1440   Ph: (317)637-9200

Indianapolis, IN 46206-1440   Fax: (317)634-7817

E-mail: pubacsm@acsm.org

Contact: David Brewer, Editor.

Desc: Lists international jobs for positions relating to sports medicine and exercise science. *Type:* Newsletter.

Affirmative Action Compliance Manual for Federal Contractors

Bureau of National Affairs, Inc. (BNA)

1231 25th St. NW   Ph: (202)452-4323

Washington, DC 20037   Free: 800-372-1033

    Fax: (202)452-7773

E-mail: bnaplus@bna.com

Contact: Jeff Day, Editor.

Desc: Provides text of the compliance manual issued by the Office of Federal Contract Compliance Programs and information on developments affecting affirmative action programs. *Type:* Newsletter.

Affirmative Action Register

Affirmative Action, Inc.

8356 Olive Blvd.   Ph: (314)991-1335

St. Louis, MO 63132   Free: 800-537-0655

    Fax: (314)997-1788

URL: http://www.aar-eeo.com.

Contact: Joyce R. Green, Editor.

Desc: In each issue, about 300 positions at a professional level (most requiring advanced study) available to women, minorities, veterans, and the handicapped; listings are advertisements placed by employers with affirmative action programs. *Type:* Directory.

The Almanac of American Employers

Plunkett Research, Ltd.

PO Drawer 541737   Ph: (713)932-0000

Houston, TX 77254-1737   Fax: (713)932-7080

E-mail: sales@plunkettresearch.com

URL: http://www.plunkettresearch.com.

Contact: Jack W. Plunkett, Editor.

Desc: Over 500 of the largest and fastest growing firms with 2,500 employees or more in America. Principal content of publication is Ranks and ratings for financial stability, salaries, benefits, hiring, corporate culture, special hiring/training programs, women and minorities in top posts, human resources contacts, complete financial records, advancement opportunity. *Type:* Directory.

American Association of School Personnel Administrators

3080 Brickhouse Ct.   Ph: (757)340-1217

Virginia Beach, VA 23452   Fax: (757)340-1889

E-mail: aaspa@aaspa.org

URL: http://www.aaspa.org

Contact: Herb Salinger, Exec.Dir.

Desc: Persons employed in school personnel administration in the U.S. and Canada. Establishes acceptable school personnel standards, techniques, and practices. *Type:* Association.

American Compensation Association

14040 N. Northsight Blvd.   Ph: (602)951-9191

Scottsdale, AZ 85260   Fax: (602)483-8352

E-mail: aca@acaonline.org

URL: http://www.acaonline.org

Contact: Wallace J. Nichols, CCP, Exec.Dir.

Desc: Managerial, professional, and executive level administrative personnel in business, industry, and government who are responsible for the design, establishment, execution, administration, or application of total compensation practices (including benefits) and policies in their organizations. Conducts surveys, research, and certification program; confers Certified Compensation Professional (CCP) designation and Certified Benefits Professional (CBP) designation. Furthers the exchange of information on current practice and research in all phases of employee compensation including wages, salaries, pensions, group insurance, and other related forms of employee remuneration. *Type:* Association.

American Jobs Abroad

Gale Group Inc.

27500 Drake Rd.   Ph: (248)699-4253

Farmington Hills, MI 48331-   Free: 800-877-GALE

3535   Fax: (248)699-8070

E-mail: galeord@galegroup.com

URL: http://www.galegroup.com.

Contact: Edward Knappman, Editor.

Desc: Over 800 U.S. corporations and 100 government agencies, associations, and other organizations that employ Americans overseas, generally on an ongoing or long-term basis at wages or salaries comparable to those in the U.S. *Type:* Directory.

American Payroll Association

30 E. 33rd St., 5th Fl.   Ph: (212)686-2030

New York, NY 10016   Fax: (212)686-4080

E-mail: apa@apa-ed.com

URL: http://www.americanpayroll.org

Contact: Daniel J. Maddux, Exec.Dir.

Desc: Payroll employees. Works to increase members' skills and professionalism through education and mutual support. *Type:* Association.

American Society of Employers

23815 Northwestern Hwy.   Ph: (810)353-4500

Southfield, MI 48075   Fax: (810)353-1224

Contact: William A. Sebastian, Pres.

Type: Association.

Asian Resources

5709 Stockton Blvd.   Ph: (916)454-1892

Sacramento, CA 95824   Fax: (916)454-1895

Contact: May O. Lee, Exec.Dir.

Desc: Provides information on employment opportunities to individuals who are unemployed with no other means of income and to disadvantaged individuals. *Type:* Association.

At Work

Berrett-Koehler Communications Inc.

8 California St., Ste. 610   Ph: (415)288-0260

San Francisco, CA 94111-4825   Free: 800-929-2929

    Fax: (415)362-2512

E-mail: bkpub@bkpub.com

URL: http://www.ReadersNdex.com;   http://www.atworknews.com.

Contact: Alis Valencia, Editor, (510)339-6700, fax: (510)339-6722, editor@atworknews.com.

Desc: Reports the "radical" changes transforming in the workplace. Describes how organizations put into practice "our most deeply held values—democracy, service, participation, integrity, partnership, empowerment, stewardship, environmental consciousness, etc." Recurring features include letters to the editor, book reviews, and columns titled Visions, Hearts & Minds, Reports on Innovative Practicies, and Resources. *Type:* Newsletter.

Bay Area Employer Directory

James R. Albin

431 Bridgeway   Ph: (415)332-6438

Sausalito, CA 94965   Fax: (415)332-6468

URL: http://www.albin.com.

Contact: James R. Albin, Editor, albin@sausalito.com.

Desc: Over 2,000 employers in the San Francisco Bay Area each having 100 or more employees; includes both private and government employers. *Type:* Directory.

Benefits Watch

Applied Benefits Research

34125 U.S. Highway 19N   Ph: (813)785-2819

Palm Harbor, FL 34684   Fax: (813)785-4306

Contact: Patrick Mandberg, Editor.

Desc: Concerned with the management of employee benefit compliance issues. *Type:* Newsletter.

The Better-Work Supervisor

Clement Communications, Inc.

Concord Industrial Park   Ph: (610)459-1700

10 LaCrue Ave.   Free: 800-345-8101

Concordville, PA 19331   Fax: (610)459-0936

Desc: Provides advice and suggestions for supervisors on how to handle their employees and potential problems in the workplace. Features proven case histories, examples of typical management problems and solutions, ways to promote teamwork, and methods of inspiring confidence in workers. *Type:* Newsletter.

BLR's Job Descriptions Encyclopedia

Business & Legal Reports, Inc.

39 Academy St.   Ph: (203)318-0000

Madison, CT 06443   Free: 800-727-5257

    Fax: (203)245-2559

E-mail: service@blr.com

Contact: Judith A. Ruddy, Editor, judyr@blr.com.

Desc: Profiles job descriptions and offers guidelines. *Type:* Newsletter.

BNA Policy and Practice Series

Bureau of National Affairs, Inc. (BNA)
1231 25th St. NW   Ph: (202)452-4323
Washington, DC 20037   Free: 800-372-1033
                          Fax: (202)452-7773
E-mail: bnaplus@bna.com
Contact: Jeff Day, Managing Editor.
Desc: Offers a notification and reference service concerning employer-employee relations. Covers personnel management, labor relations, fair employment practices, compensation, and wages and hours. *Type:* Newsletter.

BNA/PPF Surveys

Bureau of National Affairs, Inc. (BNA)
1231 25th St. NW   Ph: (202)452-4323
Washington, DC 20037   Free: 800-372-1033
                          Fax: (202)452-7773
E-mail: bnaplus@bna.com
Contact: J. Michael Reidy, Editor, mreidy@bna.com.
Desc: Reports on human resources topics derived from responses to questionnaires sent to the BNA's Personnel Policies Forum. Includes topics on recruiting and selection policies, promotion and transfer procedures, wage and salary administration, employee benefits and services, communication programs, grievance procedures, performance evaluation and motivation programs, training, staffing and scheduling strategies, the Internet, human resource staff and expenditures, reference checks, human resource priorities, and discipline and discharge policies. *Type:* Newsletter.

BNAC Communicator

BNA Communications, Inc.
Bureau of National Affairs, Inc. (BNA)
9493 Key West Ave.   Ph: (301)948-0540
Rockville, MD 20850   Free: 800-233-6067
                          Fax: (301)948-2085
URL: http://www.bna.com/bnac.
Contact: Tony Cornish, Editor; Theresa McGrail, Circulation Mgr.
Desc: Tabloid providing news and information to human resource professionals, safety, environment, and EEO compliance officers. *Type:* Periodical.

BNA's Human Resources Report

The Bureau of National Affairs, Inc. (BNA)
1231 25th St. NW   Ph: (202)452-4200
Washington, DC 20037
E-mail: bnaplus@bna.com
URL: http://bna.com/mkt/hrl/hrlwdec.htm
Desc: Contains the complete text of BNA Employee Relations Weekly, a newsletter on developments and trends affecting employee relations. Covers relevant national news, legislative and regulatory developments, labor economics, developments in training and technology, health benefits, employee-management relations, compensation, and legal developments. *Type:* Database.

Business and Finance Career Directory

Gale Group Inc.
27500 Drake Rd.   Ph: (248)699-4253
Farmington Hills, MI 48331- Free: 800-877-GALE
  3535   Fax: (248)699-8070
E-mail: galeord@galegroup.com
URL: http://www.galegroup.com.
Contact: Bradley J. Morgan, Editor.
Desc: Approximately 300 companies in accounting, banking, investment banking, stock brokerage, and insurance offering entry-level positions and internships; sources of help-wanted ads, professional associations, producers of videos, databases, career guides, and professional guides and handbooks. *Type:* Directory.

California Employer Advisor

Employer Resource Institute, Inc.
9 Main St., Ste. 700   Free: 800-695-7178
Tiburon, CA 94920   (415)435-9679
Contact: Larry J. Shapiro, Esq., Editor.
Desc: Serves as a guide to California employment law and employee relations. *Type:* Newsletter.

California Employer, MIC 84

California State Employment Development Department
PO Box 826880   Ph: (916)654-7079
Sacramento, CA 94280-0001 Fax: (916)654-5843
URL: http://www.edd.cahwnet.gov.
Contact: Kevin Callori, Editor.
Desc: Contains news and notes for California employers subject to the provisions of the California Unemployment Insurance Code. *Type:* Newsletter.

California Job Journal

California Job Journal
1800 Tribute Rd.   Ph: (916)925-0800
Sacramento, CA 95815-4314 Free: 800-655-JOBS
                          Fax: (916)925-0101
E-mail: cjj@jobjournal.com.
Contact: Clayton Babcock, Editor; Jay Verdoorn, Editor, editor@jobjournal.com.
Desc: Job openings in California from entry-level to executive positions. *Type:* Directory.

California State Council of Service Employees

1007 Seventh St., 4th Floor Ph: (916)442-3838
Sacramento, CA 95814-3407 Fax: (916)442-0976
Contact: Dean C. Tipps, Exec.Sec./Treas.
Type: Association.

Canadian Employment Law Letter

M. Lee Smith Publishers LLC
5201 Virginia Way   Ph: (615)373-7517
PO Box 5094   Free: 800-274-6774
Brentwood, TN 37024-5094 Fax: 800-785-9212
E-mail: custserv@mleesmith.com
URL: http://www.mleesmith.com.
Contact: Nancy A. Eber, Editor; Brian Smeenk, Editor.
Desc: Contains information on Canadian employment law. *Type:* Newsletter.

Canadian HR Reporter

MPL Communications Inc.
133 Richmond St., Ste. 700 Ph: (416)869-1177
Toronto, ON, Canada M5H   Fax: (416)869-0616
  3M8
E-mail: chrr@mplcomm.com.
Contact: George Pearson, Editor; John Hobel, Managing Editor; S. Pepper, Publisher; B. Martland, Publisher.
Desc: Provides Canadian human resource industry news and advice. *Type:* Newsletter.

Career Confidential

Bureau of Business Practice
24 Rope Ferry Rd.   Ph: (860)442-4365
Waterford, CT 06386   Free: 800-243-0876
                          Fax: (860)437-3555
URL: http://www.bbpnews.com
Contact: Deborah Cottrill, Editor, deborah_cottrill@prenhall.com; Elaine Stattler, Managing Editor.
Desc: Provides strategies for career management. Recurring features include interviews. *Type:* Newsletter.

The Career Guide—Dun's Employment Opportunities Directory

Dun & Bradstreet
3 Sylvan Way   Ph: (973)605-6442
Parsippany, NJ 07054-3896 Free: 800-526-0651
                          Fax: (973)605-6911
E-mail: dnbmdd@dnb.com
Desc: More than 5,000 companies on leading employers throughout the U.S. that provide career opportunities in sales, marketing, management, engineering, life and physical sciences, computer science, mathematics, statistics planning, accounting and finance, liberal arts fields, and other technical and professional areas; based on data supplied on questionnaires and through personal interviews. Also covers personnel consultants; includes some public sector employers (governments, schools, etc.) usually not found in similar lists. *Type:* Directory.

Career Opportunities News

Ferguson Publishing Co.
200 W. Madison, Ste. 300 Ph: (312)580-5480
Chicago, IL 60606   Fax: (312)580-4948
E-mail: fergpub@aol.com; connews@aol.com.
URL: http://www.fergpubco.com
Contact: Robert Calvert, Jr., Editor.
Desc: Examines career trends and occupations of the future, as well as current career opportunities. Carries information on job leads, information sources, salaries and comparable worth, internships, and grant programs. *Type:* Newsletter.

Career Planning & Adult Development Network Newsletter

Career Planning & Adult Development Network
4965 Sierra Rd.   Ph: (408)559-4945
San Jose, CA 95132   Fax: (408)559-8211
Contact: Richard Knowdell, Editor, knowdell@best.com.
Desc: Contains features and news items on career development and human resources: theory, methodology, research, practices, and techniques. Deals with manpower, organizational planning, counseling, training, equal opportunity, career transition, marketing skills, and adult learning. *Type:* Newsletter.

Careers for Dreamers and Doers: A Guide to Management Careers in the Nonprofit Sector

Foundation Center
79 5th Ave.   Ph: (212)620-4230
New York, NY 10003-3076   Free: 800-424-9836
                          Fax: (212)807-3677
Contact: Lilly Cohen, Editor; Dennis R. Young, Editor.
Desc: Nonprofit management programs at colleges and universities. Principal content of publication is job search advice and strategies, career histories of nonprofit C.E.O.s, development officers, and foundation officials, and compensation patterns in the field. *Type:* Directory.

The Caretaker Gazette

Gary C. Dunn
PO Box 5887   Ph: (602)488-1970
Carefree, AZ 85377-5887
E-mail: caretaker@uswest.com
URL: http://www.angelfire.com/wa/caretaker.
Contact: Thea K. Dunn, Editor.
Desc: Covers the property caretaking field. Recurring features include job listings, letters to the editor, interviews, and a column titled Caretaker Profile. *Type:* Newsletter.

Cartoon Opportunities

Cartoon Opportunities
PO Box 248   Ph: (215)822-9158
Chalfont, PA 18914   Fax: (215)723-9788
E-mail: billkeo@erols.com

Contact: Bradley Keough, Editor-in-Chief.

Desc: Functions as a marketplace to list work opportunities for cartoonists. *Type:* Newsletter.

Changing Course

Making Waves, Publishers
137 Barrett St.   Ph: (413)585-0451
Northampton, MA 01060   Free: 800-267-6388
    Fax: (413)584-6506
URL: http://www.changingcourse.com.

Contact: Valerie Young, Editor.

Desc: Contains alternative ideas and advisement on changing and choosing employment that suits ones lifestyle. Recurring features include letters to the editor, interviews, book reviews, notices of publications available, and columns titled Opportunities Knock: Creative Alternatives to Working 9-5, Resources for a Change, and Dollar/Sense. *Type:* Newsletter.

Checkpoint

Russell Staffing Resources
PO Box 6279   Ph: (415)781-1444
San Rafael, CA 94903-0279   Free: 800-616-JOBS
    Fax: (415)986-6003
E-mail: rsrjobs@netdex.com

Contact: Mark C. Simmons, Editor.

Desc: Designed to meet the needs of persons responsible for hiring and employment. Includes updates on hot trends, technologies, laws, new human resource tools, techniques, advice, and columns titled You Heard It Here First and It's Enough to Drive You Batty. *Type:* Newsletter.

The Chronicle of Higher Education

Merit Network, Inc.
4251 Plymouth Rd.   Ph: (313)764-9430
Ste. C   Fax: (313)647-3185
Ann Arbor, MI 48105-2785
E-mail: editor@.chronicle.com
URL: http://chronicle.com/jobs/

Desc: Provided by the Chronicle of Higher Education, this web site provides a number of services available only to subscribers, including: a full report of daily briefings on developments in higher education; reports on developments in information technology of interest to faculty members and administrators; daily updates on available grants; the full text of the current issue of The Chronicle, as well as an archive of back issues dating back over 8 years; and job announcements. Free services online include access to Colloquy, an open forum on issues in higher education, and job announcements from the previous issue of The Chronicle. *Type:* Database.

CJA Forum

CJA
17852 17th St., Suite 209   Ph: (714)731-0867
Tustin, CA 92780-2143

Contact: Lou Adler, Editor.

Desc: Covers employment issues, including hiring, selection, interviewing, and career management. *Type:* Newsletter.

The Classified News

Metroland Printing & Publishing
9350 Yonge St.   Ph: (905)881-3373
PO Box 390   Free: 800-565-6357
Richmond Hill, ON, Canada   Fax: (905)881-9924
L4C 4Y6

Contact: Judith Bullis, Editor.

Desc: Weekly employment newspaper. *Alt. Contact:* 3145 Wolfedale Rd., Mississauga, ON, Canada L5C 1W1; telephone: (416)273-8111; fax: (416)273-4991. *Type:* Periodical.

College and University Personnel Association

1233 20th St. NW, Ste. 301   Ph: (202)429-0311
Washington, DC 20036-1250   Fax: (202)429-0149
URL: http://www.cupa.org

Contact: Susan Jurow, Exec.Dir.

Desc: Professional organization made up of colleges and universities interested in the improvement of campus Human Resource administration. *Type:* Association.

Colorado Employment Law Letter

M. Lee Smith Publishers LLC
5201 Virginia Way   Ph: (615)373-7517
PO Box 5094   Free: 800-274-6774
Brentwood, TN 37024-5094   Fax: 800-785-9212
E-mail: custserv@mleesmith.com

Contact: John M. Husband, Editor; Sandra R. Goldman, Editor; Jude Biggs, Editor.

Desc: Addresses litigation and court decisions affecting employment issues. *Type:* Newsletter.

Colorado Job Finder

Colorado Municipal League
1660 Lincoln St., Ste. 2100   Ph: (303)831-6411
Denver, CO 80264   Fax: (303)860-8175

Contact: Barb Major, Contact.

Desc: Consists of local government employment opportunities in Colorado and surrounding area. *Type:* Newsletter.

Computing and Software Design Career Directory

Gale Group Inc.
27500 Drake Rd.   Ph: (248)699-4253
Farmington Hills, MI 48331-   Free: 800-877-GALE
3535   Fax: (248)699-8070
E-mail: galeord@galegroup.com
URL: http://www.galegroup.com.

Contact: Bradley J. Morgan, Editor; Joseph M. Palmisano, Editor.

Desc: Over 200 companies and organizations with entry-level opportunities as computer programmers, software engineers, technical writers, information center analysts, and similar positions; sources of help-wanted ads, professional associations, producers of videos, databases, career guides, and professional guides and handbooks. *Type:* Directory.

Connecticut Employment Law Letter

M. Lee Smith Publishers LLC
5201 Virginia Way   Ph: (615)373-7517
PO Box 5094   Free: 800-274-6774
Brentwood, TN 37024-5094   Fax: 800-785-9212
E-mail: custserv@mleesmith.com

Contact: Mike E. Foley, Editor; Fritz Morches, Editor.

Desc: Addresses legislation and court decisions affecting employment issues. *Type:* Newsletter.

Connecticut Labor Situation

Office of Research and Information
Connecticut State Department of Labor
200 Folly Brook Blvd.   Ph: (860)566-3462
Wethersfield, CT 06109   Fax: (860)566-7963

Contact: Salvatore DiPillo, Editor, salvatore.dipillo@po. state.ct.us.

Desc: Covers statewide employment, unemployment, earnings and hours, personal income of state residents, average manufacturing workweek hours, and other labor-related topics. *Type:* Newsletter.

County Employment and Wages

The WEFA Group
1110 Vermont Ave., NW   Ph: (202)775-0610
Washington, DC 20005
URL: http://www.fdic.gov

Desc: Contains more than 81,000 monthly and quarterly time series on employment and wages for all 3140 U.S. counties. *Available:* The WEFA Group. *Type:* Database.

County Personal Income, Population, and Employment

The WEFA Group
1110 Vermont Ave., NW   Ph: (202)775-0610
Washington, DC 20005
URL: http://www.fdic.gov

Desc: Contains approximately 180,000 annual time series from the Bureau of Economic Analysis for all U.S. counties. *Available:* The WEFA Group. *Type:* Database.

Creative Training Techniques

Lakewood Publications, Inc.
50 S. 9th St.   Ph: (612)333-0471
Minneapolis, MN 55402   Free: 800-328-4329
    Fax: (612)333-6521
E-mail: justask@lakewoodpub.com
URL: http://www.lakewoodpub.com.

Contact: Bob Pike, Editor; Randy Johnson, Editor.

Desc: Provides basic, quick-results-oriented ideas, techniques, and delivery methods for training employees. Covers programs, training aids, and equipment. *Type:* Newsletter.

Cultural Diversity at Work Newsletter

The GilDeane Group, Inc.
13751 Lake City Way NE, Ste.   Ph: (206)362-0336
210   Fax: (206)363-5028
Seattle, WA 98125-8612
E-mail: 75364.2356@compuserve.com; editors@ diversityhotwire.com.
URL: http://www.diversityhotwire.com.

Contact: Barbara R. Deane, Editor-in-Chief; Alison Peacock, Managing Editor.

Desc: Focuses on how diverse people can work together and conduct business effectively. Articles contain information on recruiting diverse employees, working with upper management, designing diversity training, facilitating diversity task forces, building productive multicultural teams, and marketing to diverse groups. *Type:* Newsletter.

Current Employment

Publishing and Business Consultants
4427 W. Slauson Ave.
Los Angeles, CA 90043-2717

Contact: Atia Napoleon, Editor and Publisher.

Desc: Magazine featuring updated information on current government jobs and industry trends. *Type:* Periodical.

Directory of Outplacement Firms

Kennedy Information
One Kennedy Place, Route 12   Ph: (603)585-6544
South   Free: 800-531-0007
Fitzwilliam, NH 03447   Fax: (603)585-9221
E-mail: bookstore@kennedyinfo.com
URL: http://www.kennedyinfo.com

Desc: 200 outplacement-management consulting firms. *Type:* Directory.

Disabled Businesspersons Association

SDSU Institute   Ph: (619)594-8805
5850 Hardy Ave., No. 112   Fax: (619)594-4208
San Diego, CA 92182-5313
E-mail: dbanet@ix.netcom.com
URL: http://www.web-link.com/dba/dba.htm

Contact: Urban Miyares, Pres.

Desc: Persons with disabilities, corporations, organizations, government agencies, and interested individuals. Works to help disabled entrepreneurs and professionals maximize their potential in the business world. *Type:* Association.

DISCovering Careers & Jobs

Gale Group Inc.
27500 Drake Rd.　　　　　Ph: (248)699-4253
Farmington Hills, MI 48331-　Free: 800-877-GALE
3535　　　　　　　　　　Fax: (248)699-8070
E-mail: galeord@galegroup.com
URL: http://www.galegroup.com.; http://www.gale.com.
Desc: Descriptions of over 1,400 job titles in some 250 career areas; over 1,000 abstracts, excerpts, and selected articles on various job issues; listings of informational and training programs, trade directories, certification agencies, profesional associations, periodicals, career and test guides, employment agencies, sources of want ads, scholarships and awards. *Type:* Directory.

DISCovering Careers & Jobs Plus

Gale Group Inc.
27500 Drake Rd.　　　　　Ph: (248)699-4253
Farmington Hills, MI 48331-　Free: 800-877-GALE
3535　　　　　　　　　　Fax: (248)699-8070
E-mail: galeord@galegroup.com
URL: http://www.galegroup.com.
Desc: Approximately 41,000 potential employers; profiles and application procedures for all major two- and four-year U.S. colleges and universities, vocational schools, financial aid and scholarships. *Type:* Directory.

EEO Review

John Wiley and Sons, Inc.
605 3rd Ave.　　　　　　Ph: (212)850-6000
New York, NY 10158　　　Free: 800-225-5945
　　　　　　　　　　　　Fax: (212)850-6049
E-mail: subinfo@wiley.com
Contact: Sarah Magee, Editor; Jean Stephenson, Managing Editor, jstephenson@qm.jwiley.com.
Desc: Provides information for personnel managers and supervisors who want to handle EEO (Equal Employment Opportunity) and other personnel policy responsibilities more effectively and keep their company out of jeopardy. Offers approaches to dealing with substance abuse, AIDS, hiring and firing, promotions, employee discipline, counseling, and supervising the handicapped. *Type:* Newsletter.

EEOC Compliance Manual

Bureau of National Affairs, Inc. (BNA)
1231 25th St. NW　　　　Ph: (202)452-4323
Washington, DC 20037　　Free: 800-372-1033
　　　　　　　　　　　　Fax: (202)452-7773
E-mail: bnaplus@bna.com
Contact: Jeff Day, Managing Editor; Gail Moorstein, Asst. Managing Editor.
Desc: Summarizes and analyzes policies, procedures, and standards followed by the staff of the Equal Employment Opportunity Commission (EEOC). Contains text of compliance procedures, interpretive manual, conciliation standards, and EEOC regional attorneys' deskbook. *Type:* Newsletter.

EMA Reporter

Society for Human Resource Management
606 N. Washington St.　　Ph: (703)548-3440
Alexandria, VA 22314　　　Fax: (703)836-0367
E-mail: shrm@shrm.org
Contact: Llyod Pernell, Editor.
Desc: Facilitates the exchange of information and ideas among members of the Association, which aims to "advance professionalism within the area of employment and associated resources functions." Alerts members to employment trends and issues and to employment litigation. Recurring features include member and Association news and meeting reports. *Type:* Newsletter.

Employee Benefits and Executive Compensation Counselor

Business Laws Inc.
11630 Chillicothe Rd.　　Ph: (440)729-7996
Chesterland, OH 44026　　Free: 800-759-0929
　　　　　　　　　　　　Fax: (440)729-0645
E-mail: hancock@counsel.com
URL: http://www.Businesslaws.com
Contact: W.M. Hancock, Editor.
Desc: Contains discussions of employee benefit issues, ERISA enforcement, benefit claims, and executive compensation issues such as employment agreements. Recurring features include reports of meetings. *Type:* Newsletter.

EMPLOYEE BENEFITS INFOSOURCE™

International Foundation of Employee Benefit Plans (IFEBP)
18700 W. Bluemound Rd.　Ph: (414)786-6710
PO Box 69
Brookfield, WI 53008-0069
E-mail: ebinfo@ifebp.org
URL: http://www.ifebp.org
Contact: Employee Benefits Inforsource Department, (414)786-6710, fax: (414)786-8780, ebinfo@ifebp.org.
Desc: Contains more than 80,000 citations, with abstracts, to the worldwide literature on employee benefit plans. Covers surveys, statistics, trends, and background information in these areas: corporate, union, and public employee benefit plans, group insurance, international benefits, pension investments, health care, compensation, human resources, and benefit plan service providers. *Available:* The Dialog Corporation, DIALOG; West Group, WESTLAW. *Type:* Database.

Employee Health & Fitness

American Health Consultants, Inc.
3525 Piedmont Rd., Bldg. 6,　Ph: (404)262-7436
Ste. 400　　　　　　　　　Free: 800-688-2421
Atlanta, GA 30305　　　　　Fax: (404)262-7837
E-mail: customerservice@ahcpub.com
Contact: Stephen E. Lewis, Editor.
Desc: Contains updates on corporate health promotion programs, and information on weight loss, exercise, smoking cessation, high blood pressure, and wellness activities. Also includes information on employee assistance programs and suggestions from experts on improving wellness programs in the workplace. *Type:* Newsletter.

Employee Relocation Council

1720 N St. NW　　　　　　Ph: (202)857-0857
Washington, DC 20036　　　Fax: (202)467-4012
E-mail: info@erc.org
URL: http://www.erc.org
Contact: H. Cris Collie, Exec.VP.
Desc: Representatives of major corporations that transfer personnel and representatives from the relocation service industry. Seeks to study, evaluate, and communicate information on practices and procedures in relocation of employees, so that the transfer may be accomplished with maximum efficiency and minimum disruption to the employee, his or her family, and the employer. *Type:* Association.

Employee Terminations Law Bulletin

Quinlan Publishing Company
23 Drydock Ave.　　　　Ph: (617)542-0048
Boston, MA 02210　　　Free: 800-229-2084
　　　　　　　　　　　　Fax: (617)345-9646
E-mail: quinlanp@quinlan.com
Contact: Alfred Gordon, Esq., Editor.
Desc: Advises employers on preventable errors and lawful procedure regarding employee dismissal. Reports on court decisions involving employee terminations. *Type:* Newsletter.

Employment Bulletin

Rhode Island Department of Labor and Training
101 Friendship St.　　　　Ph: (401)222-3706
Providence, RI 02903-3740　Fax: (401)222-2731
URL: http://www.dlt.state.rieus; http://www.det.state.ri.us/webdev/lmi/lmihome.html.
Contact: Maria Ferreira, Editor, mferreira@dlt.state.ri.us.
Desc: Focuses on employment and unemployment activity in Rhode Island. Recurring features include news of research and notices of publications available. *Type:* Newsletter.

Employment Discrimination Law Update

Oakstone Legal & Business Publishing
4635 Nicols Rd., Ste. 100　Ph: (651)452-8267
Eagan, MN 55122-3337　　Free: 800-365-4900
　　　　　　　　　　　　Fax: (651)452-8694
Desc: Contains judicial decisions, legislation, administrative regulations, and Law Review articles impacting employment issues, specifically on discrimination. *Type:* Newsletter.

Employment Guide

The Bureau of National Affairs, Inc. (BNA)
1231 25th St. NW　　　　Ph: (202)452-4200
Washington, DC 20037
E-mail: bnaplus@bna.com
URL: http://www.bna.com/mkt/hrl/hrlwdec.htm
Desc: Contains the complete text of Employment and Policy Guide, providing information on trends and developments in employment policies and employee relations. Covers drug and alcohol abuse, holidays, leaves, polygraph testing, performance appraisals, use of references, retirement, use of company car, and workplace smoking. *Type:* Database.

Employment Guide Newsletter

The Bureau of National Affairs, Inc. (BNA)
1231 25th St. NW　　　　Ph: (202)452-4200
Washington, DC 20037
E-mail: bnaplus@bna.com
URL: http://bna.com/mkt/hrl/hrlwdec.htm
Desc: Contains the complete text of the Employment Guide Newsletter, providing news and information on developments in the workplace. Covers legal and regulatory changes that affect workplace policies, solutions to employee relations problems, and innovative employment practices. *Type:* Database.

Employment Law Update

Rutkowski & Associates, Inc.
Box 15250　　　　　　　　Ph: (812)476-4520
Evansville, IN 47716-0250
Contact: Arthur D. Rutkowski, Editor; Barbara Rutkowski, Editor.
Desc: Covers legislation, court cases, and current trends in employment law. Contains sample policies. *Type:* Newsletter.

Employment in New York State

Department of Labor
W. Averell Harriman Office
  Bldg. 12, Rm. 480
Albany, NY 12240
URL: http://www.labor.state.ny.us/html/newsletr/
current/index.htm.
Desc: Contains information on employment and unemployment in the state of New York. *Type:* Newsletter.

Employment Opportunities, USA

Washington Research Associates
1660 S. Albion, Ste. 390   Ph: (303)756-9038
Denver, CO 80222   Fax: (303)758-9203
E-mail: wra@aol.com
Contact: Joseph Ryan, Editor.
Desc: List of over 1,000 employment contacts in companies and agencies in the banking, arts, telecommunications, education, and 14 other industries and professions, including the federal government. *Type:* Directory.

Employment Practices Newsletter

CCH Inc.
2700 Lake Cook Rd.   Ph: (847)267-7000
Riverwoods, IL 60015   Free: 800-449-8114
                                 Fax: (847)224-8299
URL: http://www.cch.com; http://www.cch.com; http://
hr.cch.com.
Contact: Vernon Fitch, JD, Editor; Catherine Long, BA, Editor; Michele Pointer, JD, Editor; Melisa L. Premer, JD, Editor; James Taylor, JD, Editor.
Desc: Report letter summary that highlights the latest trends, cases and legislative changes. *Type:* Newsletter.

Employment Research

W.E. Upjohn Institute for Employment Research
300 S. Westnedge Ave.   Ph: (616)343-5541
Kalamazoo, MI 49007-4686   Fax: (616)343-7310
E-mail: publications@we.upjohninst.org
URL: http://www.upjohninst.org.
Contact: David Nadziejka, nadziejka@we.upjohninst.org.
Desc: Highlights research performed by staff economists at the W.E. Upjohn Institute. *Type:* Newsletter.

Environmental Career Directory

Gale Group Inc.
27500 Drake Rd.   Ph: (248)699-4253
Farmington Hills, MI 48331-   Free: 800-877-GALE
  3535   Fax: (248)699-8070
E-mail: galeord@galegroup.com
URL: http://www.galegroup.com.
Contact: Bradley J. Morgan, Editor; Joseph M. Palmisano, Editor.
Desc: Over 250 companies and organizations offering entry-level positions in environment-related careers, including forestry management, fish and wildlife management, and air and water quality control; sources of help-wanted ads, professional associations, producers of videos, databases, career guides, and professional guides and handbooks. *Type:* Directory.

ERI Update

Economic Research Institute
16770 NE 79th St., Ste. 104   Ph: (206)556-0205
Redmond, WA 98052   Free: 800-627-3697
                                 Fax: 800-753-4415
E-mail: eri-redmond@msn.com
URL: http://www.erieri.com/~eri.
Contact: David Thomsen, Editor; Briana Bennitt, Editor.
Desc: Discusses relocation, geographic, and salary assessor software. Provides tips, solutions, and guidelines for users. *Type:* Newsletter.

ESOP Association

1726 M St. NW, Ste. 501   Ph: (202)293-2971
Washington, DC 20036   Fax: (202)293-7568
E-mail: esop@the-esop.emplowner.org
URL: http://www.the-esop-emplowner.org
Contact: J. Michael Keeling, Pres.
Desc: Companies with employee stock ownership plans (1300); associate members are lawyers, accountants, appraisers, actuaries, brokers, management and benefit consultants, and bankers specializing in working with ESOP (800). Acts as national information clearinghouse for the press and public interested in the concept of employee ownership; provides forum for the exchange of ideas, experience, and advice among members; lobbies for favorable legislation and regulation on national and state levels; produces and distributes communications material to educate employees on stock ownership. *Type:* Association.

Executive Recruiter News

Kennedy Information
One Kennedy Place, Route 12   Ph: (603)585-6544
  South   Free: 800-531-0007
Fitzwilliam, NH 03447   Fax: (603)585-9221
E-mail: bookstore@kennedyinfo.com
URL: http://www.kennedyinfo.com;   http://www.
kennedypub.com/ern.html.
Contact: Joseph Daniel McCool, Editor, ern-editor@
kennedyinfo.com.
Desc: The authoritative voice of the recruiting industry, covering news, analysi s, practice advice, proprietary data and opinion. *Type:* Newsletter.

Executive Search Review

Hunt-Scanlon Publishing Co. Inc.
1 E. Putnam Ave.   Ph: (203)629-3629
Greenwich, CT 06830   Fax: (203)629-3701
E-mail: hsp@interport.net
URL: http://www.hunt-scanlon.com.
Contact: Scott A. Scanlon, Editor.
Desc: Provides information about the executive search industry. *Type:* Newsletter.

ExecutiveSelect - Finance Executives Edition

Hunt-Scanlon Publishing
One East Putnam Ave.   Ph: (203)629-3629
Greenwich, CT 06830   Free: 800-477-1199
                                 Fax: (203)629-3701
E-mail: hsp@interport.net
URL: http://www.hunt-scanlon.com
Desc: More than 25,000 finance executives in over 9,500 companies in the U.S. *Type:* Directory.

ExecutiveSelect Gold

Hunt-Scanlon Publishing
One East Putnam Ave.   Ph: (203)629-3629
Greenwich, CT 06830   Free: 800-477-1199
                                 Fax: (203)629-3701
E-mail: hsp@interport.net
URL: http://www.hunt-scanlon.com
Desc: More than 100,000 top and middle management professionals in human resources, finance, sales and marketing, and information technology at over 10,000 companies in the U.S. *Type:* Directory.

ExecutiveSelect - Human Resource Executives Edition

Hunt-Scanlon Publishing
One East Putnam Ave.   Ph: (203)629-3629
Greenwich, CT 06830   Free: 800-477-1199
                                 Fax: (203)629-3701
E-mail: hsp@interport.net
URL: http://www.hunt-scanlon.com
Desc: More than 23,000 human resource professionals in over 9,500 public and private companies in the U.S. *Type:* Directory.

ExecutiveSelect - Information Technology Executives Edition

Hunt-Scanlon Publishing
One East Putnam Ave.   Ph: (203)629-3629
Greenwich, CT 06830   Free: 800-477-1199
                                 Fax: (203)629-3701
E-mail: hsp@interport.net
URL: http://www.hunt-scanlon.com
Desc: More than 10,000 information technology professionals in over 9,000 public and private companies. *Type:* Directory.

Fair Employment Practice

Warren, Gorham & Lamont, Inc.
RIA Group
PO Box 6159   Free: 800-950-1216
Carol Stream, IL 60197
Contact: Michael O'Toole, Editor.
Desc: Offers advice on how to protect a company from potential bias charges. *Type:* Newsletter.

Fair Employment Practices

Bureau of National Affairs, Inc. (BNA)
1231 25th St. NW   Ph: (202)452-4323
Washington, DC 20037   Free: 800-372-1033
                                 Fax: (202)452-7773
E-mail: bnaplus@bna.com
Contact: Nancy J. Sedmak, Managing Editor.
Desc: Provides a notification and reference service covering developments affecting fair employment practices. Includes federal laws, orders, and regulations; policy guides and discussions of federal court decisions; and state and local fair employment practice laws. *Type:* Newsletter.

Fair Employment Practices Guidelines

Bureau of Business Practice
24 Rope Ferry Rd.   Ph: (860)442-4365
Waterford, CT 06386   Free: 800-243-0876
                                 Fax: (860)437-3555
URL: http://www.bbpnews.com
Contact: Mary Lou Devine, Editor, mary_lou-devine@
pren.com.
Desc: Provides information on legislative, administrative, and judicial developments in the fair employment practices field. Recurring features include columns that track legislative, regulatory, and court developments. *Type:* Newsletter.

Fair Employment Practices Newsletter

The Bureau of National Affairs, Inc. (BNA)
1231 25th St. NW   Ph: (202)452-4200
Washington, DC 20037
E-mail: bnaplus@bna.com
URL: http://bna.com/mkt/hrl/hrlwdec.htm
Desc: Contains the complete text of Fair Employment Practices Newsletter, covering federal and state activities relating to equal employment opportunity. Covers the Equal Employment Opportunity Commission (EEOC), the Office of Federal Contract Compliance Programs (OFCCP), court action in discrimination suits, new laws and regulations, and affirmative action programs. *Type:* Database.

Fair Employment Practices Summary of Latest Developments

Bureau of National Affairs, Inc. (BNA)
1231 25th St. NW   Ph: (202)452-4323
Washington, DC 20037   Free: 800-372-1033
                                 Fax: (202)452-7773
E-mail: bnaplus@bna.com
Contact: Jeff Day, Managing Editor.
Desc: Highlights developments in employment opportunity and affirmative actions, and affirmative action pro-

grams. Reports on federal and state court decisions, Equal Employment Opportunity Commission (EEOC) rulings and Office of Federal Contract Compliance Programs (OFCCP) decisions, new laws, regulations, and agency directives. *Type:* Newsletter.

Fair Employment Report
Business Publishers, Inc.
8737 Colesville Rd., Ste. 1100   Ph: (301)589-5103
Silver Spring, MD 20910   Free: 800-274-6737
   Fax: (301)587-4530
E-mail: bpinews@bpinews.com
URL: http://www.bpinews.com.
Contact: Chuck Knebl, Editor.
Desc: Focuses on developments on the state and national levels regarding employment practices and discrimination. Emphasizes important legal decisions and governmental activities, particularly those of the Equal Employment Opportunity Commission, the Office of Federal Contract Compliance Programs, the supreme court, federal courts, congress and state legislatures. *Type:* Newsletter.

Federal Career Opportunities
Federal Research Service, Inc.
370 Maple Ave. NW   Ph: (703)281-0200
PO Box 1059   Free: 800-822-5627
Vienna, VA 22183-1059   Fax: (703)281-7639
E-mail: info@fedjobs.com
URL: http://www.fedjobs.com.
Contact: Marcia LeFavour, Managing Editor.
Desc: Lists current federal jobs. Contains articles relevant to the federal application process and hiring trends. *Type:* Newsletter.

Federation Employment and Guidance Service
114 5th Ave., 11th Fl.   Ph: (212)366-8400
New York, NY 10011   Fax: (212)366-8441
Contact: Alfred P. Miller, Exec.VP.
Desc: Voluntary, nonsectarian community human service agency. Serves more than 50,000 persons annually in over 117 locations with individual and group career development services, including psychological testing, job placement, and vocational rehabilitation, as well as mental health, residential, developmental, clinical, and youth services. Provides programs in economic development and criminal justice. *Type:* Association.

FERA—Focus
FERA, Inc.
6111 Jackson Rd., Ste. 118   Ph: (313)994-9060
Ann Arbor, MI 48103   Fax: (313)998-1378
URL: http://www.knowledgeworks.com/.
Contact: John A. Seeley, Editor.
Desc: Discusses consulting work and research on evaluation of corporate training, human resource development programs, community-based social services, and educational programs. *Type:* Newsletter.

The Fordyce Letter
The Kimberly Organization
PO Box 31011   Ph: (314)965-3883
Des Peres, MO 63131   Fax: (314)965-8177
E-mail: fordyceltr@aol.com.
Contact: Paul Hawkinson, Editor and Publisher.
Desc: Provides information for the personnel and placement industry. *Type:* Newsletter.

From Nine to Five
The Dartnell Corp.
360 Hiatt Dr.   Free: 800-621-5463
Palm Beach Gardens, FL 33418   Fax: (561)622-2423
E-mail: dartnell@dartnellcorp.com
URL: http://www.dartnellcorp.com; http://www.lrp.com.

Contact: Kim Anderson, Editor, kanderson@dartnellcorp.com.
Desc: Provides "tips, shortcuts, and helpful information for success in the office," particularly secretaries and office workers. Recurring features include columns titled titled Business Skills Clinic, Shortcuts, and The Coffee Break. *Type:* Newsletter.

Green Thumb
2000 N. 14th St., Ste. 800   Ph: (703)522-7272
Arlington, VA 22201   Fax: (703)522-0141
E-mail: p.r.directoraliceanne_toole@greenthumb.org
URL: http://www.greenthumb.org
Contact: Andrea J. Wooten, Pres.
Desc: Seeks to strengthen families, communities, and our nation by providing older and disadvantaged adults with opportunities to learn, work, and serve others. *Type:* Association.

Guide to Background Investigations
T.I.S.I.
4110 S. 100th East Ave.   Ph: (918)664-8799
Tulsa, OK 74146-3639   Free: 800-247-8713
   Fax: (918)664-9074
E-mail: comments@usetheguide.com; products@usetheguide.com.
URL: http://www.usetheguide.com.
Desc: Federal, state, and local government offices and over 4,000 higher educati on institutions that provide emloyers and investigators with background information on job applicants, including criminal records, driving records, military records, G.E.D. test score sources, nurse aide registries, child care licensing boards, worker's compensation records, federal records, state licensing boards and educational histories; includes departments of education for verifying teaching credentials, medical licensing for M.D.s and nurses, and secretaries of state for corporation information. *Type:* Directory.

Healthcare Career Directory—Nurses and Physicians
Gale Group Inc.
27500 Drake Rd.   Ph: (248)699-4253
Farmington Hills, MI 48331-   Free: 800-877-GALE
3535   Fax: (248)699-8070
E-mail: galeord@galegroup.com
URL: http://www.galegroup.com.
Contact: Bradley J. Morgan, Editor.
Desc: Over 300 hospitals and companies offering entry-level positions for nurses and physicians; sources of help-wanted ads, professional associations, producers of videos, databases, career guides, and professional guides and handbooks. *Type:* Directory.

High Technology Careers Magazine
HTC
4701 Patrick Henry Dr., No.   Ph: (408)970-8800
1901   Fax: (408)980-5103
Santa Clara, CA 95054
E-mail: htc@vjf.com
URL: http://www.vjf.com; http://www.hightechcareers.com.
Contact: Paul J. Burrowes, Publisher, burrowes@vjf.com.
Desc: Magazine (tabloid) containing employment opportunity information for the engineering and technical community. *Alt. Contact:* 4701 Patrick Henry Dr., No. 1901, Santa Clara, CA 95054; telephone: (408)970-8800; fax: (408)980-5103. *Type:* Periodical.

Hiring & Firing
Carswell
Thomson Professional Publishing
One Corporate Plaza
2075 Kennedy Rd.   Ph: (416)609-3800
Scarborough, ON, Canada M1T   Free: 800-387-5164
3V4   Fax: (416)298-5082
E-mail: orders@carswell.com
Contact: Cindy Moser, Editor; Mark Rogers, Editor.
Desc: Monitors hiring and firing issues as they relate to the law. Covers such topics as sexual harassment, discrimination, and labor relations. *Type:* Newsletter.

HR Briefing
Bureau of Business Practice
24 Rope Ferry Rd.   Ph: (860)442-4365
Waterford, CT 06386   Free: 800-243-0876
   Fax: (860)437-3555
URL: http://www.bbpnews.com
Contact: Valerie Bolden-Barrett, Editor, valerie_bolden-barrett@prenhall.com.
Desc: Provides how-to information, legal developments, and trends in human resources. Recurring features include interviews, legal citations, workplace news, experts' viewpoints. *Type:* Newsletter.

HR Fact Finder
Jamestown Area Labor-Management Committee Inc.
PO Box 819   Ph: (716)665-3654
1093 E 2 St. No. 309   Free: 800-542-7869
Jamestown, NY 14702-0819   Fax: (716)665-8060
E-mail: njalmc@cecomet.net
URL: http://www.jalmc.org.
Contact: Karen France, Editor.
Desc: Summarizes articles from various publications on such topics as company benefits, health, the Family Leave Act, Americans with Disabilities Act, hiring practices, employment law, workers compensation, budgets, and sexual harassment. *Type:* Newsletter.

HR Focus
American Management Association
1601 Broadway   Ph: (212)586-8100
New York, NY 10019-7420   Free: 800-313-8650
   Fax: (212)903-8083
E-mail: cust-serv@amanet.org; hrfocus@amanet.org.
URL: http://www.amanet.org/periodicals/hrf/.
Contact: Genevieve Capowski, Editor.
Desc: Focuses on personnel management. *Type:* Newsletter.

HR Manager's Legal Reporter
Ransom & Benjamin Publishers LLC
PO Box 160   Ph: (860)536-2000
Mystic, CT 06355   Free: 800-334-3352
   Fax: (860)536-1545
E-mail: rbpubs@aol.com
URL: http://www.rbpubs.com.
Contact: Maureen Gallagher, Editor.
Desc: Provides information, news, and how-to articles on employment law. Recurring features include columns titled Washington Watch, You Be the Judge, From the States, and In Brief. *Type:* Newsletter.

HR Reporter
LRP Publications
747 Dresher Rd.   Ph: (215)784-0941
PO Box 980   Free: 800-341-7874
Horsham, PA 19044-0980   Fax: (215)784-0870
E-mail: custserve@lrp.com
Contact: Linda Segall, Editor.

Employment

Desc: Covers issues in human relations, corporate policies and programs, and new concepts, theories, and trends. Recurring features include a two-page Update with notes on new reports and publications, tips, and a calendar of events. *Type:* Newsletter.

HRMagazine
Society for Human Resource Management
606 N. Washington St. Ph: (703)548-3440
Alexandria, VA 22314 Fax: (703)836-0367
E-mail: shrm@shrm.org; hemagazine@shrm.org.
URL: http://www.shrm.org.
Contact: John T. Adams, III, Editor and Publisher, john@shrm.org; Leon Rubis, Editor, leon@shrm.org; Patrick Mirza, Managing Editor, mirza@shrm.org; Phaedra Brotherton, Assoc. Ed.; Alice M. Starcke, Assoc. Ed., alice@shrm.org; Stacy Van Derwall, Asst. Ed.; Caroline A. Foster, Dir. of Design & Prod.; Susan Montgomery, Production Mgr., susan@shrm.org; Keith Harlow, Production Coordinator, keith@shrm.org; Shirley E.M. Raybuck, Desktop Publishing Coordinator. *Desc:* Magazine for human resource management professionals. *Type:* Periodical.

Human Resource Management News
Kennedy Information
One Kennedy Pl., Rte. 12 S. Ph: (603)585-6544
Fitzwilliam, NH 03447 Free: 800-531-0007
  Fax: (603)585-9555
E-mail: bookstore@kennedy.info.com; hrmn-editor@kennedyinfo.com.
Contact: Miles Z. Epstein, Editor; David G. Epstein, Editor.
Desc: The source for HR news, analysis, trends and technology, since 1951. Now includes "What's ahead in HR" as a regular feature. *Type:* Newsletter.

Human Resource Management Today
Center for Personnel and Human Resource Management
Florida State University
College of Business Fax: (850)644-7843
Tallahassee, FL 32306
Contact: Dr. Micki Kacmar, Ph.D., Editor.
Desc: Offers information on the Center's Advisory Board, conferences, and meetings; tracks pertinent legislation. Recurring features include notices of publications available. *Type:* Newsletter.

Human Resource Professional
LRP Publications
747 Dresher Rd. Ph: (215)784-0941
PO Box 980 Free: 800-341-7874
Horsham, PA 19044-0980 Fax: (215)784-0870
E-mail: custserve@lrp.com
Contact: Marilyn Schaefer, Editor.
Desc: Provides human resource information. *Type:* Newsletter.

Human Resources
Lafferty Publications Ltd.
420 Lexington Ave., Ste. 1745 Ph: (212)557-6726
New York, NY 10170 Fax: (212)557-7266
Contact: Ciaran Brennan, Editor; Paul Byrne, Publisher.
Desc: Provides human resource information for the financial service industry. *Type:* Newsletter.

Human Resources Executive Review
The Conference Board, Inc.
845 3rd Ave. Ph: (212)759-0900
New York, NY 10022-6679 Fax: (212)980-7014
E-mail: info@conference-board.org
URL: http://www.conference-board.org

Contact: Chuck Mitchell, Editor.
Desc: Contains news of research and information on human resources issues. *Type:* Newsletter.

Human Resources Management Ideas and Trends
CCH Inc.
2700 Lake Cook Rd. Ph: (847)267-7000
Riverwoods, IL 60015 Free: 800-449-8114
  Fax: (847)224-8299
URL: http://www.cch.com; http://www.cch.com; http://hhr.cch.com.
Contact: Lamon Lampley, Jr., Managing Editor.
Desc: Covers general human resources management issues. *Type:* Newsletter.

Human Resources Measurements
Wonderlic Personnel Test Inc.
1509 N. Milwaukee Ave. Ph: (847)680-4900
Libertyville, IL 60048 Free: 800-323-3742
  Fax: (847)680-9492
E-mail: contact@wonderlic.com
URL: http://www.wonderlic.com.
Contact: Paul G. Coutre, Editor; Kristine Neiman, Editor.
Desc: Presents information on hiring and employee testing. Covers recruiting, technology, and hiring techniques. *Type:* Newsletter.

Human Resources Practice Ideas
Warren, Gorham & Lamont, Inc.
RIA Group
PO Box 6159 Free: 800-950-1216
Carol Stream, IL 60197
Contact: Kelly Leisten, Editor.
Desc: Provides information about employment laws and regulations. *Type:* Newsletter.

Hunt-Scanlon's Select Guide to Finance Executives
Hunt-Scanlon Publishing
One East Putnam Ave. Ph: (203)629-3629
Greenwich, CT 06830 Free: 800-477-1199
  Fax: (203)629-3701
E-mail: hsp@interport.net
URL: http://www.hunt-scanlon.com
Desc: More than 25,000 finance professionals in 9,500 public and private companies. *Type:* Directory.

Hunt-Scanlon's Select Guide to Human Resource Executives
Hunt-Scanlon Publishing
One East Putnam Ave. Ph: (203)629-3629
Greenwich, CT 06830 Free: 800-477-1199
  Fax: (203)629-3701
E-mail: hsp@interport.net
URL: http://www.hunt-scanlon.com
Desc: More than 23,000 human resource executives, personnel managers, and compensation, benefits, and training professionals in 9,500 companies in the U.S. *Type:* Directory.

Hunt-Scanlon's Select Guide to Sales & Marketing Executives
Hunt-Scanlon Publishing
One East Putnam Ave. Ph: (203)629-3629
Greenwich, CT 06830 Free: 800-477-1199
  Fax: (203)629-3701
E-mail: hsp@interport.net
URL: http://www.hunt-scanlon.com
Desc: More than 13,000 sales and marketing professionals at 9,500 public and private companies in the U.S. *Type:* Directory.

Ideas & Ideals
Project Equality of Wisconsin, Inc.
1442 N. Farwell Ave., Ste. 210 Ph: (414)272-2642
Milwaukee, WI 53202 Fax: (414)272-2644
Contact: Betty J. Thompson, Editor.
Desc: Newsletter for project Equality of Wisconsin, a nonprofit organization, dedicated to promoting justice and equality especially in those issues relating to the workplace. A coalition of interfaith organizations and businesses. *Type:* Newsletter.

Independent Educational Services
1101 King St. Ph: (703)548-9700
Alexandria, VA 22314-2944 Free: 800-257-5102
  Fax: (703)548-7171
E-mail: info@ies-search.org
URL: http://www.ies-search.org
Contact: John W. Sanders, Pres.
Desc: Nonprofit consulting, head search, and teacher recruitment organization. Furnishes to independent (private) schools dossiers of qualified candidates for teaching and administrative positions. Offers to teachers and prospective teachers information concerning current requirements and qualifications for positions in the field of education and vacancies for which they qualify. *Type:* Association.

Individual Employment Rights
Bureau of National Affairs, Inc. (BNA)
1231 25th St. NW Ph: (202)452-4323
Washington, DC 20037 Free: 800-372-1033
  Fax: (202)452-7773
E-mail: bnaplus@bna.com
Contact: Nancy J. Sedmak, Managing Editor.
Desc: Provides case reference and notification on individual employment rights issues. Covers employment at will, privacy, polygraph testing, and other employee rights issues outside the traditional labor-management relations sphere. *Type:* Newsletter.

Individual Employment Rights Newsletter
The Bureau of National Affairs, Inc. (BNA)
1231 25th St. NW Ph: (202)452-4200
Washington, DC 20037
E-mail: bnaplus@bna.com
URL: http://bna.com/mkt/hrl/hrlwdec.htm
Desc: Contains the complete text of Individual Employment Rights Newsletter, a publication covering employee rights typically not addressed by traditional labor/management policies and practices. Focuses on litigation involving issues of employment-at-will, privacy, character defamation, and polygraph, drug, and alcohol testing. *Available:* LEXIS-NEXIS, LEXIS; West Group, WESTLAW. *Type:* Database.

InPractice
American Productivity & Quality Center
123 N. Post Oak Ln., 3rd Fl. Ph: (713)681-4020
Houston, TX 77024 Free: 800-776-9676
  Fax: (713)681-8578
E-mail: apqcinfo@apqc.org
URL: http://www.apqc.org; http://www.apqc.org.
Contact: Susan Elliott, Editor, (713)685-4641, selliott@apqc.org; Vicki Powers, Contact; Craig Henderson, Contact.
Desc: Focuses on best practice companies in the areas of benchmarking, customer satisfaction, measurement, and knowledge management; education; excellence. *Type:* Newsletter.

Inside NAPS

National Association of Personnel Services
3133 Mount Vernon Ave.   Ph: (703)684-0180
Alexandria, VA 22305-2540   Fax: (703)684-0071
E-mail: naps@vni.net.
URL: http://www.napsweb.org.
Contact: Beth Rogers, Editor; Dianne B. Callis, Publisher.
Desc: Concerned with the private placement industry.
Type: Newsletter.

International Association for Human Resource Information Management—Membership Directory

International Association for Human Resource Information Management
401 N. Michigan Ave.   Ph: (312)321-5141
Chicago, IL 60611   Fax: (312)627-6636
E-mail: moreinfo@ihrim.org
URL: http://www.ihrim.com.
Contact: Carl Nielson, Editor.
Desc: 5,900 listings; provides name, industry, company, and special interest groups. *Type:* Directory.

International Association of Personnel in Employment Security

1801 Louisville Rd.   Ph: (502)223-4459
Frankfort, KY 40601   Fax: (502)223-4127
E-mail: iapes@aol.com
URL: http://www.iapes.org
Contact: Roger Detweiler, Exec.Dir.
Desc: Officials and others engaged in job placement, unemployment compensation, and labor market information administration through municipal, state, provincial, and federal government employment agencies and unemployment compensation agencies. Conducts workshops and research. Offers professional development program of study guides and tests. *Type:* Association.

International Employment Hotline

Carlyle Corp.
1088 Middle River Rd.   Ph: (804)985-6444
Stanardsville, VA 22973   Free: 800-291-4618
    Fax: (804)985-6828
E-mail: cindy@internationaljobs.org
Contact: Lisa L. Law, Editor, Lisa@internationaljobs.org.
Desc: Covers the latest developments in the international job market. Summarizes hiring cycles of major employers. *Type:* Newsletter.

International Personnel Management Association

1617 Duke St.   Ph: (703)549-7100
Alexandria, VA 22314   Fax: (703)684-0948
E-mail: ipma@ipma-hr.org
URL: http://www.ipma-hr.org
Contact: Neil E. Reichenberg, Exec.Dir.
Desc: Public personnel agencies (1400); individuals, including personnel workers, consultants, and professors (4400). Seeks to improve personnel practices in government through provision of testing services, advisory service, conferences, professional development programs, research, and publications. *Type:* Association.

IOMA's Report on Reducing Benefits Costs

Institute of Management & Administration, Inc.
29 W. 35th St., 5th Fl.   Ph: (212)244-0360
New York, NY 10001-2299   Fax: (212)564-0465
E-mail: subserve@ioma.com
URL: http://www.ioma.com
Contact: Rebecca Morrow, Editor; Perry Patterson, Publisher.
Desc: Provides information about benefits cost reduction strategies. *Type:* Newsletter.

Job Express

FVI & Wendy Vandamme
105 N. Main St.   Ph: (201)299-1535
Boonton, NJ 07005   Free: 800-836-0667
    Fax: (201)335-4866
Contact: Wendy Vandame, Editor.
Desc: Contains surveys of billing rates for contract computer services, listings of open assignments and contracts, and situations wanted. Covers tradeshows and seminars. *Type:* Newsletter.

Job Hunters' Sourcebook

Gale Group Inc.
27500 Drake Rd.   Ph: (248)699-4253
Farmington Hills, MI 48331-   Free: 800-877-GALE
3535   Fax: (248)699-8070
E-mail: galeord@galegroup.com
URL: http://www.galegroup.com.
Contact: Kathleen Maki, Editor.
Desc: Job hunting-related information resources for 193 high-interest occupations, including manuals, directories, sources of help-wanted ads, employment agencies, placement services, and trade journals. *Type:* Directory.

The Job Seeker

The Job Seeker
28672 Cty EW   Ph: (608)378-4290
Warrens, WI 54666   Fax: (608)378-4290
E-mail: jobseeker@tomah.com
Contact: Becky Potter.
Desc: Specializes "in environmental and natural resource vacancies nationwide." Lists current vacancies from federal, state, local, private, and non-profit employers. *Type:* Newsletter.

Job Seeker's Guide to Socially Responsible Companies

Gale Group Inc.
27500 Drake Rd.   Ph: (248)699-4253
Farmington Hills, MI 48331-   Free: 800-877-GALE
3535   Fax: (248)699-8070
E-mail: galeord@galegroup.com
URL: http://www.galegroup.com.
Contact: Job opportunities at companies deemed to be socially responsible. *Type:* Directory.

Job Training and Placement Report

Impact Publications, Inc.
1300 Royalton   Ph: (715)258-2448
Waupaca, WI 54981   Fax: (715)258-9048
E-mail: impact@gglbbs.com
Contact: Scott Kolpien, Publisher; Tari Aderhold, Managing Editor.
Desc: A newsletter for professionals who support employment for people with disabilities. Monthly issues cover Job Development, Funding Resources, Legal Issues, Advocacy, and much more. *Type:* Newsletter.

JobMart

American Planning Association
122 S. Michigan Ave., Ste. 1600   Ph: (312)431-9100
Chicago, IL 60603-6107   Fax: (312)431-9985
E-mail: jschwab@planning.org
Contact: Grace Williams, Editor.
Desc: Reports on jobs in the planning field, covering urban and regional opportunities and related jobs in community development and transportation. Recurring features include educational opportunities and internships. *Type:* Newsletter.

Jobs for America's Graduates

1729 King St., Ste. 200   Ph: (703)684-9479
Alexandria, VA 22314   Fax: (703)684-9489
E-mail: jqk@jaq.org
URL: http://www.jag.org
Contact: Jimmy G. Kocninger, Ph.D., Exec.VP.
Desc: Develops statewide systems dedicated to serving at-risk youth who are most likely to leave school before graduation or who have already left school. The national organization is responsible for implementing the JAG model and the appropriate program applications. JAG programs are targeted for at-risk and disadvantaged students who have limited work experience, do not plan to attend college immediately upon graduation or are at risk of dropping out. *Type:* Association.

Jobs from Recyclables Possibility Newsletter

Prosperity & Profits Unlimited, Distribution Services
PO Box 416   Ph: (303)575-5676
Denver, CO 80201-0416
Contact: A.C. Doyle, Editor.
Desc: Describes employment options. *Type:* Newsletter.

Kansas Monthly Employment Review

Labor Market Information Services
Kansas Department of Human Resources
401 SW Topeka Blvd.   Ph: (785)296-5058
Topeka, KS 66603-3182   Fax: (785)296-5286
E-mail: laborstats@hr.state.ks.us; wlayes@hr.state.ks.us.
Desc: Covers the employment market in Kansas. *Type:* Newsletter.

Kennedy's Career Strategist

Career Strategies
1150 Willmette Ave.   Ph: (847)251-1661
Wilmette, IL 60091   Free: 800-728-1709
    Fax: (847)251-5191
Contact: Marilyn Moats Kennedy, Editor, mmkcareer@aol.com.
Desc: Offers advice on job hunting and discusses such topics as "how to win at office politics." Follows employment trends in various industries. Recurring features include interviewing techniques, salary strategies, and advice column. *Type:* Newsletter.

Labor Market Review

Office of Research and Information
Connecticut State Department of Labor
200 Folly Brook Blvd.   Ph: (860)566-3462
Wethersfield, CT 06109   Fax: (860)566-7963
Contact: Maryann Przyhysz, Editor.
Desc: Covers "the major labor market areas of Bridgeport, Hartford, New Haven-Meriden, Stamford, and Waterbury. Separate write-ups are published for the minor labor market areas of Bristol, Danbury, Danielson, Lower River, Middletown, New Britain, New London-Norwich, Norwalk, Torrington, and Willimantic." Discusses the local labor force, total employment, unemployment, nonagricultural wage and salary employment, manufacturing workers' hours and wages, characteristics of the insured unemployed, available Job Bank opportunities, and the employment and unemployment outlook for the future. *Type:* Newsletter.

Labor Trends

Alignmark Information Publishing
1340 Braddock Pl., Ste. 400   Ph: (703)706-0207
Alexandria, VA 22314   Fax: (703)683-4852
Contact: Matthew Tallmer, Editor.
Desc: The Premier Weekly Labor Affairs Newsletter focusing on NLRB issues, labor contracts and union negotiations. *Type:* Newsletter.

Laborwatch

Berens & Tate, P.C.
10050 Regency Circle, Ste. 400   Ph: (402)391-1991
Omaha, NE 68135   Free: 800-729-1441
                      Fax: (402)391-7363
Desc: Provides information about labor and employment law, management, and human resources. *Type:* Newsletter.

The Lakewood Report on Positive Employee Practices

Lakewood Publications, Inc.
50 S. 9th St.   Ph: (612)333-0471
Minneapolis, MN 55402   Free: 800-328-4329
                      Fax: (612)333-6521
E-mail: justask@lakewoodpub.com
Contact: Brian McDermott, Editor; Philip G. Jones, Publisher.
Desc: Provides information about providing quality products and services. *Type:* Newsletter.

Leads

Leads
Box 9333   Ph: (613)746-2292
Ottawa, ON, Canada K1G 3V1
Contact: Tom Kennedy, Editor and Publisher.
Desc: Explores opportunities for second incomes. *Type:* Newsletter.

The Lean Production Report

Productivity, Inc.
541 NE 20th Ave., Ste. 108   Free: 800-966-5423
Portland, OR 97232-2862
URL: http://www.mpgnet.com.
Contact: Chet Marchwinski, Editor, cmarchwi@prodinc.com.
Desc: Discusses ways to implement lean and agile manufacturing. Includes analyses, reports, a calendar of events, editorials, news of research, and columns titled Just-In-Time, technology, supplier relations, employee involvement, Kanban. *Type:* Newsletter.

Louisiana Employment Law Letter

M. Lee Smith, Publishers LLC
5201 Virginia Way   Ph: (615)373-7517
PO Box 5094   Free: 800-274-6774
Brentwood, TN 37024-5094   Fax: (615)373-5183
E-mail: custserv@mleesmith.com
URL: http://www.mleesmith.com.
Contact: H. Mark Adams, Editor; Mary Ellen Jordan, Editor.
Desc: Addresses legislation and court decisions affecting employment issues. *Type:* Newsletter.

Louisiana Labor Market Information

Office of Employment Security
Louisiana State Department of Labor
PO Box 94094   Ph: (504)342-3141
Baton Rouge, LA 70804-9094
Contact: Leonard King.
Desc: Supplies data on civilian labor force, employment and unemployment for the current month, the previous month, and for the same month a year ago. Covers all labor market areas within the state of Louisiana. *Type:* Newsletter.

Magazines Career Directory

Gale Group Inc.
27500 Drake Rd.   Ph: (248)699-4253
Farmington Hills, MI 48331-   Free: 800-877-GALE
   3535   Fax: (248)699-8070
E-mail: galeord@galegroup.com

URL: http://www.galegroup.com.
Contact: Bradley J. Morgan, Editor.
Desc: Approximately 300 companies offering job opportunities, internships, and training possibilities for those seeking a career in magazine publishing; sources of help-wanted ads, professional associations, videos and databases, career guides, and professional guides and handbooks. *Type:* Directory.

Managing Your Career

Dow Jones & Co., Inc.
PO Box 300   Ph: (609)520-4305
Princeton, NJ 08543   Free: 800-JOB-
                            HUNT
                      Fax: (609)520-7315
Contact: Tony Lee, Editor, (609)520-4306.
Desc: Career guidance magazine for college students. *Type:* Periodical.

MarketPlace

iMarket Inc.
460 Totten Pond Rd.   Ph: (617)672-9200
Waltham, MA 02154   Free: 800-590-0065
                      Fax: (617)672-9290
E-mail: acctmgr@imarketinc.com
URL: http://www.imarketinc.com;   http://www.
imarketinc.com.
Desc: Over 10 million U.S. businesses. *Type:* Directory.

MBA Employment Guide Report

Association of MBA Executives Inc
5 Summit Place   Ph: (203)315-5221
Branford, CT 06405   Fax: (203)483-6186
Desc: More than 4,000 firms that employ persons with Master of Business Administration degrees. More detailed profiles are given for 100 firms selected on the basis of their on-campus recruitment activity. Custom reports are issued upon request at $10.00 per report. *Type:* Directory.

Medical Technologists and Technicians Career Directory

Gale Group Inc.
27500 Drake Rd.   Ph: (248)699-4253
Farmington Hills, MI 48331-   Free: 800-877-GALE
   3535   Fax: (248)699-8070
E-mail: galeord@galegroup.com
URL: http://www.galegroup.com.
Contact: Bradley J. Morgan, Editor; Joseph M. Palmisano, Editor.
Desc: Over 300 hospitals and companies offering entry-level positions in medical technology specialties; sources of help-wanted ads, professional associations, producers of videos, databases, career guides, and professional guides and handbooks. *Type:* Directory.

Mental Health and Social Work Career Directory

Gale Group Inc.
27500 Drake Rd.   Ph: (248)699-4253
Farmington Hills, MI 48331-   Free: 800-877-GALE
   3535   Fax: (248)699-8070
E-mail: galeord@galegroup.com
URL: http://www.galegroup.com.
Contact: Bradley J. Morgan, Editor; Joseph M. Palmisano, Editor.
Desc: Over 300 agencies, organizations, and companies offering entry-level positions in mental health, social work, counseling, psychology, etc.; sources of help-wanted ads, professional associations, producers of videos, databases, career guides, and professional guides and handbooks. *Type:* Directory.

MFG Net

Productivity, Inc.
541 NE 20th Ave., Ste. 108   Free: 800-966-5423
Portland, OR 97232-2862
URL: http://www.mfgnet.com.
Contact: Chet Marchwinski, Editor, cmarchwi@prodinc.com.
Desc: Focuses on how manufacturers are using internet tools to cut costs, manage supply chains, grow sales, and improve teamwork. *Type:* Newsletter.

Michigan Employer Advisor

Unemployment Agency
7310 Woodward Ave., Rm. 606   Ph: (313)876-5491
Detroit, MI 48202   Fax: (313)876-5225
URL: http://www.miua.com.
Contact: Bill DiSessa, Editor, (313)876-5488, bill.disessa@ua.cis.state.mi.us.
Desc: Provides information on Unemployment Agency (UA) activities and the issues with which the UA is concerned, such as unemployment insurance, unemployment taxes, and a healthy Michigan economy with rapid reemployment. *Type:* Newsletter.

Minnesota Employment Review

Minnesota Department of Economic Security,
Research and Statistics Office
390 N. Robert St.   Ph: (651)296-8688
St. Paul, MN 55101   Fax: (651)282-5429
URL: http://www.dis.state.mn.us/lmi/other.htm.
Contact: Judith Trent, Editor, jtrent@state.mn.us; Debbie Morrison, Circulation Mgr.
Desc: Details Minnesota's employment and unemployment situation. *Type:* Newsletter.

MSA Employment

The WEFA Group
1110 Vermont Ave., NW   Ph: (202)775-0610
Washington, DC 20005
URL: http://www.fdic.gov
Desc: Contains approximately 24,000 monthly time series on employment, hours, and earnings for 270 Metropolitan Statistical Areas (MSAs). Source of data is the Bureau of Labor Statistics 790 Survey. *Available:* The WEFA Group. *Type:* Database.

NACO Update on Job Training

National Association of Counties
440 1st St. NW, 8th Fl.   Ph: (202)393-6226
Washington, DC 20001   Fax: (202)393-2630
Contact: Cynthia Kenny, Editor.
Desc: Provides federal, state, and local information on the operation of the Job Training Partnership Act (JTPA). Highlights other issues on employment and training ranging from economic development to welfare. *Type:* Newsletter.

NASEA News

National Association of Student Employment
Administrators (NASEA)
1156 15th St. NW, Ste. 502   Ph: (202)530-0053
Washington, DC 20005-1704
Contact: Bob Cunningham, Editor.
Desc: Offers information on student employment, discussing issues such as job development, summer employment, and student financial aid. Carries news of Association activities, book reviews, announcements of awards, and a column titled Federal Relations. *Type:* Newsletter.

National Alliance of Business

1201 New York Ave. NW, Ste.   Ph: (202)289-2888
  700   Free: 800-787-2848
Washington, DC 20005   Fax: (202)289-1303

Contact: Robert Jones, Pres. & CEO.

Desc: Dedicated to building a quality workforce by providing business leadership and expertise at the national, state, and local levels to educate, train, and prepare all Americans to succeed in today's internationally competitive workplaces. *Type:* Association.

National Association of Colleges and Employers—Spotlight

National Association of Colleges and Employers
62 Highland Ave.   Ph: (610)868-1421
Bethlehem, PA 18017   Free: 800-544-5272
                            Fax: (610)868-0208

E-mail: kathy@jobweb.org
URL: http://www.jobweb.org/; http://www.jobweb.org.
Contact: Mimi Collins, Editor; Claudia Allen, Editor, claudia@jobweb.org.

Desc: Devoted to career planning and employment of college graduates. Recurring features include news of regulations and legislation, technological developments statistics, research, trends, publications, and events related to career development and employment. *Type:* Newsletter.

National Association of Personnel Services

3133 Mt. Vernon Ave.   Ph: (703)684-0180
Alexandria, VA 22305   Fax: (703)684-0071

E-mail: info@napsweb.org
URL: http://www.napsweb.org
Contact: Dianne B. Callis, Pres.

Desc: Private employment and temporary service firms. Compiles statistics on professional agency growth and development; conducts certification program and educational programs. Association is distinct from former name of National Association of Personnel Consultants. *Type:* Association.

National Association of Professional Employer Organizations

901 N. Pitt St., Ste. 350
Alexandria, VA 22314-1536
URL: http://www.napeo.org
Contact: Milan P. Yager, Exec.VP.

Desc: Professional employer organizations. Seeks to enhance professionalism in the professional employer industry. *Type:* Association.

National Association of Temporary and Staffing Services

119 S. St. Asaph St.   Ph: (703)549-6287
Alexandria, VA 22314-3119   Fax: (703)549-4808
E-mail: natss@natss.org
URL: http://www.natss.org
Contact: Richard A. Wahlquist, Exec.VP.

Desc: Companies supplying workers to other firms on a temporary and long term staffing basis. Sponsors 20 to 30 regional workshops, in-depth industry studies and comprehensive website. *Type:* Association.

National Job Corps Alumni Association

1333 H St., NW Ste. 300 W   Free: 800-733-5627
Washington, DC 20005   Fax: (202)638-3807
URL: http://www.jobcorp.org/njcaa
Contact: Lutricia Brooks, Contact.

Desc: Former members of the Job Corps and its supporters. Objectives are to: enhance the public awareness and image of the Job Corps (a nationwide federally-sponsored training program offering education, vocational training, and work experience in urban, rural, or inner city residen-

tial centers to disdvantaged youth aged 16 to 24) and its alumni; conduct programs and provide services in response to the needs and interests of the Job Corps; support the educational and career development of Job Corps members; provide a forum for social interaction and group support for Job Corps alumni. Conducts educational programs on communications, job search skills, public relations, and community service; sponsors social programs such as local reunions, dances, theme parties, and dinners; coordinates benefits program which include club membership and automobile discounts; makes available employment information. *Type:* Association.

National JobBank

Adams Media Corp.
260 Center St.   Ph: (781)767-8100
Holbrook, MA 02343   Free: 800-872-5627
                            Fax: (781)767-0994
E-mail: jobbank@adamsonline.com
URL: http://www.adamsmedia.com;   http://www.careercity.com; http://www.adamsmedia.com/reference.
Contact: Steven Graber, Editor.
Desc: Over 21,000 employers nationwide. *Type:* Directory.

New Jersey Employment Law Letter

M. Lee Smith Publishers LLC
5201 Virginia Way   Ph: (615)373-7517
PO Box 5094   Free: 800-274-6774
Brentwood, TN 37024-5094   Fax: 800-785-9212
E-mail: custserv@mleesmith.com
URL: http://www.mleesmith.com.
Contact: S. Joseph Fortunato, Editor; Edward P. Lynch, Editor; Gregory C. Parliman, Editor; Patrick J. McCarthy, Editor; Theresa Donahue Egler, Editor.
Desc: Addresses legislation and court decisions affecting employment issues. *Type:* Newsletter.

News and Notes (Washington)

International Society for Performance Improvement
1300 L St. NW, Ste. 1250   Ph: (202)408-7969
Washington, DC 20005   Fax: (202)408-7972
E-mail: info@ispi.org
Contact: Megan Spillane, Dir. of Marketing.
Desc: Contains information on the activities of the International Society for Performance Improvement. Includes chapter news and job openings. *Type:* Newsletter.

North Carolina Employment Security Commission—Area Labor Market Newsletter

North Carolina Employment Security Commission
PO Box 25903   Ph: (919)733-2936
Raleigh, NC 27612   Fax: (919)733-8662
Desc: Provides narrative information concerning local employment office program activities and operations. Contains civilian labor force estimates for the counties in the area. *Type:* Newsletter.

North Carolina Employment Security Commission—Labor Area Summary

North Carolina Employment Security Commission
PO Box 25903   Ph: (919)733-2936
Raleigh, NC 27612   Fax: (919)733 8662
Desc: Summarizes month-by-month changes in the composition of the labor force in the following Standard Metropolitan Statistical Areas in North Carolina: Asheville, Charlotte-Gastonia-Rock Hill, Greensboro-Winston-Salem-High Point, and Raleigh-Durham. Analyzes developments in employment, unemployment, labor supply and demand, training program activities, and related issues. *Type:* Newsletter.

NRPA Job Bulletin

National Recreation and Park Association, Professional Services Division
22377 Belmont Ridge Rd.   Ph: (703)858-0784
Ashburn, VA 20148   Free: 800-626-6772
                            Fax: (703)858-0707
E-mail: info@nrpa.org
URL: http://www.nrpa.org.
Contact: Georgina F. Cosens, Editor, (703)858-2155, gcosens@nrpa.org.
Desc: Provides listings of employment opportunities in the park, recreation, and leisure services field. *Type:* Newsletter.

Oklahoma Employment Law Letter

M. Lee Smith Publishers LLC
5201 Virginia Way   Ph: (615)373-7517
PO Box 5094   Free: 800-274-6774
Brentwood, TN 37024-5094   Fax: 800-785-9212
E-mail: custserv@mleesmith.com
Contact: Charles S. Plumb, Editor; Lynn Paul Mattson, Editor; Kathy R. Neal, Editor.
Desc: Addresses legislation and court decisions affecting employment issues. *Type:* Newsletter.

Organizations and Change

International Registry of Organization Development Professionals
Organization Development Institute
11234 Walnut Ridge Rd.   Ph: (440)729-7419
Chesterland, OH 44026   Fax: (440)729-9319
E-mail: aa563@cleveland.freenet.edu.
URL: http://members.aol.com/odinst.
Contact: Dr. Donald W. Cole, RODC, Publisher/Editor, donwcole@aol.com.
Desc: Serves organization development professionals, teachers of organizational behavior, management consultants, personnel directors and executives by carrying news items, interest surveys, economic information, and committee reports. Recurring features include announcements of conferences, meetings, publications, consulting opportunities, and employment openings. *Type:* Newsletter.

Overseas Employment Newsletter

Overseas Employment Services
1255 Laird, Ste. 208   Ph: (514)739-1108
Mount Royal, PQ, Canada H3P Fax: (514)739-0795
  2T1
Contact: Leonard Simcoe, Editor.
Desc: Contains approximately 300 job openings for a broad range of skills, careers, and positions in developing and industrialized nations worldwide. Remarks: Entries occasionally written in French. *Type:* Newsletter.

People Trends

The Strategy Group Inc.
290 Beckley Ln.   Free: 800-728-0967
Dublin, OH 43017-1346   Fax: (614)761-0967
Contact: Carl Crawford, Editor and Publisher, carl@thestrategygroup.com.
Desc: Provides information about human resources. Includes research and market trends. *Type:* Newsletter.

The Personnel Assistant

Council on Education in Management
321 Lennon Ln.   Ph: (510)988-1835
Walnut Creek, CA 94598
Contact: Ruth Locher, Editor.
Desc: Provides information and advice about human resources. *Type:* Newsletter.

Personnel Executives Contactbook

Gale Group Inc.
27500 Drake Rd.   Ph: (248)699-4253
Farmington Hills, MI 48331-   Free: 800-877-GALE
3535   Fax: (248)699-8070
E-mail: galeord@galegroup.com
URL: http://www.galegroup.com.
Contact: Cynthia Russell Spomer, Editor.
Desc: 30,000 personnel and human resources officials in the U.S. *Type:* Directory.

Personnel Legal Alert

Alexander Hamilton Institute
70 Hilltop Rd.   Ph: (201)825-3377
Ramsey, NJ 07446-1119   Free: 800-879-2441
     Fax: (201)825-8696
E-mail: custsvc@ahipubs.com; pla@ahipubs.com.
URL: http://www.ahipubs.com; http://www.ahipubs.com.
Contact: Gloria Ju, Editor.
Desc: Provides information about employment law. Topics include court opinions and government regulations. *Type:* Newsletter.

Personnel Postscript

Medical Group Management Association
104 Inverness Terr. E.   Ph: (303)799-1111
Englewood, CO 80112-5306   Free: 888-608-5601
     Fax: (303)397-1824
URL: http://www.mgma.com.
Contact: Marilee Aust, Editor.
Desc: Supplements personnel policies manuals in the medical field. Provides updates on employment and personnel issues, including legislative matters, performance management, performance evaluation policies, and employee involvement. *Type:* Newsletter.

Peterson's Internships

Peterson's
202 Carnegie Center   Ph: (609)243-9111
PO Box 2123   Free: 800-338-3282
Princeton, NJ 08543-2123   Fax: (609)243-9150
URL: http://www.peterson.com; http://www.petersons.com.
Contact: Karen Hansen, Editor.
Desc: 40,000 career-oriented internship positions with over 1,700 organizations in the U.S. ranging from business to theater, communications to science. *Type:* Directory.

Peterson's Job Opportunities for Business Majors

Peterson's
202 Carnegie Center   Ph: (609)243-9111
PO Box 2123   Free: 800-338-3282
Princeton, NJ 08543-2123   Fax: (609)243-9150
URL: http://www.peterson.com; http://www.petersons.com.
Contact: Karen Hansen, Editor.
Desc: The 2,000 largest U.S. employers hiring in several fields, including financial services, management consulting, consumer products, and media/ entertainment. *Type:* Directory.

Peterson's Job Opportunities for Health and Science Majors

Peterson's
202 Carnegie Center   Ph: (609)243-9111
PO Box 2123   Free: 800-338-3282
Princeton, NJ 08543-2123   Fax: (609)243-9150
URL: http://www.peterson.com; http://www.petersons.com.
Contact: Karen Hansen, Editor.

Desc: About 1,300 research, consulting, government, and non-profit and profit service organizations that hire college and university graduates in science and health-related majors. *Type:* Directory.

Physical Science Career Directory

Gale Group Inc.
27500 Drake Rd.   Ph: (248)699-4253
Farmington Hills, MI 48331-   Free: 800-877-GALE
3535   Fax: (248)699-8070
E-mail: galeord@galegroup.com
URL: http://www.galegroup.com.
Contact: Bradley J. Morgan, Editor; Joseph M. Palmisano, Editor.
Desc: Over 210 chemical companies, testing and research laboratories, and consulting firms in the U.S. offering entry-level positions and internships; sources of help-wanted ads, professional associations, producers of videos, databases, career guides, and professional guides and handbooks. *Type:* Directory.

Pilots Rights Association

1440 N St. NW, Ste. 911 W
Washington, DC 20005
Contact: Jack H. Young, Pres.
Desc: Airline pilots opposed to age discrimination in employment. Objective is to overturn the Federal Aviation Administration's age 60 mandatory retirement rule. *Type:* Association.

Plunkett's Companion to The Almanac of American Employers: Mid-Size Firms

Plunkett Research, Ltd.
PO Drawer 541737   Ph: (713)932-2000
Houston, TX 77254-1737   Fax: (713)932-7080
URL: http://www.plunkettresearch.com.
Contact: Jack W. Plunkett, Editor.
Desc: Profiles of 500 rapid growing mid-size firms. *Type:* Directory.

Plunkett's Employers Internet Sites with Careers Information

Plunkett Research, Ltd.
PO Drawer 541737   Ph: (713)932-2000
Houston, TX 77254-1737   Fax: (713)932-7080
URL: http://www.plunkettResearch.com.
Desc: Hundreds of major employers Internet sites that contain career information and job postings. *Type:* Directory.

Practical Supervision

Professional Training Associates, Inc.
210 Commerce Blvd.   Ph: (512)255-6006
Round Rock, TX 78664-2189   Free: 800-424-2112
E-mail: demwit@protrain.com
Contact: Robert Moskowitz, Editor.
Desc: Supplies practical advice and new ideas for solving daily problems of managing people and becoming an effective supervisor. Covers such topics as improving employee attitudes and motivation, correcting performance problems, interviewing and evaluating job applicants, and training employees. *Type:* Newsletter.

Professional Careers Sourcebook

Gale Group Inc.
27500 Drake Rd.   Ph: (248)699-4253
Farmington Hills, MI 48331-   Free: 800-877-GALE
3535   Fax: (248)699-8070
E-mail: galeord@galegroup.com
URL: http://www.galegroup.com.
Contact: Christine Maurer, Editor.
Desc: Approximately 8,500 career planning resources, covering 122 careers including job descriptions, publishers of

professional and trade periodicals, career guides, test guides, educational directories, and reference guides and handbooks; professional associations; standards/ certification agencies; sponsors of programs, scholarships, grants, fellowships, and awards; professional meetings and conventions; and other sources of career planning information. *Type:* Directory.

Project Equality—Update

Project Equality, Inc.
6301 Rockhill Rd., Ste. 315   Ph: (816)361-9222
Kansas City, MO 64131   Free: 877-PEISEED
     Fax: (816)361-8997
URL: http://members.aol.com/pequality/pedirectory.html1.
Contact: Kirk P. Perucca, Editor.
Desc: Reports on program activities of the Project and Advocacy issues. Focuses on issues related to the achievement of equal employment opportunities. *Type:* Newsletter.

The PSIC Listing

Protective Services Information Center
PO Box 3831   Ph: (217)364-5711
Springfield, IL 62708
E-mail: psic@famvid.com
Contact: James D. Allen, Editor.
Desc: Provides listings of jobs and career advancement opportunities in the protective service professions, such as security, law enforcement, and investigation. Entries include contact information. *Type:* Newsletter.

Public Administration Career Directory

Gale Group Inc.
27500 Drake Rd.   Ph: (248)699-4253
Farmington Hills, MI 48331-   Free: 800-877-GALE
3535   Fax: (248)699-8070
E-mail: galeord@galegroup.com
URL: http://www.galegroup.com.
Contact: Bradley J. Morgan, Editor; Joseph M. Palmisano, Editor.
Desc: Over 210 U.S. federal government departments and agencies and other public organizations offering entry-level positions and internships; sources of help-wanted ads, professional associations, producers of videos, databases, career guides, and professional guides and handbooks. *Type:* Directory.

Public Employment Reporter

NYPER Publications, LLC
887 Birchwood Ln.   Ph: (518)786-1654
Niskayuna, NY 12309   Fax: (518)456-8582
E-mail: nyper@capital.net; editor@nyper.com.
Desc: Provides information and statistics on employment. *Type:* Newsletter.

Public Interest Employment Service Job Alert

Public Interest ClearingHouse
100 McAllister St.   Ph: (415)255-1714
San Francisco, CA 94102-4929   Fax: (415)255-3042
E-mail: picorg@pic.org; pies@pic.org.
Contact: Odilla Sidime-Brazier, Editor.
Desc: Lists job openings in legal aid offices, public interest law firms, and nonprofit organizations. Remarks: also available via e-mail. *Type:* Newsletter.

QI/TQM

American Health Consultants, Inc.
3525 Piedmont Rd., Bldg. 6,   Ph: (404)262-7436
Ste. 400   Free: 800-688-2421
Atlanta, GA 30305   Fax: (404)262-7837
E-mail: customerservice@ahcpub.com
Contact: Mary Kouri, Editor, (303)771-8424.
Desc: Presents information on continuous quality improvement in health care facilities and implementing management principles. Recurring features include interviews and news of research. *Type:* Newsletter.

The Quality Management Sourcebook

Routledge, Inc.
29 W. 35th St.   Ph: (212)216-7800
New York, NY 10001-2291   Free: 800-634-7064
    Fax: (212)564-7854
E-mail: reference@routledge-ny.com
URL: http://www.routledge-ny.com; http://www.routledge-ny.com.
Contact: Christine Avery, Editor; Diane Zabel, Editor.
Desc: Quality management organizations, training materials, and resource people. *Type:* Directory.

Quality Manager's Alert

Progressive Business Publications
370 Technology Dr.   Ph: (610)695-8600
Malvern, PA 19355   Free: 800-220-5000
    Fax: (610)651-2981
URL: http://www.pbp.com.
Contact: Jim McCanney, Editor.
Desc: Communicates the latest information on changing quality standards and how companies get buy-in on quality from employees. Recurring features include interviews, news of research, a calendar of events, news of educational opportunities, and a column titled Sharpen Your Judgment. *Type:* Newsletter.

The Recruiting & Search Report

Kenneth J. Cole
PO Box 9433   Ph: (904)235-3733
Panama City Beach, FL 32417
Contact: Kenneth J. Cole, Publisher.
Desc: Emphasizes analytical and academic issues relating to executive search techniques, procedures, research, and developments. Recurring features include news of research. *Type:* Newsletter.

Recruiting Trends

Remy Publishing Company
401 N. Franklin St., 3rd Fl.   Ph: (312)464-0300
Chicago, IL 60610   Free: 800-542-6670
    Fax: (312)464-0166
Contact: Catherine Davis, Editor.
Desc: Covers trends and practices in recruiting people for jobs in science, engineering, management, and hard-to-fill technical positions, including hourly and part-time work. Reports on successful techniques, new developments in interviewing and testing, and regulatory agencies and government requirements affecting employment. *Type:* Newsletter.

Resume Pro Newsletter

Damn Good Resume Service
PO Box 3289   Ph: (510)540-5876
Berkeley, CA 94703   Fax: (510)658-9614
Contact: Yana Parker, Editor and Publisher.
Desc: Provides information and examples on creating resumes. Topics include news, samples, and technology. *Type:* Newsletter.

Runzheimer Reports on Relocation

Runzheimer International
Runzheimer Park   Ph: (414)767-2200
Rochester, WI 53167   Free: 800-558-1702
    Fax: (414)767-2476
URL: http://www.rumzheimer.com
Contact: Nat Workman, Sr. Editor, niw@runzheimer.com.
Desc: Reports on employer relocation and relocation management, trends in corporate policy development and methods employed by companies that relocate employees, and the complexities of transfers and relocation policies. Recurring features include survey results with commentary and a monthly report on mortgage rates and home value changes. *Type:* Newsletter.

Saludos Web: Careers, Employment & Culture

Saludos Hispanos
73-121 Fred Waring Dr., Ste. 100
Palm Desert, CA 92260
E-mail: saludos@well.net
URL: http://www.saludos.com
Desc: Supported by Saludos Hispanos magazine, this site is devoted to promoting Hispanic careers and education. Online job postings and resume services are offered. *Type:* Database.

SER - Jobs for Progress National

100 Decker Dr., Ste. 200   Ph: (972)541-0616
Irving, TX 75062   Free: 800-427-2306
E-mail: hguajardo@sernational.org
URL: http://www.sernational.org
Contact: Hugo Cardona, Pres. & CEO.
Desc: Aims to provide employment training and opportunities for Spanish-speaking and disadvantaged Americans. Seeks to increase business and economic opportunities for minority communities and ensure optimum participation by the Hispanic community in public policy forums. Most SER performance contracts are funded by the federal government. *Type:* Association.

SIGCPR Newsletter

Special Interest Group on Programming Languages (SIGPLAN)
Association for Computing Machinery
1515 Broadway   Ph: (212)869-7440
New York, NY 10036   Free: 800-342-6626
    Fax: (212)302-5826
E-mail: acmhelp@acm.org
URL: http://www.acm.org/sigcpr/.
Contact: George Schell, Editor.
Desc: Provides items of interest to individuals involved in selection, training, supervision, evaluation, and associated aspects of computer personnel management. *Type:* Newsletter.

Smart Workplace Practices

Independent Small Business Employers of America
520 S. Pierce, Ste. 224   Ph: (515)424-3187
Mason City, IA 50401   Free: 800-728-3187
    Fax: (515)424-1673
Contact: Jim Collison, Editor.
Desc: Helps employers, managers, and supervisors stay out of trouble by adopting and maintaining the best possible workplace policies and practices. *Type:* Newsletter.

Society for Human Resource Management

1800 Duke St.   Ph: (703)548-3440
Alexandria, VA 22314-3499   Free: 800-283-7476
    Fax: (703)836-0367
E-mail: shrm@shrm.org
URL: http://www.shrm.org
Contact: Michael R. Losey, CEO.
Desc: Professional organization of human resource, personnel, and industrial relations professionals and executives. Promotes the advancement of human resource management. *Type:* Association.

Sound Opportunities

Sound Opportunities
PO Box 16722   Ph: (206)933-6556
Seattle, WA 98116   Fax: (206)933-6566
E-mail: soundop@soundop.com
URL: http://www.soundop.com
Contact: Karen Rudd, karen@soundop.com.
Desc: Lists current employment, volunteer and internship opportunities for nonprofit organizations in the Pacific Northwest. *Type:* Newsletter.

The Source

Rachel P.R. Services
1650 S. Pacific Coast Hwy., Ste. 200-C
Redondo Beach, CA 90277
Contact: Janis Brett-Elspas, Editor.
Desc: Features nationwide employment opportunities in advertising, public relations, journalism, and marketing. *Type:* Newsletter.

South Carolina Employment Law Letter

M. Lee Smith Publishers LLC
5201 Virginia Way   Ph: (615)373-7517
PO Box 5094   Free: 800-274-6774
Brentwood, TN 37024-5094   Fax: 800-785-9212
E-mail: custserv@mleesmith.com
URL: http://www.mleesmith.com.
Contact: Carl B. Carruth, Editor; Edwin W. Johnson, II, Editor; Richard J. Morgan, Editor.
Desc: Addresses legislation and court decisions affecting employment issues. *Type:* Newsletter.

Staffing Industry Report

Staffing Industry Analysts, Inc.
2235 Grant Rd., No. 3   Ph: (650)903-9494
Los Altos, CA 94024   Fax: (650)903-9811
E-mail: subservices@sireport.com
URL: http://www.sireport.com.
Contact: Peter Yessne, Editor, editor@sireport.com; Theresa Daly, Editor.
Desc: Focuses on the temporary help and employment services industry. Provides information on economic forecasts, employment indicators, finance, labor and market trends, stocks, and statistics. *Type:* Newsletter.

State Personnel Review

Council of State Governments
2760 Research Park Dr.   Ph: (606)244-8000
PO Box 11910   Free: 800-800-1910
Lexington, KY 40578-1910   Fax: (606)244-8001
E-mail: info@csg.org
Contact: Julie Billips, Editor; Deana Lykins, Editor.
Desc: Offers news on personnel information exchanges among state agencies. Recurring features include interviews, news of research, a calendar of events, reports of meetings, news of educational opportunities, and notices of publications available. *Type:* Newsletter.

Success Today

Stewart Associates
12625 Frederick St., No.I-5   Ph: (714)247-4726
Moreno Valley, CA 92553-5216
Desc: Geared toward business professionals who want to advance in their companies. *Type:* Newsletter.

The Successful Benefits Communicator

Lawrence Ragan Communications, Inc.
316 N. Michigan Ave., Ste. 300   Ph: (312)960-4100
Chicago, IL 60601   Free: 800-878-5331
    Fax: (312)960-4105
E-mail: cservice@ragan.com
Contact: Lawrence Ragan, Publisher; Forrest Cates, Editor; Susan Weston, Circulation Mgr.; Sharon Giankos, Art Director; Melissa Eckhardt, Marketing Director.
Desc: Offers ideas, techniques, and tips for those who communicate benefits information. *Type:* Newsletter.

Supervisor's Guide to Employment Practices

Clement Communications, Inc.
Concord Industrial Park   Ph: (610)459-1700
10 LaCrue Ave.   Free: 800-345-8101
Concordville, PA 19331   Fax: (610)459-0936
Desc: Provides information to managers and supervisors regarding sensitive human resource issues. *Type:* Newsletter.

Supported Employment InfoLines

Training Resource Network, Inc.
PO Box 439 Ph: (904)823-9800
Saint Augustine, FL 32085-0439 Fax: (904)823-3554
E-mail: trninc@aol.com
URL: http://www.trninc.com.
Contact: Dawn Langton, Editor, (904)824-7121; Dale Dileo, Publisher.
Desc: Discusses training and employment opportunities, techniques and news. *Type:* Newsletter.

TeamLeader

The Dartnell Corp.
360 Hiatt Dr. Free: 800-621-5463
Palm Beach Gardens, FL 33418 Fax: (561)622-2423
E-mail: dartnell@dartnellcorp.com; teamldr@dartnellcorp.com.
URL: http://www.dartnellcorp.com
Desc: Training newsletter that provides information and instruction to guide team leaders of both functional and self-directed work teams in effective team leadership skills. Topics covered include employee relations, productivity, cost control, quality/customer service, and safety. *Type:* Newsletter.

Texoma Workforce Development Board

Janie Bates
305 W Woodard, Ste. 217 Ph: (903)465-7408
Denison, TX 75020-6202 Fax: (903)465-1745
E-mail: janie.bates@twc.state.tx.us
URL: http://texomaworkforce.com
Contact: Janie Bates, Exec.Dir.
Type: Association.

Training and Development Organizations Directory

The Gale Group
27500 Drake Rd. Ph: (248)699-4253
Farmington Hills, MI 48331-3535
URL: http://www.galegroup.com
Contact: Customer Service. Toll-free: 800-877-GALE.
Desc: Contains descriptions of more than 2600 organizations that offer more than 10,000 seminars, workshops, and training programs. Covers a wide variety of topics for personnel training and personal development, including interpersonal communication, negotiation, decision making, leadership, productivity, public speaking, stress management, team building, and human resource development. *Available:* The Gale Group, InfoTrac Web. *Type:* Database.

Training Directors' Forum Newsletter

Lakewood Publications, Inc.
50 S. 9th St. Ph: (612)333-0471
Minneapolis, MN 55402 Free: 800-328-4329
Fax: (612)333-6521
E-mail: justask@lakewoodpub.com; mhequet@lakewoodpub.com.
Contact: Dave Zielinski, Editor.
Desc: Carries discussions of issues and developments related to managing the training function, such as training's role in organizational change and computer training programs. Serves as a forum for the exchange of information and ideas among executives in the field. *Type:* Newsletter.

Training Media Review

TMR Publications
PO Box 381822 Ph: (617)661-1095
Cambridge, MA 02238-1822 Fax: (617)661-1797
E-mail: tmr1@tmreview.com
URL: http://www.tmreview.com.
Contact: Bill Ellet, Editor and Publisher.

Desc: Provides information for business trainers. Recurring features include software, video, Internet, and book reviews. *Type:* Newsletter.

Tulsa Area Large Employers

Metropolitan Tulsa Chamber of Commerce
616 S. Boston Ave. Ph: (918)585-1201
Tulsa, OK 74119 Free: 800-624-6822
Fax: (918)585-8386
Desc: About 275 companies in Tulsa, Oklahoma with a hundred or more employees. *Type:* Directory.

United Nations Jobs Newsletter

Thomas F. Burola & Associates
6477 Telephone Rd., Ste. 7R Fax: (805)654-1708
Ventura, CA 93003
Desc: Focuses on employment conditions within the United Nations System and lists vacancy notices. Covers the World Bank, Canadian International Development Agency (CIDA), Overseas Development Agency (ODA), United States Agency for International Development (USAID), Asian Development Bank, European Bank for Reconstruction and Development, International Red Cross, and related private sector consulting companies. *Type:* Newsletter.

Virginia Court Reporters Association Newsletter

Virginia Court Reporters Association
RR 74, Box 1034 Ph: (804)556-4726
Plain View, VA 23156 Fax: (804)556-2533
E-mail: 75551.2702@compuserve.com
Contact: Carol Hill Switzer, Editor.
Desc: Publishes anything educational, entertaining, or enlightening about court reporting. Recurring features include interviews, news of research, a calendar of events, reports of meetings, news of educational opportunities, job listings, and notices of publications available. *Type:* Newsletter.

Vocational Careers Sourcebook

Gale Group Inc.
27500 Drake Rd. Ph: (248)699-4253
Farmington Hills, MI 48331-3535 Free: 800-877-GALE
Fax: (248)699-8070
E-mail: galeord@galegroup.com
URL: http://www.galegroup.com.
Contact: Christine Maurer, Editor.
Desc: Approximately 134 careers designated as "vocational" in "Occupational Outlooks Handbook"; lists organizations that offer career planning assistance; publishers of related periodicals, career guides, and test guides; industry associations; standards and certification agencies; sponsors of programs, scholarships, grants, and other financial aid programs; professional meetings and conventions. *Type:* Directory.

Vocational Foundation, Inc.

902 Broadway, 15th Fl. Ph: (212)777-0700
New York, NY 10010 Fax: (212)673-8975
Contact: Rebecca Taylor, Exec.Dir.
Desc: Seeks to aid high school dropouts and young people with correctional and drug abuse histories. *Type:* Association.

W. E. Upjohn Institute for Employment Research

300 S. Westnedge Ave. Ph: (616)343-5541
Kalamazoo, MI 49007-4686 Fax: (616)343-3308
E-mail: publications@we.upjohninst.org
URL: http://www.upjohninst.org
Contact: Richard Wyrma, Mktg.Mgr.
Desc: The institute is the major activity of the W. E. Upjohn Unemployment Trustee Corporation, a private non-

profit organization formed in 1932 "for research into the causes and effects of unemployment and to study and investigate the feasibility and methods of insuring against unemployment and devise ways and means of preventing and alleviating the distress and hardship caused by unemployment." Research is conducted by the staff and by grant-funded scholars. *Type:* Association.

WAVE

501 School St. SW, Ste. 600 Ph: (202)484-0103
Washington, DC 20024 Free: 800-274-2005
Fax: (202)488-7595
Contact: Lawrence C. Brown, Jr., Pres.
Desc: Organization, funded in part by the U.S. Department of Labor and grants from corporations and foundations, that helps disadvantaged 16-21 year old high school dropouts and students at risk of dropping out to find unsubsidized jobs and careers. Dropouts attend classes to prepare for their high school equivalency diplomas and to learn basic living skills, such as how to find an apartment, how to dress for a job interview, and how to balance a checkbook. *Type:* Association.

What's New in Benefits & Compensation

Progressive Business Publications
370 Technology Dr. Ph: (610)695-8600
Malvern, PA 19355 Free: 800-220-5000
Fax: (610)651-2981
URL: http://www.pbp.com.
Contact: John T. Hiatt, Editor.
Desc: Communicates the latest legal, tax and policy developments that help benefits executives address cost concerns while meeting complex needs of employees. Recurring features include interviews, news of research, a calendar of events, and a column titled Sharpen Your Judgment. *Type:* Newsletter.

What's Working in Human Resources

Progressive Business Publications
370 Technology Dr. Ph: (610)695-8600
Malvern, PA 19355 Free: 800-220-5000
Fax: (610)651-2981
URL: http://www.pbp.com.
Contact: Tom Gorman, Editor.
Desc: Reports on the latest trends in Human Resources, including the latest employment law rulings. Recurring features include interviews, news of research, a calendar of events, news of educational opportunities, and a column titlted Sharpen Your Judgment. *Type:* Newsletter.

Wider Opportunities for Women

815 15th St. NW, Ste. 916 Ph: (202)638-3143
Washington, DC 20005 Fax: (202)638-4885
E-mail: ldobbs@w-o-w.org
Contact: Lina Frescas-Dobbs, Exec.Dir.
Desc: To expand employment opportunities for women through information, employment training, technical assistance, and advocacy. Works to overcome barriers to women's employment and economic equity, including occupational segregation, sex stereotypic education and training, discrimination in employment practices and wages. Sponsors Women's Work Force Network, a national network of 500 women's employment programs and advocates. *Type:* Association.

Wildcat Service Corporation

161 Hudson St. Ph: (212)219-9700
New York, NY 10013 Fax: (212)941-5793
Contact: Amalia V. Betanzos, Pres.
Desc: Provides transitional employment and training for chronically unemployed persons (former substance abusers, ex-offenders, welfare mothers, out-of-school youth, and illiterate and delinquent youth). Systematically prepares and grooms employees to accept the full responsibility of full-time work within a 12-month time period. Placement rate of terminees is about 70% in a variety of industries. *Type:* Association.

WorkAmerica

National Alliance of Business (NAB)

1201 New York NW, Ste. 700   Ph: (202)289-2888
Washington, DC 20005-3917   Free: 800-787-2848
                             Fax: (202)289-1303

E-mail: info@nab.com

Contact: Lawrence Spinelli, Editor.

Desc: Provides coverage of issues affecting the quality of the American work force. Discusses education, "second-chance systems" for the economically disadvantaged, and workplace training. *Type:* Newsletter.

Workforce Diversity

Remy Publishing Company

401 N. Franklin St., 3rd Fl.   Ph: (312)464-0300
Chicago, IL 60610   Free: 800-542-6670
                      Fax: (312)464-0166

Contact: Catherine Davis, Editor.

Desc: Reports on innovative diversity programs, surveys, and resources used to develop or enhance efforts to meet the challenges of today's changing workforce and global workplace. *Type:* Newsletter.

Workforce Stability Alert

M. Lee Smith, Publishers LLC

PO Box 5094   Ph: (615)373-7517
Brentwood, TN 37024-5094   Free: 800-274-6774
                            Fax: (615)373-5183

Contact: Roger Herman, Editor; Joyce Gioia, Editor.

Desc: Provides information on employee recruitment and retention, management techniques, and human resource issues. Recurring features include book reviews and columns titled Crazy Idea of the Month, Leadership, Ask HR Henrietta, Recruitment, and Best Corporate Practices. *Type:* Newsletter.

Working Options

Association of Part-Time Professionals

Crescent Plaza   Ph: (703)734-7975
7700 Leesburg Pike, Ste. 216   Fax: (703)734-7405
Falls Church, VA 22043

E-mail: lemans@erols.com

URL: http://www.aptp.org

Contact: Margaret Volpe, Editor.

Desc: Advocates alternative work schedules, particularly part-time employment for professionals. Topics include job sharing, older workers, personnel policies, employee benefits, insurance, chapter news, and legislative news. *Type:* Newsletter.

Working Together

The Dartnell Corp.

360 Hiatt Dr.   Free: 800-621-5463
Palm Beach Gardens, FL 33418   Fax: (561)622-2423

E-mail: dartnell@dartnellcorp.com;   worktog@
dartnellcorp.com.

URL: http://www.dartnellcorp.com

Contact: Kim Antersen, Editor.

Desc: Provides non-management level employees motivational information to promote loyalty, cooperation, teamwork, and productivity. Contains articles with suggestions on work habits, customer relations, work safety, and similar topics. *Type:* Newsletter.

WorkPlace America

Hunt-Scanlon Publishing Co. Inc.

1 E. Putnam Ave.   Ph: (203)629-3629
Greenwich, CT 06830   Fax: (203)629-3701

E-mail: hsp@interport.net

URL: http://www.hunt-scanlon.com.

Contact: Christopher W. Hunt, Editor; Scott A. Scanlon, Publisher.

Desc: Provides information on the current state of the American workplace. *Type:* Newsletter.

Wrongful Discharge Report

Andrews Publications

175 Strafford Ave., Bldg. 4, Ste.   Ph: (610)225-0510
   140   Free: 800-345-1101
Wayne, PA 19087   Fax: (610)225-0501

Contact: Linda Coady, Editor.

Desc: Summarizes state and federal appellate court decisions, providing complete legal citations, and analyzing each decision as it affects personnel policy and management. *Type:* Newsletter.

Energy

Advanced Battery Technology

Seven Mountains Scientific, Inc.

913 Tressler St.   Ph: (814)466-6559
PO Box 650   Fax: (814)466-2777
Boalsburg, PA 16827

E-mail: sevmtnsci@csrlink.com

Contact: Dr. E. Thomas Chesworth, P.E., Technical Editor.

Desc: Follows developments in the international battery industry, including research, engineering, manufacturing, sales, and financial news. Recurring features include news of the industry, battery & fuel cell patents, research, book reviews, a calendar of events, and columns titled Electric Vehicles and New Products. *Type:* Newsletter.

American Council for an Energy Efficient Economy

1001 Connecticut Ave. NW,   Ph: (202)429-0063
   Ste. 801   Fax: (202)429-0193
Washington, DC 20036

E-mail: ace3pubs@ix.netcom.com

URL: http://www.aceee.org

Contact: Howard Geller, Exec.Dir.

Desc: Collects, evaluates, and disseminates information to encourage the implementation of energy-efficient technologies and practices. Conducts research on energy conservation and links to environmental and economic issues. Sponsors conferences to facilitate the exchange of information among all interested groups. *Type:* Association.

American Gas Association

444 N. Capitol St. NW   Ph: (703)841-8400
Washington, DC 20001   Fax: (703)841-8406

URL: http://www.aga.com

Contact: David N. Parker, Pres. and CEO.

Desc: Corporate members include any entity that, as a principal or agent, conducts activities in sales, transportation or storage of natural gas and gas-related activities. Provides information on sales, finance, utilization, research, management, safety, accounting, and all phases of natural gas transmission and distribution. *Type:* Association.

American Solar Energy Society

2400 Central Ave., G-1   Ph: (303)443-3130
Boulder, CO 80301   Fax: (303)443-3212

E-mail: ases@ases.org

URL: http://www.ases.org/solar

Contact: Larry Sherwood, Dir.

Desc: Professional energy society organized to promote a wide utilization of solar energy through the application of science and technology. Encourages basic and applied research and development. Conducts workshops; organizes forums inviting researchers, policymakers, practitioners and consumers for discussion, analysis, and debate. *Type:* Association.

American Wind Energy Association

122 C St. NW, 4th Fl.   Ph: (202)383-2500
Washington, DC 20001   Fax: (202)383-2505

E-mail: windmail@awea.org

URL: http://www.econet.org/awea/

Contact: Randall Swisher, Exec.Dir.

Desc: Wind energy equipment manufacturers; project developers and dealers; individuals from industry, government, and academia; interested others. Works to: advance the art and science of using energy from the wind for human purposes; encourage the use of wind energy conversion systems as alternatives to current energy systems that depend on depletable fuels; facilitate the widespread use of wind as a renewable, nonpolluting energy source by fostering communication within the field of wind energy and between the technical community and the public. *Type:* Association.

API EnCompass: News

American Petroleum Institute (API)

API EnCompass

275 Seventh Ave., 9th Floor   Ph: (212)366-4040
New York, NY 10001-6708

E-mail: info@apiencompass.org

URL: http://www.apiencompass.org

Contact: Dorthy Eska, Online Coordinator, (212)206-2224, fax: (212)366-4298, esko@apiencompass.org.

Desc: Contains business and economic news taking place in the petroleum and energy-related industries. Includes abstracts and detailed indexing of upstream and downstream articles selected from a list of worldwide industry trade publications. *Available:* The Dialog Corporation, DIALOG; Questel • Orbit; Cambridge Scientific Abstracts (CSA), Internet Database Service; Dow Jones Interactive Publishing; infoMarket, KnowledgeLink; American Petroleum Institute (API), API EnCompass. *Type:* Database.

APIPAT

American Petroleum Institute (API)

API EnCompass

275 Seventh Ave., 9th Floor   Ph: (212)366-4040
New York, NY 10001-6708

E-mail: info@apiencompass.org

URL: http://www.apiencompass.org

Contact: Dorothy Eska, Online Coordinator, (212)206-2224, eska@apiencompass.org.

Desc: Contains abstracts (from 1980), of patents related to the petroleum refining and petrochemical industries issued in all industrial countries, as well as European patents issued under the European Patent Procedure (December 1978), and world patents issued under the Patent Cooperation Treaty. Beginning in January 1981, also covers patents related to oilfield chemicals. *Available:* The Dialog Corporation, DIALOG; STN International. *Type:* Database.

Brown's Directory of North American & International Gas Companies

Advanstar Communications

7500 Old Oak Blvd.   Ph: (440)243-8100
Cleveland, OH 44130-3369   Free: 800-225-4569
                            Fax: (440)891-2733

E-mail: directories@advanstar.com

URL: http://www.advanstar.com.

Contact: Karen Eagle, Editor.

Desc: Operating gas companies (utilities, including municipal systems, and transmission companies), brokers, holding companies, state public service commissions, and industry associations, and suppliers includes major gas companies outside the United States. *Type:* Directory.

California Solar Energy Industries Association—Membership Directory

California Solar Energy Industries Association
PO Box 782   Ph: (916)649-9858
Rio Vista, CA 94571   Fax: (916)649-9757
URL: http://www.calseia.org; http://www.calseia.com.

Contact: Les Nelson, Editor, (949)837-7430, fax: (949)586-2357, lanelson@worldnet.att.net.

Desc: About 100 member companies and professionals. *Type:* Directory.

Coal Week

McGraw-Hill, Inc.
1221 Avenue of the Americas   Ph: (212)512-6410
New York, NY 10020

Desc: Contains the complete text of the Coal Week newsletter on the production, transportation, and marketing of steam coal. Covers coal land leasing and legal and regulatory developments affecting coal mining, coal prices and availability, and corporate developments in the electric utilities industry. *Available:* LEXIS-NEXIS, NEXIS; The Dialog Corporation, DIALOG; Dow Jones Interactive Publishing. *Type:* Database.

Coal Week International

McGraw-Hill, Inc.
1221 Avenue of the Americas   Ph: (212)512-6410
New York, NY 10020

Desc: Contains the complete text of Coal Week International, a newsletter on the international market for steam and coking coal. Covers governmental activity, markets and prices, freight rates, demand, production, and research. *Available:* LEXIS-NEXIS, NEXIS; The Dialog Corporation, DIALOG; Dow Jones Interactive Publishing. *Type:* Database.

Compressed Gas Association

1725 Jefferson Davis Hwy., Ste.   Ph: (703)412-0900
    1004   Fax: (703)412-0128
Arlington, VA 22202-4100
E-mail: cga@cganet.com
URL: http://www.cganet.com

Contact: Carl T. Johnson, CEO & Pres.

Desc: Firms producing and distributing compressed, liquefied, and cryogenic gases; manufacturers of related equipment. Submits recommendations to appropriate government agencies to improve safety standards and methods of handling, transporting, and storing gases; acts as advisor to regulatory authorities and other agencies concerned with safe handling of compressed gases; collaborates with national organizations to develop specifications and standards of safety; compiles information. Maintains 25 technical committees. *Type:* Association.

DRI Canadian Energy Forecast

Standard & Poor's DRI
Data Products Division
24 Hartwell Ave.   Ph: (781)863-5100
Lexington, MA 02421
E-mail: client_services@dri.mcgraw-hill.com
URL: http://www.dri.mcgraw-hill.com

Contact: Client Resource Center, (781)860-6527.

Desc: Contains more than 2000 annual energy forecasts for Canada and these 7 regions: Alberta, the Atlantic Provinces, British Columbia, Manitoba, Ontario, Quebec, and Saskatchewan. Covers production, stocks, exports, and domestic consumption and prices by sector (e.g., residential, electric utility) for crude oil, petroleum products, natural gas, coal, and electricity. *Available:* Standard & Poor's DRI, Data Products Division. *Type:* Database.

DRI European Energy Forecast

Standard & Poor's DRI
Data Products Division
24 Hartwell Ave.   Ph: (781)863-5100
Lexington, MA 02421
E-mail: client_services@dri.mcgraw-hill.com
URL: http://www.dri.mcgraw-hill.com

Desc: Contains country-specific forecasts of energy supply, demand, and prices for Austria, Belgium, Denmark, Finland, France, Germany, Greece, Ireland, Italy, the Netherlands, Norway, Spain, Sweden, Switzerland, the United Kingdom, and total Europe. Subject coverage includes production, net imports, change in stocks, and final consumption for each of these energy sources: crude oil, electricity and delivered hydro/geothermal and nuclear electricity; natural gas, refinery gas, blast furnace gas oven and works gas; gasoline, kerosene, gas/diesel oil, LPG, Naptha, residual fuel oil, jet fuel, other petroleum products; hard coal, coke, and lignite. *Type:* Database.

DRI Natural Gas Forecast

Standard & Poor's DRI
Data Products Division
24 Hartwell Ave.   Ph: (781)863-5100
Lexington, MA 02421
E-mail: client_services@dri.mcgraw-hill.com
URL: http://www.dri.mcgraw-hill.com

Contact: Client Resource Center, (781)860-6527, fax: (781)860-6416.

Desc: Contains more than 600 annual forecasts of U.S. oil and natural gas supply, prices, and production costs. *Available:* Standard & Poor's DRI, Data Products Division. *Type:* Database.

DRI U.S. Long-Term Energy Forecast

Standard & Poor's DRI
Data Products Division
24 Hartwell Ave.   Ph: (781)863-5100
Lexington, MA 02421
E-mail: client_services@dri.mcgraw-hill.com
URL: http://www.dri.mcgraw-hill.com

Contact: Client Services, (617)860-6527, fax: (617)860-6416.

Desc: Contains approximately 3500 annual forecasts of U.S. energy supply, demand, and prices. *Available:* Standard & Poor's DRI, Data Products Division. *Type:* Database.

Electrical Marketing

Intertec Publishing Corp.
9800 Metcalf Ave.   Ph: (913)341-1300
Overland Park, KS 66212   Free: 800-400-5945
                                        Fax: (913)967-1328
Contact: Ms. Dale Funk, Editor; Timothy Kasen, Editor.

Desc: Focuses on market developments, mergers and acquisitions, price trends, legislation, law suits, and executive changes affecting the electrical industry. Recurring features include news of members, news of research, an electrical price index, and a calendar of events. *Type:* Newsletter.

Energy

The WEFA Group
1110 Vermont Ave., NW   Ph: (202)775-0610
Washington, DC 20005
URL: http://www.fdic.gov

Desc: Contains 15,000 weekly, monthly, quarterly, and annual time series of detailed supply and demand statistics for the major forms of energy, including petroleum, oil, natural gas, coal and electricity. Coverage includes supply and demand, including weekly rig count and gasoline prices by state; reserves, stocks, production, consumption,

trade, and prices of petroleum and petroleum products; wells by depth, and estimated costs and completions by type of well for drilling; annual and monthly supply, demand, trade, and prices of natural gas; coal production, consumption, stocks, trade, and average mine price by state or coal producing district; electricity sales, revenues, prices, and industrial electric power use; state data on energy consumption by major economic sector and by principal energy type. *Available:* The WEFA Group; STN International. *Type:* Database.

Energy Engineering—Directory of Software for Energy Managers and Engineers Issue

Fairmont Press, Inc.
700 Indian Trail   Ph: (770)925-9388
Lilburn, GA 30047   Fax: (770)381-9865
Contact: Dr. Anna F. Williams, Editor.

Desc: Directory of 60 manufacturers of computer software for energy engineering including sizing for energy systems, office management and accounting, costing, and project management. *Type:* Directory.

Energy Information Administration New Releases

National Energy Information Center
EI-30   Ph: (202)586-8800
1000 Independence Ave. SW,   Fax: (202)586-0727
    Rm. 1F-048
Washington, DC 20585
URL: http://www.eia.doe.gov/neic/newrel.html.

Contact: Ingrid Springer, Editor, ispringe@eia.doe.gov; Jonathan Cogan, Energy Information Administrator.

Desc: Lists reports and publications regarding energy, electricity, coal, petroleum, natural gas, and nuclear energy. Recurring features include news of research and notices of publications available. *Type:* Newsletter.

Energy Research in Progress

U.S. Department of Energy
Office of Scientific and Technical Information (OSTI)
PO Box 62   Ph: (423)574-1000
Oak Ridge, TN 37831
E-mail: ostiwebmaster@apollo.osti.gov
URL: http://www.osti.gov

Desc: Contains approximately 40,000 summaries of energy-related research projects conducted or sponsored by the U.S. Department of Energy. *Type:* Database.

Energyline

Congressional Information Service, Inc. (CIS)
4520 East-West Hwy., Suite   Ph: (301)654-1550
    800
Bethesda, MD 20814-3389
E-mail: 12425 (DIALMAIL)
URL: http://www.cispubs.com

Desc: Contains more than 80,000 citations (with abstracts, from 1971) to literature relating to energy issues and problems. Aspects of the area that are covered include economics; government policy and planning; international political and economic issues; research and development; petroleum, natural gas, and coal resources and reserves; solar energy; unconventional energy sources; electric, nuclear, and thermo-nuclear power; fuel production, transport, and storage; consumption; conservation; and environmental impact. *Available:* The Dialog Corporation, DIALOG; The Dialog Corporation, DIALOG; Questel • Orbit; Questel • Orbit; FIZ Technik (Fachinformationszentrum Technik e.V.). *Type:* Database.

EPRI

3412 Hillview Ave.   Ph: (650)855-2000
Palo Alto, CA 94304-1395   Fax: (650)855-2900
URL: http://www.epri.com

Contact: Kurt Yeager, Pres.

Desc: All sectors of the electric utility industry. Purpose is to conduct a broad economically and environmentally acceptable program of research and development in technologies for electric power production, transmission, distribution, and utilization. Primary areas of research are: advanced power systems; coal combustion systems; electrical systems; energy analysis and environment; energy management and utilization; nuclear power. *Type:* Association.

Hearth Products Association

1601 N. Kent St., Ste. 1001   Ph: (703)522-0086
Arlington, VA 22209   Fax: (703)522-0548
E-mail: hpamail@hearthassoc.org
URL: http://www.hearthassoc.org
Contact: Carter E. Keithley, Pres./CEO.
Desc: Trade association representing manufacturers, dealers, and suppliers. Promotes the use of alternative fuels as sources of energy; encourages safety in the use of alternative fuels; fosters the highest level of design, quality, and performance in appliances using alternative fuels. Activities include legislative monitoring. *Type:* Association.

Hydro Review Worldwide—Industry Directory Issue

HCI Publications
410 Archibald St.   Ph: (816)931-1311
Kansas City, MO 64111   Fax: (816)931-2015
E-mail: hci@aol.com
Contact: Carl Vansant, Editor-in-Chief.
Desc: List of over 250 manufacturers and suppliers of products and services to the hydroelectric industry worldwide; related trade organizations. *Type:* Directory.

Industrial Bioprocessing Alert

Technical Insights
John Wiley and Sons, Inc.
32 N. Dean St.   Ph: (201)568-4744
Englewood, NJ 07631
E-mail: TIInf@wiley.com
URL: http://www.wiley.comm/technicalinsights
Contact: Kristine Swain, Director of Operations, ibainfo@insights.com.
Desc: Contains the complete text of Industrial Bioprocessing Alert, a monthly newsletter on the commercial and technical aspects of biotechnology, applied to the production of energy and chemicals from renewable organic materials. *Available:* CompuServe Information Service. *Type:* Database.

Inside Energy/With Federal Lands

McGraw-Hill, Inc.
1221 Avenue of the Americas   Ph: (212)512-6410
New York, NY 10020
Desc: Contains the complete text of Inside Energy/With Federal Lands, a newsletter on U.S. federal energy policy, legislation, and regulations. *Available:* LEXIS-NEXIS, NEXIS; The Dialog Corporation, DIALOG; Dow Jones Interactive Publishing. *Type:* Database.

Inside N.R.C.

McGraw-Hill, Inc.
1221 Avenue of the Americas   Ph: (212)512-6410
New York, NY 10020
Desc: Contains the complete text of the Inside N.R.C. newsletter, covering activities of the U.S. Nuclear Regulatory Commission and issues affecting the nuclear power industry. *Available:* LEXIS-NEXIS, NEXIS; The Dialog Corporation, DIALOG; Dow Jones Interactive Publishing. *Type:* Database.

Institute of Gas Technology

1700 S. Mount Prospect Rd.   Ph: (847)768-0500
Des Plaines, IL 60018-1804   Fax: (847)768-0501
URL: http://www.igt.org
Contact: Bernard S. Lee, Pres.
Desc: Educational and research facility sponsored by companies engaged in the production, processing, transmission, and distribution of natural gas and related fuels; engineering firms; large energy consumers. Conducts contract research for government and industry in the field of nonnuclear energy technology. *Type:* Association.

International Association for Energy Economics

28790 Chagrin Blvd., Ste. 350   Ph: (216)464-5365
Cleveland, OH 44122-4630   Fax: (216)464-2737
E-mail: iaee@iaee.org
URL: http://www.iaee.org
Contact: David Williams, Exec.Dir.
Desc: Individuals employed by consulting and research organizations, government, universities, and the energy industries who are professionally interested in energy economics. Provides a forum for professional communication and exchange of experience among energy economists from different countries. *Type:* Association.

International Institute for Energy Conservation

750 1st St. NE, Ste. 940   Ph: (202)842-3388
Washington, DC 20002   Fax: (202)842-1565
E-mail: iiec@iiec.org
URL: http://www.iiec.org
Contact: Kelly Gordon, Program Dir.
Desc: Works to encourage, implement, and improve energy efficiency in developing countries. Facilitates the acquisition of energy conserving technologies and policies. Disseminates information; conducts training and education programs. *Type:* Association.

Interstate Natural Gas Association of America

10 G St., NE, Ste. 700   Ph: (202)216-5900
Washington, DC 20002   Fax: (202)216-0877
URL: http://www.ingaa.org
Contact: Jerald V. Halvorsen, Pres.
Desc: Transporters of natural gas. *Type:* Association.

LEXIS® Energy Library

LEXIS-NEXIS
9443 Springboro Pike   Ph: (937)865-6800
PO Box 933
Dayton, OH 45401-0933
URL: http://www.lex-nexis.com
Desc: Contains federal and state case law, federal and state statutes, the Federal Register, federal and state energy- and utility-related materials, including bill tracking, federal agency material from the Department of the Interior, materials from the Federal Energy Regulatory Commission (FERC0), Federal Power Commission (FPC), and the Nuclear Regulatory Commission (NRC), several states' Public Utilities Commission decisions, a number of publications from The Bureau of National Affairs (BNA), industry reports from Investext, and more than 40 leading energy and utility industry publications. *Available:* LEXIS-NEXIS, LEXIS. *Type:* Database.

LP/Gas—Industry Buying Guide Issue

Advanstar Communications
131 W. First St.   Free: 800-346-0085
Duluth, MN 55802
E-mail: fulfill@superfil.com
Contact: Zane Chastain, Editor.
Desc: List of about 1,000 liquid propane gas equipment manufacturers and suppliers; list of about 700 distributors of gas appliances and equipment. *Type:* Directory.

Moody's Public Utility Manual

Financial Information Services (FIS)
60 Madison Ave., 6th Fl.   Ph: (212)413-7601
New York, NY 10010   Free: 800-342-5647
                              Fax: (212)413-7777
E-mail: fis@fisonline.com
URL: http://www.fisonline.com.
Contact: John Ieraci, Editor.
Desc: About 560 electric and gas utility companies, gas transmission companies, and telephone and water companies. *Type:* Directory.

Motion Systems Handbook

Penton Media Inc.
1100 Superior Ave.   Ph: (216)696-7000
Cleveland, OH 44114-2543   Fax: (216)931-9524
E-mail: corpcomm@penton.com
Contact: Larry Berardinis, Editor.
Desc: Over 1,000 manufacturers, distributors, and suppliers of pt/motion control equipment and components (bearings, controls, drives, motors, and accessories). *Type:* Directory.

National Directory of Propane Refilling Stations

National Propane Gas Association
1600 Eisenhower Ln., Ste. 100   Ph: (630)515-0600
Lisle, IL 60532   Fax: (630)515-8774
E-mail: npga@propanegas.com
URL: http://www.propaneqas.com/npga
Desc: Over 2,500 sources of propane fuel in the United States. *Type:* Directory.

National Energy Foundation

5225 Wiley Post Way, Ste. 170   Ph: (801)539-1406
Salt Lake City, UT 84116   Fax: (801)539-1451
E-mail: info@nef1.org
URL: http://www.nef1.org
Contact: Edward Dalton, Ed.D., Pres.
Desc: Works to stimulate interest and increase knowledge of the current energy situation through nationwide educational programs for teachers and students. Focuses on usage, conservation, economics, renewable energy resources, new sources of energy, projected changes in lifestyle (economic, scientific, social, and political), and creation of dialogue among corporate and educational communities. Creates and distributes economic instruction materials dealing with energy, water, mining, science, technology, conservation, the environment, and other natural resource topics. *Type:* Association.

National Propane Gas Association

1600 Eisenhower Ln., Ste. 100   Ph: (630)515-0600
Lisle, IL 60532   Free: 800-457-4772
                                 Fax: (630)515-8774
E-mail: npga@propanegas.com
URL: http://www.propanegas.com/npga
Contact: D. N. Myers, Exec.VP.
Desc: Producers and distributors of propane gas; manufacturers and distributors of equipment and utilization appliances. Objectives are to promote safety in all phases of storage, handling, and utilization of propane gas; formulate materials and programs to educate industry personnel, fire services, and the consumer. *Type:* Association.

Nuclear Energy Institute

1776 I St. NW, Ste. 400   Ph: (202)739-8000
Washington, DC 20006   Fax: (202)785-1898
E-mail: webmaster@nei.org
URL: http://www.nei.org
Contact: Joe Colvin, CEO & Pres.
Desc: Electric utilities, manufacturers, industrial firms, research and service organizations, educational institutions, labor groups, and governmental agencies engaged in development and utilization of nuclear energy, especially nuclear-produced electricity, and other energy matters. Maintains speakers' bureau; compiles statistics and public attitude data. *Type:* Association.

Nucleonics Week

McGraw-Hill, Inc.
1221 Avenue of the Americas   Ph: (212)512-6410
New York, NY 10020

Contact: Circulation Dept., (212)512-6410 or 2743, fax: (212)512-2723, eweil@mhenergy.com.

Desc: Contains the complete text of Nucleonics Week newsletter, covering worldwide technical, corporate, and regulatory developments for the nuclear power industry. One edition each month includes statistics for the previous month's electric power generation. *Available:* LEXIS-NEXIS, NEXIS; The Dialog Corporation, DIALOG; Dow Jones Interactive Publishing. *Type:* Database.

Nucleus

Union of Concerned Scientists
2 Brattle Sq.   Ph: (617)547-5552
PO Box 9105   Fax: (617)864-9405
Cambridge, MA 02238-9105
E-mail: ucs@ucsusa.org
URL: http://www.ucsusa.org
Contact: Janet S. Wager, Editor.

Desc: Covers energy policy, international security, and global resources, including global climate change, renewable energy, energy efficiency, transportation policy, nuclear nonproliferation, international security, and nuclear reactor safety. Recurring features include information on UCS's work, and a list of publications and films available through UCS. *Type:* Newsletter.

Oil & Gas Journal Energy Database

PennWell Publishing Co.
1421 S. Sheridan   Ph: (918)832-9346
Tulsa, OK 74112
E-mail: sandram@pennwell.com
Contact: Sandra Meyer, Database Mgr., (918)832-9346, fax: (918)831-9497, sandram@pennwell.com.

Desc: Contains more than 100,000 weekly, monthly, quarterly, and annual time series on the oil and natural gas industry. Covers drilling, exploration, production, reserves, imports, exports, consumption, demand, and prices. *Available:* GE Information Services (GEIS); Haver Analytics, HaverSelect. *Type:* Database.

Oxygenated Fuels Association

1300 17th St. N. Ste. 1850   Ph: (703)841-7100
Arlington, VA 22209-3801   Fax: (703)841-7720
URL: http://www.ofa.net
Contact: Carrie Wigglesworth, Exec.Dir.

Desc: International manufacturers of motor fuel oxygenates such as methanol and methyl-tertiary-butyl-ether (MTBE). Oxygenates are a major component of reformulated gasoline (RFG). Purposes are to: address the legislative, environmental, and regulatory issues related to oxygenated fuel use; develop safe procedures for blending, handling, and distributing oxygenated fuels; conduct and sponsor research; make available to the public technical and scientific information about the use of fuel blends; provide a forum for the exchange of technical information about the use of these fuels in turbine and internal combustion engines. *Type:* Association.

Pacific Russian Oil and Gas Report

Russian Far East Advisory Group LLC
PO Box 22126   Ph: (206)477-2668
Seattle, WA 98122   Fax: (206)628-0979
E-mail: update@russianfareast.com
URL: http://www.russianfareast.com.
Contact: Elisa Miller, Ph.D., Editor.

Desc: Contains commercial intelligence and analysis on business in Russia. Recurring features include interviews, news of research, and a calendar of events. *Type:* Newsletter.

Plunkett's Energy Industry Almanac

Plunkett Research, Ltd.
PO Drawer 541737   Ph: (713)932-0000
Houston, TX 77254-1737   Fax: (713)932-7080
E-mail: sales@plunkettresearch.com
URL: http://www.plunkettresearch.com.
Contact: Jack W. Plunkett, Publisher.

Desc: 500 companies in the energy, petroleum energy services, and utilities field. Principal content of publication is statistics, trends, finance, and individuals of the energy and utilities industries. *Type:* Directory.

Power—Buyers' Guide Issue

McGraw-Hill, Inc.
11 W. 19th St., 2nd Fl.   Ph: (212)337-4062
New York, NY 10011   Fax: (212)627-3811
Contact: Marie Leone, Editor.

Desc: List of about 1,000 manufacturers and suppliers of equipment, products, and services for the power generation and energy processing, supply, and control industries. *Type:* Directory.

Power Generation Markets Quarterly

Energy and Business Newsletters
McGraw-Hill Companies   Ph: (212)904-6410
2 Penn Plaza, 5th Fl.   Free: 800-223-6180
New York, NY 10121   Fax: (212)904-2723
E-mail: mdiaz@mnenergy.com.
URL: http://www.mhenergy.com.
Contact: Ron Dionne, Editor, (212)904-3486, fax: (212)904-2723, rdionne@mnenergy.com; Gail Roberts, Assoc. Editor, (212)904-2306, fax: (212)904-2723.

Desc: Provides updates on project development activities, solicitations, power needs, regulation, and utility avoided-cost rates in the U.S. and Canada. *Type:* Newsletter.

Renewable Fuels Association

1 Massachusetts Ave. NW, Ste.   Ph: (202)289-3835
820   Free: 800-542-3835
Washington, DC 20001   Fax: (202)289-7519
E-mail: etohrfa@erols.com
URL: http://www.ethanolrfa.org
Contact: Eric Vaughn, Pres.

Desc: Engineering and financial firms, marketers, producers, and state governments working toward developments in biomass fuel technology, mainly alcohol fuels. Represents the renewable fuels industry before the government and throughout the U.S. Is active in areas encompassing every facet of biomass fuel production from agricultural crops to finished product. *Type:* Association.

Report on Gas Customer Satisfaction

Hart Publications
1201 Seven Locks Rd., Ste. 200   Ph: (301)340-1520
Potomac, MD 20854   Free: 800-897-4278
    Fax: (301)309-9473
E-mail: hartinfo@phillips.com
URL: http://www.hartpub.com
Contact: Stephen Munro, Editor.

Desc: Focuses on customer satisfaction in the natural gas industry. Covers topics such as top performers, customer satisfaction initiatives, marketing, regulation, pipelines, and other related issues. *Type:* Newsletter.

Royale Energy Report

Royale Energy, Inc.
7676 Hazard Center Dr., Ste.   Ph: (619)297-8505
1500   Fax: (619)297-0438
San Diego, CA 92108
URL: http://www.royl.com.
Contact: Jack Connolly, Editor.

Desc: Contains news of domestic and international events that affect the oil and gas industry. *Type:* Newsletter.

Rural Arkansas

Arkansas Electric Cooperative, Inc.
8000 Scott Hamilton Dr.   Ph: (501)570-2200
PO Box 510   Fax: (501)570-2205
Little Rock, AR 72203-0510
Contact: Ouida H. Cox, Editor and Publisher.

Desc: Magazine for cooperative members and consumers. *Type:* Periodical.

Solar Energy Industries Association

122 C St. NW, 4th Fl.   Ph: (202)383-2600
Washington, DC 20001   Fax: (202)383-2670
URL: http://www.seia.org
Contact: Scott Sklar, Exec.Dir.

Desc: Manufacturers, installers, distributors, contractors, and engineers of solar energy systems and components. Purpose is to accelerate and foster commercialization of solar energy conversion for economic purposes. Maintains Solar Energy Research and Education Foundation. *Type:* Association.

Texas Co-op Power

Texas Electric Cooperatives, Inc.
PO Box 9589   Ph: (512)454-0311
Austin, TX 78766-9589   Fax: (512)467-9442
Contact: Martin Bevins, Advertising Mgr., (512)459-0311, bevins@texas-ec.org; Karen Nejtek, Circulation Mgr., knejtek@texas-ec.org.

Desc: Local consumer magazine. *Type:* Periodical.

TULSA

Petroleum Abstracts PA
600 S. College   Ph: (918)631-2297
Tulsa, OK 74104-3189
E-mail: QUESTION@TUred.pa.utulsa.edu
URL: http://www.pa.utulsa.edu
Contact: Customer Service, (918)631-2297, QUESTION@ TURED.PA.UTULSA.EDU.

Desc: Contains more than 230,000 citations, most with abstracts, to worldwide literature and patents on the exploration, development, and production of petroleum resources, particularly oil and natural gas. Covers the areas of geology; geophysics; geochemistry; well drilling, completion, and servicing; well logging; transport and storage; environmental impact; alternate fuels and energy sources; supplemental technology; and mineral commodities. *Available:* Questel • Orbit; The Dialog Corporation, DIALOG; STN International. *Type:* Database.

U.S. Department of Energy - Office of Energy Research Home Page

U.S. Department of Energy - Office of Energy Research
Washington, DC 20585   Ph: (202)586-5430
    Fax: (202)586-4120
E-mail: webmaster@www.er.doe.gov
URL: http://www.er.doe.gov
Desc: The U.S. Department of Energy, Office of Energy Research WWW page provides information by and about the DOE and OER. *Type:* Database.

U.S. Energy Association

1620 Eye St. NW, Ste. 1000   Ph: (202)331-0415
Washington, DC 20006   Fax: (202)331-0418
Contact: Barry K. Worthington, Exec.Dir.

Desc: One of 100 national committees representing the energy interests of industry, government, professional and technical societies, educational institutions, and legal and other professional service organizations. Supports World Energy Council objectives, which are: to provide for broad consideration of energy resources, policy, management, technology, use, and conservation as they relate to the total energy picture of the U.S. *Type:* Association.

WESTLAW® Energy
West Group
620 Opperman Dr.   Ph: (651)687-7000
St. Paul, MN 55164-0526
URL: http://www.westgroup.com
Desc: Contains the complete text of U.S. federal and state court decisions, statutes and regulations, Federal administrative law publications, specialized files and texts and periodicals dealing with energy and utilities, including the development, distribution, allocation, ownership, production, and conservation of fuels and alternative energies. *Available:* West Group, WESTLAW. *Type:* Database.

Engineering

AACE International—Directory of Members
AACE International
209 Prairie Ave. Ste. 100   Ph: (304)296-8444
Morgantown, WV 26501   Free: 800-858-COST
                              Fax: (304)291-5728
E-mail: info@aacei.org
URL: http://www.aacei.org; http://www.aacei.com.
Contact: Kathy Deweese, Editor.
Desc: 6,000 cost engineers, estimators, and cost management professionals worldwide. *Type:* Directory.

Access Newsletter
National Center for Supercomputing Applications (NCSA)
University of Illinois
152 Computing Applications   Ph: (217)244-0072
  Bldg.   Fax: (217)244-1987
605 E. Springfield Ave.
Champaign, IL 61820
URL: http://www.ncsa.uiuc.edu.
Contact: Melissa LaBorg-Johnson, Managing Editor.
Desc: Informs users, potential users, and sponsoring agencies of the Center's research and technology, as well as activities, services, and products. Available online only. *Type:* Newsletter.

Accreditation Board for Engineering and Technology
111 Market Pl., Ste. 1050   Ph: (410)347-7700
Baltimore, MD 21202-4012   Fax: (410)625-2238
E-mail: eandis@abet.org
URL: http://www.abet.org
Contact: George D. Peterson, Exec.Dir.
Desc: Professional societies representing over one million engineers are participating bodies (22); affiliate bodies (5); board of directors has 44 representatives. Is responsible for the quality control of engineering education. Accredits college curricula in engineering, engineering technology, and engineering-related areas. *Type:* Association.

Alpha Pi Mu
Dr. Robert D. Dryden
PO Box 773   Ph: (503)297-3604
Portland, OR 97207-0773   Fax: (503)297-3694
E-mail: jdryden@eas.pdx.edu
Contact: Dr. Robert D. Dryden, Exec.Dir.
Desc: Honor society - men and women, industrial engineering. *Type:* Association.

American Association of Engineering Societies
1111 19th St. NW, Ste. 403   Ph: (202)296-2237
Washington, DC 20036   Fax: (202)296-1151
E-mail: pleon@aaes.org
URL: http://www.aaes.org
Contact: Tom Price, Exec.Dir.
Desc: Coordinates the efforts of the member societies in the provision of reliable and objective information to the

general public concerning issues which affect the engineering profession and the field of engineering as a whole; to collect, analyze, document, and disseminate data which will inform the general public of the relationship between engineering and the national welfare; to provide a forum for the engineering societies to exchange and discuss their views on matters of common interest; and to represent the U.S. engineering community aborad through representation in WFEO and UPADI. *Type:* Association.

American Consulting Engineers Council
1015 15th St. NW   Ph: (202)347-7474
Suite 802   Fax: (202)898-0068
Washington, DC 20005
Contact: Howard M. Messner, Exec.VP.
Desc: Consulting engineering firms engaged in private practice. Conducts programs concerned with public relations, business practices, governmental affairs, international practice, and professional liability. Compiles statistics on office practices, insurance, employment, insurance clients served, and services provided. *Type:* Association.

American Consulting Engineers Council— Membership Directory
American Consulting Engineers Council (ACEC)
35 Technology Pky., No. 150
Norcross, GA 30092-2901
Contact: Teresa Peterson, Editor.
Desc: Approximately 5,200 consulting engineering firms with a total of over 180,000 employees; affiliated state consulting engineer associations and related engineering organizations. *Type:* Directory.

American Indian Science and Engineering Society
5661 Airport Blvd.   Ph: (303)939-0023
Boulder, CO 80301-2339   Fax: (303)939-8150
E-mail: info@aises.org
URL: http://www.aises.org
Contact: Norbert S. Hill, Jr., Exec.Dir.
Desc: American Indian and non-Indian students and professionals in science, technology, and engineering fields; corporations representing energy, mining, aerospace, electronic, and computer fields. Seeks to motivate and encourage students to pursue undergraduate and graduate studies in science, engineering, and technology. Sponsors science fairs in grade schools, teacher training workshops, summer math/science sessions for 8th-12th graders, professional chapters, and student chapters in colleges. *Type:* Association.

American Society of Agricultural Engineers
2950 Niles Rd.   Ph: (616)429-0300
St. Joseph, MI 49085-9659   Fax: (616)429-3852
E-mail: hq@asae.org
URL: http://www.asae.org
Contact: Melissa Moore, Exec.VP.
Desc: Professional and technical organization of individuals interested in engineering and technology for agriculture. Develops engineering standards used in agriculture. Sponsors technical meetings and continuing education programs. *Type:* Association.

American Society of Civil Engineers
1801 Alexander Bell Dr.   Ph: (703)295-6000
Reston, VA 20191-4400   Free: 800-548-2723
                               Fax: (703)295-6222
E-mail: webmaster@asce.org
URL: http://www.asce.org
Contact: James E. Davis, Exec.Dir.
Desc: 4Professional society of civil engineers. Enhances the welfare of humanity by advancing the science and profession of engineering. Offers continuing education courses and technical specialty conferences. *Type:* Association.

American Society for Engineering Education
1818 N St., NW, Ste.600   Ph: (202)331-3500
Washington, DC 20036   Fax: (202)265-8504
Contact: Frank Huband, Exec.Dir.
Desc: Professional educational society of college and university engineering deans, administrators, and teachers; practicing engineers; corporate executives; persons interested in engineering education; engineering colleges; technical colleges and institutes; junior colleges; government agencies; industrial organizations. Seeks to advance education and research in engineering, science, and related fields. Administers annual College-Industry Education Conference and Engineering Research Forum; sponsors summer schools, workshops, and effective teaching institutes. *Type:* Association.

American Society for Engineering Education
American Society for Engineering Education
1818 N St. NW, Ste. 600   Ph: (202)331-3500
Washington, DC 20036-2479   Fax: (202)265-8504
URL: http://www.asee.org/
Contact: David Hesprich, webmaster@asee.org.
Desc: Site contains information on ASEE, its publications and projects, and a "Quick-Select Index" which conveniently lists the page's links. This is followed by a more thorough outline of these links. *Type:* Database.

American Society of Heating, Refrigerating and Air-Conditioning Engineers
1791 Tullie Cir. NE   Ph: (404)636-8400
Atlanta, GA 30329   Free: 800-5-ASHRAE
                               Fax: (404)321-5478
E-mail: ashrae@ashrae.org
URL: http://www.ashrae.org
Contact: Frank M. Coda, Exec.V.P.
Desc: Technical society of heating, ventilating, refrigeration, and air-conditioning engineers. Sponsors numerous research programs in cooperation with universities, research laboratories, and government agencies on subjects such as human and animal environmental studies, effects of air-conditioning, quality of inside air, heat transfer, flow, and cooling processes. Research and general technical programs are conducted through 90 technical committees organized in 10 sections. *Type:* Association.

American Society of Mechanical Engineers
3 Park Ave., Lbby. 2   Ph: (212)705-7722
New York, NY 10016-5902   Free: 800-THE-
                                     ASME
                               Fax: (212)705-7674
E-mail: infocentral@asme.org
URL: http://www.asme.org
Contact: Dr. David Belden, Exec.Dir.
Desc: Technical society of mechanical engineers and students. Conducts research; develops boiler, pressure vessel, and power test codes. *Type:* Association.

American Society of Naval Engineers— Membership Directory
American Society of Naval Engineers
1452 Duke St.   Ph: (703)836-6727
Alexandria, VA 22314   Fax: (703)836-7419
E-mail: asnehq.asne@mcimail.com
URL: http://www.jhuapl.edu/ASNE
Contact: Robert L. Steele, Editor.
Desc: Naval Engineers Journal. 7,000 civilian and U.S. Navy engineers engaged in or interested in design, construction, operation, and maintenance of naval and maritime craft, navigation, motive power, etc., as related to Navy needs. *Type:* Directory.

American Society of Plumbing Engineers

3617 Thousand Oaks Blvd., No. 210
Westlake Village, CA 91362-3649
Ph: (805)495-7120
Fax: (805)495-4861
E-mail: aspehq@aol.com
URL: http://www.aspe.org
Contact: Stanley M. Wolfson, Exec.Dir.
Desc: Consulting engineers involved in the design and specification of plumbing systems; manufacturers, governmental officials, contractors, and publishers related to the industry may become members on a limited basis. Seeks to resolve professional problems in plumbing engineering; advocates greater cooperation among members and plumbing officials, contractors, laborers, and the public. Code committees examine regulatory codes pertaining to the industry and submit proposed revisions to code writing authorities to simplify, standardize, and modernize all codes. *Type:* Association.

American Solar Energy Society Fact File

American Solar Energy Society
2400 Central Ave., G-1
Boulder, CO 80301
Ph: (303)443-3130
Fax: (303)443-3212
E-mail: ases@ases.org
URL: http://www.ases.org/solar/factbase.htm
Contact: Todd Stewart, Writer and Researcher.
Desc: This site is a very good introduction to solar energy technology and the use of solar power as an alternate energy source. You'll find historical information and considerable material on statistics and market assessments, business briefs, environmental issues, government and regulatory involvement, and the economic impact of renewable energy sources. *Type:* Database.

APICS -- The Educational Society for Resource Management

5301 Shawnee Rd.
Alexandria, VA 22312
Ph: (703)354-8851
Free: 800-444-2742
Fax: (703)354-8106
URL: http://www.apics.org
Contact: Jeffry W. Raynes, CAE, Exec.Dir. and COO.
Desc: Offers programs and materials on resource management concepts and techniques. Develops and provides education on materials for all areas of manufacturing and service industries. Recognizes persons certified in production and inventory management (CPIM) and integrated resource management (CIRM). *Type:* Association.

Application Development Strategies

Cutter Information Corporation
37 Broadway, Ste. 1
Arlington, MA 02174-5552
Ph: (781)648-8702
Free: 800-325-3717
Fax: (781)648-1950
E-mail: klovering@cutter.com
Contact: Paul Harmon, Editor.
Desc: Contains hands-on tool reviews, industry news and trends, product developments, and application case studies. Recurring features include a calendar of events and notices of publications available. *Type:* Newsletter.

ASCE News

American Society of Civil Engineers
1801 Alexander Bell Dr.
Reston, VA 20191-4400
Ph: (703)295-6000
Free: 800-548-2723
Fax: (703)295-6222
E-mail: asce@asce.org
URL: http://www.asce.org.
Contact: Charles F. Hemming, Editor, chemming@asce.org.
Desc: Newspaper reporting on the activities of the ASCE and news of the civil engineering profession in general. *Type:* Periodical.

ASFE: Professional Firms Practicing in the Geosciences—Membership Directory

ASFE: Professional Firms Practicing in the Geosciences
8811 Colesville Rd., Ste. G106
Silver Spring, MD 20910
Ph: (301)565-2733
Fax: (301)589-2017
E-mail: info@asfe.org
URL: http://www.asfe.org.
Contact: John P. Bachner, Editor.
Desc: About 300 firms offering consulting services in the geosciences. *Type:* Directory.

ASME News

American Society of Mechanical Engineers (ASME)
3 Park Ave.
New York, NY 10016-5990
Ph: (212)591-7722
Free: 800-843-2763
Fax: (212)591-7674
E-mail: infocentral@asme.org; smithem@asme.org.
Contact: John Falcioni, Editor-in-Chief.
Desc: Engineering tabloid. *Type:* Periodical.

Association for Facilities Engineering

8180 Corporate Park Dr., Ste. 305
Cincinnati, OH 45242
Ph: (513)489-2473
Free: 888-222-0155
Fax: (513)247-7422
E-mail: mail@afe.org
URL: http://www.afe.org
Contact: Bruce Medaris, Managing Dir.
Desc: Professional society of plant engineers and facilities managers engaged in the management, engineering, maintenance, and operation of industrial, institutional, and commercial facilities. *Type:* Association.

The Bent of Tau Beta Pi

Tau Beta Pi Association
PO Box 2697
Knoxville, TN 37901-2697
Ph: (423)546-4578
Fax: (423)546-4579
E-mail: tbp@tbp.org; bent@tbp.org.
Contact: J.D. Froula, Editor; R.E. Hawks, Advertising Mgr.
Desc: National engineering honor society magazine. *Type:* Periodical.

Billet Forming

Engineering Research Center for Net Shape Manufacturing, Ohio State University
339 Baker Systems/1971 Neil Ave.
Columbus, OH 43210
Ph: (614)292-5063
Fax: (614)292-7219
URL: http://nsmwww.eng.ohio-state.edu/.
Contact: Sabine Toennesmann, Editor; Victor Vazquez, Editor.
Desc: Discusses recent events and research into net shape manufacturing at the ERC. Includes announcements of upcoming metal forming conferences and meetings. *Type:* Newsletter.

Chi Epsilon

Dr. Robert L. Henry
University Texas at Arlington
Box 19316
Arlington, TX 76019-0316
Ph: (817)272-2752
Fax: (817)272-2826
E-mail: rhenry@utarlg.uta.edu
Contact: Dr. Robert L. Henry, Natl.Sec.-Treas.
Desc: National honor society - civil engineering. *Type:* Association.

Chi Epsilon, National Civil Engineering Honor Society

3100 Premier Dr., No. 200
Irving, TX 75063
Ph: (817)272-2752
Fax: (817)272-2826
E-mail: rhenry@utarlg.uta.edu
Contact: Robert L. Henry, Sec.-Treas.
Desc: Honor society. *Type:* Association.

Civil Engineering-ASCE

American Society of Civil Engineers
1801 Alexander Bell Dr.
Reston, VA 20191-4400
Ph: (703)295-6000
Free: 800-548-2723
Fax: (703)295-6222
E-mail: asce@asce.org; cemag@ny.asce.org.
URL: http://www.pubs.asce.
Contact: Virginia Fairweather, Editor-in-Chief; William N. Jensen, Advertising Mgr.
Desc: Professional magazine. *Type:* Periodical.

Computer-Aided Engineering—Reference Issue

Penton Media Inc.
1100 Superior Ave.
Cleveland, OH 44114-2543
Ph: (216)696-7000
Fax: (216)931-9524
E-mail: corpcomm@penton.com; caenetmaster@penton.com.
URL: http://www.penton.com/cae.
Contact: Robert Mills, Editor.
Desc: List of more than 900 suppliers, consulting firms, and organizations that provide products and services for computer aided design and manufacturing. *Type:* Directory.

Computer Design

PennWell Publishing Co.
98 Spit Brook Rd.
Nashua, NH 03062-5737
Ph: (603)891-0123
Fax: (603)891-0574
Contact: John Miklosz, Editor-in-Chief; Dave Allen, Publisher; Tim Tobeck, Assoc. Publisher.
Desc: Printed in two editions: magazine covers microprocessor-based systems design; news edition covers the systems time-to-market team. *Type:* Periodical.

Design News

Cahners Publishing Company
275 Washington St.
Newton, MA 02458
Ph: (617)558-2119
Fax: (617)558-4700
E-mail: dn@chners.com.
Contact: Larry Maloney, Publisher.
Desc: Magazine covering design engineering. *Alt. Contact:* fax: (617)558-4402. *Type:* Periodical.

Designfax

Adams Business Media
29100 Aurora Rd., Ste. 200
Solon, OH 44139-1855
Ph: (440)248-1125
Fax: (440)248-0187
Contact: Michael Malley, Editor; Fred C. Rodgers, Publisher.
Type: Periodical.

Die Casting

Engineering Research Center for Net Shape Manufacturing, Ohio State University
339 Baker Systems/1971 Neil Ave.
Columbus, OH 43210
Ph: (614)292-5063
Fax: (614)292-7219
URL: http://msmwww.eng.ohio-state.edu.
Contact: Sabine Tonnesmann, Editor; Ryan Zinn, Editor.
Desc: Covers net shape manufacturing of die casting project descriptions and plans. Also contains die casting reports. *Type:* Newsletter.

Die & Mold Design and Manufacturing
Engineering Research Center for Net Shape Manufacturing, Ohio State University
339 Baker Systems/1971 Neil   Ph: (614)292-5063
   Ave.   Fax: (614)292-7219
Columbus, OH 43210
URL: http://nsmwww.eng.ohio-state.edu.
Contact: Sabine Toennesmann, Editor; Peter Fallboehmer, Editor.
Desc: Covers net shape manufacturing design project descriptions and plans. Recurring features include news of research. *Type:* Newsletter.

Directory of Contract Staffing Firms—Engineering
C.E. Publications
PO Box 16490   Ph: (818)907-7351
Encino, CA 91416
Desc: 1,015 employment staffing agencies which offer worldwide temporary engineering and technical jobs openings. *Type:* Directory.

Directory of Engineering and Engineering Technology Co-Op Programs
Cooperative Education Division (CED)
American Society for Engineering Education (ASEE)
c/o Cooperative Education   Ph: (601)325-3823
   Program   Fax: (601)325-8733
Mississippi State University
Box 6046
Mississippi State, MS 39762
E-mail: ceddir@coop.msstate.edu.
Contact: Mike Mathews, Editor, mike@coop.msstate.edu; Beth Callahan, Editor, beth@coop.msstate.edu.
Desc: About 150 colleges and universities with cooperative education programs in engineering and engineering technology; coverage includes the United States and Canada. *Type:* Directory.

Directory of Minority and Women-Owned Architectural & Engineering Firms
American Consulting Engineers Council
1015 15th St. NW, Ste. 802   Ph: (202)347-7474
Washington, DC 20005   Fax: (202)898-0068
E-mail: acec@acec.org
Desc: More than 520 minority and women-owned architectural and engineering firms. *Type:* Directory.

ECN (Electronic Component News)
Cahners Business Information
201 King of Prussia Rd.   Ph: (610)964-4000
Radnor, PA 19087-5114   Fax: (610)964-2915
E-mail: marketaccess@cahners.com; ecninfo@chilton.net.
URL: http://www.ecnmag.com.
Contact: G. Frueh, Editor, (610)964-4972, gfrueh@chilton.net; Joseph Breck, Publisher, (610)964-4345, jbreck@chilton.net.
Desc: Magazine (tabloid) for electronics design engineers and engineering management. *Type:* Periodical.

EDN Magazine Edition
Cahners Publishing Co.
275 Washington St.   Ph: (617)964-3030
Newton, MA 02158   Fax: (617)558-4700
URL: http://www.ednmag.com.
Contact: Michael Markowitz, Editor, (617)558-4214, fax: (617)558-4470, m.markowitz@cahners.com; Tom Tobeck, Publisher, (617)558-4454, fax: (617)558-4470, ttobek@edn.cahners.com; Lauren Elsaesser, Promotion Coordinator.
Desc: Magazine for electronic design engineers and engineering managers. *Type:* Periodical.

EE Product News
Penton Media Inc.
1100 Superior Ave.   Ph: (216)696-7000
Cleveland, OH 44114-2543   Fax: (216)931-9524
E-mail: corpcomm@penton.com
Contact: Joseph V. DelGatto, Editor, (201)393-6072, jdelgatto@penton.com; Matthew Reseska, Publisher, (201)393-6067, mreseska@penton.com; David Maliniak, Editor-in-Chief, (201)393-6051, dmaliniak@pentin.com.
Desc: Trade magazine (tabloid). *Alt. Contact:* 611 Rte 46 West, Hasbrouck Heights, NJ 07604; telephone: (201)393-6051; fax: (201)393-6043. *Type:* Periodical.

Ei COMPENDEX*PLUS™
Engineering Information Inc. (Ei)
1 Castle Point Terrace   Ph: (201)216-8500
Hoboken, NJ 07030
E-mail: ei@ei.org
URL: http://www.ei.org
Desc: Contains more than three million citations, with abstracts, from more than 2600 journals, reports, books, and conference proceedings covering fields of engineering and technology. Sources include approximately 4500 journals, reports, books, and conference proceedings. *Available:* The Dialog Corporation, DataStar; The Dialog Corporation, DIALOG; CompuServe Information Service, Knowledge Index; Questel • Orbit; FIZ Technik (Fachinformationszentrum Technik e.V.); STN International; France Ministry of Defense, Delegation Generale pour l'Armement, Centre de Documentation de l'Armement (CEDOCAR); SilverPlatter Education, Inc.; Ovid Technologies, Inc. *Type:* Database.

Ei Page One™
Engineering Information Inc. (Ei)
1 Castle Point Terrace   Ph: (201)216-8500
Hoboken, NJ 07030
E-mail: ei@ei.org
URL: http://www.ei.org
Desc: Contains table of contents listings providing citations to more than 2 million journal articles and conference papers and proceedings annually in all fields of engineering. Sources include more than 5,400 leading journals and conference proceedings in engineering and technology issued by major engineering societies, commercial publishers, research and development organizations, university presses, and government agencies. *Available:* Research Libraries Group, Inc. (RLG), Research Libraries Information Network (RLIN); Research Libraries Group, Inc. (RLG), CitaDel™ Service. *Type:* Database.

Electrical Construction and Maintenance (EC&M)
Intertec Publishing Corp.
9800 Metcalf Ave.   Ph: (913)341-1300
Overland Park, KS 66212   Free: 800-400-5945
   Fax: (913)967-1328
Contact: John DeDad, Editor; Rich Hathaway, Group Publisher; Bob MacArthur, Publisher.
Desc: Magazine focusing on electrical engineering, construction, and maintenance. *Type:* Periodical.

Electronic Engineering Times
CMP Media Inc.
600 Community Dr.   Ph: (516)562-5000
Manhasset, NY 11030
URL: http://www.cmp.com
Desc: Contains the complete text of Electronic Engineering Times, a weekly newsletter for technical managers and engineers in the electronics industry. Covers analyses and information on current events and trends in technology and business, design practices, and professional development. *Available:* LEXIS-NEXIS, NEXIS; LEXIS-NEXIS, NEXIS. *Type:* Database.

Engineered Materials Abstracts®
Cambridge Scientific Abstracts (CSA)
7200 Wisconsin Ave., Ste. 601   Ph: (301)961-6700
Bethesda, MD 20814-4823
E-mail: sales@csa.com
URL: http://www.csa.com
Desc: Contains more than 145,000 citations, with abstracts, to worldwide literature on the development, processing, and production of ceramic, composite, and polymeric materials for engineering uses. Sources include more than 1600 technical journals, books, technical reports, dissertations, conference proceedings, and U.S., British, and European Patent Office patents. *Available:* The Dialog Corporation, DIALOG; Questel • Orbit; STN International; European Information Network Services (EINS). *Type:* Database.

Engineering Department Management and Administration Report
Institute of Management & Administration, Inc.
29 W. 35th St., 5th Fl.   Ph: (212)244-0360
New York, NY 10001-2299   Fax: (212)564-0465
E-mail: subserve@ioma.com
URL: http://www.ioma.com
Contact: Joe Mazel, Editor; Perry Patterson, Publisher.
Desc: Provides information on managing engineering departments. Includes budgeting, finances, and cost reduction. *Type:* Newsletter.

Engineering Foundation
United Engineering Center
3 Park Ave., 27th Fl.   Ph: (212)705-7835
New York, NY 10016-5902   Fax: (212)705-7441
E-mail: engfnd@aol.com
URL: http://www.enfnd.org
Contact: Charles Freiman, Dir.
Desc: Members of the board of this endowed foundation are appointed by the 5 founder societies: American Society of Civil Engineers; American Institute of Mining, Metallurgical and Petroleum Engineers; American Society of Mechanical Engineers; Institute of Electrical and Electronics Engineers; American Institute of Chemical Engineers. Supports research in engineering, conducts 25 leading-edge interdisciplinary conferences per year, and generally seeks to advance the profession of engineering and "the good of mankind." *Type:* Association.

ENR: Engineering News-Record
McGraw-Hill, Inc.
2 Penn Plaza   Ph: (212)904-2000
New York, NY 10121   Free: 800-223-6180
   Fax: (212)904-6068
URL: http://www.mcgraw-hill.com; http://www.enr.com.
Contact: Howard Stussman, Editor-in-Chief; Howard Mager, Publisher.
Desc: Magazine focusing on engineering and construction. *Type:* Periodical.

ESD Technology—Corporate/Sustaining Membership Issue
ANCAR Publishing
21700 Northwestern Hwy., Ste. 565
Southfield, MI 48075
Contact: Karen Shellie, Editor.
Desc: List of over 465 firms in engineering and related fields; most firms are located in the Detroit, Michigan area. *Type:* Directory.

IEEE Industry Applications Society

IEEE Corporate Office
3 Park Ave., 17th Fl.   Ph: (212)419-7900
New York, NY 10016-5997

Contact: Dan Senese, Gen.Mgr.

Desc: A society of the Institute of Electrical and Electronics Engineers . Studies the application of electrical systems, apparatus, devices, and control to the processes and equipment of industry and commerce. *Type:* Association.

IEEE Signal Processing Society

445 Hoes Ln.   Ph: (732)562-3888
PO Box 1331   Fax: (732)235-1627
Piscataway, NJ 08855-1331
E-mail: sp.info@ieee.org
URL: http://www.ieee.org/sp/index.html

Desc: Promotes the theory and application of "filtering, coding, transmitting, estmating, detecting, analyzing, recognizing, synthesizing, recording, and reproducing signals by digital or analog devices or techniques." *Type:* Association.

IEEE Spectrum

Institute of Electrical and Electronics Engineers, Inc.
305 E. 47th St.   Ph: (212)417-7900
New York, NY 10017   Free: 800-678-4333
    Fax: (212)419-7579
E-mail: society@comsoc.org
URL: http://www.spectrum.leee.org.

Contact: Anthony Durniak, Publisher, (212)419-7560, fax: (212)419-7579, a.durniak@ieee.org; William R. Saunders, Associate Pulisher, (212)705-7760, fax: (212)708-7579, w.saunders@ieee.org.

Desc: Magazine for the scientific and engineering professional. Provides information on developments and trends in engineering, physics, mathematics, chemistry, medicine/biology, and the nuclear sciences. *Type:* Periodical.

Illuminating Engineering Society of North America

120 Wall St., 17th Fl.   Ph: (212)248-5000
New York, NY 10005-4001   Fax: (212)248-5017
E-mail: bbay@iesna.org
URL: http://www.iesna.org

Contact: William Hanley, Exec.VP.

Desc: Technical society whose members include engineers, architects, designers, educators, students, contractors, distributors, utility personnel, scientists, and manufacturers dealing with the art, science, or practice of illumination. Provides speakers, referrals, and assistance with technical problems. Maintains liaison with schools and colleges. *Type:* Association.

Institute of Industrial Engineers

25 Technology Park/Atlanta   Ph: (770)449-0460
Norcross, GA 30092   Free: 800-494-0460
    Fax: (770)441-3295
URL: http://www.iienet.org

Contact: David Levy, Dir. of Operations.

Desc: Professional society of industrial engineers and student members. Concerned with the design, improvement, and installation of integrated systems of people, materials, equipment, and energy. Draws upon specialized knowledge and skill in the mathematical, physical, and social sciences together with the principles and methods of engineering analysis and design, to specify, predict, and evaluate the results obtained from such systems. *Type:* Association.

Instrumentation & Automation News

Instrumentation & Automation News
201 King of Prussia Rd.   Ph: (610)964-4419
Radnor, PA 19089   Fax: (610)964-2919
E-mail: chilton.net/ppool.
URL: http://www.chilton.net/ian.

Contact: Pat Pool, Editor.

Desc: Magazine (tabloid) for designers, specifiers, and users of control and instrumentation products and systems. *Type:* Periodical.

Instrumentation & Control Systems (I&CS)

Cahners Business Information
201 King of Prussia Rd.   Ph: (610)964-4000
Radnor, PA 19087-5114   Fax: (610)964-2915
E-mail: marketaccess@cahners.com
URL: http://www.chilton.net/ics.

Contact: Ron Kuhfeld, Editor, rkuhfeld@chilton.net; Richard E. Dute, Publisher; Matt DeJulio, Advertising Mgr.

Desc: Magazine serving control engineers and specialists. *Type:* Periodical.

International Council on Systems Engineering

2150 N 107th St. Ste.205   Ph: (206)361-6607
Seattle, WA 98133-9009   Free: 800-366-1164
    Fax: (206)367-8777
E-mail: incose@halcyon.com
URL: http://www.incose.org

Contact: Shirley Bishop, Mng. Dir.

Desc: Encourages use of the systems engineering approach to solving large-scale problems in industry, academia, and government. *Type:* Association.

International Federation of Professional and Technical Engineers

8630 Fenton St., No. 400   Ph: (301)565-9016
Silver Spring, MD 20910-3803   Fax: (301)565-0018
E-mail: 71363.77@compuserve.com

Contact: Paul Almeida, Pres.

Desc: AFL-CIO. *Type:* Association.

International Gas Turbine Institute, ASME

5775B Glenridge Dr., Ste. 370   Ph: (404)847-0072
Atlanta, GA 30328-5380   Fax: (404)847-0151
E-mail: igti@asme.org
URL: http://www.asme.org/igti

Contact: Ann E. McClure, CAE, Dir.

Desc: Educational and technical institute of the American Society of Mechanical Engineers. *Type:* Association.

International Society of Explosives Engineers

29100 Aurora Rd.   Ph: (216)349-4004
Cleveland, OH 44139-1800   Fax: (216)349-3788
E-mail: isee@isee.org
URL: http://www.isee.org

Contact: Jeffrey L. Dean, Exec.Dir. and Gen.Counsel.

Desc: Persons engaged in, or who have been engaged in, explosives engineering; interested persons and organizations, including those involved in the fields of construction, quarrying, mining, demolition, geophysical prospecting, vibration control, drilling and blasting, and the use and handling of explosives in general. Offers services in matters affecting the manufacture, transportation, storage, and use of explosives and related equipment. Acts as a repository for all information, both inside and outside of the U.S., on explosives engineering. *Type:* Association.

ISA

PO Box 3561   Ph: (919)549-8411
67 Alexander Dr.   Fax: (919)549-8288
Durham, NC 27702
E-mail: info@isa.org

URL: http://www.isa.org

Contact: James E. Pearson, Exec.Dir.

Desc: Fosters advancement in the theory, design, manufacture, and use of instruments, computers, and systems for measurement and control. *Type:* Association.

Junior Engineering Technical Society

1420 King St., Ste. 405   Ph: (703)548-5387
Alexandria, VA 22314-2794   Fax: (703)548-0769
E-mail: jets@nae.edu
URL: http://www.jets.org

Contact: Michael Peralta, Exec.Dir.

Desc: High school students interested in mathematics, science, technology, and engineering. *Type:* Association.

Korean Scientists and Engineers Association in America

1952 Gallows Rd., Ste. 300   Ph: (703)748-1221
Vienna, VA 22182   Fax: (703)748-1331
E-mail: sejong@ksea.org
URL: http://www.ksea.org

Contact: Ki Dong Lee, Pres.

Desc: Scientists and engineers holding single or advanced degrees. Goals are to: promote friendship and mutuality among Korean and American scientists and engineers; contribute to Korea's scientific, technological, industrial, and economic developments; strengthen the scientific, technological, and cultural bonds between Korea and the U.S. Sponsors symposium. *Type:* Association.

Machine Design

Penton Media Inc.
1100 Superior Ave.   Ph: (216)696-7000
Cleveland, OH 44114-2543   Fax: (216)931-9524
E-mail: corpcomm@penton.com; mdeditor@penton.com.
URL: http://www.machinedesign.com.

Contact: Ron Khol, Editor, rkhol@penton.com; Joe DiFranco, Publisher, jdifranco@penton.com.

Desc: Magazine on design engineering function. *Type:* Periodical.

Maintenance Management Newsletter

Springfield Resources
902 Oak Lane Ave.   Ph: (215)924-0270
Philadelphia, PA 19126-3336   Free: 800-242-5656
    Fax: (215)424-4284
URL: http://www.maintrainer.com.

Contact: Joel Levitt, Editor.

Desc: Provides information of interest to maintenance professionals and plant engineers. Recurring features include interviews, a calendar of events, book reviews, news of educational opportunities, and notices of publications available. *Type:* Newsletter.

Material Handling Engineering

John Davis
1100 Superior Ave.   Ph: (216)931-9414
Cleveland, OH 44114   Free: 800-366-1901
    Fax: (216)696-7658
Contact: Bernard Knill, Editor; John Davis, Publisher, jdavis@penton.com.

Desc: Magazine for managers of material handling systems in warehouses and manufacturing plants. *Type:* Periodical.

Materials Research Society

506 Keystone Dr.   Ph: (724)779-3003
Warrendale, PA 15086-7537   Fax: (724)779-8313
E-mail: info@mrs.org
URL: http://www.mrs.org/

Contact: John B. Ballance, Exec.Dir.

Desc: Professionals involved in materials science and engineering; students. Objectives are to foster interaction among researchers working on different classes of inorganic and organic materials and to promote interdisciplinary basic research on materials. *Type:* Association.

Mechanical Engineering

American Society of Mechanical Engineers (ASME)
3 Park Ave.   Ph: (212)591-7722
New York, NY 10016-5990   Free: 800-843-2763
    Fax: (212)591-7674
E-mail: infocentral@asme.org; memag@asme.org.
Contact: John Falconi, Editor.
Desc: Mechanical engineering. *Type:* Periodical.

Mechanical Engineering Abstracts

Cambridge Scientific Abstracts (CSA)
7200 Wisconsin Ave., Ste. 601   Ph: (301)961-6700
Bethesda, MD 20814-4823
E-mail: sales@csa.com
URL: http://www.csa.com
Desc: Contains more than 300,000 citations, with abstracts, to the literature in mechanical engineering, production engineering, engineering management, and related areas. Topics covered include energy and power; mechanics; materials and devices; measurement and control; production processes; tools and equipment; and transport and handling. *Available:* The Dialog Corporation, DIALOG; STN International; Cambridge Scientific Abstracts (CSA), Internet Database Service. *Type:* Database.

Missouri Engineer—Directory of Professional Services Issue

Missouri Society of Professional Engineers
200 E. McCarty St., Ste. 200   Ph: (314)636-4861
Jefferson City, MO 65101
Contact: Cherie L. Bishop, Editor.
Desc: List of about 100 companies legally authorized to practice engineering, architecture, or surveying in Missouri; list of 4,000 members of the architectural, land surveying, and professional engineering societies. *Type:* Directory.

MTM Association for Standards and Research

1111 E. Touhy Ave.   Ph: (847)299-1111
Des Plaines, IL 60018   Fax: (847)299-3509
E-mail: mtm@mtm.org
URL: http://www.mtm.org
Contact: Dirk J. Rauglas, Exec.Dir.
Desc: Persons interested in the fields of industrial engineering, industrial psychology, and human engineering. Conducts research at accredited institutions on human motion (the physical movement of body and limb), with emphasis on examining: internal velocity, acceleration, tension, and control characteristics of a given motion under several conditions; external regularities of given groups of motion as they vary under several conditions of performance; the proper use of motion information in measuring, controlling, and improving manual activities. Also studies ergonomics and the effects of workplace environment on productivity. *Type:* Association.

NACE International: The Corrosion Society

PO Box 218340   Ph: (281)228-6223
Houston, TX 77218-8340   Fax: (281)228-6300
E-mail: msd@mail.nace.org
URL: http://www.nace.org
Contact: G. M. Shankel, Exec.Dir.
Desc: NACE International is a professional technical society dedicated to reducing the economic impact of corrosion, promoting public safety, and protecting the environment by advancing the knowledge of corrosion engineering and science. With more than 15,000 members worldwide, NACE conducts programs for technical training, sponsors technical conferences, and produces standards, publications, and software. Maintains certification program for engineers, technicians, and coating inspectors. *Type:* Association.

National Action Council for Minorities in Engineering

Empire State Bldg., Ste. 2212   Ph: (212)279-2626
350 Fifth Ave.   Fax: (212)629-5178
New York, NY 10118-2299
URL: http://www.nacme.org
Contact: Dr. George Campbell, Jr., Pres.
Desc: Leads the national effort to increase access to careers in engineering and other science-based disciplines. Supported by the nation's leading technology-intensive companies, NACME conducts research and public policy analysis, develops and operates national demonstration programs at precollege and university levels, and disseminates information through publications, conferences, and electronic media. NACME is also the nation's largest privately funded source of scholarships for minority students in engineering. *Type:* Association.

National Council of Examiners for Engineering and Surveying

PO Box 1686   Ph: (864)654-6824
Clemson, SC 29633   Fax: (864)654-6033
E-mail: editor@ncees.org
URL: http://www.ncees.org
Contact: Betsy Browne, Exec.Dir.
Desc: Service organization for engineering and land surveying registration boards. Works to promote uniform standards of registration and to coordinate interstate registration of engineers. Maintains 17 standing and 5 special committees; operates speakers' bureau; compiles statistics. *Type:* Association.

National Institute for Certification in Engineering Technologies

1420 King St.   Free: 888-476-4238
Alexandria, VA 22314-2794
URL: http://www.nicet.org
Contact: John D. Antrim, Gen.Mgr.
Desc: Grants and issues certificates to engineering technicians and technologists who voluntarily apply for certification and satisfy competency criteria through examinations and verification of work experience. (More than 90,000 technicians and 900 technologists have been certified.) Requirements for certification involve work experience in terms of job task proficiency and length of progressively more responsible experience. Levels of certification are Associate Engineering Technician, Engineering Technician, Senior Engineering Technician, Associate Engineering Technologist, and Certified Engineering Technologist. *Type:* Association.

National Society of Black Engineers

1454 Duke St.   Ph: (703)549-2207
PO Box 25588   Fax: (703)683-5312
Alexandria, VA 22313-5588
URL: http://www.nsbe.org
Contact: Charles E. Walker, Exec. Dir.
Desc: Engineering and science students. Seeks to increase the number of minority graduates in engineering and technology. *Type:* Association.

National Society of Professional Engineers

1420 King St.   Ph: (703)684-2800
Alexandria, VA 22314   Free: 888-285-6773
    Fax: (703)836-4875
E-mail: customer.service@nspe.org
URL: http://www.nspe.org
Contact: Patrick J. Natale, Exec.Dir.
Desc: Professional engineers and engineers-in-training in all fields registered in accordance with the laws of states or territories of the U.S. or provinces of Canada; qualified graduate engineers, student members, and registered land surveyors. Is concerned with social, professional, ethical, and economic considerations of engineering as a profession; encompasses programs in public relations, employment practices, ethical considerations, education, and career guidance. *Type:* Association.

Newsletter of Engineering Analysis Software

Frank Maga & Associates
PO Box 6805   Ph: (805)242-6950
Frazier Park, CA 93222   Fax: (805)242-6953
Contact: Frank B. Maga, Editor.
Desc: Offers computer solutions to problems in structural analysis, encompassing the fields of civil, mechanical, and aerospace engineering design and analysis. Presents capsules of information gleaned from research in journals and publications around the world; government agencies; universities; private firms; and from symposia. *Type:* Newsletter.

Omega Chi Epsilon

Kansas State University   Ph: (913)532-4318
Department of Chemical   Fax: (913)532-7372
Engineering
Manhattan, KS 66506-5102
Contact: Walter P. Walawender, Acting Exec.Sec.
Desc: Honor society - chemical engineering. Undergraduate and graduate students enrolled in chemical engineering curricula who display high academic achievement. Recognizes academic excellence, leadership, and service; encourages original investigation in chemical engineering; promotes student-faculty dialogue. *Type:* Association.

Optics Education Directory

International Society for Optical Engineering (SPIE)
1000 20th St.   Ph: (360)676-3290
PO Box 10   Fax: (360)647-1445
Bellingham, WA 98227
E-mail: opticsed@spie.org; opticsed@spie.org.
URL: http://www.spie.org/web/education_home.html.
Contact: Pascale Barnett, Editor.
Desc: More than 250 colleges and universities worldwide offering courses in optical engineering. *Type:* Directory.

Penetrant Progress

Sherwin, Inc.
5530 Borwick Ave.   Ph: (562)861-6324
South Gate, CA 90280   Fax: (562)923-8370
E-mail: sherwininc@aol.com
Desc: Carries information on and specifications on liquid penetrants. *Type:* Newsletter.

Peterson's Job Opportunities for Engineering and Computer Science Majors

Peterson's
202 Carnegie Center   Ph: (609)243-9111
PO Box 2123   Free: 800-338-3282
Princeton, NJ 08543-2123   Fax: (609)243-9150
URL: http://www.peterson.com
Contact: Karen Hansen, Editor.
Desc: Approximately 2,000 research, consulting, manufacturing, government, and technical services organizations hiring colleges graduates in the fields of engineering, telecommunications, biotechnology, software, and consumer electronics. *Type:* Directory.

Photonics Spectra

Laurin Publishing Co. Inc.
Berkshire Common   Ph: (413)499 0514
PO Box 4949   Free: 800-553-0051
Pittsfield, MA 01202-4949   Fax: (413)442-3180
E-mail: photonics@laurin.com
URL: http://www.PhotonicsNet.com
Contact: Stephanie Weiss, Senior Editor; T.C. Laurin, Exec. Publisher; Wendy Laurin, Vice Pres. Mktg.
Desc: Magazine covering optics, fiber, electro-optics, lasers, imaging and optical computing. *Type:* Periodical.

Plant Engineering

Cahners Business Information

1350 E. Touhy Ave.
Des Plaines, IL 60018

Ph: (847)635-8800
Free: 800-446-6551
Fax: (847)635-6856

E-mail: bkinross@cahners.com

Contact: Richard Dunn, Editor, (847)390-2691, t.dunn@pe.cahners.com; Rick Schwer, Publisher, (847)390-2078.

Desc: Magazine focusing on engineering support and maintenance in industry. *Type:* Periodical.

Plant Services

Putman Publishing Co.

555 W. Pierce Rd., Ste. 301
Itasca, IL 60143

Ph: (630)467-1300
Fax: (630)467-1109

E-mail: chuck.boyles@publishers.com.

URL: http://www.plantservices.com.

Contact: John Blatnik, Publisher, fax: (630)467-1120, john.blatnik@publishers.com; Larry Howe, Assoc. Publisher; Chuck Boyles, Editor-in-Chief, chuck.boyles@publishers.com.

Desc: Magazine on plant maintenance professionals. *Type:* Periodical.

Processing of Polymeric Composites and Injection Molding

Engineering Research Center for Net Shape Manufacturing, Ohio State University

339 Baker Systems/1971 Neil Ave.
Columbus, OH 43210

Ph: (614)292-5063
Fax: (614)292-7219

URL: http://nsmwww.eng.ohio-state.edu.

Contact: Sabine Toennesmann, Editor; Oliver Becker, Editor.

Desc: Covers net shape manufacturing project descriptions and plans. Contains improvement of processing techniques for manufacturing polymeric materials. *Type:* Newsletter.

Product Design and Development

Cahners Business Information

201 King of Prussia Rd.
Radnor, PA 19087-5114

Ph: (610)964-4000
Fax: (610)964-2915

E-mail: marketaccess@cahners.com

URL: http://www.pddnet.com.

Contact: Tom King, Publisher, (610)964-4361, fax: (610)964-4947; Lisa Arrigo, Editor.

Desc: Features product news for the design engineering market. *Type:* Periodical.

Sigma Gamma Tau

Dr. Stephen M. Batill

University of Notre Dame
Department of Aerospace & Mechanical Engineering
04 Hessert Center
Notre Dame, IN 46556-5684

Ph: (219)631-7007
Fax: (219)631-8355

E-mail: marilyn.k.walker.4@nd.edu

URL: http://www.aoe.vt.edu/sgt/

Contact: Dr. Frederick H. Lutze, Pres.

Desc: National honor society - aerospace engineering. *Type:* Association.

Simulation Technical Committee Newsletter

Simulation Technical Committee
IEEE Computer Society

1730 Massachusetts Ave. NW
Washington, DC 20036-1992

Contact: Adel Elmaghraby, Editor.

Desc: Carries technical articles on applications of computer simulation and modeling and advances in the field. Contains Society reports, news of research, book reviews, calls for papers, and a calendar of events. *Type:* Newsletter.

Society for the Advancement of Material and Process Engineering

PO Box 2459
Covina, CA 91722-8459

Ph: (626)331-0616
Free: 800-562-7360
Fax: (626)332-8929

E-mail: sampeibo@aol.com

URL: http://www.et.byu.edu/~sampe

Contact: Daun E. White, Exec.Dir.

Desc: Material and process engineers, scientists, and other professionals engaged in development of advanced materials and processing technology in airframe, missile, aerospace, propulsion, electronics, life sciences, management, and related industries. International and local chapters sponsor scholarships for science students seeking financial assistance. Provides placement service for members. *Type:* Association.

Society of American Military Engineers

607 Prince St.
Alexandria, VA 22314-2289

Ph: (703)549-3800
Free: 800-336-3097
Fax: (703)684-0231

E-mail: same@same.org

URL: http://www.same.org

Contact: Vadm. A. Bruce Beran, Exec.Dir.

Desc: Military engineers, architects, construction equipment manufacturers, building materials suppliers, and construction and engineering firms. Works to advance the science of military engineering. *Type:* Association.

Society of Cable Telecommunications Engineers

140 Philips Rd.
Exton, PA 19341-1318

Ph: (610)363-6888
Free: 800-542-5040
Fax: (610)363-5898

E-mail: info@scte.org

URL: http://www.scte.org

Contact: John D. Clark, Jr., Pres.

Desc: Persons engaged in engineering, construction, installation, technical direction, management, or administration of cable television and broadband communications technologies. Also eligible are students in communications, educators, government and regulatory agency employees, and affiliated trade associations. Dedicated to the technical training and further education of members. *Type:* Association.

Society of Logistics Engineers

8100 Professional Pl., Ste. 211
Hyattsville, MD 20785

Ph: (301)459-8446
Fax: (301)459-1522

Contact: Barbara King, Exec.Dir.

Desc: Corporate and individual management and technical practitioners in the field of logistics, including scientists, engineers, educators, managers, and other specialists in commerce, aerospace, and other industries, government, and the military. (Logistics is the art and science of management engineering and technical activities concerned with requirements, and designing, supplying, and maintaining resources to support objectives, plans, and operations.) Covers every logistics specialty, including maintainability, systems and equipment maintenance, maintenance support equipment, human factors, training and training equipment, spare parts, overhaul and repair, handbooks, field site activation and operation, field engineering, facilities, packaging, materials handling, and transportation. Sponsors job referral service; conducts specialized education programs; operates speakers' bureau. *Type:* Association.

Society of Manufacturing Engineers

1 SME Dr.
PO Box 930
Dearborn, MI 48121-0930

Ph: (313)271-1500
Free: 800-733-4763
Fax: (313)271-2861

URL: http://www.sme.org

Contact: Philip Trimble, Exec.Dir.

Desc: Professional society of manufacturing engineers, practitioners, and management executives concerned with manufacturing technologies for improved productivity. Seeks to advance the science of manufacturing through the continuing education of manufacturing engineers, practitioners, and management. Conducts expositions, international seminars and clinics. *Type:* Association.

Society of Motion Picture and Television Engineers

595 W. Hartsdale Ave.
White Plains, NY 10607

Ph: (914)761-1100
Fax: (914)761-3115

E-mail: smpte@smpte.org

URL: http://www.smpte.org

Contact: Frederick C. Motts, Exec.Dir.

Desc: Professional engineers and technicians in motion pictures, television, motion imaging and allied arts and sciences. To advance engineering technology, disseminate scientific information, and sponsor lectures, exhibitions, and conferences to advance the theory and practice of engineering. Develops standards for motion pictures and television and sponsors standards promulgated by the American National Standards Institute, to promote interchangeability and provide for operating efficiency; provides standards subscription service. *Type:* Association.

Society of Naval Architects and Marine Engineers

601 Pavonia Ave., Ste. 400
Jersey City, NJ 07306

Contact: Francis M. Cagliari, Exec.Dir.

Desc: Naval architects and marine and ocean engineers. Seeks to advance the art, science, and practice of naval architecture, shipbuilding, marine engineering, and all ied fields. Objectives are to exchange information and ideas among its members; to disseminate the results of research, experience, and information; to promote the professional integrity and status of its members and advancement in their knowledge; to further education in naval architecture, marine, and ocean engineering; to encourage and sponsor research and other inquiries important to the advancement of the art. *Type:* Association.

Society of Tribologists and Lubrication Engineers

840 Busse Hwy.
Park Ridge, IL 60068-2376

Ph: (847)825-5536
Fax: (847)825-1456

Contact: Edward Salek, Exec.Dir.

Desc: Engineers and others united to: advance the science of lubrication tribology and related arts and sciences; stimulate the study and development of lubrication tribology techniques; accumulate and disseminate information; promote higher standards in the field. Sponsors joint committees, councils, and several courses held in conjunction with annual meeting. Courses include: Basic Lubrication; Bearings; EHD; Hydraulics; Metalworking; Seals; Solid Lubrication; Synthetic Lubricants; Tribology Ceramics. *Type:* Association.

Society of Women Engineers

120 Wall St., 11th Fl.
New York, NY 10005

Ph: (212)509-9577
Fax: (212)509-0224

Contact: Christine Burke, Exec.Dir.

Desc: Educational service society of women engineers; membership is also open to men. Supplies information on the achievements of women engineers and the opportunities available to them; assists women engineers in preparing for return to active work following temporary retirement. Serves as an informational center on women in engineering. *Type:* Association.

The Soo Locks

U.S. Army Corps of Engineers - Detroit District
477 Michigan Ave.   Ph: (313)226-4680
Detroit, MI 48226
URL: http://sparky.nce.usace.army.mil/SOO/soohmpg.
html
Contact: Mark Paasche, markp@superior.lre.usace.army.
mil.
Desc: The Soo Locks database provides information about
the Soo Locks, Sault Ste. Marie, Michigan. *Type:* Database.

Tau Alpha Pi

1818 N St., NW   Ph: (202)331-3514
Washington, DC 20036
Contact: Prof. Frederick J. Berger, D.Sc., Founding Exec.
Dir.
Desc: National honor society for engineering technology.
Type: Association.

Tau Beta Pi Association

PO Box 2697   Ph: (423)546-4578
Knoxville, TN 37901-2697   Fax: (423)546-4579
E-mail: tbp@tbp.org
URL: http://www.tbp.org
Contact: James D. Froula, Sec.-Treas.
Desc: Honor society - engineering. Grants student loans.
Honors students for non-engineering activities as Laure-
ates. *Type:* Association.

Technology Review

Technology Review
201 Vassar St.   Ph: (617)253-8250
Cambridge, MA 02139   Fax: (617)258-5850
E-mail: trcomments@mit.edu.
Contact: John Benditt, Editor, (617)258-7888, fax:
(617)258-8778; R. Bruce Journey, Publisher/CEO,
(617)253-2708.
Desc: Magazine reviewing new developments in technology with an emphasis on economic, political, and social implications. Not a new product publication. *Type:*
Periodical.

Theta Tau

655 Craig Rd., Ste. 128   Ph: (314)994-1904
St. Louis, MO 63141-7168   Free: 800-264-1904
                                      Fax: (314)997-3234
E-mail: central@thetatau.org
URL: http://www.thetatau.org
Contact: Michael T. Abraham, Exec. Dir.
Desc: Professional fraternity - engineering. Maintains hall
of fame. *Type:* Association.

United Engineering Foundation

3 Park Ave., 27th Fl.   Ph: (212)591-7829
New York, NY 10016-5902   Fax: (212)705-7441
URL: http://www.engfnd.org
Contact: Charles Freiman, Exec.Dir.
Desc: Federation of 5 major national engineering societies:
American Institute of Chemical Engineers; American In-
stitute of Mining, Metallurgical and Petroleum Engineers;
American Society of Civil Engineers; American Society of
Mechanical Engineers; Institute of Electrical and Electron-
ics Engineers. Supports research in engineering and ad-
vances the engineering arts and sciences through its
conference program. *Type:* Association.

Welding Innovation

James F. Lincoln Arc Welding Foundation
PO Box 17035   Ph: (216)481-4300
Cleveland, OH 44117   Fax: (216)486-1751
URL: http://www.lincolnelectric.com.
Contact: Duane Miller, Editor; Scott Funderburk, Asst.
Editor, scott_funderburk@lincolnelectric.com.

Desc: Magazine covering arc welding design, engineering,
and fabrication. *Type:* Periodical.

www.industry.net

Industry.net Inc.
15 Inverness Way E., B106   Ph: (303)397-2383
Englewood, CO 80112-5776   Fax: (303)705-4205
E-mail: newseditor@industry.net.
URL: http://www.industry.net.

Contact: Liz Maynard Prigge, Director, Editorial Content;
Marty Farrell, VP, Sales; Eileen Quirk, COO; Rich Remington, Director of Technical and Prod.

Desc: News web site covering manufacturing and industrial equipment for engineering professionals. *Type:* Periodical.

English

**Conference on College Composition and
Communication**

1111 W. Kenyon Rd.   Ph: (217)328-3870
Urbana, IL 61801   Free: 800-369-6283
                                      Fax: (217)328-0977
URL: http://www.ncte.org/cccc
Contact: Faith Schullstrom, Sec./Treas.
Desc: College and university educators involved in teach-
ing composition and communica tion. *Type:* Association.

English-Speaking Union of the United States

16 E. 69th St.   Ph: (212)879-6800
New York, NY 10021   Fax: (212)772-2886
E-mail: info@english-speakingunion.org
URL: http://www.english-speakingunion.org
Contact: David Olyphant, Exec.Dir.
Desc: Fosters mutual understanding and friendship among
English-speaking people worldwide; seeks to expand chan-
nels of communication. Administers information pro-
grams and English in Action program. Maintains 7500
volume library of materials pertaining to Britain. *Type:* As-
sociation.

National Council of Teachers of English

1111 Kenyon Rd.   Ph: (217)328-3870
Urbana, IL 61801-1096   Free: 800-369-6283
                                      Fax: (217)328-9645
URL: http://www.ncte.org
Contact: Faith Schullstrom, Exec.Dir.
Desc: Teachers of English at all school levels. Works to in-
crease the effectiveness of instruction in English language
and literature. Sponsors Conference on College Composi-
tion and Communication, Conference on English Educa-
tion, Conference on English Leadership, Whole Language
Umbrella, and Two-Year College English Association.
Type: Association.

National Writing Project

University of California   Ph: (510)642-0963
5511 Tolman Hall, No. 1670   Fax: (510)642-4545
Berkeley, CA 94720-1670
E-mail: nwp@socrates.berkeley.edu
URL: http://www.nwp.berkeley.edu
Contact: Richard Sterling, Exec.Dir.
Desc: Teachers at universities and colleges that sponsor
separate writing projects. Provides teachers with the skills
necessary to teach students how to write. *Type:* Associa-
tion.

**Sigma Tau Delta, the International English
Honor Society**

c/o Dr. William C. Johnson   Ph: (815)753-1612
Department of English
Northern Illinois University
DeKalb, IL 60115
E-mail: sigmatd@niu.edu
URL: http://www.english.org
Contact: Dr. William C. Johnson, Exec.Dir.
Desc: Honor society - men and women, English. *Type:* As-
sociation.

**Teachers of English to Speakers of Other
Languages**

1600 Cameron St., Ste. 300   Ph: (703)836-0774
Alexandria, VA 22314-2751   Fax: (703)836-7864
E-mail: tesol@tesol.edu
URL: http://www.tesol.edu
Desc: School, college, and adult education teachers who
teach English as a second or foreign language; students and
professional people in the field; colleges and schools are institutional members. Aims to improve the teaching of English as a second or foreign language by promoting
research, disseminating information, developing guidelines and promoting certification, and serving as a clearinghouse for the field. Offers placement service; operates
speakers' bureau. *Type:* Association.

Entertainers

David Copperfield International Fan Club

11777 San Vincente Blvd., No.   Ph: (619)592-0843
  601
Los Angeles, CA 90049
Contact: Hy Kotkin, Exec. Officer.
Desc: Fans of magician/illusionist David Copperfield
(1957-). Informs members about Copperfield's activities
and Project Magic . Sponsors competitions. *Type:* Association.

Joni James International Fan Club

PO Box 7207
Westchester, IL 60154-7207
Contact: Wayne Michael Brasler, Pres. & Editor.
Desc: Admirers of Joni James. *Type:* Association.

Entertainment

Actors' Fund of America

729 Seventh Ave., 10th Fl.   Ph: (212)221-7300
New York, NY 10019   Fax: (212)764-0238
E-mail: jbeninca@actorsfund.org
URL: http://www.actorsfund.org
Contact: Joseph P. Benincasa, Exec.Dir.
Desc: Human service organization of the entertainment industry. Provides emergency financial assistance to those in
need; makes available social services, counseling and psychotherapy, health and education services, and nursing
home care and retirement housing. Conducts substance
abuse programs and blood drives; sponsors survival jobs
program to provide employment for those between engagements. *Type:* Association.

American Kitefliers Association

320 Hungerford Dr.   Free: 800-525-2550
Rockville, MD 20850   Fax: 800-252-2550
E-mail: aka@aka.kite.org
URL: http://www.aka.kite.org
Contact: Mel Hickman, Exec.Dir.
Desc: Persons interested in kite building, kiting events, and
the advancement of kites. Sponsors specialized education
and competitions; provides teachers' packets on kites and
kite building. *Type:* Association.

Argonaut Entertainment Inc.
455 Delta Ave.   Ph: (513)871-2746
Ste. 204   Fax: (513)871-0793
Cincinnati, OH 45226
Contact: Harold A. Tieger, President; Lenny Dave, Creative Dir.; Barry Elkus, Mktg. Dir.
Desc: Distributes comic books. *Alt. Contact:* 455 Delta Ave., Ste. 204, Cincinnati, OH 45226; telephone: (513)871-2746; fax: (513)871-0793. *Type:* Periodical.

Arts and Leisure Times
EWA Publications
2446 E. 65th St.   Ph: (718)763-7034
Brooklyn, NY 11234   Fax: (718)763-7035
Contact: Kevin Browne, Editor; Justin Baron, Publisher; Bill Tarrington, Advertising Mgr.
Desc: Community newspaper. *Type:* Periodical.

At the Shore
South Jersey Publishing Co.
1000 W. Washington Ave.   Ph: (609)272-7000
Pleasantville, NJ 08232-3806   Free: 800-651-8279
     Fax: (609)272-7086
E-mail: atshore@pressplus.com.
Contact: Bob McCormick, Publisher, (609)272-7110.
Desc: Community newspaper. *Type:* Periodical.

Auditions U.S.A.-Models & Talent
The John King Network
244 Madison Ave., Ste. 393   Ph: (212)969-8715
New York, NY 10016   Fax: (212)969-8715
Contact: John King, Publisher.
Desc: Journal providing audition information for people in show business and modeling. *Alt. Contact:* telephone: (516)763-7499; fax: (516)763-7499. *Type:* Periodical.

Austin Chronicle
Austin Chronicle
PO Box 49066   Ph: (512)454-5766
Austin, TX 78765   Fax: (512)458-6910
E-mail: mail@auschron.com.
URL: http://www.auschron.com.
Contact: Louis Black, Editor; Nick Barbaro, Publisher.
Desc: Newspaper (tabloid) covering local entertainment and political activities. *Type:* Periodical.

Avenue
Avenue
950 3rd Ave.   Ph: (212)758-9517
New York, NY 10022   Fax: (212)758-7395
Contact: Craig Bromberg, Editor; Michelle Sonkin, Publisher.
Desc: Lifestyle magazine. *Type:* Periodical.

Baltimore City Paper
Scranton Times
812 Park Ave.   Ph: (410)889-6600
Baltimore, MD 21201-4847   Fax: (410)523-2222
Contact: Donald Farley, V.P./Gen. Mgr.
Desc: Lifestyle and entertainment newspaper (tabloid). *Type:* Periodical.

BASELINE
BASELINE II INC.
838 Broadway   Ph: (212)254-8235
4th Fl.
New York, NY 10003
E-mail: bios@pkbaseline.com
URL: http://www.pkbaseline.com.
Desc: Contains information on the U.S. entertainment industry, with an emphasis on films, television, and cable television. *Available:* BASELINE II INC. *Type:* Database.

Better Living
American Business
80 Central Park West, Ste. 16B   Ph: (212)581-2000
New York, NY 10023
Contact: Joe Queenan, Editor; Ralph Ginzburg, Publisher; Richard K. Greene, Advertising Mgr.
Desc: Lifestyle magazine focusing on the working rich. *Type:* Periodical.

The Billennium®: The Official Celebration of the Year 2000™
Billennium Organizing Committee
1335 W. Altgeld St.   Ph: (773)327-2000
Chicago, IL 60614   Fax: (773)327-1999
E-mail: information@billennium.com
URL: http://www.billennium.com/
Contact: information@billennium.com.
Desc: In contrast to the negative doomsaying so prevalent everywhere now, this site looks at the Year 2000 in a very optimistic way. It serves as the headquarters for the celebration of the millennium - not only the accomplishments of the past 2000 years but also for the hope and promise of the next 1000. *Type:* Database.

Biography
A & E Television Networks
235 E. 45th St.   Ph: (212)210-9750
New York, NY 10017   Fax: (212)210-1326
Contact: Paulette McLeod, Publisher; Anne Rieschick, Editor; Diane Lowman, Marketing Dir.
Desc: Consumer entertainment magazine covering biographies. *Type:* Periodical.

BPI Entertainment News Wire
100 Boylston St. Ste. 210   Ph: (617)482-9447
Boston, MA 02116   Fax: (617)482-9562
Contact: John Morgan, VP News and Photo Serv.; Don Gallagher, Managing Editor; Judy Webb, Sales Mgr.
Desc: Distributes magazine, newspaper, and feature articles. *Alt. Contact:* 100 Boylston St. Ste. 210, Boston, MA 02116; telephone: (617)482-9447; fax: (617)482-9562. *Type:* Periodical.

Bride's Magazine
Conde Nast Publications, Inc.
140 E. 45th St., 39th Fl.   Ph: (212)880-8800
New York, NY 10017   Free: 800-223-0780
     Fax: (212)880-8248
E-mail: letters@brides.com.
Contact: Millie Martini Bratten, Editor-in-Chief; Deborah I. Fine, Publisher; Kit Logan, Advertising Mgr.
Desc: Magazine presenting information to engaged couples on finance, travel, liquor, cars, electronics, entertaining, home furnishings, fashion, fitness, health, and beauty. *Alt. Contact:* 140 E. 45th St., 39th Fl., New York, NY 10017; fax: (212)880-8644. *Type:* Periodical.

Burlington Liars Club
179 Beth Ct.   Ph: (414)763-4640
Burlington, WI 53105
Contact: John Soeth, Pres.
Desc: "To perpetuate the American heritage of telling humorous tall tales." Originally founded in 1929 as the Liars Club, which disbanded in 1980 and was reestablished in 1981 under the current name. *Type:* Association.

Buying & Dining Guide
Community Publications of America Inc.
80 8th Ave., Ste. 315   Ph: (212)243-6800
New York, NY 10011   Fax: (212)243-7457
Contact: Allan Horwitz, Publisher.
Desc: Shopping and dining guide. Separate editions throughout the country. *Type:* Periodical.

Buzz
Buzz Inc.
11845 W. Olympic Blvd., Ste.   Ph: (310)473-2721
800   Fax: (310)473-2876
Los Angeles, CA 90064
URL: http://www.buzzmag.com.
Contact: Eden Collinsworth, CEO; Scott Kramer, President; Mark Smelzer, Publisher; Marilyn Bethany, Editor-in-Chief; C. Montgomery, Advertising Mgr.
Desc: City magazine for and about Los Angeles, focusing on art, politics, culture, and entertainment. *Alt. Contact:* fax: (310)473-5091. *Type:* Periodical.

Campus Canada Magazine
Canadian Controlled Media Communications
287 MacPherson Ave.   Ph: (416)928-2909
Toronto, ON, Canada M4V   Free: 800-320-6420
1A4   Fax: (416)966-1181
Contact: Sarah Moore, Managing Editor; Harvey Wolfe, Publisher; Andrew Feldman, Sales.
Desc: Student lifestyle magazine covering entertainment, travel, careers, sports, health, and campus issues. *Type:* Periodical.

Cannery Row Creations
69 Pasa Hondo   Ph: (408)659-1845
Carmel Valley, CA 93924   Fax: (408)659-1399
Contact: Yavor Bachev, Self-Syndicator/Owner.
Desc: Distributes humor column. *Alt. Contact:* 69 Pasa Hondo, Carmel Valley, CA 93924; telephone: (408)659-1845; fax: (408)659-1399. *Type:* Periodical.

Carolina Country
North Carolina Association of Electric Corp.
3400 Sumner Blvd. 27616   Ph: (919)872-0800
PO Box 27306   Free: 800-662-8835
Raleigh, NC 27611-7306   Fax: (919)878-3970
E-mail: carolina.country@ncemcs.com.
URL: www.ncemcs.com.
Contact: Micheal E.C. Gery, Editor; Monica Russell, Business Mgr.
Desc: General interest magazine. *Type:* Periodical.

Casino News & Entertainment Review
William J. Rondeau
PO Box 5678, Sta. A
Toronto, ON, Canada M5W
1N8
Contact: William J. Rondeau, Editor.
Desc: Presents articles on new hotel openings, innovations, and games. Recurring features include news of research, a calendar of events, news of educational opportunities, book reviews, and notices of publications available. *Type:* Newsletter.

Casting News
The John King Network
244 Madison Ave., Ste. 393   Ph: (212)969-8715
New York, NY 10016   Fax: (212)969-8715
Contact: John King, Publisher.
Desc: Trade magazine featuring news of television, film, print, video, fashion and stage castings. *Alt. Contact:* telephone: (516)763-7499; fax: (516)763-7499. *Type:* Periodical.

Chicago Cigar Smoker Magazine
Jonathan Scott's Cigar Smoker Magazine
PO Box 2323   Ph: (630)790-3433
Glen Ellyn, IL 60138   Fax: (630)986-0369
E-mail: ccsm1@aol.com.
URL: http://www.chicagocigar.com.
Contact: Jonathan Scott, Publisher/CEO; Gregory S. Bayer, Technical Svcs.

Desc: Men's lifestyle magazine featuring articles on cigar smoking, celebrities, fashion, food, and the media. *Type:* Periodical.

Cigar Aficionado

Cigar Aficionado
387 Park Ave. S   Ph: (212)684-4224
New York, NY 10016   Fax: (212)684-5424
URL: http://www.cigaraficionado.com.
Contact: Marvin R. Shanken, Editor and Publisher; Gordon Mott, Managing Editor.
Desc: Men's lifestyle magazine directed toward those who wish to expand their knowledge of premium cigars. *Type:* Periodical.

Circus Magazine

Circus Enterprises
6 W. 18th St., 2nd Fl.   Ph: (212)242-4902
New York, NY 10011   Fax: (212)242-5734
Contact: Gerald Rothberg, Editor and Publisher; Gary Victor, Advertising Mgr.
Desc: Magazine covering popular music news and rock-and-roll personalities. *Type:* Periodical.

City Pages

City Pages, Inc.
401 N. 3rd St., Ste. 550 Ph: (612)375-1015
Minneapolis, MN 55401   Fax: (612)372-3737
E-mail: adinfo@citypages.com.
URL: http://www.citypages.com.
Contact: Tom Finkel, Editor, tfinkel@citypages.com; Mark Bartel, Publisher, mbartel@citypages.com; Jerry Gloe, Advertising Dir., (612)372-3743, fax: (612)372-3737, jgloe@citypages.com.
Desc: News and art information. *Alt. Contact:* PO Box 59183, Minneapolis, MN 55459-0183; telephone: (612)375-1015; fax: (612)372-3737. *Type:* Periodical.

Colorado Country Life

Colorado Rural Electric Association
1313 W. 46th Ave.   Ph: (303)455-4111
Denver, CO 80211   Fax: (303)455-2807
Contact: Frank McCrea, Editor and Publisher; Mona Neeley, Managing Editor.
Desc: Association journal. *Alt. Contact:* PO Box 11338, Denver, CO 80211; telephone: (303)455-4111; fax: (303)455-4807. *Type:* Periodical.

The Country Club

The Country Club
16 Forest St.   Ph: (203)972-3892
New Canaan, CT 06840   Fax: (203)966-7268
Contact: E. MacFarlan Moore, Editor and Publisher.
Desc: Magazine edited exclusively for private country club members. *Type:* Periodical.

Country Extra

Reiman Publications, LLC
5400 S. 60th St.   Ph: (414)423-0100
Greendale, WI 53129-1404 Free: 800-682-9019
                         Fax: (414)423-8463
Contact: Tom Curl, Editor.
Desc: Rural lifestyle magazine for individuals living or wishing to live in the country. *Type:* Periodical.

Country Journal

Cowles Enthusiast Media
4 High Ridge Park   Ph: (203)322-2400
Stamford, CT 06905   Fax: (203)322-1966
E-mail: cntryjrnl@aol.com.
Contact: Toni Apgar, Publishing Dir.; Maryann Merion, Ad. Dir., mmerion@erols.com; Josh Garskof, Managing Editor.

Desc: General resource publication on rural life, providing practical advice for the country dweller. *Type:* Periodical.

Cowboys & Indians

Cowboys & Indians
8214 Westchester Dr., Ste. 800 Ph: (214)750-8222
Dallas, TX 75225   Fax: (214)750-4522
Contact: Charlotte Berney, Editor; Reid Slaughter, Publisher; Susan Stanton, Assoc. Publisher.
Desc: Western lifestyle magazine for general consumers. *Alt. Contact:* 128 Grant Ave., Santa Fe, NM 87501; telephone: (505)989-3400; fax: (505)989-3434. *Type:* Periodical.

Creative Loafing

Creative Loafing
750 Willoughby Way   Ph: (404)688-5623
Atlanta, GA 30312   Free: 800-953-5623
                         Fax: (404)614-3599
E-mail: webmaster.creativeloafing@.com.
URL: http://www.creativeloafing.com.
Contact: Deborah Eason, Publisher; Ken Edlestin, Editor; Howard Landsman, General Sales Mgr., (404)614-1227, fax: (404)614-1227, howard.landsman@cln.com.
Desc: Alternative news weekly newspaper (tabloid). *Type:* Periodical.

Details

Conde Nast Publications, Inc.
140 E. 45th St., 39th Fl. Ph: (212)880-8800
New York, NY 10017   Free: 800-223-0780
                           Fax: (212)880-8248
E-mail: letters@brides.com
URL: http://www.swoon.com.
Contact: Jonathan Newhouse, Publisher; Julie McGowan, Advertising Dir.
Desc: Magazine covering talents and trends in fashion, beauty, art, music, night life, and restaurants. *Alt. Contact:* 632 Broadway, 12th Fl., New York, NY 10012; telephone: (212)420-0689; fax: (212)598-0284. *Type:* Periodical.

Directory of Funparks & Attractions

Amusement Business
PO Box 24970   Ph: (615)321-4250
Nashville, TN 37202   Free: 800-999-3322
                         Fax: (615)327-1575
URL: http://www.amusementbusiness.com; http://www.amusementbusiness.com.
Contact: Karen Oertley, Editor.
Desc: Over 2,100 amusement parks, zoos, kiddie lands, theme parks, family entertainment centers, and other tourist attractions with revenue-producing activities worldwide. *Type:* Directory.

Dr. Mildred Culp

Universal Press Syndicate
4520 Main St., Ste. 700
Kansas City, MO 64111-7701
URL: http://www.work-wise.com.
Contact: Mildred Culp, Contact.
Desc: Distributes WorkWise. Using survey related material, discusses evolving workplace issues of interest to managers and executives. Focuses on improving workplace relationships and job effectiveness. *Alt. Contact:* Universal Press Syndicate 4520 Main St., Ste. 700, Kansas City, MO 64111-7701. *Type:* Periodical.

Easy Living Magazine

Eagle Promotions Ltd.
201-20039 96th Ave.   Ph: (604)882-9380
Langley, BC, Canada V1M 3C6 Fax: (604)852-2894
Desc: Magazine covering family interest issues. *Type:* Periodical.

Elvis International Forum

Creative Radio Network
PO Box 3373   Ph: (818)991-3892
Thousand Oaks, CA 91359   Fax: (818)991-3894
Contact: Darwin L. Lamm, Editor.
Desc: Consumer magazine covering entertainment. *Type:* Periodical.

Entertainment Lifestyles

EWA Publications
2446 E. 65th St.   Ph: (718)763-7034
Brooklyn, NY 11234   Fax: (718)763-7035
Contact: Kevin Browne, Editor; Justin Baron, Publisher; Bill Tarrington, Advertising Mgr.
Desc: Community newspaper. *Type:* Periodical.

Entertainment Marketing Letter

EPM Communications, Inc.
160 Mercer St., 3rd Fl.   Ph: (212)941-0099
New York, NY 10012-3212   Fax: (212)941-1622
E-mail: epmcommun@aol.com; EML@pipeline.com.
Contact: Ira Mayer, Editor.
Desc: Reports on techniques used in the marketing of films, music, videos, television, radio, and cable features. Covers tie-in campaigns, sponsorship, in-theatre advertising, and interactive telephone promotions. *Type:* Newsletter.

Entertainment News Calendar

250 W. 57th St.   Ph: (212)421-1370
Ste. 1517-132   Fax: (212)563-3488
New York, NY 10107
Contact: Evelyn Heyward, Bureau Chief.
Desc: Distributes news service for entertainment features. *Alt. Contact:* 250 W. 57th St., Ste. 1517-132, New York, NY 10107; telephone: (212)421-1370; fax: (212)563-3488. *Type:* Periodical.

Entertainment News Syndicate

Dag Hammarskjold Comm. Ctr. Ph: (212)223-1821
PO Box 20481   Fax: (212)223-3737
New York, NY 10017
Contact: Lee Canaan, Theatre and Travel Ed.; Jed Canaan, Sports Ed.; Barbara Marsten, Fashion/Beauty Ed.; Marilyn Kirk, Hospitality Ed.; Robert Michaels, Music Film Ed.
Desc: Distributes gossip, theatre, and travel reviews. *Alt. Contact:* Dag Hammarskjold Comm. Ctr., PO Box 20481, New York, NY 10017; telephone: (212)223-1821; fax: (212)223-3737. *Type:* Periodical.

Entertainment Today

Best Publishing, Inc.
801 S. Main St., Ste. L   Ph: (818)566-4030
Burbank, CA 91506   Fax: (818)566-4295
E-mail: enttoday@artnet.net.
URL: http://www.ent-today.com.
Contact: John Salazar, Publisher, (808)841-4030.
Desc: Entertainment newspaper covering film, music, arts, video, theater, multimedia, and dining. *Type:* Periodical.

Entertainment Weekly

Time Inc.
Time-Life Bldg., Rockefeller Ph: (212)522-1212
  Center   Fax: (212)522-0315
1271 Avenue of the Americas
New York, NY 10020
URL: http://www.PathFinder.com/ew.
Contact: Michael J. Klingensmith, Publisher; Jason McManus, Editor; Richard B. Stolley, Advertising Mgr.; James W. Seymore, Jr., Managing Editor.
Desc: Magazine reporting on trends in TV, video, music, movies, books, and multimedia . *Type:* Periodical.

Esquire

Hearst Magazines
959 8th Ave.   Ph: (212)649-2000
New York, NY 10019-5905
Contact: David Granger, Editor-in-Chief; Valerie Sembalier, Publisher.
Desc: Magazine reporting on men's interests and fashions. *Alt. Contact:* 250 W. 55th St., 7th Fl., New York, NY 10019; telephone: (212)649-4020; fax: (212)977-3158. *Type:* Periodical.

Essence

Essence Communications, Inc.
1500 Broadway, 6th Fl.   Ph: (212)642-0600
New York, NY 10036   Free: 800-274-9398
     Fax: (212)921-5173
Contact: Susan Taylor, Editor-in-Chief; Edward Lewis, Publisher; Clarence O. Smith, President.
Desc: Magazine for contemporary black women. *Type:* Periodical.

The Fear Finder

Halloween Events, Inc.
36393 Dequindre   Ph: (248)524-9782
Troy, MI 48083   Fax: (248)524-1320
Contact: Edward Terebus, Owner.
Desc: Newspaper covering local Halloween events and news. *Type:* Periodical.

Florida Living Magazine

Florida Media, Inc.
3235 Duff Rd.   Ph: (941)858-7244
Lakeland, FL 33810   Fax: (941)859-5297
E-mail: flliving@earthlink.net.
URL: http://www.floridaliving.org.
Contact: E. Douglas Cifers, Publisher, fax: (941)859-3197; Kristen Crane, Managing Editor.
Desc: Statewide lifestyle magazine. *Type:* Periodical.

Forum

General Media
11 Penn Plaza, 12th Fl.   Ph: (212)702-6000
New York, NY 10001   Fax: (212)702-6262
Contact: Don Myrus, Editorial Dir.; Bob Guccione, Publisher.
Desc: Magazine of human relations and sexuality. *Type:* Periodical.

Friendly Exchange

Farmers Insurance Group of Companies
PO Box 2120   Ph: (810)558-7026
Warren, MI 48090-2120   Fax: (810)558-5897
URL: http://www.friendlyexchange.com.
Contact: Dan Grantham, Editor, (810)558-7225, dgrantha@cecom.com; Tom Krempel, Advertising Mgr., (810)558-7148; Deanne Olive, Managing Editor, (810)558-7272; Rebecca Yops, Art Dir., (810)558-7254.
Desc: General interest lifestyle magazine. *Alt. Contact:* 30400 Van Dyke, Warren, MI 48093-2316. *Type:* Periodical.

The Gadget Guru

95 White Bridge Rd.   Ph: (615)356-9595
Ste. 212   Fax: (615)356-9596
Nashville, TN 37205
Contact: Andy Pargh, President.
Desc: Distributes information on new consumer products. *Alt. Contact:* 95 White Bridge Rd., Ste. 212, Nashville, TN 37205; telephone: (615)356-9595; fax: (615)356-9596. *Type:* Periodical.

Gallery Magazine

Montcalm Publishing Corp.
401 Park Ave. S., 3rd Fl.   Ph: (212)779-8900
New York, NY 10016-8802   Fax: (212)725-7215
Contact: Barry Janoff, Editor; Russell T. Orenstein, Publisher.
Desc: Men's interest magazine. *Type:* Periodical.

Georgia Straight

Vancouver Free Press
1770 Burrard St., 2nd Fl.   Ph: (604)730-7000
Vancouver, BC, Canada V6J   Fax: (604)730-7010
3G7
E-mail: info@straight.com.
Contact: Charles Campbell, Editor; Dan McLeod, Publisher.
Desc: Magazine (tabloid). *Alt. Contact:* 2nd Fl., 1770 Burrard St, Vancouver, BC, Canada V6J 3G7; telephone: (604)730-7000; fax: (604)730-7010. *Type:* Periodical.

Get Up & Go! Magazine

Age Wave Communications
500 Felsen St., Ste. 101
El Cajon, CA 92020
E-mail: npti@retirehouse.com.
Contact: Laura Impastato, Editor, (619)593-2910, fax: (619)442-4043; Terri Teahune, Publisher.
Desc: Niche publication (50-plus). *Type:* Periodical.

GQ (Gentlemen's Quarterly)

Conde Nast Publications, Inc.
140 E. 45th St., 39th Fl.   Ph: (212)880-8800
New York, NY 10017   Free: 800-223-0780
     Fax: (212)880-8248
E-mail: letters@brides.com
Contact: Arthur Cooper, Editor; Michael Clinton, Publisher; Steve Shepherd, Advertising Mgr.
Desc: Magazine featuring fashions and style for men. *Type:* Periodical.

Harper's Bazaar

Hearst Magazines
959 8th Ave.   Ph: (212)649-2000
New York, NY 10019-5905
Contact: Liz Tilberis, Editor; Jeannette Chang, Publisher.
Desc: Fashion and beauty magazine. *Alt. Contact:* 1700 Broadway, New York, NY 10019. *Type:* Periodical.

Harper's Magazine

McArthur Foundation
666 Broadway   Ph: (212)614-6500
New York, NY 10012   Free: 800-444-4653
     Fax: (212)228-5889
Contact: Lewis H. Lapham, Editor; John R. MacArthur, Publisher.
Desc: General editorial magazine. *Type:* Periodical.

Harrowsmith Country Life

Malcolm Publishing Inc.
11 450 Albert Hudon Blvd.   Ph: (514)327-4464
Montreal-Nord, PQ, Canada   Free: 800-563-6738
H1G 3J9   Fax: (514)327-0514
E-mail: hclmag@globetrotter.net.
Contact: Tom Cruickshank, Editor, (416)481-2657, fax: (416)481-4179; Michel Paradis, Publisher; Yolanda Thornton, Advertising Mgr.
Desc: A country lifestyle magazine. *Type:* Periodical.

Have Fun at the Movies

10717 Bushire Dr.   Ph: (214)902-0942
Dallas, TX 75229   Fax: (214)350-3063
E-mail: nreagan@aol.com.
Contact: Gail Reagan, Columnist; Sophie Redditt, Ed./ Computer Layout.
Desc: Distributes film and video recommendations. *Alt. Contact:* 10717 Bushire Dr., Dallas, TX 75229; telephone: (214)902-0942; fax: (214)350-3063. *Type:* Periodical.

Hemispheres

Pace Communications, Inc.
1301 Carolina St.   Ph: (336)378-6065
Greensboro, NC 27401-1001   Fax: (336)378-8261
Contact: Kate Greer, Editor; Bonnie McElveen-Hunter, Publisher; John Ballantyne, Vice President; Karen Finley, Advertising Service Mgr.
Desc: Magazine for frequent travelers, United Airlines. *Type:* Periodical.

Hollywood Hotline

Hollywood Hotline
3727 W. Magnolia Blvd 803   Ph: (818)845-8400
Burbank, CA 91505-2818
Desc: Contains news of the entertainment industry, including motion pictures, television, music, and home entertainment. Covers programming, production, deals and contracts, unions and guilds, new scripts, celebrities, and reviews. *Available:* America Online, Inc.; CompuServe Information Service; Delphi Internet Services Corporation; AT&T EasyLink Services; Youvelle Renaissance Group, GEnie. *Type:* Database.

Hollywood Inside Syndicate

PO Box 49957   Ph: (909)672-8459
Los Angeles, CA 90049-0957   Fax: (909)672-8459
E-mail: holywood@ez2.net.
URL: http://www.ez2.net/hollywood.
Contact: John Austin, Editor-in-Chief.
Desc: Distributes Books of the Week, Celebrity-Quotes, and Hollywood Inside weekly columns. *Alt. Contact:* PO Box 49957, Los Angeles, CA 90049-0957; telephone: (909)672-8459; fax: (909)672-8459. *Type:* Periodical.

Hollywood News Calendar

15030 Ventura Blvd.   Ph: (818)986-8168
Ste. 742   Fax: (818)789-8047
Sherman Oaks, CA 91403
Contact: Carolyn Fox, Editor-in-Chief; Susan Fox-Davis, Editor.
Desc: Distributes entertainment news and features. *Alt. Contact:* 15030 Ventura Blvd., Ste. 742, Sherman Oaks, CA 91403; telephone: (818)986-8168; fax: (818)789-8047. *Type:* Periodical.

Home Focus

2140 Sul Ross   Ph: (713)630-0049
Houston, TX 77098
Contact: Gay Elliott McFarland, Author; Blair Pittman, Photographer.
Desc: Distributes interior design and decoration column. *Alt. Contact:* 2140 Sul Ross, Houston, TX 77098; telephone: (713)630-0049. *Type:* Periodical.

Hometown Flavor

25874 Blanca Way   Ph: (805)255-6605
Valencia, CA 91355
Contact: Kevin Hoover, Ed./Mgr.
Desc: Distributes columns and anecdotes. *Alt. Contact:* 25874 Blanca Way, Valencia, CA 91355; telephone: (805)255-6605. *Type:* Periodical.

HUMOR Project

480 Broadway, Ste. 210   Ph: (518)587-8770
Saratoga Springs, NY 12866-   Free: 800-600-4242
2288   Fax: (518)587-8771
E-mail: questions@humorproject.com

URL: http://www.humorproject.com
Contact: Dr. Joel Goodman, Pres.

Desc: Health care professionals, educators, counselors, therapists, business executives, and others interested in developing their sense of humor. Believes humor can be used as a constructive tool, personally and professionally. Provides speeches, training, grants, and programs on how to improve and apply one's sense of humor. *Type:* Association.

Hustler Busty Beauties
L.F.P., Inc.
8484 Wilshire Blvd., Ste. 900   Ph: (323)651-5400
Beverly Hills, CA 90211   Fax: (323)651-2741
E-mail: hustler@lfp.com; busty@lfp.com.

Contact: N. Morgen Hagen, Editor; Larry Flynt, Publisher; Allen Maine, Advertising Dir., (213)951-7907, fax: (213)651-5400.

Desc: Adult magazine. *Type:* Periodical.

Hustler Magazine
L.F.P., Inc.
8484 Wilshire Blvd., Ste. 900   Ph: (323)651-5400
Beverly Hills, CA 90211   Fax: (323)651-2741
E-mail: hustler@lfp.com
URL: http://www.hustler.com.

Contact: Allan MacDonell, Editor, amacdonell@lfp.com; Larry Flynt, Publisher; Allen Maine, Advertising Dir., (323)951-7907, fax: (323)651-0651, amaine@ifp.com.

Desc: Men's entertainment magazine. *Type:* Periodical.

IEG Sponsorship Report
IEG Sponsorship Report
640 North LaSalle, Ste. 600   Ph: (312)944-1727
Chicago, IL 60610-3777   Free: 800-834-4850
   Fax: (312)944-1897
E-mail: ieg@sponsorship.com
Contact: Lesa Ukman, Editor.

Desc: Monitors corporate sponsorship of sports, music, festivals, causes and the arts. Recurring features include a column titled Assertions and Who Does What in Sponsorship. *Type:* Newsletter.

The Improper Bostonian
Improper Publications, Inc.
45 Newbury St., Ste. 509   Ph: (617)859-1446
Boston, MA 02116   Fax: (617)859-1446
E-mail: improperb@aol.com.

Contact: Mark Semonian, Publisher; Nancy Gaines, Editor; Jim Pite, VP Sales/Marketing.

Desc: Newspaper. *Type:* Periodical.

Infotainment World
Game Pro Media Group
951 Mariners Island Blvd., No.   Ph: (415)349-4300
700   Fax: (415)349-7482
San Mateo, CA 94404-1561
E-mail: gpmg@gamepro.com
Contact: John Rousseau, Pres./CEO, (415)286-2525; Cyndy Sandor, VP/Assoc. Publisher, (415)286-2515; Elaine Starling, Marketing Dir., (415)286-2590; Wes Nihei, Editor-in-Chief, (415)286-2543; Suzanne McCloskey, Circulation Dir.

Desc: Video game magazine. *Type:* Periodical.

Interactive Update
Alexander & Associates
38 E. 29th St., 10th Fl.   Ph: (212)684-2333
New York, NY 10016   Fax: (212)684-0291
Contact: Michael Peck, Editor; Sally Plourde, Publisher.

Desc: Provides information on the interactive entertainment industry, focusing on software. *Type:* Newsletter.

The International American Sunbeam
Gerald L. Sprouse Publishing Co.
PO Drawer 830
Ooltewah, TN 37363
Contact: Gerald L. Sprouse, Editor and Publisher.
Desc: Alternative newspaper. *Type:* Periodical.

International Brotherhood of Magicians
11155 South Towne Sq.   Ph: (314)845-9200
St. Louis, MO 63123-7823   Fax: (314)845-9220
E-mail: no1inmagic@aol.com
URL: http://www.magician.org
Contact: Darleen Eads, Office Mgr., Exec.Sec.
Desc: Professional and semiprofessional magicians; suppliers, assistants, agents, and others interested in magic. Seeks to advance the art of magic in the field of amusement, entertainment, and culture. Promotes proper means of discouraging false or misleading advertising of effects, tricks, literature, merchandise, or actions appertaining to the magical arts; opposes exposures of principles of the art of magic, except in books on magic and magazines devoted to such art for the exclusive use of magicians and devotees of the art; encourages humane treatment and care of live animals whenever employed in magical performances. *Type:* Association.

International Pen Friends
Leslie Fox
PO Box 159
Hackensack, NJ 07602
Contact: Leslie Fox, Regional Rep.
Desc: Individuals who wish to correspond with people from different nations or cultures; correspondents are matched by age, sex, and language. Participants live in 188 countries and include speakers of 5 languages (English, German, Spanish, French, and Portuguese) send self-addressed stamped envelope for information to Leslie Fox c/o IPF. *Type:* Association.

Journal America
Journal America
PO Box 459   Ph: (973)728-8355
Hewitt, NJ 07421   Fax: (973)728-7128
E-mail: journal@warwick.net
URL: http://www.ajournal.com.
Contact: Glen Malmgren, Contact.
Desc: Consumer lifestyle magazine covering family living and the home. *Type:* Periodical.

Just for Men
721 Shore Acres Dr.   Ph: (914)698-0721
Mamaroneck, NY 10543
Contact: Lois Fenton, Editor.
Desc: Distributes men's clothing column. *Alt. Contact:* 721 Shore Acres Dr., Mamaroneck, NY 10543; telephone: (914)698-0721. *Type:* Periodical.

Kentucky Living
Kentucky Association of Electric Cooperatives
PO Box 32170   Ph: (502)451-2430
Louisville, KY 40232   Free: 800-595-4846
   Fax: (502)459-1611
Contact: Paul Wesslund, Editor and Publisher; Stephanie Dumeyer, Advertising Mgr.
Desc: Magazine on people, places, events, and history of Kentucky. *Type:* Periodical.

Kinky Fetishes
AJA Publishing
PO Box 70
Port Chester, NY 10573
Contact: Julie Silver, Editor; Wayne Shuster, Advertising Mgr.; Sean Michael, Circulation Mgr.

Desc: Consumer magazine covering erotica. *Type:* Periodical.

Koopersmith's Kreative Kingdom & Kalendar
1437 W. Rosemont Ste. 1W   Ph: (773)743-5341
Chicago, IL 60660-1319   Fax: (773)743-5395
E-mail: kooper@interaccess.com.
Contact: Adrienne Sioux Koppersmith, Founder/CEO.
Desc: Distributes daily, weekly, and monthly material focusing on goodwill, humanitarian, altruistic, and fun "holidates." *Alt. Contact:* 1437 W. Rosemont Ste. 1W, Chicago, IL 60660-1319; telephone: (773)743-5341; fax: (773)743-5395. *Type:* Periodical.

Las Vegas Insider
Donald Currier
PO Box 29274   Ph: (520)636-1649
Las Vegas, NV 89126   Free: 800-628-1686
   Fax: (520)636-5514
E-mail: amchb@primnet.com
Contact: Donald Currier, Editor.
Desc: Offers advice on low cost hotels, room bargains, food, gaming tips, and tourist information in Las Vegas, Reno, and Atlantic City. Recurring features include news of research, a calendar of events, job listings, book reviews, and notices of publications available. *Type:* Newsletter.

Lew Little Enterprises Inc.
42-C Spring Canyon   Ph: (520)432-8003
PO Box 47   Fax: (520)432-8004
Bisbee, AZ 85603-0047
Contact: Mary Ellen Corbett, Managing Editor; Lewis A. Little, Editor.
Alt. Contact: 42-C Spring Canyon, PO Box 47, Bisbee, AZ 85603-0047; telephone: (520)432-8003; fax: (520)432-8004. *Type:* Periodical.

Lifestyle
Alpha General Corp.
421 W. MacArthur Blvd.   Ph: (510)420-1381
Oakland, CA 94609   Fax: (510)420-1383
Contact: Brian Eastman, Editor; Marc Horwitz, Advertising Mgr.; Dave Sawle, Publisher; Gary Gold, Editor.
Desc: Magazine catering to the singles lifestyle. *Type:* Periodical.

Living in South Carolina
The Electric Cooperatives of South Carolina
808 Knox Abbott Dr.   Ph: (803)796-6060
Cayce, SC 29033   Fax: (803)796-6064
E-mail: livinginsc@aol.com.
Contact: John B. Bruce, Editor.
Desc: Electric cooperative magazine. *Type:* Periodical.

Llewellyn's New Worlds of Mind and Spirit
Llewellyn Publications
PO Box 64383   Ph: (651)291-1970
St. Paul, MN 55164-0383   Free: 800-843-6666
   Fax: (651)291-1908
E-mail: kitty@llewellyn.com; lwlpc@llewellyn.com.
URL: http://www.llewellyn.com; http://www.llewellyn.com.
Contact: Carl Llewellyn Weschcke, Publisher; Stephanie Clement, Marketing Mgr.
Desc: Catalog for readers interested in practical applications of astrology, psychology, occult philosophy, and inner awareness techniques. Includes reviews, articles, and news for the New Age community. *Type:* Periodical.

Maclean's

Maclean Hunter Ltd.
777 Bay St., 6th Fl.　　　　Ph: (416)596-5000
Toronto, ON, Canada M5W　Fax: (416)596-5552
1A7
E-mail: letters@macleans.ca.

Contact: Robert Lewis, Editor-in-Chief.

Desc: Newsmagazine. *Type:* Periodical.

Man Watchers

12308 Darlington Ave.
Los Angeles, CA 90089

Contact: Suzy Mallery, Pres. & Founder.

Desc: Women aged 18 and older. Presents "Well Worth Watching" cards to men; selects "ten top men in the world" annually. Conducts woman-man opinion research; maintains speakers' bureau and hall of fame; compiles statistics; sponsors Man of the 90s competitions. *Type:* Association.

Marie Claire

Hearst Magazines
959 8th Ave.　　　　　　Ph: (212)649-2000
New York, NY 10019-5905

Contact: Glenda Bailey, Editor-in-Chief; Cynthia Lewis, Publisher.

Desc: Lifestyle publication. *Alt. Contact:* 1790 Broadway, New York, NY 10019; telephone: (212)649-5000. *Type:* Periodical.

Men's Journal

Wenner Media
1290 Avenue of the Americas　Ph: (212)484-1616
New York, NY 10104　　　　Fax: (212)767-8209

Contact: Jann S. Wenner, Editor-in-Chief; John Rasmus, Editor; Kevin C. O'Malley, Publisher; Kent Brownridge, General Mgr.; Christopher Sachs, Advertising Dir.

Desc: Magazine focusing on men's leisure activities. *Type:* Periodical.

Miami New Times

New Times
2800 Biscayne Blvd., Ste. 100　Ph: (305)576-8000
PO Box 011591　　　　　　Fax: (305)571-7677
Miami, FL 33137
URL: http://www.miaminewtimes.com.

Contact: Jim Mullin, Editor; Tom Finkel, Managing Editor; Michael B. Cohen, Publisher.

Desc: Alternative Weekly. *Type:* Periodical.

Midwest Living Magazine

Meredith Corp.
1716 Locust St.　　　　　Ph: (515)284-3000
Des Moines, IA 50309-3023　Free: 800-678-2674
　　　　　　　　　　　　Fax: (515)284-3697

Contact: Dan Kaercher, Editor; Tom E. Benson, Publisher; Lyle C.R. Landon, Advertising Mgr.

Desc: Midwest regional lifestyle magazine featuring travel, food, home, and garden. *Type:* Periodical.

Mikero Entertainments

HC 4 Box 50-A　　　　　Ph: (210)833-5861
Blanco, TX 78606-9511

Contact: Mike Sheedy, Owner.

Desc: Distributes games, puzzles, and weekly publications. *Alt. Contact:* HC 4 Box 50-A, Blanco, TX 78606-9511; telephone: (210)833-5861. *Type:* Periodical.

The Moneybook

TeeVee Moneysaver, Inc., Publications
52 West Main St.　　　　Ph: (908)722-6270
PO Box 954　　　　　　Fax: (908)722-7303
Somerville, NJ 08876

Contact: George E. Vedrook, Publisher; Richard E. Schmelz, Editor.

Desc: Community shopping magazine. *Type:* Periodical.

Motion Picture and Television Fund

23388 Mulholland Dr.　　Ph: (818)876-1888
Woodland Hills, CA 91364　Fax: (818)876-1079

Contact: William Haug, Exec.Dir.

Desc: Welfare agency of the motion picture and television industry, supported by contributions (1-2% of salary) from employees in the industry. Conducts drug and alcohol abuse programs; provides maintenance and medical care. Operates Motion Picture Country House/Hospital, permanent home for the elderly, and five outpatient health centers. *Type:* Association.

Movie Reviews Data Base

Cineman Syndicate
PO Box 4433　　　　　Ph: (914)692-4572
Middletown, NY 10941-4433
E-mail: MCI Mail: 213-9111
URL: http://www.minireviews.com

Contact: Jay A. Brown, Publisher., (914)692-4572, fax: (914)692-8311, cineman@frontiernet.net.

Desc: Contains more than 7000 movie reviews written for syndication by film critic Jay A. Brown. *Available:* America Online, Inc.; Bloomberg Financial Markets; Infonautics Corporation; SoftLine Information, Inc. *Type:* Database.

National Arbor Day Foundation

100 Arbor Ave.　　　　Ph: (402)474-5655
Nebraska City, NE 68410　Fax: (402)474-0820
URL: http://www.arborday.org

Contact: Gary Brienzo, Infomation Coor.

Desc: National associations, corporations, communities, state government agencies, and individuals dedicated to tree planting and environmental stewardship. Organized to: properly and officially promote the observance of Arbor Day each year; create an awareness and appreciation among all peoples through all forms of communication of the fundamental role that trees play in day-to-day existence; endorse, support, or otherwise implement education programs that will stimulate and inspire youth to better understand the bounty and joy of trees; recognize achievement among all elements of society through an annual awards program for contributions made to the understanding, appreciation, conservation, and wise use of trees; initiate programs that encourage the planting of trees and create an awareness of those resource programs that will assure the perpetuation and growing abundance of this basic resource; establish and maintain the Arbor Day Farm at Nebraska City, Nebraska, to educate Americans about Arbor Day, trees as a natural resource, and tree planting; raise and collect funds through gifts, contributions, and other funding programs. *Type:* Association.

National Fantasy Fan Club for Disneyana Enthusiasts

PO Box 19212　　　　　Ph: (714)731-4705
Irvine, CA 92623-9212

Contact: Frank Pascale, III, Pres.

Desc: Fans and collectors of anything to do with Walt Disney products. Promotes enjoyment of any past, present, or future Disney cartoon characters, films, amusement parks, and merchandise. *Type:* Association.

National Frumps of America

PO Box 1047　　　　　Ph: (407)644-3431
Winter Park, FL 32790

Contact: Barbara Hovanetz, Pres. & Founder.

Desc: "Ordinary, average, grass roots" people organized to celebrate the joys of things mundane. Believes that "ordinary" people can be extraordinary. Bestows Frump of the Year award. *Type:* Association.

National Lampoon

J 2 Communications
10850 Wilshire Blvd., Ste. 1000　Ph: (310)474-5252
Los Angeles, CA 90024　　　　Fax: (310)474-1219

Contact: Duncan Murray, Publisher.

Desc: Magazine featuring humor and satire. *Type:* Periodical.

New Times

New Time
1201 E. Jefferson　　　　Ph: (602)271-0040
PO Box 2510　　　　　　Fax: (602)340-8806
Phoenix, AZ 85002
URL: http://www.phoenixnewtimes.com.

Contact: Jeremy Voas, Editor; Joe Larkin, Advertising Dir., (602)258-1073, fax: (602)495-9954, joe_larkin@newtimes.com; Michele Laven, Publisher.

Desc: Weekly newspaper serving as a comprehensive news, arts, entertainment and resta urant guide for Phoenix. *Type:* Periodical.

New York Entertainment Scene

EWA Publications
2446 E. 65th St.　　　　Ph: (718)763-7034
Brooklyn, NY 11234　　　Fax: (718)763-7035

Contact: Kevin Browne, Editor; Justin Baron, Publisher; Bill Tarrington, Advertising Mgr.

Desc: Community newspaper. *Type:* Periodical.

The New Yorker

Advance Publications
20 W. 43rd St.　　　　　Ph: (212)840-3800
New York, NY 10036　　　Fax: (212)536-5735

Contact: Tina Brown, Editor.

Desc: Magazine publishing news editorials, short fiction, poetry, and art reviews. *Type:* Periodical.

Now

Now Communications Inc.
150 Danforth Ave.　　　Ph: (416)461-0871
Toronto, ON, Canada M4K　Fax: (416)461-2886
1N1
E-mail: letters@now.com.
URL: http://www.now.com.

Contact: Alice Klein, CEO & Exec. Editor, alicek@now.com; Michael Hollett, Editor and Publisher, michaelh@now.com; David Logan, Operations Mgr., davidl@now.com; Marina Glogovac, Human Resources Mgr., marinag@now.com.

Desc: Alternative newspaper (tabloid). *Type:* Periodical.

Official Gumby Fan Club

PO Box 3905　　　　　Ph: (847)352-6565
Schaumburg, IL 60168　　Fax: (847)352-9607
Contact: A. J. Marsiglia, Dir.

Desc: Fans of the animated character Gumby who was created in 1956 by Art Clokey and currently appears in a syndicated cartoon series. Makes available discounts on Gumby-related items; keeps members informed of the character's public and media appearances. *Type:* Association.

Ohio Magazine

Ohio Magazine
62 E. Broad Street   Ph: (614)461-5083
Columbus, OH 43215   Free: 800-426-4624
                                          Fax: (614)461-8717
URL: http://www.ohiomagazine.com.
Contact: Roy Wolford, General Mgr.; Shannon Jackson,
Editor.
Desc: Regional magazine. *Type:* Periodical.

Oklahoma Living Magazine

Oklahoma Living Magazine
PO Box 54309   Ph: (405)478-1455
Oklahoma City, OK 73154-   Fax: (405)478-0246
    1309
Contact: Lu Hollander, Editor; Cly de D. Blythe, Publish-
er; Linda Haneborg, Advertising Mgr.
Desc: Lifestyle magazine. *Type:* Periodical.

The Onion

Onion, Inc.
33 University Square, Ste. 270   Ph: (608)256-1372
Madison, WI 53715   Free: 800-695-4376
                                          Fax: (608)256-2535
URL: http://www.theonion.com.
Contact: Scott Dikkers, Editor; Peter Haise, Publisher; An-
drew Smith, National Advertising Mgr., smith@theonion.
com.
Desc: Humor, satire, and entertainment newspaper. *Type:*
Periodical.

Orange County Living

Affluent Target Marketing
1219 N Tustin Ave.   Ph: (714)632-9810
Anaheim, CA 92807   Free: 800-662-5577
                                          Fax: (714)632-3435
Contact: Morris Miller, Contact.
Desc: Consumer magazine covering home improvement
for an affluent audience. *Type:* Periodical.

Pacific News Group

Pacific News Group
206 N. Kennebec Dr.   Ph: (714)637-5342
Anaheim, CA 92807   Fax: (714)637-4701
E-mail: pacnewgr@aol.com
Contact: Randy Matin, Editor; William Preston, Travel;
Candace Chambers, Fashion; Tim Adams, Theatre; C.B.
George, Books; Randy Matin, Elec., Interactive Media,
Video/Music.
Desc: Entertainment and travel features syndicate. *Type:*
Periodical.

Parent's Guide

Penn Media Group, LLC
366 Easton Rd.   Ph: (215)343-8400
Warrington, PA 18976   Fax: (215)343-8406
Contact: Mary Arsenault, Editor, rgmary@aol.com; Stephen J. Arsenault, Editor, rgstevea@aol.com; Eugene Ter-
ramani, Sales Mgr., rggene@aol.com.
Desc: Magazine focused on parenting. Includes advice columns and lists of activities in the Philadelphia, PA metropolitan area. *Type:* Periodical.

Pensez-Y Bien!

Editions E.J.S. and Edibec
325 Marais St., Ste. 227   Ph: (418)686-1940
Vanier, PQ, Canada G1M 3R3   Fax: (418)686-1942
Desc: Consumer magazine for public employees in Que-
bec, Canada. Official publication of Services Financiers
MFQ Inc. *Type:* Periodical.

Penthouse

Penthouse International Ltd.
General Media Communications
11 Penn Plaza, 12th Fl.   Ph: (212)702-6000
New York, NY 10001-2006   Fax: (212)702-6262
E-mail: webmaster@penthousemag.com.
URL: www.penthousemag.com.
Contact: Peter Bloch, Editor, peter.bloch@generalmedia.
com; Bruce Garfunkel, Assoc. Pub., fax: (212)702-6275,
bruce.garfunkel@generalmedia.com.
Desc: Men's monthly magazine. *Type:* Periodical.

Penthouse Variations

General Media
11 Penn Plaza, 12th Fl.   Ph: (212)702-6000
New York, NY 10001   Fax: (212)702-6262
E-mail: variations@generalmedia.com.
URL: http://www.penthousemag.com/variations.
Contact: VK McCarty, v.k.mccarty@generalmedia.com.
Desc: Consumer magazine covering erotica for men and
couples. *Type:* Periodical.

People Weekly

Time Inc.
Time-Life Bldg., Rockefeller   Ph: (212)522-1212
    Center   Fax: (212)522-0315
1271 Avenue of the Americas
New York, NY 10020
Contact: Ann Moore, President; Nora McAniff, Publisher;
Jeremy Koch, Vice President.
Desc: Magazine featuring personalities and entertainment
news. *Type:* Periodical.

Play Meter—Directory Issue

Skybird Publishing Co., Inc.
PO Box 24170   Ph: (504)488-7003
New Orleans, LA 70184   Fax: (504)488-7083
E-mail: news@playmeter.com.
URL: http://www.playmeter.com.
Contact: Valerie Cognevich, Editor; Bonnie Theard, Editor; Carol P. Lally, Publisher; Steve White, Special Projects Editor.
Desc: About 500 firms that manufacture and distribute
coin-operated video and electronic games and other
amusement machines; 300 firms that supply the industry;
state and national trade associations; exporters and importers; foreign manufacturers and distributors. *Type:* Directory.

Playboy

Playboy
680 N. Lake Shore Dr.   Ph: (312)751-8000
Chicago, IL 60611   Fax: (312)751-2818
URL: http://www.playboy.com.
Contact: Arthur Kretchmer, Editorial Dir.; Richard Kins-
ler, Exec. VP & Publisher; Hugh M. Hefner, Editor-in-
Chief.
Desc: Entertainment magazine for men. *Type:* Periodical.

Playgirl

Playgirl, Inc.
801 2nd Ave.   Ph: (212)661-7878
New York, NY 10017   Free: 800-877-6139
                                          Fax: (212)697-6343
URL: www.playgirlmag.com.
Contact: Judy Cole, Editor-in-Chief; Patrice Baldwin,
Managing Editor.
Desc: Adult entertainment magazine for women. *Type:* Pe-
riodical.

Plunkett's Entertainment and Media Industry Almanac

Plunkett Research, Ltd.
PO Drawer 541737   Ph: (713)932-0000
Houston, TX 77254-1737   Fax: (713)932-7080
E-mail: sales@plunkettresearch.com
URL: http://www.plunkettresearch.com.
Contact: Jack W. Plunkett, Publisher.
Desc: 400 companies in radio, television, film, publishing,
electronic media, new media, and entertainment. Princi-
pal content of publication is statistics, trends, finance, and
individuals of the media industries. *Type:* Directory.

Popular Mechanics

Hearst Magazines
959 8th Ave.   Ph: (212)649-2000
New York, NY 10019-5905
URL: http://www.popularmechanics.com.
Contact: Joe Oldham, Editor, joldham@Hearst.com; Jay
McGill, Publisher, fax: (212)956-5457, jmcgill@Hearst.
com.
Desc: Magazine focusing on autos, the home, and leisure.
Prints Latin American Edition. *Alt. Contact:* 224 W. 57th
St., New York, NY 10019; telephone: (212)649-3098;
fax: (212)586-5562. *Type:* Periodical.

Portland Rose Festival Association

220 NW 2nd Ave.   Ph: (503)227-2681
Portland, OR 97209   Fax: (503)227-6603
URL: http://www.rosefestival.org
Contact: Dick Clark, Exec.Mgr.
Desc: Businesses and individuals promoting local civic
Rose Festival. *Type:* Association.

Pre-Vue Entertainment Magazine

National Pre-Vue Network Inc.
7825 Fay Ave.   Ph: (619)456-5577
La Jolla, CA 92037   Fax: (619)542-0114
E-mail: prevuemag@aol.com.
Desc: Movie magazine. *Type:* Periodical.

Puzzle Feature Syndicate

29971 Pebble Beach Dr.   Free: 800-292-4308
Sun City, CA 92586
Contact: Jackie Mathews, Editor.
Desc: Distributes crossword puzzles and word puzzles. *Alt.
Contact:* 29971 Pebble Beach Dr., Sun City, CA 92586;
toll-free: 800-292-4308. *Type:* Periodical.

Recreation News

Recreation News
PO Box 32335   Ph: (202)965-6960
Washington, DC 20007-0635   Fax: (202)965-6964
E-mail: recreation_news@mcimail.com.
Contact: Henry Dunbar, Editor; Michael T. Kapsa, Pub-
lisher.
Desc: Newspaper focusing on recreational activities in the
Washington, D.C. area. *Type:* Periodical.

Restaurant/Food Review

EWA Publications
2446 E. 65th St.   Ph: (718)763-7034
Brooklyn, NY 11234   Fax: (718)763-7035
Contact: Kevin Browne, Editor; Justin Baron, Publisher;
Bill Tarrington, Advertising Mgr.
Desc: Community newspaper. *Type:* Periodical.

Right On!

Sterling/Macfadden Partnership
233 Park Ave. S.   Ph: (212)780-3500
New York, NY 10003   Fax: (212)780-3555
Contact: Cynthia Horner, Editor, (212)780-3519, fax:
(212)780-3571; Allen Tuller, Publisher; Mitch Hers-
kowitz, Advertising Dir., (212)490-1715.

Desc: Black young adult entertainment magazine. *Type:* Periodical.

Robb Report

Robb Report
1 Acton Pl.　　　　　　　　Ph: (978)263-7749
Acton, MA 01720　　　　　Free: 800-229-7622
　　　　　　　　　　　　　Fax: (978)263-0722

E-mail: robb@robbreport.com.
URL: http://www.robbreport.com.

Contact: Steven Caste, Editor; Dan Phillips, Publisher, fax: (978)263-3812; Rick Sedler, Advertising Dir., fax: (978)263-3812.

Desc: Lifestyle magazine focusing on vintage and exotic automobiles, lifestyle and interiors, upscale travel, boating, investment opportunities, technology, profiles, and recreation. *Type:* Periodical.

The Rocket

BAM Media, Publishers
2028 5th Ave.　　　　　　Ph: (206)728-7625
Seattle, WA 98121　　　　Fax: (206)728-8827
E-mail: rocketsea@aol.com.
URL: http://www.musicuniverse.com.

Contact: Charles Cross, Editor; Joe Ehrban, Music Editor; Wendy Geldien, Advertising Mgr.

Desc: Music entertainment magazine. *Type:* Periodical.

Rural Living

Virginia, Maryland, and Delaware Association of Electric Cooperatives
4201 Dominion Blvd., Ste. 101　Ph: (804)346-3344
Glen Allen, VA 23060　　　　　Fax: (804)346-3448
URL: http://www.odec.com/aec/aecmagazine.

Contact: Richard G. Johnstone, Jr., Editor, (804)968-4087, fax: (804)346-3448, rjohnstone@odec.com.

Desc: Magazine featuring articles on energy efficiency, electrical saftey, and other utility issues as well as offering features on people and places in rural and suburban Virginia. *Type:* Periodical.

Ruralite

Ruralite Services, Inc.
2040 A St.　　　　　　　　Ph: (503)357-2105
PO Box 558　　　　　　　 Fax: (503)357-8615
Forest Grove, OR 97116
E-mail: ruralite@europa.com.

Contact: Curtis Condon, Editor.

Desc: Consumer magazine for customers of specific consumer-owned utilities throughout Alaska, Washington, Wyoming, California, Idaho, Nevada, and Utah. *Type:* Periodical.

The San Francisco and Bay Area Guide

San Francisco Guide, Inc.
2087 Union St. No. 1　　　Ph: (415)775-2212
San Francisco, CA 94123-4102　Fax: (415)441-7773
E-mail: info@sfguide.com.

Contact: Eric Symons, Sales Mgr.; Linda Schreibman, Publisher/Contact.

Desc: Entertainment guide magazine. *Type:* Periodical.

San Francisco Style International

PO Box 330063　　　　　　Ph: (415)788-6589
San Francisco, CA 94133-4063

Alt. Contact: PO Box 330063, San Francisco, CA 94133-4063; telephone: (415)788-6589. *Type:* Periodical.

Saturday Night

Saturday Night
184 Front St. E., Ste. 400　Ph: (416)368-7237
Toronto, ON, Canada M5A　Free: 800-267-6568
　4N3　　　　　　　　　 Fax: (416)368-5112
E-mail: editorial@saturdaynight.ca.
URL: http://www.enews.ca.

Contact: Paul Tough, Editor, tough@saturdaynight.ca; Maureen Cavan, Publisher, mcavan@saturdaynight.ca; Kathryn Brownlie, V.P. of Advertising Sales, brownlie@saturdaynight.ca; Geoffrey Dawe, Advertising Mgr.

Desc: Magazine presenting opinion and comment on Canadian politics, business, and culture. *Type:* Periodical.

Scrambl-Gram Inc.

1772 State Rd.　　　　　　Ph: (216)923-2397
Cuyahoga Falls, OH 44223　Fax: (216)923-4346

Contact: Charles R. Elum, President; Scott Bowers, General Mgr.; Mary Elum, Sales Dir.; R.A. Faloon, Sales Dev.

Desc: Distributes crosswords and other puzzles; promotions to radio and print media. *Alt. Contact:* 1772 State Rd., Cuyahoga Falls, OH 44223; telephone: (216)923-2397; fax: (216)923-4346. *Type:* Periodical.

Seattle Weekly

Quickfish Media, Inc.
1008 Western Ave., Ste. 300　Ph: (206)623-0500
Seattle, WA 98104-1006　　　Fax: (206)467-4338
URL: http://seattleweekly.com.

Contact: Michael Crystal, Publisher, (206)467-4334, mcrystal@seattleweekly.com; Ellen Cole, Advertising Dir., (206)467-4341, fax: (206)467-4355.

Desc: Alternative news magazine (tabloid) focusing on public affairs, arts, entertainment, and lifestyle in Seattle. *Type:* Periodical.

SF Weekly

SF Weekly
185 Berry St., No. 3800　　Ph: (415)541-0700
San Francisco, CA 94107　 Fax: (415)777-1839

Contact: Jim Rizzi, Publisher; John Mecklin, Editor-in-Chief; Bill Wyman, Arts & Entertainment Editor; Chris Brand, Art Dir.

Desc: Newsmagazine. *Type:* Periodical.

Sioux Falls Shopping News Informer

Sioux Falls Shopping News, Inc.
4005 S. Western Ave.　　　Ph: (605)339-3633
PO Box 5184　　　　　　　Free: 800-843-6805
Sioux Falls, SD 57117-5148　Fax: (605)335-6873

Contact: K.A. Lesnar, Publisher.

Desc: TV and entertainment supplement. *Type:* Periodical.

SLAM Magazine

Imp-Press Publications
509 St. Clair Ave. W.
PO Box 73585
Toronto, ON, Canada M6C
　1C0

Desc: Alternative arts magazine. *Type:* Periodical.

Soaring Spirit

Valley of the Sun Publishing Co.
PO Box 38　　　　　　　　Ph: (562)488-7880
Malibu, CA 90265　　　　 Fax: (562)488-7870
URL: http://www.sutphenpublishing.com.

Contact: Dick Sutphen, Editor.

Desc: Magazine covering metaphysical New Age philosophy with complete catalog listing of Valley of the Sun products. *Type:* Periodical.

South Dakota High Liner

South Dakota Highliner
222 West Pleasant Dr.　　Ph: (605)224-8823
PO Box 1138　　　　　　　Free: 800-201-8823
Pierre, SD 57501　　　　　Fax: (605)224-4430

Contact: Jennifer Stalley, Editor, jenniferl@sdvca.com.

Desc: Magazine for South Dakota. *Type:* Periodical.

Southern Living

Southern Progress
2100 Lakeshore Dr.　　　 Ph: (205)877-6000
Birmingham, AL 35209-6721　Free: 888-737-3529
　　　　　　　　　　　　　Fax: (205)877-6600

Contact: John A. Floyd, Jr., Editor; Michael Carlton, Exec. Editor; Eleanor Griffin, Exec. Editor; Kaye Mabry Adams, Exec. Editor; Scott Sheppard, Group Publisher; Kevin Lynch, Publisher; Greg Keyes, VP, Marketing; Rich Smyth, Advertising Dir.

Desc: Magazine featuring food, homes, garden, travel, and features edited for southern tastes. *Type:* Periodical.

Stereophile

Stereophile Inc.
208 Delgado St.　　　　　Ph: (505)982-2366
Santa Fe, NM 87501　　　Fax: (505)989-8791
E-mail: jatkinson@sterophile.com.
URL: http://www.stereophile.com.

Contact: Larry Archibald, Publisher; John Atkinson, Editor; Pip Tannenbaum, Ad Copy Mgr.; Mary Olivern, Circulation Dir.

Desc: Consumer magazine covering hi-fi equipment and audio and recording news. *Type:* Periodical.

Suffolk County Life

Suffolk Life Newspapers
PO Box 9167　　　　　　　Ph: (516)369-0800
Riverhead, NY 11901　　　Fax: (516)369-5390
E-mail: stnewsroom@hamptons.com

Contact: David J. Willmott, Editor and Publisher; Lou Grasso, Managing Editor.

Desc: Community newspaper. *Type:* Periodical.

*Surface

*Surface
7 Isadora Duncan　　　　　Ph: (415)929-5100
San Francisco, CA 94102　 Fax: (415)929-5103
E-mail: surfacemag@surfacemag.com.

Contact: Richard Klein, Publisher, rklein@surfacemag.com; Riley John-Donnell, Publisher; Jeremy Lin, Editorial Dir.; Steve McDonald, Advertising Dir.

Desc: Magazine covering fashion, arts, and entertainment. *Type:* Periodical.

Swank

Swank Publications
210 Rte. 4E, Ste. 401　　　Ph: (201)843-4004
Paramus, NJ 07652　　　　Fax: (201)843-8636
E-mail: genesismag@aol.com

Contact: Paul Gamblio, Editor; John Dee, Advertising Mgr.

Desc: Men's magazine featuring erotica, sports, and adventure. *Type:* Periodical.

Symbol

Pasco Publishing, Inc.
120 Interstate N. Pkwy. E., No.　Ph: (770)956-1207
　445　　　　　　　　　　　　　Free: 888-679-6265
Atlanta, GA 30339　　　　　　 Fax: (770)988-8976
E-mail: symbolmag@aol.com.

Contact: Jane Gaston, Managing Editor, gastonpeac@aol.com; Gregory A. Caccavale, Publisher.

Desc: Lifestyle magazine. *Type:* Periodical.

'TEEN

Petersen Publishing Co., L.L.C.

6420 Wilshire Blvd.
Los Angeles, CA 90048-5515

Ph: (323)782-2350
Fax: (323)782-2704

Contact: Linda Platzner, Executive Publisher, (212)886-3600; Launlanne Murphy, Advertising Dir.

Desc: Magazine covering beauty, health, fashion, and self-improvement. *Type:* Periodical.

TeeVee Moneysaver (Edition 1)

TeeVee Moneysaver, Inc., Publications

52 West Main St.
PO Box 954
Somerville, NJ 08876

Ph: (908)722-6270
Fax: (908)722-7303

Contact: George E. Vedrook, Publisher; Frank Cardell, Editor.

Desc: Free shopper. *Type:* Periodical.

Tennessee Magazine

Tennessee Electric Cooperative Association

710 Spence Ln.
PO Box 100912
Nashville, TN 37224

Ph: (615)367-9284
Fax: (615)367-2495

E-mail: thetennmag@aol.com

Contact: Cathleen Swiney, Editor, cswiney@juno.com; Robin Conover, Production Mgr.; Ron Bell, Art Director; Susan Pilgreen, Advertising Mgr.; Trish Milburn, Staff Writer.

Desc: Rural electric magazine. *Type:* Periodical.

Texas Southern University

Biochemistry and Molecular Biology Laboratory

3201 Wheeler Ave.
Houston, TX 77004

Ph: (713)313-7990
Fax: (713)313-7932

Contact: Dr. Sunday Fadulu, chm.

Desc: Cell biology and genetics, emphasizing control of gene expression in normal cells and carcinogenesis, particularly isolation and purification of deprimerones (low molecular-weight peptides). *Type:* Research center.

This Side of 60

PO Box 332
North Newton, KS 67117

Ph: (316)283-2309
Fax: (316)284-0500

E-mail: thisside60@aol.com.

Contact: Marie Snider, Self-Syndicator.

Desc: Distributes weekly column--This Side of 60. *Alt. Contact:* PO Box 332, North Newton, KS 67117; telephone: (316)283-2309; fax: (316)284-0500. *Type:* Periodical.

Time Out New York

Time Out New York

627 Broadway, 7th Fl.
New York, NY 10012

Ph: (212)539-4495

E-mail: letters@timeoutny.com.

Contact: Cyndi Stivers, Editor-in-Chief, cyndis@timeoutny.com; Alison Tocci, Publisher, fax: (212)677-9665, alisont@timeoutny.com.

Desc: Arts and entertainment magazine. *Type:* Periodical.

Toronto Life

Key Publishers Co. Ltd.

59 Front St. E.
Toronto, ON, Canada M5E
1B3

Ph: (416)364-3334
Fax: (416)861-1169

E-mail: lifeline@for-lifelin; online@torontolife.com.
URL: http://www.lifeline.com; http://www.torontolife.com.

Contact: William Duron, Publisher; John Macfarlane, Editor; Martin White, Advertising Dir.

Desc: City, business, politics, lifestyle, entertainment, and general interest magazine. *Type:* Periodical.

Tournament of Roses Association

391 S. Orange Grove Blvd.
Pasadena, CA 91184

Ph: (626)449-4100
Fax: (626)449-9066

Contact: John H. B. French, CEO.

Desc: Individuals living or working within 15 miles of Pasadena, CA who volunteer their services to help organize and stage the annual Tournament of Roses Parade and Rose Bowl football game (935). Maintains 33 committees including, Community Relations, Coronation, Equestrian, Float Construction, Float Entry, Football, Judging, Music, Press Relations, Television and Radio, and University Entertainment. *Type:* Association.

Tribute

Tribute Publishing Co.

900-A Don Mills Rd., Ste. 1000
Don Mills, ON, Canada N3C
1V6

Ph: (416)445-0544
Fax: (416)445-2894

Contact: Sandra I. Stewart, Publisher/Editorial Dir.; Brian A. Stewart, Publisher.

Desc: Movie/entertainment magazine for theater patrons. *Type:* Periodical.

Troika

Lone Tout Publications, Inc.

PO Box 1006
Weston, CT 06883

Ph: (203)227-5377
Fax: (203)222-9332

E-mail: etroika@aol.com
URL: troikamagazine.com.

Contact: Celia Meadow, Editor; Greg Weber, Advertising Mgr.; Alvin Averill, Circulation Mgr.

Desc: Consumer lifestyle magazine. *Type:* Periodical.

Turtle Force - The Official Fan Club of the Teenage Mutant Ninja Turtles

Box 3974
Schaumburg, IL 60168-3974

Ph: (847)352-6565
Fax: (847)352-9607

Contact: A. J. Marsiglia, Exec. Officer.

Desc: Represents those interested in the Teenage Mutant Ninja Turtles. Promotes Teenage Mutant Ninja Turtles paraphenalia. *Type:* Association.

TV Crosswords

Hachette Filipacchi Magazines, Inc.

1633 Broadway, 41st Fl.
New York, NY 10019

Ph: (212)767-6000
Fax: (212)989-4561

Contact: Linda Montera, Editor; Patrice Listfield, Publisher.

Desc: TV-theme crossword puzzles magazine. *Type:* Periodical.

Us

Wenner Media

1290 Avenue of the Americas
New York, NY 10104

Ph: (212)484-1616
Fax: (212)767-8209

Contact: Barbara O'Dair, Editor; Andrew Amill, Publisher; Lisa Kennedy, Managing Editor; Kent Brownridge, General Mgr.

Desc: Magazine containing articles on entertainment personalities and current events. Features television and film, fashion, fads, politics, business, travel, and trends. *Type:* Periodical.

USA Weekend

Gannett Co., Inc.

1100 Wilson Blvd.
Arlington, VA 22234

Ph: (703)284-6000
Free: 800-872-0001

E-mail: usaw@usaweekend.com.
URL: http://www.usaweekend.com.

Contact: Marcia Bullard, Editor/Pres.; Chuck Gabrielson, Publisher; William Coakley, VP, Operations; Beth Lawrence, VP, Advertising; Dave Barber, VP, Newspaper Relations; Thomas Meisel, VP, Production.

Desc: General interest Sunday newspaper magazine. *Alt. Contact:* 1100 Wilson Blvd., Arlington, VA 22234-0001; telephone: (703)276-3400; fax: (703)276-5518; toll-free: 800-729-2992. *Type:* Periodical.

Vanity Fair

Conde Nast Publications, Inc.

140 E. 45th St., 39th Fl.
New York, NY 10017

Ph: (212)880-8800
Free: 800-223-0780
Fax: (212)880-8248

E-mail: letters@brides.com

Desc: General editorial magazine. *Type:* Periodical.

Vermont Life

Vermont Life Magazine

6 Baldwin St.
Montpelier, VT 05602

Ph: (802)828-3241
Fax: (802)828-3366

E-mail: vtlife@lif.state.vt.us
URL: http://www.state.vt.us/vtlife.

Contact: Thomas K. Slayton, Editor, (802)828-5538, tslayton@lif.state.vt.us; Andrew Jackson, Advertising Mgr., (802)828-3244, ajackson@lif.state.vt.us.

Desc: Regional interest magazine featuring the people, events, and heritage that make Vermont unique. *Type:* Periodical.

Western Itasca Review & Deerpath Shopper

Lebhar-Friedman, Inc.

425 Park Ave.
New York, NY 10022-3556

Ph: (212)756-5228
Free: 800-453-2427
Fax: (212)756-5120

Contact: Rick Van Warner, Editor; James C. Doherty, Publisher.

Desc: Local newspaper and shopper *Type:* Periodical.

Western Living

Telemedia Publishing

555 W. 12th Ave, Ste. 300
SouthEast Tower
Vancouver, BC, Canada V5Z
4L4

Ph: (604)877-7732
Fax: (604)877-4848

Contact: Carol Ann Rule, Editor; Greg Hrychorchuk, Publisher; Joanne Owens, Advertising Mgr.

Desc: Lifestyle magazine. *Alt. Contact:* 10301 108th St., Ste. 201, Edmonton, AB, Canada T5J 1L7; telephone: (403)424-7171; fax: (403)425-6488. *Type:* Periodical.

What's On Magazine

What's On Magazine

4425 S. Industrial Rd.
Las Vegas, NV 89103

Ph: (702)891-8811
Free: 800-494-2876
Fax: (702)891-8804

E-mail: whatson@wizard.com.
URL: http://www.whats-on.com; http://www.ilovevegas.com.

Contact: Haley Hertz, Exec. Editor, haley@ilovevegas.com; Murray Hertz, Publisher; Stacey Hertz, Managing Editor, stacey@ilovevegas.com; Michael Dunn, Art Dir., michael@ilovevegas.com; Mel Carter, Distribution Dir.; Barry Berlin, Acct. Exec.

Desc: Guiding people to the best of Las Vegas *Type:* Periodical.

Wilton Lifestyles

Brooks Community Newspapers, Inc.

542 Westport Ave.
Norwalk, CT 06851

Ph: (203)226-6311
Fax: (203)227-6864

E-mail: bcnews3@netakis.com

Contact: Louise Lancaster-Keim, Editor; Kevin Lally, President; Ida Culhane, Sales Mgr.; B. V. Brooks, Publisher.

Desc: Community newspaper. *Type:* Periodical.

Wisconsin REC News

Wisconsin Federation of Co-ops
30 W. Mifflin St. No. 401
Madison, WI 53703

Contact: Perry Baird, Editor.

Desc: Magazine (tabloid) focusing on farm and home electrification. *Type:* Periodical.

Your Life Matters

Your Life Matters
8058 Pinnacle Peak Ave.   Ph: (702)222-1998
Las Vegas, NV 89113   Fax: (702)222-1940
URL: http://janetgreeson.com.

Contact: Janet Greeson, Editor, janetgreeson@aol.com;
Eugene Boyle, Editor.

Desc: Lifestyles magazine. *Type:* Periodical.

Environment

Acid Rain

Congressional Information Service, Inc. (CIS)
4520 East-West Hwy., Suite   Ph: (301)654-1550
    800
Bethesda, MD 20814-3389
E-mail: 12425 (DIALMAIL)
URL: http://www.cispubs.com

Contact: User Support.

Desc: Contains more than 4000 citations and abstracts of the world's published literature relating to acid rain research, development, policy, causes, and effects worldwide. *Available:* European Information Network Services (EINS). *Type:* Database.

America the Beautiful Fund

1730 K St. NW, Ste. 1002   Ph: (202)638-1649
Washington, DC 20006   Free: 800-522-3557

Contact: Nanine Bilski, Pres.

Desc: Offers recognition, technical support, and small seed grants to private citizens and community groups to initiate new local action projects that improve the quality of the environment. Projects affect environmental design, land preservation, green plantings, civic arts, and historical and cultural preservation, through citizens' volunteer services. *Type:* Association.

Arizona Health Services Department

Public Health Services

Epidemiology and Disease Control

Environmental Health Office

3815 N. Black Canyon Hwy.   Ph: (602)230-5808
Phoenix, AZ 85015   Fax: (602)230-5959

Contact: Lee A. Bland, Chf.

Desc: Environmental health. *Type:* Research center.

Arizona Health Services Department

Public Health Services

State Laboratory Services

Environmental and Analytical Chemistry Office

1520 W. Adams   Ph: (602)542-1188
Phoenix, AZ 85007-2698   Fax: (602)542-1169

Contact: Patricia Adler, Mgr.

Desc: Environmental and analytical chemistry. *Type:* Research center.

Arizona Health Services Department

Public Health Services

State Laboratory Services

Environmental and Clinical Microbiology Office

1520 W. Adams   Ph: (602)542-1188
Phoenix, AZ 85007-2698   Fax: (602)542-1169
URL: http://www.hs.state.az.us

Contact: William Slanta, Chf.

Desc: Microbiology and environmental microbiology. *Type:* Research center.

BNA Daily Environment Report

The Bureau of National Affairs, Inc. (BNA)
1231 25th St. NW   Ph: (202)452-4200
Washington, DC 20037
E-mail: bnaplus@bna.com
URL: http://bna.com/mkt/hrl/hrlwdec.htm
Contact: BNA PLUS, (202)452-4323, fax: (202)822-8092, bnaplus@bna.com.

Desc: Contains information on legislation, regulation, litigation, budget matters, enforcement and industry actions on national, state, and international environmental issues. Topics covered include air and water pollution control, hazardous substances, solid waste, recycling, drinking water, oil and gas, radioactive wastes. *Available:* LEXIS-NEXIS, LEXIS; West Group. *Type:* Database.

BNA International Environment Daily

The Bureau of National Affairs, Inc. (BNA)
1231 25th St. NW   Ph: (202)452-4200
Washington, DC 20037
E-mail: bnaplus@bna.com
URL: http://bna.com/mkt/hrl/hrlwdec.htm
Desc: Contains information on pollution control activity by federal and international courts and legislatures, regulatory agencies, and private organizations that affect air pollution, water pollution, solid waste mangement, hazardous waste, oil pollution, natural resources utilization, and mining policies. Subject coverage also includes world climate change, environmental policy trends, and debt-for-nature issues. *Available:* LEXIS-NEXIS, NEXIS; West Group, WESTLAW; LEXIS-NEXIS, LEXIS. *Type:* Database.

Center for International Development and Environment

1709 New York Ave. NW   Ph: (202)462-0900
Washington, DC 20006
Contact: Thomas Fox, Dir.

Desc: Seeks to achieve balance between the long-term conservation of natural resources, the environment, and human needs. Conducts research, education, and field services in such areas as human settlements, the marine environment, sustainable agriculture, energy, and forestry and land use. Maintains IIED-Earthscan, a media information unit providing books on environmental and developmental problems for nongovernmental organizations and government agencies. *Type:* Association.

The Chemical Scorecard

Environmental Defense Fund
287 Park Ave. S.
New York, NY 10010
URL: http://www.scorecard.org/
Contact: Bill Pease, Bill_Pease@edf.org.

Desc: An excellent source of environmental and pollutant information, the Chemical Scorecard offers you data on the chemicals, hazards, and pollutants you'll find in your own community. Use the Polluter Locator to find out what's being released into your community's environment and who's responsible. *Type:* Database.

Citizens for Animals, Resources and Environment

PO Box 18772   Ph: (414)466-1250
Milwaukee, WI 53218
Contact: Debi Zweifel, Dir. & Founder.

Desc: Informational network for those interested in promoting humane treatment for all animals, wise use of the earth's resources, and environmental protection. Compiles and disseminates information on national and worldwide organizations. *Type:* Association.

CJE Newsletter

Coalition for Jobs and the Environment
PO Box 645   Ph: (703)628-8996
Abingdon, VA 24210-0645
Desc: Covers issues relating to employment, jobs, and environmental safety. Recurring features include letters to the editor, news, interviews, a calendar of events, news of members, and columns titled Action Needed and Resources. *Type:* Newsletter.

Co-op America's National Green Pages

Co-op America
1612 K St., NW, Ste. 600   Ph: (202)872-5307
Washington, DC 20006   Free: 800-584-7336
                               Fax: (202)331-8166

E-mail: info@coopamerica.org
URL: http://www.greenpages.org.
Contact: Don Beaulieu, Editor, don@coopamerica.org.
Desc: 2,000 businesses and nonprofit organizations in the U.S. that produce environmentally benign products such as non-toxic household products, plant based paints, cruelty free body care products, organic foods, and energy saving devices. Also companies that offer socially responsible financial services. *Type:* Directory.

Colorado State University

Institute of Rural Environmental Health

College of Veterinary Medicine Ph: (970)491-6074
Department of Environmental   Fax: (970)491-2940
    Health
Fort Collins, CO 80523-1676
E-mail: jreif@cvmbs.colostate.edu
Contact: Dr. John S. Reif, Dir.
Desc: Rural environmental health and safety, focusing on the health and well-being of agricultural workers in Colorado and the Rocky Mountain region. Studies applications of preventive medicine through chemical epidemiology, toxicology, occupational health and safety, comparative medicine, and zoonoses. *Type:* Research center.

Conservation Technology Information Center

Jim Mitchell
1220 Porter Dr., Rm. 170   Ph: (765)494-9555
West Lafayette, IN 47906-1383 Fax: (765)494-5969
E-mail: ctic@ctic.purdue.edu
URL: http://www.ctic.purdue.edu/
Contact: John Hebblethwaite, Contact.
Desc: Individuals (20,000), corporations (70), and institutions (42) concerned with environmentally responsible agriculture and farming. Promotes environmentally and ecibinucally responsible decision making by farmers through dissemination of information. *Type:* Association.

The Cousteau Society

870 Greenbrier Cir., Ste. 402 Ph: (757)523-9335
Chesapeake, VA 23320   Free: 800-441-4395
                               Fax: (757)523-2747

E-mail: cousteau@infi.net
URL: http://www.cousteau.org
Contact: Francine Cousteau, Pres.
Desc: Environmental education organization dedicated to the protection and improvement of the quality of life for present and future generations. Objectives are education and evaluation of man-nature interrelationships. *Type:* Association.

Earth Island Institute
300 Broadway, Ste. 28   Ph: (415)788-3666
San Francisco, CA 94133   Fax: (415)788-7324
E-mail: earthisland@earthisland.org
URL: http://www.earthisland.org
Contact: David R. Brower, Chm.
Desc: Individuals working to coordinate environmental and wildlife protection projects. Seeks to develop innovative projects for the conservation, preservation, and restoration of the global environment; promotes ecologically and socially sound development. *Type:* Association.

EDF Letter
Environmental Defense Fund
257 Park Ave. S, 16th Fl.   Ph: (212)505-2100
New York, NY 10010   Fax: (212)505-0892
URL: http://www.edf.org.
Contact: Norma H. Watson, Editor.
Desc: Reports on EDF actions concerning a range of national and global environmental problems in the areas of air quality, energy and resource conservation, wildlife protection, water resource management, and toxic substance use and regulation. Recurring features include editorials and news of research. *Type:* Newsletter.

Encyclopedia of Endangered Species
Gale Group Inc.
27500 Drake Rd.   Ph: (248)699-4253
Farmington Hills, MI 48331-   Free: 800-877-GALE
3535   Fax: (248)699-8070
E-mail: galeord@galegroup.com
URL: http://www.galegroup.com.
Contact: Bill Freedman, Editor.
Desc: Contact information on wildlife and conservation organizations. Principal content of publication is approximately 700 reports on endangered species worldwide. *Type:* Directory.

Encyclopedia of Environmental Information Sources
Gale Group Inc.
27500 Drake Rd.   Ph: (248)699-4253
Farmington Hills, MI 48331-   Free: 800-877-GALE
3535   Fax: (248)699-8070
E-mail: galeord@galegroup.com; science@gale.com.
URL: http://www.galegroup.com.; http://www.gale.com.
Contact: Sarojini Balachandran, Editor.
Desc: 20,000 sources of information on environmental topics, including abstracting and indexing services, almanacs and yearbooks, bibliographies, directories, encyclopedias and dictionaries, online databases, periodicals, newsletters, research centers and institutes, statistical sources, and associations and societies. *Type:* Directory.

Enviroline
Congressional Information Service, Inc. (CIS)
4520 East-West Hwy., Suite   Ph: (301)654-1550
800
Bethesda, MD 20814-3389
E-mail: 12425 (DIALMAIL)
URL: http://www.cispubs.com
Contact: Alistair Morrison, Customer Support, (301)951-4529, fax: (301)654-4033.
Desc: Contains approximately 300,000 citations with abstracts to a broad range of issues and topics related to the environment and the management and use of natural resources. Major topic areas included are air, water, and noise pollution; management of renewable and nonrenewable resources of the land and water; environmental impact of agriculture, chemicals, and biological and radiological contaminants; weather modification; and population planning and control. *Available:* The Dialog

Corporation, DataStar; The Dialog Corporation, DIALOG; The Dialog Corporation, DIALOG; DIMDI (Deutsches Institut fuer Medizinische Dokumentation und Information); DIMDI (Deutsches Institut fuer Medizinische Dokumentation und Information); Questel • Orbit; Questel • Orbit; FIZ Technik (Fachinformationszentrum Technik e.V.); European Information Network Services (EINS). *Type:* Database.

Environment Abstracts
Congressional Information Service, Inc. (CIS)
4520 East-West Hwy., Suite   Ph: (301)654-1550
800
Bethesda, MD 20814-3389
E-mail: 12425 (DIALMAIL)
URL: http://www.cispubs.com
Contact: User Support.
Desc: Provides some 250,000 citations and abstracts of the world's periodical and other published and unpublished literature dealing with environmental and energy-related topics. Comprises the following 3 databases: • Acid Rain Abstracts--contains about 4000 citations, with abstracts, to the worldwide literature on the environment and human life. *Available:* LEXIS-NEXIS; The Dialog Corporation, DIALOG; The Dialog Corporation, DataStar. *Type:* Database.

Environment Reporter
The Bureau of National Affairs, Inc. (BNA)
1231 25th St. NW   Ph: (202)452-4200
Washington, DC 20037
E-mail: bnaplus@bna.com
URL: http://bna.com/mkt/hrl/hrlwdec.htm
Contact: BNA PLUS, (202)452-4323, fax: (202)822-8092, bnaplus@bna.com.
Desc: Contains the complete text of the current developments section of Environment Reporter, covering state and federal legislative, regulatory, judicial, industrial, and technical activities and developments related to pollution control and the environment. Includes air and water pollution, hazardous and solid wastes, land use and reclamation, and sewage treatment. *Available:* LEXIS-NEXIS, LEXIS; West Group, WESTLAW; LEXIS-NEXIS, NEXIS. *Type:* Database.

Environmental Action Foundation
6930 Carroll Ave., Ste. 600   Ph: (301)891-1100
Takoma Park, MD 20912   Fax: (301)891-1100
Contact: Margaret Morgan-Hubbard, Exec.Dir.
Desc: Environmental research and educational organization that serves as a resource for concerned citizens and organizations in the areas of energy policy, toxic substances, and solid waste reduction. *Type:* Association.

Environmental Assessment Association
1224 N. Nokomis NE   Ph: (320)763-4320
Alexandria, MN 56308-5072   Fax: (320)763-9290
E-mail: eaa@iami.org
URL: http://www.iami.org/eaa.html
Contact: Kenneth Twichell, Mng.Dir.
Desc: Environmental professionals. Dedicated to providing members with information and education in the environmental industry concerning environmental inspections, testing and hazardous material removal. *Type:* Association.

Environmental Careers Organization
179 South St.   Ph: (617)426-4375
Boston, MA 02111   Fax: (617)423-0998
URL: http://www.eco.org
Contact: John R. Cook, Jr., Pres.
Desc: Seeks to protect and enhance the environment through the development of professionals, the promotion

of careers, and the inspiration of individual action. Offers paid internships, career development educational programs and related publications. Participants in programs are mostly upper-level undergraduate, graduate, and doctoral students, or recent graduates seeking professional experience relevant to careers in the environmental fields. *Type:* Association.

Environmental Defense Fund
257 Park Ave. S   Ph: (212)505-2100
New York, NY 10010   Free: 800-684-3322
                                    Fax: (212)505-2375
E-mail: contact-edf@edf.org
URL: http://www.edf.org
Contact: Fred D. Krupp, Exec.Dir.
Desc: Links science, law, economics, and engineering to create innovative and economically viable solutions to environmental problems. Four areas of focus include protecting and restoring biodiversity (with an emphasis on rivers and watersheds); stabilizing climate by developing policies to reduce dependence on fossil fuels; reducing risks to human health from exposure to toxic chemicals; and protecting oceans from pollution and overfishing. *Type:* Association.

Environmental Health News
University of Washington
Department of Environmental Health
PO Box 354695   Ph: (206)543-9711
Seattle, WA 98105-6099   Fax: (206)685-3872
E-mail: ahidy@uwashington.edu.
Contact: Sharon Morris, Managing Editor, smorris@u.washington.edu.
Desc: Informs researches, teachers, and workers about current news and issues in environmental health. *Type:* Newsletter.

Environmental Health Service
Rancho Los Amigos Med. Ctr.   Ph: (562)401-7561
Med. Sci. Bldg., Rm. 51   Fax: (562)803-6883
7601 E. Imperial Hwy.
Downey, CA 90242
E-mail: hgong@dhs.co.la.ca.us
Contact: Dr. Henry Gong, Jr., Contact.
Desc: Drug studies of patients with asthma or COPD; air pollution, including effects of ozone on healthy subjects and patients with mild asthma; physiological and cellular responses to acute exposures to ozone, sulfur dioxide, nitrogen dioxide, carbon monoxide, and particulates; health effects of acid aerosols; pharmaceutical drugs; and development of field study programs, including in-home method for self-testing and lung function performance using research quality instrumentation and personal computers, and documentation of typical hourly and daily activity to assess potential effects of air pollution on those activities. *Type:* Research center.

Environmental Industries Marketplace
Gale Group Inc.
27500 Drake Rd.   Ph: (248)699-4253
Farmington Hills, MI 48331-   Free: 800-877-GALE
3535   Fax: (248)699-8070
E-mail: galeord@galegroup.com
URL: http://www.galegroup.com.
Desc: Nearly 11,000 companies involved in environment-related activities such as air pollution control, hazardous waste treatment, asbestos abatement, landfills, recycling, and noise pollution control; includes consultants, attorneys, engineering firms, surveyors, research facilities, manufacturers and distributors, retailers and wholesalers, transportation and disposal firms, and analysis and treatment facilities. *Type:* Directory.

Environmental Law Reporter®

Environmental Law Institute
1616 P St. NW, Ste. 200   Ph: (202)939-3800
Washington, DC 20036
URL: http://www.eli.org
Desc: Contains information on U.S. environmental law.
Available: West Group, WESTLAW; LEXIS-NEXIS,
LEXIS. *Type:* Database.

Environmental and Occupational Health Sciences Institute

681 Frelignhuysen Rd.   Ph: (732)445-0200
PO box 1179   Fax: (732)455-0131
Piscataway, NJ 08855-1179
E-mail: robson@eohsi.rutgers.edu
URL: http://www.eohsi.rutgers.edu
Contact: Mark G. Robson, PhD, Exec.Dir.
Desc: Toxicology, public education and risk communication, occupational health, exposure measurement and assessment, environmental health, and environmental policy. Studies the basic mechanisms by which environmental exposures harm the body, investigates methods for measuring and reducing exposure and improving health including clinical evaulation of individuals potentially affected adversely by environmental agents, and develops and analyzes ways to communicate information. *Type:* Research center.

Environmental Periodicals Bibliography

International Academy at Santa Barbara
Environmental Studies Institute
800 Garden St., Suite D   Ph: (805)965-5010
Santa Barbara, CA 93101-1552
E-mail: iasb@igc.apc.org
Contact: Rosalyn Cordero, (805)683-4927, fax: (805)683-4657, info@iasb.org.
Desc: Contains 584,000 citations to scientific, technical, and popular periodical literature (more than 500 titles) dealing with the environment, including public policy and legal issues, water, air, soil, and noise pollution, solid waste management, recycling and reduction, health hazards, and urban planning. Also covers the discovery, development, transportation, and consumption of traditional and alternative energy resources. *Available:* The Dialog Corporation, DIALOG; Cambridge Scientific Abstracts (CSA). *Type:* Database.

Environmental Policy Institute

218 D St. SE   Ph: (202)544-2600
Washington, DC 20003   Fax: (202)543-4710
Contact: Michael S. Clark, Pres.
Desc: A division of Friends of the Earth . Public interest environmental organization engaged in research, education, and lobbying activities. Works for energy conservation, environmental protection, and the increased use of renewable sources of energy. *Type:* Association.

Environmental Portection Agency
Office of Research and Development
National Health and Environmental Effects Research Laboratory
Gulf Ecology Division

Durham, NC 27711   Ph: (919)541-2281
                               Fax: (919)541-4324
E-mail: reiter.larry@epmail.epa.gov
Contact: Lawrence W. Reiter, Dir.
Desc: Responsible for the study of the physical, chemical, and biological dynamics of coastal wetlands, estuaries, and near-shore marine environments. The goal is to protect and preserve the living resources of the Gulf of Mexico and similar environments by providing descriptive data and developing diagnostic procedures to characterize the ecological condition of near-coastal areas and corresponding watersheds, describing sources and causes and evaluating rates of environmental decline. *Type:* Research center.

Environmental Protection Agency

401 M St. SW   Ph: (202)260-2090
Washington, DC 20460
URL: http://www.epa.gov/
Contact: Carol M. Browner, Dir of Admin.
Desc: The EPA functions to protect human health and to safeguard the natural environment in cooperation with state and local governments. Its mission is to control and abate pollution in the areas of air, water, solid waste, pesticides, radiation, and toxic substances. *Type:* Government agency, office, or program.

Environmental Protection Agency
Office of Research and Development
Office of Health and Environmental Assessment
Human Health Assessment Group

Mail Code 6103   Ph: (202)260-5898
401 M St., SW   Fax: (202)260-9766
Washington, DC 20460
Contact: Robert Brenner, Dir.
Desc: Health assessments for carcinogens, genotoxic agents, and reproductive and developmental toxicants as encountered in environmental exposure scenarios. *Type:* Research center.

Environmental Resources Technology

Petroleum Abstracts PA
600 S. College   Ph: (918)631-2297
Tulsa, OK 74104-3189
E-mail: QUESTION@TUred.pa.utulsa.edu
URL: http://www.pa.utulsa.edu
Contact: David Brown, Marketing Manager, (918)631-2297, fax: (918)599-9361, dbrown@utulsa.edu.
Desc: Contains more than 32,000 citations, most with abstracts, to the worldwide literature and patents dealing with environmental, health and safety, and ecological issues related to petroleum exploration, production, and transportation. Includes descriptions of environmental-technology patents, government reports, and conference papers. *Available:* Questel • Orbit. *Type:* Database.

Environmental Services Directory for Washington State

Jeremy Mattox & Associates, Inc.
PO Box 99486   Ph: (206)282-2591
Seattle, WA 98199   Fax: (206)284-6570
E-mail: esdwa@aol.com.
URL: http://www.enviroindustry.com/esdwa/.
Contact: Jeremy Mattox, Editor.
Desc: Over 350 companies and organizations supplying environmental services and products in Washington state, and related government agencies. *Type:* Directory.

For Mother Earth

Community Organizing Center
Old First Presbyterian Church Ph: (614)252-9255
1101 Bryden Rd.   Fax: (614)443-6125
Columbus, OH 43205
E-mail: walk@igc.apc.org
Desc: Works to: repeal Public Law 93-531 which advocates forced relocation of the Dine (Navajo) from their homelands; end nuclear testing, which occurs on the land of indigenous persons; support the inclusion of indigenous nations into the United Nations ; train community organizers; conduct educational series on interrelated issues. *Type:* Association.

Forest Service Employees for Environmental Ethics

PO Box 11615   Ph: (541)484-2692
Eugene, OR 97403   Fax: (541)484-3004
E-mail: afseee@afseee.org

URL: http://www.afseee.org
Contact: Andy Stahl, Exec.Dir.
Desc: Present, former, and retired U.S. Forest Service employees, workers from other land management agencies, and concerned citizens. Works to create a responsible value system for the Forest Service based on a land ethic which ensures ecologically and economically sustainable resource management. *Type:* Association.

Gale Environmental Sourcebook

Gale Group Inc.
27500 Drake Rd.   Ph: (248)699-4253
Farmington Hills, MI 48331-   Free: 800-877-GALE
3535   Fax: (248)699-8070
E-mail: galeord@galegroup.com
URL: http://www.galegroup.com.
Desc: Approximately 12,000 organizations, government agencies, research facilities, educational programs, scholarships and awards, consumer organizations, corporate contacts, products, and publications concerned with the environment. *Type:* Directory.

Global Response

PO Box 7490   Ph: (303)444-0306
Boulder, CO 80306-7490   Fax: (303)449-9794
E-mail: globresponse@igc.apc.org
URL: http://www.globalresponse.org
Contact: Paula Palmer, Exec.Dir.
Desc: Individuals concerned with ecology and the environment. Responds to environmental emergencies around the world by writing letters. *Type:* Association.

Global Warming International Center

22W381 75th St.   Ph: (630)910-1551
Naperville, IL 60565-9245   Fax: (630)910-1561
E-mail: syshen@megsinet.net
URL: http://www.globalwarming.net/
Contact: Dr. Sinyan Shen, Dir.
Desc: Ministerial agencies and industrial corporations. Concerned with impacts and effects of global warming. *Type:* Association.

Greenpeace

847 W. Jackson Blvd., Ste. 7   Ph: (312)563-6060
Chicago, IL 60607   Free: 800-326-0959
                               Fax: (312)563-6099
Contact: Patricia Sumner, Office Mgr.
Desc: Concerned citizens united to preserve and protect threatened and endangered species, halt the dumping of toxic chemicals into the environment, and stop production of ozone depleting chemicals. Involved in the nuclear and conventional weapons disarmament movement. *Type:* Association.

Greenpeace Minneapolis

57 Cleveland Ave. S
Saint Paul, MN 55105-1004
URL: http://www.greenpeace.org/~usa
Contact: Bill Busse, Dir.
Type: Association.

Greenpeace U.S.A.

1436 U St. NW   Ph: (202)462-1177
Washington, DC 20009   Free: 800-326-0959
                               Fax: (202)462-4507
E-mail: info@wdc.greenpeace.org
URL: http://www.greenpeaceusa.org
Contact: Barbara Dudley, Exec.Dir.
Desc: Conservationists who believe that verbal protests against threats to environmental quality are not adequate. Initiates active, though nonviolent, measures to aid endangered species such as placing boats between harpoonists and whales and placing themselves bodily between hunters and seal pups. Monitors conditions of environmental concern including the greenhouse effect, radioactive and toxic waste dumping, and a comprehensive test ban for nuclear weapons. *Type:* Association.

Hawaii Heptachlor Research and Education Foundation
250 Ward Ave., Ste. 217   Ph: (808)589-2963
Honolulu, HI 96814-4007   Fax: (808)589-2964
E-mail: hhref@lava.net
Contact: Dr. Willis Butler, Pres.
Desc: Sponsors and supports medical research and medical treatment programs, including research on the effects of pesticides and other toxic substances on humans, and methods and treatment of medical problems caused by exposure to such substances. Current research projects include a medical monitoring program, which will examine the health effects of chronic exposure of Oahu's residents to Heptachlor in dairy products. *Type:* Research center.

Human Ecology Action League
PO Box 29629   Ph: (404)248-1898
Atlanta, GA 30359   Fax: (404)248-0162
E-mail: healnatnl@aol.com
URL: http://members.aol.com/healnatnl/index.html
Contact: Muriel A. Dando, Pres.
Desc: Individuals and organizations interested in the study of human ecology and multiple chemical sensitivities, specifically how human health may be affected by synthetic and natural substances in the environment. Objectives are: to collect and disseminate information on human ecology and ecological illness to persons suffering from such illness, and to government agencies, scientists, and health care professionals; to raise public awareness about potential dangers from substances in the environment. *Type:* Association.

In Brief
Earthjustice Legal Defense Fund
180 Montgomery St., Ste. 1400   Ph: (415)627-6700
San Francisco, CA 94104   Free: 800-584-6460
        Fax: (415)627-6740
E-mail: eajus@earthjustice.org
URL: http://www.earthjustice.org.
Contact: Tom Turner, Editor, tturner@earthjustice.org.
Desc: Provides news of the Fund's litigation activities. *Type:* Newsletter.

Kemper Research Foundation
429 Mill St.   Ph: (513)249-2489
Milford, OH 45150-1027
Contact: Richard Kemper, Dir.
Desc: Building related illnesses, focusing on the effects of microorganisms on man and the environment, including heating, ventilating, and air conditioning equipment. *Type:* Research center.

Kids for a Clean Environment
PO Box 158254   Ph: (615)331-7381
Nashville, TN 37215   Free: 800-952-3223
        Fax: (615)333-9879
E-mail: kidsface@mindspring.com
URL: http://www.kidsface.org
Contact: Trish Poe, Exec.Dir.
Desc: Children, parents, teachers, and others working to improve the environment. Focus is on children organizing and implementing ideas and programs on their own, supported and assisted by parents and teachers (membership free to children). *Type:* Association.

Kids for a Clean Environment
Patricia Poe
PO Box 158254   Ph: (615)331-7381
Nashville, TN 37215-8254   Free: 800-952-3223
        Fax: (615)333-9879
E-mail: kidsface@mindspring.com
URL: http://www.kidsface.org
Contact: Trish Poe, Exec.Dir.

Desc: Children promoting environmental protection. Conducts charitable activities. *Type:* Association.

Kids for Saving Earth
PO Box 421118   Ph: (612)559-1234
Minneapolis, MN 55442   Fax: (612)559-6980
E-mail: kseww@aol.com
URL: http://www.kidsforsavingearth.org
Contact: Tessa Hill, Pres.
Desc: Formed by individual members and other groups interested in environmental issues. Consists of several clubs. Works to educate and empower kids to unite and take positive and peaceful action to help protect the earth's environment. *Type:* Association.

LEXIS® Environmental Law Library
LEXIS-NEXIS
9443 Springboro Pike   Ph: (937)865-6800
PO Box 933
Dayton, OH 45401-0933
URL: http://www.lex-nexis.com
Desc: Provides federal and state case law, federal and state statutes, EPA and state site records, the Federal Register, legislative histories, the Congressional Record, federal bill tracking and federal agency materials from the Department of the Interior, Environmental Protection Agency (EPA), and the National Oceanic & Atmospheric Administration (NOAA). Also includes materials from the Environmental Law Institute, environmental law reviews, a number of publications from the Bureau of National Affairs (BNA), and more than 70 leading industrial publications. *Available:* LEXIS-NEXIS, LEXIS. *Type:* Database.

Massachusetts Institute of Technology
Center for Environmental Health Sciences
50 Ames St., Rm. E18-666   Ph: (617)253-6220
Cambridge, MA 02139   Fax: (617)258-5424
E-mail: thilly@mit.edu
URL: http://web.mit.edu/cehs/www/
Contact: William G. Thilly, ScD, Dir.
Desc: Mutagens and carcinogens in fuel combustion, cooking processes, fungal contamination, and losses from hazardous waste sites. Studies include direct measurement of chemicals and genetic change in humans. *Type:* Research center.

Michigan Out-of-Doors
Michigan United Conservation Clubs
2101 Wood St.   Ph: (517)346-6493
PO Box 30235   Free: 800-777-6720
Lansing, MI 48909   Fax: (517)371-1505
E-mail: mucc@mucc.org
Contact: Dennis Knickerbocker, Editor; Richard L. Jameson, Publisher; William Donahue, Advertising Mgr.
Desc: Magazine focusing on conservation, hunting, and fishing. *Alt. Contact:* Box 30235, Lansing, MI 48909; telephone: (517)371-1041; fax: (517)371-1505. *Type:* Periodical.

National Environmental Health Association
720 S. Colorado Blvd., Ste. 970,   Ph: (303)756-9090
  S. Tower   Fax: (303)691-9490
Denver, CO 80246-1925
E-mail: staff@neha.org
URL: http://www.neha.org
Contact: Nelson E. Fabian, Exec.Dir.
Desc: Represents all professionals in environmental health and protection, including Registered Sanitarians, Registered Environmental Health Specialists, Registered Environmental Technicians, Certified Environmental Health Technicians, Registered Hazardous Substances Professionals and Registered Hazardous Substances Specialists.

NEHA's mission is to advance the environmental health and protection profession for the purpose of providing a healthful environment for all. Educational materials, publications, credentials and meetings are available to NEHA members and non-member professionals who strive to improve the environment. *Type:* Association.

National Foundation for the Chemically Hypersensitive
4407 Swinson Rd.   Ph: (517)689-6369
Rhodes, MI 48652   Fax: (517)689-6369
Contact: Fred Nelson, Dir.
Desc: Individuals suffering from chemical hypersensitivity, their families, and friends; health care professionals; interested others. Promotes public awareness of chemical hypersensitivity disorders, such as multiple chemical sensitivities, environmental illness, food intolerance, total allergy syndrome, candida, and chronic fatigue. *Type:* Association.

National Registry of Environmental Professionals
PO Box 2099   Ph: (847)724-6631
Glenview, IL 60025   Fax: (847)724-4223
E-mail: nrep@primenet.com
URL: http://www.nrep.org
Contact: Richard A. Young, Exec.Dir.
Desc: Certifies auditors, property assessors, lending analysts, indoor air quality specialists, hazardous and chemical material managers, ISO 14000 program administrators, environmental managers, engineers, technologists, scientists, and technicians. Promotes legal and professional recognition through professional registration credentialing. *Type:* Association.

New York University
Institute of Environmental Medicine
550 1st Ave.   Ph: (212)998-1212
New York, NY 10016
E-mail: costam@charlotte.med.nyu.edu
Contact: Max Costa, PhD, Dir.
Desc: Toxicology, chemical carcinogenesis, radiation carcinogenesis and dosimetry, respiratory disease and aerosol physiology, environmental pollution and ecology, epidemiology, and biostatistics and biomathematics, including studies on skin, bladder, and lung cancer from environmental sources, environmental hazards to which industrial and community populations are exposed, industrial and environmental health hazards and means for their control, and sources of human exposures to radiation. *Type:* Research center.

North American Association for Environmental Education
1255 23rd St. NW, Ste. 400   Ph: (202)884-8912
Washington, DC 20037-1199   Fax: (202)884-8701
E-mail: beager410@aol.com
URL: http://www.naaee.org
Contact: Edward McCrea, Exec.Dir.
Desc: Individuals associated with colleges, schools, nature centers, government agencies, and environmental organizations; associates include students in environmental education and environmental studies. *Type:* Association.

Oregon State University
Environmental Health Sciences Center
Agriculture and Life Science   Ph: (541)737-3608
  1011 ALS   Fax: (541)737-4371
Corvallis, OR 97331-7302
URL: http://www.ehsc.orst.edu
Contact: William Baird, Dir.
Desc: Provides and stimulates coordinated multidisciplinary research to assess the impact of environmental chemi-

cals on human health and to predict associated short- and long-term effects. Specific research draws upon capabilities of faculty, staff, and graduate students in chemistry, biochemistry, agricultural chemistry, biology, food science, fisheries and wildlife, veterinary medicine, pharmacology, toxicology, immunology, and statistics. *Type:* Research center.

Pollution Engineering Buyer's Guide

Cahners Business Information
1350 E. Touhy Ave.   Ph: (847)635-8800
Des Plaines, IL 60018   Free: 800-446-6551
     Fax: (847)635-6856
E-mail: bkinross@cahners.com; polengineering@cahners.com.
URL: http://www.manufacturing.net.
Contact: John Krukowski, Editor; Diane Pirocanac, Editor.
Desc: Lists of about 32,000 suppliers of equipment and services for the environmental control field, and about 2,500 companies providing independent services as consultants, contractors, or managers for the pollution control industry and other industries concerned with the environment. *Type:* Directory.

Pollution Equipment News—Buyer's Guide Issue

Rimbach Publishing, Inc.
8650 Babcock Blvd.   Ph: (412)364-5366
Pittsburgh, PA 15237   Free: 800-245-3182
     Fax: (412)369-9720
E-mail: rimbach@sgi.net
Contact: David C. Lavender, Editor.
Desc: Over 3,000 manufacturers of pollution control equipment and products. *Type:* Directory.

Quebec-Labrador Foundation/Atlantic Center for the Environment

55 S. Main St.   Ph: (978)356-0038
Ipswich, MA 01938   Fax: (978)356-7322
E-mail: atlantic@qlf.org
URL: http://www.qlf.org
Contact: Lawrence B. Morris, Pres.
Desc: Environmental education professionals, students, and others interested in conservation and improving the environment. Promotes education and involvement of the public in resource management and other environmental issues. Conducts research and educational programs. *Type:* Association.

Rutgers University

Noise Technical Assistance Center

Cook College   Ph: (732)932-8065
Department of Env. Sci.   Fax: (732)932-8644
14 College Farm Rd.
New Brunswick, NJ 08901
E-mail: zwerling@envsi.rutgers.edu
URL: http://envsci.rutgers.edu/estc/rntac
Contact: Eric M. Zwerling, Contact.
Desc: Health effects of noise and community noise enforcement. *Type:* Research center.

Sierra

Sierra Club
85 Second St., 2nd Fl.   Ph: (415)977-5500
San Francisco, CA 94105-3441   Fax: (415)977-5793
E-mail: planet@sierraclub.org; sierra.letters@sierraclub.org.
URL: http://www.sierraclub.org.
Contact: Joan Hamilton, Editor, (415)977-5794; Robert Schildgen, Managing Editor, (415)977-5691, robert.schildgen@sieraclub.org; Frank Noto, Nat'l Adv. Dir., (415)977-5606, frank.noto@sierraclub.org.

Desc: Magazine on conservation and the environment. *Type:* Periodical.

Simon Fraser University

Environmental Physiology Unit

Sch. of Kinesiology   Ph: (604)291-3782
Burnaby, BC, Canada V5A 1S6   Fax: (604)291-3040
E-mail: ablaber@sfu.ca
URL: http://fas.sfu.ca/research/epu.html
Contact: Andrew P. Blaber, Co-Dir.
Desc: Professional divers response to carbon dioxide and nitrogin narcosis, models of thermoregulatory control, altitude acclimation, health hazard appraisal, design and performance evaluation of underwater breathing apparatus, hyperbaric oxygen toxicity, evaluation of personal flotation devices, hypothermia protection, environmental testing of equipment, and pressure testing of diving equipment. *Type:* Research center.

Society of Environmental Toxicology and Chemistry

1010 N. 12th Ave.   Ph: (850)469-1500
Pensacola, FL 32501-3367   Fax: (850)469-9778
E-mail: setac@setac.org
URL: http://www.setac.org
Contact: Rodney Parrish, Exec.Dir.
Desc: Professionals in the fields of chemistry, toxicology, biology, and ecology; atmospheric, health, and earth sciences; and environmental engineering. Promotes the use of multidisciplinary approaches to examine the impacts of chemicals and technology on the environment. *Type:* Association.

South Carolina Health and Environmental Control Department

Health Services Division

Division of Environmental Health

2600 Bull Street   Ph: (803)935-7945
Columbia, SC 29201   Fax: (803)935-7825
E-mail: vaughajh@columb72.dhec.state.sc.us
Contact: Jack H. Vaughan, Jr., Dir.
Desc: Environmental pollution and its effects. *Type:* Research center.

UCLA Center for Clean Technology

University of California, Los Angeles
Center for Clean Technology
7440 Boelter Hall
PO Box 951600
Los Angeles, CA 90024-1600
E-mail: cct@seas.ucla.edu
URL: http://cct.seas.ucla.edu
Contact: Selim Senkan, Director.
Desc: The UCLA Center for Clean Technology (CCT) server contains access to information about the CCT's environmental research, education, and outreach efforts, including an announcement of a new program to retrain displaced defense engineers for environmental careers. There are also links to other environmental activities at UCLA and related WWW Virtual Libraries servers. *Type:* Database.

U.S. Department of Defense

Army Medical Research and Materiel Command

Army Research Institute of Environmental Medicine

42 Kansas St.   Ph: (508)233-4811
Natick, MA 01760-5007   Fax: (508)233-5298
URL: http://www.usariem.army.mil
Contact: Col. Marie Stephens, Contact.
Desc: Effects of temperature, altitude, work, chemical defense, and military nutrition on the soldier's life processes,

performance, and health; defining the complex interaction of environmental stress, the body's defenses, and the techniques, equipment, and procedures best calculated to protect the soldier and make the soldier operationally effective; assessing decrements to soldier performance caused by the synergy of environmental extremes and protective measures against chemical agents; and conducting research in the physiology and health effects of Army physical fitness training. *Type:* Research center.

U.S. Department of Defense

Army Medical Research and Materiel Command

Army Research Institute of Environmental Medicine

Natick, MA 01760-5007   Fax: (508)651-5298
Desc: DOD premier laboratory for human physiology and environmental medicine research. Its mission is to sustain and maximize the health and performance of individual service members, military crews, and troop populations. *Type:* Research center.

U.S. Department of Energy

Office of the Environment, Safety, and Health

1000 Independence Ave. SW   Ph: (202)586-4704
Washington, DC 20585   Fax: (202)586-0956
URL: http://www.doe.gov/
Contact: Peter N. Brush, Acting Assistant Secretary.
Desc: Provides independent oversight of departmental execution of environmental, occupational safety and health, and nuclear/nonnuclear safety and security laws, regulations, and policies; ensures that departmental programs are in compliance with environmental, health, and nuclear/nonnuclear safety protection plans, regulations, and procedures; exercises independent review and approval of environmental impact statements prepared within the Department; and carries out the legal functions of the nuclear safety civil penalty and criminal referral activities. *Type:* Government agency, office, or program.

U.S. Department of Health and Human Services

Agency for Toxic Substances and Disease Registry

1600 Clifton Rd. NE, MS E-60   Ph: (404)639-0501
Atlanta, GA 30333   Fax: (404)639-7000
URL: http://www.atsdr1.atsdr.cdc.gov:8080/
Contact: Claire V. Broome, Acting Administrator.
Desc: The Agency, in cooperation with states and other federal and local official agencies, collects, maintains, analyzes, and disseminates information relating to serious diseases, mortality, and human exposure to toxic or hazardous substances; establishes appropriate registries necessary for long-term follow up or specific scientific studies; establishes and maintains a complete listing of areas closed to the public or otherwise restricted in use because of toxic substance contamination; assists, consults, and coordinates with private or public health care providers in the provision of medical care and testing of exposed individuals; assists the Environmental Protection Agency in identifying hazardous waste substances to be regulated; develops scientific and technical procedures for evaluating public health risks from hazardous substance incidents and for developing recommendations to protect the public health; and provides medical, epidemiological, technical, and administrative advice and consultation to protect public health and worker safety and health in instances of exposure or potential exposure to hazardous substances, and arranges for program support to ensure adequate response to public health emergencies. *Type:* Government agency, office, or program.

U.S. Department of Health and Human Services

Agency for Toxic Substances and Disease Registry

1600 Clifton Rd., N.E.   Ph: (404)639-0700
Mail Stop E-28   Fax: (404)639-0744
Atlanta, GA 30333

Contact: Peter J. McCumiskey, PhD, Actg.Dir.

Desc: Epidemiologic studies on human health effects related to hazardous substance exposure, emphasizing substance-specific research on priority hazardous substances. Comprises Division of Health Studies, Division of Toxicology, Division of Health Assessment and Consultation, and Division of Health Education. *Type:* Research center.

U.S. Department of Health and Human Services

Centers for Disease Control and Prevention

National Center for Environmental Health

4770 Buford Hwy. NE (MS   Ph: (770)488-7231
F-29)   Fax: (770)488-7742
Atlanta, GA 30341-3724
E-mail: mym5@cdc.gov
URL: http://www.cdc.gov

Contact: Melinda Moore, Assoc.Dir. for Global Health.

Desc: Administers national programs that promote a healthy environment and prevent premature death and avoidable illness and disability caused by non-infectious, non-occupational, environmental, and related factors. The Center is to be reorganized into divisions on Birth Defects and Pediatric Genetics, Childhood Development Disabilities and Health Environmental Hazards and Health Effects, and Laboratory Sciences. *Type:* Research center.

U.S. Department of Health and Human Services

Centers for Disease Control and Prevention

National Center for Environmental Health

1600 Clifton Rd. NE   Ph: (404)639-3311
Atlanta, GA 30333   Fax: (404)488-7015
URL: http://www.cdc.gov/

Contact: Richard J. Jackson, Director.

Desc: The Center administers national programs that promote a healthy environment and prevent premature death and avoidable illness and disability caused by non-infectious, non-occupational, environmental and related factors. *Type:* Government agency, office, or program.

U.S. Department of Health and Human Services

National Center for Environmental Health

Birth Defects and Developmental Disabilities Division

Health Studies Branch

4770 Buford Hwy, NE, F34   Ph: (770)488-7150
Atlanta, GA 30341-3724   Fax: (770)488-7156
E-mail: gpo1@cec.gov
URL: http://www.cdc.gov

Contact: Dr. Colleen Boyle, Dir.

Desc: Surveillance research, intervention methods, and technical consultations leading to the design, conduct, analysis, and evaluation of epidemiologic studies of adverse reproductive outcomes (i.e., birth defects, developmental disabilities, genetic abnormalities, mental retardation, and spontaneous abortion). Activities include population-based surveillance, use of case-control methods, and randomized controlled trails. *Type:* Research center.

U.S. Department of Health and Human Services

National Center for Environmental Health

Environmental Hazards and Health Effects Division

4770 Buford Hwy., NE, F28   Ph: (770)488-7300
Atlanta, GA 30341-3724   Fax: (770)488-7310
E-mail: HXF1@CEHDEH1.EM.CDC.GOV

Contact: Dr. Henry Falk, Dir.

Desc: Environmental public health problems and their prevention. Specific areas of interest include toxic chemicals, natural environmental hazards, environmentally-induced disease, international environmental health, and indoor air pollution. *Type:* Research center.

U.S. Department of Health and Human Services

National Center for Environmental Health

Environmental Hazards and Health Effects Division

Health Studies Branch

4770 Buford Hwy. F-46   Ph: (404)488-7359
Atlanta, GA 30333
E-mail: mam7@cdc.gov

Contact: Michael A. McGeehin, Contact.

Desc: Epidemiologic studies on environmental exposure and health effects. Also studies the epidemiology of natural disasters. *Type:* Research center.

U.S. Department of Health and Human Services

National Center for Environmental Health

Environmental Health Laboratory Sciences Division

CDC   Ph: (770)488-7950
4770 Buford Hwy.   Fax: (770)488-4839
Atlanta, GA 30341-3724
E-mail: EJSI@cdc.gov
URL: http://inside.nceh.cdc.gov/ehls/ehlshome.htm

Contact: Dr. Eric J. Sampson, Dir.

Desc: Chronic disease and toxicant exposure. Laboratory methods development accounts for most of the activities related to problem definition in chronic disease. *Type:* Research center.

U.S. Department of Health and Human Services

National Institute of Environmental Health Sciences

PO Box 12233   Ph: (919)541-3201
Research Triangle Park, NC   Fax: (919)541-2260
27709
E-mail: olden@niehs.nih.gov
URL: http://www.niehs.nih.gov

Contact: Dr. Kenneth Olden, Dir.

Desc: Environmental health sciences in the NIEHS laboratories at Research Triangle Park, NC, and supports research through its extramural and intramural programs. The Institute's Extramural Research and Training Division supports research within educational institutions, research institutes, and other public and private nonprofit organizations through individual grants, contracts, and Research Career Development Awards. *Type:* Research center.

U.S. Department of Health and Human Services

National Institute of Environmental Health Sciences

Division of Environmental Carcinogenesis

Experimental Carcinogenesis and Mutagenesis Laboratory

PO Box 12233   Ph: (919)541-4141
Research Triangle Park, NC   Fax: (919)541-1460
27709
E-mail: tennant@niehs.nih.gov
URL: http://www.niehs.nih.gov/diredmp/home.htm

Contact: Dr. Raymond Tennant, Chf.

Desc: Central role played by genetic and epigenetic events in the processes of carcinogenesis. Seeks to; understand the involvement of specific gene mutations and epigenetic events in cancer development; understand the role of chemicals and other environmental factors in the induction of cancer; derive insights into relationships between mutagenicity, chemical structure, and mechanisms of mutagenesis and carcinogenesis; and minimize the risks to human health by improving the ability to rapidly identify, classify, or quantitate the effects of potential mutagens and carcinogens. *Type:* Research center.

U.S. Department of Health and Human Services

National Institute of Environmental Health Sciences

Division of Extramural Research and Training

PO Box 12233   Ph: (919)541-7723
Research Triangle Park, NC   Fax: (919)541-2843
27709
E-mail: SASSAMAN@NIEHS.NIH.GOV
URL: http://www.niehs.nih.gov

Contact: Anne P. Sassaman, PhD, Dir.

Desc: Consequences of the exposure of humans and other biological systems to potentially toxic or harmful agents in the environment. Investigators at colleges, universities, and research foundations are supported through individual research grants, program project grants, and other support mechanisms. *Type:* Research center.

U.S. Department of Health and Human Services

National Institute of Environmental Health Sciences

Division of Intramural Research

PO Box 12233   Ph: (919)541-3205
Research Triangle Park, NC   Fax: (919)541-5002
27709
E-mail: barrett@niehs.nih.gov

Contact: Dr. J. Carl Barrett, Sci.Dir.

Desc: Plans and conducts the Institute's basic laboratory and clinical research, which encompasses the environmental areas of medicine, biology, pharmacology, neurosciences and pulmonary pathobiology, chemistry, toxicology, genetics, and biophysics. Plans and conducts a program of toxicology and carcinogenesis studies to establish and characterize the toxicity of chemicals and other environmental agents, and to develop, validate, and evaluate such methods. *Type:* Research center.

U.S. Department of Health and Human Services

National Institute of Environmental Health Sciences

Division of Intramural Research

Comparative Medicine Branch

PO Box 12233   Ph: (919)541-4400
Research Triangle Park, NC   Fax: (919)541-4076
27709
E-mail: forsythe@niehs.nih.gov

Contact: Dr. Diane Forsythe, Chf.

Desc: Experimental animal procurement, housing, and utilization for the Institute; advises Institute scientists of appropriate animal models for use in research programs; maintains a laboratory for the diagnosis and research of animal diseases; operates a rodent genetics resource, including gnotobiotic capability. *Type:* Research center.

U.S. Department of Health and Human Services

National Institute of Environmental Health Sciences

Division of Intramural Research

Environmental Toxicology Program

PO Box 12233, MD A3-01   Ph: (919)541-3802
Research Triangle Park, NC   Fax: (919)541-0295
27709

URL: http://ntp-server.niehs.nih.gov
Contact: Dr. George W. Lucier, Dir.
Desc: Environmental toxicology. *Type:* Research center.

U.S. Department of Health and Human Services

National Institute of Environmental Health Sciences

Division of Intramural Research

Epidemiology Branch

Mail Drop A3-05   Ph: (919)541-7703
PO Box 12233   Fax: (919)541-2511
Research Triangle Park, NC
27709

Contact: Allen J. Wilcox, Chf.
Desc: Field studies of human disease (particularly chronic diseases) attributable to environmental pollutants; investigates the effects of environmental toxins on fetal and child development; and conducts basic and applied research in laboratory support methodology involved in the monitoring of human populations. *Type:* Research center.

U.S. Department of Health and Human Services

National Institutes of Health

National Institute of Environmental Health Sciences

PO Box 12233   Ph: (919)541-3211
Research Triangle Park, NC
27709

URL: http://www.niehs.nih.gov/
Contact: Kenneth Olden, Director.
Desc: NIEHS conducts and supports basic and applied research on how the environment interacts with genetic factors to cause disease and dysfunction. The primary emphasis is on disease prevention through identification and assessment of risks. *Type:* Government agency, office, or program.

U.S. Department of Transportation

Coast Guard

Office of Health and Safety

Safety and Environmental Health Division

Coast Headquarters Bldg.   Ph: (202)267-1883
2100 2nd St. SW   Fax: (202)267-4355
Washington, DC 20593

Contact: William K. Lowry, Chf.
Desc: Responsible for all internal mishap prevention, environmental health, and occupational health within the Coast Guard, including aircraft crashes, vessel collisions, fires, explosions, and chemical exposures. *Type:* Research center.

U.S. Government Books

U.S. Government Bookstore
T.P. O'Neill, Jr., Federal Bldg.   Ph: (617)720-4180
10 Causeway St., Rm. 169   Fax: (617)720-5753
Boston, MA 02222

Desc: Provides a listing of books on commercial fisheries, marine and coastal recreation, environments, safety and standards, natural history, marine industries, boating, and sports. *Type:* Newsletter.

University of California, Irvine

Air Pollution Health Effects Laboratory

Department of Community &   Ph: (949)824-5860
  Environmental Medicine   Fax: (949)824-4763
Irvine, CA 92697-1825

E-mail: rfphalen@uci.edu
Contact: Dr. Robert F. Phalen, Dir.
Desc: Lung development and defenses, particle deposition in the lungs, inhalation exposure to oxidant, fine particulate and acidic aerosol mixtures, inhalation exposure methodology, and environmental and occupational inhalation toxicology, emphasizing particle plus gas mixtures. Also develops and validates mathematical models of inhaled particle deposition. *Type:* Research center.

University of Connecticut

Center for Environmental Health

3636 Horsebarn Rd.   Ph: (860)486-2480
Box U-39   Fax: (860)486-5067
Storrs, CT 06269-4039

E-mail: lsilbart@ansc1.cag.uconn.edu
URL: http://www.lib.uconn.edu/canr/ansci/ceh/cehpage.htm
Contact: Dr. Lawrence Silbart, Actg.Dir.
Desc: Interdisciplinary studies of environmental health problems of concern to Connecticut, emphasizing carcinogenesis, pesticides, epidemiology and biostatistics, and genetic biomonitoring. *Type:* Research center.

University of Miami

Pesticide Residue, Toxic Waste and Basic Research Analytical Laboratory

Bldg. B   Ph: (305)284-7020
12500 SW 152 St.   Fax: (305)232-7461
Miami, FL 33177-1411

Contact: Chip Walls, Lab.Mgr.
Desc: Pesticides, air pollutants, carcinogens, and chemicals, with emphasis on biological, agricultural, and environmental samples. *Type:* Research center.

University of Michigan

Michigan Institute for Environmental and Health Sciences

Sch. of Public Health   Ph: (734)764-3188
1420 Washington Heights   Fax: (734)936-7283
Ann Arbor, MI 48109-2029

E-mail: hmancy@umich.edu
Contact: Khalil H. Mancy, PhD, Ch.
Desc: Environmental and health sciences, including studies on the safety of air, water, and food supply, human nutrition, toxicology, and industrial health and safety. Areas include basic research on the impact of chemicals, including dietary constituents on biological systems, environmental toxicology and epidemiology, relationships between diet and disease, studies of water and air pollution; and identification and management of radiation, chemical and other hazards in the workplace. *Type:* Research center.

University of Minnesota

Center for Environment and Health Policy

Box 807 UMHC   Ph: (612)626-0900
420 Delaware St., SE   Fax: (612)626-0650
Minneapolis, MN 55455

E-mail: ksexton@mail.eoh.umn.edu
Contact: Ken Sexton, Dir.
Desc: Center promotes the use of environmental, biological, and social science knowledge in the development of public policies relevant to environmental agents and their effects on the health of people. Center's focus is on applying existing scientific data to analyze environmental risks while considering economic, social, and political implications. *Type:* Research center.

University of North Alabama

Occupational and Environmental Health Laboratory

Department of Chemistry and   Ph: (205)765-4474
  Industrial Hygiene   Fax: (205)765-4329
UNA Box 5049
Florence, AL 35632-0001

E-mail: mmoeller@unanov.una.edu
Contact: Dr. Michael Moeller, Contact.
Desc: Conducts research in the areas of environmental health, industrial hygiene, and risk assessment. *Type:* Research center.

University of North Carolina at Chapel Hill

Center for Environmental Medicine and Lung Biology

104 Mason Farm Rd.   Ph: (919)962-0126
CB 7310   Fax: (919)966-9863
Chapel Hill, NC 27599-7310

E-mail: pwspar@med.unc.edu
URL: http://www.med.unc.edu/envLung/welcome1.htm
Contact: Philip A. Bromberg, MD, Dir.
Desc: Environmental impacts on human health, including effects of inhaled agents on the respiratory system in diseased and healthy human subjects and on human cell lines and basic and clinical studies in environmental health sciences. *Type:* Research center.

University of Pennsylvania

Institute for Environmental Medicine

1 John Morgan Bldg.   Ph: (215)898-9100
36th St. & Hamilton Walk   Fax: (215)898-0868
Philadelphia, PA 19104-6068

E-mail: abf@mail.med.upenn.edu
URL: http://www.med.upenn.edu/~ifem
Contact: Dr. Aron B. Fisher, Dir.
Desc: Cellular and molecular biology of lung function with special emphasis on the lung surfactant system, undersea physiology, physiological and toxic effects of oxygen, isobaric gas counterdiffusion, and hyperbaric oxygen therapy. *Type:* Research center.

University of Quebec at Montreal

Centre for Study of Biological Interactions Between Environment and Health

PO Box 8888, Downtown Sta.   Ph: (514)987-3915
Montreal, PQ, Canada H3C   Fax: (514)987-6183
  3P8

E-mail: mergler.donna@uqam.ca
URL: http://www.unites.uqam.ca/cinbiose/anglais/
Contact: Donna Mergler, Dir.
Desc: Occupational health, ergonomics. *Type:* Research center.

University of Utah

Rocky Mountain Center for Occupational and Environmental Health

Bldg. 512   Ph: (801)581-8719
Salt Lake City, UT 84112   Fax: (801)581-7224

E-mail: rmoser@rmcoeh.utah.edu
URL: http://www.rmcoeh.utah.edu/
Contact: Dr. Royce Moser, Dir.
Desc: Occupational and environmental health and safety with emphasis on PM10 quantification, international studies, environmental epidemiology, asbestos-related health problems, musculoskeletal and other injury evaluation and prevention, and ergonomic aspects of the work environment. *Type:* Research center.

Wayne State University

C.S. Mott Center for Human Growth and Development

275 E. Hancock St.
Ph: (313)577-1485
Detroit, MI 48201
Fax: (313)577-8554
E-mail: mitch@mdix.obgyn.wayne.edu

Contact: Dr. Marappa G. Subramanian, Dir. of Oper.

Desc: Human growth and development, including causative factors, identification, prevention, and remedy of birth defects. Uses mechanical, chemical, and hormonal devices as well as acceptable social, psychological, ethical, and moral approaches. *Type:* Research center.

We Care About New York

1333 President St.
Ph: (212)686-1001
Brooklyn, NY 11213-4217
Fax: (212)725-5897

Contact: Emory N. Jackson, Exec. Officer.

Desc: Volunteer environmental awareness organization advocating for a cleaner New York City, particularly the prevention and removal of litter and graffiti. Conducts direct-action neighborhood projects. *Type:* Association.

WESTLAW® Environmental Law

West Group

620 Opperman Dr.
Ph: (651)687-7000
St. Paul, MN 55164-0526
URL: http://www.westgroup.com

Desc: Contains the complete text of U.S. federal and state court decisions, statutes and regulations, administrative law publications, specialized files, and texts and periodicals dealing with environmental protection and conservation, including radioactive, solid and toxic waste management, pollution, clean air and water acts, and the impact of administrative and zoning law on the environment. *Available:* West Group, WESTLAW. *Type:* Database.

Ethnic Studies

A. Magazine

Metro East Publications, Inc.

677 5th Ave., 3rd Fl.
Ph: (212)593-8089
New York, NY 10022
Free: 800-446-6235
Fax: (212)593-8082

E-mail: amag@amagazine.com.
URL: http://www.amagazine.com.

Contact: Jeff Yang, Publisher, jyang@amagazine.com; Gilbert Cheah, Assoc. Publisher, gcheah@amagazine.com; Karen Wang, Advertising Dir., kbwang@amagazine.com; Karen Lam, Editor-in-Chief, karenlam@amagazine.com.

Desc: Magazine reporting on Asian American life, culture, politics, fashion, entertainment. *Type:* Periodical.

American Indian Libraries Newsletter

The American Indian Library Association

School of Library and
Ph: (405)325-3921
Information Studies
Fax: (405)325-7648
The University of Oklahoma
Norman, OK 73019
E-mail: lpatterson@uoknor.edu.

Contact: Dr. Rhonda Harris Taylor, Editor.

Desc: Reports news and events related to American Indian libraries/services. Reviews publications related to Native Americans. *Type:* Newsletter.

American Ireland Education Foundation-Political Education Committee

54 S. Liberty Dr., Ste. 401
Ph: (914)947-2726
Stony Point, NY 10980
Free: 800-777-6807
Fax: (914)947-2599

E-mail: aipec@aol.com

Contact: John Finucane, Pres.

Desc: Supporters of the peaceful reunification of Ireland. Seeks to educate the American public on the nationalist point of view concerning Northern Ireland, which, according to the group, is that the reunification of Ireland is the best solution to the political, human rights, and economic problems of Northern Ireland. Advocates endorsement of the MacBride Principles, which describe fair employment practices to be exercised by U.S. companies conducting business in Northern Ireland. Promotes American Irish awareness and a campaign to end negative Irish stereotypes. *Type:* Association.

American Ireland Fund

211 Congress St., 10th Fl.
Ph: (617)574-0720
Boston, MA 02110
Free: 800-475-3863
Fax: (617)574-0730

E-mail: irlfund@aol.com
URL: http://www.irlfunds.org

Contact: Kingsley Aikins, Exec.Dir.

Desc: Seeks to promote "peaceful, constructive change" in Ireland by "aiding projects of Peace, Culture and Charity in Ireland, North and South." Supports integrated schools and cross-community jobs and skills training, and projects that protect the environment, create jobs, serve the elderly, and care for the children affected by sectarian violence. *Type:* Association.

American Latvian Association in the United States

400 Hurley Ave.
Ph: (301)340-1914
Rockville, MD 20850-3121
Fax: (301)340-8732

Contact: Anita Terauds, Sec.Gen.

Desc: Persons of Latvian ancestry or birth. Works to unite Americans of Latvian descent, to strengthen their ethnic heritage, and to acquaint the American public with the Republic of Latvia by making available tapes, records, books, and movies about the Republic of Latvia. Provides assistance to Republic of Latvia. *Type:* Association.

American Mutual Life Association

19424 S. Waterloo Rd.
Ph: (216)531-1900
Cleveland, OH 44119
Fax: (216)531-8123

Contact: Joseph F. Petric, Jr., Sec.Treas.

Desc: Fraternal benefit life insurance society. Maintains recreation center. *Type:* Association.

American-Scandinavian Foundation

15th East 65th St.
Ph: (212)879-9779
New York, NY 10021
Fax: (212)249-3444
E-mail: asf@amscan.org
URL: http://www.amscan.org

Contact: Edward P. Gallagher, Pres.

Desc: Americans, Scandinavians, and Americans of Scandinavian descent. *Type:* Association.

Ancient Order of Hibernians in America

31 Logan St.
Ph: (315)252-3895
Auburn, NY 13021
Fax: (315)252-6996

Contact: Thomas McNabb, Sec.

Desc: Fraternal benefit insurance society of American Catholics who are Irish by birth or descent. Maintains speakers' bureau; compiles statistics. *Type:* Association.

Aramco World

Aramco Services Company

Box 2106
Houston, TX 77252-2106

Contact: Robert Arndt, Editor, rarndt@aramco.com; Dick Doughty, Asst. Editor.

Desc: Magazine covering Arab and Muslim culture. *Type:* Periodical.

Armenian Assembly of America

122 C St. NW, Ste. 350
Ph: (202)393-3434
Washington, DC 20001
Fax: (202)638-4904
E-mail: info@aaainc.org
URL: http://www.aaainc.org

Contact: Ross Vartian, Exec.Dir.

Desc: Purposes: to serve as a forum for the promotion of communication, cooperation, and coordination of activities within the Armenian-American community; to foster an awareness and appreciation of the Armenian cultural heritage and to promote the preservation of significant Armenian cultural materials and monuments; to advance research and data collection and to disseminate accurate information regarding the Armenian people; to provide the means by which the Armenian community can speak effectively on issues of importance and concern; to gather and disseminate information to the Armenian-American community; to promote greater Armenian-American participation in the American democratic process; to assist persons of Armenian ancestry subject to infringement or violation of basic human and civil rights; to engage in charitable, humanitarian, and educational efforts to alleviate human suffering of Armenians. *Type:* Association.

Armenian General Benevolent Union

55 E. 59th St.
Ph: (212)765-8260
New York, NY 10022-1112
Fax: (212)319-6507
E-mail: agbuny@aol.com

Contact: Louise Simone, Pres.

Desc: Charitable humanitarian and educational organization established to promote Armenian heritage. Operates 55 schools and centers worldwide, provides summer intern programs, and has established the American University of Armenia, along with other major medical, educational, and cultural institutions in Armenia. *Type:* Association.

Armenian Missionary Association of America

31 W. Century Road
Ph: (201)265-2607
Paramus, NJ 07652
Fax: (201)265-6015
E-mail: amaainc@aol.com

Contact: Rev. Moses B. Janbazian, Exec. Dir.

Desc: Maintains a range of educational, evangelism, relief, social service, church and child care ministries in 20 countries around the world. Emphasizes full financial disclosure, accountability and careful stewardship of funds. *Type:* Association.

Armenian Research Center Home Page

University of Michigan, Dearborn

4901 Evergreen Rd.
Ph: (313)593-5000
Dearborn, MI 48128
E-mail: gottenbr@umich.edu
URL: http://www.umd.umich.edu/dept/armenian/

Desc: This site provides access to the electronic database of the Armenian Research and Publication Center. The database currently contains 3684 books; 18,969 newspaper articles; 2500 items from the Armenian Assembly of America including clipped and translated articles from international newspapers; images; and bibliographies of holdings in other collections. *Type:* Database.

The Asia Foundation

465 California St., 14th Fl.
Ph: (415)982-4640
San Francisco, CA 94104
Fax: (415)392-8863
E-mail: webmaster@asiafound.org
URL: http://www.asiafoundation.org

Contact: Carolyn Iyoya Irving, Communications & Outreach Mgr.

Desc: Supported by U.S. government grants and private contributions. Works to: strengthen government and institutions in Asia and the Pacific Islands; promote Asian-Pacific cooperation; and develop closer Asian-American relations. *Type:* Association.

Asia Society

725 Park Ave.
Ph: (212)288-6400
New York, NY 10021
Fax: (212)517-8555
Contact: Ambassador Nicholas Platt, Pres.

Desc: Dedicated to fostering understanding of Asia and communication between Americans and the peoples of Asia and the Pacific. Presents a wide range of programs including high-level conferences, symposia, international study missions, press briefings, publications, major art exhibitions and performing arts productions. *Type:* Association.

Assembly of Turkish American Associations

1601 Connecticut Ave. NW,
Ph: (202)483-9090
Ste. 303
Fax: (202)483-9092
Washington, DC 20009
E-mail: assembly@ataa.org
URL: http://www.ataa.org
Contact: Guler Koknar, Exec.Dir.

Desc: Associations (53) and individuals (10,000) who coordinate activities of regional Turkish-American associations for the purpose of presenting an objective view of Turkey and the Turkish-American and Turkish people and enhancing understanding between these people and Americans. Provides educational materials and organizational assistance to Turkish-American community schools and their teachers. Provides speakers to the Turkish-American community and other interested groups concerning issues on the history, culture, and language of Turks. *Type:* Association.

Baltic American Freedom League

PO Box 29657
Ph: (213)255-4215
Los Angeles, CA 90029
Fax: (213)255-8730
E-mail: valdisp@aol.com
URL: http://www.bafl.com
Contact: Valdis Pavlovskis, Pres.

Desc: Americans of Baltic ancestry; human rights activists in the Baltic nations of Estonia, Latvia, and Lithuania. Disseminates information on Baltic history, culture, and current events. *Type:* Association.

Belgian American Educational Foundation

195 Church St.
Ph: (203)777-5765
New Haven, CT 06510
Contact: Emile L. Boulpaep, Pres.

Desc: Promotes closer relations and the exchange of intellectual ideas between Belgium and the U.S. through fellowships granted to graduate students of one country for study and research in the other. Assists higher education and scientific research and commemorates the work of the Commission for Relief in Belgium and associated organizations during the First World War, 1914-1918. *Type:* Association.

Chicano/Latino Net

University of California, Los Angeles
c/o mail Services
Ph: (310)825-4321
Box 951361
Los Angeles, CA 90095-1361
E-mail: webadmin@ucla.edu
URL: http://latino.sscnet.ucla.edu/

Desc: The Chicano/Latino Net database provides access to networked information of interest to the Latino community. The database includes research guides, bibliographies, statistical data sets, information resources, library data, a Latino virtual museum, directories of organizations, a job center, and serves as a gateway between faculty, staff, and students. *Type:* Database.

Croatian Fraternal Union of America

100 Delaney Dr.
Ph: (412)351-3909
Pittsburgh, PA 15235
Fax: (412)823-1594
Contact: Bernard M. Luketich, Pres.

Desc: Persons of Croatian or Slavic descent or origin and their relatives. Fraternal benefit insurance society. Maintains Ethnic Museum. *Type:* Association.

CSA Fraternal Life

122 W. 22nd
Ph: (630)472-0500
Oak Brook, IL 60523-1557
Fax: (630)472-1100
Contact: Vera A. Wilt, Pres.

Desc: Fraternal benefit life insurance society. Sponsors sports, photo, poster, and Miss National CSA competitions; coordinates scholarship program. Maintains museum, biographical archives, and 1500 volume library of magazines and Czech books dating back to the 1860s. *Type:* Association.

Czech World Union

39 Hillside Dr.
Ph: (303)232-7856
Lakewood, CO 80215-6639
Fax: (303)232-7856
Contact: Prof. Libor Brom, Ph.D., Pres.

Desc: Athletic, charitable, political, recreational, religious, and scientific organizations. Advocates the restoration of all human rights in Czechoslovakia; promotes the freedom and self-determination of Slavic nations. Coordinates efforts of member groups; individual organizations specialize in politics, science, or theology. *Type:* Association.

Diversity Database

University of Maryland
College Park, MD 20742
Ph: (301)405-1000
URL: http://www.inform.umd.edu/EdRes/Topic/Diversity/
Contact: diversity@umail.umd.edu.

Desc: The University of Maryland's Diversity Database is a significant compilation of documents, links, and associated resources on the topic of multicultural and cultural diversity, specifically in the areas of age, class, disability, ethnicity, gender, national origin, race, religion & sexual orientation. Here you will find local, national, and international academic resources including dictionaries and glossaries defining diversity terms, issue-specific resources, samples of diversity initiatives in other institutions, and general reference sources. *Type:* Database.

First Catholic Slovak Union of the U.S.A. and Canada

6611 Rockside Rd.
Ph: (216)642-9406
Independence, OH 44131
Free: 800-JED-NOTA
Fax: (216)642-4310
Contact: Kenneth A. Arendt, National Sec.

Desc: Fraternal benefit life insurance society for Catholic Americans of Slovak descent. Conducts field seminars; sponsors competitions and children's services. Operates museum. *Type:* Association.

Holland Society of New York

122 E. 58th St.
Ph: (212)758-1675
New York, NY 10022
Fax: (212)758-2232
Contact: Annette Van Rooy, Exec.Sec.

Desc: Descendants in the direct male line of settlers in the Dutch Colonies in North America prior to 1675. Collects and preserves data on the early history of the Dutch Colonies and the genealogy of descendants of early settlers. Has translated baptismal, marriage, and death records of early Dutch churches. *Type:* Association.

Hungarian Reformed Federation of America

2001 Massachusetts Ave. NW
Ph: (202)328-2630
Washington, DC 20036-1011
Fax: (202)328-7984
Contact: George Dozsa, Pres.

Desc: Fraternal benefit insurance society primarily for Americans of Hungarian descent. Sponsors competitions; provides student aid funds. Maintains museum and biographical archives. *Type:* Association.

Independent Newspaper from Russia

Independent Newspaper From Russia
7338 Dartford, Ste. 9
Ph: (703)827-0414
Mc Lean, VA 22102
Fax: (703)827-8923
Contact: Cynthia Neu, Editor.

Desc: Tabloid featuring stories from Moscow's political newspapers. *Type:* Periodical.

India Network Foundation

Bowling Green State University - Department of Sociology - India Network Foundation
PO Box 556
Ph: (419)352-9335
Bowling Green, OH 43402
Fax: (419)352-9334
E-mail: inf@indnet.org
URL: http://india.bgsu.edu
Contact: Dr. K. V. Rao, kvrao@indnet.org.

Desc: The India Network Foundation is a non-profit charitable organization that serves the Asian and Indian communities. Included are archives, news, literature, discussions of social and cultural issues, research data, and much more. *Type:* Database.

Irish American Cultural Association

10415 S. Western
Ph: (773)238-7150
Chicago, IL 60643
Contact: Thomas R. McCarthy, Pres.

Desc: People interested in all areas of Irish culture, especially as it relates to their ethnic identity. Promotes the study and appreciation of Irish culture. Provides funds for Irish writers, painters, musicians, and craftsmen. *Type:* Association.

Irish American Unity Conference

529 14th St. NW, No. 837
Ph: (202)662-8830
Washington, DC 20045
Free: 800-947-IAUC
Fax: (202)662-8831
E-mail: 104543.3677@compuserve.com
URL: http://www.iauc.org
Contact: Andrew L. Somers, Pres.

Desc: American human rights organization working for peace with justice in a united Ireland. *Type:* Association.

Irish National Caucus

413 E. Capitol St. SE
Ph: (202)544-0568
Washington, DC 20003
Fax: (202)543-2491
URL: http://www.knight-hub.cob/nc/
Contact: Fr. Sean McManus, Pres.

Desc: Persons concerned with the protection of human rights in Northern Ireland. Through lobbying and public education efforts, seeks to make human rights in Ireland an American issue, both legally and morally. Ultimate goal is the promotion of just and lasting peace in Ireland, free from English rule. *Type:* Association.

Knights of Equity

Harry J. Cummings
37 Meadowvale Rd., No.
Ph: (412)828-8770
2
Cheswick, PA 15024-9425
E-mail: james1@wwnet.com
Contact: Harry J. Cummings, Supreme Sir Knight.

Desc: Americans who are of Irish ancestry and are practicing Roman Catholics. Seeks to: advance members spiritually, materially, and socially; teach Irish history and culture; help the cause of liberty and freedom for the people of Ireland. Assists orphan homes, homes for the aged, and young men interested in priesthood. *Type:* Association.

Lithuanian Regeneration Association

c/o V. Jokubaitis Ph: (216)481-7161
3000 Hadden Rd.
Euclid, OH 44117-2122
Contact: V. Jokubaitis, Pres.
Desc: Political-cultural organization dedicated to supporting the independence of "democratic Lithuania in her ethnographic territory." Maintains speakers' bureau and biographical archives. *Type:* Association.

National Association of Americans of Asian Indian Descent

Dr. Ahmed Kutty
3320 Ave. A Ph: (308)865-2263
Kearney, NE 68847-1666 Fax: (308)865-2263
Contact: Dr. Sridltart Kazil, Pres.
Desc: Business and professional people of Asian Indian origin or descent. Promotes and protects the economic, political, social, and educational interests of citizens of Indian origin. Seeks to unite the Indian community. *Type:* Association.

National Council for Eurasian and East European Research

910 17th St., NW Ph: (202)822-6950
Ste. 300 Fax: (202)822-6955
Washington, DC 20006
E-mail: nceeer@aol.com
URL: http://www.netcom.com/~ncseer/main.html
Contact: Christopher Bowe, Exec.Dir.
Desc: Conducts a peer review of funding proposals for postdoctoral research (U.S. only). Aims to develop and sustain a long-term and high-quality research program dealing with major policy issues and questions of Eastern Europe, the USSR, and its successor states' social, political, economic, and historical development. *Type:* Association.

National Federation of American Hungarians

717 2nd St. NE Ph: (202)546-3003
Washington, DC 20002 Fax: (202)547-0392
Contact: Laszlo Pasztor, Contact.
Desc: Americans of Hungarian descent. Seeks to ease the transition of recently-arrived Hungarian immigrants to the U.S. Educates Hungarian Americans regarding Hungarian culture and history. *Type:* Association.

National Hispanic Marketplace Review

Center for Hispanic American Studies
PO Box 13404 Ph: (303)871-8583
Denver, CO 80201
Contact: George Autobee, Editor; Lure Copoda, Publisher.
Desc: Provides information on marketing to Hispanic consumers. *Type:* Newsletter.

National Slavic Convention

16 S. Patterson Park Ave. Ph: (410)276-7676
Baltimore, MD 21231 Fax: (410)276-1233
Contact: Rev. I. Dornic, Pres.
Desc: Individuals and organizations of persons of East European, particularly Slavic descent. Seeks to coordinate efforts of various organizations to help individuals with legal, social, economic, educational, and health problems. Conducts specialized education programs. *Type:* Association.

National Slovak Society of the United States of America

333 Technology Dr., Ste. 112 Ph: (412)488-1890
Canonsburg, PA 15317 Free: 800-488-1890
 Fax: (412)488-0327
E-mail: nsslisa@usaor.net

Contact: David G. Blazek, Pres.
Desc: Fraternal benefit life insurance society for men and women of Slovak descent and their families in the United States. Offers aid to orphans, widows, the aged, and disabled persons. *Type:* Association.

National Spiritual Assembly of the Baha'is of the U.S.

536 Sheridan Rd. Ph: (847)869-9039
Wilmette, IL 60091 Fax: (847)869-0247
E-mail: secretariat@usbnc.org
URL: http://www.bahai.org
Contact: Robert C. Henderson, Sec.Gen.
Desc: National governing body and administrative agency for U.S. adherents of the Baha'i Faith, an independent worldwide religion. The Baha'i Faith, which follows the writings of Baha'u'llah, teaches the oneness of God, the common foundation of the world's religions, and the oneness of all the races of mankind. *Type:* Association.

Palestine Congress of North America

PO Box 9621 Ph: (301)652-0052
Washington, DC 20016
Contact: Said Ari Kat, Exec.Dir.
Desc: Goals are to build a better image for all Arab peoples and to develop a stronger political lobby on behalf of a Middle East solution that will provide Palestinians with their own homeland. Supports Palestine Liberation Organization efforts to establish an independent Palestinian state. *Type:* Association.

Philippine News

Philippine News
PO Box 2767 Ph: (415)872-3000
South San Francisco, CA Free: 800-432-5877
 94083-2767 Fax: (415)872-0217
E-mail: pnewshq@aol.com.
URL: http://www.philippinenews.com.
Contact: Alex A. Esclamado, Publisher.
Desc: Newspaper for the Filipino community (six U.S. editions). *Type:* Periodical.

Polynesian Cultural Center

55-370 Kamehameha Hwy. Ph: (808)293-3333
Laie, HI 96762 Free: 800-367-7060
 Fax: (808)293-3339
Contact: Lester W. B. Moore, CEO.
Desc: Presents, preserves, and perpetuates the arts, crafts, culture, and lore of Fijian, Hawaiian, Maori, Marquesan, Tahitian, Tongan, Samoan, and other Polynesian peoples. Seeks to preserve and dramatize ancient cultures in a manner that is entertaining, informative, and educational. Polynesian islanders demonstrate traditional ways of life in villages of authentic huts at the center, which is located on a 42-acre site on the north shore of the island of Oahu, 38 miles from Waikiki. *Type:* Association.

Portuguese Society Queen St. Isabel

3031 Telegraph Ave. Ph: (510)658-0983
Oakland, CA 94609 Fax: (510)658-6517
Contact: Maria A. Rego, Treas./Sec. Pro-Temp.
Desc: Sponsors annual charity project. *Type:* Association.

Providence Association of Ukrainian Catholics in America

817 N. Franklin St. Ph: (215)627-4984
Philadelphia, PA 19123 Fax: (215)238-1933
Contact: Ihor Smolij, Rec.Sec.
Desc: Fraternal benefit life insurance society. *Type:* Association.

Pueblo to People

PO Box 2545 Free: (713)956-1172
Houston, TX 77252-2545
Contact: Cathie Chilson, Co-Dir.
Desc: Individuals concerned with socioeconomic conditions. Objectives are to sponsor activities that will improve Central American socioeconomic conditions and present the U.S. public with what the group considers to be a more realistic picture of Central American issues. *Type:* Association.

Raoul Wallenberg Committee of the United States

575 Lexington Ave., 7th Fl. Ph: (212)350-4875
New York, NY 10022 Fax: (212)350-4240
E-mail: rachel@raoulwallenberg.org
Contact: Rachel Oestreicher Bernheim, Chm. & Pres.
Desc: Educates the American public about the life and deeds of Raoul Wallenberg (1912-), a Swedish diplomat and honorary citizen of the United States responsible for saving over 100,000 Jews in Budapest, Hungary from the Nazi concentration camps during World War II. (Wallenberg disappeared in 1945 at the hands of the Soviet forces but has reportedly been seen in Soviet Gulag prisons and mental institutions and is believed to be alive.) Works to secure Wallenberg's freedom or to establish the truth of his fate. Serves as an information clearinghouse and provides background materials on Wallenberg to schools, universities, churches, and synagogues. *Type:* Association.

Russian and East European Studies Database

University of Pittsburgh
University Center for Ph: (412)648-7390
 International Studies Fax: (412)648-4672
4G Forbes Quadrangle
Pittsburgh, PA 15260
E-mail: ucis+@pitt.edu
URL: http://www.ucis.pitt.edu/reesweb/
Contact: Karen Rondestvedt, Slavic Bibliographer, rondest+@pitt.edu.
Desc: The Russian and Eastern European Studies database is a comprehensive index of electronic resources on the Balkans, the Baltic states, the Caucasus, Central Asia, Central Europe, Eastern Europe, the Russian Federation, and the former Soviet Union. Data can be accessed by discipline or type of resource (interactive databases, software, discussion groups, etc.) Shortcuts to popular destinations are provided. *Type:* Database.

Selfreliance Association of American Ukrainians

98 2nd Ave. Ph: (212)777-1336
New York, NY 10003 Fax: (212)777-1336
Contact: Natalia Duma, Pres.
Desc: Americans of Ukrainian birth or descent. Aids Ukrainian immigrants. Offers courses in Ukrainian literature and history. *Type:* Association.

Serb National Federation

1 5th Ave., 7th Fl. Ph: (412)642-7372
Pittsburgh, PA 15222-3126 Fax: (412)642-1372
E-mail: snf@serbnathlfed.org
URL: http://www.serbnathfed.org
Contact: George Martich, Pres.
Desc: Fraternal benefit life insurance society. *Type:* Association.

Slovak-American National Council

HVASTA
PO Box 4197 Ph: (703)281-0334
St. Augustine, FL 32085-4197 Fax: (703)281-0002
Contact: John Hvasta, Pres.
Desc: Slovak-Americans. Purpose is to act as an issue-oriented public advocate for Slovak interests in the U.S.

Seeks to address and educate Congress on issues including immigration, refugees, resettlement, human rights abuses, and religious persecution in former Czechoslovakia. *Type:* Association.

Slovak Catholic Sokol
205 Madison St.   Ph: (973)777-2605
Passaic, NJ 07055   Free: 800-886-7656
                         Fax: (973)779-8245
Contact: Steven M. Pogorelec, Supreme Sec.

Desc: Americans of Slovak or Slav descent. *Type:* Association.

Slovene National Benefit Society
247 W. Allegheny Rd.   Free: 800-843-7675
Imperial, PA 15126-9774
E-mail: snpj@snpj.com
URL: http://www.snpj.com
Contact: Karen A. Valencic, Sec.

Desc: Fraternal benefit life insurance society. Maintains scholarship fund, museum, juvenile department, youth circles, and youth and young adult programs. Sponsors sports and team activities. *Type:* Association.

SOKOL U.S.A.
276 Prospect St.   Ph: (973)676-0280
PO Box 189   Fax: (973)676-3348
East Orange, NJ 07019
Contact: Milan S. Kovac, Supreme Sec.

Desc: Fraternal benefit life insurance society. Promotes physical fitness through gymnastic competitions and exhibitions. Maintains camps and halls in several states. *Type:* Association.

Sons of Norway
1455 W. Lake St.   Ph: (612)827-3611
Minneapolis, MN 55408   Fax: (612)827-0658
E-mail: fraternal@sofn.com
URL: http://www.sofn.com
Contact: Lee A. Rowe, CEO.

Desc: Fraternal benefit insurance society for persons of Norwegian and other Nordic birth, descent, or affiliation by marriage. Promotes preservation of Norwegian cultural heritage; sponsors Norwegian language and crafts classes and camps; produces slide programs on Norwegian folk culture and fine arts. Maintains Sons of Norway Foundation, which provides educational, charitable, and cultural support for programs promoting the preservation of Norwegian culture. *Type:* Association.

Tibet Fund
241 E. 32nd St.   Ph: (212)213-5011
New York, NY 10016   Fax: (212)779-9245
E-mail: tibetfund@tibetfund.org
URL: http://www.tibetfund.org
Contact: Rinchen Dharlo, Pres.

Desc: Purposes are to: assist in the preservation of Tibetan culture; further ongoing development of Tibetan arts and sciences; promote Tibetan contributions to the modern world. Funds Tibetan institutions in exile such as the Tibetan Medical Institute, the Institute of Higher Tibetan Studies, and the Tibetan Institute of Performing Arts, in addition to Tibetan Buddhist monastic institutions now reestablished in India and Nepal. Maintains speakers' bureau; conducts charitable program; compiles statistics. *Type:* Association.

Tolstoy Foundation
104 Lake Rd.   Ph: (914)268-6140
Valley Cottage, NY 10989 Fax: (914)268-6937
E-mail: tfhq@aol.com
Contact: Xenia Woyevodsky, Exec.Dir.

Desc: Voluntary agency "to assist refugees from countries under oppression in the area of welfare, to preserve and promote the finest traditions of Russian art, history, and thought, and generally the best humanitarian ideals of Russian culture." Operates old age homes and a nursing home. *Type:* Association.

Turkish-American Association
1600 Broadway   Ph: (212)956-1560
48th St., Ste. 318   Fax: (212)956-1562
New York, NY 10019-7413
Contact: Inci Fenik, Sec.

Desc: Promotes cultural relations between the United States and Turkey. Sponsors Turkish radio program in the New York/New Jersey area, films, concerts, music festivals, conferences, and lectures; arranges charter flights to Turkey. *Type:* Association.

Ukrainian National Association
2200 Route 10   Ph: (973)292-9800
Parsippany, NJ 07054-0280 Free: 800-253-9862
                         Fax: (973)292-0900
E-mail: webmaster@brama.com
Contact: Ulana M. Diachuk, Pres.

Desc: Fraternal benefit life insurance society for persons of Ukrainian and Slavic ancestry and their relatives. *Type:* Association.

Union of Councils
1819 H St. NW, Ste. 230 Ph: (202)775-9770
Washington, DC 20006   Fax: (202)775-9776
E-mail: ucsj@ucsj.com
URL: http://www.fsumonitor.com
Contact: Yosef Abramowitz, Pres.

Desc: Educates the public about the situation facing Jews and human rights activists in the former Soviet Union, such as denial of emigration requests and anti-Semitism. Maintains daily contact with refusenik community (those who applied for, and were denied, emigration visas from the Soviet Union) and sets policy and makes program decisions in consultation with refusenik leaders. Works with professional groups of scientists, doctors, and lawyers to bring attention to violations of professional ethics such as psychiatric abuse and illegal detainment. *Type:* Association.

United Hellenic Voters of America
525 W. Lake St.   Ph: (708)628-1721
Addison, IL 60101   Fax: (708)543-7001
Contact: Dr. Dimitrios Kyriazopoulos, Supreme Chm.

Desc: Persons of Greek descent united to: establish and promote citizenship among people of Hellenic descent; encourage these people to participate in politics or public service, and in the political affairs of their communities; aid members in the exercise of their rights and responsibilities as U.S. citizens. Recommends and supports candidates for elected or appointed office. *Type:* Association.

Western Fraternal Life Association
1900 1st Ave. NE   Ph: (319)363-2653
Cedar Rapids, IA 52402   Fax: (319)363-8806
Contact: Ray Miller, Pres.

Desc: Fraternal benefit society. *Type:* Association.

World Association of Upper Silesians
c/o Dr. Karol H. Sitko
PO Box 3
Tafton, PA 18464
Contact: Dr. Karol H. Sitko, Pres.

Desc: Individuals interested in or from the area known as Upper Silesia. (Silesia is a region of approximately 20,000 square miles in east Central Europe divided between north central Czechoslovakia and southwest Poland; it was formerly a province of Prussia and a crownland of Austria.) Promotes Polish-German reconciliation. Cooperates with Upper Silesian organizations throughout the western world. *Type:* Association.

World Federation of Taiwanese Associations
PO Box 2736, Sta. F   Ph: (416)292-4030
Scarborough, ON, Canada Fax: (416)470-1545
M1W 3P3
Contact: Dr. Shane Lee, Pres.

Desc: Individuals interested in Taiwan and those who consider Taiwan their homeland. Promotes friendship and Taiwanese culture; conducts seminars related to Taiwanese economics, politics, environment, and arts. *Type:* Association.

Zgoda
Polish National Alliance of North America
7526 Broadway   Ph: (216)641-4900
Cleveland, OH 44105   Fax: (216)271-0079
Contact: Dr. Wojciech Wierzewski, Editor.

Desc: Fraternal organization magazine printed in English and Polish. *Type:* Periodical.

Evangelism

AMF International
Box 5470   Ph: (708)418-0020
Lansing, IL 60438-5470   Fax: (708)418-0132
E-mail: amfi@iname.com
URL: http://www.amfi.org
Contact: Wesley N. Taber, Exec.Dir.

Desc: Persons who make contributions and pray for evangelization and welfare of Jewish people. Seeks to: present Jesus of Nazareth as Israel's Messiah; improve relations between Jews and Christians; oppose anti-Semitism in all its forms; encourage informed support of Israel. Sponsors Bible classes; maintains missionaries in the U.S. *Type:* Association.

Athletes in Action
PO Box 588   Ph: (513)933-2421
Lebanon, OH 45036   Fax: (513)933-2424
E-mail: AIAcom@aol.com
URL: http://www.athletesinaction.org
Contact: Wendel Deyo, Dir.

Desc: Athletic ministry of Campus Crusade for Christ International. Maintains national and international athletic teams in men's and women's basketball, men's baseball, women's softball, gymnastics, track and field, wrestling, soccer, cycling, men's and women's volleyball, and swimming. Seeks to present the message of Jesus Christ worldwide through the platform of sports. *Type:* Association.

Bible Christian Union
PO Box 969   Ph: (630)279-5516
Wheaton, IL 60189-0969
Contact: George W. Murray, Exec.Dir.

Desc: Evangelical missionaries. Nondenominational evangelical mission agency operating in 12 Western and Central European countries. Establishes local evangelical churches; provides religious and leadership training. *Type:* Association.

Bible Holiness Movement
PO Box 1643   Ph: (250)498-3895
Oroville, WA 98844
Contact: Mrs. M. J. Wakefield, Exec. Officer.

Desc: Christian missionary denomination with emphasis on evangelism. Areas of concern include civil rights, racial equality, pacifism, food relief, and alcoholic and addict rehabilitation. *Type:* Association.

Bill Glass Ministries
PO Box 9000   Ph: (972)291-7895
Cedar Hill, TX 75106-2349 Fax: (972)293-0173
E-mail: gene@glassweb.com

URL: http://www.glassweb.com/

Contact: Bill Glass, Evangelist/CEO.

Desc: Evangelistic crusade founded by Bill Glass (1935-), former professional football player for the Detroit Lions and the Cleveland Browns. *Type:* Association.

Billy Graham Evangelistic Association

1300 Harmon Pl.   Ph: (612)338-0500
Minneapolis, MN 55403   Fax: (612)335-1289
URL: http://www.graham-assn.org

Contact: John R. Corts, Pres. & COO.

Desc: International evangelical organization. Conducts evangelistic crusades; broadcasts ministries over radio and television. Promotes Bible study. *Type:* Association.

Campus Crusade for Christ International

100 Sunport Ln.   Ph: (407)826-2000
Orlando, FL 32807
URL: http://www.ccci.org

Contact: William R. Bright, Founder & Pres.

Desc: Presents the gospel of Jesus Christ to individuals, groups, and protectorates in 152 countries. "To help fulfill the Great Commission of Christ in this generation and to work with other members of the Body of Christ." Activities focus on major discipleship/evangelism related events and include: Bible study groups for students, conferences for students, families, pastors, and laity. Operates over 40 ministries including: Andre Kole; Athletes in Action ; Business Executive; Campus (university/college); Christian Embassy; Christian Leadership (faculty); Drama; Family; Here's Life, World (special discipleship/evangelism outreach that has sponsored training by radio in 12 languages and translated the film "Jesus" into 236 languages); Here's Life, America (lay); Here's Life, Black America Now Heritage; Here's Life Christian Resource Centers; Here's Life Inner City; Here's Life Training Centers; Hispanic; International; International Christian Graduate University; International Student; Jesus Film Project; Josh McDowell; Mass Media; Military; Music; Paragon Productions (multimedia); Prayer; Prison; Student Venture (high school). *Type:* Association.

Child Evangelism Fellowship

Box 348   Ph: (314)456-4321
Warrenton, MO 63383   Free: 800-748-7710
                         Fax: (314)456-2078

Contact: Reese Kauffman, Pres.

Desc: Maintains local chapters throughout U.S. and Canada. Seeks to "take the Gospel of the Lord Jesus Christ to the world's children" by such means as home Bible classes, summer Bible classes, school-related classes, and camps. *Type:* Association.

Evangelical Friends International

5350 Broadmoor Cr. NW   Ph: (330)493-1660
Canton, OH 44709   Fax: (330)493-0852
E-mail: efcer@aol.com

Contact: Dr. John P. Williams, Jr., Regional Dir.

Desc: Coalition of Evangelical Friends churches. *Type:* Association.

Fellowship of Christian Athletes

8701 Leeds Rd.   Ph: (816)921-0909
Kansas City, MO 64129   Free: 800-289-0909
                         Fax: (816)921-8755

E-mail: fca@fca.org
URL: http://www.fca.org

Contact: Dal Shealy, Pres.

Desc: Professional and student athletes, present and former; clergy and laypersons. "To present to athletes and coaches and all whom they influence, the challenge and adventure of receiving Jesus Christ as Savior and Lord,

serving Him in their relationships and in the fellowship of the church." Sponsors rallies, retreats, summer sports camps, meetings of junior and senior high school and college athletes during the academic year, coaches meetings, athletic clinics, and school assemblies. Maintains National Conference Center in Indiana for retreats and leadership training. *Type:* Association.

Gideons International

2900 Lebanon Rd.   Ph: (615)883-8533
Nashville, TN 37214   Fax: (615)889-6877

Contact: Jerry Burden, Exec.Dir.

Desc: Christian business and professional men in 172 countries who seek "to win others for the Lord Jesus Christ" by distributing the Bible or portions thereof to individuals, hotels, hospitals, schools, and institutions. *Type:* Association.

International Students

PO Box C   Ph: (719)576-2700
Colorado Springs, CO 80901 Free: 800-ISI-TEAM
                         Fax: (719)576-5363

E-mail: team@isionline.org
URL: http://www.isionline.org

Contact: Tom Phillips, Pres.

Desc: Organizes friendship and hospitality programs for international students. *Type:* Association.

Inter-Varsity Christian Fellowship of the United States of America

PO Box 7895   Ph: (608)274-9001
Madison, WI 53707-7895   Fax: (608)274-7882
URL: http://www.ivcf.org

Contact: Stephen A. Hayner, Pres.

Desc: Students and faculty who are members of affiliated groups in universities, colleges, nursing schools, and other educational institutions. Provides evangelistic, spiritual growth, Bible study, prayer, and missionary activities. *Type:* Association.

Laymen's Home Missionary Movement

1156 St. Matthews Rd.   Ph: (610)827-7665
PO Box 67
Chester Springs, PA 19425-0067

Contact: Bernard W. Hedman, Exec.Dir.

Desc: Interdenominational, nonsectarian movement of individuals united to preach the Gospel and foster Christian behavior; stimulate a greater interest in individual and group Bible study; disseminate information and encourage others to spread knowledge of the Bible, particularly as it pertains to the modern world. *Type:* Association.

Life Action Ministries

2000 Morris Dr.   Ph: (616)684-5905
Niles, MI 49120   Fax: (616)684-0923
E-mail: bpaulus@lifeaction.org
URL: http://www.lifeaction.org

Contact: Rev. Byron Paulus, Exec.Dir.

Desc: Nationwide revival ministry devoted to America's return to living standards communicated through the Bible. Seeks the rebuilding and strengthening of the home and family through various ministries including Life Action Singers. *Type:* Association.

Life Outreach International

PO Box 982000   Ph: (817)267-4211
Fort Worth, TX 76182-8000 Fax: (817)685-1977
E-mail: feedback@lifetoday.com
URL: http://www.lifetoday.org

Contact: James Robison, Bd.Chm.

Desc: Christian ministry founded by James Robison (1963-). Sponsors daily (Monday-Friday) and weekly (Sunday) Christian television programs in the U.S. and Canada. *Type:* Association.

Luis Palau Evangelistic Association

PO Box 1173   Ph: (503)614-1500
Portland, OR 97207   Fax: (503)614-1599
E-mail: lpea@palau.org
URL: http://www.gospelcom.net/lpea

Contact: Luis Palau, Pres.

Desc: Mission organization founded by Luis Palau (1934-), Argentinian-born evangelist. Conducts evangelistic campaigns and outreach programs to bring the word of Christ to the world. Supports service to the church through: Bible teaching; counseling by mail; evangelism training. *Type:* Association.

Morris Cerullo World Evangelism

Dr. Morris Cerullo
PO Box 85277   Ph: (619)277-2200
San Diego, CA 92186   Fax: (619)277-5111
E-mail: morriscerullo@mcwe.com
URL: http://www.mcwe.com/

Contact: Dr. Morris Cerullo, Pres.

Desc: Christian missionary organization that functions through ministers in 133 countries. Sponsors Morris Cerullo evangelistic crusades around the world and in major cities of North America. Conducts minister training seminars in various countries, training approximately 50,000 ministers annually. *Type:* Association.

Pentecostal Evangel

General Council of the Assemblies of God Gospel Publishing House
1445 Boonville Ave.   Ph: (417)862-2781
Springfield, MO 65802-1894 Fax: (417)862-0416
E-mail: pevangel@ag.org.

Contact: Hal Donaldson, Editor; Jodi Harmon, Advertising Mgr.; Ken Horn, Managing Editor.

Desc: Assemblies of God official magazine. *Type:* Periodical.

Revival Fires (Christian Evangelizers Association)

PO Box 1008   Ph: (417)338-2422
Branson West, MO 65737   Fax: (417)338-8605
URL: http://www.revivalfires.org

Contact: Cecil Todd, Pres.

Desc: Religious congregations. Seeks to spread the gospel worldwide through missionary work. Sponors television programs and crusades; operates two orphanages, one hospital and out-patient clinic in Kerala State India. *Type:* Association.

Southern Missioner

Sacred Heart Southern Missions
PO Box 300   Ph: (601)781-1360
Walls, MS 38680-0300   Fax: (601)781-3340
URL: http://www.sacredheartleague.org.

Contact: Paul Bauer, Editor, pbauer@sacredheartleague.org.

Desc: Highlights the activities of the Sacred Heart Southern Missionaries, a Roman Catholic group that works in the nine northern counties of Mississippi. Recurring features include reports of social service programs, educational improvements, human interest stories, and a column titled Father Charles Writes.. *Type:* Newsletter.

WEC International

PO Box 1707   Ph: (215)646-2322
Fort Washington, PA 19034 Fax: (215)646-6202
E-mail: 105501.3520@compuserve.com
URL: http://www.wec-usa.org

Contact: James G. Raymo, Jr., USA Dir.

Desc: "Purpose is to evangelize the remaining unevangelized areas of the world by establishing churches, and sometimes hospitals and schools." *Type:* Association.

Word of Life Fellowship

PO Box 600
Schroon Lake, NY 12870   Ph: (518)532-7111
URL: http://www.wol.org   Fax: (518)532-7421
Contact: George Theis, Exec.Dir.

Desc: Religious, evangelistic organization particularly interested in "winning young people to Christ and Christian living." Activities include Bible clubs, rallies, radio and television programs, Bible institutes, and distribution of literature. Has missionaries in 47 countries. Maintains summer camps throughout the world. *Type:* Association.

World Evangelical Fellowship

PO Box WEF   Ph: (630)668-0440
Wheaton, IL 60189-8004   Fax: (630)668-0498
E-mail: wef-na@xc.org
URL: http://www.worldevangelical.org
Contact: Agustin B. Vencer, Jr., Dir.

Desc: Works to establish and help regional and national evangelical alliances empower and mobilize local churches and Christian organizations to "disciple the nations for Christ." Seeks to: strengthen evangelical leadership; develop a "world evangelical identity"; enhance the interdependence of churches through sharing of information and resources. *Type:* Association.

World Relief

PO Box WRC   Ph: (630)665-0235
Wheaton, IL 60189   Free: 800-535-5433
   Fax: (630)665-4473
E-mail: worldrelief@xc.org
URL: http://www.worldrelief.org
Contact: Dr. Clive Calver, Pres.

Desc: Emergency aid, development assistance, and refugee service of the National Association of Evangelicals. Conducts programs of disaster relief; refugee relief and resettlement; community development programs, including public health, education, and economic assistance. Carries out programs in Asia, Africa, Latin America, and the U.S. *Type:* Association.

Youth Evangelism Association

George Dooms
Tri-State Youth for Christ   Ph: (812)867-2418
13000 U.S. 41 N   Fax: (812)867-8933
Evansville, IN 47711
Contact: George Dooms, Pres.

Desc: Youth leaders and ministries. Works to provide youth activities and promote family ministries. Conducts educational and charitable programs. *Type:* Association.

Families

Alliance for Children and Families

11700 W. Lake Park Dr.   Ph: (414)359-1040
Milwaukee, WI 53224   Free: 800-221-3726
   Fax: (414)359-1074
URL: http://www.fsanet.org
Contact: Peter Goldberg, CEO & Pres.

Desc: Federation of local agencies in more than 1000 communities providing family counseling, family life education and family advocacy services, and other programs to help families with parent-child, marital, mental health, and other problems of family living. Assists member agencies in developing and providing effective family services. Works with the media, government, and corporations to promote strong family life. *Type:* Association.

Family Research Council

801 G St. NW   Ph: (202)393-2100
Washington, DC 20001   Free: 800-225-4008
   Fax: (202)393-2134
E-mail: corrdept@frc.org

URL: http://www.frc.org
Contact: Gary Bauer, Pres.

Desc: Provides expertise and information to government agencies, members of Congress, policymakers, the media, and the public. Focuses on issues such as: parental autonomy and responsibility; the impact of parental absence; community support for single parents; effects of the tax system on families; families assisting less fortunate families; the sanctity of life; adolescent pregnancy; teen suicide; family strengths; parental choice in education; divorce reform; military family issues. *Type:* Association.

Family Resource Coalition of America

20 N. Wacker Dr. Ste. 1100   Ph: (312)338-0900
Chicago, IL 60606   Fax: (312)338-1522
E-mail: frca@frca.org
URL: http://www.frca.org
Contact: Shay Riley, Media Relations Dir.

Desc: Membership, consulting, and advocacy organization that has been advancing the movement to strengthen and support families since 1981. The family support movement and FRCA seek to strengthen and empower families and communities so that they can foster the optimal development of children, youth and adult family members. Builds networks, produces resources, advocates for public policy, provides consulting services, and gathers knowledge to help the family support movement grow. *Type:* Association.

Family Violence Awareness Page: Let's Stop Domestic Violence And Child Abuse

famvi.com
PO Box 17186   Ph: (317)888-1318
Indianapolis, IN 46217-0186   Fax: (317)888-3091
E-mail: comments@famvi.com
URL: http://www.famvi.com/
Contact: Gary Templeton, gtemp@iquest.net.

Desc: The Domestic Violence Home Page is dedicated to preventing family violence and to providing information about services available to families in need of assistance. This site includes articles, essays, and readers' comments on all aspects of domestic violence. *Type:* Database.

Focus on the Family

8605 Explorer Dr.   Ph: (719)531-3400
Colorado Springs, CO 80920   Free: 800-A-FAMILY
   Fax: (719)548-4525
URL: http://www.fotf.org
Contact: Dr. James C. Dobson, Pres.

Desc: Promotes traditional Judeo-Christian values and strong family ties. *Type:* Association.

Focus on the Family Magazine

Focus on the Family
8605 Explorer Dr.   Ph: (719)531-3400
Colorado Springs, CO 80920-   Free: 800-232-6459
1051   Fax: (719)548-5860
E-mail: tifeditor@fotf.org
URL: http://www.family.org.
Contact: James C. Dobson, Ph.D, Publisher; Tom Neven, Editor, (719)548-5881, fax: (719)548-3499; Kurt Bruner, Vice President of Periodicals; Timothy Jones, Senior Art Dir.

Desc: Magazine containing marriage and parenting articles from a Christian perspective. *Type:* Periodical.

Homelink

PO Box 650   Ph: (305)294-7766
Key West, FL 33041   Free: 800-638-3841
   Fax: (305)294-1448
E-mail: usa@homelink.org
URL: http://www.swapnow.com
Contact: Karl Costabel, Exec. Officers.

Desc: Individuals and families interested in exchanging homes (apartments, cottages, or farms) temporarily for holiday and vacation purposes. Members write to each other to make their own exchange or rental arrangements. The club is linked with Homelink International, Cambridge, England; International Home Exchange, Manly, Australia; Sejours, Aix-en-Provence, France; Holiday Service, Memmelsdorf, Germany; LOVW, Groningen, Netherlands; Intercambio de Casas, Madrid, Spain; Taxi-Stop, Ghent, Belgium; Casa Vacanza, Padova, Italy; and West World Holiday Exchange, Vancouver, Canada; these groups issue combined directories of U.S. and European home exchange offerings. *Type:* Association.

International Chili Society

6755 Speedway Blvd.   Ph: (702)643-5700
Las Vegas, NV 89115   Fax: (702)643-8300
E-mail: chiliics@earthlink.net
URL: http://www.chilicookoff.com
Contact: Jim West, Exec.Dir.

Desc: Chili enthusiasts who believe that chili cooking is "as American as apple pie." Sponsors chili cook-offs in search of the best chili. Holds 350 competitions with winners proceeding to one of 97 regional or state competitions. Regional and state champions compete at annual cook-off where the winner receives a $25,000 prize. *Type:* Association.

LEXIS® Family Law Library

LEXIS-NEXIS
9443 Springboro Pike   Ph: (937)865-6800
PO Box 933
Dayton, OH 45401-0933
URL: http://www.lex-nexis.com

Desc: Contains the state and federal case law addressing family-related law issues. Also has federal regulatory materials, state and federal statutes, and bill tracking information from all 50 states and the District of Columbia. *Available:* LEXIS-NEXIS, LEXIS. *Type:* Database.

San Diego Family Magazine

San Diego Family Magazine
PO Box 23960   Ph: (619)685-6970
San Diego, CA 92193
E-mail: sandiegofamily@family.com.
URL: http://www.sandiegofamily.com.
Contact: Sharon Bay, Publisher.

Desc: Magazine. *Type:* Periodical.

Save a Family Plan

PO Box 611832
Port Huron, MI 48061-1832
E-mail: safpinfo@safp.org
URL: http://www.safp.org
Contact: Fr. Sebastian Adayanthrath, Exec.Dir.

Desc: Seeks to assist families in developing regions in India and Haiti. *Type:* Association.

Teaching-Family Association

910 Charles St.   Ph: (540)370-0102
Fredericksburg, VA 22401-5810   Fax: (540)370-0015
Contact: Michael P. Hussey, Pres.

Desc: Practitioners (individuals trained in providing family services to youths living in group home situations); others include evaluators, trainers, program consultants, and administrators not involved in a live-in group home situation. Ensures that minimum standards of quality are met in all of the programs throughout the U.S. *Type:* Association.

TV-Free America
1611 Connecticut Ave. NW,   Ph: (202)887-0436
Ste. 3A   Fax: (202)518-5560
Washington, DC 20009
E-mail: tvfa@essential.org
URL: http://www.essential.org/orgs/tvfa
Contact: Henry Labalme, Exec.Dir.

Desc: Works to encourage Americans to drastically reduce the amount of time spent watching television to promote family interaction and community involvement. *Type:* Association.

Family Planning

Advocates for Youth
1025 Vermont Ave. NW, Ste.   Ph: (202)347-5700
200   Fax: (202)347-2263
Washington, DC 20005
E-mail: info@advocatesforyouth.org
URL: http://www.advocatesforyouth.org
Contact: James Wagoner, Exec.Dir. & Pres.

Desc: Objectives are to: reduce the incidence of unintended teenage pregnancy and childbearing and promote adolescent health through education; to prevent the proliferation of the human immunodeficiency virus (HIV) among adolescents; motivate teens to think and act responsibly about birth control and parenting; conduct programs and advocacy campaigns to assure minors' access to family planning information and services. *Type:* Association.

Alan Guttmacher Institute
120 Wall St., 21st Fl.   Ph: (212)248-1111
New York, NY 10005   Fax: (212)248-1951
E-mail: info@agi-usa.org
URL: http://www.agi-usa.org
Contact: Jeannie I. Rosoff, Pres.

Desc: Fosters sound public policies on voluntary fertility control and population issues and encourages responsive reproductive health programs through policy analysis, public education, and research in the U.S. and internationally. Compiles statistics and conducts policy-relevant research on the provision of services relating to reproductive health care. *Type:* Association.

American Society for Reproductive Medicine
1209 Montgomery Hwy.   Ph: (205)978-5000
Birmingham, AL 35216-2809   Fax: (205)978-5005
E-mail: asrm@asrm.com
URL: http://www.asrm.com
Contact: Nancy C. Hayley, Adm.Dir.

Desc: Gynecologists, obstetricians, urologists, reproductive endocrinologists, veterinarians, research workers, and others interested in reproductive health in humans and animals. Seeks to extend knowledge of all aspects of fertility and problems of infertility and mammalian reproduction; provides a rostrum for the presentation of scientific studies dealing with these subjects. Offers patient resource information and placement service. *Type:* Association.

Association of Reproductive Health Professionals
2401 Pennsylvania Ave. NW,   Ph: (202)466-3825
Ste. 350   Fax: (202)466-3826
Washington, DC 20037-1718
E-mail: arhp@arhp.org
URL: http://www.arhp.org
Contact: Wayne C. Shields, Pres.

Desc: Professionals in reproductive health, including obstetricians, gynecologists, family practitioners, pediatricians, nurse clinicians, researchers, educators, counselors, and administrators. Interested in contraception, sexually transmitted diseases, HIV/AIDS, menopause, urogenital disorders, sexuality, cancer prevention/detection, abortion and infertility. *Type:* Association.

Association for Voluntary Surgical Contraception
79 Madison Ave.   Ph: (212)561-8000
New York, NY 10016   Fax: (212)779-9439
Contact: Hugo Hoogenboom, Pres.

Desc: Aim is to make safe and effective voluntary surgical contraception a known and real choice for all men and women everywhere. Surgical contraception includes female sterilization, vasectomy, hormonal implants, intrauterine devices, injectables and other methods that require medical procedures. Helps countries and institutions around the world establish, expand, or improve surgical contraception services. *Type:* Association.

AVSC International
79 Madison Ave.   Ph: (212)561-8000
New York, NY 10016-7802   Fax: (212)779-9489
E-mail: info@avsc.org
URL: http://www.avsc.org
Contact: Amy E. Pollack, Pres.

Desc: Seeks to provide women and men with access to voluntary and safe contraception. Helps countries and institutions develop, improve, and expand systems for the provision of clinic-based contraception services. Special expertise in female sterilization and vasectomy. *Type:* Association.

Catholics for a Free Choice
1436 U St. NW, No. 301   Ph: (202)986-6093
Washington, DC 20009   Fax: (202)332-7995
E-mail: cffc@igc.apc.org
URL: http://www.cath4choice.org/catholicvote
Contact: Frances Kissling, Pres.

Desc: Seeks shape and advance sexual and reproductive ethics that are based on justice, reflect a commitment to women's well-being, and respect and affirm the moral capacity of women and men to make sound and responsible decisions about their lives. *Type:* Association.

Family Health International
PO Box 13950   Ph: (919)544-7040
Durham, NC 27709   Fax: (919)544-7261
URL: http://www.fhi.org
Contact: Willard Cates, MD MPH, Pres.

Desc: Biomedical researchers and technical assistants. Promotes increased availability, safety, effectiveness, acceptability, and ease of using family planning methods. Works to improve the delivery of voluntary fertility planning and primary health care services, and reduce the spread of sexually transmitted diseases, especially HIV infection. *Type:* Association.

Fertility Research Foundation
877 Park Ave.   Ph: (212)744-5500
New York, NY 10021   Fax: (212)744-6536
E-mail: frfbaby@msn.com
Contact: Masood A. Khatamee, M.D., Exec.Dir.

Desc: Specializes in human reproduction. Provides therapeutic, diagnostic, and consultation service for childless couples. Conducts comprehensive infertility surveys which include: endoscopy, sperm antibodies determination, bacteriological assessment, endocrine studies, laboratory facilities for complete hormone assays, surgical correction of genital diseases, artificial donor insemination, and ovulation induction. *Type:* Association.

International Planned Parenthood Federation, Western Hemisphere Region
120 Wallstreet, 9th Fl.   Ph: (212)248-6400
New York, NY 10005   Fax: (212)248-2441
E-mail: info@ippfwhr.org
URL: http://www.ippfwhr.org
Contact: Hernan Sanhueza, Regional Dir.

Desc: Independent family planning organizations in Canada, Latin America, Caribbean Islands, and the United States. Views family planning as "the expression of the human right of couples to have only the children they want and to have them when they want them." Works to extend the practice of voluntary family planning by providing information, education, and services to couples. *Type:* Association.

Pathfinder International
9 Galen St., Ste. 217   Ph: (617)924-7200
Watertown, MA 02472   Fax: (617)924-3833
URL: http://www.pathfind.org
Contact: Daniel E. Pellegrom, Pres.

Desc: Established to find, demonstrate, and promote new and more efficient family planning programs in developing countries. Objectives are to introduce and expand the availability of effective family planning services; improve the welfare of families in developing countries; assist developing countries in implementing population policies favorable to national development. Conducts activities with a concern for upholding human rights, enhancing the status and role of women, and respecting the views of family planning clients. *Type:* Association.

Planned Parenthood Federation of America
810 7th Ave.   Ph: (212)261-4560
New York, NY 10019   Fax: (212)245-1845
URL: http://www.plannedparenthood.org/
Contact: Gloria Feldt, Pres.

Desc: Organizations providing leadership in making effective means of voluntary fertility regulation, including contraception, abortion, sterilization, and infertility services, available and fully accessible to all as a central element of reproductive health; stimulating and sponsoring relevant biomedical, socioeconomic, and demographic research; developing appropriate information, education, and training programs to increase knowledge about human reproduction and sexuality. Supports and assists efforts to achieve similar goals worldwide. Operates more than 900 centers that provide medically supervised reproductive health services and educational programs. *Type:* Association.

Resolve
1310 Broadway   Ph: (617)623-1156
Somerville, MA 02144-1731   Fax: (617)623-0252
E-mail: resolveinc@aol.com
URL: http://www.resolve.org
Contact: Diane D. Aronson, Exec.Dir.

Desc: Persons with problems of infertility and associated professionals who work with infertile couples such as adoption workers, physicians, and counselors. Seeks to provide "timely, compassionate support and information to people who are experiencing infertility, and to increase awareness of infertility issues." *Type:* Association.

Farming

Agriview
Vermont Department of Agriculture
116 State St., Drawer 20   Ph: (802)828-2500
Montpelier, VT 05602-2901   Fax: (802)828-2361
URL: http://www.cit.state.vt.us/agric.
Contact: Justin Johnson, Editor, justin@agr.state.vt.us.

Desc: Contains news on the Vermont farm community. Recurring features include a calendar of events. *Type:* Newsletter.

All Around Kentucky

Kentucky Farm Bureau Federation
9201 Bunsen Park Way   Ph: (502)495-5000
Louisville, KY 40220   Fax: (502)495-5114
E-mail: info@kyfb.win.net.
Contact: Gary Huddleston, Editor and Publisher; Judy Crask, Advertising Mgr.
Desc: Agriculture magazine reporting farm policy news and information on rural living. *Type:* Periodical.

American Farm Bureau Federation

225 Touhy Ave.   Ph: (847)685-8600
Park Ridge, IL 60068   Fax: (847)685-8896
URL: http://www.fb.com
Contact: Dean R. Kleckner, Pres.
Desc: Federation of 50 state farm bureaus and Puerto Rico, with membership on a family basis. Analyzes problems of members and formulates action to achieve educational improvement, economic opportunity, and social advancement. Maintains speakers' bureau; sponsors specialized education program. *Type:* Association.

American Farmland

American Farmland Trust
1200 18th St. NW, Ste. 800   Ph: (202)331-7300
Washington, DC 20036   Free: 800-886-5170
                         Fax: (202)659-8339
E-mail: info@farmland.org
URL: http://www.farmland.org.
Contact: Christina Soto, Editor, csoto@farmland.org.
Desc: Offers information on establishing voluntary land protection programs to protect American farmland from development pressure and soil erosion, and to reduce the environmental impacts of farming. Recurring features include model land projects, preservation policies, and accounts of endangered agricultural regions. *Type:* Newsletter.

American Harvest

Cornucopia Press/Special Interest Publishing
3 Golf Center, Ste. 221
Hoffman Estates, IL 60195
Contact: Tamara Sellman, Editor.
Desc: Provides information regarding meatless low-fat cooking, organic farming and gardening, sustainable agriculture, and natural foods. Recurring features include columns titled FoodNotes, From Scratch, Season to Taste, and Good For You. *Type:* Newsletter.

American Society of Agricultural Consultants Newsletter

American Society of Agricultural Consultants (ASAC)
900 S. Cherry St., Ste. 508   Ph: (303)759-5091
Denver, CO 80246-2664   Fax: (303)758-0190
E-mail: asfmra@aol.com; asac@agrl-associations.org
Contact: Mia Peterson, Editor.
Desc: Features American Society for Agricultural Consultants member news and events. Recurring features include interviews, news of research, book reviews, a calendar of events, news of educational opportunities, notices of publications available, and job listings. *Type:* Newsletter.

Arkansas Farm Bureau Federation

Farm Bureau Center   Ph: (501)224-4400
PO Box 31
Little Rock, AR 72203
URL: http://www.arfb.com
Contact: Dennis Robertson, Exec.VP.
Desc: Represents the interests of members. Lobbies on their behalf. *Type:* Association.

Bio-Dynamic Farming and Gardening Association

PO Box 29135   Ph: (415)561-7797
San Francisco, CA 94129-0135   Free: 888-516-7797
                                 Fax: (415)561-7796
Contact: Charles Beedy, Exec.Dir.
Desc: Farmers, gardeners, consumers, physicians, and scientists interested in improving nutrition and health through the production of high quality food using bio-dynamic farming. (Bio-dynamic farming stresses restoration of organic matter to the soil, use of special preparations to stimulate biological activity of soil and plant growth, crop rotation, proper cultivation to avoid structural damage to soil, and establishment of beneficial environmental conditions such as forests, wind protection, and water regulation.) *Type:* Association.

C & A

American Anthropological Association
4350 N. Fairfax Dr., Ste. 640   Ph: (703)528-1902
Arlington, VA 22203-1620   Fax: (703)528-3546
URL: http://www.ameranthassn.org
Contact: Jeffrey L. Longhofer, Editor.
Desc: Features articles on agriculture development and agrarian transformation. Recurring features include news of research, news of educational opportunities, book reviews, notices of publications available, and a calendar of events. *Type:* Newsletter.

California Farm Bureau Federation

1601 Exposition Blvd.   Ph: (916)924-4075
Sacramento, CA 95815   Fax: (916)923-5318
Contact: Bob L. Vice, Pres.
Desc: Farmers. Represents members' interests; conducts lobbying activities. *Type:* Association.

Cooperative Farmer

Southern States Cooperative, Inc.
PO Box 26234   Ph: (804)281-1369
Richmond, VA 23260   Fax: (804)281-1119
Contact: Charles I. Batchelor, Editor and Publisher.
Desc: Agricultural magazine. *Type:* Periodical.

Farm Bureau Journal

Oklahoma Farm Bureau, Inc.
2501 N. Stiles   Ph: (405)523-2300
Oklahoma City, OK 73105   Free: 800-299-2412
                            Fax: (405)523-2362
URL: http://www.fb.com/okfb.
Contact: Mike Nichols, Editor, (405)523-2345, fax: (405)523-2362, mike_nichols@okfb.fb.com.
Desc: Agriculture magazine (tabloid). *Type:* Periodical.

Farm Bureau Press

Arkansas Farm Bureau Federation
10720 Kanis Rd.   Ph: (501)224-4400
PO Box 31   Fax: (501)228-1557
Little Rock, AR 72211-3825
Contact: A. Audie Ayer, Editor; James M. Kester, Advertising Mgr., (501)228-1274.
Desc: Association newspaper covering farm issues in Arkansas and nationally. *Alt. Contact:* Box 31, Little Rock, AR 72203-0031; telephone: (501)228-1307; fax: (501)228-1557. *Type:* Periodical.

Farm News & Views

Oklahoma Farmers Union
6200 N.W. 2nd   Ph: (405)789-5666
PO Box 24000   Fax: (405)491-1599
Oklahoma City, OK 73127-6521
Contact: Phil Klutts, Editor; H. Lee Streetman, Advertising Mgr.

Desc: Tabloid reporting on and promoting the family farm system of agriculture. Official publication of the Oklahoma Farmers Union. *Type:* Periodical.

Farm Tax Saver

Sara Wyant
191 S. Gary Ave.   Ph: (708)462-2861
Carol Stream, IL 60188   Fax: (708)462-2869
E-mail: swyant@formprogress.com
Contact: Trenna Grabowski, Editor.
Desc: Monitors changes in tax laws and analyzes how they affect farm families. Covers areas such as social security tax, tax shelters, tax on investments, and tax records required on transportation costs. *Type:* Newsletter.

Farming for Profit

Doane Agricultural Services
11701 Borman Dr., Ste. 100   Ph: (314)569-2700
St. Louis, MO 63146-4199   Fax: (314)569-1083
Contact: Allen Dever, Editor.
Desc: Provides information on farm commodities. *Type:* Newsletter.

FarmWeek

Illinois Agricultural Association
1701 Towanda Ave.   Ph: (309)557-3140
Bloomington, IL 61701   Fax: 800-998-6090
E-mail: lagoltz@aol.com.
Contact: Dave McClelland, Editor, (309)557-3156, fax: (800)640-1995; Richard Verdery, Advertising Mgr., rverdery@ilfb.org.
Desc: Agricultural publication (tabloid) for Illinois farmers. *Type:* Periodical.

FFA UPDATE

The National FFA Organization
6060 FFA Dr.   Ph: (317)802-6060
PO Box 68960   Fax: (317)802-6061
Indianapolis, IN 46268-0960
Desc: Designed for National FFA Organization members. Recurring features include a calendar of events, news of educational opportunities, job listings, and notices of publications available. *Type:* Newsletter.

FloridAgriculture

Florida Farm Bureau Federation
PO Box 147030   Ph: (352)374-1523
Gainesville, FL 32614-7030   Fax: (352)374-1530
Contact: Mary Ward, Editor, (352)374-1521; G.B. Crawford, Asst. Editor, (352)374-1517; Judy Plock, (904)374-1521; Mary Griffis, Advertising Mgr.; Tom Lampert, Advertising Representative.
Desc: Newspaper for members of the Florida Farm Bureau Federation. *Type:* Periodical.

FMRA News

American Society of Farm Managers and Rural Appraisers (ASFMRA)
950 S. Cherry St., Ste. 508   Ph: (303)758-3513
Denver, CO 80246-2664   Fax: (303)758-0190
E-mail: asfmra@agri-associations.org; publications@agri-associations.org
Contact: Mia Peterson, Editor, mpeterson@agri-associations.org.
Desc: Considers such topics as environmental issues, governmental regulation, technological advances, relative legislation, and other issues pertinent to rural resource properties. Recurring features include news of Society activities, educational offerings, and membership updates. *Type:* Newsletter.

Georgia Farm Bureau Federation

PO Box 7068   Ph: (912)474-8411
Macon, GA 31298   Fax: (912)474-8750
Contact: Wayne Dollar, Contact.
Desc: Provides services to farmers. *Type:* Association.

The Hoosier Farmer

Indiana Farm Bureau, Inc.
225 South East St.   Ph: (317)692-7822
PO Box 1290   Fax: (317)692-7854
Indianapolis, IN 46206
E-mail: infbinfo@farmbureau.com
Contact: Tom Asher, Editor; Paul Miner, Managing Editor, (317)692-7822.
Desc: Agricultural magazine. *Type:* Periodical.

Iowa Farm Bureau Federation

5400 W. University Ave.   Ph: (515)225-5400
West Des Moines, IA 50265   Fax: (515)225-5419
E-mail: comments@ifbf.org
URL: http://www.ifbf.org
Contact: Richard Harris, Exec.Dir.
Desc: Farms. Promotes agriculture and protects the general welfare of its members. *Type:* Association.

Kansas Country Living

Kansas Electric Cooperative, Inc.
PO Box 4267   Ph: (913)478-4554
Gage Center Sta.   Fax: (913)478-4852
Topeka, KS 66604-0267
Contact: Larry Freeze, Editor.
Desc: Magazine for members of Kansas' electric cooperatives that promotes the uses of electrical energy around the farm and home. *Type:* Periodical.

Kansas Living

Kansas Farm Bureau
2627 KFB Plaza   Ph: (913)587-6000
Manhattan, KS 66502   Fax: (913)587-6914
Contact: Steve Logback, Editor; John Schlageck, Managing Editor; Debbie Hargrave, Business Mgr.
Desc: Farm news magazine. *Type:* Periodical.

Linder Farm Network

1929 Cedar Ave. S   Ph: (507)444-0167
Owatonna, MN 55060   Fax: (507)444-9080
Contact: Lynn Ketelson, Farm Dir.; Terri Weldele, Farm Broadcaster.
Alt. Contact: 1929 Cedar Ave. S, Owutonnu, MN 55060; telephone: (507)444-0167; fax: (506)444-9080. *Type:* Periodical.

Michigan Farm Bureau

7373 W. Saginaw Hwy.   Ph: (517)323-7000
PO Box 30960   Fax: (517)323-6558
Lansing, MI 48909
URL: http://www.fb.com/mifb
Contact: Jack Laurie, Pres.
Desc: Farmer advocacy organization. Provides buyer services and insurance. *Type:* Association.

Michigan Farm Radio Network

PO Box 269   Ph: (313)439-1522
Milan, MI 48160-0269
Contact: Robert Driscoll, President; John Stommen, Vice President; Patrick Driscoll, Exec. and Farm Dir.
Desc: Agricultural radio network format. *Alt. Contact:* PO Box 269, Milan, MI 48160-0269; telephone: (313)439-1522. *Type:* Periodical.

National Association of Farmer Elected Committeemen

Verner Magnusson
2030 County Rd. N   Ph: (402)377-2236
Oakland, NE 68045
Contact: Verner Magnusson, Pres.
Desc: Works to: build a sound farm program; promote conservation; preserve the family farm; develop an export market; promote parity for farmers. *Type:* Association.

National Farmers Union

11900 E. Cornell Ave.   Ph: (303)337-5500
Aurora, CO 80014-3194   Free: 800-347-1961
    Fax: (303)368-1390
E-mail: nfu.denver@nfu.org
URL: http://www.nfu.org
Contact: Leland H. Swenson, Pres.
Desc: Farm families interested in agricultural welfare. Carries on educational, cooperative, and legislative activities. *Type:* Association.

National Farmers Union Newsletter

National Farmers Union/Canada
250-C 2nd Ave., S.   Ph: (306)652-9465
Saskatoon, SK, Canada S7K   Fax: (306)664-6226
2M1
E-mail: nfu@sk.sympatico.ca
URL: http://www.nfu.ca.
Contact: Darrin Qualman, Editor.
Desc: Contains information on agricultural and rural issues. *Type:* Newsletter.

National Grange

1616 H St. NW   Ph: (202)628-3507
Washington, DC 20006   Fax: (202)347-1091
URL: http://www.nationalgrange.org
Contact: Kermit W. Richardson, Master.
Desc: Rural family service organization with a special interest in agriculture. Promotes mission and goals through legislative, social, educational, community service, youth, and member services programs. *Type:* Association.

Nebraska Union Farmer

Nebraska Farmers Union
PO Box 22667   Ph: (402)476-8815
Lincoln, NE 68542-2667   Fax: (402)476-8859
E-mail: nefusal@aol.com.
Contact: Sally Herrin, Editor.
Desc: Presents news of the Union and information that affects farmers and rural communities. Recurring features include news of research, a calendar of events, reports of meetings, and news of educational opportunities. *Type:* Newsletter.

Nevada Farm Bureau Agriculture and Livestock Journal

Nevada Farm Bureau Federation
1300 Marietta Way   Ph: (702)358-3276
Sparks, NV 89431   Free: 800-922-1106
    Fax: (702)358-2107
E-mail: ednufb@aol.com
URL: http://www.fb.com/nufb.
Contact: Norman F. Cardoza, Editor.
Desc: Provides news, features, and editorials of interest to Nevada farmers and ranchers. Recurring features include news of research. *Type:* Newsletter.

New England Farm Bulletin & Garden Gazette

Jacob's Meadow, Inc.
PO Box 67   Ph: (508)998-5424
Taunton, MA 02780-0067
Contact: Pam Comstock, Editor.

Desc: Features articles and information on gardening and farming. *Type:* Newsletter.

No-Till Farmer

No-Till Farmer
PO Box 624   Ph: (414)782-4480
Brookfield, WI 53008   Fax: (414)782-1252
Contact: Frank Lessiter, Editor.
Desc: Provides news and information to farmers interested in any aspect of reduced tillage and the farming environment. *Type:* Newsletter.

Nova Scotia Department of Agriculture and Marketing—Extension Newsletter

Nova Scotia Department of Agriculture & Marketing
PO Box 550   Ph: (902)893-6589
Truro, NS, Canada B2N 5E3
URL: http://www.nsac.ns.ca/e/newsletters.
Contact: George MacKenzie, Editor; Elizabeth Crouse, Editor; Cheryl Chandler, Editor.
Desc: Publishes brief articles on farming and news from each of the six 4-H regions in Nova Scotia. Recurring features include a section titled Agricultural Awareness. *Type:* Newsletter.

Ohio Farm Bureau Federation

PO Box 479   Ph: (614)249-2400
Columbus, OH 43216   Fax: (614)249-2200
Contact: John C. Fisher, Exec.V.Pres.
Desc: Farmers and others involved in agriculture and related businesses. Represents members' interests. *Type:* Association.

Oklahoma Farm Bureau Journal

Oklahoma Farm Bureau, Inc.
2501 N. Stiles   Ph: (405)523-2300
Oklahoma City, OK 73105   Free: 800-299-2412
    Fax: (405)523-2362
Contact: Mike Nichols, Editor, mike_nichols@okfb.fb.com.
Desc: Newspaper covering organizational issues relating to agriculture and rural interests. *Type:* Periodical.

Oregon Farm Bureau News

Oregon Farm Bureau Federation
3415 Commercial St. SE, Ste. G   Ph: (503)399-1701
Salem, OR 97302-4668
Contact: Dave Dillon, Editor.
Desc: Contains information of interest to Bureau members. *Type:* Newsletter.

Organic Crop Improvement Association

1001 Y St., Ste. B   Ph: (402)477-2323
Lincoln, NE 68508-1172   Fax: (402)477-4325
E-mail: info@ocia.org
URL: http://www.ocia.org
Contact: Betty Kananen, Exec.Dir.
Desc: Certification organization representing growers, processors, and manufacturers worldwide. Seeks to improve credibility of certified products through audit trail and crop improvement. *Type:* Association.

Pro Farmer

Professional Farmers of America, Inc.
219 Parkade   Ph: (319)277-1278
PO Box 6   Fax: (319)277-7896
Cedar Falls, IA 50613
URL: http://www.profarmer.com.
Contact: Chip Flory n, Editor, fax: (319)277-7892, editors@profarmer.com.
Desc: Provides industry news, marketing advice, hedging recommendations, and analysis of the effects of potential market makers in crops and livestock, particularly soybeans, wheat, corn, cotton, beef, and hogs. Contains weekly market outlook with specific marketing recommendations. *Type:* Newsletter.

Professional Farmers of America

Box 6   Ph: (319)277-1271
219 Parkade   Free: 800-635-3931
Cedar Falls, IA 50613   Fax: (319)277-7982
E-mail: editors@profarmer.com
URL: http://www.profarmer.com
Contact: Merrill J. Oster, Pres.

Desc: Provides farmers with marketing strategies, data on market trends, and analyses of market-impacting developments worldwide. Offers seminars and home study courses. Sponsors commercial exhibits. *Type:* Association.

Progressive Farmer Network

1004 N. Jackson St.   Ph: (601)324-0949
Box 2000   Fax: (601)324-0972
Starkville, MS 39759
Alt. Contact: 1004 N. Jackson St., Box 2000, Starkville, MS 39759; telephone: (601)324-0949; fax: (601)324-0972. *Type:* Periodical.

Show Me Missouri Farm Bureau News

Missouri Farm Bureau Federation
Box 658   Ph: (573)893-1400
Jefferson City, MO 65102   Free: 800-922-4MFB
    Fax: (573)893-1470
E-mail: mo@momail.com; fbinfo@computerland.net.
Contact: Chris Fennewald, Editor, (573)893-1469.

Desc: Agricultural magazine for members of the Missouri Farm Bureau. *Alt. Contact:* 701 S. Country Club Dr., Jefferson City, MO 65102; telephone: (573)893-1400; fax: (573)893-1470. *Type:* Periodical.

Small Farm News

Small Farm Center
University of California   Ph: (530)752-8136
One Shields Ave.   Fax: (530)752-7716
Davis, CA 95616-8699
E-mail: sfcenter@ucdavis.edu
Contact: Susan McCue, Editor, (530)752-7849, semccue@ucdavis.edu.

Desc: Covers topics of interest to small farmers. Includes government actions and crop information. *Type:* Newsletter.

South Carolina Farm Bureau Federation

PO Box 754   Ph: (803)796-6700
Columbia, SC 29202   Fax: 800-421-6515
Contact: David Winkles, Pres.

Desc: Promotes the general welfare of its members. Lobbies and conducts workshops and seminars. *Type:* Association.

Soybean Digest

Soybean Digest
7900 International Dr., 3rd Fl.   Ph: (612)851-9329
Minneapolis, MN 55425   Free: 800-722-5334
    Fax: (612)851-4601
E-mail: sbd@intertec.com.
Contact: Ron Sorensen, Publisher, (612)851-4690, ron_sorensen@intertec.com; Syl Marking, Editor, (612)851-4640, syl_marking@intertec.com; Neil Tietz, Managing Editor, (612)851-4677, neil_tietz@intertec.com; Lynn Chadek, Production Coord., (612)851-4622, lynn_chadek@intertec.com.

Desc: Magazine offering production, marketing, and management information for farmers who grow soybeans in rotation with other crops. *Type:* Periodical.

Spokesman

Iowa Farm Bureau Federation
406 Stevens   Ph: (515)648-2521
Iowa Falls, IA 50126   Free: 800-442-3276
    Fax: (515)648-4606
Contact: Darryl Jahn, Editor, (515)225-5413, fax: (515)225-5419; Mark Hamilton, Publisher; Jo E. Martin, General Mgr.; Don Dauterive, National Account Mgr.; Larry Tucker, Co-op Account Manager.

Desc: Agricultural newspaper. *Type:* Periodical.

Tennessee Farm Bureau Federation

PO Box 313   Ph: (615)388-7872
Columbia, TN 38402-0313   Fax: (615)381-3540
Contact: Flavins Barker, Pres.

Desc: Represents the interests of rural families. Disseminates information of interest to farmers. *Type:* Association.

Tennessee Farm Bureau News

Tennessee Farm Bureau Federation
147 Bear Creek Pike   Ph: (931)388-7872
PO Box 313   Fax: (931)388-5818
Columbia, TN 38402
Contact: Pettus Read, Editor.

Desc: Agricultural and consumer newspaper (tabloid). *Type:* Periodical.

Virginia Farm Bureau News

Virginia Farm Bureau Federation
12580 W. Creek Parkway   Ph: (804)784-1234
PO Box 27552   Fax: (804)784-2588
Richmond, VA 23238
URL: http://www.vafo.com.
Contact: Eric Miller, Editor, (804)784-1322.

Desc: Newspaper covering Farm Bureau policies and activities; national and state agricultural trends, legislative activities, markets, and consumer information. *Type:* Periodical.

The Western Producer

The Western Producer
2310 Millar Ave.   Ph: (306)665-3500
PO Box 2500   Fax: (306)653-1255
Saskatoon, SK, Canada S7K 2C4
E-mail: newsroom@producer.com.
URL: http://www.producer.com.
Contact: Barb Glen, Editor, (306)665-3537, fax: (306)934-2401, fairbairn@producer.com; Allan W. Laughland, Publisher, laughland@producer.com; Darryl Thompson, Advertising Dir., dthompson@producer.com.

Desc: Agricultural newspaper. *Alt. Contact:* fax: (306)934-2401; toll-free: 800-667-6978. *Type:* Periodical.

Federal Government

A.G.A. GasNet

American Gas Association (A.G.A.)
1515 Wilson Blvd.   Ph: (703)841-8400
Arlington, VA 22209
URL: http://www.aga.com

Desc: Provides access to news and information on the natural gas industry in the following modules: NEWS AND COMMUNICATIONS BUREAU. • Media Watch--highlights articles concerning the gas industry. *Available:* American Gas Association (A.G.A.). *Type:* Database.

Alliance

Public Service Alliance of Canada
233 Gilmour St.   Ph: (613)560-4235
Communications and Political   Fax: (613)236-1654
   Action Section
Ottawa, ON, Canada K2P 0P1
URL: http://www.psac.com.
Contact: Nancy Mitchell, Editor.

Desc: Public service magazine on labor. *Type:* Periodical.

The Almanac of the Unelected

Maximov Publications
200 E. 32nd St., Ste. 13B   Ph: (212)251-0819
New York, NY 10016   Fax: (212)251-1042
E-mail: maximov@usa.net
URL: http://www.maximov.com/

Contact: Steve Piacente, Editor; Todd E. Keeler, Editor.

Desc: 700 administrative and legislative committee staff members and information on legislative committees. *Type:* Directory.

Americans United for God and Country

PO Box 183
Merion Station, PA 19066

Contact: Leslie Harris, Exec.Dir.

Desc: "To promote patriotism and the love of God and country in accordance with the principles and purposes of the framers of the Constitution of the United States, and the amendments known as the Bill of Rights." Seeks to revitalize the Judeo-Christian concepts in America with the use of federal tax credits and grants to help finance private schools. Believes that since Judeo-Christian citizens provide support for public schools through their tax funds, their concepts should be taught in these schools. *Type:* Association.

BNA Daily News from Washington

The Bureau of National Affairs, Inc. (BNA)
1231 25th St. NW   Ph: (202)452-4200
Washington, DC 20037
E-mail: bnaplus@bna.com
URL: http://bna.com/mkt/hrl/hrlwdec.htm

Desc: Contains the complete text of 24 BNA electronic-only publications that provide coverage of news of news on national and international government and private sector activities. The file contains the following publications: BNA Antitrust & Trade Regulation Daily (ATD); BNA Banking Daily (BBD); BNA Bankruptcy Law Daily (BLD); BNA California Environment Daily (CED); BNA Chemical Regulation Daily (CRD); BNA Corporate Counsel Daily (CCD); BNA Employment Policy & Law Daily; BNA Federal Contracts Daily (FCD); BNA Health Care Daily (HCD); BNA International Business and Finance Daily (IBF); BNA International Environment Daily (IED); BNA International Trade Daily (ITD); BNA Labor Daily (BLD); BNA Management Briefing (MBD); BNA National Environment Daily; BNA Occupational Safety & Health Daily (OSD); BNA Patent, Trademark & Copyright Daily (PTD); BNA Pensions & Benefits Daily (PBD); BNA Product Liability Daily (PLD); BNA Securities Law Daily (SLD); BNA State Environment Daily (SED); BNA Tax Updates (BTU); BNA Toxics Law Daily (TLD); and BNA Washington Insider (BWI). *Available:* The Dialog Corporation, DIALOG; CompuServe Information Service, Knowledge Index; LEXIS-NEXIS, NEXIS; West Group. *Type:* Database.

BNA Federal Contracts Daily

The Bureau of National Affairs, Inc. (BNA)
1231 25th St. NW   Ph: (202)452-4200
Washington, DC 20037
E-mail: bnaplus@bna.com
URL: http://bna.com/mkt/hrl/hrlwdec.htm

Desc: Contains current information on legislative, regulatory, and judicial activities that affect federal contracts and grants. Includes analyses of controversies related to contract awards and profits, grant programs, minority contracting and sub-contracting, procurement policies, and research and development procedures. *Available:* LEXIS-NEXIS, LEXIS; West Group, WESTLAW. *Type:* Database.

BNA Presidential Calendar

The Bureau of National Affairs, Inc. (BNA)
1231 25th St. NW   Ph: (202)452-4200
Washington, DC 20037
E-mail: bnaplus@bna.com
URL: http://bna.com/mkt/hrl/hrlwdec.htm
Desc: Contains a calendar of daily activities in the U.S. Congress and the Office of the President. *Available:* BT North America, Inc.; West Group, WESTLAW. *Type:* Database.

BNA Washington Insider

The Bureau of National Affairs, Inc. (BNA)
1231 25th St. NW   Ph: (202)452-4200
Washington, DC 20037
E-mail: bnaplus@bna.com
URL: http://bna.com/mkt/hrl/hrlwdec.htm
Desc: Contains news and information dealing with federal legislative and regulatory developments. Includes pending business, labor, and trade legislation, proposed regulations, and related federal agency actions. *Available:* LEXIS-NEXIS, LEXIS; LEXIS-NEXIS, NEXIS; West Group, WESTLAW. *Type:* Database.

Board of Examiners Newsletter

The American Institute of Certified Public Accountants
Harborside Financial Ctr.   Ph: (201)938-3287
201 Plaza 3   Free: 800-TOA-ICPA
Jersey City, NJ 07311-3881   Fax: (201)398-3741
Contact: Mary Moore, Editor.
Desc: Provides information for State Boards of Accountancy. Recurring features include a calendar of events, book reviews, and notices of publications available. *Type:* Newsletter.

Catalog of Federal Domestic Assistance

Federal Domestic Assistance Catalog Staff
General Services Administration
300 7th St. SW, Reporters Bldg.   Ph: (202)708-5126
Washington, DC 20407   Free: 800-669-8331
                                  Fax: (202)401-8233
URL: http://www.gsa.gov.
Contact: Robert Brown, Director.
Desc: Federal programs and activities that provide assistance or benefits to state and local governments, Indian tribes, profit and nonprofit organizations and institutions, and individuals. *Type:* Directory.

Center for Public Integrity

910 17th St. NW, 7th Fl.   Ph: (202)466-1300
Washington, DC 20006   Fax: (202)466-1101
URL: http://www.publicintegrity.org
Contact: Charles Lewis, Exec.Dir.
Desc: Promotes a higher standard of integrity in the American political process and in government. *Type:* Association.

Citizens Against Government Waste

1301 Connecticut Ave. NW   Ph: (202)467-5300
Washington, DC 20036   Free: 800-BE-ANGRY
                             Fax: (202)467-4253
E-mail: webmaster@cagw.org
URL: http://www.cagw.org
Contact: Thomas A. Schatz, Pres.
Desc: Nonpartisan organization that seeks to educate the public, individuals in public administration, and Congress on eliminating waste, mismanagement, and inefficiency in government spending. Promotes the need to reduce the federal deficit and seeks to create public support for programs designed to reduce waste in spending. Seeks to expose cases of mismanagement which may occur at any level of government. *Type:* Association.

Commerce Business Daily

Commerce Business Daily (CBD)
11300 Rockville Pike, Ste. 1100   Ph: (301)287-2700
Rockville, MD 20852-3030
URL: http://www.cbd.com
Desc: Contains the complete text of the Commerce Business Daily, covering business news; contract awards of $25,000 or more by civil agencies and $100,000 or more by military agencies; proposed U.S. government procurements for services, supplies, equipment, and material of $25,000 or more for civilian and military agencies; research and development sources sought; special notices, including some international information, e.g., foreign government standards; and surplus property sales. *Available:* The Dialog Corporation, DIALOG; United Communications Group, PERISCOPE; Commerce Business Daily (CBD); McGraw-Hill Companies, Inc., Aviation Week Group, Aviation/Aerospace Online; Delphi Internet Services Corporation; Knowledge Express Data Systems, Knowledge Express; CompuServe Information Service, Knowledge Index; Telescan, Inc.; LEXIS-NEXIS, NEXIS; U.S. Department of Commerce, Economics and Statistics Administration, STAT-USA; Federal Information & News Dispatch, Inc. (FIND). *Type:* Database.

Committee to Restore the Constitution

2218 W. Prospect Rd.
PO Box 986
Fort Collins, CO 80522
Contact: Col. Archibald E. Roberts, Dir.
Desc: Individuals united for: motivating Americans to act within authority of the Constitution to restore interest-free money, repudiate unpayable national debt, and eliminate federal deficits. Seeks to provide public education on the facts "behind the constitutional crisis"; organization of conscientious citizens in patriotic action centers; motivation of elected officials at county and state levels of government to correct excesses of federal agents. *Type:* Association.

Congressional Record

U.S. Government Printing Office (GPO)
Office of Electronic Information Dissemination Services (SDE)
732 N. Capitol St.   Ph: (202)512-1530
Washington, DC 20402
URL: http://www.access.gpo.gov/su_docs/aces/aces140.html
Desc: Provides the complete text of the Congressional Record (House, Senate, Extension of Remarks, and Digest sections). Includes bills and resolutions, amendments, committee and subcommittee reports, public laws, floor actions, schedules of committee and floor activities, executive communications, speeches, and materials inserted into the Record by members of Congress. *Available:* LEXIS-NEXIS, LEXIS; West Group, WESTLAW. *Type:* Database.

Congressional Research Report

Penny Hill Press
6440 Wiscasset Rd.   Ph: (301)229-8229
Bethesda, MD 20816-2115   Fax: (301)229-6988
E-mail: pennyhill@clark.net
URL: http://www.clark.net/pub/pennyhill/pennyhill.html.
Contact: Walter Seager, Editor.
Desc: Acts as an information source for clients seeking news of research reports distributed by the Library of Congress' Congressional Research Service (CRS). Offers a synopsis describing each report listed; reports may be obtained through a member of Congress at no cost. *Type:* Newsletter.

The Consortium

The Consortium for Independent Journalism
2200 Wilson Blvd., Ste. 102-   Ph: (703)920-1802
231   Free: 800-738-1812
Arlington, VA 22201
E-mail: rparry@ix.netcom.com
URL: http://www.delve.com/consort
Desc: This site represents The Consortium for Independent Journalism. Links include a free look at recent stories, the Consortium bookstore, and What we are about. *Type:* Database.

Council for Excellence in Government

1301 K St., NW, Ste. 450 W   Ph: (202)728-0418
Washington, DC 20036   Fax: (202)728-0422
Contact: Patricia McGinnis, President.
Desc: Business leaders with executive-level government experience who wish to promote and support excellence in government. *Type:* Association.

Directory of Federal Libraries

Oryx Press
4041 N. Central Ave., Ste. 700   Ph: (602)265-2651
Phoenix, AZ 85012-3397   Free: 800-279-6799
                                 Fax: 800-279-4663
E-mail: info@oryxpress.com
URL: http://www.oryxpress.com
Contact: William R. Evinger, Editor.
Desc: Nearly 3,000 libraries serving branches of the federal government. *Type:* Directory.

DMS/FI Contract Awards

Forecast International Inc./DMS
22 Commerce Rd.   Ph: (203)426-0800
Newtown, CT 06470
E-mail: sales@forecast1.com
URL: http://www.forecast1.com
Contact: Monty Nebinger, Data Products Manager.
Desc: Contains procurement outlay information on more than 4.0 million non-classified military, aerospace, and general contracts in excess of $25,000 awarded by the U.S. government. *Available:* The Dialog Corporation, DIALOG. *Type:* Database.

Documents to the People

Government Documents Round Table (GODORT)
American Library Association (ALA)
1301 Pennsylvania Ave. NW,   Ph: (202)628-8410
Ste. 403   Free: 800-941-8478
Washington, DC 20004   Fax: (202)628-8419
E-mail: plm@alawash.org; maxymuk@zodiac.rutgers.edu.
URL: http://www.ala.org.
Contact: John Shuler, Editor, (312)996-2738, fax: (312)413-0424.
Desc: Concerned with all aspects of government documents. Provides information about new developments in areas such as acquisition, bibliographic control, and use of federal, state, local, international, and foreign government publications; organization and administration of collections; and government publishing and information policies and activities. *Type:* Newsletter.

Economic Reports of the President

The Libraries of the University of Missouri, St. Louis
8001 Natural Bridge Rd.   Ph: (314)516-5451
St. Louis, MO 63121
URL: http://www.umsl.edu/services/govdocs/
Contact: R. Muns, Reference Librarian, srcmuns@umslvma.umsl.edu.
Desc: The Economic Report of the President contains the Administration's domestic and international economic policies. The gopher site contains the ERP's of the years 1992-1994. *Type:* Database.

Encyclopedia of Governmental Advisory Organizations

Gale Group Inc.

27500 Drake Rd.	Ph: (248)699-4253
Farmington Hills, MI 48331-	Free: 800-877-GALE
3535	Fax: (248)699-8070

E-mail: galeord@galegroup.com
URL: http://www.galegroup.com.
Contact: Donna Batten, Editor, donna_batten@gale.com.
Desc: More than 7,000 boards, panels, commissions, committees, presidential conferences, and other groups that advise the President, Congress, and departments and agencies of federal government; includes interagency committees and federally sponsored conferences. Also includes historically significant organizations. *Type:* Directory.

Federal Acquisition Regulations

The Dialog Corporation
DIALOG

11000 Regency Pkwy., Ste. 400	Ph: (919)462-8600
Cary, NC 27511	

URL: http://www.dialog.com
Contact: Marketing.
Desc: Contains the complete text of acquisition, procurement, and contracting regulations covering the provision of goods and services to the U.S. federal government. *Available:* The Dialog Corporation, DIALOG. *Type:* Database.

Federal Contracts Report

The Bureau of National Affairs, Inc. (BNA)

1231 25th St. NW	Ph: (202)452-4200
Washington, DC 20037	

E-mail: bnaplus@bna.com
URL: http://bna.com/mkt/hrl/hrlwdec.htm
Contact: BNA PLUS, (202)452-4323, fax: (202)822-8092, bnaplus@bna.com.
Desc: Contains the complete text of Federal Contracts Report, covering significant developments in government agencies, including the U.S. Department of Defense, General Accounting Office, executive agencies, courts, and the Congress. *Available:* LEXIS-NEXIS, LEXIS; LEXIS-NEXIS, NEXIS; West Group, WESTLAW. *Type:* Database.

Federal/Federal Regional Directory Annual Edition

Carroll Publishing

4701 Sangamore Rd., No. S155	Ph: (301)263-9800
Bethesda, MD 20816	Free: 800-336-4240
	Fax: (301)263-9801

E-mail: custsvc@carrollpub.com
URL: http://www.carrolpub.com
Desc: 40,000 federal government and 22,000 federal regional government officials. *Type:* Directory.

Federal Managers Association

1641 Prince St.	Ph: (703)683-8700
Alexandria, VA 22314-2818	Fax: (703)683-8707

URL: http://www.fpmj.com
Contact: Frances Webb, Chief Operating Officer.
Desc: Managers and supervisors in all federal agencies. Goals are to increase the efficiency of the work force, and to promote and support legislation beneficial to members. Examples of previous legislation that have benefited members include: the retirement of federal employees with 30 years of service at age 55; the Supervisory (Wage Board) Job Grading Standards of 1968; increased government contributions to health and life insurance programs. *Type:* Association.

The Federal Register

U.S. Government Printing Office (GPO)
Office of Electronic Information Dissemination Services (SDE)

732 N. Capitol St.	Ph: (202)512-1530
Washington, DC 20402	

URL: http://www.access.gpo.gov/su_docs/aces/aces140.html
Desc: Contains the complete text of the Federal Register, a daily publication covering U.S. governmental agency actions. *Available:* The Dialog Corporation, DIALOG; LEXIS-NEXIS, LEXIS; LEXIS-NEXIS, NEXIS; West Group, WESTLAW. *Type:* Database.

Federal Regulatory Directory

Congressional Quarterly

1414 22nd St. NW	Ph: (202)887-8500
Washington, DC 20037	Free: 800-638-1710
	Fax: 800-380-3810

URL: http://books.cq.com
Contact: Mary Burke Marshall, Editor.
Desc: Over 100 federal regulatory agencies including about 15 major agencies, about 15 smaller independent agencies, and agencies within federal departments. *Type:* Directory.

The Federal Web Locator

Villanova University - School of Law - The Center for Information Law and Policy

Garey Hall	Ph: (610)519-7000
299 Spring Mill Rd.	
Villanova, PA 19085	

E-mail: cilp@mail.cilp.org
URL: http://www.law.vill.edu/fed-agency/fedwebloc.html
Contact: Ken Mortensen.
Desc: With the stated goal of being "the one stop shopping point for federal government information on the World Wide Web," The Federal Web Locator serves effectively as the gateway to those agencies and organizations that are part of, or are connected with, the U.S. federal government. *Type:* Database.

Forecast International/DMS Contracts Awards/Online

Forecast International, Inc.

22 Commerce Rd.	Ph: (203)426-0800
Newtown, CT 06470	Free: 800-451-4975
	Fax: (203)426-1964

E-mail: sales@forecast1.com
URL: http://www.forecast1.com; http://www.dialog.com.
Contact: Stacey Downer, Editor, stacey.downer@forecast1.com.
Desc: Over three million non-classified military, aerospace, and civil contract outlays of more than $25,000 awarded by the federal government for research and development, services, or procurement of supplies and equipment. *Type:* Directory.

Goods & Services Bulletin

Commonwealth of Massachusettes
State Bookstore, Rm. 116
State House
Boston, MA 02133
Desc: Contains notices of invitations to bid and requests for proposals of Massachusetts state contracts. *Type:* Newsletter.

Governing Magazine

Times Publishing Co.

490 1st Ave. S.	Ph: (727)893-8111
PO Box 1121	Free: 800-333-7505
St. Petersburg, FL 33701	Fax: (727)893-8675

E-mail: mailbox@governing.com.
Contact: Peter Harkness, Publisher.

Desc: Magazine serving the public sector of federal, state and local government. *Alt. Contact:* 1100 Conneticut Ave. NW, Ste. 1300, Washington, DC 20036; telephone: (202)862-8802; fax: (202)862-0032; toll-free: 800-944-0922. *Type:* Periodical.

Government Affairs Yellow Book

Leadership Directories, Inc.

104 5th Ave.	Ph: (212)627-4140
New York, NY 10011	Fax: (212)645-0931

E-mail: info@leadershipdirectories.com; governmentaffairs@leadershipdirectories.com.
URL: http://www.leadershipdirectories.com; http://www.leadershipdirectories.com.
Contact: Andrew Neusner, Editor.
Desc: More than 19,000 government affairs professionals who lobby at the state and federal level. *Type:* Directory.

Government Contracts & Subcontract Leads Directory

Government Data Publications, Inc.

1661 MacDonald Ave.	Ph: (718)627-0819
Brooklyn, NY 11230	Fax: (718)998-5960

Contact: Siegfried Lobel, Editor.
Desc: Firms which received prime contracts for production of goods or services from federal government agencies during the preceding twelve months. *Type:* Directory.

Government Documents Catalog Service DocsFinder

Auto-Graphics, Inc.

3201 Temple Ave.	Ph: (909)595-7204
Pomona, CA 91768	

E-mail: info@auto-graphics.com
URL: http://www.auto-graphics.com
Contact: Leslie Carter, Government Documents Specialist, (206)952-0190, fax: (206)952-0480, lac@auto-graphics.com.
Desc: Contains citations to all publications of U.S. government agencies, including the U.S. Congress, cumulated monthly since 1976. GPO Shipping list records are included. *Available:* Auto-Graphics, Inc. *Type:* Database.

Government Primecontracts Monthly

Government Data Publications, Inc.

1661 MacDonald Ave.	Ph: (718)627-0819
Brooklyn, NY 11230	Fax: (718)998-5960

Contact: Siegfried Lobel, Publisher.
Desc: Recently awarded government contracts in the production/manufacturing/service fields. *Type:* Directory.

Government Product News

Penton Media Inc.

1100 Superior Ave.	Ph: (216)696-7000
Cleveland, OH 44114-2543	Fax: (216)931-9524

E-mail: corpcomm@penton.com
URL: http://www.govgroup-online.com.
Contact: Leslie Drahos, Editor-in-Chief, ldrahos@penton.com; Vaughn Rockhold, Publisher, vrockhold@penton.com; Robert Marinez, Advertising Mgr., bmarinez@penton.com.
Desc: Magazine (tabloid) containing information on products, services, systems, and applications of interest to government procurement officials at municipal, county, special district, state, and federal levels. *Type:* Periodical.

Government Product News—Buyers Guide for Office Equipment Issue

Penton Media Inc.

1100 Superior Ave.	Ph: (216)696-7000
Cleveland, OH 44114-2543	Fax: (216)931-9524

E-mail: corpcomm@penton.com
Contact: Leslie Drahos, Editor.

Desc: List of over 1,000 manufacturers of office equipment. *Type:* Directory.

Government Programs

Publishing and Business Consultants
4427 W. Slauson Ave.
Los Angeles, CA 90043-2717
Contact: Atia Napoleon, Editor and Publisher.
Desc: Magazine presenting special government programs covering education, employment, housing, etc. *Type:* Periodical.

Government Research Directory

Gale Group Inc.
27500 Drake Rd.   Ph: (248)699-4253
Farmington Hills, MI 48331-   Free: 800-877-GALE
3535   Fax: (248)699-8070
E-mail: galeord@galegroup.com
URL: http://www.galegroup.com.; http://www.gale.com.
Contact: Anthony L. Gerring, Editor.
Desc: Over 4,330 research and development facilities operated or sponsored by the United States or Canadian governments, including research centers, bureaus, and institutes; testing and experiment stations; data collection and analysis centers; government-supported user facilities; cooperative research programs; and major research-supporting service units. *Type:* Directory.

GPO Monthly Catalog

U.S. Government Printing Office (GPO)
Office of Electronic Information Dissemination
Services (SDE)
732 N. Capitol St.   Ph: (202)512-1530
Washington, DC 20402
URL: http://www.access.gpo.gov/su_docs/aces/aces140.html
Desc: Contains more than 375,000 citations to the publications of U.S. government agencies, including the U.S. Congress. Covers Senate and House hearings on bills and laws, as well as agency-sponsored studies, fact sheets, maps, handbooks, subject bibliographies, and conference proceedings. *Available:* The Dialog Corporation, DIALOG; OCLC Online Computer Library Center, Inc., OCLC EPIC; OCLC Online Computer Library Center, Inc., OCLC FirstSearch Catalog; CARL Corporation. *Type:* Database.

GPO Publications Reference File

U.S. Government Printing Office (GPO)
Office of Electronic Information Dissemination
Services (SDE)
732 N. Capitol St.   Ph: (202)512-1530
Washington, DC 20402
URL: http://www.access.gpo.gov/su_docs/aces/aces140.html
Desc: Contains citations to approximately 27,000 public documents published by the executive, judicial, and legislative branches of the U.S. federal government and currently sold by the Superintendent of Documents. *Available:* The Dialog Corporation, DIALOG; CompuServe Information Service, Knowledge Index. *Type:* Database.

Initiators

806 Devon Rd.   Ph: (941)497-3887
Venice, FL 34293
Contact: Marie G. McAfee, Chm.
Desc: "Patriotic members for constitutional government as set by our forefathers." Aims "to inform and educate the American public to the annihilation that is facing it." Opposes "internationalist" organizations; advocates that Congress "buy back the Federal Reserve." Initiators is so named because individual citizens are encouraged "to act on their own initiative and constitutional rights, where and when action is needed." *Type:* Association.

Judicial Yellow Book

Leadership Directories, Inc.
104 5th Ave.   Ph: (212)627-4140
New York, NY 10011   Fax: (212)645-0931
E-mail: info@leadershipdirectories.com; judicial@leadershipdirectories.com.
URL: http://www.leadershipdirectories.com; http://www.leadershipdirectories.com.
Contact: Claudia Finney, Editor.
Desc: More than 2,000 U.S. federal court judges, including the U.S. Supreme Court, U.S. Court of Appeals and U.S. District Courts, U.S. Tax Court, U.S. Court of International Trade, U.S. Court of Veterans' Appeals, and U.S. Court of Appeals for the Armed Forces; more than 1,200 state judges, including state supreme courts and state courts of appeals; complete staff for each judge's chambers, including law clerks; and complete listings of administrative staff for each court. *Type:* Directory.

Lesko's Info-Power III

Visible Ink Press
27500 Drake Rd.   Ph: (248)699-4253
Farmington Hills, MI 48331-   Free: 800-776-6265
3535   Fax: (248)699-8067
E-mail: galeord@gale.com
URL: http://www.gale.com
Contact: Matthew Lesko, Editor.
Desc: Over 45,000 sources of free information and materials on a wide range of subjects, such as business, finance, fine art, education, careers, science and technology, energy, the environment, agriculture, and economics; includes state government agencies, Federal Public Information Offices, Freedom of Information Act offices, other federal government agencies, and their publications. *Type:* Directory.

LEXIS® General Federal Library

LEXIS-NEXIS
9443 Springboro Pike   Ph: (937)865-6800
PO Box 933
Dayton, OH 45401-0933
URL: http://www.lex-nexis.com
Desc: Contains a comprehensive collection of federal legal materials of a general nature, including case law from all federal courts. Legislative materials include the United States Code Service, United States Public Laws, pending federal legislation, legislative histories, and the Congressional Record. *Available:* LEXIS-NEXIS, LEXIS. *Type:* Database.

Marketing Moves

U.S. Government Printing Office
PO Box 371954
Pittsburgh, PA 15250-7954
Contact: Kathryn McConnell, Managing Editor; Lorena Beauchesne, Editor.
Desc: Concerned with the marketing of government publications. Includes "how-to" pieces, success stories, and tips for successful marketing plans. *Type:* Newsletter.

National Association of Hispanic Federal Executives

PO Box 469   Ph: (703)787-0291
Herndon, VA 20172-0469   Fax: (703)787-4675
E-mail: oliverez@compuserve.com
URL: http://www.nahfe.org
Contact: Manuel Oliverez, Pres. and CEO.
Desc: Hispanic and other federal employees ranked GS-12 and above; individuals in the private sector whose positions are equivalent to rank GS-12. Promotes the federal government as a model employer by encouraging qualified individuals to apply for federal government positions. *Type:* Association.

National Association of Retired Federal Employees

606 N. Washington St.   Ph: (703)838-7760
Alexandria, VA 22314   Free: 800-627-3394
                                   Fax: (703)838-7785
E-mail: natlhq@narfe.org
Contact: Frank G. Atwater, Pres.
Desc: Retired U.S. Government civilian and District of Columbia employees, their spouses, persons drawing annuities as survivors of retired U.S. government employees, present employees eligible for optional retirement, and federal employees with at least 5 years' service. *Type:* Association.

National Auctions and Sales

Publishing and Business Consultants
4427 W. Slauson Ave.
Los Angeles, CA 90043-2717
Contact: Andeson Napoleon Atia, Editor and Publisher.
Desc: Magazine containing specific information on routine government auctions. *Type:* Periodical.

National Center for Constitutional Studies

HC-61 Box 1056   Ph: (208)645-2625
Malta, ID 83342   Free: 800-388-4512
                                   Fax: (208)645-2667
E-mail: nccs@xmission.com
URL: http://www.xmission.com/~nccs
Contact: Zeldon Nelson, Exec.Dir.
Type: Association.

National Contract Management Association

1912 Woodford Rd.   Ph: (703)448-9231
Vienna, VA 22182   Free: 800-344-8096
                                   Fax: (703)448-0939
URL: http://www.ncmahq.org
Contact: James W. Goggins, CACM, CAE, Exec. VP.
Desc: Professional individuals concerned with administration, procurement, acquisition, negotiation, and management of contracts and subcontracts. Works for the education, improvement, and professional development of members and nonmembers through national and chapter programs, symposia, and educational materials. Develops training materials to serve the acquisition community. *Type:* Association.

National Legal and Policy Center

1309 Vincent Pl.   Ph: (703)847-3088
Mc Lean, VA 22101   Fax: (703)847-6969
Contact: Ken Boehm, Chm.
Desc: Legal foundation promoting ethics in government. *Type:* Association.

National Partnership for Reinventing Government

The White House - Office of the Vice President - National Partnership for Reinventing Government
750 17th St. NW, Ste. 200   Ph: (202)632-0150
Washington, DC 20006   Fax: (202)632-0390
E-mail: lee.wexel@npr.gsa.gov
URL: http://www.npr.gov/
Desc: The National Partnership for Reinventing Government (NPR) collection provides information about the Reinventing Government initiative (Clinton-Gore Administration's initiative to reform the way the federal government works). The database allows access to NPR reports; agency, executive, and legislative actions; missions, objectives, and current activities of NPR Reinvention Councils and working groups; NPR implementation activities; the NPR Reinvention Roundtable Newsletter; agency reinvention success stories; related speeches and links to other sources of pertinent federal, state, local, and international information. *Type:* Database.

NetVet

Washington University - Division of Comparative Medicine
Box 8061, 660 S. Euclid Ave.   Ph: (314)362-3700
St. Louis, MO 63110   Fax: (314)362-6480
URL: http://netvet.wustl.edu/vet.htm
Contact: Ken Boschert, Associate director, ken@wudcm.wustl.edu.
Desc: NetVet provides extensive and well-organized links to information on colleges of veterinary medicine from around the world. This site also offers career information concerning veterinary specialties, organizations, meetings, and a directory as well as mailing lists, links to publications and references, animal laws and regulations, and commerce and businesses listings. *Type:* Database.

Office of Economic Conversion Information

U.S. Department of Commerce - Economic Development Administration
HCHB Rm. 7321   Free: 800-345-1222
Washington, DC 20230
E-mail: jlavery@doc.gov
URL: http://netsite.esa.doc.gov/oeci
Desc: The Economic Conversion Information Exchange (OECI) is a clearinghouse of information needed to anticipate, plan for, and respond to defense downsizing. The database contains a compendium of government programs and a host of other materials designed to assist businesses, communities and workers affected by defense budget cutbacks and other economic development challenges. *Type:* Database.

Regulatory Report

America's Community Bankers
900 19th St. NW, Ste. 400   Ph: (202)857-3100
Washington, DC 20006   Fax: (202)857-5581
E-mail: info@acbankers.org
Contact: Bill Marshall, Editor; Brian Nixon, Editor and Publisher.
Desc: Provides information about government regulation of finance. Topics include real estate, lending, and mortgages. *Type:* Newsletter.

U. S. Federal Government Agency Directory

Louisiana State University - Middleton Library
Baton Rouge, LA 70803-1412   Ph: (225)388-6825
                                      Fax: (225)388-6825
URL: http://www.lib.lsu.edu/gov/fedgov.html
Contact: Smittie Bolner, sbolner@lsu.edu.
Desc: The Federal Government Agency Directory is a directory of federal agencies on the Internet. The listing is very extensive, covering almost every office and agency with a prescence on the Internet. *Type:* Database.

U.S. Bureau of Justice Statistics

U.S. Department of Justice
810 Seventh St.   Ph: (202)307-0703
Washington, DC 20531
E-mail: askbjs@ojp.usdoj.gov
URL: http://www.ojp.usdoj.gov/bjs/
Desc: The U.S. Bureau of Justice Statistics collects, analyzes, publishes, and disseminates information on crime, criminal offenders, victims, and the justice system. *Type:* Database.

U.S. Code of Federal Regulations

U.S. Government Printing Office (GPO)
Office of Electronic Information Dissemination Services (SDE)
732 N. Capitol St.   Ph: (202)512-1530
Washington, DC 20402
URL: http://www.access.gpo.gov/su_docs/aces/aces140.html

Desc: Contains the complete text of all titles of the U.S. Code of Federal Regulations. *Available:* LEXIS-NEXIS, LEXIS; West Group, WESTLAW. *Type:* Database.

U.S. Department of State Press Briefings

U.S. Department of State
2201 C St. NW   Ph: (202)647-4000
Washington, DC 20520   Fax: (202)647-7120
E-mail: publicaffairs@panet.us-state.gov
URL: http://secretary.state.gov/www/briefings/index.html
Desc: The U.S. Department of State Press Briefings database contains the transcripts as well as audio files of daily briefings. *Type:* Database.

United States Government Manual

Office of the Federal Register (NFP)
National Archives and Records Administration
Washington, DC 20408   Ph: (202)523-5230
                                      Fax: (202)523-6866
E-mail: info@fedreg.nara.gov
URL: http://www.access.gpo.gov/su_docs/.
Contact: Karen L. Ashlin, Editor.
Desc: The "Manual" is the official handbook of the United States government, and includes descriptions and lists of principal personnel of agencies and other bodies in the legislative, judicial, and executive branches; the executive branch is covered in greatest depth. (The "Manual" devotes roughly 40 of 860 pages to the legislative branch and 20 to the judicial; the "Congressional Directory," described in a separate listing, devotes roughly 260 of 1,200 pages to the executive branch and 60 to the judicial.) Text of the listings is primarily concerned with programs and activities rather than administrative structure, but general organization charts are given. *Type:* Directory.

U.S. Government Purchasing and Sales Directory

Office of Government Contracting
Small Business Administration
409 3rd St. SW   Ph: (202)205-6460
Washington, DC 20416
Desc: Major military and civilian purchasing offices, military installations, and field offices of the General Services Administration, Small Business Administration, and Commerce Department. *Type:* Directory.

U.S. Immigration

Publishing and Business Consultants
4427 W. Slauson Ave.
Los Angeles, CA 90043-2717
Contact: Atia Napoleon, Editor and Publisher.
Desc: Magazine containing general information on Visas and Green Cards. *Type:* Periodical.

U.S. Newswire

U.S. Newswire
National Press Bldg., Ste. 1272   Ph: (202)347-2770
Washington, DC 20045
E-mail: newsdesk@usnewswire.com
URL: http://www.usnewswire.com
Contact: Mark Bagley, fax: (202)347-2767, bagley@usnewswire.com.
Desc: Contains the complete text of news releases and statements from the U.S. federal government and other national newsmakers to the Washington press corps. *Available:* Bell & Howell Information and Learning; LEXIS-NEXIS, NEXIS; NewsEdge Corporation; Dow Jones Interactive Publishing; The Dialog Corporation, DIALOG; Reuters Information Services Inc. *Type:* Database.

The Washington Post

The Washington Post News Research Center
1150 15th St., NW, 5th Fl.   Ph: (202)334-6762
Washington, DC 20071
E-mail: belton@washpost.com
URL: http://www.washingtonpost.com
Desc: Contains the complete text of local, national, and international news items appearing in The Washington Post. *Available:* The Dialog Corporation, DIALOG; Dow Jones Interactive Publishing; LEXIS-NEXIS, NEXIS; FT PROFILE; Legi-Slate, Inc.; European Information Network Services (EINS); Bell & Howell Information and Learning; NewsBank, Inc. *Type:* Database.

WETA/CapAccess Community Network

WETA/CapAccess - Greater Washington's Community Network
2775 S. Quincy St.   Ph: (703)998-2430
Arlington, VA 22206-2226   Fax: (703)824-7350
URL: http://www.capaccess.org/
Desc: The WETA/CapAccess Community Network is a local, nonprofit, community network, established to provide community service organizations, including schools, governmental agencies, libraries and others with technical assistance on interactive technology to serve their constituents. The site contains links and info about community services, resources and interests. *Type:* Database.

Worldwide Assurance for Employees of Public Agencies

7651 Leesburg Pike   Ph: (703)790-8010
Falls Church, VA 22043   Free: 800-368-3484
                                      Fax: (703)790-4606
E-mail: waepa@waepa.org
URL: http://www.waepa.org
Contact: William C. Gratz, Exec.Dir.
Desc: Federal civilian employees. Provides group life, accidental death and dismemberment, dependent group life insurance coverage and long-term care insurance to federal civilian employees at reasonable cost. *Type:* Association.

Feminism

ERA Impact Project

c/o NOW Legal Defense and   Ph: (212)925-6635
   Educ. Fund
99 Hudson St.
New York, NY 10013
Desc: A special project of NOW Legal Defense and Education Fund and Women's Law Project. Objectives are: to serve as a national information clearinghouse on state Equal Rights Amendment litigation; to implement national educational outreach; to conduct pilot litigation in Pennsylvania; to develop a state ERA litigation strategy. Has participated in cases involving employment discrimination, education equity, family issues, and insurance. *Type:* Association.

Global Fund for Women

425 Sherman Ave., Ste. 300   Ph: (650)853-8305
Palo Alto, CA 94306   Fax: (650)328-0384
E-mail: gfw@globalfundforwomen.org
URL: http://www.globalfundforwomen.org
Contact: Kavita N. Ramdas, Pres.
Desc: Grantmaking organization providing support to women's groups working on emerging, controversial, or difficult issues. *Type:* Association.

Inter-American Commission of Women

c/o Organization of American   Ph: (202)458-6084
  States   Fax: (202)458-6094
1889 F St. NW, Rm. 880
Washington, DC 20006
Contact: Carmen Lomellin, Exec.Sec.

Desc: Specialized agency of the Organization of American States dealing with issues concerning women. Commission is composed of one delegate for each member country of OAS. Mobilizes, trains, and organizes women "so that they may fully participate in all fields of human endeavor, on a par with men, as two beings of equal value, coresponsible for the destiny of humanity." Informs the OAS general assembly and member governments on: civil, political, social, economic, and cultural status of women in the Americas; progress achieved in the field as well as problems to be considered; development of a plan of action following the Decade of Women (1976-85) of strategies for full and equal participation by women by the year 2000. *Type:* Association.

International Center for Research on Women

1717 Massachusetts Ave. NW,   Ph: (202)797-0007
  Ste. 302   Fax: (202)797-0020
Washington, DC 20036
E-mail: icrw@igc.apc.org
Contact: Dr. Geeta Rao Gupta, Pres.

Desc: Purpose is to promote social and economic development with women's full participation. Conducts research programs and provides technical services for the design, implementation, and evaluation of development projects that integrate women into mainstream economic roles. Disseminates research findings to policymakers and others throughout the world who are concerned with economic and socioeconomic issues of developing countries. *Type:* Association.

Ms. Foundation for Women

120 Wall St., 33rd Fl.   Ph: (212)742-2300
New York, NY 10005   Fax: (212)742-1653
E-mail: info@ms.foundation.org
URL: http://www.ms.foundation.org
Contact: Marie C. Wilson, Pres.

Desc: Supports the efforts of women and girls to govern their own lives and influence the world around them. Funds and assists women's self-help organizing efforts, and pursues changes in public conciousness, law, philanthropy, and social policy. Directs resources to break down barriers based on race, class, age, disability, sexual orientation, and culture. *Type:* Association.

National Association of Commissions for Women

D.C. Commission for Women
Reeves Center, Rm. N-354   Ph: (202)839-8083
2000 14th St. NW   Fax: (202)939-8763
Washington, DC 20009
Contact: Carrolena Key, Exec. Dir.

Desc: State, city, and county commissions that focus on the status of women. To strengthen and coordinate the vital work of the state and local commissions, in seeking to further the legal, social, political, economic, and educational equality of American women, that they may make their fullest contribution in our nation. Works to: eliminate discrimination based on sex, race, age, religion, national origin, or marital status in all phases of American society; foster the dissemination of information and provide counsel on opportunities for the effective participation of women in the private and public sector; create greater public awareness of the role and function of commissions on the status of women and provide a national focus on issues affecting women; strenghten commissions, coordinate their efforts nationwide, and provide a unified

voice; act as a central clearinghouse and networking resource for information and activities of commissions across the country; foster a closer relationship and fuller exchange of ideas among members. *Type:* Association.

National Association of Cuban-American Women of the U.S.A.

PO Box 614   Ph: (201)864-4879
Union City, NJ 07087   Fax: (201)223-0036
Contact: Ziomara Sanchez, Pres.

Desc: Addresses current issues, concerns, and problems affecting Hispanic and minority women, and to achieve goals such as equal education and training, fair immigration policy, and meaningful work with adequate compensation. Coordinates activities with national Hispanic and other minority organizations; responds to female concerns from minority and majority populations; encourages participation in related task forces, legislative activities, and professional endeavors; acts as clearinghouse and referral center. Supports bilingual and bicultural education at the local, state, and national levels. *Type:* Association.

National Congress of Neighborhood Women

249 Manhattan Ave.   Ph: (718)388-8915
Brooklyn, NY 11211   Free: 888-777-5776
     Fax: (718)388-0285
E-mail: nghldwmn@aol.com

Desc: Low-and moderate-income women from diverse ethnic and racial backgrounds united to: bring about neighborhood stabilization and revitalization; raise awareness of women's roles in neighborhood activities and organizations as well as on issues affecting low-income women; provide a voice for a new women's movement that reflects family and neighborhood values while promoting women's empowerment. *Type:* Association.

National Council of Negro Women

633 Pennsylvania Ave. NW   Ph: (202)628-0015
Washington, DC 20004-2605   Fax: (202)785-8733
Contact: Dorothy I. Height, Pres.

Desc: A coalition of 31 national organizations and concerned individuals. Assists in the development and utilization of the leadership of women in community, national, and international life. Provides a center of information for and about women in the black community; stimulates cooperation among women in diverse economic and social interests; acts as a catalyst for constructive advocacy on a number of women's issues. *Type:* Association.

National Federation of Business and Professional Women's Clubs

2012 Massachusetts Ave. NW   Ph: (202)293-1100
Washington, DC 20036   Fax: (202)861-0298
URL: http://www.bpwwusa.org
Contact: Gail Shaffer, Exec.Dir.

Desc: Men and women of every age, religion, political party, and socioeconomic background. Works to achieve equity for all women in the workplace through advocacy, education, and information. Provides professional development, networking, and career advancement opportunities for working women. *Type:* Association.

National Organization for Women

1000 16th St. NW, Ste. 700   Ph: (202)331-0066
Washington, DC 20036   Fax: (202)785-8576
E-mail: now@now.org
URL: http://www.now.org
Contact: Patricia Ireland, Pres.

Desc: Men and women who support "full equality for women in truly equal partnership with men." Seeks to end prejudice and discrimination against women in government, industry, the professions, churches, political parties, the judiciary, labor unions, education, science, medicine,

law, religion, "and every other field of importance in American society." Promotes passage of an Equal Rights Amendment and enforcement of federal legislation prohibiting discrimination on the basis of sex. Engages in lobbying and litigation. Works to increase the number of women elected to local, county, and state offices, the House of Representatives, and the Senate. *Type:* Association.

National Partnership for Women and Families

1875 Connecticut Ave. NW,   Ph: (202)986-2600
  Ste. 710   Fax: (202)986-2539
Washington, DC 20009
E-mail: info@nationalpartnership.org
URL: http://www.nationalpartnership.org
Contact: Judith L. Lichtman, Pres.

Desc: Attorneys, administrators, publicists, and secretaries. Purpose is to secure equal rights for women through advocacy and monitoring, and public education. Works for women's rights in family law, employment, women's health, and other areas. *Type:* Association.

National Women's Political Caucus

1211 Connecticut Ave. NW,   Ph: (202)785-1100
  Ste. 425   Free: 800-729-NWPC
Washington, DC 20036   Fax: (202)785-3605
E-mail: nwpcmail@aol.com
Contact: Anita Perez Ferguson, Pres.

Desc: Individuals supporting increased political influence of women. Multipartisan caucus seeking to gain an equal voice and place for women in the political process at local, state, and national levels. Supports women candidates for elective and appointive political offices. *Type:* Association.

9 to 5, National Association of Working Women

231 W. Wisconsin Ave., Ste.   Ph: (414)274-0925
  900   Fax: (414)272-2870
Milwaukee, WI 53203
E-mail: naww9to5@execpc.com
Contact: Ellen Bravo, Exec.Dir.

Desc: Women office workers. Seeks to build a national network of local office worker chapters that strives to gain better pay, proper use of office automation, opportunities for advancement, elimination of sex and race discrimination, and improved working conditions for women office workers. Works to introduce legislation or regulations at state level to protect video display terminal operators. *Type:* Association.

NOW Legal Defense and Education Fund

395 Hudson St., 5th Fl.   Ph: (212)925-6635
New York, NY 10014-3669   Fax: (212)226-1066
URL: http://www.nowldef.org
Contact: Kathryn J. Rodgers, Exec.Dir.

Desc: Now LDEF, the country's oldest women's rights organization, is committed to achieve equality for women and girls by transforming the institutions and values of our society through legal advocacy, public policy development, education and strategic alliances. Current areas of forms are economic empowerment, physical safety, the inclusion of women's voices and perspectives in the media and the elimination of gender bias in the justice system. *Type:* Association.

United Nations Development Fund for Women

304 E. 45th St., 6th Fl.   Ph: (212)906-6400
New York, NY 10017   Fax: (212)906-6705
Contact: Noeleen Heyzer, Dir.

Desc: Autonomous fund operating in association with the United Nations Development Programme and created by the UN General Assembly following the International Women's Year, 1975. The Fund's purpose is to support the efforts of women in the developing world to achieve their objectives for economic and social development and for equality, and by doing so, to improve the quality of life for all. The Fund works in three key program areas of strategic importance to women: Agriculture, Trade and Industry, and Macro Policy and National Planning. *Type:* Association.

Film

Abbott and Costello International Fan Club
PO Box 262
Carteret, NJ 07008-0262
URL: http://www.citynet.com/abbottandcostellofc/
Contact: Billy Wolfe, Founder & Dir.
Desc: Fans and admirers of the comedy team of Bud Abbott (1896-1974) and Lou Costello (1906-59), which attained peak popularity on both the stage and screen, as well as on radio, from 1941 to 1951. Seeks to keep alive the spirit of good-natured buffoonery which characterized their works. *Type:* Association.

Academy of Motion Picture Arts and Sciences
8949 Wilshire Blvd.   Ph: (310)247-3000
Beverly Hills, CA 90211   Fax: (310)247-2600
Contact: Bruce Davis, Exec.Dir.
Desc: Motion picture producers, directors, writers, cinematographers, editors, actors, and craftsmen. *Type:* Association.

Adam Film World Guide
Knight Publishing Corp.
8060 Melrose Ave.   Ph: (323)653-8060
Los Angeles, CA 90046   Fax: (323)655-9452
E-mail: psi@loop.com.
Contact: Jeremy Stone, Editor; Tim Connelly, Advertising Mgr.; Mitchell Neal, Marketing Dir.
Desc: Magazine. *Type:* Periodical.

AMAMA news
The Recruiting Network, Inc.
PO Box 68366   Ph: (847)524-8487
Schaumburg, IL 60168-0366   Free: 800-562-6593
E-mail: rpipeline@aol.com
Contact: Carol Johnson, Publisher; Mershon Shrigley, Editor.
Desc: Covers the real estate recruiting and retention industry. *Type:* Newsletter.

American Film Institute
John F. Kennedy Center for the   Ph: (202)416-7816
   Performing Arts   Free: 800-774-4234
Washington, DC 20566   Fax: (202)416-8421
Contact: Jean Firstenberg, Dir.
Desc: Nonprofit, nongovernmental corporation dedicated to preserving and developing the nation's artistic and cultural resources in film and video. Catalogs and preserves America's film heritage. Acts as a bridge between learning a craft and practicing a profession, through an intensive two-year course in filmmaking and film theory. *Type:* Association.

American Film Marketing Association
10850 Wilshire Blvd., 9th Fl.   Ph: (310)446-1000
Los Angeles, CA 90024-4321   Fax: (310)446-1600
E-mail: info@afma.com
URL: http://www.afma.com
Contact: Mike Frischkorn, Pres.
Desc: Independent producers and distributors of feature length theatrical films involved in selling film rights to domestic and foreign territories. Contributes to negotiations with foreign producer associations; has developed standardized theatrical and video contracts in English, French, Italian, and Spanish. Established and maintains the AFMA International Arbitration Tribunal, a system through which prominent entertainment attorneys throughout the world assist members and consenting clients in reaching equitable and binding agreements. *Type:* Association.

AMIA Newsletter
Association of Moving Image Archivists (AMIA)
8949 Wilshire Blvd.   Ph: (310)550-1300
Beverly Hills, CA 90211   Fax: (310)550-1363
E-mail: amia@ix.netcom.com; glukow@pacbell.net.
Contact: Sally Hubbard, (310)825-2592, shubbard@ucla.edu.
Desc: Presents information on the preservation of film and video materials, and the moving image archival profession. REC news of research, a calendar of events, reports of meetings, job listings, book reviews, and notices of publications available. *Type:* Newsletter.

AV Guide Newsletter
Educational Screen, Inc.
380 E. Northwest Hwy.   Ph: (847)298-6622
Des Plaines, IL 60016-2282   Fax: (847)390-0408
Contact: Natalie Ferguson, Editor, (842)391-1024.
Desc: Furnishes news and information about audio-visual materials. *Type:* Newsletter.

AV Market Place
R. R. Bowker
A Unit of Cahners Business Information
121 Chanlon Rd.   Ph: (908)464-6800
New Providence, NJ 07974   Free: 888-269-5372
                             Fax: (908)771-7704
E-mail: info@bowker.com
Contact: Karen Hallard, Managing Editor.
Desc: Over 7,000 producers and distributors of audiovisual materials, including production companies, production services, and manufacturers and dealers handling equipment and supplies. Also includes awards and festivals, associations, film & TV commercials, periodicals, and reference books. *Type:* Directory.

Bowker's Complete Video Directory
R. R. Bowker
A Unit of Cahners Business Information
121 Chanlon Rd.   Ph: (908)464-6800
New Providence, NJ 07974   Free: 888-269-5372
                             Fax: (908)771-7704
E-mail: info@bowker.com
URL: http://www.bowker.com.
Contact: Doreen Gravesande, Editor; B. Lamar, Editor; Barbara Holton, Editor.
Desc: In four volumes, over 151,000 theatrical and non-theatrical videocassette titles. *Type:* Directory.

Bowker's Directory of Videocassettes for Children
R. R. Bowker
121 Chanlon Rd.   Ph: (908)464-6800
New Providence, NJ 07974   Free: 800-521-8110
                             Fax: (908)665-6688
E-mail: techsupport@bowker.com
URL: http://www.bowker.com
Desc: More than 23,000 educational and entertainment videocassette titles for children. *Type:* Directory.

Boxoffice—Buyers Directory Issue
RLD Communications, Inc.
155 S. El Molino Ave., Ste. 100   Ph: (626)396-0250
Pasadena, CA 91101   Fax: (626)396-0248
E-mail: boxoffice@earthlink.net
URL: http://www.boxoffice.com.
Contact: Kim Williamson, Editor.
Desc: Comprehensive listing of motion picture theatrical distributors, and manufacturers and suppliers of equipment, services and supplies for motion picture theaters. *Type:* Directory.

Film Bill
Film Bill, Inc.
250 W 54th St.   Ph: (212)977-4140
New York, NY 10019   Fax: (212)977-4404
Contact: George Fenmore, Editor and Publisher; Toddy Gelfand, Food & Restaurant Editor; Thelma Fenmore, Reviews Editor.
Desc: Consumer magazine covering all aspects of film and film making. *Type:* Periodical.

Film and Video Career Directory
Gale Group Inc.
27500 Drake Rd.   Ph: (248)699-4253
Farmington Hills, MI 48331- Free: 800-877-GALE
   3535   Fax: (248)699-8070
E-mail: galeord@galegroup.com
URL: http://www.galegroup.com.
Contact: Bradley J. Morgan, Editor; Joseph M. Palmisano, Editor.
Desc: Over 210 U.S. film and video production companies, postproduction facilities, and other companies providing services related to film and video that offer entry-level positions and internships; sources of help-wanted ads, professional associations, producers of videos, databases, career guides, and professional guides and handbooks. *Type:* Directory.

Hollywood Reporter Blu-Book Production Directory
The Hollywood Reporter
5055 Wilshire Blvd., 6th Fl.   Ph: (213)525-2000
Los Angeles, CA 90036   Fax: (213)525-2390
E-mail: thrscoh@hollywoodreporter.com
Contact: Randall Tierney, Editor.
Desc: Over 12,000 companies in the Los Angeles and other companies worldwide providing products and services to the entertainment industry, including motion picture and television studios, studio executives listings, production companies, distribution companies, equipment rental and sales companies, interactive/multimedia, special effects, actors, musicians, and celebrities, foreign press representatives, entertainment festivals, composers and lyricists, performers' and writers' agents, and film commissions worldwide. *Type:* Directory.

Independent Feature Project
104 W. 29th St., 12th Fl.   Ph: (212)465-8200
New York, NY 10001-5310   Fax: (212)465-8525
E-mail: ifpny@ifp.org
URL: http://www.ifp.org
Contact: Michelle Byrd, Exec.Dir.
Desc: Independent film producers and directors. Promotes the production and distribution of independent feature films. Maintains information service on development, financing, and distribution. *Type:* Association.

International Animated Film Society, ASIFA - Hollywood
725 S. Victory   Ph: (818)842-8330
Burbank, CA 91502   Fax: (818)842-5645
E-mail: asifa@earthlink.net
Contact: Antran Manoogian, Pres.
Desc: Professional animation artists, fans, and students of animation. Works to promote and advance the art of animation. *Type:* Association.

International Association of Audio Visual Communicators
9531 Jamacha Blvd., Ste. 263   Ph: (619)461-1600
Spring Valley, CA 91977   Fax: (619)461-1606
URL: http://www.iaavc.org
Contact: Phillip N. Shuey, Exec.Dir.
Desc: Media producers, managers, and creative and technical people in industry, government, education, and technical, promotional, and enrichment fields. *Type:* Association.

International Association of Audio Visual Communicators—Membership Roster

International Association of Audio Visual Communicators
9531 Jamacha Blvd., Ste. 263   Ph: (619)461-1600
Spring Valley, CA 91977   Fax: (619)461-1606
E-mail: sheemonW@cindys.com.
URL: http://www.iaavc.org.
Contact: Phillip N. Shuey, Editor.
Type: Directory.

International Dictionary of Films and Filmmakers

St. James Press, Inc.
27500 Drake Rd.   Ph: (248)699-4253
Farmington Hills, MI 48331-   Free: 800-877-4253
3535   Fax: (248)699-8069
E-mail: galeord@gale.com
Contact: Nicolet V. Elert, Editor; Aruna Vasudevan, Editor; Laurie C. Hillstrom, Editor; Amy L. Unterburger, Editor; Grace Jeromski, Editor.
Desc: In an illustrated multi-volume set, approximately 500 directors and filmmakers, 650 actors and actresses, and 520 writers and production artists (in volumes 2, 3, and 4 respectively). Both historical and contemporary artists are listed, chosen on the basis of international importance in film history. *Type:* Directory.

International Directory of Educational Audiovisuals

National Information Center for Educational Media
PO Box 8640   Ph: (505)265-3591
Albuquerque, NM 87198   Free: 800-926-8328
                                      Fax: (505)256-1080
E-mail: nicem@nicem.
URL: http://www.nicem.com
Desc: Approximately 300,000 records of educational and training materials produced since 1984, or those still in print, covering all age levels, subject areas, and media types from more than 20,000 U.S. and international distributors. *Type:* Directory.

International Teleproduction Society

527 Maple Ave. E., Ste. 204   Ph: (703)319-0800
Vienna, VA 22180   Fax: (703)319-1120
URL: http://www.itsnet.org
Contact: Mr. Terry Rainey, Pres.
Desc: Companies involved in teleproduction and post production for video and audio, film-to-tape transfer, graphics, color correction, duplication, animation, electronic imaging. *Type:* Association.

Magill's Survey of Cinema

The Gale Group
27500 Drake Rd.   Ph: (248)699-4253
Farmington Hills, MI 48331-
3535
URL: http://www.galegroup.com
Contact: Customer Service. Toll-free: 800-877-GALE.
Desc: Contains descriptions of more than 34,000 films worldwide, dating from the silent era to the present. Provides title, plot summary, release date, country of origin, cast, production credit, running time, type (color or black & white), major awards (e.g., Academy, Cannes Film Festival, and Golden Globe awards for Best Picture, Best Director, Best Actor, Best Actress, Best Screenplay), 1500-word full text critical review, citations to additional reviews, Motion Picture Association of America rating, and awards. *Available:* The Dialog Corporation, DIALOG; CompuServe Information Service; NIFTY Corporation, NIFTY-SERVE; CompuServe Information Service, Knowledge Index. *Type:* Database.

Marquee

Marquee Media Inc.
1325 Burnhamthorpe Rd. E.   Ph: (905)274-7174
Mississauga, ON, Canada L4Y   Fax: (905)274-9799
3V8
Contact: David Haslam, Publisher; Fred Hussey, Advertising Mgr., (905)281-0003, fax: (905)281-8884; Alexandra Lenhoff, Managing Editor, alenhoff@marquee.ca.
Desc: Entertainment magazine containing upcoming film and music previews. *Type:* Periodical.

Motion Picture Association of America

1600 Eye St. NW   Ph: (202)293-1966
Washington, DC 20006   Fax: (202)296-7410
URL: http://www.mpaa.org
Contact: Jack J. Valenti, Pres.
Desc: Represents principal producers and distributors of motion pictures in the U.S. Member companies include Buena Vista Pictures Distribution, Inc. (The Walt Disney Co., Hollywood Pictures, Touchstone Pictures); Metro-Goldwyn-Mayer Inc. *Type:* Association.

Movieline

Movieline, Inc.
1141 S. Beverly Dr.   Ph: (310)282-0711
Los Angeles, CA 90035   Fax: (310)282-0859
Contact: Anne Volokh, Publisher.
Desc: Film magazine reporting on those who make the movies. *Type:* Periodical.

The National Casting Guide

Peter Glenn Publications
42 W. 38th St.   Ph: (212)869-2020
New York, NY 10018   Free: 888-332-6700
                                      Fax: (212)354-4099
E-mail: gj-pgp@stealth.net
URL: http://www.peterglennpublications.com.
Contact: David Vardo, Editor.
Desc: Includes nationwide production companies, film commisions, coaches, schools, theaters, and other artists' resources. *Type:* Directory.

New York Council of Motion Picture and Television Unions

75 9th Ave. Fl 7   Ph: (212)989-8441
New York, NY 10011-7006   Fax: (212)741-2679
Contact: Danny Robert, Exec. Coord.
Desc: Writers, performers, artists, technicians, craftsmen, musicians, directors, assistant directors, production managers and coordinators, script supervisors, cameramen, and service personnel. Serves as an umbrella organization for unions and guilds. *Type:* Association.

The Oracle of Bacon at Virginia

University of Virginia - Department of Computer Science
Charlottesville, VA 22903
E-mail: webman@cs.virginia.edu
URL: http://www.cs.virginia.edu/~bct7m/bacon.html
Contact: Brett Tjaden, oracle@virginia.edu.
Desc: The Kevin Bacon game involves choosing a motion picture actor or actress and linking him or her to a movie in which Kevin Bacon appeared with the fewest number of links possible. Take Mel Brooks, for instance. *Type:* Database.

Premiere

Hachette Filipacchi
PO Box 55394   Ph: (303)604-7455
Boulder, CO 80323
URL: http://www.premiere.com.
Contact: Marian Schwindeman, Publisher; Susan Lyne, Editor.

Type: Periodical.

Reel Directory

Bonnie Carroll
PO Box 866   Ph: (707)584-8083
Cotati, CA 94931
URL: http://www.reeldirectory.com.
Contact: Bonnie Carroll, Editor.
Desc: About 4,000 firms and organizations, including actor and model agencies, advertising agencies, trade unions, trade associations; suppliers of audiovisual, photographic, and motion picture equipment and materials; graphic services; sound studios, film laboratories, and other services in the San Francisco and northern California area. *Type:* Directory.

Scene at the Movies

Scene, Inc.
930 5th Ave.   Ph: (212)737-8100
New York, NY 10021-2651   Fax: (212)737-8884
Desc: Magazine. *Type:* Periodical.

Screen's Production Bible

Screen Enterprises, Inc.
16 W. Erie St.   Ph: (312)664-5236
Chicago, IL 60610   Fax: (312)664-8425
E-mail: screen@screenmag.com
URL: http://screenmag.com.
Contact: Ruth L. Ratny, Editor.
Desc: About 3,500 firms and 18,000 persons working in the motion picture and television industry in Chicago, Illinois. *Type:* Directory.

Star Trek Communicator

ST Communicator
Box 111000   Ph: (303)574-0907
Aurora, CO 80011   Free: 800-TRUE-
                                             FAN
                                      Fax: (303)547-9442
E-mail: stcustservice@fanmedia.com
Contact: Jon Bradley Snyder, Editor-in-Chief; David Latimer, Advertising Dir.; Dan Madsen, President/Publisher.
Desc: Consumer entertainment magazine covering all aspects of the film and television show, Star Trek. *Type:* Periodical.

Star Wars Insider

Official Star Wars Fan Club
Box 111000   Ph: (303)574-0907
Aurora, CO 80042   Fax: (303)574-9442
Contact: Jon Bradley Snyder, Editor-in-Chief; David Latimer, Advertising Dir./Circulation Mgr.
Desc: Consumer magazine for Star Wars motion picture enthusiasts. *Alt. Contact:* 3720 Revere St., Denver, CO 80239. *Type:* Periodical.

Sundance Institute

PO Box 16450   Ph: (801)328-3456
Salt Lake City, UT 84116   Fax: (801)575-5175
E-mail: institute@sundance.org
URL: http://www.sundance.org
Contact: Ken Brecher, Exec.Dir.
Desc: Resource center for independent filmmakers and other artists. Works to support the production of well-crafted, low-budget films for a variety of markets; educate individuals on aspects of their craft; provide a disciplined and professional environment for participants, including the opportunity to collaborate with professionals. Sponsors programs in film, theatre, dance, and music. *Type:* Association.

Take One

Connell Communications Inc.

86 Elm St.   Ph: (603)924-7271

Peterborough, NH 03458-1052   Fax: (603)924-7013

Contact: James H. Faulkner, Editor; Gloria Redman, Advertising Mgr.

Desc: Cinema publication (tabloid) listing and announcing major new movie titles released each month on videocassette and the latest music release information. *Type:* Periodical.

Training Media Association—Pre-Views

Training Media Association (TMA)

198 Thomas Johnson Dr., Ste.   Ph: (301)662-4268

206   Fax: (301)695-7627

Frederick, MD 21702

Contact: Frank Russell, Editor.

Desc: Consists of news specifically of interest to members of TMA, including notices of meetings, news of seminars, introductions to new members, and film and tape festival schedules. Discusses issues of media piracy. *Type:* Newsletter.

Video Investor

Paul Kagan Associates, Inc.

126 Clock Tower Pl.   Ph: (831)624-1536

Carmel, CA 93923   Fax: (831)625-3225

E-mail: info@kagan.com

Contact: George Niesen, Editor.

Desc: Reports videocassette industry developments, including sales statistics and forecasts. Provides news of related conventions and events and focuses on sales and rentals of film product, performance of retail outlets, market shares of suppliers and distributors, the sale of chains and outlets, hardware revenues and sales, and laser disk technologies. *Type:* Newsletter.

Video Source Book

Gale Group Inc.

27500 Drake Rd.   Ph: (248)699-4253

Farmington Hills, MI 48331-   Free: 800-877-GALE

3535   Fax: (248)699-8070

E-mail: galeord@galegroup.com

URL: http://www.galegroup.com.; http://www.gale.com.

Contact: Jim Craddock, Editor, craddock@gale.com; Michelle Banks, Editor, michelle_banks@gale.com.

Desc: Approximately 150,000 videos covering approximately 175,000 programs available from more than 2,100 distributors. *Type:* Directory.

Video Technology News

Phillips Business Information, Inc.

1201 Seven Locks Rd., Ste. 300   Ph: (301)340-1520

Potomac, MD 20854   Free: 888-707-5809

    Fax: (301)340-3847

E-mail: clientservices.pbi@phillips.com

URL: http://www.ijumpstart.com.

Contact: Arthur Cole, Editor, acole@phillips.com.

Desc: Reports on video technologies from a business point of view. Provides industry analyses and forecasts, reports on new products and emerging media trends. *Type:* Newsletter.

VideoHound's Complete Guide to Cult Flicks and Trash Pics

Visible Ink Press

27500 Drake Rd.   Ph: (248)699-4253

Farmington Hills, MI 48331-   Free: 800-776-6265

3535   Fax: (248)699-8067

E-mail: galeord@gale.com

URL: http://www.gale.com

Contact: Carol Schwartz, Editor, carol.schwartz@gale.com.

Desc: 1,085 alternative films. *Type:* Directory.

VideoHound's Golden Movie Retriever

Visible Ink Press

27500 Drake Rd.   Ph: (248)699-4253

Farmington Hills, MI 48331-   Free: 800-776-6265

3535   Fax: (248)699-8067

E-mail: galeord@gale.com

URL: http://www.gale.com

Contact: Jim Craddock, Editor, craddock@gale.com.

Desc: Approximately 25,000 movie videos. *Type:* Directory.

Videomaker—Desktop Video Product Directory

Videomaker, Inc.

920 Main St.   Ph: (530)891-8410

PO Box 4591   Free: 800-284-3226

Chico, CA 95927   Fax: (530)891-8443

E-mail: editor@videomaker.com

URL: http://www.videomaker.com.

Contact: Stephen Muratore, Editor, smuratore@videomaker.com.

Desc: Listing of 250 computer/video hardware and software products available for consumer and low-end professional applications. *Type:* Directory.

VIDION/International Association of Video

1440 N St. NW, Ste. 601   Ph: (202)328-9346

Washington, DC 20005   Fax: (202)347-5829

Contact: David H. Rice, Exec.Dir.

Desc: Individuals and firms in the video industry. Keeps members updated on industry developments and the release of new video games, equipment, and videocassette movies. *Type:* Association.

Finance

AACE International

Barry G. McMillan

209 Prairie Ave.   Ph: (304)296-8444

Morgantown, WV 26501   Free: 800-858-2678

    Fax: (304)291-5728

E-mail: 76543.1216@compuserve.com

URL: http://www.aacei.org

Contact: Barry G. McMillan, Exec.Dir.

Desc: Professional society of cost managers, cost engineers, estimators, schedulers and planners, project managers, educators, representatives of all branches of engineering, engineering students, and others. Conducts technical and educational programs. Offers placement service. *Type:* Association.

AAII Journal

American Association of Individual Investors

625 N. Michigan Ave., Ste.   Ph: (312)280-0170

1900   Free: 800-428-2244

Chicago, IL 60611   Fax: (312)280-1625

E-mail: journal@aaii.com

URL: http://www.aaii.com.

Contact: Maria Crawford Scott, Editor, mcs@aaii.com.

Desc: Journal containing practical information on personal finance and investment. *Type:* Periodical.

ACA Advocate

American Collectors Association, Inc.

4040 W. 70th St.   Ph: (612)926-6547

Minneapolis, MN 55435

E-mail: aca@collector.com

Contact: Stephen L. Albrecht, Editor.

Desc: Provides the collection industry with information on regulatory happenings and legislative issues at state and federal levels. *Type:* Newsletter.

AIMR Exchange

Association for Investment Management & Research

PO Box 3668   Ph: (804)980-3668

Charlottesville, VA 22903   Free: 800-247-8132

    Fax: (804)980-9755

E-mail: info@aimr.org; aimrexchange@aimr.org.

URL: http://www.aimr.org; http://www.aimr.com/aimr.html.

Contact: Derik L. Rice, Editor.

Desc: Offers articles on the ongoing activities and educational programs and publications of the Association. Recurring features include member profiles and interviews, news of upcoming educational opportunities for members and the investment community, coverage of Association led initiative, CFA examination information, and announcements of recent publications. *Type:* Newsletter.

American Association of Individual Investors

625 N. Michigan Ave., Ste.   Ph: (312)280-0170

1900   Free: 800-428-2244

Chicago, IL 60611   Fax: (312)280-9883

E-mail: members@aaii.com

URL: http://www.aaii.com

Contact: James B. Cloonan, Chm.

Desc: Individuals who make their own investment decisions. Assists individuals in becoming effective managers of their own assets through educational programs and research. Programs help individuals develop an investment philosophy and decision-making process based on their objectives, capabilities and attitudes. *Type:* Association.

America's Corporate Finance Directory

National Register Publishing Co.

121 Chanlon Rd.   Ph: (908)464-6800

New Providence, NJ 07974   Free: 800-521-8110

    Fax: (908)508-7671

E-mail: info@renp.com

URL: http://www.reedref.com

Contact: Patricia Flinsch-Rodriguez, Editor.

Desc: Financial personnel and outside financial services relationships of 5,000 leading United States corporations and their wholly-owned United States subsidiaries; includes New York and American stock exchange firms, companies with largest 2,000 pension funds, and 2,500 of the largest private corporations. *Type:* Directory.

Associated Credit Bureaus—Communicator

Associated Credit Bureaus, Inc.

1090 Vermont Ave. NW, Ste.   Ph: (202)371-0910

200   Fax: (202)371-0134

Washington, DC 20005

Contact: Kitson Flynn, Editor.

Desc: Covers news affecting the credit reporting and collection service industries. Reports on regulatory trends, court decisions, legislation, and Association news. *Type:* Newsletter.

Audit Wire

Institute of Internal Auditors, Inc.

249 Maitland Ave.   Ph: (407)830-7600

Altamonte Springs, FL 32701-   Free: 877-867-4957

4201   Fax: (407)831-5171

E-mail: iiapubs@pbd.com

URL: http://www.theiia.org

Contact: Leah Miller, Editor.

Desc: Covers internal auditing's role in a global business environment; communicates the IIA's perspectives on current and emerging issues; and delivers news about the people, places, and events that shape the profession. Columns include: Feedback; Cusiness & Industry; Close-Up; IS Saavy; Newsmakers; Classifieds; Affiliates; Tribute; and Calendar. *Type:* Newsletter.

Bankruptcy Case Update

Matthew Bender & Company, Inc.
1275 Broadway   Free: 800-223-1940
Albany, NY 12204   Fax: 800-544-6572
URL: http://www.bender.com.

Contact: Ellen Siegel, Editor.

Desc: Provides Congressional updates, tracking bankruptcy-related legislation from the proposal through the enactment stage. Features recent developments in the area of bankruptcy law, including synopses of Supreme Court cases. *Type:* Newsletter.

Bankruptcy Current Awareness Alert

West Group
50 Broad St. E.   Ph: (716)546-1490
Rochester, NY 14694-0001   Free: 800-327-2665
    Fax: (716)258-3768
URL: http://www.westgroup.com.

Contact: David M. Holliday, Editor.

Desc: Highlights developments in the law of bankruptcy under the Bankruptcy Reform Act of 1978. *Type:* Newsletter.

Barron's

Dow Jones & Co., Inc.
200 Liberty St.   Ph: (212)416-3675
New York, NY 10281   Free: 800-622-ASIA
    Fax: (212)416-2676
E-mail: editors@news.barrons.com.
URL: http://www.barrons.com.

Contact: Edwin A. Finn, Jr., Editor/Pres., (212)416-2157, fax: (212)416-2829; Robert R. Paradise, Publisher, (212)416-2626, fax: (212)416-3206; Geoffrey E. Meyer, Advertising Sales Dir., (212)597-5928, fax: (212)597-5688.

Desc: Business and finance magazine. *Type:* Periodical.

Best's Market Guide

A.M. Best Company
Ambest Rd.   Ph: (201)439-2200
Oldwick, NJ 08858
E-mail: bestweek@ambest.com

Desc: Corporate stocks, bonds, and municipal bonds; insurance-backed companies or municipality securities; insurance company investment officers. *Type:* Directory.

Blue Chip Financial Forecasts

Capitol Publications, Inc.
1101 King St., Ste. 444   Ph: (703)683-4100
Alexandria, VA 22314   Free: 800-655-5597
    Fax: (703)739-6517

Contact: Randell E. Moore, Editor.

Desc: Makes predictions five quarters in advance regarding future trends in U.S. and foreign interest rates, exchange rates, inflation, economic growth, and monetary policy. *Type:* Newsletter.

Canadian Treasury Management Review

Royal Bank of Canada
Royal Bank Plaza   Ph: (416)974-6268
South Tower
200 Bay St.
Toronto, ON, Canada M5J 2J5

Contact: Colleen Killeavy, Editor.

Desc: Features product information, trends, and issues in treasury management. Recurring features include a calendar of events and columns titled Viewpoint, Back to Basics, and Treasury Tip. *Type:* Newsletter.

Card News

Phillips Business Information, Inc.
1201 Seven Locks Rd., Ste. 300   Ph: (301)340-1520
Potomac, MD 20854   Free: 888-707-5809
    Fax: (301)340-3847
E-mail: clientservices.pbi@phillips.com

Contact: Lurdes da Maia, Editor, ldamala@phillips.com.

Desc: Provides comprehensive coverage of transaction card developments, the market position of automatic teller machines, debit and credit cards, marketing strategies, new products, competition, regulations, and security. Absorbed Credit Card Insider Report, 1992. *Type:* Newsletter.

Cardfax

Faulkner & Gray, Inc.
300 S. Wacker Dr., 18th Fl.   Ph: (312)913-1334
Chicago, IL 60606   Fax: (312)913-1365
E-mail: order@faulknergray.com; ccm@faulknergray.com; cardfax@aol.com.

Contact: Andrea McKenna Findlay, Editor.

Desc: Contains news of the credit and debit card industry. Emphasizes company plans, ventures, programs, performance, competition, and legal and regulatory issues. *Type:* Newsletter.

CardTrak

CardWeb Inc.
1270 Fairfield Rd., Ste. 51   Ph: (717)338-1885
Gettysburg, PA 17325   Fax: (717)338-1509
E-mail: cardstaff@cardweb.com
URL: http://www.cardtrak.com.

Contact: Robert B. McKinley, Editor.

Desc: Reviews credit card offers and trends, surveying more than 500 issuers nationally. Divides surveys into several categories, including gold cards, secured cards, no-fee cards, and no-interest cards; lists co-branded and affinity cards. *Type:* Newsletter.

Center on Budget and Policy Priorities

777 N. Capitol St. NE, Ste. 705   Ph: (202)408-1080
Washington, DC 20002   Fax: (202)408-1056
E-mail: center@center.cbpp.org

Contact: Robert Greenstein, Exec. Dir.

Desc: Promotes better public understanding of the impact of federal and state governmental spending policies and programs primarily affecting low and moderate income families and individuals; acts as resource center and information clearinghouse for the media, national and local organizations (including major church denominations), and individuals. Areas of research include national poverty trends, tax policy, housing affordability, effectiveness and funding for social programs, hunger and nutrition issues, unemployment, minimum wage, and state budget and tax policies. Conducts special studies on minorities and poverty. *Type:* Association.

Center for Financial Freedom and Accuracy in Financial Reporting

PO Box 37812   Ph: (513)475-0100
Cincinnati, OH 45222   Free: 800-543-0486
    Fax: (513)475-6014
E-mail: crimpol@eos.net

Contact: Lawrence T. Patterson, Exec. Officer.

Desc: Individuals interested in financial freedom and in reporting on laws that they believe financially hurt the working population. Seeks to protect Social Security retirement benefits against "government confiscation." Advocates a return to the gold standard. Conducts research on IRA accounts and government sponsored programs. *Type:* Association.

Certified Financial Planner Board of Standards

1700 Broadway, Ste. 2100   Ph: (303)830-7500
Denver, CO 80290-2101   Free: 888-CFPMARK
    Fax: (303)860-7388
E-mail: Mail@cfp.board.org
URL: http://www.cfp-board.org

Contact: Noel Maye, Media Relations Dir.

Desc: Licenses financial planners who have completed educational, examination, work experience, and ethics requirements to use the Certified Financial Planner and CFP federally registered trademarks. Has developed a code of ethics for the financial planning profession. Cooperates with regulatory agencies; fosters public awareness of the CFP mark. *Type:* Association.

CFO & Controller Alert

Progressive Business Publications
370 Technology Dr.   Ph: (610)695-8600
Malvern, PA 19355   Free: 800-220-5000
    Fax: (610)651-2981
URL: http://www.pbp.com.

Contact: Ron McRae, Editor.

Desc: Assists buy financial executives boost cash flow, control expenses, manage resources, and comply with changing regulations. Recurring features include interviews, a calendar of events, news of educational opportunities, and columns titled Management and Sharpen Your Judgment. *Type:* Newsletter.

Chapter 11 Update

Andrews Publications
175 Strafford Ave., Bldg. 4, Ste.   Ph: (610)225-0510
140   Free: 800-345-1101
Wayne, PA 19087   Fax: (610)225-0501

Contact: Donna M. Higgins, Editor.

Desc: Monitors all major developments in today's corporate bankruptcies and examines pertinent court decisions related to Chapter 11 filings. *Type:* Newsletter.

Charitable Gift Planning News Newsletter

Charitable Gift Planning News
PO Box 214373   Ph: (214)328-4244
Dallas, TX 75221-4373   Fax: (214)328-4244
E-mail: carolcgpn@aol.com

Contact: Jerry J. McCoy, Editor, (202)466-6941, fax: (202)466-6942, mccoylaw@aol.com; Terry L. Simmons, Editor, (214)969-1419, fax: (214)969-1751, simmonst@tklaw.com.

Desc: Updates information on income, gifts, estate tax cases, ruling laws, and financial planning. Recurring features include columns titled Cases in the News, Private Letter Rulings, Washington Report, Reader's Guide, and Planner's Forum. *Type:* Newsletter.

CLU Comment

Institute of Chartered Life Underwriters & Financial Consultants (CLU)
41 Lesmill Rd.   Ph: (416)444-5251
Don Mills, ON, Canada M3B   Free: 800-563-5822
2T3   Fax: (416)444-8031

Desc: Disseminates information on business and estate planning. Remarks: Also available in a separate French edition called Commentaires. *Type:* Newsletter.

Collection Agency Report

First Detroit Corp.
PO Box 5025   Ph: (810)573-0045
Warren, MI 48090-5025   Free: 800-366-5995
    Fax: (810)573-9219
E-mail: firstdetroit@usa.com

Contact: Albert W. Scace, Editor and Publisher.

Desc: Provides news and analysis about the collection industry. *Type:* Newsletter.

The Collection Quarterly

Voss, Michaels, Lee & Associates
PO Box 1829
Holland, MI 49422-1829
Ph: (616)772-2345
Free: 800-253-4646
Contact: Tammy S. Rhoades, Editor.
Desc: Offers information on commercial collection services, including credit inquiry, pre-collection letter, legal forwarding, and special services for project work, consulting, and seminars. Also provides answers to frequently asked questions and financial data. *Type:* Newsletter.

Consumer Trends

International Credit Association
243 N. Lindbergh Blvd.
PO Box 419057
St. Louis, MO 63141-1757
Ph: (314)991-3030
Fax: (314)991-3029
E-mail: icahdqtrs@stlnet.com
Contact: Michael E. Staten; Robert W. Johnson.
Desc: Deals with consumer and commercial credit and economics. *Type:* Newsletter.

The Controller's Report

Institute of Management & Administration, Inc.
29 W. 35th St., 5th Fl.
New York, NY 10001-2299
Ph: (212)244-0360
Fax: (212)564-0465
E-mail: subserve@ioma.com
URL: http://www.ioma.com
Contact: Tim Harris, Editor; Perry Patterson, Publisher.
Desc: Provides information for corporate controllers. Includes cost benchmarks and tips. *Type:* Newsletter.

Corporate EFT Report

Phillips Business Information, Inc.
1201 Seven Locks Rd., Ste. 300
Potomac, MD 20854
Ph: (301)340-1520
Free: 888-707-5809
Fax: (301)340-3847
E-mail: clientservices.pbi@phillips.com
URL: http://www.phillips.com
Contact: Lisa Hane, Editor.
Desc: Discusses cash management and money transfer issues. *Type:* Newsletter.

Corporate Finance Network

Corporate Finance Network
One Kendall Sq.
Bldg. 200
Cambridge, MA 02139
Ph: (617)225-2900
E-mail: infoplease@corpfine
URL: http://www.corpfinet.com/
Desc: CorpiNet define's its mission as providing professionals and executives in the financial services industry the information and resources they need to develop and implement competitive strategies in a wired world. Written for an audience of executives and decisions makers in the financial services industry, their web site is an excellent resource for finding financial-related sites on the web. *Type:* Database.

Corporate Finance Sourcebook

National Register Publishing Co.
121 Chanlon Rd.
New Providence, NJ 07974
Ph: (908)464-6800
Free: 800-521-8110
Fax: (908)508-7671
E-mail: info@renp.com
URL: http://www.reedref.com
Contact: Patricia Flinsch-Rodriguez, Editor.
Desc: Securities research analysts; major private lenders; investment banking firms; commercial banks; United States-based foreign banks; commercial finance firms; leasing companies; foreign investment bankers in the United States; pension managers; banks that offer master trusts; cash managers; business insurance brokers; business real estate specialists; lists about 3,550 firms; 15,000 key financial experts. *Type:* Directory.

Corporate Financing Week

Institutional Investor, Inc.
488 Madison Ave.
New York, NY 10022
Ph: (212)224-3300
Free: 800-543-4444
Fax: (212)224-3490
Contact: Tom Lamont, Editor.
Desc: Covers all aspects of corporate capital raising, including mergers and acquisitions, taxation issues, new products, market-trends, and activities at investment banks. *Type:* Newsletter.

Cred-Alert

American Collectors Association, Inc.
4040 W. 70th St.
Minneapolis, MN 55435
Ph: (612)926-6547
E-mail: aca@collector.com
Contact: James Hoskyn, Editor.
Desc: Monitors credit and collection court decisions, legislative decisions, and other general credit matters of interest to credit grantors and collectors. Remarks: Serves as a public relations tool that members may imprint with their agency's name for distribution to their clientele. *Type:* Newsletter.

Credit

American Financial Services Association (AFSA)
Government Affairs Department
919 18th St. NW
Washington, DC 20006
Ph: (202)296-5544
Fax: (202)223-0321
E-mail: afsa@afsamail.com
Contact: Lynne B. Strang, Editor.
Desc: Provides decision-makers of financial services companies with information and brief news reports pertaining to the industry. Reports on current events of interest, including legislative and regulatory activities, news of research, industry trends and forecasts, and industry developments relating to consumer finance, mergers, and sales. *Type:* Newsletter.

Credit Card News

Faulkner & Gray, Inc.
11 Penn Plaza, 17th Fl.
New York, NY 10001-2006
Ph: (212)967-7000
Free: 800-535-8403
Fax: (212)967-7180
E-mail: order@faulknergray.com
Contact: Linda Punch, Editor.
Desc: Provides analyses of the credit card industry. Covers market strategies, trends, cost factors, bad debt losses, and interest-rate spreads. *Type:* Newsletter.

Credit Line

Bureau of Business Practice
24 Rope Ferry Rd.
Waterford, CT 06386
Ph: (860)442-4365
Free: 800-243-0876
Fax: (860)437-3555
URL: http://www.bbpnews.com
Contact: Brendan Johnston, Editor, brendan_johnston@prenhall.com; Joyce Anne Grabel, Managing Editor.
Desc: Provides advice for credit and collection staff. Recurring features include interviews. *Type:* Newsletter.

Credit Manager

Warren, Gorham & Lamont, Inc.
RIA Group
PO Box 6159
Carol Stream, IL 60197
Free: 800-950-1216
Contact: D. Cummings, Editor.
Desc: Focuses on providing "new ways to manage accounts receivable cash flow to speed up collections and reduce bad debt." *Type:* Newsletter.

Credit Risk Management Report

Phillips Business Information, Inc.
1201 Seven Locks Rd., Ste. 300
Potomac, MD 20854
Ph: (301)340-1520
Free: 888-707-5809
Fax: (301)340-3847
E-mail: clientservices.pbi@phillips.com
Contact: Lurdes da Maia, Editor, blamaia@phillips.com.
Desc: Analyzes the consumer credit marketplace. Covers hardware and software developments as well as delinquincy rates. *Type:* Newsletter.

CreditWeek

Standard & Poor's
25 Broadway
New York, NY 10004-1064
Ph: (212)208-8000
Free: 800-221-5277
Fax: (212)208-0040
URL: http://www.stockinfo.standardpoor.com
Contact: Alex Poletsky, Editor.
Desc: Standard & Poor's flagship print information and news publication that covers the global credit markets. Includes insightful feature articles on market events and trends, plus columns titled Rating News and Credit Watch. *Type:* Newsletter.

CreditWeek Municipal

Standard & Poor's
25 Broadway
New York, NY 10004-1064
Ph: (212)208-8000
Free: 800-221-5277
Fax: (212)208-0040
URL: http://www.stockinfo.standardpoor.com
Contact: Jeffrey E. Dunsavage, Editor; Alex Poletsky, Managing Editor.
Desc: Offers news, analysis, and coverage of credit trends in the municipal bond market. Recurring features include news of research, a calendar of events, notices of publications available, and a DRI Regional Economic Barometer. *Type:* Newsletter.

CRIS Commentary

Frederick Research Corporation
1441 Prospect Ave.
Plainfield, NJ 07060
Ph: (908)753-4514
Contact: Carl R. Frederick, Editor.
Desc: Profiles selected companies for investors, with information on the company's background, management, facilities and personnel, retail operations and markets, and financial state. Recurring features include economic analysis and forecasts, editorials, news of research, and a calendar of events. *Type:* Newsletter.

CRIS Report

Frederick Research Corporation
1441 Prospect Ave.
Plainfield, NJ 07060
Ph: (908)753-4514
Desc: Carries information on corporations, focusing on items helpful to investors. Remarks: CRIS is an acronym for Corporate Research Information Service. *Type:* Newsletter.

Currencies and Credit Markets

Investment Rarities, Inc.
7850 Metro Pkwy., No. 106/121
Minneapolis, MN 55425
Free: 800-328-1860
Contact: Kurt Richebacher, Editor.
Desc: Provides information on the currencies and credit markets. *Type:* Newsletter.

CUSIP Master Directory
Standard & Poor's
25 Broadway   Ph: (212)208-8000
New York, NY 10004-1064   Free: 800-221-5277
                               Fax: (212)208-0040
URL: http://www.stockinfo.standardpoor.com
Contact: Harry J. Lopez, Editor, hlopez@mgh.com.
Desc: Standard nine character numbers and descriptions of more than 1,500,000 stocks, bonds, warrants, etc. of 100,000 issuers, including corporations and municipalities of the United States and Canada. "CUSIP Corporate Directory" covers corporate securities only. *Type:* Directory.

Directory of Bond Agents
Standard & Poor's
25 Broadway   Ph: (212)208-8000
New York, NY 10004-1064   Free: 800-221-5277
                               Fax: (212)208-0040
URL: http://www.stockinfo.standardpoor.com
Desc: Processing information on over 30,000 publicly held bonds, including corporate, municipal, convertible, foreign, and Canadian bonds. *Type:* Directory.

Directory of Municipal Bond Dealers of the United States
American Banker/Bond Buyer Inc.
International Thomson Publishing Corp.
1 State St. Plaza   Ph: (212)803-8200
New York, NY 10004   Free: 800-362-3807
                               Fax: (212)843-9612
Desc: Municipal bond dealers, finance officers, attorney and finance consultants in the U.S. *Type:* Directory.

Dow Jones Financial News Service
200 Liberty St.   Ph: (212)416-2414
14th Fl.   Free: 800-223-2274
New York, NY 10281
Contact: Craig O. Allsopp, Vice President; Bob Williams, Dir.-Admin.; Robert Prinsky, Managing Editor; Neal Lipschutz, Deputy Mng. Ed.
Desc: Distributes international financial and corporate business news. *Alt. Contact:* 200 Liberty St., 14th Fl., New York, NY 10281; telephone: (212)416-2414; toll-free: 800-223-2274. *Type:* Periodical.

Dowline
Dow Jones & Co., Inc.
PO Box 300   Ph: (609)520-4305
Princeton, NJ 08543   Free: 800-JOB-HUNT
                               Fax: (609)520-7315
URL: http://bis.dowjones.com.
Contact: Catherine Jo Ward, Editor, (609)520-4656; Carl M. Valenti, Publisher.
Desc: Online information service periodical. *Type:* Periodical.

Downtown
315 E. 5th St.   Ph: (212)529-2255
No. 2H   Fax: (212)529-2269
New York, NY 10003-8855
Contact: James Rosenbrick, Publisher; Mary Hyatt, Manager.
Alt. Contact: 315 E. 5th St., No. 2H, New York, NY 10003-8855; telephone: (212)529-2255; fax: (212)529-2269. *Type:* Periodical.

Emerging Markets Debt Report
American Banker - Bond Buyer
One State Street Plaza, 27th Fl.   Ph: (212)803-8366
New York, NY 10004
URL: http://www.americanbanker.com

Desc: Contains the complete text of LDC Debt Report, a newsletter on less developed country (LDC) debt and debt restructuring. Covers debt reduction policies and programs; negotiations between debtor and lender nations; news from the International Monetary Fund (IMF), Third World Bank, and other multinational financial organizations; and the effects of LDC debt on earnings in the financial services industry. *Available:* Bell & Howell Information and Learning; LEXIS-NEXIS, NEXIS; LEXIS-NEXIS, NEXIS. *Type:* Database.

Estate and Financial Planners Alert
Research Institute of America
PO Box 5159   Free: 800-431-9025
Carol Stream, IL 60197
Desc: Spotlights critical developments in estate and financial planning. *Type:* Newsletter.

Everybody's Money
Credit Union National Association, Inc. (CUNA)
Publications and Web Services   Ph: (608)231-4082
  Dept.   Free: 800-356-9655
5710 Mineral Point Rd.   Fax: (608)231-4370
PO Box 431
Madison, WI 53701
E-mail: askem@cuna.org.
Contact: Susan Tiffany, Editor.
Desc: Money management magazine for credit union members. *Type:* Periodical.

Excellence in Leadership
Manager's Association of Insurance & Financial Advisors of Canada (MAIFAC)
41 Lesmill Rd.   Ph: (416)444-2852
North York, ON, Canada M3B   Fax: (416)444-8031
  2T3
E-mail: renee@caifa.com
Contact: Renee Maksymin, Editor.
Desc: Carries news of the Association, follows trends, laws, and legislation affecting life insurance, and offers tips to enhance the managerial effectiveness of Association members. Recurring features include interviews, news of research, a calendar of events, reports of meetings, and articles on management. *Type:* Newsletter.

Finance & Development
International Monetary Fund
700 19th St. NW   Ph: (202)623-7430
Washington, DC 20431   Fax: (202)623-7201
E-mail: jlavin@imf.org; fandd@imf.org; pgleason@imf.org.
URL: http://www.imf.org; http://www.imf.org/fandd.
Contact: Ian S. McDonald, Editor-in-Chief, (202)623-7090, fax: (202)623-6149, imcdonald@imf.org; Linda Marx, Dir. of Sales, (212)252-0222, fax: (212)252-1020.
Desc: Magazine explaining work and policies of the Bretton Woods institutions. Carries articles and book reviews on financial and developmental issues. Published in seven languages (English, French, Spanish, Arabic, and Chinese). *Alt. Contact:* Finance & Development International Monetary Fund, Washington, DC 20431; telephone: (202)623-6639; fax: (202)623-6149. *Type:* Periodical.

Financial Executives Institute
10 Madison Ave.   Ph: (973)898-4600
PO Box 1938   Fax: (973)898-4649
Morristown, NJ 07962-1938
Desc: Professional organization of corporate financial executives performing duties of chief financial officer, controller, treasurer, or vice-president-finance. *Type:* Association.

Financial Focus
Jack W. Everett, CFP, AIMC
2140 Professional Dr., No. 105   Ph: (916)791-1447
Roseville, CA 95661   Free: 800-678-FTPC
                                 Fax: (916)791-3444
Contact: Jack W. Everett, Editor, jeverett@quiknet.com.
Desc: Provides information about investments, taxes, and estate planning. *Type:* Newsletter.

Financial Management Association International
College of Business   Ph: (813)974-2084
  Administration   Fax: (813)974-3318
University of South Florida
Tampa, FL 33620-5500
E-mail: fma@coba.usf.edu
URL: http://www.fma.org
Contact: Jack S. Rader, Executive Dir.
Desc: Professors of financial management; corporate financial officers. Facilitates exchange of ideas among persons involved in financial management or the study thereof. *Type:* Association.

Financial Manager's Report of Cost Cutting
Institute of Management & Administration, Inc.
29 W. 35th St., 5th Fl.   Ph: (212)244-0360
New York, NY 10001-2299   Fax: (212)564-0465
E-mail: subserve@ioma.com
URL: http://www.ioma.com
Contact: Ann Podolske, Editor; Lee Rath, Publisher.
Desc: Provides information about cost control. Topics include labor costs, benefits, insurance, and tax. *Type:* Newsletter.

Financial Managers Society
230 W. Monroe, Ste. 2205   Ph: (312)578-1300
Chicago, IL 60606   Free: 800-ASK-4FMS
                               Fax: (312)578-1308
E-mail: lauriek@fmsinc.org
URL: http://www.fmsinc.org
Desc: Technical information exchange for financial managers of financial institutions. *Type:* Association.

Financial Managers Update
Financial Managers Society, Inc. (FMS)
230 W. Monroe, Ste. 2205   Ph: (312)578-1300
Chicago, IL 60606-4703   Free: 800-275-4367
                               Fax: (312)578-1308
E-mail: fms@fmsinc.org
Contact: Lynn W. Adkins, Editor-in-Chief; Laurie Kaczmar, Managing Editor, lauriek@frmsinc.org.
Desc: Provides financial managers of savings and loan institutions with the latest industry news. Features legislative and regulatory updates and thrift industry accounting issues reports regularly. *Type:* Newsletter.

Financial Market Trends
Organization for Economic Cooperation and Development (OECD)
2001 L St. NW, Ste. 650   Ph: (202)785-6323
Washington, DC 20036-4922   Free: 800-456-6323
                               Fax: (202)785-0350
E-mail: washington.contact@oecd.org
URL: http://www.oecdwash.org
Desc: Provides analysis of U.S. and international financial markets. *Type:* Newsletter.

Financial Monitor
American Society of Chartered Life Underwriters and Chartered Financial Consultants
270 Bryn Mawr Ave.   Ph: (215)526-2500
Bryn Mawr, PA 19010
Contact: Roslyn Myers, Editor.

Desc: Financial newsletter covering investments, financial and retirement planning. *Type:* Newsletter.

Financial News Network
2200 Fletcher Ave.   Ph: (201)585-2622
Fort Lee, NJ 07024
Alt. Contact: 2200 Fletcher Ave., Fort Lee, NJ 07024; telephone: (201)585-2622. *Type:* Periodical.

Financial Planning Digest
Harcourt Brace Professional Publishing
525 B St., No. 1900   Ph: (619)699-6716
San Diego, CA 92101-4495   Free: 800-831-7799
                                      Fax: (619)699-6716
URL: http://www.hbpp.com; http://www.hbpp.com.
Desc: Provides coverage on various topics related to financial planning. Includes tips and time-saving strategies. *Type:* Newsletter.

The Financial Post
Toronto Sun Publishing Corp.
333 King St. E.   Ph: (416)947-2191
Toronto, ON, Canada M5A   Fax: (416)947-2450
   3X5
URL: http://www.canoe.ca/FP.
Contact: Doug Knight, Publisher.
Type: Periodical.

Financial Women International
200 N. Glebe Rd., Ste. 820   Ph: (703)807-2007
Arlington, VA 22203-3728   Fax: (703)807-0111
E-mail: fwistaff@erols.com
URL: http://www.fwi.org
Contact: Gale S. Wood, CAE, Exec.Dir.
Desc: Women officers and managers in the financial industry. *Type:* Association.

Financial World
Financial World Partners
1328 Broadway, 3rd Fl.   Ph: (212)594-5030
New York, NY 10001   Free: 800-829-5916
                                     Fax: (212)629-0026
URL: http://www.enews.com/magazines/financial world; http://www.financialworld.com.
Contact: Barry L. Rupp, Chairman and CEO; Seth E. Hoyt, President/Publisher; Stephen Taub, Editor-in-Chief; John Kennelly, Advertising Mgr.
Desc: Magazine focusing on finance and business that provides useful information to individual and professional investors and corporate managers. *Type:* Periodical.

Financial Yellow Book
Leadership Directories, Inc.
104 5th Ave.   Ph: (212)627-4140
New York, NY 10011   Fax: (212)645-0931
E-mail: info@leadershipdirectories.com; financial@leadershipdirectories.com.
URL: http://www.leadershipdirectories.com; http://www.leadershipdirectories.com.
Contact: Don Doyle, Editor.
Desc: Over 31,000 key executives from leading financial organizations in the United States, and over 5,800 board members and their outside affiliations. *Type:* Directory.

FINSTAT - Global Financial Databank
The WEFA Group
1110 Vermont Ave., NW   Ph: (202)775-0610
Washington, DC 20005
URL: http://www.fdic.gov
Desc: Contains approximately 1400 time series of daily and end-of-month data on international exchange rates, Eurocurrency interest rates, London money rates, and gold prices. Also contains London and overseas stock indexes, including the Financial Times Actuaries and Financial Times Actuaries Fixed Interest indexes and some commodity prices. *Available:* The WEFA Group. *Type:* Database.

Foundation for Economic Education
30 S. Broadway   Ph: (914)591-7230
Irvington, NY 10533   Free: 800-452-3518
                                     Fax: (914)591-8910
E-mail: freeman@westnet.com
URL: http://www.fee.org
Contact: Janette Brown, Contact.
Desc: Sponsors economic studies for those requesting them in the fields of free market theory and limited government. Encourages the study and promotion of private ownership, free exchange, open competition, and limited government. Conducts seminars; maintains speakers' bureau and 8500 volume library of materials on Henry Hazlitt, Ludwig von Mises, individual rights, private property, history, economics, free markets, government, and philosophy. *Type:* Association.

Funds Transfer Report
Bankers Research Publications, Inc.
34 Imperial Ave.   Ph: (203)227-1237
PO Box 431   Fax: (203)227-1237
Westport, CT 06881
Contact: Theodore G. Volckhausen, Editor.
Desc: Provides consumer credit and funds transfer information for bank trade. *Type:* Newsletter.

Futures Magazine SourceBook
Financial Communications Co., Inc.
250 S. Wacker Dr., Ste. 1150   Ph: (312)977-0999
Chicago, IL 60606   Free: 800-972-9316
                                     Fax: (312)977-1042
URL: http://www.futuresmag.com.
Contact: Ginger Szala, Editor-in-Chief, gszala@futuresmag.com.
Desc: Exchanges dealing in futures and options contracts, including commodities, foreign currencies, stock indexes, and financial instruments; international coverage. Also includes about 2,000 advisory services, brokerage firms, consultants, research firms, management services, etc., specializing in futures, options, and derivatives trading. *Type:* Directory.

Galante's Venture Capital and Private Equity Directory
Asset Alternatives, Inc.
170 Linden St., 2nd Fl.   Ph: (781)304-1400
Wellesley, MA 02482   Fax: (781)304-1440
E-mail: info@assetnews.com; info@assetalt.com.
URL: http://www.assetnews.com.
Contact: Steven P. Galante, Editor, (781)431-2353.
Desc: More than 2,000 venture capital, buyout, and mezzanine firms; international coverage. *Type:* Directory.

The Global Directory of Financial Information Vendors
Irwin Professional Publishing
1333 Burr Ridge Pkwy   Ph: (708)789-4000
Burr Ridge, IL 60521   Free: 800-634-3966
                                     Fax: (708)798-6933
Contact: James Essinger, Editor; Joseph Rosen, Editor.
Desc: On-line financial services vendors and their operating systems. *Type:* Directory.

Global Financial Data Sample Data Series
Global Financial Data Sample Data Series
500 North Atlantic, Ste. 208   Ph: (626)284-0341
Alhambra, CA 91801
E-mail: btaylor@globalfindata.com
URL: http://globalfindata.com/samples.htm
Contact: Bryan Taylor, II, President, btaylor@globalfindata.com.
Desc: This page offers several sample tables from Global Financial Data's long-term historical financial database on stock market indices, exchange rates, inflation rates, and other historical economic data. You can inspect almost three dozen table and charts containing such historical data as consumer price inflation rates from 1899 to 1997; dollar exchange rates from 1899 to 1997; end-of-decade stock market indices for 38 countries from 1900 to 1997, as well as current-month indices for the same countries; and an index of English consumer prices from the year 1264 (yes, 1264) to 1997. *Type:* Database.

Government Finance Officers Association of United States and Canada
180 N. Michigan Ave., Ste. 800   Ph: (312)977-9700
Chicago, IL 60601   Fax: (312)977-4806
URL: http://www.gfoa.org
Contact: Jeffrey L. Esser, Exec.Dir.
Desc: Finance officers from city, county, state, provincial, and federal governments, schools, and other special districts; retirement systems, colleges, universities, public accounting firms, financial institutions, and others in the United States and Canada interested in government finance. Maintains five centers: Finance & Operations; Federal Liaison; Research, Professional Development; and Technical Services. *Type:* Association.

High Yield Report
American Banker/Bond Buyer Inc.
International Thomson Publishing Corp.
1 State St. Plaza   Ph: (212)803-8200
New York, NY 10004   Free: 800-362-3807
                                     Fax: (212)843-9612
Contact: Ken Hunter, Editor.
Desc: Examines markets for high-yield corporate bonds, work-outs, bankruptcies, and secondary markets for distressed securities. Contains pricing information for primary and secondary markets and analysis of the high-yield sector. *Type:* Newsletter.

Institute of Certified Financial Planners
3801 East Florida Ave., Ste. 708   Ph: (303)759-4900
Denver, CO 80210-2571   Free: 800-322-4237
                                     Fax: (303)759-0749
Contact: David Brand, Exec.Dir.
Desc: Individuals who have been designated Certified Financial Planner (CFP) Licensees and those who are enrolled in programs accredited by the CFP Board of Standards. Seeks to: establish and maintain professionalism in the field of financial planning; provide a forum for the interchange of ideas; insure the integrity of the profession through enforcement of a rigorous code of ethics. Sponsors continuing education programs; conducts regional conferences maintains referral service. *Type:* Association.

Institute of Financial Education
55 Monroe St., Ste. 2800   Ph: (312)364-0100
Chicago, IL 60603   Free: 800-946-0488
                                     Fax: (312)364-0190
E-mail: ifego@theinstitute.com
URL: http://www.THEINSTITUTE.com
Contact: E. Dennis Graham, Pres.
Desc: Nationwide educational organization conducting courses for personnel of savings institutions, commercial banks, and credit unions. *Type:* Association.

Institute of International Finance
2000 Pennsylvania Ave. NW,   Ph: (202)857-3600
   Ste. 8500   Fax: (202)775-1430
Washington, DC 20006-1812
Contact: Charles H. Dallara, Mng.Dir.
Desc: Financial institutions. Seeks to improve upon the process of sovereign lending, trade and project financing, and the long-term efficiency of international credit markets. *Type:* Association.

International Association for Financial Planning

5775 Glenridge Dr. NE, Ste.   Ph: (404)845-0011
  B-300   Free: 800-945-IAFP
Atlanta, GA 30328-5364   Fax: (404)845-3660
E-mail: info@iafp.org
URL: http://www.iafp.org

Contact: Janet McCallen, Exec.Dir.

Desc: Individuals in 22 countries involved in the financial planning aspects of the financial services industry. Seeks to increase members' expertise and professional standing in financial planning by assisting them in obtaining ideas and educational opportunities that would otherwise not be available. Promotes standards of business ethics, personal integrity, and professional conduct in the financial planning field. *Type:* Association.

Journal of Financial Planning

Institute of Certified Financial Planners
3801 E. Florida Ave., Suite 708   Ph: (303)759-4900
Denver, CO 80210   Free: 800-322-4237
  Fax: (303)759-0749
E-mail: icfp@icfp.org; journal@icfp.org.

Contact: Marv Tuttle, Editor, mtuttle@icfp.org.

Desc: Provides coverage of industry events and developments as well as happenings within the association. Carries articles on regulatory, ethical, and public relations aspects of the industry. *Type:* Newsletter.

Kiplinger's Personal Finance Magazine

Kiplinger Washington Editors, Inc.
1729 H St. NW   Ph: (202)887-6491
Washington, DC 20006   Free: 800-544-0155
  Fax: (202)887-6542
E-mail: magazine@kiplinger.com.

Contact: Theodore J. Miller, Editor; Knight Kiplinger, Publisher; Roger Steckler, Advertising Mgr.

Desc: Personal finance magazine featuring new and existing products and services providing information on investments, insurance, taxes, home ownership, recreation, education, automobiles, healthcare, and career and retirement planning. *Type:* Periodical.

Knight-Ridder Financial News

2020 W. 89th St.   Ph: (913)642-7373
Leawood, KS 66206

Contact: Angus Robertson, Mng. Dir./Exec. Ed.; Kara Bennett, Managing Editor; Sally Heinemann, Managing Editor.

Desc: Distributes worldwide financial and commodity news. *Alt. Contact:* 2020 W. 89th St., Leewood, KS 66206; telephone: (913)642-7373. *Type:* Periodical.

The Leahy Newsletter

Leahy Newsletter, Inc.
PO Box 467
Tustin, CA 92781   Ph: (714)665-2270
  Fax: (714)665-2271
E-mail: bleahy@aol.com

Contact: Robert Leahy, Editor.

Desc: Provides information on treasury management. *Type:* Newsletter.

Managing Credit, Receivables, and Collections

Institute of Management & Administration, Inc.
29 W. 35th St., 5th Fl.   Ph: (212)244-0360
New York, NY 10001-2299   Fax: (212)564-0465
E-mail: subserve@ioma.com
URL: http://www.ioma.com

Contact: Mary Ludwig, Editor, mludwig@ioma.com; Perry Patterson, Publisher, ppatterson@ioma.com.

Desc: Provides information on managing credits and collections departments. Remarks: also available via e-mail. *Type:* Newsletter.

Manhattan Institute for Policy Research

52 Vanderbuit Ave., 2nd Fl.   Ph: (212)599-7000
New York, NY 10017   Fax: (212)599-3494
URL: http://www.manhattan-institute

Contact: Larry Mone, Pres.

Desc: Corporations, foundations, and individuals. Purpose is to assist scholars, government officials, and the public in obtaining a better understanding of economic processes and the effect of government programs on the economic situation. Sponsors policy forums, conferences, lectures, and debates. *Type:* Association.

Money

Time Inc.
Time-Life Bldg., Rockefeller   Ph: (212)522-1212
  Center   Fax: (212)522-0315
1271 Avenue of the Americas
New York, NY 10020

Contact: Landon Y. Jones, Editor; William M. Kelly, Jr., Publisher; Charles Rubens, II, Advertising Mgr.

Desc: Magazine focusing on personal and family finance. *Type:* Periodical.

Money Management Letter

Institutional Investor, Inc.
488 Madison Ave.   Ph: (212)224-3300
New York, NY 10022   Free: 800-543-4444
  Fax: (212)224-3490

Contact: Tom Lamont, Editor; Ciaran Spillane, Managing Editor.

Desc: Serves as an information source for professionals involved in U.S. pension fund management. *Type:* Newsletter.

Money Matters

Christian Financial Concepts
601 Broad St. SE   Ph: (770)534-1000
Gainesville, GA 30501   Free: 800-722-1976
  Fax: (770)536-7226
URL: http://www.cfcministry.org.

Contact: Chuck Thompson, Editor-in-Chief, (770)534-0529, fax: (770)503-9447, joab@concentric.net.

Desc: Aims to "teach biblical principles of finance." Informs readers about legislation and regulation that affects them financially. Topics include state of the economy, legislation, and budgeting. *Type:* Newsletter.

Moneyworld

Gulf/Atlantic Publishing, Inc.
1947 Lee Rd.   Ph: (407)628-5700
Winter Park, FL 32789-2165   Free: 800-444-4980
  Fax: (407)628-0807
E-mail: money_world@money-world.net.

Contact: Donald R. Philpott, Managing Editor, don_philpott@money-world.net; Roberto E. Veitia, Publisher; Jessica Klarp, Editor, jessica_klarp@money-world.net.

Desc: Investment magazine (tabloid). *Type:* Periodical.

Municipal Issuers Registry

The Bond Buyer's Municipal Marketplace Group
A Thomson Financial Services Company
1330 Greenwood Ave.   Ph: (847)920-1928
Wilmette, IL 60091   Fax: (847)920-1929
URL: http://www.munimarketplace.com.

Contact: Marjorie S. Mizes, Publisher, mmizes@thomson.com.

Desc: Top 6,000 municipal issuers based on long-term debt issued in past four years. *Type:* Directory.

National Association of Credit Management

8815 Centre Park Dr., Ste. 200   Ph: (410)740-5560
Columbia, MD 21045-2158   Free: 800-955-8815
  Fax: (410)740-5574
URL: http://www.nacm.org

Contact: Paul J. Mignini, CAE, Pres.

Desc: Credit and financial executives representing manufacturers, wholesalers, financial institutions, insurance companies, utilities, and other businesses interested in business credit. Promotes sound credit practices and legislation. Conducts Graduate School of Credit and Financial Management at Dartmouth College, Hanover, NH. *Type:* Association.

National Association of State Auditors, Comptrollers, and Treasurers

2401 Regency Rd., Ste. 302   Ph: (606)276-1147
Lexington, KY 40503   Fax: (606)278-0507
E-mail: nasact@mis.net
URL: http://www.sso.org/nasact

Contact: Relmond P. Van Daniker, Exec.Dir.

Desc: Auditors, comptrollers, and treasurers of state fiscal agencies. Objective is to study government, particularly finance, financial reporting, taxation, and administration; and to study office methods, procedures, and general administration of state government. Offers training program and peer review and technical services. *Type:* Association.

National Bankruptcy Reporter

Andrews Publications
175 Strafford Ave., Bldg. 4, Ste.   Ph: (610)225-0510
  140   Free: 800-345-1101
Wayne, PA 19087   Fax: (610)225-0501

Contact: Rosemary MacDonald, Editor.

Desc: Serves as notification of bankruptcy reports filed in federal courts on the East and West Coasts (with the exception of New York, regarding which only court proceedings in the southern part of the state are covered). *Type:* Newsletter.

The National Financial News Service

1210 Ashbridge Rd.   Ph: (610)344-7380
Ste. 3   Free: 800-939-NFNS
West Chester, PA 19380   Fax: (610)696-1184
URL: http://www.nfns.com.

Contact: Ronald S. Shur, CEO; Bruce A. Myers, Dir.-Mktg., bruce@nfns.com.

Alt. Contact: 1210 Ashbridge Rd., Ste. 3, West Chester, PA 19380; telephone: (610)344-7380; fax: (610)696-1184; toll-free: 800-939-NFNS. *Type:* Periodical.

National Institute of Credit

Credit Research Foundation of   Ph: (410)740-5560
  the NACM   Fax: (410)740-5574
8815 Centre Park Dr., Ste. 200
Columbia, MD 21045

Contact: Robin Schaseil, Exec.Pres.

Desc: A division of the National Association of Credit Management. Offers, through local chapter classes (independently and in cooperation with local colleges), courses in credit and financial management to students; grants certificates, and Credit Business Associate, Credit Business Fellow, and Certified Credit Executive designations to persons satisfactorily completing the required points courses and examinations. Also offers the NIC Credit Administration Certificate program, which provides new members with the basic principles of business credit and financial management. *Type:* Association.

National Rural Utilities Cooperative Finance Corporation

2201 Cooperative Way   Ph: (703)709-6700
Herndon, VA 20171-3024   Free: 800-424-2954
    Fax: (703)709-6777
E-mail: izdepse@mail.nrucfc.org
URL: http://www.nrucfc.org
Contact: Sheldon C. Petersen, CEO.
Desc: Rural electric cooperative distribution systems, power supply systems, regional and statewide associations, one national association, and associate members. Based on the concepts of member-ownership and selfhelp, the purpose of the cooperative is to arrange financing for the programs and projects of its rural electric system members. Provides rural electric system members with a continuing source of private capital to supplement loan funds made available by the Rural Utilities Service. *Type:* Association.

Newsletter/Credit/Canada

Credit Association of Canada
62 Barrymore Rd.   Ph: (416)267-9673
Scarborough, ON, Canada M1J   Fax: (416)431-2275
1W3
Contact: P.H. (Phil) Etter, F.C.I., Editor.
Desc: Provides news of developments affecting the credit industry. *Type:* Newsletter.

The Nilson Report

HSN Consultants Inc.
300 Esplanade Dr., Ste. 1790   Ph: (805)983-0448
Oxnard, CA 93030   Fax: (805)983-0792
Contact: H. Spencer Nilson, Editor and Publisher.
Desc: Provides information about the credit card industry. *Type:* Newsletter.

Not-for-Profit Financial Strategies

Harcourt Brace Professional Publishing
525 B St., No. 1900   Ph: (619)699-6716
San Diego, CA 92101-4495   Free: 800-831-7799
    Fax: (619)699-6716
URL: http://www.hbpp.com; http://www.hbpp.com.
Desc: Contains advice on tax law compliance, broad coverage of new standards from FASB and GASB, and tips and strategies for using new technology. *Type:* Newsletter.

Notables

National Foundation for Consumer Credit (NFCC)
8611 2nd Ave., Ste. 100   Ph: (301)589-5600
Silver Spring, MD 20910-3372   Fax: (301)495-5623
E-mail: nfcc@nfcc.org
Contact: William Furmanski, Editor.
Desc: Covers issues concerning consumer credit counseling, family finances, and debt counseling. Recurring features include news of research, reports of meetings, book reviews, and notices of publications available. *Type:* Newsletter.

Peak to Peak

The Berger Funds
PO Box 5005   Ph: (303)329-0200
Denver, CO 80217   Fax: (303)336-4691
URL: http://www.bergerfunds.com.
Desc: Newsletter for shareholders in Berger funds. Recurring features include letters to the editor, interviews, and articles on IRA and taxes. *Type:* Newsletter.

A Penny Saved

Diane M. Rosener
PO Box 3471   Ph: (402)556-5655
Omaha, NE 68103-0471
E-mail: apnnysvd@juno.com.
Contact: Diane M. Rosener, Editor, apnnusvd@juno.com.

Desc: Focuses on saving money and spending wisely. Highlights how to be thrifty without being cheap, and living well without going broke in the process. *Type:* Newsletter.

People and Smart Money

Smith Barney
140 E. Ridgewood Ave. 3NT   Ph: (201)967-6338
Paramus, NJ 07652   Free: 800-526-0829
    Fax: (201)262-3761
Contact: Barbara Bruce-Ross, Editor.
Desc: Created to "provide financial information for people of all walks of life." Addresses readers questions and at times provides outside legal, accountant, and insurance representative's advice. Recurring features include notices of publications available and book reviews. *Type:* Newsletter.

Personal Finance

Lombardi Publishing Co.
51 Toro Rd.   Ph: (416)633-1600
North York, ON, Canada M3J   Fax: (416)633-6188
2A4
Contact: Don Sutton, Editor.
Desc: Provides articles on tax and financial planning, investing, and money management. Recurring features include columns titled Your Mutual Funds, PF Model Portfolio, and Talking Money. *Type:* Newsletter.

Personal Finance

KCI Communications, Inc.
1750 Old Meadow Rd.   Ph: (703)905-8000
Mc Lean, VA 22102
Contact: Stephen Leeb, Editor.
Desc: Contains articles on subjects of interest to those investigating personal finance strategies. Provides news, information, and suggestions on investment decisions. *Type:* Newsletter.

Planning Matters

International Association for Financial Planning
5775 Glenridge Dr. NE, Ste.   Ph: (404)845-0011
B-300   Free: 800-945-4237
Atlanta, GA 30328   Fax: (404)845-3660
E-mail: info@iafp.org
URL: http://www.iafp.org.
Contact: Bruce Lloyd, Editor, brucel@iafp.org.
Desc: Carries general news for the financial services industry. Covers such topics as current trends and developments in financial planning, banking, and insurance. *Type:* Newsletter.

Private Placement Letter

Securities Data Publishing Inc.
1290 Avenue of the Americas   Ph: (212)765-5311
New York, NY 10104   Free: 800-455-5844
    Fax: (212)937-0420
E-mail: sdp@tfn.com
Contact: Clint Winstead, Editor.
Desc: Profiles current private financings. Includes information concerning the company, offers details, security type, dollar amount, names of broker/dealers and investors, and use of proceeds. *Type:* Newsletter.

PSI Global Abstracts

Payment Systems Inc.
3030 N. Rocky Point Dr. W.,   Ph: (813)287-2774
Ste. 800   Fax: (813)286-7377
Tampa, FL 33607
Contact: James L. Belcher, Editor.
Desc: Provides summaries on research of publications of the U.S. financial industry. *Type:* Newsletter.

Public Finance/Washington Watch

American Banker - Bond Buyer
One State Street Plaza, 27th Fl.   Ph: (212)803-8366
New York, NY 10004
URL: http://www.americanbanker.com
Desc: Contains the complete text of Public Finance/Washington Watch, a newsletter providing analyses of federal government activities that affect state and local finance and municipal bond markets. Covers Congressional legislation, Securities and Exchange Commission (SEC) regulations, and Internal Revenue Service (IRS) and Treasury Department arbitrage rules. *Available:* LEXIS-NEXIS, NEXIS. *Type:* Database.

Royal Trust MoneyGuide

Ariad Custom Publishing
119 Spadina Ave., No. 1005   Ph: (416)971-9294
Toronto, ON, Canada M5V   Free: 800-668-1990
2L1   Fax: (416)971-9292
URL: http://www.royalbank.com/english/wealth.
Contact: Kathryn Choppe, Managing Editor, kchopp@ariad-ltd.com.
Desc: Provides information and advice on money and personal finances, in particular asset management, investments, retirement, and estate planning. *Type:* Newsletter.

SmartMoney

Hearst Magazines/Dow Jones & Co., Inc.
1755 Broadway, 4th Fl.   Ph: (212)373-9300
New York, NY 10019
Contact: Steven Swartz, Editor-in-Chief; Chris Lambiase, Publisher, fax: (212)246-3790; Robert Fritze, Associate Publisher.
Desc: SmartMoney is a personal business magazine edited for discriminating investors, featuring practical and imaginative ideas for investing, spending and saving. *Alt. Contact:* 1755 Broadway, 2nd Fl., New York, NY 10019; telephone: (212)765-7323; toll-free: 800-444-4204. *Type:* Periodical.

Standard & Poor's Directory of Bond Agents

Standard & Poor's
25 Broadway   Ph: (212)208-8000
New York, NY 10004-1064   Free: 800-221-5277
    Fax: (212)208-0040
URL: http://www.stockinfo.standardpoor.com; http://www.stockinfo.standard&poor.com.
Contact: Robert M. Sterenson, Managing Editor.
Desc: List of paying agents, registrars, co-registrars, trustees and conversion agents for approximately 30,000 corporate and municipal bonds. *Type:* Directory.

The Tax Directory

Tax Analysts
6830 N. Fairfax Dr.   Ph: (703)533-4400
Arlington, VA 22213   Free: 800-955-3444
    Fax: (703)533-4444
E-mail: cservice@tax.org; taxdir@tax.org.
URL: http://www.tax.org.
Contact: Tamera L. Wells-Lee, Editor.
Desc: Volume One—Approximately 15,000 federal and state government tax legislators, policymakers, adminstrators, and employees; tax regulation attorneys; over 500 international tax officials with central banks, ministries of finance, foreign embassies and consulate, and chambers of commerce. Volume Two—Over 6,800 private sector tax professionals; about 2,000 accounting, law, enrolled agent, and actuarial firms; over 300 tax and business journalists and editors working for magazines, journals, newspapers, television, and radio; tax sections of nearly 100 trade and professional associations; state CPA, bar, and enrolled agent associations; over 2,300 corporate tax managers of large U.S. firms. *Type:* Directory.

The TaxLetter

Hume Publishing Co. Ltd.
604-2200 Yonge St.　　　　Ph: (416)440-8260
Toronto, ON, Canada M4S　Free: 800-733-4863
2C6　　　　　　　　　　　Fax: (416)440-8268
E-mail: humenewsletters@mindspring.com
Contact: David Louis, Editor.
Desc: Acts as a consumer newsletter that specializes in personal tax-planning, offering timely advice, information, and recommendations on personal and business tax-planning strategies. Features columns titled ShelterWatch, RRSP Watch, Looking Out for No. *Type:* Newsletter.

Techno-Fundamental Ranks

Ned Davis Research, Inc.
600 Bird Bay Dr.　　　　Ph: (941)484-6107
Venice, FL 34292　　　　Free: 800-241-0621
　　　　　　　　　　　 Fax: (941)484-8693
URL: http://www.ndr.com.
Contact: Richard J. Sprague, Sr. Equity Selection Analyst, rich@ndr.com.
Desc: Ranks stocks based on computer-derived formulae that include technical, sentiment, and fundamental data. *Type:* Newsletter.

TELL

Association for Governmental Leasing and Finance
1200 19th St. NW, Ste. 300　　Ph: (202)429-5135
Washington, DC 20036　　　　 Fax: (202)429-5113
E-mail: aglf@sba.com; aglf@dc.sba.com.
Contact: Degra Podrut, debra-podral@dc.sbg.com.
Desc: Covers a broad range of subjects affecting the municipal leasing industry, including alternative finance methods available to state and local governments. Reports changes in legislation and case laws regarding leasing and finance and notifies members of upcoming meetings and conferences. *Type:* Newsletter.

Think Yourself Rich

Cossman International, Inc.
PO Box 4480　　　　　　Ph: (619)320-7717
Palm Springs, CA 92263　Fax: (619)320-9247
Contact: E. Jos Cossman, Editor and Publisher.
Desc: Explores how to increase one's wealth. *Type:* Newsletter.

Thomson National Directory of Mortgage Brokers

Thomson Financial Publishing
4709 Golf Rd., 6th Fl.　　Ph: (847)676-9600
Skokie, IL 60076-1253　　Free: 800-321-3373
　　　　　　　　　　　 Fax: (847)933-8101
URL: http://www.tfp.com; http://www.bankinfo.com
Contact: Nancy Zukowski, Editor.
Desc: Over 11,000 mortgage broker firms in the United States. *Type:* Directory.

Treasury Management Association

7315 Wisconsin Ave., Ste.　　Ph: (301)907-2862
600W　　　　　　　　　　　Fax: (301)907-2864
Bethesda, MD 20814-3211
Contact: James Kaitz, Pres.
Desc: Seeks to establish a national forum for the exchange of concepts and techniques related to improving the management of treasury and the careers of professionals through research, education, publications, and recognition of the treasury management profession through a certification program. *Type:* Association.

Trust Letter

American Bankers Association
Products Group
1120 Connecticut Ave. NW　　Ph: (202)663-5374
Washington, DC 20036　　　　Free: 800-338-0626
　　　　　　　　　　　　　 Fax: (202)828-4540
Contact: Larry Price, Publisher.
Desc: Contains updates of national legislation and regulation that impacts the trust and investment businesses. Reports on significant industry happenings, important research, and provides coverage of ABA legislative/regulatory testimony and committee activities, especially in the areas of taxation, securities, and employee benefits. *Type:* Newsletter.

Turnarounds & Workouts

Beard Group, Inc.
PO Box 9867　　　　　　Ph: (301)951-6400
Washington, DC 20016　　Fax: (301)951-3621
E-mail: chris@beard.com
Contact: Nina Novak, Editor, nina@beard.com.
Desc: Reports on important bankruptcy cases, major new filings, the ramifications of new taxation laws, and on federal agencies affected by or affecting bankruptcies. Recurring features include legislative and regulatory alerts; reviews of books, and surveys on specific troubled industries. *Type:* Newsletter.

12 Credit Card Secrets Banks Don't Want You to Know

Massachusetts Executive Office of Consumer Affairs and Business Regulation
1 Ashburton Pl.
Boston, MA 02108
URL: http://www.consumer.com/consumer/CREDITC.html
Desc: This website contains 12 valuable tips concerning credit cards from a consumer agency. *Type:* Database.

Valuation Researcher

Valuation Research Corp.
330 E. Kilbourn Ave., Ste. 1020　Ph: (414)271-8662
Milwaukee, WI 53202-3141　　　 Fax: (414)271-3240
Contact: James Marciniak, Editor.
Desc: Publishes valuation news and information for use in asset management, finance, and tax planning. *Type:* Newsletter.

Value Forecaster

Robert A. Freitas Jr.
PO Box 50　　　　　　　Ph: (916)939-9140
Pilot Hill, CA 95664
Contact: Robert A. Freitas, Jr., Editor.
Desc: Provides original investment and economics research. *Type:* Newsletter.

Vanderwicken's Financial Digest

Plumstead Group Inc.
PO Box 545　　　　　　Ph: (215)297-8222
New Hope, PA 18938　　Free: 800-892-6280
E-mail:　subscriptions@vanfinance.com;　editor@vanfinance.com.
URL: http://www.vanfinance.com.
Contact: Peter Vanderwicken, Editor and Publisher.
Desc: Publishes abstracts of financial articles compiled from journals and magazines. *Type:* Newsletter.

The Venture Capital Directory on CD-ROM

Infon
15600 NE 8th, B1-161　　Free: 800-654-6366
Bellevue, WA 98008　　　Fax: (425)746-4655
Desc: Over 500 venture capital firms and over 2,000 investors. *Type:* Directory.

The Wall Street Journal Interactive Edition

Dow Jones & Company, Inc.
PO Box 300　　　　　　Free: 800-396-2834
Princeton, NJ 08543
E-mail: inquiries@interactive.wsj.com.
URL: http://update.wsj.com/
Desc: The Wall Street Journal Interactive addition, updated daily, contains many of the features of the news stand edition. Features include market data, technology reports, global news, and more. *Type:* Database.

Who's Who in Asian Banking & Finance

Baron's Who's Who
412 N. Coast Hwy., Ste. B110　Ph: (949)497-8615
Laguna Beach, CA 92651　　　 Fax: (949)786-8918
E-mail: info@baronswhoswho.com
URL:　http://www.baronswhoswho.com;　http://baronswhoswho.com/wwwabfdet.htm.
Contact: John L. Pellam, Editor.
Desc: 1,851 prominent and influential bankers and investors and 1,552 banks and financial institutions in Asia. *Type:* Directory.

Who's Who in Electronic Commerce

Phillips Publishing International, Inc.
7811 Montrose Rd.　　　Ph: (301)340-2100
Potomac, MD 20854　　　Fax: (301)424-0245
Desc: Firms, organizations, and individuals in the electronic commerce industry including VANs, vendors, and user groups. *Type:* Directory.

Who's Who in Finance and Industry

Marquis Who's Who
Reed Elsevier
121 Chanlon Rd.　　　　Ph: (908)464-6800
New Providence, NJ 07974　Free: 800-521-8110
　　　　　　　　　　　　 Fax: (908)771-8645
E-mail: info@marquiswhoswho.com
Contact: Samuel J. Dempsey, Managing Editor.
Desc: Over 21,000 individuals. *Type:* Directory.

Who's Who in the Securities Industry

Economist Publishing Co.
11 E. Hubbard, Ste. 3A　　Ph: (312)467-1888
Chicago, IL 60610　　　　 Free: 800-843-3266
　　　　　　　　　　　　 Fax: (312)467-0225
Contact: John C. Cutler, Publisher.
Desc: About 1,000 investment bankers. *Type:* Directory.

Woodrow Wilson National Fellowship Foundation

CN 5281　　　　　　　　Ph: (609)452-7007
Princeton, NJ 08543-5281　Fax: (609)452-0066
URL: http://www.woodrow.org
Contact: Robert Weisbuch, Pres.
Type: Association.

World's Emerging Stock Markets

Probus Publishing Co.
1333 Burr Ridge Pkwy.
Burr Ridge, IL 60521-6489
Contact: Keith K. H. Park, Editor; Antoine W. Van Agtmael, Editor.
Desc: Directories of stock markets in Central and South America, Asia, the Middle East, and Europe. Principal content of publication is analysis of the workings of the stock exchanges in the countries covered, including investment strategies, opportunities and risks, and profiles of the top companies in each market. *Type:* Directory.

Worth Magazine

Capital Publishing Co.
575 Lexington Ave.   Ph: (212)223-3100
New York, NY 10022   Free: 800-777-1851
   Fax: (212)223-1598
E-mail: toworth@aol.com.
URL: http://www.worth.com.
Contact: John Koten, Editor; Dann Ferrara, Editor; Jane Berentson, Editor; Susan Goodall, Managing Editor; Philip Bratter, Art Dir.
Desc: Investment and personal finance magazine. *Type:* Periodical.

Your Money

Consumers Digest Inc.
8001 N. Lincoln Ave.   Ph: (847)763-9200
Skokie, IL 60077-3657   Free: 800-727-4438
   Fax: (847)763-0200
Contact: Dennis Fertig, Editor; Randy Weber, Publisher; Howard S. Plissner, VP/Dir. of Advertising, (212)685-9489, fax: (212)685-9528.
Desc: Magazine containing personal finance and investment advice. *Type:* Periodical.

Fire Fighting

International Association of Fire Chiefs

4025 Fair Ridge Dr.   Ph: (703)273-0911
Fairfax, VA 22033   Fax: (703)273-9363
E-mail: dircomm@iafc.org
URL: http://www.iafc.org
Contact: Dale Smith, Dir.
Desc: Fire Dept. cheif officers, emergency services administrators and emergency medical services directors/managers and supervisors, career, volunteer, municipal and private, who are interested in improving fire, rescue, and EMS coverage to the general public. Provides leadership to career and volunteer chiefs, chief fire officers and managers of emergency service organizations throughout the international community through vision, information, education, services and representation to enhance their professionalism and capabilities. *Type:* Association.

International Association of Fire Fighters

1750 New York Ave. NW, 3rd   Ph: (202)737-8484
Fl.   Fax: (202)737-8418
Washington, DC 20006-5395
Contact: Alfred K. Whitehead, Pres.
Desc: AFL-CIO, Canadian Labour Congress. *Type:* Association.

International Fire Fighter

International Association of Fire Fighters
1750 New York Ave. NW   Ph: (202)737-8484
Washington, DC 20006-5395   Fax: (202)737-8418
Contact: Alfred K. Whitehead, Editor; Kelly Press, Publisher; George Burke, Communications Dir.
Desc: Union tabloid. *Type:* Periodical.

International Society for Fire Service Instructors

PO Box 2320   Ph: (508)881-5800
Stafford, VA 22554-2320   Free: 800-435-0005
   Fax: (508)881-6829
URL: http://www.afem.org/afem/
Contact: Edward McCormack, CEO.
Desc: Umbrella organization for emergency management membership groups. Seeks to provide information, training, and education to fire officers, fire fighters, rescue, and emergency personnel. *Type:* Association.

National Conference of Firemen and Oilers

1900 L St., Ste. 502   Ph: (202)872-3600
Washington, DC 20036   Fax: (202)872-1222
Contact: George Francisco, Pres.
Desc: Union of boiler operators. *Type:* Association.

Newsline

National Burglar and Fire Alarm Association (NBFAA)
7101 Wisconsin Ave., Ste. 901   Ph: (301)907-3202
Bethesda, MD 20814-4805   Fax: (301)907-7897
E-mail: staff@alarm.org
URL: http://www.alarm.org; http://www.alarm.org.
Contact: David Saddler, Editor.
Desc: Provides news on the security industry, including marketing tips for small businesses and false alarm prevention ideas. Recurring features include interviews, a calendar of events, reports of meetings, news of educational opportunities, book reviews, and notices of publications available. *Type:* Newsletter.

Society for the Preservation and Appreciation of Antique Motor Fire Apparatus in America

PO Box 2005   Ph: (914)343-4219
Syracuse, NY 13220-2005
Contact: George Valrance, Sec.
Desc: Individuals interested in old fire fighting methods and apparatus, or who own or wish to own antique (defined as at least 25 years old) fire fighting apparatus. Chartered by the New York State Education Department as a nonprofit, educational, and historical society dedicated to fire service history and to preserving, restoring, and operating antique fire service apparatus. Conducts research; provides maintenance information and historical data. *Type:* Association.

Firearms

American Rifleman

National Rifle Association of America
11250 Waples Mill Rd.   Ph: (703)267-1300
Fairfax, VA 22030-9400   Free: 800-672-3888
   Fax: (703)267-3971
URL: http://www.nra.org.
Contact: E.G. Bell, Jr., Editor, (703)267-1339; Diane Senesac, Advertising Dir., (703)267-1316, fax: (703)267-3800; Diane Senesac, Mailing contact.
Desc: Magazine covering firearms ownership and use. *Type:* Periodical.

Arms & the World

PO Box 32221   Ph: (202)337-1560
Washington, DC 20007   Fax: (202)625-1999
Contact: Russell Warren Howe, Author.
Desc: Distributes weekly column on defense and security. *Alt. Contact:* PO Box 32221, Washington, DC 20007; telephone: (202)337-1560; fax: (202)625-1999. *Type:* Periodical.

Center to Prevent Handgun Violence

1225 Eye St. NW, Ste. 1100   Ph: (202)289-7319
Washington, DC 20005   Fax: (202)408-1851
URL: http://www.cphv.org
Contact: Sarah Brady, Chm.
Desc: Sponsors prevention programs for parents and youth on the risks associated with guns; legal representation for gun violence victims; and out reach to the entertainment community to encourage deglamorization of guns in the media. *Type:* Association.

Coalition to Stop Gun Violence

1000 16th St NW Ste 603   Ph: (202)530-0340
Washington, DC 20036   Fax: (202)530-0331
E-mail: noguns@aol.com
URL: http://www.gunfree.org
Contact: Michael K. Beard, Pres.
Desc: National educational, professional, and religious organizations, representing 120,000 individuals, united to seek a ban on the private sale and possession of handguns in America. (Exceptions to the ban would include the police, active military personnel, federally licensed collectors, and target shooters whose handguns are used and kept only at shooting clubs). Works to enact restrictive handgun controls at the national, state, and local levels; assists state and local handgun control organizations. *Type:* Association.

Gun Owners Incorporated

10100 Fair Oaks Blvd., Ste. I   Ph: (916)967-4970
Fair Oaks, CA 95628   Fax: (916)967-4974
E-mail: gunownca@aol.com
URL: http://www.gunownersca.com
Contact: Carolyn Herbertson, Contact.
Desc: Persons contributing funds to the defense of Americans' right to "safely and legally" own firearms. Advocates harsher punishment for criminals misusing firearms. Keeps members informed on legislation concerning gun control. *Type:* Association.

Gun World

Gallant/Charger Publications, Inc.
34249 Camino Capistrano   Ph: (714)493-2101
Capistrano Beach, CA 92624   Free: 800-767-1017
   Fax: (714)240-8680
Contact: Jack Lewis, Editor and Publisher; Jack Mitchell, Advertising Mgr.
Desc: Magazine for gun enthusiasts. *Type:* Periodical.

Guns and Ammo

Petersen Publishing Co., L.L.C.
6420 Wilshire Blvd.   Ph: (323)782-2350
Los Angeles, CA 90048-5515   Fax: (323)782-2704
Contact: Doug Hamlin, Publisher; Geoff Steer, Publisher; Peter Clancey, Senior Vice President.
Desc: Magazine on firearms for beginners and experts. Features articles on target shooting, defensive techniques, plinking, hunting, law enforcement. *Type:* Periodical.

Guns Magazine

Publishers Development Corp.
591 Camino de la Reina, Ste.   Ph: (619)297-8520
200   Free: 800-633-8001
San Diego, CA 92108   Fax: (619)297-5353
Contact: Scott Farrel, Editor; George E. von Rosen, Publisher; Denny Fallon, Advertising Mgr.
Desc: Magazine on firearms and shooting sports. *Type:* Periodical.

Handgun Control, Inc.

1225 Eye St. NW, Ste. 1100   Ph: (202)898-0792
Washington, DC 20005   Fax: (202)371-9615
URL: http://www.handguncontrol.org
Contact: Robert Walker, President.
Desc: Public citizens' lobby working for legislative controls and governmental regulations on the manufacture, importation, sale, transfer, and civilian possession of guns. Compiles up-to-date information on the gun issue, including approaches, statistics, legislation, and research. Maintains speakers' bureau. *Type:* Association.

Handgun Control—Progress Report

Handgun Control, Inc.
1225 Eye St. NW, Rm. 1100   Ph: (202)898-0792
Washington, DC 20005   Fax: (202)682-4462
Contact: Robin Terry, Editor.
Desc: Presents an on-going discussion of the proposals and developments of national handgun control legislation and news of governmental and administrative actions relevant to handgun control. Suggests activities for member activists. *Type:* Newsletter.

HandGunning

Primedia Special Interest Publication
2 News Plaza   Ph: (309)682-6626
PO Box 1790   Free: 800-521-2885
Peoria, IL 61656-1790   Fax: (309)682-7394
Contact: John Crowley, Editor.
Desc: Magazine for handgunners; includes reports, techniques, and event coverage. *Type:* Periodical.

Handguns

Petersen Publishing Co., L.L.C.
6420 Wilshire Blvd.   Ph: (323)782-2350
Los Angeles, CA 90048-5515   Fax: (323)782-2704
Contact: Jan Liboruel, Editor; Ken Elliott, Publisher; Thomas J. Siatos, Editor.
Desc: Gun enthusiast magazine emphasizing coverage on handguns. *Alt. Contact:* 6420 Wilshire Blvd., Los Angeles, CA 90048. *Type:* Periodical.

Handloader

Wolfe Publishing Co.
6471 Airpark Dr.   Ph: (520)445-7810
Prescott, AZ 86301   Free: 800-899-7810
   Fax: (520)778-5124
E-mail: wolfepub@futureone.com
URL: http://www.riflemagazine.com; handloadermagazine.com;   http://www. handloadermagazine.com.
Contact: Dave Scovill, Editor; Mark Harris, Publisher; Don Polacek, Advertising Mgr.
Desc: Magazine covering ammunition handloading. *Type:* Periodical.

National Association of Federally Licensed Firearms Dealers

2455 E. Sunrise Blvd., Ste. 916   Ph: (954)561-3505
Fort Lauderdale, FL 33304   Fax: (954)561-4129
URL: http://www.amfire.com
Contact: Andrew Molchan, Pres.
Desc: Persons licensed by the federal government to sell firearms. Provides firearm retailers with low-cost liability insurance, current information on new products for the industry, and retail business guidance. *Type:* Association.

Point Blank

Citizens Committee for the Right to Keep and Bear Arms
Liberty Park   Ph: (206)454-4911
12500 N.E. 10 Pl.   Fax: (206)451-3959
Bellevue, WA 98005
E-mail: jhvg@liberty.seanet.com.
URL: http://www.ccrkba.org.
Contact: John M. Snyder, Editor, (202)326-5259, fax: (202)898-1939.
Desc: Fosters public awareness of the citizen's right to bear arms. Reports on gun control legislation, pro-gun candidates, Committee activities, and news stories relating to gun control. *Type:* Newsletter.

Rifle

Wolfe Publishing Co.
6471 Airpark Dr.   Ph: (520)445-7810
Prescott, AZ 86301   Free: 800-899-7810
   Fax: (520)778-5124
E-mail: wolfepub@futureone.com
URL: http://www.riflemagazine.com; handloadermagazine.com; http://www.riflemagazine.com.
Contact: Dave Scovill, Editor; Mark Harris, Publisher; Don Polacek, Advertising Mgr.
Desc: Covers all types of rifles-centerfires, rimfires, air rifles and muzzle loaders. *Type:* Periodical.

Shooting Times

Primedia Special Interest Publication
2 News Plaza   Ph: (309)682-6626
PO Box 1790   Free: 800-521-2885
Peoria, IL 61656-1790   Fax: (309)682-7394
Contact: Beth Nelson, Advertising Mgr.; Joel Hutchcroft, Editor, (309)679-5402.
Desc: Magazine focusing on guns and shooting sports. *Type:* Periodical.

Shotgun News

Primedia Special Interest Publication
2 News Plaza   Ph: (309)682-6626
PO Box 1790   Free: 800-521-2885
Peoria, IL 61656-1790   Fax: (309)682-7394
E-mail: SGNewsamerica online, inc.com.
Contact: Robert W. Hunnicurt, General Mgr.; Chuck Boysen, Circulation Mgr.; Debi Fontaine, Class. Adv.
Desc: Advertising magazine for gun collectors, dealers and hunters. *Type:* Periodical.

Fish

The Aquaculture Industry

The Davlin Corporation
PO Box 2250   Ph: (760)749-7600
Valley Center, CA 92082-2250   Fax: (760)749-7674
Contact: Andrew Daylin, Jr., Editor, aquaandy@aol.com.
Desc: Reports on visits to aquaculture companies and offers reviews by financial and security analysts, along with comments on factors that may influence investors and potential investors of the industry. Recurring features include news of research and reports of meetings. *Type:* Newsletter.

Aquatic Farming Newsletter

California Aquaculture Association
PO Box 1004   Ph: (760)359-3474
Niland, CA 92257   Fax: (760)359-3308
E-mail: fish@brawleyonline.com; fish@cts.com.
URL: http://aqua.ucdavis.edu/organizations/caa.html.
Contact: George Ray, Editor.
Desc: Covers aquaculture techniques, industry trends, and current concerns. *Type:* Newsletter.

Commercial Fisheries Newsline

Michigan Sea Grant Extension
702 Chippewa Square   Ph: (906)228-4830
Marquette, MI 49855   Fax: (906)228-4572
URL: http://www.ansc.purdue.edu/aquanic/.
Contact: Ron Kinnunen, Editor, kinnunen@msue.msu. edu.
Desc: Covers current research, issues, and regulations affecting the Great Lakes commercial fishing and aquaculture industries. Recurring features include news of research, reports of meetings, news of educational opportunities, and notices of publications available. *Type:* Newsletter.

The Davlin Report

The Davlin Corporation
PO Box 2250   Ph: (760)749-7600
Valley Center, CA 92082-2250   Fax: (760)749-7674
E-mail: AquaAndy@aol.com or AquaAndy@alumni. princeton.edu.
Contact: Andrew Davlin, Jr., Editor, aquaandy@aol.com.
Desc: Reports on the managed culture of aquatic organisms in water for economic profit. *Type:* Newsletter.

Fish & Fisheries Worldwide

National Information Services Corporation (NISC)
Wyman Towers   Ph: (410)243-0797
3100 St. Paul St.
Baltimore, MD 21218
E-mail: sales@nisc.com
URL: http://www.nisc.com
Contact: Achala M, Directories Manager, ( )91 40 782-1517, fax: ( )91 40 782-2538, achala@nisc.co.in.
Desc: Covers the world's literature on fish and fisheries. Comprises 225,000 total citations broken out in the following files: • Fisheries Review--contains more than 110,000 citations, with abstracts, to published and unpublished literature on fish and fisheries. *Available:* National Information Services Corporation (NISC), NISC DISCover. *Type:* Database.

Fisheries Market News Report

Urner Barry Publications, Inc.
Box 389   Ph: (732)240-5330
Toms River, NJ 08754   Free: 800-932-0617
   Fax: (732)341-0891
E-mail: mail@urnerbarry.com
URL: http://www.seafoodnet.
Contact: Joseph Soja, Editor.
Desc: Summarizes five National Marine Fisheries Service reports and provides comparisons on cold storage, imports and exports, holdings, and landings. Monitors segments of the fishery market via news briefs. *Type:* Newsletter.

For Fish Farmers

Mississippi Cooperative Extension Service Extension Wildlife & Fisheries Department
PO Box 9690   Ph: (601)325-3174
Mississippi State, MS 39762   Fax: (601)325-8750
Contact: Dr. Martin W. Brunson, Editor.
Desc: Addresses concerns of fish farmers. Includes such information as fish farm acreage in Mississippi, catfish biology, disease prevention and control, and equipment evaluation. *Type:* Newsletter.

Great Lakes Troller

Great Lakes Troller
District Extension Sea Grant   Ph: (616)846-8250
   Agent   Fax: (616)846-0655
333 Clinton
Grand Haven, MI 49417
Contact: Charles Pistis, Editor, pistis@msue.msu.edu.
Desc: Reports on issues concerning Great Lakes fisheries. *Type:* Newsletter.

ICA Communicae

International Center for Aquaculture and Aquatic Environments (ICAAE)
Auburn University
Swingle Hall   Ph: (205)844-4786
Auburn University
Auburn, AL 36849
URL: http://www.ag.auburn.edu/dept/faa.
Contact: Dr. Bryan, Editor, bduncan@ausag.auburn.edu.
Desc: Highlights international aquaculture development including the research, staff activities, and training programs in aquaculture at the Center's warm water fisheries station. Catalogs international operation of the Center's staff involved in conferences, study tours, and overseas programs. *Type:* Newsletter.

IIFET Newsletter

International Institute of Fisheries Economics and Trade (IIFET)
Oregon State University, AREC   Ph: (503)737-1416
Dept.   Fax: (503)737-2563
220 Ballard Hall
Corvallis, OR 97331-3601
Contact: Ann L. Shriver, Editor, shrivera@cmail.orst.org; Debi Mandigo, Editorial Asst.
Desc: Keeps members abreast of events in the fisheries sectors around the world and facilitates cooperative research in the field. Also covers association workshops, conferences, and training programs. *Type:* Newsletter.

National Fisheries Institute

1901 N. Fort Myer Dr., Ste.   Ph: (703)524-8881
  700   Fax: (703)524-4619
Arlington, VA 22209
E-mail: office@nfi.org
URL: http://www.nfi.org
Contact: Richard E. Gutting, Jr., Exec.VP.
Desc: Producers (boat owners), distributors, processors, wholesalers, importers and exporters, and canners of fish and shellfish. *Type:* Association.

Shrimp Notes

Shrimp World, Inc.
417 Eliza St.   Ph: (504)368-1571
New Orleans, LA 70114   Fax: (504)368-1573
URL: http://www.shrimpcom.com.
Contact: William D. Chauvin, Editor, chauvin@shrimpcom.com; Karen Chauvin, Editor, chauvin@shrimpcom.com.
Desc: Analyzes factors determining the shrimp market status, including U.S. shrimp imports, domestic production, and economic factors. *Type:* Newsletter.

Fishing

American Bass Association

PO Box 896   Ph: (540)386-2109
Gate City, VA 24251-0896
E-mail: aba@mounet.com
URL: http://www.aba-usa.com
Contact: Bob Barker, Pres.
Desc: Individuals interested in bass angling. Promotes bass fishing through regional two-person fishing events. *Type:* Association.

American Fisheries Society

5410 Grosvenor Ln., Ste. 110   Ph: (301)897-8616
Bethesda, MD 20814   Fax: (301)897-8096
E-mail: main@fisheries.org
URL: http://www.fisheries.org
Contact: Robert Kendall, Actg.Exec.Dir.
Desc: International scientific organization of fisheries and aquatic science professionals, including fish culturists, fish biologists, water quality scientists, fish health professionals, fish technologists, educators, limnologists, and oceanographers. Promotes the development of all branches of fishery science and practice, and the conservation, development, and wise utilization of fisheries, both recreational and commercial. Strengthens professional standards by certifying fisheries scientists, stressing professional ethics, and providing forums for the exchange of scientific and management information. *Type:* Association.

American Fisheries Society—Membership Directory and Handbook

American Fisheries Society
5410 Grosvenor Ln., Ste. 110   Ph: (301)897-8616
Bethesda, MD 20814   Fax: (301)897-5080
E-mail: main@fisheries.org

URL: http://www.fisheries.org/
Contact: Susan Bowman Monseur, Editor; Trisha Milburn, Editor.
Desc: About 9,300 member individuals, firms, and others concerned with fishery sciences and the fishery industry worldwide, including fish culturists, fish biologists, water quality scientists, hatchery personnel, limnologists, and oceanographers. *Type:* Directory.

Atlantic Offshore Fisherman's Association Newsletter

Atlantic Offshore Fisherman's Association
221 3rd St.   Ph: (401)849-3232
PO Box 3001   Fax: (401)847-9966
Newport, RI 02840
Contact: Susan Cortis, Editor; Richard Allen, Editor.
Desc: Discusses news and concerns of the organization, fishing policies, and trade news affecting the fishing industry. Recurring features include news of members. *Type:* Newsletter.

Bass Anglers Sportsman Society

PO Box 17900   Ph: (334)272-9530
Montgomery, AL 36141   Fax: (334)279-7148
Contact: Helen Sevier, Chm. & CEO.
Desc: Individuals who enjoy the sport of bass fishing. Promotes interest in fishing, particularly bass fishing; works to help members improve their fishing skills; strives to enhance fishery resources through management, conservation, and other environmental measures. *Type:* Association.

Bassmaster Magazine

B.A.S.S. Inc.
5845 Carmichael Rd.   Ph: (334)272-9530
Montgomery, AL 36117-2329   Fax: (334)279-7148
E-mail: bassinc@mindspring.com; bmadv@mindspring.com.
URL: http://www.bassmaster.com.
Contact: Dave Precht, Editor; Helen Sevier, Publisher; Ken Woodard, Advertising Dir.; JoAnna Pitts, Asst. to the Editor.
Desc: Magazine covering boating and freshwater bass fishing. *Type:* Periodical.

Crappie

NatCom Inc.
5300 CityPlex Tower   Ph: (918)491-6100
2448 E. 81st St.   Fax: (918)491-9424
Tulsa, OK 74137-4207
E-mail: 73172,2054@compuserve.com.
URL: http://www.golfillustated.
Contact: Mark Chestnut, Executive editor; Ellie Shimer, Associate Publisher; Bill Cork, V.P. Communication; Gerald Pope, Publisher.
Desc: How-to magazine for recreational fishermen. *Type:* Periodical.

Federation of Fly Fishers

PO Box 1595   Ph: (406)585-7592
Bozeman, MT 59771   Fax: (406)585-7596
Contact: Tom Jindra, Pres.
Desc: Promotes fly fishing as the most enjoyable and sportsmanlike method of fishing and as the method most consistent with the preservation and conservation of fishing waters and game fish. *Type:* Association.

The Fisherman

L.I. Fisherman Publishing Corp.
14 Ramsey Rd.   Ph: (516)345-5200
Shirley, NY 11967-4704   Fax: (516)345-5304
Contact: Tim Coleman, Editor; Rich Reina, Publisher.
Desc: Regional magazine on sport fishing. *Type:* Periodical.

The Fisherman-Long Island Edition

L.I.F. Publishing Corp.
14 Ramsey Rd.   Ph: (516)345-5200
Shirley, NY 11967   Fax: (516)345-5304
Contact: Tom Melton, Editor; Fred Golofaro, Publisher; Mike Caruso, Advertising Mgr.
Desc: Magazine covering local fresh and salt water sportfishing. *Type:* Periodical.

Fishing Smart!

Aqua-Field Publishing Company, Inc.
66 W. Gilbert St., Ste. FL-2   Ph: (908)935-1222
Red Bank, NJ 07701   Fax: (908)935-9846
Contact: Edward Montague, Editor; Steve Ferber, Publisher.
Desc: Magazine on fishing. *Type:* Periodical.

Fly Fisherman

Cowles Enthusiast Media
4 High Ridge Park   Ph: (203)322-2400
Stamford, CT 06905   Fax: (203)322-1966
Contact: John Randolph, Editor and Publisher; Linda Walter, Advertising Dir.
Desc: Magazine of interest to fly fishermen. *Alt. Contact:* 6405 Flank Dr., Harrisburg, PA 17112; telephone: (717)657-9555; fax: (717)657-9526. *Type:* Periodical.

Fly Fishing Made Easy

Aqua-Field Publishing Company, Inc.
66 W. Gilbert St., Ste. FL-2   Ph: (908)935-1222
Red Bank, NJ 07701   Fax: (908)935-9846
Contact: Edward.Montague, Editor; Steve Ferber, Publisher.
Desc: Magazine on flyfishing. *Type:* Periodical.

Fly Fishing in Saltwater

Aqua-Field Publishing Company, Inc.
66 W. Gilbert St., Ste. FL-2   Ph: (908)935-1222
Red Bank, NJ 07701   Fax: (908)935-9846
Contact: Edward Montague, Editor; Steve Ferber, Publisher.
Desc: Magazine on flyfishing in saltwater. *Type:* Periodical.

Fly Fishing for Trout

Aqua-Field Publishing Company, Inc.
66 W. Gilbert St., Ste. FL-2   Ph: (908)935-1222
Red Bank, NJ 07701   Fax: (908)935-9846
Contact: Edward Montague, Editor; Steve Ferber, Publisher.
Desc: Magazine on flyfishing for trout. *Type:* Periodical.

Flyfishing Quarterly

Aqua-Field Publishing Company, Inc.
66 W. Gilbert St., Ste. FL-2   Ph: (908)935-1222
Red Bank, NJ 07701   Fax: (908)935-9846
Contact: Edward Montague, Editor; Steve Ferber, Publisher.
Desc: Magazine on flyfishing. *Type:* Periodical.

Game & Fish Magazine

Game & Fish Publications, Inc.
2250 Newmarket Pkwy., Ste.   Ph: (770)953-9222
  110   Fax: (770)933-9510
PO Box 721
Marietta, GA 30061-0741
Contact: David Morris, Editor; C.W. "Chuck" Larsen, Publisher; Curtis Richison, Advertising Mgr.
Desc: Magazine with specific state editions providing in-depth information on the wheres, whens, and hows of hunting and fishing in these states. *Type:* Periodical.

Great Lakes Sport Fishing Council

Dan Thomas
PO Box 297   Ph: (630)941-1351
Elmhurst, IL 60126   Fax: (630)941-1196
E-mail: glsfC@msn.com
URL: http://www.great-lakes.org
Contact: Dan Thomas, Pres.
Desc: Great Lakes sport fishermen and their families. Disseminates information and provides educational programs on conservation and sport fishing in the Great Lakes. Represents the interests of members before state and federal agencies. *Type:* Association.

The In-Fisherman

In-Fisherman
Two In-Fisherman Dr.   Ph: (218)829-1648
Brainerd, MN 56425-8098   Fax: (218)829-2371
E-mail: scottl@in-fisherman.com.
URL: http://www.in-fisherman.com.
Contact: Stu Legaard, Publisher, (218)825-2548, stul@in-fisherman.com.
Desc: For Freshwater Anglers; from beginners to professionals. *Alt. Contact:* Two In-Fisherman Dr., Brainerd, MN 56425; telephone: (218)829-1648; fax: (218)829-3091. *Type:* Periodical.

Inter-American Tropical Tuna Commission

Scripps Institution of Oceanography
8604 La Jolla Shores Dr.   Ph: (619)546-7100
La Jolla, CA 92037-1508   Fax: (619)546-7133
E-mail: JJoseph@iattc.ucsd.edu
Contact: Dr. James Joseph, Dir.
Desc: Appointed commissioners representing Japan, France, Nicaragua, Ecuador, El Salvador, Costa Rica, Panama, Vanuatu, Venezuela and the United States. Conducts studies on Pacific Ocean tunas and dolphins associated with tunas. *Type:* Association.

International Game Fish Association

1GFA World Fishing Center   Ph: (954)927-2628
300 Gulf Stream Way   Fax: (954)924-4299
Dania Beach, FL 33004
E-mail: igfahq@aol.com
URL: http://www.igfa.org
Contact: Michael Leech, Pres.
Desc: Federation of freshwater and saltwater anglers and angling clubs; interested individuals. Goals are to: promote the study of game fish angling, related species, and habitat requirements of such species; analyze the effects of sports fishing and commercial fishing upon game fish species; represent the sport fisherman in decisions concerning conservation and management of game fish populations. *Type:* Association.

International Pacific Halibut Commission

PO Box 95009   Ph: (206)634-1838
Seattle, WA 98145-2009   Fax: (206)632-2983
URL: http://www.iphc.washington.edu/
Contact: Dr. Bruce M. Leaman, Dir.
Desc: Intergovernmental organization of commissioners appointed by the United States (3) and Canada (3) to be responsible for management of the halibut fishery in the North Pacific and Bering Sea. *Type:* Association.

North American Fisherman

North American Outdoor Group, Inc.
12301 Whitewater Dr., Ste. 260   Ph: (612)988-7117
Minnetonka, MN 55343   Free: 800-688-7611
    Fax: (612)936-9169
E-mail: addept@naoginc.com; fishingclub@pclink.com.
URL: http://www.fishingclub.com.
Contact: Steve Pennaz, Editor, (612)988-7228; Rich Sundberg, Publisher; Russell Nolan, Group Publisher.

Desc: Fishing magazine. *Type:* Periodical.

North American Fishing Club

12301 Whitewater Dr., Ste. 260   Ph: (612)936-0555
Minnetonka, MN 55343   Free: 800-843-6232
    Fax: (612)988-7154
Contact: Steven F. Burke, CEO.
Desc: Fishermen. Seeks to improve the fishing skills of members and promotes enjoyment of the sport. *Type:* Association.

Sport Fishing

World Publications, Inc.
330 W. Canton Ave.   Ph: (407)628-4802
Winter Park, FL 32789   Fax: (407)628-7061
E-mail: sportfish@worldzine.com.
Contact: Terry Snow, President; Dean Travis Clarke, Exec. Editor; Glenn Hughes, Publisher, gh1@worldzine.com.
Desc: Magazine about saltwater fishing. *Type:* Periodical.

Sport Fishing Institute

1033 N. Fairfax St.
Alexandria, VA 22314-1540
Contact: Dr. Gilbert C. Radonski, Pres.
Desc: Sport fish conservation agency supported by manufacturers of fishing tackle, accessories, and other related equipment and products as well as individual anglers. Sponsors symposia on fisheries science and sport fisheries management; conducts staff research on fish conservation and economics. Maintains placement service; compiles statistics. *Type:* Association.

Florists

American Floral Marketing Council

Society of American Florists
1601 Duke St.   Ph: (703)836-8700
Alexandria, VA 22314-3406   Free: 800-336-4743
    Fax: (703)836-8705
Contact: Mary Anne Hansan, Dir.
Desc: A committee of the Society of American Florists. Florists, flower growers, wholesalers, and hard goods suppliers. Dedicated to increasing flower and plant sales during nonholiday periods through the implementation of national advertising and promotional programs. *Type:* Association.

Florists' Transworld Delivery Association

29200 Northwestern Hwy.   Ph: (810)355-9300
Southfield, MI 48034   Fax: (810)351-7764
Contact: Bob Norton, Pres.
Desc: Retail florist shops in North America selling flowers, gifts, candy, and fruit by wire. Conducts specialized advertising, education, and research programs; compiles statistics. Conducts ZIP code marketing service. *Type:* Association.

Interflora

3113 Woodcreek Rd.   Fax: (630)719-6183
Downers Grove, IL 60515
Desc: Floral retail shops belonging to: Florists' Transworld Delivery Association (North, Central, and South America), Interflora British Unit, and Fleurop (Europe). Represents retail florists. Serves as a world clearinghouse for members' floral orders and services. *Type:* Association.

Membership Directory of the New Jersey State Florists' Association, Inc. and the New Jersey Plant and Flower Growers Associations, Inc.

New Jersey State Florists' Association, Inc.
7 Toucan Ct.   Ph: (201)696-4087
Wayne, NJ 07470
Contact: Charles J. Marvinny, Editor.

Desc: About 600 member florists and growers, and manufacturers and suppliers of florist-related products and services in New Jersey. *Type:* Directory.

Ohio Florists' Association Bulletin

Ohio Florists' Association
2130 Stella Ct., Ste. 200   Ph: (614)487-1117
Columbus, OH 43215-1033   Fax: (614)487-1216
E-mail: ofa@ofa.org
Contact: Michelle Gaston, Managing Editor.
Desc: Covers issues in the floral industry, including crop production, management, marketing, and care and handling. Recurring features include notices of publications available. *Type:* Newsletter.

Society of American Florists

1601 Duke St.   Ph: (703)836-8700
Alexandria, VA 22314-3406   Free: 800-336-4743
    Fax: (703)836-8705
Contact: Peter J. Moran, Exec.VP.
Desc: Growers, wholesalers, retailers, and allied tradesmen in the floral industry. Lobbies Congress on behalf of the industry; sponsors educational programs; promotes the floral industry; prepares materials for consumers and for high school and college students; provides business resources. Sponsors Floricultural Hall of Fame, American Academy of Floriculture, American Floral Marketing Council , and Professional Floral Commentators - International. *Type:* Association.

Wholesale Florists and Florist Suppliers of America

410 Pine St.   Ph: (703)242-7000
Vienna, VA 22180   Fax: (703)319-1647
E-mail: j.wanko@wffsa.org
Contact: Jim Wanko, Exec.VP.
Desc: Proprietorships, partnerships, or corporations conducting wholesale businesses in fresh flowers, greens, or plants, or engaged in the manufacture and/or wholesaling of florist supplies; others actively engaged in the floral industry are associate members. Preserves and strengthens the wholesale florists' position in the floral industry. Provides a unified voice to promote the wholesalers' contributions to the industry. *Type:* Association.

Food

Ahimsa

American Vegan Society
PO Box H   Ph: (609)694-2887
Malaga, NJ 08328   Fax: (609)694-2288
Contact: H. Jay Dinshah, Editor.
Desc: Provides information on maintaining a vegan lifestyle. Recurring features include interviews, news of members, and book reviews. *Type:* Newsletter.

Alliance of Warehouses and Federations

Desc: Food cooperatives and federations. To provide mutual support among member food cooperatives and to promote the development of cooperative businesses and education. *Type:* Association.

American Culinary Federation

10 San Bartola Dr.   Ph: (904)824-4468
PO Box 3466   Fax: (904)825-4758
St. Augustine, FL 32085-3466
E-mail: acf@acfchefs.net
URL: http://www.acfchefs.org
Contact: Terri Picttaro, Contact.
Desc: National and local chapters of professional chefs and cooks. Works to advance the culinary profession by sponsoring a continuing education program to keep members informed on food preparation and new equipment, apprenticeship training, and demonstrations for charitable and professional groups. Has sent a United States team of chefs to the International Culinary Olympic Competition in Frankfurt, Germany since 1960. *Type:* Association.

American Institute of Food Distribution

28-12 Broadway   Ph: (201)791-5570
Fair Lawn, NJ 07410-3913   Fax: (201)791-5222
E-mail: 70473.741@compuserve.com
URL: http://www.foodinstitute.com
Contact: Rick Pfaff, Pres.
Desc: Canners, packers, freezers, manufacturers, brokers, wholesalers, retailer-cooperatives, chains, independent retailers, growers, trade associations, banks, advertising and government agencies, supply houses, and others working for or with the food trades. Serves as central information service for the food trades. *Type:* Association.

American School Food Service Association

1600 Duke St., 7th Fl.   Ph: (703)739-3900
Alexandria, VA 22314   Fax: (703)739-3915
URL: http://www.asfsa.org
Contact: Barbara S. Borschow, CAE, Exec.Dir.
Desc: Persons engaged in school food service or related activities in public or private schools, preschools, colleges, and universities. Seeks to encourage and promote the maintenance and improvement of the school food and nutrition program. Sponsors National School Lunch Week in October and National School Breakfast week in March. *Type:* Association.

American Seafood Institute REPORT

Rhode Island Seafood Council
212 Main St., Ste. No. 3   Ph: (401)783-4200
Wakefield, RI 02879-3512   Free: 800-328-3474
                                  Fax: (401)789-9727
E-mail: seafood@seafoodrus.org; rboragine@seafoodrus.org.
Contact: Colleen Coyne-Boragine, Editor.
Desc: Gives news on the seafood industry. Recurring features include letters to the editor, news of research, calendar of events, reports of meetings, job listings, and book reviews. *Type:* Newsletter.

Baking/Snack Directory & Buyer's Guide

Sosland Publishing Co.
4800 Main St., Ste. 100   Ph: (816)756-1000
Kansas City, MO 64112-2513   Fax: (816)756-0494
URL: http://www.sosland.com.
Contact: Laurie Gorton, Editor, lgorton@sosland.com.
Desc: Wholesale bakers of bread, cake, cookies, crackers, pasta; manufacturers of snack foods, mixes, and frozen dough; licensors of proprietary brands; manufacturers of equipment and products and suppliers of services used in wholesale baking. For bakers—Company name, address, phone, principal headquarters and plant personnel, principal products, sales volume, production method, and number of employees. For manufacturers—Company name, address, phone, name and title of contact. *Type:* Directory.

The Bread Basket

Quality Professional Services
1655 County Rd. 2   Ph: (613)923-2116
Mallorytown, ON, Canada K0E   Fax: (613)923-2116
  1R0
E-mail: bread@recorder.ca
Desc: Provides information on bread machines. Offers suggestions on purchasing grains and flours, details bread-making and ingredient storage tips, includes seven recipes in each issue. *Type:* Newsletter.

The Candy Dish

National Candy Brokers Association
710 E. Ogden Ave., Ste. 600   Ph: (630)369-2406
Naperville, IL 60563
E-mail: ncba@bonline.com
Contact: Michael Hansen, Editor.
Desc: Supports the mission of the Association to provide a single voice for the industry. Concentrates on Association activities and events such as elections, conventions, and awards. *Type:* Newsletter.

Candy Industry Buying Guide

Stagnito Communications Inc.
1935 Shermer Rd., No. 100   Ph: (847)205-5660
Northbrook, IL 60062-5354   Fax: (847)205-5680
Contact: Susan Tiffany, Editor.
Desc: List of approximately 600 suppliers of ingredients, equipment, services, and supplies to the candy industry. *Type:* Directory.

Canned Food Information Council

c/o National Food Processing   Ph: (202)639-5900
  Association
1401 New York Ave. NW, Ste.
  400
Washington, DC 20005
Contact: Roger Coleman, Sr.VP.
Desc: A council of National Food Processors Association. Seeks to enhance the image of canned foods by conducting programs and promotional activities funded by food processors, steel makers, and can manufacturers. Televises cooking demonstrations using canned foods. *Type:* Association.

Canned Fruit Promotion Service

PO Box 7111   Ph: (415)495-7714
San Francisco, CA 94120   Fax: (415)541-0107
Contact: T. J. Elliott, Contact.
Desc: Promotes the interests of the fruit canning industry. Provides product information. Maintains speakers' bureau. *Type:* Association.

Cereal Foods World

American Association of Cereal Chemists
3340 Pilot Knob Rd.   Ph: (651)454-7250
St. Paul, MN 55121-2097   Free: 800-328-7560
                                  Fax: (651)454-0766
E-mail: aacc@scisoc.org
URL: http://www.scisoc.org/aacc
Contact: Jody Grider, Editor.
Desc: Contains brief news items about the cereal industry, including news of imports/exports and legislation. Focuses on the use, processing, and marketing of cereal grains and cereal-based foods. *Type:* Newsletter.

Chocolate Manufacturers Association of the U. S.A.

7900 Westpark Dr., Ste. A-320   Ph: (703)790-5011
Mc Lean, VA 22102   Fax: (703)790-5752
URL: http://www.candyusa.org
Contact: Lawrence T. Graham, Pres.
Desc: Manufacturers of cocoa and chocolate products, including solid chocolate products with added fruit, nuts, cereals, or other foods. Finances American Cocoa Research Institute. Compiles statistics. *Type:* Association.

Chocolatier

Haymarket Group, Ltd.
45 W. 34th St., Ste. 600   Ph: (212)239-0855
New York, NY 10001   Fax: (212)967-4184
Contact: Michael Schneider, Editor-in-Chief; Elizabeth Hall, Advertising Dir.; Elizabeth Hall, Advertising Mgr.
Desc: Magazine focusing on chocolate in cooking and baking. Includes information on cookbooks, entertaining, and restaurants. *Type:* Periodical.

Cleveland Food Dealer

Cleveland Food Dealers Association, Inc.
5800 Grant Ave.   Ph: (216)641-2444
Cuyahoga Heights, OH 44105   Fax: (216)641-2446
Contact: Joan Sanford, Editor.
Desc: Covers issues related to the food and grocery industry. Contains information on food store equipment and machinery. *Type:* Newsletter.

The Co-op Newsletter

North Coast Co-op
940 9th St.   Ph: (707)826-8667
Arcata, CA 95521-6112   Fax: (707)826-8666
E-mail: co-optaz@northcoastco-op.com
URL: http://www.northcoastco-op.com.
Contact: Karen Jeffries, Editor.
Desc: Provides news of food co-ops, natural foods, and lifestyles. *Type:* Newsletter.

Concessionworks

National Association of Concessionaires (NAC)
35 E. Wacker Dr., Ste. 1816   Ph: (312)236-3858
Chicago, IL 60601   Fax: (312)236-7809
Contact: Susan Cross, Editor, smcross@earthlink.net; Meredith Ely, Asst. Editor.
Desc: Publishes news of the Association and its activities in the concession industry. Provides reports of meetings and conferences, features on individuals and companies, a calendar of events, and general news of the industry. *Type:* Newsletter.

Delta Pride News

Delta Catfish Processors, Inc.
Industrial Park   Ph: (601)887-5401
PO Box 850
Indianola, MS 38751
Contact: Walter Harrison, Editor.
Desc: Informs customers and stockholders of new developments and techniques within Delta Catfish Processors and within the fresh fish processing industry. Recurring features include news of research, staff news, items on the annual Brokers' Conference and on awards won by Delta Catfish, new product introductions, information on training materials available, and columns titled A Message From the President and Outlook on Supply and Demand. *Type:* Newsletter.

Dickinson's FDA Review

Ferdic Inc.
PO Box 28   Ph: (717)731-1426
Camp Hill, PA 17011   Fax: (717)731-1427
E-mail: ferdic@ix.netcom.com
Contact: James G. Dickinson, Editor.
Desc: Recurring features include interviews, news of research, a calendar of events, reports of meetings, and notices of publications available. *Type:* Newsletter.

Directline

International Jelly & Preserve Association
5775 Peachtree-Dunwoody Rd.,   Ph: (404)252-3663
  Ste., 500G   Fax: (404)252-0774
Atlanta, GA 30342
E-mail: ijpa@assnhq.com
Contact: Pam Chumley, Editor; Sue Taylor, Editor.
Desc: Reports on pesticides, organic food production, product liability, and health issues of food stuffs. *Type:* Newsletter.

Earthstar Examiner

Missouri Mycological Society
2888 Ossenfort Rd.   Ph: (314)458-1458
Glencoe, MO 63038   Fax: (314)458-1458
Contact: Ken Gilberg, Editor.
Desc: Reports on mushroom hunting and Society activities. Disseminates information on locating, identifying, and cooking mushrooms. *Type:* Newsletter.

END

National Environmental Health Association
720 S. Colorado Blvd., Ste. 970,   Ph: (303)756-9090
    South Tower   Fax: (303)691-9490
Denver, CO 80246-1904
E-mail: staff@neha.org
URL: http://www.neha.org
Contact: Julie Collins, Editor.
Desc: Concerned with sanitation in food service facilities, including school lunchrooms and restaurants. Covers food preparation equipment and products, sanitation procedures, and inspection techniques. *Type:* Newsletter.

FDA Week

Inside Washington Publishers
PO Box 7167   Ph: (703)416-8500
Ben Franklin Sta.   Free: 800-424-9068
Washington, DC 20044-7167
E-mail: iwp@iwpnews.com
Contact: Donna Haseley, Editor; Tara Meltzer, Associate Editor; April E. Fulton, Associate Editor.
Desc: Reports on Food and Drug Administration policy, regulation, and enforcement. *Type:* Newsletter.

Focus on Food and Beverage

Food Processing Machinery and Supplies Association
200 Daingerfield Rd.   Ph: (703)684-1080
Alexandria, VA 22314   Free: 800-331-8816
                Fax: (703)548-6563
E-mail: fpmsa@clark.net
Contact: Janet Palmisano, Editor; Ron McNally, Editor.
Desc: Covers the canning, freezing, packaging, beverage, pharmaceutical and food processing industries. Recurring features include editorials, trade statistics, guest columnists, news of members, and product releases. *Type:* Newsletter.

The Food Channel

Noble & Associates
515 State St., 29th Fl.   Ph: (312)644-4600
Chicago, IL 60610   Fax: (312)644-0493
E-mail: foodchannel@noble.net.
URL: http://www.foodchannel.com.
Contact: Joshua Isenberg, Editor.
Desc: Covers trends in food processing, grocery and convenience store retailing, distribution, restaurant management, and other food-related businesses. Reports on new food products and trends in the food industry. *Type:* Newsletter.

Food Chemical News

CRC Press, LLC
2000 Corporate Blvd. NW   Ph: (561)994-0555
Boca Raton, FL 33431
URL: http://www.crcpress.com.
Contact: Paul Shread, Editor.
Desc: Provides in-depth, timely coverage of the laws affecting food regulation, including additives, colors, pesticides, and allied products. Recurring features include news of research. *Type:* Newsletter.

Food Distributors International—Membership Directory & Buyers Guide

Food Distributors International
201 Park Washington Ct.   Ph: (703)532-9400
Falls Church, VA 22046   Fax: (703)538-4673
E-mail: staff@fdi.org
URL: http://www.fdi.org.
Contact: Sarah Ely, Editor.
Desc: Association members; suppliers of software packages applicable to the grocery wholesale and foodservice distribution industries; suppliers of warehouse and distribution equipment used in the food industry. *Type:* Directory.

Food History News

Sandra L. Oliver
1061 Main Rd.   Ph: (207)734-8140
Islesboro, ME 04848   Fax: (207)734-8140
E-mail: fhnslo@midcoast.com
Contact: Sandra L. Oliver, Editor.
Desc: Provides information about the history of food in North America. Recurring features include book reviews, and news. *Type:* Newsletter.

Food Industry Futures

Food Industry Futures
PO Box 430   Ph: (315)682-7455
Fayetteville, NY 13066-0430   Fax: (315)682-7455
Contact: Ian D.H. Cuthill, Editor.
Desc: Reports on long range trends and development in the food industry. *Type:* Newsletter.

The Food Industry Informer

Mid-Atlantic Food Dealers Association
7484 Candlewood Rd., Ste. R   Ph: (410)859-2777
Hanover, MD 21076   Fax: (410)859-8948
Contact: Brenda Corn, Editor; Denis Zegar, Publisher.
Desc: Focuses on food distribution in the Mid-Atlantic region. *Type:* Newsletter.

The Food Industry Newsletter

Newsletters, Inc.
PO Box 342730   Ph: (301)469-8507
Bethesda, MD 20827-2730   Fax: (301)469-7271
Contact: Ray Marsili, Editor.
Desc: Serves food manufacturers at the management level. Covers marketing, sales, distribution, and marketing research areas. *Type:* Newsletter.

Food Ingredient News

Business Communications Co., Inc.
25 Van Zant St.   Ph: (203)853-4266
Norwalk, CT 06855-1781   Fax: (203)853-0348
E-mail: buscom2@aol.com
URL: http://www.buscom.com; http://www.buscom.com/.
Contact: Dorothy Kroll, Editor.
Desc: Analyzes new products, patents, and industry trends of new food ingredients. Also covers new technologies, regulations, and research. *Type:* Newsletter.

The Food Institute Report

American Institute of Food Distribution, Inc.
28-12 Broadway   Ph: (201)791-5570
Fair Lawn, NJ 07410   Fax: (201)791-5222
E-mail: foodl@foodinstitution.com
URL: http://www.foodinstitute.com; http://www.foodinstitute.com.
Contact: Brian Todd, Sr. VP, bTodd@foodinstitute.com; Rick Pfaff, Pres.; Jim Gawley, Vice President.
Desc: Reports on developments in the food industry, including new products, the food service industry, mergers and acquisitions, current legislation and regulations, judicial decisions, and financial and marketing information. *Type:* Newsletter.

Food Labeling & Nutrition News

CRC Press, LLC
2000 Corporate Blvd. NW   Ph: (561)994-0555
Boca Raton, FL 33431
URL: http://www.crcpress.com.
Contact: Brendan McDonell, Editor.
Desc: Concerned with labeling, advertising, and packaging news from the FDA, USDA, FTC, and other federal and state agencies involved nutrition policy and labeling of foods, beverages and dietary supplements. *Type:* Newsletter.

Food Nutrition Health News

1712 Taylor St. NW   Ph: (202)723-2477
Washington, DC 20111   Fax: (202)882-9335
Contact: Goody L. Solomon, Author/Owner/Exec. Ed., goody@cpcuq.org; German Solomon, Asst. Ed.
Desc: Distributes features and special reports. *Alt. Contact:* 1712 Taylor St. NW, Washington, DC 2011; telephone: (202)723-2477; fax: (202)882-9335. *Type:* Periodical.

Food Processing—Annual Guide & Directory

Putman Publishing Co.
555 W. Pierce Rd., Ste. 301   Ph: (630)467-1300
Itasca, IL 60143   Fax: (630)467-1109
E-mail: hbeck88177@aol.com.
URL: http://www.foodprocessing.com.
Contact: Bob Messenger, Editor.
Desc: List of food equipment and ingredient companies. *Type:* Directory.

Food Processing Guide & Directory

Putman Publishing Co.
555 W. Pierce Rd., Ste. 301   Ph: (630)467-1300
Itasca, IL 60143   Fax: (630)467-1109
Contact: Mike Pehanich, Editor; Diane Toops, Editor.
Desc: Lists of over 5,390 food ingredient and equipment manufacturers (Standard Industrial Classification (SIC) codes 201-209). Also includes government agencies, about 283 food laboratories, 370 national associations, about 141 architects and engineers, and more than 696 special services. *Type:* Directory.

Food Processing Worldwide Guide & Directory of Ingredients, Equipment & Supplies

Putman Publishing Co.
555 W. Pierce Rd., Ste. 301   Ph: (630)467-1300
Itasca, IL 60143   Fax: (630)467-1109
Desc: 4,127 international companies serving the food industry, as well as 3,052 products. *Type:* Directory.

Food Protection Report

Charles Felix Associates
4600 East West Hwy., Ste. 200
Bethesda, MD 20814-3415
E-mail: foodprotec@aol.com.
Contact: Charles W. Felix, Editor.
Desc: Addresses developments in food protection that will have an impact on safety programs. Incorporates a four-page insert titled Inside Report that provides features, editorials, and analysis, and discusses innovations in the industry. *Type:* Newsletter.

The Food Resource

Oregon State University - Nutrition and Food Management
Corvallis, OR 97331-5103   Ph: (541)737-3561
E-mail: food@mail.orst.edu
URL: http://www.orst.edu/food-resource/food.html
Contact: ZoeAnn Holmes, Ph.D., holmesz@ucs.orst.edu.
Desc: This database contains a wide range of food-related information, including images, other food references, and related documents. It is the intention of the site to provide as much information about food as possible. *Type:* Database.

Food Review

USDA's Economic Research Service
1800 M St. NW, Rm. 3100   Ph: (202)694-5050
Washington, DC 20036   Free: 800-999-6779
                Fax: (202)694-5718
URL: http://www.econ.ag.gov.
Contact: Mary E. Maher, Managing Editor.
Desc: Provides analysis, data, and trends on domestic and foreign food consumption, food prices, export opportunities, product safety, nutrition, marketing, and processing technology. Also includes updates on domestic food assistance programs. *Type:* Newsletter.

Food Safety Notebook

Lyda Associates Inc.
PO Box 700
Palisades, NY 10964
Ph: (914)359-8282
Fax: (914)359-1229
Contact: Lillian Langseth, Ph.D., Editor.
Desc: Contains articles on food safety from journals, experts in the field. *Type:* Newsletter.

Food Talk

Charles Felix Associates
4600 East West Hwy., Ste. 200
Bethesda, MD 20814-3415
E-mail: foodprotec@aol.com.
Contact: Charles W. Felix, Editor.
Desc: Meant to be distributed by health departments, food companies and distributions to restaurant and retail food store operators in their jurisdictions. Offers articles dealing with the sanitary handling of foods, based on news reports on foodborne outbreaks, contaminations, court cases, U.S. Food and Drug Administration (FDA) regulatory decisions, and epidemiological notes from the Centers for Disease Control (CDC). *Type:* Newsletter.

Food for Thought

Life Sciences Library
Pennsylvania State University
University Park, PA 16802
Ph: (814)865-3703
Fax: (814)863-6370
Contact: Heather K. Moberly, Editor, hkm1@psu.edu.
Desc: Publishes briefs on nutrition and agriculture librarianship, and reports on meetings and activities in SLA. Recurring features include news of members, news of research, a calendar of events, statistics, obituaries, and a column titled Executive Chef (by the Division president). *Type:* Newsletter.

Food Writer

Page One
20 W. Athens Ave.
Ph: (610)896-2879
Ardmore, PA 19003
E-mail: pageone1@aol.com; foodwriter@aol.com.
Contact: Lynn Kerrigan, Editor.
Desc: Provides ideas, media contracts, and marketing listings to individuals who write about food. Recurring features include letters to the editor, interviews, news of educational opportunities, book reviews, job listings, notices of publications available, and columns titled Food Trends, Self-Publishing, and Newsletter Editor's Corner. *Type:* Newsletter.

FOODS ADLIBRA

FOODS ADLIBRA Publications
9000 Plymouth Ave. N.
Ph: (612)540-4759
Minneapolis, MN 55427
E-mail: oxcon002@mail.genmills.com
Contact: Judith O'Connell, Editor, (612)540-4759, fax: (612)540-3166, oxcon002@mail.genmills.com.
Desc: Contains more than 280,000 citations, with abstracts, to more than 500 food industry trade publications on research and development in food technology and packaging. Covers nutritional and toxicological information. *Available:* The Dialog Corporation, DIALOG. *Type:* Database.

Foodservice Product News

Young Conway Publications, Inc.
1101 Richmond Ave., Ste. 201
Ph: (732)295-5959
Point Pleasant Beach, NJ
Fax: (732)295-5979
08742-3049
E-mail: foodserviceproductnews.asia.latino@worldnet.att.net.
Contact: Judy Ann Young, Editor; Mark Conway, Publisher.

Desc: Magazine serving the restaurant food service market. *Type:* Periodical.

Fresh Views

C.H. Robinson Company
8100 Mitchell Rd., Ste. 1700
Ph: (612)937-8500
Eden Prairie, MN 55344-2285
Fax: (612)937-6740
Contact: Wendy Carson.
Desc: Explores produce marketing issues and ideas. *Type:* Newsletter.

Grocery Manufacturers of America

1010 Wisconsin Ave. NW, Ste.
Ph: (202)337-9400
900
Fax: (202)337-4508
Washington, DC 20007
Contact: C. Manly Molpus, Pres. & CEO.
Desc: Manufacturers of food and nonfood products sold through grocery trade. *Type:* Association.

HACCP Management News

CRC Press, LLC
2000 Corporate Blvd. NW
Ph: (561)994-0555
Boca Raton, FL 33431
URL: http://www.crcpress.com.
Contact: Paul Shread, Editor; John Briley, Editor.
Desc: Provides information on laws and regulations of HAACP regarding meat, poultry, and seafood. Includes upcoming regulation for other foods. *Type:* Newsletter.

Horn of Plenty

St. Mary's Food Bank
2841 N. 31st Ave.
Ph: (602)352-3640
Phoenix, AZ 85009
Fax: (602)352-3659
URL: http://www.smfb.org.
Contact: Sandy Schimmel, Editor, sandy@smfb.org.
Desc: Concerned with happenings at St. Mary's Food Bank in Phoenix, Arizona. *Type:* Newsletter.

HRI Buyers Guide

Urner Barry Publications, Inc.
Box 389
Ph: (732)240-5330
Toms River, NJ 08754
Free: 800-932-0617
Fax: (732)341-0891
E-mail: mail@urnerbarry.com
Contact: Joseph Fackenthal, Editor.
Desc: Quotes prices paid for perishable food items by restaurants and other "mass feeding outlets" in the U.S. Prices, which are based on prompt payment and delivery charge, vary according to quality, quantity, size, service needed, and special preparation. *Type:* Newsletter.

Ice News

Packaged Ice Association
4101 Lake Boone Trail, Ste. 201
Fax: (919)787-4916
Raleigh, NC 27607
Contact: Pamela Sproul, Editor.
Desc: Reports on the Association's activities in the areas of government relations, technology, merchandising, sanitation, and plant operations. Also carries pertinent industry and legislative news. *Type:* Newsletter.

IFDA Food Distributor

International Foodservice Distributors Association (IFDA)
201 Park Washington Court
Ph: (703)532-9400
Falls Church, VA 22046
Fax: (703)538-4673
E-mail: kewuxvn@aol.com.
URL: http://nawga-ifda.org.
Contact: David Alan Coia, Editor, dacoia@erols.com.
Desc: Carries news of the food service industry, including activities of manufacturers, brokers, and distributors, as well as trends in food service operation. Recurring features include profiles of food service distribution companies in the U.S. and Canada, a calendar of events, and reports of conventions and conferences. *Type:* Newsletter.

IFMA World

International Foodservice Manufacturers Association (IFMA)
Two Prudential Plaza
Ph: (312)540-4400
180 N. Stetson Ave., Ste. 4400
Fax: (312)540-4401
Chicago, IL 60601
E-mail: ifma@prodigy.com
URL: http://www.foodserviceworld.com/IFMA
Contact: Mary Neil Crosby, Editor.
Desc: Covers Association activities and conferences. Reports on market research, regulations and legislation, and other industry issues. *Type:* Newsletter.

Institute of Food Technologists

221 N. LaSalle St., Ste. 300
Ph: (312)782-8424
Chicago, IL 60601
Fax: (312)782-8348
E-mail: info@ift.org
URL: http://www.ift.org
Contact: Daniel Weber, Exec.Dir.
Desc: Scientific educational society of technical personnel in food industries, production, product development, research, and product quality. Promotes application of science and engineering to the evaluation, production, processing, packaging, distribution, preparation, and utilization of foods. Aids educational institutions in developing curricula for training in this area. *Type:* Association.

International Food Information Council

International Food Information Council Foundation
1100 Connecticut Ave. NW,
Ste. 430
Washington, DC 20036
E-mail: foodinfo@ific.health.org
URL: http://ificinfo.health.org/
Desc: A nonprofit organization based in Washington, D.C., the International Food Information Council Foundation is dedicated to disseminating "sound, scientific information on food safety and nutrition to journalists, health professionals, educators, government officials and consumers." Its official Web site goes a long way toward achieving that goal, reaching thousands of Web surfers interested in learning more about the food they eat. Among the many topics explored in great detail here are food labeling, fats and fat replacers, sweeteners, and nutrition and health for children, adolescents, and adults. *Type:* Database.

International Food Information Council

1100 Connecticut Ave. NW,
Ph: (202)296-6540
Ste. 430
Fax: (202)296-6547
Washington, DC 20036
E-mail: foodinfo@ific.health.org
URL: http://www.ificinfo.health.org
Contact: Sylvia Rowe, Pres.
Desc: Serves as an information and educational resource on nutrition and food safety. Provides science-based information to journalists, health professionals, educators, government officials and other opinion leaders who communicate with the public. *Type:* Association.

International Foodservice Editorial Council— News

International Foodservice Editorial Council
PO Box 491
Ph: (914)452-4345
Hyde Park, NY 12538-0491
Fax: (914)452-0532
E-mail: ifec@aol.com
Contact: Carol Metz, Editor.
Desc: Offers news of the activities and members of the Council, which aims to improve communications among leading food service magazines, food companies, and educational institutions. Recurring features include a calendar of events. *Type:* Newsletter.

International Jelly and Preserve Association

5775 Peachtree-Dunwoody Rd.,   Ph: (404)252-3663
Ste. 500-G   Fax: (404)252-0774
Atlanta, GA 30342
E-mail: ijpa@assnhq.com
URL: http://www.jelly.org

Contact: Pamela A Chumley, Exec.Dir.

Desc: Manufacturers of fruit spreads, such as fruit butters, jams, jellies, marmalades, pie fillings, and preserves; producers of bakers' supplies; brokers; suppliers of packaging materials. Works to maintain standards for the preserve industry. *Type:* Association.

International Maple Syrup Institute

Larry Myott, Exec.Sec.
PO Box 53010   Ph: (802)656-5417
Burlington, VT 05405-3010   Fax: (802)656-5422
E-mail: larry.myott@uvm.edu

Contact: Larry Myott, Exec.Sec.

Desc: Maple syrup producers, packers, equipment suppliers, government representatives, and extension officers. Promotes the development of the pure maple syrup industry through promotional activities and the improvement of production techniques. *Type:* Association.

Jersey Directory

American Jersey Cattle Association
6486 E. Main St.   Ph: (614)861-3636
Reynoldsburg, OH 43068-2362   Fax: (614)861-8040
E-mail: usjersey@iwaynet.net
URL: http://www.jerseydirectory.com.

Contact: Cherie L. Bayer, Ph.D., Editor.

Desc: 700 breeders of Jersey cattle and suppliers of industry services, such as stud-service businesses, marketers, embryo transfer labs, sales managers, auctioneers, associations; international coverage. *Type:* Directory.

The Kashrus Newsletter

Yeshiva Birkas Reuven
PO Box 204   Ph: (718)336-8544
Brooklyn, NY 11204
URL: http://www.kosherinfo.com.

Contact: Rabbi Yosef Wikler, Editor.

Desc: Monitors the food industry for kosher food consumers. Updates readers on the unauthorized use of kosher symbols, mislabeled products, supervision changes, and new products. *Type:* Newsletter.

Les Amis d'Escoffier

Dr. Stanley J. Nicas
1230 Main St.   Ph: (508)892-8000
Leicester, MA 01524   Fax: (508)892-3620

Contact: Dr. Stanley J. Nicas, Chm.

Desc: An educational organization of professionals in the food and wine industries. *Type:* Association.

Manufacturers' Agents for Food Service Industry

2402 Mt. Vernon Rd., Ste. 110   Ph: (770)698-8994
Dunwoody, GA 30338   Fax: (770)698-8043
E-mail: bparcells@mindspring.com
URL: http://www.mafsi.org

Contact: Brad Parcells, Exec.Dir.

Desc: Independent manufacturers' representative firms selling equipment, furnishings, and supplies to dealers and users. Sponsors annual mini manufacturer sales meetings. Conducts specialized education programs. *Type:* Association.

Meat Business Magazine—Directory Issue

Printing & Publishing, Inc.
109 W. Washington St.   Ph: (618)476-7770
Millstadt, IL 62260   Free: 800-451-0914
   Fax: (618)476-1616

E-mail: bizmag@stlmo.com.

Contact: Paul Stoecklein, Editor.

Desc: List of manufacturers and other suppliers of equipment and materials used in the meat packing industry. *Type:* Directory.

Mexican Food and Beverage Board

314 E. 41st St.   Ph: (212)682-3770
New York, NY 10017

Contact: Thomas Brenker, Pres.

Desc: International trade association originally established by the Mexican government to promote and improve the image of Mexican food in the U.S. and to increase exports of Mexican food products. Represents chain and independent Mexican restaurants and producers and manufacturers of Mexican food and related products. *Type:* Association.

Monthly Price Review

Urner Barry Publications, Inc.
PO Box 389   Ph: (732)240-5330
Toms River, NJ 08754   Free: 800-932-0617
   Fax: (732)341-0891

E-mail: mail@urnerbarry.com

Contact: Richard Brown, Editor.

Desc: Provides daily price information and monthly averages on dairy, egg, and poultry products. Remarks: Subscription includes a supplement titled Annual Price Review. *Type:* Newsletter.

The Mycophile

The North American Mycological Association
10 Lynn Brooke Pl.   Ph: (304)744-1654
Charleston, WV 25312-9521

Contact: Judy Roger, Editor, (503)657-7358, judyr@hevanet.com.

Desc: Contains information on wild mushrooms and fungi including "subjects having to do with the collection, study, preserving, eating, distribution, and scientific description" of these fungi. Recurring features include book reviews, items on club activities and programs, a calendar of events, and news of research and of members, obituaries, mycologists of the past and items of general interest about fungi. *Type:* Newsletter.

NACUFS First Monday

National Association of College & University Food Services
1405 S. Harrison Rd., Ste. 305   Ph: (517)332-2494
East Lansing, MI 48824-5242   Fax: (517)332-8144
E-mail: webmaster@nacufs.org
URL: http://www.nacufs.org/nacufs; http://www.nacufs.org/nacufs.

Contact: Lee Chaharyn, R.D., Editor, chaharyn@pilot.msu.edu.

Desc: Covers news of interest to food service industry personnel in academic institutions. Also reports on regional Association activities. *Type:* Newsletter.

National Confectioners Association of the U.S.

7900 Westpark Dr., Ste. A-320   Ph: (703)790-5750
Mc Lean, VA 22102   Fax: (703)790-5752
E-mail: smith@candyusa.org
URL: http://www.candyusa.org

Contact: Susan Smith, Contact.

Desc: Manufacturers of confectionery products; suppliers to the industry. Conducts research and technical and governmental services; provides information to the public; conducts annual confectionery technology course at the University of Wisconsin, Madison; gathers statistics on the industry. *Type:* Association.

National Food Processors Association

1301 I St.   Ph: (202)639-5900
Washington, DC 20005   Fax: (202)639-5932
E-mail: nfpa@nfpa-food.org
URL: http://www.nfpa-food.org

Contact: John R. Cady, President & CEO.

Desc: Leading authority on food science and food safety for the food industry. Members produce processed and packaged fruits and vegetables, meat and poultry, seafood, cereals, dairy products, drinks, juices, and other specialty items or provide supplies and services to food manufacturers. *Type:* Association.

National Food Processors Association—Information Letter

National Food Processors Association
1401 New York Ave. NW   Ph: (202)639-5994
Washington, DC 20005   Fax: (202)637-8068
URL: http://www.nfpa-food.org.

Contact: Michelle P. Spring, Editor.

Desc: Provides information about the food processing industry. Covers such topics as actions of Congress, federal standards for food products, sanitary inspection, industry statistics and research, consumer and trade regulations, procurement, farm programs, labor, marketing, taxation, and business ethics. *Type:* Newsletter.

National Food Service Management Institute

Beth King
P.O. Drawer 188   Ph: (601)232-7658
University, MS 38677-0188   Free: 800-321-3054
   Fax: (601)232-5615

E-mail: nfsmi@sunset.backbone.olemiss.edu
URL: http://www.olemiss.edu/depts/nfsmi

Contact: Dr. Jane Logan, Exec.Dir.

Desc: Works for the improvement of child nutrition programs and services that promote healthy eating behaviors in children. *Type:* Association.

National Honey Market News

U.S. Department of Agriculture
Agricultural Marketing Service
Fruit and Vegetable Market News
21 N. 1st Ave., Ste. 224   Ph: (509)575-2494
Yakima, WA 98902-2663   Fax: (509)457-7132

Contact: Linda Verstrate, Editor.

Desc: Provides information on colony, honey plant, and market conditions for honey-producing states and regions. Includes specific pricing information for each type of unprocessed honey sold in each state, import and export comparisons, and updates on federal price-support programs. *Type:* Newsletter.

National Packing News

National Packing News
PO Box 1349   Ph: (209)728-1455
Murphys, CA 95247   Fax: (209)728-3277

Contact: Jack W. Soward, Editor.

Desc: Discusses topics that affect the food processing industry in the nation, including production, marketing, new developments and products, new plants and plant expansions, and professional appointments. Recurring features include news of research, statistics, book reviews, and obituaries. *Type:* Newsletter.

New Product News

I.I.S.
936 Merchandise Mart   Ph: (312)464-8501
Chicago, IL 60654   Fax: (312)464-8550

Contact: Lynn Dornblaser, Editorial Dir.

Desc: Provides information about the retail food market. Includes industry news and analysis. *Type:* Newsletter.

NNFA Today

National Nutritional Foods Association (NNFA)
3931 MacArthur Blvd., Ste. 101
Newport Beach, CA 92660-3013
Ph: (949)622-6272
Free: 800-966-6632
Fax: (949)622-6266
E-mail: nnfa@nnfa.org
URL: http://www.nnfa.org.
Contact: Tracy A. Taylor, Editor, ttaylor@nnfa.org.
Desc: Supplies professionals in the health foods industry with analysis of business, legislative, social, technological, scientific, and economic developments affecting the industry. Provides information and suggestions on marketing, merchandising, public relations, and business management. *Type:* Newsletter.

North American Truffling Society Newsletter

North American Truffling Society, Inc.
PO Box 296
Corvallis, OR 97339
Ph: (541)752-2243
E-mail: sprawlinson@proaxis.com.
Desc: Designed for those interested in learning how to harvest their own truffles (an underground fungi popular as a gourmet food). Highlights rare truffle specimens found by Society members, including the scientific name and the conditions under which the truffle was found. *Type:* Newsletter.

Organic Food Business News

Hotline Printing & Publishing
PO Box 161132
Altamonte Springs, FL 32716
Ph: (407)628-1377
Fax: (407)628-9935
Contact: Dennis Blank, Editor.
Desc: Provides information about the organic food industry. Includes news, analysis, and commodity reports. *Type:* Newsletter.

Pacific Epicure

John Doerper
610 Donovan Ave.
Bellingham, WA 98225-7315
Ph: (206)733-6174
Contact: John Doerper, Editor.
Desc: Focuses on West Coast food and wine. *Type:* Newsletter.

Prepared Foods—Source Book

Cahners Business Information
1350 E. Touhy Ave.
Des Plaines, IL 60018
Ph: (847)635-8800
Free: 800-446-6551
Fax: (847)635-6856
E-mail: bkinross@cahners.com
Contact: Dave Fusaro, Editor; Bob Swientek, Editor.
Desc: About 600 food and beverage companies. *Type:* Directory.

Progressive Grocer's Trade Dimensions Database

National Decision Systems Inc. (NDS)
5375 Mira Sorrento Place, Ste. 400
San Diego, CA 92121
Ph: (619)622-0800
URL: http://www.natdecsys.com
Contact: Robert Galvin, Production Mgr.
Desc: Contains descriptive data on more than 36,000 U.S. supermarkets and superettes. *Available:* LEXIS-NEXIS, NEXIS. *Type:* Database.

Quebec Maple Syrup Producers Federation

Makaera Vir Inc.
1751 Richardson, Ste. 5513
Montreal, PQ, Canada H3K 1G6
Ph: (514)679-0530
Fax: (514)679-0139
E-mail: info@vir.ca
URL: http://www.maple-erable.qc.ca/

Desc: This multi language site provides a moderate amount of information concerning the maple syrup industry in Canada, how maple syrup is made, equipment suppliers, production statistics, and nutritional values. Several recipes are available here as well. *Type:* Database.

Quick Topics Newsletter

American Wholesale Marketers Association
1128 16th St. NW
Washington, DC 20036-4802
Ph: (202)463-2124
Free: 800-482-2962
Fax: (202)463-6467
Contact: Barbara Valakos, Editor, barbarav@awmanet.org.
Desc: Provides wholesalers of candy and tobacco products, brokers, salespersons, and manufacturers with industry news. Recurring features include news of members and notices of Association activities, events, awards, and research and educational programs. *Type:* Newsletter.

Ram's Horn

Nutrition Policy Institute
125 Highfield Rd.
Toronto, ON, Canada M4L 2T9
Contact: Brewster Kneen, Publisher; Cathleen Kneen, Editor.
Desc: Monitors and analyzes food systems. Recurring features include news of research, book reviews, notices of publications available. *Type:* Newsletter.

The Reporter

Division of Food and Drugs
Massachusetts Department of Public Health
305 South St.
Jamaica Plain, MA 02130
Ph: (617)983-6764
Fax: (617)983-6770
Contact: Joan L. Gancarski, Editor, joan.gancarski@state.ma.us.
Desc: Provides news and information on federal and Massachusetts food regulations, microbiology and epidemiology related to food borne illnesses, community sanitation, analysis of food safety issues, and local food inspection programs and concerns. *Type:* Newsletter.

Seafood Price-Current

Urner Barry Publications, Inc.
Box 389
Toms River, NJ 08754
Ph: (732)240-5330
Free: 800-932-0617
Fax: (732)341-0891
E-mail: mail@urnerbarry.com
URL: http://www.seafoodnet.com.
Contact: Paul B. Brown, Jr., Editor.
Desc: Provides seafood market price quotations for fresh and frozen fin and shell fish throughout the United States. *Type:* Newsletter.

Seafood Source

National Fisheries Institute
1901 N. Ft. Myer Dr., No. 700
Arlington, VA 22209
Ph: (703)524-8880
Fax: (703)524-4619
Contact: Linda Candler, Editor.
Desc: Covers a variety of consumer-oriented subjects: cooking tips, recipes, and restaurant trends related to seafood. *Type:* Newsletter.

Seafood Trend Newsletter

Ken Talley
8227 Ashworth Ave. N
Seattle, WA 98103
Ph: (206)523-2283
Fax: (206)526-8719
Contact: Ken Talley, Editor.
Desc: Provides information about the seafood industry. *Type:* Newsletter.

Snack Food Association

1711 King St., Ste. 1
Alexandria, VA 22314
Ph: (703)836-4500
Free: 800-628-1334
Fax: (703)836-8262
E-mail: sfa@sfa.org
URL: http://www.snax.com
Contact: James W. Shufelt, Pres.
Desc: Manufacturers of potato chips, pretzels, corn chips, tortilla chips, popcorn, parched corn, cheese twists, popped pork rinds, processed nuts, meat snacks, fruit snacks, and grain-based snacks; associate members are suppliers and distributors of fats and oils, packaging supplies, machinery, seasonings, and potato and corn growers. *Type:* Association.

Snack Food—Buyer's Guide Issue

Stagnito Publishing Co., an MWC Company
1935 Shermer Rd., Ste. 100
Northbrook, IL 60062
Ph: (847)205-5660
Fax: (847)205-5680
Contact: Bernard Pacyniak, Editor.
Desc: Monthly, business publication serving the snack food industry. List of approximately 900 suppliers of products and services to the snack food processing industry. *Type:* Directory.

Sugar Association

1101 15th St. NW, Ste. 600
Washington, DC 20005
Ph: (202)785-1122
Fax: (202)785-5019
E-mail: sugar@sugar.org
URL: http://www.sugar.org
Contact: Dr. Richard Keelor.
Desc: Represents processors, refiners and growers of beet sugar and cane sugar. Disseminates scientifically based information on the nutritional and health aspects of sucrose. Promotes research. *Type:* Association.

Supermarket Savvy Information & Resource Service

Linda McDonald Associates, Inc.
11102 Lakeside Forest Ln.
Houston, TX 77042
Ph: (713)978-6960
Free: 888-577-2889
Fax: (713)478-7044
E-mail: info@supermarketsavvy.com.
Contact: Linda McDonald, Editor.
Desc: Presents information and resources about new food products in supermarkets, natural food stores, and gourmet food stores. *Type:* Newsletter.

Trend/Wire

The Credenza Co.
PO Box 6217
Leawood, KS 66211
Ph: (913)648-7492
Fax: (913)648-7492
Contact: Art Siemering, Publisher and Executive Editor.
Desc: Advises on food and consumer trends by providing competitive marketing strategies based on current and horizon trends. Recurring features include interviews, news of research, reports of meetings, and notices of publications available. *Type:* Newsletter.

Turkey World—Leading Companies Issue

Watt Publishing Co.
122 S. Wesley Ave.
Mt. Morris, IL 61054-1497
Ph: (815)734-4171
Fax: (815)734-4201
URL: http://www.wattnet.com.
Contact: Bernard E. Heffernan, Editor, hefferna@wattmm.mhs.compuserve.com.
Desc: List of leading turkey processing firms in terms of live weight of processed birds. *Type:* Directory.

Uker's International Tea & Coffee Directory & Buyers' Guide
Lockwood Trade Journal, Inc.
130 W. 42nd St., 10th Fl.   Ph: (212)391-2060
New York, NY 10036   Fax: (212)827-0945
E-mail: teacof@aol.com
Contact: Jane McCabe, Editor; Leonard Emerson, Editor.
Desc: Firms that export and import tea and coffee; processing and packaging firms; manufacturers and suppliers of processing equipment and materials; related government agencies; specialty roasters and their suppliers. *Type:* Directory.

United Food and Commercial Workers International Union
1775 K St. NW   Ph: (202)223-3111
Washington, DC 20006   Fax: (202)466-1562
URL: http://www.ufcw.org/
Contact: Douglas H. Dorgay, Pres.
Desc: AFL-CIO. *Type:* Association.

Vegetarian Journal's Foodservice Update
The Vegetarian Resource Group
PO Box 1463   Ph: (410)366-8343
Baltimore, MD 21203   Fax: (410)366-8804
E-mail: vrg@vrg.org
URL: http://www.vrg.org
Desc: Provides information about serving vegetarian meals in institutions. Includes advice and recipes. *Type:* Newsletter.

Vegetarian Voice—Local Vegetarian Organizations Section
North American Vegetarian Society
PO Box 72   Ph: (518)568-7970
Dolgeville, NY 13329   Fax: (518)568-7979
E-mail: navs@telenet.net
URL: http://www.cyberveg.org/navs
Contact: Brian Graff, Editor, navs@telenet.net; Maribeth Abrams-McHenry, Editor, (860)652-8089, 73231.171@compuserve.com.
Desc: List of over 180 affiliated vegetarian societies and information centers. *Type:* Directory.

VFDA Update
Virginia Food Dealers Association, Inc. (VFDA)
4121 Meadowdale Blvd., Ste. D   Ph: (804)271-5964
Richmond, VA 23234   Free: 800-552-9819
      Fax: (804)271-5991
E-mail: vfda@mindspring.com
Contact: Nadine Kadlubowski, Editor.
Desc: Carries news and items of interest to those in retail food industries. *Type:* Newsletter.

Vinegar Institute
5775 Peachtree-Dunwoody Rd.,   Ph: (404)252-3663
Ste. 500-G   Fax: (404)252-0774
Atlanta, GA 30342
E-mail: vi@assnhq.com
Contact: Pamela A. Chumley, Exec.Dir.
Desc: Manufacturers and bottlers of vinegar and suppliers to the industry. Seeks to improve the quality of vinegar and increase its acceptance to the consumer. *Type:* Association.

Who's Who in the Egg and Poultry Industries
Watt Publishing Co.
122 S. Wesley Ave.   Ph: (815)734-4171
Mt. Morris, IL 61054-1497   Fax: (815)734-4201
URL: http://www.wattnet.com.
Contact: Robert Tuten, Editor, tuten@wattmm.mhs.compuserve.com.

Desc: Producers, processors, and distributors of poultry meat and eggs in the United States; manufacturers of supplies and equipment for the poultry industry; breeders and hatcheries; refrigerated public warehouses; food chain buyers of poultry meat and eggs; related government agencies; poultry associations. *Type:* Directory.

World Coffee & Tea—OCS Buyer's Guide
GCI Publishing Co., Inc.
PO Box 1110
Olney, MD 20830-1110
Contact: Colin A. Campbell, Editor.
Desc: Directory of manufacturers and suppliers of equipment and products for the office coffee service industry. *Type:* Directory.

World Food Chemical News
CRC Press, LLC
2000 Corporate Blvd. NW   Ph: (561)994-0555
Boca Raton, FL 33431
E-mail: newsdiv@crcpress.com.
URL: http://www.crcpress.com.
Contact: Declan Conroy, Editor.
Desc: Provides information about global food chemical regulation. *Type:* Newsletter.

Forest Industries

Alberta Forestry Association—Bulletin
Alberta Forestry Association
10526 Jasper Ave., Ste. 101
Edmonton, AB, Canada T5J
1Z7
Contact: Audrey Ruff, Editor.
Desc: Monitors current developments within and affecting the Alberta forestry industry and updates members on the programs and activities of the Association. Recurring features include a calendar of events. *Type:* Newsletter.

American Forest and Paper Association
1111 19th St., NW   Ph: (202)463-2700
Washington, DC 20036   Fax: (202)463-2785
URL: http://www.afpa.org
Contact: W. Henson Moore, Pres. & CEO.
Desc: Represents approximately 400 member companies and related trade associations which grow, harvest, and process wood and wood fiber, manufacture pulp, paper and paperboard from both virgin and recycled fiber, and produce solid wood products. *Type:* Association.

American Forest & Paper Association—Statistical Roundup
American Forest and Paper Association
Forest & Paper Information   Ph: (202)463-2700
Center   Fax: (202)463-2785
1111 19th St. NW, Ste. 700
Washington, DC 20036
Contact: Kathy Shaffer, Editor.
Desc: Provides monthly statistical data on the wood products industry, with coverage of each major hardwood and softwood lumber-producing region. *Type:* Newsletter.

American Pulpwood Association
600 E. Jefferson St., Ste. 350   Ph: (301)838-9385
Rockville, MD 20852-1157   Fax: (301)838-9481
E-mail: nward@apulpa.org
URL: http://www.apulpa.org
Contact: Richard Lewis, Pres.
Desc: Consumers and suppliers of pulpwood. Conducts programs on new methods and machines in growing, protecting, harvesting, and utilizing pulpwood; labor training and safety; utilization of mill and woods wastes; management of company forest lands; cooperation with conservation agencies; the viewpoint of the pulpwood harvesting industry on national legislation and federal regulations. Disseminates statistics on receipts, consumption, and inventories of pulpwood. *Type:* Association.

APA: The Engineered Wood Association
PO Box 11700   Ph: (253)565-6600
Tacoma, WA 98411   Fax: (253)565-7265
URL: http://www.apawood.org
Contact: David L. Rogoway, Pres.
Desc: Manufacturers of structural panel products, oriented strand board and composites. Conducts trade promotion through advertising, publicity, merchandising, and field promotion. *Type:* Association.

Association of Western Pulp and Paper Workers
PO Box 4566   Ph: (503)228-7486
1430 SW Clay   Fax: (503)228-1346
Portland, OR 97208
Contact: Lenard Roberts, Pres.
Desc: Independent. Workers in the pulp, paper, paper converting, lumber, and chemical industries. Lobbies in Oregon, Washington, and California; prepares position papers on related political issues; sponsors research and educational projects; conducts collective bargaining; operates library. *Type:* Association.

CINTRAFOR News
Center for International Trade in Forest Products (CINTRAFOR)
University of Washington
College of Forest Resources   Ph: (206)543-8684
P.O. Box 352100   Fax: (206)685-0790
Seattle, WA 98195-2100
E-mail: cintra4@u.washington.edu
Contact: Rosemarie Braden, Editor, (206)543-0700, rbraden@u.washington.edu.
Desc: Summarizes research and related activities in the area of forest products trade, including international symposiums, workshops, publications, and new technology trends sponsored by the Center. *Type:* Newsletter.

Composite Panel Association
18928 Premiere Ct.   Ph: (301)670-0604
Gaithersburg, MD 20879   Fax: (301)840-1252
E-mail: info@pbmdf.com
URL: http://www.pbmdf.com
Contact: Richard Margosian, Pres.
Desc: The North American trade association for the particleboard, medium density fiberboard (MDF) industries, and for other compatible products. Dedicated to increasing the acceptance and use of industry products and providing for the general welfare of the industry. *Type:* Association.

Crow's Weekly Market Report of Lumber & Panel Products
C.C. Crow Publications, Inc.
PO Box 25749   Ph: (503)646-8075
Portland, OR 97298-0749   Free: 800-800-9510
      Fax: (503)646-9971
URL: http://www.crows.com.
Contact: Sam Sherrill, Editor, ssherrill@crows.com.
Desc: Serves as a market report on lumber, plywood, and panel wood products, supplying news, analysis, and price information as a guide to sales. Carries market data on the transportation industry as it pertains to the shipment of forest products. *Type:* Newsletter.

Forest Industries Council on Taxation
1111 19th St. NW, No. 800   Ph: (202)463-2757
Washington, DC 20036   Fax: (202)463-2057
Contact: Katherene Elsen, Exec.Dir.
Desc: Policy coordinating organization for private industrial and nonindustrial timberland owners on federal timber tax issues. *Type:* Association.

Forest Log

Oregon Department of Forestry
2600 State St.   Ph: (503)945-7421
Salem, OR 97310   Fax: (503)945-7212

Contact: Rosemary Hardin, Editor.

Desc: Discusses forestry issues on state and private lands, laws reguarding forest management, and practices. Recurring features include interviews, news of research, report of meetings, and notices of publications available. *Type:* Newsletter.

Forest Products Abstracts

CAB International
CABI Publishing
10 E. 40th St., Ste. 3203
New York, NY 10016   Ph: (212)481-7018
E-mail: cabi-nao@cabi.org
URL: http://www.cabi.org

Contact: Sue Hill, Product Manager, Crop Production and Natural Resources, s.hill@cabi.org.

Desc: Contains citations, with abstracts, to current periodical and other published literature relating to the extraction, utilization, and marketing of wood and other forest products. Corresponds to Forest Products Abstracts and in part to the online CAB ABSTRACTS and CAB FORESTRY databases and the TREECD CD-ROM product. *Type:* Database.

Forest Products Society

2801 Marshall Ct.   Ph: (608)231-1361
Madison, WI 53705-2295   Fax: (608)231-2152
E-mail: info@forestprod.org
URL: http://www.forestprod.org

Contact: Arthur B. Brauner, Exec.VP.

Desc: Individuals interested in wood industry research, development, production, utilization, and distribution, from logging operations through finished products and utilization of residue as by-products. Maintains 30 technical committees. *Type:* Association.

Forestry Abstracts

CAB International
CABI Publishing
10 E. 40th St., Ste. 3203
New York, NY 10016   Ph: (212)481-7018
E-mail: cabi-nao@cabi.org
URL: http://www.cabi.org

Contact: Sue Hill, Product Manager, Crop Production and Natural Resources, s.hill@cabi.org.

Desc: Contains citations, with abstracts, to current periodical and other published literature relating to forestry. Corresponds to Forestry Abstracts and in part to the online CAB ABSTRACTS and CAB FORESTRY databases and the TREECD CD-ROM product. *Type:* Database.

Forestry in the Appalachian Hardwoods of Kentucky

Web Communications
125 Water St., Ste. A1
Santa Cruz, CA 95060   Ph: (408)457-9671
E-mail: info@webcom.com
URL: http://www.webcom.com/duane/duanefor.html

Contact: Duane Bristow, oldky@webcom.com.

Desc: The Forestry in the Appalachian Hardwoods of Kentucky web site provides access to information about forestry, especially in the Appalachians of Kentucky. Data covers such topics as forest management and timber growth. *Type:* Database.

Forestry Update

Oregon State University Extension Service
College of Forestry   Ph: (541)737-3700
Peavy Hall 119   Fax: (541)737-3008
Corvallis, OR 97331-5712
E-mail: reeds@ccmail.orst.edu.

Contact: Steve Clements, Editor.

Desc: Reports on developments in forestry research and extension. Recurring features include notices of publications available, news of research, a calendar of events, and news of educational opportunities. *Type:* Newsletter.

Hardwood Research Bulletin

National Hardwood Lumber Association
PO Box 34518   Ph: (901)382-1818
Memphis, TN 38184-0518   Fax: (901)382-6419
E-mail: nhla@natlhoodwood.org

Contact: Dan A. Meyer, Editor.

Desc: Provides abstracts and digests of current research information concerning hardwood forest management, silviculture, insects, diseases, resource utilization, product development, manufacturing technology, and economics. Lists upcoming events, workshops, short courses, and seminars of interest to members. *Type:* Newsletter.

Illinois Forest Management Newsletter

Cooperative Extension Service
University of Illinois at Urbana-Champaign
1301 W. Gregory Dr.   Ph: (217)333-2666
Urbana, IL 61801

Desc: Features "management information and timely tips for woodland owners on silviculture, tree planting, wildlife management, forest investments and taxes, marketing, harvesting and utilization, forest insect and disease problems, residential tree care, and the care of wood products." *Type:* Newsletter.

ISTF News

International Society of Tropical Foresters, Inc. (ISTF)
5400 Grosvenor Ln.   Ph: (301)897-8720
Bethesda, MD 20814   Fax: (301)897-3690
E-mail: istfiu5f@igc.apl.org.

Contact: Frank H. Wadsworth, Editor, (787)766-5335, fax: (787)766-6302.

Desc: Covers developments in tropical forestry. Recurring features include book reviews, notices of upcoming meetings, lists of members, and notes on member activities. *Type:* Newsletter.

Kentucky's Growing Gold

Natural Resources and Environmental Protection Cabinet
Department for Natural Resources
Kentucky Division for Forestry
627 Comanche Trail   Ph: (502)564-4496
Frankfort, KY 40601

Contact: Larry Lowe, Editor.

Desc: Lists privately owned timber for sale that has been marked for cutting. Provides occasional articles and items of interest on the forest industry. *Type:* Newsletter.

Le Papetier

Quebec Forest Industries Association
1200, ave. Germain-des-Pres, Ph: (418)651-9352
  bur. 102   Fax: (418)651-4622
Ste-Foy, PQ, Canada G1V 3M7
E-mail: info@aifq.qc.ca

Contact: Benot Massicotte.

Desc: Provides news and information regarding the paper industry in Quebec. Recurring features include letters to the editor, news of research, and news of educational opportunities. *Type:* Newsletter.

Madison's Canadian Lumber Reporter Newsletter

Macmillan Publishing Co.
Macmillan Library Reference Group
PO Box 159   Free: 800-257-5157
Thorndike, ME 04986

Contact: Ward Johnson, Editor.

Desc: Analyzes the North American lumber market trends and conditions. *Type:* Newsletter.

National Woodland Owners Association

374 Maple Ave. E., Ste. 310 Ph: (703)255-2300
Vienna, VA 22180   Free: 800-476-8733

Contact: Dr. Keith A. Argow, Pres.

Desc: A member of the Natural Resources Council of America and the National Council on Private Forests . Woodland owners united to promote wise management of nonindustrial private forest lands. Works with cooperating and affiliated state woodland owners' associations and serves as voice for private landowners on forestry, wildlife, and resource conservation issues. *Type:* Association.

New Brunswick Tree and Forest

Canadian Forestry Association of New Brunswick
124 St. John St.   Ph: (506)452-1339
Fredericton, NB, Canada E3B Fax: (506)452-7950
  4A7

Contact: David Folster, Editor.

Desc: Provides information on various programs that focus on trees and forestry topics. *Type:* Newsletter.

Northeastern Lumber Manufacturers Association—Information Log

Northeastern Lumber Manufacturers Association
272 Tuttle Rd.   Ph: (207)829-6901
PO Box 87A   Fax: (207)829-4293
Cumberland Center, ME 04021
E-mail: nelma@javanet.com

Contact: Donna J. Reynolds, Editor.

Desc: Discusses the growth, harvesting, production, and marketing of Northeastern lumber. Includes news of federal and state activities and of business of the Association. *Type:* Newsletter.

Northwestern Scene

Northwestern Lumber Association
1405 Lilac Dr. N, Ste. 130   Ph: (612)544-6822
Minneapolis, MN 55422   Free: 800-331-0193
                             Fax: (612)544-0820

Contact: Gary L. Smith, Editor.

Desc: Concentrates on providing retail lumber dealers in Iowa, Minnesota, North Dakota, and South Dakota with information and news relating to the lumber industry. Also contains information of interest to distributors, manufacturers, and allied industries. *Type:* Newsletter.

OFA Newsletter

Ontario Forestry Association
200 Consumers Rd., Ste. 307 Ph: (416)493-4565
Willowdale, ON, Canada M2J   Fax: (416)493-4608
  4R4
E-mail: forestry@oforest.on.ca

Contact: Jim Coats, Editor.

Desc: Provides news on forestry and conservation. Recurring features include letters to the editor, a calendar of events, reports of meetings, news of research and educational opportunities, and notices of publications available. *Type:* Newsletter.

Out of the Woods

Independent Forest Products Association
14780 SW Osprey Dr., Ste. 270   Ph: (503)590-5559
Beaverton, OR 97007   Fax: (503)590-1555
Contact: Laura Cleland, Editor.
Desc: Covers news of the forest products industry, including significant government and legislative actions and business statistics and trends. Recurring features include reprints of relevant articles from newspapers around the country. *Type:* Newsletter.

Random Lengths

Random Lengths Publications, Inc.
450 Country Club Rd., Ste. 240   Ph: (541)686-9925
Eugene, OR 97401   Fax: (541)686-9629
E-mail: rlmail@randomlengths.com
URL: http://www.randomlengths.com
Contact: Burrle Elmore, Editor.
Desc: Publishes market reports on North American forest products (lumber, softwood panels, shingles, shakes, particleboard, and MDF) plus a price guide covering 1,500 items. Contains articles on topics affecting the economy of the industry and analyses of the major North American softwood species. *Type:* Newsletter.

Random Lengths Export

Random Lengths Publications, Inc.
450 Country Club Rd., Ste. 240   Ph: (541)686-9925
Eugene, OR 97401   Fax: (541)686-9629
E-mail: rlmail@randomlengths.com
URL: http://www.randomlengths.com; http://www.randomlengths.com.
Contact: Shawn Church, Editor.
Desc: Focuses on overseas export markets for North American softwood products and competing suppliers. Provides statistics and market commentary, as well as price guides listing prices to exporters, importers, and wholesalers in North American markets. *Type:* Newsletter.

Random Lengths Weekly Report

Random Lengths Publications, Inc.
450 Country Club Rd., Ste. 240   Ph: (541)686-9925
Eugene, OR 97401   Fax: (541)686-9629
E-mail: rlmail@randomlengths.com
URL: http://www.randomlengths.com; http://www.randomlengths.com.
Contact: Burrle Elmore, Editor.
Desc: Covers the North American softwood markets, including lumber, plywood, oriented strand board, and related products. Includes price guides. *Type:* Newsletter.

Random Lengths Yardstick

Random Lengths Publications, Inc.
450 Country Club Rd., Ste. 240   Ph: (541)686-9925
Eugene, OR 97401   Fax: (541)686-9629
E-mail: rlmail@randomlengths.com
URL: http://www.randomlengths.com; http://www.randomlengths.com.
Contact: Joseph Heitz, Editor.
Desc: Provides information on the forest products industry and related statistics. *Type:* Newsletter.

The Seattle Post-Intelligencer

The Seattle Post-Intelligencer
101 Elliott Ave. W   Ph: (206)448-8000
Seattle, WA 98119
URL: http://www.seattle-pi.com
Desc: Contains the complete text of news items, feature stories, and editorials from the Seattle Post-Intelligencer newspaper. Regional coverage emphasizes high technology, aviation, maritime and timber industries, and the environment. *Available:* The Dialog Corporation, DIALOG; Dow Jones Interactive Publishing; Bell & Howell Information and Learning. *Type:* Database.

Seedling News

TreePeople
12601 Mulholland Dr.   Ph: (818)753-4600
Beverly Hills, CA 90210   Fax: (818)753-4635
Desc: Covers environmental topics, such as urban forestry and sustainable communities. Recurring features include a Collection and reports of meetings. *Type:* Newsletter.

SF Newsletter

Southern Forest Products Association
PO Box 641700   Ph: (504)443-4464
Kenner, LA 70064-1700   Fax: (504)443-6612
Contact: David Kellogg, Editor.
Desc: Concerned with forest products, timber resources, home building, transportation, lumber manufacturing, and business and Association news. *Type:* Newsletter.

Society of American Foresters

5400 Grosvenor Ln.   Ph: (301)897-8720
Bethesda, MD 20814   Fax: (301)897-3690
E-mail: safweb@safnet.org
URL: http://www.safnet.org
Contact: William H. Banzhaf, Exec.VP.
Desc: Professional society of foresters and scientists working in related fields. Serves as accrediting agency for professional forestry education. Provides professional training. *Type:* Association.

Southeastern Lumber Manufacturers Association

PO Box 1788   Ph: (404)361-1445
Forest Park, GA 30298   Fax: (404)361-5963
URL: http://www.slma.org
Contact: Stephen H. Rountree, Pres.
Desc: Independent southeastern lumber manufacturers. Represents and coordinates efforts of membership to alleviate local, regional, and national problems that affect independent southeastern lumber manufacturing industry. *Type:* Association.

Southern Forest Products Association

PO Box 641700   Ph: (504)443-4464
Kenner, LA 70064   Fax: (504)443-6612
URL: http://www.sfpa.org
Contact: Karl W. Lindberg, Pres.
Desc: Southern pine lumber manufacturers. Conducts market development and product promotional programs and government affairs activities. *Type:* Association.

Timber Mart-South

University of Georgia
Daniel B. Warnell School of Forest Resources
Athens, GA 30602-2152   Ph: (706)542-4756
    Fax: (706)542-1670
E-mail: tmart@arches.uga.edu
Contact: Tom Harris, Editor.
Desc: Reports market prices for raw forest products. Data includes current prices (stumpage) plus current F.O.B. Mill delivered prices actually paid for sawtimber, pulpwood, veneer, chip-n-saw, poles, and chips, both pine and hardwood. *Type:* Newsletter.

The Timberline

New England Forestry Foundation, Inc.
PO Box 1099   Ph: (508)448-8380
283 Old Dunstable Rd
Groton, MA 01450
E-mail: krossneff@aol.com.
Contact: Christina Petersonly, Editor.
Desc: Contains forestry-related articles. *Type:* Newsletter.

TOC Management Services

6825 SW Sandburg St.   Ph: (503)620-1710
Tigard, OR 97223   Fax: (503)620-3935
E-mail: toc@toc.org
Contact: Rodger M. Glos, Pres.
Desc: Employers' association formed to serve its membership and the industry in the fields of labor, industrial, and employee relations. Provides practical counsel, assistance, and representation in wage and contract negotiations, contract administration, interpretations and grievance handling, and arbitration proceedings. Provides qualified assistance in problems concerning safety, affirmative action, federal and state labor laws, and productivity services. *Type:* Association.

Two-Way Transmissions

Forest Industries Telecommunications
871 Country Club Rd., A   Ph: (541)485-8441
Eugene, OR 97401-2200   Fax: (541)485-7556
E-mail: license@landmobile.com
URL: http://www.landmobile.com.
Contact: Kenton Sturdevant, Exec. Vice-Pres., kenton@landmobile.com.
Desc: Distributes telecommunication information to forest industries. Covers current dockets before the Federal Communications Commission involving the landmobile industry. *Type:* Newsletter.

Under the Canopy—Forestry & Forest Products Newsletter

Alaska Cooperative Extension
PO Box 756180   Ph: (907)474-6363
University of Alaska Fairbanks   Fax: (907)474-5139
Fairbanks, AK 99775-6180
E-mail: fnals@aurora.alaska.edu
Contact: Dr. Robert Wheeler, Editor.
Desc: Focuses on forestry in Alaska, including legislation, tree diseases, forest fires, wood use, and tree farms. Recurring features include news from the Board of Forestry, the 4-H Forestry Camp, and state forests in Alaska and a list of free publications from the Cooperative Extension Service. *Type:* Newsletter.

United Paperworkers International Union

3340 Perimeter Hill Dr.   Ph: (615)834-8590
Nashville, TN 37211   Fax: (615)834-7741
Contact: Boyd D. Young, Pres.
Desc: AFL-CIO; Canadian Labour Congress. *Type:* Association.

Western Wood Products Association

522 SW 5th Ave.   Ph: (503)224-3930
Ste. 500   Fax: (503)224-3934
Portland, OR 97204-2122
E-mail: info@wwpa.org
URL: http://www.wwpa.org
Contact: Walter M. Wirfs, Pres.
Desc: Lumber manufacturers in 12 western states and Alaska. Maintains lumber grade inspection bureau to assure grading standards on a uniform basis. Provides technical support and statistical services. *Type:* Association.

Xi Sigma Pi

University of Tennessee   Ph: (423)522-9455
Department of Forestry, Wildlife
    and Fishery
Knoxville, TN 37901
Contact: Dr. David M. Ostermeier, Natl.Sec.
Desc: Honorary society - forestry. *Type:* Association.

France/French

L'Actualite

Maclean Hunter Ltd.

1001 Maisonneuve Blvd. W,   Ph: (514)843-2542
Ste. 1000   Fax: (514)845-2063
Montreal, PQ, Canada H3A
3E1

E-mail: ucteour@maclean-hunter-quebec.qc.ca.

URL: http://cedrom-sni.qc.ca/3.1.html; http://www.maclean-hunter.quebec.qc.ca.

Contact: Jean Pare, Publisher; Donald A. Ladkin, Editor.

Desc: Current and public affairs magazine for Quebec (French). *Type:* Periodical.

Agence France-Presse

1015 15th St. NW   Ph: (202)414-0535
Ste. 500   Fax: (202)414-0634
Washington, DC 20005

E-mail: afp@cais.com.

Contact: Pierre Lesourd, Exec. Dir.; Carol DeHaven, Reg. Mktg./Sales Dir North America; Steve Messere, Mktg./Sales Mgr.; Jacques Rigolage, U.S. Admin.; Francis Pajot, Tech. Dir. for Americas.

Desc: Distributes news photographs and text. *Alt. Contact:* 1015 15th St. NW, Ste. 500, Washington, D. 20005; telephone: (202)414-0535; fax: (202)414-0634. *Type:* Periodical.

ARCHIE

Les Editions Heritage, Inc.

300, rue Arran   Ph: (514)875-0327
St.-Lambert, PQ, Canada J4R   Fax: (514)672-5448
1K5

E-mail: heritage@mlink.net

Contact: Bob St-Martin, Editor; Jacques Payette, Publisher.

Desc: French adaptation of ARCHIE comics. *Type:* Periodical.

Association Canado Americaine

PO Box 989   Ph: (603)625-8577
Manchester, NH 03105-0989   Fax: (603)625-1214

Contact: Eugene A. Lemieux, Pres.Gen.

Desc: Fraternal benefit life insurance society of American and Canadian Roman Catholics of French descent. Operates cultural and linguistic summer camps. *Type:* Association.

Chatelaine

Maclean Hunter Ltd.

1001 Maisonneuve Blvd. W,   Ph: (514)843-2542
Ste. 1000   Fax: (514)845-2063
Montreal, PQ, Canada H3A
3E1

Contact: Micheline Lachance, Editor and Publisher; Reg Finlayson, Editor.

Desc: Women's magazine (French). *Type:* Periodical.

Club Francais d'Amerique

1051 Divisadero St.   Ph: (415)921-5100
San Francisco, CA 94115   Fax: (415)921-0213

E-mail: fpress@hooked.net

Contact: Lisel Fay, Office Mgr.

Desc: Subscribers and friends of Le *Journal Francais and France Today* (*The French Newspaper*); individuals interested in the French language and culture. Seeks to assist teachers and students of French in defining practical applications for foreign language ability. *Type:* Association.

Committee of French Speaking Societies

54 W. 55th St., No. 3R   Ph: (212)830-4103
New York, NY 10019   Ph: (212)830-4109

Contact: Jean-Jacques de Saint Andrieu, Pres.

Desc: Federation of French and French-speaking societies. Sponsors celebrations of French holidays (Bastille Day, Armistice Day). *Type:* Association.

Contact-Laval

Les Hebdos Select

625 Blvd. Rene Levesque O.   Ph: (514)866-3131
Bureau 800   Fax: (514)866-3030
Montreal, PQ, Canada H3B
1R2

Contact: Richard Fontaine, V.P. & / Editor; Claude La-Belle, Sales Director.

Desc: Community newspaper (French and English). *Alt. Contact:* 189 Ave. Laval, Laval, PQ, Canada H7N 3V8. *Type:* Periodical.

Courrier-Laval

Les Hebdos Select

625 Blvd. Rene Levesque O.   Ph: (514)866-3131
Bureau 800   Fax: (514)866-3030
Montreal, PQ, Canada H3B
1R2

Contact: Claude LaBelle, Sales Dir., (514)667-4360, fax: (514)667-9498.

Desc: Community newspaper (French). *Type:* Periodical.

Echos-Vedettes

Echos-Vedettes

801 Sherbrooke Est., Ste. 202   Ph: (514)528-7111
Montreal, PQ, Canada H2L   Fax: (514)528-7115
4X9

E-mail: echos@accent.net.

Contact: Marc Chatelle, Editor; Louise Branchaud, Managing Editor.

Desc: TV and theater newspaper (French). *Type:* Periodical.

French Institute/Alliance Francaise

22 E. 60th St.   Ph: (212)355-6100
New York, NY 10022-1077   Fax: (212)935-4119

E-mail: tbechara@fiaf.org

URL: http://www.fiaf.org

Contact: David Black, Dir.

Desc: Dedicated to promoting and enhancing the knowledge of French culture and the mutual understanding between French and American people. *Type:* Association.

La Presse

La Presse Ltee.

7, rue St-Jacques   Ph: (514)285-7272
Montreal, PQ, Canada H2Y   Fax: (514)845-8129
1K9

Contact: Roger D. Landry, Editor and Publisher; Fernand Lacourse, Advertising Mgr.

Desc: General newspaper (French). *Type:* Periodical.

Le Courrier Laval

Le Reseau Select

625 Rene Levesque West Blvd.,   Ph: (514)866-3131
Bur. 1410   Fax: (514)866-3030
Montreal, PQ, Canada H3B
1R2

Contact: P. Venir, Editor.

Desc: Community newspaper. *Alt. Contact:* 189 Avenue Laval, Laval, PQ, Canada H7N 3V8. *Type:* Periodical.

Le Courrier du Sud (The South Shore Courier)

Cie Imprimerie & Pub. Rive Sud Ltee.

267 St-Charles Ouest   Ph: (450)646-3333
Longueuil, PQ, Canada J4H   Fax: (450)674-0205
1E3

Contact: Jean-Paul Auclair, Editor; Lucie Masse, Advertising Mgr.

Desc: Newspaper (French and English). *Type:* Periodical.

Le Journal de Montreal

Journal de Montreal

4545, rue Frontenac   Ph: (514)521-4545
Montreal, PQ, Canada H2H   Free: 800-521-4545
2R7   Fax: (514)521-4416

URL: http://www.journaldemontreal.com.

Contact: Paul Beaugrand-Champagne, Editor; P. Francoeur, Publisher; Gilles Lamoureux, Advertising Mgr.; Louise Blanchard, Editor, (514)521-4545; Claire Harting, Editor, (514)521-4545; Jean-Philippe Decarie, Editor, (514)521-4545; Pierre Francoeur, Publisher.

Desc: General newspaper (French). *Type:* Periodical.

Le Journal de Quebec

Groupe Quebecor Inc.

450, rue Bechard, Vanier   Ph: (418)683-1573
Quebec, PQ, Canada G1M 2E9   Fax: (418)683-1027

Contact: Jean-Clau de l'Abbee, Editor; Daniel Houde, Advertising Mgr.

Desc: General newspaper (tabloid) (French). *Type:* Periodical.

Le Magazine Affaires Plus

Transcontinental Publishing

1100 Rene-Levesque Blvd. W,   Ph: (514)392-9000
24th Fl.   Free: 800-461-3773
Montreal, PQ, Canada H3B   Fax: (514)392-4723
4X9

E-mail: commerce.pub@mail.transcontinental.ca

Contact: Pierre Duhanel, Editor; Lyne Rivard, Advertising Mgr.

Desc: General business magazine emphasizing personal finance management and lifestyles (French). *Type:* Periodical.

Le Soleil

UniMedia Inc.

925 Chemin St. Louis   Ph: (418)686-3270
PO Box 1547   Fax: (418)686-3260
Quebec, PQ, Canada G1K 7J6

URL: http://www@lescleil.com.

Contact: Gilbert Lacasse, Editor and Publisher; Jasmin Gilbert, Advertising Mgr.; Gilbert Lavoie, Managing Editor; Michael Samsmon, News Editor, (418)626-3360, fax: (418)686-3374, msamson@lesoleil.com; Gilles Ouellet, Business Editor, (418)686-3420, fax: (418)626-3429; Berthold Landry, City Editor, (418)686-3357; Magella Soucy, Feature/Lifestyle and Fashion Editor, (418)686-3412; Maurice Dumas, Sports Editor; Gilles Carignan, Entertainment Editor, (418)686-3369.

Desc: General newspaper (French). *Alt. Contact:* 925 Chemin St. Louis, PO Box 1547, Quebec, PQ, Canada G1K 7J6; telephone: (418)686-3394; fax: (418)686-3374; toll-free: 800-463-1892. *Type:* Periodical.

LES AFFAIRES

Transcontinental Publishing

1100 Rene-Levesque Blvd. W,   Ph: (514)392-9000
24th Fl.   Free: 800-461-3773
Montreal, PQ, Canada H3B   Fax: (514)392-4723
4X9

E-mail: commerce.pub@mail.transcontinental.ca

URL: http://www.lesaffaires.com.

Contact: Jean-Paul Gagne, Contact, gagnejp@mail.transcontinentsl.ca; Andre Prefontaine, Editor-in-Chief, prefontainea@mail.transcontinental.ca; Yvon Tremblay, Contact, tremblayy@transcontinental.ca.

Desc: Tabloid covering finance, development, business. *Type:* Periodical.

Magazine Le Clap

Cinema Le Clap
2360, Chemin Ste-Foy Ph: (418)653-2470
Sainte-Foy, PQ, Canada G1V Free: 800-361-2470
4H2 Fax: (418)653-6018
E-mail: leclap@medom.qc.ca.
URL: http://www.clap.qc.ca.

Contact: Michel Aube, Publisher; Sylvie Nicol, Editor.

Desc: Magazine featuring information about current movies (French). *Type:* Periodical.

Reader's Digest Magazine

Reader's Digest Magazines Ltd.
215 Redfern Ave. Ph: (514)934-0751
Westmount, PQ, Canada H3Z Free: 800-465-0780
2V9 Fax: (514)932-3637

Contact: Katherine Walker, Editor-in-Chief; Larry Thomas, Advertising Mgr.

Desc: General interest magazine (English and French). *Type:* Periodical.

Revue Notre-Dame du Cap

Revue Notre-Dame du Cap
626 Notre-Dame Ph: (819)374-2441
Cap-de-la-Madeleine, PQ, Fax: (819)374-2441
Canada G8T 4G9

Contact: Paul Arsenault, Editor; Jerome Martineau, Editor-in-Chief, jerome.martineau@sympatico.ca.

Desc: Catholic magazine (French). *Type:* Periodical.

RND (Revue Notre-Dame)

Les Missionnaires du Sacre-Coeur
2215 Marie-Victorin Ph: (418)681-3581
Sillery, PQ, Canada G1T 1J6 Fax: (418)681-1139
E-mail: rnd@indestron.ca.

Contact: Paul Desaulniers, Editor.

Desc: Catholic magazine (French). *Type:* Periodical.

Selection du Reader's Digest (Canadian-French Edition)

Reader's Digest Magazines Ltd.
215 Redfern Ave. Ph: (514)934-0751
Westmount, PQ, Canada H3Z Free: 800-465-0780
2V9 Fax: (514)932-3637
URL: http://www.selectionrd.ca.

Contact: Lise Verschelden, Editor; Larry Thomas, Advertising.

Desc: General interest consumer magazine. *Type:* Periodical.

Tabaret

University of Ottawa
Alumni and Development Ph: (613)562-5857
178 Laurier E. Free: 800-465-1888
Ottawa, ON, Canada K1N 6N5 Fax: (613)562-5113
E-mail: alumninfo@uottawa.ca.

Contact: Linda Scales, Editor, (613)562-5800, lscales@uottawa.com.

Desc: Alumni magazine (French and English). *Alt. Contact:* University of Ottawa, Alumni Relations Office, 178 Laurier E., Ottawa, ON, Canada K1N 6N5; telephone: (613)562-5857; fax: (613)562-5113; toll-free: 800-465-1888. *Type:* Periodical.

TV Hebdo

Trustmedia Inc.
2020 University, Ste. 2000 Ph: (514)848-7000
Montreal, PQ, Canada H3A Fax: (514)848-7070
2A5
E-mail: tv@trustar.com.

Contact: Jean-Louis Podlesak, Editor, (514)848-7164, jean.louis_podlesak@trustar.com.

Desc: Television entertainment magazine (French). *Type:* Periodical.

Union Saint-Jean-Baptiste

Box F Ph: (401)769-0520
Woonsocket, RI 02895 Free: 800-225-USJB
  Fax: (401)766-3014

Contact: Charles Boisvert, Asst.VP.

Desc: Fraternal benefit life insurance society of Roman Catholics of French origin. *Type:* Association.

VOILA QUEBEC

Les Publications Vacances (Quebec), Inc.
185 Saint Paul St. Ph: (418)694-1272
Quebec, PQ, Canada G1K 3W2 Fax: (418)692-3392

Contact: Lynn Magee, Editor; Curtis J. Sommerville, Publisher; Marco Beaulieu, Dir./Sales & Marketing; Isabelle Dion, Sales Rep.

Desc: Magazine for visitors to Quebec City (English and French). *Type:* Periodical.

Free Enterprise

American Business Conference

1730 K St. NW, Ste. 1200 Ph: (202)822-9300
Washington, DC 20006 Fax: (202)467-4070

Contact: Barry K. Rogstad, Pres.

Desc: Chief executive officers of midsize, high-growth companies. Concerns itself with tax policy, regulatory reform, and international trade issues; works to preserve the free enterprise system. *Type:* Association.

Center for the Defense of Free Enterprise

Liberty Park Ph: (425)455-5038
12500 NE 10th Pl. Fax: (425)451-3959
Bellevue, WA 98005

Contact: Ron Arnold, VP.

Desc: Defends and promotes the principles of the American free enterprise system and relates their application to contemporary American society. *Type:* Association.

Citizens for a Sound Economy

1250 H St., NW, Ste. 700 Ph: (202)783-3870
Washington, DC 20005-3908 Fax: (202)783-4687

Contact: Paul Beckner, Pres.

Desc: Foundations, corporations, and individuals. Strives to advance understanding of the market process in order to restore a sound economy. Seeks to return economic decision-making to citizens by reducing government interference in the economy. *Type:* Association.

Fisher Institute

PO Box 530689 Ph: (972)660-1733
Grand Prairie, TX 75053 Fax: (972)660-1245

Contact: John McCuistion, Pres.

Desc: Nonpartisan research organization whose primary goal is to direct government, business, and public attention toward the use of competitive markets and good health as the best solution to America's long-range economic problems. *Type:* Association.

Free the Eagle

7526 Diplomat Dr. Ph: (703)257-4782
Manassas, VA 20109 Fax: (703)257-4758

Contact: Tammy J. Lyles, Dir.

Desc: Serves as a citizen's lobbying organization to encourage legislation in Congress to maintain and encourage free enterprise and individual freedom. Supports legislation to reduce government waste and to assist and recognize the legitimacy of antidictatorship democratic resistance movements throughout the world. Initiates campaigns to reform Congressional policies toward multilateral lending institutions which support developing countries. *Type:* Association.

The Heritage Foundation

214 Massachusetts Ave. NE Ph: (202)546-4400
Washington, DC 20002 Fax: (202)546-8328
URL: http://www.heritage.org

Contact: Edwin J. Feulner, Jr., Pres.

Desc: Public policy research institute dedicated to the principles of free competitive enterprise, limited government, individual liberty, and a strong national defense. Programs include analysis of current public policy subjects. Maintains Heritage Resource Bank, which provides for communication among 2000 academics and several hundred other policy research groups. *Type:* Association.

Made in the U.S.A. Foundation

1828 L St. NW No. 1000 Ph: (202)822-6060
Washington, DC 20036 Fax: (202)822-6062

Contact: Joel Joseph, Exec.Dir.

Desc: Consumers, unions, manufacturers, and trade associations committed to improving American competitiveness and preserving American economic leadership. Supports actions to reduce American reliance on imports, increase purchases of American products domestically and overseas, and ensure that the standard of fair trade is applied worldwide. Promotes changes in consumer behavior, government policies, and corporate practices that the foundation believes have contributed to America's decline in the international marketplace. *Type:* Association.

Students in Free Enterprise

The Jack Sheumaker SIFE Ph: (417)831-9505
  World Headquarters Free: 800-677-7433
1959 E. Kerr Fax: (417)831-6165
Springfield, MO 65803
E-mail: sifehq@sife.org
URL: http://www.sife.org

Contact: Alvin Rohrs, CEO & Pres.

Desc: Supports student teams on over 600 college campuses and universities worldwide, providing students the opportunity to make a difference, and to devel. *Type:* Association.

Friends

Friends General Conference

1216 Arch St., No. 2B Ph: (215)561-1700
Philadelphia, PA 19107 Free: 800-966-4556
  Fax: (215)561-0759
E-mail: fgc@fgcquaker.org

Contact: Bruce Birchard, Gen.Sec.

Desc: Association of 14 yearly meetings, which include 540 local meetings of the Religious Society of Friends (Quakers). Sponsors retreats and conferences. Offers teacher training for First-day Schools. *Type:* Association.

Friends United Meeting

101 Quaker Hill Dr. Ph: (765)962-7573
Richmond, IN 47374-1980 Fax: (765)966-1293
E-mail: fuminfo@xc.org
URL: http://www.fum.org

Contact: Johan Maurer, Gen.Sec.

Desc: Association of 27 Friends yearly meetings cooperate in education, missions, peace, evangelism, and publications. *Type:* Association.

Quaker Service Bulletin

American Friends Service Committee
1501 Cherry St.   Ph: (215)241-7049
Philadelphia, PA 19102   Free: 888-588-AFSC
          Fax: (215)241-7275
E-mail: TPfueller@mail.afsc.org; qsbeditor@afsc.org.
URL: http://www.ofsc.org; http://www.afsc.orglqsb.htm.
Contact: Melissa K. Elliott, Editor, (215)241-7051, fax: (241)241-7525, melliott@atsc.com.

Desc: Concerned with the issues of peace, reconciliation, nonmilitary solutions to conflicts, social change, and other issues of international concern. Also covers domestic issues, such as education, youth and militarism, social justice, minority rights, criminal justice, rights of immigrants, the homeless, Indian rights, and hunger, "focusing particularly on empowerment." Recurring features include news of the current work of the Committee, editorials, and news of AFSC staff members. *Type:* Newsletter.

Fruits and Vegetables

America West Airlines Magazine

Skyword Marketing Inc.
4636 E. Elwood St.   Ph: (602)997-7200
Suite 5   Fax: (602)997-9875
Phoenix, AZ 85040-1963
Contact: Michael Derr, Editor; Mark Cipriani, Advertising/Traffic Asst.

Desc: Inflight magazine for America West. *Type:* Periodical.

American Fruit Grower—Source Book Issue

Meister Publishing Co.
37733 Euclid Ave.   Ph: (440)942-2000
Willoughby, OH 44094   Free: 800-572-7740
          Fax: (440)942-0662
E-mail: info@meisternet.com; afg-edit@meisterpubl.com.
Contact: Laurie Grubich, Editor.

Desc: List of manufacturers and distributors of equipment and supplies for the commercial fruit growing industry. *Type:* Directory.

Apple Processing Report

U.S. Department of Agriculture
Agricultural Marketing Service
Fruit and Vegetable Market News
21 N. 1st Ave., Ste. 224   Ph: (509)575-2494
Yakima, WA 98902-2663   Fax: (509)457-7132
Desc: Compiles prices of apples used for juice and peeler products and the number of tons delivered weekly to processors. *Type:* Newsletter.

Asparagus Fax Report

U.S. Department of Agriculture
Agricultural Marketing Service
Fruit and Vegetable Market News
2202 Monterey St., Ste. 104-A   Ph: (559)487-5178
Fresno, CA 93721-3129   Free: 800-487-8796
          Fax: (559)487-5199
URL: http://www.ams.usda.gov/marketnews.htm.
Contact: Kevin Morris, Officer-in-Charge.

Desc: Deals with asparagus. Covers the major growing areas, rail and truck shipment information, and FOB shipping point prices. *Type:* Newsletter.

Atlanta Wholesale Fruit and Vegetable Report

U.S. Department of Agriculture
Agricultural Marketing Service
Fruit and Vegetable Market News
2202 Monterey St., Ste. 104-A   Ph: (559)487-5178
Fresno, CA 93721-3129   Free: 800-487-8796
          Fax: (559)487-5199
URL: http://www.ams.usda.gov/marketnews.htm.
Contact: John Kerrens, Officer-in-Charge.

Desc: Reports wholesale prices on fruits and vegetables in the Atlanta metropolitan area. *Type:* Newsletter.

Baltimore Wholesale Fruit and Vegetable Report

Fruit and Vegetable Market News Service
Agricultural Marketing Service
U.S. Department of Agriculture (USDA)
Maryland Wholesale Produce   Ph: (410)799-4840
  Market   Fax: (410)799-8442
7460 Conowingo Ave., B-101
Jessup, MD 20794
Contact: Holly R. Mozal, Editor.

Desc: Contains daily wholesale demand, supply, and price information on fresh fruits and vegetables at the Maryland Wholesale Produce Market in Jessup. *Type:* Newsletter.

Benton Harbor Fruit & Vegetable Report

Michigan Department of Agriculture
PO Box 1204   Ph: (616)925-3270
Benton Harbor, MI 49023-1204   Fax: (616)925-3272
Desc: Reports cash prices paid to growers of various fruits and vegetables from the trading lanes of the Benton Harbor Fruit Market. Recurring features include Wholesale terminal market reports from U.S.D.A Market News Service. *Type:* Newsletter.

Blue Anchor, Inc.

PO Box 367   Ph: (209)591-6030
Dinuba, CA 93618   Fax: (209)531-7181
Contact: Patrick Sanguinetti, Pres.

Desc: Cooperative marketing organization distributing deciduous tree fruits and table grapes. *Type:* Association.

Boston Wholesale Fruit and Vegetable Report

U.S. Department of Agriculture
Agricultural Marketing Service
Fruit and Vegetable Market News
2202 Monterey St., Ste. 104-A   Ph: (559)487-5178
Fresno, CA 93721-3129   Free: 800-487-8796
          Fax: (559)487-5199
URL: http://www.ams.usda.gov/marketnews.htm.
Contact: James J. Calnan, Officer-in-Charge.

Desc: Reports wholesale prices on fruits and vegetables in the Boston metropolitan area. *Type:* Newsletter.

Calavo Growers of California

2530 Red Hill Ave.
Santa Ana, CA 92705-5542
Contact: Allen J. Vangelos, Pres. & CEO.

Desc: Cooperative marketing organization. Activities include packaging, promotion, and marketing of avocados, other fresh specialty fruits, and fresh frozen avocado products. Conducts research; compiles statistics; offers computerized services. *Type:* Association.

California Avocado Commission

1251 E. Dyer Rd., No. 200   Ph: (714)558-6761
Santa Ana, CA 92705   Fax: (714)641-7024
E-mail: vweaver@avocad.org
URL: http://www.avocado.org
Contact: Mark Affleck, Pres. & CEO.

Desc: Marketing organization for growers and packers of California avocados. *Type:* Association.

California Iceberg Lettuce Commission

PO Box 3354   Ph: (408)375-8277
Monterey, CA 93942   Fax: (408)375-8593
Contact: Wade A. Whitfield, Pres.

Desc: Commissioners who represent California's growers and shippers of iceberg lettuce. (California produces 75% of the iceberg lettuce grown in the U.S.) Aims to make available to consumers a high quality year-round supply of iceberg lettuce at more stable prices; to increase U.S. consumption of lettuce so that growers and shippers can benefit from a growing market where prices better reflect production and sales costs. *Type:* Association.

California Kiwifruit Commission

9845 Horn Rd., Ste. 160   Ph: (916)362-7490
Sacramento, CA 95827   Fax: (916)362-7993
E-mail: info@kiwifruit.org
URL: http://www.kiwifruit.org
Contact: E. Scott Horsfall, Pres.

Desc: California kiwifruit growers. *Type:* Association.

California Prune News

California Prune Board
5990 Stoneridge Dr., Ste. 101   Ph: (925)734-0150
Pleasanton, CA 94588-3234   Fax: (925)734-0525
E-mail: pam@prunes.org
Contact: Richard Peterson, Editor.

Desc: Reports news of concern to California prune growers and packers. Contains promotion program description and production information. *Type:* Newsletter.

Calyx Newsletter

North American Blueberry Council
4995 Golden Foothill Pkwy.   Ph: (916)933-9399
  No. 2   Fax: (916)933-9777
El Dorado Hills, CA 95762
E-mail: 104361.2253@compuserve.com

Desc: Supports the Council's function as a clearinghouse for research and development activities in blueberry production. Publicizes and promotes all production areas and monitors developments affecting blueberry growers and marketers. *Type:* Newsletter.

Chicago Wholesale Fruit and Vegetable Report

U.S. Department of Agriculture
Agricultural Marketing Service
Fruit and Vegetable Market News
2202 Monterey St., Ste. 104-A   Ph: (559)487-5178
Fresno, CA 93721-3129   Free: 800-487-8796
          Fax: (559)487-5199
URL: http://www.ams.usda.gov/marketnews.htm.
Contact: Kevin Morris, Officer-in-Charge.

Desc: Reports wholesale fruit and vegetable prices in the Chicago metropolitan area. *Type:* Newsletter.

Chilean Fruit and Vegetable Report

U.S. Department of Agriculture
Agricultural Marketing Service
Fruit and Vegetable Market News
2202 Monterey St., Ste. 104-A   Ph: (559)487-5178
Fresno, CA 93721-3129   Free: 800-487-8796
          Fax: (559)487-5199
URL: http://www.ams.usda.gov/marketnews.htm.
Contact: Kevin Morris, Officer-in-Charge.

Desc: Contains information on prices, volume, and related data on fruits and vegetables imported to the U.S. from Chile. *Type:* Newsletter.

Cranberry Station Newsletter

Cranberry Experiment Station
Glen Charlie Rd.   Ph: (508)295-2212
PO Box 569   Fax: (508)295-6387
East Wareham, MA 02538
Contact: Martha Sylvia, Editor, martys@umext.umass.edu.
Desc: Provides information on cranberry culture. Discusses weed control, herbicides, fungicides, insects, and cultivation of cranberries. *Type:* Newsletter.

The Cranberry Vine

Washington State University
2907 Pioneer Rd.   Ph: (360)642-2031
Long Beach, WA 98631
Contact: Kim Patten, Editor, pattenk@cahe.wsu.edu.
Desc: Carries general information for cranberry growers. Recurring features include news of research, a calendar of events, reports of meetings, news of educational opportunities, and notices of publications available. *Type:* Newsletter.

Dallas Wholesale Fruit and Vegetable Report

U.S. Department of Agriculture
Agricultural Marketing Service
Fruit and Vegetable Market News
2202 Monterey St., Ste. 104-A   Ph: (559)487-5178
Fresno, CA 93721-3129   Free: 800-487-8796
    Fax: (559)487-5199
URL: http://www.ams.usda.gov/marketnews.htm.
Contact: Kevin Morris, Officer-in-Charge.
Desc: Reports wholesale fruit and vegetable prices in the Dallas metropolitan area. *Type:* Newsletter.

Detroit Wholesale Fruit and Vegetable Report

U.S. Department of Agriculture
Agricultural Marketing Service
Fruit and Vegetable Market News
2202 Monterey St., Ste. 104-A   Ph: (559)487-5178
Fresno, CA 93721-3129   Free: 800-487-8796
    Fax: (559)487-5199
URL: http://www.ams.usda.gov/marketnews.htm.
Contact: Michael Rann, Officer-in-Charge.
Desc: Reports wholesale prices on fruits and vegetables in the Detroit metropolitan area. *Type:* Newsletter.

Eastern Vegetable and Fruit Report

U.S. Department of Agriculture
Agricultural Marketing Services
Fruit and Vegetable Market News
State Farmer's Market   Ph: (912)226-9511
Thomasville, GA 31792
URL: http://www.ams.usda.gov/marketnews.htm.
Contact: Richard DeMenna, Officer-in-Charge.
Desc: Reports on vegetables and fruit. Covers the major growing areas on the east coast of the U.S., and provides information on rail and shipment, and FOB shipping points. *Type:* Newsletter.

Florida Citrus Commission/Florida Department of Citrus

1115 E. Memorial Blvd.   Ph: (941)499-2500
PO Box 148   Fax: (941)284-4300
Lakeland, FL 33802-0148
E-mail: dsantang@fdochq.mail2.wise.net
URL: http://www.floridajuice.com
Contact: Daniel L. Santangelo, Exec.Dir.
Desc: Executive agency of state government, established in 1935 to regulate, conduct research for, and promote Florida citrus industry. *Type:* Association.

Florida Citrus Mutual

Citrus Mutual Bldg.   Ph: (813)682-1111
PO Box 89   Fax: (813)682-1074
Lakeland, FL 33801
URL: http://www.fl-citrus-mutual.com
Contact: Bobby F. McKown, Exec.VP/CEO.
Desc: Florida citrus growers' organization supplying market and price information to its members. Marketing of fruit is handled by affiliated shippers and processors. *Type:* Association.

Florida Department of Citrus

PO Box 148   Ph: (941)499-2500
Lakeland, FL 33802   Fax: (941)284-4300
URL: http://www.floridajuice.com
Contact: Daniel L. Santangelo, Exec.Dir.
Desc: Established by an act of the Florida legislature and governed by the Florida Citrus Commission, a body of 12 citrus industry members appointed by the governor to staggered 3-year terms. Administers the citrus laws of the state; has regulatory authority over the packing, processing, labeling, and handling of citrus fruits and products. Conducts advertising and merchandising activities, and product marketing, scientific, and economic research. *Type:* Association.

Florida Gift Fruit Shippers Association

521 N. Kirkman Rd.   Ph: (407)295-1491
Orlando, FL 32808   Free: 800-432-8607
    Fax: (407)290-0918
Contact: Joseph E. Ball, Exec.VP.
Desc: Firms packing and shipping gift fruit packages. *Type:* Association.

Fraser's Potato Newsletter

Harry Fraser
R.R. 1
Charlottetown, PE, Canada C1A   Ph: (902)569-2685
7J6   Fax: (902)569-5589
Contact: Harry Fraser, Editor.
Desc: Features information about the potato industry in North America. *Type:* Newsletter.

Fresh Facts

Fresh Produce & Floral Council
6301 Beach Blvd., No. 150   Ph: (714)739-0177
Buena Park, CA 90621   Fax: (714)739-0226
Contact: Linda Stine, Editor.
Desc: Discusses trends and issues in fresh fruit, vegetable, and floral supply. *Type:* Newsletter.

Fresh Fruits, Vegetables and Ornamental Crops

U.S.D.A. Agricultural Marketing Service, Fruit & Vegetable Market News
PO Box 96456, Rm. 2503-5   Ph: (202)720-2175
Washington, DC 20090-6456   Fax: (202)720-0547
URL: http://www.ams.usda.gov.
Contact: Douglas Edwards, Head, Transportation Reports.
Desc: Summarizes seasonal movement of fresh fruits, vegetables, and ornamental crops with comparison to the previous season. *Type:* Newsletter.

Fruit & Nut Review

California Agricultural Statistics Service
U.S. Department of Agriculture (USDA)
PO Box 1258   Ph: (916)654-0895
Sacramento, CA 95812
Desc: Features information on the fruit and nut industry. Covers berry, grape, citrus, deciduous and nut acreage, production, price, and utilization. *Type:* Newsletter.

Grape Crush Report

California Agricultural Statistics Service
U.S. Department of Agriculture (USDA)
PO Box 1258   Ph: (916)654-0895
Sacramento, CA 95812
Desc: Reports on California's grape industry. Features information on grape tonnage and prices, processing, weighted average grower returns, and brix adjustment factors. *Type:* Newsletter.

Idaho Potato Commission

PO Box 1068   Ph: (208)334-2350
Boise, ID 83701   Fax: (208)334-2274
URL: http://www.idahopotatoes.com
Contact: M. B. Anderson, Dir.
Desc: A department of the State of Idaho; commissioners are appointed by the governor. Five commissioners are active potato growers who represent five growers' organizations; two commissioners are shippers or handlers of Idaho potatoes; and two represent the Idaho potato processors and their associations. Commission is charged with the advertising, public relations, and field merchandising of Idaho-grown potatoes. *Type:* Association.

Incider

Processed Apples Institute
5775 Peachtree-Dunwoody Rd.   Ph: (404)252-3663
    NE, Ste. G500
Atlanta, GA 30342-1507
Contact: Larry Davenport, Editor; Sue Taylor, Editor.
Desc: Compiles information on the apple industry. Discusses pesticide usage, industry relations, and technology. *Type:* Newsletter.

International Produce Federation

PO Box 176   Ph: (703)690-2100
Fairfax Station, VA 22039   Fax: (703)690-8129
Contact: Dr. Charles H. Emely, CAE & Mng.Dir.
Desc: Works to increase the global fruit and vegetable trade. *Type:* Association.

Los Angeles Wholesale Fruit and Vegetable Report

U.S. Department of Agriculture
Agricultural Marketing Service
Fruit and Vegetable Market News
2202 Monterey St., Ste. 104-A   Ph: (559)487-5178
Fresno, CA 93721-3129   Free: 800-487-8796
    Fax: (559)487-5199
URL: http://www.ams.usda.gov/marketnews.htm.
Contact: Kevin Morris, Officer-in-Charge.
Desc: Reports wholesale fruit and vegetable prices in the Los Angeles metropolitan area. *Type:* Newsletter.

Marketing Michigan Fruit

Michigan Department of Agriculture
PO Box 1204   Ph: (616)925-3270
Benton Harbor, MI 49023-1204   Fax: (616)925-3272
Desc: Provides summaries of the year's fruit crops in Michigan. *Type:* Newsletter.

Miami Fruit and Vegetable Report

U.S. Department of Agriculture
Agricultural Marketing Service
Fruit and Vegetable Market News
2202 Monterey St., Ste. 104-A   Ph: (559)487-5178
Fresno, CA 93721-3129   Free: 800-487-8796
    Fax: (559)487-5199
URL: http://www.ams.usda.gov/marketnews.htm.
Contact: James E. Cunningham, Officer-in-Charge.
Desc: Reports wholesale prices on fruits and vegetables in the Miami metropolitan area. *Type:* Newsletter.

National Apple and Pear Report

U.S. Department of Agriculture
Agricultural Marketing Service
Fruit and Vegetable Market News
2202 Monterey St., Ste. 104-A   Ph: (559)487-5178
Fresno, CA 93721-3129   Free: 800-487-8796
                                  Fax: (559)487-5199

Desc: Lists daily prices on various fruits. *Type:* Newsletter.

National Berry Report

U.S. Department of Agriculture
Agricultural Marketing Service
Fruit and Vegetable Market News
2202 Monterey St., Ste. 104-A   Ph: (559)487-5178
Fresno, CA 93721-3129   Free: 800-487-8796
                                  Fax: (559)487-5199

URL: http://www.ams.usda.gov/marketnews.htm.

Contact: Kevin Morris, Officer-in-Charge.

Desc: Deals with berries. Covers the major growing areas, rail and truck shipment information, and FOB shipping point prices. *Type:* Newsletter.

National Corn Growers Association

1000 Executive Pky., Ste. 105   Ph: (314)275-9915
St. Louis, MO 63141-6397   Fax: (314)275-7061
E-mail: corn info@ncga.com
URL: http://www.ncga.com/

Contact: Christine L. Wehrman, CEO, Exec.VP.

Desc: Growers of corn. Furthers the use, proper marketing, legislative position, and efficient production of corn. Conducts research and educational programs. *Type:* Association.

National Potato Council

5690 DTC Blvd., Ste. 230E   Ph: (303)773-9295
Englewood, CO 80111-3200   Fax: (303)773-9296
E-mail: npcspud@ix.netcom.com
URL: http://www.npcspud.com

Contact: A. R. Middaugh, Exec.Dir.

Desc: Commercial potato growers. Takes action on national potato legislative, regulatory, and environmental issues. *Type:* Association.

The National Potato and Onion Report

U.S. Department of Agriculture
Agricultural Marketing Service
Fruit and Vegetable Market News
1820 E. 17th St.   Ph: (208)525-0166
Idaho Falls, ID 83404   Fax: (208)525-5546

Desc: Lists daily prices on various vegetables. *Type:* Newsletter.

National Potato Promotion Board

7555 E. Hampden Ave., Ste.   Ph: (303)369-7783
   412   Fax: (303)369-7718
Denver, CO 80231

Contact: Tim O'Conner, Pres. & CEO.

Desc: Growers of five or more acres of potatoes. Provides a way to organize and finance a national promotion program for potatoes, to increase consumption, expand markets, and make the growing and marketing of potatoes a better business for all; carries out effective and continuous coordinated marketing research, retail marketing, consumer advertising, public relations, and export programs. *Type:* Association.

National Watermelon Report

Federal-State Market News
PO Box 1447   Ph: (912)228-1208
State Farmers Market-Stall No.   Fax: (912)225-1516
   39
Thomasville, GA 31792

Desc: Reports on f.o.b. shipping point prices from Arizona, California, Florida, Georgia, Indiana, Missouri, North Carolina, South Carolina, Texas, and Virginia for domestically produced watermelons. *Type:* Newsletter.

National Wholesale Herb Market News Report

U.S. Department of Agriculture
Agricultural Marketing Service
Fruit and Vegetable Market News
2202 Monterey St., Ste. 104-A   Ph: (559)487-5178
Fresno, CA 93721-3129   Free: 800-487-8796
                                  Fax: (559)487-5199

URL: http://www.ams.usda.gov/marketnews.htm.

Contact: Steven D. Daily, Officer-in-Charge.

Desc: Reports wholesale prices on herbs from 15 major cities. *Type:* Newsletter.

New York Wholesale Fruit and Vegetable Report

U.S. Department of Agriculture
Agricultural Marketing Service
Fruit and Vegetable Market News
2202 Monterey St., Ste. 104-A   Ph: (559)487-5178
Fresno, CA 93721-3129   Free: 800-487-8796
                                  Fax: (559)487-5199

URL: http://www.ams.usda.gov/marketnews.htm.

Contact: Kevin Morris, Officer-in-Charge.

Desc: Reports wholesale fruit and vegetable prices in the New York City metropolitan area. *Type:* Newsletter.

Northwest Berry Processing Report

U.S. Department of Agriculture
Agricultural Marketing Service
Fruit and Vegetable Market News
21 N. 1st Ave., Ste. 224   Ph: (509)575-2494
Yakima, WA 98902-2663   Fax: (509)457-7132

Desc: Compiles statistics on the berry processing industry. *Type:* Newsletter.

Online Processing Tomato Database

Ohio State University
Columbus, OH 43210-1096
URL: http://www.hcs.ohio-state.edu/hcs/EM/
ProcTomato/SearchProctom.html

Desc: This database will provide historical information for the horticulturalist or produce grower specializing in tomatoes. Search the database for data from 1960 to 1995 on such topics as volume and value of production, acres planted and harvested, average price, average yield per acre, and other information. *Type:* Database.

Philadelphia Wholesale Fruit and Vegetable Report

U.S. Department of Agriculture
Agricultural Marketing Service
Fruit and Vegetable Market News
2202 Monterey St., Ste. 104-A   Ph: (559)487-5178
Fresno, CA 93721-3129   Free: 800-487-8796
                                  Fax: (559)487-5199

URL: http://www.ams.usda.gov/marketnews.htm.

Contact: Michael E. Cramer, Officer-in-Charge.

Desc: Reports wholesale prices on fruits and vegetables in the Philadelphia metropolitan area. *Type:* Newsletter.

Pittsburgh Wholesale Fruit and Vegetable Report

U.S. Department of Agriculture
Agricultural Marketing Service
Fruit and Vegetable Market News
2202 Monterey St., Ste. 104-A   Ph: (559)487-5178
Fresno, CA 93721-3129   Free: 800-487-8796
                                  Fax: (559)487-5199

URL: http://www.ams.usda.gov/marketnews.htm.

Contact: Dennis Jemmerson, Officer-in-Charge.

Desc: Reports wholesale prices of fruits and vegetables in the Pittsburgh metropolitan area. *Type:* Newsletter.

PMA Freshline

Produce Marketing Association
1500 Casho Mill Rd.   Ph: (302)738-7100
PO Box 6036   Fax: (302)731-2409
Newark, DE 19714-6036
E-mail: pma@mail.pma.com
URL: http://www.pma.com; www.pma.com.

Contact: Lee Mannering, Editor.

Desc: Provides information on PMA Division and task force activities, new Association programs and projects, Association meetings and tours. Also features research reports, surveys, and other industry news. *Type:* Newsletter.

Pome News

Home Orchard Society, Inc.
PO Box 230192   Ph: (503)639-6250
Tigard, OR 97281-0192
URL: http://www.wvi.com/~dough/HOS/HOSI.html.

Contact: Ted L. Swensen, Editor, (503)296-1468, fax: (503)977-9330, tswensen@jps.net.

Desc: Reflects the aims of the Society, which include promoting the "science, culture, and pleasure of fruit-bearing trees, shrubs, vines, and plants in the home landscape." Recurring features include news of members, suggestions on growing and care of fruit trees, and recipes. *Type:* Newsletter.

Processed Apples Institute

5775 Peachtree-Dunwoody Rd.,   Ph: (404)252-3663
   Ste. 500-G   Fax: (404)252-0774
Atlanta, GA 30342
E-mail: pai@assnhq.com

Contact: Andrew G. Ebert, PhD, Exec.Dir.

Desc: Processors of apple products and suppliers to the industry. Conducts program to improve business conditions in the apple products industry and to enable the industry to serve the interests of consumers. Conducts research programs. *Type:* Association.

St. Louis Wholesale Fruit and Vegetable Report

U.S. Department of Agriculture
Agricultural Marketing Service
Fruit and Vegetable Market News
2202 Monterey St., Ste. 104-A   Ph: (559)487-5178
Fresno, CA 93721-3129   Free: 800-487-8796
                                  Fax: (559)487-5199

URL: http://www.ams.usda.gov/marketnews.htm.

Contact: Charles M. Gore, Officer-in-Charge.

Desc: Reports wholesale prices on fruits and vegetables in the St. Louis metropolitan area. *Type:* Newsletter.

Seattle Wholesale Fruit and Vegetable Report

U.S. Department of Agriculture
Agricultural Marketing Service
Fruit and Vegetable Market News
2202 Monterey St., Ste. 104-A   Ph: (559)487-5178
Fresno, CA 93721-3129   Free: 800-487-8796
                                  Fax: (559)487-5199

URL: http://www.ams.usda.gov/marketnews.htm.

Contact: Peter Echanove, Officer-in-Charge.

Desc: Provides report of wholesale prices on fruits and vegetables in the Seattle metropolitan area. *Type:* Newsletter.

Sun Growers of California

PO Box 9024   Ph: (925)463-8200
Pleasanton, CA 94566   Fax: (925)463-7492
URL: http://www.sungrowers.com
Contact: William Beaton, Pres.

Desc: Walnut, hazelnut, pecan, Brazil nut, almond, raisin, prune, fig, and dried apricot, peach, pear, and apple marketing organization. Acts as an administrative and marketing service organization for Diamond Walnut Growers, Sun-Maid Growers of California, Sunsweet Growers, Valley Fig Growers, and Sun-Land Products of California. *Type:* Association.

Sunkist Growers

PO Box 7888   Ph: (818)986-4800
Van Nuys, CA 91409-7888   Fax: (818)379-7511
Contact: Vince Lupinacci, Pres. & CEO.

Desc: Citrus fruit marketing cooperative. *Type:* Association.

Sun-Maid Growers of California

13525 S. Bethel Ave.   Ph: (209)896-8000
Kingsburg, CA 93631   Free: 800-272-4746
   Fax: (209)897-2362
E-mail: gmcbee@sunmaid.com
Contact: Barry Kriebel, Pres.

Desc: Agricultural processing and marketing cooperative. Processes and markets all types and varieties of raisins in bulk and consumer packages, raisin bread, dried fruits, fruit bits (a mixture of dried fruits), and beverage alcohol. *Type:* Association.

Tomato Fax Report

U.S. Department of Agriculture
Agricultural Marketing Service
Fruit and Vegetable Market News
2202 Monterey St., Ste. 104-A   Ph: (559)487-5178
Fresno, CA 93721-3129   Free: 800-487-8796
   Fax: (559)487-5199
URL: http://www.ams.usda.gov/marketnews.htm.
Contact: Kevin Morris, Officer-in-Charge.

Desc: Provides information on tomatoes, covering the major growing areas. Includes rail and truck shipment information, and FOB shipping point prices representing the most uniform level of trading. *Type:* Newsletter.

Triangle

Florida Citrus Mutual
PO Box 89   Ph: (941)682-1111
Lakeland, FL 33802   Fax: (941)682-1074
E-mail: fcmutual@gte.net
Contact: Lisa Backman, Editor.

Desc: Contains items of interest to citrus growers, including statistical data, market information, ongoing scientific research, and action by various government agencies. Recurring features include weather forecasts, market information, production statistics, news of research, a calendar of events, and reports of meetings. *Type:* Newsletter.

Tuber News

National Potato Promotion Board
7555 E. Hampden Ave., No. 412
Denver, CO 80231
Contact: Lisa Cutter, Editor.

Desc: Provides news and information about the promotional activities of the Potato Board for persons in trade and industry. *Type:* Newsletter.

United Fresh Fruit and Vegetable Association

727 N. Washington St.   Ph: (703)836-3410
Alexandria, VA 22314   Fax: (703)836-7745
E-mail: uffva@uffva.org
Contact: Thomas E. Stenzel, Pres.

Desc: Represents the interests of producers and distributors of commercial quantities of fresh fruits and vegetables. Represents the business interests of growers, shippers, processors, brokers, wholesalers and distributors of produce, working together with our customers at retail and foodservice, our suppliers at every step in the distribution chain, and international partners. *Type:* Association.

U.S. Apple Association

6707 Old Dominion Dr., Ste. 320   Ph: (703)442-8850
   Fax: (703)790-0845
Mc Lean, VA 22101
URL: http://www.usapple.org
Contact: Kraig R. Naasz, Pres.

Desc: Represents all segments of the apple industry; over 600 individual firms involved in the apple business, as well as 36 state and regional apple asociations representing the 9000 apple growers throughout the country. Seeks to provide the means for all segments of the apple industry to join in appropriate collective efforts to profitably produce and market apples and apple products. *Type:* Association.

Vegetable Review

California Agricultural Statistics Service
U.S. Department of Agriculture (USDA)
PO Box 1258   Ph: (916)654-0895
Sacramento, CA 95812

Desc: Covers processing and fresh market vegetable, potato acreage, production, and prices. *Type:* Newsletter.

Vegetarian Newsletter

University of Florida, Horticultural Sciences Dept.
PO Box 110690   Ph: (352)392-2134
Gainesville, FL 32611-0690   Fax: (352)392-5653
Contact: Prof. George Hochmuth, Editor, gjh@gnv.ifas.ufl.edu.

Desc: Focuses on vegetable crops extension in Florida, including commercial vegetables, vegetable gardening, and pesticide updates. Recurring features include news of research, a calendar of events, news of educational opportunities, and notices of publications available. *Type:* Newsletter.

Western Fruit Report

U.S. Department of Agriculture
Agricultural Marketing Service
Fruit and Vegetable Market News
2202 Monterey St., Ste. 104-A   Ph: (559)487-5178
Fresno, CA 93721-3129   Free: 800-487-8796
   Fax: (559)487-5199
URL: http://www.ams.usda.gov/marketnews.htm.
Contact: Kevin Morris, Officer-in-Charge.

Desc: Covers tree fruit and grapes from California and its competitive areas. Provides information on prices, volume of movement, crop estimates, storage figures, etc. *Type:* Newsletter.

Western Growers Association

17620 Fitch St.   Ph: (949)863-1000
Irvine, CA 92614   Free: 800-949-4704
E-mail: dmoore@wga.com
URL: http://www.wga.com
Contact: David L. Moore, Pres.

Desc: California and Arizona growers, shippers, and packers of fresh produce; brokers, distributors, jobbers, and members of allied industries. Represents members' concerns in areas including: transportation; legislation; standardization; labor relations; marketing services; public relations; legal services; insurance compensation. *Type:* Association.

Western Melon and Vegetable Report

U.S. Department of Agriculture
Agricultural Marketing Service
Fruit and Vegetable Market News
2202 Monterey St., Ste. 104-A   Ph: (559)487-5178
Fresno, CA 93721-3129   Free: 800-487-8796
   Fax: (559)487-5199
URL: http://www.ams.usda.gov/marketnews.htm.
Contact: Stephen Skuba, Officer-in-Charge.

Desc: Reports on melons and vegetables. Covers the major growing areas on the west coast of the U.S. *Type:* Newsletter.

Wild Blueberry Bulletin

Wild Blueberry Association of North America
Kentville Agricultural Ctr.   Ph: (207)288-2655
Kentville, NS, Canada B4N 1J5   Fax: (207)288-2656
Contact: P.J. Rideout, Editor.

Desc: Reports on activities and programs of the Association as well as recipes and other items of interest to the wild blueberry industry. Recurring features include reports of meetings and a calendar of events. *Type:* Newsletter.

Fuel

International Coal Review

National Mining Association
1130 17th St. NW   Ph: (202)463-2625
Washington, DC 20036-4677   Fax: (202)833-9636
URL: http://www.nma.org.
Contact: Leslie Coleman, Editor, (202)463-9780, lcoleman@nma.org; Tom Hutchcraft, Editor, (202)463-2638, thutchcraft@nma.org.

Desc: Follows coal imports and exports by month, weight (in tons), value, coal type, and country of destination. *Type:* Newsletter.

Fundraising

Channels

PR Publishing Company, Inc.
Dudley House   Ph: (603)778-0514
PO Box 600   Fax: (603)778-1741
Exeter, NH 03833-0600
Contact: June Barber, Editor.

Desc: Carries news items on public relations and organizational management, fund raising, and volunteerism. Discusses what local and national organizations are doing to help people through improved communication, and offers ideas for improving communication. *Type:* Newsletter.

European Foundation Centre Profiles

Foundation Center
79 5th Ave.   Ph: (212)620-4230
New York, NY 10003-3076   Free: 800-424-9836
   Fax: (212)807-3677

Desc: European and international foundations offering grants in Europe. *Type:* Directory.

Financial Aid for Minorities

Todd Publications
PO Box 635   Ph: (914)358-6213
Nyack, NY 10960   Free: 800-747-1056
   Fax: (914)358-1059
E-mail: toddpub@aol.com
URL: http://www.toddpublications.com

Desc: Scholarships, fellowships, loans, and other sources available to help minority students in these six areas: business; education; engineering and science; health fields; and journalism and mass communications. *Type:* Directory.

Foundations of the 1990s

Foundation Center
79 5th Ave.   Ph: (212)620-4230
New York, NY 10003-3076   Free: 800-424-9836
    Fax: (212)807-3677
Desc: Over 9,000 independent, community, and corporate foundations incorporated since 1989. *Type:* Directory.

Fund Raiser's Guide to Human Service Funding

The Taft Group
27500 Drake Rd.   Ph: (248)699-4253
Farmington Hills, MI 48331-   Free: 800-347-GALE
3535   Fax: (248)699-8097
E-mail: galeord@gale.com
URL: http://www.gale.com/taft/
Contact: Laurie Fundukian, Editor.
Desc: More than 1,860 corporations and foundations that contribute to human service projects. *Type:* Directory.

Fund Raising Management—Non-Profit Software Package Directory Issue

Hoke Communications, Inc.
224 7th St.   Ph: (516)746-6700
Garden City, NY 11530   Free: 800-229-6700
    Fax: (516)294-8141
E-mail: frmmag@aol.com
Contact: George R. Reis, Editor.
Desc: List of approximately 100 suppliers of computer software designed for use in the field of nonprofit fund raising. *Type:* Directory.

Guide to Greater Washington D.C. Grantmakers

Foundation Center
79 5th Ave.   Ph: (212)620-4230
New York, NY 10003-3076   Free: 800-424-9836
    Fax: (212)807-3677
Contact: Carrie Ann Sabato, Copywriter.
Desc: Over 1,100 foundations in Washington D.C. that provide funding to nonprofit organizations. *Type:* Directory.

Jewish Federation of Metropolitan Chicago

1 S. Franklin St.   Ph: (312)346-6700
Ben Gurion Way   Fax: (312)444-2086
Chicago, IL 60606-4694
Contact: Steven B. Nasatir, Ph.D., Pres.
Desc: Allocates funds received from the Jewish United Fund, United Way, and other sources to benefit social welfare, health and education agencies. *Type:* Association.

Montgomery Area United Way

Charles G. Colvin
532 S. Perry St.   Ph: (334)264-7318
Montgomery, AL 36104   Fax: (334)264-7485
Contact: Charles G. Colvin, Exec.Dir.
Desc: Health and human service agencies serving Autauga, Elmore, and Montgomery counties. Coordinates problem solving, fundraising, and planning among members. *Type:* Association.

National Guide to Funding for the Economically Disadvantaged

Foundation Center
79 5th Ave.   Ph: (212)620-4230
New York, NY 10003-3076   Free: 800-424-9836
    Fax: (212)807-3677
Desc: Over 1,400 foundations and corporate direct giving programs that have a history of giving grants to projects and institutions that aid the economically disadvantaged. *Type:* Directory.

National Guide to Funding for Elementary and Secondary Education

Foundation Center
79 5th Ave.   Ph: (212)620-4230
New York, NY 10003-3076   Free: 800-424-9836
    Fax: (212)807-3677
Desc: More than 2,300 foundations and corporate direct giving programs with a history of awarding grant monies to elementary and secondary education. *Type:* Directory.

National Guide to Funding for Libraries and Information Services

Foundation Center
79 5th Ave.   Ph: (212)620-4230
New York, NY 10003-3076   Free: 800-424-9836
    Fax: (212)807-3677
Desc: 600 foundations and corporate direct giving programs that typically offer funding to libraries and information centers. *Type:* Directory.

National Guide to Funding in Religion

Foundation Center
79 5th Ave.   Ph: (212)620-4230
New York, NY 10003-3076   Free: 800-424-9836
    Fax: (212)807-3677
Desc: Over 4,400 foundation and direct giving programs that historically offer funding to churches, synagogues, mosques, and other religious-affiliated programs. *Type:* Directory.

Taft Group Corporate Giving Directory

Gale Group Inc.
27500 Drake Rd.   Ph: (248)699-4253
Farmington Hills, MI 48331-   Free: 800-877-GALE
3535   Fax: (248)699-8070
E-mail: galeord@galegroup.com
URL: http://www.galegroup.com.; http://www.taftgroup.com; http://www.gale.com.
Contact: Lori Schoenenberger, Editor, lori.schoenenberger@gale.com.
Desc: Top 1,000 major corporation- and company-sponsored foundations and direct-giving programs. *Type:* Directory.

United Way of the Bluegrass

101 East Vine St., No. 720   Ph: (606)233-4460
Lexington, KY 40507-1417   Fax: (606)259-3397
Contact: H. Winston Faircloth, Pres. & CPO.
Desc: Volunteers working to raise and allocate funds to help solve community problems. *Type:* Association.

United Way of Central Florida

PO Box 1357   Ph: (813)648-1500
Highland City, FL 33846   Free: 800-881-UWAY
    Fax: (813)648-1535
E-mail: uwcf@aol.com
URL: http://www.uwcf.org
Contact: Terry Worthington, Pres.
Desc: To assist in fundraising by conducting company-wide employee campaigns and by encouraging corporate contributions. *Type:* Association.

United Way of East Central Iowa

1030 5th Ave. SE   Ph: (319)398-5372
Cedar Rapids, IA 52403-2428   Free: 800-332-8182
    Fax: (319)398-5381
E-mail: aweci@inav.com
URL: http://www.cedar-rapids.ia.unitedway.org
Contact: Mr. Lynn Nichols, Pres.
Desc: Provides training and technical assistance to area not-for-profit organizations, volunteer recruitment and matching program. Maintains information and referral services linking those in need with area programs. *Type:* Association.

United Way of Genesee and Lapeer Counties

202 E Boulevard Dr.   Ph: (810)232-8121
Flint, MI 48503-1866   Fax: (810)232-2898
Contact: Michael K. Brown, Pres.
Type: Association.

United Way of Greater Knoxville

1301 Hannah Ave.   Ph: (423)523-9131
PO Box 326   Fax: (423)522-7312
Knoxville, TN 37901-0326
URL: http://www.unitedwayknox.org
Contact: Ben Landers, Pres.
Desc: Works to raise and distribute funds within Knox County in an ongoing effort to meet local health and human service needs in our community. *Type:* Association.

United Way of Greater St. Louis

1111 Olive St.   Ph: (314)421-0700
St. Louis, MO 63101   Fax: (314)539-4154
E-mail: @stl.unitedway.org
URL: http://www.stl.unitedway.org
Contact: Charmaine S. Chapman, Pres./CEO.
Desc: To assist in fundraising by conducting company-wide employee campaigns and by encouraging corporate contributions. Works to improve the quality of life by ensuring effective delivery of human services in metropolitan St. *Type:* Association.

United Way of Marshall County

PO Box 392   Ph: (219)936-3366
2701 N. Michigan St.   Fax: (219)936-8040
Plymouth, IN 46563
E-mail: rhonzik@skyenet.net
Contact: Jeff Honzik, Exec. Dir.
Type: Association.

United Way of New York City

99 Park Ave.   Ph: (212)973-3800
New York, NY 10016-1550   Fax: (212)490-9477
URL: http://www.uwnyc.org
Contact: Ralph Dickerson, Jr., Pres./CPO.
Type: Association.

United Way of Oakland County

50 Wayne St.   Ph: (810)456-8805
Pontiac, MI 48342-2159   Fax: (810)456-8809
Contact: J. Thomas Laing, Exec. Dir.
Desc: To unite the community in an organized effort to plan, coordinate, support and monitor effective human service programs that address changing needs. *Type:* Association.

United Way Services of Cleveland

1331 Euclid Ave.   Ph: (216)436-2100
Cleveland, OH 44115-2577   Fax: (216)436-2109
E-mail: larriem@pop.cybergate.net
URL: http://www.virtcity.com/organiza/unitedwa
Contact: Mike Benz, Pres.
Desc: Funds health and human service organizations in Cuyohoga and Geauga counties. *Type:* Association.

United Way of Southeastern New England

229 Waterman St.   Ph: (401)521-9000
Providence, RI 02906
Contact: Dennis M. Murphy, Pres.
Desc: Sponsors fundraising and fund distribution programs on behalf of social service organizations in Rhode Island and surrounding communities in Massachusetts and Connecticut. *Type:* Association.

United Way of Summit County
90 N Prospect St.   Ph: (330)762-7601
PO Box 1260   Fax: (330)762-0317
Akron, OH 44309-1260
E-mail: uwsc@compuserve.com
Contact: Gerard J. Cerny, Pres.
Desc: Conducts annual fund drive to support local health and human service agencies. *Type:* Association.

United Way of York County
800 E King St.   Ph: (717)843-0957
York, PA 17403-1772   Fax: (717)843-4082
E-mail: info@unitedway-york.org
URL: http://www.unitedway-york.org
Contact: Robert Woods, Pres.
Type: Association.

Who Gets Grants: Foundation Grants to Nonprofit Organizations
Foundation Center
79 5th Ave.   Ph: (212)620-4230
New York, NY 10003-3076 Free: 800-424-9836
                  Fax: (212)807-3677
Desc: More than 20,000 nonprofit organizations that received more than 65,000 grants. *Type:* Directory.

Furniture

Bench Press
Workbench
180 Pulaski St.
Bayonne, NJ 07002
Contact: Warren Rubin, Contact.
Desc: Contains information on the Workbench company and its products and customers. *Type:* Newsletter.

The Furniture Executive
American Furniture Manufacturers Association
PO Box HP-7   Ph: (336)884-5000
High Point, NC 27261   Fax: (336)884-5306
E-mail: afmahp@aol.com
Contact: Nancy High, Editor.
Desc: Reports on the activities of the American Furniture Manufacturers Association and on issues impacting on the industry. *Type:* Newsletter.

Furniture Transporter
Bohman Industrial Traffic Consultants, Inc.
PO Box 889   Ph: (508)632-1913
Gardner, MA 01440   Fax: (508)630-2917
Contact: Ray Bohman, Jr., Editor.
Desc: Reports important news and developments in shipping, packaging, and transporting that affect the furniture and allied products industries. *Type:* Newsletter.

International Home Furnishings Representatives Association
209 S. Main, M-1405   Ph: (336)889-3920
PO Box 670   Fax: (336)883-8245
High Point, NC 27261
E-mail: ihfra@aol.com
URL: http://www.ihfra.org
Contact: Kelly R. Crisco, CHR, Exec.Dir.
Desc: Local affiliated organizations of approximately 3200 home furnishings representatives. Provides services to affiliates and individual members, including information exchange, listing manufacturers seeking representatives in all territories and representatives seeking manufacturers' lines in specific territories. Conducts certified home furnishings educational program. *Type:* Association.

National Home Furnishings Association
PO Box 2396   Ph: (336)883-1650
High Point, NC 27261   Free: 800-888-9590
                  Fax: (336)883-1195
E-mail: mail@nhfa.org
URL: http://www.nhfa.org
Contact: Patricia Bowling, Exec.VP.
Desc: Retailers of home furnishings. Provides educational programs for retail sales managers and trainers; for middle management; for owners and executives; for family businesses; and for residential interior designers. *Type:* Association.

United Furniture Workers Insurance Fund
1910 Airlane Dr.   Ph: (615)889-8860
PO Box 100037   Fax: (615)391-0865
Nashville, TN 37224
Contact: Willie Rudd, Chm.
Desc: AFL-CIO. A division of International Union of Electronic, Electrical, Salaried, Machine, and Furniture Workers. *Type:* Association.

Wood Digest-Showcase
Cygnus Publishing Inc.
1233 Janesville Ave.   Ph: (920)563-6388
Fort Atkinson, WI 53538 Free: 800-547-7377
                  Fax: (920)563-1699
Contact: Steve Ehle, Editor.
Desc: List of suppliers of materials, machinery, tools, and services for woodworking, cabinetry, casegoods, and furniture manufacturing processes (SIC 24, 25, 37, and 39). *Type:* Directory.

Games

American Bridge Association
Gloria Christler
2828 Lakewood Ave. SW Ph: (404)768-5517
Atlanta, GA 30315   Fax: (404)767-1871
Contact: Gloria Christler, Exec.Sec.
Desc: Individuals, primarily blacks, interested in the game of bridge. Encourages the playing of duplicate bridge. Sponsors annual tournaments as benefits for charitable organizations. *Type:* Association.

Basic Chess Features
PO Box 140   Ph: (212)586-3700
South Gibson, PA 18842
Contact: Shelby Lyman, President.
Desc: Distributes chess features. *Alt. Contact:* PO Box 140, South Gibson, PA 18842; telephone: (212)586-3700. *Type:* Periodical.

Chess Life
U.S. Chess Federation
3054 NYS Rt., 9W   Ph: (914)562-8350
New Windsor, NY 12553   Free: 800-388-KING
                  Fax: (914)561-2437
E-mail: chesslife_uscf@juno.com.
Contact: Glenn Petersen, Editor; Alan Kontor, Advertising Mgr., tla_uscf@juno.com.
Desc: Technical magazine for chess players. *Type:* Periodical.

Chesstours
PO Box 1182   Ph: (702)786-3178
Reno, NV 89504
E-mail: 72142.335@atscompuserve.com.
Contact: Larry Evans, Author/Owner.
Alt. Contact: PO Box 1182, Reno, NV 89504; telephone: (702)786-3178. *Type:* Periodical.

Diehard Game Fan
Game Fan
5137 Clareton Dr., No. 210 Ph: (818)706-3260
Agoura, CA 91301   Fax: (818)706-1367
URL: http://www.gamefan.com.
Contact: Jay Puryear, Editor and Publisher, jpuryear-metropolitanropolismedia.com.
Desc: Consumer magazine covering video games. *Type:* Periodical.

Double Eagle Newsletter
American Darts Organization
230 N. Crescent Way, No. K Ph: (714)254-0212
Anaheim, CA 92801   Fax: (714)254-0214
E-mail: adooffice@aol.com
Contact: Katie Harris, Editor.
Desc: Monitors developments and events in the sport of darts for dart players, manufacturers, and suppliers. Discusses equipment and techniques of the game. *Type:* Newsletter.

The Duelist
The Duelist
PO Box 707   Ph: (425)204-8000
Renton, WA 98057   Fax: (425)204-5928
E-mail: duelist@wizards.com
URL: http://www.wizards.com.
Contact: Rob Hahn, Editor; Wendy Noritake, Publisher, (425)204-7230, wendy@wizards.com; Bob Henning, Advertising Mgr., (425)204-7262, bob@wizards.com.
Desc: Consumer magazine for players of the game Magic: The Gathering, and other trading card and electronic games. *Type:* Periodical.

EGM2
Ziff Davis Video Game Group
1920 Highland Ave., No. 222 Ph: (630)916-7222
Lombard, IL 60148   Fax: (630)916-7227
URL: http://www.videogames.com.
Contact: Joe Funk, Editorial Dir.; Howard Grossman, Editor-in-Chief; Joan McInerney, Circulation Director, jmcinern@zd.com; Jonathan Lane, Publisher.
Desc: Consumer magazine covering video games. *Type:* Periodical.

Electronic Gaming Monthly
Ziff Davis Video Game Group
1920 Highland Ave., No. 222 Ph: (630)916-7222
Lombard, IL 60148   Fax: (630)916-7227
E-mail: egm@zd.com.
URL: http://www.videogames.com.
Contact: Joe Funk, Editorial Dir.; Joan McInerney, Circulation Dir., jmcinern@zd.com; Jonathan Lane, Publisher; John Davison, Editor-in-Chief.
Desc: Consumer magazine covering video gaming. *Type:* Periodical.

Game Informer Magazine
Sunrise Publications, Inc.
10120 W. 76th St.   Ph: (612)946-7256
Eden Prairie, MN 55344-3744 Fax: (612)946-8155
E-mail: gamers@winternet.com
URL: http://www.gameinformer.com.
Contact: Andy McNamara, Editor; Kim Benike, Advertising Sales; Terrie Maley, Circulation and Marketing Mgr.; Rich Cihak, Publisher.
Desc: Consumer magazine covering video and computer game information and reviews. *Type:* Periodical.

Gaming Products and Services—Buyers Guide Issue
RCM Enterprises, Inc.
2233 University Ave. W., Ste. 410   Ph: (612)523-0666
                                     Fax: (612)523-0665
St. Paul, MN 55114
E-mail: rcmpub@aol.com
Contact: Dawn Skully, Editor.
Desc: List of companies providing products and services for the gaming industry; international coverage. *Type:* Directory.

Inquest, The Gaming Magazine
Wizard Entertainment
151 Wells Ave.   Ph: (914)268-2000
Congers, NY 10920   Fax: (914)268-6357
URL: http://www.wizardworld.com.
Contact: Mike Searle, Editor, mikesearle@aol.com; Ken Scrudato, Advertising Dir.; Paul Rolnick, Circ. and Dist. Director.
Desc: Consumer magazine covering games, including collectible card, role playing and board games. *Type:* Periodical.

National Indian Gaming Association
Richard G. Hill
224 Second St. SE   Ph: (202)546-7711
Washington, DC 20003   Free: 800-286-6442
                        Fax: (202)546-1755
URL: http://www.indiangaming.org
Contact: Richard G. Hill, Chm.
Desc: Indian nations operating gambling establishments (142) are members; tribes, organizations, and businesses supporting Indian gaming establishments (63) are associate members. Works to protect and preserve the welfare of tribes seeking to achieve economic self-sufficiency through the operation of gaming establishments. *Type:* Association.

National Mah Jongg League
250 W. 57th St.   Ph: (212)246-3052
New York, NY 10107   Fax: (212)246-4117
Contact: Ruth Unger, Pres.
Desc: Promotes the game of Mah Jongg. *Type:* Association.

National Scrabble Association
c/o Williams & Co.   Ph: (516)477-0033
PO Box 700   Fax: (516)477-0294
Greenport, NY 11944
E-mail: info@scrabble-assoc.com
URL: http://www.scrabble-assoc.com
Contact: John D. Williams, Exec.Dir.
Desc: Scrabble players. Sanctions, organizes, and publicizes Scrabble crossword game tournaments in the U.S. *Type:* Association.

Official U.S. PlayStation Magazine
Ziff Davis Video Game Group
1920 Highland Ave., No. 222   Ph: (630)916-7222
Lombard, IL 60148   Fax: (630)916-7227
URL: http://www.videogames.com.
Contact: Joe Funk, Editorial Dir.; Wataru Maruyama, Editor-in-Chief; Joan McInerney, Circulation Dir., jmcinern@zd.com; Jonathan Lane, Publisher.
Desc: Consumer magazine covering video gaming for the Sony PlayStation. *Type:* Periodical.

OGR.com: Computer Gaming Reviews, Previews, News, and Features
Online Gaming Review
100 East Ridge   Ph: (203)431-9000
Ridgefield, CT 06877   Fax: (203)431-3000
E-mail: letters@ogr.com

URL: http://www.ogr.com/
Contact: Doug Radcliffe, Site Manager, doug@ogr.com.
Desc: A site devoted to computer games, OGR.com offers the latest reviews and detailed analysis of current titles, as well as previews of up-and-coming releases. It also provides news and current events about games and the gaming industry. *Type:* Database.

PSExtreme
PSExtreme
1175 Chess Dr., E   Ph: (415)372-0942
Foster City, CA 94404   Fax: (415)372-0753
Contact: Dave Winding, Publisher; Mark Winding, Advertising Mgr.; Mike Gerrardo, Circulation Mgr.
Desc: Gaming publication focusing on the Sony Play Station. *Type:* Periodical.

Puzzle Buffs International
41 Park Dr.   Ph: (216)923-2397
Port Clinton, OH 43452-2072
Contact: Charles R. Elum, Pres.
Desc: Individuals who share an interest in word puzzles and word games. Seeks to showcase the puzzle-solving skills of members and to inform the public about the mental exercise and enjoyment of puzzling. *Type:* Association.

United States Chess Federation
3054 NYS Rte. 9   Ph: (914)562-8350
New Windsor, NY 12553   Free: 800-388-KING
                         Fax: (914)561-2437
URL: http://www.uschess.org
Contact: Mike Cavallo, Exec.Dir.
Desc: Governing body of United States chessplayers unit of the World Chess Federation. Conducts all championship events, including National Open, U.S. Championship, U.S. Junior, U.S. Open, and U.S. Women's. Sends teams abroad to compete in international events and maintains rating system for every U.S. Chess tournament. *Type:* Association.

Where to Gamble
Visible Ink Press
27500 Drake Rd.   Ph: (248)699-4253
Farmington Hills, MI 48331-3535   Free: 800-776-6265
                   Fax: (248)699-8067
E-mail: galeord@gale.com
URL: http://www.gale.com
Contact: George Cantor, Editor.
Desc: Gaming venues for casino and riverboat gambling, horse racing, jai alai, and the lottery. *Type:* Directory.

World Bocce Association
1098 W. Irving Park Rd.   Ph: (630)860-2623
Bensenville, IL 60106   Free: 800-OKB-OCCE
                         Fax: (630)595-2541
E-mail: mrbocce@worldbocce.org
URL: http://www.worldbocce.org/usa
Contact: Philip Ferrari, Pres.
Desc: Works to introduce the game of bocce to the public to promote and preserve Italian heritage. *Type:* Association.

Gardening

African Violet Society of America
2375 North   Ph: (409)839-4725
Beaumont, TX 77702   Free: 800-770-AVSA
                      Fax: (409)839-4329
E-mail: avsa@avsa.org
URL: http://www.avsa.org
Contact: Jenny Daugeneau.

Desc: Amateur and commercial African violet growers interested in the propagation and culture of African violets. *Type:* Association.

American Gloxinia and Gesneriad Society
c/o Jon Dixon   Ph: (413)323-6661
PO Box 14
Fremont, NH 03044-0014
Contact: Leslie Milide, Contact.
Desc: Amateur and semi-professional gardeners who grow gloxinias or related plants indoors in a window garden, under fluorescent lights, or in home greenhouses. Provides information on new and known gesneriads. Funds research on gesneriads and related topics; seeks to educate the public about gesneriads and their culture. *Type:* Association.

American Homestyle and Gardening
The New York Times Co.
229 W. 43rd St.   Ph: (212)556-1234
New York, NY 10036-3913
E-mail: name@nytimes.com
Contact: Karen Saks, Editor-in-Chief; George Fields, Publisher.
Desc: Ideas for home-improvement. *Type:* Periodical.

American Horticultural Society
7931 E. Boulevard Dr.   Ph: (703)768-5700
Alexandria, VA 22308   Free: 800-777-7931
                        Fax: (703)768-8700
E-mail: info@ahs.org
URL: http://www.ahs.org
Contact: Linda Hallman, Pres./CEO.
Desc: Membership includes amateur and professional gardeners. Missing is to educate and inspire people of all ages to became successful and environmentally responsible gardeners by advancing the art and science of horticulture. Operates free seed exchange, discount book service, and gardeners' information service for members. *Type:* Association.

American How-To
North American Outdoor Group, Inc.
12301 Whitewater Dr., Ste. 260   Ph: (612)988-7117
Minnetonka, MN 55343   Free: 800-688-7611
                        Fax: (612)936-9169
E-mail: addept@naoginc.com; addept@naoginc.com.
URL: http://www.handymanclub.com.
Contact: Tom Sweeney, Editor, (612)988-7290; Sheila Riley Becker, Publisher, (612)988-7114; Russell M. Nolan, Group Publisher.
Desc: Do-it-yourself home improvement magazine. *Type:* Periodical.

American Rose Society
PO Box 30000   Ph: (318)938-5402
Shreveport, LA 71130-0030   Free: 800-637-6534
                             Fax: (318)938-5405
E-mail: ars@ars-hq.org
URL: http://www.ars.org
Contact: Michael C. Kromer, Exec.Dir.
Desc: Amateur gardeners, commercial growers, related dealers, and local rose societies and garden clubs. Establishes rules and sponsors national and district rose shows; conducts school for and accredits rose show judges; sponsors research on rose growing problems; conducts a rose name registration system; provides rose growing/culture referrals. *Type:* Association.

Better Homes and Gardens: Garden, Deck and Landscape

Meredith Corp.

1716 Locust St.	Ph: (515)284-3000
Des Moines, IA 50309-3023	Free: 800-678-2674
	Fax: (515)284-3697

Contact: Glenn DiNella, Editor; Stephen Levinson, Publisher; Pat Tomlinson, Advertising Dir.

Desc: Consumer magazine covering gardening and landscaping. *Type:* Periodical.

Better Homes and Gardens: Garden Ideas & Outdoor Living

Meredith Corp.

1716 Locust St.	Ph: (515)284-3000
Des Moines, IA 50309-3023	Free: 800-678-2674
	Fax: (515)284-3697

Contact: Kate Carter Frederick, Editor; Pat Tomlinson, Advertising Dir.; Jerry Ward, VP/Publishing Director.

Desc: Consumer magazine covering gardening in the U.S. and Canada. *Type:* Periodical.

Canadian Gardening

Camar Publications Ltd.

210-340 Ferrier St.	Ph: (905)475-8440
Markham, ON, Canada L3R 2Z5	Fax: (905)475-9246

URL: http://www.canadiangardening.com.

Contact: Jacqueline Howe, Publisher, jacquelinehowe@camarpublications.com; Beckie Fox, Editor.

Desc: Canadian gardening magazine. *Type:* Periodical.

Country Accents

Goodman Media Group, Inc.

1700 Broadway, 34th Fl.	Ph: (212)541-7100
New York, NY 10019	Fax: (212)245-1241

Contact: Lorraine Shea, Editor; Jason Goodman, Publisher; Irwin Linker, Vice President; Louisa Kearney, Advertising Dir.

Desc: Home service and decorating magazine covering topics relevant to country living. *Type:* Periodical.

Country Home Country Gardens

Meredith Corp.

125 Park Ave.	Ph: (212)551-7117
New York, NY 10017	Fax: (212)551-6918

Contact: LuAnn Brandsen, Editor; Sue Katzen, Advertising Mgr.; David Ball, Circulation Mgr.

Desc: Consumer magazine covering gardening. *Alt. Contact:* 1716 Locust St., Des Moines, IA 50309-3023; telephone: (515)284-3515; fax: (515)284-2552. *Type:* Periodical.

Country Living

Hearst Magazines

959 8th Ave.	Ph: (212)649-2000
New York, NY 10019-5905	

URL: http://www.homearts.com; http://www.countryliving.com.

Contact: Nancy Mernit Soriano, Editor-in-Chief; Peg Farrell, Publisher.

Desc: Home decorating and lifestyle magazine. *Alt. Contact:* 224 W. 57th St., 7th floor, New York, NY 10019; telephone: (212)649-3501; fax: (212)956-3857. *Type:* Periodical.

Decks & Backyard Projects

Aqua-Field Publishing Company, Inc.

66 W. Gilbert St., Ste. FL-2	Ph: (908)935-1222
Red Bank, NJ 07701	Fax: (908)935-9846

Contact: Edward Montague, Editor; Cheryl Ferber, Publisher; Cheryl Ferber, Account Exec.

Desc: Magazine on building backyard projects. *Type:* Periodical.

Dynamics International Gardening Association

Drawer 1165	Ph: (919)625-4790
Asheboro, NC 27204-1165	

Contact: William A. Barnes, Exec.Dir.

Desc: Educators, scientists, horticulturists, arborists, hobbyists, and youth groups. Promotes gardening in elementary schools. *Type:* Association.

Fine Gardening

Taunton Press

63 S. Main St., Box 5506	Free: 800-926-8776
Newtown, CT 06470-5506	Fax: (203)270-6751

E-mail: jchilds@taunton.com

URL: http://www.taunton.com; http://www.taunton.com.

Contact: Suzanne Roman, Publisher, sueroman@taunton.com; Lee Ann White, Editor, fg@taunton.com; Jodie Delohery, Art Dir., jdelohery@art.taunton.com.

Desc: Hands-on magazine for avid gardeners of all skill levels. Filled with tips, ideas, information, and inspiration on garden design, gardening techniques, garden structures, and plants for the home landscape. *Type:* Periodical.

Flower & Garden

KC Publishing Inc.

4645 Belleview	Ph: (816)531-5730
Kansas City, MO 64112	Free: 800-878-7855
	Fax: (816)531-3873

E-mail: kcpublishing@earthlink.net

Contact: Angela Hughes, Editor; John C. Prebich, Publisher; Connie Moss, V.P. Production & Adv. Support.

Desc: Magazine covering home gardening and landscaping. *Type:* Periodical.

Garden Club of America

14 E 60th St. Fl 3	
New York, NY 10022-1006	

Contact: Cathy Kilroy, Exec.Dir.

Desc: Amateur gardeners. Seeks to stimulate the knowledge and love of gardening among amateurs, aid in the protection of native plants and birds, and encourage civic planting. *Type:* Association.

Germinations

Butterbrooke Farm

78 Barry Rd.	Ph: (203)888-2000
Oxford, CT 06478	

Contact: Dr. Thomas M. Butterworth, Editor.

Desc: Provides information about gardening, sustainable agriculture, food, nutrition, and related items of interest to gardeners and seed-savers. Recurring features include editorials, news of research, letters to the editor, news of members, book reviews and a calendar of events. *Type:* Newsletter.

Government Product News—Buyers Guide for Grounds Maintenance Issue

Penton Media Inc.

1100 Superior Ave.	Ph: (216)696-7000
Cleveland, OH 44114-2543	Fax: (216)931-9524

E-mail: corpcomm@penton.com

Contact: Leslie A. Drahos, Editor.

Desc: List of over 1,000 manufacturers of grounds maintenance equipment. *Type:* Directory.

The Green Thumb

PO Box 579	Ph: (716)374-5400
Naples, NY 14512	

Contact: George Abraham, Editor; Katherine Abraham, Asst. Ed.

Desc: Distributes gardening questions and answers. *Alt. Contact:* PO Box 579, Naples, NY 14512; telephone: (716)374-5400. *Type:* Periodical.

Herb Gatherings

Herb Gatherings

10949 East 200 South	Ph: (765)296-4116
Lafayette, IN 47905-9453	

E-mail: hrbgthrngs@aol.com

Contact: Carla J. Nelson, Editor and Publisher.

Desc: Shares "in the pursuance of knowledge and the enjoyment of the passions and pleasures of herbs." Offers articles on gardening, recipes, fairy and plant folklore, and a calendar of herb events. Recurring features include columns titled Rues and Eclectic Mix of Herb Information. *Type:* Newsletter.

Herbal Earth

Herbal Earth

PO Box 56	Ph: (603)226-1927
Epsom, NH 03234	Fax: (603)463-7230

Contact: Christine McKenna, Editor; Michelle Parker.

Desc: Promotes the use of herbs in daily life for cooking, medicine, cosmetics, and crafts. Recurring features include a calendar of events, news of educational opportunities, book reviews, and columns titled Garden Spotlight, Craft Corner, and Featured Herbs. *Type:* Newsletter.

Home Gardener's Newsletter

Moore Consulting

Box 9527	Ph: (415)524-1163
Berkeley, CA 94709	

Contact: Dr. Wayne S. Moore, Editor.

Desc: Contains seasonal gardening tips and suggestions. *Remarks:* May be customized to include the name of the subscribing nursery or gardening center on the masthead. *Type:* Newsletter.

Home Magazine

Hachette Filipacchi Magazines, Inc.

1633 Broadway, 41st Fl.	Ph: (212)767-6000
New York, NY 10019	Fax: (212)989-4561

Contact: John Miller, Publisher, (212)767-6266, fax: (212)489-4576, jjmhfm@aol.com; Edward Abramson, Publisher, (212)767-5519, fax: (212)767-5568; Gale Steves, Editor-in-Chief, (212)767-6810, fax: (212)767-5595.

Desc: Consumer magazine. *Type:* Periodical.

Home, Yard & Garden Pest Newsletter

University of Illinois

ACES Newsletter Service

69 Mumford Hall	Ph: (217)244-5166
1301 W. Gregory Dr.	
Urbana, IL 61801	

Contact: Phil Nixon, Editor.

Desc: Discusses insect, weed, and plant disease pests of the yard and garden. Covers current pest controls, application equipment and methods, and storage and disposal of pesticides for the yard and garden. *Type:* Newsletter.

Kitchen Garden

Taunton Press

63 S. Main St., Box 5506	Free: 800-926-8776
Newtown, CT 06470-5506	Fax: (203)270-6751

E-mail: jchilds@taunton.com

URL: http://www.taunton.com; http://www.taunton.com.

Contact: Mary Morgan, Editor, (230)426-8191, kg@taunton.com; Suzanne Roman, Publisher, sueroman@taunton.com; Rosalind Wanke, Art Dir.

Desc: Gardening magazine for people who take pleasure and pride in their gardens and the food they prepare from them. Contains how-to information on growing, cooking, and preserving vegetables, herbs, and fruits. *Type:* Periodical.

National Council of State Garden Clubs

4401 Magnolia Ave.
St. Louis, MO 63110-3492
Ph: (314)776-7574
Fax: (314)776-5108
Contact: Mrs. Francis Mantler, Office Mgr.
Desc: Federation of garden clubs. Seeks to protect and conserve natural resources through teacher-training environmental education workshops; encourages the improvement of roadsides and parks; assists in establishing botanical gardens and horticultural centers. Conducts Landscape Design Schools. *Type:* Association.

National Gardening

National Gardening Association
180 Flynn Ave.
Burlington, VT 05401
Ph: (802)863-1308
Free: 800-538-7476
Fax: (802)863-5962
E-mail: nga@garden.org
URL: http://www.garden.org; http://www.garden.org.
Contact: Michael MacCaskey, Editor-in-Chief, mikem@garden.org; Larry Sommers, Vice Pres., Publishing, larrys@garden.org.
Desc: Magazine covering fruit, vegetable, and ornamental gardening for home and community gardeners. *Type:* Periodical.

National Gardening Association

180 Flynn Ave.
Burlington, VT 05401
Ph: (802)863-1308
Free: 800-538-7476
Fax: (802)863-5962
E-mail: nga@garden.org
URL: http://www.garden.org
Contact: David E. Els, Pres.
Desc: Home gardeners, community garden groups, nursing and rehabilitation homes, schools, youth clubs, and camps. Works to sustain the essential values of life and community, renewing the fundamental links between people, plants and the earth. *Type:* Association.

National Junior Horticultural Association

Joe Maxson
702 W. Elm
Durant, OK 74701-2602
Ph: (580)924-0771
Contact: Joe Maxson, Exec.Sec.
Desc: Conducts educational programs for young people interested in horticulture. Maintains separate divisions for junior members (14 and under) and senior members (15-22). Sponsors projects and contests in production and marketing, demonstration, horticulture, achievement and leadership, gardening, experimental horticulture, environmental beautification, and public speaking. *Type:* Association.

North American Rock Garden Society

Jacques Mommens
PO Box 67
Millwood, NY 10546
Ph: (914)762-2948
E-mail: mommens@ibm.net
URL: http://www.nargs.org
Contact: Jacques Mommens, Exec.Sec.
Desc: Persons interested in cultivation of alpine and saxatile plants. Membership includes gardeners from 32 countries. Goals are to increase knowledge of rock garden plants, their value, habits, and geographical distribution and to promote good design and construction of rock gardens. *Type:* Association.

The Old Farmer's Almanac Gardener's Companion

Yankee Publishing Inc.
PO Box 520
Dublin, NH 03444-0520
Ph: (603)563-8111
Fax: (603)563-8252
E-mail: almanac@yankeepub.com
URL: http://www.almanac.

Contact: Georgia Orcatt, Editor; Sherin Wight, Publisher.
Desc: Consumer magazine covering all levels of gardening. *Type:* Periodical.

Organic Gardening

Rodale Books
400 S. 10th St.
Emmaus, PA 18098-0099
Ph: (610)967-5171
Fax: (610)967-7722
E-mail: ddonche1@rodalepress.com
URL: http://www.rodalepress.com; http://www.rodalepress.com.
Contact: Nancy Beaubaire, Editor, (610)967-7907, fax: (610)967-7846; Anne Marie Crown, Assoc. Publisher, (610)967-8617, acrown1@rodalepress.com; Dolly Donchez, Advertising Asst., (610)967-8715, ddonche1@rodalepress.com.
Desc: Horticulture and gardening magazine. *Type:* Periodical.

The Potting Shed

Richboro Press
1280 Stump Rd.
Southampton, PA 18966-0947
Ph: (215)355-6084
Fax: (215)364-2212
Contact: Charles Moore, Editor.
Desc: Provides information and advice on greenhouse growing the year around. Supplies a month-by-month schedule of which vegetables and flowers to plant in a greenhouse and when to transplant outdoors. *Type:* Newsletter.

SLI Newsletter

Society for Louisiana Irises (SLI)
c/o Elaine Bourque
1812 Broussard Rd. E.
Lafayette, LA 70508
Ph: (318)856-5859
Contact: Farron Campbell, Editor; Dennis Vercher, Editor.
Desc: Reports on the breeding and care of Louisiana irises. Covers Society activities. *Type:* Newsletter.

Southwest Organic News

New Mexico Organic Growers & Associates
2 Rincon de Cholla
Corrales, NM 87048
Ph: (505)898-2308
Fax: (505)299-8883
E-mail: soilutions@aol.com; kking0524@aol.com.
Contact: Kathy King, Editor, kking0524@aol.com.
Desc: Promotes "sustainable organic growing techniques in New Mexico and the Southwestern United States." Provides articles on tips for yard and garden care, low water landscaping, herbicide symptoms, and other topics for environmentally sound gardening. *Type:* Newsletter.

Veranda

Veranda Publications Inc.
455 East Paces Ferry Rd., Ste. 216
Atlanta, GA 30305
Ph: (404)261-3603
Free: 800-767-5863
Fax: (404)364-9772
Contact: Lisa Newsom, Editor.
Desc: Consumer magazine featuring interiors, gardens, flowers, antiques, architecture, cuisine, designer interviews, travel and literary excerpts. *Type:* Periodical.

Gay/Lesbian

The Advocate

Liberation Publications, Inc.
6922 Hollywood Blvd., 10th Fl.
Los Angeles, CA 90028
Ph: (213)871-1225
Fax: (213)467-0173
E-mail: newsroom@advocate.com.
URL: http://www.advocate.com.
Desc: National gay and lesbian news and lifestyle magazine. *Alt. Contact:* PO Box 4371, Los Angeles, CA 90078-4371; fax: (213)467-6805. *Type:* Periodical.

The Center Voice

Lesbian & Gay Community Services Center, Inc.
One Little W. 12th St.
New York, NY 10014
Ph: (212)620-7310
Fax: (212)924-2657
E-mail: info@gaycenter.org
URL: http://www.gaycenter.org.
Contact: Daniel Willson, Editor, daniel@gaycenter.org.
Desc: Spotlights news, programs, and services of the Center. Recurring features include a calendar of events. *Type:* Newsletter.

Courage

St. John the Baptist Church
210 W. 31st St.
New York, NY 10001
Ph: (212)268-1010
Fax: (212)268-7150
E-mail: nycourage@aol.com
URL: http://www.world.std.com/~courage
Contact: Fr. John F. Harvey, Dir.
Desc: Provides spiritual support for men and women with homosexual tendencies who desire to live chaste lives in accordance with the teachings of the Roman Catholic Church. *Type:* Association.

Gay Lesbian Alliance Against Defamation

150 W. 26th St., Ste. 503
New York, NY 10001
Ph: (212)807-1700
Free: 800-429-6334
Fax: (212)807-1806
E-mail: glaad@glaad.org
URL: http://www.glaad.org
Contact: Joan M. Garry, Exec. Dir.
Desc: The Gay & Lesbian Alliance Against Defamation (GLADD) is a national organization dedicated to promoting fair, accurate and inclusive representation of individuals and events in all media as a means of combating homphobia and all forms of discrimination based on sexual orientation and identity. In pursuit of its mission, GLADD focuses on five main strategies: To organize the lesbian, gay, bisexual and transgender cmmunity to respond to negative and positive portrayals of our community in media through its Monitoring and Mobilization program; To work directly with media professionals to improve their understanding of th lesbian, gay, bisexual and transgender community by providing accurate information and offering seminars as part of its Outreach to Media Professionals program; To work continually with lesbian, gay, bisexual and transgender organizations and individuals to refine and expand their understanding of the media and skills needed to work with them by offering training interventions and technical assistance through its Community Relations program; To study and articulate cultural and media-specifc trends issues and controversies to inform the work of GLADD and other organizations through its Research and Analysis program; and To promote lesbian, gay, bisexual and transgender Visibility by designing and implementing public education cmapaigns with positive lesbian, gay, bisexual and transgender images. *Type:* Association.

Gay, Lesbian, and Straight Education Network

Gay, Lesbian, and Straight Education Network
121 W. 27th. St., Ste. 804
New York, NY 10001
Ph: (212)727-0135
Fax: (212)727-0254
E-mail: webdiva@glsen.org
URL: http://www.glsen.org/
Desc: GLSEN strives to bring attention to gay and lesbian issues in the educational community. Their Web site provides news stories, information on their conferences and training seminars, a listing of chapters across the U.S, and more. *Type:* Database.

The GP Reporter

Star Reporter Publishing Company, Inc.

050167 Rosebank Sta.   Ph: (718)981-5703
Staten Island, NY 10305-0004   Fax: (718)981-5713

Contact: R.A. Lindberg, Editor.

Desc: Focuses on journalism, mass communication, advertising, and marketing "to promote the growth of a professional journalistic approach to the legitimate concerns of Gay men and women." Recurring features include editorials and news briefs. *Type:* Newsletter.

Honcho Magazine

MMG, Inc.

462 Broadway, Ste. 4000   Ph: (212)966-8400
New York, NY 10013   Free: 888-664-7827
    Fax: (212)966-9366

E-mail: honchomag@aol.com.

Contact: Douglas McClemont, Editor-in-Chief.

Desc: Magazine for adult gay males. *Type:* Periodical.

Human Rights Campaign

919 18th St. NW, No. 800   Ph: (202)628-4160
Washington, DC 20006   Fax: (202)347-5323
E-mail: hrc@hrc.org
URL: http://www.hrc.org

Contact: Elizabeth Birch, Dir.

Desc: Purpose is to lobby Congress: to prevent enactment of national legislation adversely affecting the civil rights of gay and lesbian individuals and people living with AIDS/HIV; to encourage funding for AIDS education, patient care, and research; to support legislation favorable to gays, lesbians, and AIDS patients. Directs messages to senators and representatives prior to legislative action on gay/lesbian, AIDS or choice issues; organizes a support network on the state, congressional district, and local levels; maintains a congressional alert system to inform local leaders and organizations about legislative developments. *Type:* Association.

Just for the Record

Just for the Record

1824 E. English St.   Ph: (316)264-4889
Wichita, KS 67211-1918
E-mail: jftr@valdalewis.com

Contact: Valda Lewis, Editor, vlewis@valdlewis.com.

Desc: Covers issues and events of interest to the gay and lesbian community, such as AIDS, alcohol/drug abuse, equality legislation, arts, and fellowship. Recurring features include a calendar of events. *Type:* Newsletter.

Lambda Legal Defense and Education Fund

120 Wall St., Ste. 1500   Ph: (212)809-8585
New York, NY 10005   Fax: (212)809-0055
E-mail: lambda@lambdalegal.org
URL: http://www.lambdalegal.org

Contact: Kevin M. Cathcart, Contact.

Desc: Purpose is to defend the civil rights of gay persons and people with AIDS in areas such as employment, housing, education, child custody, and the delivery of medical and social services. Engages in test case litigation as counsel or cocounsel; files briefs as "a friend of the court" to present statistical and educational information and to help inform the court of the needs of gay men and lesbians and people with AIDS. Provides resources and assistance to attorneys working on behalf of gay clients. *Type:* Association.

The Lesbian News

The Lesbian News

PO Box 55   Ph: (310)787-8658
Torrance, CA 90507   Free: 800-458-9888
    Fax: (310)787-1965
E-mail: theln@earthlink.net.

URL: http://www.lesbiannews.com.

Contact: Ella Matthes, Publisher; Claudia Piras, Editor, (562)438-4444, fax: (562)439-3375; Claudia Piras, Advertising Dir.

Desc: Magazine of lesbian and gay-oriented articles, features, and cartoons. *Alt. Contact:* PO Box 55, Torrance, CA 90507. *Type:* Periodical.

Mandate Magazine

MMG, Inc.

462 Broadway, Ste. 4000   Ph: (212)966-8400
New York, NY 10013   Free: 888-664-7827
    Fax: (212)966-9366

E-mail: malemags@aol.com.

Contact: Douglas McClemont, Editor-in-Chief.

Desc: Magazine for adult gay males. *Type:* Periodical.

MEN

SL, Inc.

PO Box 4356   Ph: (323)468-1919
Los Angeles, CA 90078-4356   Fax: (323)957-9219
E-mail: info@men-to-men.com

Contact: Austin Foxxe, Editor-in-Chief, afoxxe@men-to-men.com.

Desc: Magazine featuring gay, male erotica. *Type:* Periodical.

National Gay and Lesbian Task Force

2320 17th St. NW   Ph: (202)332-6483
Washington, DC 20009   Fax: (202)332-0207

Contact: Kerry Lobel, Dir.

Desc: Dedicated to the elimination of prejudice against persons based on their sexual orientation. Lobbies U.S. Congress; organizes on the "grass roots" level; demonstrates and engages in direct action for gay freedom and full civil rights. *Type:* Association.

National Gay Youth Network

PO Box 846
San Francisco, CA 94101-0846

Contact: M. Nulty, Exec. Officer.

Desc: Gay youth support groups, gay student unions, and their sponsors; other interested groups. Serves as a networking resource for the exchange of information among members. Conducts research and educational programs; offers technical assistance. *Type:* Association.

Out Magazine

The Soho Building

110 Greene St., Ste. 600   Ph: (212)334-9119
New York, NY 10012-3836   Free: 800-792-2760
    Fax: (212)334-9227

E-mail: outadv@aol.com.

Contact: James Collard, Editor-in-Chief; Henry Scott, President; Louis M. Fabrizio, Publisher.

Desc: Consumer magazine for gay men and lesbians. Features articles on culture, people, and current issues of concern to the gay community. *Type:* Periodical.

Parents, Families, and Friends of Lesbians and Gays

1101 14th St. NW, Ste. 1030   Ph: (202)638-4200
Washington, DC 20005   Fax: (202)638-0243
E-mail: info@pflag.org
URL: http://www.pflag.org

Desc: Promotes the health and well-being of gay, lesbian, bisexual, and transgendered persons and their family and friends. Works to educate the public, end discrimination, and secure equal civil rights. Offers support, education, and advocacy. *Type:* Association.

Playguy Magazine

MMG, Inc.

462 Broadway, Ste. 4000   Ph: (212)966-8400
New York, NY 10013   Free: 888-664-7827
    Fax: (212)966-9366

E-mail: malemags@aol.com.

Contact: Douglas McClemont, Editor-in-Chief.

Desc: Magazine for adult gay males. *Type:* Periodical.

Queer Nation

Box 34773
Washington, DC 20043

Desc: Dedicated to the "subversion of heterosexism and homophobia in all of its various cultural, political, and economic manifestations." Uses nonviolent actions to "celebrate and flaunt sexual diversity." *Type:* Association.

United Lesbian and Gay Christian Scientists

1200 Laurel Ave., Ste. 105   Ph: (323)654-4867
West Hollywood, CA 90046-
    5115

Contact: Pastor John W. Vondouris, Founder.

Desc: Gay and lesbian Christian Scientists. Works to "stimulate confrontation with the church policy of censorship," to challenge the church to publish diverse opinions on controversial topics, and to try to help overcome stereotypes that incite anger and hatred against homosexuals. *Type:* Association.

Universal Fellowship of Metropolitan Community Churches

8704 Santa Monica Blvd., 2nd   Ph: (310)360-8640
Fl.   Fax: (310)360-8680
Los Angeles, CA 90069-4548
E-mail: ufmcchq@aol.com
URL: http://www.ufmcc.com

Contact: Rev. Troy D. Perry, Moderator.

Desc: Christian group ministering to primarily gay/lesbian communities in 15 countries through worship services and social action. Maintains Board of Global Outreach. Conducts research and educational programs. *Type:* Association.

Genealogy

Allison Family Association

c/o Sandy Allison   Ph: (314)341-3549
10095 County Rd. 5120   Fax: (314)364-5310
Rolla, MO 65401
E-mail: sandy@rollenet.org

Contact: Sandy Allison, Pres.

Desc: Individuals with the surname Allison; interested members of other family lines. Conducts genealogical research; sponsors history seminars. Provides indexing service; operates speakers' bureau; compiles statistics. *Type:* Association.

American Heritage

American Heritage

60 5th Ave.   Ph: (212)206-5500
New York, NY 10011-8882   Fax: (212)620-2332
E-mail: mail@americanheritage.com
URL: http://www.americanheritage.com.

Contact: Richard F. Snow, Editor; Edward Z. Hughes, Publisher.

Desc: Magazine on the political, cultural, and social aspects of American history. *Type:* Periodical.

Asian American Genealogical Sourcebook

Gale Group Inc.
27500 Drake Rd.   Ph: (248)699-4253
Farmington Hills, MI 48331-   Free: 800-877-GALE
  3535   Fax: (248)699-8070
E-mail: galeord@galegroup.com
URL: http://www.galegroup.com.
Contact: Paula K. Byers, Editor.
Desc: Information sources on Asian American genealogy.
Type: Directory.

Biography and Genealogy Master Index

Gale Group Inc.
27500 Drake Rd.   Ph: (248)699-4253
Farmington Hills, MI 48331-   Free: 800-877-GALE
  3535   Fax: (248)699-8070
E-mail: galeord@galegroup.com
URL: http://www.galegroup.com.; http://galenet.gale.
com; http://www.gale.com.
Contact: Frank Castronova, Editor.
Desc: BGMI and its updates provide consolidated indexes
that indicate whether a biographical sketch being sought
is contained in one or more of about 3,000 volumes and
editions of more than 1,000 biographical dictionaries and
who's who listing contemporary and historical personalities; the indexes contain more than 12 million citations.
Publications indexed include "Who's Who in America,"
the Marquis "Who's Who" regional publications, "American Men and Women of Science," "Standard & Poor's
Register of Corporations, Directors, and Executives," and
other standard biographical reference works. *Type:* Directory.

Biography Master Index

The Gale Group
27500 Drake Rd.   Ph: (248)699-4253
Farmington Hills, MI 48331-
  3535
URL: http://www.galegroup.com
Contact: Customer Service. Toll-free: 800-877-GALE.
Desc: Contains more than 10.6 million citations to biographical information appearing in more than 2300 editions and volumes of more than 700 source publications,
including English-language general and geographical
Who's Who-type publications, major biographical dictionaries, handbooks, and directories. Covers more than 4
million current and historical persons. *Available:* The Dialog Corporation, DIALOG; The Gale Group, GaleNet.
Type: Database.

British Heritage

Cowles Enthusiast Media
4 High Ridge Park   Ph: (203)322-2400
Stamford, CT 06905   Fax: (203)322-1966
Contact: Gail Huganir, Editor and Publisher; Suzanne
Kradel, Editor.
Desc: Magazine covering travel, history, profiles, antiques,
food, and cultural heritage in England, Scotland, Ireland,
and Wales. *Alt. Contact:* PO Box 8200, Harrisburg, PA
17105-8200; telephone: (717)657-9555; fax: (717)657-
9552. *Type:* Periodical.

Clan Shaw Society

3031 Appoxmattox Ave. Apt.
  102
Olney, MD 20832-1498
Contact: Mr. Meredith L. Shaw, Pres.
Desc: Persons bearing the surname Shaw and/or descen-
dants of a Shaw or one of the septs of the clan, including
relationships by marriage. The septs of Clan Shaw include:
Ayson (New Zealand), Adamson, Esson, MacAy,
MacHay, Sheach, Shiach, Sheath, Seith, Seth, Scaith,
Skaith, and Shay, with variant spellings of each. (Clan

Shaw is based principally on the Scottish Clan Shaw heritage, but welcomes all Shaws regardless of believed national origin.). Seeks to provide opportunities for
communication between and socializing among members,
to further genealogical research on the Shaw lineage, and
to bring credit to Clan Shaw and the family name. *Type:*
Association.

Family History Department of the Church of Jesus Christ of Latter-Day Saints

50 E. North Temple   Ph: (801)240-2331
Salt Lake City, UT 84150   Fax: (801)240-5551
E-mail: fhl@ldschurch.org
URL: http://www.lds.org
Contact: Richard E. Turley, Jr., Mng. Dir.
Desc: A department of the Church of Jesus Christ of Lat-
ter-day Saints Promotes local and family history (genea-
logical) research; microfilms and preserves genealogical
data, genealogical researchers. Maintains 3000 family his-
tory centers in 64 countries. *Type:* Association.

Genealogical Computing

Ancestry, Inc.
PO Box 990   Ph: (801)426-3500
Orem, UT 84057   Free: 800-262-3787
                                   Fax: (801)426-3501
E-mail: support@ancestry-inc.com; gceditor@ancestry-
inc.com.
URL: http://www.ancestry.com.
Contact: Matthew & April Helm, Editor.
Desc: Focuses on the uses of personal computers for genea-
logical records management. Reviews and discusses the ap-
plications of various computer software and offers how-to
articles and tips from users. *Type:* Newsletter.

Genealogical Computing

Ancestry, Inc.
PO Box 990   Ph: (801)426-3500
Orem, UT 84057   Free: 800-262-3787
                                   Fax: (801)426-3501
E-mail: support@ancestry-inc.com
Contact: Matthew Helm, Editor, gceditor@ancestry.com;
April Lelsh-Helm, Senior Editor.
Desc: Genealogical computer databases, bulletin boards,
and interest groups in the United States, Australia, and
Great Britain. *Type:* Directory.

General Society of Mayflower Descendants

PO Box 3297   Ph: (508)746-3188
Plymouth, MA 02361   Fax: (508)746-2488
Contact: Caroline L. Kardell, Historian Gen.
Desc: Descendants of passengers of the Mayflower, the ves-
sel that transported the Pilgrims from England to Plym-
outh, MA in 1620. Conducts research into descendants
of the Mayflower Pilgrims through the fifth generation.
Type: Association.

Harden - Hardin - Harding Family Association

2500 Winningham Rd.   Ph: (804)645-8595
Crewe, VA 23930
E-mail: oranhj@nottwayez.net
Contact: James Oran Harding, Contact.
Desc: Individuals with the surname Harden and its variant
spellings; other members of the Harden family. Promotes
study of family history and genealogy. *Type:* Association.

International Society Daughters of Utah Pioneers

300 N. Main St.   Ph: (801)538-1050
Salt Lake City, UT 84103-1699   Fax: (801)535-1119
Contact: Mary A. Johnson, Pres.
Desc: Descendants of Utah pioneers. *Type:* Association.

Jacob Horning Family Organization

1665 Hartland Woods Dr.   Ph: (810)632-5763
Howell, MI 48843-9044   Fax: (810)632-5427
Contact: Kathleen Horning, Contact.
Desc: Maintains genealogical records tracing all Horning
family members back to Germany. *Type:* Association.

John More Association

9831 Sidehill Rd.   Ph: (814)725-4915
North East, PA 16428
E-mail: jmaprez@erie.net
Contact: Eric More Marshall, Pres.
Desc: Direct descendants and spouses of Betty Taylor
More (1738-1823), and John More (1745-1840). Works
to preserve genealogical records of the More family and
perpetuate the family ties. *Type:* Association.

Lillard Family Association

1669 Mountain View Rd.   Ph: (423)338-5777
Benton, TN 37307   Fax: (423)338-0332
E-mail: rlill55941@wingnet.net
Contact: Ralph Emerson Lillard, Sec.-Treas.
Desc: Members of the Lillard and related families. Pro-
motes study of Lillard family history and genealogy; seeks
to identify and unite Lillard family members. *Type:* Associ-
ation.

Medical University of South Carolina

General Clinical Research Center

171 Ashley Ave.   Ph: (803)792-3256
Charleston, SC 29425   Fax: (803)792-2601
E-mail: keyl@musc.edu
URL: http://www.gcrc.musc.edu
Contact: Dr. L. Lyndon Key, Jr., Prog.Dir.
Desc: Bone and mineral metabolism, cardiology, diabetes,
endocrinology, gastroenterology, hypertension, nutrition,
obstetrics and gynecology, oncology, hematology, phar-
macology, pulmonary medicine, and rheumatology and
immunology. Provides medical scientists with the oppor-
tunity for clinical research in all aspects of biomedicine.
Type: Research center.

The Mountain Institute

Main & Dogwood Sts.   Ph: (304)358-2401
PO Box 907   Fax: (304)358-2400
Franklin, WV 26807
Contact: Dr. Jane Pratt, Pres. and CEO.
Desc: Educational and scientific organization dedicated to
advancing mountain cultures and preserving mountain
environments. *Type:* Association.

National Genealogical Society

4527 17th St. N.   Ph: (703)525-0050
Arlington, VA 22207-2399   Free: 800-473-0060
                                   Fax: (703)525-0052
E-mail: ngs@ngsgenealogy.org
URL: http://www.ngsgenealogy.org
Contact: Francis Shane, Exec.Dir.
Desc: Individuals, families, societies and organizations.
Promotes genealogical research and education; stimulates
and fosters preservation and publication of records of ge-
nealogical interest including national, state, county, town-
ship, city, town, church, cemetery, Bible, and family
records. *Type:* Association.

National Society Colonial Dames XVII Century

1300 New Hampshire Ave. NW   Ph: (202)293-1700
Washington, DC 20036-1595   Fax: (202)466-6099
Contact: Mrs. Dougas Swanson, Pres.Gen.
Desc: American women who are lineal descendants of per-
sons who lived and served prior to 1701 in one of the
Original Colonies in the geographical area of the present
United States of America. *Type:* Association.

National Society, Daughters of the American Colonists

2205 Massachusetts Ave. NW Ph: (202)667-3076
Washington, DC 20008
Contact: Mrs. Harold N. Ottaway, Pres.
Desc: Women descended from men and women who gave civil or military service to the Colonies prior to the Revolutionary War. *Type:* Association.

National Society of New England Women

Desc: Patriotic, educational, and charitable society of individuals descended from ancestors born in New England prior to 1789. Sponsors student loan funds. *Type:* Association.

Native Daughters of the Golden West

543 Baker St. Ph: (415)563-9091
San Francisco, CA 94117-1405 Fax: (415)563-4230
Contact: Tamara Malberg, Exec.Sec.
Desc: Native born Californian women. Works to promote the history of the State of California, venerate California pioneers, promote child welfare programs, assist in marking and restoring historic landmarks, and participate in civic affairs. Presents annual scholarship. *Type:* Association.

Native Sons of the Golden West

414 Mason St., Ste. 300 Ph: (415)392-1223
San Francisco, CA 94102 Fax: (415)392-1224
Contact: Ronald W. Koeper, Grand Sec.
Desc: Fraternal society of men born in California. Dedicated to the preservation of the history and landmarks of California and the West. Gives financial assistance to St. *Type:* Association.

New England Historic Genealogical Society

101 Newbury St. Ph: (617)536-5740
Boston, MA 02116-3007 Free: 888-906-3447
  Fax: (617)536-7307
E-mail: membership@nehgs.org
URL: http://www.nehgs.org
Contact: Ralph J. Crandall, Exec.Dir.
Desc: Collects and preserves materials relating to family history and local history. Conducts lectures on local and national levels. *Type:* Association.

Online Genealogy Library at Ancestry.com

Ancestry.com
P.O. Box 990 Ph: (801)426-3500
Orem, UT 84059-0990 Fax: (801)426-3501
E-mail: techmail@ancestry-inc.com
URL: http://www.ancestry.com/ancestry/search.asp
Contact: database@ancestry-inc.com
Desc: Ancestry.com, which calls itself "the largest online genealogy search engine," has considerable resources available on-site to back up that claim. It makes available several free databases for the genealogy researcher, including the Social Security Death Index (updated to June 1998), the Ancestry World Tree (which contains over 7 million names), and a selection of other databases such as The Source, A Guidebook for Genealogy; WWI Civilian Draft Registrations; and 50,000 Bibliographic Sources from the Library of Congress. *Type:* Database.

The Record

National Archive and Records Administration
National Archive at College Park
8601 Adelphi Rd. Ph: (301)713-6000
College Park, MD 20740-6001
Contact: Roger A. Bruns, Editor.
Desc: Describes the activities and issues surrounding the National Archive and Records Administration, and serves to promote discussion and dialogue among its constituents. Provides information on preservations, Archive issues, the electronic documentary highway, teaching approaches, and family and genealogical history. *Type:* Newsletter.

Sons of Confederate Veterans

PO Box 59 Ph: (615)380-1844
Columbia, TN 38401 Free: 800-697-6884
  Fax: (615)381-6712
E-mail: exedir@scv.org
URL: http://www.scv.org
Contact: Maitland O. Westbrook, III, Exec.Dir.
Desc: Lineal and collateral descendants of Confederate Civil War veterans. *Type:* Association.

United Daughters of the Confederacy

328 N Blvd. Ph: (804)355-1636
Richmond, VA 23220-4057 Fax: (804)359-1325
Contact: Ms. Marion Giannasi, Exec.Sec.
Desc: Women descendants of Confederate veterans of the Civil War. *Type:* Association.

William Armstrong and Mary Kirk Family Organization

2421 N 750 E Ph: (801)375-4390
Provo, UT 84604
Contact: Elizabeth Fletcher Hunter, Sec.
Desc: Descendants of William Armstrong and Mary Kirk; other individuals with an interest in Armstrong and Kirk family history. Promotes study of, and interest in, Armstrong and Kirk family history and genealogy. *Type:* Association.

William Hutchinson and Jane Penman Family Organization

2421 N 750 E Ph: (801)375-4390
Provo, UT 84604
Contact: Elizabeth Fletcher Hunter, Sec.
Desc: Descendants of William Hutchinson and Jane Penman; other individuals with an interest in Hutchinson and Penman family history. Promotes study of, and interest in, Hutchinson and Penman family history and genealogy. *Type:* Association.

Genetics

Albany Medical College

Pediatric Pulmonary and Cystic Fibrosis Care, Research & Teaching Center

47 New Scotland Ave. - A112 Ph: (518)262-6880
Albany, NY 12208 Fax: (518)262-6884
E-mail: rkaslovsky@ccgateway.amc.edu
Contact: Robert Kaslovsky, MD, Dir.
Desc: Cystic fibrosis, asthma clinical studies of patients. Also performs studies on lung vascular injury. *Type:* Research center.

Alberta Children's Hospital Research Centre

1820 Richmond Rd. SW Ph: (403)229-7241
Calgary, AB, Canada T2T 5C7
Contact: Dr. R. Brent Scott, Dir.
Desc: Centre houses two research groups: the Medical Genetics Research Group which conducts research on genetic epidemiology, genetic linkage, molecular genetics, human sperm chromosome analysis, experimental mammalian teratology, developmental genetics, cytogenetics, and birth defects; and the Behavioural Research Group with programs in childhood conditions such as hyperactivity, diet and behavior, learning disorders, and stress-related disorders. Research and development of diagnostic services in biochemical genetics, cytogenetic and molecular genetics are supported through the Alberta Hereditary Diseases Program and are integrated in the Centre. *Type:* Research center.

Alberta Children's Hospital Research Centre

Medical Genetics Group

1820 Richmond Rd. SW Ph: (403)229-7373
Calgary, AB, Canada T2T 5C7 Fax: (403)229-7624
URL: http://www.ucalgary.ca/uofc/faculty/medicine/medgenetics/index.htm
Contact: Dr. Floyd Snyder, Dir.
Desc: Genetics, including mammalian developmental genetics, genetic control of meiosis, gene mapping and linkage, population genetics, genetic susceptibility to multifactorial inherited disorders such as insulin-dependent diabetes mellitus, use of recombinant DNA methods in clinical medicine, syndrome identification, congenital anomaly surveillance and epidemiology, chromosomal abnormalities in human sperm and eggs, asymmetry, metacarpophalangeal pattern profile studies, regulatory and genetic aspects of nucleotide metabolism, molecular characterization of inherited enzyme abnormalities, and MSAFP - Down Syndrome screen. *Type:* Research center.

American Society of Human Genetics

9650 Rockville Pke. Ph: (301)571-1825
Bethesda, MD 20814-3998 Fax: (301)530-7079
E-mail: society@genetics.faseb.org
URL: http://www.faseb.org/genetics
Contact: Elaine Strass, Exec.Dir.
Desc: Professional society of physicians, researchers, genetic counselors, and others interested in human genetics. *Type:* Association.

Baylor College of Medicine

Baylor DNA Diagnostic Laboratory

Department of Molecular & Ph: (713)798-6536
  Human Genetics Fax: (713)798-6584
1 Baylor Plz., Rm. T538
Houston, TX 77030
E-mail: carolynr@bcm.tmc.edu
URL: http://www.bcm.tmc.edu/medgen/dna-index.html
Contact: C. Sue Richards, PhD, Dir.
Desc: DNA-based testing for diagnosis, including carrier detection, prenatal diagnosis of more than 15 genetic diseases, densitometric detection of deletion and duplication mutations, estimations of carrier risk for cystic fibrosis, and rapid diagnosis of Duchenne muscular dystrophy with the multiplex amplication assay. *Type:* Research center.

Baylor College of Medicine

Department of Molecular and Human Genetics

1 Baylor Plz., Rm. 904E Ph: (713)798-6522
Houston, TX 77030 Fax: (713)798-6521
E-mail: abeaudet@bcm.tmc.edu
URL: http://ginger.bcm.tmc.edu:8088/
Contact: Dr. Arthur L. Beaudet, Dir.
Desc: Basic research in genetics includes determination of the molecular organization of the HPRT gene, gene replacement therapy, gene expression, structure of human chromosome, molecular studies of cystic fibrosis, gene mapping, glycerol kinase deficiency, cell protein synthesis, recombinant DNA techniques, teratology, dysmorphology, clinical cytogenetics, somatic gene transfer, human lipid storage diseases, molecular biology of immune development and human immunodeficiencies, DNA repair and replication, mechanisms of regulation and expression of liver specific genes, molecular genetics of heritable eye diseases, prenatal diagnosis of congenital malformations and in utero therapy of these lesions, and characterization of families of transgenic mice that show mutant phenotypes. Also coordinates research and patient services in the field of molecular genetics. *Type:* Research center.

Baylor College of Medicine

Kleberg Cytogenetic Laboratory

1 Baylor Plz., Rm 15E Ph: (713)798-4984
Houston, TX 77030 Fax: (713)798-3157
E-mail: kcl@bcm.tmc.edu
URL: http://www.bcm.tmc.edu/kcl/
Contact: Lisa Shaffer, PhD, Dir.

Desc: High-resolution chromosome analysis and development of molecular diagnostic methods for cytogenetic disorders and chromosomal studies. *Type:* Research center.

Boston University

Center for Human Genetics

715 Albany St. Ph: (617)638-7083
Boston, MA 02118-2394 Fax: (617)638-7092
E-mail: amilunsk@bu.edu
URL: http://www.med-info.bu.edu/dna-labs.htm
Contact: Aubrey Milunsky, MD, Dir.

Desc: Routine and specialized chromosome studies, prenatal diagnosis of genetic disorders, molecular genetic (DNA) analysis for diagnosis and carrier detection, maternal serum triple screening, biochemical genetic studies, cancer cytogenetics, paternity testing with DNA analysis, and genetic counseling and birth defects evaluation. *Type:* Research center.

Canadian Genetic Diseases Network

NCE Bldg. Ph: (604)822-7886
2125 East Mall, Rm. 348 Fax: (604)822-7945
Vancouver, BC, Canada V6T
 1Z4
Contact: Dr. Ron Woznow, Dir.

Desc: Genetic causes of diseases, including myotonic dystrophy, Huntington's disease, and Wilson's disease; genetic predisposition to cancer, including colerectal cancer, tuberculosis, and diabetes; carrier screening and mutation and distribution in populations, including cystic fibrosis, cleft palate, thalassemia, and ricketts; cost effective diagnostic testing, including retinoblastoma and alkaline phosphatase definciency; biochemical genetics and models of disease, including Huntington's disease, Tay Sachs, lipoprotein lipase deficiency, retinal myopathies, and metabolic diseases; and new therapy trials, including muscular dystrophy and DNA modification strategies. *Type:* Research center.

Case Western Reserve University

Center for Human Genetics

Univ. Hospitals of Cleveland Ph: (216)844-3936
11100 Euclid Ave., Lakeside Fax: (216)844-7497
 1500
Cleveland, OH 44106
URL: http://mediswww.meds.cwru.edu/dept/genetics/
Contact: Huntington F. Willard, PhD, Dir.

Desc: Human genetics, clinical genetics, molecular genetics, and cytogenetics. *Type:* Research center.

Case Western Reserve University

Center for Inherited Disorders of Energy Metabolism

Rainbow Babies and Childrens Ph: (216)844-1286
 Hosp. Fax: (216)844-8005
Department of Pediatrics, Rm.
 4010
11100 Euclid Ave.
Cleveland, OH 44106
E-mail: cidem@po.cwru.edu
URL: http://www.cwru.edu/CWRU/Med/CIDEM/
cidem.htm
Contact: Dr. Douglas Kerr, Dir.

Desc: Defects of human energy metabolism, focusing on diagnosis and management. Emphasis is on disorders of pyruvate fatty acid oxidation, and mitochondrial function. *Type:* Research center.

Case Western Reserve University

Cystic Fibrosis and Pediatric Pulmonary Center

Rainbow Babies and Childrens Ph: (216)844-3267
 Hospital, Rm. 3001 Fax: (216)844-5916
11100 Euclid Ave.
Cleveland, OH 44106
Contact: Dr. Pamela B. Davis, Dir.

Desc: Cystic fibrosis and pulmonary physiology in children, including basic and clinical studies on evolution and pathology of pulmonary lesion in cystic fibrosis, abnormal mucous secretions of patients with cystic fibrosis, developmental biology of the lung, pulmonary physiology, treatment of chronic obstructive pulmonary disease, intracellular signalling, electrolyte transport and membrane permeability of intestinal, sweat, and respiratory epithelial and individual cells and membrane biopotentials, gene therapy of pulmonary diseases, and inflammation in the cystic fibrosis lung. Asthma studies include basic cell biology of airways and studies of therapeutic regimens for safety and efficacy. *Type:* Research center.

Center for Human Genetics

PO Box 770 Ph: (207)288-5815
Bar Harbor, ME 04609-0770
Contact: Melba Wilson, Dir.

Desc: Epidemiological and laboratory studies in human genetics, including studies on retinitis pigmentosa, hemochromatosis, hemophilia, Down's syndrome, and cystic fibrosis. *Type:* Research center.

Center for the Improvement of Human Functioning International, Inc.

Research Division

3100 N. Hillside Ph: (316)682-3100
Wichita, KS 67219 Fax: (316)682-5054
E-mail: riordan@southwind.net
URL: http://www.brightspot.org
Contact: Hugh Riordan, MD, Dir.

Desc: Human genetic variability and its effects on body chemistry, health and disease, and diagnosis and treatment, especially cancer. Also investigates the measurement of naturally occurring low-energy emission from the human body and effects of extracorporeal subtle energies. *Type:* Research center.

Children's Hospital

Cystic Fibrosis Research Center

3705 5th Ave. Ph: (412)692-5630
Pittsburgh, PA 15213 Fax: (412)692-6645
Contact: David M. Orenstein, MD, Dir.

Desc: Cystic fibrosis and related diseases, including pediatric pulmonary and pediatric gastrointestinal diseases. Also studies pediatric exercise physiology, and lung cellular immunology. *Type:* Research center.

Children's Hospital

Molecular Diagnostics Lab

Pathology Dept., B120 Ph: (303)837-2725
1056 E. 19th Ave. Fax: (303)831-4112
Denver, CO 80218
E-mail: wei.qi@tchden.org
Contact: Qi Wei, PhD, Dir.

Desc: Research and testing for genetic diseases, focusing on cancer. DNA diagno stics testing services include both major and minor breakpoint cluster region (BCR) rearrangments; pre-B cell ALL t(1;19) PCR analysis; Y DNA PCR and probe analysis; retinoblastoma gene deletion and linkage analysis; Wilms' tumor gene deletion analysis; and DNA and RNA isolation for special studies. *Type:* Research center.

Children's Hospital and Medical Center

Cystic Fibrosis Research Center

4800 Sand Point Way NE Ph: (206)526-2024
PO Box C5371 Fax: (206)528-2639
Mail Stop CH18
Seattle, WA 98105
E-mail: bramsey@u.washington.edu
Contact: Bonnie W. Ramsey, Dir.

Desc: Cystic fibrosis, particularly cardiopulmonary and infectious disease-related pathophysiology, gene therapy, and evaluation of treatment of patients with cystic fibrosis and cardiorespiratory diseases, including clinically oriented research on lung mechanics, and sputum microbiology. *Type:* Research center.

Children's Memorial Hospital

Cystic Fibrosis Research Center

Northwestern University Ph: (773)880-4382
2300 Children's Plz. Fax: (773)880-6300
Box 43
Chicago, IL 60614
E-mail: smccolley@nwu.edu
URL: http://www.childmmc.edu/cmhweb/cmhdepts/
pulmonaryweb/cfweb/cfhome.htm
Contact: Dr. Susanna McColley, Dir.

Desc: Cystic fibrosis, (airways inflammation, exercise, psychosocial, outcomes research, nutrition, multicenter trials of microbiology and epidemiology). *Type:* Research center.

Colorado State University

Macromolecular Resources

Department of Biochemistry, Ph: (970)491-0424
 355 MRB Fax: (970)491-0239
Fort Collins, CO 80523
E-mail: macromolres@mmr.bmb.colostate.edu
URL: http://mmr.bmb.colostate.edu/
Contact: Carol J. Fiol, PhD, Dir.

Desc: Produces custom oligonucleotides for DNA researchers and custom peptides. Also offers mass spectrophotometry, protein sequencing and DNA sequencing services. *Type:* Research center.

Columbia University

Center for Reproductive Sciences

Columbia Presbytarian Medical Center

630 W. 168th St. Ph: (212)305-2377
New York, NY 10032 Fax: (212)305-3869
E-mail: tmm1@columbia.edu
URL: http://cmpcnet.columbia.edu/research/campus/
camp0059.html
Contact: Dr. Rogerio A. Lobo, MD, Dir.

Desc: Biology of reproduction, including neurondocrinology, male and female gametogenesis, reproductive endrocrinology, genetics, perinatology, and reproductive oncology. *Type:* Research center.

Columbia University

Molecular Genetics Laboratory

722 W. 168th St., Box 23 Ph: (212)543-5000
New York, NY 10032 Fax: (212)543-6002
E-mail: tcg1@columbia.edu
Contact: Dr. Conrad Gilliam, Dir.

Desc: Human molecular genetics, including genetic and physical mapping of human chromosomes, and the mapping and characterization of human disease genes. *Type:* Research center.

Cooperative Human Linkage Center

University of Iowa
Iowa City, IA 52242
E-mail: help@chlc.org
URL: http://www.chlc.org/
Contact: Jeff Murray, M.D., jeff-murray@umaxc.weeg.uiowa.edu.
Desc: The goal of the Cooperative Human Linkage Center is to "develop statistically rigorous, high heterozygosity genetic maps of the human genome that are greatly enriched for the presence of easy-to-use PCR-formatted microsatellite markers." The center uses this site to present genomics information as it becomes available and to link geneticists to other genomics resources. A glossary of terms used in the documents is included. *Type:* Database.

Cystic Fibrosis Center

Cedars-Sinai Med. Ctr., Rm.   Ph: (310)855-6310
   4310 North Tower   Fax: (310)657-1778
8700 Beverly Blvd.
Los Angeles, CA 90048
Contact: Gail Walenga, RN PhD, Contact.
Desc: Sputum in cystic fibrosis of the pancreas, including studies of nature of sputum and liquefaction, lysozyme content, L-forms of bacteria, and observations on new antimicrobial agents. *Type:* Research center.

Cystic Fibrosis Center

Pediatric Pulmonary Division,   Ph: (503)494-8023
   UHN 56   Fax: (503)494-8898
3181 SW Sam Jackson Park Rd.
Portland, OR 97201
E-mail: eisenbej@ohsu.edu
Contact: Jay D. Eisenberg, MD, Res.Dir.
Desc: Cystic fibrosis, including laboratory and clinical studies of molecular abnormalities in cystic fibrosis and lyses of pulmonary mucus. *Type:* Research center.

Cystic Fibrosis Foundation

6931 Arlington Rd., Ste. 200   Ph: (301)951-4422
Bethesda, MD 20814   Free: 800-344-4823
   Fax: (301)951-6378
E-mail: info@cff.org
URL: http://www.cff.org
Contact: Robert Beall, PhD, Pres./CEO.
Desc: Causes and treatment of cystic fibrosis. The Research Development Program involves a network of research centers supported by the Foundation; also supports many care centers thoughout the United States. *Type:* Research center.

Cystic Fibrosis Research Center/Pediatric Pulmonary Disease Center

1430 Tulane Ave.   Ph: (504)588-5601
Tulane University   Fax: (504)588-5490
New Orleans, LA 70112
E-mail: rbecker@tmcpop.tmc.tulane.edu
Contact: Dr. Robert C. Beckerman, Dir.
Desc: Cystic fibrosis, bronchopulmonary dysplasia, apnea, sleep disordered breathing, SIDS, and other acute and chronic pulmonary diseases, including basic and clinical studies on their causes and treatment, conducted in the three medical schools. *Type:* Research center.

Dalhousie University

Atlantic Research Centre

5849 University Ave., Rm.   Ph: (902)494-6491
   C-304   Fax: (902)494-1394
Halifax, NS, Canada B3H 4H7
E-mail: h.cook@dal.ca
URL: http://www.mcms.dal.ca/ticu/arc/archome.html
Contact: Dr. Harold W. Cook, Dir.
Desc: Biochemistry and genetics, including human cytogenetics, human inherited metabolic diseases, epidemiological studies of mental retardation, biochemistry and metabolism in the developing brain, and lipid second messengers, signal transduction, and membrane metabolism in normal and diseased human cells in culture. Provides special biomedical services relating to the causes and prevention of mental handicap. *Type:* Research center.

Duke University

Cystic Fibrosis Research Center

PO Box 2994   Ph: (252)684-3364
Durham, NC 27710   Fax: (252)684-2292
Contact: Marc Majure, MD, Dir.
Desc: Cystic fibrosis and related respiratory diseases of children. *Type:* Research center.

Eleanor Roosevelt Institute

1899 Gaylord St.   Ph: (303)333-4515
Denver, CO 80206   Fax: (303)333-8423
E-mail: davepatt@eri.uchsc.edu
URL: http://www-eri.uchsc.edu
Contact: David Patterson, PhD, Pres.
Desc: Biochemistry and mammalian genetics. Investigates human and other mammalian cell systems, biosynthetic pathways of purines and pyrimidines, biochemical structure and function of cell surface membranes, cytogenetics, cancer genetics, genetic biochemistry, mutagenesis, carcinogenesis, down syndrome, Lou Gehrig's disease (ALS), and arthritis. *Type:* Research center.

Emory University

Cystic Fibrosis Care, Teaching and Research Center

1547 Clifton Rd. NE   Ph: (404)727-5728
Atlanta, GA 30322   Fax: (404)727-4828
E-mail: dcaplan@emory.edu
Contact: Dr. Daniel B. Caplan, Dir.
Desc: Cystic fibrosis and respiratory and gastrointestinal diseases of children. *Type:* Research center.

GenBank®

U.S. National Library of Medicine (NLM)
National Center for Biotechnology Information (NCBI)
8600 Rockville Pike   Ph: (301)496-2475
Bldg.38A, Room 8N-803
Bethesda, MD 20894
E-mail: info@ncbi.nlm.nih.gov
Contact: User Services, GenBank, info@ncbi.nlm.nih.gov.
Desc: Contains descriptions of DNA and RNA sequences with 25 or more nucleotide bases. Includes more than 2,209,00 reported sequences, totalling more than 1.5 million bases. *Available:* STN International; U.S. National Library of Medicine (NLM), National Center for Biotechnology Information (NCBI). *Type:* Database.

GENE-TOX

U.S. National Library of Medicine (NLM)
Specialized Information Services Division
8600 Rockville Pike   Ph: (301)496-6531
Bethesda, MD 20894
E-mail: toxmail@toxnetmail.nlm.nih.gov
URL: http://toxnet.nlm.nih.gov
Desc: Contains genetic toxicology (mutagenicity) data on about 3,000 chemicals. Data are extracted from reviews by work panels of experts knowledgeable about specific test systems and references select papers from the open scientific literature. *Available:* U.S. National Library of Medicine (NLM), Toxicology Information Program (TIP). *Type:* Database.

Genetic Technology Alert

Technical Insights
John Wiley and Sons, Inc.
32 N. Dean St.   Ph: (201)568-4744
Englewood, NJ 07631
E-mail: TIInf@wiley.com
URL: http://www.wiley.comm/technicalinsights
Contact: Lyn Schmidt, Sales & Marketing Manager, gt-nainfo@insights.com.
Desc: Contains the complete text of Genetic Technology Alert, a monthly newsletter covering commercial applications in the chemical, energy, food, and pharmaceutical industries of products resulting from genetic engineering. Includes market forecasts, business news from leading biotechnology firms, announcements of investment opportunities, reports on research activities at universities and research institutions, and reports of new products. *Available:* CompuServe Information Service. *Type:* Database.

Genetics Abstracts

Cambridge Scientific Abstracts (CSA)
7200 Wisconsin Ave., Ste. 601   Ph: (301)961-6700
Bethesda, MD 20814-4823
E-mail: sales@csa.com
URL: http://www.csa.com
Contact: Anthea Gotto, Manager, Electronic Services, (301)961-6795, fax: (301)961-6720, anthea@csa.com.
Desc: Contains more than 200,000 citations, with abstracts, to the worldwide literature on genetics. Sources include specialist literature such as journals, books, conference proceedings, and reports. *Available:* Cambridge Scientific Abstracts (CSA). *Type:* Database.

Human Genome Abstracts

Cambridge Scientific Abstracts (CSA)
7200 Wisconsin Ave., Ste. 601   Ph: (301)961-6700
Bethesda, MD 20814-4823
E-mail: sales@csa.com
URL: http://www.csa.com
Desc: Contains more than 15,000 citations, with abstracts, to international periodical and other literature covering human genomes (chromosomes with the genes they contain). Sources include specialist literature such as journals, books, conference proceedings, and reports. *Type:* Database.

Indiana University Bloomington

Howard Hughes Medical Institute Research Laboratory

Jordan Bldg., Rm. A507   Ph: (812)855-3033
Bloomington, IN 47405
URL: http://www.indiana.edu/~rugs/ctrdir/hhmirl.html
Contact: Thomas C. Kaufman, Dir.
Desc: Understanding the genetic basis of the developmental program of higher organisms. Efforts focus on the homeotic genes that play a crucial role in the development of the fruit fly Drosphilia melanogaster. *Type:* Research center.

Indiana University-Purdue University at Indianapolis

Cystic Fibrosis and Pediatric Pulmonary Clinic

702 Barnhill Dr., Rm. 2750   Ph: (317)274-3434
Indianapolis, IN 46202-5225   Fax: (317)274-9773
E-mail: heigen@iupui.edu
Contact: Howard Eigen, MD, Dir.
Desc: Cystic fibrosis and chronic lung diseases, including clinical studies of pediatric pulmonary, gastrointestinal, genetic problems, and lung inflammation. *Type:* Research center.

International Center for Skeletal Dysplasia

St. Joseph Med. Ctr.   Ph: (410)337-1250
7620 York Rd.   Fax: (410)337-1042
Towson, MD 21204

Contact: Dr. Steven Kopits, Dir.

Desc: Skeletal dysplasia, particularly dwarfism. Studies include metatropic dysplasia, a rare form of dwarfism identified in 1966. *Type:* Research center.

Jackson Laboratory

600 Main St.   Ph: (207)288-6000
Bar Harbor, ME 04609-1500   Free: 800-422-6423
    Fax: (207)288-6076
E-mail: pubinfo@jax.org
URL: http://www.jax.org

Contact: Kenneth Paigen, PhD, Dir.

Desc: Formal genetics, molecular genetics, developmental genetics, physiological genetics, immunology, cell biology, and biochemistry as related to cancer, diabetes, anemias, other human diseases, as well as normal growth and development. Annually produces 2,000,000 genetically standardized mutant and inbred mice strains for its own research staff and research workers throughout the world. *Type:* Research center.

Jeanette Kennelly Kroch Center for Twin Studies

Northwestern Memorial   Ph: (312)926-7519
    Hospital   Fax: (312)926-0367
Prentice Pavilion
333 E. Superior St., Rm. 410
Chicago, IL 60611

Contact: Alan M. Peaceman, MD, Dir.

Desc: Multiple births. Conducts ultrasound and genetic research for the early detection of identical or fraternal twins; longitudinal ultrasound studies to determine normal growth patterns in multiple-birth pregnancies; clinical studies of methods to prevent premature labor and delivery, which result in low-birthweight twins; and studies related to specific aspects of twin development, such as speech patterns. *Type:* Research center.

Johns Hopkins University

Adolescent Idiopathic Scoliosis Laboratory

Ross Bldg., Rm. 229   Ph: (410)614-3717
720 Rutland Ave.   Fax: (410)502-6414
Baltimore, MD 21205
E-mail: dschwab@welchlink.welch.jhu.edu
URL: http://www.med.jhu.edu/ais/

Contact: Dr. Nancy H. Miller, Contact.

Desc: Genetics of adolescent idiopathic scoliosis, a condition characterized by a lateral curvature of the spine. *Type:* Research center.

Johns Hopkins University

Center for Hereditary Eye Diseases

Wilmer Ophthalmological   Ph: (410)955-5214
    Institute   Fax: (410)614-4363
Maumenee Bldg., Rm. 517
600 N. Wolfe St.
Baltimore, MD 21287-9237
E-mail: jhched@jhmi.edu

Contact: Dr. Irene Hussels Maumenee, Dir.

Desc: Studies of molecular mechanisms underlying genetic eye diseases. Emphasis on diagnosis and management of common as well as rare genetic eye diseases, and the prevention of vision loss through early medical or surgical intervention. *Type:* Research center.

Johns Hopkins University

Cystic Fibrosis Research Center

202 Physiology   Ph: (410)955-7166
725 N. Wolfe St.   Fax: (410)955-0461
Baltimore, MD 21205
E-mail: wguggino@orion.bs.jhmi.edu

Contact: Dr. William B. Guggino, Dir.

Desc: Cystic fibrosis and related fields, including epithelial cell transport, molecular genetics, respiratory cell biology, and biochemistry. *Type:* Research center.

Laval University

Medical Research Centre

Human Genetics Unit

2705, boulevard Laurier   Ph: (418)654-2103
Ste. Foy, PQ, Canada G1V 4G2   Fax: (418)654-2207
E-mail: jackpuymirat@crchul.ulaval.ca

Contact: Jack Puymirat, MD, Dir.

Desc: Molecular mechanisms controlling genetic expression; thyroid hormones and central nervous system development; molecular genetics of myotonic dystrophy; implication of cytoskeletal and nucleoskeletal proteins in morphonogenetic and differentiation processes; molecular genetics of Charcot-Marie-Tooth disease; control of cell cycle; gene therapy; myoblasts transplantation for Duchenne's disease, Myotonia congenita. *Type:* Research center.

Lawrence Berkeley National Laboratory

Life Sciences Division

1 Cyclotron Rd.   Ph: (510)486-4365
Mail Stop 83-101   Fax: (510)486-5586
Berkeley, CA 94720
E-mail: mjbissell@lbl.gov
URL: http://www.lbl.gov/lifesciences/

Contact: Mina J. Bissell, PhD, Div.Dir.

Desc: Human Genome Project; mutagenesis and carcinogenesis, emphasizing DNA repair and recombination; mechanisms of tissue-specific gene expression, focusing on mammary gland cells and hemopoiesis; structural biology, concentrating on the three-dimensional structure of integral membrane proteins; and radiobiology, stressing molecular and cellular mechanisms and the risks associated with radiation as an environmental hazard. *Type:* Research center.

Leland Stanford Junior University

Stanford Human Genome Center

Department of Genetics   Ph: (650)812-1915
855 California Ave.   Fax: (650)812-1916
Palo Alto, CA 94304-5120
E-mail: webmaster@www-shgc.stanford.edu
URL: http://shgc.stanford.eud/

Contact: Construction of high resolution Radiation Hybrid maps of the human genome and the sequencing of large, contiguous genomic relations. *Type:* Research center.

Louisiana State University in Shreveport

Genetics Section of Pediatrics

Med. Ctr.   Ph: (318)675-6088
1501 Kings Hwy.   Fax: (318)675-4669
Shreveport, LA 71130

Contact: T.F. Thurmon, MD, Dir.

Desc: Clinical applications of genetics, biochemical genetics, and cytogenetics. Studies include chromatographic diagnostic techniques, heredity of dysmorphic syndromes, and chromosome aberrations in cancer. *Type:* Research center.

McGill University

Laboratory of Molecular Genetics

3801 University St., Rm. 651   Ph: (514)398-1979
Montreal, PQ, Canada H3A   Fax: (514)398-1509
    2B4
E-mail: cxph@music.mcgill.ca

Contact: Dr. Kenneth Hastings, Dir.

Desc: Biological significance and molecular mechanisms of proliferation-related gene regulation, including cDNA clones corresponding to mRNAs, which are more abundant in rapidly proliferating cells (including myoblasts and fibroblasts) than in quiescent or postmitotic cells. The chief method of analysis has been through the use of DNA sequencing. *Type:* Research center.

McGill University

Montreal Neurological Institute

Laboratory of Muscle Biochemistry

3801 University St., Rm. 665   Ph: (514)398-8502
Montreal, PQ, Canada H3A   Fax: (514)398-1509
    2B4
E-mail: cxhp@musica.mcgill.ca

Contact: Dr. Paul Holland, Dir.

Desc: Collagen binding proteins of muscle cells in culture, the effect of contractile activity of cultured muscle on the biosynthesis of proteins of the sarcoplasmic reticulum, and the role of different types of glycoproteins in the process of myoblast fusion. *Type:* Research center.

McMaster University

Regional Cytogenetics Laboratory

1200 Main St. W.   Ph: (905)521-5084
Hamilton, ON, Canada L8S 4J9   Fax: (905)521-2651
E-mail: carter@fhs.mcmaster.ca

Contact: Dr. Ronald F. Carter, Dir.

Desc: Human genetics and cytogenetics, etiology of chromosomal aberrations, and retroviral and ademoviral gene therapy. *Type:* Research center.

MCP Hahnemann University of the Health Sciences

Center for Gene Therapy

School of Medicine   Ph: (215)762-7284
245 N. 15 St., Mail Stop 421   Fax: (215)762-7408
Philadelphia, PA 19102-1192
E-mail: prockop@auhs.edu

Contact: Dr. Darwin J. Prockop, Dir.

Desc: Gene therapy of bone and cartilage diseases, Parkinson's Disease and brain tumors. *Type:* Research center.

MCP Hahnemann University of the Health Sciences

Institute for Human Genetics

320 E. North Ave.   Ph: (412)359-6388
Pittsburgh, PA 15212   Free: 800-520-6344
    Fax: (412)359-6488
URL: http://www.pgh.auhs.edu/genetics/brochure/au/index.html

Contact: Prof. Reed E. Pyeritz, PhD, Chm.

Desc: Mammalian genetics. *Type:* Research center.

Medical College of Wisconsin

Cystic Fibrosis Research Center

Milwaukee Children's Hosp. of   Ph: (414)266-6730
    Wisc.   Fax: (414)266-3653
Specialty Clinic
9000 W. Wisconsin
Milwaukee, WI 53226
E-mail: splaingard@mcw.edu

Contact: Dr. M. L. Splaingard, Dir.

Desc: Cystic fibrosis, chest impedance measurements, and newborn screening studies. Provides patient care as a service to referring physicians and instruction for small groups of medical students from the College. *Type:* Research center.

MetroHealth Medical Center

Department of Epidemiology and Biostatistics

Human Genetic Analysis Resource

2500 MetroHealth Dr. Ph: (216)778-3863
Cleveland, OH 44109 Fax: (216)778-3280
E-mail: rce@hal.cwru.edu
URL: http://darwin.mhmc.cwru.edu/
Contact: Robert Elston, Dir.

Desc: Identification and chromosome mapping of genes involved in common diseases that may be primarily environmentally-influenced, as well as the genes underlying rarer monogenic diseases with much smaller environmental influence. Research focuses on theoretical development of statistical methods for analysis of family data, especially to detect and identify genetic components that underlie disease susceptibility. *Type:* Research center.

Michael Fund/International Foundation for Genetic Research

500 A Garden City Dr. Ph: (412)823-6380
Pittsburgh, PA 15236 Fax: (412)373-7713
E-mail: tmf@pennet.com
URL: http://www.pennet.com/chuckdet/index.html
Contact: Ms. Randy Engel, Contact.

Desc: Down's Syndrome and related genetic disorders with a pro-life philosophy, focusing on funding, prevention, cure or reducing the effects of Down's Syndrome. Also opposes abortion of the unborn, including deliberate euthanasia of children and adults with birth defects. *Type:* Research center.

Molecular Diagnostics Laboratory

Cedars-Sinai Medical Center Ph: (310)855-7627
110 George Burns Rd. Fax: (310)652-8010
Davis, 2069
Los Angeles, CA 90048
E-mail: jkorenberg@xchg.peds.csmc.edu
URL: http://www.csmc.edu/genetics/korenberg/korenberg.html
Contact: Dr. Julie Korenberg, Contact.

Desc: DNA isolation and diagnostics, including Southern blotting, libraryscreening, subcloning, probe growth, and preparation. *Type:* Research center.

National Science Foundation

Directorate for Biological Sciences

Division of Molecular and Cellular Biosciences

Genetics Program

4201 Wilson Blvd., Rm. 655 Ph: (703)306-1439
Arlington, VA 22230 Fax: (703)306-0355
E-mail: dnasser@nsf.gov
Contact: Dr. Delill Nasser, Dir.
Desc: Genetics. *Type:* Research center.

National Science Foundation

Directorate for Biological Sciences

Division of Molecular and Cellular Biosciences

Microbial Genetics Program

4201 Wilson Blvd., Rm. 655 Ph: (703)306-1439
Arlington, VA 22230 Fax: (703)306-0355
E-mail: pharrima@nsf.gov
URL: http://www.nsf.gov
Contact: Philip D. Harriman, Prog.Dir.

Desc: Supports research focused on the organization, function, transmission, mutation, regulation, and recombination of genetic information of microorganisms. Other topics supported include gene evolution, genetics of microbial interactions with eukaryotic organisms, and genetics of microbial plasmids and viruses. *Type:* Research center.

New York University

Rusk Institute of Rehabilitation Medicine

400 E. 34th St. Ph: (212)263-6150
New York, NY 10016 Fax: (212)263-8815
Contact: Dr. Mathew Lee, Dir.

Desc: Conducts clinical and basic research on neuromuscular diseases, head trauma, stroke, and music therapy. *Type:* Research center.

North York General Hospital

North York Regional Genetics Centre

4001 Leslie St. Ph: (416)756-6345
Toronto, ON, Canada M2K Fax: (416)756-6727
1E1
E-mail: pwyaH@nygh.on.ca
Contact: Dr. Philip Wyatt, Dir.

Desc: Clinical genetics, prenatal biology, and chromosomal and metabolic diseases. *Type:* Research center.

Oregon Health Sciences University

Biochemical Genetics Laboratory

Department of Molecular and Ph: (503)494-8392
Med. Genetics Fax: (503)494-7645
3181 SW Sam Jackson Park
Rd., BH-2029
Portland, OR 97201
E-mail: gibsonm@ohsu.edu
URL: http://www.ohsu.edu/som-MedGen/bcgenlab.htm
Contact: K. Michael Gibson, PhD, Dir.

Desc: Inborn errors of metabolism and mitochondrial myopathies. *Type:* Research center.

Pope Paul VI Institute for the Study of Human Reproduction, Inc.

6901 Mercy Rd. Ph: (402)390-6600
Omaha, NE 68106-2621 Fax: (402)390-9851
URL: http://www.popepaulvi.com
Contact: Jean Packard, Contact.
Desc: Human reproduction and Down's Syndrome. *Type:* Research center.

Queen's University at Kingston

Cytogenetics and DNA Research Laboratory

Ongwanada Resource Ctr. Ph: (613)548-4417
191 Portsmouth Ave. Fax: (613)548-8135
Kingston, ON, Canada K7M
8A6
E-mail: holdenj@post.queensu.ca
Contact: Jeanette J.A. Holden, PhD, Dir.

Desc: Cytogenetics, DNA markers, linkage studies, fragile-X syndrome, X-linked mental retardation, x-linked hydrocephalus, Down's syndrome, autism, affective disorders, schizophrenia, melanoma, and chromosome instability. *Type:* Research center.

REBASE

Dr. Richard Roberts
New England Biolabs Ph: (978)927-3382
32 Tozer Road
Beverly, MA 01915
E-mail: roberts@neb.com
URL: http://www.neb.com/rebase
Contact: R.J. Roberts, (978)927-3382, fax: (978)921-1527, roberts@neb.com.

Desc: Contains descriptions of more than 3000 restriction enzymes. Includes over 218 prototypes and their isoschizomers, recognition sequence, and site of cleavage. *Available:* Dr. Richard Roberts. *Type:* Database.

Rockefeller University

Laboratory of Biochemical Genetics and Metabolism

1230 York Ave. Box 179 Ph: (212)327-7700
New York, NY 10021 Fax: (212)327-7165
E-mail: stewaco@rockvax.rockefeller.edu
URL: http://www.rockefeller.edu

Contact: Prof. Jan L. Breslow, MD, Contact.

Desc: Human genetic susceptibility to atherosclerosis, especially the molecular genetics and clincial significance of the apolipoproteins, a group of proteins that coat the lipoprotein particles and determine their metabolism. *Type:* Research center.

Rockefeller University

Laboratory of Human Genetics and Hematology

1230 York Ave. Ph: (212)327-8000
New York, NY 10021
URL: http://www.rockefeller.edu/labheads/auerbach/auerbach.html

Contact: Arleen D. Auerbach, Dir.

Desc: Fanconi anemia (FA), an autosomal recessive disorder characterized clinically by progressive pancytopenia, variable skeletal and other congenital abnormalities, predisposition to malignancy, particularly acute myelogenous leukemia (AML), prenatal diagnosis of FA, and identification of genes that cause FA. *Type:* Research center.

Rockefeller University

Starr Center for Human Genetics

1230 York Ave. Ph: (212)327-8000
New York, NY 10021
URL: http://www.rockefeller.edu/graduate/censtarr.htm

Contact: Dr. Jeffrey M. Friedman, Dir.

Desc: Genetic analysis of human disease and biology, including heart disease, obesity, diabetes, schizophrenia, and Alzheimer's disease. *Type:* Research center.

Saginaw Valley State University

Genetic Research Laboratory

7400 Bay Rd. Ph: (517)790-4358
University Center, MI 48710 Fax: (517)790-2717
E-mail: cfp@svsu.edu

Contact: Dr. Charles F. Pelzer, Hd.

Desc: Molecular genetics, emphasizing electrophoresis and Southern Blots of human DNA, isoelectric focusing of blood proteins in health and disease such as breast cancer, and biochemical genetics of red cell isozymes in the mouse. Performs restriction fragment length polymorphism (RFLP) analysis to help map human chromosone number 10 and Southern blotting to identify tumor suppressor genes. *Type:* Research center.

St. Christopher's Hospital for Children

Cystic Fibrosis Center

Erie Ave. at Front St. Ph: (215)427-4801
Philadelphia, PA 19134 Fax: (215)427-4805
E-mail: schidlow@auhs.edu

Contact: Daniel Schidlow, MD, Dir.

Desc: Cystic fibrosis and other chronic respiratory diseases, including cystic fibrosis of the pancreas in children, epidemiology of lung infections, airway injury in children, lung mechanics in infants, developmental respiratory physiology, and clinical trials for new therapies against cystic fibrosis. *Type:* Research center.

Sherbrooke University

Molecular Biology Research Centre

Departement de Microbiologie   Ph: (819)564-5321
et infectiologie   Fax: (819)564-5392
Faculte de Medecine
3001, 12e Ave. N.
Sherbrooke, PQ, Canada J1H
   5N4
E-mail: p.bourgaux@courrier.usherb.ca
Contact: P. Bourgaux, Contact.
Desc: Gene expression in vitro and in vivo, including the recombination of viral and cellular genes, alternative splicing of RNA, expression and function of transformation genes, replication of telomeres and clinical applications of PCR. *Type:* Research center.

Southwest Foundation for Biomedical Research

Molecular Genetics Laboratory

Department of Genetics   Ph: (210)674-1410
PO Box 760549   Fax: (210)670-3316
San Antonio, TX 78245-0147
Contact: James E. Hixson, Chm.
Desc: Molecular genetics of heart disease in humans and nonhuman primates. *Type:* Research center.

Stanford University

Beckman Center for Molecular and Genetic Medicine

Sch. of Med.   Ph: (650)723-7184
Stanford, CA 94305   Fax: (650)725-4951
E-mail: pberg@cmgm.stanford.edu
URL: http://www.cmgm.stanford.edu
Contact: Dr. Paul Berg, Dir.
Desc: Molecular understanding of critical biological functions and how these are affected by disease, including study of genes related to human disease, development of new diagnostic tests for known and newly recognized diseases, and development of therapies based on gene or cell replacement models. *Type:* Research center.

Stanford University

Interdepartmental Medical Genetics Program

Howard Hughes Med. Inst.   Ph: (650)725-8089
Beckman Ctr.   Fax: (650)725-8112
Stanford, CA 94305-5323
E-mail: francke@cmgm.stanford.edu
Contact: Dr. Uta Francke, Training Prog.Dir.
Desc: Molecular basis of heritable disorders, including polygenic and multi-factorial diseases, chromosome structure and function, and genome and gene mapping. Develops methods to manipulate and study large fragments of DNA and animal models and new treatment modalities of human genetic disease by homologous recombination. *Type:* Research center.

State University of New York Health Science Center at Syracuse

Robert C. Schwartz Cystic Fibrosis Center and Pediatric Pulmonary Center

750 E. Adams, 5th Fl.-Pediatrics   Ph: (315)464-6323
Syracuse, NY 13210   Fax: (315)464-6322
E-mail: anbarr@vax.cs.hscsyr.edu
Contact: Dr. Ran D. Anbar, Dir.
Desc: Cystic fibrosis, asthma, including clinical studies. *Type:* Research center.

Sudden Arrythmia Death Syndromes Foundation

508 E. South Temple 20   Ph: (801)531-0937
Salt Lake City, UT 84102-1013   Free: 800-STO-PSAD
   Fax: (801)531-0945
E-mail: sads@aros.net
URL: http://www.sads.org

Contact: Lynne Godfrey, Prg.Dir.
Desc: Seeks to save the lives of children and young adults who are genetically predisposed to sudden death by cardia arrhythmias. *Type:* Association.

Texas A&M University

Alkek Institute of Biosciences and Technology

Center for Genome Research

2121 W. Holcombe Blvd.   Ph: (713)677-7651
Houston, TX 77030-3303   Fax: (713)677-7689
E-mail: rwells@ibt.tamu.edu
URL: http://keck.tamu.edu/~wells/wellslab.html
Contact: Dr. Robert D. Wells, Dir.
Desc: Structure and biology of DNA in living cells and viruses and its role in the developmental expression of genetic information. Specific research areas include cancer and other human genetic diseases, maintenance and stability of chromosome ends, and the processing of information from DNA into functional messenger ribonucleic acid (RNA) for expression into proteins. *Type:* Research center.

Trinity University

Genetics Laboratory for Typing Nonhuman Primates

Department of Biology   Ph: (210)736-8347
715 Stadium Dr.   Fax: (210)736-7229
San Antonio, TX 78212-7200
E-mail: wstone@trinity.edu
URL: http://www.trinity.edu/nwstoneindex.htm
Contact: William H. Stone, PhD, Dir.
Desc: Genetic typing of nonhuman primates of various species. The aim is to define as many genetic markers as possible in nonhuman primates. *Type:* Research center.

United Cerebral Palsy Research and Educational Foundation

1660 L St. NW, Ste. 700   Ph: (202)776-0406
Washington, DC 20036   Free: 800-872-5827
   Fax: (202)776-0414
E-mail: ucpa@ucpa.org
URL: http://ucpa.org
Contact: Murray Goldstein, DO, Contact.
Desc: Cerebral palsy, focusing on improving the treatment, management, and functioning of persons with cerebral palsy. Also provides research grants. *Type:* Research center.

U.S. Department of Health and Human Services

Food and Drug Administration

Center for Biologics Evaluation and Research

Molecular Medical Genetics Staff

1401 Rockville Pike   Ph: (301)443-1544
Rockville, MD 20852   Fax: (301)496-7027
Contact: Gerald Marti, Actg.Chf.
Desc: Molecular medical genetics. *Type:* Research center.

U.S. Department of Health and Human Services

National Cancer Institute

Divison of Cancer Epidemiology and Genetics

Biostatistics Branch

EPN-431   Ph: (301)496-4153
Bethesda, MD 20892   Fax: (301)402-0081
Contact: Mitchell H. Gail, Chf.
Desc: Biometric and mathematical approaches to investigate the distribution, causes, and natural history of cancer. New statistical methods are developed for designing and analyzing epidemiologic, clinical, and experimental studies of cancer. *Type:* Research center.

U.S. Department of Health and Human Services

National Cancer Institute

Laboratory of Genetics

NIH Bldg. 37, Rm. 2B04   Ph: (301)496-1734
9000 Rockville Pike   Fax: (301)402-1031
Bethesda, MD 20892
Contact: Dr. Michael Potter, Chf.
Desc: Role of genes that determine susceptibility and resistance to neoplastic development and special genes and their products that are associated with the neoplastic state (oncogenes, retroviral gene products, tumor associated antigens). Past activities have involved studies of the plasma cell tumor system in mice, and research continues on the organization of immunoglobulin genes and gene families and structure-function correlations with monoclonal antibodies. *Type:* Research center.

U.S. Department of Health and Human Services

National Center for Infectious Diseases

Division of Parasitic Diseases

Entomology Branch

4770 Buford Hwy., MS F22   Ph: (770)488-4799
Chamblee, GA 30341-3724   Fax: (770)488-7794
Desc: Vector characteristics using anopheles gambiae as the primary research model; develops and uses molecular methods to describe the genetic composition of vector populations; and seeks to control vector-borne disease transmission through genetic manipulation of natural vector populations. *Type:* Research center.

U.S. Department of Health and Human Services

National Center for Research Resources

Biological Modesl and Materials Resource Program

Caenorhabditis Genetics Center

Univ. of Minnesota   Ph: (612)625-2265
250 Biological Sciences Center   Fax: (612)625-5754
1445 Gortner Ave.
St. Paul, MN 55108-1095
E-mail: stier@biosci.cbs.umn.edu
Contact: Bob Herman, Dir.
Desc: Provides genetic stocks of Caenorhabditis elegans and other Caenorhabditis species for use by investigators initiating or continuing research on this nematode. The Center also acquires new strains described in current literature and evaluates methods for permanent storage of genetic stocks. *Type:* Research center.

U.S. Department of Health and Human Services

National Heart, Lung, and Blood Institute

Molecular Hematology Branch

NIH Bldg. 10, Rm. 7D18   Ph: (301)496-5844
9000 Rockville Pike   Fax: (301)496-9985
Bethesda, MD 20892
E-mail: besafer@helix.nih.gov
Contact: Brian Safer, Actg.Chf.
Desc: Mechanism and regulation of mammalian gene expression to develop the understanding and technology necessary to carry out human gene therapy. The types of diseases being targeted are genetic cancer, viral, and cardiovascular. *Type:* Research center.

U.S. Department of Health and Human Services

National Institute of Dental Research

Division of Intramural Research

Gene Therapy and Theraptics Branch

NIH Bldg. 10, Rm. 1N113   Ph: (301)496-1363
10 Center Dr, MSC 1190   Fax: (301)402-1228
Bethesda, MD 20892-1190
Contact: Dr. Bruce J. Baum, Chf.

Desc: Oral and dental diseases. Primary efforts are directed at understanding neurotransmitter receptor regulation of events involved in salivary secretion, such as water movement, ion fluxes, and protein synthesis and processing. *Type:* Research center.

U.S. Department of Health and Human Services
National Institute of Diabetes and Digestive and Kidney Diseases
Division of Intramural Research
Genetics and Biochemistry Branch

NIH Bldg. 10, Rm. 9D15 Ph: (301)496-2710
10 Center Dr. MSC 1810 Fax: (301)496-9878
Bethesda, MD 20892-1810
Contact: Dr. R. Daniel Camerini-Otero, Chf.

Desc: Clinical, biochemical, developmental, and molecular genetics. The range of current projects covers a wide field, from the very basic (e.g., mechanisms of genetic recombination and gene conversion in mammalian cells, DNA-mediated gene transfer, the regulation of gene expression, the molecular biology of early development in itXenopus laevis/it, biosynthesis and transport of lysosomal proteins, the molecular mechanisms of endocytosis, and the biochemical and molecular bases of human genetic disorders) to the more applied (i.e., development of new diagnostic tests and carrier detection for a number of human genetic diseases and the development of new techniques for gene purification and transfer). *Type:* Research center.

U.S. Department of Health and Human Services
National Institute of Diabetes and Digestive and Kidney Diseases
Laboratory of Chemical Biology

NIH Bldg. 10, Rm. 9N307 Ph: (301)496-5408
10 Center Dr. MSC-1822 Fax: (301)402-0101
Bethesda, MD 20892-1822
E-mail: aschecht@helix.nih.gov
Contact: Dr. Alan N. Schechter, Chf.

Desc: Chemical biology, including protein chemistry; and molecular genetics, including sickle cell anemia and thassemia. Research focuses on the control of gene expression, folding of proteins, and therapy of genetic diseases. *Type:* Research center.

U.S. Department of Health and Human Services
National Institute of Environmental Health Sciences
Division of Intramural Research
Environmental Biology and Medicine Program

PO Box 12233 Ph: (919)541-3535
Research Triangle Park, NC Fax: (919)541-7593
27709
Contact: Dr. John Drake, Chf.

Desc: Mutagenesis on a subcellular level and whole animal genetics. Focuses on the mechanisms of mutation, the nature of genes and how they function, and a greater understanding of mutation events and their impacts on reproduction and development in multicellular organisms. *Type:* Research center.

U.S. Department of Health and Human Services
National Institute of General Medical Sciences
Division of Genetics and Developmental Biology

Bldg. 45, Rm. 2AS-25 Ph: (301)594-0943
45 Center Drive, MSC 6200 Fax: (301)480-2228
Bethesda, MD 20892-6200
E-mail: greenbej@nigms.nih.gov
URL: http://www.nih.gov/nigms
Contact: Judith H. Greenberg, PhD, Dir.
Desc: Genetics research and developmental biology to better understand the fundamental processes and mechanisms

of inheritance. An objective of the program is the eventual prevention and improved treatment of genetic ills in man, including multifactoral diseases with a strong hereditary component, such as diabetes, atherosclerosis, hypertension, and schizophrenia. *Type:* Research center.

U.S. Department of Health and Human Services
National Institute of Mental Health
Intramural Research Programs Division (Clinical Research)
Clinical Neurogenetics Branch

NIH Bldg. 10, Rm. 3N-218 Ph: (301)496-3465
9000 Rockville Pike Fax: (301)402-0859
Bethesda, MD 20892
E-mail: elliotg@helix.nih.gov
URL: http://www.nimh.nih.gov/~cmg/
Contact: Elliot S. Gershon, MD, Chf.

Desc: Clinical and basic biologic and pharmacologic studies relating to the genetics of manic-depressive illness and schizophrenia. *Type:* Research center.

U.S. Department of Health and Human Services
National Institutes of Health
National Human Genome Research Institute

9000 Rockville Rd. Ph: (301)496-0844
Bethesda, MD 20892
URL: http://www.nhgri.nih.gov/
Contact: Francis S. Collins, MD, Director.

Desc: The Center provides leadership for and formulates research goals and long-range plans, including the study of ethical, legal, and social implications of human genome research. It supports and administers research and research training programs and the systemic, targeted effort to create detailed maps of the genomes of organisms. *Type:* Government agency, office, or program.

U.S. Department of Health and Human Services
National Institutes of Health
Office of Recombinant DNA Activities

6000 Executive Blvd. Ste. 302 Ph: (301)496-9838
Bethesda, MD 20892-7010 Fax: (301)496-9839
E-mail: orda@odepsm2.od.nih.gov
URL: http://www.nih.gov/od/orda/
Contact: Debra Knorr, Actg.Dir.

Desc: Administers the recombinant DNA research activities supported and monitored by the National Institutes of Health. (Recombinant DNA is prepared through laboratory transplantation or splicing of genes from one organism to another.) ORDA reviews all special requests submitted to NIH involving recombinant DNA technology and implements NIH policies and procedures for conducting this research. *Type:* Research center.

University of Alabama at Birmingham
Gregory Fleming James Cystic Fibrosis Research Center

1918 University Blvd. Ph: (205)934-9640
MCLM 796 Fax: (205)934-7593
Birmingham, AL 35294-0005
E-mail: sorscher@phybio.bhs.uab.edu
Contact: Dr. Eric J. Sorscher, Dir.

Desc: Cystic fibrosis, including electrolyte transport and metabolism, mucin secretion and biochemistry, genetics, regulation of immune mechanisms, membrane traffic regulation, gene therapy, and pharmacologic therapy. *Type:* Research center.

University of Alabama at Birmingham
Laboratory of Medical Genetics

908 S. 20th, Rm. 336 Ph: (205)934-4983
Birmingham, AL 35294 Fax: (205)975-6389
Contact: Dr. Andrew Carroll, Int.Dir.

Desc: Medical genetics. Performs cell culture and cytogenetic studies of cells derived by means of culture from tissue biopsies, leukocytes, and bone marrow. *Type:* Research center.

University of Arkansas at Little Rock
Arkansas Children's Hospital Cystic Fibrosis Center

800 Marshall Ph: (501)320-1018
Little Rock, AR 72202-3591 Fax: (501)320-3930
Contact: Dr. Robert Warren, Dir.

Desc: Cystic fibrosis and related respiratory diseases of children, including aerosol deposition and pulmonary function testing in children. *Type:* Research center.

University of California, Davis
Division of Agriculture and Natural Resources
Genetic Resources Conservation Program

1 Shields Ave. Ph: (530)754-8501
Davis, CA 95616 Fax: (530)754-8505
E-mail: grcp@ucdavis.edu
URL: http://www.grcp.ucdavis.edu
Contact: Dr. Calvin O. Qualset, Dir.

Desc: Facilitates the collection and maintenance of animal, plant, and microbial genetic resources; identifies animal, plant, and microbial genetic resources critical to California and supports their conservation; and develops improved methods and strategies for procuring and maintaining genetic resources. *Type:* Research center.

University of California, San Diego
Pediatric Pulmonary and Cystic Fibrosis Center

200 W. Arbor Ph: (619)294-6125
MC 8448 Fax: (619)296-3758
San Diego, CA 92103
Contact: Dr. Michael J. Light, MD, Dir.

Desc: Neonatal and pediatric pulmonary medicine, including cystic fibrosis, chronic illness, neonatal pulmonary mechanics and control of breathing, and pulmonary surfactant. *Type:* Research center.

University of Colorado
B.F. Stolinsky Research Laboratories

4200 E. 9th Ave., Box C233 Ph: (303)315-7301
Denver, CO 80262 Fax: (303)315-8080
Contact: Stephen I. Goodman, MD, Dir.

Desc: Biochemical genetics and nutrition. The Laboratories are federally designated as a center for research in mental retardation or related aspects of human development. *Type:* Research center.

University of Colorado
Cystic Fibrosis Center

4200 E. Ninth Ave., C-220 Ph: (303)315-6026
Denver, CO 80262
Contact: Frank J. Accurso, Dir.

Desc: Cystic fibrosis and related respiratory diseases of children. Conducts studies of airway inflammation. *Type:* Research center.

University of Colorado at Boulder
Institute for Behavioral Genetics

CB 447 Ph: (303)492-2839
Boulder, CO 80309 Fax: (303)492-8063
E-mail: smolent@ibg.colorado.edu
Contact: Dr. Toni N. Smolen, Assr.Dir.

Desc: Application of behavioral genetics to pharmacogenetics, learning disabilities, cognitive development, and vulnerability to drug abuse. Specific interests include genetics of aging, reading disability, genetic and neurobiological correlates of animal behavior, human alcohol studies, and genetic factors in personality and cognitive development of twins and adopted children. *Type:* Research center.

University of Iowa

Birth Defects and Genetic Disorders Unit

2614 JCP   Ph: (319)335-9901
Iowa City, IA 52242   Fax: (319)356-3347
E-mail: jim-smith@uiowa.edu
Contact: James M. Smith, Contact.

Desc: Causes, prevention, and treatment of birth defects and genetic disorders. Coordinates University clinical service programs and related educational programs throughout the state of Iowa with afflicted individuals. *Type:* Research center.

University of Louisville

Louisville Twin Study

Med.-Dental Res. Bldg.   Ph: (502)852-1090
Health Sci. Ctr.   Fax: (502)852-1093
Louisville, KY 40292
E-mail: apmath01@ulkyvm.louisville.edu
Contact: Dr. Adam P. Matheny, Jr., Dir.

Desc: Human behavior genetics, including a longitudinal study of twins and siblings from birth to early adulthood, assessment of temperament and mental development, biomedical studies of twins, and multivariate analyses of their cognitive, perceptual, and motor skills. *Type:* Research center.

University of Miami

Cystic Fibrosis Research Center

PO Box 016820   Ph: (305)243-6641
Miami, FL 33101   Fax: (305)243-6708
E-mail: gpiedimo@mednet.med.miami.edu
Contact: Dr. Giovanni Piedimonte, Dir.

Desc: Cystic fibrosis, asthma, pulmonary manifestations of pediatric AIDS, and respiratory diseases of children. Also studies pediatric exercise physiology. *Type:* Research center.

University of Minnesota

Caenorhabditis Genetics Center

250 Biological Science Center   Ph: (612)625-2265
1445 Gortner Ave.   Fax: (612)625-5754
St. Paul, MN 55108-1095
E-mail: stier@biosci.cbs.umn.edu
URL: http://elegans.swmed.edu/
Contact: Dr. Robert K. Herman, Dir.

Desc: Acquisition, banking, distribution, and coordination of genetic nomenclature of Caenorhabditis elegans strains maintained for distribution to researchers. *Type:* Research center.

University of Minnesota

Cystic Fibrosis Center

University of Minnesota   Ph: (612)626-4440
  Hospital   Fax: (612)624-0696
420 Delaware St. SE
Minneapolis, MN 55455
E-mail: warwi001@tc.umn.edu
Contact: Dr. Warren J. Warwick, Dir.

Desc: Cystic fibrosis, pediatric pulmonary diseases, pulmonary physiology, infant pulmonary function, biochemistry of cystic fibrosis, nutrition, liver disease, inflammation, psychosocial intervention, home monitoring, heart-lung and lung transplantation, sweat test, bioengineering, biophysics, and physical therapy. Activities include development of high frequency compression therapy. *Type:* Research center.

University of Minnesota

Institute of Human Genetics

420 Delaware St. SE   Ph: (612)624-9180
Box 206 MAYO   Fax: (612)626-7031
Minneapolis, MN 55455-0392
E-mail: faras@gene.med.umn.edu
URL: http://www.ihg.med.umn.edu/index.html
Contact: Prof.Dr. Anthony J. Faras, Dir.

Desc: Human genetics and developmental biology, including biochemical, molecular, and clinical genetics, cytogenetics, metabolism, and genetic counseling. Current research involves tumor viruses; gene transfer; eukaryotic gene regulation; rearrangement and regulation of immunoglobulin genes; molecular genetics of the major histocompatibility complex; genetic defects of human pigment genes; and bone marrow transplantation. *Type:* Research center.

University of Missouri--Columbia

Cystic Fibrosis Research Center

Health Sci. Ctr.   Ph: (573)882-6978
Department of Child Health   Fax: (573)882-2742
Columbia, MO 65212
E-mail: PeterKonig@muccmail.missouri.edu
Contact: Peter Konig, MD, Dir.

Desc: Intracellular control mechanisms of secretion as they relate to cystic fibrosis, secretory mechanisms for water and electroytes in exocrine glands, structure and function of pulmonary glycoproteins in cystic fibrosis and other chronic pulmonary diseases, and therapies for pulmonary disease in cystic fibrosis. *Type:* Research center.

University of Nebraska Medical Center

Hattie B. Munroe Center for Human Genetics

4420 Dewey St.   Ph: (402)559-5070
Omaha, NE 68198-5440   Fax: (402)559-9463
E-mail: wgsanger@unmc.edu
URL: http://www.unmc.edu/mrimedia/cytolab.html
Contact: Warren G. Sanger, PhD, Dir.

Desc: Research and treatment concentrating in cancer cytogenetics and prenatal diagnosis, including lymphoma, leukemia, and solid tumor research, chromosome changes in response to treatment, diagnostics of chromosome abnormalities, and treatment of prenatal genetic conditions associated with mental retardation and disability. *Type:* Research center.

University of Nebraska at Omaha

Pediatric Pulmonary and Cystic Fibrosis Research Center

600 S. 42 St.   Ph: (402)559-6275
PO Box 985190   Fax: (402)559-7062
Omaha, NE 68198-5190
E-mail: jcolombo@unmc.edu
Contact: Dr. John L. Colombo, Dir.

Desc: Cystic fibrosis, including optimal use of antibiotics and respiratory therapy modalities; optimal use of aerosolized drug therapy; pancreatic function; effects of chronic aspiration, particularly on airway hyperactivity and inflammation; and bronchoalveolar lavage cytology in acute and chronic pediatric diseases. *Type:* Research center.

University of Oklahoma

Pulmonary and Cystic Fibrosis Center

Children's Hospital of   Ph: (405)271-6390
  Oklahoma, Rm. 3316B   Fax: (405)271-5055
940 NE 13th St.
Oklahoma City, OK 73104
E-mail: james-royall@ouhsc.edu
Contact: James Royall, Dir.

Desc: Cystic fibrosis and other respiratory diseases of children. *Type:* Research center.

University of Texas--Houston Health Science Center

Genetic Marker Laboratory

Genetic Ctr. GSBS   Ph: (713)500-9800
PO Box 20334   Fax: (713)500-0900
Houston, TX 77225
URL: http://www.hgc.sph.uth.tmc
Contact: Dr. Eric Boerwinkle, Dir.

Desc: Investigates DNA polymorphisms to find genetic bases for diseases, with special emphasis on common chronic diseases such as diabetes and heart disease. Approaches include linkage and pedigree analysis, DNA automated typing, and sequencing. *Type:* Research center.

University of Texas--Houston Health Science Center

Human Genetics Center

PO Box 20334   Ph: (713)500-9800
Houston, TX 77225   Fax: (713)500-0900
E-mail: hgc@utsph.sph.uth.tmc.edu
URL: http://hgc.sph.uth.tmc.edu
Contact: Dr. Eric Boerwinkle, Dir.

Desc: Genetic analysis of the common chronic diseases to identify and characterize the genes contributing to morbidity and mortality in most westernized populations. Research involves genetic linkage studies to localize and characterize genes contributing to disease susceptibility. *Type:* Research center.

University of Texas Southwestern Medical Center at Dallas

Eugene McDermott Center for Human Growth and Development

6000 Harry Hines Blvd.   Ph: (214)648-1600
Dallas, TX 75235-8591   Fax: (214)648-1666
E-mail: gevans@utsw.swmed.edu
URL: http://mcdermott.swmed.edu
Contact: Dr. Glen A. Evans, Dir.

Desc: Physical mapping of human chromosomes and genomes of other complex organisms, technology development to support genome science, and engineering and computational development for DNA sequencing of the human genome. *Type:* Research center.

University of Toronto

Centre for Cardiovascular Research

Cardiac Gene Unit

Department of Clinical   Ph: (416)978-8758
  Biochemistry and Med.   Fax: (416)978-5650
100 College St., Rm. 418A
Toronto, ON, Canada M5G
  1L5
E-mail: liewcc@tcgu.med.utoronto.ca
URL: http://www.tcgu.med.utoronto.ca
Contact: C.C. Liew, Hd.

Desc: Genes that may be associated with cardiovascular disease. *Type:* Research center.

University of Utah

DNA Diagnostic Laboratory

Center for Advanced Medical   Ph: (801)581-8334
  Technology   Free: 888-DNA-
729 S. Arapeen Dr.   MAPS
Salt Lake City, UT 84108   Fax: (801)585-3876
E-mail: ken@genetics.utah.edu
URL: http://www.genetics.utah.edu
Contact: Kenneth Ward, MD, Dir.

Desc: Gene mapping, genetic diagnosis, preimplantation testing, pregnancy loss, birth defect genes, and preeclampsia genes. *Type:* Research center.

University of Utah
Intermountain Cystic Fibrosis Center
School of Medicine   Ph: (801)581-2410
50 N. Medical Dr., Rm 2A120   Fax: (801)581-4920
Salt Lake City, UT 84132
E-mail: dennis.nielson@hsc.utah.edu
Contact: Dr. Dennis W. Nielson, Pediatrics Dir.
Desc: Cystic fibrosis and pulmonary disease, including studies electrolyte metabolism in the lung, lung mechanics, clinical studies of new therapies, and antibiotic pharmacology. *Type:* Research center.

University of Vermont
Genetics Laboratory
Vermont Cancer Ctr.   Ph: (802)656-8346
32 N. Prospect St.   Fax: (802)656-8333
Burlington, VT 05401-3498
E-mail: ralberti@zoo.uvm.edu
Contact: Dr. Richard Albertini, Dir.
Desc: Genetic toxicology, including investigations of the mechanisms of mutation, development of tests for detecting the consequences of exposure to environmental toxicants which damage genes (genotoxicants), definition of human populations which are unusually susceptible to certain mutations, and correlation of the presence of indicators of genotoxicant exposure and/or genetic damage with subsequent health outcomes of monitored human populations. *Type:* Research center.

Usher Syndrome Self-Help Network
Foundation Fighting Blindness
Exec. Plaza 1, Ste. 800   Ph: (410)785-1414
11350 McCormick Rd.   Free: 888-394-3937
Hunt Valley, MD 21031-1014   Fax: (410)771-9470
URL: http://www.blindness.org
Contact: Stephanie Horney, Coordinator.
Desc: A self-help network for individuals diagnosed with Usher Syndrome and their families and friends. (Usher Syndrome is a genetic disorder causing hearing loss at birth and eventual retinal degeneration.). *Type:* Association.

Washington University in St. Louis
Cystic Fibrosis Research Center
1 Children's Pl.   Ph: (314)454-2694
St. Louis, MO 63110   Fax: (314)454-2515
E-mail: mallory@a1.kids.wustl.edu
Contact: Dr. George Mallory, Dir.
Desc: Cystic fibrosis and pulmonary diseases, plus nutrition and malabsorption in relation to cystic fibrosis and liver diseases and effects of mechanisms of inflammatory response in cystic fibrosis-related diseases. Conducts research on lung transplantation and nutrition in cystic fibrosis, as well as basic studies of immune mechanisms. *Type:* Research center.

Wayne State University
Center for Molecular Medicine and Genetics
540 E. Canfield   Ph: (313)577-5323
Detroit, MI 48201   Fax: (313)577-5218
E-mail: cmmg@cmb.biosci.wayne.edu
URL: http://cmmg.biosci.wayne.edu
Contact: George Grunberger, MD, Dir.
Desc: Development and differentiation, including studies into meiotic differentiation, cell type-specific gene regulation, protein structure and function, and genome organization and stability; cancer and metastasis, including mapping of cancer genes, induction of carcinogenesis, gene regulation in cancer, and mechanisms of metastasis; human genetics and disease, comprising the genetic cause of Huntington's disease, arthritis and tissue remodeling, and diabetes and insulin action; viral disease, including mother-fetus transmission of AIDS, and papilloma viruses in cervical cancer; and gene therapeutics, including fetal gene therapy, and gene therapy for lymphoma and leukemia. *Type:* Research center.

Wayne State University
Cystic Fibrosis Care, Teaching and Resource Center
Children's Hospital of Michigan   Ph: (313)745-5541
3901 Beaubien   Fax: (313)993-2948
Detroit, MI 48201
E-mail: dtoder@med.wayne.edu
Contact: Debbie Toder, MD, Dir.
Desc: Cystic fibrosis and pediatric pulmonary diseases. Also participates in multi-centered clinical trials. *Type:* Research center.

Wayne State University
Cytogenetics Laboratory
Department of Pathology   Ph: (313)577-1208
3800 Woodward LL1   Fax: (313)966-0687
Detroit, MI 48201
Contact: Dr. Salah Ebrahim, MD, Dir.
Desc: Cytogenetics, including studies in the areas of neonatal development and endocrinology. Performs tests on amniotic fluids, CVS, bloods, bone marrows, and solid tissues. *Type:* Research center.

Wayne State University
Sickle Cell Center
Children's Hospital of Michigan   Ph: (313)745-5613
3901 Beaubien   Fax: (313)745-5237
Detroit, MI 48201
E-mail: ssarnaik@wayne.med.edu
Contact: Dr. S. Sarnaik, Dir.
Desc: Sickle cell diseases, including clinical trials of new drugs, psychosocial research, and newborn screening and follow-up of infants with sickle cell diseases. *Type:* Research center.

West Virginia University
Cystic Fibrosis Center
Department of Pediatrics   Ph: (304)293-1216
Health Sci. Ctr.   Fax: (304)293-4341
PO Box 9214
Morgantown, WV 26506
Contact: Stephen C. Aronoff, MD, Dir.
Desc: Efficacy of exercise programs in cystic fibrosis and attachment of pseudomonas to cells in cystic fibrosis. *Type:* Research center.

Geography

American Congress on Surveying and Mapping
5410 Grosvenor Ln., Ste. 100   Ph: (301)493-0200
Bethesda, MD 20814-2144   Fax: (301)493-8245
E-mail: infoacsm@mindspring.com
URL: http://www.survmap.com
Contact: John Lisack, Jr., C, Exec.Dir.
Desc: Professionals, technicians, and students in the field of surveying and mapping including surveying of all disciplines, land and geographic information systems, cartography, geodesy, photogrammetry, engineering, geophysics, geography, and computer graphics; American Association for Geodetic Surveying, American Cartographic Association, and National Society of Professional Surveyors. Objectives are to: advance the sciences of surveying and mapping; promote public understanding and use of surveying and mapping; speak on the national level as the collective voice of the profession; provide publications to serve the surveying and mapping community. *Type:* Association.

Association of American Geographers
1710 16th St. NW   Ph: (202)234-1450
Washington, DC 20009-3198   Fax: (202)234-2744
E-mail: gaia@aag.org

URL: http://www.aag.org
Contact: Ronald F. Abler, Exec.Dir.
Desc: Professional society of educators and scientists in the field of geography. Seeks to further professional investigations in geography and to encourage the application of geographic research in education, government, and business. Conducts research; compiles statistics. *Type:* Association.

Equinox
Equinox
11 450 boul. Albert-Hudon
Montreal-Nord, PQ, Canada
    H1G 3J9
Contact: Michel Paradis, Publisher; Alan Morantz, Editor.
Desc: Magazine featuring The Human Community, the Natural World, Science & Technology . *Alt. Contact:* 11450 boul. Albert-Hudon, Montreal-Nord, PQ, Canada H1G 3J9; telephone: (514)327-4464; fax: (514)327-0514. *Type:* Periodical.

Facts On File World News Digest
Facts on File, Inc.
11 Penn Plaza   Ph: (212)896-4287
New York, NY 10001
E-mail: newmedia@factsonfile.com
URL: http://www.factsonfile.com
Desc: Contains the complete text of Facts on File World News Digest, providing news summaries of current events worldwide. 250,000 hyperlinks connect the user to everything of importance in the news from January 1980 to the present. *Available:* CARL Corporation; EBSCOhost; Auto-Graphics, Inc.; OCLC Online Computer Library Center, Inc.; Ameritech Library Services, Vista. *Type:* Database.

Gamma Theta Upsilon
Department of Geography   Ph: (608)785-8333
La Crosse, WI 54601   Fax: (608)785-8332
E-mail: holde_vh@mail.uwlax.edu
Contact: Virgil Holder, Exec.Sec.
Desc: Cosponsors Visiting Geographical Scientist Program with Association of American Geographers. *Type:* Association.

Great Lakes Information Network
Great Lakes Commission
400 4th St.   Ph: (734)665-9135
Ann Arbor, MI 48103-4816   Fax: (734)665-4370
E-mail: glc@glc.org
URL: http://www.great-lakes.net/
Contact: Christine Manninen, manninen@glc.org.
Desc: The Great Lakes Information Network web site contains data and information concerning environmental quality, resource management, transportation, demographic and economic development data, information, resources, human health, tourism, news, events and weather, and other information about the Great Lakes region of the United States and Canada. *Type:* Database.

LC MARC: Maps
U.S. Library of Congress
Cataloging Distribution Service
101 Independence Ave., S.E.   Ph: (202)707-6100
Washington, DC 20541-4912
E-mail: cdsinfo@loc.gov
URL: http://www.lcweb/loc.gov/cds
Contact: Customer Support Unit.
Desc: Provides full bibliographic descriptions and cataloging information for more than 170,000 single and multi-sheet maps, map sets, and maps treated as serials that are currently cataloged by the Library of Congress. Records are in US MARC format. *Type:* Database.

National Geographic

National Geographic Society
1145 17th St. NW
Washington, DC 20036

Ph: (202)857-6112
Free: 800-638-6400
Fax: (202)775-6141

E-mail: natgeo1@aol.com
URL: http://www.nationalgeographic.com; http://www.nationalgeographic.com.

Contact: Gilbert M. Grosvenor, Chairman of the Board of Trustees; Reg Murphy, President; William L. Allen, Editor.

Desc: Magazine designed to teach individuals about history, culture, the environment, science, and themselves. *Type:* Periodical.

National Geographic Society Education Foundation

1145 17th St. NW
Washington, DC 20036

Ph: (202)857-7363
Fax: (202)429-5701

URL: http://www.nationalgeographic.com/
Contact: Gilbert Grosvenor, Chair.

Desc: A foundation of the National Geographic Society . Funds and develops geography programs in U.S. school curricula. *Type:* Association.

Professional Land Surveyors of Oregon

15108 SE River Rd.
Milwaukie, OR 97267

Ph: (503)654-3646
Fax: (503)654-3646

E-mail: plsoxsec@teleport.com
URL: http://www.plso.org
Contact: Bert Mason, Jr., Exec.Sec.

Desc: Licensed land surveyors and associates. Promotes the improvement of the profession and the modernization of statutes. *Type:* Association.

U.S. Geological Survey Cartographic Data

U.S. Geological Survey
MS804 National Center
Reston, VA 20192
E-mail: webmaster@www.usgs.gov
URL: http://info.er.usgs.gov/data/cartographic/index.html
Contact: webmaster@usgs.gov.

Desc: USGS Cartographic Data contains digital elevation models and data for mapping purposes. A database variety of cartographic, geographic, earth science, and remotely sensed data, products, and services in support of Federal, State, and public interests can be accessed to include information about the Earth's natural and cultural features, base maps and special maps in several scales, digital cartographic data, aerial photographs and other remotely sensed data. *Type:* Database.

Geology

American Association of Petroleum Geologists

Box 979
Tulsa, OK 74101

Ph: (918)584-2555
Fax: (918)560-2665

E-mail: postmaster@aapg.org
URL: http://www.aapg.org
Contact: Lyle Bair, Exec.Dir.

Desc: Professional society of geologists teaching at the college level and engaged in exploration for hydrocarbons research. *Type:* Association.

American Geological Institute

4220 King St.
Alexandria, VA 22302-1502

Ph: (703)379-2480
Fax: (703)379-7563

E-mail: agi@agiweb.org
URL: http://www.agiweb.org
Contact: Dr. Marcus E. Milling, Exec.Dir.

Desc: Federation of national scientific and technical societies in the earth sciences. Seeks to: stimulate public under-

standing of geological sciences; improve teaching of the geological sciences in schools, colleges, and universities; maintain high standards of professional training and conduct; work for the general welfare of members. *Type:* Association.

American Geophysical Union

2000 Florida Ave. NW
Washington, DC 20009

Ph: (202)462-6900
Free: 800-966-AGU1
Fax: (202)328-0566

E-mail: service@kosmos.agu.org
URL: http://www.agu.org
Contact: A. F. Spilhaus, Jr., Exec.Dir.

Desc: Individuals professionally associated with the field of geophysics; supporting institutional members are companies and other organizations whose work involves geophysics. Promotes the study of problems concerned with the figure and physics of the earth; initiates and coordinates research that depends upon national and international cooperation and provides for scientific discussion of research results. *Type:* Association.

Association of Engineering Geologists

Texas A & M University
MS-3115
College Station, TX 77843-3115

Ph: (409)443-4639
Fax: (409)443-2948

E-mail: aeghq@aol.com
Contact: Edwin A. Blackey, Jr., Exec. Dir.

Desc: Graduate geologists and geological engineers; full members must have five years experience in the field of engineering geology. Seeks to: provide a forum for the discussion and dissemination of technical and scientific information; encourage the advancement of professional recognition, scientific research, and high ethical and professional standards. *Type:* Association.

Earth Science Computer Applications

Gibbs Associates
PO Box 706
Boulder, CO 80306

Ph: (303)444-6032
Free: 800-378-5089
Fax: (303)444-6032

URL: http://www.csn.net/~bgibbs; http://www.info-mine.com/.
Contact: Betty Gibbs, Editor, bgibbs@csn.org.

Desc: Contains information about developments in computer software for mining, geology, and other earth sciences. Topics include new software reviews, Internet resources, hardware, vendors, and applications. *Type:* Newsletter.

Geological Society of America

3300 Penrose Pl.
PO Box 9140
Boulder, CO 80301-9140

Ph: (303)447-2020
Free: 800-472-1988
Fax: (303)447-1133

E-mail: web@geosociety.org
URL: http://www.geosociety.org
Contact: Donald Davidson, Exec.Dir.

Desc: Professional society of geologists. Promotes the science of geology. Maintains placement service. *Type:* Association.

GeoRef™ (Geological Reference File)

American Geological Institute (AGI)
GeoRef Information System
4220 King St.
Alexandria, VA 22302-1502

Ph: (703)379-2480

E-mail: kyost@agiweb.org
Contact: Kay Yost, Assistant to the Director., (703)379-2480, fax: (703)379-7563, kyost@jei.umd.edu.

Desc: Contains approximately 2 million citations to the literature of geology and geophysics: areal geology, economic geology, extraterrestrial geology, geochemistry, geochro-

nology, geomorphology, marine geology, mineralogy, paleontology, petrology, solid-earth geophysics, stratigraphy, and structural geology. Corresponds to the following publications: Bibliography and Index of North American Geology (1785-1970), Bibliography and Index of Geology Exclusive of North America (1933-1968), Geophysical Abstracts (1966-1971), Bibliography of Theses in Geology (1965-1966), Bibliography and Index of Geology (1969-present), and Bibliography and Index of Micropaleontology (1972-present). *Available:* The Dialog Corporation, DIALOG; Questel • Orbit; OCLC Online Computer Library Center, Inc., OCLC EPIC; OCLC FirstSearch Electronic Collections Online; Community of Science, Inc. *Type:* Database.

GIS Newsletter

Geoscience Information Society (GIS)
c/o American Geological
   Institute
4220 King St.
Alexandria, VA 22302

Contact: Mary Frances Lembo, Editor, (509)372-7441, fax: (509)372-7431, mf.lembo@pnl.gov.

Desc: Covers news of geosciences libraries and information retrieval services, facilitating an exchange of information in the field. Recurring features include news of members and listings of new publications and job openings. *Type:* Newsletter.

Global Land Information System

U.S. Geological Survey - Global Land
Information System - EROS Data Center - Karl
Mundt Federal Center
Sioux Falls, SD 57198

Ph: (605)594-6151
Free: 800-252-4547
Fax: (605)594-6589

E-mail: edcweb@edcwww.cr.usgs.gov
URL: http://sun1.cr.usgs.gov/glis/glis.html

Desc: The Global Land Information System (GLIS) is an interactive computer system, developed by the U.S. Geological Survey, through which scientists can collect and study information about geographic areas using metadata (descriptive information about data sets). *Type:* Database.

National Council for GeoCosmic Research

9307 Thornewood Dr.
Baltimore, MD 21234-3219

Ph: (410)243-0100

E-mail: annen@prodigy.com
URL: http://www.geocosmic.org

Contact: Gayle Herskovitz, Exec.Sec.

Desc: Works to further study of the interaction of man and the universe. *Type:* Association.

National Geographic Society

1145 17th St. NW
Washington, DC 20036

Ph: (202)857-7000
Fax: (202)775-6141

E-mail: askngs@nationalgeographic.com
URL: http://www.nationalgeographic.com

Contact: Gilbert M. Grosvenor, Cmn.

Desc: Persons interested in increasing and diffusing geographic knowledge. Sponsors expeditions and research in geography, natural history, archaeology, astronomy, ethnology, and oceanography; sends writers and photographers throughout the world; disseminates information through its magazines, maps, books, television documentaries, films, educational media, and information services for media. Maintains National Geographic Society Geography Education Program to enhance geographic education in grades K-12; also maintains Explorers Hall museum. *Type:* Association.

NSF Geosciences Integrated Earth Information Server

U.S. National Science Foundation - University Corporation for Atmospheric Research Unidata Program Center

PO Box 3000   Ph: (303)497-8644
Boulder, CO 80307
E-mail: support@unidata.ucar.edu
URL: http://atm.geo.nsf.gov
Contact: Ben Domenico, ben@unidata.ucar.edu.
Desc: The National Science Foundation supports research, education, and infrastructure to advance the state of knowledge about Earth, including its atmosphere, continents, oceans, interior, and the processes the modify them as well as link them together. NSF Geosciences Integrated Earth Information Server contains a range of earth-related data in a variety of forms and includes current local weather maps and bulletins; oceanographic, seismic, and other environmental information (sea surface temperature maps, polar observations, high-resolution images of atmospheric events, and ozone measurements) and instructional materials (diagrams, lesson plans, charts, contests, observation instructions, a cloud catalog, and instructional modules). *Type:* Database.

Sigma Gamma Epsilon

University of Oklahoma   Ph: (405)325-3031
100 E. Boyd, Rm. N-131   Fax: (405)325-7069
Norman, OK 73019
E-mail: bbellis-sge@ou.edu
URL: http://www.nitro9.earth.uni.edu.SGE.html
Contact: Charles J. Mankin, Sec.-Treas.
Desc: Honorary society recognizing scholarship and professionalism in the earth sciences. Seeks: scholastic, scientific, and professional advancement of its members; cooperation between colleges and universities devoted to the advancement of earth science. *Type:* Association.

Society of Exploration Geo-physicists

PO Box 702740   Ph: (918)497-5500
Tulsa, OK 74170   Fax: (918)497-5557
URL: http://www.seg.org
Contact: Paul Hummel, Exec.Dir.
Desc: Individuals having eight years of education and experience in exploration geophysics or geology. Promotes the science of geophysics, especially as it applies to the exploration for petroleum and other minerals. Encourages high professional standards among members; supports the common interests of members. *Type:* Association.

USGS Digital Data Series DDS-6

U.S. Geological Survey
MS964 Box 25046   Ph: (303)236-1317
Denver Federal Center
Denver, CO 80225-0046
E-mail: webmaster@www.usgs.gov
URL: http://www.usgs.gov/reports/digital_data_series/DDS-6/DDS-6.html
Desc: The Geologic Names of the United States database contains data on nomenclature applied to stratigraphic units used in the United States, its territories, and possessions. Data include a summary of present day usage and the historical record. *Type:* Database.

World Data Center - A for Marine Geology and Geophysics

U.S. National Oceanic and Atmospheric Administration - National Geographic Data Center
Mail Code E/GC3   Ph: (303)497-6826
325 Broadway   Fax: (303)497-6513
Boulder, CO 80303-3328
E-mail: info@ngdc.noaa.gov
URL: http://www.ngdc.noaa.gov/mgg/aboutmgg/wdcamgg.html

Contact: cmoore@ngdc.noaa.gov.
Desc: The World Data Center-A for Marine Geology and Geophysics gathers extensive data from the sea floor including both on-site measurements such as seafloor cores, and remotely sensed data such as marine magnetics, gravity, seismic reflection/refraction, and bathymetry. There are also datasets available from seafloor samples, cores, sediments, a selection of unique of images, and more. *Type:* Database.

Germany/German

American Institute for Contemporary German Studies

1400 16th St. NW, Ste. 420   Ph: (202)332-9312
Washington, DC 20036   Fax: (202)265-9531
E-mail: aicgsdoc@jhunix.hcf.jhu.edu
URL: http://www.jhu.edu/~aicgsdoc/
Contact: Jackson Janes, Exec.Dir.
Desc: Established to develop and conduct a systematic and comprehensive effort to promote a better understanding of developments in Germany and Europe since World War II, and to train and develop a new generation of American experts on Germany. *Type:* Association.

Delta Phi Alpha

College of Languages,   Ph: (808)956-8516
  Linguistics, and Literature   Fax: (808)956-9879
2545 The Mall, Bilger 101
University of Hawaii at Manoa
Honolulu, HI 96822
Contact: Dr. Cornelia Moore, Dean.
Desc: Honor society - men and women, German studies. *Type:* Association.

German-American National Congress

4740 N. Western Ave., 2nd Fl.   Ph: (773)275-1100
Chicago, IL 60625   Fax: (773)275-4710
Contact: Ernst Ott, Pres.
Desc: Americans of German ancestry; noncitizens may join if willing to become U.S. citizens. A nonpartisan, civic organization that seeks to maintain German culture, art, and customs and affect the extended promotion and dissemination of the German language in educational institutions in the U.S. *Type:* Association.

German Society of the City of New York

6 E. 87th St.   Ph: (212)360-6022
New York, NY 10128   Fax: (212)360-6027
Contact: Wolfgang Hamel, Exec.Dir.
Desc: Individuals and firms interested in assisting German immigrants. Provides German-American families and individuals with welfare services, employment, and professional counseling. Sponsors activities for senior citizens. *Type:* Association.

Society for German-American Studies

Dr. Don Heinrich Tolzmann
University of Cincinnati   Ph: (513)556-1955
Blegen Library   Fax: (513)556-2113
PO Box 210113
Cincinnati, OH 45221
Contact: Dr. Don Heinrich Tolzmann, Pres.
Desc: Academicians, students, and individuals and organizations interested in German-American studies. Works to advance the field, improve cross-cultural relations, and to assist those interested in studying, researching, or teaching German-Americana. Conducts and disseminates studies on German-American history, literature, and culture. *Type:* Association.

Gerontology

AARP, Utah State Office

6975 Union Park Center, Ste.   Ph: (801)561-1037
320   Fax: (801)561-2209
Midvale, UT 84047-4184
Contact: Kirsten T. Ball, State Rep.
Desc: Individuals 50 years of age or over living in the state of Utah. *Type:* Association.

AgeLine

American Association of Retired Persons (AARP) Research Information Center
601 E St., NW   Ph: (202)434-6231
Washington, DC 20049
E-mail: ageline@aarp.org
Contact: Margaret Eccles, AgeLine Database Manager, (202)434-6231, fax: (202)434-6408, ageline@capcon.net.
Desc: Contains more than 50,000 citations, with abstracts, to the literature on social gerontology, with a focus on the social, psychological, and economic aspects of middle age and aging. Covers demographics, economics, employment, health and health care services, housing, intergenerational relationships, social and family relationships, psychological aspects, retirement, transportation, consumer aspects, and leisure. *Available:* Ovid Technologies, Inc.; The Dialog Corporation, DIALOG; CompuServe Information Service, Knowledge Index; HeathGate Data Corporation. *Type:* Database.

American Federation for Aging Research

1414 Avenue of the Americas,   Ph: (212)752-2327
18th Fl.   Free: 800-330-4660
New York, NY 10019   Fax: (212)832-2298
E-mail: amfedaging@aol.com
URL: http://www.afar.org
Contact: Stephanie Lederman, Exec.Dir.
Desc: Physicians, scientists, and other individuals involved or interested in research in aging and associated diseases. Purpose is to stimulate and fund research on aging. *Type:* Association.

American Geriatrics Society

770 Lexington Ave., Ste. 300   Ph: (212)308-1414
New York, NY 10021   Free: 800-247-4779
   Fax: (212)832-8646
E-mail: info.amger@americangeriatrics.org
URL: http://www.americangeriatrics.org
Contact: Linda Hiddemen Barondess, Exec.VP.
Desc: Professional society of physicians and other health care professionals interested in problems of the aged. Encourages and promotes the study of geriatrics; stresses the importance of medical research in the field of aging. Conducts seminars. *Type:* Association.

The American Senior

Publishing and Business Consultants
4427 W. Slauson Ave.
Los Angeles, CA 90043-2717
Contact: Atia Napoleon, Editor and Publisher.
Desc: Magazine covering breakthroughs in health care for seniors. *Type:* Periodical.

Gerontological Society of America

1030 15th St. NW, Ste. 250   Ph: (202)842-1275
Washington, DC 20005-1503   Fax: (202)842-1150
E-mail: geron@geron.org
URL: http://www.geron.org
Contact: Elizabeth Bergen, Contact.
Desc: Physicians, physiologists, psychologists, anatomists, biochemists, sociologists, social workers, psychiatrists, pharmacologists, nurses, geneticists, zoologists, en-

docrinologists, economists, administrators, and other professionals interested in improving the well-being of older people by promoting scientific study of the aging process, publishing information for professionals about aging, and bringing together groups interested in aging research. Encourages research and education on the aging process. *Type:* Association.

MCP Hahnemann University of the Health Sciences

Center for Gerontological Research
2900 Queen Ln. Ph: (215)991-8460
Philadelphia, PA 19129 Fax: (215)843-1192
E-mail: cristofalo@auhs.edu
URL: http://www.auhs.edu
Contact: Vincent J. Cristofalo, PhD, Dir.
Desc: Bone metabolism and aging, cell cycle kinetics and dynamics, cell proliferation and signal transduction, growth factor regulatory mechanisms, growth/senescence regulatory genes, cellular transformation and immortalization, immunosenescence, neural plasticity, osteoporosis, problems associated with aging skin, regulation of gene expression, role of free radicals in aging and structural and molecular changes in aged brains. *Type:* Research center.

National Institute on Aging

Gerontology Research Center
5600 Nathan Shock Dr. Ph: (410)558-8110
Baltimore, MD 21224 Fax: (410)558-8137
E-mail: longod@grc.nia.nih.gov
Contact: Dr. Dan L. Longo, MD, Dir.
Desc: Gerontology research, including molecular genetics, human physiology, personality, behavioral research, and Alzheimer's disease studies. *Type:* Research center.

Glass

American Flint Glass Workers Union
1440 S. Byrne Rd. Ph: (419)385-6687
Toledo, OH 43614 Free: 800-742-8213
  Fax: (419)385-8839
Contact: Richard Morgan, Pres.
Desc: AFL-CIO. *Type:* Association.

Fenton Art Glass Collectors of America
PO Box 384 Ph: (304)375-6196
Williamstown, WV 26187 Fax: (304)375-4679
Contact: Cheryl Robinson, Pres.
Desc: Collectors of Fenton Art glass. (Fenton is the family name of a contemporary glass-making company.) Encourages appreciation of the glass-making industry and the history of Fenton glass. *Type:* Association.

Glass Reflections
Glass Association of North America
2945 SW Wanamaker Dr., Ste. Ph: (785)271-0208
  A Fax: (785)271-0166
Topeka, KS 66614-5321
E-mail: gana@glasswebsite.com
URL: http://www.glasswebsite.com/gana
Contact: Vicki Louvier, Editor.
Desc: Relates information on flat glass (plate, window, building, and industrial) products to independent glass distributors and contractors, as well as architects and the building industry in general. Reports on current industry trends and Association activities, including educational programs. *Type:* Newsletter.

National Glass Association
8200 Greensboro Dr., 3rd Fl. Ph: (703)442-4890
Mc Lean, VA 22102 Fax: (703)442-0630
E-mail: nga@glass.org

URL: http://www.glass.org
Contact: Philip J. James, CAE, CEO.
Desc: Manufacturers, installers, retailers, distributors, and fabricators of flat, architectural, automotive, and specialty glass and metal products, mirrors, shower and patio doors, windows, and table tops. *Type:* Association.

SIGMA Newsletter
Sealed Insulating Glass Manufacturers Association (SIGMA)
401 N. Michigan Ave. Ph: (312)644-6610
Chicago, IL 60611-4267 Fax: (312)321-6869
E-mail: sigma@sba.com.
Contact: Daniel Consiglio, Editor.
Desc: Publishes news of activities and members of the Association, which aims to "upgrade product performance through mandatory certification testing, new technological research and current problem-solving and educational seminars." Contains industry news, product information from member companies, notices of personnel changes, and feature articles about the industry. *Type:* Newsletter.

Society of Glass and Ceramic Decorators—Directory
Society of Glass Ceramic Decorators
1627 K St., NW, Ste. 800 Ph: (202)728-4132
Washington, DC 20006 Fax: (202)728-4133
E-mail: sgcd@sgcd.org
Contact: Sandra Spence, Editor.
Desc: More than 700 member manufacturers, suppliers, decorators, and designers of glass and ceramics; international coverage. *Type:* Directory.

Golf

Executive Golfer
Pazdur Publishing, Inc.
2171 Campus Dr. Ph: (949)752-6474
Irvine, CA 92612 Fax: (949)752-0398
Contact: Edward F. Pazdur, Publisher; Mark Pazdur, Advertising Dir.; Theda Ahern Pazdur, Editor.
Desc: Magazine providing private country club golfers with information on resorts for meetings, guest policies at private clubs, and golf communities for investment and retirement. Contains instructive articles for executives over 40. *Type:* Periodical.

Florida State Golf Association
5714 Draw Ln. Ph: (941)921-5695
Sarasota, FL 34238 Fax: (941)923-1254
E-mail: fsga@usga.org
Contact: Jim Demick, Exec.Dir.
Desc: To promote and preserve amateur golf. Conducts championships. *Type:* Association.

Fore Magazine
Southern California Golf Association
PO Box 8386 Ph: (818)980-3630
North Hollywood, CA 91618- Free: 800-554-7242
  8386 Fax: (818)980-1808
E-mail: bthomas@scga.org.
Contact: Robert D. Thomas, Editor and Publisher, bthomas@scga.org.
Desc: Southern California Golf Association magazine. *Alt. Contact:* 3740 Cahuenga Blvd., North Hollywood, CA 91604; telephone: (818)980-3630; fax: (818)980-1808. *Type:* Periodical.

Golf America Online
ACR Publications
2535 25th Ave. S. Ph: (612)722-7733
Minneapolis, MN 55406 Fax: (612)722-9996
E-mail: editor@acrpub.com
URL: http://golfamerica.com/
Desc: An online publication devoted to golf, resources include improving an individual's game, info on courses around the nation, travel tips, jokes, games, links to related sites, and more. The site offers lots of links for golfers, from golf lessons to an online proshop, complete with order forms. *Type:* Database.

Golf Course Superintendents Association of America
1421 Research Park Dr. Ph: (785)841-2240
Lawrence, KS 66049-3859 Free: 800-472-7878
  Fax: (785)832-4488
E-mail: infobox@gcsaa.org
Contact: Stephen F. Mona, CAE, CEO.
Desc: Golf course superintendents, agronomists, and research and commercial interests concerned with golf course maintenance and improvement. *Type:* Association.

Golf Digest
New York Times Magazine Group
5520 Park Ave. Ph: (203)373-7000
Trumbull, CT 06611 Fax: (203)373-7111
URL: http://www.golfdigest.com.
Contact: Jerry Tarde, Editor, (203)373-7198, fax: (203)371-2162; Tom Brown, Publisher, (212)739-3019; Dan Govern, VP/National Sales Mgr., (203)371-2117.
Desc: International magazine for golfers. *Type:* Periodical.

Golf Journal
U.S. Golf Association
Golf House Ph: (908)234-2300
PO Box 708 Free: 800-336-4446
Far Hills, NJ 07931-0708 Fax: (908)781-5497
E-mail: golfjournal@usga.org.
Contact: Brett Avery, Editor, (908)781-5497, fax: (908)781-1112, bavery@usga.org; Rich Skyzinski, Managing Editor, (972)539-5992, fax: (972)539-5993, rskyzinski@usga.org; Donna Panagakos, Art Dir., (908)781-1032, fax: (908)781-1112, dpanagakos@usga.org.
Desc: Magazine for golf enthusiasts. *Type:* Periodical.

Golf Magazine
Times Mirror Magazines, Inc.
2 Park Ave. Ph: (212)779-5000
New York, NY 10016-5601 Fax: (212)779-5522
URL: http://www.golfonline.com.
Contact: George Peper, Editor-in-Chief, fax: (212)779-5522, gpeper@golfonline.com; James A. Frank, Editor, (212)779-5040, fax: (212)779-5522, jfrank@golfonline.com; James D. Kahn, Publisher, (212)779-5056.
Desc: Magazine devoted to golf. *Type:* Periodical.

Golf Publishing Syndicate
2743 Saxon St. Ph: (610)437-4982
Allentown, PA 18103 Fax: (610)437-4982
Contact: Karl Gilbert, President.
Desc: Distributes columns concerning golf, trends, equipment, etiquette, instruction, and analysis. *Alt. Contact:* 2743 Saxon St., Allentown, PA 18103; telephone: (610)437-4982; fax: (610)437-4982. *Type:* Periodical.

Golf Resort Directory
Adams Business Media
60 Main St. Ph: (978)897-5552
Maynard, MA 01754-2011 Fax: (978)897-6824
E-mail: amueller@mail.aip.com.
URL: http://www.meetingsnet.com.

Contact: Alison Hall, Editor, ahall@mail.aip.com.
Desc: Hotels and resorts with golf facilities for corporate events. *Type:* Directory.

Golf Resorts—The Complete Guide

Lanier Publishing International
PO Box D Ph: (707)763-0271
Petaluma, CA 94953 Fax: (707)763-5762
E-mail: lanier@travelguides.com; office01@travelguides.com.
URL: http://www.travelguides.com; http://www.travelguides.com/.
Contact: Pamela Lanier, Editor.
Desc: Over 1,000 golf resorts; also includes state tourist bureaus. *Type:* Directory.

Golf Today

Golf Today
204 Industrial Way Ph: (650)802-8165
San Carlos, CA 94070 Free: 800-GOLF-PUTT
Fax: (650)802-8114
URL: http://www.golftodaymagazine.com.
Contact: Bob Koczor, Editor and Publisher.
Type: Periodical.

Golf World

Billian Publishing, Inc.
2100 Powers Ferry Rd., Ste. 300 Ph: (770)955-5656
Atlanta, GA 30339 Free: 800-533-8484
Fax: (770)952-0669
E-mail: ati@billian.com
Contact: Richard S. Taylor, Editor; Douglas C. Billian, Publisher.
Desc: Magazine covering tournament golf at all levels of play internationally; also features travel articles, analysis, and instruction. *Type:* Periodical.

GOLFWEEK

Golfweek
7657 Commerce Center Dr. Ph: (407)345-5500
Orlando, FL 32819 Fax: (407)345-9404
URL: http://www.golfweek.com.
Contact: Ken Henson, President, (407)345-5510, fax: (407)345-9404, khanson@golfweek.com; Jim Nugent, Publisher, jnugent@golfweek.com; Dave Seanor, Editor, (407)345-5536, fax: (407)345-9945, dseanor@golfweek.com.
Desc: Journal of record for competitive golf. Delivers the most complete news and information about the game, the people and the industry, to golf's most important audience. *Type:* Periodical.

Ladies Professional Golf Association

100 International Golf Dr. Ph: (904)274-6200
Daytona Beach, FL 32124-1092 Fax: (904)274-1099
Contact: H. James Ritts, III, Commissioner.
Desc: Professional women golfers and educators. *Type:* Association.

Links Magazine

Purcell Enterprises
1040 William Hilton Pkwy., Ph: (803)842-6200
Ste. 200 Fax: (803)842-6233
PO Box 7628
Hilton Head Island, SC 29938
E-mail: sales@linksmagazine.com.
URL: http://www.linksmagazine.com.
Contact: Joe Passov, Editor, passov@linksmagazine.com; John R. Purcell, Jr., Publisher, purlinks@aol.com.
Desc: Magazine covering golf tradition and lifestyle. *Type:* Periodical.

The McGolf Update

The McGulf Company
821 Lone Pine Rd. Ph: (248)647-4669
Bloomfield Hills, MI 48302 Fax: (248)647-2879
Contact: Sally McHenry, Editor.
Desc: Features news and tips on increasing golf course revenues. *Type:* Newsletter.

National Golf Foundation

1150 S. U.S. Hwy. 1, Ste. 401 Ph: (561)744-6006
Jupiter, FL 33477 Free: 800-733-6006
Fax: (561)744-6107
E-mail: ngf@ngf.org
URL: http://www.ngf.org
Contact: Dr. Joseph F. Beditz, CEO & Pres.
Desc: Golf-oriented businesses including: equipment and apparel companies; golf facilities; golf publications; golf course architects, developers, and builders; companies offering specialized services to the golf industry; golf associations; teachers, coaches and instructors and other interested individuals. Serves as a market research and strategic planning organization for the golf industry and promotes public golf course development in the U.S. *Type:* Association.

Nevada Magazine—Nevada Golf Statewide Directory

State of Nevada
Capitol Complex Ph: (702)687-5416
Carson City, NV 89710 Fax: (702)687-6159
E-mail: editor@nevadamagazine.com; nevmag@aol.com.
Contact: David Moore, Editor; Richard Moreno, Publisher.
Desc: About 75 golf courses in Nevada, the Tahoe Basin, and the surrounding area. *Type:* Directory.

PGA Tour Tournaments Association

13000 Sawgrass Village Circle, Ph: (606)278-7095
Ste. 36
Pointe Verda Beach, FL 32082
Contact: Barry Palm, Exec.Dir.
Type: Association.

Pocket Pro Golf Magazine

Longhurst Golf Corp.
85 W. Wilmot St., Unit 14 Ph: (905)764-5409
Richmond Hill, ON, Canada Fax: (905)764-5462
L4B 1K7
Contact: B.A. Longhurst, Editor; Bruce A. Longhurst, Publisher.
Desc: Golf magazine (English and French). *Type:* Periodical.

Professional Golfers' Association of America

100 Ave. of Champions Ph: (561)624-8400
Palm Beach Gardens, FL 33410 Fax: (561)624-8430
URL: http://www.pga.com/
Contact: Jim Awtrey, CEO.
Desc: Golf professionals and apprentices associated with golf clubs, courses, and tournaments. *Type:* Association.

Score

Canadian Controlled Media Communications
287 MacPherson Ave. Ph: (416)928-2909
Toronto, ON, Canada M4V Free: 800-320-6420
1A4 Fax: (416)966-1181
Contact: Bob Weeks, Managing Editor, weeksy@1direct.com; Kim Locke, Publisher; Peter Simpson, Advertising Dir.
Desc: Canada's Foremost Consumer Golf Magazine, now in its 17th year. *Type:* Periodical.

Southern California Golf Association

3740 Cahuenga Blvd., West Ph: (818)980-3630
North Hollywood, CA 91604 Fax: (818)980-1808
URL: http://www.scga.org
Contact: Thomas A. Morgan, Exec.Dir.
Desc: Association of amateur golfers. *Type:* Association.

United States Golf Association

PO Box 708 Ph: (908)234-2300
Far Hills, NJ 07931 Fax: (908)234-9687
E-mail: usga@usga.org
URL: http://www.usga.org
Contact: David B. Fay, Exec.Dir.
Desc: Regularly organized golf clubs and golf courses. Serves as governing body for golf in the United States. *Type:* Association.

Western Golf Association

1 Briar Rd. Ph: (847)724-4600
Golf, IL 60029 Fax: (847)724-7133
Contact: Donald D. Johnson, Exec.Dir.
Desc: More than 500 golf and country clubs. Conducts three national golf championships: the Western Open, Western Amateur, and Western Junior. Supports and administers the Evans Scholars Foundation, which awards four-year college scholarships to caddies on a competitive basis. *Type:* Association.

Government Employees

AFGE

American Federation of Government Employees, AFL-CIO
80 F St. NW Ph: (202)639-6419
Washington, DC 20001 Fax: (202)639-6441
E-mail: communications@afge.org.
Contact: Magda Seymour, Editor; John Irvine, Managing Editor.
Desc: Provides news and information on federal government and DC government workers. *Type:* Newsletter.

American Federation of Government Employees

80 F St. NW Ph: (202)737-8700
Washington, DC 20001 Fax: (202)639-6441
E-mail: communications@afge.org
URL: http://www.afge.org
Contact: Bobby L. Harnage, Sr., Nat'l Pres.
Desc: Federal employees including food inspectors, nurses, printers, cartographers, lawyers, police officers, census workers, OSHA inspectors, janitors, truck drivers, secretaries, artists, plumbers, immigration inspectors, scientists, doctors, cowboys, botanists, park rangers, computer programmers, foreign service workers, airplane mechanics, environmentalists, and writers. Seeks to help provide good government services, while ensuring that government workers are treated fairly and with dignity. *Type:* Association.

American Federation of State, County and Municipal Employees

1625 L St. NW Ph: (202)429-1000
Washington, DC 20036
URL: http://www.afscme.org
Contact: Gerald W. McEntee, Pres.
Desc: AFL-CIO. *Type:* Association.

American Foreign Service Association

2101 E St. NW Ph: (202)338-3687
Washington, DC 20037 Fax: (202)338-6820
Contact: Susan Reardon, Exec.Dir.
Desc: Associate membership is open to individuals and international organizations and corporations interested in foreign affairs, international trade, and economic policy. *Type:* Association.

Association of Civilian Technicians

12510-B Lake Ridge Dr.   Ph: (703)494-4845
Lake Ridge, VA 22192   Fax: (703)494-0961
URL: http://www.actnat.com
Contact: John T. Hunter, Pres.
Desc: Civilian technicians of the National Guard. Aided in having National Guard technicians recognized as federal employees (their salaries are paid by the federal government, but they had previously been considered state employees). Full retirement credit for past technician service has been gained; is still seeking to have National Guard technicians considered civilian technicians. *Type:* Association.

Association of Government Accountants

2208 Mount Vernon Ave.   Ph: (703)684-6931
Alexandria, VA 22301-1314   Free: 800-AGA-7211
                                Fax: (703)548-9367
URL: http://www.agacgfm.org
Contact: Thomas C. Raevis, Comptroller.
Desc: Professional society of financial managers employed by federal, state, county, and city governments in financial management and administrative positions. Conducts research; offers education and professional development programs. *Type:* Association.

Carroll's Municipal Directory

Carroll Publishing
4701 Sangamore Rd., No. S155   Ph: (301)263-9800
Bethesda, MD 20816   Free: 800-336-4240
                                 Fax: (301)263-9801
E-mail: custsvc@carrollpub.com
URL: http://www.carrolpub.com
Contact: Mike Tangney, Editor.
Desc: About 43,000 officials in more than 7,800 cities towns and village: includes top elected, council or elected board members. *Type:* Directory.

Civil Service Employees Association

143 Washington Ave.   Ph: (518)434-0191
PO Box 125   Free: 800-342-4146
Albany, NY 12210   Fax: (518)462-3639
Contact: Daniel Donahue, Pres.
Desc: AFL-CIO. Members are state and local government employees from all public employee classifications. Negotiates work contracts; represents members in grievances; provides legal assistance for on-the-job problems; provides advice and assistance on federal, state, and local laws affecting public employees. *Type:* Association.

Congressional Directory

Capitol Advantage
PO Box 1223
Order Department   Ph: (703)734-3266
Mc Lean, VA 22101   Free: 800-659-8708
                                Fax: (703)847-0573
URL: http://congress.nw.dc.us.
Contact: Dr. John Hansan, Ph.D., Editor.
Desc: 100 current senators and 440 House of Representative members. *Type:* Directory.

Congressional Staff Directory

CQ Press
Congressional Quarterly Inc.
815 Slaters Ln.   Ph: (703)739-0900
Alexandria, VA 22314   Free: 800-638-1710
                                Fax: (703)739-0234
E-mail: staffdir@staffdirectories.com
URL: http://www.staffdirectories.com; http://www. cqdirectories.com; http://csd.cq.com.
Contact: Joel Treese, Editor.
Desc: 18,000 members of the legislative branch, including senators, representatives, their staffs, and key personnel of the executive branch of the federal government. Includes 3,200 biographies of congressional staff, lists of committees and subcommittees with members and staffs, and lists of members showing their committee and subcommittee assignments. *Type:* Directory.

Congressional Yellow Book

Leadership Directories, Inc.
104 5th Ave.   Ph: (212)627-4140
New York, NY 10011   Fax: (212)645-0931
E-mail: info@leadershipdirectories.com; congressional@ leadershipdirectories.com.
URL: http://www.leadershipdirectories.com; http://www. leadershipdirectories.com.
Contact: Eric Birkholz, Editor.
Desc: Members of Congress and their principal aides, Congressional committees, leadership, and congressional support arms. *Type:* Directory.

Council of Jewish Organizations in Civil Service

45 E. 33rd St., Rm. 310   Ph: (212)689-2015
New York, NY 10016
Contact: Louis Weiser, Pres.
Desc: Jewish civil servants employed at city, state, or federal levels. Seeks to prevent discrimination and to actively promote a merit system based on individual ability regardless of race, color, creed, or national origin. Activities include Hebrew and Yiddish cultural programs. *Type:* Association.

The Federal Employee

National Federation of Federal Employees
1016 16th St. NW   Ph: (202)862-4400
Washington, DC 20036   Fax: (202)862-4432
Contact: Lisa Harris Kelly, Editor; Laura Pearlman, Editor.
Desc: Provides news and information on issues (legislative and regulatory) affecting federal employees. *Type:* Newsletter.

Federal Employees Education and Assistance Fund

8441 W. Bowles Ave., Ste. 200   Ph: (303)933-7580
Littleton, CO 80123   Free: 800-323-4140
                                Fax: (303)933-7587
URL: http://www.fpmi.com/feea/feeahome.html
Contact: Steve Bauer, Exec.Dir.
Desc: Civilian federal and postal employees and their families. Provides educational and emergency assistance grants and loans to qualified federal employees and their dependents. *Type:* Association.

Federal Human Resources Week

LRP Publications
747 Dresher Rd.   Ph: (215)784-0941
PO Box 980   Free: 800-341-7874
Horsham, PA 19044-0980   Fax: (215)784-0870
E-mail: custserve@lrp.com
Contact: Kenneth F. Kahn, Esq., Publisher; Ken Hughes, Managing Editor.
Desc: Provides information about news and events related to federal human resources. Topics covered include discrimination, compensation, and overtime. *Type:* Newsletter.

Federal Jobs Digest

Federal Jobs Digest
325 Pennsylvania Ave. SE   Ph: (914)762-5111
Washington, DC 20003   Free: 800-824-5000
                                Fax: (914)762-4818
E-mail: fjdwebmaster@jobsfed.com; fjdeditor@jobsfed. com.
URL: http://www.jobsfed.com.
Contact: Peter E. Ognibene, Editor.
Desc: Over 10,000 specific job openings in the federal government in each issue. *Type:* Directory.

Federal Yellow Book

Leadership Directories, Inc.
104 5th Ave.   Ph: (212)627-4140
New York, NY 10011   Fax: (212)645-0931
E-mail: info@leadershipdirectories.com;   federal@ leadershipdirectories.com.
URL: http://www.leadershipdirectories.com; http://www. leadershipdirectories.com.
Contact: Forrest Fisanich, Editor.
Desc: Federal departments, including the Executive Office of the President, the Office of the Vice President, the Office of Management and Budget, the Cabinet, and the National Security Council, and over 38,000 key personnel; over 70 independent federal agencies. *Type:* Directory.

Government Employee Relations Report

The Bureau of National Affairs, Inc. (BNA)
1231 25th St. NW   Ph: (202)452-4200
Washington, DC 20037
E-mail: bnaplus@bna.com
URL: http://bna.com/mkt/hrl/hrlwdec.htm
Contact: BNA PLUS, (202)452-4323, fax: (202)822-8092, bnaplus@bna.com.
Desc: Contains the complete text of the current developments section of Government Employee Relations Report, covering federal, state, and local issues and developments in employment by the public sector. Covers collective bargaining, grievance settlements, union activities, and decisions and appealed cases by the Federal Labor Relations Authority (FLRA). *Available:* LEXIS-NEXIS, LEXIS; LEXIS-NEXIS, NEXIS; West Group, WESTLAW. *Type:* Database.

Government Employee Relations Report

Bureau of National Affairs, Inc. (BNA)
1231 25th St. NW   Ph: (202)452-4323
Washington, DC 20037   Free: 800-372-1033
                                Fax: (202)452-7773
E-mail: bnaplus@bna.com
Contact: James F. Fitzpatrick, Managing Editor.
Desc: Provides notification and reference services covering developments affecting federal, state, and municipal government employee relations. Recurring features include texts of selected agreements, regulations, administrative rulings, and executive orders. *Type:* Newsletter.

Government Manager

The Bureau of National Affairs, Inc. (BNA)
1231 25th St. NW   Ph: (202)452-4200
Washington, DC 20037
E-mail: bnaplus@bna.com
URL: http://bna.com/mkt/hrl/hrlwdec.htm
Desc: Contains the complete text of Government Manager, a newsletter providing advice to federal government supervisors on handling employee relations problems, including employee discipline, absenteeism, morale, productivity, union organizing, and collective bargaining. Also covers personnel management, labor relations, grievances, court and National Labor Relations Board rulings, and equal employment opportunity issues. *Type:* Database.

Government Training News

Ronald G. Rago
PO Box 1036   Ph: (304)535-2355
Harpers Ferry, WV 25425   Fax: (304)535-9914
Contact: Ronald G. Rago, Editor.
Desc: Reports on the latest training trends and opportunities, best practices, and overall learning and training policy. Serves as a source of information and ideas about training techniques and career development programs among training professionals at the federal, state, and local levels. *Type:* Newsletter.

Guideposts for Effective Leadership - Tackling Federal Workplace Issues

LRP Publications
747 Dresher Rd.
PO Box 980
Horsham, PA 19044-0980
E-mail: custserve@lrp.com
Ph: (215)784-0941
Free: 800-341-7874
Fax: (215)784-0870

Contact: Rick Grant, Editor.

Desc: Provides information about federal employment law concerning government employees. *Type:* Newsletter.

International Association of Assessing Officers—Membership Directory

International Association of Assessing Officers
130 E. Randolph, Ste. 850
Chicago, IL 60601-6217
E-mail: webmaster@iaao.org
URL: http://www.iaao.org; http://www.iaao.org.
Ph: (312)819-6100
Fax: (312)819-6149

Contact: Annie Aubrey, Editor.

Desc: About 8,500 state and local officials concerned with valuation of property for tax purposes. *Type:* Directory.

IPMA News

International Personnel Management Association
1617 Duke St.
Alexandria, VA 22314
E-mail: ipma@ipma-hr.org
URL: http://www.ipma-hr.org.
Ph: (703)549-7100
Fax: (703)684-0948

Contact: Karen D. Smith, Editor, ksmith@ipma-hr.org.

Desc: Provides news of the Association at the national, regional, and chapter levels. Presents labor relations and court developments dealing with public sector personnel management. *Type:* Newsletter.

Massachusetts Municipal Directory

Massachusetts Municipal Association
60 Temple Pl.
Boston, MA 02111
Ph: (617)426-7272
Free: 800-882-1498
Fax: (617)695-1314

Contact: John Ouelette, Editor; Lise Giekes, Editor; Patricia Mikes, Communication Director.

Desc: Massachusetts municipal and county governments; regional agencies; state and national professional associations; selected state government offices. *Type:* Directory.

Messenger

Unemployment Agency
7310 Woodward Ave., Rm. 606
Detroit, MI 48202
Ph: (313)876-5491
Fax: (313)876-5225

Contact: Lynda Robinson, Editor.

Desc: Features news of interest to current and retired Commission employees. Recurring features include columns titled Branch Office News, MESC people and Customer Service Honor Roll. *Type:* Newsletter.

National Association of Civil Service Employees

7185 Navajo Rd., Ste. C
San Diego, CA 92119

Contact: S. K. Gossman, Sec.

Desc: Federal, state, county, and city civil service employees; association employees and counselors. Assists nonprofit charitable, educational, and scientific organizations in promoting social welfare. Conducts service and product consumer research and educational programs and symposia; sponsors competitions; maintains placement service. *Type:* Association.

National Association of Government Employees

159 Burgin Pkwy.
Quincy, MA 02169
E-mail: nage@erols.com
URL: http://www.nage.org
Ph: (617)376-0220
Fax: (617)376-0285

Contact: Kenneth T. Lyons, Pres.

Desc: Union of civilian federal government employees with locals and members in military agencies, Internal Revenue Service, Post Office, Veterans Administration, General Services Administration, Federal Aviation Administration, and other federal agencies, as well as state and local agencies. *Type:* Association.

National Federation of Federal Employees

1016 16th St. NW, Ste. 300
Washington, DC 20036
Ph: (202)862-4400
Fax: (202)862-4432

Contact: James Cunningham, Pres.

Desc: Independent. Opposes Social Security coverage for civil service workers. Conducts seminars on labor relations. *Type:* Association.

National Treasury Employees Union

901 E. St. NW, Ste. 600
Washington, DC 20004
Ph: (202)783-4085
Fax: (202)783-4085

Contact: Robert M. Tobias, Pres.

Desc: Employees of the federal government. Conducts research and educational training programs. Sponsors Federal Employees Education and Assistance Fund. *Type:* Association.

New York Civil Service Update

NYPER Publications, LLC
887 Birchwood Ln.
Niskayuna, NY 12309
E-mail: nyper@capital.net
Ph: (518)786-1654
Fax: (518)456-8582

Contact: Harvey Randall, Editor.

Desc: Covers matters of interest to personnel administrators, union leaders, and attorneys involved in public personnel law. *Type:* Newsletter.

PERB News

New York State Public Employment Relations Board (PERB)
80 Wolf Rd., 5th Fl.
Albany, NY 12205-2604
Ph: (518)457-2676
Fax: (518)457-2664

Contact: Rosemarie V. Rosen, Editor.

Desc: Covers board and hearing officer decisions and fact-finding reports. Recurring features include a calendar of events and reports of meetings. *Type:* Newsletter.

The Professional Manager

Professional Managers Association
Box 895, Ben Franklin Sta.
Washington, DC 20044
E-mail: pmaoffice@aol.com.
Fax: (202)927-4979

Contact: Matthew Chase, Editor.

Desc: Provides information of interest to federal civil service employees in mid-level management positions. Discusses issues such as fairness of pay and appraisal systems and innovative management practices. *Type:* Newsletter.

Public Employee Dismissals Bulletin

Quinlan Publishing Company
23 Drydock Ave.
Boston, MA 02210
Ph: (617)542-0048
Free: 800-229-2084
Fax: (617)345-9646
E-mail: quinlanp@quinlan.com

Contact: Anil Adyanthaya, Esq., Editor-in-Chief.

Desc: Provides summaries of recent state and federal court decisions in the area of public employee dismissals. Coverage includes discrimination, free speech, disability, drug testing, misconduct, and sexual misconduct. *Type:* Newsletter.

The Public Employee Magazine

American Federation of State, County & Municipal Employees
1625 L St. NW
Washington, DC 20036-5687
E-mail: pubaffairs@afscme.org.
URL: http://www.asscme.org.
Ph: (202)429-1144
Fax: (202)429-1120

Contact: Jeff Rubin, Editor.

Desc: Magazine providing news and features of concern to members of AFSCME. *Type:* Periodical.

State Yellow Book

Leadership Directories, Inc.
104 5th Ave.
New York, NY 10011
E-mail: info@leadershipdirectories.com; state@leadershipdirectories.com.
URL: http://www.leadershipdirectories.com; http://www.leadershipdirectories.com.
Ph: (212)627-4140
Fax: (212)645-0931

Contact: Howard Hammerman, Editor.

Desc: Over 37,000 elected and appointed officials in the executive branch, and state legislators and their committees. *Type:* Directory.

Taylor's Encyclopedia of Government Officials: Federal and State

Political Research, Inc.
Tegoland at Bent Tree
16850 Dallas Pkwy.
Dallas, TX 75248
E-mail: clientservices@politicalresearch.com
URL: http://www.politicalresearch.com; http://www.politicalresearch.com.
Ph: (972)931-8827
Free: 800-782-9002
Fax: (972)248-7159

Contact: John Clements, Editor.

Desc: Over 20,000 federal and state government officials. *Type:* Directory.

United States Senate Telephone Directory

Government Printing Office
Washington, DC 20510
Ph: (202)512-1800

Desc: Members of the Senate and their staffs; Senate committees and their staffs; Senate subcommittees and their staffs; and Senate leadership and support offices. *Type:* Directory.

The Unsung Heroes

Public Employees Roundtable
Box 14270
Washington, DC 20044-4270
E-mail: permail@patriot.net
URL: http://www.patriot.net/users/permail.

Contact: Jo A. Wright, Editor; Gretchen Hakola, Editor.

Desc: Represents the interests of and seeks to develop stronger bonds among public employees with an aim toward improving their performance and productivity. Reports on the organization's efforts to educate the public and legislators about the contributions of public employees to the nation's security and well-being and promotes interest in public service careers. *Type:* Newsletter.

Want's Federal-State Court Directory

Want Publishing Co.
Graybar Bldg. - Grand Central
420 Lexington Ave., Suite 300
New York, NY 10170
URL: http://www.wantpublishing.com.
Ph: (212)687-3774
Fax: (212)687-3779

Contact: Robert S. Want, Editor, rwant@msn.com.

Desc: All federal court judges and clerks of court, and United States attorneys and magistrates, judges; state supreme court chief justices and state court administrators; Supreme Court Chief Justices of Canada and other nations. *Type:* Directory.

Who's Who in American Politics
Marquis Who's Who
Reed Elsevier
121 Chanlon Rd.   Ph: (908)464-6800
New Providence, NJ 07974   Free: 800-521-8110
    Fax: (908)771-8645
E-mail: info@marquiswhoswho.com
Contact: Beverley McDonough, Managing Editor.
Desc: Over 27,000 persons ranging from principal local, state, and federal officials to men and women active and influential behind the scenes. *Type:* Directory.

Who's Who in the United Nations and Related Agencies
Omnigraphics Inc.
2500 Penobscot Bldg.   Ph: (313)961-1340
Detroit, MI 48226   Free: 800-234-1340
    Fax: (313)961-1383
E-mail: info@omnigraphics.com
URL: http://www.omnigraphics.com; http://www.omnigraphics.com.
Contact: Stanley R. Greenfield, Editor.
Desc: Approximately 3,000 members of the United Nations and related agencies, including officials and ambassadors. *Type:* Directory.

Graphic Arts/Design

Advanced Imaging—Buyers Guide Issue
Cygnus Publishing Inc.
445 Broad Hollow Road, Ste.   Ph: (516)845-2700
21   Free: 800-308-6397
Melville, NY 11747-3601   Fax: (516)845-2736
E-mail: info@advancedimagingmag.com
Contact: Barry Mazor, Editor-in-Chief.
Desc: List of about 800 electronic imaging companies and their products. *Type:* Directory.

American Ink Maker—Buyers' Guide Issue
Cygnus Publishing Inc.
445 Broad Hollow Road, Ste.   Ph: (516)845-2700
21   Free: 800-308-6397
Melville, NY 11747-3601   Fax: (516)845-2736
E-mail: info@advancedimagingmag.com; inckmaker@erols.com.
Contact: Linda M. Casatelli, Editor.
Desc: Guide to suppliers of raw materials, equipment, and services for manufacturers of printing ink, pigments, varnishes, graphic chemicals, and similar products; includes members of the National Association of Printing Ink Manufacturers. *Type:* Directory.

American Printer
Intertec Publishing Co.
29 N. Wacker Dr.   Ph: (312)726-2802
Chicago, IL 60606   Free: 800-621-9907
    Fax: (312)726-2574
Contact: Jill Roth, Editorial Dir., (312)609-4232, fax: (312)726-3091, jill_roth@intertec.com; Scott Bieda, Publisher, (312)609-4252, fax: (312)726-3091, scott_bieda@intertec.com.
Desc: Magazine covering the printing and publishing market. *Type:* Periodical.

Archie Comics
Archie Comic Publications, Inc.
325 Fayette Ave.   Ph: (914)381-5155
Mamaroneck, NY 10543   Fax: (914)381-2335
E-mail: archiecom@aol.com; archiecomics@mindspring.com.
URL: http://www.archiecomics.com.
Contact: Michael Silberkleit, Chairman, mikes@archiecomics.com; Richard Goldwater, President, richg@archiecomics.com.

Desc: Comics and comic digests. *Type:* Periodical.

Association of Graphic Communications
W.A. Dirzulaitis
330 7th Ave., 9th Fl.   Ph: (212)279-2100
New York, NY 10001-5010   Fax: (212)279-5381
E-mail: bd@accomm.org
URL: http://www.agcomm.org
Contact: William A. Dirzulaitis, Pres.
Desc: Works to promote and protect the interests of member companies and increase their graphic capabilities and corporate exposure. *Type:* Association.

Board Report for Graphic Artists
Board Report for Graphic Artists
PO Box 300789   Ph: (303)839-9058
Denver, CO 80203   Fax: (303)839-1272
Contact: Drew Allen Miller, Editor.
Desc: Serves graphic artists, designers, desktop publishers and advertising agencies. Consists of four publications: The Art Director's Newsletter, the Designer's Compendium, Logo Ideas and Trademark Trends. *Type:* Newsletter.

The Capital Letter
Printing Industries of America, Inc.
100 Daingerfield Rd.   Ph: (703)519-8100
Alexandria, VA 22314   Fax: (703)548-3227
URL: http://www.printing.org.
Contact: Bethany Culpepper, Manager, (703)519-8114, bculpepper@printing.org.
Desc: Covers events in Washington, D.C., concerning the printing and graphic arts industry. Focuses on labor/management, environmental, health and safety, procurement, trade, and copyright issues of interest to graphic arts management. *Type:* Newsletter.

Cartoonews Inc.
9 Mountain Laurel Dr.   Ph: (203)622-1547
Greenwich, CT 06831   Fax: (203)622-1648
Contact: T.R. Fletcher, President; L. Raymond, VP Sales; Stephen Castagneto, Dir-Admin.; Steve Lefkowitz, Graphic Asst.
Desc: Distributes Lurie's World and Lurie's Business World. *Alt. Contact:* 9 Mountain Laurel Dr., Greenwich, CT 06831; telephone: (203)622-1547; fax: (203)622-1648. *Type:* Periodical.

Cartoonists and Writers Syndicate
67 Riverside Dr.   Ph: (212)362-9256
Ste. 1-D   Fax: (212)595-4218
New York, NY 10024
E-mail: cmedia67@aol.com.
Contact: Jerry Robinson, Pres./Edit. Dir.; Jens Robinson, VP/Ed.; Susan Monagan, Features Sales; Patricia Gregory, Asst. Ed. Bus. Spec. Servs.; Sihanouk Mariona, Asst. Ed.; David Sung, Asst. Ed.
Desc: Distributes political and humor cartoons. *Alt. Contact:* 67 Riverside Dr., Ste. 1-D, New York, NY 10024; telephone: (212)362-9256; fax: (212)595-4218. *Type:* Periodical.

Computer Aided Design Report
CAD/CAM Publishing
1010 Turquoise St., Ste. 320   Ph: (619)488-0533
San Diego, CA 92109   Fax: (619)488-6052
E-mail: cadcentral@cadcamnet.com
URL: http://www.cadcamnet.com
Contact: Jeanette De Wyze, Editor.
Desc: "Learn how other firms are using CAD to improve productivity—and how you can avoid their mistakes." Provides an analysis of developments in the CAD/CAM (Computer-Aided Design/Computer-Aided Manufacturing) field. Highlights advances in CAD/CAM technology and monitors industry trends. *Type:* Newsletter.

Continuous Improvement Update
GATF SPC Users Group
Technical Services Group
Graphic Arts Technical Foundation (GATF)
4615 Forbes Ave.   Fax: (412)621-3049
Pittsburgh, PA 15213
Contact: Pamela Groff, Editor; Donna Mangold, Editor.
Desc: Covers continuous improvement in the printing industry. *Type:* Newsletter.

CyberInk
National Association of Printers & Lithographers
75 W. Century Rd.   Ph: (201)634-9600
Paramus, NJ 07652   Free: 800-642-6215
    Fax: (201)634-0324
E-mail: publications@napl.org
Contact: Dawn Lospaluto, Editor.
Desc: Offers information relating to NAPL's (National Association of Printers and Lithographers) Profit Connection website and its sponsors. *Type:* Newsletter.

Dan's Cartoons & Graphic Humor
PO Box 410   Ph: (906)482-6234
Chassell, MI 49916-0410
Contact: Dan Rosandich, President.
Desc: Distributes cartoons. *Alt. Contact:* PO Box 410, Chassell, MI 49916-0410; telephone: (906)482-6234. *Type:* Periodical.

Design Firm Management & Administration Report
Institute of Management & Administration, Inc.
29 W. 35th St., 5th Fl.   Ph: (212)244-0360
New York, NY 10001-2299   Fax: (212)564-0465
E-mail: subserve@ioma.com
URL: http://www.ioma.com
Contact: Ned Godfrey, Editor.
Desc: Advises consulting firms on practice management. *Type:* Newsletter.

Designer
University and College Designers Association
209 Commerce St.   Ph: (703)548-1770
Alexandria, VA 22314
Contact: Jody Zamirowski, Editor; Jean Springer, Editor.
Desc: Focuses on different areas of visual communication design, including graphics, photography, signage, films, and other related fields. Reviews communication and design technologies and techniques. *Type:* Newsletter.

The Eagle
Fitzpatrick Management, Inc.
522 Lilac Rd.   Ph: (704)542-2685
Charlotte, NC 28209-1425
Contact: Robert L. Fitzpatrick, Editor.
Desc: Serves as a publication about issues pertaining to dealer/manufacturer relations in the graphic arts industry. Recurring features include interviews, reports of meetings, and the analysis and interpretation of topical issues in North America and internationally. *Type:* Newsletter.

Flexographic Technical Association
900 Marconi Ave.   Ph: (516)737-6020
Ronkonkoma, NY 11779   Fax: (516)737-6813
URL: http://www.fta-ffta.org
Contact: William C. Dowdell, Pres.
Desc: Firms engaged in printing by flexographic process suppliers to the industry; end users. Seeks to advance the art and science of flexographic printing and assist and recommend developments in flexography. *Type:* Association.

Gambill Arts & Graphix Syndicate
66435 Pierson Blvd. Ph: (619)251-2401
Desert Hot Springs, CA 92240 Fax: (619)251-2401
Contact: George Gambill, Creator/Owner/Artist; Suzanne Gambill, Feature Ed.
Desc: Distributes cartoon panels. *Alt. Contact:* 66435 Pierson Blvd., Desert Hot Springs, CA 92240; telephone: (619)251-2401; fax: (619)251-2401. *Type:* Periodical.

George's Tips
George Hartman
2776 California Ct. Ph: (402)435-3191
Lincoln, NE 68510-3116
Contact: George Hartman, Editor.
Desc: Provides information for cartoonists ranging from general articles on the profession to suggestions on art technique or the creation of ideas. Covers art and cartoon markets. *Type:* Newsletter.

Ghost Rider
Marvel Entertainment, Inc.
387 Park Ave. S. Ph: (212)696-0808
New York, NY 10016 Fax: (212)576-8598
Desc: Comic book. *Type:* Periodical.

Graphic Arts Blue Book
A. F. Lewis & Co.
245 5th Ave. Ph: (212)679-0770
New York, NY 10016 Fax: (212)545-7963
E-mail: gartsbb@village.ios.com; gartsbb@village.ios.com.
URL: http://www.d-net.com/graphartsbb.
Contact: Linda Curran, Editor, (630)323-9777, fax: (630)323-9379; Doris Reyes, Editor; MaryKay Zobjeck, Editor, (630)323-9777, fax: (630)323-9379.
Desc: Printing plants, bookbinders, imagesetters, platemakers, paper merchants, paper manufacturers, printing machinery manufacturers and dealers, and others serving the graphic arts industry (Standard Industrial Classification (SIC) code 2600, 2700). Seven editions: New York edition (7,000 establishments) covers metropolitan New York and the state of New Jersey; Southeastern edition (10,500 establishments) covers Kentucky, Tennessee, Alabama, Mississippi, Virginia (except Washington suburbs), North Carolina, South Carolina, Georgia, and Florida; Northeastern edition (6,000 establishments) covers Connecticut, Maine, Massachusetts, New Hampshire, New York (upstate only), Rhode Island, and Vermont; Delaware Valley-Ohio edition (8,500 establishments) covers Pennsylvania, Maryland, Delaware, District of Columbia and its Virginia suburbs, and Ohio; Midwestern edition (13,000 establishments) covers Illinois, Indiana, Iowa, Michigan, Minnesota, Missouri, Wisconsin, North and South Dakota; Western edition (11,000 establishments) covers Arizona, California, Nevada, Oregon, Washington, Montana, Idaho, Wyoming, Utah, Alaska, Hawaii. Texas central edition (8000 establishments) covering Texas, Colorado, New Mexico, Oklahoma, Louisiana, Kansas and Nebraska. *Type:* Directory.

Graphic Arts Monthly
Cahners Business Information
345 Hudson St., 4th Fl. Ph: (212)519-7200
New York, NY 10014-4502 Fax: (212)519-7700
URL: http://www.gammag.com.
Contact: Roger Ynostroza, Editor, (212)519-7326, fax: (212)519-7489, r.ynostroza@cahners.com; Ronald Andriani, Group VP, (212)519-7225, fax: (212)519-7225, randriani@cahners.com; Adam Strominger, Classified Ad. Mgr., (212)519-7322, fax: (212)519-7491, astrominger@cahners.com; Christopher Lyons, Group Publisher, (212)519-7320, fax: (212)519-7485, lyonscope@aol.com; Earl Wilken, Assoc. Editor, (212)519-7324, fax: (212)519-7489, e.wilken@cahners.com; Rani Levy, Creative D

Desc: Magazine featuring commercial printing and graphic arts, including digital technologies. *Type:* Periodical.

Graphic Arts Monthly Sourcebook
Cahners Publishing Co.
245 W. 17th St. Ph: (212)463-6828
New York, NY 10014 Free: 800-523-9654
 Fax: (212)463-6530
URL: http://www.gammag.com.
Contact: Roger Ynostroza, Editor, r.ynostroza@cahners.com; Jo Ann Powell, Editor, jpowell@cahners.com.
Desc: About 1,400 manufacturers and distributors of graphic arts equipment, supplies, and services, and 700 graphic arts dealers. *Type:* Directory.

Graphic Arts Technical Foundation
200 Deer Run Rd. Ph: (412)741-6860
Sewickley, PA 15143-2600 Free: 800-910-GATF
 Fax: (412)741-2311
E-mail: info@gatf.org
URL: http://www.gatf.org
Contact: George H. Ryan, Pres.
Desc: Scientific, research, technical, and educational organization serving the international graphic communications industries. Conducts research in all graphic processes and their commercial applications. Conducts seminars, workshops, and forums on graphic arts and environmental subjects. *Type:* Association.

Graphic Communications Association
100 Daingerfield Rd. Ph: (703)519-8160
Alexandria, VA 22314-2888 Fax: (703)548-2867
E-mail: info@gca.org
URL: http://www.gca.org
Contact: Norman W. Scharpf, Pres.
Desc: Printers, publishers, advertising agencies, prepress services, manufacturers, fulfillment houses, service bureaus, electronic publishers, document managers, and software and hardware vendors to the industry. Objectives are to coordinate research and procedures relating to graphic arts print production; to provide for exchange of information and experience; to develop and disseminate educational and training materials relating to computer utilization and activities; to establish standard terminology in connection with computer usage in the graphic communications and electronic publishing industries; to provide specifications and guidance to the suppliers of equipment and systems in arriving at products and services suited to the needs of the graphic communications industry; to establish a favorable climate for the achievement of graphic communications systems goals. *Type:* Association.

Graphic Communications International Union
1900 L St. NW Ph: (202)462-1400
Washington, DC 20036 Fax: (202)721-0600
URL: http://www.gciu.org
Contact: James J. Norton, Pres.
Desc: AFL-CIO; Canadian Labour Congress. *Type:* Association.

Graphic Communications Today
Graphic Communications Association
100 Daingerfield Rd. Ph: (703)519-8160
Alexandria, VA 22314 Fax: (703)548-2867
URL: http://www.gca.org/headline/index.htm.
Contact: Alan Kotok, Editor, (703)579-8173, fax: (703)548-2867, editor@gca.org.
Desc: Provides current information on the graphic communications industry. Available online only. *Type:* Newsletter.

Graphics Update
Printing Association of Florida, Inc.
PO Box 170010 Ph: (305)558-4855
Miami, FL 33017-0010 Fax: (305)823-8965
Contact: Gene Strul, Editor.
Desc: Concerned with developments within the field of graphic arts. Covers aspects of the industry with an emphasis on Florida, including news of exhibitions, statistics, new technologies and products, and events affecting the ancillary industries. *Type:* Newsletter.

GrayPrint
The Gray Printing Company
401 E. North St. Ph: (419)435-6638
PO Box 840 Free: 800-837-4729
Fostoria, OH 44830 Fax: (419)435-9410
E-mail: grayprint@aol.com
URL: http://www.graypaint.com.
Contact: Scott Gray, Editor; Robert Gray, Editor.
Desc: Provides news of developments in printing. Includes articles on camera-ready art and photograph development, letters to the editor, and a column titled Printer's Ink. *Type:* Newsletter.

Heavy Metal
Metal Mammoth Inc.
100 Merrick Rd., Ste. 400 E. Ph: (516)594-2130
 Bldg. Fax: (516)594-2133
Rockville Centre, NY 11570
E-mail: hvymt2@freewwweb.com.
Contact: Debra Jurofsky, Managing Editor; Howard Jurofsky, Director.
Desc: Consumer magazine of illustrated fantasy. *Type:* Periodical.

The Hulk
Marvel Entertainment, Inc.
387 Park Ave. S. Ph: (212)696-0808
New York, NY 10016 Fax: (212)576-8598
Contact: Bobbie Chase, Editor.
Desc: Comic book. *Type:* Periodical.

ImageMaker
Screen Printing Association International (SPAI)
10015 Main St. Ph: (703)385-1335
Fairfax, VA 22031 Fax: (703)273-0456
Contact: Bruce H. Joffe, Editor.
Desc: Carries short items on interesting, informative, and innovative uses of screen printing. *Type:* Newsletter.

Imaging Service Bureau Newsletter
Image Publishing
PO Box 3149 Ph: (203)222-9310
Westport, CT 06880 Free: 800-347-9310
 Fax: (203)222-7871
E-mail: imagepub@futuris.net
Contact: David J. Miles, Editor.
Desc: Features news and company profiles of micrographics, data entry, and optical disc conversion service bureaus. Recurring features include letters to the editor, interviews, job listings, book reviews, and notices of publications available. *Type:* Newsletter.

Imaging Update
Worldwide Videotex
PO Box 3273 Ph: (561)738-2276
Boynton Beach, FL 33424-3273
E-mail: markedit@gnn.com; markedit@juno.com.
URL: http://www.wvpubs.com.
Desc: Updates on imaging and computer graphics industry. Reports on news of research and development, new products, markets and strategies, and management information systems. *Type:* Newsletter.

Impressions—Sourcebook

Miller Freeman, Inc.
13760 Noel Rd., Ste. 500   Ph: (972)239-3060
Dallas, TX 75240   Free: 800-527-0207
    Fax: (972)419-7825
URL: http://www.impressionsmag.com.
Contact: Deborah Sexton, Editor.
Desc: List of more than 1,500 suppliers of products, services, and equipment used in the imprinted sportswear industry. *Type:* Directory.

In-Plant Profiles

North American Publishing Co.
401 N. Broad St.   Ph: (215)238-5300
Philadelphia, PA 19108   Free: 800-777-8074
    Fax: (215)238-5270
URL: http://www.napco.com
Desc: In-plant printing and graphic arts facilities, managers, graphic arts dealers and associations in the U.S. *Type:* Directory.

Industrial Designers Society of America

1142 E Walker Rd., Ste. E   Ph: (703)759-0100
Great Falls, VA 22066   Fax: (703)759-7679
E-mail: idsa@erols.com
URL: http://www.idsa.org
Contact: Robert T. Schwartz, Exec.Dir.
Desc: Professional society of industrial designers. Represents the profession in its relations with business, education, government, and international designers; promotes the industrial design profession. *Type:* Association.

Ink on Paper

Graphic Arts Publishing Inc.
3100 Bronson Hill Rd.   Ph: (716)346-2776
Livonia, NY 14487   Free: 800-724-9476
    Fax: (716)346-2776
E-mail: mfsppr@rit.edu.
Contact: M.F. Southworth, Editor, fax: (716)346-6978; D.K. Southworth, Editor.
Desc: Describes "procedures and equipment to improve quality and productivity" for graphic arts practitioners and companies. Provides information on references, control tools, trends, and relevant quality control and scanner facts. *Type:* Newsletter.

International Association of Printing House Craftsmen

7042 Brooklyn Blvd.   Ph: (612)560-1620
Minneapolis, MN 55429-1370   Free: 800-466-4274
    Fax: (612)560-1350
E-mail: kkeane1069@aol.com
URL: http://www.iaphc.org
Contact: Kevin Keane, Exec.Dir.
Desc: Individuals employed in any facet of the graphic arts. *Type:* Association.

International Reprographic Association

800 Enterprise Dr., Ste. 202   Ph: (630)571-4685
Oak Brook, IL 60523   Fax: (630)571-4731
Contact: Brian McCarthy, Exec.Dir.
Desc: Commercial blue print and photocopy firms, engineering supply stores, and materials and equipment suppliers. *Type:* Association.

Just the Fax

International Association of Presentation Professionals
294 Arden Rd.   Ph: (412)531-7739
Pittsburgh, PA 15216   Free: 800-688-2748
Contact: Lesley Hayes, Editor, lesley@vicom.ca.
Desc: Provides tips and techniques to members of the association. Informs of association activities and news. *Type:* Newsletter.

Leadership Excellence

National Association of Printers & Lithographers
75 W. Century Rd.   Ph: (201)634-9600
Paramus, NJ 07652   Free: 800-642-6215
    Fax: (201)634-0324
E-mail: publications@napl.org
Contact: Dawn Lospaluto, Editor.
Desc: Offers print management information from NAPL (National Association of Printers and Lithographers) consultants and other experts in almost every business discipline. *Type:* Newsletter.

Letterspace

Type Directors Club
60 E. 42nd St., Ste. 721   Ph: (212)983-6042
New York, NY 10165-0799   Fax: (212)983-6043
E-mail: director@tdc.org
URL: http://www.tdc.org.
Contact: Carol Wahler, Editor.
Desc: Highlights interests of the Type Directors Club, an organization devoted to graphic arts and typography. Recurring features include book reviews, a calendar of events, news of educational opportunities, and news of members. *Type:* Newsletter.

Management Portfolio

Printing Industries of America, Inc.
100 Daingerfield Rd.   Ph: (703)519-8100
Alexandria, VA 22314   Fax: (703)548-3227
Contact: Scott Brisoce, Editor, sbriscoe@printing.org.
Desc: Analyzes trends and offers advice to graphic arts companies so that they may operate and compete more effectively in the marketplace. Recurring features include interviews, news of research, reports of meetings, news of educational opportunities, and notices of publications available. *Type:* Newsletter.

Mastering CorelDRAW Newsletter

Kazak Communications
16 Ottawa St.
Toronto, ON, Canada M4T
   2B6
URL: http://www.corelnet.com.
Contact: Chris Dickman, Editor.
Desc: Covers CorelDRAW graphics applications. Offers "tips and tricks with a hands-on focus." Remarks: Also available on diskette. *Type:* Newsletter.

Morbius

Marvel Entertainment, Inc.
387 Park Ave. S.   Ph: (212)696-0808
New York, NY 10016   Fax: (212)576-8598
Contact: Bobbie Chase, Editor.
Desc: Comic Book. *Type:* Periodical.

Musick Toons

PO Box 1215   Ph: (419)562-4778
Bucyrus, OH 44820-4215   Fax: (419)562-4778
Contact: Earl T. Musick, Managing Editor.
Desc: Distributes cartoons and comic strips. *Alt. Contact:* PO Box 1215, Bucyrus, OH 44820-4215; telephone: (419)562-4778; fax: (419)562-4778. *Type:* Periodical.

NAPL Economic Edge

National Association of Printers & Lithographers
75 W. Century Rd.   Ph: (201)634-9600
Paramus, NJ 07652   Free: 800-642-6215
    Fax: (201)634-0324
E-mail: publications@napl.org; perc@napl.org.
Desc: Provides current economic data for the printing industry. Also covers sales growth projections, capital spending, and employment. *Type:* Newsletter.

National Association of Printers and Lithographers

75 W. Century Rd.   Ph: (201)634-9600
Paramus, NJ 07652-1408   Free: 800-642-NAPL
    Fax: (201)634-0324
URL: http://www.napl.org
Contact: I. Gregg van Wert, Pres.
Desc: Firms engaged in printing. *Type:* Association.

NSPA Newsletter

National State Publishing Association (NSPA)
48 Liberty Pl., No. 2   Ph: (601)264-3442
Hattiesburg, MS 39402   Fax: (601)264-3442
E-mail: ams@access-net.com
Contact: Linda Carroll, Editor.
Desc: Tracks innovations in state printing programs and other developments of interest to state printing officials. Covers Association activities. *Type:* Newsletter.

Ontario Industrial Arts Bulletin

Westminster Word Processing
64 Smith St.   Ph: (416)734-7447
Welland, ON, Canada L3C
   4H4
Contact: Brian Carswell, Editor.
Desc: Reports on the industrial arts industry in Ontario. *Type:* Newsletter.

Piercy & Barclay Designers Inc.

7080 SW Fir Loop   Ph: (503)620-4551
Ste. 100   Fax: (503)684-7032
Tigard, OR 97223
URL: http://www.teleport.com/~piercy.
Contact: Janet Piercy, Self-Syndicator.
Alt. Contact: 7080 SW Fir Loop, Ste. 100, Tigard, OR 97223; telephone: (503)620-4551; fax: (503)684-7032. *Type:* Periodical.

Principal's Report

Institute of Management & Administration, Inc.
29 W. 35th St., 5th Fl.   Ph: (212)244-0360
New York, NY 10001-2299   Fax: (212)564-0465
E-mail: subserve@ioma.com
URL: http://www.ioma.com
Contact: Kneeland Godfrey, Editor; Lee Rath, Publisher.
Desc: Provides information and advice for design firms. Topics include market strategies and compensation. *Type:* Newsletter.

Print Media Production Source

SRDS
1700 Higgins Rd.   Ph: (847)375-5000
Des Plaines, IL 60018-5605   Free: 800-851-7737
    Fax: (847)375-5001
E-mail: contact@srds.com
Contact: Peter Spina, Editor.
Desc: Production listings for business, consumer, and farm periodicals and daily newspapers. *Type:* Directory.

The Printer's Apprentice

The Printer's Apprentice
88 E. Main St., Ste. 457
Mendham, NJ 07945-1832
Contact: David Smith, Editor.
Desc: Directed toward the printing business, services, and supplies. *Type:* Newsletter.

Printer's Ink

Thomson-Shore, Inc.
7300 W. Joy Rd.   Ph: (734)426-3939
Dexter, MI 48130-9701   Fax: (734)426-6219
E-mail: rickg@tshore.com; donnaf@tshore.com.

Contact: Ned Thomson, Editor, nedt@tshore.com.

Desc: Provides information on developments in printing and binding and other ten ets of book manufacturing. Includes a feature article, company news, informatio n on printing prices, and a column titled Trivia. *Type:* Newsletter.

PrintImage International

401 N. Michigan Ave.   Ph: (312)321-6886
Chicago, IL 60611-4267   Free: 800-234-0040
   Fax: (312)527-6789

E-mail: printimage@printimage.org

URL: http://www.printimage.org

Contact: David Steinhardt, Exec.Dir.

Desc: Owners and managers of printing companies; industry suppliers. Seeks to bring recognition, improved quality, and increased profits to the entire quick printing field. Compiles statistics; sponsors specialized user groups and research programs; Provides speakers' bureau. *Type:* Association.

Printing Impressions

North American Publishing Co.
401 N. Broad St.   Ph: (215)238-5300
Philadelphia, PA 19108   Free: 800-777-8074
   Fax: (215)238-5270

URL: http://www.napco.com; http://www.piworld.com.

Contact: Mark Michelson, Editor, (215)238-5329, fax: (215)238-5484, mmichelson@napco.com; Carl Lock, Publisher, (215)238-5348.

Desc: Trade magazine. *Type:* Periodical.

Printing Impressions Executive Briefing

North American Publishing Co.
401 N. Broad St.   Ph: (215)238-5300
Philadelphia, PA 19108   Free: 800-777-8074
   Fax: (215)238-5270

URL: http://www.napco.com; http://www.piworld.com.

Contact: Christopher Cornell, Editor.

Desc: Provides current news on the commercial printing, business forms printing, package printing, and related industries. Includes acquisitions and mergers, equipment installations, and industry trends. *Type:* Newsletter.

Printing Impressions—Top 500 Printers Issue

North American Publishing Co.
401 N. Broad St.   Ph: (215)238-5300
Philadelphia, PA 19108   Free: 800-777-8074
   Fax: (215)238-5270

E-mail: editor.pi@napco.com.

URL: http://www.napco.com

Contact: Mark Michelson, Editor.

Desc: List of the leading 500 commercial, financial, directory, publication, check, book, business form, packaging, and specialty printers. *Type:* Directory.

Printing Industries of America

100 Daingerfield Rd.   Ph: (703)519-8100
Alexandria, VA 22314   Free: 800-742-2666
   Fax: (703)548-3227

E-mail: jsass@printing.org

URL: http://www.printing.org

Contact: Ray Roper, Pres./CEO.

Desc: Commercial printing firms (lithography, letterpress, gravure, platemakers, typographic houses); allied firms in the graphic arts. Provides extensive management services for member companies, including government relations, industry research and statistical information, technology information and assistance, and management education and publications. Compiles statistical and economic data, including annual ratio study which provides a benchmark for printers to compare profits as a basis for improving individual member company and industry profits. *Type:* Association.

Printing Industry Gold Book

North American Publishing Co.
401 N. Broad St.   Ph: (215)238-5300
Philadelphia, PA 19108   Free: 800-777-8074
   Fax: (215)238-5270

E-mail: pgbeditoc@napco.com.

URL: http://www.napco.com

Contact: Lisa A. Denshuick, Editor, (215)238-5335, fax: (215)238-5099, ldenshuick@napco.com.

Desc: Printing buyers, advertising agencies, design firms, commercial/inplant printers, Printing Industries of America membership list, graphic arts executives, industry suppliers, dealers, paper mills, and merchants, products of manufacturers, associations, consulting services, research organizations, graphic arts educational facilities, converting companies, and award winners in the U.S. *Type:* Directory.

Printing, Publishing, and Media Workers Sector of the CWA

501 E. 3rd St. NW   Ph: (202)434-1238
Washington, DC 20001-2797   Fax: (202)434-1245

Contact: William J. Boarman, Pres.

Desc: AFL-CIO; CWA. *Type:* Association.

PRINTOUT

Association of Graphic Communications
330 Seventh Ave., 9th Fl.   Ph: (212)279-2100
New York, NY 10001-5010   Fax: (212)279-5381
E-mail: bd@agcomm.org

Contact: William A. Dirzulaitis, Editor.

Desc: Seeks to communicate to the graphic communications industry in the New York/New Jersey metropolitan area on economic/business news, education/training support, public affairs, regulatory issues, human resources, labor issues, technical trends, sales, marketing, and customer relation techniques that affect all aspects of graphic arts. Features news of the programs of the Association, which include seminars, courses, and hands-on training, group insurance plans, an annual exhibition, and consulting services. *Type:* Newsletter.

printRIT Update

Technical & Education Center of the Graphic Arts
Rochester Institute of Technology
66 Lomb Memorial Dr.   Ph: (716)475-7090
Rochester, NY 14623-5604   Free: 800-724-2536
   Fax: (716)475-7000

E-mail: webmail@rit.edu

URL: http://www.rit.edu/CIMS/TE.

Contact: Sandy Richolson, Editor, (716)475-2549, fax: (716)475-7052, slrtec@rit.edu.

Desc: Reports on testing activities, training seminars, conferences, workshops, and programs of the Center. *Type:* Newsletter.

PSMJ Principal Strategies

PSMJ Resources, Inc.
10 Midland Ave.   Ph: (617)965-0055
Newton, MA 02158   Free: 800-537-PSMJ
   Fax: (617)965-5152

E-mail: psmj@ixnetcom.com

Contact: C. Winslow Pettingell, Editorial Director; Susan A. Yoder, Editor.

Desc: Focuses on service excellence in the design professions. *Type:* Newsletter.

Quick Printing—Source Guide

Cygnus Publishing Inc.
445 Broad Hollow Road, Ste.   Ph: (516)845-2700
21   Free: 800-308-6397
Melville, NY 11747-3601   Fax: (516)845-2736

E-mail: info@advancedimagingmag.com; quickptg@aol.com.

Contact: William C. Lewis, Editor.

Desc: List of national suppliers to the quick printing business and small commercial printing industry, including suppliers of paper, copiers, design services, presses, software, pre-press, and camera and platemaking equipment. *Type:* Directory.

Roll Call

TEKRA direct
1435 S. Osprey   Ph: (941)330-1210
Sarasota, FL 34239   Free: 800-453-9538
   Fax: (941)330-1220

E-mail: info@tekradirect.com

URL: http://www.tekradirect.com.

Contact: Linda Jennings, Contact, (941)351-1005, fax: (941)351-0846, jennings@netline.net.

Desc: Designed to provide solutions for the wide format ink jet printing community. Includes articles on issues and problems affecting this industry, and possible solutions. *Type:* Newsletter.

Rothco Cartoons

1463 44th St.   Ph: (718)853-5435
Brooklyn, NY 11219

Contact: Steven Weiss, President.

Desc: Distributes single panel cartoons. *Alt. Contact:* 1463 44th St., Brooklyn, NY 11219; telephone: (718)853-5435. *Type:* Periodical.

Schwadron Cartoon & Illustration Service

PO Box 1347   Ph: (313)426-8433
Ann Arbor, MI 48106   Fax: (313)426-8433

Contact: Harley Schwadron, Editor; Sally Booth, Sec.

Desc: Distributes cartoons. *Alt. Contact:* PO Box 1347, Ann Arbor, MI 48106; telephone: (313)426-8433; fax: (313)426-8433. *Type:* Periodical.

Screenprinting and Graphic Imaging Association International

10015 Main St.   Ph: (703)385-1335
Fairfax, VA 22031-3489   Fax: (703)273-0456
E-mail: sgia@sgia.org
URL: http://www.sgia.org

Contact: John M. Crawford, CAE, Pres.

Desc: Printers who use the screen process of printing and/or digital (electronic) printing; associate members are suppliers and manufacturers; educational institutions. Provides training, workshops, and educational seminars; technical, managerial, educational, informational, governmental, safety, and research services. *Type:* Association.

Sheetfed Operations Quarterly

National Association of Printers & Lithographers
75 W. Century Rd.   Ph: (201)634-9600
Paramus, NJ 07652   Free: 800-642-6215
   Fax: (201)634-0324

E-mail: publications@napl.org

Contact: Cynthia L. Shaw, Editor.

Desc: Features articles based on presentations made at the GATF/NAPL (National Association of Printers and Lithographers) Sheetfed Pressroom Conference. *Type:* Newsletter.

SIGGRAPH Computer Graphics

Special Interest Group on Computer Graphics &
Interactive Techniques
Association for Computing Machinery
1515 Broadway   Ph: (212)869-7440
New York, NY 10036   Free: 800-342-6626
E-mail: acmhelp@acm.org

Contact: Gordon Cameron, Editor.

Desc: Treats all aspects of graphical person/machine communication and image processing and manipulation. Discusses graphics theory, raster graphics, algorithms, languages, animation, and applications to such fields as publishing, cartography, biomedicine, and Computer-Aided Design (CAD). *Type:* Newsletter.

Society for Environmental Graphic Design— Messages

Society for Environmental Graphic Design
(SEGD)
401 F St. NW, Ste. 333   Ph: (202)638-5555
Washington, DC 20001   Fax: (202)638-0891
E-mail: segdoffice@aol.com; segdoffice@aol.com.

Contact: Elisabeth Banks, Editor.

Desc: Reports on Society program news, member services, resources, job opportunities, and product news. Recurring features include an ADA column. *Type:* Newsletter.

Sourcebook: El Directorio Internacional Flexografico de Productos y Servicios

Foundation of Flexographic Technical Association
900 Marconi Ave.   Ph: (516)737-6020
Ronkonkoma, NY 11779-7212   Fax: (516)737-6813
URL: http://www.fta-ffta.org.

Contact: Graciela I. Gilbride, Editor, ggilbride@vax.fta-ffta.org.

Desc: Products and services to the International Flexographic industry in Spanish. *Type:* Directory.

Step-By-Step Electronic Design

Step-By-Step Publishing
c/o Dynamic Graphics Inc.   Ph: (309)688-2300
6000 N. Forest Park Dr.   Free: 800-255-8800
Peoria, IL 61614   Fax: (309)688-8515

Contact: Sara Booth, Editor.

Desc: Contains how-to articles on electronic graphic design and production via real-world projects. Recurring features include columns titled The Graphic Eye, Design Workshop, In the Trenches, and Q & A. *Type:* Newsletter.

Tattoo Club of America

Spider Webb Tattoo Gallery
158 W 15th St.   Ph: (212)255-1490
No. BSMT   Fax: (212)691-6643
New York, NY 10011-6718

Contact: Spider Webb, Pres.

Desc: Tattoo artists and individuals worldwide who have been tattooed. Seeks to promote the art of tattooing and make it more acceptable to the public. *Type:* Association.

Trademark Trends

Trademark Trends
PO Box 300789   Ph: (303)839-9058
Denver, CO 80203   Fax: (303)839-1272

Contact: Drew Allen Miller, Editor.

Desc: Features recently registered trademarks in an indexed and categorized format. Recurring features include a calendar of events. *Type:* Newsletter.

U & Ic

International Typeface Corp.
805 3rd Ave.   Ph: (212)371-0699
New York, NY 10022-7513   Fax: (212)752-4752

Contact: Margaret Richardson, Editor; Joyce Rutter Kaye, Managing Editor.

Desc: Upper and Lowercase. Graphic arts magazine for designers and graphic artists. *Type:* Periodical.

XPLOR International

24238 Hawthorne Blvd.   Ph: (310)373-3633
Torrance, CA 90505-6505   Free: 800-669-7567
     Fax: (310)375-4240
E-mail: info@xplor.org
URL: http://www.xplor.org

Contact: Keith T. Davidson, Ph.D., Pres.

Desc: An independent industry association (not sponsored by computer manufacturers). *Type:* Association.

Greece/Greek

American Hellenic Educational Progressive Association

1909 Q St. NW, Ste. 500   Ph: (202)232-6300
Washington, DC 20009   Fax: (202)232-2140

Contact: Timothy Maniatis, Exec.Dir.

Desc: Fraternal organization composed primarily of persons of Greek descent. U.S. citizenship (or declared intention to achieve citizenship) is required. *Type:* Association.

Daughters of Penelope

1909 O St. NW, No. 500   Ph: (202)234-9741
Washington, DC 20009   Fax: (202)483-6983
E-mail: daughters@ahopea.org

Contact: Helen G. Pappas, Exec.Dir.

Desc: Women's fraternal organization. Participates in other philanthropic activities. Sponsors Daughters of Penelope Foundation. *Type:* Association.

Greek Catholic Union of the U.S.A.

5400 Tuscarawas Rd.   Ph: (412)495-3400
Beaver, PA 15009   Free: 800-722-4GCU
     Fax: (724)495-3421

Contact: Michael Roman, Pres.

Desc: Fraternal benefit life insurance society. Provides aid to unemployed individuals and funding to religious education programs. Sponsors competitions. *Type:* Association.

Greek Orthodox Ladies Philoptochos Society, Inc.

345 E. 74th St.   Ph: (212)744-4390
New York, NY 10021-3701   Fax: (212)861-1956

Contact: Eve C. Condakes, Pres.

Desc: Women 18 years or older of the Greek Orthodox faith. Aim is to preserve the sacredness of the Orthodox family and perpetuate and promote the charitable and philanthropic purposes of the Greek Orthodox Archdiocese of North America. *Type:* Association.

Greek Orthodox Young Adult League

8 E. 79th St.   Ph: (212)570-3560
New York, NY 10021   Fax: (212)861-2183

Desc: Greek Orthodox youth throughout the Americas. Conducts leadership and religious education workshops, athletic tournaments, summer camps, and other activities to assist the church program locally and nationally. Distributes religious films. *Type:* Association.

Panepirotic Federation of America, Canada, and Australia

1790 Broadway, Ste. 1315   Ph: (212)582-5095
New York, NY 10019   Fax: (212)582-5098

Contact: Nicholas Gage, Pres.

Desc: Americans, Canadians, and Australians of Epirotic origin. (Epirus is located in the northwest region of ancient Greece, half of which remains Greek, while the other half is now occupied by Albania.) Seeks to protect freedom of religion and speech, cultural autonomy, and language for persons living in northern Epirus (that which is under Albanian control). Promotes respect for the law; cultivates spirit of brotherhood between Epirotans, Americans, Canadians, and Australians; defends Greeks of northern Epirus through legal means. *Type:* Association.

Hardware

Associated Locksmiths of America

3003 Live Oak St.   Ph: (214)827-1701
Dallas, TX 75204   Free: 800-532-2562
     Fax: (214)827-1810
E-mail: convtion@anet-dfw.com
URL: http://www.aloa.org

Contact: Charles W. Gibson, Jr., Exec.Dir.

Desc: Retail locksmiths; associate members are manufacturers and distributors of locks, keys, safes, and burglar alarms. Objective is to educate and provide current information to individuals in the physical security industry. *Type:* Association.

Door and Hardware Institute

14170 Newbrook Dr.   Ph: (703)222-2010
Chantilly, VA 20151-2232   Fax: (703)222-2410
URL: http://www.dhi.org

Contact: Jerry Heppes, CAE, Exec.Dir.

Desc: Commercial distributors, manufacturers and specifiers involved in doors and builders' hardware (locks, door hardware, latches, hinges, and electrified products). Works with architects, contractors, and building owners. Conducts management and technical courses and membership-related surveys. *Type:* Association.

Hardware Age Home Improvement Market Who Makes It Buyer's Guide Issue

Cahners Business Information
201 King of Prussia Rd.   Ph: (610)964-4000
Radnor, PA 19087-5114   Fax: (610)964-2915
E-mail: marketaccess@cahners.com; homeimpvmt@aol.com.
URL: http://www.homemkt.com.

Contact: Jim Cory, Editor.

Desc: About 4,400 manufacturers of automotive, electrical, lawn and garden, and plumbing products; building supplies, hardware, housewares, paint, sporting goods, tools, and warehouse equipment. *Type:* Directory.

Houseware Industry News and Topics

International Pot and Kettle Clubs
c/o Mildred Johnson   Ph: (206)927-6003
4107 Harbor Ridge Rd. N.E.
Tacoma, WA 98422

Contact: Mildred Johnson, Editor.

Desc: Represents the manufacturers of housewares, hardware and allied products, and houseware buyers for wholesalers and retail stores. Reports on the status of the industry in general and provides a forum for the consideration of topics pertinent to the industry and to membership. *Type:* Newsletter.

National Retail Hardware Association
5822 W. 74th St.   Ph: (317)290-0338
Indianapolis, IN 46278 Free: 800-772-4424
                        Fax: (317)328-4354
E-mail: nrha@iquest.net
URL: http://www.nrha.org
Contact: John P. Hammond, Mng.Dir.

Desc: Represents independent family-armed hardware/home improvement retailers. Sponsors correspondence courses in hardware and building materials retailing; conducts annual cost-of-doing-business study. *Type:* Association.

Precision Machined Products Association
6700 W. Snowville Rd.   Ph: (440)526-0300
Brecksville, OH 44141   Fax: (440)526-5803
URL: http://www.pmpa.org
Contact: Jack D. McNaughton, Exec.VP.

Desc: Manages the information, training, and technical needs of manufacturers of component parts to customer's order, machined from rod, bar, or tube stock, of metal, fiber, plastic, or other material, using automatic or hand screw machines, automatic bar machines, and CNC machines. *Type:* Association.

Pump News & Patents
IMPACT Publications
PO Box 3113
Ketchum, ID 83340   Ph: (208)622-3210
                        Fax: (208)726-2115
Contact: Mary Jo Helmeke, Editor.

Desc: Examines new pump products, software, and technical developments. Includes literature reviews and manufacturers' addresses. *Type:* Newsletter.

Valve Manufacturers Association of America
1050 17th St. NW, Ste. 280   Ph: (202)331-8105
Washington, DC 20036   Fax: (202)296-0378
E-mail: vma@vma.org
URL: http://www.vma.org
Contact: William S. Sandler, Pres.

Desc: Manufacturers of industrial valves and actuators including gate valves, globe valves, check valves, water works, IBBM gate valves, tapping sleeves and crosses, fire hydrants, ball valves, butterfly valves, nonmetal valves, corrosion resistant valves, thru-conduit valves, plug valves, automatic control and regulating valves, solenoid valves, and safety and relief valves. *Type:* Association.

Valve Variations
Valve Manufacturers Association of America (VMA)
1050 17th St. NW, Ste. 280   Ph: (202)331-8105
Washington, DC 20036   Fax: (202)296-0378
E-mail: vma@vma.org
Contact: William S. Sandler, Editor, wsandler@vma.org.

Desc: Provides industry statistics and forecasts. *Type:* Newsletter.

VMA Update
Valve Manufacturers Association of America (VMA)
1050 17th St. NW, Ste. 280   Ph: (202)331-8105
Washington, DC 20036   Fax: (202)296-0378
E-mail: vma@vma.org
Contact: Lisa Cherubini, Editor.

Desc: Provides Association and member company news. Reports on current legislative and regulatory action concerning the industry. *Type:* Newsletter.

Wire Industry News
CRU International
7474 Greenway Center Dr., Ste.   Ph: (301)441-8997
820   Fax: (301)441-9091
Greenbelt, MD 20770
E-mail: cru_sales@compuserve.com
Contact: Karen Chasez, Editor.

Desc: Monitors business activities in the wire industry, including mergers, restructurings, management appointments, and start-ups. Studies major marketing shifts and technological developments of interest to upper and middle industry management. *Type:* Newsletter.

Health

Agent Orange Review
V.A. Headquarters
Department of Veterans Affairs
Environmental Agents Service--131
810 Vermont Ave. NW   Ph: (202)273-8580
Washington, DC 20420   Fax: (202)273-9080
Contact: Donald J. Rosenblum, Editor.

Desc: Provides information regarding health concerns of Vietnam veterans, concentrating on news, legislation, policies, and procedures on the long-term health consequences of Agent Orange exposure. *Type:* Newsletter.

alive
ALIVE Magazine
7436 Fraser Park Dr.   Ph: (604)435-1919
Burnaby, BC, Canada V5J 5B9 Free: 800-663-6580
                             Fax: (604)435-4888
E-mail: editorial@ultranet.ca.
Contact: Lorna Vanderhaggae, Editor; Siegfried Gursche, Publisher; Charlene Beckman, Art Dir.

Desc: Magazine promoting healthy living, alternative health, and nutrition. *Type:* Periodical.

Allergy Alert
Allergy Foundation of Canada
PO Box 1904   Ph: (306)652-1608
Saskatoon, SK, Canada S7K 3S5 Fax: (306)373-7591
Contact: Sandy Woynarski, Editor, sswoynarski@sk.sympatico.ca.

Desc: Covers topics of interest to allergic persons and their families. Recurring features include letters to the editor, news of research, book reviews, and columns titled Hints, Helps, How-To's, Food Facts Product Reviews, Environmentally Yours, and Doctor Talk. *Type:* Newsletter.

Allergy/Asthma Quarterly
Allergy/Asthma Information Association
30 Eglinton Ave. W, Ste. 750   Ph: (905)712-2242
Mississauga, ON, Canada L5R   Fax: (905)712-2245
3E7
Contact: Susan Daglish, Editor.

Desc: Disseminates information on allergies and asthma. Answers questions submitted by adults and children. *Type:* Newsletter.

ALTERNATIVES for the Health Conscious Individual
Mountain Home Publishing
PO Box 829   Ph: (210)367-4492
Ingram, TX 78025   Free: 800-527-3044
                         Fax: (210)424-5059
Contact: Dr. David G. Williams.

Desc: Emphasizes natural therapies and self-help techniques to obtain optimal health without the use of drugs or surgery. Provides information regarding specific nutritional supplements, diets, exercises, and therapies for the prevention and/or treatment of various health conditions. *Type:* Newsletter.

American Academy of Pain Management
13947 Mono Way, No. A   Ph: (209)533-9744
Sonora, CA 95370   Fax: (209)533-9750
E-mail: aapm@aapainmanage.org
URL: http://www.aapainmanage.org
Contact: Richard S. Weiner, PhD, Exec.Dir.

Desc: To establish the core body of knowledge necessary to become a pain management professional. *Type:* Association.

American Association for Health Education
1900 Association Dr.   Ph: (703)476-3437
Reston, VA 20191   Free: 800-213-7193
                         Fax: (703)476-6638
E-mail: aahe@aahperd.org
URL: http://www.aahperd.org/aahe.aahe.html
Contact: Becky J. Smith, Ph.D., Exec.Dir.

Desc: Professionals who have responsibility for health education in schools, colleges, communities, hospitals and clinics, and industries. Purposes are advancement of health education through program activities and federal legislation; encouragement of close working relationships between all health education and health service organizations; achievement of good health and well-being for all Americans automatically, without conscious thought and endeavor. *Type:* Association.

American Association for the Study of Headache
19 Mantua Rd.   Ph: (609)423-0043
Mount Royal, NJ 08061   Fax: (609)423-0082
E-mail: aashhq@talley.com
URL: http://www.aash.org
Contact: Linda McGillicuddy, Exec. Dir.

Desc: Physicians, dentists, and related scientists interested in the study of headaches. Brings together practitioners in different fields of medicine to discuss ideas and beliefs about headache and head pain. *Type:* Association.

American Council for Headache Education
19 Mantua Rd.   Ph: (609)423-0258
Mount Royal, NJ 08061   Free: 800-255-ACHE
                         Fax: (609)423-0082
E-mail: achehq@talley.com
URL: http://www.achenet.org
Contact: Linda McGillicuddy, Exec.Dir.

Desc: Individuals suffering from headaches; physicians. Seeks to advance the study and treatment of headache. *Type:* Association.

American Council for Health Care Reform
712 W. Broad St., Ste. B2   Ph: (703)908-9220
Falls Church, VA 22046-3222 Free: 800-240-6423
                             Fax: (703)908-9467
Contact: William Shaker, Pres.

Desc: Organized to eliminate what the council terms unnecessary and costly federal and state health care regulations and laws, such as certificate of public need restrictions that limit public choice in the selection of health care providers. Supports health care reform, based on Consumer choice. Testifies before congressional and state legislative committees. *Type:* Association.

American Foundation for Health
2107 Dwight Way   Ph: (510)644-3366
Berkeley, CA 94704
Contact: Dr. Ken Matsumura, Exec.Dir.

Desc: Individuals interested in improving the delivery of health care services. Encourages recording of personal medical data. Conducts educational research projects and activities. *Type:* Association.

American Health Care Advisory Association

PO Box 11369
Robinson, TX 76706

Contact: Nick Keeling, Pres.

Desc: Acts as an advisory organization promoting improved health care and reduction in medical costs. Gathers information concerning medical and insurance costs. *Type:* Association.

American Health Care Association

1201 L St. NW   Ph: (202)842-4444
Washington, DC 20005   Fax: (202)842-3860
URL: http://www.ahca.org

Contact: Dr. Paul R. Willging, Exec.VP.

Desc: Federation of state associations of long-term health care facilities. Promotes standards for professionals in long-term health care delivery and quality care for patients and residents in a safe environment. Focuses on issues of availability, quality, affordability, and fair payment. *Type:* Association.

American Health Foundation

320 E. 43rd St.   Ph: (212)953-1900
New York, NY 10017   Fax: (212)687-2339

Contact: Dr. Ernst Wynder, Pres.

Desc: Devoted to promoting preventive medicine, emphasizing four major fields: research (nutrition, environmental carcinogenesis, molecular biology, experimental pathology, and epidemiology); clinical research and service for children (through screening and intervention); public health action (educating laymen and medical and government personnel in the principles of preventive medicine); health economics research (investigating direct and indirect costs of major diseases and comparing them with preventive approaches). Maintains Naylor Dana Institute for Disease Prevention and the Child Health Center in Valhalla, NY and The Mahoney Institute for Health Promotion Research in New York City. *Type:* Association.

American Health and Temperance Association

DeWitt Williams
12501 Old Columbia Pike   Ph: (301)680-6733
Silver Spring, MD 20904-6600 Fax: (301)680-6464

Contact: DeWitt Williams, Exec.Dir.

Desc: Seeks to publicize, through popular education, the effects of alcoholic beverages, tobacco, and narcotics; foster health; promote an alcohol- and drug-free way of life. *Type:* Association.

American Health for Women

American Health
19 W. 22nd St.   Ph: (212)366-8900
New York, NY 10010   Free: 800-365-5005
URL: http://www.americanhealth.com.

Contact: Freddi Greenberg, Editor-in-Chief, editor@americanhealth.com; Susan Buckley, Publisher.

Desc: Health magazine. *Alt. Contact:* 28 W. 23rd St., New York, NY 10010; fax: (212)627-3833. *Type:* Periodical.

American Massage Therapy Association

820 Davis St., Ste. 100   Ph: (847)864-0123
Evanston, IL 60201-4444   Fax: (847)864-1178
E-mail: info@inet.amtamassage.org
URL: http://www.amtamassage.org

Contact: Ronald Precht, Communications Mgr.

Desc: Massage therapists and massage schools. Promotes standards for the professions, has a Code of Ethics, and supports chapter efforts for state regulation of massage. *Type:* Association.

American Public Health Association

800 I St., N.W.   Ph: (202)777-2742
Washington, DC 20001-3710 Fax: (202)789-5661
E-mail: comments@apha.org
URL: http://www.apha.org

Contact: Mohammad Akhter, MD, Exec.Dir.

Desc: Professional organization of physicians, nurses, educators, academicians, environmentalists, epidemiologists, new professionals, social workers, health administrators, optometrists, podiatrists, pharmacists, dentists, nutritionists, health planners, other community and mental health specialists, and interested consumers. Seeks to protect and promote personal, mental, and environmental health. *Type:* Association.

American Social Health Association

PO Box 13827   Ph: (919)361-8400
Research Triangle Park, NC Fax: (919)361-8425
  27709
URL: http://www.ashastd.org

Contact: Linda Alexander, PhD, Pres./CEO.

Desc: A national voluntary health agency dedicated to stopping sexually transmitted diseases and their harmful consequences to individuals, families and communities. Works to expand biomedical research, provide information and education programs, upgrade clinical care, and improve public policy. Provides leadership in public policy issues. *Type:* Association.

American University

National Center for Health Fitness

Nebraska Hall, Lower Level   Ph: (202)885-6275
4400 Massachusetts Ave. NW   Fax: (202)885-6288
Washington, DC 20016-8037
E-mail: nchfaa@american.edu
URL: http://www.healthy.american.edu

Contact: Robert C. Karch, Dir.

Desc: Worksite health promotion programs, focusing on costs, benefits, and cost-effectiveness, and including international health promotion and special populations. Consulting activities include health promotion program design, implementation, and management. *Type:* Research center.

Arizona Health Services Department

Public Health Services

State Laboratory Services

1520 W. Adams   Ph: (602)542-1188
Phoenix, AZ 85007-2698   Fax: (602)542-1169
URL: http://www.hs.state.oz.us

Contact: Barbara Erickson, PhD, Bureau Chf.

Desc: State health laboratory. *Type:* Research center.

Arizona Health Services Department

Public Health Services

State Laboratory Services

Flagstaff Regional Laboratory

2500 N. Fort Valley Rd.   Ph: (520)226-1154
Flagstaff, AZ 86001   Fax: (520)774-9419

Contact: Daniel Crough, Mgr.

Desc: Public health laboratory. *Type:* Research center.

Arizona Health Services Department

Public Health Services

State Laboratory Services

Tucson Regional Laboratory

416 W. Congress, Ste. 119   Ph: (520)628-6360
Tucson, AZ 85701   Fax: (520)628-6356

Contact: Judy Fordyce, Mgr.

Desc: Public health regional lab. *Type:* Research center.

Associated Bodywork and Massage Professionals

28677 Buffalo Park Rd.   Ph: (303)674-8478
Evergreen, CO 80439-7347 Free: 800-458-2267
                         Fax: (303)674-0859
E-mail: expectmore@abmp.com
URL: http://www.abmp.com

Contact: Katie Armitage, Exec.Dir.

Desc: Professional massage therapists and bodyworkers, sports massage therapists, estheticians, skin care professionals, reflexologists, orthobionomists, and infant massage instructors; massage therapy schools; affiliated organizations. Promotes the art and science of massage and bodywork. *Type:* Association.

Associated Health Foundation

99 Madison Ave.   Ph: (212)889-4455
New York, NY 10016   Free: 800-722-8668

Contact: Edward Birnbaum, Pres.

Desc: Extends life-saving services to members through incentive benefits. Contributes to hospitals and institutions that carry on research. *Type:* Association.

Association of Cosmetologists and Hairdressers

2547 Monroe   Ph: (313)563-0360
Dearborn, MI 48124   Fax: (248)669-0636

Contact: Mary Ann Neuman, Pres.

Desc: Cosmetologists and beauticians; beauty product manufacturers, wholesalers, buyers, and retailers. Seeks to keep members informed of current trends in the beauty culture industry. Conducts demonstrations. *Type:* Association.

Association for Health Services Research

1130 Connecticut Ave. NW,   Ph: (202)223-2477
  Ste. 700   Fax: (202)835-8972
Washington, DC 20036
E-mail: info@ahsr.org
URL: http://www.ahsr.org

Desc: Individuals and organizations concerned with health services research. Objectives are to educate the public concerning the need for and contribution of health services research in improving health care in the U.S.; to foster productive cooperation among researchers, public and private funding agencies, health professionals, policymakers, and the public; to represent the views of members in the development and implementation of national legislative and administrative policies concerning health services research. *Type:* Association.

Association of State and Territorial Health Officials

1275 K St., NW, Ste. 800   Ph: (202)371-9090
Washington, DC 20005-4006 Fax: (202)371-9797
E-mail: cbeversd@astho.org
URL: http://www.astho.org

Contact: Cheryl A. Beversdorf, Exec.VP.

Desc: Represents the executive officer of the department of public health of each of the U.S. states, territories and possessions and is engaged in a wide range of legislative, educational, scientific and programmatic issues and activities on behalf of public health. Seeks to "formulate and influence sound national public health policy and to assist state health officials in the development and implementation of programs and policies to promote health and prevent disease, injury and disability." Serves as a primary information resource to state health agencies on a wide range of issues, including HIV/AIDS, immunizations, tobacco-use control, primary care, maternal and child health, school health and the environment. *Type:* Association.

Asthma Update

Asthma Update
123 Monticello Ave.　　　Ph: (301)267-8329
Annapolis, MD 21401

Contact: David C. Jamison, Editor, dcjamison@toad.net.

Desc: Presents medical information on asthma treatment, household air control measures, and exertional asthma. Includes annotated abstracts from current medical journals and perspectives on asthma by health professionals. *Type:* Newsletter.

Atlanta Reproductive Health Centre WWW

Atlanta Reproductive Health Centre
Georgia Baptist Medical Center　　Ph: (404)265-3662
　Office
285 Blvd. NE, Ste. 320
Atlanta, GA 30312
E-mail: feedback@ivillage.com
URL: http://www.ivf.com/

Contact: Dr. Mark Perloe, M.D., mperloe@ivf.com.

Desc: The Atlanta Reproductive Health Centre Databases contain information in the areas of womens' health including: infertility, polycystic ovaries, IVF, endometriosis and pelvic pain treatment options. Also online is the complete contents of *Miracle Babies and Other Happy Endings*, a book for couples with fertility problems. *Type:* Database.

Ball State University

Human Performance Laboratory
Muncie, IN 47306　　　　　Ph: (765)285-1156
　　　　　　　　　　　　　Fax: (765)285-8596
URL: http://www.bsu.edu/hpl

Contact: Dr. David L. Costill, Dir.

Desc: Human performance, including studies on effects of physical training on skeletal muscular metabolism, nutritional demands during muscular activity, fluid replacement during and following acute dehydration, muscle glycogen utilization during prolonged exertion, and swimming research. *Type:* Research center.

Baylor College of Medicine

Center for Allergy and Immunological Disorders
1 Baylor Plz.　　　　　　Ph: (713)770-1319
Houston, TX 77030　　　　Fax: (713)770-1260
E-mail: wshearer@bcm.tmc.edu

Contact: William T. Shearer, Dir.

Desc: Allergy and immunological disorders, including basic and clinical projects in cancer immunology, immunoreconstitution of immunodeficient children, immunoregulation of cellular and humoral immune responses, immune complex diseases, immunotherapy of neoplastic diseases, pulmonary immunology, rheumatic diseases, allergic diseases of children, and AIDS. Facilities available for specialty training of pre- and postdoctoral students on either a research or clinical level. *Type:* Research center.

Benjamin Franklin Literary and Medical Society
1100 Waterway Blvd.　　　Ph: (317)636-8881
Indianapolis, IN 46202　　Fax: (317)634-1791

Contact: Cory SerVaas, M.D., Pres. & CEO.

Desc: Individuals, industries, and businesses united to support research and promote sciences, literature, and the arts in order to achieve greater public understanding of science and the humanities. Major emphasis is on the dissemination of health, preventive medicine, and nutrition information to the health community and the public. Advocates a preventive approach to health care including proper nutrition, daily exercise, and good health habits. *Type:* Association.

Body Bulletin

Rodale Books
400 S. 10th St.　　　　　Ph: (610)967-5171
Emmaus, PA 18098-0099　　Fax: (610)967-7722
E-mail: ddonche1@rodalepress.com
URL: http://www.rodalepress.com

Contact: Chris Hill, Editor.

Desc: Touches on all aspects of health, including exercise, nutrition, stress control, disease prevention, and staying free of drugs. Treats "real issues that affect real people." Recurring features include book reviews, and news of research. *Type:* Newsletter.

Boston University

Arthritis Center
Conte Bldg., 5th Fl.　　　Ph: (617)638-4310
71 E. Newton St.　　　　　Fax: (617)638-5226
Boston, MA 02118
E-mail: jkorn@med-med1.bu.edu
URL: http://medicine.bu.edu/arth.htm

Contact: Dr. Joseph Korn, Dir.

Desc: Biophysical, biochemical, immunologic, and clinical aspects of scleroderma amyloidosis, experimental lupus, rheumatoid arthritis, infectious arthritis, and nonarticular rheumatic diseases, particularly fibromyalgia. Also conducts health services research in rheumatology and performs epidemiological studies. *Type:* Research center.

Brigham and Women's Hospital

Asthma and Allergic Diseases Cooperative Research Center
Smith Bldg., 6th Fl.　　　Ph: (617)525-1300
1 Jimmy Fund Way　　　　Fax: (617)525-1310
Boston, MA 02115

Contact: K. Frank Austen, MD, Contact.

Desc: Clinical areas include allergy, clinical immunology, rheumatology, nephrology, immunodermatology, and infectious diseases; pre-clinical areas include mast cell biology, biology of human peripheral blood, leukocytes including eosinophils, neutrophils and monocytes, arachidonic acid metabolism by the 5-lipoxygenase pathway, and complement biology. *Type:* Research center.

Canadian Fitness and Lifestyle Research Institute
201-185 Somerset W.　　　Ph: (613)233-5528
Ottawa, ON, Canada K2P 0J2　Fax: (613)233-5536
E-mail: info@cflri.ca
URL: http://activeliving.ca/cflri/cflri.html

Contact: Cora Lynn Craig, Pres.

Desc: Population fitness levels, recreation habits, and link between physical activity and other life-style patterns of Canadians; benefits and costs of a physically active lifestyle. Offers a national research contribution award program to support studies on physical activity and fitness. *Type:* Research center.

CCH Health Law Focus

CCH Inc.
2700 Lake Cook Rd.　　　Ph: (847)267-7000
Riverwoods, IL 60015　　Free: 800-449-8114
　　　　　　　　　　　　Fax: (847)224-8299
URL: http://www.cch.com

Contact: Mary Frances Korenjack, Editor.

Desc: Covers legal topics of interest to health care providers, including Medicare/Medicaid, antitrust law, tax-exempt status, medical malpractice, job safety, human resource management, licensing, and health planning. *Type:* Newsletter.

CDC Wonder - Public Health Information

Centers for Disease Control and Prevention
1600 Clifton Rd. NE　　　Ph: (404)639-3311
Atlanta, GA 30333
URL: http://wonder.cdc.gov/

Contact: WONDER User Support, cwus@cdc.gov.

Desc: The CDC WONDER database is the access point for the Centers for Disease Control and Prevention's numerous reports, guidelines, and public health data. Find data on such topics as AIDS, mortality and natality, prevention guidelines, fluoridation, sexually transmitted diseases, cancer epidemiology, and other disease and health related information. *Type:* Database.

Chronic Pain Letter

Robert J. Fabian Memorial Foundation
PO Box 1303
Old Chelsea Sta.
New York, NY 10011

Contact: Alice DeLury, Editor; Dorothy Fabian, Exec. Editor.

Desc: Provides information on the causes and management of chronic pain. Covers such topics as Phantom Limb Pain, rheumatoid arthritis, and various treatments including medications, marijuana as a pain reducer, and acupressure. *Type:* Newsletter.

Common Ground: Resources for Personal Transformation

Common Ground
305 San Anselmo Ave.　　Ph: (415)459-4900
San Anselmo, CA 94960　Free: 800-442-4922
　　　　　　　　　　　　Fax: (415)459-4974
URL: http://www.comngrnd.com.

Contact: Baha'Uddin Alpine, Publisher.

Desc: Music schools; art instructors; educational programs; conferences and festivals; natural and health food restaurants and suppliers; medicine and dentistry professionals who emphasize preventive health care; holistic health practitioners; individuals engaged in the psychic arts, psychology, and psychic healing; retreat sites, camps, hot springs, and inns; publications, book publishers, and other sources of materials; gyms, dance studios, yoga instructors, and instructors in the martial arts; palmists and astrologists. All listings are paid. Coverage is primarily of northern California. *Type:* Directory.

Community Health Services (Saskatoon) Association Ltd.—Focus

Community Health Services Saskatoon Association Ltd.
455 2nd Ave. N.　　　　Ph: (306)652-0300
Saskatoon, SK, Canada S7K　Fax: (306)664-4120
　2C2
E-mail: ad136@stn.saskatoon.sk.ca.

Contact: Ingrid Larson, Editor.

Desc: Profiles Association events and programs. Discusses health issues. *Type:* Newsletter.

Consumer Product Safety Commission
East West Towers　　　　Ph: (301)504-0580
4330 East West Hwy.　　Free: 800-638-CPSC
Bethesda, MD 20814
URL: http://www.cpsc.gov/

Contact: Ann Brown, Chairman of the Board.

Desc: The purpose of the Consumer Product Safety Commission is to protect the public against unreasonable risks of injury from consumer products; to assist consumers in evaluating the comparative safety of consumer products; to develop uniform safety standards for consumer products and minimize conflicting state and local regulations; and to promote research and investigation into the causes and prevention of product-related deaths, illnesses, and injuries. It also collects information on consumer product-related injuries and maintains a comprehensive Injury Information Clearinghouse. *Type:* Government agency, office, or program.

Consumer Product Safety Commission

Epidemiology and Health Sciences Directorate

4330 East-West Hwy.	Ph: (301)504-0957
Bethesda, MD 20814-4408	Fax: (301)504-0124

URL: http://www.cpsc.gov

Contact: Dr. Mary Ann Danello, Dir.

Desc: Determines exposure to hazardous chemicals from consumer products. This includes investigation of children's products; pollutant emissions (both chemical and biological) from structural materials, consumer products, and indoor combustion sources and their impact on indoor air quality; bioavailability and potential for consumer exposure to carcinogenic and other chemical hazard-containing commercial substances; and acute and chemical toxicity of various household products to determine proper precautionary and first aid labeling. *Type:* Research center.

Consumer Product Safety Commission

Epidemiology and Health Sciences Directorate

Hazard Analysis Division

4330 East-West Hwy.	Ph: (301)504-0470
Bethesda, MD 20814	Fax: (301)504-0124

E-mail: sahmed@cpsc.gov

URL: http://cpsc.gov

Contact: Susan W. Ahmed, PhD, Dir.

Desc: Analyses of product-related injury data to the Commission and other organizations to guide and support remedial strategy development and decision-making. As a part of this function, Division analysts and statisticians participate in the selection and planning of projects; develop guidelines for investigations and surveys and monitor their progress; compile and analyze data and information available from established Commission projects, other health and safety-oriented organizations, and computer searches of medical, scientific, and technical literature databases; prepare issue-oriented data summaries, reports, and memoranda describing the frequency and severity of injuries and major hazard patterns related to specific types of products; participate in oral briefings of the Commission on the nature and scope of injuries to be addressed by each remedial option considered; participate in the identification of injury reductions related to past Commission actions; and identify emerging hazards through continuous monitoring of injury trends. *Type:* Research center.

Consumer Reports on Health

Consumers Union of U.S., Inc.

101 Truman Ave.	Ph: (914)378-2000
Yonkers, NY 10703-1057	Free: 800-234-2188
	Fax: (914)378-2904

Contact: Michael Leff, Editor, (802)860-2262, fax: (802)860-2966, leffmi@consumer.org.

Desc: Presents information on health and medicine from a consumer's point of view. Recurring features include news of research. *Type:* Newsletter.

Cooper Institute for Aerobics Research

12330 Preston Rd.	Ph: (972)341-3200
Dallas, TX 75230	Free: 800-635-7050
	Fax: (972)341-3224

URL: http://www.cooperinst.org

Contact: Dr. Charles L. Sterling, Exec.Dir.

Desc: Cardiovascular disease, stress management, women's health, exercise physiology, health promotion, nutrition, youth fitness, hypertension, aging, and epidemiology. Using data from the affiliated Cooper Clinic, the Institute conducts the Aerobics Center Longitudinal Study, which monitors 25,000 subjects over their lifetime to study the effects of exercise and health habits on death and disability rates from chronic diseases. *Type:* Research center.

Coping

Media America, Inc.

PO Box 682268	Ph: (615)790-2400
Franklin, TN 37068-2268	Fax: (615)794-0179

E-mail: copingmag@aol.com.

Contact: Kay Thomas, Editor; Michael Holt, Publisher; Paula Chadwell, Advertising Mgr., (615)791-3834.

Desc: Consumer magazine for people whose lives have been touched by cancer. *Type:* Periodical.

CPA Health Niche Advisor

Harcourt Brace & Company

525 B St., Ste. 1900	Ph: (619)231-6616
San Diego, CA 92101-4495	Free: 800-831-7799
	Fax: (619)699-6593

E-mail: propub@harcourtbrace.com; newsletters@hbpp.com.

URL: http://healthniche.hbpp.com.

Contact: Reed Tinsley, Editor.

Desc: Covers strategies and techniques for CPAs serving the healthcare profession. Recurring features include calendar of events, reports of meetings, news of educational opportunities, and book reviews. *Type:* Newsletter.

CPHA Health Digest

Canadian Public Health Association

1565 Carling Ave., Ste. 400	Ph: (613)725-3769
Ottawa, ON, Canada K1Z 8R1	Fax: (613)725-9826

Contact: Mrs. Karen Craven, Editor.

Desc: Features updates on Association's activities and conference announcements. Recurring features include columns titled Executive Director's Page, CPHA in Action, Feature Article, and Resolutions and Motions. *Type:* Newsletter.

Creighton University

Allergic Disease Center

2500 California	Ph: (402)280-2940
Omaha, NE 68178	Fax: (402)280-1843

E-mail: rtownley@creighton.edu

URL: http://www.medicine.ereighton.edu/allergic/home.html

Contact: Robert G. Townley, MD, Ch.

Desc: Multidisciplinary research in asthma, allergic rhinitis, allergic diseases, clinical and basic immunology, clinical and basic pharmacology and physiology, airway reactivity in patients with asthma, and allergies. Laboratory research consists of studies of human lung, eosinophils, mast cells, lymphocytes, and platelets to correlate adrenergic and cholinergic receptors and receptor mechanisms; and role of pro-inflamatory cytokines, leukotrienes and platelet activating factor on airway reactivity and in asthma and animal models of asthma. *Type:* Research center.

Delicious! Magazine

New Hope Communications

1301 Spruce St.	Ph: (303)939-8440
Boulder, CO 80302	Free: 800-839-7263
	Fax: (303)939-9559

E-mail: sales@newhope.com; delicious@newhope.com.

URL: http://www.newhope.com/delicious.

Contact: Kathryn Arnold, Editorial Director-Consumer Publications, ka@newhope.com; Nicola Ferrell, Production Dir.; Kim Paulsen, VP Publishing Division, kp@newhope.com.

Desc: Magazine designed to be used as a merchandising and educational tool by natural food stores. *Type:* Periodical.

DME Bulletin Special Issue

Department of Medical Education

University of Illinois at Chicago

Medical Education, M/C 591,	Ph: (312)996-5899
Box 6998, 986 CME	Fax: (312)413-2048
Chicago, IL 60612	

URL: http://www.uic.edu/com/mcme/.

Contact: Eve Fine, Editor.

Desc: Provides a forum for essays on human values in the health-science industry. Promotes programs, activities, and events in the medical humanities and bioethic community. *Type:* Newsletter.

Education Special Interest Section Quarterly

American Occupational Therapy Association, Inc. (AOTA)

PO Box 31220	Ph: (301)652-2682
Bethesda, MD 20824-1220	Free: 800-877-1383
	Fax: (301)652-7711

E-mail: ajotsis@aota.org.

Contact: Elizabeth Holcomb, Managing Editor.

Desc: Focuses on issues concerning the education of occupational therapy practitioners. Recurring features include columns titled From the Editor and From the Chairperson. *Type:* Newsletter.

EMF Health Report

Information Ventures, Inc.

42 S. 15th St., Ste. 700	Ph: (215)569-2300
Philadelphia, PA 19102-2299	Fax: (215)569-2575

E-mail: ivi@infoventures.com

URL: http://infoventures.com

Contact: Robert B. Goldberg, Editor.

Desc: Provides information on the health effects of electromagnetic fields (EMFs) in nontechnical language. Surveys the ongoing debate surrounding claims that EMFs pose a threat to the public. *Type:* Newsletter.

Energy Times

Energy Times, Inc.

548 Broadhollow Rd.	Ph: (516)777-7773
Melville, NY 11747	

Contact: Gerard McIntee, Editor and Publisher; Carl Lowe, Managing Editor.

Desc: Consumer magazine for health food store shoppers. *Type:* Periodical.

Executive Health's Good Health Report

Executive Health

383 Rte. 46 W.	Ph: (201)227-5599
Fairfield, NJ 07004-2402	Fax: (201)575-5366

Contact: Deborah Hauss, Editor.

Desc: Feature articles on personal health, nutrition, preventative medicine, weight reduction, and exercise. Gives primary consideration to one health topic per issue. *Type:* Newsletter.

Fitness Plus Magazine

Focus Publishing Ltd.

PO Box 168

Seymour, TN 37865-0168

Contact: Steve Raimondi, Editor; H. McQueeney, Publisher; John Wilson, Advertising Dir.

Desc: Health and fitness magazine. *Type:* Periodical.

Free Stress Free Newsletter

Institute for Transformational Studies

Wolf Creek Productions

PO Box 1181	Ph: (920)921-6991
Fond du Lac, WI 54936-1181	Fax: (920)921-7691

E-mail: stress@wolfcrk.com.

URL: http://www.wolfcrk.com.

Contact: Anthony S. Dallmann-Jones, Ph.D., Editor, asd-jones@wolfcrk.com.

Desc: Aims to raise awareness of stress management techniques in our daily lives through primary thought forms. Remarks: Available online only. *Type:* Newsletter.

A Friend Indeed

A Friend Indeed Publications, Inc.

419 Graham Ave., Main 71   Ph: (204)989-8028
Winnipeg, MB, Canada R3C   Fax: (204)989-8029
0M3

E-mail: afi@pangea.ca

URL: http://www.afriendindeed.ca.

Contact: Janine O'Leary Cobb, Editor, janine@odyssee.net.

Desc: Deals with menopause and women's midlife issues. Recurring features include letters to the editor, news of research, a calendar of events, reports of meetings, book reviews, and notices of publications available. *Type:* Newsletter.

George Washington University

Biostatistics Center

6110 Executive Blvd., Ste. 750   Ph: (301)881-9260
Rockville, MD 20852   Fax: (301)881-3742

E-mail: vicki@biostat.bsc.gwu.edu

URL: http://biostat.bsc.gwu.edu/staff/staf.addar.html

Contact: Vicki Zell, Dir. of Admin.

Desc: Biostatistics, focusing on data management and analysis for medical research projects. *Type:* Research center.

Georgia Southern University

Center for Rural Health and Research

PO Box 8148   Ph: (912)681-0260
Statesboro, GA 30460-8148   Fax: (912)681-0816

E-mail: jstrick@gasou.edu

URL: http://www2.gasou.edu/crhr/crhr.htm

Contact: W. Jay Strickland, PhD, Dir.

Desc: Rural health in Georgia. Currently conducting a census of programs promoting well-being of children and families in the state and a study of the impact of social support on the well being of HIV/AIDS patients. *Type:* Research center.

Georgia State University

Viral Immunology Center

NIH B Virus Resource Laboratory

PO Box 4118   Ph: (404)651-0808
Atlanta, GA 30302-4118   Fax: (404)651-0814

E-mail: bvirus@gsu.edu

URL: http://www.gsu.edu/bvirus

Contact: Dr. Julia Hilliard, Dir.

Desc: B-virus infections, basic pathogenesis mechanisms of this and other neurotropic herpesviruses, control and prevention strategies. It provides rapid virological and serological analyses and collaborates in studies of Herpes virus simiae and B-virus infections in humans and nonhuman primates, particularly macaques. *Type:* Research center.

Good Health Bulletin

Harvey W. Watt & Co., Inc.

PO Box 20787   Ph: (404)767-7501
Atlanta, GA 30320   Free: 800-241-6103
   Fax: (404)761-8326

Contact: Bill Maness, Editor.

Desc: Contains up-to-date helpful medical and related information concerning health, fitness, and longevity. Recurring features include news of research. *Type:* Newsletter.

Harvard Health Letter

Harvard Health Publications Group

164 Longwood Ave.   Ph: (617)432-1485
Boston, MA 02115   Fax: (617)432-1506

E-mail: hwhw@warren.med.harvard.edu

Contact: Stephen Goldfinger, M.D., Editor-in-Chief; Leah R. Garnett, Editor.

Desc: Provides information on medicine and health to the general public in layperson's terms. Features concise reviews of current health topics such as Parkinson's disease, how to choose an HMO, vitamin use, heart disease, and prostate cancer. *Type:* Newsletter.

Harvard Heart Letter

Harvard Health Publications Group

164 Longwood Ave.   Ph: (617)432-1485
Boston, MA 02115   Fax: (617)432-1506

E-mail: hwhw@warren.med.harvard.edu

URL: http://www.hms.harvard.edu.

Contact: Thomas H. Lee, Editor.

Desc: Contains articles and information on cardiovascular health. *Type:* Newsletter.

Harvard University

Kresge Center for Environmental Health

665 Huntington Ave.   Ph: (617)432-1272
Boston, MA 02115   Fax: (617)277-2382

E-mail: brain@hsph.harvard.edu

URL: http://www.hsph.harvard.edu/Register/Kresge.html

Contact: Joseph D. Brain, Dir.

Desc: Environmental health, including interdisciplinary studies on effects and control of air pollutants, occupational health and medicine, safeguards for nuclear power reactors, environmental and respiratory physiology, radiation biology, toxicology and air sampling, exposure/dose assessment, water microbiology, and personnel protection. Serves as a focus for envi activities within the School. *Type:* Research center.

Harvard Women's Health Watch

Harvard Health Publications Group

164 Longwood Ave.   Ph: (617)432-1485
Boston, MA 02115   Fax: (617)432-1506

E-mail: hwhw@warren.med.harvard.edu

Contact: Beverly Merz, Editor.

Desc: Address issues unique to women's health, such as mammography and hormone replacement therapy and other topics in medicine, psychology, and health science policy that are of particular interest to women. Recurring features include columns titled, By the Way, Doctor (questions from reader answered by a physician), Update (discussing recently publicized issues), Mental Health, Chronic Conditions, and Alternative Therapies. *Type:* Newsletter.

Health

Time Inc. Health

2 Embarcadero Center, Ste. 600   Ph: (415)248-2700
San Francisco, CA 94111   Fax: (415)248-2779

Contact: Barbara Paulsen, Editor-in-Chief, editor@health.com; Sheridan Warrick, Executive Editor.

Desc: Consumer magazine covering medicine, health, and fitness issues. *Type:* Periodical.

Health Care

National Technical Information Service (NTIS)
U.S. Department of Commerce

5285 Port Royal Rd.   Ph: (703)605-6000
Springfield, VA 22161-0001   Free: 800-553-NTIS
   Fax: (703)605-6900

E-mail: orders@ntis.fedworld.gov

Desc: Consists of abstracted reports covering planning methodology, health services, facilities utilization, and health needs. Also covers health care assessment, quality assurance, forecasting and measurement methods, and legislation and regulations. *Type:* Newsletter.

Health Education Reports

Chester Associates, Inc.

4401-A Connecticut Ave. NW,   Ph: (703)960-6859
Ste. 212   Fax: (703)960-0189
Washington, DC 20008

Contact: Lawrence M. O'Rourke, Editor.

Desc: Focuses on developments relating to public health and wellness programs and government health policy. *Type:* Newsletter.

Health Exchange

Medical Group Management Association

104 Inverness Terr. E.   Ph: (303)799-1111
Englewood, CO 80112-5306   Free: 888-608-5601
   Fax: (303)397-1824

URL: http://www.mgma.com.

Contact: Kelli Davis, Editor.

Desc: Contains general articles related to health and wellness on frequently discussed medical subjects. Includes exercise tips, diet recommendations, and lifestyle features. *Type:* Newsletter.

Health Perspective

Clayton-Davis & Associates

8229 Maryland Ave.   Ph: (314)862-7800
St. Louis, MO 63105   Fax: (314)721-5171

Contact: Ruth Sirko, Editor; Mary Brown, Advertising Mgr.

Desc: Consumer health tabloid. *Type:* Periodical.

Health Planning and Administration

U.S. National Library of Medicine (NLM)
MEDLARS Management Section

8600 Rockville Pike   Ph: (301)496-3147
Bethesda, MD 20894

URL: http://www.sis.nlm.nih.gov/dirline

Desc: Contains approximately 620,000 citations to the worldwide literature on health care delivery. Covers budgeting, finance, organization, administration, management, planning, facilities, and personnel resource development. *Available:* The Dialog Corporation, DIALOG; CompuServe Information Service, Knowledge Index; U.S. National Library of Medicine (NLM), TOXNET; PaperChase; Swiss Academy of Medical Sciences, Documentation Service (DOKDI); The Dialog Corporation, DataStar; The Dialog Corporation, DataStar. *Type:* Database.

Health Promotion Features & Training Consultants

PO Box 920   Ph: (702)852-0754
Verdi, NV 89439   Fax: (702)852-OSKI

Contact: John Yacenda, Ed./Dir., jyacenda@intercomm.com; Benita Crocco, Assoc. Ed.

Alt. Contact: PO Box 920, Verdi, NV 89439; telephone: (702)852-0754; fax: (702)852-OSKI. *Type:* Periodical.

Health Sentry

Performance Resource Press, Inc.

1270 Rankin Dr., Ste. F   Ph: (248)588-7733
Troy, MI 48083   Free: 800-453-7733
   Fax: (248)588-6633

E-mail: sapeap@ix.netcom.com

Contact: Brent Chartier, Editor.

Desc: Offers information on behavioral and lifestyle issues that can impede job performance. Includes discussion of topics such as mental health, alcohol and other drug dependency, and family and relationships. *Type:* Newsletter.

HEALTH & YOU

Health Ink Communications

1245 N. Church St.   Ph: (609)778-0011
Moorestown, NJ 08057   Fax: (609)778-4422
E-mail: healthlink@healthlink.com
URL: http://www.healthink.com.
Contact: Craig Ammerman, President.
Desc: Consumer-oriented health publications distributed
by hospitals, corporations, and managed care companies.
Type: Periodical.

HEALTHletter

American Association of Retired Persons (AARP)

601 E St. NW   Ph: (202)434-2277
Washington, DC 20049   Fax: (202)434-6451
E-mail: aarp1@aol.com
Desc: Provides health and medicine information, focusing
especially on older people. Published by the American As-
sociation of Retired Persons. *Type:* Newsletter.

Healthline

Healthline Magazine

830 Menlo Ave., Ste. 100   Ph: (415)325-6457
Menlo Park, CA 94025   Fax: (415)322-2436
URL: http://www.health_line.com.
Contact: Paul M. Insel, Editor.
Desc: Features easy-to-read articles by physicians on gener-
al health topics. *Type:* Newsletter.

Heart & Soul

Rodale Books

400 S. 10th St.   Ph: (610)967-5171
Emmaus, PA 18098-0099   Fax: (610)967-7722
E-mail: ddonche1@rodalepress.com
URL: http://www.rodalepress.com
Contact: Stephanie Stokes Oliver, Editor-in-Chief; Teresa
L. Ridley, Managing Editor.
Desc: Health and fitness magazine for African-American
women. *Alt. Contact:* 733 3rd Ave., 15th Fl., New York,
NY 10017; telephone: (212)573-0358; fax: (212)338-
9194. *Type:* Periodical.

the helper

Herpes Resource Center
American Social Health Association

PO Box 13827   Ph: (919)361-8421
Research Triangle Park, NC   Fax: (919)361-8425
  27709
Contact: Sheryl Crabtree, Director.
Desc: Covers the latest research and news on herpes infection, including symptoms, psychosocial issues, treatment
options, and natural therapies. *Type:* Newsletter.

Home and Community Health Special Interest Section Quarterly

American Occupational Therapy Association, Inc. (AOTA)

PO Box 31220   Ph: (301)652-2682
Bethesda, MD 20824-1220   Free: 800-877-1383
                                        Fax: (301)652-7711
E-mail: ajotsis@aota.org.
Contact: Amy Eutsey, Managing Editor, amye@aota.org.
Desc: Focuses on issues concerning the provision of occu-
pational therapy services in home and community health
care settings. *Type:* Newsletter.

Home Health Business Report

American Health Consultants, Inc.

3525 Piedmont Rd., Bldg. 6,   Ph: (404)262-7436
  Ste. 400   Free: 800-688-2421
Atlanta, GA 30305   Fax: (404)262-7837
E-mail: customerservice@ahcpub.com

Contact: Tim Fay, Editor; Caralyn Davis, Editor, caralyn_
davis@medic.com.
Desc: Recurring features include News, interviews, company profiles, technology updates, and notices of industry
meetings and conferences. *Type:* Newsletter.

HSS Mentor

Herpes Social Solutions

PO Box 1001   Ph: (302)998-6960
New Castle, DE 19720
Contact: Jennifer S. Wolynetz, Editor.
Desc: Provides social aid and support for those inflicted
with the herpes virus, as well as advice and information
about the disease. Recurring features include letters to the
editor and book reviews. *Type:* Newsletter.

Humor & Health Letter

Humor & Health Letter

PO Box 16814   Ph: (601)957-0075
Jackson, MS 39236   Fax: (601)977-0423
Contact: Joseph R. Dunn, Editor, jrdd@worldnet.ah.net.
Desc: Dedicated to humor and communicating its relationships with health-medical, psychological, social, and
spiritual well-being. Informs readers on clinical, research,
and program developments and discoveries. *Type:* Newsletter.

Indiana University-Purdue University at Indianapolis

Institute of Action Research for Community Health

1111 Middle Dr., Rm. 235   Ph: (317)274-0026
Indianapolis, IN 46202
URL: http://www.indiana.edu/~rugs/ctrdir/iarch.html
Contact: Beverly C. Flynn, Dir.
Desc: Community health issues in Indiana as well as na-
tionally and internationally. *Type:* Research center.

The Informer

The Simon Foundation for Continence

PO Box 835   Ph: (847)864-3913
Wilmette, IL 60091   Free: 800-237-4666
                                        Fax: (847)864-9758
Desc: Discusses topics concerned with bladder or bowel in-
continence. *Type:* Newsletter.

The Informer

The Simon Foundation for Continence

PO Box 835   Ph: (847)864-3913
Wilmette, IL 60091   Free: 800-237-4666
                                        Fax: (847)864-9758
URL: http://www.simonfoundation.org.
Desc: Magazine for persons with bladder or bowel inconti-
nence. *Type:* Periodical.

Institute for Positive Weight Management Newsletter

Institute for Positive Weight Management

Box 1271   Ph: (407)750-7004
Boca Raton, FL 33429-1271
Contact: Dr. Lynn Brown, Editor.
Desc: Reflects the Institute's philosophy of weight manage-
ment. Recurring features include columns titled The
PWM Philosophy and You, Health Corner, Practical
Tips, Research Corner, and Answer to Your Question.
Type: Newsletter.

Intergovernmental Health Policy Project

444 N. Capital St. Ste 515   Ph: (202)624-8698
Washington, DC 20001   Fax: (202)737-1069
E-mail: dick.merritt@ncsl.org
Contact: Richard E. Merritt, Dir.

Desc: Provides information on state health legislation and
programs to state executive officials, legislators, legislative
staff, and others. *Type:* Association.

International Health and Temperance Association

12501 Old Columbia Pike   Ph: (301)680-6719
Silver Spring, MD 20904   Fax: (301)680-6707
E-mail: 74617.2242@compuserve.com
Contact: Thomas R. Neslund, Exec.Sec.
Desc: Seeks to "enlighten the public concerning the harmful effects of alcohol, tobacco, and narcotics and to mount
an educational campaign to solve these problems." Promotes principles of health and temperance. *Type:* Association.

International Massage Association

3000 Connecticut Ave NW, Ste.   Ph: (202)387-6555
  308   Fax: (202)332-0531
Washington, DC 20008
Contact: Will Green, Pres.
Desc: Professional massage practitioners and massage
schools. Promotes unification of massage practitioners, regardless of technique or training. *Type:* Association.

International Medical Services for Health

45449 Severn Way, Ste. 161   Ph: (703)444-4477
Sterling, VA 20166   Free: 800-521-1175
                                        Fax: (703)444-4471
E-mail: inmed@ix.netcom.com
URL: http://www.inmed.org
Contact: Linda Pfeiffer, Ph.D., Pres.
Desc: Works to help disadvantaged people worldwide to
improve the health of their families and communities.
Type: Association.

Internet Food and Drug Administration

U.S. Food and Drug Administration

HFE-88   Ph: (301)827-4420
5600 Fishers Ln.   Free: 800-532-4440
Rockville, MD 20857   Fax: (301)443-9767
E-mail: execsec@oc.fda.gov
URL: http://www.fda.gov
Desc: Internet FDA provides information on matters of
public health and safety, including product recalls, drug
approvals for humans and animals, legislation, news, summaries of relevant Federal Register announcements, and
delayed imports. *Type:* Database.

Ironman

Ironman Publishing

1701 Ives Ave.   Ph: (805)385-3500
Oxnard, CA 93033   Free: 800-447-0008
                                        Fax: (805)385-3515
E-mail: ironmagagazine@aol.com.
URL: http://www.ironmanmagazine.com.
Contact: Steve Holman, Editor, ironchief@aol.com; John
Balik, Publisher, ironleader@aol.com.
Desc: Magazine on bodybuilding and fitness. *Type:* Period-
ical.

Johns Hopkins Medical Letter—Health After 50

Medletter Associates Inc.

632 Broadway   Ph: (212)505-2255
New York, NY 10012
E-mail: health-after-50@enews.com.
Contact: Rodney Friedman, Editor.
Desc: Covers physical and medical health issues of interest
to persons over fifty years old. Recurring features include
a column titled Our Readers Ask. *Type:* Newsletter.

Johns Hopkins University

Center for Communication Programs

111 Market Pl., Ste. 310   Ph: (410)659-6300
Baltimore, MD 21202-4024   Fax: (410)659-6266
E-mail: ccp@jhuccp.org
URL: http://www.jhuccp.org
Contact: Phyllis T. Piotrow, PhD, Dir.

Desc: Health communications in the areas of family health, reproductive health, maternal and child health, and AIDS/STD prevention. Develops communication programs using mass media, interpersonal communication and community mobilization. *Type:* Research center.

Let's Live

Franklin Publications

320 N. Larchmont Blvd., 3rd   Ph: (323)469-3901
Fl.   Free: 800-225-6473
Box 74908   Fax: (323)469-9597
Los Angeles, CA 90004
E-mail: letslive@earthlink.net; letslivelb@aol.com.
Contact: Beth Salmon, Editor; Paul D. Wolff, Publisher; Laura Barnaby, Managing Editor, nuinsights@asl.com; Laila Bomis, Media Coord.
Desc: Publication focuses on natural, holistic health, fitness, sports nutrition, herbs and vitamins/minerals. Articles are mostly written by industry experts. *Type:* Periodical.

Looking Forward

The Hope Heart Institute

c/o Exclusive Distributor   Ph: (616)343-0770
350 E. Michigan Ave., Ste. 301   Free: 800-334-4094
Kalamazoo, MI 49007-3851   Fax: (616)343-6260
Contact: Carol P. Garzona, Editor.
Desc: Offers health tips for persons over age 50. Emphasizes preventive measures and discusses health issues such as nutrition, weight loss, exercise, self-care, medical care, safe driving, stress management, and family and lifestyle issues. *Type:* Newsletter.

Lupus Sun

Shreveport Chapter

Lupus Foundation of America, Inc.

2013 S. Brookwood Dr.   Ph: (318)686-2528
Shreveport, LA 71118-2744
Contact: Bill Wheeler, Editor.
Desc: Serves as a support and information network for lupus patients and their families. Contains news of research and Chapter activities. *Type:* Newsletter.

Marshall University

Center for Rural Health Research

Sch. of Med.   Ph: (304)696-7255
Huntington, WV 25703   Fax: (304)696-7048
E-mail: rwalker@musom02.mu.wvnet.edu
Contact: Robert Walker, MD, Chm.
Desc: Rural health problems. Also guides predoctoral and postdoctoral research on rural health, rural geriatrics, and prevention in rural populations. *Type:* Research center.

Massachusetts Health Data Consortium

460 Totten Pond Rd., 3rd Fl.   Ph: (781)890-6040
Waltham, MA 02451   Fax: (781)768-2510
E-mail: masshdc@aol.com
URL: http://www.mahealthdata.org
Contact: Elliot M. Stone, Exec.Dir. & CEO.
Desc: Health services research, including studies of hospitals, patient and physician databases, and discharged patients since 1978. *Type:* Research center.

Mayo Clinic Health Letter

Mayo Foundation for Medical Education and Research

200 1st St. SW   Ph: (507)284-0773
Rochester, MN 55905   Free: 800-333-9037
                                 Fax: (507)284-8018
Contact: Christopher Frye, Editor.

Desc: Features articles on practical health information, timely topics, and developments in prevention and treatment of illness. Aims to help subscribers achieve healthier lives by providing useful, reliable, easy-to-understand health information. *Type:* Newsletter.

Med News

Cypress Publishing

PO Box 777   Ph: (713)256-4318
Cypress, TX 77429-0777   Fax: (713)373-4450
Contact: Lisa M. Lyle, Editor.
Desc: Provides upbeat, short, and timely articles on how to be healthier and healthier. Topics include diet, exercise, stress management, and other healthy lifestyle habits. *Type:* Newsletter.

Medical Society of Nova Scotia News

Medical Society of Nova Scotia

5 Spectacle Lake Dr.   Ph: (902)468-1866
City of Lakes Business Park   Free: 800-563-3427
Dartmouth, NS, Canada B3B   Fax: (902)468-6578
  1X7
Contact: Janet Robertson, Managing Editor; Donna Christopher, Editor; Pam Fancy, Asst. Ed.; Debra Girandy, Production Asst.
Desc: Covers health-related issues in Nova Scotia, such as acquired immunodeficiency syndrome (AIDS), poverty, nutrition, and health politics regarding The Royal Commission on Health Care. *Type:* Newsletter.

Men's Health

Rodale Books

400 S. 10th St.   Ph: (610)967-5171
Emmaus, PA 18098-0099   Fax: (610)967-7722
E-mail: ddonche1@rodalepress.com; ltrolli1@rodalepress.com.
URL: http://www.rodalepress.com;   http://www.menshealth.com.
Contact: Michael Lafavore, Editor; Jeffrey Morgan, Publisher, (212)573-0348.
Desc: Magazine offering health advice for men. *Type:* Periodical.

The Mirkin Report

The Mirkin Report

PO Box 10   Ph: (301)951-0906
Kensington, MD 20895   Fax: (301)951-0557
Contact: Mary Singer, Editor.
Desc: Provides the latest information on fitness, nutrition, health, and sexuality matters. Also provides low-fat recipes. *Type:* Newsletter.

NAPWHP News

Council of State Governments

2760 Research Park Dr.   Ph: (606)244-8000
PO Box 11910   Free: 800-800-1910
Lexington, KY 40578-1910   Fax: (606)244-8001
E-mail: info@csg.org
Contact: Deana Lykins, Editor.
Desc: Provides information on public wellness programs initiatives. Recurring features include interviews, news of research, a calendar of events, reports of meetings, news of educational opportunities, and notices of publications available. *Type:* Newsletter.

Narcolepsy & Sleep Disorders

NASD

PO Box 51113   Ph: (415)856-7564
Palo Alto, CA 94303   Free: 800-829-1933
E-mail: path2pub@aol.com
URL: http://members-aol.com/pathzpub/home.htm; http://www.narcolepsy.com.

Contact: William Baird, Editor.

Desc: Provides information enabling informed treatment choices and the securing of rights and entitlements, unbiased reviews of patient care topics, and findings of peer-reviewed published research. Recurring features include letters to the editor, news of research, and cartoon commentary. *Type:* Newsletter.

National Alopecia Areata Foundation

PO Box 150760   Ph: (415)456-4644
San Rafael, CA 94915-0760   Fax: (415)456-4274
E-mail: naaf@compuserve.com
URL: http://www.alopeciaareata.com

Contact: Vicki Kalabokes, CEO.

Desc: Individuals concerned about alopecia areata, a disease causing partial scalp hair loss, total scalp hair loss (alopecia totalis), or total loss of body hair (alopecia universalis); cause and cure are unknown and the course of the disease is unpredictable. Objectives are to: develop public awareness of the disease; provide a support network; raise funds for research; keep patients medically informed with explanations about AA and the latest treatments. Maintains medical advisory board; operates information booth at meetings of the American Academy of Dermatology. *Type:* Association.

National Association of Health Unit Coordinators

1211 Locust St.   Ph: (215)545-3310
Philadelphia, PA 19107-5400   Free: 888-22-
                                       NAHUC
                                 Fax: (215)545-8107
E-mail: nahuc@nursecominc.com

Contact: Rosemary Boisselle, Pres.&CEO.

Desc: Coordinators of nonclinical nursing unit activities; educators, supervisors, students, and graduates in the field. Promotes the professional practice of unit coordinating. *Type:* Association.

National Beauty Culturists' League

25 Logan Cir. NW   Ph: (202)332-2695
Washington, DC 20005   Fax: (202)332-0940

Contact: Dr. Wanda J.W Nelson, CEO/Pres.

Desc: Beauticians, cosmetologists, and beauty products manufacturers. Encourages standardized, scientific, and approved methods of hair, scalp, and skin treatments. *Type:* Association.

National Certification Commission for Acupuncture and Oriental Medicine

11 Canal Center Plaza, Ste. 300 Ph: (703)548-9004
Alexandria, VA 22314   Fax: (703)548-9079
E-mail: info@nccaom.org
URL: http://www.nccaom.org

Contact: Dr. Christina Herlihy, CEO.

Desc: Establishes and maintains standards of competence for the safe and effective practice of acupuncture and Oriental medicine; to evaluate an applicant's qualifications in relation to these established standards through the administration of national board examinations; to certify practitioners who meet these standards. *Type:* Association.

National Cosmetology Association

3510 Olive St. Ph: (314)534-7982
St. Louis, MO 63103 Free: 800-527-1683
 Fax: (314)534-8618
E-mail: nca1@sba.com
URL: http://www.nca-now.com
Contact: Diane Sherrill White, Pres.
Desc: Owners of cosmetology salons; cosmetologists. *Type:* Association.

National Farm Medicine Center

1000 N. Oak Ave. Ph: (715)387-5107
Marshfield, WI 54449-5790 Fax: (715)389-4950
E-mail: gundersp@mfldclin.edu
URL: http://www.marshmed.org/nfmc/
Contact: Paul D. Gunderson, PhD, Contact.
Desc: Agriculture-related health problems, including injury, respiratory diseases, noise-induced hearing loss, migrant health, and cancer. *Type:* Research center.

National Headache Foundation

428 W. Saint James Pl., 2nd Fl. Ph: (773)388-6399
Chicago, IL 60614-2750 Free: 888-NHF-5552
 Fax: (773)525-7357
URL: http://www.headaches.org
Contact: Suzanne Simons, M.D., Exec.Dir.
Desc: Headache sufferers, physicians, health care professionals. Serves as an information resource to headache sufferers, their families, and the physicians who treat them. *Type:* Association.

National Health Policy Forum

2021 K St. NW, Ste. 800 Ph: (202)872-1390
Washington, DC 20052 Fax: (202)862-9837
Contact: Judith Miller Jones, Dir.
Desc: Nonpartisan education program serving primarily senior federal legislative and regulatory health staff but also addressing the interests of state officials and their Washington representatives. Seeks to foster more informed government decision making. Helps decision makers forge the personal acquaintances and understanding necessary for cooperation among government agencies and between government and the private sector. *Type:* Association.

National Women's Health Network—Network News

National Women's Health Network
514 10th St. NW, Ste. 400 Ph: (202)347-1140
Washington, DC 20004 Fax: (202)347-1168
Contact: Cynthia A. Pearson, Exec. Dir.
Desc: Carries timely health information and medical alerts for women. Emphasizes matters affecting reproductive rights and occupational and environmental health. *Type:* Newsletter.

Natural Health

Natural Health Books
70 Lincoln St., Fl. 5 Ph: (617)232-1000
Boston, MA 02111-8661 Fax: (617)232-1572
Contact: Ann D'Alesandro, Advertising Dir.; Chris Kimball, Publisher; Anne Alexander, Editor.
Desc: Magazine of alternative medicine, natural foods and products, and self-care. *Alt. Contact:* PO Box 1200, Brookline Village, MA 02147; telephone: (617)232-1000; fax: (617)232-1572. *Type:* Periodical.

Natural Way Magazine

Natural Way Publications, Inc.
1 Bridge St. 125 Ph: (914)591-2011
Irvington, NY 10533 Free: 800-697-2267
 Fax: (914)591-2017
E-mail: NatWay@aol.com
URL: http://www.naturalwaymagazine.com.

Contact: Cathy Raymond, Editor-in-Chief; Warren Tabatch; Arthur Maxwell, Advertising Dir.
Desc: Consumer magazine covering alternative health news & views. *Type:* Periodical.

New Living

New Living
PO Box 1519 Ph: (516)751-8819
Stony Brook, NY 11790 Fax: (516)751-8910
E-mail: newliving@aol.com.
URL: http://www.newliving.com.
Contact: Christine Harvey, Editor-in-Chief; Mark Kalaygian, Editor.
Desc: Largest health and fitness newsmagazine on Long Island. *Type:* Periodical.

New York State Department of Health

New York State Department of Health
Corning Tower Ph: (518)474-7354
Empire State Plaza Fax: (518)473-1326
Albany, NY 12237
E-mail: nyhealth@health.state.ny.us
URL: http://www.health.state.ny.us
Desc: The New York State Department of Health database provides users with information about the department and its services. Some features available include consumer information, a directory of departmental phone numbers, New York State vital statistics access, medical information for consumers and providers, a public health forum, a section devoted to research, and more. *Type:* Database.

New York State Department of Health

Wadsworth Center
PO Box 509 Ph: (518)474-7592
Albany, NY 12201-0509 Fax: (518)474-3439
E-mail: sturman@wadsworth.org
URL: http://www.wadsworth.org
Contact: Lawrence S. Sturman, MD,PhD, Dir.
Desc: Health of the citizens of the state of New York, focusing on laboratory investigations related to disease and environmental hazards of public health concern. Programs are conducted through 21 major laboratories organized within four scientific divisions: the Division of Environmental Disease Prevention includes the Laboratory of Environmental Biology, Laboratory of Environmental Immunology, Laboratory of Human Toxicology and Molecular Epidemiology, Laboratory of Organic Analytical Chemistry, and Laboratory of Inorganic and Nuclear Chemistry; the Division of Genetic Disorders includes the Laboratory of Newborn Screening and Genetic Services, Laboratory of Clinical Genetics and Genetic Epidemiology, Laboratory of Human Molecular Genetics, Laboratory of Developmental Genetics, Laboratory of Reproductive and Metabolic Disorders, and Laboratory of Nervous Systems Disorders; the Division of Infectious Disease includes the Laboratory of Bacterial Disease, Laboratory of Infectious Disease Immunology, Laboratory of Mycobacterial, Fungal, and Parasitic Disease, Laboratory of Viral Disease, and Laboratory of Zoonotic Disease and Epidemiology; and the Division of Molecular Medicine includes the Laboratory of Structural Pathology, Laboratory of Cellular Regulation, Laboratory of Computational Biology and Molecuar Imaging, Laboratory of Molecular Diagnostics, and Laboratory of Diagnostic Oncology. *Type:* Research center.

News/Noticias

U.S.-Mexico Border Health Association (USMBHA)
Pan American Health Organization
6006 N. Mesa, Ste. 600 Ph: (915)581-6645
El Paso, TX 79912 Fax: (915)833-4768
E-mail: mail@usmbha.org; officer@usmbha.org

URL: http://www.usmbha.org.
Contact: Gerardo De Cosio, M.D., Editor.
Desc: Membership information journal of the U.S.-Mexico Border Health Association. Aims to promote the improvement of the health status of border communities. *Type:* Newsletter.

NSF International

PO BOX 130140 Ph: (734)769-8010
Ann Arbor, MI 48113-0140 Free: 800-673-6275
 Fax: (734)769-0109
E-mail: info@nsf.org
URL: http://www.nsf.org
Contact: Dr. Dennis Mangino, Pres. & CEO.
Desc: Specializes in the areas of public health and environmental quality focusing on water quality, food safety, indoor air health and the environment. Develops standards, operates product certification and listings programs for products that meet or exceed public health safety standards. Maintains a worldwide network of auditors who conduct unannounced inspections of manufacturer facilities to ensure compliance and to protect the integrity of the NSF Certification Mark. *Type:* Association.

NYCAMH

Bassett Healthcare Ph: (607)547-6023
1 Atwell Rd. Free: 800-343-7527
Cooperstown, NY 13326 Fax: (607)547-6087
E-mail: jmay@lakenet.org
URL: http://www.bassetthealthcare.org
Contact: John J. May, MD, Dir.
Desc: Studies barn dusts, mites, health needs of agricultural workers in New York, dosimetry on farms, agricultural lung hazards, farm machinery safety, and migrant health. *Type:* Research center.

NYSDOH - Communicable Disease Fact Sheets

New York State Department of Health
125 Worth St. Ph: (212)788-5261
ESP Corning Tower, Rm. 651 Fax: (212)964-0472
New York, NY 10012
E-mail: nyhealth@health.state.ny.us
URL: http://www.health.state.ny.us/nysdoh/consumer/commun.htm
Desc: The Communicable Disease Fact Sheets, developed by the New York State Department of Health, maintains an alphabetical listing of dozens of communicable diseases. The entry for each disease contains information about the condition, including who gets the disease, method of transmittal, symptoms, how long the disease is spread in infected individuals, vaccine availability, treatment information, including effects of non-treatment, and prevention information. *Type:* Database.

Oakland University

Meadowbrook Health Enhancement Institute
Rochester, MI 48309-4401 Ph: (248)370-3198
 Fax: (248)370-4522
E-mail: fwstrans@oakland.edu
Contact: Dr. Fred Stransky, Dir.
Desc: Exercise physiology and the health profile enhancement of residents in internal medicine. *Type:* Research center.

Occupational Medicine Rehabilitation Clinic

2400 Moore Park, Ste. 100 Ph: (408)885-5920
San Jose, CA 95128 Fax: (408)885-4728
Desc: Injuries due to repetitive motion, especially job-related injuries, and treatment. *Type:* Research center.

Ohio Health Letter

Ohio Health Letter
224 Pleasant St.   Fax: (937)767-9361
Yellow Springs, OH 45387

Contact: Jeffrey Simons, Editor.

Desc: Summarizes news of Ohio medical centers, state doctor and nurse associations, and individual patients and their medical/social problems. Includes state health statistics. *Type:* Newsletter.

Ordinary Miracles

Brain Injury Association, Inc.
1127 S. Mannheim Rd., Ste.   Ph: (708)344-4646
    213   Free: 800-699-6443
Westchester, IL 60154-2562   Fax: (708)344-4680
E-mail: biail@yahoo.com
URL: http://www.biausa.org/illinois/bia.htm.

Contact: Cheryl Burda, Editor.

Desc: Publicizes the activities of the Association, which provides the crucial supports to individuals with brain injuries and their families. Provides information about available programs and services, prevention and treatment, resources, support groups, and recreational events. *Type:* Newsletter.

Pan American Health Organization

525 23rd St. NW   Ph: (202)974-3000
Washington, DC 20037   Fax: (202)338-0869
URL: http://www.paho.org

Contact: Dr. Bryna Brennan, Dir., Public Information.

Desc: Governments of Western Hemisphere nations united to improve physical and mental health in the Americas. Coordinates regional activities combating disease including exchange of statistical and epidemiological information, development of local health services, and organization of disease control and eradication programs. Encourages development in health systems and technology; provides consulting services; conducts educational courses on public health topics including environmental health, food and nutrition, and tropical diseases. *Type:* Association.

PCC Sound Consumer

Puget Consumers Co-op
4201 Roosevelt Way NE   Ph: (206)547-1222
Seattle, WA 98105-6008   Fax: (206)545-7131

Contact: Kim Runcinan, Editor.

Desc: Provides information on food, nutrition, and health news for members of Puget Consumers Co-op. *Type:* Newsletter.

Pennsylvania Health Department

Public Health Assessment

Epidemiology Bureau

Health & Welfare Bldg., Rm.   Ph: (717)783-4677
    907   Fax: (717)772-6975
PO Box 90
Harrisburg, PA 17108
E-mail: hers103w@wonder.em.cdc.gov

Contact: Joel Hersh, Dir.

Desc: Disease control and incidences in populations for the purposes of intervention. Specific programs include: communicable disease epidemiology, environmental health assessment, HIV/AIDS epidemiology, cancer epidemiology, and chronic disease epidemiology. *Type:* Research center.

Pennsylvania Health Department

Public Health Assessment

Laboratories Bureau

Health and Welfare Bldg.   Ph: (717)787-5901
PO Box 90   Fax: (717)772-6959
Harrisburg, PA 17108

Contact: Bruce Kleger, Dir.

Desc: Public health issues. *Type:* Research center.

People's Medical Society

462 Walnut St.   Ph: (610)770-1670
Allentown, PA 18102   Free: 800-624-8773
    Fax: (610)770-0607

E-mail: mad1@peoplesmed.org
URL: http://www.peoplesmed.org

Contact: Charles B. Inlander, Pres.

Desc: Promotes citizen involvement in the cost, quality, and management of the American health care system. Seeks to: train and encourage individuals to study local health care systems, practitioners, and institutions and promote preventive health care and medical cost control by these groups; address major policy issues and control health costs; encourage more preventive practice and research; promote self-care and alternative health care procedures; launch an information campaign to assist individuals in maintaining personal health and to prepare them for appointments with medical professionals. *Type:* Association.

Personal Health Advisor News

Empire BlueCross BlueShield
PO Box 1740
New York, NY 10163-1740

Desc: Provides health information. Includes health advice and information about doctors. *Type:* Newsletter.

Phil Kaplan's Health & Wealth Newsletter

Philip A. Kaplan
1304 SW 160th Ave.   Ph: (954)389-0280
Fort Lauderdale, FL 33326
URL: http://PhilKaplan.com.

Contact: Phil Kaplan, Editor, phil@philkaplan.com.

Desc: Discusses topics related to fitness, nutrition, and exercise. *Type:* Newsletter.

Physicians Committee for Responsible Medicine

PO Box 6322   Ph: (202)686-2210
Washington, DC 20015   Fax: (202)686-2216
E-mail: pcrm@pcrm.org
URL: http://www.pcrm.org

Contact: Neal D. Barnard, M.D., Pres.

Desc: Physicians, scientists, healthcare professionals, and interested others. Increases public awareness about the importance of preventive medicine and nutrition, and raises scientific and ethical questions pertaining to the use of humans and animals in medical research. *Type:* Association.

Prevention

Rodale Books
400 S. 10th St.   Ph: (610)967-5171
Emmaus, PA 18098-0099   Fax: (610)967-7722
E-mail: ddonche1@rodalepress.com; preventiondm@aol.com
URL: http://www.rodalepress.com

Contact: Mark Bricklin, Editor; Ken Wallace, Publisher.

Desc: Magazine containing articles on wellness, preventive medicine, self-care, and fitness. *Type:* Periodical.

Prevention at Work

Worker's Compensation Board of BC
6951 Westminster Hwy.   Ph: (604)279-7572
Richmond, BC, Canada V7C   Free: 800-661-2112
    1C6   Fax: (604)279-7696
URL: http://www.wcb.bc.ca.

Contact: Heather Prime, Editor.

Desc: Focuses on issues, changes, and events of the Worker's Compensation Board of British Columbia. Publication also explores workplace health and safety initiatives, issues, and solutions including safety education, injury and fatality statistics, and health and safety programs in the workplace. *Type:* Newsletter.

Proactive Risk Management

Lippincott Williams & Wilkins
227 E. Washington Sq.   Ph: (215)238-4200
Philadelphia, PA 19106-3780   Free: 800-777-2295
    Fax: (215)238-4227
URL: http://www.lrpub.com.

Contact: Tim Baker, Editor.

Desc: Dedicated to proactive healthcare risk management. Covers safety, training, policies, and quality programs. *Type:* Newsletter.

Program for Appropriate Technology in Health

4 Nickerson St., Ste. 300   Ph: (206)285-3500
Seattle, WA 98109-1699   Fax: (206)285-6619
E-mail: info@path.org
URL: http://www.path.org

Contact: Gordon W. Perkin, M.D., Pres.

Desc: Works to improve reproductive and child health, immunization programs, and diagnostic technologies in developing countries. Focuses on the effectiveness, availability, safety, and appropriateness of technologies for health and family planning. Conducts research and development, field assessment, communications, and technology transfer programs. *Type:* Association.

Public Citizen Health Research Group

1600 20th St. NW   Ph: (202)588-1000
Washington, DC 20009
URL: http://www.citizen.org
Contact: Sidney M. Wolfe, MD, Dir.

Desc: Health care delivery, workplace safety and health, drug regulation, food additives, medical device safety, and environmental influences on health. Conducts consumer advocacy and lobbying on health matters and monitors the enforcement of health and safety legislation. *Type:* Research center.

Public Health Centre

2400 D'Estimauville St.   Ph: (418)666-7000
Beauport, PQ, Canada G1E   Fax: (418)666-2776
    7G9
Contact: Michel Vezina, Dir.

Desc: Operational research, including effectiveness of interventions of sexual behavior of seropositive individuals; psychological stress of homosexual AIDS patients; and studies on organochlorinated contaminants. *Type:* Research center.

Public Health Foundation Newsletter

Public Health Foundation
1220 L St. NW, Ste. 350   Ph: (202)898-5600
Washington, DC 20005   Fax: (202)898-5609
Contact: Molly Pickett, Editor.

Desc: Serves to promote the aim of the Foundation, which is to strengthen health activities "in order to improve the health of all Americans." Reports on Public Health Foundation's projects, including workshops, grants to states, hotlines, and publications on timely health policy and health data issues. Recurring features include a calendar of events. *Type:* Newsletter.

Public Health Institute

2001 Addison St., Ste. 210   Ph: (510)644-8200
Berkeley, CA 94704-1103   Fax: (510)644-9319
E-mail: ktabor@publichealth.org
URL: http://www.publichealth.org/phipage
Contact: Joseph M. Hafey, Pres./CEO.

Desc: Conducts research on a broad range of public health issues, including alcohol problems, women's health issues, epidemiology, occupational health, toxic chemicals, genetics, diet and nutrition, and cancer prevention. *Type:* Research center.

Regulatory Affairs Professionals Society

12300 Twinbrook Pky., Ste.   Ph: (301)770-2920
  350   Fax: (301)770-2924
Rockville, MD 20852
E-mail: feedback@raps.org
URL: http://www.raps.org
Contact: Sherry Keramidas, PhD, CAE.

Desc: Represents the regulatory affairs profession and the individuals who are part of this dynamic field. RAPS members are the health regulatory leaders of today and tomorrow in areas such as medical devices, pharmaceuticals, biologics, biotechnology and in vitro diagnostics. *Type:* Association.

Resource News

National Wellness Association
PO Box 827   Ph: (715)342-2969
Stevens Point, WI 54481-0827   Free: 800-244-8922
   Fax: (715)342-2979
E-mail: nwa@wellnessnwi.org
URL: http://www.wellnesshwi.org/nwa/.
Desc: Lists and describes current resources on health and wellness promotion, including books, CDs, audiotapes, videos, posters, pamphlets, reports, guidebooks, and newsletters. *Type:* Newsletter.

Saint Raphaels' Better Health

St. Raphael's Better Health
1450 Chapel St.   Ph: (203)789-3972
New Haven, CT 06511   Fax: (203)789-4053
Contact: Magaly Olivero, Publishing Dir.
Desc: Health magazine. *Type:* Periodical.

Satsang

Fivefold Path, Inc.
Rt. 8 Box 369   Ph: (540)948-5463
Madison, VA 22727   Fax: (540)948-5214
URL: http://www.summit.net/home/agnihotra.
Contact: Lisa C. Powers, President.
Desc: Provides information about agnihotra, ayurvedic healing fire, and other homa therapy practices. Describes how these techniques are used in healing the environment, improving agriculture, in holistic healing, and stress reduction. *Type:* Newsletter.

School System Special Interest Section Quarterly

American Occupational Therapy Association, Inc. (AOTA)
PO Box 31220   Ph: (301)652-2682
Bethesda, MD 20824-1220   Free: 800-877-1383
   Fax: (301)652-7711
E-mail: ajotsis@aota.org.
Contact: Amy Eutsey, Managing Editor, amye@aota.org.
Desc: Focuses on issues concerning the delivery of occupational therapy services in school settings. Recurring features include columns titled From the Editor and From the Chairperson. *Type:* Newsletter.

Science/Health Abstracts

Yuchi Pines Institute
Box 319   Ph: (205)288-5495
Ft. Mitchell, AL 36856
Contact: Phylis Austin, Editor.
Desc: Provides news of interest regarding science and health. *Type:* Newsletter.

Second Opinion

Second Opinion Publishing Inc.
7100 Peachtree Dunwoody Rd.,   Ph: (770)668-0432
  Ste. 100   Free: 800-728-2288
Atlanta, GA 30328   Fax: (770)668-0692
Contact: Dr. William Campbell Douglass, Editor.
Desc: "Provides a 'skeptic's view' of today's 'accepted' health and medicine procedures from a classically trained MD." Offers readers suggestions to "make themselves healthier, not their doctors richer." Discusses alternative medical treatments and inexpensive cures. Provides "outspoken critiques" of the current system of established medicine and warnings of unpublished health risks. *Type:* Newsletter.

Smoking and Health

U.S. Centers for Disease Control and Prevention (CDC)
Office on Smoking and Health
Technical Information Center
Rhodes Bldg., Mailstop K50   Ph: (770)488-5708
Atlanta, GA 30333
URL: http://www.cdc.gov/tobacco
Contact: Alice A. Devierno, Assistant Director, Technical Information Center.
Desc: Contains more than 50,000 citations, with some abstracts, to worldwide scientific and technical literature on tobacco, tobacco use, and smoking. Sources include scientific and translated journals, technical reports, bibliographies, books and book reviews, monographs, annual reports, and patents. *Available:* U.S. National Library of Medicine (NLM), TOXNET. *Type:* Database.

State Health Notes

Forum for State Health Policy Leadership
444 N. Capital St., NW, Ste.   Ph: (202)624-3574
  515   Fax: (202)737-1069
Washington, DC 20001
Contact: Linda Demkovich, Editor, linda.demkovich@ncsl.org.
Desc: Deals with a wide range of state health policy issues: Medicaid, public health issues, health planning and insurance, licensure, staffing in the health-care field, mental health, and substance abuse. Features include legislative/program updates, innovative public/private sector initiatives, interviews of key policy officials, and publication summaries and highlights. *Type:* Newsletter.

State University of New York Health Science Center at Brooklyn

Scientific/Academic Computing Center

450 Clarkson Ave.   Ph: (718)270-7475
Box 7
Brooklyn, NY 11203
Contact: Dr. Jack Lubowsky, Dir.
Desc: Applications of computing to biomedical research. Provides consulting services to the Health Sciences Center in the fields of statistical analysis, experimental design and methodology, signal analysis, data acquisition techniques, and analytical methods. *Type:* Research center.

Stratis Health

2901 Metro Dr., Ste. 400   Ph: (612)854-3306
Bloomington, MN 55425   Fax: (612)853-8503
Contact: David M. Ziegenhagen, CEO.

Desc: Physicians interested in ensuring the availabilty of quality health care at reasonable costs. Evaluates health care services at hospitals, retirement homes, and other facilities. Develops health care standards for hospitals and offers consultation services to operators of health care facilities to improve efficiency in services. *Type:* Association.

Stroke Club International Bulletin

Stroke Clubs International
805 12th St.   Ph: (409)762-1022
Galveston, TX 77550
E-mail: strokeclubs@aol.com
Contact: Ellis Williamson, Editor.
Desc: Provides information on Stroke Clubs International as well as stroke-related topics such as stroke prevention, returning to work after having a stroke, and insurance policies. Also addresses public awareness issues. *Type:* Newsletter.

Synergy

Canadian Society for International Health
170 Laurier Ave. W, Ste. 902   Ph: (613)230-2654
Ottawa, ON, Canada K1P 5V5   Fax: (613)230-8401
E-mail: csih@fox.nstn.ca
Contact: Mary Bridgeo, Editor.
Desc: Provides information on international health, emphasizing Canadian initiatives. Serves to inform international health professionals and to provide awareness of Canadian expertise and activities related to improving health in developing countries. *Type:* Newsletter.

Take a Breather

Lung Association - Metropolitan Toronto and York Region
365 Bloor St. E., Ste. 601   Ph: (416)922-9440
Toronto, ON, Canada M4W   Fax: (416)922-9430
  3L4
Contact: Andre C. Roberts, Editor, aroberts@terraport.net.
Desc: Covers Association issues; provides financial updates and volunteer news. Offers information on health and environmental concerns, especially air pollution. *Type:* Newsletter.

Taking Care

United Health Care Services, Inc.
8201 Greensboro Dr., Ste. 500   Ph: (703)394-7600
Mc Lean, VA 22102   Fax: (703)394-7584
E-mail: tkngcare@uhc.com
Contact: Melanie Lutz, Editor.
Desc: Contains articles on health care education, fitness, nutrition, family and mental health, workplace issues, and informed use of the medical care system. Includes recipes, product comparisons, reader contests, health news updates, and a columns titled Doctor Q & A. *Type:* Newsletter.

The Tampon Health Website

CritPath
2062 Lombard St.   Ph: (215)545-2212
Philadelphia, PA 19146   Fax: (215)735-2762
E-mail: rich@critpath.org
URL: http://critpath.org/~tracy/spot.html
Contact: Tracy Bannett, tracy@critpath.org.
Desc: S.P.O.T. is a group of women dedicated to informing other women about the dangers of major brand tampon use. *Type:* Database.

Texas A&M University

Center for Urban and Structural Entomology

Department of Entomology   Ph: (409)845-5855
College Station, TX 77843-2475   Fax: (409)845-5926
E-mail: r-gold@tamu.edu

URL: http://entowww.tamu.edu

Contact: Dr. Roger Gold, Dir.

Desc: Urban and public health entomology, focusing on investigations of the parasites and predators of cockroaches. *Type:* Research center.

Tipsheet

Minnesota Chapter
Arthritis Foundation
830 Transfer Rd.   Ph: (612)644-4108
St. Paul, MN 55114-1460   Free: 800-333-1380
                          Fax: (612)644-4219
E-mail: ddressel@arthritis.org.
URL: http://www.arthritis.org.

Desc: Provides tips for people with arthritis such as medical information and coping suggestions. *Type:* Newsletter.

TopHealth

TopHealth
PO Box 381116   Free: 800-871-9525
Birmingham, AL 35238-1116 Fax: (205)991-2870

Contact: Donald L. Deye, M.D., Editor.

Desc: Provides information, news, and techniques to achieve and maintain "a healthier lifestyle." *Type:* Newsletter.

TOPS Club

Susan Trones
4575 S. 5th St.   Ph: (414)482-4620
PO Box 07360   Free: 800-932-8677
Milwaukee, WI 53207
E-mail: comm@globaldialog.com
URL: http://www.tops.org

Contact: Betty Domenoe, Pres.

Desc: Weight control self-help association using group dynamics, competition, and recognition to help members lose weight. TOPS is medically oriented, requiring physician-approved individual diet programs, and physician-set weight goals. *Type:* Association.

TOPS News

TOPS Club, Inc.
PO Box 07360   Ph: (414)482-4620
Milwaukee, WI 53207-0360
URL: http://www.tops.org

Contact: Kathleen Davis, Editor.

Desc: Membership magazine containing articles on nutrition, dieting, and fitness. *Type:* Periodical.

Union of American Physicians and Dentists

1330 Broadway, Ste. 730   Ph: (510)839-0193
Oakland, CA 94612   Free: 800-622-0909
                          Fax: (510)763-8756
E-mail: uapd@uapd.com

Contact: Robert Weinmann, M.D., Pres.

Desc: Independent national labor organization made up of self-employed medical doctors and dentists as well as those employed by hospitals, teaching institutions, counties, and municipalities. Seeks to: provide optimum medical care for the people; ensure quality facilities for the provision of medical care; enable physicians to give of themselves, unhindered by extraneous forces, for the welfare of their patients; ensure reasonable compensation for physicians commensurate with their training, skill, and the responsibility they bear for the life and health of their fellow human beings. *Type:* Association.

U.S. Department of Agriculture
Food Safety and Inspection Service

14th St. & Independence Ave.   Ph: (202)720-7943
  SW   Fax: (202)720-1843
Washington, DC 20250
URL: http://www.usda.gov/agency/fsis/homepage.htm/

Desc: The service is responsible for ensuring that meat and poultry products moving in interstate and foreign commerce for human consumption are safe, wholesome, and accurately labeled. *Type:* Government agency, office, or program.

U.S. Department of Health and Human Services
Agency for Health Care Policy and Research

2101 E Jefferson St.   Ph: (301)594-1364
Rockville, MD 20852
E-mail: info@ahcpr.gov
URL: http://www.ahcpr.gov/

Contact: John M. Eisenberg, Dir of Admin.

Type: Government agency, office, or program.

U.S. Department of Health and Human Services
Centers for Disease Control and Prevention

1600 Clifton Rd. NE   Ph: (404)639-3311
Atlanta, GA 30333
URL: http://www.cdc.gov/

Contact: Claire V. Broome, Acting Director.

Desc: The Centers for Disease Control administers national programs for the prevention and control of communicable and vector-borne diseases and other preventable conditions. It develops and implements programs to deal with environmental health problems, including responding to environmental, chemical, and radiation emergencies. *Type:* Government agency, office, or program.

U.S. Department of Health and Human Services
Centers for Disease Control and Prevention
Epidemiology Program Office

1600 Clifton Rd. NE   Ph: (404)639-3311
Atlanta, GA 30333
URL: http://www.cdc.gov/

Contact: Barbara Holloway, Acting Director.

Type: Government agency, office, or program.

U.S. Department of Health and Human Services
Centers for Disease Control and Prevention
National Center for Health Statistics

1600 Clifton Rd. NE   Ph: (404)639-3311
Atlanta, GA 30333
URL: http://www.cdc.gov/

Contact: Edward J. Sondik, Director.

Desc: The NCHS mission is to collect, analyze, and disseminate national health statistics; conduct research in survey and statistical methodology; provide specialized training programs and technical assistance; and coordinate cooperative programs with state, national, and international organizations. NCHS maintains data systems that produce data in the following areas: extent of illness and disability in the population; distribution and normative standards for physiological and nutritional measurements; national vital statistics, including births, deaths, marriages, and divorces; hospital, nursing home, and ambulatory care utilization; health expenditures; family formation, growth, and dissolution; and other major health topics. *Type:* Government agency, office, or program.

U.S. Department of Health and Human Services
Centers for Disease Control and Prevention
National Immunization Program Office

1600 Clifton Rd. NE   Ph: (404)639-3311
Atlanta, GA 30333
URL: http://www.cdc.gov/

Contact: Walter A. Orenstein, Director.

Type: Government agency, office, or program.

U.S. Department of Health and Human Services
Centers for Disease Control and Prevention
Public Health Practice Program Office

1600 Clifton Rd. NE   Ph: (404)639-3311
Atlanta, GA 30333

Contact: Edward L. Baker, Director.

Type: Government agency, office, or program.

U.S. Department of Health and Human Services
Food and Drug Administration

5600 Fishers Ln.   Ph: (301)443-1544
Rockville, MD 20857
URL: http://www.fda.gov/

Contact: Jerold R. Mande, Contact.

Desc: The mission of the Food and Drug Administration is to protect the public health of the nation as it may be impaired by foods, drugs, biological products, cosmetics, medical devices, ionizing and nonionizing radiation-emitting products and substances, poisons, pesticides, and food additives. Its regulatory functions are geared to insure that foods are safe, pure, and wholesome; that drugs, medical devices, and biological products are safe and effective; that cosmetics are harmless; that all of the above are honestly and informatively packaged; and that exposure to potentially injurious radiation is minimized. *Type:* Government agency, office, or program.

U.S. Department of Health and Human Services
Food and Drug Administration

Rm. 1471   Ph: (301)827-2410
5600 Fishers Ln.   Fax: (301)443-3100
Rockville, MD 20857
URL: http://www.fda.gov

Contact: Michael A. Friedman, MD, Lead Dep.Commnr.

Desc: Public health of the nation as it may be impaired by foods, drugs, biological products, cosmetics, medical devices, ionizing and nonionizing radiation-emitting products and substances, poisons, pesticides, and food additives. FDA's functions are to ensure that: foods are safe, pure, and wholesome; drugs, medical devices, and biological products are safe and effective; cosmetics are harmless; that all of the above are honestly and informatively packaged; and that exposure to potentially injurious radiation is minimized. *Type:* Research center.

U.S. Department of Health and Human Services
Food and Drug Administration
Center for Biologics Evaluation and Research

c/o Food and Drug   Ph: (301)827-2000
  Administration   Fax: (301)827-0440
5600 Fishers Ln.
Rockville, MD 20857
URL: http://www.fda.gov/

Contact: Kathryn C. Zoon, Director.

Desc: Center administers regulation of biological products under the biological product control provisions of the Public Health Service Act and applicable provision of the Federal Food, Drug, and Cosmetic Act. It provides dominant focus in the Administration for coordination of the AIDS program, works to develop an AIDS vaccine and AIDS diagnostic tests, and conducts other AIDS-related activities. *Type:* Government agency, office, or program.

U.S. Department of Health and Human Services

Food and Drug Administration

Center for Devices and Radiological Health

c/o Food and Drug	Ph: (301)443-4690
Administration	Free: 800-638-2041
5600 Fishers Ln.	Fax: (301)594-1320
Rockville, MD 20857	
URL: http://www.fda.gov	

Contact: D. Bruce Burlington, Director.

Desc: The Center develops and carries out a national program designed to control unnecessary exposure of humans to, and assure the safe use of, potentially hazardous ionizing and non-ionizing radiation. It also develops policy and priorities relating to the safety, effectiveness, and labeling of medical devices for human use; conducts an electronic product radiation control program; develops, plans, and evaluates surveillance and compliance programs for medical devices and radiation exposure; plans, conducts, and supports research and testing relating to medical devices and to the health effects of radiation exposure; reviews and evaluates medical devices premarket approval applications, product development protocols, and exemption requests for investigational devices; develops, promulgates, and enforces performance standards for appropriate categories of medical devices and Good Manufacturing Practice (GMP) regulations for manufacturers; provides technical and other nonfinancial assistance to small manufacturers of medical devices; develops regulations, standards, and criteria and recommends changes in FDA legislative authority necessary to protect the public health; provides scientific and technical support to other components within FDA and other agencies on matters relating to radiological health and medical devices; and maintains appropriate liaison with other federal, state, and international agencies, with industry, and with consumer and professional organizat

U.S. Department of Health and Human Services

Food and Drug Administration

Center for Drug Evaluation and Research

c/o Food and Drug	Ph: (301)827-4573
Administration	
5600 Fishers Ln.	
Rockville, MD 20857	
URL: http://www.fda.gov/	

Contact: Janet Woodcock, Director.

Desc: Center develops FDA policy with regard to the safety, effectiveness, and labeling of all drugs for human use; reviews and evaluates new drug applications and notices of claimed investigational exemption of new drugs; develops and implements standards for the safety and effectiveness of all over-the-counter drugs; monitors the quality of marketed drugs through product testing, surveillance, and compliance programs; develops guidelines on current Good Manufacturing Practices for use by the drug industry; develops and disseminates information and educational material on drugs to the medical community and the public; conducts research and develops scientific standards on the composition, quality, safety, and efficacy of human drugs; collects and evaluates information on the effects and use trends of marketed drugs; monitors prescription drug advertising and promotional labeling to assure their accuracy and integrity; analyzes data on accidental poisonings; and disseminates toxicity and treatment information on medicines. *Type:* Government agency, office, or program.

U.S. Department of Health and Human Services

National Center for Chronic Disease Prevention and Health Promotion

Division of Adult and Community Health

Mail Stop K-45	Ph: (770)488-5269
4770 Buford Hwy., NE	Fax: (770)488-5964
Atlanta, GA 30341-3724	

Contact: Dr. James S. Marks, Dir.

Desc: Chronic disease morbidity, mortality, and behavioral risk factors; develops surveillance tools and provides assistance to state and local health departments, universities, and voluntary agencies; administers and reports to Congress on the Preventive Health and Health Services Block Grant; and studies health status of special populations, including women, minorities, and the elderly. *Type:* Research center.

U.S. Department of Health and Human Services

National Institute for Occupational Safety and Health

Biomedical and Behavioral Science Division

Physical Agents Effects Branch

Robert A. Taft Laboratories, MS	Ph: (513)533-8153
C-27	Fax: (513)533-8510
4676 Columbia Pkwy.	
Cincinnati, OH 45226-1998	
E-mail: wgl0@niobbs1.en.cdc.gov	
URL: http://www.cdc.gov/niosh/homepage.html	

Contact: W. Gregory Lotz, PhD, Br.Chf.

Desc: Health effects of non-ionizing radiation and noise in the workplace. *Type:* Research center.

U.S. Department of Health and Human Services

National Institute for Occupational Safety and Health

Education and Information Division

Information Resources Branch

Robert A. Taft Laboratories	Ph: (513)533-8326
4676 Columbia Pkwy.	Free: 800-356-4674
Cincinnati, OH 45226-1998	Fax: (513)533-8588
E-mail: vepl@cdc.gov	
URL: http://www.cdc.gov/niosh	

Contact: Vern Anderson, Chf.

Desc: Provides technical information support for NIOSH research programs. Its activities include collecting, organizing, and retrieving published and unpublished technical literature related to the field of occupational safety and health. *Type:* Research center.

U.S. Department of Health and Human Services

National Institute for Occupational Safety and Health

Physical Sciences and Engineering Division

Robert A. Taft Laboratories	Ph: (513)841-4500
4676 Columbia Pkwy.	Fax: (513)841-4321
Cincinnati, OH 45226-1998	
E-mail: lxd3@niopse1.em.cdc.gov	

Contact: Laurence J. Doemeny, Actg.Dir.

Desc: Performance criteria for environmental (industrial hygiene) monitoring equipment; assessing control technology for occupational health hazards; conducting research and developing equipment for control of occupational health hazards; conducting research and developing sampling and analytical methods for occupational toxic substances; providing analytical chemistry support for the Institute's laboratory and field research programs; and providing assistance to the industrial hygiene community in operating a quality control reference program for industrial hygiene laboratories. Division comprises branches for Engineering Control Technology, Measurements Research Support, Methods Research, and Quality Assurance and Statistics. *Type:* Research center.

U.S. Department of Health and Human Services

National Institute for Occupational Safety and Health

Physical Sciences and Engineering Division

Methods Research Branch

Robert A. Taft Laboratories	Ph: (513)841-4241
Mail Stop R-7	Fax: (513)841-4500
4676 Columbia Pkwy.	
Cincinnati, OH 45226-1998	
E-mail: MTA1@NIOPSE1.EM.CDC.GOV	

Contact: Mr. Martin Abell, Chf.

Desc: Research that develops, improves and evaluates analytical methods for the evaluation of levels of toxic materials found in the work environment, and in industrial and biologic materials; providing expert consultation for the development of occupational health criteria and standards on methods for microbiological and chemical analytical procedures; providing special consultation to the National Institute for Occupational Safety and Health and other government agencies; and providing validated NIOSH procedures for sampling and analytical methods. Branch comprises one section for the development and evaluation of field instruments and two sections for laboratory methods development. *Type:* Research center.

U.S. Department of Health and Human Services

National Institute for Occupational Safety and Health

Physical Sciences and Engineering Division

Quality Assurance and Statistics Activity

Robert A. Taft Laboratories	Ph: (513)841-4266
4676 Columbia Pkwy.	Fax: (513)841-4545
Cincinnati, OH 45226-1998	
E-mail: pcs1@cdc.gov	

Contact: Paul Schlecht, Chf.

Desc: Quality of NIOSH industrial hygiene laboratory services; conduct with the American Industrial Hygiene Association (AIHA) a proficiency testing program for industrial hygiene laboratories (the Proficiency Analytical Testing Program, covering a variety of metal and organic analyses, silica, and asbestos analyses); conduct with the U.S. Environmental Protection Agency and AIHA a proficiency testing program for environmental labs, including the Environmental Lead Proficiency Analytical Testing Program, which covers lead analyses in paint chips, soil, and dust wipes; and provide statistical support for NIOSH industrial hygiene chemistry and engineering control research. *Type:* Research center.

U.S. Department of Health and Human Services

National Institute for Occupational Safety and Health

Respiratory Disease Studies Division

Appalachian Laboratory for	Ph: (304)285-5749
Occupational Safety and	Fax: (304)285-5861
Health, R	
1095 Willowdale Road.	
Morgantown, WV 26505-2888	

Contact: Gregory Wagner, MD, Dir.

Desc: Clinical and epidemiological research on occupational respiratory disease; provides medical, surveillance, and autopsy services; conducts medical and environmental research; conducts health hazard evaluations in mining industries; designs and conducts research programs in agricultural and noncoal mining health; and plans, coordinates, and conducts energy research relating to occupational safety and health, including research in the areas of synthetic fuel production and occupational hazards associated with solar and other new energy sources. Division comprises the Clinical Investigations Branch, Environmental Investigations Branch, Epidemiological Investigations Branch, Examination Processing Branch, and Laboratory Investigations Branch. *Type:* Research center.

U.S. Department of Health and Human Services
National Institute for Occupational Safety and Health
Respiratory Disease Studies Division
Clinical Investigations Branch

Appalachian Laboratory for   Ph: (304)291-4755
Occupational Safety and   Fax: (304)291-4067
Health
944 Chestnut Ridge Rd.
Morgantown, WV 26505-2888
Contact: John L. Hankinson, PhD, Chf.

Desc: Occupational lung diseases. *Type:* Research center.

U.S. Department of Health and Human Services
National Institute for Occupational Safety and Health
Respiratory Disease Studies Division
Environmental Investigations Branch

Appalachian Laboratory for   Ph: (304)285-6131
Occupational Safety and   Fax: (304)285-5861
Health
1095 Willowdale Rd.
Morgantown, WV 26505
E-mail: fjh1@cdc.gov
URL: http://www.cdc.gov/niosh/homepage.html
Contact: Frank J. Hearl, Chf.

Desc: Industrial hygiene, particularly as related to sampling and analytical methods, survey protocols, epidemiology, and surface physics. Conducts basic industrial hygiene research on agents causing or likely to cause respiratory disease. *Type:* Research center.

U.S. Department of Health and Human Services
National Institute for Occupational Safety and Health
Surveillance, Hazard Evaluations, and Field Studies Division

Mail Stop R-12   Ph: (513)841-4428
Robert A. Taft Laboratories   Fax: (513)841-4483
4676 Columbia Pkwy.
Cincinnati, OH 45226-1998
E-mail: ljf4@nioshe2.em.cdc.gov
Contact: Dr. Lawrence J. Fine, Dir.

Desc: Epidemiologic field research and national surveillance in occupational health. Activities are carried out in three branches: Hazard Evaluations and Technical Assistance, Industrywide Studies, and Surveillance. *Type:* Research center.

U.S. Department of Health and Human Services
National Institute for Occupational Safety and Health
Surveillance, Hazard Evaluations, and Field Studies Division
Hazard Evaluations and Technical Assistance Branch

Robert A. Taft Laboratories   Ph: (513)841-4428
Mail Stop R-9   Fax: (513)841-4483
4676 Columbia Pkwy.
Cincinnati, OH 45226-4382
E-mail: dss2@nioshe1.em.cdc.gov
URL: http://www.cdc.gov/niosh/homepage.html
Contact: Mr. Dave Sundin, Chf.

Desc: General industry requests for assistance in evaluating potential health hazard situations, including requests from employers, employees, employee representatives, other federal agencies, and state and local agencies. Branch evaluates whether or not chemical, biological, or physical agents are hazardous as used or found in the workplace and makes recommendations for control procedures, improved work practices, and medical screening to reduce exposure levels and subsequent health effects. *Type:* Research center.

U.S. Department of Health and Human Services
National Institute for Occupational Safety and Health
Surveillance, Hazard Evaluations, and Field Studies Division
Industrywide Studies Branch

Robert A. Taft Laboratories   Ph: (513)841-4203
4676 Columbia Pkwy., Rm. 13   Fax: (513)841-4486
Cincinnati, OH 45226-1998
URL: http://www.cdc.gov/niosh
Contact: Dr. Elizabeth M. Ward, Chf.

Desc: Industrywide studies, through record studies and clinical/environmental studies, to: identify occupational causes of disease in the working population and their offspring; determine the incidence and prevalence of acute and chronic effects from work-related exposures to toxic and hazardous substances; and provide information needed to develop standards to control occupational health hazards. Branch comprises sections for industrial hygiene and epidemiology. *Type:* Research center.

U.S. Department of Health and Human Services
National Institute for Occupational Safety and Health
Surveillance, Hazard Evaluations, and Field Studies Division
Surveillance Branch

Robert A. Taft Laboratories   Ph: (513)841-4303
4676 Columbia Pkwy., ML-R19   Fax: (513)841-4489
Cincinnati, OH 45226-1998
E-mail: jps4@cdc.gov
URL: http://www.cdc.gov/niosh/homepage.html
Contact: John Sestito, Chf., Surveillance Branch.

Desc: Surveillance system of the nation's work force and its environs and to make an early detection and continuous assessment of the magnitude and extent of job-related illnesses, exposures, and hazardous agents. Branch comprises sections for medical activity, hazards, and illness effects. *Type:* Research center.

U.S. Department of Health and Human Services
National Institutes of Health
National Institute of Allergy and Infectious Diseases

9000 Rockville Pike   Ph: (301)496-5717
Bethesda, MD 20892   Fax: (301)496-4409
URL: http://www.niaid.nih.gov/
Contact: Anthony S. Fauci, MD, Director.

Desc: NIAID conducts and supports broadly based research and research training on the causes, characteristics, prevention, control, and treatment of a wide variety of diseases believed to be attributable to infectious agents, including bacteria, viruses, and parasites; to allergies; or to other deficiencies or disorders in the responses of the body's immune mechanisms. Among areas of special emphasis are: AIDS, asthma and allergic disease, sexually transmitted diseases, clinical immunology, disease control measures, research and development, antiviral substances, and hospital-associated infections. *Type:* Government agency, office, or program.

U.S. Department of Health and Human Services
National Institutes of Health
Research Grants Division

9000 Rockville Pike   Ph: (301)435-1111
Bethesda, MD 20892
URL: http://www.nih.gov/
Desc: Division provides staff support to the Office of the Director, NIH, in the formulation of grant and award policies and procedures, central receipt of all Public Health Service applications for research training support, and makes initial referral to Service components. *Type:* Government agency, office, or program.

U.S. Department of Health and Human Services
Public Health Service
Office of the Assistant Secretary for Health and Surgeon General

200 Independence Ave. SW   Ph: (202)619-0257
Washington, DC 20201
Contact: David Satcher, Contact.

Desc: The Office consists of general and special staff offices that support the Assistant Secretary for Health in planning and directing the activities of the Public Health Service. Components include the Office of the Surgeon General, the Office of Disease Prevention and Health Promotion, the Office of Health Communications, the Office of Health Operations, the Office of Health Planning and Evaluation, the Office of Intergovernmental Affairs, and the Office of Population Affairs. *Type:* Government agency, office, or program.

University of California at Berkeley
Center for Occupational and Environmental Health

School of Public Health   Ph: (510)642-0761
Berkeley, CA 94720-7360   Fax: (510)642-5815
E-mail: llew@uclink4.berkeley.edu
URL: http://ehs.sph.berkeley.edu/coeh/
Contact: Dr. Robert C. Spear, Dir.

Desc: Occupational medicine, toxicology, industrial hygiene, epidemiology, occupational health nursing, and ergonomics. Specific research includes studies on the causes, diagnosis, and prevention of occupational and environmental injuries and illnesses. *Type:* Research center.

University of Colorado
Center for Health Services Research

1355 S. Colorado Blvd., Ste.   Ph: (303)756-8350
306   Fax: (303)759-8196
Denver, CO 80222
Contact: Peter W. Shaughnessy, PhD, Dir.

Desc: Health services research and health policy research for federal and state governments, foundations, and related organizations, emphasizing general health policy topics and issues in long-term care quality, access, cost and cost effectiveness. Studies emphasize Medicare and Medicaid quality assurance and reimbursement for long-term care providers, including home health agencies, subacute care facilities, swing-bed hospitals, and traditional nursing homes. *Type:* Research center.

University of Connecticut Health Center
Center for International Community Health Studies

Department of Community   Ph: (860)679-1570
Medicine   Fax: (860)679-1581
263 Farmington Ave.
Farmington, CT 06030-6330
E-mail: schensul@nso2.uchc.edu
URL: http://www.commed.uchc.edu/cichs/cichs.htm
Contact: Stephen L. Schensul, PhD, Dir.

Desc: The health of underprivileged people in the U.S. and abroad, emphasizing international primary health care and community health, including international health policy, urban health in developing and developed countries, maternal and child health, health programs and problems in Peru, Sri Lanka, Kenya, Mauritius, and Connecticut, effects of economic development on health, and the role of the hospital in the developing world. *Type:* Research center.

University of Iowa

Great Plains Center for Agricultural Health

Inst. for Rural and	Ph: (319)335-4212
Environmental Health	Fax: (319)335-4225
Iowa City, IA 52242	

E-mail: stephen-reynolds@uiowa.edu
URL: http://info.pmch.uiowa.edu/gpcah/gpc.htm
Contact: Dr. Stephen Reynolds, Contact.

Desc: Training of agricultural health professionals; farm safety chapter development; education of health professionals; production of materials; industrial hygiene, including respirator evaluation, anhydrous ammonia, pesticide exposure, composting exposure, and dust reduction studies; toxicology, including organic dust induced lung inflammation, molecular biology methods for bioaerosol exposure assessment, reference organic dust repository, and inhalation toxicology models; ergonomics, including a database for guidelines for children's agricultural tasks, and evaluation of assistive technologies; and rural health, including respiratory disease, dermatologic and allergic disease, hearing loss, neurologic disease and mental health, reproductive health outcomes, and the determinants of these disease outcomes in a random sample of farm, rural non-farm and town households in the Keokuk County, Iowa. *Type:* Research center.

University of Iowa

Injury Prevention Research Center

College of Med.	Ph: (319)335-4418
100 Oakdale Campus, No. 134	Fax: (319)335-4225
IREH	
Iowa City, IA 52242-5000	

E-mail: john-lundell@uiowa.edu
URL: http://info.pmeh.uiowa.edu/iprc/iprc.htm
Contact: Dr. Craig Zwerling, Dir.

Desc: Control and prevention of rural injuries in these high risk populations through research, education and training, and public policy targeting especially ruraal motor vehicle injuries and farm and other occupational injuries. The specific aims of the research projects include examining the rates and risk factors of farm-related injuries among Iowa farmers; evaluating the effectiveness of trauma care in Iowa; and examining driving avoidance behavior in drivers with traumatic brain injuries. *Type:* Research center.

University of Iowa

Institute for Rural and Environmental Health

Preventive Med. & Env. Health	Ph: (319)335-4415
Dept.	Fax: (319)335-4225
IREH, Oakdale Campus	
Iowa City, IA 52242-5000	

E-mail: craig-zwerling@uiowa.edu
URL: http://info.pmeh.uiowa.edu/
Contact: Dr. Craig Zwerling, Dir.

Desc: Occupational injury and disease research and prevention and environmental health among farmers, those living in rural areas, and general industry. Conducts multidisciplinary studies of health effects due to modern agricultural and industrial practices, particularly in the areas of agricultural medicine, occupational medicine, industrial hygiene, environmental health, and environmental chemistry. *Type:* Research center.

University of Iowa

State Hygienic Laboratory

102 Oakdale Campus H101	Ph: (319)335-4500
OH	Fax: (319)335-4600
Iowa City, IA 52242-5002	

E-mail: director@uhl.uiowa.edu
URL: http://www.uhl.uiowa.edu
Contact: Mary J.R. Gilchrist, PhD, Dir.

Desc: Virology, limnology, industrial hygiene, neonatal metabolic and prenatal diseases detection, microbiology,

and organic, inorganic, and radiation chemistry. Conducts research and service in all areas relating to the environment and public health, including rapid diagnosis of disease agents by molecular methods and enzyme immunoassay, and monitoring immune status by flow cytometry. *Type:* Research center.

University of Maryland at College Park

Minority Health Research Laboratory

HHP Bldg. 1241	Ph: (301)405-2467
College Park, MD 20742	Fax: (301)314-9167

E-mail: cadholli@aol.com

Contact: Chalene Day, Dir., Minority Hea.

Desc: Promotes health and disease prevention among poorly served, underserved, and never served populations in the U.S., by researching issues that impact diverse populations. *Type:* Research center.

University of Montreal

Centre for Occupational Stress and Health

School of Industrial Relations	Ph: (514)343-7320
Montreal, PQ, Canada H3C 3J7	Fax: (514)343-5764

E-mail: dolan@ere.umontreal.ca

Contact: Dr. Shimon L. Dolan, Dir.

Desc: Diagnosis and intervention in the field of occupational stress, focusing on stress in police officers, social workers, hospital workers, executive personnel, and workers in other stressful occupations. *Type:* Research center.

University of North Dakota

Center for Rural Health

School of Medicine and Health	Ph: (701)777-3848
Sciences	Fax: (701)777-2389
PO Box 9037	
Grand Forks, ND 58202-9037	

E-mail: bgibbens@mail.med.und.nodak.edu
URL: http://www.med.und.nodak.edu/depts/Rural/director.htm

Contact: Brad Gibbens, Assoc.Dir.

Desc: Rural health issues. *Type:* Research center.

University of Quebec

National Institute for Scientific Research

Armand-Frappier Institute

Virology Research Centre

531 Blvd. des Prairies	Ph: (514)686-5515
Case Postale 100	Fax: (514)686-5626
Laval, PQ, Canada H7N 4Z3	

Contact: Dr. Max Arella, Dir.

Desc: Molecular virology, ecovirology, and biotechnology, including studies on the mechanisms of viral transmission, interactions between viruses-hosts and environment, new viral vaccines, applications of monoclonal antibodies and DNA probes to viral diagnostics, use of insect viruses as expression vectors and biological control agents. *Type:* Research center.

University of Rochester

Strong Children's Research Center

Medical Center	Ph: (716)275-8447
Box 777	Fax: (716)271-7512
601 Elmwood Ave.	
Rochester, NY 14642	

E-mail: scrc@urmc.rochester.edu
URL: http://www.urmc.rochester.edu/smd/scrc

Contact: Dr. Richard Insel, Dir.

Desc: Pediatrics. *Type:* Research center.

The University of Texas Lifetime Health Letter

Health Science Center
University of Texas

1100 Holcombe Blvd.	Ph: (713)792-4265
PO Box 20036	Free: 800-274-6377
Houston, TX 77225	

E-mail: sdeaner@uthouston.edu.

Contact: Linda Barth, Editor.

Desc: Designed to promote proactive health, fitness, nutrition, and mental well-being for consumers. Recurring features include news of research and columns titled Ask the Doctor and Health Notes. *Type:* Newsletter.

University of Vermont

McClure Musculoskeletal Research Center

Department of Orthopaedic and	Ph: (802)656-2250
Rehabilitation	Fax: (802)656-4247
Stafford Hall, 4th Fl.	
Burlington, VT 05405-0084	

E-mail: beynnon@salus.med.uvm.edu
URL: http://www.vtmednet.org/-g136911
Contact: Bruce D. Beynnon, PhD, Dir.

Desc: Occupational and sports injuries and nontraumatic and congenital disorders, including how musculoskeletal structures are injured and how they heal. Research focuses on lower back pain, including studies of lifting, posture, seating, vehicle vibration, exercise, and different low back pain treatments; sports medicine, including knee, shoulder, and ankle injuries; scoliosis, including the etiology of idiopathic scoliosis and growth asymmetry research; and joint replacement studies. *Type:* Research center.

University of Western Ontario

OSHTECH Inc.

Bio-Engineering Bldg.	Ph: (519)661-3044
London, ON, Canada N6A 5B9	Fax: (519)661-3934

E-mail: oshtech@julian.uwo.ca
URL: http://www.ohsrc
Contact: Dr. Peter Pityn, Dir.

Desc: Occupational health and safety, occupational epidemiology, residential and office air quality, ergonomics, inhalational studies, and occupational hygiene. *Type:* Research center.

University of Wisconsin--Madison

State Laboratory of Hygiene

465 Henry Mall	Ph: (608)262-1293
Madison, WI 53706	Free: 800-442-4618
	Fax: (608)262-3257

E-mail: rhl@mail.slh.wisc.edu
URL: http://www.slh.wisc.edu
Contact: Dr. R.H. Laessig, Dir.

Desc: Bacteriology, cancer cytology, cytogenetics, immunology, industrial hygiene, environmental health, pathology, clinical chemistry, toxicology, and virology, including respiratory and enterovirus infections, a survey of zoonosis in Wisconsin, especially California encephalitis virus, and chromosomal studies in congenital anomalies. *Type:* Research center.

University of Wisconsin--Madison

Wisconsin Occupational Health Laboratory

2601 Agriculture Dr.	Ph: (608)224-6210
PO Box 7996	Free: 800-446-0403
Madison, WI 53707-7996	Fax: (608)262-6213

E-mail: director@wohl.slh.wisc.edu

Desc: Industrial hygiene. *Type:* Research center.

Vegetarian Resource Group

PO Box 1463	Ph: (410)366-8343
Baltimore, MD 21203	Fax: (410)366-8804

E-mail: vrg@vrg.org

URL: http://www.vrg.org

Contact: Charles Stahler, Sec.

Desc: Health professionals, activists, and educators who work with businesses and individuals to bring about healthy changes in schools, workplaces, and communities. *Type:* Association.

Vegetarian Times

Cowles Enthusiast Media

4 High Ridge Park	Ph: (203)322-2400
Stamford, CT 06905	Fax: (203)322-1966

Contact: Susan Tauster, (708)848-8100, fax: (708)848-8175, susant@cowles.com.

Desc: Magazine devoted to vegetarian food and related topics such as health, fitness, and the environment. *Alt. Contact:* PO Box 570, Oak Park, IL 60303; telephone: (708)848-8100; fax: (708)848-8175. *Type:* Periodical.

Veggie Life

EGW Publishing Co.

1041 Shary Cir.	Ph: (925)671-9852
Concord, CA 94518	Fax: (925)671-0692

E-mail: veggieed@aol.com.

Contact: Sharon Barela, Editor; Robert Marshall, Advertising Mgr.; Lea Reiter, Advertising Mgr.

Desc: Consumer magazine covering health, nutrition, and vegetarian cooking. *Type:* Periodical.

VNA Health Care Services

Towne Centre Offices	Ph: (412)256-6910
1789 South Braddock Ave.	Free: 800-640-4862
PO Box 82550	Fax: (412)256-6920
Pittsburgh, PA 15218	

E-mail: homecare@vna-pqh.org

URL: http://www.vna-pqh.org

Contact: Andrew R. Peacock, Exec.Dir.

Desc: Provides multidisciplinary home health care service to homebound patients regardless of ability to pay. *Type:* Association.

Voice of the Diabetic

National Federation of the Blind

Diabetes Action Network	Ph: (573)875-8911
811 Cherry St., Ste. 309	Fax: (573)875-8902
Columbia, MO 65201	

URL: http://www.nfb.org/voice.htm.

Contact: Ed Bryant, Editor.

Desc: Magazine presenting personal stories, practical guidance by blind diabetics and medical professionals, medical news, resource column, and a recipe corner. *Type:* Periodical.

Weight Watchers Magazine

Southern Progress

2100 Lakeshore Dr.	Ph: (205)877-6000
Birmingham, AL 35209-6721	Free: 888-737-3529
	Fax: (205)877-6600

URL: http://www.mag@mindspring.com.

Contact: Kate Greer, Editor, (205)877-5730, kate_greer@spc.com; Jeff Ward, Publisher, (205)877-6489, fax: (205)877-6469.

Desc: Magazine promoting self-esteem through healthy eating, fitness and weight-control. Reports on health, nutrition, fitness, food, healthful recipes, fashion and beauty. *Type:* Periodical.

Wellness Program Management Advisor

American Business Publishing

PO Box 456	Ph: (732)292-1100
Allenwood, NJ 08720	Free: 800-516-4343
	Fax: (732)292-1111

E-mail: hrp@healthrespubs.com; info@wellnessjunction.com.

Contact: Robert K. Jenkins, Publisher.

Desc: Covers wellness programs. Provides analyses of various programs, including information on expenses, return on investments, and strategies adopted. *Type:* Newsletter.

Women's Health Letter

Kerri Bodmer

2245 E. Colorado Blvd., No.	Ph: (818)798-0638
104	Fax: (818)798-0639
Pasadena, CA 91107	

Contact: Kerri Bodmer, Editor.

Desc: Publishes articles and news relevant to women's health issues. *Type:* Newsletter.

Women's Health Weekly

C.W. Henderson Publications

Subscription Office	Free: 800-633-4931
PO Box 830409	Fax: (205)995-1588
Birmingham, AL 35283-0409	

E-mail: whw@yourhealthnet.com.

URL: http://www.newsfile.com/1w.htm; http://www.newsfile.com.

Contact: Michelle Marble, Editor.

Desc: Contains news concerning women's health issues, focusing on research published from both government and private sectors. The information is from both a clinical and non-clinical perspective. *Type:* Newsletter.

Women's International Public Health Network

7100 Oak Forest Ln.	Ph: (301)469-9210
Bethesda, MD 20817	Fax: (301)469-8423

Contact: Dr. Naomi Baumslag, Pres.

Desc: Individuals and organizations with an interest in women's health issues. Promotes adoption of public health policies and programs providing greater access to health care for women. *Type:* Association.

WorkFit

SharpVandercook, Inc.

209 Tenth Ave. S, Ste. 525	Ph: (615)259-2059
Nashville, TN 37203	Fax: (615)251-3142

Desc: Focuses on health issues. Provides information on such topics as nutrition, fitness, vitamin supplements, and disease prevention. *Type:* Newsletter.

World Research News

World Research Foundation

41 Bell Rock Plaza

Sedona, AZ 86351-8804

Contact: Steve Ross, Ph.D., Editor; Robert Maver, F.S.A., Editor; Julianne Balistren, Editor; LaVerne Ross Boeckmann, Editor; Heidemarie Kleber, Editor; Prof. Dr. Karl Walter, Editor.

Desc: Reviews alternative therapies. Offers books and health information packs (traditional and non-traditional). *Type:* Newsletter.

Yoga Journal

California Yoga Teachers Association

2054 University Ave., Suite 600	Ph: (510)841-9200
Berkeley, CA 94704	Free: 800-IDO-YOGA
	Fax: (510)644-3101

E-mail: yoga@sirius.com.

URL: http://www.yogajournal.com.

Contact: Rick Fields, Editor; John Abbott, Interim Pub.; Deena Brown, Advertising Dir.

Desc: Magazine devoted to holistic living and yoga. *Type:* Periodical.

Your Health Report

General Learning Communications

900 Skokie Blvd., Ste. 200	Ph: (847)205-3000
Northbrook, IL 60062	Fax: (847)564-8197

Contact: Carol Lezak, Editor.

Desc: Encourages good health habits and preventive care among community members, managed care group members, and company employees and their families. Seeks to "empower readers to be wise consumers of health care services." Remarks: Masthead designed to be personalized with a client's title, logo, and information about services offered (hospitals), benefits news and guidelines (managed care plans), and company news and benefits (corporations). *Type:* Newsletter.

Health Care

Advances

Alzheimer's Association

919 N. Michigan Ave., Ste.	Ph: (312)335-8700
1000	Free: 800-272-3900
Chicago, IL 60611-1676	Fax: (312)335-1110

Contact: Michele Pellissier, Editor.

Desc: Promotes the work of the Association, which is dedicated to supporting research into the causes, cure, and treatment of Alzheimer's disease, and to provide support and assistance to Alzheimer patients, their families and caregivers. Recurring features include articles on research, patient care, legal and financial issues, public policy, advocacy updates, and Association fundraising news. *Type:* Newsletter.

AHA Guide to the Health Care Field

American Hospital Association (AHA)

1 N. Franklin, St. 27	Ph: (312)422-3000
Chicago, IL 60606	Free: 800-424-4301
	Fax: (312)422-4796

Desc: Hospitals, networks, multi-health care systems, freestanding ambulatory surgery centers, psychiatric facilities, long-term care facilities, substance abuse programs, hospices, Health Maintenance Organizations (HMOs), and other health-related organizations. *Type:* Directory.

American College Health Association

PO Box 28937	Ph: (410)859-1500
Baltimore, MD 21240-8937	Fax: (410)859-1510

E-mail: acha@access.digex.net

URL: http://www.clbalt/acha.org

Contact: Doyle Randol, Exec.Dir.

Desc: Institutions (930) and individuals (2500). Provides an organization in which institutions of higher education and interested individuals may work together to promote health in its broadest aspects for students and all other members of the college community. *Type:* Association.

American Dental Directory

American Dental Association

211 E. Chicago Ave.	Ph: (630)440-4649
Chicago, IL 60611	Free: 800-947-4746
	Fax: (630)443-9970

Desc: Over 170,000 dentists. Also includes list of active and historic dental schools, dental organizations, and state dental examining boards. *Type:* Directory.

American Health Quality Association

1140 Conneticut Ave. NW, Ste.	Ph: (202)331-5790
1050	Fax: (202)331-9334
Washington, DC 20036	

E-mail: information@ahqa.org

URL: http://www.ahqa.org

Contact: Josef Reum, Exec.VP.

Desc: Institutions and individuals. Purpose is to develop communications programs for physicians, institutions, and others interested in peer review organizations (PROs). Provides a national forum for the interchange of ideas, techniques, and information relating to medical quality assessment. *Type:* Association.

American Lung Association of Eastern Missouri

1118 Hampton Ave.　　　Ph: (314)645-5505
St. Louis, MO 63139-3196　　　Free: 800-LUN-
　　　　　　　　　　　GUSA
　　　　　　　　　Fax: (314)645-7128
E-mail: alaem@mail1.il.net
URL: http://www.lungusa.org
Contact: Susan K. Glassman, Exec.Dir.
Desc: Works toward the prevention and control of lung disease. Focuses on public health education programs, advocacy, and research. *Type:* Association.

American Medical Group Association

1422 Duke St.　　　Ph: (703)838-0033
Alexandria, VA 22314-3430　　Fax: (703)548-1890
E-mail: amga@amga.org
URL: http://www.amga.org
Contact: Dr. Donald W. Fisher, CEO.
Desc: Trade association for group practice integrate a delivery systems and IPAS representing more than 45,000 physicians. Fosters accreditation of medical clinics; compiles statistics on group practice; sponsors research, patient education, insurance programs, and capitation management assistance. Conducts symposia; makes available consulting services. *Type:* Association.

Asthma and Allergy Advocate

American Academy of Allergy, Asthma and Immunology
611 E. Wells St., 4th Fl.　　Ph: (414)272-6071
Milwaukee, WI 53202　　　Fax: (414)272-6070
E-mail: info@aaaai.org
URL: http://www.aaaaii.org.
Contact: Rebecca Dinan, Managing Editor.
Desc: Informs patients of physicians and allergists about asthma and allergies. Contains information on asthma, allergy, allergy treatments and research, and seasonal, insect-related, and other allergies. *Type:* Newsletter.

The Back Letter

Lippincott-Raven Publishers
12107 Insurance Way　　Ph: (301)714-2300
Hagerstown, MD 21740　　Free: 800-638-3030
　　　　　　　　　Fax: (301)714-2398
Contact: Sam W. Wiesel, MD, Editor; Mark L. Schoene, Editor.
Desc: Covers all aspects of spine function, disease and injury. *Type:* Newsletter.

BNA's Health Care Facilities Guide

Bureau of National Affairs, Inc. (BNA)
1231 25th St. NW　　　Ph: (202)452-4323
Washington, DC 20037　　Free: 800-372-1033
　　　　　　　　　Fax: (202)452-7773
E-mail: bnaplus@bna.com
Contact: Randy Kubetin, Managing Editor, rkubetin@bna.com.
Desc: Explains environmental, worker safety, and health regulations that affect health care facilities. *Type:* Newsletter.

Bottomline/Health

Boardroom Reports, Inc.
55 Railroad Ave.　　　Ph: (203)625-5900
Greenwich, CT 06830　　Fax: (203)861-7443
E-mail: BLHealth@boardroom.com.
Contact: David Freeman, Editor.
Desc: Provides information and current news on health issues. *Type:* Newsletter.

Briefings on Assisted Living

Opus Communications
100 Hoods Ln.　　　Ph: (781)639-1872
PO Box 1168　　　Free: 800-650-6787
Marblehead, MA 01945　　Fax: (781)639-2982
E-mail: customer_service@opuscomm.com
URL: http://www.opuscomm.com
Contact: Suzanne Perney, Publisher; Tricia Long, Assoc. Editor.
Desc: Covers topics of interest to developers and managers of assisted living facilities. Recurring features include interviews and news of research. *Type:* Newsletter.

Briefings on JCAHO

Opus Communications
100 Hoods Ln.　　　Ph: (781)639-1872
PO Box 1168　　　Free: 800-650-6787
Marblehead, MA 01945　　Fax: (781)639-2982
E-mail: customer_service@opuscomm.com
URL: http://www.opuscomm.com; http://www.opuscomm.com.
Contact: Ilene MacDonald, Editor.
Desc: Reports on Joint Commission on Accreditation of Healthcare Organizations (JCAHO) standards and subjects and regulations. Recurring features include interviews, notices of publications available, and a column titled Ask the Experts. *Type:* Newsletter.

Briefings on JCAHO: Home Health & Hospice

Opus Communications
100 Hoods Ln.　　　Ph: (781)639-1872
PO Box 1168　　　Free: 800-650-6787
Marblehead, MA 01945　　Fax: (781)639-2982
E-mail: customer_service@opuscomm.com
URL: http://www.opuscomm.com
Desc: Provides strategies and solutions needed to achieve and maintain JCAHO accreditation. Includes information on topics such as correcting and preventing problems and Type I recommendations and tips on how to prepare a staff for survey. *Type:* Newsletter.

Buyers' Guide for the Health Care Market

Health Forum, Inc.
One North Franklin, 27th Fl.　Ph: (312)893-6844
Chicago, IL 60606　　　Free: 800-821-2039
　　　　　　　　　Fax: (312)422-4600
URL: http://www.ahapress.com; http://www.healthforum.com.
Contact: Jennifer Hornberger, Special Projects Editor.
Desc: 1,200 manufacturers and suppliers of equipment, products, and services to the health care industry. *Type:* Directory.

Case Management Resource Guide

Center for Healthcare Information
4000 Birch St., No. 112　　Ph: (949)752-2335
Newport Beach, CA 92660　　Free: 800-627-2244
　　　　　　　　　Fax: (949)752-8433
E-mail: chi@healthcare-info.com
URL: http://www.healthcare-info.com
Contact: Diane S. Liebenson, Editor; Kevin F. O'Grady, M.D., Editor.
Desc: In four regional volumes, lists 110,000 health care facilities and support services, including homecare, rehabilitation, psychiatric, and addiction treatment programs; hospices, adult day care, and burn and cancer centers. *Type:* Directory.

Center for Health Economics Research

Waverley Oaks Rd., Ste. 330　Ph: (781)788-8100
Waltham, MA 02452-8414　　Fax: (781)788-8101
E-mail: jan@her-cher.org
Contact: Dr. Janet B. Mitchell, Pres.
Desc: Health economics, including alternative ways of reimbursing capital under the Medicare prospective payment system, access to care, physician payment, hospital costs, black-white treatment differences, and cost-effectiveness of technology. *Type:* Research center.

Corporate Compliance Officer

Opus Communications
100 Hoods Ln.　　　Ph: (781)639-1872
PO Box 1168　　　Free: 800-650-6787
Marblehead, MA 01945　　Fax: (781)639-2982
E-mail: customer_service@opuscomm.com
URL: http://www.opuscomm.com
Contact: Margaret Dragon, Exec. Dir.
Desc: Provides information on how to establish and maintain a compliance program. Includes the latest government investigations on Medicare and Medicaid regulatory changes and professional development. *Type:* Newsletter.

Creative HealthCare News

AARP Pharmacy Service
601 E. St. NW
Washington, DC 20049
Contact: Marie Manthey, President.
Desc: Provides news on "creative healthcare" from a management slant. Topics include healthcare reform, work redesign, case management, and patient-focused services. *Type:* Newsletter.

Current Health 1

Weekly Reader Corp.
200 First Stamford Pl.　　Ph: (203)705-3500
PO Box 120023　　　Fax: (203)705-1661
Stamford, CT 06912-0023
Contact: Carole Rubenstein, Editor, (847)205-3141, ruben@glcomm.com; Peter E. Berger, Pres./CEO.
Desc: Magazine for elementary school children. *Alt. Contact:* 900 Skokie Blvd., Northbrook, IL 60062-4028; telephone: (847)205-3000; fax: (847)564-8197. *Type:* Periodical.

Current Health 2

Weekly Reader Corp.
200 First Stamford Pl.　　Ph: (203)705-3500
PO Box 120023　　　Fax: (203)705-1661
Stamford, CT 06912-0023
Contact: Carole Rubenstein, Editor, (847)205-3141, fax: (847)564-8197, ruben@glcomm.com; Peter E. Bergen, Pres./CEO.
Desc: Magazine for middle and secondary school students. *Alt. Contact:* 900 Skokie Blvd., Ste. 200, Northbrook, IL 60062-4028; telephone: (847)205-3000; fax: (847)564-8197. *Type:* Periodical.

Detwiler's Directory of Health and Medical Resources

The Detwiler Group
PO Box 15308　　　Ph: (219)749-6534
Fort Wayne, IN 46885　　Fax: (219)493-6717
Contact: Susan Detwiler, Editor, (219)749-6534, smdetwiler@detwiler.com.
Desc: Over 2,000 federal agencies, commercial research firms, associations, publishers, and other sources of information on the medical and healthcare industry; limited international coverage. *Type:* Directory.

Directions: Looking Ahead in Healthcare

Health Resources Publishing
1913 Atlantic Ave., Ste. F4　Ph: (732)292-1100
Manasquan, NJ 08736　　Free: 800-516-4343
　　　　　　　　　Fax: (732)292-1111
E-mail: hrp@healthrespubs.com
Contact: Robert K. Jenkins, Publisher.

Desc: Deals with healthcare. Covers such topics as forecasts, trends, innovations, facts, and statistics. *Type:* Newsletter.

Directory of Biomedical and Health Care Grants

Oryx Press
4041 N. Central Ave., Ste. 700   Ph: (602)265-2651
Phoenix, AZ 85012-3397   Free: 800-279-6799
    Fax: 800-279-4663
E-mail: info@oryxpress.com
URL: http://www.oryxpress.com;   http://www.
higheredconnect.com/grantselect.
Contact: Jennifer Ashley, Editor.
Desc: Support for postgraduate resarch and laboratory investigations and describes funding for studies in health care delivery, internships, assistantships, faculty fellowships and development, and individual project support. *Type:* Directory.

Directory of Nurse-Midwifery Practices

American College of Nurse-Midwives
818 Connecticut Ave., NW, Ste.   Ph: (202)728-9860
900   Fax: (202)728-9897
Washington, DC 20006
E-mail: info@acnm.org
URL: http://www.midwife.org; http://www.midwife.org.
Contact: John Boggess, Editor.
Desc: Over 3,000 nurse-midwifery practices. *Type:* Directory.

Directory of Nursing Homes

HCIA Inc.
300 E. Lombard St.   Ph: (410)576-9600
Baltimore, MD 21202   Free: 800-568-3282
    Fax: (410)752-6309
E-mail: pubs@hcia.com; info@hcia.com; pubs@hcia.com.
Contact: Beth Waibel, Editor.
Desc: Over 16,000 state-licensed long-term care facilities. *Type:* Directory.

DRI Health Care Cost Forecasting

Standard & Poor's DRI
Data Products Division
24 Hartwell Ave.   Ph: (781)863-5100
Lexington, MA 02421
E-mail: client_services@dri.mcgraw-hill.com
URL: http://www.dri.mcgraw-hill.com
Contact: Client Services, (617)860-6527, fax: (617)860-6416.
Desc: Contains approximately 100 quarterly forecast indexes of U.S. health-care costs. *Available:* Standard & Poor's DRI, Data Products Division. *Type:* Database.

Encyclopedia of Health Information Sources

Gale Group Inc.
27500 Drake Rd.   Ph: (248)699-4253
Farmington Hills, MI 48331-   Free: 800-877-GALE
3535   Fax: (248)699-8070
E-mail: galeord@galegroup.com
URL: http://www.galegroup.com.
Contact: Alan Rees, Editor.
Desc: Over 13,000 sources of information of interest to health care personnel, such as publications, health organizations, research centers, and databases. *Type:* Directory.

Executive Briefings on Health Care Regulations

Opus Communications
100 Hoods Ln.   Ph: (781)639-1872
PO Box 1168   Free: 800-650-6787
Marblehead, MA 01945   Fax: (781)639-2982
E-mail: customer_service@opuscomm.com
URL: http://www.opuscomm.com

Desc: Reports on accreditation regulations in both acute and post-acute care facilities. Includes topics such as medical laws, JCAHO, HCFA, OIG, DOJ, EPA, FDA, OSHA, reimbursement/Medicare updates, managed care, and regulatory updates. *Type:* Newsletter.

Executive Report on Integrated Care & Capitation

Managed Care Information Center
PO Box 456   Ph: (732)292-1100
Allenwood, NJ 08720   Free: 888-843-6242
    Fax: (732)292-1111
E-mail: info@themcic.com
URL: http://www.hin.com.
Contact: Joseph Schmidt, Editor.
Desc: Provides market facts as well as information on network alliances, economics, mergers and acquisitions, and other issues related to integrated care and capitation. *Type:* Newsletter.

The Executive Report on Managed Care

Managed Care Information Center
PO Box 456   Ph: (732)292-1100
Allenwood, NJ 08720   Free: 888-843-6242
    Fax: (732)292-1111
E-mail: info@themcic.com
URL: http://www.hin.com.
Contact: Joseph Schmidt, Editor.
Desc: Disseminates news of employers implementing managed care programs. *Type:* Newsletter.

The Executive Report on Physician Organizations

Managed Care Information Center
PO Box 456   Ph: (732)292-1100
Allenwood, NJ 08720   Free: 888-843-6242
    Fax: (732)292-1111
E-mail: info@themcic.com
Contact: Melanie Matthews, Editor.
Desc: Contains trends, legislation, and affecting physicians organization's mergers, acquisitions, and joint ventures. *Type:* Newsletter.

Family Health Care Clinic

George Spann
PO Box 6227   Ph: (601)825-7280
Pearl, MS 39288-6227   Fax: (601)825-8130
Contact: Margaret A. Gray, DPA, CEO.
Type: Association.

Federation of Nurses and Health Professionals

555 New Jersey Ave. NW   Ph: (202)879-4491
Washington, DC 20001   Free: 800-238-1133
    Fax: (202)879-4597
E-mail: fnhpaft@aft.org
URL: http://www.aft.org/fnhp/index.html
Contact: Mary Lehman Mac Donald, Dir.
Desc: Collective bargaining organization of registered nurses, licensed practical nurses, and other professional and technical employees in the health field. Works to improve members' professional standards through promoting continuing education, advancing their economic status, and securing working conditions conducive to optimum performance and the most effective delivery of health care. *Type:* Association.

Gift of Sight

Operation Eyesight Universal
4 Parkdale Crescent NW   Ph: (403)283-6323
Calgary, AB, Canada T2N 3T8   Free: 800-585-8265
    Fax: (403)270-1899
E-mail: oevca@giftofsight.com; ocuca@cadvision.ca.
URL: http://www.giftofsight.com.

Contact: Dawna Crawford, Fund Development Dir., dawna@giftofsight.com.
Desc: Provides information and case histories on eye care programs in the developing world funded by the Operation Eyesight. *Type:* Newsletter.

God's Love We Deliver

166 Avenue of the Americas   Ph: (212)294-8100
New York, NY 10013-1207   Free: 800-747-2023
    Fax: (212)294-8101
URL: http://www.glwd.com
Contact: Kathy Spahn, Exec.Dir.
Desc: Delivers nutritional meals to men, women, and children with AIDS. *Type:* Association.

Good Medicine

BEST Medical Publications Inc.
87 Browning Ave.   Ph: (416)461-1932
Toronto, ON, Canada M4K   Fax: (416)465-4801
1W1
Contact: T. J. O'Brien, Publisher.
Desc: Promotes preventive medicine and good health through personal knowledge and awareness. *Type:* Newsletter.

The Guide to the Nation's Hospices

National Hospice Organization
1901 N. Moore St., Ste. 901   Ph: (703)243-5400
Arlington, VA 22209   Free: 800-658-8898
    Fax: (703)525-5762
E-mail: drsnho@cais.com.
Contact: Audra Kelly, Editor.
Desc: About 3,000 hospices, palliative care centers, and other programs serving terminally ill persons. *Type:* Directory.

Health Care Human Resources Alert

Opus Communications
100 Hoods Ln.   Ph: (781)639-1872
PO Box 1168   Free: 800-650-6787
Marblehead, MA 01945   Fax: (781)639-2982
E-mail: customer_service@opuscomm.com
URL: http://www.opuscomm.com
Desc: Contains news on rules and regulations on compliance programs. Includes topics such as JCAHO, DOL, OSHA, compliance, workplace safety, ADA, training on abuse, sexual harassment, credentialing and privileging, criminal checks, Medicare fraud, NCQA standards, ERISA, and fraud training. *Type:* Newsletter.

Health Care Labor Manual Bulletin

Aspen Publishers, Inc.
200 Orchard Ridge Dr., No.   Ph: (301)417-7500
200   Free: 800-638-8437
Gaithersburg, MD 20878   Fax: (301)417-7650
E-mail: customer.service@aspenpubl.com
URL: http://www.aspenpub.com
Contact: Terri Miner, Production Coord.; Trudi Graham, Marketing Mgr ; Laureece Woodson, Permissions Editor.
Desc: Reports on recent cases, legislation, and developments affecting the health community and its employees. *Type:* Newsletter.

Health Care Law Monthly

Matthew Bender & Company
Two Park Ave.   Ph: (212)448-2118
New York, NY 10016   Free: 800-252-9257
    Fax: (212)448-2749
Contact: Scott Becker, Editor, (312)750-6016, scott. becker@rosshardies.com; Michael Cassidy, Editor, (412)392-5593, cassidm@dmclaw.com; Shana Siegel, Legal Editor, (212)448-2647, fax: (212)448-2570, Shana. Siegel@bender.com.

Desc: Provides information on legislative, regulatory, and judicial changes in the health care field. Covers transactional and regulatory issues, fraud, abuse, provider contracting, antitrust, tax-exempt entities, corporate compliance, managed care, and integrated services. *Type:* Newsletter.

Health Governance Report

Opus Communications
100 Hoods Ln.   Ph: (781)639-1872
PO Box 1168   Free: 800-650-6787
Marblehead, MA 01945   Fax: (781)639-2982
E-mail: customer_service@opuscomm.com
URL: http://www.opuscomm.com

Desc: Provides news on trends and issues pertaining to health care. Offers analysis on the responsibilities of directors and trustees in the health care industry. *Type:* Newsletter.

Health Issues Update

National Wellness Association
PO Box 827   Ph: (715)342-2969
Stevens Point, WI 54481-0827   Free: 800-244-8922
                                    Fax: (715)342-2979
E-mail: nwa@wellnessnwi.org
URL: http://www.wellnessnwi.org/nwa/; http://www.wellnessnwi.org/nwa/.
Contact: Linda R. Chapin, DDS, Editor.
Desc: Provides updates on the changes occuring at the federal level regarding health care, health promotion, and health policy. Information and resources of key importance to professionals in health and wellness highlighted. *Type:* Newsletter.

Health Letter

Public Citizen's Health Research Group
2000 P St. NW, Ste. 700   Fax: (202)296-1727
Washington, DC 20036
Contact: Sidney M. Wolfe, Editor.
Desc: Designed as a personal health guide for "reducing preventable illnesses and also avoiding needless and unnecessarily dangerous or overpriced medical care." Discusses specific diseases and treatments and other issues, including Medicare, health maintenance organizations (HMOs), government regulations, and getting a second medical opinion. *Type:* Newsletter.

Health News Daily

F-D-C Reports, Inc.
5550 Friendship Blvd., Ste. 1   Ph: (301)657-9830
Chevy Chase, MD 20815   Free: 800-332-2181
                                    Fax: (301)656-3094
E-mail: fdcr@clarknet.com
Contact: John Zakotnik, Editor.
Desc: Tracks developments in health care policy, legislation and regulation, insurance, pharmaceuticals, delivery, manufacturing, technology and treatment, funding, and research. *Type:* Newsletter.

Health News Daily

FDC Reports, Inc.
5550 Friendship Blvd., Suite 1   Ph: (301)657-9830
Chevy Chase, MD 20815
E-mail: fdcr@clark.net
URL: http://www.fdcreports.com
Desc: Contains the complete text of Health News Daily, a daily newsletter on health-care delivery. Covers policy and legislation, insurance, funding, manufacturing and technology, pharmaceuticals, and medical treatments. *Available:* The Dialog Corporation, DataStar; The Dialog Corporation, DIALOG; The Dialog Corporation, DIALOG. *Type:* Database.

Health Research and Educational Trust of New Jersey

760 Alexander Rd.   Ph: (609)275-4145
Princeton, NJ 08543-0001   Fax: (609)275-4228
E-mail: fvali@njha.com
URL: http://www.njha.com
Contact: Valerie Sellers, VP, Health Plan. & Res.
Desc: Health services, access to primary healthcare in New Jersey; geographic variations of hospitalizations for ambulatory care sensitive conditions; domestic violence, medical and social management of care for the victims. *Type:* Research center.

Health Research, Inc.

1 University Place   Ph: (518)431-1200
Rensselaer, NY 12144-3456   Fax: (518)431-1234
E-mail: eam01@health.state.ny.us
Contact: Michael Barth, Exec.Dir.
Desc: Public health and cancer, including basic and clinical research in cause and treatment of cancer and related malignancies; environmental studies to determine long-range health hazards of pesticides, industrial discharge, and radioactive and sewage wastes; and detection and prevention of infectious diseases, including AIDS and tuberculosis. Also studies rehabilitation, biology, immunology, hematology, virology, chemistry, toxicology, and environment. *Type:* Research center.

Health and Stress

The American Institute of Stress
124 Park Ave.   Ph: (914)963-1200
Yonkers, NY 10703   Free: 800-24-RELAX
                                    Fax: (914)965-6267
E-mail: stress124@earthlink.net
URL: http://www.stress.org.
Contact: Paul J. Rosch, Editor.
Desc: Focuses on the Institute's concern for development of methods for the measurement and reduction of stress. Recurring features include a calendar of events, news of research, book reviews, and reports of meetings and conferences related to stress. *Type:* Newsletter.

Health Watch Canada

Multi-Vision Publishing, Inc.
655 Bay St., Ste. 1100
Toronto, ON, Canada M5G
    2K4
Contact: Ashley Harvey, Publisher; Constance Droganes, Editor.
Desc: Trade journal covering family health. *Type:* Periodical.

Health and Wellness Database

The Gale Group
27500 Drake Rd.   Ph: (248)699-4253
Farmington Hills, MI 48331-
    3535
URL: http://www.galegroup.com
Contact: (650)378-5000, fax: (800)676-2345.
Desc: Contains more than 295,000 records representing citations, nontechnical abstracts, author abstracts, and/or the complete text of articles appearing in international consumer-oriented health periodicals and newsletters, medical journals, general-interest magazines, newspapers, and pamphlets published by medical associations and societies. Records are added first to Newsearch and are then transferred to this database monthly. *Available:* CompuServe Information Service; The Dialog Corporation, DIALOG; Ovid Technologies, Inc. *Type:* Database.

Healthcare Advertising Review

The Business Word
5350 S. Roslyn St., Ste. 400   Ph: (303)967-0130
Englewood, CO 80111-2125   Free: 800-328-3211
                                    Fax: (303)290-9025
Contact: Jeanette Herreria, Editor; Tom Rees, Editor; Donald E.L. Johnson, Publisher.
Desc: Provides information about health care advertising. Topics include print, radio, television, and direct mail advertising. *Type:* Newsletter.

Healthcare Information Management

Healthcare Information and Management Systems Society (HIMSS)
230 E. Ohio St., Ste. 500   Ph: (312)664-4467
Chicago, IL 60611   Fax: (312)664-6143
Contact: Julie Foreman, Manager; Katrina Young, Publications Assistant.
Desc: Reports on health care information management systems, including the latest management trends in information systems, management engineering, and telecommunications. *Type:* Newsletter.

Healthcare Intranet Report

COR Healthcare Resources
PO Box 40959   Ph: (805)564-2177
Santa Barbara, CA 93140-0959   Fax: (805)564-2146
E-mail: corinfo@corhealth.com
Contact: Chuck Appleby, Editor.
Desc: Contains information on health information systems. *Type:* Newsletter.

Healthcare IS/IT Market Reporter

Managed Care Information Center
PO Box 456   Ph: (732)292-1100
Allenwood, NJ 08720   Free: 888-843-6242
                                    Fax: (732)292-1111
E-mail: info@themcic.com
URL: http://www.themcic.com.
Contact: Jodi L. Kastel, jkastel@themcic.com; Robert K. Jenkins, Publisher.
Desc: Covers the healthcare information technology market. Provides information on products, contracts, licensing agreements, and Internet/Intranet applications. *Type:* Newsletter.

Healthcare Marketer's Executive Briefing

Health Resources Publishing
1913 Atlantic Ave., Ste. F4   Ph: (732)292-1100
Manasquan, NJ 08736   Free: 800-516-4343
                                    Fax: (732)292-1111
E-mail: hrp@healthrespubs.com
URL: http://www.healthrespubs.com.
Contact: Jodi L. Kastel, Editor, jkastel@healthrespubs.com; Robert K. Jenkins, Publisher.
Desc: Designed to keep professionals abreast of the newest marketing and public relations techniques and strategies within the field of health care. *Type:* Newsletter.

Healthcare Marketing Abstracts

COR Healthcare Resources
PO Box 40959   Ph: (805)564-2177
Santa Barbara, CA 93140-0959   Fax: (805)564-2146
E-mail: corinfo@corhealth.com
Contact: Mark Hagland, Editor.
Desc: Contains summaries of articles on healthcare marketing selected from more than 140 publications. *Type:* Newsletter.

Healthcare Perspective

Gartner Group, Inc.
401 Edgewater Pl., Ste. 580   Ph: (617)246-7585
Wakefield, MA 01880-6210   Fax: (617)246-8263

Contact: Sandy Cummings, Editor, sandra.cummings@
gartner.com.

Desc: Explores topics relevant to information systems development and strategy in healthcare organizations. Features market research summary reports on HMOs, PPOs, local delivery systems, insurance companies, TPAs, and physician contracting organizations. *Type:* Newsletter.

The Healthcare Strategist

COR Healthcare Resources
PO Box 40959   Ph: (805)564-2177
Santa Barbara, CA 93140-0959   Fax: (805)564-2146
E-mail: corinfo@corhealth.com

Contact: Susan J. Anthony, Editor.

Desc: Provides information on healthcare industry. *Type:* Newsletter.

Hog Market News

New Brunswick Hog Marketing Board
259 Brunswick St., Ste. 302   Ph: (506)458-8051
Fredericton, NB, Canada E3B   Fax: (506)453-1985
1G8
E-mail: nbhog@nbnet.nb.ca

Contact: Paul LeBlanc, Editor.

Desc: Updates weekly hog prices, marketing news, and other news briefs. Recurring features include news of research and reports of meetings. *Type:* Newsletter.

Home Health Agency Insider

American Federation of Home Health Agencies
1320 Fenwick Ln., Ste. 100   Ph: (301)588-1454
Silver Spring, MD 20910   Fax: (301)588-4732

Contact: Robert B. Raible, Editor.

Desc: Provides information on regulatory and legislative issues of concern to home health agencies. Discusses employment topics and the issues of providing care. *Type:* Newsletter.

Home Health Line

United Communications Group
11300 Rockville Pike, Ste. 1100   Ph: (301)287-2700
Rockville, MD 20852-3030   Free: 800-929-4824
Fax: (301)287-2049

E-mail: customer@ucg.com; hhl@ucg.com; homehlth@
ucg.com.

Contact: Jason Huffman, Editor, (301)287-2476, fax: (301)816-8945, huffman@ucg.com.

Desc: Reports on Medicare, Medicaid, and other federal and managed care coverage and payment for home health care, including home health agencies, hospice care, home medical equipment, home infusion therapy, and the home care industry as a business. *Type:* Newsletter.

Home Infusion Therapy Management

American Health Consultants, Inc.
3525 Piedmont Rd., Bldg. 6,   Ph: (404)262-7436
Ste. 400   Free: 800-688-2421
Atlanta, GA 30305   Fax: (404)262-7837
E-mail: customerservice@ahcpub.com

Contact: Rob Hamel, Editor.

Desc: Provides professional guidance on every aspect of home infusion therapy management. Offers cost effective alternatives to lengthy hospital stays. *Type:* Newsletter.

Homecare Clinical Advisor

Beacon Health Corp.
12308 N. Corporate Pkwy., Ste.   Ph: (414)243-6100
100   Free: 800-553-2041
Mequon, WI 53092-3380   Fax: (414)243-1207
E-mail: info@beaconhealth.org

Contact: Diane Omdahl.

Desc: Provides clinical practice updates, solutions and tips for home health care professionals. Recurring features include columns titled What's New, Q & A, Troubleshooting, Teaching Tips, and Resource Tips. *Type:* Newsletter.

Hope Health Letter

The Hope Heart Institute
c/o Exclusive Distributor   Ph: (616)343-0770
350 E. Michigan Ave., Ste. 301   Free: 800-334-4094
Kalamazoo, MI 49007-3851   Fax: (616)343-6260

Contact: Carol Garzona, Editor.

Desc: Offers brief, carefully researched articles focusing on factors affecting employee health and corporate health care cost containment. Emphasizes preventive measures and discusses health issues, including AIDS, smoking, self-care, safety, nutrition, weight loss, exercise, substance abuse, stress, and safe driving. *Type:* Newsletter.

HOPE News

Project HOPE
People-to-People Health   Ph: (540)837-2100
Foundation, Inc.   Free: 800-544-HOPE
Millwood, VA 22646

Contact: Laura Petrosian, Editor, lpetrosi@projhope.org.

Desc: Carries news of Project HOPE's international and domestic programs, which promote better world health through the training of medical, dental, and allied health personnel in developing areas of the world. Provides reports on program activities and results, headquarters conferences and meetings, personnel briefs, fund-raising activities, and volunteer events. *Type:* Newsletter.

Hospice of Michigan

Barbara Lewis
16250 Northland Dr., Ste. 212   Ph: (248)559-9209
Southfield, MI 48075   Fax: (248)559-4649

Contact: Carolyn J. Cassin, Pres.

Desc: Provides home-based care to terminally ill individuals and support for their families. Conducts charitable activities. *Type:* Association.

Hospital Blue Book

Billian Publishing, Inc.
2100 Powers Ferry Rd., Ste. 300   Ph: (770)955-5656
Atlanta, GA 30339   Free: 800-533-8484
Fax: (770)952-0669

E-mail: ati@billian.com; blu-book@billian.com.

Contact: Sandra McBrayer, Editor.

Desc: More than 6,687 hospitals; some listings also appear in a separate southern edition of this publication. *Type:* Directory.

Hospital Home Health

American Health Consultants, Inc.
3525 Piedmont Rd., Bldg. 6,   Ph: (404)262-7436
Ste. 400   Free: 800-688-2421
Atlanta, GA 30305   Fax: (404)262-7837
E-mail: customerservice@ahcpub.com

Contact: Park Morgan, Editor, parkmorgan@medec.com.

Desc: Provides clinical, legal, and management information pertinent to hospital-based home health agencies. Also monitors government regulation and profiles successful or unique programs. *Type:* Newsletter.

Illinois State Dental Society Source Book & Directory of Members

Illinois State Dental Society
1010 S. 2nd St.   Ph: (217)525-1406
PO Box 376   Fax: (217)525-8872
Springfield, IL 62705
E-mail: ildent@isds.org.

Contact: D. Milton Salzer, Editor.

Desc: List of members of the Illinois Dental Society and member services. *Type:* Directory.

Industrial Hygiene News—Buyer's Guide Issue

Rimbach Publishing, Inc.
8650 Babcock Blvd.   Ph: (412)364-5366
Pittsburgh, PA 15237   Free: 800-245-3182
Fax: (412)369-9720

E-mail: rimbach@sgi.net

Contact: David C. Lavender, Editor.

Desc: List of about 1,000 manufacturers and suppliers of products, equipment, and services to the occupational health, industrial hygiene, and safety industry. *Type:* Directory.

Inside MS

National Multiple Sclerosis Society
733 3rd Ave.   Ph: (212)986-3240
New York, NY 10017   Free: 800-FIGHT-MS
Fax: (212)986-7981
E-mail: info@nmss.org; editor@nmss.org.
URL: http://www.nmss.org.

Contact: Martha King, Editor; Bill Rosen, Advertising Rep., (201)222-0123; Lorna Smedman, Managing Editor.

Desc: Magazine for people with multiple sclerosis, their families, attending professionals, and interested donors. Provides information on coping, research, legislation, medical advances and disability rights advocacy. *Type:* Periodical.

Iowa Medical Directory

Jola Publications
2933 N. 2nd St.   Ph: (612)529-5001
Minneapolis, MN 55411   Fax: (612)521-2289
E-mail: jolapub@aol.com

Contact: Dennis Schapiro, Publisher.

Desc: Approximately 6,000 health care facilities and professionals in Iowa including clinics, hospitals, nursing homes, and doctors. *Type:* Directory.

Johns Hopkins School of Public Health

Risk Sciences and Public Policy Institute

615 N. Wolfe St., Rm. 6033   Ph: (410)614-4962
Baltimore, MD 21205   Fax: (410)955-0863
E-mail: mschwab@jhsph.edu
URL: http://www.jhsph.edu/Research/Centers/rsppi

Contact: Dr. Jonathan M. Samet, Dir.

Desc: Interpretation, synthesis, and organization of scientific information for analysis risk; evaluation of the implications of risk assessments for alternative management decisions; and evaluation of risk management outcomes for public health. *Type:* Research center.

Laval University

Health Services Research Group

Pavillon des sciences de   Ph: (418)656-3503
l'administration   Fax: (418)656-2624
Cite universitaire
Ste. Foy, PQ, Canada G1K 7P4

Contact: Prof. Clermont Begin, Contact.

Desc: Health care organizations, including planning, financing, decision making, information systems, evaluation of health policies, socio-political aspects of organization and evaluation of health services. *Type:* Research center.

LEXIS® Health Law Library

LEXIS-NEXIS
9443 Springboro Pike Ph: (937)865-6800
PO Box 933
Dayton, OH 45401-0933
URL: http://www.lex-nexis.com
Desc: Contains health-care related decisions from the U.S. Supreme Court since 1955, from the Federal Courts of Appeal since 1955, from the Federal Circuit Appeals Court since 1982, from the District Courts since 1955, and from all state Supreme Courts and from some state Courts of Appeal, with earliest state cases since 1955. *Available:* LEXIS-NEXIS, LEXIS. *Type:* Database.

Lifeline

National Chronic Pain Outreach Association
PO Box 274 Ph: (540)862-9437
Millboro, VA 24460-0274 Fax: (540)862-9485
E-mail: ncpoa1@aol.com
Contact: Mike Troyer, Editor.
Desc: Contains features, book and other media reviews, personal profiles, research news, and commentary on topics relating to chronic pain and its management. *Type:* Newsletter.

Managed Behavioral Health News

Atlantic Information Services, Inc.
1100 17th St. NW, No. 300 Ph: (202)775-9008
Washington, DC 20036 Free: 800-521-4323
  Fax: (202)331-9542
Contact: Terry Rudd, Editor.
Desc: Provides information and news on behavioral healthcare. *Type:* Newsletter.

Managed Health and You

Physician Link
A Division of Wentworth Publishing Co., Inc.
PO Box 11177 Ph: (717)393-1000
Lancaster, PA 17605-1177 Free: 800-331-5196
  Fax: (717)393-4702
URL: www.wentworth.com.
Contact: Ann Mead Ash, Senior Ed.; Nancy Sabulsky, Circulation Mgr.
Desc: Provides information for physicians on managed care. Recurring features include interviews and a column titled Dr. *Type:* Newsletter.

Managing Today's Health Care Worker

Clement Communications, Inc.
Concord Industrial Park Ph: (610)459-1700
10 LaCrue Ave. Free: 800-345-8101
Concordville, PA 19331 Fax: (610)459-0936
E-mail: editor@clement.com.
Contact: Leslie Schwartz, Sr.Ed.; Jeff Hall, Managing Editor; Maureen Solon, Exec.Ed.
Desc: Provides health care managers with information and techniques. Topics include recruiting and training volunteers, new technology, patient care developments, and staff conflict resolutions. *Type:* Newsletter.

Medical and Health Care Books and Serials in Print

R. R. Bowker
A Unit of Cahners Business Information
121 Chanlon Rd. Ph: (908)464-6800
New Providence, NJ 07974 Free: 888-269-5372
  Fax: (908)771-7704
E-mail: info@bowker.com
URL: http://www.bowker.com.
Contact: Barbara Holton, Editor; D. Gravesande, Editor.
Desc: List of 2,500 publishers and distributors of books, micropublishers of serials, and abstracting and indexing services concerned with health sciences and health care, including medicine, dentistry, psychiatry, nursing, etc. *Type:* Directory.

Medical and Health Information Directory

Gale Group Inc.
27500 Drake Rd. Ph: (248)699-4253
Farmington Hills, MI 48331- Free: 800-877-GALE
3535 Fax: (248)699-8070
E-mail: galeord@galegroup.com
URL: http://www.galegroup.com.
Contact: Lynn Pearce, Editor.
Desc: In Volume 1, more than 20,000 medical and health oriented associations, organizations, institutions, and government agencies, including health maintenance organizations (HMOs), preferred provider organizations (PPOs), insurance companies, pharmaceutical companies, research centers, and medical and allied health schools. In Volume 2, over 11,000 medical book publishers; medical periodicals, directories, audiovisual producers and services, medical libraries and information centers, electronic resources, and health-related internet search engines. In Volume 3, more than 28,000 clinics, treatment centers, care programs, and counseling/diagnostic services for 31 subject areas. *Type:* Directory.

Medicare Compliance Alert

United Communications Group
11300 Rockville Pike, Ste. 1100 Ph: (301)287-2700
Rockville, MD 20852-3030 Free: 800-929-4824
  Fax: (301)287-2049
E-mail: customer@ucg.com
URL: http://www.ucg.com.
Contact: Michael Peck, Editor; Robert Sperber, Publisher.
Desc: Disseminates news and guidance for keeping health care business arrangements within bounds of changing Medicare rules on patient referrals, physician investments, limited partnerships, and other joint ventures. Reports latest developments of "safe harbors" regulations, legislation, and enforcement of civil money penalty laws. *Type:* Newsletter.

The MIHOW Networker

Center for Health Services
Vanderbilt Medical Center
Sta. 17 Ph: (615)322-4773
Nashville, TN 37232-8180 Fax: (615)343-0325
Contact: Kelen F. Taylor, Editor.
Desc: Focuses on the Center's community service work in the Kentucky, Tennessee, Virginia, West Virginia, and Alabama region. Carries the reports of staff members on their ongoing research and outreach projects. *Type:* Newsletter.

Minority Health Resources Directory

ANROW Publishing
1700 Research Blvd., Ste. 400 Ph: (301)294-5400
Rockville, MD 20852-3142 Fax: (301)294-5401
Contact: Patricia President, Editor.
Desc: 360 federal government programs and agencies, organizations, and foundations offering health services and products to minority group members. *Type:* Directory.

Modern Healthcare

Crain Communications Inc.
740 N. Rush St. Ph: (312)649-5200
Chicago, IL 60611
URL: http://www.crain.com
Desc: Contains the complete text of Modern Healthcare, a weekly magazine covering the business side of the health care industry. *Available:* Dow Jones Interactive Publishing; Bell & Howell Information and Learning; LEXIS-NEXIS, NEXIS; Reuters Information Services Inc.; The Gale Group, InfoTrac Web; Medical Data Exchange (MDX). *Type:* Database.

Modern Healthcare

Crain Communications, Inc.
740 N. Rush St. Ph: (312)649-5200
Chicago, IL 60611-2590 Fax: (312)649-5360
URL: http://www.modernhealthcare.com.
Contact: Clark Bell, Editor, (312)649-5342, fax: (312)280-3183, mhceditamerica online, inc.com; Charles S. Lauer, Publisher, (312)649-5297; Sheryl Bull, Advertising Dir.
Desc: Weekly Business news magazine for Healthcare Management *Type:* Periodical.

National Association for Healthcare Quality

4700 W. Lake Ave. Ph: (847)375-4720
Glenview, IL 60025-1485 Free: 800-966-9392
  Fax: (847)375-6320
E-mail: info@nahq.org
URL: http://www.nahq.org
Contact: Diane Burgher, Exec.Dir.
Desc: Healthcare professionals in quality assessment and improvement, utilization and risk management, case management, infection control, managed care, nursing, and medical records. Objectives are: to encourage, develop, and provide continuing education for all persons involved in health care quality; to give the patient primary consideration in all actions affecting his or her health and welfare; to promote the sharing of knowledge and encourage a high degree of professional ethics in health care quality. Offers accredited certification in the field of healthcare quality, utilization, and risk management. *Type:* Association.

National Association for Home Care

228 7th St. SE Ph: (202)547-7424
Stanton Park Fax: (202)547-3540
Washington, DC 20003
E-mail: clc@nahc.org
URL: http://www.nahc.org
Contact: Val J. Halamandaris, Pres.
Desc: Providers of home health care, hospice, and homemaker-home health aide services; interested individuals and organizations. Develops and promotes high standards of patient care in home care services. Seeks to affect legislative and regulatory processes concerning home care services; gathers and disseminates home care industry data; develops public relations strategies; works to increase political visibility of home care services. *Type:* Association.

National Center for Homeopathy: Directory of Practitioners, Study Groups, Pharmacies, and Resources

National Center for Homeopathy
801 N. Fairfax St., Ste. 306 Ph: (703)548-7790
Alexandria, VA 22314 Fax: (703)548-7792
E-mail: nchinfo@igc.apc.org
URL: http://www.homeopathic.org.
Desc: About 450 doctors of medicine and osteopathy, dentists, chiropractors, acupuncturists, and veterinarians who include homeopathy in their practices. *Type:* Directory.

National Institute of Allergy and Infectious Diseases: National Institutes of Health

U.S. Department of Health and Human Services - National Institutes of Health National Institute of Allergy and Infectious Diseases
Office of Communications Ph: (301)496-5717
Bldg. 31, Rm. 7A-50
31 Center Dr. MSC 2520
Bethesda, MD 20892-2520
E-mail: ocpostoffice@flash.niaid.nih.gov
URL: http://www.niaid.nih.gov
Desc: The National Institute of Allergy and Infectious Diseases (NIAID), a component of the National Institutes of

Health (NIH), independently operates this Web site to disseminate information pertaining to the conduct and support of federally-sponsored research to prevent, diagnose and treat illnesses such as AIDS and other sexually transmitted diseases, tuberculosis and malaria, as well as asthma and allergies. This site exits to offer an information exchange for public- and private-sector scientists and health care professionals with respect to available research data/outcomes and research opportunities. *Type:* Database.

National Union of Hospital and Health Care Employees/SEIU
310 W. 43rd St.　　　　Ph: (212)582-1890
New York, NY 10036

Contact: Jerome Brown, Acting Pres.

Desc: An affiliate of the Service Employees International Union , Health Care Division. Works to organize hospital and health care employees into a labor union. *Type:* Association.

Nebraska Medical Directory
Jola Publications
2933 N. 2nd St.　　　　Ph: (612)529-5001
Minneapolis, MN 55411　　Fax: (612)521-2289
E-mail: jolapub@aol.com

Contact: Dennis Schapiro, Publisher.

Desc: Approximately 6,000 health care facilities and professionals in Nebraska including clinics, hospitals, pharmacies, nursing homes, and doctors. *Type:* Directory.

New Age
New Age Publishing
42 Pleasant St.　　　　Ph: (617)926-0200
Watertown, MA 02172　　Fax: (617)926-5021
E-mail: editor@newage.com.
URL: http://www.newage.com/home/newage/.

Contact: Joan Duncan Oliver, Editor; David H. Thorne, Publisher.

Desc: New Age Journal reports on leading-edge ideas in the areas of health, natural living, self-improvement, psychology, publishing and music. It is written for readers who are not limited by conventional thinking and are seeking to improve their lives and society. *Type:* Periodical.

New Jersey Health and Senior Services Department
Health Planning and Regulation
Health Care Systems Analysis
Research and Development
Health & Agricultural Bldg.,　Ph: (609)292-9354
Rm. 601　　　　　Fax: (609)292-6523
PO Box 360
Trenton, NJ 08625-0360
E-mail: ean@doh.state.nj.us

Contact: Emmanuel Noggoh, Dir.

Desc: Health care. *Type:* Research center.

News and Strategies for Managed Medicare and Medicaid
Atlantic Information Services, Inc.
1100 17th St. NW, No. 300　Ph: (202)775-9008
Washington, DC 20036　　Free: 800-521-4323
　　　　　　　　Fax: (202)331-9542

Contact: Chris Gearon, Editor.

Desc: Reports on developments on Medicare and Medicaid. *Type:* Newsletter.

Occupational Health & Safety Purchasing Sourcebook
Stevens Publishing Corp.
5151 Belt Line Road, Ste. 1010　Ph: (972)687-6700
Dallas, TX 75240　　　Fax: (972)687-6799

Contact: Blake Smith, Editor; Mark Hartley, Editor; Teri Eisman, Editor.

Desc: Over 1,500 manufacturers, distributors, and consultants of products and services in the field of safety, health, and environmental protection. *Type:* Directory.

Oley Foundation for Home Parenteral and Enteral Nutrition
214 Hun Memorial, A-23　Ph: (518)262-5079
Albany Medical Center　　Free: 800-776-OLEY
Albany, NY 12208　　　Fax: (518)262-5528
E-mail: joan_bishop@ccgateway.amc.edu
URL: http://www.wizvax.net/oleyfdn

Contact: Joan Bishop, Exec.Dir.

Desc: Promotes optimal care for persons requiring infused nutrition at home. *Type:* Association.

The Open Minds Practice Advisor
Behavioral Health Industry News, Inc.
10 York St., Ste. 200　　Ph: (717)334-1329
Gettysburg, PA 17325　　Fax: (717)334-0538
E-mail: openminds@openminds.com.
URL: http://www.openminds.com.

Contact: Monica E. Oss, Editor.

Desc: Covers topics related to mental health, including substance abuse. *Type:* Newsletter.

Orthodontic Directory of the World
Orthodontic Directory of the World
4525 Harding Rd., No. 110　Ph: (615)373-8165
Nashville, TN 37205　　　Fax: (615)383-2362
E-mail: odw@bellsouth.net

Contact: William H. Oliver, D.M.D., Editor.

Desc: 9,000 main and 5,750 branch orthodontic offices in the U.S. and Canada, and 7,500 main office listings for orthodontists overseas. *Type:* Directory.

Patient Care and Nursing Products
Card-Zine Communications, Inc.
8912 Ewing Ave.
Evanston, IL 60203

Contact: Ira Lieb, Publisher; Julie Euler, Editor.

Desc: Journal for health-care professionals reporting products that serve the needs of limited mobility and immobilized patients. *Type:* Periodical.

Pittsburgh Research Institute
5th Ave. Pl., Ste. 1711　　Ph: (412)255-7000
Pittsburgh, PA 15222　　Fax: (412)255-7503
E-mail: wwy@pittvms.cis.pitt.edu

Contact: Wanda W. Young, ScD, Pres.

Desc: Health services research, particularly in health care delivery and financing systems, including hospital cost analyses/case mix measurement, case mix reporting to the health care industry, hospital and physician payment systems, hospital cost/product line analyses, quality assessment/utilization monitoring, clinical outcomes assessment, and information systems design. *Type:* Research center.

Portable Practitioner: Opportunities in the Healing Arts
Monica Gruler & Company
PO Box 2095　　　　Ph: (616)347-8591
Petoskey, MI 49770　　Free: 800-968-2877
　　　　　　　　Fax: (616)347-8591
E-mail: mgruler1@aol.com; portprac@freeway.net.
URL: http:www.cybersytes.com/portprac.

Contact: Monica Gruler, Editor.

Desc: Features marketing and practice-growing suggestions for massage therapists and bodyworkers. Recurring features include interviews, a calendar of events, news of educational opportunities, job listings, and notices of publications available. *Type:* Newsletter.

Primary Care Newsletter
Lippincott Williams & Wilkins
351 W. Camden St.　　Ph: (410)528-8517
Baltimore, MD 21201-2436　Free: 800-882-0483
　　　　　　　　Fax: (410)528-4312
URL: http://www.wwilkins.com

Contact: Dr. Michael K. Rees, Editor-in-Chief; Kerry O'Rourke, Managing Editor.

Desc: Reports on the contents of the Core Curriculum Committee's lecture series, A Core Curriculum in Primary Care Medicine. Also includes supplemental information helpful to the practice of adult primary care medicine in the office and ambulatory setting. *Type:* Newsletter.

Prime Health & Fitness
Weider Publications
21100 Erwin St.　　　Ph: (818)884-6800
Woodland Hills, CA 91367-　Free: 800-423-5590
3712　　　　　　Fax: (818)704-5734
E-mail: jweider@weiderpub.com; primefit1@aol.com.
URL: http://www.primehealth-fitness.com.

Contact: Bill Bush, Editor; David Kalmansohn, Senior Editor, (818)595-0572, fax: (818)595-0575; Mike Carlson, Assoc. Editor.

Desc: Consumer magazine covering health, fitness, and lifestyle for men over 35 years. *Type:* Periodical.

Profiles in Healthcare Marketing
The Business Word
5350 S. Roslyn St., Ste. 400　Ph: (303)967-0130
Englewood, CO 80111-2125　Free: 800-328-3211
　　　　　　　　Fax: (303)290-9025

Contact: Jeannette Herreria, Editor; Donald E.L. Johnson, Publisher; Tom Rees, Editor.

Desc: Provides information about medical and hospital marketing. *Type:* Newsletter.

Proofs—Buyers' Guide and U.S. Manufacturers' Directory Issue
Dental Economics Division
PennWell Publishing Co.
Box 3408　　　　　Ph: (918)835-3161
Tulsa, OK 74101　　　Fax: (918)831-9804

Contact: Julie Harris, Editor, julieh@pennwell.com.

Desc: List of over 600 manufacturers of dental products and equipment; coverage includes foreign listings. *Type:* Directory.

Rate Controls
Rate Controls Publications, Inc.
PO Box 35425　　　Ph: (602)995-9435
Phoenix, AZ 85069　　Free: 800-975-8100
　　　　　　　　Fax: (602)995-9458
E-mail: rcpubs@primenet.com

Contact: Arnold P. Silver, Publisher; Glenn Pearl, Editor.

Desc: Analyzes health care trends and developments. Provides an economic analysis service for health care management. *Type:* Newsletter.

Reimbursement Advisor
Aspen Publishers, Inc.
200 Orchard Ridge Dr., No.　Ph: (301)417-7500
200　　　　　　Free: 800-638-8437
Gaithersburg, MD 20878　Fax: (301)417-7650
E-mail: customer.service@aspenpubl.com
URL: http://www.aspenpub.com

Contact: Dennis Barry, Esq., Editor.

Desc: Provides information on health care spending and Medicare reimbursement. Deals with universal health insurance, physician payments, preventative services, and the industry's regulations. *Type:* Newsletter.

Report on Medical Guidelines & Outcomes Research

Aspen Publishers, Inc.

200 Orchard Ridge Dr., No. 200   Ph: (301)417-7500
Free: 800-638-8437
Gaithersburg, MD 20878   Fax: (301)417-7650
E-mail: customer.service@aspenpubl.com
URL: http://www.aspenpub.com

Contact: Jane Lowers, Editor.

Desc: Provides news, information, analysis, and advice concerning medical guidelines and outcomes research development and applications. Remarks: Also available via e-mail. *Type:* Newsletter.

The Saturday Evening Post

The Saturday Evening Post Society

1100 Waterway Blvd.   Ph: (317)636-8881
Indianapolis, IN 46202   Fax: (317)637-0126
E-mail: silverbob@juno.com.
URL: http://www.satevepost.org.

Contact: Dr. Cory J. SerVaas, Editor.

Desc: General interest magazine. *Type:* Periodical.

School Health Alert

School Health Alert

PO Box 150127   Ph: (615)255-3609
Nashville, TN 37215-0127   Fax: (615)255-6956

Contact: Richard Adams, M.D., Editor; Jan Ozias, Ph.D., Editor; Robert Andrews, Publisher.

Desc: Provides reviews from many medical and nursing journals containing current news for nurses. Recurring features include letters to the editor, interviews, and news of research. *Type:* Newsletter.

Sneeze The Day!

Good Communications, Inc.

PO Box 10069   Ph: (512)454-6090
Austin, TX 78766   Free: 800-968-1738
Fax: (512)454-3420
E-mail: gooddogmag@aol.com

Contact: Judi Sklar, Editor.

Desc: Provides news and product test reports on allergy products, asthma and allergy medications, air cleaner, HEPA Filters, and vacuum cleaners. Recurring features include news of research. *Type:* Newsletter.

Spencer's Compliance Guide for Health & Benefit Plans

Charles D. Spencer & Associates, Inc.

250 S. Wacker Dr., Ste. 600   Ph: (312)993-7900
Chicago, IL 60606-5834   Free: 800-555-5490
Fax: (312)993-7910
E-mail: spencernet@mindspring.com

Contact: Miriam B. Scott, Assoc. Editor.

Desc: Publishes news and reports about federal laws and rules regarding employer- provided health and welfare benefits. Recurring features include news of research. *Type:* Newsletter.

Strategic Health Care Marketing

Health Care Communications

11 Heritage Ln.   Ph: (914)967-6741
Rye, NY 10580   Fax: (914)967-3054
E-mail: healthcomm@aol.com

Contact: Michele von Dambrowski, Editor.

Desc: Provides news and analysis on health care services marketing, and business development. Covers strategies and techniques used by marketing innovators. *Type:* Newsletter.

Strategies for Healthcare Excellence

COR Healthcare Resources

PO Box 40959   Ph: (805)564-2177
Santa Barbara, CA 93140-0959   Fax: (805)564-2146
E-mail: corinfo@corhealth.com

Contact: Judith Jenna, Editor.

Desc: Contains case studies detailing how health care organizations are achieving productivity and quality in the delivery of health care services. Recurring features include interviews, book reviews, and notices of publications available. *Type:* Newsletter.

Unique Opportunities

UO Inc.

455 S. 4th Ave., No. 1236   Ph: (502)589-8250
Louisville, KY 40202   Fax: (502)587-0848
E-mail: UNOP@aol.com

Contact: Mollie Hudson, Editor; Mel Weinberger, Publisher/Advertising; Bett Coffman, Assoc. Ed.

Desc: Professional magazine covering career development for physicians. *Type:* Periodical.

U.S. Department of Health and Human Services

Public Health Service

5600 Fishers Ln.   Ph: (301)443-3921
Rockville, MD 20857

Desc: The mission of the Public Health Service is to promote the protection and advancement of the nation's physical and mental health. This is accomplished by coordinating with the states to set and implement national health policy and pursue effective intergovernmental relations; generating and upholding cooperative international health-related agreements, policies, and programs; conducting medical and biomedical research; sponsoring and administering programs for the development of health resources, prevention and control of diseases, and alcohol and drug abuse; providing resources and expertise to the states and other public and private institutions in the planning, direction, and delivery of physical and mental health care services; and enforcing laws to assure the safety and efficacy of drugs and protection against impure and unsafe foods, cosmetics, medical devices, and radiation-producing projects. *Type:* Government agency, office, or program.

University of Alaska Anchorage

Institute for Circumpolar Health Studies

3211 Providence Dr., Ste.   Ph: (907)786-6575
K103-1   Fax: (907)786-6576
Anchorage, AK 99508
E-mail: ayichs@uaa.alaska.edu
URL: http://cwolf.uaa.alaska.edu/~ayichs/main.html

Contact: Brian Saylor, PhD, Dir.

Desc: Health problems and issues facing Alaskans and other populations in the circumpolar north, including epidemiologic studies of population health problems; studies of health services need, access and utilization; and evaluation of health policy and the effectiveness of new health programs. *Type:* Research center.

University of Houston

Institute for Health Care Marketing

College of Business   Ph: (713)743-4558
Administration   Fax: (713)743-4572
Department of Marketing
Houston, TX 77204-6283
E-mail: gelb@uh.edu
URL: http://www.cba.uh.edu/dept/mark/inst/health/intro.html

Contact: Prof. Betsy D. Gelb, Dir.

Desc: Health care marketing and health promotion. *Type:* Research center.

University of Montreal

Interdisciplinary Health Research Group

C.P. 6128, Succursale Centre-   Ph: (514)343-6185
ville   Fax: (514)343-2207
Montreal, PQ, Canada H3C 3J7
E-mail: gris@ere.umontreal.ca
URL: http://alize.ere.umontreal.ca/gris/sp

Contact: Raynald Pineault, PhD, Dir.

Desc: Health services, including analysis of health care system, evaluation of interventions, studies of determinants of health in populations, and investigations of methodological and conceptual developments in the field of health services research. Specific projects conducted in areas of curative and preventive practices, global health care, behavior of professionals and organizations, health education, health promotion, and maternal and child health. *Type:* Research center.

Visiting Nurse Association of Texas

1440 W Mockingbird Ln., Ste.   Ph: (214)689-0000
500   Free: 800-442-4490
Dallas, TX 75247-6911   Fax: (214)689-0010

Contact: Mary Suther, Pres. & CEO.

Desc: Strives to provide high quality health and support services in the home to the ill, frail, disabled and dying. Promotes health, dignity, comfort and independence, regardless of ability to pay to the extent of the agency's resources. *Type:* Association.

Wellness Management

National Wellness Association

PO Box 827   Ph: (715)342-2969
Stevens Point, WI 54481-0827   Free: 800-244-8922
Fax: (715)342-2979
E-mail: nwa@wellnessnwi.org; nwa@wellnessnwi.org.
URL: http://www.wellnessnwi.org/nwa/; http://www.wellnessnwi.org/nwa/.

Contact: Linda R. Chapin, D.D.S., M.S., Editor.

Desc: Serves as a forum for the National Wellness Association. Provides information on recent developments, resources, programming, events, and educational opportunities in the wellness and health promotion fields. *Type:* Newsletter.

Wellness Resource Directory

National Wellness Association

PO Box 827   Ph: (715)342-2969
Stevens Point, WI 54481-0827   Free: 800-244-8922
Fax: (715)342-2979
E-mail: nwa@wellnessnwi.org
URL: http://www.wellnessnwi.org/nwa/; http://www.wellnessnwi.org/wrd/.

Desc: Wellness and health promotion resources and services. *Type:* Directory.

York University

Centre for Health Studies

4700 Keele St., Rm. 214   Ph: (416)736-5941
Toronto, ON, Canada M3J 1P3   Fax: (416)736-5986
E-mail: ychs@yorku.ca
URL: http://www.yorku.ca

Contact: Georgina Feldberg, PhD, Dir.

Desc: Political economy of health; health policy, institutions and professions; women and health; culture, ethnicity and health; mental and physical fitness; and health and the environment. *Type:* Research center.

Health Care Products

American Orthotic and Prosthetic Association
1650 King St., Ste. 500 Ph: (703)836-7116
Alexandria, VA 22314 Fax: (703)836-0838
URL: http://www.theaopa.org
Contact: Robert T. Van Hook, Exec.Dir.
Desc: Represents more than 1,800 member companies that custom fit or manufacture componentry for patients with prostheses (artificial limbs) and orthoses (braces). *Type:* Association.

The Beauty Industry Report
The Beauty Industry Report
21704 Devonshire St., No. 343 Ph: (818)678-4495
Chatsworth, CA 91311 Fax: (818)998-0375
E-mail: beautyrprt@aol.com
Contact: Mike Nave, Editor and Publisher.
Desc: Dedicated to the professional beauty salon and store industry. Recurring features include columns titled Guest Column. *Type:* Newsletter.

Cosmetic Insiders' Report
Cosmetic Insider's Report
270 Madison Ave. Ph: (212)951-6600
New York, NY 10016 Fax: (212)481-6563
Contact: Don Davis, Editor.
Desc: Carries news and current insider views of the cosmetic, toiletries, and fragrance industries. Includes items on marketing, advertising, regulation, technology, consumer buying patterns, new products, company developments, and people in the industry. *Type:* Newsletter.

Cosmetic, Toiletry and Fragrance Association
1101 17th St. NW, Ste. 300 Ph: (202)331-1770
Washington, DC 20036 Fax: (202)331-1969
URL: http://www.ctfa.org/
Contact: E. Edward Kavanaugh, Pres.
Desc: Manufacturers and distributors of finished cosmetics, fragrances, and personal care products; suppliers of raw materials and services. Provides scientific, legal, regulatory, and legislative services. *Type:* Association.

Cosmetics Counter Update
Beginning Press
13075 Gateway Dr., No. 300 Ph: (206)444-1616
Tukwila, WA 98168-3335 Free: 800-831-4088
 Fax: (206)444-1625
URL: http://www.cosmeticscop.com; http://www.cosmeticscop.com.
Contact: Paula Begoun, Editor, paulab@accessone.com.
Desc: Seeks to dispel myths around the cosmetic industry and strives to give consumers the straight facts about cosmetics, cosmetic lines, and skin care products. Recurring features include columns titled Readers Answers & Questions and Product Reviews. *Type:* Newsletter.

Health Industry Distributors Association
66 Canal Center Plza., Ste. 520 Ph: (703)549-4432
Alexandria, VA 22314-1591 Fax: (703)549-6495
Contact: S. Wayne Kay, Pres.
Desc: Distributors of medical, laboratory, surgical, and home health care equipment and supplies to hospitals, physicians, nursing homes, and industrial medical departments. Conducts sales training, management seminars, and research through the HIDA Educational Foundation. *Type:* Association.

Health Industry Manufacturers Association
1200 G St. NW, Ste. 400 Ph: (202)783-8700
Washington, DC 20005 Fax: (202)783-8750
Contact: Alan H. Magazine, Pres.
Desc: Represents domestic (including U.S. territories and possessions) manufacturers of medical devices, diagnostic products, and healthcare information systems. Develops programs and activities on economic, technical, medical, and scientific matters affecting the industry. *Type:* Association.

Infusium
Members Only
2365 Cote de Liesse
Saint-Laurent, PQ, Canada
 H4N 2M7
Desc: Passes along "new developments in haircare, offers its customers discount incentives, exciting makeovers, and provides a forum for the sharing of haircare secrets, ideas, and tips." Recurring features include letters to the editor. *Type:* Newsletter.

National Association for Medical Equipment Services
625 Slaters Ln., Ste. 200 Ph: (703)836-6263
Alexandria, VA 22314-1171 Fax: (703)836-6730
E-mail: info@names.org
URL: http://www.names.org
Contact: William D. Coughlan, CAE, Pres. & CEO.
Desc: Home medical equipment, oxygen suppliers, and rehabilitation technology suppliers. To represent professionals in the home medical equipment service industry; to support legislation and regulations that are beneficial to the home health care industry and provide incentives for suppliers to continue to serve Medicare/Medicaid beneficiaries. *Type:* Association.

Optical Laboratories Association
PO Box 2000 Ph: (703)359-2830
Merrifield, VA 22116-2000 Fax: (703)359-2834
Contact: Robert L. Dziuban, CAE, Exec. Dir.
Desc: Independent, wholesale ophthalmic laboratories and suppliers serving the ophthalmic field. *Type:* Association.

Vision Council of America
1655 Ft. Myer Dr. Suite 200 Ph: (703)243-1508
Arlington, VA 22209-3108 Free: 800-424-8422
 Fax: (703)243-1597
E-mail: vica@visionsite.org
URL: http://www.visionsite.org
Contact: Susan Burton, Exec.VP.
Desc: Trade association of optical industry companies that sponsor exhibits at industry trade shows. Works to serve the collective interests of the ophthalmic community; encourages the public to visit eye care practitioners regularly. Seeks to produce top quality trade shows. *Type:* Association.

World International Nail and Beauty Association
1221 N. Lake View Ph: (714)779-9883
Anaheim, CA 92807 Fax: (714)779-9972
Contact: Jim George, Pres.
Desc: Professionals in the nail and skin care industries. Objectives are to: represent the manicure and skin care industry; promote the effective use and application of manicuring and skin care products and equipment; provide a means for mutual communication and joint study; represent the industry before state boards, the Food and Drug Administration, and other regulatory agencies. *Type:* Association.

Health Plans

American Association of Health Plans
1129 20th St. NW, Ste. 600 Ph: (202)778-3200
Washington, DC 20036 Fax: (202)331-7487
URL: http://www.aahp.org
Contact: Karen Ignagni, Pres.
Desc: Supports the managed health care industry. *Type:* Association.

Delta Dental Plans Association
1515 W. 22nd St., No. 1200 Ph: (630)574-6001
Oak Brook, IL 60523 Fax: (630)574-6999
URL: http://www.deltadental.com
Contact: Kim Volk, Pres.
Desc: Active state dental service corporations; inactive state dental service corporations; state dental societies; foreign dental service plans. Seeks to increase the availability of dental service to the public by assisting state dental societies in the formation of dental service corporations and by coordinating the activities of dental service corporations and helping them in the development of dental care programs for application to multistate and national accounts. A dental service corporation (or dental service plan) refers to a nonprofit corporation organized by the dental profession to provide prepaid dental care coverage to the public on a group basis. *Type:* Association.

FOCUS - The Computer Society for Doctors
PO Box 15579 Ph: (415)626-4600
San Francisco, CA 94115
Desc: Physicians, dentists, office managers, and other individuals interested in the utilization of computers in the medical office. *Type:* Association.

Hearing Impaired

a.b.c. Reports
League for the Hard of Hearing
71 W. 23rd St. Ph: (212)741-7650
New York, NY 10010 Fax: (212)255-4413
E-mail: abc@lhh.org.
URL: http://www.lhh.org/abc.
Contact: Arlene Romoff, Editor-in-Chief, (201)444-2240, fax: (201)670-8776, aromoff@aol.com.
Desc: Advocates better communication for the hearing impaired. Reports on the latest advances in technology, computers, broadcasting, travel healthcare the arts, and other services that assist deaf & hard of hearing people. *Type:* Newsletter.

Association of Late-Deafened Adults
10310 Main St., No. 274 Ph: (404)289-1596
Fairfax, VA 22030-2410 Fax: (404)284-6862
E-mail: ldmpoppins@aol.com
URL: http://www.alda.org
Contact: Mary Clarke, Pres.
Desc: People who have become deaf adventitiously and rely on visual systems to communicate effectively. Provides information, support, and social opportunities through self-help groups, general membership meetings, and social events. Advocates for the needs of late-deafened people. *Type:* Association.

Central Institute for the Deaf
818 S. Euclid Ave. Ph: (314)977-0000
St. Louis, MO 63110 Fax: (314)977-0025
E-mail: nielsen@cid.wustl.edu
URL: http://www.cid.wustl.edu
Contact: Donald W. Nielsen, Dir.
Desc: Auditory communication and its disorders, including studies of hearing function, auditory physiology, sensory neuroscience, auditory biophysics and biomechanics, effects of noise, and regeneration in the auditory nervous system. Also performs clinical studies of speech and linguistics, communication in infants, characteristics of deaf speech, evaluation of cochlear implants in children, and audiology. *Type:* Research center.

Deafness Research Foundation

575 5th Ave., 11th Fl.
New York, NY 10017-2422

Ph: (212)599-0027
Free: 800-535-3323
Fax: (212)599-0039

E-mail: drf@drf.org
URL: http://www.drf.org
Contact: John Wheeler, Pres./CEO.

Desc: Participates in the National Temporal Bone and Balance Pathology Resource Registry Program of the National Institute on Deafness and Other Communication Disorders. Approximately 1000 physicians and other professionals in ear medicine and research and 52 medical societies underwrite the foundation's fundraising costs through membership in the Centurions of the Deafness Research Foundation; approximately 300 other interested individuals raise funds through membership in the Deafness Research Foundation Alliance. *Type:* Association.

Hear Now

9745 E. Hampden Ave., No.
300
Denver, CO 80231-4329

Ph: 800-648-4327
Free: 800-648-HEAR
Fax: (303)695-7789

E-mail: jostelter@aol.com
URL: http://www.leisurelan.com/~hearnow/
Contact: Joanita Stelter, PR Officer.

Desc: Provides hearing aids for very low income hard of hearing individuals of all ages. Offers financial and fund raising assistance for hard of hearing and deaf individuals who need cochlear implants. Collects broken and used hearing aids through its HEAR-O Recycling Program to support assistance programs. *Type:* Association.

Hearing Loss

Self Help for Hard of Hearing People

7910 Woodmont Ave., Ste.
1200
Bethesda, MD 20814

Ph: (301)657-2248
Fax: (301)913-9413

E-mail: national@shhh.org
URL: http://www.shhh.org; http://www.shhh.org; http://www.shhh.org.
Contact: Barbara Kelley, Editor; Donna L. Sorkin, Executive Dir.

Desc: Magazine covering all aspects of hearing loss as well as new technology. *Type:* Periodical.

Helen Keller National Center for Deaf-Blind Youths and Adults

111 Middle Neck Rd.
Sands Point, NY 11050

Ph: (516)944-8900
Fax: (516)944-7302

E-mail: hkncpr@aol.com
Contact: Joseph J. McNulty, Dir.

Desc: Established to provide and develop maximum support and training to deaf-blind individuals. Objectives are to: evaluate the degree of physical and psychosocial functioning of deaf-blind individuals; determine rehabilitation needs, interests, and potential; design and improve rehabilitation techniques. Provides: rehabilitation to achieve meaningful contact with the environment, effective means of communication, and constructive participation in the home and community; community education programs; job placement for students who are deaf-blind; placement in residential settings. *Type:* Association.

International Hearing Society

16880 Middlebelt Rd., Ste. 4
Livonia, MI 48154-3367

Ph: (734)522-7200
Free: 800-521-5247
Fax: (734)522-0200

URL: http://www.hearingihs.org
Contact: Robin Clowers, Exec.Dir.

Desc: Hearing aid specialists who test hearing for the selection, adaptation, fitting, adjusting, servicing, and sale of hearing aids. *Type:* Association.

National Association of the Deaf

814 Thayer Ave.
Silver Spring, MD 20910

Ph: (301)587-1788
Fax: (301)587-1791

E-mail: nadinfo@nad.org
URL: http://www.nad.org
Contact: Nancy J. Bloch, Exec.Dir.

Desc: Adult deaf persons, parents of deaf children, professionals and students in the field of deafness, and interested individuals; organizations of and for deaf people. Seeks to "safeguard the accessibilit y and civil rights of 28 million deaf and hard of hearing Americans in education, employment, health care and telecommunications". *Type:* Association.

Ohio School for the Deaf Alumni Association

901 S. Sunbury Rd.
Westerville, OH 43081

Ph: (614)890-5533
Fax: (614)890-5534

E-mail: osdaa@aol.com
Contact: Richard D. Huebner, Pres.

Desc: Provides services to the elderly deaf, deaf-blind, and multi-handicapped persons. Advocates on behalf of the disabled; conducts charitable programs; sponsors festival. *Type:* Association.

Self Help for Hard of Hearing People

Martin J. McNamara

7910 Woodmont Ave., Ste.
1200
Bethesda, MD 20814

Ph: (301)657-2248
Fax: (301)913-9413

E-mail: national@shhh.org
URL: http://www.shhh.org
Contact: Donna L. Sorkin, Exec.Dir.

Desc: Volunteer organization of hard-of-hearing people and their relatives and friends; professionals working with hearing impaired persons. *Type:* Association.

The Sign Writer

The Deaf Action Committee for Sign Writing

Center for Sutton Movement
Writing
Box 517
La Jolla, CA 92038-0517

Ph: (619)456-0098
Fax: (619)456-0020

E-mail: dac@signwriting.org.
URL: http://www.signwriting.org.

Desc: Contains articles in both printed and sign written format for hearing impaired individuals. Available online only. *Type:* Newsletter.

Southern California TDD Community Directory

EF Training Center, Inc.

7712 Lankershim Blvd.
North Hollywood, CA 91605

Ph: (818)764-4311
Free: 888-877-5379
Fax: (818)764-4066

E-mail: eftc@aol.com
Contact: David Rosenbaum, President.

Desc: Approximately 2,800 individuals, businesses, government agencies, and non-profit organizations in the southern California area with accessible TDD phone service. *Type:* Directory.

Tinnitus Today

American Tinnitus Association (ATA)

PO Box 5
Portland, OR 97207

Ph: (503)248-9985
Free: 800-634-8978
Fax: (503)248-0024

E-mail: tinnitus@ata.org.
Contact: Gloria Reich, Editor.

Desc: Studies tinnitus, the presence of ringing in the ears, or head noises, which "can appear in a variety of forms such as buzzing, roaring, whistling, hissing, or high-pitched screeches." Recurring features include Association news, news of research, analysis of treatments, statistics, book reviews, and convention and meeting news. *Type:* Newsletter.

Heating and Cooling

Air Conditioning Contractors of America

1712 New Hampshire Ave.,
NW
Washington, DC 20009

Ph: (202)483-9370
Fax: (202)588-1217

E-mail: comm@acca.org
URL: http://www.acca.org
Contact: Roger Jask, CEO/Exec.VP.

Desc: Contractors involved in installation and service of heating, air conditioning, and refrigeration systems. Associate members are utilities, manufacturers, wholesalers, and other market-oriented businesses. Monitors utility competition and operating practices of HVAC manufacturers and wholesalers. *Type:* Association.

Air-Conditioning and Refrigeration Institute

4301 N. Fairfax Dr., Ste. 425
Arlington, VA 22203

Ph: (703)524-8800
Fax: (703)528-3816

E-mail: ari@ari.org
URL: http://www.ari.org
Contact: Clifford H. Rees, Jr., Pres.

Desc: Manufacturers of air conditioning, refrigeration, and heating products and components. Develops and establishes equipment and application standards and certifies performance of certain industry products; provides credit and statistical services to members. *Type:* Association.

Air Movement and Control Association

30 W. University Dr.
Arlington Heights, IL 60004-
1893

Ph: (847)394-0150
Fax: (847)253-0088

E-mail: amca@amca.org
URL: http://www.AMCA.org
Contact: Peter N. Hanly, Exec.VP & CEO.

Desc: Manufacturers of air moving and control equipment and related air systems equipment. Conducts research on improvement of methods of testing; develops standard codes for fans, louvers, dampers, shutters, and similar equipment. *Type:* Association.

ARW Supplier News

Air-Conditioning and Refrigeration Wholesalers Association

1650 S. Dixie Hwy., 5th Fl.
Boca Raton, FL 33432-7462

Ph: (305)755-7000
Fax: (305)491-8100

E-mail: e-mail@arwi.org
Contact: James S. McMullen, Editor.

Desc: Informs supplier members of pertinent Association and industry news. Recurring features include announcements of companies accepted into the Association, meeting reports, and a column titled News From and About ARW Suppliers. *Type:* Newsletter.

ARW Wholesaler News

Air-Conditioning and Refrigeration Wholesalers Association

1650 S. Dixie Hwy., 5th Fl.
Boca Raton, FL 33432-7462

Ph: (305)755-7000
Fax: (305)491-8100

E-mail: e-mail@arwi.org
Contact: James S. McMullen, Editor.

Desc: Focuses on Association news and industry information of concern to member wholesalers and suppliers. Recurring features include information on Association programs and services, notices of educational materials available, a calendar of events, and news of members. *Type:* Newsletter.

Heating/Piping/Air Conditioning—Info-Dex Issue

Penton Media Inc.
1100 Superior Ave.   Ph: (216)696-7000
Cleveland, OH 44114-2543   Fax: (216)931-9524
E-mail: corpcomm@penton.com
Contact: Robert T. Korte, Editor.
Desc: Listing of 1,400 manufacturers in the heating/piping/air conditioning industry, and 200 associations and government agencies concerned with standards for the industry. *Type:* Directory.

IHEA News

Industrial Heating Equipment Association (IHEA)
1901 N. Myer Dr.   Ph: (703)525-2513
Arlington, VA 22209   Fax: (703)535-2515
Contact: James J. Houston, Editor.
Desc: Supplies news for industrial heating equipment manufacturers. Reports on governmental and legislative actions, studies conducted by the Association, seminars and meetings, and Association activities. *Type:* Newsletter.

International Association of Heat and Frost Insulators and Asbestos Workers

William G. Bernard
1776 Massachusetts Ave. NW,   Ph: (202)785-2388
   Ste. 301   Fax: (202)429-0568
Washington, DC 20036-1989
Contact: William G. Bernard, Gen.Pres.
Desc: AFL-CIO. *Type:* Association.

MACS Action!

Mobile Air Conditioning Society Worldwide
PO Box 100   Ph: (215)679-2220
East Greenville, PA 18041-0100   Fax: (215)541-4635
E-mail: info@macsw.org
Contact: Elvis Hoffpauir, Editor; Amy Kline, Editor.
Desc: Serves as the publication of the Mobile Air Conditioning Society Worldwide. Recurring features include news of research, a calendar of events, news of educational opportunities, and notices of publications available. *Type:* Newsletter.

MACS Service Reports

Mobile Air Conditioning Society Worldwide
PO Box 100   Ph: (215)679-2220
East Greenville, PA 18041-0100   Fax: (215)541-4635
E-mail: info@macsw.org
Contact: Elvis Hoffpauir, Editor; Amy Kline, Editor.
Desc: Serves as the information publication of the Mobile Air Conditioning Society Worldwide. Recurring features include news of research, a calendar of events, news of educational opportunities, and notices of publications available. *Type:* Newsletter.

NRCA Refrigeration News

National Refrigeration Contractors Association
1900 Arch St.   Ph: (215)564-3484
Philadelphia, PA 19103-1498   Fax: (215)963-9785
E-mail: nrca@femley.com
Contact: June M. Bretz, Editor.
Desc: Covers developments and activities in the refrigeration industry and within the Association. Provides information on industry regulations and business management and development. *Type:* Newsletter.

Refrigeration Service Engineers Society

1666 Rand Rd.   Ph: (847)297-6464
Des Plaines, IL 60016-3552   Fax: (847)297-5038
E-mail: rses@starnetinc.com
URL: http://www.rscs.org
Contact: Joe Ziemba, Exec.VP.

Desc: Persons engaged in refrigeration, air-conditioning and heating installation, service, sales, and maintenance. *Type:* Association.

Sheet Metal and Air Conditioning Contractors' National Association

4201 Lafayette Center Dr.   Ph: (703)803-2980
Chantilly, VA 20151-1209   Fax: (703)803-3732
E-mail: info@smacna.org
URL: http://www.smacna.org
Contact: John W. Sroka, Exec.VP.
Desc: Ventilating, air handling, warm air heating, architectural and industrial sheet metal, kitchen equipment, testing and balancing, siding, and decking and specialty fabrication contractors. Prepares standards and codes; sponsors research and educational programs on sheet metal duct construction and fire damper (single and multiblade) construction. *Type:* Association.

Shop Talk

International Mobile Air Conditioning Association
PO Box 9000   Ph: (817)338-1100
Fort Worth, TX 76147-2000   Fax: (817)338-1451
E-mail: imaca@iamerica.net
Contact: William F. Allison, Exec. Dir.
Desc: Carries news briefs on happenings in the motor vehicle air conditioning and installed accessories industry. Publishes technical as well as management-oriented articles and listings of manuals, technical services, and training opportunities available. *Type:* Newsletter.

Hispanic

American Association of Teachers of Spanish and Portuguese

University of Northern Colorado   Ph: (303)351-1090
Butler-Hancock, Rm. 210   Fax: (303)351-1095
Greeley, CO 80639
E-mail: lsandste@bentley.unco.edu
URL: http://www.aatsp.org
Contact: Dr. Lynn A. Sandstedt, Exec.Dir.
Desc: Teachers of Spanish and Portuguese languages and literatures and others interested in Hispanic culture. Operates placement bureau and maintains pen pal registry. Sponsors honor society, Sociedad Honoraria Hispanica and National Spanish Examinations for secondary school students. *Type:* Association.

Daily Word

Unity School of Christianity
1901 NW Blue Pkwy.   Ph: (816)524-3550
Unity Village, MO 64065-0001
E-mail: info@unityworldhq.org.
URL: http://www.dailyword.org.
Contact: Colleen Zuck, Editor.
Desc: Religious magazine. Prints edition in Spanish, La Palabra Diaria; also prints edition in large type. *Type:* Periodical.

El Economico

Media News Group, Inc.
604 Pine Ave.   Ph: (562)499-1415
Long Beach, CA 90844   Fax: (562)499-1484
E-mail: bruno512@ptconnect.infi.net; ptconnect.com/eleconomico.
Contact: Bruno Larosa, General Mgr., (562)499-1415, fax: (562)499-1484.
Desc: Spanish newspaper. *Type:* Periodical.

El Nuevo Dia

El Dia Inc.
PO Box 712   Ph: (787)793-7070
San Juan, PR 00906-7512   Fax: (787)793-8850
Contact: Antonio L. Ferre, Editor and Publisher.
Desc: Newspaper (Spanish). *Type:* Periodical.

El Nuevo Herald

Hometown Herald
1520 E. Sunrise Blvd.   Ph: (954)527-8940
Fort Lauderdale, FL 33304   Fax: (954)527-8955
Contact: Barbara Gutierrez, Editor; Robert Suarez, Publisher; Roberto Oliva, Advertising Dir.
Desc: Spanish-language newspaper. *Type:* Periodical.

El Vocero de Puerto Rico

Gastar Roca Inc.
PO Box 9023831   Ph: (809)721-2300
San Juan, PR 00902-3831   Fax: (809)725-8422
Contact: Gaspar Roca, Editor and Publisher; Alfredo Arias, Advertising Mgr.
Desc: Newspaper (tabloid) (Spanish). *Type:* Periodical.

Embarazo (Pregnancy)

Gruner & Jahr USA Publishing
375 Lexington Ave., 10th Fl.   Ph: (212)499-2000
New York, NY 10017-4024   Free: 800-599-8489
                                            Fax: (212)499-2159
Contact: Joceline Frank, Editor.
Desc: Magazine educating Hispanic mothers-to-be about pregnancy and birth. *Type:* Periodical.

Grand Council of Hispanic Societies in Public Service

PO Box 636, Stuyvesant Sta.   Ph: (212)615-6625
New York, NY 10009
Contact: Debra Martinez, Pres.
Desc: Umbrella organization for 22 Hispanic societies. Advocates affirmative action, equal employment, and economic opportunities for Hispanics. *Type:* Association.

HISPANIC

Hispanic Publishing Corp.
98 San Jacinto Blvd., Ste.1150   Ph: (512)476-5599
Austin, TX 78701   Fax: (512)320-1942
URL: http://www.hisp.com.
Contact: Alfredo J. Estrada, Editor and Publisher, editor@hisp.com; aestrada@hisp.com; Romeo Perez, Advertising Dir., rperez@hisp.com; Cory Ostos, Circulation Dir., cory@hisp.com.
Desc: General internet magazine covering Hispanic issues and people. *Type:* Periodical.

Hispanic American Almanac

Gale Group Inc.
27500 Drake Rd.   Ph: (248)699-4253
Farmington Hills, MI 48331-   Free: 800-877-GALE
   3535   Fax: (248)699-8070
E-mail: galeord@galegroup.com
URL: http://www.galegroup.com.
Contact: Nicolas Kanellos, Editor.
Desc: Lists of Hispanic associations, historic landmarks, and public interest law and political organizations. *Type:* Directory.

Hispanic Americans Information Directory

Gale Group Inc.
27500 Drake Rd.   Ph: (248)699-4253
Farmington Hills, MI 48331-   Free: 800-877-GALE
   3535   Fax: (248)699-8070
E-mail: galeord@galegroup.com
URL: http://www.galegroup.com.

Contact: Charles Montney, Editor.

Desc: About 5,400 sources of information on a variety of aspects of Hispanic American life and culture, including national, state, and local organizations; publishers of newspapers, periodicals, newsletters, and other publications and videos; television and radio stations; library collections; museums and other cultural institutions; Hispanic studies programs and research centers; federal and state government agencies; the leading 500 Hispanic-owned businesses in terms of revenue; awards, honors, and prizes; and educational scholarships, fellowships, and loans. *Type:* Directory.

Hispanic Link News Service

1420 N St. NW
Ste. 101   Ph: (202)234-0280
Washington, DC 20005   Fax: (202)234-4090
E-mail: zapotec@aol.com.
Contact: Patricia Guadalupe, Editor; Charles Ericksen, Publisher; Jonathan Higuera, Editor and Publisher.

Desc: Distributes Hispanic news. *Alt. Contact:* 1420 N St. NW, Ste. 101, Washington, DC 20005; telephone: (202)234-0280; fax: (202)234-4090. *Type:* Periodical.

Hispanic Yearbook

T.I.Y.M. Publishing Co., Inc.
1489 Chain Bridge Rd., Ste.   Ph: (703)734-1632
200   Fax: (703)356-0787
Mc Lean, VA 22101
E-mail: tiym@aol.com
URL: http://www.tiym.com.
Contact: Juan Ovidio Zavala, Editor; Angela Zavala, Editor.

Desc: Over 7,250 organizations, 1,900 publications, and other institutes and individuals of interest to the Hispanic community in the U.S., including government agencies, embassies, and consulates and private companies. *Type:* Directory.

Hispanic Yellow Pages of Central Florida

La Prensa Newspaper
685 S. CR 427   Ph: (407)767-0070
Longwood, FL 32750   Fax: (407)767-5478
Contact: Manuel A. Toro, Editor.

Desc: Over 5,000 Hispanic businesses and organizations in the central Florida counties of Brevard, Lake, Volusia, Orange, Osceola, and Seminole. *Type:* Directory.

La Estrella De Puerto Rico

La Estrella De Puerto Rico
Paris St., No. 165   Ph: (809)754-4440
Floral Park   Fax: (809)754-4457
Hato Rey, PR 00917
Contact: Pete Curras, Publisher; Diana Santiago, Director.
Desc: Newspaper about North, West, and South Puerto Rico. *Type:* Periodical.

La Guia Familiar

Latin Publications, Inc.
19804 Nordhoff Pl.   Ph: (818)882-9200
PO Box 9190   Fax: (818)882-7200
Van Nuys, CA 91406-1309
Contact: Arthur Lerner, Publisher.
Desc: Community newspaper (Spanish). *Type:* Periodical.

La Informacion

La Informacion Publishing Co., Inc.
6065 Hillcroft, Ste. 400   Ph: (713)272-0100
PO Box 740426   Fax: (713)272-0011
Houston, TX 77274
Contact: Emilio Martinez-Paula, Editor and Publisher; Lina Koscak, Editor.
Desc: Spanish language newspaper (tabloid). *Type:* Periodical.

La Raza

Rossi Publications, Inc.
3909 N. Ashland Ave.   Ph: (773)525-9400
Chicago, IL 60613   Fax: (773)525-5350
E-mail: adsales@laraza.com
URL: http://www.laraza.com.
Contact: Jorge Oclander, Editor, (773)525-1763, fax: (773)525-7747, joclander@laraza.com; Luis H. Rossi, Publisher, (773)327-6500, fax: (773)327-3822, lrossi@laraza.com; Robert J. Armband, Publisher, (773)525-6285, fax: (773)525-6449, armband@laraza.com.
Desc: Community newspaper (tabloid) (Spanish). *Type:* Periodical.

La Subasta

La Subasta
6120 Tarnef, Ste. 110   Ph: (214)951-9500
Houston, TX 77074
Contact: Orlando R. Budini, Editor.
Desc: Newspaper (Spanish tabloid) for the Hispanic community in Houston. *Type:* Periodical.

Latina

Latina
PO Box 581546   Ph: (612)623-4305
Minneapolis, MN 55458-1546   Fax: (612)623-4305
Contact: Randy Melcher, Editor.
Desc: Bilingual magazine on the economy, people, entertainment, and the arts. *Type:* Periodical.

League of United Latin American Citizens

221 N. Kansas, Ste. 1200   Ph: (915)577-0726
El Paso, TX 79901   Fax: (915)577-0914
Contact: Rick Dovalina, Pres.
Desc: Hispanic Americans, including Mexican-Americans, Puerto Ricans, and Central and South Americans, concerned with seeking full social, political, economic, and educational rights for Hispanics in the U.S. Supports LULAC National Educational Service Centers . Offers employment and training programs. *Type:* Association.

Mexican American Legal Defense and Educational Fund

634 S. Spring St., 11th Fl.   Ph: (213)629-2512
Los Angeles, CA 90014   Fax: (213)629-0266
E-mail: maldesla@aol.com
URL: http://www.maldes.org
Contact: Antonia Hernandez, Pres.
Desc: Funded through a range of sources including foundations, corporations, and individuals. *Type:* Association.

Mexican-American Opportunity Foundation

401 N. Garfield Ave.   Ph: (213)890-9600
Montebello, CA 90640   Fax: (213)890-9637
Contact: Dionicio Morales, Pres.
Desc: Seeks to create solutions to the needs and problems of Spanish-speaking and Hispanic Americans; conducts programs of benefit to all U.S. minorities. Activities include child care services, bilingual and bicultural development, training and assistance to senior citizens, apprenticeship preparation for women and minorities, home exterior painting and home repairs, employment services, educational and vocational training, counseling, information and referral for child care services, and musical entertainment. *Type:* Association.

Mexican American Unity Council

2300 W. Commerce, Ste. 300   Ph: (210)978-0500
San Antonio, TX 78207   Fax: (210)978-0547
E-mail: ftexan@mauc.org
Contact: Frances J. Teran, Pres./CEO.
Desc: Dedicated to the ideal of improving opportunities and promoting economic development in the low income Hispanic neighborhoods of San Antonio. Empowers the people to take control of their lives and their community. *Type:* Association.

Movimiento Familiar Cristiano

3570 Thompson Pl.
Hayward, CA 94541-5756
Contact: Rodrigo & Stella Agudelo, Co-Pres.
Desc: Husbands and wives working together in small groups to improve the quality of family life in the Spanish-speaking communities of the U.S. Program involves a cycle of four years of study based on three areas of family life: relations between spouses, relations between parents and children, and the family's relations with society. Material for each year consists of 15 themes for group dialogue and husband-wife dialogue. *Type:* Association.

Mundo L.A.

Latin Publications, Inc.
19804 Nordhoff Pl.   Ph: (818)882-9200
PO Box 9190   Fax: (818)882-7200
Van Nuys, CA 91406-1309
Contact: Arthur Lerner, Publisher.
Desc: Newspaper. *Type:* Periodical.

National Association for Hispanic Elderly - Los Angeles Branch

234 E Colorado Blvd Ste 300   Ph: (213)487-1922
Pasadena, CA 91101-2213   Free: 800-953-8553
    Fax: (213)385-3014
Contact: Carmelia G Lacayo, Pres./Ceo.
Type: Association.

National Council of La Raza

810 1st St. NE, 3rd Fl.   Ph: (202)289-1380
Washington, DC 20002   Fax: (202)289-8173
Contact: Raul Yzaguirre, Pres.
Desc: National umbrella organization working for civil rights and economic opportunities for Hispanics. Provides technical assistance to Hispanic community-based organizations in comprehensive community development, including economic development, housing, employment and training, business assistance, health, and other fields. Conducts research programs; compiles statistics; advocates on behalf of Hispanics. *Type:* Association.

National Network of Hispanic Women

PO Box 4223   Ph: (650)497-2733
Stanford, CA 94305
Contact: Sylvia Castillo, Exec. Editor.
Desc: Promotes the identification and advancement of outstanding Hispanic women for leadership positions in the public and private sectors. *Type:* Association.

National Puerto Rican Coalition

1700 K St. NW, Ste. 500   Ph: (202)223-3915
Washington, DC 20006   Fax: (202)429-2223
E-mail: nprc@aol.com
Contact: Manuel Mirabal, Pres.
Desc: Local and national Puerto Rican organizations (105) and individuals (451) interested in national programs and issues affecting the Puerto Rican community. Objectives are to: foster the social, economic, and political well-being of Puerto Ricans; evaluate the potential impact on Puerto Rican communities of legislative and governmental proposals and policies; represent interests of Puerto Ricans to the public and private sectors; develop a network of Puerto Rican organizations. Conducts public policy analysis, research, and community networking; sponsors educational seminars; collects and compiles statistics on housing, employment, education, and social welfare. *Type:* Association.

National Puerto Rican Forum

31 E. 32nd St., 4th Fl.   Ph: (212)685-2311
New York, NY 10016-5536   Fax: (212)685-2349
URL: http://www.nprf.org

Contact: Kofi A. Boateng, Exec.Dir.

Desc: Concerned with the overall improvement of Puerto Rican and Hispanic communities throughout the U.S. Seeks to identify the obstacles preventing the advancement of the Puerto Rican and Hispanic communities and to develop strategies to remove them. Designs and implements programs in areas of job counseling, training and placement, and English language skills, to deal effectively with the problems of Puerto Ricans and other Hispanics. *Type:* Association.

Puerto Rican Association for Community Affairs

853 Broadway, 5th Fl. Ph: (212)614-2900
New York, NY 10003 Fax: (212)529-8917
Contact: Yolanda Sanchez, Exec.Dir.

Desc: Strives to preserve Puerto Rican language, history, and art; develops a positive self-image among Puerto Ricans and creates an awareness of self, in and outside of the Puerto Rican community; develops leadership potential of the Puerto Rican community; shares resources with other Puerto Rican organizations in the U.S.; advocates human rights and civil liberties. Conducts Criemos Los Nuestros, a foster care and adoption program designed to provide services to Puerto Rican and Latin American children; an emergency boarding house to protect children during temporary crisis situations; operates PRACA Day Care Center, which offers bilingual and bicultural curriculum to children three to 12 years of age in preschool and after-school programs. Sponsors day care services to homeless families living in New York City hotels. *Type:* Association.

Puerto Rican Family Institute

145 W. 15th St. Ph: (212)924-6320
New York, NY 10011 Fax: (212)691-5635
Contact: Maria Elena Girone, Exec.Dir.

Desc: Established for the preservation of the health, well-being, and integrity of Puerto Rican and Hispanic families in the U.S. Programs include: Program to Preserve the Integration of the Puerto Rican Migrant Family, which combines social work, educational, psychiatric, and psychological services on behalf of the newly arrived migrants and immigrants; child placement prevention programs in Manhattan and Brooklyn, NY, which seek to remove barriers that make attaining family stability difficult; Placement Prevention Program for Juveniles on Probation. Operates Bronx, Brooklyn, Queens, and Manhattan mental health clinics, three community residences for 25 severely retarded young adults, and a branch office in Rio Piedras, Puerto Rico to assist returned migrant families. *Type:* Association.

Saludos Hispanos

Saludos Hispanos
73121 Fred Waring Dr., No. Ph: (619)776-1206
100 Free: 800-371-4456
Palm Desert, CA 92260 Fax: (619)776-1214
URL: http://www.saludos.com.
Contact: Mona DeCrinis, Editor.

Desc: Magazine showcasing successful Hispanic Americans and promoting higher education (English and Spanish). *Type:* Periodical.

Ser Padres

Gruner & Jahr USA Publishing
375 Lexington Ave., 10th Fl. Ph: (212)499-2000
New York, NY 10017-4024 Free: 800-599-8489
  Fax: (212)499-2159
Contact: Molly Ingram, Dir. Sales & Ops, (212)499-2094, fax: (212)499-2097; Jane Traulsen, Editor, (212)499-2084, fax: (212)499-2097.

Desc: Hispanic magazine providing information on parenting. *Type:* Periodical.

Sun

Sun
800 S. Valley View Ph: (702)385-3111
Box 4275 Fax: (702)383-7264
Las Vegas, NV 89127-0275
Contact: Brian Greenspun, Editor; Bill Schaul, Advertising Mgr.

Desc: Community newspaper. *Type:* Periodical.

Temas

Temas Corp. Inc.
300 West 55th St., Apt. 14 Ph: (212)582-4750
New York, NY 10019-5172 Fax: (212)541-7910
Contact: Jose de la Vega, Editor and Publisher.

Desc: General interest magazine for Spanish speaking people. *Type:* Periodical.

TV y Novelas

Editorial Televisa
6355 NW 36th St. Ph: (305)871-6400
Miami, FL 33166-7099 Fax: (305)871-4939
E-mail: cosmo@editorial-televisa.com
Contact: Dora Luz Vargas, Editor; Enrique J Perez, Advertising Mgr.; Mario A. Freude, Editor.

Desc: Magazine covering the spanish-language soap operas lifestyles of entertainers; including photos and interviews (Spanish). *Type:* Periodical.

Vanidades Continental

Editorial Televisa
6355 NW 36th St. Ph: (305)871-6400
Miami, FL 33166-7099 Fax: (305)871-4939
E-mail: cosmo@editorial-televisa.com
Contact: Sara Barcelo de Castany, Editor; Enrique J. Perez, Advertising Sales Dir.; Mario A. Freude, V.P. Sales.

Desc: Women's fashion and beauty magazine (Spanish). *Type:* Periodical.

Vida Nueva

The Tidings Corp.
3424 Wilshire Blvd., 6th Fl. Ph: (213)637-7360
Los Angeles, CA 90010 Fax: (213)637-6360
E-mail: editorial@vida-nueva.com.
Contact: Victor Aleman, Editor.

Desc: Neawspaper. *Type:* Periodical.

Vista Magazine

Vista Publications
999 Ponce de Leon Blvd., Ste. Ph: (305)442-2462
  600 Fax: (305)443-7650
Coral Gables, FL 33134
Contact: Gustavo Godoy, Publisher; Carmen Teresa Roiz, Regional Editor, carmentere@aol.com; Julia Lobaco, Editor, jlobaco@aol.com.

Desc: Magazine supplement in major daily English language newspapers. *Type:* Periodical.

Historic Preservation

American Antiquarian Society

185 Salisbury St. Ph: (508)755-5221
Worcester, MA 01609-1634 Fax: (508)753-3311
URL: http://www.mark.mwa.org
Contact: Ellen S. Dunlap, Pres.

Desc: Gathers, preserves, and promotes serious study of the materials of early American history and life. Conducts program on the history of the book in American culture. Maintains research library specializing in the period of American history through 1876. *Type:* Association.

Association for Preservation of Civil War Sites

11 Public Sq., Ste. 200 Ph: (301)665-1400
Hagerstown, MD 21740 Fax: (301)665-1416
E-mail: apcws@intrepid.com
Contact: Robert K. Edmiston, COO.

Desc: American Civil War enthusiasts. Works to preserve historic Civil War sites by donation, easement, and fee-simple purchase. *Type:* Association.

Association for the Preservation of Civil War Sites Nationwide and Non-Profit

11 Public Sq., Ste. 200 Ph: (301)665-1400
Hagerstown, MD 21740 Fax: (301)665-1416
E-mail: apcws@intrepid.net
URL: http://www.apcws.org
Contact: Dennis E. Frye, Pres.

Desc: Fosters interest in the preservation of Civil War sites. *Type:* Association.

Association for the Preservation of Virginia Antiquities

204 West Franklin St. Ph: (804)648-1889
Richmond, VA 23220 Fax: (804)775-0802
E-mail: apva@apva.org
URL: http://www.apva.org
Contact: Peter Dun Grover, Exec.Dir.

Desc: Owns and/or maintains over 35 historical properties, some of which are open to the public. Presents annual awards for significant contributions to historic preservation in Virginia. Conducts seminars; offers professional training for docents. *Type:* Association.

Frank Lloyd Wright Home and Studio Foundation

951 Chicago Ave. Ph: (708)848-1976
Oak Park, IL 60302 Fax: (708)848-1248
Contact: Joan Mercuri, Exec.Dir.

Desc: Individuals interested in the work of architect Frank Lloyd Wright (1867-1959). Founded through a co-stewardship arrangement with the National Trust for Historic Preservation to restore and preserve Wright's Oak Park, IL home and studio, in which he developed the style known as the Prairie school of architecture. *Type:* Association.

Friends of the National Parks at Gettysburg

PO Box 4622 Ph: (717)334-0772
Gettysburg, PA 17325 Fax: (717)334-3118
E-mail: fnpg@mail.cvn.net
Contact: Vickey Monrean, Exec.Dir.

Desc: Citizens interested in protecting, preserving, and maintaining the two national parks at Gettysburg: Gettysburg National Military Park and the Eisenhower National Historic Site. *Type:* Association.

Heritage Institute of Ellis Island

19 E. 48th St., Ste. 502 Ph: (212)308-9580
New York, NY 10017-1009 Fax: (212)750-0323
E-mail: stens@mail.idt.net
Contact: Sten Sture Nordin, Chm.

Desc: Seeks to foster and promote public awareness of Ellis Island. *Type:* Association.

Historic Deerfield

PO Box 321 Ph: (413)774-5581
Deerfield, MA 01342 Fax: (413)773-7415
E-mail: grace@historic-deerfield.org
URL: http://www.historic-deerfield.org
Contact: Donald R. Friary, Exec.Dir.

Desc: Owns and maintains 52 buildings on 93 acres in Deerfield, MA, including the Deerfield Inn (1884), 14 houses open daily to the public and furnished with antique furniture, textiles, ceramics, and other early American decorative arts. Offers educational programs and special events for families. *Type:* Association.

Hudson River Sloop Clearwater

112 Market St.   Ph: (914)454-7673
Poughkeepsie, NY 12601   Fax: (914)454-7953
E-mail: office@mail.clearwater.org
URL: http://www.clearwater.org
Contact: Lew Eisenberg, Exec.Dir.
Desc: Owners of the 106-foot sloop Clearwater. Promotes
interest in the restoration and preservation of the Hudson
River and related waters. Promotes environmental educa-
tion and action programs; sponsors waterfront festivals,
school programs, and day sails for camps and scouts,
schools, community groups, historical societies, and indi-
viduals. Type: Association.

National Trust for Historic Preservation

1785 Massachusetts Ave. NW   Ph: (202)588-6000
Washington, DC 20036   Free: 800-944-6847
                                  Fax: (202)588-6038
E-mail: members@nthp.org
URL: http://www.nationaltrust.org
Contact: Richard Moe, Pres.
Desc: National private organization chartered by the U.S.
Congress to facilitate public participation in the preserva-
tion of buildings, sites, and objects significant in American
history and culture. Gives direct assistance in the form of
low-interest loans, matching grants, and expert counsel.
Type: Association.

Royal Oak Foundation

285 W. Broadway   Ph: (212)966-6565
New York, NY 10013   Free: 800-913-6565
                                  Fax: (212)966-6619
E-mail: oakroyal@aol.com
URL: http://www.royal-oak.org
Contact: Mrs. Damaris Horan, Exec.Dir.
Desc: Professionals, students, and laypeople who are inter-
ested in architecture, nature conservation, and historic
preservation areas. Seeks to further the preservation and
understanding of Anglo-American cultural and architec-
tural heritage. Conducts symposia; presents lecture series
and special lectures given by foreign speakers visiting the
U.S.; sponsors exhibits emphasizing historic preservation.
Type: Association.

Society for the Preservation of New England Antiquities

141 Cambridge St.   Ph: (617)570-9105
Boston, MA 02114
URL: http://www.spnea.org
Contact: Jane Nylander, Pres.
Desc: Seeks to preserve, interpret, and collect building,
landscapes, and objects relecting New England's daily life
from the 17th century to the present. Owns and operates
35 historic properties in five states which tell about the
people and stories of New England. Offers educational
programs. Type: Association.

Statue of Liberty - Ellis Island Foundation

52 Vanderbilt Ave., Dept. W   Ph: (212)883-1986
New York, NY 10017-3898   Fax: (212)883-1069
URL: http://www.ellisisland.org
Contact: Stephen A. Briganti, Pres.
Desc: Objectives are: to foster and promote public knowledge of and interest in the history of the Statue of Liberty
and Ellis Island and to restore both monuments. More
than $400 million has been raised for the restoration,
which included the creation of an exhibit on the Statue's
history and construction. The restored Main Registry
Building on Ellis Island contains a 100,000 square foot
museum telling the story of the peopling of America. Type:
Association.

Thomas Jefferson's Poplar Forest

PO Box 419   Ph: (804)525-1806
Forest, VA 24551   Fax: (804)525-7252
URL: http://www.poplarforest.org
Contact: Lynn A. Beebe, Exec.Dir.
Desc: Seeks to preserve and restore Poplar Forest, the
house Thomas Jefferson (1743-1826), third president of
the U.S., built as his year-round retreat on his plantation
in Bedford County, VA. Type: Association.

United States Historical Society

1st and Main Sts.   Ph: (804)648-4736
Richmond, VA 23219   Free: 800-788-4478
                                  Fax: (804)648-0002
URL: http://www.ushsdolls.com
Contact: Robert H. Kline, Chairman.
Desc: Dedicated to historical research and the sponsorship
of projects which are artistically and historically signifi-
cant. Type: Association.

United States Lighthouse Society

244 Kearny St., 5th Fl.   Ph: (415)362-7255
San Francisco, CA 94108   Fax: (415)362-7464
Contact: Wayne C. Wheeler, Pres. & Exec.Dir.
Desc: Promotes restoration and preservation of America's
lighthouses. Seeks to unite public agencies, private corporations, and individuals interested in preserving lighthouses and promoting maritime heritage. Collects lore
and artifacts for maritime and lighthouse museums. Type:
Association.

Walden Woods Project

44 Baker Farm Rd.   Ph: (617)367-3787
Lincoln, MA 01773-3004   Free: 800-554-3569
                                  Fax: (617)367-6292
Contact: Kathi Anderson, Dir.
Desc: Works to protect 2 historical land tracts surrounding
Walden Pond, in Concord, Massachusetts, where author
Henry David Thoreau (1817-62) conducted his conserva-
tion studies from 1845-47. (The areas where Thoreau
maintained a retreat during his stay at Walden are current-
ly protected by the state of Massachusetts as historical
landmarks). Disseminates information. Type: Association.

History

Adirondack Historical Association

Adirondack Museum   Ph: (518)352-7311
Blue Mountain Lake, NY   Fax: (518)352-7653
  12812-0099
URL: http://www.adkmuseum.org
Contact: Jacqueline Day, Museum Dir.
Desc: Preserves and promotes the history of the Adiron-
dack area. Type: Association.

America: History and Life

ABC-CLIO
130 Cremona Dr.   Ph: (805)968-1911
PO Box 1911
Santa Barbara, CA 93116-1911
E-mail: library@abc-clio.com
URL: http://www.abc-clio.com
Contact: Judith L. Burnstein, Online Services Coordina-
tor.
Desc: Contains citations, with abstracts, to social science
and humanities literature on all aspects of U.S. and Cana-
dian history, culture, and current affairs from prehistoric
times to the present. Available: CompuServe Information
Service, Knowledge Index; ABC-CLIO. Type: Database.

The American Civil War Homepage

University of Tennessee, Knoxville
Knoxville, TN 37996   Ph: (423)974-1900
E-mail: sunsite@utk.edu
URL: http://sunsite.utk.edu/civil-war/
Contact: Dr. George Hoemann, hoemann@utk.edu.
Desc: The American Civil War Homepage provides hun-
dreds of links to the most useful identified online informa-
tion about the American Civil War (1861-1865). An
outline of resources acts as a table of contents for the site.
Type: Database.

American Historical Association

400 A St. SE   Ph: (202)544-2422
Washington, DC 20003   Fax: (202)544-8307
E-mail: aha@theaha.org
URL: http://www.theaha.org
Contact: Sandria Freitag, Exec.Dir.
Desc: Professional historians, educators, and others inter-
ested in promoting historical studies and collecting and
preserving historical manuscripts. Type: Association.

American History

Primedia Enthusiast Publications
6405 Flank Dr.   Ph: (717)657-9555
Harrisburg, PA 17112-2753   Fax: (717)657-9552
Contact: Tom Huntington, Editor; Diane Myers, Adver-
tising Mgr.
Desc: Magazine for general audiences, featuring articles on
American cultural, social , political, and military history
Alt. Contact: telephone: (717)657-9555; fax: (717)657-
9552. Type: Periodical.

Biography Index

H.W. Wilson Company
950 University Ave.   Ph: (718)588-8400
Bronx, NY 10452
E-mail: custserv@hwwilson.com
URL: http://www.hwwilson.com
Contact: Technical Support Department., techmail@info.
hwwilson.com.
Desc: Contains citations to biographical information in
some 2700 biographies, autobiographies, critical studies,
and biographical fiction as well as periodicals, newspaper
obituaries, and other printed sources. Information, on
both current and historical persons, includes person's
name, dates of birth (and death), profession, and the
names and dates of biographical source publications that
list the individual. Available: Ovid Technologies, Inc.;
OCLC Online Computer Library Center, Inc., OCLC
EPIC; OCLC Online Computer Library Center, Inc.,
OCLC FirstSearch Catalog; SilverPlatter Information,
Inc.; H.W. Wilson Company, WilsonWeb. Type: Database.

Black History Month Resource Book

Gale Group Inc.
27500 Drake Rd.   Ph: (248)699-4253
Farmington Hills, MI 48331-   Free: 800-877-GALE
  3535   Fax: (248)699-8070
E-mail: galeord@galegroup.com
URL: http://www.galegroup.com.
Desc: Listings of African American organizations. Type:
Directory.

Blue Ridge Country

Leisure Publishing Co.
3424 Brambleton Ave.   Ph: (540)989-6138
PO Box 21535   Free: 800-548-1672
Roanoke, VA 24018-1535   Fax: (540)989-7603
E-mail: leisure@roanoke.infi.net
URL: http://www6.roanoke.infi.net/~leisure/brc.html.;
http://www.infi.net/leisure/brc.html; http://www.
blueridgecountry.com.

Contact: Kurt Rheinheimer, Editor; Richard Wells, Publisher; Patty Jackson, Production Dir.; Denise Koff, Circulation Dir.

Desc: Magazine celebrating the beauty and heritage of the mountain regions of GA, KY, MD, NC, SC, TN, VA, and WV. *Type:* Periodical.

The Book

Program in the History of the Book in American Culture
American Antiquarian Society
185 Salisbury St.   Ph: (508)755-5221
Worcester, MA 01609-1634   Fax: (508)754-9069
Contact: Robert A. Gross, Editor; John B. Hench, Editor, jbh@mwa.org; Caroline F. Sloat, Managing Editor, cfs@mwa.org.

Desc: Focuses on the Society's History of the Book Program, which deals with the period from 1639-1876 in American culture. Contains notes on archival and research collections, authors' queries, and reports on Program seminars and lectures. *Type:* Newsletter.

Bowker Biographical Directory

R.R. Bowker
121 Chanlon Rd.   Ph: (908)464-6800
New Providence, NJ 07974
URL: http://www.bowker.com

Desc: Contains biographical information on more than 160,000 leading North Americans in the fields of engineering, the physical and biological sciences, art, and politics. Covers some 119,600 scientists and engineers; approximately 11,800 artists, critics, curators, administrators, librarians, historians, collectors, and dealers; and more than 27,600 political decision-makers at all levels from federal to local government. *Available:* The Dialog Corporation, DIALOG; LEXIS-NEXIS, NEXIS. *Type:* Database.

Chemical Heritage Foundation

315 Chestnut St.   Ph: (215)925-2178
Philadelphia, PA 19106-2702 Fax: (215)925-1954
E-mail: joneb@chemheritage.org
URL: http://www.chemheritage.org
Contact: Arnold Thackray, Pres.

Desc: Serves as the primary source for the history of chemical science and technology. Encourages research, scholarship, and writing on history of chemical science, chemical engineering, and the chemical process industries. Locates archival records of organizations and individuals important in the history of chemistry and chemical engineering. *Type:* Association.

Chicago Historical Society

Clark St. at North Ave.   Ph: (312)642-4600
Chicago, IL 60614   Fax: (312)266-2077
URL: http://www.chicagohs.org
Contact: Douglas Greenberg, Pres.-Dir.

Desc: Individuals dedicated to collecting, preserving, and interpreting the history of Chicago, IL and selected areas of American history. Sponsors: lecture series, guest speakers; programs; exhibits. *Type:* Association.

Civil War Times Illustrated

Primedia Enthusiast Publications
6405 Flank Dr.   Ph: (717)657-9555
Harrisburg, PA 17112-2753 Fax: (717)657-9552
E-mail: cwt@cowles.com.
URL: http://www.historynet.com
Contact: Jim Kushlan, Editor, (717)540-6694, fax: (717)657-9552; Diane Myers, Advertising Dir.
Desc: Nonpartisan magazine covering the Civil War period. *Alt. Contact:* 6405 Flank Dr., Harrisburg, PA 17112-2753; telephone: (717)540-6694; fax: (717)657-9552. *Type:* Periodical.

Colorado Historical Society

1300 Broadway   Ph: (303)866-3682
Denver, CO 80203   Fax: (303)866-5739
E-mail: pie@sni.net
URL: http://aclin.org/other/historic/chs/index.html
Contact: Georgianna Contiguglia, Pres.

Desc: Individuals interested in collecting, interpreting, and preserving the history of Colorado and the American West. Offers student internships. *Type:* Association.

The Conference of Patriotic and Historic Societies

122 East 58th St.   Ph: (212)755-7082
New York, NY 10022   Fax: (212)755-7962
Desc: Patriotic or historical societies. Promotes patriotic and historic societies. *Type:* Association.

Facing History and Ourselves National Foundation

16 Hurd Rd.   Ph: (617)232-1595
Brookline, MA 02146   Fax: (617)232-0281
URL: http://www.facing.org
Contact: Margot Stern Strom, Exec.Dir.

Desc: Assists teachers and administrators in educating students about 20th century genocide, racism, human rights, and related issues of human behavior. Has developed an interdisciplinary curriculum, geared to junior high, high school, and university levels, that centers on the Holocaust and the genocide of Armenians committed during World War I; this curriculum is designed to encourage critical thinking about the lessons of history and the means for realizing a better future world. Investigates adolescent development; works to increase understanding of how adolescents view the world; studies and promotes voluntary activity such as community service and youth participation programs. *Type:* Association.

Good Old Days

House of White Birches
306 E. Parr Rd.   Ph: (219)589-4000
Berne, IN 46711   Fax: (219)589-8093
Contact: Ken Tate, Editor.

Desc: Magazine on the nostalgic past; including authentic photos, drawings, cartoons, memories, features, songs, poems, and advertising. *Type:* Periodical.

Guide to American Studies Resources

Journals Publishing Division
Johns Hopkins University Press
2715 N. Charles St.   Ph: (410)516-6987
Baltimore, MD 21218   Free: 800-548-1784
                          Fax: (410)516-6968
E-mail: jlorder@jhupress.jhu.edu; jlinfo@mail.press.jhu.edu
Contact: John F. Stephens, Editor.

Desc: List of colleges and universities which offer undergraduate and graduate degrees in American studies. *Type:* Directory.

Historic Landmarks of Black America

Gale Group Inc.
27500 Drake Rd.   Ph: (248)699-4253
Farmington Hills, MI 48331- Free: 800-877-GALE
3535   Fax: (248)699-8070
E-mail: galeord@galegroup.com
URL: http://www.galegroup.com.
Contact: George Cantor, Editor.

Desc: 300 sites significant in African-American history. *Type:* Directory.

Historical Abstracts

ABC-CLIO
130 Cremona Dr.   Ph: (805)968-1911
PO Box 1911
Santa Barbara, CA 93116-1911
E-mail: library@abc-clio.com
URL: http://www.abc-clio.com
Contact: Judith L. Burnstein, Online Services Coordinator.

Desc: Contains citations and abstracts of the worldwide literature from approximately 2000 journals and, since 1980, books and dissertations on political, diplomatic, economic, social, cultural, and intellectual history and related areas of the social sciences and humanities. Covers the history of the world since 1450 except for the United States and Canada. *Available:* CompuServe Information Service, Knowledge Index. *Type:* Database.

Horatio Alger Association of Distinguished Americans

99 Canal Center Plz.   Ph: (703)684-9444
Alexandria, VA 22314   Fax: (703)548-3822
URL: http://www.horatioalger.com
Contact: Terrence J. Giroux, Exec.Dir.

Desc: Objectives are to recognize modern-day individuals whose own initiative and efforts led to significant achievement; promote appreciation of the contribution business makes to the economic stability and quality of life for all Americans; serve as a channel of communication between business and education; promote the free enterprise system to the youth of America. *Type:* Association.

Kansas State Historical Society

6425 SW 6th Ave.   Ph: (785)272-8681
Topeka, KS 66615-1099   Fax: (785)272-8682
E-mail: reference@hspo.wpo.state.ks.us
URL: http://www.kshs.org
Contact: Ramon Powers, Exec.Dir.

Desc: Individuals interested in preserving the history of the state of Kansas. Operates state museum, preservation office, archeology office, and 15 historic sites. *Type:* Association.

Landmarks of American Presidents

Gale Group Inc.
27500 Drake Rd.   Ph: (248)699-4253
Farmington Hills, MI 48331- Free: 800-877-GALE
3535   Fax: (248)699-8070
E-mail: galeord@galegroup.com
URL: http://www.galegroup.com.
Contact: Dr. Carl Wheeless, Editor.

Desc: Historic sites associated with the 41 U.S. presidents. *Type:* Directory.

Marquis Who's Who®

Reed Elsevier Inc.
Marquis Who's Who
121 Chanlon Rd.   Ph: (908)771-6800
New Providence, NJ 07974
URL: http://www.marquiswhoswho.com

Desc: Contains biographical information on notable persons worldwide from the present and the past. Covers more than 790,000 prominent individuals. *Available:* The Dialog Corporation, DIALOG; The Dialog Corporation, DIALOG; CompuServe Information Service, Knowledge Index; NIFTY Corporation, NIFTY-SERVE. *Type:* Database.

Monmouth Antiquarian Society

13998 McCaleb Rd.
Monmouth, OR 97361
Contact: Steven Gagnon, Pres.

Desc: Worldwide membership is by election and limited to 600 heads of households and their immediate families. Dedicated to discovering, developing, and perpetuating the inventions and projects of antiquity using state-of-the-art technology. *Type:* Association.

National Cowboy Hall of Fame and Western Heritage Center

1700 NE 63rd St.   Ph: (405)478-2250
Oklahoma City, OK 73111   Fax: (405)478-4714
E-mail: nchf@aol.com
URL: http://www.cowboyhalloffame.org
Contact: Ken W. Townsend, Exec.Dir.
Desc: Persons interested in preserving the heritage of the American West and in honoring the pioneers who developed the West. *Type:* Association.

National Register of Historic Places

U.S. National Parks Service
1849 C St. NW   Ph: (202)208-6843
PO Box 37127
Washington, DC 20240
URL: http://www.cr.nps.gov/nr/nrhome.html
Contact: John P. Byrne, John_P._Byrne@nps.gov.
Desc: The National Register of Historic Places Database contains the official federal list of more than 68,000 listings including all historic areas in the National Park System; more than 2,200 National Historic Landmarks, which have been designated by the Secretary of the Interior because of their importance to all Americans; properties across the country that have been nominated by governments, organizations, and individuals because they are significant to the nation, to a state, or to a community. *Type:* Database.

New-York Historical Society

170 Central Park, W.   Ph: (212)873-3400
New York, NY 10024   Fax: (212)874-8706
URL: http://www.nyhistory.or
Contact: Betsy Gotbaum, Pres.
Desc: Individuals interested in preserving the history of New York. Maintains museum documenting city, state, and national history. *Type:* Association.

Organization of American Historians

112 N. Bryan Ave.   Ph: (812)855-7311
Bloomington, IN 47408-4199   Fax: (812)855-0696
E-mail: oah@indiana.edu
URL: http://www.indiana.edu/~oah
Contact: Arnita A. Jones, Exec.Dir.
Desc: Professional historians, including college faculty members, secondary school teachers, graduate students, and other individuals in related fields; institutional subscribers are college, university, high school and public libraries, and historical agencies. Promotes historical research and study. Sponsors 12 prize programs for historical writing; maintains speakers' bureau. *Type:* Association.

Phi Alpha Theta

50 College Dr.   Ph: (610)433-4140
Allentown, PA 18104-6100   Free: 800-394-8195
   Fax: (610)433-4661
E-mail: phialpha@ptd.net
Contact: Graydon A. Tunstall, Jr., Exec.Dir.
Desc: Honor society - men and women, history. *Type:* Association.

Pyramids, the Inside Story

Public Broadcasting Service
1320 Braddock Place
Alexandria, VA 22314
E-mail: www@pbs.org
URL: http://www.pbs.org/wgbh/nova/pyramid/
Contact: nova@wgbh.org.
Desc: You can leave your trowel in your toolbag when you visit this site on the pyramids of ancient Egypt. Discover historical details and new findings about these immense ancient structures. *Type:* Database.

Randolph County Historical Society

223 N. Clark   Ph: (660)263-5621
Moberly, MO 65270   Fax: (660)263-0646
Contact: Carla Brockman, Pres.
Desc: Individuals interested in preserving the history of Randolph County, MO. Maintains historical center and railroad museum. *Type:* Association.

Reminisce

Reiman Publications, LLC
5400 S. 60th St.   Ph: (414)423-0100
Greendale, WI 53129-1404   Free: 800-682-9019
   Fax: (414)423-8463
Desc: Magazine featuring vintage photos and recollections of events in the 20's, 30's, 40's, and 50's. *Type:* Periodical.

Society for Creative Anachronism

PO Box 360789   Ph: (408)263-9305
Milpitas, CA 95036-0789   Fax: (408)263-0641
E-mail: ea@sca.org
Contact: Andrew Smith.
Desc: People interested in learning about the Middle Ages by means of theoretical and practical research into various aspects of the culture and technology of the time. Primary activity is staging events that provide an opportunity for members to exercise and display skills in medieval music, dancing, cooking, and martial arts, and to display artifacts such as clothing, manuscripts, armor, pavilions, and furniture which members have created or commissioned. Seeks to provide a total environment in which everyone can be a participant rather than a spectator. *Type:* Association.

Sons and Daughters of the Soddies

c/o Vivian D. Phillips
PO Box 393
Colby, KS 67701-0393
Contact: Vivian D. Phillips, Pres.
Desc: Persons who have had experience with a sod house, part sod building, dugout, or adobe structure; direct descendants of former sod house dwellers. Gathers and preserves documents, pictures, history, and items pertaining to the era of prairie settlement in North America, circa 1840-1940. Conducts research activities on use, construction, and location of pioneer sod houses. *Type:* Association.

State Historical Society of Wisconsin

816 State St.   Ph: (608)264-6400
Madison, WI 53706-1488   Fax: (608)264-6404
E-mail: shsw.membership@ccmail.adp.wisc.edu
URL: http://www.shsw.wisc.edu/
Contact: George L. Vogt, Dir.
Desc: Promotes wider appreciation of the American heritage, with particular emphasis on the collection, advancement, and dissemination of knowledge of the history of Wisconsin. Maintains state historical museum and seven historic sites. *Type:* Association.

United States Capitol Historical Society

200 Maryland Ave. NE   Ph: (202)543-8919
Washington, DC 20002   Fax: (202)544-8244
E-mail: uschs@uschs.org
URL: http://www.uschs.org
Contact: Clarence J. Brown, Pres.
Desc: A private non-profit, non-patisan educational organization chartered by Congress to preserve and communicate the history and heritage of the U.S. Capital, its institutions, and the individuals who have served in Congress. Society activities include tours and programs, popular & scholarly symposia & publications, and enhancement of the Capitol's collection of art & artifacts. *Type:* Association.

Holocaust

American Gathering of Jewish Holocaust Survivors

122 W. 30th St., Ste. 205   Ph: (212)239-4230
New York, NY 10001   Fax: (212)279-2926
Contact: Max Lieberman, Exec.Dir.
Desc: Holocaust survivors; related associations. To perpetuate the remembrance of the Holocaust and of responsibility for Nazi crimes against the Jews; to combat anti-Semitism. Holds commemorative programs and gatherings periodically. *Type:* Association.

Braun Center for Holocaust Studies

c/o Anti-Defamation League of   Ph: (212)490-2525
    B'nai B'rith   Fax: (212)867-0779
823 United Nations Plz.
New York, NY 10017
Contact: Abraham H. Foxman, Dir.
Desc: A program of the Anti-Defamation League of B'nai B'rith . Serves as a central resource for information on the Holocaust. Develops curricula; organizes teacher-training workshops. *Type:* Association.

International Network of Children of Jewish Holocaust Survivors

c/o Rosita Kenigsberg   Ph: (305)919-5690
Florida International University   Fax: (305)919-5691
North Miami Campus
3000 NE 151st St.
North Miami Beach, FL 33181
Contact: Rosita Kenigsberg, Exec. VP.
Desc: Seeks to: provide a liaison among organizations of children of Holocaust survivors and coordinate their activities; provide these groups with a unified voice on issues including the rise of neo-Nazism, anti-Semitism, and desecration of the Holocaust. *Type:* Association.

Response

Simon Wiesenthal Center
9760 W. Pico Blvd.   Ph: (310)553-9036
Los Angeles, CA 90035   Fax: (310)553-8007
URL: http://www.@wiesenthal.com.
Contact: Rabbi Abraham Cooper, Editor-in-Chief; Lydia C. Springer, Editor.
Desc: Contains news of the Center's efforts to fight contemporary worldwide antisemitism, neo-Nazism, and prejudice, and to promote tolerance and Holocaust education. Remarks: Also published every 2-3 months is Beit Hashoa/Museum of Tolerance Update, providing information on the Center's Beit Hashoa/Museum of Tolerance, a 165,000-square foot human rights complex. *Type:* Newsletter.

Simon Wiesenthal Center

9760 W. Pico Blvd.   Ph: (310)553-9036
Los Angeles, CA 90035-4792   Free: 800-900-9036
   Fax: (310)553-8007
URL: http://www.wiesenthal.com
Contact: Rabbi Marvin Hier, Dean.
Desc: Dedicated to the preservation of the memory of the Holocaust through education and awareness, with the goal that "no people shall ever again fall victim to an atrocity of such magnitude." Develops programs in the areas of Holocaust Studies and Research, Educational Outreach to schools and various organizations, International Social Action and Media. *Type:* Association.

Home Economics

American Association of Family and Consumer Sciences

1555 King St.   Ph: (703)706-4600
Alexandria, VA 22314-2752   Fax: (703)706-4663
E-mail: info@aafcs.org
URL: http://www.aafcs.org

Contact: Ann Collins Chadwick, CFCS, Exec.Dir.

Desc: Elementary, secondary, post-secondary and extension educators and administrators; other professionals in government, business and nonprofit sectors; and students preparing for the field. Works to improve the quality of individual and family life through programs that "educate, influence public policy, disseminate information and publish research findings". *Type:* Association.

Phi Upsilon Omicron

PO Box 329   Ph: (304)368-0612
Fairmont, WV 26555-0329

Contact: Dr. Shirley Chase, Exec.Sec.

Desc: Honor society of women and men in family and consumer sciences. *Type:* Association.

Honor Societies

Alpha Chi

Harding University   Ph: (501)279-4443
HU Box 12249   Fax: (501)279-4589
Searcy, AR 72149-0001
E-mail: alphachi@harding.edu
URL: http://www.harding.edu/~alphachi

Contact: Dennis M. Organ, Exec.Dir.

Desc: Honor society - college students ranking in the upper ten percent of their class, invited into membership by their local Alpha Chi chapter as juniors, seniors, or graduating seniors. *Type:* Association.

Alpha Kappa Mu

2401 Corprew Ave.   Ph: (757)624-9668
Norfolk State University   Fax: (757)683-2849
Norfolk, VA 23504

Contact: Dr. Ann McKinney, Exec.Sec.-Treas.

Desc: Honor society - men and women, scholarship. *Type:* Association.

Alpha Sigma Nu

Peg Finucan Fennig
Marquette University   Ph: (414)288-7542
201 Brooks   Fax: (414)288-3259
PO Box 1881
Milwaukee, WI 53201-1881
E-mail: fennigp@vms.csd.mu.edu
URL: http://www.mu.edu/dept/ASN

Contact: Peg Finucan Fennig, Exec.Dir.

Desc: Scholastic honor society - students at 30 Jesuit colleges, universities and theologates in the U.S and one in the Republic of Korea. *Type:* Association.

Beta Phi Mu Newsletter

Beta Phi Mu
School of Information Studies
Florida State University
Tallahassee, FL 32306-2100   Ph: (850)644-3907
     Fax: (850)644-6253

E-mail: beta_phi_mu@lis.fsu.edu

Contact: Mary Upshaw Rhodes, Editor.

Desc: Updates member and chapter news for the international library and information science honor society. *Type:* Newsletter.

Delta Epsilon Sigma

Dr. J. Patrick Lee
11300 NE 2nd Ave.   Ph: (305)899-3020
Barry University   Fax: (305)899-3026
Miami, FL 33161
E-mail: jplee@mail.barry.edu

Contact: Dr. J. Patrick Lee, Sec.-Treas.

Desc: Honorary scholastic fraternity - men and women. *Type:* Association.

Gamma Beta Phi

575 Oak Ridge Tpke., Ste. A4   Ph: (423)483-6212
Oak Ridge, TN 37830-7100   Free: 800-628-9920
     Fax: (423)483-9801

E-mail: gbphqs@aol.com

Contact: Margaret McCauley, Exec.Dir.

Desc: College honor-service society. College and university students who are in the top 10-20% of their class academically, and who are committed to scholarship, service, and good character. Recognizes excellence in education, promotes leadership ability and character, and aims to foster and improve education through service projects. *Type:* Association.

Golden Key National Honor Society

James W. Lewis
1189 Ponce de Leon Ave.   Ph: (404)377-2400
Atlanta, GA 30306-4624   Fax: (404)373-7033
URL: http://www.gknhs.gsu.edu/

Contact: James W. Lewis, Exec.Dir.

Desc: Honor society - men and women, scholarship. Recognizes and encourages scholastic excellence and achievement at the undergraduate level. *Type:* Association.

Intercollegiate Knights

PO Box 7264, University Sta.   Ph: (801)489-0458
Provo, UT 84602-7264

Contact: Nolan Smith, Exec.Dir.

Desc: Honor society - men and women, scholarship, leadership, and service. Maintains national archives at Brigham Young University. Sponsors charitable programs administered through the Intercollegiate Knights Foundation. *Type:* Association.

Kappa Gamma Pi National Office

10215 Chardon Rd.   Ph: (440)286-3764
Chardon, OH 44024-9700   Fax: (440)286-4379
E-mail: kgpnews@aol.com

Contact: Christine S. Walick, Natl. Exec.Sec.

Desc: National Catholic College Graduate Honor Society. *Type:* Association.

Mortar Board

1250 Chambers Rd., No. 170   Ph: (614)488-4094
Columbus, OH 43212   Fax: (614)488-4095
E-mail: mortar0board@osu.edu
URL: http://www.mortarboard.org

Contact: Diane M. Selby, Exec.Dir.

Desc: National honor society for recognizing college seniors (students) who have achieved outstanding scholarship, leadership, and service. Mortar Board National Foundation awards annual fellowships to members for graduate study. Offers project grants to selected chapters for service projects. *Type:* Association.

National Alpha Lambda Delta

Box 4403   Ph: (912)752-4324
Macon, GA 31208-4403   Fax: (912)752-4387
E-mail: ald@mercer.edu
URL: http://www.mercer.edu/~ald

Contact: Dr. Glenda Earwood-Smith, Exec.Dir.

Desc: Freshman Honor society. *Type:* Association.

National Honor Society

1904 Association Dr.   Ph: (703)860-0200
Reston, VA 20191-1537   Fax: (703)476-5432
E-mail: nhs@nassp.org
URL: http://www.nassp.org

Contact: Rocco Marano, Dir.

Desc: Secondary school students in grades 10, 11, and 12, excelling in scholarship, leadership, service, and character. Founded and directed by National Association of Secondary School Principals. Bestows awards and scholarships. *Type:* Association.

National Junior Honor Society

1904 Association Dr.   Ph: (703)860-0200
Reston, VA 20191-1537   Fax: (703)476-5432
E-mail: njhs@nassp.org
URL: http://www.nassp.org

Contact: Rocco Morano, Dir.

Desc: Students in middle or junior high school excelling in scholarship, leadership, service, character, and citizenship. Founded and directed by National Association of Secondary School Principals. *Type:* Association.

News, Notes, and Quotes

Phi Delta Kappa International
408 N. Union   Ph: (812)339-1156
PO Box 789   Free: 800-766-1156
Bloomington, IN 47402-0789   Fax: (812)339-0018
E-mail: headquarters@pdkintl.org
URL: http://www.pdkintl.org; http://www.pdkintl.org.

Contact: Donovan R. Walling, Editor.

Desc: Publicizes events and projects of the chapters of this honorary society. Reports on the society's work to enhance quality education through research and leadership activities. *Type:* Newsletter.

Omicron Delta Kappa Society

118 Bradley Hall   Ph: (606)257-5000
Lexington, KY 40506-0058   Fax: (606)323-1014
E-mail: odknhdq@pop.uky.edu
URL: http://www.uky.edu/otherorgs/odk

Contact: John D. Morgan, Exec.Dir.

Desc: Honor society - college men and women in their junior or senior year. Maintains Omicron Delta Kappa Foundation. *Type:* Association.

Order of the Coif

Wayne McCormack
College of Law   Ph: (801)446-6574
University of Utah   Fax: (801)581-2190
Salt Lake City, UT 84112-0730
E-mail: strong@law.arizona.edu

Contact: Wayne McCormack, Sec.-Treas.

Desc: Honorary scholastic society - men and women, law. *Type:* Association.

Phi Beta Delta

The University of Georgia   Ph: (706)542-7903
Office of International   Fax: (706)542-6622
     Education
201 Barrow Hall
Athens, GA 30602-2407
E-mail: rreiff@arches.uga.edu
URL: http://www.sa.sdsu.edu/isc/pbd.home

Contact: Dr. Richard Reiff, Exec.Dir.

Desc: Honor society - international education. Chapters hold educational and social programs related to international education and exchange. *Type:* Association.

Phi Kappa Phi

PO Box 16000   Free: 800-804-9880
Louisiana State University   Fax: (225)388-4900
Baton Rouge, LA 70893-6000
URL: http://www.phikappaphi.org/
Contact: John W. Warren, Exec.Dir.
Desc: Honor society - men and women, scholarship. Maintains Phi Kappa Phi Foundation. *Type:* Association.

Horse Racing

Harness Horsemen International

Bank Plaza Bldg.   Ph: (609)259-3717
14 Main St.   Fax: (609)259-3778
Robbinsville, NJ 08691
Contact: Michael Izzo, Exec.Dir.
Desc: Owners, drivers, trainers, and breeders engaged in harness racing. Works to better harness racing standards. Promotes welfare, insurance, and better purses. *Type:* Association.

Horsemen's Benevolent and Protective Association

1001 North Schmeer Road   Ph: (503)285-4941
Portland, OR 97217-9505
E-mail: tbking@imagine.com
Contact: Scott Savin, Exec.Dir.
Desc: Owners and trainers of thoroughbred horses. Promotes the sport of horse racing. *Type:* Association.

The Jockey Club

40 E. 52nd St.   Ph: (212)371-5970
New York, NY 10022   Fax: (212)371-6123
Contact: Hans J. Stahl, Exec.Dir.
Desc: Acts as the official breed registry for U.S. and Canadian Thoroughbreds. Establishes regulations governing Thoroughbred breeding and the importation of foreign Thoroughbreds for racing purposes. *Type:* Association.

Thoroughbred Racing Protective Bureau

420 Fair Hill Dr., Ste. 2   Ph: (410)398-2261
Elkton, MD 21921   Fax: (410)398-1499
Contact: Paul Berube, Pres.
Desc: National investigative bureau financed by the Thoroughbred Racing Associations. Conducts character investigations of racing licenses and of applicants for positions in racing. Investigates reports of malpractice. *Type:* Association.

United States Trotting Association

750 Michigan Ave.   Ph: (614)224-2291
Columbus, OH 43215   Fax: (614)224-4575
URL: http://www.ustrotting.com
Contact: Fred J. Noe, Exec.VP.
Desc: Owners, trainers, and drivers of Standardbred horses, officials of harness racing, track officers, sponsors of fairs, and other track organizations. Works to improve the breed of trotting and pacing horses, establish rules regulating standards and registration of such horses, licensed drivers and officials, and register drivers' colors. *Type:* Association.

Horseback Riding

American Association of Sheriff Posses and Riding Clubs

7312 Monterrey Dr.   Ph: (817)451-5061
Fort Worth, TX 76112   Fax: (817)496-7808
Contact: Garland Hargis, Pres.
Desc: Federation of sheriff posses and riding clubs. Standardizes parade rules for judging; holds Seven-Man Relay, Spring Roundup, and play days; promotes keeping alive the spirit of "Old West." *Type:* Association.

American Horse Shows Association

220 E. 42nd St., Ste. 409   Ph: (212)972-2472
New York, NY 10017-5876   Fax: (212)983-7286
Contact: Katherine E. Jackson, Exec.Dir.
Desc: Individuals and horse shows. Promotes interest in equestrian sports; establishes and enforces rules governing equestrian competitions; maintains records and sanctions dates for competitions. Administers drugs and medication testing program and research. *Type:* Association.

Back Country Horsemen of America

PO Box 1367   Ph: (360)832-2461
Graham, WA 98338   Free: 800-893-5161
     Fax: (360)832-2471
Contact: Peg Greiwe, Exec.Sec.
Desc: Individuals who enjoy riding horses in wilderness and back country areas. Promotes the common sense use and enjoyment of horses in the wilderness; seeks to ensure availability of back country horse trails. *Type:* Association.

United States Combined Training Association

525 Old Waterford Rd., NW   Ph: (703)779-0440
Leesburg, VA 20176   Fax: (703)779-0550
E-mail: uscta4u@aol.com
URL: http://www.eventingusa.com
Contact: Jo Whitehouse, Exec.Dir.
Desc: Horsemen and others supporting the objectives of the USCTA. Formulates, distributes, and explains standards, rules, and regulations for the proper conduct of combined training instruction and equestrian combined training competitions. *Type:* Association.

United States Dressage Federation

PO Box 6669   Ph: (402)434-8550
Lincoln, NE 68506-0669   Fax: (402)434-8570
E-mail: usdressage@navix.net
URL: http://www.usdf.org/
Contact: Robin Gifford, Exec.Dir.
Desc: Members of local dressage organizations and other interested individuals. Promotes and encourages a high standard of accomplishment in dressage throughout the U.S., primarily through educational programs, and to improve understanding of dressage through educational clinics, forums, and seminars. (In dressage, a horse is trained to execute intricate and highly refined steps and maneuvers. Ideally, the signals from rider to horse are not visible to the spectator.). *Type:* Association.

United States Equestrian Team

Gladstone, NJ 07934   Ph: (908)234-1251
     Fax: (908)234-9417
URL: http://www.uset.org
Contact: James Hastie, Dir. Of Communications.
Desc: Contributors supporting the work of USET, which trains, equips, and finances teams of horses, riders, and drivers to represent the U.S. in the equestrian events of the Pan American and Olympic Games, World Championships, and other international competitions in dressage, endurance, show jumping, three-day eventing, and combined driving. Holds Olympic trials, and regional screening trials to select team riders and drivers; sponsors National Open Three Day, Show Jumping, Combined Driving, and Dressage events; maintains training center at Gladstone, NJ. *Type:* Association.

United States Pony Clubs

The Kentucky Horse Park
4071 Iron Works Pike   Ph: (606)254-7669
Lexington, KY 40511   Fax: (606)233-4652
E-mail: uspc@ponyclub.org
URL: http://www.ponyclub.org
Contact: Catherine M. Lerza, Exec.Dir.
Desc: Provides education in riding, mounted sports, horse management, and the care of horses and ponies. Grants certificates of proficiency. Promotes responsibility, moral judgment, leadership, and self-confidence in youth. *Type:* Association.

Horses

American Equine Association

Box 658   Ph: (973)697-9668
Newfoundland, NJ 07435   Fax: (973)697-1538
Contact: Carole Winterberger, Exec.Dir.
Desc: Individuals interested in maintaining a place for the horse in American society. Seeks to unite horsepeople. Makes available credit cards and horse-related products to members. *Type:* Association.

American Horse Shows Association— Competition Calendar

American Horse Shows Association Inc.
220 E. 42nd St.   Ph: (212)972-2472
New York, NY 10017-5806   Fax: (212)983-7286
Desc: List of about over 2,500 horse shows held throughout the year in the United States and Canada. *Type:* Directory.

American Junior Paint Horse Association

c/o American Paint Horse   Ph: (817)834-2746
  Association   Fax: (817)834-3152
PO Box 961023
Fort Worth, TX 76161-0023
URL: http://www.APHA.com.
Contact: Patty Reiber, Youth Coord.
Desc: Young men and women 18 years of age or younger. Seeks to improve and promote the American Paint Horse, a breed characterized by markings of irregular patterns of white on the horse's body. Aims to enhance the capabilities of members in the breeding, raising, and exhibition of horses; also aims to develop members' academic and leadership skills. *Type:* Association.

American Morgan Horse Association

PO Box 960   Ph: (802)985-4944
Shelburne, VT 05482   Fax: (802)985-8897
E-mail: info@morganhorse.com
URL: http://www.morganhorse.com
Contact: Jesse Smith, Exec.Dir.
Desc: Breeders and owners of purebred Morgan horses. Maintains registry showing ownership, transfers, and pedigree records. Promotes and sponsors youth programs. *Type:* Association.

American Paint Horse Association

PO Box 961023   Ph: (817)834-2742
Fort Worth, TX 76161   Fax: (817)834-3152
URL: http://www.apha.com/
Contact: Ed Roberts, Exec.Sec.
Desc: Owners of Paint horses, a breed characterized by markings or irregular patterns of white on the horse's body. Collects, records, and preserves the pedigrees of Paint horses; conducts genetic research; stimulates and regulates matters pertaining to the history, breeding, exhibition, publicity, sale, racing, or improvement of the breed. *Type:* Association.

American Quarter Horse Association

1600 Quarter Horse Dr.   Ph: (806)376-4811
Amarillo, TX 79104   Fax: (806)349-6409
E-mail: aqhamail@aqha.org
URL: http://www.aqha.com
Contact: Bill Brewer, Exec.VP.
Desc: Breeders, owners, trainers, and others interested in the American Quarter Horse. *Type:* Association.

American Quarter Horse Youth Association

1600 Quarter Horse Dr.   Ph: (806)376-4888
PO Box 200   Fax: (806)349-6409
Amarillo, TX 79168
URL: http://www.aqha.com

Contact: Robin Devin, Dir. of Youth Activities.

Desc: Youth division of the American Quarter Horse Association. Quarter horse enthusiasts 18 years old and younger. Promotes expanded involvement between young people and the quarter horse. *Type:* Association.

American Saddlebred Horse Association—Membership Directory

American Saddlebred Horse Association
4093 Iron Works Pike   Ph: (606)259-2742
Lexington, KY 40511   Fax: (606)259-1628
E-mail: asha@saddlebred.net
Contact: Lynn Weatherman, Editor.
Desc: Members, charter clubs, and breeder's futurities of the American Saddlebred Horse Association, bylaws, rules. *Type:* Directory.

Appaloosa Horse Club

5070 Hwy. 8 West   Ph: (208)882-5578
Moscow, ID 83843   Fax: (208)882-8150
E-mail: aphc@appaloosa.com
URL: http://www.appaloosa.com
Contact: Roger Klamfoth, CEO.
Desc: Works to promote and preserve Appaloosa breed. Serves as a registry; sets official standards and establishes guidelines for acceptance and classification for the breed; issues and records certificates of registration. Sponsors four trail rides per year. *Type:* Association.

Arabian Horse Registry of America

12000 Zuni St.   Ph: (303)450-4748
Westminster, CO 80234
URL: http://www.theregistry.org
Contact: Ralph F. Clark, Resident Officer.
Desc: Maintains purebred Arabian registry. *Type:* Association.

Denver Catholic Register

Arch Bishop Newspaper
200 Josephine St.   Ph: (303)388-4411
Denver, CO 80206-4710   Fax: (303)321-3693
Contact: Charlene Scott, Editor; J. Francis Stafford, Archbi, Publisher; Frank Vecchiarelli, Advertising Dir.
Desc: Catholic newspaper (tabloid). *Type:* Periodical.

Equus

Primedia Equine Group
656 Quince Orchard Rd., Ste.   Ph: (301)977-3900
600   Fax: (301)990-9015
Gaithersburg, MD 20878
E-mail: dletters@aol.com; equuslts@aol.com.
Contact: Ami Shinitzky, Editor and Publisher; Susan Harding, Publisher.
Desc: Magazine featuring health, care, and understanding of horses. *Type:* Periodical.

Horses—National and Horse Show Service Directory

Horses Magazine
21 Greenview
Carlsbad, CA 92009
Contact: John Quirk, Editor.
Desc: About 130 horse stables, farms, trainers, and riding schools and clubs; 40 suppliers of services to horses shows, including announcers, course designers, managers, photographers, and transporters. *Type:* Directory.

International Arabian Horse Association

10805 E. Bethany Dr.   Ph: (303)450-4500
Aurora, CO 80014-2605   Fax: (303)696-4599
URL: http://www.iaha.com
Contact: Carol Alm, Exec.VP.

Desc: Federation of state/local (270) and regional (18) associations representing 28,000 Arabian horse owners, breeders, and enthusiasts. Maintains Half-Arabian and Anglo-Arabian registries and promotes the entire Arabian breed. Maintains show records of Arabian horse placings. *Type:* Association.

Missouri Fox Trotting Horse Breed Association

PO Box 1027   Ph: (417)683-2468
Ava, MO 65608   Fax: (417)683-6144
E-mail: foxtrot@goin.missouri.org
URL: http://www.MFTHBA.com
Contact: Tom Owen, Pres.
Desc: Promoters, breeders, trainers, and owners of Missouri fox trotting horses. Seeks to gain acceptance of the Missouri fox trotting horse as a family horse. Sponsors sales, trail rides, and promotional activities. *Type:* Association.

National Cutting Horse Association

4704 Hwy. 377 S.   Ph: (817)244-6188
Fort Worth, TX 76116-8805   Fax: (817)244-2015
E-mail: ncha@startext.net
URL: http://www.nchacutting.com
Contact: Henry Conley, Exec.Dir.
Desc: Persons interested in the cutting horse (a saddle horse used to separate cattle from a herd). Promotes exhibition and breeding activities. *Type:* Association.

Palomino Horse Breeders of America

15253 E. Skelly Dr.   Ph: (918)438-1234
Tulsa, OK 74116-2637   Fax: (918)438-1232
E-mail: yellahrses@aol.com
URL: http://www.palominohba.com
Contact: Cindy Chilton, Gen.Mgr.
Desc: Owners, breeders, and exhibitors of purebred Palomino horses. Maintains registry of pedigrees. *Type:* Association.

Peruvian Paso Horse Registry of North America

3077 Wiljan Ct., Ste. A   Ph: (707)579-4394
Santa Rosa, CA 95407
E-mail: info@pphrna.org
URL: http://www.pphrna.org
Contact: Janetta Michael, Exec.Dir.
Desc: Breeders and owners of Peruvian Paso horses; others interested in the breed. Seeks to: aid and encourage traditional breeding, training, and showing of the Peruvian Paso; maintain an authentic registry for purebred Peruvian Pasos; institute and standardize rules for judging; promote the uniqueness of the Peruvian Paso. *Type:* Association.

Pinto Horse Association of America

1900 Samuels Ave.   Ph: (817)336-7842
Fort Worth, TX 76102   Fax: (817)336-7416
URL: http://www.pinto.org
Contact: Joe E. Grissom, Exec.Mgr.
Desc: Persons interested in the promotion and improvement of the Pinto breed of horses. Maintains registry. Offers Register of Merit Programs including: ROM; Certificate of Achievement; Certificate of Ability; Championship; Supreme Champion. *Type:* Association.

The Quarter Horse Journal

American Quarter Horse Association
1600 Quarter Horse Dr.   Ph: (806)376-4888
PO Box 32470   Free: 800-291-7323
Amarillo, TX 79120   Fax: (806)349-6400
E-mail: aqhajrnl@arn.net.
Contact: Jim Jennings, AQHA Dir. of Publications; Doug Hayes, Advertising Dir., (806)376-1284; Lesli Groves, Editor, (806)376-4888.
Desc: Magazine promoting advancement and improvement of the breeding and performance of the American Quarter Horse. *Type:* Periodical.

Tennessee Walking Horse Breeders' and Exhibitors' Association

PO Box 286   Ph: (615)359-1574
Lewisburg, TN 37091   Free: 800-359-1574
                             Fax: (615)359-2539
URL: http://www.twhbea.com
Contact: Bob Cherry, Exec.Dir.
Desc: Owners, breeders, trainers, exhibitors, and others interested in the Tennessee Walking horse. Maintains registry of pedigrees and ownership. Operates speakers' bureau. *Type:* Association.

Horticulture

AABGA Newsletter

American Association of Botanical Gardens and Arboreta (AABGA)
351 Longwood Rd.   Ph: (610)925-2500
Kennett Square, PA 19348   Fax: (610)925-2700
E-mail: aahga@aol.com
Contact: Victoria Mattern, Editor.
Desc: Covers news and issues affecting North American botanical gardens and arboreta, their professional staffs and their work. Recurring features include profiles of gardens, news of members, book reviews, a calendar of events, notices of publications and videos, job listings, and funding news. *Type:* Newsletter.

AgInfo

University of Arizona - College of Agriculture
Forbes Bldg., Rm. 306   Ph: (520)621-7621
Tucson, AZ 85721-0036   Fax: (520)621-7196
E-mail: webmaster@ag.arizona.edu
URL: http://ag.arizona.edu/
Desc: AgInfo contains a wealth of information about the University of Arizona's College of Agriculture. From research details and staff data to departmental and publications information, this site contains anything a prospective student needs to know about this institute of higher learning. *Type:* Database.

American Conifer Society—Bulletin

American Conifer Society
PO Box 360   Ph: (804)984-3660
Keswick, VA 22947-0360   Fax: (804)984-3660
Contact: Charlene Harris, ED.
Desc: Describes conifers, collections, events. *Type:* Newsletter.

American Rhododendron Society—Membership List

American Rhododendron Society
11 Pinecrest Dr.   Ph: (707)725-3043
Fortuna, CA 95540   Fax: (707)725-1217
E-mail: deedaneri@aol.com.
URL: http://www.rhodedendron.org.
Contact: Sonja Nelson, Editor, snelson@cnw.com.
Desc: About 6,000 gardeners of rhododendron plants (azaleas and heather), and rhododendron nurseries that serve local chapters; members are both hobbyists and horticulturists. *Type:* Directory.

American Society for Horticultural Science

600 Cameron St.   Ph: (703)836-4606
Alexandria, VA 22314-2562   Fax: (703)836-2024
E-mail: ashs@ashs.org
Contact: Michael W. Neff, Exec.Mgt. Team Leader.
Desc: Educators and government workers engaged in research, teaching, or extension work in horticultural science; firms, associations, and others interested in horticulture. Promotes and encourages interest in scientific research and education in horticulture. *Type:* Association.

Arbor Day

National Arbor Day Foundation
100 Arbor Ave.
Nebraska City, NE 68410
Ph: (402)474-5655
Fax: (402)474-0820
URL: http://www.arborday.org.

Contact: John Rosenow, Editor.

Desc: Promotes trees and the tree-related activities of the Foundation and other groups and individuals nationwide. Profiles specific trees and reports on the educational efforts of the Foundation. *Type:* Newsletter.

Arboriculture Consultant

American Society of Consulting Arborists
15245 Shady Grove Rd., Ste. 130
Rockville, MD 20850-3222
Ph: (301)947-0483
Fax: (301)990-9771
E-mail: asca@mgmt.sol.com

Contact: Beth W. Palys, Exec. Dir.; Anne Trone, Director.

Desc: Contains information on trees. *Type:* Newsletter.

The Boxwood Bulletin

American Boxwood Society
134 Methodist Church Ln.
West Augusta, VA 24485
Ph: (540)939-4646

Contact: John S. McCarthy, Editor.

Desc: Promotes the care and enjoyment of the boxwood shrub, "man's oldest garden ornamental," with items on its planting, winter protection, nurture, varieties, propagation, pruning, and history. Recurring features include scientific articles reprinted from recognized sources. *Type:* Newsletter.

Business Management Newsletter

Turfgrass Producers International
1855 A Hicks Rd.
Rolling Meadows, IL 60008-1215
Ph: (847)705-9898
Free: 800-405-8873
Fax: (847)705-8347
E-mail: turf-grass@msn.com

Contact: Thomas G. Ford, Editor.

Desc: Considers the industry involving sod producers, equipment manufacturers, and sod suppliers with a specific emphasis on business and managerial perspectives. Promotes, from an administrative angle, the Association's desire to advance efficient and economical production of quality sod, to develop standards within the industry, and to increase public awareness of the industry. *Type:* Newsletter.

California Ornamental Crops Report

Federal-State Market News
630 Sansome St., Rm. 727
San Francisco, CA 94111
Ph: (415)705-1300
Fax: (415)705-1301

Contact: Fred Teensma, Editor.

Desc: Covers national wholesale markets, local auctions, and shipping information for cut flowers in the state of California. *Type:* Newsletter.

Dawes Arboretum Newsletter

Dawes Arboretum
7770 Jacksontown Rd. SE
Newark, OH 43055
Ph: (740)323-2355
Free: 800-443-2937
Fax: (740)323-4058

Contact: Luke E. Messinger, Editor, lemessinger@ee.net.

Desc: Publishes news of the Arboretum and its programs, including hikes, classes, and workshops. Comments on horticulture, nature, and history as they apply to the Arboretum. *Type:* Newsletter.

Garden Clippings Horticulture Newsletter

UMASS Extension
University of Massachusetts
French Hall
Amherst, MA 01003-0099
Ph: (508)831-1223
Fax: (508)831-0120

Contact: Kathleen M. Carroll, Editor, kcarroll@umext.umass.edu.

Desc: Offers advice on lawn and garden care, covering such areas as weeding, tilling, plant selection, and pests. Recurring features include research updates, a garden calendar, and notices of publications available. *Type:* Newsletter.

Green World News

Bonsai & Orchid Association
26 Pine St.
Dover, DE 19901
Ph: (302)736-6781
Fax: (302)736-6763

Desc: Updates members of the bonsai and orchid industry on the latest technical information in the field. Reviews new products, growing methods, pertinent regulations, and industry trends. *Type:* Newsletter.

Grow Letter

SunPorch Structures, Inc.
495 Post Rd. E
Westport, CT 06880
Ph: (203)454-0040
Fax: (203)454-0020

Contact: Fred Schwartz, Editor.

Desc: Devotes articles to growing and/or cultivation of flowers, vegetables, and succulents. Recurring features include letters to the editor, news of research, news of educational opportunities, book reviews, and notices of publications available. *Type:* Newsletter.

The Grower

Wholesale Nursery Growers of America
1250 I St. NW, Ste. 500
Washington, DC 20005
Ph: (202)789-2900
Fax: (202)789-1893
URL: http://www.anla.org.

Contact: Craig Regelbrugge, Editor.

Desc: Reports news and information regarding the wholesale nursery industry. *Type:* Newsletter.

Heather News

North American Heather Society
c/o Karla Lortz
502 E. Haskell Hill Rd.
Shelton, WA 98584
Ph: (360)427-5318
Fax: (360)427-5318
E-mail: handh@heathsandheathers.com

Contact: Donald Mackay, Editor, (914)769-6553, fax: (914)741-2833, lemackay@aol.com.

Desc: Provides information and articles on heather. *Type:* Newsletter.

Hort News

UMASS Extension
University of Massachusetts
French Hall
Amherst, MA 01003-0099
Ph: (508)831-1223
Fax: (508)831-0120

Contact: Kathleen M. Carroll, Editor.

Desc: Contains horticultural information. *Type:* Newsletter.

Horticultural Abstracts

CAB International
CABI Publishing
10 E. 40th St., Ste. 3203
New York, NY 10016
Ph: (212)481-7018
E-mail: cabi-nao@cabi.org
URL: http://www.cabi.org

Desc: Contains citations, with abstracts, to worldwide journal articles and other published literature relating to horticulture. Covers temperate tree fruits and nuts, small fruits, viticulture, vegetables (temperate, tropical, and greenhouse), ornamental plants, minor industrial crops, and tropical and subtropical fruit and plantation crops. *Type:* Database.

Inside

National Sunflower Association
4023 State St.
Bismarck, ND 58501
Ph: (701)328-5105
Free: 888-718-7033
Fax: (701)328-5101

Contact: Larry Kleingartner, Editor.

Desc: Provides information on the sunflower industry. Carries articles on sunflower production, research, markets, and education. *Type:* Newsletter.

International Society of Arboriculture

PO Box 3129
Champaign, IL 61826-3129
Ph: (217)355-9411
Fax: (217)355-9516
E-mail: isa@isa-arbor.com
URL: http://www.ag.uiuc.edu/~isa/

Contact: William P. Kruidener, Exec.Dir.

Desc: Individuals engaged in commercial, municipal, and utility arboriculture; city, state, and national government employees; municipal and commercial arborists; others interested in shade tree welfare. Disseminates information on the care and preservation of shade and ornamental trees. Supports research projects at educational institutions. *Type:* Association.

Landscape Nursery Council

1689 Glens Dr.
Florence, KY 41042
Ph: (606)525-1809
Fax: (606)525-9114

Contact: Steve Wills, Exec.Dir.

Desc: Encourages the exchange of information. *Type:* Association.

Magnolia Magazine

Magnolia Society, Inc.
6616 81st St.
Cabin John, MD 20818
Ph: (301)320-4296
Fax: (301)320-4296
URL: http://www.tallahassee.net/~magnolia.

Contact: Larry W. Langford, Editor.

Desc: Discusses aspects of magnolia culture. Covers hybridization, seed collection, storing, mailing, genetics, the search for new species abroad, and similar subjects. *Type:* Newsletter.

Minnesota Landscape Arboretum News

Minnesota Landscape Arboretum Foundation
3675 Arboretum Dr.
PO Box 39
Chanhassen, MN 55317-0039
Ph: (612)443-2460

Contact: Maria Klein, Editor, maria@arboretum.umn.edu; klein023@gold.tc.umn.edu.

Desc: Focuses on educational activities, cultural events, and classes at the Arboretum. Carries items on horticultural research, gardening advice, volunteer opportunities, gift ideas, and tours. *Type:* Newsletter.

Missouri Botanical Garden Bulletin

Missouri Botanical Garden
PO Box 299
St. Louis, MO 63166
Ph: (314)577-5123
Fax: (314)577-9598

Contact: Susan W. Caine, Editor, scaine@lehmann.mobot.org.

Desc: Discusses horticulture, botanical research, gardening, environmental concerns, science education, economic plants, and Garden events. Functions as an extension of the Garden, which is concerned with research and education. *Type:* Newsletter.

NAA Reporter

National Arborist Association, Inc.
PO Box 1094
Amherst, NH 03031
Ph: (603)673-3311
Free: 800-733-2622
Fax: (603)672-2613
E-mail: narbor1@jlc.net

Contact: Peter Gerstenberger, Editor.

Desc: Concerned with the profession of arboriculture. *Type:* Newsletter.

National Arborist Association

The Meeting Place Mall   Ph: (603)673-3311
Rte. 101, PO Box 1094   Fax: (603)672-2613
Amherst, NH 03031
E-mail: 76142.463@compuserve.com
URL: http://www.natlarb.com
Contact: Amelia Reinert, Deputy Exec.Dir.
Desc: Commercial tree service companies. Works to improve arboricultural practices and inform the public of the need for preservation and proper care of shade trees. Conducts specialized education programs. *Type:* Association.

Native Plants

Lady Bird Johnson Wildflower Center
4801 La Crosse Ave.   Ph: (512)292-4200
Austin, TX 78739   Fax: (512)292-4627
E-mail: wildflower@wildflower.org
Contact: Karen Bassett, Editor/Writer, bassett@wildflower.org.
Desc: Educates people about the environmental necessity, economic value, and natural beauty of native plants. Recurring features include news of national events, projects, and developments, conservation and preservation of native plants, and individuals who champion native plants. *Type:* Newsletter.

New England Wild Flower

New England Wild Flower Society (NEWFS)
Garden in the Woods   Ph: (508)877-7630
180 Hemenway Rd.   Fax: (508)877-3658
Framingham, MA 01701
E-mail: newfs@newfs.org
URL: http://www.newfs.org.
Contact: Sarah Blair Shonbrun, Editor, shonbrun@newfs.org.
Desc: Contains news of the New England Wild Flower Society, including conservation of native New England plants, plant conservation research, general plant conservation, horticulture, especially native plant gardening and landscaping with native plants. Also includes a listing of the society's catalogue of seasonal courses for adults and children in conservation, gardening, field trips, garden tours, and nature-related arts and crafts. *Type:* Newsletter.

New Horizons

Horticultural Research Institute
1250 I St. NW, Ste. 500   Ph: (202)789-2900
Washington, DC 20005   Fax: (202)789-1893
Contact: Ashby P. Ruden, Editor, aruden@anla.org.
Desc: Explores research of the science and art of nursery, retail garden center, and landscape plant production, marketing, and care. *Type:* Newsletter.

North American Lily Society—Quarterly Bulletin

North American Lily Society, Inc.
PO Box 272   Ph: (507)451-2170
Owatonna, MN 55060   Fax: (507)455-0087
E-mail: gilman@ll.net
Contact: Mary Hoffman, Editor.
Desc: Carries information on the activities of the Society and articles about lilies. *Type:* Newsletter.

Ornamental Crops National Market Trends

Federal-State Market News
630 Sansome St., Rm. 727   Ph: (415)705-1300
San Francisco, CA 94111   Fax: (415)705-1301
Contact: Fred Teensma, Editor.
Desc: Covers regional production, wholesale markets, and imports of cut flowers. *Type:* Newsletter.

Ornamental Horticulture

CAB International
CABI Publishing
10 E. 40th St., Ste. 3203   Ph: (212)481-7018
New York, NY 10016
E-mail: cabi-nao@cabi.org
URL: http://www.cabi.org
Contact: Sue Hill, Product Manager, Crop Production and Natural Resources, s.hill@cabi.org.
Desc: Contains citations, with abstracts, to current periodical and other published literature related to ornamental horticulture for gardens and public parks. Corresponds to Ornamental Horticulture and in part to the online CAB ABSTRACTS database and the HORTCD and CAB ABSTRACTS CD-ROM products. *Type:* Database.

The Plant Press

Arizona Native Plant Society
Box 41206, Sun Sta.
Tucson, AZ 85717
Contact: Karen Enyedy Breunig, Editor.
Desc: Contains on about desert plants and news of the Society. Recurring features include book reviews. *Type:* Newsletter.

Plants & Gardens News

Brooklyn Botanic Garden
1000 Washington Ave.   Ph: (718)622-4433
Brooklyn, NY 11225   Fax: (718)622-7839
Contact: Elizabeth McGowan, Editor.
Desc: Discusses gardening, planting tips, news of gardening products, sources for new seeds and plants, and book reviews. Recurring features include plantprofile, news of research, and fun for kids. *Type:* Newsletter.

Review of Plant Pathology

CAB International
CABI Publishing
10 E. 40th St., Ste. 3203   Ph: (212)481-7018
New York, NY 10016
E-mail: cabi-nao@cabi.org
URL: http://www.cabi.org
Desc: Contains citations, with abstracts, to current periodical and other published literature relating to plant pathology, including diseases of crop plants, ornamental plants, and forest trees caused by fungi, bacteria, viruses, mycoplasma-like organisms and nonparasitic factors and their control; fungicides and antibiotics in relation to the control of plant diseases; and general and systematic mycology as it refers to fungi of agricultural importance. Corresponds to Review of Plant Pathology and in part to the online CAB ABSTRACTS and CAB PLANT PROTECTION databases and the CAB ABSTRACTS on CD-ROM and CABPESTCD products. *Type:* Database.

San Francisco Wholesale Ornamental Crops Report

Federal-State Market News
630 Sansome St., Rm. 727   Ph: (415)705-1300
San Francisco, CA 94111   Fax: (415)705-1301
Contact: Fred Teensma, Editor.
Desc: Reports price information for San Francisco's wholesale flower market. Provides prices from the same date a year previously for selected cut flowers. *Type:* Newsletter.

Seasons

Morris Arboretum of the University of Pennsylvania
9414 Meadowbrook Ave.   Ph: (215)247-5777
Philadelphia, PA 19118   Fax: (215)248-4439
Contact: Andrea D'Asaro, Editor, kms@pobox.upenn.edu.
Desc: Describes Arboretum programs and activities and provides popular horticultural and botanical information. Carries articles on events or topics related to the display, education, and research functions of the Morris Arboretum. *Type:* Newsletter.

The Sego Lily

Utah Native Plant Society
3631 S. Carolyn St.   Ph: (801)581-5322
Salt Lake City, UT 84106
Contact: Marjorie Stolhand, Editor.
Desc: Promotes knowledge and appreciation of native Utah flora. Recurring features include editorials, news of research, a calendar of events, news of members, book reviews, and columns titled Wildflower Watch, Wildflower Photography, and Native Plants in Home Landscaping. *Type:* Newsletter.

The Shade Tree

New Jersey Shade Tree Foundation
Blake Hall   Ph: (732)246-3210
PO Box 231   Fax: (732)246-3210
New Brunswick, NJ 08903
Contact: Richard Wolowicz, Editor.
Desc: Discusses community environment programs, the impact of chemicals used on vegetation, and news of members. Recurring features include a column titled Secretary's Corner. *Type:* Newsletter.

Soil-Plant Analysts

Soil and Plant Analysis Council, Inc.
621 Rose St.
Lincoln, NE 68502-2040
E-mail: spcouncil@aol.com
Contact: J. Benton Jones, Jr., Editor.
Desc: Provides a clearinghouse of information on soil testing and plant analysis for individuals from industry, public institutions, and independent laboratories. Advises on proposed federal legislation and regulations topics. *Type:* Newsletter.

Tree City USA Bulletin

National Arbor Day Foundation
100 Arbor Ave.   Ph: (402)474-5655
Nebraska City, NE 68410   Fax: (402)474-0820
Contact: John E. Rosenow, Publisher; James R. Fazio, Editor.
Desc: Provides tree planting and care instructions and information. *Type:* Newsletter.

The Treeworker

National Arborist Association, Inc.
PO Box 1094   Ph: (603)673-3311
Amherst, NH 03031   Free: 800-733-2622
    Fax: (603)672-2613
E-mail: narbor1@jlc.net
Contact: Robert Rouse, Editor.
Desc: Provides practical information on worker safety, tree care techniques, skills development, and general knowledge of trees. *Type:* Newsletter.

Turf News

Turfgrass Producers International
1855 A Hicks Rd.   Ph: (847)705-9898
Rolling Meadows, IL 60008-   Free: 800-405-8873
1215   Fax: (847)705-8347
E-mail: turf-grass@msn.com
Contact: Wendell Mathews, Editor.
Desc: Publishes information in support of the Association's efforts to encourage the efficient economical production of quality sod, promote an increased awareness of standards within the industry, and broaden public awareness. Recurring features include news of members, news of research, news of Association events and educational programs, and specific industry news of interest. *Type:* Newsletter.

Weed Control Manual

Meister Publishing Co.
37733 Euclid Ave. Ph: (440)942-2000
Willoughby, OH 44094 Free: 800-572-7740
 Fax: (440)942-0662
E-mail: info@meisternet.com; wcm_edit@meisterpubl.
com.
URL: http://www.meisterpro.com.
Contact: Charlotte Sine, Editor; Laurie Moses, Editor.
Desc: List of herbicides registered for use in the U.S. Information is listed by crop. *Type:* Directory.

Hospital

American College of Healthcare Executives

1 N. Franklin, Ste. 1700 Ph: (312)424-2800
Chicago, IL 60606-3491 Fax: (312)424-0023
E-mail: geninfo@ache.org
URL: http://www.ache.org
Contact: Thomas C. Dolan, Ph.D., Pres.

Desc: Healthcare executives. Conducts credentialing and educational programs and an annual Congress on Healthcare Management. Conducts, as well ground-breaking research and career development and public policy programs. *Type:* Association.

American Hospital Association

1 N. Franklin, Ste. 27 Ph: (312)422-3000
Chicago, IL 60606 Fax: (312)422-4519
URL: http://www.aha.org
Contact: Richard J. Davidson, Ph.D., Pres.

Desc: Health care provider organizations. Seeks to advance the health of individuals and communities. Leads, represents, and serves health care provider organizations that are accountable to the community and committed to health improvement. *Type:* Association.

American Society for Healthcare Engineering of the American Hospital Association

American Hospital Association
One N. Franklin, Ste. 2700 Ph: (312)422-3800
Chicago, IL 60606 Fax: (312)422-4571
E-mail: dporter@ashe.org
URL: http://www.ashe.org
Contact: Joseph J. Martori, Exec.Dir.

Desc: Hospital engineers, facilities managers, directors of buildings and grounds, assistant administrators, directors of maintenance, directors of clinical engineering, design and construction professionals, and safety officers. Works to: promote better patient care by encouraging and assisting members to develop their knowledge and increase their competence in the field of facilities management; cooperate with hospitals and allied associations in matters pertaining to facilities management; bring about closer cooperation among members; provide a medium for interchange of material relative to facilities management. Maintains library; conducts educational programs. *Type:* Association.

Association for Healthcare Philanthropy

313 Park Ave., Ste. 400 Ph: (703)532-6243
Falls Church, VA 22046 Fax: (703)532-7170
E-mail: ahp@go-ahp.org
URL: http://www.go-ahp.org
Contact: Dr. William C. McGinly, Pres.,CEO.

Desc: Persons employed by healthcare organizations in the field of healthcare resource development and fundraising; hospital administrators and trustees; hospitals; interested individuals. Purposes are to create a cohesive body of healthcare development executives to advance the interests and knowledge of healthcare fund development; to encourage and stimulate better understanding of healthcare needs; to accomplish common goals through an exchange of ideas and information. Conducts educational programs. *Type:* Association.

Association for Healthcare Resource and Materials Management

American Hospital Association
1 N. Franklin Ph: (312)422-3840
Chicago, IL 60606 Fax: (312)422-4573
E-mail: awharff1@aha.org
Contact: Albert Sunseri, Exec.Dir.

Desc: Individuals active in the field of purchasing, inventory and distribution, and materials management as performed in hospitals, related patient care institutions, or government and voluntary health organizations, and who are employed by an organization eligible for institutional membership in the American Hospital Association; associate members are individuals active in the areas of health care supply manufacturing, distributing, and consulting. Purposes are to: assist members with their responsibilities; provide access to the latest ideas, methods, developments, information, and techniques in the field of hospital purchasing and materials management; establish associations with others in the profession; provide recognition in the profession through participation in policy-making; provide a link with the AHA. Conducts certification program in health care management. *Type:* Association.

Catholic Health Association of the United States

4455 Woodson Rd. Ph: (314)427-2500
St. Louis, MO 63134-3797 Fax: (314)427-0029
E-mail: mplace@chausa.org
URL: http://www.chausa.org
Contact: Rev. Michael D. Place, Pres. & CEO.

Desc: Catholic hospitals, health care facilities, religious orders, health care systems, and extended care facilities. Aims to participate in the life of the Church by advancing the healthcare ministry and assert leadership within the Church and society through programs of advocacy, facilitation, and education. *Type:* Association.

The Connecticut Hospice Newsletter

The Connecticut Hospice, Inc.
61 Burban Dr. Ph: (203)481-6231
Branford, CT 06405 Free: 800-846-7742
 Fax: (203)483-9539
E-mail: cthospc@interserv.com
URL: http://www.hospice.com.
Contact: Rev. John Abbott, Editor; Althea B. Porcher, Editor.

Desc: Covers the "interdisciplinary team approach" to caring for patients and families coping with a terminal illness (team members include individuals with expertise in arts, bereavement, pastoral care, nursing, medicine, pharmacy, as well as volunteers). Recurring features include interviews, a calendar of events, and news of educational opportunities. *Type:* Newsletter.

Downtown Update

New York Downtown Hospital
170 William St.
New York, NY 10038-2649
Desc: Covers the news of New York Downtown Hospital. Provides information on new procedures and programs, as well as new hires and employee promotions. *Type:* Newsletter.

Federation of American Health Systems

1405 N. Pierce, No. 311 Ph: (501)661-9555
Little Rock, AR 72217-8708 Fax: (501)663-4903
URL: http://www.fahs.com
Contact: Thomas A. Scully, Pres.

Desc: Privately- or investor-owned (for-profit) hospitals. *Type:* Association.

Floating Hospital

Pier 11 Wall at South St. Ph: (212)514-7440
New York, NY 10005 Fax: (212)785-0290
Contact: Kathleen Lopez, Exec.Dir.

Desc: Provides medical, dental and health education services. Programs occur within a 4-deck ship, docked in the East River at Wall Street. Provides health services to homeless children and their families, children in kinship foster care and their kinship families, and adolescents who engage in high risk behaviors. *Type:* Association.

Friend to Friend

St. Mary's Hospital
Development Office
1200 W. Walnut St. Ph: (501)636-0200
Rogers, AR 72756
Contact: Michael Packnett, President.

Desc: Provides information about St. Mary's Hospital in Rogers, Arkansas. *Type:* Newsletter.

Healthcare Association of New York State

74 N. Pearl St. Ph: (518)431-7732
Albany, NY 12207 Fax: (518)431-7915
E-mail: mwurth@hanys.org
URL: http://www.hanys.org
Contact: Maryjane Worth, Exec.Dir.

Desc: Nonprofit, voluntary, and public hospitals, nursing facilities, home health agencies, hospice and adult day care programs, and other related health care facilities. Acts as key advocate with the state and federal governments for health facilities. *Type:* Association.

Healthcare Information and Management Systems Society

230 E. Ohio St., Ste. 500 Ph: (312)664-4467
Chicago, IL 60611-3269 Fax: (312)664-6143
E-mail: himss@himss.org
URL: http://www.himss.org/
Contact: John A. Page, Exec.Dir.

Desc: Persons who, by education and/or appropriate experience, are professionally qualified to engage in the analysis, design, and operation of health care information systems, management engineering, telecommunications, and clinical systems professions. Provides leadership in health care for the management of systems, information, and change, while striving for high quality, efficient and effective patient care through analysis and technology implementation. Maintains speakers' bureau. *Type:* Association.

Healthcare PR and Marketing News

Phillips Business Information, Inc.
1201 Seven Locks Rd., Ste. 300 Ph: (301)340-1520
Potomac, MD 20854 Free: 888-707-5809
 Fax: (301)340-3847
E-mail: clientservices.pbi@phillips.com
Contact: Sharmi Banik, Editor.

Desc: Concerned with market communications, target-audience education, community relations, employee communications, public affairs, crisis management, investor relations, and corporate communications of health care Industry. *Type:* Newsletter.

Healthcare Resource & Materials Management News

Association for Healthcare Resource & Materials Management (AHRMM)
American Hospital Association (AHA)
One N. Franklin Ph: (312)422-3840
Chicago, IL 60606 Fax: (312)422-4573
E-mail: ahrmm@aha.org; dspaag1@aha.org.
URL: http://www.ahrmm.org.
Contact: Deborah Sprindzunas, Editor, dsprind1@aha.
org.

Desc: Provides information about hospital purchasing and materials management. Includes reviews of educational programs, current legal and legislative problems, and new materials management techniques. *Type:* Newsletter.

Healthcare Risk Management

American Health Consultants, Inc.
3525 Piedmont Rd., Bldg. 6,   Ph: (404)262-7436
   Ste. 400   Free: 800-688-2421
Atlanta, GA 30305   Fax: (404)262-7837
E-mail: customerservice@ahcpub.com
Contact: Greg Freeman, Editor.

Desc: Analyzes specific legal cases and trends relevant to healthcare liability. Discusses malpractice, liability for patients, staff and visitor injury, injury prevention, biomedical engineering, and medical staff credentials. *Type:* Newsletter.

Herman Hospital

Department of Research

John Freedman Bldg., G-700   Ph: (713)500-5828
PO Box 20036   Fax: (713)500-5830
Houston, TX 77225
Contact: Paula Knudson, Exec.Off.

Desc: Evaluates and supervises the quality and conduct of all research involving patients, property, personnel, and facilities of the Hospital. Collaborates with graduate programs on multidisciplinary studies and projects. *Type:* Research center.

Hospice Foundation of America

777 17th St., No. 401   Free: 800-854-3402
Miami Beach, FL 33139   Fax: (305)538-0092
E-mail: hfa@hospicefoundation.org
URL: http://www.hospicefoundation.org
Contact: David Abrams, Senior V.Pres.

Desc: Works to promote the philosophy and application of hospice care for terminally ill people and improve the American health system. *Type:* Association.

Hospice Management Advisor

American Health Consultants, Inc.
3525 Piedmont Rd., Bldg. 6,   Ph: (404)262-7436
   Ste. 400   Free: 800-688-2421
Atlanta, GA 30305   Fax: (404)262-7837
E-mail: customerservice@ahcpub.com
Contact: Jan Pogue, Managing Editor.

Desc: Covers cost management, quality assurance, infection control, and risk management issues in relation to hospices. Recurring features include interviews and news of research. *Type:* Newsletter.

Hospital Employee Health

American Health Consultants, Inc.
3525 Piedmont Rd., Bldg. 6,   Ph: (404)262-7436
   Ste. 400   Free: 800-688-2421
Atlanta, GA 30305   Fax: (404)262-7837
E-mail: customerservice@ahcpub.com
Contact: Barric S. Rissman, Editor; Coles McKagen, Managing Editor.

Desc: Provides information on how to protect hospital employees from work-related hazards. Discusses prevention, treatment, detection, and the degree of risk, as well as government regulations and employee's legal rights. *Type:* Newsletter.

The Hospital and Healthsystem Association of Pennsylvania(HA)

4750 Lindle Rd.   Ph: (717)564-9200
PO Box 8600   Fax: (717)561-5333
Harrisburg, PA 17105-8600
URL: http://www.hap2000.org
Contact: Carolyn F. Scanlan, Pres. & CEO.

Desc: Approved or licensed hospitals. Promotes the provision of quality health care and related services in a cost-effective manner. *Type:* Association.

Hospital Materials Management

The Business Word
5350 S. Roslyn St., Ste. 400   Ph: (303)967-0130
Englewood, CO 80111-2125   Free: 800-328-3211
    Fax: (303)290-9025
Contact: Paula DeJohn, Editor.

Desc: Covers issues surrounding price and purchasing patterns in U.S. hospitals. *Type:* Newsletter.

Hospital Outlook

Federation of American Health Systems
1405 N. Pierce St., Ste. 311   Ph: (501)661-9555
Little Rock, AR 72207   Fax: (501)663-4903
Contact: Craig Havighurst, Editor.

Desc: Focuses on administrative and financial topics of interest to privately-owned or investor-owned hospitals. Carries legislative updates and news of developments in the industry. *Type:* Newsletter.

Hospital Practice

McGraw-Hill Healthcare Information Group
4530 W. 77th St.   Ph: (612)835-3222
Minneapolis, MN 55435   Fax: (612)835-3460
URL: http://www.hosppract.com.
Contact: Janis Cohen, VP/Publisher, (212)512-2125; Gretchen Drasner, Senior Mktg. Mgr., (612)832-7877; M. James Dougherty, Group Vice President, (612)832-7876; Lee Powers, Exec. Editor, (612)832-7839; Nancy Souza, Director of Sales, (212)512-3492; Rita Beale, Vice President of Sales, (212)512-3634; Monica Brent, Acct. Mgr., (312)616-3308; Brett Talbott, Mktg. Assoc., btalbott@mcgraw-hill.com.

Desc: Magazine providing information on developments and problem areas in medicine and clinical research. Emphasizes application of medical knowledge to the direct care of patients. *Type:* Periodical.

Hospital Research and Educational Trust

1 N. Franklin   Ph: (312)422-2600
Chicago, IL 60606   Fax: (312)422-4568
E-mail: dbohr1@aha.org
Contact: Deborah Bohr, VP.

Desc: Encourages and engages in educational, research, and demonstration activities to improve the management of hospital and health services. *Type:* Association.

Joint Commission on Accreditation of Healthcare Organizations

1 Renaissance Blvd.   Ph: (630)792-5889
Oakbrook Terrace, IL 60181   Fax: (630)792-5005
E-mail: cmyers@jcaho.org
URL: http://www.jcaho.org
Contact: Dennis S. O'Leary, M.D., Pres.

Desc: Strives to improve the quality of care provided to the public through the provision of health care accreditation and related services that support performance improvement in health care organizations. Evaluates and accredits nearly 18,000 health care organizations and programs in the United States, including hospitals, networks, home care, long term care, behavioral health care, laboratory and ambulatory care services. *Type:* Association.

LifeTimes

St. Luke's - Roosevelt Hospital Center
1111 Amsterdam Ave.
New York, NY 10025
Desc: Disseminates information on health care issues and activities, programs, and services provided by St. Luke's-Roosevelt Hospital Center. *Type:* Newsletter.

Medical News Report

Standish Publishing Co.
PO Box 335   Ph: (610)519-9220
Ardmore, PA 19003   Fax: (610)519-9221
Contact: Kim Standish, Editor.

Desc: Provides information about hospital public relations activities. Recurring features include interviews, a calendar of events, and columns titled Across the Country, Story Ideas, The Weeks Ahead, and Media Tactics. *Type:* Newsletter.

Michigan Health and Hospital Association

6215 W. St. Joseph Hwy.   Ph: (517)323-3443
Lansing, MI 48917   Fax: (517)323-0946
URL: http://www.mah.org
Contact: Spencer Johnson, Pres.

Desc: Hospitals, inpatient institutions, clinics, and hospital auxiliaries. Acts as the industry's major advocate and promotes community education. *Type:* Association.

Monday Report

Massachusetts Hospital Association (MHA)
5 New England Executive Park   Ph: (781)272-8000
Burlington, MA 01803
URL: http://www.mhalink.org.
Contact: Lisa Derbyshire, Editor, fax: (781)272-0048, lderbyshire@mhalink.org.

Desc: Carries hospital-related news, access and quality-of-care concerns, healthcare finance policies and regulations. *Type:* Newsletter.

Multi-Hospital Systems and Group Purchasing Organizations Directory

SMG Marketing Group, Inc.
875 N. Michigan Ave.   Ph: (312)642-3026
Chicago, IL 60611   Free: 800-678-3026
    Fax: (312)642-9729
Contact: John Henderson, President.

Desc: Over 480 multi-hospital systems and group purchasing organizations. *Type:* Directory.

National Association of Children's Hospitals and Related Institutions

401 Wythe St.   Ph: (703)684-1355
Alexandria, VA 22314   Fax: (703)684-1589
Contact: Lawrence A. McAndrews, Pres. & CEO.

Desc: Children's hospitals and related institutions whose programs are clinical (as opposed to social or custodial). Purposes are: to promote the quality of child health care through the dissemination of information and the promotion of research and education programs related to such care; to participate in related charitable, scientific, and educational endeavors. *Type:* Association.

National Certification Board Perioperative Nursing

Diane T. Howery
2170 S. Parker Rd., Ste. 295   Ph: (303)369-9566
Denver, CO 80231   Fax: (303)695-8464
URL: http://www.certiboard.org
Contact: Diane I. Howery, Exec.Dir.

Desc: Works to promote registered nurses. *Type:* Association.

National Hospice Organization

1901 N. Moore St., Ste. 901   Ph: (703)243-5900
Arlington, VA 22209   Free: 800-658-8898
    Fax: (703)525-5762
E-mail: drsnho@cais.com
URL: http://www.nho.org
Contact: John J. Mahoney, Pres.

Desc: Hospice organizations and individuals interested in the promotion of the hospice concept and program of care. (Hospice is a concept of caring for the terminally ill and their families which enables the patient to live as fully as possible, makes the entire family the unit of care, and centers the caring process in the home whenever appropriate. Inpatient facilities are available for those unable to be cared for at home.) Promotes standards of care in program planning and implementation; monitors health care legislation and regulation relevant to hospice care. *Type:* Association.

National Institute for Jewish Hospice

8723 Alden Dr., Ste. 5107   Ph: (323)467-7423
Los Angeles, CA 90048   Free: 800-446-4448
                                    Fax: (619)322-3817

Contact: LeVana Lev, Exec.Dir.

Desc: Individuals, business firms, and organizations concerned about terminally ill Jewish people. Serves as a resource center that seeks to help terminal patients and their families deal with their grief by providing information on traditional Jewish views on death, dying, and managing the loss of a loved one. Offers guidance and training to patients and interested hospice personnel, health care professionals, clergy, and family members who work with terminally ill Jewish people. *Type:* Association.

New York City Health and Hospitals Corporation

Public Affairs and Special   Ph: (212)566-6000
  Projects
125 Worth St., Rm. 502
New York, NY 10013

Contact: Jo Ivey Boufford, M.D., Pres.

Desc: Created by the New York State Legislature to replace the City's Department of Hospitals; the largest municipal hospital system in the United States. Manages 16 hospitals with over 10,000 beds, five Neighborhood Family Care Centers, 40 community-based clinics, and New York City's Emergency Medical Service. Seeks to provide "high quality medical and mental health services." *Type:* Association.

New York City Health and Hospitals Corporation

Public Affairs

125 Worth St., Rm. 504   Ph: (212)788-3357
New York, NY 10013   Fax: (212)788-3358

Desc: Created by the New York State Legislature to replace the City's Department of Hospitals; the largest municipal hospital system in the United States. Manages 11 acute care hospitals, 5 long-term care hospitals, 6 primary care hospitals, 6 certified home health agencies, over 40 community-based clinics, and New York City's Emergency Medical Service. *Type:* Association.

NHO NewsLine

National Hospice Organization

1901 N. Moore St., Ste. 901   Ph: (703)243-5400
Arlington, VA 22209   Free: 800-658-8898
                                    Fax: (703)525-5762

Contact: Jennifer Morales, Editor.

Desc: Advocates the importance of hospice care, a specialized health care program emphasizing the management of pain, fear, and loneliness associated with terminal illness while providing care and support for the family as well as the patient. Contains news and information about hospice programs in the United States and laws and regulations imparting them. *Type:* Newsletter.

Ohio Hospital Association

155 E. Broad St.
Columbus, OH 43215

Contact: James R. Castle, Pres.

Desc: Hospitals (250); individuals and organizations that support hospitals (4000). Assists hospitals and related organizations in serving community health care needs. *Type:* Association.

RPNAM Update

Registered Psychiatric Nurses Association of Manitoba (RPNAM)

1854 Portage Ave.   Ph: (204)888-4841
Winnipeg, MB, Canada R3J   Fax: (204)888-8638
  0G9

E-mail: rpnam@escape.ca

URL: http://www.rpnam.mb.ca.

Contact: A.D. Osted, Editor, aosted@pyschiatricnurses. mb.ca.

Desc: Provides a forum for communications among psychiatric nurses in Manitoba. Recurring features include letters to the editor, a calendar of events, research news, reports of meetings, notices of educational and employment opportunities, publication announcements, and a column titled Current Trends & Issues. *Type:* Newsletter.

Society for Healthcare Strategy and Market Development of the American Hospital Association

1 N. Franklin, Ste. 3100   Ph: (312)422-3888
Chicago, IL 60606   Fax: (312)422-4579

E-mail: stratsoc@aha.org

URL: http://www.stratsociety.org

Contact: Lauren Barnett, Exec. Dir.

Desc: Persons in hospitals, health systems and networks, managed care plans, and physician groups who are engaged in strategic planning, business development, marketing, or public relations activities. *Type:* Association.

Spectrum

Society for Healthcare Strategy and Market Development

American Hospital Association

1 N. Franklin, 31st Fl.   Ph: (312)422-3738
Chicago, IL 60606   Fax: (312)422-4577

E-mail: stratsoc@aha.org

Contact: Lauren Barnett, Exec. Editor; Elizabeth J. Liwazck, Managing Editor.

Desc: Examines issues, strategies, and methods of health care marketing, public relations, public affairs, and related disciplines. Reports on successful programs and trends in the field. *Type:* Newsletter.

U.S. Department of Health and Human Services
Office of Research and Demonstrations
Office of Demonstrations and Evaluations
Hospital Experimentation Division

2302 Oak Meadows Bldg.   Ph: (410)966-6670
6325 Security Blvd.
Baltimore, MD 21207

Contact: Michael Hupfer, Actg.Dir.

Desc: Design, testing, and evaluation of alternative health care payment systems for hospitals and other types of providers. *Type:* Research center.

VHA

220 E. Las Colinas Blvd.   Ph: (972)830-0000
Irving, TX 75039-5500   Fax: (972)830-0141

E-mail: feedback@vha.com

URL: http://www.vha.com

Contact: C. Thomas Smith, Pres. & CEO.

Desc: Health care alliance that represents 1,600 healthcare organizations nationwide, offering its members programs and services to help them improve their operational and clinical efficiency as well as community health. *Type:* Association.

Wings of Hope

Hope Hospice

9470 HealthPark Cir.
Fort Myers, FL 33908

Contact: Anthony J. Palumbo, Editor.

Desc: Provides information about hospice care. Recurring features include columns titled In Perspective, Spotlight, and Memorials, Honorariums and Donations. *Type:* Newsletter.

Hospitality Industries

American Hotel & Motel Association

1201 New York Ave. NW, Ste.   Ph: (202)289-3100
  600   Fax: (202)289-3199
Washington, DC 20005-3931

E-mail: info@ahma.com

URL: http://www.ahma.com

Contact: William P. Fisher, Pres. & CEO.

Desc: Federation of 52 state lodging associations, representing over 1.4 million hotel and motel rooms. Promotes business of hotels and motels through publicity and promotion programs. Works to improve operating methods through dissemination of information on industry methods. *Type:* Association.

America's Future Foods Report

Technomic Information Services

A Division of Technomic, Inc.

300 S. Riverside Plz., Ste. 1940   Ph: (312)876-0004
  S   Fax: (312)876-1158
Chicago, IL 60606

Contact: John Hofer, Editor.

Desc: Analyzes and predicts food trends in the retail and food service industry. *Type:* Newsletter.

Cameron's Hospitality Marketing Reporter

Cameron's Publications

5325 Sheridan Dr.   Ph: (716)833-4369
PO Box 1160   Fax: (716)834-4159
Williamsville, NY 14231-1160

E-mail: campub@cameronpub.com

URL: http://www.cameronpub.com/.

Contact: Nina Cameron, Editor, ninac@cameronpub. com; Bob McClelland, Publisher.

Desc: Profiles and comments on actual restaurant and hotel marketing; offers marketing ideas for each day of the upcoming month. Recurring features include reproductions of advertisements, columns on marketing related to specific holidays, and a column titled Best Marketing Idea of the Month. *Type:* Newsletter.

Catering Industry Employee

Hotel Employees and Restaurant Employees International Union

1219 28th St. NW   Ph: (202)393-4373
Washington, DC 20007-3389   Fax: (202)965-2958

URL: http://www.hereunion.org.

Contact: Ted T. Hansen, Editor; Donald J. Byers, Managing Editor.

Desc: Trade journal for culinary and hospitality workers. Official publication of the Hotel Employees and Restaurant Employees International Union. *Type:* Periodical.

Catering Service Idea Newsletter

Prosperity & Profits Unlimited, Distribution Services

PO Box 416   Ph: (303)575-5676
Denver, CO 80201-0416

Contact: A.C. Doyle, Editor.

Desc: Presents ideas for those in the catering business. *Type:* Newsletter.

Cheers

Adams Business Media
1180 Avenue of the Americas,   Ph: (212)827-4700
   11th Fl.   Fax: (212)827-4720
New York, NY 10036
E-mail: cheers@mail.aip.com.
URL: http://www.cheersonline.com.

Contact: Doug Martin, Publisher, (212)827-4707; Jack Robertiello, Publisher, (212)827-4709, fax: (212)827-4720.

Desc: Full service restaurant and bar magazine. *Type:* Periodical.

ConcepTrac

Technomic Information Services
A Division of Technomic, Inc.
300 S. Riverside Plz., Ste. 1940   Ph: (312)876-0004
S   Fax: (312)876-1158
Chicago, IL 60606

Desc: Provides news on chain restaurant development. Includes information on decor, atmosphere, service styles, cooking preparation methods, and unit economics. *Type:* Newsletter.

CRFA National Hospitality News

Canadian Restaurant and Foodservices
Association (CRFA)
316 Bloor St. S.W.   Ph: (416)923-8416
Toronto, ON, Canada M5S   Free: 800-387-5649
   1W5   Fax: (416)923-1450

Contact: David Harris, Editor.

Desc: Informs members of association activities and industry concerns, including labor shortages, sales tax reform, and government issues. Recurring features include news of research, reports of meetings, notices of publications available, statistics, and the columns titled National Infostats, The Personnel File, and Focus on Ottawa. *Type:* Newsletter.

Educational Foundation of the National Restaurant Association

1200 17th st. NW., No. 1400   Ph: (202)331-5900
Washington, DC 20036-3097   Free: 800-424-5156
                            Fax: (202)331-5946
E-mail: info@dineout.org
URL: http://www.restaurant.org

Contact: Daniel A. Gescheidle, Pres.

Desc: Educational foundation supported by the National Restaurant Association and all segments of the foodservice industry including restaurateurs, foodservice companies, food and equipment manufacturers, distributors, and trade associations. Dedicated to the advancement of professional standards in the industry through education and research. Offers video training programs, management courses, and careers information. *Type:* Association.

Florida Hotel & Motel Journal—Buyer's Guide Issue

Accommodations, Inc., Subsidiary
Florida Hotel & Motel Association
200 W. College Ave.   Ph: (850)224-2888
Tallahassee, FL 32301   Free: 800-476-FHMA
                            Fax: (850)222-1752

Contact: S. Jayleen Woods, Editor.

Desc: List of approximately 300 allied member suppliers to the hotel and motel industry in Florida. *Type:* Directory.

Hospitality Law

Magna Publications, Inc.
2718 Dryden Dr.   Ph: (608)246-3580
Madison, WI 53704   Free: 800-433-0499
                            Fax: (608)246-3597
E-mail: custserv@magnapubs.com
Contact: Doris Green, Editor.

Desc: Discusses legal issues pertaining to the hospitality industry, using actual cases as illustration. Offers articles on liability, contract law, tax codes, and legal trends relevant to the lodging industry. *Type:* Newsletter.

Hospitality Sales and Marketing Association International

1300 L St. NW, Ste. 1020   Ph: (202)789-0089
Washington, DC 20005   Fax: (202)789-1725
E-mail: bghsmai@aol.com
URL: http://www.hsmai.org
Contact: Robert A. Gilbert, CHME, Exec. VP/CEO.

Desc: Sales and marketing executives, managers, owners, and other hospitality industry executives; people from allied fields; other individuals and firms. "An international organization devoted wholly to education of executives employed by the hospitality industry." Cooperates with American Hotel and Motel Association and other organizations. *Type:* Association.

Hotel Employees and Restaurant Employees International Union

1219 28th Sr. NW   Ph: (202)393-4373
Washington, DC 20007   Fax: (202)333-0468
Contact: John W. Willhelm, Gen.Sec.-Treas.
Desc: AFL-CIO. *Type:* Association.

Hotel & Travel Index

Cahners Travel Group
500 Plaza Dr.   Ph: (201)902-2000
Secaucus, NJ 07094-3626   Fax: (201)319-1797
URL: http://www.cahners.com; http://www.traveler.net.
Contact: Ray Costa, Assoc. Publisher; Susan Weinstock, Editor.

Desc: Over 41,000 hotels, resorts, inns, and guest houses, worldwide; hotel representatives and reservations services. *Type:* Directory.

Hotels—Worldwide Product Source Issue

Cahners Business Information
1350 E. Touhy Ave.   Ph: (847)635-8800
Des Plaines, IL 60018   Free: 800-446-6551
                            Fax: (847)635-6856
E-mail: bkinross@cahners.com
Contact: Jeff Weinstein, Editor.

Desc: List of manufacturers of equipment, suppliers of services, and their restaurant, hotel, and institutional products; international coverage. *Type:* Directory.

Inside Preferred of America

Preferred Hotels & Resorts Worldwide
311 S. Wacker Dr., No. 1900   Ph: (312)913-0400
Chicago, IL 60606-6618   Free: 800-323-7500
                            Fax: (312)913-0444
Contact: Shane O'Flaherty, Editor.

Desc: Provides information for executives and general managers of the independently-owned Preferred Hotels. Reports personnel changes, statistics, and meeting and convention dates and locations. *Type:* Newsletter.

National Association of Catering Executives

60 Revere Dr., Ste. 500   Ph: (847)480-9080
Northbrook, IL 60062   Fax: (847)480-9282
URL: http://www.nace.net
Contact: John R. Waxman, Exec.Dir.
Desc: Professional caterers in North America; affiliate members, the local and national suppliers and vendors in the many disciplines that impact and influence the catering business. Addresses banquet facilities, off-premise, country club, military and resort catering. *Type:* Association.

National Association of Pizza Operators

PO Box 1347   Ph: (812)949-0909
New Albany, IN 47151   Fax: (812)941-9711
Contact: Gerry Durnell, Exec.Dir.

Desc: Independent and franchised pizza operators; manufacturers and suppliers of pizza equipment; research organizations; schools with hotel and restaurant management programs; similar establishments in foreign countries. Promotes the advancement of marketing and product technology in the pizza industry. Provides educational references and seminars; conducts product research and development programs. *Type:* Association.

National Domestic Workers Union

643 Delbridge St., NW   Ph: (404)523-5800
Atlanta, GA 30314-4151
Contact: Dorothy Bolden, Founder & Pres.

Desc: Works to provide insurance benefits and improve the relationship between employer and domestic employee. Represents members' interests in wage, transportation, and shorter work week negotiations. Offers senior citizen and employment placement services. *Type:* Association.

National Restaurant Association

1200 17th St., NW   Ph: (202)331-5900
Washington, DC 20036   Fax: (202)331-2429
E-mail: isal@restaurant.org
URL: http://www.restaurant.org
Contact: Herman Cain, CEO .

Desc: Restaurants, cafeterias, clubs, contract foodservice management, drive-ins, caterers, institutional food services, and other members of the foodservice industry; also represents establishments belonging to nonaffiliated state and local restaurant associations in governmental affairs. Supports foodservice education and research in several educational institutions; conducts traveling management courses and seminars for restaurant personnel. Affiliated with the Educational Foundation of the National Restaurant Association to provide training and education for operators, food and equipment manufacturers, distributors, and educators. *Type:* Association.

Newsline

Ontario Accommodation Association
347 Pido Rd., Unit 2   Ph: (705)745-4982
RR 6   Fax: (705)745-4983
Peterborough, ON, Canada K9J
   6X7
E-mail: info@ontarioaccommodation.com
Contact: Bruce M. Gravel, Editor.

Desc: Provides news of Association activities, government lobbying and regulatory changes. *Type:* Newsletter.

Official Hotel Guide

Cahners Travel Group
500 Plaza Dr.   Ph: (201)902-2000
Secaucus, NJ 07094-3626   Fax: (201)319-1797
URL: http://www.cahners.com.
Contact: Wilma Goldenberg, Editor.

Desc: In three volumes, 30,000 hotels, motels, and resorts worldwide. Volume 1 covers most of the U.S.; Volume 2 covers the rest of the U.S. and the Western Hemisphere; Volume 3 covers Europe, the Middle East, Asia, and Africa. Includes separate lists of golf resorts and tennis resorts; health spas, dude ranches, bed and breakfasts, and casino & hotels in the United States; also includes lists of hotels in the Caribbean with golf, tennis, casinos, and all-inclusive. *Type:* Directory.

Pennsylvania Hospitality Directory

Pennsylvania Travel Council
902 N. 2nd St., Dept. 201   Ph: (717)232-8880
Harrisburg, PA 17102   Fax: (717)232-8948
E-mail: info@patravel.org
URL: http://www.patravel.org.
Contact: Eric Adams, Editor.
Desc: Over 500 Pennsylvania travel related businesses, including hotels/motels, meeting facilities, bed and breakfasts, farm vacations, attractions, ski areas, campgrounds, tour operators, restaurants, suppliers to the hospitality industry, etc. *Type:* Directory.

Preferred Hotels Association

311 S. Wacker Dr., No. 1900   Ph: (312)913-0400
Chicago, IL 60606-6618   Free: 800-323-7500
                                  Fax: (312)913-0444
Contact: Peter Cass, Pres.
Desc: Independent luxury hotels and resorts united to compete with the marketing power of chain operations. Promotes the individuality, high standards, hospitality, and luxury of member hotels. *Type:* Association.

Resort Management Report

Rouge Et Noir Inc.
PO Box 1146
Midlothian, VA 23113   Ph: (804)230-0736
                                  Fax: (804)230-4931
Desc: Analyzes the financial operations of casinos. *Type:* Newsletter.

Restaurant Business

Bill Communications, Inc.
355 Park Ave. S.   Ph: (212)592-6200
New York, NY 10010-1789   Free: 800-266-4712
                                  Fax: (212)592-6339
E-mail: 200-4782@mcimail.com.
URL: http://ww.restaurantbiz.com.
Contact: Peter Romeo, Editor, (212)592-6524, p.romeo@restaurantbiz.com; Michael Charlton, Publisher, (212)592-6504.
Desc: Trade magazine for restaurants and commercial food service. *Type:* Periodical.

Restaurant Hospitality

Penton Media Inc.
1100 Superior Ave.   Ph: (216)696-7000
Cleveland, OH 44114-2543   Fax: (216)931-9524
E-mail: corpcomm@penton.com; rheditors@aol.com.
Contact: Mike DeLuca, Group Publisher, (216)931-9254, fax: (216)696-0836, mdeluca@penton.com; Mike Keefe, Jr., Publisher, (216)931-9731, fax: (216)696-0836, mkeefe@penton.com; Michael Sanson, Editor-in-Chief, (216)931-9571, fax: (216)696-0836, msanson@penton.com.
Desc: Magazine for managers and other executives of restaurant chains, independent restaurants, and hotels - foodservice operations. *Type:* Periodical.

Restaurants & Institutions

Cahners Business Information
1350 E. Touhy Ave.   Ph: (847)635-8800
Des Plaines, IL 60018   Free: 800-446-6551
                                  Fax: (847)635-6856
E-mail: bkinross@cahners.com; riedit@cahners.com.
URL: http://www.rimag.com.
Contact: Patricia Dailey, Editor-in-Chief, (847)390-2028, fax: (847)390-2031, pdailey@cahners.com.
Desc: Magazine focusing on foodservice and lodging management. *Type:* Periodical.

Spas: The International Spa Guide

Bain-Dror International Travel, Inc.
PO Box 1405   Ph: (516)944-5508
Port Washington, NY 11050   Free: 800-252-5344
                                  Fax: (516)944-7540
E-mail: bditusa@aol.com
URL: http://www.bdit.com
Contact: Eli Dror, Editor; Joseph Bain, Editor.
Desc: Over 600 spas and spa resort hotels worldwide. *Type:* Directory.

TECHNOMIC Foodservice Digest

Technomic Information Services
A Division of Technomic, Inc.
300 S. Riverside Plz., Ste. 1940   Ph: (312)876-0004
S   Fax: (312)876-1158
Chicago, IL 60606
Contact: Jan Sneesby, Editor.
Desc: Contains abstracted citations from 100 publications on business developments in the foodservice industry. Recurring features include a column titled I See It on forces and factors shaping the industry. *Type:* Newsletter.

TECHNOMIC Restaurant Information Services

Technomic Information Services
A Division of Technomic, Inc.
300 S. Riverside Plz., Ste. 1940   Ph: (312)876-0004
S   Fax: (312)876-1158
Chicago, IL 60606
Contact: Jan Sneesby, Director of Publications; Jan Sneesby, Editor.
Desc: Provides business profiles and abstracted news on nearly 300 restaurant chains and companies. *Type:* Newsletter.

Travel and Hospitality Career Directory

Gale Group Inc.
27500 Drake Rd.   Ph: (248)699-4253
Farmington Hills, MI 48331-   Free: 800-877-GALE
3535   Fax: (248)699-8070
E-mail: galeord@galegroup.com
URL: http://www.galegroup.com.
Contact: Bradley J. Morgan, Editor.
Desc: Over 400 airlines, cruise lines, hotels, motels, resorts, major attractions, meeting planning firms, convention facilities, visitors' bureaus, tourist boards, and travel agencies offering careers in the travel industry; sources of help-wanted ads, professional associations, videos, databases, career guides, and professional guides and handbooks. *Type:* Directory.

USFA Hotel-Motel National Master List

United States Fire Administration
Federal Emergency Management   Ph: (301)447-1000
  Agency
16825 S. Seton Ave.
Emmitsburg, MD 21727
URL: http://www.usfa.fema.gov/hotel/index.htm
Desc: This database lets you search for hotels and motels nationwide that meet the strict requirements of the Hotel and Motel Fire Safety Act of 1990. Search the master list by hotel identification number, name, location, and other criteria. *Type:* Database.

Wisconsin Dells Visitor and Convention Bureau

701 Superior St.   Ph: (608)254-8088
PO Box 390   Free: 800-22-DELLS
Wisconsin Dells, WI 53965-   Fax: (608)254-4293
0390
E-mail: wisdells@midplains.net
URL: http://www.wisdells.com
Contact: Romy A. Snyder, Exec.Dir.
Desc: Businesses involved in tourism. Seeks to promote the Wisconsin Dells, WI area as a major vacation destination. *Type:* Association.

Housing

Abbeyfield Houses Society of Canada Newsletter

Abbeyfield Houses Society of Canada
427 Bloor St. W., Box 1   Ph: (416)920-7483
Toronto, ON, Canada M5S   Fax: (416)920-6956
1X7
Contact: Robert McMullan, Editor; Helen Walsh, Editor.
Desc: Reports on news of Abbeyfield Houses Society of Canada, a provider of care and companionship for the elderly. Also features articles related to aging, housing, and lifestyle. *Type:* Newsletter.

Assisted Housing Management Insider

Brownstone Publishers, Inc.
149 Fifth Ave., 16th Fl.   Ph: (212)473-8200
New York, NY 10010-6801   Free: 800-643-8095
                                  Fax: (212)473-8786
E-mail: assisthous@aol.com.
Contact: Lynne Glass, Editor.
Desc: Explains U.S. Department of Housing and Urban Development (HUD) regulatory requirements for federally-assisted housing, and gives advice on how to stay in compliance. *Type:* Newsletter.

Assisted Living Federation of America

10300 Eaton Place, Ste. 400   Ph: (703)691-8100
Fairfax, VA 22030   Fax: (703)691-8106
E-mail: info@alfa.org
URL: http://www.alfa.org
Contact: Karen A. Wayne, President/CEO.
Desc: Providers of assisted living, state associations of providers, and others interested or involved in the industry. Promotes the interests of the assisted living industry and works to enhance the quality of life for the population it serves. *Type:* Association.

Common Ground Community Housing Development Fund Corp.

Rosanna Haggerty
255 W 43rd St.   Ph: (212)768-8989
New York, NY 10036-3917
Contact: Jaime Chapin, Dir. of Dev.
Type: Association.

Cooperative Housing Foundation

8300 Colesville Rd., Ste. 420   Ph: (301)587-4700
Silver Spring, MD 20910   Fax: (301)587-2626
E-mail: mailbox@chfhq.com
URL: http://www.chfhq.org
Contact: Michael E. Doyle, Pres./CEO.
Desc: Leaders in housing cooperative, labor, business and civic organizations who are interested in improving the quality of housing and communities, especially for persons of modest income. Provides private-sector assistance directed at economic development, settlements and planning. Sponsors the development of cooperative and self-help housing. Strives to enable families to invest their own resources to improve their income situation and their living conditions; strengthens new capabilities of host governments and communities, donor agencies, small and medium-sized private businesses, non-governmental organizations in more than 25 countries worldwide. *Type:* Association.

DRI Housing Forecast

Standard & Poor's DRI
Data Products Division
24 Hartwell Ave.   Ph: (781)863-5100
Lexington, MA 02421
E-mail: client_services@dri.mcgraw-hill.com
URL: http://www.dri.mcgraw-hill.com

Desc: Contains 13 quarterly historical and forecast time series of U.S. housing sales and prices. *Type:* Database.

Enterprise Foundation

10227 Wincopin Cir., Ste. 500   Ph: (410)964-1230
Columbia, MD 21044-3400   Free: 800-624-4298
   Fax: (410)964-1918
URL: http://www.enterprisefoundation.org
Contact: Rey Ramsey, Pres.

Desc: Assists nonprofit neighborhood housing organizations that provide "decent, affordable housing" as well as other basic human needs for low-income families. Provides technical assistance and training directly to neighborhood based nonprofit organizations to increase their capacity to provide housing and related human services in the cities in which the Enterprise works. Advises on planning and management systems. *Type:* Association.

Habitat for Humanity International

121 Habitat St.   Ph: (912)924-6935
Americus, GA 31709-3498   Fax: (912)924-6541
E-mail: public_info@habitat.org
URL: http://www.habitat.org
Contact: Millard Fuller, Pres. & Founder.

Desc: Ecumenical Christian housing organization. Works in partnership with people in need throughout the world to build shelter that is sold to them at no profit through no-interest loans. Funds, building materials and labor are donated by individuals, churches, corporations and other organizations who share the goal of eliminating substandard housing in the world. *Type:* Association.

Habitat for Humanity International

Habitat for Humanity International
121 Habitat St.   Ph: (912)924-6935
Americus, GA 31709
URL: http://www.habitat.org/

Desc: Describes the Habitat for Humanity organization, its accomplishments, supporters, and mission. There are online directories which are updated to list special Habitat builds, trips, and events. *Type:* Database.

The Housing Authority Journal

New York City Housing Authority
250 Broadway, Rm. 917   Ph: (212)306-3327
New York, NY 10007   Fax: (212)306-6482
Contact: Patricia A. Gonzales, Director of Publications.

Desc: Journal on public housing in New York City. *Type:* Periodical.

Ledger Quarterly

Community Associations Institute Research Foundation
1630 Duke St.   Ph: (703)548-8600
Alexandria, VA 22314   Fax: (703)684-1581
Contact: Gary A. Porter, Editor.

Desc: Reports on issues affecting the financial affairs of co-operative, condominium, homeowner, and other community associations. *Type:* Newsletter.

Manufactured Housing Institute

2101 Wilson Blvd., Ste. 610   Ph: (703)558-0400
Arlington, VA 22201-3062   Free: 800-505-5500
   Fax: (703)558-0401
E-mail: info@mfghome.org
URL: http://www.mfghome.org
Contact: Blake Brophy, Dir., Fin., Adm., and Info.Svcs.

Desc: Manufacturers of manufactured homes; suppliers of equipment, components, furnishings and services, financial services companies, state association organizations, retailers and community owners. Promotes sales of manufactured homes through programs and services in six key areas: government relations, technical activities, financing, public relations, site development, and community operations. *Type:* Association.

Mobilehome Parks Report

Thomas P. Kerr, Inc.
3807 Pasadena Ave., Ste. 100   Ph: (916)971-0489
Sacramento, CA 95821-2815   Fax: (916)971-1849
Contact: Thomas P. Kerr, Editor, tkerr@aol.com.

Desc: Provides information and analysis of legislation, court decisions, and trends affecting mobile home park investment and management. Discusses such topics as rent control, housing for the elderly, HUD regulations, real estate development, and affordable housing. *Type:* Newsletter.

National Association of Housing and Redevelopment Officials

630 Eye St. NW   Ph: (202)289-3500
Washington, DC 20001   Fax: (202)289-8181
E-mail: nahro@nahro.org
URL: http://www.nahro.org
Contact: Richard Y. Nelson, Exec.Dir.

Desc: Individuals (6400) and public agencies (2600) engaged in community rebuilding by community development, public housing, large-scale private or cooperative housing rehabilitation, and conservation of existing neighborhoods through housing code enforcement, voluntary citizen action, and government action. To develop new techniques in administrative practices, finance, design, construction, management, and community relations. Consults with federal government agencies and other policy-making bodies on questions of national and local policy. *Type:* Association.

National Council of State Housing Agencies

444 N. Capitol St., Ste. 438   Ph: (202)624-7710
Washington, DC 20001   Fax: (202)624-5899
URL: http://www.ncsha.org
Contact: John McEvoy, Exec.Dir.

Desc: State Housing Finance Agencies from 50 states, Puerto Rico, and the Virgin Islands; affiliate members include investment bankers, housing development firms, and other public and private agencies involved with low and moderate income single- and multi-family housing finance, development, and management. *Type:* Association.

National Housing Conference

815 15th St. NW, Ste. 538   Ph: (202)393-5772
Washington, DC 20005   Fax: (202)393-5656
E-mail: nhc@nhc.org
URL: http://www.nhc.org
Contact: Robert J. Reid, Exec.Dir.

Desc: Housing authority officials, community development specialists, builders, bankers, lawyers, accountants, owners, residents, insurers, architects and planners, religious organizations, labor groups, and national housing and housing related organizations. Mobilizes support for effective programs in housing and community development as well as affordable and accessible housing for all Americans. Holds educational programs. *Type:* Association.

National Low Income Housing Coalition/Low Income Housing Information Service

1012 14th St. NW, Ste. 610   Ph: (202)662-1530
Washington, DC 20005   Fax: (202)393-1973
E-mail: hn0053@handsnet.org
Contact: Shelia Crowley, Pres.

Desc: Seeks to educate the public and organizations about low-income housing through meetings, conferences, literature, and technical assistance. *Type:* Association.

Northwest Minnesota Community Housing Development Organization

PO Box 128   Ph: (218)637-2431
Mentor, MN 56736-0000   Fax: (218)637-2433
E-mail: imeier@means.net

Contact: Lee Meier, Exec.Dir.

Type: Association.

Professional Apartment Management

Brownstone Publishers, Inc.
149 Fifth Ave., 16th Fl.   Ph: (212)473-8200
New York, NY 10010-6801   Free: 800-643-8095
   Fax: (212)473-8786
E-mail: profaptmgt@aol.com.

Contact: Geoffrey Goldberg, Editor.

Desc: Provides apartment managers strategies, techniques, and methods for attracting and retaining tenants and avoiding legal disputes. Includes model lease language and sample ads, forms, and letters. *Type:* Newsletter.

The Robert L. Siegel Letter

Robert L. Siegel & Associates
26 Chateau Trianon Dr.   Ph: (504)471-2040
Kenner, LA 70065-2040   Fax: (504)471-0526
Contact: Robert L. Siegel, Editor and Publisher.

Desc: Provides information about housing and the economy. *Type:* Newsletter.

Self-Help Enterprises

PO Box 351   Ph: (209)733-9091
Visalia, CA 93279
Contact: Robert Marshall, Exec.Dir.

Desc: Board members include low-income participants in the program and local business and professional persons. Assists eligible low-income people in selfhelp housing techniques in the San Joaquin Valley and provides ancillary services in the areas of housing, counseling, and community development. *Type:* Association.

Statewide Independent Living Council of Tennessee

480 Craighead St., Ste. 200   Ph: (615)297-2666
Nashville, TN 37204-2343   Free: 888-THE-SILC
   Fax: (615)383-1176
E-mail: the-silc@mindspring.com
Contact: Kimberly Hines, Exec.Dir.

Desc: Works to promote independent living in Tennessee and to support the independent living philosophy, its practices, and its values. *Type:* Association.

United Homeowners' Association

1511 K St. NW, Ste. 326   Ph: (202)408-8842
Washington, DC 20005   Fax: (202)408-8156
E-mail: a.clark@uha.org
URL: http://www.uha.org
Contact: Jordan Clark, Pres.

Desc: Works to promote and protect the interests of homeowners. *Type:* Association.

Urban Homesteading Assistance Board

120 Wall St., 20th Fl.   Ph: (212)479-3300
New York, NY 10005   Fax: (212)344-6457
E-mail: info@uhab.org
URL: http://www.uhab.org
Contact: Andrew Reicher, Exec.Dir.

Desc: Assists low-income neighborhood housing groups and tenant organizations. Works to develop nonprofit, co-operative, resident-controlled housing. Provides technical assistance and services to low- and moderate-income families seeking selfhelp solutions to their housing needs; assists in developing and implementing sweat equity rehabilitation and homesteading projects throughout New York City. *Type:* Association.

Human Development

Aloha International

PO Box 665
Kilauea, HI 96754

Ph: (808)828-0302
Fax: (808)828-2839

E-mail: huna@aloha.net
URL: http://huna.org/~huna
Contact: Serge King, Ph.D., Exec.Dir.
Desc: Nondenominational religious order of individuals dedicated to creating peace and environmental harmony through the use of Huna (Hawaiian word meaning "hidden" or "secret"). Huna is a system of psychology used to remedy emotional and physical problems based on the knowledge of how the physical, mental, and spiritual levels of consciousness function effectively when used properly. Conducts classes, courses, lectures, tour groups, seasonal celebrations, and workshops; administers training in Huna techniques to individuals, group leaders, and counselors; offers Hawaiian shaman training. *Type:* Association.

Churchman Associates

4300 N.W. 23rd Ave., No. 203
Gainesville, FL 32606-6541

Ph: (352)378-3871
Fax: (352)378-3871

E-mail: chasmagg@aol.com
Contact: Charles Gregg, Managing Ed.
Desc: Idealists who support *The Human Quest*, an independent journal of liberalism and religious humanism founded in 1804 by Episcopal leadership. Seeks to uphold the conviction that religious journalism must provide a forum for the free exchange of ideas and opinions. Believes that "religion is consonant with the most advanced revelations in every department of knowledge; that we are in a fraternal world community; and that the moral and spiritual evolution of man is only at the beginning." Supports education for world peace. *Type:* Association.

Directory of Human Resources-Maricopa County

Community Information & Referral
1515 E. Osborn Rd., Annex
Phoenix, AZ 85014

Ph: (602)263-8856
Fax: (602)263-0979

E-mail: cirs@cirs.org
URL: http://www.cirs.org.
Contact: John Herman, Editor, john@cirs.org.
Desc: More than 1,000 governmental and private nonprofit human service organizations in Maricopa County, Arizona. *Type:* Directory.

Esalen Institute

Highway 1
Big Sur, CA 93920

Ph: (408)667-3000
Fax: (408)667-2724

E-mail: friends@esalen.org
URL: http://www.esalen.org
Desc: A nonprofit educational center that explores trends in the sciences, art, religion, and philosophy, with emphasis on the potentialities and values of human existence. *Type:* Association.

Human Resource Development Inst

222 South Jefferson
Chicago, IL 60661

Ph: (312)441-9009
Fax: (312)441-9019

Contact: C. Vincent Bakeman, PhD, Pres./CEO.
Type: Association.

Humanist Movement of Iranian People

Contact: Dr. Adnan Mazarei, Sec.Gen.
Desc: Established in Iran, RAMA claims to be the first attempt to organize a humanist group as a political party. Goal is to "liberate humanism from its philanthropic, only moral, academic meaning and transform it into a solid, tangible socio-economic doctrine." Also referred to as "applied humanism." Believes that people are living in a transitory historical period and will soon witness an "unprecedented economic, social, political and intellectual mutation" that will "transform the entire living condition of mankind." Attempts to apply humanist principles to what it sees as "the new human society." Maintains library of 5000 volumes. *Type:* Association.

HUNA Research

1760 Anna St.
Cape Girardeau, MO 63701

Ph: (573)334-3478

Contact: Dr. E. Otha Wingo, Pres.
Desc: Teachers of Huna and others from the healing professions; individuals wishing to develop and improve their lives; others interested in Huna. (Huna is a system of psychology used by the Kahunas of ancient Hawaii to remedy emotional and physical problems. The system is based on the knowledge of how the physical, mental, and spiritual levels of consciousness function effectively when used properly.) Works to assist members and others in taking charge of their own destiny and making a better life for themselves and their friends. *Type:* Association.

Inner Peace Movement

PO Box 4900
Washington, DC 20008

Free: 800-336-8008

Contact: Francisco Coll, Founder.
Desc: A leadership training program designed "to help man identify and balance the physical, mental and spiritual forces in life so he can mold his own destiny and become the architect of his own success." Believes that meditation and inner guidance will help individuals make mature decisions. *Type:* Association.

Institute of Cultural Affairs

1054 25th Ave.
Seattle, WA 98122

Ph: (206)323-2100

E-mail: icaseattle@igc.apc.org
URL: http://www.ica-usa.org
Contact: Louise Singleton, Pres.
Desc: U.S. branch of the Institute of Cultural Affairs International . Global research, training, and demonstration group concerned with the human factor in world development. *Type:* Association.

Institute of HeartMath

PO Box 1463
14700 W. Park Ave.
Boulder Creek, CA 95006

Ph: (408)338-8500
Fax: (408)338-9861

E-mail: info@heartmath.org
URL: http://www.webcom.com/hrtmath
Contact: Katharine Florindo, Exec.Dir.
Desc: Works to create a cultural shift in how organizations view people, and how people view each other and themselves. *Type:* Association.

Institute of Noetic Sciences

475 Gate 5 Rd., Ste. 300
Sausalito, CA 94965-0909

Ph: (415)331-5650
Fax: (415)331-5673

E-mail: membership@noetic.org
URL: http://www.noetic.org
Contact: Winston O. Franklin, Pres.
Desc: Promotes research and education on the noetic sciences and the subject of human consciousness. (Noetic sciences encompass diverse ways of knowing including intellectual, sensate, and intuitive). Seeks to broaden knowledge of the nature and abilities of the mind and consciousness and to apply that knowledge toward the enhancement of human well-being and the quality of life. *Type:* Association.

Joygerms Unlimited

PO Box 219, Eastwood Sta.
Syracuse, NY 13206

Ph: (315)472-2779

Contact: Joan E. White, Founder.
Desc: Churches, schools, organizations, health and wholeness centers, and interested individuals dedicated to "spreading joy and cheer" throughout the world. Seeks to "eliminate doom and gloom" and "rid the world of gruff and grumpy grouches" by promoting goodwill and humor. Conducts Smile Check Up Clinics in hospitals, nursing homes, schools, and fraternal organizations. *Type:* Association.

The ManKind Project

PO Box 230
Malone, NY 12953-0230

Free: 800-870-4611
Fax: (514)624-2527

E-mail: dhnwmtl@aol.com
URL: http://www.mkp.org
Contact: Drury Heffernan, Admin.
Desc: Seeks to help men reclaim their warrior masculine sides in order to reach a healthy balance between the individual and community. *Type:* Association.

Moral Re-Armament

1156 15th St. NW, Ste. 910
Washington, DC 20005-1704

Ph: (202)872-9077
Fax: (202)872-9137

E-mail: mrawash@aol.com
URL: http://www.mra.org.uk
Contact: Richard W. B. Ruffin, Exec.Dir.
Type: Association.

School of Metaphysics Associates

Dr. Barbara Condron
HCR 1, Box 15
Windyville, MO 65783

Ph: (417)345-8411
Fax: (417)345-6668

E-mail: som@som.org
URL: http://www.som.org
Contact: Dr. Barbara Condron, Bd.Chm.
Desc: Individuals supporting the research, educational, and service operations of the School of Metaphysics . Promotes the "spiritual evolution" of humanity through "bringing the insights and benefits of metaphysical research to all of mankind." *Type:* Association.

Unarius Academy of Science, California Center

145 S. Magnolia Ave.
El Cajon, CA 92020-4522

Ph: (619)444-7062
Free: 800-475-7062
Fax: (619)444-9637

E-mail: unel@unarius.org
URL: http://www.umzvius.org
Contact: Charles L. Spiegel, Dir.
Desc: Promotes the theory of past life therapy; works to liberate individuals from the "psychic amnesia" of the past. Believes all humans have lived on other worlds in the past and will do so again; we draw on energies and experiences of past lives, but are unaware of doing so; one functions at "half-potential" until psychic awareness is achieved. *Type:* Association.

Human Rights

Amnesty Action

Amnesty International USA
322 8th Ave.
New York, NY 10001

Ph: (212)807-8400
Free: 800-266-3789
Fax: (212)627-1451

E-mail: lberg@aiusa.org
URL: http://www.amnesty-usa.org
Contact: Ron Lajoie, Editor, rlajoie@aiusa.org.
Desc: Contains national and international news on human rights issues and on efforts to end human rights abuses. *Type:* Newsletter.

Amnesty International On-line

Amnesty International
304 Pennsylvania Ave. SE   Ph: (202)807-8400
Washington, DC 20003   Fax: (202)463-9193
E-mail: admin-us@aiusa.org
URL: http://www.amnesty.org/

Contact: WebDeveloper@amnesty.org.

Desc: Amnesty International Online contains information concerning Amnesty International (AI), an organization concerned with the protection of human rights. It includes facts and figures about AI, reports of human rights violations, and the Universal Declaration of Human Rights, among other features. *Type:* Database.

Amnesty International of the U.S.A.

322 8th Ave.   Ph: (212)807-8400
New York, NY 10001   Free: 800-AMN-
                ESTY
                Fax: (212)627-1451

Contact: William F. Schulz, Exec.Dir.

Desc: Works impartially for the release of men, women, and children detained anywhere for their conscientiously held beliefs, color, ethnic origin, sexual orientation, religion, or language, provided they have neither used nor advocated violence. Opposes torture, "disappearances," and executions without reservation and advocates fair and prompt trials for all political prisoners. Has consultative status with the United Nations and the Council of Europe, has cooperative relations with the Inter-American Commission on Human Rights, and has observer status with the Organization of African Unity. *Type:* Association.

Amnesty International of the U.S.A., Midwest Regional Office

53 W. Jackson, Rm. 1162   Ph: (312)427-2060
Chicago, IL 60604-3507   Free: 800-AMN-
                ESTY
                Fax: (312)427-2589
URL: http://www.amnesty-usa.org

Contact: Nancy Bothne, Dir.

Desc: Individuals in the midwestern U.S. interested in promoting human rights throughout the world. *Type:* Association.

The Aspen Institute

1333 New Hampshire Ave.   Ph: (202)736-5800
NW, Ste. 1070
Washington, DC 20036
URL: http://www.aspenist.org

Contact: Dr. Charles Knapp, Pres.

Desc: Organizes seminars, workshops, and conferences to bring together business, educational, and cultural leaders from the United States and abroad to discuss issues and initiate action on human, social, and other vital problems in our society and the world. Work is based on consideration of cultural, historical, spiritual, and moral values. Conducts meetings throughout the year, including executive seminars for business leaders. *Type:* Association.

Choice In Dying

1035 30th St., NW   Ph: (202)338-9790
Washington, DC 20007   Free: 800-989-9455
                Fax: (202)338-0242
E-mail: cid@choices.org
URL: http://www.choices.org

Contact: Karen Kaplan, Exec.Dir.

Desc: Seeks to foster communication about end-of-life decisions among individuals, their family and those in the healthcare profession. Publishes educational materials. *Type:* Association.

Choices

Choice in Dying
1035 30th St.   Ph: (202)338-9790
Washington, DC 20007-3823   Free: 800-989-WILL
                Fax: (202)338-0242

E-mail: cid@choices.org
URL: http://www.choices.org; http://www.choices.org.

Contact: Mary Meyer, Editor.

Desc: Reports on issues related to end-to-life health care and developments in legislation, case law, public policy, and professional perspectives. Recurring features include letters to the editor and columns titled Legal Briefs and On Balance. *Type:* Newsletter.

Committee on Human Rights for the People of Nicaragua

17413 Collier Way
Poolesville, MD 20837-2126

Contact: Carlos Anzoategui, Chm. & Exec.Dir.

Desc: Monitors, reports, documents, and records violations of the human rights of the people of Nicaragua. Advocates for the human rights of Indian tribes on the east coast of Nicaragua such as Miskitos, Sumos Ramas, and Creoles. Provides information and referrals to needy refugees. *Type:* Association.

Hemlock Society U.S.A.

PO Box 101810   Ph: (303)639-1202
Denver, CO 80250   Free: 800-247-7421
                Fax: (303)639-1224
E-mail: hemlock@privatei.com
URL: http://www.hemlock.org/hemlock

Contact: Faye Girsh, Ed.D., Exec.Dir.

Desc: Maximizes options for dignified death, including voluntary physician aid in dying for mentally competent, terminally ill adults who request it, within the context of legal safeguards. Through education, research, and legislation, serves as the voice of a national grassroots movement, providing materials and information to the public, the media, health care professionals, and legislators. A legislative arm, PRO-USA, funnels funds directly into efforts to change the law to legalize physician aid in dying. *Type:* Association.

Human Rights Library

University of Minnesota
Minneapolis, MN 55455   Ph: (612)625-5000
E-mail: hoffm019@maroon.tc.umn.edu
URL: http://www.umn.edu/humanrts/

Contact: http://www.umn.edu/humanrts/index.html.

Desc: A repository of full-text official documents, arranged according to issuing organization; plus educational materials, profiles of information sources; and bibliographies. Treaties and such are presented with their dates of passage and other pertinent details. *Type:* Database.

Human Rights Watch

350 5th Ave., 34th Fl.
New York, NY 10118-3299
E-mail: hrwnyc@hrw.org
URL: http://www.hrw.org

Contact: Kenneth Roth, Exec.Dir.

Desc: Organization which promotes and monitors human rights worldwide. Evaluates the human rights practices of governments in accordance with standards recognized by international laws and agreements including the United Nations Declaration of Human Rights and the Helsinki Accords. Identifies government abuses of human rights such as kidnapping, torture, and imprisonment for nonviolent association, exile, psychiatric abuse, and censorship; publicizes and protests against these violations. *Type:* Association.

Inter-American Commission on Human Rights

1889 F St. NW, 8th Fl.   Ph: (202)458-6002
Washington, DC 20006   Fax: (202)458-3992
URL: http://www.oas.org/en/prog/hrights.htm

Contact: Dr. Jorge Taiana, Exec.Sec.

Desc: Citizens of member nations of the Organization of American States . Promotes and protects human rights in the Caribbean, and North, Central, and South America. Maintains 5000 volume library specializing in human rights law. *Type:* Association.

International Association of Former Soviet Political Prisoners and Victims of the Communist Regime

1310 Avenue R, Ste. 6-F   Ph: (718)339-4563
Brooklyn, NY 11229   Fax: (718)339-4563
E-mail: bolonkin@aol.com
URL: http://members.aol.com/bolonkin/info.htm

Contact: Alexander Bolonkin, Ph.D., Pres.

Desc: Works to protect former Soviet political prisoners and victims of the Communist regime from human rights abuses. *Type:* Association.

International Human Rights Law Group

1200 18th St. NW, Ste. 602   Ph: (202)822-4600
Washington, DC 20036   Fax: (202)822-4606
E-mail: humanrights@hrlawgroup.org

Contact: Gay J. McDougall, Exec.Dir.

Desc: Human rights and legal professionals engaged in human rights advocacy, litigation and training around the world. Supports and helps empower advocates to expand the scope of human rights protection for men and women and promotes broad participation in building human rights standards and procedures at the national, regional and international levels. *Type:* Association.

International League for Human Rights

432 Park Ave. S., Ste. 1103   Fax: (212)684-1696
New York, NY 10016
E-mail: ilhr@ilhr.org
URL: http://www.ilhr.org

Contact: Catherine Q. Fitzpatrick, Exec.Dir.

Desc: Individuals and national affiliates promoting human rights, including political and civil rights, racial and religious freedom, and the implementation of the Universal Declaration of Human Rights. Serves as nongovernmental agency accredited by the United Nations, International Labor Organization, United Nations Educational, Scientific and Cultural Organization, and Council of Europe . Participates in studies and programs on human rights. *Type:* Association.

International Right of Way Association

13650 S. Gramercy Pl.   Ph: (310)538-0233
Gardena, CA 90249   Fax: (310)538-1471
E-mail: rosenberg@irwa.com
URL: http://www.irwa.com

Contact: Raymond H. Rosenberg, CAE, Exec.VP.

Desc: International professional society of appraisers, attorneys, engineers, negotiators, property managers, title examiners, and others whose principal interest is in the purchase of land and rights in land for the construction of transportation, utility, and other public service facilities. *Type:* Association.

Irish Lobby

Irish National Caucus (INC)
413 E. Capitol St. SE   Ph: (202)544-0568
Washington, DC 20003   Fax: (202)543-2491

Contact: Fr. Sean McManus, Editor.

Desc: Carries information on the work of the Irish National Caucus to "get the U.S. to adapt a proper foreign policy on unity, freedom, justice and peace in Ireland." Reports on human rights issues and violations in Northern Ireland and the Caucus' boycott of the Ford Motor Company. *Type:* Newsletter.

Lawyers Committee for Human Rights

333 7th Ave., 13th Fl.   Ph: (212)845-5200
New York, NY 10001   Fax: (212)845-5299
Contact: Michael Posner, Exec.Dir.
Desc: Public interest law center that works to promote international human rights and refugee law and legal procedures. Focuses on cases where volunteer lawyers may help promote international human rights standards. Is involved in the pro bono representation of indigent political asylum applicants in the U.S. *Type:* Association.

The Lifestyles Organization

2641 W. La Palma, Ste. A   Ph: (714)821-9939
Anaheim, CA 92801   Fax: (714)821-1465
E-mail: playcouples-info@playcouples.com
URL: http://www.playcouples.com
Contact: Robert L. McGinley, Ph.D., Pres.
Desc: Participants are persons living an alternative lifestyle. Holds seminars, workshops, and panel presentations on topics including ways of living, social recreation, marriage and other interpersonal relationships, swinging, communes, legal and medical aspects of human behavior, and human sexuality. *Type:* Association.

Male Liberation Foundation

701 NE 67th St.   Ph: (305)756-6249
Miami, FL 33138   Fax: (305)756-6006
Contact: Frank Bertels, Founder & Dir.
Desc: Individuals who seek to publicize the "new discrimination" against men, including discrimination which caused men "to become the coffee boys, floor sweepers, and delivery boys in the 1990s." Believes that men and women have real biological and psychological differences and that public awareness, education, and acceptance of these differences will reduce the divorce rate. Seeks to educate men about their economic and political losses and solutions; supports joint custody and paternal leave for fathers of newborn children. Seeks to defend homemakers (traditional women) from "screaming radical feminists." Lobbies for changes in Affirmative Action policies, abortion laws, divorce inequities, and sexual harassment rulings. *Type:* Association.

Men's Defense Association

17854 Lyons   Ph: (651)464-7887
Forest Lake, MN 55025   Fax: (651)464-7135
E-mail: mensdefens@aol.com
URL: http://www.mensdefense.org/
Contact: Richard F. Doyle, Pres.
Desc: Male victims of sex discrimination, actual or potential. Purposes are: to obtain equal rights under the law for all male persons; to promote and foster the just and competent administration of government, especially of the judicial branch; to study, promote, and engage in activities that will strengthen the marriage relationship and family life; to foster, promote, and undertake activities that will restore and maintain the dignity of male persons; to engage in, foster, and promote continuing public education in the aforesaid areas; to aid and assist individuals in areas consistent with the purposes of the organization. *Type:* Association.

National Organization for Men

11 Park Pl.   Ph: (212)686-6253
New York, NY 10007   Fax: (212)791-3056
URL: http://www.tnom.com
Contact: Richard Bogash, Pres.
Desc: Men and women united in efforts to promote and advance the equal rights of men in matters such as affirmative action programs, alimony, child custody, men's health, child abuse, battered husbands, divorce, educational benefits, military conscription, and veterans' benefits. Maintains Institute for the Study of Matrimonial Laws , established as a research and education foundation for the study of the nation's divorce, alimony, and custody and visitation laws. Offers support group; lobbies for equal rights for men; compiles statistics. *Type:* Association.

National Organization for Men Legal Defense and Education Fund

11 Park Pl.   Ph: (212)686-6253
New York, NY 10007   Fax: (212)791-3056
Contact: Dr. Allan Boudreau, Contact.
Desc: Supporters of National Organization for Men, a heterosexual men's rights advocacy group. Initiates legislation for reform of state and national family law courts. *Type:* Association.

Physicians for Human Rights

100 Boylston St., Ste. 702   Ph: (617)695-0041
Boston, MA 02116   Fax: (617)695-0307
E-mail: phrusa@phrusa.org
URL: http://www.phrusa.org
Contact: Leonard Rubenstein, Exec.Dir.
Desc: Mobilizes the health professions and enlists the support of the general public to protect and promote the human rights of all people. *Type:* Association.

Humanities

Academic Index™

The Gale Group
27500 Drake Rd.   Ph: (248)699-4253
Farmington Hills, MI 48331-3535
URL: http://www.galegroup.com
Contact: Jim Knight.
Desc: Expanded Academic ASAP offers balanced full text coverage of every academic concentration- from advertising and microbiology to history, political science, and art history. It also incorporates many interdisciplinary journals, national news magazines, and The New York Times. *Available:* The Dialog Corporation, DIALOG; CompuServe Information Service, Knowledge Index; The Dialog Corporation, DataStar; CARL Corporation; The Gale Group, InfoTrac Web. *Type:* Database.

ACH Newsletter

Association for Computers and the Humanities (ACH)
Humanities Computing Facility   Ph: (213)825-6759
Univ. Of California
Santa Barbara, CA 93106-3170
Contact: Vicky Walsh, Editor.
Desc: Carries news of activities in the field of computer-related research in humanities. Recurring features include news of the Association and a calendar of events. *Type:* Newsletter.

Arts & Humanities Search®

Institute for Scientific Information (ISI)
3501 Market St.   Ph: (215)386-0100
Philadelphia, PA 19104
E-mail: isiorder@isinet.com
URL: http://www.isinet.com
Desc: Contains bibliographic data on items from more than 1140 arts and humanities journals. Also includes individually selected relevant items from more than 7000 science and social sciences journals. *Available:* The Dialog Corporation, DIALOG; The Dialog Corporation, DIALOG; OCLC Online Computer Library Center, Inc., OCLC EPIC; OCLC Online Computer Library Center, Inc., OCLC FirstSearch Catalog; The Dialog Corporation, DataStar; Institute for Scientific Information (ISI). *Type:* Database.

Denver Arts Center Programs

The Publishing House, Inc.
7380 Lowell Blvd.   Ph: (303)428-9529
PO Box 215   Fax: (303)430-1676
Westminster, CO 80030
Contact: Melanie Simonet, Editor; Wilbur Flachman, Publisher; Frank Debolt, Advertising Mgr.
Desc: Magazine covering events held at the Denver Center for the Performing Arts. *Type:* Periodical.

Essay and General Literature Index

H.W. Wilson Company
950 University Ave.   Ph: (718)588-8400
Bronx, NY 10452
E-mail: custserv@hwwilson.com
URL: http://www.hwwilson.com
Contact: Technical Support Department., techmail@info.hwwilson.com.
Desc: Contains 70,000 citations to English-language essay collections and anthologies in the humanities and social sciences. Covers a variety of subject areas (e.g., economics, history, politics), with an emphasis on literature and critical works. *Available:* H.W. Wilson Company, WilsonWeb; OCLC Online Computer Library Center, Inc., OCLC EPIC; Ovid Technologies, Inc.; SilverPlatter Information, Inc. *Type:* Database.

Humanities Index

H.W. Wilson Company
950 University Ave.   Ph: (718)588-8400
Bronx, NY 10452
E-mail: custserv@hwwilson.com
URL: http://www.hwwilson.com
Contact: Technical Support Department., (718)588-8400, custserv@info.hwwilson.com.
Desc: Contains citations to articles and book reviews in 400 general-interest periodicals and periodicals in the humanities. Covers theology, religion, performing arts, literary and political criticism, language and literature, philosophy, history, folklore, classical studies, and archaeology. *Available:* H.W. Wilson Company, WilsonWeb; H.W. Wilson Company, WilsonWeb; OCLC Online Computer Library Center, Inc., OCLC EPIC; OCLC Online Computer Library Center, Inc., OCLC FirstSearch Catalog; Ovid Technologies, Inc.; Ameritech Library Services, Vista; NlightN. *Type:* Database.

LetsFindOut.com: The Knowledge Adventure Encyclopedia

Knowledge Adventure, Inc.
1311 Grand Central Ave.   Free: 800-556-5141
Glendale, CA 91201   Fax: (818)246-5604
URL: http://www.letsfindout.com/
Desc: Sure to appeal to the tech savvy student in the house, this encyclopedia has a decided emphasis on cool. Topics covered are broad, but unlike some other encyclopedias seem to hit only the highlights of history, etc. *Type:* Database.

Lingo Magazine

Hard Press, Inc.
PO Box 184   Ph: (413)232-4690
West Stockbridge, MA 01266-0184   Fax: (413)232-4675
E-mail: editors@hardpress.com.
URL: http://www.handpress.com.
Contact: Jon Gams, Editor, jongams@handpress.com; Chad Odefey, Asst. Editor; Ned Depew, Mktg.
Desc: Magazine including poetry, art, photographs, music, and fiction. *Type:* Periodical.

Pen & Ink

Pen & Ink Press
PO Box 517
Metairie, LA 70004-0517
Contact: Ann Hoyt, Editor; Francis Nordan, Editor; Sharida Rizzuto, Editor.
Desc: Publishes poetry, news, fiction and non-fiction articles, and reviews. *Type:* Newsletter.

The Poetry Explosion Newsletter (PEN)

Poet Band Co.
3392 Webster Ave.
Pittsburgh, PA 15219-3975
Contact: Arthur C. Ford, Editor.
Desc: Publishes poetry, both rhyming and non-rhyming, and prose. *Type:* Newsletter.

Poets' Roundtable

Esther Alman
826 S. Center St.   Ph: (812)234-0819
Terre Haute, IN 47807
Contact: Esther Alman, Editor.
Desc: Provides information for members of Poets' Study Club. Sponsors annual open poetry competition. *Type:* Newsletter.

Texas Young Writers' Newsletter

Texas Young Writers
PO Box 942
Adkins, TX 78101-0942
Contact: Susan Currie, Editor.
Desc: Publishes short stories and poetry of young authors ages 12-19 from all over U.S. Features articles on the art and business of writing. *Type:* Newsletter.

USIC Educational Foundation

220 National Press Bldg.   Ph: (202)662-8744
14th & F Sts. NW   Fax: (202)662-8754
Washington, DC 20045
Contact: Anthony Harrigan, Pres.
Desc: A lecture series program dedicated to bringing an understanding of private enterprise, individual liberty, and the traditional values that underlie society to college campuses. *Type:* Association.

World Databases in the Humanities

National Register Publishing Co.
121 Chanlon Rd.   Ph: (908)464-6800
New Providence, NJ 07974   Free: 800-521-8110
                          Fax: (908)508-7671
E-mail: info@renp.com
URL: http://www.reedref.com
Contact: C.J. Armstrong, Editor.
Desc: Humanities information on databases, including CD-ROM, magnetic tape, diskette, online, fax, or databroadcast worldwide. *Type:* Directory.

Hunger

Benson Institute Review

Benson Institute
Brigham Young University
110 B-49   Ph: (801)378-2607
Provo, UT 84602   Fax: (801)378-0099
E-mail: Benson_Institute@byu.edu
Contact: Linda Hunter Adams, Editor, (801)378-4455, linda_adams@byu.edu.
Desc: Focuses on the activities and issues of the Ezra Taft Benson Agriculture and Food Institute. Provides information on nutrition and agricultural research, with an emphasis on malnutrition in underdeveloped areas. *Type:* Newsletter.

Bread for the World

1100 Wayne Ave., Ste. 1000   Ph: (301)608-2400
Silver Spring, MD 20910   Free: 800-822-7323
                            Fax: (301)608-2401
E-mail: bread@igc.org
URL: http://www.bread.igc.org
Contact: David Beckmann, Pres.
Desc: Christians united against hunger and poverty. *Type:* Association.

Food for the Hungry, Inc.

7729 E. Greenway Rd.   Ph: (602)998-3100
Scottsdale, AZ 85260   Free: 800-248-6437
                           Fax: (602)443-1420
URL: http://www.fh.org
Contact: Ted Yamamori, CEO.
Desc: Organized to offer both disaster relief and long-range selfhelp assistance. *Type:* Association.

Food Research and Action Center

1875 Connecticut Ave. NW,   Ph: (202)986-2200
  Ste. 540   Fax: (202)986-2525
Washington, DC 20009-5728
E-mail: foodresearch@frac.org
URL: http://www.frac.org
Contact: James D. Weill, Pres.
Desc: Renders technical assistance, training, research, information, and community organizing assistance to low-income organizations endeavoring to make federal food assistance programs more responsive to the acute needs of millions of hungry Americans. Seeks to enhance public awareness of problems of hunger and poverty. Researches, writes, and publishes analyses of federal food programs; offers strategies for local and statewide antihunger activities. *Type:* Association.

Freedom from Hunger

1644 DaVinci Ct.   Ph: (530)758-6200
PO Box 2000   Fax: (530)758-6241
Davis, CA 95617
E-mail: info@freefromhunger.org
URL: http://www.freefromhunger.org
Contact: Dr. Christopher Dunford, Pres.
Desc: Promotes "self-help for a hungry world." Works to build the capacity of individuals and communities to overcome the root causes of chronic hunger and malnutrition. Committed to having a major long-term impact on hunger by improving on the record of traditional development approaches. Poor, rural women are the primary target of the Credit with Education program, which provides them with opportunities to invest in their own small businesses and to save for emergency needs. *Type:* Association.

Institute for Food and Development Policy

398 60th St.   Ph: (510)654-4400
Oakland, CA 94618   Free: 800-274-7826
                          Fax: (510)654-4551
E-mail: foodfirst@foodfirst.org
URL: http://www.foodfirst.org
Contact: Peter Rosset, Exec.Dir.
Desc: Investigates the root causes of hunger and food problems in the U.S. *Type:* Association.

International Food Policy Research Institute

1200 17th St. NW   Ph: (202)862-5600
Washington, DC 20036-3006   Fax: (202)467-4439
E-mail: ifpri_info@cgnet.com
Contact: Dr. Per Pinstrup-Andersen, Dir.Gen.
Desc: Research center established to analyze alternative national and international strategies and policies for meeting the food needs in developing countries with a view toward reducing hunger and malnutrition. Conducts policy research on the problems of food production, consumption, and trade in developing countries. Addresses issues of increasing sustainable food production and improving the equity of its distribution. *Type:* Association.

Love is Feeding Everyone

310 N. Fairfax, 2nd Fl.   Ph: (323)936-0895
Los Angeles, CA 90036   Fax: (323)936-5162
Contact: Brenda Pierce, Operations Dir.
Desc: Works to alleviate hunger in Los Angeles, CA and surrounding areas by directing surplus food to needy individuals through network with other social service agencies. Encourages supermarkets, manufacturers, and trade associations to donate to LIFE still-edible food that cannot be sold due to printed expiration dates or packaging defects. Holds food drives outside of supermarkets in order to encourage shoppers to purchase an item and donate it to LIFE to help feed hungry people. *Type:* Association.

Presbyterian Hunger Program

Presbyterian Church (U.S.A.)   Ph: (502)569-5832
100 Witherspoon St.   Fax: (502)569-8963
Louisville, KY 40202-1396
E-mail: php@pcusa.org
Contact: Diane Hockenberry, Associate.
Desc: Promotes "the integrity of creation" and global interdependence by encouraging personal and corporate responsibility and increased understanding of the causes of global hunger. Provides funds to over 350 hunger-related projects annually including direct hunger relief, hunger-related development assistance, public policy advocacy, lifestyle integrity, including environmental justice, and education and interpretation. Focuses on issues such as global debt, the environment, homelessness, and women and development. *Type:* Association.

Second Harvest

116 S. Michigan Ave., Ste. 4   Ph: (312)263-2303
Chicago, IL 60603   Free: 800-532-FOOD
                           Fax: (312)236-5626
URL: http://www.secondharvest.org
Contact: Christine Vladimiroff, Exec. Officer.
Desc: Network of food banks that distribute millions of pounds of donated food and grocery products to the hungry through food pantries, soup kitchens, and homeless shelters. *Type:* Association.

Senior Gleaners, Inc.

3185 Longview Dr.   Ph: (916)971-1530
North Highlands, CA 95660   Fax: (916)482-3450
E-mail: sgi@seniorgleaners.org
URL: http://www.seniorgleaners.org
Contact: James E. Magel, Pres.
Desc: Retired senior citizens who salvage edible but often unsalable foods. The gleaners collect what farmers cannot harvest or cannot sell after the harvest, not only for themselves, but also to distribute to charitable organizations. (It is estimated that in one year's time, the amount of food wasted during production and distribution could have fed 49 million people.) Although Senior Gleaners Inc., is a local California organization, many similar groups have been organized across the nation. *Type:* Association.

Share Our Strength

Bill Shore
733 15th St. NW, Ste. 640   Ph: (202)393-2925
Washington, DC 20005   Free: 800-969-4767
                            Fax: (202)347-5868
Contact: Bill Shore, Exec. Dir.
Desc: Chefs, restaurateurs, creative professionals, and interested volunteers. Seeks to alleviate hunger in the U.S. *Type:* Association.

Immigration

American Immigration Control Foundation

Box 525   Ph: (540)468-2022
Main St.   Fax: (540)468-2024
Monterey, VA 24465
Contact: John Vinson, Pres.

Desc: American citizens concerned about what the AICF views as uncontrolled immigration into the U.S. Objective is to educate Americans and their leaders about the need for immigration control and problems the AICF believes are caused by illegal immigration. *Type:* Association.

Close Up Foundation

44 Canal Center Plz.   Ph: (703)706-3300
Alexandria, VA 22314   Free: 800-256-7387
    Fax: (703)706-0000
E-mail: webmaster@closeup.org
URL: http://www.closeup.org
Contact: Stephen A. Janger, Pres.

Desc: Encourages responsible participation in the democratic process by citizens of all ages and backgrounds; promotes increased civic awareness, involvement, and achievement through non-partisan educational programs in government and citizenship. Operates Close Up Washington, a government studies program for middle school and high school students and teachers from the U.S. and other countries, including hearing and visually impaired students. *Type:* Association.

Ethics Resource Center

1747 Pennsylvania Ave. NW,   Ph: (202)737-2258
    Ste. 400   Free: 800-777-1285
Washington, DC 20006   Fax: (202)737-2227
E-mail: ethics@ethics.org
URL: http://www.ethics.org
Contact: Michael G. Daigneault, Esq., Pres.

Desc: Seeks to serve as a catalyst to improve the ethical practices of individuals and organizations from the classroom to the boardroom. The organization fulfills its mission through three distinct areas of expertise: as a leader in the fields of organizational/business ethics consulting; as a provider and facilitator of character education programs; and as an ethics information clearinghouse. *Type:* Association.

Federation for American Immigration Reform

1666 Connecticut Ave. NW,   Ph: (202)328-7004
    Ste. 400   Free: 800-395-0890
Washington, DC 20009   Fax: (202)387-3447
E-mail: fair@fairus.org
URL: http://www.fairus.org
Contact: Daniel Stein, Exec.Dir.

Desc: Advocates comprehensive reform of present immigration policies to conform with present-day demographic, environmental, and labor-force realities; promotes active enforcement of laws against illegal immigration. *Type:* Association.

Immigration and Refugee Services of America

1717 Massachusetts Ave., NW,   Ph: (202)347-3507
    Ste. 701   Free: 800-307-4712
Washington, DC 20036   Fax: (202)347-3418
E-mail: irsa@irsa-uscr.org
URL: http://www.irsa-uscr.org
Contact: Roger P. Winter, Exec.Dir.

Desc: Service organization that promotes cultural pluralism and assists refugees and immigrants in adjusting to American life and becoming fully participating citizens. Has member agencies, usually called International Institutes, in 33 cities that act as centers of service and fellowship for all nationalities. Advises its affiliated agencies on program and policy developments affecting the foreign born. *Type:* Association.

Industrial Equipment

American Gear Manufacturers Association

1500 King St., Ste. 201   Ph: (703)684-0211
Alexandria, VA 22314-2730   Fax: (703)684-0242
E-mail: webmaster@agma.org
URL: http://www.agma.org
Contact: Joe T. Franklin, Jr., Pres.

Desc: Manufacturers of gears, geared speed changers, and related equipment; manufacturers of gear cutting and checking equipment; teachers of mechanical engineering and gearing. Conducts educational and research programs; compiles statistics and financial data. *Type:* Association.

American Machine Tool Distributors' Association

1445 Research Blvd., No. 450   Ph: (301)738-1200
Rockville, MD 20850-8125   Free: 800-878-2683
    Fax: (301)738-9499
E-mail: jallen@amtda.org
URL: http://www.amtda.org
Contact: Ralph J. Nappi, Pres.

Desc: Distributors and builders of manufacturing technology. *Type:* Association.

American Paint and Coatings Journal— Directory of Raw Material Distributors & Manufacturers' Agents Issue

Douglas Publications, Inc.
4113 Fawn Trail   Ph: (970)663-0241
Loveland, CO 80537   Fax: (970)663-0172
E-mail: creittr@aol.com.
Contact: Mary Benke, Editor, mbenke@oneimage.com.

Desc: List of about 400 manufacturers' agents and distributors of raw materials and equipment for the paint manufacturing industry. *Type:* Directory.

Assembly Buyers Guide Issue

Cahners Publishing
2000 Clearwater Dr.   Ph: (630)320-7000
Oak Brook, IL 60523   Free: 800-826-6270
Contact: Donald E. Hegland, Editor.

Desc: List of manufacturers of equipment used to assemble manufactured products. *Type:* Directory.

Automatic I.D. News—Buyer's Guide Issue

Advanstar Communications
131 W. First St.   Free: 800-346-0085
Duluth, MN 55802
E-mail: fulfill@superfil.com
URL: http://www.autoidnews.com.
Contact: Mark David, Editor.

Desc: List of manufacturers, suppliers, consultants, value added resellers, and dealers/distributors of automatic identification and data capture software, technology, equipment, and products for bar code, biometric identification, electronic data interchange, machine vision, magnetic stripe, optical character recognition, radio frequency data communications, radio frequency identification, smart cards, and voice data entry; also includes related organizations, and sources for industry standards. *Type:* Directory.

Compressed Air

Compressed Air
253 E. Washington Ave.   Ph: (908)850-7817
Washington, NJ 07882-2495   Fax: (908)689-3095
E-mail: camag@ingersoll-rand.com.
URL: http://www.ingersoll-rand.com.
Contact: Thomas McAloon, Editor, (908)850-7818; Paul Dickard, Publisher; Kelly Spiece, Editorial Asst., (908)850-7840.

Desc: General Industrial Publication. *Type:* Periodical.

Construction Industry Manufacturers Association

111 E. Wisconsin Ave., Ste.   Ph: (414)272-0943
    1000   Fax: (414)272-1170
Milwaukee, WI 53202
E-mail: cima@cimanet.com
URL: http://www.cimanet.com
Contact: Dennis Slater, Pres.

Desc: Manufacturers of off-highway earthmoving and construction machinery and allied equipment and components. Compiles statistics. *Type:* Association.

Directory and Guide to Industry Products

Door and Hardware Institute
14170 Newbrook Dr.   Ph: (703)222-2010
Chantilly, VA 20151-2233   Fax: (703)222-2410
E-mail: publications@dhi.org.
URL: http://www.dhi.org.
Contact: Donna Munari, Editor.

Desc: More than 700 firms which supply doors, hinges, locks, cabinet and closet hardware, door motors, smoke closing and detection devices, washroom accessories, and similar accessories; includes products for the handicapped; international coverage. *Type:* Directory.

DRI Plant and Equipment Expenditures Forecast

Standard & Poor's DRI
Data Products Division
24 Hartwell Ave.   Ph: (781)863-5100
Lexington, MA 02421
E-mail: client_services@dri.mcgraw-hill.com
URL: http://www.dri.mcgraw-hill.com
Contact: Client Resource Center, (781)860-6527, fax: (781)860-6416.

Desc: Contains 78 quarterly and annual historical and forecast time series of plant and equipment expenditures 26 U.S. industries ranging from food and beverages to trade and services. *Available:* Standard & Poor's DRI, Data Products Division. *Type:* Database.

High Tech Ceramics News

Business Communications Co., Inc.
25 Van Zant St.   Ph: (203)853-4266
Norwalk, CT 06855-1781   Fax: (203)853-0348
E-mail: buscom2@aol.com
URL: http://www.buscom.com; http://www.buscom.com.
Contact: Dr. Thomas Abraham, Editor, tombcc@aol.com.

Desc: Analyses products, patents, and trends in the high-tech ceramics industry. *Type:* Newsletter.

ID Systems Buyer's Guide

Helmers Publishing, Inc.
174 Concord St.   Ph: (603)924-9631
PO Box 874   Fax: (603)924-7408
Peterborough, NH 03458
E-mail: editors@idsystems.com.
URL: http://www.idsystems.com.
Contact: David Andrews, Editor-in-Chief.

Desc: Over 750 companies that provide complete automated data collection systems, bar code scanners, printers, data collection terminals, etc. *Type:* Directory.

Industrial Distribution Association

3 Corporate Sq., Ste. 201   Ph: (404)261-3991
Atlanta, GA 30329   Fax: (404)266-8311
E-mail: idainc@pop.mindspring.com
URL: http://www.ida-assoc.org
Contact: Gary L. Buffington, Exec.VP.

Desc: Distributers of industrial equipment and supplies. *Type:* Association.

Industrial Equipment News

Thomas Publishing Co.

5 Penn Plaza   Ph: (212)695-0500
New York, NY 10001   Fax: (212)290-7206
E-mail: ordertr@thomasregister.com; ienedit@iennet.com.
Contact: Mark F. Devlin, Editor-in-Chief; Jack O'Toole, Publisher; Robert Clark, Art Director; Deborah R. Maskin, Managing Editor; Larry I. Bernstein, Exec. Editor.
Desc: Magazine containing new product information for manufacturing industries. *Type:* Periodical.

Industrial Market Place

Wineberg Publications

7842 N. Lincoln Ave.   Ph: (847)676-1900
Skokie, IL 60077   Free: 800-323-1818
     Fax: (847)676-0063
E-mail: imp@wwa.com.
URL: http://www.industrialmktpl.com.
Contact: Adrienne Gallender, Publisher.
Desc: Trade magazine focusing on metal and metalworking machinery, and plant & factory equipment. *Type:* Periodical.

Industrial Surfactants Electronic Handbook

Ashgate Publishing Co.

Old Post Rd.   Ph: (802)276-3162
Brookfield, VT 05036   Fax: (802)276-3837
E-mail: info@ashgatechem.com
Contact: Michael Ash, Editor; Irene Ash, Editor.
Desc: Manufacturers of more than 16,000 tradenamed surface-active agents for industrial applications. *Type:* Directory.

Institute of Caster Manufacturers

104 S. Michigan Ave., Ste. 1500   Ph: (312)201-0101
Chicago, IL 60603   Fax: (312)201-0214
Contact: Jack Lagershausen, Exec.Dir.
Desc: Trade association representing manufacturers of casters and wheels for material handling equipment. *Type:* Association.

Locator

Machinery Dealers National Association

315 S. Patrick St.   Ph: (703)836-9300
Alexandria, VA 22314-3501   Free: 800-872-7807
     Fax: (703)836-9303
E-mail: office@mdna.org; bcross@locatoronline.com.
URL: http://www.mdna.org; http://www.usedequip.com.
Contact: Darryl McEwen, Publisher.
Desc: Magazine on metalworking, plastic and electrical machinery, and power equipment. *Type:* Periodical.

The Maintenance Journal

International Maintenance Institute

PO Box 751896   Ph: (281)481-0869
Houston, TX 77275-1896   Fax: (281)481-8337
Contact: Barbara Walters, Editor.
Desc: Covers in-house and contract maintenance services for chemical refineries, manufacturing firms, government agencies, and institutions. Also concerned with the distributors of maintenance products and services, as well as allied industries. *Type:* Newsletter.

Manufacturers Alliance for Productivity and Innovation

1525 Wilson Blvd., Ste. 900   Ph: (703)841-9000
Arlington, VA 22209   Fax: (703)841-7104
Contact: Kenneth McLennan, Pres.
Desc: Manufacturing and related business service companies. Membership concentrated in the following sectors:

aerospace; automotive; scientific instruments; electronics; computers and telecommunication equipment; chemicals/pharmaceuticals; oil and oil-related equipment; electrical equipment farm, construction, food, material handling, and other machinery; primary and fabricated metals. *Type:* Association.

Material Handling Industry

8720 Red Oak Blvd., Ste. 201   Ph: (704)676-1190
Charlotte, NC 28217   Free: 800-345-1815
     Fax: (704)676-1199
E-mail: vwheller@mhia.org
URL: http://www.mhia.org
Contact: A. L. Leffler, CEO.
Desc: Consultants, integrators, and manufacturers of industrial material handling equipment and systems. Promotes education in the use of material handling equipment. *Type:* Association.

Microtechnology News

Business Communications Co., Inc.

25 Van Zant St.   Ph: (203)853-4266
Norwalk, CT 06855-1781   Fax: (203)853-0348
E-mail: buscom2@aol.com
URL: http://www.buscom.com; http://www.buscom.com/.
Contact: Patrick Wier, Editor.
Desc: Reports on patents and provides market analysis in the areas of thin films and diamond materials. Covers such topics as plastics and polymer coatings, optical films and coverings, composite films, and developments in electronics technology. *Type:* Newsletter.

National Fluid Power Association

3333 N. Mayfair Rd.   Ph: (414)778-3344
Milwaukee, WI 53222-3219   Fax: (414)778-3361
E-mail: nfpa@nfpa.com
URL: http://www.nfpa.com
Contact: Dennis Mcguirk, Exec.Dir.
Desc: Manufacturers of components such as hydraulic and pneumatic pumps, valves, cylinders, filters, seals, hoses, and fittings used in transmitting power by means of a fluid (gas or liquid) under pressure; the components are used in industrial and mobile machinery in the material-handling, automotive, railway, aircraft, marine, aerospace, construction, agricultural, and other industries. Works to develop: American National Standards Institute and International Organization for Standardization; fluid power technical standards; fluid power index (industry sales); management and marketing studies. *Type:* Association.

National Welding Supply Association

1900 Arch St.   Ph: (215)564-3484
Philadelphia, PA 19103   Fax: (215)564-2175
URL: http://www.nwsa.com
Contact: G. A. Taylor Fernley, Mng.Dir.
Desc: Manufacturers and distributors of welding equipment, supplies, and industrial and medical gases. *Type:* Association.

North American Die Casting Association

9701 W. Higgins Rd., Ste. 880   Ph: (847)292-3600
Rosemont, IL 60018   Fax: (847)292-3620
Contact: Daniel L. Twarog, CAE, Exec.VP.
Desc: Producers of die castings and suppliers to the industry, product and die designers, metallurgists, and students. Develops product standards; compiles trade statistics on metal consumption trends; conducts promotional activities; provides information on chemistry, mechanics, engineering, and other arts and sciences related to die casting. Provides training materials and short, intensive courses in die casting. *Type:* Association.

OPEDA Outlook

Outdoor Power Equipment Distributors Association (OPEDA)

1900 Arch St.   Ph: (215)564-3484
Philadelphia, PA 19103   Fax: (215)963-9784
E-mail: opeda@fernley.com
Contact: Joe Koury, Editor, jkoury@fernley.com.
Desc: Covers Association and industry news, personnel changes, new products, and corporate developments. *Type:* Newsletter.

Partners for Democratic Change

823 Uloa St.   Ph: (415)665-0652
San Francisco, CA 94127   Fax: (415)665-2732
E-mail: pdci@ix.netcom.com
URL: http://www.partners-intl.org
Contact: Raymond Shonholtz, J.D., Pres.
Desc: Committed to advancing the democratic management of conflict and the building of civil society in transitioning democracies through developing indigenous capacities to address in-country conficts. *Type:* Association.

Power Transmission Distributors Association

6400 Shafer Ct., Ste. 670   Ph: (847)825-2000
Rosemont, IL 60018-4909   Fax: (847)825-0953
E-mail: ptda@ptda.org
URL: http://www.ptda.org
Contact: Mary Sue Lyon, Exec.VP.
Desc: Distributors and manufacturers of power transmission/motion and position control equipment. Maintains business management and continuing education resources; conducts educational programs; compiles statistics, sponsors industry convention, conducts research, co-sponsors industry tradeshows. *Type:* Association.

Rock and Dirt

TAP Publishing Co.

174 Fourth St.   Ph: (931)484-5137
PO Box 3079   Free: 800-251-6776
Crossville, TN 38557   Fax: (931)484-2532
Contact: Mike Stone, Publisher, mstone@rockanddirt.com; M. S. Ironside, Editor, mironside@rockanddirt.com.
Desc: Buy and sell trade newspaper (tabloid) for heavy construction earth moving machinery. *Type:* Periodical.

Scrubber/Adsorber Newsletter

McIlvaine Co.

2970 Maria Ave.   Ph: (847)272-0010
Northbrook, IL 60062   Fax: (847)272-9673
E-mail: editor@mcilvainecompany.com
URL: http://www.mcilvainecompany.com
Contact: Virginia Grimse, Editor.
Desc: Focuses on applications for particulate scrubbing, absorption, adsorption, odor control, wet dust suppression, and distillation. Offers information on trends in the field, systems and auxiliaries, and patents. *Type:* Newsletter.

Specialty Tools and Fasteners Distributors Association

500 Elm Grove Rd.   Ph: (414)784-4774
Box 44   Free: 800-352-2981
Elm Grove, WI 53122   Fax: (414)784-5059
E-mail: stafda@execpc.com
URL: http://www.stafda.org
Contact: Morrie E. Halvorsen, Exec.Dir.
Desc: Distributors and suppliers of power tools, power-actuated tools, anchors, fastening systems, diamond drilling, and related construction equipment. Encourages legal, ethical, and friendly business relations within the industry. *Type:* Association.

Stark's Truck & Off-Highway Ledger

J-C Communications Company, Inc.

318 W. Adams St.   Ph: (312)236-5122
Chicago, IL 60606   Fax: (312)236-3297
E-mail: jccomm@starks-news.com
Contact: John A. Stark, President.
Desc: Provides updated news on production, sales, and stocks of light, medium and heavy-duty trucks, and farm and construction machines. Recurring features include statistical surveys, vehicle design trends, late-breaking business news, periodic two-page market closeups, and executive interviews. *Type:* Newsletter.

Used Equipment Directory

Penton Media Inc.

611 Rte. 46 W.   Ph: (201)393-6060
Hasbrouck Heights, NJ 07604   Free: 800-526-6052
    Fax: (201)393-6242
E-mail: info@buyused.com
URL: http://www.buyused.com.
Contact: James Mack, Editor, jmack@buyused.com; Robert Tannen, Editor.
Desc: List of 800 dealers in used metalworking, electrical, power, process, and material handling equipment and machine tools. *Type:* Directory.

Valve News & Patents

IMPACT Publications

PO Box 3113   Ph: (208)622-3210
Ketchum, ID 83340   Fax: (208)726-2115
Contact: Mary Jo Helmeke, Editor.
Desc: Reviews new valve products, software, and current literature in the field. Recurring features include news of research, a calendar of events, reports of meetings, news of educational opportunities, book reviews, notices of publications available, notices of upcoming seminars, and technical reports. *Type:* Newsletter.

Industrial Workers

AFL-CIO

815 16th St. NW, Rm 703   Ph: (202)637-5000
Washington, DC 20006   Fax: (202)637-5058
URL: http://www.aflcio.org/home.htm
Contact: John Sweeney, Pres.
Desc: Federation of national unions, state federations, city central bodies, and directly affiliated local unions. *Type:* Association.

Industrial Union Department (of AFL-CIO)

815 16th St. NW   Ph: (202)842-7800
Washington, DC 20006   Fax: (202)842-7938
Contact: Pete Dicicco, Pres.
Desc: Federation of steel, automotive, electrical, clothing, governmental, glass, and rubber labor unions. *Type:* Association.

International Union Allied Industrial Workers of America

3520 W. Oklahoma Ave.   Ph: (414)645-9500
PO Box 343913   Fax: (414)645-5530
Milwaukee, WI 53234
Contact: Nick Serraglio, Pres.
Desc: AFL-CIO. Coordinates activities of local unions. Sponsors steward training, collective bargaining, and annual summer school programs. *Type:* Association.

Machinists Non-Partisan Political League

9000 Machinists Pl.   Ph: (301)967-4575
Upper Marlboro, MD 20772   Fax: (301)967-4595
Contact: Rich Michalski, Dir.
Desc: To elect labor's friends to Congress. Compiles statistics. *Type:* Association.

Maryland State and District of Columbia AFL-CIO

7 School St.   Ph: (410)269-1940
Annapolis, MD 21401   Fax: (410)280-2956
Contact: Edward A. Mohler, Pres.
Desc: Labor unions. Represents the interests of labor; lobbies for favorable legislation. *Type:* Association.

Metropolitan Detroit AFL-CIO

2550 W. Grand Blvd., 2nd Fl.   Ph: (313)896-2600
Detroit, MI 48208   Fax: (313)896-1078
Contact: Edgar A. Scribner, Pres.
Desc: Labor unions. Represents the interests of labor; lobbies for favorable legislation. *Type:* Association.

National Organization of Industrial Trade Unions

148-06 Hillside Ave.   Ph: (718)291-3434
Jamaica, NY 11435   Fax: (718)526-2920
Contact: Daniel Lasky, Emeritus Pres.
Desc: Industrial trade unions representing 8,500 individuals. Advocates better wages, hours, and conditions for members. Operates medical and dental centers in Manhattan and Long Island, NY for members and their families. *Type:* Association.

Information Management

Alabama Archivist

University of South Alabama Archives

USA Springhill, Rm. 0722   Ph: (334)434-3800
Mobile, AL 36688   Fax: (334)434-3622
Contact: Elisa Baldwin, Editor, ebaldwin@jaguar1. ushouthal.edu.
Desc: Provides news of archival activities in Alabama, covering archival repositories and significant historical collections, special work by archivists, legislative matters relating to historical records, and general information concerning the archival profession and standards. Recurring features include Society reports, news of research, and a calendar of events. *Type:* Newsletter.

APDU Newsletter

Association of Public Data Users (APDU)

Division of Business &   Ph: (504)280-3154
    Economic Research   Fax: (504)280-6094
University of New Orleans
New Orleans, LA 70148
E-mail: apdudb@uno.edu; apdudb@uno.edu.
Contact: Deirdre Gaquin, Editor.
Desc: Designed to "facilitate the utilization of public data through sharing knowledge about files and applicable software, exchange of documentation, and joint purchasing of data." Informs readers as to what is accessible and the media on which it is available, problems or advantages of the product, and issues affecting the collection and dissemination of public data. Serves as a forum for members to share data and its uses and reports the needs of public data users to statistical agencies of the federal government. *Type:* Newsletter.

Association for Information and Image Management

1100 Wayne Ave., Ste. 1100   Ph: (301)587-8202
Silver Spring, MD 20910   Fax: (301)587-2711
E-mail: resource.center@aiim.org
URL: http://www.aiim.org
Contact: John Mancini, Pres.
Desc: Manufacturers, vendors, and individual users of information and image management equipment, products, and services. Holds special meetings for trade members and companies. *Type:* Association.

Association of Records Managers and Administrators

4200 Somerset, Ste. 215   Ph: (913)341-3808
Prairie Village, KS 66208   Free: 800-422-2762
    Fax: (913)341-3742
E-mail: hq@arma.org
URL: http://www.arma.org/hq
Contact: Peter R. Hermann, CAE, Exec.Dir./CEO.
Desc: Provides education, reseach, and networking opportunities to information professionals, to enble them to use their skills and experience to leverage the value of records, information and knowledge as corporate assets and as contributors to organizational success. *Type:* Association.

Charles Babbage Institute Newsletter

Charles Babbage Institute of the History of Computing

103 Walter Library   Ph: (612)624-5050
117 Pleasant St., S.E.   Fax: (612)625-8054
University of Minnesota
Minneapolis, MN 55455
E-mail: cbi@tc.umn.edu
URL: http://www.cbi.umn.edu/.
Contact: Robert W. Seidel, Editor.
Desc: Covers news of Institute activities relating to the history of computing as well as archival acquisitions. Recurring features include news of research, book notices, and notices of workshops. *Type:* Newsletter.

The Clearinghouse Directory: A Guide to Information Clearinghouses and Their Resources, Services, and Publications

Gale Group Inc.

27500 Drake Rd.   Ph: (248)699-4253
Farmington Hills, MI 48331-   Free: 800-877-GALE
    3535   Fax: (248)699-8070
E-mail: galeord@galegroup.com
URL: http://www.galegroup.com.
Contact: Donna Batten, Editor, donna_batten@gale.com.
Desc: Over 600 clearinghouses in the U.S. and Canada. *Type:* Directory.

Conference of Intermountain Archivists(CIMA) Newsletter

Conference of Intermountain Archivists (CIMA)

PO Box 2048   Ph: (801)975-4023
Salt Lake City, UT 84114-2048   Fax: (801)974-0336
URL: http://www.lib.utah.edu/cima.
Contact: Glen Fairclough, Editor, gfairclo@tate.ut.us; Jeff Kintop, Assistant Editor, (702)687-5210, jmkintop@clan. lib.nv.us.
Desc: Concerned with the preservation and use of archival and manuscript materials in the Intermountain West and adjacent areas. Disseminates information on research materials and archival methodology; provides a forum for the discussion of common concerns; and cooperates with similar cultural and educational organizations. *Type:* Newsletter.

The DATA BASE for Advances in Information Systems

Association for Computing Machinery
Special Interest Group on Management Information Systems

1515 Broadway
New York, NY 10036
URL: http://wwwcis.gsu.edu/~dbase/.
Contact: Ephraim R. McLean, Co-Ed.; Mark Keil, Co-Ed.; Natalie Bailey, Managing Editor.
Desc: Presents articles on practical research relating to business uses of information systems. *Type:* Newsletter.

Data Base Alert

Knowledge Industry Publications, Inc.
701 Westchester Ave.   Ph: (914)328-9157
White Plains, NY 10604   Free: 800-800-5474
                              Fax: (914)328-9093

E-mail: kipimktg@kipi.com
URL: http://www.kipinet.com

Contact: Judy Duke, Editor.

Desc: Provides updates on publicly available online services. Contains a "listing of distributors of new or revised data bases with data bases listed alphabetically under the appropriate distributor along with information about pricing, updates, and number of records." Remarks: Newsletter is part of DataBase Directory Service, which includes an annual directory and supplement. *Type:* Newsletter.

Data to Knowledge Newsletter

Database Research Group, Inc.
2476 Bolsover, Ste. 488
Houston, TX 77005
E-mail: 75401.174@compuserve.com

Contact: Ronald G. Ross, Editor.

Desc: Covers topics in data administration and Information Resource Management (IRM). Recurring features include letters to the editor, interviews, and columns titled Executive Forum, Data Base Advisor, and Business Rules Forum. *Type:* Newsletter.

Dat@Line

Dun & Bradstreet
3 Sylvan Way   Ph: (973)605-6442
Parsippany, NJ 07054-3896   Free: 800-526-0651
                              Fax: (973)605-6911

E-mail: dnbmdd@dnb.com

Contact: Jean Fitzgerald, Editor, fitzjean@mail.dnb.com.

Desc: Informs online users of database contents and applications. Also provides general information on Dun & Bradstreet. *Type:* Newsletter.

DIALOG Bluesheets

The Dialog Corporation
DIALOG
11000 Regency Pkwy., Ste. 400   Ph: (919)462-8600
Cary, NC 27511
URL: http://www.dialog.com

Contact: Marketing.

Desc: Contains descriptions and guidelines for searching all databases that are currently accessible online through Knight-Ridder Information Services, Inc., DIALOG. Corresponds to DIALOG's printed Bluesheets, excluding sample records. *Available:* The Dialog Corporation, DIALOG. *Type:* Database.

DIALOG CHRONOLOG® Newsletter™

The Dialog Corporation
DIALOG
11000 Regency Pkwy., Ste. 400   Ph: (919)462-8600
Cary, NC 27511
URL: http://www.dialog.com

Contact: Marketing.

Desc: Contains the complete text of the international edition of the monthly newsletter of Knight-Ridder Information Inc. Provides information on new and reloaded databases, DIALOG special services, database search aids, telecommunications, DIALOG user meetings and workshops, regional service activities, and new system features. *Available:* The Dialog Corporation, DIALOG. *Type:* Database.

DIALOG Journal Name Finder™

The Dialog Corporation
DIALOG
11000 Regency Pkwy., Ste. 400   Ph: (919)462-8600
Cary, NC 27511
URL: http://www.dialog.com

Contact: Marketing.

Desc: Contains more than 1.7 million citations to journal names contained in DIALOG databases. Covers journals in bibliographic, full-text, and news source files in all subject disciplines. *Available:* The Dialog Corporation, DIALOG. *Type:* Database.

DIALOG Product Name Finder

The Dialog Corporation
DIALOG
11000 Regency Pkwy., Ste. 400   Ph: (919)462-8600
Cary, NC 27511
URL: http://www.dialog.com

Contact: Marketing.

Desc: Designed as a search aid to locate product information in DIALOG databases. Contains product names from databases accessible online through DIALOG shown in the form in which they appear in the original database index, including abbreviations, punctuation, and spelling variations. *Available:* The Dialog Corporation, DIALOG. *Type:* Database.

DIALOG Publications™

The Dialog Corporation
DIALOG
11000 Regency Pkwy., Ste. 400   Ph: (919)462-8600
Cary, NC 27511
URL: http://www.dialog.com

Contact: Marketing.

Desc: Provides descriptions of DIALOG system and database publications that are available for purchase. Enables the user to place an order online and have items sent automatically to the subscriber's "mail to" address and billed to the subscriber account. *Available:* The Dialog Corporation, DIALOG. *Type:* Database.

DIRLINE

U.S. National Library of Medicine (NLM)
MEDLARS Management Section
8600 Rockville Pike   Ph: (301)496-3147
Bethesda, MD 20894
URL: http://www.sis.nlm.nih.gov/dirline

Desc: Contains information on more than 15,000 organizations that provide information in their areas of specialization. Each record contains the organization name, address, telephone number(s), descriptions of broad and specific subject areas covered, holdings (e.g., databases or document collections), list of representative publications, types of information services provided, and any fees or restrictions on use. *Type:* Database.

Document Center—Update

Document Center
111 Industrial Rd. Ste. 9   Ph: (650)591-7600
Belmont, CA 94002   Fax: (650)591-7617
E-mail: info@doccenter.com
URL: http://www.document-center.com.

Contact: Claudia Bach, President.

Desc: Informs of the Center's specifications and standards services available to customers. *Type:* Newsletter.

Electronic Information Report

SIMBA Information Inc.
11 Riverbend Dr. S.   Ph: (203)358-4100
PO Box 4234   Free: 800-307-2529
Stamford, CT 06907-0234   Fax: (203)358-5824
E-mail: info@simbanct.com

URL: http://www.simbanet.com

Contact: Matt Bechard, Editor, (203)358-4346, fax: (203)358-5826, matthew_bechard@simbanet.com; Ben de la Cruz, Managing Editor, (202)986-6917; Linda Kopp, Sr. Managing Editor, (203)358-4285.

Desc: Monitors, analyzes and reports on trends and developments in the business and professional information services market. Features timely news, analysis and statistics written from a product, financial and marketing viewpoint; expert interpretations on underlying trends; and strategic view of major issues. *Type:* Newsletter.

Executive Brief

Society for Information Management
401 N. Michigan Ave.
Chicago, IL 60611-4267
URL: http://www.simnet.org.

Contact: Katie Fries, Editor.

Desc: Serves as a member benefit for the Society for Information Management. Includes IT issues from a General Manager's perspective. *Type:* Newsletter.

Federal Information Center Program

Gen. Services Admin.   Free: 800-688-9889
1800 F St. NW, Rm G-242
Washington, DC 20405
URL: http://www.fic.info.gov

Contact: Warren D. Snaider, Contracting Officers Tech. Rep.

Desc: Nationwide toll-free service providing vital assistance to those "lost in a maze of federal programs and services" by answering their questions or by directing them to the proper office to help with the problem. Persons with phone inquiries may obtain a brochure on the program from the Consumer Information Center. *Type:* Association.

Federation Facts

Federation of Government Information Processing Councils, Inc.
c/o General Services   Ph: (404)331-5106
   Administration   Fax: (404)331-3628
401 W. Peachtree St., Ste. 2700
Atlanta, GA 30365-2550

Desc: Distributed to federal, state, and local government information resource managers. Disseminates data on information policy and regulations and provides a forum for information technology managers to discuss issues and solve mutual problems. *Type:* Newsletter.

Federation of Government Information Processing Councils

U.S. General Services Admin.
Atth: 4KTH-A, Ste. 2700
401 W. Peachtree St.
Atlanta, GA 30365-2550

Contact: Mary Ann Enely, Contact.

Desc: Federal, state, and local government information resource managers; government information processing line and staff managers. Reviews and comments on proposed legislation such as the Paperwork Reduction Act, Federal Procurement Regulations, and Federal Information Resources Management Regulations. Disseminates information to operating personnel in field installation on information policy and regulations. *Type:* Association.

FYI/IM

Association for Information and Image Management
1100 Wayne Ave., Ste. 1100   Ph: (301)587-8202
Silver Spring, MD 20910   Free: 800-477-2246
                                 Fax: (301)587-2711

URL: http://www.aiim.org.

Contact: Beth S. Rosenberg, Editor.

Desc: Offers news about industry leaders in information and image management. Reports on the Association's programs, members, and conferences. *Type:* Newsletter.

Gale Directory of Databases

The Gale Group
27500 Drake Rd.   Ph: (248)699-4253
Farmington Hills, MI 48331-
3535
URL: http://www.galegroup.com

Desc: Contains detailed descriptions of more than 13,500 publicly available databases and database products accessible through an online vendor or batch processor or available for direct lease, license, or purchase as a CD-ROM, diskette, magnetic tape, or handheld product, or on another computer-readable recording/storage medium. Covers databases of all types in all subject areas produced worldwide in English and other languages. *Available:* The Dialog Corporation, DataStar; The Gale Group, GaleNet. *Type:* Database.

Gale Directory of Databases

Gale Group Inc.
27500 Drake Rd.   Ph: (248)699-4253
Farmington Hills, MI 48331-   Free: 800-877-GALE
3535   Fax: (248)699-8070
E-mail: galeord@galegroup.com; infoindu@gale.com.
URL: http://www.galegroup.com.; http://www.gale.com.

Contact: Marc Faerber, Editor.

Desc: Approximately 13,000 publicly available electronic databases. Volume 1 covers approximately 5,700 databases available online; volume 2 CD-ROM, magnetic tape, diskette, handheld, and batch access database products. Includes 700 databases that are defunct or no longer publicly available. Also covers over 3,600 database producers and over 2,500 online services and database vendors. *Type:* Directory.

Hard Sciences

Cambridge Scientific Abstracts (CSA)
7200 Wisconsin Ave., Ste. 601   Ph: (301)961-6700
Bethesda, MD 20814-4823
E-mail: sales@csa.com
URL: http://www.csa.com

Desc: Contains more than 500,000 citations, with abstracts, to international periodical and other research literature covering all fields of engineering and science and technology, including computer and information systems science, electronics and communications, safety science, mechanical engineering, and solid state materials and superconductivity science. Sources include journals, books, government and technical reports, dissertations, and conference proceedings. *Available:* The Dialog Corporation, DIALOG; European Information Network Services (EINS). *Type:* Database.

Indexing & Abstracting Society of Canada—Bulletin

Indexing and Abstracting Society of Canada (IASC)
PO Box 744, Sta. F
Toronto, ON, Canada M4Y
2N6

Contact: James Turner, Vice President.

Desc: Focuses on news and information of indexing and abstracting in Canada. Recurring features include news of research, a calendar of events, news of educational opportunities, book reviews, and notices of publications available. *Type:* Newsletter.

Info Outlook

Information Plus, Inc.
2 Bloor St. W., Ste. 404   Ph: (416)968-1062
Toronto, ON, Canada M4W   Fax: (416)968-2591
3E2

Contact: Deborah C. Sawyer, Editor.

Desc: Furnishes and interprets future trends in the information industry, focusing on the North American market. Features articles on the advantageous use of information by corporations, including interviews with key individuals in the information industry. *Type:* Newsletter.

InfoManage

SMR International
527 3rd Ave., No. 105   Ph: (212)683-6285
New York, NY 10016-4168   Fax: (212)683-2987
E-mail: 73042.67@compuserve.com
URL: http://www.mindspring.com/~smrintl/smr.html.

Contact: Guy St. Clair, Editor and Publisher.

Desc: Focuses on international information management. Covers industry trends, new directions in management, personnel issues, relationships with vendors, independent information brokers, publishers, and consultants, financial planning, education and professional development, and other issues that affect the delivery of information and the information executive's role in delivering information. *Type:* Newsletter.

The Information Bank Abstracts

The New York Times Index
16th Fl.   Ph: (212)221-3471
1133 Avenue of the Americas
New York, NY 10036

Contact: Alan Greengrass, Director, Index Operations, (212)221-3471, fax: (212)221-5052, agreengrass@nytimes.com.

Desc: Contains abstracts of all news and editorial matter from the final late edition of The New York Times as well as all original news and feature stories appearing in the The Wall Street Journal, The Asian Wall Street Journal Weekly, Miami Herald, and Philadelphia Inquirer. Items covered include general news articles, forecasts, analyses, surveys, biographies, features, columns, and editorials. *Available:* LEXIS-NEXIS, NEXIS; The Dialog Corporation, DataStar; Dow Jones Interactive Publishing; Bell & Howell Information and Learning; OCLC Online Computer Library Center, Inc. *Type:* Database.

Information Broker

Burwell Enterprises, Inc.
5619 Plumtree Dr.
Dallas, TX 75252-4928
E-mail: burwellinfo@burwellinc.com
URL: http://www.burwell.com

Contact: Helen P. Burwell, Editor; Joanne Paulino, Managing Editor.

Desc: Covers companies that offer fee-based information services and issues related to "the business" of information brokering. *Type:* Newsletter.

Information Council of the Americas

PO Box 53371   Ph: (504)641-2166
New Orleans, LA 70153

Contact: Ed Butler, Pres.

Desc: "To manifest truth through the media of communications." Maintains library of 10,000 volumes on communism, fascism, capitalism, and socialism. *Type:* Association.

Information Executive

Association of Information Technology Professionals
315 S. Northwest Hwy., Ste.   Ph: (847)825-8124
200   Free: 800-224-9371
Park Ridge, IL 60068   Fax: (847)825-1693
E-mail: 70430.35@compuserve.com.
Contact: Susan Smith, Editor, 110737.266@compuserve.com.

Desc: Provides up-to-date information on the changes and developments of the information systems industry. *Type:* Newsletter.

Information Industry Association

1625 Massachusetts Ave. NW,   Ph: (202)986-0280
Ste. 700   Fax: (202)638-4403
Washington, DC 20036
E-mail: info@infoindustry.org
URL: http://www.infoindustry.org
Contact: Joe M. Carmack, Membership Service Assoc.

Desc: Provides a forum for networking, education, and government relations activities supporting the needs of creators and packages of information content, otherwise known as "content providers." *Type:* Association.

Information Management

Idea Group Publishing
1331 E. Chocolate Ave.   Ph: (717)533-8845
Hershey, PA 17033   Free: 800-345-4332
                               Fax: (717)533-8661
E-mail: jtravers@idea-group.com.
URL: http://www.idea-group.com.
Contact: Mehdi Khosrowpour, Editor.

Desc: Follows trends and issues in the field of information technology and information resources technology. Strives to "enhance the overall knowledge and understanding of effective information resources management in the 1990s and beyond." Recurring features include interviews, news of research, a calendar of events, book reviews, news of product releases, and columns titled Technology Talk, An Information Management Tool, and End User Attitudes. *Type:* Newsletter.

Information Please

Information Please LLC
31 Saint James Ave., 6th Fl.   Ph: (617)832-0300
Boston, MA 02116-4101   Fax: (617)956-2696
E-mail: info@infoplease.com
URL: http://www.infoplease.com
Contact: Paul Evenson, Webmaster, pevenson@infoplease.com.

Desc: The classic print almanacs arrive online, and in their full glory! Information Please provides a veritable plethora of statistical, textual, and graphical information on everything under the sun. Broad subject areas covered correspond to the print editions: World, Sports, Entertainment, Business, US, People, Science and Technology, Living, Society. *Type:* Database.

The Information Report

Washington Researchers
416 Hungerford Dr., Ste. 315   Ph: (301)251-9550
Rockville, MD 20850   Fax: (301)251-9526
E-mail: research@researchers.com
Contact: Laurie Schlagel, Editor.

Desc: Contains 40-140 items in each issue identifying little-known sources of information. Lists and describes directories, special libraries, booklets, seminars, studies, and other research sources available on markets, competition, federal regulation, and economic conditions. *Type:* Newsletter.

Information Solutions

Information Plus, Inc.
14 Lafayette Square, Ste. 2000   Ph: (716)852-2220
Buffalo, NY 14203-1920   Fax: (716)852-1653
Contact: Deborah C. Sawyer, Editor.
Desc: Discusses the use of competitive intelligence as well as customer, supplier, and market intelligence. Focuses on North America and global information. *Type:* Newsletter.

Information Standards Quarterly

National Information Standards Organization
4733 Bethesda Ave., Ste. 300   Ph: (301)654-2512
Bethesda, MD 20814   Fax: (301)654-1721
E-mail: nisohq@niso.org; nisopress@niso.org.
URL: http://www.niso.org.
Desc: Reports development of new and revised technical standards for library information systems, products, and services. Includes a list of published voluntary consensus standards. *Type:* Newsletter.

Information Technology Report

Atlantic Information Services, Inc.
1100 17th St. NW, No. 300   Ph: (202)775-9008
Washington, DC 20036   Free: 800-521-4323
   Fax: (202)331-9542
Contact: Susan Namovicz-Peat, Editor.
Desc: Provides news on information technology. *Type:* Newsletter.

Information Today

Information Today, Inc.
143 Old Marlton Pike   Ph: (609)654-6266
Medford, NJ 08055-9936
E-mail: custserv@infotoday.com
Contact: Heather Rudolph.
Desc: Contains the complete text of Information Today, a monthly newspaper covering developments in the electronic information industry. Covers online databases and services, optical disk products and technologies, telecommunications systems, and computer equipment for information storage and retrieval. *Available:* Information Today, Inc. *Type:* Database.

International Information Management Congress

1650 38th St., No. 205W   Ph: (303)440-7085
Boulder, CO 80301   Fax: (303)440-7234
E-mail: info@iimc.org
URL: http://www.iimc.org
Contact: John A. Lacy, Pres. & CEO.
Desc: Trade association for the document imaging/management industry. Seeks to communicate document-based technologies and applications to an international audience through conferences, exhibitions, publications, and various membership interactions. Promotes understanding and cooperation among organizations engaged in furthering the progress and application of document-based information systems. *Type:* Association.

IT Cost Management Strategies

Computer Economics, Inc.
5841 Edison Pl.   Ph: (760)438-8100
Carlsbad, CA 92008-6519   Free: 800-326-8100
   Fax: (760)431-1126
E-mail: info@compecan.com; custserv@compecon.com.
URL: http://www.computereconomics.com; http://www.computereconomics.com.
Contact: Anne Zalatan, Editor-in-Chief.
Desc: Provides financial advice and analysis to data processing executives in charge of the data processing budget. Includes research of line-item cost comparisons by type of industry, installation size, company revenue, and type of expenditure. *Type:* Newsletter.

Key Words

American Society of Indexers
PO Box 39366
Phoenix, AZ 85069-9366
E-mail: asi@well.com
URL: http://www.well.com/user/asi/.
Contact: Paula Presley, Editor.
Desc: Contains information for members of the Society and interested freelance and salaried indexers, publishers, and editors. Recurring features include announcements of seminars, meetings, software tools for indexing, and standards development. *Type:* Newsletter.

LIMS/Letter

Write Away Communications
PO Box 935   Ph: (707)833-6885
Kenwood, CA 95452   Fax: (707)833-6865
E-mail: limsletter@aol.com.
URL: http://www.limsource.com.
Contact: Helen Coillespie, Editor.
Desc: Provides information for Information Management Systems (LIMS) professionals. Recurring features include interviews, news of research, and a calendar of events. *Type:* Newsletter.

Managing System Development

Applied Computer Research
PO Box 82266   Ph: (602)216-9100
Phoenix, AZ 85071-2266   Free: 800-234-2227
   Fax: (602)216-9200
E-mail: 72603.2553@compuserve.com
URL: http://www.acrhq.org
Contact: Janet Butler, Editor.
Desc: Designed for data processing professionals who need to know the latest findings in system development productivity. Covers such topics as effective program testing, quality circles, prototyping, and improving productivity with software tools. *Type:* Newsletter.

Mid-Atlantic Archivist

Mid-Atlantic Regional Archives Conference
c/o George Washington   Ph: (202)994-7283
   University   Fax: (202)463-6205
The Gelman Library
2130 H St. NW
Washington, DC 20052
Contact: G. David Anderson, Editor.
Desc: Contains news and information for and about members of the Conference. Seeks exchange of information between colleagues, improvement of competence among archivists, and encourages professional involvement of persons actively engaged in the preservation and use of historical research materials. *Type:* Newsletter.

NASIRE Exchange

NASIRE: Representing Chief Information Officers of the States
167 W. Main St., Ste. 600   Ph: (606)231-1971
Lexington, KY 40507   Fax: (606)231-1928
E-mail: nasire@amrinc.net
URL: http://www.nasire.org.
Contact: Amy Hughes, Program Mgr.
Desc: Provides news on issues involving state information resource management and of the Association. Recurring features include news of research, a calendar of events, reports of meetings, and notices of publications available. *Type:* Newsletter.

National Environmental Satellite, Data, and Information Service

2069 Federal Bldg. 4, Rm. 2069
Washington, DC 20233
Contact: Gregory W. Withee, Deputy Asst.Admin.

Desc: A major line component of the National Oceanic and Atmospheric Administration, U.S. Department of Commerce. Is responsible for acquiring, processing, archiving, recalling, and disseminating worldwide environmental data and environmental science information concerning the atmosphere, oceans, solid earth, and near space. *Type:* Association.

News/Retrieval Online Newsletter

Dow Jones & Company, Inc.
P.O. Box 300   Ph: (609)520-4000
Princeton, NJ 08543-0300
URL: http://www.dj.com
Desc: Contains information of interest to users of Dow Jones News/Retrieval. Covers system and service enhancements, tutorial materials, current prices and operating hours, software products, reference information, and ordering information on available user aids and software. *Available:* Dow Jones & Company, Inc. *Type:* Database.

NewsNet Action Letter

NewsNet, Inc.
945 Haverford Rd.   Fax: (610)527-0338
Bryn Mawr, PA 19010
E-mail: info@newsnet.com
URL: http://www.newsnet.com.
Contact: Raia King, Editor.
Desc: Functions to keep subscribers up-to-date on NewsNet's services and online publications. Provides application features, sample searches, and news on system enhancements. *Type:* Newsletter.

NFAIS Newsletter

National Federation of Abstracting and Information Services (NFAIS)
1518 Walnut St.   Ph: (215)893-1561
Suite 307   Fax: (215)893-1564
Philadelphia, PA 19102
E-mail: nfais@nfais.org
URL: http://www.pa.utulsa.edu/nfais.html; http://www.pa.utulsa.edu/NFAIS.HTML.
Contact: Wendy Wicks, Editor; Richard T. Kaser, Exec. Editor.
Desc: Contains information about "abstracting and indexing, secondary services and systems, thesaurus development, user education, online-copyright, international issues, new technologies," and other subjects of significance to the information community. Recurring features include Federation news and statistics; editorials; book reviews; a calendar of events; and columns on Washington news, international news, and people in the industry. *Type:* Newsletter.

NTIS NewsLine

National Technical Information Service (NTIS)
U.S. Department of Commerce
5285 Port Royal Rd.   Ph: (703)605-6000
Springfield, VA 22161-0001   Free: 800-553-NTIS
   Fax: (703)605-6900
E-mail: orders@ntis.fedworld.gov
Desc: NewsLine is a corporate outreach publication with an audience in both the private and public sectors. Published on a quarterly schedule, it announces new product development and describes trends in the world of electronic information dissemination where NTIS is a recognized leader. *Type:* Newsletter.

Optical Memory News

Phillips Business Information, Inc.
1201 Seven Locks Rd., Ste. 300   Ph: (301)340-2100
Potomac, MD 20854-2958   Free: 800-777-5006
   Fax: (301)424-4297
URL: http://www.phillips.com.

Contact: Shahida Sweeney, Editor.

Desc: Focuses on industries developing and producing optical memory technology. Provides specialized reports on Compact Disk Read-Only Memory (CD-ROM) technology, profiles key industry personnel and major companies, and explores issues relating to the manufacture of optical memory technology. *Type:* Newsletter.

SIGBIT Database

Special Interest Group on Programming Languages (SIGPLAN)
Association for Computing Machinery
1515 Broadway   Ph: (212)869-7440
New York, NY 10036   Free: 800-342-6626
                         Fax: (212)302-5826
E-mail: acmhelp@acm.org

Contact: James Wetherbe, Editor; Leslie Maggi McKenzie, Editor.

Desc: Disseminates information relating to office and business applications of databases (including very large databases) and decision support systems. *Type:* Newsletter.

SIGMOD Record

Special Interest Group on Programming Languages (SIGPLAN)
Association for Computing Machinery
1515 Broadway   Ph: (212)869-7440
New York, NY 10036   Free: 800-342-6626
                         Fax: (212)302-5826
E-mail: acmhelp@acm.org

Contact: Jennifer Widom, Editor.

Desc: Discusses current topics relating to a range of interests in database management, including data models, management systems, user interfaces, restructuring, and translation and design methodologies. Also covers techniques and methods used in analysis design, testing maintenance, and computer-based information systems. *Type:* Newsletter.

SIM Network

Society for Information Management
401 N. Michigan Ave.
Chicago, IL 60611-4267
URL: http://www.simnet.org.

Contact: Vanessa Glener, Editor.

Desc: Covers IT management issues and SIM events, programs, and activities. *Type:* Newsletter.

Society of Competitive Intelligence Professionals

1700 Diagonal Rd., Ste. 600   Ph: (703)739-0696
Alexandria, VA 22314   Fax: (703)739-2524
E-mail: info@scip.org
URL: http://www.scip.org

Contact: Guy Kolb, CAE, Exec.Dir.

Desc: Acts as a forum for the exchange of news and ideas among professionals involved in competitive intelligence and analysis. *Type:* Association.

Yardstick Quarterly

Gartner Group
56 Top Gallant Rd.   Ph: (203)964-0096
Stamford, CT 06904   Fax: (203)324-7901

Contact: Randall F. Brophy, Editor.

Desc: Covers revenue, market share, and segmentation of 240 information industry vendors. Contains notification of industry performance. *Type:* Newsletter.

Insurance

AAIS Viewpoint

American Association of Insurance Services (AAIS)
1035 S. York Rd.   Ph: (630)595-3225
Bensenville, IL 60106   Free: 800-564-AAIS
                          Fax: (630)595-4647

E-mail: AAISinsure@aais.org
URL: http://www.aais.org.
Contact: Joseph S. Harrington, Editor, Joe-H@aais.org.
Desc: Contains news of current insurance issues, AAIS activities, insurance legislation, and other subjects of interest. *Type:* Newsletter.

ACORD

1 Blue Hill Plz., 15th Fl.   Ph: (914)620-1700
PO Box 1529   Fax: (914)620-3600
Pearl River, NY 10965-8529
URL: http://www.acord.org
Contact: Gregory A. Maciag, Pres. & CEO.
Desc: ACORD is the insurance industry's nonprofit standards developer--a resource for information about object technology, EDI and electronic commerce in the U.S. and abroad. More than 1,000 financial service institutions are affiliated with ACORD, as are 29,000 agencies, software providers, producer associations, user groups, and other industry organizations. *Type:* Association.

Actuarial Digest

Actuarial Digest
PO Box 1127   Ph: (904)273-1245
Ponte Vedra Beach, FL 32004
Contact: Gene Hubbard, Editor.
Desc: Covers issues of concern to working actuaries. Recurring features include letters to the editor, interviews, news of research, a calendar of events, news of educational opportunities, job listings, book reviews, notices of publications available, and a column titled What's New. *Type:* Newsletter.

Actuarial Futures

Society of Actuaries
475 N. Martingale Rd., Ste. 800   Ph: (847)706-3500
Schaumburg, IL 60173-2226   Fax: (847)706-3599
E-mail: bhaynes@soa.org
URL: http://www.soa.org; http://www.soa.org.
Contact: Kathleen S. Elden, Editor.
Desc: Facilitates the professional development of Society members in the field of futurism. Recurring features include letters to the editor and a column titled Chairperson's Corner. *Type:* Newsletter.

The Actuary

Society of Actuaries
475 N. Martingale Rd., Ste. 800   Ph: (847)706-3500
Schaumburg, IL 60173-2226   Fax: (847)706-3599
E-mail: bhaynes@soa.org
URL: http://www.soa.org; http://www.soa.org.
Contact: Jacqueline Bitowt, Staff Ed., jbitowt@soa.org.
Desc: Features information about actuaries practicing in life and health insurance, pensions, and investments in the U.S. and Canada. *Type:* Newsletter.

Actuary of the Future

Society of Actuaries
475 N. Martingale Rd., Ste. 800   Ph: (847)706-3500
Schaumburg, IL 60173-2226   Fax: (847)706-3599
E-mail: bhaynes@soa.org
URL: http://www.soa.org; http://www.soa.org.
Contact: John C. Christensen, Editor.
Desc: Encourages and facilitates communication and professional development of members of the Society who have nontraditional experience or have an interest in exploring nontraditional roles and opportunities for actuaries. Recurring features include a column titled Editor's Note. *Type:* Newsletter.

The Advisor

America's Community Bankers
900 19th St. NW, Ste. 400   Ph: (202)857-3100
Washington, DC 20006-5002   Fax: (202)296-8716
E-mail: info@acbankers.org
URL: http://www.acbankers.org.
Desc: Relates information on crime trends, case histories, and guidelines for security risk management. *Type:* Newsletter.

ALTA Update

American Land Title Association (ALTA)
1828 L St. NW, Ste. 705   Ph: (202)296-3671
Washington, DC 20036   Free: 800-787-ALTA
                           Fax: (202)223-5843
E-mail: service@alta.org
Contact: Ann vom Eigen, Editor.
Desc: Provides the title insurance industry with information on the Association's federal legislative and agency activities. Reviews significant events and trends and comments on how they may affect the industry. *Type:* Newsletter.

American Academy of Actuaries

1100 17th St., NW, 7th Fl.   Ph: (202)223-8196
Washington, DC 20036   Fax: (202)872-1948
Desc: Ensures that the American public recognizes and benefits from the independent expertise of the actuarial profession in the formulation of public policy and the adherence of actuaries to high professional standards in discharging their responsibilities. The academy was founded in 1965 by 4 specialty actuarial associations in the U.S. to represent the entire profession: Casualty Actuarial Society; Conference of Actuaries in Public Practice (now Conference of Consulting Actuaries); Society of Actuaries; Fraternal Actuarial Association (now defunct). *Type:* Association.

American Council of Life Insurance

1001 Pennsylvania Ave. NW   Ph: (202)624-2000
Washington, DC 20004-2599   Fax: (202)624-2319
E-mail: acli@acli.com
URL: http://www.acli.com
Contact: Carroll A. Campbell, Jr., Pres.CEO.
Desc: National trade association that represents the interests of legal reserve life insurance companies in legislative, regulatory and judicial matters at the federal, state and municipal levels of government and at the NAIC. Its member companies hold more than 90 percent of the life insurance force in the United States. *Type:* Association.

American Foreign Service Protective Association

1716 N St. NW   Ph: (202)833-4910
Washington, DC 20036   Fax: (202)833-4918
Contact: John P. Shumate, Exec.VP.
Desc: Insurance society for employees of the American Foreign Service. *Type:* Association.

American Fraternal Union

111 4th Ave. S.   Ph: (218)365-3143
PO Box 59   Fax: (218)365-3181
Ely, MN 55731
Contact: John L. Cheenik, Sec.-Treas.
Desc: Fraternal benefit life insurance society. Persons up to 80 years of age may join, regardless of race, creed, or national background. *Type:* Association.

American Institute for CPCU

720 Providence Rd.   Ph: (610)644-2100
PO Box 3016   Free: 800-644-2101
Malvern, PA 19355-0716   Fax: (610)640-9576
E-mail: cserv@cpcuiia.org

URL: http://www.aicpcu.org

Contact: Lawrence G. Brandon, CPCU, Chm.

Desc: Determines qualifications for professional certification of insurance personnel; conducts examinations and awards designation of Chartered Property Casualty Underwriter (CPCU). *Type:* Association.

American Insurance Association

1130 Connecticut Ave. NW Ste. 1000
Washington, DC 20036
Ph: (202)828-7100
Fax: (202)293-1219

Contact: Robert E. Vagley, Pres.

Desc: Represents companies providing property and casualty insurance and suretyship. *Type:* Association.

American Insurance Services Group, A Unit of Insurance Services Office

85 John St.
New York, NY 10038
Ph: (212)669-0400
Fax: (212)669-0535

Contact: Richard Boehning, Pres.

Desc: Subscribers are companies involved in property casualty insurance. Provides a forum for discussion of problems; promotes safety and security of persons and property; assists in the effective disposition of property claims. Serves as clearinghouse for insurance claims and information; offers training and education, informational materials, and catastrophe support regarding premium audit problems. *Type:* Association.

American Society of Chartered Life Underwriters and Chartered Financial Consultants—Query

American Society of Chartered Life Underwriters and Chartered Financial Consultants

270 Bryn Mawr Ave.
Bryn Mawr, PA 19010
Ph: (215)526-2500

Contact: Roslyn Myers, Editor.

Desc: Contains news of interest to clients of chartered life underwriters. Covers such topics as life insurance, trusts, taxation, and financial planning. *Type:* Newsletter.

American Society of Chartered Life Underwriters and Chartered Financial Consultants—Society Page

American Society of Chartered Life Underwriters and Chartered Financial Consultants

270 Bryn Mawr Ave.
Bryn Mawr, PA 19010
Ph: (215)526-2500

Contact: Roslyn Myers, Editor.

Desc: Reports Society and member news, notices of the Society's upcoming conferences and seminars, and continuing education information. Features signed insurance, finance, and management articles. *Type:* Newsletter.

Artisans Order of Mutual Protection

PO Box 52779
Philadelphia, PA 19115-7779
Ph: (215)708-1000
Fax: (215)708-1779

Contact: William E. Swirsding, Admin.

Desc: Fraternal benefit life insurance society. Offers children's services; maintains charitable and educational programs; compiles statistics. *Type:* Association.

Austin Insurance Report

Report Publications

PO Box 12368
Austin, TX 78711
Ph: (512)478-5663
Fax: (512)478-2345

Contact: Homer Olsen, Editor.

Desc: Focuses on developments in the Texas insurance industry. *Type:* Newsletter.

Auto Insurance Report

Risk Communications

33 Lindall St.
Laguna Niguel, CA 92677
Ph: (714)443-0330
Fax: (714)443-0331

Contact: Brian P. Sullivan, Editor and Publisher, bpsullivan@aol.com.

Desc: Provides information about the auto insurance industry. Includes news and analysis about private and commercial auto insurance. *Type:* Newsletter.

Baptist Life Association

8555 Main St.
Buffalo, NY 14221
Ph: (716)633-4393
Free: 800-227-8543

Contact: Sterling Knowka, Pres.

Desc: Fraternal benefit life insurance society. Provides orphan benefits and automatic newborn coverage. Sponsors annual scholarship contests for insured members; offers branch activities. *Type:* Association.

Barger & Wolen Newsletter

Barger & Wolen

515 S. Flower St., 34th Fl.
Los Angeles, CA 90071-2205
Ph: (213)680-2800
Fax: (213)614-7399

Contact: Robert J. Cerny, Editor.

Desc: Discusses current events in the legal field relating to insurance. Carries decision briefs. *Type:* Newsletter.

Best's Insurance Reports--Life/Health

A.M. Best Company

Ambest Rd.
Oldwick, NJ 08858
Ph: (908)439-2200

URL: http://www.ambest.com

Desc: Contains the complete text of Best's Insurance Reports--Life/Health, an industry standard providing ratings and commentary. Comprises the following 3 files: • Preface--contains industry information and an explanation of Best's Ratings. *Available:* LEXIS-NEXIS, LEXIS; LEXIS-NEXIS, NEXIS. *Type:* Database.

Best's Insurance Reports--Property/Casualty

A.M. Best Company

Ambest Rd.
Oldwick, NJ 08858
Ph: (908)439-2200

URL: http://www.ambest.com

Desc: Contains the complete text of Best's Insurance Reports--Property/Casualty, an industry standard providing ratings and commentary. Comprises the following 3 files: • Preface--contains industry information and an explanation of Best's Ratings. *Available:* LEXIS-NEXIS, LEXIS; LEXIS-NEXIS, NEXIS. *Type:* Database.

Best's Intelligencer

A.M. Best Company

Ambest Rd.
Oldwick, NJ 08858
Ph: (201)439-2200

E-mail: bestweek@ambest.com

Contact: Patricia Forsythe, Editor.

Desc: "Provides a brief description of insurance filings that have been approved/processed by state insurance departments in the prior month." *Type:* Newsletter.

Best's State/Line Databases--Property/Casualty

A.M. Best Company

Ambest Rd.
Oldwick, NJ 08858
Ph: (908)439-2200

URL: http://www.ambest.com

Contact: A.M. Best Customer Service.

Desc: Contains complete market share and underwriting premium and loss data for individual property/casualty lines in each state or U.S. territory. *Available:* A.M. Best Company. *Type:* Database.

Best's Statement File--Life/Health

A.M. Best Company

Ambest Rd.
Oldwick, NJ 08858
Ph: (908)439-2200

URL: http://www.ambest.com

Contact: A.M. Best, Customer Service.

Desc: Contains financial data on more than 1600 U.S. life and health insurance companies. *Available:* A.M. Best Company. *Type:* Database.

Best's Statement File--Property/Casualty

A.M. Best Company

Ambest Rd.
Oldwick, NJ 08858
Ph: (908)439-2200

URL: http://www.ambest.com

Contact: A.M. Best, Customer Service.

Desc: Contains financial data on more than 2400 U.S. property and casualty insurance companies. *Available:* A.M. Best Company. *Type:* Database.

Best's Underwriting Newsletter

A.M. Best Company

Ambest Rd.
Oldwick, NJ 08858
Ph: (201)439-2200

E-mail: bestweek@ambest.com

Contact: Joseph Mangan, CPCU, Editor.

Desc: Focuses on current developments in the field of insurance underwriting. Suggests solutions for specific problems in the field. *Type:* Newsletter.

BestWeek Life/Health Edition

A.M. Best Company

Ambest Rd.
Oldwick, NJ 08858
Ph: (201)439-2200

E-mail: bestweek@ambest.com

Contact: Brendan Noonan, Editor.

Desc: Contains annotated news articles and staff-written perspectives on current events in the life/health insurance industry. Reports on legislative developments, new products, and corporate changes. *Type:* Newsletter.

BestWeek Property/Casualty Editions

A.M. Best Company

Ambest Rd.
Oldwick, NJ 08858
Ph: (201)439-2200

E-mail: bestweek@ambest.com

Contact: Brendan Noonan, Editor.

Desc: Contains articles and staff-written perspectives on current events in the property/casualty and life/health insurance industries, statistical studies and special reports by A.M Best financial analysts. Reports on legislative developments, industry meetings, new products, and corporate changes. *Type:* Newsletter.

Business Insurance

Crain Communications Inc.

740 N. Rush St.
Chicago, IL 60611
Ph: (312)649-5200

URL: http://www.crain.com

Desc: Contains the complete text of Business Insurance, a newspaper providing information on the purchase and administration of corporate insurance and self-insurance programs, including property and liability insurance, reinsurance, and employee benefit and risk management programs. Includes reports on major commercial insurance claim settlements, legal and regulatory developments affecting the industry, and major losses resulting from fires, explosions, natural disasters, and litigation. *Available:* LEXIS-NEXIS, NEXIS; Dow Jones Interactive Publishing; Bell & Howell Information and Learning; NewsEdge Corporation; Profound Inc., The Dialog Corporation; Reuters Information Services Inc.; The Gale Group, InfoTrac Web. *Type:* Database.

Business Insurance—Agent/Broker Profiles Issue

Business Insurance

740 N. Rush St. Ph: (312)649-5279
Chicago, IL 60611-2590 Fax: (312)280-3174
Contact: Sandra L. Budde, Editor.
Desc: List of approximately 250 insurance agents and brokers specializing in commercial insurance. *Type:* Directory.

Business Insurance—Captive Managers Issue

Business Insurance

740 N. Rush St. Ph: (312)649-5279
Chicago, IL 60611-2590 Fax: (312)280-3174
Contact: Sandra L. Budde, Editor.
Desc: List of over 150 captive managers worldwide. *Type:* Directory.

Business Insurance—Directory of HMOs, POSS and PPOs Issue

Crain Communications, Inc.

740 N. Rush St. Ph: (312)649-5200
Chicago, IL 60611-2590 Fax: (312)649-5360
Contact: Sandra L. Budde, Editor.
Desc: More than 1,500 regional and national health maintenance, point of service and preferred provider organizations. *Type:* Directory.

Business Insurance—Directory of Property Loss Control Consultants

Business Insurance

740 N. Rush St. Ph: (312)649-5279
Chicago, IL 60611-2590 Fax: (312)280-3174
Contact: Sandra L. Budde, Editor.
Desc: Listing of 100 companies that provide loss prevention inspection and research, building plan reviews, training seminars, and other loss control consulting services. *Type:* Directory.

Business Insurance—Directory of Reinsurance Intermediaries

Crain Communications, Inc.

740 N. Rush St. Ph: (312)649-5200
Chicago, IL 60611-2590 Fax: (312)649-5360
Contact: Sandra L. Budde, Editor.
Desc: List of nearly 100 reinsurance intermediaries, also known as reinsurance brokers, in the United States and Bermuda. *Type:* Directory.

Business Insurance—Employee Benefit Consultants Issue

Crain Communications, Inc.

740 N. Rush St. Ph: (312)649-5200
Chicago, IL 60611-2590 Fax: (312)649-5360
Contact: Sandra L. Budde, Editor.
Desc: List of about 130 firms that offer employee benefit consulting services. *Type:* Directory.

Business Insurance—Environmental Risk Management Consultants Issue

Crain Communications, Inc.

740 N. Rush St. Ph: (312)649-5200
Chicago, IL 60611-2590 Fax: (312)649-5360
Contact: Sandra L. Budde, Editor.
Desc: Directory of over 120 environmental risk management consultants in the United States. *Type:* Directory.

Business Insurance—International Insurers & Benefits Networks Issue

Crain Communications, Inc.

740 N. Rush St. Ph: (312)649-5200
Chicago, IL 60611-2590 Fax: (312)649-5360
Contact: Sandra L. Budde, Editor.

Desc: Lists of approximately 20 international insurers and 10 international benefit networks around the world. *Type:* Directory.

Business Insurance—International Reinsurers Issue

Business Insurance

740 N. Rush St. Ph: (312)649-5279
Chicago, IL 60611-2590 Fax: (312)280-3174
Contact: Sandra L. Budde, Editor.
Desc: Directory of approximately 50 reinsurance companies around the world. *Type:* Directory.

Business Insurance—Risk Management Consultants Issue

Business Insurance

740 N. Rush St. Ph: (312)649-5279
Chicago, IL 60611-2590 Fax: (312)280-3174
Contact: Sandra L. Budde, Editor.
Desc: List of about 250 firms that provide risk management consulting. *Type:* Directory.

Business Insurance—Risk Management Information Systems Issue

Crain Communications, Inc.

740 N. Rush St. Ph: (312)649-5200
Chicago, IL 60611-2590 Fax: (312)649-5360
Contact: Sandra L. Budde, Editor.
Desc: Listing of approximately 50 risk management information system developers in the United States. *Type:* Directory.

Business Insurance—Third-Party Claims Administrators Issue

Business Insurance

740 N. Rush St. Ph: (312)649-5279
Chicago, IL 60611-2590 Fax: (312)280-3174
Contact: Sandra L. Budde, Editor.
Desc: List of approximately 225 third-party claims administration, adjusting, and auditing firms that process claims for self-insured clients, including employee benefit-and property/casualty claims. *Type:* Directory.

Business Insurance—Utilization Review/Case Management Providers Issue

Crain Communications, Inc.

740 N. Rush St. Ph: (312)649-5200
Chicago, IL 60611-2590 Fax: (312)649-5360
Contact: Sandra L. Budde, Editor.
Desc: Directory of approximately 140 utilization review service providers and case managers in the U.S. *Type:* Directory.

CALUnderwriter

California Association of Life Underwriters

70 Washington St., No. 325 Ph: (510)834-2258
Oakland, CA 94607
E-mail: califalu@aol.com
Contact: Daniel L. Crouch, Editor.
Desc: Covers Association news and events, and legislative, legal and regulatory issues affecting life and health insurance agents and managers. Provides news of industry trends and sales ideas. *Type:* Newsletter.

Casualty Actuarial Society

1100 N. Glebe Rd., Ste. 600 Ph: (703)276-3100
Arlington, VA 22201 Fax: (703)276-3108
E-mail: office@casact.org
URL: http://www.casact.org
Contact: James H. Tinsley, Exec. Dir.
Desc: Professional society of actuaries. Seeks to advance the body of knowledge of actuarial science in applications other than life insurance, maintains qualification standards, promote high standards of conduct and competence, and increase awareness of actuarial science. Examinations required for membership. *Type:* Association.

CCIA Newsletter

Consumer Credit Insurance Association (CCIA)

542 S. Dearborn, No. 400 Ph: (312)939-2242
Chicago, IL 60605-1522 Fax: (312)939-8287
Contact: William Burfeind, Editor.
Desc: Focuses on consumer credit insurance in the areas of life insurance, accident and health insurance, and property insurance. Includes news of the Association. *Type:* Newsletter.

Chartered Property Casualty Underwriter Society

PO Box 3009 Ph: (610)251-2728
Malvern, PA 19355-0709 Free: 800-932-2728
  Fax: (610)251-2775
Contact: James R. Marks, CPCU, Contact.
Desc: Dedicated to meeting the needs of professionals who have earned the CPCU designation so that they may serve the public, property, and casualty insurance industry in a competent and ethical manner. *Type:* Association.

COBRA Guide—Connections

CCH Inc.

2700 Lake Cook Rd. Ph: (847)267-7000
Riverwoods, IL 60015 Free: 800-449-8114
  Fax: (847)224-8299
URL: http://www.cch.com
Contact: Jan Gerstein, Product Group Leader.
Desc: Provides information on pending legislation, significant cases, rulings, regulations, trends, surveys, and tips to help the COBRA practitioner keep abreast of the law and comply with its regulations. *Type:* Newsletter.

CompAct

Society of Actuaries

475 N. Martingale Rd., Ste. 800 Ph: (847)706-3500
Schaumburg, IL 60173-2226 Fax: (847)706-3599
E-mail: bhaynes@soa.org
URL: http://www.soa.org; http://www.soa.org.
Contact: Brian Pollack, Editor.
Desc: Disseminates information concerning developments in computer science as it relates to the work of actuaries. Recurring features include a column titled Sound Bytes. *Type:* Newsletter.

Construction Insurance and Risk Management

Insurance Marketing and Management Services (IMMS)

12424 Wilshire Blvd., Ste. 600 Ph: (310)442-6000
Los Angeles, CA 90025 Free: 800-753-4467
  Fax: (310)207-2111
E-mail: plus@imms.com
URL: http://www.imms.com
Contact: George Nordhaus, Publisher.
Desc: Addresses construction insurance issues, including laws, liabilities, and activities. Remarks: Subscribers receive 1,000 copies per edition. *Type:* Newsletter.

Council of Insurance Agents & Brokers

701 Pennsylvania Ave. NW, Ste. Ph: (202)783-4400
750 Fax: (202)783-4410
Washington, DC 20004-2608
E-mail: ciab@ciab.com
URL: http://www.ciab.com
Contact: Ken A. Crerar, Pres.
Desc: Represents the interests of the leading commercial property and casualty insurance agencies and brokerage firms. *Type:* Association.

CPCU News

Society of Chartered Property & Casualty Underwriters (CPCU)
PO Box 3009   Ph: (610)251-2764
720 Providence Rd.   Fax: (610)251-2761
Malvern, PA 19355
URL: http://www.CPCUsociety.org.
Contact: Jane Greiner, Editor.
Desc: Publishes news of the Society, its members, and its services. *Type:* Newsletter.

CPCU Society

720 Providence Rd.   Ph: (610)251-2727
PO Box 3009   Free: 800-932-CPCU
Malvern, PA 19355-0709   Fax: (610)251-2775
E-mail: cpcu@ansiweb.com
URL: http://www.cpcusociety.org
Contact: James R. Marks, Exec.VP.
Desc: Professional society of individuals who have passed ten national examinations of the American Institute for Chartered Property Casualty Underwriters, have 3 years of work experience, have agreed to be bound by a code of ethics, and have been awarded CPCU designation. Promotes education, research, social responsibility, and professionalism in the field. Holds seminars, symposia, videoconferences, and workshops; conducts research projects. *Type:* Association.

CUNA Mutual Group

5910 Mineral Point Rd.   Ph: (608)238-5851
PO Box 391   Free: 800-937-2644
Madison, WI 53705   Fax: (608)238-2449
URL: http://www.cunamutual.com/
Contact: Michael B. Kitchen, Chief Exec. Officer.
Desc: Promotes credit unions, insurance, and finance-related products. Provides products and services designed to support the development of the credit union system. Promotes a positive public perception of credit unions. *Type:* Association.

Defense Reseach International

750 N. Lake Shore Dr., Ste.   Ph: (312)944-0575
  500   Free: 800-423-7059
Chicago, IL 60611   Fax: (312)944-2003
E-mail: dri@mcs.net
URL: http://www.dri.org
Contact: Donald Hirsch, Dir.
Desc: Lawyers, claims people, adjusters, insurance companies, trade associations, corporations, and "target" defendants in civil litigation, such as doctors, pharmacists, engineers, manufacturers, and other professional and skilled personnel. Seeks to increase the knowledge and improve the skills of defense lawyers and to improve the adversary system of justice. Maintains research facilities, including files of speeches, briefs, and names of expert witnesses in various fields. *Type:* Association.

Degree of Honor Protective Association

445 Minnesota St., No. 1600   Ph: (612)224-7436
St. Paul, MN 55101-1080   Fax: (612)224-7446
Contact: Jacqueline A. Felling, Natl.Pres.
Desc: Fraternal benefit life insurance society. Provides children's services; operates charitable and educational programs. *Type:* Association.

Disability Insurance Training Council

1000 Connecticut Ave., NW,   Ph: (202)223-5533
  Ste. 810   Fax: (202)785-2274
Washington, DC 20036
Desc: Educational arm of the National Association of Health Underwriters. Provides institutional advanced disability income and health insurance research seminars as well as marketing and underwriting clinics. NAHU maintains Health Insurance Training Council (HITC), Disability Training Insurance Council (DTIC), and Foundation for Promotion of Consumer Health Education. *Type:* Association.

Equitable Reserve Association

Box 448   Ph: (920)722-1574
Neenah, WI 54957-0448   Free: 800-722-1574
    Fax: (920)722-5400
Contact: Robert E. Miller, Pres.
Desc: Fraternal benefit insurance society. *Type:* Association.

Excess & Surplus Market News

Examco
5728 Jefferson Hwy.   Ph: (504)733-8400
New Orleans, LA 70123   Free: 800-638-7597
    Fax: (504)729-4450
Contact: Juan Hovey, Editor.
Desc: Reports and analyzes news regarding the excess and surplus/specialty lines insurance market. Covers competitors, products, and legal developments. *Type:* Newsletter.

Expanding Horizons

Society of Actuaries
475 N. Martingale Rd., Ste. 800   Ph: (847)706-3500
Schaumburg, IL 60173-2226   Fax: (847)706-3599
E-mail: bhaynes@soa.org
URL: http://www.soa.org; http://www.soa.org.
Contact: Margie Rosenberg, Editor.
Desc: Facilitates the professional development of Society members in the areas of actuarial education and research. Recurring features include letters to the editor, news of educational opportunities, news of research, and a calendar of events. *Type:* Newsletter.

Federal & State Insurance Week

JR Publishing Inc.
PO Box 6654   Ph: (703)532-2235
Mc Lean, VA 22106   Fax: (703)532-2236
Contact: John V. Reistrup, Editor.
Desc: Covers political and legislative developments affecting general insurance issues. *Type:* Newsletter.

Financial Reporter

Society of Actuaries
475 N. Martingale Rd., Ste. 800   Ph: (847)706-3500
Schaumburg, IL 60173-2226   Fax: (847)706-3599
E-mail: bhaynes@soa.org
URL: http://www.soa.org; http://www.soa.org.
Contact: G. Thomas Mitchell, Editor.
Desc: Encourages the professional development of Society members in the field of life insurance company financial reporting. Recurring features include letters to the editor, news of research, news of educational opportunities, and a calendar of events. *Type:* Newsletter.

GAMA International

1922 F St., NW   Ph: (202)331-6088
Washington, DC 20006   Free: 800-345-2687
    Fax: (202)785-5712
E-mail: gamamail@gama.nalu.org
URL: http://www.gamaweb.com
Contact: Renee Pietrangelo, Acting Exec.VP.
Desc: Life insurance general agents and managers, assistant agency heads, home office officials, and others interested in life insurance related financial field management. Works to improve quality of management and of life insurance selling through educational programs, code of ethical practices, and research programs. Maintains hall of fame and speakers' bureau. *Type:* Association.

Gleaner Life Insurance Society

5200 W. U.S. 223   Ph: (517)263-2244
Box 1894   Free: 800-992-1894
Adrian, MI 49221   Fax: (517)265-7745
E-mail: gleaner@gleanerlife.com
URL: http://www.gleanerlife.com

Contact: Frank Dick, Pres. & Chm.
Desc: Fraternal benefit life insurance society. *Type:* Association.

Grand Lodge Order of the Sons of Hermann in Texas

PO Box 1941   Ph: (210)226-9261
San Antonio, TX 78297   Free: 800-234-4124
    Fax: (210)226-3055
URL: http://www.texasshermansons.org
Contact: Leroy Muehlstein, Grand Pres.
Desc: Fraternal benefit life insurance society. *Type:* Association.

Grand Lodge Order of the Sons of Hermann in Texas

PO Box 1941   Ph: (210)226-9261
San Antonio, TX 78297   Free: 800-234-4124
    Fax: (210)226-3055
Contact: Leroy P. Muehlstein, Grand Pres./CEO.
Desc: Fraternal benefit life insurance society. *Type:* Association.

Health Insurance Association of America

555 13th St., NW, Ste. 600 E.   Ph: (202)824-1600
Washington, DC 20004-1109   Fax: (202)824-1722
URL: http://www.hiaa.org
Contact: Charles Kahn, Pres.
Desc: Represents commercial health insurers in the states and in Washington, DC. Works to create a positive image of the industry. Issues data on benefits and products, tracks legislation and regulations, and offers insurance education. *Type:* Association.

Health Section News

Society of Actuaries
475 N. Martingale Rd., Ste. 800   Ph: (847)706-3500
Schaumburg, IL 60173-2226   Fax: (847)706-3599
E-mail: bhaynes@soa.org; smartz@soa.org.
URL: http://www.soa.org; http://www.soa.org.
Contact: Leigh Wachenheim, Editor.
Desc: Encourages the professional development of Society members specializing in the field of health insurance benefit plans. Recurring features include letters to the editor, news of research, and a calendar of events. *Type:* Newsletter.

Hine's Directory of Insurance Adjusters, Investigators, and Appraisers

Hine's Inc.
Box 143   Ph: (630)365-1630
Geneva, IL 60134   Fax: (630)365-1631
Contact: Stephen E. Walter, Editor.
Desc: 1,200 independent insurance adjuster offices in the United States and Canada. *Type:* Directory.

Honorable Order of the Blue Goose, International

12940 Walnut Rd.   Ph: (414)782-7608
Elm Grove, WI 53122   Fax: (414)782-7608
Contact: Terry Maloney, Exec.Dir.
Desc: Fraternal organization of property and casualty insurance people. *Type:* Association.

How to Get Paid

Wentworth Publishing Company
PO Box 11177   Ph: (717)393-7197
Lancaster, PA 17605-1177   Free: 800-331-5196
    Fax: (717)393-4702
E-mail: dellb@classroom.net.
Contact: Ann Mead Ash, Editor.
Desc: Offers suggestions for collection of payment from Medicare and other third-party payers, for health care practices. Recurring features include Medicare hotline, advice column. *Type:* Newsletter.

IBA West

101 Market St., Ste. 702   Ph: (415)957-1212
San Francisco, CA 94105   Free: 800-772-8998
    Fax: (415)541-9184
URL: http://www.ibawest.com
Contact: Jerry W. O'Kane, CAE, CEO.
Desc: Trade Association of Independent Insurance Brokers in the 5 most western states. *Type:* Association.

I.I.I. Data Base Search

Insurance Information Institute (I.I.I.)
110 William St.   Ph: (212)669-9200
New York, NY 10038
E-mail: consumer@iii.org
URL: http://www.iii.org
Contact: Marjorie Gordon, Director, Information Services.
Desc: Provides citations and abstracts of insurance-related literature appearing in magazines, newspapers, and trade publications and books. *Available:* Reuters Information Services Inc. *Type:* Database.

I.I.I. Insurance Daily

Insurance Information Institute (I.I.I.)
110 William St.   Ph: (212)669-9200
New York, NY 10038
E-mail: consumer@iii.org
URL: http://www.iii.org
Desc: Provides summaries of news articles relating to the property and casualty insurance industry. *Available:* Insurance Information Institute (I.I.I.). *Type:* Database.

Illinois Insurance

Illinois Department of Insurance
320 W. Washington   Ph: (217)782-4515
Springfield, IL 62767-0001   Fax: (217)782-5020
URL: http://www.state.il.us/ins.
Contact: Nan Nases, Editor.
Desc: Serves as a regulatory newsletter for the state of Illinois insurance industry. Recurring features include news of hearings, rules summaries and producer regulatory actions. *Type:* Newsletter.

IMMS Weekly Marketeer

Insurance Marketing and Management Services (IMMS)
12424 Wilshire Blvd., Ste. 600   Ph: (310)442-6000
Los Angeles, CA 90025   Free: 800-753-4467
    Fax: (310)207-2111
E-mail: plus@imms.com
URL: http://www.imms.com
Contact: George Nordhaus, Publisher.
Desc: Furnishes IMMS members with news of marketing and financial services in the area of property/casualty and life insurance. Contains management features, profiles of insurance operations, discussion of marketing techniques, product news, and news of members. *Type:* Newsletter.

Independent Insurance Agents of America

127 S. Peyton   Ph: (703)683-4422
Alexandria, VA 22314   Free: 800-221-7917
    Fax: (703)683-7556
Contact: Jeffrey M. Yates, CEO.
Desc: Sales agencies handling property, fire, casualty, and surety insurance. Organizes technical and sales courses for new and established agents. Sponsors Insurance Youth Golf Classic. *Type:* Association.

Independent Order of Foresters

PO Box 179   Ph: (416)429-3000
Niagara Sta.   Free: 800-828-1540
Buffalo, NY 14201   Fax: (416)429-0089
E-mail: info@iof.org

URL: http://www.iof.org/
Contact: J. Robert Heatley, VP & Exec.Sec.
Desc: Fraternal benefit life insurance society with local branches (courts) in Canada, the United States, and the British Isles. *Type:* Association.

The INFORMER

Transportation, Loss, Prevention, & Security Council
American Trucking Associations, Inc.
2200 Mill Rd.   Ph: (703)838-1864
Alexandria, VA 22314   Free: 800-ATA-LINE
    Fax: (703)683-9752
E-mail: tlpsc@trucking.org
URL: http://www.truckline.com/tlpsc.
Contact: Linda Simpson, Editor, lsimpson@trucking.org.
Desc: Concerned with loss and damage claims and loss prevention in the transport and freight industries. Discusses new developments and legislation, legal and arbitration decisions, packaging, liability, insurance, security, and related issues. *Type:* Newsletter.

Inland Marine Underwriters Association— Impact

Inland Marine Underwriters Association
111 Broadway, 15th Fl.   Ph: (212)233-7958
New York, NY 10006   Fax: (212)732-3451
E-mail: imua@worldnet.att.net
URL: http://www.imua.org.
Contact: Melissa Kalt, Editor.
Desc: Disseminates news and views of interest to insurance companies transacting inland marine insurance in the U.S. Provides a forum for the discussion of problems which are of common concern. *Type:* Newsletter.

Insider Update

Delta Dental Plan of California
PO Box 7736   Ph: (415)972-8487
San Francisco, CA 94120   Fax: (415)972-8466
E-mail: corpcomms@delta.org.
URL: http://www.deltadentalca.org/bro/bro-iu-index.html.
Contact: Natasha Curry, Editor, ncurry@delta.org.
Desc: Provides information on Delta's products and how they compare in the dental benefits market. Covers legislative issues pertaining to dental benefits carriers and tracks industry trends. *Type:* Newsletter.

InSITE

Society of Insurance Trainers and Educators (SITE)
2120 Market St., Ste. 107   Ph: (415)621-2830
San Francisco, CA 94114-1395   Fax: (415)621-0889
E-mail: socinsedtr@aol.com
Contact: Lois A. Markovich, CPCU, Editor.
Desc: Reports news and information on insurance education and training. Presents case problems for discussion and new training techniques. *Type:* Newsletter.

Insurance Accountant

American Banker/Bond Buyer Inc.
International Thomson Publishing Corp.
1 State St. Plaza   Ph: (212)803-8200
New York, NY 10004   Free: 800-362-3807
    Fax: (212)843-9612
Contact: Michelle Clayton, Editor.
Desc: Summarizes current changes in accounting policies that affect insurers. Monitors developments at FASB, AICPA, NAIC, and inside the federal government. *Type:* Newsletter.

Insurance Crime Prevention Institute

15 Franklin St.   Ph: (203)226-6347
Westport, CT 06880   Free: 800-221-5715
    Fax: (203)227-4663
Contact: Arnold Schlossberg, Jr., Dir.
Desc: Insurance companies united to investigate and secure prosecution of fraud in connection with casualty and property insurance claims. Conducts limited, industry-wide training programs related to insurance fraud, using films, speakers, and brochures to aid in instructing property and casualty insurance industry and public law enforcement bodies interested in the detection and prosecution of insurance fraud. Address unknown since 1994 edition. *Type:* Association.

Insurance Forum

Insurance Forum, Inc.
PO Box 245   Ph: (812)876-6502
Ellettsville, IN 47429
Contact: Joseph M. Belth, Editor.
Desc: Provides analyses and information on the insurance business. *Type:* Newsletter.

Insurance Industry Newsletter

Smith & Associates
PO Box 3006   Ph: (912)355-4117
Savannah, GA 31402-3006
Contact: George V.R. Smith, Editor, gvrs@aol.com.
Desc: Provides news and comment on the insurance industry in the U.S. Contains information on legislation and regulation, trends, promotions, and new products. *Type:* Newsletter.

Insurance Information Institute

110 William St.   Ph: (212)669-9200
New York, NY 10038   Fax: (212)732-1916
E-mail: info@iii.org
URL: http://www.iii.org
Contact: Gordon C. Stewart, Pres.
Desc: Property and liability insurance companies. Provides information and educational services to mass media, educational institutions, trade associations, businesses, government agencies, and the public. Conducts public opinion surveys. *Type:* Association.

Insurance Information Institute Database

Insurance Information Institute
110 William St.   Ph: (212)669-9200
New York, NY 10038   Free: 800-331-9146
    Fax: (212)791-1807
E-mail: consumer@iii.org
URL: http://www.iii.org/home.html
Desc: The Insurance Information Institute Database provides: the full text of many of their consumer brochures, explaining such topics as how to save money on auto insurance, how to select homeowners insurance, home security, how to prepare for a hurricane, and how to file a claim; recent financial results for the property/casualty insurance industry; a catalog of publications; and a description of the services provided to consumers and the media. New features include video and audio news releases on various insurance topics. *Type:* Database.

Insurance Institute of America

720 Providence Rd.   Ph: (610)644-2100
PO Box 3016   Free: 800-644-2101
Malvern, PA 19355-0716   Fax: (610)640-9576
E-mail: cserv@cpcuiia.org
URL: http://www.aicpu.org
Contact: Jerne E. Troxel, Ph.D., Chm. & CEO.
Desc: Sponsors 23 educational programs for property and liability insurance personnel. Conducts exams and awards certificates and diplomas. Maintains library of over 8600 volumes on insurance, management, finance, and economics. *Type:* Association.

Insurance Institute of Southern Alberta Newsletter

Insurance Institute of Southern Alberta
1015 4th St. SW, Ste. 801   Ph: (403)266-3427
Calgary, AB, Canada T2R 1J4   Fax: (403)269-3199
Contact: F.A. Lang, Editor.
Desc: Covers insurance education. *Type:* Newsletter.

Insurance Issues Update

Insurance Information Institute (I.I.I.)
110 William St.   Ph: (212)669-9200
New York, NY 10038
E-mail: consumer@iii.org
URL: http://www.iii.org
Contact: Ruth Gastel, Director, Issues Analysis, (212)669-9228, fax: (212)267-9591, ruthg@iii.org.
Desc: Contains the complete text of 25 Insurance Issues Update, covering current developments in property and casualty insurance. Covers insurance-related issues, including automobile insurance fraud, auto safety and drunk driving, catastrophies, the civil justice system, medical cost control, environmental liability, financial and market conditions, insolvencies, rate regulation, and residual markets. *Available:* Reuters Information Services Inc.; LEXIS-NEXIS. *Type:* Database.

Insurance Market Place

Rough Notes Co., Inc.
11690 Technology Dr.   Ph: (317)582-1600
Carmel, IN 46032-5600   Free: 800-428-4384
    Fax: (317)816-1001
E-mail: rnc@in.net
URL: http://www.roughnotes.com.
Contact: Larry France, Editor.
Desc: List of specialty, excess, and surplus lines insurance company home offices, and nationwide agencies and managing underwriters handling these lines; local Lloyd's of London qualified representatives and specialty managing general agencies are listed in regional inserts. *Type:* Directory.

Insurance Periodicals Index

NILS Publishing Company
P.O. Box 2507
Chatsworth, CA 91313-2507   Ph: (818)998-8830
E-mail: insource@nils.com
URL: http://www.nils.com
Contact: Barbara Booth, Vice President Editorial, (818)998-8830, fax: (818)718-8482, bbooth@nils.com.
Desc: Contains more than 180,000 citations, with abstracts, to literature on the insurance industry, employee benefit plans, pensions, and risk management. Covers all lines (e.g., life, health, property and casualty) and business aspects (e.g., marketing, financing, underwriting) of insurance. *Available:* LEXIS-NEXIS, LEXIS; LEXIS-NEXIS, NEXIS; West Group, WESTLAW. *Type:* Database.

Insurance Phone Book and Directory

U.S. Directory Service, Publishers
121 Chanlon Rd.   Ph: (908)464-6800
New Providence, NJ 07974   Free: 800-521-8110
    Fax: (908)665-6688
Contact: Erica Milowitz, Editor; Elizabeth Kizar, Editor; Maria Ganduglia-Pirovano, Editor.
Desc: About 4,000 life, accident and health, worker's compensation, auto, fire and casualty, marine, surety, and other insurance companies. *Type:* Directory.

Insurance Regulation

Wakeman/Walworth, Inc.
300 N. Washington St.   Ph: (703)549-8606
Alexandria, VA 22314   Free: 800-876-2545
URL: http://statecapitals.com.

Contact: Keyes Walworth, Editor.

Desc: Details state regulation of policies, rates, and benefits for all types of insurance, including life, health, automobile, homeowner, and malpractice. Covers tort reform, malpractice, licensing, self insurance, and innovations such as lifestyle considerations. *Type:* Newsletter.

Insurance Regulator

American Banker/Bond Buyer Inc.
International Thomson Publishing Corp.
1 State St. Plaza   Ph: (212)803-8200
New York, NY 10004   Free: 800-362-3807
    Fax: (212)843-9612
URL: http://www.americanbanker.com.

Contact: Miles Maguire, Managing Editor; David G. Schutt, Publisher.

Desc: Monitors federal and national initiatives to regulate the insurance industry. Covers the National Association of Insurance Commissioners, Congress, the courts, and federal agencies such as the SEC and the Department of Labor. *Type:* Newsletter.

Insurance Services Office

7 World Trade Center   Ph: (212)898-6000
New York, NY 10048   Fax: (212)898-5525

Contact: Fred R. Marcon, Pres. & CEO.

Desc: Property and liability insurance companies. Seeks to: make available to any insurer, on a voluntary basis, statistical, actuarial, policy forms, and other related services; function as an insurance advisory organization and statistical agent. *Type:* Association.

Insurance Society of New York

c/o The College of Insurance   Ph: (212)815-9237
101 Murray St.   Fax: (212)815-9208
New York, NY 10007
E-mail: library@tci.edu
URL: http://www.tci.edu

Contact: Ellen Thrower, Pres.

Desc: Parent organization of The College of Insurance, a fully accredited, undergraduate and graduate degree-granting educational institution located in New York City. Offers courses in risk management, actuarial science, and insurance and financial services. Maintains insurance library of 100,000 books, periodicals, pamphlets, and historic documents. *Type:* Association.

Insurance Testing Institute

720 Providence Rd.   Ph: (215)251-9966
Malvern, PA 19355

Contact: Norman A. Baglini, Ph.D., Pres.

Desc: A division of the Insurance Institute of America. Provides testing services for insurance agents and brokers. *Type:* Association.

International Section News

Society of Actuaries
475 N. Martingale Rd., Ste. 800   Ph: (847)706-3500
Schaumburg, IL 60173-2226   Fax: (847)706-3599
E-mail: bhaynes@soa.org; smartz@soa.org.
URL: http://www.soa.org; http://www.soa.org.

Contact: Kevin Law, Editor; John Nigh, Editor.

Desc: Encourages the professional development of Society members in international areas of practice, including insurance pensions and social security programs. Recurring features include letters to the editor, news of research, news of educational opportunities, and a calendar of events. *Type:* Newsletter.

IRM Services

4401 Barclay Downs Dr.   Ph: (704)551-3000
Charlotte, NC 28209   Free: 800-RISK-IRM
    Fax: (704)551-3111
Contact: R. Bruce Jamieson, Pres. and CEO.
Desc: Mutual and stock insurance companies. Reinsures large property risks for its member companies and their affiliates and subsidiaries. Offers engineering training with an emphasis on commercial property protection. *Type:* Association.

The John Liner Letter

Standard Publishing Corp.
155 Federal St.   Ph: (617)457-0600
Boston, MA 02110-9637   Free: 800-682-5759
    Fax: (617)457-0608
E-mail: stnd@earthlink.net
Contact: Robert Montgomery, Editor.
Desc: Provides advice on insurance for business firms, such as broadening coverage, cutting costs, and anticipating special insurance problems. *Type:* Newsletter.

John Liner Review

Standard Publishing Corp.
155 Federal St.   Ph: (617)457-0600
Boston, MA 02110-9637   Free: 800-682-5759
    Fax: (617)457-0608
E-mail: stnd@earthlink.net
Contact: Meike Olin, Editor.
Desc: Examines issues in the fields of business insurance and risk management. Alerts readers to key problems confronting them and spells out methods for their solution. *Type:* Newsletter.

The Journal

Society of Insurance Trainers and Educators (SITE)
2120 Market St., Ste. 107   Ph: (415)621-2830
San Francisco, CA 94114-1395   Fax: (415)621-0889
E-mail: socinsedtr@aol.com
Contact: Lois Markovich, Exec. Dir.
Desc: Provides information on training and education within the insurance industry. Recurring features include book reviews. *Type:* Newsletter.

LAN Life Association News

National Association of Life Underwriters
1922 F St. NW   Ph: (202)331-6070
Washington, DC 20006-4387   Free: 800-247-4074
    Fax: (202)835-9608
E-mail: lanadv@nalu.org; lanedit@nalu.org.
Contact: Afsoon Namini, Publisher; Jeffery R. Kosnett, Editor.
Desc: Service and Educational magazine for life insurance agents and financial advisors. *Type:* Periodical.

LEXIS® Insurance Law Library

LEXIS-NEXIS
9443 Springboro Pike   Ph: (937)865-6800
PO Box 933
Dayton, OH 45401-0933
URL: http://www.lex-nexis.com
Desc: Contains the complete text of the insurance statutes for 50 states, the District of Columbia, and Puerto Rico, state regulations, attorney general opinions, case law, and National Association of Insurance Commissioners (NAIC) proceedings, reports, and model legislation. Also contains abstracts of articles from more than 35 journals covering the insurance industry. *Available:* LEXIS-NEXIS, LEXIS. *Type:* Database.

Liability Week

JR Publishing Inc.
PO Box 6654   Ph: (703)532-2235
Mc Lean, VA 22106   Fax: (703)532-2236
Contact: John V. Reistrup, Editor.
Desc: Reports on weekly judicial, regulatory, and legislative developments affecting liability issues at the state and federal levels of government. *Type:* Newsletter.

Life Office Management Association

2300 Windy Ridge Pkwy., Ste.   Ph: (770)951-1770
   600   Fax: (770)984-0441
Atlanta, GA 30339-8443
E-mail: marketing@loma.org
URL: http://www.loma.org/
Contact: Thomas P. Donaldson, Pres. & CEO.
Desc: Life and health insurance companies and financial services in the U.S. and Canada; and overseas in 45 countries; affiliate members are firms that provide professional support to member companies. Provides research, information, training, and educational activities in areas of operations and systems, human resources, financial planning and employee development. *Type:* Association.

Life Underwriter Training Council

7625 Wisconsin Ave.   Ph: (301)913-5882
Bethesda, MD 20814   Fax: (301)913-0123
Contact: Dennis Storks, Pres.
Desc: Members are students who are life underwriters taking part in sales training courses sponsored by local life underwriters associations. Promotes improved quality of life insurance marketing by providing training, a clearinghouse for information on life underwriter education and training, and assistance to anyone interested in the life insurance sales and service training. *Type:* Association.

LIMRA International

Box 208   Ph: (860)688-3358
Hartford, CT 06141   Free: 800-235-4672
                                Fax: (860)298-9555
URL: http://www.limra.org
Contact: Richard A. Wecker, Pres. & CEO.
Desc: Life insurance and financial services companies. Conducts market, consumer, economic, financial, and human resources research; monitors industry distribution systems and product and service developments. *Type:* Association.

Lloyd's Insurance International

L.L.P. Inc.
41-21 28th St., No. RM-D   Ph: (212)529-9500
Long Island City, NY 11101-   Free: 800-955-6937
   3732
Contact: Robert Cox, Editor.
Desc: Features summaries on global insurance news. *Type:* Newsletter.

Loyal Christian Benefit Association

PO Box 13005   Ph: (814)453-4331
Erie, PA 16514-1305   Free: 800-234-5222
                                Fax: (814)453-3211
E-mail: lcaba@erie.net
URL: http://www.lcba.com
Contact: Jacqueline Sobania-Robison, Pres.
Desc: Fraternal benefit life insurance society. Practicing Christian men, women, and children. Sponsors orphans' benefits. *Type:* Association.

Luso-American Fraternal Federation

Luso-American Plz.   Ph: (510)828-4884
7080 Donlon Way   Fax: (510)828-4554
Dublin, CA 94568
Contact: Rodrigo Alvernaz, Exec.V.Pres.

Desc: Division of Luso-American Life Insurance Society. Sponsors Luso-American Education Foundation. *Type:* Association.

Luso-American Life Insurance Society

Luso-American Plz.   Ph: (510)828-4884
7080 Donlon Way   Fax: (510)828-4554
Dublin, CA 94568
E-mail: lusoweb@aol.com
URL: http://www.luso-american.org
Contact: Rodrigo Alvernaz, CEO.
Desc: Promotes Luso-American cultural, social, educational and charitable activities of its members, their families and others. *Type:* Association.

Managed Care Outlook

Aspen Publishers, Inc.
200 Orchard Ridge Dr., No.   Ph: (301)417-7500
   200   Free: 800-638-8437
Gaithersburg, MD 20878   Fax: (301)417-7650
E-mail: customer.service@aspenpubl.com
URL: http://www.aspenpub.com
Contact: Gregory Galdabini, Editor.
Desc: Features information on opportunities and developments in the managed care industry. Recurring features include Industry Insights, at-a-glance charts with the information readers need to know, and Regional Briefs, a quick read of the important news in relevant markets across the country. *Type:* Newsletter.

Mealey's Insurance Supplement

Mealey Publications, Inc.
PO Box 62090   Ph: (610)768-7800
King of Prussia, PA 19406-0230 Free: 800-MEA-LEYS
                                Fax: (610)768-0880
E-mail: news@mealeys.com
URL: http://www.mealeys.com.
Contact: Colleen Keenan, Editor.
Desc: Provides summaries and text of complaints, motions, and appellate briefs in latent disease and property damage insurance litigation. *Type:* Newsletter.

Mealey's Litigation Report: Insurance Fraud

Mealey Publications, Inc.
PO Box 62090   Ph: (610)768-7800
King of Prussia, PA 19406-0230 Free: 800-MEA-LEYS
                                Fax: (610)768-0880
E-mail: news@mealeys.com
URL: http://www.mealeys.com.
Contact: Teresa Zink, Editor.
Desc: Reviews civil and criminal cases arising from efforts by policyholders and third parties to defraud insurance carriers. Topics include exaggerated and suspicious claims, arson, reverse bad faith, restitution, indictments, RICO and mail fraud. *Type:* Newsletter.

Merritt Insurance Report

Merritt Publishing
6133 Bristol Pkwy., Ste. 140   Ph: (310)450-7234
Culver City, CA 90230-6613   Free: 800-638-7597
                                Fax: (310)396-4563
E-mail: merritt2@interserve.com
Contact: Sue Sink, Senior Editor; James Walsh, Managing Editor, jwalsh@merrittpub.com.
Desc: Offers commentary on "trends and events of interest to professionals in insurance risk management, loss prevention, and loss control." Recurring features include news of research, regulatory actions, and legislative updates. *Type:* Newsletter.

The Merritt Insurance Report

Examco
5728 Jefferson Hwy.   Ph: (504)733-8400
New Orleans, LA 70123   Free: 800-638-7597
                                Fax: (504)729-4450
URL: http://www.examco.com.
Contact: Pat Sheppard, Editor.
Desc: Presents approaches to selling insurance, managing an agency, and succeeding in the industry. *Type:* Newsletter.

Million Dollar Round Table

325 W. Touhy   Ph: (847)692-6378
Park Ridge, IL 60068   Fax: (847)518-8921
URL: http://www.agents-online.com
Contact: John J. Prast, CAE, Exec.VP.
Desc: Life insurance agents who earn $54,200 in eligible commissions at least 60% in life insurance annuities, or disability income up to 40% may come from health coverage, long-term care or mutual funds. Members from the U.S. must belong to the National Association of Life Underwriters must requalify for membership annually. *Type:* Association.

National Association of Health Underwriters

1000 Connecticut Ave. NW,   Ph: (703)276-0220
   Ste. 810   Fax: (703)841-7797
Washington, DC 20036
E-mail: kcorcoran@nahu.org
URL: http://www.nahu.org
Contact: Kevin Corcoran, Exec.VP.
Desc: Insurance agents and brokers engaged in the promotion, sale, and administration of disability income and health insurance. Sponsors advanced health insurance underwriting and research seminars. Testifies before federal and state committees on pending health insurance legislation. *Type:* Association.

National Association of Independent Insurers

2600 River Rd.   Ph: (847)297-7800
Des Plaines, IL 60018   Fax: (847)297-5064
Contact: Jack Ramirez, Pres.
Desc: Independent property and liability insurance companies. Provides advocacy and technical information. *Type:* Association.

National Association of Insurance Brokers

1300 I St., NW, Ste. 490 E   Ph: (202)783-4400
Washington, DC 20005   Fax: (202)628-6707
Contact: Carl A. Modecki, CAE, Pres.
Desc: Full-service commercial insurance brokers and regional and specialty companies which administer coverage in the property/casualty market and provide insurance brokerage and risk management services around the world. Seeks to take an active part in shaping the legislative and regulatory environment as it concerns the insurance brokerage industry. *Type:* Association.

National Association of Insurance Commissioners

120 W. 12th St., Ste. 1100   Ph: (816)842-3600
Kansas City, MO 64105   Fax: (816)471-7004
URL: http://www.naic.org
Contact: Catherine J. Weatherford, Exec.V.P.
Desc: State officials supervising insurance. Promotes uniformity of legislation and regulation affecting insurance to protect interests of policyholders. *Type:* Association.

National Association of Insurance Women International

1847 E. 15th   Ph: (918)744-5195
PO Box 4410   Free: 800-766-6249
Tulsa, OK 74159   Fax: (918)743-1968
E-mail: contact@naiw.org
URL: http://www.naiw.org

Desc: Insurance industry professionals. Promotes continuing education and networking for the professional advancement of its members. *Type:* Association.

National Association of Life Companies

1455 Pennsylvania Ave. NW,   Ph: (202)783-6252
Ste. 1250   Fax: (202)783-1636
Washington, DC 20004
Contact: S. Roy Woodall, Jr., Pres.

Desc: Life and life health insurance companies. Works to provide a forum for "younger progressive companies" to discuss, study, and solve common problems. Keeps members informed on pertinent legislative matters. *Type:* Association.

National Association of Life Underwriters

1922 F St. NW   Ph: (202)331-6000
Washington, DC 20006-4387   Fax: (202)835-9601
URL: http://www.nalu.com
Contact: Auther Kraus, Exec.VP/CEO.

Desc: Federation of state (50) and local associations (942) representing 108,000 life insurance agents, general agents, and managers; associate members are independent insurance agents, general managers of life companies and other life and health insurance professionals. Objectives are to support and maintain the highest principles and standards of life and health insurance; to promote high ethical standards; to inform the public, render community service, and promote public goodwill. Sponsors public service programs. *Type:* Association.

National Association of Professional Insurance Agents

400 N. Washington St.   Ph: (703)836-9340
Alexandria, VA 22314   Fax: (703)836-1279
E-mail: piaweb@pianet.org
URL: http://www.pianet.com
Contact: Douglas S. Culkin, CAE, Contact.

Desc: Insurance agencies. Activities are educational, representative, and service-oriented. Sponsors over 200 educational programs and seminars each year on all aspects of property and casualty insurance, ranging from the novice to specialist level. *Type:* Association.

National Association of Professional Surplus Lines Offices

6405 N. Cosby, Ste. 201   Ph: (816)741-3910
Kansas City, MO 64151   Fax: (816)741-5409
Contact: Richard M. Bouhan, Exec.Dir.

Desc: Wholesale insurance brokers and agents. Develops standards for the surplus lines industry. *Type:* Association.

National Association of Surety Bond Producers

5225 Wisconsin Ave. NW, Ste.   Ph: (202)686-3700
600   Fax: (202)686-3656
Washington, DC 20015-2015
URL: http://www.nasbp.org
Contact: Richard A. Foss, Exec.VP.

Desc: Insurance agents and brokers writing surety bonds. *Type:* Association.

National Association for Variable Annuities

12030 Sunrise Valley Dr., Ste.   Ph: (703)620-0674
110   Fax: (703)620-6362
Reston, VA 20191
URL: http://www.navanet.org

Contact: Mark Mackey, Pres.CEO.

Desc: Seeks to promote knowledge of variable annuities and variable life insurance products among members and the public. *Type:* Association.

National Council on Compensation Insurance

750 Park of Commerce Dr.   Free: 800-622-4123
Boca Raton, FL 33487
URL: http://www.ncci.com
Contact: David A. Kocher, Pres.CEO.

Desc: Insurance providers of all types writing workers' compensation insurance. Conducts ratemaking, research, and statistical programs. *Type:* Association.

National Crop Insurance Services

7201 W. 129th St., No. 200   Ph: (913)685-2767
Overland Park, KS 66213   Free: 800-951-6247
    Fax: (913)685-3080
URL: http://www.ag/risk.org
Contact: Robert Parkerson, Pres.

Desc: NCIS was organized for three primary purposes: to gather and analyze crop statistics; to develop standard policy terms and conditions so that agents and consumers need to understand only a few basic program options; and, to develop loss adjustment methods and adjuster training to support the appraisal of crop damage so that losses can be settled fairly. *Type:* Association.

National Insurance Crime Bureau

10330 S. Roberts Rd.   Ph: (708)430-2430
Palos Hills, IL 60465   Free: 800-447-6282
    Fax: (708)430-2446
URL: http://www.nicb.org
Contact: John Diliberto, Pres. & CEO.

Desc: Property-casualty insurance companies; self-insured firms, works in detecting, preventing and deterring insurance-related crime. *Type:* Association.

National Motorist Association

402 W. Second St.   Ph: (608)849-6000
Waunakee, WI 53597-1342   Free: 800-882-2785
    Fax: (608)849-8697
E-mail: nma@motorists.com
Contact: Todd Franklin, Contact.

Desc: Automotive insurance company. *Type:* Association.

National Underwriter Life & Health/Financial Services Edition

National Underwriter Co.
505 Gest St.   Ph: (513)721-2140
Cincinnati, OH 45203
URL: http://www.nuco.com
Contact: Mary C. Hall, J.D., Multi-Media Products Manager, fax: (513)721-0126, marych4382@aol.com (America Online).

Desc: Provides information pertinent to the life and health insurance industry, including current events coverage, trade association meetings, new product introductions, technology updates, and coverage of state, federal, and legislative affairs. Searchable by date, author, keywords, and headlines. *Available:* LEXIS-NEXIS, NEXIS; LEXIS-NEXIS, NEXIS; The Dialog Corporation, DataStar; Dow Jones & Company, Inc.; CompuServe Information Service. *Type:* Database.

National Underwriter Property & Casualty/Risk and Benefits Management Edition

National Underwriter Co.
505 Gest St.   Ph: (513)721-2140
Cincinnati, OH 45203
URL: http://www.nuco.com
Contact: Mary C. Hall, J.D., Multi-Media Products Manager, fax: (513)721-0126, marych4382@aol.com.

Desc: Provides information pertinent to the property and casualty insurance industry, including current events coverage, trade association meetings, new product introductions, technology updates, and in-depth coverage of state, federal and legislative affaires pertaining to the insurance industry. Coverage also includes risk management, employee benefits, stocks and marketing, and industry trends. *Available:* LEXIS-NEXIS, NEXIS; LEXIS-NEXIS, NEXIS; The Dialog Corporation, DataStar; Dow Jones & Company, Inc.; CompuServe Information Service. *Type:* Database.

Neighbors of Woodcraft

PO Box 1897   Ph: (503)656-8118
Oregon City, OR 97045-0052   Free: 800-456-1771
    Fax: (503)656-7656
E-mail: jcollier@nowfts.com
Contact: James B. Collier, Pres.

Desc: Men and women's fraternal benefit life insurance society operating in nine western states. Conducts research and educational programs; makes available student loan fund. *Type:* Association.

NewsDirect

Society of Actuaries
475 N. Martingale Rd., Ste. 800   Ph: (847)706-3500
Schaumburg, IL 60173-2226   Fax: (847)706-3599
E-mail: bhaynes@soa.org; jadduci@.soa.org.
URL: http://www.soa.org; http://www.soa.org.
Contact: Kixan Desai, Editor.

Desc: Encourages the professional development of Society members in the fields of nontraditional marketing and product delivery. Recurring features include letters to the editor, news of research, news of educational opportunities, and a calendar of events. *Type:* Newsletter.

Order of United Commercial Travelers of America

632 N. Park St.   Ph: (614)228-3276
PO Box 159019   Free: 800-848-0123
Columbus, OH 43215   Fax: (614)228-1898
Contact: Thomas Luffy, COO.

Desc: Fraternal benefit insurance organization. Aids local units for retarded citizens; sponsors youth activities; grants scholarships to teachers of the mentally retarded. Provides benevolent funds to widows and orphans of deceased members, to members who are victims of natural disasters, and to terminally ill cancer patients. *Type:* Association.

Parmafacts

Public Agency Risk Managers Association (PARMA)
PO Box 6810   Ph: (408)865-6930
San Jose, CA 95150
URL: http://www.parma.com.

Desc: Considers, discusses, and exchanges ideas for the improvement and functioning of risk management in government agencies. Tells of the Association's assistance to agencies in fostering education, communication, and mutual cooperation. *Type:* Newsletter.

The Pennsylvania Insurance Advisor

Martin & Company, Publisher
PO Box 70   Ph: (610)558-1516
Edgemont, PA 19028-0070   Fax: (610)558-1568
Contact: Paul P. Martin, Editor.

Desc: Provides information about the Pennsylvania Insurance Department. *Type:* Newsletter.

Pension Section News

Society of Actuaries
475 N. Martingale Rd., Ste. 800   Ph: (847)706-3500
Schaumburg, IL 60173-2226   Fax: (847)706-3599
E-mail: bhaynes@soa.org; smartz@soa.org.
URL: http://www.soa.org; http://www.soa.org.

Contact: Dan Arnold, Editor.

Desc: Encourages the professional development of Society members in the field of pension planning. *Type:* Newsletter.

Personal Perspective

Insurance Marketing and Management Services (IMMS)
12424 Wilshire Blvd., Ste. 600   Ph: (310)442-6000
Los Angeles, CA 90025   Free: 800-753-4467
Fax: (310)207-2111

E-mail: plus@imms.com
URL: http://www.imms.com

Contact: George Nordhaus, Publisher; Pamela Grieman, Editor.

Desc: Provides a resource for insurance agents to explain homeowners, auto, personal property, health, and life coverages and related issues to clients. Recurring features include news of research and a column titled Short Shots. *Type:* Newsletter.

Physician Focus

Blue Shield of California
50 Beale St.   Ph: (415)229-5000
San Francisco, CA 94105

Contact: Marty Jeffcock, Editor.

Desc: Provides information pertaining to Blue Shield of California's private healthcare plans in the areas of new coverage, expenditures, policy guidelines, and items of general healthcare financing affecting physicians in California. *Type:* Newsletter.

Physician Insurers Association of America

2275 Research Blvd., Ste. 250   Ph: (301)947-9000
Rockville, MD 20878   Fax: (301)947-9090
URL: http://www.thepiaa.org

Contact: Lawrence E. Smarr, Pres.

Desc: Physician liability insurance companies, including domestic physician and dental liability insurers, international affiliates, and reinsurers. Seeks to further the best interests of member companies in areas related to physician liability insurance. *Type:* Association.

Policies in Review

Standard Publishing Corp.
155 Federal St.   Ph: (617)457-0600
Boston, MA 02110-9637   Free: 800-682-5759
Fax: (617)457-0608

E-mail: stnd@earthlink.net

Contact: Robert Montgomery, Editor.

Desc: Provides in-depth analysis of significant nonstandard Property/Casualty policies and programs. Deals with such coverages as professional liability of architects and engineers, asbestos removal liability, association professional liability, automobile dealers physical damage, claims-made general liability, convention cancellation insurance, data processing insurance, directors/officers liability, errors/omissions liability, excess/umbrella liability, IBNR coverage, kidnap/ransom insurance, liquor liability, mortgage protection insurance, occurance form general liability, pollution legal liability, products/completed operations liability, railroad protective liability, and self-storage operations. *Type:* Newsletter.

Producer News

Smith & Associates
PO Box 3006   Ph: (912)355-4117
Savannah, GA 31402-3006

Contact: George V.R. Smith, Editor, gvrs@aol.com.

Desc: Published as a confidential report for independent agents and brokers who deal in property and liability insurance. Provides commentary and news on developments in legislation, regulation, court cases, marketing, and industry associations. *Type:* Newsletter.

Product Development News

Society of Actuaries
475 N. Martingale Rd., Ste. 800   Ph: (847)706-3500
Schaumburg, IL 60173-2226   Fax: (847)706-3599
E-mail: bhaynes@soa.org; jadduci@soa.org.
URL: http://www.soa.org; http://www.soa.org.

Contact: Dave Whittemore, Editor.

Desc: Encourages the professional development of Society members involved in new product development. Recurring features include letters to the editor, news of research, news of educational opportunities, and a calendar of events. *Type:* Newsletter.

Professional Insurance

Insurance Marketing and Management Services (IMMS)
12424 Wilshire Blvd., Ste. 600   Ph: (310)442-6000
Los Angeles, CA 90025   Free: 800-753-4467
Fax: (310)207-2111

E-mail: plus@imms.com
URL: http://www.imms.com

Contact: George Nordhaus, Publisher.

Desc: Updates and reviews the personal lines of home owners, auto, personal property, and health and life insurance coverage. Covers commercial lines, reviewing property and liability coverage and finance, business, management, and workers' compensation issues. *Type:* Newsletter.

Professional Insurance Communications of America—The Communique

Professional Insurance Communications of America
c/o National Association of   Ph: (317)875-5250
    Mutual Insurance Companies   Free: 800-336-2642
3601 Vincennes Rd.   Fax: (317)879-8408
PO Box 68700
Indianapolis, IN 46268

Contact: Janet E.H. Wright, Editor.

Desc: Presents "technical 'how to' articles slanted to insurance company publications editors," along with news of the association. *Type:* Newsletter.

Property Insurance Report

Risk Communications
33 Lindall St.   Ph: (714)443-0330
Laguna Niguel, CA 92677   Fax: (714)443-0331
Contact: Brian P. Sullivan, Editor and Publisher, bpsullivan@aol.com.

Desc: Provides information about residential and commercial property insurance. Includes news and regulatory information. *Type:* Newsletter.

Property Loss Research Bureau

3025 Highland Parkway, Ste.   Ph: (630)724-2200
    800   Fax: (630)724-2260
Downers Grove, IL 60515-1291
Contact: Wallace R. Hanson, Pres.

Desc: Sponsored by mutual and stock insurance companies. *Type:* Association.

Public Risk Management Association

1815 Fort Myer Dr., Ste. 1020   Ph: (703)528-7701
Arlington, VA 22209-1805   Fax: (703)528-7966
E-mail: info@primacentral.org
URL: http://www.primacentral.org
Contact: James Coyle, Exec.Dir.

Desc: Public agency risk, insurance, human resources, attorneys, and/or safety managers from cities, counties, villages, towns, school boards, and other related areas. To provide an information clearinghouse and communications network for public risk managers to share resources, ideas, and experiences. Offers information on risk, insurance, and safety management. *Type:* Association.

Quotesmith: Term Life Insurance Quote Page

Quotesmith Corporation
8205 S. Cass Ave., Ste. 102   Free: 800-556-9393
Darien, IL 60561
URL: http://www.quotesmith.com/

Desc: In the market for a term life insurance policy? Unless you've never bought any type of insurance before, you probably already appreciate how difficult it is to gather comparative rate information from all those insurers who market the coverage in which you're interested. This site takes a lot of the hassle out of getting term life insurance rate quotes. *Type:* Database.

Register of North American Insurance Companies

American Preeminent Registry, Publishers
PO Box 822   Ph: (908)651-1650
Old Bridge, NJ 08857-0822   Free: 800-229-1650
Fax: (908)651-1126

Contact: Brian Axelrod, Publisher.

Desc: Over 4,500 insurance companies in the U.S. and Canada. *Type:* Directory.

Reinsurance Section News

Society of Actuaries
475 N. Martingale Rd., Ste. 800   Ph: (847)706-3500
Schaumburg, IL 60173-2226   Fax: (847)706-3599
E-mail: bhaynes@soa.org; jadduci@soa.org.
URL: http://www.soa.org; http://www.soa.org.

Contact: Bernard Goebel, Editor.

Desc: Encourages the professional development of Society members in the field of reinsurance. Recurring features include letters to the editor, news of research, news of educational opportunities, and a calendar of events. *Type:* Newsletter.

Report on Healthcare Information Management

Capitol Publications, Inc.
1101 King St., Ste. 444   Ph: (703)683-4100
Alexandria, VA 22314   Free: 800-655-5597
Fax: (703)739-6517

Contact: Justin McGuire, Managing Editor.

Desc: Provides news, information, analysis, and advice concerning hospital and physician group management information systems. *Type:* Newsletter.

Risk Financing Newsletter

International Risk Management Institute, Inc.
12222 Merit Dr., Ste. 1450   Ph: (972)960-7693
Dallas, TX 75251-2276   Free: 800-827-4242
Fax: (972)960-6037

E-mail: info@irmi.com
URL: http://www.irmi.com
Contact: Don Riggin, Editor.

Desc: Concentrates on funding alternatives (such as captives, risk retention groups, pooling, self insurance, and retrospective rating) and provides information on tax and legal considerations. Remarks: Included with subscription to Risk Financing Manual Service (not available separately). *Type:* Newsletter.

Risk & Insurance Magazine's Managing Risk for Loss Prevention and Cost Control

LRP Publications
747 Dresher Rd.   Ph: (215)784-0941
PO Box 980   Free: 800-341-7874
Horsham, PA 19044-0980   Fax: (215)784-0870
E-mail: custserve@lrp.com

Contact: Donald R. Kinsley, Esq, Editor.

Desc: Discusses the function of loss prevention and risk management for businesses. Contains articles on responsibility to employees and the public, product liability and safety, worker's compensation, and computer security. *Type:* Newsletter.

Risk and Insurance Management Society

655 3rd Ave., 2nd Fl.   Ph: (212)286-9292
New York, NY 10017   Fax: (212)986-9716
URL: http://www.rims.org

Contact: Linda H. Lamel, Exec.Dir.

Desc: Corporate risk and insurance managers. Dedicated to advancing the practice of risk management, a discipline that protects physical, financial, and human resources. *Type:* Association.

Risk Management News

Examco
5728 Jefferson Hwy.   Ph: (504)733-8400
New Orleans, LA 70123   Free: 800-638-7597
                                    Fax: (504)729-4450

Contact: James Walsh, Managing Editor, jwalsh@merrittpubcom.

Desc: Serves corporate risk managers, covering insurance industry changes, trends and issues in risk management, workers compensation, product liability, and environmental impact judgments. Recurring features include book reviews, notices of publications available, case law studies, news of research and legal and legislative developments. *Type:* Newsletter.

Risk Manager Law Bulletin

Quinlan Publishing Company
23 Drydock Ave.   Ph: (617)542-0048
Boston, MA 02210   Free: 800-229-2084
                                    Fax: (617)345-9646
E-mail: quinlanp@quinlan.com

Desc: Presents the latest information on liability insurance. *Type:* Newsletter.

The Risk Report

International Risk Management Institute, Inc.
12222 Merit Dr., Ste. 1450   Ph: (972)960-7693
Dallas, TX 75251-2276   Free: 800-827-4242
                                   Fax: (972)960-6037
E-mail: info@irmi.com
URL: http://www.irmi.com

Contact: Kathie Clark, Asst. Ed.

Desc: Deals with risk management and commercial insurance. Monitors trends in loss exposures, insurance pricing, and coverage. *Type:* Newsletter.

Risk Retention Reporter

Insurance Communications
PO Box 50147   Ph: (626)796-4972
Pasadena, CA 91115   Fax: (626)796-2363

Contact: Karen Cutts, Editor and Publisher, cutts@rrr.com.

Desc: Provides information about risk retention groups and purchasing groups. *Type:* Newsletter.

Risks and Rewards

Society of Actuaries
475 N. Martingale Rd., Ste. 800   Ph: (847)706-3500
Schaumburg, IL 60173-2226   Fax: (847)706-3599
E-mail: bhaynes@soa.org; jadduci@soa.org.
URL: http://www.soa.org; http://www.soa.org.

Contact: Richard Wendt, Editor; Luke Girard, Editor.

Desc: Encourages the professional development of Society members in the field of investment. Recurring features include letters to the editor, news of research, news of educational opportunities, and a calendar of events. *Type:* Newsletter.

RiskWatch

Public Risk Management Association (PRIMA)
1815 Ft. Myer Dr., Ste. 1020   Ph: (703)528-7701
Arlington, VA 22209   Fax: (703)528-7966
E-mail: info@primacentral.org

Contact: Liz Lobert, Editor, liz@primacentral.org.

Desc: Provides a review of legislation and current events affecting public agency risk managers. Recurring features include news on federal and state legislation, insurance issues, court cases, upcoming seminars and meetings, and relevant job openings across the country. *Type:* Newsletter.

Royal Neighbors of America

230 16th St.   Ph: (309)788-4561
Rock Island, IL 61201   Free: 800-627-4762
E-mail: rnafield@ix.netcom.com
URL: http://www.royalneighbors.org

Contact: Jonni E. Miklos, Natl.Pres.

Desc: Fraternal life insurance society administered by women that insures men, women, and children. *Type:* Association.

Self-Insurance Institute of America

12241 Newport Ave., Ste. 100   Ph: (714)508-4920
Santa Ana, CA 92705   Free: 800-851-7789
                                    Fax: (714)508-4904
E-mail: webmaster@siia.org
URL: http://www.siia.org

Contact: James A. Kinder, CEO.

Desc: Actuaries, attorneys, claims adjusters, consultants, corporations, employers, insurance companies, risk managers, third party administrators, and others involved or interested in self-insurance. Purpose is to foster and promote alternative methods of risk protection as opposed to conventional insurance. Seeks to advance the concept of self-insurance characterized by the transfer of risk from an insurance company to the individual employer. *Type:* Association.

SIR News

Society of Insurance Research
691 Crossfire Ridge   Ph: (770)426-9270
Marietta, GA 30064   Fax: (770)426-9298
E-mail: 103336.2226@compuserve.com; 104355.2510@compuserve.com
URL: http://www.connectyou.com/ins/sir.htm.

Contact: Jack Ward, Editor.

Desc: Discusses problems, solutions, and perspectives of life/health and property/casualty insurance. Recurring features include columns titled Member News, Mark Your Calendars, Issues Focus, and editorials. *Type:* Newsletter.

Slavonic Benevolent Order of the State of Texas

PO Box 100   Ph: (254)773-1575
Temple, TX 76503   Free: 800-727-7578
                                    Fax: (254)774-7447

Contact: Leonard D. Mikeska, VP.

Desc: Fraternal benefit life insurance society. Supports rest home for aged members. Sponsors youth clubs. *Type:* Association.

Small Talk

Society of Actuaries
475 N. Martingale Rd., Ste. 800   Ph: (847)706-3500
Schaumburg, IL 60173-2226   Fax: (847)706-3599
E-mail: bhaynes@soa.org
URL: http://www.soa.org; http://www.soa.org.

Contact: James R. Thompson, Editor.

Desc: Encourages the professional development of Society members employed by small life insurance companies. Recurring features include letters to the editor, news of research, news of educational opportunities, and a calendar of events. *Type:* Newsletter.

Smart's Insurance Bulletin

James Whitaker & Associates
951 Old County Rd., No. 137   Ph: (415)982-1480
Belmont, CA 94002-2760   Free: 800-500-7627
                                    Fax: (415)341-3304
E-mail: 76060.2700@compuserve.com; smarts@smarts.pub.com.
URL: http://www.smartspob.com; http://www.insweb.com; http://www.riskinfo.com.

Contact: Frederick L. Pilot, Editor.

Desc: Covers California legislative, regulatory, and judicial concerns on property and casualty insurance. *Type:* Newsletter.

Society of Actuaries

475 N. Martingale Rd., Ste. 800   Ph: (847)706-3500
Schaumburg, IL 60173-2226   Fax: (847)706-3599
URL: http://www.soa.org

Contact: John E. O'Connor, Jr., Exec.Dir.

Desc: Professional organization of individuals trained in the application of mathematical probabilities to the design of insurance, pension, and employee benefit programs. Sponsors series of examinations leading to designation of fellow or associate in the society. Maintains speakers' bureau; conducts educational and research programs. *Type:* Association.

Society of Certified Insurance Counselors

PO Box 27027   Ph: (512)345-7932
Austin, TX 78755-2027   Free: 800-633-2165
                                    Fax: (512)343-2167
E-mail: alliance@scic.com
URL: http://www.scic.com/alliance

Contact: William T. Hold, Ph.D., Pres.

Desc: Holders of the Certified Insurance Counselor designation, which is acquired through the successful completion of the Society's five institutes and accompanying examinations. Licensed agents, brokers, solicitors, corporate risk managers, and members of the insurance faculty of an accredited college or university are eligible for examination and certification; to retain the CIC designation, one must complete an annual update each year. *Type:* Association.

Society of Financial Service Professionals

270 S. Bryn Mawr Ave.   Ph: (610)526-2500
Bryn Mawr, PA 19010-2195   Free: 888-243-2258
                                    Fax: (610)527-4010
URL: http://www.financialpro.org

Contact: Donald Manger, CEO.

Desc: Professional society of insurance and financial advisors. *Type:* Association.

Society of Insurance Research—Research Review

Society of Insurance Research
691 Crossfire Ridge   Ph: (770)426-9270
Marietta, GA 30064   Fax: (770)426-9298
E-mail: 103336.2226@compuserve.com; 104355.2510@compuserve.com

URL: http://www.sirnet.com.

Contact: Jack Ward, Editor, (860)633-1422, fax: (860)659-8664, jackward@javanet.com.

Desc: Carries professional papers or articles related to insurance research. Recurring features include conference presentations, insurance research sources, and CEO perspectives. *Type:* Newsletter.

Supreme Council of the Royal Arcanum

PO Box 392   Ph: (617)426-4135
Boston, MA 02101   Fax: (617)426-2322

Contact: Kenneth J. Kolek, Supreme Sec.

Desc: Fraternal benefit life insurance society. *Type:* Association.

Teachers Insurance and Annuity Association

730 3rd Ave.   Ph: (212)490-9000
New York, NY 10017   Fax: (212)916-5100

Contact: John H. Biggs, CEO.

Desc: Active and retired staff members of nonprofit colleges, universities, junior colleges, independent schools, foundations, libraries, scientific and research organizations, and teaching hospitals. Aids and strengthens nonproprietary and nonprofit colleges, universities, and related nonprofit institutions engaged primarily in education and research by providing annuities, individual life insurance/group life, mutual funds, long-term total disability insurance, and long-term care insuranc suited to the needs of such institutions and of their faculty and staff. *Type:* Association.

Title News

American Land Title Association (ALTA)
1828 L St. NW, Ste. 705   Ph: (202)296-3671
Washington, DC 20036   Free: 800-787-ALTA
          Fax: (202)223-5843

E-mail: service@alta.org
URL: http://www.alta.org.

Contact: Lisa Cole, Editor.

Desc: Provides information for title companies and property investors. *Type:* Newsletter.

Travelers Protective Association of America

3755 Lindell Blvd.   Ph: (314)371-0533
St. Louis, MO 63108   Fax: (314)371-0537

Contact: W.J. Karle, Jr., Exec.Secy.

Desc: Fraternal benefit society for men and women between the ages of 18 and 60. *Type:* Association.

Unemployment Insurance Reports with Social Security

CCH Inc.
2700 Lake Cook Rd.   Ph: (847)267-7000
Riverwoods, IL 60015   Free: 800-449-8114
          Fax: (847)224-8299

URL: http://www.cch.com; http://www.cch.com; http://hhr.cch.com.

Contact: Jan Gerstein, Manager.

Desc: Issues of CCH's Unemployment Insurance Reports with Social Security provide timely information on social security and federal/state unemployment insurance taxes, coverage, and benefits. Pertinent federal and state laws are reported promptly and reflected in place in the explanatory guides, as are regulations, judicial and administrative decisions, rulings, releases, and forms. *Type:* Newsletter.

United Societies of the United States of America

613 Sinclair St.   Ph: (412)672-3196
Mc Keesport, PA 15132   Fax: (412)672-3183

Contact: Rev. Eugene P. Yackanich, Sec.

Desc: Fraternal benefit life insurance society. *Type:* Association.

U.S. Letter Carriers Mutual Benefit Association

100 Indiana Ave. NW, Ste. 510   Ph: (202)638-4318
Washington, DC 20001   Fax: (202)783-6123

Contact: Michael J. O'Connor, Dir.

Desc: Fraternal benefit life insurance society. *Type:* Association.

Vasa Order of America

24 Crestmont Dr.   Ph: (401)364-9177
Carolina, RI 02812

E-mail: ksgomez@netsense.net

Contact: Karen Soderberg-Gomez, Contact.

Desc: A Swedish-American fraternal society offering sick and old-age benefits. Sponsors youth clubs. *Type:* Association.

The Weekly Insider (IBA West)

Insurance Brokers and Agents of the West
1000 Broadway, Ste. 600   Ph: (510)663-7800
Oakland, CA 94607-4041   Free: 800-772-8998
          Fax: (510)663-7835

E-mail: ibawest@aol.com
URL: http://ibawest.com.

Contact: Amy E. Komazec, Editor, akomazec@aol.com.

Desc: Carries insurance industry news, legislative developments, and insurance technical reviews of workers compensation and commercial and personal lines. Recurring features include interviews, an education calendar of events, and legislative and legal reports. *Type:* Newsletter.

William Penn Association

709 Brighton Rd.   Ph: (412)231-2979
Pittsburgh, PA 15233-1821   Fax: (412)231-8535

Contact: George S. Charles, Jr., Pres.

Desc: Fraternal benefit life insurance society. *Type:* Association.

Woman's Life Insurance Society

PO Box 5020   Ph: (810)985-5191
1338 Military St.   Free: 800-521-9292
Port Huron, MI 48061-5020   Fax: (810)985-6970

Contact: Janice U. Whipple, Pres.

Desc: Fraternal benefit life insurance society focusing on the needs of women. Each review or local club engages in local charitable community projects. *Type:* Association.

Workers' Comp

Insurance Marketing and Management Services (IMMS)
12424 Wilshire Blvd., Ste. 600   Ph: (310)442-6000
Los Angeles, CA 90025   Free: 800-753-4467
          Fax: (310)207-2111

E-mail: plus@imms.com
URL: http://www.imms.com

Contact: George Nordhaus, Publisher.

Desc: Contains information on insurance policies and coverages. Remarks: Personal subscribers receive 1,000 copies per issue; commercial subscribers, 1,500 copies. *Type:* Newsletter.

Workmen's Benefit Fund of the U.S.A.

99 N. Broadway   Ph: (516)938-6060
Hicksville, NY 11801-2905   Fax: (516)938-6882

Contact: Charles L. Grossman, Sec. & CEO.

Desc: Fraternal benefit life insurance society. *Type:* Association.

Workmen's Circle

45 E. 33rd St.   Ph: (212)889-6800
New York, NY 10016   Fax: (212)532-7518

E-mail: member@circle.org
URL: http://www.circle.org

Contact: Robert Kestenbaum, Exec.Dir.

Desc: Jewish (but not exclusively) men, women, and children. *Type:* Association.

Interior Design

American Society of Interior Designers

4035 E. Fanfol Dr.
Phoenix, AZ 85028-5103

E-mail: asid@asid.org
URL: http://www.interiors.org

Contact: Robert H. Angle, Exec.Dir.

Desc: Practicing professional interior designers and affiliate members in allied design fields. ASID Educational Foundation sponsors scholarship competitions, finances educational research, and awards special grants. Operates speakers' bureau; maintains placement service. *Type:* Association.

ARIDO

Association of Registered Interior Designers of Ontario
717 Church St.   Ph: (416)921-2127
Toronto, ON, Canada M4W   Free: 800-334-1180
2M5   Fax: (416)921-3660

E-mail: adminoffice@arido.on.ca

Contact: Lori Theoret, Editor, ltheoret@arido.on.ca.

Desc: Covers issues affecting the interior design profession. Contains information on association news as well as design resources. *Type:* Newsletter.

Canadian Home Workshop

Camar Publications Ltd.
210-340 Ferrier St.   Ph: (905)475-8440
Markham, ON, Canada L3R   Fax: (905)475-9246
2Z5

E-mail: letters@canadianworkshop.ca.

Contact: Tom Hopkins, Sr. V.P./Editorial, (905)475-8440, fax: (905)475-9560, tomhopkins@camarpublications.com; Jacqueline Howe, Publisher, (905)475-8440, fax: (905)475-9246, jacquelinehowe@camarpublications.com.

Desc: Magazine on woodworking, home improvement, and home repairs. *Type:* Periodical.

Canadian House & Home Magazine

Canadian Home Publishers, Inc.
511 King St. W., Ste. 120   Ph: (416)593-0204
Toronto, ON, Canada M5V   Free: 800-559-8868
2Z4   Fax: (416)591-1630

E-mail: homepub@inforamp.net

Contact: Cobi Ladner, Editor; Lynda Reeves, Publisher; Alexandra Cooper, Circulation Director, acooper@canhomepub.com; Marvela Yarhi, Advertising Dir., myarhi@canhomepub.com.

Desc: Magazine presenting current trends in home design and decorating. *Type:* Periodical.

CAUS News

Color Association of the United States (CAUS)
409 W. 44th St.   Ph: (212)582-6884
New York, NY 10036   Fax: (212)757-4557

E-mail: cau@colorassociation.com

Contact: Margaret Walch, Editor.

Desc: Explores aspects of color design, discussing applications to a wide variety of fields, including fashion, textiles, interior decorating, environmental construction, marketing, and advertising. Contains news of research, book reviews, and editorials. *Type:* Newsletter.

Colonial Homes

Hearst Magazines
959 8th Ave.   Ph: (212)649-2000
New York, NY 10019-5905

Contact: Annette Stramesi, Editor, (212)830-2950, astramesi@hearst.com; Brian J. Doyle, Publisher, (212)830-2901, bdoyle@hearst.com; Al Berman, Advertising Dir., (212)830-2902, aberman@hearst.com.

Desc: Magazine's unique editorial approach combines history and heritage to present leaders with an updated interpretation of classic American style. Editorial features include elegant and practical ideas beautifully photographes to encourage home enthusiasts to enhance their personal style. *Alt. Contact:* 1790 Broadway, New York, NY 10019; telephone: (212)830-2959; fax: (212)586-3455. *Type:* Periodical.

Contract Design Source Guide

Miller Freeman, Inc.
1 Penn Plaza, 10th Fl.   Ph: (212)714-1300
New York, NY 10119-1198   Fax: (212)643-5612
URL: http://www.contractdesign.com.

Contact: Regina Quinn, Editor, rquinn@mfi.com.

Desc: List of manufacturers and suppliers of commercial-grade furniture, fabric, carpet, lighting, and other furnishings for commercial and institutional settings, showroom marts. *Type:* Directory.

Country Sampler's Decorating Ideas

Sampler Publications, Inc.
707 Kautz Rd.   Ph: (630)377-8000
St. Charles, IL 60174   Fax: (630)377-8914

Contact: Ann Wilson, Editor; Dawn Wiggerman, Nat'l. Sales Mgr.; Robert Sexton, Circulation Mgr.

Desc: Do-it-yourself decorating magazine. *Type:* Periodical.

Elle Decor

Hachette Filipacchi Magazines, Inc.
1633 Broadway, 41st Fl.   Ph: (212)767-6000
New York, NY 10019   Fax: (212)989-4561

Contact: Marian McEvoy, Editor; Charles C. Bricker, Jr., Exec. Dir.; Elizabeth Sverbeyeff Byron, Advertising Mgr.; Brenda G. Saget, Publisher; Caroline Bowyer, Editor.

Desc: Architecture and interior design magazine. *Type:* Periodical.

The Family Handyman

Home Service Publications, Inc.
28 W. 23rd St.   Ph: (212)366-8686
New York, NY 10016   Fax: (212)366-8618

Contact: Gary Havens, Editor; Thomas Ph. Witschi, Publisher.

Desc: Do-it-yourself home improvement magazine. *Alt. Contact:* 7900 International Dr., Ste. 950, Minneapolis, MN 55425; telephone: (612)854-3000; fax: (612)854-8009. *Type:* Periodical.

Good Housekeeping

Hearst Magazines
959 8th Ave.   Ph: (212)649-2000
New York, NY 10019-5905

Contact: Ellen Levine, Editor-in-Chief; Patricia Haegele, Publisher; T.R. Shepard, Advertising Mgr.

Desc: Magazine focusing on women and the home. *Alt. Contact:* telephone: (212)649-2200. *Type:* Periodical.

Home Improvement Time

7425 Steubenville Pike   Ph: (412)787-2881
PO Box 247   Fax: (412)787-3233
Oakdale, PA 15071

Contact: James A. Stewart, Jr., President; Carole C. Stewart, Vice President.

Desc: Distributes home and property improvement information. *Alt. Contact:* 7425 Steubenville Pike, PO Box 247, Oakdale, PA 15071; telephone: (412)787-2881; fax: (412)787-3233. *Type:* Periodical.

Home Magazine

Hachette Publications
5670 Wilshire Blvd., Ste. 500   Ph: (213)954-0500
Los Angeles, CA 90036   Fax: (213)954-4800

Contact: Joseph C. Ruggiero, Editor; William F. Bondlow, Jr., Publisher; George H. Oestreich, Advertising Mgr.

Desc: Magazine focusing on home building, remodeling, design, and decorating. *Type:* Periodical.

House Beautiful

Hearst Magazines
959 8th Ave.   Ph: (212)649-2000
New York, NY 10019-5905

Contact: Louis Oliver Gropp, Editor; Cindy Sperling Spengler, Publisher; Kate Kelly Smith, Advertising Mgr., (212)903-5250.

Desc: Magazine focusing on architecture, building, interior decorating, gardening, and landscaping. *Alt. Contact:* 1700 Broadway, New York, NY 10019; telephone: (212)903-5084. *Type:* Periodical.

House Beautiful Kitchen/Baths

Hearst Magazines
959 8th Ave.   Ph: (212)649-2000
New York, NY 10019-5905

Contact: Kelly Reardon-Taavre, Editor-in-Chief, (212)649-4456, fax: (212)265-6718.

Desc: Publication covering kitchen and bath design. *Alt. Contact:* 250 W. 55th Street, New York, NY 10019; telephone: (212)649-4336, (212)265-6218; 1700 Broadway, New York, NY 10019; telephone: (212)830-2911; fax: (212)586-3455. *Type:* Periodical.

Interior Design—Buyers Guide Issue

Cahners Publishing Co.
245 W. 17th St.   Ph: (212)463-6828
New York, NY 10014   Free: 800-523-9654
                                Fax: (212)463-6530

Contact: Ben Velez, Editor.

Desc: Lists of 4,000 manufacturers and suppliers of furniture, furnishings, and services to contract and residential designers; trade buildings and marts; trade associations; carpet guide. *Type:* Directory.

Interior Design Sourcebook

Omnigraphics Inc.
2500 Penobscot Bldg.   Ph: (313)961-1340
Detroit, MI 48226   Free: 800-234-1340
                                Fax: (313)961-1383
E-mail: info@omnigraphics.com
URL: http://www.omnigraphics.com

Contact: Susan A. Lewis, Editor.

Desc: Interior design resources for academics and professionals, including, competitions and scholarships, magazines and publishers, trade associations, governmental agencies and research centers, conferences, design theory, programming and planning, furniture, finishes and textiles, building and interior systems, project types, visual communication methods, and business and professional practice. *Type:* Directory.

Interior Fashion News

Cygnus Publishing Inc.
445 Broad Hollow Road, Ste.   Ph: (516)845-2700
   21   Free: 800-308-6397
Melville, NY 11747-3601   Fax: (516)845-2736
E-mail: info@advancedimagingmag.com

Contact: Lori Stones-Feuer, Editor-in-Chief.

Desc: Functions as a source of news and information for the wallcoverings and window coverings industry. Covers areas of interest to those involved directly or indirectly with wallcoverings, window coverings, and interior cordinates, including current trends affecting the industry, new markets, market shifts, mergers and acquisitions, automation information, and news of people within the industry. *Type:* Newsletter.

International Society of Interior Designers

1933 S. Broadway, Ste. 138   Ph: (213)744-1313
Los Angeles, CA 90007   Fax: (213)744-1252

Contact: Michael D. Temple, Pres.

Desc: Professional interior designers, assistant interior designers, educators, and students devoted to establishing and maintaining professional standards for the field of interior design. Restores and redecorates community projects such as hospitals. Maintains biographical archives and placement service; operates speakers' bureau. *Type:* Association.

Metropolitan Home

Hachette Filipacchi Magazines, Inc.
1633 Broadway, 41st Fl.   Ph: (212)767-6000
New York, NY 10019   Fax: (212)989-4561

Contact: Donna Warner, Editor-in-Chief; John Miller, Publisher.

Desc: Magazine on home interior design and decorating. *Type:* Periodical.

Michigan Design Center Directory

Michigan Design Center
1700 Stutz   Ph: (248)649-4772
Troy, MI 48084   Fax: (248)649-1224
E-mail: mdescenter@aol.com; info@michigandesign.com.

Contact: Ginger Vintzel, Editor.

Desc: About 1,400 manufacturers represented at 40 showrooms in the Center; suppliers of furniture, fabrics, wall coverings, floor coverings, lighting, accessories, kitchen, and tile merchandise. *Type:* Directory.

Midwest Home & Garden

Minnesota Monthly Publications, Inc.
10 S. 5th St., Ste. 1000   Ph: (612)371-5800
Minneapolis, MN 55402-1012   Fax: (612)371-5801

Contact: Jan Senn, Editor, (612)371-5833, jsenn@mnmo.com; Steve Fox, Publisher.

Desc: Supplement to Minnesota Monthly. *Type:* Periodical.

National Kitchen and Bath Association

687 Willow Grove St.   Ph: (908)852-0033
Hackettstown, NJ 07840   Fax: (908)852-1695
URL: http://www.nkba.org

Contact: Robert O. Hirsch, Ph.D., CAE, Chief Exec. Officer.

Desc: Manufacturers and firms engaged in retail kitchen sales; manufacturers' representatives and wholesale distributors; utilities, publications, and other firms supplying products or services to the kitchen and bathroom industry. Protects and promotes the interest and welfare of members by fostering a better business climate in the industry. *Type:* Association.

Old-House Interiors

Gloucester Publishers
2 Main St.   Ph: (978)283-3200
Gloucester, MA 01930-5726   Fax: (978)283-4629
URL: http://www.oldhouseinteriors.com.

Contact: Patricia Poore, Editor; William O'Donnell, Publisher; Becky Bernie, National Sales Mgr.

Desc: Consumer magazine covering interior design. *Type:* Periodical.

Paint and Decorating Retailers Association

403 Axminister Dr. Ph: (314)326-2636
St. Louis, MO 63026 Free: 800-737-0107
 Fax: (314)326-1823
E-mail: info@pdra.org
URL: http://www.pdra.org
Contact: Ernest W. Stewart, Exec.VP.
Desc: Independent retailers of wall-covering, window, and floor coverings and paint. *Type:* Association.

Romantic Homes

Sampler Publications, Inc.
707 Kautz Rd. Ph: (630)377-8000
St. Charles, IL 60174 Fax: (630)377-8914
Contact: Peg Short, Editor-in-Chief; Dawn Anderson, National Sales Mgr.
Desc: Home and garden magazine. *Type:* Periodical.

Southern Accents

Southern Progress
2100 Lakeshore Dr. Ph: (205)877-6000
Birmingham, AL 35209-6721 Free: 888-737-3529
 Fax: (205)877-6600
Contact: Mark Mayfield, Editor; Bill Carey, Publisher.
Desc: Consumer magazine. *Type:* Periodical.

Style at Home

Telemedia Communications, Inc.
25 Sheppard Ave. W, Ste. 100 Ph: (416)733-7600
North York, ON, Canada M2N Fax: (416)733-7981
6S7
Contact: Gail Johnston Habs, Editor; Kerry Mitchell, Publisher; Monica Drexler, Advertising Mgr.; Darlene Storey, Circulation Dir.
Desc: Consumer magazine covering home decoring and interior design. *Type:* Periodical.

Victorian Homes

Vintage Publications, Inc.
PO Box 61 Ph: (413)659-3785
Millers Falls, MA 01349 Fax: (413)659-3113
Contact: Carolyn Flaherty, Editor; Donna Jeanloz, Publisher.
Desc: Magazine featuring Victorian home decoration. *Alt. Contact:* 550 7th St., Brooklyn, NY 11215; telephone: (718)499-5789. *Type:* Periodical.

W.D. Farmer Residence Designer Inc.

2007 Montreal Rd. Ph: (770)934-7380
Tucker, GA 30084 Fax: (770)934-1700
E-mail: wdfarmer@wdfarmerplans.com.
Contact: W.D. Farmer, President; Vickie F. Starkey, Asst. Sec.-Treas./Dir. Advertising.
Desc: Distributes weekly feature, homes, releases. *Alt. Contact:* 2007 Montreal Rd., Tucker, GA 30084; telephone: (770)934-7380; fax: (770)934-1700. *Type:* Periodical.

Internal Medicine

American Board of Internal Medicine

501 Walnut St., Ste. 1700 Ph: (215)446-3500
Philadelphia, PA 19106-3699 Free: 800-441-2246
 Fax: (215)446-3470
URL: http://www.abim.org
Contact: Harry R. Kimball, Pres.
Desc: Certification board established to determine the qualifications of, administer examinations to, and certify as specialists in internal medicine those doctors meeting its standards of clinical competence. Board members are elected from certified leaders in internal medicine. The board has certified approximately 121,000 internists and 54,000 subspecialist diplomates and issued 10,000 recertification certificates. *Type:* Association.

American College of Physicians

190 N. Independence Mall West Ph: (215)351-2600
Philadelphia, PA 19106-1572 Free: 800-523-1546
 Fax: (215)351-2448
E-mail: interpub@mail.acponline.org
URL: http://www.acponline.org
Contact: Walter J. McDonald, Exec. VP.
Desc: Professional society of medical doctors specializing in internal medicine and closely related specialties such as dermatology, neurology, psychiatry, cardiology, gastroenterology, and public health. Sponsors annual postgraduate courses for practicing physicians. Sponsors teaching and research scholarship competition. *Type:* Association.

American Society of Internal Medicine

2011 Pennsylvania Ave. NW, Ph: (202)835-2746
Ste. 800 Fax: (202)835-0443
Washington, DC 20006-1834
Contact: Alan R. Nelson, M.D., Exec.VP.
Desc: Professional society of physicians specializing in internal medicine. Is concerned with the social, economic, and political factors affecting the delivery of high quality care. Focuses on the delivery and financing of medical care in areas including access to care, appropriate reform of American health care system, medical and public education, issues affecting the elderly, private and public sector, health insurance and reimbursement, managed care, documentation of physician performance, and medical technology and computerization aimed at maintaining and promoting high quality medical care at a reasonable cost. *Type:* Association.

International Development

Ashoka: Innovators for the Public

1700 N. More St., Ste. 1920 Ph: (703)527-8300
Arlington, VA 22209 Fax: (703)527-8383
URL: http://www.ashoka.org
Contact: William Drayton, Pres.
Desc: Entrepreneurs, scientists, educators, attorneys, and activists; churches, schools, and private institutions; concerned individuals. Seeks to bring about change and provide assistance to economically and socially disadvantaged citizens in the Third World, in Bangladesh, Brazil, India, Indonesia, Mexico, Nepal, Thailand, South Africa, Senegal, Cofe D'Ivoire, Burkina Faso, Ghana, Nigeria, Cameroun, Mali, and Zimbabwe, through education, legal advocacy, environmental programs, income-generation projects, health and medicine, and applied technology. *Type:* Association.

Caribbean/Latin American Action

1818 N St. NW, Ste. 500 Ph: (202)466-7464
Washington, DC 20036 Fax: (202)822-0075
E-mail: info@claa.org
URL: http://www.claa.org
Contact: Antonio Colorado, Exec.Dir.
Desc: Caribbean Basin and United States leaders from corporate, international, government, and nonprofit organizations. *Type:* Association.

Centre for Development and Population Activities

1400 16th St. NE Ph: (202)667-1142
Washington, DC 20036 Fax: (202)332-4496
E-mail: cmail@cedpa.org
URL: http://www.cedpa.org
Contact: Peggy Curlin, Pres.
Desc: Administers community-based development projects in Africa, Asia, Latin America, the Middle East and Eastern Europe in partnership with local woman-run organizations. *Type:* Association.

Christian Reformed World Relief Committee

2850 Kalamazoo Ave. SE Ph: (616)246-0740
Grand Rapids, MI 49560 Free: 800-552-7972
 Fax: (616)224-0834
Contact: Andy Ryskamp, Dir.
Desc: Administers worldwide relief and development work in 30 countries. *Type:* Association.

Concern America Newsletter

Concern America
2020 N. Broadway Ph: (714)953-8575
PO Box 1790 Fax: (714)953-1242
Santa Ana, CA 92702
E-mail: concamerinc@earthlink.net
Desc: Covers the organization's development programs in Third World countries. *Type:* Newsletter.

Consultative Group on International Agricultural Research

1818 H St. NW Ph: (202)473-8918
Washington, DC 20433 Fax: (202)473-8110
E-mail: cgiar@cgnet.com
URL: http://www.cgiar.org
Contact: Alexander Von Der Osten, Exec.Sec.
Desc: Countries, multilateral development agencies, regional development banks, and private foundations. Supports network of 18 agricultural research centers purporting to improve the quality and quantity of food production and protect natural resources in developing countries. Supports research on critical aspects of food production in these countries that are not covered by other research facilities and that are of wide usefulness regionally or globally. *Type:* Association.

Counterpart International

1200 18th st. NW, Suite 1100 Ph: (202)296-9676
Washington, DC 20036 Fax: (202)296-9679
E-mail: info@counterpart.org
URL: http://www.counterpart.org
Contact: Stanley W. Hosie, Exec.Dir.
Desc: Manages civic, social and economic development, and humanitarian relief projects with partner nongovernment organizations (NGOs) in the South Pacific, Former Soviet Republics and Vietnam. *Type:* Association.

Financial Services Volunteer Corps

10 E 53rd St., 24th Fl
New York, NY 10022
Contact: J. Andrew Spindler, Exec.Dir.
Desc: Assists emerging democracies in establishing financial systems. *Type:* Association.

Heifer Project International

PO Box 808 Ph: (501)376-6836
Little Rock, AR 72203 Free: 800-422-0474
 Fax: (501)376-8906
E-mail: info@heifer.org
URL: http://www.heifer.org
Contact: Jo Luck, Exec.Dir.
Desc: A nonsectarian, selfhelp organization that provides livestock, poultry, technical aid, and related agricultural services to people in developing areas of the world. *Type:* Association.

International Human Assistance Programs

Desc: Helps raise the living standards of impoverished people in developing countries of Africa, Asia, and the Pacfic with innovative selfhelp programs. Major projects focus on helping disadvantaged rural families meet their needs in areas of food production, health care, nutrition, family planning, environmental sanitation, vocational training, community leadership training, physical rehabilitation, and income-creating projects for women and young people. Many of these services are combined with total community development projects that are cooperatively planned and executed with the village people and designed to be self-supporting when IHAP phases out its development aid. *Type:* Association.

International Voluntary Services
1901 Pennsylvania Ave. NW, Ph: (202)387-5533
  Ste. 501 Fax: (202)466-5669
Washington, DC 20006
E-mail: ivs@pacthq.org

Contact: Anne D. Shirk, Chief Operating Officer.

Desc: Supported by church groups, universities, research organizations, foundations, corporations, and former volunteers. Motto is "Poverty in a world of plenty, hunger in a world of abundance, and exploitation of the weak by the powerful are unacceptable and unnecessary." Provides skilled technicians for projects addressed to the needs of low-income rural people in developing countries. Provides a channel, independent of national or religious affiliation, through which skilled and motivated volunteers may serve as a development resource. *Type:* Association.

Just Act: Youth Action for Global Justice
333 Valencia St., No. 101 Ph: (415)431-4204
San Francisco, CA 94103 Free: 800-743-3808
  Fax: (415)431-5953
E-mail: info@justact.org
URL: http://www.justact.org

Contact: Mark Rand, Exec.Dir.

Desc: Campus student organizations, primarily undergraduates, united to learn more about global development issues and help to alleviate hunger, disease, and poverty in the third World and in the U.S. Focuses efforts through four major programs: the Partnership in Development Program, which allows American college students direct contact with communities in the Third World and allows them to help raise funds for specific village-based development projects overseas. *Type:* Association.

Katalysis North/South Development Partnership
1331 N. Commerce St. Ph: (209)943-6165
Stockton, CA 95202 Fax: (209)943-7046
E-mail: Katalysis2@aol.com

Contact: X Gerald Hildebrand, Pres. & CEO.

Desc: Supports low income people to gain self-reliance by helping them to improve their economic and social conditions. Works through multilateral partnerships with community based organizations using participatory processes to provide training and technical assistance in microenterprise development, women's community banking, and institutional strengthening. Practices a partnership model of international development which allows all participants to relate as equals, relaxing the hierarchical mindset and replacing power with process as the means of effecting organizational goals. *Type:* Association.

Oxfam America
26 West St. Ph: (617)482-1211
Boston, MA 02111-1206 Free: 800-225-5800
  Fax: (617)728-2594
E-mail: oxfamusa@oxfamamerica.org

Contact: Raymond Offenheiser, Pres.

Desc: Autonomous development and disaster assistance organization cooperating in a worldwide network known as Oxfam, a name derived from the Oxford Committee for Famine Relief, which began in England in 1942. Funds self-help projects in the poorer countries of Asia, Africa, and the Americas. Emphasis is on promoting economic and food self-reliance. *Type:* Association.

PACT
1901 Pennsylvania Ave. NW, Ph: (202)466-5666
  5th. Fl. Fax: (202)466-5669
Washington, DC 20006

Contact: Louis L. Mitchell, CEO.

Desc: Believes that "the foundation of civil society is pluralism--where citizens acting together can express their interests, exchange information, strive for mutual goals and influence government." Seeks to strengthen the community-focused nonprofit sector worldwide. *Type:* Association.

PLAN International
PO Box 7670 Ph: (401)294-3693
Warwick, RI 02887 Fax: (401)295-7062

Contact: John GreenSmith, Inter.Exec.Dir.
Type: Association.

Planning Assistance
1832 Jefferson Pl. NW Ph: (202)466-3290
Washington, DC 20036 Fax: (202)466-3293

Contact: Robert Learmonth, Exec.Dir.

Desc: Assists voluntary and governmental organizations in developing countries and the U.S. *Type:* Association.

Science and Technology Branch
Science, Tech., Energy, Ph: (212)963-8807
  Environment & Natural Fax: (212)963-1267
  Resources
Department of Economic and
  Social Development
1 United Nations Plz., DC1-
  10th Fl.
New York, NY 10017

Contact: Carlos Nones, Exec.Dir.

Desc: Branch of the UN; promotes science and technology for development. Provides developing countries with technology assessment and forecasting services for New and Emerging Sciences and Technologies (Nest) using the Advance Technology Alert-System (ATAS). Coordinates the UN system in science and technology for development, especially at national level through interagency country missions. *Type:* Association.

Seva Foundation
1786 5th St. Ph: (510)845-7382
Berkeley, CA 94710-1716 Free: 800-223-7382
  Fax: (415)845-7410
E-mail: admin@seva.org
URL: http://www.seva.org

Contact: James O'Den, Exec.Dir.

Desc: Seva (a Sanskrit word for service) works to prevent blindness in India, Nepal, and Tibet; community development in Mexico and Guatemala; and provides diabetes treatment for Native Americans on reservations. In addition, Seva provides small grants for local projects that serve homelessness, youth at risk, and persons with HIV/AIDS. *Type:* Association.

SourceMex
Latin American Data Base (LADB)
Latin American Institute
University of New Mexico
801 Yale NE Ph: (505)277-6839
Albuquerque, NM 87131-1016 Free: 800-472-0888
  Fax: (505)277-6837
E-mail: info@ladb.unm.edu
URL: http://www.ladb.unm.edu/sourcemex.

Contact: Carlos Navarro, Editor.

Desc: Provides information on private investments, trade debt, inflation, public policy, maquiladoras, petroleum, agriculture, pollution, social wellfare, etc. Remarks: Available online only. *Type:* Newsletter.

Technoserve
49 Day St. Ph: (203)852-0377
Norwalk, CT 06854 Free: 800-99-
  WORKS
  Fax: (203)838-6717
E-mail: technoserve@tns.org
URL: http://www.technoserve.org

Contact: Peter A. Reiling, Pres. & CEO.

Desc: Works to improve the economic and social well-being of low-income people in Latin America, Africa, and Eastern Europe. *Type:* Association.

Trickle Up Program
121 W 27th St., Ste. 504 Ph: (212)362-7958
New York, NY 10001 Fax: (212)877-7464
E-mail: info@trickleup.org
URL: http://www.trickleup.org

Contact: Suzan Habachy, Exec.Dir.

Desc: Dedicated to creating new opportunities for self-employment and economic and social well-being among the low-income populations of the world. *Type:* Association.

United Nations Development Programme
1 United Nations Plz. Ph: (212)906-5315
New York, NY 10017 Fax: (212)906-5364
URL: http://www.undp.org

Contact: James Gustave Speth, Admin.

Desc: Formed as a result of United Nations General Assembly vote to merge 2 existing development operations, the Expanded Programme of Technical Assistance and the Special Fund. Currently funds 6000 projects in more than 170 developing countries and territories. Through a network of 132 offices in developing countries it cooperates with governments, at their request, and with 40 specialized and technical UN agencies and non-governmental organizations. *Type:* Association.

International Exchange

AFS Intercultural Programs
71 W. 23rd St., 17th Fl. Ph: (212)807-8686
New York, NY 10010 Free: 800-AFS-INFO
  Fax: (212)807-1001
E-mail: info@afs.org
URL: http://www.afs.org

Contact: Richard Spencer, Pres.

Desc: Former American Field Service ambulance drivers, students, and host families in 80 countries who have participated in AFS programs. Promotes international understanding, primarily through exchange of secondary school students, 16 to 18 years of age. Conducts a variety of exchange programs providing family living experiences to fit the needs of the participants. *Type:* Association.

American Council for International Studies
19 Bay State Rd. Ph: (617)236-2051
Boston, MA 02215 Fax: (617)236-4703

Contact: Peter Jones, Pres.

Desc: Teachers and students in the U.S. who wish to study abroad; foreign students studying in the U.S. Promotes international educational experience for high school teachers and students. *Type:* Association.

American Development Group
2318 Cleveland St., No. 1 Ph: (954)964-4463
Hollywood, FL 33020-3046 Fax: (954)964-4133
E-mail: adgusacigi@prodigy.net

Contact: Elias T. Samaha, Exec. Officer.

Desc: Manufacturers of cigarettes and suppliers of cigars. *Type:* Association.

American Institute for Foreign Study

102 Greenwich Ave.   Ph: (203)869-9090
Greenwich, CT 06830   Free: 800-727-2437
                            Fax: (203)869-9615

Contact: Robert J. Brennan, Pres.

Desc: Students and teachers at all levels. Encourages the understanding of foreign countries, and their languages and cultures among American students and teachers. Sponsors courses in Australia, Asia, Europe, and Mexico at renowned universities using local faculty and professors from participating United States institutions. *Type:* Association.

Antitrust & Trade Regulation Report

The Bureau of National Affairs, Inc. (BNA)
1231 25th St. NW   Ph: (202)452-4200
Washington, DC 20037
E-mail: bnaplus@bna.com
URL: http://bna.com/mkt/hrl/hrlwdec.htm

Contact: BNA PLUS, (202)452-4323, fax: (202)822-8092, bnaplus@bna.com.

Desc: Contains the complete text of Antitrust & Trade Regulation Report, covering legislative, regulatory, and judicial activities related to laws on restrictive trade practices, including litigation, negotiations, and civil and criminal investigations. Also covers competition law developments in the European Community (EC) and Japan. *Available:* LEXIS-NEXIS, LEXIS; LEXIS-NEXIS, NEXIS; West Group, WESTLAW. *Type:* Database.

Asian Business Link

Asian Business League
233 Sansome, Ste. 1108   Ph: (415)788-4664
San Francisco, CA 94104   Fax: (415)788-4756

Desc: Promotes local business and trade in the Pacific basin. Serves as a forum for networking, discussion of business development issues, acknowledgement of members' successes, and personnel placement. *Type:* Newsletter.

Asian Economic News

Kyodo News International, Inc.
50 Rockefeller Plaza, Ste. 803   Ph: (212)397-3723
New York, NY 10020   Free: 800-536-3510

Desc: Provides information on companies and ventures in Asian regions and countries. Covers business, trade, and economic policies. *Type:* Newsletter.

Association for International Practical Training

10400 Little Patuxent Pky. Ste.   Ph: (410)997-2200
   250   Fax: (410)992-3924
Columbia, MD 21044
E-mail: aipt@aipt.org
URL: http://www.aipt.org

Contact: Elizabeth Chazottes, CEO.

Desc: Helps coordinate training around the world in fields such as travel, the culinary arts, hotel management, engineering, and business administration. *Type:* Association.

Association for World Travel Exchange

38 W. 88th St.   Ph: (212)787-7706
New York, NY 10024   Fax: (212)580-9283

Contact: Robert L. Tesdell, Exec.Dir.

Desc: Sponsors a camp counselor program and low-cost study-hospitality tours for foreign student visitors to the U.S. Operates the International Student Center (youth hostel) in New York City. Conducts placement service. *Type:* Association.

BNA Antitrust Database

The Bureau of National Affairs, Inc. (BNA)
1231 25th St. NW   Ph: (202)452-4200
Washington, DC 20037
E-mail: bnaplus@bna.com
URL: http://bna.com/mkt/hrl/hrlwdec.htm

Desc: Contains information covering antitrust legislation, banking, and securities regulation. *Available:* West Group, WESTLAW. *Type:* Database.

BNA International Trade Daily

The Bureau of National Affairs, Inc. (BNA)
1231 25th St. NW   Ph: (202)452-4200
Washington, DC 20037
E-mail: bnaplus@bna.com
URL: http://bna.com/mkt/hrl/hrlwdec.htm

Desc: Contains information on federal judicial, legislative, and regulatory activities affecting U.S. trade. *Available:* LEXIS-NEXIS, LEXIS; West Group, WESTLAW; LEXIS-NEXIS, NEXIS. *Type:* Database.

BNA's Eastern Europe Reporter

Bureau of National Affairs, Inc. (BNA)
1231 25th St. NW   Ph: (202)452-4323
Washington, DC 20037   Free: 800-372-1033
                           Fax: (202)452-7773
E-mail: bnaplus@bna.com; beer@bna.com.
URL: http://www.newsstand.lotus.com.

Contact: Basco Eszeki, Managing Editor.

Desc: Covers legislative, regulatory, and legal developments affecting business, trade, and investment in Eastern Europe and the former Soviet Union. *Type:* Newsletter.

Brazil Watch

Orbis Publications, LLC
3201 New Mexico Ave. NW,   Ph: (202)237-0155
   Ste. 249   Fax: (202)237-0596
Washington, DC 20016
E-mail: orbis@orbispub.com
URL: http://www.orbispub.com.

Contact: Richard W. Foster, Editor.

Desc: Focuses on political, economic, and business events in Brazil. Features interviews with government officials and provides coverage of the Brazilian Congress, political parties, economic policy, environmental issues, and foreign debt. *Type:* Newsletter.

Brazilian-American Chamber of Commerce— News Bulletin

Brazilian-American Chamber of Commerce, Inc.
509 Madison Ave., Ste. 304   Ph: (212)751-4691
New York, NY 10022   Fax: (212)751-7692
E-mail: info@brazilcham.com
URL: http://www.brazilcham.com

Contact: Sueli Bonaparte, Editor.

Desc: Provides up-to-date information on the economy of Brazil and on Brazil's economic relations with the U.S. Concerned with economic data, energy, imports/exports, industry, shipping, and agriculture. *Type:* Newsletter.

British Universities North America Club

PO Box 430   Ph: (203)264-0901
Southbury, CT 06488   Free: 800-GO-
                                 BUNAC
                           Fax: (203)264-0251
URL: http://www.bunac.org
Contact: Jim Buck, Gen.Mgr.

Desc: Promotes educational and cultural, work/travel, exchange programs between British and North American students and around the world. Coordinates employment opportunities, including camp counseling, in the United States, Canada, and Jamaica for British students and in Great Britain and Australia for American students. Offers scholarships to British students studying in North America. *Type:* Association.

Business Europe

Treasury & Risk Management
111 W. 57th St., 11th Fl.   Ph: (212)459-3004
New York, NY 10019-2211   Fax: (212)459-3007
E-mail: newyork@eiu.com
Contact: Nicholas Stevenson, Editor.

Desc: Discusses current news, trends, and developments about trade and investment in European markets. *Type:* Newsletter.

Business Opportunities from Israel

Israel Economic Mission
800 2nd Ave., 16th Fl.   Ph: (212)499-5600
New York, NY 10017-4709   Fax: (212)564-8964
Contact: Beth Belhin, Editor.

Desc: Describes new products and product lines made in Israel suitable for export to the U.S. Lists the Israeli manufacturer. *Type:* Newsletter.

Canada Letter

S & S Press Co., Ltd.
13964 Tallon Pl.   Ph: (604)588-0727
Surrey, BC, Canada V3V 5X8
Contact: Akira Shigematsu, Editor.

Desc: Provides news on Canadian business activity in Japan. *Type:* Newsletter.

Consumers for World Trade Newsletter

Consumers for World Trade (CWT)
2000 L St. NW, Ste. 200   Ph: (202)785-4835
Washington, DC 20036   Fax: (202)416-1734
E-mail: cwt@cwt.org
URL: http://www.cwt.org.
Contact: Doreen L. Brown, Editor, dbrown@cwt.org.

Desc: Supplies information on trade issues following the issues through the legislative process to conclusion. Reports on International Trade Commission actions, carries interviews with trade leaders, and provides news of organization activities. *Type:* Newsletter.

Council on International Educational Exchange

205 E. 42nd St.   Ph: (212)822-2600
New York, NY 10017   Fax: (212)822-2699
Contact: Stevan Trooboff, Pres/CEO.

Desc: Dedicated to helping people gain understanding, acquire knowledge, and develop skills for living in a globally interdependent and culturally diverse world. *Type:* Association.

Countertrade & Offset

DP Publications
PO Box 7188   Fax: (703)425-7911
Fairfax Station, VA 22039
Contact: Michael Morrison, Editor; James Thomas, Assistant Editor.

Desc: Remarks: Telex: 263 128 CTO UR. *Type:* Newsletter.

The Cuba Report

The Cuba Report
501 Brickell Key Dr., No. 200   Ph: (305)381-8685
Miami, FL 33131
E-mail: cubarpt@icanect.net
Contact: James D. Whisenand, Editor.

Desc: Focuses on domestic economic developments, future economic reconstruction of Cuba, economic transformation, and investment in Cuba. Recurring features include interviews, news of research, and a calendar of events. *Type:* Newsletter.

C.V. Starr Newsletter
C.V. Starr Center for Applied Economics
New York University
269 Mercer St., 3rd Fl.   Ph: (212)998-8936
New York, NY 10003   Fax: (212)995-3932
Contact: Tracy Ryan, Editor, fax: (212)995-3932, tracy.
ryan@nyu.edu.
Desc: Focuses on economic developments, privatization,
macro- and microeconomics, exchange rate systems, and
household wealth patterns. Recurring features include a
calendar of events and columns titled Focal Research Projects, New Appointments, Visitors, Policy Luncheons,
Publications, Seminars, Activities and Awards, and Conference Participation. *Type:* Newsletter.

Doing Business in Asia
CCH Inc.
2700 Lake Cook Rd.   Ph: (847)267-7000
Riverwoods, IL 60015   Free: 800-449-8114
    Fax: (847)224-8299
URL: http://www.cch.com
Desc: Publishes information in a question and answer for-
mat pertaining to trade with major Asian nations. *Type:*
Newsletter.

Doing Business in Eastern Europe
CCH Inc.
2700 Lake Cook Rd.   Ph: (847)267-7000
Riverwoods, IL 60015   Free: 800-449-8114
    Fax: (847)224-8299
URL: http://www.cch.com
Desc: Covers current information about doing business in
Eastern Europe, including banking, currency, tax laws, re-
sources, and regulations. *Type:* Newsletter.

Doing Business in Europe
CCH Inc.
2700 Lake Cook Rd.   Ph: (847)267-7000
Riverwoods, IL 60015   Free: 800-449-8114
    Fax: (847)224-8299
URL: http://www.cch.com
Contact: James Rooney, Editor; Joan Goode, Advertising
Dir.
Desc: Provides an overview of business operations in Eu-
rope, including finance, tax, and labor requirements. *Type:*
Newsletter.

DRI Canadian Primary Source
Standard & Poor's DRI
Data Products Division
24 Hartwell Ave.   Ph: (781)863-5100
Lexington, MA 02421
E-mail: client_services@dri.mcgraw-hill.com
URL: http://www.dri.mcgraw-hill.com
Contact: Client Services, (617)860-6527, fax: (617)860-
6416.
Desc: Contains more than 1100 series of industrial sector
detail and regional and provincial aggregates for capital ex-
penditures, housing, banking and money markets activity.
Includes investment, labor income, wages and salaries, for-
eign exchange and trade. *Available:* Standard & Poor's
DRI, Data Products Division. *Type:* Database.

DRI/TBS World Trade Forecast
Standard & Poor's DRI
Data Products Division
24 Hartwell Ave.   Ph: (781)863-5100
Lexington, MA 02421
E-mail: client_services@dri.mcgraw-hill.com
URL: http://www.dri.mcgraw-hill.com
Contact: Client Services, (617)860-6527, fax: (617)860-
6416.
Desc: Contains approximately 82,000 annual historical
and forecast time series on import and export volumes,
and prices in current U.S. dollars. *Available:* Standard &
Poor's DRI, Data Products Division. *Type:* Database.

East Asian Business Intelligence
NVST.COM
717 D St. NW, No. 300   Ph: (202)628-7767
Washington, DC 20004-2807   Free: 800-809-0666
    Fax: (202)628-6618
Contact: Anne Phelan, Editor.
Desc: Furnishes "early, accurate reports on sales, contracting and private trade opportunities in East Asia," along
with names of key contacts, addresses, and telephone and
fax numbers. Features the latest government tender offers
in each issue and alerts readers to future business opportunities. *Type:* Newsletter.

East Asian Executive Reports
NVST.COM
717 D St. NW, No. 300   Ph: (202)628-7767
Washington, DC 20004-2807   Free: 800-809-0666
    Fax: (202)628-6618
Contact: William C. Hearn, Editor.
Desc: Features legal, financial, and practical aspects of
doing business in East Asia. Features articles on local requirements for agents and sponsors, branch offices, joint
ventures, importing, government tendering, licensing, and
sourcing. *Type:* Newsletter.

East/West Business & Trade
Welsh Pony and Cob Society of America
PO Box 2977   Ph: (703)667-6195
Winchester, VA 22601
Contact: Justin Ford, Editor.
Desc: Examines recent developments in the former Soviet
republics and Eastern Europe that affect business and
trade. Interested in topics such as nuclear energy, intra-
German trade, Hungary's offshore bank, and the Siberian-
West European gas pipeline. *Type:* Newsletter.

East West Report
United States Pan Asian American Chamber of
Commerce (USPAACC)
1329-18th St. NW   Ph: (202)296-5221
Washington, DC 20036   Fax: (202)296-5225
E-mail: uspaacc@his.com
Contact: Susan Au Allen, Editor.
Desc: Provides advocacy, education, information, and net-
work opportunities for Asian Pacific American business
owners and professionals. Furnishes information on chari-
table, scientific, and educational programs. *Type:* Newslet-
ter.

EF Foundation for Foreign Study
One Education St.   Ph: (617)619-1000
Cambridge, MA 02141   Free: 800-44S-HARE
    Fax: (617)619-1401
E-mail: foundation@ef.com
URL: http://www.effoundation.org
Contact: Tineke Van Dam, Pres.
Desc: Network of representatives throughout Europe, Asia,
and the Americas. Seeks to further international under-
standing through cultural and academic exchange. *Type:*
Association.

Emerging Markets Week
Institutional Investor, Inc.
488 Madison Ave.   Ph: (212)224-3300
New York, NY 10022   Free: 800-543-4444
    Fax: (212)224-3490
Contact: Tom Lamont, Editor.
Desc: Reports news on the financial markets in Latin
America, including who's buying what and why, and how
local trading, clearance, and settlement mechanisms are
developing. *Type:* Newsletter.

Export Communications
ARISTO Marketing Corp.
10 Newman Ave., M/S 16432   Ph: (401)435-3717
East Providence, RI 02916   Fax: (401)435-7093
E-mail: export@aristonet.com
URL: http://www.aristonet.com.
Contact: Patricia J. Epple, Editor, patricia@aristonet.com.
Desc: Provides practical information and trade leads on ex-
port opportunities and developments in foreign markets.
Recurring features include letters to the editor, a calendar
of events, job listings, and a column titled Internet Re-
source Guide. *Type:* Newsletter.

Export Finance Letter Quarterly
Richard Barovick
4938 Hampden Ln., Ste. 346   Ph: (301)907-8647
Bethesda, MD 20814   Fax: (301)907-8650
E-mail: barovick@erols.com
Contact: Richard Barovick, Editor.
Desc: Provides news and information on exporting. *Type:*
Newsletter.

Export News
Canadian Exporters' Association
99 Bank St., Ste. 250   Ph: (613)238-8888
Ottawa, ON, Canada K1P 6B9   Fax: (613)563-9218
Contact: Greg MacDonald, Dir. of Public Relations &
Communication.
Desc: Provides news and information on exporting. *Type:*
Newsletter.

The Export Practitioner
M.K. Technology
1920 N St., Ste. 750   Ph: (202)463-1250
Washington, DC 20036   Fax: (202)429-9812
E-mail: exp@mk.ibek.com.
URL: http://www.exportprac.com.
Contact: Erik C. Wemple, Editor, erik@mk.lbek.com.
Desc: Focuses on regulatory policy and legal trends regard-
ing export of products and services. Covers planning strat-
egies for marketability. *Type:* Newsletter.

The Exporter
Trade Data Reports, Inc.
90 John St.   Ph: (212)587-1340
New York, NY 10038   Fax: (212)587-1344
E-mail: exporter@exporter.com.
URL: http://www.exporter.com.
Desc: Covers export operations, markets, training re-
sources, and world trade information. *Type:* Newsletter.

The Financial Times Currency Forecaster
Capitol Publications, Inc.
1101 King St., Ste. 444   Ph: (703)683-4100
Alexandria, VA 22314   Free: 800-655-5597
    Fax: (703)739-6517
Contact: Alan Teck, Editor; David Kenning, Publisher.
Desc: Provides forecasts and analysis on currency and eco-
nomic indicators. *Type:* Newsletter.

Foreign Affairs
Council on Foreign Relations Press
58 E. 68th St.   Ph: (212)434-9400
New York, NY 10021   Fax: (212)861-2759
E-mail: foraff@email.cfr.org.
Contact: James F. Hoge, Jr., Editor; David Kellogg, Pub-
lisher; David Hilmer, Advertising Dir.
Desc: Magazine on international relations, trade, and eco-
nomics. *Type:* Periodical.

Foreign Trade Fairs New Products Newsletter

Printing Consultants, Publishers

Box 636, Federal Sq.   Ph: (908)686-2382
Newark, NJ 07101

Contact: John E. Felber, Editor.

Desc: Provides descriptions of and manufacturer's addresses for new foreign products. Remarks: Included in subscription to I.I.I: International Intertrade Index, to which this newsletter serves as a supplement. *Type:* Newsletter.

Free Market

Ludwig von Mises Institute for Austrian Economics

Auburn University   Ph: (334)844-2500
Auburn, AL 36849   Fax: (334)844-2583
E-mail: lvmises@mail.auburn.edu

Contact: L.H. Rockwell, Publisher; Jeffrey Tucker, Editor.

Desc: Discusses issues and controversies in economic policies from the point of view of the Austrian School of economics. *Type:* Newsletter.

FX Week

Waters Information Services, Inc.

PO Box 2248   Ph: (607)770-9242
Binghamton, NY 13902-2248   Free: 800-947-7947
E-mail: kmiller@watersinfo.com.

Contact: Julie Ros, Editor.

Desc: Reports on developments in currency trading and the foreign exchange market, including products, personnel movement, and strategies of major participants. Remarks: Alternate fax number: (607) 770-9435. *Type:* Newsletter.

German Academic Exchange Service

950 3rd Ave., 19th Fl.   Ph: (212)758-3223
New York, NY 10022   Fax: (212)755-5780
E-mail: daadny@daad.org
URL: http://www.daad.org

Contact: Britta Baron, Dir.

Desc: Promotes international relations among institutions of higher education, specifically in the area of academic and scientific exchange. *Type:* Association.

Iberoamerican Cultural Exchange Program

13920 93rd Ave. NE   Ph: (425)821-1463
Kirkland, WA 98034   Fax: (425)821-1849
E-mail: icepbpm@aol.com

Contact: Bonnie P. Mortell, Contact.

Desc: Educational service organization that arranges long- and short-term exchange programs between the U.S. and Spanish-speaking countries. *Type:* Association.

Idol Money Review and World Monitor

Mulberry Press Inc.

PO Box 300   Ph: (905)957-0602
Smithville, ON, Canada L0R   Fax: (905)957-5263
2A0

E-mail: idolmoney@aol.com.

Contact: Wilfred J. Hahn, Editor; Joyce Hahn, Subscription Mgr.

Desc: Provides information on the economy and investment markets worldwide. Includes topics such as social security and pensions, market trends, and population/age statistics. *Type:* Newsletter.

Importweek

Canadian Importers Association, Inc.

438 University Ave., Ste. 1618   Ph: (416)595-5333
Box 60   Fax: (416)595-8226
Toronto, ON, Canada M5G
2K8

E-mail: info@importers.ca; mmccormack@importers.ca
URL: http://www.importeres.ca; http://www.importers.ca.

Contact: Catherine McPherson, Editor.

Desc: Examines the import trade industry. *Type:* Newsletter.

India Business and Investment Report

PSi, Inc.

75 Maiden Ln.   Ph: (212)806-8840
New York, NY 10038   Fax: (212)514-9766

Contact: M. Puri, Editor.

Desc: Covers India's role in international trade and investment and the affect of political developments upon these areas. Recurring features include cross-border transactions (mergers, acquisitions, joint ventures, direct investment), market information, and a calendar of meetings and expositions in India. *Type:* Newsletter.

Institute of International Education

809 United Nations Plz.   Ph: (212)883-8200
New York, NY 10017-3580   Fax: (212)984-5452
URL: http://www.iie.org

Contact: Dr. Allan E. Goodman, Pres./CEO.

Desc: Seeks to develop better understanding between the people of the U.S. and the peoples of other countries through higher educational exchange and training programs for students, scholars, artists, leaders, and specialists; assists in developing educational programs to serve the economic and social needs of emerging nations. *Type:* Association.

Institute for the International Education of Students

223 W. Ohio St.   Ph: (312)944-1750
Chicago, IL 60610-4196   Free: 800-955-2300
          Fax: (312)944-1448

E-mail: info@iesabroad.org
URL: http://www.iesabroad.org

Contact: Dr. Mary Dwyer, Pres.

Desc: Provides international educational programs in Europe, Asia, Australia, and South America for college students. *Type:* Association.

Inter-American Trade Report

National Law Center for Inter-American Free Trade

111 S. Church Ave., Ste. 200   Ph: (520)622-1200
Tucson, AZ 85701-1602   Fax: (520)622-0957
E-mail: natlaw@natlaw.com
URL: http://www.natlaw.com.

Contact: Felipe Garcia, Editor; Tim Baker, Contact.

Desc: Summarizes the latest developments in the trade and investment industries in Latin America. *Type:* Newsletter.

Interactive Global News

PANGAEA Communications

630 Ninth Ave., Ste. 1000   Ph: (212)445-8580
New York, NY 10036   Fax: (212)445-2542
URL: http://www.pangaea.net/ign/news.htm.

Contact: Beth Stone, Editor.

Desc: Covers international business, global marketing trends, and consumer product and service industries. Recurring features include news of research, a calendar of events, book reviews, job listings, notices of publications available, and columns titled Bargain Travel, Country Profiles & Updates. *Type:* Newsletter.

Interexchange

161 6th Ave.   Ph: (212)924-0446
New York, NY 10013   Fax: (212)924-0575
E-mail: info@interexchange.org
URL: http://www.interexchange.org

Contact: Uta Christianson, Exec.Dir.

Desc: Serves American students traveling abroad and foreign students visiting America. *Type:* Association.

Interflo

Interflo

PO Box 42   Ph: (201)763-9483
Maplewood, NJ 07040   Fax: (201)763-9493
E-mail: interflo@aol.com.

Contact: Paul R. Surovell, Editor.

Desc: Contains abstracts and indexes on foreign trade and investment in the former Soviet republics, including Russia, Ukraine, Kazakhstan, Belarus, Azerbaijan, Turkmenistan, and others. *Type:* Newsletter.

International Country Risk Guide

The PRS Group

6320 Fly Rd., Ste. 102   Ph: (315)431-0511
PO Box 248   Fax: (315)431-0200
East Syracuse, NY 13057-0248
E-mail: custserv@prsgroup.com

Contact: Tom Sealy, Editor.

Desc: Covers politics, economics, and financial risk for 130 countries. Includes write-ups and statistics for individual countries and regions. *Type:* Newsletter.

International Currents

Ned Davis Research, Inc.

600 Bird Bay Dr.   Ph: (941)484-6107
Venice, FL 34292   Free: 800-241-0621
          Fax: (941)484-8693

Contact: Neil Leeson, Editor; Tim Hayes, Co-Editor.

Desc: Covers global currency flows. Identifies prospects for currencies and gold, and tracks stock markets using timing models. *Type:* Newsletter.

International Economic Scoreboard

The Conference Board, Inc.

845 3rd Ave.   Ph: (212)759-0900
New York, NY 10022-6679   Fax: (212)980-7014
E-mail: info@conference-board.org
URL: http://www.conference-board.org

Contact: Robert G. Taylor, Editor; Marilyn Mitchell.

Desc: Provides current data on the business outlook in 11 major industrial countries: Australia, Canada, France, West Germany, Italy, Japan, Korea, New Zealand, Taiwan, the United Kingdom, and the U.S. Remarks: A source for additional information on this indicator system and its uses is available at the Center for International Business Cycle Research, Columbia University Business School. *Type:* Newsletter.

International Intertrade Index

Printing Consultants, Publishers

Box 636, Federal Sq.   Ph: (908)686-2382
Newark, NJ 07101

Contact: John E. Felber, Editor.

Desc: Lists new imported products that have been displayed at foreign trade fairs and that are available to U.S. importers and distributors. *Type:* Newsletter.

International Market Alert

United Communications Group

11300 Rockville Pike, Ste. 1100   Ph: (301)287-2700
Rockville, MD 20852-3030   Free: 800-929-4824
          Fax: (301)287-2049

E-mail: customer@ucg.com

Contact: Dan Weil, Editor.

Desc: Provides a fax service covering financial markets, world economy developments, foreign exchange, and U.S. interest rates. *Type:* Newsletter.

International Schools Services

15 Roszel Rd.   Ph: (609)452-0990
PO Box 5910   Fax: (609)452-2690
Princeton, NJ 08543
E-mail: iss@iss.edu

URL: http://www.iss.edu

Contact: Dr. John M. Nicklas, Pres.

Desc: Purpose is to provide educational services for American and international schools overseas. Operates a number of schools on behalf of U.S. industry abroad and recruits and recommends personnel. *Type:* Association.

International Trade Alert

American Association of Exporters and Importers
11 W. 42nd St.   Ph: (212)944-2230
New York, NY 10036   Fax: (212)382-2606

Contact: Elizabeth Stern Bayer, Editor.

Desc: Reports on trade issues as they affect importers and exporters. Contains news of actions by Customs, the Federal Drug Administration (FDA), and the Department of Commerce, CITA, CPSC, FTC, and the USDA, as well as other federal agencies and departments; and the status of regulations on imported/exported products. *Type:* Newsletter.

International Trade Reporter

Bureau of National Affairs, Inc. (BNA)
1231 25th St. NW   Ph: (202)452-4323
Washington, DC 20037   Free: 800-372-1033
   Fax: (202)452-7773

E-mail: bnaplus@bna.com

Contact: Linda G. Botsford, Managing Editor.

Desc: Covers current international trade policies of the U.S. and of major U.S. trading partners. Topics include bilateral negotiations, customs, export/import policy, foreign investment, standards, taxation, and other related issues. *Type:* Newsletter.

International Trade Reporter

The Bureau of National Affairs, Inc. (BNA)
1231 25th St. NW   Ph: (202)452-4200
Washington, DC 20037

E-mail: bnaplus@bna.com

URL: http://bna.com/mkt/hrl/hrlwdec.htm

Contact: BNA PLUS, (202)452-4323, fax: (202)822-8092, bnaplus@bna.com.

Desc: Contains the complete text of the current developments section of International Trade Reporter, covering developments in international trade and actions of U.S. courts and federal agencies related to imports and exports. *Available:* LEXIS-NEXIS, LEXIS; West Group, WESTLAW. *Type:* Database.

International Trade Reporter Current Reports

Bureau of National Affairs, Inc. (BNA)
1231 25th St. NW   Ph: (202)452-4323
Washington, DC 20037   Free: 800-372-1033
   Fax: (202)452-7773

E-mail: bnaplus@bna.com

URL: http://www.bna.com.

Contact: Linda G. Botsford, Editor.

Desc: Reports and analyzes legislative, regulatory, and legal developments affecting U.S. trade policies and the policies of major U.S. trading partners. Recurring sections include World News, Asia-Pacific Rim, Americas/NAFTA, Legal Action, East-West Trade, and Africa/Middle East. *Type:* Newsletter.

International Trade Reporter Decisions

Bureau of National Affairs, Inc. (BNA)
1231 25th St. NW   Ph: (202)452-4323
Washington, DC 20037   Free: 800-372-1033
   Fax: (202)452-7773

E-mail: bnaplus@bna.com

Contact: Linda G. Botsford, Editor.

Desc: Carries digested, classified, and indexed judicial and administrative decisions dealing with legal issues arising from U.S. trade law. *Type:* Newsletter.

The International Trader

GMS Publications
76 Mamaroneck Ave., Ste. 6   Ph: (914)946-2734
White Plains, NY 10601   Free: 800-206-5656
   Fax: (914)946-3093

E-mail: centre@juno.com; gmspub@aol.com

URL: http://www.ourworld.compuserve.com/homepages/CENTRETRADE; http://ourworld.compuserve.com/homepages/CENTRETRADE; http://forwarders.com/resource/gmspub/gmspub.html; http://www.centretrade.com/www/gmspub

Contact: Warren Hasting, Editor; Rose Budd, Editor, centre@fcc.net.

Desc: Devoted to international trade, finance, transportation, and logistics. Provides current information on import/export matters, plus new ways to finance and market them. *Type:* Newsletter.

International Traders Association

c/o The Mellinger Co.   Ph: (805)257-2700
25620 Rye Canyon Rd., Unit B   Fax: (805)257-4840
Valencia, CA 91355

E-mail: mellco@tradezone.com

URL: http://www.tradezone.com

Contact: Brainerd L. Mellinger, III, Pres. & CEO.

Desc: Individuals and firms involved in the import and export, and/or mail order business. Objectives are to promote world trade and international business between members and educate foreign suppliers, manufacturers, and governments about the trader's role in the marketplace through publications and personal visits. Sponsors trade show. *Type:* Association.

International Traders' Mailbag

ICS Group
PO Box 4082   Ph: (949)552-8494
Irvine, CA 92710-4082

E-mail: ibis-info@juno.com

Contact: Adair Wyett, Editor.

Desc: Focuses on international trade. Covers new trade regulations, restrictions, and opportunities. *Type:* Newsletter.

International Traders Newsletter

International Business Information Service
PO Box 3271   Ph: (714)552-8494
Tustin, CA 92781-3271

Desc: Offers current information and ideas for active international traders. Recurring features include letters to the editor, news of research, a calendar of events, book reviews, notices of publications available, and columns titled Q & A and JUST IN. *Type:* Newsletter.

Internationalist

Assist International
90 John St., Rm. 505   Ph: (212)725-3312
New York, NY 10038-3202

Contact: Peter J. Robinson, Jr., Editor.

Desc: Communicates international trade events, conferences, seminars, and trade shows occuring in the New York/Connecticut/New Jersey region. Recurring features include a calendar of events and a listing of international trade resources available in the tri-state region. *Type:* Newsletter.

Japan-U.S. Business Report

Japan Economic Institute
1000 Connecticut Ave. NW,   Ph: (202)296-5633
Ste. 211   Fax: (202)296-8333
Washington, DC 20036

E-mail: jei@jei.org

Contact: Susan MacKnight, Editor.

Desc: Monitors what Japanese companies are doing in the U.S. and activities of American businesses in Japan. *Type:* Newsletter.

Japan Weekly Monitor

Kyodo News International, Inc.
50 Rockefeller Plaza, Ste. 803   Ph: (212)397-3723
New York, NY 10020   Free: 800-536-3510

E-mail: gorok@kyodonews.com.

Desc: Contains information on Japanese economic activity and indicators from government agencies and trade associations. Covers the country's stock market, currency exchanges, and foreign relations. *Type:* Newsletter.

JEI Report

Japan Economic Institute
1000 Connecticut Ave. NW,   Ph: (202)296-5633
Ste. 211   Fax: (202)296-8333
Washington, DC 20036

E-mail: jei@jei.org

Contact: Arthur J. Alexander, Editor.

Desc: Covers Japanese economics, politics, international relations, and relations with the U.S. using objective analyses for a primarily U.S. readership. *Type:* Newsletter.

Journal of Commerce

Journal of Commerce, Inc.
Two World Trade Center, 27th   Ph: (212)837-7051
Fl.
New York, NY 10048-0662

URL: http://www.piers.com

Desc: Contains the complete text of more than 102,000 articles from The Journal of Commerce, covering water, air, truck, and rail freight transportation industries. Also covers news and legislation affecting international trade, the insurance industry, commodities markets, and the chemical, petroleum, and plastics industries. *Available:* The Dialog Corporation, DIALOG. *Type:* Database.

Lagniappe Monthly on Latin America Projects & Finance

Latin American Information Services Inc.
159 W. 53rd St., 28th Fl.   Ph: (212)765-5520
New York, NY 10019-6090   Free: 800-278-7043
   Fax: (212)765-2927

URL: http://www.lais.com; http://www.lais.cais.

Contact: Rosemary H. Werrett, Editor, rwerrett@pipeline.com; Trudy Balch, Managing Editor.

Desc: Tracks business opportunities arising in Latin America as a result of new project development and privatization. Focuses on activity in electric energy, oil and gas, telecommunications, mining, transportation, and water treatment. *Type:* Newsletter.

Leadership Montreal

Board of Trade of Metropolitan Montreal
5 Place Ville Marie   Ph: (514)871-4000
Plaza Level, Ste. 12500   Fax: (514)871-1255
Montreal, PQ, Canada H3B 4Y2

Contact: Madeleine Murdock, Editor.

Desc: Features news on business, legislation, and international trade. Recurring features include interviews, news of research, a calendar of events, reports of meetings, and notices of publications available. *Type:* Newsletter.

LEXIS® International Trade Library

LEXIS-NEXIS
9443 Springboro Pike   Ph: (937)865-6800
PO Box 933
Dayton, OH 45401-0933

URL: http://www.lex-nexis.com

Desc: Contains a comprehensive collection of federal case law, statutes, regulations, and agency decisions all related to the importing of goods and services, exporting of goods and services, licensing of intellectual property, payment of taxes, or investment and banking at the international level. *Available:* LEXIS NEXIS, LEXIS. *Type:* Database.

Machinery Outlook

Manfredi & Associates
20934 W. Lakeview Pkwy.   Ph: (847)949-9080
Mundelein, IL 60060   Fax: (847)949-9910
E-mail: info@manfredi.com
Contact: Frank Manfredi, Editor.
Desc: Provides news of interest on construction and mining machinery. *Type:* Newsletter.

Main Economic Indicators

Organization for Economic Cooperation and Development (OECD)
2001 L St. NW, Ste. 650   Ph: (202)785-6323
Washington, DC 20036-4922   Free: 800-456-6323
                                 Fax: (202)785-0350
E-mail: washington.contact@oecd.org
URL: http://www.oecdwash.org; http://www.washcont.org.
Desc: Covers general and foreign business and general economics. Gives statistics and/or indicators for the Gross National Product (GNP), industrial production, deliveries, stocks and orders, construction, wholesale and retail sales, employment, wages, prices, finance, foreign trade, and balance of payments for OECD countries. *Type:* Newsletter.

Management Contents®

The Gale Group
27500 Drake Rd.   Ph: (248)699-4253
Farmington Hills, MI 48331-3535
URL: http://www.galegroup.com
Contact: (650)378-5000, fax: (800)676-2345.
Desc: Contains more than 283,000 citations, with abstracts, to the worldwide English-language literature on business and management from more than 140 journals. Covers finance and economics (including accounting, banking, and managerial economics); industry (including commodities and goods, production, industrial relations); and management and administration (including public administration, planning, decision science, human resource development, management philosophy, operations research, and marketing). *Available:* The Dialog Corporation, DataStar; The Dialog Corporation, DIALOG. *Type:* Database.

Market: Asia Pacific

The PRS Group
6320 Fly Rd., Ste. 102   Ph: (315)431-0511
PO Box 248   Fax: (315)431-0200
East Syracuse, NY 13057-0248
E-mail: custserv@prsgroup.com
Contact: Robin Bromby, Editor.
Desc: Concerned with demographics, lifestyles, and business opportunities in the Asia Pacific region. Profiles a particular city or country in each issue, providing consumer market trends, surveys results, and articles on direct marketing and marketing management. *Type:* Newsletter.

Middle East Executive Reports

NVST.COM
717 D St. NW, No. 300   Ph: (202)628-7767
Washington, DC 20004-2807   Free: 800-809-0666
                                 Fax: (202)628-6618
Contact: Colin MacKinnon, Contributing Editor; William Hearn, Publisher; Mimi Mann, Editor.
Desc: Covers legal, financial, and practical aspects of doing business in the Middle East. Features articles on local requirements for agents and sponsors, branch offices, joint ventures, importing, government tendering, licensing, and sourcing, technology transfer, labor, product liability, taxes, marketing, investment, and repatriation of profits, and financing. *Type:* Newsletter.

Monthly Import Detention List

National Technical Information Service (NTIS)
U.S. Department of Commerce
5285 Port Royal Rd.   Ph: (703)605-6000
Springfield, VA 22161-0001   Free: 800-553-NTIS
                                 Fax: (703)605-6900
E-mail: orders@ntis.fedworld.gov
URL: http://www.ntis.gov.
Desc: Tabulates items of imported food-stuffs and pharmaceuticals that have been detained. Arranges the detentions by product code, sample number, the product, district and port of entry, manufacturer's and shipper's name, city and country of entry, the primary and secondary reasons for detention, and unit type, quantity, and value. *Type:* Newsletter.

NACEL Open Door

3410 Federal Dr., Ste. 101   Fax: (612)686-9601
St. Paul, MN 55122
Contact: Richard Banasikowski, Contact.
Desc: International high school student exchange between high school age students from the U.S. and those from Asia, Australia, Europe, Latin America, and the Middle East. *Type:* Association.

National Customs Brokers and Forwarders Association of America

1200 18th St., NW, Ste. 901   Ph: (202)466-0222
Washington, DC 20036   Fax: (202)466-0226
E-mail: staff@ncbfaa.org
URL: http://www.ncbfaa.org
Contact: Barbara Reilly, Exec.VP.
Desc: Treasury-licensed customs brokers, FMC-licensed independent ocean freight forwarders, and CNS-registered air cargo agents; associate members in 25 foreign countries. Seeks to maintain high standards of business practice throughout the industry. *Type:* Association.

Newsearch™

The Gale Group
27500 Drake Rd.   Ph: (248)699-4253
Farmington Hills, MI 48331-3535
URL: http://www.galegroup.com
Contact: (650)378-5000, fax: (800)676-2345.
Desc: Contains citations, with selected abstracts, to the current 2 to 6 weeks of articles and stories indexed and abstracted by The Gale Group. Sources include more than 5000 general-interest, legal, trade, computer, health, and business publications, newspapers, BusinessWire, and other wire services. *Available:* The Dialog Corporation, DIALOG; CompuServe Information Service, Knowledge Index. *Type:* Database.

The Orange Report

Netherlands Chamber of Commerce in the U.S., Inc.
1 Rockefeller Plaza, Ste. 1420   Ph: (212)265-6460
New York, NY 10020   Fax: (212)265-6402
Contact: Rinus Oosthoek, Editor.
Desc: Reports on issues affecting the transatlantic trade and investment environment. *Type:* Newsletter.

Pacific American Institute

49 Stevenson St., Ste. 525   Ph: (415)512-9760
San Francisco, CA 94105   Fax: (415)512-9765
Contact: Janet Holyko, Pres.
Desc: Seeks to provide high-quality travel and educational experiences for students from overseas. Contracts with overseas companies to recruit students for travel-study programs. Provides living arrangements for international students with families in American communities. *Type:* Association.

PacificScope

International Relations & Pacific Studies Library
University of California, San Diego
0175-W, 9500 Gilman Dr.   Ph: (619)534-1413
La Jolla, CA 92093-0175   Fax: (619)534-8526
URL: http://irpslibrary.ucsd.edu.
Contact: Maria Reinalda Adams, Editor, mradams@ucscl.edu.
Desc: Serves as a forum for information on the Library's collections and services. Provides news of the Library's computer database resources and new additions to the general collection. *Type:* Newsletter.

PAIS International

Public Affairs Information Service, Inc. (PAIS)
521 W. 43rd St.   Ph: (212)736-6629
New York, NY 10036-4396
E-mail: inquiries@pais.org
URL: http://www.pais.org
Contact: Barbara Preschel, inquiries@pais.org.
Desc: Contains more than 400,000 citations, with brief abstracts, to literature on business and the social sciences with emphasis on contemporary social, economic, and political issues and the making and evaluating of public policy. *Available:* The Dialog Corporation, DIALOG; CompuServe Information Service, Knowledge Index; OCLC Online Computer Library Center, Inc., OCLC EPIC; Research Libraries Group, Inc. (RLG), Research Libraries Information Network (RLIN); The Gale Group, InfoTrac Web; Ovid Technologies, Inc.; EBSCO Publishing; SilverPlatter Information, Inc. *Type:* Database.

Pring Market Review

International Institute for Economic Research
PO Box 624   Ph: (804)696-0415
Gloucester, VA 23061   Fax: (804)694-0028
Contact: Martin J. Pring, Editor.
Desc: Provides information about the world's financial markets. *Type:* Newsletter.

ProfitSouth ProfitGram

James Cotton Associates
2943 Tall Pines Way, NE   Ph: (770)938-6058
Atlanta, GA 30345-1404   Fax: (770)938-6058
E-mail: jacotton@bellsouth.net
Contact: Jim Cotton, Editor.
Desc: Reports on international and domestic business and marketing issues. Covers client profitability, new market development, and strategic planning. *Type:* Newsletter.

Russian Far East Update

Russian Far East Advisory Group LLC
PO Box 22126   Ph: (206)477-2668
Seattle, WA 98122   Fax: (206)628-0979
E-mail: update@russianfareast.com
URL: http://www.russianfareast.com.
Contact: Elisa B. Miller, Editor.
Desc: Provides business briefings on trade and economic developments in the Russian Far East, with the intention of addressing the unique problems of doing business in the region. Covers such industries as communications, mining, forestry, fishing, oil and gas, transportation, and banking. *Type:* Newsletter.

Scandinavian Seminar

24 Dickinson St.   Ph: (413)253-9736
Amherst, MA 01002   Fax: (413)253-5282
URL: http://www.scandinavianseminar.com
Contact: Jacqueline Waldman, Oper.Officer.
Desc: Seeks to promote life-long learning and cultural exchange. *Type:* Association.

Southeast Asia Weekly Fax Bulletin

Orbis Publications, LLC

3201 New Mexico Ave. NW,   Ph: (202)237-0155
    Ste. 249   Fax: (202)237-0596
Washington, DC 20016
E-mail: orbis@orbispub.com

Desc: Provides information on political, economic, and business events in Cambodia, Laos, Malaysia, Myanmar, The Philippines, Singapore, Thailand, and Vietnam. *Type:* Newsletter.

Trade and Development Bi-Weekly

Congressional Information Bureau, Inc.

3030 Clarendon Blvd. No. 202   Ph: (703)516-4801
Arlington, VA 22201-2845   Fax: (703)516-4804
E-mail: info@cibpubs.com

Contact: Robert P. Cazalas, Contact.

Desc: Reports on export opportunities for U.S. companies with U.S. and international bank financial aid. *Type:* Newsletter.

Trade & Industry Index™

The Gale Group

27500 Drake Rd.   Ph: (248)699-4253
Farmington Hills, MI 48331-
    3535
URL: http://www.galegroup.com

Contact: (650)378-5000, fax: (800)676-2345.

Desc: Contains more than 5.5 million citations, with abstracts (since 1992), to worldwide business, trade, and industry journal literature, as well as the complete text of 650 sources. Provides comprehensive coverage of more than 1500 business and industry publications, specialized trade journals, regional business publications, international periodicals, newspapers, BusinessWire, and other newswires. *Available:* The Dialog Corporation, DataStar; The Dialog Corporation, DIALOG; CompuServe Information Service, Knowledge Index. *Type:* Database.

U.K. Venture Capital Journal

Venture Economics, Inc.

40 W. 57th St., 11th Fl.   Ph: (212)765-5311
New York, NY 10019   Free: 800-455-5844
      Fax: (212)765-6123

Contact: Kathleen Devlin, Editor-in-Chief, devlin@tfn.com; Jennifer Jury, Editor.

Desc: Contains news, analysis, and data on UK's venture capital/buyout industries. *Type:* Newsletter.

UniSpeak

Unicon Systems

126 LaSalle Ave.
Buffalo, NY 14217-2630

Contact: David Albanese, Editor.

Desc: Provides new of economic, social, and political events throughout the world, with an emphasis on international business. Recurring features include letters to the editor, news of research, a calendar of events, and notices of publications available. *Type:* Newsletter.

United Nations Development Programme

United Nations

New York, NY 10017
E-mail: webmaster@undp.org
URL: http://www.undp.org

Desc: The United Nations Development Programme gopher and web server contains information about and by the UN. Included is the UN charter, information about the UNDP focus areas of poverty, environment, gender, and governance, current news pertaining to UN activity around the world. *Type:* Database.

U.S. ITC Update

Worldwide Videotex-Telcom

PO Box 3273   Ph: (561)738-2276
Boynton Beach, FL 33424
E-mail: markedit@juno.com

Contact: Mark Wright, Publisher.

Desc: Contains the complete text of U.S. ITC Update, a monthly newsletter on U.S. International Trade Commission (ITC) decisions affecting the import of foreign products. *Type:* Database.

USA-ROC Economic Council—Fax Update

USA-ROC Economic Council

1726 M St. NW, Ste. 601   Ph: (202)331-8966
Washington, DC 20036   Fax: (202)331-8985
E-mail: usaroc@aol.com

Desc: Seeks to promote business relations between the U.S. and Taiwan. *Type:* Newsletter.

Vietnam Business Infotrack

Vietnam Access

PO Box 1210   Ph: (805)985-7126
Port Hueneme, CA 93044-1210   Fax: (805)985-0839
E-mail: vietnamaccess@vcnet.com
URL: http://www.vcnet.com/vietnamaccess./va.html.

Contact: Kahn Le, Manager/Editor.

Desc: Covers recent commercial and economic developments in Vietnam and their effect on trade and investment. *Type:* Newsletter.

Washington Export Letter

Richard Barovick

4938 Hampden Ln., Ste. 346   Ph: (301)907-8647
Bethesda, MD 20814   Fax: (301)907-8650
E-mail: barovick@erols.com

Contact: Richard Barovick, Editor.

Desc: Provides news and information to small and mid-sized exporters. Covers developments in export promotion, export finance, export taxes, and export regulations. *Type:* Newsletter.

Washington International Business Report

International Business-Government Counsellors, Inc.

818 Connecticut Ave., 12th Fl.   Ph: (202)872-8181
Washington, DC 20006   Fax: (202)872-8696
E-mail: wibr@ibgc.com.
URL: http://www.ibgc.com.

Contact: Solveig B. Spielmann, Editor.

Desc: Analyzes the effect of government policies on international business operations, including marketing opportunities, competition, production sourcing, and financing costs. Discusses foreign trade and investment policy, multinational corporations, taxes, technology transfer, human rights, foreign boycotts, international finance, and East-West trade. *Type:* Newsletter.

Washington Tariff & Trade Letter

Gilston Communications Group

PO Box 467   Ph: (301)570-4544
Washington, DC 20044   Free: 800-270-9989
      Fax: (301)570-4545

Contact: Samuel M. Gilston, Editor.

Desc: Provides information on trends affecting a wide range of industries and products, trade statistics, international trade negotiations, and related subjects. *Type:* Newsletter.

What's Working for American Companies in International Sales & Marketing

Progressive Business Publications

370 Technology Dr.   Ph: (610)695-8600
Malvern, PA 19355   Free: 800-220-5000
      Fax: (610)651-2981

URL: http://www.pbp.com.

Contact: Julie Power, Editor.

Desc: Offers real world examples and the latest news from around the world to supply sales and marketing professionals an edge in international business. Recurring features include interviews, news of research, a calendar of events, news of educational opportunities, and a column titled Sharpen Your Judgment. *Type:* Newsletter.

World Industrial Reporter (Reportero Industrial)

Keller International Publishing, LLC

150 Great Neck Rd.   Ph: (516)829-9210
Great Neck, NY 11021   Fax: (516)829-5414
E-mail: kellpub@world.att.net

Contact: Felicia Morales, Editor; Robert Herlihy, Publisher.

Desc: World-wide industrial manufacturing magazine (tabloid) (English, Arabic, Spanish). *Type:* Periodical.

World Learning

U.S. Headquarters, Kipling Rd.   Ph: (802)257-7751
PO Box 676   Free: 800-451-4465
Brattleboro, VT 05302-0676   Fax: (802)258-3248
E-mail: info@worldlearning.org
URL: http://www.worldlearning.org

Contact: Dr. James A. Cramer, Pres. And CEO.

Desc: Provides individuals and institutions ability to develop the leadership capabilities and cross-cultural competence needed to function effectively in the global arena. Administers social and economic development activities under U.S. government and international contracts and grants. *Type:* Association.

World Trade Center of New Orleans

2 Canal St., Ste. 2900   Ph: (504)529-1601
New Orleans, LA 70130   Fax: (504)529-1691

Contact: Eugene Schreiber, Mng.Dir.

Desc: U.S. and foreign business leaders united for the promotion of international trade, friendship, and understanding. Programs visits for foreign VIPs; sends trade and cultural missions of business and civic leaders abroad each year. *Type:* Association.

The WorldPaper

World Times, Inc.

210 World Trade Center   Ph: (617)439-5400
Boston, MA 02210   Fax: (617)439-5415
E-mail: editorial@worldtimes.com.
URL: http://www.worldpaper.com.

Contact: Crocker Snow, Jr., Pres./Editor-in-Chief, (617)439-5410, csnow@worldtimes.com; Cameron Brandt, Editor, (617)439-5442, cbrandt@worldtimes.com; Lena Granberg, Publisher, (617)439-5413, lgranberg@worldtimes.com.

Desc: An international editorial supplement to newspapers and magazines featuring writers who write about their native countries (English, Spanish, Russian, Chinese, Japenese). *Type:* Periodical.

Worldwide Business Exchange

Phlander Company

PO Box 5385   Ph: (706)259-2280
Cleveland, TN 37320-5385   Fax: (706)259-2291

Contact: J.F. Straw, Editor.

Desc: Provides information for the global business community. Includes worldwide contacts and business opportunities. *Type:* Newsletter.

Youth For Understanding International Exchange
3501 Newark St. NW   Ph: (202)966-6808
Washington, DC 20016   Free: 800-424-3691
                            Fax: (202)895-1104
E-mail: pio@yfu.org
URL: http://www.youthforunderstanding.org
Contact: Stephen M. Johnson, President and CEO.
Desc: Groups and individuals. Provides educational opportunities for young people and adults who want to learn more about other people, language, and culture through international student exchange. *Type:* Association.

International Health

African Medical and Research Foundation, U.S.A.
19 W. 44th St., Ste. 1708   Ph: (212)768-2440
New York, NY 10036   Fax: (212)768-4230
E-mail: amrefusa@aol.com
URL: http://www.amref.org
Desc: U.S. branch of the African Medical and Research Foundation. Voluntary organization providing medical services to aid and augment health programs in developing nations and in rural areas of East Africa. *Type:* Association.

Foundation for the Support of International Medical Training
417 Center St.   Ph: (716)754-4883
Lewiston, NY 14092   Fax: (519)836-3412
E-mail: iamat@sentex.net
URL: http://www.sentex.net/~iamat
Contact: Mrs. M. A. Uffer, Pres.
Desc: Individuals and corporations organized to provide information regarding the availability of competent medical care overseas and information concerning sanitary conditions, health hazards, and climatic conditions in various parts of the world. *Type:* Association.

Hesperian Foundation
1919 Addison Ave., Ste. 304   Ph: (510)845-1447
Palo Alto, CA 94303   Fax: (510)845-4507
E-mail: hesperianfdn@igc.apc.org
URL: http://www.hesperian.org
Contact: Sarah Shannon, Exec.Dir.
Desc: Promotes good health in the developing world and in poor communities in the U.S. countries through community-based, informed self-care. Fosters constructive dialogue on health care and social change. *Type:* Association.

People-to-People Health Foundation
Project HOPE Health Sciences   Ph: (540)837-2100
Educ. Center   Free: 800-544-HOPE
Carter Hall   Fax: (540)837-1813
Millwood, VA 22646
Contact: William B. Walsh, Jr., Pres.&CEO.
Desc: Promotes better world health and understanding through the training of medical, nursing, dental, and allied health personnel in developing areas of the world. Operates the Center for Health Affairs, which provides research and policy analysis to help develop solutions to problems in worldwide health systems. Develops programs which include the use of volunteer doctors, nurses, and allied health professionals to teach modern techniques in health sciences education, health services delivery systems, health facilities management, and health-related humanitarian assistance. *Type:* Association.

Project Concern International
3550 Afton Rd.   Ph: (619)279-9690
San Diego, CA 92123   Fax: (619)694-0294
E-mail: postmaster@projcon.cts.com
URL: http://www.serve.com/pci

Contact: Heather Girard, Event/Media Coord.
Type: Association.

International Understanding

Atlantic Council of the United States
910 17th St. NW, Ste. 1000   Ph: (202)463-7226
Washington, DC 20006   Fax: (202)463-7241
URL: http://www.acus.org
Contact: David C. Acheson, Pres.
Desc: Conducts programs to: promote better understanding of major international security, political, and economic problems; foster informed public debate on these issues; make substantive policy recommendations to both the Executive and Legislative branches of the U.S. government, as well as to appropriate international organizations. Sponsors young leaders seminars; offers counselors program for high-level senior advisers. *Type:* Association.

Center for Citizen Initiatives
PO Box 29912   Ph: (415)561-7777
San Francisco, CA 94129-0912   Fax: (415)561-7778
E-mail: ccibrad@igc.apc.org
URL: http://www.igc.org/cci
Contact: Sharon Tennison, Pres.
Desc: Works to develop the private business sector and offer solutions to environmental problems in the former USSR. Maintains the Economic Development Program which matches Soviet entrepreneurs with American business administrators for one-month placement in U.S. businesses. *Type:* Association.

China Facts & Figures Annual
Academic International Press
PO Box 1111   Fax: (850)934-0953
Gulf Breeze, FL 32562-1111
E-mail: aipress@aol.com
URL: http://sites.gulf.net/aip/; http://www.ai-press.com.
Contact: Robert Perrins, Editor, (902)585-1782, fax: (902)585-1070, robert.perrins@acadiau.ca.
Desc: Statistical information about leading organizations, corporations, and other institutions in China in the military, foreign affairs, political affairs, and economy, including industrial and agricultural production, energy, foreign trade, communications, transportation, population, international relations, foreign aid, finance, science, technology and space law, cultural life, health, education, and welfare. Each annual volume supplements and updates previous volumes. *Type:* Directory.

CUBANEWS
Target Research
611 Pennsylvania Ave. SE, Ste.   Ph: (202)543-5076
341   Free: 800-376-3324
Washington, DC 20003   Fax: (202)546-8929
E-mail: latinenergy@compuserve.com
Contact: M. Feer, Editor.
Desc: Covers business and economic issues involving Cuba, including an economic overview, monthly developments, and industrial analysis. *Type:* Newsletter.

Educators for Social Responsibility
23 Garden St.   Ph: (617)492-1764
Cambridge, MA 02138   Free: 800-370-2515
                               Fax: (617)864-5164
E-mail: educators@national.org
URL: http://www.esrnational.org
Contact: Larry Dieringer, Exec.Dir.
Desc: Educators for Social Responsibility's primary mission is to help young people develop the convictions and skills to shape a safe, sustainable, and just world. Promotes children's ethical and social development through leadership in conflict resolution, violence prevention, intergroup relations and character education. *Type:* Association.

ISAR: Initiative for Social Action and Renewal in Eurasia
1601 Connecticut Ave. NW,   Ph: (202)387-3034
Ste. 301   Fax: (202)667-3291
Washington, DC 20009
E-mail: postmaster@isar.org
URL: http://.www.isar.org
Contact: Eliza K. Klose, Exec.Dir.
Desc: Promotes citizen participation and the development of the nongovernmental sector in the countries of the former Soviet Union. Supports citizen activists and grassroots nongovernmental organizations(NGOs) in their efforts to create just and sustainable societies. Programs emphasize information exchange, cooperative activities and networking. *Type:* Association.

Leadership Education for Asian Pacifics
327 E. 2nd St., Ste. 226   Ph: (213)485-1422
Los Angeles, CA 90012   Fax: (213)485-0050
E-mail: leap90012@aol.com
URL: http://www.leap.org/leap
Contact: J.D. Hokoyama, Pres. & Exec.Dir.
Desc: Strives to achieve full participation and equality for Asian Pacific Americans through leadership, empowerment, and policy. *Type:* Association.

National Democratic Institute for International Affairs
1717 Massachusetts Ave. NW,   Ph: (202)328-3136
5th Fl.   Fax: (202)939-3166
Washington, DC 20036
E-mail: demos@ndi.org
URL: http://www.ndi.org
Contact: Kenneth D. Wollack, Pres.
Desc: Workes to strengthen and expand democracy worldwide. Provides practical assistance to civic and political leaders advancing democratic values, practices and institutions. Works with democrats in every region of the world to build political and civic organizations, safeguard elections, and promote citizen participation, openness and accountability in government. *Type:* Association.

Neighbor to Neighbor
1611 Telegraph Ave. Ste. 1111   Ph: (510)419-0101
Oakland, CA 94612   Free: 800-366-8289
                                Fax: (510)419-0202
Contact: Jeff Robinson, Exec.Dir.
Desc: Began as a project of the Institute for Food and Development Policy . Publicized, organized, and lobbied to change U.S. policy in Central America. *Type:* Association.

Overseas Development Council
1875 Connecticut Ave. NW,   Ph: (202)234-8701
Ste. 1012   Fax: (202)745-0067
Washington, DC 20009
URL: http://www.odc.org
Contact: John W. Sewell, Pres.
Desc: Seeks to improve deision making on multilateral cooperation, development, and the better management of related global problems; conduct studies on current and emerging problems; provide a forum through conferences, seminars, and discussions for those directly concerned with development; distribute information among those working on development problems and among those citizens concerned with the development of poor nations; keep the urgency of the challenges of development before the public and responsible authorities. Conducts seminars, discussion groups, special conferences, and workshops for government officials, political figures, business executives, scholars, and labor and church representatives. Works with congressional groups and other organizations on matters pertaining to development issues. *Type:* Association.

Internet

CyberHound's Guide to Internet Discussion Groups
Gale Group Inc.
27500 Drake Rd.   Ph: (248)699-4253
Farmington Hills, MI 48331-   Free: 800-877-GALE
3535   Fax: (248)699-8070
E-mail: galeord@galegroup.com
URL: http://www.galegroup.com.; http://www.cyberhound.com/.
Desc: Nearly 4,500 listservs and newsgroups on the Internet. *Type:* Directory.

Gale Guide to Internet Databases
Gale Group Inc.
27500 Drake Rd.   Ph: (248)699-4253
Farmington Hills, MI 48331-   Free: 800-877-GALE
3535   Fax: (248)699-8070
E-mail: galeord@galegroup.com
URL: http://www.galegroup.com.; http://www.gale.com.
Contact: John Krol, Editor, john.krol@gale.com.
Desc: Approximately 5,500 Internet databases, including government, business, academic, research, educational databases, pop culture. *Type:* Directory.

Net Guide: Your Map to the Services, Information and Entertainment on the Electronic Highway
Random House, Inc.
201 E. 50th St.   Free: 800-726-0600
New York, NY 10022   Fax: (212)848-2436
Contact: Tracy Smith, Editor; Charles Levine, Editor.
Desc: More than 4,000 databases, bulletin board systems, and other online services; includes business, entertainment, science and technology, and recreational services. *Type:* Directory.

Investments

The Acker Letter
Bob Acker
2718 E. 63rd St.   Ph: (718)531-8981
Brooklyn, NY 11234
Contact: Bob Acker, Editor.
Desc: Focuses on under-researched companies for the professional and individual investor. Recurring features include coverage of the American Stock Exchange, the New York Stock Exchange, and the O.T.C. *Type:* Newsletter.

The Addison Report
Addison Investment Management Company
PO Box 402   Ph: (508)528-8678
Franklin, MA 02038-0402
Contact: Andrew L. Addison, Editor.
Desc: Provides investment recommendations for stocks, bonds, mutual fund timing, and commodities. Monitors two investment portfolios: one for the conservative investor, the other for the speculative investor. *Type:* Newsletter.

AIC Investment Bulletin
AIC Investment Advisors, Inc.
30 Stockbridge Rd.   Ph: (413)499-1111
Great Barrington, MA 01230-1226
Contact: Richard F. Maloney, Editor.
Desc: Serves investors by covering current business conditions, gold, silver, and the Tax Reform Act. Also covers securities markets, South African socio-economic conditions, interest rates, bonds, and domestic common stocks. *Type:* Newsletter.

Al Hanson's Economic Newsletter
Allen D. Hanson
PO Box 9   Ph: (218)367-2404
Ottertail, MN 56571
Contact: Al Hanson, Editor.
Desc: Offers advice on trading stocks, bonds, and commodities. Discusses the ramifications of tax law changes. *Type:* Newsletter.

The American Advisor
Goldline International, Inc.
100 Wilshire Blvd., 3rd Fl.   Ph: (818)501-3600
Santa Monica, CA 90401-1104
Contact: Joseph C. Battaglia, Editor.
Desc: Makes recommendations for building successful wealth-builing portfolios and surveys market developments pertaining to collecting and investing in gold and silver coins and bullion. Spotlights undervalued and overvalued coins and provides insight on economic trends. *Type:* Newsletter.

American Cash Flow Institute
255 S. Orange Ave., Ste. 624   Ph: (407)843-2032
PO Box 2668   Free: 800-253-1294
Orlando, FL 32802   Fax: (407)648-9470
URL: http://www.acfi_online.com
Contact: Deborah Bracknell, Exec.Dir.
Desc: Individuals who sell and trade debt instruments, such as mortgages, accounts receivables, annuities, structured settlements, and lottery winnings. *Type:* Association.

American Stock Exchange Radio AMEX
86 Trinity Pl.   Ph: (212)306-1637
New York, NY 10006
Contact: Yolanda Cain, Contact.
Desc: Business news/stock report format. *Alt. Contact:* 86 Trinity Pl., New York, NY 10006; telephone: (212)306-1637. *Type:* Periodical.

The Amernick Market Report
Amernick Publishing Company
PO Box 10065   Ph: (510)525-3055
Berkeley, CA 94709-5065
E-mail: amernick@home.com; amernick@ix.netcom.com.
Contact: Larry Amernick, Editor-in-Chief.
Desc: Provides information on international stock market events. *Type:* Newsletter.

Armstrong Report
Princeton Economic Institute, Inc.
PO Box 7227   Ph: (609)987-9522
Princeton, NJ 08543-7227   Fax: (609)987-0726
Desc: Analysis of financial and commodity markets. *Type:* Newsletter.

Asia Pacific Media Investor
Paul Kagan Associates, Inc.
126 Clock Tower Pl.   Ph: (831)624-1536
Carmel, CA 93923-8734   Fax: (831)625-3225
E-mail: info@kagan.com
Contact: Jeffrey Rago, Senior Asia Pacific Analyst.
Desc: Provides investors with information on Asia Pacific Cable/pay TV. *Type:* Newsletter.

Asset Sales Report
American Banker - Bond Buyer
One State Street Plaza, 27th Fl.   Ph: (212)803-8366
New York, NY 10004
URL: http://www.americanbanker.com
Desc: Contains the complete text of Asset Sales Report, a newsletter on the loan sales industry, including commercial loans and asset- and mortgage-backed securities. Covers legal and regulatory developments, market news and analyses, and information about industry leaders. *Available:* Bell & Howell Information and Learning; LEXIS-NEXIS, NEXIS; LEXIS-NEXIS, NEXIS. *Type:* Database.

Association for Investment Management and Research
5 Boar's Head Ln.   Ph: (804)980-3668
PO Box 3668   Free: 800-247-8132
Charlottesville, VA 22903-0668   Fax: (804)980-9755
E-mail: info@aimr.org
URL: http://www.aimr.org
Contact: Thomas A. Bowman, CFA, Pres. & CEO.
Desc: Security and financial analyst association whose members are practicing investment analysts. Includes private, voluntary self-regulation program in which AIMR members are enrolled. Promotes education, uniform performance presentation standards, improved accounting and disclosure of corporate information, and development of improved standards of investment research and portfolio management. *Type:* Association.

The Astute Investor Newsletter
Charles E. Cardwell
135 Beechwood Ln.   Ph: (423)376-2732
Kingston, TN 37763-4708
E-mail: astute_investor@compuserve.com.
Contact: Charles E. Cardwell, Editor.
Desc: Identifies and provides financial facts on stocks which meet classic value criteria established by Benjamin Graham: (1) Lists all widely traded stocks which sell below book value and have an earnings yield in excess of sixteen percent. (2) Lists all widely traded stocks which sell thirty percent or more below Net Current Assets(NCA), the minimum breakup value estimated by subtracting all liabilities from current assets. *Type:* Newsletter.

Bacard's Global Investor
Ferney Scribes Inc.
PO Box 1118   Ph: (415)257-6162
Mill Valley, CA 94942
E-mail: investor@crl.com.
URL: http://www.crl.com/~investor.
Contact: Andre Bacard, Editor.
Desc: Provides monthly updates of select no-load global and international funds, model portfolios, foreign market graphs, monthly analysis and current recommendations. Recurring features include news of research and a column titled Mutual Fund in the Spotlight. *Type:* Newsletter.

Bahamas Dateline
Caribbean Dateline Publications, Ltd.
PO Box 23276   Ph: (703)404-0894
Washington, DC 20026
Contact: N. Poteat Day, Editor.
Desc: Provides information on investments, laws, incorporation, tax haven information, tourism, business, and real estate in the Bahamas for foreign investors. Recurring features include news, a periodic directory of properties for sale or rent, and a column titled Review of the News. *Type:* Newsletter.

Barclay Managed Futures Report
Barclay Managed Futures Report
508 N. 2nd St., Ste. 201   Ph: (515)472-3456
Fairfield, IA 52556   Fax: (515)472-9514
E-mail: info@barclaygrp.com; barclay@fairfield.com.
Contact: Sol Waksman, Editor, sol@barclaygrp.com.
Desc: Presents an overview of performance of money managers specializing in futures markets. *Type:* Newsletter.

Bert Dohmen's Special Bulletin
Dohmen Capital Research Institute
1132 Bishop St., Ste. 1500   Ph: (808)545-2243
Honolulu, HI 96813   Free: 800-992-9989
              Fax: (808)545-1994
Contact: Bert Dohmen-Ramirez, Editor.
Desc: Functions as a supplement to the Wellington Letter. Provides immediate alert-type analysis of economic events as they occur and their effect on the market. *Type:* Newsletter.

Bert Dohmen's Wellington Letter

Dohmen Capital Research Institute
1132 Bishop St., Ste. 1500   Ph: (808)545-2243
Honolulu, HI 96813   Free: 800-992-9989
   Fax: (808)545-1994
E-mail: dohmcap@aol.com.
Contact: Bert Dohmen-Ramirez, Editor.
Desc: Provides a comprehensive monthly analysis of the major U.S. and world investments. *Type:* Newsletter.

Better Investing

National Association of Investors Corporation
PO Box 220   Ph: (810)543-0612
Royal Oak, MI 48068
URL: http://www.better-investing.org.
Contact: Donald E. Danko, Editor.
Desc: Features investment information on various corporations as seen by 10 different columnists. *Type:* Newsletter.

Better Investing

National Association of Investors Corp.
711 W. 13 Mile Rd.   Ph: (810)583-6242
Madison Heights, MI 48071   Fax: (810)583-4880
URL: http://www.better-investing.org.
Contact: Donald E. Danko, Editor; Martha F. Stephens, Advertising Mgr.
Desc: Magazine focusing on investing in long-term common stock. *Alt. Contact:* 711 West Thirteen Mile Rd., Madison Heights, MI 48071; telephone: (810)583-6242; fax: (810)583-4880. *Type:* Periodical.

BI Research Newsletter

BI Research, Inc.
PO Box 133   Ph: (203)270-9244
Redding, CT 06875
E-mail: birstocks@aol.com
Contact: Thomas C. Bishop, Editor.
Desc: Contains 7-8 in-depth investment recommendations per year, featuring common stocks judged likely to double over the next 1-3 years, primarily from OTC, but also from VSE, ASE, and NYSE. Updates each open recommendation in detail approximately every 6 weeks. *Type:* Newsletter.

Billington's Stock Focus II

Billington Publications Inc.
1660 Benson Rd.   Ph: (360)945-1490
Point Roberts, WA 98281   Free: 800-721-5726
   Fax: (360)945-1089
E-mail: info@billingtons.com; stockmkt@whidbey.com
URL: http://www.billingtons.com;   http://www.billingtons.com.
Contact: Lance Fortt, Editor.
Desc: Deals with international companies that are publicly traded. Provides advice to help companies become public and raise public monies. *Type:* Newsletter.

BioTech Navigator

Wong & Wong Inc.
PO Box 7274   Ph: (503)649-1355
Beaverton, OR 97007-7274   Fax: (503)649-4490
E-mail: wong@biotechnav.com
URL: http://www.biotechnav.com.
Contact: Nadine Wong, Editor, wong@biotechnav.com.
Desc: Provides investors with information and recommendations on biotechnology stocks. Recurring features include news of research and columns titled Bio Analysis, Bio Background, BioTech Stock Updates, Bio Pod Stocks, Bio Portfolio, and Bio Indices. *Type:* Newsletter.

The Blue Book of CBS Stock Reports

MPL Communications Inc.
133 Richmond St., Ste. 700   Ph: (416)869-1177
Toronto, ON, Canada M5H   Fax: (416)869-0616
3M8
Contact: Marc Johnson, Editor.
Desc: Profiles potential stock investments. Offers investors recommendations for investments based on a given company's performance relative to market, recent developments and outlook, current performance, and performance in the previous fiscal year. *Type:* Newsletter.

Blue Chip Stocks

Elton Stephens
4016 S. Michigan St.   Ph: (219)291-3823
South Bend, IN 46614-2544   Free: 800-553-5866
   Fax: (219)291-3823
Contact: Elton Stephens, Editor.
Desc: Lists blue chip stocks that "have good earnings and dividends." *Type:* Newsletter.

The Blue List of Current Municipal and Corporate Offerings

Standard & Poor's
65 Broadway   Ph: (212)770-4300
New York, NY 10006   Free: 800-221-5277
   Fax: (212)770-0220
URL: http://www.bluelist.com.
Contact: Malcolm Conner, Editor, (212)770-0444, fax: (212)425-6859, mconner@mcgraw-hill.com.
Desc: Provides municipal bond offerings. Remarks: For subscription information, call (212) 770-4354. *Type:* Newsletter.

BNA Securities Law Daily

The Bureau of National Affairs, Inc. (BNA)
1231 25th St. NW   Ph: (202)452-4200
Washington, DC 20037
E-mail: bnaplus@bna.com
URL: http://bna.com/mkt/hrl/hrlwdec.htm
Desc: Contains reports on state and federal legislative, regulatory, and judicial actions affecting securities, commodities, and corporate activities. *Available:* LEXIS-NEXIS, LEXIS; West Group, WESTLAW. *Type:* Database.

Bob Brinker's Marketimer

Robert J. Brinker Investment Advisory Services, Ltd.
2023 N. Atlantic Ave., Ste. 301   Free: 800-700-1030
Cocoa Beach, FL 32931
URL: http://www.adpad.com/marketimer;   http://www.bobbrinker.com.
Contact: Robert J. Brinker, Editor.
Desc: Serves as a stock market timing device. Recurring features include forecasts, plus the columns titled No Load Recommended List and Model Investment Portfolios. *Type:* Newsletter.

Bob Nurock's Advisory/Private Elves Report

Investor's Analysis, Inc.
PO Box 460   Ph: (505)820-2737
Santa Fe, NM 87504-0460   Free: 800-227-8883
Contact: Robert J. Nurock, Editor, nurock@elfhollow.com.
Desc: Advises investors on planning stock market strategies and provides specific ideas for fulfilling the strategy. Carries followups on past recommendations. *Type:* Newsletter.

The Bond Buyer Full Text

American Banker - Bond Buyer
One State Street Plaza, 27th Fl.   Ph: (212)803-8366
New York, NY 10004
URL: http://www.americanbanker.com
Desc: Contains more than 193,000 articles reporting news and information on the fixed-income securities market. Provides information on municipal bond issues available for negotiated and competitive bidding in each state, including name of borrowing entity, purpose of issue, issue and maturity dates, amount, interest cost to borrower, and underwriter. *Available:* The Dialog Corporation, DIALOG; The Dialog Corporation, DIALOG; LEXIS-NEXIS, NEXIS; LEXIS-NEXIS, NEXIS; Dow Jones & Company, Inc.; LEXIS-NEXIS, LEXIS; Thomson Financial Services, Inc., I/PLUS Direct; Bell & Howell Information and Learning. *Type:* Database.

Bondweek

Institutional Investor, Inc.
488 Madison Ave.   Ph: (212)224-3300
New York, NY 10022   Free: 800-543-4444
   Fax: (212)224-3490
Contact: Tom Lamont, Editor; Greg Joslyn, Exec. Editor; Victor Kramer, Managing Editor.
Desc: Focuses exclusively on the taxable fixed-income markets. Covers investment strategies, emerging trends, interest rate analysis and forecasts, economic regulatory developments, and new technology, and the effects of all the preceding on the U.S. *Type:* Newsletter.

The Bowser Directory of Small Stocks

R. Max Bowser
PO Box 6278   Ph: (757)877-5979
Newport News, VA 23606   Fax: (757)595-0622
E-mail: ministocks@aol.com
Contact: Cindy Bowser, Editor.
Desc: Provides extensive information on stocks valued at $3/share or less. *Type:* Newsletter.

The Bowser Report

R. Max Bowser
PO Box 6278   Ph: (757)877-5979
Newport News, VA 23606   Fax: (757)595-0622
E-mail: ministocks@aol.com
Contact: R. Max Bowser, Editor.
Desc: Recommends and reports on stocks priced $3 per share or less on the New York and American stock exchanges (NYSE and ASE) and similar-priced Over-the-Counter stocks (OTC). Recurring features include a feature article and columns titled Insider Trading, Best Buys, Minipriced Stocks in Buying Range, Follow-Through, Notes By the Editor, and Subscriber Forum. *Type:* Newsletter.

The Bowser Warrant Register

R. Max Bowser
PO Box 6278   Ph: (757)877-5979
Newport News, VA 23606   Fax: (757)595-0622
E-mail: ministocks@aol.com
Contact: Max Bowser, Editor and Publisher.
Desc: Provides information about warrants valued at $3/share or less. *Type:* Newsletter.

Bull and Bear Financial Report

David J. Robinson
PO Box 917179   Ph: (407)682-6170
Longwood, FL 32791
URL: http://www.thebullandbear.com.
Contact: David J. Robinson, Editor.
Desc: Provides a wide range of investment advisory opinion by leading investment advisors, including stocks, mutual funds, precious metals, real estate, currencies, and tax strategies. Recommends and summarizes top investment advisory newsletters. *Type:* Newsletter.

Bull & Bear's Directory of Investment Advisory Newsletters

Bull & Bear Financial Newspaper
PO Box 917179   Ph: (407)682-6170
Longwood, FL 32791   Free: 800-336-BULL
                                  Fax: (407)775-1760
Contact: David J. Robinson, President.
Desc: Approximately 400 investment advisory newsletters from various investment areas. *Type:* Directory.

The Bullion and Mutual Fund Advisory

Moneypower
1304 Edgewood Ave.   Ph: (313)537-8096
Ann Arbor, MI 48103-5522
Contact: James H. Moore, Editor.
Desc: Advises on investments in gold, silver, and platinum, including which metal is at a bargain price, when to buy, when to exchange for other bullion to multiply ounces free, reputible dealers, safe storage, and fair prices. *Type:* Newsletter.

Business Network

Opportunity Hot-Line
c/o Business Network   Ph: (440)442-5600
5420 Mayfield Rd., No. 205   Fax: (440)449-3227
Cleveland, OH 44124
Contact: Irwin Friedman, Editor.
Desc: Discusses various types of funding for business from private investors. *Type:* Newsletter.

Business Opportunities Digest

Straw Enterprises
301 Plymouth Dr.   Fax: (404)259-4013
Dalton, GA 30721-8366
Contact: Jim Straw, Publisher; Bob Riemke, Editor; D. Straw, Circulation Mgr.
Desc: Discusses business and investment opportunites around the world. *Type:* Newsletter.

Cable Network Investor

Paul Kagan Associates, Inc.
126 Clock Tower Pl.   Ph: (831)624-1536
Carmel, CA 93923-8734   Fax: (831)625-3225
E-mail: info@kagan.com
Contact: Dwight Beach, Managing Editor.
Desc: Provides financial analysis of cable networks. *Type:* Newsletter.

The Cabot Market Letter

Cabot Heritage Corporation
PO Box 3067   Ph: (978)745-5532
Salem, MA 01970   Fax: (978)745-1283
E-mail: office@cabotm.com
Contact: Carlton G. Lutts, Editor; Timothy W. Lutts, Editor.
Desc: Analyzes and recommends stock investments. Emphasizes that "optimum profits depend upon good market timing and good stock selection." Each issue follows a model portfolio made up of 12 stocks from lesser known companies chosen for their high potential for rapid, long-term growth. *Type:* Newsletter.

California Investment Review

International Capital Resources
388 Market St., Ste. 500   Ph: (415)296-2519
San Francisco, CA 94111   Fax: (415)296-2529
Contact: Gerald A. Benjamin, Publisher.
Desc: "Profiles venture capital and expansion financing opportunities, and provides equity investors a confidential procedure for examining participation in venture capital deals typically available only to established investment funds and partnerships." *Type:* Newsletter.

California Municipal Bond Advisor

California Municipal Bond
1037 S. Palm Canyon Dr.   Ph: (760)320-7997
Palm Springs, CA 92264-8378   Fax: (760)320-7202
Contact: Zane B. Mann, Editor.
Desc: Analyzes information on California bonds and bond funds. *Type:* Newsletter.

California Public Finance

American Banker Newsletters
510 W. 6th St., No. 320   Ph: (213)627-8350
Los Angeles, CA 90014
Desc: Covers developments affecting municipal bonds and public finance in California. *Type:* Newsletter.

California Technology Stock Letter

Murenove, Inc.
PO Box 308   Ph: (650)726-8495
Half Moon Bay, CA 94019   Fax: (650)726-8494
E-mail: subs@ctsl.com
Contact: Michael Murphy, Editor.
Desc: Analyzes technology companies in industries such as semiconductors, computers, software, and biotechnology. Focuses on Rgrowth flowS—earnings plus R&D per share—as the driving force for growth. *Type:* Newsletter.

Canada Stockwatch

Canjex Publishing, Ltd.
700 W. Georgia St.   Ph: (604)687-1500
Box 10371, Pacific Centre   Fax: (604)687-2304
Vancouver, BC, Canada V7Y
1J6
Contact: John Woods, Editor.
Desc: Publishes information on all various public companies listed on the Vancouver Stock Exchange, such as reviews of annual and semiannual reports, announcements of changes of control and share consolidations, notices from regulatory authorities, and daily news. Recurring features include letters to the editor and columns titled Market Summary and The Regulators. *Type:* Newsletter.

Canadian Investor

Lombardi Publishing Co.
51 Toro Rd.   Ph: (416)633-1600
North York, ON, Canada M3J   Fax: (416)633-6188
2A4
Contact: George Leong, Editor.
Desc: Provides information on blue-chip and conservative stocks. Includes a market outlook, corporate performance reports, companies to watch, and an advisory digest. *Type:* Newsletter.

Canadian MoneySaver

Dale Ennis
PO Box 370   Ph: (613)352-7448
Bath, ON, Canada K0H 1G0   Fax: (613)352-7700
E-mail: moneyinfo@canadianmoneysaver.ca.
URL: http://www.canadianmoneysaver.ca.
Contact: Dale Ennis, Editor.
Desc: Examines taxes, investment, and financial planning in Canada. Recurring features include interviews, book reviews, and notices of publications available. *Type:* Newsletter.

Canadian Penny Stock Reporter

Lombardi Publishing Co.
51 Toro Rd.   Ph: (416)633-1600
North York, ON, Canada M3J   Fax: (416)633-6188
2A4
Contact: George Leong, Editor.
Desc: Gives recommendations on BE penny stocks between $1.00 - $5.00. (Does not recommend gold or resource stocks.) Details a model portfolio and lists the top 10 penny stocks in each issue. *Type:* Newsletter.

Cappiello's Closed-End Fund Digest

Madent Publishing Inc.
1224 Coast Village Circle, Ste.
11
Santa Barbara, CA 93105
Contact: Patrick Winton, Editor.
Desc: Provides market insights and specific fund recommendations. Recurring features include interviews with fund managers and industry analysts, news of research, and statistical analyses of more than 480 closed-end funds. *Type:* Newsletter.

Caribbean Dateline

Caribbean Dateline Publications, Ltd.
PO Box 23276   Ph: (703)404-0894
Washington, DC 20026
Contact: N. Poteat Day, Editor.
Desc: Highlights investment opportunities, business, tourism, real estate, business law, tax havens, and IRS rulings relevant to foreign investors in that area. Recurring features include statistics, book reviews, and columns titled Front Page, For the Record, Country Updates, and Stock Markets. *Type:* Newsletter.

CDN Reporter

Lombardi Publishing Co.
51 Toro Rd.   Ph: (416)633-1600
North York, ON, Canada M3J   Fax: (416)633-6188
2A4
Contact: Mitchell Clark, Editor.
Desc: Provides recommendations on speculative stocks traded on the Canadian Dealer Network. Recurring features include a quote of the month. *Type:* Newsletter.

Certified Coin Dealer Newsletter

Ron Downing
PO Box 7939   Ph: (310)515-7369
Torrance, CA 90504   Fax: (310)515-7534
E-mail: cdn@greysheet.com.
Desc: Provides current prices and market commentary on certified coins (Mint State Grades of MS61-MS67 and PR61-PR67) of Professional Coin Grading Service (PCGS), Numismatic Guaranty Corporation of America (NGC) Weekly, ANACS, and Numismatic Certification Institute (NCI) Monthly. *Type:* Newsletter.

Chartcraft Technical Indicator Review

Chartcraft, Inc.
30 Church St.   Ph: (914)632-0422
PO Box 2046
New Rochelle, NY 10801
Contact: Michael Burke, Editor.
Desc: Provides a concise review of the stock market. Each stock in the Dow-Jones Industrial Averages is listed and marked bullish or bearish. *Type:* Newsletter.

Chartcraft Weekly Options Service

Chartcraft, Inc.
30 Church St.   Ph: (914)632-0422
PO Box 2046
New Rochelle, NY 10801
Contact: Michael Burke, Editor.
Desc: Features a computer printout listing option stock. *Type:* Newsletter.

Chartcraft Weekly Service

Chartcraft, Inc.
30 Church St.   Ph: (914)632-0422
PO Box 2046
New Rochelle, NY 10801
Contact: Michael Burke, Editor.
Desc: Offers recommendations to investors in New York and American Stock Exchange securities, including buy and sell signals and relative strength. Discusses industry groups and option indexes. *Type:* Newsletter.

The Chartist

The Chartist
PO Box 758   Ph: (310)596-2385
Seal Beach, CA 90740
Contact: Dan Sullivan, Editor.
Desc: Provides general financial information, including the ratings of over 2,000 stocks, focusing on the top 24 buys. *Type:* Newsletter.

The Cheap Investor

Mathews and Associates, Inc.
2545 W. Golf Rd., Ste. 350
Hoffman Estates, IL 60194
Contact: Bill Mathews, Editor.
Desc: Aims to "recommend stocks that have at least a 50% to 100% increase potential." Provides three to six stock recommendations in each issue, with information on and analysis of each company. Carries updates on previously recommended stocks. *Type:* Newsletter.

Churchill Group—Monthly Report

Churchill-Hemisphere Inc.
120 Rte. 59   Ph: (914)368-0633
Suffern, NY 10901   Free: 800-571-3857
                               Fax: (914)357-7439
E-mail: churchill.22@aol.com.
Contact: Dr. Gerald P. Hirsch, Editor.
Desc: Covers related investments news, including stocks, bonds, money funds, government securities, numismatics, real estate, insurance, limited and tax advantaged partnerships, and mortgages. *Type:* Newsletter.

Citizens Network for Foreign Affairs

1111 19th St. NW, Ste. 900   Ph: (202)296-3920
Washington, DC 20036   Fax: (202)296-3948
URL: http://www.cfna.com
Contact: John H. Costello, Pres.
Desc: Commited to stimulating international economic growth and development. *Type:* Association.

Commercial Paper Guide

Standard & Poor's
25 Broadway   Ph: (212)208-8000
New York, NY 10004-1064   Free: 800-221-5277
                               Fax: (212)208-0040
URL: http://www.stockinfo.standardpoor.com
Contact: Alex Poletsky, Editor.
Desc: Serves as a guide to approximately 2,000 commercial paper ratings. *Type:* Newsletter.

COMPUSTAT

Standard & Poor's Compustat
7400 S. Alton Court   Ph: (303)771-6510
Englewood, CO 80112
URL: http://compustat.com
Desc: Contains annual, quarterly, and monthly income statement, balance sheet, statement of cash flows, and line of business and market data for publicly held U.S. and selected non-U.S. corporations. *Available:* ADP Network Services, Inc.; CompuServe Information Service; Interactive Data Corporation; FactSet Data Systems, Inc.; Standard & Poor's Compustat; Vestek Systems, Inc. *Type:* Database.

Computerized Investing

American Association of Individual Investors
625 N. Michigan Ave., Ste.   Ph: (312)280-0170
  1900   Free: 800-428-2244
Chicago, IL 60611   Fax: (312)280-1625
Contact: John Bajkowski, Editor.
Desc: Furnishes articles on computer-aided investment analysis and investment-related software programs and database. Contains information on hardware and software, new product announcements, and editorial commentary. *Type:* Newsletter.

Consensus of Insiders

Consensus of Insiders
PO Box 493
Pompano Beach, FL 33061
E-mail: wysong@gate.net
Contact: W. H. Casson, Editor.
Desc: Acts as a stock market advisory, based upon analysis of transactions by corporate insiders, members of the stock exchanges, specialists, and traders. Provides advice on market timing, and stock selection. *Type:* Newsletter.

Conservative Speculator

Guidera Publishing Corporation
39 Sheridan Park Cir., No. 6-7   Ph: (803)681-3399
Bluffton, SC 29910-6025
Contact: Lawrence C. Oakley, Editor.
Desc: Contains investment information to help "readers make more money with the 10% they put into our special situations than they make with the 90% they put into everything else." Recurring features include profiles of companies in which investment is recommended and columns titled Ken Coleman's Market Timing, Bond Advisory, Special Situations, Update Briefs, and Sneak Previews. *Type:* Newsletter.

The Contrary Investor

Fraser Management Associates, Inc.
309 S. Willard St.   Ph: (802)658-0322
PO Box 494   Fax: (802)658-0260
Burlington, VT 05402
E-mail: info@fraser.com
Contact: James L. Fraser, Editor.
Desc: Analyzes stock market trends based on a theory of contrary values. Makes specific recommendations, guiding the investor away from popular, "overbought" investments. *Type:* Newsletter.

The Contrary Investor Follow-Up

Fraser Management Associates, Inc.
309 S. Willard St.   Ph: (802)658-0322
PO Box 494   Fax: (802)658-0260
Burlington, VT 05402
E-mail: info@fraser.com
Contact: James L. Fraser, Editor.
Desc: Contains analysis and regular reports on all stock selections found in The Contrary Investor until each has closed at a definite selling price. *Type:* Newsletter.

Conversion Watch

SNL Securities
321 E. Main St.   Ph: (804)977-1600
PO Box 2124   Fax: (804)977-4466
Charlottesville, VA 22902
E-mail: subscriptions@snl.com
URL: http://www.snl.com.
Contact: Chris Smith, Editor; John Racine, Contact.
Desc: Informs readers by fax whenever new activity is announced. Provides all relevant data on conversion related filings and important conversion dates. *Type:* Newsletter.

Coolcat Explosive Small Cap Growth Stock Report

Kevin Kennedy
2408 Tamarack   Ph: (209)875-0613
Sanger, CA 93657
Contact: Kevin Kennedy, Publisher.
Desc: Provides selection and rankings, current price and volume information, and recommended buy and stop loss sell points for variables including price momentum, earning strength, and industry strength. Includes variations of CANSLIM investment model. *Type:* Newsletter.

Corporate Governance Bulletin

Investor Responsibility Research Center, Inc. (IRRC)
1350 Connecticut Ave., NW,   Ph: (202)833-0700
  Ste. 700   Fax: (202)833-3555
Washington, DC 20036
E-mail: heidi.salceld@irrc.org.
URL: http://www.irrc.org; http://www.irrc.org.
Contact: Rosemary Lally, Editor.
Desc: Monitors policy developments in Congress, federal regulatory agencies, the courts, and other government bodies affecting institutional and corporate investing. Highlights significant actions by companies and major institutional investors. *Type:* Newsletter.

Crawford Perspectives

Arch Crawford
1382 3rd Ave., No. 403   Ph: (212)744-6973
New York, NY 10021-0403
Contact: Arch Crawford, Editor.
Desc: Publishes information on the stock market based on a "unique cycle approach using elipses instead of pure cycles to gain higher resolution in determining turning points." Employs technical analyses to back up astronomic cycles. "Ranked 1 market timer 5 year period by independent rating service". *Type:* Newsletter.

Creative Investment Advisor

M. Jane Garvey
PO Box 495   Ph: (630)858-4663
Glen Ellyn, IL 60138-0495   Fax: (630)858-4357
E-mail: garveyjane@aol.com
Contact: M. Jane Garvey, Publisher.
Desc: Offers educational and legislative information and advises small real estate investors on how to become more successful. Recurring features include columns titled The House Doctor and Dr. *Type:* Newsletter.

The Cricket Letter

Cricket Communications Inc.
PO Box 527   Ph: (215)747-6684
Ardmore, PA 19003   Fax: (215)747-7082
E-mail: crcktinc@aol.com
Contact: E.A. Stern, Editor; Mark Battersby, Publisher.
Desc: Provides information about United States tax and business regulations for foreign investors. *Type:* Newsletter.

CSI Technical Journal

Commodity Systems, Inc. (CSI)
200 W. Palmetto Park Rd.   Ph: (561)392-8663
Boca Raton, FL 33432   Free: 800-274-4727
                               Fax: (561)392-7761
E-mail: marketing@scidata.com
URL: http://www.csidata.com.
Contact: Robert C. Pelletier, Editor; Sabrine Carle, Editor.
Desc: Informs investors on new markets, investment opportunities, technical analysis, trading know-how, money management principals, and spread trading. Recurring features include news of research. *Type:* Newsletter.

Cumulative Stock Profits

CSP Advisor
PO Box 246   Ph: (212)896-8760
Forest Hills, NY 11375-0246
Contact: S. J. Rifkin, Editor.
Desc: Provides advice to investors trying "for small but quick gains that will accumulate to large profits." *Type:* Newsletter.

Currency Market Perspective

Elliott Wave International
200 Main St., Hunt Tower, Ste.   Ph: (770)536-0309
    400   Free: 800-336-1618
Gainesville, GA 30501   Fax: (770)536-2514
E-mail: customerservice@elliottwave.com

Contact: Jim Chorek, Director.

Desc: Provides information on the currency markets. Recurring features include news of research. *Type:* Newsletter.

David Hall's Inside View

David Hall's North American Trading
1936 E. Deere Ave., Ste. 102   Ph: (714)261-0509
Santa Ana, CA 92705-5723   Free: 800-359-4255
    Fax: (714)252-0541
E-mail: info@davidhall.com

Contact: David Hall, Editor.

Desc: Provides advisory information on collecting and investing in rare coins. *Type:* Newsletter.

Defined Contribution News

Institutional Investor, Inc.
488 Madison Ave.   Ph: (212)224-3300
New York, NY 10022   Free: 800-543-4444
    Fax: (212)224-3490

Contact: Tom Lamont, Editor.

Desc: Covers all aspects of the defined contribution pension plan market from the plan sponsor and vendor points of view. Discusses topics such as searches for investment managers; record keepers, administrators, and trustees; legislative and regulatory developments; plan profiles; sponsor forums; new vendor products; and personnel changes and DC Database. *Type:* Newsletter.

Derivatives Tactics

Derivative Strategy & Tactics
153 Waverley Pl., Ste. 1200   Ph: (212)366-9578
New York, NY 10014   Fax: (212)366-0551

Contact: Joe Kolman, Editor and Publisher.

Desc: Provides information for institutional investors. Topics include options, swaps, and other financial derivatives. *Type:* Newsletter.

Derivatives Week

Institutional Investor, Inc.
488 Madison Ave.   Ph: (212)224-3300
New York, NY 10022   Free: 800-543-4444
    Fax: (212)224-3490

Contact: Tom Lamont, Editor; Greg Joslyn, Editor; Carolina Bernardez, Managing Editor.

Desc: Offers competitive intelligence on new products, regulations, market opportunities, and people relating to derivatives (instruments linked to equities, interest rates, commodities and currencies worldwide). *Type:* Newsletter.

Dick Davis Digest

Steven Halpern
PO Box 350630   Ph: (954)467-8500
Ft. Lauderdale, FL 33335-0630   Free: 800-654-1514
    Fax: (954)467-6444

Contact: Steven Halpern, Editor; Steven Lord, Publisher.

Desc: Carries excerpts from over 400 stock market letters and stock, bond, and mutual fund recommendations from leading analysts on Wall Street. Provides overview of general market trends and news of specific industries and companies. *Type:* Newsletter.

The Dines Letter

James Dines & Company, Inc.
PO Box 22   Free: 800-84-LUCKY
Belvedere, CA 94920

Contact: James Dines, Editor.

Desc: Provides investment advice based on the interdependent use of fundamentals, Technical Analysis and mass psychology. Includes economic predictions, short-term trading advice, and analysis of the stock market as a whole. *Type:* Newsletter.

Directory of Alternative Investment Programs

Asset Alternatives, Inc.
170 Linden St., 2nd Fl.   Ph: (781)304-1400
Wellesley, MA 02482   Fax: (781)304-1440
E-mail: info@assetnews.com
URL: http://www.assetnews.com.

Contact: Steven P. Galante, Editor, (617)431-2353.

Desc: More than 400 institutional investors engaged in alternative investment partnerships. *Type:* Directory.

Directory of Registered Investment Advisors

Money Market Directories, Inc.
320 E. Main St.   Ph: (804)977-1450
PO Box 1608   Free: 800-446-2810
Charlottesville, VA 22902   Fax: (804)979-9962

Contact: Jesse Noel, Editor.

Desc: Over 12,000 financial investment advisory firms that are registered with the United States Securities and Exchange Commission or state registered, including some overseas and Canadian firms; professional and financial industry associations. *Type:* Directory.

Dividend & Income Investor

Lombardi Publishing Co.
51 Toro Rd.   Ph: (416)633-1600
North York, ON, Canada M3J   Fax: (416)633-6188
    2A4

Desc: Provides advice for investors. Recommends portfolio options for income investors. *Type:* Newsletter.

Dow Jones Business and Finance Report

Dow Jones & Company, Inc.
P.O. Box 300   Ph: (609)520-4000
Princeton, NJ 08543-0300
URL: http://www.dj.com

Desc: Contains financial news, statistics, and information on developments in business and industry, domestic and international economies, and the stock market. Includes headline news; summaries of The Wall Street Journal's "Heard On The Street" column; Dow Jones Capital Market Report newswires; volume, indexes, and actives for New York and American Stock Exchange and NASDAQ Over-the-Counter issues; and credit market, precious metal, foreign exchange, petroleum industry, and stock-index futures reports. *Available:* Dow Jones & Company, Inc. *Type:* Database.

Dow Jones Futures and Index Quotes

Dow Jones & Company, Inc.
P.O. Box 300   Ph: (609)520-4000
Princeton, NJ 08543-0300
URL: http://www.dj.com

Desc: Provides current and historical stock quotations for more than 80 contracts from major North American stock exchanges (with a 10-30 minute delay during market hours). Includes daily open, high, low, last, and settlement prices as well as daily volume and open interest and lifetime high and low prices. *Available:* Dow Jones & Company, Inc. *Type:* Database.

Dow Jones Historical Quotes

Dow Jones & Company, Inc.
P.O. Box 300   Ph: (609)520-4000
Princeton, NJ 08543-0300
URL: http://www.dj.com

Desc: Provides historical quotes for common and preferred stocks. Includes daily high, low, close, and volume for stock prices and composites during the preceding year; monthly stock summaries from 1979 to date; and quarterly summaries from 1978 to date. *Available:* Dow Jones & Company, Inc. *Type:* Database.

Dow Jones Investment Advisor

Dow Jones Financial Publishing
179 Ave. at the Common   Ph: (908)389-8700
Shrewsbury, NJ 07702   Fax: (908)389-8701
E-mail: bvinocur@ix.netcom.com.
URL: http://www.djfpc.com.

Contact: Robert Clark, Editor; Angie Finch, Managing Editor; David Smith, Advertising Dir.; Charles Stroller, President.

Desc: Investment magazine for financial professionals. Includes coverage of mutual funds, insurance products and partnerships combined with feature articles for financial planners. *Type:* Periodical.

Dow Jones Real-Time Quotes

Dow Jones & Company, Inc.
P.O. Box 300   Ph: (609)520-4000
Princeton, NJ 08543-0300
URL: http://www.dj.com

Contact: Maggie Landis, P.R. Liaison.

Desc: Provides stock prices (with no delay) from major North American exchanges. Includes composite and NASDAQ National Market system stock quotes. *Available:* Dow Jones & Company, Inc. *Type:* Database.

Dow Theory Forecasts Newsletter

Horizon Publishing Company LLC
7412 Calumet Ave.   Fax: (219)931-6487
Hammond, IN 46324-2692
E-mail: chris@dowtheory.com.
URL: http://www.dowtheory.com.

Contact: Richard J. Moroney, Editor, rmorney@horizonpublishing.com.

Desc: Interprets stock market movements based on the Dow Theory. Features anticipations of future trends and includes information and recommendations on individual stock and industry groups. *Type:* Newsletter.

Dowbeaters

Dow Beaters, Inc.
PO Box 284   Ph: (201)273-0120
Ironia, NJ 07845

Contact: Peter DeAngelis, Editor.

Desc: Identifies stocks selected for above average performance with an emphasis on low-priced (single digit) equities. *Type:* Newsletter.

DRI Business Fixed Investment Forecast

Standard & Poor's DRI
Data Products Division
24 Hartwell Ave.   Ph: (781)863-5100
Lexington, MA 02421
E-mail: client_services@dri.mcgraw-hill.com
URL: http://www.dri.mcgraw-hill.com

Contact: Client Services, (617)860-6527, fax: (617)860-6416.

Desc: Contains about 200 historical and forecast time series of U.S. expenditures for durable equipment and construction. *Available:* Standard & Poor's DRI, Data Products Division. *Type:* Database.

DRI Financial Market Indexes

Standard & Poor's DRI
Data Products Division
24 Hartwell Ave.   Ph: (781)863-5100
Lexington, MA 02421
E-mail: client_services@dri.mcgraw-hill.com
URL: http://www.dri.mcgraw-hill.com
Contact: Client Resource Center, (781)860-6527, fax: (781)860-6416.
Desc: Contains more than 1200 indexes reflecting the performance of financial markets worldwide. Covers equities, fixed income securities, futures and options, and other financial instruments. *Available:* Standard & Poor's DRI, Data Products Division. *Type:* Database.

DRI U.S. and Canadian Equities

Standard & Poor's DRI
Data Products Division
24 Hartwell Ave.   Ph: (781)863-5100
Lexington, MA 02421
E-mail: client_services@dri.mcgraw-hill.com
URL: http://www.dri.mcgraw-hill.com
Contact: Client Services, (617)860-6527, fax: (617)860-6416.
Desc: Contains daily time series of current and historical prices, dividends, and fundamental financial information for more than 50,000 equity issues listed on the New York, American, NASDAQ Over-The-Counter, Toronto, Vancouver, Alberta, and Montreal exchanges. *Available:* Standard & Poor's DRI, Data Products Division. *Type:* Database.

DRIP Investor

Horizon Publishing Company LLC
7412 Calumet Ave.   Fax: (219)931-6487
Hammond, IN 46324-2692
E-mail: custserv@dripinvestor.com.
Contact: Charles Carlson, Editor, ccarlson@horizonpublishing.com.
Desc: Covers stocks that can be purchased directly from the company as well as changes in their plans. *Type:* Newsletter.

DRP Report

SAM Designs
PO Box 7696   Ph: (903)592-5465
Tyler, TX 75711
Contact: Suzanne Mitchell, Editor and Publisher.
Desc: Provides information about dividend reinvestment plan stocks. Includes company addresses and investing tips. *Type:* Newsletter.

Earnings Power Report

Prominent Investment Research
521 5th Ave., Ste. 1740   Fax: (212)573-6355
New York, NY 10175
Contact: Jeff Marcus, President & CEO.
Desc: Aims to help individuals make money by taking advantage of stocks that consistently report actual earnings significantly above forecasted earnings. Provides buy and sell recommendations of select companies, data on major domestic equity markets, economic insights, market commentaries, and company reviews. *Type:* Newsletter.

East-West Center

1601 East-West Rd.   Ph: (808)944-7111
Honolulu, HI 96848-1601   Fax: (808)944-7376
E-mail: ewcinfo@ewc.hawaii.edu
URL: http://www.ewc.hawaii.edu
Contact: Kenji Sumida, Pres.
Desc: Established by Congress as a cooperative institution to promote better relations and understanding among the nations and peoples of Asia, the Pacific, and the U.S. through cooperative study, training, and research. Multidisciplinary, problem-oriented programs are conducted on international relations, environment and policy, population, resources, economic development, journalism, and Pacific Islands development. *Type:* Association.

Eisenhower Exchange Fellowships

256 S. 16th St.   Ph: (215)546-1738
Philadelphia, PA 19102   Free: 800-275-1333
                                Fax: (215)546-4567
E-mail: ike@eef.org
URL: http://www.eef.org
Contact: Adrian A. Basora, Pres.
Desc: Established as a nonpartisan tribute to former U.S. President Dwight D. Eisenhower (1890-1969) to foster international development and understanding. *Type:* Association.

The Elliott Wave Theorist

Elliott Wave International
200 Main St., Hunt Tower, Ste.   Ph: (770)536-0309
400   Free: 800-336-1618
Gainesville, GA 30501   Fax: (770)536-2514
E-mail: customerservice@elliottwave.com
Contact: Robert R. Prechter, Jr., Editor.
Desc: Published to "outline the progress of markets in terms of the Elliott Wave Principle" and to educate interested persons in its successful application. Analyzes Elliott waves, Fibonacci relationships, fixed time cycles, momentum, sentiment, and supply-demand factors; covers stocks, bonds, gold, and the economy. *Type:* Newsletter.

Equities Special Situations

Equities Magazine Inc.
160 Madison Ave., 3rd Fl.   Ph: (212)213-1300
New York, NY 10016-5412
Contact: Robert J. Flaherty, Editor.
Desc: Offers stock recommendations. *Type:* Newsletter.

Fabian Premium Investment Resources

Fabian Investment Resources
2100 Main St., Ste. 300   Ph: (714)536-1931
Huntington Beach, CA 92647   Free: 800-950-8765
                                    Fax: (714)536-7066
E-mail: service@fabian.com
URL: http://www.fabian.com.
Contact: Doug Fabian, Editor.
Desc: Provides advice on mutual fund timing with the goal of 15-20% compounded annualized growth over the long term. Covers domestic common stock funds. *Type:* Newsletter.

Fament Stock Advisory Service

Gordon D. Mors
9157 Trujillo Way   Ph: (916)363-2138
Sacramento, CA 95826   Fax: (916)366-7326
E-mail: fament1@prodigy.net.
Contact: Gordon D. Mors, Editor.
Desc: Offers advice for those interested in stock market investment. *Type:* Newsletter.

Favorably Positioned Stocks

Barrow Investment Management
3800 W. Bay to Bay Blvd., Ste.   Ph: (813)831-4191
21
Tampa, FL 33629-6826
Contact: Alston "Mac" Barrow, Editor.
Desc: "Invests two real $50,000 portfolios for aggressive growth and conservative growth." Carries investment advice and Wall Street news items. Picks top mutual funds and highlights stocks and funds. *Type:* Newsletter.

Fidelity Insight

Mutual Fund Investors Association
PO Box 9135   Ph: (617)369-2500
Wellesley, MA 02181   Fax: (617)369-2510
Contact: Eric M. Kobren, Editor.
Desc: Covers Fidelity Mutual Funds, offering information and advice, performance statistics, and fund analysis. Recurring features include 4 model portfolios, new fund announcements, and a performance scorecard. *Type:* Newsletter.

Fidelity Investor

Phillips Publishing
7811 Montrose Rd.   Free: 800-992-9989
Potomac, MD 20854
Contact: James H. Lowell, III, Editor; David J. Durham, Publisher.
Desc: Contains investment advice covering Fidelity mutual funds. Recurring features include interviews, model portfolios, performance reviews, and best buys. *Type:* Newsletter.

Fidelity Monitor

Independent Fidelity Investors, Inc.
PO Box 1270   Ph: (916)624-0191
Rocklin, CA 95677   Free: 800-397-3094
                           Fax: 800-290-4630
URL: http://www.fidelitymonitor.com.
Contact: Jack Bowers, Editor.
Desc: Covers Fidelity's stocks and mutual funds. Offers strategies and recommendations. *Type:* Newsletter.

Finance Over 50

Ron Jackson Company
22 Yankee Hill   Ph: (510)704-9490
Oakland, CA 94618   Free: 800-769-6310
                           Fax: (510)704-0177
Contact: Jeff Carter, Editor.
Desc: Provides finance and investment (stocks and mutual funds) advice for investors over age 50, retired or nearly retired. Recurring features include news of research. *Type:* Newsletter.

Financial Services Report

Phillips Business Information, Inc.
1201 Seven Locks Rd., Ste. 300   Ph: (301)340-1520
Potomac, MD 20854   Free: 888-707-5809
                           Fax: (301)340-3847
E-mail: clientservices.pbi@phillips.com
Contact: Lurdes daMala Abruscato, Assis. Managing Editor, ldamala@phillips.com.
Desc: Follows the banking, savings and loan, and financial services industries at the state and national levels. Reports on actions in congress, state legislatures, banking commissions, and the courts. *Type:* Newsletter.

Fitch Insights

Fitch IPCA, Inc.
1 State St. Plaza   Ph: (212)908-0500
New York, NY 10004   Free: 800-753-4824
                            Fax: (212)344-2052
Contact: Barbara A. Besen, Publisher, bbesen@fitchinv.com.
Desc: Provides ratings actions, comments, criteria, and surveillance via fax. Includes explanations of ratings decisions as well as Fitch's views on market actions and events. *Type:* Newsletter.

Forbes—Mutual Fund Survey Issue

Forbes Magazine
60 5th Ave.   Ph: (212)620-2200
New York, NY 10011   Fax: (212)206-5174
E-mail: letters@forbesdigital.com

URL: http://www.forbes.com.
Contact: William Baldwin, Editor.
Desc: List of nearly 2,000 mutual funds rated according to historical performance (if time in business permits); list of mutual fund distributors. *Type:* Directory.

Forbes Special Situation Survey

Forbes Investors Advisory Institute
60 5th Ave.   Ph: (212)620-2210
New York, NY 10011   Fax: (212)206-5174
E-mail: letters@forbesdigital.com
Contact: Vahan Janjigian, Editor, (212)620-2214, vjanjigian@forbes.com.
Desc: Covers investment in "unusual equity securities .. for sophisticated investors seeking potential above-average capital gains and able to take a degree of risk." Specifies that it is not for "traders." Recommends the individual speculative equity securities. *Type:* Newsletter.

Ford Equity Research Data Bases

Ford Investor Services, Inc.
11722 Sorrento Valley Rd., Ste.   Ph: (619)755-1327
1
San Diego, CA 92121
E-mail: info@fordinv.com
URL: http://www.fordinv.com
Contact: Tim Alward, Director of Marketing.
Desc: Contains more than 100 financial data items for each of 4000 leading common stocks. Primary data include company name, CUSIP number, ticker symbol, quality rating, growth persistence rating, 12-month earnings per share, normal earnings per share, dividend rate, projected earnings growth rate, standard deviation of annual earnings, book value, debt/equity ratio, end-of-month share price, previous month share price, shares outstanding, percent of shares held by institutions, beta, quarterly earnings series for the past 4 quarters, an estimate for the coming quarter, an industry classification, and company annual revenues. *Available:* Vestek Systems, Inc.; The DAIS Group, Inc. *Type:* Database.

Ford Investment Management Report

Ford Investor Services, Inc.
11722 Sorrento Valley Rd., Ste.   Ph: (619)755-1327
I   Fax: (619)455-6316
San Diego, CA 92121
Contact: David C. Morse, Editor.
Desc: Summarizes financial and market data for 2,680 common stocks in the Ford Data Base to provide investment managers with information for selection. Includes news of research, investment reviews, and special study reports covering research projects. *Type:* Newsletter.

Ford Value Report

Ford Investor Services, Inc.
11722 Sorrento Valley Rd., Ste.   Ph: (619)755-1327
I   Fax: (619)455-6316
San Diego, CA 92121
Contact: D.C. Morse, Editor.
Desc: Provides tabulations of financial data and investment analysis results for 2,000 common stocks. Also includes a commentary on stock market fundamentals, summary data on market trends, and a selected list of recommended stocks. *Type:* Newsletter.

The Forecaster

Forecaster Publishing Co., Inc.
19623 Ventura Blvd.   Ph: (818)345-4421
Tarzana, CA 91356
Contact: John V. Kamin, Editor.
Desc: Presents forecasts, business strategies, and personal money management information. Covers gold and silver coins, real estate, diamonds, old cars, distressed property, proprietary business, art, plus wholesale auctions, rare coins, stamps, and guns (does not cover stocks, bonds, or commodities). *Type:* Newsletter.

Foreign Activity Report

Securities Industry Association
120 Broadway, 35th Fl.   Ph: (212)608-1500
New York, NY 10271   Fax: (212)608-1604
E-mail: info@sia.com
Contact: David G. Strongin, Editor.
Desc: Examines U.S. activity in foreign securities and foreign activity in U.S. securities. Discusses the U.S. dollar in comparison to foreign currencies and changes in the stock price indices and the Gross National Product. Reports country by country investment in U.S. securities. *Type:* Newsletter.

401(k) Dimensions

Hearst Business Communications, Inc.
645 Stewart Ave.   Ph: (516)229-3601
Garden City, NY 11530   Free: 800-659-9878
                              Fax: (516)229-3636
E-mail: raionline@hearst.com
Contact: Beth Helfont, Editor, bhelfont@raionline.com.
Desc: Educates 401(k) participants on the value of 401(k) plans and sound investment principles. *Type:* Newsletter.

Franklin Research's Insight

Franklin Research and Development Corporation
711 Atlantic Ave.   Ph: (617)423-6655
Boston, MA 02111   Free: 800-548-5684
                              Fax: (617)482-6179
E-mail: insight@frdc.com.
Contact: Patrick McVeigh, Editor.
Desc: Provides socially concerned investors with investment advice that will have a positive impact on society and the economy. Includes a kids page. *Type:* Newsletter.

French-American Foundation

509 Madison Ave. Ste. 310   Ph: (212)288-4400
New York, NY 10022-5501   Fax: (212)288-4769
E-mail: french_amerfon@msn.com
Contact: Mr. Michael Iovenko, Pres.
Desc: Works to strengthen relations between the United States and France by creating opportunities for French and American professionals to discuss and address problems of major concern to both societies and to stimulate change through cooperation. Projects include exchange of specialists, internships, study tours, conferences, fellowships, surveys, and special studies. *Type:* Association.

Friendship Ambassadors Foundation

110 Mamaroneck Ave.   Ph: (914)328-8589
White Plains, NY 10601   Free: 800-526-2908
                              Fax: (914)328-8578
E-mail: friendlyam@aol.com
URL: http://www.faf.org
Contact: Patrick L. Sciarratta, Exec.Dir.
Desc: Individuals active in culture and the performing arts (choral groups, jazz ensembles, orchestras, and dance groups) united to promote international understanding. Develops cultural exchanges (performing and concert tours) between the U.S., Europe, Latin America and Asia. *Type:* Association.

The Friendship Force

57 Forsythe St. NW, Ste. 900   Ph: (404)522-9490
Atlanta, GA 30303   Fax: (404)688-6148
Contact: Dr. Wayne Smith, Pres.
Desc: Private organization, with members in 42 countries and throughout the U.S., whose purpose is promoting understanding in the world through the "force of friendship," accomplished by creating an environment for establishing friendships through exchange visits. A group of citizens are flown to a city in another nation to stay in private homes for an exchange period of approximately 14 days. Goal is to exchange a cross-section from each community, representative of occupation, race, age, and sex. *Type:* Association.

Fund Exchange

Paul A. Merriman & Associates, Inc.
1200 Westlake Ave. N., Ste.   Ph: (206)285-8877
700   Fax: (206)286-2079
Seattle, WA 98109-3530
Contact: Paul Merriman, Editor.
Desc: Provides market timing advice in the areas of aggressive growth funds, conservative growth-income funds, municipal bonds, fixed income, and gold. Remarks: Subscription includes a twenty-four hour telephone hotline. *Type:* Newsletter.

The FundLetter

Hume Publishing Co. Ltd.
604-2200 Yonge St.   Ph: (416)440-8260
Toronto, ON, Canada M4S   Free: 800-733-4863
2C6   Fax: (416)440-8268
E-mail: humenewsletters@mindspring.com
Contact: A. Michael Keerma, Editorial Dir.
Desc: Provides advice and recommendations on investing in mutual funds. *Type:* Newsletter.

Fundline Advisory Service

David H. Menashe & Company
PO Box 663   Ph: (818)346-5637
Woodland Hills, CA 91365
Contact: David H. Menashe, Editor.
Desc: Serves as an investment advisory for no-load mutual funds. Presents market analysis based on the "Trading Oscillator" and a 39-week momentum schedule. *Type:* Newsletter.

Futures Industry Association

2001 Pennsylvania Ave. NW,   Ph: (202)466-5460
Ste. 600   Fax: (202)296-3184
Washington, DC 20006-1807
E-mail: info@fiafii.org
URL: http://www.fiafii.org
Contact: John M. Damgard, Pres.
Desc: Acts as a principal spokesman for the futures and options industry. Represents all facets of the futures industry, including many international exchanges. Actively works to preserve the system of free and competitive markets by representing the interests of the industry in connection with legislative and regulatory issues. *Type:* Association.

F.X.C. Newsletter

FXC Investers Corporation
62-19 Cooper Ave.   Ph: (718)417-1330
Glendale, NY 11385   Free: 800-FXC-0992
                              Fax: (718)417-5950
E-mail: fxcmgt@aol.com
Contact: Sabine Boehm, Manager; Francis X. Curzio, Editor.
Desc: Focuses on investments and comments on the market, interest rates, the economy, precious metals, oil, gas, and real estate. Discusses equity and fixed income situations. *Type:* Newsletter.

FXC Report

FXC Investers Corporation
62-19 Cooper Ave.   Ph: (718)417-1330
Glendale, NY 11385   Free: 800-FXC-0992
                              Fax: (718)417-5950
E-mail: fxcmgt@aol.com
URL: http://www.fxcinv.com.
Contact: Francis Curzio, Editor.
Desc: Reports on the securities of companies that have the potential for extreme capital appreciation. Offers news of research for investors with risk capital, conservative and speculative investment recommendations, and performance reports. *Type:* Newsletter.

Gerald Perritt's Mutual Fund Letter

Investment Information Services, Inc.
12514 Starkey Rd. Ph: (813)585-3801
Largo, FL 33773 Free: 800-326-6941
Fax: (813)585-3909
E-mail: perrittcap@aol.com; mutletter@aol.com.
Contact: Gerald W. Perritt, Editor, gwperritt@aol.com.
Desc: Analyzes mutual funds in light of current economic trends, tailoring recommendations to various investment objectives. Contains articles on mutual fund investing, portfolio maintenance, and investment strategies. *Type:* Newsletter.

Global Investing

Agorot Ltd.
1040 1st Ave., Ste. 305 Ph: (212)758-9480
New York, NY 10022-2902 Free: 800-388-4237
Fax: (212)758-0407
E-mail: advs@compuserve.com
URL: http://www.global-investing.com.
Contact: Vivian Lewis, Editor.
Desc: Covers American depositary receipts, country funds, and investing internationally "without leaving Wall Street or changing brokers." Recurring features include stock recommendations, model portfolios, interviews, news of research, and book reviews. *Type:* Newsletter.

Global Investment Technology

Investment Media, Inc.
820 Second Ave., 4th Fl. Ph: (212)370-3700
New York, NY 10017 Fax: (212)370-4606
Contact: Pavan Sahgal, Editor; Michael Honton, Publisher; Mark Anerd, Managing Editor.
Desc: Analyzes strategic issues concerning domestic and international investment institutions and plan sponsors. *Type:* Newsletter.

Global Money Management

Institutional Investor, Inc.
488 Madison Ave. Ph: (212)224-3300
New York, NY 10022 Free: 800-543-4444
Fax: (212)224-3490
Contact: Tom Lamont, Editor.
Desc: Reports on international fund management, including investment strategies; pension fund searches; hires for consultants, managers, and custodians; performance measurement; developing markets, and significant personnel changes. *Type:* Newsletter.

Global Volunteers

375 E. Little Canada Rd. Ph: (612)407-6100
St. Paul, MN 55117-1627 Free: 800-487-1074
Fax: (651)482-0915
E-mail: email@globalvolunteers.org
URL: http://www.globalvolunteers.org
Contact: Burnham Philbrook, Pres.
Desc: Seeks to establish global understanding through volunteer work experience. *Type:* Association.

The Globalist

Globalist, Inc.
2974 Bucklin Hill Rd., Ste. 179
PO Box 3544
Silverdale, WA 98383
URL: http://www.telebyte.com/money.html.
Contact: Joe DeBeauchamp, Editor, joedebo@kendaco.telebyte.com.
Desc: Tracks developments in international stock markets and investment opportunities. *Type:* Newsletter.

Going Public

IDD Enterprises LP
Harborside Financial Center
600 Plaza II, 4th Fl.
Jersey City, NJ 07311
E-mail: ipo@iddis.com.
Contact: Mark Kollar, Editor.
Desc: Publishes information on initial public offerings pertaining to investments such as securities, franchises, municipal funds, restaurants, and pharmaceuticals. *Type:* Newsletter.

Gold Mining Stock Report

Robert Bishop
PO Box 1217 Ph: (510)283-4848
Lafayette, CA 94549 Free: 800-759-7677
Fax: (510)283-8901
Contact: Bob Bishop, Editor.
Desc: Offers analysis and specific recommendations for investors interested in gold mining stocks, emphasizing junior companies. Carries discussions of market strategy. *Type:* Newsletter.

Gold Stocks Advisory

Marketing & Publishing Associates, Ltd.
1217 St. Paul St.
Baltimore, MD 21202
Contact: Paul Sarnoff, Editor.
Desc: Covers on stock investments in gold and gold mining. *Type:* Newsletter.

Good Money Quarterly Reports

Good Money Publications, Inc.
Calais Stage Rd.
PO Box 363
Worcester, VT 05682
E-mail: ympp41b@prodigy.com.
Contact: Dr. Ritchie P. Lowry, Editor; Peter R. Lowry, Editor.
Desc: Provides "sufficient information so that informed investors and consumers can make their own judgments based upon their own investing and consuming goals and values." *Type:* Newsletter.

Good News

Investment & Speculation SIG, MENSA
11160 Glade Dr. Ph: (703)620-4480
Reston, VA 22091-4709
Contact: Ben Perchik, Editor, perchikb@aol.com.
Desc: Shares information on investments, primarily stocks, funds, real estate, taxes, precious metals, and collectibles. Recurring features include letters to the editor, book reviews, notices of publications available, investment portfolios, market predictions, and columns titled Questions & Answers, Stock Tips, Mutual Fund Recommendations, and Foreign Stocks. *Type:* Newsletter.

The Grandich Letter

Grandich Publications
PO Box 354 Ph: (732)905-3822
Perrineville, NJ 08535-0354
Contact: Peter Grandich, Editor.
Desc: Covers markets in banking and finance, commodities, bonds, currencies, energy, estate planning, business, futures, economics, metals, insurance, medical research, new issues, oil, gas, mining, options, penny stocks, precious metals, real estate, securities, taxes and tax shelters, technology, and treasury bills. *Type:* Newsletter.

The GreenMoney Journal & Online Guide

The Greenmoney Journal
W. 608 Glass Ave. Ph: (509)328-1741
Spokane, WA 99205 Fax: (509)328-9422
URL: http://www.greenmoney.com.
Contact: Cliff Feigenbaum, Editor and Publisher, cliffgmj@ior.com; Tom Kliewer, Editor.
Desc: "Encourages and promotes the awareness of socially and environmentally responsible business, investing and consumer resources in publications and online. Our goal is to educate and empower individuals and businesses to make informed financial decisions through aligning their personal, corporate and financial principles." Recurring features include a calendar of events. *Type:* Newsletter.

Growth Fund Guide

Growth Fund Research, Inc.
Growth Fund Research Bldg. Ph: (605)341-1971
PO Box 6600 Free: 800-621-8322
Rapid City, SD 57709
Contact: Walter J. Rouleau, Editor.
Desc: Specializes in analysis of No-Load (no broker fee) Mutual Funds. Provides "forecasts, ratings, charts, risk ratios, market analysis, strength studies, and buy and sell signals of top performing funds." Includes telephone hot-line and Valueratio program. *Type:* Newsletter.

Growth Stock Outlook

Growth Stock Outlook, Inc.
PO Box 15381 Ph: (301)654-5205
Chevy Chase, MD 20825 Fax: (301)986-0722
Contact: Charles Allmon, Editor.
Desc: Provides data on stock earnings, sales, price-earnings ratios, dividends, book values, returns on shareholder equity, and institutional holdings. Recommends specific companies for long-term investment. *Type:* Newsletter.

Handbook for No-Load Fund Investors

No-Load Fund Investor, Inc.
PO Box 318 Ph: (914)693-7420
Irvington on Hudson, NY Free: 800-252-2042
10533 Fax: (914)693-8067
E-mail: noloadfund@aol.com
Contact: Sheldon Jacobs, Editor; Layne Aurand, Editor.
Desc: List of over 2,565 mutual funds that do not charge commissions or have low sales fees. *Type:* Directory.

High Yield Quarterly

Standard & Poor's
25 Broadway Ph: (212)208-8000
New York, NY 10004-1064 Free: 800-221-5277
Fax: (212)208-0040
URL: http://www.stockinfo.standardpoor.com
Contact: David Gibson, Editor.
Desc: Contains news, analysis, and features concerning trends in the junk bond market. Recurring features include news of research. *Type:* Newsletter.

Historical Dow Jones Averages

Dow Jones & Company, Inc.
P.O. Box 300 Ph: (609)520-4000
Princeton, NJ 08543-0300
URL: http://www.dj.com
Desc: Provides historical stock averages, including daily high, low, close, and volume available, for industrials, transportation, utilities, and 65-stock composite indexes for the preceding year. *Available:* Dow Jones & Company, Inc. *Type:* Database.

Hulbert Financial Digest

Hulbert Financial Digest
5051-B Backlick Rd.   Ph: (703)683-5905
Annandale, VA 22003-6045
URL: http://www.hulbertdigest.com.
Contact: Mark Hulbert, Editor.
Desc: Provides performance ratings on more than 400 portfolios recommended by more than 145 financial newsletters, calculated on the basis of model portfolios constructed according to each newsletter's advice. Includes a timing scoreboard, analysis of newsletter performance, list of mutual funds most frequently recommended for sale or purchase, a stock market sentiment index, and a question and answer section. *Type:* Newsletter.

IBC's Money Fund Expense Report

IBC Financial Data, Inc.
290 Eliot St.   Ph: (508)881-2800
PO Box 9104   Free: 800-343-5413
Ashland, MA 01721-9104   Fax: (508)881-0001
E-mail: info@ibcdata.com
URL: http://www.ibcdata.com
Contact: Peter Crane, Managing Editor, pcrane@ibcdata.com; Connie Bugbee, Editor, cbugbee@ibcdata.com; Marie Albin, Associate Editor, malbin@ibcdata.com.
Desc: Contains charged and incurred expense ratios, net and gross quarterly yields, and quarterly expense ratio averages for more than 1,300 money funds. Offers commentary on relevant trends. *Type:* Newsletter.

IBC's Money Fund Report

IBC Financial Data, Inc.
290 Eliot St.   Ph: (508)881-2800
PO Box 9104   Free: 800-343-5413
Ashland, MA 01721-9104   Fax: (508)881-0001
E-mail: info@ibcdata.com
URL: http://www.ibcdata.com; http://www.ibcdata.com.
Contact: Connie Bugbee, Editor, cbugbee@ibcdata.com; Peter Crane, Managing Editor, pcrane@ibcdata.com.
Desc: Publishes weekly data on more than 1,300 taxable and tax-free money market mutual funds. Provides summary of money fund activity, including average 7-day, 30-day, 7-day compound yields, assets, and average maturities. *Type:* Newsletter.

IBC's MONEY FUND REPORT/ELECTRONIC

IBC Financial Data, Inc.
290 Eliot St.   Ph: (508)881-2800
PO Box 9104
Ashland, MA 01721-9104
URL: http://ibcdata.com
Contact: (508)881-2800, fax: (508)881-0982.
Desc: Contains information and analyses of trends and developments in the money market mutual funds industry. *Available:* IBC Financial Data, Inc.; Delphi Internet Services Corporation. *Type:* Database.

IBC's Money Market Insight

IBC Financial Data, Inc.
290 Eliot St.   Ph: (508)881-2800
PO Box 9104   Free: 800-343-5413
Ashland, MA 01721-9104   Fax: (508)881-0001
E-mail: info@ibcdata.com
URL: http://www.ibcdata.com
Contact: Peter Crane, Managing Editor, pcrane@ibcdata.com; Connie Bugbee, Editor, cbugee@ibcdata.com; Marie Albin, Associate Editor, malbin@ibcdata.com.
Desc: Presents articles on money market issues and data on more than 1,300 money market mutual funds. Covers money market trends, money market instruments, 12-month trend analysis, summaries of money fund activity, and top performing funds. *Type:* Newsletter.

IBC's Rated Money Fund Report

IBC Financial Data, Inc.
290 Eliot St.   Ph: (508)881-2800
PO Box 9104   Free: 800-343-5413
Ashland, MA 01721-9104   Fax: (508)881-0001
E-mail: info@ibcdata.com
URL: http://www.ibcdata.com
Contact: Peter Crane, Managing Editor, fax: (508)881-0982, perane@ibcdata.com.
Desc: Provides information on yield, return, asset, maturity, and other topics related to money market mutual funds. Includes top money fund listings. *Type:* Newsletter.

Income Fund Outlook

Institute for Econometric Research
2200 SW 10th St.   Ph: (954)421-1000
Deerfield Beach, FL 33442   Free: 800-442-9000
          Fax: 800-338-4528
Contact: Norman G. Fosback, Editor.
Desc: Provides information on safety ratings, yield forecasts, and recommendations for money market mutual funds and insured money market accounts and bond and income funds. Remarks: Maintains a telephone hotline. *Type:* Newsletter.

Income Stocks

Elton Stephens
4016 S. Michigan St.   Ph: (219)291-3823
South Bend, IN 46614-2544   Free: 800-553-5866
          Fax: (219)291-3823
Contact: Elton Stephens, Editor.
Desc: Lists income stocks that "have good earnings & dividends." *Type:* Newsletter.

The Independent Adviser

Fund Family Shareholder Association
7811 Montrose Rd.   Free: 800-435-3372
Potomac, MD 20854   Fax: (301)424-5059
Contact: Daniel P. Wiener, Editor.
Desc: Provides investment information and news on Vanguard mutual funds. Recurring features include letters to the editor, interviews, news of research, and buy/hold/sell recommendations. *Type:* Newsletter.

The Independent Adviser for Vanguard Investors

Phillips Business Information, Inc.
1201 Seven Locks Rd., Ste. 300   Ph: (301)340-1520
Potomac, MD 20854   Free: 888-707-5809
          Fax: (301)340-3847
E-mail: clientservices.pbi@phillips.com
Contact: Daniel P. Weiner, Editor; David J. Durham, Publisher.
Desc: Provides information and investing advice about the Vanguard family of mutual funds. Recurring features include letters to the editor, interviews, and news of research. *Type:* Newsletter.

Individual Investor

Individual Investor's Group
125 Broad St., 14th Fl.   Ph: (212)742-2277
New York, NY 10004
Desc: Provides investment information on growth stocks. Selects stocks of companies based on records of rapidly expanding sales and earnings, analyzing the progress and growth prospects for each stock on a regular basis. *Type:* Newsletter.

Inside Market Data

Waters Information Services, Inc.
PO Box 2248   Ph: (607)770-9242
Binghamton, NY 13902-2248   Free: 800-947-7947
E-mail: kmiuer@watersinfo.com.
Contact: Andrew Delaney, Editorial Dir.
Desc: Focuses on market data and financial news services, including coverage of digital data feeds, quote terminals, brokerage branch systems, and product marketing. Remarks: Alternate fax number: (607) 770-9435. *Type:* Newsletter.

Insider Trading Monitor

CDA/Investnet
1455 Research Blvd.   Ph: (954)384-1500
Rockville, MD 20850
E-mail: insiderwatch@cda.com
URL: http://www.cda.com
Contact: Customer Service, (305)384-1500, fax: (305)384-1540.
Desc: Contains information on open market sales, purchases, and option exercises of stocks by more than 300,000 corporate insiders (e.g., officers, directors and major shareholders holding 10 percent or more of all shares) in approximately 14,000 companies. Enables the user to retrieve information by individual and by company. *Available:* The Dialog Corporation, DIALOG; CDA/Investnet; Dow Jones Interactive Publishing. *Type:* Database.

Institutional Investor

Institutional Investor, Inc.
488 Madison Ave.   Ph: (212)224-3300
New York, NY 10022   Free: 800-543-4444
          Fax: (212)224-3490
Contact: David Wachtel, Publisher.
Desc: Magazine for the investment or financial industry. *Type:* Periodical.

Interactive Multimedia Investor

Paul Kagan Associates, Inc.
126 Clock Tower Pl.   Ph: (831)624-1536
Carmel, CA 93923   Fax: (831)625-3225
E-mail: info@kagan.com
Desc: Tracks public stocks and private deals in the media industry. Analyzes interactive multimedia companies and projects growth of new TV and data networks. *Type:* Newsletter.

Interinvest Review and Outlook

Interinvest Corporation
84 State St., 7th Fl.   Ph: (617)723-7870
Boston, MA 02109   Fax: (617)723-1966
Contact: Dr. Hans Black, Editor.
Desc: Provides a review of domestic and international markets. Includes information on the U.S. stock market and currency exchange rates. *Type:* Newsletter.

International Campaign for Tibet

1825 K St. NW, Ste. 520   Ph: (202)785-1515
Washington, DC 20006   Fax: (202)785-4343
E-mail: ict@igc.apc.org
URL: http://www.savetibet.org
Contact: John Ackerly, Pres.
Desc: Promotes human rights and democratic freedoms for the people of Tibet. *Type:* Association.

International Capital Markets and Securities Regulation

West Group
620 Opperman Dr.   Ph: (651)687-7000
St. Paul, MN 55164-0526
URL: http://www.westgroup.com
Desc: Contains the complete text of the treatise entitled International Capital Markets and Securities Regulation. Covers regulations in the United States, Canada, United Kingdom, France, the Netherlands, Belgium, Luxemburg, Germany, Australia, Japan, and Hong Kong. *Available:* West Group, WESTLAW. *Type:* Database.

International Insiders Report

Alan Shawn Feinstein Associates
37 Alhambra Circle   Ph: (401)467-5155
Cranston, RI 02905-3416   Fax: (401)941-0988
URL: http://www.feinsteinfoundation.com.
Contact: Alan Shawn Feinstein, Editor.
Desc: Supplies news and tips on financial opportunities outside the securities field to readers "who want to make money or make their savings grow." Discusses such topics as collectibles, error stamps, gems, and the gold standard. *Type:* Newsletter.

International Society for Intercultural Education, Training and Research

1444 I St. NW, No. 700   Ph: (202)712-9045
Washington, DC 20005-2210   Fax: (202)216-9646
E-mail: sietar@bostromdc.com
Contact: David L. Santini, Account Exec.
Desc: Persons concerned with intercultural education, training, and research in public and private agencies. Aim is to foster communication, cooperation, and understanding between persons with differing national, cultural, racial, and ethnic backgrounds through the promotion of intercultural education, training, and research. Attempts to bring persons of differing and sometimes conflicting perspectives together in fruitful communication and collaboration across disciplinary and professional boundaries. *Type:* Association.

InvesTech Market Analyst

InvesTech Research
2472 Birch Glen   Ph: (406)862-7777
Whitefish, MT 59937-3349   Free: 800-955-8500
                                    Fax: (406)862-7707
E-mail: investec@digisys.net
URL: http://www.investech.com.
Contact: James B. Stack, Editor.
Desc: Provides monetary analysis of the Federal Reserve and technical analysis of the stock market. Monitors key monetary statistics, including money supply growth, bank liquidity, and loan demand. *Type:* Newsletter.

InvesTech Mutual Fund Advisor

InvesTech Research
2472 Birch Glen   Ph: (406)862-7777
Whitefish, MT 59937-3349   Free: 800-955-8500
                                    Fax: (406)862-7707
E-mail: investec@digisys.net
URL: http://www.investech.com.
Contact: James B. Stack, Editor.
Desc: Research and analysis of topics critical to the mutual fund investor, with precise investment instructions and model portfolio. Also includes Advisory Digest and Economic Diary. *Type:* Newsletter.

Investing for a Better World

Franklin Research and Development Corporation
711 Atlantic Ave.   Ph: (617)423-6655
Boston, MA 02111   Free: 800-548-5684
                                    Fax: (617)482-6179
E-mail: insight@frdc.com.
Contact: Patrick McVeigh, Editor.
Desc: Provides general financial and social investment advice and equity briefs of companies for investors wishing to make socially responsible investments. Reviews socially responsible mutual funds quarterly. *Type:* Newsletter.

Investing for Growth

Lombardi Publishing Co.
51 Toro Rd.   Ph: (416)633-1600
North York, ON, Canada M3J   Fax: (416)633-6188
  2A4
Contact: Don Sutton, Editor.

Desc: Provides advice concerning the stocks that are included in the TSE 300 Composite. Focuses on one industry per issue. *Type:* Newsletter.

Investment Column Quarterly

NAR Publications
PO Box 233   Ph: (914)557-8713
Barryville, NY 12719   Free: 800-759-4969
                                    Fax: (914)557-6770
E-mail: narpublish@aol.com
Contact: Nicholas A. Roes, Editor.
Desc: Provides information for investors. Includes articles, news, and reviews. *Type:* Newsletter.

The Investment Funds Newsletter

Investment Funds Institute of Canada
151 Youn St., 5th Fl.   Ph: (416)363-2158
Toronto, ON, Canada M5C   Fax: (416)861-9937
  2W7
Contact: Selwyn B. Kossuth, Editor.
Desc: Offers current news and information to people involved with the investment funds industry, including news of related legislation, statistics on industry growth, and news of members and products offered by the Institute. Recurring features include articles on aspects of investment funds, letters to the editor, notices of publications available, and a column titled Comment. *Type:* Newsletter.

Investment Guide

American Investment Services, Inc.
Division St.   Ph: (413)528-1216
Great Barrington, MA 01230   Fax: (413)528-0103
Contact: Louis A. Moscatello, Editor.
Desc: Contains analyses of stock market activity and strategies for investment. Recurring features include market statistics, Dow high-yield stock investing. *Type:* Newsletter.

Investment Management Consultants Association

9101 E. Kenyon Ave., Ste. 3000   Ph: (303)770-3377
Denver, CO 80237   Fax: (303)770-1812
URL: http://www.imca.org
Contact: Evelyn Brust, Exec.Dir.
Desc: Consultants, money managers, and others in the investment management consultant business. Purposes are to increase public awareness of investment management consultants, provide educational programs to members, and encourage high business standards. Operates consulting industry certification program. *Type:* Association.

Investment Management Technology

Waters Information Services, Inc.
PO Box 2248   Ph: (607)770-9242
Binghamton, NY 13902-2248   Free: 800-947-7947
E-mail: kmiller@watersinfo.com.
Contact: Peter Harris, Editorial Director.
Desc: Reports on the information and technology concerns of the institutional investor marketplace. *Type:* Newsletter.

Investment Program Association

1101 17th St. HW, Ste. 703   Ph: (202)775-9750
Washington, DC 20036   Fax: (202)331-8446
Contact: Christopher L. Davis, Pres.
Desc: Partnership sponsors and investors in energy, leasing, research and development, real estate, and communications. Goal is to promote and preserve the investment partnership as a vehicle for capital formation. *Type:* Association.

Investment Quality Trends

Geraldine S. Weiss
7440 Girard St., Ste. 4   Ph: (619)459-3818
La Jolla, CA 92037   Fax: (619)459-3819
E-mail: iqtrends@pacbell.net.
URL: http://www.iqtrends.com.
Contact: Gregory Weiss, Editor.
Desc: Provides a computer analysis of 350 select blue-chip stocks. Features write-ups with charts on three featured stocks. *Type:* Newsletter.

The Investment Reporter

MPL Communications Inc.
133 Richmond St., Ste. 700   Ph: (416)869-1177
Toronto, ON, Canada M5H   Fax: (416)869-0616
  3M8
Contact: David Driscoll, Editor.
Desc: Profiles specific companies and market trends and developments, making recommendations to assist in formulating investment strategies. Includes short articles offering advice on investment decisions. *Type:* Newsletter.

Investment Strategy Letter

Birkelbach Investments/Securities, Inc.
208 S. LaSalle, Ste. 1700   Ph: (312)853-2820
Chicago, IL 60604   Free: 800-458-2358
                                     Fax: (312)853-3183
Contact: Carl M. Birkelbach, Editor.
Desc: Provides strategies for the conservative and aggressive investor, predicting future movements in the market and recommends wise investments and financial planning suggestions. *Type:* Newsletter.

Investor Relations Newsletter

Remy Publishing Company
401 N. Franklin St., 3rd Fl.   Ph: (312)464-0300
Chicago, IL 60610   Free: 800-542-6670
                                     Fax: (312)464-0166
Contact: Gerald E. Murray, Editor.
Desc: Carries information on all facets of investor relations, offering practical data for corporate financial officers. *Type:* Newsletter.

Investor Responsibility Research Center

1755 Massachusetts Ave. NW,   Ph: (202)234-7500
  Ste. 600   Fax: (202)332-8570
Washington, DC 20036
Contact: Margaret Carroll, Exec.Dir.
Desc: Publishes reports and analyses on proxy voting and other business issues affecting corporations and investors. Focuses on the areas of South Africa, the environment, social issues, and corporate governance. *Type:* Association.

Investor, U.S.A.

Seahorse Financial Advisers Inc.
437 Shunpike   Ph: (914)677-6865
Millbrook, NY 12545   Fax: (914)677-0317
Contact: Edvard Jorgensen, Editor, edjo001@ibm.net.
Desc: Discusses investment from a global perspective. Recurring features include portfolio updates and columns titled Market Performances, Timing Indicators, and Investment Strategy. *Type:* Newsletter.

Investor's Digest

MPL Communications Inc.
133 Richmond St. W., Ste. 700   Ph: (416)869-1177
Toronto, ON, Canada M5H   Fax: (416)869-0456
  3M8
Contact: Joseph Chrysdale, Managing Editor.
Desc: Presents news and analysis on stocks, bonds, and mutual funds. Recurring features include interviews, news of research, brokers' reports, and market letters. *Type:* Newsletter.

Investors Intelligence

Chartcraft, Inc.
30 Church St.   Ph: (914)632-0422
PO Box 2046
New Rochelle, NY 10801
Contact: Michael Burke, Editor.
Desc: Serves as a "comprehensive and authoritative Stock Market Advisory Service dedicated to bringing the investor facts, original projections, and a cross section of the recommendations of other leading Services." *Type:* Newsletter.

Investors' Update

Richard J. Schwary
525 W. Manchester   Free: 800-225-7531
Inglewood, CA 90301   Fax: (310)330-3766
Desc: Contains precious metal projections, rare coin market, and the economy. *Type:* Newsletter.

IOMA's Report on Managing 401(K) Plans

Institute of Management & Administration, Inc.
29 W. 35th St., 5th Fl.   Ph: (212)244-0360
New York, NY 10001-2299   Fax: (212)564-0465
E-mail: subserve@ioma.com
URL: http://www.ioma.com
Contact: Rebecca Morrow, Editor; Perry Patterson, Publisher.
Desc: Provides information for managing 401(K) retirement plans. *Type:* Newsletter.

The IRA Reporter

Universal Pensions, Inc.
431 Golf Course Rd. N.   Ph: (218)829-4781
PO Box 979   Free: 800-346-3860
Brainerd, MN 56401   Fax: (218)829-2106
Contact: Jennifer Olsen, Editor.
Desc: Carries information on legislation and procedures relating to all types of individual retirement arrangements (IRAs), SIMPLES and MSAs. *Type:* Newsletter.

IRA - Stocks

Elton Stephens
4016 S. Michigan St.   Ph: (219)291-3823
South Bend, IN 46614-2544   Free: 800-553-5866
          Fax: (219)291-3823
Contact: Elton Stephens, Editor.
Desc: Lists Individual Retirement Account (IRA) stocks that "have good earnings and dividends." *Type:* Newsletter.

IWB-FAX

James Dines & Company, Inc.
PO Box 22   Free: 800-84-LUCKY
Belvedere, CA 94920
Desc: Provides investment advice between issues of the Dines Letter for sudden change between issues as market conditions warrant. *Type:* Newsletter.

J. Taylor's Gold and Gold Stocks

Taylor Hard Money Advisors, Inc.
33-42 61st St.   Ph: (718)457-1426
Woodside, NY 11377
Contact: Jay L. Taylor, Editor.
Desc: Provides buying and selling recommendations for gold stocks. *Type:* Newsletter.

Jackpotunities

Jackpotunities, Inc.
Box 393, Centuck Sta.   Ph: (914)664-5242
Yonkers, NY 10710
Desc: Covers various opportunities to win prizes, providing readers a means to "increase the odds for winning sweepstakes and contests." Lists contests/sweepstakes and includes hints where appropriate, along with general information on related issues such as disqualifications and taxes on winnings. Includes complete instructions necessary to enter those contests listed. *Type:* Newsletter.

Japan Weekly Monitor

Kyodo News International, Inc.
50 Rockefeller Plaza, Rm. 803   Ph: (212)397-3723
New York, NY 10020
URL: http://www.kyodonews.com
Desc: Contains summary data and analyses of activity on the Tokyo Stock Exchange and the Tokyo foreign exchange market, news of business developments affecting U.S. and Japanese trade, and economic data released by the Japanese government and industrial organizations. *Type:* Database.

Jay Schabacker's Mutual Fund Investing

Phillips Business Information, Inc.
1201 Seven Locks Rd., Ste. 300   Ph: (301)340-1520
Potomac, MD 20854   Free: 888-707-5809
          Fax: (301)340-3847
E-mail: clientservices.pbi@phillips.com
URL: http://www.phillips.com; http://www.phillips.com/mutual.htm.
Contact: Jay Schabacker, Editor.
Desc: Offers advice concerning the mutual fund market using "a proven safety-first investment method." Makes specific recommendations and discusses related financial management issues. Recurring features include information on current investment, fund performances, and a column titled Sectors. *Type:* Newsletter.

John Bollinger's Capital Growth Letter

Bollinger Capital Management, Inc.
PO Box 3358   Ph: (310)798-8855
Manhattan Beach, CA 90266   Fax: (310)798-8858
E-mail: bband@bollingerbands.com
URL: http://www.bollingesbands.com.
Contact: John Bollinger, Editor.
Desc: Provides investors with specific investment advice on stocks, bonds, precious metals, oil, and the dollar. *Type:* Newsletter.

The John Martone Letter

John Martone
PO Box 228
Mahopac, NY 10541
Contact: John Martone, Editor.
Desc: Recommends stock market investments, especially stock options. Remarks: Available online only. *Type:* Newsletter.

Jumbo Rate News

Bauer Communications, Inc.
2655 LeJeune Rd., PH-1   Ph: (305)445-9500
Coral Gables, FL 33114-5510   Free: 800-388-6686
          Fax: (305)445-6775
Contact: Paul A. Bauer, Editor; Caroline P. Jervey, Managing Editor.
Desc: Reports on high-yielding, insured Jumbo CD (Certificate of Deposit) rates nationwide. Analyzes each institution by current credit-worthiness, and lists current assets and capital ratios. *Type:* Newsletter.

Junior Growth Stocks

Growth Stock Outlook, Inc.
PO Box 15381   Ph: (301)654-5205
Chevy Chase, MD 20825   Fax: (301)986-0722
Contact: Charles Allmon, Editor.
Desc: Serves experienced investors with information on "the risk and possible rewards of investing in small, emerging growth companies." Provides data on earnings, sales, shares outstanding, compound growth rates, book values, and price-earnings ratios for approximately 210 companies. Recurring features include columns titled Stock Study Guide and New Issue Digest. *Type:* Newsletter.

The Kirkpatrick Market Strategist

Kirkpatrick & Company, Inc.
PO Box 699
Chatham, MA 02633-0699
E-mail: kirkco@nh.ultranet.com
Contact: Charles D. Kirkpatrick, Editor.
Desc: Focuses on the technical, institutional, and individual stock and bond markets. Discusses market timing and stock selections based on earning's growth and "price behavior." Remarks: Subscription includes weekly facimiles and monthly longer-term services. *Type:* Newsletter.

The Konlin Letter

Kon-Lin Research & Analysis Corporation
5 Water Rd.   Ph: (516)744-8536
Rocky Point, NY 11778   Fax: (516)744-3096
Contact: Konrad Kuhn, Editor.
Desc: Provides investment advice on stocks under $10, especially Emerging Growth and Special Situations stock "poised for Explosive Price Appreciation Potential." Makes specific buy and sell recommendations and monitors "a broad range of technical indicators for the best possible market timing advice." *Type:* Newsletter.

The Lancz Letter

Alan B. Lancz & Associates, Inc.
2400 N. Reynolds Rd.   Ph: (419)536-5200
Toledo, OH 43615   Fax: (419)536-5401
E-mail: abl@ablonline.com
Contact: Alan B. Lancz, Editor.
Desc: "Gives current advice on stocks, bonds, precious metals, currencies and other related investment vehicles." Analyzes interest rate and general investment trends and suggests investments for both aggressive and conservative investors. Recurring features include portfolio performance statistics and columns titled Investor's Corner and New Recommendations. *Type:* Newsletter.

LANSA

Latin American Paper Money Society
3304 Milford Mill Rd.   Ph: (410)655-3109
Baltimore, MD 21244-2041
Contact: Arthur C. Matz, Editor.
Desc: Discusses Latin American and Iberian paper money, including history and new issues. Recurring features include letters to the editor, news of research, a calendar of events, book reviews, and notices of publications available. *Type:* Newsletter.

Lanston Letter

Aubrey G. Lanston & Company, Inc.
1 Chase Manhattan Plaza, 53rd   Ph: (212)612-1676
Fl.   Fax: (212)363-3423
New York, NY 10005
E-mail: aubrey@pipeline.com
URL: http://www.lanston.com.
Contact: David M. Jones, Editor.
Desc: Analyzes the factors influencing the financial market, especially government securities prices. Focuses on possible shifts in Federal Reserve policy and resulting movements in market interest rates. *Type:* Newsletter.

LEXIS® Federal Securities Library

LEXIS-NEXIS
9443 Springboro Pike   Ph: (937)865-6800
PO Box 933
Dayton, OH 45401-0933
URL: http://www.lex-nexis.com
Desc: Contains more than 60 separately searchable files covering federal case law; Securities Exchange Commission (SEC) no-action interpretative and exemptive letters, decisions, orders, releases, administrative proceedings, rul-

ings and SEC filings (both EDGAR and pre-EDGAR); Commodities Futures Trading Commission (CFTC) decisions, orders, releases; no action, interpretative, and exemptive letters, National Association of Securities Dealers (NASD) rules, disciplinary actions and notices to members; legislative materials; statutory and regulatory materials; selected RICO, class derivative, and collateralized mortgage obligations case law, rules, and regulations; Federal Reserve Board materials; AICPA annual reports and accounting and auditing literature files; Standard & Poors company information; state administrative decisions, orders, releases, and no-action letters; and company news and analysis information. *Available:* LEXIS-NEXIS, LEXIS. *Type:* Database.

LEXIS® State Securities Library

LEXIS-NEXIS
9443 Springboro Pike   Ph: (937)865-6800
PO Box 933
Dayton, OH 45401-0933
URL: http://www.lex-nexis.com
Desc: Contains state case law, administrative decisions, orders, releases, no-action letters, and Bureau of National Affairs (BNA) materials relating to state securities legislation. *Available:* LEXIS-NEXIS, LEXIS. *Type:* Database.

Litigation and Practice Under Rule 10b-5

West Group
620 Opperman Dr.   Ph: (651)687-7000
St. Paul, MN 55164-0526
URL: http://www.westgroup.com
Desc: Contains the complete text of the treatise entitled Litigation and Practice Under Rule 10b-5 by Arnold S. Jacobs. *Available:* West Group, WESTLAW. *Type:* Database.

Lombardi Investment Club

Lombardi Publishing Co.
51 Toro Rd.   Ph: (416)633-1600
North York, ON, Canada M3J   Fax: (416)633-6188
    2A4
Desc: Provides recommendations on the top rated Lombardi stock picks. Includes expert financial advice. *Type:* Newsletter.

Lombardi's Mutual Fund Picks

Lombardi Publishing Co.
51 Toro Rd.   Ph: (416)633-1600
North York, ON, Canada M3J   Fax: (416)633-6188
    2A4
Contact: Mitchell Clark, Editor.
Desc: Provides advice on mutual fund investing. Includes details on model mutual fund portfolios. *Type:* Newsletter.

Long Term Investing

Concept Publishing
PO Box 500   Ph: (716)243-3148
York, NY 14592-0500   Fax: (716)243-3148
Contact: David Coleman, Editor.
Desc: Profiles conservative and value-bases investing. *Type:* Newsletter.

Lovejoy's MarketBrief Ratings

Lovejoy Corporation
PO Box 1442   Ph: (609)989-9484
Palmer Sq.
Princeton, NJ 08542
E-mail: marketbrief@earthlink.net.
Contact: David Luciano, Editor.
Desc: Gives "fundamental, technical, and psychological investment analysis of stocks, mutual funds, and industries transformed into ratings (BestBuy, Buy, Caution, Sell, Avoid) on a scale from one to three. Provides timing strategy for stock, bond, and gold markets." Recurring features include letters to the editor. *Type:* Newsletter.

The Low Priced Stock Survey

Horizon Publishing Company LLC
7412 Calumet Ave.   Fax: (219)931-6487
Hammond, IN 46324-2692
E-mail: lpssurvey@aol.com.
Contact: Randall Roeing, Editor.
Desc: Reviews and analyzes stocks offered at a price of $20 or less. Analysis is divided into sections: Emerging Growth Opportunities, The Fundamentalist, Bargain Spotlight, Stock of the Month, and Master List Highlights. *Type:* Newsletter.

Low Priced Stocks

Elton Stephens
4016 S. Michigan St.   Ph: (219)291-3823
South Bend, IN 46614-2544   Free: 800-553-5866
                          Fax: (219)291-3823
Contact: Elton Stephens, Editor.
Desc: Lists approximately 50 low priced stocks that "have good earnings and dividends." *Type:* Newsletter.

Managing Your Future

Money Magazine
Time & Life Blgd.   Ph: (212)522-2651
New York, NY 10020   Fax: (212)522-1802
E-mail: 76702.1026@compuserve.com
Contact: Eric Schurenberg, Editor.
Desc: Offers independent advice on retirement saving and basic investing principles. *Type:* Newsletter.

Mansfield Stock Chart Service

R.W. Mansfield Company
2973 Kennedy Blvd.   Ph: (201)795-0630
Jersey City, NJ 07306-3884   Fax: (201)795-5476
E-mail: iwilkow@aol.com
Desc: Published in nine editions covering individual companies on the New York Stock Exchange; the American Stock Exchange; Over-The-Counter trading; International and Long Term S & P Industry Groups; S & P 500; and S & P Mid-Cap. *Type:* Newsletter.

Margo's Market Monitor

Margo Parrish
175 Bedford St., Ste. 14   Ph: (781)861-0302
Lexington, MA 02173   Fax: (781)861-1489
Contact: Margo Parrish, Editor.
Desc: Concentrates primarily on the 35 Fidelity Sector Funds. Discusses past and future stock market trends and the impact and ramifications of inflation and deflation, then makes specific recommendations for buying and selling. *Type:* Newsletter.

Market Insider Bulletin

Lombardi Publishing Co.
51 Toro Rd.   Ph: (416)633-1600
North York, ON, Canada M3J   Fax: (416)633-6188
    2A4
Contact: Tony Jasansky, Editor.
Desc: Monitors the stock market and provides predictions on the market direction. Provides analysis of the TSE and the NYSE. *Type:* Newsletter.

Market Logic

Institute for Econometric Research
2200 SW 10th St.   Ph: (954)421-1000
Deerfield Beach, FL 33442   Free: 800-442-9000
                          Fax: 800-338-4528
Contact: Norman G. Fosback, Editor.
Desc: Serves as an advisory, covering technical fundamental and monetary indicators, specific stock recommendations, market timing, and general investment. Remarks: Maintains a telephone hotline. *Type:* Newsletter.

Market Maneuvers

Market Maneuvers
305 Madison Ave., Ste. 1166   Ph: (212)592-4141
New York, NY 10165
Contact: David Wanetick, Editor.
Desc: Describes the current activities and future prospects for the most favorably-positioned stocks. *Type:* Newsletter.

Market Month

Standard & Poor's
25 Broadway   Ph: (212)208-8000
New York, NY 10004-1064   Free: 800-221-5277
                          Fax: (212)208-0040
URL: http://www.stockinfo.standardpoor.com
Contact: Jean M. Kozlowski, Editor.
Desc: Supplies individual investors with current market information and offers specific stock recommendations to buy and sell. Recurring features include reviews of previous recommendations and columns titled Company Spotlight, Report Card, and Industry Spotlight. *Type:* Newsletter.

Market Timing Report

Ted C. Earle
PO Box 225   Ph: (520)795-9552
Tucson, AZ 85702
Contact: Ted C. Earle, Editor.
Desc: Aims to "provide recommendations which will result in a real return on your investment portfolio while minimizing risk and restricting the portfolio to high liquidity investments. A real return means a positive return after taxes and inflation." Recurring features include reports on the Federal Reserve and the markets covered, statistics, and news of research. *Type:* Newsletter.

Market Watch

Board of Trade of Kansas City, Missouri
4800 Main St., Ste. 303   Ph: (816)753-7500
Kansas City, MO 64112   Free: 800-821-5228
                          Fax: (816)531-0627
E-mail: kcbt@kcbt.com
URL: http://www.kcbt.com.
Desc: Provides market analysis and trading strategies for Kansas City Board of Trade (KCBT) contracts including Value Line Stock Index futures, hard red winter wheat futures and options, and western natural gas futures and options. *Type:* Newsletter.

Media General Financial Services Common Stock Database

Media General Financial Services, Inc. (MGFS)
301 E. Franklin St.   Ph: (804)775-8000
PO Box 85333
Richmond, VA 23293
E-mail: info@mgfs.com
URL: http://www.mgfs.com
Contact: Charles Blackburn, VP Marketing/Business Development.
Desc: Contains detailed daily, monthly, quarterly, and annual financial and trading data on more than 8000 U.S. companies. *Available:* The Dialog Corporation, DIALOG; Dow Jones Interactive Publishing; Track Data Corporation; Data Downlink Corporation. *Type:* Database.

Medical Technology Stock Letter

Medical Technology Stock Letter
PO Box 40460   Ph: (510)843-1857
Berkeley, CA 94704   Fax: (510)843-0901
E-mail: mtsl@aol.com
Contact: James McCamant, Editor.
Desc: Specializes in investments in health care companies. Offers news of the industry and recommendations for buying, selling, and holding stocks. *Type:* Newsletter.

Meridian International Center

1630 Crescent Pl. NW   Ph: (202)667-6800
Washington, DC 20009   Fax: (202)667-1475
Contact: Hon. Walter Cutler, Pres.
Desc: Cultural and educational organization in the field of international affairs dedicated to the promotion of international understanding through the excange of people, ideas, and the arts. Provides services to international visitors, diplomats, and Americans interested in international issues. Owns and operates Meridian House and White-Meyer House, both listed in the National Register of Historic Places. *Type:* Association.

Michael Lombardi Line

Lombardi Publishing Co.
51 Toro Rd.   Ph: (416)633-1600
North York, ON, Canada M3J   Fax: (416)633-6188
2A4
Contact: George Leong, Editor.
Desc: Provides recommendations on long and short positions. Includes a weekly updated hotline. *Type:* Newsletter.

The Middle/Fixed Income Letter

MASTCA Publishing Corporation
PO Box 55   Ph: (914)794-5793
Loch Sheldrake, NY 12759-   Free: 800-345-7526
0055
Contact: Joel Lerner, Editor.
Desc: Provides current financial information for the "unsophisticated middle income investor." *Type:* Newsletter.

MMA Cycles Report

Merriman Market Analyst (MMA)
PO Box 250012   Ph: (810)737-5409
West Bloomfield, MI 48325-   Free: 800-962-4613
0012
E-mail: mmacycles@email.msm.com.
Contact: Raymond A. Merriman, Editor, fax: (248)626-3037.
Desc: Presents summaries and strategies on the stock market, precious metals, T-bonds, currencies, and grains. *Type:* Newsletter.

MMS Weekly Economic Survey

MMS International
1301 Shoreway Rd.   Ph: (650)595-0610
Belmont, CA 94002   Free: 800-227-7304
    Fax: (650)637-4303
Contact: Louis Radovich, Editor.
Desc: Covers market expectations and the effect of market sentiment on key financial variables. *Type:* Newsletter.

Monetary Digest

David J. Robinson
PO Box 917179   Ph: (407)682-6170
Longwood, FL 32791
URL: http://www.thebullandbear.com.
Desc: Offers a comprehensive digest of top-performing investment newsletters. *Type:* Newsletter.

Money Market Directory of Pension Funds and Their Investment Managers

Money Market Directories, Inc.
320 E. Main St.   Ph: (804)977-1450
PO Box 1608   Free: 800-446-2810
Charlottesville, VA 22902   Fax: (804)979-9962
URL: http://www.mmdaccess.com.
Contact: Jesse Noel, Editor.
Desc: Over 48,000 tax-exempt funds (corporate, union, government and endowment) with over $1,000,000 in assets, and about 1,800 investment management services, bank trust departments, and insurance companies handling at least $10,000,000 in tax-exempt funds. *Type:* Directory.

Money Reporter

MPL Communications Inc.
133 Richmond St., Ste. 700   Ph: (416)869-1177
Toronto, ON, Canada M5H   Fax: (416)869-0616
3M8
Contact: Marc Johnson, Editor.
Desc: Offers investors current information on investment topics ranging from recommended stocks to income reinvestment. Also includes informational items on investment perspectives and a weekly Fact Sheets supplement, providing preferred share prices and recommendations. *Type:* Newsletter.

Money Talks

Titan Value Equities Group, Inc.
520 N. Brookhurst St., Ste. 130   Ph: (714)778-4375
Anaheim, CA 92801   Free: 800-675-3269
    Fax: (714)778-6187
Contact: Stewart Case, Editor.
Desc: Covers financial planning, investing, news and views. Recurring features include interviews, news of research, reports of meetings, and columns titled Investment Ideas, News Briefs, and Commentary. *Type:* Newsletter.

The Moneychanger

Franklin Sanders
PO Box 341753   Ph: (901)853-6136
Memphis, TN 38184-1753
Contact: Franklin Sanders, Editor.
Desc: Makes investment recommendations congruent with the editors' attempts to "help Christians prosper with their principles intact in an age of monetary and moral chaos." Focuses on the gold and silver markets. Recurring features include interviews and columns titled Current Market Projections and Unforgettable (quotes and commentary). *Type:* Newsletter.

Moneyletter

Agora, Inc.
1217 St. Paul St.   Ph: (410)223-2510
Baltimore, MD 21202   Free: 800-433-1528
    Fax: (410)223-2559
E-mail: 75127.1411@compuserve.com
Contact: Walter Frank, Chief Investment Officer.
Desc: "Provides assertive, do-it-yourself, individual investors with a unique market timing system, specific buy and sell recommendations, and portfolio allocation advice on no-load mutual funds." *Type:* Newsletter.

The MoneyLetter

Hume Publishing Co. Ltd.
604-2200 Yonge St.   Ph: (416)440-8260
Toronto, ON, Canada M4S   Free: 800-733-4863
2C6   Fax: (416)440-8268
E-mail: humenewsletters@mindspring.com
Contact: Gordon Pape, Senior Editor.
Desc: Designed to offer financial planning advice and investment and tax-planning strategies to a broad range of investors. Recommends specific stocks, bonds, mutual funds, and occasional esoteric investments. *Type:* Newsletter.

The Moneypaper

Temper of the Times Communications, Inc.
1010 Mamaroneek Ave.   Ph: (914)381-5400
Mamaroneck, NY 10543   Free: 800-388-9993
    Fax: (914)381-7206
E-mail: moneypaper@aol.com;   moneypaper@moneypaper.com.
Contact: Vita Nelson, Editor.
Desc: Contains strategies to minimize sales costs and articles on investing and market trends. Includes a summary of monthly financial news drawn from over 70 financial publications and advisory services. *Type:* Newsletter.

MoniResearch Newsletter

MoniResearch Corp.
PO Box 19146   Ph: (360)225-0703
Portland, OR 97280   Free: 800-615-6664
    Fax: (360)225-0703
E-mail: moninews@compuserve.com
Contact: Steve Shellans, Editor.
Desc: Provides performance rankings of market timers and tactical asset allocators. Recurring features include performance tables, interviews, news of research, and reports of meetings. *Type:* Newsletter.

Monthly Market Report

SNL Securities
321 E. Main St.   Ph: (804)977-1600
PO Box 2124   Fax: (804)977-4466
Charlottesville, VA 22902
E-mail: subscriptions@snl.com
URL: http://www.snl.com.
Contact: Steve Tomasi, Editor; Wendy Cholbi, Editor; John Racine, Editor.
Desc: Contains expert articles on timely issues in the thrift industry. Includes analysis of important thrift activity, conversion information, and stock highlights. *Type:* Newsletter.

Morningstar Investor

Morningstar Inc.
225 W. Wacker Dr., Ste. 400   Ph: (312)696-6000
Chicago, IL 60606   Free: 800-735-0700
    Fax: (312)696-6001
URL: http://www.morningstar.com
Contact: Susan Dziubinski, Editor.
Desc: Contains in-depth articles intended to help individuals develop their mutual fund strategies. Includes data on the Morningstar 500, a select list of leading mutual funds. *Type:* Newsletter.

Motion Picture Investor

Paul Kagan Associates, Inc.
126 Clock Tower Pl.   Ph: (831)624-1536
Carmel, CA 93923   Fax: (831)625-3225
E-mail: info@kagan.com
URL: http://www.pkbaseline.com.
Contact: George Niesen, Editor.
Desc: Concerned with motion picture investment, financing, and limited partnerships. Analyzes trends in movie exhibitor and motion picture stocks of publicly held companies, makes projections, and reports industry news. *Type:* Newsletter.

MPT Review

Navellier-MPT Review, Inc.
1 E. Liberty, 3rd Fl.   Ph: (775)785-2300
Reno, NV 89501   Free: 800-454-1395
    Fax: (775)785-2321
E-mail: info@navellier.com; jerryr@navellier.com.
URL: http://www.mptreview.com.
Contact: Louis G. Navellier, Editor.
Desc: Provides extensive quantitative analysis on nearly 400 stocks and the market environment. *Type:* Newsletter.

Muniweek

American Banker - Bond Buyer
One State Street Plaza, 27th Fl.   Ph: (212)803-8366
New York, NY 10004
URL: http://www.americanbanker.com
Desc: Contains the complete text of Muniweek, a weekly newspaper covering the fixed-income securities market. Provides reviews of fixed-income bonds and securities, including Treasury bonds and bills, mortgage-backed securities, financial futures, taxable issues, and corporate and municipal bonds. *Available:* Bell & Howell Information and Learning. *Type:* Database.

Investments

Mutual Fund Advisor
The Mutual Fund Advisor, Inc.
1 Sarasota Tower, Ste. 602 Ph: (941)954-5500
2 N. Tamiami Trail
Sarasota, FL 34236
Contact: Donald H. Rowe, Editor.
Desc: Covers top performing mutual funds, U.S. and world stock markets, precious metals, income funds, international equity funds, sector funds, and no-load funds. *Type:* Newsletter.

Mutual Fund Digest
Hirsch Organization
PO Box 2069 Ph: (201)767-4100
River Vale, NJ 07675 Fax: (201)767-7337
Contact: Warren Boroson, Editor, (201)444-3583.
Desc: Provides information and recommendations on mutual funds and related topics. Includes a model stock portfolio and quotes in each issue. *Type:* Newsletter.

Mutual Fund Directory
Securities Data Publishing
Circulation Dept. Ph: (212)432-0045
40 W. 57th St., 11th Fl.
New York, NY 10019
Contact: Michele Stibgen, Editor.
Desc: Organizational information on more than 6,900 open end mutual funds, covering load, no-load, institutional and money market funds. *Type:* Directory.

Mutual Fund Forecaster
Institute for Econometric Research
2200 SW 10th St. Ph: (954)421-1000
Deerfield Beach, FL 33442 Free: 800-442-9000
Fax: 800-338-4528
Contact: Norman G. Fosback, Editor.
Desc: Forecasts performance for more than 500 mutual funds and rates best buys. Recurring features include a Directory of Mutual Funds, listing performance data, one-year profit projections, and risk rating. *Type:* Newsletter.

Mutual Fund Market News
Dalbar Publishing, Inc.
Federal Reserve Plaza Ph: (617)723-6400
30th Fl.
Boston, MA 02210
Contact: Susan Weiner, Editor.
Desc: Provides persons in the mutual fund industry with critical information, breaking news, industry developments, new product analyses, and changes in market share. Covers all major changes of distribution for mutual funds and related products, with emphasis on banks, broker/dealers, captive sales forces, corporate and nonprofit pensions, and direct markets. *Type:* Newsletter.

Mutual Fund Trends
Growth Fund Research, Inc.
Growth Fund Research Bldg. Ph: (605)341-1971
PO Box 6600 Free: 800-621-8322
Rapid City, SD 57709
Contact: Walter J. Rouleau, Editor.
Desc: Provides high quality semi-log charts with multiple moving averages and relative strength line on approximately 180 top performing funds. Statistics include lows to current time and high to low. *Type:* Newsletter.

Mutual Funds Performance Report
Media General Financial Services, Inc. (MGFS)
301 E. Franklin St. Ph: (804)775-8000
PO Box 85333
Richmond, VA 23293
E-mail: info@mgfs.com
URL: http://www.mgfs.com

Desc: Contains performance rankings for the top 25 mutual funds for the current week, 4 weeks, year-to-date, 12 months, and 3, 5, and 10 years. Also contains quarterly time series on return, income yield, beta values, and shares outstanding for 4800 mutual funds, as well as address and telephone number of fund manager. *Available:* Dow Jones Interactive Publishing. *Type:* Database.

Mutual Funds Report
Wiesenberger
1455 Research Blvd. Ph: (301)545-4000
Rockville, MD 20851 Free: 800-232-2285
Fax: (301)545-6400
E-mail: wies@cda.com
Contact: Stephanie Kendall, Editor; Dawn Kahler, Managing Editor.
Desc: Provides information on more then 9,800 mutual funds. *Type:* Newsletter.

National Association of Investors Corporation
711 W. 13 Mile Rd. Ph: (810)583-6242
Madison Heights, MI 48071 Fax: (810)583-4880
URL: http://www.better_investing.org
Desc: Federation of independent investment clubs ranging from ten to 20 members each; interested individuals. Members contribute 20 dollars or more per month, which is invested in securities as a group. Has councils staffed by volunteers in 65 cities to counsel and teach investing techniques and sound investment procedures to interested people. *Type:* Association.

National Futures Association
200 W. Madison St. Ph: (312)781-1410
Chicago, IL 60606-3447 Free: 800-621-3570
Fax: (312)781-1467
E-mail: public_affairs@nfa.futures.org
URL: http://www.nfa.futures.org
Contact: Robert K. Wilmouth, CEO & Pres.
Desc: Futures commission merchants; commodity trading advisors; commodity pool operators; brokers and their associated persons. Works to: strengthen and expand industry self-regulation to include all segments of the futures industry; provide uniform standards to eliminate duplication of effort and conflict; remove unnecessary regulatory constraints to aid effective regulation. Conducts member qualification screening, financial surveillance, and registration. *Type:* Association.

National Investment Company Service Association
36 Washington St., Ste. 70 Ph: (781)416-7200
Wellesley Hills, MA 02181- Fax: (781)416-7065
1904
E-mail: bgoldberg@nicsa.org
URL: http://www.nicsa.org
Contact: Robert L. Goldberg, Pres.
Desc: Mutual fund investment managers, distributors, custodians, transfer agents, accounting and legal firms, broker/dealers, and general providers of services and products to the mutual fund industry. Seeks to address future service needs and trends by providing a forum on operational and technological developments. *Type:* Association.

National Investor Relations Institute
8045 Leesburg Pike, Ste. 600 Ph: (703)506-3570
Vienna, VA 22182 Fax: (703)506-3571
E-mail: info@niri.org
URL: http://www.niri.org
Contact: Louis M. Thompson, Jr., Pres. & Ceo.
Desc: Executives engaged in investor relations. To identify the role of the investor relations practitioner; to protect a free and open market with equity and access to investors of all kinds; to improve communication between corporate management and shareholders, present and future. *Type:* Association.

National Quotation Service
National Quotation Bureau, LLC (NQB)
11 Penn Plaza, 15th Fl. Ph: (212)868-7100
New York, NY 10001 Free: 800-732-7868
Fax: (212)868-3828
Type: Newsletter.

National Real Estate Investors Association
89 S Riverview Ave. Ph: (513)866-6200
Miamisburg, OH 45342 Free: 800-922-2214
Fax: 800-525-6410
Contact: Sue Brawn, Sec.
Desc: Investors in real estate. Promotes appreciation of real estate investments. *Type:* Association.

The Neatest Little FundLetter
Jason Kelly
11032 Moorpark St., No. 17 Ph: (818)752-1934
North Hollywood, CA 91602 Free: 800-339-5671
URL: http://www.jasonkelly.com.
Contact: Jason Kelly, Editor.
Desc: Aims to help readers "use the various tools to create and manage their own mutual fund portfolio better than professional managers." Also includes how-to articles and model portfolios. Columns titled Kelly's Quicklist, Fund-Folio, and FundFilter. *Type:* Newsletter.

New Issues
Institute for Econometric Research
220 SW 10th St. Ph: (954)421-1000
Deerfield Beach, FL 33442 Free: 800-442-9000
Fax: (954)570-8200
Contact: Norman G. Fosback, Editor.
Desc: Serves as a guide to initial public offerings. Includes a calendar of events and specific buy and sell recommendations. *Type:* Newsletter.

Newspaper Investor
Paul Kagan Associates, Inc.
126 Clock Tower Pl. Ph: (831)624-1536
Carmel, CA 93923 Fax: (831)625-3225
E-mail: info@kagan.com
Contact: George Niesen, Editor.
Desc: Provides valuations of private and public newspapers and companies and analysis of newspaper industry economics and trends. *Type:* Newsletter.

Nielsen's International Investment Letter
Nielsen & Nielsen, Inc.
PO Box 7532
Olympia, WA 98507
Contact: Thor Nielsen, Editor.
Desc: Tracks domestic and international stockmarkets and economies, precious metals, and other commodities, U.S. and foreign bonds, interest rates, foreign currencies, and real estate. *Type:* Newsletter.

The No-Load Fund Investor
No-Load Fund Investor, Inc.
PO Box 318 Ph: (914)693-7420
Irvington on Hudson, NY Free: 800-252-2042
10533 Fax: (914)693-8067
E-mail: noloadfund@aol.com
URL: http://www.adpad.com/noload/.
Contact: Sheldon Jacobs, Editor.
Desc: Predicts which no-load and low-load funds will perform best overall in the coming year. Provides performance data for 995 no- and low-loads and recommends funds and analyzes promising new funds. *Type:* Newsletter.

NoLOAD Fund X

DAL Investment Company
235 Montgomery St., Ste. 662   Ph: (415)986-7979
San Francisco, CA 94104   Free: 800-763-8639
                                      Fax: (415)986-1595
E-mail: dal@dal-investment.com; fundxcfundx.
Contact: Janet Brown, Editor, janet@dal-investment.com.
Desc: Provides performance data on over 740 noload and
loload mutual funds, including advice on which funds to
buy, when to move your money in response to changing
market conditions, and predictions on future top performers. Features include letters to the editor, summary of leading indexes, market commentary, fund news and analysis.
Type: Newsletter.

NQB Monthly Price Report

National Quotation Bureau, LLC (NQB)
11 Penn Plaza, 15th Fl.   Ph: (212)868-7100
New York, NY 10001   Free: 800-732-7868
                                      Fax: (212)868-3828
Desc: Includes information about 9,000 National Association of Securities Dealers Automated Quotations (NAS-
DAQ) stock market and non-NASDAQ securities
extracted from the Pink Sheets of all over-the-counter
traded equities. Recurring features include weekly and annual high and low bids, final bid and ask for the current
month's period, historic high and low bids, notations for
capital changes, marginability, bankruptcy, or receiver-
ship, and a report of the period's statistics showing number of advancing, declining, unchanged, new highs and
lows, and the number of securities traded for the first time.
Type: Newsletter.

NQB Price Digest

National Quotation Bureau, LLC (NQB)
11 Penn Plaza, 15th Fl.   Ph: (212)868-7100
New York, NY 10001   Free: 800-732-7868
                                      Fax: (212)868-3828
Desc: Includes information about 9,000 National Association of Securities Dealers Automated Quotations (NAS-
DAQ) stock market and non-NASDAQ securities
extracted from the Pink Sheets of all over-the-counter
traded equities. Recurring features include weekly and annual high and low bids, final bid and ask for the current
week's period, historic high and low bids, notations for
capital changes, marginability, bankruptcy, or receiver-
ship, and a report of the period's statistics showing number of advancing, declining, unchanged, new highs and
lows, and the number of securities traded for the first time.
Type: Newsletter.

NYSE Weekly Stock Buys

Elton Stephens Investments
4016 S. Michigan St.   Ph: (219)291-3823
South Bend, IN 46614   Free: 800-553-5866
                                      Fax: (219)291-3823
Contact: Elton Stephens, Editor.
Desc: Identifies stocks with increases in dividends, earn-
ings, and price appreciation. *Type:* Newsletter.

Oberweis Report—A Monthly Review

Oberweis Asset Management, Inc.
951 Ice Cream Dr., Ste. 200   Ph: (630)801-6000
North Aurora, IL 60542-1472   Free: 800-323-6166
                                      Fax: (630)896-5282
URL: http://www.oberweisfunds.com.
Contact: Jim Oberweis, Editor.
Desc: Provides stock market and financial market analyses,
reviews of individual stocks, and stock news. Identifies
small, rapidly growing companies, especially high technology stocks. *Type:* Newsletter.

Operations Update

Securities Industry Association
120 Broadway, 35th Fl.   Ph: (212)608-1500
New York, NY 10271   Fax: (212)608-1604
E-mail: info@sia.com
Contact: Thomas J. Monahan, Editor.
Desc: Examines the operations of brokerage businesses. Re-
curring features include a calendar of events. *Type:* News-
letter.

Opinion Letters in Securities Matters

West Group
620 Opperman Dr.   Ph: (651)687-7000
St. Paul, MN 55164-0526
URL: http://www.westgroup.com
Desc: Contains the complete text of Opinion Letters In Securities Matters: Text - Clauses - Law by Arnold S. Jacobs,
covering the definition, purpose, and content of opinion
letters relating to securities matters. *Available:* West
Group, WESTLAW. *Type:* Database.

The Option Advisor

Schaeffer's Investment Research, Inc.
PO Box 46709   Ph: (513)589-3800
Cincinnati, OH 45246-9906   Free: 800-327-8833
                                      Fax: (513)589-3810
E-mail: info@optionadvisor.com.
URL: http://www.optionadvisor.com.
Contact: Bernard G. Schaeffer, Sr. Ed., fax: (800)967-
7461, bernie@sir-inc.com.
Desc: Makes "both aggressive and conservative recommendations on listed stock options" for the individual investor. Reports on news pertinent to the options market
including new options listings, tax tips, and "attractive
brokerage firms." Remarks: Subscription includes a telephone hotline service and approximately six special bulletins per year. *Type:* Newsletter.

The Option Strategist

McMillan Analysis Corporation
PO Box 1323   Ph: (973)328-1674
Morristown, NJ 07962-1323   Free: 800-724-1817
                                      Fax: (973)328-1303
E-mail: mac19@ix.netcom.com
URL: http://www.optionstrategist.com.
Contact: Lawrence G. McMillan, Editor.
Desc: Discusses options on stocks, indices, and futures. In-
cludes investment recommendations and educational arti-
cles. *Type:* Newsletter.

Options Trading Bulletin

Lombardi Publishing Co.
51 Toro Rd.   Ph: (416)633-1600
North York, ON, Canada M3J   Fax: (416)633-6188
2A4
Contact: Don Sutton, Editor.
Desc: Provides information and advice on U.S. options.
Type: Newsletter.

OTC Growth Stock Watch

Geoffrey J. Eiten
1040 Great Plain Ave.   Ph: (781)444-6100
Needham, MA 02192   Free: 888-268-2479
                                      Fax: (781)444-6101
E-mail: info@otcgsw.com
URL: http://www.otcgsw.com.
Contact: Geoffrey J. Eiten, Editor and Publisher.
Desc: Focuses on companies on NASDAQ in the $5 to
$100 million sales range. Contains news on past recom-
mendations and commentary on current market condi-
tions. *Type:* Newsletter.

OTC Insight

Insight Capital Management Inc.
2121 N. California Blvd., No.   Ph: (925)274-5037
560   Fax: (925)946-4054
Walnut Creek, CA 94596
E-mail: info@icrm.com
URL: http://www.investools.com/cgi-bin/server.pl/
newsletters/otcn.
Contact: James O. Collins, Editor.
Desc: Reports on financial investments concentrating on
over-the-counter growth stocks. Recurring features in-
clude statistics on 100 stocks, model portfolios, and col-
umns titled How to Start a Portfolio, New Buys,
Additions and Deletions to the Buy List, and Investment
Outlook and Strategy. *Type:* Newsletter.

Over Priced Stock Bulletin

Lombardi Publishing Co.
51 Toro Rd.   Ph: (416)633-1600
North York, ON, Canada M3J   Fax: (416)633-6188
2A4
Desc: Provides recommendations on short sales. Disseminates current information on a short-position portfolio of
four to five stocks. *Type:* Newsletter.

Overpriced Stock Service (OSS)

Murenove, Inc.
PO Box 308   Ph: (650)726-8495
Half Moon Bay, CA 94019   Fax: (650)726-8494
E-mail: subs@ctsl.com
Contact: Michael Murphy, Editor.
Desc: "Specializes in short selling based on fundamental
analysis. Focuses on overvalued, overhyped companies of
all sizes, often with deteriorating balance sheets, adverse
business environments, and earnings disappointments."
Recurring features include news of research. *Type:* News-
letter.

Patient Investor

Ariel Capital Management, Inc.
307 N. Michigan Ave., 5th Fl.   Ph: (312)726-0140
Chicago, IL 60601   Free: 800-725-0140
                                      Fax: (312)726-7473
Contact: John W. Rogers, Editor.
Desc: Abstracts several companies traded on the New York
Stock Exchange, AMEX, and/or OTC. *Type:* Newsletter.

The Pearson Investment Letter

Walter D. Pearson
1628 White Arrow Dr.   Ph: (813)659-2560
Dover, FL 33527
Contact: Walter D. Pearson, Publisher, pearsoncap@aol.
com; R. Scott Pearson, Editor.
Desc: Selects 8 or more low risk stocks per month and for
each provides background and company history, describes
the stock, and tries to project the growth potential. Recurring features include updates on previous recommendations and short notes on other subjects. *Type:* Newsletter.

Penny Mines

Lombardi Publishing Co.
51 Toro Rd.   Ph: (416)633-1600
North York, ON, Canada M3J   Fax: (416)633-6188
2A4
Desc: Provides recommendations on speculative penny
mine stocks listed on Canadian stock exchanges. *Type:*
Newsletter.

Penny Stocks Newsletter

Vello Kulbin
31731 Outer Hwy. 10
Redlands, CA 92373-8610
Contact: Vello Kulbin, Editor.

Desc: Focuses on low-priced stocks selling for less than one dollar per share. Lists penny stocks and "performs extensive research to locate, investigate and report on specific growth companies." Studies international as well as domestic trends affecting penny stocks. *Type:* Newsletter.

Pensions & Investments

Crain Communications Inc.
740 N. Rush St.   Ph: (312)649-5200
Chicago, IL 60611
URL: http://www.crain.com

Desc: Contains the complete text of Pensions & Investments, a biweekly newspaper providing news of corporate and institutional capital management. Covers corporate financing; capital markets; cash, portfolio, and pension fund management; real estate investing; and international investments. *Available:* LEXIS-NEXIS, NEXIS; Dow Jones Interactive Publishing; Bell & Howell Information and Learning; NewsEdge Corporation; Reuters Information Services Inc.; The Gale Group, InfoTrac Web; Profound Inc., The Dialog Corporation. *Type:* Database.

People to People International

501 E. Armour Blvd.   Ph: (816)531-4701
Kansas City, MO 64109   Fax: (816)561-7502
E-mail: ptpi@vaxl.umkc.edu

Desc: Professionals and university and secondary school students. Founded by President Dwight D. *Type:* Association.

The Personal Capitalist

The Personal Capitalist
6911 S. 66th East Ave., Ste. 101
Tulsa, OK 74133-1748
Contact: Sean Christian, Editor.

Desc: Serves as an education/information service for investing. Includes the newsletters World Update, Capitalist Commentary, Investment Strategies, and Portfolio Review. *Type:* Newsletter.

Peter Dag Portfolio Strategy and Management

Peter Dag & Associates, Inc.
65 Lake Front Dr.   Ph: (330)644-2782
Akron, OH 44319-3698   Free: 800-833-2782
                         Fax: (330)644-2798
URL: http://www.peterdag.com.
Contact: Dr. George Dagnino, Editor.

Desc: Provides forecasts on stock market trends, interest rates, bonds, gold, commodities, crude oil, inflation, the economy, the U.S. dollar, and foreign stock markets. *Type:* Newsletter.

Peter Eliades' Stockmarket Cycles

Peter Eliades
PO Box 6873   Ph: (707)579-8444
Santa Rosa, CA 95406-0873   Free: 800-888-4351
                         Fax: (707)579-0274
E-mail: info@stockmarketcycles.com; cycles@metro.net.
Contact: Peter Eliades, Editor.

Desc: Focuses on future trends in overall market through cycles and technical analysis. Gives daily entry and exit points on the stock index futures and occasional projections for bond futures, gold, T-bills, and silver. *Type:* Newsletter.

Platt's Metals Price Alert

McGraw-Hill, Inc.
2 Penn Plaza   Ph: (212)904-2000
New York, NY 10121   Free: 800-223-6180
                         Fax: (212)904-6068
E-mail: metals@platts.com.
URL: http://www.mcgraw-hill.com
Contact: Andy Blamey, Editor-in-Chief.

Desc: Faxes current metal news and price information from London and New York at the close of the exchanges. *Type:* Newsletter.

Power Markets Week

Energy and Business Newsletters
McGraw-Hill Companies   Ph: (212)904-6410
2 Penn Plaza, 5th Fl.   Free: 800-223-6180
New York, NY 10121   Fax: (212)904-2723
E-mail: ymiranda@mhenergy.com.
URL: http://www.mhenergy.com.
Contact: Karen Larsen, Editor-in-Chief.

Desc: Provides 17 daily price indexes from emerging locations in the Southeast and Midwest, new monthly indexes in industries that assist traders in managing risk and creating more liquidity at COB, Palo Verde, PJM, Cinergy, Entergy, and New England. Includes market commentary. *Type:* Newsletter.

The Primary Trend

Arnold Investment Counsel, Inc.
700 N. Water St.   Ph: (414)271-2726
Milwaukee, WI 53202
Contact: Barry Arnold, Editor; Lilli Gust, Editor.

Desc: Comments on general market conditions and makes recommendations to buy, sell, or hold specific stocks based on the investment philosophy of Arnold Investment Counsel. Recurring features include a listing of current recommendations. *Type:* Newsletter.

The Private Equity Analyst

Asset Alternatives, Inc.
170 Linden St., 2nd Fl.   Ph: (781)304-1400
Wellesley, MA 02482   Fax: (781)304-1440
E-mail: info@assetnews.com
URL: http://www.assetalt.com.
Contact: Steven P. Galante, Editor.

Desc: Purposes to be the "leading source of news and analysis of institutional participation in venture capital, management buyouts, and other types of alternative assets." Recurring features include a collection and columns titled The Fund Raisers Roundup and News Briefs. *Type:* Newsletter.

Professional Investor Report

Dow Jones & Company, Inc.
PO Box 300   Ph: (609)520-4000
Princeton, NJ 08543-0300
URL: http://www.dj.com

Desc: Contains information on news, trading alerts, and statistical reports on active stocks, plus coverage of overall market activity. Covers more than 5000 stocks traded on the New York Stock Exchange (NYSE), American Stock Exchange (AMEX), and National Market System (major companies) of the NASDAQ Over-the-Counter market. *Available:* Dow Jones & Company, Inc.; Track Data Corporation. *Type:* Database.

The Professional Tape Reader

RADCAP, Inc.
PO Box 2407   Free: 800-868-7857
Hollywood, FL 33022
Contact: Stan Weinstein, Editor.

Desc: Functions as a stock market advisory service. Offers forecasts for long- and short-term trends and the most promising and vulnerable stocks and groups. *Type:* Newsletter.

Professional Timing Service

Curtis J. Hesler
PO Box 7483   Ph: (406)543-4131
Missoula, MT 59807
Contact: Curtis J. Hesler, Editor.

Desc: Offers advice on market timing, including the buying and selling of individual stocks and gold, no-load fund switching, interest rate instruments, and index options. Recurring features include news of research and book reviews. *Type:* Newsletter.

Profitable Investing

Profitable Investing
7811 Montrose Rd.
Potomac, MD 20854
Contact: Richard E. Band, Editor.

Desc: Advises individuals seeking low-risk growth by providing "a wealth of information." Discusses various stocks, mutual funds, interest income, and tax issues. Contains lists of best investments. *Type:* Newsletter.

The Prudent Speculator

Al Frank Asset Management, Inc.
PO Box 1438   Ph: (714)497-7687
Laguna Beach, CA 92652   Free: 800-258-7786
Contact: Al Frank, Editor.

Desc: Presents a fundamental approach to stock selection and buying strategies for long-term capital gains appreciation. Provides technical analysis to aid market timing for both speculators and conservative investors. *Type:* Newsletter.

PSA NOW

PSA: The Bond Market Trade Association
40 Broad St.   Ph: (212)809-7000
New York, NY 10004   Fax: (212)742-1549
URL: http://www.psa.com/news.htm.
Contact: Caroline Benn, SVP Communications.

Desc: Reports current developments regarding all bond markets securities, including regulation, legislation, and market practices and operations. Recurring features include a calendar of events and reports of meetings. *Type:* Newsletter.

Recon For Investors (RFI)

Echo 4 Communications
2490 Black Rock Turnpike, Ste.   Ph: (203)368-1862
422
Fairfield, CT 06430-2404
URL: http://www.geocities.com/wallstrett/7744.
Contact: Robert K. Morgan, Editor, rkm-echo4@worldnet.att.net.

Desc: Provides updates on financial, investment, political and other "Recon" that has the potential to impact the financial markets and the economy. *Type:* Newsletter.

The Research Bulletin

Frederick Research Corporation
1441 Prospect Ave.   Ph: (908)753-4514
Plainfield, NJ 07060

Desc: Carries investment research data. Remarks: Available only online. *Type:* Newsletter.

Richard C. Young's Intelligence Report

Phillips Business Information, Inc.
1201 Seven Locks Rd., Ste. 300   Ph: (301)340-1520
Potomac, MD 20854   Free: 888-707-5809
                         Fax: (301)340-3847
E-mail: clientservices.pbi@phillips.com
Contact: Richard C. Young, Editor.

Desc: Provides information for "serious, conservative investors (buy and hold as opposed to active traders)." Features investing advice and recommendations for best funds, stocks, and bonds for current or retirement income. *Type:* Newsletter.

Richard Croft's Money Matters

Lombardi Publishing Co.
51 Toro Rd.   Ph: (416)633-1600
North York, ON, Canada M3J   Fax: (416)633-6188
2A4

Desc: Offers investment advice and specific stock, mutual fund, and bond recommendations for investors. Includes updated model portfolios. *Type:* Newsletter.

The Richland Report

Richland Report
PO Box 222   Ph: (619)459-2611
La Jolla, CA 92038   Fax: (619)459-2612
Contact: Kennedy Gammage, Editor.

Desc: Analyzes and interprets direction of overall market using McClellan Oscillator, Summation Index, and Nominal Market Cycles. Recommends stocks, mutual funds, mining issues, and short sales using fundamental and technical analysis. *Type:* Newsletter.

Risk Factor Method of Investing

Invest/O - Registered Investment Advisors
65575 Sisemore Rd.   Ph: (541)389-3676
PO Box 5996
Bend, OR 97708-5996
Contact: William John Kuhn, Editor.

Desc: Provides stock market advice, investment risk information, and financial planning perspectives. Contains sample portfolios and quotes from other investment advisors. *Type:* Newsletter.

Roman Reports

Roman Reports
12600 Rockside Rd., Ste. 107 Ph: (216)662-4593
Garfield Heights, OH 44125
Contact: Dave Roman.

Desc: Educates individuals on "get rich quick" scams and schemes. *Type:* Newsletter.

The Ron Warmoth Newsletter

R.W. Enterprises
PO Box 4037   Ph: (213)389-3483
Los Angeles, CA 90078   Fax: (213)389-6211
Contact: Ron Warmoth, Editor.

Desc: Provides "intuitive impressions on all aspects of personal prosperity" by psychic Ron Warmoth, who employs "intuition, hunches and remote viewing" to predict how world events will affect the stock market, gold prices, energy, interest rates, mineral and buried treasure exploration, real estate, and inflation. *Type:* Newsletter.

Ronald Sadoff's Major Trends

Ronald Sadoff
250 W. Coventry Ct.   Ph: (414)352-8460
Milwaukee, WI 53217-3961
Contact: Ronald Sadoff, Editor.

Desc: Provides stock and bond market summaries and trends, advice on when and how to invest for optimum growth and minimal risk. Interprets losses or gains in the stock market as resulting from the changes in four "environments": monetary, psychological, technical, and the economic/business cycle. *Type:* Newsletter.

Rosen Numismatic Advisory

Numismatic Counseling Inc.
PO Box 38   Ph: (516)433-5800
Plainview, NY 11803   Fax: (516)433-5801
Contact: Maurice Rosen, Editor.

Desc: In-depth analysis for rare coin investors. Comprehensive coverage of all active areas, key interviews and no-holes-barred examination of controversial subjects. *Type:* Newsletter.

RRSP Letter

Lombardi Publishing Co.
51 Toro Rd.   Ph: (416)633-1600
North York, ON, Canada M3J   Fax: (416)633-6188
2A4

Contact: Marisha Roman, Editor.

Desc: Offers advice on self-directed and standard RRSPs. Suggests portfolios for different age groups. *Type:* Newsletter.

The Ruff Times

Phoenix Ink
PO Box 887   Ph: (801)489-8681
Springville, UT 84663-0887   Free: 800-773-7833
                              Fax: (801)489-7877

E-mail: service@rufftimes.com.
URL: http://www.rufftimes.com.
Contact: Howard J. Ruff, Editor.

Desc: Provides current financial and investment information and advice. And offers conservative political, social, and economic opinions. *Type:* Newsletter.

The Ruta Financial Newsletter

Philip Ruta
PO Box 3056   Free: 800-832-1891
Stamford, CT 06905-0056

E-mail: ruta.financial@worldnet.att.net.
Contact: Philip R. Ruta, Editor.

Desc: Covers stock activities and provides recommendations. Features stock exchanges, energy market, and securities investment. *Type:* Newsletter.

SCIP Investment Survey

Frederick Research Corporation
1441 Prospect Ave.   Ph: (908)753-4514
Plainfield, NJ 07060

Desc: Provides short investment reports on public companies. Remarks: Available by fascimile only. *Type:* Newsletter.

SEC Today

Washington Service Bureau, Inc.
655 15th St. NW   Ph: (202)508-0600
Washington, DC 20005   Free: 800-955-5219
                              Fax: (202)508-0694

URL: http://www.wsb.com/sectoday; http://www.wsb.com.
Contact: Jackie Lumb, Editor, (202)508-0648, jacquelynlumb@notrs.lis.cch.com.

Desc: Reports on activities within the securities industry. Provides notices of Securities and Exchange Commission (SEC) meetings, administrative proceedings, investment companies, holding company, and corporation finance releases. *Type:* Newsletter.

Section 16 of the Securities Exchange Act

West Group
620 Opperman Dr.   Ph: (651)687-7000
St. Paul, MN 55164-0526
URL: http://www.westgroup.com

Desc: Provides the complete text of the treatise entitled Section 16 of the Securities Exchange Act by Arnold S. Jacobs. *Available:* West Group, WESTLAW. *Type:* Database.

Sector Fund Newsletter

Sector Funds Newsletter
PO Box 239   Ph: (619)748-0805
Poway, CA 92074-0239
Contact: Dr. Cato B. Ohrn, Editor.

Desc: Provides information and advice on stock market investing. *Type:* Newsletter.

Securities and Federal Corporate Law

West Group
620 Opperman Dr.   Ph: (651)687-7000
St. Paul, MN 55164-0526
URL: http://www.westgroup.com

Desc: Contains the complete text of the treatise entitled Securities and Federal Corporate Law by Harold S. Bloomenthal. *Available:* West Group, WESTLAW. *Type:* Database.

Securities Industry Trends

Securities Industry Association
120 Broadway, 35th Fl.   Ph: (212)608-1500
New York, NY 10271   Fax: (212)608-1604
E-mail: info@sia.com

Contact: George R. Monahan, Editor.

Desc: Examines economic developments affecting securities firms, including tax policy, the changing composition of the securities industry, and major trends in the industry. Supplies a series of security industry statistics tables covering areas such as trading volume, yields on a monthly average, end of month prices, underwriting, mutual funds, margin debt, and financial data for New York Stock Exchange firms doing a public business. *Type:* Newsletter.

Securities & Partnership Law for MLPs & Other Investment Limited Partnerships

West Group
620 Opperman Dr.   Ph: (651)687-7000
St. Paul, MN 55164-0526
URL: http://www.westgroup.com

Desc: Contains the complete text of Securities & Partnership Law for MLP's & Other Investment Limited Partnerships by Linda A. Wertheimer and John C. *Available:* West Group, WESTLAW. *Type:* Database.

Securities Pro

Securities Pro
PO Box 248   Ph: (212)534-7180
New York, NY 10029

Contact: Tony Chapelle, Editor and Publisher.

Desc: Reports on African-American firms and individuals involved in the investments industry. Covers hirings, firings, job promotions, new accounts, and trends. *Type:* Newsletter.

Securities Regulation & Law Report

Bureau of National Affairs, Inc. (BNA)
1231 25th St. NW   Ph: (202)452-4323
Washington, DC 20037   Free: 800-372-1033
                              Fax: (202)452-7773
E-mail: bnaplus@bna.com

Contact: Susan Raleigh Jenkins, Managing Editor.

Desc: Covers regulation of securities and commodities activity at federal and state levels. Includes developments from the courts, Congress, the Administration, Securities and Exchange Commission, Commodity Futures Trading Commission, banking regulations, Financial Accounting Standards Board, professional associations, and industry. *Type:* Newsletter.

Sentinel Investment Letter

Hanover Investment Management Corporation
853 2nd St. Pike, No. A-2
Richboro, PA 18954-1082

Desc: Provides an overview of stock market action and other issues of interest to investors. *Type:* Newsletter.

Small Cap Trader

Lombardi Publishing Co.
51 Toro Rd.   Ph: (416)633-1600
North York, ON, Canada M3J   Fax: (416)633-6188
2A4
Contact: George Leong, Editor.
Desc: Offers investment advice on stocks priced under $1.
00. Includes technical and fundamental analysis on companies, stock charts, and model portfolios. *Type:* Newsletter.

Smart Money Tracker

Lombardi Publishing Co.
51 Toro Rd.   Ph: (416)633-1600
North York, ON, Canada M3J   Fax: (416)633-6188
2A4
Contact: Marisha Roman, Editor.
Desc: Reports on the strategies of Canada's foremost portfolio managers. Includes detailed information on Canada's mutual fund managers and gives tips on how to become successful in the field. *Type:* Newsletter.

SMR Stock Service

SMR Inc.
PO Box 7476
Boulder, CO 80306-7476
E-mail: charts@smr.com
Contact: Jerry Hodges, Editor.
Desc: Functions as a charting service providing daily highs, lows, and closing marks as well as short- and long-term oscillators that indicate buy and sell signals on stocks and options. Also plots the NYSE (New York Stock Exchange), Institutional and S&P (Standard & Poor's Corp.) 100 stock indexes. *Type:* Newsletter.

SNL Financial Services Daily

SNL Securities
321 E. Main St.   Ph: (804)977-1600
PO Box 2124   Fax: (804)977-4466
Charlottesville, VA 22902
E-mail: subscriptions@snl.com
URL: http://www.snl.com.
Contact: Debra Davenport, Editor, fax: (804)984-8020, ddavenport@snl.com; John W. Milligan, Editor-in-Chief, jmilligan@snl.com.
Desc: Summarizes by email or fax daily news headlines on finance companies, mortgage banks, investment advisors, and brokers/dealers, plus dividend and earnings announcements, stock highlights and index values, registration statements, and ownership filings. *Type:* Newsletter.

Society of Depreciation Professionals Newsletter

Society of Depreciation Professionals
5505 Connecticut Ave., NW,   Ph: (202)362-0680
No. 280   Fax: (202)966-2283
Washington, DC 20015
Contact: Ronald Daniel, Editor.
Desc: Focuses on perspectives on the state of capital recovery and Society activity. Recurring features include interviews, a calendar of events, reports of meetings, news of members, and software developments. *Type:* Newsletter.

South Africa Investor

Investor Responsibility Research Center, Inc. (IRRC)
1350 Connecticut Ave., NW,   Ph: (202)833-0700
Ste. 700   Fax: (202)833-3555
Washington, DC 20036
E-mail: mktg@irrc.org.
URL: http://www.irrc.org
Contact: Meg Voorhes, Editor.
Desc: Reports on events and trends that will shape the future of South Africa and analyzes how these developments affect multinational corporations with investments in South Africa. *Type:* Newsletter.

Southern African Analysis & Advice

Southern African Analysis & Advice
PO Box 1587   Ph: (203)966-9645
New Canaan, CT 06840   Fax: (203)966-6350
Contact: Dr. Les de Villiers, Publisher, lesdv@aol.com.
Desc: Monitors investment related developments in and around South Africa. Offers comprehensive data and expert analysis, as well as specific advice on opportunities in this market. *Type:* Newsletter.

Special Investment Situations

George W. Southerland
PO Box 4254   Ph: (423)886-1628
Chattanooga, TN 37405-0254   Fax: (423)886-3537
E-mail: mrsis@aol.com.
Contact: George W. Southerland, Editor.
Desc: Provides stock market investment recommendations. Focuses on companies that "offer the prospect of a substantial capital gain in a relatively short time with comparatively small risk." Includes a description of the company, pertinent financial data, and factors influencing the recommendation. *Type:* Newsletter.

Special Situations Newsletter

Charles H. Kaplan
26 Broadway, Ste. 200   Ph: (201)418-4411
New York, NY 10004   Free: 800-756-1811
        Fax: (201)418-5085
Contact: Charles H. Kaplan, Editor and Publisher.
Desc: Analyzes undiscovered, small-cap, low-priced stocks with outstanding capital appreciation potential. Reports on good comapnies with strong fundamentals including earnings track record, strong balance sheet with little long-term debt, good financial record and no inside selling. *Type:* Newsletter.

Standard & Poor's Corporation Newsletter

Standard & Poor's
25 Broadway   Ph: (212)208-8000
New York, NY 10004-1064   Free: 800-221-5277
        Fax: (212)208-0040
URL: http://www.stockinfo.standardpoor.com; http://www.standardpoor.com/ratings.
Desc: Collects data from several publications and corporations which specialize in stocks and investments. *Type:* Newsletter.

Standard & Poor's Corporation—Outlook

Standard & Poor's
65 Broadway   Ph: (212)770-4300
New York, NY 10006   Free: 800-221-5277
        Fax: (212)770-0220
Contact: Arnold Kaufman, Editor.
Desc: Supplies investment advice, recommending specific stocks and reviewing past recommendations and carries company profiles. Recurring features include columns titled In the Limelight, 5-Star Stock of the Month, Stocks for Total Return, and Statistical Highlights. *Type:* Newsletter.

Standard & Poor's Dividend Record

Standard & Poor's
Dividend Record Department
25 Broadway, 19th Fl.   Ph: (212)208-8369
New York, NY 10004-1064
URL: http://www.standardandpoors.com/ratings
Contact: Robert Sterenson, Director, (212)208-1121, fax: (212)208-8284.
Desc: Contains dividend disbursement data for more than 12,000 stocks listed on the New York Stock Exchange (NYSE) and American Stock Exchange (AMEX), the NASDAQ market and the Toronto and Montreal stock exchanges. Also contains data on American Depository Receipts, mutual funds, closed-end investment companies, limited partnerships, and real-estate investment trusts. *Available:* Standard & Poor's. *Type:* Database.

Standard & Poor's Emerging & Special Situations

Standard & Poor's
25 Broadway   Ph: (212)208-8000
New York, NY 10004-1064   Free: 800-221-5277
        Fax: (212)208-0040
URL: http://www.stockinfo.standardpoor.com
Contact: Robert S. Natale, Editor.
Desc: Designed "to serve investors who seek maximum capital gains through equity investments in emerging growth companies, new issues and special situations." Provides model portfolios and investment screens recommendations on prospective new issues. *Type:* Newsletter.

Standard & Poor's Industry Surveys

Standard & Poor's
25 Broadway   Ph: (212)208-8000
New York, NY 10004-1064   Free: 800-221-5277
        Fax: (212)208-0040
URL: http://www.stockinfo.standardpoor.com; http://www.advisorinsight.com.
Contact: Eileen M. Bossong-Martines, Editor, (212)208-8506, fax: (212)412-0395, eileen_martines@mcgraw-hill.com.
Desc: Broad reviews of major U.S. industries, including current environment, background information, major issues, opportunities, and forecasting of major trends. *Type:* Newsletter.

Standard & Poor's Security Dealers of North America

Standard & Poor's
25 Broadway   Ph: (212)208-8000
New York, NY 10004-1064   Free: 800-221-5277
        Fax: (212)208-0040
URL: http://www.stockinfo.standardpoor.com
Contact: Thomas A. Lupo, Publisher.
Desc: Over 12,000 security dealers; includes over 300 offices outside North America. *Type:* Directory.

Standard & Poor's Stock Reports—New York Stock Exchange, American Stock Exchange, Nasdaq Stock Market and Regional Exchanges

Standard & Poor's
25 Broadway   Ph: (212)208-8000
New York, NY 10004-1064   Free: 800-221-5277
        Fax: (212)208-0040
URL: http://www.stockinfo.standardpoor.com; http://www.stockinfo.standardpoor.com.
Contact: John Schemitsch, Editor; Peter Wilson, Editor.
Desc: Over 4,600 companies whose securities are traded on the New York Stock Exchange, American Stock Exchange and Nasdaq Stock Market and Regional Exchanges. *Type:* Directory.

The Stanger Review

Robert A. Stanger & Co., Inc.
PO Box 7490   Ph: (732)389-3600
Shrewsbury, NJ 07702   Fax: (732)544-0779
Contact: Nancy Schabel Mahon, Editor-in-Chief.
Desc: Reports partnership sales and market information. *Type:* Newsletter.

The Staton Institute Advisory

The Staton Institute, Inc.
300 East Blvd., B-4   Ph: (704)332-7514
Charlotte, NC 28203-4784   Free: 800-779-7175
        Fax: (704)332-0427
URL: http://Investools.com.
Contact: Bill Staton, Editor.
Desc: Explains ways to make money, including how to become a maillionaire by buying a less expensive car and how to convert pocket change into a small fortune. *Type:* Newsletter.

Stock Guide

Standard & Poor's
25 Broadway
New York, NY 10004-1064

Ph: (212)208-8000
Free: 800-221-5277
Fax: (212)208-0040

URL: http://www.stockinfo.standardpoor.com
Contact: Frank LoVaglio, Editor; Shauna Morrison, Publisher.
Desc: Financial summary of over 7,000 issues. *Type:* Periodical.

Stock Market Strategy

Ned Davis Research, Inc.
600 Bird Bay Dr.
Venice, FL 34292

Ph: (941)484-6107
Free: 800-241-0621
Fax: (941)484-8693

Contact: Tim Hayes, Editor.
Desc: Advises on timing model readings and offers strategy for market timing. Covers technical analysis of the stock market and monetary conditions. *Type:* Newsletter.

The Stock Picture

M.C. Horsey & Company, Inc.
PO Box H
Salisbury, MD 21801-1130

Ph: (301)742-3700

Desc: Features over 1,900 stocks on the American and New York Stock Exchanges and charts their successes and setbacks over a ten-year period. *Type:* Newsletter.

The Strategic Investor

Bank of Montreal Investment Management Ltd.
302 Bay St., 10th Fl.
Toronto, ON, Canada M5X
1A1

Free: 800-665-7700

Desc: Offers timely and practical information for becoming a more strategic investor of First Canadian Mutual Funds. Discusses financial strategies, economic forecasts, and performance reviews. *Type:* Newsletter.

Structured Finance

Standard & Poor's
25 Broadway
New York, NY 10004-1064

Ph: (212)208-8000
Free: 800-221-5277
Fax: (212)208-0040

URL: http://www.stockinfo.standardpoor.com
Contact: Jennifer Lachanski, Managing Editor.
Desc: Provides news, analysis, and coverage of trends in the structured finance market. Recurring features include news of research, a calendar of events, and notices of publications available. *Type:* Newsletter.

Subscriber Bulletin

National Association of Securities Dealers, Inc.
1735 K St. NW
Washington, DC 20006

Ph: (202)728-6900
Fax: (202)728-8882

Desc: Covers developments in The Nasdaq Stock Market. Emphasizes new trading technologies, regulations, enhancements to Nasdaq services, and future developments. *Type:* Newsletter.

The Swiatek Report

Minerva-Swiatek
PO Box 218
Manhasset, NY 11030

Ph: (516)365-4120
Free: (516)365-4121

Contact: Anthony Swiatek, Editor.
Desc: Contains consumer-oriented information on how to avoid getting "shafted" when investing in coins and jewelry. Discusses various numismatic and coin topics, including current market status, opinion on what is "for real" and what is being "unjustly promoted," and how behind-the-scene activities affect the investor. *Type:* Newsletter.

Systems and Forecasts

Signalert Corporation
150 Great Neck Rd.
Great Neck, NY 11021

Ph: (516)829-6444

Contact: Gerald Appel, Editor.
Desc: Provides stock market advice regarding general timing in the stock, bond, and currency markets as well as specific recommendations regarding stocks, options, stock index futures, and mutual funds. Examines research into stock market timing methods and indicators and offers book and product reviews. *Type:* Newsletter.

T Theory Update

Laundry and Company, Inc.
3 Thurstons Ct.
Nantucket, MA 02554

Free: 888-228-2995

URL: http://www.ttheory.com.
Contact: Terrence Laundry, Editor, tlaundry@nantucket.net.
Desc: Provides management's strategy for long-term growth using fidelity mutual funds. Remarks: Available online only. *Type:* Newsletter.

Taipan

Agora, Inc.
1217 St. Paul St.
Baltimore, MD 21202-4702

Ph: (410)234-0515
Fax: (410)837-1999

URL: http://www.agoraworldwide.com.
Contact: Christoph Amberger, Editor.
Desc: Discusses business and investment with a "high-tech global approach." Recurring features include letters to the editor. *Type:* Newsletter.

Talking Gold with WIL-ARM

WIL-ARM Inc.
PO Box 730
Hudson, PQ, Canada J0P 1H0

Ph: (514)458-1540
Fax: (514)458-2114

E-mail: techtalk@wil-arm.com
Contact: Mervyn Burak, Editor.
Desc: Provides commentary, analysis, and recommendations (based on technical analysis techniques) on gold and 160 Canadian gold stocks. *Type:* Newsletter.

the Target 2000 and beyond Investor

Brattin Capital Management, Inc.
PO Box 8429
Bartlett, IL 60103-8429

Ph: (708)736-1094
Fax: (708)213-2274

Contact: Bruce A. Brattin, President.
Desc: Concentrates on emerging growth stocks and closed-end funds as a way to participate in emerging markets internationally. Provides information on investment research topics and market commentary, including a recommended model portfolio and a watch list of potential additions to the model portfolio. *Type:* Newsletter.

Tax Avoidance Letter

Lombardi Publishing Co.
51 Toro Rd.
North York, ON, Canada M3J
2A4

Ph: (416)633-1600
Fax: (416)633-6188

Contact: Marisha Roman, Editor.
Desc: Offers advice on tax minimization strategies for individuals. Includes updates on changing tax legislation, analysis of tax regulations and procedures, tax planning, and tax planned investments. *Type:* Newsletter.

Tax Management Real Estate Journal

Tax Management Inc.
Bureau of National Affairs, Inc.
1250 23rd St. NW
Washington, DC 20037

Ph: (202)833-7240
Free: 800-372-1033

URL: http://taxmanagement.bna.com.
Contact: Glenn B. Davis, Managing Editor.
Desc: Offers analyses of judicial, legislative, and administrative developments in the real estate tax area. Recurring features include columns titled Washington Items and Practitioners' Comments. *Type:* Newsletter.

Technical Analysis of Canadian Stocks

Lombardi Publishing Co.
51 Toro Rd.
North York, ON, Canada M3J
2A4

Ph: (416)633-1600
Fax: (416)633-6188

Contact: Roman Franko, Editor.
Desc: Provides educational tips on the science of technical analysis of stocks. Recurring features include a column on Hot Stocks and market and sector reviews. *Type:* Newsletter.

Technical Trends

John R. McGinley
PO Box 792
Wilton, CT 06897

Ph: (203)762-0229
Free: 800-736-0229
Fax: (203)761-1504

E-mail: jmcgoo@juno.com.
URL: http://capecod.net/techtrends.
Contact: John R. McGinley, Editor.
Desc: Provides charts and data on "the most accurate, publicly available stock market indicators," based on frequent testing. Includes commentary on indicators and on the market in general. *Type:* Newsletter.

Timer Digest

James H. Schmidt
PO Box 1688
Greenwich, CT 06836

Ph: (203)629-3503
Free: 800-356-2527
Fax: (203)629-2175

Contact: James H. Schmidt, Editor.
Desc: Compiles and ranks the performance of intermediate and long-term stock market, gold, and bond timing signals by monitoring advisory services. Includes articles on mutual fund switch programs, fidelity sector funds, Dow Jones Industrials, and profiles of investment advisors of 80 services. *Type:* Newsletter.

Today's Options

Techno-Fundamental Investments, Inc.
PO Box 14111
Scottsdale, AZ 85267

Ph: (602)996-2908

Contact: Bob Jubb, Editor.
Desc: Contains information on and recommendations for stock options investment. *Type:* Newsletter.

Tomorrow's Stocks

Techno-Fundamental Investments, Inc.
PO Box 14111
Scottsdale, AZ 85267

Ph: (602)996-2908

Contact: Bob Jubb, Editor.
Desc: Contains information and recommendations on stock market investing. *Type:* Newsletter.

Trade Like a Bookie

Opportunities in Options
300 Esplanade Dr., No. 200
Oxnard, CA 93030

Ph: (805)278-4350
Free: 800-456-9699
Fax: (805)278-4364

E-mail: oio@mail.westnet
URL: http://www.oio.com.
Contact: David L. Caplan, Editor.
Desc: Provides information about commodities and stock options. *Type:* Newsletter.

Tradeline

IID Information Services, Inc. (IDDIS)
Harborside Financial Center   Ph: (201)938-5900
600 Plaza II, 5th Fl.
Jersey City, NJ 07311
E-mail: sales@iddis.com
URL: http://www.idd.net

Contact: Josefina Voyantzis, Sales and Marketing Coordinator, (201)938-5876, jvoyantzis@iddis.com.

Desc: Contains historical and current securities market data for more than 150,000 issues traded on the major North American exchanges. Covers corporate stocks, bonds, options, warrants, units (i.e., two or more securities sold as a package), mutual funds, indexes (bond yields, exchange rates, market advances), government securities (Federal National Mortgage Association securities), and government agency issues (Federal Intermediate Credit Banks bonds). *Available:* National Computer Network Corporation (NCN); IDD Enterprises LP, IDD Plus; IDD Enterprises LP, IDD Plus; LEXIS-NEXIS. *Type:* Database.

Tradeline International

IID Information Services, Inc. (IDDIS)
Harborside Financial Center   Ph: (201)938-5900
600 Plaza II, 5th Fl.
Jersey City, NJ 07311
E-mail: sales@iddis.com
URL: http://www.idd.net

Contact: Lori Miller, Product Manager, (201)938-5876, sales@iddis.com.

Desc: Contains current and historical securities market data for more than 70,000 issues traded on about 117 exchanges in 59 countries outside of North America. Includes average daily, weekly, monthly, quarterly, and yearly prices, historical dividends, capital changes, and more than 900 international stock market indexes. *Available:* The Dialog Corporation, DIALOG; Dow Jones & Company, Inc.; IDD Enterprises LP, IDD Plus. *Type:* Database.

Trade*Plus

E Trade Group
4 Embarcadero Pl.   Ph: (415)842-2500
2400 Geng Rd.
Palo Alto, CA 94303
E-mail: service@etrade.com
URL: http://www.etrade.com

Contact: Tom Tisch, Vice President of Marketing.

Desc: Contains current and historical price information for securities traded on the New York and American Stock Exchanges, as well as NASDAQ National Market System and over-the-counter stocks. Also includes prices for options traded on the Chicago Board of Exchange and the American, Philadelphia, and Pacific Exchanges. *Available:* CompuServe Information Service; The Dialog Corporation, DIALOG; America Online, Inc.; Trade*Plus, Inc. *Type:* Database.

The Traveling Investor

The Traveling Investor Inc.
3998 NW 7th Pl.   Ph: (954)421-6264
Deerfield Beach, FL 33442

Contact: Larry Unterbrink, Editor; Mary Unterbrink, Editor.

Desc: Covers issues pertaining to international investment and travel. Recurring features include interviews, book reviews, and columns titled Stock of the Month, Model Portfolios, and Performance Records. *Type:* Newsletter.

Trendvest Ratings

Trendvest Corporation
1168 First Colonial Rd., Ste. 12   Ph: (757)412-4301
Virginia Beach, VA 23454-2419   Fax: (757)412-4302
E-mail: editor@trendvest.com.
URL: http://www.trendvest.com.

Contact: Larry T. Christy, Editor.

Desc: Provides a single numerical rating to summarize the relative attractiveness of investment possibilities. *Type:* Newsletter.

Turning Points

Concept Publishing
PO Box 500   Ph: (716)243-3148
York, NY 14592-0500   Fax: (716)243-3148

Contact: David Coleman, Editor.

Desc: Reports on and assesses the conditions of the stock and bond market for buying and/or selling. Makes long and short term forecasts, and offers financial and tax planning advice. *Type:* Newsletter.

21st Century Investments

21st Century Publishers
1320 Curt Gowdy Dr.   Ph: (307)635-5511
Cheyenne, WY 82009

Contact: Richard J. Maturi, Editor.

Desc: Covers investments poised to do well in the next century and beyond. Includes analysis updates of investment candidates covered in The 105 Best Investments for the 21st Century. *Type:* Newsletter.

UNISTOX

United Press International (UPI)
1510 H St. NW   Ph: (202)898-8000
Washington, DC 20005
URL: http://www.upi.com

Desc: Contains current and historical information on stock market and commodity market prices. Provides opening prices, closing prices, annual price ranges, most active, and odd lots as well as specialized reports. *Available:* BT North America, Inc. *Type:* Database.

United and Babson Investment Report

Babson-United Investment Advisors, Inc.
101 Prescott St.   Ph: (617)235-0900
Wellesley Hills, MA 02181   Fax: (617)235-8834

Contact: Donald Fox, Editor.

Desc: Provides "a concise summary of business and investment developments, including Washington news, commodity price trends, industry surveys, the outlook for the stock market, and specific buy-hold-sell advice on stocks and bonds for growth, income, and profit." Registered with SEC. *Type:* Newsletter.

The Value Line Convertibles Survey

Value Line, Inc.
220 E. 42nd St.   Ph: (212)907-1500
New York, NY 10017   Free: 800-634-3583
    Fax: (212)907-1911
E-mail: vlconv@valueline.com.

Contact: George Graham, Contact, (212)907-1595, ggraham@valueline.com.

Desc: Shows the investor how to build and maintain a convertible portfolio, how to decide upon the appropriate amount of risk, and how to select issues that fall within those risk limitations. Concerned with convertible debentures, convertible preferred stocks, and warrants. *Type:* Newsletter.

The Value Line Investment Survey

Value Line, Inc.
220 E. 42nd St.   Ph: (212)907-1500
New York, NY 10017   Free: 800-634-3583
    Fax: (212)907-1911
URL: http://www.valueline.com.

Contact: J. Bernhard, Editor.

Desc: Presents "specific investment advice, including year-ahead and 3- to 5-year performance evaluations, projections of key financial measures, and concise, objective commentary on current operations and future prospects" for 1,700 stocks. Also offers analysis of the economy and stock market overall. *Type:* Newsletter.

The Value Line Options Survey

Value Line, Inc.
220 E. 42nd St.   Ph: (212)907-1500
New York, NY 10017   Free: 800-634-3583
    Fax: (212)907-1911

Contact: Richard Cunniffe, Editor.

Desc: Designed to show the investor how to build and maintain an option portfolio, how to decide on the appropriate amount of risk, and how to select issues that fall within those risk limitations. Provides weekly evaluations of over 8,000 options, investment strategies, and market news. *Type:* Newsletter.

Vello Kulbin's Investments Newsletter

Vello Kulbin
31731 Outer Hwy. 10
Redlands, CA 92373-8610

Contact: Vello Kulbin, Editor.

Desc: Contains information on investments other than stocks. *Type:* Newsletter.

Venture Capital Journal

Venture Economics, Inc.
40 W. 57th St., 11th Fl.   Ph: (212)765-5311
New York, NY 10019   Free: 800-455-5844
    Fax: (212)765-6123

Contact: Kathleen Devlin, Editor-in-Chief.

Desc: Hard news, analysis and data on the North American private equity market. *Type:* Newsletter.

Venture Capital and Small Business Financings

West Group
620 Opperman Dr.   Ph: (651)687-7000
St. Paul, MN 55164-0526
URL: http://www.westgroup.com

Desc: Contains the complete text of the treatise entitled Venture Capital and Small Business Financings by Robert J. Haft. *Available:* West Group, WESTLAW. *Type:* Database.

Vickers Weekly Insider Report

Vickers Stock Research Corp.
226 New York Ave.   Ph: (516)423-7710
Huntington, NY 11743   Free: 800-645-5043
    Fax: (516)423-7715
E-mail: vickers2@ix.com; smokesigel@aol.com.

Contact: Richard Chneo, Editor.

Desc: Reports on stock insider transactions and maintains portfolios based on insider buy signals-96 up 68%. *Type:* Newsletter.

The Volume Reversal Survey

Almarco LLC
PO Box 1451   Ph: (520)282-1275
Sedona, AZ 86339   Fax: (520)282-6364
URL: http://www.vrsurvey.com.

Contact: Mark Leibovit, Editor, leibovit@vrsurvey.com.

Desc: Predicts sudden shifts among buyers and sellers by utilizing the editors's approach to cyclicol and volume analysis as applied to stocks, and financial markets. *Type:* Newsletter.

VSE Review

Vancouver Stock Exchange (VSE)
Stock Exchange Tower   Ph: (604)689-3334
609 Granville St.   Fax: (604)688-6051
PO Box 10333
Vancouver, BC, Canada V7Y
   1H1
E-mail: information@vse.ca; subscriptions@vse.ca.
URL: http://www.vse.ca/billing/publicationlist.asp.
Contact: Wade Murray, Editor, (604)643-6592, wmurray@vse.ca.
Desc: Provides "a complete and official summary on the month's transactions on equities and options; pertinent cumulative figures; recaps details of listing changes, options, and financing transactions by listed companies." *Type:* Newsletter.

The Wall Street Digest

Donald H. Rowe
1 Sarasota Tower, No. 602   Ph: (941)954-5500
2 N. Tamiami Trail   Free: 800-785-5050
Sarasota, FL 34236   Fax: (941)364-8447
Contact: Donald H. Rowe, Editor.
Desc: Covers major investment areas, including stocks and bonds; foreign currencies; gold, silver, and other precious metals; real estate; tax shelters; and estate planning. Recurring features include "a digest of the month's best" investment and financial seminars, newsletter reviews, and statistics. *Type:* Newsletter.

Wall Street Letter

Institutional Investor, Inc.
488 Madison Ave.   Ph: (212)224-3300
New York, NY 10022   Free: 800-543-4444
                            Fax: (212)224-3490
URL: http://www.news.com.
Contact: Justin Schack, Managing Editor.
Desc: Features breaking news, industry trends, and personnel changes of interest to the financial world's leading players. *Type:* Newsletter.

Wall Street S.O.S. Options Alert

Security Objective Services
17175 N. Lake Dr.
Bay Minette, AL 36507
Desc: Covers index options trading, including specific recommendations and trading strategy for the four most popular options. *Type:* Newsletter.

Wall Streetwise

Wilson Enterprise, Inc.
PO Box 12451   Ph: (919)419-1318
Durham, NC 27709-2451   Free: 800-419-1318
                           Fax: (919)544-0234
E-mail: wswstaff@wall-streetwise.com; wstreetw@aol.com.
URL: http://www.wall-streetwise.com.
Contact: Chris Wilson, Editor, fax: (919)493-9870, cwilson@wall-streetwise.com.
Desc: Publishes financial information and provides stock market investment recommendations. Remarks: Available online only. *Type:* Newsletter.

Water Investment Newsletter

U.S. Water News, Inc.
230 Main St.   Ph: (316)835-2222
Halstead, KS 67056-9983   Free: 800-251-0046
                           Fax: (316)835-2223
Contact: Mary DeSena, Editor.
Desc: Analyzes and profiles water stocks and investments. *Type:* Newsletter.

Western Pacific Stock Exchange Guide

CCH Inc.
2700 Lake Cook Rd.   Ph: (847)267-7000
Riverwoods, IL 60015   Free: 800-449-8114
                           Fax: (847)224-8299
URL: http://www.cch.com
Desc: Concentrates on procedures, business regulations, and listing requirements of the principal stock exchanges in the Oceania region. *Type:* Newsletter.

WESTLAW® Securities and Blue Sky Law

West Group
620 Opperman Dr.   Ph: (651)687-7000
St. Paul, MN 55164-0526
URL: http://www.westgroup.com
Desc: Contains the complete text of U.S. federal and state court decisions, statutes and regulations, administrative law publications, specialized files, and texts and periodicals dealing with securities and blue sky law. *Available:* West Group, WESTLAW. *Type:* Database.

Whisper on Wall Street

George Brooks
221 West Ave.   Ph: (203)656-0261
Darien, CT 06820
Contact: George Brooks, Editor.
Desc: Covers investments on all exchanges as well as emerging companies, promising speculations, and special situations. *Type:* Newsletter.

Wiesenberger Mutual Funds Update

Wiesenberger
1455 Research Blvd.   Ph: (301)545-4000
Rockville, MD 20851   Free: 800-232-2285
                           Fax: (301)545-6400
E-mail: wies@cda.com
Contact: Stephanie Kendall, Editor.
Desc: Lists performance, risk statistics, portfolio composition, and dividend information on more than 9,800 mutual funds. Funds are listed by investment objective categories. *Type:* Newsletter.

Wireless Cable Investor

Paul Kagan Associates, Inc.
126 Clock Tower Pl.   Ph: (831)624-1536
Carmel, CA 93923   Fax: (831)625-3225
E-mail: info@kagan.com
Desc: "The original bible of the wireless cable, multipoint distribution pay TV industry." Provides an overview of the cable competition. *Type:* Newsletter.

Women's Investment Newsletter

Phoenix Communications Group, Ltd.
1837 S. Nevada Ave.   Ph: (719)576-9200
Colorado Springs, CO 80906
Contact: Suzanne Fortune, Editor.
Desc: Presents in-depth analysis and trading strategies concerning common stocks, options, mutual funds, income/fixed securities, and tax-advantaged investments. Also considers such topics as tax planning and life insurance as they apply to investments. *Type:* Newsletter.

World Money Analyst

Newstar Orient Ltd.
824 E. Baltimore St.   Fax: (410)837-3879
Baltimore, MD 21202
Contact: Stephen Sjuggerud, Editor.
Desc: Advises the "sophisticated international investor." Covers stocks and currencies. Recurring features include columns titled Currency Trends, Interest Rate Trends, and Market Trends. *Type:* Newsletter.

World Neighbors

4127 NW 122 St.   Ph: (405)752-9700
Oklahoma City, OK 73120-   Free: 800-242-6387
   9933   Fax: (405)752-9393
E-mail: info@wn.org
URL: http://www.wn.org
Contact: Ron Burkard, Exec.Dir.
Desc: Seeks to eliminate hunger, disease, and poverty in Asia, Africa, and Latin America. Helps people to analyze and solve their own problems by developing and testing simple technologies at the community level and training local leaders to spread successful methods. Programs focus on food production, community-based health, family planning, water and sanitation, environmental conservation, and small business. *Type:* Association.

Wright Bankers' Service

Wright Investors' Service
1000 Lafayette Blvd.   Ph: (203)330-5000
Bridgeport, CT 06604   Fax: (203)330-5001
Contact: Michael Flament, Editor.
Desc: Carries economic and stock market analyses and forecasts. Provides specific recommendations for investment, and updates previous recommendations. *Type:* Newsletter.

The Yamamoto Forecast

The Yamamoto Forecast
PO Box 573   Ph: (808)877-2690
Kahului, HI 96733
Contact: Irwin T. Yamamoto, Editor.
Desc: Analyzes and reports on undervalued stocks, selling at bargain prices and ready to emerge market timing and economy. *Type:* Newsletter.

Zacks Earnings Estimates

Zacks Investment Research, Inc.
155 N. Wacker Dr.   Ph: (312)630-9880
Chicago, IL 60606
URL: http://www.zacks.com
Desc: Contains reports on projected earnings for approximately 6000 major U.S. corporations based on a consensus of financial analysts. *Available:* ADP Network Services, Inc.; Bridge Information Systems, Inc., Knight-Ridder Financial Information Group; Dow Jones Interactive Publishing; LEXIS-NEXIS, LEXIS; Quotron Systems, Inc.; Track Data Corporation; Zacks Investment Research, Inc.; The DAIS Group, Inc.; The Dialog Corporation, DIALOG; Knowledge Express Data Systems, Knowledge Express. *Type:* Database.

Israel

America-Israel Cultural Foundation

51 E. 42nd St., Ste. 400   Ph: (212)557-1600
New York, NY 10017   Fax: (212)557-1611
URL: http://www.aicf.webnet.org
Contact: Kathleen Mellon, Exec.Dir.
Desc: Encourages, promotes, and sustains cultural excellence in Israel. *Type:* Association.

America Israel Friendship League

134 E. 39th St.   Ph: (212)213-8630
New York, NY 10016   Fax: (212)683-3475
URL: http://www.usa50israel.org
Contact: Ms. Ilana Artman, Exec.VP.
Desc: Seeks to maintain and strengthen the mutually supportive relationship between people of the United States and Israel. Seeks to promote the friendship between the two democracies. *Type:* Association.

Americans for Peace Now

1835 K St., NW, Ste. 500 Ph: (202)728-1893
Washington, DC 20006 Fax: (202)728-1895
E-mail: apndc@peacenow.org
URL: http://www.peacenow.org
Contact: Debra DeLee, Pres.

Desc: A support group of American Jews representing the Peace Now movement in Israel. (Peace Now, also known as Shalom Achshav, is an Israeli peace movement that supports a negotiated peace settlement between the Israeli government and Palestinian leaders based on exchanging territories for peace and security.) Purposes are to help familiarize American Jews with Peace Now, its history and goals, and its impact on the peace struggle in Israel. Promotes solidarity with Israel. *Type:* Association.

Friends of the IDF

21 W. 38th St., 5th Fl. Ph: (212)575-5030
New York, NY 10018 Fax: (212)575-7815
E-mail: fitf@fitf.org
Contact: Marvin Josephson, Chrm.

Desc: Fundraising organization which provides for the social, educational, and recreational needs of the the soldiers of the Israel Defense Forces by providing educational centers, rest camps, clubs, gyms, gift packages, and other items. Works with the Association for the Well-Being of Israels Soldiers. *Type:* Association.

Israel Humanitarian Foundation

276 5th Ave., Ste. 901 Ph: 800-443-5699
New York, NY 10001 Fax: (212)213-9233
E-mail: info@ihf.net
Contact: Stanley J. Abrams, Exec.VP.

Desc: Provides assistance and support for medical, vocational, educational, and social service institutions in Israel and fosters and supports philanthropy and educational activities in the United States and Israel. *Type:* Association.

National Christian Leadership Conference for Israel

43422 W. Oaks Dr., No. 300 Ph: (248)557-4540
Novi, MI 48377 Fax: (248)557-4527
E-mail: nclci@msn.com
URL: http://www.nclci.org
Contact: David Blewett, Exec.Dir.

Desc: Christian clergy and laity with a concern in reaffirming American Christian support for "the people, land, and State of Israel." Efforts are aimed toward helping coordinate, unify, and support the activities of many local and regional Christian groups in the U.S. working on behalf of Israel. Acts as clearinghouse for American Christian organizations advocating support to Israel through their educational programs. *Type:* Association.

New Israel Fund

1625 K St. NW, Ste. 500 Ph: (202)223-3333
Washington, DC 20006 Fax: (202)659-2789
E-mail: info@nif.org
URL: http://www.nif.org
Contact: Norman S. Rosenberg, Exec.Dir.

Desc: International philanthropic partnership of North Americans, Israelis, and Europeans which supports activities in Israel that defend civil and human rights, promote Jewish-Arab equality and coexistence, advance the status of women, nurture tolerance and religious pluralism, reduce social and economic gaps, pursue enviromental justice and promote government accountability. *Type:* Association.

United Israel Appeal

111 8th Ave. Ph: (212)339-6900
New York, NY 10011-5201 Fax: (212)754-4293
Contact: Rabbi Daniel Allen, Acting Chr.

Desc: Allocates funds for Israel's immigration and resettlement program. *Type:* Association.

United Israel World Union

1123 Broadway, Ste. 723 Ph: (212)688-7557
New York, NY 10010 Fax: (212)688-7557
Contact: David Horowitz, Pres.

Desc: Individuals from all faiths in 12 countries who have accepted Mosaism as the one workable code which can bring peace to mankind. Encourage study and education of Mosaic law with the aim of finding a common religious denominator based on the Hebrew Bible that will satisfy all people. Motto is "one God, one Law, for all humanity." Sponsors biblical research and archaeology. *Type:* Association.

Italy/Italian

Italian Catholic Federation Central Council

675 Hegenberger Rd., No. 110 Ph: 888-423-1924
Oakland, CA 94621 Fax: (510)633-9758
URL: http://www.home.earthlink.net/~icf1924/
Contact: Thomas E. Sarnicola, Exec.Dir.

Desc: Catholics of Italian birth or descent. Conducts religious, patriotic, social, cultural, and charitable activities. *Type:* Association.

National Italian American Foundation

1860 19 St., NW Ph: (202)387-0600
Washington, DC 20009 Free: 800-989-NIAF
  Fax: (202)387-0800
E-mail: info@niaf.org
URL: http://www.niaf.org
Contact: Alfred M. Rotondaro, Exec.Dir.

Desc: U.S. citizens of Italian ancestry. *Type:* Association.

Order Sons of Italy in America

219 E St. NE Ph: (202)547-2900
Washington, DC 20002 Fax: (202)546-8168
Contact: Philip R. Piccigallo, Ph.D., Exec.Dir.

Desc: Fraternal society for American men and women of Italian descent. Works to keep alive the rich cultural heritage of Italy and the Italian people; has helped to enrich the diversified culture through educational, charitable, social, civic, and philanthropic activities; founded the Commission for Social Justice, the anti-defamation arm of the Italian-American movement, and the Tax-Exempt Sons of Italy Foundation. *Type:* Association.

Japan/Japanese

COSMOS 1

Teikoku Databank America, Inc.
747 Third Ave., 25th Fl. Ph: (212)421-9805
New York, NY 10017
E-mail: koshi@teikoku.com
URL: http://www.teikoku.com/

Desc: Contains financial data on approximately 350,000 small- and medium-sized Japanese firms. Covers balance statements, sales, profits and losses, and dividends and capital investment for the most recent 4 years. *Available:* G-Search Ltd.; Knight-Ridder, Inc.; LEXIS-NEXIS; Profound Inc., The Dialog Corporation; Thomson Financial Securities Data (TFSD). *Type:* Database.

COSMOS 2

Teikoku Databank America, Inc.
747 Third Ave., 25th Fl. Ph: (212)421-9805
New York, NY 10017
E-mail: koshi@teikoku.com
URL: http://www.teikoku.com/
Contact: Koshi Komatsuzaki, Manager.

Desc: Contains financial and descriptive data on more than 1,100,000 Japanese companies (English version, 230,000 companies). For each company, provides name, address, telephone number, industrial classification, principal activities, number of employees, capital, credit rating, and sales, profits, dividends, and corporate income for the most recent 2 years. *Available:* Teikoku Databank, Ltd., COSMOSNET; Profound Inc., The Dialog Corporation; LEXIS-NEXIS; Thomson Financial Securities Data (TFSD); The Dialog Corporation, DIALOG; The Dialog Corporation, DataStar; Nikkei Telecom; Infocheck. *Type:* Database.

Gochiso-Sama!

Gochiso-Sama!
631 Watersedge Dr. Fax: (313)662-4212
Ann Arbor, MI 48105
Contact: Lucy Seligman, Editor.

Desc: Reviews Japan restaurants, food, original recipes, and cookbooks through articles. *Type:* Newsletter.

Jane's Defence Weekly

Jane's Information Group
1340 Braddock Pl., Ste. 300 Ph: (703)683-3700
Alexandria, VA 22314-1657
E-mail: info@janes.com
URL: http://www.janes.com
Contact: Rahul Belani, (703)683-3700, fax: (800)836-0297, info@janes.com.

Desc: Contains the complete text of Jane's Defence Weekly, a weekly magazine covering defense industries worldwide. Includes military developments, personnel changes, business news, and information on equipment, intelligence, and contracts. *Available:* Bell & Howell Information and Learning; The Dialog Corporation, DIALOG; Dow Jones Interactive Publishing; NewsEdge Corporation; LEXIS-NEXIS; Reuters Ltd.; Profound Inc., The Dialog Corporation; Jane's Information Group. *Type:* Database.

Japan Economic Newswire Plus

Kyodo News International, Inc.
50 Rockefeller Plaza, Rm. 803 Ph: (212)397-3723
New York, NY 10020
URL: http://www.kyodonews.com

Desc: Contains the complete text of more than 283,000 English-language news items reported by the Kyodo News Service of Tokyo, Japan. Provides coverage of economic, political, trade, and social news in Japan and the Pacific Rim countries. *Available:* The Dialog Corporation, DIALOG; LEXIS-NEXIS, NEXIS; Dow Jones Interactive Publishing; The Gale Group, InfoTrac Web. *Type:* Database.

Japan National Tourist Organization

1 Rockefeller Plz., Ste. 1250 Ph: (212)757-5640
New York, NY 10020 Fax: (212)307-6754
Contact: Mr. Naohiko Sasaki, Dir.

Desc: Instrument of the Japanese government to promote Japan's tourist industry through overseas publicity, information services, and other related activities. Prepares videos and publicity materials; provides technical assistance to the tourist industry of Japan; conducts market surveys and participates in overseas fairs and exhibitions. Maintains tourist information centers in Tokyo and Kyoto, Japan to aid foreign tourists. *Type:* Association.

Japan Policy & Politics

Kyodo News International, Inc.
50 Rockefeller Plaza, Rm. 803 Ph: (212)397-3723
New York, NY 10020
URL: http://www.kyodonews.com

Desc: Contains the complete text of Japan Policy and Politics, a newsletter covering Japanese policy and politics affecting domestic and international affairs. Covers activities and statements of the prime minister, the Diet, ministries, and political parties. *Type:* Database.

Japan Science Scan

Kyodo News International, Inc.
50 Rockefeller Plaza, Rm. 803   Ph: (212)397-3723
New York, NY 10020
URL: http://www.kyodonews.com

Desc: Contains the complete text of Japan Science Scan, a weekly newsletter on current Japanese scientific research, environmental policy, medical news, and health-related articles. *Type:* Database.

Japan Society

333 E. 47th St.   Ph: (212)832-1155
New York, NY 10017   Fax: (212)755-6752
E-mail: gen@jpnsoc.com
URL: http://www.jpnsoc.com
Contact: William Clark, Jr., Pres.

Desc: Individuals, institutions, and corporations representing the business, professional, and academic worlds in Japan and the United States. Promotes the exchange of ideas between Americans and Japanese in order to enhance their mutual understanding. Organizes exchange programs and offers courses in Japanese and English. *Type:* Association.

Japan Transportation Scan

Kyodo News International, Inc.
50 Rockefeller Plaza, Rm. 803   Ph: (212)397-3723
New York, NY 10020
URL: http://www.kyodonews.com

Desc: Contains the complete text of Japan Transportation Scan, a weekly newsletter on the Japanese automotive industry. Covers company news and financial performances, manufacturing, shipments, marketing, and licensing. *Type:* Database.

Japanese American Citizens League

1765 Sutter St.   Ph: (415)921-5225
San Francisco, CA 94115   Fax: (415)931-4671
E-mail: jacl@jacl.org
Contact: Herbert Yamanishi, Nat.Dir.

Desc: Educational, civil, and human rights organization. Works to defend the civil and human rights of all peoples, particularly Japanese Americans. Seeks to preserve the cultural and ethnic heritage of Japanese Americans. *Type:* Association.

Japanese-American Yellow Pages

Abcotek Technologies Companies, Inc.
15123 34th Ave.   Ph: (212)751-6000
Flushing, NY 11354   Fax: (718)358-3298
Contact: Marcello Valenzano, President.

Desc: Approximately 6,000 Japanese-owned and other companies, associations, and societies that serve the Japanese community and Japanese tourists and business visitors in the metropolitan New York, New Jersey, and Connecticut areas. *Type:* Directory.

Japanese Investment in the Midwest

Japan America Society of Greater Cincinnati
Greater Cincinnati Chamber of Commerce
300 Carew Tower   Ph: (513)579-3114
441 Vine St.   Fax: (513)579-3102
Cincinnati, OH 45202

Desc: More than 400 Japanese manufacturing companies in Illinois, Indiana, Kentucky, Michigan, Ohio, and Tennessee. *Type:* Directory.

Teikoku Japanese Companies

Teikoku Databank America, Inc.
747 Third Ave., 25th Fl.   Ph: (212)421-9805
New York, NY 10017
E-mail: koshi@teikoku.com
URL: http://www.teikoku.com/

Contact: Tamatsu Inami.

Desc: Contains descriptive and financial data on more than 186,000 Japanese companies that conduct business overseas and have official English company names. For each company, provides name, address, telephone number, Teikoku Databank Standard Industrial Classification (TIC) codes, incorporation date, number of employees, sales, profits, dividends, major trading banks, credit rating, and names of executive officers. *Available:* The Dialog Corporation, DIALOG; The Dialog Corporation, DIALOG; Nikkei Telecom; The Dialog Corporation, DataStar; G-Search Ltd.; LEXIS-NEXIS, NEXIS. *Type:* Database.

Jewelry

American Gem Society

8881 W. Sahara   Ph: (702)255-6500
Las Vegas, NV 89117   Fax: (702)255-7420
E-mail: agsbennet@aol.com
URL: http://www.ags.org
Contact: Ruth Bennet, Interim Exec.Dir.

Desc: Representatives from 1500 retail jewelry firms in North America dedicated to proven ethics, knowledge and consumer protection. Encourages members to pursue studies in gemology; confers titles of Registered Jeweler, Registered Supplier, Certified Gemologist, and Certified Gemologist Appraiser upon those taking recognized courses and passing extensive examinations. *Type:* Association.

Diamond Dealers Club

580 5th Ave.   Ph: (212)869-9777
New York, NY 10036   Fax: (212)869-5164
Contact: Martin Hochbaum, Mgr.

Desc: Seeks to foster the interests of the diamond industry, promote equitable trade principles, eliminate abuses and unfair trade practices, disseminate accurate and reliable information concerning the industry, establish uniform business ethics, and cooperate with other persons and organizations for the advancement of the trade. Maintains active trading floor for all categories of wholesale diamonds and offers all members arbitration tribunals for dispute settlement. Operates charitable program. *Type:* Association.

Diamond Insight

Tryon Mercantile Inc.
790 Madison Ave.   Ph: (212)570-4180
New York, NY 10021   Fax: (212)772-1286
Contact: Guido Giovannini-Torelli, Editor.

Desc: Serves as a source of "vital intelligence on the world's important stones, future price indicators and key individuals behind the trends." Addresses issues in the diamond industry worldwide. Covers the wholesale and retail market, major jewelry auctions, and De Beers/Centenary/Central Selling Organization (CSO) activities. *Type:* Newsletter.

The Diamond Registry Bulletin

Joseph Schlussel
580 5th Ave., Ste. 806   Ph: (212)575-0444
New York, NY 10036   Free: 800-223-7955
    Fax: (212)575-0722
E-mail: diamond58@aol.com.
URL: http://www.diamondregistry.com.
Contact: Joseph Schlussel, Editor; Joyce Lempel, Editor.

Desc: Supplies current data on the present and future outlook of the diamond market. Provides information concerning trends in jewelry and investment companies and actual wholesale prices by size, quality, and shape for certified and commercial diamonds. *Type:* Newsletter.

Gem and Jewelry Fact Sheets Quarterly Supplement

American Gem Society
8881 W. Sahara Ave.   Ph: (702)255-6500
Las Vegas, NV 89117   Fax: (702)255-7420
Contact: Angela B. White, Editor.

Desc: Highlights jewelry industry developments. Discusses market projections, new sources of gemstones, and major marketing ideas. *Type:* Newsletter.

Gemological Institute of America

5345 Armada Dr.   Ph: (760)603-4000
Carlsbad, CA 92008   Free: 800-421-7250
    Fax: (760)603-4080
E-mail: selliott@qia.edu
URL: http://www.gia.edu
Contact: William E. Boyajian, Pres.

Desc: Alumni are sustaining members. Conducts home study programs, resident courses, and traveling seminars in identification and quality analysis of diamonds and other gemstones and pearls, and in jewelry making and repair, jewelry designing, and jewelry sales. Through subsidiaries, manufactures and sells gem testing and diamond grading equipment and audiovisual gemstone presentations. *Type:* Association.

Independent Jewelers Organization

25 Seir Hill Rd.   Ph: (203)226-6941
Norwalk, CT 06850-1322   Free: 800-624-9252
    Fax: (203)454-4371
Contact: Jeffrey Roberts, Pres.CEO.

Desc: Works to aid independent jewelers in competing in local markets through advertising, promotion, and buyers' assistance. *Type:* Association.

Jewelers of America

1185 6th Ave., 30th Fl.   Ph: (212)768-8777
New York, NY 10036   Free: 800-223-0673
    Fax: (212)768-8087
E-mail: jewelersam@aol.com
URL: http://www.Jewelers.org
Contact: Matthew Runci, Exec.Dir.

Desc: Retailers of jewelry, watches, silver, and allied merchandise. *Type:* Association.

Jewelers Board of Trade

PO Box 6928
Providence, RI 02940
Contact: Nathaniel C. Earle, Pres.

Desc: Credit reporting agency for manufacturers, wholesalers, and importers of jewelry. Maintains branch offices in New York City, Chicago, IL, and Los Angeles, CA. *Type:* Association.

Jewelers Security Alliance of the U.S.

6 E. 45th St.   Ph: (212)687-0328
New York, NY 10017   Free: 800-537-0067
    Fax: (212)808-9168
E-mail: jsa@polygon.net
Contact: John J. Kennedy, Pres.

Desc: Principal activity is crime prevention for the jewelry industry. *Type:* Association.

Jewelers Shipping Association

125 Carlsbad St.   Ph: (401)943-6020
Cranston, RI 02920   Fax: (401)943-1490
Contact: Jim Sell, Gen.Mgr.

Desc: Primarily jewelry and silverware manufacturers; others whose freight complements jewelry-type freight. Purpose is to provide surface and air freight shipping services for members. *Type:* Association.

The Jewelry Appraiser

National Association of Jewelry Appraisers, Inc.
PO Box 6558   Ph: (301)261-8270
Annapolis, MD 21401-0558
Contact: James V. Jolliff, Editor.
Desc: Provides information on jewelry and gem appraising. Carries items on current appraisal practices and standards, and a wholesale price guide titled the Price Reporter. *Type:* Newsletter.

Jewelry Newsletter International

Newsletters International, Inc.
2600 S. Gessner Rd.   Ph: (713)783-0100
Houston, TX 77063
Contact: Len Fox, Editor.
Desc: Reports news and developments in the jewelry industry, with brief items on people, companies, products, the changing scene and tastes, retailers, jobbers, and manufacturers. Recurring features include cost-cutting tips, listings of recommended books, professional opportunity notices, and items on economic trends. *Type:* Newsletter.

The Loupe

Gemological Institute of America
5355 Armada Dr., Ste. 300   Ph: (760)603-4000
Carlsbad, CA 92008   Free: 800-421-7250
   Fax: (760)603-4262
URL: http://www.gia.org
Contact: Tom Byrnes, Editor.
Desc: Provides information on activities, events, courses, and products of the Institute. Includes student achievements. *Type:* Newsletter.

Manufacturing Jewelers and Silversmiths of America

1 State St., 6th Fl.   Ph: (401)274-3840
Providence, RI 02908-5035   Free: 800-444-MJSA
   Fax: (401)274-0265
E-mail: mjsa@internetmci.com
Contact: James F. Marquart, Pres./CEO.
Desc: Manufacturers of jewelry, silverware, and allied items; suppliers to the industry; jewelry salesmen. Conducts wage and company policy survey annually and the Export Development Assistance Program. *Type:* Association.

MJSA Benchmark

Manufacturing Jewelers & Suppliers of America
1 State St., 6th Fl.   Ph: (401)274-3840
Providence, RI 02908-5035   Free: 800-444-6572
   Fax: (401)274-0265
Contact: Tom Viola, Editor.
Desc: Informs members, jewelry manufacturers of legislative news concerning their industry, expositions around the country, export news, tax news, and advances in technology. Presents information in the form of brief updates. *Type:* Newsletter.

Rapaport Diamond Report

Rapaport Diamond Corporation
15 W. 47th St.   Ph: (212)354-0575
New York, NY 10036   Fax: (212)840-0243
E-mail: rap@diamonds.net
URL: http://www.diamonds.net.
Contact: Amber Michelle, Editor, (212)535-2283, fax: (212)249-0595, amber@diamond.com.
Desc: Lists "approximate cash New York asking price indications" for diamonds. Also lists stones at no charge for which Rapaport is broker, approximate broker sell indications, and diamond industry news. *Type:* Newsletter.

Spectra

American Gem Society
8881 W. Sahara Ave.   Ph: (702)255-6500
Las Vegas, NV 89117   Fax: (702)255-7420
Contact: Angela B. White, Editor.
Desc: Informs members of Society activities promoting ethical business standards and professional excellence in the retail jewelry industry. Features articles about technical advances in the field and profiles of members. *Type:* Newsletter.

Jewish

Academic Committee on Soviet Jewry

Dr. Harris O. Schoenberg
345 E. 46th St.   Ph: (212)557-9013
New York, NY 10017
Contact: Dr. Harris O. Schoenberg, Exec. Sec.
Desc: To alert and mobilize the academic community on the situation of Jews in the former Soviet Union. *Type:* Association.

Agudath Israel of America

84 William St., 12th Fl.   Ph: (212)797-9000
New York, NY 10038   Fax: (212)269-2843
Contact: B. Borchardt, Exec.Dir.
Desc: Members of the Orthodox Jewish faith. To organize Jews for religious, educational, and philanthropic purposes. Maintains legislative and public affairs bureaus and biographical archives; provides placement service, speakers' bureau, research programs, religious and educational programs, and children's services. *Type:* Association.

American Friends of the Jerusalem Institute for Talmudic Research

Desc: Yeshiva scholars. To research Talmudic laws and apply them to current situations. Conducts professional training seminars; compiles statistics; sponsors charitable programs; bestows awards. *Type:* Association.

American Jewish Committee

Institute of Human Relations
165 E. 56th St.   Ph: (212)751-4000
New York, NY 10022   Fax: (212)838-2120
E-mail: info@ajc.org
URL: http://www.ajc.org
Contact: David Harris, Exec.Dir.
Desc: American citizens from more than 600 communities. Conducts program of education, research, and human relations; combats bigotry; seeks to protect religious and civil rights; supports security for Israel. *Type:* Association.

American Jewish Congress

15 E. 84th St.   Ph: (212)879-4500
New York, NY 10028   Fax: (212)249-3672
Contact: Phil Baum, Exec.Dir.
Desc: American Jews opposed to all forms of racism and committed to the unity, security, dignity, and creative survival of Jews in Israel, the USSR, and wherever they may be threatened. Maintains library. Sponsors the Institute for Jewish-Christian Relations. *Type:* Association.

American Jewish Joint Distribution Committee

711 3rd Ave.   Ph: (212)687-6200
New York, NY 10017-4014   Fax: (212)682-7262
E-mail: info@jdcny.org
Contact: Michael Schneider, Exec.VP.
Desc: Maintains health, welfare, assistance and social programs for needy Jews in nearly 60 countries in Asia, Africa, Europe, the former Soviet Union, and Latin America. *Type:* Association.

American Jewish Organizations Directory

H. Frenkel, Publisher
75 Montgomery St., No. 3D   Ph: (212)227-7957
New York, NY 10002
Contact: H. Frenkel, Editor.
Desc: Lists of Jewish organizations, synagogues, and schools. *Type:* Directory.

American ORT

817 Broadway   Ph: (212)353-5800
New York, NY 10003-4756   Free: 800-364-9678
   Fax: (212)979-9545
URL: http://www.aort.org
Contact: Brian J. Strum, Exec.Dir.
Desc: Provides quality technical education and training to students in the international ORT network of schools in 60 countries around the world. Teaches the skills of more than 100 trades and professions ranging from auto mechanics and welding to biotechnology, robotics, computers, and fiber optics. *Type:* Association.

American Sephardi Federation

305 7th Ave.   Ph: (212)366-7223
New York, NY 10001   Fax: (212)366-7263
E-mail: asf@amsephfed.org
URL: http://www.amsephfed.org
Contact: Jayne Rosengarten, Exec.Dir.
Desc: Umbrella organization representing congregations, organizations, and individual Sephardic Jews. Works to promote and strengthen Sephardic identity and awareness. Seeks to educate other Jews and non-Jews on the Sephardim. *Type:* Association.

Amit Women

817 Broadway   Ph: (212)477-4720
New York, NY 10003   Free: 800-989-2648
   Fax: (212)353-2312
Contact: Evelyn Blachor, Pres.
Desc: Religious-Zionist organization of Jewish women. Provides child care, social welfare education, and vocational training programs for youth and newcomers to Israel in an atmosphere of Jewish tradition. Serves as Israel Ministry of Education's Official Reshet (network) for religious secondary technological and vocational education. *Type:* Association.

Association of Reform Zionists of America

633 3rd Ave.   Ph: (212)249-0100
New York, NY 10017   Fax: (212)650-4289
Contact: Rabbi Ammiel Hirsch, Exec.Dir. & Editor.
Desc: Individuals seeking to stimulate Zionist commitment among American Reform Jews and to promote Reform Judaism in Israel. Maintains Israel Religious Action Center. Operates speakers' bureau; conducts specialized education; sponsors leadership workshops, travel department. *Type:* Association.

Bialystoker Stimme

Bialystoker Center
228 E. Broadway   Ph: (212)475-7755
New York, NY 10002
Contact: Sol Krim, Editor; Rabbi Irving Rosner, Editor.
Desc: Presents current and past news concerning the Center and nursing home. Features articles on Bialystok, Poland. *Type:* Newsletter.

B'nai B'rith International

1640 Rhode Island Ave. NW   Ph: (202)857-6600
Washington, DC 20036   Fax: (202)857-1099
Contact: Dr. Sidney M. Clearfield, Exec.VP.
Desc: Jewish men, women, and youth "of good moral character." Offers religious, cultural, civic, and social programs for teenagers and Jewish students and faculty of some 400 college campuses in 12 countries. Maintains museum, and speakers' bureau. Conducts programs on important Jewish issues. *Type:* Association.

B'nai B'rith International Jewish Monthly

B'nai B'rith

1640 Rhode Island Ave. NW   Ph: (202)857-6600
Washington, DC 20036   Fax: (202)296-1092
E-mail: ijm@bnaibrith.org
URL: http://bnaibrith.org/ijm
Contact: Eric Rozenman, Executive Editor, (202)857-6646, erozenman@bnaibrith.org; Stacey Free, Managing Editor, (202)857-2708.
Desc: Jewish family interest magazine. *Type:* Periodical.

B'nai B'rith Senior Citizens Housing Committee

1640 Rhode Island Ave. NW   Ph: (202)857-6581
Washington, DC 20036   Fax: (202)857-0980
E-mail: seniors@bnaibrith.org
URL: http://www.bnaibrith.org
Contact: Mark D. Olshan, Ph.D., Dir.
Desc: Provides housing facilities in six countries for elderly and handicapped people with low incomes. *Type:* Association.

B'nai B'rith Youth Organization

1640 Rhode Island Ave. NW   Ph: (202)857-6633
Washington, DC 20036   Fax: (202)857-6568
Contact: Sam Fisher, Contact.
Desc: A commission of B'nai B'rith International. Jewish youth organization with members from orthodox, conservative, and reform backgrounds. Offers Richard Klutznick Social Work Training Fund for graduate training in social work in return for future work commitment in organization. *Type:* Association.

Bnai Zion

136 E. 39th St.   Ph: (212)725-1211
New York, NY 10016   Free: 800-JOIN-399
    Fax: (212)684-6327
E-mail: bzf@mail.idt.net
Contact: Mel Parness, Exec.VP.
Desc: Fraternal benefit life insurance society of Jewish individuals and families. Conducts activities supporting growth and development of Israel and Jewish education. *Type:* Association.

Broward Jewish Journal

SFNN, Inc.

601 Fairway Dr.   Ph: (954)574-5300
Deerfield Beach, FL 33441   Free: 800-275-8820
    Fax: (954)429-1207
E-mail: bukley@gate.net; ptom@netrunner.net.
Contact: Andrew Polin, Editor; Rabbi Bruce Warshal, Publisher.
Desc: Jewish interest newspaper (tabloid). *Type:* Periodical.

Central Organization for Jewish Education

770 Eastern Pky.   Ph: (718)953-2353
Brooklyn, NY 11213
Contact: Dr. Nissan Mindel, Sec.
Desc: Educational arm of the Lubavitch Movement. Promotes Jewish education and religious observance as a daily experience for all Jews. Develops curricula that will stimulate concern for and active interest in Jewish education. *Type:* Association.

Chai Today

Chai Publications

420 Lincoln Rd., Ste. 409   Ph: (305)672-1937
Miami Beach, FL 33139   Fax: (305)673-1283
Contact: Michael Lozenik, Editor.
Desc: Magazine promoting an understanding of the principles of Judaism. *Type:* Periodical.

Coalition for the Advancement of Jewish Education

261 W. 35th St., Fl. 12A   Ph: (212)268-4210
New York, NY 10001   Fax: (212)268-4214
E-mail: 500-8447@mcimail.com
URL: http://www.caje.org
Contact: Eliot G. Spack, Dir.
Desc: People concerned with all aspects of Jewish education at all levels of the religion. Sponsors Curriculum Bank program network which serves as a resource for teachers and principals. *Type:* Association.

Congress for Jewish Culture

25 E. 21st St.   Ph: (212)505-8040
New York, NY 10010   Fax: (212)505-8044
Contact: Prof. Yonia Fain, Co-Pres.
Desc: Federation of organizations of writers, educators, publishers, cultural departments, and fraternal organizations promoting Jewish cultural activities such as literary events, concerts of Jewish music, and art exhibits and publication of works in Yiddish. *Type:* Association.

Directory of Jewish Resident Summer Camps

JWB Jewish Book Council

15 E. 26th St.   Ph: (212)532-4949
New York, NY 10010
Desc: 200 camps run by Jewish community organizations. *Type:* Directory.

Emunah Women of America

7 Penn Plz.   Ph: (212)564-9045
New York, NY 10001   Free: 800-368-6440
    Fax: (212)643-9731
E-mail: info@emunah.org
URL: http://www.emunah.org
Contact: Shirley Singer, Exec. Vice Pres.
Desc: A network of chapters throughout North America, with affiliated branches in 33 countries throughout the world. Supports and maintains 225 institutions in Israel where over 20,000 needy children are cared for in kindergartens, day care centers, nurseries, girls' homes, vocational training schools, and community colleges. Sponsors tours to Israel. *Type:* Association.

Federation of Jewish Men's Clubs

475 Riverside Dr., Ste. 450   Ph: (212)749-8100
New York, NY 10115-0022   Free: 800-288-3562
    Fax: (212)316-4271
E-mail: fjmc@jtsa.edu
URL: http://www.jtsa.edu/fjmc/fjmchmpg.html
Contact: Rabbi Charles E. Simon, Exec.Dir.
Desc: Federation of men's clubs in Conservative Jewish congregations. Cosponsors Laymen's Institute for adult study courses; sponsors Hebrew Literacy Campaign, Art of Jewish Living Family Education program, and Holocaust Memorial program. Promotes Ramah camps for children. *Type:* Association.

Free Sons of Israel

250 5th Ave., Ste. 201   Ph: (212)725-3690
New York, NY 10001   Fax: (212)725-5874
URL: http://www.freeson.upg.com
Contact: Richard Reiner, Grand Sec.
Desc: Jewish fraternal benefit society. *Type:* Association.

Hadassah Magazine

Hadassah, The Women's Zionist Organization of America

50 W. 58th St.   Ph: (212)688-2656
New York, NY 10019   Fax: (212)446-9521
E-mail: hadamags@aol.com.
Contact: Alan Tigay, Editor, (212)688-2906; Ruth Kinney, Adv. Coord., nadiing5@aol.com.

Desc: Magazine covering Jewish economic, educational, political, and cultural issues in the U.S. and Israel. *Type:* Periodical.

Hadassah, The Women's Zionist Organization of America

50 W. 58th St.   Ph: (212)355-7900
New York, NY 10019   Free: 800-664-JOIN
    Fax: (212)303-8282
URL: http://www.hadassah.org
Contact: Dr. Laura Schor, Exec.Dir.
Desc: Largest women's and Jewish membership organization in the United States. Promotes health education, social action and advocacy, community volunteerism, Jewish education and research and commections with Israel. Supports the International Research Institute on Jewish Women at Brandeis University, the Hadassah Foundation and Hadassah Leadership Academy. *Type:* Association.

Hebrew Immigrant Aid Society

333 7th Ave.   Ph: (212)967-4100
New York, NY 10001-5004   Fax: (212)967-4483
Contact: Leonard S. Glickman, Exec.VP.
Desc: Assists refugees and migrants from Europe, North Africa, the Middle East, and other trouble areas resettle in the United States, Canada, Latin America, and Australia. Maintains offices and committees around the world to: help locate relatives and friends; prepare documents; arrange for transportation; provide reception and resettlement services. *Type:* Association.

Hineni

232 West End Ave.   Ph: (212)496-1660
New York, NY 10023   Fax: (212)496-1908
Contact: Barbara Janov, Exec.Dir.
Desc: Jewish families and individuals. Seeks to make Jews aware of and knowledgeable about their heritage. *Type:* Association.

Histadruth Ivrith of America

426 W. 58th St., Rm. 409   Ph: (212)957-5811
New York, NY 10019-1102
Contact: Rabbi Abraham Kupchik, Exec.VP.
Desc: Promotes renewed interest in Hebrew language and culture. *Type:* Association.

Jewish Chautauqua Society

633 3rd Ave.   Ph: (212)570-0707
New York, NY 10017   Fax: (212)650-4189
Contact: Doug Barden, Dir.
Desc: Sponsored by the National Federation of Temple Brotherhoods comprising 450 men's clubs with 50,000 members in the United States, Canada, and abroad. Conducts a six-phase educational program for better understanding and appreciation of Jews and Judaism by people of all faiths; assigns rabbis to lecture at colleges, private and parochial schools, and seminars; endows resident lectureships on Judaism for college credit; donates Jewish reference books to college libraries. Sponsors institutes for Christian clergy. *Type:* Association.

Jewish Community Centers Association of North America

15 E. 26th St.   Ph: (212)532-4949
New York, NY 10010   Fax: (212)481-4174
E-mail: info@jcca.org
URL: http://www.jcca.org
Contact: Allan Finkelstein, Exec.VP.
Desc: Affiliated Jewish Community Centers including The 92nd Street Young Men's and Young Women's Hebrew Association and their branches and camps in the U.S. and Canada which have a combined membership of more than 1,000,000; local Armed Services committees; full- and

part-time Jewish chaplains and lay leaders in all branches of the Armed Forces. Through community consultants and program specialists, aids Jewish community centers in planning programs, personnel recruitment, building construction, camping, health and physical education, administration, research publications, and public relations. *Type:* Association.

Jewish Cultural Clubs and Societies

1133 Broadway, Rm. 1203   Ph: (212)675-8854
New York, NY 10010

Contact: Gedalia Sandler, Gen.Sec.

Desc: Yiddish and English speaking individuals, most of whom are retired. Conducts fraternal, cultural, social action, and senior citizens activities. Conducts lectures and concerts; contributes to Jewish children's schools. *Type:* Association.

The Jewish Herald

The Jewish Herald, Inc.
1689 46th St.   Ph: (718)972-4000
Brooklyn, NY 11204   Fax: (718)972-9400
E-mail: 71263.257@compuserve.com.

Contact: Leon J. Sternheim, Editor and Publisher; Mark Stern, Editor.

Desc: Newspaper reporting Jewish community, local, and national news. *Type:* Periodical.

Jewish Press

Jewish Press, Inc.
338 3rd Ave.   Ph: (718)330-1100
Brooklyn, NY 11215   Free: 800-992-1600
                                 Fax: (718)935-1215
URL: http://www.jpeditor.com.

Contact: Jacob Klass, Vice President/Advertising Dir.; Sholom Klass, Editor and Publisher, jpeditor@aol.com; Jerry Greenwald, Vice President/General Mgr.

Desc: Jewish national newspaper. *Type:* Periodical.

Jewish Publication Society

1930 Chestnut St.   Ph: (215)564-5925
Philadelphia, PA 19103-4599   Free: 800-234-3151
                                 Fax: (215)564-6640
E-mail: jewishbook@aol.com
URL: http://www.jewishpub.org
Contact: Dr. Ellen Frankel, Editor-in-Chief.

Desc: Individuals and institutions, predominantly Jewish, interested in publication and dissemination of books on Jewish history, religion, and literature. *Type:* Association.

Jewish Reconstructionist Federation

7804 Montgomery Ave, No.9   Ph: (215)782-8500
Elkins Park, PA 19027   Fax: (215)782-8805
E-mail: jrfnatl@aol.com
URL: http://www.shamash.org/jrf
Contact: Mordechai Leibling, Rabbi.

Desc: Federation of synagogues and fellowships committed to the philosophy and program of the Jewish Reconstructionist Movement. Coordinates rabbinical and educational training. Maintains placement service and speakers' bureau. *Type:* Association.

Jewish Telegraphic Agency

330 7th Ave., 11th Fl.   Ph: (212)643-1890
New York, NY 10001-5010   Fax: (212)643-8498
E-mail: jtainfo@aol.com
URL: http://www.JTA.org
Contact: Mark J. Joffe, Exec. Ed. and Publisher.

Desc: Purpose is to report worldwide news concerning Jewish people. *Type:* Association.

The Jewish Week

The Jewish Week
1501 Broadway   Ph: (212)921-7822
New York, NY 10036   Fax: (212)921-8420
E-mail: comr@jewishweek.org.

Contact: Phillip Ritzenberg, Publisher; Conrad Berke, Advertising Mgr.

Desc: Jewish interest newspaper. *Type:* Periodical.

Jewish Woman

Jewish Women International
1828 L. St. NW Ste. 250   Ph: (202)857-1300
Washington, DC 20036   Fax: (202)857-1380
E-mail: jwi@jwi.org; editor@jwi.org.

Contact: Susan Tomchin, Editor.

Desc: Jewish women's magazine. *Type:* Periodical.

Jewish Women International

1828 L St. NW, Ste. 250   Ph: (202)857-1300
Washington, DC 20036   Free: 800-343-2823
                                 Fax: (202)857-1380
E-mail: jwi@jwi.org
URL: http://www.jewishwomen.org
Contact: Gail Rubinson, Exec.Dir.

Desc: Jewish Women International strengthens the lives of women, children, and families through education, advocacy and action. Focusing on family violence and the emotional health of children, JWI serves as an agent for change. Community activities include domestic violence awareness, self-esteem projects, interfaith forums, holocaust awareness, hospital humor carts, and other youth projects. *Type:* Association.

Jews for Jesus

60 Haight St.   Ph: (415)864-2600
San Francisco, CA 94102   Fax: (415)552-8325
E-mail: jfj@jewsforjesus.org
URL: http://www.jewsforjesus.org
Contact: David Brickner, Exec.Dir.

Desc: Jewish people who believe that Y'shua (Jesus) is the Messiah and claim their lives have been changed as a result of that belief. Promotes understanding and reconciliation; helps Christians appreciate the Jewish heritage of the church. Provides Jewish evangelism seminars and Messianic music and drama workshops. *Type:* Association.

Kadima

155 5th Ave.   Ph: (212)533-7800
New York, NY 10010   Fax: (212)353-9439
E-mail: youth@uscj.org
URL: http://www.uscj.org/uscj
Contact: Robert Gamer, Dir.

Desc: Jewish boys and girls in grades five through eight who are members of conservative synagogues. Sponsored by the Department of Youth Activities of the United Synagogue of America. To involve young people in informal, cultural, educational, recreational, religious, and social activities through their synagogues. *Type:* Association.

Kolel Chibas Jerusalem

1282 49th St.   Ph: (718)633-7112
Brooklyn, NY 11219   Fax: (718)633-5783
Contact: Rabbi Berish Rubin, Exec.Dir.

Desc: Collects contributions and fixed payments for religious services and memorial prayers; provides charity for over 2 thousand neddy families and individuals in Israel. Maintains three free dental clinics in Israel. *Type:* Association.

Lubavitch International

Lubavitch News Service
770 Eastern Pkwy.   Ph: (718)774-4000
Brooklyn, NY 11213   Fax: (718)774-2718
Contact: Yosef B. Friedman, Editor; Baila Olidort, Editor.

Desc: Reports on various Chabad-Lubavitch activities around the world. Recurring features include columns titled Message From Lubavitcher Rebbe, Issue at Hand, Milestones, Then and Now, Lubavitch Bookshelf, Lubavitch on Campus, A Time to Build, Focus on Education, and New Chabad-Lubavitch Centers. *Type:* Newsletter.

Lubavitch Movement

770 Eastern Pky.   Ph: (718)774-4000
Brooklyn, NY 11213   Fax: (718)774-2718
Contact: Rabbi Krinsky, Exec. Officer.

Desc: International movement founded for the purpose of proclaiming Judaism and the observance of the Torah worldwide. (The Torah is the body of law and wisdom contained in Jewish scripture and other sacred literature and oral tradition.) Maintains the Kehot Publications Society, through which the group publishes primarily the literature and philosophy of Hasidic teachings. Operates speakers' bureau and 125,000 volume library; offers children's services. *Type:* Association.

Lubavitch Women's Organization

325 Kingston Ave.   Ph: (718)493-1773
Brooklyn, NY 11213   Fax: (718)604-0594
Contact: Shterna Spritzer, Pres.

Desc: Jewish women and girls. Sponsored by the Lubavitch Movement. Purposes are: to bring Jewish heritage and culture to Jewish women and girls; to enhance their knowledge and practice of Jewish traditions and customs, including religious candle lighting rituals, establishment and maintenance of Kosher homes, family and marriage laws, and holidays; to increase public awareness of Jewish culture, heritage, and tradition. *Type:* Association.

Lubavitch Youth Organization

770 Eastern Pky.   Ph: (718)953-1000
Brooklyn, NY 11213   Fax: (718)771-6315
Contact: Rabbi D. Raskin, Chm.

Desc: Jewish individuals and organizations dedicated to strengthening Jewish identity and commitment. Sponsors youth activities, educational programs, campus activities, chabad houses (retreat homes where Jews can go to rekindle their faith), and mitzvah mobiles (religious caravans meant to provide spiritual uplifting). Operates speakers' bureau and placement service; compiles statistics. *Type:* Association.

Machne Israel

770 Eastern Pky.   Ph: (718)774-4000
Brooklyn, NY 11213   Fax: (718)774-2718
Contact: Rabbi Yehuda Krinsky, Exec.Dir.

Desc: Social service arm of the Lubavitch Movement . To materially and spiritually aid Jewish and non-Jewish persons. *Type:* Association.

Na'amat U.S.A.

200 Madison Ave., 21st Fl.   Ph: (212)725-8010
New York, NY 10016   Fax: (212)447-5187
E-mail: naamat@naamat.org
Contact: Sheila Guston, CAE, Exec.Dir.

Desc: Cooperates with Na'amat Movement of Working Women and Volunteers to enhance the status of women, children and families in Israel and the United States as a part of a worldwide progressive Jewish women's organization and the Labor Zionist Movement. *Type:* Association.

National Committee for the Furtherance of Jewish Education

824 Eastern Pky.　　　　Ph: (718)735-0200
Brooklyn, NY 11213　　　Free: 800-33N-CFJE
　　　　　　　　　　　　Fax: (718)735-4455
E-mail: survival9@aol.com
URL: http://www.iltsp.org
Contact: Rabbi Sholem B. Hecht, Chm.
Desc: Works to disseminate the ideals of Torah-true education among the Jewish youth of America, and to strengthen their identity, committment, and pride. *Type:* Association.

National Conference of Synagogue Youth

333 7th Ave., 18th Fl.　　Ph: (212)563-4000
New York, NY 10001　　　Fax: (212)564-9058
Contact: Rabbi Raphael B. Butler, Dir.
Desc: Teenage synagogue youth movement of the Union of Orthodox Jewish Congregations of America. To strengthen and deepen the loyalty of Jewish youth to Torah and Mitzvoth, to the Jewish people, and to the orthodox synagogue. Sponsors Yachad, which conducts program for the developmentally disabled. *Type:* Association.

National Council of Jewish Women

53 W. 23rd St.　　　　　Ph: (212)645-4048
New York, NY 10010　　　Fax: (212)645-7466
Contact: Nan Rich, Nat.Dir.
Desc: Sponsors programs of education, social action, and community service for youth, the elderly, and women. *Type:* Association.

National Council of Young Israel

3 W. 16th St.　　　　　　Ph: (212)929-1525
New York, NY 10011　　　Free: 800-617-NCYI
　　　　　　　　　　　　Fax: (212)727-9526
Contact: Rabbi Pesach Lerner, Exec.VP.
Desc: Families of traditional Jewish faith in the U.S., Canada, Mexico, and Israel. Seeks "to perpetuate traditional Judaism; instill a love for Americanism and the principles of democracy; bring Jewish youth back to the synagogue; educate the youth and adults in the heritage and culture of the Jewish people." Benevolent Association in the New York City area; conducts programs nationwide for adults and youths. *Type:* Association.

National Federation of Temple Brotherhoods

838 5th Ave.　　　　　　Ph: (212)570-0707
New York, NY 10021　　　Free: 800-765-6200
　　　　　　　　　　　　Fax: (212)650-4189
Contact: Doug Barden, Exec.Dir.
Desc: Dedicated to enhancing the world through the ideal of brotherhood. Involved in education, social action, youth activities, and other programs which contribute to temple and community life. Sponsors Jewish Chautauqua Society, which sponsors accredited college courses and one-day lectures on Judaic topics, provides book grants to educational institutions, produces educational videotapes on interfaith topics, and sponsors interfaith institutes. *Type:* Association.

National Jewish Community Relations Advisory Council

443 Park Ave. S　　　　　Ph: (212)684-6950
New York, NY 10016　　　Fax: (212)686-1353
E-mail: contactus@thejcpa.org
Contact: Dr. Lawrence Rubin, Exec.V.Chm.
Desc: National Jewish agencies (13) and local Jewish community relations councils (123) jointly developing policies such as: interpretation of Israel, oppression of Jews abroad, combating anti-Semitism, equal opportunity, equal rights, civil liberties, religious freedom, and other democratic practices. Encourages friendly relationships among groups. Conducts placement services for member agencies. *Type:* Association.

National Yiddish Book Center

Harry & Jeanette Weinberg　Ph: (413)256-4900
　Bldg.　　　　　　　　　Fax: (413)256-4700
1021 West St.
Amherst, MA 01002-3375
E-mail: yiddish@bikher.org
URL: http://www.yiddishbookcenter.org
Contact: Aaron Lansky, Pres.
Desc: Jewish cultural activists; students and scholars of Yiddish literature; other interested persons. Dedicated to the revitalization of Jewish life through the preservation and promotion of Yiddish culture. Collects discarded Yiddish books; catalogs, and makes the books available to teachers, students, and university and institution libraries. *Type:* Association.

New York Association for New Americans

17 Battery Pl.　　　　　　Ph: (212)425-2900
New York, NY 10004-1102　Fax: (212)514-6938
Contact: Mark Handelman, Exec.VP.
Desc: Resettlement and rehabilitation agency for Jewish newcomers and other refugees in the greater New York area. *Type:* Association.

New York Association for New Americans

17 Battery Pl.　　　　　　Ph: (212)425-2900
New York, NY 10004-1102　Fax: (212)425-7160
Contact: Mark Handelman, Exec.VP.
Type: Association.

The 92nd Street Young Men's and Young Women's Hebrew Association

1395 Lexington Ave.　　　Ph: (212)996-1100
New York, NY 10128　　　Fax: (212)828-3077
URL: http://www.92ndsty.org
Contact: Sol Adler, Exec.Dir.
Desc: Jewish community and cultural center in New York serving the educational and recreational needs of more than 500,000 members and nonmembers each year. *Type:* Association.

North American Conference on Ethiopian Jewry

32 Nassau St.　　　　　　Ph: (212)233-3200
New York, NY 10038　　　Fax: (212)233-5243
E-mail: nacoej@aol.com
URL: http://www.cais.com/nacoej
Contact: Barbara Ribakove Gordon, Exec.Dir.
Desc: Works for the welfare and advancement of the Ethiopian Jewish community in Israel. Sponsors educational, vocational, and cultural preservation programs in Israel. Assists Jews still in Ethopia. *Type:* Association.

North American Federation of Temple Youth

46 Bowen Rd.　　　　　　Ph: (914)987-6300
PO Box 443　　　　　　　Fax: (914)986-7185
Warwick, NY 10990
E-mail: rjyouth@warwick.net
URL: http://www.uahc.org
Contact: Rabbi Dennis Eisner, Dir.
Desc: Members of local Temple Youth groups (ages 15-18) affiliated with Reform Jewish congregations. Purpose is to instill Jewish identity in young people and foster commitment to the ideals and values of Reform Judaism. Offers programs in the areas of worship, religious education, community service, and social action. *Type:* Association.

North American Jewish Youth Council

515 Park Ave.　　　　　　Ph: (212)751-6070
New York, NY 10022
Contact: Jonathan Goldstein, Pres.
Desc: Jewish (Zionist and non-Zionist) youth movements and youth organizations. To serve as an umbrella organization for its constituent organizations, regarding common activities and NAJYC conference. Represents American Jewish youth in all official bodies. *Type:* Association.

Ozar Hatorah

625 Broadway 5th Fl.　　　Ph: (212)253-7245
New York, NY 10012　　　Fax: (212)473-4773
E-mail: ozartora@shemayisreal.com
Contact: Joseph Shalom, Pres.
Desc: To establish and maintain schools for Jewish youth in Europe and North Africa, providing a combined program of religious and secular education. *Type:* Association.

Pirchei Agudath Israel

84 William St., 11th Fl.　　Ph: (212)797-9000
New York, NY 10038　　　Fax: (212)269-2843
Contact: Rabbi Shimon Grama, National Dir.
Desc: Children's division of Agudath Israel of America. Educates Orthodox male Jewish children in the traditional Orthodox Jewish way of life and thought, with emphasis on Torah concepts and values. Membership composed mainly of Yeshiva students. *Type:* Association.

Reform Judaism

Union of American Hebrew Congregations
633 3rd Ave., 6th Fl.　　　Ph: (212)650-4240
New York, NY 10017-6778
URL: http://uahc.org/rjmag/.
Contact: Aron Hirt-Manheimer, Editor; Joy Weinberg, Managing Editor & Advertising Mgr.
Desc: Magazine covering issues of importance to the Jewish community (particularly to the Reform Jewish community). *Type:* Periodical.

The Religious Zionist Youth Movement - Bnei Akiva of the United States and Canada

25 W. 26th St.　　　　　　Ph: (212)889-5260
New York, NY 10010　　　Fax: (212)213-3053
Contact: Judy Srebro, Exec. Officer.
Desc: Religious Zionist youth movement of boys and girls aged ten to 18, with an older group (ages 18-25) serving as the leadership. Promotes Jewish culture and religion with emphasis placed on Israel in modern-day society. Conducts study programs in Israel; operates five regional summer camps; holds annual leadership training seminars in over 20 North American cities. *Type:* Association.

The Reporter

Women's American ORT
315 Park Ave. S.　　　　　Ph: (212)505-7700
New York, NY 10010　　　Fax: (212)674-3057
E-mail: avivap@waort.org.
Contact: Aviva Patz, Editor, avivap@waort.org.
Desc: Magazine reporting on women's issues, education, and Jewish affairs. Includes feature articles, opinion, and book reviews. *Type:* Periodical.

Southern California Council for Soviet Jews

3755 Goodland Ave.　　　Ph: (818)984-1424
Studio City, CA 91604　　Fax: (818)766-4321
Contact: Si Frumkin, Chm.
Desc: Educates the public about the situation facing Jews in the former Soviet Union. *Type:* Association.

Tzivos Hashem

332 Kingston　　　　　　Ph: (718)467-6630
Brooklyn, NY 11213　　　Fax: (718)467-8257
E-mail: tzivos@aol.com
URL: http://www.tzivos-hashem.org
Contact: Rabbi Benjaminson, Dir.
Desc: Children under 13 years of age. Seeks to foster among Jewish youth an appreciation of their Jewish heritage. Maintains educational resource center, educational toy and book store, Tzivos Hashem Book Club, and Hachai (a publishing house). *Type:* Association.

Union of American Hebrew Congregations

633 3rd St.   Ph: (212)650-4000
New York, NY 10017-6778
E-mail: uahc@uahc.org
URL: http://www.uahc.org
Contact: Rabbi Eric H. Yoffie, Pres.
Desc: Central congregational body of Reform Judaism in the Western Hemisphere. Provides religious, educational, cultural, and administrative programs to more than 870 affiliated synagogues. *Type:* Association.

Union of Orthodox Jewish Congregations of America

333 7th Ave., 19th Fl.   Ph: (212)563-4000
New York, NY 10001   Fax: (212)564-9058
Contact: Rabbi Raphael Butler, Exec.VP.
Desc: Federation of Orthodox Jewish synagogues representing 600,000 members. "For the perpetuation and advancement of traditional Judaism." Serves as national central agency to provide guidance to congregations, youth groups, and individuals; conducts national authoritative Kosher Certification Service, certifying foods through all phases of production as "Kosher" in compliance with Orthodox Jewish dietary laws. Maintains speakers' bureau; offers counseling and assistance in establishing new communities and synagogues; provides childrens' services; conducts retreats and lecture services. *Type:* Association.

United Jewish Appeal

National Office   Ph: (212)284-6500
Eigth Ave., Ste. 11 E   Fax: (212)818-9509
New York, NY 10011
E-mail: marketing@uja.org
URL: http://www.uja.com
Contact: Bernard C. Moscouitz, CEO.
Desc: Principal fundraising organization in the U.S. on behalf of Jewish needs overseas. Works in conjunction with the American Jewish Joint Distribution Committee and the United Israel Appeal to provide humanitarian programs and social services for Jews worldwide and in Israel. *Type:* Association.

United Jewish Appeal - Federation of Jewish Philanthropies of New York

111 8th Ave., East-11   Ph: (212)980-1000
New York, NY 10011-5201   Fax: (212)888-7538
Contact: Stephen D. Solender, Exec.VP.
Desc: Federation of agencies that provide hospital, health, geriatric, vocational, family and child care services, and Jewish education to individuals in the greater New York area, Israel, and 34 countries. Conducts fundraising and communal planning programs; maintains biographical archives. *Type:* Association.

United Synagogue Youth

United Synagogue of Conservative Judaism
Department of Youth Activities   Ph: (212)533-7800
155 5th Ave.   Fax: (212)353-9439
New York, NY 10010
E-mail: youth@uscj.org
URL: http://www.uscj.org/usy/
Contact: Jules A. Gutin, Dir.
Desc: Jewish youth (ages 13-17) interested in continuing and strengthening their identification with Judaism through study and discussion groups, leadership training, and special interest groups. *Type:* Association.

Women of Reform Judaism, The Federation of Temple Sisterhoods

838 5th Ave.   Ph: (212)650-4050
New York, NY 10021   Fax: (212)650-4059
E-mail: wrj@vahc.org

Contact: Ellen Y. Rosenberg, Exec.Dir.
Desc: Women of Reform or liberal Jewish congregations. Works "to intensify Jewish knowledge and to translate religious ideals into practical service to Jewish and humanitarian causes." Activities include: providing services to local affiliates; creating study material for Jewish parents and other adults; encouraging an appreciation of Jewish ceremonials and art; stimulating interest and actively participating in modern Jewish and social problems; working for the blind; supporting Israel and Jewry in the former Soviet Union. Also involved in youth activities, service to the elderly, education on UN affairs, and efforts to improve international understanding. *Type:* Association.

Women's American ORT

315 Park Ave., S   Ph: (212)505-7700
New York, NY 10010   Free: 800-51-WAORT
   Fax: (212)674-3057

E-mail: waort@waort.org
URL: http://www.waort.org
Contact: Amy Stone, Marketing Dir.
Desc: Seeks to end anti-Semitism and ensure democracy and pluralism in the U.S; promotes women's rights and issues. *Type:* Association.

Women's League for Conservative Judaism

48 E. 74th St.   Ph: (212)628-1600
New York, NY 10021   Free: 800-628-5083
   Fax: (212)772-3507

E-mail: wleague74@aol.com
URL: http://www.jtsa.edu/wlcj
Contact: Bernice Balter, Exec.Dir.
Desc: Composed of Sisterhoods affiliated with the Conservative movement, dedicated to the perpetuation of traditional Judaism and the translation of its ideals into practice. Purposes are: to guide its affiliates in local, national, and international activities, making them aware of their civic responsibilities; to foster Jewish education through study courses, Jewish Family Living Institutes and through the establishment of Synagogue and Sisterhood libraries. Supports Torah Fund - a Campaign for the Jewish Theological Seminary. *Type:* Association.

World Confederation of United Zionists

130 E. 59th St., 12th Flr.   Ph: (212)371-1452
New York, NY 10022   Fax: (212)371-3265
Contact: Kalman Sultanik, Exec.Co-Pres.
Desc: Unaffiliated with any Israeli political party, group promotes Zionist education, information, and welfare activities on behalf of Israel. Encourages private and collective agriculture and industry in Israel; strives for an "Israel-centered creative Jewish survival in Diaspora." *Type:* Association.

World Union for Progressive Judaism

633 3rd Ave.   Ph: (212)650-4090
New York, NY 10017-6778   Fax: (212)650-4289
E-mail: 5448032@mcimail.com
URL: http://www.rj.org/wupj/index.html
Contact: Rabbi Imiel Hirsh, North American Dir.
Desc: Congregations of Reform, Liberal, and Progressive Jews in 29 countries. Promotes the cause of Progressive Judaism; establishes new congregations and national constituencies; arranges for the training of rabbis and teachers; coordinates activity between constituencies. *Type:* Association.

YIVO Institute for Jewish Research

555 W. 57th St., 11th Fl.   Ph: (212)246-6080
New York, NY 10019   Fax: (212)292-1892
URL: http://www.baruch.cuny.edu/yivo
Contact: Tom Freudenheim, Exec.Dir.
Desc: Engages in research in East European Jewish social and historical studies, and in Yiddish language, literature, and folklore as they relate to East European Jews and their descendants. *Type:* Association.

Zionist Organization of America

4 E. 34th St.   Ph: (212)481-1500
New York, NY 10016   Fax: (212)481-1515
Contact: Bertram Koyn, Exec.Dir.
Desc: Conducts an educational and informational program for Israel and Jewry. Maintains speakers' bureau. *Type:* Association.

Journalism

ACME Features Syndicate

147 NE Yamhill   Ph: (503)843-4555
Sheridan, OR 97378   Fax: (503)843-4001
E-mail: acmefeat@aol.com.
Contact: Sondra Gatewood, Exec. Ed.
Desc: Distributes various columns and comics including Life in Hell. *Alt. Contact:* 147 NE Yamhill, Sheridan, OR 97378; telephone: (503)843-4555; fax: (503)843-4001. *Type:* Periodical.

ACT Newsletter

American Association of Agricultural Communicators of Tomorrow
67 Mumford Hall   Ph: (217)333-4782
1301 W. Gregory
Urbana, IL 61801
Desc: Promotes the Association's aim to advance the field of agricultural communications and to encourage professional exchange of information. Recurring features include news of members and a calendar of events. *Type:* Newsletter.

The Advocate

Capital City Press
525 Lafayette St.   Ph: (504)383-1111
Baton Rouge, LA 70802-5410   Free: 800-960-6397
   Fax: (504)388-0348
Contact: Douglas L. Manship, Publisher; David C. Manship, Publisher.
Desc: General newspaper. *Type:* Periodical.

AEJMC News

Association for Education in Journalism & Mass Communication (AEJMC)
234 Outlet Pointe Blvd., Ste. A   Ph: (803)798-0271
Columbia, SC 29210-5667   Fax: (803)772-3509
E-mail: aejmc@sc.edu
Contact: Kyshia Brown, Editor.
Desc: Monitors developments in the field of journalism education. Recurring features include news of members; a job placement service; news of schools/departments of journalism, mass communications, and affiliate organizations; and columns titled Update from the President, Update from the Executive Director, and Briefs. *Type:* Newsletter.

AIM Report

Accuracy in Media, Inc. (AIM)
4455 Connecticut Ave., NW   Ph: (202)364-4401
   No. 330   Fax: (202)364-4098
Washington, DC 20008
E-mail: ar@take.aim.org; aim@aim.org
URL: http://take.aim.org; http://www.aim.org/aim.html.
Contact: Reed Irvine, Editor.
Desc: Publicizes biased, inaccurate, or unbalanced reporting in the media. Seeks to bring accountability to all forms of the media through citizen action, public awareness, and factual reporting to responsible media leaders. *Type:* Newsletter.

A.J. Cook
6785 Slash Pine   Ph: (901)754-8925
Memphis, TN 38119
Contact: A.J. Cook, Author/Owner.
Desc: Distributes federal tax columns. *Alt. Contact:* 6785
Slash Pine, Memphis, TN 38119; telephone: (901)754-
8925. *Type:* Periodical.

Akron Beacon Journal
Knight-Ridder, Inc.
50 W. Fernando St.   Ph: (408)938-7700
San Jose, CA 95113
E-mail: bjeditor@akron.infi.net.
URL: http://www.beaconjournal.com.
Contact: John Dotson, Jr., Publisher; Glenn Guzzo, Managing Editor.
Desc: General newspaper. *Alt. Contact:* 44 E. Exchange,
PO Box 640, Akron, OH 44328-0001; telephone:
(330)996-3000; fax: (330)376-9235. *Type:* Periodical.

Akron Beacon Journal
The Beacon Journal Publishing Co.
44 E. Exchange St.   Ph: (330)996-3000
P.O. Box 640
Akron, OH 44309-0640
URL: http://www.ohio.com
Contact: Cathy Tierney, Chief Librarian, (216)996-3898.
Desc: Contains the complete text of news items and feature
articles from the Akron Beacon Journal (Ohio) newspaper.
Regional coverage emphasizes the rubber, steel, and automotive industries. *Available:* The Dialog Corporation, DIALOG; CompuServe Information Service, Knowledge
Index. *Type:* Database.

Albuquerque Journal
Albuquerque Publishing Co.
7777 Jefferson NE   Ph: (505)823-3393
Albuquerque, NM 87109   Free: 800-641-3451
                                   Fax: (505)823-3369
E-mail: journal@abqjournal.com.
URL: http://www.abqjournal.com.
Contact: Jerry Crawford, Editor; T.H. Lang, Publisher;
Gene McGehee, Advertising Mgr.
Desc: General newspaper. *Type:* Periodical.

**American Auto Racing Writers & Broadcasters
Newsletter**
*American Auto Racing Writers & Broadcasters
Association*
922 N. Pass Ave.   Ph: (818)842-7005
Burbank, CA 91505   Fax: (818)842-7020
Contact: Dusty Brandel, Editor.
Desc: Provides information about writing and broadcasting contests, pertinent publications, and activities of the
Association and its local chapters. *Type:* Newsletter.

**American Press Service and Features
Syndicate**
PO Box 917   Ph: (818)997-6497
Van Nuys, CA 91408-0917   Fax: (818)988-4337
E-mail: iibick@aol.com.
Contact: Israel Bick, VP/Gen. Mgr.
Desc: Distributes news features and entertainment columns. *Alt. Contact:* PO Box 917, Van Nuys, CA 91408-
0917; telephone: (818)997-6497; fax: (818)988-4337.
Type: Periodical.

**American Society of Journalists and Authors
Newsletter**
American Society of Journalists & Authors
1501 Broadway, Ste. 302   Ph: (212)997-0947
New York, NY 10036   Fax: (212)768-7414
E-mail: 75227.1650@compuserve.com

Contact: Dodi Schultz, Editor.
Desc: Reports on the business meetings of the Society and
provides market news as well as news of members, publishers, editors, and association chapters. Recurring features
include professional market reports and discussions of
magazines, books, and other media. *Type:* Newsletter.

American Visions
American Visions Media, Inc.
1156 15th St. NW, Ste 615   Ph: (202)496-9593
Washington, DC 20005   Fax: (202)496-9851
Contact: Gary Puckrein, President; Joanne Harris, Editor;
Mel Fellis, Advertising Mgr.
Type: Periodical.

The American Way Features
128 Lighthouse Dr.   Ph: (561)746-7815
Jupiter, FL 33469-3511
Contact: Thomas J. Anderson, Publisher; Linda Parton,
Mng. Ed./Circulation Mgr.
Alt. Contact: 128 Lighthouse Dr., Jupiter, FL 33469-
3511; telephone: (561)746-7815. *Type:* Periodical.

Anchorage Daily News
Anchorage Daily News
1001 Northway Dr.   Ph: (907)257-4200
PO Box 149001   Fax: (907)258-2157
Anchorage, AK 99514-9001
E-mail: newsroom@pop.adn.com.
URL: http://www.adn.com.
Contact: Mike Dunham, Art Editor; Fuller Cowell, Publisher; Ken Carter, Production Dir.; Pat Dougherty, Acting Editor; Kathleen McCoy, Feature Editor; Bill White,
Business Editor; Gene Gilbert, TV Editor; David Hulen,
City Editor; Michael Carey, Editorial Page Editor.
Desc: General newspaper. *Type:* Periodical.

Anchorage Daily News
Anchorage Daily News
1001 Northway Dr.   Ph: (907)257-4200
P.O. Box 14-9001
Anchorage, AK 99508
E-mail: subscription@pop.adn.com
URL: http://www.adn.com
Desc: Contains the complete text of news items and feature
articles from the Anchorage Daily News (Alaska) newspaper. *Available:* The Dialog Corporation, DIALOG; The
Dialog Corporation, DIALOG; Bell & Howell Information and Learning; LEXIS-NEXIS, NEXIS. *Type:* Database.

AP DataStream
The Associated Press (AP)
50 Rockefeller Plaza   Ph: (212)621-1585
New York, NY 10020
URL: http://www.ap.org
Desc: Contains the complete text of more than 1.28 million items from AP's DataStream newswire service. *Available:* CompuServe Information Service; Bell & Howell
Information and Learning; The Dialog Corporation, DIALOG; FT PROFILE; U.S. Videotel, Inc. *Type:* Database.

AP Online
The Associated Press (AP)
50 Rockefeller Plaza   Ph: (212)621-1585
New York, NY 10020
URL: http://www.ap.org
Desc: Contains the complete text of news stories covering
international, national, sports, business, and weather
news. Contains approximately 400 stories daily. *Available:*
CompuServe Information Service; BT North America,
Inc.; Prodigy Services Company, PRODIGY. *Type:* Database.

Arab-American Press Guild Newsletter
Arab-American Press Guild
PO Box 291250   Ph: (818)507-0333
Los Angeles, CA 90027   Fax: (818)246-1936
E-mail: newscirc@pacbell.net
Contact: Samir Shami, Editor.
Desc: Focuses on issues pertaining to the Arab-American
Press Guild and its activities. AAPG is designed to "organize and serve Arab-American journalists, assist the Arab-American community in its press needs, (and) to coordinate Arab press-related conferences and and issues in the
United States." Recurring features include a calendar of
events and notices of publications available. *Type:* Newsletter.

Arcadia Feature Syndicate
PO Box 1205   Ph: (309)341-0737
Galesburg, IL 61402
Contact: Clarice Anders, Managing Editor.
Desc: Distributes stamp column. *Alt. Contact:* PO Box
1205, Galesburg, IL 61402; telephone: (309)341-0737.
Type: Periodical.

The Arizona Daily Star
Star Publishing Co.
4850 S. Park Ave.   Ph: (520)573-4400
Tucson, AZ 85726-6807
Contact: Michael Pulitzer, Publisher; Stephen Auslander,
Editor; Bobbie Jo Buel, Managing Editor; Elaine Raines,
Librarian, (602)573-4130.
Desc: General newspaper. *Type:* Periodical.

The Arizona Republic
Phoenix Newspapers, Inc.
200 E. Van Buren St.   Ph: (602)271-8632
PO Box 85004   Fax: (602)271-8004
Phoenix, AZ 85004-2227
URL: http://www.a3central.com.
Contact: John Oppedahl, Managing Editor; H. Kenneth
Clouse, Advertising Dir.; Conrad Kloh, Dir. of Sales/
Marketing; Louis A. Weil, III, Publisher.
Desc: General newspaper. *Type:* Periodical.

Arizona Republic
Phoenix Newspapers, Inc. - Library, LI-18
PO Box 100   Ph: (602)444-8114
Phoenix, AZ 85001
URL: http://www.azcentral.com
Desc: Contains the complete text of news items and feature
articles from the daily Arizona Republic newspaper. Regional coverage emphasizes the aerospace industry, high
technology, tourism, real estate development, military
contracts, and Native American issues. *Available:* Bell &
Howell Information and Learning; LEXIS-NEXIS,
NEXIS. *Type:* Database.

Arkansas Democrat Gazette
Little Rock Newspapers, Inc.
Capitol Ave. & Scott St.   Ph: (501)378-3400
PO Box 2221
Little Rock, AR 72203
URL: http://www.ardemgaz.com
Desc: Contains the complete text of the Arkansas Democrat Gazette, a general circulation statewide newspaper reporting local, national, and international news. Covers all
news stores, features, editorials, and sports. *Available:*
LEXIS-NEXIS. *Type:* Database.

Arkansas Democrat-Gazette

Arkansas Democrat-Gazette, Inc.

Capitol Ave. & Scott St.   Ph: (501)378-3400
PO Box 2221   Fax: (501)372-3908
Little Rock, AR 72203
URL: http://www.ardemgaz.com.
Contact: Griffin Smith, Jr., Exec. Editor, (501)399-3610;
W.E. Hussman, Jr., Publisher, (501)378-3402; Dick
Browning, National Advertising, (501)378-3447,
dbrowning@ardemgaz.com; David Bailey, Managing Editor, (501)378-3594; Phyllis Brandon, High Profile Ed.,
(501)378-3574; John Mobbs, Advertising Dir., (501)378-3437; Ron Beach, Classified Advertising Mgr.
Desc: General newspaper. *Type:* Periodical.

Asbury Park Press

Asbury Park Press, Inc.

3601 Hwy. 66   Ph: (732)922-6000
PO Box 1550   Free: 800-822-9770
Neptune, NJ 07754-1550   Fax: (732)918-9144
E-mail: editors@app.com.
URL: http://www.app.com.
Contact: E. Donald Lass, Editor and Publisher, fax:
(732)922-6326; W. Raymond Ollwerther, Executive Editor, fax: (732)922-4818, wro@app.com; Jody Calendar,
Deputy Executive Editor, fax: (732)922-4818, jodyc@
app.com; Peter E. Donoghue, Night Editor, fax:
(732)922-4818; Charles W. Ritscher, Senior Vice Pres. for
Corporate Develop., fax: (732)922-6326; Daniel Curtis,
Regional Advertising Mgr., fax: (732)918-1298; Diane
Rogala, National Advertising Mgr., fax: (732)918-1298;
Sam Sic
Desc: General newspaper. *Type:* Periodical.

Ascher Features Syndicate

214 Boston Ave.   Ph: (609)927-1842
Egg Harbor Twp., NJ 08234
Contact: Sidney Ascher, President; Evelyn Ascher, Sec./
Treas.
Alt. Contact: 214 Boston Ave., Egg Harbor Twp., NJ
08234; telephone: (609)927-1842. *Type:* Periodical.

Ashleigh Brilliant

117 W. Vallerio St.   Ph: (805)682-0531
Santa Barbara, CA 93101
E-mail: ashleigh@west.net.
URL: http://www.west.net/~ashleigh.
Contact: Ashleigh Brilliant, President; Dorothy Brilliant,
Vice President.
Desc: Distributes cartoon feature. *Alt. Contact:* 117 W.
Vallerio St., Santa Barbara, CA 93101; telephone:
(805)682-0531. *Type:* Periodical.

Ask Aunt Madge

5420 Oraibi Dr.   Ph: (602)561-5632
Glendale, AZ 85308
Contact: Jack Anderson, Editor.
Alt. Contact: 5420 Oraibi Dr., Glendale, AZ 85308; telephone: (602)561-5632. *Type:* Periodical.

Associated Press

50 Rockefeller Plz.   Ph: (212)621-1500
New York, NY 10020   Fax: (212)621-1723
Contact: Susan Clark, Corp. Communications.
Desc: News cooperative that gathers and disseminates
world, national, regional, and state news, pictures, and
audio reports. Information travels via satellites and landlines to 1500 newspapers and 5700 radio and television
stations in the United States, and to more than 10,000
newspapers and broadcast stations worldwide. *Type:* Association.

Associated Press/AP Newsfeatures

50 Rockefeller Plaza   Ph: (212)621-1821
New York, NY 10020
Contact: Louis Boccardi, Pres./CEO; James Kennedy,
Business Ed.; William Ahearn, VP/Exec. Ed.; Norm
Goldstein, Dir./APN Spec. Proj.
Desc: Distributes news wire service. *Alt. Contact:* 50
Rockefeller Plaza, New York, NY 10020; telephone:
(212)621-1821. *Type:* Periodical.

Associated Press Network

1825 K St. NW   Ph: (202)736-1100
Ste. 710   Free: 800-821-4747
Washington, DC 20006   Fax: (202)736-1199
Contact: Louis D. Boccardi, President; Jim Williams, Vice
President.
Alt. Contact: 1825 K St. NW, Ste. 710, Washington, DC
20006; telephone: (202)736-1100; fax: (202)736-1199;
toll-free: 800-821-4747. *Type:* Periodical.

Associated Press/Wide World Photo

50 Rockefeller Plaza   Ph: (212)621-1930
New York, NY 10020   Fax: (212)621-1955
Contact: Patricia Lantis, Director.
Alt. Contact: 50 Rockefeller Plaza, New York, NY 10020;
telephone: (212)621-1930; fax: (212)621-1955. *Type:* Periodical.

Asterisk Features

RR 2 Mallard Rd.   Ph: (604)468-7584
Box 9   Fax: (604)468-7520
Nanoose Bay, BC, Canada V0R
    2R0
Contact: John Somerville, President.
Desc: Distributes comic strips. *Alt. Contact:* RR 2 Mallard
Rd., Box 9, Nanoose Bay, BC, Canada V0R 2R0; telephone: (604)468-7584; fax: (604)468-7520. *Type:* Periodical.

The Atlanta Constitution/The Atlanta Journal

Atlanta Journal-Constitution

P.O. Box 4689   Ph: (404)526-5240
P.O. Box 4689
Atlanta, GA 30302
Contact: Virginia Everett, Director of News Research Services, (404)526-5213, geverett@ajc.com.
Desc: Contains stories from The Atlanta Constitution and
The Atlanta Journal, two general circulation newspapers
reporting local, national, and international news. Regional
coverage emphasizes the food and beverage, tobacco, telecommunications, and transportation industries. *Available:*
The Dialog Corporation, DIALOG; LEXIS-NEXIS,
NEXIS; CompuServe Information Service, Knowledge
Index; Dow Jones Interactive Publishing; West Group,
WESTLAW; Prodigy Services Company, PRODIGY;
NewsBank, Inc. *Type:* Database.

The Atlanta Journal and Constitution

The Atlanta Journal and Constitution

72 Marietta St. NW   Ph: (404)526-5151
PO Box 4689   Free: 800-846-6672
Atlanta, GA 30302-4689   Fax: (404)526-5746
E-mail: constitution@ajc.com; journal@ajc.com.
URL: http://www.accessatlanta.com.
Contact: Ron Martin, Editor; Roger Kintzel, Publisher;
Susan Soper, Asst. Mng. Editor, (404)526-5441.
Desc: General newspaper. *Type:* Periodical.

The Atlanta Voice

The Atlanta Voice

633 Pryor St. SW   Ph: (404)524-6426
Box 92405   Fax: (404)523-7853
Atlanta, GA 30314-0405
Contact: Stan Washington, Editor; Janis Ware, Publisher.
Desc: Black community newspaper. *Type:* Periodical.

Atlantic Feature Syndicate

16 Slayton Rd.   Ph: (617)665-4442
Melrose, MA 02176
Contact: Mark Parisi, President; Lynn Reznick, Mktg. Dir.
Alt. Contact: 16 Slayton Rd., Melrose, MA 02176; telephone: (617)665-4442. *Type:* Periodical.

The Atlantic Monthly

The Atlantic Monthly Co.

77 N. Washington St.   Ph: (617)854-7700
Boston, MA 02114   Fax: (617)854-7876
URL: http://www.theatlantic.com.
Contact: William Whitworth, Editor-in-Chief.
Desc: General interest magazine. *Type:* Periodical.

The Augusta Chronicle

The Augusta Chronicle

News Bldg.   Ph: (706)724-0851
725 Broad St.   Fax: (706)722-7403
PO Box 1928
Augusta, GA 30903
E-mail: newsroom@augustachronicle.com
URL: http://www.augustachronicle.com.
Contact: Dennis Sodomka, Exec. Editor; W.S. Morris, III,
Publisher.
Desc: Daily newspaper. *Type:* Periodical.

Austin American-Statesman

Cox Texas Publications, Inc.

PO Box 670   Ph: (512)445-3500
Austin, TX 78767   Free: 800-444-4382
    Fax: (512)445-3800
E-mail: news@statesman.com.
URL: http://www.austin360.com.
Contact: Michael Laosa, Publisher; James Ripley, Vice
Pres./CFO; Susan Davidson, HR/Dir.; Robert Stewart,
Controller; Richard Apperley, ITS Dir.; Connie Salinas,
Mktg. Dir.
Desc: General newspaper. *Type:* Periodical.

Austin American-Statesman

Austin American-Statesman

305 S. Congress Ave.   Ph: (512)445-3676
P.O. Box 670
Austin, TX 78767
URL: http://www.austin36.com
Desc: Contains the complete text of the Austin American-
Statesman, a general circulation newspaper reporting local,
national, and international news. Special areas of interest
include extensive coverage of state government news and
issues. *Available:* Bell & Howell Information and Learning. *Type:* Database.

Authenticated News International

34 High St.   Ph: (914)232-7726
Katonah, NY 10536-1117
Desc: Distributes photographs. *Alt. Contact:* 34 High St.,
Katonah, NY 10536-1117; telephone: (914)232-7726.
Type: Periodical.

Avanti NewsFeatures

29106 Palomino Dr.   Ph: (810)573-2755
Warren, MI 48093-3505   Fax: (810)573-2755
E-mail: avanti1054@aol.com.

Contact: Hawke Fracassa, Sr. Mng. Ed.; Anne Fracassa, Sr. Ed./Auto; Craig Oldani, Tech. Ed.; Michael Raveane, Politics Ed.; Tracey Lee-Petri, Parenting Columnist; Bob Gramer, Music Ed.; Anthony W. Guerrero, Motorcycle Ed.; Francesca Fracassa, Food Ed.; Becca Fracassa, Medical Ed; Karen Oldani, Arts & Crafts Ed.; Tony Oldani, Tools Ed.; Filip Fracassa, Travel Ed.; Karen Pearlman, Sports Ed.; A.M. Schlosser, Lifestyle Ed.

Alt. Contact: 29106 Palomino Dr., Warren, MI 48093-3505; telephone: (810)573-2755; fax: (810)573-2755. *Type:* Periodical.

The Baltimore Sun

The Baltimore Sun
501 N. Calvert St.   Ph: (410)332-6000
Baltimore, MD 21278-0001   Free: 800-829-8000
                                         Fax: (410)752-6049

Contact: Michael Waller, Publisher; John Carroll, Editor, (410)332-6496; William Marimow, Managing Editor, (410)332-6088; Steve Proctor, Assistant Managing Editor, (410)332-6120.

Desc: General newspaper. *Type:* Periodical.

The Baltimore Sun

The Baltimore Sun
501 N. Calvert St.   Ph: (410)332-6800
Baltimore, MD 21278
URL: http://www.sunspot.net/recy/

Desc: Contains the complete text of The Baltimore Sun, a general circulation newspaper reporting local, national, and international news. Special areas of interest include area and state industries, including defense and electronics, service, commercial fishing, agriculture, and tourism; and topics such as government issues, taxes, and proposed legislation. *Available:* Bell & Howell Information and Learning; The Dialog Corporation, DIALOG; The Dialog Corporation, DIALOG; LEXIS-NEXIS, NEXIS; CompuServe Information Service, Knowledge Index. *Type:* Database.

Bangor Daily News

Bangor Daily News
491 Main St.   Ph: (207)990-8000
PO Box 1329   Free: 800-432-7964
Bangor, ME 04402-1329   Fax: (207)941-0885
E-mail: bdnmail@bangornews.infi.net; Bangornews@aol.com.

Contact: Richard J. Warren, Publisher, (207)990-8221, fax: (207)941-9476; Robert W. Stairs, VP, Administration, (207)990-8223, fax: (207)990-8095; A. Mark Woodward, Exec. Ed., (207)990-8239, fax: (207)941-9476; Wayne A. Lawton, Advertising Dir., (207)990-8061; James M. Spox, Circulation Mgr., (207)990-8280, fax: (207)990-8027; Charles Campo, Librarian, (207)990-8160, fax: (207)990-8160, bdnlib@bangornews.infi.net.

Desc: General newspaper. *Type:* Periodical.

The Bascome Syndicate

62 Cobbetts Ln.   Ph: (516)749-0111
Shelter Island, NY 11964
Contact: Rosemary Bascome, Editor.
Desc: Distributes "Along the Food Trail." *Alt. Contact:* 62 Cobbetts Ln., Shelter Island, NY 11964; telephone: (516)749-0111. *Type:* Periodical.

Bay City News Service

1390 Market St.   Ph: (415)552-8900
Ste. 324   Fax: (415)552-8912
San Francisco, CA 94102
Contact: Dick Fogel, Editor; Marcia Fogel, Entertainment Ed.; Joann Sutro, News Ed.; Wayne Futak, General Mgr.
Desc: Distributes regional wire service. *Alt. Contact:* 1390 Market St., Ste. 324, San Francisco, CA 94102; telephone: (415)552-8900; fax: (415)552-8912. *Type:* Periodical.

Bay Shore Suffolk Life

Suffolk Life Newspapers
PO Box 9167   Ph: (516)369-0800
Riverhead, NY 11901   Fax: (516)369-5390
E-mail: stnewsroom@hamptons.com
Contact: David J. Willmott, Editor and Publisher; Joe MacLellan, Managing Editor.
Desc: Community newspaper. *Type:* Periodical.

Beaver Creek Features

3508 W. 151 St.   Ph: (216)259-1389
Cleveland, OH 44111-2105
E-mail: deann@cybergate.net.
URL: http://www.cybergate.net-deann.
Contact: Dean Norman, Artist/Owner.
Desc: Distributes cartoon features about wildlife and outdoor recreation. *Alt. Contact:* 3508 W. 151 St., Cleveland, OH 44111-2105; telephone: (216)259-1389. *Type:* Periodical.

Better Homes & Gardens Features Syndicate

1716 Locust St.   Free: 800-678-8135
Des Moines, IA 50309-3023   Fax: 800-678-5994
Contact: Jerry Ward, VP Pub. Group; Gary Fees, Business Mgr.; Dennis Christensen, Western Rep.; Robert Krisch, Northeast Rep.
Alt. Contact: 1716 Locust St., Des Moines, IA 50309-3023; fax: 800-678-5994; toll-free: 800-678-8135. *Type:* Periodical.

Bettman Archive

902 Broadway   Ph: (212)777-6200
New York, NY 10010   Fax: (212)533-4034
Contact: Herbert Gstalder, President; Anne Rudden, Assoc. Dir.; Darby Harper, Res. Mgr.; Dann Peirce, Mktg. Dir.
Alt. Contact: 902 Broadway, New York, NY 10010; telephone: (212)777-6200; fax: (212)533-4034. *Type:* Periodical.

Big Red Hen Productions

Box 807   Free: 888-BIG-REDH
45 Tudor City Pl.
New York, NY 10017
Contact: Frances K. Grace, Self-Syndicator.
Alt. Contact: Box 807, 45 Tudor City Pl., New York, NY 10017; toll-free: 888-BIG-REDH. *Type:* Periodical.

The Birmingham News

The Birmingham News
2200 4th Ave. N.   Ph: (205)325-2222
PO Box 2553   Free: 800-283-4051
Birmingham, AL 35202-2553   Fax: (205)325-3246
E-mail: 70550.3405@compuserve.com.
Contact: Victor H. Hanson, II, Publisher, (205)325-2411; Victor H. Hanson, III, General Mgr., (205)325-3126; Thomas V. Scarritt, Editor, (205)325-2205, fax: (205)325-3278; Carol F. Nunnelley, Managing Editor, (205)325-2111, fax: (205)325-2283.
Desc: General newspaper. *Alt. Contact:* PO Box 2553, Birmingham, AL 35202; telephone: (205)325-2444; fax: (205)325-2283; toll-free: 800-283-4144. *Type:* Periodical.

Black Press Service Inc.

166 Madison Ave.   Ph: (212)686-6850
New York, NY 10016   Fax: (212)686-7308
Contact: Jay R. Levy, President; Roy Thompson, Editor; Bill Baldwin, Assoc. Ed.; Peter Knight, Sales Mgr.
Desc: Distributes news wire service. *Alt. Contact:* 166 Madison Ave., New York, NY 10016; telephone: (212)686-6850; fax: (212)686-7308. *Type:* Periodical.

The Blade

The Toledo Blade Co.
541 N. Superior St.   Ph: (419)724-6000
Toledo, OH 43660-1000   Fax: (419)724-6439
URL: http://www.toledoblade.com.
Contact: Paul Block, Publisher; William Block, Publisher; Paul Block, Jr., Publisher; John Robinson Block, Co-Publisher/Ed. in Chief; Thomas Walton, VP/Editor; Gary J. Blair, VP of Administration; David M. Beihoff, VP/General Mgr.
Desc: General newspaper. *Type:* Periodical.

Boston Features Syndicate

42 Eugenia St.   Ph: (617)963-5073
Randolph, MA 02368
Contact: Harry Privette, President; Martin Hanna, Director.
Desc: Distributes Mini-Bopper cartoon. *Alt. Contact:* 42 Eugenia St., Randolph, MA 02368; telephone: (617)963-5073. *Type:* Periodical.

The Boston Globe

New York Times Co./Globe Newspaper Co.
135 Morrissey Blvd.   Ph: (617)929-2935
PO Box 2378   Fax: (617)929-3192
Boston, MA 02107-3310
Contact: Matthew V. Storen, Editor; William O. Taylor, Publisher; Benjamin B. Taylor, President; Mary Jane Patrone, Vice Pres. of Marketing.
Desc: General newspaper. *Type:* Periodical.

The Boston Globe

Globe Newspaper Co.
PO Box 2378   Ph: (617)929-2000
Boston, MA 02107
E-mail: desisto@boston.com
URL: http://www.boston.com
Desc: Contains the complete text of staff-written news items, feature stories, columns, and editorials from The Boston Globe (Massachusetts) newspaper. Regional coverage emphasizes area politics, the high technology industry, real estate, and the arts. *Available:* Bell & Howell Information and Learning; The Dialog Corporation, DIALOG; CompuServe Information Service, Knowledge Index; LEXIS-NEXIS, NEXIS. *Type:* Database.

Boston Herald

Boston Herald
PO Box 2096   Ph: (617)426-3000
Boston, MA 02106-2096   Free: 800-225-2040
                               Fax: (617)542-1315
URL: http://www.bostonherald.com.
Contact: Ken Chandler, Editor, (617)542-1315; Patrick Purcell, Publisher; Shaun Butler, Advertising Vice Pres.; Bill Weber, Asst. Managing Editor; Andrew F. Costello, Jr., Executive Editor; Kevin Convey, Managing Editor; Andrew Gully, Managing Editor; Sonia Turek, Deputy Managing Editor; Andy Tomolonis, Deputy Managing Editor; Ted Bunker, Asst. Managing Editor; Gwen Gage, Vice Pres., Promotions; Randy Hano, National Sales Mgr.; Bob Sheehan, Retail Advertising Mgr.; Tom Libby, Dir., I
Desc: General newspaper. *Type:* Periodical.

Boston Magazine

Boston Magazine
300 Massachusetts Ave.   Ph: (617)262-9700
Boston, MA 02115   Fax: (617)262-4925
E-mail: artj@bostonmagazine.com.
URL: http://www.bostonmagazine.com.
Contact: Craig Vnger, Editor; Alan J. Klein, Publisher; Susan Watson, Marketing Director; Mary Kaye Chryssicas, Advertising Dir.

Desc: Magazine covering business, politics, and lifestyle in the Boston metropolitan area. *Type:* Periodical.

Bradford Journal/Miner

Bradford Journal
265 S. Ave.　　　　　　　　Ph: (814)362-6563
PO Box 17　　　　　　　　Fax: (814)368-8202
Bradford, PA 16701
E-mail: journal@penn.com.
Contact: Grant Nichols, Publisher.
Desc: Community newspaper. *Type:* Periodical.

Brenafeatures

PO Box 233　　　　　　　　Ph: (617)444-8244
Needam, MA 02192-2820
Contact: John Brennan, Pres./Ed.; Alice F. Brennan, VP/ Assoc. Ed.
Alt. Contact: PO Box 233, Needam, MA 02192-2820; telephone: (617)444-8244. *Type:* Periodical.

Briargate Media

PO Box 998　　　　　　　　Ph: (719)531-3304
Colorado Springs, CO 80901　　Fax: (719)531-3302
Contact: James C. Dobson, Ph.D, Author.
Alt. Contact: PO Box 998, Colorado Springs, CO 80901; telephone: (719)531-3304; fax: (719)531-3302. *Type:* Periodical.

The Broward Informer

The Broward Informer
PO Box 130207　　　　　　Ph: (954)370-6009
Sunrise, FL 33313
E-mail: informer@interpoint.net.
URL: http://www.browardinformer.com.
Contact: Steve Mangerian, Editor of food, travel, entertainment; Mayda Mangerian, Editor-in-Chief; Michael Gaines, Office Mgr.
Desc: Local with empyhasis on travel and consumer protection, and seniors' affairs news. *Type:* Periodical.

Bucks County Courier Times

Greater Philadelphia Newspapers
8400 Rte. 13　　　　　　　Ph: (215)949-4000
Levittown, PA 19057　　　　Fax: (215)949-4114
URL: http://www.bcct-gpn.com.
Contact: Timothy J. Birch, Editor.
Desc: Newspaper. *Type:* Periodical.

Buddy Basch Feature Syndicate

771 West End Ave.　　　　　Ph: (212)666-2300
New York, NY 10025-5572
Contact: Buddy Basch, Editor and Publisher; Frances Scott, Asst. Pub./Women's Ed.; Murri Barber, Reporter; Charles J. Brand, Reporter; Peter Mallon, Reporter; Michael Flaster, Photographer; G. Godfrey, Esq., Atty.
Desc: Distributes travel, entertainment, medical, and health columns. *Alt. Contact:* 771 West End Ave., New York, NY 10025-5572; telephone: (212)666-2300. *Type:* Periodical.

The Buffalo News

Stanford Lipsey Publishers
1 News Plaza　　　　　　　Ph: (716)849-3434
Buffalo, NY 14203-2994　　Free: 800-777-8680
　　　　　　　　　　　　Fax: (716)849-3409
URL: http://www.buffnews.com.
Contact: Murray Light, Editor; Stanford Lipsey, Publisher; Warren Colville, Exec. Vice Pres.
Desc: Daily newspaper. *Type:* Periodical.

The Buffalo News

The Buffalo News
One News Plaza　　　　　　Ph: (716)849-3434
Box 100
Buffalo, NY 14240
Contact: Eliot Shapiro, Library Director.
Desc: Contains the complete text of the Buffalo News (New York) newspaper covering Allegany, Cattaraugus, Chautauqua, Erie, Genesee, Niagara, Orleans, and Wyoming counties. Regional coverage emphasizes the automotive, banking, and insurance industries, local sports and government news, and news from Buffalo State University. *Available:* The Dialog Corporation, DIALOG; LEXIS-NEXIS, NEXIS; Dow Jones Interactive Publishing. *Type:* Database.

The Calgary Herald

Southam, Inc.
Calgary Herald
215-16 St. SE　　　　　　Ph: (403)235-7100
PO Box 2400, Station M
Calgary, AB, Canada T2P 0W8
E-mail: online@theherald.southam.ca
URL: http://www.southam.com/calgaryherald
Desc: Contains the complete text of news items and feature articles from the Calgary Herald (Alberta) newspaper. Regional coverage emphasizes the oil and gas, energy, and consumer electronics industries; agriculture; local businesses; political issues; real estate and housing construction; and sports. *Available:* Infomart Assistant, Infomart Online; LEXIS-NEXIS, NEXIS; Infomart Dialog Limited; Infomart Online. *Type:* Database.

Calgary Herald

Southam, Inc.
999 8th St. SW, Ste. 300　　Ph: (403)209-3500
Calgary, AB, Canada T2R 1N7　Free: 800-387-2446
　　　　　　　　　　　　(403)245-8666
URL: http://www.calgaryherald.com.
Contact: Ken King, Publisher, (403)235-7422, fax: (403)235-7575; Crosbie Cotton, Editor-in-Chief, (403)235-7525, fax: (403)235-7379; Francesca Briggs, VP, Advertising & Sales, (403)235-7175, fax: (403)235-7772; Joan Crockatt, Managing Editor, (403)235-7516, fax: (403)235-7379; Shelley Knapp, Editor, Computers/ Technology, (403)235-7553, fax: (403)235-7358; Neil Haeslar, Observer/New Media Editor, (403)235-7588, fax: (403)235-7379.
Desc: General newspaper. *Alt. Contact:* 215-16 St. S.E., Calgary, AB, Canada T2P 0W8; telephone: (403)235-7433; fax: (403)235-7438. *Type:* Periodical.

The Calgary Mirror (Northside and Southside)

Net Mirror, Inc.
2615 12th St., NE　　　　　Ph: (403)250-4200
Calgary, AB, Canada T2E 7W9　Fax: (403)250-4258
Contact: Edith DiPalma, Editor; Ken King, Publisher; Wayne Kennelly, General Mgr.
Desc: Local newspaper. *Type:* Periodical. ⌐

The Calgary Sun

The Calgary Sun
2615 12th St. NE　　　　　Ph: (403)250-4200
Calgary, AB, Canada T2E 7W9　Fax: (403)250-4180
E-mail: calnews@sunpub.com; callet@sunpub.com.
URL: http://www.canoe.ca/calgarysun; http://www.canoe.ca.
Contact: Chris Nelson, Editor-in-Chief, (403)250-4121; Les Pyette, Publisher, (403)250-4100, fax: (403)250-4213, lpyette@sunpub.com; Ed Huculak, Advertising Dir., (403)250-4240, fax: (403)250-4258, ehuculak@sunpub.com; Anika Van Wyk, Assistant Today Ed., (403)250-4308; Paul Jackson, Assoc. Ed., (403)250-4120; Rick Bell, Columnist, (403)250-4305, rbell@sunpub.com; Licia Corbella, Editor, (403)250-4129, lcorbell@sunpub.com.

Desc: Newspaper (tabloid). *Type:* Periodical.

California Features International Inc.

PO Box 58　　　　　　　　Ph: (310)441-0565
Beverly Hills, CA 90213　　Fax: (310)441-4544
Contact: Brad Eltermann, P; Stan Findellem, Vice President.
Desc: Distributes celebrity, lifestyle, and travel features. *Alt. Contact:* PO Box 58, Beverly Hills, CA 90213; telephone: (310)441-0565; fax: (310)441-4544. *Type:* Periodical.

California News Service

121 N. Gate Hall　　　　　Ph: (510)642-9054–
Berkeley, CA 94720　　　　Fax: (510)643-9136
Contact: Susan Rasky, Editor.
Desc: Distributes political features. *Alt. Contact:* 121 N. Gate Hall, Berkeley, CA 94720; telephone: (510)642-9054; fax: (510)643-9136. *Type:* Periodical.

Canada Wide Feature Service Limited

Box 345　　　　　　　　　Ph: (416)947-2191
Sta. A　　　　　　　　　　Fax: (416)947-2450
Toronto, ON, Canada M5W 1C2
Contact: Richard Vroom, Sales Rep./Miller Feat. Syn.; Wanda Goodwin, Photo Sales; Glenn Garnett, Editor; Joe Marino, General Mgr.; Kevin Taite, Project Coord.
Desc: Distributes comic strips, crosswords, and news features. *Alt. Contact:* Box 345, Sta. A, Toronto, ON, Canada M5W 1C2; telephone: (416)947-2191; fax: (416)947-2450. *Type:* Periodical.

The Canadian Press & Broadcast News

36 King St. E　　　　　　Ph: (416)364-0321
Toronto, ON, Canada M5C 2L9　Fax: (416)364-0207
E-mail: cp@canpress.ca.
URL: http://www.xe.net/canpress.
Contact: Donald Jarrett, VP Fin. & Admin.; Jim Poling, VP Editorial/Acting GM; Wayne Waldroff, VP Broadcasting; Denis Tremblay, VP French Svcs.; M. Sifton, Chm.; W. Waldroff, VP Broadcasting/GM Broadcast News.
Alt. Contact: 36 King St. E, Toronto, ON, Canada M5C 2L9; telephone: (416)364-0321; fax: (416)364-0207. *Type:* Periodical.

Canadian Press Newstex

The Canadian Press (CP)
36 King St. E.　　　　　　Ph: (416)364-0321
Toronto, ON, Canada M5C 2L9
E-mail: pn@cp.org
URL: http://www.cp.org
Desc: Contains the the complete text of more than 2 million English-language news stories from the CP newswire service. Includes stories from CP bureaus in Canada, CP reporters abroad, and local stories from CP's member newspapers. *Available:* QL Systems Limited, QUICK-LAW; The Canadian Press (CP). *Type:* Database.

The Capital Times/Wisconsin State Journal

Madison Newspapers, Inc.
1901 Fish Hatchery Rd.　　Ph: (608)252-6412
P.O. Box 8058
Madison, WI 53708
E-mail: lybrary@madison.com
URL: http://www.madison.com
Contact: Ron Larson, Library Director, (608)252-6113, fax: (608)252-6119, lybrary@madison.com.
Desc: Contains selected text of the Capital Times and Wisconsin State Journal (Madison) newspapers. Regional cov-

erage emphasizes University of Wisconsin news, research, sports, state government, dairy and other agriculture, paper and other manufacturing, and the insurance industry. *Available:* The Dialog Corporation, DIALOG; LEXIS-NEXIS, NEXIS; Bell & Howell Information and Learning; LEXIS-NEXIS. *Type:* Database.

Capitol News Service

1713 J St. Ste. 202   Ph: (916)445-6336
Sacramento, CA 95814   Fax: (916)443-5871
Contact: David A. Kline, Exec.Ed.

Desc: Distributes news service. *Alt. Contact:* 1713 J St. Ste. 202, Sacramento, CA 95814; telephone: (916)445-6336; fax: (916)443-5871. *Type:* Periodical.

Capper's

Capper's
1503 SW 42nd St.   Ph: (785)274-4300
Topeka, KS 66609-1265   Free: 800-678-5779
          Fax: (785)274-4305
E-mail: cappers@kspress.com.

Contact: Ann Crahan, Editor, (785)274-4346; Bryan Welch, Publisher, (785)274-4305; Keith Chartier, Advertising Mgr., (785)274-4330.

Desc: Human interest magazine (tabloid). *Type:* Periodical.

Carberry Columns

1349 Douglas Ave.   Ph: (708)799-6360
Flossmoor, IL 60422
Contact: Mary Margaret Carberry, Author/Owner.

Desc: Distributes personal opinion, social commentary, and humor pieces. *Alt. Contact:* 1349 Douglas Ave., Flossmoor, IL 60422; telephone: (708)799-6360. *Type:* Periodical.

The Caruba Organization

9 Brookside Dr.   Ph: (201)763-6392
PO Box 40   Fax: (201)763-4287
Maplewood, NJ 07040-0040
Contact: Alan Caruba, President.

Desc: Distributes The Boring Institute media spoof, National Anxiety Center book reviews, and other features. *Alt. Contact:* 9 Brookside Dr., PO Box 40, Maplewood, NJ 07040-0040; telephone: (201)763-6392; fax: (201)763-4287. *Type:* Periodical.

Central News Agency

2 Penn Plaza 18th Fl.   Ph: (212)643-9332
c/o UPI   Fax: (212)643-9334
New York, NY 10001
Contact: Kwang-Chun Huang, Corr.; David Yin-Chi Wang, NY Bureau Chief.

Desc: Distributes news articles. *Alt. Contact:* 2 Penn Plaza 18th Fl., c/o UPI, New York, NY 10001; telephone: (212)643-9332; fax: (212)643-9334. *Type:* Periodical.

Central Newspapers Inc.

1000 National Press Bldg.   Ph: (202)662-7260
Washington, DC 20045   Fax: (202)662-7268
Desc: Distributes congressional reporting. *Alt. Contact:* 1000 National Press Bldg., Washington, DC 20045; telephone: (202)662-7260; fax: (202)662-7268. *Type:* Periodical.

Central Press Features of London

400 Madison Ave.   Ph: (212)832-2839
Ste. 1704
New York, NY 10017
Contact: Jeffrey Blyth, US Ed.

Alt. Contact: 400 Madison Ave., Ste. 1704, New York, NY 10017; telephone: (212)832-2839. *Type:* Periodical.

Century News Service

929 W. Broad St.   Ph: (703)532-3267
Ste. 200   Fax: (703)532-3396
Falls Church, VA 22046

Desc: Distributes Eye on Washington. *Alt. Contact:* 929 W. Broad St., Ste. 200, Falls Church, VA 22046; telephone: (703)532-3267; fax: (703)532-3396. *Type:* Periodical.

Changing Times-The Kiplinger Washington Editors Inc.

1729 H St. NW   Ph: (202)887-6400
Washington, DC 20006

Desc: Distributes Kiplinger Finance Magazine, Washington Letter, Tax Letter, Agriculture Letter, Florida Letter, and California Letter. *Alt. Contact:* 1729 H St. NW, Washington, DC 20006; telephone: (202)887-6400. *Type:* Periodical.

Charleston Daily Mail

Charleston Daily Mail
1001 Virginia St. E.   Ph: (304)348-5140
Charleston, WV 25331   Fax: (304)348-4847
E-mail: dmnews@dailymail.com.
URL: http://www.dailymail.com.
Contact: David Greenfield, Editor; Terry Horne, Publisher.

Desc: General newspaper. *Type:* Periodical.

Charleston Gazette

Gazette Daily Inc.
1001 Virginia St. E.   Ph: (304)348-5100
Box 2993   Free: 800-982-6397
Charleston, WV 25301-2895   Fax: (304)348-5133
Contact: Craig Selby, Publisher, (304)348-5199, fax: (308)348-1233, cselby@wvgazette.com.

Desc: General newspaper. *Type:* Periodical.

Charlotte Observer

Knight-Ridder, Inc.
50 W. Fernando St.   Ph: (408)938-7700
San Jose, CA 95113
URL: http://www.charlotte.com.
Contact: Jennifer Bucbaer, Editor, (704)358-5001; Peter Ridder, Publisher, (704)358-5834; Maggie Krust, Advertising Mgr., (704)358-5333.

Desc: General newspaper. *Alt. Contact:* 600 S. Tryon St., PO Box 32188-28232, Charlotte, NC 28202-1842; telephone: (704)358-5040; fax: (704)358-5036. *Type:* Periodical.

The Charlotte Observer

The Charlotte Observer
600 S. Tryon St.   Ph: (704)358-5777
Charlotte, NC 28202
E-mail: charcom@charlotte.infi.net
URL: http://www.charlotte.com/
Contact: Marion Paynter, Library Manager, (704)358-5212, fax: (704)358-5203, paynter@charlotte.com.

Desc: Contains the complete text of news items and feature articles from The Charlotte Observer (North Carolina) newspaper. Regional coverage emphasizes the banking, construction, textile, and transportation industries, sports, and religion. *Available:* The Dialog Corporation, DIALOG; CompuServe Information Service, Knowledge Index. *Type:* Database.

Chattanooga Times & Free Press

Chattanooga Publishing Co.
400 E. 11th St.   Ph: (423)756-1234
PO Box 1447   Fax: (423)752-3388
Chattanooga, TN 37401-1447
URL: http://www.chattimes.com.

Contact: Walter E. Hussman, Publisher; Paul Neely, Assoc. Publisher.
Desc: Newspaper. *Type:* Periodical.

Chicago

K-III Magazine Corp.
500 N. Dearborn, Ste. 1200
Chicago, IL 60610
Contact: Richard Babcock, Editor; John Carroll, Publisher; George Gretser, Advertising Dir.

Desc: Metropolitan magazine for the Chicago area. *Type:* Periodical.

Chicago Reader

Chicago Reader, Inc.
11 E. Illinois   Ph: (312)828-0350
Chicago, IL 60611   Fax: (312)828-0305
E-mail: mail@chireader.com.
URL: http://www.chicagoreader.com.
Contact: Alison True, Editor; Jane Levine, Publisher; Don Humberton, Advertising Dir.

Desc: Alternative newspaper covering urban issues and politics, arts and entertainment. *Type:* Periodical.

Chicago Sun-Times

Chicago Sun-Times Inc.
401 N. Wabash Ave.   Ph: (312)321-3000
Chicago, IL 60611-3593   Fax: (312)321-3084
Contact: F. David Radler, Publisher; Joe Sherman, Asst. Publisher; J. David Dodd, Executive VP; Nigel Wade, Editor-in-Chief; Larry Green, Exec. Editor.

Desc: General newspaper. *Type:* Periodical.

Chicago Sun-Times

Chicago Sun-Times
401 N. Wabash Ave.   Ph: (312)321-2593
Chicago, IL 60611
Contact: Terri Golembiewski, Library Director, (312)321-2592, fax: (312)321-3084.

Desc: Contains the complete text of news items and feature articles from the Chicago Sun-Times (Illinois) newspaper. Regional coverage emphasizes business, political, and social issues and local events. *Available:* LEXIS-NEXIS, NEXIS; LEXIS-NEXIS, LEXIS; Dow Jones Interactive Publishing; Bell & Howell Information and Learning. *Type:* Database.

Chicago-Sun Times Features Inc.

401 N. Wabash Ave.   Ph: (312)321-2890
Ste. 532-A   Fax: (312)321-2336
Chicago, IL 60611
E-mail: elschiele@aol.com.
URL: http://www.suntimes.com.
Contact: Elizabeth Owens-Schiele, Syndicate Mgr.

Alt. Contact: 401 N. Wabash Ave., Ste. 532-A, Chicago, IL 60611; telephone: (312)321-2890; fax: (312)321-2336. *Type:* Periodical.

Chicago Tribune

Tribune Publishing
435 N. Michigan Ave.   Ph: (312)222-3232
Chicago, IL 60611-4022
URL: http://www.chicago.tribune.com.
Contact: Jac Fuller, V.P./Editor; John W. Madigan, Publisher.

Desc: General newspaper. *Type:* Periodical.

The Chicago Tribune

Chicago Tribune Co.
435 N. Michigan Ave.   Ph: (312)222-3232
Chicago, IL 60611
URL: http://www.chicago.tribune.com

Desc: Contains the complete text of The Chicago Tribune, a general circulation newspaper reporting local, national, and international news. Special areas of interest include services, such as advertising, marketing, banking, options and commodity trading and finance; industries, including energy, food, high technology, manufacturing, retail, steel and transportation; and topics such as agriculture, architecture, city government, the arts and entertainment, and sports. *Available:* Bell & Howell Information and Learning; The Dialog Corporation, DIALOG; CompuServe Information Service, Knowledge Index; LEXIS-NEXIS, NEXIS; NIFTY Corporation, NIFTY-SERVE. *Type:* Database.

Chorpus Christi Caller-Times

Caller-Times
820 N. Lower Broadway   Ph: (512)884-2011
PO Box 9136
Corpus Christi, TX 78469
E-mail: cteds@caller.com.
URL: http://www.caller.com.
Contact: Larry Rose, Editor; Steve Sullivan, Publisher, (512)886-3666.
Desc: General newspaper. *Alt. Contact:* telephone: (512)886-3732. *Type:* Periodical.

The Christian Science Monitor

Christian Science Publishing Society
One Norway St.   Ph: (617)450-2000
Boston, MA 02115
E-mail: support@monitor.com
URL: http://www.csmonitor.com
Desc: Contains the complete text of news items, feature articles, and editorials from The Christian Science Monitor newspaper. Covers current national and international issues and events, and trends in world politics, business, industry, and popular culture, with an emphasis on news analysis. *Available:* Bell & Howell Information and Learning; The Dialog Corporation, DIALOG; LEXIS-NEXIS, NEXIS; CompuServe Information Service, Knowledge Index. *Type:* Database.

Chronicle Features

870 Market St.   Ph: (415)777-7212
San Francisco, CA 94102   Fax: (415)362-0279
E-mail: cfeatures@aol.com.
Contact: Stuart Dodds, Ed./Gen. Mgr.; Rennie Kirby, Office Mgr.; Susan Peters, Assoc. Ed.; Harley Colbert, Prod. Mgr.; Sue Fenstermaker, Ed. Prod. Mgr.; Hilda Bloom, Perm. Ed.
Desc: Distributes cartoons, columns, and news articles. *Alt. Contact:* 870 Market St., San Francisco, CA 94102; telephone: (415)777-7212; fax: (415)362-0279. *Type:* Periodical.

The Chronicle Herald

The Halifax Herald Ltd.
260 Brownlow Ave.   Ph: (902)426-3329
PO Box 610   Free: 800-563-1187
Dartmouth, NS, Canada B3B   Fax: (902)426-1164
1V9
Contact: G.W. Dennis, Publisher; Fred Buckland, Editor.
Desc: Newspaper. *Type:* Periodical.

The Cincinnati Enquirer

Gannett Co., Inc.
1100 Wilson Blvd.   Ph: (703)284-6000
Arlington, VA 22234   Free: 800-872-0001
Contact: George R. Blake, Editor; Harry M. Whipple, Publisher; David L. Hunke, Advertising Mgr.
Desc: General newspaper. *Alt. Contact:* 312 Elm St., Cincinnati, OH 45202; telephone: (513)721-2700; fax: (513)721-2703. *Type:* Periodical.

The Cincinnati Enquirer

The Cincinnati Enquirer
312 Elm St.   Ph: (513)721-2700
Cincinnati, OH 45202
URL: http://www.enquirer.com

Desc: Contains the complete text of The Cincinnati Enquirer, a general circulation newspaper reporting local, national, and international news. Covers all news stories, features, editorials, arts, and sports. *Available:* Bell & Howell Information and Learning; LEXIS-NEXIS, NEXIS. *Type:* Database.

Cincinnati/Kentucky Post

E.W. Scripps Co.
Cincinnati Post
125 E. Court St.   Ph: (513)977-3825
Cincinnati, OH 45202
URL: http://www.scripps.com

Desc: Contains the complete text of news items, feature articles, columns, and editorials from The Cincinnati Post (Ohio) and The Kentucky Post newspapers. Regional coverage emphasizes industries engaged in the manufacture of aircraft engines, auto parts, food products, industrial machinery, chemicals, metal products, toys, and apparel. *Available:* The Dialog Corporation, DIALOG; The Dialog Corporation, DIALOG; Bell & Howell Information and Learning. *Type:* Database.

The Cincinnati Post

E.W. Scripps Co.
125 E. Court St.   Ph: (513)352-2000
Cincinnati, OH 45202   Fax: (513)621-3962
E-mail: cpost@one.net.
URL: http://www.cincypost.com.
Contact: Paul F. Knue, Editor.
Desc: Newspaper. *Type:* Periodical.

Cineman Syndicate

PO Box 4433   Ph: (914)692-4572
Middletown, NY 10941   Fax: (914)692-8311
E-mail: cineman@ny.frontiercomm.net.
Contact: Jay A. Brown, Editor; John P. McCarthy, Assoc. Ed.; Robert Edelstein, Assoc. Ed.
Desc: Distributes book, movie, and music reviews; horoscopes; trivia quiz. *Alt. Contact:* PO Box 4433, Middletown, NY 10941; telephone: (914)692-4572; fax: (914)692-8311. *Type:* Periodical.

City News Bureau of Chicago

35 E. Wacker Dr.   Ph: (312)782-8100
Ste. 792   Fax: (312)201-0603
Chicago, IL 60601
Contact: Joseph Reilly, General Mgr.; Paul Zimbrakos, City Ed.
Desc: Distributes news wire service. *Alt. Contact:* 35 E. Wacker Dr., Ste. 792, Chicago, IL 60601; telephone: (312)782-8100; fax: (312)201-0603. *Type:* Periodical.

City News Service Inc.

1900 Avenue of the Stars   Ph: (310)201-9120
Ste. 1870   Fax: (310)201-9124
Los Angeles, CA 90067
Contact: Vicki Psomas, Business Mgr.; Douglas Faigin, President; Yet Lock, Vice President; Pat Teague, Editor.
Desc: Distributes news wire service. *Alt. Contact:* 1900 Avenue of the Stars, Ste. 1870, Los Angeles, CA 90067; telephone: (310)201-9120; fax: (310)201-9124. *Type:* Periodical.

City Paper

City Paper
Philadelphia City Paper   Ph: (215)735-8444
123 Chestnut St., 3rd Fl.   Fax: (215)735-8535
Philadelphia, PA 19106
E-mail: adinfo@citypaper.net
URL: http://www.citypaper.net.
Contact: Paul Curci, Publisher, fax: (215)875-1820, paul@citypaper.net; Amy Stoller, Advertising Dir.; Claudia Lippman, Production Mgr., fax: (215)875-1834, claudia@citypaper.net.
Desc: Alternative newsweekly. *Type:* Periodical.

The Clarion Ledger

Gannett Co., Inc.
1100 Wilson Blvd.   Ph: (703)284-6000
Arlington, VA 22234   Free: 800-872-0001
URL: http://www.gannett.com.
Contact: John Johnson, Editor; Robert E. Robbins, Publisher; William M. Joyner, Jr., Advertising Mgr.
Desc: General newspaper. *Alt. Contact:* 311 E. Pearl St., PO Box 40, Jackson, MS 39205; telephone: (601)961-7000; fax: (601)961-7047. *Type:* Periodical.

Clear Creek Features

PO Box 35   Ph: (916)272-7176
Rough and Ready, CA 95975
Contact: Mike Drummond, Author/Self-Syndicator.
Desc: Distributes features and columns. *Alt. Contact:* PO Box 35, Rough and Ready, CA 95975; telephone: (916)272-7176. *Type:* Periodical.

Clio Among the Media

Association for Education in Journalism & Mass Communications
Dept. of Journalism
St. Michael's College
Colchester, VT 05439
Contact: David Mindich, Editor.
Desc: Provides news of interest regarding the study and history of journalism and mass communications. *Type:* Newsletter.

CMA Newsletter

College Media Advisers, Inc.
University of Memphis   Ph: (901)678-2403
Dept. of Journalism   Fax: (901)678-4798
3711 Veterans Ave.
Memphis, TN 38152-6661
E-mail: cma-l@latech; spielberger@cc.memphis.edu; rsplbrgr@cc.memphis.edu.
URL: http://www.spub.edu/~cma; http://www.college-media.org.
Contact: Kenneth L. Rosenauer, Editor, (816)271-4322, fax: (816)271-4543, klr9015@griffon.mwsc.edu.
Desc: Provides an exchange of information and ideas for advisors of college publications. Contains news items and a list of recommended publications. *Type:* Newsletter.

The Cole Papers

The Cole Group
PO Box 3426   Ph: (650)994-2100
Daly City, CA 94015-0426   Fax: (650)994-2108
E-mail: info@colegroup.com
URL: http://www.colegroup.com.
Contact: David M. Cole, Editor.
Desc: Emphasizes professional publishing systems for newspapers and magazines. Covers industry meetings, including NEXPO, Digital Photography, and the Seybold Seminars. *Type:* Newsletter.

Colorado Springs Gazette

Freedom Newspapers Inc.
Gazette
30 S. Prospect   Ph: (719)632-5511
P.O. Box 1779
Colorado Springs, CO 80901
E-mail: gazette@usa.net
URL: http://www.gazette.com
Desc: Contains the complete text of news items and feature articles from the Colorado Springs Gazette (Colorado) newspaper. *Available:* Bell & Howell Information and Learning. *Type:* Database.

Colorado Springs Gazette Telegraph

Freedom Newspapers, Inc.
37 Prospect   Ph: (719)636-0266
PO Box 1779   Free: 800-800-2748
Colorado Springs, CO 80901   Fax: (719)636-0202
URL: http://www.usa.net/gazette/.
Contact: Steven A. Smith, Editor, (719)636-0105; Wayne Stewart, Asst. Editor, (719)636-0189; Gary Blakeley, Operations Dir., (719)636-0200; Mary Jacobus, Sales and Marketing Dir., (719)636-0104; Jane Ellis, Retail Advertising Dir., (719)636-0310; Cliff Foster, City Editor, (719)636-0363; Todd Hegert, Features Editor, (719)636-0273; Terri Fleming, Managing Editor; Jim Wright, Business Editor.
Desc: General newspaper. *Alt. Contact:* 30 S. Prospect, Colorado Springs, CO 80903; telephone: (719)636-0266; fax: (719)636-0202. *Type:* Periodical.

The Columbus Dispatch

The Dispatch Printing Co.
34 S. 3rd St.   Ph: (614)461-5000
Columbus, OH 43215-4241   Fax: (614)461-7580
URL: http://www.dispatch.com.
Contact: Mike Curtin, Editor, (614)461-5069, fax: (614)461-7580; John F. Wolfe, Publisher, (614)461-5141, fax: (614)461-5017; Gary Merrell, Advertising Dir., (614)461-5194, fax: (614)469-6087; James Gilmour, CFO, (614)461-8788, fax: (614)461-5017.
Desc: General newspaper. *Type:* Periodical.

The Columbus Dispatch

The Dispatch Printing Company
345 3rd South St.   Ph: (614)461-5000
Columbus, OH 43215
URL: http://www.dispatch.com
Contact: Jim Hunter, Librarian, (612)461-5039.
Desc: Contains the complete text of news items and feature articles from The Columbus Dispatch (Ohio) newspaper. Regional coverage emphasizes the banking and insurance industries, information technologies research, and state government and legislative activity. *Available:* The Dialog Corporation, DIALOG; The Dialog Corporation, DIALOG; Bell & Howell Information and Learning; CompuServe Information Service, Knowledge Index. *Type:* Database.

The Commercial Appeal

Memphis Publishing Co.
495 Union Ave.   Ph: (901)529-2322
Memphis, TN 38103   Free: 800-444-6397
    Fax: (901)529-5833
URL: GOMEMPHIS.COM.
Contact: Angus McEachran, President, (901)529-2390, fax: (901)529-2522; Richard Remmert, General Mgr., (901)529-2205, fax: (901)529-5833; David Enstad, Advertising Dir., (901)529-2250, fax: (901)529-2245; Warren Funk, Personnel Dir., (901)529-2631, fax: (901)529-2618; Jimmy Hamilton, Operations Dir., (901)529-2410, fax: (901)529-2705; Darrell Jones, Circulation Dir., (901)529-2663, fax: (901)529-6539; Janice Earheart, Controller, (901)529-2210, fax: (901)529-5833; Elena Cainas, Marketin

Desc: General newspaper. *Type:* Periodical.

The Commercial Appeal (Memphis, Tennessee)

Memphis Publishing Co.
495 Union Ave.   Ph: (901)529-2211
Memphis, TN 38103
Contact: (901)529-2782, fax: (901)529-6460, library@gomemphis.com.
Desc: Contains the complete text of locally-written articles; locally-written columns; most wire service stories; some freelance materials; some letters, some op-ed, some public forum; obituaries; recipes, restaurant reviews; captions of graphics and photos; corrections; full text of charts from The Commercial Appeal. Corresponds in part to the The Commercial Appeal online database. *Available:* The Dialog Corporation, DIALOG; CompuServe Information Service; Dow Jones Interactive Publishing; LEXIS-NEXIS, NEXIS. *Type:* Database.

Communications International/National News

1423 N. Orange Grove Ave.   Ph: (213)876-1668
PO Box 46-181   Fax: (213)876-1404
Los Angeles, CA 90046
URL: http://www.bchurchill.com.
Contact: Bonnie Churchill, Lead Columnist; Stuart Allengham, Editor; Hillary Bekins, President.
Desc: Distributes Bonnie Churchill Reporting Leisure Time and Youth Parade. *Alt. Contact:* 1423 N. Orange Grove Ave., PO Box 46-181, Los Angeles, CA 90046; telephone: (213)876-1668; fax: (213)876-1404. *Type:* Periodical.

Community Features

PO Box 172   Ph: (770)287-3798
Oakwood, GA 30566   Fax: (770)287-0112
Contact: Bill Johnson, President; Kim Calhoun, Graphic Arts; Christina Hollingsworth, Business Mgr.
Alt. Contact: PO Box 172, Oakwood, GA 30566; telephone: (770)287-3798; fax: (770)287-0112. *Type:* Periodical.

Community and Suburban Press Service

117 W. 2nd St.   Ph: (502)223-1736
PO Box 639   Fax: (502)223-2679
Frankfort, KY 40602
Contact: Eugene Combs, President.
Desc: Distributes horoscopes, editorials, cartoons, and crosswords. *Alt. Contact:* 117 W. 2nd St., PO Box 639, Frankfort, KY 40602; telephone: (502)223-1736; fax: (502)223-2679. *Type:* Periodical.

Compass Syndicate

PO Box 395   Ph: (317)844-1188
Carmel, IN 46032
Contact: Peggy Gisler, Owner/Ed.; Marge Eberts, Owner/Ed.
Desc: Distributes pamphlets. *Alt. Contact:* PO Box 395, Carmel, IN 46032; telephone: (317)844-1188. *Type:* Periodical.

Connecticut Post

Connecticut Post
410 State St.   Ph: (203)333-0161
Bridgeport, CT 06604-4501   Free: 800-423-8058
    Fax: (203)366-3373
E-mail: ctnews@snet.net.
Contact: Rick Sayers, Editor/Assoc. Publisher, (203)330-6325, fax: (203)367-8158; Mike Daly, Managing Editor, (203)330-6394; Todd Hollis, Asst. M.E./Technology, (203)330-6480; John Schwing, Fairfield County Editor, (203)330-6248; Mary Moran, New Heaven County/Valley Editor, (203)330-6224; Jim Shay, Sunday/Travel Editor, (230)330-6242; Linda Pinto, State Editor, (203)330-6496; Tom Caruso, Business Editor, (203)330-6351; Elaine Ficarra, F.E./Real Estate Editor, (203)330-6227; Gary Rogo

Desc: General newspaper. *Alt. Contact:* fax: (203)367-8158. *Type:* Periodical.

Connecticut Traveler

Connecticut Motor Club AAA
2276 Whitney Ave.   Ph: (203)288-7441
Hamden, CT 06518-3505   Fax: (203)230-0182
Contact: Annette Cormany, Director.
Desc: Published for members of the Connecticut Motor Club-AAA who reside in some of Connecticut's most affluent areas. Editorial focuses on travel, with features ranging from regional daytrips to international destinations. Other regualr columns cover insurance, car care, traffic safety, local events and exclusive member savings. *Type:* Periodical.

Continental Features/ Continental News Service

501 W. Broadway   Ph: (619)492-8696
Ste. 265
Plaza A
San Diego, CA 92101
Contact: Gary Salamone ED.
Desc: Distributes items of world and national news/analysis. *Alt. Contact:* 501 W. Broadway, Ste. 265, Plaza A, San Diego, CA 92101; telephone: (619)492-8696. *Type:* Periodical.

Continental Newstime

Continental Features/Continental News Service
501 W. Broadway, Ste. 265,   Ph: (619)492-8696
    Plaza A
San Diego, CA 92101
E-mail: newstime@hotbot.com
Contact: Gary P. Salamone, Editor-in-Chief.
Desc: Magazine featuring news and commentary on national and world affairs. *Type:* Periodical.

Contra Costa Times

Contra Costa Newspapers, Inc.
2640 Shadelands Dr.   Ph: (925)935-2525
Walnut Creek, CA 94598-2513   Free: 800-465-0780
    Fax: (925)943-8362
Contact: George Riggs, Publisher & CEO; Pamela Henson, Vice Pres./Advertising; John Armstrong, Editor & Vice Pres. News; Mona Hatfield, News Research Manager.
Desc: General newspaper. *Type:* Periodical.

Copley News Service

123 Camino de la Reina   Ph: (619)293-1818
Ste. E-250   Free: 800-238-6196
PO Box 190   Fax: (619)297-0537
San Diego, CA 92108
E-mail: cnssd@aol.com.
Contact: David C. Copley, President; Charles Ohl, Ed./Gen. Mgr.; Robert M. Witty, Exec. VP/Ed.; Patricia E. Gonzalez, VP/Bus. Mgr.; Gabriel Bradford, Sales Mgr.; Glenda Winders, Ed. Mgr.; Nanette Wiser, Mktg. and Ed. Dir.
Desc: Distributes feature stories and political cartoons. *Alt. Contact:* 123 Camino de la Reina, Ste. E-250, PO Box 190, San Diego, CA 92108; telephone: (619)293-1818; fax: (619)297-0537; toll-free: 800-238-6196. *Type:* Periodical.

County Star

Suburban Newspapers of Greater St. Louis
1714 Deer Tracks Trail   Ph: (314)822-2292
St. Louis, MO 63131   Fax: (314)821-0843
Contact: Michael T. Cody, Editor; Paul Winans, Publisher.
Desc: Community newspaper. *Alt. Contact:* 4426 Woodson Rd., St. Louis, MO 63134-3702; telephone: (314)426-2222; fax: (314)821-3652. *Type:* Periodical.

The Courier-Journal

Courier-Journal Co.
525 W. Broadway St.   Ph: (502)582-4011
Louisville, KY 40202-2137   Fax: (502)582-4075
URL: http://www.courier-journal.com.
Contact: David V. Hawpe, Editor; Edward Manassah, Publisher; Stephen Bernard, Advertising Dir.
Desc: General newspaper. *Type:* Periodical.

The Courier-Journal (Louisville, Kentucky)

Courier-Journal Co.
525 W. Broadway   Ph: (502)582-4184
PO Box 740031
Louisville, KY 40201-7431
E-mail: sbidwell@louisv02.gannett.com
Contact: Sharon Bidwell, Reference Librarian, (502)582-4184.
Desc: Contains the complete text of news items and feature articles from The Courier-Journal (Louisville, Kentucky) newspaper. Regional coverage emphasizes the automobile, horse racing, liquor, and tobacco industries. *Available:* Bell & Howell Information and Learning; LEXIS-NEXIS, NEXIS. *Type:* Database.

Courier-Post

Gannett Co., Inc.
1100 Wilson Blvd.   Ph: (703)284-6000
Arlington, VA 22234   Free: 800-872-0001
Contact: Dan Martin, Pres./Publisher; Skip Hidlay, Exec. Editor; Calvin Stovall, Managing Editor; Stevan Ecken, Dir. of Circulation; Robert Schaad, Production Dir.; John Ziomek, Advertising Dir.; Don Lemire, Controller; Carl Lovern, Market Development Dir.; Lori Trasmondi, Dir./Human Res.; Robert Ringham, Dir. of Photography.
Desc: General newspaper. *Alt. Contact:* 301 Cuthbert Blvd., Cherry Hill, NJ 08002; telephone: (609)486-2411; fax: (609)663-2831. *Type:* Periodical.

Crain News Service

740 N. Rush St.   Ph: (312)649-5464
Chicago, IL 60611   Fax: (312)397-5500
Contact: Henry Bernstein, Editor; Melanie Glover, Admin. Asst.; Joseph Hanley, Sales Mgr.
Desc: Distributes news service. *Alt. Contact:* 740 N. Rush St., Chicago, IL 60611; telephone: (312)649-5464; fax: (312)397-5500; New York Office 220 E. 42nd St., New York, NY 10010; telephone: (212)254-0890; fax: (212)254-7646. *Type:* Periodical.

Creative Syndication Services

PO Box 40   Ph: (314)938-4486
Eureka, MO 63025
Contact: Edward E. Baldwin, Publisher.
Alt. Contact: PO Box 40, Eureka, MO 63025; telephone: (314)938-4486. *Type:* Periodical.

Creators Syndicate

5777 W. Century Blvd.   Ph: (310)337-7003
Ste. 700   Fax: (310)337-7625
Los Angeles, CA 90045
E-mail: cr8ors@aol.com.
Contact: Richard S. Newcombe, President; Anita Tobias, Exec. VP; Mike Santiago, Exec.; Katherine Searcy, VP/Edit. Dir.; Peter Alcan, Sales Exec.; Jennifer Turner, Sales Admin.; Margo Sugrue, Sales Exec.; Tony Rossi, Sales Exec.; Dominique Dubois, Sales Admin.
Desc: International distribution of cartoons and editorials including Ann Landers, BC, and Wizard of Id. *Alt. Contact:* 5777 W. Century Blvd., Ste. 700, Los Angeles, CA 90045; telephone: (310)337-7003; fax: (310)337-7625. *Type:* Periodical.

Crete/University Park Star

Star Newspapers
6901 W 159th St.   Ph: (708)802-8800
Tinley Park, IL 60477   Fax: (708)802-8899
Contact: Lester Sons, Editor; Norman Rosinski, Publisher; Jim Meidell, Advertising Mgr.; Jay Frederickson.
Desc: Newspaper group serving 51 communities in Chicago's southern suburbs. *Type:* Periodical.

Cricket Communications

PO Box 527   Ph: (215)747-6684
Ardmore, PA 19003   Fax: (215)747-7082
E-mail: 76550.42@compuserve.com.
Contact: Edwin Marks, Pres./Pub.; Mark E. Battersby, Editor.
Alt. Contact: PO Box 527, Ardmore, PA 19003; telephone: (215)747-6684; fax: (215)747-7082. *Type:* Periodical.

Cromley News-Features

1912 Martha's Rd.   Ph: (703)695-5118
Alexandria, VA 22307   Fax: (703)693-7206
Contact: Ray Cromley, President.
Alt. Contact: 1912 Martha's Rd., Alexandria, VA 22307; telephone: (703)695-5118; fax: (703)693-7206. *Type:* Periodical.

Cronin Features Syndicating Inc.

1000 Parkview Dr.   Ph: (305)376-6057
No. 631
Hallandale, FL 33009
Contact: Sylvia Cronin, VP/Author; Edward Wallace Dresner, Sales Mgr.
Alt. Contact: 1000 Parkview Dr., No. 631, Hallandale, FL 33009; telephone: (305)376-6057. *Type:* Periodical.

Crown Syndicate Inc.

3817 W. Parkmount Pl.   Ph: (206)285-1888
PO Box 99126
Seattle, WA 98199
Contact: L.M. Boyd, President; Patricia Boyd, Vice President.
Alt. Contact: 3817 W. Parkmount Pl., PO Box 99126, Seattle, WA 98199; telephone: (206)285-1888. *Type:* Periodical.

Current Digest of the Post-Soviet Press

Current Digest of the Soviet Press
3857 N. High St.   Ph: (614)292-4234
Columbus, OH 43214
Contact: Stephanie Fowler, Business Mgr., (614)292-4234, fax: (614)267-2161, fowler.40@osk.edu.
Desc: Contains the full text of all issues of the Current Digest of the Soviet/Post-Soviet Press for 15 years. Emphasis is on politics, foreign affairs, and economics, although other social and cultural issues are covered. *Available:* LEXIS-NEXIS, NEXIS; LEXIS-NEXIS, LEXIS. *Type:* Database.

Daily Challenge

Daily Challenge
1360 Fulton St.   Ph: (718)643-1162
Brooklyn, NY 11216   Fax: (718)857-9115
Contact: Thomas H. Watkins, Jr., Publisher.
Desc: Black community newspaper. *Type:* Periodical.

Daily Herald

Paddock Publications
PO Box 280   Ph: (847)427-4300
Arlington Heights, IL 60006   Fax: (847)427-1301
URL: http://www.dailyherald.com.
Contact: Douglas Ray, Vice President; John Lampinen, Managing Editor; David Beery, Editorial Page Editor; Jim Slusher, Editor; Pamela DeFiglio, Writer; Colin O'Donnell, Metro Editor; Tom Quinlan, Sports Editor; Madeleine Doubek, Political Editor; Diane Dungey, Projects Editor; James Kane, Business Editor; Don Thompson, State Gov't Writer; Richard Klicki, News Editor; Theresa Schmedding, Asst. News Editor; Colleen Thomas, Metro News Editor; Jim Harvey, Copy Editor-Neighbor; Tom Jachim.
Desc: General newspaper. *Alt. Contact:* PO Box 280, Arlington Heights, IL 60006; telephone: (847)427-4300; fax: (847)427-1301. *Type:* Periodical.

Daily News

Daily News
21221 Oxnard St.   Ph: (818)713-3000
Woodland Hills, CA 91367   Fax: (818)713-0058
Contact: Robert W. Burdick, Editor; David J. Auger, Publisher; Bob McCroy, Advertising Dir.
Desc: General newspaper. *Type:* Periodical.

Daily Press

Tribune, Co.
PO Box 746   Ph: (757)247-4600
Newport News, VA 23607   Free: 800-543-8980
                                Fax: (757)245-8618
E-mail: dpedlt@aol.com.
URL: http://www.dailyxpress.com; http://www.dpxpress.com.
Contact: Will Corbin, VP/Editor, (757)247-4713, wcorbin@dailypress.com; Kathy Waltz, Pres./Publisher, (757)247-4612, kwaltz@dailypress.com; Mike Asher, Technology Dir., (757)247-4930, masher@dailypress.com; Lisa Bohnaker, Dir. of Business Development, (757)247-4878, lbohnaker@dailypress.com; Tony Farley, VP/Circ. Dir., (757)247-4817, tfarley@dailypress.com; Kristine Faulkner, Dir. of Internet Publishing, (757)247-4983, kfaulkner@dailypress.com; George McDaniel, VP/A
Desc: General newspaper. *Type:* Periodical.

The Daily Press (Newport News, Virginia)

Tribune Co.
Daily Press
7505 Warwick Blvd.   Ph: (757)245-4882
P.O. Box 746
Newport News, VA 23607
E-mail: news@dailypress.com
URL: http://www.dailypress.com
Contact: Melissa Simpson, Library Manager, (757)247-4879, fax: (757)247-4882, msimpson@tribune.com.
Desc: Contains the complete text of all editions of The Daily Press (Virginia) newspaper covering Hampton, Newport News, Gloucester, Williamsburg, and James City, Isle of Wight, Middlesex and New Kent counties. Provides regional coverage emphasis on the activities at the NASA Research Center, military affairs, and the automobile, banking, brewing, office machines, and shipbuilding industries. *Available:* The Dialog Corporation, DIALOG; Tribune Co., Daily Press. *Type:* Database.

The Daily Texan

Texas Student Publications/University of Texas
P.O. Box D   Ph: (512)471-1865
Austin, TX 78713-7209
E-mail: TEXAN@utxvms.cc.utexas.edu
URL: http://stumedia.tsp.utexas.edu/webtexan/
Contact: Michelle Carlson, Systems Analyst, (512)471-5887, fax: (512)471-1576, mcarlson@mail.utexas.edu.
Desc: Contains the complete text of news items and feature articles from The Daily Texan newspaper. Regional coverage emphasizes state government, politics, and activities of the University of Texas. *Type:* Database.

The Daily Tribune News
Cartersville Newspapers
PO Box 70   Ph: (404)382-4545
251 South Tenn. St.   Fax: (404)382-2711
Cartersville, GA 30120-0070
Contact: Charles Hurley, Editor and Publisher.
Desc: General newspaper. *Type:* Periodical.

The Dallas Morning News
Dallas Tribune
508 Young St.   Ph: (214)977-8222
PO Box 655237   Free: 800-431-0010
Dallas, TX 75265   Fax: (214)977-8638
Contact: Burl Osborne, Editor and Publisher; Jeremy L. Halbreich, President & General Manager; J. William Cox, Sr. VP/Administration & Operations; Ralph Langer, Sr. VP/Executive Editor; Richard Starks, Sr. VP/Sales & Marketing; Barry Peckham, VP/ Circulation; Reggie Brown, VP Finance.
Desc: General newspaper. *Type:* Periodical.

The Dallas Morning News
The Dallas Morning News
508 Young St.   Ph: (214)977-8222
P.O. Box 655237
Dallas, TX 75265
Contact: Gerry Barker, (214)977-4036, fax: (214)977-8177.
Desc: Contains the complete text of The Dallas Morning News, a general circulation newspaper reporting local, national, and international news. Contains all articles published since August of 1984, representing more than 830,000 pieces. *Available:* Bell & Howell Information and Learning; LEXIS-NEXIS, NEXIS. *Type:* Database.

DANY News Service
22 Lesley Dr.   Ph: (516)921-8313
Syosset, NY 11791
Contact: David Nydick, President; Robert Manhemer, Editor.
Desc: Distributes education, sports, and entertainment features. *Alt. Contact:* 22 Lesley Dr., Syosset, NY 11791; telephone: (516)921-8313. *Type:* Periodical.

Dayton Daily News
Dayton Newspapers Inc.
45 S. Ludlow St.   Ph: (937)225-2321
Dayton, OH 45402   Free: 800-686-NEWS
                             Fax: (937)225-2334
URL: http://www.activedayton.com.
Contact: Max Jennings, Editor; Brad Tillson, Publisher; Pat Keil, Advertising Mgr.
Desc: General newspaper. *Type:* Periodical.

Dayton Daily News
Dayton Newspapers, Inc.
45 S. Ludlow St.
Dayton, OH 45402   Ph: (937)225-2000
URL: http://www.activedayton.com
Desc: Contains the complete text of news items and feature articles from the Dayton Daily News (Ohio) newspaper, but does not include some syndicated material. Regional coverage emphasizes the aerospace, aviation, automotive, and manufacturing industries. *Available:* The Dialog Corporation, DIALOG; The Dialog Corporation, DIALOG; LEXIS-NEXIS, LEXIS; Bell & Howell Information and Learning. *Type:* Database.

Democrat and Chronicle
Gannett Co., Inc.
1100 Wilson Blvd.   Ph: (703)284-6000
Arlington, VA 22234   Free: 800-872-0001
Contact: Steven Brandt, Publisher/Pres.; Thomas Callinan, Editor/VP, News; Carolyn Washburn, Managing Editor; Cheryl Elzey, Newsroom Mgr.; Matt Dudek, Asst. Managing Editor/Admin.; Dennis Floss, Asst. Managing Editor/Presentation; Sebby Wilson Jacobson, Special Projects Editor; Cynthia Benjamin, Outreach/Training Mgr.; Richard Moss, Copy Chief; Steve Boerner, Asst. Features Editor; Steve Snider, Dir. of Newsroom Technology; Gini Wheeler, Library Mgr.; Mary Ellin Arch, "Our Towns" Edi
Desc: General newspaper. *Alt. Contact:* 55 Exchange Blvd., Rochester, NY 14614-2001; telephone: (716)232-7100; fax: (716)258-3027. *Type:* Periodical.

The Denver Post
MediaNews Group, Inc.
Denver Post
1560 Broadway   Ph: (303)820-1010
Denver, CO 80202
URL: http://www.denverpost.com
Contact: Vickie Makings, Manager, (303)820-1691.
Desc: Contains the locally produced text of The Denver Post, a general circulation newspaper reporting local, national, and international news. Excludes news obtained from the Associated Press and other wire services. *Available:* Bell & Howell Information and Learning; LEXIS-NEXIS, NEXIS. *Type:* Database.

The Des Moines Register
Gannett Co., Inc.
1100 Wilson Blvd.   Ph: (703)284-6000
Arlington, VA 22234   Free: 800-872-0001
Contact: Dennis Ryerson, Vice President & Editor, (515)284-8502, fax: (515)286-2511, dryerson@dmreg.com; Randy Brubaker, Sr. Asst. Mng. Editor, (515)284-8564, fax: (515)286-2804, brubakerr@news.dmreg.com; Randy Essex, Iowa Editor, (515)284-8065, essexr@news.dmreg.com; Diane Graham, Managing Editor, (515)284-8530, dgraham@news.dmreg.com; Nancy Clark, Suburban Editor, (515)284-8039, clarkn@news.dmreg.com.
Desc: General newspaper. *Alt. Contact:* PO Box 957, Des Moines, IA 50304; telephone: (515)284-8000; fax: (515)286-2511. *Type:* Periodical.

Detroit Free Press
Knight-Ridder, Inc.
50 W. Fernando St.   Ph: (408)938-7700
San Jose, CA 95113
URL: http://www.freep.com.
Contact: Joe Stroud, Editor, (313)222-6583, fax: (313)222-6774; Heath J. Meriwether, Publisher, (313)222-5794, fax: (313)222-8874; Robert G. McGruder, Exec. Editor, (313)222-6821, fax: (313)222-5981; Chip Visci, Managing Editor, (313)222-8850, fax: (313)222-5981; Jerry Teagan, Vice President and Business Mgr., (313)222-6595, fax: (313)222-8874; Laura Varon Brown, Graphics Dir., (313)222-5002, fax: (313)222-5981; Ron Dzwonkowski, Projects Editor, (313)222-6635, fax: (313)222-5981; Car
Desc: General newspaper. Publishes combined weekend and holiday editions with the Detroit News under 1989 Joint Operating Agreement. *Alt. Contact:* 321 W. Lafayette Blvd., Detroit, MI 48226; telephone: (313)222-6400; fax: (313)222-5981; toll-free: 800-678-6400. *Type:* Periodical.

Detroit Free Press
Knight-Ridder, Inc.
600 Fort St.   Ph: (313)222-6400
Detroit, MI 48226
E-mail: library@freepress.com
Contact: Alice Pepper, Library Technology Coordinator, (313)222-5135, fax: (313)222-8770.
Desc: Contains the complete text of the Detroit Free Press, a general circulation newspaper reporting local, national, and international news. Special areas of interest include the automobile industry and labor issues and Great Lakes industry and environment. *Available:* The Dialog Corporation, DIALOG; CompuServe Information Service, Knowledge Index; VU/TEXT Information Services, DIALOG Information Services; Detroit Free Press Library. *Type:* Database.

The Detroit News
Detroit News
615 Lafayette Blvd.   Ph: (313)222-2300
Detroit, MI 48226
E-mail: letter@detnews.com
URL: http://www.detnews.com
Contact: Patricia Zacharias, Library Manager., (313)222-2040, letter@detnews.com.
Desc: Contains the complete text of news items and feature articles from The Detroit News, a daily general circulation newspaper providing coverage of local, state, and national news. Regional coverage emphasizes the automotive industry and related local business and industry. *Available:* Bell & Howell Information and Learning; LEXIS-NEXIS, NEXIS; Detroit News. *Type:* Database.

The Detroit News
Gannett Co., Inc.
1100 Wilson Blvd.   Ph: (703)284-6000
Arlington, VA 22234   Free: 800-872-0001
Contact: Mark Silverman, Editor and Publisher; Robert Giles, Editor; Christina Bradford, Managing Editor.
Desc: General newspaper. Publishes combined weekend and holiday editions with the Detroit Free Press under 1989 Joint Operating Agreement. *Alt. Contact:* 615 W. Lafayette Blvd., Detroit, MI 48226-3197; telephone: (313)222-2300; fax: (313)222-2335; toll-free: 800-678-4115. *Type:* Periodical.

DIALOG Headlines
The Dialog Corporation
DIALOG
11000 Regency Pkwy., Ste. 400   Ph: (919)462-8600
Cary, NC 27511
URL: http://www.dialog.com
Contact: Marketing.
Desc: Provides the complete text of national and international news articles dealing with general news, business and finance, and sports, with special emphasis on late-breaking stories. Data are derived from the Reuters newswire, Agence France Presse, and The Independent newspapers. *Available:* The Dialog Corporation, DIALOG. *Type:* Database.

Dispatch Features
703 Ridgemark Dr.   Ph: (408)637-9795
Hollister, CA 95023
Contact: George Crenshaw, President.
Desc: Distributes cartoons. *Alt. Contact:* 703 Ridgemark Dr., Hollister, CA 95023; telephone: (408)637-9795. *Type:* Periodical.

Dona Z. Meilach Features
2018 Saliente Way   Ph: (619)436-4395
Carlsbad, CA 92009   Fax: (619)436-1402
E-mail: dmeilach@msn.com.
Contact: Dona Z. Meilach, President.
Alt. Contact: 2018 Saliente Way, Carlsbad, CA 92009; telephone: (619)436-4395; fax: (619)436-1402. *Type:* Periodical.

Donrey Washington News Bureau
937 National Press Bldg.   Ph: (202)783-1760
Washington, DC 20045   Fax: (202)783-1955
Desc: Distributes news features. *Alt. Contact:* 937 National Press Bldg., Washington, DC 20045; telephone: (202)783-1760; fax: (202)783-1955. *Type:* Periodical.

Dorsey Communications
9239 Doheny Rd. Ph: (310)273-2245
Los Angeles, CA 90069 Fax: (310)273-6967
Contact: Helen Dorsey, CEO.
Alt. Contact: 9239 Doheny Rd., Los Angeles, CA 90069;
telephone: (310)273-2245; fax: (310)273-6967. *Type:* Periodical.

Down East Magazine
Down East Enterprise, Inc.
PO Box 679 Ph: (207)594-9544
Camden, ME 04843-0679 Free: 800-766-1670
 Fax: (207)594-7215
E-mail: downeast@midcoast.com; advertising@downeast.com.
Contact: Dale Kuhnert, Editor, dkuhnert@downeast.com; H. Allen Fernald, President, afernald@downeast.com; Kit Parker, Publisher, kparker@downeast.com.
Type: Periodical.

Duluth News-Tribune
Knight-Ridder, Inc.
50 W. Fernando St. Ph: (408)938-7700
San Jose, CA 95113
E-mail: newstrib@duluth.infi.net.
URL: http://www.duluthnews.com.
Contact: Craig Gemoules, Managing Editor, (218)720-4167; Mary Jacobus, Pres./Publisher, (218)723-5420, fax: (218)723-5339; Curt Peterson, Circulation Dir., (218)723-5252, fax: (218)720-4150; Bill Albrecht, Advertising Dir., (800)456-7979, fax: (218)723-5295; Andrea Novel, Exec. City Editor, (218)723-4120; Connie Wirta, City Editor, (218)723-5341; Diana Faherty, City Editor, (218)723-5310; Chris Miller, Sports Editor, (218)723-5312; Bob King, Chief Photographer, (218)723-5363; Virgil
Desc: General newspaper. *Alt. Contact:* 424 W. 1st St., Duluth, MN 55802-1516; telephone: (218)723-5313; fax: (218)720-4120; toll-free: 800-456-8282. *Type:* Periodical.

Dunkel Sports Research Service News-Journal
PO Box 2831 Ph: (904)252-1511
Daytona Beach, FL 32120 Fax: (904)258-8465
URL: http://www.n-jcenter.com.
Contact: Dick Dunkel, Author/Owner.
Desc: Distributes college and high school football features and a statistical basketball rating system. *Alt. Contact:* PO Box 2831, Daytona Beach, FL 32120; telephone: (904)252-1511; fax: (904)258-8465. *Type:* Periodical.

Eagle Newspaper
Spectrum Press
1370 South 500 West Ph: (801)292-1088
Bountiful, UT 84010 Fax: (801)261-5623
Contact: Michele Bartmess, Editor; Peter Bernhard, Publisher; Bill Olsen, Advertising Mgr.
Desc: Community newspaper. *Type:* Periodical.

Ebony
Johnson Publishing Co., Inc.
820 S. Michigan Ave. Ph: (312)322-9200
Chicago, IL 60605-2191 Fax: (312)322-9375
Contact: John H. Johnson, Publisher.
Desc: General editorial magazine geared toward African-Americans. *Type:* Periodical.

Editorial Consultant Service
PO Box 524 Ph: (516)481-5487
West Hempstead, NY 11552 Fax: (516)481-5487
Contact: Richard Kiley, Vice President; Arthur A. Ingoglia, Editorial Dir.; John Riley, Auto Ed./Columnist.
Desc: Distributes Let's Talk About Your Car automotive column, motoring and trade columns, book reviews, auto features. *Alt. Contact:* PO Box 524, West Hempstead, NY 11552; telephone: (516)481-5487; fax: (516)481-5487. *Type:* Periodical.

Editorials on File
Facts On File News Services
Division of PRIMEDIA Reference Corporation
11 Penn Plaza, 15th Fl. Ph: (212)290-8090
New York, NY 10001-2006 Free: 800-363-7976
 Fax: (212)967-9051
E-mail: info@facts.com
Contact: Oliver Trager, Editor.
Desc: Contains compilation of actual newspaper editorials on controversies of the day and background essays. *Type:* Newsletter.

Editor's Copy Syndicate
3803 Pin Oaks St. Ph: (941)366-2169
Sarasota, FL 34232
Contact: Edward H. Sims, Editor and Publisher; Bente Christensen, Business Mgr.; Frederik Sims, Circulation Mgr.
Desc: Distributes current editorials, newspaper fillers. *Alt. Contact:* 3803 Pin Oaks St., Sarasota, FL 34232; telephone: (941)366-2169. *Type:* Periodical.

Editors Press Service Inc.
330 W. 42nd St. Ph: (212)563-2252
15th Fl. Fax: (212)563-2517
New York, NY 10036
Contact: Kerry Slagle, President; Mario Lorenzo, Vice President; Jorge Martinez, Latin American Sales Rep.
Alt. Contact: 330 W. 42nd St., 15th Fl., New York, NY 10036; telephone: (212)563-2252; fax: (212)563-2517. *Type:* Periodical.

The Edmonton Examiner
Bowes Publishers
12040 149 St. Ph: (780)453-9001
Edmonton, AB, Canada T5V 1P2
Contact: Maurice Tougas, Editor, (780)453-7097, fax: (780)451-4574, mtougas@edmontonexaminer.com; Don Sinclair, Publisher; Brenda Colbourn, Advertising Mgr.
Desc: Community newspaper. *Type:* Periodical.

The Edmonton Journal
The Edmonton Journal
10006-101st St. Ph: (403)429-5100
Edmonton, AB, Canada T5J Fax: (403)429-5500
2S6
URL: http://www.southam.com/edmontonjournal.
Contact: Linda Hughes, Publisher/Pres., (403)429-5129, fax: (403)429-5536; Murdoch Davis, Editor-in-Chief, (403)429-5201, fax: (403)429-5677, mdavis@thejournal.southam.ca; Sheila Pratt, Managing Editor, (403)498-5671, fax: (403)429-5677, spratt@thejournal.southam.ca; Allan Mayer, Asst. Managing Editor, (403)498-5669, fax: (403)429-5677, amayer@thejournal.southam.ca; Ray Wood, Asst. Managing Editor, (403)429-5668, fax: (403)429-5677, rwood@thejournal.southam.ca; Malcolm Ma
Desc: General newspaper. *Alt. Contact:* PO Box 2421, Edmonton, AB, Canada T5J 0S1; telephone: (403)429-5200; fax: (403)498-5677. *Type:* Periodical.

The Edmonton Journal
The Edmonton Journal
10006-101st St. Ph: (403)429-5100
Edmonton, AB, Canada T5J 2S6
E-mail: business@thejournal.southam.co
URL: http://www.edmontonjournal.com
Desc: Contains the complete text of The Edmonton Journal (Alberta) newspaper. Regional coverage emphasizes provincial political and business news, the Alberta stock exchange, agriculture, forestry, and oil industries, aboriginal rights, environmental issues, and the local arts. *Available:* Infomart Online; Infomart Assistant, Infomart Online; Infomart Dialog Limited. *Type:* Database.

The Edmonton Sun
Sun Media Corp.
333 King St. E Ph: (416)947-2222
Toronto, ON, Canada M5A Fax: (416)947-2441
3X5
Contact: Craig Martin, Publisher; David Black, General Mgr., dblack@sunpub.com; Paul Stanway, Editor-in-Chief; Grahham Dalziel, Managing Editor; Tom Elsworthy, Assoc. Editor.
Desc: General newspaper (tabloid). *Alt. Contact:* 4990 92nd Ave., Ste. 250, Edmonton, AB, Canada T6B 3A1; telephone: (403)468-0100; fax: (403)468-0214. *Type:* Periodical.

El Paso Herald-Post
Herald-Post Publishing Co.
300 N. Campbell Ph: (915)546-6340
PO Box 20 Fax: (915)546-6349
El Paso, TX 79999-0020
E-mail: hp@gte.net.
Contact: Georgiana Vines, Editor.
Desc: General newspaper. *Type:* Periodical.

El Paso Times
El Paso Times
Times Plaza Ph: (915)546-6104
El Paso, TX 79901-1470 Free: 800-351-1677
 Fax: (915)546-6496
Contact: Tom Fenton, Editor and Publisher; Bill Berryhill, Editor.
Desc: General newspaper. *Type:* Periodical.

Elizabethtown Mt. Joy Merchandiser
Engle Publishing Co.
PO Box 500 Ph: (717)653-4300
Mount Joy, PA 17552-0500 Free: 800-800-1833
 Fax: (717)653-1833
Contact: Monica Koons, Editor; Pauline H. Engle, Publisher; Donald Musser, Advertising Mgr.
Desc: Community newspaper. *Type:* Periodical.

EM: Ebony Man
Johnson Publishing Co., Inc.
820 S. Michigan Ave. Ph: (312)322-9200
Chicago, IL 60605-2191 Fax: (312)322-9375
Contact: Ooloong J. Smith, Editor; John H. Johnson, Publisher; Errol Griffiths, Advertising Dir.
Desc: Black men's magazine featuring regular columns on health, fashion, and sports. *Type:* Periodical.

enRoute
Maclean Hunter Ltd.
777 Bay St., 6th Fl. Ph: (416)596-5000
Toronto, ON, Canada M5W Fax: (416)596-5552
1A7
Contact: Karen Hanley, Editor; Donald C. Coote, Publisher; Avril Higgins, Advertising Mgr.
Desc: In-flight magazine (English and French). *Alt. Contact:* 150 John St., Ste. 900, Toronto, ON, Canada M5V 3E3; telephone: (416)591-1550; fax: (416)591-3511. *Type:* Periodical.

Erie Daily Times
Times Publishing Co.
205 W. 12th St. Ph: (814)870-1600
Erie, PA 16534-0001 Free: 800-352-0043
 Fax: (814)870-1615
Contact: Tony Pasquale, Editor; Edward Mead, Publisher; Michael Mead, Publisher; John Andersen, Editor.
Desc: General newspaper. *Type:* Periodical.

The Evansville Courier

Evansville Courier Co., Inc.
300 Walnut St. Ph: (812)424-7711
Evansville, IN 47713 Free: 800-288-3200
Fax: (812)422-8196

E-mail: vhue@evansville.net.
URL: http://www.evansville.net.

Contact: Thomas W. Tuley, Editor and Publisher; Robert K. Savage, Natl. Administration.

Desc: General newspaper. *Type:* Periodical.

Evening News Broadcasting/ Willis News Service

PO Box 25615 Ph: (202)333-3007
Washington, DC 20007

Contact: Clayton Willis, White House Corr./Photojournalist.

Alt. Contact: PO Box 25615, Washington, DC 20007; telephone: (202)333-3007. *Type:* Periodical.

Exclusive Press Syndicate

108 E. 66th St. Ph: (212)988-5190
Ste. 6A Fax: (212)628-1153
New York, NY 10021

Contact: Dina Dellale, Managing Editor.

Desc: Distributes news features. *Alt. Contact:* 108 E. 66th St., Ste. 6A, New York, NY 10021; telephone: (212)988-5190; fax: (212)628-1153. *Type:* Periodical.

Exhibitor Relations Co.

116 N. Robertson Blvd. Ph: (310)657-2005
Ste. 606 Fax: (310)657-7283
Los Angeles, CA 90048

Contact: John Krier, President; Paul Dergarabedian, Exec. VP.

Alt. Contact: 116 N. Robertson Blvd., Ste. 606, Los Angeles, CA 90048; telephone: (310)657-2005; fax: (310)657-7283. *Type:* Periodical.

Exito

Sun Sentinel
8323 NW 12 St., No. 212 Ph: (305)597-5000
Miami, FL 33126 Fax: (305)597-5035

Contact: Cristina Beauvoir, Advertising Dir.; Alfredo Duran, Publisher.

Desc: Community newspaper. *Alt. Contact:* 8323 NW 12 St. No. 212, Miami, FL 33126; telephone: (305)597-5000; fax: (305)597-5035. *Type:* Periodical.

Express-News

Express News
PO Box 2171 Ph: (210)225-7411
San Antonio, TX 78297-2171 Free: 800-456-7411
Fax: (210)225-8351

Contact: Jim Moss, Editor; Mark Kilpatrick, Managing Editor; Bob Lange, Advertising Mgr.; Lawrence Walker, Publisher.

Desc: General newspaper. *Type:* Periodical.

Extra Newspaper Features

18 1st Ave. SE Ph: (507)285-7671
PO Box 6118 Fax: (507)285-7666
Rochester, MN 55903-6118

Contact: Kelly J. Boldan, Ed./Dir.

Alt. Contact: 18 1st Ave. SE, PO Box 6118, Rochester, MN 55903-6118; telephone: (507)285-7671; fax: (507)285-7666. *Type:* Periodical.

EXTRA! Update

FAIR
130 W. 25 St., 8th Fl. Ph: (212)633-6700
New York, NY 10012 Free: 800-847-3993
Fax: (212)727-7668

E-mail: fair@fair.org
Contact: Jim Naurekas, Editor.

Desc: Offers well-documented criticism of the establishment media by a national progressive media watch group. Recurring features include news of research. *Type:* Newsletter.

Eye Weekly

Eye Communications, Ltd.
471 Adelaide St. W. Ph: (416)971-8421
Toronto, ON, Canada M5V Fax: (416)971-9697
1T1

E-mail: eye@eye.net.
URL: http://www.eye.net.
Contact: Bill Reynolds, Editor, (416)504-4339, fax: (416)504-4348, reynolds@eye.net; Carol McDowall, Associate Publisher, (416)504-4339, fax: (416)504-4341, mcdowall@eye.net.

Desc: Newspaper. *Type:* Periodical.

Fairchild News Service

Capital Cities/ABC Inc.
7 W. 34th St. Ph: (212)630-4000
New York, NY 10001

Contact: Olivia Thompson, Exec. VP Publishing.

Desc: Distributes fashion and lifestyle photographs and articles. *Alt. Contact:* Capital Cities/ABC Inc. 7 W. 34th St., New York, NY 10001; telephone: (212)630-4000. *Type:* Periodical.

Family Features Editorial Services Inc.

8309 Melrose Dr. Ph: (913)888-3800
Shawnee Mission, KS 66214 Fax: (913)888-3503
URL: http://www.culinary.net.

Contact: Dianne S. Hogerty, President, dhogerty@culinary.net; Ken Glaser, Mgr. Media & Member Svcs.

Alt. Contact: 8309 Melrose Dr., Shawnee Mission, KS 66214; telephone: (913)888-3800; fax: (913)888-3503. *Type:* Periodical.

Fayetteville Observer-Times

Fayetteville Publishing Co.
PO Box 849 Ph: (910)323-4848
458 Whitfield St. Fax: (910)486-3531
Fayetteville, NC 28306-1698
URL: http://www.fayettevillenc.com.

Contact: Ramon L. Yarborough, Publisher, (910)486-3501, fax: (910)433-3431; Charles Broadwell, Editor, (910)486-3503, fax: (910)486-3545, cbwell@fayehevillenc.com; Michelle Valenzuela, Editor, fax: (910)486-3545.

Desc: General newspaper. *Type:* Periodical.

Feature Service Syndicate

855 Moulin Ave. Ph: (810)544-0470
Madison Heights, MI 48071-
0654

Contact: William R. Hatch, President; Glenn E. Dibble, Exec. VP/Sr. Ed.; Alex Cedo, Sales Mgr.

Alt. Contact: 855 Moulin Ave., Madison Heights, MI 48071-0654; telephone: (810)544-0470. *Type:* Periodical.

Features International of London

400 Madison Ave. Ph: (212)832-2839
Ste. 1704
New York, NY 10017
Contact: Jeffrey Blyth, U.S. Ed.

Desc: Distributes news, features, and stories from the UK. *Alt. Contact:* 400 Madison Ave., Ste. 1704, New York, NY 10017; telephone: (212)832-2839. *Type:* Periodical.

The Federal Register

Counterpoint Publishing
610 Opperman Dr
Eagan, MN 55123-1340
Desc: Contains the complete text of the Federal Register, a daily publication covering U.S. governmental agency actions. *Type:* Database.

Feeley News Bureau

3141 Washington Ave. Ph: (708)251-7191
Wilmette, IL 60091-2082
Contact: Jim Feeley, Bureau Chief.

Desc: Distributes general news. *Alt. Contact:* 3141 Washington Ave., Wilmette, IL 60091-2082; telephone: (708)251-7191. *Type:* Periodical.

Financial News Syndicate

22115 O'Connell Rd. Ph: (815)568-8267
Marengo, IL 60152 Fax: (815)568-0487
Desc: Distributes consumer news and personal finance. *Alt. Contact:* 22115 O'Connell Rd., Marengo, IL 60152; telephone: (815)568-8267; fax: (815)568-0487. *Type:* Periodical.

The 5th Wave

16 Rowe Pt. Ph: (508)546-2448
Rockport, MA 01966 Fax: (508)546-7747
E-mail: the5wave@tiac.net.

Contact: Rich Tennant, Cartoonist; Debbie Clarke, Asst.

Alt. Contact: 16 Rowe Pt., Rockport, MA 01966; telephone: (508)546-2448; fax: (508)546-7747. *Type:* Periodical.

The Flint Journal

The Flint Journal
200 E. 1st St. Ph: (313)766-6100
Flint, MI 48502 Fax: (313)767-7518
Contact: Carlton Winfrey, Opinion Page Editor; Dave Poniers, Sports Editor; John Dickson, Photo Director; Marcia Mattson, Health Writer, (313)766-6326; Ron Krueger, Food Writer, (313)766-6241; Tom Lindley, Editor, (313)766-6189; Danny R. Gaydou, Publisher, (313)766-6324; Roger Samuel, Advertising Dir., (313)766-6330; Roger Van Noord, Managing Editor, (313)766-6241; Michael Riha, Metro Editor, (313)766-6374; Rhonda Sanders, Features Editor, (313)766-6241; Brooke Rausch, Assoc. Editor.

Desc: General newspaper. *Type:* Periodical.

The Florida Times-Union

Morris Communications Corp.
PO Box 936 Ph: (706)540-0123
Augusta, GA 30903 Fax: (706)823-3440
E-mail: 73711.1232@compuserve.com
URL: http://www.jacksonville.com.

Contact: Richard T. Allport, Exec. Editor; Frederick W. Hartmann, Editor; Carl N. Cannon, Publisher; Raymond P. Dallman, Dir. of Advertising & Marketing.

Desc: General newspaper. *Alt. Contact:* 1 Riverside Ave., Jacksonville, FL 32202-4904; telephone: (904)359-4111; fax: (904)359-4478. *Type:* Periodical.

Florida Today

Cape Publications, Inc.
Gannett Plaza Ph: (407)242-3500
PO Box 419000 Free: 800-633-8449
Melbourne, FL 32941-9000 Fax: (407)242-6620
Contact: Bennie Ivory, Editor; Michael Coleman, Publisher.

Desc: General newspaper. *Type:* Periodical.

FNA News

PO Box 11999   Ph: (801)355-3336
Salt Lake City, UT 84147   Free: (801)355-1901
Contact: Richard Goldberger, Managing Editor; Francine Modderno, Wash. Bureau Chief; Pamela Teplick, Society Ed.; Connie Terry, Health Ed./ Bureau Chief Los Angeles; M.F. Heyrend, Legal Affs. Ed.; Marlon U. Stones, Tech Ed.; K. Rossi, Energy Ed./Acting Bureau Chief Houston. *Alt. Contact:* PO Box 11999, Salt Lake City, UT 84147; telephone: (801)355-3336; toll-free: (801)355-1901. *Type:* Periodical.

Followup File

Roger Scott
2222 Foothill Blvd., Ste. 344   Ph: (818)957-5511
La Canada, CA 91011
Contact: Roger Scott, Editor, rdscott@pacbell.net.
Desc: Provides news-feature ideas for radio and television news departments and newspapers to follow up. Each item includes basic facts, questions to investigate, suggested sources for research or interview, and possible tie-ins with related events or subjects. *Type:* Newsletter.

Foreign Press News

Foreign Press Association
110 E. 59th St., 2nd Fl.   Ph: (212)826-4452
New York, NY 10022-1304   Fax: (212)826-4657
Contact: Karl Grun, Editor.
Desc: Reports Association events, including special conferences and meetings, presentations of scholarships and other awards, and news of members. *Type:* Newsletter.

Fort Worth Star-Telegram

Capital Cities/ABC, Inc.
825 7th Ave., 6th Fl.   Ph: (212)887-8400
New York, NY 10019   Fax: (212)887-8484
URL: http://www.star-telegram.com.
Contact: Wes Turner, President, (817)390-7453, fax: (336)-2790; Mac Tully, Sr.VP Arlington ed. Editor, (817)548-5433; Craig Diebel, Vice President, (817)390-7877, fax: (390)-7869; Jim Witt, Vice President, jwitt@star.telegram.com; Paul Harral, Reader Advocates, (817)390-7836; Gary M. Hardee, Deputy Exec. Editor, (817)390-7957; Roland Lindsay, State Editor, (817)390-7981; Rex Seline, Sr. Business Editor, (817)390-7729, fax: (390)-7774; Phyllis Stone, Tarrant Bus. Editor, (817)390-7
Desc: Newspaper with a Democratic orientation. *Alt. Contact:* 400 W. 7th St., Fort Worth, TX 76102; telephone: (817)390-7400; fax: (817)390-7831. *Type:* Periodical.

Fotopress Independent News Service International

Box 1268 Sta. Q   Ph: (416)441-1405
Toronto, ON, Canada M4T   Fax: (416)445-4953
  2P4
E-mail: fotopress@enterprise.ca.
URL: http://www.enterprise.ca/~fotopress.
Contact: John M. Kubik, Ops. Dir.; Steven Brown, Accts. Admin.; Robert O'Connor, United Kingdom Photographer; Wes Jonasson, Europe Photographer; Y. Kenditos, Middle East Photographer; David Tam-Baryohi, Africa Photographer; Mulenga Chola, Africa Photographer; Obafimi Oredein, Africa Photographer; Pin Chek Chong, Indochina Photographer; Nohiro Kimura, Japan Photographer; Alfoso Tobar, South America Photographer; Vincent Delgado, Central America Photographer; David Margolis, Southern E
Alt. Contact: Box 1268 Sta. Q, Toronto, ON, Canada M4T 2P4; telephone: (416)441-1405; fax: (416)445-4953. *Type:* Periodical.

The Fresno Bee

McClatchy Newspapers, Inc.
3425 N. 1st St., Ste. 201   Ph: (209)441-6111
Fresno, CA 93726-6819   Fax: (209)441-6436
Contact: Beverly Kees, Exec. Editor; Gary B. Pruitt, Publisher; Ray Steele, Jr., General Mgr.; Alan Truax, Advertising Dir.
Desc: General newspaper. *Type:* Periodical.

The Fresno Bee

McClatchy Newspapers
1626 E St.   Ph: (916)321-1846
Fresno, CA 93786
E-mail: mwilson@fresnobee.com
Desc: Contains the complete text of news items, feature articles, stories, and editorials from the Fresno Bee (California) newspaper. Regional coverage emphasizes government, environment, agriculture, and agribusiness. *Available:* Bell & Howell Information and Learning; LEXIS-NEXIS, NEXIS; Dow Jones Interactive Publishing. *Type:* Database.

Future Features Syndicate

1923 N. Wickham Rd.   Ph: (407)259-3822
Ste. 117   Fax: (407)259-1471
Melbourne, FL 32935
E-mail: futrfeat@iu.net.
URL: http://www.spindata.com/futrfeat.
Contact: Ada Lewis Forney, President; Jerome L. Forney, Creative Dir.
Desc: Distributes cartoon panels and strips, editorial cartoon services, caricatures, illustrations, and cartoon graphics. *Alt. Contact:* 1923 N. Wickham Rd., Ste. 117, Melbourne, FL 32935; telephone: (407)259-3822; fax: (407)259-1471. *Type:* Periodical.

Gannett News Service

1000 Wilson Blvd.   Ph: (703)276-5800
10th Fl.   Fax: (703)558-3813
Arlington, VA 22229-0001
Contact: Robert W. Ritter, Editor; J. Ford Huffman, Man. Ed. Features, Graphics, & Photograp; Jefferey Stinson, Reg. Ed.; Ron Cohen, Natl. Ed.; Judi Austin, Reg. Ed./West; Phil Pruitt, Reg. Ed./East; Jerry Langdon, Mng. Ed. /Sports; Emilie Davis, Copy Desk Chief; Craig Schwed, Bus. Ed.
Desc: Distributes news wire service. *Alt. Contact:* 1000 Wilson Blvd., 10th Fl., Arlington, VA 22229-0001; telephone: (703)276-5800; fax: (703)558-3813. *Type:* Periodical.

Gannett News Service

Gannett New Media Services
1100 Wilson Blvd., 24th Fl.   Ph: (703)276-3400
Arlington, VA 22234
Desc: Contains the complete text of national and international news, features, finance, and sports stories transmitted over the Gannett News Service wire service. Emphasis is on state and regional stories. *Available:* Bell & Howell Information and Learning; LEXIS-NEXIS, NEXIS. *Type:* Database.

The Gazette

Southam, Inc.
250 St-Antoine St. W.   Ph: (514)987-2350
Montreal, PQ, Canada H2Y   Free: 800-363-6765
  3R7   Fax: (514)987-2323
URL: http://www.gazette.gc.ca.
Contact: Michael Goldbloom, Publisher; Robert Attala, VP of Advertising; Alan Allnutt, Editor-in-Chief; Raymond Brassard, Managing Editor.
Desc: General newspaper. *Type:* Periodical.

The Gazette (Montreal, Quebec)

Southam, Inc.
44 Frid St.   Ph: (905)526-3333
PO Box 300
Hamilton, ON, Canada L8N
  3G3
URL: http://www.hamiltonspectator.com
Desc: Contains the complete text of news items and feature articles from The Gazette (Montreal) newspaper. Covers international, national, regional, political, business, sports, entertainment, and fashion news. *Available:* Infomart Online; Infomart Online; Infomart Assistant, Infomart Online; LEXIS-NEXIS, NEXIS; LEXIS-NEXIS, NEXIS; Infomart Dialog Limited. *Type:* Database.

The Gelman Feature Syndicate

826 E. 14th St.   Ph: (718)434-6050
Brooklyn, NY 11230
Contact: Bernard Gelman, Owner/Ed.
Alt. Contact: 826 E. 14th St., Brooklyn, NY 11230; telephone: (718)434-6050. *Type:* Periodical.

Gemini News Service

400 Madison Ave.   Ph: (212)832-2839
Ste. 1704
New York, NY 10017
Desc: Distributes news and features for the United Kingdom. *Alt. Contact:* 400 Madison Ave., Ste. 1704, New York, NY 10017; telephone: (212)832-2839. *Type:* Periodical.

German Press Agency

405 E. 42nd St.   Ph: (212)355-0318
United Nations Rm. S-352   Fax: (212)753-6168
New York, NY 10017
Contact: Helmut Raether, Chief Corr.
Alt. Contact: 405 E. 42nd St., United Nations Rm. S-352, New York, NY 10017; telephone: (212)355-0318; fax: (212)753-6168. *Type:* Periodical.

Global Features Syndicate

6326 Matte   Ph: (514)322-4578
North Montreal, PQ, Canada
  H1G 2E8
Contact: Nick Trezza, President.
Alt. Contact: 6326 Matte, North Montreal, PQ, Canada H1G 2E8; telephone: (514)322-4578. *Type:* Periodical.

Global Horizons

1330 New Hampshire Ave. NW   Ph: (202)659-1921
Ste. 609
Washington, DC 20036
Contact: Edward Flattau, President; Pamela Ebert, Columnist.
Desc: Distributes environmental column. *Alt. Contact:* 1330 New Hampshire Ave. NW, Ste. 609, Washington, DC 20036; telephone: (202)659-1921. *Type:* Periodical.

Global Information Network

777 United Nations Plz.   Ph: (202)662-7171
New York, NY 10017   Fax: (202)662-7164
Contact: Lisa Vives, Exec. Dir.; Andrew Whitehead, English Ed.; Patricia Correge, Spanish Ed.
Desc: Distributes Third World news features and abstracts in English and Spanish. *Alt. Contact:* 777 United Nations Plz., New York, NY 10017; telephone: (202)662-7171; fax: (202)662-7164. *Type:* Periodical.

The Global Media Report—Europe

Robert L. Keyser, III
2744 Cortinna Ln.   Ph: (303)674-5003
Evergreen, CO 80439-9451   Fax: (303)674-2935
E-mail: gmr-europe@worldnet.att.com.

Contact: Robert L. Keyser, III, Editor and Publisher. *Desc:* Aims to help businesses, agencies, and individuals better understand and work with European news media outlets. Recurring features include a monthly contact directory. *Type:* Newsletter.

The Globe and Mail

The Globe & Mail
444 Front St. W.   Ph: (416)585-5000
Toronto, ON, Canada M5V   Fax: (416)585-5705
2S9
URL: http://www.globeandmail.com.
Contact: Roger Parkinson, Publisher; Grant Crosbie, V.P. of Advertising Sales; William Thorsell, Editor-in-Chief; Dimitri Chrus, V.P. of Circulation.
Desc: General newspaper. *Type:* Periodical.

Globe Syndicate

499 Richardson Rd.   Ph: (540)635-3229
Strasburg, VA 22657-5236   Fax: (540)635-3229
E-mail: bourjfam@atsdelphi.com.
Contact: Monte Bourjaily, Jr., Editor and Publisher; Monte Bourjaily, III, Ed./Assoc. Pub.
Desc: Distributes editorial commentary columns. *Alt. Contact:* 499 Richardson Rd., Strasburg, VA 22657-5236; telephone: (540)635-3229; fax: (540)635-3229; 218 S. Fairfax St., Alexandria, VA 22314; telephone: (703)549-2322; fax: (703)519-8275. *Type:* Periodical.

Graham News Syndicate

2770 W. 5th St.   Ph: (718)372-1920
Ste. G-20
Brooklyn, NY 11224
Contact: Paula Royce Graham, Pres./Ed.; Lane W. Hall, Corr.; Liz Clifton, Corr.
Desc: Distributes columns on food, restaurants, travel, lifestyles, fashion, and consumer products. *Alt. Contact:* 2770 W. 5th St., Ste. G-20, Brooklyn, NY 11224; telephone: (718)372-1920. *Type:* Periodical.

The Grand Rapids Press

Booth Newspapers, Inc.
155 Michigan St. NW   Ph: (616)459-1400
Grand Rapids, MI 49503-2302   Fax: (616)459-1502
Contact: Michael Lloyd, Editor.
Desc: General newspaper. *Type:* Periodical.

Graphic Syndicate

1000 Gerrard St. E.   Ph: (416)463-3824
PO Box 98098   Fax: (416)463-7854
Toronto, ON, Canada M4M
3L9
E-mail: info@hotgraphics.com.
URL: http://www.hotgraphics.com.
Contact: Michael Lea, General Mgr.; Catherine Farley, Ed. Mgr.; Cindy Vatour, Syn. Rep.
Desc: Distributes weekly information graphics including On the Money, Lifeline, Ecoline, The Book Lady, and The Village Vet. *Alt. Contact:* 1000 Gerrard St. E., PO Box 98098, Toronto, ON, Canada M4M 3L9; telephone: (416)463-3824; fax: (416)463-7854. *Type:* Periodical.

Green Bay Press-Gazette

Green Bay Press-Gazette
435 E. Walnut
PO Box 19430
Green Bay, WI 54301-5001
Contact: John D. Gibson, Editor; William T. Nusbaum, Publisher; Susan Lindsey, Advertising Dir.
Desc: General newspaper. *Type:* Periodical.

The Greenville News

Greenville News
PO Box 1688   Ph: (864)298-4100
Greenville, SC 29602   Free: 800-274-7879
    Fax: (864)298-4395
URL: http://www.greenvilleonline.com.
Contact: Thomas Hutchison, Editor; Steven Brandt, Publisher; Louisa Koken, Advertising Mgr.; John Pittman, Editor; John Higgins, General Mgr.
Desc: General newspaper. *Type:* Periodical.

Griffin-Larrabee News Bureau

PO Box 1042   Ph: (202)554-3579
Washington, DC 20013
Desc: Distributes news features. *Alt. Contact:* PO Box 1042, Washington, DC 20013; telephone: (202)554-3579. *Type:* Periodical.

Grit

Ogden Publications
1503 SW 42nd St.   Ph: (913)274-4300
Topeka, KS 66609-1265   Fax: (913)274-4305
E-mail: grit@kspress.com.
URL: http://www.grit.com.
Contact: Donna Doyle, Editor-in-Chief; Bryan Welch, Publisher; Keith Chartier, Advertising Mgr.
Desc: Family oriented tabloid. *Type:* Periodical.

GSM News Service

PO Box 104   Ph: (201)385-2000
Oradell, NJ 07649-0104
Alt. Contact: PO Box 104, Oradell, NJ 07649-0104; telephone: (201)385-2000. *Type:* Periodical.

Harbor City Star

Harbor City Star
2575 McCollough Rd., Ste. B1   Ph: (250)758-4917
Nanaimo, BC, Canada V9E   Fax: (250)758-4513
5W5
Contact: Steve Jenkisen, Editor; Clyde Wicks, Publisher; Roy Fisher, Advertising Mgr.
Desc: Community newspaper. *Type:* Periodical.

The Harrisburg Patriot/The Evening News

The Patriot-News
812 Market St.   Ph: (717)255-8100
P.O. Box 2265
Harrisburg, PA 17101
E-mail: newsroom@patriot.microserve.com
Contact: Deanna Mills, Chief Librarian, (717)255-8402, fax: (717)255-8456, library@pn.microserve.com.
Desc: Contains the complete text of selected news items and feature articles from the Harrisburg Patriot and Sunday Patroit-News (Pennsylvania), two general circulation newspapers reporting local, national, and international news. Special areas of interest include the Pennsylvania state government. *Available:* Bell & Howell Information and Learning; Dow Jones Interactive Publishing. *Type:* Database.

Harte-Hanks Newspapers

958 National Press Bldg.   Ph: (202)628-1585
Washington, DC 20045
Desc: Distributes news covering Texas affairs. *Alt. Contact:* 958 National Press Bldg., Washington, DC 20045; telephone: (202)628-1585. *Type:* Periodical.

The Hartford Courant

The Hartford Courant
285 Broad St.   Ph: (860)241-6200
Hartford, CT 06115   Fax: (860)520-3176
Contact: Michael E. Waller, Publisher and CEO; Marty Petty, GM/Senior V-P; David S. Barrett, Editor and Vice-President.

Desc: General newspaper. *Type:* Periodical.

The Hartford Courant

The Hartford Courant Company
285 Broad St.   Ph: (860)241-6200
Hartford, CT 06115
URL: http://www.courant.com
Desc: Contains the complete text of selected news items and feature articles from The Hartford Courant (Connecticut) newspaper. Special areas of interest include the insurance industry, manufacturing, and cultural events. *Available:* Bell & Howell Information and Learning; LEXIS-NEXIS, NEXIS. *Type:* Database.

Hartford Inquirer

Inquires Newspaper Group
PO Box 1260   Ph: (860)522-1462
Hartford, CT 06143   Fax: (860)522-3014
Contact: Edward Laiscell, Editor; William R. Hales, Publisher.
Desc: Black community newspaper. *Type:* Periodical.

Hearst News Service

1701 Pennsylvania Ave. NW   Ph: (202)298-6920
Washington, DC 20006   Fax: (202)333-1184
Contact: Charles Lewis, Wash. Bureau Chief; Susanna McBee, Asst. Bureau Chief/News Ed.; Katie Harrison, Office Mgr.
Desc: Distributes news columns. *Alt. Contact:* 1701 Pennsylvania Ave. NW, Washington, DC 20006; telephone: (202)298-6920; fax: (202)333-1184. *Type:* Periodical.

Herald Tribune

Herald Tribune Co., LLC
2793 E. Foothill Blvd.   Ph: (626)585-9060
Pasadena, CA 91107-3444   Fax: (626)585-9860
E-mail: htsales1@aol.com
URL: http://www.heraldtribune.com.
Contact: Alex Suh, CEO; Rob Clyde, Advertising and Marketing; Gary McCarty, Managing Editor, htnews1@aol.com.
Desc: Newspaper covering local and community news in San Gabriel Valley, California. *Type:* Periodical.

The Home News & Tribune

Asbury Park Press, Inc.
3601 Hwy. 66   Ph: (732)922-6000
PO Box 1550   Free: 800-822-9770
Neptune, NJ 07754-1550   Fax: (732)918-9144
E-mail: letter@thnt.com.
URL: http://www.thnt.com.
Desc: General newspaper. *Type:* Periodical.

The Honolulu Advertiser

The Honolulu Advertiser
News Bldg.   Ph: (808)525-8090
605 Kapiolani Blvd.   Fax: (808)525-8037
PO Box 3110
Honolulu, HI 96802
Contact: Jim Gatti, Editor, (808)525-8080, jgatti@aloha.net; Dick Adair, Cartoonist, (808)525-8067; Wanda Adams, Living Section Editor, (808)525-8034; Judi Erickson, Money Section Editor, (808)525-8063; Dennis Anderson, Sports Writer, (808)525-8067; Jerry Burris, Editorial Page Editor, (808)525-8090; Hugh Clark, Big Isle Bureau Chief; Bev Creamer, Staff Writer, (808)525-8013; Kevin Dayton, Government Bureau Writer, (808)525-8070; Wayne Harada, Entertainment Editor, (808)525-8034;
Desc: Metropolitan newspaper. *Type:* Periodical.

Hope Springs Press

849 Hermitage Rd.
Manakin-Sabot, VA 23103
Ph: (804)784-5025
Fax: (804)784-3713
E-mail: catbird@webpointers.com.
URL: http://www.webpointers.com.
Contact: Robin Lind, Mng. Dir.; Kitty Williams, Ed. Dir.
Desc: Distributes feature columns about the Internet and World Wide Web. *Alt. Contact:* 849 Hermitage Rd., Manakin-Sabot, VA 23103; telephone: (804)784-5025; fax: (804)784-3713. *Type:* Periodical.

Hopkins Syndicate Inc.

802 S. Washington
Bloomington, IN 47401
Ph: (812)331-7753
Contact: S.L. Abram, Ed./Gen. Mgr.
Desc: Distributes psychology material. *Alt. Contact:* 802 S. Washington, Bloomington, IN 47401; telephone: (812)331-7753. *Type:* Periodical.

Houston Chronicle

Houston Chronicle
801 Texas Ave.
Houston, TX 77002
Ph: (713)220-7171
Free: 800-735-3800
Fax: (713)220-6677
URL: http://www.houstonchronicle.com.
Contact: Jack Loftis, Editor; Tony Pederson, Managing Editor; Tommy Miller, Deputy Managing Ed.; Susan Bischoff, Asst. Managing Ed.; Dan Cunningham, Asst. Managing Ed.; Fernando Dovalina, Asst. Managing Ed.; Walter Johns, Asst. Managing Ed.
Desc: General newspaper. *Type:* Periodical.

Houston Chronicle

Houston Chronicle
801 Texas Ave.
Houston, TX 77002
Ph: (713)220-7171
URL: http://www.houstonchronicle.com
Desc: Contains the complete text of news items and feature articles from the Houston Chronicle (Texas) newspaper. Regional coverage emphasizes the aerospace, energy, gas and oil, international finance, medical research, and shipping industries. *Available:* Bell & Howell Information and Learning; LEXIS-NEXIS, NEXIS. *Type:* Database.

Houston Post

Houston Post Company
4747 Southwest Fwy.
Houston, TX 77027
Ph: (713)840-5600
Desc: Contains the complete text of news items and feature articles from The Houston Post (Texas) newspaper. Regional coverage emphasizes energy, petrochemicals, aerospace, and medicine. *Available:* The Dialog Corporation, DIALOG; The Dialog Corporation, DIALOG; CompuServe Information Service, Knowledge Index; LEXIS-NEXIS, NEXIS. *Type:* Database.

Humor Books Syndicate

28 Clare St.
Stafford, VA 22554
Ph: (540)720-6300
Fax: (540)720-6877
Contact: Al Brooks, Cartoonist/Columnist.
Alt. Contact: 28 Clare St., Stafford, VA 22554; telephone: (540)720-6300; fax: (540)720-6877. *Type:* Periodical.

Humornet

313 E. 6th St.
2d Fl.
New York, NY 10003
Ph: (212)614-1591
Fax: (212)614-9563
Contact: Larry Litt, Editor.
Desc: Distributes humor items and social commentary. *Alt. Contact:* 313 E. 6th St., 2d Fl., New York, NY 10003; telephone: (212)614-1591; fax: (212)614-9563. *Type:* Periodical.

The Huntsville Times

The Huntsville Times
PO Box 1487, West Sta.
Huntsville, AL 35807-0487
Ph: (205)532-4000
Free: 800-240-8463
Fax: (205)532-4420
Contact: Bob Ward, Editor; William C. Green, Jr., Publisher; William Cooper Green, III, General Mgr.; Chris Welch, Sports Dir.
Desc: General newspaper. *Type:* Periodical.

IAPA News

Inter American Press Association (IAPA)
2911 NW 39th St.
Miami, FL 33142
Ph: (305)634-2465
Fax: (305)635-2272
E-mail: siptroti@aol.com.
Contact: Ricardo Trotti, Editor; Julio E. Munoz, Editor; Michael Hayes, Editor.
Desc: Publishes news of the Association, an organization devoted to protecting "freedom of the press in Americas." Recurring features include news of members, statistics on press freedoms throughout North, Central, and South America and the Caribbean, announcements of awards and Association elections, and a page of news briefs and obituaries called News People & Events. *Type:* Newsletter.

The Idaho Statesman

Gannett Co., Inc.
1100 Wilson Blvd.
Arlington, VA 22234
Ph: (703)284-6000
Free: 800-872-0001
E-mail: news@idstates.com.
URL: http://www.accessatlanta.com.
Contact: Margaret Buchanan, Publisher, (208)377-6301, fax: (208)377-6303, mbuchana@boise.gannett.com; Steve Silberman, Managing Editor, (208)377-6406, ssilberm@boise.gannett.com; Robert Pedersen, Circulation Mgr., pbederse@boise.gannett.com.
Desc: General newspaper. *Alt. Contact:* 1200 N. Curtis Rd., PO Box 40, Boise, ID 83707; telephone: (208)377-6200; fax: (208)377-6309; toll-free: 800-635-8934. *Type:* Periodical.

Independence Feature Syndicate

14142 Denver W. Pkwy.
Ste. 185
Golden, CO 80401-3134
Ph: (303)279-6536
Fax: (303)279-4176
Contact: David Kopel, Editor.
Desc: Distributes opinion columns. *Alt. Contact:* 14142 Denver W. Pkwy., Ste. 185, Golden, CO 80401-3134; telephone: (303)279-6536; fax: (303)279-4176. *Type:* Periodical.

The Indianapolis Star

Indianapolis Newspapers, Inc.
307 N. Pennsylvania St.
Indianapolis, IN 46204-1811
Ph: (317)633-1240
Free: 800-669-7827
Fax: (317)633-1038
Contact: Frank Caperton, Exec. Editor, (317)633-9169; Nancy Comiskey, Managing Editor, Features/Photo/Graphics, (317)633-9104; Ted Daniels, Managing Editor, News, (317)633-9266; Chip Maury, Dir. of Photography, (317)633-9279; Tom Peyton, Art Dir., (317)633-9853; Mark Rochester, Projects Editor, (317)633-9288; Alex Wadell, A.M. News Editor, (317)633-9277; Tom Swenson, P.M. News Editor, (317)656-1397; John H. Lyst, Editor, (317)633-9172; Eugene S. Pulliam, Publisher, (317)633-1298.
Desc: General newspaper. *Type:* Periodical.

The Indianapolis Star/The Indianapolis News

Indianapolis Newspapers Inc.
307 N. Pennsylvania St.
Indianapolis, IN 46206-0145
Ph: (317)633-1240
E-mail: webmaster@stanews.com.

URL: http://www.news.com
Desc: Contains the complete text of The Indianapolis Star and The Indianapolis News. Covers all news stories, local columns, syndicated columns, features, editorials, obituaries, the arts, and sports. *Available:* Bell & Howell Information and Learning; LEXIS-NEXIS, NEXIS. *Type:* Database.

Ink

Association of Free Community Papers
401 N. Michigan Ave., Ste. 2300
Chicago, IL 60611
Ph: (312)644-6610
Fax: (312)321-6869
Contact: Vikki Fox, Editor.
Desc: Provides publishers and suppliers of free community papers with information on related areas, including programs, services, and meetings available to members of the Association. Covers promotions, acquisitions, supplier news, legislative items, postal rulings, and all news of interest to members. *Type:* Newsletter.

Inman News Features

5335 College
Ste. 25
Oakland, CA 94618
Ph: (510)658-9252
Fax: (510)658-9317
E-mail: inmannews@aol.com.
URL: http://www.inman.com.
Contact: Bradley Inman, Owner.
Desc: Distributes real estate news. *Alt. Contact:* 5335 College, Ste. 25, Oakland, CA 94618; telephone: (510)658-9252; fax: (510)658-9317. *Type:* Periodical.

Insight

The Washington Times Corp.
3600 New York Ave. NE
Washington, DC 20002-1947
Ph: (202)636-3000
Free: 800-822-2822
Fax: (202)636-3000
Contact: Paul Rodriguez, Managing Editor; Peter Gogan, Business Dir.
Desc: General interest news magazine covering geopolitics, business, science, health, law, and culture. *Type:* Periodical.

INSIGHT News

17 St. Joseph St.
Ste. 309
Toronto, ON, Canada M4Y 1J8
Ph: (416)413-4900
Fax: (416)413-4887
Contact: Richard W. Reynolds, Exec. Ed.
Alt. Contact: 17 St. Joseph St., Ste. 309, Toronto, ON, Canada M4Y 1J8; telephone: (416)413-4900; fax: (416)413-4887. *Type:* Periodical.

Inter Press Service Distributed by Global Information Network

1293 National Press Bldg.
Washington, DC 20045
Ph: (202)662-7171
Fax: (202)662-7164
Contact: Yvette Collymore, Bureau Chief.
Desc: Distributes Third World news wire service. *Alt. Contact:* 1293 National Press Bldg., Washington, DC 10045; telephone: (202)662-7171; fax: (202)662-7164. *Type:* Periodical.

Inter Press Service International Database

Global Information Network, Ltd. (GIN)
275 Seventh Ave. 1206
New York, NY 10001-6708
Ph: (212)647-0123
E-mail: ipsgin@igc.apc.org
URL: http://www.ips.org
Contact: Lisa Vives, Executive Director, ipsgin@igc.apc.org.
Desc: Contains the complete text of news items issued over the Inter Press Service International newswire service.

Covers international news, including regional coverage of Africa, Asia, the sub-continent, Latin America and the Caribbean, as well as general news concerning the United States, Europe, and the countries of the former Soviet Union. *Available:* LEXIS-NEXIS, NEXIS; Dow Jones Interactive Publishing; NewsBank, Inc.; Responsive Database Services, Inc.; Reuters Information Services Inc.; Profound Inc., The Dialog Corporation; SIRS, Inc.; NewsEdge Corporation; The Dialog Corporation, DIALOG; Infonautics Corporation; Internet Financial Network. *Type:* Database.

International Features Inc.

184 Kanan Dume Rd.　　Ph: (818)889-6988
Malibu, CA 90265
Contact: Colin Dangaard, President; Linda Fox, Vice President; Rod Barrand, Editor.
Desc: Distributes news features. *Alt. Contact:* 184 Kanan Dume Rd., Malibu, CA 90265; telephone: (818)889-6988. *Type:* Periodical.

International Motor Press Association—Impact

International Motor Press Association
1756 Broadway, Rm. 26J　　Ph: (212)315-4900
New York, NY 10019　　Fax: (212)315-4903
Contact: Nancy Coggins, Editor.
Desc: Reports on Association activities. *Type:* Newsletter.

International News Agency

2445 Pine Tree Dr.　　Ph: (305)674-9746
Ste. 20　　Fax: (305)674-1939
Miami Beach, FL 33140-4611
Contact: C.H. Garvey, Bureau Chief; R.J. Sherker, Exec. Ed.; T.M. Mosburg, Asst. Ed.; Larry Lowis, Managing Editor; Donna Shaw, Arts Dept.; Ed Dever, Bus. Dept.; Ed Hayden, Charity Dept.; Roz Sholin, Food; Pat Simpson, Sports; Judy Putnam, Travel.
Desc: Distributes features on conventions, conferences, trade shows, expositions, sporting events, cruise ships, hotels, restaurants, and attractions in the southeast U.S. and the Caribbean islands. *Alt. Contact:* 2445 Pine Tree Dr., Ste. 20, Miami Beach, FL 33140-4611; telephone: (305)674-9746; fax: (305)674-1939. *Type:* Periodical.

Interpress of London and New York

400 Madison Ave.　　Ph: (212)832-2839
Ste. 1704
New York, NY 10017
Contact: Jeffrey Bly, Editor-in-Chief.
Desc: Distributes news features. *Alt. Contact:* 400 Madison Ave., Ste. 1704, New York, NY 10017; telephone: (212)832-2839. *Type:* Periodical.

Interpress Service

1293 National Press Bldg.　　Ph: (202)662-7160
Washington, DC 20045　　Fax: (202)662-7164
Contact: James Lobe, Bureau Chief.
Desc: Distributes Third World economic activity, news, features. *Alt. Contact:* 1293 National Press Bldg., Washington, DC 20045; telephone: (202)662-7160; fax: (202)662-7164. *Type:* Periodical.

Interstate News Service

237 S. Clark Ave.　　Ph: (314)522-1300
St. Louis, MO 63135　　Free: 800-522-1301
　　Fax: (314)522-1999
Contact: Michael J. Olds, Pres./Mng. Ed.; James J. Olds, Vice President; Ellen M. Olds, Sec./Treas.; Diane Ross, Asst. Mng. Ed.
Desc: Distributes general travel and state capital news. *Alt. Contact:* 237 S. Clark Ave., St. Louis, MO 63135; telephone: (314)522-1300; fax: (314)522-1999; toll-free: 800-522-1301. *Type:* Periodical.

Interview

Interview
575 Broadway　　Ph: (212)941-2800
New York, NY 10012　　Free: 800-925-9574
　　Fax: (212)941-2885
Contact: Ingrid Sischy, Editor; Sandra J. Brant, Publisher; Victoria Melekson, Director.
Desc: Magazine featuring famous personalities in fashion, film, art, photography, politics, and music. *Type:* Periodical.

The IRE Journal

Investigative Reporters and Editors, Inc. (IRE)
University of Missouri　　Ph: (573)882-2042
138 Neff Annex　　Fax: (573)882-5431
School of Journalism
Columbia, MO 65211
E-mail: info@ire.org
URL: http://www.ire.org; http://www.nicar.org.
Contact: Steve Weinberg, Editor.
Desc: Promotes better investigative journalism. Covers sources of information, techniques of award-winning journalists, and issues of journalism. *Type:* Newsletter.

J Features

PO Box 70　　Ph: (617)383-9858
Cohasset, MA 02025-0070
Contact: Charles A. Jaffe, Columnist; Susan Biddle Jaffe, Syn. Mgr.
Desc: Distributes personal finance and investment features. *Alt. Contact:* PO Box 70, Cohasset, MA 02025-0070; telephone: (617)383-9858. *Type:* Periodical.

Jack Posner Syndicate

216 Ellesmere E.　　Ph: (954)427-8068
Deerfield Beach, FL 33442
Alt. Contact: 216 Ellesmere E., Deerfield Beach, FL 33442; telephone: (954)427-8068. *Type:* Periodical.

Jandon Features

53961 222nd St.　　Ph: (712)527-9517
Glenwood, IA 51534　　Fax: (712)527-5063
E-mail: driggenbach@mcimail.com.
Contact: Don Riggenbach, Manager.
Desc: Distributes gardening information. *Alt. Contact:* 53961 222nd St., Glenwood, IA 51534; telephone: (712)527-9517; fax: (712)527-5063. *Type:* Periodical.

J.D. Crowe

2400 Kettner Blvd.　　Ph: (619)582-2769
Studio 216
San Diego, CA 92101
Contact: J.D. Crow, Self-Syndicator.
Alt. Contact: 2400 Kettner Blvd., Studio 216, San Diego, CA 92101; telephone: (619)582-2769. *Type:* Periodical.

The Jerusalem Post Foreign Service

211 E. 43rd St.　　Ph: (212)599-3666
New York, NY 10017　　Fax: (212)599-4743
E-mail: jpedt@jpost.co.il.
URL: http://www.jpost.co.il.
Contact: Marilyn Henry, NY Corr.; Nina Keren-David, Electronic Publishing; Hillel Kuttler, Wash. Corr.
Alt. Contact: 211 E. 43rd St., New York, NY 10017; telephone: (212)599-3666; fax: (212)599-4743. *Type:* Periodical.

Jet

Johnson Publishing Co., Inc.
820 S. Michigan Ave.　　Ph: (312)322-9200
Chicago, IL 60605-2191　　Fax: (312)322-9375
Contact: John H. Johnson, Publisher.
Desc: Newsmagazine for the black community. *Type:* Periodical.

Jewish Telegraphic Agency Inc.

330 7th Ave.　　Ph: (212)643-1890
11th Fl.　　Fax: (212)643-8498
New York, NY 10001-5010
E-mail: jtany@aol.com.
URL: http://www.jta.org.
Contact: Mark Joffe, Exec. Ed./Pub.; Caryn Rosen Adelman, President; Lisa Hostein, Editor; Kenneth Bandler, Managing Editor; Marshall Weinberg, Chm.
Desc: Distributes Jewish news articles. *Alt. Contact:* 330 7th Ave., 11th Fl., New York, NY 10001-5010; telephone: (212)643-1890; fax: (212)643-8498. *Type:* Periodical.

Jiji Press America Ltd.

120 W. 45th St.　　Ph: (212)575-5830
Ste. 1401　　Fax: (212)764-3950
New York, NY 10036
Contact: Kunji Oguro, President; S. Yamazaki, Managing Editor.
Alt. Contact: 120 W. 45th St., Ste. 1401, New York, NY 10036; telephone: (212)575-5830; fax: (212)764-3950. *Type:* Periodical.

Johnson County Sun

Sun Publications, Inc.
7373 W. 107th St.　　Ph: (913)648-4620
Overland Park, KS 66212-2547　　Fax: (913)381-1402
Contact: Jack Lovelace, Editor; John Yates, V.P. of Operations; Steve Rose, Publisher; Jo Stapleton, Advertising Mgr.
Desc: Newspaper. *Type:* Periodical.

The Journal Friday Home Report

The Journal Newspapers
6408 Edsall Rd.　　Ph: (703)560-4000
Alexandria, VA 22312　　Free: 800-531-1223
　　Fax: (703)846-8505
Contact: James McCormick, Editor; Dorothy Ralph, Advertising Mgr.
Desc: Newspaper carrying real estate advertising and articles. *Type:* Periodical.

The Journal Gazette

The Journal Gazette Co.
600 W. Main St.　　Ph: (219)461-8444
Fort Wayne, IN 46802　　Fax: (219)461-8648
E-mail: jgnews@jg.net.
URL: http://www.jg.net/jg.
Contact: Craig Klugman, Editor, (219)461-8853, cklugman@jg.net; Julie Inskeep Walda, Publisher, (219)461-8490, jwalda@jg.net; Sherry Skufca, Managing Editor, (219)461-8201, sskufca@jg.net; Ed Breen, Graphics Editor, (219)461-8771, fax: (219)461-8893, ebreen@jg.net; Tom Pellegrene, Jr., Mgr. of News Technologies, (219)461-8377, tpellegrene@jg.net; Tracy Warner, Metro Editor, (219)461-8428, twarner@jg.net; Jim Touvell, Sports Editor, (219)461-8260, jtouvell@jg.net;
Desc: General newspaper. *Type:* Periodical.

Journal Press Syndicate

PO Box 931　　Ph: (212)580-8559
Grand Central Sta.　　Fax: (202)764-4384
New York, NY 10163-0931
Contact: Donald Finck, Director; John Lynker, Managing Editor; William Kresse, Art Dir.; Eugene R. Smith, Editor.
Desc: Distributes columns, comic strips, and news features. *Alt. Contact:* PO Box 931, Grand Central Sta., New York, NY 10163-0931; telephone: (212)580-8559; fax: (202)764-4384. *Type:* Periodical.

The Journal Record (Oklahoma City, Oklahoma)
The Journal Publishing Co.
PO Box 26370   Ph: (405)235-3100
Oklahoma City, OK 73126
E-mail: dpage@journalrecord.com
URL: http://www.journalrecord.com
Desc: Contains the complete text of news items and feature articles from The Journal Record (Oklahoma City, Oklahoma) newspaper. *Available:* Bell & Howell Information and Learning. *Type:* Database.

Journal Star
The Peoria Journal Star, Inc.
1 News Plaza   Ph: (309)686-3000
Peoria, IL 61643   Free: 800-225-5757
                           Fax: (309)686-3296
URL: http://www.pjstar.com.
Contact: Barb Drake, Editorial Page Ed., (309)686-3133; Clare Howard, Business Reporter, (309)686-3250; Dennis Dmond, Ed. Systems Man., (309)686-3243; Eric Behrens, Photo/Graphics Ed., (309)686-3137; Mike Miller, Religion/TV Editor, (309)686-3120; Ken Kirchoefer, State Editor, (309)686-3041.
Desc: General newspaper. *Type:* Periodical.

Kalamazoo Gazette
Booth Newspapers
401 S. Burdick St.   Ph: (616)345-3511
Kalamazoo, MI 49007-5279   Fax: (616)345-0583
URL: http://www.mlive.com.
Contact: James R. Mosby, Jr., Editor; James Pulliam, Advertising Mgr.
Desc: General newspaper. *Type:* Periodical.

The Kansas City Star
Kansas City Star Co.
1729 Grand Blvd.   Ph: (816)234-4280
Kansas City, MO 64108   Free: 800-726-2340
                           Fax: (816)234-4267
URL: http://www.kansascity.com.
Contact: Art Brisbane, Editor; Bob Woodworth, Publisher; Mark Johnston, Advertising Mgr.
Desc: General newspaper. *Type:* Periodical.

Kansas Scholastic Press Association—Courier
Kansas Scholastic Press Association
University of Kansas   Ph: (913)864-0605
200 Stauffer-Flint Hall   Fax: (913)864-5945
Lawrence, KS 66045
E-mail: kspa@kuhub.cc.ukans.edu
Contact: John Hudnall, Editor.
Desc: Provides information on the development of high school publications and student press legislation. Discusses headlines, computer graphics, journalistic professionalism, and photography. *Type:* Newsletter.

Kappa Tau Alpha
c/o Dr. Keith P. Sanders   Ph: (573)882-7685
University of Missouri   Fax: (573)884-1720
School of Journalism
Columbia, MO 65211
E-mail: ktahq@showme.missouri.edu
Contact: Dr. Keith P. Sanders, Exec.Dir.
Desc: Honor society - men and women, in the field of journalism and mass communications. *Type:* Association.

Keister-Williams Newspaper Services
PO Box 8005   Ph: (804)293-4709
Charlottesville, VA 22906 Fax: (804)293-4884
Contact: Jean Lindsay, Author; Meta L. Nay, Mktg. Dir.; Ky Lindsay, Sales VP.
Desc: Distributes religious features. *Alt. Contact:* PO Box 8005, Charlottesville, VA 22906; telephone: (804)293-4709; fax: (804)293-4884. *Type:* Periodical.

Keystone Press Agency Inc.
202 E. 42nd St.   Ph: (212)924-8123
4th Fl.   Fax: (212)924-8123
New York, NY 10017
E-mail: balpert@worldnet.att.com.
Contact: Brian F. Alpert, Managing Editor.
Alt. Contact: 202 E. 42nd St., 4th Fl., New York, NY 10017; telephone: (212)924-8123; fax: (212)924-8123. *Type:* Periodical.

King Features Syndicate Inc.
235 E. 45th St.   Ph: (212)455-4000
New York, NY 10017   Free: 800-526-5464
                           Fax: (212)455-4119
Contact: Joseph F. D'Angelo, President; Lawrence T. Olsen, Exec. VP & Gen. Mgr.; Ted Hannah, Dir. Adv. & PR; Jay Kennedy, Comics Ed.; Paul G. Eberhart, Dir. Ops.; Maria Carmicino, Managing Editor; George Haeberlein, Dir. Sales; Mary Anne Miller, Intl. Sales Mgr.; John Killian, Asst. Sales Mgr./Midwest Sales; Dick Lafave, Southwest Sales; John Perry, Southeast Sales; Richard Heimlich, Southwest Sales; Dennis Danko, Telemarketing Sales Mgr.; Chris Monahan, Telemarketing Sales Rep.; Jam
Desc: Distributes automotive, business, and personal finance commentary; entertainment, graphic services, humor, lifestyle, advice. mental and physical fitness, and sports columns; comics, games, and puzzles. *Alt. Contact:* 235 E. 45th St., New York, NY 10017; telephone: (212)455-4000; fax: (212)455-4119; toll-free: 800-526-5464. *Type:* Periodical.

Knight-Ridder/Tribune Information Services
790 National Press Bldg.   Ph: (202)383-6080
Washington, DC 20045   Fax: (202)393-2460
URL: http://www.online.presslink.com.
Contact: Mike Duggan, Mng. Ed News Serv. & KRT Kids; Jane Scholz, Editor; Charles Borst, Dir. Photo Serv.; George Rorick, Dir. Graphic Serv. & News in Motion; Robert Harris, Dir. Bus. News; Lily Dow, Dir. Interactives; Walter Mahoney, Sales. Dir. Chicago Office.
Desc: Distributes news wire service, photos, and graphics. *Alt. Contact:* 790 National Press Bldg., Washington, DC 20045; telephone: (202)383-6080; fax: (202)393-2460; 435 N. Michigan Ave., Ste.1500, Chicago, IL 60611; telephone: (312)222-4695. *Type:* Periodical.

The Knoxville News-Sentinel
Knoxville News Sentinel Co.
208 W. Church Ave.   Ph: (423)523-3131
PO Box 59038   Fax: (423)673-3478
Knoxville, TN 37902-1683
E-mail: kns@knoxnews.com
URL: http://www.knoxnews.com.
Contact: Harry Moskos, Editor, (423)521-8142; Bruce Hartmann, Advertising Mgr., (423)521-8192; Frank Cagle, Managing Editor, (423)521-8139.
Desc: General newspaper. *Type:* Periodical.

KRTN News Wire
790 National Press Bldg.   Ph: (202)383-6080
Washington, DC 20045
Contact: Jane Scholz, Editor; Walter Mahoney, Sales Dir.
Desc: Distributes news, business, and sports features. *Alt. Contact:* 790 National Press Bldg., Washington, DC 20045; telephone: (202)383-6080. *Type:* Periodical.

Kyodo News Serivce
50 Rockefeller Plaza   Ph: (212)603-6600
Ste. 816   Fax: (212)603-6621
New York, NY 10020
E-mail: kyodony@aol.com.
URL: http://www.kyodo.co.jp.
Contact: Kunihiko Suzuki, NY Bureau Chief; Akihiro Onoda, Dep Bureau Chief; Masaru Imai, Dept. Bureau

Chief; Shitaro Nishiyama, Office Mgr.; Toru Maruyama, Corr.; Hitoshi Kawahara, Coor.; Hiroki Sugita, Corr.; Yasuki Matsumoto, Corr.; Miho Tabuchi, Corr.; Hajime Miyagawa, Corr.; Manabu Matsuse, Corr.; Takaya Uno, Editor.
Desc: Distributes American news forwarded to Japanese wire service and newspapers. *Alt. Contact:* 50 Rockerfeller Plaza, Ste. 816, New York, NY 10020; telephone: (212)603-6600; fax: (212)603-6621. *Type:* Periodical.

La Opinion
Lozano Enterprises
411 W. 5th St.   Ph: (213)622-8332
Los Angeles, CA 90013-1028 Fax: (213)896-2151
Contact: Monica Lozano, Editor, (213)622-8332, fax: (213)896-2151; Jose I. Lozano, Publisher.
Desc: General newspaper (Spanish). *Type:* Periodical.

L.A. Weekly
L.A. Weekly
6715 Sunset Blvd.   Ph: (213)465-9909
Los Angeles, CA 90028   Free: 800-304-4414
                           Fax: (213)465-3220
E-mail: webmaster@laweekly.com.
URL: http://www.laweekly.com.
Contact: Sue Horton, Editor; Mike Sigman, Publisher; Tom Christie, Arts Editor.
Desc: Newspaper (tabloid) featuring news, people, entertainment, and the arts. *Type:* Periodical.

Lakes Area Advertiser
Lakes Area Advertiser, Inc.
236 Rte. 173   Ph: (847)395-4444
Antioch, IL 60002   Fax: (847)395-8480
Contact: Carol Anderson, President.
Desc: Newspaper. *Type:* Periodical.

Lansing State Journal
Lansing State Journal
120 E. Lenawee   Ph: (517)377-1000
Lansing, MI 48919-0001   Fax: (517)377-1298
URL: http://www.lansinglife.com.
Contact: Zack Binkley, Editor; W. Curtis Riddle, Publisher; Ron Carpretia, Advertising Mgr.
Desc: General newspaper. *Type:* Periodical.

Las Vegas Review-Journal
Donrey Media Group
PO Box 17017   Ph: (501)785-7810
Fort Smith, AR 72917-7017 Fax: (501)785-9467
Contact: Sherman Frederick, Publisher, (702)383-0237, fax: (702)383-0402; Jim Hannah, Human Resources Dir.; Jack Harpster, Advertising Dir., (702)383-0223, fax: (702)383-0435; Allan Fleming, General Mgr., (702)383-0365, fax (702)383-0389; Terry Duck, Production Dir., (702)383-0466, fax: (702)383-4699; Tom Mitchell, Editor, (702)383-0261, Tom_Mitchell@lvrj.com; Patricia Johnson, Business Mgr., (702)383-0215, fax: (702)383-4665; Charles Zobell, Managing Editor, (702)383-0293, Charl
Desc: General newspaper. *Alt. Contact:* PO Box 70, Las Vegas, NV 89125; 1111 W. Bonanza, Las Vegas, NV 89106; telephone: (702)383-0211, (702)383-0302. *Type:* Periodical.

The Las Vegas Review-Journal
The Las Vegas Review-Journal
PO Box 70   Ph: (702)383-0211
Las Vegas, NV 89125
E-mail: padmini_pai@lvrj.com
URL: http://www.lvrj.com
Contact: Padmini P. Pai, Librarian.
Desc: Contains the complete text of news items and feature articles from the Las Vegas Review Journal (Nevada) news-

paper. *Available:* Bell & Howell Information and Learning; LEXIS-NEXIS; The Dialog Corporation, DIALOG; Dow Jones Interactive Publishing; The Las Vegas Review-Journal. *Type:* Database.

Leawood Sun

Sun Publications, Inc.
7373 W. 107th St.   Ph: (913)648-4620
Overland Park, KS 66212-2547   Fax: (913)381-1402
Contact: Jack Lovelace, Editor; Steve Rose, Publisher; Jo Stapleton, Advertising Mgr.
Desc: Newspaper. *Type:* Periodical.

Leawood Sun, Blue Valley Edition

Sun Publications, Inc.
7373 W. 107th St.   Ph: (913)648-4620
Overland Park, KS 66212-2547   Fax: (913)381-1402
Contact: Jack Lovelace, Editor; Steve Rose, Publisher; Jo Stapleton, Advertising Manager.
Desc: Newspaper. *Type:* Periodical.

The Ledger

The Ledger
33815 W. Lime St.   Ph: (941)802-7000
PO Box 408   Fax: (941)687-7090
Lakeland, FL 33802
E-mail: online@theledger.com.
URL: http://www.theledger.com.
Contact: Louis Michael Perez, Exec. Editor; Don R. Whitworth, Publisher.
Desc: General newspaper. *Type:* Periodical.

Lenexa Sun

Sun Publications, Inc.
7373 W. 107th St.   Ph: (913)648-4620
Overland Park, KS 66212-2547   Fax: (913)381-1402
E-mail: sunnews@sunpublications.com.
Contact: Jack Lovelace, Editor; Steve Rose, Publisher.
Desc: Newspaper. *Type:* Periodical.

Lester Syndicate

PO Box 1183   Ph: (408)257-9567
Cupertino, CA 95015
Contact: Mary Lester, Publisher; William Lester, Exec. Ed.
Desc: Distributes information on food, wine, religion, and politics. *Alt. Contact:* PO Box 1183, Cupertino, CA 95015; telephone: (408)257-9567. *Type:* Periodical.

Lexington Herald-Leader

Knight-Ridder, Inc.
50 W. Fernando St.   Ph: (408)938-7700
San Jose, CA 95113
Contact: Ann Cawlkins, Advertising Dir., (606)231-3172, fax: (606)231-3454; Tim Kelly, Publisher, (606)231-3257, fax: (606)231-3454; David Holwerk, Managing Editor, (606)231-3224, fax: (606)231-3326; Sharon Thompson, (606)231-3321; Bettye Lee Mastin, (606)231-3250; Todd Van Campen, Religion Reporter, (606)231-3252; Beverly Fotune, Gardening Reporter, (606)231-3251; Liz Petros, Regional Editor, (606)231-3305; Angie Muhs, Frankfort Bureau Chief (Politics), (502)227-4390; Mary O'Doherty
Desc: General newspaper. *Alt. Contact:* , 100 Midland Ave., Lexington, KY 40508; telephone: (606)231-3100; fax: (606)254-9738. *Type:* Periodical.

Lexington Herald-Leader

Lexington Herald-Leader Company
100 Midland Ave.   Ph: (606)231-3200
Lexington, KY 40508
E-mail: hllib@.infi.net
Desc: Contains the complete text of news items and feature stories from The Lexington Herald-Leader (Kentucky)

newspaper. Regional coverage includes the coal industry, automotive manufacturing, collegiate sports, government, and horse breeding and racing. *Available:* The Dialog Corporation, DIALOG; The Dialog Corporation, DIALOG. *Type:* Database.

Lincoln Journal

Journal-Star Printing Co.
926 P St.   Ph: (402)475-4200
PO Box 81609   Fax: (402)473-7291
Lincoln, NE 68508
URL: http://www.nebweb.com.
Contact: W. Earl Dyer, Editor.
Desc: General newspaper. *Type:* Periodical.

Lincoln Star

Journal-Star Printing Co.
926 P St.   Ph: (402)475-4200
PO Box 81609   Fax: (402)473-7291
Lincoln, NE 68508
Contact: W. Earl Dyer, Editor.
Desc: General newspaper. *Type:* Periodical.

The London Free Press

Blockburn Group
369 York St.   Ph: (519)679-1111
London, ON, Canada N6A 4G1 Fax: (519)667-4523
Contact: Philip R. McLeod, Editor; James E. Armitage, Publisher.
Desc: General newspaper. *Type:* Periodical.

Los Angeles Daily News

Los Angeles Daily News
21221 Oxnard St.   Ph: (818)713-3000
P.O. Box 4200
Woodland Hills, CA 91367
Contact: Margaret Douglas, Chief Librarian, (818)713-3657, fax: (818)713-0058.
Desc: Contains the complete text of the Daily News, a general circulation newspaper reporting Los Angeles area local news as well as national and international news. Special areas of interest include high technology, aerospace industry and the entertainment industry. *Available:* The Dialog Corporation, DIALOG; CompuServe Information Service; LEXIS-NEXIS, NEXIS; Dow Jones Interactive Publishing. *Type:* Database.

Los Angeles Features Syndicate

650 Winnetka Mews   Ph: (847)446-4082
Ste. 110   Fax: (847)446-4804
Winnetka, IL 60093
E-mail: oneillword@aol.com.
Contact: Alice O'Neill, Managing Editor; A.V. Licht, President.
Desc: Distributes Hollywood Behind the Scenes. *Alt. Contact:* 650 Winnetka Mews, Ste. 110, Winnetka, IL 60093; telephone: (847)446-4082; fax: (847)446-4804. *Type:* Periodical.

Los Angeles Independent

National Media, Inc.
4201 Wilshire Blvd., Ste. 600 Ph: (323)932-6397
Los Angeles, CA 90010   Fax: (323)932-8285
E-mail: laingroup@aol.com.
URL: http://www.laindependent.com.
Contact: Brian Lewis, Managing Editor; Stephen Laxineta, President; Bruce M. Wood, Publisher.
Desc: Community newspaper. *Alt. Contact:* 4201 Wilshire Blvd., Ste. 600, Los Angeles, CA 90010; telephone: (323)932-6397; fax: (323)932-8285. *Type:* Periodical.

Los Angeles Magazine

Los Angeles Magazine
1888 Century Park E., Ste. 920 Ph: (310)557-7569
Los Angeles, CA 90067   Fax: (310)557-7517
Contact: Lew Harris, Editor; Geoff Miller, Publisher; Katie Marin, Advertising Dir.
Desc: Metropolitan magazine. *Type:* Periodical.

Los Angeles Times

Los Angeles Times, Inc.
Times Mirror Sq.   Ph: (213)237-7811
Los Angeles, CA 90053   Free: 800-528-4637
                    Fax: (213)237-7386
Contact: Shelby Coffey, III, Managing Editor; Dave Laventhol, Publisher.
Desc: General newspaper. *Type:* Periodical.

The Los Angeles Times

The Los Angeles Times
Times Mirror Sq.   Ph: (213)237-5000
Los Angeles, CA 90053
URL: http://www.latimes.com
Desc: Contains the complete text of all editorial content, including news items, feature stories, and editorials from all sections and editions of The Los Angeles Times (California) newspaper. Regional coverage includes the entertainment industry, high-technology industries, and Pacific Rim commerce. *Available:* The Dialog Corporation, DIALOG; The Dialog Corporation, DIALOG; CompuServe Information Service, Knowledge Index; NIFTY Corporation, NIFTY-SERVE; Dow Jones & Company, Inc. *Type:* Database.

Los Angeles Times Magazine

Los Angeles Times, Inc.
Times Mirror Sq.   Ph: (213)237-7811
Los Angeles, CA 90053   Free: 800-528-4637
                    Fax: (213)237-7386
Contact: Alice Short, Editor, (213)237-3408; Mark Willes, Publisher.
Desc: General interest magazine. *Type:* Periodical.

Los Angeles Times Syndicate

218 S. Spring St.   Ph: (213)237-5485
Los Angeles, CA 90012   Fax: (213)237-3698
Contact: Willard Colston, Chm.; Jesse E. Levine, Pres./CEO; Steven Christensen, VP/Gen. Mgr.; Jim Lomenzo, Sales Exec./East & Ohio; Beth Barber, Dir. Acct. Relations & Article Sales; Tom Griffiths, Sales Exec./West & South; Lupe Salazar, Reprints & Perms.; Gary Neeleman, VP/Dir.-Sales-LATSI; Grant Armendariz, Sales Exec./Midwest & South; Cathryn Irvine, Promo. Mgr.
Desc: Distributes advice, art, authoritative commentary, business, humor, lifestyle, politics, and sports columns, comic strips, puzzles, and news services. *Alt. Contact:* 218 S. Spring St., Los Angeles, CA 90012; telephone: (213)237-5485; fax: (213)237-3698. *Type:* Periodical.

Los Angeles Times Syndicate International

2 Park Ave.   Ph: (212)447-1450
Ste. 1802   Fax: (212)447-1454
New York, NY 10016
Contact: Jesse E. Levine, Pres./CEO; Gary Neeleman, VP Dir of Sales Utah Office; Beth Barber, Dir. Acct Relations and Article Sales Ne; Charles Curmi, Sales-Europe Middle East Near East & Afr; Maryann Grau, Sales-Europe London Office.
Desc: Distributes international sales of the Los Angeles Times Syndicate material. *Alt. Contact:* 2 Park Ave., Ste. 1802, New York, NY 10016; telephone: (212)447-1450; fax: (212)447-1454; 143 S. Main St., Salt Lake City, UT 84111; telephone: (801)363-4934; fax: (801)363-4941; Atrium Unit Jupiter House, Triton Ct. 14, Finsbury Sq., London, En EC2A 1BR; telephone: (447)1 588 7588; fax: (447)4 638 3011. *Type:* Periodical.

Los Angeles Times/Washington Post News Service

1150 15th St. NW   Ph: (202)334-6173
Washington, DC 20071   Fax: (202)334-5096
E-mail: latwp@atsnewsservice.com.
URL: http://www.newsservice.com.
Contact: Al Leeds, Pres./Ed. Dir.; John W. Payne, VP/Gen. Mgr.; Charles R. Carter, Business Mgr.; Dick Preston, VP/Comm. Dir.; Bao N. Dang, Treas.; Kate Carlisle, Mng. Ed. Wash.; Robert S. Cleland, Mktg. Mgr.; Michael J. Kaese, Mng. Ed. LA.
Desc: Distributes celebrity, commentary, entertainment, food, gardening, health, hobbies, humor, media, money, and travel columns; book reviews, and photographs. *Alt. Contact:* 1150 15th St. NW, Washington, DC 20071; telephone: (202)334-6173; fax: (202)334-5096. *Type:* Periodical.

Lynch News Service

5805 Wilson Ln.   Ph: (301)229-3123
Bethesda, MD 20817-6204
Contact: David Lynch, Bureau Chief.
Desc: Distributes news features. *Alt. Contact:* 5805 Wilson Ln., Bethesda, MD 20817-6204; telephone: (301)229-3123. *Type:* Periodical.

MacLean's, Canada's Weekly Newsmagazine

The Financial Post Datagroup
333 King St. E.   Ph: (416)350-6440
Toronto, ON, Canada M5A
    4N2
E-mail: fpdg@fpdata.finpost.com
URL: http://www.fpdata.finpost.com
Desc: Contains the complete text of Maclean's, a magazine covering national and international political, economic, scientific, and cultural events and trends. Includes reviews of books, movies, plays, and art. *Available:* Infomart Online; Infomart Assistant, Infomart Online; Globe Information Services, Info Globe Online; Infomart Dialog Limited. *Type:* Database.

The Macomb Daily

The Macomb Daily
100 Macomb Daily Dr.   Ph: (810)469-4510
PO Box 707   Fax: (810)469-2892
Mount Clemens, MI 48046
E-mail: edit@macombdaily.com
Contact: Phil Van Hulle, Editor, (810)783-0226; Ken Kish, Managing Editor, News, (810)783-0228; Niky Hachigian, Lifestyles Editor, (810)783-0323.
Desc: General newspaper. *Type:* Periodical.

The Macon Telegraph

Knight-Ridder, Inc.
50 W. Fernando St.   Ph: (408)938-7700
San Jose, CA 95113
URL: http://www.macontelegraph.com.
Contact: Edmund E. Olson, Publisher, (912)744-4290, fax: (912)744-4469; Richard D. Thomas, Vice-President/Editor, (912)744-4340, fax: (912)744-4385; Ron Woodgeard, General Mgr., (912)744-4319, fax: (912)744-4385; Barbara Stinson, Managing Editor, Features, (912)744-4221, fax: (912)744-4385; Bill Weaver, Assistant Managing Editor, News, (912)744-4330, fax: (912)744-4385; Jane Self, Assistant Features Editor, (912)744-4225, fax: (912)744-4385; Ella Haynes, Television Editor, (912)744-4
Desc: General newspaper. *Alt. Contact:* 120 Broadway, Macon, GA 31201-3444; telephone: (912)744-4200; fax: (912)744-4269; 120 Broadway, Macon, GA 31201-3444. *Type:* Periodical.

Magazine Article Summaries

EBSCO Publishing
10 Estes St.   Ph: (978)356-6500
Ipswich, MA 01938
E-mail: ep@epnet.com
Desc: Contains citations, with abstracts, to articles published in more than 400 general-interest periodicals. Covers the arts, consumer issues, business, computers, current events, education, health, literature, politics, and science. *Available:* CARL Corporation; Ameritech Library Services, Vista. *Type:* Database.

Maine Sunday Telegram

The Portland Newspapers
390 Congress St.   Ph: (207)791-6650
PO Box 1460   Free: 800-442-6036
Portland, ME 04101-3514   Fax: (207)791-6920
E-mail: portlandpaper@scryer.nlis.net; porlandpaper@server.nlis.net.
URL: http://www.portland.com.
Contact: Madeline Corson, Editor; Amanda Schumaker, Publisher; Jodie Krueger, Circulation Mgr.; Bruce Gensmer, President; Steve Coreenlec, feature editor.
Desc: General newspaper. *Type:* Periodical.

Manhattan Spirit

New York Press, Inc.
333 7th Ave., 14th Fl.   Ph: (212)941-1130
New York, NY 10001   Fax: (212)941-7824
Contact: Tom Allon, Publisher.
Desc: Community newspaper. *Type:* Periodical.

Market Guide Database

Market Guide Inc.
2001 Marcus Ave., Suite S200   Ph: (516)327-2400
Lake Success, NY 11042
URL: http://www.marketguide.com
Contact: Jeff Geisenheimer, (516)759-1253, fax: (516)-676-9240.
Desc: Contains information on more than 10,000 public companies traded on the New York and American stock exchanges, National Association of Securities Dealers Automated Quotations, and over-the-counter exchanges. It includes detailed historical annual and quarterly financial statements in the same format used by the reporting company when it files with the SEC, company description, financial ratios, growth rates, company to industry comparisons, institutional ownership, insider trading statistics, and short interest information. *Available:* Bridge Information Systems, Inc., Knight-Ridder Financial Information Group; Quotron Systems, Inc.; Track Data Corporation; Market Guide Inc.; Argus Research Corporation; CDA Investment Technologies, CDA/Wiesenberger; Interactive Data Corporation; Shark Information Systems; Telescan, Inc.; ADP Financial Information Services (ADP/FIS); Telerate Systems Inc.; Thomson Financial Securities Data (TFSD). *Type:* Database.

Market News Service

100 William St.   Ph: (212)509-4444
3rd Fl.   Fax: (212)509-5520
New York, NY 10038-3284
URL: http://www.economeister.com.
Contact: Tony Mace, Managing Editor, tony@atsmktnews.com; Ron Corday, Editor; Denis Guino, Wash. Bureau Chief; Jon Hurdle, London Bureau Chief; John Carter, Euro. Ed.; Mark Pender, Media Ed.
Desc: Distributes financial and Washington news, including politics. *Alt. Contact:* 100 William St., 3rd Fl., New York, NY 10038-3284; telephone: (212)509-4444; fax: (212)509-5520. *Type:* Periodical.

MDDC Press News

Maryland-Delaware-D.C. Press Association
4201 Northview Dr., Ste. 219   Ph: (301)352-0600
Bowie, MD 20716   Fax: (301)352-0606
E-mail: mddcpress@aol.com
Contact: James Donahue, Exec. Dir.; Chuck Boteler, Advertising Dir.
Desc: Publishes on topics for newspaper personnel. *Type:* Newsletter.

Medill News Service

1325 G St. NW   Ph: (202)347-8700
Ste. 730   Fax: (202)662-1814
Washington, DC 20005-3195
Desc: Distributes political/federal government news. *Alt. Contact:* 1325 G St. NW, Ste. 730, Washington, DC 20005-3195; telephone: (202)347-8700; fax: (202)662-1814. *Type:* Periodical.

Metro

Metro Publishing, Inc.
550 S. 1st St.   Ph: (408)298-8000
San Jose, CA 95113   Fax: (408)298-0602
URL: http://www.metroactive.com.
Contact: Dan Pulcrano, Editor; David Cohen, Publisher; Scott Levander, Ad Dir.
Desc: Newspaper (tabloid) covering regional news, arts, and entertainment. *Type:* Periodical.

Metro Reporter

Metro Reporter
270 Francisco St.   Ph: (415)391-2030
San Francisco, CA 94133-2120   Fax: (415)391-2527
Contact: Charles E. Belle, Editor; Carlton B. Goodlett, Publisher.
Desc: Black community newspaper. *Type:* Periodical.

Metro Times

Metro Times, Inc.
733 Saint Antoine St.   Ph: (313)961-4060
Detroit, MI 48226-2936   Fax: (313)961-6598
E-mail: metrotimes@metrotimes.com; metrotimes@aminc.com.
URL: http://www.metrotimes.com.
Contact: Jim McCarter, Publisher, jmccarter@aminc.com; Larry Gabriel, Editor, lgabriel@aminc.com.
Desc: Newspaper. *Type:* Periodical.

Metropolitan News

EWA Publications
2446 E. 65th St.   Ph: (718)763-7034
Brooklyn, NY 11234   Fax: (718)763-7035
Contact: Kevin Browne, Editor; Justin Baron, Publisher; Bill Tarrington, Advertising Mgr.
Desc: Community newspaper. *Type:* Periodical.

The Miami Herald

Knight-Ridder, Inc.
50 W. Fernando St.   Ph: (408)938-7700
San Jose, CA 95113
Contact: Jim Hampton, Editor, (305)376-2287; David Lawrence, Publisher; Jim Roos, V.P./Marketing.
Desc: General newspaper. *Alt. Contact:* 1 Herald Plaza, Miami, FL 33132-1693; telephone: (305)350-2111. *Type:* Periodical.

Miami Herald

The Miami Herald Publishing Co.
One Herald Plaza   Ph: (305)376-3434
Miami, FL 33132-1693
URL: http://www.herold.com
Desc: Contains the complete text of news articles and feature stories from the final and regional editions (Broward

County, Keys, and Florida) of the Miami Herald (Florida) newspaper. Covers local, national, and international (especially Latin American) news. *Available:* The Dialog Corporation, DIALOG; CompuServe Information Service, Knowledge Index; LEXIS-NEXIS, NEXIS; LEXIS-NEXIS, NEXIS. *Type:* Database.

Michaels News

Rte. 5 Box 367   Ph: (715)284-5638
Black River Falls, WI 54615-9160

Contact: Marion Michaels, Pres./Ed.

Desc: Distributes columns on the environment, health, safety, folk cures, travel, parenting, and teaching reviews. *Alt. Contact:* Rte. 5 Box 367, Black River Falls, WI 54615-9160; telephone: (715)284-5638. *Type:* Periodical.

Midwest Features

PO Box 9907   Ph: (608)274-8925
Madison, WI 53725-9907

Contact: Mary Bergin, Founder/Ed.

Desc: Distributes feature material and columns with a strong Wisconsin emphasis. *Alt. Contact:* PO Box 9907, Madison, WI 53725-9907; telephone: (608)274-8925. *Type:* Periodical.

Miller Features Syndicate Inc.

480 University Ave.   Ph: (416)979-9588
No. 802   Free: 800-388-1356
Toronto, ON, Canada M5G   Fax: (416)979-0303
1V2

Contact: Richard Vroom, President; Michelle Brem, Sales Mgr.; Agnes Christie, Sales Mgr.

Desc: Distributes news. *Alt. Contact:* 480 University Ave., No. 802, Toronto, ON, Canada M5G 1V2; telephone: (416)979-9588; fax: (416)979-0303; toll-free: 800-388-1356. *Type:* Periodical.

Milwaukee Journal Sentinel

Journal Sentinel, Inc.
333 W. State St.   Ph: (414)224-2000
Milwaukee, WI 53203-1305   Fax: (414)224-2469
URL: http://www.jsonline.com.

Contact: Steven Smith, Chairman, (414)224-2425; Keith Spore, Pres./Pub., (414)224-2475; W. Martin Kaiser, Editor, (414)224-2345; Mark Thomas, Circulation Mgr., (414)224-2201; Richard Dobson, VP, Adv., (414)224-2932, fax: (414)224-0777, rdobson@onwis.com; George Stanley, Managing Editor, (414)224-2345; Heidi Reuter Lloyd, Senior Editor/Adminstration, (414)224-2185; Gerry Hinkley, Deputy Mng. Editor, (414)224-2016; Carl Schwartz, Senior Editor, National, (414)224-2877; Dave Vogel, S

Desc: General newspaper. *Type:* Periodical.

Milwaukee Journal Sentinel

Journal Sentinel, Inc.
PO Box 661   Ph: (414)224-2376
Milwaukee, WI 53201

Desc: Contains selected text of news items and feature articles from The Milwaukee Journal and The Milwaukee Sentinel newspapers of Wisconsin, as well as the Milwaukee Journal Sentinel after the two newspapers merged in 1995. *Available:* LEXIS-NEXIS; Dow Jones Interactive Publishing. *Type:* Database.

Minority Features Syndicate

PO Box 421   Ph: (412)342-5300
Farrell, PA 16121   Fax: (412)342-6244

Contact: Bill Murray, President; Merry Frable, Editor.

Desc: Distributes columns and cartoons. *Alt. Contact:* PO Box 421, Farrel, PA 16121; telephone: (412)342-5300; fax: (412)342-6244. *Type:* Periodical.

Mission Sun

Sun Publications, Inc.
7373 W. 107th St.   Ph: (913)648-4620
Overland Park, KS 66212-2547   Fax: (913)381-1402

Contact: Jack Lovelace, Editor; Steve Rose, Publisher; Joseph Mickelson, Vice Pres. of Sales & Marketing.

Desc: Newspaper. *Type:* Periodical.

The Mississauga Booster

The Mississauga Booster
5650 Keaton Cres., Unit A   Ph: (905)890-4606
Mississauga, ON, Canada L5R   Fax: (905)890-3999
3G3

E-mail: booster@idirect.com.

Contact: Kristy Elik, Editor; Paul McCallion, Publisher.

Desc: Good news community newspaper *Type:* Periodical.

The Mississauga News

The Mississauga News
3145 Wolfedale Rd.   Ph: (905)273-8111
Mississauga, ON, Canada L5C   Fax: (905)273-9119
3A9

Contact: Judy Hughes, Editor; Ronald Lenyk, Publisher; Dave Robinson, Advertising Mgr.

Desc: Community newspaper. *Type:* Periodical.

The Mobile Register

The Mobile Press
304 Government St.   Ph: (334)433-1551
PO Box 2488   Free: 800-239-1659
Mobile, AL 36630   Fax: (334)434-8662

E-mail: register@bibbs.com.

URL: http://www.mobileregister.com.

Contact: Stan Tiner, Editor; Howard Bronson, Publisher; John W. Winter, Advertising Mgr.

Desc: General newspaper. Combined weekend edition with the Mobile Press as the The Mobile Press Register. *Type:* Periodical.

The Modesto Bee

McClatchy Newspapers, Inc.
3425 N. 1st St., Ste. 201   Ph: (209)441-6111
Fresno, CA 93726-6819   Fax: (209)441-6436

Contact: Sanders LaMont, Editor-in-Chief; Cheryl Ebright, Advertising Dir.; Judy Sly, Asst. Mng. Editor; Susan Windemoth, Asst. Mng. Editor; Mark Vasche, Managing Editor; Jim Lawrence, Graphics Editor.

Desc: General newspaper. *Alt. Contact:* 1325 H St., Modesto, CA 95354; telephone: (209)578-2351; fax: (209)578-2207. *Type:* Periodical.

Monitor News & Features Services

PO Box 160 CSL   Ph: (514)482-1628
Montreal, PQ, Canada H4V
2Y3

Contact: David Moulton, General Mgr.

Desc: Distributes mail order design patterns for woodworking. *Alt. Contact:* PO Box 160 CSL, Montreal, PQ, Canada H4V 2Y3; telephone: (514)482-1628. *Type:* Periodical.

The Morning Call

The Morning Call
101 N. 6th St., No. 1260   Ph: (215)820-6500
Allentown, PA 18101-1403   Fax: (215)820-6617

Contact: Lawrence Hymans, Editor; Gary K. Shorts, Publisher; Robert Richelderfer, Advertising Mgr.

Desc: General newspaper. *Type:* Periodical.

The Morning Call (Allentown, Pennsylvania)

Times-Mirror Newspapers, Inc.
101 N. 6th St.   Ph: (610)820-6523
P.O. Box 1260
Allentown, PA 18105

E-mail: doncevic@mcall.com

Contact: Lois A. Doncevic, Director, (610)820-6523, doncevic@mcall.com.

Desc: Contains the complete text of The Morning Call, a general circulation newspaper reporting Pennsylvania and metro Allentown area news, and the Call's Sunday edition known as the Sunday Morning-Call. Special areas of interest include local industry, business and economy, sports, travel, and the arts. *Available:* The Dialog Corporation, DIALOG; LEXIS-NEXIS. *Type:* Database.

Morning News

Times Publishing Co.
205 W. 12th St.   Ph: (814)870-1600
Erie, PA 16534-0001   Free: 800-352-0043
     Fax: (814)870-1615

URL: http://www.timesnews.com.

Contact: Jeff Pinski, Editor; Michael Mead, Publisher; John Andersen, Advertising Dir.

Desc: General newspaper. *Type:* Periodical.

Morris News Service

229 Peachtree St. NE   Ph: (404)589-8424
202 Cain Tower
Atlanta, GA 30303

Desc: Distributes news. *Alt. Contact:* 229 Peachtree St. NE, 202 Cain Tower, Atlanta, GA 30303; telephone: (404)589-8424. *Type:* Periodical.

Mother Jones

Foundation for National Progress
731 Market St., Ste. 600   Ph: (415)665-6637
San Francisco, CA 94103-2027   Fax: (415)665-6696

URL: http://www.motherjones.com.

Contact: Jeffrey Klein, Editor; Jay Harris, Publisher.

Desc: Magazine covering news, politics, and culture. *Type:* Periodical.

NABJ Update

National Association of Black Journalists
University of Maryland   Ph: (301)405-0439
3100 Taliaferro Hall   Fax: (301)405-8555
College Park, MD 20742-7717

URL: http://www.nabj.org.

Contact: Debbie Chase, Editor.

Desc: Reports on activities of the National Association of Black Journalists. *Type:* Newsletter.

National Enquirer

National Enquirer
600 East Coast Ave.   Ph: (561)586-1111
Lake Worth, FL 33464-0002   Fax: (561)540-1009

E-mail: letters@nationalenquirer.com.

URL: http://www.nationalenquirer.com.

Contact: Steve Coz, Editor, fax: (561)540-1010; Tony Hoyt, Publisher, (212)888-3320.

Desc: General editorial. *Type:* Periodical.

National Examiner

Globe Communications
5401 NW Broken Sound Blvd.   Ph: (561)997-7733
Boca Raton, FL 33487-3587   Free: 800-749-7733
     Fax: (561)241-5689

Contact: William Burt, Editor; Tony Miles, Exec. Publisher; Jack Linder, Advertising Mgr.

Desc: Tabloid featuring articles on celebrities, human interest, and the supernatural. *Type:* Periodical.

National Forum Inc.

PO Box 7099   Ph: (703)764-0496
Fairfax Station, VA 22039

Contact: Douglas Cohn, Sr. Ed. and Pub.; Ralph Nader, Consumer Affairs/Political Columnist; Jack Kemp, Political Columnist.

Desc: Distributes national columns. *Alt. Contact:* PO Box 7099, Fairfax Sta., VA 22039; telephone: (703)-764-0496. *Type:* Periodical.

National News Bureau

PO Box 43039   Ph: (215)546-8088
Philadelphia, PA 19129

Contact: Andrea Diehl, Vice President; Andy Edelman, Vice President; Harry Jay Katz, Publisher.

Desc: Distributes entertainment and leisure-oriented features. *Alt. Contact:* PO Box 43039, Philadelphia, PA 19129; telephone: (215)546-8088. *Type:* Periodical.

National Newspaper Association

1525 Wilson Blvd., Ste. 550   Ph: (703)907-7900
Arlington, VA 22209   Free: 800-829-4662
                                 Fax: (703)907-7901

E-mail: info@nna.org
URL: http://www.nna.org

Contact: Kenneth B. Allen, Exec. VP & CEO.

Desc: Representatives of community newspapers. *Type:* Association.

National Newspaper Index™

The Gale Group
27500 Drake Rd.   Ph: (248)699-4253
Farmington Hills, MI 48331-
   3535
URL: http://www.galegroup.com

Contact: (650)3678-5000, fax: (800)676-2345.

Desc: Contains more than 2.8 million citations to articles, news reports, editorials, letters to the editor, obituaries, biographies, and reviews appearing in the following 5 newspapers: The Christian Science Monitor, The Los Angeles Times, The New York Times, The Wall Street Journal, and The Washington Post as well as items transmitted over BusinessWire and PR Newswire. Corresponds to the online National Newspaper Index database. *Available:* The Dialog Corporation, DIALOG; CompuServe Information Service, Knowledge Index; The Dialog Corporation, DataStar; CARL Corporation; Ameritech Library Services, Vista; The Gale Group, InfoTrac Web. *Type:* Database.

National Press Club

National Press Bldg.   Ph: (202)662-7500
529 14th St. NW   Fax: (202)662-7512
Washington, DC 20045

Contact: John Bloom, Gen.Mgr.

Desc: Reporters, writers, and newspeople employed by newspapers, wire services, magazines, radio and television stations, and other forms of news media; former newspeople and associates of newspeople are nonvoting members. *Type:* Association.

National Press Club—Record

National Press Club
National Press Bldg.   Ph: (202)662-7500
Washington, DC 20045

Contact: Dennis S. Feldman, Editor.

Desc: Covers only Club activities and programs. Recurring features include a calendar of events and a column titled Job Opportunities. *Type:* Newsletter.

National Press Foundation—Update

National Press Foundation (NPF)
1282 National Press Bldg.   Ph: (202)662-7350
Washington, DC 20045   Fax: (202)662-1232

Contact: Frank Holeman, Editor.

Desc: Publishes news of the National Press Foundation, a professional organization working toward "excellence in journalism." Reports on NPF meetings, conferences, and member activities and accomplishments. *Type:* Newsletter.

National Press Syndicate

401 E. 74th St.   Ph: (212)744-4623
Ste. 15-M   Fax: (212)744-4623
New York, NY 10021
E-mail: romresorts@aol.com.
URL: http://www.romresorts.com.

Contact: Paulette Cooper, Publisher.

Alt. Contact: 401 E. 74th St., Ste. 15-M, New York, NY 10021; telephone: (212)744-4623; fax: (212)744-4623. *Type:* Periodical.

National Press Writers Group

7200 Wisconsin Ave.   Ph: (301)657-1616
Ste. 212   Fax: (301)657-8475
Bethesda, MD 20814

Contact: Joel Joseph, Publisher.

Desc: Distributes controversial nonfiction. *Alt. Contact:* 7200 Wisconsin Ave., Ste. 212, Bethesda, MD 20814; telephone: (301)657-1616; fax: (301)657-8475. *Type:* Periodical.

New Canaan Lifestyles

Brooks Community Newspapers, Inc.
542 Westport Ave.   Ph: (203)226-6311
Norwalk, CT 06851   Fax: (203)227-6864
E-mail: bcnews3@netakis.com

Contact: Louise Lancaster-Keim, Editor; Kevin Lally, President; B. V. Brooks, Publisher.

Desc: Community newspaper. *Type:* Periodical.

New England News Service Inc.

66 Alexander Rd.   Ph: (617)969-4102
Newton, MA 02161

Contact: Eleanor Gun, Pres./CEO; Milton J. Gun, Bureau Chief/Sports Ed.; Eleanor Margolis, Living/Leisure; Steven Richards, Computer/Tech.; Howard Neal, Business.

Desc: Distributes information on U.S. District court general news and overseas interests. *Alt. Contact:* 66 Alexander Rd., Newton, MA 02161; telephone: (617)969-4102. *Type:* Periodical.

The New Federalist

KMW Publishing Co. Inc.
PO Box 889   Ph: (703)777-9451
Leesburg, VA 20175   Fax: (703)771-3099
E-mail: eirns@larouchepub.com.

Contact: Nancy Spannaus, Editor-in-Chief; William F. Wertz, Jr., Editor; Alan Yue, Editor; Stuart Lewis, Photo Editor.

Desc: National newspaper associated with the LaRouche political movement. *Type:* Periodical.

New Haven Register

New Haven Register
Long Wharf, 40 Sargent Dr.   Ph: (203)789-5200
New Haven, CT 06511   Fax: (203)865-7894
URL: http://www.ctcentral.com.

Contact: William Rush, Publisher; Hank Misiak, Advertising Dir.; Abram Katz, Editor; Charles Kochakian, Editor; Jack Kramer, Editor; Michael Lynch, Marketing Director; Dave Butler, Editor; Michael Vanacore, National Manager; Tina Goodwin, Research Manager.

Desc: General newspaper. *Type:* Periodical.

The New Orleans Times-Picayune

Times-Picayune Publishing Corporation
3800 Howard Ave.   Ph: (504)826-3300
New Orleans, LA 70140
URL: http://www.molalive.com

Desc: Contains the complete text of news items and feature stories from The Times-Picayune (New Orleans) newspaper. Regional coverage emphasizes the oil, marine, aerospace, nuclear, shipping, agriculture, seafood, tourism, and music industries. *Available:* The Dialog Corporation, DIALOG; The Dialog Corporation, DIALOG; Bell & Howell Information and Learning; CompuServe Information Service, Knowledge Index; LEXIS-NEXIS, NEXIS. *Type:* Database.

The New Republic

New Republic, Inc.
1220 19th St. NW   Ph: (202)331-7494
Suite 600   Fax: (202)331-0275
Washington, DC 20036
E-mail: tnr@aol.com.

Contact: Martin Peretz, Editor-in-Chief; Joan M. Stapleton, Publisher.

Desc: Journal featuring current events comments and reviews. *Type:* Periodical.

New Times

The Burnside Group, Inc.
1950 Sawtelle Blvd., No. 200   Ph: (310)477-0403
Los Angeles, CA 90025   Fax: (310)477-8428

Contact: James Vowell, Editor and Publisher, editor@newtimesla.com.

Type: Periodical.

New Wave Syndication

PO Box 232   Ph: (617)471-8733
North Quincy, MA 02171

Contact: Tim Lynch, President.

Desc: Distributes comics columns. *Alt. Contact:* PO Box 232, North Quincy, MA 02171; telephone: (617)471-8733. *Type:* Periodical.

New York Daily News

New York News, Inc.
450 W. 33rd St.   Ph: (212)210-2100
New York, NY 10001   Fax: (212)210-2049
URL: http://www.mostnewyork.com.

Contact: Martin Dunn, Editor-in-Chief; Debby Krenek, Exec. Editor; Fred Drasner, Publisher; Arthur Browne, Managing Editor; Michael Goodwin, Editorial Page Editor; Fran Wood, Features Editor; Kevin Whitmer, Sports Dir.; Jeff Weingran, TV Editor; Hap Hairston, Business Editor; Susan Jordan, National Editor; Michael Lipack, Photo Editor.

Desc: General newspaper. *Type:* Periodical.

New York Post

New York Post Corp.
1211 6th Ave.   Ph: (212)930-8000
New York, NY 10036

Contact: Ken Chandler, Editor; Marc Kalech, Managing Editor; Steve Cuozzo, Executive Editor; Anne Aquilina, Admin. Editor.

Desc: General newspaper. *Type:* Periodical.

New York Press

New York Press, Inc.
333 7th Ave., 14th Fl.   Ph: (212)941-1130
New York, NY 10001   Fax: (212)941-7824

Contact: Russ Smith, Editor.

Desc: Newspaper. *Type:* Periodical.

New York Press Association

1681 Western Ave.   Ph: (518)464-6483
Albany, NY 12203-4305   Fax: (518)464-6489
URL: http://www.nynewspapers.com

Contact: Michelle K. Rea, Exec.Dir.

Desc: Promotes the general welfare of its member newspapers and the quality of community journalism. Sponsors competitions, seminars, and libel hotline. *Type:* Association.

New York Press Photographers Association

225 E. 36th St.   Ph: (212)889-6633
New York, NY 10016   Fax: (212)889-6634

Contact: Bill Turnbull, President.

Alt. Contact: 225 E. 36th St., New York, NY 10016; telephone: (212)889-6633; fax: (212)889-6634. *Type:* Periodical.

The New York Times

The New York Times Co.
229 W. 43rd St.   Ph: (212)556-1234
New York, NY 10036-3913
E-mail: name@nytimes.com
URL: http://www.nytimes.com.

Contact: Arthur O. Sulzberger, Jr., Publisher and Chairman, (212)556-3588; Joseph Lelyveld, Exec.Ed., (212)556-1157; Bill Keller, Managing Editor, (212)556-1219; Soma Golden Behr, Asst. Managing Ed., (212)556-4418; Gerald Boyd, Deputy Managing Ed., (212)556-7756; Carolyn Lee, Asst. Managing Ed., (212)556-1250; Jack Rosenthal, Asst. Managing Ed./Editor-in-Chief, (212)556-7740; Allan M. Siegal, Asst. Managing Ed., (212)556-1049; Tom Bodkin, Assoc. Managing Ed., (212)556-1035; Dennis L.

Desc: General newspaper. *Type:* Periodical.

The New York Times

The New York Times Company
New York Times On-Line Services
520 Speedwell Ave.   Ph: (973)829-0036
Morris Plains, NJ 07950

Desc: Contains the complete text of each day's final edition of The New York Times, a general circulation newspaper reporting local, national, and International news. Covers all news stories, features, editorials, letters to the editor, obituaries, and sports. *Available:* LEXIS-NEXIS, NEXIS; LEXIS-NEXIS, NEXIS; Dow Jones & Company, Inc.; America Online, Inc.; OCLC Online Computer Library Center, Inc., OCLC FirstSearch Catalog; OCLC Online Computer Library Center, Inc., OCLC EPIC; The Dialog Corporation, DIALOG; The Dialog Corporation, DIALOG; The Dialog Corporation, DataStar. *Type:* Database.

The New York Times Abstracts

The New York Times Index
16th Fl.   Ph: (212)221-3471
1133 Avenue of the Americas
New York, NY 10036

Contact: Alan Greengrass, Director, Index Operations, (212)221-3471, fax: (212)221-5052, agreengrass@nytimes.com.

Desc: Contains citations, with abstracts, to articles appearing in the daily final edition of The New York Times, a general circulation newspaper reporting local, national, and international news. *Available:* The Dialog Corporation, DIALOG; The Dialog Corporation, DataStar; LEXIS-NEXIS, NEXIS; Dow Jones Interactive Publishing; OCLC Online Computer Library Center, Inc. *Type:* Database.

The New York Times Biographical File

The New York Times Company
New York Times On-Line Services
520 Speedwell Ave.   Ph: (973)829-0036
Morris Plains, NJ 07950

Desc: Contains the complete text of selected biographical articles from The New York Times newspaper. Includes obituaries, interviews, profiles, and "Man in the News" columns on more than 15,000 individuals, including artists, business and civic leaders, politicians, sports figures, and other newsmakers. *Available:* LEXIS-NEXIS, NEXIS. *Type:* Database.

New York Times News Service

229 W. 43rd St.   Ph: (212)556-1927
Rm. 943   Fax: (212)556-3535
New York, NY 10036
E-mail: robison@nytimes.com.

Contact: James Robison, Exec. Ed.; Lila Locksley, Assoc. Ed.; Deborah Marchand, Dir. Graphics/Photo; Barbara Mancuso, Dir. Permissions.

Desc: Distributes news. *Alt. Contact:* 229 W. 43rd St., Rm. 943, New York, NY 10036; telephone: (212)556-1927; fax: (212)556-3535. *Type:* Periodical.

New York Times Syndication Sales Corporation

122 E. 42nd St.   Ph: (212)499-3300
14th Fl.   Free: 800-972-3550
New York, NY 10168   Fax: (212)499-3382
URL: http://www.yourhealthdaily.com.

Contact: John Brewer, Pres./Ed-in-Chief; Karl Horwitz, Pres.-Intl.; Paul Finch, VP Central & South America; Gloria Brown Anderson, VP/Exec. Ed.; Bab Farnell, Sales Exec. North America; Connie White, Sales Exec. North America; Patrick Vance, Dir. Spec. Proj.; Peter Trigg, Dir. Comm. & Tech.

Desc: Distributes features, graphics service, magazines, news services, and photographs. *Alt. Contact:* 122 E. 42nd St., 14th Fl., New York, NY 10168; telephone: (212)499-3300; fax: (212)499-3382; toll-free: 800-972-3550. *Type:* Periodical.

Newhouse News Service

1101 Connecticut Ave. NW   Ph: (202)383-7800
Washington, DC 20036

Contact: Deborah Howell, Wash. Bureau Chf/Ed., debhowell@aol.com; Robert Hodierne, Natl. Ed./Dept. Bureau Chief; Hope Horman, Office Mgr.

Desc: Distributes news service. *Alt. Contact:* 1101 Connecticut Ave. NW, Washington, DC 20036; telephone: (202)383-7800. *Type:* Periodical.

News Herald

Heritage Newspapers, Inc.
1 Heritage Pl., Ste. 100   Ph: (313)246-0800
Southgate, MI 48195   Fax: (313)284-2028
URL: http://www.heritage.com.

Contact: Karl Ziomek, Editor; Donald W. Thurlow, Publisher; Bill Dillingham, Advertising Mgr.; Lynn Hemphill, Editor; Sue Nations, Circulation Mgr.; Bonnie Klimowicz, Circulation Mgr.

Desc: Community newpaper. *Type:* Periodical.

The News-Journal

The News-Journal Corp.
901 6th St.   Ph: (904)252-1511
Daytona Beach, FL 32117-8099   Fax: (904)258-8465

Contact: Tippen Davidson, Publisher & Co-Editor; Josephine Davidson, Editor; Georgia Kaney, General Mgr.; Dick Dunkel, Managing Editor; Mike Czeczot, Managing Editor; Don Lindley, Managing Editor; Tom Brown, Business Editor; Natalie Dix, Editoral page editor; Linda Trimble, Education Editor; Suzy Kridner, Entertainment & Home editor; Judy Liberi, Fashion editor; Suzy Kridner, Travel & Women's editor; Cathy Klasne, Food editor; Suzy Kridner, Lifestyle editor; Warren Baslee, Outdoor editor; Lyd

Desc: Newspaper with a Democratic orientation. *Type:* Periodical.

The News Journal

The News Journal
950 W. Basin Rd.   Ph: (302)324-2617
PO Box 15505   Free: 800-235-9100
New Castle, DE 19720   Fax: (302)324-5518
E-mail: newsroom@newsjournal.com.

Desc: General newspaper. *Type:* Periodical.

The News-Leader

The News-Leader
651 N. Boonville Ave.   Ph: (417)836-1100
Springfield, MO 65806-1005   Fax: (417)836-1147
URL: http://www.ozarksgateway.com.

Contact: Andy McMills, Exec. Editor; Fritz Jacobi, Publisher.

Desc: General newspaper. *Type:* Periodical.

The News and Observer

The News & Observer
215 S. McDowell St.   Ph: (919)829-4500
PO Box 191   Fax: (919)829-4529
Raleigh, NC 27602
URL: http://www.nando.net.

Contact: Fred Crisp, Publisher, (919)829-4651, fax: (919)829-4872; Jim McClure, Advertising Dir., (919)836-2822, fax: (919)829-4808; Anders Gyllenhall, Sr. Managing Ed., (919)829-8958, fax: (919)836-5911; Judy Bolch, Asst. Managing Ed., (919)829-4556, fax: (919)836-5911; Mile Yopp, Asst. Managing Editor, (919)829-4543, fax: (919)836-5911; Will Sutton, Asst. Managing Editor; Melanie Sill, Asst. Managing Editor.

Desc: General newspaper. *Type:* Periodical.

The News & Observer (Raleigh, North Carolina)

The News & Observer
P.O. Box 191   Ph: (919)829-4868
Raleigh, NC 27602
E-mail: croberts@nando.com

Contact: Colline Roberts, Archive Operations Manager, (919)829-4868, fax: (919)829-8916, croberts@nando.net.

Desc: Contains the complete text of The News & Observer, a general circulation newspaper reporting local, national, and international news. Covers all news stories, features, editorials, arts, and sports. *Available:* Bell & Howell Information and Learning; Dow Jones Interactive Publishing; LEXIS-NEXIS, NEXIS. *Type:* Database.

News & Record

Landmark Communications, Inc.
150 W. Brambleton Ave.   Ph: (757)446-2000
Norfolk, VA 23510-2018   Free: 800-446-2004

Contact: Ben J. Bowers, Editor; Carl Mangum, Jr., Publisher; Joe Antle, Advertising Dir.

Desc: General newspaper. *Alt. Contact:* 200 E. Market St., PO Box 20848, Greensboro, NC 27401-2910. *Type:* Periodical.

News/Retrieval Worldwide Report

Dow Jones & Company, Inc.
P.O. Box 300   Ph: (609)520-4000
Princeton, NJ 08543-0300
URL: http://www.dj.com

Desc: Covers selected front-page U.S. national and international news stories from the Associated Press, Dow Jones' newswires, and broadcast media. *Available:* Dow Jones & Company, Inc. *Type:* Database.

The News-Sentinel (Fort Wayne, Indiana)

The News-Sentinel (Fort Wayne, Indiana)
600 W. Main St.　　　　Ph: (219)461-8222
Fort Wayne, IN 46802
E-mail: nseditor@fortwayne.infi.net
Desc: Contains the complete text of locally-produced news items from The News-Sentinel (Fort Wayne, Indiana) newspaper. Regional coverage emphasizes the agribusiness, automotive, defense, financial, insurance, medical, and transportation industries. *Available:* The Dialog Corporation, DIALOG. *Type:* Database.

The News Transcript

Greater Media Newspapers
2 Kennedy Blvd.　　　　Ph: (732)247-6161
East Brunswick, NJ 08816　　Fax: (732)247-0215
Contact: Greg Bean, Exec. Editor; Kevin Witman, Publisher; Elaine Cusham, Advertising Dir.; Kathy Herban, Circulation Mgr.; Mark Rosman, Managing Editor.
Desc: Suburban community newspaper. *Alt. Contact:* 25 Kilmer Dr., Ste. 109, Morganville, NJ 07751; telephone: (732)972-6740; fax: (732)972-6746. *Type:* Periodical.

The News Tribune

McClatchy Newspapers
PO Box 15779　　　　Ph: (916)321-1000
Sacramento, CA 95852
URL: http://www.tribnet.com.
Contact: David Zeeck, Executive Editor, (253)597-8434, david.zeeck@mail.tribnet.com; Elizabeth Brenner, Publisher, (253)597-8854, brenner.betsy@m.tribnet.com; David Seago, Editorial Page Editor, (253)597-8634, sds@p.tribnet.com; Cathy J. Brewis, Employee & Community Relations Dir., (253)274-7344, cathy.brewis@mail.tribnet.com; Suki Dardarian, Coord. Editor, (253)597-8257; Don Ruiz, Contact, (253)597-8676; Karen Baker, Coord. Editor, (253)597-8606; Tara Cady, Asst Circulat
Desc: General newspaper. *Alt. Contact:* PO Box 11000, Tacoma, WA 98411-0008; telephone: (206)597-8688; fax: (206)597-8274; toll-free: 888-597-TRIB. *Type:* Periodical.

News USA Inc.

8300 Boone Blvd.　　　　Ph: (703)827-5800
No. 810　　　　　　　Free: 800-355-7800
Vienna, VA 22182　　　　Fax: (703)827-5814
E-mail: vpmedia@newsusa.com.
URL: http://www.newsusa.com.
Contact: Richard D. Smith, Chm./CEO; Jackie Teare, Managing Editor; Chris Petersen, Pres./COO; William H. Watson, VP Media Servs.; Denny Townsend, Managing Editor; John Pitts, Asst. Mng. Ed.; Kate Bentley, Production Mgr.; Victoria Jancek, Media Relations.
Desc: Distributes news features. *Alt. Contact:* 8300 Boone Blvd., No. 810, Vienna, VA 22182; telephone: (703)827-5800; fax: (703)827-5814; toll-free: 800-355-7800. *Type:* Periodical.

Newsbytes News Network

Carriage House　　　　Ph: (612)430-1100
406 W. Olive St.　　　　Fax: (612)430-0441
Stillwater, MN 55082
Contact: Wendy Woods, Ed./Gen. Mgr.
Desc: Distributes news. *Alt. Contact:* Carriage House, 406 W. Olive St., Stillwater, MN 55082; telephone: (612)430-1100; fax: (612)430-0441. *Type:* Periodical.

Newsday

Newsday
235 Pinelawn　　　　Ph: (516)843-2020
Melville, NY 11747-4250　　Fax: (516)843-2953
URL: http://www.newsday.com.
Contact: Raymond Jansen, Publisher; Anthony Marro, Editor; Bob Brandt, Managing Editor; Howard Schneider, Managing Editor; Charlotte Hall, Managing Editor.

Desc: General newspaper. *Type:* Periodical.

Newsday

Newsday, Inc.
235 Pinelawn Rd.　　　　Ph: (516)843-2335
Melville, NY 11747
E-mail: library@newsday.com
URL: http://www.newsday.com
Contact: Theresa Kiely, Library Director, (516)843-2338, kiely@newsday.com.
Desc: Contains the complete text of Newsday, general circulation newspapers reporting local, national, and international news. Covers all news stories, local columns, features, editorials, obituaries, arts, sports, and letters to the editor. *Available:* Bell & Howell Information and Learning; LEXIS-NEXIS, NEXIS; LEXIS-NEXIS, NEXIS; CompuServe Information Service, Knowledge Index. *Type:* Database.

Newsday.com

Newsday, Inc.
235 Pinelawn Rd.　　　　Ph: (516)843-2335
Melville, NY 11747
E-mail: library@newsday.com
URL: http://www.newsday.com
Desc: Provides access to Long Island and New York City news headlines, computer news briefs and software reviews, a Long Island bulletin board directory, sports and business updates, weather reports, reviews, and other information. *Type:* Database.

Newspaper Abstracts

Bell & Howell Information and Learning
300 N. Zeeb Rd.　　　　Ph: (734)761-4700
PO Box 1346
Ann Arbor, MI 48106-1346
E-mail: info@umi.com
URL: http://www.umi.com
Contact: UMI Help Line.
Desc: Contains more than 2.6 million citations, with abstracts, to articles from 19 major daily newspapers: American Banker, Atlanta Constitution, Atlanta Journal (selected articles only), Boston Globe, Chicago Tribune, The Christian Science Monitor, Denver Post, Detroit News, Guardian and Guardian Weekly (London), Houston Post, The Los Angeles Times, New York Times, St. Louis Post-Dispatch, San Francisco Chronicle, Times-Picayune (New Orleans), USA Today, Wall Street Journal, The Washington Post, and Washington Times. *Available:* The Dialog Corporation, DIALOG; The Dialog Corporation, DIALOG; OCLC Online Computer Library Center, Inc., OCLC FirstSearch Catalog; Ovid Technologies, Inc.; Ovid Technologies, Inc. *Type:* Database.

Newspaper Enterprise Association

200 Madison Ave.　　　　Ph: (212)293-8500
4th Fl.　　　　　　　Free: 800-221-4816
New York, NY 10016　　　Fax: (212)293-8600
URL: http://www.unitedmedia.com.
Contact: Robert Levy, Exec. Ed.; Ben Wattenberg, Edit./Op/Ed Columnist; Douglas R. Stern, Pres./CEO; Diana B. Loevy, VP/Edit. Dir.; Lisa Klem Wilson, VP Sales & Mktg.; John B. Matthews, Natl. Sales Dir.; Amy Lago, Mng. Ed. Comic Art; Rose Novotny, Mgr. Intl. Syndications; Rebecca Shannonhouse, Mng. Ed. UFS & NEA; Mary Anne Grimes, Promotions Mgr.; Peter Hultberg, Customer Serv. Mgr.
Desc: Distributes various features including children's commentary, consumer, business, entertainment, food, graphics, health, sports, comic strips, and editorial cartoons. *Alt. Contact:* 200 Madison Ave., 4th Fl., New York, NY 10016; telephone: (212)293-8500; fax: (212)293-8600; toll-free: 800-221-4816. *Type:* Periodical.

Newspaper Features Council Inc.

376 Arch St.　　　　Ph: (203)661-3386
Greenwich, CT 06830　　Fax: (203)661-7337
E-mail: cnck@aol.com.
Contact: Richard S. Newcombe, Creators Syndicate Pres.; Jane amari, Kansas City Star First VP; Steven Christensen, Los Angeles Times Syndicate Second VP; Sue Smith, Dallas Morning News Sec./Treas.; Corinta Kotula, Exec. Dir.
Alt. Contact: 376 Arch St., Greenwich, CT 06830; telephone: (203)661-3386; fax: (203)661-7337. *Type:* Periodical.

Newspaper Features Inc.

14 High St.　　　　Ph: (516)759-9709
Locust Valley, NY 11560
Alt. Contact: 14 High St., Locust Valley, NY 11560; telephone: (516)759-9709. *Type:* Periodical.

The Newspaper Guild

501 3rd St. NW 2nd Fl.
Washington, DC 20001-2760
E-mail: lgildersleeve@cwa-union.org
URL: http://www.newsguild.org
Contact: Linda Foley, Pres.
Desc: AFL-CIO; Canadian Labour Congress, and International Federation of Journalists. *Type:* Association.

Newspaper & Periodical Abstracts

Bell & Howell Information and Learning
300 N. Zeeb Rd.　　　　Ph: (734)761-4700
PO Box 1346
Ann Arbor, MI 48106-1346
E-mail: info@umi.com
URL: http://www.umi.com
Contact: Maria Keller.
Desc: Contains more than 2.5 million citations, with abstracts, to articles from more than 25 major newspapers; approximately 1600 general-interest, professional, and scholarly periodicals; and 70 television news and current affairs programs. Subjects include business, science, education, current affairs, arts, health, sports, economics, health, fitness, social problems, government, technology, history, literature, psychology, and sociology. *Available:* The Dialog Corporation, DIALOG; OCLC Online Computer Library Center, Inc., OCLC EPIC; OCLC Online Computer Library Center, Inc., OCLC FirstSearch Catalog; CARL Corporation; Research Libraries Group, Inc. (RLG), CitaDel™ Service. *Type:* Database.

Newsportraits Syndicate

PO Box 564　　　　Ph: (201)342-2985
Hackensack, NJ 07602-0564
Contact: Y.L. Tiajcliff, Exec. Ed.; Martin Sager, Business Mgr.
Desc: Distributes news. *Alt. Contact:* PO Box 564, Hackensack, NJ 07602-0564; telephone: (201)342-2985. *Type:* Periodical.

Newsprints

Essential Information, Inc.
PO Box 19405　　　　Ph: (202)387-8030
Washington, DC 20036　　Fax: (202)234-5176
Contact: Cynthia Renfro, Editor.
Desc: Reprints "the best in local, hard-hitting, investigative journalism." Publishes local reports on labor, the environment, consumer news, and business. Recurring features include letters to the editor. *Type:* Newsletter.

Newsweek
Newsweek, Inc.
251 W. 57th St.   Ph: (212)445-4000
New York, NY 10019   Free: 800-634-6850
                                 Fax: (212)445-5068
Contact: Richard M. Smith, Editor-in-Chief; Richard M. Smith, President; Harold Shain, US Publisher/General Mgr; Maynard Parker, Editor; Mark Whitaker, Managing Editor.
Desc: Current news magazine. *Type:* Periodical.

Newsweek
Newsweek, Inc.
251 W. 57th St.   Ph: (212)445-4000
New York, NY 10019-1802
URL: http://www.newsweek.com
Desc: Each disk is devoted to a specific topic of general interest. *Available:* LEXIS-NEXIS, NEXIS. *Type:* Database.

Newsweek International - Latin America Edition
Newsweek, Inc.
251 W. 57th St.   Ph: (212)445-4000
New York, NY 10019   Free: 800-634-6850
                                 Fax: (212)445-5068
URL: http://www.newsweek.com.
Contact: Deborah Barry, Advertising Dir., (212)445-4190, fax: (212)445-4142, deborah_barry@newsweekmag.com.
Desc: Current news magazine. *Type:* Periodical.

North County Times
North County Times
207 E. Pennsylvania Ave.   Ph: (619)745-6611
Escondido, CA 92025   Fax: (619)745-8809
Contact: Richard K. Peterson, Editor; Richard High, President; Scott Putnicki, Advertising Dir.
Desc: Newspaper for Inland North County, CA. *Type:* Periodical.

The North County Times
Howard Publications Inc.
207 E. Pennsylvania Ave.   Ph: (619)745-6611
Escondido, CA 92025   Fax: (619)740-5433
Contact: Kent Davy, Editor; S. Scott Putnicki, Advertising Dir.; Richard High, Publisher.
Desc: General newspaper. *Alt. Contact:* PO Box 90, Oceanside, CA 92049-0090; telephone: (714)433-7333. *Type:* Periodical.

North Shore Sunday
Community Newspaper Company
240A Elm St   Ph: (617)733-8200
Somerville, MA 02144   Free: 800-880-1812
                                 Fax: (617)433-8285
Contact: Taylor Armerding, Editor; Chuck Goodrich, Publisher; Robert Tisi, Ad. Mgr.
Desc: Community newspaper (tabloid). *Alt. Contact:* 152 Sylvan St., Danvers, MA 01923; telephone: (508)774-0505; fax: (508)762-0450. *Type:* Periodical.

North York Mirror
Metroland
10 Tempo Ave.   Ph: (416)493-4400
Willowdale, ON, Canada M2H   Fax: (416)493-4703
  2N8
E-mail: scm@metrodiv.com.
Contact: Debby Dupuis, Managing Editor, fax: (416)493-6190; Betty Carr, Publisher; Eugene Dupuis, Advertising Dir.
Desc: Community newspaper (tabloid). *Type:* Periodical.

Northeast Johnson County Sun
Sun Publications, Inc.
7373 W. 107th St.   Ph: (913)648-4620
Overland Park, KS 66212-2547   Fax: (913)381-1402
Contact: Jack Lovelace, Editor; Steve Rose, Publisher; Jo Stapleton, Advertising Manager.
Desc: Newspaper. *Type:* Periodical.

Northeast Sun Commerce Comet
Eastern Group Publications Inc.
2500 S. Atlantic Blvd., No. A   Ph: (213)263-5743
Los Angeles, CA 90040-2004   Fax: (213)263-9169
Contact: Dolores Sanchez, Editor and Publisher; Jonathan Sanchez, Advertising Mgr.
Desc: Bilingual community newspaper concentrating on Hispanic issues. *Type:* Periodical.

Northeast Times
Times Newspapers, Inc.
2512 Metropolitan Dr.   Ph: (215)355-9009
Trevose, PA 19053   Fax: (215)355-4812
E-mail: promedpub@aol.com; pronedpub@aol.com.
URL: http://www.northeasttimes.com.
Contact: John Scanlon, Editor; Timothy Smylie, Advertising Mgr.
Desc: Newspaper. *Type:* Periodical.

Northside Recorder-Times - Prime Time, Inc.
Fisher Publications, Inc.
8603 Botts Ln.   Ph: (210)828-3321
PO Box 17947   Fax: (210)828-3787
San Antonio, TX 78217
Contact: Steve Henry, Editor, shenry@onr.com; Robt. Jones, Publisher.
Desc: Suburban community newspaper. *Type:* Periodical.

Northwest Press
Press Community Newspapers
5552 Cheviot Rd.   Ph: (513)923-3111
Cincinnati, OH 45247   Fax: (513)923-1806
Contact: Everett L. Rudisell Publisher; Thomas F. Noonan, Editor; Anthony E. Schad, Advertising Mgr.; Sheri R. Celesti, Advertising Dir.
Desc: Local newspaper. *Type:* Periodical.

Oakland Press
Oakland Press Co.
48 W. Huron St., No. 436009   Ph: (248)332-8181
PO Box 9   Fax: (248)332-8284
Pontiac, MI 48342-2101
Contact: William Thomas, Editor; Bruce H. McIntyre, Publisher.
Desc: General newspaper. *Type:* Periodical.

The Oakland Tribune
Oakland Tribune Inc.
66 Jack London Sqr.   Ph: (510)208-6300
Oakland, CA 94607
URL: http://www.newschoice.com
Desc: Contains the complete text of news items and feature articles from The Oakland Tribune (California) newspaper. Covers all news stories, features, editorials, arts, and sports. *Available:* Bell & Howell Information and Learning. *Type:* Database.

Ocean County Reporter
Ocean County Newspapers, Inc.
8 Robbins St.   Ph: (732)349-1501
Toms River, NJ 08753   Fax: (732)240-0545
E-mail: ocreportr@aol.com.
Contact: Robert J. Juzwiak, Publisher, fax: (732)349-8636; Paul Haney, Advertising Dir.

Desc: Newspaper. *Alt. Contact:* PO Box 2449, Toms River, NJ 08754. *Type:* Periodical.

Ohio Washington News Service
529 14th St. NW   Ph: (202)737-1888
Washington, DC 20009
Alt. Contact: 529 14th St. NW, Washington, DC 20009; telephone: (202)737-1888. *Type:* Periodical.

Oklahoman
Oklahoma Publishing Co.
9000 N. Broadway   Ph: (405)475-3311
PO Box 25125   Free: 800-375-6397
Oklahoma City, OK 73114   Fax: (405)475-3970
URL: http://www.oklahoma.net.
Contact: Edward L. Gaylord, Editor and Publisher.
Desc: General newspaper. *Type:* Periodical.

Olathe Sun
Sun Publications, Inc.
7373 W. 107th St.   Ph: (913)648-4620
Overland Park, KS 66212-2547   Fax: (913)381-1402
Contact: Jack Lovelace, Editor; Steve Rose, Publisher; Jo Stapleton, Advertising Mgr.
Desc: Newspaper. *Type:* Periodical.

Omaha World-Herald
Omaha World-Herald Co.
1334 Dodge St.   Ph: (402)444-1000
Omaha, NE 68102-1122   Free: 800-284-6397
                                 Fax: (402)345-0183
Contact: G. Woodson Howe, Vice President and Editor; Mike Finney, Exec. News Editor; Deanna Sands, Managing Editor; Bob Gerken, Nat'l Advertising Mgr., (402)444-1000; Gerald Wade, Action Editor, (402)444-1000; Jim Bresette, Entertainment Magazine Editor, (402)444-1000; Pat Waters, Editor, (402)444-1000; Larry King, Asst. Managing Editor, (402)444-1000.
Desc: General newspaper. *Type:* Periodical.

Omaha World-Herald
Omaha World-Herald Company
World-Herald Sq.   Ph: (402)444-1000
1334 Dodge
Omaha, NE 68102
E-mail: webmaster@omaha.com
URL: http://www.theadvocate.com
Desc: Contains the complete text of news items and feature articles from the Omaha World-Herald (Nebraska) newspaper. Covers all news stories, features, editorials, arts, and sports. *Available:* Bell & Howell Information and Learning; LEXIS-NEXIS, NEXIS; The Dialog Corporation, DIALOG. *Type:* Database.

The 1960 Sun
Sun Newspapers, Inc.
1136 Sheldon Rd.   Ph: (281)452-0530
PO Box 280   Fax: (281)333-2800
Channelview, TX 77530
E-mail: jmjscribe@aol.com
Contact: Mark Jones, Editor; Pam Winder, General Mgr.
Desc: Community newspaper. *Alt. Contact:* 3730 FM 1960 W, Ste. 108, Houston, TX 77068; telephone: (281)333-4900; fax: (281)333-2800. *Type:* Periodical.

Online USA
PO Box 75   Ph: (310)587-0025
Beverly Hills, CA 90213-0075   Fax: (310)587-0027
URL: http://www.onlineusa.com.
Contact: Brad Elterman, Photo Desk; Paul Harris, Features Desk.
Alt. Contact: PO Box 75, Beverly Hills, CA 90213-0075; telephone: (310)587-0025; fax: (310)587-0027. *Type:* Periodical.

OPC Bulletin

Overseas Press Club of America, Inc. (OPC)
320 E. 42nd St.   Ph: (212)983-4655
New York, NY 10017   Fax: (212)983-4692
Contact: Lee Townsend, Editor.
Desc: Carries articles on world journalism, freedom of the press, and international events and personalities in the field. Recurring features include reports on exhibits and films, book reviews, letters from readers, Club news, a calendar of events, and news of foreign correspondents. *Type:* Newsletter.

Orange County Register

Freedom Communications Inc.
625 N. Grand Ave.   Ph: (714)835-1234
PO Box 11626   Fax: (714)543-3904
Santa Ana, CA 92701-4347
E-mail: ocregister@link.freedom.com.
URL: http://www.ocregister.com.
Contact: R. David Threshie, Publisher; Tonnie Katz, Editor; N. Christian Anderson, Assoc. Publisher; John Schueler, Assoc. Publisher; Dick Cheverton, Managing Editor; Ken Brusic, Managing Editor.
Desc: General newspaper. *Type:* Periodical.

The Orange County Register

The Orange County Register
625 N. Grand Ave.   Ph: (714)835-1234
PO Box 11626
Santa Ana, CA 92701
Contact: Sharon Ostmann, Director of News Research.
Desc: Contains the complete text of news items and feature articles from The Orange County Register (California) newspaper. Regional coverage emphasizes the aerospace, computer, defense, medical research, and tourism industries. *Available:* Bell & Howell Information and Learning; NewsBank, Inc., CD News; Dow Jones Interactive Publishing. *Type:* Database.

Oregon Publisher

Oregon Newspaper Publishers Association
7150 SW Hampton, Ste. 111   Ph: (503)624-6397
Portland, OR 97223   Fax: (503)639-9009
Contact: LeRoy Yorgason, Publisher, fax: (405)624-9811, leroy@orenews.com; Lexi Witt, Editor, fax: (503)624-9811, lexi@orenews.com.
Desc: Covers journalism and publishing topics. *Type:* Newsletter.

The Oregonian

The Oregonian Publishing Co.
1320 S.W. Broadway   Ph: (503)221-8327
Portland, OR 97201
Contact: The Oregonian Library, (503)221-8132, fax: (503)294-4021.
Desc: Contains the complete text of news items and feature articles from The Oregonian newspaper. Regional coverage emphasizes the agriculture, commercial fishing, electronics, forestry, manufacturing, shipping and ship building, and tourism industries and environmental issues. *Available:* Bell & Howell Information and Learning; The Dialog Corporation, DIALOG; CompuServe Information Service, Knowledge Index. *Type:* Database.

The Oregonian

Oregonian Publishing Co.
1320 SW Broadway   Ph: (503)221-8327
Portland, OR 97201-3469 Free: 800-452-1420
                         Fax: (503)221-5306
URL: http://oregonlive.com.
Contact: Sandra Mims Rowe, Editor; Fred A. Stickel, Publisher; Denny Atkin, Advertising Mgr., (503)221-8279, fax: (503)594-5094, dennya1@aol.com.

Desc: General newspaper. *Type:* Periodical.

The Orlando Sentinel

Orlando Sentinel Communications
633 N. Orange Ave.   Ph: (407)420-5000
Orlando, FL 32801-1300   Fax: (407)420-5661
Contact: Jane Healy, Managing Editor, jhealy@orlandosentinel.com; Manning Pynn, Editor of Editorial Page, mpynn@orlandosentinel.com; Bill Dunn, Associate Managing Editor, bdunn@orlandosentinel.com; Jim Clark, Staff Development Editor, jclark@orlandosentinel.com; John Huff, Editor of New Technology, jhuff@orlandosentinel.com.
Desc: General newspaper. *Type:* Periodical.

The Orlando Sentinel

Sentinel Communications Co.
633 N. Orange Ave.   Ph: (407)420-5000
Orlando, FL 32801
URL: http://www.orlandosentinel.com
Desc: Contains news items and feature articles from The Orlando Sentinel (Florida) newspaper. Regional coverage emphasizes tourism, agriculture, business, and high technology industries. *Available:* The Dialog Corporation, DIALOG; The Dialog Corporation, DIALOG; Bell & Howell Information and Learning; LEXIS-NEXIS, NEXIS; CompuServe Information Service, Knowledge Index; NewsBank, Inc., CD News. *Type:* Database.

Oshawa-Whitby-Clarington-Port Perry This Week

Metroland Printing & Publishing
865 Farewell Ave. S   Ph: (905)579-4400
Oshawa, ON, Canada L1H 7L5   Fax: (905)579-1809
E-mail: newsroom@durham.net.
URL: http://www.durhamnews.net.
Contact: Timothy J. Whittaker, Publisher, fax: (905)579-2238; Bruce Danford, Advertising Mgr.; Joanne Burghardt, Editor-in-Chief, joannebe durham.net.
Desc: Local newspaper. *Alt. Contact:* 865 Farewell Ave. S., Oshawa, ON, Canada L1H 7L5; telephone: (416)579-4400; fax: (416)579-2238. *Type:* Periodical.

The Ottawa Citizen

Southam, Inc.
1101 Baxter Rd.   Ph: (613)829-9100
PO Box 5020   Free: 800-267-6100
Ottawa, ON, Canada K2C 3M4
Contact: Russell Mills, Publisher and President, (613)596-3500, fax: (613)596-8436, rmills@thecitizen. southam.ca; Neil Reynolds, Editor, (613)596-3554, fax: (613)596-3788, nreynolds@thecitizen.southam.ca; James Orban, VP Marketing, (613)596-3726, fax: (613)596-8436, jorban@thecitizen.southam.ca; Scott Anderson, Managing Editor, (613)596-8503, fax: (613)596-3788; Don Butler, Exec. Editor, (613)596-3671, fax: (613)596-3788.
Desc: General newspaper. *Alt. Contact:* 1101 Baxter Rd., PO Box 5020, Ottawa, ON, Canada K2C 3M4; telephone: (613)596-3664; fax: (613)726-1198. *Type:* Periodical.

The Ottawa Citizen

Southam, Inc.
Ottawa Citizen Newspaper
1101 Baxter Rd.   Ph: (613)829-9100
P.O. Box 5020
Ottawa, ON, Canada K2C 3M4
E-mail: letters@thecitizen.southam.ca
URL: http://www.ottawacitizen.com
Desc: Contains the complete text of news items, feature articles, and editorials from The Ottawa Citizen (Ontario) newspaper. Covers national and international news, federal government activities, and local business. *Available:* Infomart Online; Infomart Assistant, Infomart Online; LEXIS-NEXIS, NEXIS. *Type:* Database.

Ottaway Newspapers

1025 Connecticut Ave. NW   Ph: (202)828-3390
Ste. 310
Washington, DC 20036
Contact: William Schmick, III, Bureau Chief; Winston Wood, Dept. Chief; Kevin McCaney, Feature Ed.
Desc: Distributes news service. *Alt. Contact:* 1025 Connecticut Ave. NW, Ste. 310, Washington, DC 20036; telephone: (202)828-3390. *Type:* Periodical.

Overland Park Sun

Sun Publications, Inc.
7373 W. 107th St.   Ph: (913)648-4620
Overland Park, KS 66212-2547   Fax: (913)381-1402
Contact: Jack Lovelace, Editor; Jo Stapleton, Advertising Mgr.; Steve Rose, Publisher.
Desc: Newspaper. *Type:* Periodical.

Overland Park Sun, Blue Valley Edition

Sun Publications, Inc.
7373 W. 107th St.   Ph: (913)648-4620
Overland Park, KS 66212-2547   Fax: (913)381-1402
Contact: Jack Lovelace, Editor; Steve Rose, Publisher; Jo Stapleton, Advertising Manager.
Desc: Newspaper. *Type:* Periodical.

Pacific News Service

450 Mission St.   Ph: (415)243-4364
Ste. 204
San Francisco, CA 94105-2526
E-mail: pacificnews@pacificnews.org.
URL: http://www.pacificnews.org/jinn
Contact: Sandy Close, Exec. Ed.; Franz Schurmann, Associate Ed.; Richard Rodriguez, Associate Ed.; Andrew Lam, Associate Ed.; Kris Schell, Pub. Mgr.; Nell Bernstein, Youth Outlook Ed.
Desc: Distributes news service. *Alt. Contact:* 450 Mission St., Ste. 204, San Francisco, CA 94105-2526; telephone: (415)243-4364. *Type:* Periodical.

The Palm Beach Post

The Palm Beach Post
2751 S. Dixie Hwy.   Ph: (407)820-4401
West Palm Beach, FL 33405   Free: 800-432-7595
                         Fax: (407)820-4407
Contact: Tom Guiffrida, Publisher, (407)820-4124; Edward Sears, Editor, (407)820-4133; Jan Tuckwood, Assoc. Editor, (407)820-4519, fax: (407)820-4445.
Desc: General newspaper. *Type:* Periodical.

The Palm Beach Post

Palm Beach Newspapers, Inc.
PO Box 24700   Ph: (561)820-4495
West Palm Beach, FL 33416-4700
E-mail: library@gate.net
URL: http://www.gopbi.com
Contact: Sammy Alzofon, Library Director.
Desc: Contains the complete text of news items and feature stories from the Palm Beach Post (Florida) newspaper, a daily general circulation newspaper reporting local, national, and international news. Special areas of interest include regional business, including financial, agricultural, real estate, and utilities. *Available:* The Dialog Corporation, DIALOG; The Dialog Corporation, DIALOG; CompuServe Information Service, Knowledge Index; LEXIS-NEXIS, NEXIS. *Type:* Database.

The Pantagraph (Bloomington, Illinois)

The Pantagraph (Bloomington, Illinois)
301 W. Washington St.   Ph: (309)829-9411
Bloomington, IL 61701
E-mail: pantagra@pantagraph.com

URL: http://www.pantagraph.com

Desc: Contains the complete text of news items and feature articles from The Pantagraph (Bloomington, Illinois) newspaper. Regional coverage emphasizes the insurance industry, issues of state government, and activities of Illinois State University and Illinois Wesleyan University. *Available:* Bell & Howell Information and Learning. *Type:* Database.

Parade

Parade Publications
711 3rd Ave.   Ph: (212)450-7000
New York, NY 10017   Fax: (212)450-7087
Contact: Walter Anderson, Editor; Carlo Vittorini, Publisher; John Beni, President.

Desc: Sunday magazine for newspaper readers. Covers current events, human interest stories and food, beauty, fitness, health and science. *Type:* Periodical.

The Patriot Ledger

The Patriot Ledger
PO Box 9159   Ph: (617)786-7000
Quincy, MA 02269-9159   Free: 800-972-5070
                                Fax: (617)786-7298
E-mail: newsroom@ledger.com.
Contact: William Ketter, Editor; K. Prescott Low, Publisher.

Desc: General newspaper. *Type:* Periodical.

The Patriot-News

The Patriot News
812 Market St.   Ph: (717)255-8100
Harrisburg, PA 17105   Fax: (717)255-8456
E-mail: newsroom@patriot.microserve.com.
Contact: John A. Kirkpatrick, Publisher, (717)255-8178; Caroline Harrison, General Mgr., (717)255-8272; John A. Kirkpatrick, Editor, (717)255-8178; Tom Baden, Managing Editor, (717)255-8104; Jim Stephanak, Advertising Dir., (717)255-8201; Betty Way, Circulation Mgr., (717)255-8437.

Desc: General newspaper. *Type:* Periodical.

Pen Tip International Features Inc.

PO Box 3789   Ph: (207)775-4211
Portland, ME 04104-3789   Fax: (207)775-4280
E-mail: pentip@maine.com.
Contact: Paul A. Kolsti, President.

Desc: Distributes editorial illustrations. *Alt. Contact:* PO Box 3789, Portland, ME 04104-3789; telephone: (207)775-4211; fax: (207)775-4280. *Type:* Periodical.

Pensacola News Journal

Pensacola News Journal
1 News-Journal Plaza   Ph: (904)435-8500
Pensacola, FL 32501-5670   Fax: (904)435-8633
Contact: Anne Saul, Exec. Editor; Kenneth W. Andrews, Publisher; George Gutierrez, Advertising Mgr.; Gayle Pryor.

Desc: General newspaper. *Type:* Periodical.

Philadelphia Daily News

Knight-Ridder, Inc.
50 W. Fernando St.   Ph: (408)938-7700
San Jose, CA 95113
Contact: Zachary Stalberg, Editor; Herbert W. Moloney, III, Contact.

Desc: Newspaper (tabloid). *Alt. Contact:* 400 N. Broad St., Philadelphia, PA 19130-4015; telephone: (215)854-5900; fax: (215)854-5105. *Type:* Periodical.

Philadelphia Daily News

Philadelphia Newspapers, Inc.
400 N. Broad St.   Ph: (215)854-5000
P.O. Box 8527
Philadelphia, PA 19130
Desc: Contains the complete text of news items and feature stories from the Philadelphia Daily News (Pennsylvania) newspaper. Regional coverage emphasizes politics, industry, crime and crime prevention, education, banking, and transportation. *Available:* The Dialog Corporation, DIALOG. *Type:* Database.

Philadelphia Inquirer

Philadelphia Newspapers, Inc.
400 N. Broad St.   Ph: (215)854-5000
P.O. Box 8527
Philadelphia, PA 19130
Desc: Contains the the complete text of news items and feature stories from the Philadelphia Inquirer (Pennsylvania) newspaper. Regional coverage emphasizes the insurance, banking, health care, legal services, shipping, and transportation industries. *Available:* The Dialog Corporation, DIALOG; The Dialog Corporation, DIALOG; CompuServe Information Service, Knowledge Index; LEXIS-NEXIS, NEXIS; LEXIS-NEXIS, NEXIS. *Type:* Database.

Philadelphia Inquirer

Philadelphia Newspapers, Inc.
400 N. Broad St.   Ph: (215)854-2000
Philadelphia, PA 19130   Fax: (215)854-4794
Contact: Maxwell E.P. King, Editor; Todd Brownrout, Contact.

Desc: General newspaper. *Type:* Periodical.

The Philadelphia Tribune Metro Edition

Philadelphia Tribune Co.
522 S. 16th St.   Ph: (215)893-4097
Philadelphia, PA 19146   Fax: (215)735-3612
Contact: Paul A. Bennett, Editor; Robert W. Bogle, Advertising Mgr.

Desc: Black community newspaper. *Type:* Periodical.

Philadelphia Weekly

Review Publishing Ltd.
1701 Walnut St.   Ph: (215)563-7400
Philadelphia, PA 19103   Fax: (215)563-6799
E-mail: mail@philaweekly.com.
URL: http://www.philadelphiaweekly.com.
Contact: Anthony A. Clifton, President; Tim Whitaker, Editor; Joseph H. Trachman, Publisher; Mark Evans, Art Dir.; Alicia Goldblum, Production Mgr.

Desc: Alternative newspaper. *Type:* Periodical.

PitchWeekly

Pitch Publishing, Inc.
3535 Broadway, Ste. 400   Ph: (816)561-6061
Kansas City, MO 64111   Fax: (816)756-0502
E-mail: pitch@pitch.com.
URL: http://www.pitch.com.
Contact: Hal Brody, Publisher, halb@pitch.com; Bruce Rodgers, Editor, brodgers@pitch.com; Michael Gruenenfelder, Classified Mgr., classified@pitch.com.

Desc: Alternative weekly focusing on Kansas City's news and entertainment. *Type:* Periodical.

The Pittsburgh Post-Gazette

The Pittsburgh Post-Gazette
34 Blvd. of the Allies   Ph: (412)263-1100
Pittsburgh, PA 15222
URL: http://www.post-gazette.com
Desc: Contains the complete text of news items and feature articles from The Pittsburgh Post-Gazette, a general-

circulation daily newspaper covering Pennsylvania and regional business, finance, banking, the arts, and sports, as well as selected national and international news. NOTE: This database also contains a two-year backfile of The Pittsburgh Press, which, following a recent labor strike, was sold to the PG Publishing Company; and Allegheny Bulletin, the newspaper published by the Pittsburgh Press Company during the strike. *Available:* The Dialog Corporation, DIALOG; The Dialog Corporation, DIALOG; CompuServe Information Service, Knowledge Index; Bell & Howell Information and Learning; LEXIS-NEXIS, NEXIS. *Type:* Database.

Plain Dealer

Newhouse Services
1801 Superior Ave. E.   Ph: (216)999-6000
Cleveland, OH 44114   Free: 800-362-0727
                                Fax: (216)344-4620
URL: http://www.cleveland.com.
Contact: Thomas Vail, Editor and Publisher; John Moloney, Editor.

Desc: General newspaper. *Type:* Periodical.

The Plain Dealer (Cleveland, Ohio)

The Plain Dealer (Cleveland, Ohio)
1801 Superior Ave., N.E.   Ph: (216)999-4195
Cleveland, OH 44114
Contact: Patti Graziano, Library Director., (216)999-4195, fax: (216)999-6363.

Desc: Contains the complete text of news items and feature articles from The Plain Dealer (Cleveland, Ohio) newspaper. Regional coverage emphasizes the financial services, health care, and manufacturing industries. *Available:* Bell & Howell Information and Learning; The Dialog Corporation, DIALOG. *Type:* Database.

Portland Press Herald

The Portland Newspapers
390 Congress St.   Ph: (207)791-6650
PO Box 1460   Free: 800-442-6036
Portland, ME 04101-3514   Fax: (207)791-6920
E-mail: portlandpaper@scryer.nlis.net; herald@portland.com.
URL: http://www.portland.com.
Contact: Madeline Corson, Publisher; Amanda Schumaker, Advertising Mgr.; Bruce Ceensmer, President; Jodie Krueger, Director.

Desc: General newspaper. *Type:* Periodical.

The Post and Courier

Evening Post Publishing Co.
134 Columbus St.   Ph: (803)577-7111
Charleston, SC 29403   Fax: (803)937-5579
E-mail: editorial@duesouth.net
URL: http://www.charleston.net.
Contact: Larry Tarleton, Editor; Ivan V. Anderson, Jr., Publisher; Ken Burger, Columnist; Elsa McDowell, Columnist; Dan Conover, City editor; Barbera S. Williams, Editorial page editor, (803)577-7111; Malcolm DeWitt, Sports editor; Teresa Taylor, Business Editor; Michelle Harmon, Librarian; Ann Burger, Food Editor, (803)577-7111.

Desc: General newspaper. *Type:* Periodical.

Post/Dispatch Features

703 Ridgemark Dr.   Ph: (408)637-9795
Hollister, CA 95023   Fax: (408)636-1225
Contact: George Crenshaw, President; Van Masters, Managing Editor; Al Otis, Sales Promotion.

Desc: Distributes magazine cartoons including Belvedere. *Alt. Contact:* 703 Ridgemark Dr., Hollister, CA 95023; telephone: (408)637-9795; fax: (408)636-1225. *Type:* Periodical.

Post-Gazette

Post Gazette
PO Box 957 Ph: (412)263-1100
Pittsburgh, PA 15230-0957 Fax: (412)391-8452
URL: http://www.post-gazette.com.
Contact: John G. Craig, Jr., Editor, (412)263-1641,
jcraig@post-gazette.com; William Block, Jr., Co-Pub.,
(412)263-1430; John R. Block, Co-Pub., (412)263-1946.
Desc: General newspaper. *Type:* Periodical.

The Post-Standard

The Syracuse Newspapers, Inc.
Clinton Sq. Ph: (315)470-0011
PO Box 4818 Free: 800-765-4335
Syracuse, NY 13221 Fax: (315)470-3081
Contact: Michael J. Connor, Executive Editor; Stephen A.
Rogers, Editor and Publisher; James F. Kleinklaus, Advertising Dir.
Desc: General newspaper. *Alt. Contact:* PO Box 4915, Syracuse, NY 13221; telephone: (315)470-0011; fax:
(315)470-3081; toll-free: 800-765-4335. *Type:* Periodical.

The Post-Tribune (Gary, Indiana)

Post-Tribune Publishing, Inc.
1065 Broadway Ph: (219)881-3055
Gary, IN 46402
Desc: Contains the complete text of news items and feature
articles from the Post-Tribune (Indiana), a general circulation newspaper reporting local, national, and international
news. Regional coverage emphasizes the steel industry and
agribusiness. *Type:* Database.

PR Newswire

810 7th Ave. Free: 800-832-5522
35th Fl.
New York, NY 10019
URL: http://www.prnewswire.com.
Contact: Ian Capps, President; John Williams, Senior VP;
Ken Dowell, Ed. Dir.; Fred Ferguson, Features Coord.
Desc: Distributes news wire service. *Alt. Contact:* 810 7th
Ave., 35th Fl., New York, NY 10019; toll-free: 800-832-
5522. *Type:* Periodical.

Prairie Village Sun

Sun Publications, Inc.
7373 W. 107th St. Ph: (913)648-4620
Overland Park, KS 66212-2547 Fax: (913)381-1402
Contact: Jack Lovelace, Editor; Steve Rose, Publisher; Jo
Stapleton, Advertising Mgr.
Desc: Newspaper. *Type:* Periodical.

Press Associates Inc.

815 15th St. NW Ph: (202)638-0444
Ste. 1102-N Fax: (202)638-0955
Washington, DC 20005-2201
Contact: Mark J. Gruenberg, Ed./Pres; Robert B. Cooney,
Ed. Emeritus; Dennis B. Dons, Jr. Ed.
Desc: Distributes news concerning legislative issues, politics, unemployment, court decisions, labor cases, national
health, Social Security, and Medicare; The Washington
Window, a commentary column; Work & Health, a job
safety column; How to Buy, a consumer column. *Alt. Contact:* 815 15th St. NW, Ste. 1102-N, Washington, DC
20005-2201; telephone: (202)638-0444; fax: (202)638-
0955. *Type:* Periodical.

The Press of Atlantic City

South Jersey Publishing Co.
1000 W. Washington Ave. Ph: (609)272-7000
Pleasantville, NJ 08232-3806 Free: 800-651-8279
Fax: (609)272-7086
E-mail: acpress@acy.digex.net.
URL: http://www.pressplus.com.

Contact: Paul A. Merkoski, Editor, (609)272-1100; Robert M. McCormick, Publisher; Keith Dawn, Advertising
Mgr.; Charles A. Bryant, Jr., Dir. of Finance & Admin.;
Robert Mawhinney, Dir. of Sales & Mktng.; Jayne Doherty, Classified Mgr.; Larry West, At the Shore Business
Mgr.; John Rodney, Production Dir.; Vito Cicero, Circulation Dir.; Kathleen Leonard, Personnel Dir.; Maryjane
Briant, Managing Editor; Steve Warren, Deputy Mng.
Ed.; David Benson, Production Editor; Mark Melhorn, At
th
Desc: General newspaper. *Alt. Contact:* 11 Devins Ln.,
Pleasantville, NJ 08232-3806; telephone: (609)272-1234;
fax: (609)645-7224. *Type:* Periodical.

The Press Democrat

The Press Democrat
427 Mendocino Ave. Ph: (707)546-2020
PO Box 569 Free: 800-675-5056
Santa Rosa, CA 95402 Fax: (707)546-2437
URL: http://www.pressdemo.com.
Contact: Bruce Kyse, Exec. Editor, (707)521-5256,
bkyse@pressdemo.com; Michael J. Parman, Publisher,
(707)526-8596, fax: (707)521-5302; Ken Svanum, Advertising Dir., (707)526-8575, fax: (707)521-5493,
ksvanum@pressdemocrat.com; Bob Swofford, Managing
Editor, (707)521-5251, bswofford@pressdemo.com; Brad
Bollinger, Business Editor, (707)521-5283, fax: (707)521-
5418, bbollinger@pressdemo.com; Jim Fremgen, News
Editor, (707)521-5298, jfremgen@pressdemocrat.com;
George Mane
Desc: General newspaper. *Alt. Contact:* PO Box 910, Santa
Rosa, CA 95402; telephone: (707)526-8585; fax:
(707)546-7538; toll-free: 800-675-5056. *Type:* Periodical.

The Press-Enterprise

The Valley Times
PO Box 9700 Ph: (909)242-7614
Moreno Valley, CA 92552 Fax: (909)247-1920
URL: http://www.pe.net.
Contact: Sue Barry, Classified Advertising Sales Manager;
Joel Blain, Editor; Jim Maurer, Sales Mgr.; Joe Frederickson, Marketing Dir.; Dave Cornwall, Advertising Dir.;
Rich DeAtley, Entertainment Editor; T.E. Foreman, Theater Editor; John Garrett, Sports Editor; Judith Graffam,
Editor; Michael Schuerman, Marketing Research Mgr.;
Howard Hayes, Jr., Chairman; Robert Hirt, TV Week
Editor; Laurie Lucas, Editor; Sally Ann Maas, Assistant
Managing Editor Features; Andrew McCue, Business E
Desc: Local newspaper. *Type:* Periodical.

The Press-Enterprise

The Press-Enterprise
3512 14th St. Ph: (909)684-1200
P.O. Box 792
Riverside, CA 92501
Desc: Contains selected text of The Press-Enterprise, a
general circulation newspaper reporting local, national,
and international news with an emphasis on southern California. *Available:* Bell & Howell Information and Learning; LEXIS-NEXIS. *Type:* Database.

Press News Ltd.

36 King St. E. Ph: (416)364-0321
Toronto, ON, Canada M5C Fax: (416)594-2163
2L9
Contact: Jim Poling, General Mgr.; Michael Sifton, Chm.
Alt. Contact: 36 King St. E., Toronto, ON, Canada M5C
2L9; telephone: (416)364-0321; fax: (416)594-2163.
Type: Periodical.

Press Photo Service

79-14 Parsons Blvd. Ph: (718)526-9069
Flushing, NY 11366
Contact: Harris Sutter, Pres./Ed.; Mike Weber, Vice President; Charles Phillips, General Mgr.; Jeff Hollander, Entertainment/Sports Ed.

Alt. Contact: 79-14 Parsons Blvd., Flushing, NY 11366;
telephone: (718)526-9069. *Type:* Periodical.

Press & Sun-Bulletin

Gannett Co., Inc.
1100 Wilson Blvd. Ph: (703)284-6000
Arlington, VA 22234 Free: 800-872-0001
URL: http://www.pressconnects.com.
Contact: Martha Steffens, Exec. Editor, (607)798-1186;
William Monopoli, Publisher, (607)798-1111; Nancy
Solliday, Advertising Mgr.
Desc: General newspaper. *Alt. Contact:* Binghamton Press
Co., Vestal Pkwy. E., PO Box 1270, Binghamton, NY
13902; telephone: (607)798-1151; fax: (607)798-1113;
toll-free: 800-365-0077. *Type:* Periodical.

Press-Telegram (Long Beach, California)

Twin Coast Newspapers, Inc.
604 Pine Ave. Ph: (310)435-1161
Long Beach, CA 90844
Desc: Contains the complete text of news items and feature
articles from the Press-Telegram Long Beach newspaper.
Regional coverage emphasizes aerospace, petroleum,
chemical, motion picture, television , defense, international trade, and shipbuilding industries in Los Angeles and
Orange counties. *Type:* Database.

Professional Hockey Writers' Association

Sherry L. Ross
1480 Pleasant Valley Way, No. Ph: (973)669-8607
44 Fax: (973)669-8607
West Orange, NJ 07052
Contact: Sherry L. Ross, Sec.-Treas.
Desc: Writers who cover member teams of the National
Hockey League. Encourages high standards among professional hockey writers. *Type:* Association.

The Providence Journal

The Providence Journal Co.
75 Fountain St. Ph: (401)277-7000
Providence, RI 02902-0050 Fax: (401)277-7889
Contact: Stephen Hamblett, Publisher; Howard G. Sutton, President; Joel Rawson, Sr. VP; Donald Ross, V.P.
Advertising.
Desc: Newspaper. *Type:* Periodical.

The Province

Pacific Press
A Southam Company
1-200 Granville St. Ph: (604)605-2222
Vancouver, BC, Canada V6C Fax: (604)605-2323
3N3
URL: http://www.vancouverprovince.com.
Contact: Malcolm Kirk, Managing Editor; Chris Baker,
Vice Pres., of Manufacturing; Michael Cook, Editor; Joey
Thompson, Editoral Page Editor; Renee Blackstone, Living Editor; Lorne Smith, Money Editor, (604)732-2022;
Bill Holden, News Dir.; John Denniston, Photo Editor,
(604)732-2034.
Desc: General newspaper. *Alt. Contact:* BC, Canada; fax:
(604)605-2720. *Type:* Periodical.

The Province (Vancouver, British Columbia)

Pacific Press Ltd.
2250 Granville St. Ph: (604)732-2111
Vancouver, BC, Canada V6H
3G2
URL: http://www.southam.com/vancouversun
Desc: Contains the complete text of The Province (Vancouver) newspaper. Regional coverage emphasizes politics,
entertainment, sports, and business, including the Vancouver Stock Exchange. *Available:* Infomart Online; Infomart Online; Infomart Assistant, Infomart Online;
Infomart Dialog Limited. *Type:* Database.

Quad-City Times

Quad-City Times
500 E. 3rd St.　　　　　　Ph: (319)383-2200
PO Box 3828　　　　　　Free: 800-437-4641
Davenport, IA 52801-1708　Fax: (319)383-2433
E-mail: qctimes@aol.com.
URL: http://www.qctimes.com.
Contact: Dave Foselier, Publisher; Beth Clark, Publisher;
Mark Ridolfi, General Mgr./Managing Editor, (319)383-
2450; Jim Thompson, Circulation Mgr.; Roy Booker, Li-
brarian, (319)383-2293.
Desc: General newspaper. *Type:* Periodical.

Quarryville Advertiser

Engle Publishing Co.
PO Box 500　　　　　　Ph: (717)653-4300
Mount Joy, PA 17552-0500　Free: 800-800-1833
　　　　　　　　　　　Fax: (717)653-1833
Contact: C. A. Engle, Publisher; Patrick Lee, Advertising
Mgr.; J. R. Rutt, Circulation Mgr.
Desc: Shopper. *Type:* Periodical.

Quaternary Features

PO Box 72　　　　　　Ph: (212)744-1867
New York, NY 10021
E-mail: tomdbug@aol.com.
Contact: Ken Fisher, Manager.
Alt. Contact: PO Box 72, New York, NY 10021; tele-
phone: (212)744-1867. *Type:* Periodical.

Queens Chronicle

Mark I. Publications, Inc.
62-33 Woodhaven Blvd.　Ph: (718)205-8000
Rego Park, NY 11374　　Fax: (718)205-0150
E-mail: qchron@aol.com.
Contact: Betty Cooney, Senior editor; Susan Merzon, Pub-
lisher; Mark Weidler, Assoc. Publisher; Raymond Sito,
General Mgr.
Desc: Community newspaper (tabloid). *Type:* Periodical.

Queens Tribune Publications

Tripco Inc.
17415 Horace Harding Expy.　Ph: (718)357-7400
Fresh Meadows, NY 11365-　Fax: (718)357-9417
　1527
Contact: David Keisman, Publisher; Stu Bukofzer, Editor.
Desc: General newspaper. *Type:* Periodical.

Quill and Scroll Society

University of Iowa　　　Ph: (319)335-5795
School of Journalism
Iowa City, IA 52242
E-mail: quill-scroll@uiowa.edu
URL: http://www.uiowa.edu/~quill-sc
Contact: Richard P. Johns, Exec. Dir.
Desc: Honor Society high school journalism students recommended for membership by their schools. Seeks to reward individual achievements and to encourage individual
initiative in high school journalism, creative writing, and
allied fields. Provides information to editors, staffs, and
advisers on all phases of publication work. *Type:* Association.

Quiz Features

4007 Connecticut Ave. NW　Ph: (202)966-0025
Washington, DC 20008　　Fax: (202)966-4074
Contact: Donald Saltz, Author; Mozelle Saltz, Research
Dir.
Desc: Distributes question and answer quizzes. *Alt. Con-
tact:* 4007 Connecticut Ave. NW, Washington, DC
20008; telephone: (202)966-0025; fax: (202)966-4074.
Type: Periodical.

QV

Scribe Media
5606 Medical Circle　　Ph: (608)271-1025
Madison, WI 53719　　Free: 800-373-9692
　　　　　　　　　　Fax: (608)271-1150
E-mail: scribe@xc.org
Contact: Gordon Govier, Editor.
Desc: Publishes topics of interest by and for Christians
working in the news media. *Type:* Newsletter.

Reader's Digest

Reader's Digest Association, Inc.
28 W. 23rd St.　　　　Ph: (212)366-8700
New York, NY 10010　　Fax: (212)366-8799
E-mail: readersdigest@notes.compuserve.com.
Contact: Greg Coleman, Publisher; Chris Willcox, Editor
in Chief.
Desc: General interest non-fiction magazine. *Type:* Period-
ical.

Reader's Guide Abstracts Select Edition

H.W. Wilson Company
950 University Ave.　　Ph: (718)588-8400
Bronx, NY 10452
E-mail: custserv@hwwilson.com
URL: http://www.hwwilson.com
Contact: Technical Support Department., techmail@info.
hwwilson.com.
Desc: Contains citations, with abstracts, to selected articles
cited in the Readers' Guide to Periodical Literature. Covers topics of general interest, including the arts, business,
computers, crafts, current events, education, fashion, food
and cooking, health, history, home improvement, news,
photography, politics, science, and sports. *Available:* H.W.
Wilson Company, WilsonWeb; H.W. Wilson Company,
WilsonWeb; SilverPlatter Information, Inc. *Type:* Database.

Reading Eagle

Eagle Times
PO Box 582　　　　　Free: 800-633-7222
Reading, PA 19603-0582
Contact: Charles M. Gallagher, Managing Editor; William
S. Flippin, Publisher; Robert Wanner, Editor, edit@
prolog.net.
Desc: General newspaper. *Type:* Periodical.

Real People

Main St. Publishing Co., Inc.
450 7th Ave., Ste. 1701　Ph: (212)244-2351
New York, NY 10123　　Free: 800-237-9851
　　　　　　　　　　Fax: (212)244-2367
Contact: Alex Polner, Editor, (212)244-2351, fax:
(212)244-2367, mrs-2@idt.net; Brad Hamilton, Editor,
bradhamilton@mindspring.com; Philip Reccchia, Editor;
Margaret Saraco, Editor, mrs@idt.net; Curt Schleier, Editor, curt_s@compuserve.com; Michael Szymanski, Editor,
mikeszy@aol.com.
Desc: Entertainment & Personality Publication *Type:* Periodical.

The Record

Bergen Record Corp.
150 River St.　　　　　Ph: (201)646-4000
Hackensack, NJ 07601-7172　Fax: (201)646-4135
Contact: Glenn Ritt, Vice Pres./Editor; Robert Sapanara,
President; Vivian Waixel, Managing Editor.
Desc: General newspaper. *Type:* Periodical.

The Record (Hackensack, New Jersey)

Bergen Record Corporation
150 River St.　　　　　Ph: (201)646-4000
Hackensack, NJ 07602
E-mail: newsroom@bergen.com
URL: http://www.bergen.com
Desc: Contains the complete text of news items and feature
articles from The Record (Hackensack, New Jersey) news-
paper. Regional coverage emphasizes economic, political,
and social issues of Bergen, Essex, Hudson, Morris, and
Passaic counties. *Available:* Bell & Howell Information
and Learning; The Dialog Corporation, DIALOG. *Type:*
Database.

The Register-Guard

Guard Publishing Co.
975 High St.　　　　　Ph: (541)485-1234
PO Box 10188
Eugene, OR 97440-2188
Contact: A.F. Baker, III, Editor and Publisher; Fletcher
Little, General Mgr.; Don Robinson, Editor; Janelle Hart-
man, Reporter; Kimber Williams, Reporter; Carl Davaz,
Graphic Ed.; Jim Godbold, Managing Editor.
Desc: General newspaper. *Type:* Periodical.

Religion Newswriters Association Newsletter

Religion Newswriters Association
c/o Debra Mason　　　Ph: (614)891-9001
88 W. Plum St.　　　　Fax: (614)891-9001
Westerville, OH 43081
E-mail: rnastuff@aol.com
Contact: Debra Mason, Editor.
Desc: Seeks to "advance the professional standards of religion journalism in the secular press." Informs members of
Association activities, meetings, contests, and awards. Recurring features include news of research, guest columns,
and obituaries. *Type:* Newsletter.

Reno Gazette-Journal

Gannett Co., Inc.
1100 Wilson Blvd.　　Ph: (703)284-6000
Arlington, VA 22234　　Free: 800-872-0001
URL: http://www.nevadanet.com.
Contact: Tonia Cunning, Executive Editor, (702)788-
6299; Sue Clark-Johnson, Publisher, (702)788-6208;
John Zidich, Sales Mgr., (702)788-6293, fax: (702)788-
6516, jzidich@reno.garnett.com; Clare Wood, Editor,
(775)788-6322, fax: (775)788-6458; Linda Dono, Editor,
(775)788-6302, fax: (775)788-6458; Mark Lundahl, Editor, (775)788-6230, fax: (775)788-6458; Tim Dunn, Editor, (775)788-6355, fax: (775)788-6458; Ray Hagar,
Editor, (775)788-6345, fax: (775)788-6458.
Desc: General newspaper. *Alt. Contact:* PO Box 22000,
Reno, NV 89520-2000; telephone: (702)788-6397; fax:
(702)788-6458. *Type:* Periodical.

The Repository

The Repository
500 Market Ave. S.　　Ph: (216)454-5611
Canton, OH 44702-2112　Fax: (216)454-5610
Contact: Michael E. Hanke, Editor; Michael J. Miller, Ad-
vertising Dir.
Desc: General newspaper. *Type:* Periodical.

Retail News Bureau

Div. of Retail Reporting Corp.　Ph: (212)279-7000
302 5th Ave.　　　　　Fax: (212)279-7014
New York, NY 10001
Contact: John Burr, Publisher; Bridget Biggane, Editor.
Desc: Distributes women's fashion news. *Alt. Contact:* Div.
of Retail Reporting Corp., 302 5th Ave., New York, NY
10001; telephone: (212)279-7000; fax: (212)279-7014.
Type: Periodical.

Reuters America Inc.

1700 Broadway 31st Fl. Ph: (212)603-3400
New York, NY 10019 Fax: (212)603-3446
Alt. Contact: 1700 Broadway 31st Fl., New York, NY 10019; telephone: (212)603-3400; fax: (212)603-3446. *Type:* Periodical.

Richmond Times-Dispatch

Richmond Newspapers, Inc.
333 E. Grace St. Ph: (804)649-6000
PO Box 85333 Fax: (804)775-8059
Richmond, VA 23293-1000
URL: http://www.gatewayva.com.
Contact: William Millsaps, Managing Editor; J. Stewart Bryan, III, Publisher; Louise Seals, Managing Editor; Pam Feibish, Business Editor.
Desc: General newspaper. *Type:* Periodical.

Richmond Times-Dispatch/Richmond News/ Virginia Business

Richmond Newspapers, Inc.
333 E. Grace St. Ph: (804)649-6000
P.O. Box 85333
Richmond, VA 23293
URL: http://www.gateway-va.com
Desc: Contains the complete texts of the Richmond Times-Dispatch and the Richmond News-Leader, two general circulation newspapers reporting local, national, and international news, as well as the complete text of the monthly Virginia Business. Special areas of interest include the tobacco industry. *Available:* Bell & Howell Information and Learning; The Dialog Corporation, DIALOG; The Dialog Corporation, DIALOG; CompuServe Information Service, Knowledge Index. *Type:* Database.

The Riverfront Times

Hartmann Publishing Co.
6358 Delmar Blvd., Ste. 200 Ph: (314)615-6666
St. Louis, MO 63130-4719 Fax: (314)615-6655
URL: http://www.rftstl.com.
Contact: Safir Ahmed, Editor, (314)615-6713, fax: (314)615-6716, safir_ahmed@rftstl.com; Terry Coe, Publisher, (314)615-6717, terry_coe@rftstl.com; Cheryl Schaeffer, Ad Director, (314)615-6613, cheryl_schaeffer@rftstl.com.
Desc: Alternative newspaper (tabloid) with political articles, in-depth features, entertainment, and classified and personal ads. *Type:* Periodical.

RMS Syndication

14713 Pleasant Hill Rd. Ph: (704)588-2453
Charlotte, NC 28278-7927
Contact: David A. Butler, President.
Alt. Contact: 14713 Pleasant Hill Rd., Charlotte, NC 28278-7927; telephone: (704)588-2453. *Type:* Periodical.

The Roanoke Times

The Roanoke Times
PO Box 2491 Ph: (540)981-3100
Roanoke, VA 24010-2491 Fax: (703)981-3391
E-mail: roatimes@infi.net
URL: http://www.roanoke.com.
Contact: Mike Riley, Editor, (703)981-3227, fax: (703)981-3446, mikeri@roanoke.com; Walter Rugaber, Publisher, (703)981-3246, walterr@roanoke.com; Cathy Greenberg, Advertising Mgr., cathyg@roanoke.comp.
Desc: General newspaper. *Alt. Contact:* PO Box 2491, Roanoke, VA 24010-2491; telephone: (703)981-3257; fax: (703)981-3391; toll-free: 800-346-1234. *Type:* Periodical.

Rockford Register Star

Gannett Co., Inc.
1100 Wilson Blvd. Ph: (703)284-6000
Arlington, VA 22234 Free: 800-872-0001
URL: http://www.gannett.com.
Contact: Linda G. Cunningham, Exec. Editor; Mary P. Stier, Publisher.
Desc: General newspaper. *Alt. Contact:* 99 E. State St., Rockford, IL 61104; telephone: (815)987-1302; fax: (815)962-6578. *Type:* Periodical.

Rocky Mountain Motorist

AAA Colorado, Inc.
4100 E. Arkansas Ave. Ph: (303)753-8800
Denver, CO 80222 Fax: (303)758-8515
Contact: Kelly Eastlund, Managing Editor; Steve Seay, Publisher/President.
Desc: Magazine for members of the Colorado American Automobile Association. Contains articles on domestic and foreign travel as well as automotive issues. *Type:* Periodical.

Rocky Mountain News

Rocky Mountain News
400 W. Colfax Ave. Ph: (303)892-2300
Denver, CO 80204
E-mail: newsquest@denver-rmn.com
URL: http://www.InsideDenver.com
Desc: Contains the complete text of news stories, columns, feature articles, editorials, and letters from all daily editions of The Rocky Mountain News (Denver) newspaper. Regional coverage emphasizes university research in medicine and aerospace, the aerospace industry, agriculture, cable television and entertainment, computer technology, manufacturing, mining, oil and other energy related industries, telecommunications, state and federal government, and professional sports and outdoor activities. *Available:* Bell & Howell Information and Learning; LEXIS-NEXIS; Dow Jones Interactive Publishing. *Type:* Database.

Roeland Park Sun

Sun Publications, Inc.
7373 W. 107th St. Ph: (913)648-4620
Overland Park, KS 66212-2547 Fax: (913)381-1402
Contact: Jack Lovelace, Editor; Stan Rose, Publisher; Shirley Rose, Publisher; Steve Rose, Publisher; Mike Lomario, Editor.
Desc: Newspaper. *Type:* Periodical.

Roll Call Report Syndicate

Thomas Reports Inc. Ph: (202)737-1888
1257-B National Press Bldg.
Washington, DC 20045
E-mail: roll-call-votes@atsmsu.com.
URL: http://www.roll-call-votes.com.
Contact: Richard G. Thomas, Editor and Publisher; Cora Hoopes, Associate Ed.; David K. Martin, Associate Ed.; Patrick Harden, Associate Ed.
Desc: Distributes congressional news. *Alt. Contact:* Thomas Reports Inc., 1257-B National Press Bldg., Washington, DC 20045; telephone: (202)737-1888. *Type:* Periodical.

Royal Features

PO Box 58174 Ph: (713)532-2145
Houston, TX 77258-8714
Contact: Fay W. Henry, Exec. Dir.
Alt. Contact: PO Box 58174, Houston, TX 77258-8714; telephone: (713)532-2145. *Type:* Periodical.

The Sacramento Bee

The Sacramento Bee
2100 Q St. Ph: (916)321-1000
PO Box 15779 Free: 800-876-8700
Sacramento, CA 95852 Fax: (916)321-1524
URL: http://www.sacbee.com.
Contact: Gregory Favre, Exec. Editor, (916)321-1006, fax: (916)321-1109, gfavre@sacbee.com; Rick Rodriquez, Managing Editor, (916)321-1002, rrodriquez@sacbee.com; Pam Dinsmore, Exec. News Editor, (916)321-1024, pdinsmore@sacbee.com; Amy Chance, Capitol Bureau Chief, (916)326-5535, achance@sacbee.com; Howard Shintaku, Art/Graphics Dir., (916)321-1027, hshintaku@sacbee.com.
Desc: General newspaper. *Type:* Periodical.

The Sacramento Bee

The Sacramento Bee
2100 Q St. Ph: (916)321-1475
P.O. Box 15779
Sacramento, CA 95816
URL: http://www.sacramentobee.com
Desc: Contains the complete text of news items, feature articles, stories, and editorials from The Sacramento Bee (California) newspaper. Covers local, state, and national news, including government, law, business and industry, economics, transportation, education, sports, leisure, and the arts. *Available:* The Dialog Corporation, DIALOG; Bell & Howell Information and Learning; LEXIS-NEXIS, NEXIS; LEXIS-NEXIS, NEXIS; CompuServe Information Service, Knowledge Index. *Type:* Database.

St. Louis Post-Dispatch

St. Louis Post-Dispatch
900 N. Tucker Blvd. Ph: (314)340-8274
St. Louis, MO 63101-9990
URL: http://www.stlnet.com/
Contact: Gerald Brown, Library Director, (314)340-8274, fax: (314)340-3050.
Desc: Contains the complete text of news items and feature articles from the St. Louis Post-Dispatch newspaper. *Available:* The Dialog Corporation, DIALOG; The Dialog Corporation, DIALOG; Bell & Howell Information and Learning; LEXIS-NEXIS, NEXIS; CompuServe Information Service, Knowledge Index; NewsBank, Inc., CD News. *Type:* Database.

St. Louis Post-Dispatch

Pulitzer Publishing Co.
900 N. Tucker Blvd. Ph: (314)340-8000
St. Louis, MO 63101 Free: 800-365-0820
 Fax: (314)340-3050
URL: http://www.sto.net.com.
Contact: William F. Woo, Editor; Nicholas G. Penninman, IV, Publisher; Gerald F. Anderson, Advertising Mgr.
Desc: General newspaper. *Type:* Periodical.

St. Paul Pioneer Press

Knight-Ridder, Inc.
50 W. Fernando St. Ph: (408)938-7700
San Jose, CA 95113
E-mail: pioneerpress.com.
URL: http://www.pioneerplanet.com.
Contact: Rick Sadowski, President, (612)228-5404, fax: (612)228-5416, rsadowski@pioneerpress.com; Walker Lundy, Editor, (612)228-5480, fax: (612)228-5500, wlundy@pioneerpress.com; Ron Clark, Editorial Pages Editor, (612)228-5544, fax: (612)228-5564, rclark@pioneerpress.com; Mary Altuvilla, Vice President, (612)228-5302, maltuvilla@pioneerpress.com; Scott Frantzen, Vice President, (612)228-5150, sfrantzen@pioneerpress.com.
Desc: General newspaper. *Alt. Contact:* 345 Cedar St., St. Paul, MN 55101; telephone: (612)222-5011; fax: (612)228-5500; toll-free: 800-950-9080. *Type:* Periodical.

St. Paul Pioneer Press

St. Paul Pioneer Press
345 Cedar St.   Ph: (651)228-5192
St. Paul, MN 55101-1057
Contact: Ruth Ehmcke, Library Researcher, (651)222-6397, infodesk@pioneerpress.com.
Desc: Contains the complete text of the St. Paul Pioneer Press (Minnesota) newspaper. *Available:* The Dialog Corporation, DIALOG; CompuServe Information Service, Knowledge Index; St. Paul Pioneer Press; St. Paul Pioneer Press. *Type:* Database.

St. Petersburg Times

Times Publishing Co.
490 First Ave., S.   Ph: (813)893-8111
P.O. Box 1121
St. Petersburg, FL 33731
URL: http://www.sptimes.com
Contact: Caroline Ziadia, Information Station.
Desc: Contains the complete text of news items and feature articles from the St. Petersburg Times (Florida) newspaper. *Available:* The Dialog Corporation, DIALOG; LEXIS-NEXIS, NEXIS; CompuServe Information Service; America Online, Inc.; Dow Jones Interactive Publishing. *Type:* Database.

St. Petersburg Times

Times Publishing Co.
490 1st Ave. S.   Ph: (727)893-8111
PO Box 1121   Free: 800-333-7505
St. Petersburg, FL 33701   Fax: (727)893-8675
URL: http://www.sptimes.com.
Contact: Andy Barnes, Editor, (727)893-8625; Paul Tash, Exec. Editor, (727)893-8887; Tom Rawlins, Senior Editor, (727)893-8420; Chris Lavin, World Editor, (727)893-8739; Ron Dupont, Web Editor/Asst. Metro Editor, (727)893-8628; Phil Gailey, Editor, (727)893-8268; Margo Hammond, Editor, (727)893-8768; Jack Sheppard, AME/Sports, (727)893-8495; Nancy Waclawek, AME/Features, (727)893-8780; Rob Hooker, Metro Editor/Business Editor, (727)893-8780; Sonya Doctorian, AME/Photo, (727)893-8231;
Desc: General newspaper. *Type:* Periodical.

Salmon Syndication

PO Box 4272   Ph: (707)552-1699
Vallejo, CA 94590-9991   Fax: (707)644-2680
E-mail: salsyndusa@aol.com.
Contact: Ray Salmon, Author; Donna Salmon, Editor; Stephen Salmon, Production.
Desc: Distributes single panel cartoons. *Alt. Contact:* PO Box 4272, Vallejo, CA 94590-9991; telephone: (707)552-1699; fax: (707)644-2680. *Type:* Periodical.

The Salt Lake Tribune

Dominic Welch
400 Tribune Bldg.   Ph: (801)237-2031
Salt Lake City, UT 84111   Fax: (801)237-2022
URL: http://www.sltrib.com.
Contact: James E. Shelledy, Editor, (801)237-2011, editor@sltrib.com; David Ledford, Deputy Editor, (801)237-2011, ledford@sltrib.com; Tom McCarthey, Deputy Editor, (801)237-2011, tcm@sltrib.com; Judy Rollins, Deputy Editor, (801)237-2075, rollins@sltrib.com; Terri Ellefsen, News Editor, terrie@sltrib.com; Shia Kapos, News Editor, skapos@sltrib.com; Tim Fitzpatrick, Exec. VP/News Editor, fitz@sltrib.com; Dawn House, News Editor, dawn@sltrib.com; Peg McEntee, N
Desc: General newspaper. *Alt. Contact:* The Salt Lake Tribune 143 S. Main St., Salt Lake City, UT 84111; telephone: (801)237-2045; fax: (801)521-9418. *Type:* Periodical.

The Salt Lake Tribune

The Salt Lake Tribune
143 S. Main St.   Ph: (801)237-2083
P.O. Box 867
Salt Lake City, UT 84110
URL: http://www.sltrib.com
Desc: Contains the complete text of The Salt Lake Tribune (Utah), a general circulation newspaper reporting local, national, and International news. Covers all news stories, features, editorials, arts, and sports. *Available:* Bell & Howell Information and Learning; The Dialog Corporation, DIALOG. *Type:* Database.

The San Bernardino County Sun

The San Bernardino County Sun
399 N. D St.   Ph: (714)889-9666
San Bernardino, CA 92401-1518   Fax: (714)381-3976
E-mail: sbsun@earthlink.net.
Contact: O. Ricardo Pimentel, Exec. Editor, fax: (919)885-8741; Mark Adkins, Publisher; Jeannine Duvall, Advertising Dir., (909)386-3045.
Desc: General newspaper. *Type:* Periodical.

San Diego Reader

San Diego Reader
1703 India   Ph: (619)235-3000
San Diego, CA 92101   Fax: (619)231-0489
E-mail: hrosen@spreader.com.
URL: http://www.sdreader.com.
Contact: Jim Holman, Editor and Publisher; Janis Walsh, Advertising Mgr.
Desc: Newspaper covering San Diego lifestyle emphasizing the arts, entertainment, and politics. Features comprehensive listings of movies, events, theater, and pop music; restaurant and film reviews; and free classified advertisements for its readers. *Alt. Contact:* P.O. Box 85803, San Diego, CA 92186; telephone: (619)235-3000; fax: (619)231-0489. *Type:* Periodical.

The San Diego Union-Tribune

Union-Tribune Publishing Co.
PO Box 191   Ph: (619)299-3131
San Diego, CA 92112-4106   Free: 800-244-6397
    Fax: (619)293-2064
URL: http://www.uniontrib.com.
Contact: Helen K. Copley, Publisher, (619)293-1106; Gene Bell, Pres./CEO, (293)-1101; Mack Quintana, Sales & Mrkt. Director, (293)-1500; Dexter La Pierre, Display Advertising Dir., (293)-1421; Rick Ott, Marketing Dir., (293)-1580; Karin Winner, Editor, (293)-1201; Neil Morgan, Assoc. Editor/Sr. Columnist, (293)-1301; Bill Gaspard, Sr. Editor/Visuals, (293)-1274; Doug Hope, Sr. Editor/Administration, (293)-1216; Todd Merriman, Sr. Editor/News, (293)-1049; Gina Lubrano, Readers Rep.
Desc: International, national, and local news. *Alt. Contact:* 350 Camino de la Renta, San Diego, CA 92108 3092; telephone: (619)293-1211; fax: (619)293-1440. *Type:* Periodical.

The San Diego Union-Tribune

Union-Tribune Publishing Company
PO Box 191   Ph: (619)299-3131
San Diego, CA 92112-4106
URL: http://www.uniontrib.com
Desc: Contains the complete text of news items and feature articles from The San Diego Union-Tribune newspaper reporting local, state (California), national, and international news. *Available:* Bell & Howell Information and Learning; Dow Jones Interactive Publishing; Union-Tribune Publishing Company. *Type:* Database.

The San Francisco Bay Guardian

The San Francisco Bay Guardian
520 Hampshire St.   Ph: (415)255-3100
San Francisco, CA 94110   Fax: (415)255-8955
URL: http://www.spbg.com.
Contact: Bruce B. Brugmann, Editor and Publisher.
Desc: Alternative Newsweekly. *Type:* Periodical.

San Francisco Chronicle

Chronicle Publishing Co.
901 Mission St.   Ph: (415)777-1111
San Francisco, CA 94103   Fax: (415)896-1107
Contact: Michael Bauer, Food Editor; John Carman, Television.
Desc: General newspaper. *Type:* Periodical.

San Francisco Chronicle

San Francisco Chronicle Newspaper
901 Mission St.   Ph: (415)777-8482
San Francisco, CA 94103
URL: http://www.sfgate.com
Contact: Richard Geiger, Library Director, geigerr@sfgate.com.
Desc: Contains the complete text of news items, feature articles, columns, editorials, and letters from the San Francisco Chronicle (California) newspaper. Regional coverage emphasizes Pacific Rim trade, as well as San Francisco Bay area and Silicon Valley industries, including biotechnology, computers, robotics, and semiconductors. *Available:* Bell & Howell Information and Learning; The Dialog Corporation, DIALOG; The Dialog Corporation, DIALOG; CompuServe Information Service, Knowledge Index; LEXIS-NEXIS, NEXIS; NewsBank, Inc., CD News. *Type:* Database.

The San Francisco Examiner

The San Francisco Examiner
925 Mission St.   Ph: (415)777-5700
San Francisco, CA 94103
URL: http://www.sfgate.com
Contact: Judy Canter, (415)777-7845, fax: (415)512-9486.
Desc: Contains the complete text of news and feature articles from the San Francisco Examiner (California) newspaper. Regional coverage emphasizes northern California business news, politics, environmental action, the Silicon Valley, Pacific Rim news, the wine industry, earthquakes, AIDS news, and northern California university research. *Available:* The Dialog Corporation, DIALOG; The Dialog Corporation, DIALOG; Bell & Howell Information and Learning; LEXIS-NEXIS, NEXIS. *Type:* Database.

San Francisco Examiner

San Francisco Examiner
110 5th St.   Ph: (415)777-2424
San Francisco, CA 94103-2918
URL: http://www.sfgate.com.
Contact: William R. Hearst, III, Publisher; Frank Flood, Advertising Mgr.
Desc: General newspaper. *Type:* Periodical.

San Francisco Independent

San Francisco Independent
1201 Evans Ave.   Ph: (415)826-1100
San Francisco, CA 94124   Fax: (415)826-5371
Contact: Zoran Basich, Managing Editor; Wayne Wedgeworth, Advertising Dir.; Tom Trent, Natl. Ad. Mgr.
Desc: Community newspaper. *Type:* Periodical.

San Francisco Magazine

San Francisco Magazine
243 Vallejo St.   Ph: (415)398-2800
San Francisco, CA 94111   Fax: (415)398-6777
URL: http://www.sanfran.com.
Contact: Dale Eastman, Editor-in-Chief; Barney Fonzi, VP/Advertising Dir.; Steven Rivera, Publisher.
Desc: Regional interest magazine covering personalities, places, and events in the San Francisco Bay area. *Type:* Periodical.

San Jose Mercury News

Knight-Ridder, Inc.
50 W. Fernando St.   Ph: (408)938-7700
San Jose, CA 95113
Contact: Robert Ingle, Editor; Larry Jinks, Publisher.
Desc: General newspaper. *Alt. Contact:* 750 Ridder Park Dr., San Jose, CA 95190-0001; telephone: (408)920-5000; fax: (408)288-8060. *Type:* Periodical.

San Jose Mercury News

San Jose Mercury News
750 Ridder Park Dr.   Ph: (408)920-5000
San Jose, CA 95190
E-mail: blaing@sjmercury.com
URL: http://www.sjmercury.com/help/mcstaff.htm
Desc: Contains the complete text of the San Jose Mercury News (California), a general circulation newspaper reporting local, national, and international news. Special areas of interest include developments of high-tech industries located in California's Silicon Valley, business and economic developments that link the countries around the Pacific Basin, commercial and residential real estate in the San Jose area, and scientific studies and medical breakthroughs from Stanford University Medical School and Stanford Research Institute. *Available:* The Dialog Corporation, DIALOG; CompuServe Information Service, Knowledge Index. *Type:* Database.

Savannah Morning News

Savannah Morning News
PO Box 1088   Ph: (912)236-9511
Savannah, GA 31402-1088   Free: 800-533-1150
                                   Fax: (912)234-6522
E-mail: letted@savannahnow.com.
URL: http://www.savannahnow.com.
Contact: Frank Anderson, Publisher, (912)652-0265; Tom Barton, Editor, (912)652-0300, fax: (912)234-6522; Donald Bailey, Advertising Dir., (912)652-0238, fax: (912)652-0260.
Desc: General newspaper. *Type:* Periodical.

The Scarborough Mirror

Metroland
10 Tempo Ave.   Ph: (416)493-4400
Willowdale, ON, Canada M2H   Fax: (416)493-4703
   2N8
E-mail: scm@metrodiv.com.
Contact: David Fuller, Editor, (418)493-6190; Betty Carr, Publisher; Eugene Dupuis, Advertising Mgr.
Desc: Community newspaper. *Type:* Periodical.

Schlein News Bureau

308 E. Capitol St. NE   Ph: (202)544-5893
Ste. 9
Washington, DC 20003
Alt. Contact: 308 E. Capitol St. NE, Ste. 9, Washington, DC 20003; telephone: (202)544-5893. *Type:* Periodical.

Schmidt Services Inc.

720 Creek Rd.   Ph: (716)591-3010
Attica, NY 14011
Contact: Stephen P. Schmidt, President.

Alt. Contact: 720 Creek Rd., Attica, NY 14011; telephone: (716)591-3010. *Type:* Periodical.

Science Features Service

8758 Sophia Ave.   Ph: (818)892-9433
North Hills, CA 91343
Contact: Chuck Gordon, Managing Editor; Steve Russell, Editor.
Desc: Distributes science and technology features. *Alt. Contact:* 8758 Sophia Ave., North Hills, CA 91343; telephone: (818)892-9433. *Type:* Periodical.

The Scranton Times

The Scranton Times
149 Penn Ave.   Ph: (717)348-9100
PO Box 3311   Fax: (717)348-9135
Scranton, PA 18505-3311
Contact: Edward Lynett, Editor and Publisher; William Lynett, Publisher; George Lynett, Publisher; Harold F. Marion, Jr., General Mgr.; Robert L. Burke, Managing Editor.
Desc: General newspaper. *Type:* Periodical.

Scripps League Newspaper

PO Box 1109   Ph: (703)713-1920
Herndon, VA 22070
Desc: Distributes information including space, defense, forest, national parks, and education news. *Alt. Contact:* PO Box 1109, Herndon, VA 22070; telephone: (703)713-1920. *Type:* Periodical.

Scripps-McClatchy Western Service

1090 Vermont Ave. NW   Ph: (202)408-2730
Ste. 1000
Washington, DC 20005
URL: http://www.shns.com.
Contact: Dan Thomasson, Ed./Bureau Chief; Marvin West, Managing Editor; Sid Goldberg, Ed. Dev.; Irwin Breslauer, Gen. Exec.
Desc: Distributes general news. *Alt. Contact:* 1090 Vermont Ave. NW, Ste. 1000, Washington, DC 20005; telephone: (202)408-2730. *Type:* Periodical.

Seattle Post-Intelligencer

Seattle Post Intelligencer
101 Elliott Ave. W.   Ph: (206)448-8000
Seattle, WA 98119-4220   Fax: (206)448-8166
E-mail: editor@seattle-pi.com.
URL: http://www.seattle-pi.com.
Contact: J.D. Alexander, Editor and Publisher, (206)448-8308, jdalexander@seattle-pi.com; Kenneth Bunting, Managing Editor, (206)448-8210, kenbunting@seattle-pi.com; Kathy Best, Metro Editor, (206)448-8031, kathybest@seattle-pi.com; Robert Schenet, National and Foreign Editor, (206)448-8037, robertschenet@seattlepi.com.
Desc: General newspaper. Combined Sunday edition with the Seattle Times as the Times/ Post-Intelligencer. *Type:* Periodical.

Seattle Times

Knight-Ridder, Inc.
50 W. Fernando St.   Ph: (408)938-7700
San Jose, CA 95113
URL: http://www.scattletimes.com.
Contact: Michael R. Fancher, Editor, (206)464-2330, mfancher@seattletimes.com; F.A. Blethen, Publisher, (206)464-8502; Roy G. Schaefer, Advertising Mgr., (206)464-2558, rschaefer@seattletimes.com.
Desc: General newspaper. Combined Sunday edition with the Seattle Post-Intelligencer as the Times/Post-Intelligencer. *Alt. Contact:* Fairview Ave. N. & John, PO Box 70, Seattle, WA 98111-0070; telephone: (206)464-2132; fax: (206)382-6760. *Type:* Periodical.

The Seattle Times

The Seattle Times
P.O. Box 70   Ph: (206)464-2310
Seattle, WA 98111
URL: http://www.seattletimes.com
Contact: Barbara Davis, News Library Database Coordinator.
Desc: Contains the complete text of news items and feature articles from The Seattle Times (Washington) newspaper. Regional coverage emphasizes the aerospace, high technology and biotechnology, and retail industries, as well as Pacific Rim business, trade, and cultural issues. *Available:* Bell & Howell Information and Learning; The Dialog Corporation, DIALOG; LEXIS-NEXIS, NEXIS; CompuServe Information Service, Knowledge Index. *Type:* Database.

Second Ring Syndicate

1515 Dobson St.   Ph: (847)475-0457
PO Box 22
Evanston, IL 60204-0022
E-mail: jpera@sungard.com.
Contact: Jim Pera, Artist/Owner.
Desc: Distributes comic strips, comic panels, and fine art illustrations. *Alt. Contact:* 1515 Dobson St., PO Box 22, Evanston, IL 60204-0022; telephone: (847)475-0457. *Type:* Periodical.

Shawnee-Merriam Sun

Sun Publications, Inc.
7373 W. 107th St.   Ph: (913)648-4620
Overland Park, KS 66212-2547   Fax: (913)381-1402
Contact: Jack Lovelace, Editor; Jo Stapleton, Advertising Manager; Steve Rose, Publisher.
Desc: Newspaper. *Type:* Periodical.

SIPA News Service

59 E. 54th St.   Ph: (212)759-5571
New York, NY 10022   Fax: (212)593-5194
Contact: Henry O. Dormann, Chm./Ed.; Darrell Brown, Pres./Exec. Ed.
Desc: Distributes photographs. *Alt. Contact:* 59 E. 54th St., New York, NY 10022; telephone: (212)759-5571; fax: (212)593-5194. *Type:* Periodical.

Skintalk

32905 W. 12 Mile Rd.   Ph: (248)553-2900
Ste. 330
Farmington Hills, MI 48334
Contact: Jon H. Blum, M.D., President.
Desc: Distributes dermatology information. *Alt. Contact:* 32905 W. 12 Mile Rd., Ste. 330, Farmington Hills, MI 48334; telephone: (248)553-2900. *Type:* Periodical.

Skoglund Features

HC 35 Box 249   Ph: (207)372-8052
St. George, ME 04857   Fax: (207)372-8052
E-mail: humblefarmer@midcoast.com.
URL: http://www.midcoast.com/ ~humblfmr.
Contact: Robert Skoglund, Columnist.
Alt. Contact: HC 35 Box 249, St. George, ME 04857; telephone: (207)372-8052; fax: (207)372-8052. *Type:* Periodical.

Slightly Off

1168 Sagebrush Trail   Ph: (847)639-1232
Cary, IL 60013   Fax: (847)639-1232
E-mail: sltlyoff@mc.net.
URL: http://www.mc.net/slightlyoff.
Contact: Deb DiSandro, Author/Owner.
Desc: Distributes family humor columns. *Alt. Contact:* 1168 Sagebrush Trail, Cary, IL 60013; telephone: (847)639-1232; fax: (847)639-1232. *Type:* Periodical.

Small Newspapers Group Inc.

1183 National Press Bldg.   Ph: (202)662-7240
Washington, DC 20045

Desc: Distributes news. *Alt. Contact:* 1183 National Press Bldg., Washington, DC 20045; telephone: (202)662-7240. *Type:* Periodical.

Society for Collegiate Journalists

School of Journalism
1000 Regent University Dr.
Virginia Beach, VA 23464-5041

Contact: Dr. J. Douglas Tarpley, Exec.Dir.

Desc: Recognition society - men and women, collegiate print and broadcast journalism. Evaluates college and university broadcast, film, and print journalism programs; sponsors research programs. Conducts national contests among members. *Type:* Association.

Society of Professional Journalists

16 S. Jackson   Ph: (765)653-3333
Greencastle, IN 46135   Fax: (765)653-4631
E-mail: spj@spjhq.org
URL: http://www.spj.org

Contact: Gregory A. Christopher, Exec.Dir.

Desc: Professional society - journalism. Promotes a free and unfettered press; high professional standards and ethical behavior; journalism as a career. *Type:* Association.

The Something Better News

Something Better Publications, Inc.
3300 28th St. SW   Ph: (616)530-3957
Grandville, MI 49418   Fax: (616)530-0728
URL: http://www.somebetnews.com.

Contact: Jerry Fennell, President and Editor.

Desc: Christian community newspaper. *Type:* Periodical.

South Bay's Shopping Newspaper

Excel Promotions Corp.
150 W. Hoffman Ave.   Ph: (516)226-2636
Lindenhurst, NY 11757

Contact: Richard Freedman, Publisher.

Desc: Community newspaper. *Type:* Periodical.

South Bend Tribune

Schurz Communications Inc./South Bend Tribune
225 W. Colfax Ave.   Ph: (219)235-6474
South Bend, IN 46626   Fax: (219)239-2646

Contact: John J. McGann, Editor and Publisher.

Desc: General newspaper. *Type:* Periodical.

Southam News

Infomart Dialog Limited
1450 Don Mills Rd.   Ph: (416)442-2198
Don Mills, ON, Canada M3B
    2X7
E-mail: helpdesk@infomart.ca
URL: http://www.infomart.com/

Contact: Client Service Consultants, (416)442-2198, fax: (416)442-2126, helpdesk@infomart.ca.

Desc: Contains the complete text of news items from the Southam News newswire service. Covers general interest, business, sports, science and medicine, lifestyles, and fashion news. *Available:* Infomart Online; Infomart Assistant, Infomart Online; Infomart Dialog Limited. *Type:* Database.

Southam Syndicate

151 Sparks St.   Ph: (613)236-0491
Ste. 200   Fax: (613)236-1788
Ottawa, ON, Canada K1P 5E3

Contact: Ros Guggi, Manager, rguggi@southam.ca; Dan Smythe, Ed. Coord.; Allison McLean, Business Mgr.

Desc: Distributes features and wire stories for seven of Canada's major newspapers including the Calgary Herald, Edmonton Journal, Montreal Gazette, Ottawa Citizen, Vancouver Province, and the Vancouver Sun. *Alt. Contact:* 151 Sparks St., Ste. 200, Ottawa, ON, Canada K1P 5E3; telephone: (613)236-0491; fax: (613)236-1788. *Type:* Periodical.

Specialty Features Syndicate

17255 Redford Ave.   Ph: (313)533-1846
Detroit, MI 48219

Contact: Lewis Kaye, President; Verdice Kordel, Food Ed.; L.E. Crandall, Manager.

Desc: Distributes literary condensations, health, and nutrition columns. *Alt. Contact:* 17255 Redford Ave., Detroit, MI 48219; telephone: (313)533-1846. *Type:* Periodical.

The Spectator

Southam, Inc.
44 Frid St.   Ph: (905)526-3333
PO Box 300   Fax: (905)522-1696
Hamilton, ON, Canada L8N
    3G3
URL: http://www.hamiltonspectator.com.

Contact: Ron Austin, Editor; Gordon Bullock, Publisher; David Copeland, Advertising Mgr.; Doug Foley, Editor, (416)526-3242.

Desc: Newspaper. *Alt. Contact:* 44 Frid St., PO Box 300, Hamilton, ON, Canada L8N 3G3; telephone: (905)526-3333; fax: (905)526-1054. *Type:* Periodical.

The Spectator

Southam, Inc.
44 Frid St.   Ph: (905)526-3333
PO Box 300
Hamilton, ON, Canada L8N
    3G3
URL: http://www.hamiltonspectator.com

Contact: John E. Lawrence, Chief Librarian, (905)526-3209.

Desc: Contains the complete text of The Spectator, a general circulation newspaper covering local and national news. *Available:* Infomart Online; Infomart Assistant, Infomart Online; Infomart Dialog Limited. *Type:* Database.

Spectrum Features

400 E. 2nd St.   Ph: (717)389-4825
BCH 106   Fax: (717)389-2094
Bloomsburg, PA 17815
E-mail: brasch@planetx.bloomu.edu.
URL: http://hubble.bloomu.edu/~spectrum.

Contact: Jen Boscia, Exec. Ed.; John Michaels, Associate Ed.; Angela Elliott, Business Mgr.; Mark Steinruck, Prod. Dir.

Desc: Distributes humor, political, and regional features. *Alt. Contact:* 400 E. 2nd St., BCH 106, Bloomsburg, PA 17815; telephone: (717)389-4825; fax: (717)389-2094. *Type:* Periodical.

SPLC Report

Student Press Law Center
1101 Wilson Blvd., Ste. 1910   Ph: (703)807-1904
Arlington, VA 22209   Fax: (703)807-2109
E-mail: splc@splc.org

Desc: Summarizes current controversies involving student press rights. Discusses publication advisors, libel, advertising and economics, and publications in colleges and high schools. *Type:* Newsletter.

The Spokesman-Review

Cowles Publishing Co.
999 W. Riverside Ave.   Ph: (509)459-5000
PO Box 2160
Spokane, WA 99210
URL: http://www.spokane.net.

Contact: Christopher Peck, Editor; W.H. Cowles, III, Publisher; Shaun O'L. Higgins, Advertising Mgr.; W. Duane Harter, Editor.

Desc: General newspaper. *Type:* Periodical.

The Spotlight

Liberty Lobby
300 Independence Ave. SE   Ph: (202)544-1794
Washington, DC 20003
E-mail: libertylob@aol.com
URL: http://www.spotlight.org.

Contact: Frederick V. Blahut, Managing Editor; Andrew Arnold, Editor.

Desc: Newspaper covering public affairs. *Type:* Periodical.

Stadium Circle Features

335 Court St.   Ph: (718)797-0210
Ste. 85   Fax: (718)797-0210
Brooklyn, NY 11231-4335
E-mail: newyorkbob@aol.com.

Contact: Robert S. Anthony, Ed./Columnist.

Desc: Distributes weekly personal computer column. *Alt. Contact:* 335 Court St., Ste. 85, Brooklyn, NY 11231-4335; telephone: (718)797-0210; fax: (718)797-0210. *Type:* Periodical.

Stampede Features

114 E. Bridge St.   Ph: (307)326-9852
PO Box 1647   Fax: (307)326-5709
Saratoga, WY 82331

Contact: Ann Palen, Office Mgr.; Jerry Palen, President. *Alt. Contact:* 114 E. Bridge St., PO Box 1647, Saratoga, WY 82331; telephone: (307)326-9852; fax: (307)326-5709. *Type:* Periodical.

Star

Star Editorial, Inc.
660 White Plains Rd.   Ph: (914)332-5000
Tarrytown, NY 10591-5182   Fax: (914)332-5044

Contact: Phil Bunton, Editor-in-Chief; Stephen LeGrice, Exec. Editor; Alistar Duncan, Photo Dir.; Dick Belsky, News Editor; Rob DeMarco, Photo Editor; Peter Burt, National Editor; Reed Sparling, Books Editor; Marion Collins, Deputy News Editor; Lisa Arcella, Assoc. News Editor; Carolyn Callahan, Asst. News Editor; Steve Herz, Articles Editor; Steve Tinney, L.A. Bureau Chief; Richard Gooding, Sr. Editor; Bob Smith, Sr. Editor; Roger Hitts, Sr. Reporter; Ira Berger, Deputy Photo Editor

Desc: Magazine with creatively embellished news and entertainment features. *Type:* Periodical.

Star-Ledger

Newark Morning Ledger Co.
Star-Ledger Plaza   Ph: (201)877-4141
Newark, NJ 07101   Fax: (201)877-5845

Contact: Jim Willse, Editor; Rick Everett, Advertising Mgr.; Martin Bartner, Publisher; Jack Elliott, Editorial Editor, (201)877-4040; Roger Harris, Theatre Editor, (201)877-4134; Neal Cocchia, Editor, (201)877-4169; Robert Braun, Education Editor, (201)877-4005; David Allen, Financial Editor, (201)877-4281; Arthur Lenehan, Picture Editor, (201)877-4229; David Wald, Politics Editor, (201)877-4040; Monica Maske, Religion Editor, (201)877-4167; Tony Verga, Sunday Editor, (201)877-4167;

Desc: General newspaper. *Type:* Periodical.

Star-Ledger (Newark, New Jersey)

Newark Morning Ledger Co.
Star-Ledger Plaza   Ph: (973)877-4141
Newark, NJ 07102
URL: http://www.nnj.com

Desc: Contains the complete text of news items and feature articles from The Star-Ledger (Newark, New Jersey) newspaper. Special areas of interest include business and industry; research and development companies (Bell Laboratories and RCA Research); pharmaceutical companies (Johnson & Johnson, Hoffman LaRoche, Merck, Sandoz, Ciba Geigy, and Squibb); insurance companies (Prudential Insurance); banking; and transportation (both air and cargo shipping). *Available:* Bell & Howell Information and Learning. *Type:* Database.

Star Tribune

Star Tribune
425 Portland Ave. S.   Ph: (612)673-4000
Minneapolis, MN 55488   Fax: (612)673-7138
URL: http://www.startribune.com.

Contact: Tim J. McGuire, Exec. Editor; Joel Kramer, Publisher.

Desc: General newspaper. *Type:* Periodical.

Star Tribune (Minneapolis, Minnesota)

The McClatchy Company
425 Portland Ave.   Ph: (612)673-7398
Minneapolis, MN 55488

Desc: Contains the complete text of the Star Tribune, a general circulation newspaper reporting local Minneapolis and St. Paul (Minnesota), national, and international news. *Available:* The Dialog Corporation, DIALOG. *Type:* Database.

The State

Knight-Ridder, Inc.
50 W. Fernando St.   Ph: (408)938-7700
San Jose, CA 95113
E-mail: state@cyberstate.infi.net.
URL: http://www.thestate.com.

Contact: Fred Mott, President & Publisher, (803)771-8324, fax: (803)771-8446; Brad Warthen, Editorial Page Editor, (803)771-8468, fax: (803)771-8639, edcyber@cyberstate.infi.net; Mark Lett, Vice President & Executive Editor, (803)771-8451, mlett@thestate.infi.net; Glen Nardi, Vice President Operations, (803)771-8639, fax: (803)771-8446; Carol Hanner, Managing Editor, (803)771-8508, fax: (803)771-8430, channer@thestate.infi.net; Holly Rogers, Human Resources Director, (803)77

Desc: General newspaper. *Alt. Contact:* 1401 Shop Road, PO Box 1333, Columbia, SC 29202; telephone: (803)771-6161, (803)771-8415; fax: (803)771-8430. *Type:* Periodical.

The State (Columbia, South Carolina)

The State-Record Co., Inc.
P.O. Box 1333   Ph: (803)771-6161
Columbia, SC 29202
E-mail: lhemphill@thestate.com
URL: http://www.thestate.com

Contact: Dargan Richards, Librarian, (803)771-8493, fax: (803)771-8430, drichards@thestate.com.

Desc: Contains the complete text of The State, a general circulation newspaper reporting local, national, and international news. Special areas of interest include South Carolina government, business, and industry. *Available:* The Dialog Corporation, DIALOG. *Type:* Database.

Staten Island Advance

Advance Publications, Inc.
950 Fingerboard Rd.   Ph: (718)981-1234
Staten Island, NY 10305   Fax: (718)982-5789
Contact: Brian Laline, Editor; Richard Diamond, Publisher; Mark Hanley, Editorial Page Editor.

Desc: General newspaper. *Alt. Contact:* 950 Fingerboard Rd., Staten Island, NY 10305. *Type:* Periodical.

States News Service

NY Times Subscriber Service   Ph: (202)628-3100
1333 F St. NW
Ste. 400
Washington, DC 20004
Contact: Leland Schwartz, Editor.

Desc: Distributes general news. *Alt. Contact:* NY Times Subscriber Service, 1333 F St. NW, Ste. 400, Washington, DC 20004; telephone: (202)628-3100. *Type:* Periodical.

The Suburban

Michael Publishing Inc.
8170 Wavell Rd.   Ph: (514)484-1107
Cote St.-Luc, PQ, Canada H4W   Fax: (514)484-9616
   1M3
Contact: Gilnes Morin, Editor.

Desc: Community newspaper (tabloid). *Type:* Periodical.

Sun Features Inc.

45 Kennedy Pkwy.   Ph: (619)431-1660
PO Box 45   Fax: (619)431-1669
Cardiff, CA 92007
Contact: Joyce Lain Kennedy, President, jlk@sunfeatures.com; Tim K. Horrell, Vice President.

Alt. Contact: 45 Kennedy Pkwy., PO Box 45, Cardiff, CA 92007; telephone: (619)431-1660; fax: (619)431-1669. *Type:* Periodical.

Sun Newspaper

Sun Publications, Inc.
7373 W. 107th St.   Ph: (913)648-4620
Overland Park, KS 66212-2547   Fax: (913)381-1402
Contact: Jack Lovelace, Editor; Stan Rose, Publisher; Shirley Rose, Publisher; Steve Rose, Publisher; Mike Lomario, Editor.

Desc: Newspaper. *Type:* Periodical.

Sun-Sentinel

Sun-Sentinel Co.
200 E. Las Olas Blvd.   Ph: (954)356-4000
Fort Lauderdale, FL 33301-2293   Fax: (954)356-4559
URL: http://www.sunsentinel.com;   http://www.sun-sentinel.com.
Contact: Earl Maucker, Editor, (954)356-4600; Ellen Soeteber, Managing Editor, (954)356-4602.

Desc: Newspaper. *Alt. Contact:* telephone: (954)356-4500; fax: (954)356-4559. *Type:* Periodical.

Sun-Sentinel of Fort Lauderdale

Sun-Sentinel Co.
200 E. Las Olas   Ph: (954)356-4741
Fort Lauderdale, FL 33301-2293
E-mail: bhikek@tribune.co
Contact: Dean Perry, (954)356-4752, fax: (954)356-4748, perry@sunsent.com.

Desc: Contains the complete text of news items and feature articles from Sun-Sentinel (Florida) newspaper. Regional coverage emphasizes politics and government and the construction, health, leisure and recreation, and tourism industries. *Available:* The Dialog Corporation, DIALOG; CompuServe Information Service, Knowledge Index; Bell & Howell Information and Learning; LEXIS-NEXIS; Dow Jones Interactive Publishing; America Online, Inc. *Type:* Database.

Sunday Gazette-Mail

Charleston Newspapers
1001 Virginia St. E.   Ph: (304)348-5140
Charleston, WV 25301
Contact: Robert L. Smith, Publisher; Terry L. Horne, Publisher; William Birt, Editor.

Desc: Newspaper. *Type:* Periodical.

Sunshine Press Services

325 Pennsylvania Ave. SE   Ph: (202)544-3647
Washington, DC 20003   Fax: (202)544-4887
Contact: Edward Roeder, Editor.

Alt. Contact: 325 Pennsylvania Ave. SE, Washington, DC 20003; telephone: (202)544-3647; fax: (202)544-4887. *Type:* Periodical.

The Surrey/North Delta Leader

The Surrey Leader
PO Box 276
Surrey, BC, Canada V3T 4W8
Contact: Frank Bucholtz, Editor; Andrew Holota, Advertising Mgr.; Duane Geddes, Regional Vice Pres.; Ed Galenzoski, Advertising Mgr.

Desc: Community newspaper. *Type:* Periodical.

Sylvia Syndicate

1440 N. Dayton   Ph: (312)943-4862
Chicago, IL 60622
Contact: Nicole Hollander, President.

Desc: Distributes Sylvia cartoon strip. *Alt. Contact:* 1440 N. Dayton, Chicago, IL 60622; telephone: (312)943-4862. *Type:* Periodical.

Syndication Associates Inc.

2502 E. 71st   Ph: (918)481-6050
Ste. A   Fax: (918)481-6380
Tulsa, OK 74136
Contact: Ann M. Wyland, Mktg.

Alt. Contact: 2502 E. 71st, Ste. A, Tulsa, OK 74136; telephone: (918)481-6050; fax: (918)481-6380. *Type:* Periodical.

Taipei Economic & Cultural Office Information Div.

1230 Avenue of the Americas   Ph: (212)373-1800
2nd Fl.   Fax: (212)373-1866
New York, NY 10020-1513
Contact: Ben Shao, Senior Info. Officer.

Alt. Contact: 1230 Avenue of the Americas, 2nd Fl., New York, NY 10020-1513; telephone: (212)373-1800; fax: (212)373-1866. *Type:* Periodical.

The Tampa Tribune

Tampa Tribune
202 S. Parker St.   Ph: (813)259-7711
PO Box 191   Free: 800-382-5588
Tampa, FL 33606-2395   Fax: (813)259-7676
URL: http://www.tampatrib.com.
Contact: Jack Butcher, Publisher.

Desc: General newspaper. *Type:* Periodical.

Tass News Agency

50 Rockefeller Plaza   Ph: (212)245-4250
Ste. 501
New York, NY 10020
Contact: Alex Berezhkov, Bureau Chief.

Desc: Distributes general news. *Alt. Contact:* 50 Rockefeller Plaza, Ste. 501, New York, NY 10020; telephone: (212)245-4250. *Type:* Periodical.

Telegram & Gazette

Telegram & Gazette
20 Franklin St.   Ph: (508)793-9100
PO Box 15012   Fax: (508)793-9281
Worcester, MA 01615-0012
E-mail: info@telegram.com
URL: http://www.telegram.com.

Contact: Bruce S. Bennett, President and Publisher; Robert Z. Nemeth, Editorial Page Editor; Harry T. Whitin, Editor; Thomas F.X. Cole, Marketing Services Director; Robert N. Recore, Advertising Dir.; Nancy Cahalen-Bayley, Asst. Advertising Sales Dir.; Anthony J. Simollardes, Advertising Operations Mgr.; Maurice J. Guarini, National Advertising Mgr.; Edward J. Bauer, Classified Display Mgr.; Ron Wolfram, Zone Sales Division Mgr.; Barry R. LaRoche, Circulation Mgr.; Peter H. Horstmann

Desc: General newspaper. *Type:* Periodical.

The Tennessean

Gannett Co., Inc.
1100 Wilson Blvd.   Ph: (703)284-6000
Arlington, VA 22234   Free: 800-872-0001

Contact: Craig Moon, Publisher, (615)259-8303, fax: (615)259-8875, cmoon@tennessean.com; Frank Sutherland, Editor, (615)259-8003, fax: (615)259-8093; David Green, Mng. Ed., Days, (615)726-5989, fax: (615)259-8093, dgreen@tennessean.com; Cindy Smith, Mng. Ed., Nights, (615)259-5989, fax: (615)259-8093, csmith@tennessean.com; Sandra Roberts, Mng. Ed., Opinion, (615)259-8095, fax: (615)726-8928, sroberts@tennessean.com; D'Anna Sharon, Art Dir., (615)726-8911, fax: (615)259-8

Desc: Newspaper. *Alt. Contact:* 1100 Broadway St., Nashville, TN 37203; telephone: (615)259-8000; fax: (615)259-8093. *Type:* Periodical.

Texas Monthly

Texas Monthly
PO Box 1569   Ph: (512)320-6900
Austin, TX 78767   Fax: (512)476-9007
URL: http://www.texasmonthly.com.

Contact: Gregory Curtis, Editor; Michael R. Levy, Publisher; Jalaene A. Levi-Garza, Sr. VP/Advertising Dir., advertising@texasmonthly.com.

Desc: Magazine covering Texas politics, sports, business, culture, and changing lifestyles. *Type:* Periodical.

Thomson News Service

1331 Pennsylvania Ave. NW   Ph: (202)628-2157
Ste. 524   Fax: (202)347-5017
Washington, DC 20004

Contact: William Sternberg, Bureau Chief; Randy Wynn, News Ed.; Bob Mitchell, News Exchange Ed.

Desc: Distributes political and national news. *Alt. Contact:* 1331 Pennsylvania Ave. NW, Ste. 524, Washington, DC 20004; telephone: (202)628-2157; fax: (202)347-5017. *Type:* Periodical.

Time

Time Inc.
Time-Life Bldg., Rockefeller   Ph: (212)522-1212
    Center   Fax: (212)522-0315
1271 Avenue of the Americas
New York, NY 10020

Contact: E. Bruce Hallett, President; Norman Pearlstine, Editor-in-Chief; Walter Isaacson, Managing Editor.

Desc: Current news magazine. *Type:* Periodical.

Time (Asia)

Time Inc.
Time-Life Bldg., Rockefeller   Ph: (212)522-1212
    Center   Fax: (212)522-0315
1271 Avenue of the Americas
New York, NY 10020

Contact: Henry Muller, Editor; Robert L. Miller, Publisher.

Desc: Current news magazine. *Type:* Periodical.

Time (Atlantic)

Time Inc.
Time-Life Bldg., Rockefeller   Ph: (212)522-1212
    Center   Fax: (212)522-0315
1271 Avenue of the Americas
New York, NY 10020

Contact: Henry Muller, Editor; Robert L. Miller, Publisher.

Desc: Current news magazine. *Type:* Periodical.

Time (Canada)

Time Inc.
Time-Life Bldg., Rockefeller   Ph: (212)522-1212
    Center   Fax: (212)522-0315
1271 Avenue of the Americas
New York, NY 10020
URL: http://www.time.com.

Contact: Walter Isaacson, Managing Editor; Don F. Brown, President; Norman Pearlstine, Editor-in-Chief.

Desc: Current news magazine. *Type:* Periodical.

Time Data Syndicate

PO Box 717   Free: 800-322-5101
Manchester, NH 03105-0717

Contact: Larry White, Director; Marcia White, Treas.

Desc: Distributes astrology features. *Alt. Contact:* PO Box 717, Manchester, NH 03105-0717; toll-free: 800-322-5101. *Type:* Periodical.

Time (Latin America)

Time Inc.
Time-Life Bldg., Rockefeller   Ph: (212)522-1212
    Center   Fax: (212)522-0315
1271 Avenue of the Americas
New York, NY 10020

Contact: Hugh Wiley, Vice President.

Desc: Current news magazine. *Type:* Periodical.

Times

Times of Trenton Publishing Corp.
500 Perry St.   Ph: (609)989-5454
Trenton, NJ 08605   Free: 800-753-3088
                        Fax: (609)396-3633
E-mail: 76666.1313@compuserve.comp.

Contact: Brian S. Malone, Editor; Richard Bilotti, Publisher; Lynn Orr, Advertising Mgr.; Martin Griff, Photo editor, (609)396-3232; Jim Gauger, Sports editor, (609)396-3232.

Desc: General newspaper. *Type:* Periodical.

The Times

The Times
222 Lake St.   Ph: (318)459-3200
Shreveport, LA 71101   Free: 800-551-8892
                        Fax: (318)459-3301

Contact: Mike Whitehead, Editor; Bob Bryan, Managing Editor.

Desc: General newspaper. *Type:* Periodical.

The Times

Howard Publications
601 45th St.   Ph: (219)933-3327
Munster, IN 46321   Fax: (219)933-3249
URL: http://www.thetimesonline.com.

Contact: Wm. Nangle, Exec. Editor; Wm. Howard, Publisher; Don Caldwell, Advertising Dir.

Desc: General newspaper. *Type:* Periodical.

Times Colonist

Times Colonist
2621 Douglas St.   Ph: (604)380-5211
PO Box 300   Fax: (604)380-5353
Victoria, BC, Canada V8W
    2N4
E-mail: timesc@interlink.bc.ca.

Contact: P. Baillie, Publisher, (250)380-5202; V. Williams, Advertising Mgr., (250)380-5240; B. Poole, Managing Editor, (250)380-5207.

Desc: General newspaper. *Type:* Periodical.

Times News Service

Army Times Publishing Co.
6883 Commercial Dr.   Ph: (703)750-8125
Springfield, VA 22159-0200   Fax: (703)750-8781

Alt. Contact: Army Times Publishing Co. 6883 Commercial Dr., Springfield, VA 22159-0200; telephone: (703)750-8125; fax: (703)750-8781. *Type:* Periodical.

The Times-Picayune

Times-Picayune Publishing Corp.
3800 Howard Ave.   Ph: (504)826-3729
New Orleans, LA 70125-1429   Free: 800-925-0000
                        Fax: (504)826-3007
E-mail: webmaster@neworleans.net.
URL: http://www.neworleans.net.

Contact: Jim Amoss, Editor; Ashton Phelps, Jr., Publisher; Robert O'Neill, Advertising Mgr.

Desc: General newspaper. *Type:* Periodical.

The Times-Union

Hearst Publishing Group
Capital Newspapers Division
News Plaza   Ph: (518)454-5694
Box 1500
Albany, NY 12212
E-mail: mhuber@hearst.com
URL: http://www.timesunion.com

Contact: Richard Matturro, Librarian, (518)454-5734.

Desc: Contains the complete text of news items and feature articles from two Albany, New York general circulation newspapers: The Times-Union and The Knickerbocker News. Covers all news stories, local columns, features, editorials, sports, and letters to the editor. *Available:* The Dialog Corporation, DIALOG; LEXIS-NEXIS, NEXIS; Bell & Howell Information and Learning. *Type:* Database.

TJFR Business News Reporter

TJFR Publishing Company
2020 Arpahoe St.   Ph: (303)296-1200
Denver, CO 80205   Fax: (303)296-0059
E-mail: e-tjfr@tjfr.com
URL: http://www.tjfr.com.

Contact: Dean Rotbart, Editor.

Desc: Covers news and developments in the business and financial media. Includes profiles of editors and reporters and policy changes at major news organizations. *Type:* Newsletter.

Today's News

Infomart Dialog Limited
1450 Don Mills Rd.   Ph: (416)442-2198
Don Mills, ON, Canada M3B
2X7
E-mail: helpdesk@infomart.ca
URL: http://www.infomart.com/

Contact: Elaine Robertson, (416)442-2223, fax: (416)445-3508, erobertson@infomart.ca.

Desc: Contains the complete text of daily news stories from several sources, including The Financial Post, The Ottawa Citizen, The Vancouver Sun, The Province (Vancouver), The Toronto Star, The Toronto Sun, The Gazette (Montreal), The Daily News, Calgary Herald, Canadian Press News Wire, Presse Canadienne Service Francais, Canada Newswire, Canadian Corporate News, Business Information Wire, ISDN. Coverage includes general news, business, editorial, and sports stories. *Available:* Infomart Online; Infomart Assistant, Infomart Online; Infomart Dialog Limited. *Type:* Database.

Tom & Joanne O'Toole Travel Journalists/ Photographers

4603 Wood St.   Ph: (216)942-5455
Willoughby, OH 44094-5821

Contact: Thomas J. O'Toole, Journalist/Photogrpaher; Joanne R. O'Toole, Journalist.

Desc: Distributes worldwide and cruise ship travel features. *Alt. Contact:* 4603 Wood St., Willoughby, OH 44094-5821; telephone: (216)942-5455. *Type:* Periodical.

The Toronto Star

Toronto Star Newspapers Ltd.
1 Yonge St., 5th Fl.   Ph: (416)367-2000
Toronto, ON, Canada M5E
1E6
URL: http://www.thestar.com.

Contact: John Honderich, Editor; David Jolley, Publisher; P.J. (Ian) Bain, Advertising Mgr.

Desc: General newspaper. *Type:* Periodical.

The Toronto Star

Toronto Star Newspapers Ltd.
One Yonge St.   Ph: (416)367-2000
Toronto, ON, Canada M5E
1E6
E-mail: newsroom@inforamp.net
URL: http://www.thestar.com

Desc: Contains the complete text of news items, feature articles, and editorials from The Toronto Star (Ontario) newspaper. Covers national and regional general and financial news. *Available:* Infomart Online; Infomart Online; LEXIS-NEXIS, NEXIS; LEXIS-NEXIS, NEXIS; Infomart Assistant, Infomart Online; Infomart Dialog Limited; European Information Network Services (EINS). *Type:* Database.

Toronto Star Syndicate

1 Yonge St.   Ph: (416)869-4989
Toronto, ON, Canada M5E   Fax: (416)869-4587
1E6

Contact: Peter W. Taylor, Manager; Robin Graham, Sales; Dolores Johnstone, Sales; Ted Cowan, Sales; Jean Bradshaw, Photo Sales.

Desc: Distributes general news. *Alt. Contact:* 1 Yonge St., Toronto, ON, Canada M5E 1E6; telephone: (416)869-4989; fax: (416)869-4587. *Type:* Periodical.

Toronto Sun

Toronto Sun Publishing Corporation
333 King St.   Ph: (416)947-2258
Toronto, ON, Canada M5A
3X5
E-mail: sundown@io.org
URL: http://www.canoe.ca

Desc: Contains the complete text of The Toronto Sun, a daily newspaper providing local, provincial, national, and International news. Covers all news stories, features, columns, and editorials. *Available:* Infomart Online; Infomart Online; LEXIS-NEXIS, NEXIS; LEXIS-NEXIS, NEXIS; Infomart Dialog Limited; Infomart Assistant, Infomart Online. *Type:* Database.

Town Talk

Town Talk
24 Baltimore Pike   Ph: (215)566-6755
Media, PA 19063   Fax: (215)566-1261
E-mail: towntalknp@aol.com

Contact: Chris Parker, Editor; David Alpher, Publisher. *Desc:* Community newspaper (tabloid). *Alt. Contact:* P.O. Box 110, Media, PA 19063; telephone: (610)566-6755; fax: (610)566-1261. *Type:* Periodical.

Trade News Service

Published by Parmax Inc.
3701 Rte. 21 S.   Ph: (716)396-0027
Canandaigua, NY 14424-9020   Fax: (716)396-3057
E-mail: 76073.1205@compuserve.com.
Contact: Dennis C. Maxfield, Senior Ed.
Desc: Distributes edible and inedible fats and oils pricing and fundamental and trade data. *Alt. Contact:* Published by Parmax Inc. 3701 Rte. 21 S., Canandaigua, NY 14424-9020; telephone: (716)396-0027; fax: (716)396-3057. *Type:* Periodical.

Trans America Syndicate

311 S. Wacker   Ph: (312)876-0500
Ste. 6200   Fax: (312)362-0700
Chicago, IL 60606
Contact: William Barrett, Director.
Alt. Contact: 311 S. Wacker, Ste. 6200, Chicago, IL 60606; telephone: (312)876-0500; fax: (312)362-0700. *Type:* Periodical.

Trends in College Media

National Scholastic Press Association
620 Rarig Center   Ph: (612)625-8335
330 21st Ave. S.   Fax: (612)626-0720
Minneapolis, MN 55455
E-mail: info@studentpress.journ.uun.edu.
URL: http://studentpress.journ.uun.edu.
Contact: Tom E. Rolnicki, Executive Editor; Ross Namaste, Editor.
Desc: Advises editors and advisors of college newspapers, yearbooks, and magazines. Recurring features include interviews, a calendar of events, news of educational opportunities, book reviews, and columns titled Trendsline, Technobabble, Online Update, News Briefly and It's the Law. *Type:* Newsletter.

Trends in High School Media

National Scholastic Press Association
620 Rarig Center   Ph: (612)625-8335
330 21st Ave. S.   Fax: (612)626-0720
Minneapolis, MN 55455
E-mail: info@studentpress.journ.uun.edu.
URL: http://studentpress.journ.uun.edu.
Contact: Tom E. Rolnicki, Editor; Ross Namaste, Editor.
Desc: Advises editors and advisors of high school newspapers, yearbooks, and magazines. Recurring features include interviews, a calendar of events, news of educational opportunities, book reviews, and columns titled Trendsline, News Briefly, Technobabble, Online Update, and It's the Law. *Type:* Newsletter.

The Tribune

Thomson Newspapers
120 W. 1st Ave.   Ph: (602)898-6500
Mesa, AZ 85210   Fax: (602)898-6463
URL: http://www.tribaz.com.
Contact: Alan Geere, Editor, (602)898-6305; Karen Wittmer, COO/Publisher, (602)898-6504; Mike Romero, VP of Circulation, (602)898-6560; Jim Ripley, Managing Editor.

Desc: General newspaper. *Type:* Periodical.

Tribune Media Services Inc.

435 N. Michigan Ave.   Ph: (312)222-4444
Ste. 1500   Free: 800-245-6536
Chicago, IL 60611   Fax: (312)222-8620
E-mail: tms@tribune.com.
Contact: David D. Williams, Pres./CEO; Walter F. Mahoney, VP-Sales Syndicate & KRT Products; Barbara Needleman, VP-Data Base & Advertising; Michael A. Silver, VP-Editorial & Business Dev.
Desc: Distributes political, medical, and financial columns. *Alt. Contact:* 435 N. Michigan Ave., Ste. 1500, Chicago, IL 60611; telephone: (312)222-4444; fax: (312)222-8620; toll-free: 800-245-6536. *Type:* Periodical.

Tribune-Review

Tribune Review Publishing Co.
622 Cabin Hill Dr.   Ph: (724)834-1151
Greensburg, PA 15601   Free: 800-433-3046
     Fax: (724)838-5171
E-mail: letters@tribune.review.com.
URL: http://www.tribune-review.com/trio/; http://www.trbune-review.com/trib/.
Contact: George A. Beidler, Editor; Edward H. Harrell, Advertising Mgr.; Kraig Cawley, Advertising Dir.
Desc: Newspaper. *Type:* Periodical.

Tufty News Service

2107 National Press Bldg.   Ph: (202)347-8998
Washington, DC 20045
Desc: Distributes environmental and bio-engineering management information. *Alt. Contact:* 2107 National Press Bldg., Washington, DC 20045; telephone: (202)347-8998. *Type:* Periodical.

The Tulsa Tribune

World Publishing Co.
315 S. Boulder Ave.   Ph: (918)581-8583
P.O. Box 1770
Tulsa, OK 74102
E-mail: worldlib@ionet.net
Contact: Austin Farley, Library Director., (918)581-8583, fax: (918)581-8425, worldlib@ionet.net.
Desc: Contains the complete text of The Tulsa Tribune, a general circulation newspaper reporting local, national, and international news. Special areas of interest include energy, aerospace, computer, healthcare/medical services, and financial services. *Available:* Bell & Howell Information and Learning. *Type:* Database.

Tulsa World

World Publishing Co.
315 S. Boulder Ave.   Ph: (918)581-8583
P.O. Box 1770
Tulsa, OK 74102
E-mail: worldlib@ionet.net
Contact: Austin Farley, Library Director, (918)581-8583, fax: (918)581-8425, worldlib@ionet.net.
Desc: Contains the complete text of Tulsa World, a general circulation newspaper reporting local, national, and international news. Special areas of interest include extensive coverage of local business news such as the oil and aerospace industries. *Available:* Bell & Howell Information and Learning; LEXIS-NEXIS, NEXIS. *Type:* Database.

Tulsa World

World Publishing Co.
315 S. Boulder Ave.   Ph: (918)581-8300
PO Box 1770   Free: 800-999-6297
Tulsa, OK 74103   Fax: (918)581-8353
E-mail: tulsa@mail.webtek.
URL: http://www.tulsa.com.
Contact: Robert Haring, Editor.
Desc: General newspaper. *Type:* Periodical.

U-Bild Newspaper Features

PO Box 2383   Free: 800-828-2453
Van Nuys, CA 91409   Fax: (818)785-3229
E-mail: ubild@aol.com.
Contact: Kevin Taylor, President; Gina Rosa, General
Mgr.; Jeffrey Reeves, Feature Ed.
Desc: Distributes information about woodworking and
handicraft items. *Alt. Contact:* PO Box 2383, Van Nuys,
CA 91409; fax: (818)785-3229; toll-free: 800-828-2453.
Type: Periodical.

The Union Leader

Union Leader Corp.
100 William Loeb Dr.   Ph: (603)668-4321
PO Box 9555   Fax: (603)668-0382
Manchester, NH 03109-5309
E-mail: theul@aol.com.
Contact: J.W. McQuaid, Editor-in-Chief; Nackey S. Loeb,
Publisher; Charles Perkins, Executive Editor; James Line-
han, Managing Editor.
Desc: General newspaper. *Type:* Periodical.

Union-News & Sunday Republican

Union News & Sunday Republican
1860 Main St.   Ph: (413)788-1000
Springfield, MA 01101   Fax: (413)788-1301
URL: http://www.masslive.com.
Contact: Arnold Friedman, Editor; David Starr, Publisher;
Dwight Brouillard, Advertising Dir.
Desc: General newspaper. *Type:* Periodical.

United Feature Syndicate Inc.

200 Madison Ave.   Ph: (212)293-8500
New York, NY 10016   Free: 800-221-4816
                             Fax: (212)293-8760
URL: http://www.unitedmedia.com.
Contact: Douglas R. Stern, Pres./CEO; Sidney Goldberg,
Sr. VP/Gen. Mgr.-Syndication; Diana B. Loevy, VP/Ed.
Dir.; Lisa Klem Wilson, VP-Sales & Mktg.; John B. Mat-
thews, Natl. Sales Dir.; Robert Levy, Exed. Ed.-UFS &
NEA; Amy Lago, Mng. Ed.-Comic Art; Rose Novotny,
Mgr.-International Syndication; Rebecca Shaunohouse,
Mng. Ed-UFS & NEA; Mary Anne Grimes, Promotions
Mgr.; Peter Hultberg, Customer Service Mgr.
Alt. Contact: 200 Madison Ave., New York, NY 10016;
telephone: (212)293-8500; fax: (212)293-8760; toll-free:
800-221-4816. *Type:* Periodical.

United Media

Feature Syndicates: Newspaper Enterprise
Association United Features Syndicate
200 Madison Ave.   Ph: (212)293-8500
New York, NY 10016   Free: 800-221-4816
                             Fax: (212)293-8760
URL: http://www.unitedmedia.com.
Contact: Douglas R. Stern, Pres./CEO; Kevin Ryan, Sr.,
VP-Finance & Admin.; Sidney Goldberg, Sr., VP/Gen.
Mgr.-Syndication; Diane Shaib, Sr. VP-U.S. Licensing;
Diana B. Loevy, VP/Ed. Dir.; Lisa Klem Wilson, VP-Sales
& Mktg.; John B. Matthews, Natl. Sales Dir.; Robert
Levy, Exed. Ed.-UFS & NEA; Amy Lago, Mng. Ed.-
Comic Art; Rose Novotny, Mgr.-International Syndica-
tion; Diane Iselin, Dir.-Communications; Mary Anne
Grimes, Promotion Mgr.

Desc: Distributes comics, general features. *Alt. Contact:*
Feature Syndicates: Newspaper Enterprise Association
United Features Syndicate 200 Madison Ave., New York,
NY 10016; telephone: (212)293-8500; fax: (212)293-
8760; toll-free: 800-221-4816. *Type:* Periodical.

United Press International

1400 I St. NW   Ph: (202)898-8000
Washington, DC 20005   Fax: (202)898-8057
Contact: John R. Hayes, CEO; Peter Leach, VP-
Operations; Ron MacIntyre, VP-Sales & Mktg.; Anthony
Jay, Jr., CFO; Robert Martin, Mng. Ed.-International;
Tobin Beck, Mng. Ed.-North America; Raphael Calis,
Exec. Ed.; Kathleen Silvassy, Washington Bureau Mgr.;
Helen Thomas, UPI White House Bureau Mgr.; Lin Cop-
pedge-Martin, Dir.-HR; Larry Shuster, Science Ed.; Ian
Love, Sports Ed.; Valerie Kuklenski, Entertainment Ed.

Desc: Distributes general news, graphics, and photographs.
Alt. Contact: 1400 I St. NW, Washington, DC 20005;
telephone: (202)898-8000; fax: (202)898-8057. *Type:* Periodical.

U.S. Newswire

1272 National Press Bldg.   Ph: (202)347-2770
Washington, DC 20045   Fax: (202)347-2767
E-mail: newsdesk@usnewswire.com.
URL: http://www.usnewswire.com.

Desc: Distributes general news advisories and statements.
Alt. Contact: 1272 National Press Bldg., Washington, DC
20045; telephone: (202)347-2770; fax: (202)347-2767.
Type: Periodical.

Universal Press Syndicate

4520 Main St.   Ph: (816)932-6600
Kansas City, MO 64111-7701   Free: 800-255-6734
                             Fax: (816)932-6648
Contact: John McMeel, Pres./CEO; Kathleen Andrews,
VP/Co. Chm.; Thomas Thornton, Vice President; Lee
Salem, VP/Ed. Dir.; Elena Fallon, VP-Finance; Donna
Martin, VP/Contributing Ed.; George Diggs, VP-
Creative; Harriet Choice, VP/Ed. Special Services; Robert
Duffy, VP-Sales & New Media; Bill Mitchell, Ed./Dir.-
Dev./New Media; Nancy Meis, Dir.-Mktg./New Media;
Alan McDermott, Asst. VP/Sr. Ed.; Dan Dalton, Asst.
VP/Sales Mgr.; Sue Roush, Managing Editor; Jake Mor-
rissey, Assoc. Ed.; Eliza

Desc: Distributes cartoons, general news. *Alt. Contact:*
4520 Main St., Kansas City, MO 64111-7701; telephone:
(816)932-6600; fax: (816)932-6648; toll-free: 800-255-
6734. *Type:* Periodical.

The Upper East Side Resident

Resident Publications
215 Lexington Ave., 13th Fl. Ph: (212)679-1740
New York, NY 10016-5023   Fax: (212)679-4886
E-mail: residentp@aol.com
Contact: Carin Smilk, Editor; Larry Gelfand, Publisher.

Desc: Tabloid for residents of New York's upper East side.
Type: Periodical.

USA Today

Gannett Co., Inc.
1100 Wilson Blvd.   Ph: (703)284-6000
Arlington, VA 22234   Free: 800-872-0001
URL: http://www.gannett.com.

Contact: Peter S. Prichard, Editor, (703)276-3400; Thomas Curley, Publisher.

Desc: General newspaper with national perspective. *Type:*
Periodical.

USA TODAY

Gannett New Media Services
1100 Wilson Blvd., 24th Fl. Ph: (703)276-3400
Arlington, VA 22234

Desc: Contains the complete text of USA TODAY, a daily
general-interest newspaper reporting national and state
news. Covers all stories appearing in the News, Money,
Sports, Life, and Bonus sections as well as the USA Week-
end magazine. *Available:* The Dialog Corporation, Data-
Star; Bell & Howell Information and Learning; LEXIS-
NEXIS, NEXIS; LEXIS-NEXIS, NEXIS; The Dialog
Corporation, DIALOG; The Dialog Corporation, DIA-
LOG; CompuServe Information Service, Knowledge
Index; NIFTY Corporation, NIFTY-SERVE. *Type:* Data-
base.

USC Today

University of Southern Colorado
Dept. of Mass Communications Ph: (303)549-2818
2200 Bonforte Blvd.   Fax: (719)549-2120
Pueblo, CO 81001-4901
Contact: Patricia Bowie Orman, Advertising Mgr.; Gail
Binkly, Faculty Adviser.

Desc: Collegiate newspaper. *Type:* Periodical.

Utah County Journal

Oldham Associates, Inc.
500 West 1200 South   Ph: (801)226-1983
Orem, UT 84058   Fax: (801)226-3624
Contact: Levor Oldham, Publisher, (801)226-1983, fax:
(801)226-3624, ucjournal@dtint.com; Levor Oldham,
Managing Editor.

Desc: Newspaper. *Type:* Periodical.

Valley Scene

Gannett Co., Inc.
1100 Wilson Blvd.   Ph: (703)284-6000
Arlington, VA 22234   Free: 800-872-0001
Contact: Mark Adkins, Publisher, (909)386-4259; Jeannine Duvall, Advertising Dir., (909)386-3945.

Desc: Community newspaper. *Type:* Periodical.

The Vancouver Courier

Vancouver Courier
1574 W. 6th Ave.   Ph: (604)738-1411
Vancouver, BC, Canada V6J   Fax: (604)731-1474
1R2
E-mail: editor@courier.mnis.com.

Contact: Mick Maloney, Managing Editor; Peter Ballard,
Publisher; Phil Hager, Publisher; Sylvia Talbot, Sales
Mgr.; Jack Lymburner, General Mgr.

Desc: Community newspaper. *Type:* Periodical.

The Vancouver Sun

Pacific Press
A Southam Company
1-200 Granville St.   Ph: (604)605-2222
Vancouver, BC, Canada V6C   Fax: (604)605-2323
3N3
Contact: John Cruickshank, Editor-in-Chief, (604)605-
2319; Donald Babick, Publisher, (604)605-2868, fax:
(604)605-2308; Vivienne Sosnowski, Managing Editor;
Patricia Graham, Sr. Editor; Shelley Fralic, Deputy Managing Editor; Daphne Bramham, Associate Editor; Nicholas Palmer, Chief News Editor.

Desc: General newspaper. *Alt. Contact:* BC, Canada; telephone: (604)605-2111. *Type:* Periodical.

The Vancouver Sun

Pacific Press Ltd.
2250 Granville St.　　Ph: (604)732-2111
Vancouver, BC, Canada V6H
　3G2
URL: http://www.southam.com/vancouversun
Desc: Contains the complete text of news items and feature articles from The Vancouver Sun (British Columbia) newspaper. Regional coverage emphasizes the fishing, forestry, mining, and shipping industries; environmental, labor, and political issues; finance; tourism; and trade between Canada, the western United States, Japan, and other Pacific Rim countries. *Available:* Infomart Online; Infomart Online; Infomart Assistant, Infomart Online; LEXIS-NEXIS, NEXIS; LEXIS-NEXIS, NEXIS; Infomart Dialog Limited; European Information Network Services (EINS). *Type:* Database.

Ventura County Star

Ventura County Star
5250 Ralston St.　　Ph: (805)650-2900
Ventura, CA 93003　　Fax: (805)650-2944
Contact: Tim Gallagher, Editor, (805)655-5838, fax: (805)650-2950; Joe Howry, Managing Editor, (805)655-5801, fax: (805)650-2950.
Desc: General newspaper. *Alt. Contact:* CA; telephone: (805)655-5837; fax: (805)650-2950. *Type:* Periodical.

The Victoria Advocate

Victoria Advocate Publishing Co.
311 E. Constitution　　Ph: (512)575-1451
Victoria, TX 77901-8140　　Fax: (512)574-1220
Contact: John M. Roberts, Editor; John M. Roberts, Publisher.
Desc: General newspaper. *Type:* Periodical.

The Village Voice

VV Publishing Co.
36 Cooper Sq.　　Ph: (212)475-3300
New York, NY 10003-7149　　Free: 800-825-0061
　　Fax: (212)475-8944
Contact: Jon Z. Larsen, Editor; Michael Ellerin, Publisher; Petee Weinberger, Display Advertising Dir.
Desc: Newspaper (tabloid) on politics and the arts. *Type:* Periodical.

The Vindicator

The Vindicator Printing Co.
Vindicator Sq. No. 107　　Ph: (216)747-1471
PO Box 780　　Free: 800-686-5003
Youngstown, OH 44501　　Fax: (216)747-6712
Contact: Paul C. Jagnow, Managing Editor; Betty H. Brown Jagnow, Publisher.
Desc: General newspaper. *Type:* Periodical.

Virginia Pilot

Landmark Communications, Inc.
150 W. Brambleton Ave.　　Ph: (757)446-2000
Norfolk, VA 23510-2018　　Free: 800-446-2004
URL: http//www.pilotline.com.
Contact: Sandra Rowe, Editor; Robert Benson, Publisher; Dale Bowen, Advertising Mgr.
Desc: General newspaper. *Type:* Periodical.

Walter Cronkite School of Journalism and Telecommunication

Arizona State University
PO Box 871305　　Ph: (602)965-5011
Tempe, AZ 85287-1305
E-mail: at@asu.edu
URL: http://www.asu.edu/cronkite/
Contact: jtschool@asu.edu.
Desc: The Walter Cronkite School of Journalism home page offers easy access to links related to ASU and the

School of Journalism. Site visitors can access information about the school, faculty, alumni organization, admissions criteria and application procedures, and links to journalism sites. *Type:* Database.

The Washington Post

The Washington Post
1150 15th St. NW　　Ph: (202)334-6160
Washington, DC 20071-2400　　Free: 800-627-1150
　　Fax: (202)334-5693
E-mail: ffwd@washpost.com
Contact: Donald E. Graham, Publisher; Boisfeuillet Jones, Jr., President & General Manager; Leonard Downie, Exec. Editor; Meg Greenfield, Editorial Page Editor; Stephen S. Rosenfeld, Deputy Editorial Page Editor; Robert Kaiser, Managing Editor; Michael Getler, Deputy Managing Editor; Ben Bradlee, Vice-President.
Desc: General newspaper. *Type:* Periodical.

The Washington Post Magazine

The Washington Post
1150 15th St. NW　　Ph: (202)334-6160
Washington, DC 20071-2400　　Free: 800-627-1150
　　Fax: (202)334-5693
E-mail: ffwd@washpost.com
Contact: Anne Karalekas, Publisher; Steve Coll, Editor.
Desc: Magazine covering Washington personalities and issues affecting the city, the Virginia and Maryland suburbs, and the nation. *Type:* Periodical.

The Washington Post Writers Group

1150 15th St. NW　　Ph: (202)334-6375
Washington, DC 20071-9200　　Free: 800-879-9794
E-mail: writersgrp@washpost.com.
Contact: Alan Shearer, Editorial Dir./Gen. Mgr.; Anna Karavangelo, Assoc. Ed.; Mary Fleming, Sales Mgr./International; Grace Hill, Sales Mgr./North America; Suzanne Whelton, Operations Mgr./Comics Ed.; Kim Arrington, Permissions Ed.; Michael Metz, Sales Rep.
Alt. Contact: 1150 15th St. NW, Washington, DC 20071-9200; telephone: (202)334-6375; toll-free: 800-879-9794. *Type:* Periodical.

The Washington Times

News World Communications
3600 New York Ave. NE　　Ph: (202)636-3000
Washington, DC 20002　　Fax: (202)529-2471
E-mail: wtnews@wt.infi.net.
URL: http://www.washtimes.com.
Contact: Wesley Pruden, Editor-in-Chief; Bill Giles, Managing Editor; Preston E. Innerst, Sr., Deputy Managing Editor; Francis Coombs, Deputy Managing Editor; Ted Agres, Deputy Asst. Managing Editor; Barbara Taylor, Asst. Managing Editor; Mary Lou Forbes, Communentary Editor; Tod Lindberg, Editorial Page Editor; Kenneth Hanner, National Desk Editor; David Jones, Foreign Desk Editor; Ken McIntyre, Metro Desk Editor; Bob Menaker, Business Desk Editor; Gary Hopkins, Sports Editor; Glen
Desc: Newspaper with a Report orientation. *Type:* Periodical.

The Washington Times

The Washington Times
3600 New York Ave., N.E.　　Ph: (202)636-4918
Washington, DC 20002
E-mail: wtnews@wt.nifi.net
URL: http://www.washtimes.com
Desc: Contains the complete text of news items and feature articles from The Washington Times newspaper. Covers local, national, and world news, entertainment, business, and sports. *Available:* Bell & Howell Information and Learning; The Dialog Corporation, DIALOG; The Dialog Corporation, DIALOG; NlightN. *Type:* Database.

Washingtonian Magazine

Washington Magazine, Inc.
1828 L St. NW, Ste. 200　　Ph: (202)296-1246
Washington, DC 20036-5104
E-mail: editorial@washtonian.com.
URL: http://www.washtonian.com.
Contact: John A. Limpert, Editor, (202)296-3600; Philip Merrill, Publisher; Eleanor Merrill, Assoc. Publisher; Edward P. Mansfield, Jr., Advertising Dir.
Desc: Metropolitan interest magazine. *Type:* Periodical.

West Coast Syndicate

320 Vista Linda Dr.　　Ph: (415)388-2024
Mill Valley, CA 94941
Contact: Carol Townsend, Pres./Exec. Ed.
Desc: Distributes business, food, and wine features; puzzles. *Alt. Contact:* 320 Vista Linda Dr., Mill Valley, CA 94941; telephone: (415)388-2024. *Type:* Periodical.

Western Horseman

Western Horseman, Inc.
PO Box 7980　　Ph: (719)633-5524
Colorado Springs, CO 80933　　Free: 800-874-6774
　　Fax: (719)633-1392
Contact: Pat Close, Editor; Randy Witte, Publisher; Corliss Palmer, Advertising Dir.
Desc: Magazine covering forms of horsemanship and all breeds of horses; emphasizing western stock horses and western lifestyle. *Type:* Periodical.

The Western Producer Newsfeature Service

2310 Millar Ave.　　Ph: (306)665-3591
PO Box 2500　　Fax: (306)934-2401
Saskatoon, SK, Canada S7K
　2C4
Contact: Michael Gillgannon, Managing Editor; Sean Pratt, Reporter/Ed.
Alt. Contact: 2310 Millar Ave., PO Box 2500, Saskatoon, SK, Canada S7K 2C4; telephone: (306)665-3591; fax: (306)934-2401. *Type:* Periodical.

Westword

Westword Corp.
PO Box 5970　　Ph: (303)296-7744
Denver, CO 80217　　Fax: (303)296-5416
E-mail: denver.editorial@westword.com.
URL: http://www.westword.com.
Contact: Patricia Calhoun, Editor; Amy Cobb, Publisher, fax: (303)296-5415, acobb@westword.com; Scott Tobias, Advertising Dir., fax: (303)296-2457, stobias@westword.com.
Desc: Metro newsweekly. *Type:* Periodical.

Whitegate Features Syndicate

71 Faunce Dr.　　Ph: (401)274-2149
Ste. 1
Providence, RI 02906
Contact: Ed Issac, President; Steve Corey, VP/Gen. Mgr.; Eve Green, Talent Mgr./Special Sales; Mary Howard, Office Mgr.
Alt. Contact: 71 Faunce Dr., Ste. 1, Providence, RI 02906; telephone: (401)274-2149. *Type:* Periodical.

Wichita Eagle

Knight-Ridder, Inc.
50 W. Fernando St.　　Ph: (408)938-7700
San Jose, CA 95113
URL: http://www.wichitaeagle.com.
Contact: Rick Thames, Jr., Editor, (316)268-6694, fax: (316)268-6627, rthames@wichitaeagle.com; Peter Pitz, Publisher, (316)268-6503, fax: (316)268-6609, ppitz@wichitaeagle.com; Sheri Dill, VP/Marketing, (316)268-6633, fax: (316)268-6609, sdill@wichitaeagle.com; Ron Davidson, VP/Advertising, (316)268-6291, fax: (316)268-6658, rdavidson@wichitaeagle.com; Karen Magnuson, Managing Editor, (316)268-6405, fax: (316)268-6627, kmagnuson@wichitaeagle.com.

Desc: General newspaper. *Alt. Contact:* PO Box 820, Wichita, KS 67201; telephone: (316)268-6000, (316)268-6351; fax: (316)268-6627. *Type:* Periodical.

Wichita Eagle
Wichita Eagle and Beacon Publishing Co., Inc.
825 E. Douglas Ph: (316)268-6000
P.O. Box 820
Wichita, KS 67202
E-mail: dbagby@wichitaeagle.com
Contact: Deb Bagby, (316)268-6551, fax: (316)268-6646, sdill@wichitaeagle.com
Desc: Contains the complete text of news items, columns, feature articles, and editorials from the Wichita Eagle (Kansas) newspaper. Regional coverage emphasizes agriculture, aviation, financial services, and petroleum industries, sports, and the arts. *Available:* The Dialog Corporation, DIALOG. *Type:* Database.

The Windsor Star
Southam, Inc.
44 Frid St. Ph: (905)526-3333
PO Box 300
Hamilton, ON, Canada L8N 3G3
URL: http://www.hamiltonspectator.com
Contact: Windsor Star Library, (519)255-5711, fax: (519)255-5515.
Desc: Contains the complete text of news items and feature articles from The Windsor Star (Ontario) newspaper. Regional coverage emphasizes the automobile and agricultural industries and labor issues. *Available:* Infomart Online; Infomart Assistant, Infomart Online; Infomart Dialog Limited. *Type:* Database.

WINGS: Women's International News Gathering Service
PO Box 33220 Ph: (512)416-9000
Austin, TX 78764
Contact: Frieda Werden, Producer; Mary O'Grady, Health and Humor Editor.
Desc: Distributes radio news and current affairs programs by and about women around the world. *Alt. Contact:* PO Box 33220, Austin, TX 78764; telephone: (512)416-9000. *Type:* Periodical.

The Winnipeg Free Press
The Winnipeg Free Press
1355 Mountain Ave. Ph: (204)697-7001
Winnipeg, MB, Canada R2X 3B6 Fax: (204)697-7465
Contact: Rudy Redekop, Publisher; Nicholas Hirst, Editor; Laurie Finley, Advertising Dir.; Steve Pona, News Editor; Julian Rachey, Sports Editor; Morley Walker, Entertainment Editor.
Desc: General newspaper. *Type:* Periodical.

Winston-Salem Journal
Piedmont Publishing Co.
PO Box 3159 Ph: (336)727-7211
Winston-Salem, NC 27102-3159 Fax: (336)727-7315
URL: http://www.journalnow.com.
Contact: Jon Witherspoon, Publisher, (336)727-7350, fax: (336)727-7354, jwitherspoon@w-s-journal.com; V.C. Taylor III, General Mgr., (336)727-7348, fax: (336)727-7354, vtaylor@w-s-journal.com; Raymond McDowell, Controller, (336)727-7232, fax: (336)727-7245, rmcdowell@w-s-journal.com; Bill Downey, Advertising Mgr., (336)727-7335, fax: (336)727-7268, wdowney@w-s-journal.com; Carl Crothers, Managing Editor, (336)727-7277, ccrothers@w-s-journal.com; Jim Laughrun, Asst. Mgr
Desc: General newspaper. *Type:* Periodical.

Wisconsin State Journal
Madison Newspapers, Inc.
1901 Fish Hatchery Rd. Ph: (608)252-6100
PO Box 8058 Fax: (608)252-6119
Madison, WI 53713
E-mail: info@krause.com
URL: http://www.madison.com.
Contact: Frank Denton, Editor; James E. Burgess, Publisher; David Stoeffler, Editor, (608)252-6118.
Desc: General newspaper. *Type:* Periodical.

Worcester Telegram & Gazette
The Chronicle Publishing Company
Worcester Telegram & Gazette
20 Franklin St. Ph: (508)793-9100
P.O. Box 15012
Worcester, MA 01615-0012
E-mail: info@telegram.com
URL: http://www.telegram.com
Desc: Contains the complete text of two general circulation newspapers, the daily Telegram & Gazette and the Sunday Telegram, reporting local, national, and international news. Regional coverage emphasizes the arts, the environment, high technology industries, medicine, and politics. *Available:* Bell & Howell Information and Learning. *Type:* Database.

Working Press of the Nation
R. R. Bowker
121 Chanlon Rd. Ph: (908)464-6800
New Providence, NJ 07974 Free: 800-521-8110
  Fax: (908)665-6688
E-mail: techsupport@bowker.com
URL: http://www.bowker.com
Contact: Judith Salk, Editor; Elizabeth Onaran, Editor.
Desc: In three separate volumes, syndicates and over 7,200 daily and weekly newspapers; 1,500 newsletters; over 14,000 radio and television stations; 5,500 magazines; 2,500 internal publications. *Type:* Directory.

World Features Syndicate
5842 Sagebrush Rd. Ph: (619)468-1099
La Jolla, CA 92037 Fax: (619)456-6264
Contact: Ronald A. Sataloff, President; Karl A. Van Asselt, Assoc. Ed.
Desc: Distributes daily and weekly columns. *Alt. Contact:* 5842 Sagebrush Rd., La Jolla, CA 92037; telephone: (619)468-1099; fax: (619)456-6264. *Type:* Periodical.

World Federation of Travel Writers and Journalists
Don Bonhaus
One Ballinswood Rd. Ph: (732)291-2840
Atlantic Highlands, NJ 07716-1510 Fax: (732)291-9272
E-mail: donbonhaus@aol.com
Contact: Don Bonhaus, Commissioner, The Americas.
Desc: Travel journalists. Promotes professional advancement of members. *Type:* Association.

World Images News Service
6520 China Grove St. Ph: (703)922-1756
Alexandria, VA 22310 Fax: (703)922-1756
URL: http://www.winsphoto.com.
Contact: Jack W. Sykes, CEO/Chief Photographer, jack@winsphoto.com; Donna L. Southard, Photo Ed.; Robert H. Williams, News Ed.
Desc: Distributes daily and special news photos and stock photos. *Alt. Contact:* 6520 China Grove St., Alexandria, VA 22310; telephone: (703)922-1756; fax: (703)922-1756. *Type:* Periodical.

World News Connection
National Technical Information Service (NTIS)
U.S. Department of Commerce
5285 Port Royal Rd. Ph: (703)605-6000
Springfield, VA 22161-0001 Free: 800-553-NTIS
  Fax: (703)605-6900
E-mail: orders@ntis.fedworld.gov
URL: http://wnc.Fedworld.gov.
Desc: Provides an online publication featuring news accounts, commentaries, and government statements from foreign broadcasts, press agency transmissions, newspapers, and periodicals published in the previous 48 to 72 hours. Regions covered include the People's Republic of China, Eastern Europe, the Soviet Union, East Asia, Near East and South Asia, Latin America, Western Europe, and Sub Saharan Africa. *Type:* Newsletter.

World News Syndicate Ltd.
PO Box 419 Ph: (213)469-2333
Hollywood, CA 90078 Fax: (213)469-2333
Contact: William C. Lane, Managing Editor; Laurie A. Williams, Entertainment Ed.; William P. Jenkins, General Mgr.
Desc: Distributes beauty, book review, entertainment, and medical columns. *Alt. Contact:* PO Box 419, Hollywood, CA 90078; telephone: (213)469-2333; fax: (213)469-2333. *Type:* Periodical.

World Press
2547 Monroe St. Ph: (313)563-0360
Dearborn, MI 48124-3013 Fax: (313)563-1448
Contact: Stephen R. Castor, Editor.
Alt. Contact: 2547 Monroe St., Dearborn, MI 48124-3013; telephone: (313)563-0360; fax: (313)563-1448. *Type:* Periodical.

World Press Review
200 Madison Ave. Ph: (212)889-5155
Rm. 2104 Fax: (212)889-5634
New York, NY 10016
E-mail: wpr@panix.com.
Contact: Barry Shelby, Sr. Ed.; Larry Martz, Editor; Gail Robinson, Managing Editor; B.J. Kowalski, Sr. Ed.
Alt. Contact: 200 Madison Ave., Rm. 2104, New York, NY 10016; telephone: (212)889-5155; fax: (212)889-5634. *Type:* Periodical.

World Union Press
Rm. 373 Ph: (212)688-7557
Press Section Fax: (212)688-7557
United Nations
New York, NY 10017
Contact: David Horowitz, Editor; Gregg Sitrin, Assoc. Ed.; Raymond Reuven Solomon, Staff.
Desc: Distributes political news, United Nations and world events. *Alt. Contact:* Rm. 373, Press Section, United Nations, New York, NY 10017; telephone: (212)688-7557; fax: (212)688-7557. *Type:* Periodical.

World Watch/Foreign Affairs Syndicate
144-21 Charter Rd. Ph: (718)591-7246
Ste. 5C
Kew Gardens Hills, NY 11435
Contact: John J. Metzler, Editor.
Desc: Distributes political and foreign affairs news. *Alt. Contact:* 144-21 Charter Rd., Ste. 5C, Kew Gardens Hills, NY 11435; telephone: (718)591-7246. *Type:* Periodical.

Writers Clearinghouse
PO Box 340 Ph: (610)873-8946
Downingtown, PA 19335
Contact: Richard D. Carreno, Mng. Dir., carrenr@staff.richmond.ac.uk; Gillian Williams, VP-USA.

Desc: Distributes men's fashion and equestrian activities information. *Alt. Contact:* PO Box 340, Downington, PA 19335; telephone: (610)873-8946; 92 Kew Rd., Richmond, London, En TW9 2PQ; telephone: (018)1 332 8266; fax: (018)1 332 3050. *Type:* Periodical.

York Community Courier East

Engle Publishing Co.
PO Box 500   Ph: (717)653-4300
Mount Joy, PA 17552-0500   Free: 800-800-1833
                                    Fax: (717)653-1833
Contact: C. A. Engle, Publisher; Patrick Lee, Advertising Mgr.
Desc: Community newspaper. *Type:* Periodical.

York Community Courier West

Engle Publishing Co.
PO Box 500   Ph: (717)653-4300
Mount Joy, PA 17552-0500   Free: 800-800-1833
                                    Fax: (717)653-1833
Contact: C. A. Engle, Publisher; Patrick Lee, Advertising Mgr.
Desc: Community newspaper. *Type:* Periodical.

Yossarian News Service

PO Box 236   Ph: (415)588-5990
Millbrae, CA 94030
Contact: Charlie Chase, Exec. Ed.; Elio Ligi, Managing Editor; Paul Fericano, Editor; Pamela Meuser, Managing Editor; Katherine Daly, Edit. Dir.; Bruce Pryor, Assoc. Ed.
Desc: International distribution of parody news stories, political and social satire. *Alt. Contact:* PO Box 236, Millbrae, CA 94030; telephone: (415)588-5990. *Type:* Periodical.

Zondervan Press Syndicate

5300 Patterson Ave. SE   Ph: (616)698-3425
Grand Rapids, MI 49530   Fax: (616)698-3223
E-mail: zpub@zph.com.
URL: http://www.zondervan.com.
Contact: Judy Waggoner, Managing Editor.
Desc: Distributes feature articles, short quotes, money columns, cartoons, and puzzles. *Alt. Contact:* 5300 Patterson Ave. SE, Grand Rapids, MI 49530; telephone: (616)698-3425; fax: (616)698-3223. *Type:* Periodical.

Korea/Korean

The Korea Society

950 3rd Ave., 8th Fl.   Ph: (212)759-7525
New York, NY 10022   Fax: (212)759-7530
E-mail: korea.ny@koreasociety.org
URL: http://www.koreasociety.org
Contact: Ambassador Donald P. Gregg, Chm. of the Board/Pres.
Desc: Works to foster increased understanding between the people of the United States and Korea. Promotes improved economic, cultural, and educational exchange through seminars, educational programs, and research. *Type:* Association.

Korean National Association

141 S. New Hampshire Ave.   Ph: (213)382-9345
Los Angeles, CA 90004-5805   Fax: (213)382-1678
Contact: Woon-Ha Kim, Pres.
Desc: Operates Korean language school for children and young adults. *Type:* Association.

Labor

Archives of Labor and Urban Affairs Newsletter

Archives of Labor and Urban Affairs
Wayne State University
Walter P. Reuther Library   Ph: (313)577-4024
5401 Cass Ave.
Detroit, MI 48202
Contact: Mike Smith, Editor.
Desc: Lists Archives' accessions, activities, and programs. Compiles manuscript collections on the subjects of labor and urban-related fields. *Type:* Newsletter.

BNA Labor Daily

The Bureau of National Affairs, Inc. (BNA)
1231 25th St. NW   Ph: (202)452-4200
Washington, DC 20037
E-mail: bnaplus@bna.com
URL: http://bna.com/mkt/hrl/hrlwdec.htm
Contact: BNA PLUS, (202)452-4323, fax: (202)822-8092, bnaplus@bna.com.
Desc: Provides information on developments and trends in labor and human resources, including collective bargaining, fair employment practices, management and union activities, pension benefits, and arbitration. Data are derived from new and proposed legislation, National Labor Relations Board (NLRB) decisions, congressional reports, federal agency directives, and key speeches from industrial relations meeting and conferences. *Available:* The Dialog Corporation, DIALOG. *Type:* Database.

BNAC Communicator

BNA Communications, Inc.
Bureau of National Affairs, Inc. (BNA)
9493 Key West Ave.   Ph: (301)948-0540
Rockville, MD 20850   Free: 800-233-6067
                                    Fax: (301)948-2085
E-mail: bnac@bna.com.
URL: http://www.bna.com/bnac.
Contact: Tony Cornish, Editor.
Desc: Disseminates information on issues, topics, and trends in human resource training and development. *Type:* Newsletter.

California-Employee Relations Report

M. Lee Smith Publishers LLC
5201 Virginia Way   Ph: (615)373-7517
PO Box 5094   Free: 800-274-6774
Brentwood, TN 37024-5094   Fax: 800-785-9212
E-mail: custserv@mleesmith.com
URL: http://www.mleesmith.com.
Contact: Barrett W. McBride, Editor.
Desc: Provides news and analysis of fundamental employment issues in California. Covers legislative and regulatory activities, litigation, and legal developments. *Type:* Newsletter.

California Labor and Employment ALERT Newsletter

Castle Publications Ltd.
PO Box 580   Ph: (818)708-3208
Van Nuys, CA 91408   Fax: (818)708-9287
E-mail: info@castlepublications.com
URL: http://www.castlepublications.com.
Contact: Richard Simmons, President.
Desc: Reports on current developments in California and federal laws concerning personnel and employment issues. Recurring features include notices of publications available. *Type:* Newsletter.

California Labor and Employment Law Quarterly

State Bar of California
Labor and Employment Law Section
555 Franklin St.
San Francisco, CA 94102
Contact: Bonnie G. Bogue, Editor; Judy B. Freeman, Managing Editor; Michael J. Egan, Managing Editor; Timothy B. Sotille, Editor; Carol Vendrillo, Editor.
Desc: Contains information and news on California's labor and employment laws and regulations. *Type:* Newsletter.

Canadian Federation of Labour—Federation Update

Canadian Federation of Labour
107 Sparks St., Ste. 300   Ph: (613)234-4141
Ottawa, ON, Canada K1P 5B5   Fax: (613)234-5188
Desc: Advises on recent involvements within the Federation. *Type:* Newsletter.

Canadian Labour Arbitration Summaries

Canada Law Book, Inc.
240 Edward St.   Ph: (905)841-6472
Aurora, ON, Canada L4G 3S9   Free: 800-263-3269
                                    Fax: (905)841-5085
E-mail: webmaster@canadalawbook.ca
URL: http://www.canadalawbook.ca
Contact: E.B. Willis, Editor.
Desc: Covers labor arbitration awards in Canada. *Type:* Newsletter.

Canadian Labour Arbitration Summaries

Canada Law Book Inc.
240 Edward St.   Ph: (905)841-6472
Aurora, ON, Canada L4G 3S9
URL: http://www.canadalawbook.com
Desc: Contains approximately 25,300 summaries of published Canadian labor arbitration decisions. Includes significant French-language awards from the province of Quebec. *Available:* QL Systems Limited, QUICKLAW; LEXIS-NEXIS. *Type:* Database.

CLEAR Newsletter

Center for Labor Education and Research (CLEAR)
University of Hawaii
1420-A Lower Campus Dr.   Ph: (808)956-7145
Honolulu, HI 96822-2313   Fax: (808)956-2023
URL: http://www.uhwo.haw.edu/clear/.
Contact: Adrienne Valdez, Editor; William Puette, Editor.
Desc: Updates national and local information of concern to working people and union leaders. Includes legal decisions, health and safety issues, current trends in labor, collective bargaining, and discrimination laws. *Type:* Newsletter.

CLEAR Report

Center for Labor Education and Research (CLEAR)
University of Alabama at Birmingham
1044 11th St. S.   Ph: (205)934-2101
Birmingham, AL 35216   Fax: (205)975-5087
E-mail: csturgis@uab.edu
URL: http://www.uab.edu/clear.
Contact: Edwin Brown, Editor, (205)934-8753, edlbrown@uab.edu.
Desc: Covers labor and industrial relations. Announces conferences. *Type:* Newsletter.

CLUW News

Coalition of Labor Union Women (CLUW)
1126 16th St. NW   Ph: (202)466-4610
Washington, DC 20036   Fax: (202)776-0537
URL: http://www.cluw.org.
Contact: Connie Kopelov, Editor.
Desc: Contains information on the activities of the Coalition and news items relevant to union women. Recurring features include a schedule of events. *Type:* Newsletter.

Coalition of Labor Union Women

1126 16th St. NW   Ph: (202)466-4610
Washington, DC 20036   Fax: (202)776-0537
Contact: Chrystl Lindo-Bridgeforth, Exec.Dir.
Desc: Aims to: unify all union women in order to determine common problems within unions and deal effectively with objectives; promote unionism and encourage unions to be more aggressive in their efforts to bring unorganized women under collective bargaining agreements; inform members about what can be done within the labor movement to achieve equal opportunity and correct discriminatory job situations; educate and inspire union brothers to help achieve affirmative action in the workplace. *Type:* Association.

Collective Bargaining Bulletin

Bureau of National Affairs, Inc. (BNA)
1231 25th St. NW   Ph: (202)452-4323
Washington, DC 20037   Free: 800-372-1033
                               Fax: (202)452-7773
E-mail: bnaplus@bna.com
Contact: Leslie Goldman, Managing Editor.
Desc: Presents news of developments in collective bargaining, including contract settlements, bargaining techniques and trends, and contract interpretations by the courts. Recurring features include columns titled Clause Talk, Arbitrating the Contract, Facts & Figures, and Perspective. *Type:* Newsletter.

Comparative Industrial Relations Newsletter

McGroote School of Business/ McMaster University
Hamilton, ON, Canada L8S   Ph: (905)525-9140
   4C7   Fax: (905)521-8995
E-mail: pringlep@mcmaster.ca.
Contact: Prof. Roy J. Adams, Editor.
Desc: Designed to "foster cross disciplinary communication among those interested in comparative, international labor issues." Also spotlights people in the news, organizations, and conferences. Recurring features include news of research, book reviews, and notices of publications available. *Type:* Newsletter.

Concerned Educators Against Forced Unionism

8001 Braddock Rd., Ste. 500   Ph: (703)321-8519
Springfield, VA 22160   Free: 800-325-7892
                               Fax: (703)321-7342
E-mail: clj@nrtw.org
Contact: Cathy Jones, Coor.
Desc: Works to inform educators about compulsory unionism by developing and disseminating accurate, timely, and relevant information. *Type:* Association.

Congress of Independent Unions

303 Ridge St.   Ph: (618)462-2447
Alton, IL 62002   Fax: (618)462-5579
Contact: R. Richard Davis, Pres.
Desc: Members of independent labor unions. Objectives are: to organize nonunionized employees into independent labor unions; to represent independent labor unions; to act as a bargaining agent between labor unions and management. Maintains library. *Type:* Association.

Council Courier

Montgomery County Council of Supporting Services Employees, Inc.
973A Russell Ave.   Ph: (301)948-8766
Gaithersburg, MD 20879   Fax: (301)948-8769
Desc: Discusses the economy, business privatization, and unions. Recurring features include a calendar of events, and news of members. *Type:* Newsletter.

Daily Labor Report

The Bureau of National Affairs, Inc. (BNA)
1231 25th St. NW   Ph: (202)452-4200
Washington, DC 20037
E-mail: bnaplus@bna.com
URL: http://bna.com/mkt/hrl/hrlwdec.htm
Contact: BNA PLUS, (202)452-4323, fax: (202)822-8092, bnaplus@bna.com.
Desc: Contains the complete text of Daily Labor Report, covering legislative, regulatory, and judicial activities related to labor relations and employment practices. Covers fair employment practices, immigration, pension benefits, collective bargaining, arbitration, Social Security reform, occupational safety, and job training. *Available:* LEXIS-NEXIS, LEXIS; West Group, WESTLAW. *Type:* Database.

Daily Labor Report

Bureau of National Affairs, Inc. (BNA)
1231 25th St. NW   Ph: (202)452-4323
Washington, DC 20037   Free: 800-372-1033
                               Fax: (202)452-7773
E-mail: bnaplus@bna.com
Contact: Jerome Ashton, Managing Editor.
Desc: Covers labor developments in Congress, the courts, federal agencies, unions, management, and the National Labor Relations Board. *Type:* Newsletter.

Decisions of Boards Database

The Bureau of National Affairs, Inc. (BNA)
1231 25th St. NW   Ph: (202)452-4200
Washington, DC 20037
E-mail: bnaplus@bna.com
URL: http://bna.com/mkt/hrl/hrlwdec.htm
Desc: Contains selected text from case decisions of the National Labor Relations Board (NLRB). Topics include collective bargaining, labor relations legislation, management strategy, and mediation and conciliation. *Type:* Database.

Decisions of Courts Database

The Bureau of National Affairs, Inc. (BNA)
1231 25th St. NW   Ph: (202)452-4200
Washington, DC 20037
E-mail: bnaplus@bna.com
URL: http://bna.com/mkt/hrl/hrlwdec.htm
Desc: Contains selected text of all federal and state court decisions on any issue involving labor relations. *Type:* Database.

Economic Notes

Labor Research Association, Inc.
145 W. 28th St.   Ph: (212)714-1677
New York, NY 10001   Free: 800-875-8775
                               Fax: (212)714-1674
Contact: Gregory Tarpinian, Editor.
Desc: Discusses economic and political trends of interest to the labor movement. Covers issues such as bargaining, industrial trends, corporate strategies, and productivity. *Type:* Newsletter.

Ed Welch on Worker's Compensation—Michigan Edition

Edward M. Welch
2875 Northwind Dr., Ste.   Ph: (517)332-5266
   210-A   Fax: (517)332-5273
East Lansing, MI 48823
Contact: Edward M. Welch, Editor and Publisher.
Desc: Provides information on worker's compensation, focusing especially on Michigan regulations. *Type:* Newsletter.

Ed Welch on Worker's Compensation—National Edition

M. Lee Smith Publishers LLC
5201 Virginia Way   Ph: (615)373-7517
PO Box 5094   Free: 800-274-6774
Brentwood, TN 37024-5094   Fax: 800-785-9212
E-mail: custserv@mleesmith.com
Contact: Edward M. Welch, Editor and Publisher.
Desc: Provides information on worker's compensation. Includes news and regulations. *Type:* Newsletter.

1199 News

1199, National Health and Human Service Employees Union SEIU, AFL-CIO
310 W. 43rd St.   Ph: (212)631-4561
New York, NY 10036   Fax: (212)244-4568
Contact: Daniel North, Editor.
Desc: Describes attempts to organize hospital and health care employees into a labor union. Discusses related developments, problems, and issues. *Type:* Newsletter.

Employee Policy for the Public and Private Sector

Wakeman/Walworth, Inc.
300 N. Washington St.   Ph: (703)549-8606
Alexandria, VA 22314   Free: 800-876-2545
URL: http://statecapitals.com.
Contact: Keyes Walworth, Editor.
Desc: Provides nationwide coverage of state actions on employees' rights to organize and strike, as well as on working conditions, grievances, right of appeal, bargaining procedures, arbitration and hiring, and disciplinary practices. Discusses state government in relation to wages in private industry; contains a digest of state policies concerning unemployment and workers' compensation benefits. *Type:* Newsletter.

Employee Relations in Action

Alignmark Information Publishing
1340 Braddock Pl., Ste. 400   Ph: (703)706-0207
Alexandria, VA 22314   Fax: (703)683-4852
Contact: Elmer Ellentuck, Editor, (718)549-0414; Diane Roberts, Assoc. Editor, (212)367-6417.
Desc: Publishes case studies of employee problems and management reactions. Provides details and analysis of the events, arbitration, and ruling. *Type:* Newsletter.

Employee Relations Bulletin

Bureau of Business Practice
24 Rope Ferry Rd.   Ph: (860)442-4365
Waterford, CT 06386   Free: 800-243-0876
                               Fax: (860)437-3555
URL: http://www.bbpnews.com
Contact: Christine Kotrba, Editor, christine_kotrba@ prenhall.com.
Desc: Provides information about trends, ways to effectively manage staff, legislation affecting business organizations, and methods for staying competitive. Recurring features include interviews, news of research, reports of meetings, and book reviews. *Type:* Newsletter.

Employer Bargaining Objectives

The Bureau of National Affairs, Inc. (BNA)
1231 25th St. NW   Ph: (202)452-4200
Washington, DC 20037
E-mail: bnaplus@bna.com
URL: http://bna.com/mkt/hrl/hrlwdec.htm
Desc: Contains information from surveys of employers on goals to be sought at upcoming collective bargaining negotiations. Covers employers in the aerospace, communications, fabricated and primary metals, food, glass, textile, and utilities industries with contract renewals due in the current year. *Type:* Database.

The Employment Bulletin

Canada Law Book, Inc.
240 Edward St.   Ph: (905)841-6472
Aurora, ON, Canada L4G 3S9   Free: 800-263-3269
   Fax: (905)841-5085
E-mail: webmaster@canadalawbook.ca
URL: http://www.canadalawbook.ca
Contact: Brian A. Grosman, Editor.
Desc: Contains news and analysis of policy, legislation, and court decisions that affect employer-employee relationships, and offers strategies for coping with legislative changes and policy initiatives. Addresses employee benefits, discipline and termination, contracts, performance evaluation, discrimination and harrassment, occupational health and safety, and ethics. *Type:* Newsletter.

Employment and Labour Law Reporter

Butterworths
75 Clegg Rd.   Ph: (905)479-2665
Markham, ON, Canada L6G   Free: 800-668-6481
   1A1   Fax: (905)479-2826
E-mail: ellr@butterworths.ca.
URL: http://www.butterworths.ca
Contact: Margaret Manley, Managing Editor.
Desc: Provides information about employment and labor law in Canada. *Type:* Newsletter.

Fact Sheet Newsletter

Labor Studies Center
College of Professional Studies
University of the District of Columbia
Dept. of Management   Ph: (202)282-3718
4200 Connecticut Ave. NW
MB 5200
Washington, DC 20008
Contact: Isadore Goldberg, Ph.D., Coord.
Desc: Concerned with labor relations, human resources, and civil rights in higher education. Reports on faculty, graduate students, administrators, and civil service employees. *Type:* Newsletter.

Florida Workers' Compensation Law Bulletin

LRP Publications
747 Dresher Rd.   Ph: (215)784-0941
PO Box 980   Free: 800-341-7874
Horsham, PA 19044-0980   Fax: (215)784-0870
E-mail: custserve@lrp.com
Contact: Joan Grossman, Editor.
Desc: Publishes decisions of Florida courts regarding worker's compensation issues. *Type:* Newsletter.

Glass Molders, Pottery, Plastics, and Allied Workers International Union

608 E. Baltimore Pike   Ph: (610)565-5051
PO Box 607   Fax: (610)565-0983
Media, PA 19063
Contact: James H. Rankin, Pres.
Desc: AFL-CIO; CLC. *Type:* Association.

Government Training and Development

National Association for Government Training & Development
167 W. Main St., Ste. 600   Ph: (606)231-1925
Lexington, KY 40507   Fax: (606)231-1928
E-mail: naftdd@aol.com
Contact: Carol Roberts, Association Mgr.; Adrielle Craft, Editor.
Desc: Presents coverage of events and activities regarding job training and development. Recurring features include interviews, a calendar of events, reports of meetings, news of educational opportunities, notices of publications available, and a column titled President's Corner. *Type:* Newsletter.

GraphiCommunicator

Graphic Communications International Union
1900 L St. NW   Ph: (202)462-1400
Washington, DC 20036   Fax: (202)331-9516
Contact: James J. Norton, Editor; Herald Grandstaff, Managing Editor.
Desc: Trade newspaper of the Graphic Communications International Union. *Type:* Periodical.

Health Labor Relations Reports

Opus Communications
100 Hoods Ln.   Ph: (781)639-1872
PO Box 1168   Free: 800-650-6787
Marblehead, MA 01945   Fax: (781)639-2982
E-mail: customer_service@opuscomm.com
URL: http://www.opuscomm.com
Contact: Frank J. Bardack, Editor.
Desc: Focuses on employee and labor relations in the health care field. Reports on court and National Labor Relations Board (NLRB) decisions in the areas of wrongful discharge, employment-at-will, discrimination, and union organizing. *Type:* Newsletter.

Highlander Reports

Highlander Research and Education Center, Inc.
1959 Highlander Way   Ph: (615)933-3443
New Market, TN 37820   Fax: (615)933-3424
E-mail: hrec@igc.apc.org
Contact: Mary Thom Adams, Editor; Tami Elkins, Editor.
Desc: Reports on the Center's efforts "to develop leadership for democracy in labor unions and community organizations struggling for justice and social change in Appalachia." Concerned with such issues as environmental and occupational health hazards, the educational needs of rank and file union members, voter registration/education, community-based health clinics, and land and energy resources. Recurring features include news of the Center, news of members and supporters, and a calendar of events. *Type:* Newsletter.

HR Tool Kit Blueprint

CCH Inc.
2700 Lake Cook Rd.   Ph: (847)267-7000
Riverwoods, IL 60015   Free: 800-449-8114
   Fax: (847)224-8299
URL: http://www.cch.com; http://www.cch.com; http://www.hr.cch.com.
Contact: Phyllis N. Green, Editor, phyllis_green@cch.com.
Desc: A monthly newsletter that provides timely coverage of company practices and government developments. *Type:* Newsletter.

Human Resources Report

Bureau of National Affairs, Inc. (BNA)
1231 25th St. NW   Ph: (202)452-4323
Washington, DC 20037   Free: 800-372-1033
   Fax: (202)452-7773
E-mail: bnaplus@bna.com
Contact: Gail Moorstein, Managing Editor.
Desc: Monitors employee and labor relations in the United States. Follows private sector developments in compensation, health benefits, Equal Employment Opportunity (EEO), labor economics, legislation, and regulatory issues. *Type:* Newsletter.

IBEW Journal

International Brotherhood of Electrical Workers, AFL-CIO
1125 15th St. NW   Ph: (202)728-6014
Washington, DC 20005   Fax: (202)728-7664
Contact: C. James Spellane, Director.
Desc: Labor magazine for local union members. *Type:* Periodical.

Idaho Employment

Idaho State Department of Labor
317 Main St.   Ph: (208)334-6168
Boise, ID 83735-0670   Free: 800-772-2553
E-mail: jadams@doe.state.id.us.
Desc: Discusses unemployment rates, workers, hours and salary, economic updates, and the agricultural influence of the state. *Type:* Newsletter.

Illinois Workers' Compensation Law Bulletin

LRP Publications
747 Dresher Rd.   Ph: (215)784-0941
PO Box 980   Free: 800-341-7874
Horsham, PA 19044-0980   Fax: (215)784-0870
E-mail: custserve@lrp.com
Contact: Teri Danik, Editor; Kenneth Kahn, Publisher.
Desc: Publishes court opinions regarding Illinois workers' compensation. *Type:* Newsletter.

Impact

Canada Law Book, Inc.
240 Edward St.   Ph: (905)841-6472
Aurora, ON, Canada L4G 3S9   Free: 800-263-3269
   Fax: (905)841-5085
E-mail: webmaster@canadalawbook.ca
URL: http://www.canadalawbook.ca
Contact: Lynn H. Harnden, Editor; Simon Ouellet.
Desc: Addresses issues in employer/employee relations from legal and managerial perspectives. Remarks: Additional toll-free telephone number: 800-263-3269 (in Canada only). *Type:* Newsletter.

Improving Employee Productivity

Institute of Management & Administration, Inc.
29 W. 35th St., 5th Fl.   Ph: (212)244-0360
New York, NY 10001-2299   Fax: (212)564-0465
E-mail: subserve@ioma.com
URL: http://www.ioma.com
Contact: Ann Podolske, Editor; Lee Rath, Publisher.
Desc: Provides tips on motivating employees and improving business productivity. *Type:* Newsletter.

Inside Labor Relations

Alignmark Information Publishing
1340 Braddock Pl., Ste. 400   Ph: (703)706-0207
Alexandria, VA 22314   Fax: (703)683-4852
Contact: Matthew Tallmer, Editor.
Desc: Provides intelligence for the executive tracking legal, political and regulartory developments affecting national labor policy. Recurring features include a column titled Hard News. *Type:* Newsletter.

Institute for Improvement in Quality and Productivity Newsletter

Institute for Improvement in Quality and Productivity
University of Waterloo
200 University Ave. W
Waterloo, ON, Canada N2L
 3G1
E-mail: brodgers@jeeves.uwaterloo.ca.
Contact: G. Dennis Beecroft, Editor.
Desc: Provides continuing education and information for industries interested in productivity and quality management. Recurring features include news of educational opportunities. *Type:* Newsletter.

Interchange (Rockville)

Transportation Communications International Union
3 Research Pl.   Ph: (301)948-4910
Rockville, MD 20850   Fax: (301)330-7661
Contact: R. A. Scardelletti, Editor; L.E. Bosher, Managing Editor; D. S. Curry, Executive Dir.
Desc: Trade magazine for transportation union members. *Type:* Periodical.

International Leather Goods, Plastic and Novelty Workers' Union

265 W. 14th St., Ste. 711   Ph: (212)675-9240
New York, NY 10011   Fax: (212)675-6896
Contact: Rosemary Behrman, Pres.
Desc: AFL-CIO. *Type:* Association.

IRC Newsletter

Industrial Relations Center (IRC)
University of Hawaii
2425 Campus Rd.   Ph: (808)956-8132
Honolulu, HI 96822   Fax: (808)956-3609
E-mail: uhirc@hawaii.edu
Desc: Focuses on industrial relations and collective bargaining, with summaries of court decisions in the field and of decisions of the National Labor Relations Board and other boards and commissions. Covers pending legislation pertaining to work, labor-management relations, and similar subjects. *Type:* Newsletter.

IRRA Newsletter

Industrial Relations Research Association (IRRA)
University of Wisconsin -   Ph: (608)262-2762
 Madison   Fax: (608)265-4591
4233 Social Science Bldg.
1180 Observatory Dr.
Madison, WI 53706-1393
E-mail: irra@macc.wisc.edu
URL: http://www.irra.ssc.wisc.edu
Contact: Kay B. Hutchison, Editor, kbhutchi@facstaff.wisc.edu.
Desc: Presents news of meetings, elections, and programs of this Association of business, labor, and government leaders interested in researching labor and management relationships. *Type:* Newsletter.

IUE News

International Union of Electronic, Electrical, Salaried, Machine and Furniture Workers, AFL-CIO
1126 16th St. NW   Ph: (202)785-7208
Washington, DC 20036-4866   Fax: (202)785-7448
E-mail: info@iue.org; iuenews@iue.org.
Contact: Lauren Asplen, Editor, (202)785-7230.
Desc: Labor newspaper. *Type:* Periodical.

Label Letter

Union Label & Services Trades
815 16th St. NW   Ph: (202)628-2131
Washington, DC 20006   Fax: (202)638-1602
Contact: Charlie Mercer, Editor.
Desc: Provides news and information in support of unionized labor, often highlighting injustices experienced by non-unionized members of the work force. Recurring features include a list of products and companies currently under boycott by the AFL-CIO. *Type:* Newsletter.

Labor Arbitration and Dispute Settlements

Bureau of National Affairs, Inc. (BNA)
1231 25th St. NW   Ph: (202)452-4323
Washington, DC 20037   Free: 800-372-1033
                       Fax: (202)452-7773
E-mail: bnaplus@bna.com
URL: http://www.bna.com.
Contact: Nancy J. Sedmak, Editor.
Desc: Contains the full text of arbitration cases and digests of court decisions involving arbitration. *Type:* Newsletter.

Labor Arbitration in Government

American Arbitration Association
140 W. 51st St.   Ph: (212)484-4000
New York, NY 10020-1203   Fax: (212)541-4041
URL: http://www.adr.org
Contact: Susan Zuckerman, Editor.
Desc: Contains a summary of labor arbitration awards involving agencies of government. Covers city, county, state, and federal employment issues. *Type:* Newsletter.

Labor Area Summary

Bureau of Labor Market Information
New York State Department of Labor
State Office Bldg. Campus
Albany, NY 12240
Desc: Deals with employment and unemployment in major metropolitan areas. *Type:* Newsletter.

Labor Center Reporter

Center for Labor Research and Education
Institute of Industrial Relations
University of California, Berkeley
2521 Channing Way   Ph: (510)642-0323
Berkeley, CA 94720   Fax: (510)642-6432
E-mail: clre@violet.berkley.edu
URL: gopher:violet.berkeley.eduport2521; http://violet.berkeley.edu/~iir/clre/lcr/lcr.html.
Desc: Supplies economic and social analysis of issues of concern to the trade union community. *Type:* Newsletter.

Labor and Employment Law

Section of Labor and Employment Law
American Bar Association (ABA)
750 N. Lake Shore Dr.   Ph: (312)988-6076
Chicago, IL 60611-3319 Fax: (312)988-6081
Contact: Elliott Brehoff, Editor; Timothy O'Reilly, Editor; Joel O'Alba, Editor.
Desc: Discusses labor and employment law. Recurring features include a calendar of events, reports of meetings, news of educational opportunities, and notices of publications available. *Type:* Newsletter.

Labor Institute of Public Affairs

815 16th St. NW, Ste. 206   Ph: (202)637-5334
Washington, DC 20006   Free: 800-242-UNION
                            Fax: (202)508-6962
Contact: Bill Wagner, Exec.Dir.
Desc: Sponsored by the AFL-CIO. Produces educational programs for labor unions; also produces news programs for broadcast and public television. *Type:* Association.

Labor-Management Relations Analysis/News and Background

Bureau of National Affairs, Inc. (BNA)
1231 25th St. NW   Ph: (202)452-4323
Washington, DC 20037   Free: 800-372-1033
                       Fax: (202)452-7773
E-mail: bnaplus@bna.com
Contact: Nancy J. Sedmark, Editor.
Desc: Summarizes developments and rulings in the field of labor law. Covers major non-decisional developments and recent significant arbitration awards and offers in-depth analysis and evaluation of the week's labor news. *Type:* Newsletter.

Labor Notes

Labor Education and Research Project
7435 Michigan Ave.   Ph: (313)842-6262
Detroit, MI 48210   Fax: (313)842-0227
E-mail: labornote@igc.apc.org; labornotes@labornotes.org.
Contact: Jim West, Editor, jimwlaboratoryornotes.org; Martha Gruelle, Editor, marhtaglaboratoryornotes.org.
Desc: Carries news of the labor movement from the grassroots perspective of rank-and-file union members. Recurring features include letters to the editor, a resources column which lists publications, films, calendars, and other materials available, and columns titled NewsWatch, Steward's Corner, Review, Speaking for Ourselves, Viewpoint, Solidarity Network, and Resources. *Type:* Newsletter.

Labor Relations

Bureau of National Affairs, Inc. (BNA)
1231 25th St. NW   Ph: (202)452-4323
Washington, DC 20037   Free: 800-372-1033
                       Fax: (202)452-7773
E-mail: bnaplus@bna.com
Contact: Bill L. Manville, Editor.
Desc: Contains full text and summaries of federal labor laws and summaries of state labor laws, National Labor Relations Board and court rulings, and policy guides for employer-employee relations. Discusses the employer's legal rights and obligations concerning labor relations matters. *Type:* Newsletter.

Labor Relations Bulletin

Bureau of Business Practice
24 Rope Ferry Rd.   Ph: (860)442-4365
Waterford, CT 06386   Free: 800-243-0876
                       Fax: (860)437-3555
URL: http://www.bbpnews.com
Contact: Robert Halprin, Editor, robert_halprin@prenhall.com.
Desc: Provides information and insight to management and labor officials to help them avoid or resolve conflicts. Recurring features include reports on current developments in labor law and relations, discipline and grievance cases based on actual arbitration, a question and answer column on labor and employment relations, and a column titled Reflections of an Arbitrator, offering the insight and experience of prominent national arbitrators. *Type:* Newsletter.

Labor Relations Reporter

Bureau of National Affairs, Inc. (BNA)
1231 25th St. NW   Ph: (202)452-4323
Washington, DC 20037   Free: 800-372-1033
                       Fax: (202)452-7773
E-mail: bnaplus@bna.com
Contact: Nancy J. Sedmak, Editor.
Desc: Covers labor-management relations, wages and hours, labor arbitration, fair employment practices, and individual employment rights using multi-part notification and reference format. Remarks: Also available diskette. *Type:* Newsletter.

Labor Relations Week

The Bureau of National Affairs, Inc. (BNA)
1231 25th St. NW   Ph: (202)452-4200
Washington, DC 20037
E-mail: bnaplus@bna.com
URL: http://bna.com/mkt/hrl/hrlwdec.htm
Desc: Contains the complete text of Labor Relations Week, a magazine on congressional, judicial, legislative, and economic developments affecting private-sector labor relations. Replaces two BNA products: Retail/Services Labor Report and White Collar Report. *Type:* Database.

Labor Relations Week

Bureau of National Affairs, Inc. (BNA)
1231 25th St. NW   Ph: (202)452-4323
Washington, DC 20037   Free: 800-372-1033
                          Fax: (202)452-7773
E-mail: bnaplus@bna.com
Contact: Susan Sala, Managing Editor.
Desc: Provides a comprehensive overview of developments influencing labor relations in the private sector. *Type:* Newsletter.

Labor World

Labor World Publishing Company
E. 102 Boone Ave.   Ph: (509)327-7637
Spokane, WA 99202   Fax: (509)327-2331
Contact: John Leinen, Editor.
Type: Newsletter.

Labour Arbitration Cases

Canada Law Book Inc.
240 Edward St.   Ph: (905)841-6472
Aurora, ON, Canada L4G 3S9
URL: http://www.canadalawbook.com
Desc: Contains the complete text of more than 2000 Canadian labor arbitration decisions. Summaries of decisions are available in Canadian Labour Arbitration Summaries. *Available:* LEXIS-NEXIS, LEXIS; QL Systems Limited, QUICKLAW. *Type:* Database.

LEXIS® Employment Law Library

LEXIS-NEXIS
9443 Springboro Pike   Ph: (937)865-6800
PO Box 933
Dayton, OH 45401-0933
URL: http://www.lex-nexis.com
Desc: Contains state and federal case law, fair employment practices, and individual employment rights decisions, wage and hour decisions, state and federal codes, state public employee relations board decisions for a number of states, an employment law treatise, labor arbitration materials, social security rulings, health care materials, and relevant topical publications. *Available:* LEXIS-NEXIS, LEXIS. *Type:* Database.

LEXIS® State Employment Law Library

LEXIS-NEXIS
9443 Springboro Pike   Ph: (937)865-6800
PO Box 933
Dayton, OH 45401-0933
URL: http://www.lex-nexis.com
Desc: Contains employment-related decisions from all state Supreme Courts and from most state Courts of Appeals. Also includes relevant federal cases and agency decisions from the LEXIS Labor Library and the complete text of the current developments sections of BNA Daily Labor Report, Government Employee Relations Report, BNA Pensions & Benefits Daily, and BNA Pension Reporter. *Available:* LEXIS-NEXIS, LEXIS. *Type:* Database.

LMI News Release

Pennsylvania State Employment Service
140 N. Duke St.   Fax: (717)771-4402
York, PA 17401-1110
Contact: L. Baugher, Editor.
Desc: Furnishes labor force and unemployment statistics, along with average factory hours and earnings. *Type:* Newsletter.

Local 876 News

United Food & Commercial Workers
Local 876
876 Horace Brown Dr.
Madison Heights, MI 48071
Contact: Katie Shullman, Managing Editor; Andy Johnson, Editor.
Desc: Union Magazine. *Type:* Newsletter.

Management Report for Nonunion Organizations

John Wiley and Sons, Inc.
605 3rd Ave.   Ph: (212)850-6000
New York, NY 10158   Free: 800-225-5945
                          Fax: (212)850-6049
E-mail: subinfo@wiley.com
Contact: Sarah Magee, Editor; Alfred T. DeMaria, Editor; Susan Malowski, Subscription Mgr.
Desc: Features news on current activities; employers' responses; NLRB rulings; court cases; pending legislation; government policies; and advice and opinions from Alfred T. DeMaria, "one of the country's foremost labor lawyers" representing management. *Type:* Newsletter.

Migrant Dropout Reconnection Program

Robert Lynch
BOCES Geneseo Migrant   Ph: (716)245-5681
   Center   Fax: (716)245-5680
Holcomb Bldg., Rm. 210
Geneseo, NY 14454
Contact: Robert Lynch, Dir.
Desc: A program of the BOCES Geneseo Migrant Center . Migrant farmworker youth who have dropped out of the U.S. public education system. *Type:* Association.

Milwaukee Labor Press, AFL-CIO

Milwaukee County Labor Council AFL-CIO
633 S. Hawley Rd.   Ph: (414)771-7070
Milwaukee, WI 53214   Fax: (414)771-0509
E-mail: lbnprscc@execpc.com.
Contact: Carole Casamento, Editor.
Desc: Newspaper (tabloid) on issues concerning labor unions and members. *Type:* Periodical.

The MOICC Newsletter

Minnesota Occupational Information
Coordinating Committee (MOICC)
Dept. of Economic Security   Ph: (612)296-2072
390 N. Robert St.
St. Paul, MN 55101
Contact: John Cosgrove, Editor.
Desc: Promotes communication and cooperation among those who produce and use occupational information. Monitors local, state, and national developments and programs of interest to planners, counselors, and placement staff in education, employment, and training programs. *Type:* Newsletter.

National Business News

National Business Association
PO Box 870728
Dallas, TX 75287-0728
Desc: Gives the self-employed business owner advice on productivity and growth. *Type:* Newsletter.

National Federation of Independent Unions

1166 S. 11th St.   Ph: (215)336-3300
Philadelphia, PA 19147   Fax: (215)755-3542
Contact: F. J. Chiappardi, Pres.
Desc: Federation of more than 300 independent labor unions. Seeks to obtain national recognition and equal representation for independent unions in Washington, DC and elsewhere. Conducts legislative conference. *Type:* Association.

National Right to Work Committee

8001 Braddock Rd., Ste. 500   Ph: (703)321-9820
Springfield, VA 22160   Free: 800-325-7892
                               Fax: (703)321-7342
E-mail: info@nrtw.org
URL: http://www.nrtw.org/
Contact: Reed E. Larson, Pres.
Desc: Individuals seeking to promote the principle that "everyone must have the right but not be compelled to join labor unions." *Type:* Association.

National Right to Work Legal Defense and Education Foundation

8001 Braddock Rd., Ste. 600   Ph: (703)321-8510
Springfield, VA 22160   Free: 800-336-3600
                               Fax: (703)321-9319
Contact: Reed E. Larson, Pres.
Desc: Assists employees whose human and civil rights are being violated under compulsory union membership arrangements. Provides free legal aid to individual workers and conducts in-depth research aimed at developing new legal theories based on existing law and legal precedents which may be effectively utilized to assist employees whose rights have been infringed by compulsory unionism. General case classifications include: misuse of compulsory union dues for political and ideological purposes; violations of the constitutional right of free speech and assembly and other civil rights; violations of the merit principle in public employment and academic freedom in public education; injustice of compulsory union hiring hall "referral system"; violations of existing protections against compulsory unionism; victimization of persons and property of employees by outright union violence. *Type:* Association.

National Right to Work Newsletter

National Right to Work Committee
8001 Braddock Rd., Ste. 500   Ph: (703)321-9820
Springfield, VA 22160   Free: 800-325-7892
                               Fax: (703)321-7143
Contact: Reed Larson, Editor.
Desc: Provides information on compulsory unionism, labor law, politics, and economics. *Type:* Newsletter.

New Unionist

New Union Party
1821 University Ave. W., No.   Ph: (651)646-5546
S-116
St. Paul, MN 55104
E-mail: nup@minn.net
Contact: Jeff Miller, Editor.
Desc: Enunciates the program of the New Union Party. Focuses on issues of industrial organization, labor, economics, and politics. *Type:* Newsletter.

New York Taylor Law Update

NYPER Publications, LLC
887 Birchwood Ln.   Ph: (518)786-1654
Niskayuna, NY 12309   Fax: (518)456-8582
E-mail: nyper@capital.net
Contact: Harvey Randoll, Editor.
Desc: Summarizes court and administrative rulings affecting labor relations in public employment. *Type:* Newsletter.

NLS News

National Longitudinal Surveys
2 Massachusetts Ave. NE, Rm.   Ph: (202)606-7388
4945   Fax: (202)606-6425
Washington, DC 20212-0001
E-mail: nls_info@bls.gov
Contact: Donna S. Rothstein, Editor, rothstein_d@bls.gov.
Desc: Contains the status and availability of NLS (National Longitudinal Surveys) data tapes and CD-ROMs for the seven NLS cohorts (Older Men, Mature Women, Young Men, Young Women, Youth 79 and children, and Youth 97); notices to researchers of data file or documentation errors; summaries of in-progress and completed NLS research; and other information of general interest to the NLS research community. Remarks: Also available hard copy. *Type:* Newsletter.

NY Workers Compensation Law Reporter

LRP Publications
747 Dresher Rd.   Ph: (215)784-0941
PO Box 980   Free: 800-341-7874
Horsham, PA 19044-0980   Fax: (215)784-0870
E-mail: custserve@lrp.com
Contact: Joan Grossman, Editor.
Desc: Provides full text of the workers compensation decisions in New York, including statutes, rules, regulations, and applicable forms. All are fully indexed and summarized for fast, accurate researching. *Type:* Newsletter.

Our Ontario

Ontario Public Service Employees Union
100 Lesmill Rd.   Ph: (416)443-8888
North York, ON, Canada M3B   Free: 800-268-7376
3P8   Fax: (416)443-1702
E-mail: opseu@opseu.org
URL: http://www.opseu.org.
Contact: Kafie FitzRandolph, Editor, kfitzrandolph@opseu.org.
Desc: Union magazine. *Type:* Periodical.

Paperworkers International Union, United, AFL-CIO, LU 315

PO Box 1475   Ph: (615)834-8590
Nashville, TN 37202   Fax: (615)834-7741
URL: http://www.upiu.org
Contact: Boyd Young, Intl.Pres.
Type: Association.

Payroll Manager's Letter

Bureau of Business Practice
24 Rope Ferry Rd.   Ph: (860)442-4365
Waterford, CT 06386   Free: 800-243-0876
                                 Fax: (860)437-3555
URL: http://www.bbpnews.com
Contact: Joanne Mitchell-George, Managing Editor, joanne_mitchell-george@prenhall.com; Julia Muino Russell, Senior Editor.
Desc: Provides information payroll professionals require to comply with IRS, SSA, and other government regulations. Includes reports on court cases and their impact on payroll, relevant technology updates, and innovations in the payroll field. *Type:* Newsletter.

Pennsylvania AFL-CIO/COPE Newsletter

Pennsylvania AFL-CIO
230 State St.   Ph: (717)238-9351
Harrisburg, PA 17101-1138   Fax: (717)238-8541
Contact: James H. Deegan, Editor.
Desc: Communicates news and information on labor issues. Recurring features include news of research. *Type:* Newsletter.

Personnel Practice Ideas

Warren, Gorham & Lamont, Inc.
RIA Group
PO Box 6159   Free: 800-950-1216
Carol Stream, IL 60197
Contact: Gerard Panaro, Editor.
Desc: Considers the range of issues facing those engaged in personnel management. Concentrates on discussing legislative and regulatory developments related to personnel and labor topics. *Type:* Newsletter.

Planning Newsletter

Sachnoff & Weaver, Ltd.
30 S. Wacker Dr., No. 2900   Ph: (312)207-1000
Chicago, IL 60606   Fax: (312)207-6400
E-mail: swltd@aol.com
Contact: Jeff London, Editor.
Desc: Reviews developments in a variety of areas of law affecting closely-held businesses, including labor and employment issues, tax issues, intellectual property, and employee benefits. Discusses recent court decisions and new laws passed. *Type:* Newsletter.

Profiles of American Labor Unions (PALU)

Gale Group Inc.
27500 Drake Rd.   Ph: (248)699-4253
Farmington Hills, MI 48331-   Free: 800-877-GALE
3535   Fax: (248)699-8070
E-mail: galeord@galegroup.com
URL: http://www.galegroup.com.; http://www.gale.com.
Contact: Terrance Peck, Editor; Donna Craft, Editor.
Desc: Over 313 national and nearly 33,000 independent, regional, state, and local unions in the United States; companies, plants, and other facilities with labor agreements. *Type:* Directory.

Public Employee Reporters

LRP Publications
747 Dresher Rd.   Ph: (215)784-0941
PO Box 980
Horsham, PA 19044
E-mail: custserve@lrp.com
URL: http://www.lrp.com
Contact: Lee Ann Kurzinsky, Product Group Mgr., (215)784-0941, fax: (215)784-9639, custserv@lrp.com.
Desc: Covers labor relations in the public sector for the following states: California, Florida, Illinois, Indiana, Michigan, New Jersey, Ohio, New York, and Pennsylvania. Provides summaries by state and subject, all legal decisions, and orders of public employment boards and commissions and related appellate court decisions. *Available:* LEXIS-NEXIS, LEXIS. *Type:* Database.

Quality First

The Dartnell Corp.
360 Hiatt Dr.   Free: 800-621-5463
Palm Beach Gardens, FL 33418   Fax: (561)622-2423
E-mail: dartnell@dartnellcorp.com
URL: http://www.dartnellcorp.com
Contact: David Dee, Editor.
Desc: Provides information on producing quality products and services. *Type:* Newsletter.

Report on Salary Surveys

Institute of Management & Administration, Inc.
29 W. 35th St., 5th Fl.   Ph: (212)244-0360
New York, NY 10001-2299   Fax: (212)564-0465
E-mail: subserve@ioma.com
URL: http://www.ioma.com
Contact: Laime Vaitkus, Editor, lvaitkus@ioma.com; Perry Patterson, Publisher, ppatterson@ioma.com.
Desc: Provides information about setting and controlling compensation levels. Remarks: Also available via e-mail. *Type:* Newsletter.

Resistor

IBM Workers United
19 Julian St.   Ph: (607)797-6911
Binghamton, NY 13905-1911
Contact: Lee Conrad, Editor.
Desc: Reports news on IBM and its effect on employees from a worker and union perspective. *Type:* Newsletter.

RWDSU Record

Retail, Wholesale and Dept. Store Union-AFL-CIO
30 E. 29th St.   Ph: (212)684-5300
New York, NY 10016-7997   Fax: (212)779-2809
Contact: Stuart Appelbeum, Editor.
Desc: Labor union newspaper. *Type:* Periodical.

St. Louis/Southern Illinois Labor Tribune

St. Louis/Southern Illinois Tribune
505 S. Ewing Ave.   Ph: (314)535-9660
St. Louis, MO 63103   Fax: (314)535-2700
Contact: Dana Spitgev, Editor; Edward M. Finkelstein, Publisher; Don Chesley, Marketing Dir.
Desc: Labor newspaper (AFL-CIO). *Type:* Periodical.

School of Labor and Industrial Relations Newsletter

School of Labor and Industrial Relations
College of Social Science
Michigan State University
East Lansing, MI 48824-1032   Ph: (517)355-1800
                                 Fax: (517)355-7656
Contact: Sally Pratt, Editor.
Desc: Reports news of the School, including the status of various programs and services and statistics on growth. Contains articles on manpower, organizational behavior and personnel management, international and comparative labor and industrial relations, social structure and community organization, and social and industrial psychology. *Type:* Newsletter.

Screen Actor

Screen Actor
5757 Wilshire Blvd.   Ph: (213)549-6652
Los Angeles, CA 90036   Fax: (213)549-6656
Contact: Katherine Moore, Director/Supervising Editor; Greg Krizman, Managing Editor.
Desc: Publishes news of the Screen Actors Guild (SAG) for national members. Concerned with labor issues in the motion picture industry, legislation relative to the industry, union benefits, retirement plans, and news of local performers and performances in film and television. *Type:* Newsletter.

Solidarity

International Union, U.A.W.
8000 E. Jefferson Ave.   Ph: (313)926-5291
Detroit, MI 48214   Fax: (313)331-1520
E-mail: uaw@uaw.org
URL: http://www.uaw.org
Contact: David Elsila, Editor.
Desc: Labor magazine. *Type:* Periodical.

Southwest Statistical Summary

U.S. Bureau of Labor Statistics
525 Griffin St., Rm. 221   Ph: (214)767-6970
Dallas, TX 75202   Fax: (214)767-3720
URL: http://www.stats.bls.gov/rogecon.htm.
Contact: Cheryl R. Abbot, Economist.
Desc: Consists of consumer price indexes for the U.S., Dallas-Ft. Worth, and Houston, Texas. *Type:* Newsletter.

State County & Municipal Employees AFL-CIO, Dc, DC 33

3001 Walnut St, 9th Fl.   Ph: (215)895-3300
Philadelphia, PA 19104
Contact: Franklin Wallace, Controller.
Type: Association.

State Labor Laws

Bureau of National Affairs, Inc. (BNA)
1231 25th St. NW   Ph: (202)452-4323
Washington, DC 20037   Free: 800-372-1033
     Fax: (202)452-7773
E-mail: bnaplus@bna.com
Contact: Jeff Day, Editor, (202)452-4474, fax: (202)452-4603, jday@bna.com.
Desc: Provides full texts, digests, and charts of state labor laws, covering their scope, jurisdiction, administration, and enforcement. Also discusses how state labor law relates to federal laws affecting labor relations and employment regulation and provides directories of state agencies that administer and enforce these laws. *Type:* Newsletter.

Sugar World

International Commission for Coordination of Solidarity Among Sugar Workers (ICCSASW)
2084 Danforth Ave., Ste. 3   Ph: (416)467-8621
Toronto, ON, Canada M4C 1J9   Fax: (416)467-9143
E-mail: iccsasw@web.apc.org
URL: http://www.web.apc.org/sugarworker.
Contact: R. McQuaid, Editor.
Desc: Features reports of meetings and current legislation. *Remarks:* Also available in Spanish. *Type:* Newsletter.

Summary of Labor Arbitration Awards

American Arbitration Association
140 W. 51st St.   Ph: (212)484-4000
New York, NY 10020-1203   Fax: (212)541-4041
URL: http://www.adr.org
Contact: Susan Lukerman.
Desc: Provides information on private-sector labor arbitration decisions, discipline, discharge, sexual harassment, drug and alcohol testing, absenteeism, and safety in the workplace. *Type:* Newsletter.

The Teamster

International Brotherhood of Teamsters
25 Louisiana Ave. NW   Ph: (202)624-6800
Washington, DC 20001-2198   Fax: (202)624-6918
URL: http://www.teamster.org.
Contact: Matt Witt, Editor.
Desc: Labor union magazine. *Type:* Periodical.

32E Events

Service Employees International Union Local 32E (SEIU)
4234 Bronx Blvd.   Ph: (718)324-6556
Bronx, NY 10466   Fax: (718)994-2932
Contact: Diana D. DeGroat, Editor.
Desc: Educates and informs members, retirees, and their families. Notifies of meetings and benefit changes. *Type:* Newsletter.

Total Productive Maintenance

Productivity, Inc.
541 NE 20th Ave., Ste. 108   Free: 800-966-5423
Portland, OR 97232-2862
Contact: Norman Bodek, Publisher; Lloyd Resnick, Editor-in-Chief; Antionette Saloomey, Circulation Mgr.
Desc: Spotlights productivity. *Type:* Newsletter.

Trade Union Advisor

Labor Research Association, Inc.
145 W. 28th St.   Ph: (212)714-1677
New York, NY 10001   Free: 800-875-8775
     Fax: (212)714-1674
Contact: Greg Tarpinian, Editor.
Desc: Covers economic and political issues as they affect American workers and trade union leaders. *Type:* Newsletter.

U.A. Journal

United Association of Journeymen & Apprentices of the Plumbing & Pipefitting Industry of the U.S. & Canada
901 Massachusetts Ave. NW   Ph: (202)628-5823
Washington, DC 20001   Fax: (202)628-5024
URL: http://www.ua.org.
Contact: Thomas H. Patchell, Editor.
Desc: Labor magazine. *Type:* Periodical.

The Union Craftsman

Reilly/Echols Printing, Inc.
1710 S. Harwood   Ph: (214)428-8385
PO Box 152358   Free: 800-874-5863
Dallas, TX 75315-2358   Fax: (214)426-2548
Contact: Mrs. Wallace C. Reilly, Editor.
Desc: Discusses labor issues. *Type:* Newsletter.

Union Democracy Review

Association for Union Democracy, Inc.
500 State St.   Ph: (718)855-6650
Brooklyn, NY 11217-1803   Fax: (718)855-6799
E-mail: aud@igc.apc.org
Contact: Herman Benson, Editor.
Desc: Supports the Association's aim to promote democratic principles and practice in the American labor movement and organizations. Provides reports on union developments and reform, analysis of union democracy legislation, and discussion of the pros and cons of various aspects of union democracy. *Type:* Newsletter.

Union Labor Journal

Kern-Inyo-Mono County Central Labor Council
200 W. Jeffrey   Ph: (805)324-6451
Bakersfield, CA 93305   Fax: (805)327-8379
E-mail: kernclc@lightspeed.net
URL: http://www.kernlabor.org.
Desc: Focuses on labor issues. *Type:* Newsletter.

Union Labor Report

Bureau of National Affairs, Inc. (BNA)
1231 25th St. NW   Ph: (202)452-4323
Washington, DC 20037   Free: 800-372-1033
     Fax: (202)452-7773
E-mail: bnaplus@bna.com
Contact: Jeff Day, Managing Editor.
Desc: Provides a notification and reference service covering labor relations questions and reporting on employee relations and union developments. Carries a section titled Reference File, which includes the subsections: In General; Steward's Guide to Shop Problems; Union Organizing; Rights of Strikers; Collective Bargaining; When NLRB Steps In; Bargaining Elections; Procedure in Complaint Cases; State Labor Relations Laws, Wages, Hours, Overtime, Child Labor; Occupational Safety and Health; Arbitration Awards; and Union Administration. *Type:* Newsletter.

Union Labor Report Weekly Newsletter

Bureau of National Affairs, Inc. (BNA)
1231 25th St. NW   Ph: (202)452-4323
Washington, DC 20037   Free: 800-372-1033
     Fax: (202)452-7773
E-mail: bnaplus@bna.com
Contact: Jeff Day, Managing Editor.
Desc: Provides a roundup of developments of concern to organized labor. Includes summaries of arbitration awards and court cases. *Type:* Newsletter.

Union Labor Report Weekly Newsletter

The Bureau of National Affairs, Inc. (BNA)
1231 25th St. NW   Ph: (202)452-4200
Washington, DC 20037
E-mail: bnaplus@bna.com
URL: http://bna.com/mkt/hrl/hrlwdec.htm
Desc: Contains the complete text of Union Labor Weekly Newsletter, a publication covering developments and trends in union activity and labor laws. Covers federal and state legislative action, contract disputes related to complaints and grievances, union financial data, and summaries of significant labor arbitration awards. *Type:* Database.

Union Labor Report's On the Line

Bureau of National Affairs, Inc. (BNA)
1231 25th St. NW   Ph: (202)452-4323
Washington, DC 20037   Free: 800-372-1033
     Fax: (202)452-7773
E-mail: bnaplus@bna.com
Contact: Jeff Day, Managing Editor.
Desc: Reports on shop floor issues affecting union stewards. Includes summaries of arbitration awards, court cases, and problem-solving tips. *Type:* Newsletter.

UNITE!

Union of Needletrades, Industrial & Textile Employees
1710 Broadway   Ph: (212)265-7000
New York, NY 10019   Fax: (212)582-3175
Contact: Jo-Ann Mort, Director; Michael Yellin, Editor.
Desc: Disseminates information on the Union; concerned with legislation, safety, and labor bargaining practices. Recurring features include columns titled Washington Watch, Retirees, and President's Column. *Type:* Newsletter.

Unite! Magazine

Union of Needletrades, Industrial & Textile Employees
1710 Broadway   Ph: (212)265-7000
New York, NY 10019   Fax: (212)582-3175
Contact: Michael Yellin, Editor, myell@uniteunion.org.
Desc: Tabloid magazine for union members. Contains news of union activities and reports on organizing, collective bargaining, union policy, and legislative positions. *Type:* Periodical.

United Nations Staff Union

Muhammud Oummih
UN, Rm. S-525   Ph: (212)963-7076
New York, NY 10017   Fax: (212)963-3367
Contact: Rose Marie Waters, Pres.
Desc: Individuals employed by the United Nations . Engages in collective bargaining to represent the interests of UN employees. *Type:* Association.

Utah Labor Market Report

Utah Department of Workforce Services
140 East 300 South   Ph: (801)536-7800
PO Box 45249   Fax: (801)536-7869
Salt Lake City, UT 84145-0249
URL: http://udesb.state.ut.us/lmi; http://www.udesb.state.us.

Contact: Kenneth E. Jensen, Editor.

Desc: Provides economic analysis and data concerning Utah's labor market. Recurring features include news of research and notices of publications available. *Type:* Newsletter.

UTU News

United Transportation Union (UTU)
14600 Detroit Ave.   Ph: (216)228-9400
Cleveland, OH 44107   Fax: (216)228-5755
E-mail: utu@compuserve.com; 74407.576@compuserve.com.
URL: http://www.utu.org.
Contact: C.L. Little, Editor, c.little@utu.org.
Desc: Railroad, mass transit and bus labor newspaper (tabloid). *Type:* Periodical.

Voice of Local 399

Hospital and Service Employees Union
1247 W. 7th St.   Ph: (213)680-9567
Los Angeles, CA 90017   Fax: (213)488-0328
E-mail: seiu399@aol.com
Contact: Tom Ramsay, Editor.
Desc: Discusses issues of concern to the Local 399 hospital and service employees union of the Los Angeles area. Deals with wages, politics, health care, and member news. *Type:* Newsletter.

WDL News

Workers Defense League, Inc. (WDL)
218 W. 40th St., Rm. 205-209   Ph: (212)730-7412
New York, NY 10018
Contact: Jon Bloom, Editor.
Desc: Reports on the current projects of the League. *Type:* Newsletter.

West Virginia AFL-CIO Observer

West Virginia Labor Federation, AFL-CIO
501 Broad St.
Charleston, WV 25301
Contact: Cindy Pauley, Editor.
Desc: An informational tool for union members. *Type:* Newsletter.

WESTLAW® Labor and Employment

West Group
620 Opperman Dr.   Ph: (651)687-7000
St. Paul, MN 55164-0526
URL: http://www.westgroup.com
Desc: Contains the complete text of U.S. federal and state court decisions, statutes and regulations, administrative law publications, specialized files, and texts and periodicals dealing with labor law. *Available:* West Group, WESTLAW. *Type:* Database.

What's New in Collective Bargaining Negotiations and Contracts

The Bureau of National Affairs, Inc. (BNA)
1231 25th St. NW   Ph: (202)452-4200
Washington, DC 20037
E-mail: bnaplus@bna.com
URL: http://bna.com/mkt/hrl/hrlwdec.htm
Desc: Contains the complete text of the newsletter, What's New in Collective Bargaining Negotiations and Contracts. Includes case studies of problem-solving approaches to collective bargaining. *Type:* Database.

Workers' Comp Advisor - California Edition

Genesis Publishing, Inc.
12626 High Bluff Dr., Ste. 325   Ph: (619)453-0858
San Diego, CA 92130-2073
Contact: Donna Hawkins, Editor.

Desc: Covers workers' compensation and occupational medicine issues in California. Recurring features include letters to the editor, interviews, news of research, a calendar of events, reports of meetings, news of educational opportunities, book reviews, notices of publications available, and columns titled Med-Legal Briefs, Hotline Qs and As, and Case Law Updates. *Type:* Newsletter.

Workers' Comp Advisor - Ohio Edition

Genesis Publishing, Inc.
12626 High Bluff Dr., Ste. 325   Ph: (619)453-0858
San Diego, CA 92130-2073
Contact: Donna M. Buys, Editor.
Desc: Contains information on workers' compensation and occupational medicine in Ohio. Recurring features include letters to the editor, interviews, news of research, a calendar of events, reports of meetings, news of educational opportunities, book reviews, notices of publications available, and columns titled Med-Legal Briefs and Case Law Update. *Type:* Newsletter.

Workers' Comp Managed Care

Aspen Publishers, Inc.
200 Orchard Ridge Dr., No.   Ph: (301)417-7500
    200   Free: 800-638-8437
Gaithersburg, MD 20878   Fax: (301)417-7650
E-mail: customer.service@aspenpubl.com
URL: http://www.aspenpub.com
Contact: Jane Anderson, Editor.
Desc: Covers trends in workers' comp managed care, new state laws, and pilot projects involving workers' comp, 24-hour care, accreditation, employer case studies, and workers' comp acquisitions. Recurring features include interviews, news of research, and reports of meetings. *Type:* Newsletter.

Workers' Comp News

Examco
5728 Jefferson Hwy.   Ph: (504)733-8400
New Orleans, LA 70123   Free: 800-638-7597
    Fax: (504)729-4450
Contact: Pat Sheppard, Editor; Jan King, Publisher.
Desc: Provides information on workers' compensation. Recurring features include cost saving ideas, examples, and questions and answers. *Type:* Newsletter.

Workers' Compensation Business Management Guide

CCH Inc.
2700 Lake Cook Rd.   Ph: (847)267-7000
Riverwoods, IL 60015   Free: 800-449-8114
    Fax: (847)224-8299
URL: http://www.cch.com
Contact: Troy Hanson, Editor, hansont@cch.com.
Desc: Features timely reporting quick answers, case studies, and state law summaries. Remarks: Includes CCH Workers' Compensation Newsletter every two weeks and Workers' Compensation Business Management Guide Newsletter (issued seminmonthly); both are available separately as well. *Type:* Newsletter.

Workers' Compensation Monitor

LRP Publications
747 Dresher Rd.   Ph: (215)784-0941
PO Box 980   Free: 800-341-7874
Horsham, PA 19044-0980   Fax: (215)784-0870
E-mail: custserve@lrp.com
Contact: Gary Magel, Editor.
Desc: Suggest ways to reduce workers' compensation costs and improve your return -to-work programs. Provides proven solutions your colleagues have implemented to resolve their challenges. *Type:* Newsletter.

Working America

United Food and Commercial Workers International Union
1775 K St. NW   Ph: (202)223-3111
Washington, DC 20006
Contact: Douglas H. Dority, Editor; Greg Denier, Managing Editor.
Desc: Labor union magazine. *Type:* Periodical.

Working Smart

National Institute of Business Management
1750 Old Meadow Rd., Ste.   Ph: (703)905-8000
    302   Free: 800-543-2049
Mc Lean, VA 22102   Fax: (703)905-8042
Contact: Morey Stettner, Editor.
Desc: Provides advice, ideas and answers to help today's managers work more effectively and efficiently. *Type:* Newsletter.

Workplace News

Workplace News
240 Edward St.   Ph: (905)841-6481
Aurora, ON, Canada L4G 3S9   Free: 800-263-3269
    Fax: (905)841-5078
E-mail: workplace@canadalawbook.ca
Contact: Beth Marlin, Editor.
Desc: Covers labor and employment issues in Canada. Contains analyses of the impact of court and tribunal rulings as well as profiles of union and management personalities. *Type:* Newsletter.

Wyoming Labor Force Trends

Employment Resources Division
Research and Planning
PO Box 2760   Ph: (307)473-3808
246 S. Center   Fax: (307)473-3834
Casper, WY 82602
URL: http://wyjobs.state.wy.us/lmi/rphone.htm.
Contact: Gayle C. Edlin, Editor, gedlin@missc.state.wy.us; David Bullard, Assoc. Ed.; Valerie Davis, Assoc. Ed.
Desc: Reports on labor market developments and related issues in Wyoming. Contains employment statistics and economic analysis. *Type:* Newsletter.

Laboratory

Analytical Chemistry—Lab Guide

American Chemical Society
1155 16th St. NW   Ph: (202)872-4562
Washington, DC 20036   Free: 800-227-5558
    Fax: (202)776-8166
E-mail: cpt@acs.org; labguide@acs.org.
URL: http://pubs.acs.org/.
Desc: List of about 2,200 manufacturers of scientific instruments, equipment, chemicals, and other supplies for scientific research and chemical laboratories; laboratory supply houses; analytical and research services. *Type:* Directory.

Biomedical Products—Life Science Lab Reference

Cahners Business Information
New Product Information Division
301 Gibraltar Dr.   Ph: (973)292-5100
Morris Plains, NJ 07950   Fax: (973)539-3476
URL: http://www.bioprodmag.com
Contact: Stephen C. Ernst, Editor, sernst@gordon.cahners.com; Pamela H. Ahlberg.
Desc: List of over 1000 manufacturers of equipment and supplies for laboratories using animals in research. *Type:* Directory.

Laboratory

Clinical Laboratory Management Association
989 Old Eagle School Rd., Ste. 815
Wayne, PA 19087
Ph: (610)995-9580
Fax: (610)995-9568
URL: http://www.clma.org
Contact: George Linial, Exec. VP.
Desc: Individuals holding managerial or supervisory positions with clinical laboratories; persons engaged in eduation of such individuals; manufacturers or distributors of equipment or services to clinical laboratories. Objectives are: to enhance management skills and promote more efficient and productive department operations; to further exchange of professional knowledge, new technology, and colleague experience; to encourage cooperation among those engaged in management or supervisory functions. Activities include: workshops, seminars, and expositions; dissemination of information about legislation and other topics. *Type:* Association.

Directory of International and Regional Organizations Conducting Standards-Related Activities
National Technical Information Service (NTIS)
U.S. Department of Commerce
5285 Port Royal Rd.
Springfield, VA 22161-0001
Ph: (703)605-6000
Free: 800-553-NTIS
Fax: (703)605-6900
E-mail: orders@ntis.fedworld.gov
URL: http://www.ntis.gov.
Desc: 338 international and regional organizations which conduct standardization, certification, laboratory accreditation, and other standards-related activities. *Type:* Directory.

Linscott's Directory of Immunological & Biological Reagents
William D. Linscott
4877 Grange Rd.
Santa Rosa, CA 95404
Ph: (707)544-9555
Fax: (415)389-6025
E-mail: linscottsdirectory@compuserve.com.
Contact: William D. Linscott, Editor.
Desc: Approximately 500 suppliers of reagents used in biomedical research, worldwide. *Type:* Directory.

National Committee for Clinical Laboratory Studies
940 W. Valley Rd., Ste. 1400
Wayne, PA 19087-1898
Ph: (610)688-0100
Fax: (610)688-0700
E-mail: exoffice@nccls.org
URL: http://www.nccls.org
Contact: John V. Bergen, Ph.D., Exec.Dir.
Desc: Government agencies, professional societies, clinical laboratories, and industrial firms with interests in medical testing. Purposes are to promote the development of national and international standards for medical testing and to provide a consensus mechanism for defining and resolving problems that influence the quality and cost of laboratory work performed. *Type:* Association.

Landscaping

Associated Landscape Contractors of America
150 Elden St., Ste. 270
Herndon, VA 20170
Ph: (703)736-9666
Fax: (703)736-9668
E-mail: @alca.org
URL: http://www.alca.org
Contact: Debra Holder, Exec.Dir.
Desc: Landscape contractors. Works to represent, lead, and unify the interior and exterior landscape industry by working together on a national basis; addressing environmental and legislative issues; and creating increased opportunities in business. *Type:* Association.

City Trees
Society of Municipal Arborists
PO Box 364
Wellesley Hills, MA 02181
Ph: (781)235-7600
Fax: (978)535-3899
Contact: Leonard E. Phillips, Jr., Editor, lenp@ci.wellesley.ma.us.
Desc: Addresses all aspects of municipal (urban) forestry. Contains technical articles on species of trees, pest control, conservation, planning, design, and equipment. *Type:* Newsletter.

Garden Council
10210 Bald Hill Rd.
Mitchellville, MD 20721-2836
Contact: Gary Mariani, CEO.
Desc: Retailers, growers, manufacturers, distributors, suppliers, and trade association executives. Conducts nationwide consumer education, promotion, and advertising campaigns. Promotes the sale and use of lawn and garden products. *Type:* Association.

Garden Design
Meigher Communications
100 Avenue of the Americas
New York, NY 10013
Ph: (212)334-1212
Fax: (212)334-1260
Contact: Dorothy Kalins, Editor-in-Chief; Joe Armstrong, Publisher; Douglas Brenner, Editor.
Desc: Magazine on garden design, featuring individual gardens, design trend stories, design history, profiles, horticulture coverage, and book reviews. *Type:* Periodical.

Grounds Maintenance—Buyers' Guide Issue
Intertec Publishing Corp.
9800 Metcalf Ave.
Overland Park, KS 66212
Ph: (913)341-1300
Free: 800-400-5945
Fax: (913)967-1328
E-mail: gm_editorial@intertec.com.
URL: http://www.grounds-mag.com.
Contact: Mark Welterlen, Editor.
Desc: List of manufacturers, growers, and suppliers of materials for landscaping design, construction, and maintenance; landscaping associations. *Type:* Directory.

Landscape Management Greenbook—Buyers Guide Issue
Advanstar Communications
7500 Old Oak Blvd.
Cleveland, OH 44130-3369
Ph: (440)243-8100
Free: 800-225-4569
Fax: (440)891-2733
E-mail: directories@advanstar.com
URL: http://www.advanstar.com.
Contact: Terry McIver, Editor, tmciver@advanstar.com.
Desc: List of about 1200 manufacturers, dealers/distributors, and suppliers of landscaping and grounds maintenance equipment, chemicals, seeds, and supplies. *Type:* Directory.

Professional Grounds Management Forum
Professional Grounds Management Society
120 Cockeysville Rd., Ste. 104
Hunt Valley, MD 21030
Ph: (410)584-9754
Free: 800-609-7467
Fax: (410)584-9756
E-mail: ppgms@aol.com
Contact: John Gillan, Editor.
Desc: Reports news of the Society and its members. Provides information on upcoming conferences, recent government action, and on current topics of interest to members. *Type:* Newsletter.

Turf Notes
UMASS Extension
University of Massachusetts
French Hall
Amherst, MA 01003-0099
Ph: (508)831-1223
Fax: (508)831-0120
Contact: Mary C. Owen, Editor.
Desc: Promotes the profession of turfgrass manager. *Type:* Newsletter.

TurfGrass TRENDS
Advanstar Communications
7500 Old Oak Blvd.
Cleveland, OH 44130-3369
Ph: (440)243-8100
Free: 800-225-4569
Fax: (440)891-2733
E-mail: obmpbp@en.com
URL: http://www.lib.msu.edu/tgif; http://www.plcaa.org.
Contact: Terry McIver, Editor; John Payne, Publisher.
Desc: Provides current research articles provided by turf management schools in a practical format for turf managers. *Type:* Newsletter.

Vitis Vine
The Green Guerillas
625 Broadway, 9th Fl.
New York, NY 10012
Ph: (212)674-8124
Fax: (212)505-8613
Contact: Steve Frillmann, Editor.
Desc: Discusses gardening and the association's volunteer activities and events. Seeks to help low-income communities in New York City improve their landscape. *Type:* Newsletter.

Languages

American Association of Teachers of German
112 Haddontowne Ct., No. 104
Cherry Hill, NJ 08034
Ph: (609)795-5553
Fax: (609)795-9398
E-mail: aatg@bellatlantic.net
URL: http://www.aatg.org
Contact: Helene Zimmer-Loew, Exec.Dir.
Desc: Teachers of German at all levels; individuals interested in German language and culture. Offers in-service teacher-training workshops. *Type:* Association.

American Council of Teachers of Russian/American Council for Collaboration and Language Study
1776 Massachusetts Ave. NW, Ste. 700
Washington, DC 20036
Ph: (202)833-7522
Fax: (202)833-7523
E-mail: general@actr.org
URL: http://www.actr.org
Contact: Dan Davidson, Exec.Dir.
Desc: Private, non-profit educational association and exchange organization devoted to improving education, professional training, and research within and about the Russian-speaking world, including both the Russian Federation and the many scores of non-Russian cultures and populations inhabiting the regions of central and eastern Europe and Eurasia. Strongly committed to the principle that an international perspective in scholarship and education contributes to the development of new critical frames of reference and strengthens conceptual and methodological approaches in many disciplines. Provides special support for regional language research and training, textbook development for Russian and the other languages of the region, the teaching of English as a foreign language, faculty and curriculum development, and in-country immersion programs as the historic and core mission of the organization. *Type:* Association.

American Council on the Teaching of Foreign Languages

6 Executive Plz. Ph: (914)963-8830
Yonkers, NY 10701-6801 Fax: (914)963-1275
E-mail: actflhq@aol.com
URL: http://www.actfl.org
Contact: C. Edward Scebold, Exec.Dir.
Desc: Individuals interested in the teaching of classical and modern foreign languages in schools and colleges throughout America. Included in the ACTFL structure are state, regional, and national organizations of foreign language teachers and supervisors from all levels of education. Operates materials center which produces inexpensive classroom and professional materials. *Type:* Association.

American Translators Association

1800 Diagonal Rd., Ste. 220 Ph: (703)683-6100
Alexandria, VA 22314 Fax: (703)683-6122
E-mail: ata@atanet.org
URL: http://www.atanet.org
Contact: Walter W. Bacak, Jr., Exec.Dir.
Desc: Fosters the professional development of translators and interpreters and promotes the translation and interpretation professions. *Type:* Association.

Center for Applied Linguistics

4646 40th St. NW Ph: (202)362-0700
Washington, DC 20016 Fax: (202)362-3740
E-mail: info@cal.org
URL: http://www.cal.org
Contact: Donna Christian, Pres.
Desc: Serves as a national and international resource center in the application of linguistic science to social, cultural, and educational problems. *Type:* Association.

Intercultural Development Research Association

5835 Callaghan Rd., Ste. 350 Ph: (210)684-8180
San Antonio, TX 78228-1190 Fax: (210)684-5389
E-mail: contact@idra.org
URL: http://www.idra.org
Contact: Dr. Maria Robledo Montecel, Exec.Dir.
Desc: Professionals who have extensive field, research, and development-based experience in education, especially bilingual minority education and dropout prevention programs. Dedicated to the principle that all children are entitled to an equal educational opportunity. Strives for the elimination of educational inequities through involvement in the areas of training and technical assistance and research. *Type:* Association.

Linguistics and Language Behavior Abstracts

Sociological Abstracts, Inc.
Cambridge Scientific Abstracts
PO Box 22206 Ph: (619)695-8803
San Diego, CA 92192-0206
E-mail: socio@cerfnet.com
Contact: Terry M. Owen, Electronic Products Manager, (619)695-8803, fax: (619)695-0416, socio@cerfnet.com.
Desc: Contains more than 238,000 citations, with abstracts, to the world's published literature on the nature, use, and teaching of language as well as linguistics, speech, communication, and related topics from 1973 to the present. Includes citations to book reviews appearing in serials abstracted for Linguistics and Language Behavior Abstracts. *Available:* The Dialog Corporation, DIALOG; Cambridge Scientific Abstracts (CSA), Internet Database Service. *Type:* Database.

Modern Language Association of America

10 Astor Pl., 5th Fl. Ph: (212)475-9500
New York, NY 10003 Fax: (212)477-9863
E-mail: info@mla.org

URL: http://www.mla.org
Contact: Phyllis Franklin, Exec.Dir.
Desc: College and university teachers of English and of modern foreign languages. Seeks to advance all aspects of literary and linguistic study. *Type:* Association.

Modern Language Association of America—Job Information List

Modern Language Association of America
10 Astor Pl. Ph: (212)614-6349
New York, NY 10003-6981 Fax: (212)533-0680
Contact: Roy Chustek, Editor.
Desc: Available positions for college teachers of English and foreign languages in four-year colleges and universities; February issue includes separate section of openings in two-year institutions. Separate editions for English and American language and literature and for foreign language openings. *Type:* Directory.

National Association for Bilingual Education

1220 L St. NW, Ste. 605 Ph: (202)898-1829
Washington, DC 20005-4018 Fax: (202)789-2866
E-mail: nabe@nabe.org
Contact: Nancy Zelasko, Contact.
Desc: Educators, administrators, paraprofessionals, community and laypeople, and students. Purposes are to recognize, promote, and publicize bilingual education. *Type:* Association.

Phi Sigma Iota

5211 Essen Ln., Ste. 2 Ph: (504)769-7100
Baton Rouge, LA 70809-3593 Fax: (504)769-7105
Contact: Dr. Santiago Vilas, Exec.Dir.
Desc: Honor society - foreign languages. *Type:* Association.

Spectra

National Communication Association
5105 Backlick Rd., No. E Ph: (703)750-0533
Annandale, VA 22003 Fax: (703)914-9471
E-mail: members@natcom.org
Contact: James L. Gaudino, Editor.
Desc: Discusses forensics, interpretation, interpersonal communication, rhetoric and public address, communication theory, mass media, theater, and speech and language sciences. Recurring features include official business of the Association, news briefs concerning members, and notices of available materials. *Type:* Newsletter.

Laundry

CLA Member News

Coin Laundry Association
1315 Butterfield Rd., Ste. 212 Ph: (630)963-5547
Downers Grove, IL 60515 Fax: (630)963-5864
E-mail: info@coinlaundry.org
Contact: Brian Wallace, Dir. of Communications.
Desc: Provides management and technical information for members of the self-service (coin-operated) laundry and drycleaning industry. *Type:* Newsletter.

Cycles

Service Directions, Inc.
PO Box 380 Ph: (914)738-3800
Pelham, NY 10803 Free: 800-666-0505
  Fax: (914)738-3863
E-mail: SDIWECARE@aol.com
Desc: Describes new laundry equipment, advances in laundryroom management, and analyzes problems in residential laundryrooms. Recurring features include interviews. *Type:* Newsletter.

Fabricare

International Fabricare Institute
12251 Tech Rd. Ph: (301)622-1900
Silver Spring, MD 20904 Free: 800-638-2627
  Fax: (301)236-9320
E-mail: communications@ifi.org
Contact: Jillian Handman, Contributing Editor.
Desc: Informs drycleaners and launderers of industry developments and Institute activities. Carries legislative updates, technical data, management ideas, and tips on problem fabrics and garments. *Type:* Newsletter.

NAILM News

National Association of Institutional Linen Management
2130 Lexington Rd., Ste. H Ph: (606)624-0177
Richmond, KY 40475 Free: 800-669-0863
  Fax: (606)624-3580
Contact: Kathleen Lane, Managing Editor; Adrienne Grizzell, Editor.
Desc: Covers management and technical information, governmental activity, and upcoming educational events related to the institutional laundry industry. Recurring features include news of the Association and its members and calendar of events. *Type:* Newsletter.

National Association of Institutional Linen Management

2130 Lexington Rd., Ste. H Ph: (606)624-0177
Richmond, KY 40475 Fax: (606)624-3580
E-mail: nailm@iclub.org
URL: http://www.nailm.com
Contact: Adrienne Grizzell, CEO.
Desc: Managers of laundries serving institutions such as hospitals, nursing homes, hotels, schools, and correctional facilities. Seeks improvement of laundry technology and management through exchange of information and educational programs. *Type:* Association.

Uniform and Textile Service Association

1300 N. 17th St., Ste. 750 Ph: (703)247-2600
Arlington, VA 22209 Fax: (703)841-4750
E-mail: info@utsa.com
URL: http://www.utsa.com
Contact: David F. Hobson, Pres. & CEO.
Desc: Conducts research in improved processes, materials, and marketing practices. *Type:* Association.

Law

ABA Journal

American Bar Association
750 N. Lake Shore Dr. Ph: (312)988-5000
Chicago, IL 60611-4497 Free: 800-285-2221
  Fax: (312)988-6881
E-mail: abajournal@abanet.org.
Contact: Gary Hengstler, Editor and Publisher, (312)988-5999, fax: (312)988-6026, hengstler@staff.abanet.org; Robert A. Brouwer, Associate Publisher, (312)988-5993, fax: (312)988-6014, brouwer@staff.abanet.org.
Desc: Legal publication. *Type:* Periodical.

Accounting for Law Firms

Leader Publications
New York Law Publishing Company
345 Park Ave., South Ph: (212)545-6170
New York, NY 10010 Free: 800-888-8300
  Fax: (212)696-1848
E-mail: leader@ljextra.com; leader@ljextra.com.
Contact: Mark Hopkins, Editor, (917)256-2019, fax: (212)481-8161, mhopkins@ljextra.com.
Desc: Offers information on accounting practices, arbitration, contingency fees, and revenue rulings for law firms. *Type:* Newsletter.

The Advocate

Capital City Press
525 Lafayette St. Ph: (504)383-1111
Baton Rouge, LA 70802-5494
E-mail: jarnold@communique.net
Desc: Contains the complete text of news items and feature articles from The Advocate (formerly The Morning Advocate), a general-circulation daily. Regional coverage emphasizes Louisiana state and local business, government, and politics, as well as consumer affairs, crime, education, entertainment, real estate, religion, and sports. *Available:* Bell & Howell Information and Learning; LEXIS-NEXIS, NEXIS. *Type:* Database.

All-Canada Weekly Summaries

Canada Law Book Inc.
240 Edward St. Ph: (905)841-6472
Aurora, ON, Canada L4G 3S9
URL: http://www.canadalawbook.com
Desc: Contains more than 127,000 summaries of judgments in civil cases tried in the supreme, federal, and provincial courts in Canada. Includes cases deemed to be of particular importance in county courts. *Available:* QL Systems Limited, QUICKLAW; LEXIS-NEXIS. *Type:* Database.

Alliance for Justice

2000 P St. NW, Ste. 712 Ph: (202)822-6070
Washington, DC 20036 Fax: (202)822-6068
Contact: Nan Aron, Exec.Dir.
Desc: Public interest law firms, university clinical law programs, legal defense funds, and other public interest organizations and individuals dedicated to providing equal access to government forums for all groups and individuals. Objectives are to: focus the resources and talents of members on key issues that affect the impact and survival of the public interest movement; provide a forum for discussing critical issues; coordinate and catalyze action by alerting members of key developments in the courts, Congress, and federal agencies. Advocates and provides technical support on attorneys' fees and other funding issues; reports on regulatory issues; and monitors federal judicial selection procedures and potential nominees. *Type:* Association.

The Altman Weil Pensa Report to Legal Management

Altman Weil Pensa Publications, Inc.
8555 W. Forest Home Ave., Ph: (414)886-1304
No. 202
Milwaukee, WI 53228-3408
Contact: James Wilber, Editor, jameswilber@prodigy.com.
Desc: Reports on economic, management and technology trends affecting the legal profession. Contains articles on equipment, systems, publications, insurance, and services used in law offices, providing evaluations, descriptions, and purchasing information when that is helpful. *Type:* Newsletter.

American Arbitration Association

1633 Broadway No. 10 Fl. Ph: (212)484-4000
New York, NY 10019-6708 Free: 800-778-7879
 Fax: (212)765-4874
URL: http://www.adv.org
Contact: William K. Slate, II, Pres.
Desc: Corporation, unions, trade and educational associations, law firms, arbitrators, and interested individuals. Dedicated to the resolution of disputes through the use of mediation, arbitration, democratic elections, and other voluntary methods. Provides administrative services for arbitrating, mediating, or negotiating disputes and impartial administration of elections. *Type:* Association.

American Association of Testifying Physicians

2330 S. Brentwood Blvd. Ph: (314)961-2300
St. Louis, MO 63144-2096 Fax: (314)961-9828
Contact: Maven A. Goniff, Sr., VP.
Desc: Professional society of physicians (2487); associate members are insurance companies (66). Dedicated to the improvement of the judicial system as it relates to the practice of medicine. Trains doctors to effectively testify in court. *Type:* Association.

American Bankruptcy Institute

44 Canal Center Plaza, Ste. 404 Ph: (703)739-0800
Alexandria, VA 22314 Fax: (703)739-1060
E-mail: info@abiworld.org
URL: http://www.abiworld.org
Contact: Samuel J. Gerdano, Exec.Dir.
Desc: Attorneys, accountants, and other providers of financial services, lending institutions, credit organizations, consumer groups, federal and state governments, and other interested individuals. Provides a multidisciplinary forum for the exchange of information on bankruptcy and insolvency issues. Fosters dialogue among lawyers, businesspersons, and legislators on current and potential bankruptcy problems. *Type:* Association.

American Bar Association

750 N. Lake Shore Dr. Ph: (312)988-5000
Chicago, IL 60611 Free: 800-285-2221
 Fax: (312)988-5528
URL: http://www.abanet.org
Contact: Robert A. Stein, Exec.Dir.
Desc: Attorneys in good standing of the bar of any state. Conducts research and educational projects and activities to: encourage professional improvement; provide public services; improve the administration of civil and criminal justice; increase the availability of legal services to the public. Sponsors Law Day USA. *Type:* Association.

American Bar Association Section of International Law and Practice

740 15th St. NW Ph: (202)662-1660
Washington, DC 20005-1022 Fax: (202)662-1669
URL: http://www.abanet.org/intlaw
Contact: Mara Flynn, Publications Dir.
Desc: Attorneys (13,000) licensed to practice law in the U.S.; attorneys (1000) admitted to the bar in foreign countries; law students (2000). Seeks to advance the rule of law worldwide; assists attorneys in practice involving international issues. Conducts continuing education programs; maintains over 60 committees including International Trade, International Banking, Soviet and Eastern European Law, Human Rights, and Environmental Law. *Type:* Association.

American Bar Association Young Lawyers Division

750 N. Lake Shore Dr. Ph: (312)988-5000
Chicago, IL 60611 Fax: (312)988-6231
E-mail: younglawyers@abanet.org
URL: http://www.abanet.org/yld
Contact: Bo Landrum, Staff Dir.
Desc: Members of the American Bar Association who are under the age of 36 or have been accepted to the bar for 5 years or less. Provides information to lawyers who are beginning their legal careers; assists state bar associations to facilitate public service initiatives. *Type:* Association.

American Corporate Counsel Association

1025 Connecticut Ave. NW, Ph: (202)293-4103
Ste. 200 Fax: (202)331-7454
Washington, DC 20036-5425
URL: http://www.acca.com
Contact: Frederick J. Krebs, Pres.
Desc: Lawyers practicing law in corporate law departments. Represents corporate counsel on public policy issues before the courts, legislatures, and agencies at the local, state, and national levels. *Type:* Association.

American Federation of Police and Concerned Citizens

3801 Biscayne Blvd. Ph: (305)573-0070
Miami, FL 33137 Fax: (305)573-9819
E-mail: policeinfo@aphf.org
URL: http://www.aphf.org
Contact: Lt. Morton Feldman, Exec.VP.
Desc: Governmental and private law enforcement officers (paid, part-time, or volunteer) united for the prevention of crime and the apprehension of criminals. Offers death benefits and training programs to members. *Type:* Association.

American Health Lawyers Association

1120 Connecticut Ave. NW, Ph: (202)833-1100
Ste. 950 Fax: (202)833-1105
Washington, DC 20036-3902
E-mail: info@healthlawyers.org
URL: http://www.healthlawyers.org
Contact: Marietta Gaden, Dir.
Desc: Attorneys who represent or are employees of hospitals or other health organizations. Works to disseminate information on health care law and legislation; keep members abreast of court decisions in the health care field; conduct legal seminars and institutes. *Type:* Association.

American Immigration Lawyers Association

1400 Eye St. NW, Ste. 1200 Ph: (202)371-9377
Washington, DC 20005 Fax: (202)371-9449
Contact: Jean Butterfield, Exec.Dir.
Desc: Lawyers specializing in the field of immigration and nationality law. Fosters and promotes the administration of justice with particular reference to the immigration and nationality laws of the United States. *Type:* Association.

American Intellectual Property Law Association

2001 Jefferson Davis Hwy., Ste. Ph: (703)415-0780
203 Fax: (703)415-0786
Arlington, VA 22202
E-mail: aipla@aipla.org
URL: http://www.aipla.org
Contact: Nancy A. Haley, Dir. of Operations.
Desc: Voluntary bar association of lawyers practicing in the fields of patents, trademarks, and copyrights. Aids in the operation and improvement of U.S. patent, trademark, and copyright systems, including the laws by which they are governed and rules and regulations under which federal agencies administer those laws. *Type:* Association.

American Journal of International Law

American Society of International Law
2223 Massachusetts Ave., N.W. Ph: (202)939-6000
Washington, DC 20008-2864
URL: http://www.asl.org
Desc: Contains the complete text of the American Journal of International Law, a quarterly journal featuring articles, editorials, notes, and comments by scholars on developments on international law and international relations. Covers summaries of relevant decisions by national and international courts and arbitral or other tribunals. *Available:* West Group, WESTLAW; LEXIS-NEXIS, LEXIS. *Type:* Database.

American Judicature Society

180 N. Michigan Ave., Ste. 600 Ph: (312)558-6900
Chicago, IL 60601 Fax: (312)558-9175
E-mail: members@ajs.org
Contact: Sandra Ratcliff Dafron, Exec.VP/Dir.

Desc: Lawyers, judges, law teachers, government officials, and citizens interested in the effective administration of justice. Conducts research; presents educational programs; offers a consultation service; sponsors and organizes citizens' conferences on judicial improvement. Coordinates the work of states in judicial discipline and removal through its Center for Judicial Conduct Organizations. *Type:* Association.

American Law Institute

4025 Chestnut St.	Ph: (215)243-1600
Philadelphia, PA 19104-3099	Free: 800-253-6397
	Fax: (215)243-1664

URL: http://www.ali.org
Contact: Geoffrey C. Hazard, Dir.

Desc: Judges, law teachers, and lawyers. Promotes the clarification and simplification of the law and its better adaptation to social needs by continuing work on the Restatement of the Law, model and uniform codes, and model statutes. Conducts a program of continuing legal education jointly with the American Bar Association called "ALI-ABA". *Type:* Association.

American Lawyers Auxiliary

541 N. Bairbanks, 15th Fl.	Ph: (312)988-6387
Chicago, IL 60611-3314	Fax: (312)988-5032

Contact: Lynn Dunagan, Pres.

Desc: Acts as a clearinghouse for state and local groups throughout the country, promoting educational programs pertaining to the law. Encourages members to volunteer their services to legal services programs and to juvenile courts. Cooperates with the organized bar in public service activities and programs such as Law Day and courthouse tours; promotes public service programs such as Advocacy for a Barrier Free Environment. *Type:* Association.

American Society of Composers, Authors and Publishers

1 Lincoln Plz.	Ph: (212)621-6000
New York, NY 10023	Fax: (212)724-9064

URL: http://www.ascap.com
Contact: Marilyn Bergman, Pres.Chmn. of the Board.

Desc: Composers, lyricists, and publishers. Serves as clearinghouse in the field of music performing rights. Grants licenses and distributes royalties for the public performance of the copyrighted musical works of its members by broadcasters, symphony orchestras, and other users. *Type:* Association.

American Society of International Law

2223 Massachusetts Ave. NW	Ph: (202)939-6000
Washington, DC 20008-2864	Fax: (202)797-7133

E-mail: members@asil.compuserve.com
URL: http://www.asil.org
Contact: Charlotte Ku, Exec.Dir. and Exec.VP.

Desc: Scholars, practitioners, government officials, political scientists, and specialists in subjects. Such as human rights, law of the sea, disarmament and more. Provides access to insight and information on the world of international law. *Type:* Association.

American Tort Reform Association

1850 M St., NW, Ste 1095	Ph: (202)682-1163
Washington, DC 20036	Fax: (202)682-1022

E-mail: sjoyce@atra.org
URL: http://www.atra.org/atra/atra.htm
Contact: Sherman Joyce, Pres.

Desc: Membership include professional groups and businesses, nonprofits and trade associations. Advocates changes in the current tort system, returning fairness, efficiency, and predictability to the civil justice system. *Type:* Association.

Antitrust & Trade Regulation Report

Bureau of National Affairs, Inc. (BNA)

1231 25th St. NW	Ph: (202)452-4323
Washington, DC 20037	Free: 800-372-1033
	Fax: (202)452-7773

E-mail: bnaplus@bna.com; atrr@bna.com.

Contact: Sheldon B. Richman, Managing Editor.

Desc: Monitors enforcement developments in competition and deceptive trade practice fields. Reviews these developments on the federal, state, and international levels. *Type:* Newsletter.

Aspen Law & Business Directory of Corporate Counsel

Aspen Law & Business

1165 Avenue of the Americas 37	Ph: (212)894-8484
New York, NY 10036-2601	

Desc: Contains biographies of legal counsel for corporations and non-profit organizations. Includes lawyer's name, position, year of appointment (if available), specialization (e.g., job practice, function, legal matter managed), year and location of bar passage, education history, offices held in professional organizations, previous employment, and current employer's name, address, and telephone number. *Available:* West Group, WESTLAW. *Type:* Database.

Association of American Law Schools— Placement Bulletin

Association of American Law Schools

1201 Connecticut Ave. NW,	Ph: (202)296-8851
Ste. 800	Fax: (202)296-8869
Washington, DC 20036-2605	

E-mail: aals@aals.org
URL: http://www.aals.org.

Contact: Janet L. Kulick, Editor.

Desc: Lists faculty and administrative job positions available at law schools and government positions. Focuses on openings in the U.S., but includes occasional listings in Canada, Australia, and New Zealand. *Type:* Newsletter.

Association of Legal Administrators

175 E. Hawthorn Pky., Ste. 325	Ph: (847)816-1212
Vernon Hills, IL 60061-1428	Fax: (847)816-1213

URL: http://www.alanet.org

Contact: John J. Michalik, Exec.Dir.

Desc: Administrators of private law firms and corporate and governmental law departments. Promotes the exchange of information regarding administration and management problems particular to legal organizations; provides information on the value and availability of professional administrators; improves standards and qualifications; develops continuing education programs; participates in the advancement of legal administration. Offers classified advertising service. *Type:* Association.

Association of Trial Lawyers of America

1050 31st St. NW	Ph: (202)965-3500
Washington, DC 20007	Free: 800-424-2725
	Fax: (202)625-7312

Contact: Thomas H. Henderson, Jr., Exec.Dir.

Desc: Lawyers, judges, law professors, paralegals, and students engaged in civil plaintiff or criminal defense advocacy. Objectives include: advancing jurisprudence and the law as a profession; encouraging mutual support and cooperation among members of the bar; advancing the cause of persons seeking redress for damages against person or property; training in advocacy; upholding and improving the adversary system and trial by jury. Holds year-round educational programs. *Type:* Association.

Attorney Jobs

Federal Reports Inc.

1010 Vermont Ave. NW, Ste.	Ph: (202)393-3311
408	Free: 800-296-9611
Washington, DC 20005	Fax: (202)393-1553

E-mail: lawcareers@attorneyjobs.com
URL: http://www.attorneyjobs.com.
Contact: Linda Sutherland, Managing Editor.

Desc: Details listings of hundreds of attorney and law-related positions in the United States and internationally, at all levels and with various types of employers. Recurring features include job listings and notices of contacts for legal and law-related services. *Type:* Newsletter.

Auto-Cite

West Group

620 Opperman Dr.	Ph: (651)687-7000
St. Paul, MN 55164-0526	

URL: http://www.westgroup.com

Desc: Contains information regarding U.S. federal case law, the case law of all 50 states, administrative decisions, and tax materials. *Available:* LEXIS-NEXIS, LEXIS. *Type:* Database.

Barclays Official California Code of Regulations

Barclay's Law Publishers

PO Box 95767	Ph: (312)732-8800
Chicago, IL 60694-5767	

URL: http://www.westgroup.com

Contact: Craig Solomon, Marketing Coordinator, (415)244-0402, fax: (415)588-5486.

Desc: Contains all authorized regulations of California's 200-plus state agencies, boards, commissions, and departments except the California Building Standards Code. Organized into 26 subject categories. *Available:* Barclay's Law Publishers; West Group, WESTLAW; LEXIS-NEXIS, LEXIS. *Type:* Database.

Billcast™ Archive

George Mason University
Center for the Study of Public Choice

MSN 1D3 Carow Hall	Ph: (703)993-2330
4400 University Dr.	
Fairfax, VA 22030-4444	

Desc: Contains information on public bills introduced in the U.S. House of Representatives and Senate during the preceding session of Congress. *Available:* Information for Public Affairs, Inc. (IPA), StateNet; West Group, WESTLAW; LEXIS-NEXIS, LEXIS. *Type:* Database.

Billcast™ Legislative Forecasts

George Mason University
Center for the Study of Public Choice

MSN 1D3 Carow Hall	Ph: (703)993-2330
4400 University Dr.	
Fairfax, VA 22030-4444	

Desc: Contains information on public bills introduced in the U.S. House of Representatives and Senate during the current session of Congress. *Available:* LEXIS-NEXIS, LEXIS; Information for Public Affairs, Inc. (IPA), StateNet; West Group, WESTLAW. *Type:* Database.

Black's Law Dictionary®

West Group

620 Opperman Dr.	Ph: (651)687-7000
St. Paul, MN 55164-0526	

URL: http://www.westgroup.com

Desc: Contains the complete text of the Centennial (6th) edition of Black's Law Dictionary published by West Group. Provides definitions of some 35,000 terms and phrases, including more than 5000 new and revised entries, covering words, terms, and phrases used in American and English jurisprudence, both ancient and modern. *Available:* West Group, WESTLAW. *Type:* Database.

BNA Bankruptcy Law Daily

The Bureau of National Affairs, Inc. (BNA)
1231 25th St. NW   Ph: (202)452-4200
Washington, DC 20037
E-mail: bnaplus@bna.com
URL: http://bna.com/mkt/hrl/hrlwdec.htm

Desc: Contains the complete text of articles covering judicial decisions, legislation, and administrative actions relating to bankruptcy law. *Available:* LEXIS-NEXIS, LEXIS; West Group, WESTLAW. *Type:* Database.

BNA's Directory of State and Federal Courts, Judges, and Clerks

BNA Books
1250 23rd St. N.W   Ph: (202)833-7470
Washington, DC 20037-1165   Free: 800-960-1220
                          Fax: (202)833-7490
E-mail: books@bna.com
URL: http://www.bna.com/bnabooks

Contact: Kamla J. King, Editor; Judith Miller, Editor.

Desc: More than 21,000 judges and judicial officials in more than 2,300 state and federal courts; coverage includes U.S. territories. *Type:* Directory.

BNA's Patent, Trademark & Copyright Journal

The Bureau of National Affairs, Inc. (BNA)
1231 25th St. NW   Ph: (202)452-4200
Washington, DC 20037
E-mail: bnaplus@bna.com
URL: http://bna.com/mkt/hrl/hrlwdec.htm

Contact: BNA PLUS, (202)452-4323, fax: (202)822-8092, bnaplus@bna.com.

Desc: Contains the complete text of BNA's Patent, Trademark & Copyright Journal, covering legislation, committee reports, international developments (e.g., treaties, conventions), and court and federal agency rulings on patents, trademarks, copyright, and unfair competition. *Available:* LEXIS-NEXIS, LEXIS; West Group, WESTLAW. *Type:* Database.

The Bottom Line

Law Office Economics Section
Illinois State Bar Association
Illinois Bar Center   Ph: (217)525-1760
Springfield, IL 62701

Contact: Jeffrey M. Simon, Editor.

Desc: Offers information on law office management. *Type:* Newsletter.

California Lawyer

Daily Journal Corp.
915 E. 1st St.   Ph: (213)229-5300
Los Angeles, CA 90012-4050   Free: 800-652-1700
                          Fax: (213)680-3682

Contact: Peter Allen, Editor; Tema Goodwin, Managing Editor, tema_goodwin@dailyjournal.com.

Desc: Law magazine. *Alt. Contact:* 1145 Market St., 8th Fl., San Francisco, CA 94103; telephone: (415)252-0500; fax: (415)252-0288. *Type:* Periodical.

Campbell's List

Campbell's List, Inc.
PO Box 428   Ph: (407)644-8298
Maitland, FL 32751   Fax: (407)740-6494
E-mail: camplist@sprynet.com

Contact: John A. Campbell, Editor.

Desc: About 1,000 law firms in general practice that will handle referrals; international coverage. *Type:* Directory.

Canada Statute Service on CD-ROM

Canada Law Book Inc.
240 Edward St.   Ph: (905)841-6472
Aurora, ON, Canada L4G 3S9
URL: http://www.canadalawbook.com

Contact: General Sales, Canada Law Book Inc.

Desc: Contains the consolidated Revised Statutes of Canada and the Revised Regulations of Canada with all subsequent amendments, new Acts and regulations, plus the Canada Statute Citator. *Available:* Infomart Online. *Type:* Database.

Canadian Criminal Cases

Canada Law Book Inc.
240 Edward St.   Ph: (905)841-6472
Aurora, ON, Canada L4G 3S9
URL: http://www.canadalawbook.com

Desc: Contains more than 9750 criminal case decisions from all Canadian provincial courts and the Supreme Court of Canada. Includes the complete text of judgments since 1987. *Available:* QL Systems Limited, QUICK-LAW; LEXIS-NEXIS, LEXIS. *Type:* Database.

Canadian Patent Index

University of British Columbia Library
1956 Main Hall   Ph: (604)822-5404
Vancouver, BC, Canada V6T
1Z1
E-mail: rsimmer@unixg.ubc.ca
URL: http://www.datalib.ubc.ca

Desc: Contains about 200,000 citations to Canadian patents. Users can search by patent or application number, classification, and keywords. *Type:* Database.

Canadian Patent Reporter

Canada Law Book Inc.
240 Edward St.   Ph: (905)841-6472
Aurora, ON, Canada L4G 3S9
URL: http://www.canadalawbook.com

Desc: Contains the complete text and headnotes of approximately 6600 decisions covered in Canadian Patent Reporter. Covers significant cases on patents, industrial design, copyrights, and trademarks from the Commissioner of Patents, Registrar of Trade Marks, and various Canadian courts. *Available:* QL Systems Limited, QUICKLAW; LEXIS-NEXIS, LEXIS. *Type:* Database.

Center for Law and Social Policy

1616 P St. NW, Ste. 150   Ph: (202)328-5140
Washington, DC 20036   Fax: (202)328-5195
E-mail: info@clasp.org
URL: http://www.clasp.org

Contact: Alan Houseman, Dir.

Desc: To improve the economic conditions of low-income families with children and to secure access for low-income households to our civil justice system. *Type:* Association.

Center for Reproductive Law and Policy

120 Wall St.   Ph: (212)514-5534
New York, NY 10005   Fax: (212)514-5538
E-mail: info@crlp.org
URL: http://www.crlp.org

Contact: Janet Benshoof, Pres.

Desc: Reproductive rights attorneys and activists. Dedicated to secure women's reproductive freedoms in the U.S. *Type:* Association.

Center for Research of Public Law

Universite de Montreal - Centre de Recherche en Droit Public Facult, de droit
C.P. 6128, Succ. Centre-ville   Ph: (514)343-7210
Montreal, PQ, Canada H3C 3J7   Fax: (514)343-7508
E-mail: infodroit@droit.umontreal.ca

URL: http://www.droit.umontreal.ca

Contact: Guy Huard, Editor, huard@crdp.umontreal.ca.

Desc: The CRDP (Centre for Research in Public Law) Web site aims at making Quebec and Canadian law more accessible. Amongst legal documents of interest at this site, the Civil Code of Quebec and the Quebec Charter of Personal Rights and Freedoms deserve special mention. *Type:* Database.

Christic Institute

PO Box 845   Ph: (310)287-1556
Malibu, CA 90265-0845   Fax: (310)287-1559

Contact: Sara M. Nelson, Nat.Dir.

Desc: Public law and policy center. Engages in legal work on political issues; informs the public on the importance of these issues. Functions also as an interfaith public policy center. *Type:* Association.

CIS

Congressional Information Service, Inc. (CIS)
4520 East-West Hwy., Suite   Ph: (301)654-1550
800
Bethesda, MD 20814-3389
E-mail: 12425 (DIALMAIL)
URL: http://www.cispubs.com

Desc: Contains more than 254,000 citations, with abstracts, to publications produced by the committees and subcommittees of the U.S. Congress. *Available:* The Dialog Corporation, DIALOG. *Type:* Database.

Citizens Legal Protective League

5456 Lake Ave.   Ph: (407)322-7011
Sanford, FL 32773

Contact: Dr. Merle E. Parker, Chm.

Desc: U.S. residents wishing to represent themselves in court without hiring lawyers. Objectives are to acquaint Americans with their right to use all courts in person without hiring a lawyer and to provide basic training in general court procedures, preparations for suits, and answers to suits and motions. *Type:* Association.

CLAIMS™/CITATION

IFI/Plenum Data Corporation
3202 Kirkwood Highway Ste.   Ph: (302)998-0478
203
Wilmington, DE 19808
E-mail: ifiplenum@aol.com

Contact: Jim Brown, Customer Service, (302)998-0478, fax: (302)998-0733.

Desc: Contains information on every U.S. and non-U.S. patent (over 5 million patent numbers) cited in U.S. patents granted after 1947. *Available:* The Dialog Corporation, DIALOG; Questel • Orbit; STN International; ChemWeb, Inc. *Type:* Database.

CLAIMS™/Comprehensive Database

IFI/Plenum Data Corporation
3202 Kirkwood Highway Ste.   Ph: (302)998-0478
203
Wilmington, DE 19808
E-mail: ifiplenum@aol.com

Contact: Jim Brown, Customer Service, (302)998-0478, fax: (302)998-0733.

Desc: Contains enhanced indexing of the U.S. chemical and chemically related patents included in CLAIMS/UNITERM. *Available:* Questel • Orbit; STN International; The Dialog Corporation, DIALOG; ChemWeb, Inc. *Type:* Database.

CLAIMS™/Reassignment & Reexamination

IFI/Plenum Data Corporation
3202 Kirkwood Highway Ste.   Ph: (302)998-0478
203
Wilmington, DE 19808
E-mail: ifiplenum@aol.com
Contact: Jim Brown, Customer Service, (302)998-0478, fax: (302)998-0733.
Desc: Contains more than 370,000 records for which ownership has transferred from one party to another or a security interest has been issued. Contains over 2800 reexamined records for which patentability has been reviewed and rejected, reaffirmed or modified. *Available:* The Dialog Corporation, DIALOG; Questel • Orbit; STN International; ChemWeb, Inc. *Type:* Database.

CLAIMS™/Reference

IFI/Plenum Data Corporation
3202 Kirkwood Highway Ste.   Ph: (302)998-0478
203
Wilmington, DE 19808
E-mail: ifiplenum@aol.com
Contact: Jim Brown, Customer Service, (302)998-0478, fax: (302)998-0733.
Desc: Contains U.S. classification codes and titles for classes and subclasses provided in the U.S. Patent Office *Manual of Classification* and the *Index to the U.S. Patent Classification.* Covers approximately 400 main classes and 115,000 subclasses that pertain to patents issued for mechanical, electrical, and chemical inventions. *Available:* The Dialog Corporation, DIALOG; Questel • Orbit; STN International; ChemWeb, Inc. *Type:* Database.

CLAIMS™/U.S. Patent Abstracts

IFI/Plenum Data Corporation
3202 Kirkwood Highway Ste.   Ph: (302)998-0478
203
Wilmington, DE 19808
E-mail: ifiplenum@aol.com
Contact: Jim Brown, Customer Service, (302)998-0478, fax: (302)998-0733.
Desc: Contains more than 2.7 million records for granted and reissued U.S. patents, including chemical patents since 1950, mechanical and electric patents since 1963, and design patents since 1976 as well as defensive publications, and statutory invention registrations. *Available:* The Dialog Corporation, DIALOG; Questel • Orbit; STN International; Questel • Orbit; ChemWeb, Inc. *Type:* Database.

CLAIMS™/UNITERM

IFI/Plenum Data Corporation
3202 Kirkwood Highway Ste.   Ph: (302)998-0478
203
Wilmington, DE 19808
E-mail: ifiplenum@aol.com
Contact: Jim Brown, Customer Service.
Desc: Contains more than 2.3 million citations, with abstracts, to all granted U.S. utility patents, reissue patents, and defensive publications. *Available:* The Dialog Corporation, DIALOG; Questel • Orbit; STN International; Questel • Orbit; ChemWeb, Inc. *Type:* Database.

Clearing House Quarterly Lawyers (CHQ)

Attorneys' National Clearing House Co.
PO Box 8688   Ph: (941)263-0840
Naples, FL 34101-8688   Free: 800-231-6736
      Fax: (941)263-1033
E-mail: anch@attorneyreferral.com; chq@attorneyreferral.com.
URL: http://www.attorneyreferral.com/chq.
Contact: John M. Birk, President.
Desc: Attorneys handling collection matters (commercial & retail), creditors' rights and creditor bankruptcy issues. *Type:* Directory.

Commission on Accreditation for Law Enforcement Agencies

10306 Eaton Pl., Ste. 320   Ph: (703)352-4225
Fairfax, VA 22030-2201   Free: 800-368-3757
      Fax: (703)591-2206
URL: http://www.calea.org
Contact: Richard F. Kitterman, Jr., Exec.Dir.
Desc: Objective is to administer an accreditation program by which law enforcement agencies at local, county, state, national, and international levels can voluntarily demonstrate their compliance with professional criteria; has established a body of over 400 standards of evaluation. Overall purpose of the accreditation program is to improve the delivery of law enforcement services. Recruits, selects, and trains assessors who conduct on-site assessments of agency compliance with standards. *Type:* Association.

Copyright Clearance Center

222 Rosewood Dr.   Ph: (978)750-8400
Danvers, MA 01923   Fax: (508)750-4744
Contact: Joseph S. Alen, Pres.
Desc: Photocopy users (corporations, academic and research libraries, information brokers, government agencies, and others who systematically utilize or distribute photocopy material) and publishers, authors, or other owners of copyrights. Established in response to 1978 copyright law which requires that permission of copyright owners be obtained by anyone doing systematic photocopying or photocopying not permitted under the fair use provision of the law. *Type:* Association.

copyRights

The Permissions Group
1247 Milwaukee Ave., Ste. 303
Glenview, IL 60025
Contact: Cheryl Besenjak, Publisher.
Desc: Provides the latest legislative updates, electronic rights information, copyright infringement cases, and rights resources to all areas of intellectual property—from film to software. *Type:* Newsletter.

Current Index to Legal Periodicals

University of Washington
Marian Gould Gallagher Law Library
1100 N.E. Campus Pkwy.   Ph: (206)543-4097
Seattle, WA 98105
URL: http://lib.law.washington.edu/cilp/cilp.html
Desc: Indexes articles from more than 490 American academic legal publications. Provides subject access to all academic law school law review articles. *Available:* West Group, WESTLAW; University of Washington, Marian Gould Gallagher Law Library. *Type:* Database.

Delta Theta Phi

21330 Center Ridge Rd., 32   Ph: (440)895-9990
Rocky River, OH 44116-3251   Free: 800-783-2600
      Fax: (440)895-9994
URL: http://www.deltathetaphi.org
Contact: Catherine K. Smith, Exec.Dir.
Desc: Professional fraternity - law. *Type:* Association.

Directory of Corporate Counsel

Aspen Law & Business/Panel Publishers
1185 Avenue of the Americas,   Ph: (212)597-0200
37th Fl.   Free: 800-447-1777
New York, NY 10036   Fax: (212)597-0338
Contact: Linda D. Humphries, Editor.
Desc: Provides information on the organization, structure and personnel of the corporate and non-profit law departments of the U.S. and Canada. *Type:* Directory.

Dominion Law Reports

Canada Law Book Inc.
240 Edward St.   Ph: (905)841-6472
Aurora, ON, Canada L4G 3S9
URL: http://www.canadalawbook.com
Desc: Contains the fully edited text of all the cases of the 4th series from 1984 to the present. Also contains the head notes for the 2nd and 3rd series of the Dominion Law Reports. *Available:* QL Systems Limited, QUICKLAW; LEXIS-NEXIS, LEXIS. *Type:* Database.

DYNIS

Control Data Systems Canada, Ltd.
Information Services
4201 Lexington Ave. N.
St. Paul, MN 55123
Contact: Mark Steinert, Manager.
Desc: Contains the complete text of registered and pending trademark applications in Canada. *Available:* Control Data Systems Canada, Ltd., Information Services. *Type:* Database.

Economic Equity Insider

National Network for Women's Employment
1625 K. St. NW, Ste. 300   Ph: (202)467-6346
Washington, DC 20006   Free: 800-235-2732
      Fax: (202)467-5366
E-mail: ww@immsys.immsys.com.
Contact: Carol Hamilton, Editor.
Desc: Provides updates on legislation and legislative issues affecting women, women in transition, women's job training and education, and women's economic status. *Type:* Newsletter.

Encyclopedia of Legal Information Sources

Gale Group Inc.
27500 Drake Rd.   Ph: (248)699-4253
Farmington Hills, MI 48331-   Free: 800-877-GALE
3535   Fax: (248)699-8070
E-mail: galeord@galegroup.com
URL: http://www.galegroup.com
Contact: Brian Baker, Editor; Patrick Petit, Editor.
Desc: Over 29,000 books, periodicals, newsletters, law reviews and digests, newspapers, audiovisual materials, and other publications; research centers, institutes, and clearinghouses; professional associations and societies; databases; and other organizations and sources of information on 480 legal topics. *Type:* Directory.

Environmental Law Institute

1616 P St. NW, Ste. 200   Ph: (202)939-3800
Washington, DC 20036   Fax: (202)939-3868
E-mail: widholm@eli.org
URL: http://www.eli.org
Contact: J. William Futrell, Pres.
Desc: Launched by the Public Law Education Institute and the Conservation Foundation. Seeks to: conduct and sponsor research on environmental law and policy; maintain a clearinghouse for information regarding environmental law; engage in related educational activities, including conferences, seminar programs, and workshops. Has conducted environmental law courses with law schools, governmental agencies, and other nonprofit organizations. *Type:* Association.

EPA Civil Enforcement Docket

U.S. Environmental Protection Agency (EPA)
Center for Environmental Information and
Statistics (CEIS)
401 M St. SW   Ph: (202)260-2090
Washington, DC 20460-0003
URL: http://www.epa.gov/ceis/
Contact: Stephanie Myers, CIS User Support Specialist.

Desc: Contains case information for all civil judicial cases (more than 4206) filed by the U.S. Department of Justice on behalf of the U.S. Department of Justice on behalf of the U.S. Environmental Protection Agency's Office of Enforcement. *Available:* Oxford Molecular Group, Chemical Information Systems. *Type:* Database.

Estate Planning Review

CCH Inc.

2700 Lake Cook Rd.	Ph: (847)267-7000
Riverwoods, IL 60015	Free: 800-449-8114
	Fax: (847)224-8299

URL: http://www.cch.com; http://www.cch.com; http://tax.cch.com.

Desc: Monthly newsletter covering estate and financial planning issues for individuals. Includes coverage of retirement planning, insurance planning and investments. *Type:* Newsletter.

The Expert and the Law

National Forensic Center

17 Temple Terrace   Ph: (609)883-0550
Lawrenceville, NJ 08648
E-mail: forenexpts@att.net
URL: http://www.expertindex.com

Desc: Contains the complete text of The Expert and the Law, a newsletter covering the application of scientific, medical, and technical knowledge to litigation. Includes news about the use of consultants by attorneys and feature articles on the effective use of experts and consultants (e.g., ethical considerations when expert witnesses incur out-of-pocket expenses). *Available:* LEXIS-NEXIS, NEXIS. *Type:* Database.

ExpertNet

ExpertNet, Ltd.

2514 Royal Ridge Dr.   Ph: (708)672-3078
Crete, IL 60417
E-mail: 44: ABA375 (Dialcom)

Desc: Contains information on more than 1300 physicians available to serve as expert trial witnesses or consultants to attorneys in medical malpractice and personal injury cases. Covers physicians in all medical specialties. *Available:* West Group, WESTLAW. *Type:* Database.

F.E.A.R. Chronicles

Forfeiture Endangers American Rights (FEAR)

20-A Sunnyside   Ph: (415)388-8128
Suite 204
Mill Valley, CA 94941
E-mail: k.bergman@genie.com.
Contact: Judy Osburn, Editor.

Desc: Publishes detailed reports on pending forfeiture legislation, analysis of Supreme Court decisions regarding forfeiture, and forfeiture law abuses. *Type:* Newsletter.

Federal Bar Association

2215 M St. NW   Ph: (202)785-1614
Washington, DC 20037-1416   Fax: (202)785-1568
E-mail: fba@fedbar.org
URL: http://www.fedbar.org
Contact: Michael Campiglia, Exec.Dir.

Desc: Attorneys employed by the federal government as legislators, judges, lawyers, or members of quasi-judicial boards and commissions; those with previous government legal experience; and those with a substantive interest in federal law and who practice before a federal court or agency. Over 100 specialized committees, operating through 24 Sections and Divisions, provide various programs such as continuing legal education and professional and community service. *Type:* Association.

Federalist Society for Law and Public Policy Studies

1015 18th St., NW, Ste. 425   Ph: (202)822-8138
Washington, DC 20036   Fax: (202)296-8061
E-mail: fedsoc@radix.net
URL: http://www.fed-soc.org
Contact: Eugene B. Meyer, Exec.Dir.

Desc: Conservative and libertarian lawyers, law students, law school faculty, and individuals interested in the current state of the legal order. *Type:* Association.

Florida Bar Journal—Directory Issue

The Florida Bar

650 Apalachee Pkwy.	Ph: (850)561-5600
Tallahassee, FL 32399-2300	Free: 800-342-8060
	Fax: (850)561-5817

URL: http://www.flabar.org
Contact: Judson H. Orrick, Editor, (850)561-5682, jorrick@flabar.org.

Desc: List of about 60,000 members of The Florida Bar, legal and lawyer associations, courts, government officials, members of the judiciary, and the Rules Regulating The Florida Bar. *Type:* Directory.

Food and Drug Law Institute

1000 Vermont Ave. NW, Ste.   Ph: (202)371-1420
   200   Fax: (202)371-0649
Washington, DC 20005-4903
E-mail: comments@fdli.org
URL: http://www.fdli.org
Contact: John C. Villforth, Pres.

Desc: Manufacturers and distributors of food, drugs, cosmetics, and devices are industrial members; law firms and others are associate members. Promotes the development of essential knowledge about the laws that regulate the research for, production, and sale of food, drugs, medical devices, and cosmetics. *Type:* Association.

Foreign Assets Litigation Reporter

Andrews Publications

175 Strafford Ave., Bldg. 4, Ste.   Ph: (610)225-0510
   140   Free: 800-345-1101
Wayne, PA 19087   Fax: (610)225-0501
Contact: Michelle Sarnocinski, Editor.

Desc: Covers developments in U.S. and foreign courts regarding the attachment of foreign assets and reports on the complex litigation and international arbitration that has resulted. *Type:* Newsletter.

Guide to Computer Law

CCH Inc.

2700 Lake Cook Rd.	Ph: (847)267-7000
Riverwoods, IL 60015	Free: 800-449-8114
	Fax: (847)224-8299

URL: http://www.cch.com

Desc: Cover computer law, including such areas as copyrights, patents, and sales. Contains full-text of court cases and laws. *Type:* Newsletter.

HALT - Americans for Legal Reform

1612 K St. NW, Ste. 510   Ph: (202)887-8255
Washington, DC 20006   Free: 888-FOR-HALT
          Fax: (202)887-9699
E-mail: halt@halt.org
URL: http://www.halt.org
Contact: James C. Turner, Exec.Dir.

Desc: Citizens of diverse socioeconomic and age groups dedicated to legal reform. Purposes are to: reform the system and educate the public to allow simple, affordable, and equitable disposition of legal affairs; make consumers sophisticated shoppers of legal services and increase their self-reliance and ability to handle their own affairs; simplify the language and procedures of the law; develop and support alternative means for resolving legal disputes; improve the quality and reduce the cost of available legal services. Works on reform legislation in attorney regulation, tort law, probate, divorce, real estate, and related areas at the state and federal levels; encourages increased citizen participation on attorney grievance commit tees. *Type:* Association.

Hine's Insurance Counsel

Hine's Inc.

Box 143   Ph: (630)365-1630
Geneva, IL 60134   Fax: (630)365-1631
Contact: Stephen E. Walter, Editor.

Desc: 2,500 law firms in the United States and Canada that handle defense in litigation involving insurance and transportation companies. *Type:* Directory.

InProReport

Intellectual Property Law Center

702 Marshall St., No. 410
Redwood City, CA 94063
E-mail: inprocb@aol.com

Desc: Covers all queries regarding intellectual property rights, with an emphasis on trademarks. *Type:* Newsletter.

International Association of Chiefs of Police

515 N. Washington St.   Ph: (703)836-6767
Alexandria, VA 22314   Free: 800-THE-IACP
          Fax: (703)836-4543
URL: http://www.theiacp.org
Contact: Dan Rosenblatt, Exec.Dir.

Desc: Police executives who are commissioners, superintendents, chiefs, and directors of national, state, provincial, and municipal departments; assistant and deputy chiefs; division or district heads. Provides consultation and research services in all phases of police activity. *Type:* Association.

International Association of Defense Counsel

1 N. Franklin St., No. 2400   Ph: (312)368-1494
Chicago, IL 60606-3401   Fax: (312)368-1854
E-mail: office@iadclaw.org
URL: http://www.iadclaw
Contact: Richard J. Hayes, Exec.Dir.

Desc: Attorneys practicing defense trial law in 13 countries. Organizes research projects; offers continuing legal education programs including the Defense Counsel Trial Academy for young trial lawyers. Conducts annual legal writing contest. *Type:* Association.

International Association for Identification

2535 Pilot Knob Rd., Ste. 117   Ph: (651)681-8566
Mendota Heights, MN 55120-   Fax: (651)681-8443
   1120
E-mail: iaisecty@aol.com
URL: http://www.iaibbs.org
Contact: Ashley R. Crooker, Jr., Sec.-Treas.

Desc: Individuals engaged in forensic identification, investigation, and scientific crime detection. Strives to improve methods of scientific identification techniques used in criminal investigations. *Type:* Association.

International Center for Not-for-Profit Law

1511 K St. NW, Ste. 723   Ph: (202)624-0766
Washington, DC 20005-1401   Fax: (202)624-0767
E-mail: dcincnl@aol.com
URL: http://www.icnl.org
Contact: Karla Simon, Exec.VP.

Desc: Seeks to assist in the formation of laws and regulatory systems that stimulate activities of nonprofit organizations worldwide. *Type:* Association.

International Economic Law Documents

American Society of International Law
2223 Massachusetts Ave., N.W.   Ph: (202)939-6000
Washington, DC 20008-2864
URL: http://www.asl.org
Contact: David A. Levi, Editor, (202)939-6036.

Desc: Contains the complete text of international agreements and other documents dealing with the international economic law. For each document, includes an introduction and a bibliography. *Available:* West Group, WESTLAW; LEXIS-NEXIS, LEXIS. *Type:* Database.

International Law Institute

1615 New Hampshire Ave. NW   Ph: (202)483-3036
Washington, DC 20009   Fax: (202)483-3029
URL: http://www.ili.org
Contact: Stuart Kerr, Exec.Dir.
Type: Association.

International Law Students Association

2223 Massachusetts Ave. NW   Ph: (202)939-6030
Washington, DC 20008-2864   Fax: (202)265-0386
E-mail: ilsa@access.digex.net
URL: http://www.kentlaw.edu/ilsa
Contact: Yvette Roozenbeek, Exec.Dir.

Desc: Law societies at law schools worldwide; interns and associate members. Seeks to promote interest in international legal problems through cooperative development of programs. Provides support to local groups for on-campus programming and coordinates regional, national, and international events. *Type:* Association.

International Legal Materials

American Society of International Law
2223 Massachusetts Ave., N.W.   Ph: (202)939-6000
Washington, DC 20008-2864
URL: http://www.asl.org
Contact: David A. Levy, Interim Editor, (202)939-6036.

Desc: Contains the complete text of the International Legal Materials, a bimonthly publication providing basic legal documents for use in research and analysis. Contains the complete texts of important treaties and agreements, judicial and arbitral decisions, national legislation, international organization resolutions, and other similar documents. *Available:* LEXIS-NEXIS, LEXIS; West Group, WESTLAW. *Type:* Database.

International Licensing Industry Merchandisers' Association

350 5th Ave., Ste. 2309   Ph: (212)244-1944
New York, NY 10118   Fax: (212)563-6552
E-mail: info@licensing.org
URL: http://www.licensing.org
Contact: Charles M. Riotto, Exec.Dir.

Desc: Companies and individuals engaged in the marketing and servicing of licensed properties, both as agents and as property owners; manufacturers and retailers in the licensing business; supporters of the licensing industry. Objectives are to establish a standard reflecting a professional and ethical management approach to the marketing of licensed properties; to become the leading source of information in the industry; to communicate this information to members and others in the industry through publishing, public speaking, seminars, and an open line; to represent the industry in trade and consumer media and in relationships with the government, retailers, manufacturers, other trade associations, and the public. *Type:* Association.

International Trademark Association

1133 Avenue of the Americas   Ph: (212)768-9887
New York, NY 10036   Fax: (212)768-7796
URL: http://www.inta.org

Contact: Robin A. Rolfe, Exec.Dir.

Desc: Trademark owners; associate members are lawyers, law firms, advertising agencies, designers, market researchers, and others in the trademark industries. Seeks to: protect the interests of the public in the use of trademarks and trade names; promote the interests of members and of trademark owners generally in the use of their trademarks and trade names; disseminate information concerning the use, registration, and protection of trademarks in the United States, its territories, and in foreign countries. *Type:* Association.

Inventors Workshop International Education Foundation

1029 Castillo St.   Ph: (805)967-5722
Santa Barbara, CA 93101-3736   Fax: (805)899-4927
URL: http://www.ideahelp.com
Contact: Alan Tratner, Pres.

Desc: Amateur and professional inventors in the U.S. Provides instruction, assistance, and guidance in areas including: patent protection; patent searches for inventions; offering inventions for sale; getting inventions and products designed, produced, and manufactured; choosing experts when required; performing as many of these vital actions as capabilities and resources provide. Organizes seminars and semiannual programs on invention promotion and "Reduction to Practice." Conducts research. *Type:* Association.

IOMA's Report on Controlling Law Firm Costs

Institute of Management & Administration, Inc.
29 W. 35th St., 5th Fl.   Ph: (212)244-0360
New York, NY 10001-2299   Fax: (212)564-0465
E-mail: subserve@ioma.com
URL: http://www.ioma.com
Contact: Ann Podolske, Editor; Lee Rath, Publisher.

Desc: Provides information about controlling costs in law firms. Topics include taxes, insurance, employees, and office equipment. *Type:* Newsletter.

Judicature

American Judicature Society
180 N. Michigan, Ste. 600   Ph: (312)558-6900
Chicago, IL 60601
E-mail: ipilchen@ajs.org

Desc: Contains the complete text of Judicature, a magazine covering reports and opinions on the administration of justice and its improvement. Includes articles, book reviews, and letters to the editor. *Available:* West Group, WESTLAW. *Type:* Database.

The Judicial Conduct Reporter

American Judicature Society
180 N. Michigan, Ste. 600   Ph: (312)558-6900
Chicago, IL 60601
E-mail: ipilchen@ajs.org

Desc: Contains the complete text of Judicial Conduct Reporter, a quarterly publication covering commentary and analysis of matters relating to judicial conduct. Includes reviews of law articles, summaries of relevant cases and advisory opinions, news of judicial appointments, notices of conferences, and information on grants, alliances, and personnel changes at the American Judicature Society (AJS). *Available:* West Group, WESTLAW. *Type:* Database.

Judicial Discipline and Disability Digest

American Judicature Society
180 N. Michigan, Ste. 600   Ph: (312)558-6900
Chicago, IL 60601
E-mail: ipilchen@ajs.org

Desc: Contains the complete text of Judicial Discipline & Disability Digest, a publication of summaries and editorial

enhancements covering published and unpublished final decisions from federal and state courts and commissions in cases involving disability retirement, judicial conduct, and collateral matters. Includes the majority opinion, concurrences or dissents, constitutional or statutory changes occurring after the decision, and a discussion of any ambiguities within the decision. *Available:* West Group, WESTLAW. *Type:* Database.

The Know-How Report

Euromoney Law Publishers Inc.
36 W. 44th St., Ste. 1101   Fax: (212)921-2480
The Bar Bldg.
New York, NY 10036

Contact: Sidney Bernstein, President and Publisher.

Desc: Reports on news concerning copyright, trademark, patent, and other intellectual property issues. *Type:* Newsletter.

The LAMA Manager

Legal Assistant Management Association
638 Prospect Ave.   Ph: (203)586-7507
Hartford, CT 06105-4250   Fax: (203)586-7550

Contact: Casey Anderson, Newsletter Liaison.

Desc: Intends "to be the primary source of information regarding legal assistant management. . .". Serves to "maximize legal assistant managers' contributions to quality, efficiency, and economy in the delivery of legal services." Recurring features include a collection. *Type:* Newsletter.

Law Books and Serials in Print

R. R. Bowker
A Unit of Cahners Business Information
121 Chanlon Rd.   Ph: (908)464-6800
New Providence, NJ 07974   Free: 888-269-5372
     Fax: (908)771-7704
E-mail: info@bowker.com
URL: http://www.bowker.com.

Contact: Barbara Holton, Editor; D. Gravesande, Editor.

Desc: List of publishers and producers of over 55,000 legal reference publications, periodicals, software, audio cassette titles and video cassettes under 6,608 headings. Principal content of publication is annotated listings of legal reference sources arranged by subject, title, and author. *Type:* Directory.

Law Firm Marketing & Profit Report

IOMA
29 W. 35th St., 5th Fl.
New York, NY 10001-2299

Contact: Sarah Pate, Editor.

Desc: Provides marketing and management information for lawyers in private practice. *Type:* Newsletter.

Law Firms Yellow Book

Leadership Directories, Inc.
104 5th Ave.   Ph: (212)627-4140
New York, NY 10011   Fax: (212)645-0931
E-mail: info@leadershipdirectories.com; lawfirms@leadershipdirectories.com
URL: http://www.leadershipdirectories.com; http://www.leadershipdirectories.com.

Contact: Janet Nelson-Henry, Editor.

Desc: Approximately 800 large law firms and over 23,000 attorneys and administrators at more than 3,000 domestic and foreign offices, subsidiaries, and affiliates. *Type:* Directory.

Law and Legal Information Directory

Gale Group Inc.
27500 Drake Rd.
Farmington Hills, MI 48331-3535
Ph: (248)699-4253
Free: 800-877-GALE
Fax: (248)699-8070
E-mail: galeord@galegroup.com
URL: http://www.galegroup.com.

Contact: Steven Wasserman, Editor; Jacqueline Wasserman O'Brien, Editor; Bonnie Shaw Pfaff, Editor.

Desc: More than 34,000 national and international organizations, bar associations, federal and highest state courts, federal regulatory agencies, law schools, firms and organizations offering continuing legal education, paralegal education, sources of scholarships and grants, awards and prizes, special libraries, information systems and services, research centers, publishers of legal periodicals, books, and audiovisual materials, lawyer referral services, legal aid offices, public defender offices, legislature manuals and registers, small claims courts, corporation departments of state, law enforcement agencies, state agencies, including disciplinary agencies, and state bar requirements. *Type:* Directory.

Laws and Ordinances of the Republic of Poland

University of Florida
Center for Governmental Responsibility
College of Law
230 Bruton-Geer
PO Box 117629
Gainesville, FL 32611
Ph: (352)392-2237

Contact: JoAnn Kelin, Devel. Dir.

Desc: Contains the complete text of the original English-language texts of the treaties and international agreements with Poland, and the original English-language translations of Polish laws, ordinances, and orders. *Available:* West Group, WESTLAW. *Type:* Database.

Lawyers' Committee for Civil Rights Under Law

1450 G St. NW, Ste. 400
Washington, DC 20005
Ph: (202)662-8600
Fax: (202)783-0857
E-mail: barnwine@lawyerscomm.org

Contact: Barbara R. Arnwine, Dir.

Desc: Operates through local committees of private lawyers in eight major cities to provide legal assistance to poor and minority groups living in urban centers. National office undertakes reform efforts in such fields as employment, voting rights, and housing discrimination. *Type:* Association.

Lawyer's Register International by Specialties and Fields of Law Including a Directory of Corporate Counsel

Lawyer's Register Publishing Co.
4555 Renaissance Pkwy., Ste. 101
Cleveland, OH 44128
Ph: (216)591-1492
Free: 800-477-6345
Fax: (216)591-0265
E-mail: info@sportsref.com
URL: http://www.sportsref.com

Contact: Jeannine Dreimiller, Editor.

Desc: Corporate legal staffs worldwide; legal firms; independent practicing attorneys each identified as a specialist in one or more fields of law. *Type:* Directory.

Legal Information Alert

Alert Publications, Inc.
401 W. Fullerton Pkwy.
Chicago, IL 60614-2810
Ph: (773)525-7594
Fax: (773)525-7015
E-mail: alertpub@compuserve.com
URL: http://www.alertpub.com.

Contact: Donna Tuke Heroy, Editor.

Desc: Presents reviews of recent publications in law, criminal justice, and legal research, including books, CD-ROM videotapes, and microform. Provides an abstract/critical review for each publication, cost, publication date, and name and address of publisher. *Type:* Newsletter.

Legal Resource Index™

The Gale Group
27500 Drake Rd.
Farmington Hills, MI 48331-3535
Ph: (248)699-4253
URL: http://www.galegroup.com

Contact: (650)378-5000, fax: (800)676-2345.

Desc: Provides indexing for some 800 of the most highly-regarded legal publications, such as law reviews, legal newspapers, law specialty publications, bar association journals, and international legal journals. Also includes law-related, indexed articles from more than 1,000 additional business and general interest titles. *Available:* The Dialog Corporation, DIALOG; CompuServe Information Service, Knowledge Index; LEXIS-NEXIS, LEXIS; West Group, WESTLAW; The Dialog Corporation, DataStar; CARL Corporation. *Type:* Database.

Legal Tech

Leader Publications
New York Law Publishing Company
345 Park Ave., South
New York, NY 10010
Ph: (212)545-6170
Free: 800-888-8300
Fax: (212)696-1848
E-mail: leader@ljextra.com; leader@ljextra.com.

Contact: Adam Schagman, ESQ., Editor.

Desc: Reports on recent developments in technology for the law office. Contains information in the areas of word processing, billing and timekeeping, document control, interoffice communications, and legal research. *Type:* Newsletter.

Legal Times

American Lawyer Media, L.P.
1730 M St. NW, Ste. 802
Washington, DC 20036
Ph: (202)457-0686
Fax: (202)785-4539
E-mail: legal.times@counsel.com.

Contact: Eric Effron, Editor and Publisher; Tom Watson, Exec. Editor; Jon Groner, Managing Editor; Ann Pelham, Associate Publisher; Mari Hotchkiss, Production Dir.; Laura McFarland, Advertising Mgr.

Desc: Legal magazine covering law, lobbying, and politics in Washington, DC. *Type:* Periodical.

Legal & Word Briefs

PO Box 414253
Miami, FL 33141
Ph: (305)372-0933
Fax: (305)372-0836

Contact: John Ritter, Pres./Writer; Anne Colby, Writer.

Alt. Contact: PO Box 414253, Miami, FL 33141; telephone: (305)372-0933; fax: (305)372-0836. *Type:* Periodical.

LEGI-SLATE

Legi-Slate, Inc.
10 G St. NE, Ste. 500
Washington, DC 20002
Ph: (202)898-2300
URL: http://www.legi-slate.com

Desc: A database system containing complete descriptions, histories, and updates of Congressional and regulatory activity. The legislative service includes the complete text of the Congressional Record, committee reports, and all bills and resolutions introduced in the U.S. *Available:* Legi-Slate, Inc.; Legi-Slate, Inc. *Type:* Database.

LEGI-SLATE Inc.

777 N. Capitol
Washington, DC 20002
Ph: (202)898-2300
Free: 800-733-1131
Fax: (202)898-3030

Contact: Mark L. Capaldini, President; Nancy Schwerzler, VP/Ed.

Desc: Distributes federal legislative and regulatory news. *Alt. Contact:* 777 N. Capitol, Washington, DC 20002; telephone: (202)898-2300; fax: (202)898-3030; toll-free: 800-733-1131. *Type:* Periodical.

LEXIS® Bankruptcy Library

LEXIS-NEXIS
9443 Springboro Pike
PO Box 933
Dayton, OH 45401-0933
Ph: (937)865-6800
URL: http://www.lex-nexis.com

Desc: Contains a comprehensive collection of primary and secondary legal research materials that includes case law, rules, statutory and regulatory materials, legal publications, accounting literature, and other resources pertaining to bankruptcy issues. 1986, and the Retiree Benefits Bankruptcy Protection Act of 1987; selected Congressional Record documents from February 1978; Bankruptcy Datasource profiles, news, and plans for reorganization; state case law for the states of California, Delaware, Florida, Illinois, Michigan, New Jersey, New York, Ohio, Pennsylvania, and Texas; Canadian case law from the Ontario Court of Justice General Division in Bankruptcy from January 1989; UCC filings; selected accounting and auditing literature; and the complete text of such publications as Bankruptcy Law Journal, Bankruptcy Development Journal, BNA Bankruptcy Law Daily, Directory of Bankruptcy Attorneys, Bankruptcy Litigation Manual, and Liquidation Alert. *Available:* LEXIS-NEXIS, LEXIS. *Type:* Database.

LEXIS® Federal Sentencing Library

LEXIS-NEXIS
9443 Springboro Pike
PO Box 933
Dayton, OH 45401-0933
Ph: (937)865-6800
URL: http://www.lex-nexis.com

Desc: Contains sentencing-related decisions from the Supreme Court since 1970, the Court of Appeals since 1789, and the District Courts since 1789. Also includes notices, rules, and decisions from the Federal Sentencing Commission since 1986, the Parole Commission since 1980, the Bureau of Prisons since 1980, and the Drug Enforcement Administration (DEA) since 1980; selected notices from the Federal Bureau of Investigation (FBI) since 1981, and the Department of Justice since 1981; and the complete text of the Federal Sentencing guidelines since 1987, Federal Rules of Criminal Procedure, Title 18 from the United States Code, and Title 28 from the Code of Federal Regulations. *Available:* LEXIS-NEXIS, LEXIS. *Type:* Database.

LEXIS® Law Reviews Library

LEXIS-NEXIS
9443 Springboro Pike
PO Box 933
Dayton, OH 45401-0933
Ph: (937)865-6800
URL: http://www.lex-nexis.com

Desc: Consists of more than 200 law reviews, several American Bar Association publications and the American Institute of Certified Public Accountants periodicals, an Environmental Law Institute publication, ALR and Led2d annotations, leading legal indices, and a number of Warren Gorham & Lamont tax journals. *Available:* LEXIS-NEXIS, LEXIS. *Type:* Database.

LEXIS® Legal Reference Library

LEXIS-NEXIS
9443 Springboro Pike
PO Box 933
Dayton, OH 45401-0933
Ph: (937)865-6800
URL: http://www.lex-nexis.com

Desc: Contains abstract materials and directories from structured information sources which add value and complement materials available in other specialized libraries. Also includes a citation manual, government information, and a legal usage dictionary, as well as abstracts from more than 700 legal journals, yearbooks, institutes, bar association organizations, university publications, specialty journals, and legal newspapers. *Available:* LEXIS-NEXIS, LEXIS. *Type:* Database.

LEXIS® Patent, Trademark, & Copyright Libraries

LEXIS-NEXIS
9443 Springboro Pike   Ph: (937)865-6800
PO Box 933
Dayton, OH 45401-0933
URL: http://www.lex-nexis.com

Desc: Contains patent, trademark, and copyright case decisions from the Supreme Court since 1790, from the Courts of Appeals since 1789, from the Federal Circuit Court of Appeals since 1982, from the District Courts since 1789, from the Court of Claims from 1940 to 1982, and from the Claims Court since October 1982. *Available:* LEXIS-NEXIS, LEXIS. *Type:* Database.

LEXSEE

LEXIS-NEXIS
9443 Springboro Pike   Ph: (937)865-6800
PO Box 933
Dayton, OH 45401-0933
URL: http://www.lex-nexis.com

Desc: Contains the complete text of state and federal court opinions, administrative decisions, Attorney General opinions, Internal Revenue Service (IRS) materials, law reviews, and the complete text of annotations from American Law Reports. Also includes the complete text of Federal Tax Coordinator 2D. *Available:* LEXIS-NEXIS, LEXIS. *Type:* Database.

LEXSTAT

LEXIS-NEXIS
9443 Springboro Pike   Ph: (937)865-6800
PO Box 933
Dayton, OH 45401-0933
URL: http://www.lex-nexis.com

Desc: Contains the complete text of the Internal Revenue Code, United States Code Service (USCS), and Deering's California Code. Also provides Consolidated Law Service covering the statutes of Colorado, Connecticut, Florida, Iowa, Michigan, Minnesota, Missouri, Montana, Nebraska, Oregon, Washington, and Wisconsin. *Available:* LEXIS-NEXIS, LEXIS. *Type:* Database.

Licensing Executives Society

1800 Diagonal Rd., Ste. 280   Ph: (703)836-3106
Alexandria, VA 22314-2840   Fax: (703)836-3107
URL: http://www.usa-canadian.les.org
Contact: Margaret Steven, Exec.Dir.

Desc: U.S. and foreign businessmen, scientists, engineers, and lawyers having direct responsibility for the transfer of technology. Maintains placement service. *Type:* Association.

Martindale-Hubbell Canadian Law Directory

Martindale-Hubbell, Inc.
LEXIS-NEXIS Group
121 Chanlon Rd.   Ph: (908)464-6800
New Providence, NJ 07974   Free: 800-526-4902
          Fax: (908)771-7792
E-mail: info@martindale.com

Desc: Thousands of Canadian attorneys, law firms, and corporate law departments, as well as U.S. laywers interested in receiving referrals from Canada. *Type:* Directory.

Martindale-Hubbell Law Directory

Martindale-Hubbell, Inc.
LEXIS-NEXIS Group
121 Chanlon Rd.   Ph: (908)464-6800
New Providence, NJ 07974   Free: 800-526-4902
          Fax: (908)771-7792
E-mail: info@martindale.com
URL: http://www.martindale.com; http://www.lawyers.com.

Contact: Louis J. Andreozzi, Editor.

Desc: Lawyers and law firms in the United States, its possessions, and Canada, plus leading law firms worldwide; includes a biographical section by firm, and a separate list of patent lawyers, attorneys in government service, inhouse counsel, and services, suppliers, and consultants to the legal profession. *Type:* Directory.

Martindale-Hubbell Law Directory Online

Martindale-Hubbell, Inc.
Reed Reference Publishing   Ph: (908)464-6800
    Group
121 Chanlon Rd.
New Providence, NJ 07974
URL: http://www.martindale.com

Desc: Contains information on more than 900,000 legal firms, banks, corporate legal departments, and special legal services for lawyers. Listings provide name, firm name and address, telephone number, date of birth, college of first and additional degrees, law school, fields of law, court admissions (e.g., local, state, federal), scholastic and legal honors, Martindale-Hubbell rating (when available), membership(s) in bar associations, clients, languages, biography, firm size, and legal services. *Available:* LEXIS-NEXIS, LEXIS; LEXIS-NEXIS, LEXIS. *Type:* Database.

Minnesota State Legislator

Minnesota Legislative Reference Library
645 State Office Bldg.
St. Paul, MN 55155-1050
E-mail: www@library.leg.state.mn.us
URL: http://www.leg.state.mn.us/

Desc: The Minnesota State Legislator database contains information about the legislative branch of Minnesota government, including the House of Representatives and Senate, Minnesota laws, statutes, and rules. Historical information about the legislature can be found, as well as employment opportunities, and links to other Minnesota governmental sites. *Type:* Database.

Morality in Media Newsletter

Morality in Media, Inc.
475 Riverside Dr., Ste. 239   Ph: (212)870-3222
New York, NY 10115   Fax: (212)870-2765
E-mail: mimnyc@ix.netcom.com.
Contact: Patrick McGrath, Editor.

Desc: Concerned with illegal pornography and broadcasting indecency. Provides articles on obscenity laws, court cases, community action, and the role of organized crime in pornography traffic. *Type:* Newsletter.

National Academy of Conciliators

PO Box 560366
Dallas, TX 75356-0366
Contact: Lester B. Wolff, Pres.

Desc: Professionals dealing with dispute settlement consulting and training services. Promotes alternatives to litigation; provides skills development programs for independent third parties involved in dispute settlements; promotes preventive dispute settlement programs. Offers training and certification programs and establishes professional standards. *Type:* Association.

National Association of American School Employees and Retirees Legal Defense Counsel

William Bert Johnson
1890 Schoolcraft
Detroit, MI 48223
Contact: William Bert Johnson, Chief Counsel.

Desc: Legal counsellors (600) representing school employees and retirees (195,000). Works to ensure equal justice under law for members and to secure members' rights; seeks to improve access to justice and the efficiency and effectiveness of the appellate process. Solicits the aid of attorneys to defend the interests of members. *Type:* Association.

National Association of Criminal Defense Lawyers

1025 Connecticut Ave., NW,   Ph: (202)872-8600
    Ste. 901   Fax: (202)872-8690
Washington, DC 20036
E-mail: assist@nacdl.com
URL: http://www.criminaljustice.org
Contact: Stuart M. Statler, Exec.Dir.

Desc: Advances the mission of the nation's criminal defense lawyers to ensure justice and due process for persons accused of crime or other misconduct. A professional bar association that includes private criminal defense lawyers, public defenders, law professors, and judges committed to preserving fairness within America's criminal justice system. *Type:* Association.

National Association for Law Placement Directory of Legal Employers

National Association for Law Placement (NALP)
1666 Connecticut Ave., Suite   Ph: (202)667-1666
    325
Washington, DC 20009
E-mail: info@nalp.org
Contact: Julie P. Hamre, Deputy Director, (202)667-1666, jhamre@nalp.org.

Desc: Tains information on more than 1200 employers of legal professionals. Covers law firms, corporate legal departments, and local and federal government and public interest agencies. *Available:* LEXIS-NEXIS. *Type:* Database.

National Association of Police Organizations

750 1st St. NW, Ste. 920   Ph: (202)842-4420
Washington, DC 20002-4241   Fax: (202)842-4396
E-mail: napo@erols.com
URL: http://www.napo.org
Contact: Robert Scully, Exec.Dir.

Desc: Police officers united to promote the needs of members on a national level. *Type:* Association.

National Bar Association

1225 11th St. NW   Ph: (202)842-3900
Washington, DC 20001   Fax: (202)289-6170
URL: http://www.nationalbar.org
Contact: John Crump, Exec.Dir.

Desc: Professional association of minority (predominantly African-American) attorneys, members of the judiciary, law students, and law faculty. Represents the interests of members and the communities they serve. *Type:* Association.

National Black Police Association

3251 Mt. Pleasant St. NW   Ph: (202)986-2070
Washington, DC 20010-2103   Fax: (202)986-0410
URL: http://www.blackpolice.org
Contact: Ronald E. Hampton, Exec.Dir.

Desc: Male and female black police officers. Seeks to: improve relationships between police departments and the black community; recruit minority police officers on a national scale; eliminate police corruption, brutality, and racial discrimination. Maintains speakers' bureau. *Type:* Association.

National Center for State Courts

300 Newport Ave.   Ph: (757)253-2000
Williamsburg, VA 23185   Fax: (757)220-0449
Contact: Roger K. Warren, Pres.

Desc: Provides assistance to state and local trial and appellate courts in improving their structure and administration. Furnishes consultant services; conducts national studies and projects; acts as a clearinghouse for exchange of information on court problems; coordinates activities of other organizations involved in judicial improvement, providing secretariat services for several. Conducts conferences and training courses. *Type:* Association.

National Center for Youth Law

114 Sansome St., Ste. 900   Ph: (415)543-3307
San Francisco, CA 94104   Fax: (415)956-9024
E-mail: info@youthlaw.org
Contact: John F. O'Toole, Dir.

Desc: Employs eight attorneys on a full-time basis to provide assistance to legal services programs and private attorneys representing poor children and youth across the U.S. Assistance includes consultation, training, legal research, drafting of pleadings and motions, aid in writing trial and appellate briefs, and participation in litigation in selected cases. Maintains collection of pleadings, memoranda, motions, briefs, and other specialized materials. *Type:* Association.

National Clearinghouse for Legal Services

205 W. Monroe, 2 Systems Fl.   Ph: (312)263-3830
Chicago, IL 60606   Free: 800-621-3256
                                   Fax: (312)263-3846
URL: http://www.nclsplp.com
Contact: Rita McLennon, Exec.Dir.

Desc: Legal services attorneys and programs; private attorneys; law universities and libraries; court judges and libraries; government organizations. Makes available information on case law with respect to issues relating to poor people. Operates extensive brief bank of cases and publications relating to poverty law and the consumer. *Type:* Association.

National Council of Juvenile and Family Court Judges

PO Box 8970   Ph: (702)784-6012
University of Nevada   Fax: (702)784-6628
Reno, NV 89507
Contact: Louis W. McHardy, Exec.Dir.

Desc: Judges with juvenile and family court jurisdiction and others with a professional interest in the nation's juvenile justice system. Works to further more effective administration of justice for young people through the improvement of juvenile and family court standards and practices. *Type:* Association.

National Court Reporters Association

8224 Old Courthouse Rd.   Ph: (703)556-6272
Vienna, VA 22182   Free: 800-272-6272
                                   Fax: (703)556-6291
E-mail: msic@ncrahq.org
URL: http://www.verbatimreporters.com
Contact: Mark Golden, CAE, Exec.Dir.

Desc: Independent state, regional, and local associations. Verbatim court reporters who work as official reporters for courts and government agencies, as freelance reporters for independent contractors, and as captioners for television programmings; retired reporters, teachers of court reporting, and school officials; student court reporters. Conducts research; compiles statistics; offers several certification programs, publishes journal. *Type:* Association.

National Directory of Prosecuting Attorneys

National District Attorneys Association
99 Canal Center Plaza, Ste. 510   Ph: (703)549-9222
Alexandria, VA 22314   Fax: (703)836-3195
E-mail: jean.holt@ndaa-apri.org
Contact: Newman Flanagan, Editor.

Desc: About 2,800 elected or appointed local prosecuting attorneys. *Type:* Directory.

National Employment Lawyers Association

600 Harrison St., Ste. 535   Ph: (415)227-4655
San Francisco, CA 94107   Fax: (415)495-7465
E-mail: nelahq@nela.org
URL: http://www.nela.org
Contact: Terisa E. Chaw, Exec.Dir.

Desc: Attorneys who represent individual employees in cases involving employment discrimination, wrongful termination, benefits, and other employment-related matters. Promotes the professional development of members through networking, publications, technical assistance, and education. Supports the workplace rights of individual employees via lobbying and other activities. *Type:* Association.

National Federation of Paralegal Associations

Lu Hangley
PO Box 33108   Ph: (816)941-4000
Kansas City, MO 64114-0108   Fax: (816)941-2725
E-mail: info@paralegals.org
URL: http://www.paralegals.org
Contact: Lu Hangley, Mng.Dir.

Desc: State and local paralegal associations and other organizations supporting the goals of the federation (55); individual paralegals (17,000). To serve as a national voice of the paralegal profession; to advance, foster, and promote the paralegal concept; to monitor and participate in developments in the paralegal profession; to maintain a nationwide communications network among paralegal associations and other members of the legal community. *Type:* Association.

National Health Lawyers Association

1120 Connecticut Ave. NW,   Ph: (202)833-1100
   Ste. 950   Fax: (202)833-1105
Washington, DC 20036
E-mail: healthlaw@nhla.org
URL: http://www.nhla.org
Contact: Marilou King, Exec.Dir.

Desc: Private, corporate, institutional, and governmental lawyers, and health professionals. Seeks to establish a forum for nonpartisan objective treatment of issues in the field of health law and to disseminate differing points of view. Conducts research; sponsors educational programs for lawyers, their clients, and other professional and technical personnel in the health field. *Type:* Association.

National Institute for Trial Advocacy

PO Box 6500   Ph: (219)239-7770
Notre Dame, IN 46556-6500   Free: 800-225-NITA
                                   Fax: (219)282-1263
E-mail: nita.1@nd.edu
URL: http://www.nd.edu/~nita
Contact: Raymond M. White, COO.

Desc: Lawyers and judges dedicated to improvement of the trial bar in the U.S. Trains lawyers in trial advocacy skills; develops methods for teaching and learning such skills in law schools and in continuing education programs. Sponsors regional training programs featuring student performance in a courtroom atmosphere augmented by team teaching, videotape review of the students' performances, demonstrations, and lectures. *Type:* Association.

National Jewish Law Students Association

233 Bay State Rd.   Fax: (617)353-7214
Boston, MA 02215
E-mail: dansudit@spiritmail.com
Contact: David A. Blansky, Pres.

Desc: Seeks to foster a Jewish identity in legal professionals and students and to promote their active involvement in the community. *Type:* Association.

The National Law Journal

New York Law Publishing Company
345 Park Ave. South   Ph: (212)779-9200
New York, NY 10010

Desc: Contains the complete text of The National Law Journal, a weekly newspaper for the legal profession. Feature articles cover trends in case law, employment, criminal investigations, and law office management techniques. *Available:* LEXIS-NEXIS, NEXIS; West Group, WESTLAW. *Type:* Database.

The National Notary

National Notary Association
9350 DeSoto Ave.   Ph: (818)739-4000
PO Box 2402   Free: 800-876-6827
Chatsworth, CA 91313-2402   Fax: (818)700-0920
E-mail: natlnotary@aol.com; nna@nationalnotary.org.
Contact: Charles N. Faerber, Editor, (818)739-4015;
Deborah M. Thaw, Publisher, (818)739-4015.

Desc: Legal trade magazine. *Type:* Periodical.

National Organization of Black Law Enforcement Executives

4609 Pinecrest Office Park Dr.,   Ph: (703)658-1529
   Ste. 2-F   Fax: (703)658-9479
Alexandria, VA 22312-1442
E-mail: noble@noblenatl.org
URL: http://www.noblenatl.org
Contact: Robert Stewart, Exec.Dir.

Desc: Law enforcement executives above the rank of lieutenant; police educators; academy directors; interested individuals and organizations. Goals are: to provide a platform from which the concerns and opinions of minority law enforcement executives and command-level officers can be expressed; to facilitate the exchange of programmatic information among minority law enforcement executives; to increase minority participation at all levels of law enforcement; to eliminate racism in the field of criminal justice; to secure increased cooperation from criminal justice agencies; to reduce urban crime and violence. *Type:* Association.

National Paralegal Association

Box 406   Ph: (215)297-8333
Solebury, PA 18963   Fax: (215)297-8358
URL: http://www.nationalparalegal.org
Contact: H. Jeffrey Valentine, Exec.Dir.

Desc: Paralegals, paralegal students, educators, supervisors, paralegal schools, administrators, law librarians, law clinics, and attorneys. Objective is to advance the paralegal profession by promoting recognition, economic benefits, and high standards. Registers paralegals; maintains speakers' bureau, job bank, and placement service; offers resume preparation assistance. *Type:* Association.

National Sheriffs' Association

1450 Duke St.   Ph: (703)836-7827
Alexandria, VA 22314-3490   Free: 800-424-7827
                                   Fax: (703)683-6541
E-mail: nsamail@sheriffs.org
URL: http://www.sheriffs.org
Contact: A.N. Moser, Jr., Exec.Dir.

Desc: Serves the law enforcement/criminal justice professionals of the nation by raising the level of professionalism among those in the field of criminal justice. NSA has been involved in numerous programs to enable sheriffs, their deputies, chiefs of police, and others in the field of criminal justice and public safety to perform their jobs in the best possible manner and to better serve the people of their city/counties and jurisdictions. NSA has offered training, information, and other services to sheriffs, deputies, and others throughout the nation and has worked to forge cooperative relationships with local, state, and federal criminal justice professionals across the nation to network and form partnerships about numerous programs and projects. *Type:* Association.

The New York Law Journal

New York Law Publishing Company
345 Park Ave. South   Ph: (212)779-9200
New York, NY 10010

Desc: Contains the complete text of the New York Law Journal, a daily publication providing information of interest to the New York legal community. *Available:* LEXIS-NEXIS, NEXIS; West Group, WESTLAW. *Type:* Database.

Nolo News

Nolo Press
950 Parker St.　　　　　　Ph: (510)549-1976
Berkeley, CA 94710　　　　Free: 800-992-6656
　　　　　　　　　　　　　Fax: 800-645-0895
E-mail: noloinfo@nolopress.com; nolonews@nolo.com.
URL: http://www.nolo.com; http://www.nolo.com.

Contact: Ralph Warner, Editor; Mary Randolph, Editor.

Desc: Publishes consumer interest articles on self-help law and on the self-help law movement. Offers reviews, law materials, and updates of books published by Nolo Press. *Type:* Newsletter.

Oceana's Law Library Newsletter

Oceana Publications, Inc.
75 Main St.　　　　　　　Ph: (914)693-8100
Dobbs Ferry, NY 10522-1601　Free: 800-831-0758
　　　　　　　　　　　　　Fax: (914)693-0402
E-mail: info@oceanalaw.com
URL:　　http://www.oceanalaw.com;　　http://www.oceanalaw.com.

Contact: Stephen Smith, Editor, ssmith@oceanalaw.com.

Desc: Contains information on legal books, services, and conferences of interest to law librarians. Recurring features include books reviewed and received, descriptions of other recommended books, listings of specific retrospective monographs and sets, news of members, and other news of interest concerning Oceania publications. *Type:* Newsletter.

Of Counsel

Law & Business, Inc.
Prentice-Hall, Inc.
1185 Avenue of the Americas,　Ph: (212)597-0200
　No. 37
New York, NY 10036-2601

Contact: Larry Smith, Editor.

Desc: Discusses law firm management. Features insights on subjects ranging from marketing to compensation systems. *Type:* Newsletter.

Pacific Legal Foundation

2151 River Plaza Dr. Ste. 305　Ph: (916)641-8888
Sacramento, CA 95833　　　Fax: (916)920-3444
E-mail: plf@jps.net
URL: http://www.pacificlegal.org

Contact: Robert K. Best, Pres.

Desc: Litigates in state and federal courts challenging government actions, laws, and regulations that infringe on individual and economc freedoms. Defends and espouses the principles of private property rights, constitutionally limited government, free market enterprise, and individual responsibility. Opposes unfair tax assessment policies; challenges hiring and contracting quotas and preferences; supports education, tort, and welfare reforms. *Type:* Association.

Partner's Report

Institute of Management & Administration, Inc.
29 W. 35th St., 5th Fl.　　Ph: (212)244-0360
New York, NY 10001-2299　Fax: (212)564-0465
E-mail: subserve@ioma.com
URL: http://www.ioma.com; http://www.ioma.com/.

Contact: Lisa Isom-Rodriguez, Editor, lisom-rodriguez@toma-hql.mhs.compuserve.com.

Desc: Covers subjects relevant to the ownership, profitability, and management of law firms. *Type:* Newsletter.

PATDATA

U.S. Patent and Trademark Office (PTO)
Office of Electronic Information Products
Crystal Plaza 3, Ste. 441　　Ph: (703)306-2600
Washington, DC 20231
E-mail: oeip@uspto.gov
URL: http://www.uspto.gov

Desc: Contains citations, with abstracts, to approximately 700,000 U.S. utility patents issued since 1971 and all reissue patents and defense publications issued by the United States Patent and Trademark Office since 1975. *Available:* Ovid Technologies, Inc.; Ovid Technologies, Inc. *Type:* Database.

Patent Status File

The Gale Group
27500 Drake Rd.　　　　Ph: (248)699-4253
Farmington Hills, MI 48331-3535
URL: http://www.galegroup.com

Desc: Contains more than 300,000 references to post-issue actions affecting U.S. patents. *Available:* Questel • Orbit. *Type:* Database.

Phi Alpha Delta

345 N. Charles St.　　　　Ph: (410)347-3118
Baltimore, MD 21201　　　Fax: (410)347-3119
E-mail: padoffice@aol.com
URL: http://www.pad.org

Contact: Frank C. Patek, II, Exec.Dir.

Desc: Professional fraternity - law. *Type:* Association.

Phi Delta Phi International Legal Fraternity

1750 N St., NW　　　　　Ph: (202)628-0148
Washington, DC 20036　　Free: 800-368-5606
　　　　　　　　　　　　Fax: (202)296-7619
E-mail: phideltaphi@worldnet.att.net
URL: http://www.phideltaphi.org

Contact: Sam S. Crutchfield, Exec.Dir.

Desc: Professional fraternity - law. Promotes professional development and legal ethics. *Type:* Association.

Police Executive Research Forum

1120 Connecticut Ave. NW,　Ph: (202)466-7820
　Ste. 930　　　　　　　　Fax: (202)466-7826
Washington, DC 20036
E-mail: perf@policeforum.org
URL: http://www.policeforum.org

Contact: Chuck Wexler, Exec.Dir.

Desc: General members are executive heads of large public police agencies who have completed at least four years of college; subscribing members are executives other than department heads and executives of criminal justice agencies; sustaining members are former members who no longer qualify for general membership. Stresses cooperation with other professionals and organizations in the criminal justice system. Seeks to stimulate public understanding and discussion of important criminal justice issues. *Type:* Association.

Police Marksman Association

6000 E. Shirley Ln.　　　Ph: (334)271-2010
Montgomery, AL 36117　　Fax: (334)279-9267
E-mail: pma@policemarksman.com
URL: http://www.policemarksman.com

Contact: Mr. Charles Leslie Dees, Pres.

Desc: Law enforcement personnel. Provides firearms training and survival knowledge for effective performance in the line of duty. *Type:* Association.

Post-Soviet Media Law & Policy Newsletter

Benjamin N. Cardozo School of Law/Yeshiva University
Jacob Burns Institute for Advanced Legal Studies
Brookdale Center
55 5th Ave.
New York, NY 10003
URL: http://www.vii.org/monroe.

Contact: Monroe E. Price, Editor, (212)790-0402, fax: (212)790-0205, price@ymail.yu.edu; Peter Yu, Managing Editor, peter_yu@msn.com.

Desc: Contains in-depth articles about media law in the former U.S.S.R. *Type:* Newsletter.

Punitive Damages: A State-by-State Guide to Law and Practice

West Group
620 Opperman Dr.　　　　Ph: (651)687-7000
St. Paul, MN 55164-0526
URL: http://www.westgroup.com

Desc: Contains the full text of Punitive Damages: A State-by-State Guide to Law and Practice, written by Richard L. Blatt, Robert W. *Available:* West Group, WESTLAW. *Type:* Database.

Securities Regulation & Law Report

The Bureau of National Affairs, Inc. (BNA)
1231 25th St. NW　　　　Ph: (202)452-4200
Washington, DC 20037
E-mail: bnaplus@bna.com
URL: http://bna.com/mkt/hrl/hrlwdec.htm

Desc: Contains the complete text of Securities Regulation & Law Report, covering federal and state regulations and laws on securities. Includes corporate governance and attorney responsibility, enforcement activities, commodity futures regulation, and accounting standards and practices. *Available:* LEXIS-NEXIS, LEXIS; West Group, WESTLAW; LEXIS-NEXIS, NEXIS. *Type:* Database.

Shepard's Citations

Shepard's/McGraw-Hill, Inc.
555 Middle Creek PKWY　　Ph: (719)488-3000
Colorado Springs, CO 80921-3622
URL: http://www.shepards.com

Desc: Provides a comprehensive list of citations to a given case, statute or administrative decision. Includes analyses of the cited case, or other legal authority, covering the history (e.g., affirmed, dismissed, superseded); treatment (e.g., criticized, harmonized, overruled); and operation of orders (e.g., amended, revoked, revised). *Available:* American Institute of Certified Public Accountants (AICPA), Total On-Line Tax and Accounting Library (TOTAL); West Group, WESTLAW; LEXIS-NEXIS, LEXIS. *Type:* Database.

Sierra Club Legal Defense Fund

Desc: Purposes are to use existing legal remedies to protect the natural environment of the U.S. and develop a realistic and enforceable body of environmental law through the implementation of existing statutes, regulations, and common law principles. Maintains library. *Type:* Association.

Sigma Delta Kappa

5315 18th St. N
Arlington, VA 22205-3046

Contact: Norris Shealy, Grand Sec. & Editor.

Desc: Professional fraternity - law. *Type:* Association.

Technical Advisory Service for Attorneys

Technical Advisory Service, Inc.
1166 DeKalb Pike   Ph: (610)275-8272
Blue Bell, PA 19422
E-mail: experts@tasanet.com
URL: http://www.tasanet.com

Contact: Kathy Walters, Westlaw Service Info., (612)687-1734, walters@westgroup.com.

Desc: Contains information on approximately 20,000 individuals in a variety of occupations available to serve as expert witnesses or as consultants to attorneys and insurance firms. Includes a TASA Expert Number, state or province in which the expert works or resides, educational and employment histories, area of expertise, and other relevant information. *Available:* West Group, WESTLAW. *Type:* Database.

Texas Bar Journal

State Bar of Texas
1414 Colorado   Ph: (512)463-1463
Austin, TX 78701   Free: 800-204-2222
                         Fax: (512)463-1475

Contact: Kelley Jones-King, Managing Editor; Homer Williams, Pub. Rep., hwilliams@austin.rr.com.

Desc: Legal news journal for the legal profession. *Type:* Periodical.

TRADEMARKSCAN® - Canada

Thomson & Thomson
500 Victory Rd.   Ph: (617)479-1600
North Quincy, MA 02171-3145
URL: http://www.Thomson-Thomson.com

Contact: Electronic Information Services, 11541 (DIALOG - DIALMAIL).

Desc: Contains information on more than 627,000 trademark registrations and applications filed with Canadian Intellectual Property Office. Includes trademark; International Classification number; current status; dates of first use, filing, advertisement, registration, and renewal; goods/services description; mark type; owner history; registration number; and application number. *Available:* The Dialog Corporation, DIALOG; Thomson & Thomson. *Type:* Database.

TRADEMARKSCAN® - U.S. Federal

Thomson & Thomson
500 Victory Rd.   Ph: (617)479-1600
North Quincy, MA 02171-3145
URL: http://www.Thomson-Thomson.com

Contact: Electronic Information Services, 11541 (DIALOG - DIALMAIL).

Desc: Contains information on more than 2 million federal trademark registrations and applications (including "Intent to Use") filed with the U.S. Patent and Trademark Office (USPTO). *Available:* The Dialog Corporation, DIALOG; Thomson & Thomson. *Type:* Database.

TRADEMARKSCAN® - U.S. State

Thomson & Thomson
500 Victory Rd.   Ph: (617)479-1600
North Quincy, MA 02171-3145
URL: http://www.Thomson-Thomson.com

Desc: Contains information on more than 970,000 commercial trademarks, excluding corporate names, registered with the offices of the Secretaries of State of individual U.S. states, American Samoa, and Puerto Rico. *Available:* The Dialog Corporation, DIALOG; Thomson & Thomson. *Type:* Database.

Trial Lawyers for Public Justice

1717 Massachusetts Ave. NW,   Ph: (202)797-8600
    Ste. 800   Fax: (202)232-7203
Washington, DC 20036
E-mail: tlpj@tlpj.org
URL: http://www.tlpj.org

Contact: Arthur H. Bryant, Exec.Dir.

Desc: National public interest care firm dedicated to using trial lawyers' skills and resources to advance to public good. *Type:* Association.

Uniform Commercial Code Cases

West Group
620 Opperman Dr.   Ph: (651)687-7000
St. Paul, MN 55164-0526
URL: http://www.westgroup.com

Desc: Contains court decisions from the Uniform Commercial Code Reporting Service. Covers attorney general, county general, U.S. *Type:* Database.

United States Bar Directory

Attorneys' National Clearing House Co.
PO Box 8688   Ph: (941)263-0840
Naples, FL 34101-8688   Free: 800-231-6736
                              Fax: (941)263-1033
E-mail: anch@attorneyreferral.com; usbd@attorneyreferral.com.
URL: http://www.attorneyreferral.com/usbd.

Contact: John M. Birk, Vice President.

Desc: Over 3,000 general and specialized practice attorneys employed through correspondence (letter, phone, fax or e-mail). *Type:* Directory.

U.S. Copyrights

The Dialog Corporation
DIALOG
11000 Regency Pkwy., Ste. 400   Ph: (919)462-8600
Cary, NC 27511
URL: http://www.dialog.com

Contact: Marketing.

Desc: Contains registration, renewal, and ownership information for more than 8.5 million active copyright and mask-work registrations on file at the U.S. Copyright Office. *Available:* The Dialog Corporation, DIALOG; The Dialog Corporation, DIALOG. *Type:* Database.

U.S. FullText

MicroPatent
250 Dodge Ave.   Ph: (203)466-5055
East Haven, CT 06512-3358
E-mail: info@micropat.com
URL: http://www.micropat.com

Contact: Sue Kelly, Sales & Technical Support.

Desc: Contains the complete text of patent documents issued by world, European, and US patent and trademark offices. For each patent, includes front-page bibliographic data and abstract, as well as descriptions of drawings, background and summary of the invention, examples, and claims. *Type:* Database.

United States Law Week

The Bureau of National Affairs, Inc. (BNA)
1231 25th St. NW   Ph: (202)452-4200
Washington, DC 20037
E-mail: bnaplus@bna.com
URL: http://bna.com/mkt/hrl/hrlwdec.htm

Contact: BNA PLUS, (202)452-4323, fax: (202)822-8092, bnaplus@bna.com.

Desc: Contains the complete text of Sections 1, 2, and 3 of United States Law Week, providing an overview of precedent-setting cases in all areas of law and from all jurisdictions. *Available:* LEXIS-NEXIS, LEXIS; LEXIS-NEXIS, NEXIS; West Group, WESTLAW. *Type:* Database.

United States Law Week, Daily Edition

The Bureau of National Affairs, Inc. (BNA)
1231 25th St. NW   Ph: (202)452-4200
Washington, DC 20037
E-mail: bnaplus@bna.com
URL: http://bna.com/mkt/hrl/hrlwdec.htm

Contact: BNA PLUS, (202)452-4323, fax: (202)822-8092, bnaplus@bna.com.

Desc: Provides comprehensive reports and analysis of the Supreme Court's case docket, orders, calendars, motions, arguments, and general news. Includes an overview of the nation's most important state supreme court and federal legal developments. *Available:* LEXIS-NEXIS, NEXIS; LEXIS-NEXIS, LEXIS; West Group, WESTLAW; The Dialog Corporation, DIALOG. *Type:* Database.

U.S. Patent Search Plus

MicroPatent
250 Dodge Ave.   Ph: (203)466-5055
East Haven, CT 06512-3358
E-mail: info@micropat.com
URL: http://www.micropat.com

Contact: Sue Kelly, Sales & Technical Support., fax: (203)495-6909.

Desc: Contains citations, with abstracts and exemplary claim to U.S., EPO, and PCT patents. Software enables the user to search by title, patent number, date of issue, inventor(s), state or country of residence of first inventor, assignee, application serial number and filing date, classification, keyword, abstract, exemplary claim, and status. *Type:* Database.

Volunteer Lawyers for the Arts

1 E. 53rd St., 6th Fl.   Ph: (212)319-2787
New York, NY 10022   Fax: (212)752-6575
E-mail: vlany@bway.net

Contact: Amy Schwartzman, Exec.Dir.

Desc: Volunteer lawyers who provide free legal services to artists and art organizations in art-related legal matters. Works to familiarize the legal profession and the arts community with legal problems confronting artists and provide them with available solutions. *Type:* Association.

Washington Legal Foundation

2009 Massachusetts Ave. NW   Ph: (202)588-0302
Washington, DC 20036   Fax: (202)588-0386
URL: http://www.wlf.org

Contact: Daniel J. Popeo, Chmn.

Desc: Public interest law and policy center. Holds monthly media briefings on current issues and publishes a bi-weekly op-ed feature in the national edition of the *New York Times*. *Type:* Association.

Western Center on Law and Poverty

3701 Wilshire Blvd., Ste. 208   Ph: (213)487-7211
Los Angeles, CA 90010   Fax: (213)487-0242

Contact: Mary Burdick, Exec.Dir.

Desc: Provides legal counsel and representation to individuals and groups whose actions may effect change in institutions affecting the poor. Specializes in poverty law in California, offering litigation assistance and services to all neighborhood legal services programs. Concentrates on substantive areas of law including housing, health, employment, welfare, and education. *Type:* Association.

Western Legal Publications Database

Western Legal Publications Ltd.
200-856 Homer St.   Ph: (604)687-5671
Vancouver, BC, Canada V6B
    2W5
E-mail: wlp@mindlink.bc.ca
URL: http://www.westernlegal.com

Desc: Contains digests of more than 80,000 Canadian federal and selected civil and criminal judicial decisions, including the following: British Columbia civil and criminal court and B.C. Labour Relations Board decisions from 1979 to date; B.C. Labour Arbitration decisions from 1982 to date; civil and criminal court decisions for Manitoba, Saskatchewan, and Alberta from 1980 to date; Supreme Court of Canada decisions from 1980 to date; and Federal Court of Appeal decisions from 1981 to date. *Available:* QL Systems Limited, QUICKLAW. *Type:* Database.

WESTLAW® Administrative Law Databases
West Group
620 Opperman Dr.   Ph: (651)687-7000
St. Paul, MN 55164-0526
URL: http://www.westgroup.com
Desc: Contains documents that relate to the quasi-judicial and quasi-legislative proceedings of administrative agencies. Among the subjects included are the status, organization, and powers of government agencies. *Available:* West Group, WESTLAW. *Type:* Database.

WESTLAW® Bankruptcy Library
West Group
620 Opperman Dr.   Ph: (651)687-7000
St. Paul, MN 55164-0526
URL: http://www.westgroup.com
Desc: Contains the complete text of U.S. federal court decisions, statutes and regulations, specialized files, and texts and periodicals dealing with bankruptcy, including the administration of debtor estates and insolvency. *Available:* West Group, WESTLAW. *Type:* Database.

WESTLAW® Bicentennial of the Constitution Database
West Group
620 Opperman Dr.   Ph: (651)687-7000
St. Paul, MN 55164-0526
URL: http://www.westgroup.com
Desc: Contains the complete text of documents that report or explain the events surrounding the United States' origins. *Available:* West Group, WESTLAW. *Type:* Database.

WESTLAW® Bulletin
West Group
620 Opperman Dr.   Ph: (651)687-7000
St. Paul, MN 55164-0526
URL: http://www.westgroup.com
Desc: Contains documents prepared by the editorial staff of West Publishing Company that summarize recent developments in the law that apply generally or are not covered in one of the Westlaw Topical Highlights or Westlaw State Bulletin databases. *Available:* West Group, WESTLAW. *Type:* Database.

WESTLAW® Communications
West Group
620 Opperman Dr.   Ph: (651)687-7000
St. Paul, MN 55164-0526
URL: http://www.westgroup.com
Desc: Contains the complete text of U.S. federal court decisions, statutes and regulations, administrative law publications, and texts and periodicals dealing with communications law. *Available:* West Group, WESTLAW. *Type:* Database.

WESTLAW® Delaware Corporation Law
West Group
620 Opperman Dr.   Ph: (651)687-7000
St. Paul, MN 55164-0526
URL: http://www.westgroup.com
Desc: Contains the complete text of cases, decisions, and orders interpreting Delaware statutory law relating to corporation law and practice from the Delaware state courts, U.S. Supreme Court, Court of Appeals, district courts, bankruptcy courts, claim courts, and related federal courts. *Available:* West Group, WESTLAW. *Type:* Database.

WESTLAW® Family Law Databases
West Group
620 Opperman Dr.   Ph: (651)687-7000
St. Paul, MN 55164-0526
URL: http://www.westgroup.com
Contact: WEST Reference Attorneys. Toll-Free No.: (800) REF-ATTY.
Desc: Contains the complete text of U.S. federal court decisions, statutes and regulations, state court decisions, and specialized files, and texts and periodicals dealing with family law, including such topics as abortion, adoption, custody, divorce, juvenile delinquency, marriage, and minors' rights. *Available:* West Group, WESTLAW. *Type:* Database.

WESTLAW® Federal Case Law Library
West Group
620 Opperman Dr.   Ph: (651)687-7000
St. Paul, MN 55164-0526
URL: http://www.westgroup.com
Desc: Contains the complete text of U.S. federal laws, statutes and regulations, executive documents, court decisions. *Available:* West Group, WESTLAW. *Type:* Database.

WESTLAW® First Amendment Databases
West Group
620 Opperman Dr.   Ph: (651)687-7000
St. Paul, MN 55164-0526
URL: http://www.westgroup.com
Desc: Contains documents that relate to the protections guaranteed by the First Amendment to the Federal Constitution. Among the subjects included are expressions of the freedom of speech, religion, and of the press, and the rights of petition and to assemble peacefully. *Available:* West Group, WESTLAW. *Type:* Database.

WESTLAW® Government Benefits Databases
West Group
620 Opperman Dr.   Ph: (651)687-7000
St. Paul, MN 55164-0526
URL: http://www.westgroup.com
Desc: Contains documents that relate to federal, state, and local government assistance and entitlement programs. Among the subjects included are Aid to Families with Dependent Children, care for the homeless and indigent, food stamps, housing assistance, old-age and survivors benefits, Railroad Retirement Act and Social Security Act benefits, Supplemental Security Income, and other disability and welfare programs. *Available:* West Group, WESTLAW. *Type:* Database.

WESTLAW® Government Contracts
West Group
620 Opperman Dr.   Ph: (651)687-7000
St. Paul, MN 55164-0526
URL: http://www.westgroup.com
Desc: Contains the complete text of U.S. federal and state court decisions; statutes and regulations; administrative law; specialized materials; and texts and periodicals that relate to contracts with governments or their political subdivisions. *Available:* West Group, WESTLAW. *Type:* Database.

WESTLAW® Health Law Databases
West Group
620 Opperman Dr.   Ph: (651)687-7000
St. Paul, MN 55164-0526
URL: http://www.westgroup.com
Contact: WEST Reference Attorneys. Toll-Free No.: (800) REF-ATTY.
Desc: Contains the complete text of U.S. federal court decisions, statutes and regulations, state court decisions, and law reviews, texts, bar journals, and specialized legal sources covering health services and medical malpractice. *Available:* West Group, WESTLAW. *Type:* Database.

WESTLAW® Immigration
West Group
620 Opperman Dr.   Ph: (651)687-7000
St. Paul, MN 55164-0526
URL: http://www.westgroup.com
Desc: Contains the complete text of U.S. federal court decisions, statutes and regulations, and texts and periodicals dealing with immigration law. *Available:* West Group, WESTLAW. *Type:* Database.

WESTLAW® Insurance
West Group
620 Opperman Dr.   Ph: (651)687-7000
St. Paul, MN 55164-0526
URL: http://www.westgroup.com
Desc: Contains the complete text of U.S. state court decisions, state statutes, and specialized files, texts, and periodicals dealing with insurance, including policyholder rights and liabilities, industry regulation, and the issuance of policies and sale of insurance. *Available:* West Group, WESTLAW. *Type:* Database.

WESTLAW® Intellectual Property
West Group
620 Opperman Dr.   Ph: (651)687-7000
St. Paul, MN 55164-0526
URL: http://www.westgroup.com
Desc: Contains the complete text of U.S. federal court decisions, statutes and regulations, specialized files, and texts and periodicals dealing with intellectual property law, including the rights of artist, authors, composers, and designers of creative works, and the significance of copyright, patent, or trademark protection. *Available:* West Group, WESTLAW. *Type:* Database.

WESTLAW® International Law
West Group
620 Opperman Dr.   Ph: (651)687-7000
St. Paul, MN 55164-0526
URL: http://www.westgroup.com
Desc: Contains the complete text of U.S. federal court decisions, statutes and regulations, administrative law publications, specialized files, and texts and periodicals dealing with international law. *Available:* West Group, WESTLAW. *Type:* Database.

WESTLAW® Jurisprudence & Constitutional Theory Texts and Periodicals Database
West Group
620 Opperman Dr.   Ph: (651)687-7000
St. Paul, MN 55164-0526
URL: http://www.westgroup.com
Desc: Contains documents from law reviews, texts, CLE course materials, bar journals, and legal practice-oriented periodicals. *Available:* West Group, WESTLAW. *Type:* Database.

WESTLAW® Legal Ethics & Professional Responsibility Databases
West Group
620 Opperman Dr.   Ph: (651)687-7000
St. Paul, MN 55164-0526
URL: http://www.westgroup.com
Contact: WEST Reference Attorneys. Toll-Free No.: (800) REF-ATTY.
Desc: Contains the complete text of U.S. federal and state court decisions, statutes and regulations, state court decisions, law reviews, bar association journals, and law-related texts that relate to the regulation of the practice of law and bar associations and their members. *Available:* West Group, WESTLAW. *Type:* Database.

WESTLAW® Litigation

West Group
620 Opperman Dr.   Ph: (651)687-7000
St. Paul, MN 55164-0526
URL: http://www.westgroup.com

Desc: Contains the complete text of law reviews, bar association journals, and law-related texts dealing with U.S. federal litigation law. *Available:* West Group, WESTLAW. *Type:* Database.

WESTLAW® Maritime Law

West Group
620 Opperman Dr.   Ph: (651)687-7000
St. Paul, MN 55164-0526
URL: http://www.westgroup.com

Desc: Contains the complete text of U.S. federal court decisions, statutes and regulations, admistrative law publications, and texts and periodicals that relate to the regulation of maritime commerce, navigation, and navigable waters. *Available:* West Group, WESTLAW. *Type:* Database.

WESTLAW® Professional Malpractice Library

West Group
620 Opperman Dr.   Ph: (651)687-7000
St. Paul, MN 55164-0526
URL: http://www.westgroup.com

Desc: Contains the complete text of U.S. state court decisions, specialized files, and texts and periodicals dealing with professional malpractice. *Available:* West Group, WESTLAW. *Type:* Database.

WESTLAW® State Ethics Opinions Databases

West Group
620 Opperman Dr.   Ph: (651)687-7000
St. Paul, MN 55164-0526
URL: http://www.westgroup.com

Desc: Contains the complete text of opinions issued by the state bar associations or their committees on ethics, concerning attorney professional ethics and conduct. Currently covers ten states: California from 1977, Florida from 1977, Michigan from 1988, Minnesota from 1972, New Jersey from 1968, New York from 1977, Ohio from 1977, Oregon from July 1991, Pennsylvania from 1987, and Texas from 1977. *Available:* West Group, WESTLAW. *Type:* Database.

WESTLAW® Texts and Periodicals

West Group
620 Opperman Dr.   Ph: (651)687-7000
St. Paul, MN 55164-0526
URL: http://www.westgroup.com

Desc: Contains the complete text of selected articles from more than 450 law review publications, bar association journals, and other law-related publications relating to federal law and other major practice topics. Covers administrative law, antitrust and trade regulation, bankruptcy, business organizations, civil rights, communications, commercial law and contracts corporations, criminal justice, education, energy, environmental law, estate planning and probate law, family law, financial services, First Amendment, government benefits, government contracts, health services, immigration, insurance, intellectual property, international law, jurisprudence and constitutional theory, labor and employment, legal services, litigation, maritime law, military law, pension and retirement benefits, products liability, professional malpractice, real property, securities and blue sky law, taxation, tort law, transportation, and workers' compensation. *Available:* West Group, WESTLAW. *Type:* Database.

WESTLAW® Topical Highlights Databases

West Group
620 Opperman Dr.   Ph: (651)687-7000
St. Paul, MN 55164-0526
URL: http://www.westgroup.com
Contact: WEST Reference Attorneys. Toll Free No. (800) REF-ATTY.

Desc: Contains more than 8500 summaries of recent state and federal court decisions and legal activities in these areas:. Covers antitrust, bankruptcy, corporations and securities, criminal justice, education, employment law, energy and utilities, environmental law, family law, federal practice and procedure, financial services, insurance, intellectual property, maritime, medical malpractice, multistate taxation, products liability, and real property. *Available:* West Group, WESTLAW. *Type:* Database.

WESTLAW® Tort Law Library

West Group
620 Opperman Dr.   Ph: (651)687-7000
St. Paul, MN 55164-0526
URL: http://www.westgroup.com

Desc: Contains the complete text of texts and law review and bar association journal articles dealing with tort law. Includes Restatement of the Law of Torts First and Second. *Available:* West Group, WESTLAW. *Type:* Database.

WESTLAW® Workers' Compensation Library

West Group
620 Opperman Dr.   Ph: (651)687-7000
St. Paul, MN 55164-0526
URL: http://www.westgroup.com

Desc: Contains the complete text of U.S. federal administrative law decisions issued by the Benefits Review Board; U.S. state court decisions for all 50 states and the District of Columbia; individual state administrative workers' compensation board decisions for 17 states; and relevant law reviews, texts, and bar journals relating to workers' compensation issues, including programs that compensate employees and their families for employment-related injuries, the Federal Employees' Compensation Act, the Longshore and Harbor Workers' Compensation Act, and similar state acts. *Available:* West Group, WESTLAW. *Type:* Database.

West's Legal Directory

West Group
620 Opperman Dr.   Ph: (651)687-7000
St. Paul, MN 55164-0526
URL: http://www.westgroup.com

Desc: Contains over 675,000 profiles of attorneys and law firms located throughout the United States, Puerto Rico, the Virgin Islands, Canada, and England. For each, provides name, company or government agency, address and telephone number, current position, court and bar admissions and years, areas of practice, date of birth, educational background, fraternities/sororities, current/past affiliations or offices held, qualifications, specialty areas, published works, professional affiliations, and representative cases and clients. *Available:* West Group, WESTLAW. *Type:* Database.

Who's Who in American Law

Marquis Who's Who
Reed Elsevier
121 Chanlon Rd.
New Providence, NJ 07974   Ph: (908)464-6800
                            Free: 800-521-8110
                            Fax: (908)771-8645
E-mail: info@marquiswhoswho.com
Contact: Lisa Weissbard, Managing Editor.

Desc: Over 27,800 lawyers, judges, law school deans and professors, and other legal professionals. *Type:* Directory.

Law Enforcement

Fraternal Order of Police, Grand Lodge

1410 Donelson Pike, No. A17   Ph: (615)399-0900
Nashville, TN 37217-2933   Fax: (615)399-0400
E-mail: glsop@grandlodgefop.org
URL: http://www.grandlodgefop.org
Contact: Jerry W. Atnip, National Sec.

Desc: Fraternal order of full-time law enforcement officers. Seeks social and economic benefits for members and professional advancement of policemen. Conducts seminars, research, educational, and charitable programs; compiles statistics. *Type:* Association.

International Association of Arson Investigators—Constitution and Bylaws, Membership Directory

International Association of Arson Investigators, Inc.
300 S. Broadway, No. 100   Ph: (314)621-1966
St. Louis, MO 63102-2808   Fax: (314)621-5125
E-mail: iaaihq@aol.com
Contact: Benny King, Editor.

Desc: 8,000 member arson investigators. *Type:* Directory.

International Union of Police Associations

1421 Prince St., Ste. 330   Ph: (703)549-7473
Alexandria, VA 22314   Free: 800-247-4872
                             Fax: (703)683-9048
E-mail: sam@iupa.org
URL: http://www.iupa.org/iupa.html
Contact: Sam A. Cabral, Pres.

Desc: AFL-CIO. Police officers organized to secure just compensation for their service and equitable settlement of their grievances, promote the establishment of just and reasonable work conditions, and encourage the formation of local unions, state and provincial associations, and joint councils. Seeks professionalization of the police officer through collective bargaining seminars and research. *Type:* Association.

Law Enforcement Alliance of America

7700 Leesburg Pike, Ste. 421   Ph: (703)847-2677
Falls Church, VA 22043   Fax: (703)556-6485
Contact: James J. Fotis, Exec.Dir.

Desc: Works to improve the criminal justice system and keep citizens safe from violent crime. *Type:* Association.

National Crime Prevention Council

1700 K St. NW, 2nd Fl.   Ph: (202)466-6272
Washington, DC 20006-3817   Fax: (202)296-1356
URL: http://www.weprevent.org
Contact: John A. Calhoun, Exec.Dir.

Desc: Seeks to educate the public to enable citizens to prevent crime and build safer, more caring communities. Sponsors public service advertising, featuring McGruff the Crime Dog and the slogan "Take a Bite Out of Crime," in cooperation with the Advertising Council and the U.S. Department of Justice. *Type:* Association.

National Directory of Law Enforcement Administrators and Correctional Institutions

National Public Safety Information Bureau
3273 Church St., Ste. 201   Ph: (715)345-2772
PO Box 365   Free: 800-647-7579
Stevens Point, WI 54481   Fax: (715)345-7288
E-mail: info@safetysource.com
URL: http://www.npsib.com.
Contact: Laura Gross, Editor; Steve Cywinski, Publisher.

Desc: Police departments, sheriffs, coroners, criminal prosecutors, child support agencies, state law enforcement and criminal investigation agencies; federal criminal investigation and related agencies; state and federal correctional institutions; campus law enforcement departments; airport and harbor police, Bureau of Indian Affairs officials, and Canadian law enforcement personnel. *Type:* Directory.

National Juvenile Detention Directory

American Correctional Association
4380 Forbes Blvd. Ph: (301)918-1800
Lanham, MD 20706-4322 Free: 800-222-5646
  Fax: (301)918-1900
E-mail: admin@aca.org
URL: http://www.corrections.com/aca
Contact: Alice Fins, Editor, afins@aca.org.
Desc: Juvenile detention centers in the United States at the state, county and local level. *Type:* Directory.

Police—Buyer's Guide Issue

Bobit Publishing
21061 S Western Ave. Ph: (310)533-2400
Torrance, CA 90501 Fax: (310)533-2503
E-mail: sbf@bobit.com
Contact: Randall C. Resch, Editor.
Desc: List of suppliers of police products and services. *Type:* Directory.

Police and Firemen's Insurance Association

101 E. 116th St. Ph: (317)581-1913
Carmel, IN 46032 Free: 800-221-7342
  Fax: (317)571-5946
Contact: Jerry Davis, Pres.
Desc: Fraternal benefit insurance society. *Type:* Association.

WETIP

PO Box 1296 Ph: (909)987-5005
Rancho Cucamonga, CA 91730- Fax: (909)987-2477
1296
Contact: Bill Brownell, CEO.
Desc: Business, industry, service clubs, private citizens, foundations, insurance companies, chambers of commerce, and veterans' and fraternal groups. Serves as a citizens' selfhelp program designed to eliminate drug trafficking and major crimes. Organization has aided in murder arrests and successful apprehensions of criminals who have committed robbery, burglary, fraud, rape, drug trafficking, auto theft, or assault. Anonymous tips are conveyed to law officers and arrests are made only after verified law enforcement investigations. Rewards of up to $1000 are given upon verified factual reports from law enforcement agencies that WeTIP information was received prior to arrest and that the information was helpful in the arrest and conviction. Conducts Witness Anonymous Program, which includes corporations, insurance companies, and institutions. Program is dedicated to reducing crime and fear of crime in business communities by providing crime information directly to the concerned corporation, as well as the appropriate law enforcement agency. Maintains speakers' bureau; compiles statistics; conducts educational programs. *Type:* Association.

Leadership

INROADS

10 S. Broadway, Ste. 700 Ph: (314)241-7488
St. Louis, MO 63102 Fax: (314)241-9325
URL: http://www.inroadsinc.org
Contact: Charles I. Story, Pres. & CEO.
Desc: Participants are U.S. corporations that sponsor internships for minority students and pledge to develop career opportunities for the interns. Prepares black, Hispanic, and Native American high school and college students for leadership positions within major American business corporations and in their own communities. *Type:* Association.

Legal Education

ALI-ABA Committee on Continuing Professional Education

4025 Chestnut St. Ph: (215)243-1600
Philadelphia, PA 19104-3099 Free: 800-CLE-
  NEWS
  Fax: (215)243-1664
URL: http://www.ali-aba.org
Contact: Richard E. Carter, Exec.Dir.
Desc: Representatives from American Bar Association and American Law Institute. Assists in the development, organization, and implementation of educational programs for lawyers who have been admitted to practice. Programs run from 1-day institutes to advanced and specialized training courses of 1 or more weeks. *Type:* Association.

ALI/ABA Continuing Legal Education

American Law Institute - American Bar Association (ALI-ABA)
4025 Chestnut St. Ph: (215)243-1600
Philadelphia, PA 19104
E-mail: publications@ali-aba.org
URL: http://www.ali-aba.org
Desc: Contains the complete text of selected articles from the American Law Institute -- American Bar Association Course of Study Materials, Video Law Materials, and Resource Materials providing continuing legal education materials on a full range of topics. *Available:* West Group, WESTLAW; LEXIS-NEXIS. *Type:* Database.

Association of American Law Schools

1201 Connecticut Ave. NW, Ph: (202)296-8851
Ste. 800 Fax: (202)296-8869
Washington, DC 20036-2605
E-mail: aals@aals.org
URL: http://www.aals.org
Contact: Carl C. Monk, Exec.Dir.
Desc: Law schools association. Seeks to improve the legal profession through legal education. Interacts for law professors with state and federal government, other legal education and professional associations, and other national higher education and learned society organizations. *Type:* Association.

Council on Legal Education Opportunity

740 1st St. NW 9th Fl. Ph: (202)662-8630
Washington, DC 20005 Fax: (202)662-1032
Contact: Cassandra Sneed, Exec.Dir.
Desc: Federally funded program that assists economically and educationally disadvantaged students gain entrance to American Bar Association approved law schools. Sponsors six-week summer institutes for selected college graduates and provides a 5000 annual living stipend to those certified summer institute graduates who continue in law school. *Type:* Association.

Law School Admission Council

PO Box 2000-M Ph: (215)968-1001
Newtown, PA 18940 Fax: (215)968-1169
E-mail: lsacinfo@lsac.org
URL: http://www.lsac.org
Contact: Philip D. Shelton, Exec.Dir.
Desc: Law schools in the U.S. and Canada. Develops and administers the Law School Admission Test (LSAT). *Type:* Association.

Law Student Division

American Bar Association Ph: (312)988-5623
750 N. Lake Shore Dr. Fax: (312)988-6033
Chicago, IL 60611
E-mail: abalsd@abanet.org
URL: http://www.abanet.org/ls
Contact: Sherry Gouwens, Dir.

Desc: National law student association. Seeks to: further academic excellence through participation by law students in the efforts of the organized bar; achieve awareness and promote the involvement of law students in the solutions of problems confronted in today's changing society; promote professional responsibility. Sponsors nationwide Client Counseling Competition, National Appellate Advocacy Competition, and Negotiation Competition. *Type:* Association.

Practising Law Institute

810 7th Ave. Ph: (212)824-5700
New York, NY 10019 Free: 800-260-4754
  Fax: (212)581-4670
Contact: Victor J. Rubino, Exec.Dir.
Desc: Provides through publications, courses, videotapes, forums, and seminars, training for lawyers throughout the country in new developments in the law and new legal techniques. Presents over 250 seminars annually. *Type:* Association.

Practising Law Institute Course Handbooks Database

Practising Law Institute (PLI)
810 Seventh Ave. Ph: (212)824-5700
New York, NY 10019
URL: http://www.pli.edu
Desc: Contains the complete text of selected articles published in Practising Law Institute (PLI) course handbooks. Covers 9 subject areas: commercial law and practice; corporate law and practice; criminal law and urban problems; estate planning and administration; litigation and administrative practice; New York law; patents, copyrights, trademarks, and literary property; real estate law and practice; and tax law and practice. *Available:* West Group, WESTLAW. *Type:* Database.

Libraries

AACL Newsletter

Alberta Association of College Librarians (AACL)
c/o Canadian University College Ph: (403)782-3381
50 Ramona Ave. Fax: (403)782-3977
College Heights, AB, Canada
T4L 2B7
E-mail: library@cauc.ab.ca
Contact: Joyce Van Scheik, Editor, juansche@cauc.ab.ca.
Desc: Provides a forum for communication among member libraries. *Type:* Newsletter.

ACA Bulletin

Association of Canadian Archivists (ACA)
Box 2596, Sta. D Ph: (613)443-0251
Ottawa, ON, Canada K1P 5W6 Free: 888-443-2243
  Fax: (613)443-0261
E-mail: ltaraif@magmacom.com; Hardif@magmacom.com.
Contact: Elizabeth Diamond, Editor.
Desc: Functions as a forum for all persons who are engaged in the discipline and practice of archival science. Publishes brief articles on archives and activities of archivists and the Association. *Type:* Newsletter.

Access

Library of Michigan
717 W. Allegan St. Ph: (517)373-5578
PO Box 30007 Free: 800-992-9012
Lansing, MI 48909 Fax: (517)373-5700
URL: http://www.libofmich.lib.mi.us.
Contact: Carey L. Draeger, Editor, cdraeger@libofmich.;lib.mi.us.
Desc: Covers current activities of library staff. Deals primarily with projects and events of Michigan Library Law, Library Development and Special Services, and Information and Government Services of the library. *Type:* Newsletter.

Access AMICUS Search Service

National Library of Canada
Client Information Centre
395 Wellington St. Ph: (613)997-7227
Ottawa, ON, Canada K1A 0N4
E-mail: cic@nlc-bnc.ca
URL: http://www.nlc-bnc.ca
Contact: Client Information Centre, (819)997-7227, fax: (819)994-6835, cic@nls-bnc.ca.
Desc: Contains more than 15 million full bibliographic descriptions of monographs, serials, newspapers, theses, federal and provincial documents, microforms, music, sound recordings, and other publications or media available in more than 700 Canadian libraries. The system provides access for Canadian libraries and researchers. *Available:* National Library of Canada, Information Technology Services. *Type:* Database.

ACCESS Newsletter

Ohio Library Council
35 E. Gay St. Ph: (614)221-9057
Columbus, OH 43220-3879 Fax: (614)221-6234
Contact: Wayne Piper, Editor, wpiper@olc.org.
Desc: Carries Association news and announcements of awards, gifts, and grants. Includes membership list updates, a calendar of events, summaries of talks or lectures of interest, and notices of available materials, such as bookmarks or posters. *Type:* Newsletter.

Action for Libraries

Bibliographical Center for Research, Rocky Mountain Region, Inc.
14394 E. Evans Ave. Ph: (303)751-6277
Aurora, CO 80014-1478 Free: 800-392-1552
  Fax: (303)751-9787
E-mail: admin@bcr.org
URL: http://www.bcr.org.
Contact: Sharon Hoffhines, Editor, shoffhin@ber.org.
Desc: Monitors news of information industry developments that affect library cataloging and research services. Includes such topics as micro services and systems, online bibliographies, new information access systems, information security, and disaster planning. *Type:* Newsletter.

Ad Libs

Metropolitan Library System
131 Dean A. McGee Ph: (405)231-8618
Oklahoma City, OK 73102- Fax: (405)236-5219
6499
Contact: Julia Fresonke, Editor, fresonke_julia@mail.mls.lib.ok.us.
Desc: Covers Oklahoma County library activities, programs, grants awarded, and other items of interest to the library system. *Type:* Newsletter.

Administrative Notes

U.S. Government Printing Office (GPO)
Superintendent of Documents Ph: (202)512-1119
Washington, DC 20401 Fax: (202)512-1432
URL: http://www.access.gpo.gov/su_docs/dpos/adnotes.html.
Contact: Marian W. MacGilvray, Editor.
Desc: Publishes information on seminars, library program services, and search capabilities for products. *Type:* Newsletter.

Administrative Notes Technical Supplement

U.S. Government Printing Office (GPO)
Superintendent of Documents Ph: (202)512-1119
Washington, DC 20401 Fax: (202)512-1432
URL: http://www.access.gpo.gov/su_docs/dpos/techsup.html.
Contact: Laurie Beyer Hall, Editor.

Desc: Includes columns titled, Classification/Cataloging Update, Update to the List of Classes, etc. *Type:* Newsletter.

Advanced Technology/Libraries

Macmillan Publishing Co.
Macmillan Library Reference Group
PO Box 159 Free: 800-257-5157
Thorndike, ME 04986
Contact: Judy Duke, Editor, fax: (914)941-8773; Fred Olsen, Publisher.
Desc: Covers library automation, resource sharing, and the economics of new technological developments affecting libraries. Discusses grants, contracts, and government funding of libraries. *Type:* Newsletter.

ALA/SRRT Newsletter

ALA Social Responsibilities Round Table
c/o Eubanks
Brooklyn College Library
Brooklyn, NY 11210
Desc: Provides information for libraries regarding book purchasing. Focuses on small press and movement press books. *Type:* Newsletter.

ALA Washington News

American Library Association (ALA)
1301 Pennsylvania Ave., NW Ph: (202)628-8410
Washington, DC 20004 Fax: (202)628-8419
Contact: Lynne E. Bradley, Editor.
Desc: Describes federal and regulatory actions originated in Washington that affect the ALA and library programs. *Type:* Newsletter.

ALAWON

American Library Association (ALA)
1301 Pennsylvania Ave., NW Ph: (202)628-8410
Washington, DC 20004 Fax: (202)628-8419
Contact: Lynn E. Bradley, Editor.
Desc: Concerned with legislation impacting the library profession. *Type:* Newsletter.

ALCTS Network News

Association for Library Collections and Technical Services (ALCTS)
50 E. Huron St. Ph: (312)944-6780
Chicago, IL 60611 Free: 800-545-2433
  Fax: (312)280-5033
E-mail: alcts@ala.org
Contact: Karen Muller, Editor.
Desc: Contains advance copy of articles and features that will appear later in the print publication ALCTS Newsletter. Features current legislative news, news from the library technical services and publishing world, and ALCTS candidates for office and election results, as well as conference schedules (including meeting room locations) and reports shortly after the conference of major actions and events. *Type:* Newsletter.

ALCTS Newsletter

Association for Library Collections and Technical Services (ALCTS)
50 E. Huron St. Ph: (312)944-6780
Chicago, IL 60611 Free: 800-545-2433
  Fax: (312)280-5033
E-mail: alcts@ala.org
URL: http://www.ala.org/alcts/alcts_news.
Contact: Dale Swensen, Editor, dale_swensen@byu.edu.
Desc: Concerned with collection development, cataloging, acquisitions, microform management, serials management, and preservation of materials in libraries. Contains news of activities of the Division and news items contributed by press releases from agencies and publishers. *Type:* Newsletter.

ALSC Newsletter

Association for Library Service to Children
American Library Association
50 E. Huron St. Ph: (312)280-2163
Chicago, IL 60611 Free: 800-545-2433
  Fax: (312)944-7671
E-mail: alsc@ala.org; rsinger@ala.org
URL: http://www.ala.org.
Contact: Anitra Steele, Editor.
Desc: Publishes news of the Association, its activities, meetings, and conferences. Provides information on awards, grants, and scholarships. *Type:* Newsletter.

American Association of Law Libraries

53 W Jackson Blvd., Ste. 940 Ph: (312)939-4764
Chicago, IL 60604 Fax: (312)431-1097
E-mail: aallhq@aall.org
URL: http://www.aallnet.org
Contact: Roger Parent, Exec.Dir.
Desc: Librarians who serve the legal profession in the courts, bar associations, law societies, law schools, private law firms, federal, state, and county governments, and business; associate members are legal publishers and other interested persons. Seeks to advance the profession of law librarianship. *Type:* Association.

American Library Association

50 E. Huron St. Ph: (312)944-6780
Chicago, IL 60611 Free: 800-545-2433
  Fax: (312)280-3255
URL: http://www.ala.org
Contact: William Gordon, Exec.Dir.
Desc: Librarians, libraries, trustees, friends of libraries, and others interested in the responsibilities of libraries in the educational, social, and cultural needs of society. Promotes and improves library service and librarianship. *Type:* Association.

American Library Directory

R.R. Bowker
121 Chanlon Rd. Ph: (908)464-6800
New Providence, NJ 07974
URL: http://www.bowker.com
Contact: Yvette Berthel, Manager-Online Services, (908)665-2854.
Desc: Contains information on more than 37,000 U.S., Canadian and Mexican public, academic, government, and special libraries, library consortia and networks, and library schools. For each organization, provides name, library type, address, Standard Address Number (SAN), telephone number, personnel (names, titles, and title codes), staff size and status, total number of staff, number of professional staff, number of clerical staff, year library founded, year building constructed, size of population served, annual circulation, subject interests and codes, fiscal year, annual budget, expenditure figures (books, periodicals, preservation, materials), salaries, projected fiscal year, projected budget and expenditures, library holdings (book titles, book volumes, periodical subscriptions, periodical volumes bound, special collections), library automation, acquisitions systems used, cataloging systems used, circulation systems used, interlibrary loan systems used, online reference searches conducted, special collections maintained, special services offered, library publications titles and codes, library system membership, and library network membership. *Available:* The Dialog Corporation, DIALOG; LEXIS-NEXIS, NEXIS. *Type:* Database.

American Library Directory

R. R. Bowker

A Unit of Cahners Business Information

121 Chanlon Rd.   Ph: (908)464-6800
New Providence, NJ 07974   Free: 888-269-5372
                          Fax: (908)771-7704

E-mail: info@bowker.com

Contact: Beverley McDonough, Managing Editor.

Desc: Over 36,000 U.S. and Canadian academic, public, county, provincial, and regional libraries; library systems; medical, law, and other special libraries; and libraries for the blind and physically handicapped. Separate section lists over 350 library networks and consortia and 220 accredited and unaccredited library school programs. *Type:* Directory.

American Theological Library Association

820 Church St., Ste. 400   Ph: (847)869-7788
Evanston, IL 60201-5603   Free: 800-665-2852
                          Fax: (708)869-8513

Contact: Dennis Norlin, Exec.Dir./CEO.

Desc: Professional theological librarians; persons interested in theological librarianship; institutions. "To study problems of theological libraries, increase professional competence of the membership and improve the quality of library service to theological education." Seeks to: foster professional growth of members; provide continuing education programs; publish, preserve, and disseminate theological literature, research tools, and aids; develop and implement standards for theological libraries; promote theological research; facilitate communication among members. Provides consultation service to member institutions. *Type:* Association.

American Theological Library Association Newsletter

American Theological Library Association

820 Church St., Ste. 400   Ph: (847)869-7788
Evanston, IL 60201-5613   Free: 888-665-ATLA
                          Fax: (847)869-8513

E-mail: atla@atla.com
URL: http://www.atla.com

Contact: Margret Tacke Collins, Editor.

Desc: Presents news of interest to library professionals at theological schools. Recurring features include notices of publications available and job listings. *Type:* Newsletter.

Among Michigan Friends

Friends of Michigan Libraries, Livonia Civic Center Library

32777 Five Mile Rd.   Ph: (313)421-8306
Livonia, MI 48154

Contact: Annie Brewer, Editor.

Desc: Profiles the interests, issues, news, and activities of the Friends which aim to support Michigan libraries. Recurring features include a calendar of events. *Type:* Newsletter.

ANLA Newsletter

Association Newfoundland & Labrador Archives (ANLA)

Colonial Bldg., Military Rd. Ph: (709)726-2869
St. Johns, NF, Canada A1C   Fax: (709)729-0578
  2C9

Contact: Joe Le Clair, Editor.

Desc: Concerned with the activities of archives and archivists in the province and generally. Recurring features include calendar of events, reports of meetings, book reviews, notices of publications available, and column titled Preservation Pickles. *Type:* Newsletter.

APLA Bulletin

Atlantic Provinces Library Association (APLA)

Dalhousie University   Ph: (902)424-5264
School of Library and   Fax: (902)542-2128
  Information Studies
Halifax, NS, Canada B3H 4H8

Contact: John Neilson, Editor, (506)453-4595, fax: (506)453-4752, neilson@unb.ca; Linda Hansen, Asst. Editor, (506)648-5701, fax: (506)648-5788, lhansen@unbsj.ca.

Desc: Disseminates information to promote library service in the provinces of New Brunswick, Newfoundland, Nova Scotia, and Prince Edward Island. Recurring features include research articles, feature stories on regional libraries and library issues, job listings, interviews, a calendar of events, reports of conferences and meetings, brief news stories, letters to the editor, and columns titled From the Editor's Desk, From the President's Desk, User Education Mailbox and News from the Regions. *Type:* Newsletter.

Archival Outlook

Society of American Archivists

527 S. Wells St., 5th Fl.   Ph: (312)922-0140
Chicago, IL 60617-3922   Fax: (312)347-1452
E-mail: info@archivists.org

Contact: Teresa Brinati, Editor.

Desc: Publishes news of relevance to the professional archival community. Recurring features include a calendar of events, quick tips feature, news from constituent groups, news of educational opportunities, and job listings. *Type:* Newsletter.

Archives Society of Alberta Newsletter

Archives Society of Alberta (ASA)

PO Box 21080   Ph: (403)228-0827
Dominion Postal Outlet   Fax: (403)244-5173
Calgary, AB, Canada T2P 4H5
URL: http://www.glenbow.org/asa/newslet/welcome.htm.

Contact: Jim Bowman, Editor.

Desc: Designed to serve the interests of the professional archival community in Alberta by publishing news of the profession and the Society's activities. Provides a forum for member discussion and debate. *Type:* Newsletter.

ARLIS/NA Update

Art Libraries Society of North America

1550 S. Coast Hwy.   Ph: (949)376-3456
Laguna Beach, CA 92651   Fax: (949)497-9007

Desc: Publishes news of the Society, "the only professional organization in North America devoted exclusively to the concerns of art information specialists." Informs member art librarians and visual resources curators of upcoming meetings, elections, and conferences; grants and fellowships available; and projects sponsored by the Society. Also carries general news of interest to the art library world. *Type:* Newsletter.

Asian/Pacific American Librarians Association Newsletter

Asian/Pacific American Librarians Association

c/o Sandra Yamate   Ph: (773)478-4455
4509 N. Francisco   Fax: (773)478-0786
Chicago, IL 60625

Contact: Rama Vishvanasham, Editor; Fengua Wang-Schaefer, Editor, fwang@brick.purchase.edu.

Desc: Designed for librarians and information specialists with an interest in or focus on Asian and Pacific American librarianship. Recurring features include Association news, notices of conferences, programs, news of members, book reviews, job openings, exhibits, and current publications. *Type:* Newsletter.

Association of Canadian Map Libraries and Archives—Bulletin

Association of Canadian Map Libraries and Archives

National Archives of Canada

395 Wellington St.   Ph: (613)996-7619
Ottawa, ON, Canada K1A 0N3 Fax: (613)995-6226

Contact: Donald Lemon, Editor.

Desc: Contains articles on map librarianship, map archives, and new maps. Recurring features include book reviews. *Type:* Newsletter.

Association of College and Research Libraries

50 E. Huron St.   Ph: (312)280-3248
Chicago, IL 60611-2795   Free: 800-545-2433
                          Fax: (312)280-2520

E-mail: acrl@ala.org
URL: http://www.ala.org/acrl.html

Contact: Althea Jenkins, Exec.Dir.

Desc: Academic and research librarians. Seeks to improve the quality of service in academic libraries; promotes the professional and career development of academic and research librarians; represents the interests and supports the programs of academic and research libraries. *Type:* Association.

Association of Research Libraries

21 Dupont Cir. NW, Ste. 800 Ph: (202)296-2296
Washington, DC 20036   Fax: (202)872-0884
E-mail: ARLHQ@arl.org
URL: http://www.arl.org

Contact: Duane Webster, Exec.Dir.

Desc: University, public, private, and governmental research libraries. Seeks to: shape and influence forces affecting large research libraries so that the libraries may effectively serve the needs of students, faculty, and the research community; strengthen and extend the capacity of member libraries, in order to provide the recorded information needed, both now and in the future, by the research community. Provides library training and consulting in management and program development; collects membership data including salaries, expenditures, and materials. *Type:* Association.

Association of Research Libraries - Statistics and Measurement Program

Association of Research Libraries

21 Dupont Cir., Ste. 800   Ph: (202)296-2296
Washington, DC 20036   Fax: (202)872-0884
E-mail: darlhq@arl.org
URL: http://www.arl.org/stats/

Contact: Julia Blixrud, Senior Program Officer, jblix@arl.org.

Desc: The Association of Research Library (ARL) Statistics and Measurement Program site describes and measures the performance of research libraries and their contributions to teaching, research, scholarship and community service. It includes information on collections' size and growth, staff expenditures, materials and operating expenditures, interlibrary loan activities, an annual salary survey, ARL program and publications information and more. *Type:* Database.

Association of Specialized & Cooperative Library Agencies—Interface

Association of Specialized and Cooperative Library Agencies M/ASCLA

50 E. Huron St.   Ph: (312)280-4399
Chicago, IL 60611   Free: 800-545-2433
                          Fax: (312)944-8085

Contact: Frederick Duda, Editor, (941)921-5426, fax: (941)751-7098, fredduda@worldnet.att.net.

Desc: Covers state library agencies, multitype library cooperation, and library service to special groups such as the deaf, handicapped, blind, elderly, incarcerated, and others. Includes news of division activities and publication reviews. *Type:* Newsletter.

The Bakken

The Bakken
3537 Zenith Ave., S.   Ph: (612)927-6508
Minneapolis, MN 55416
URL: http://www.bakkenmuseum.org.

Contact: David Rhees, Editor, rhees@bakkenmuseum.org.

Desc: Publishes news of exhibits and acquisitions of the Bakken, which is committed to "documenting the history of electricity as a cultural force and as a tool and object for the study of life in health and disease." Features articles concerning the history of electricity. Recurring features include news of scholars in the field and a calendar of events. *Type:* Newsletter.

Base Line

Map and Geography Round Table (MAGERT)
American Library Association (ALA)
c/o James A. Coombs   Ph: (417)280-3205
Southwest Missouri State Univ.   Free: 800-545-2433
Maps Library   Fax: (417)280-3257
901 S. National, No. 175
Springfield, MO 65804-0095

Contact: Mark Thomas, Editor, (919)660-5853, fax: (919)684-2855, markt@duke.edu.

Desc: Provides current information on cartographic materials, publications of interest to map and geography librarians, related government activities, and map librarianship. Recurring features include conference and meeting information, news of research, job listings, and columns by the Division chair and the editor. *Type:* Newsletter.

BCLA Reporter

British Columbia Library Association (BCLA)
150-900 Howe St.   Ph: (604)683-5354
Vancouver, BC, Canada V6Z   Fax: (604)609-0707
  2M4
E-mail: bclainternalerchange.ubc.ca

Contact: Ted Benson, Editor.

Desc: Profiles library organizations in British Columbia. Contains news clippings. *Type:* Newsletter.

Beta Phi Mu

Florida State University   Ph: (850)644-3907
School of Information Studies   Fax: (850)644-6253
Tallahassee, FL 32306-2100
E-mail: beta_phi_mu@lis.fsu.edu
URL: http://www.cas.usf.edu/lis/bpm

Contact: Dr. F. William Summers, Contact.

Desc: Professional honor society - men and women, library science. *Type:* Association.

BiblioData's Price Watcher

BiblioData
PO Box 61   Ph: (781)444-1154
Needham Heights, MA 02494   Fax: (781)449-4584
E-mail: ina@bibliodata.com; ina@bibliodata.com.
URL: http://www.bibliodata.com.

Contact: Ruth Orenstein, Publisher; Linda Cooper, Editor; Susan Weiler, Contrib. Editor.

Desc: Offers information for researchers and librarians looking for the best prices for online data, including tips, cost-saving strategies, new pricing announcements, source comparisons, analysis and reviews, and case studies. *Type:* Newsletter.

Bibliographic Index

H.W. Wilson Company
950 University Ave.   Ph: (718)588-8400
Bronx, NY 10452
E-mail: custserv@hwwilson.com
URL: http://www.hwwilson.com
Contact: Technical Support Department., techmail@info. hwwilson.com.

Desc: Contains more than 133,000 citations to bibliographies with 50 or more citations that are published separately as books and pamphlets or that appear in other publications. Covers scholarly and general-interest topics. *Available:* Ovid Technologies, Inc.; OCLC Online Computer Library Center, Inc., OCLC EPIC; OCLC Online Computer Library Center, Inc., OCLC FirstSearch Catalog. *Type:* Database.

Big Sky Libraries

Montana State Library
1515 E. 6th Ave.   Ph: (406)444-3115
Helena, MT 59620   Fax: (406)444-5612
E-mail: msl@msl.state.mt.us
URL: http://www.msl.state.mt.us/admin/update.html.
Contact: Tristen Shinnick, Editor, tshinnic@msl.state.mt. us.

Desc: Covers state and library-related news. *Type:* Newsletter.

Black Caucus Newsletter

BCALA Newsletter
1000 Holt Ave., No. 2654   Ph: (407)646-2676
Rollins College   Fax: (407)646-1515
Winter Park, FL 32789
E-mail: bcnews@rollins.edu.
Contact: Dr. George C. Grant, Editor.

Desc: Reports news of interest about black librarians in library work and library education. Recurring features include notices of professional opportunities and activities of individuals within the Caucus and the American Library Association. *Type:* Newsletter.

Bluford Notes and Quotes

F.D. Bluford Library
North Carolina A&T State   Ph: (336)334-7867
  University   Fax: (336)334-7783
1601 E. Market St.
Greensboro, NC 27411
URL: http://www.library.ncat.edu.
Contact: Ednita Bullock, Editor.

Desc: Provides information on services, information sources, and automation trends at the University library. Recurring features include a calendar of events and reports of meetings. *Type:* Newsletter.

BNA's Review of What's New

Bureau of National Affairs, Inc. (BNA)
1231 25th St. NW   Ph: (202)452-4323
Washington, DC 20037   Free: 800-372-1033
                        Fax: (202)452-7773
E-mail: bnaplus@bna.com
URL: http://www.bna.com.
Contact: Norman Kerner, Managing Editor, nkerner@ bna.com.

Desc: Describes new books, looseleafs, CD-ROM products, reports, newsletters, videos, software, info-paks, and online products available from BNA. *Type:* Newsletter.

Book Marks

Ann Smith
c/o Mikkelsen Library   Ph: (605)336-4383
Augusta College   Fax: (605)336-5447
Sioux Falls, SD 57197
Contact: Ann Smith, Editor, fax: (605)336-5447, asmith@ inst.augie.edu.

Desc: Carries news by and for South Dakota public, school, academic, and special libraries. Discusses statewide library issues, reviews South Dakota books, and advises members of continuing education for small libraries. *Type:* Newsletter.

Bookends

Public Library of Youngstown and Mahoning County
305 Wick Ave.   Ph: (330)744-8636
Youngstown, OH 44503   Fax: (330)744-2258
E-mail: xxiii@yfn.ysu.edu
Contact: Janet S. Loew, Editor.

Desc: Newsletter for the public library of Youngstown and Mahoming County. Includes library news, activities, and programs. *Type:* Newsletter.

Bowker Annual: Library and Book Trade Almanac

R. R. Bowker
A Unit of Cahners Business Information
121 Chanlon Rd.   Ph: (908)464-6800
New Providence, NJ 07974   Free: 888-269-5372
                        Fax: (908)771-7704
E-mail: info@bowker.com
Contact: Dave Bogart, Editor.

Desc: Lists of accredited library schools; scholarships for education in library science; library organizations; library statistics; publishing and bookselling organizations. *Type:* Directory.

Buffalo & Erie County Public Library—Bulletin

Buffalo & Erie County Public Library
1 Lafayette Sq.   Ph: (716)858-7182
Buffalo, NY 14203   Fax: (716)858-6211
Contact: Michael C. Mahaney, Editor, mahaneym@ buffalolib.org.

Desc: Discusses new developments in library services, resources, facilities, and programs in Buffalo and Erie County. *Type:* Newsletter.

Business and Finance Division Bulletin

Business and Finance Division Special Libraries Association (SLA)
1700 18th St. NW   Ph: (202)234-4700
Washington, DC 20009-2508   Fax: (202)265-9317
Contact: Cynthia Lenox, Editor.

Desc: Provides information on business and finance libraries and librarianship. Covers subjects such as database searching, reference exchange, articles, bibliographies, and activities of the Division. *Type:* Newsletter.

Business Information from Your Public Library

Administrator's Digest Press
719 San Miguel Ln.   Ph: (415)573-5474
Foster City, CA 94404
Contact: Robert S. Alvarez, Editor.

Desc: "Designed to let business people know that their public library is eager and able to serve them." Lists new business books, news bits, and a how-to article. *Type:* Newsletter.

California Libraries

California Library Association
717 K St., Ste. 300   Ph: (916)447-8541
Sacramento, CA 95814-3477   Fax: (916)447-8394
E-mail: info@cla-net.org
Desc: Reports on news of the Association, whose purpose is "to promote the development of library service of the highest quality and maximum availability for all residents of California." Recurring features include a calendar of events, news of research, book reviews, news of members, letters to the editor, tours and workshops, and the column President's Corner. *Type:* Newsletter.

California State Library Foundation Newsletter
California State Library
Library Development Services Bureau
PO Box 942837 Ph: (916)653-5217
Sacramento, CA 95814 Fax: (916)653-8443
Contact: Catherine Lewis, Editor.

Desc: Publishes news of the State Library, along with services and programs having an impact on California libraries. Contains articles on workshops, grant programs, and technological developments. *Type:* Newsletter.

Canadian Association of Music Libraries Newsletter
Canadian Association of Music Libraries, Archives & Documentation Centres
Huntington College Library Ph: (705)673-4148
935 Ramsey Lake Rd. Fax: (705)673-6917
Sudbury, ON, Canada P3E 2C6
Contact: Desmond Maley, Librarian, dmaley@nickel.laurentian.ca.

Desc: Encourages and promotes the activities of Canadian music libraries, archives, and documentation centers. Recurring features include a calendar of events, news of research, reports of meetings, and book reviews. *Type:* Newsletter.

Canadiana
Canadian Centre for Occupational Health and Safety (CCOHS)
250 Main St. E. Ph: (905)570-8094
Hamilton, ON, Canada L8N 1H6
E-mail: custserv@ccohs.ca
URL: http://www.ccohs.ca/

Desc: Contains more than 45,000 citations, with abstracts, to documents published in Canada, about Canadian subjects, or by Canadian authors, and relating to occupational health and safety. Sources include books, monographs, periodicals, journal articles, and conference proceedings, covering published, unpublished, and limited distribution materials held by the Canadian Centre for Occupational Health and Safety. *Type:* Database.

CANUC:S
National Library of Canada
Acquisitions and Bibliographic Services Branch
Union Catalogue Division
395 Wellington St. Ph: (613)997-7990
Ottawa, ON, Canada K1A 0N4
E-mail: union.catalogue@nlc-bnc.ca
Contact: Louise Cloutier, Library Technical Assistant, (819)997-7386, Louise.Cloutier@nlc-bnc.ca.

Desc: Contains bibliographic descriptions of more than 180,000 serials in the social sciences and humanities included in the collection of more than 500 Canadian libraries. Also contains general-interest serials in science, technology, and interdisciplinary serials. *Type:* Database.

CEMA Update
CEMA
C/O Anne Weimann Ph: (203)372-2260
25 Elmwood Ave. Fax: (203)579-4413
Trumbull, CT 06611
Contact: Carole Braunschweig, Editor.

Desc: Focuses on news of the Association. Recurring features include interviews, news of research, a calendar of events, reports of meetings, news of educational opportunities, job listings, and notices of publications available. *Type:* Newsletter.

Centennial State Libraries Newsletter
Colorado State Library
201 E. Colfax Ave., Rm. 309 Ph: (303)866-6900
Denver, CO 80203 Fax: (303)866-6940
URL: http://www.cde.state.co.us/libnews.htm.
Contact: Kathleen D. Parent, Editor, parent_k@cde.state.co.us.

Desc: Publishes general news of library issues, local happenings, and state and federal actions affecting Colorado libraries. *Type:* Newsletter.

Center for Electronic Records of the U.S. National Archives and Records Administration
National Archives at College Park - Center for Electronic Records
8601 Adelphi Rd. Ph: (301)713-6645
College Park, MD 20740-6001
E-mail: webmaster@nara.gov
URL: http://www.nara.gov/nara/electronic/homensx.html
Contact: cer@nara.gov.

Desc: The Center for Electronic Records of the U.S. National Archives and Records Administration (NARA) database contains directory information to over 30,000 electronic records covering a wide subject scope of data gathered from 19 departments of the federal government. *Type:* Database.

Center for Research Libraries
James Green
VP for Member Services Ph: (773)955-4545
6050 S. Kenwood Ave. Fax: (773)955-4339
Chicago, IL 60637-2804
E-mail: green@crlmail.uchicago.edu
URL: http://www.crl.uchicago.edu
Contact: Donald B. Simpson, Pres.

Desc: Institutions with large research libraries. Aids libraries in their efforts to improve and increase the amount of and access to scholarly materials needed to support research. *Type:* Association.

Channel
Division for Libraries and Community Learning (DLCL)
Wisconsin Department of Public Instruction
125 S. Webster St., 5th Fl. Ph: (608)266-3374
PO Box 7841
Madison, WI 53707
Contact: Mark Ibach, Editor, ibachme@mail.state.wi.us.
Desc: Reports news of the Division for Library Services in Wisconsin. Carries information about library and media center services in general, continuing education opportunities for librarians, and Wisconsin professional materials. *Type:* Newsletter.

The Charleston Report
Charleston Group
164 Market St., Ste. 213
Charleston, NC 29401
Contact: Linda Crismond, Editor, (813)937-2974, fax: (813)937-1370, crismond.
Desc: Aims to assist publishers and vendors in improving their sales in the library market. Remarks: Editorial address: 303 Mariner Dr., Tarpon Springs, FL 34689. *Type:* Newsletter.

Church and Synagogue Library Association
PO Box 19357 Ph: (503)244-6919
Portland, OR 97280 Free: 800-LIB-CSLA
Fax: (503)977-3734
E-mail: csla@worldaccessnet.com
URL: http://www.worldaccessnet.com/~csla
Contact: Judith Janzen, Administrator.

Desc: Church and synagogue librarians; religious groups interested in promoting church or synagogue libraries. Co-operates with library schools providing educational opportunities for church and synagogue librarians, and with religious publishers providing material useful to these librarians. *Type:* Association.

Civilization
Civilization
666 Pennsylvania Ave. SE, Ste. Ph: (202)546-6600
303 Fax: (202)546-6632
Washington, DC 20003
E-mail: letters@civmag.com.
Contact: Sara Sklaroff, Managing Editor.
Desc: Magazine for members of the Library of Congress. *Type:* Periodical.

CLENexchange
Continuing Library Education Network and Exchange
American Library Association
50 E. Huron Ph: (312)944-6780
Chicago, IL 60611 Fax: (312)280-3256
Contact: Gail McGovern, Editor.
Desc: Publishes information on continuing library education: staff development, program ideas, and new concepts. Recurring features include CLENE news, book reviews, news of research, and a column titled Idea Forum. *Type:* Newsletter.

Connecticut Libraries
Connecticut Library Association
Franklin Commons Ph: (860)486-3278
106 Rte. 32 Fax: (860)486-0584
Franklin, CT 06254-1811
E-mail: kzoller@connix.com.
Contact: David Kapp, Editor, dkapp@aol.com.
Desc: Covers library news in Connecticut. *Type:* Newsletter.

CORMOSEA Bulletin
Committee on Research Materials on Southeast Asia
University of Wisconsin
278E Memorial Library Ph: (608)262-5493
728 State St. Fax: (608)265-2754
Madison, WI 53706
URL: http://www.library.wisc.edu/guides/seasia/cormosea/.
Contact: Carol L. Mitchell, Editor.
Desc: Addresses Southeast Asian librarianship and research materials, including current bibliographies, country profiles, translations, and technology. Recurring features include news of research, a calendar of events, reports of meetings, book reviews, and notices of publications available. *Type:* Newsletter.

Corpo Clip
Corporation of Professional Librarians of Quebec
307 Ste. Catherine W., Ste. 320 Ph: (514)845-3327
Montreal, PQ, Canada H2X Fax: (514)845-1618
2A3
E-mail: cbpq@interlink.net; info@ce-q.qc.ca.
URL: http://libertel.montreal.qc.ca/info/cbpq.
Contact: Josee Saint-Marseille, Editor.
Desc: Follows the association's undertakings to safeguard the professional interests of its members, ensure the protection of the public, and regulate the use of the title professional librarian. Carries material on the professional accomplishments of members, the information field, and new technologies as applied to library and information science. *Type:* Newsletter.

Corporate Library Update

Cahners Publishing Co.

245 W. 17th St.   Ph: (212)463-6828
New York, NY 10014   Free: 800-523-9654
Fax: (212)463-6530

Contact: Susan S. DiMattia, Editor, ssdimattia@aol.com.
Desc: Deals with service techniques, marketing ideas, new developments in technology and managements trends. *Type:* Newsletter.

The Crab

Maryland Library Association

400 Cathedral St.   Ph: (410)727-7422
Baltimore, MD 21201-4401   Fax: (410)625-9594

Desc: Provides information on library programs and projects Maryland. Recurring features include letters to the editor, interviews, news of research, a calendar of events, reports of meetings, news of educational opportunities, book reviews, and notices of publications available. *Type:* Newsletter.

CyberHound's Guide to Internet Libraries

Gale Group Inc.

27500 Drake Rd.   Ph: (248)699-4253
Farmington Hills, MI 48331-   Free: 800-877-GALE
3535   Fax: (248)699-8070
E-mail: galeord@galegroup.com
URL: http://www.galegroup.com.; http://www.
cyberhound.com/.

Desc: 2,000 academic, public, corporate, nonprofit, and special libraries. *Type:* Directory.

Dacus Focus

Dacus Library

Winthrop University   Ph: (803)323-2131
Rock Hill, SC 29733   Fax: (803)323-3285
URL: http://www.winthrop.edu/docus/focus32.pdf.

Contact: Patricia I. Ballard, Editor, ballardp@winthrop.edu.

Desc: Announces programs, new acquisitions, staff news, and accomplishments of the Dacus Library. Recurring features include a column titled Den of Antiquity . *Type:* Newsletter.

Directions for Utah Libraries

Utah State Library Division

250 North 1950 West, Ste. A   Ph: (801)466-5888
Salt Lake City, UT 84116-7901

Contact: Chip Ward, Editor.

Desc: Contains news, events and issues concerning Utah's libraries. Recurring features include a calendar of events and news of educational opportunities. *Type:* Newsletter.

Directory of Special Libraries and Information Centers

Gale Group Inc.

27500 Drake Rd.   Ph: (248)699-4253
Farmington Hills, MI 48331-   Free: 800-877-GALE
3535   Fax: (248)699-8070
E-mail: galeord@galegroup.com; infoindustry@gale.com.
URL: http://www.galegroup.com.; http://www.gale.com.
Contact: Matthew Miskelly, Editor, matthew.miskelly@gale.com.

Desc: Over 23,000 special libraries, information centers, documentation centers, etc.; about 500 networks and consortia; major special libraries abroad also included. Volume 1 part 2 contains 6 other appendices (besides networks and consortia): Regional and Subregional Libraries for the Blind & Physically Handicapped, Patent & Trademark Depository Libraries, Regional Government Depository Libraries, United Nations Depository Libraries, World Bank Depository Libraries, and European Community Depository Libraries. *Type:* Directory.

DLA Bulletin

Division of Library Automation (DLA)
University of California

300 Lakeside Dr., 8th Fl.   Ph: (510)987-0564
Oakland, CA 94612-3550   Fax: (510)839-3573
URL: http://ftp.dla.ucop.edu/pub/dlabulletin/.

Contact: Mary Jean Moore, Editor, mj.moore@ucop.edu.

Desc: Focuses on systemwide library automation at the University of California. Discusses subjects such as online catalog studies and research, record processing and consolidation, and retrospective conversion. *Type:* Newsletter.

DOCUSER

U.S. National Library of Medicine (NLM)
MEDLARS Management Section

8600 Rockville Pike   Ph: (301)496-3147
Bethesda, MD 20894
URL: http://www.sis.nlm.nih.gov/dirline

Desc: Contains information on approximately 14,000 libraries and other organizations that use the interlibrary loan (ILL) service of the National Library of Medicine (NLM) or are part of the Regional Document Delivery Network. Each record includes the institutional identification (organization name, library name, library telephone numbers, type of institution, library identifier); interlibrary loan service (type of materials loaned, charges, instructions, limitations on services, participation in DOCLINE, other electronic services used); Regional Medical Library participation (network membership and level of library within the network); SERHOLD (NLM's National Biomedical Serials Holdings Database) and participation (indicates whether serials holdings are reported to the MEDLARS, reporting agency, SERHOLD reporting level, and SERHOLD code). *Available:* U.S. National Library of Medicine (NLM), TOXNET; U.S. National Library of Medicine (NLM), TOXNET. *Type:* Database.

Downtown Promotion Reporter

Alexander Research & Communications, Inc.

215 Park Ave. S, Ste. 1301   Ph: (212)228-0246
New York, NY 10003   Fax: (212)228-0376
Contact: Mary Barr, Editor.

Desc: Focuses primarily on helping downtown areas be as competitive and successful as possible on a day-to-day basis. Reports on market research, retailing, advertising approaches, public relations techniques, budgeting, and organization. *Type:* Newsletter.

Dusty Shelf

Kansas City Area Archivists
The Nazarene Archives

6401 The Paseo   Ph: (816)333-7000
Kansas City, MO 64131
URL: http://cctr.umkc.edu/WHMCKC/KCAA/
KCAAHOME.HTM.

Contact: Stan Ingersol, Editor.

Desc: Contains essays and editorials on local and national archives. Recurring features include a calendar of events, reports of meetings, news of educational opportunities, job listings, notices of publications available, and a column titled Conservation Notes. *Type:* Newsletter.

Easy Access

Oregon Historical Society Press

1200 Park Ave. SW   Ph: (503)222-1741
Portland, OR 97205   Fax: (503)221-2035
Contact: M.C. Cuthill, Editor; Kris White, Editor.

Desc: Reports news for archival professionals. Recurring features include letters to the editor, news of research, a calendar of events, reports of meetings, news of educational opportunities, job listings, book reviews, and notices of publications available. *Type:* Newsletter.

EMIE Bulletin

Ethnic Materials & Information Exchange
Round Table (EMIE)
American Library Association (ALA)

Queens College, Rosenthal 305   Ph: (718)997-3626
Flushing, NY 11367   Fax: (718)997-3797

Contact: David Cohen, Publisher, dco$lib@qci.qc.edu;
James McShane, Editor, (785)231-0519, fax: (785)231-0519, jmcshane@tscpe.lib.ks.us.

Desc: Reports on programs and activities of the Round Table and news of related ethnic organizations. Focuses on multicultural librarianship. *Type:* Newsletter.

ERIC/IT Update

ERIC Clearinghouse on Information and Technology

Syracuse University   Ph: (315)443-3640
4-194 Center for Science and   Free: 800-464-9107
Technology   Fax: (315)443-5448
Syracuse, NY 13244-4100
E-mail: eric@ericir.syr.edu
URL: http://ericlr.syr.edu/ithome.

Contact: Susann Wurster, Editor.

Desc: Concentrates on the areas of education technology and library/information science. Offers informational resources and annotated bibliographies on topics of current interest in the areas of bibliographic instruction, microcomputers, computers and libraries, and television, visual literacy, and videotaping. *Type:* Newsletter.

Ex Libris

The Johns Hopkins University

Milton S. Eisenhower Library   Ph: (410)516-8327
Baltimore, MD 21218   Fax: (410)516-5080

Contact: Timothy Fiteh, Editor.

Desc: Focuses on the activities, needs, and interests of the John Hopkins University libraries. Recurring features include a calendar of events. *Type:* Newsletter.

Federal Library and Information Center Committee

701 Penn. Ave., Ste. 725   Ph: (202)707-4800
Washington, DC 20540-5100   Fax: (202)707-4848
URL: http://www.lcweb.loc.gov/flicc

Contact: Susan Tarr, Exec.Dir.

Desc: Representatives of departments and agencies of the federal government. Makes recommendations on federal library and information policies, programs, and procedures; coordinates cooperative activities and services among federal libraries and information centers. *Type:* Association.

FEDLINK Technical Notes

Federal Library and Information Network (FEDLINK)
Federal Library and Information Center Committee (FLICC)

Library of Congress   Ph: (202)707-4800
Washington, DC 20540-4930   Fax: (202)707-4825
E-mail: fliccfpe@loc.gov
URL: http://www.lcweb.loc.gov/flicc.

Contact: Susan M. Tarr, Exec. Dir.; Robin Hatziyannis, Editor-in-Chief.

Desc: Carries technical information about the Federal Library and Information Center Committee and its network component FEDLINK, its programs and services, and items of interest to those in library science and information fields. *Type:* Newsletter.

Finger Lakes Library System Newsletter

Finger Lakes Library System
314 N. Cayuga St.　　　　　Ph: (607)273-4074
Ithaca, NY 14850　　　　　Fax: (607)273-3618
Contact: Carol Hendrix, Editor, chendrix@lakenet.org.
Desc: Published to keep member librarians, trustees, and local politicians informed of System activities. Carries departmental reports, member library news, and public relations tips. *Type:* Newsletter.

FLICC Newsletter

Federal Library and Information Network (FEDLINK)
Federal Library and Information Center Committee (FLICC)
Library of Congress　　　　Ph: (202)707-4800
Washington, DC 20540-4930　Fax: (202)707-4825
E-mail: fliccfpe@loc.gov
URL: http://www.lcweb.loc.gov/flicc.
Contact: Susan M. Tarr, Exec. Dir.; Robin Hatziyannis, Editor-in-Chief.
Desc: Provides news and items of interest for federal librarians, information specialists, and administrators. Recurring features include reports on FLICC meetings, descriptions of its programs and projects, working group updates, announcements of educational programs for federal library and information center personnel. *Type:* Newsletter.

Flickertale

North Dakota State Library
604 E. Boulevard Ave., Dept.　Ph: (701)328-2492
　j50　　　　　　　　　　Free: 800-472-2104
Bismarck, ND 58505-0800　　Fax: (701)328-2040
E-mail: cboganow@state.nd.us.
URL: http://ndjl.lib.state.nd.us.
Contact: Cynthia C. Larson, Editor; Mike Jaugstetter, Editor.
Desc: Presents news and information regarding the North Dakota State Library system. Recurring features include news of educational opportunities, notices of publications available, and a calendar of events. *Type:* Newsletter.

Focus

Ruth O'Donnell
3509 Trillium Ct.　　　　　Ph: (850)942-4869
Tallahassee, FL 32312　　　Fax: (850)668-6911
Contact: Ruth O'Donnell, Contact, odonnellr@worldnet. att.net.
Desc: Contains news and advice for libraries serving adults with disabilities and older adults. *Type:* Newsletter.

Focus: Library Service to Older Adults, People With Disabilities

Ruth O'Donnell
3509 Trillium Ct.　　　　　Ph: (850)942-4869
Tallahassee, FL 32312　　　Fax: (850)668-6911
Contact: Ruth O'Donnell, Editor.
Desc: Discusses library programs for older adults and people with disabilities and presents new programs and approaches for meeting their needs. *Type:* Newsletter.

Focus: On the Center for Research Libraries

Center for Research Libraries
6050 S. Kenwood Ave.　　　Ph: (773)955-4545
Chicago, IL 60637-2804　　Fax: (773)955-4339
URL: http://www.crl.uchicago.edu; http://wwwcrl. uchicago.edu.
Contact: Linda Naru, Editor, naru@crimail.uchicago.edu.
Desc: Serves as a report to research libraries throughout the U.S and Canada. Recurring features include research library acquisitions, information on Center activities, news for and about Center staff, and related items. *Type:* Newsletter.

Folger News

The Folger Shakespeare Library
201 E. Capitol St. SE　　　Ph: (202)544-7077
Washington, DC 20003-1094　Fax: (202)544-4623
Contact: Kristi Berg, Head of Public Relations.
Desc: Newsletter for donors, friends, and members of the Folger Shakespeare Library. *Type:* Newsletter.

Footnotes

State Library of Iowa
E 12th and Grand
Des Moines, IA 50319
Contact: Annette Wetteland, Editor, awettel@mail.lib. state.ia.us.
Desc: Covers the activities of the State Library of Iowa, and news pertaining to libraries and librarians. *Type:* Newsletter.

Friends of Amherst College Library Newsletter

Friends of Amherst College Library
Robert Frost Library　　　　Ph: (413)542-2212
Amherst College　　　　　　Fax: (413)542-2662
PO Box 5000
Amherst, MA 01002-5000
E-mail: library@unix.amherst.edu
URL: http://www.amherst.edu/~library/friends/.
Contact: John Lancaster, Editor, (413)542-2299, fax: (413)542-2692, jlancaster@amherst.edu.
Desc: Details activities of the Friends and of the College Library. Contains feature literary articles, news of Library gifts and accessions, accounts of speakers who have appeared at the Library, and background on special collections. *Type:* Newsletter.

Friends of Libraries U.S.A.

1420 Walnut St., Ste. 450　Ph: (215)790-1674
Philadelphia, PA 19102　　　Free: 800-936-5872
　　　　　　　　　　　　Fax: (215)545-3821
E-mail: folusa@libertynet.org
URL: http://www.folusa.com
Contact: Sandy Dolnick, Exec.Dir.
Desc: Friends groups, libraries, clubs, associations, corporations, and interested individuals. Works to encourage the development of excellent library service to all residents of the U.S. *Type:* Association.

Friends of Libraries U.S.A. News Update

Friends of Libraries U.S.A.
1420 Walnut St., Ste. 450　Ph: (215)790-1674
Philadelphia, PA 19102　　　Free: 800-9FO-LUSA
　　　　　　　　　　　　Fax: (215)545-3821
E-mail: folusa@libertynet.org
Contact: Jane Rutledge, Editor.
Desc: Informs members on activities of benefit to them, including organizing, fundraising, literacy programs, and book and author events. Recurring features include book reviews. *Type:* Newsletter.

Friendscript

Board of Trustees
Library Office of Development and Public Affairs
University of Illinois at Urbana-Champaign
227 Library　　　　　　　Ph: (217)333-5682
1408 W. Gregory　　　　　Fax: (217)333-2214
Urbana, IL 61801
Contact: Terry Maher, Editor.
Desc: Contains information on the library's collections and services. Recurring features include interviews, news of research, and a calendar of events. *Type:* Newsletter.

Gale's Ready Reference Shelf

Gale Group Inc.
27500 Drake Rd.　　　　　Ph: (248)699-4253
Farmington Hills, MI 48331-　Free: 800-877-GALE
　3535　　　　　　　　　Fax: (248)699-8070
E-mail: galeord@galegroup.com
URL: http://www.galegroup.com.; http://www.gale.com.
Desc: Contain descriptions and contact information for more than 320,000 organizations, publications, and databases, including associations, religious organizations, research centers, directories, publishing and broadcast firms, newsletters, libraries and information centers, and government advisory organizations. *Type:* Directory.

Get Ready Sheet

Mid-York Library System
1600 Lincoln Ave.　　　　　Ph: (315)735-8328
Utica, NY 13502-5395　　　Fax: (315)735-0943
Contact: Diana Norton, Editor; Nancy Hotaling, Manager, hotaling@midyork.lib.ny.us.
Desc: Lists books and audio visual materials that will be promoted or shown on national television or radio, made into a broadcast television movie or motion picture, become a finalist in a national book award contest, or are seasonal. Includes title, author, publisher, ISBN, and price; promotion show name and date aired; and producer, director, and cast names. *Type:* Newsletter.

Golda Meir Library Newsletter

Golda Meir Library
PO Box 604　　　　　　　Ph: (414)229-6980
University of Wisconsin -　　Fax: (414)229-3605
　Milwaukee
Milwaukee, WI 53201
Contact: Tim Ericson, Editor, tle@gml.lib.uwm.edu.
Desc: Carries articles on the resources, activities, special services, and programs of this urban university library, named to honor the late prime minister of Israel, Golda Meir (1898-1978). Provides details on the content and use of special collections among the Library holdings. *Type:* Newsletter.

Granite State Libraries

New Hampshire State Library
20 Park St.　　　　　　　Ph: (603)271-2081
Concord, NH 03301-6314　　Fax: (603)271-6826
URL: http://www.state.nh.us/gsl.
Contact: Michael York, Editor, myork@finch.nhsl.lib.nh. us.
Desc: Focuses on New Hampshire libraries and librarians. Carries book reviews, lists of new items contributed to the Library, funding information, a calendar of events, and columns titled Vox Chilis and Editorial Notice. *Type:* Newsletter.

The Grist Newsletter

James M. Milne Library
State University College at　Ph: (607)436-2722
　Oneonta　　　　　　　　Fax: (607)436-3081
Oneonta, NY 13820
Desc: Newsletter of Milne Library at SUNY College at Oneonta. *Type:* Newsletter.

Harris Library Report

Harris InfoSource
2057 E. Aurora Rd.　　　　Ph: (330)425-9000
Twinsburg, OH 44087-1999　Free: 800-888-5900
　　　　　　　　　　　　Fax: (330)425-7150
E-mail: customerservice@harrisinfo.com; catknapp@aol. com.
URL: http://www.harrisinfo.com
Contact: Jenifer Minozzi, Editor.
Desc: Carries news on the manufacturing sector from Harris InfoSource International for public, business, and academic libraries and allied organizations. Furnishes updates on manufacturing directories, software, statistics, networking, resource tools, and contests. *Type:* Newsletter.

Harvard Librarian

Harvard University Library
Wadsworth House   Ph: (617)495-7793
Cambridge, MA 02138   Fax: (617)495-0370

Contact: Timothy Hanke, Editor.

Desc: Reports news and information concerning Harvard University libraries. Recurring features include librarian profiles, book reviews, notices of publications available, exhibition announcements, news of library appointments and grants. *Type:* Newsletter.

Hennepin County Library Cataloging Bulletin

Hennepin County Library
12601 Ridgedale Dr.   Ph: (612)541-8562
Minnetonka, MN 55343-5648   Fax: (612)541-8600

Contact: Sanford Berman, Editor.

Desc: Provides information about changes and updates in the Hennepin County Library catalog. *Type:* Newsletter.

Hitchhiker

New Mexico State Library
325 Don Gaspar   Ph: (505)827-3813
Santa Fe, NM 87501-2777   Fax: (505)827-3888
URL: http://www.stlib.state.nm.us.

Contact: Robert Upton, Editor, rupton@stlib.state.nm.us.

Desc: Carries brief items concerning libraries and librarians in New Mexico, jobs listings, notes on personnel, and listings of additions to the State Library's collection of professional reading material. Recurring features include announcements of conferences, workshops, resources, and continuing education opportunities, items on developments in the State Library Commission, and news of awards granted. *Type:* Newsletter.

IASL Newsletter

International Association of School Librarianship
Box 34069, Dept. 300   Ph: (206)925-0266
Seattle, WA 98124-1069   Fax: (206)925-0566
E-mail: iasl@rockland.com

Contact: Judy O'Connell, Editor.

Desc: Covers Association activities and developments in school library programs worldwide. Recurring features include book reviews, a schedule of activities, news of research, and reports from IASL Directors. *Type:* Newsletter.

Idaho Librarian

Idaho Library Association
University of Idaho Library   Ph: (208)885-2509
Moscow, ID 83844-2350   Fax: (208)885-6817

Contact: Karen Schlegl, Editor; Christine Dezelar-Tiedman, Editor, chrisd@belle.lib.uidaho.edu.

Desc: Contains information on Idaho Library Association's activities. *Type:* Newsletter.

Illinois State Library—Insight

Illinois State Library
300 S. 2nd St.   Ph: (217)785-0052
Springfield, IL 62701-1796   Free: 800-665-5576
    Fax: (217)782-8261
E-mail: nkrah@library.sos.state.il.us.

Contact: Catherine O'Connor, Editor; Kristie Metrow, Editor.

Desc: Covers issues of interest to the library and trustee community, releases news from the Illinois Secretary of State, as State Librarian, and focuses on topics including telecommunications, grants announcements and development. *Type:* Newsletter.

In JCB

John Carter Brown Library
Brown University
Box 1894   Ph: (401)863-2725
Providence, RI 02912   Fax: (401)863-3477

Desc: Provides news of Library publications, programs, acquisitions, building news, gifts, and exhibitions. Recurring features include a calendar of events and a donor list. *Type:* Newsletter.

Infinity

Preservation Section
Society of American Archivists (SAA)
527 S. Wells St., 5th Fl.   Ph: (312)922-0140
Chicago, IL 60607   Fax: (312)347-1452
E-mail: info@archivists.org

Desc: Informs members of Society and archives news and events. Recurring features include news of research, a calendar of events, reports of meetings, news of educational opportunities, book reviews, notices of publications available, and a column titled From the Chair. *Type:* Newsletter.

Information Retrieval & Library Automation

Lomond Publications
PO Box 88   Ph: (301)694-0123
Mount Airy, MD 21771   Free: 800-443-6299
    Fax: (301)694-5151
E-mail: thattery@aol.com

Contact: Maxine Hattery, Editor.

Desc: Supplies "librarians and information specialists with international coverage of new technologies, products/equipment, literature, professional meetings and other significant developments which improve information systems and library services for science, social science, law and medicine." Covers library and information networks, computer technology and systems, and policy issues. *Type:* Newsletter.

Information Science Abstracts

Information Today, Inc.
143 Old Marlton Pike   Ph: (609)654-6266
Medford, NJ 08055-9936
E-mail: custserv@infotoday.com

Contact: Jim Brown, Customer Service.

Desc: Contains more than 165,000 citations, with abstracts, to the worldwide literature on information science and such related areas as documentation, library science, and information services. Coverage extends to education issues relating to information and library science. *Available:* The Dialog Corporation, DIALOG. *Type:* Database.

Information Technology Newsletter

Idea Group Publishing
1331 E. Chocolate Ave.   Ph: (717)533-8845
Hershey, PA 17033   Free: 800-345-4332
    Fax: (717)533-8661
E-mail: jtravers@idea-group.com.
URL: http://www.idea-group.com

Contact: Greg Crawford, Editor; Cary White, Editor.

Desc: Discusses cybrary networks, library practices, information access, and new technology product releases. Recurring features include letters to the editor, interviews, news of research, a calendar of events, news of educational opportunities, and book reviews. *Type:* Newsletter.

Intellectual Freedom Action News

American Library Association (ALA)
50 E. Huron St.   Ph: (312)280-5038
Chicago, IL 60611   Free: 800-545-2433
    Fax: (312)280-5033
E-mail: oif@ala.org.
URL: http://www.ala.org/alaorg/oif/ifan_pub.html.

Contact: Judith F. Krug, Editor, (312)280-4222, jkrug@ala.org; Richard Matthews, Editor, (312)280-4224, rmatthew@ala.org; Don Wood, Editor, (312)280-4225, dwood@ala.org.

Desc: Serves as an update for "intellectual freedom issues." Recurring features include news of research, a calendar of events, reports of meetings, news of educational opportunities, and notices of publications available. *Type:* Newsletter.

Inter-Com

District of Columbia Library Association (DCLA)
7117 Poplar Ave.
Takoma Park, MD 20912

Contact: Jacque-Lynne Schulman, Editor.

Desc: Deals with libraries and librarians in the Washington D.C., area. Recurring features include a calendar of events, reports of meetings, job listings, and notices of publications available. *Type:* Newsletter.

International Directory of News Libraries

LDA Publishers
42-36 209 St.   Ph: (718)224-9484
Bayside, NY 11361-2747   Free: 888-388-9887
    Fax: (718)224-9487

Contact: Andrew V. Ippolito, Editor, andyippolito@mindspring.com.

Desc: Nearly 800 global newspaper, magazine, broadcast libraries, and International News bureau offices; identifies the members of the News Division of the Special Libraries Association and members of the Association of U.K. Media Librarians (AUKML). *Type:* Directory.

International Leads

American Library Association (ALA)
50 E. Huron St.   Ph: (312)280-5038
Chicago, IL 60611   Free: 800-545-2433
    Fax: (312)280-5033

Contact: Ron Chepesiuk, Editor, chepesiukr@winthrop.edu.

Desc: Presents news about international library activities, the international work of ALA and other organizations, and people and publications in the field. Recurring features include interviews, reports of meetings, and news of educational opportunities. *Type:* Newsletter.

ISL Newsletter

Idaho State Library (ISL)
325 W. State St.   Ph: (208)334-2150
Boise, ID 83702   Fax: (208)334-4016
URL: http://www.lili.org/isl.

Contact: Stephanie Bailey-White, Editor, swhite@isl.state.id.us.

Desc: Provides news of individual libraries and other information of interest to public, academic, and special libraries in Idaho. Covers State Library Board activities, new library programs and promotions, reference and technical services, and budgets. *Type:* Newsletter.

John F. Kennedy Library Newsletter

John F. Kennedy Library Foundation
Boston, MA 02125   Ph: (617)436-9986
    Fax: (617)436-3395

Contact: Donna Smerlas, Editor.

Desc: Reports on Library programs, exhibits, and archives. *Type:* Newsletter.

Journal of Youth Services in Libraries

Association for Library Service to Children
American Library Association
50 E. Huron St.   Ph: (312)280-2163
Chicago, IL 60611   Free: 800-545-2433
                              Fax: (312)944-7671
E-mail: alsc@ala.org; rsinger@ala.org
Contact: Donald J. Kenney, Editor; Linda J. Wilson, Editor.

Desc: Reflects the aims of the Division, which is "responsible for the evaluation and selection of materials for teenagers and young adults." Reports on information and developments relevant to strengthening library services to teenagers. Reviews recommended books. *Type:* Newsletter.

Kansas Libraries

State Library of Kansas
300 SW 10th Ave., Rm. 343N   Ph: (785)296-3875
Topeka, KS 66612-1593   Free: 800-432-3919
                              Fax: (785)296-6650
URL: http://skyways.lib.ks.us/kansas/.
Contact: Eric Hansen, Editor, erich@ink.org.

Desc: Contains news and information on legislative matters and state and federal issues which concern Kansas libraries and the State Library. Also covers resource sharing, automation and technology, and library literacy. *Type:* Newsletter.

LC MARC: Books All

U.S. Library of Congress
Cataloging Distribution Service
101 Independence Ave., S.E.   Ph: (202)707-6100
Washington, DC 20541-4912
E-mail: cdsinfo@loc.gov
URL: http://www.lcweb.loc.gov/cds
Contact: Customer Support Unit.

Desc: Contains bibliographic and cataloging information on more than 5 million monographs published worldwide since 1968. Covers books in English since 1968; in French, since 1973; in German, Portuguese, and Spanish, since 1975; in other Roman alphabet languages, since 1976-77; in South Asian and Cyrillic alphabet languages (in Romanized form), since 1979; and in Greek (in Romanized form), since 1980. *Available:* The Dialog Corporation, DIALOG; The Dialog Corporation, DIALOG; British Library, National Bibliographic Service, BLAISE; University of Tsukuba, Science Information Processing Center; H.W. Wilson Company, WilsonWeb; NlightN. *Type:* Database.

LC MARC: Name Authorities

U.S. Library of Congress
Cataloging Distribution Service
101 Independence Ave., S.E.   Ph: (202)707-6100
Washington, DC 20541-4912
E-mail: cdsinfo@loc.gov
URL: http://www.lcweb.loc.gov/cds
Contact: Customer Support Unit.

Desc: Contains the complete Library of Congress (LC) name authority file. Covers more than 3.9 million personal, corporate, series, and title authority records. *Type:* Database.

LC MARC: Serials

U.S. Library of Congress
Cataloging Distribution Service
101 Independence Ave., S.E.   Ph: (202)707-6100
Washington, DC 20541-4912
E-mail: cdsinfo@loc.gov
URL: http://www.lcweb.loc.gov/cds
Contact: Customer Support Unit.

Desc: Provides full bibliographic descriptions and cataloging information on more than 800,000 serials cataloged and/or authenticated by the U.S. Library of Congress or by CONSER (Cooperative Online Serials Program) participants. *Type:* Database.

LC MARC: Subject Authorities

U.S. Library of Congress
Cataloging Distribution Service
101 Independence Ave., S.E.   Ph: (202)707-6100
Washington, DC 20541-4912
E-mail: cdsinfo@loc.gov
URL: http://www.lcweb.loc.gov/cds
Contact: Customer Support Unit.

Desc: Contains the complete Library of Congress (LC) subject authority file. Includes more than 240,000 records, representing subject headings established by the Library of Congress. *Type:* Database.

LC MARC: Visual Materials

U.S. Library of Congress
Cataloging Distribution Service
101 Independence Ave., S.E.   Ph: (202)707-6100
Washington, DC 20541-4912
E-mail: cdsinfo@loc.gov
URL: http://www.lcweb.loc.gov/cds
Contact: Customer Support Unit.

Desc: Provides full bibliographic descriptions and cataloging information for more than 135,000 audiovisual items, including projected media, two-dimensional non-projectable graphic representations, and kits. Covers materials in all languages; titles are in Romanized form. *Type:* Database.

Liaison

New Brunswick Library Service
PO Box 6000, Marysville Pl.   Ph: (506)453-2354
Fredericton, NB, Canada E3B   Fax: (506)453-2416
  5H1
Contact: Jocelyne Thompson, Editor.

Desc: Provides information on current events in public libraries and public school libraries in New Brunswick. Also details activities of the New Brunswick Library Trustee Association, and The New Brunswick Library Service. *Type:* Newsletter.

Librarians Collection Letter

Librarians Collection Letter
PO Box 223   Ph: (509)935-0769
Chewelah, WA 99109
Contact: Regan Robinson, Editor, regan@stevcolib.org.

Desc: Combines interviews, articles, news, and reviews to provide solutions to problems facing collection development staff members in libraries. Covers budgeting, selection, weeding, policies procedures, assessment, vendors, publishers, and new technologies. *Type:* Newsletter.

Library Administrator's Digest

BC PL Foundation Inc.
320 York Rd.   Ph: (410)887-4622
Towson, MD 21204   Fax: (410)887-6103
E-mail: lad@mail.bcpl.lib.md.us.
Contact: Charles W. Robinson, Editor.

Desc: Designed to keep library administrators abreast of new ideas and developments, particularly in the public library field. Recurring features include editorials and letters to the editor. *Type:* Newsletter.

The Library Cat

The Library Cat
PO Box 274   Ph: (218)236-7205
Moorhead, MN 56560
Contact: Phyllis Lahti, Editor.

Desc: Aims to encourage the establishment of cats in a library setting; to improve the image and the well-being of the library cat; and to unite library cat advocates everywhere. *Type:* Newsletter.

Library of Congress—Information Bulletin

Library of Congress
Printing and Processing Section,   Ph: (202)707-2905
  Rm. LM G-14   Fax: (202)707-9199
Washington, DC 20540
URL: gopher://marvel.loc.gov/ii/loc/pubs/lcib.
Contact: Guy Lamolinara.

Desc: Carries news from and about the Library of Congress and its services. Includes limited information on activities beyond the Library which may be of interest to staff and the library world. *Type:* Newsletter.

Library Developments

Library Development Division
Texas State Library
PO Box 12927   Ph: (512)463-5465
Austin, TX 78711   Fax: (512)463-8800
URL:
  http://link.tsl.state.tx.us/dir/ldnews.dir/.files/
  nwslttr.txt.
Contact: Sue Polanka, Editor, jeanette.larson@tsl.state.tx.us.

Desc: Reports the activities of the Texas State Library and other groups which affect the Library. Recurring features include listings of continuing education opportunities for Texas librarians, listings of new titles available for loan from the Library Science Collection, statistics, and updates on federal, state, and private funding. *Type:* Newsletter.

Library Hi Tech News

Pierian Press
5000 Washtenaw Ave.   Ph: (734)434-5530
Ann Arbor, MI 48106   Free: 800-678-2435
                              Fax: (734)434-6409
E-mail: pubinfo@pierianpress.com
Contact: C. Edward Wall, Editor.

Desc: Offers "timely and late-breaking news about all aspects of technology related to library operations." Includes "news of new products, database developments, cooperative networks, technology vendors." Recurring features include book reviews and a calendar of events. *Type:* Newsletter.

Library Hotline

Cahners Publishing Co.
245 W. 17th St.   Ph: (212)463-6828
New York, NY 10014   Free: 800-523-9654
                              Fax: (212)463-6530
Contact: Susan S. DiMattia, Editor, ssdimattia@aol.com.

Desc: Features news of libraries and information science. Deals with coverage of related and relevant topics, such as governmental influence on information availability and special library programs. *Type:* Newsletter.

Library Issues

Mountainside Publishing, Inc.
321 S. Main St.   Ph: (734)662-3925
PO Box 8330   Fax: (734)662-4450
Ann Arbor, MI 48107
URL: http://www.libraryissues.com.
Contact: Richard M. Dougherty, Editor, apdougherty@compuserve.com.

Desc: Offers overviews of the trends and problems affecting campus libraries. *Type:* Newsletter.

Library Journal Sourcebook

Cahners Business Information
245 W. 17th St.   Ph: (212)463-6823
New York, NY 10011   Fax: (212)463-6734
URL: http://www.libraryjournal.com.
Contact: Eric Bryant, Managing Editor, bryant@lj.cahners.com.

Desc: List of over 500 suppliers of products and services used by libraries from abstracting to word processing equipment. *Type:* Directory.

Library Literature

H.W. Wilson Company
950 University Ave.   Ph: (718)588-8400
Bronx, NY 10452
E-mail: custserv@hwwilson.com
URL: http://www.hwwilson.com
Contact: Technical Support Department., techmail@info.hwwilson.com.
Desc: Contains citations to articles and reviews of books, periodicals, and audiovisual materials in the library and information science area. Sources include 234 library and general periodicals, more than 600 new monographs yearly, conference proceedings, pamphlets, and library school theses. *Available:* H.W. Wilson Company, WilsonWeb; H.W. Wilson Company, WilsonWeb; Ovid Technologies, Inc.; OCLC Online Computer Library Center, Inc., OCLC EPIC; OCLC Online Computer Library Center, Inc., OCLC FirstSearch Catalog; CARL Corporation; SilverPlatter Information, Inc.; The Dialog Corporation, DIALOG; Bell & Howell Information and Learning. *Type:* Database.

Library Matters

Queens Borough Public Library
89-11 Merrick Blvd.   Ph: (718)990-0705
Jamaica, NY 11432   Fax: (718)291-2695
Contact: Joe Catrambone, Jr., Exec. Editor; Donna Hill, Managing Editor.
Desc: Provides news about the Library. Recurring features include a calendar of events. *Type:* Newsletter.

Library Notes

Academic Affairs Library
University of North Carolina at Chapel Hill
Davis Library   Ph: (919)962-0171
CB No. 3914   Fax: (919)962-0484
Chapel Hill, NC 27599-3914
Contact: David C. Taylor, Editor.
Desc: Contains news on library services and resources available to faculty and students. Covers trends in libraries and information. *Type:* Newsletter.

Library PR News

Library Educational Institute, Inc.
Box 219, RD 1   Ph: (717)746-1842
New Albany, PA 18833   Fax: (717)746-1114
E-mail: parrot@epix.net.
Contact: Phil Bradbury, Editor.
Desc: Concerns library public relations, publicity, graphic arts, and display. Includes how-to articles on library promotion. *Type:* Newsletter.

Library Systems Newsletter

Library Technology Reports
American Library Association (ALA)
50 E. Huron St.   Free: 800-545-2433
Chicago, IL 60611   Fax: (312)440-9374
Contact: Howard S. White, Editor-in-Chief, (312)280-4271, hwhite@ala.org; Richard W. Boss, Contributing Editor, (301)946-2240, fax: (301)946-6505.
Desc: Reports on technological developments in library automation systems. Covers vendor services, computer disc technology, and other areas of interest. *Type:* Newsletter.

Library Times International

Future World Publishing Company
PO Box 125   Ph: (304)776-6994
Institute, WV 25112   Fax: (304)776-6994
Contact: R.N. Sharma, Editor, (304)766-3117, fax: (304)766-4103, sharmarn@mail.wvsc.edu.
Desc: Monitors international developments and events related to library and information science. Carries items on countries worldwide. *Type:* Newsletter.

The Library User

University Library
University of Nebraska, Omaha
6001 Dodge St.   Ph: (402)554-2640
Omaha, NE 68182-0237   Fax: (402)554-3215
URL: http://library.unomaha.edu/.
Contact: Janice S. Boyer, Editor, jboyer@unomaha.edu.
Desc: Publishes information about the services and activities of the Library. Includes articles about collections, staff, resource tools, special events, and other items of interest to users of the University Library. *Type:* Newsletter.

The Library of Virginia

The Library of Virginia
800 E. Broad St.   Ph: (804)692-3592
Richmond, VA 23219-8000   Fax: (804)692-3594
URL: http://vsla.edu
Contact: Janice M. Hathcock, Editor.
Desc: Carries articles on LVA resources and services and on other libraries in the state of Virginia. Includes brief items from American Library Association releases. *Type:* Newsletter.

LITA Newsletter

Library and Information Technology Association (LITA)
50 E. Huron St.   Ph: (312)280-4270
Chicago, IL 60611   Free: 800-545-2433
    Fax: (312)280-3257
E-mail: lita@ala.org
URL: http://www.lita.org
Contact: Walt Crawford, Editor.
Desc: Reports on technology in libraries, including technical standards, online catalogs, expert systems, telecommunications, optical systems, and conference programs and discussions within LITA. Remarks: Editor's address is RLG, 1200 Villa St., Mountain View, CA 94041-1100, (415) 691-2227; fax (415) 964-0943. *Type:* Newsletter.

LOEX News

LOEX Clearinghouse
Eastern Michigan University
c/o Linda Shirato   Ph: (734)487-0168
University Library   Fax: (734)487-8861
Ypsilanti, MI 48197
Contact: Linda Shirato, Editor, lib_shirato@online.emich.edu.
Desc: Provides information on bibliographic instruction and serves as a forum for exchange of ideas. Includes list of clearinghouse items for lending, job openings, bibliographies, and conference schedules. *Type:* Newsletter.

Long Island Archives Conference Newsletter

Long Island Archives Conference
History Department   Ph: (718)990-6229
St. John's University   Fax: (718)380-0353
Jamaica, NY 11439
Contact: Richard Harmond, Editor.
Desc: Covers upcoming events and acquisitions of the Department, including national and state government and nongovernment archives. Recurring features include reports of meetings, job listings, and columns titled President's Column and What's New. *Type:* Newsletter.

Lutheran Church Library Association

122 W. Franklin Ave., No. 604   Ph: (612)870-3623
Minneapolis, MN 55404-2474   Fax: (612)870-0170
E-mail: lclahq@aol.com
Contact: Leanna Kloempken, Exec.Dir.
Desc: Individuals, church libraries, and church organizations. Seeks to further the growth of church libraries. Assists members in establishing and operating a church library; furnishes lists of books and audio visuals recommended for church libraries. *Type:* Association.

Macomb County Library Newsletter

Macomb County Library
16480 Hall Rd.   Ph: (810)286-6660
Clinton Township, MI 48038
Contact: Peg Lamont, Editor.
Desc: Covers activities, events, and other news connected with the Macomb County Library and libraries in general. Occasionally includes an annotated bibliography of library holdings on a specific subject. *Type:* Newsletter.

Madison Public Library Newsletter

Madison Public Library
39 Keep St.   Ph: (973)377-0722
Madison, NJ 07940   Fax: (973)377-3142
Contact: Nancy S. Vernon, Editor; Jan Sendell, Editor.
Desc: Reports on Library fundraising efforts, day trips, donations, new acquisitions, concerts, and other activities. Recurring features include a calendar of events and staff news. *Type:* Newsletter.

The Maine Entry

Maine State Library
Sta. 64   Ph: (207)287-5620
Augusta, ME 04333-0064   Fax: (207)287-5624
E-mail: slecoms@state.me.us.
Contact: Edna Comstock, Editor, edna.comstock@state.me.us; Linda Gustafson, Editor.
Desc: Features stories on aspects of librarianship and public and school library service. Covers district and state library news. *Type:* Newsletter.

Maine Memo

Maine Library Association
Warren Memorial Library   Ph: (207)854-5891
479 Main St.
Westbrook, ME 04092
URL: http://www.mainelibraries.org/mainememo2.html.
Contact: Anastasia S. Weigle, Editor, aweigle@warren.lib.me.us.
Desc: Provides the Maine Library community informed on activities and events of significance and interest. Recurring features include a calendar of events, job listing, and notices of publications available. *Type:* Newsletter.

Manitoba League of the Physically Handicapped—Update

Manitoba League of the Physically Handicapped
200-294 Portage Ave.   Ph: (204)943-6099
Winnipeg, MB, Canada R3C 0B9
Contact: Dave Martin, Editor.
Desc: Reports on League activities, issues, and priorities. Provides a forum for events and other concerns of the disabled. *Type:* Newsletter.

Marian Library Newsletter

Marian Library
University of Dayton
300 College Park Ave.   Ph: (513)229-4214
Dayton, OH 45469
Contact: Rev. Thomas A. Thompson, Editor.
Desc: Provides information about significant acquisitions to the Marian Library, which houses "the world's most comprehensive collection of materials related to the theology and cult of the Virgin Mary." Also offers details of exhibits arranged by the Library. Recurring features include news of staff members, acknowledgement of contributions, and news of research undertaken by visiting scholars. *Type:* Newsletter.

Marketing to Libraries Through Library Associations

American Library Association (ALA)
50 E. Huron St.　　　Ph: (312)280-5038
Chicago, IL 60611　　Free: 800-545-2433
　　　　　　　　　　Fax: (312)280-5033
Desc: National, international, and state library associations. *Type:* Directory.

Marketing Treasures

Chris Olson & Associates
857 Twin Harbor Dr.　　Ph: (410)647-6708
Arnold, MD 21012-1027　Fax: (410)647-0415
E-mail: olson@access.digex.net
URL: http://www.chrisolson.com.
Contact: Chris Olson, Editor.
Desc: Aims to help librarians promote the services of their libraries. Provides creative ideas, helpful hints, and insights on how other libraries promote their services. *Type:* Newsletter.

MBLC Notes

Massachusetts Board of Library Commissioners (MBLC)
648 Beacon St.　　　Ph: (617)267-9400
Boston, MA 02215　　Free: 800-952-7403
　　　　　　　　　　Fax: (617)421-9833
Contact: Louise Kanus, Editor.
Desc: Covers the activities and policies of the state library development agency in Massachusetts. Recurring features include columns titled Legislative Update, At Your Service, and Preservation Inquirer. *Type:* Newsletter.

Medical Library Association

65 E. Wacker Pl., Ste. 1900　Ph: (312)419-9094
Chicago, IL 60601-7298　　　Fax: (312)419-8950
E-mail: info@mlahq.org
URL: http://www.mlanet.org
Contact: Carla J. Funk, Contact.
Desc: Librarians and others engaged in professional library or bibliographical work in medical and allied scientific libraries. Purposes are to foster medical and allied scientific libraries, to promote the educational and professional growth of health science librarians, and to exchange medical literature among members. Offers continuing education courses, certification and recertification programs, and placement service. *Type:* Association.

MHLS News

Mid-Hudson Library System (MHLS)
103 Market St.　　　Ph: (914)471-6060
Poughkeepsie, NY 12601
E-mail: mhls@ulysses.sebridge.org
URL: http://www.midhudson.org.
Contact: Dr. Fred Stielow, Editor, stielow@sebridge.com; Deborah Begley, Editor.
Desc: Serves as a forum for information, suggestions, problems, and successes for library trustees and others in the region. Covers library programs, fundraising, public relations, and pertinent legislation. *Type:* Newsletter.

Michigan Librarian Newsletter

Michigan Library Association
6810 South Cedar, Ste. 6　　Ph: (517)694-6615
Lansing, MI 48911　　　　　Fax: (517)694-4330
E-mail: mla@mlc.lib.mi.us
URL: http://www.mla.lib.mi.us
Contact: Marianne Hartzell, Editor.
Desc: Devoted to librarians and libraries in the state of Michigan, with news of legislation, reports of workshops and continuing education events, and regular columns for the various divisions and roundtables of the Association. *Type:* Newsletter.

Michigan Library Consortium

6810 S. Cedar, Ste. 8　　Ph: (517)694-4242
Lansing, MI 48911　　　Free: 800-530-9019
　　　　　　　　　　　Fax: (517)694-9303
E-mail: helpserv@mlc.lib.mi.us
URL: http://www.mlc.lib.mi.us
Contact: Randy Dykhuis, Exec.Dir.
Desc: Provides libraries with OCLC, an international on-line database. Provides discounts for other reference databases including Ovid Online, DIALOG, and WILSONLINE; and CD-ROM reference products including Knight-Ridder on Disc, SilverPlatter, and WILSONDISC. *Type:* Association.

Microfilming Projects Newsletter

Seminar on the Acquisition of Latin American Library Materials (SALALM)
General Library
University of New Mexico
Albuquerque, NM 87131
Contact: Basil Malish, Editor.
Desc: Lists original microreproduction projects in progress or recently completed on Latin American or Iberian topics. *Type:* Newsletter.

Mid-Hudson Library System—Bulletin

Mid-Hudson Library System (MHLS)
103 Market St.　　　Ph: (914)471-6060
Poughkeepsie, NY 12601
E-mail: mhls@ulysses.sebridge.org
URL: http://www.midhudson.org.
Contact: Jane Daniels, Editor, Janed@scbridge.org.
Desc: Contains current news and information for librarians in the Mid-Hudson Library System. *Type:* Newsletter.

MLA News

Medical Library Association
65 E. Wacker Dr., Ste. 1900　Ph: (312)419-9094
Chicago, IL 60601-7298　　　Fax: (312)419-8950
E-mail: info@mlahq.org
URL: http://www.mlanet.org
Contact: Jean Demas, Editor, fax: (630)724-2091, jdemas@allianceai.org.
Desc: Covers topics about the association, the health sciences information industry, legislation, and international events. Regular features include updates and reviews of new information technology, medical publication trends, classifieds, and educational opportunities. *Type:* Newsletter.

MLA Newsletter

Minnesota Library Association
1315 Lowry Ave. N.　　Ph: (612)521-1735
Minneapolis, MN 55411
E-mail: mnla@augsburg.edu
Contact: Margaret Maes Axtmann, Editor; Deborah K. Sales, Editor.
Desc: Reports MLA efforts in obtaining increased state aid to libraries, working towards interlibrary cooperation legislation, and providing continuing education for librarians. Recurring features include news of events, programs, and meetings of MLA, and a list of job openings in the state. *Type:* Newsletter.

MLS: Marketing Library Services

Information Today, Inc.
143 Old Marlton Pike　　Ph: (609)654-6266
Medford, NJ 08055　　　Free: 800-300-9868
　　　　　　　　　　　Fax: (609)654 4309
E-mail: custserv@infotoday.com
URL: http://www.infotoday.com
Contact: Kathy Miller, Editor, kmiller@infotoday.com.
Desc: Tells librarians and information professionals how to actively market their services to gain clients and to justify their existence. Discusses communication skills, fundraising, marketing events, and technology. *Type:* Newsletter.

MO Info

Missouri Library Association
1306 Business 63 S., Ste. B　Ph: (573)449-4627
Columbia, MO 65201　　　　Fax: (573)449-4655
Contact: Jean Ann McCartney, Editor, jmccartn@mail.more.net.
Desc: Reports on the Association and library activities at the local, state, and federal levels. Recurring features include a calendar of events, reports of meetings, news of educational opportunities, notices of publications available, and columns titled ALA News, Around the State and Members in the News. *Type:* Newsletter.

MPLA Newsletter

Mountain Plains Library Association (MPLA)
c/o University of South Dakota　Ph: (605)677-6088
　Library　　　　　　　　　　Fax: (605)677-5488
414 E. Clark St.
Vermillion, SD 57069-2390
E-mail: jedelen@usd.edu
Contact: Heidi M. Nickisch, Editor, nickisch@usd.edu.
Desc: Announces library news from Arizona, Utah, Nebraska, Kansas, New Mexico, North Dakota, South Dakota, Nevada, Wyoming, Montana, Colorado, and Oklahoma. Discusses various aspects of libraries, librarianship, continuing education for librarians, and new technology in its application to libraries and to the dissemination of information. *Type:* Newsletter.

MPLnow

Muncie Public Library (MPL)
315 W. Adams St.　　Ph: (765)747-8209
Muncie, IN 47305-2304　Fax: (765)747-8211
Contact: Roslyn Modzelewski, Editor.
Desc: Reports news and activities of the library. Recurring features include a calendar of events. *Type:* Newsletter.

National Library of Medicine—News

National Library of Medicine
National Institutes of Health
U.S. Department of Health and Human Services
8600 Rockville Pike, Bldg. 38　Ph: (301)496-7771
Bethesda, MD 20894　　　　　Free: 800-272-4787
　　　　　　　　　　　　　　Fax: (301)496-7831
URL: gopher://gopher.nlm.nih.gov.
Contact: Melanie Modlin, Editor, melanie-modlin@nlm.nih.gov.
Desc: Reports on Library programs, policies, services, exhibits, and collections. Recurring features include notices of publications available, staff notes, and a list of references citing works that discuss the products and services of the Library. *Type:* Newsletter.

National Library News

National Library of Canada
395 Wellington St.　　　Ph: (613)995-7969
Ottawa, ON, Canada K1A 0N4　Fax: (613)991-9871
E-mail: publications@nlc-bnc.ca
URL: http://www.nbc-bnc.ca; http://www.nlc-bmc.ca/pubs/nl-news/enlnuvs.htm.
Contact: Jean-Marie Briere, Editor.
Desc: Provides information on the National Library of Canada. Reports on events and the library's collections. *Type:* Newsletter.

National Library Service for the Blind and Physically Handicapped—News

National Library Service for the Blind and Physically Handicapped
Library of Congress
1291 Taylor St., NW   Ph: (202)707-5100
Washington, DC 20542   Free: 800-424-8567
                             Fax: (202)707-0712
E-mail: nls@loc.gov

Contact: Vicki Fitzpatrick, Editor.

Desc: Covers the programs and projects of the Service, which publishes books and magazines in braille and in recorded form for readers who cannot read conventional print materials. Reports on related programs around the country and worldwide. *Type:* Newsletter.

National Library Service for the Blind and Physically Handicapped—Update

National Library Service for the Blind and Physically Handicapped
Library of Congress
1291 Taylor St., NW   Ph: (202)707-5100
Washington, DC 20542   Free: 800-424-8567
                             Fax: (202)707-0712
E-mail: nls@loc.gov

Contact: Freddie Peaco, Editor.

Desc: Reports on volunteer activities related to library services for the blind and physically handicapped, including braille and recorded book production and machine repair. Carries profiles of the work of specific volunteer organizations and answers by braille instructors to questions about literary braille rules. *Type:* Newsletter.

NCompass

Nebraska Library Commission (NLC)
1200 N St., Ste. 120   Ph: (402)471-2045
Lincoln, NE 68508-2023   Free: 800-307-2665
                             Fax: (402)471-2083
URL: http://www.nlc.state.ne.us/public/ncom.html; http://www.nlc.state.ne.us/public/newslet.html.

Contact: Mary Jo Ryan, Editor, mjryan@neon.nlc.state.ne.us.

Desc: Serves as a medium of communication for libraries in Nebraska. Contains articles on programs and policies of the Commission, legislative developments, funding, interlibrary networking, and activities of local and regional libraries. *Type:* Newsletter.

Nevada Libraries

Nevada Library Association
Nevada State Library & Archives   Ph: (702)687-8322
100 N. Stewart St.   Fax: (702)687-8311
Carson City, NV 89701-4285

Contact: Holly Van Valkenburgh, Editor, hvanvalk@clan.lib.nv.us.

Desc: Serves as a vehicle of communication for the Association. Contains brief articles by members on aspects of librarianship, as well as news releases from the American Library Association and the Mountain Plains Library Association. *Type:* Newsletter.

New York Public Library News

New York Public Library
5th Ave. & 42nd St.   Ph: (212)221-7676
New York, NY 10018   Fax: (212)768-7439

Contact: Esther Harriott, Editor.

Desc: Informs re activities and developments at the Library, including educational programs, exhibitions, and recent acquisitions. *Type:* Newsletter.

A Newberry Newsletter

Newberry Library
60 W. Walton St.   Ph: (312)943-9090
Chicago, IL 60610   Fax: (312)943-1013
URL: http://www.newberry.org.

Contact: Vivienne Jones, Editor.

Desc: Reports on Library news of interest to the community: programs, projects, grants, fellowships, research, holdings, and discoveries in the collection. Contains items on the Library's four research centers: the Center for Renaissance Studies, the D'Arcy McNickle Center for the History of the American Indian, the Hermon Dunlap Smith Center for the History of Cartography, and the Family and Community History Center. *Type:* Newsletter.

News About Library Services for the Blind & Physically Handicapped

Department for the Blind & Physically Handicapped
South Carolina State Library
PO Box 821   Ph: (803)898-5900
Columbia, SC 29202   Free: 800-922-7818
                             Fax: (803)898-5907
E-mail: guynell@leo.SCSL.state.SC.US.

Contact: Naomi Bradey, Editor, naomi@leo.scsl.state.sc.us.

Desc: Provides information on services and products available to visually and physically impaired individuals. Includes information on new books available on cassette, record, and large print. *Type:* Newsletter.

News and Clues

San Joaquin Valley Library System
2420 Mariposa St.   Ph: (209)488-3229
Fresno, CA 93721
E-mail: sjvis@sjvls.lib.ca.us

Contact: David DeLaurant, Editor.

Desc: Newsletter for members of San Joaquin Valley library system. *Type:* Newsletter.

News for South Carolina Libraries

South Carolina State Library
PO Box 11469   Ph: (803)734-8666
Columbia, SC 29211   Fax: (803)734-8676
URL: http:///www.state.sc.us/scsl/.

Contact: Ann Addy, Editor, ann@leo.scsi.state.sc.us; Georgia Gillens, Layout.

Desc: Offers state-wide coverage of library news and developments, including adult and children's services. Carries brief notes on conferences, workshops, library courses, and grants. *Type:* Newsletter.

Newsletter of the Society of Maine Archivists

Society of Maine Archivists
The Edmund S. Muskie Archives
Bates College   Ph: (207)786-6354
70 Campus Ave.   Fax: (207)786-6035
Lewiston, ME 04240
E-mail: muskie@abacus.bates.edu

Contact: Chris Beam, Editor.

Desc: Reports on acquisitions, events relating to historical documentation, and grant information. Recurring features include a calendar of events, letters to the editor, news of research, reports of meetings and columns titled From the SMA President, From the Editor, and Tips for Archivists. *Type:* Newsletter.

Newspoke

Alaska Library Association
PO Box 81084   Ph: (907)479-4784
Fairbanks, AK 99708   Fax: (907)479-4784

Contact: Patience Frederickson, Editor.

Desc: Remarks: Computer Alaska State Library. *Type:* Newsletter.

Northern New Jersey Chapter of the CLA Newsletter

Catholic Library Association
Northern New Jersey Unit
Essex Catholic High School
135 Glenwood Ave.   Ph: (201)674-4200
East Orange, NJ 07017   Fax: (201)674-9121

Contact: Sr. Monica Donohoe, CSJP, Editor.

Desc: Provides information and news of interest to New Jersey chapter librarians in the Catholic Library Association. Recurring features include news of research, a calendar of events, reports of meetings, news of educational opportunities, and notices of publications available. *Type:* Newsletter.

Northwest Territories Registered Nurses' Association Newsletter

Northwest Territories Registered Nurses' Association (NWTRNA)
PO Box 2757   Ph: (867)873-2745
Yellowknife, NT, Canada X1A Fax: (867)873-2336
2R1

Contact: Donna Stanley, Editor.

Desc: Informs registered nurses of Association activities, provides a forum for discussion, and disseminates information of interest. Recurring features include notices of community education courses, a calendar of events, and reports of meetings. *Type:* Newsletter.

Nova Scotia Library Association Newsletter

Nova Scotia Library Association
c/o Nova Scotia Provincial   Ph: (902)424-2400
   Library   Fax: (902)424-0633
3770 Kempt Rd.
Halifax, NS, Canada B3K 4X8

Desc: Contains reports of meetings and columns titled President's Message, What's New, NSLA Board of Directors, and Interest Group Reports. *Type:* Newsletter.

NYLA Bulletin

New York Library Association
252 Hudson Ave.   Ph: (518)432-6952
Albany, NY 12210-1802   Free: 800-252-6952
                             Fax: (518)427-1697
E-mail: nyla.communications@pobox.com; nyla.communications@pobox.com.

Contact: Bruce Robertson, Editor.

Desc: Provides information of interest to library professionals. Brings news of legislation. *Type:* Newsletter.

OCLC Newsletter

OCLC Online Computer Library Center, Inc.
6565 Frantz Rd.   Ph: (614)764-6000
Dublin, OH 43017-0702   Free: 800-848-5878
                             Fax: (614)764-6096
E-mail: oclc@oclc.org
URL: http://www.oclc.org/; http://www.oclc.org.

Contact: Nita Dean, Editor, (614)761-5002, nita_dean@oclc.org; Bob Murphy, Editor, (614)761-5136, bob_murphy@oclc.org; George Promenschenkel, Editor, (614)761-5170, promensg@oclc.org.

Desc: Published as a service to users and potential users of OCLC automated library and information systems. Includes client news and information on Center activities. *Type:* Newsletter.

OCLC Online Union Catalog

OCLC Online Computer Library Center, Inc.
6565 Frantz Rd.   Ph: (614)764-6000
Dublin, OH 43017
E-mail: job@oclc.org
URL: http://www.oclc.org

Desc: Contains full bibliographic descriptions and cataloging information for more than 39 million books, serials, manuscripts, sound records, audiovisual materials, maps, music scores, and computer-readable files published worldwide. *Available:* OCLC Online Computer Library Center, Inc.; OCLC Online Computer Library Center, Inc., OCLC EPIC; OCLC Online Computer Library Center, Inc., OCLC FirstSearch Catalog; OCLC Online Computer Library Center, Inc., OCLC FirstSearch Catalog; STN International; STN International. *Type:* Database.

ODL Source

Oklahoma Department of Libraries
200 NE 18th St.   Ph: (405)521-2502
Oklahoma City, OK 73105   Free: 800-522-8116
    Fax: (405)348-0886
Contact: William Young, Editor; William Petrie, Contributor; Michelle Webb, Editor, mwebb@oltn.odl.state.ok. us.
Desc: Concerned with libraries and librarianship. Recurring features include news items, descriptions of library projects and programs, announcements, and a column titled Oklahoma Authors. *Type:* Newsletter.

OHIONET

1500 W. Lane Ave.   Ph: (614)486-2966
Columbus, OH 43221   Free: 800-686-8975
URL: http://www.ohionet.org
Contact: Michael P. Butler, Exec.Dir.
Desc: Libraries. Shares information services and resources; provides training for library automation systems. *Type:* Association.

The One-Person Library

Information Bridges International, Inc.
477 Harris Rd.   Ph: (216)486-7443
Cleveland, OH 44143   Fax: (216)486-8810
Contact: Judith A. Siess, Editor, jsiess@en.com.
Desc: Provides reports on the literature, management thoughts, case studies, book reviews, and general information for the librarian who works alone. Functions as a forum for the exchange of ideas and information for the reader. *Type:* Newsletter.

Online Libraries and Microcomputers

Information Intelligence, Inc. (III)
P.O. Box 31098   Ph: (602)996-2283
Phoenix, AZ 85046
E-mail: rhuleatt@infointelligence.com
URL: http://www.infointelligence.com/www/iii-info
Desc: Contains the complete text of Online Libraries and Microcomputers, a newsletter covering library online and automation applications (including the Internet), online databases, and microcomputers. Features news and trends, reviews of software and hardware, editorials, forthcoming meetings, publications, and new online/CD-ROM databases of interest to libraries. *Available:* The Dialog Corporation, DIALOG; The Dialog Corporation, DataStar; STN International; Bell & Howell Information and Learning; LEXIS-NEXIS; Dow Jones Interactive Publishing; Bell & Howell Information and Learning; European Information Network Services (EINS); Infonautics Corporation; CARL Corporation. *Type:* Database.

Open Mike

Lutheran Church Library Association
122 W. Franklin Ave.   Ph: (612)870-3623
Minneapolis, MN 55404   Fax: (612)870-0170
E-mail: lclahq@aol.com
Contact: Leanna Kloempken, Editor.
Desc: Serves as a liaison between chapter leaders and the Association's national office. Offers librarians program and workshop ideas, general library information, author lists, conference information, and free catalogs and bookmarks. *Type:* Newsletter.

Orange Seed

State Library of Florida
Florida Department of State
R. A. Gray Bldg.   Ph: (850)487-2651
Tallahassee, FL 32399-0250   Fax: (850)488-2746
URL: http://www.dlis.dos.state.fl.us/orange/index.htm.
Contact: Larry Nash White, Editor, lwhitemainel.dos. state.fl.us.
Desc: Reports the activities in libraries in Florida. Covers programs, awards, new publications funding, and staff news. *Type:* Newsletter.

The Outrider

Wyoming State Library
2301 Capitol Ave.   Ph: (307)777-5915
Cheyenne, WY 82009-0060   Fax: (307)777-6289
URL: http://www.wsl.state.wy.us/slpub/outrider/index. html.
Contact: Linn Rounds, Editor, lround@missc.state.wy.us.
Desc: Provides news about the activities of the Wyoming State Library, its board, other tax-supported libraries in the state, the American Library Association, and the library field in general. Recurring features include job listings, meetings, workshops, and other events; personnel news; reports on consultant activities and acquisitions news; and columns titled News Briefs, Around the State. *Type:* Newsletter.

PAM Bulletin

Physics-Astronomy-Mathematics Division
Special Libraries Association (SLA)
c/o Irene Laursen
Wellesley College
Science Library
Wellesley, MA 02181-8289
Contact: Thurston Miller, Editor; Irene Laursen, Asst. Ed.
Desc: Serves as the Division bulletin, providing news relating to "all aspects of librarianship in the fields of physics, astronomy, and mathematics," emphasizing "the control, dissemination, and retrieval of knowledge and information in these areas." Publishes notices of events of interest to members, including calls for papers, workshops, conferences, and relevant publications. Recurring features include news of research and of members, job listings, news of educational opportunities, and a column titled Message From the Chair. *Type:* Newsletter.

Pennsylvania Citizens for Better Libraries Newsletter

Pennsylvania Citizens for Better Libraries
502 Ellen Rd.   Free: 800-870-3858
Camp Hill, PA 17011-2018
E-mail: pcbl@shrsys.hslc.org
Contact: Lois Smith, Editor.
Desc: Monitors the various sources of support for Pennsylvania libraries. Provides reports on organization activities and members, an exchange of library program and resource ideas, and a calendar of events. *Type:* Newsletter.

PLL Perspectives

Sabrina I. Pacifici
1722 Eye St. NW   Ph: (202)736-8510
Washington, DC 20006   Fax: (202)736-8711
Contact: Sabrina I. Pacifici, Editor, spacific@cais.com.
Desc: Features articles and columns on management, technology, online research, legal research, and technical services for private firm and corporate librarians. Covers current federal legislation, copyright laws, and law librarianship. *Type:* Newsletter.

Polar Libraries Bulletin

Polar Libraries Colloquy
Byrd Polar Research Center
The Ohio State Univ.
1090 Carmack Rd., 176 Scott
    Hall
Columbus, OH 43210-1002
Contact: Lynn Lay, Editor.
Desc: Covers news and events of the Colloquy and the Alaska State Library. Recurring features include reports of meetings, notices of publications available and columns titled Polar News Notes and People in the News. *Type:* Newsletter.

The Primary Source

Society of Mississippi Archivists
PO Box 1151   Ph: (601)359-6889
Jackson, MS 39215-1151   Fax: (601)359-6964
E-mail: sboyd@mdah.state.ms.us; irmgard.wolfe@usm. edu
Contact: Mattie Sink, Editor.
Desc: Focuses on activities and trends in the archival and library community both regionally and nationally. Includes information on conservation and articles on state repositories and their holdings. *Type:* Newsletter.

Prospect Researcher's Guide to Biographical Research Collections

The Taft Group
27500 Drake Rd.   Ph: (248)699-4253
Farmington Hills, MI 48331-   Free: 800-347-GALE
    3535   Fax: (248)699-8097
E-mail: galeord@gale.com
URL: http://www.gale.com/taft/
Contact: Jane Kokernak, Editor.
Desc: Approximately 1,000 geographical, biographical, business, fund raising, newspaper, foundation, historical, and other special libraries in the U.S. with holdings on individuals and companies. *Type:* Directory.

The Public Library of Cincinnati and Hamilton County—Staff Notes

Staff Association
The Public Library of Cincinnati and Hamilton County
800 Vine St.   Ph: (513)369-6900
Cincinnati, OH 45202-2009
Contact: Uri Toch, Editor.
Desc: Reports Association meeting results, retiree news, and other staff information. Recurring features include a calendar of events, reports of meetings. *Type:* Newsletter.

The Reading Light

Library for the Blind and Physically Handicapped
Mississippi Library Commission
5455 Executive Pl.   Ph: (601)354-7208
Jackson, MS 39206-4104   Free: 800-446-0892
    Fax: (601)354-6077
E-mail: mlbph@mlc.lib.ms.us
Contact: Rahye Puckett, Editor, rahyep@mlc.lib.ms.us; John Whitlock, Editor, jwhit@mlc.lib.ms.us.
Desc: Provides information on special services, aids, recent publications, and locally-produced talking books which are not available through the Library of Congress. Reviews new aids and appliances, pertinent activities and events, staff members, and related organizations. *Type:* Newsletter.

REMARC

ISM Library Information Services
3300 Bloor St. W., 16th Fl.,   Ph: (416)236-7171
    West Tower
Etobicoke, ON, Canada M8X
    2X2
URL: http://www.ism.ca/lis/

Contact: Brian Morrell, Manager of Bibliographic Services, (416)236-7171, fax: (416)236-7489, bam@ag-canada.com.

Desc: A companion file to LC MARC that contains more than 3.7 million bibliographic records on works cataloged by the Library of Congress (LC) prior to 1979 that are not included in LC MARC. Covers items in English prior to 1968; in French, prior to 1973; in German, Spanish, and Portuguese, prior to 1975; in Dutch, Scandinavian, Italian, and Rumanian, prior to 1976; in other Roman alphabet languages, prior to 1977; and in non-Roman alphabet languages, prior to 1979. *Available:* The Dialog Corporation, DIALOG. *Type:* Database.

Research Libraries Group

1200 Villa St.   Ph: (650)962-9951
Mountain View, CA 94041-   Free: 800-537-RLIN
    1100   Fax: (650)964-0943
E-mail: bl.ric@rlg.bitnet

Contact: James P. Michalko, Pres.

Desc: Universities, archives, historical societies, museums, and related institutions devoted to improving access to information that supports research and learning. Maintains the Research Libraries Information Network (RLIN), an online bibliographic database of more than 22 million items, including books, serials, archival materials, maps, music scores, sound recordings, films, photographs, and computer-readable files. RLIN contains the Library of Congress Name Authority and Subject Authority Files, the Art and Architecture thesaurus, and special databases for 18th-century printed material, art auction catalogs, and library collection management. *Type:* Association.

Research Libraries Group News

Research Libraries Group
1200 Villa St.   Ph: (650)691-2208
Mountain View, CA 94041-   Fax: (650)964-0943
    1100

Contact: Hilary Hannon, Editor.

Desc: Reports news of the organization. *Type:* Newsletter.

River City Library Times

Evansville-Vanderburgh County Public Library
22 SE 5th St.   Ph: (812)428-8200
Evansville, IN 47708   Fax: (812)428-8397
E-mail: mau@evans.evcpl.lib.in.us.
URL: http://www.evcpl.lib.in.us.

Contact: Evelyn Walker, Editor, (812)428-8241, evelynw@evans.evcpl.lib.in.us.

Desc: Covers library news and events. Recurring features include a calendar of events and focus on different branches or departments. *Type:* Newsletter.

RLIN Focus

Research Libraries Group
1200 Villa St.   Ph: (650)691-2208
Mountain View, CA 94041-   Fax: (650)964-0943
    1100
URL: http://www.rig.org/r-focus.html.

Contact: Karen Smith-Yoshimura, Editor.

Desc: Contains information on computer-based services for libraries, archives, and their patrons. *Type:* Newsletter.

RUSA Update

Reference and User Services Association (RUSA)
American Library Association (ALA)
50 E. Huron St.   Ph: (312)280-4397
Chicago, IL 60611   Free: 800-545-2433
    Fax: (312)944-8085
E-mail: rusa@ala.org
URL: http://www.ala.org/rusa/update.

Contact: Beth Woodard, Editor, (217)244-1882, fax: (217)333-1116, bswoodar@uiuc.edu.

Desc: Serves as a vehicle for communication among RASD members, focusing on librarianship in areas of reference and adult services. Publishes news of the Division's activities and state, regional, and national news items of interest. *Type:* Newsletter.

SALALM Newsletter

SALALM Secretariat
Benson Latin American   Fax: (512)495-4488
    Collection
Sid Richardson Hall 1.109
The University of Texas at
    Austin
Austin, TX 78713

Contact: Laurence Hallewell, Editor.

Desc: Provides an international forum focused exclusively on Latin American library collection development and service. Recurring features include news about the Seminar; a message from the president; informational notes; book-dealer/publisher news; items on significant acquisitions, new periodicals, and reference tools; and reports on the annual conference. *Type:* Newsletter.

Saskatoon Public Library—Preface

Saskatoon Public Library
311 23rd St. E.   Ph: (306)975-7530
Saskatoon, SK, Canada S7K 0J6   Fax: (306)975-7766
Contact: Lynne Townsend, Editor, lynnet@charly.publib.saskatoon.sk.ca.

Desc: Lists and describes Library programs. Recurring features include a calendar of events and library news. *Type:* Newsletter.

School of Library and Information Science Newsletter

School of Library and Information Science
University of Iowa
3087 Library   Ph: (319)335-5707
Iowa City, IA 52242-1420   Fax: (319)335-5374
Contact: Ethel Bloesch, Editor, ethel-bloesch@uiowa.edu.

Desc: Publishes news of the Library School, including personnel changes, faculty notes, obituaries, awards, and fellowships received by students, and course information. Recurring features include a calendar of events and columns titled From the Director and Alumni Notes. *Type:* Newsletter.

SCRLC Reports Regional

South Central Research Library Council (SCRLC)
215 N. Cayuga St.   Ph: (607)273-9106
Ithaca, NY 14850   Fax: (607)272-0740
E-mail: scrlc@lakenet.org
Contact: Jean Currie, Editor, jcurric@lakenet.org.

Desc: Serves the reference and research needs of libraries in 14 counties in New York state. Includes regional news relating to council and member libraries. *Type:* Newsletter.

The Serials Directory, 13th Edition

EBSCO Publishing
10 Estes St.   Ph: (978)356-6500
Ipswich, MA 01938
E-mail: ep@epnet.com

Contact: Technical Support, fax: (508)535-8523, eptech@epnet.com.

Desc: Contains bibliographic and ordering information for more than 155,000 serials, annuals, and irregular serials published worldwide. Includes the complete CONSER Machine Readable Cataloging (MARC) record for each title, as well as publisher name, address, and price. *Available:* EBSCOhost. *Type:* Database.

SLA Chapter Notes

Special Libraries Association
1700 18th St. NW   Ph: (202)234-4700
Washington, DC 20009-2514   Fax: (202)234-2442
E-mail: sla@sla.org
URL: http://www.sla.org

Contact: Penny Heavner, Editor; Mary Nell Bryant, Editor.

Desc: Updates members on plans, accomplishments, and upcoming events of the Association. *Type:* Newsletter.

SLA Social Science Division - Special Libraries Association—Bulletin

SLA Social Science Division
Special Libraries Association (SLA)
c/o Jo-Ellen Vernall-Knoerl   Ph: (202)434-6244
American Association of Retired   Fax: (202)434-6408
    Persons
601 E St. NW
Washington, DC 20049
E-mail: jknoerl@aarp.org.

Contact: Olivia Pickett, Editor.

Desc: Contains news of the Division, the Association, and members. Recurring features include book reviews. *Type:* Newsletter.

Smiletter

Southcentral Minnesota Inter-Library Exchange (SMILE)
PO Box 3031   Ph: (507)625-7555
Mankato, MN 56002-3031   Fax: (507)625-4049

Contact: Lucy Lowry, Editor.

Desc: Highlights the programs and services of SMILE, a network of information centers and libraries in southcentral Minnesota. Recurring features include news of members and member libraries and a calendar of events. *Type:* Newsletter.

South End

Wayne State University
Reuther Library
5401 Cass Ave.   Ph: (313)577-4024
Detroit, MI 48202   Fax: (313)577-4300

Contact: William R. Gulley, Editor.

Desc: Reports Association news and news from national archives and repositories in Michigan. Carries feature items of interest to archivists. *Type:* Newsletter.

The Southeastern Librarian

Southeastern Library Association
PO Box 987
Tucker, GA 30085
E-mail: joe_b_forsee@solinet.net.

Desc: Discusses topics of interest to librarians in the Southeastern states, including children's literature, literacy, and the needs of special groups. Recurring features include news of members and a calendar of events. *Type:* Newsletter.

    Where To Go / Who To Ask

The Southwestern Archivist

Society of Southwest Archivists (SSA)
c/o Glenn L. McMullen   Ph: (504)388-6501
Louisiana State University   Fax: (504)334-1695
Hill Memorial Library
Special Collections
Baton Rouge, LA 70803
URL: http://www.tulane.edu//miller/speccoghomepage.
html.

Contact: Glenn L. McMullen, Editor.

Desc: Supports the aims of the Society, which include: "to
provide a means for effective cooperation among people
concerned with the documentation of human experience,"
and "to promote the adoption of sound principles and
standards for the preservation and administration of records." Recurring features include news of research, news
of members, and a calendar of events. *Type:* Newsletter.

Special Libraries Association

1700 18th St. NW   Ph: (202)234-4700
Washington, DC 20009-2514   Fax: (202)265-9317
E-mail: sla@sla.org
URL: http://www.sla.org/

Contact: David R. Bender, Ph.D., Exec.Dir.

Desc: International association of information professionals who work in special libraries serving business, research,
government, universities, newspapers, museums, and institutions that use or produce specialized information.
Seeks to advance the leadership role of special librarians.
Offers consulting services to organizations that wish to establish or expand a library or information services. *Type:*
Association.

Spotlight on Your Library

Dayton and Montgomery County Public Library
215 E. 3rd St.   Ph: (513)227-9500
Dayton, OH 45402

Contact: Mark Willis, Editor.

Desc: Provides current information on library services and
involvement in Montgomery County, Ohio. *Type:* Newsletter.

SRRT Newsletter

Social Responsibilities Round Table (SRRT)
American Library Association (ALA)
50 E. Huron St.   Ph: (312)944-6780
Chicago, IL 60611   Free: 800-545-2433
                             Fax: (312)440-9374

Contact: Carol Reid, Editor.

Desc: Reports on the efforts of the Round Table to increase
awareness about the responsibilities of libraries in relation
to current social problems which affect libraries and ways
in which they serve the public. Recurring features include
reports on Round Table task forces, book and periodical
reviews, and a column titled Coordinator's Memo. *Type:*
Newsletter.

State Library of Iowa—Footnotes

State Library of Iowa
E. 12th & Grand   Ph: (515)281-7574
Des Moines, IA 50319   Free: 800-248-4483
                             Fax: (515)281-6191

Contact: Annette Wetteland, Editor, awettel@mail.lib.
state.ia.us.

Desc: Reports on programs and services of the State Library of Iowa and carries news of interest to Iowa librarians and trustees. *Type:* Newsletter.

**Subject Directory of Special Libraries and
Information Centers**

Gale Group Inc.
27500 Drake Rd.   Ph: (248)699-4253
Farmington Hills, MI 48331- Free: 800-877-GALE
  3535   Fax: (248)699-8070
E-mail: galeord@galegroup.com
URL: http://www.galegroup.com.; http://www.gale.com.
Contact: Matthew Miskelly, Editor, matthew.miskelly@
gale.com.
Desc: In three volumes, approximately 14,000 special and
research libraries, information centers, archives, and data
centers maintained by government agencies, business, industry, newspapers, educational institutions, nonprofit organizations, and societies. Volume 1 covers business,
government, and law libraries; volume 2, computers, engineering, and science libraries; and volume 3, health science
libraries. *Type:* Directory.

TALL Newsletter

Toronto Association of Law Librarians (TALL)
c/o Toronto Document   Ph: (416)963-9723
  Exchange   Fax: (705)789-3671
PO Box 90
111 Richmond St. W, Ste. 200
Toronto, ON, Canada M5H
  2T4
E-mail: biculw@fmgmt.mgmt.utoronto.ca.
Desc: Emphasizes current developments in law librarianship, member news, and articles of interest to Toronto's
law library community. *Type:* Newsletter.

Technicalities

Media Periodicals
1102 Grand, 23rd Fl.   Ph: (816)842-8111
Kansas City, MO 64106   Free: 800-243-5201
                             Fax: (816)842-8188
E-mail: trozzolo@aol.com.
Contact: Sheila S. Intner, Editor.
Desc: Presents discussion, opinions, and reviews on library
management topics, including computer applications, online services, library budgets, serials and preservation management, collection building, automation, software,
library marketplace trends, and the Library of Congress.
Type: Newsletter.

Tennessee Archivist

Society of Tennessee Archivists
c/o Tennessee State Library & Ph: (615)741-2561
  Archives   Fax: (615)741-6471
403 Seventh Ave. N.
Nashville, TN 37243-0312
E-mail: dmartinson@juno.com
URL: http://www.arkay.net/tnarchivist/.
Contact: David R. Sowell, Editor, drsowell@earthlink.net.
Desc: Provides information on state and national archival
activities. Announces professional meetings and work-
shops, archival job openings, and new collections. *Type:*
Newsletter.

Third Indicator

*Bibliographical Center for Research, Rocky
Mountain Region, Inc.*
14394 E. Evans Ave.   Ph: (303)751-6277
Aurora, CO 80014-1478   Free: 800-392-1552
                             Fax: (303)751-9787
E-mail: admin@bcr.org
URL: http://www.bcr.org.
Contact: Janice Mitchell Campau, Editor, jcampau@bcr.
org.
Desc: Provides articles and information concerning the
Online Computer Library Center (OCLC) and library au-
tomation. *Type:* Newsletter.

Tracings

School of Library and Information Studies
University of Oklahoma
401 W. Brooks, Rm. 120   Ph: (405)325-3921
Norman, OK 73019   Free: 800-522-0772
                             Fax: (405)325-7648
E-mail: slisinfo@lists.ou.edu
Contact: Linda Pye, Editor.
Desc: Provides news and information about the library
school and its faculty, students, and alumni. Recurring
features include notices of grants and scholarships, reports
of various library association meetings, and a calendar of
events. *Type:* Newsletter.

Trails

Texas State Library and Archives Commission
PO Box 12927   Ph: (512)936-4636
Austin, TX 78711   Fax: (512)463-5436
E-mail: info@tsl.state.tx.us
URL: http://www.tsl.state.tx.us/plo/about/news.html;
www.tsl.state.tx.us.
Contact: Nancy Webb, Editor.
Desc: Covers library technology and techniques. Reports
general statewide library news. *Type:* Newsletter.

Treasures

Reynolds Historical Library
University of Alabama at Birmingham
1700 University Blvd.   Ph: (205)934-4475
Birmingham, AL 35294   Fax: (205)975-8476
E-mail: sbabinsa@uab.edu; fharkins@uab.edu.
Desc: Provides news of the Library, a collection of rare
books on the health sciences. Carries notices of financial
donations, lists of new books, a calendar of events, and a
column focusing on the Library's lecture series. *Type:*
Newsletter.

Trustee Voice

American Library Trustee Association (ALTA)
50 E. Huron St.   Ph: (312)280-2161
Chicago, IL 60611   Free: 800-545-2433
                             Fax: (312)280-3257
Contact: Tari Marshall Sliz, Editor.
Desc: Carries articles on the various responsibilities and
duties of library trustees and public library trusteeship.
Provides news of Association programs. *Type:* Newsletter.

UCSD Libraries Newsletter

Friends of the UCSD Libraries
University of California, San Ph: (619)534-2533
  Diego   Fax: (619)534-5950
9500 Gilman Dr.
La Jolla, CA 92093-0175
Contact: Lynda Claassen, Editor.
Desc: Covers the intellectual, social, and business activities
of the Library and the Friends of the Libraries. Reports on
library issues, lectures, staff appointments, new acquisi-
tions, and library events. *Type:* Newsletter.

ULC Exchange

ULC Exchange
1603 Orrington Ave., Ste. 1080 Ph: (847)866-9999
Evanston, IL 60201   Fax: (847)866-9989
E-mail: ulc@gpl.glenview.lib.il.us
Contact: Linda Crusimond, Editor, (727)937-2974, fax:
(727)943-7508.
Desc: Covers federal, state, and local developments con-
cerning urban libraries. Reports projects and programs un-
dertaken by urban libraries and items of interest to
Council members. *Type:* Newsletter.

UMI Info Store

Bell & Howell Information and Learning
300 N. Zeeb Rd.   Ph: (734)761-4700
PO Box 1346
Ann Arbor, MI 48106-1346
E-mail: info@umi.com
URL: http://www.umi.com
Desc: Contains full bibliographic descriptions of more than 15,000 periodicals and serials from which articles can be ordered from UMI. Publications cover such topics as chemistry, computer science, earth sciences, engineering, life sciences, mathematics, medicine, physics, arts, business and management, communications, current events, economics, education, general interest, history, and nursing. *Available:* Ovid Technologies, Inc.; BT North America, Inc.; The Dialog Corporation, DIALOG; STN International. *Type:* Database.

The U*N*A*B*A*S*H*E*D Librarian

Marvin H. Scilken
GPO Box 2631   Ph: (212)255-2429
New York, NY 10116-2631   Fax: (212)691-3807
Contact: Marvin H. Scilken, MLS, Editor; Mary P. Scilken, Ph.D., Editor.
Desc: Carries practical library ideas and library humor, with innovative ideas concerning library procedures and forms. Recurring features include parodies and poetry. *Type:* Newsletter.

United States Newspaper Program (USNP) Database

U.S. National Foundation on the Arts and the Humanities
National Endowment for the Humanities
Division of Preservation and Access
OPO 411   Ph: (202)606-8570
1100 Pennsylvania Ave., N.W.
Washington, DC 20506
E-mail: preservation@neh.gov
Contact: Jeffrey Field, Deputy Director, Division of Preservation and Access, (202)606-8570, fax: (202)606-8639, preservation@neh.gov.
Desc: Contains complete bibliographic descriptions and holdings information for newspaper titles published in the United States from 1690 to date. Expected to hold more than 150,000 unique titles when the database is completed. *Available:* OCLC Online Computer Library Center, Inc. *Type:* Database.

University of Iowa Libraries Newsletter

Friends of the University of Iowa Libraries
University of Iowa
c/o Main Library   Ph: (319)335-5871
Iowa City, IA 52242
Contact: Jeffrey Dodd, Editor.
Desc: Supplies news of recent noteworthy events within the library system. Carries articles on special collections, specific titles, private presses, cataloging, automation, and developments in the consortium Research Libraries Group, Inc. *Type:* Newsletter.

USBE

United States Book Exchange (USBE)
2969 W. 25th St.   Ph: (216)241-6960
Cleveland, OH 44113-5332   Fax: (216)241-6966
E-mail: usbe@usbe.com
Contact: Victoria Nann, Editor.
Desc: Features the activities of the Exchange. Recurring features include letters to the editor, interviews, and reports of meetings. *Type:* Newsletter.

Vermont Department of Libraries Newsletter

Vermont Department of Libraries
109 State St.   Ph: (802)828-3261
Montpelier, VT 05609-0601   Fax: (802)828-2199
URL: http://dol.state.vt.us.
Contact: Marianne Kotch, Editor, mkotch@dol.state.vt.us.
Desc: Specializes in library-related news of interest to librarians, legislators, and citizens of Vermont. Recurring features include a calendar of events, a list titled Changes to Vermont Library Directory, and columns focusing on children's and special services. *Type:* Newsletter.

The Volunteer Libraries and Volunteer Librarians

Association of Private Libraries, Residential Collections
66 Frankfort St., Apt. 2G   Ph: (212)732-4461
New York, NY 10038-1622
Contact: Sophie Mitrisin, Editor.
Desc: Provides news items and views on topics concerning the development and application of book ownership and personal libraries, including such issues as arrangement and organizational problems, housing, use, and eventual disposition of books. Recurring features include news of members, news of research, and news of educational opportunities. *Type:* Newsletter.

WCLC News & Views

Western Connecticut Library Council (WCLC)
PO Box 1284   Ph: (203)577-4010
Middlebury, CT 06762   Fax: (203)577-4015
Contact: Anita Barney, Editor, abarney@wclc.org.
Desc: Functions as a vehicle for the Council, which seeks "to improve and expand the library services and the associated cultural, educational, and informational facilities available to the residents of western Connecticut." Covers concerns of interest to Council members, including national, regional, and local activities, workshops, and meetings. *Type:* Newsletter.

Western Plains Library System Newsletter

Western Plains Library System
PO Box 1027   Ph: (405)323-0974
Clinton, OK 73601
E-mail: wplssc@brightoh.net
Contact: Dee Ann Ray, Editor.
Desc: Covers activities and service programs of the Library system. Recurring features include a calendar of events and book reviews. *Type:* Newsletter.

Who's Who in Special Libraries

Special Libraries Association
1700 18th St. NW   Ph: (202)234-4700
Washington, DC 20009-2514   Fax: (202)234-2442
E-mail: sla@sla.org; whoswho@sla.org.
URL: http://www.sla.org; http://www.sla.org.
Contact: Susan Broughton, Editor, susan-b@sla.org.
Desc: About 14,000 librarians of libraries and special collections having a specific subject focus. *Type:* Directory.

Wilson Name Authority File

H.W. Wilson Company
950 University Ave.   Ph: (718)588-8400
Bronx, NY 10452
E-mail: custserv@hwwilson.com
URL: http://www.hwwilson.com
Contact: Technical Support Department., techmail@info.hwwilson.com.
Desc: Contains more than 650,000 references to the preferred forms of personal names, corporate names, and selected publication titles as they are used in databases and publications of The H.W. Wilson Company. *Available:* H.W. Wilson Company, WilsonWeb. *Type:* Database.

Wisconsin Library Association Newsletter

Wisconsin Library Association
5250 E. Terrace Dr., Ste. A1   Ph: (608)245-3640
Madison, WI 53718-5215   Fax: (608)245-3646
Contact: James A. Gollata, Editor.
Desc: Provides news of Association activities, meetings, conferences, and awards and honors involving the members. Recurring features include reports on officers and units of the Association. *Type:* Newsletter.

Literacy

Children's Literacy Initiative

Linda Katz and Marcia Moon
2314 Market St.   Ph: (215)561-4676
Philadelphia, PA 19103   Fax: (215)561-4677
E-mail: clibooks@aol.com
Contact: Linda Katz, Co-Dir.
Desc: Works to encourage emergent literacy skills of young children by providing training workshops for teachers, parents, and caregivers who serve low-income children. *Type:* Association.

Laubach Literacy International

Box 131, 1320 Jamesville Ave.   Ph: (315)422-9121
Syracuse, NY 13210   Free: 888-528-2224
                            Fax: (315)422-6369
E-mail: info@laubach.org
URL: http://www.laubach.org
Contact: Robert F. Caswell, Pres. & CEO.
Desc: Seeks to reduce adult illiteracy worldwide. Motivates and supports teaching of the world's estimated 965 million illiterate adults and older youths to a level of listening, speaking, reading, writing, and basic computational skills enabling them to solve their daily problems. Laubach sponsors more than 1100 literacy programs in the US and 71 partner programs in 36 developing countries worldwide. *Type:* Association.

Literacy Volunteers of America

635 James St.   Ph: (315)472-0001
Syracuse, NY 13203-2241   Fax: (315)472-0002
E-mail: lvanat@aol.com
Contact: Marsha L. Tait, Pres.
Desc: Trains and aids individuals and organizations to tutor adults in basic literacy and English as a second language. Provides training materials and services on national scale to literacy tutorial programs utilizing volunteers. Compiles statistics. *Type:* Association.

Literature

B.C. Bookworld

B.C. Bookworld
3516 West 13th Ave.   Ph: (604)736-4011
Vancouver, BC, Canada V6R   Fax: (604)736-4011
2S3
E-mail: bcbook@portal.ca.
Contact: Alan Twigg, Publisher; David Lester, Editor.
Desc: Newspaper presenting lively news coverage of books related to British Columbia. *Type:* Periodical.

Books

San Diego Union-Tribune
PO Box 191   Ph: (619)293-1531
San Diego, CA 92112   Free: 800-244-6397
                            Fax: (619)293-2432
Contact: Arthur Salm, Books Ed., (619)293-1321, fax: (619)293-2436, arthur.salm@uniontrib.com; Al Lacranaga, Advertising Mgr.
Desc: Newspaper covering current trends in books. *Type:* Periodical.

Children's Literature Awards and Winners: A Directory of Prizes, Authors, and Illustrators

Gale Group Inc.

27500 Drake Rd.   Ph: (248)699-4253
Farmington Hills, MI 48331-   Free: 800-877-GALE
3535   Fax: (248)699-8070
E-mail: galeord@galegroup.com
URL: http://www.galegroup.com.

Contact: Dolores B. Jones, Editor.

Desc: 300 awards granted for children's literature, including discontinued awards. *Type:* Directory.

Colorado Review

Colorado State Unversity
Department of English
Fort Collins, CO 80523   Ph: (970)491-5449
E-mail: creview@vines.colostate.edu.

Contact: David Milofsky, Editor; Karen Olson, Managing Editor; Nanette Rogers, Managing Editor; Jorie Graham, Poetry Editor; Donald Revell, Poetry Editor.

Desc: Magazine covering poetry, fiction, nonfiction, and reviews. *Type:* Periodical.

IDEALS

Ideals Publications Inc.
535 Metroplex Dr., Ste. 250   Ph: (615)333-0478
Nashville, TN 37211   Fax: (615)781-1447

Contact: Lisa Ragan, Editor; Patricia Pingry, Publisher.

Desc: Magazine containing poetry and short prose pieces thematically related to seasons and holidays. *Type:* Periodical.

International Graphoanalysis Society

111 N. Canal St.   Ph: (312)930-9446
Chicago, IL 60606   Fax: (312)930-5903
E-mail: headquarters@igas.com
URL: http://www.igas.com

Contact: Kathleen Kusta, Pres.

Desc: Handwriting analysts and identification experts. Maintains hall of fame, speakers' bureau, and 5000 volume library on subjects such as psychology and identification. Compiles statistics; conducts research programs, specialized education, and placement service. *Type:* Association.

Lambda Iota Tau

Bruce W. Hozeski
Ball State University   Ph: (765)285-8456
Department of English   Fax: (765)285-3765
2000 W. University Ave.
Muncie, IN 47306-0460
E-mail: 00bwhozeski@bsuvc.bsu.edu
URL: http://www.bsu.edu/english/lit

Contact: Prof. Bruce W. Hozeski, Exec.Sec. Treas.

Desc: Literature honor society comprised of men and women. Literature of all modern languages. *Type:* Association.

Mississippi Review

University of Southern Mississippi
Box 5144, Southern Sta.
Hattiesburg, MS 39406-5144

Contact: Frederick Barthelme, Editor; Rie Fortenberry, Managing Editor.

Desc: Literary magazine covering poetry, fiction and interviews. *Type:* Periodical.

MLA International Bibliography

Modern Language Association of America (MLA)
10 Astor Place   Ph: (212)614-6350
New York, NY 10003
E-mail: danielle.uchitelle@mla.org

Contact: Daniel Uchitelle, Director, Center for Information Services, (212)614-6350, fax: (212)477-9863, daniel@mla.org.

Desc: Contains more than one million citations to scholarly (both theoretical and descriptive) literature in linguistics, modern languages, literature, and folklore gathered from 3500 journals, series, books, and essay collections. Provides information on comparative and historical linguistics, specific languages (including composite and derivative languages), and other communicative behavior. *Available:* OCLC Online Computer Library Center, Inc., OCLC EPIC; OCLC Online Computer Library Center, Inc., OCLC FirstSearch Catalog; Ovid Technologies, Inc. *Type:* Database.

The Monthly

Klaber Publishing Corp.
1301 59th St.   Ph: (510)658-9811
Emeryville, CA 94608   Fax: (510)658-9902
E-mail: themonthly@aol.com.

Contact: Tim Devaney, Editor; Karen Klaber, Publisher.

Desc: General interest magazine emphasizing food, health, science, the environment, entertainment, personal essays, interviews, investigative features, and local history. *Type:* Periodical.

National Story League

c/o Virginia Dare Shope   Ph: (814)942-3449
1342 4th Ave. Juniata
Altoona, PA 16601-6131

Contact: Alice Brynteson, Pres.

Desc: Teachers, social workers, librarians, Sunday school teachers, and others interested in children's work. "To encourage the creation and appreciation of the good and beautiful in life and literature through the art of storytelling." Seeks to discover the "best" stories in the world's literature and tell them to young people with love and sympathy. *Type:* Association.

The New York Review of Books

The New York Review of Books
1755 Broadway, 5th Fl.   Ph: (212)757-8070
New York, NY 10019-3780   Fax: (212)333-5374
E-mail: nyrev@nybooks.com; nyrev@panix.com.
URL: http://www.nybooks.com.

Contact: Robert Silvers, Editor; Barbara Epstein, Editor; Rea S. Hederman, Publisher; Catherine Tice, Assoc. Pub.

Desc: Literary, cultural, and political magazine. *Type:* Periodical.

Papyrus

Papyrus Literary Enterprises
102 LaSalle Rd.
PO Box 27097
West Hartford, CT 06127-0797
E-mail: readersndex.com/ple
URL: http://www.readersndex.com/papyrus.

Contact: Ginger Whitaker, Contact, gwhitaker@imagine.com.

Desc: Magazine featuring African American poetry, fiction, and non-fiction. Accepts book reviews. *Type:* Periodical.

Tiptoe Literary Service

27 Wildwood Ln.   Ph: (360)484-7722
PO Box 206
Naselle, WA 98638-0206
E-mail: anne@willapabay.org.

Contact: Anne Grimm-Richardson, Author.

Desc: Distributes title updates and manuscript information. *Alt. Contact:* 27 Wildwood Ln., PO Box 206, Naselle, WA 98638-0206; telephone: (360)484-7722. *Type:* Periodical.

Utne Reader

Lens Publishing Co., Inc.
1624 Harmon Pl., Ste. 330   Ph: (612)338-5040
Minneapolis, MN 55403
E-mail: info@utne.com.

Contact: Cathy Madison, Editor, editor@utne.com; Eric Utne, Chm., utne@utne.com; Jeanne Gallaher, Circulation Dir., gallaher@utne.com; Tom McKusick, Advertising Dir., mctom@utne.com; Robert Welsch, President.

Desc: Digest of original articles and material reprinted from alternative and independent media. Keeps readers abreast of new ideas and emerging issues. *Type:* Periodical.

Livestock

The AAMP Capitol Line Up

American Association of Meat Processors
1 Meating Pl.   Ph: (717)367-1168
PO Box 269   Fax: (717)367-9096
Elizabethtown, PA 17022-2883
E-mail: aamp@aamp.com

Contact: Stephen F. Krut, Editor.

Desc: Provides information for Association members on legislative news and topics affecting the industry. *Type:* Newsletter.

AAMPlifier

American Association of Meat Processors
1 Meating Pl.   Ph: (717)367-1168
PO Box 269   Fax: (717)367-9096
Elizabethtown, PA 17022-2883
E-mail: aamp@aamp.com

Contact: Anne B. Tantum, Editor, anntan@aamp.com; Bernard Shire, Editor.

Desc: Covers association meetings, news of members, industry trends and guidelines, the activities of related organizations, legislative happenings, and regulatory affairs. *Type:* Newsletter.

The American CattleWoman

American National CattleWomen, Inc.
5420 S. Quebec   Ph: (303)694-0313
PO Box 3881   Fax: (303)694-0313
Englewood, CO 80155

Contact: Julie Walker, Exec. Dir.

Desc: Promotes ANCW programs and membership. *Type:* Newsletter.

American Cavy Breeders Association

Lenore J. Gergen
16540 Hogan Ave.   Ph: (651)437-9746
Hastings, MN 55033-9576   Fax: (651)438-9928
E-mail: cavyclub@aol.com
URL: http://www.dfs.netten.net/ACBA

Contact: Rachel Fair, Pres.

Desc: Promotes cavies (guinea pigs) and cavy breeding. Sponsors youth club. *Type:* Association.

American Dairy Goat Association

PO Box 865   Ph: (828)286-3801
Spindale, NC 28160   Fax: (828)287-0476
E-mail: adgajdw2@aol.com
URL: http://www.adga.org

Contact: Ronald E. Gelvin, Sec.-Treas.

Desc: Breeders, owners, and dairymen interested in French Alpine, Nubian, Saanen, Toggenburg, LaMancha, and Oberhasli dairy goats. Maintains registry for purebred dairy goats, showing ownership, transfers, and pedigree records. *Type:* Association.

American Donkey and Mule Society

2901 N. Elm St. Ph: (940)382-6845
Denton, TX 76201 Fax: (940)484-8417
E-mail: adms@juno.com
URL: http://www.donkeys.com
Contact: Leah Patton, Off.Mgr.
Desc: Individuals and local organizations working to protect and promote the donkey and the mule and to provide services for their owners and clubs, disseminate information, and coordinate international activities. Maintains American Mule and Donkey Register (stud book) and national show standards; certifies inspector-judges and conducts teaching clinics for them. *Type:* Association.

American Egg Board

1460 Renaissance Dr., Ste. 301 Ph: (708)296-7043
Park Ridge, IL 60068 Fax: (708)296-7007
Contact: Louis B. Raffel, Pres.
Desc: Board of American egg producers appointed by the Secretary of Agriculture. Offers advertising, educational, research, and promotional programs designed to increase consumption of eggs and egg products. *Type:* Association.

American Meat Institute Newsletter

American Meat Institute
PO Box 3556 Ph: (703)841-2400
Washington, DC 20007 Fax: (703)527-0938
Contact: Janet M. Riley, Editor.
Desc: Contains news of legislative and government regulations and actions relevant to the meat industry. Recurring features include Institute news and livestock and slaughter reports. *Type:* Newsletter.

American Rabbit Breeders Association

PO Box 426 Ph: (309)664-7500
Bloomington, IL 61702 Fax: (309)664-0941
E-mail: arbapost@aol.com
URL: http://www.arba.net
Contact: Glen C. Carr, Sec.
Desc: Promotes, encourages, and development of the domestic rabbit industry and fancy which includes registration, showing, pets, and commerical purposes. *Type:* Association.

American Royal Association

1701 American Royal Ct. Ph: (816)221-9800
Kansas City, MO 64102 Fax: (816)221-8189
E-mail: americanroyal@americanroyal.com
URL: http://www.americanroyal.com
Contact: James D. Taylor, Exec.VP.
Desc: Business firms and individuals are sponsors. Seeks to further livestock breeds and the agricultural industry through the annual American Royal Livestock, Horse Show and Rodeo. *Type:* Association.

American Sheep Industry Association

6911 S. Yosemite St., Ste. 200 Ph: (303)771-3500
Englewood, CO 80112-1414 Fax: (303)771-8200
URL: http://www.sheepusa.org
Contact: Peter Orwick, Exec.Dir.
Desc: Producers of sheep and wool. Goal is to advance the standards and profitability of the sheep industry. *Type:* Association.

American Silkie Bantam Club Newsletter

American Silkie Bantam Club
14920 Nation Rd. Ph: (816)628-3690
Kearney, MO 64060-8115
E-mail: asbc@onehst.com
Contact: Valerie Hirvela, Editor, (813)676-0066, fax: (813)621-2510, vhirvela@mindspring.com.
Desc: Carries news items on the American Silkie Bantam chicken and the people involved in raising and showing them. *Type:* Newsletter.

BEEF

Webb Division, Intertec Publishing Corp.
7900 International Dr., 3rd Fl. Ph: (612)851-9329
Minneapolis, MN 55425-1510 Free: 800-722-5334
  Fax: (612)851-4601
E-mail: beef@intertec.com.
URL: http://www.homefarm.com.
Contact: Joe Roybal, Editor; Wayne Bollum, Publisher.
Type: Periodical.

Beef Business Bulletin

National Cattlemen's Association
5420 S. Quebec St. Ph: (303)694-0305
Greenwood Village, CO 80111 Fax: (303)694-2851
URL: http://www.beef.org.
Contact: Curt Olson, Editor; Brett Erickson, Advertising Mgr.
Desc: Covers the cattle industry. *Type:* Newsletter.

Beef Today

Farm Journal, Inc.
Centre Square W. Ph: (215)557-8900
1500 Market St., 28th Fl. Free: 800-523-1538
Philadelphia, PA 19102-2148 Fax: (215)568-4238
Contact: Dale E. Smith, President; Roger D. Randall, Publisher; Bill Miller, Editor.
Desc: Magazine for farmers and ranchers raising beef cows, feeders, and backgrounder cattle. *Alt. Contact:* RR 1, Box 51, Council Grove, KS 66846; telephone: (316)767-7041; fax: (316)767-7028. *Type:* Periodical.

Capitol Line-Up

American Association of Meat Processors
1 Meating Pl. Ph: (717)367-1168
PO Box 269 Fax: (717)367-9096
Elizabethtown, PA 17022-2883
E-mail: aamp@aamp.com
Contact: Bernard F. Shire, Editor, bernie@aamp.com.
Desc: Features news and information on meat products, issues brought up by the United States Department of Agriculture (USDA) and its Food Safety and Inspection Service (FSIS), and current market conditions. Recurring features include news of research, a calendar of events, reports of meetings, and legislative and regulatory news. *Type:* Newsletter.

Dairy Goat Journal

Dave Thompson
PO Box 10 Ph: (920)648-8285
128 E. Lake St. Fax: (920)648-3770
Lake Mills, WI 53551
Contact: Dave Thompson, Publisher.
Type: Directory.

Drovers

Vance Publishing Corp.
10901 W. 84th Terrace Ph: (913)438-8700
Lenexa, KS 66214 Free: 800-252-1925
  Fax: (913)438-0690
E-mail: ghenderson@drovers.com.
Contact: Greg Henderson, Assoc. Pub./Editor; Warren E. Morse, Publisher.
Desc: Trade magazine on beef cattle production and marketing. *Type:* Periodical.

Egg Report

Poultry Division
Market News Branch
U.S. Department of Agriculture (USDA)
210 Walnut St., Rm. 951 Ph: (515)284-4471
Des Moines, IA 50309 Fax: (515)284-4468
URL: http://www.ams.usda.gov/marketnews.htm.

Type: Newsletter.

Finnsheep Short Tales

Finnsheep Breeders Association
PO Box 260 Ph: (414)646-5845
Dousman, WI 53118 Fax: (414)646-5845
Contact: Sandra M. De Master, Editor.
Desc: Covers the raising, breeding, and marketing of Finnsheep, a breed of sheep known for prolificacy, early sexual maturity, out of season lambing, lambing ease and vigor, and soft, lustrous wool. Reports on sales of sheep and provides information on purebred and crossbred Finnsheep. *Type:* Newsletter.

Georgia Livestock

Livestock and Seed Division
Agricultural Marketing Service
U.S. Department of Agriculture (USDA)
South Bldg., Rm. 2613 Ph: (202)720-6231
PO Box 96456 Fax: (202)690-3732
Washington, DC 20090-6456
Contact: Ernie Morgan, Editor.
Desc: Reports on meat statistics in Georgia. Provides information on cattle auctions, slaughter and feeder classes, direct sales, and price and markets. *Type:* Newsletter.

Hogs Today

Farm Journal, Inc.
Centre Square W. Ph: (215)557-8900
1500 Market St., 28th Fl. Free: 800-523-1538
Philadelphia, PA 19102-2148 Fax: (215)568-4238
Contact: Dale E. Smith, President; Roger D. Randall, Publisher; Dean Houghton, Editor.
Desc: Agricultural magazine for hog managers and producers. *Alt. Contact:* PO Box 164A, Polo, MO 64671; telephone: (816)586-5641. *Type:* Periodical.

International Single Comb Black Minorca Club

Gerald Franklin Wright
721 Church St. Ph: (716)287-4417
Medina, NY 14103
Contact: Gerald Franklin Wright, Sec.-Treas.
Desc: Breeders of exhibition black minorca poultry. Sponsors competitions; compiles statistics. *Type:* Association.

Interstate Producers Livestock Association

1705 W. Luthy Dr. Ph: (309)691-5360
Peoria, IL 61615 Fax: (309)691-3891
Contact: E. J. Strasma, Exec.VP.
Desc: Cooperative marketing organization for livestock producers in the Midwest. *Type:* Association.

Iowa Pork Producers

Iowa Pork Producers Association
Box 71009 Ph: (515)225-7675
Clive, IA 50325 Free: 800-372-7675
  Fax: (515)225-0563
Contact: Peter Theodore, IPPA, Editor and Publisher.
Desc: Reports on news and activities of the Association. *Type:* Newsletter.

Lean Trimmings

National Meat Association
1970 Broadway, Ste. 825 Ph: (510)763-1533
Oakland, CA 94612 Fax: (510)763-6186
E-mail: nma@hooked.net
URL: http://www.nmaonline.org.
Contact: Jeremy Russell, Editor.
Desc: Deals with the latest regulatory and business news on the meat industry. Recurring features include news of research, a calendar of events, reports of meetings, job listings, and sections on members, labor relations, and marketing trends. *Type:* Newsletter.

Livestock Marketing Association

7509 Tiffany Springs Pky.   Ph: (816)891-0502
Kansas City, MO 64153-2315   Free: 800-821-2048
    Fax: (816)891-0552
Contact: James E. Frost, Gen.Mgr.
Desc: Livestock marketing businesses and livestock dealers. Sponsors annual World Livestock Auctioneer Championships. Offers management and promotional services. *Type:* Association.

Livestock Price Outlook

University of Illinois
ACES Newsletter Service
69 Mumford Hall   Ph: (217)244-5166
1301 W. Gregory Dr.
Urbana, IL 61801
Contact: Chris Hurt, Editor.
Desc: Provides "forecasts of prices and production for hogs and cattle following inventory reports. Includes inventory data, forecasting methods and discussions of pricing strategies." Remarks: Devotes four issues to hogs; two to cattle; and two issues to developments in livestock markets and marketing methods. *Type:* Newsletter.

Livestock Publications Council—Actiongram

Livestock Publications Council (LPC)
910 Currie St.   Ph: (817)336-1130
Fort Worth, TX 76107   Fax: (817)336-5233
Contact: Diane Johnson, Editor, diane@weblifepro.com.
Desc: Concentrates on news, personalities, and developments in the livestock publishing industry. Carries job listings, news of educational opportunities, and information on Council activities and members. *Type:* Newsletter.

Livestock Review

California Agricultural Statistics Service
U.S. Department of Agriculture (USDA)
PO Box 1258   Ph: (916)654-0895
Sacramento, CA 95812
Desc: Presents information on livestock inventories, intentions and prices, pasture, slaughter, and on-feed data for cattle and sheep. *Type:* Newsletter.

Meat Sheet

Dr. William Albanos Jr.
Box 124   Ph: (630)963-2252
Westmont, IL 60559-0124   Fax: (630)963-2980
Contact: Ann Fisher, Editor; Deborah Ash, Editor; Bob Brown, Editor; Tiffany Albanos, Sales Mgr.
Desc: Reports meat prices and statistical information. Recurring features include news of research. *Type:* Newsletter.

Mohair Council of America

BOX 5337   Ph: (915)655-3161
San Angelo, TX 76902   Free: 800-583-3161
    Fax: (915)655-4761
Contact: Zane Willard, Exec.Dir.
Desc: Mohair growers throughout the U.S. Promotes the use of mohair. Maintains fabric library; conducts cooperative advertising and promotion with mills, manufacturers, and retailers. *Type:* Association.

National Carlot Meat Trade Report

Livestock and Seed Division
Agricultural Marketing Service
210 Walnut St., Rm. 767   Ph: (515)284-4460
Des Moines, IA 50309-2106   Fax: (515)284-4231
Contact: Mike Erwin, Editor.
Desc: Reports on meat and hide statistics. Include markets and prices. *Type:* Newsletter.

National Chicken Council

1015 15th ST. NW, Ste. 930   Ph: (202)296-2622
Washington, DC 20005   Fax: (202)293-4005
E-mail: wroenigk@chickenusa.org
Contact: George B. Watts, Pres.
Desc: Membership includes producers and processors of broiler chickens; distributors and allied industry. *Type:* Association.

National Chicken Council—Washington Report

National Chicken Council
1015 15th St. NW, Ste. 930   Ph: (202)296-2622
Washington, DC 20005   Fax: (202)293-4005
E-mail: ncc@chickenusa.org
Contact: Margaret Ernst, Editor.
Desc: Centers on issues affecting the marketing of poultry for the broiler processing industry. Covers government actions, export markets, and grain supplies. *Type:* Newsletter.

National Hereford Hog Record Association Newsletter

National Hereford Hog Record Association
Rte. 1   Ph: (605)997-2116
Box 37   Fax: (605)997-2116
Flandreau, SD 57028-0037
Contact: Ruby Schrecengost, Editor.
Desc: Features national sale results and hog breeder's winnings. Lists transfers and registrations. *Type:* Newsletter.

National Hog Farmer

Webb Division, Intertec Publishing Corp.
7900 International Dr., 3rd Fl.   Ph: (612)851-9329
Minneapolis, MN 55425-1510   Free: 800-722-5334
    Fax: (612)851-4601
E-mail: nhf@intertec.com.
URL: http://www.homefarm.com.
Contact: Dale Miller, Editor; Wayne Bollum, Publisher.
Desc: Trade magazine for pork producers. *Type:* Periodical.

National Pork Producers Council

PO Box 10383   Ph: (515)223-2600
Des Moines, IA 50306   Fax: (515)223-2646
E-mail: pork@nppc.org
URL: http://www.nppc.org/
Contact: Al Tank, CEO.
Desc: Federation of state pork producer associations. Promotes the pork industry through research programs, consumer education, and lobbying activities. Compiles statistics; maintains speakers' bureau and hall of fame. *Type:* Association.

National Pork Report

Pork Publications, Inc.
PO Box 10383   Ph: (515)223-2600
Des Moines, IA 50306   Fax: (515)223-2646
Contact: Jan Tayloe, Editor; Don Frankson, Advertising Mgr.
Desc: Official magazine of the National Pork Producers Council, presenting industry news. *Type:* Periodical.

National Swine Registry

PO Box 2417   Ph: (765)463-3594
West Lafayette, IN 47906   Fax: (765)497-2959
Contact: Darrell D. Anderson, Exec.Sec.
Desc: Maintains registry for purebred Duroc, Yorkshire, Hampshire, and Landrace swine showing ownership, transfers, and pedigree records. *Type:* Association.

Nutrition Abstracts and Reviews, Series B: Livestock Feeds and Feeding

CAB International
CABI Publishing
10 E. 40th St., Ste. 3203   Ph: (212)481-7018
New York, NY 10016
E-mail: cabi-nao@cabi.org
URL: http://www.cabi.org
Contact: Tania Fisher, Product Manager, t.fisher@cabi.org.
Desc: Contains citations, with abstracts, to current periodical and other published literature relating to the nutritional aspects of livestock feeds and feeding. Animals covered include horses, cattle, sheeps, goats, pigs, poultry, deer, rabbits, domestic mammals and birds, game, and fish. *Type:* Database.

Pork

Vance Publishing Corp.
10901 W. 84th Terrace   Ph: (913)438-8700
Lenexa, KS 66214   Free: 800-252-1925
    Fax: (913)438-0690
E-mail: porkmag@aol.com.
Contact: Marlys Miller, Editor, mmpork@aol.com; Bill Newham, Publisher, bnpork@aol.com.
Desc: Magazine on pork production and marketing. *Alt. Contact:* WI; telephone: (608)278-9211; fax: (608)278-9311. *Type:* Periodical.

The Pork Report

SPI Marketing Group
502 45th St. W., 2nd Fl.   Ph: (306)653-3014
Saskatoon, SK, Canada S7L   Free: 800-667-2003
6H2   Fax: (306)244-2918
E-mail: spi@sk.sympatico.ca
URL: http://agri-infolink.com/spi.
Contact: Patty Martin, Editor, (306)933-4404, fax: (306)244-4497, agribusiness@sk.sympatico.ca.
Desc: Covers items of interest to the Saskatchewan pork industry, including weekly prices. Recurring features include letters to the editor, interviews, news of research, a calendar of events, reports of meetings, news of educational opportunities, job listings, and book reviews. *Type:* Newsletter.

Poultry Abstracts

CAB International
CABI Publishing
10 E. 40th St., Ste. 3203   Ph: (212)481-7018
New York, NY 10016
E-mail: cabi-nao@cabi.org
URL: http://www.cabi.org
Contact: Tania Fisher, Product Manager.
Desc: Contains citations, with abstracts, to current periodical and other published literature related to poultry. Covers fowls, turkeys, ducks, geese, and game and other birds. *Type:* Database.

Poultry Report

California Agricultural Statistics Service
U.S. Department of Agriculture (USDA)
PO Box 1258   Ph: (916)654-0895
Sacramento, CA 95812
Desc: Provides information on chicken and turkey settings, hatchings, eggs produced, inventory, prices, and cold storage. *Type:* Newsletter.

The Saskatchewan Stockgrower

The Saskatchewan Stock Growers Association
PO Box 4752
Regina, SK, Canada S4P 3Y4
E-mail: ssga@sk.sympatico.ca
Contact: Pamela Mitchell, Editor.

Desc: Reports on Saskatchewan's commercial cattle operations, feedlots, pure bred associations, and sheep and hog operations. *Type:* Newsletter.

Shaver Focus
Shaver Poultry Breeding Farms Ltd.
PO Box 400   Ph: (519)621-5191
Cambridge, ON, Canada N1R   Fax: (519)621-9407
5V9

Contact: Dr. Peter Hunton, Editor.

Desc: Provides technical information on egg production, poultry meat production, and poultry breeding. Recurring features include news of research. *Type:* Newsletter.

Sheep Industry Development Program
American Sheep Industry Association
6911 S. Yosemite St.   Ph: (303)771-3500
Englewood, CO 80112   Fax: (303)771-8200
E-mail: amsheep@rmii.org
URL: http://www.sheepusa.org

Contact: Peter Orwick, Exec.Dir.

Desc: A program of the American Sheep Industry Association . Develops production and management systems to make lamb and wool production consistently profitable and to encourage research that will benefit the sheep industry. *Type:* Association.

Tun-Us-In
National Tunis Sheep Registry
819 Lyon St.   Ph: (413)589-9653
Ludlow, MA 01056-1161

Desc: Publishes news and information of interest to breeders of registered Tunis sheep. Carries news of research, reports on Registry activities, notes on members, and a calendar of events. *Type:* Newsletter.

United States Meat Export Federation
1050 17th St., Ste. 2200   Ph: (303)623-6328
Denver, CO 80265-2073   Fax: (303)623-0297
URL: http://www.usmef.org

Contact: Philip M. Seng, Pres. & CEO.

Desc: Meat producers, packers, purveyors, exporters, and processors; livestock breeding associations; manufacturers of meat industry equipment and supplies; others related to the industry. Seeks to develop and identify overseas markets for U.S. beef, pork, lamb, and other meats. *Type:* Association.

U.S. Poultry News
U.S. Poultry and Egg Association
1530 Cooledge Rd.   Ph: (770)493-9401
Tucker, GA 30084   Fax: (770)493-9257

Contact: Larry Brown, Editor.

Desc: Discusses common problems in the poultry industry. Summarizes the results of research programs studying solar energy, vaccines, noise abatement, cholesterol, and recycling. *Type:* Newsletter.

Urner Barry Publications, Inc.—Yellow Sheet
Urner Barry Publications, Inc.
Box 389   Ph: (732)240-5330
Toms River, NJ 08754   Free: 800-932-0617
                              Fax: (732)341-0891
E-mail: mail@urnerbarry.com
URL: http://www.urnerbarry.com.

Contact: Joseph Muldowney, Editor.

Desc: Lists daily U.S. market prices for beef, pork, lamb, veal, and by-products. *Type:* Newsletter.

Urner Barry's Price-Current
Urner Barry Publications, Inc.
Box 389   Ph: (732)240-5330
Toms River, NJ 08754   Free: 800-932-0617
                              Fax: (732)341-0891
E-mail: mail@urnerbarry.com
URL: http://www.urnerbarry.com.

Contact: Richard A. Brown, Editor.

Desc: Reports national base price on turkeys, chickens, eggs, egg products, and other related items. Recurring features include special editions for events such as the Southeastern Poultry & Egg Association convention. *Type:* Newsletter.

Urner Barry's Price-Current, West Coast Edition
Urner Barry Publications, Inc.
Box 389   Ph: (732)240-5330
Toms River, NJ 08754   Free: 800-932-0617
                              Fax: (732)341-0891
E-mail: mail@urnerbarry.com
URL: http://www.urnerbarry.com.

Contact: Richard Brown, Editor.

Desc: Reports on West Coast-based prices for turkeys, eggs and egg products, and chickens. Examines market situations for each commodity segment. *Type:* Newsletter.

Weekly Insiders Poultry Report
Urner Barry Publications, Inc.
Box 389   Ph: (732)240-5330
Toms River, NJ 08754   Free: 800-932-0617
                              Fax: (732)341-0891
E-mail: mail@urnerbarry.com

Contact: Russell Whitman, Editor.

Desc: Carries market information and statistics on poultry products. *Type:* Newsletter.

Weekly Insiders Turkey Letter and Weekly Hatch Report
Urner Barry Publications, Inc.
Box 389   Ph: (732)240-5330
Toms River, NJ 08754   Free: 800-932-0617
                              Fax: (732)341-0891
E-mail: mail@urnerbarry.com

Contact: Russell Whitman, Editor.

Desc: Contains market statistics on turkey prices. Serves as a market guide by its inclusion of retrospective as well as current turkey prices and figures on storage holdings. *Type:* Newsletter.

World Ark
Heifer Project International (HPI)
PO Box 808   Ph: (501)376-6836
Little Rock, AR 72203   Free: 800-422-0474
                              Fax: (501)376-8906
E-mail: ahb@heifer.org; worldark@heifer.org.

Contact: Anna H. Bedford, Editor.

Desc: Highlights the Project's livestock development efforts carried on as part of the struggle against hunger in the U.S. and in other countries. *Type:* Newsletter.

Lutheran

Aid Association for Lutherans
4321 N. Ballard Rd.   Ph: (920)734-5721
Appleton, WI 54919-0001   Free: 800-225-5225
                              Fax: (920)730-4757
E-mail: aalmail@aal.org
URL: http://www.aal.org

Contact: John O. Gilbert, Pres./CEO.

Desc: Fraternal benefit society providing life, disability income, and retirement insurance for Lutherans and their families throughout the U.S. Local branch structure permits development and pursuit of volunteer activities by members, which help others. Provides wellness and educational programs. *Type:* Association.

Concordia Mutual Life Association
PO Box 9230   Ph: (630)971-8000
Downers Grove, IL 60515-9230 Free: 800-342-5265
                              Fax: (630)971-9332
E-mail: cmlife@cmlife.com

Contact: Robert O. Gettinger, Pres. & CEO.

Desc: Fraternal benefit society. Provides financial planning with life insurance and annuity products to individuals and their families. Offers scholarships to members. *Type:* Association.

Department for Campus Ministry, Division for Education, Evangelical Lutheran Church in America
Evangelical Lutheran Church in   Ph: (312)380-2847
   America   Fax: (312)380-1465
8765 W. Higgins Rd.
Chicago, IL 60631

Contact: Rev. James R. Carr, Dir.

Desc: Members are representatives of national church body; staff members are religious workers on campuses. Sponsors support, development, and interpretation of ministries in higher education. *Type:* Association.

International Lutheran Laymen's League
2185 Hampton Ave.   Ph: (314)951-4000
St. Louis, MO 63139   Free: 800-944-3450
                              Fax: (314)951-4295
URL: http://www.lhm.org

Contact: Roger Hebermehl, Exec.Dir.

Desc: Members are of the Lutheran Church-Missouri Synod and Lutheran Church-Canada Communicant members interested in lay activities of the church. Sponsors the "Worldwide Lutheran Hour" radio program, "Woman to Woman" radio program, "On Main Street" videos, and television specials. Provides special program materials for affiliated groups. *Type:* Association.

International Lutheran Women's Missionary League
3558 S. Jefferson Ave.   Ph: (314)268-1531
St. Louis, MO 63118-3910   Free: 800-252-LWML
                              Fax: (314)268-1532
E-mail: ilwml@ilwml.org

Contact: Norine Stumpf, Office Mgr.

Desc: Women's groups within the congregations of the Lutheran Church-Missouri Synod in the U.S. Works to develop a program of mission education, inspiration, and service for the women of the Lutheran Church-Missouri Synod, and to gather voluntary funds for mission projects. *Type:* Association.

Lutheran Council in the U.S.A.
360 Park Ave. S.   Ph: (212)532-6350
New York, NY 10010

Contact: John R. Houck, Gen.Sec.

Desc: Joint agency of the American Lutheran Church, Lutheran Church in America, Association of Evangelical Lutheran Churches, Lutheran Church-Missouri Synod, and Latvian Evangelical Lutheran Church in America. Seeks to achieve theological consensus among Lutherans; conducts ecumenical dialogues; coordinates Lutheran planning in American missions and social ministries; resettles refugees; serves as a pastoral arm to Lutheran clergy in specialized ministries; advocates on behalf of American Indians; administers programs in campus ministry; handles Lutheran relationships with Boy Scouting and other civic youth groups; provides services to Lutheran military personnel; interprets Lutheranism through the media; and alerts Lutherans to public issues and h andles their interests before the federal government. Maintains inter-Lutheran archives; compiles membership statistics. *Type:* Association.

Lutheran Men in Mission

Evangelical Lutheran Church in America
Division for Congregational Ministries, 9th Fl.
8765 W. Higgins
Chicago, IL 60631
Ph: (773)380-2566
Free: 800-638-3522
Fax: (773)380-2588

Contact: Doug Haugen, Director.

Desc: Male members of congregations of the Evangelical Lutheran Church of America. Seeks to involve men in the work of the church. *Type:* Association.

Lutheran World Relief

390 Park Ave. S.
New York, NY 10016
Ph: (212)532-6350
Free: 800-LWR-LWR2
Fax: (212)213-6081

E-mail: lwr@lwr.org
URL: http://www.lwr.org/

Contact: Kathryn F. Wolford, Pres.

Desc: Works on behalf of the Lutheran churches of the U.S. in overseas programs of community and agricultural development, social service, primary health care, and material aid. Provides aid regardless of race, creed, or political affiliation. *Type:* Association.

Lutheran Youth Fellowship

c/o Lutheran Church-Missouri Synod
1333 S. Kirkwood Rd.
St. Louis, MO 63122
Ph: (314)965-9000
Fax: (314)822-8307

Contact: Rev. Terry K. Dittmer, Dir.

Desc: Young adults ranging from junior high age through age 25. To support youth groups within the Lutheran Church-Missouri Synod and to provide young people with the opportunity to carry out their role as Christ's disciples. Fosters fellowship among Lutheran Church-Missouri Synod youth and other youth groups; enables youths to share their faith through evangelistic and mission projects; develops leadership skills; increases dialogue between the church and its young people; encourages the exchange of ideas and resources for improving youth ministry. *Type:* Association.

Wheat Ridge Ministries

1 Pierce Pl., Ste. 250E
Itasca, IL 60143
Ph: (630)766-9066
Free: 800-762-6748
Fax: (630)766-9622

E-mail: wrmbimlerrw@wheatridge.org
URL: http://www.wheatridge.org

Contact: Richard W. Bimler, Pres.

Desc: Independent Lutheran organization. Provides "seed-money" grants for church-related health and social service projects in nine countries. Raises funds through contributions and by annual distribution of Christmas Seals. *Type:* Association.

World Mission Prayer League

232 Clifton Ave.
Minneapolis, MN 55403-3497
Ph: (612)871-6843
Fax: (612)871-6844

E-mail: wmpl@aol.com
URL: http://www.wmpl.org

Contact: Charles Lindquist, Gen.Dir.

Desc: Provides opportunity for lay members, as well as for pastors, to preach the Gospel and labor for its successful propagation among the unevangelized peoples of the earth. *Type:* Association.

Management

ABI/INFORM®

Bell & Howell Information and Learning

300 N. Zeeb Rd.
PO Box 1346
Ann Arbor, MI 48106-1346
Ph: (734)761-4700

E-mail: info@umi.com
URL: http://www.umi.com

Contact: Search Assistance, (502)583-4111, fax: (502)589-5572.

Desc: Contains complete bibliographic information and abstracts to more than 1000 publications in business and management information. Contains more than 530,000 records from more than 1000 leading Business and management publications, including over 350 English-language titles from outside the United States. *Available:* Ovid Technologies, Inc.; The Dialog Corporation, Data-Star; The Dialog Corporation, DIALOG; CompuServe Information Service, Knowledge Index; Questel • Orbit; Gesellschaft fur Betriebswirtschaftliche Information mbH (GBI); STN International; CARL Corporation; FT PROFILE; Research Libraries Group, Inc. (RLG); CitaDel™ Service; OCLC Online Computer Library Center, Inc., OCLC EPIC; OCLC Online Computer Library Center, Inc., OCLC FirstSearch Catalog; LEXIS-NEXIS, NEXIS; Ameritech Library Services, Vista; Bell & Howell Information and Learning; European Information Network Services (EINS). *Type:* Database.

Academy of Management

PO Box 3020
Briarcliff Manor, NY 10510-8020
Ph: (914)923-2607
Fax: (914)923-2615

E-mail: aom@fsmail.pace.edu
URL: http://www.aom.pace.edu

Contact: Nancy Urbanowicz, Exec.Dir.

Desc: Professors in accredited universities and colleges who teach management; selected business executives who have made significant written contributions to the literature in the field of management and organization. Offers placement service. *Type:* Association.

Academy of Management News

Academy of Management

Pace University
PO Box 3020
Briarcliff Manor, NY 10510-8020
Ph: (914)923-2607
Fax: (914)923-2615

E-mail: aom@fsmail.pace.edu

Contact: Jo Ann Duffy, Editor.

Desc: Provides notice of officer elections, meetings and conferences of interest, calls for papers, and member publications and accomplishments. Recurring features include news of research, a calendar of events, and reports of meetings. *Type:* Newsletter.

Administration & Management Special Interest Section Quarterly

American Occupational Therapy Association, Inc. (AOTA)

PO Box 31220
Bethesda, MD 20824-1220
Ph: (301)652-2682
Free: 800-877-1383
Fax: (301)652-7711

E-mail: ajotsis@aota.org.

Contact: Elizabeth Holcomb, Managing Editor.

Desc: Focuses on the administration and management issues of occupational therapy services. *Type:* Newsletter.

Administrative Management Society

1101 14th St. NW, No. 1100
Washington, DC 20005-5601
Ph: (202)371-8299
Fax: (202)371-1090

Contact: M. Sutherland, Exec.Dir.

Desc: Professional administrators in administrative services and financial, personnel, systems, and information man-

agement; educators, management consultants, and small business owners. Promotes application of management methods to commerce and industry for the purpose of increasing productivity, lowering costs, and improving quality; encourages and participates in research; promotes sound employee and employer relationships; aids managers in career development. Sponsors professional accreditation for Certified Administrative Manager (CAM). *Type:* Association.

Advance Business Reports

Advance Business Reports, Inc.

130 W. 42nd St., Ste. 702
New York, NY 10036-7802

Contact: Murray Ansell, Editor.

Desc: Provides information on occupancy and expansion of new business facilities. Published in multiple editions by geographic area. *Type:* Newsletter.

Affiliated Warehouse Companies Newsletter

Affiliated Warehouse Companies, Inc.

54 Village Ct.
PO Box 295
Hazlet, NJ 07730
Ph: (732)739-2323
Fax: (732)739-4154

E-mail: sales@awco.com
URL: http://www.awco.com

Contact: Jim McBride, Editor.

Desc: Relates news and points of interest involving clients, industry updates, trends and activities of the warehouse industry. Recurring features include news of research, a calendar of events, reports of meetings, and news of educational opportunities. *Type:* Newsletter.

American Management Association

1601 Broadway
New York, NY 10019-7420
Ph: (212)586-8100
Free: 800-262-9699
Fax: (212)903-8168

URL: http://www.amanet.org

Contact: George B. Weathersby, Pres. & CEO.

Desc: American Management Association provides educational forums worldwide where members and their colleagues learn superior, practical business skills and explore best practices of world-class organizations through interaction with each other and expert faculty practitioners. AMA's publishing program provides tools individuals use to extend learning beyond the classroom in a process of life-long professional growth and development through education. *Type:* Association.

Applied Management Newsletter

National Association for Management

5920 E Central No. 205
Wichita, KS 67208
Ph: (316)668-0763

Type: Newsletter.

Association for Systems Management

PO Box 38370
Cleveland, OH 44138-0370

Contact: Robert C. La Prad, Exec.Dir.

Desc: International professional organization of executives and specialists in management information systems serving business, commerce, education, government, and the military. Expresses concern with communications, electronics, equipment, forms control, human relations, organization, procedure writing, and systems applications. *Type:* Association.

Board Leadership

Jossey-Bass Inc., Publishers

350 Sansome St.
San Francisco, CA 94104
Ph: (415)433-1767
Free: 888-378-2537
Fax: 800-605-2665

E-mail: webperson@jbp.com

URL: http://www.josseybass.com

Contact: John Carver, Editor.

Desc: Covers all aspects of a Board's job, including drafting a mission statement, conducting meetings, hiring, and strategic planning. *Type:* Newsletter.

Bulletin to Management

Bureau of National Affairs, Inc. (BNA)
1231 25th St. NW   Ph: (202)452-4323
Washington, DC 20037   Free: 800-372-1033
     Fax: (202)452-7773
E-mail: bnaplus@bna.com

Contact: Jeff Day, Managing Editor.

Desc: Features summaries of current developments in human resource/personnel management and labor relations, including key court decisions, legislation, and collective bargaining. Provides information on "real-life job situations" and ready-to-use policy guides. *Type:* Newsletter.

Bureau of Business Practice Management Letter

Prentice Hall, Inc.
1 Lake St.   Ph: (201)236-7000
Upper Saddle River, NJ 07458

Desc: Covers aspects of business practice management. *Type:* Newsletter.

Business Coaching Practice Builder

National Association of Business Coaches
11954 Big Spring Rd.   Ph: (301)791-9332
Clear Spring, MD 21722   Fax: (301)582-3639
E-mail: cnrc@erols.com

Contact: J. Stephen Lanning, Editor.

Desc: Provides business coaches and other business professionals with educational and training information, including marketing techniques and client enrichment opportunities. Recurring features include a calendar of events and book reviews. *Type:* Newsletter.

Capacity Management Review

Institute for Computer Capacity Management (ICCM)
1020 8th Ave. S, Ste. 6   Ph: (941)261-8945
Naples, FL 34102   Fax: (941)261-5456
E-mail: editor@demandtech.com.

Contact: Mark B. Friedman, Publisher.

Desc: Emphasizes information systems management issues over technical details. Covers information on responsibilities for enterprise-wide performance improvement and capacity planning, as well as technical staff involved. *Type:* Newsletter.

Center for Creative Leadership

PO Box 26300   Ph: (336)545-2810
Greensboro, NC 27438-6300   Fax: (336)282-3284
E-mail: info@leaders.ccl.org
URL: http://www.ccl.org

Contact: John Alexander, Pres.

Desc: Promotes behavioral science research and leadership education. *Type:* Association.

CEO Job Opportunities Update

Don J. DeBolt
1575 Eye. St. NW, Ste. 1190   Ph: (202)408-7900
Washington, DC 20005   Fax: (202)408-7907
E-mail: info@associationjobs.com; ceoupdate@associationjobs.com

Contact: Mark Graham, Editor; Don DeBolt, Publisher Emeritus; Lynn McNutt, Editor.

Desc: Lists management-level job openings in associations and nonprofit organizations. *Type:* Newsletter.

CFO

CFO Publishing
253 Summer St.   Ph: (617)345-9700
Boston, MA 02210   Fax: (617)951-9306

Contact: Julia Homer, Editor; David Laird, Publisher; Laurie Finnie, Advertising Mgr.

Desc: Business magazine for small to mid-sized companies. *Type:* Periodical.

Chief Executive Officer's Newsletter

Center for Entrepreneurial Management, Inc.
180 Varick St., 17th Fl.   Ph: (212)633-0060
New York, NY 10014   Fax: (212)633-0063
E-mail: ceoclubs@bway.net
URL: http://www.ceo-clubs.org

Contact: Joe Manuso, Editor.

Desc: "Designed to provide accurate and authoritative information relative to subjects of concern to entrepreneurial managers." Covers management, taxes, finance, marketing, information sources, and educational programs. Recurring features include news of seminars, book reviews, news of research and survey results, and columns titled Entrepreneurs's Hall of Fame, Mind Your Own Business, Resources, Accounting, Personal, Miscellaneous, and The Business Exchange. *Type:* Newsletter.

Consortium for Graduate Study in Management

200 S. Hanley Rd., Ste. 1102   Ph: (314)935-6324
St. Louis, MO 63105-3415   Fax: (314)935-5014
E-mail: cgsm@simon.wustl.edu

Contact: Phyllis Scott Buford, CEO.

Desc: Graduate fellowship program operated by Indiana University, New York University, University of Michigan, University of North Carolina, University of Virginia, Washington University, University of Rochester, University of Southern California, University of Texas-Austin, University of California-Berkely, and the University of Wisconsin to hasten the entry of minorities into managerial positions in business. Program includes three-day orientation program, summer business internships and career placement, and involves minority groups such as American Indians, Afro-Americans, Mexican-Americans, Puerto Ricans, and Dominicians who hold U.S. citizenship. *Type:* Association.

Continuous Improvement Newsletter

Continuous Improvement
8460 Dygert Dr.   Ph: (616)891-9114
Alto, MI 49302   Fax: (616)891-9114
E-mail: isogroup@cris.com.
URL: http://www.cris.com/~isogroup/.

Contact: Richard Clements, Editor.

Desc: Contains tips and techniques for effective management in business, service industries, and manufacturing. Recurring features include interviews, software and book reviews, notices of publications available, and columns titled ISO 9000, QS-9000, ISO-14000 Tutorials, and Intelligence Briefings. *Type:* Newsletter.

Council of Logistics Management

2805 Butterfield Rd., No. 200   Ph: (630)574-0985
Oak Brook, IL 60523   Fax: (630)574-0989
E-mail: clmadmin@clm1.org
URL: http://www.clm1.org

Contact: George A. Gecowets, Exec.VP.

Desc: Business executives with a professional interest in logistics and physical distribution management; includes members from industrial concerns as well as consultants and educators. Concerned with advancing and promoting the management science of integrating transportation, warehousing, material handling, protective packaging, inventory size and location, and other areas of customer service, to reduce overall costs of selling and marketing, while improving competitive status. *Type:* Association.

Development Director's Newsletter

CD Publications
8204 Fenton St.   Ph: (301)588-6380
Silver Spring, MD 20910   Free: 800-666-6380
     Fax: (301)588-6385
E-mail: cdpubs@clark.net

Contact: Cele Garrett, Editor; Stephanie Roeske.

Desc: Covers management techniques for directors of nonprofit organizations. *Type:* Newsletter.

Dollars & Cents

Finance and Administration Section
American Society of Association Executives (ASAE)
1575 I St. NW   Ph: (202)626-2781
Washington, DC 20005-1168
URL: http://www.asaenet.org/SECTIONS/FINANCE/.

Contact: Brenda Luper, C.P.A., Section Manager; Joseph S. Cavarretta, Editor; Steven Washington, Asst. Editor; Tamara Faggen, Asst. Editor.

Desc: Addresses topics of interest to association specialists in the areas of finance, human resources, technology applications, and staff administration; including changing tax laws, getting the most from a CPA firm, budgeting and resource allocation, office automation, office services administration, personnel management, financial management, and accounting software. *Type:* Newsletter.

The Don Hawk Executive Report

Hawk Enterprises
5400 Memorial Dr., Ste. 514   Ph: (713)880-3236
Houston, TX 77007   Fax: (713)880-0427
E-mail: hawkent@ibm.net

Contact: Don Hawk, Editor and Publisher.

Desc: Provides information about executive leadership, corporate management, and organization. *Type:* Newsletter.

The Economic Home Owner

Publishing and Business Consultants
4427 W. Slauson Ave.
Los Angeles, CA 90043-2717

Contact: Atia Napoleon, Editor and Publisher.

Desc: Magazine featuring tips on home maintenance and repair. *Type:* Periodical.

Employers Group

1150 S. Olive St., Ste. 2300   Ph: (213)748-0421
PO Box 15013   Fax: (213)742-0301
Los Angeles, CA 90015
URL: http://www.hronline.org

Contact: William A. Dahlman, Pres. & CEO.

Desc: Provides human resources management services including wage, salary, and benefit surveys; personnel practices surveys; management counseling; management education programs; litigation surveillance; government relations; and research library service. Provides customized human resources services including employee opinion surveys and employee communications programs through its subsidiary, The Employers Group Service Corp. Offers unemployment insurance services, workers' compensation programs, and in-house management training programs. *Type:* Association.

Executive Edge

Select Press
PO Box 37   Ph: (415)924-1612
Corte Madera, CA 94976-0037

Contact: Rick Crandall, Editor.

Desc: Contains articles and tips designed to improve managerial styles and careers. Covers customer service, quality, leadership, time management, office politics, and personal fitness. *Type:* Newsletter.

Executive Excellence

Executive Excellence
1344 E. 1120 S.   Ph: (801)375-4014
Provo, UT 84606-6379   Free: 800-304-9782
                        Fax: (801)377-5960

E-mail: info@eep.com
URL: http://www.eep.com.
Contact: Kenneth M. Shelton, Editor.
Desc: Provides articles by CEOs, educators, consultants, and trainers for individuals interested in developing management and leadership skills and find excellence in the workplace. *Type:* Newsletter.

FACILITY fast facts

Cash-Callahan & Company, Inc.
PO Box 770
Provincetown, MA 02657-0770
Contact: Connacht Cash, Editor.
Desc: Discusses facility management issues and legislation related to facility and office management. Provides updates on national and state codes and regulations. *Type:* Newsletter.

Facility Manager's Alert

Progressive Business Publications
370 Technology Dr.   Ph: (610)695-8600
Malvern, PA 19355   Free: 800-220-5000
                        Fax: (610)651-2981
URL: http://www.pbp.com.
Contact: Bill Hatton, Editor.
Desc: Offers cost-saving strategies to help managers operate more efficient facilities. Recurring features include interviews, news of research, a calendar of events, news of educational opportunities, and a column titled Sharpen Your Judgment. *Type:* Newsletter.

Front Line Management

Economics Press, Inc.
12 Daniel Rd.   Ph: (973)227-1224
Fairfield, NJ 07004-2565   Free: 800-526-2554
                        Fax: (973)526-2554
E-mail: info@epinc.com; order@epinc.com
URL: http://www.epinc.com
Contact: Phil Hall, Editor, edit@epinc.com.
Desc: Offers ideas and suggestions to provide a foundation in the principles of supervisory management. Remarks: Closed series of 48 issues offered in bulk or over 48 weeks. *Type:* Newsletter.

Harvard Management Update

Harvard Business School Press
Harvard Business School Publishing
60 Harvard Way   Ph: (617)495-6700
Boston, MA 02163   Free: 800-545-7685
                        Fax: (617)496-8066
E-mail: custserv@hbsp.harvard.edu
URL: http://www.hbsp.harvard.edu; http://www.hbsp.harvard.edu.
Contact: John Case, Exec.Ed.
Desc: Provides information on current management techniques and trends. *Type:* Newsletter.

Human Resource Management News

Remy Publishing Company
401 N. Franklin St., 3rd Fl.   Ph: (312)464-0300
Chicago, IL 60610   Free: 800-542-6670
                        Fax: (312)464-0166
Contact: John V. Hickey, Editor.
Desc: Reports on employee relations, personnel administration, and industrial relations. *Type:* Newsletter.

Human Resource Planning Society

317 Madison Ave., Ste. 1509   Ph: (212)490-6387
New York, NY 10017   Fax: (212)682-6851
Contact: Walter J. Cleaver, Exec.Dir.
Desc: Human resource planning professionals representing 160 corporations and 3000 individual members, including strategic human resources planning and development specialists, staffing analysts, business planners, line managers, and others who function as business partners in the application of strategic human resource management practices. Seeks to increase the impact of human resource planning and management on business and organizational performance. *Type:* Association.

IFMA News

International Facility Management Association
1 E. Greenway Plaza, 11th Fl.   Ph: (713)623-4362
Houston, TX 77046-0194   Free: 800-359-4362
                        Fax: (713)623-6124
Contact: Allison Tilly Carswell, Editor.
Desc: Provides information on the Association's activites and on the facility management profession. Recurring features include news of research, a calendar of events, news of educational opportunities, job listings, book reviews, notices of publications available, and columns titled President's Column, Codes & Regulations Report, and Research Review. *Type:* Newsletter.

Industry Week

Penton Media Inc.
1100 Superior Ave.   Ph: (216)696-7000
Cleveland, OH 44114-2543   Fax: (216)931-9524
E-mail: corpcomm@penton.com; webmaster@penton.com; www@industryweek.com.
URL: http://www.industryweek.com.
Contact: John R. Brandt, Editor-in-Chief, (216)931-9443, fax: (216)696-7670, jbrandt@industryweek.com; Carl T. Marino, Publisher, (216)931-9561, fax: (216)696-7670, cmarino@industryweek.com.
Desc: Magazine containing articles to help industry executives sharpen their managerial skills and increase their effectiveness. *Type:* Periodical.

Innovative Leader

Winston J. Brill Associates
4134 Cherokee Dr.   Ph: (608)231-6766
Madison, WI 53711   Fax: (608)231-6794
E-mail: wjbrill@facstaff.wisc.edu
Contact: Winston J. Brill, Contact.
Desc: Serves as a resource for managers on developments and innovations. *Type:* Newsletter.

Institute for Operation Research and the Management Sciences

901 Elkridge Landing Rd., Ste.   Ph: (401)274-2525
400   Fax: (401)274-3189
Linthicum Heights, MD 21090-2909
Contact: Randall Robinson, Exec.Dir.
Desc: Professional society for scientists and management in business, labor, government, teaching, and research. Aim is to advance scientific knowledge and improve management practices; members contribute to or learn about important findings in management technology, applied mathematics, psychology, economics, and other sciences. Compiles statistics; conducts research programs; maintains speakers' bureau. *Type:* Association.

International Facility Management Association

Diana Steinman
1 E. Greenway Plz., Ste. 1100   Ph: (713)623-4362
Houston, TX 77046-0194   Free: 800-359-4362
                        Fax: (713)623-6124
E-mail: diana.steinman@ifma.org
URL: http://www.ifma.org
Contact: Dennis L. Longworth, CFM, Pres.
Desc: Facility managers worldwide representing all types of organizations including banks, insurance companies, hospitals, colleges and universities, utility companies, electronic equipment manufacturers, petroleum companies, museums, auditoriums, and federal, state, provencial, and local governments. Purposes are to enhance the professional goals of persons involved or interested in the field of facility management (the planning, designing, and managing of workplaces); to cultivate cooperation, foster understanding, and create interest among firms, individuals, and other associations and professions as they may affect facility management; to engage in the interchange of views regarding legislation, regulation, and procedures that affect facility management. *Type:* Association.

INTIX Newsletter

The International Ticketing Association
250 W. 57th, Ste. 722   Ph: (212)581-0600
New York, NY 10107   Fax: (212)581-0885
E-mail: info@intix.org
URL: http://www.intix.org.
Contact: Patricia Spira, Editor, pspira@intix.org; Kerry O'Donnell, Editor.
Desc: Seeks to keep readers informed of current trends and technological advances in technology in the ticketing industry. Covers activities of INTIX and its members, career opportunities, and results of INTIX surveys. *Type:* Newsletter.

Issue Barometer

Issue Action Publications, Inc.
207 Loudoun St. SE   Ph: (703)777-8450
Leesburg, VA 20175-3115
Contact: Teresa Yancey Crane, Editor.
Desc: Informs business, government, and opinion leaders of the objectives and activities of issue-oriented organizations. Profiles activists and their programs in order to facilitate dialogue between business and its publics. *Type:* Newsletter.

Just in Time Management Journal

Industrial Distribution Association
3 Corporate Sq., Ste. 201   Ph: (404)325-2776
Atlanta, GA 30329
URL: http://www.ida.assoc.org.
Contact: Sarah Green, Editor.
Desc: Provides information and news of interest in industrial distribution. *Type:* Newsletter.

Leadership

Prentice Hall, Inc.
1 Lake St.   Ph: (201)236-7000
Upper Saddle River, NJ 07458
Contact: David Deffley, Publisher; Patricia Thunberg, Editor; Denise Fedeli, Art Director.
Desc: Directed toward first line supervisors. Discusses the role of the supervisor and problem solving. *Type:* Newsletter.

Leadership in Action

Jossey-Bass Inc., Publishers
350 Sansome St.   Ph: (415)433-1767
San Francisco, CA 94104   Free: 888-378-2537
                        Fax: 800-605-2665
E-mail: webperson@jbp.com

URL: http://www.josseybass.com

Contact: Martin Wilcox, Editor, (316)286-4404, fax: (336)286-4434, wilcoxm@leaders.ccl.org.

Desc: Presents information on applied creativity, organizational psychology, executive development and leadership, and psychometrics. Recurring features include interviews, news of research, news of educational opportunities, and a column titled Inklings. *Type:* Newsletter.

Leadership for the Front Lines

Bureau of Business Practice
24 Rope Ferry Rd.   Ph: (860)442-4365
Waterford, CT 06386   Free: 800-243-0876
                           Fax: (860)437-3555

URL: http://www.bbpnews.com

Contact: Kathy Cipriani, Editor, kathleen_cipriani@prehall.com; Joyce Anne Grabel, Managing Editor.

Desc: Provides information about supervisory problems, and how supervisors can become more effective in their current positions. Recurring features include interviews. *Type:* Newsletter.

Leadership Strategies

Georgetown Publishing House
1101 30th St. NW   Ph: (202)337-8096
Washington, DC 20007   Free: 800-915-0022
                           Fax: (202)337-1512

Contact: Nona Aguilar, Editor.

Desc: Offers information and advice for effective business leadership. *Type:* Newsletter.

Logistics Comment

Council of Logistics Management
2805 Butterfield Rd., Ste. 200   Ph: (630)574-0985
Oak Brook, IL 60523-1170   Fax: (630)574-0989

E-mail: clmadmin@clm1.org
URL: http://www.clm1.org

Contact: Elaine M. Winter, Editor.

Desc: Designed for business personnel interested in improving logistics management skills. Alerts readers to upcoming conferences and seminars and reports briefly on past conferences. *Type:* Newsletter.

Maintenance Management

Bureau of Business Practice
24 Rope Ferry Rd.   Ph: (860)442-4365
Waterford, CT 06386   Free: 800-243-0876
                           Fax: (860)437-3555

URL: http://www.bbpnews.com; http://www.bbpnews.com.

Contact: Peter Hawkins, Editor, Peter_Hawkins@prenhall.com.

Desc: Dedicated to promoting the best practices in the industrial maintenance and facilities fields. Shares information from successful managers whose organizations have achieved outstanding performance. *Type:* Newsletter.

The Management Forum

International Management Council
430 S. 20th St.   Ph: (402)345-1904
Omaha, NE 68102-2506   Fax: (402)345-4480

E-mail: imcoffice@msn.com
URL: http://www.imc/ymca.org.

Contact: Jodeen Sterba, Editor.

Desc: Provides information about leadership and management in business. Recurring features include news of research, a calendar of events, reports of meetings, news of educational opportunities, and book reviews. *Type:* Newsletter.

Management Matters

CCH Canadian Ltd.
90 Sheppard Ave., Ste. 300   Ph: (416)441-0086
North York, ON, Canada M2N   Free: 800-268-4522
6X1   Fax: 800-461-4131

URL: http://www.ca.cch.com

Desc: Provides information on management issues. *Type:* Newsletter.

Management Matters

Merton Allen Associates (MAA)
PO Box 15640   Ph: (954)473-9560
Plantation, FL 33318-5640 Fax: (954)473-0544

E-mail: infoteamma@aol.com

Contact: David Allen, Editor.

Desc: Covers areas, disciplines, and subjects related to effective, professional, business management. Reviews available information, workshops, theses, and other documentation from world-wide governments, industry, business, and academic sources pertaining to such areas as sales, finances, management techniques, employment, manufacturing, quality, and procedures. *Type:* Newsletter.

Management Strategy

Sagamore Publishing Inc.
PO Box 647   Ph: (217)359-5940
Champaign, IL 61824-0647   Free: 800-327-5557
                           Fax: (217)359-5975

E-mail: books@sagamorepub.com
URL: http://www.sagamorepub.com

Contact: Julie Blauwkamp, Managing Editor, julieb@sagamorepub.com.

Desc: Provides information to assist managers in keeping abreast of current management issues, especially in the parks and recreation field. Recurring features include book reviews and columns titled You Be the Judge, 20/20 Management, Leisure View, Trend Sense, On the Shortside, For Your Health, Resource Review. *Type:* Newsletter.

The Manager's Intelligence Report

Lawrence Ragan Communications, Inc.
316 N. Michigan Ave., Ste. 300   Ph: (312)960-4100
Chicago, IL 60601   Free: 800-878-5331
                                  Fax: (312)960-4105

E-mail: cservice@ragan.com
URL: http://www.ragan.com.

Contact: Steve Crescenzo, Editor; Mark Ragan, Publisher; Carol Jackson, Managing Editor, carolj@ragan.com; Dan Oswald, President.

Desc: Provides strategies and ideas to help boost employee morale, save time on the job, and aid career advancement. *Type:* Newsletter.

Managing Automation

Thomas Publishing Co.
5 Penn Plaza   Ph: (212)695-0500
New York, NY 10001   Fax: (212)290-7206

E-mail: ordertr@thomasregister.com

Contact: David Broujell, Editor, (212)629-1510, fax: (212)629-1559, dbroujell@tpmgnet.com; Ralph E. Richardson, Group Pub.; Lia Kelerchian, Production Mgr., (212)629-1540, fax: (212)629-1500, lkelerchian@tmpgnet.com; Donald E. Fagan, Publisher, (212)629-1507.

Desc: Managing automation covers manufacturing business, operations, loggistics and product development within the process, batch and discrete manufacturing environments. *Type:* Periodical.

MBA Track

Jeffrey D. Halpern
1 Kendall Sq., Bldg. 600, Ste.   Fax: (617)494-1540
201
Cambridge, MA 02139

Contact: Candace C. Cline, Editor; Jeffrey D. Halpern, Publisher.

Desc: Publishes employment information for those with masters of business administration degrees. *Type:* Newsletter.

Meeting and Conference Executives Alert

MPA Communications
554 Strawberry Hill Rd.   Ph: (508)771-5200
Centerville, MA 02632   Fax: (508)775-5658

E-mail: mcea@banet.net.

Contact: Joan Mather, Editor and Publisher.

Desc: Provides information on planning meetings and special events. *Type:* Newsletter.

Meeting Planners MarketPlace

Market Place Publications
89 Access Rd.   Ph: (617)762-6600
Norwood, MA 02062   Fax: (617)762-1300

Contact: Kevin M. Curran, Editor.

Desc: Direct response service for meeting planners. *Type:* Periodical.

The Motivational Manager

Lawrence Ragan Communications, Inc.
316 N. Michigan Ave., Ste. 300   Ph: (312)960-4100
Chicago, IL 60601   Free: 800-878-5331
                                  Fax: (312)960-4105

E-mail: cservice@ragan.com
URL: http://www.ragan.com.

Contact: Steve Crescenzo, Editor; Mark Ragan, Publisher; Carol Jackson, Managing Editor, carolj@ragan.com; Dan Oswald, President.

Desc: Provides strategies and ideas to help inspire employees. Covers hiring, training, and recognizing and retaining strong employees through participative management. *Type:* Newsletter.

National Management Association

2210 Arbor Blvd.   Ph: (937)294-0421
Dayton, OH 45439   Fax: (937)294-2374

Contact: K. Stephen Bailey, Pres.

Desc: Business and industrial management personnel; membership comes from supervisory level, with the remainder from middle management and above. Seeks to develop and recognize management as a profession and to promote the free enterprise system. Prepares chapter programs on basic management, management policy and practice, communications, human behavior, industrial relations, economics, political education, and liberal education. *Type:* Association.

NOI News

Sales & Marketing Magic, Inc.
36473 U.S. Highway, 19 North   Ph: (813)784-9469
Palm Harbor, FL 34684   Fax: (813)784-7978

Contact: Douglas D. Chasick, Editor.

Desc: Addresses practical management and maintenance for apartment professionals. Offers tips and articles on apartment management issues, such as taking service bids, security, residents' service requests, inspections, staff motivation and controlling operating expenses. *Type:* Newsletter.

Nonprofit World

Society for Nonprofit Organizations
6314 Odana Rd., Ste. 1   Ph: (608)274-9777
Madison, WI 53719   Free: 800-424-7367
          Fax: (608)274-9978

E-mail: snpo@danenet.wicip.org
Contact: Jill Muehrcke, Editor.
Desc: Covers leadership and management practices, communication skills, organizational renewal, and legislative developments as they affect nonprofit organizations. Recurring features include columns titled Ask the Experts, First Alert, Entrepreneurial Spirit, People and Technology, Fundraising Forum, Relevant Reviews, Nonprofit Profiles, Nonprofit Briefs, The Board Room, Legal Counsel, and Food for Thought. *Type:* Newsletter.

Open-Book Management Bulletin

Open-Book Management: Bulletin
11 Bay State Ave.   Ph: (617)625-7095
Somerville, MA 02144   Fax: (617)666-3385
Contact: Karen Carney, Editor; John Case, Editor.
Desc: Consists of news and case studies related to open-book management. Recurring features include interviews, a calendar of events, and book reviews. *Type:* Newsletter.

Personnel Management

Bureau of National Affairs, Inc. (BNA)
1231 25th St. NW   Ph: (202)452-4323
Washington, DC 20037   Free: 800-372-1033
          Fax: (202)452-7773
E-mail: bnaplus@bna.com
Contact: Jeff Day, Managing Editor.
Desc: Provides legal clarification and practical advice on employers' pay and benefit policies, including detailed discussions of pertinent federal and state laws. Discusses such topics as health care compensation laws, pension law (ERISA), job evaluation, benefit plans, compensation administration, incentive systems, and independent contractors. *Type:* Newsletter.

Positive Leadership

Lawrence Ragan Communications, Inc.
316 N. Michigan Ave., Ste. 300   Ph: (312)960-4100
Chicago, IL 60601   Free: 800-878-5331
          Fax: (312)960-4105

E-mail: cservice@ragan.com
URL: http://www.ragan.com.
Contact: John Cowan, Editor; Mark Ragan, Publisher; Carol Jackson, Managing Editor, carolj@ragan.com.
Desc: Provides information about hiring and motivating top employees, dealing with work/family issues, giving back to your community, and becoming a more respected, ethical manager. *Type:* Newsletter.

Product Management Insight

Advanced Business Concepts, Inc.
39 Sequoia Rd.   Ph: (708)566-8420
Hawthorn Woods, IL 60047
Contact: Patricia A. Katzfey, Editor.
Desc: Focuses on product management, including new product development, organization, market focus, and product line maintenance. Recurring features include a calendar of events, book reviews, and notices of publications available. *Type:* Newsletter.

The Professional Advisor

National Training Center
123 NW 2nd Ave., No. 405
Portland, OR 97209
Contact: Bernard Hale Zick, Editor.
Desc: Addresses marketing and management of consulting services, seminars, training, and information products. Re-

curring features include letters to the editor, interviews, news of research, a calendar of events, reports of meetings, news of educational opportunities, book reviews, and an annual report on research regarding fees, incomes, and operating ratios of consultants and advisors. *Type:* Newsletter.

The Professionals Financial Forum

The Attorneys Group (TAG)
American Businesspersons Association (ABA)
National Association of the Professional (NAP)
Hillsboro Executive Center   Ph: (954)571-1877
North   Fax: (954)571-8582
350 Fairway Dr., Ste. 200
Deerfield Beach, FL 33441-1834
E-mail: ppsone@msn.com; youngpps@aol.com.
Contact: B. Lydia Young, Editor, youngpps@aol.com.
Desc: Offers "advice and up-to-date information on financial and tax planning, office management and other subjects of economic importance to professionals, attorneys, and business people." Provides news of membership benefits and services. *Type:* Newsletter.

Profiles in PDM

Hunt Personnel, Ltd.
1050 Wall St. W., Ste. 330   Ph: (212)997-2299
Lyndhurst, NJ 07071-3615   Fax: (212)438-8374
URL: http://www.huntLTD.com.
Contact: Alex Metz, Editor.
Desc: Published as a series of bulletins on basic principles of physical distribution management. *Type:* Newsletter.

Project Management Institute

4 Campus Blvd.   Ph: (610)356-4600
Newtown Square, PA 19073-   Fax: (610)356-4647
3200
E-mail: pmieo@ix.netcom.com
URL: http://www.pmi.org
Desc: Seeks to: foster recognition of the need for professionalism in worldwide project management; provide a forum for the free exchange of project management problems, solutions, and applications; coordinate industrial and academic research efforts; develop common terminology and techniques to improve project management communications; provide interface between users and suppliers of hardware and software computer systems; provide guidelines for instruction and career development in the field of project management. Accredits master's degree program in project management. Maintains placement service. *Type:* Association.

Promote and Prosper

Small Business Smarts, Inc.
2323 Clear Lake City Blvd., Ste.   Ph: (281)480-7069
180-211   Free: 800-480-0491
Houston, TX 77062   Fax: (281)480-7069
Contact: Donna Dulfer, President.
Desc: Contains information on marketing for business professionals. Recurring features include a calendar of events. *Type:* Newsletter.

The Pryor Report

Imagine Inc.
1440 Paddock Dr.
Northbrook, IL 60062-6811
Contact: Paul G. Friedman, Editor.
Desc: Provides brief articles on management techniques, including suggestions for their application. Includes book reviews and news of research relevant to middle and upper-level managers. *Type:* Newsletter.

PWA Newsletter

Performance Warehouse Association (PWA)
21311 Hawthorne Blvd., Ste.   Ph: (310)543-1523
103   Fax: (310)543-9623
Torrance, CA 90503-5610
Contact: John Towle, Editor.
Desc: Publishes news of the high performance/aftermarket warehouse industry for the members of this Association comprised of distributors, manufacturers, and manufacturers representatives. Identifies and lists market trends in eight different product areas. *Type:* Newsletter.

Research Recommendations

National Institute of Business Management
1750 Old Meadow Rd., Ste.   Ph: (703)905-8000
302   Free: 800-543-2049
Mc Lean, VA 22102   Fax: (703)905-8042
E-mail: resrecs@aol.com.
Contact: Pat DiDomencio, Editor.
Desc: Advisory on issues and events that affect small-business owners. Also provides tax reduction strategies. *Type:* Newsletter.

Results

National Staff Development Council
PO Box 240   Ph: (513)523-6029
Oxford, OH 45056   Free: 800-727-7288
          Fax: (513)523-0638
E-mail: nsdchavens@aol.com
URL: http://www.nsdc.org.
Contact: Joan Richardson, Editor.
Desc: Concerned with staff development programs for teachers and other educational personnel. Discusses effective staff development programs, news models of staff development, theories of adult learning, and planning and funding district-based staff development programs. *Type:* Newsletter.

Room at the Top

Ned Klumph Assocs.
100 Park Blvd., Apt. 77D   Ph: (609)667-1354
Cherry Hill, NJ 08034-3477
Desc: Publishes business news and information. *Type:* Newsletter.

Service Management

National Association of Service Managers
1030 W. Higgins Rd., No. 109
Hoffman Estates, IL 60195
E-mail: nasm@nasm.com
Contact: Kim Andersen, Editor.
Desc: Covers product service, management issues, and product liability. Recurring features include letters to the editor, a calendar of events, reports of meetings, news of educational opportunities, job listings, book reviews, notices of publications available, and a column titled President's Corner. *Type:* Newsletter.

Shopping Center Management Insider

Brownstone Publishers, Inc.
149 Fifth Ave., 16th Fl.   Ph: (212)473-8200
New York, NY 10010-6801   Free: 800-643-8095
          Fax: (212)473-8786
E-mail: scminews@aol.com.
Contact: Steven Gordon, Editor; John M. Striker, Publisher.
Desc: Provides information about managing shopping centers. Includes management techniques, legal news, model notices to tenants, letters, agreements, and rules. *Type:* Newsletter.

Sigma Iota Epsilon

Florida State University
214 Westcott Bldg.   Ph: (850)644-6003
Tallahassee, FL 32306   Fax: (850)644-4447
Contact: Mike Hankin, National Administrator.
Desc: Honorary and professional fraternity - management. Provides placement service, competitions, educational and charitable programs, and speakers' bureau on a local level. Student division of the Academy of Management. *Type:* Association.

Society for Advancement of Management

Texas A&M University- Corpus   Ph: (512)994-6045
  Christi   Free: 888-827-6077
College of Business   Fax: (512)994-2725
6300 Ocean Dr.
Corpus Christi, TX 78412
E-mail: moustafa@falcon.tamucc.edu
URL: http://www.enterprise.tamucc.edu/sam/sam.htm
Contact: Moustasa H. Abbelsamad, Pres.
Desc: Professional organization of management executives in industry commerce, government, and education. Fields of interest include management education, international management, administration, budgeting, collective bargaining, distribution, incentives, materials handling, quality control, and training. Sponsors numerous conferences, study groups, and seminars; conducts special programs on economics, material handling, distribution, industrial relations, and operation of small businesses. *Type:* Association.

Staff Leader

Aspen Publishers, Inc.
200 Orchard Ridge Dr., No.   Ph: (301)417-7500
  200   Free: 800-638-8437
Gaithersburg, MD 20878   Fax: (301)417-7650
E-mail: customer.service@aspenpubl.com
URL: http://www.aspenpub.com
Contact: Elizabeth Goehring, Editor.
Desc: Provides management tips and strategies for non-profit administrators. *Type:* Newsletter.

Storage Management/Iccm

Demand Technology
1020 8th Ave. S., Ste. 6   Ph: (941)261-8945
Naples, FL 34102   Free: 800-531-6143
                                   Fax: (941)261-5456
Contact: Mark Friedman, Publisher, markf@demandtech.com.
Desc: Provides advice for the storage management professional. Includes information on industry trends for use in capacity planning, performance, operations, and data storage administration. *Type:* Newsletter.

Strategic Edge

Economics Press, Inc.
12 Daniel Rd.   Ph: (973)227-1224
Fairfield, NJ 07004-2565   Free: 800-526-2554
                                   Fax: (973)526-2554
E-mail: info@epinc.com; order@epinc.com
URL: http://www.epinc.com
Contact: Richard Turitz, Editor, rturitz@epinc.com.
Desc: Designed to "provide accurate and authoritative information in regard to legal, accounting, and other professional services." Provides executives with tips and trends concerning their businesses. *Type:* Newsletter.

Strategic Leadership Forum

435 N. Michigan Ave., Ste.   Ph: (312)644-0829
  1717   Free: 800-873-5995
Chicago, IL 60611-4067   Fax: (312)644-8557
URL: http://www.slfnet.org
Contact: Gerard Soldner, Pres.
Desc: Professional society primarily comprised of executives involved in international strategic management and planning. *Type:* Association.

Success Secrets

Mark McCormack
IMG Center   Ph: (216)522-1200
1360 E. 9th St., Ste. 100   Fax: (216)522-1145
Cleveland, OH 44114
E-mail: successsecrets@imgwordd.com.
Contact: Mark McCormack, Editor-in-Chief; Mark Reiter, Exec. Editor, (212)772-8900, fax: (212)772-2619.
Desc: Contains stories that provide insight on success in business. *Type:* Newsletter.

Successful Supervisor

The Dartnell Corp.
360 Hiatt Dr.   Free: 800-621-5463
Palm Beach Gardens, FL 33418   Fax: (561)622-2423
E-mail: dartnell@dartnellcorp.com; sucsup@dartnellcorp.com.
URL: http://www.dartnellcorp.com
Contact: Linda Segall, Editor.
Desc: Biweekly training newsletter that features how-to ideas, success stories, and news items about supervision and management. Topics include: motivation, productivity, employee relations, communications, cost control, quality, customer service, and personal development. *Type:* Newsletter.

Supervisor's Guide to Quality & Excellence

Clement Communications, Inc.
Concord Industrial Park   Ph: (610)459-1700
10 LaCrue Ave.   Free: 800-345-8101
Concordville, PA 19331   Fax: (610)459-0936
E-mail: editor@clement.com.
Contact: Robi L. Miller, Managing Editor; George Y. Clement, Publisher; Neil J. Anderson, Sr.Ed.
Desc: Advises management professionals on techniques and information to better themselves as supervisors and to improve management-employee relations and the work environment. *Type:* Newsletter.

The Systems Thinker

Pegasus Communications, Inc.
1 Moody St.   Ph: (781)398-9700
Waltham, MA 02154-5339   Free: 800-272-0945
                                   Fax: (781)894-7175
Contact: Janice Molloy, Managing Editor.
Desc: Provides information about the theory and practice of the learning organization with an emphasis on systems thinking. Recurring features include letters to the editor, a calendar of events, book reviews, and columns titled Toolbox, Viewpoint, From the Headlines, systems Stories, Building Blocks, Systems Sleuth, and From the Resource Shelf. *Type:* Newsletter.

The Take-Charge Assistant

American Management Association
1601 Broadway   Ph: (212)586-8100
New York, NY 10019-7420   Free: 800-313-8650
                                   Fax: (212)903-8083
E-mail: cust-serv@amanet.org
Contact: Rosemary Kane Carlough, Publisher, (212)903-8103, fax: (212)903-8452; Florence Stone, Editor, (212)903-8075, fax: (212)903-8452, fstone@amanet.org; Carole Thielman, Production Mgr.; Seval Newton, Art Director; Beverly Hart, Marketing Manager, (212)903-7949.
Desc: Features career and professional guidance, tips, and problem solving. *Type:* Newsletter.

Team Management Briefings

Briefings Publishing Group
1101 King St., Ste. 110   Ph: (703)548-3800
Alexandria, VA 22314   Free: 800-888-2084
                                   Fax: (703)684-2136
E-mail: tloomis@briefings.com
Contact: Deirdre Hackett, Managing Editor, (503)274-2953, fax: (503)274-4349; Katie May, Contributing Editor; Joe McGavin, Exec. Editor.
Desc: Provides techniques and recommendations on how to improve organization or company growth through team work. Covers topics such as communication, group dynamics, empowerment, coaching, and improving meetings. *Type:* Newsletter.

Thiagi Game Letter

Jossey-Bass Inc., Publishers
350 Sansome St.   Ph: (415)433-1767
San Francisco, CA 94104   Free: 888-378-2537
                                   Fax: 800-605-2665
E-mail: webperson@jbp.com
URL: http://www.josseybass.com
Contact: Sivasailam Thiagarajan, Editor, (812)332-1478, thiagi@thiagi.com; Vincent J. Fritzsche, Managing Editor, (415)782-3198, vfritzsc@jbp.com.
Desc: Provides interactive experiential strategies to improve human performance with a wide range of training games, role-plays, and team building activities. Recurring features include letters to the editor, news of research, contests, and reproducible games. *Type:* Newsletter.

Today's Supervisor

National Safety Council
1121 Spring Lake Dr.   Ph: (630)285-1121
Itasca, IL 60143-3201   Free: 800-539-7468
                                   Fax: (630)285-1315
URL: http://www.nsc.org
Contact: Laura Coyne, Editor, (630)775-2276, fax: (630)775-2285, coynel@nsc.org; Kathleen Misovic, Assoc. Ed., (630)775-2288, fax: (630)775-2285, misovic@nsc.org; John Kennedy, Publisher, (630)775-2103, fax: (630)775-2285, kennedyj@nsc.org.
Desc: Magazine for the front-line supervisor containing articles related to safety and health. *Type:* Periodical.

Today's Team

Newsletters Ink
1866 Colonial Village Ln.   Ph: (717)393-1010
PO Box 11177   Free: 800-822-1858
Lancaster, PA 17605-1177
URL: http://www.ns.wentworth.com:80/tt/.
Contact: Gregory A. Gilson, General Mgr.
Desc: Focuses on issues related to team training. Recurring features include news of research and a column titled Team Talk. *Type:* Newsletter.

Today's Team Facilitator

Newsletters Ink
1866 Colonial Village Ln.   Ph: (717)393-1010
PO Box 11177   Free: 800-822-1858
Lancaster, PA 17605-1177
URL: http://www.ns.wentworth.com:80/tt/.
Contact: Gregory A. Gilson, General Mgr.
Desc: Acts as a companion to Today's Team newsletter. Focuses on issues related to team training, including creativity, problem solving, quality improvement, competitive intelligence, and motivation. *Type:* Newsletter.

Training Executive Update

NewsUpdate Communications Inc.
312-40 Wynford Dr.   Ph: (416)447-7638
Toronto, ON, Canada M3C 1J5   Fax: (416)447-2713
Contact: Susan Baka, Publisher; Shelley Boyces, Editor.

Desc: Directed toward the information needs of human resource development professionals. Discusses training resources, industry news, conference reports, and newsmakers. *Type:* Newsletter.

Turnaround Management Association

541 N. Fairbanks Ct. Ph: (312)822-9700
Ste. 1880 Fax: (312)822-9701
Chicago, IL 60611
E-mail: info@turnaround.org
Contact: Nancy Davis, Exec. Dir.

Desc: Practitioners (interim managers, consultants, corporate managers, and professional advisors), academics, students, judicial and legislative personnel). Promotes the image and credibility of the turnaround profession; fosters professional development opportunities for turnaround executives; serves as a clearinghouse of information and research pertinent to the profession. *Type:* Association.

Warehouse Management and Control Systems

Alexander Research & Communications, Inc.
215 Park Ave. S, Ste. 1301 Ph: (212)228-0246
New York, NY 10003 Fax: (212)228-0376
Contact: Margaret DeWitt, Publisher; Anita Rosepka, Managing Editor; Mary Pagliaroli, Marketing Director.
Desc: Provides in-depth information on warehouse management systems, as well as case studies and updates. *Type:* Newsletter.

World Confederation of Productivity Science

380 St. Antoine W, Rm. 3200 Ph: (514)878-9090
Montreal, PQ, Canada H2Y Fax: (514)987-1567
3X7
E-mail: miller@planetecom.net
Contact: Jean Claude Lauzon, Pres.
Desc: Fraternal association of manufacturing and commercial enterprises and employees, government agencies, professional institutions, and researchers. Goals are to promote productivity science, advance management techniques, and improve the quality of working life and environment. *Type:* Association.

Your New Pryor Report Managers Edge

Briefings Publishing Group
1101 King St., Ste. 110 Ph: (703)548-3800
Alexandria, VA 22314 Free: 800-888-2084
Fax: (703)684-2136
E-mail: tloomis@briefings.com; tloomis@briefings.com.
Contact: Paul Friedman, Editor.
Desc: Features information for managers. *Type:* Newsletter.

Manufacturing

Advanced Manufacturing

Center for Robotics and Manufacturing Systems (CRMS)
College of Engineering
University of Kentucky
220 CRMS Bldg. Ph: (606)257-6262
Lexington, KY 40506-0108 Fax: (606)323-1035
E-mail: info@crms.engr.uky.edu
Contact: Dorothy Rapp, Publications Mgr. & Editor, drapp@engr.uky.edu; Juanita Graves, Technology Transfer Editor, jgraves@engr.uky.edu.
Desc: Covers developments in manufacturing engineering, opportunities for business development, and CRMS projects and activities. Recurring features include news of research, news of educational opportunities, and articles on manufacturing problems solved. *Type:* Newsletter.

Alabama Industrial Directory

Alabama Development Office
401 Adams Ave. Ph: (334)242-0400
Montgomery, AL 36130 Free: 800-248-0033
Fax: (334)242-2414
E-mail: aidinfo@www.ado.sate.al.us
URL: http://www.ado.state.al.us.
Contact: Steve Nix, Editor, jostnix@aol.com.
Desc: Approximately 6,000 industrial companies in Alabama. *Type:* Directory.

Alaska Industrial Directory

Database Publishing Co.
1590 S. Lewis St. Ph: (714)778-6400
PO Box 70024 Free: 800-888-8434
Anaheim, CA 92825-0024 Fax: (714)778-6811
E-mail: sales@databasepublishing.com
URL: http://www.databasepublishing.com; http://www.databasepublishing.com/.
Desc: 800 manufacturing and mining companies and 1,087 owners, CEOs and key executives in Alaska. *Type:* Directory.

American Cutlery Manufacturers Association Newsletter

American Cutlery Manufacturers Association (ACMA)
112-J Elden St. Ph: (703)709-8253
Herndon, VA 20170 Fax: (703)709-1036
E-mail: acma@erols.com
Contact: David W. Barrack, Editor.
Desc: Provides information about the cutlery manufacturing industry. Recurring features include a calendar of events and reports of meetings. *Type:* Newsletter.

American Gear Manufacturers Association— News Digest

American Gear Manufacturers Association
1500 King St., Ste. 201 Ph: (703)684-0211
Alexandria, VA 22314-2730 Fax: (703)684-0242
E-mail: agma@agma.org
URL: http://www.agma.org
Contact: Mary Dee Bartolomei, Editor, marydee@agma.org.
Desc: Carries information of interest to gear manufacturers and suppliers. Recurring features include news of research, a calendar of events, reports of meetings, news of educational opportunities, and columns titled Economic Review, President's Corner, and Executive Director's View. *Type:* Newsletter.

American Industry

Publications for Industry
21 Russell Woods Rd. Ph: (516)487-0990
Great Neck, NY 11021 Fax: (516)487-0809
Contact: Jack S. Panes, Editor.
Desc: Provides new product releases and information on brochures and catalogs available to industrial plant managers in the largest firms in the U.S. Recurring features include interviews, news of research, and successful use of reports. *Type:* Newsletter.

American Manufacturers Directory

infoUSA
5711 S. 86th Circle Ph: (402)593-4600
PO Box 27347 Free: 800-555-6124
Omaha, NE 68127 Fax: (402)331-5481
E-mail: internet@infousa.com
URL: http://www.abii.com
Desc: More than 150,000 manufacturing companies with 20 or more employees. CD-ROM version lists all 531,000 U.S. manufacturers, in all employee size ranges. *Type:* Directory.

American Society for Quality

611 E. Wisconsin Ave. Ph: (414)272-8575
PO Box 3005 Free: 800-248-1946
Milwaukee, WI 53201-3005 Fax: (414)272-1734
E-mail: cs@asq.org
URL: http://www.asq.org
Contact: Paul E. Borawski, Exec.Dir.
Desc: Individuals and organizations dedicated to the ongoing development, advancement, and promotion of quality concepts, principles, and technologies. *Type:* Association.

Annual Survey of Manufacturers

The WEFA Group
1110 Vermont Ave., NW Ph: (202)775-0610
Washington, DC 20005
URL: http://www.fdic.gov
Desc: Contains 5650 annual time series of industry-specific economic data from the Census of Manufacturers and the Annual Survey of Manufacturers, sponsored by the U.S. Department of Commerce. *Available:* The WEFA Group. *Type:* Database.

Arizona Industrial Directory

Database Publishing Co.
1590 S. Lewis St. Ph: (714)778-6400
PO Box 70024 Free: 800-888-8434
Anaheim, CA 92825-0024 Fax: (714)778-6811
E-mail: sales@databasepublishing.com
URL: http://www.databasepublishing.com; http://www.databasepublishing.com/.
Contact: Kathleen Scott, Editor.
Desc: 8,500 manufacturing, wholesaling, and mining companies and 18,875 owners, CEOs and key executives in Arizona. *Type:* Directory.

Arizona Manufacturers Register

Manufacturers' News, Inc.
1633 Central St. Ph: (847)864-7000
Evanston, IL 60201 Free: 888-752-5200
Fax: (847)332-1100
E-mail: info@mninfo.com; sales@mninfo.com
URL: http://www.mninfo.com
Contact: Louise M. West, Editor.
Desc: 8,036 manufacturers in Arizona. *Type:* Directory.

Arkansas Manufacturers Register

Manufacturers' News, Inc.
1633 Central St. Ph: (847)864-7000
Evanston, IL 60201 Free: 888-752-5200
Fax: (847)332-1100
E-mail: info@mninfo.com; sales@mninfo.com
URL: http://www.mninfo.com
Contact: Louise M. West, Editor.
Desc: 3,721 manufacturers in Arkansas. *Type:* Directory.

Associated Industries of Massachusetts

222 Berkeley St. Ph: (617)262-1180
PO Box 763 Fax: (617)536-6785
Boston, MA 02116-0763
E-mail: jch@aimnet.org
URL: http://www.aimnet.org
Contact: John Gould, Pres./CEO.
Desc: Manufacturers trade association. Lobbies state and federal governments on behalf of members. *Type:* Association.

Association for Manufacturing Technology

7901 Westpark Dr. Ph: (703)893-2900
Mc Lean, VA 22102 Fax: (703)893-1151
E-mail: amt@mfgtech.org
URL: http://www.mfgtech.org

Contact: Don F. Carlson, Pres.

Desc: Supports and enhances the activities of American manufacturers. *Type:* Association.

Association for Quality and Participation

801-B W. 8th St., Ste. 501 Ph: (513)381-1959
Cincinnati, OH 45203-1607 Free: 800-733-3310
 Fax: (513)381-0070

E-mail: aqp@aqp.org
URL: http://www.aqp.org

Contact: Cathy Kramer, Exec.V.Pres.

Desc: A non-for-profit educational association and learning resource for individuals, teams, and organizations dedicated to promoting the ideas of involvement, empowerment and workplace democracy. AQP has been in operation for 20 years and disseminates information to members through publications, conferences and educational events. *Type:* Association.

Better Repping

Berman Publications
11718 Barrington Ct., No. 341 Ph: (818)905-5388
Los Angeles, CA 90049-2930

Contact: Jack Berman, Editor.

Desc: Addresses companies that sell through independent manufacturing representatives. *Type:* Newsletter.

Business Journal's Directory of Manufacturing

Business Journal of New Jersey, Inc.
50 Highway 9 Ph: (908)972-1170
Morganville, NJ 07751 Free: 800-678-2565
 Fax: (908)972-7965

Desc: 10,5000 manufacturing companies located in New Jersey. *Type:* Directory.

California Conference of Machinists

921 11th St., Ste. 450 Ph: (916)444-5599
Sacramento, CA 95814 Fax: (916)444-1661

Contact: Matthew R. McKinnon, Exec.Sec./Treas.

Type: Association.

CAMM News

Canadian Association of Moldmakers (CAMM)
424 Tecumseh Rd. E. Ph: (519)255-7863
Windsor, ON, Canada N8X Free: 800-567-2266
2R6 Fax: (519)255-9446
E-mail: cdnmolds@mnsi.net

Contact: Patricia Papp, Editor.

Desc: Contains items of interest to members of the moldmaking industry. Recurring features include editorials, information on education and shows, letters to the editor, a calendar of events, reports of meetings, news of educational opportunities, and columns titled Technical Corner and Members in the News. *Type:* Newsletter.

Canadian Hardware and Housewares Manufacturers' Association Newsletter

Canadian Hardware and Housewares Manufacturers' Association
1335 Morningside Ave., Ste. Ph: (416)282-0022
101 Fax: (416)282-0027
Scarborough, ON, Canada M1B
5M4

Contact: Kathryn Lee, Editor.

Desc: Provides news of activities in the hardwares and housewares in Canada. *Type:* Newsletter.

CIRAS News

Center for Industrial Research and Service (CIRAS)
Iowa State University Ph: (515)294-1507
2501 N. Loop Dr., Ste. 500 Fax: (515)294-4925
Ames, IA 50010-8286
E-mail: ciras@exnet.iastate.edu
URL: http://www.ciras.iastate.edu.

Contact: Jim Black, Editor, xljblack@exnet.iastate.edu.

Desc: Provides information on management techniques and methods for improving process operations. Describes services and agencies available. *Type:* Newsletter.

Classified Directory of Wisconsin Manufacturers

WMC Foundation
501 E. Washington Ave. Ph: (608)258-3400
PO Box 352 Free: 800-328-2567
Madison, WI 53701-0352 Fax: (608)258-3413
E-mail: wmc@wmc.org; dbm@wmc.org.

Contact: Marie A. Large, Editor; Jinger L. Mandt, Editor.

Desc: 11,000 manufacturing firms in Wisconsin, plus over 26,000 officers and key decision makers. *Type:* Directory.

Colorado Manufacturers Register

Database Publishing Co.
1590 S. Lewis St. Ph: (714)778-6400
PO Box 70024 Free: 800-888-8434
Anaheim, CA 92825-0024 Fax: (714)778-6811
E-mail: sales@databasepublishing.com
URL: http://www.databasepublishing.com; http://www.databasepublishing.com.

Desc: Over 6,800 manufacturing companies in Colorado, plus 14,500 key executives. *Type:* Directory.

Commercial Carpet Digest

RBI International Carpert Consultants
PO Box 722 Ph: (706)226-3217
Dalton, GA 30722 Free: 888-499-3212
 Fax: (706)278-3565
E-mail: rbi@alltell.net

Contact: Lew Migliore, Editor.

Desc: Covers the commercial carpet market. Recurring features include letters to the editor, interviews, news of research, and news of educational opportunities. *Type:* Newsletter.

DDIN-International

Larson Associates
95 Mt. Blue St. Ph: (781)659-2115
Norwell, MA 02061 Free: 800-229-3346
 Fax: (781)659-2411
E-mail: larson@dieco.com
URL: http://www.dieco.com.

Contact: Robert A. Larson, Editor, larson@dieco.com.

Desc: Contains technical and other information for the diemaking and diecutting industry. *Type:* Newsletter.

Delaware Manufacturers Register

Manufacturers' News, Inc.
1633 Central St. Ph: (847)864-7000
Evanston, IL 60201 Free: 888-752-5200
 Fax: (847)332-1100
E-mail: info@mninfo.com; sales@mninfo.com
URL: http://www.mninfo.com

Contact: Louise M. West, Editor.

Desc: 826 manufacturers in Delaware. *Type:* Directory.

Die Casting Industry Buyers Guide

Die Casting Industry Publications
3030 Malmo Dr. Ph: (708)364-1222
Arlington Heights, IL 60005- Fax: (708)364-1268
4726
URL: http://www.assnpubs.com.

Contact: Jarvis Scott, Editor.

Desc: Toolmakers, chemical firms, lubricant firms, new and used machinery manufacturers, furnace manufacturers, robotics and automation corporations, process controls firms, metal suppliers, product finishers, secondary operations, other material suppliers, computer and software firms, waste management and control firms, health and safety organizations, manufacturers; representatives, associations, and professionals organizations that serve die casters; international coverage. *Type:* Directory.

A Directory of Lincoln, Nebraska Manufacturers

Lincoln Chamber of Commerce
PO Box 83006 Ph: (402)436-2350
Lincoln, NE 68501-3006 Fax: (402)436-2360

Contact: Mark Essman, Editor.

Desc: Over 350 manufacturers located in Lincoln, Nebraska. *Type:* Directory.

The Distributor's & Wholesaler's Advisor

Alexander Research & Communications, Inc.
215 Park Ave. S, Ste. 1301 Ph: (212)228-0246
New York, NY 10003 Fax: (212)228-0376

Contact: Anita Rosepka, Editor.

Desc: Provides case studies, how-to-do-it reports, and industry news of interest to wholesalers and distributors. Covers management strategies, working with manufacturers, logistics and warehousing, finance, personnel issues, sales management, technology, customer service, and law and regulation. *Type:* Newsletter.

Dun & Bradstreet Directory of Key Manufacturing Companies in People's Republic of China

Dun & Bradstreet
3 Sylvan Way Ph: (973)605-6442
Parsippany, NJ 07054-3896 Free: 800-526-0651
 Fax: (973)605-6911
E-mail: dnbmdd@dnb.com

Desc: 17,000 leading manufacturing firms in People's Republic of China. *Type:* Directory.

Eastern Niagara Manufacturers Directory

Eastern Niagara Chamber of Commerce
151 W. Genesee St. Ph: (716)433-3828
Lockport, NY 14094-3686 Free: 800-433-4660
 Fax: (716)433-1154
E-mail: info@eastniagarany.org

Contact: David R. Kinyon, President.

Desc: About 85 manufacturers and financial institutions in eastern Niagara County, New York. *Type:* Directory.

Electro Manufacturing

Worldwide Videotex
PO Box 3273 Ph: (561)738-2276
Boynton Beach, FL 33424-3273
URL: http://www.wvpubs.com.

Desc: Covers research and development of products and services in manufacturing. Includes company profiles, studies in productivity, and new technology. *Type:* Newsletter.

Engine Manufacturers Association

401 N. Michigan Ave Ph: (312)644-6610
Chicago, IL 60611 Fax: (312)321-5111
E-mail: ema@sba.com
URL: http://www.engine-manufacturers.org

Contact: Glenn F. Keller, Exec.Dir.

Desc: Producers of internal combustion engines for all applications except those used exclusively for automobiles and aircraft. Conducts research and development programs on noise, smoke, and other emissions from internal combustion engines. *Type:* Association.

Equipment & Materials Update

Infoteam, Inc.
PO Box 15640   Ph: (954)473-9560
Plantation, FL 33318-5640   Fax: (954)473-0544
E-mail: infoteamma@aol.com
Contact: Walter A. Treff, Editor.

Desc: Covers all areas and subjects related to materials development and process equipment design, operation, and integrity. Remarks: Functions as a photocopied version of an electronic newsletter accessible on computer terminals and communicating word processors. *Type:* Newsletter.

The Exhibitor

Material Handling Industry
8720 Red Oak Blvd., Ste. 201   Ph: (704)676-1190
Charlotte, NC 28217   Free: 800-345-1815
   Fax: (704)676-1199
URL: http://www.mhia.org.
Contact: Heathir McElroy, Editor, hmcelroy@mhia.org;
Carol Miller, Editor, cmiller@mhia.org.

Desc: Informs potential exhibitors on Material Handling Industry of America-sponsored exhibitions and seminars. *Type:* Newsletter.

Florida Manufacturers Register

Manufacturers' News, Inc.
1633 Central St.   Ph: (847)864-7000
Evanston, IL 60201   Free: 888-752-5200
   Fax: (847)332-1100
E-mail: info@mninfo.com; sales@mninfo.com
URL: http://www.mninfo.com; http://www.manufacturersnews.com.
Contact: Louise M. West, Editor.

Desc: 19,770 manufacturers in Florida. *Type:* Directory.

FMA Connections

Fabricators & Manufacturers Association, International
833 Featherstone Rd.   Ph: (815)399-8700
Rockford, IL 61107   Fax: (815)399-7279
Contact: Jennifer Haldeman, Editor.

Desc: Provides members with the latest news about the Association, such as benefits and activities, and about news in the metal forming and fabricating industries. Recurring features include a calendar of events, news of educational opportunities, and book reviews. *Type:* Newsletter.

The GMP Letter

Washington Business Information, Inc.
1117 N. 19th St., No. 200   Ph: (703)247-3434
Arlington, VA 22209-1798   Fax: (703)247-3421
Contact: Samuel Gilston, Editor.

Desc: Focuses on Good Manufacturing Practice (GMP), especially Food and Drug Administration (FDA) regulations on production and quality control. Covers enforcement and practice as well as compliance with federal regulations. *Type:* Newsletter.

Greater Knoxville Directory of Manufacturers

Greater Knoxville Chamber of Commerce
601 W. Summit Hill Dr., Ste.
   300
Knoxville, TN 37902-2011
Desc: Manufacturing firms located in the 17-county greater Knoxville area. *Type:* Directory.

Gulf Coast Industrial Atlas/Directory

Industrial Information Resources
11011 Richmond Ave.   Ph: (713)783-5728
Houston, TX 77042   Free: 800-762-3361
   Fax: (713)783-2705
URL: http://www.iir-cismap.com.
Contact: Gene Dewree, Editor.

Desc: About 2,700 heavy industrial plants (including refineries, steel mills, power plants, pulp and paper mills, terminals, docks, storage saltdomes, gas processing plants, chemical plants) in Florida, Alabama, Mississippi, Louisiana, and Texas. *Type:* Directory.

Harris Connecticut Manufacturers Directory

Harris InfoSource
2057 E. Aurora Rd.   Ph: (330)425-9000
Twinsburg, OH 44087-1999   Free: 800-888-5900
   Fax: (330)425-7150
E-mail: customerservice@harrisinfo.com
URL: http://www.harrisinfo.com; http://harrisinfo.com.
Contact: Frances L. Carlsen, Editor.

Desc: 6,700 manufacturer firms in Connecticut. *Type:* Directory.

Harris Maryland Manufacturers Directory

Harris InfoSource
2057 E. Aurora Rd.   Ph: (330)425-9000
Twinsburg, OH 44087-1999   Free: 800-888-5900
   Fax: (330)425-7150
E-mail: customerservice@harrisinfo.com
URL: http://www.harrisinfo.com; http://www.harrisinfo.com.
Contact: Frances L. Carlsen, Editor.

Desc: 5,835 manufacturers and manufacturing services. *Type:* Directory.

Hawaii Industrial Directory

Database Publishing Co.
1590 S. Lewis St.   Ph: (714)778-6400
PO Box 70024   Free: 800-888-8434
Anaheim, CA 92825-0024   Fax: (714)778-6811
E-mail: sales@databasepublishing.com
URL: http://www.databasepublishing.com; http://www.databasepublishing.com/.
Desc: 1100 manufacturing companies in Hawaii. *Type:* Directory.

Haystack

Information Handling Services Group Inc.
15 Inverness Way E.
Englewood, CO 80112
E-mail: info@ihs.com
URL: http://www.ihs.com

Desc: Contains identification and technical data for 13 million components, equipment, and other military hardware listed in the Federal Supply Catalog. Includes, for each item, National Stock Number (NSN), National Item Identification Number (NIIN), Master Cross Reference List (MCRL) numbers, H4/H8 Commercial and Government Entity (CAGE) vendor information, manufacturer's part number, and item names and definitions, including Approved Item Name (AIN), Federal Item Identification Guide (FIIG), and Item Name Code (INC). *Available:* Information Handling Services Group Inc. *Type:* Database.

Idaho Manufacturers Register

Database Publishing Co.
1590 S. Lewis St.   Ph: (714)778-6400
PO Box 70024   Free: 800-888-8434
Anaheim, CA 92825-0024   Fax: (714)778-6811
E-mail: sales@databasepublishing.com
URL: http://www.databasepublishing.com; http://www.databasepublishing.com/; http://www.databasepublishing.com.

Desc: Approximately 3,100 manufacturing, mining, and high tech companies in Idaho, 6,100 key executives. *Type:* Directory.

Illinois Manufacturers Register

Manufacturers' News, Inc.
1633 Central St.   Ph: (847)864-7000
Evanston, IL 60201   Free: 888-752-5200
   Fax: (847)332-1100
E-mail: info@mninfo.com; sales@mninfo.com
URL: http://www.mninfo.com; http://www.manufacturersnews.com.
Contact: Louise M. West, Editor.

Desc: 23,003 manufacturers in Illinois. *Type:* Directory.

IMRA News & Views

Advertising and Public Relations Committee
Incentive Manufacturers Representatives Association, Inc. (IMRA)
1805 N. Mill St. A   Ph: (630)369-3466
Naperville, IL 60563-1275   Fax: (630)369-3773
Contact: Karen Renk, Editor.

Desc: Carries news of the incentives manufacturing industry, news of Association events, and articles on issues in the industry. Promotes improved understanding of the function of the direct factory representative in the premium and incentive market. *Type:* Newsletter.

The Industrial Advisor

Economic Development Institute
Georgia Institute of Technology   Ph: (404)894-6091
211 O'Keefe Bldg.   Fax: (404)894-6983
Atlanta, GA 30332
Contact: Lincoln Bates, Editor, lincoln.bates@edi.gatech.edu.

Desc: Provides information on how Georgia manufacturers can become more productive and competitive. Features case studies on technical assistance. *Type:* Newsletter.

Industrial Directory Pennsylvania

Harris InfoSource
2057 E. Aurora Rd.   Ph: (330)425-9000
Twinsburg, OH 44087-1999   Free: 800-888-5900
   Fax: (330)425-7150
E-mail: customerservice@harrisinfo.com
URL: http://www.harrisinfo.com
Desc: 7,581 companies. *Type:* Directory.

Industrial Purchasing Agent

Publications for Industry
21 Russell Woods Rd.   Ph: (516)487-0990
Great Neck, NY 11021   Fax: (516)487-0809
E-mail: ipa@pubforind.com.
Contact: Pearl S. Shaine, Editor.

Desc: Covers new product releases pertaining to the industrial manufacturing industry. Recurring features include interviews, news of research, a calendar of events, and reports of meetings. *Type:* Newsletter.

Inland-Northwest Manufacturers Directory

Spokane Area Economic Development Council
801 W. Riverside, Ste. 302   Ph: (509)624-9285
Spokane, WA 99201   Free: 800-SPO-KANE
   Fax: (509)624-3759
E-mail: edc@edc.spokane.net
URL: http://www.spokanedc.org
Contact: Mark Turner, Editor.

Desc: Over 2,500 manufacturing firms with Standard Industrial Classification (SIC) codes 20-39 and 737 and 8071 in a 38-county area covering eastern Washington, northern Idaho, western Montana, and northeastern Oregon. *Type:* Directory.

Intelligent Manufacturing
Lionheart Publishing Inc.
2555 Cumberland Pkwy., Ste. 299   Ph: (404)431-0867
Atlanta, GA 30339   Free: 800-392-7294
   Fax: (404)432-6969
E-mail: info@lionhrtpub.com
URL: http://www.lionheartpub.com; http://lionhrtpub.com.
Contact: David Blanchard, Editor, blanchard@lionhrtpub.com.
Desc: Provides solutions for manufacturing personnel. Includes industry news and information on specific production problems. *Type:* Newsletter.

International Association of Refrigerated Warehouses
7315 Wisconsin Ave., 1200N   Ph: (301)652-5674
Bethesda, MD 20814   Fax: (301)652-7269
E-mail: email@iarw.org
URL: http://www.iarw.org
Contact: J. William Hudson, Pres.
Desc: Public refrigerated warehouses storing all types of perishable foods and other perishable products; associate members are industry suppliers. *Type:* Association.

International Instrumentation & Controls—Buyers' Guide Issue
Keller International Publishing, LLC
150 Great Neck Rd.   Ph: (516)829-9210
Great Neck, NY 11021   Fax: (516)829-5414
E-mail: kellpub@world.att.net
Contact: Felicia Morales, Editor.
Desc: List of over 310 suppliers of precision instrument products and services. *Type:* Directory.

International Sleep Products Association
333 Commerce St.   Ph: (703)683-8371
Alexandria, VA 22314   Fax: (703)683-4503
E-mail: info@sleepproducts.org
URL: http://www.sleepproducts.org
Contact: Russell L. Abolt, Exec.VP.
Desc: Manufacturers of mattresses, bedding foundations, and dual purpose sleeping equipment and supplies. Compiles statistics. *Type:* Association.

International Warehouse Logistics Association
1300 W. Higgins, Ste. 111   Ph: (847)292-1891
Park Ridge, IL 60068   Fax: (847)292-1896
URL: http://www.warehouselogistics.org
Contact: Mike Jenkins, President & CEO.
Desc: Promtes the use of third-party warehousing and related logistics services. *Type:* Association.

Interstate Manufacturers and Industrial Directory
Interstate Publishers Corp.
1841 Broadway, Ste. 713   Ph: (212)246-8484
New York, NY 10023-5876   Fax: (212)246-8821
Contact: Frank Majorana, Editor.
Desc: 26,000 firms in 22 states, primarily in the East, South, and West. *Type:* Directory.

Inventory Reduction Report
Institute of Management & Administration, Inc.
29 W. 35th St., 5th Fl.   Ph: (212)244-0360
New York, NY 10001-2299   Fax: (212)564-0465
E-mail: subserve@ioma.com
URL: http://www.ioma.com
Contact: Joe Mazel, Editor; Perry Patterson, Publisher.
Desc: Provides information about controlling inventory. *Type:* Newsletter.

Juvenile Products Manufacturers Association
236 Rte. 38 W. Ste. 100   Ph: (609)231-8500
Moorestown, NJ 08057   Fax: (609)231-4664
E-mail: jpma@ahint.com
URL: http://www.jpma.org
Contact: William J. MacMillan, Pres.
Desc: Manufacturers of infants' furniture, baby carriages, strollers, chairs, and related products. Exchanges credit information. Conducts annual trade show, research, and surveys; provides statistical information. *Type:* Association.

Kansas Manufacturers Directory
Manufacturers' News, Inc.
1633 Central St.   Ph: (847)864-7000
Evanston, IL 60201   Free: 888-752-5200
   Fax: (847)332-1100
E-mail: info@mninfo.com; sales@mninfo.com
URL: http://www.mninfo.com
Contact: Louise M. West, Editor.
Desc: 4,488 manufacturers in Kansas. *Type:* Directory.

Leather Industries of America
1000 Thomas Jefferson St. NW,   Ph: (202)342-8086
Ste. 515   Fax: (202)342-9063
Washington, DC 20007
Contact: Charles S. Myers, Pres.
Desc: Firms engaged in leather tanning. Works for the promotion and advancement of the leather industry through government representation, environmental regulation, technical services, and public relations. Established Tanners' Council Research Laboratory. *Type:* Association.

Luggage and Leather Goods Manufacturers of America
350 5th Ave., Ste. 2624   Ph: (212)695-2340
New York, NY 10118   Free: 800-826-4224
   Fax: (212)643-8021
E-mail: llgma@llgma.org
URL: http://www.llgma.org
Contact: Anne L. DeCicco, CAE, Pres.
Desc: Manufacturers and wholesalers of luggage, briefcases, handbags, business and travel accessories, and personal leather goods. *Type:* Association.

Maine Manufacturers Register
Commerce Register, Inc.
190 Godwin Ave.   Ph: (201)445-3000
Midland Park, NJ 07432   Free: 800-221-2172
   Fax: (201)445-5806
Contact: Louise M. West, Editor.
Desc: 2,200 manufacturers in Maine. *Type:* Directory.

Maine/Vermont/New Hampshire Manufacturers Register
Commerce Register, Inc.
190 Godwin Ave.   Ph: (201)445-3000
Midland Park, NJ 07432   Free: 800-221-2172
   Fax: (201)445-5806
Contact: Louise M. West, Editor.
Desc: 4,000 manufacturers in Maine, Vermont, and New Hampshire. *Type:* Directory.

MAN—Modern Applications News—Abrasives/Grinding, Machines/Supplies, Finishing Equipment, Supplies Buyers' Guide
Nelson Publishing, Inc.
2500 Tamiami Tr. N.   Ph: (941)966-9521
Nokomis, FL 34275-3482   Fax: (941)966-2590
E-mail: nelpub@ix.netcom.com
Contact: Larry Olson, Editor.
Desc: List of companies that supply the metalworking industry with abrasives and grinding products and services. *Type:* Directory.

MAN—Modern Applications News—Coolants/Lubricants/Filters/Coatings Buyers' Guide
Nelson Publishing, Inc.
2500 Tamiami Tr. N.   Ph: (941)966-9521
Nokomis, FL 34275   Fax: (941)966-2590
E-mail: nelpub@ix.netcom.com
Contact: Larry Olson, Editor.
Desc: List of companies that supply the metalworking industry with coolant/lubricant/fluid equipment and products. *Type:* Directory.

MAN—Modern Applications News—Cutting Tools Buyers' Guide
Nelson Publishing, Inc.
2500 Tamiami Tr. N.   Ph: (941)966-9521
Nokomis, FL 34275-3482   Fax: (941)966-2590
E-mail: nelpub@ix.netcom.com
Contact: Larry Olson, Editor.
Desc: List of manufacturers and distributors of cutting tools. *Type:* Directory.

MAN—Modern Applications News—EDM/ECM/Plasma Identification/Marking Systems/Lasers Buyers' Guide
Nelson Publishing, Inc.
2500 Tamiami Tr. N.   Ph: (941)966-9521
Nokomis, FL 34275-3482   Fax: (941)966-2590
E-mail: nelpub@ix.netcom.com
Contact: Larry Olson, Editor.
Desc: List of companies that supply the metalworking industry with electronic drafting machine equipment and services. *Type:* Directory.

MAN—Modern Applications News—Holemaking/Equipment Buyers' Guide
Nelson Publishing, Inc.
2500 Tamiami Tr. N.   Ph: (941)966-9521
Nokomis, FL 34275-3482   Fax: (941)966-2590
E-mail: nelpub@ix.netcom.com
Contact: Larry Olson, Editor.
Desc: List of companies that supply the metalworking industry with holemaking/equipment and products. *Type:* Directory.

MAN—Modern Applications News—Laser Systems Buyers' Guide
Nelson Publishing, Inc.
2500 Tamiami Tr. N.   Ph: (941)966-9521
Nokomis, FL 34275-3482   Fax: (941)966-2590
E-mail: nelpub@ix.netcom.com
Contact: Larry Olson, Editor.
Desc: List of companies that supply the metalworking industry with laser equipment. *Type:* Directory.

MAN—Modern Applications News—Machining Centers
Nelson Publishing, Inc.
2500 Tamiami Tr. N.   Ph: (941)966-9521
Nokomis, FL 34275-3482   Fax: (941)966-2590
E-mail: nelpub@ix.netcom.com
Contact: Larry Olson, Editor.
Desc: List of companies that supply the metalworking industry with forging tools. *Type:* Directory.

MAN—Modern Applications News—QC/Measurement/Inspection Buyers' Guide
Nelson Publishing, Inc.
2500 Tamiami Tr. N.   Ph: (941)966-9521
Nokomis, FL 34275-3482   Fax: (941)966-2590
E-mail: nelpub@ix.netcom.com
Contact: Larry Olson, Editor.
Desc: List of companies that supply the metalworking industry with quality control and measurement and inspection products. *Type:* Directory.

MAN—Modern Applications News—Welding/Brazing/Soldering, Systems/Supplies Heat Treat Systems, Services

Nelson Publishing, Inc.
2500 Tamiami Tr. N. Ph: (941)966-9521
Nokomis, FL 34275-3482 Fax: (941)966-2590
E-mail: nelpub@ix.netcom.com
Contact: Larry Olson, Editor.
Desc: List of companies that supply the metalworking industry with holemaking/drilling advancement lasers in fastening and joining. *Type:* Directory.

MAN—Modern Applications News—Workholding/Toolholding Buyers' Guide

Nelson Publishing, Inc.
2500 Tamiami Tr. N. Ph: (941)966-9521
Nokomis, FL 34275-3482 Fax: (941)966-2590
E-mail: nelpub@ix.netcom.com
Contact: Larry Olson, Editor.
Desc: List of companies that supply the metalworks industry with cutting tools, coolants/fluids, problem solvers, and machine centers. *Type:* Directory.

Manufacturers Directory to Southeast Michigan

Greater Detroit Chamber of Commerce
1 Woodward Ave., Ste. 1700 Ph: (313)964-4000
Detroit, MI 48226 Fax: (313)964-0183
E-mail: aladetto@detroitchamber.com
URL: http://www.detroitchamber.com.
Contact: Melissa Armstrong, Editor.
Desc: 3,400 metro area manufacturers as well as over 350 name, title, address, Standard Industrial Classification (SIC) code, product, phone, fax & business parks. *Type:* Directory.

Manufacturers' Mart—Line Card Buyer's Guide Issue

Manufacturers' Mart Publications
16 High St. Ph: (401)348-0797
Westerly, RI 02891-1850 Fax: (401)348-0799
E-mail: info@manufacturesmart.com
URL: http://www.manufacturersmart.com.
Desc: List of suppliers of equipment and products for manufacturers in Connecticut, Maine, Massachusetts, New Hampshire, Rhode Island, and Vermont. *Type:* Directory.

Manufacturers Representatives of America—Newsline

Manufacturers Representatives of America
PO Box 150229 Ph: (817)561-7272
Arlington, TX 76015-6229 Fax: (817)561-7275
E-mail: assnhqtrs@aol.com
Contact: William R. Bess, Editor.
Desc: Published for member independent manufacturers' representatives handling sanitary supplies and paper and plastic disposable products. Carries articles to help improve agent sales skills, market coverage, and customer service, and to help establish more effective agent/principal communications. *Type:* Newsletter.

Manufacturing Automation

Vital Information Publications
754 Caravel Ln. Ph: (650)345-7018
Foster City, CA 94404 Fax: (650)345-7018
E-mail: vpa@pacbell.net
Contact: Peter Adrian, Editor.
Desc: Provides global information and market analysis on manufacturing automation. Topics include CADCAM, robotics, material handling, machine tools, systems integration, automation software, and manufacturing management issues. *Type:* Newsletter.

Manufacturing News

Publishers & Producers
PO Box 36 Ph: (703)750-2664
Annandale, VA 22003 Fax: (703)750-0064
E-mail: editor@manufacturingnews.com.
URL: http://www.manufacturingnews.com.
Contact: Richard McCormack, Editor.
Desc: Relates breaking news on manufacturing programs and policies, electronic commerce, new manufacturing technologies, and techniques. Carries guest editorials. *Type:* Newsletter.

Manufacturing Systems

Cahners Business Information
2000 Clearwater Dr. Ph: (630)320-7000
Oak Brook, IL 60523 Free: 800-826-6270
 Fax: (630)320-7373
URL: http://www.manufacturingsystems.com.
Contact: Kevin Parker, Editor, kparker@cahners.com.
Desc: Professional magazine covering information technology for manufacturing managers. *Type:* Periodical.

Manufacturing Technology Alert

Technical Insights
John Wiley and Sons, Inc.
32 N. Dean St. Ph: (201)568-4744
Englewood, NJ 07631
E-mail: TIInf@wiley.com
URL: http://www.wiley.comm/technicalinsights
Contact: Mark Roberts, Director of Computer Operations, (201)568-4744, 73373.51@compuserve.com.
Desc: Contains the complete text of Advanced Manufacturing Technology, a monthly newsletter on robotics and manufacturing technology. Covers artificial intelligence, automated machining, lasers, products and applications, and company news. *Available:* CompuServe Information Service. *Type:* Database.

Manufacturing USA: Industry Analyses, Statistics, and Leading Companies

Gale Group Inc.
27500 Drake Rd. Ph: (248)699-4253
Farmington Hills, MI 48331- Free: 800-877-GALE
3535 Fax: (248)699-8070
E-mail: galeord@galegroup.com; ecdi@statrom.com.
URL: http://www.galegroup.com.; http://www.gale.com.
Contact: Arsen J. Darnay, Editor, (248)356-6990, fax: (248)356-6426.
Desc: Lists of up to 75 leading companies for each manufacturing industry (Standard Industrial Classification (SIC) code range 2011 to 3999), selected on the basis of annual sales. *Type:* Directory.

Marketing Economics Key Plants: Guide to Industrial Purchasing Power

Marketing Economics Institute Ltd.
186-26 Avon Rd. Ph: (718)454-1697
Jamaica, NY 11432 Fax: (718)523-0351
Contact: Alfred Hong, Editor.
Desc: More than 40,000 key manufacturing plants with 100 or more employees (SIC 2011-3999); there are also editions for New England, Middle Atlantic, East North Central, West North Central, South Atlantic, East South Central, West South Central, and Mountain/Pacific regions. *Type:* Directory.

Maryland/Delaware Directory of Manufacturers

Commerce Register, Inc.
190 Godwin Ave. Ph: (201)445-3000
Midland Park, NJ 07432 Free: 800-221-2172
 Fax: (201)445-5806
Contact: Joel Rosano, Editor.
Desc: 4,000 industrial firms with five or more employees in Maryland and Delaware. *Type:* Directory.

Massachusetts Directory of Manufacturers

Commerce Register, Inc.
190 Godwin Ave. Ph: (201)445-3000
Midland Park, NJ 07432 Free: 800-221-2172
 Fax: (201)445-5806
Contact: Joel Rosano, Editor.
Desc: 6,000 industrial firms with five or more employees. *Type:* Directory.

Massachusetts Manufacturers Register

Commerce Register, Inc.
190 Godwin Ave. Ph: (201)445-3000
Midland Park, NJ 07432 Free: 800-221-2172
 Fax: (201)445-5806
Contact: Louise M. West, Editor.
Desc: 6,751 manufacturers in Massachusetts. *Type:* Directory.

The MFP Report

Bissett Communications Corp.
12844 Berkhamsted St. Ph: (562)809-8917
Cerritos, CA 90703 Fax: (562)809-1627
E-mail: bbissett@mfpreport.com
Contact: Brian Bissett, Editor and Publisher, bbissett@ix.netcom.com.
Desc: Offers business intelligence on the latest multifunction peripherals business, market and technology issues, and their impact. Features standards, products, trade shows, and company features. *Type:* Newsletter.

Michigan Manufacturers Directory

Pick Publications, Inc.
24293 Telegraph Rd., No. 140 Ph: (810)827-7111
Southfield, MI 48034 Free: 800-247-1558
 Fax: (810)827-7119
E-mail: pickincl@aol.com
Contact: Paul Pickell, Editor.
Desc: More than 16,000 manufacturers. *Type:* Directory.

Michigan Manufacturers Register

Manufacturers' News, Inc.
1633 Central St. Ph: (847)864-7000
Evanston, IL 60201 Free: 888-752-5200
 Fax: (847)332-1100
E-mail: info@mninfo.com; sales@mninfo.com
URL: http://www.mninfo.com
Contact: Louise M. West, Editor.
Desc: 22,000 manufacturers in Michigan. *Type:* Directory.

Minnesota Directory of Manufacturers

Harris InfoSource
2057 E. Aurora Rd. Ph: (330)425-9000
Twinsburg, OH 44087-1999 Free: 800-888-5900
 Fax: (330)425-7150
E-mail: customerservice@harrisinfo.com; mndir@kgpublishing.com.
URL: http://www.harrisinfo.com; http://www.harrisinfo.com.
Desc: Over 10,000 manufacturers in Minnesota. *Type:* Directory.

Mississippi Manufacturers Register

Manufacturers' News, Inc.
1633 Central St. Ph: (847)864-7000
Evanston, IL 60201 Free: 888-752-5200
 Fax: (847)332-1100
E-mail: info@mninfo.com; sales@mninfo.com
URL: http://www.mninfo.com
Contact: Louise M. West, Editor.
Desc: 3,714 manufacturers in Mississippi. *Type:* Directory.

Modern Machine Shop—Metalworking Technology Guide

Gardner Publications, Inc.

6915 Valley Ave. Ph: (513)527-8800
Cincinnati, OH 45244-3029 Free: 800-950-8800
  Fax: (513)527-8801

URL: http://www.gardnerweb.com; http://www.mmsonline.com.

Contact: Thomas L. Beard, Editor, tbeard@gardnerweb.com.

Desc: Products and services for the metalworking industry *Type:* Directory.

Montana Manufacturers Register

Manufacturers' News, Inc.

1633 Central St. Ph: (847)864-7000
Evanston, IL 60201 Free: 888-752-5200
  Fax: (847)332-1100

E-mail: info@mninfo.com; sales@mninfo.com
URL: http://www.mninfo.com

Contact: Louise M. West, Editor.

Desc: 2,099 manufacturers in Montana. *Type:* Directory.

Moody's Industry Review

Financial Information Services (FIS)

60 Madison Ave., 6th Fl. Ph: (212)413-7601
New York, NY 10010 Free: 800-342-5647
  Fax: (212)413-7777

E-mail: fis@fisonline.com
URL: http://www.fisonline.com.

Contact: John Ieraci, Editor-in-Chief.

Desc: Ranks 3,500 leading companies in 137 industry categories according to standard financial criteria (revenues, price-earnings ratio, net income, profit margin, return on capital). *Type:* Directory.

National Association of Manufacturers

1331 Pennsylvania Ave., NW, Ph: (202)637-3000
  Ste. 600 Free: 800-814-8468
Washington, DC 20004 Fax: (202)637-3182

E-mail: manufacting@nam.org
URL: http://www.nam.org

Contact: Jerry J. Jasinowski, Pres.

Desc: Manufacturers and cooperating nonmanufacturers having a direct interest in or relationship to manufacturing. Represents industry's views on national and international problems to government. *Type:* Association.

National Housewares Manufacturers Association

6400 Shafer Ct., Ste. 650 Ph: (847)292-4200
Rosemont, IL 60018 Free: 800-843-6462
  Fax: (847)292-4211

E-mail: cmarti@nhma.com
URL: http://www.housewares.org

Contact: Phillip Brandl, Pres.

Desc: Manufacturers and distributors of housewares and small appliances. *Type:* Association.

National Manufacturers Directory

Harris InfoSource

2057 E. Aurora Rd. Ph: (330)425-9000
Twinsburg, OH 44087-1999 Free: 800-888-5900
  Fax: (330)425-7150

E-mail: customerservice@harrisinfo.com; catknapp@aol.com.

URL: http://www.harrisinfo; http://www.harrisinfo.com.

Contact: Frances L. Carlsen, Editor.

Desc: Approximately 44,800 publicly- and privately-held manufacturing establishments that have at least 100 employees; also list firms providing services to manufacturers. *Type:* Directory.

Nevada Manufacturers Register

Database Publishing Co.

1590 S. Lewis St. Ph: (714)778-6400
PO Box 70024 Free: 800-888-8434
Anaheim, CA 92825-0024 Fax: (714)778-6811

E-mail: sales@databasepublishing.com; datapub@deltanet.com.

URL: http://www.databasepublishing.com; http://www.databasepublishing.com.

Desc: Approximately 1,900 manufacturers in Nevada plus names and titles of 3,600 key executives . *Type:* Directory.

New Equipment Digest

Penton Media Inc.

1100 Superior Ave. Ph: (216)696-7000
Cleveland, OH 44114-2543 Fax: (216)931-9524

E-mail: corpcomm@penton.com

Contact: R.F. King, Editor, (216)931-9269, fax: (216)696-8208, bking@penton.com; R.S. Carson, Publisher, (216)931-9373, fax: (216)696-8208, rcarson@penton.com.

Desc: Magazine (tabloid) showcasing new or improved equipment, products, materials, and components. *Type:* Periodical.

New Hampshire Manufacturers Register

Commerce Register, Inc.

190 Godwin Ave. Ph: (201)445-3000
Midland Park, NJ 07432 Free: 800-221-2172
  Fax: (201)445-5806

Contact: Louise M. West, Editor.

Desc: 2,772 manufacturers in New Hampshire. *Type:* Directory.

New Jersey Directory of Manufacturers

Commerce Register, Inc.

190 Godwin Ave. Ph: (201)445-3000
Midland Park, NJ 07432 Free: 800-221-2172
  Fax: (201)445-5806

Contact: Joel Rosano, Editor.

Desc: 10,500 industrial firms wih 5 or more employees. *Type:* Directory.

New Jersey Manufacturers Register

Manufacturers' News, Inc.

1633 Central St. Ph: (847)864-7000
Evanston, IL 60201 Free: 888-752-5200
  Fax: (847)332-1100

E-mail: info@mninfo.com; sales@mninfo.com
URL: http://www.mninfo.com

Contact: Louise M. West, Editor.

Desc: 10,957 manufacturers in New Jersey. *Type:* Directory.

New Mexico Manufacturers Register

Manufacturers' News, Inc.

1633 Central St. Ph: (847)864-7000
Evanston, IL 60201 Free: 888-752-5200
  Fax: (847)332-1100

E-mail: info@mninfo.com; sales@mninfo.com
URL: http://www.mninfo.com

Contact: Louise M. West, Editor.

Desc: 2,103 manufacturers in New Mexico. *Type:* Directory.

New Plant Report

Conway Data, Inc.

35 Technology Pkwy., Ste. 150 Ph: (770)446-6996
Norcross, GA 30092 Fax: (770)263-8825

E-mail: info.mgr@conway.com
URL: http://www.sitenet.com

Contact: Doris Alexander, Editor.

Desc: Covers new plants and plant expansions. Provides project location, company name, product to be manufactured or service performed, SIC code, type of facility, stage of development, and (as available) number of employees, square footage, investment amount, and contact name. *Type:* Newsletter.

New York Manufacturers Register

Manufacturers' News, Inc.

1633 Central St. Ph: (847)864-7000
Evanston, IL 60201 Free: 888-752-5200
  Fax: (847)332-1100

E-mail: info@mninfo.com; sales@mninfo.com
URL: http://www.mninfo.com

Contact: Louise M. West, Editor.

Desc: 18,000 manufacturers in metropolitan New York. *Type:* Directory.

New York Upstate Manufacturers Register

Manufacturers' News, Inc.

1633 Central St. Ph: (847)864-7000
Evanston, IL 60201 Free: 888-752-5200
  Fax: (847)332-1100

E-mail: info@mninfo.com; sales@mninfo.com
URL: http://www.mninfo.com

Contact: Louise M. West, Editor.

Desc: 4,850 manufacturers in upstate New York. *Type:* Directory.

North Dakota Manufacturers Register

Manufacturers' News, Inc.

1633 Central St. Ph: (847)864-7000
Evanston, IL 60201 Free: 888-752-5200
  Fax: (847)332-1100

E-mail: info@mninfo.com; sales@mninfo.com
URL: http://www.mninfo.com

Contact: Louise M. West, Editor.

Desc: 1,060 manufacturers in North Dakota. *Type:* Directory.

NTMA Record

National Tooling and Machining Association

9300 Livingston Rd. Ph: (301)248-6200
Fort Washington, MD 20744 Free: 800-248-NTMA
  Fax: (301)248-7104

URL: http://www.ntma.org.

Contact: Sandra S. Bailey, Editor.

Desc: Focuses on business management techniques and government relations for the contract tool, die, and precision machining industry. Supplies information on Association activities. *Type:* Newsletter.

Ohio Manufacturers Directory

Manufacturers' News, Inc.

1633 Central St. Ph: (847)864-7000
Evanston, IL 60201 Free: 888-752-5200
  Fax: (847)332-1100

E-mail: info@mninfo.com
URL: http://www.mninfo.com; http://www.manufacturersnews.com.

Contact: Louise M. West, Editor.

Desc: 22,648 manufacturers in Ohio. *Type:* Directory.

Oregon Manufacturers Register

Database Publishing Co.

1590 S. Lewis St. Ph: (714)778-6400
PO Box 70024 Free: 800-888-8434
Anaheim, CA 92825-0024 Fax: (714)778-6811

E-mail: sales@databasepublishing.com
URL: http://www.databasepublishing.com; http://www.databasepublishing.com.

Desc: Approximately 7,100 manufacturers plus 16,000 key executives Oregon. *Type:* Directory.

Pennsylvania Manufacturers Register

Manufacturers' News, Inc.
1633 Central St.   Ph: (847)864-7000
Evanston, IL 60201   Free: 888-752-5200
                                          Fax: (847)332-1100
E-mail: info@mninfo.com; sales@mninfo.com
URL: http://www.mninfo.com;   http://www.
manufacturersnews.com.

Contact: Louise M. West, Editor.

Desc: 19,939 manufacturers in Pennsylvania. *Type:* Directory.

Plasma Manufacturing Bulletin

Engineering Research Center for Plasma-Aided Manufacturing
University of Wisconsin-Madison
1410 Engineering Dr., Rm. 101   Ph: (608)262-2181
Madison, WI 53706   Fax: (608)262-3632
URL: http://www.engr.wisc.edu/centers/ercpam/ercpam.
html.

Contact: Catherine Cetrangolo, Editor.

Desc: Covers plasma-aided manufacturing, plasma spectroscopy, plasma diagnostics, materials characterization, educational outreach, plasma sources, langmuir probes, and other related topics. Recurring features include news of research, a calendar of events, reports of meetings, and news of educational opportunities. *Type:* Newsletter.

Power Press, Forging and Metal Fabricating Newsletter

National Safety Council
1121 Spring Lake Dr.   Ph: (630)285-1121
Itasca, IL 60143-3201   Free: 800-539-7468
                                          Fax: (630)285-1315
URL: http://www.nsc.org

Contact: Kathy Henderson, Editor.

Desc: Concerned with accident prevention and safety in power press and forging operations. Fosters safety awareness in the conviction that accidents are preventable. *Type:* Newsletter.

Reg Burnett's Carpet Market Newsletter

RBI International Carpert Consultants
PO Box 722   Ph: (706)226-3217
Dalton, GA 30722   Free: 888-499-3212
                                          Fax: (706)278-3565
E-mail: rbi@alltell.net

Contact: Reg Burnett, President.

Desc: Covers carpet trade shows. Includes information about styling trends, marketing techniques, and technical innovations. *Type:* Newsletter.

Regional Industrial Buying Guide Series

Thomas Regional Directory Co., Inc.
5 Penn Plaza   Ph: (212)629-2100
New York, NY 10001   Fax: (212)290-7335
E-mail: info@trdnet.com

Contact: Emilia Tomaszewski, Editor.

Desc: Guides to manufacturers of industrial products within regions of a state or within contiguous portions of two or three states; the "Greater Allegheny Regional Industrial Buying Guide," for example, covers western Pennsylvania, northern West Virginia, and eastern Ohio. Guides also include listings for related industrial services, such as trucking, maintenance services, etc., and distributors and manufacturers' representatives. *Type:* Directory.

REMAN Newsletter

APICS—The Educational Society for Resource Management
5301 Shawnee Rd.   Ph: (703)354-8851
Alexandria, VA 22312   Free: 800-444-2742
                                          Fax: (703)354-8106
URL: http://www.apics.org.

Contact: David Bowman, Editor, d_bowman@apics-hq.org.

Desc: Covers production, consulting, and manufacturing in the remanufacturing, repair, and overhaul (REMAN) fields. *Type:* Newsletter.

Repetitive Manufacturing SIG Newsletter

APICS—The Educational Society for Resource Management
5301 Shawnee Rd.   Ph: (703)354-8851
Alexandria, VA 22312   Free: 800-444-2742
                                          Fax: (703)354-8106
E-mail: d_bowman@apics-hq.org.
URL: http://www.apics.org.

Contact: Terry Burton, Editor.

Desc: Covers production, consulting, and manufacturing in the repetitive manufacturing fields. *Type:* Newsletter.

The Representative

Agricultural & Industrial Manufacturers Representatives Association
5800 Foxridge Dr., No. 115   Ph: (913)262-0317
Mission, KS 66202-2333   Fax: (913)262-0174

Contact: Betchie Bistrom, Editor.

Desc: Carries news and information of the Association. Seeks to improve marketing operations among independent manufacturers representatives of agricultural and industrial manufacturers. *Type:* Newsletter.

Rhode Island Manufacturers Register

Manufacturers' News, Inc.
1633 Central St.   Ph: (847)864-7000
Evanston, IL 60201   Free: 888-752-5200
                                          Fax: (847)332-1100
E-mail: info@mninfo.com; sales@mninfo.com
URL: http://www.mninfo.com

Contact: Louise M. West, Editor.

Desc: 2,500 manufacturers in Rhode Island. *Type:* Directory.

Screening Industry

Screen Manufacturers Association (SMA)
2850 S. Ocean Blvd., No. 114   Ph: (561)533-0991
Palm Beach, FL 33480-5535

Contact: Frank S. Fitzgerald, Editor, fscottfitzgerald@compuserve.com.

Desc: Covers the window and door screen industry. Recurring features include letters to the editor, news of research, a calendar of events, reports of meetings, and notices of publications available. *Type:* Newsletter.

Self Storage Association

4141 Crossgate Dr.   Free: 888-SELF-STG
Cincinnati, OH 45236
E-mail: ssa@selfstorage.org
URL: http://www.selfstorage.org

Contact: Michael R. Kidd, Exec.Dir.

Desc: Owners and operators of self storage facilities. Purpose is: to improve the quality of management, customer service, facilities; promote public awareness of the self storage industry. *Type:* Association.

Small Manufacturing SIG Newsletter

APICS—The Educational Society for Resource Management
5301 Shawnee Rd.   Ph: (703)354-8851
Alexandria, VA 22312   Free: 800-444-2742
                                          Fax: (703)354-8106
E-mail: d_bowman@apics-hq.org.
URL: http://www.apics.org.

Desc: Covers production, consulting, and manufacturing in the small manufacturing (SM) fields. *Type:* Newsletter.

South Carolina Industrial Directory

South Carolina Department of Commerce
Box 927   Ph: (803)737-0400
Columbia, SC 29202   Fax: (803)737-0418
URL: http://www.state.sc.us/commerce.

Contact: Susan Branson, Editor, sbranson@commerce.state.sc.us.

Desc: Over 4,000 industrial companies throughout South Carolina. *Type:* Directory.

South Carolina Manufacturers Register

Manufacturers' News, Inc.
1633 Central St.   Ph: (847)864-7000
Evanston, IL 60201   Free: 888-752-5200
                                          Fax: (847)332-1100
E-mail: info@mninfo.com; sales@mninfo.com
URL: http://www.mninfo.com

Contact: Louise M. West, Editor.

Desc: 5,014 manufacturers in South Carolina. *Type:* Directory.

South Dakota Manufacturers Register

Manufacturers' News, Inc.
1633 Central St.   Ph: (847)864-7000
Evanston, IL 60201   Free: 888-752-5200
                                          Fax: (847)332-1100
E-mail: info@mninfo.com; sales@mninfo.com
URL: http://www.mninfo.com

Contact: Louise M. West, Editor.

Desc: 1,146 manufacturers in South Dakota. *Type:* Directory.

Teamwork

The Dartnell Corp.
360 Hiatt Dr.   Free: 800-621-5463
Palm Beach Gardens, FL 33418   Fax: (561)622-2423
E-mail: dartnell@dartnellcorp.com
URL: http://www.dartnellcorp.com

Contact: Kim Andersen, Editor.

Desc: Focuses on successful teamwork in manufacturing and corporate businesses. Recurring features include columns titled What Would You Do?, Test Yourself and See, and Teamwork in Action. *Type:* Newsletter.

Tennessee Manufacturers Register

Manufacturers' News, Inc.
1633 Central St.   Ph: (847)864-7000
Evanston, IL 60201   Free: 888-752-5200
                                          Fax: (847)332-1100
E-mail: info@mninfo.com; sales@mninfo.com
URL: http://www.mninfo.com

Contact: Louise M. West, Editor.

Desc: 6,080 manufacturers in Tennessee. *Type:* Directory.

Texas Industrial Expansion
Bureau of Business Research
Graduate School of Business
University of Texas at Austin
PO Box 7459   Ph: (512)471-1616
Austin, TX 78713   Free: 888-212-4386
                                Fax: (512)471-1063
E-mail: bbr@uts.cc.utexas.edu; dhardy@mail.utexas.edu;
danhardy@mail.utexas.edu.
Contact: Mary LaMotte, Managing Editor, (512)475-
7810, mlamotte@mail.utexas.edu.
Desc: Reports on manufacturing activity in Texas, particu-
larly on new and expanding plants. Gives plant name, address, phone number, name of contact, a brief description
of the plant, estimated construction cost, and square footage and workforce numbers when available. *Type:* Newsletter.

Texas Manufacturers Register
Manufacturers' News, Inc.
1633 Central St.   Ph: (847)864-7000
Evanston, IL 60201   Free: 888-752-5200
                                Fax: (847)332-1100
E-mail: info@mninfo.com; sales@mninfo.com
URL: http://www.mninfo.com;   http://www.
manufacturersnews.com.
Contact: Louise West, Editor.
Desc: 22,955 manufacturers in Texas. *Type:* Directory.

Thomas Register of American Manufacturers
Thomas Publishing Co.
5 Penn Plaza   Ph: (212)695-0500
New York, NY 10001   Fax: (212)290-7206
E-mail: ordertr@thomasregister.com
URL: http://www.thomasregister.com.
Contact: Glenn Moore, Editor.
Desc: More than 151,000 manufacturing firms are listed
in this 34 volume set. Volumes 1-23 list the firms under
59,000 product headings. *Type:* Directory.

Thomas Register Online
Thomas Publishing Company
Thomas Online
Five Penn Plaza   Ph: (212)629-2125
New York, NY 10001
E-mail: 14016 (DIALMAIL)
URL: http://www.thomasregister.com
Desc: Contains information on more than 194,000 U.S.
and selected Canadian manufacturers and providers of ser-
vices. *Available:* The Dialog Corporation, DIALOG; The
Dialog Corporation, DIALOG; CompuServe Information
Service. *Type:* Database.

Toy Manufacturers of America
1115 Broadway, Suite 400   Ph: (212)675-1141
New York, NY 10010   Fax: (212)633-1429
E-mail: info@toy-tma.org
URL: http://www.toy-tma.com
Contact: Terri Bartlett, Communications Dir.
Desc: Provides business services to U.S. manufacturers and
importers of toys. Manages American International Toy
Fair; represents the industry before Federal, State and
Local government on issues of importance; provides legal
and legislative counsel; conducts educational programs;
compiles industry statistics. *Type:* Association.

UAMR Confidential Bulletin
United Association of Manufacturers'
Representatives (UAMR)
PO Box 986   Ph: (714)240-4966
Dana Point, CA 92629   Fax: (714)240-4966
Contact: Karen Mazzola, Editor.

Desc: Covers product lines offered for representation in all
fields. Provides details of the company and product, type
of accounts to be serviced, and the areas open for representation. *Type:* Newsletter.

Utah Manufacturers Register
Database Publishing Co.
1590 S. Lewis St.   Ph: (714)778-6400
PO Box 70024   Free: 800-888-8434
Anaheim, CA 92825-0024   Fax: (714)778-6811
E-mail: sales@databasepublishing.com
URL: http://www.databasepublishing.com; http://www.
databasepublishing.com.
Desc: Approximately 4,500 manufacturers in Utah, plus
9,700 key executives. *Type:* Directory.

Utillaje
Utillaje, Inc.
20 N. Wacker Dr.   Ph: (312)372-9077
Chicago, IL 60606   Fax: (312)372-6537
E-mail: utillaje@mail.internet.com.mx
URL: http://www.atillaje.com.
Contact: Uribe M. Fabian, Editor.
Desc: Over 10,000 listings of manufacturing and industrial
equipment listed by over 300 sellers throughout North,
Central, and South America. Equipment includes new,
used, and rebuilt machinery, chemical/food, as well as
electrical equipment. *Type:* Directory.

Vermont Manufacturers Directory and Guide to Major Businesses
Rivermont Business Magazine
2 Church St.   Ph: (802)863-8038
Burlington, VT 05401   Fax: (802)863-8069
E-mail: vtbizmag@together.net.
Contact: Timothy McQuiston, Editor.
Desc: Over 3,200 manufacturers in Vermont. *Type:* Direc-
tory.

Vermont Manufacturers Register
Commerce Register, Inc.
190 Godwin Ave.   Ph: (201)445-3000
Midland Park, NJ 07432   Free: 800-221-2172
                                Fax: (201)445-5806
Contact: Louise M. West, Editor.
Desc: 1,200 manufacturers in Vermont. *Type:* Directory.

Warehousing Education and Research Council
1100 Jorie Blvd., Ste. 170   Ph: (630)990-0001
Oak Brook, IL 60523-2243   Fax: (630)990-0256
E-mail: wercoffice@wc/c.org
URL: http://www.werc.org
Contact: Steven H. Williams, Dir. of Operations.
Desc: Warehousing executives united to promote the ware-
housing industry by increasing professionalism and im-
proving service within the industry. Conducts research
projects. *Type:* Association.

Western Industry Report International
Westnash Resources
PO Box 90665   Ph: (615)269-6165
Nashville, TN 37209-0665   Fax: (615)269-6165
Contact: Wes Crabbe, Publisher; Jacqueline Fox, Circula-
tion Director; Laura Doyle, Production Mgr.; Beatrice
Seay, Promotions Dir.
Desc: Informs international readers about western industry
and the major key players. *Type:* Newsletter.

Wyoming Manufacturers Register
Database Publishing Co.
1590 S. Lewis St.   Ph: (714)778-6400
PO Box 70024   Free: 800-888-8434
Anaheim, CA 92825-0024   Fax: (714)778-6811
E-mail: sales@databasepublishing.com
URL: http://www.databasepublishing.com; http://www.
databasepublishing.com.
Desc: 1,200 manufacturers in Wyoming. *Type:* Directory.

Marine

Alternative Aquaculture Network
Alternative Aquaculture Association
PO Box 109   Ph: (610)395-5854
Breinigsville, PA 18031   Fax: (610)395-8202
E-mail: altaqua@ptd.net
Contact: Steven Van Gorder, Editor.
Desc: Provides research and practical information on the
application of low-energy/high-productivity methods for
small and medium scale aquaculture. Covers develop-
ments in integrated and recirculating methods of aquacul-
ture, emphasizing energy efficiency and resource
conservation. *Type:* Newsletter.

American Association of Port Authorities
1010 Duke St.   Ph: (703)684-5700
Alexandria, VA 22314-3589   Fax: (703)684-6321
E-mail: info@aapa-ports.org
URL: http://www.aapa-ports.org
Contact: Kurt J. Nagle, Pres.
Desc: Port administrative organizations of the U.S., Canada, the Caribbean, and Latin America; contributing and
associate members are private firms with an interest in port
development, water transportation, or accessorial services.
Holds status as a cooperating organization with the Organization of American States. Particularly the Economic
and Social Council, in relation to hemispheric port development from an economic standpoint. *Type:* Association.

American Society of Naval Engineers
1452 Duke St.   Ph: (703)836-6727
Alexandria, VA 22314   Fax: (703)836-7491
E-mail: asnehq.asne@mcimail.com
URL: http://www.jhuapl.edu/ASNESNE
Contact: Capt. Dennis K. Kruse, CAE, Exec.Dir.
Desc: Professional civilian and Navy engineers interested
in naval engineering including ordnance, navigation, aeronautics, propulsion, hull, electrical and electronic, naval
architecture, ocean engineering, space systems, logistics,
and related subjects. *Type:* Association.

American Waterways Operators
Thomas A. Allegretti
1600 Wilson Blvd., Ste. 1000   Ph: (703)841-9300
Arlington, VA 22209   Fax: (703)841-0389
Contact: Thomas A. Allegretti, Pres.
Desc: Bulk commodities transporters, shipdocking and
harbor services operators, fueling, bunkering and lighter-
ing services operators, shipyards and affiliated service
members. Represents the inland and coastal tugboat, tow-
boat and barge industry. *Type:* Association.

Aquaculture—Buyers Guide Issue
Achill River Corp.
16 Church St., 2nd Fl.   Ph: (704)254-7334
PO Box 2329   Fax: (704)253-0677
Asheville, NC 28802
URL: aquamag@ioa.com.
Contact: Greg Gallagher, Editor.
Desc: List of about 1,400 manufacturers and suppliers of
equipment and materials used in fish farming, production,

processing, marketing, and aquaculture in general; international, national, regional, and state aquaculture associations; state extension specialists in fish and wildlife; regional aquaculture centers, diagnostic services, state aquaculture coordinators; universities and institutions offering aquaculture courses; soil conservation service and fish health biologists, sea grant programs, federal fish hatcheries, health centers, and fisheries assistance offices. *Type:* Directory.

Aquaculture Newsletter International

Aquaculture Newsletter International
3 Pinefield
Weston, CT 06883
Contact: Sandra M. Martin, Ph.D., Editor.
Desc: Covers all aspects of the farm-grown fish industry, including funding for businesses, new technologies, and marketing strategies. Recurring features include news of research and a calendar of events. *Type:* Newsletter.

AQUAFACTS

Louisiana Cooperative Extension Service
PO Box 25100   Ph: (504)388-2152
Baton Rouge, LA 70894-5100   Fax: (504)388-2478
Contact: C.G. Lutz, Editor.
Desc: Emphasizes commercial raising of alligators, catfish, and crawfish. Includes tips for practical management, marketing information, weather and weather influences. *Type:* Newsletter.

Aquaphyte

Center for Aquatic Plants
University of Florida
7922 NW 71st St.   Ph: (352)392-1799
Gainesville, FL 32653   Fax: (352)392-3462
URL: http://aquat1.ifas.ufl.edu/.
Contact: Victor Ramey, Editor, varamey@nervm.nerdc. ufl.edu; Karen Brown, Editor.
Desc: Monitors current aquatic plant research, particularly research on methods for controlling aquatic weeds. Provides news of the Aquatic Plant Information Retrieval System (APIRS). *Type:* Newsletter.

AQUIRE (Aquatic Toxicity Information Retrieval Database)

U.S. Environmental Protection Agency (EPA) NHEERL, MED
6201 Congdon Blvd.   Ph: (218)529-5225
Duluth, MN 55804-2595
E-mail: ecotox.support@epa.gov
Contact: Christine L. Russom, (218)720-5709.
Desc: Contains more than 149,000 data records of individual toxicity test results for more than 5900 chemicals and over 3000 freshwater and saltwater species, excluding bacteria, birds, and aquatic mammals. Corresponds to the on-line AQUIRE database. *Available:* Oxford Molecular Group, Chemical Information Systems; Technical Database Services, Inc. (TDS), TDS Numerica; U.S. Environmental Protection Agency (EPA), NHEERL, MED. *Type:* Database.

Industrial Union of Marine and Shipbuilding Workers of America

James Bleau
14 Maine Ste., Ste. 215   Ph: (207)721-8996
Brunswick, ME 04011
Desc: AFL-CIO. *Type:* Association.

International Longshore and Warehouse Union

1188 Franklin St.   Ph: (415)775-0533
San Francisco, CA 94109   Fax: (415)775-1302
Contact: Brian McWilliams, Pres.
Desc: AFL-CIO. *Type:* Association.

International Longshoremen's Association

17 Battery Pl., Rm. 1530   Ph: (212)425-1200
New York, NY 10004   Fax: (212)425-2928
Contact: John Bowers, Pres.
Desc: AFL-CIO. *Type:* Association.

Kilo i'a

Waikiki Aquarium
University of Hawaii
2777 Kalakaua Ave.   Ph: (808)923-9741
Honolulu, HI 96815   Fax: (808)923-1771
Contact: Alice Keesing, Editor, (808)222-5097, akessing@ hawaii.edu; Carol Hopper, Editor, chopper@waquarium. org.
Desc: Focuses on marine science and issues affecting the Aquarium. *Type:* Newsletter.

Marine Fish Management

Nautilus Press, Inc.
1059 National Press Bldg.   Ph: (202)347-6643
Washington, DC 20045
Contact: John R. Botzum, Editor.
Desc: Discusses the organizational, legislative, and ideological issues confronting fisheries management, particularly of the living resources in the U.S. 200-mile fisheries zone. *Type:* Newsletter.

Mariners World's Marine Directory

Mariners World Publishing Co., Inc.
521 Superior Ave.   Ph: (714)646-0521
Newport Beach, CA 92663   Free: 800-750-0521
                              Fax: (714)646-4157
E-mail: mwmd@pacbell.net
URL: http://www.marinersworld.com; http://www. mypid.com/marinersworld.
Contact: Jeff Overstreet, Editor.
Desc: Over 3,000 marinas, boat stores, and other suppliers of boating equipment and services in southern California. *Type:* Directory.

Maritime Newsletter

Maritime Trades Department, AFL-CIO
815 16th St. NW, 6th Fl.   Ph: (202)628-6300
Washington, DC 20006-4183   Fax: (202)637-3989
Contact: Max Hall, Editor.
Desc: Covers legislative news, affiliate updates, student activities, and member news. Recurring features include columns titled Maritime Update and Allied Trades. *Type:* Newsletter.

Muskies, Inc.

2301 7th St. N.   Ph: (701)239-9540
Fargo, ND 58102   Fax: (701)239-9540
Contact: Pat Johnson, Adm.Sec.
Desc: Fishermen united to promote and protect muskellunge sport fisheries. (The muskellunge is a large North American fish weighing up to 60 pounds.) Establishes muskellunge hatcheries; introduces muskellunge into suitable waters; supports selected conservation practices; seeks reduction in water pollution levels. Distributes information; promotes fellowship and sportsmanship among members. *Type:* Association.

Mystic Seaport

75 Greenmanville Ave.   Ph: (860)572-0711
Mystic, CT 06355-0990   Fax: (860)572-5328
URL: http://www.mysticseaport.org
Contact: J. Revell Carr, Pres. & Dir.
Desc: Persons interested in furthering the study of American maritime history. Operates Mystic Seaport, a maritime museum on 17 acres along the Mystic River in Connecticut. Conducts summer seamanship training program for teenagers who live and work aboard the Seaport's training vessel; also conducts a program with Williams College, Williamstown, MA, in which undergraduates from accredited colleges pursue a semester of maritime studies while in residence at the museum; cosponsors Frank C. *Type:* Association.

National Maritime Historical Society

5 John Walsh Blvd.   Ph: (914)737-7878
PO Box 68   Free: 800-221-NMHS
Peekskill, NY 10566   Fax: (914)737-7816
E-mail: seahistory@aol.com
Contact: Peter Stanford, Pres.
Desc: Individuals interested in maritime history, boats, ships, the art, literature, adventure, and lore and learning of the sea. Promotes public awareness and understanding of maritime heritage. *Type:* Association.

National Maritime Union of America

1150 17th St. NW, Ste. 700   Ph: (202)466-7060
Washington, DC 20036   Fax: (202)872-0912
Contact: Lioeanjie Rene, Pres.
Desc: AFL-CIO. *Type:* Association.

Offshore Rig Owners & Personnel Directory

Offshore Data Services, Inc.
PO Box 19909   Ph: (713)781-2713
Houston, TX 77224-1909   Fax: (713)781-9594
E-mail: editors@offshore-data.com
URL: http://www.offshore-data.com
Contact: Marie Sheffer, Editor.
Desc: Approximately 176 companies that own offshore oil drilling rigs; international coverage. *Type:* Directory.

Sea Education Association

PO Box 6   Ph: (508)540-3954
Woods Hole, MA 02543   Free: 800-552-3633
                              Fax: (508)457-4673
E-mail: admission@sea.edu
URL: http://www.sea.edu
Contact: Rafe E. A. Parker, Pres.
Desc: Runs academic programs focusing on the sea. Owns and operates two deep-sea research sailing vessels to increase students' understanding of the oceanic environment. Theories learned ashore are put into practice at sea aboard SSV Westward, a 125-foot staysail schooner, and SSV Corwith Cramer, a 134-foot brigantine. *Type:* Association.

Seafarers' International Union of North America

5201 Auth Way   Ph: (301)899-0675
Camp Springs, MD 20748   Fax: (301)899-7355
URL: http://www.seafarers.org
Contact: Michael Sacco, Pres.
Desc: AFL-CIO. Maintains Seafarers/Harry Lundberg School of Seamanship. *Type:* Association.

South Street Seaport Museum

207 Front St.   Ph: (212)748-8600
New York, NY 10038   Fax: (212)748-8610
URL: http://www.southseaport.org
Contact: Peter Neill, Pres.
Desc: Individuals and families interested in maritime history and the history of New York City. The state maritime museum of New York, it preserves and interprets the maritime history of New York City and state. Maintains 11 blocks of 19th century commercial, port-related buildings, five historic ships at Piers 15 and 16, and maritime art and artifacts. *Type:* Association.

United Seamen's Service

1 World Trade Center, Ste. 2161
New York, NY 10048

Ph: (212)775-1033
Fax: (212)432-5492

E-mail: ussammla@ix.netcom.com

Contact: Roger T. Korner, Exec.Dir.

Desc: Promotes the welfare of American seafarers and their dependents, seafarers of all nations, and other persons engaged in the maritime industry. *Type:* Association.

Marketing

About Women & Marketing

About Women, Inc.

33 Broad St.
Boston, MA 02109

Ph: (617)723-4337
Fax: (617)723-7107

E-mail: abtwmn@womenews.com

Contact: Jann Leeming, Executive Editor; Cindy Tripp, Editor.

Desc: Discusses market studies about women comsumers. Covers such topics as advertising, demographics, women's attitudes, family issues, consumer products, finance, media preferences, health care, employment, food/nutrition, shopping habits, working women, technology, and travel. *Type:* Newsletter.

Accutips

Accudata America

1625 Cape Coral Pkwy.
Cape Coral, FL 33904

Ph: (941)549-1111
Fax: (941)540-5200

E-mail: info@accudata-america.com

URL: http://www.accudata-america.com.

Contact: Mary Helen Hilton, Editor; Stacey Elmeer, Editor.

Desc: Discusses promotion and marketing issues relevant to businesses. *Type:* Newsletter.

ADM Flash

Association of Directory Marketing

One Thorn Run Center, Ste. 630
1187 Thorn Run Rd.
Moon Township, PA 15108-3198

Ph: (412)269-0663
Fax: (412)269-0655

Contact: Nancy Augustine, Editor, naugustine@admworks.org.

Desc: Features information about marketing directories. *Type:* Newsletter.

Advertising Specialty Institute—Briefings

Advertising Specialty Institute

1120 Wheeler Way
Langhorne, PA 19047-1785

Ph: (215)752-4200
Free: 800-326-7378
Fax: (215)752-9758

E-mail: info@asicentral.com

Contact: Kathy Huston, Editor, khuston@asicentral.com.

Desc: Provides marketing data. *Type:* Newsletter.

Advertising Via Telemarketing Script Presentations Newsletter

Prosperity & Profits Unlimited, Distribution Services

PO Box 416
Denver, CO 80201-0416

Ph: (303)575-5676

Contact: A. Doyle, Publisher.

Desc: Presents script presentations as means of advertising for various businesses. *Type:* Newsletter.

Alert!

Marketing Research Association

1344 Silas Deane Hwy., Ste. 306
Rocky Hill, CT 06067-0230

Ph: (860)257-4008
Fax: (860)257-3990

Contact: Lisa Asadourian, Editor.

Desc: Provides information about marketing industry events, trends in marketing research, management techniques, association events, and legislative activities affecting the marketing industry. Recurring features include news of research, a calendar of events, reports of meetings, news of educational opportunities, job listings, notices of publications available, business opportunities, and facilities for sale. *Type:* Newsletter.

Alliance Against Fraud in Telemarketing Focus on Fraud

National Consumers League

1701 K St. NW, Ste. 1200
Washington, DC 20006

Ph: (202)835-3323
Fax: (202)835-0747

E-mail: nclncl@aol.com

URL: http://www.nclnet.org

Contact: Susan Grant, Editor.

Desc: Provides information about latest trends in telemarketing and Internet fraud, enforcement actions, industry fraud-fighting efforts, and educational resources. *Type:* Newsletter.

AM&A Meakin/Art Newsletter

AM&A Meakin/Art

402 W. Taylor Ave., Ste. A-367
Round Rock, TX 78664-4237

Ph: (512)343-5092

Contact: Art Meakin, Publisher.

Desc: Discusses referral and multi-level networking marketing. *Type:* Newsletter.

American Marketing Association

311 S. WAcker Dr., Ste. 5800
Chicago, IL 60606

Ph: (312)542-9000
Free: 800-262-1150
Fax: (312)542-9001

E-mail: info@ama.org

URL: http://www.ama.org

Contact: Dennis Jorgensen, COO.

Desc: Professional society of marketing and market research executives, sales and promotion managers, advertising specialists, academics, and others interested in marketing. *Type:* Association.

Antin Marketing Letter

The Antin Marketing Group Inc.

11001 Delmar St.
Leawood, KS 66211

Ph: (913)663-5775
Fax: (913)663-5552

Contact: Brad Antin, Editor; Alan Antin, Publisher.

Desc: Provides information for marketing professionals and entrepreneurs. Topics include retail, wholesale, service, and professional practice information. *Type:* Newsletter.

ArtSource Quarterly

ArtNetwork

PO Box 1360
Nevada City, CA 95959-1360

Ph: (530)470-0862
Free: 800-383-0677
Fax: (530)470-0256

E-mail: info@artmarketing.com

URL: http://artmarketing.com

Contact: Constance Smith, Editor-in-Chief.

Desc: Focuses on assisting artists in marketing their fine art. Stories of other aritist's success. *Type:* Newsletter.

ASAE Membership Developments

Membership Section

American Society of Association Executives (ASAE)

1575 I St. NW
Washington, DC 20005

Ph: (202)626-2848
Fax: (202)842-1109

E-mail: mbrshpsec@asaenet.org

Contact: Melody Harrison, Section Mgr., mharrison@asaenet.org; Any Fabbri, Prod. Mgr.; Katherine Kress, Prod. Assoc.

Desc: Emphasizes direct mail, telemarketing, surveys, and member recruitment and retention. Recurring features include news of the Society. *Type:* Newsletter.

Association of Incentive Marketing News

Association of Incentive Marketing (AIM)

1620 Rte. 22, Ste. 300
Union, NJ 07083

Ph: (908)687-3090
Fax: (908)687-0977

E-mail: asnoff@ix.netcom.com

Contact: Marie Beyer, Editor.

Desc: Association newsletter. *Type:* Newsletter.

Biomedical Marketing Association

3905 Vincennes Rd., No. 304
Indianapolis, IN 46268-3026

Ph: (317)845-1321
Fax: (317)578-9073

E-mail: wmgcae@aol.com

Contact: Michael F. Ward, CAE, Exec.Dir.

Desc: Diagnostic marketers in the biomedical field. Compiles statistics. *Type:* Association.

The Business Marketing Notepad

Direct Marketing Publishers

1304 University Dr.
Yardley, PA 19067

Ph: (215)321-3068
Fax: (215)321-9647

Contact: Bernie Goldberg, Editor.

Desc: Provides information about business to business sales, generating leads, and telephone sales. *Type:* Newsletter.

Cable TV Marketing Letter

The Kerner Group, Inc.

PO Box 19
Martins Creek, PA 18063-0019

Contact: Rick Kerner, Editor.

Desc: "Guides businesses through the maze of cable TV advertising." Includes "real-life" success stories of television advertisers and their inside secrets, practical advice on crucial issues facing the TV market, and detailed information on where to get the best buys in media, video production, fulfillment services, and telemarketing. Shows what's considered "hot" in cable television ads and the best rates. *Type:* Newsletter.

Call Center Management Review

ICMI

PO Box 6523
Annapolis, MD 21401-0523

Ph: (410)267-0700
Free: 800-255-8110
Fax: (410)267-0563

E-mail: icmi.incoming; ccmr.ccmreview.com.

Contact: Brad Cleveland, Publisher, brad@incoming.com; Greg Levin, Editor, glevin@ccmreview.com.

Desc: Provides strategies and solutions for call center professionals worldwide. *Type:* Newsletter.

The Catalog Marketer

Maxwell Sroge Publishing, Inc.

522 Forest Ave.
Evanston, IL 60202

Ph: (847)866-1890
Fax: (847)866-1899

E-mail: newsletters@catalog-news.com

URL: http://www.catalog-news.com.

Contact: Ann Meyer, Editor; Maxwell Sroge, Publisher.

Desc: Provides information about producing catalogs. Topics include marketing, photography, news, and telephone marketing. *Type:* Newsletter.

Classified Communication

Agnes Franz

PO Box 4242   Ph: (520)778-6788

Prescott, AZ 86302   Fax: (520)445-0517

Contact: Agnes Franz, Editor and Publisher.

Desc: Provides information for advertising on a limited budget. *Type:* Newsletter.

Collegiate Trends

Strategic Marketing

550 N. Maple Ave.   Ph: (201)612-8100

Ridgewood, NJ 07450   Fax: (201)612-1444

URL: http://smcinc.com.

Contact: Eric Weil, Editor and Publisher, weil@smcinc. com.

Desc: Provides information for marketing to college students. *Type:* Newsletter.

Colloquy

Frequency Marketing, Inc.

PO Box 3920   Ph: (513)248-9184

Milford, OH 45150   Fax: (513)248-9084

E-mail: info@frequencymarketing.com; info@colloquy. com.

URL: http://www.collaguy.com.

Contact: Richard Barlow, Publisher; Barbara Kramer Zarins, Editor, (513)248-5033, barbara.kramer-zarins@ frequencymarketing.com.

Desc: Provides information on loyalty/relationship marketing trends and programs. Recurring features include letters to the editor, news of research, news of educational opportunities, international byline, book reviews, and columns titled Publisher's Notes and Have You Heard.. *Type:* Newsletter.

Communications Industries Report

International Communications Industries Association

11242 Waples Mill Rd., Ste.   Ph: (703)273-7200

200   Free: 800-659-7469

Fairfax, VA 22030   Fax: (703)278-8082

E-mail: icia@iciahq.org

URL: http://www.icia.org

Contact: Dick Larsen, Editor.

Desc: Carries how-to information on sales, marketing, production, management, and other business topics. Reports on communications industry news and presents case studies. *Type:* Newsletter.

The Competitive Advantage

Briefings Publishing Group

1101 King St., Ste. 110   Ph: (703)548-3800

Alexandria, VA 22314   Free: 800-888-2084

    Fax: (703)684-2136

E-mail: tloomis@briefings.com

Contact: Joe McGavin, Exec. Editor; Deirdre Hackett, Managing Editor; Katie May, Editor.

Desc: Provides "sales, marketing and management tools to make careers and companies more prosperous." Reports on the latest marketing information, trends, and ideas. Covers customer service, competition, strategies for success, motivation, and incentives. *Type:* Newsletter.

Creative Marketing

Association of Retail Marketing Services

244 Broad St.   Ph: (732)842-5070

Red Bank, NJ 07701-2003   Fax: (732)219-1938

E-mail: gerhop@aol.com

Contact: Karen Kircher, Editor, kkircher@bellafantc.net.

Desc: Provides information on the Association's activities in the retail incentive marketing field and developments within the industry. Contains announcements of premium incentive trade shows, retail promotion shows, and general industry news. *Type:* Newsletter.

The CSR Advisor

Standard Publishing Corp.

155 Federal St.   Ph: (617)457-0600

Boston, MA 02110-9637   Free: 800-682-5759

    Fax: (617)457-0608

E-mail: stnd@earthlink.net

Contact: Maureen Lane, Editor.

Desc: Advises customer service representatives (CSRs) of insurance agencies on how to increase sales, improve customer relations, build technical skills, and improve office management skills. *Type:* Newsletter.

The Customer Service Advantage

Progressive Business Publications

370 Technology Dr.   Ph: (610)695-8600

Malvern, PA 19355   Free: 800-220-5000

    Fax: (610)651-2981

URL: http://www.pbp.com.

Contact: Michele McGovern, Editor.

Desc: Presents practical methods for quantifying customer service benefits and motivating employees day in and day out. Recurring features include interviews, news of research, a calendar of events, news of educational opportunities, and a column titled Sharpen Your Judgment. *Type:* Newsletter.

Delaney Report

Delaney Report Inc.

149 5th Ave.   Ph: (212)979-7881

New York, NY 10010   Fax: (212)979-0691

Contact: Thomas F. Delaney, Editor.

Desc: Reports on developments in marketing, advertising, and media. *Type:* Newsletter.

The DeLay Letter

Whitaker Newsletters, Inc.

313 South Ave.   Ph: (908)889-6336

PO Box 340   Free: 800-359-6049

Fanwood, NJ 07023-0340   Fax: (908)889-6339

E-mail: BevNews@aol.com; DeLayLtr@aol.com.

Contact: Barbara W. Kaplowitz, Editor, (301)983-6634, fax: (301)299-2935.

Desc: Reports on news, perspectives, and trends in direct marketing. Recurring features include letters to the editor, news of research, and interviews. *Type:* Newsletter.

Direct Marketing Association

1120 Avenue of the Americas   Ph: (212)768-7277

New York, NY 10036-6700   Fax: (212)302-6714

E-mail: webmaster@the-dma.org

URL: http://www.the-dma.org

Contact: Robert Wientzen, CEO & Pres.

Desc: Manufacturers, wholesalers, public utilities, retailers, mail order firms, publishers, schools, clubs, insurance companies, financial organizations, business equipment manufacturers, paper and envelope manufacturers, list brokers, compilers, managers, owners, computer service bureaus, advertising agencies, lettershops, research organizations, printers, lithographers, creators, and producers of direct mail and direct response advertising. Studies consumer and business attitudes toward direct mail and related direct marketing statistics. *Type:* Association.

Direct Marketing Association—Direct Line

Direct Marketing Association, Inc. (DMA)

1120 Avenue of the Americas,   Ph: (212)768-7277

13th Fl.   Fax: (212)768-4547

New York, NY 10036-8096

URL: http://www.the-dma.org.

Contact: Claire Coyne, Editor.

Desc: Reports on activities of the Association regarding political, economic, and technological trends affecting direct marketing. Includes case studies, news of research, and technology. *Type:* Newsletter.

Direct Marketing Hints and Secrets

Bookfinders General Inc.

145 E. 27th St. PH C   Ph: (212)689-0772

New York, NY 10016-9067   Fax: (212)481-0552

Contact: Martin Gross, Editor.

Desc: Publishes strategy and techniques for direct marketing. *Type:* Newsletter.

Direct Marketing Success Letter

Nicholas Direct Inc.

PO Box 877   Ph: (813)596-4966

Indian Rocks Beach, FL 33785-   Fax: (813)596-6900

0877

Contact: Bethany Waller, Editor and Publisher.

Desc: Provides marketing strategy information. Topics include writing copy and sales letters, and purchasing advertising space. *Type:* Newsletter.

Direct Response

Creative Direct Marketing Group

1815 W. 213th St., Ste. 210   Ph: (310)212-5727

Torrance, CA 90501-2805   Fax: (310)212-5773

E-mail: cdmg@earthlink.net

Desc: Monitors over 100 of the top advertising and business publications and newsletters covering the latest direct marketing ideas and techniques. Covers direct response advertising, including articles on direct mail, television, media, copy, graphics, testing, buying habits, government and postal laws and regulations, telemarketing, fund raising, and computers. *Type:* Newsletter.

Direct Response Profit Report

Publishers Media

PO Box 1295   Ph: (619)282-5822

El Cajon, CA 92022-1295   Fax: (619)588-9103

E-mail: onlinemedia@accessl.com

Contact: Russ von Hoelecher, Editor, rvh@rustnet.com.

Desc: Provides information on direct response marketing. *Type:* Newsletter.

Distributive Education Clubs of America

1908 Association Dr.   Ph: (703)860-5000

Reston, VA 20191   Fax: (703)860-4013

Contact: Edward Davis, Ph.D., Exec.Dir.

Desc: High school juniors and seniors; junior college students interested in the field of marketing and distribution (retailing and wholesaling) as a vocation. *Type:* Association.

DM to Government Report

Amtower & Company

PO Box 339   Ph: (301)924-0058

Ashton, MD 20861-0339   Fax: (301)924-1565

Contact: Mark Amtower, Editor.

Desc: Provides information pertaining to direct marketing of products and services to the $200 billion/year U.S. federal government marketplace. *Type:* Newsletter.

DMA Washington Report

Direct Marketing Association, Inc. (DMA)

1111 19th St. NW, No. 1100   Ph: (202)955-5030

Washington, DC 20036   Fax: (202)955-0085

Contact: Elizabeth Scanlon, Editor, elizabethscanlon@the-dma.org.

Desc: Reviews federal and state legislative and regulatory activities affecting direct marketing. *Type:* Newsletter.

DMAW Marketing Advents

Direct Marketing Association of Washington, DC

7702 Leesburg Pike, Ste. 400   Ph: (703)821-3629

Falls Church, VA 22043-2600   Fax: (703)821-3694

E-mail: dmaw@hqstaff.com

Contact: Nancy Scott, Editor; John DeLellis, Editor.

Desc: Spotlights direct marketing topics for members in the Washington, DC area. Recurring features include interviews, a calendar of events, news of educational opportunities, and job listings. *Type:* Newsletter.

Drop Shipping News

Consolidated Marketing Services, Inc.
PO Box 1361   Ph: (212)688-8797
New York, NY 10017
URL: http://www.drop-shipping-news.com.

Contact: Nicholas T. Scheel, Editor, nscheel@drop-shipping-news.com.

Desc: Supplies data on firms that drop ship their products as a means of distribution. Contains information on sources of consumer and industrial products, formulation of marketing policy, and on the pricing, ordering, packaging, and handling of drop shipments. *Type:* Newsletter.

FINDOUT

Find/SVP
625 6th Ave.   Ph: (212)645-4500
New York, NY 10011   Free: 800-FIN-DSVP
                               Fax: (212)645-7681
E-mail: infoadvisor@findsvp.com; findout@findsup.com.
URL: http://www.findsvp.com.

Contact: Barbara Ferrara, Editor; Peggy Schlatter, Editor.

Desc: Directed toward retainer clients of FIND/SVP. Covers corporate news, advice, and tips on research and consulting, products and services, and trends. *Type:* Newsletter.

Fred Goss' What's Working in Direct Marketing

United Communications Group
11300 Rockville Pike, Ste. 1100   Ph: (301)287-2700
Rockville, MD 20852-3030   Free: 800-929-4824
                                   Fax: (301)287-2049
E-mail: customer@ucg.com
URL: http://www.ucg.com.

Contact: Fred Goss, Editor, fgoss@ucg.com.

Desc: Reports on direct marketing promotions for publishing, catalogs, finance, package goods, retail, and nonprofit. Reveals actual costs and results of programs for business and consumer markets. *Type:* Newsletter.

Friday Report

Hoke Communications, Inc.
224 7th St.   Ph: (516)746-6700
Garden City, NY 11530   Free: 800-229-6700
                               Fax: (516)294-8141
E-mail: frmmag@aol.com

Contact: Henry R. Hoke, Jr., Publisher.

Desc: Covers the range of direct marketing developments and legislative, regulatory, and postal demands or changes. Recurring features include reports on marketing speeches and seminars nationwide, news, and calendar of direct marketing events. *Type:* Newsletter.

Frohlinger's Marketing Report

Joseph Frohlinger
7 Coppell Dr.   Ph: (201)567-4447
Tenafly, NJ 07670-2903   Free: 800-962-7538

Contact: Joseph Frohlinger, Editor.

Desc: Provides information on marketing, advertising, and the media. Recurring features include interviews, news of research, a calendar of events, reports of meetings, job listings, and book reviews. *Type:* Newsletter.

Futuretech

Technical Insights/John Wiley & Sons, Inc.
32 N. Dean St.   Ph: (201)568-4744
Englewood, NJ 07631-2807   Free: 800-245-6217
                               Fax: (201)568-8247
E-mail: insights@wiley.com; ftinfo@insights.com.
URL: http://www.wiley.com/technical-insights; http://www.wiley.com/technical_insights.

Contact: Peter Savage, Editorial Dir.

Desc: Contains briefings on newly emerging technologies and the markets that they will create. Each issue focuses on one technology, analyzes its market impact, and provides access to developers looking for partners, licenses, or marketing agreements. *Type:* Newsletter.

GreenBook Worldwide—Directory of Marketing Research Companies and Services

New York AMA-Green Book
Lakewood Business Park   Ph: (941)752-4498
4301 32nd St. W., Ste. E-11   Free: 800-972-9202
Bradenton, FL 34210   Fax: 800-879-3751
E-mail: greenbook@nyama.org
URL: http://www.greenbook.org.

Contact: Camille Crifasi, Editor.

Desc: More than 2,500 marketing research companies worldwide (computer services, interviewing services, etc.) of marketing research needs; international coverage. Includes a list of computer programs for marketing research. *Type:* Directory.

Guerilla Marketing Newsletter

Jay Conrad Levinson
PO Box 1336   Ph: (415)381-8361
Mill Valley, CA 94942   Free: 800-748-6444
                               Fax: (415)381-8361

Contact: William Shea, Editor.

Desc: Explores marketing trends, tips, and technology. Recurring features include news of research. *Type:* Newsletter.

The Guerilla Selling Newsletter

The Guerilla Group, Inc.
947 Walnut   Ph: (303)938-8469
Boulder, CO 80302   Free: 800-682-8385
                               Fax: (303)938-8476
E-mail: tggboulder@aol.com; postmaster@guerrillagroup.com
URL: http://www.guerrillagroup.com.

Contact: Andrea Peterson, Dir., Client Relations.

Desc: Presents new sales and marketing techniques and technologies. Recurring features include news of research, a calendar of events, news of educational opportunities, and book reviews. *Type:* Newsletter.

Helen Hecker's Hotline: Marketing Strategies for Publishers & Entrepreneurs

Twin Peaks Press
PO Box 129   Ph: (360)694-2462
Vancouver, WA 98666-0129   Fax: (360)696-3210
E-mail: twinpeak@pacifier.com
URL: http://www.pacifier.com/~twinpeak/press/; http://www.pacifier.com/~twinpeak/press/.

Contact: Helen Hecker, Editor and Publisher.

Desc: Provides marketing strategies for publishers, audio and video producers, and small business owners. Recurring features include interviews, news of research, reports of meetings, news of educational opportunities, book reviews, and notices of publications available. *Type:* Newsletter.

The Infomercial Marketing Report

Steven Dworman and Associates
11533 Thurston Cl.   Ph: (310)472-5253
Los Angeles, CA 90049   Fax: (310)472-6004

Contact: Steve Dworman, Editor and Publisher.

Desc: Provides information on the infomercial industry. *Type:* Newsletter.

Inside Direct Mail

North American Publishing Co.
401 N. Broad St.   Ph: (215)238-5300
Philadelphia, PA 19108   Free: 800-777-8074
                               Fax: (215)238-5270
URL: http://www.napco.com

Contact: Hallie Mummert, Editor, (215)238-5437, hmummert@napco.com.

Desc: "More money is spent in direct mail advertising than any other medium. Unlike space or broadcast advertising—which become public knowledge the moment the ads break, direct mail is also secret." *Type:* Newsletter.

Inside Mass Marketing

Direct Marketing Association, Inc. (DMA)
1120 Avenue of the Americas,   Ph: (212)768-7277
   13th Fl.   Fax: (212)768-4547
New York, NY 10036-8096

Contact: Fredric D. Garmon, Publisher.

Desc: Provides information on mass marketing. Topics include retail and mail order marketing. *Type:* Newsletter.

International Information Report

Washington Researchers
416 Hungerford Dr., Ste. 315   Ph: (301)251-9550
Rockville, MD 20850   Fax: (301)251-9526
E-mail: research@researchers.com

Contact: Laurie Schlagel, Editor.

Desc: Lists sources of information on foreign companies, international/multinational industries, and markets. Provides 50-100 sources, including publications and associations, along with a synopsis and necessary contact information. *Type:* Newsletter.

Internet Marketing Report

Progressive Business Publications
370 Technology Dr.   Ph: (610)695-8600
Malvern, PA 19355   Free: 800-220-5000
                               Fax: (610)651-2981
URL: http://www.pbp.com.

Contact: Alan Field, Editor.

Desc: Communicates the latest news and trends in website marketing. *Type:* Newsletter.

Inventor's Desktop Companion: The Guide to Successfully Marketing and Protecting Your Ideas

Visible Ink Press
27500 Drake Rd.   Ph: (248)699-4253
Farmington Hills, MI 48331-   Free: 800-776-6265
3535   Fax: (248)699-8067
E-mail: galeord@gale.com
URL: http://www.gale.com

Contact: Richard C. Levy, Editor.

Desc: Agencies and organizations of interest to inventors, including national and regional associations, university innovation research centers, state and regional programs supporting inventors, business incubators, federal funding sources, publications, and electronic information services. *Type:* Directory.

IOMA's Marketing Department Management Report

Institute of Management & Administration, Inc.
29 W. 35th St., 5th Fl.　　　Ph: (212)244-0360
New York, NY 10001-2299　　Fax: (212)564-0465
E-mail: subserve@ioma.com; subserve@ioma.com.
URL: http://www.ioma.com
Contact: Laime Vaikus, Editor; Janice Prescott, Managing Editor.
Desc: Provides managers and supervisors with marketing ideas, information, and techniques. Articles topics include direct mail marketing, increasing marketing and sales productivity, website and the Internet, and vendors. *Type:* Newsletter.

Jonesreport for Shopping Center Marketing

Jonesreport, Inc.
9595 Whitley Dr., No. 100　　Free: 800-848-9024
Indianapolis, IN 46280
E-mail: ctrmktg@jonesreport.com.
URL: http://www.bit-wise.com/jonesreport/; http://www.jonesreport.com/jonesreport/.
Contact: Linda Lipp, Editor.
Desc: Reports current trends and developments in shopping center marketing. Guest articles by marketing specialists, and advice from shopping center marketing consultants. *Type:* Newsletter.

Langer Report

Langer Associates, Inc.
19 W. 44th St.　　　　　Ph: (212)391-0350
New York, NY 10036　　　Fax: (212)391-0357
Contact: Carol Clow Pye, Editor.
Desc: Provides news and information on changing values and lifestyles for marketers and informs readers of changes in the market research field. *Type:* Newsletter.

Larry Chase's Web Digest for Marketers

Chase Online Marketing Strategies
847A Second Ave., Ste. 332　　Ph: (212)876-1096
New York, NY 10017　　　　Fax: (212)876-1098
URL: http://wdfm.com.
Contact: Larry Chase, Exec. Editor, larry@wdfm.com; Dianna Husum, Editor; Eileen Shulock, Editor.
Desc: Delivers 15 short reviews of business-related websites every issue. *Type:* Newsletter.

Levin's Public Relations Report

Levin Public Relations & Marketing
30 Glenn St.　　　　　Ph: (914)997-0900
White Plains, NY 10603　　Fax: (914)997-9589
Contact: Donald Levin, Editor, levin@levinpr.com.
Desc: Offers strategy suggestions for management and vice presidents of communications and marketing firms. Seeks to "help gain competitive position, create awareness, increase sales and profits, and achieve other objectives." Analyzes current trends in public relations. *Type:* Newsletter.

The Levison Letter

Ivan Levison & Associates
14 Los Cerros Dr.　　　Ph: (415)461-0672
Greenbrae, CA 94904　　Fax: (415)461-7738
URL: http://www.evison.com.
Contact: Ivan Levison, Editor, ivan@levison.com.
Desc: Offers tips for improving public relations and marketing strategy. *Type:* Newsletter.

Magnet Marketing & Sales

John R. Graham, Inc.
40 Oval Rd.　　　　Ph: (617)328-0069
Quincy, MA 02170　　Fax: (617)471-1504
Contact: Rob Keane, Editor.

Desc: Contains information and advice on marketing, sales, and public relations. *Type:* Newsletter.

Mail-Order Marketing News

TJT Publications
26027 Tierra Dr.　　　Ph: (805)291-1289
Valencia, CA 91355　　Fax: (805)291-1289
E-mail: tjtpub@aol.com
URL: http://www.members.aol.com/tjtpub/index.html.
Contact: Terry Thomas, Editor.
Desc: Provides information, strategies, tips, and industry news for those who sell or buy via mail order. Includes reviews of money making opportunities and scam alerts. *Type:* Newsletter.

Mainly Marketing Newsletter

Mainly Marketing
403 Main St., Ste. 2-N　　Ph: (516)883-3382
PO Box 748　　　　　Free: 800-4-MAINLY
Port Washington, NY 11050　Fax: (516)883-2162
Contact: David Allen, Editor and Publisher.
Desc: Provides observations, research, analysis, and news of technical marketing. Recurring features include letters to the editor, news of research, a calendar of events, reports of meetings, book reviews, and notices of publications available. *Type:* Newsletter.

Market: Europe

The PRS Group
6320 Fly Rd., Ste. 102　　Ph: (315)431-0511
PO Box 248　　　　　Fax: (315)431-0200
East Syracuse, NY 13057-0248
E-mail: custserv@prsgroup.com
Contact: Doris L. Walsh, Editor.
Desc: Profiles European consumers and provides ideas for marketing strategies. Reports on European conferences and summarizes articles from international periodicals. *Type:* Newsletter.

Marketer's Guidepost

Medical Group Management Association
104 Inverness Terr. E.　　Ph: (303)799-1111
Englewood, CO 80112-5306　Free: 888-608-5601
　　　　　　　　　　　Fax: (303)397-1824
URL: http://www.mgma.com.
Contact: Kelli D. Davis, Editor.
Desc: Presents case studies and marketing techniques and offers advice for promotions and public relations campaigns. Recurring features include columns titled Quick tips, Guidepost-its, and What Would You Do? Remarks: Newsletter supplements a marketing manual. *Type:* Newsletter.

Marketing Advents

Direct Marketing Association of Washington
7702 Leesburg Pike, No. 400　Ph: (703)821-3629
Falls Church, VA 22043-2612　Fax: (703)821-3694
Contact: Nancy Scott, Managing Editor.
Desc: Contains news of Association activities and information on marketing issues, including those that are postal-related. Includes a calendar of events, news of members, and job listings. *Type:* Newsletter.

The Marketing Report

Progressive Business Publications
370 Technology Dr.　　Ph: (610)695-8600
Malvern, PA 19355　　Free: 800-220-5000
　　　　　　　　　Fax: (610)651-2981
URL: http://www.pbp.com.
Contact: Michael Boyette, Editor; Fred Hosier, Editor.
Desc: Presents the latest thinking from the leading marketing experts in the world. Recurring features include interviews, news of research, a calendar of events, news of educational opportunities, and a column titled Sharpen Your Judgment. *Type:* Newsletter.

The Marketing Revolution Newsletter

Clement Communications, Inc.
Concord Industrial Park　　Ph: (610)459-1700
10 LaCrue Ave.　　　　　Free: 800-345-8101
Concordville, PA 19331　　Fax: (610)459-0936
E-mail: editor@clement.com.
Contact: Maureen L. Rogers, Sr.Ed.; George Y Clement, Publisher; Maureen L. Solon, Exec.Ed.
Desc: Contains information and techniques for businesses on marketing and advertising. Includes articles on direct marketing, international business and markets, marketing and the Internet, and current marketing strategies. *Type:* Newsletter.

Marketing and Sales Career Directory

Gale Group Inc.
27500 Drake Rd.　　　Ph: (248)699-4253
Farmington Hills, MI 48331-　Free: 800-877-GALE
3535　　　　　　　　Fax: (248)699-8070
E-mail: galeord@galegroup.com
URL: http://www.galegroup.com.
Contact: Bradley J. Morgan, Editor.
Desc: Approximately 300 companies and organizations offering job opportunities, internships, and training possibilities for those seeking a career in marketing or sales; sources of help-wanted ads, professional associations, videos, databases, career guides, and professional guides and handbooks. *Type:* Directory.

Marketing Seminars and Conferences

LERN
1550 Hayes Dr.　　　Ph: (913)539-5376
Manhattan, KS 66502　Free: 800-678-5376
　　　　　　　　　Fax: (913)539-7766
E-mail: hq@lern.com
Contact: Paul Franklin, Editor; Anver Suliman, Senior Editor.
Desc: Offers advice on direct mail techniques, how to increase conference attendance, scheduling and pricing, and brochure design. Features columns by prominent seminar professionals and consultants. *Type:* Newsletter.

Marketing Signs

Research Center for Language and Semiotic Studies
Indiana University
PO Box 10　　　　Ph: (812)855-6493
Bloomington, IN 47405　Fax: (812)855-1273
Contact: Jean Umiker-Sebeok, Editor.
Desc: Contains articles, bibliographies, biographical sketches, and meeting announcements pertaining to the semiotics of marketplace behavior. *Type:* Newsletter.

Marketing Technology

Zhivago Marketing Partners
381 Seaside Dr.　　　Ph: (401)423-2400
Jamestown, RI 02835　Fax: (401)423-2700
URL: http://www.marketing-technology.com.
Contact: Kristin Zhivago, Editor, kristin@zhivago.com.
Desc: Covers the marketing of technical products and the technology used for marketing. *Type:* Newsletter.

Marketing with Technology News

Sarah Stambler
370 Central Park W., No. 210　Ph: (212)222-1713
New York, NY 10025　　　Fax: (212)678-6357
E-mail: sarah@mwt.com
URL: http://www.mwt.com.
Contact: Sarah Stambler, Editor.
Desc: Covers marketing information and techniques for businesses to increase profits and sales by using electronic delivery channels such as email, faxes, websites, and cable television. Recurring features include interviews and news of research. *Type:* Newsletter.

Marketwave

Leonard Clements
7342 N. Ivanhoe Ave.   Free: 800-688-4766
Fresno, CA 93722-2797   Fax: (559)275-5993
E-mail: mwave@aol.com.

Contact: Leonard Clements, Editor and Publisher.

Desc: Provides information on network marketing opportunities. Topics include industry news and fraud alerts. *Type:* Newsletter.

MSI Review

Marketing Science Institute
1000 Massachusetts Ave.   Ph: (617)491-2060
Cambridge, MA 02138   Fax: (617)491-2065
E-mail: pubs@msi.org
URL: http://www.msi.org

Contact: Susan Keane, Editor.

Desc: Reports on activities, research, and people of the Institute. Promotes practice-oriented research in marketing. *Type:* Newsletter.

NAMA Journal

National Account Management Association (NAMA)
150 N. Wacker Dr., Ste. 960   Ph: (312)251-3131
Chicago, IL 60606-1607   Fax: (312)251-3132

Contact: Lisa Napolitano, Editor; Maria T. Susano, Asst. Editor.

Desc: Publishes news of the Association, its activities, and its members. Furthers Association educational efforts and documents the accomplishments of the National Account Programs. *Type:* Newsletter.

National Account Management Association

Lisa Napolitano
150 N. Wacker Dr., Ste. 2222 Ph: (312)251-3131
Chicago, IL 60606   Fax: (312)251-3132
URL: http://www.nams.org/NAMA

Contact: Lisa Napolitano, Exec.Dir.

Desc: Corporation sales or marketing executives concerned with key/national/global account sales. *Type:* Association.

National Agri-Marketing Association

11020 King St., Ste. 205   Ph: (913)491-6500
Overland Park, KS 66210   Fax: (913)491-6502
E-mail: agrimktg@nama.org
URL: http://www.nama.org

Contact: Eldon J. White, CEO and Exec. V. P.

Desc: Persons engaged in agricultural marketing for manufacturers, advertising agencies, and the media. Promotes the highest standards of agricultural marketing; provides for the exchange of ideas; encourages the study and better understanding of agricultural advertising, selling, and marketing; works to broaden understanding of the economic importance of agriculture; encourages careers in agricultural marketing. *Type:* Association.

New Age Marketing Opportunities Newsletter

New Editions International
PO Box 2578   Ph: (520)282-9574
Sedona, AZ 86339   Fax: (520)282-9730
E-mail: newedit@sedona.net
URL: http://www.newagemarket.com.

Contact: Sophia Tarila, Editor.

Desc: Focuses on issues dealing with good marketing buys, resources, and pertinent marketing programs for businesses dealing in the New Age marketplace. *Type:* Newsletter.

Newspaper Marketing Report

VNU Newspaper Services Group
11 W. 42nd St., 11th Fl.   Ph: (212)789-3680
New York, NY 10036   Fax: (212)789-3644
Contact: Paul Martin, Editor.

Desc: Carries news of marketing research trends in media advertising, as well as items on desk top publishing, computer graphics, and other timely topics in media. *Type:* Newsletter.

NIMA International

1225 New York Ave. NW, Ste.   Ph: (202)289-6462
   1200   Free: 800-987-6462
Washington, DC 20005-6156   Fax: (202)682-0603
URL: http://www.nima.org
Contact: David Kinsman, VP, Public Affairs.

Desc: Infomercial producers, marketers, advertisers, telemarketers, duplication video services, home shopping networks, and cable and television networks. Promotes the electronic retailing industry in the best interests of the public and the association's membership worldwide. *Type:* Association.

Non Store Marketing Report

Maxwell Sroge Publishing, Inc.
522 Forest Ave.   Ph: (847)866-1890
Evanston, IL 60202   Fax: (847)866-1899
E-mail: newsletters@catalog-news.com
URL: http://www.catalog-news.com.
Contact: Harold Keeton, Editor.

Desc: Reports, interprets, and analyzes key developments in non store marketing. Provides profiles of leading mail order companies. *Type:* Newsletter.

ON Marketing

ON Marketing
7224 E. Kildee St., Ste. G-2 Ph: (562)425-5815
Long Beach, CA 90808   Fax: (562)425-5815
E-mail: ONuiry@aol.com
Contact: Octavio E. Nuiry, Editor.

Desc: Consists of information on Hispanic marketing. Recurring features include letters to the editor, interviews, news of research, book reviews, and news of educational opportunities. *Type:* Newsletter.

The Online Marketing Letter

Cyberwave Media
1360 Judson Dr.   Ph: (303)415-1195
Boulder, CO 80303-6337   Fax: (303)413-0911
URL: http://www.cyberwave.com.
Contact: Jonathan Mizel, Editor and Publisher, jonathan@cyberwave.com.

Desc: Direct-response marketing on the internet. *Type:* Newsletter.

PCS Direct Marketing Newsletter

PCS Mailing List Company
39 Cross St.   Ph: (978)532-7100
Peabody, MA 01960   Free: 800-532-LIST
                              Fax: (978)532-9181
E-mail: info@pcslist.com
Contact: Ann Guyer Healy, Editor; James M. Healy, Publisher.

Desc: Offers research tools, publications, and other advice on legal, medical, financial & consumer, direct marketing. Also covers mailing lists, databases, and software to assist with direct mailings. *Type:* Newsletter.

The Perceptive Report

Perceptive Marketers Agency, Ltd.
1100 E. Hector St., Ste. 301 Ph: (610)825-8710
Conshohocken, PA 19428   Fax: (610)825-9186
E-mail: perceptmkt@aol.com

Contact: Allen P. Solovitz, Editor.

Desc: Carries industry news, tips for managers, and profiles of those in the industry. *Type:* Newsletter.

Pi Sigma Epsilon

6560 S. 27th St., Ste. 203   Ph: (414)761-9350
Oak Creek, WI 53154-1016   Fax: (414)761-9351
URL: http://www.pisigmaepsilon.org
Contact: Frank C. Patek, II, Exec.Dir.

Desc: Professional fraternity - marketing, sales management, and selling. Conducts marketing, sales, and research projects at universities across the United States and works with corporations to provide employment cadidates. *Type:* Association.

Produce Marketing Association

1500 Casho Mill Rd.   Ph: (302)738-7100
PO Box 6036   Fax: (302)731-2409
Newark, DE 19714
E-mail: pma@mail.pma.com
URL: http://www.pma.com
Contact: Bryan E. Silbermann, CAE, Pres.

Desc: Trade Association serving marketers of fresh fruits, vegetables, and floral products worldwide. Members are involved in the production, distribution, retail, and food-service sectors of the industry. Works to create a favorable, responsible environment that advances the marketing of produce and floral products and services for North American buyers and sellers and their international partners. *Type:* Association.

Profile Briefings

Advertising Specialty Institute
1120 Wheeler Way   Ph: (215)752-4200
Langhorne, PA 19047-1785   Free: 800-326-7378
                              Fax: (215)752-9758
E-mail: info@asicentral.com

Desc: Reports on credit and marketing information. *Type:* Newsletter.

Promos and Premiums

New World Media
PO Box 95   Ph: (617)720-5751
Newton Centre, MA 02159   Fax: (617)367-9151
Contact: Jennifer Sawyer English, Editor and Publisher; Barbara Kalunian, Publisher.

Desc: Provides information about special offers available throughout the country. *Type:* Newsletter.

Promotion Marketing Association of America

257 Park Ave. S., 11th Fl.   Ph: (212)420-1100
New York, NY 10010-7304   Fax: (212)533-7622
E-mail: pmaa@pmaalink.org
URL: http://www.pmaalink.org
Contact: Claire Rosenzweig, CAE, Exec.Dir.

Desc: Fortune 500 marketer companies, promotion agencies, and companies using promotion programs; supplier members are manufacturers of package goods, cosmetics, and pharmaceuticals, consultants, and advertising agencies. Conducts surveys and studies of industry issues. *Type:* Association.

Promotion Marketing Association—Outlook

Promotion Marketing Association, Inc.
257 Park Ave. S. Ste. 1102   Ph: (212)420-1100
New York, NY 10010   Fax: (212)533-7622
E-mail: pma@pmalink.org
URL: http://www.pmalink.org.
Contact: Claire Rosenzweig, Exec. Dir.

Desc: Discusses issues and trends in the field of promotion marketing. Analyzes the merits of various types of promotion programs and marketing techniques. *Type:* Newsletter.

PSMJ Marketing Tactics

PSMJ Resources, Inc.
10 Midland Ave. Ph: (617)965-0055
Newton, MA 02158 Free: 800-537-PSMJ
 Fax: (617)965-5152
E-mail: psmj@ixnetcom.com
Contact: C. Winslow Pettingell, Editorial Dir.; Ernie Burden, Editor.
Desc: Contains current "information essential to the development of new business in every planning and design practice." Reports on marketing research and techniques and provides information on reference sources for marketing research. Recurring features include case studies, letters to the editor, and a commentary. *Type:* Newsletter.

Publishing for Professional Markets

SIMBA Information Inc.
11 Riverbend Dr. S. Ph: (203)358-4100
PO Box 4234 Free: 800-307-2529
Stamford, CT 06907-0234 Fax: (203)358-5824
E-mail: info@simbanet.com
URL: http://www.simbanet.com
Contact: Matt Behard, Editor.
Desc: Contains information for publishers on trends and statistics on market size, revenue, and financial information of major entities. *Type:* Newsletter.

Quirk's Marketing Research Review—Mall Research Facilities Directory Issue

Quirk Enterprises, Inc.
PO Box 23536 Ph: (612)854-5101
Minneapolis, MN 55423-0536 Fax: (612)854-8191
E-mail: quirk19@mail.idt.net
Contact: Joseph Rydholm, Editor, joeqmrr@mn.uswest.net.
Desc: Over 450 marketing research facilities located at shopping malls. *Type:* Directory.

Relationship Marketing Report

Marketing Publishers Inc.
PO Box 573 Ph: (703)494-1914
Occoquan, VA 22125-0573 Fax: (703)494-3422
E-mail: rmrinfo@dc.jones.com.
URL: http://www.relationshipmktg.com.
Contact: Jon Lowder, Editor.
Desc: Provides businesses and related organizations with techniques on how to build and maintain positive relationships with customers to increase profitability. Recurring features include columns titled Database Marketing Systems, Loyalty Programs, and Interactive Marketing. *Type:* Newsletter.

Research Alert

EPM Communications, Inc.
160 Mercer St., 3rd Fl. Ph: (212)941-0099
New York, NY 10012-3212 Fax: (212)941-1622
E-mail: epmcommun@aol.com; researchalert@pipeline.com.
Contact: Ira Mayer, Editor.
Desc: Summarizes the most current consumer marketing research reports. Includes complete contact, methodology, and price information. *Type:* Newsletter.

Sales Automation Success

Denali Group, Inc.
2815 NW Pine Cone Dr., No. 100 Ph: (425)392-3514
 Fax: (425)391-7982
Issaquah, WA 98027-8698
E-mail: rbohn@denali.com; richbohn@sellmorenow.com.
URL: http://www.sellmorenow.com.
Contact: Steve Pokin, Editor.
Desc: Reviews sales automation software. Offers advice for applying technology to sales and marketing problems, and how to sell more now through effective use of high technology. *Type:* Newsletter.

SCAN

Business Intelligence Program
SRI International
333 Ravenswood Ave. Ph: (650)859-4600
Menlo Park, CA 94025 Fax: (650)859-4544
Contact: Judith Clay Lhamon, Editor.
Desc: Reports research being performed in technical, market, and management areas. Analyzes early signs of potential social, political, economic, and technological change, and, relating these developments to one another, suggests possible implications for BIP's clients. *Type:* Newsletter.

Selling to Kids

Phillips Business Information, Inc.
1201 Seven Locks Rd., Ste. 300 Ph: (301)340-1520
Potomac, MD 20854 Free: 888-707-5809
 Fax: (301)340-3847
E-mail: clientservices.pbi@phillips.com
URL: http://www.phillips.com.
Contact: Devorah Goldman, Editor.
Desc: Publishes how-to articles and news for executives marketing to children. Also provides case studies, market research, and media box scores. *Type:* Newsletter.

Selling to Seniors

CD Publications
8204 Fenton St. Ph: (301)588-6380
Silver Spring, MD 20910 Free: 800-666-6380
 Fax: (301)588-6385
E-mail: cdpubs@clark.net
Desc: Suggests effective ways to reach the "over 50" market by emphasizing successful marketing strategies. Recurring features include interviews, case studies, and demographic data. *Type:* Newsletter.

Siedlecki's Business Benchmarks

Richard Siedlecki Consulting, Inc.
4767 Lake Forrest Dr. NE Ph: (404)303-9900
Atlanta, GA 30342-2539
E-mail: sied@mindspring.com
Contact: Richard Siedlecki, Editor.
Desc: Discusses management and marketing ideas to save time, improve productivity, boost effectiveness, and generate business growth. *Type:* Newsletter.

Strategies

Kalman Communications
11766 Wilshire Blvd., Ste. 120
Los Angeles, CA 90025
Contact: Jerry Kalman, Editor.
Desc: Serves as a forum for public relations news and ideas. *Type:* Newsletter.

Team Marketing Report

Team Marketing Report
660 W. Grand, Ste. 100E Ph: (312)829-7060
Chicago, IL 60610 Free: 888-616-1867
 Fax: (312)733-4071
E-mail: tmreditor@aol.com
Contact: Alan Friedman, Exec. Editor, Alanf@marketing.com; Sean Brenner, Editor, sbrenner@marketing.com.
Desc: Reports on innovative and successful sports marketing strategies. Recurring features include interviews, news of research, advertising spotlight, reports of meetings. *Type:* Newsletter.

Telemarketing Update

Update Publicare Co.
c/o Prosperity & Profits Ph: (303)575-5676
Unlimited
PO Box 416
Denver, CO 80201
Contact: A. Doyle, Editor.
Desc: Publishes excerpts from telemarketing books, and news of telemarketing laws; ideas & possibilities in order to "introduce readers to the vast area of telemarketing." Recurring features include telemarketing script presentations. *Type:* Newsletter.

Telephone Selling Report

Business by Phone, Inc.
13254 Stevens St. Ph: (402)895-9399
Omaha, NE 68137 Free: 800-326-7721
 Fax: (402)896-3353
E-mail: arts@businessbyphone.com
URL: http://www.businessbyphone.com.
Contact: Art Sobczak, Editor, arts@businessbyphone.com.
Desc: Offers pragmatic, how-to ideas on selling by phone. Contains original and excerpted material on telephone selling, telemarketing, communication, and motivation. *Type:* Newsletter.

The Top 100 List

Luce Press Clippings
42 S. Center Ph: (602)834-4884
Mesa, AZ 85210 Free: 800-528-8226
 Fax: (602)834-3821
E-mail: clip@lucepress.com
URL: http://www.lucepress.com.
Contact: Richard Weiner, Editor.
Desc: Presents marketing information and demographics from newspapers, magazines, and other media on U.S. cities. *Type:* Newsletter.

TOWERS Club Info Marketing Report

TOWERS Club Press Inc.
9107 NW 11th Ave. Ph: (360)574-3084
PO Box 2038 Fax: (360)576-8969
Vancouver, WA 98668
Contact: Jerry Buchanan, Editor.
Desc: Provides marketing advice and mail-order techniques for self-publishers of how-to materials and other home-based entrepreneurs. Recurring features include letters to the editor, interviews, news of research, book reviews, notices of publications available, notices of clinics and workshops, and columns titled News Tips & Sources, Reading Jerry's Mail, and Unclassified Ads. *Type:* Newsletter.

The Winning Manager

Wolf J. Rinke
PO Box 350 Ph: (410)531-9280
Clarksville, MD 21029 Free: 800-828-9653
 Fax: (410)531-9282
E-mail: wolfrinke@aol.com
Contact: Wolf J. Rinke, Ph.D., Editor.
Desc: Consists of information for management professionals. Recurring features include columns titled Cry Wolf. *Type:* Newsletter.

Worldgram Newsletter

Worldprofit, Inc.
PO Box 38-2767 Ph: (617)547-6372
Cambridge, MA 02238 Fax: (617)547-0061
E-mail: incor@oanet.com.
URL: http://www.worldprofit.com/fmcatalg.htm.
Contact: Dr. Jeffrey Lant, Editor, drjlant@worldprofit.com.
Desc: Internet newsletter with a marketing focus for businesses. Also offers tips on how to profit from the World Wide Web. *Type:* Newsletter.

Marriage

ABC Dialogue
Association of Bridal Consultants
200 Chestnutland Rd.   Ph: (860)355-0464
New Milford, CT 06776-2521 Fax: (860)354-1404
E-mail: bridalassn@aol.com
URL: http://www.weddingchannel.com; http://Bridalnet.com/abc.
Contact: Gerard J. Monaghan, Editor.
Desc: Explores the various aspects of wedding consulting, including bridal attire, jewelry, food, photography, and business management and advertising. Recurring features include business tips and profiles of members. *Type:* Newsletter.

American Divorce Association of Men International
1519 S. Arlington Heights Rd. Ph: (847)364-1555
Arlington Heights, IL 60005 Fax: (708)364-7273
Contact: Louis J. Filczer, Exec.Dir.
Desc: Individuals promoting divorce reform and the implementation of new divorce procedures. Provides individual divorce counseling and divorce mediation; educational and therapeutic meetings; investigative services; lawyer referral lists; strategic laymen and legal knowledge; educational services; guidance in legal self-representation; human relations consulting. *Type:* Association.

Fathers for Equal Rights
PO Box 010847, Flagler Sta. Ph: (305)251-7003
Miami, FL 33101   Free: (305)234-4156
Contact: Victor G. Moss, Exec.Dir.
Desc: Parents and grandparents involved in divorce and child custody disputes. Fights discrimination against and provides support for men in divorce cases involving custody issues. *Type:* Association.

Martial Arts

Black Belt Magazine
Rainbow Publications, Inc.
24715 Rockefeller   Ph: (805)257-4066
PO Box 918   Free: 800-423-2874
Santa Clarita, CA 91355 Fax: (805)257-3028
E-mail: rainbow@rsabbs.com
Contact: Jim Coleman, Editor; Michael James, Publisher; Barbara Lessard, Advertising Mgr.
Desc: Self-defense magazine featuring various martial arts, including how-to's, historical and current events in the martial arts. Audience ranges from pre-teens to 50's. *Type:* Periodical.

Japan Aikido Association U.S.A.
5752 S. Kingston Way Ph: (303)740-7424
Englewood, CO 80111 Fax: (303)337-1631
E-mail: nettles@tomiki.org
URL: http://www.tomiki.org/tomiki
Contact: Dave Nettles, Pres.
Desc: Fosters international amateur sports competition. *Type:* Association.

United States Judo
95 S. Marret St., Ste. 520 Ph: (408)271-1099
San Jose, CA 95113 Fax: (408)298-7554
URL: http://www.usjudo.org
Contact: Yoshihiro Uchida, Pres.
Desc: Judo groups and athletes, referees, judges, and interested individuals. Serves as national governing body for amateur judo in the United States. Promotes the sport of judo and trains athletes for competition. *Type:* Association.

United States Judo Association
21 N. Union Blvd. Ph: (719)633-7750
Colorado Springs, CO 80909 Fax: (719)633-4041
E-mail: usja@csprings.com
URL: http://www.csprings.com/usja
Contact: Edward N. Szrejter, Exec.Dir.
Desc: Amateur judo athletes and coaches. Promotes the recreational and physical benefits of judo; advocates practice of the sport to develop sportsmanship, good citizenship, and mental well-being. *Type:* Association.

U.S. Taekwondo Union
1 Olympic Plaza Ste. 405 Ph: (719)578-4632
Colorado Springs, CO 80909 Fax: (719)578-4642
E-mail: ustutkd1@aol.com
URL: http://www.ustu.com
Contact: Jay Warwick, Exec.Dir.
Desc: A member of the United States Olympic Committee and a Sport Supervising Committee of the Amateur Athletic Union of the United States. Amateur Taekwondo athletes and instructors. Promotes Taekwondo programs in the U.S. *Type:* Association.

U.S.A. Karate Federation
1300 Kenmore Blvd. Ph: (330)753-3114
Akron, OH 44314 Fax: (330)753-6967
E-mail: usakf@raex.com
URL: http://www.usakf.com
Contact: George E. Anderson, Pres.
Desc: Individuals, corporations, sports organizations, and karate clubs. Serves as a national federation for karate in the U.S. *Type:* Association.

Masons

Ancient Egyptian Arabic Order Nobles of the Mystic Shrine
2239 Democrat Rd. Ph: (901)395-0150
Memphis, TN 38132-1802 Fax: (901)395-0115
Contact: Marion Cheatham, Imperial Recorder.
Desc: Fraternal society of 32nd degree Masons. *Type:* Association.

Conference of Prince Hall Grand Masters
4th & State St. Ph: (870)534-5467
Pine Bluff, AR 71601 Fax: (870)535-3581
Contact: Howard L. Woods, Pres.
Desc: Black fraternal order united to coordinate efforts of member groups in providing leadership in and formulating goals for the black community. *Type:* Association.

Daughters of the Nile, Supreme Temple
c/o Geraldine Neely
104 Shore Dr.
Portland, TX 78374-1420
Contact: Geraldine Neely, Sec.
Desc: Mothers, wives, sisters, daughters, and widows of Shriners. Assists with philanthropic work of the Shriners' hospitals for crippled children. *Type:* Association.

Empire State Mason
Grand Lodge AF & AM
71 W. 23rd St. Ph: (212)741-4500
New York, NY 10010 Free: 800-362-7664
    Fax: (212)633-2639
E-mail: esmetitor@aol.com.
Contact: Ronald N. Bower, Managing Editor, ronnbower@aol.com.
Desc: Fraternal masonic magazine. *Alt. Contact:* 37 Oliver St., Lockport, NY 14094-4615; telephone: (716)434-4946; fax: (716)434-4496. *Type:* Periodical.

Federation of Eastern Stars
PO Box 1296
Austin, TX 78767
Contact: Lucille F. McCants, Pres.
Desc: Women's division of the Federation of Masons of the World. Seeks the unification of Easternism. Conducts charitable and community work. *Type:* Association.

Federation of Masons of the World
1017 E. 11th St. Ph: (512)477-5380
Austin, TX 78702
Contact: M. J. Anderson, Sr., Bd.Chm.
Desc: Masonic jurisdictions in 22 countries. *Type:* Association.

General Grand Chapter, Order of the Eastern Star
1618 New Hampshire Ave. NW Ph: (202)667-4737
Washington, DC 20009 Free: 800-648-1182
    Fax: (202)462-5162
E-mail: easternstar@erols.com
URL: http://www.easternstar.org/
Contact: Florence Adair, Most Worthy Grand Matron.
Desc: Master Masons in good standing, and their female relatives. Fraternal order dedicated to social enjoyment, civic interests, and serving the needy. *Type:* Association.

General Grand Chapter of Royal Arch Masons International
PO Box 489 Ph: (606)236-0757
Danville, KY 40423-0489 Fax: (606)236-6773
Contact: John F. Kirby, Sr., Gen. Grand Sec.
Desc: Members of symbolic Lodge of Free and Accepted Masons. Functions as a mutual service organization. Offers educational, research, promotional, and administrative aids through its Royal Arch Education Bureau. *Type:* Association.

Heroes of '76
8301 E. Boulevard Dr. Ph: (703)765-5000
Alexandria, VA 22308-1399 Fax: (703)765-8390
E-mail: nationalsdj@juno.com
Contact: Nelson O. Newcombe, Adjutant.
Desc: Fraternal organization. Supports the Collingwood Library and Museum on Americanism located in Mt. Vernon, VA. *Type:* Association.

Imperial Council of the Ancient Arabic Order of the Nobles of the Mystic Shrine for North America
PO Box 31356 Ph: (813)281-0300
Tampa, FL 33631-3356 Fax: (813)281-7103
Contact: Charles G. Cumpstone, Jr., Exec.VP/Coor.
Desc: Maintains 22 hospitals for crippled and burned children. *Type:* Association.

International Masonry Institute
823 15th St, MW, Ste. 1000 Ph: (410)280-1305
Washington, DC 20005 Free: 800-IMI-0988
    Fax: (301)261-2855
E-mail: nbradford@imiweb.org
URL: http://www.imiweb.org
Contact: Joan Baggett-Calambokidis, Pres.
Desc: Joint labor/management trust fund of the International Union of Bricklayers and Allied Craftsmen and union masonry contractors. Objective is the advancement of quality masonry construction through national and regional training, promotion, advertising and labor management relations programs in the U.S. and Canada. *Type:* Association.

International Order of Job's Daughters, Supreme Guardian Council
233 W. 6th St.   Ph: (402)592-7987
Papillion, NE 68046-2210   Fax: (402)592-2177
E-mail: sgc@iojd.org
URL: http://www.iojd.org
Contact: Susan M. Goolsby, Exec.Mgr.
Desc: Girls from 5 countries who are between the ages of 11 and 20 and are related to Master Masons. Promotes spiritual and character development. *Type:* Association.

Knights Templar, Grand Encampment, U.S.A.
5097 N. Elston Ave., Ste. 101   Ph: (773)777-3300
Chicago, IL 60630-2460   Fax: (773)777-8836
Contact: Charles R. Neumann, Grand Recorder.
Desc: Masonic order. *Type:* Association.

Masonic Relief Association of U.S.A. and Canada
3827 Canal St.   Ph: (504)482-2111
New Orleans, LA 70119   Fax: (504)486-2066
Contact: Glen H. Butler, Exec.Sec.
Desc: Coordinates and correlates the various forms of Masonic relief throughout the U.S. *Type:* Association.

Modern Free and Accepted Masons of the World
PO Box 1072   Ph: (706)322-3326
Columbus, GA 31902   Fax: (706)322-3805
Contact: Nelson Barrett, Contact.
Desc: Fellowship organization dedicated to educating members so that they may become better leaders and citizens. Holds seminars and workshops on topics such as leadership and business skills. Conducts Sunday school classes for children. *Type:* Association.

National Sojourners
8301 E. Boulevard Dr.   Ph: (703)765-5000
Alexandria, VA 22308-1399   Fax: (703)765-8390
E-mail: nationalsoj@juno.com
Contact: Nelson O. Newcombe, Sec.-Treas.
Desc: Past or present commissioned officers and warrant officers of the uniformed forces of the U.S. who are Master Masons. Supports the Collingwood Library and Museum on Americanism. *Type:* Association.

The Northern Light
Supreme Council, Scottish Rite, NMJ, USA
PO Box 519   Ph: (781)862-4410
Lexington, MA 02420   Fax: (781)863-1833
Contact: Richard H. Curtis, Editor, dcurtis@supremecouncil.org.
Desc: Magazine containing articles of interest to Masons and their families. *Type:* Periodical.

The Scottish Rite Journal (Southern Jurisdiction, USA)
Supreme Council of the 33rd Degree, A&A Scottish Rite
1733 16th St. NW   Ph: (202)232-3579
Washington, DC 20009-3103   Free: 800-776-2766
                 Fax: (202)387-1843
E-mail: council@srmason-sj.org
URL: http://www.srmason-sj.org.
Contact: C. Fred Kleinknecht, Editor-in-Chief; Dr. John W. Boettjer, Managing Editor.
Desc: Masonic magazine. *Type:* Periodical.

Supreme Assembly, International Order of Rainbow for Girls
Box 1868   Ph: (918)423-1328
McAlester, OK 74502   Fax: (918)423-1329
URL: http://www.iorg.org/

Contact: Mary Muhs, Supreme Worthy Advisor.
Desc: Girls' fraternal society composed of active members (unmarried girls from ages 11-20) and majority members (married women or members over 20 years old) in Australia, Brazil, Canada, Germany, Japan, Panama, Philippines, and the United States. *Type:* Association.

Supreme Council, Ancient Accepted Scottish Rite of Free-Masonry (Northern Masonic Jurisdiction)
33 Marrett Rd.   Ph: (781)862-4410
PO Box 519   Free: 800-814-1432
Lexington, MA 02420-0519   Fax: (781)863-1833
E-mail: whall@world.std.com
Contact: Winthrop L. Hall, Exec.Sec.
Desc: Scottish Rite Masons in 15 states east of the Mississippi River and north of the Ohio River. Supports Scottish Rite Masonic Museum of Our National Heritage in Lexington, MA and Children's Learning Centers, and the Abbott Scottish Rite Scholarship Program. Sponsors fellowships in programs related to finding the underlying cause of schizophrenia to 15 universities. *Type:* Association.

Supreme Council, Mystic Order Veiled Prophets of Enchanted Realm
1696 Brice Rd.   Ph: (614)860-9193
Reynoldsburg, OH 43068   Fax: (614)860-9099
E-mail: scgrotto@worldnet.att.net
Contact: E. Paul Howard, Exec.Sec.
Desc: Fraternal order for Master Masons. *Type:* Association.

Supreme Council Order of the Amaranth
2303 Murdoch Ave.   Ph: (304)485-0423
Parkersburg, WV 26101
E-mail: amaranth@wirefire.com
URL: http://www.amaranth.org
Contact: Ethel B. Fry, Supreme Sec.
Desc: Men and women of Masonic families. Fraternal order organized as "the apex and top of the Orders affording the privileges of Masonic principles to women and men." *Type:* Association.

Supreme Council 33rd Degree, Ancient and Accepted Scottish Rite of Freemasonry - Southern Jurisdiction
1733 16th St. NW   Ph: (202)232-3579
Washington, DC 20009-3103   Fax: (202)387-1843
E-mail: council@srmason-sj.org
URL: http://www.srmason-sj.org
Contact: C. F. Kleinknecht, Contact.
Desc: Membership composed of Scottish Rite (fourth to 33rd degrees) Masons in all states south of the Ohio River and west of the Mississippi River, all American territorial possessions. Maintains museum. *Type:* Association.

Tall Cedars of Lebanon of North America
2609 N. Front St.   Ph: (717)232-5991
Harrisburg, PA 17110   Fax: (717)232-5997
Contact: A. Ralph Horlbeck, Supreme Scribe.
Desc: Master Masons in good standing in their Masonic Lodge. Operates Tall Cedar Foundation, which supports muscular dystrophy research. *Type:* Association.

Mathematics

American Mathematical Society
PO Box 6248   Ph: (401)455-4000
Providence, RI 02940   Free: 800-321-4AMS
                 Fax: (401)331-3842
E-mail: cust-serv@ams.org
URL: http://www.ams.org/

Contact: Dr. John Ewing, Exec.Dir.
Desc: Professional society of mathematicians and educators. Promotes the interests of mathematical scholarship and research. Holds institutes, seminars, short courses, and symposia to further mathematical research; awards prizes. *Type:* Association.

e-MATH
American Mathematical Society
PO Box 6248   Ph: (401)455-4000
Providence, RI 02940-6248   Free: 800-321-4267
                 Fax: (401)331-3842
E-mail: webmaster@ams.org
URL: http://e-math.ams.org
Desc: E-MATH provides information on the American Math Society, and also allows searches of the following publications: Bulletin of the AMS, Conformal Geometry and Dynamics, Electronic Research Announcements, Journal of the AMS, Mathematics of Computation, Proceedings of the AMS, Representation Theory, Transactions of the AMS, and Notices of the AMS. Other topics of interest include employment opportunities, government affairs, education, access to the AMS online store, reviews, and much more. *Type:* Database.

Employment Information in the Mathematical Sciences/Journal
American Mathematical Society
PO Box 6248   Ph: (401)455-4000
Providence, RI 02940   Free: 800-321-4267
                 Fax: (401)331-3842
E-mail: pub@ams.org
URL: http://www.ams.org
Contact: Michael Saitas, Editor.
Desc: Provides concise listings of open positions (1,400-1,500/yr.) "suitable for mathematicians with education and experience at every level beyond the Bachelor's degree." Lists positions by state. Remarks: Computer the Mathematical Association of America (MAA) and the Society for Industrial and Applied Mathematics. *Type:* Newsletter.

Kappa Mu Epsilon
Department of Mathematics   Ph: (419)372-7454
Bowling Green, OH 43403-0221
URL: http://www.cst.cmich.edu/org/kme_nat
Contact: Waldemar Weber, Sec.
Desc: Honor society for men and women in mathematics. *Type:* Association.

Mathematical Association of America
1529 18th St. NW   Ph: (202)387-5200
Washington, DC 20036   Fax: (202)265-2384
E-mail: hq@maa.org
URL: http://www.maa.org
Contact: Marcia P. Sward, Exec.Dir.
Desc: College mathematics teachers; individuals using mathematics as a tool in a business or profession. Sponsors annual high school mathematics contests and W.L. Putnam Competition for college students. *Type:* Association.

Mathematics Lessons Database
University of Illinois at Urbana-Champaign
Urbana, IL 61801
URL: http://www.mste.uiuc.edu:591/mathed/queryform.html
Contact: mste@uiuc.edu.
Desc: This database houses downloadable Internet-based lessons in mathematics for students at the elementary, middle, secondary, and post-secondary levels. You can access lessons in algebra, geometry, trigonometry, calculus, and general math. *Type:* Database.

MathMagic

The Math Forum
500 College Ave.   Ph: (610)328-8225
Swarthmore, PA 19081   Free: 800-756-7823
                       Fax: (610)328-7824
E-mail: webmaster@forum.swarthmore.edu
URL: http://forum.swarthmore.edu/mathmagic/
Contact: Alan Hodson, ahodson@cs.utep.edu.
Desc: The MathMagic site provides extensive information concerning the MathMagic K-12 telecommunications project hosted by Swarthmore College's Math Forum. Topics include registration, current and previous challenges offered by the project, general data, more. *Type:* Database.

MathSci®

American Mathematical Society
PO Box 6248   Ph: (401)455-4000
Providence, RI 02940-6248
E-mail: cust-serv@math.ams.org
URL: http://www.ams.org
Contact: Daphne Potter, Information Specialist, mathsci@math.ams.org.
Desc: Contains more than 1.7 million citations, with abstracts (from July 1979), to articles, books, and conference proceedings that have appeared in Mathematical Reviews (MR), Current Mathematical Publications (CMP) (listing works to be reviewed in MR), Current Index to Statistics (CIS) (published by the American Statistical Association and the Institute of Mathematical Statistics), Index to Statistics and Probability (written by John Tukey and Ian Ross), Computing Reviews (CR), ACM Guide to Computing Literature (GCL) (published by the Association for Computing Machinery (ACM)), and Technical Reports in Computer Science (Stanford University, Mathematical and Computer Library). Corresponds to the online MathSci database. *Available:* The Dialog Corporation, DIALOG; CompuServe Information Service, Knowledge Index; American Mathematical Society; Maruzen Company, Ltd., Maruzen Scientific Information Service (MASIS) Center; European Information Network Services (EINS). *Type:* Database.

Mu Alpha Theta

601 Elm, Rm. 423   Ph: (405)325-4489
Norman, OK 73019   Fax: (405)325-7184
E-mail: matheta@ou.edu
Contact: Stanley B. Eliason, Exec.Sec.-Treas.
Desc: Honorary club - for high school and junior college mathematics. Sponsored by Mathematical Association of America and National Council of Teachers of Mathematics. *Type:* Association.

National Council of Teachers of Mathematics

1906 Association Dr.   Ph: (703)620-9840
Reston, VA 20191-1593 Free: 800-235-7566
                       Fax: (703)476-2970
URL: http://www.nctm.org
Contact: John A. Thorpe, Exec.Dir.
Desc: Teachers of mathematics in grades preK-12, two-year colleges, and teacher education personnel on college campuses. *Type:* Association.

Pi Mu Epsilon

c/o Robert Woodside   Ph: (919)328-4112
East Carolina University Fax: (919)328-6414
Department of Mathematics
Greenville, NC 27858
E-mail: mapme@ecuvm.cis.ecu.edu
URL: http://www.pme-math.org
Contact: Robert Woodside, Sec.-Treas.
Desc: Honorary society - men and women, mathematics. *Type:* Association.

Scholastic DynaMath

Scholastic, Inc.
555 Broadway   Ph: (212)343-6100
New York, NY 10012   Free: 800-724-6527
                       Fax: (212)343-4535
E-mail: custserv@scholastic.com; dynamath@scholastic.com.
URL: http://www.scholastic.com
Contact: Matt Friedman, Editor, (212)343-6458, fax: (212)343-6333.
Desc: Classroom magazine for math students in grades 3, 4, 5 and 6. *Type:* Periodical.

Scholastic MATH Magazine

Scholastic, Inc.
555 Broadway   Ph: (212)343-6100
New York, NY 10012   Free: 800-724-6527
                       Fax: (212)343-4535
E-mail: custserv@scholastic.com; mathmag@aol.com.
URL: http://www.scholastic.com
Contact: Sarah Jane Brian, Editor; Richard Robinson, Publisher.
Desc: Basic math magazine for grades 7-9. Includes activities and features that revolve around math. Teachers edition includes reviews of math software and number-related books. *Type:* Periodical.

SIGACT News

Association for Computing Machinery
1515 Broadway   Ph: (212)869-7440
New York, NY 10036   Free: 800-843-6626
                       Fax: (212)869-0581
URL: http://sigact.acm.org/sigactnews.
Contact: Ian Parberry, Editor.
Desc: Provides information on the practical and theoretical aspects of design, analysis, and application of algorithms, data structures, systems and languages for algebraic and symbolic mathematical computation. *Type:* Newsletter.

SIGNUM Newsletter

Association for Computing Machinery
1515 Broadway   Ph: (212)869-7440
New York, NY 10036   Free: 800-342-6626
E-mail: acmhelp@acm.org; editors_signum@acm.org.
Contact: Paul Havland, Editor.
Desc: Serves as a communications forum between members and other professional organizations. Provides news for individuals concerned with computational mathematics; covers analysis of numerical algorithms, mathematical software, scientific computation, theory of optimal algorithms, and automatic problem solving systems. *Type:* Newsletter.

SIGSAM Bulletin

Association for Computing Machinery
1515 Broadway   Ph: (212)869-7440
New York, NY 10036   Free: 800-342-6626
E-mail: acmhelp@acm.org
Contact: Robert Corless, Editor.
Desc: Concerned with "practical and theoretical aspects of the design, analysis and application of algorithms, data structures, systems and languages for algebraic and symbolic mathematical computation." *Type:* Newsletter.

SIGSIM Newsletter

Special Interest Group on Simulation and Modeling (SIGSIM)
Asociation for Computing Machinery
1515 Broadway   Ph: (212)869-7440
New York, NY   Free: 800-342-6626
E-mail: acmhelp@acm.org; acmhelp@acm.org.
URL: http://www.acm.org.
Contact: Dana Wyatt, Editor.

Desc: Focuses on the advancement of simulation and modeling and their discrete and continuous application in computer systems, industry and business networks, socioeconomics, and other fields. Covers experimental design and validation of simulations; techniques of digital, analog, and hybrid simulation; random number theory and generators; simulation languages and packages; statistical distribution analysis; and related computational mathematics. *Type:* Newsletter.

Society for Industrial and Applied Mathematics

3600 University City Science Ph: (215)382-9800
  Center   Free: 800-447-SIAM
Philadelphia, PA 19104-2688   Fax: (215)386-7999
E-mail: siam@siam.org
URL: http://www.siam.org
Contact: James M. Crowley, Exec.Dir.
Desc: Mathematicians, engineers, computer scientists, physical scientists, bioscientists, educators, social scientists, and others utilizing mathematics for the solution of problems. Purposes are to: promote research in applied mathematics and computational science; further the application of mathematics to new methods and techniques useful in industry and science; provide for the exchange of information between the mathematical, industrial, and scientific communities. Conducts workshops; offers courses; supports sections and university chapters. *Type:* Association.

Medical

Accreditation Association for Ambulatory Health Care

9933 Lawler Ave.   Ph: (847)676-9610
Skokie, IL 60077-3708 Fax: (847)676-9628
E-mail: aaahc@mcs.com
URL: http://www.aaahc.org
Contact: John E. Burke, Ph.D., Exec.Dir.
Desc: Operates a voluntary, peer-based accreditation and consulting program for ambulatory health care organizations as a means of assisting them in efficiently providing a high level of care for patients. Distributes free lists of accredited organizations. *Type:* Association.

Acoustic Neuroma Association

PO Box 12402   Ph: (404)237-8023
Atlanta, GA 30355   Fax: (404)237-2704
E-mail: anausa@aol.com
URL: http://www.anausa.org
Contact: Lois Lawery, Exec.Dir.
Desc: Persons who have had acoustic neuroma (a tumor growing in the inner ear) and others who have had tumors that affect the cranial nerves and adjacent neural tissue. Provides support and offers encouragement on overcoming effects of these tumors. *Type:* Association.

ACP Observer

American College of Physicians
Independence Mall W.   Ph: (215)351-2400
6th St. at Race   Free: 800-523-1546
Philadelphia, PA 19106-1572 Fax: (215)351-2644
URL: http://www.acponline.org.
Contact: Paula Katz, Exec. Editor; Ed Doyle, Exec. Dir.; Ara Eloian, Advertising Mgr.; Penny Quartapella, Editor.
Desc: Official membership tabloid of the American College of Physicians. *Type:* Periodical.

Acupuncture International Association

2330 S. Brentwood Blvd. Ph: (314)961-2300
St. Louis, MO 63144-2096 Fax: (314)961-9828
Contact: Dr. Carol Ann Lee, VP.
Desc: Doctors of medicine, chiropractic, and osteopathy who practice acupuncture. Conducts professional education, public health, and research programs. Maintains library of 1682 volumes. *Type:* Association.

Acupuncture Research Institute
14632 E. Whittier Blvd.   Ph: (213)722-7353
Whittier, CA 90605
Contact: David Chen, Exec.Dir.
Desc: Validity and American application of the ancient Chinese traditional healing art of acupuncture homoeopathy, including its modern innovations and international modifications. *Type:* Research center.

Advance for Respiratory Care Practitioners
Merion Publications Inc.
2900 Horizon Dr.   Ph: (610)278-1400
PO Box 61556   Free: 800-355-5627
King of Prussia, PA 19406   Fax: (610)278-1425
URL: http://www.advanceweb.com.
Contact: Vern Enge, Editor, venge@merion.com.
Desc: Provides current information on techniques and developments of respiratory care for respiratory therapists. *Type:* Newsletter.

Advanced Medical Research Foundation, Inc.
333 Longwood Ave.   Ph: (617)278-1800
Boston, MA 02115-5711   Fax: (617)566-0272
Contact: Nile L. Albright, MD, Pres.
Desc: Medical and cancer research and science education. *Type:* Research center.

Advances
The Robert Wood Johnson Foundation
PO Box 2316   Ph: (609)452-8701
Princeton, NJ 08543-2316
E-mail: advances@rwjf.org.
URL: http://www.rwjf.org.
Contact: Paul Tarini, Executive Editor, (609)243-5931, fax: (609)243-5874, ptarini@rwjf.org; Victoria D. Weisfeld, Editor, (609)951-5753, fax: (609)243-5874, weisfe@rwjf.org.
Desc: "The National Newsletter of The Robert Wood Johnson Foundation." Reports on issues related to health care. Recurring features include interviews, news of research, and columns titled Profile, Abridge, Grants, and People. *Type:* Newsletter.

African Medical and Research Foundation, U.S.A.
19 W. 44th St., Ste. 1708   Ph: (212)768-2440
New York, NY 10036   Fax: (212)768-4230
URL: http://www.amres.org
Contact: Ellen Subin, Pres.
Desc: The spread and prevention of AIDS, malaria, and hydatid disease. Also creates health care & training models used by developing countries worldwide. *Type:* Research center.

Alert
Alzheimer Society for Metropolitan Toronto
2323 Yonge St., Ste. 500   Ph: (416)322-6560
Toronto, ON, Canada M4P   Fax: (416)966-0706
2C9
E-mail: write@asmt.org
URL: http://www.asmt.org.
Contact: Nancy MacArthur, Editor.
Type: Newsletter.

Allegheny General Hospital
Allegheny-Singer Research Institute
320 E. North Ave.   Ph: (412)359-4212
Pittsburgh, PA 15212-9986   Fax: (412)359-1525
Contact: James H. McMaster, MD, Sr.Asst.Dean for Res. for AUHS.
Desc: Cardiovascular and pulmonary genetics, human genetics, cancer, neurosciences, musculoskeletal and trauma

issues. Staff specializations include molecular biology, radiobiology, cell biology, immunology, genetics, multimedia, telecommunications technology, biochemistry, surgery, mechanical engineering, electrical engineering, psychology, child development, physics, and special education. *Type:* Research center.

Alton Ochsner Medical Foundation
1516 Jefferson Hwy.   Ph: (504)842-3135
New Orleans, LA 70121   Fax: (504)842-3899
E-mail: rre@ochsner.org
Contact: Richard N. Re, MD, Vice Pres. of Div. of Res.
Desc: Hypertension, oncology, cardiovascular research, immunology, orthopedics, renal stones, gastrointestinal physiology (motility and perfusion), depression, and clinical pharmacology. *Type:* Research center.

Alzheimer Family Program Newsletter
Center for Aging/Geriatric Education Center
University of Alabama at Birmingham
933 19th St. S, Rm. 201   Ph: (205)934-7678
Birmingham, AL 35294-2041   Fax: (205)975-5930
Contact: J. Miller Piggott, Editor, (205)934-2178, fax: (205)934-7354.
Desc: Contains articles on coping with Alzheimer's Disease, strategies for care, and local resources. Recurring features include news of research and a calendar of events. *Type:* Newsletter.

Alzheimer's Association
919 N. Michigan Ave., Ste.   Ph: (312)335-8700
1100   Free: 800-272-3900
Chicago, IL 60611-1676   Fax: (312)335-1110
E-mail: info@alz.org
URL: http://www.alz.org
Contact: Edward Truschke, Pres.
Desc: Family members of sufferers of Alzheimer's disease. Combats Alzheimer's disease and related disorders. *Type:* Association.

Alzheimer's Research Review
American Health Assistance Foundation
15825 Shady Grove Rd., Ste.   Ph: (301)948-3244
140   Free: 800-437-2423
Rockville, MD 20850   Fax: (301)258-9454
Desc: Highlights the work of Alzheimer's disease researchers and provides tips for families dealing with Alzheimer's. Recurring features include news of research and columns titled From the President. *Type:* Newsletter.

American Academy of Family Physicians
8880 Ward Pky.   Ph: (816)333-9700
Kansas City, MO 64114   Free: 800-274-2237
    Fax: (816)822-0580
E-mail: fp@aafp.org
URL: http://www.aafp.org
Contact: Robert Graham, M.D., Exec.VP.
Desc: Professional society of family physicians who provide continuing comprehensive care to patients. *Type:* Association.

American Academy of Orthotists and Prosthetists
1650 King St., Ste. 500   Ph: (703)836-7118
Alexandria, VA 22314   Fax: (703)836-0838
E-mail: aaopline@aol.com
URL: http://www.oandp.org
Contact: Thomas A. Gorski, CAE, Exec.Dir.
Desc: Professional practitioners certified by the American Board for Certification in Orthotics and Prosthetics. Dedicated to the advancement of the profession and the improvement of patient care. *Type:* Association.

American Academy of Otolaryngology - Head and Neck Surgery
1 Prince St.   Ph: (703)836-4444
Alexandria, VA 22314-3357   Fax: (703)683-5100
E-mail: entnet@aol.com
URL: http://www.entnet.org
Contact: Dr. Michael D. Maves, Exec.VP.
Desc: Professional society of medical doctors specializing in otolaryngology (diseases of the ear, nose, and throat) and head and neck surgery. Represents otolaryngology in governmental and socioeconomic areas and provides high-quality medical education for otolaryngologists. Coordinates Combined Otolaryngological Spring Meetings for ten national otolaryngological societies. *Type:* Association.

American Academy of Physician Assistants
950 N. Washington St.   Ph: (703)836-2272
Alexandria, VA 22314-1552   Fax: (703)684-1924
E-mail: aapa@aapa.org
URL: http://www.aapa.org
Contact: Kevin D. Bayes, Contact.
Desc: Physician assistants who have graduated from an accredited program and/or are certified by the National Commission on Certification of Physician Assistants; individuals who are enrolled in an accredited PA educational program. Purposes are to: enhance public access to quality, cost-effective health care, educate the public about the physician assistant profession; represent physician assistants' interests before Congress, government agencies, and health-related organizations; assure the competence of physician assistants through development of educational curricula and accreditation programs; provide services for members. *Type:* Association.

American Academy of Tropical Medicine and Surgery
16126 E. Warren   Ph: (313)882-0641
PO Box 24224   Fax: (313)882-5110
Detroit, MI 48224-0224
Contact: Dr. Ben Allie, Chm.
Desc: Tropical diseases, including diarrhea and ankle edema, and evaluation of disease spectrum. *Type:* Research center.

American Association of Blood Banks
8101 Glenbrook Rd.   Ph: (301)907-6977
Bethesda, MD 20814   Fax: (301)907-6895
E-mail: aabb@aabb.org
URL: http://Www.aabb.org
Contact: Karen Lipton, JD, CEO.
Desc: Community and hospital blood centers and transfusion and transplantation services, physicians, nurses, technologists, administrators, blood donor recruiters, scientists, and individuals involved in related activities. Encourages the voluntary donation of blood and other tissues and organs through education, public information, and research. *Type:* Association.

American Association of Critical-Care Nurses
101 Columbia   Ph: (714)362-2000
Aliso Viejo, CA 92656-1491   Free: 800-899-AACN
    Fax: (714)362-2020
E-mail: info@aacn.org
URL: http://www.aacn.org
Contact: Phyllis Reading, Exec.Dir.
Desc: Professional critical care nurses. Established to provide continuing education programs for nurses specializing in critical care and to develop standards of nursing care of critically ill patients. Conducts educational programs. *Type:* Association.

American Association of Medical Assistants

20 N. Wacker Dr., Ste. 1575   Ph: (312)899-1500
Chicago, IL 60606-2903   Free: 800-228-2262
    Fax: (312)899-1259
URL: http://www.aama-ntl.org
Contact: Donald A. Balasa, Exec.Dir.

Desc: Medical assistants are allied health professionals who work primarily in anbilatory (out patient) settings and perform clinical and administrative procedures. Activities include a certification program consisting of study and an examination, passage of which entitles the individual to become credentialed as a Certified Medical Assistant. Conducts accreditation of one- and two-year programs in medical assisting in conjunction with the commission on Accreditation of Allied Health Education Programs. *Type:* Association.

American Association for Medical Transcription

PO Box 576187   Ph: (209)551-0883
Modesto, CA 95357-6187   Free: 800-982-2182
    Fax: (209)551-9317
E-mail: aamt@sna.com
URL: http://www.aamt.org
Contact: Claudia Tessier, Exec.Dir.

Desc: Medical transcriptionists, their supervisors, teachers and students of medical transcription, owners and managers of medical transcription services, and other interested health personnel. Purpose is to provide information about the profession of medical transcription and to provide continuing education for medical transcriptionists. (Medical transcriptionists translate patients' records of medical care and treatment from oral dictation to printed form.) Advocates professional recognition of medical transcriptionists in county, state, and national medical societies and in health care facilities nationwide. *Type:* Association.

American Association for the Study of Liver Diseases

1729 King St., Ste. 100   Ph: (703)299-9766
Alexandria, VA 22314-2720   Fax: (703)299-9622
E-mail: aasld@aasld.org
URL: http://hepar-sfgh.ucsf.edu
Contact: Sharon A. Meehan, Exec.Dir.

Desc: Liver disease and hepatic research. *Type:* Research center.

American Board for Certification in Orthotics and Prosthetics

1650 King St., Ste. 500   Ph: (703)836-7114
Alexandria, VA 22314   Fax: (703)836-0838
E-mail: lanceabc@aol.com
Contact: Lance O. Hoxie, Exec.Dir.

Desc: Certification board to establish qualifications, conduct examinations, and certify individuals (3900) and facilities (825) whom the board finds qualified to practice orthotics and prosthetics (the science of making and fitting artificial limbs and braces). *Type:* Association.

American Board of Medical Specialties

1007 Church St., Ste. 404   Ph: (847)491-9091
Evanston, IL 60201-5913   Fax: (847)328-3596
URL: http://www.abms.org/abms
Contact: Stephen H. Miller, M.D., M.P.H, Exec.VP.

Desc: Primary medical specialty boards and conjoint boards; organizations with related interests are associate members. Acts as spokesman for approved medical specialty boards as a group; is actively concerned with the establishment, maintenance, and elevation of standards for the education and qualification of physicians recognized as specialists through the certification procedures of its members; cooperates with other groups concerned in establishing standards, policies, and procedures for ensuring the maintenance of continued competence of such physicians. *Type:* Association.

American College of Angiology

295 Northern Blvd., Ste. 104   Ph: (516)484-6880
Great Neck, NY 11021-4701   Fax: (516)625-1174
Contact: H. E. Shaftel, M.D., Meeting Chmn.

Desc: Scientists from 17 countries interested in the field of vascular medicine and surgery and dedicated to scientific advancement and continued education in angiology (the study of the circulatory, or vascular system). Seeks to: define, represent, and foster the growth and development of the specialty practice of angiology; improve patient care by advising physicians on recent developments in the field; provide a common forum for the exchange of ideas, technical research, and clinical experiences. Conducts continuing medical education programs. *Type:* Association.

American College of Health Care Administrators

325 S. Patrick St.   Ph: (703)739-7900
Alexandria, VA 22314   Free: 888-88A-CHCA
    Fax: (703)739-7901
E-mail: info@achca.org
URL: http://www.achca.org
Contact: Karen S. Tucker, CAE, Pres. & CEO.

Desc: Persons actively engaged in the administration of long-term care facilities, such as nursing homes, retirement communities, assisted living facilities, and subacute care programs. ACHCA administers professional certification programs for assisted living, subacute and nursing home administrators. *Type:* Association.

American College of Obstetricians and Gynecologists

409 12th St. SW   Ph: (202)638-5577
PO Box 96920   Fax: (202)484-8107
Washington, DC 20090-6920
E-mail: mgraves@acog.org
URL: http://www.acog.org
Contact: Ralph Hale, M.D., Exec.VP.

Desc: Physicians specializing in childbirth and the diseases of women. Sponsors continuing professional development program. *Type:* Association.

American College of Occupational and Environmental Medicine

55 W. Seegers Rd.   Ph: (847)228-6850
Arlington Heights, IL 60005   Fax: (847)228-1856
E-mail: kcoyne@acoem.org
URL: http://www.acoem.org
Contact: Donald L. Hoops, Ph.D., Exec. VP.

Desc: Physicians specializing in occupational and environmental medicine. Promotes maintenance and improvement of the health of workers; works to increase awareness of occupational medicine as a medical specialty. Sponsors educational programs; maintains placement service. *Type:* Association.

American College of Occupational and Environmental Medicine—Membership Directory

American College of Occupational and Environmental Medicine
1114 N. Arlington Heights Rd.   Ph: (847)818-1800
Arlington Heights, IL 60004   Fax: (847)818-9266
Contact: Marianne Dreger, Editor, mdreger@acoem.org.

Desc: 6,500 medical directors and plant physicians specializing in occupational medicine and surgery; coverage includes Canada and other foreign countries. *Type:* Directory.

American College of Rheumatology

1800 Century Pl., Ste. 250   Ph: (404)633-3777
Atlanta, GA 30345   Fax: (404)633-1870
E-mail: acr@rheumatology.org

URL: http://www.rheumatology.org
Contact: Mark Andrejeski, Exec.VP.

Desc: Rheumatologists and rheumatology health professionals. Provides unified leadership in research, education, and the care of people with rheumatic diseases. *Type:* Association.

American College of Sports Medicine

PO Box 1440   Ph: (317)637-9200
Indianapolis, IN 46206-1440   Fax: (317)634-7817
URL: http://www.acsm.org
Contact: James R. Whitehead, Exec.VP.

Desc: Promotes and integrates scientific research, education, and practical applications of sports medicine and exercise science to maintain and enhance physical performance, fitness, health, and quality of life. *Type:* Association.

American Conference of Governmental Industrial Hygienists

1330 Kemper Meadow Dr.   Ph: (513)742-2020
Cincinnati, OH 45240   Fax: (513)742-3355
E-mail: mail@acgih.org
URL: http://www.acgih.org
Contact: Richard A. Strano, Exec.Dir.

Desc: Professional society of occupational and environmental safety and health professionals. Devoted to the development of administrative and technical aspects of worker health protection. Functions mainly as a medium for the exchange of ideas and the promotion of standards and techniques in industrial health. *Type:* Association.

American Council on Science and Health

1995 Broadway   Ph: (212)362-7044
2nd Fl.   Fax: (212)362-4919
New York, NY 10023-5860
E-mail: acsh@acsh.org
URL: http://www.acsh.org
Contact: Elizabeth Whelan, Pres.

Desc: Relationship between human health and chemicals, foods, nutrition, lifestyle factors, including cigarette smoking, the environment and human health. Activities include studies on animal-to-man extrapolation in laboratory testing, smoking cessation, Lyme disease, Reye's syndrome, hay fever, microwave ovens, infant mortality, life expectancy, AIDS, and automobile occupant restraint systems. *Type:* Research center.

American Epilepsy Society

342 N Main St.   Ph: (860)586-7505
West Hartford, CT 06117-2507   Fax: (860)586-7550
E-mail: info@aesnet.org
URL: http://www.aesnet.org
Contact: Suzanne C. Berry, CAE.

Desc: Clinicians, scientists investigating basic and clinical aspects of epilepsy, and related professional workers with an active interest in seizure disorders. Seeks to promote interdisciplinary communication, scientific investigation and exchange of clinical information about epilepsy. Works to prevent and treat epilepsy. *Type:* Association.

American Family Physician

American Academy of Family Physicians
11400 Tomahawk Creek Pkwy.   Ph: (913)906-6000
Leawood, KS 66211
E-mail: afpedit@aafp.org
URL: http://www.aafp.org/afp
Desc: Contains the complete text of American Family Physician, covering clinical review articles on diagnostic and therapeutic developments, abstracts from major medical journals, and reports on developments in medicine. Includes all images, graphs, tables, and figures from the original articles. *Available:* LEXIS-NEXIS, NEXIS. *Type:* Database.

American Family Physician

American Academy of Family Physicians

8880 Ward Pkwy.

Kansas City, MO 64114

Ph: (816)333-9700

Free: 800-274-2237

Fax: (816)333-9855

E-mail: fp@aafp.org; afpedit@aafp.org.

URL: http://www.aafp.org/afp.

Contact: Joetta Melton, Publisher; Dan Gowan, Sales Dir.; Kathy Mayfield, Production Mgr.; Wanda Kelsey-Mendez, Marketing Mgr.; Mary Totten, Circulation Dir.

Desc: Clinical journal for family physicians and others in primary care. Original scientific articles detail the latest diagnostic and therapeutic techniques in the medical field. Department features in each issue include "Tips from other Joirnals," CME credit opportunities and course calendar. *Type:* Periodical.

American Federation for Medical Research

1200 19th St. NW, Ste. 300

Washington, DC 20036-2422

Ph: (202)429-5161

Fax: (202)223-4579

E-mail: afmr@dc.sba.com

URL: http://www.afmr.org

Contact: Linda S. Chreno, Account Exec.

Desc: Clinical and laboratory medicine, including cardiovascular, dermatology, endocrinology, gastroenterology, genetics, hematology, immunology and connective tissue, infectious disease, metabolism, neoplastic disease, patient care, pulmonary, renal, and electrolytes. *Type:* Research center.

American Gastroenterological Association

7910 Woodmont Ave., Ste. 700

Bethesda, MD 20814

Ph: (301)654-2055

Fax: (301)654-5920

URL: http://www.gastroenterological.org

Contact: Robert B. Greenberg, JD, Exec.VP.

Desc: Physicians of internal medicine certified in gastroenterology; radiologists, pathologists, surgeons, and physiologists with special interest and competency in gastroenterology. Studies normal and abnormal conditions of the digestive organs and problems connected with their metabolism; conducts scientific research; offers placement services. *Type:* Association.

American Health Foundation

1 Dana Rd.

Valhalla, NY 10595

Ph: (914)592-2600

Fax: (914)592-6317

URL: http://www.ahf.org

Contact: Dr. Ernst L. Wynder, Pres.

Desc: Improves methods of prevention of cancer and other diseases, trains health professionals, and teaches the public how to reduce risk factors of disease. Conducts collaborative laboratory studies with hospitals in cellular and molecular biology, chemical and environmental carcinogenesis, cell genetics, and the nutritional aspects of disease. *Type:* Research center.

American Health Foundation

Naylor Dana Institute for Disease Prevention

1 Dana Rd.

Valhalla, NY 10595

Ph: (914)592-2600

Fax: (914)592-2317

URL: http://www.ahf.org

Contact: Noreen T. Sweeney, Libn.

Desc: Medicine, science, and social science, focusing on cancer, smoking and health, nutrition, and biology and chemistry. *Type:* Research center.

American Health Information Management Association

919 N. Michigan Ave., Ste. 1400

Chicago, IL 60611

Ph: (312)787-2672

Fax: (312)787-9793

E-mail: info@ahim.org

URL: http://www.ahima.org

Contact: Linda Kloss, Exec.Dir.

Desc: Registered record administrators; accredited record technicians with expertise in health information management, biostatistics, classification systems, and systems analysis. Sponsors Independent Study Programs in Medical Record Technology and coding. Conducts annual qualification examinations to credential medical record personnel as Registered Record Administrators (RRA), Accredited Record Technicians (ART) and Certified Coding Specialists (CCS). *Type:* Association.

American Industrial Hygiene Association

2700 Prosperity Ave., Ste. 250

Fairfax, VA 22031

Ph: (703)849-8888

Fax: (703)207-3561

E-mail: infonet@aiha.org

URL: http://www.aiha.org

Contact: O. Gordon Banks, Exec.Dir.

Desc: Professional society of industrial hygienists. Promotes the study and control of environmental factors affecting the health and well-being of workers. *Type:* Association.

American Institute of Ultrasound in Medicine

14750 Sweitzer Ln., Ste. 100

Laurel, MD 20707-5906

Ph: (301)498-4100

Free: 800-638-5352

Fax: (301)498-4450

E-mail: admin@aium.org

URL: http://www.aium.org

Contact: Carmine M. Valente, PhD, Exec.Dir.

Desc: Physicians, engineers, scientists, sonographers, and other professionals involved with diagnostic medical ultrasound. Promotes the application of ultrasound in clinical medicine, diagnostically, and in research; studies its effects on tissue and recommend standards for its applications. Promotes education in the use of ultrasonics for medical purposes. *Type:* Association.

American Leprosy Missions

1 ALM Way

Greenville, SC 29601

Ph: (864)271-7040

Free: 800-543-3135

Fax: (864)271-7062

E-mail: amlep@leprosy.org

URL: http://www.leprosy.org

Contact: Chris Doyle, Pres.

Desc: Provides medical, rehabilitative, and social care for people with leprosy, also known as Hansen's disease, in approximately 30 countries. Conducts specialized training for medical workers; supports medical and social rehabilitation; provides special literature on leprosy to medical personnel abroad. Sponsors research in the U.S., Brazil, India, and Ethiopia. *Type:* Association.

American Liver Foundation

75 Maiden Ln., Ste. 603

New York, NY 10038

Ph: (212)668-1000

Free: 800-223-0179

Fax: (212)483-8179

E-mail: info@liverfoundation.org

URL: http://www.liverfoundation.org

Contact: Alan P. Brownstein, Pres. and CEO.

Desc: Health agency working to fund research, promote the understanding and prevention of liver diseases, and find cures for liver diseases. Disseminates public and patient information on liver diseases, liver functions, and preventive measures. Organizes support groups for liver disease patients and their families. *Type:* Association.

American Lung Association

1740 Broadway

New York, NY 10019-4374

Ph: (212)315-8700

Free: 800-LUN-GUSA

Fax: (212)265-5642

E-mail: info@lungusa.org

URL: http://www.lungusa.org

Contact: John R. Garrison, CEO.

Desc: Federation of state and local associations of physicians, nurses, and laymen interested in the prevention and control of lung disease. Works with other organizations in planning and conducting programs in community services, public, professional and patient education, and research. Maintains the American Thoracic Society as its medical section. *Type:* Association.

American Managed Care and Review Association

1129 20th St. NW, Ste. 600

Washington, DC 20036-3403

Ph: (202)728-0506

Fax: (202)728-0609

Contact: Charles W. Stellar, Pres.

Desc: Medical organizations from the managed health care industry, including health maintenance organizations (HMOs), preferred provider organizations (PPOs), independent practice/physician associations (IPAs), utilization review organizations (UROs), and physician hospital organizations (PHOs); represents over 250,000 practicing physicians and 25 million individuals with health insurance. Seeks to provide better medical care at a reasonable cost, and to render the most appropriate and economical setting for its delivery. Conducts educational sessions and seminars. *Type:* Association.

American Medical Association

515 N. State St.

Chicago, IL 60610

Ph: (312)464-5000

Fax: (312)464-4184

URL: http://www.ama-assn.org/

Contact: E. Radcliffe Anderson, Exec.VP/CEO.

Desc: County medical societies and physicians. Disseminates scientific information to members and the public. Informs members on significant medical and health legislation on state and national levels and represents the profession before Congress and governmental agencies. *Type:* Association.

American Medical Association Alliance

515 N. State St.

Chicago, IL 60610-0174

Ph: (312)464-4470

Fax: (312)464-5020

Contact: Hazel J. Lewis, Exec.Dir.

Desc: Physicians' spouses. Serves as the volunteer arm of the American Medical Association . *Type:* Association.

American Medical Association Foundation

Education and Research Foundation

515 N. State St.

Chicago, IL 60610

Ph: (312)464-4543

Free: 800-262-3211

Fax: (312)464-5678

Contact: Kathleen Henrichs, PhD, Exec.Dir.

Desc: Receives and distributes funds to benefit medical education in the U.S. Also supports medical research and innovative health care programs. *Type:* Research center.

American Medical Directors Association

10480 Little Patuxent Pky., Ste. 760

Columbia, MD 21044

Ph: (410)740-9743

Free: 800-876-AMDA

Fax: (410)740-4572

URL: http://www.amda.com

Contact: Lorraine Tarnove, Exec.Dir.

Desc: Physicians providing care in long-term facilities including nursing homes. Sponsors continuing medical education in geriatrics and medical administration. Promotes improved long term care. *Type:* Association.

American Medical Informatics Association

4915 St. Elmo Ave., Ste. 401

Bethesda, MD 20814

Ph: (301)657-1291

Fax: (301)657-1296

E-mail: amia@camis.stanford.edu

Contact: Janice Kennedy, Exec.Dir.

Desc: Medical personnel, physicians, physical scientists, engineers, data processors, researchers, educators, hospital administrators, nurses, medical record administrators, and computer professionals. Objectives are: to apply advanced systems and information technologies to scientific, literary, and educational activities; to promote excellence in health care; to promote patient care, teaching, research, and health administration. *Type:* Association.

American Medical News

American Medical Association
515 N. State St.   Ph: (312)464-5000
Chicago, IL 60610   Free: 800-621-8335
                                Fax: (312)464-5830

E-mail: amaa@ama-assn.org
Contact: Robert L. Kennett, Publisher; Peter Murphy, Sales Mgr.
Desc: Socioeconomic trade publication. *Type:* Periodical.

American Medical Technologists

710 Higgins Rd.   Ph: (847)823-5169
Park Ridge, IL 60068   Free: 800-275-1268
                                Fax: (847)823-0458

E-mail: amtmail@aol.com
Contact: Gerard P. Boe, Ph.D., Exec.Dir.
Desc: National professional registry of medical laboratory technologists, technicians, medical assistants, dental assistants, and phlebotomists. Maintains job information service. Sponsors AMT Institute for Education, evaluates and recommends continuing education programs. *Type:* Association.

American Medical Women's Association

801 N. Fairfax St., Ste. 400   Ph: (703)838-0500
Alexandria, VA 22314   Fax: (703)549-3864
E-mail: info@amwa.doc.org
URL: http://www.amwa-doc.org
Contact: Eileen McGrath, Exec.Dir.
Desc: Women holding a M.D. or D.O. degree from approved medical colleges; women interns, residents, and medical students. Promotes women's health issues in medical education and public policy. *Type:* Association.

American Parkinson Disease Association Inc. Newsletter

American Parkinson Disease Association Inc.
1250 Hylan Blvd.   Ph: (718)981-8001
Staten Island, NY 10305   Free: 800-223-2732
                                Fax: (718)981-4399
Contact: Paul Maestrone, Editor.
Desc: Provides updates on the symptoms and treatments of Parkinson's disease and on current research in the field. Also discusses patients' problems in coping with the disease and the support services available. *Type:* Newsletter.

American Physiological Society

9650 Rockville Pike   Ph: (301)530-7164
Bethesda, MD 20814-3991   Fax: (301)571-8305
E-mail: info@aps.faseb.org
URL: http://www.faseb.org/aps/
Contact: Martin Frank, Exec.Dir.
Desc: Professional society of physiologists. *Type:* Association.

American Professional Practice Association

Hillsboro Executive Center N   Ph: (954)571-1877
350 Fairway Dr., Ste. 200   Fax: (954)571-8582
Deerfield Beach, FL 33441-1834
E-mail: appaorg@aol.com
URL: http://www.appa-assn.com
Contact: Ms. Pat Arden, Exec.Dir./CEO.
Desc: Provides physicians with economic benefits and services including the following: unsecured loan plans; group insurance discounts; accounts receivable collections; electronic creidt and services; continuing medical education. *Type:* Association.

American Registry of Diagnostic Medical Sonographers

600 Jefferson Plz., Ste. 360   Ph: (301)738-8401
Rockville, MD 20852-1150   Free: 800-541-9754
                                Fax: (301)738-0312

E-mail: administration@ardms.org
URL: http://www.ardms.org
Contact: Donald G. Gardiner, Exec.Dir.
Desc: Administers examinations in the field of diagnostic medical sonography and vascular technology throughout the U.S. and Canada and registers candidates passing those exams in the specialties of their expertise. *Type:* Association.

American Registry of Radiologic Technologists

1255 Northland Dr.   Ph: (651)687-0048
St. Paul, MN 55120
URL: http://www.arrt.org
Contact: Jerry B. Reid, Exec.Dir.
Desc: Radiologic technologist certification board that administers examinations, issues certificates of registration to radiographers, nuclear medicine technologists, and radiation therapists, and investigates the qualifications of practicing radiologic technologists. Governed by trustees appointed from American College of Radiology and American Society of Radiologic Technologists. *Type:* Association.

American Society of Anesthesiologists

520 N. Northwest Hwy.   Ph: (708)825-5586
Park Ridge, IL 60068-2573   Fax: (708)825-1692
E-mail: mail@asahq.org
URL: http://www.asahq.org
Contact: Glenn W. Johnson, Exec.Dir.
Desc: Professional society of physicians specializing or interested in anesthesiology. Seeks "to develop and further the specialty of anesthesiology for the general elevation of the standards of medical practice." Encourages education, research, and scientific progress in anesthesiology. *Type:* Association.

American Society for Bone and Mineral Research

1200 19th St. NW, Ste. 300   Ph: (202)857-1161
Washington, DC 20036   Fax: (202)223-4579
E-mail: asbmr@dc.sba.com
URL: http://www.asbmr.org
Contact: Julia Janko, Exec.Dir.
Desc: Bone, and mineral diseases, focusing on the prevention of osteoporosis. *Type:* Research center.

American Society of Cataract and Refractive Surgery and American Society of Ophthalmic Administrators—Directory

American Society of Cataract and Refractive Surgery
4000 Legato Rd., Ste. 850   Ph: (703)591-2220
Fairfax, VA 22033-4003   Free: 800-451-1339
                                Fax: (703)591-0614

E-mail: ascrs@ascrs.org
Contact: Christine Ford, Editor.
Desc: About 6,000 ophthalmologists and 1,700 ophthalmic administrators who are interested in and/or perform cataract surgery, anterior segment surgery, and intraocular lens implantation. *Type:* Directory.

American Society for Clinical Investigation

6900 Grove Rd.   Ph: (609)251-6976
Thorofare, NJ 08086   Free: 800-257-8290
                                Fax: (609)848-5274

URL: http://www.asci-jci.org/asci
Contact: David Ginsburg, M.D., Sec.Treas.
Desc: Physician scientists with meritorious original clinical investigations. Active members are doctors under age 48;

emeritus members are those over age 48. Promotes cultivation of clinical research by methods of natural sciences, correlation of science with the art of medical practice, encouragement of scientific investigation by medical practitioners, and publication of papers on the methods and results of clinical research. *Type:* Association.

American Society for Clinical Laboratory Science

7910 Woodmont Ave., Ste. 530   Ph: (301)657-2768
Bethesda, MD 20814   Fax: (301)657-2909
E-mail: ascls@ascls.org
URL: http://www.ascls.org
Contact: Elissa Passiment, EdM, Exec.Dir.
Desc: Primarily clinical laboratory personnel who have an associate or baccalaureate degree and clinical training and specialists who hold at least a master's degree in one of the major fields of clinical laboratory science such as bacteriology, mycology, or biochemistry; also includes technicians, specialists, and educators with limited certificates and students enrolled in approved programs of clinical laboratory studies and military medical technology schools. Promotes and maintains high standards in clinical laboratory methods and research and advances standards of education and training of personnel. *Type:* Association.

American Society for Histocompatibility and Immunogenetics

PO Box 15804   Ph: (913)541-0009
Lenexa, KS 66286   Fax: (913)541-0156
E-mail: mflanagan@applmeapro.com
Contact: Michael P. Flanagan, CAE, Exec.Dir.
Desc: Scientists, physicians, and technologists involved in research and clinical activities related to histocompatibility testing (a state of mutual tolerance that allows some tissues to be grafted effectively to others). *Type:* Association.

American Society of Radiologic Technologists

15000 Central Ave. SE   Ph: (505)298-4500
Albuquerque, NM 87123   Free: 800-444-2778
                                Fax: (505)298-5063

URL: http://www.asrt.org
Contact: Joan Parsons, Exec.VP, Operations.
Desc: Professional society of diagnostic radiography, radiation therapy, ultrasound, and nuclear medicine technologists. Advances the science of radiologic technology; establishes and maintains high standards of education; evaluates the quality of patient care; improves the welfare and socioeconomics of radiologic technologists. Operates ASRT Education and Research Foundation, which provides educational materials to radiologic technologists. *Type:* Association.

Annals of Internal Medicine

American College of Physicians
Independence Mall W.   Ph: (215)351-2400
6th St. at Race   Free: 800-523-1546
Philadelphia, PA 19106-1572   Fax: (215)351-2644
E-mail: interpub@mail.acponline.org.
URL: http://www.acponline.org.
Desc: Medical journal. *Type:* Periodical.

Aoki Diabetes Research Institute

1935 Stockton Blvd.   Ph: (916)455-2374
Sacramento, CA 95816   Fax: (916)455-3734
Contact: Thomas T. Aoki, MD, Dir. of Res.
Desc: Metabolic diseases, including diabetes mellitus. Current projects include clinical investigations in the treatment of Type I and II diabetic patients. *Type:* Research center.

Archives of Internal Medicine

American Medical Association
515 N. State St.   Ph: (312)464-5000
Chicago, IL 60610   Free: 800-621-8335
   Fax: (312)464-5830
E-mail: amaa@ama-assn.org
Contact: James E. Dalen, M.D., Editor; Robert L. Kennett, Publisher; Michael D. Springer, Publisher.
Desc: Educational/clinical journal for internists, cardiologists, gastroenterologists, and other internal medicine subspecialists. *Type:* Periodical.

Arizona Disease Control Research Commission

1616 W. Adams, Ste. B-25   Ph: (602)542-1028
Phoenix, AZ 85007   Fax: (602)542-6380
Contact: Dawn C. Schroeder, Exec.Dir.
Desc: Medical, behavioral, preventive and health policy. *Type:* Research center.

Arizona Health Services Department

Public Health Services

Center for Prevention and Health Promotion

1400 W. Washington   Ph: (602)542-7200
Phoenix, AZ 85007   Fax: (602)542-7226
Contact: Merril Krenitz, Contact.
Desc: Health. *Type:* Research center.

Arizona Health Services Department

Public Health Services

Epidemiology and Disease Control

3815 N. Black Canyon Hwy.   Ph: (602)230-5808
Phoenix, AZ 85015   Fax: (602)230-5959
E-mail: lbland@hs.state.az.us
URL: http://www.hs.state.az.us
Contact: Lee A. Bland, Actg.Bur.Ch.
Desc: Epidemiology and disease. *Type:* Research center.

Arizona Health Services Department

Public Health Services

Epidemiology and Disease Control

Chronic Disease Epidemiology Office

1400 W. Washington   Ph: (602)542-7333
Phoenix, AZ 85007   Fax: (602)542-7362
E-mail: rporter@hs.state.az.us
URL: http://www.hs.state.az.us/edc/cdepage.html
Contact: Richard Porter, Ch.
Desc: Chronic disease. *Type:* Research center.

Arizona Health Services Department

Public Health Services

Epidemiology and Disease Control

Infectious Disease Services Office

3815 N. Black Canyon Hwy.   Ph: (602)230-5808
Phoenix, AZ 85015   Fax: (602)230-5959
E-mail: vvaz@hs.state.az.us
Contact: Victorio J. Vaz, DVM, Chf.
Desc: Infectious diseases. *Type:* Research center.

Arizona State University

Biomedical Engineering Laboratories

Coll. of Eng.   Ph: (602)965-3676
COB, B-338   Fax: (602)965-0037
Tempe, AZ 85287
E-mail: guilbeau@asu.vax.eas.asu.edu
URL: http://www.asu.edu
Contact: Eric J. Guilbeau, Prof./Chm.
Desc: Biomechanics and bioinstrumentation, including medical devices, artificial organs, biosensors, analysis of motion, and nuclear imaging. Studies cardiovascular, biochemical, and physiological systems in relation to biomedical engineering. *Type:* Research center.

Arthritis Foundation

1330 W. Peachtree St.   Ph: (404)872-7100
Atlanta, GA 30309   Free: 800-283-7800
URL: http://www.arthritis.org
Desc: Causes, cures, and prevention of the various forms of arthritis and improved medical care and services for Americans affected by arthritis. *Type:* Research center.

Arthritis Foundation

1330 W. Peachtree St.   Ph: (404)872-7100
Atlanta, GA 30309   Free: 800-283-7800
   Fax: (404)872-0457
URL: http://www.arthritis.org
Contact: Don L. Riggin, CAE, CEO & President.
Desc: Seeks to: discover the cause and improve the methods for the treatment and prevention of arthritis and other rheumatic diseases; increase the number of scientists investigating rheumatic diseases; provide training in rheumatic diseases for more doctors; extend knowledge of arthritis and other rheumatic diseases to the lay public, emphasizing the socioeconomic as well as medical aspects of these diseases. *Type:* Association.

Arthritis Today

Arthritis Foundation
1330 W. Peachtree St.   Ph: (404)872-7100
Atlanta, GA 30309   Free: 800-283-7800
   Fax: (404)872-9559
Contact: Cindy T. McDaniel, Editor; William M. Otto, Publisher; Tracy Ballew, Managing Editor.
Desc: Consumer magazine on living with arthritis; updates on research and treatments as well as general health and lifestyle topics. *Type:* Periodical.

Association for Childbirth at Home, International

14140 Magnolia Blvd.   Ph: (818)386-1082
Sherman Oaks, CA 91423   Fax: (818)386-9374
E-mail: nbwc@ix.netcom.com
Contact: Tonya Brooks, Founder & Pres.
Desc: Parents, midwives, doctors, childbirth educators, other professionals, and interested individuals, all of whom support childbirth at home. Purposes are to bring accurate information and competent support to parents seeking home birth and safe hospital birth; to identify and implement correct obstetrical and pediatric practice. Offers parent education classes, leader training programs, international resource and referral service, and professional education seminars and programs; instructs parents, childbirth educators, midwives, and physicians in safe home birth and noninterventive alternative techniques. *Type:* Association.

Association of International Health Researchers

2665 Pleasant Valley Rd.   Ph: (334)473-3946
Mobile, AL 36606
Contact: Dr. Roy E. Kadel, Contact.
Desc: International health research, focusing on quality, education, techniques and methodologies. *Type:* Research center.

Association for Professionals in Infection Control and Epidemiology

1275 K St., NW   Ph: (202)789-1890
Washington, DC 20005
E-mail: apicinfo@apic.org
URL: http://www.apic.org
Contact: Christopher E. Laxton, Exec.Dir.
Desc: Physicians, microbiologists, nurses, epidemiologists, medical technicians, sanitarians, and pharmacists. Purpose is to improve patient care by improving the profession of infection control through the development of educational programs and standards. Promotes quality research and standardization of practices and procedures. *Type:* Association.

Association of Surgical Technologists

7108-C S. Alton Way   Ph: (303)694-9130
Englewood, CO 80112-2106   Fax: (303)694-9169
E-mail: ast@ast.org
URL: http://www.ast.org
Contact: William J. Teutsch, Exec.Dir.
Desc: Individuals who have received specific education and training to deliver surgical patient care in the operating room. Membership categories are available for both certified and student surgical technologists. Emphasis is placed on encouraging members to participate actively in a continuing education program. *Type:* Association.

Atlanta Research and Education Foundation, Inc.

1670 Clairmont Rd., 151F   Ph: (404)728-4856
Decatur, GA 30033-4004   Fax: (404)235-3061
E-mail: aref@mindspring.com
Contact: Antonio Laracuente, Exec.Dir.
Desc: Cardiology, pulmonary medicine, HIV/AIDS, infectious diseases, Alzheimer's disease, rehabilitation, and cancer. *Type:* Research center.

Atlantis

Atlantis
125 North Acacia Ave., Ste. 110   Ph: (619)298-7502
Solana Beach, CA 92075-1177   Fax: (619)633-3393
E-mail: atlantis@imagerynet.com
URL: http://www.imagerynet.com/atlantis.
Contact: Dennis J. Gersten, M.D., Editor.
Desc: Promotes guided imagery and other visualization techniques for application in the healthcare field. Recurring features include news of research and columns titled Editor Survey and Hot Tips. *Type:* Newsletter.

AVSC International

79 Madison Ave.   Ph: (212)561-8000
New York, NY 10016   Fax: (212)779-9489
E-mail: info@avsc.org
URL: http://www.avsc.org
Contact: Amy Pollack, Pres.
Desc: Conducts surveys on incidence, prevalence, quality, and trends of reproductive health worldwide. Conducts studies throughout the world on medical practices, voluntary practices, voluntary choice, informed consent, and decision making for sterilization, other family planning methods, and other reproductive health issues. *Type:* Research center.

The Bank Account

Living Bank
PO Box 6725   Ph: (713)961-9431
Houston, TX 77265   Free: 800-528-2971
   Fax: (713)961-0979
E-mail: info@livingbank.org
Contact: Jon Eiche, Editor, (713)528-2971, jeiche@livingbank.org.
Desc: Encourages the donation of organs and tissues for the purposes of transplantation, therapy, medical research, or anatomical study. Educates the public about donor registration and procedures, legislation, and presents news of the Living Bank's registry, referral, and promotional activities. *Type:* Newsletter.

Bassett Healthcare Research Institute

1 Atwell Rd.   Ph: (607)547-3048
Cooperstown, NY 13326   Fax: (607)547-3061
E-mail: research.institute@bassett.org
URL: http://www.bassetthealthcare.org/research
Contact: Allan Green, PhD, Dir.
Desc: Basic, clinical, and population studies in the following areas: obesity; biochemistry of serum albumin; molec-

ular biology of autoimmune diseases; experimental pathology of cancer; immunology and antigen processing; cardiovascular epidemiology; rural health education; neuroendocrine regulation of breast cancer; nutrition; health care delivery systems; and gut hormones. *Type:* Research center.

Baton Rouge Regional Tumor Registry

4950 Essen Ln.　　　　　　Ph: (225)767-0430
Baton Rouge, LA 70809　　Fax: (225)767-4742
E-mail: gayd@marybird.com
Contact: Gay Duke, Dir.
Desc: Provides a base of statistical information of cancer incidence in the Baton Rouge area and serves as a useful tool for physicians investigating the success rates of various forms of cancer treatment. Conducts specialized studies in conjunction with the American Cancer Society, National Cancer Institute, and the American College of Surgeons. *Type:* Research center.

Baylor College of Medicine
Biochemical Genetics Laboratory

1 Baylor Plz., Rm. T530　　Ph: (713)798-4982
Houston, TX 77030　　　　Free: 800-246-2436
　　　　　　　　　　　　Fax: (713)798-8937
E-mail: bioc@bcm.tmc.edu
URL: http://www.bcm.tmc.edu/medgen/biochem-indes.html
Contact: William E. O'Brien, PhD, Dir.
Desc: Diagnosing and monitoring patients with inborn errors of metabolism. *Type:* Research center.

Baylor College of Medicine
Birth Defects Center

1102 Bates St., Ste. 235　　Ph: (713)770-4280
Houston, TX 77030　　　　Free: 800-411-4363
　　　　　　　　　　　　Fax: (713)770-4294
E-mail: abeaudet@bcm.tmc.edu
URL: http://www.bcm.tmc.edu/medgen/
Contact: Dr. Arthur L. Beaudet, Dir.
Desc: Etiology and treatment of birth defects and genetic disorders. *Type:* Research center.

Baylor College of Medicine
Center for Experimental Therapeutics

Dept. of OB/GYN　　　　　Ph: (713)798-7593
6550 Fannin St., Ste. 901　Fax: (713)798-6956
Houston, TX 77030
Contact: Dr. Kenneth J. Moise, Jr., Dir.
Desc: Metabolic problems, including clinical laboratory studies of drug metabolism and drug toxicity. Develops new analytical biochemical methods for study of human metabolic problems and conducts laboratory studies in gas chromatography, mass spectrometry, and computer technology. *Type:* Research center.

Baylor College of Medicine
Center for Population Research and Studies in Reproduction

Dept. of Cell Biology　　　Ph: (713)798-6200
Houston, TX 77030　　　　Fax: (713)790-1275
E-mail: gaele@bcm.tcm.edu
URL: http://www.bcm.tcm.edu
Contact: Dr. Bert W. O'Malley, Chm.
Desc: Human reproduction, including studies on mechanism of hormone action, male reproduction, steroid regulation and protein synthesis, spermatogenesis, reproductive endocrinology, nucleic acid chemistry and genetic expression, steroid hormonal receptors, physical chemistry, cell proliferation and regulation, biochemistry of chromatin, ribonucleic acid, deoxyribonucleic acid, and cell biology. *Type:* Research center.

Baylor College of Medicine
Cullen Eye Institute

6565 Fannin NC205　　　Ph: (713)798-5942
Houston, TX 77030　　　　Fax: (713)798-3026
Contact: Dr. Dan B. Jones, Chm.
Desc: Restoring vision and preventing blindness through a better understanding of the structure, function, and diseases of the eye. Current areas of study include retina research, retinitis pigmentosa, amblyopia, ocular infections, corneal transplantation, genetic diseases of the eye, ocular trauma, cataract, glaucoma, ocular tumors, optic neuritis, laser treatment, and vision processing. *Type:* Research center.

Baylor College of Medicine
General Clinical Research Center--Adults

1 Baylor Plz., Rm.S103　　Ph: (713)798-6970
Houston, TX 77030　　　　Fax: (713)798-6990
Contact: Addison A. Taylor, MD, Assoc. Dean for Clinical Res.
Desc: Cardiology, endocrinology, gastroenterology, genetics, gynecology, hypertension and clinical pharmacology, immunology, infectious diseases, lipid metabolism, neurology, ophthalmology, and pulmonary diseases. The Center functions as a per diem unit within the Hospital; it accommodates inpatients as well as outpatients. *Type:* Research center.

Baylor College of Medicine
Maternal Fetal Medicine

Smith Plz., Ste. 901　　　Ph: (713)798-7593
6550 Fannin　　　　　　　Fax: (713)798-6956
Houston, TX 77030
Contact: Dr. Isabelle Wilkins, MD, Dir.
Desc: Prenatal diagnosis by ultrasonography, amniocentesis, and fetal blood sampling, chorionic villi sampling, longitudinal fetal growth, and pre/post-conceptual counseling. Conducts evaluation of intrauterine growth retardation in at-risk patients on prospective basis. *Type:* Research center.

Baylor College of Medicine
Vision Research Center

Cullen Eye Institute　　　Ph: (713)798-5942
6565 Fannin, NC200　　　Fax: (713)798-3026
Houston, TX 77030
Contact: Dr. Dan B. Jones, Hd.
Desc: Diseases of the retina and choroid, the cornea, and the sensory motor visual system, including studies of the anatomy, biochemistry, physiology, and pathology of the neural retina, retinal pigment epithelium and choroid, retinal organization and information processing, the role of herpes virus in corneal disease, endogenous fungal endophthalmitis or studies of cytomegolovirus in the ocular complications of AIDS, and visual dysfunction of strabismus and amblyopia. *Type:* Research center.

Benign Essential Blepharospasm Research Foundation, Inc.

Baptist Hospital Doctors Bldg.　Ph: (409)832-0788
2315 North St., Ste. 214　　Fax: (409)832-0890
PO Box 12468
Beaumont, TX 77726-2468
E-mail: bebrf@ih2000.net
URL: http://www.blepharospasm.org/~bebrf/
Contact: Mary Lou Thompson, Pres.
Desc: Benign Essential Blepharospasm/Meige (BEB/M) Syndrome and related disorders and infirmities of the facial musculature. BEB/M is an involuntary, uncontrollable spastic contraction of the eyelids and other facial musculature. *Type:* Research center.

Beth Israel Deaconess Medical Center
General Clinical Research Center

330 Brookline Ave., Rm. GZ　Ph: (617)667-4269
800　　　　　　　　　　　Fax: (617)667-5953
Boston, MA 02215
E-mail: kjordan@bidmc.harvard.edu
URL: http://corelan.bih.harvard.edu/purpose.html
Contact: Alan Moses, MD, Prog.Dir.
Desc: Biomedicine, cardiology, endocrinology, gastroenterology, gerontology, hematology, nephrology, neurology, nutrition, obstetrics, pulmonary physiology, psychiatry, and surgery. *Type:* Research center.

Better Health Now
Lombardi Publishing Co.

51 Toro Rd.　　　　　　　Ph: (416)633-1600
North York, ON, Canada M3J　Fax: (416)633-6188
2A4
Contact: Dr. Gabor Mate, Editor.
Desc: Provides general health tips and facts on nutrition, exercise, and disease avoidance. Includes recommendations on headache remedies and how to avoid osteoporosis. *Type:* Newsletter.

BiblioMedNews
Healthcare Information Services, Inc.

2335 American River Dr., Ste.　Free: 800-468-1128
307
Sacramento, CA 95825
Desc: Provides healthcare information through its variety of reference products, including databases, CD-ROMs, and software. Specialties include gastroenterology, cardiology, and urology. *Type:* Newsletter.

BIOETHICSLINE®
Georgetown University
Kennedy Institute of Ethics

Box 571212　　　　　　　Ph: (202)687-3885
Washington, DC 20057-1212
E-mail: medethx@gunet.georgetown.edu
Contact: National Reference Center for Bioethics Literature, T.J. Kahn, Sr. Bibliographer, medethx@guvm.georgetown.edu.
Desc: Contains more than 55,000 citations to the literature related to the ethical and public policy aspects of medicine, health care, and biomedical and behavioral research. Includes references to journal articles, books, court decisions, government reports, laws, bills, audiovisual materials, newspapers, and unpublished documents. *Available:* U.S. National Library of Medicine (NLM), TOXNET; DIMDI (Deutsches Institut fuer Medizinische Dokumentation und Information); Questel • Orbit; The Dialog Corporation, DataStar. *Type:* Database.

Biomedical Market Newsletter
David G. Anast

3237 Idaho Pl.　　　　　　Ph: (714)434-9500
Costa Mesa, CA 92626-2207　Fax: (714)434-9755
Contact: David G. Anast, Editor and Publisher.
Desc: Provides information for marketing biomedical equipment, devices, and instruments. Topics include financial, business, and regulatory information. *Type:* Newsletter.

Biomedical Research Foundation of Northwest Louisiana

1505 Kings Hwy.　　　　　Ph: (318)675-4100
Shreveport, LA 71103　　　Fax: (318)675-4120
E-mail: jsharp@biomed.org
URL: http://www.biomed.org
Contact: Jack Sharp, Pres.
Desc: Cardiovascular disease, neurobiology, stroke, medical imaging, medical information, and medical robotics development. *Type:* Research center.

Biomedical Research Institute

12111 Parklawn Dr.   Ph: (301)881-3300
Rockville, MD 20852   Fax: (301)881-7640
E-mail: biomed@internetmci.com
Contact: Dr. James L. Leef, Dir.
Desc: Conducts research on malaria and schistosomiasis, manages a low temperature repository, and performs large scale freeze-drying. *Type:* Research center.

The Blue Sheet

FDC Reports, Inc.
5550 Friendship Blvd., Suite 1   Ph: (301)657-9830
Chevy Chase, MD 20815
E-mail: fdcr@clark.net
URL: http://www.fdcreports.com
Desc: Covers developments among governmental and private biomedical research institutions. Reports major sources of funding and decision-making which govern biomedical research in the United States, including budgeting and grant policies at the National Institutes of Health (NIH) and other federal agencies, as well as the university medical centers which receive the most research funding. *Available:* LEXIS-NEXIS, LEXIS; The Dialog Corporation, DIALOG; The Dialog Corporation, DIALOG; Ovid Technologies, Inc.; Ovid Technologies, Inc. *Type:* Database.

BNA's Managed Care Reporter

Bureau of National Affairs, Inc. (BNA)
1231 25th St. NW   Ph: (202)452-4323
Washington, DC 20037   Free: 800-372-1033
                                 Fax: (202)452-7773
E-mail: bnaplus@bna.com
Contact: Deborah Spiegelman, Managing Editor, (202)452-7572, fax: (202)331-5102.
Desc: Notification service that covers legislative, legal, regulatory, and marketplace developments in the managed care industry. With a business slant, it supplies analysis and interpretation of the actions and policies of federal and state regulators. *Type:* Newsletter.

BNA's Medicare Report

Bureau of National Affairs, Inc. (BNA)
1231 25th St. NW   Ph: (202)452-4323
Washington, DC 20037   Free: 800-372-1033
                                 Fax: (202)452-7773
E-mail: bnaplus@bna.com
Contact: Mary Davis, Managing Editor.
Desc: Covers legislative, regulatory, and legal developments affecting or pertaining to the Medicare program. Provides information on developments in the Medicaid program that could have implications for Medicare. *Type:* Newsletter.

Boston Biomedical Research Institute

20 Staniford St.   Ph: (617)912-0300
Boston, MA 02114   Fax: (617)227-6053
E-mail: morgan@bbri.harvard.edu
URL: http://www.bbri.harvard.edu
Contact: Dr. Kathleen Morgan, Dir.
Desc: Biological and medical sciences, including fundamental biomedical studies on cell metabolism, developmental biology, gene regulation, recombinant DNA, monoclonal antibodies, intercellular matrix biology, muscle diseases, connective tissue diseases, and muscular dystrophy. *Type:* Research center.

Boston University

General Clinical Research Center

Boston Medical Center   Ph: (617)534-4834
One Medical Center Pl.   Fax: (617)414-1969
Boston, MA 02118
E-mail: mfholick@bu.edu

Contact: Michael F. Holick, MD, Prog.Dir.
Desc: Cardiovascular disease, collagen vascular disease, diabetes, gastrointestinal disease, nephrology, pediatrics, dermatology, AIDS, psoriasis, amyloidosis, and drug abuse. *Type:* Research center.

Boston University

Pulmonary Center

Sch. of Med.   Ph: (617)638-4860
80 E. Concord, R-304   Fax: (617)536-8093
Boston, MA 02118
Contact: Mary C. Williams, PhD, Assoc.Dir.
Desc: Development of an integrated approach to the cell and molecular biology of lung cells. *Type:* Research center.

Boston University

Robert Dawson Evans Memorial Department of Research

Evans Bldg., Rm. 107   Ph: (617)638-7269
88 E. Newton St.   Fax: (617)638-7199
Boston, MA 02118-2393
Contact: Dr. Joseph Loscalzo, Dir.

Desc: Peripheral vascular system, arthritis and connective tissue, hematology, hypertension and atherosclerosis, cardiovascular disease, gastroenterology, infectious diseases, endocrinology, metabolism, nephrology, nutrition, computers in medicine, biomolecular medicine, immunobiology, geriatrics, oncology, genetics, pulmonary, allergy and critical care medicine, obesity, women's health, community medicine, diabetes, general internal medicine, preventive medicine and epidemiology, and health services research. *Type:* Research center.

Brain Injury Association

105 N. Alfred St.   Ph: (703)236-6000
Alexandria, VA 22314   Free: 800-444-6443
                                 Fax: (703)236-6001
URL: http://www.biausa.org
Contact: George Zitnay, Ph.D, Pres.& CEO.

Desc: Strives to increase public awareness of brain injury, provide education and information about brain injury and promote linkage to support groups and local resources through toll-free Family Helpline. *Type:* Association.

Briefings on Behavioral Health Accreditation

Opus Communications
100 Hoods Ln.   Ph: (781)639-1872
PO Box 1168   Free: 800-650-6787
Marblehead, MA 01945   Fax: (781)639-2982
E-mail: customer_service@opuscomm.com
URL: http://www.opuscomm.com

Desc: A resource on the JCAHO, CARF, NCQA, and other accreditors. Covers interpretations of behavioral health care standards and changes in CARF policies and standards. *Type:* Newsletter.

Briefings on Coding Compliance Strategies

Opus Communications
100 Hoods Ln.   Ph: (781)639-1872
PO Box 1168   Free: 800-650-6787
Marblehead, MA 01945   Fax: (781)639-2982
E-mail: customer_service@opuscomm.com
URL: http://www.opuscomm.com

Desc: Provides information and advice on how to efficiently and effectively follow coding, documentation, and billing rules for health care organizations. Includes ideas on developing a coding compliance program and monitoring ancillary coding across departments. *Type:* Newsletter.

Briefings on JCAHO/AAAHC

Opus Communications
100 Hoods Ln.   Ph: (781)639-1872
PO Box 1168   Free: 800-650-6787
Marblehead, MA 01945   Fax: (781)639-2982
E-mail: customer_service@opuscomm.com
URL: http://www.opuscomm.com
Desc: Reports on the activities of ambulatory care accreditors, the JCAHO and the AAAHC. Provides information on how to obtain accreditation. *Type:* Newsletter.

Briefings on JCAHO: Home Medical Equipment

Opus Communications
100 Hoods Ln.   Ph: (781)639-1872
PO Box 1168   Free: 800-650-6787
Marblehead, MA 01945   Fax: (781)639-2982
E-mail: customer_service@opuscomm.com
URL: http://www.opuscomm.com
Desc: Assists in preparing for survey, recognizing common Type I problems, and learning practical compliance tips and strategies for HME organizations. *Type:* Newsletter.

Briefings on JCAHO: Long-Term & Subacute Care

Opus Communications
100 Hoods Ln.   Ph: (781)639-1872
PO Box 1168   Free: 800-650-6787
Marblehead, MA 01945   Fax: (781)639-2982
E-mail: customer_service@opuscomm.com
URL: http://www.opuscomm.com
Desc: Provides information on long-term and subacute care accreditation. Includes topics such as JCAHO, HCFA, and CARF standards and JCAHO and CARF survey processes. *Type:* Newsletter.

Briefings on Laboratory Safety and Accreditation

Opus Communications
100 Hoods Ln.   Ph: (781)639-1872
PO Box 1168   Free: 800-650-6787
Marblehead, MA 01945   Fax: (781)639-2982
E-mail: customer_service@opuscomm.com
URL: http://www.opuscomm.com
Desc: Reports on developments in fraud crackdowns and offers advice on how to implement government-approved compliance programs in laboratories. Includes information on changes in safety regulations and accrediting requirements for laboratories. *Type:* Newsletter.

Briefings on Long-Term Care Regulations

Opus Communications
100 Hoods Ln.   Ph: (781)639-1872
PO Box 1168   Free: 800-650-6787
Marblehead, MA 01945   Fax: (781)639-2982
E-mail: customer_service@opuscomm.com
URL: http://www.opuscomm.com
Contact: Kim Lawson, Editor; Jennifer I. Cofer, Publisher.
Desc: Provides information about regulations affecting long-term care facilities. Recurring features include interviews and news of research. *Type:* Newsletter.

Briefings on Outpatient Rehab Reimbursement and Regulations

Opus Communications
100 Hoods Ln.   Ph: (781)639-1872
PO Box 1168   Free: 800-650-6787
Marblehead, MA 01945   Fax: (781)639-2982
E-mail: customer_service@opuscomm.com
URL: http://www.opuscomm.com
Desc: Reports on changes occurring in health care delivery systems. Includes information on reimbursement policies and government regulations, managed care, workers' compensation, Medicare/Medicaid, PPS, and outpatient settings. *Type:* Newsletter.

Briefings on Practice Management

Opus Communications
100 Hoods Ln.   Ph: (781)639-1872
PO Box 1168   Free: 800-650-6787
Marblehead, MA 01945   Fax: (781)639-2982
E-mail: customer_service@opuscomm.com
URL: http://www.opuscomm.com
Contact: Claudia Hoffacker, Managing Editor, claudia_hoffacker@opuscomm.com; Jennifer I. Cofer, Publisher, jennifer_cofer@opuscomm.com.
Desc: Provides information about managing medical practices. Recurring features include interviews and news of research. *Type:* Newsletter.

Brigham and Women's Hospital

Channing Laboratory

181 Longwood Ave.   Ph: (617)525-2270
Boston, MA 02115-5804   Fax: (617)731-1541
E-mail: dennis_kasper@hms.harvard.edu
Contact: Dr. Dennis Kasper, Dir.
Desc: Chronic disease epidemiology and infectious diseases. *Type:* Research center.

Brigham and Women's Hospital

Clinical Research Center

221 Longwood Ave., 2nd Fl.   Ph: (617)732-5661
Boston, MA 02115   Fax: (617)732-5764
Contact: Dr. Gordon Williams, Prog.Dir.
Desc: Support facility for clinical investigation of diseases in humans. *Type:* Research center.

Brigham and Women's Hospital

Robert B. Brigham Multipurpose Arthritis and Musculoskeletal Diseases Center

75 Francis St.   Ph: (617)732-5356
Boston, MA 02115   Fax: (617)732-5505
E-mail: mhliang@bics.bwh.havard.edu
Contact: Dr. Matthew H. Liang, Dir.
Desc: Rheumatic disease, including technology assessment, policy studies, the relationship between clinical practice, outcome, and efficiency, and psychological, social, and economic factors. Also studies clinimetrics and epidemiology of rheumatic disease, Lyme disease, Carpal Tunnel Syndrome, spinal stenosis, doctor-patient communication, and SLE risk factors. *Type:* Research center.

Brown University

International Health Institute

Box G/B497   Ph: (401)863-1373
Providence, RI 02912   Fax: (401)863-1243
E-mail: Sharon_D'Antuono@Brown.edu
URL: http://www.biomed.brown.edu/medicine_programs/IHI/index-1.htm
Contact: Dr. Charles Carpenter, Dir.
Desc: Clinical and basic biomedical research focusing on the health problems of developing nations, including HIV/AIDS, infectious diseases and nutrition. Activities include ongoing field projects and the transfer of biomedical technology. *Type:* Research center.

The Brown University Long-Term Care Quality Advisor

Manisses Communications Group, Inc.
208 Governor St.   Ph: (401)831-6020
Providence, RI 02906-3246   Free: 800-333-7771
                                 Fax: (401)861-6370
E-mail: manissescs@manisses.com; lwjackim@manisses.com.
Contact: Vincent Mor, Ph.D., Editor; Barry Fogel, M.D., Editor.
Desc: Provides information about long-term care. Topics include public policy and treatment and management issues. *Type:* Newsletter.

Bucknell University

Immunobiology Research Laboratory

Dept. of Biology   Ph: (717)524-1135
Lewisburg, PA 17837   Fax: (717)524-3537
E-mail: pearson@bucknell.edu
URL: http://www.bucknell.edu
Contact: Dr. David D. Pearson, Dir.
Desc: Autoimmune diseases, particularly the causes of rheumatoid arthritis. Studies techniques to detect the disease, including protein blotting on nitro-cellulose, binding of oligosaccharides to lectins, and enzyme-linked immunoabsorbent assay tests. *Type:* Research center.

The Bulletin on Long-Term Care Law

Health Resources Publishing
1913 Atlantic Ave., Ste. F4   Ph: (732)292-1100
Manasquan, NJ 08736   Free: 800-516-4343
                                 Fax: (732)292-1111
E-mail: hrp@healthrespubs.com
Contact: Jodi L. Kastel, Publisher, jkastel@healthrespubs.com.
Desc: Covers topics related to long-term healthcare and the law, including compliance problems, needless litigation, fraud, and negligence. *Type:* Newsletter.

Bulletin on the Rheumatic Diseases

Arthritis Foundation
1330 W. Peachtree St.   Ph: (404)872-7100
Atlanta, GA 30309
URL: http://www.arthritis.com
Desc: Provides concise discussions on aspects of current developments in research and management of rheumatic diseases by experts in the field. *Available:* LEXIS-NEXIS, LEXIS. *Type:* Database.

Burn Trauma Center

Massachusetts General Hospital   Ph: (617)726-3447
Grb 1302   Fax: (617)367-8936
Boston, MA 02114
Contact: Ronald G. Tompkins, Hd.
Desc: Burns and burn trauma. *Type:* Research center.

Ca-A Cancer Journal for Clinicians

Lippincott Williams & Wilkins
345 Hudson St., 16th Fl.   Ph: (212)886-1200
New York, NY 10014   Fax: (212)886-1209
URL: http://www.ca-journal.org.
Contact: Gerald P. Murphy, M.D., Editor-in-Chief; Margie Miller, Managing Editor; Vickie Thaw, Publisher.
Desc: Original peer reviewed articles on all aspects of cancer management. *Type:* Periodical.

California Collaborative Treatment Group

University of California, San   Ph: (619)543-8080
    Diego   Fax: (619)298-0177
2760 5th Ave., Ste. 300
San Diego, CA 92103-6329
E-mail: jniosi@ucsd.edu
Contact: Jeanne Niosi, Admin.Anal.
Desc: Develops treatment protocols and drug therapies and recruits research volunteers for AIDS studies. Research focuses on clinical trials addressing value of phenotypic drug resistance testing. *Type:* Research center.

California Institute for Medical Research

2260 Clove Dr.   Ph: (408)998-4554
San Jose, CA 95128   Fax: (408)998-2723
Contact: Jada Lin, Mgr.
Desc: Medical research, including infectious diseases, stroke, analytical tools for pharmacokinetic study of anticoagulant drugs, neurological disorders, tumor biology, and AIDS. Also serves as a model regional center for traumatic head injury. *Type:* Research center.

California Pacific Medical Center Research Institute

2340 Clay   Ph: (415)561-1601
San Francisco, CA 94115   Fax: (415)561-1753
URL: http://www.cpmc.org
Contact: David R. Fielder, VP.
Desc: Medical sciences, including basic clinical research on heart and lung disease, organ transplantation, neurology, laboratory medicine, cancer, arthritis, neonatology, gene therapy (non-viral) and gastroenterology. *Type:* Research center.

Canadian Association of Physical Medicine and Rehabilitation News

Canadian Association of Physical Medicine and Rehabilitation
774 Echo Dr.   Ph: (613)730-6245
Ottawa, ON, Canada K1S 5N8   Fax: (613)730-1116
Contact: Dr. Kate Stolee, Editor.
Desc: Provides a forum for information exchange for the Association. Recurring features include letters to the editor, a calendar of events, reports of meetings, job listings, archive and committee reports, and editorials. *Type:* Newsletter.

Canadian Bacterial Diseases Network

Heritage Medical Research   Ph: (403)220-2562
    Bldg., Rm. 282   Fax: (403)283-5241
3300 Hospital Dr. NW
Calgary, AB, Canada T2N 2N1
E-mail: woods@acs.ucalgary.ca
URL: http://www.cbdn.ca
Contact: Dr. Donald E. Woods, Sci.Dir.
Desc: Bacterial diseases of humans, animals, fish, and plants. Eight program areas include: antibiotics, including structure/activity relationships at the molecular level, mechanisms of antibiotic resistance, and outer membrane permeability; intracellular bacteria, adherence, and macrophages; live attenuated and subcellular vaccines, including novel attenuated strains as vaccine carriers, outer membrane proteins as carriers for peptide epitopes, and vaccine projects on human and fish pathogens; diagnostics, including analysis of DNA sequences, monoclonal antibodies, and other methods for use as diagnostic agents for Chlamydia, Pseudomonas, Salmonella, Campylobacter, Anaerobes, toxins, beta-lactamases, Neisseria, Yersinia, Bordetella, and major fish, animal, and plant pathogens; fish vaccines and diagnostics; toxins, including toxic shock syndrome, pertussis toxin, and Pasteurella haemolytica toxin; helicobacter, including mechanisms of ineffectivenss of antibiotics, molecular biology and genetics, and surface molecule studies; and sexually transmitted diseases, including molecular biology of surface antigens and molecular typing methods. *Type:* Research center.

Canadian Liver Foundation

365 Bloor St. E, Ste. 200   Ph: (416)964-1953
Toronto, ON, Canada M4W   Free: 800-563-5483
    3L4   Fax: (416)964-0024
E-mail: clf@liver.ca
URL: http://www.liver.ca
Contact: Robert Hamp, Natl.Dir.Comm.
Desc: Aims to increase workforce and facilities in liver research by awarding summer studentships, graduate studentships, fellowships for Canadian doctors, and research establishment and operating grants for hepatologists and scientists. *Type:* Research center.

Cardiovascular Disease Management

COR Healthcare Resources
PO Box 40959   Ph: (805)564-2177
Santa Barbara, CA 93140-0959   Fax: (805)564-2146
E-mail: corinfo@corhealth.com
Contact: Marilyn Lang, RN.

Desc: Covers topics related to management of patients with cardiovascular disease. Recurring features include interviews, news of research, reports of meetings, and book reviews. *Type:* Newsletter.

Cardiovascular Reviews & Reports

Cardiovascular Reviews & Reports, Inc.
777 W. Putnam Ave.   Ph: (203)531-0450
Greenwich, CT 06830-5014   Fax: (203)531-0533
Contact: Louis F. LeJacq, Founder; JoAnn Kalaka, Publisher, jkalaka@aol.com; Nancy Sharp, Managing Editor, managingeditor@lejacq.com; Sarah Howell, Publishing Dir., showell@lejacq.com.
Desc: Journal. *Alt. Contact:* fax: (203)531-1713. *Type:* Periodical.

Carl Stough Institute of Breathing Coordination, Inc.

200 E. 66th St.   Ph: (212)308-7138
New York, NY 10021   Fax: (212)308-7138
E-mail: stoughinst@aol.com
URL: http://www.carlstough.org
Contact: Campbell C. Groel, Pres.
Desc: Respiratory science, especially relief of dyspnea (breathlessness) and prophylaxis. Emphasizes the Stough Method of Breathing Coordination (SIMBIC), a physiological discovery made by Carl Stough in the early 1960s during his work with emphysema patients. *Type:* Research center.

Case Western Reserve University

Center for Biomedical Ethics

Sch. of Med.   Ph: (216)368-6196
10900 Euclid Ave.   Free: 800-773-2633
Cleveland, OH 44106-4976 Fax: (216)368-8713
E-mail: xx245@po.cwru.edu
URL: http://www.cwru.edu/cwru/med/bioethics/bioethics.html
Contact: Thomas Murray, PhD, Dir.
Desc: Bioethics, including human genetics, decisions to end life, aging, and reproductive alternatives. *Type:* Research center.

Case Western Reserve University

General Clinical Research Center

10900 Euclid Ave.   Ph: (216)844-1589
Cleveland, OH 44106   Fax: (216)844-1522
E-mail: jpd@po.cwru.edu
URL: http://gcrc.meds.cwru.edu
Contact: Dr. E. Regis McFadden, Jr., Dir.
Desc: Clinical investigations in humans, including specific, carefully planned studies of illnesses of voluntarily participating adult and pediatric patients. *Type:* Research center.

Case Western Reserve University

Northeast Ohio Multipurpose Arthritis Center

Univ. Hospitals of Cleveland Ph: (216)844-3168
11100 Euclid Ave.   Fax: (216)844-5172
Cleveland, OH 44106
E-mail: rwm3@po.cwru.edu
Contact: Dr. Roland W. Moskowitz, Dir.
Desc: The causes, diagnosis, and treatment of arthritis, including biochemistry and pathophysiology of joints in osteoarthritis, models of degenerative joint disease and inflammatory arthritis, immunologic disorders such as systemic lupus erythematosus and rheumatoid arthritis, disorders of the spine, genetic control of arthritis disorders, and juvenile arthritis. Orthopedic studies include bioengineering, joint replacement, transplant surgery, and bone metabolism. *Type:* Research center.

Case Western Reserve University

Skeletal Research Center

Department of Biology   Ph: (216)368-3562
2080 Adelbert Rd.   Fax: (216)368-4077
Cleveland, OH 44106-7080
Contact: Arnold I. Caplan, PhD, Dir.
Desc: Tissue engineered regeneration and clinical aspects of skeletal tissue, includi cartilage, bones, tendons, and ligaments. *Type:* Research center.

Catholic Health World

Catholic Health Association of the United States
4455 Woodson Rd.   Ph: (314)253-3445
St. Louis, MO 63134-3797 Fax: (314)253-3540
URL: http://www.chausa.org.
Contact: Sandy Gilfillan, Editor.
Desc: Focuses on Catholic health care facilities, and news of legislation that affects the quality of Catholic and general health care. Features articles on people and programs within the field. *Type:* Newsletter.

Catholic Medical Mission Board

10 W. 17th St.   Ph: (212)242-7757
New York, NY 10011-5765 Free: 800-678-5969
              Fax: (212)807-9161
E-mail: cmmb@compuserve.com
Contact: Terry Kirch, Pres./Dir.
Desc: Provides health care assistance to clinical facilities in developing and transitional countries. Financial aid granted to students matriculated in accredited health care education programs in their own mission countries. Placement program assists health providers interested in volunteering for short- and long-term tours of service at selected clinical sites around the world. *Type:* Association.

Celiac News

Canadian Celiac Association
6519B Mississauga Rd.   Ph: (905)567-7195
Mississauga, ON, Canada L5N Free: 800-363-7296
  1A6   Fax: (905)567-0710
Contact: Judi Sennett, Editor.
Desc: Deals with celiac disease, dermatitis herpetiformis, and the gluten-free diet. Recurring features include letters to the editor, news of research, a calendar of events, reports of meetings, and book reviews. *Type:* Newsletter.

Center for Basic Research in Digestive Diseases

Guggenheim 17   Ph: (507)284-1006
Mayo Clinic   Fax: (507)284-0762
Rochester, MN 55905
E-mail: larusso.nicholas@mayo.edu
Contact: Dr. N. F. LaRusso, Dir.
Desc: Cell biology, focusing on molecular and biochemical mechanisms of secretion in digestive tissues. *Type:* Research center.

Center for Biotechnology

SUNY at Stony Brook   Ph: (516)632-8521
130 Life Sci. Bldg.   Fax: (516)632-8577
Stony Brook, NY 11794-5208
E-mail: clinton.rubin@suny.edu
URL: http://www.life.bio.sunysb.edu/biotech
Contact: Clinton Rubin, Dir.
Desc: Supports biomedical research in New York, and facilitates collaborations between small businesses and the research community within the state. Conducts sponsored research projects in biochemistry, immunology, microbiology, pharmacology, and chemistry. *Type:* Research center.

Center for Clinical and Lifestyle Research

21 North Quinsigamond Ave. Ph: (508)756-1228
Shrewsbury, MA 01545   Fax: (508)754-5098
E-mail: bporcaro@jamesrippe.com
URL: http://www.jamesrippe.com
Contact: James M. Rippe, MD, Dir.
Desc: Aging, hypertension, ischemic heart disease, osteoarthritis, psychological well being, cholesterol control, weight management, children's health and fitness, health benefits of walking, women's health issues, hydration and temperature regulation, and evaluation of exercise and medical equipment. *Type:* Research center.

Center for Emergency Medicine of Western Pennsylvania

230 McKee Pl., Ste. 500   Ph: (412)578-3204
Pittsburgh, PA 15213   Fax: (412)578-3241
E-mail: menegazz@pitt.edu
Contact: Dr. James J. Menegazzi, Dir., Office of Res.
Desc: Systems, therapy, and techniques involved in the delivery of emergency care, including monitoring and evaluation of field care, personnel training and performance, and patient outcome. Sample projects include study of resuscitation from cardiac arrest, endobronchial drug delivery, pediatric ventilation alternatives, surgical versus percutaneous cricothyrotomy, techniques used for the transport of the seriously ill or injured, and alternative methods of emergency airway management, including transillumination methods of intubation and translaryngeal jet ventilation. *Type:* Research center.

Center for Epidemiologic Research

Oak Ridge Institute for Sci. and Ph: (423)576-2866
  Education   Fax: (423)576-9557
210 Badger Rd.
PO Box 117
Oak Ridge, TN 37831-0117
E-mail: cragled@orau.gov
URL: http://www.orau.gov
Contact: Dr. Donna Cragle, Dir.
Desc: Occupational health and safety. *Type:* Research center.

Center for Human Services

7200 Wisconsin Ave., Ste. 600 Ph: (301)654-8338
Bethesda, MD 20814-4811 Fax: (301)941-8427
E-mail: dnicholas@urc-chs.com
URL: http://www.urc-chs.com
Contact: Dr. David Nicholas, Dir.
Desc: Applies quality assurance methods in health care settings around the world and conducts comparative studies of quality assessment, quality assurance costs, and quality relationship. *Type:* Research center.

Center for Medical Consumers and Health Information

237 Thompson St.   Ph: (212)674-7105
New York, NY 10012   Fax: (212)674-7100
Contact: Arthur Levin, Dir.
Desc: Mainstream and alternative medical treatments. *Type:* Research center.

Center News

Memorial Sloan-Kettering Cancer Center
1275 York Ave.   Ph: (212)639-3573
New York, NY 10021   Fax: (212)639-3576
URL: http://www.mskcc.org.
Contact: Debbie Rosenberg Bush.
Desc: Provides news of research and treatment advances and news of other Memorial Sloan-Kettering Cancer Center activities. *Type:* Newsletter.

Center for Research on Population and Security

PO Box 13067　　　　　　　　Ph: (919)933-7491
Research Triangle Park, NC　　Fax: (919)933-0348
　27709
E-mail: smumford@mindspring.com
URL: http://www.quinacrine.com
Contact: Stephen D. Mumford, Pres.
Desc: Population growth control, contraceptive method research, including international clinical trial technical support, and the relationship between population growth and national and global security. *Type:* Research center.

Center for Study of Multiple Birth

333 E. Superior St., Ste. 464　　Ph: (312)266-9093
Chicago, IL 60611　　　　　　Free: 800-825-6557
　　　　　　　　　　　　　　Fax: (312)908-8500
E-mail: LGK395@nwu.edu
URL: http://www.multiplebirth.com
Contact: Donald M. Keith, Exec.Dir.
Desc: Multiple birth, twin gestation, twin pregnancy diagnosis, and twin care. Research is aimed at decreasing the high infant mortality rate involved in multiple births. *Type:* Research center.

Center for Thanatology Research

391 Atlantic Ave.　　　　　　Ph: (718)858-3026
Brooklyn, NY 11217-1171　　Fax: (718)858-3026
E-mail: rhalporn@pipeline.com
URL: http://www.thanatology.org
Contact: Roberta Halporn, Dir.
Desc: Aging, dying, death, bereavement, and gravestone studies. *Type:* Research center.

Centers for Disease Control and Prevention

Centers for Disease Control and Prevention
1600 Clifton Rd. NE　　　　Ph: (404)639-3311
Atlanta, GA 30333
E-mail: netinfo@cdc.gov
URL: http://www.cdc.gov
Desc: The Centers for Disease Control and Prevention (CDC) website intends to promote health and quality of life. The repository of the most up-to-date information, the CDC provides information about preventing and controlling disease, injury, and disability. *Type:* Database.

CenterWatch

CenterWatch, Inc.
581 Boylston St.　　　　　　Ph: (617)247-2327
Boston, MA 02116　　　　　Fax: (617)247-2535
E-mail: cntrwatch@aol.com
URL: http://www.centerwatch.com/
Desc: CenterWatch is a site containing a wide variety of information on medical clinical trials. It is designed as a resource for both patients and researchers, with online information including detailed notices on research facilities including contact information, programs and trials, recent FDA approvals with lists of medical and brand names, manufacturers, treatment objectives, possible side effects; plus a FAQ on clinical research. *Type:* Database.

Central Society for Clinical Research

1481 W. 10th St., Ste. 111P
Indianapolis, IN 46202-2884
Contact: Dr. Mortan Arnsdorf, Contact.
Desc: Promotes correlation of science with the art of medical practice, scientific investigation, the advancement of medical science, and the diffusion of a scientific spirit. *Type:* Research center.

Central Society for Clinical Research

611 E. Wells　　　　　　　　Ph: (414)273-2209
Milwaukee, WI 53202　　　　Fax: (414)276-3349
E-mail: cfcr@exec.pc.com

Contact: Lynn Konek, Exec.Dir.
Desc: Clinical medicine. *Type:* Research center.

CFIDS Association of America

PO Box 220398　　　　　　Ph: 800-442-3437
Charlotte, NC 28222-0398　Fax: (704)365-9755
E-mail: cfids@cfids.org
URL: http://www.cfids.org
Contact: Kim Kenney, Exec. Officer.
Desc: Individuals with chronic fatigue and immune dysfunction syndrome (chronic viral illness associated with dysfunction of the immune system; formerly called chronic Epstein-Barr virus); doctors, nurses, and government officials. Advocates continued research into the cause and cure of the syndrome. Funds pilot medical research projects. *Type:* Association.

Children's Blood Foundation

333 E. 38th, Room 830　　Ph: (212)297-4336
New York, NY 10016　　　Fax: (212)297-4340
E-mail: cbf@nyh.med.cornell.edu
URL: http://www.thorn.net/~cbfound
Contact: Susan Byrne, Exec.Dir.
Desc: Seeks to raise funds to combat diseases of the blood in children, such as leukemia, hemophilia, thalassemia (Cooley's anemia), childhood cancers, sickle cell, and other anemias and diseases of the immune system, and AIDS. Supports a total patient care center in the New York Hospital-Cornell Medical Center, which includes diagnostic and treatment clinics, progressive research laboratories, and intensive training of physicians in the specialty of pediatric hematology/oncology. Also sponsors specialized social events. *Type:* Association.

CHOSEN

3642 W. 26th St.　　　　　Ph: (814)833-3023
Erie, PA 16506　　　　　　Fax: (814)833-4091
E-mail: chosew4jay@aol.com
Contact: Carl C. Eldred, Exec.Dir.
Desc: Interdenominational organization supporting overseas Christian medical mission work. Procures new and used medical equipment for mission hospitals in economically deprived nations; repairs and modifies equipment; prepares equipment for shipping. Provides training in infection control (operating room and sterile departments) and in the proper use and maintenance of equipment for all mission hospital staffs. *Type:* Association.

Christian Medical and Dental Society

PO Box 7500　　　　　　　Ph: (423)844-1000
Bristol, TN 37621-7500　　Fax: (423)844-1005
E-mail: main@christian-doctors.com
URL: http://www.cmds.org
Contact: David Stevens, M.D., Exec.Dir.
Desc: The Christian Medical & Dental Society serves as a voice and ministry for Christian doctors. Its mission is to "change the heart of healthcare." Founded in 1931, CMDS promotes positions and addresses policies on health care issues; conducts overseas and domestic mission projects; coordinates a network of Christian doctors for fellowship and professional growth; sponsors student ministries in medical and dental schools; distributes educational and inspirational resources; holds marriage and family conferences; provides Third World missionary doctors with continuing education resources; and conducts academic exchange programs overseas. *Type:* Association.

City of Hope

1500 E. Duarte Rd.　　　　Ph: (626)359-8111
Duarte, CA 91010　　　　　Fax: (626)301-8115
URL: http://www.cityofhope.org
Contact: Dr. Charles Balch, CEO.
Desc: Supports the National Pilot Medical Center and the Beckman Research Institute, which are engaged in treat-

ment, research, and medical education in catastrophic diseases including cancer; leukemia; blood, heart and lung diseases; certain hereditary maladies; and metabolic disorders, such as diabetes. *Type:* Association.

City of Hope Beckman Research Institute
Division of Immunology

1500 E. Duarte Rd.　　　　Ph: (626)359-2601
Duarte, CA 91010
URL: http://www.cityofhope.org
Contact: Charles M. Balch, MD, Pres./CEO.
Desc: The Division is divided into five sections: Protein Chemistry, Immunobiology, Structural Biochemistry, Mass Spectrometry and NMR Spectroscopy. Sections collaborate on projects in cancer, virology, endocrinology, and immunology. *Type:* Research center.

City of Hope National Medical Center

1500 E. Duarte Rd.　　　　Ph: (626)359-8116
Duarte, CA 91010　　　　　Fax: (626)301-8938
URL: http://www.cityofhope.org
Contact: Charles M. Balch, MD, Pres./CEO.
Desc: Metabolism, diabetes, genetics, cytology, hematology, physiology, pharmacology, neurology, cancer, cancer diagnosis and therapy, bone marrow transplantation, surgery, respiratory diseases, pathology, radiology, nuclear medicine, gene therapy, and developmental biology. *Type:* Research center.

City of Hope National Medical Center
Beckman Research Institute

1500 E. Duarte Rd.　　　　Ph: (626)357-9711
Duarte, CA 91010　　　　　Fax: (626)930-5300
E-mail: jkovach@smtplink.coh.org
URL: http://www.coh.org
Contact: John S. Kovach, MD, Exec.V.Pres.
Desc: Biology, including cell biology, molecular biology, developmental biology, molecular genetics, molecular immunology, gene regulation, and theoretical biology; immunology, including protein chemistry, peptide chemistry, mass spectrometry, and immunobiology; and neurosciences, including behavioral and neural genetics, cell physiology, cellular neurochemistry, cellular neurophysiology, membrane biochemistry, membrane neurochemistry, neuroanatomy and ultrastructure, neuropharmacology, neurophysiology, receptor physiology, biochemical genetics, and neurobiochemistry. *Type:* Research center.

Cleveland Clinic Foundation
Lerner Research Institute

9500 Euclid Ave.　　　　　Ph: (216)444-3900
Cleveland, OH 44195　　　Fax: (216)444-3279
E-mail: starkg@cesmtp.ccf.org
URL: http://www.lri.ccf.org/ri
Contact: George R. Stark, PhD, Chm.
Desc: Molecular biology; structure and function in regulation of viral and cellular genes and (proto)oncogenes, and interferon signaling mechanisms; cancer biology and genetics, including Wilms' tumor, cellular gene regulation, transgenic models, and use of newly patented 2-5A antisense technology; cell biology, including vessel wall pathophysiology, lipoprotein oxidation, regulation of gene expression and intracellular signaling pathways. Studies also include immunology, biologic response modifiers in tumor growth and regression, chemokines, nitric oxide synthase; neurosciences emphasizing cellular and genetic mechanisms in multiple sclerosis, effects of AIDS; epilepsy; neuronal signaling in cardiovascular neurobiology and diagnostic methods in cerebrovascular disease and hypertrophy, studies of lipoprotein(a), computerized modeling of protein structures, G-proteins, and study of the basis

of hypertension; biomedical engineering, including musculoskeletal biology, imaging research, biomaterials and biocompatibility, and total artificial heart and heart assist devices; and biostatistics and epidemiology. *Type:* Research center.

Cleveland Clinic Journal of Medicine
Cleveland Clinic Foundation
9500 Euclid Ave., EE37   Ph: (216)444-2661
Cleveland, OH 44195   Fax: (216)444-9385
E-mail: ccjm@cesmtp.ccf.org.
URL: http://www.ccf.org/ed/ccjhome.htm.
Contact: Linda K. Hengstler, Publisher/Editor, (216)444-2661, fax: (216)444-9385; John D. Clough, MD, Editor-in-Chief, (216)444-26612, fax: (216)444-9385; Phillip E. Canuto, Exec. Editor, (216)444-2661, fax: (216)444-9385; Joseph Dennehy, Dir. of Sales & Marketing, (516)365-8640, fax: (516)365-0587.
Desc: The Cleveland Clinic Journal of Medicine is a source of up-to-date clinical information for general internists and cardiologists. Articles are based on the Cleveland Clinic's accredited Continuing Medical Education (CME) programs and are written by physicians renowned in their fields and active as clinicians and educators. Authors include Cleveland Clinic staff physicians and visiting professors. Regular features: Interpreting Key Trials, Highlights from Medical Grand Rounds, Cardiology Dialogues, Current Drug Therapy, CME Credit Test, Internal Medicine Board Review, and Clinical Decision-making at the Crossroads. Peer-reviewed and indexed. *Type:* Periodical.

Clinical Research Center
Children's Hospital Medical   Ph: (617)355-7541
  Center   Fax: (617)730-0434
300 Longwood Ave.
Boston, MA 02115
E-mail: sweeney@a1.tch.harvard.edu
Contact: Cheryl Sweeney, Prog.Mgr.
Desc: Protocols in bone marrow transplantation, immunodeficiencies, pediatric endocrinology, bone and mineral metabolism, pediatric hematology, neuroimmunology, oncology, and pediatric gastroenterology. *Type:* Research center.

Clinical Research Center
Northwestern Univ.   Ph: (312)908-3192
Northwestern Memorial   Fax: (312)908-8450
  Hospital
250 E. Superior St., Wesley
  Pavilion Rm. 1625
Chicago, IL 60611
E-mail: glr388@nwu.edu
Contact: Gary L. Robertson, MD, Prog.Dir.
Desc: Diabetes insipidus, malabsorption in AIDS, cardiac arrhythmias, effects of diabetes on pregnancy, pituitary tumors, tumoral calcinosis, gastrointestinal malabsorption of carbohydrates and other nutrients, monoclonal antibodies in diagnosis and therapy of cancer, and Phase I and II drug trials. *Type:* Research center.

Clinical Research Institute of Montreal
110 Pine Ave. W.   Ph: (514)987-5516
Montreal, PQ, Canada H2W   Fax: (514)987-5677
  1R7
E-mail: guindow@ircm.umontreal.ca
URL: http://www.ircm.umontreal.ca
Contact: Dr. Yvan Guindon, CEO/Sci.Dir.
Desc: Causes, mechanisms, and more effective treatments of diseases in many fields of medicine, including research on hypertension, neurobiology and behavior, pain mechanisms, hyperlipidemias and atherosclerosis, proteins and peptides hormones, lipid metabolism, biomedical engineering, molecular biology, immunology, molecular genetics, bioethics, reproduction, chemical biology and polypeptides, hematopoiesis and leukemia, cancer, and bio-organic chemistry. *Type:* Research center.

CMT Newsletter
Charcot-Marie-Tooth Disease/Peroneal Muscular Atrophy International Association, Inc.
1 Springbank Dr.   Ph: (905)687-3630
St. Catharines, ON, Canada L2S Fax: (905)687-8753
  2K1
E-mail: cmtint@vaxxine.com
Contact: Linda Crabtree, Editor.
Desc: Provides information for patients, their families, and interested health care professionals on Charcot-Marie-Tooth (CMT) disease, a hereditary neuro-muscular condition that causes loss of feeling and/or movement from the knees down and the elbows down; breathing and other functions may also be affected. Recurring features include letters from people with CMT, interviews, two columns by doctors who answer questions about CMT, research news, a calendar of events, news of new aids for daily living, and up-to-date lists of new research papers printed around the world. *Type:* Newsletter.

Colorado State University
Hypo-Hyperbaric Chamber Facility
Department of Physiology   Ph: (970)491-6106
Fort Collins, CO 80523   Fax: (970)491-7569
E-mail: atucker@cvmbs.colostate.edu
Contact: Dr. Alan Tucker, Contact.
Desc: High altitude physiology, altitude illness, pulmonary hypertension, human performance at various altitudes, hyperbaric physiology, and human and animal studies. *Type:* Research center.

Columbia University
Irving Center for Clinical Research
Columbia-Presbyterian Med.   Ph: (212)305-9562
  Ctr.   Fax: (212)305-3213
622 W. 168th St., PH-10
New York, NY 10032
E-mail: ginsberg@cudept.cis.columbia.edu
URL: http://cpmcnet.columbia.edu/dept/irving_center
Contact: Dr. Henry Ginsberg, Prog.Dir.
Desc: Multidisciplinary studies of human disease and clinical pharmacology. Areas include arrhythmia control, heart failure, atherosclerosis, nutrition, metabolism, clinical pharmacology, dermatology, endocrinology, hypertension, immunology, mineral metabolism and skeletal disease, neuromuscular disease, physiology, pulmonary disease, pulmonary physiology, reproductive research studies, neurology (including dementia, stroke, and seizure disorders), oncology, AIDS/infectious disease, geriatrics, epidemiology, and substance abuse. *Type:* Research center.

Columbia University
New York Obesity Research Center
St. Luke's-Roosevelt Hospital Ph: (212)523-4161
1111 Amsterdam Ave., Rm.   Fax: (212)523-4830
  1020
New York, NY 10025
E-mail: fxp1@columbia.edu
URL: http://www.docnet.org/programs/weight/obesity/staff.html
Contact: Dr. Xavier Pi-Sunyer, Dir.
Desc: Obesity, including molecular genetics, regulation of food intake, nutrient uptake and oxidation, body composition, stable isotope methodology, exercise physiology, diabetes, and insulin resistance. *Type:* Research center.

Committee for Freedom of Choice in Medicine
1180 Walnut Ave.   Ph: (619)429-8200
Chula Vista, CA 91911   Free: 800-227-4473
                             Fax: (619)429-8004
E-mail: ambio@ix.netcom.com
Contact: Mike Culbert, Chm. Emeritus.

Desc: Purpose is to support freedom of choice for any therapy which shows clear evidence of efficacy and to prohibit the interference of government or any third party in the relationship between an informed patient and his or her physician. Activities include: publishing information to keep members apprised of the latest developments in research and treatment; directing people with questions concerning alternative therapy to physicians in their areas; maintaining an information service for physicians interested in expanding their knowledge of metabolic/nutritional treatment; providing educational exhibits for programs and seminars being conducted by various medical groups. Conducts research; compiles statistics on people with degenerative diseases who have been treated with metabolic therapy. *Type:* Association.

Committee for the Promotion of Medical Research
191 Hayward St.   Ph: (914)968-0262
Yonkers, NY 10704
Contact: Ellen M. Cosgrove, Contact.
Desc: Administration of medical research grants. *Type:* Research center.

Comprehensive Core Medical Library
Ovid Technologies, Inc.
333 Seventh Ave.   Ph: (212)563-3006
New York, NY 10001
E-mail: sales@ovid.com
URL: http://www.ovid.com
Contact: Elizabeth Pelowski, Communications Coord.
Desc: Contains the complete text of more than 70 major medical textbooks and medical journals. TEXTBOOKS: • American College of Obstetricians and Gynecologists' Precis III and Standards for Obstetric-Gynecologic Services (6th edition). *Available:* Ovid Technologies, Inc.; NIFTY Corporation, NIFTY-SERVE. *Type:* Database.

Comprehensive Epidemiologic Data Resource
U.S. Department of Energy - Office of Epidemiologic Studies
19901 Germantown Rd.   Ph: (301)903-4674
Germantown, MD 20874-1290   Fax: (301)903-4677
E-mail: cedr@cedr.lbl.gov
URL: http://cedr.lbl.gov
Contact: Barbara Brooks, CEDR Program Coordinator, barbara.brooks@eh.doe.gov.
Desc: The Comprehensive Epidemiologic Data Resource web site provides data sets that are the result of epidemiologic studies conducted on various groups of workers at different U.S. Department of Energy facilities during the past 30 years. *Type:* Database.

Connecticut Eye Bank & Visual Research Foundation, Inc.
100 Grand St.   Ph: (860)224-5550
New Britain, CT 06052   Free: 800-355-5520
                             Fax: (860)224-5720
Contact: Michael J. Rinehart, Pres./CEO.
Desc: Production of eye material for use in corneal transplantation surgery, surgical study, and for research on blindness. Projects include the Vision Immunology Program, a study of how the eye defends against disease. *Type:* Research center.

Connective Tissue Research Institute
Univ. City Sci. Ctr.   Ph: (215)382-7840
3624 Market St.   Fax: (215)382-1749
Philadelphia, PA 19104
E-mail: kefalide@mail.med.upenn.edu
Contact: Dr. Nicholas A. Kefalides, Dir.
Desc: Biochemistry, cell biology, immunology, and molecular biology of connective tissues, including characteriza-

tion and study of basement membranes, blood vessels, cornea and lens capsule of the eye, and cell virus interaction. Research is applied toward problems in cardiovascular disease, kidney disease, ocular disease, and genetic disease. *Type:* Research center.

Conomikes Medicare Hotline

Conomikes Reports
151 Kalmus Dr., Ste. B-150   Free: 800-421-6512
Costa Mesa, CA 92626-7955   Fax: (310)645-3224
Contact: George S. Conomikes, Editor, conomikes@aol.com; Deanna Slagle, Managing Editor.
Type: Newsletter.

Conomikes Reports on Medical Practice Management and Managed Care

Conomikes Reports
151 Kalmus Dr., Ste. B-150   Free: 800-421-6512
Costa Mesa, CA 92626-7955   Fax: (310)645-3224
Contact: George S. Conomikes, Editor, conomikes@aol.com; Sharon Wagner, Asst. Ed.
Desc: Focuses on medical practice management topics such as insurance tips, new patients, team building, recruiting, personal management and managed care, patient management, labor shortages, office technology, and staff communications. Recurring features include a calendar of events. *Type:* Newsletter.

Consultant

Cliggott Publishing Co.
55 Holly Hill Ln.   Ph: (203)661-0600
PO Box 4010   Fax: (203)661-8163
Greenwich, CT 06831-0010
Contact: Jonathan L. Bigelow, Chief Operating Mgr.; Susan K. Lotstein, Editor; David S. March, Associate Publisher; Stephen K. Muruta, Editorial Director; Sarah Williams, Ph.D., Managing Editor; Frank T. Iorio, Group Publisher.
Desc: Medical journal for primary care, office-based physicians. *Type:* Periodical.

Consultant's Newsletter

Society of Medical-Dental Management Consultants
3646 E. Gray Rd., No. B16-45   Free: 800-826-2264
Phoenix, AZ 85044
Contact: William H. Kidd, Editor.
Desc: Discusses news of the Society, including notices and reports of meetings, group activities, and information regarding members. Also covers management consulting for the health professional in such areas as taxes, medical design, retirement, medical economics, estate planning, and trends in medical and dental practices. *Type:* Newsletter.

Consumer Health Information Research Institute

300 E. Pink Hill Rd.   Ph: (816)228-4595
Independence, MO 64057   Fax: (816)228-4995
E-mail: drrenner@msn.com
Contact: Dr. John Renner, Dir.
Desc: Clinical medicine, health fraud and quakery, patient education, toxicology, history of medicine, medicine in art, and therapeutics. *Type:* Research center.

Contraceptive Research and Development Program

1611 N. Kent St., Ste. 806   Ph: (703)524-4744
Arlington, VA 22209   Fax: (703)524-4770
E-mail: info@conrad.org
URL: http://www.conrad.org
Contact: Henry L. Gabelnick, PhD, Dir.
Desc: Improvement of contraception methods, especially for use in developing countries. Studies include new barri-

er methods and spermicides; long-acting injectable and implantable contraceptives for women and men; nonsurgical and/or reversible sterilization techniques for women and men; immunocontraceptives directed against sperm, ova, or hormones; nonsteroidal gonadal proteins that regulate pituitary and/or gonadal functions; methods that are suitable for lactating women; and vaginal and transdermal delivery systems. *Type:* Research center.

Coriell Institute for Medical Research

401 Haddon Ave.   Ph: (609)757-4820
Camden, NJ 08103   Fax: (609)964-0254
E-mail: dabeck@umdnj.edu
URL: http://www.arginine.umdnj.edu
Contact: David P. Beck, PhD, Pres.
Desc: Cell and molecular biology, microbiology, genetics, aging, cancer and cancer immunology, tumor virology, antibodies, genetic disorders, vascular disorders, infectious diseases and virus/chromosome relationships, environmental mutagenesis, and genetic probes. Studies utilization of cells grown in tissue culture for isolation and characterization of tumor cell antigens, viruses, genetic abnormalities, tumor viruses, and chromosomes. *Type:* Research center.

Cortland Forum

Cortland Group
7 Skyline Dr.   Ph: (914)347-3800
Hawthorne, NY 10532 Fax: (914)347-3801
Desc: Medical review magazine. *Type:* Periodical.

Council for Accreditation in Occupational Hearing Conservation

611 E. Wells St.   Ph: (414)276-5338
Milwaukee, WI 53202   Fax: (414)276-3349
E-mail: info@caohc.org
URL: http://www.caohc.org
Contact: Janet L. Haynes, Exec.Dir.
Desc: To establish and maintain standards for the training of audiometric technicians (persons certified to conduct pure tone air conduction hearing tests and related duties as part of an occupational hearing conservation program). Approves courses in occupational hearing conservation and certifies those who pass these courses. Council members represent professional associations in the hearing conservation field. *Type:* Association.

Council of State and Territorial Epidemiologists

2872 Woodcock Blvd., No. 303   Ph: (770)458-3811
Atlanta, GA 30341-4015   Fax: (770)458-8516
URL: http://www.cste.org
Contact: Mr. Willis Forrester, Exec.
Desc: State epidemiologists. Works to establish closer working relationships among members; consults with and advises appropriate disciplines in other health agencies; provides technical advice and assistance to the Association of State and Territorial Health Officials; works closely with Centers for Disease Control on epidemiology, surveillance, and prevention activities. *Type:* Association.

Council for Tobacco Research - U.S.A.

900 3rd Ave.   Ph: (212)421-8885
New York, NY 10022
Contact: James F. Glenn, MD, Chm./Pres.
Desc: Cellular and molecular biology of cancer, cardiovascular and pulmonary systems, neuroscience, developmental biology, and genetics and immunology. *Type:* Research center.

Courage Stroke Network

c/o Courage Center   Ph: 800-553-6321
3915 Golden Valley Rd. Fax: (612)520-0577
Golden Valley, MN 55422
Contact: Pat Kasell, Exec. Officer.
Desc: Individuals recovering from a stroke, their families and friends, health care professionals, and other stroke recovery support groups. Promotes public awareness of stroke and its effects. Provides a forum for exchange of ideas, experiences, and information among members; acts as a clearinghouse for information and referrals. *Type:* Association.

CPA Health Care Client Letter

The American Institute of Certified Public Accountants
Harborside Financial Ctr.   Ph: (201)938-3287
201 Plaza 3   Free: 800-TOA-ICPA
Jersey City, NJ 07311-3881   Fax: (201)398-3741
Contact: Anne Wagenbrenner, Editor.
Desc: Provides tax tips, financial planning, and practice development for physicians and other health care professionals. Covers news on issues of health care reform, legislation, and the federal budget. *Type:* Newsletter.

Craniofacial Anomalies Research Center

267 EMRB   Ph: (319)335-9968
Iowa City, IA 52242 Fax: (319)335-6970
Contact: Dr. Jeffrey C. Murray, Dir.
Desc: Seeks to identify human genes and other risk factors in the etiology of craniofacial anomalies. Conducts five interrelated projects: collection and analysis of epidemiological data; genetic mapping of specific genes involved in craniofacial defects; cloning and sequencing of genes; differentiation between specific DNA isolated from a neural crest cell line; and study of normal functions in craniofacial development. *Type:* Research center.

Credentialing Across the Continuum

Opus Communications
100 Hoods Ln.   Ph: (781)639-1872
PO Box 1168   Free: 800-650-6787
Marblehead, MA 01945 Fax: (781)639-2982
E-mail: customer_service@opuscomm.com
URL: http://www.opuscomm.com
Desc: Contains credentialing requirements for specific nonacute care facilities. Includes information on surgical centers, group practices, home infusion centers, mammography centers, clinics, and home care. *Type:* Newsletter.

Crohn's and Colitis Foundation of America

386 Park Ave. S, 17th Fl.   Ph: (212)685-3440
New York, NY 10016-8804   Free: 800-932-2423
                               Fax: (212)779-4098
E-mail: info@ccfa.org
URL: http://www.ccfa.org
Contact: James V. Romano, Ph.D., Pres.CEO.
Desc: Supports research to find the cause and cure of Crohn's Disease (ileitis) and ulcerative colitis. Provides educational programs for patients, physicians, and the public, support groups, chapter newsletters, a national magazine, informational brochures and books, professional medical forums, and research publications, and a website. *Type:* Association.

CSA Alerts

Clinical Systems Association (CSA)
2265 Genesa Ln.   Ph: (407)231-1686
Vero Beach, FL 32963-3148
Contact: Roger A. Bremer, Editor.
Desc: Discusses clinical systems. *Type:* Newsletter.

Cystic Fibrosis Foundation
6931 Arlington Rd. Ph: (301)951-4422
Bethesda, MD 20814 Free: 800-344-4823
Fax: (301)951-6378
E-mail: info@cff.org
URL: http://www.cff.org
Contact: Robert J. Beall, Ph.D., Pres. & CEO.
Desc: Supports medical research, professional education, and care centers to benefit patients with cystic fibrosis (CF), an inherited fatal disease among children and young adults. With this disease a thick mucus clogs the lungs, creating breathing difficulties and high susceptibility to infection; the digestive system and other organs are also affected. More than 113 care centers affiliated with the foundation provide patient services. Type: Association.

Dalhousie University
Atlantic Health Promotion Research Centre
5981 University Ave., Rm. 5200 Ph: (902)494-2240
Halifax, NS, Canada B3H 3J5 Fax: (902)494-3594
E-mail: ahprc@dal.ca
URL: http://www.medicine.dal.ca/ahprc
Contact: Renee F. Lyons, Dir.
Desc: Physical, mental, social, and spiritual health of individuals and communities by increasing control over health issues by combining personal choice and social responsibility. Research focuses on self-help, coping, and social support. Type: Research center.

Dalhousie University
Population Health Research Unit
Fac. of Med. Ph: (902)494-3860
Department of Community Fax: (902)494-1597
Health & Epidemiology
5849 University Ave.
Halifax, NS, Canada B3H 4H7
E-mail: george.kephart@dal.ca
URL: http://www.mcms.dal.ca/gorgs/phru/index.html
Contact: George Kephart, Dir.
Desc: Health and social sciences, particularly population health, health services utilization and their interrelationships. Type: Research center.

Damien Dutton Society for Leprosy Aid
616 Bedford Ave. Ph: (516)221-5829
Bellmore, NY 11710 Fax: (516)221-5909
Contact: Howard E. Crouch, Pres.
Desc: Religious leaders and laypeople interested in aiding victims of Hansen's disease (leprosy). Provides relief, research, and recreation to victims of leprosy all over the world regardless of race, color, or creed. Type: Association.

Dannemiller Memorial Educational Foundation
12500 Network Blvd., Ste. 101 Ph: (210)641-8311
San Antonio, TX 78249 Free: 800-328-2308
Fax: (210)641-8329
E-mail: dmef@txdirect.net
URL: http://www.pain.com
Contact: Larry Vervack, Exec. Dir.
Desc: Conducts annual Anesthesia Review Course in June for M.D. anesthesiologists and in the fall for nurse anesthesiologists, and review course of current concepts in anesthesiology. Sponsors weekend anesthesia and pain management meetings. Type: Association.

Data Centrum
Data Centrum
21 W. 38th St., 4th Fl. Ph: (212)226-5252
New York, NY 10018-5506 Fax: (212)226-8847
Contact: Stu Chapman, Editor; Whitmore Jensen, Publisher; John van Hoven, Advertising Mgr.
Desc: Medical news magazine. Type: Periodical.

Deaconess Billings Clinic
Research Division
1500 Poly Dr., Ste. 202 Ph: (406)255-8470
Billings, MT 59102 Fax: (406)255-8499
E-mail: research@billingsclinic.org
URL: http://www.billingsclinic.org/research
Contact: Christopher J. Ellington, Dir. of Admin.Svcs.
Desc: Regulation of bone remodeling, arthritis, hormone replacement therapy and infectious diseases in man. Type: Research center.

Dean A. McGee Eye Institute
608 Stanton L. Young Blvd. Ph: (405)271-6363
Oklahoma City, OK 73104 Fax: (405)271-3013
E-mail: david-parke@uokhsc.edu
Contact: Dr. David W. Parke, II, Pres.
Desc: Basic and clinical investigation in visual sciences; studies also include retinal biochemistry, molecular biology, and ocular microbiology. Type: Research center.

Diabetes Education and Research Center
Franklin Medical Bldg. Ph: (215)829-3426
829 Spruce St., Ste. 302 Fax: (215)928-9150
Philadelphia, PA 19107
E-mail: diabetes@libertynet.org
URL: http://www.libertynet.org:80/~diabetes/
Contact: Dr. Duncan, Dir.
Desc: Diabetes, including the effects of oral diabetic medication, hypertension as an indicator of diabetes, and drug trials. Type: Research center.

Diabetes Forecast
American Diabetes Association
1660 Duke St. Ph: (703)549-1500
Alexandria, VA 22314 Fax: (703)683-2890
URL: http://www.diabetes.org/diabetesforecast.
Contact: Neal Friedman, M.D., Editor-in-Chief.
Desc: Magazine for diabetics and their families. Type: Periodical.

Diabetes Research Center
Health Sci. Ctr. Ph: (804)924-1931
Box 423 Fax: (804)982-3268
Charlottesville, VA 22908
Contact: Dr. Eugene J. Barrett, Dir.
Desc: Treatment, prevention, and cure of Type I and Type II diabetes mellitus, education and training of health care professionals and diabetics, and development of model care for diabetic patients. Conducts basic and clinical research with emphasis on hormone action and cyclic nucleotide metabolism. Type: Research center.

Diabetes Research Institute Foundation
3440 Hollywood Blvd., Ste. 100 Ph: (954)964-4040
Hollywood, FL 33021 Free: 800-321-3437
Fax: (954)964-7036
E-mail: info@drif.org
URL: http://www.drinet.org
Contact: Robert A. Pearlman, Exec.VP.
Desc: Works to improve the quality of life for individuals with diabetes and to find a cure for diabetes. Type: Association.

Diabetes Self-Management
R.A. Rapaport Publishing, Inc.
150 W. 22nd St. Ph: (212)989-0200
New York, NY 10011 Fax: (212)989-4786
E-mail: staff@diabetes-self-mgmt.com.
URL: http://www.diabetes-self-mgmt.com/.
Contact: James Hazlett, Editor, editor@diabetes-self-mgmt.com; James Moorehead, Circ. Dir.; Richard A. Rapaport, Pres./Publisher; Alison Jones Clarkson, Advertising Rep., (773)777-6801, fax: (773)777-6803; Kathy Jones, Advertising Rep.

Desc: Magazine providing medical, health, and self-help news for people with diabetes. Alt. Contact: Box 52890, Boulder, CO 80322-2890; toll-free: 800-234-0923. Type: Periodical.

Diagnostic Imaging SCAN
Miller Freeman, Inc.
600 Harrison St., 4th Fl. Ph: (415)905-2202
San Francisco, CA 94107 Free: 800-444-4881
Fax: (415)905-2235
E-mail: scan@mfi.com.
URL: http://www.discam.com.
Contact: Brian Casey, Editor, bcasey@mfi.com.
Desc: Examines medical imaging equipment supply and for-profit imaging services. Recurring features include interviews, quarterly reports and a faxed digest. Type: Newsletter.

DIOGENES
FOI Services, Inc.
11 Firstfield Rd. Ph: (301)975-9400
Gaithersburg, MD 20878
URL: http://www.foiservices.com
Contact: Brett McCoy, Database Manager, (301)975-0110, fax: (301)975-0702, help@foiservices.com.
Desc: Contains information on medical devices. Comprises the following three files: • 510k Notifications--provides citations to each of the devices cleared for marketing under section 510(k) of the Medical Device Amendments to the Federal Food, Drug and Cosmetic Act. Available: The Dialog Corporation, DataStar; The Dialog Corporation, DIALOG. Type: Database.

Direct Relief International
27 S. La Patera Ln. Ph: (805)964-4767
Santa Barbara, CA 93117 Fax: (805)681-4838
Contact: Max Goff, Exec.Dir.
Desc: Donates contributed pharmaceuticals, medical supplies, and equipment to health facilities and locally coordinated health projects in medically underdeveloped areas of the world. Provides emergency assistance to refugees and other victims of natural disaster and civil strife. Type: Association.

Directory of Physicians in the United States
American Medical Association
515 N. State St. Ph: (312)464-5000
Chicago, IL 60610 Free: 800-621-8335
Fax: (312)464-5830
E-mail: amaa@ama-assn.org
Contact: Suzanne Froker, Editor.
Desc: In four volume set, more than 686,000 physicians in the United States, Puerto Rico, Virgin Islands, and certain Pacific Islands and United States physicians temporarily located in foreign countries. Type: Directory.

Disease Management News
Business Information Services, Inc.
12811 North Point Ln. Ph: (301)604-4001
Laurel, MD 20708 Free: 800-559-8550
Fax: (301)604-5126
E-mail: businfosvc@aol.com
Contact: James Gutman, Publisher.
Desc: Devoted exclusively to business news, analysis, and advice in all aspects of disease management. Type: Newsletter.

Dr. Alexander Grant's Health Gazette
Alexander Grant Associates Inc.
PO Box 1786 Fax: (317)253-8582
Indianapolis, IN 46206
Contact: Alexander Grant, M.D., Editor.
Desc: Reports on medical news written for non-medically trained consumers. Provides references to journals used as sources. Type: Newsletter.

The Doctor's Office

Wentworth Publishing Company
PO Box 11177   Ph: (717)393-7197
Lancaster, PA 17605-1177   Free: 800-331-5196
                          Fax: (717)393-4702
E-mail: dellb@classroom.net.
Contact: Ann Mead Ash, Editor.
Desc: Contributes how-to articles intended to assist physicians and their office staff with all issues relating to practice management. Covers topics such as collections, scheduling, marketing, telephone management, and customer relations. *Type:* Newsletter.

Doctor's Shopper

Marketing Communications, Inc.
1086 Remsen Ave.   Ph: (718)257-8484
Brooklyn, NY 11236-3452   Fax: (718)257-8845
Contact: Ralph Selitzer, Editor and Publisher.
Desc: Magazine for physicians. *Type:* Periodical.

Doheny Eye Institute

1450 San Pablo St.   Ph: (323)442-6600
Los Angeles, CA 90033   Fax: (323)442-6688
E-mail: sryan@hsc.usc.edu
URL: http://www.usc.edu/hsc/doheny
Contact: Stephen J. Ryan, MD, Pres.
Desc: Eyebank, medical clinic group, tonography, electrophysiology, laser surgery center, contact lenses and ocular research facilities for experimental pathology, tissue culture, molecular biology, morphometry, and biostatistics. *Type:* Research center.

Donald Guthrie Foundation for Education and Research

1 Guthrie Sq.   Ph: (717)882-4620
Sayre, PA 18840   Fax: (717)882-5151
E-mail: raronstam@inet.guthrie.org
Contact: Dr. Robert Aronstam, Sci.Dir.
Desc: Cell communication and signal transduction and clinical research in immunology, virology, cancer biology, lung cancer, and neuroscience. *Type:* Research center.

Dorothea Dix Hospital

Clinical Research Unit

809 Ruggles Dr.   Ph: (919)733-5228
Raleigh, NC 27603   Fax: (919)733-5351
E-mail: jlieberman@css.unc.edu
Contact: Jeffery Lieberman, MD, Dir.
Desc: Conducts inpatient and outpatient clinical research on the neuroendocrinology, neurobiology, and psychopharmacology of affective disorders, alcoholism, and schizophrenia. Examines behavioral and endocrine effects of neuropeptides in healthy human subjects and investigates biological risk factors of alcoholism using young adults without the disease but with a history of familial alcoholism. *Type:* Research center.

Dry Eye and Tear Research Center

Regions Hospital   Ph: (651)221-8745
Dept. of Ophthalmology   Fax: (651)292-4040
640 Jackson St.
St. Paul, MN 55101
E-mail: jdnelson@mis2.sprmc.healthpartners.com
Contact: J. Daniel Nelson, MD, Dir.
Desc: Basic and clinical studies of dry eye and tearing disorders, focusing on ocular surface diseases, the effects of chemicals and nutrients on corneal epithelium, and the role of hormones in the development of dry eye states. *Type:* Research center.

Duke University

Eye Center

PO Box 3802   Ph: (252)684-5365
Durham, NC 27710   Fax: (252)684-2230
Contact: David Epstein, MD, Ch.
Desc: Eye disorders, with special focus on retinal detachment, corneal diseases, and proliferative diabetic retinopathy. *Type:* Research center.

Duke University

F.G. Hall Hyper-Hypo-Baric Center

Med. Ctr.   Ph: (252)684-5514
Box 3823   Fax: (252)684-6002
Durham, NC 27710
E-mail: benne005@mc.duke.edu
Contact: Dr. Peter B. Bennett, Sr.Dir.
Desc: Hypobaric and hyperbaric medicine and physiology, including studies of how increased hydrostatic pressure affects cells, tissues, organs, and intact organisms; studies of morphological and metabolic effects of oxygen pressures; clinical investigations of use of hyperbaric oxygen therapy; study of effects of pressure on respiratory and cardiovascular systems and thermal homeostasis; and investigations of causes, mechanisms, and prevention of effects of decompression sickness. *Type:* Research center.

Duke University

General Clinical Research Center

Med. Ctr.   Ph: (252)684-3806
Box 3854   Fax: (252)684-5041
Durham, NC 27710
E-mail: marke00l@mc.duke.edu
URL: http://www.duke.edu/rankincru/
Contact: Dr. M. Louise Markert, Prog.Dir.
Desc: Multidisciplinary, clinical research into the cause, progression, prevention, control, and cure of human disease. Sample projects have studied immunodeficiency diseases, Alzheimer's disease, food allergy, X-linked hypophosphatemic rickets, and cardiovascular disease. *Type:* Research center.

Duke University

Pediatric Asthma and Allergic Disease Center

Med. Ctr.   Ph: (919)684-2922
Box 2898   Fax: (919)681-7979
Durham, NC 27710
E-mail: buckl003@mcduke.edu
Contact: Rebecca H. Buckley, Chf. of Div.
Desc: As a unit of NIAID, the Center seeks to integrate the concepts of immunology, genetics, biochemistry, and pharmacology into clinical investigations of patients with asthma and allergic diseases. Specific projects include studies on immunoregulation in atopic eczema and in vitro studies of human immunoglobulin E (IgE) synthesis, including lymphocyte phenotypes and their function in humans with allergic diseases and excessively high IgE antibody production. *Type:* Research center.

Dwight David Eisenhower Army Medical Center

Department of Clinical Investigation

Bldg. 300   Ph: (706)787-4273
Fort Gordon, GA 30905-5650   Fax: (706)787-5216
E-mail: kentplowmn@aol.com
Contact: Col. Kent M. Plowman, MC, Ch.
Desc: Osteomyelitis in rat tibias, fibroblast attachment to teeth, periodontal implants, pharmacotherapy in burns, hormonal influence of bone growth, synthetic bone grafting materials, wound healing, and markers for malignancy. *Type:* Research center.

ECRI

Ed Stevenson, Communications Dept.
5200 Butler Pke.   Ph: (610)825-6000
Plymouth Meeting, PA 19462   Fax: (610)834-1275
E-mail: info@ecri.org
Contact: Joel J. Nobel, M.D., Pres.
Desc: Improves the safety, performance, reliability, and cost effectiveness of health care technology through research testing, and publication of results. *Type:* Association.

Electrophysiology Research Foundation

33 Fairway Dr.
Green Brook, NJ 08812-2064
E-mail: eprf@aol.com
Contact: Sanjeev Saksena, MD, Dir.
Desc: Medical education and research. *Type:* Research center.

Ellen Gregg Ingalls Eye Research Institute

700 S. 18th St., Ste. 300   Ph: (205)325-8507
Birmingham, AL 35233   Fax: (205)325-8654
Contact: Harold W. Skalka, MD, Chm.
Desc: Ophthalmic research, including laboratory and clinical research into causes and treatment of cataract formation, ocular metabolism, corneal diseases, and systemic diseases involving the eye. *Type:* Research center.

Emory University

Laboratory for Ophthalmic Research

1365-B Clifton Rd.   Ph: (404)778-4100
Atlanta, GA 30322   Fax: (404)778-4143
E-mail: ophthfe@emory.edu
URL: http://www.emory.edu
Contact: Dr. Henry F. Edelhauser, Dir.
Desc: Various biochemical, pathobiochemical, physiological, and pathophysiological aspects of fundamental causes of blindness-producing diseases, especially cataract, glaucoma, retinal detachment, diabetes, and diabetic vasculopathy. Maintains strong clinical liaison in research programming. *Type:* Research center.

Emory University

W. Dean Warren Clinical Research Center

Sch. of Med.   Ph: (404)712-7258
1364 Clifton Rd. Suite GG23   Fax: (404)727-5563
Atlanta, GA 30322
E-mail: L.Harker@emory.edu
Contact: Laurence Harker, Dir.
Desc: Disorders of amino acid, and protein metabolism; branch-chain ketoacid abnormalities; mitochondrial myopathies; clinical nutrition; energy metabolism; metabolic consequences of diabetes and obesity; effects of low protein diets and blood pressure control on the progression of renal disease; and growth disorders. *Type:* Research center.

Encyclopedia of Medical Organizations and Agencies

Gale Group Inc.
27500 Drake Rd.   Ph: (248)699-4253
Farmington Hills, MI 48331-   Free: 800-877-GALE
3535   Fax: (248)699-8070
E-mail: galeord@galegroup.com
URL: http://www.galegroup.com.; http://www.gale.com.
Contact: Lynn Pearce, Editor; Caryn Anders, Editor.
Desc: Over 16,800 state, national, and international medical associations, foundations, research institutes, federal and state agencies, and medical and allied health schools. *Type:* Directory.

Endocrine Society
4350 East West Hwy., Ste. 500   Ph: (301)941-0200
Bethesda, MD 20814   Fax: (301)941-0259
URL: http://www.endo-society.org

Contact: Scott Hunt, Exec.Dir.

Desc: Promotes excellence in research, education, and clinical practice in endocrinology and related disciplines. *Type:* Association.

Endocrinology Research Laboratory
Cabrini Med. Ctr.   Ph: (212)995-7081
247 3rd Ave.
New York, NY 10010

Contact: Dr. Leonid Poretsky, Dir.

Desc: Effects of insulin and insulin-like growth factors on ovarian function. Focuses on expression and regulation of insulin receptors and type I IGF receptors in human ovarian cells. *Type:* Research center.

Endometriosis Association
8585 N. 76th Pl.   Ph: (414)355-2200
Milwaukee, WI 53223   Free: 800-992-3636
   Fax: (414)355-6065
E-mail: endo@endometriosisassn.org
URL: http://www.endometriosisassn.org

Contact: Mary Lou Ballweg, Exec.Dir.

Desc: Women who have endometriosis and others interested in the condition. (Endometriosis is a disorder in which endometrial tissue, which lines the uterus, is also found in other locations in the body, usually the abdomen. Symptoms can include extremely painful menstruation, infertility, painful sexual intercourse, and heavy or irregular bleeding.) Disseminates information on the treatment, research, and attitudes concerning endometriosis. *Type:* Association.

EnVision
The Lighthouse National Center for Vision and Child Development
111 E. 59th St.   Ph: (212)821-9200
New York, NY 10022   Free: 800-829-0500
   Fax: (212)821-9705
E-mail: mbeck@lighthouse.org

Desc: Contains articles relating to vision loss in children and adolescents. *Type:* Newsletter.

Epi Notes
Epidemiology Division
North Carolina Department of Health and Human Services
PO Box 29601   Ph: (919)733-3419
Raleigh, NC 27627-0601   Fax: (919)733-0490

Contact: Hazel King, Editor.

Desc: Contains excerpts from epidemiologic studies and related feature articles. *Type:* Newsletter.

Epilepsy Foundation
4351 Garden City Dr.   Ph: (301)459-3700
Landover, MD 20785   Free: 800-EFA-1000
   Fax: (301)577-4941
E-mail: info@efa.org
URL: http://www.efa.org

Contact: Eric R. Hargis, Chief Exec.

Desc: National voluntary health agency which serves as the "focal point for the fight against epilepsy in the United States." Augmented by 64 affiliates in the U.S. committed to preventing and controlling epilepsy and improving the lives of those who have it. Provides federal government liaison. *Type:* Association.

Epilepsy Wellness Newsletter
Epilepsy Wellness Newsletter
1462 W. 5th Ave.   Ph: (541)686-9125
Eugene, OR 97402
E-mail: ewnmurphy@aol.com.

Contact: Patricia Murphy, Editor and Publisher.

Desc: Acts as a forum for people with epilepsy. Reports on issues and alternative treatments. *Type:* Newsletter.

Eye-Bank for Sight Restoration
120 Wall St.   Ph: (212)742-9000
New York, NY 10005-3902   Fax: (212)269-3139
E-mail: askus@.ebsr.org

Contact: Mary Jane O'Neill, Exec.Dir.

Desc: Collection and distribution of eye tissue to the scientific community. *Type:* Research center.

Eye Institute of New Jersey
New Jersey Medical School   Ph: (973)972-2050
90 Bergen St., 6th Fl.
Newark, NJ 07103
E-mail: heinrige@umdnj.edu

Contact: George F. Heinrich, MD, Pres.

Desc: Ophthalmology, including cornea, retina, uveitis, glaucoma, pediatric ophthalmolgy, and neuro-ophthalmology. *Type:* Research center.

F-D-C Reports
FDC Reports, Inc.
5550 Friendship Blvd., Suite 1   Ph: (301)657-9830
Chevy Chase, MD 20815
E-mail: fdcr@clark.net
URL: http://www.fdcreports.com

Contact: Wayne Rhodes.

Desc: Contains information related to the business, financial, and legal aspects of the health care and chemical industries. *Available:* The Dialog Corporation, DataStar; The Dialog Corporation, DIALOG; The Dialog Corporation, DIALOG; Ovid Technologies, Inc.; Ovid Technologies, Inc. *Type:* Database.

Family Health International
PO Box 13950   Ph: (919)544-7040
Research Triangle Park, NC   Fax: (919)544-7261
27709
E-mail: brobinson@fhi.org
URL: http://www.fhi.org

Contact: Dr. Willard Cates, Jr., Pres.

Desc: New contraceptive technology, contraceptive acceptability, contraceptive effectiveness and safety, breast-feeding practices, maternal/child health, demography, interventions to reduce the transmission of sexually transmitted diseases and AIDS, economics of family planning and financing of AIDS programming. Operates the Implementing AISA Prevention and Care (IMPACT), which seeks to support the local capacity of developing countries to prevent and control HIV. *Type:* Research center.

Family Physician
Illinois Academy of Family Physicians
4756 Main St.   Ph: (630)435-0257
Lisle, IL 60532   Fax: (630)435-0433
E-mail: iafp@ameritech.net

Contact: Christine Emerson, Editor; Kristen Lindstrom, Advertising Dir.

Desc: Professional newsletter for members of the Illinois Academy of Family Physicians. *Type:* Newsletter.

Family Practice Management
American Academy of Family Physicians
8880 Ward Pkwy.   Ph: (816)333-9700
Kansas City, MO 64114   Free: 800-274-2237
   Fax: (816)333-9855
E-mail: fp@aafp.org; fpmedit@aafp.org.
URL: http://www.aafp.org/family/fpm/index.html.

Contact: Clayton Raker Hasser, Publisher; Robert Edsall, Editor-in-Chief, bedsall@aafp.org.

Desc: Magazine covering socio-economic and management topics concerning family physicians. *Type:* Periodical.

Family Practice Recertification
Family Practice Recertification
241 Forsgate Dr.   Ph: (732)656-1140
Jamesburg, NJ 08831   Fax: (732)656-0059
E-mail: mrapub@aol.com.

Contact: Jane C. Monaghan, Editor; Lisa M. Greene, Advertising Dir., (914)722-7681, fax: (914)722-7686.

Desc: Medical magazine. *Type:* Periodical.

FDA News
Technomic Publishing Co., Inc.
851 New Holland Ave.   Ph: (717)291-5609
Box 3535   Free: 800-233-9936
Lancaster, PA 17604-3535   Fax: (717)295-4538
E-mail: customer@techpub.com
URL: http://www.techpub.com

Contact: Dr. Y.H. Hui, Editor-in-Chief; Lori Eby, Managing Editor.

Desc: Reports on major FDA announcements, as well as recalls and field corrections for drugs, cosmetics, devices, and biologics. *Type:* Newsletter.

FDA Surveillance Index for Pesticides
National Technical Information Service (NTIS)
U.S. Department of Commerce
5285 Port Royal Rd.   Ph: (703)605-6000
Springfield, VA 22161-0001   Free: 800-553-NTIS
   Fax: (703)605-6900
E-mail: orders@ntis.fedworld.gov

Desc: Alerts readers to the potential health risks of dietary exposure to individual pesticides. Provides an evaluation that includes FDA monitoring results; chemical, biological, and toxicological data; and usage estimates. *Type:* Newsletter.

Federation of State Medical Boards of the United States
Federation Pl.   Ph: (817)868-4000
400 Fuller Wiser Rd., Ste. 300   Fax: (817)868-4097
Euless, TX 76039-3855
E-mail: fsmb@fsmb.org
URL: http://www.fsmb.org

Contact: Dr. James Winn, M.D., Exec.VP.

Desc: State medical examining and licensing boards (including fourteen osteopathic boards). *Type:* Association.

The Female Patient
Quadrant HealthCom Inc.
26 Main St.   Ph: (973)701-8900
Chatham, NJ 07928-2402   Fax: (973)701-8894

Contact: Kathy McShea, Group Publisher, (973)701-2744, fax: (973)701-8894, kathy.mcshea@qhc.com; Caroline Tredway, Group Editor, (973)701-2776, fax: (973)701-8895, caroline.tredway@qhc.com.

Desc: Medical journal. *Type:* Periodical.

Fertility Research Foundation
877 Park Ave.   Ph: (212)744-5500
New York, NY 10021   Fax: (212)744-6536
E-mail: frfbaby@msn.com

Contact: Masood Khatamee, MD, Exec.Dir.

Desc: Fertility and human reproduction, including studies on microsurgery, fertilization, fallopian tube transplant, artificial embryonation, education and prevention of human infertility, in vitro fertilization gender selection, therapeutic donor insemination, and counselling. *Type:* Research center.

Fibromyalgia Alliance of America

PO Box 21990   Ph: (614)457-4222
Columbus, OH 43221-0990   Free: 888-717-6711
    Fax: (614)457-2729
E-mail: masaathoff@aol.com
Contact: Mary Anne Saathoff, R.N., Pres.

Desc: Individuals with fibromyalgia, their families and friends, health care professionals. (Fibromyalgia is a chronic condition of severe muscle aching and severe fatigue, along with a sleep disorder. Pain can be sharp and stabbing and appears in muscles, tendons, and ligaments. Treatments are often ineffective; the condition can be functionally disabling.). Serves as an international informational clearinghouse on fibromyalgia. *Type:* Association.

Fibromyalgia Network Newsletter

Health Information Network, Inc.
PO Box 31750   Fax: (520)290-5550
Tucson, AZ 85751-1750
URL: http://www.fmnetnews.com.
Contact: Kristin Thorson, President; Sonja Diaz, Project Coord.

Desc: Seeks to educate the public on Fibromyalgia Syndrome and Chronic Fatigue Syndrome and related conditions. Recurring features include news of research and book reviews. *Type:* Newsletter.

Florida Institute of Technology
Life Science Research Complex

3325 W. New Haven Ave.   Ph: (407)768-8000
Melbourne, FL 32904-3521   Fax: (407)984-8461
E-mail: jthomas@fit.edu
Contact: John Thomas, Contact.

Desc: Armadillo-leprosy animal model program and related laboratory studies: development and evaluation of specialty products and techniques for rapidly diagnosing infectious agents, conversion of biomass to fuels; development of marketable products from phosphate wastes. *Type:* Research center.

Foundation for Research in Infectious Diseases

PO Box 2734
Saratoga, CA 95070
Contact: Ruth Walzer, Pres.

Desc: Infectious diseases, particularly invasive mycoses. *Type:* Research center.

Franciscan Shared Laboratory, Inc.

Med. Science Labortories   Ph: (414)476-3400
11020 W. Plank Ct., Ste. 100   Fax: (414)256-5589
Wauwatosa, WI 53226
Contact: Dr. W. Hollister, Med.Dir.

Desc: Diagnostic and molecular virology, coagulation, molecular biology, and medical informatics. *Type:* Research center.

Frontier Science and Technology Research Foundation

1244 Boylston St.   Ph: (617)632-2000
Chestnut Hill, MA 02167   Fax: (617)632-2001
E-mail: fstrf@fstrf.org
URL: http://www.fstrf.org
Contact: Dr. Marvin Zelen, Contact.

Desc: Conducts joint research projects with cooperative clinical trial groups and other organizations. Provides biostatistical support and collaboration, data management and processing, project management, and administrative support to researchers. *Type:* Research center.

Gage Occupational and Environmental Health Unit

223 College St.   Ph: (416)978-5883
Toronto, ON, Canada M5T   Fax: (416)978-2608
1R4
URL: http://www.utoronto.ca/occmed/
Contact: Dr. Linn Holness, Actg.Dir.

Desc: Lung problems related to asthma, bronchitis, and occupational and environmental pollution. Areas of interest include development of more effective treatment for adult asthmatics, connection between asthma and air pollution, acute effects of second-hand tobacco smoke on asthmatics and other people, predictability of asthma outcome, occupational asthma, effects of indoor environments on human comfort and health, and environmental sensitivity. *Type:* Research center.

Gamble Program for Clinical Studies

Children's Hospital Med. Ctr.   Ph: (513)636-7490
333 Burnet Ave., CH1   Fax: (513)636-7682
Cincinnati, OH 45229-3039
E-mail: schigo@chmcc.org
URL: http://www.chmcc.org
Contact: Gilbert M. Schiff, MD, Dir.

Desc: Virology and immunology, including studies on rubella and rubella vaccines, anti-influenza agents, basic virology of influenza, herpes virus latency, role of complement in sickle cell disease and burn wounds, and basic and clinical studies on rotaviruses, hepatitis, and human immunodeficiency virus. *Type:* Research center.

Garfield G. Duncan Research Foundation, Inc.

829 Spruce St.   Ph: (215)829-3426
Philadelphia, PA 19107-5752   Fax: (215)928-9150
E-mail: diabetes@libertynet.org
URL: http://www.libertynet.org/~diabetes
Contact: Theodore G. Duncan, MD, Dir.

Desc: Diabetes. *Type:* Research center.

George Washington University
Center for Virology, Immunology and Infectious Disease Research

Children's National Medical   Ph: (202)884-3981
Center   Fax: (202)884-3985
111 Michigan Ave. NW
Washington, DC 20010
E-mail: chhollan@cnmc.org
Contact: Dr. Christie A. Holland, Dir.

Desc: Virologic and immunologic problems relating to infectious diseases and vaccine development, hospital acquired nosocomial infections. *Type:* Research center.

Georgetown University
International Center for Interdisciplinary Studies of Immunology

318 Kober-Cogan Bldg.   Ph: (202)687-8227
3800 Reservoir Rd. NW   Fax: (202)784-3597
Washington, DC 20007
E-mail: bellantij@gunet.georgetown.edu
Contact: Joseph A. Bellanti, MD, Dir.

Desc: Immunobiology, immunochemistry, immunogenetics, immunopharmacology, and immunopathology, including the clinical disciplines of allergy and immunology, infectious diseases, respiratory diseases, and disorders of immune regulation. The center's program emphasizes pediatrics. *Type:* Research center.

Georgetown University
Kennedy Institute of Ethics

Poulton Hall, Rm. 222   Ph: (202)687-6774
Washington, DC 20057   Fax: (202)687-8089
E-mail: veatchr@guvay.georgetown.edu

URL: http://www.georgetown.edu
Contact: Dr. Leroy Walters, Dir.

Desc: Social and ethical issues in biomedical sciences, such as resource allocation in health care, human experimentation, genetic engineering, euthanasia, death and dying, reproductive technologies, physician-patient relations, in vitro fertilization, abortion, and organ transplantation. Also researches other fields of applied ethics--international relations, government, law, journalism, business, and technology policy. *Type:* Research center.

Georgia Institute of Technology
Parker H. Petit Institute for Bioengineering and Bioscience

281 Ferst Dr.   Ph: (404)894-2768
Atlanta, GA 30332-0363   Fax: (404)894-2291
E-mail: robert.nerem@ibb.gatech.edu
URL: http://www.bioeng.gatech.edu
Contact: Prof. Robert M. Nerem, PhD, Dir.

Desc: Biomechanics research, including biaxial mechanical properties in tissue, biomechanical design, cardiovascular fluid mechanics, cellular engineering and non-invasive blood flow measurement; tissue engineering; and bioelectrical research, including electromagnetic systems for measuring the electrical properties of tissue, medical device/systems for diagnostic and therapeutic applications, and the applications of either air- or wire-coupled electromagnetic energy to stimulate biofunction; rehabilitation research, which entails developing orthotic devices for patients with lower body dysfunction, evaluating functional electrostimulation, and observance of the parvocellular division of the red nucleus for analyzing movement control; and computer applications research, which involves signal processing, image processing, and visualization, medical informatics, and simulation techniques to assist in making decisions regarding diagnostic and therapeutic strategies. *Type:* Research center.

Glaucoma Laser Trabeculoplasty Study

Sinai Hospital of Detroit   Ph: (248)353-1750
Franklin Eye Consultants   Fax: (248)353-7645
29275 Northwestern Hwy., Ste. 100
Southfield, MI 48034
Contact: Hugh Beckman, MD, Chm.

Desc: Examines the effectiveness and safety of argon laser trabeculoplasty as compared to traditional topical therapy in the treatment of newly diagnosed open-angle glaucoma. *Type:* Research center.

Graduate Hospital Research Center

415 S. 19th St.   Ph: (215)893-2000
Philadelphia, PA 19146   Fax: (215)893-4178
Contact: Dr. Robert H. Cox, Dir.

Desc: Major health problems, including heart disease, lung disease, neurological disorders, and cancer. Studies include hypertension, emphysema, Parkinson's disease, epilepsy, psychological evaluations, and gene therapy. *Type:* Research center.

The Gray Sheet

FDC Reports, Inc.
5550 Friendship Blvd., Suite 1   Ph: (301)657-9830
Chevy Chase, MD 20815
E-mail: fdcr@clark.net
URL: http://www.fdcreports.com
Desc: Monitors regulatory developments for medical devices and diagnostics at the Food and Drug Administration's Center for Devices & Radiological Health, as well as policies and congressional reform initiatives concerning pre-market approvals, 510(k) exemptions, and related policies. Also covers product innovations and industry news, including start-ups, financing deals, international develop-

ments, technology reimbursement, and other industry activities. *Available:* LEXIS-NEXIS, LEXIS; The Dialog Corporation, DIALOG; The Dialog Corporation, DIALOG; Ovid Technologies, Inc.; Ovid Technologies, Inc. *Type:* Database.

Hahnemannian Research Center, Inc.
18818 Teller Ave., Ste. 230   Ph: (949)852-9038
Irvine, CA 92612   Fax: (949)852-1353
E-mail: laiushshm@aol.com
Contact: Kattunilathu Oommen George, MD, Dir.
Desc: Homeopathic medicine and education, including biochemical analysis, micronutrition, Mother Tincture development, structural and degenerative studies, and deficiency detection (electromagnetic disturbances) with attention given to the emotional, mental, and physical aspects. *Type:* Research center.

Hamot Medical Center

Research Center
Hamot Prof. Bldg.   Ph: (814)877-6026
104 E. 2nd St.   Fax: (814)877-5089
Erie, PA 16507
E-mail: phyllis.kuhn@hamot.org
Contact: Phyllis Kuhn, PhD, Dir.
Desc: Drug evaluations, medical devices and diagnostic products, orthopedics, infection control, and microbiology. *Type:* Research center.

HANYS News
Healthcare Association of New York State (HANYS)
74 N. Pearl St.   Ph: (518)431-7600
Albany, NY 12207   Fax: (518)431-7915
E-mail: info@hanys.org
URL: http://www.hanys.org.
Desc: Presents articles on health care issues. Recurring features include reports of meetings. *Type:* Newsletter.

Harrington Arthritis Research Center
300 N. 18 St.   Ph: (602)254-0377
Phoenix, AZ 85006   Fax: (602)253-4817
E-mail: harcbonc@nonlinc.com
URL: http://www.arde.comm/harc
Contact: Robert L. Case, Dir.
Desc: Arthritis, including research and education on assistive devices, joint repair and microbial involvement. *Type:* Research center.

Harvard University

Berman-Gund Laboratory for the Study of Retinal Degenerations
Massachusetts Eye & Ear   Ph: (617)573-3600
   Infirmary   Fax: (617)573-3216
243 Charles St.
Boston, MA 02114
Contact: Eliot L. Berson, MD, Dir.
Desc: Effects of nutrition and light on the retina, gene detection of different forms of retinitis pigmentosa and gene therapy for animal models of hereditary retinal degenerations, human age-related macular degeneration. *Type:* Research center.

Hauptman-Woodward Medical Research Institute, Inc.
73 High St.   Ph: (716)856-9600
Buffalo, NY 14203-1196   Fax: (716)852-6086
E-mail: hauptman@hwi.buffalo.edu
URL: http://www.hwi.buffalo.edu
Contact: Herbert A. Hauptman, PhD, Pres.
Desc: Conducts research in molecular endocrinology to determine molecularstructures of biologically important

small and macromolecular compounds, to correlate the structures with their biological activities, and to elucidate the mechanism of hormone biosynthesis. Also has programs in space- and ground-based crystal growth and phasing methods in macromolecular structure determination. *Type:* Research center.

Health Canada

Health Protection Branch
Tunney's Pasture   Ph: (613)957-1804
Ottawa, ON, Canada K1A 0L2   Fax: (613)957-3954
E-mail: jlosos@hpb.hwc.ca
URL: http://www.hc-sc.gc.ca
Contact: Kent R. Foster, Asst.Dep.Min.
Desc: Toxicological, microbiological, and medical device research to establish the safety of the nation's foods, drugs, medical devices, to determine the toxic effects of environmental contaminants in air, water, and the work place, and to support public health disease control measures. Areas of expertise include reproductive toxicology, microbiology, chemical carcinogenesis, radiation physics, genotoxicity, behavioral toxicology, immunotoxicology, neurotoxicology, biochemical toxicology, and pathology. *Type:* Research center.

The Healthcare Forum
425 Market St., 16th Fl.   Ph: (415)356-4200
San Francisco, CA 94105   Fax: (415)421-8837
URL: http://www.thfnet.org
Contact: Kathryn E. Johnson, CEO & Pres.
Desc: Individuals and organizational leaders worldwide. *Type:* Association.

Health Devices® Alerts
ECRI
5200 Butler Pike   Ph: (610)825-6000
Plymouth Meeting, PA 19462
E-mail: info@ecri.org
URL: http://www.ecri.org
Contact: Beth Richardson, (610)825-6000 x370.
Desc: Contains information on reported medical device problems, hazards, recalls, technology assessments, evaluations, and updates. Includes citations, with abstracts, to English-language medical, legal, and technical literature, Action Items (AI) that ECRI has investigated, Problem Reporting Program (PRP) records from the U.S. Food and Drug Administration (FDA) voluntary reporting program, and Medical Device Reporting (MDR) records from the FDA's mandatory reporting system. *Available:* The Dialog Corporation, DIALOG. *Type:* Database.

Health Devices® Sourcebook
ECRI
5200 Butler Pike   Ph: (610)825-6000
Plymouth Meeting, PA 19462
E-mail: info@ecri.org
URL: http://www.ecri.org
Contact: Eileen Sykes, (610)825-6000.
Desc: Provides information on North American manufacturers, importers, and distributors of more than 30,000 new medical devices and equipment. Also includes service companies that buy, sell, and repair used equipment. *Available:* The Dialog Corporation, DIALOG; DIMDI (Deutsches Institut fuer Medizinische Dokumentation und Information). *Type:* Database.

Health Industry Today
The Business Word
5350 S. Roslyn St., Ste. 400   Ph: (303)967-0130
Englewood, CO 80111-2125   Free: 800-328-3211
   Fax: (303)290-9025
Contact: Donald E.L. Johnson, Publisher; Curt Werner, Managing Editor.

Desc: Discusses issues of interest to health industry manufacturers. Covers such topics as market trends, product strategies, industry news, and market analysis. *Type:* Newsletter.

Health Information Management Across the Continuum
Opus Communications
100 Hoods Ln.   Ph: (781)639-1872
PO Box 1168   Free: 800-650-6787
Marblehead, MA 01945   Fax: (781)639-2982
E-mail: customer_service@opuscomm.com
URL: http://www.opuscomm.com
Desc: Provides information on requirements and successful practices related to health information management in home care, ambulatory care, physician's offices, long-term care facilities, subacute care, rehabilitation units, and assisted living. *Type:* Newsletter.

The Health Strategist
U.S. Lifeline, Inc.
PO Box 1087   Ph: (717)243-3293
Carlisle, PA 17013   Fax: (717)243-1810
E-mail: info@uslifeline.com
Contact: Patrick Michael Plummer, Editor and Publisher; Kimberly J. Largent, Editor, kjlargent@uslifeline.com.
Desc: Delivers information and insights on today's toughest issues confronting health care executives at all levels within the supply chain. Facilitates communication between suppliers and providers; illuminates trends through a monthly poll; and provides strategies for an industry in reform. *Type:* Newsletter.

Health Volunteers Overseas
PO Box 65157, Washington   Ph: (202)296-0928
   Sta.   Fax: (202)296-8018
Washington, DC 20035-5157
E-mail: hvo@aol.com
Contact: Nancy Kelly, Exec.Dir.
Desc: Physicians, dentists, nurses, and physical therapists. Works to improve health care in developing countries through the participation of trained health and medical volunteers. *Type:* Association.

Healthcare Convention & Exhibitors Association—Association Alert
Healthcare Convention & Exhibitors Association
5775 Peachtree Dunwoody Rd.,   Ph: (404)252-3663
   Ste. 500G   Fax: (404)252-0774
Atlanta, GA 30342
E-mail: hcea@assnhq.com
Contact: Mary Anderson, Editor, manderson@assnhq.com.
Desc: Disseminates information to health care associations, exhibitors, and their Exhibitors Advisory Councils (EAC). Reports on EAC accomplishments, highlighting innovative ideas and focusing on specific problems and solutions pertaining the effective display of health care products. *Type:* Newsletter.

Healthcare Forum
425 Market St., 16th Fl.   Ph: (415)356-4400
San Francisco, CA 94105   Fax: (415)356-9300
URL: http://www.thfnet.org
Contact: Kathryn E. Johnson, CEO & Pres.
Desc: Healthcare leaders and executives. Promotes visionary leadership and motivation in healthcare. *Type:* Association.

Medical

Heartbeat of St. Joseph's Medical Center
St. Joseph's Medical Center
523 N Third St.
Brainerd, MN 56401
URL: http://www.stjosephsmedicalctr.com.
Contact: Barb K. Anderson, Contact; Melody L. Banks, Contact.
Desc: Provides health information *Type:* Newsletter.

Heimlich Institute
2368 Victory Pkwy., Ste. 410   Ph: (513)221-0002
Cincinnati, OH 45206   Fax: (513)221-0003
E-mail: heimlich@lglou.com
Contact: Henry J. Heimlich, MD, Pres.
Desc: Malaria therapy for cancer and Lyme disease, rehabilitation of swallowing, and transtracheal oxygen therapy for chronic lung diseases, including oxygen-dependent emphysema, black lung, cystic fibrosis, and interstitial fibrosis. Developments include Heimlich Maneuver for choking and drowning, Heimlich chest drainage valve, Heimlich Micro-Trach, and Heimlich operation for esophageal replacement. *Type:* Research center.

Hektoen Institute for Medical Research
627 S. Wood St., Ste. 201   Ph: (312)738-3100
Chicago, IL 60612-3810   Fax: (312)738-3102
E-mail: LabHektoen@aol.com
URL: http://www.hektoen.org
Contact: Peter Friedell, MD, Chm.
Desc: Medicine and surgery, including laboratory and clinical studies in cancer metabolism, kidney disease, virology, hematology, microbiology, bacteriology, endocrinology, pediatric cardiology, neurology, immunology, pathology, gastroenterology, orthopedic surgery, congenital heart diseases, infectious diseases, and hypertension. Specific investigations include treatment of cancer by new modalities, incidence of perinatal mortality and effect of neonatal care, metabolic aspects of renal disease, cell surface alterations in cancer and their effects on metastasis, effects of different hormones in breast carcinoma, influence of hormone receptors on several varieties of soft tissue sarcomas and malignant melanomas, and the immunological aspects of prostatic cancer. *Type:* Research center.

Helen Hayes Hospital
Regional Bone Center
Helen Hayes Hospital   Ph: (914)947-3000
Rte. 9W   Fax: (914)786-4878
West Haverstraw, NY 10993
E-mail: dwd1@columbia.edu
Contact: David W. Dempster, PhD, Dir.
Desc: Bone and calcium metabolism, including pathophysiology of bone and clinical research on the pathogenesis and treatment of diseases such as osteoporosis, primary hyperparathyroidism, and Paget's disease. Conducts calciotropic hormone assays, bone biopsies and histomorphometry, and bone mass measurements. *Type:* Research center.

Helen Keller International
90 Washington St., 15th Fl.   Ph: (212)943-0890
New York, NY 10006   Fax: (212)943-1220
E-mail: llore@hki.org
URL: http://www.hki.org
Contact: John M. Palmer, Pres.
Desc: Etiology, prevalence, incidence, and treatment of xerophthalmia (nutritional blindness), trachoma, cataract, onchocerciasis (river blindness), and other eye diseases in developing nations. Research and technical assistance conducted in Bangladesh, Bolivia, Brazil, Burkina Faso, Cambodia, Cameroon, China, Cote d'Ivoire, Dominican Republic, Ecuador, Eritirea, Ghana, Haiti, Honduras, India, Indonesia, Mali, Mexico, Morocco, Mozambique, Nepal, Niger, Nigeria, The Philippines, Sierra Leone, South Africa, Tanzania, United States, Vietnam, and Uzbekistan. *Type:* Research center.

Hemophilia Ontario News
Hemophilia Ontario
60 St. Clair Ave. E., Ste. 308   Ph: (416)972-0641
Toronto, ON, Canada M4T   Free: 888-838-8846
1N5   Fax: (416)972-0307
Desc: "Hemophilia Ontario is commited to improve the quality of life of people affected by hemophilia and related blood conditions, and to work towards a cure." Publishes on current events, new treatments, volunteer update, and advocacy news. Recurring features include news of research, a calendar of events, and job listings. *Type:* Newsletter.

HFM Medical Publications
3283 Casorso Rd.   Ph: (250)868-8603
Ste. 104   Fax: (250)868-8601
Kelowna, BC, Canada V1W
3L6
E-mail: dr.frank@cyberstore.com.
URL: http://www.drfrank.com.
Contact: Dr. Frank MacInnis, Author.
Alt. Contact: 3283 Casorso Rd., Ste. 104, Kelowna, BC, Canada V1W 3L6; telephone: (250)868-8603; fax: (250)868-8601. *Type:* Periodical.

HISTLINE
U.S. National Library of Medicine (NLM)
MEDLARS Management Section
8600 Rockville Pike   Ph: (301)496-3147
Bethesda, MD 20894
URL: http://www.sis.nlm.nih.gov/dirline
Desc: Contains citations to articles, books, conference proceedings and other literature on the history of medicine. Includes works on individuals, institutions, the profession, diseases, drugs, and medical techniques. *Available:* U.S. National Library of Medicine (NLM), TOXNET. *Type:* Database.

Holos Institutes of Health
1328 E. Evergreen   Ph: (417)865-5940
Springfield, MO 65803   Fax: (417)865-6111
E-mail: nshealy@shealyinstitute.com
URL: http://www.shealyinstitute.com
Contact: C. Norman Shealy, MD, Pres.
Desc: Clinical studies in holistic medicine with emphasis on neurochemical profiles and management of biochemical aspects of pain and stress. *Type:* Research center.

Homeopathic Council for Research and Education
50 Park Ave.   Ph: (212)684-2290
New York, NY 10016
Contact: William Bergman, MD, Contact.
Desc: Homeopathy, focusing on research and education. *Type:* Research center.

Horizon
Huntington Society of Canada
13 Water St. N.   Ph: (519)622-1002
Cambridge, ON, Canada N1R   Fax: (519)622-7370
7G6
E-mail: info@hsc-ca.org.
URL: http://www.hsc-ca.org.
Contact: Julie Stauffer, Editor.
Desc: Conveys information about Huntington disease, a hereditary brain disorder. Recurring features include interviews, news of research, a calendar of events, reports of meetings, and news of educational opportunities. *Type:* Newsletter.

Hospital Centre of the University of Montreal Research Centre
3850, rue Saint-Urbain   Ph: (514)843-2700
Montreal, PQ, Canada H2W   Fax: (514)843-2715
1T8
E-mail: hamethdm@ere.umontreal.ca
Contact: Dr. Pavel Hamet, Dir.
Desc: Cardiovascular diseases and hypertension, AIDS, cancer, diabetes and nutrition, pulmonary diseases and anesthesia, major burns, and gene therapy, including cardiovascular biochemistry, cellular biology of hypertension, molecular biology of growth, experimental surgery, oncology surgery, molecular targeting, metabolism and diabetes, respiratory electrophysiology, molecular endocrinology, epidemiology, nuclear medicine, neurobiology, nutrition and cancer, oncology, molecular oncopathology, molecular medicine, clinical pharmacology, pharmacoepidemiology and pharmacoeconomy, respiratory physiology, physiopathology of burns and related aftereffects, pain, microbiology, transplantation, and toxicology. *Type:* Research center.

Hospital for Joint Diseases
Orthopaedic Institute
Musculoskeletal Research Center
301 E. 17th St., 15th Fl.   Ph: (212)598-6567
New York, NY 10003   Fax: (212)598-6096
E-mail: pedicesare@aol.com
URL: http://www.hjd.edu/orthopaedics/mrc.html
Contact: Paul Di Cesare, MD, Dir.
Desc: Prevention and treatment of musculoskeletal diseases, including basic studies of biological and synthetic biomaterials, biomechanics, kinematics, mathematical modeling, arthritis and cartilage repair, and gene therapy. *Type:* Research center.

Hospital for Special Surgery
Research Division
535 E. 70th St.   Ph: (212)606-1480
New York, NY 10021   Fax: (212)717-1192
E-mail: boskeya@hss.edu
URL: http://www.hss.edu
Contact: Adele L. Boskey, PhD, Dir. of Res.
Desc: Orthopedics and rheumatic diseases, including studies on bone, cartilage, connective tissues, immune system, and related areas of musculoskeletal disease. *Type:* Research center.

Hospital for Special Surgery
Research Division
Mineralized Tissues Research Section
535 E. 70th St.   Ph: (212)606-1453
New York, NY 10021   Fax: (212)472-5331
E-mail: boskeya@hss.edu
URL: http://hss.hss.edu/research/mineral.htm
Contact: Adele L. Boskey, PhD, Sect.Hd.
Desc: Mechanisms of calcification and mineralized tissue remodeling, calcium handling by cells, cell and molecular biology of diseases of calcified tissues (including osteoporosis and osteogenesis imperfecta), and the genetics of bone density and IR imaging of connective tissues. *Type:* Research center.

House Ear Institute
2100 W. 3rd St., 5th Fl.   Ph: (213)483-4431
Los Angeles, CA 90057   Fax: (213)483-8789
E-mail: webmaster@hei.org
URL: http://www.hei.org
Contact: James D. Boswell, CEO.
Desc: Cause, treatment, and prevention of hearing and balance disorders, including investigations on cochlear implants and auditory prostheses, electrophysiology, electron microscopy, anatomy, cellular and molecular biology, and psychoacoustics. *Type:* Research center.

Howard and Georgeanna Jones Institute for Reproductive Medicine

601 Colley Ave. Ph: (757)446-5266
Norfolk, VA 23507 Fax: (757)446-5905

Contact: Dr. Gary Hodgen, Pres.

Desc: Human reproduction, including studies of reproductive physiology during the hours and days surrounding fertilization, fertilization process, gametogenesis, neuroendocrinology, ovarian follicular development, gene expression, reproductive toxicology, endocrine control of menstrual cycle, andrology, reproductive immunology, and cancer. *Type:* Research center.

Howard Hughes Medical Institute

4000 Jones Bridge Rd. Ph: (301)215-8855
Chevy Chase, MD 20815-6789 Fax: (301)215-8863
E-mail: potterr@hhmi.org
URL: http://www.hhmi.org

Contact: Purnell W. Choppin, MD, Pres.

Desc: Genetics, immunology, cell biology, structural biology, and neuroscience. Conducts research with scientists and staff at over 70 academic medical centers, hospitals, and universities. *Type:* Research center.

Iatrofon

IATROS
101 Hillside Dr. W Ph: (319)283-3491
Oelwein, IA 50662-2640

Contact: R.S. Jaggard, Editor.

Desc: Provides information for private and independent doctors who wish to practice without governmental involvement. Includes news and letters. *Type:* Newsletter.

Illinois Hospital Research and Educational Foundation

1151 E. Warrenville Rd. Ph: (630)505-7777
PO Box 3015 Fax: (630)505-9457
Naperville, IL 60566-7015
URL: http://www.ihha.org

Contact: Shirley Vukmanic, Contact.

Desc: Medical training and technology. *Type:* Research center.

Immune Deficiency Foundation

25 W. Chesapeake Ave. Ph: (410)321-6647
Towson, MD 21204 Free: 800-296-4433
  Fax: (410)321-9165
E-mail: idf@clark.net
URL: http://www.primaryimmune.org

Contact: Thomas L. Moran, Pres.

Desc: Immune deficiency patients, their families, and medical professionals. Promotes education and research in primary immune deficiency diseases. Holds medical symposia; bestows patient scholarship and research awards. *Type:* Association.

Immunology Abstracts

Cambridge Scientific Abstracts (CSA)
7200 Wisconsin Ave., Ste. 601 Ph: (301)961-6700
Bethesda, MD 20814-4823
E-mail: sales@csa.com
URL: http://www.csa.com

Desc: Contains more than 200,000 citations, with abstracts, to the worldwide literature on immunology relating to both humans and animals. Sources include specialist literature such as journals, books, conference proceedings, and reports. *Type:* Database.

In Brief. . .

Health Industry Manufacturers Association (HIMA)
1200 G St. NW, Ste. 400 Ph: (202)783-8700
Washington, DC 20005 Fax: (202)783-8750
E-mail: inbrief@himanet.com.
URL: http://www.himanet.com.

Contact: John Arnold, Editor.

Desc: Covers regulatory, legislative, and standards activities related to the medical device, health care information systems, and the diagnostic products industries. *Type:* Newsletter.

In Vivo

Windhover Information, Inc.
50 Washington St. Ph: (203)838-4401
Norwalk, CT 06854 Fax: (203)838-3214
E-mail: custserv@windhoverinfo.com

Contact: David Cassak, Editor; Roger Longman, Editor.

Desc: Provides strategic information for senior-level executives at healthcare product companies. Recurring features include interviews, news of research, and columns titled Deal Activity, Executive Changes, Diarist, Around the Industry and Alliance Watch. *Type:* Newsletter.

Independent Citizens Research Foundation for Study of Degenerative Diseases, Inc.

PO Box 97 Ph: (914)591-7090
Ardsley, NY 10502 Fax: (914)591-7090

Contact: Marc Beraday, Dir.

Desc: Causes and treatment of degenerative diseases. Current activities include the study of Acquired Immune Deficiency Syndrome (AIDS) and evaluation and development of calibrated Transcutaneous Electrical Nerve Stimulation (TENS), with focus on pain as related to degenerative diseases. *Type:* Research center.

Indiana University

School of Medicine

Division of Endocrinology and Metabolism

541 N. Clinical Dr. Ph: (317)274-1339
CL 459 Fax: (317)278-0658
Indianapolis, IN 46202-5111
E-mail: abaron@iupui.edu

Contact: Alain D. Baron, MD, Dir.

Desc: Basic and clinical aspects of endocrinology and metabolism, including bone metabolism, alcohol metabolism, role of aldosterone and renin in hypertensive states, and insulin secretion and action. *Type:* Research center.

Indiana University Bloomington

Center for the History of Medicine

Poplars 732-734 Ph: (812)855-4151
Bloomington, IN 47405
URL: http://www.indiana.edu/~rugs/ctrdir/chm.html

Contact: Ann Carmichael, Co-Dir.

Desc: History of medicine. *Type:* Research center.

Indiana University--Northwest

Northwest Center for Medical Education

Sch. of Med. Ph: (219)980-6550
3400 Broadway Fax: (219)980-6566
Gary, IN 46408
E-mail: wbaldwin@meded.iun.indiana.edu
URL: http://www.iun.indiana.edu

Contact: William W. Baldwin, PhD, Dir.

Desc: Diabetes, mitochondria enzymes, lymphocyte activation microvessels, corneal innervation, autonomic nervous system, blood coagulation, neuroglialneuron interactions, membrane-bound transport enzymes, erthrocyte membrane skeletal proteins, avian musculoskeletal funtional morphology, bacterial growth, immunoglobulin molecular biology. *Type:* Research center.

Indiana University-Purdue University at Indianapolis

Center for Human Performance Research

250 N. University Blvd. Ph: (317)274-3432
Indianapolis, IN 46202
URL: http://www.indiana.edu/~rugs/ctrdir/chpr.html

Contact: Jeffrey E. Edwards, Dir.

Desc: Exercise science, including the measurement of energy expenditure during physical activity. *Type:* Research center.

Indiana University-Purdue University at Indianapolis

Diabetes Research and Training Center

RG, 5th Fl. Ph: (317)630-6375
Indianapolis, IN 46202
URL: http://www.indiana.edu/~rugs/ctrdir/drtc.html

Contact: Charles M. Clark, Dir.

Desc: Diabetes mellitus treatment and prevention. *Type:* Research center.

Indiana University-Purdue University at Indianapolis

General Clinical Research Center

550 N. University Blvd. Ph: (317)274-4356
Indianapolis, IN 46202 Fax: (317)274-7346
E-mail: mpeacock@iupui.edu

Contact: Dr. Munro Peacock, Dir.

Desc: Clinical pharmacology, metabolic bone disease, AIDS, alcoholism, diabetes, hypertension, oncologic diseases, cardiac arrhythmias, neuroendocrinology, arthritis, and neonatal metabolism. *Type:* Research center.

Indiana University-Purdue University at Indianapolis

Huntington's Disease Research Roster

Med. Res. & Library Bldg. Ph: (317)274-2241
975 W. Walnut St., IB 130 Fax: (317)274-2387
Indianapolis, IN 46202-5251
E-mail: jgray@medgen.iupui.edu
URL: http://medgen.iupui.edu/divisions/

Contact: P. Michael Conneally, PhD, Dir.

Desc: Facilitates research in Huntington's disease (HD), spinal muscular atrophy, alcoholism, Parkinson Disease, and Alzheimers disease by providing research investigators with statistical and epidemiological information on patients and families, and/or with actual families for research projects. Data collected includes pedigree information, educational background, clinical history, psychiatric history, social history, history of treatment, and history of genetic counseling. *Type:* Research center.

Indiana University-Purdue University at Indianapolis

Multipurpose Arthritis and Musculoskeletal Diseases Center

541 Clinical Dr., Rm. 492 Ph: (317)274-4225
Indianapolis, IN 46202-5103 Fax: (317)274-7792

Contact: Dr. Kenneth D. Brandt, Dir.

Desc: Basic and clinical research related to rheumatic diseases. Activities are structured in two major areas: a Biomedical Component and an Epidemiology, Education, and Health Services Research Component. *Type:* Research center.

Institute for Gravitational Strain Pathology, Inc.

S. Shore Dr. Ph: (207)864-5511
PO Box 526
Rangeley, ME 04970

Contact: Gertrude Jungmann, Exec.Dir.

Desc: Effects of gravity on humans and the effect of special countermeasures to gravity strain. *Type:* Research center.

Institute for Jewish Medical Ethics

645 14th Ave. Ph: (415)752-7333
San Francisco, CA 94118 Fax: (415)752-5851
URL: http://www.hebrewacadamy.com
Contact: Barry L. Smail, Contact.
Desc: Jewish principles of medical ethics, including Jewish law and human and animal experimentation, physician compassion for the patient, artificial insemination, in-vitro fertilization, surrogate motherhood and abortion, allocation of health care resources, organ transplantation (with emphasis on kidney and developments in Israel), and the right to die. *Type:* Research center.

Institute for Metabolic Research

3508 Market St., Ste. 420 Ph: (215)222-1818
Philadelphia, PA 19104 Fax: (215)222-5325
E-mail: drmpcohen@AOL.com
Contact: Dr. Margo P. Cohen, Dir.
Desc: Metabolic effects, diagnosis, and management of diabetes mellitus and other metabolic diseases. Studies include the biochemistry and metabolism of glomerular and retinal microvascular basement membranes; role of polyol pathway in complications of diabetes; structure/function effects of non-enzymatic glycosylation of proteins; measurement of glycohemoglobin and glycoalbumin in biologic samples by immunologic methods; identification and purification of islet cell antigens. *Type:* Research center.

Institute of Noetic Sciences

475 Gate Five Rd., Ste. 300 Ph: (415)331-5650
Sausalito, CA 94965 Fax: (415)331-5673
E-mail: schlitz@noetic.org
URL: http://www.noetic.org
Contact: Dr. Marilyn Schlitz, Dir. of Res.
Desc: Nature and potential of the human mind and consciousness, particularly in the areas of exceptional human abilities, the mind/body link and healing, the role of intentionality, positive global change, and creative altruism. *Type:* Research center.

Institute for the Study and Treatment of Endometriosis

550 W. Webster Ave. Ph: (773)883-3880
Chicago, IL 60614-3708 Fax: (773)883-3551
E-mail: wdmowski@rpslmc.edu
URL: http://www.endometriosisinstitute.com
Contact: W. Paul Dmowski, MD, Dir.
Desc: Elucidation of pathophysiology of endometriosis, identification of new diagnostic tests and development of new treatment methods. *Type:* Research center.

Interchurch Medical Assistance

College Ave. at Blue Ridge Ph: (410)635-8720
Box 429 Fax: (410)635-8726
New Windsor, MD 21776
E-mail: ima@ecunet.org
Contact: Paul Derstine, Exec.Dir.
Desc: Denominational-founded autonomous organization for the solicitation, collection, and distribution of pharmaceutical, medical, dental, and hospital supplies for use in the overseas charity medical programs of American Protestant churches, relief agencies, and other American charitable organizations. *Type:* Association.

Internal Medicine News

International Medical News Group
51 John F. Kennedy Pkwy., 4th Ph: (973)379-8777
Fl. Fax: (973)379-8765
Short Hills, NJ 07078-2702
Contact: Mary Jo Dales, Editor.
Desc: Publication covering clinical developments for practicing internists. *Alt. Contact:* 12230 Wilkins Ave., Rockville, MD 20852; telephone: (301)816-8700. *Type:* Periodical.

Internal Medicine World Report

Medical World Communications
241 Forsgate Dr. Ph: (732)656-1140
PO Box CN505 Fax: (732)656-1142
Jamesburg, NJ 08831-0505
Contact: Mary Jo Fencel, National Acct. Mgr.; Karen Rosenberg, Editor; Susan Levey, Publisher.
Desc: Medical journal for internal medicine specialists. *Type:* Periodical.

International Anesthesia Research Society

2 Summit Park Dr., Ste. 140 Ph: (216)642-1124
Cleveland, OH 44131-2553 Fax: (216)642-1127
E-mail: iarshq@iars.org
URL: http://www.iars.org
Contact: Anne F. Maggiore, Exec.Dir.
Desc: Anesthesiologists and other doctors of medicine and dentistry in 50 countries interested in the specialty of anesthesiology; associate members are registered nurses, physician assistants, and respiratory therapists. Fosters progress and research in all phases of anesthesiology. *Type:* Association.

International Anesthesia Research Society

2 Summit Park Dr., Ste. 140 Ph: (216)642-1124
Cleveland, OH 44131-2553 Fax: (216)642-1127
E-mail: iarshq@iars.org
URL: http://www.iars.org
Contact: Anne F. Maggiore, Exec.Dir.
Desc: Anesthesiology, focusing on progress and research in all phases of this subject. *Type:* Research center.

International Association for Medical Assistance to Travellers

417 Center St. Ph: (716)754-4883
Lewiston, NY 14092 Fax: (519)836-3412
E-mail: iamat@sentex.net
URL: http://www.sentex.net/~iamat
Contact: Mrs. M. A. Uffer-Marcolongo, Pres.
Desc: Seeks to make competent medical care available to the traveller around the world by doctors who usually speak English or French and have medical training in Europe or North America. *Type:* Association.

International Association of Physicians in AIDS Care

225 W. Washington, Ste. 2200 Ph: (312)419-7512
Chicago, IL 60606 Fax: (312)419-7160
E-mail: iapac@iapac.org
URL: http://www.iapac.org
Contact: Gordon Nary, Pres.
Type: Association.

International Cesarean Awareness Network

1304 Kingsdale Ave. Ph: (310)542-6400
Redondo Beach, CA 90278- Fax: (310)542-5368
3926
E-mail: icaninc@aol.com
URL: http://www.childbirth.org/section/ican.html
Contact: April Kubachka, Pres.
Desc: Men and women concerned with the increasing rate of cesarean births. Objectives are: to promote vaginal births; to offer encouragement, information, and support for women wanting vaginal births after cesarean (VBAC); to assist in organizing and informing new parents and cesarean parents on preventing future cesareans by opposing unnecessary medical intervention during the birth process and by working to make hospital routines more responsive to women in labor. *Type:* Association.

International Childbirth Education Association

PO Box 20048 Ph: (612)854-8660
Minneapolis, MN 55420-0048 Fax: (612)854-8772
E-mail: info@icea.org
URL: http://www.icea.org/
Contact: Doris Olson, Mgr.
Desc: Purposes are: to further the educational, physical, and emotional preparation of expectant parents for childbearing and breastfeeding; to increase public awareness on current issues related to childbearing; to cooperate with physicians, nurses, physical therapists, hospitals, health, education, and welfare agencies, and other individuals and groups interested in furthering parental participation and minimal obstetric intervention in uncomplicated labors; to promote development of safe, low-cost alternatives in childbirth that recognize the rights and responsibilities of those involved. Develops, publishes, and distributes literature pertaining to family-centered maternity care. Offers a teacher certification program for childbirth educators. *Type:* Association.

International Childbirth Education Association—ICEA Membership Directory

International Childbirth Education Association, Inc. (ICEA)
PO Box 20048 Ph: (612)854-8660
Minneapolis, MN 55420-0048 Fax: (612)854-8772
Contact: Doris Olson, Office Mgr.
Desc: Cesarean educators, childbirth educators, counselors, family physicians, home birth specialists, nurses, nurses midwives, obstetricians and gynecologists, parent educators, pediatricians, and physical therapists and other individuals and associations involved in family-centered maternity care; international coverage. *Type:* Directory.

International Dyslexia Association

8600 LaSalle Rd. Ph: (410)296-0232
Baltimore, MD 21286-2044 Free: 800-ABCD-123
 Fax: (410)321-5069
E-mail: info@interdys.org
URL: http://www.interdys.org
Contact: J. Thomas Viall, Ph.D., Exec.Dir.
Desc: Offers free information to the public and referrals for diagnosis and treatment. Professionals in the fields of neurology, pediatrics, psychiatry, education, social work, and psychology; parents; other persons interested in the study, treatment, and prevention of the problems of specific language disability, often called developmental dyslexia or simply dyslexia. Provides a focal point for activities and ideas generated in various fields as they relate to problems of language development and learning. *Type:* Association.

International Federation of Sports Medicine

Desc: National federations, physicians, physiologists, and others interested in maintaining and improving physical and mental health through sporting activities, especially physical education, gymnastics, games, and other sports. Members conduct scientific studies of their effects, both normal and pathological. Bestows awards. *Type:* Association.

International Institute for the Advancement of Medicine

814 Cedar Ave. Ph: (570)343-5433
Scranton, PA 18505-1252 Free: 800-486-4426
 Fax: (570)343-6993
URL: http://www.iiam.org
Contact: Stephen Zeisloft, Dir.
Desc: Placement of non-transplantable human organs and tissues for research; serological testing for infectious diseases in donors; and fresh and frozen tissue slices, cells, and subcellular fractions. *Type:* Research center.

International Institute for Bioenergetic Analysis

144 E. 36th St., Ste. 1A   Ph: (212)532-7742
New York, NY 10016   Fax: (212)532-5331
E-mail: iibanet@aol.com
URL: http://www.bioenergetic-therapy.com
Contact: John Bustelos, Jr., Exec.Dir.

Desc: Works to promote research and education in the fields of mental and physical health as they relate to biological energy processes. Areas of interest include: the role of muscle tension in emotional and physical illness, relationship of body structure and body movement, energy dynamics, disturbances in motility as a factor in illness, genetic factors, principles and methods of therapy, and growth and development of the child in response to patterns of child rearing. Conducts lectures, 1-day patient workshops, professional weekend workshops, seminars, and exercise classes. *Type:* Association.

International League Against Rheumatism

c/o Charles M. Plotz, M.D.
SUNY Downstate Med. Center
450 Clarkson Ave.
Brooklyn, NY 11203
Contact: Charles M. Plotz, M.D., Treas.

Desc: Physicians interested in rheumatism. Promotes research and education in rheumatic disease. Facilitates communication among members and with United Nations Educational, Scientific and Cultural Organization and World Health Organization. *Type:* Association.

International Society for the Advancement of Humanistic Studies in Gynecology

7861 W. 38th Ave.   Ph: (303)756-6140
Wheat Ridge, CO 80033-6109
Contact: Bruce Richards, Contact.

Desc: Humanistic aspects of medicine, quality of medical care, and education of health practitioners working for the betterment of human reproduction and the resolution of social, political, and economic problems. *Type:* Research center.

Iowa State University of Science and Technology

Bessey Microscopy Facility

Bessey Hall, Rm. 1   Ph: (515)294-8635
Ames, IA 50011-1020   Fax: (515)294-1337
E-mail: hth@iastate.edu
Contact: Harry T. Horner, Dir.

Desc: Applications of microscopy in areas of biology, biomedicine, botany, agronomy, animal science, biotechnology, and engineering. *Type:* Research center.

Irvington Institute for Immunological Research

120 E. 56th St., Ste. 340   Ph: (212)758-8250
New York, NY 10022   Fax: (212)758-8968
E-mail: irving1@ix.netcom.com
URL: http://www.irvingtonresearch.org
Contact: Gail L. Freeman, Exec.Dir.

Desc: Diseases and dysfunctions involving the immune system, including AIDS, cancer, diabetes, rheumatoid arthritis, allergies, organ rejection, and systemic lupus erythematosus. *Type:* Research center.

Jackson Foundation for Medical Research & Education

20 S. Park St., Ste. 455   Ph: (608)287-2850
Madison, WI 53715   Free: 800-755-5667
    Fax: (608)287-2869
E-mail: dadams@meriter.com
Contact: Dorothy Adams, Exec.Dir.

Desc: Cardiovascular disease, hypertension, rheumatology, gastroenterology, diabetes, urology, cancer, and pain. Conducts medical and clinical investigations in areas of interest to multispecialty group physicians. *Type:* Research center.

Jacobs Institute of Women's Health

409 12th St. SW   Ph: (202)863-4990
Washington, DC 20024-2188   Fax: (202)488-4229
E-mail: mromans.@acog.org
URL: http://www.jiwh.org
Contact: Martha C. Romans, Exec.Dir.

Desc: Women's health care issues, focusing on the interaction of medical and social systems. *Type:* Research center.

JAMA

American Medical Association
515 N. State St.   Ph: (312)464-5000
Chicago, IL 60610   Free: 800-621-8335
    Fax: (312)464-5830
E-mail: amaa@ama-assn.org

Contact: George D. Lundberg, M.D., Editor; Robert L. Kennett, V.P. Publishing; Joseph Dennehy, Publisher.

Desc: Scientific general medical journal. *Type:* Periodical.

John L. McClellan Memorial Veterans' Hospital

Research Office

4300 W. 7th St.   Ph: (501)661-1202
Little Rock, AR 72205   Fax: (501)671-2599
Contact: George H. Gray, Jr., Dir.

Desc: Biomedicine, including studies of Histoplasmosis, the molecular biology of aging, molecular biology of tuberculosis and other mycobacterial diseases, molecular biology of diabetes, hyperthermia effects on tumors, antitumor drugs, nephrology. Also conducts clinical studies in cardiology, stroke, infectious diseases, prostate cancer, and aneurysms. *Type:* Research center.

John P. Robarts Research Institute

100 Perth Dr.   Ph: (519)663-5777
PO Box 5015   Fax: (519)663-3789
London, ON, Canada N6A 5K8
Contact: Dr. Mark J. Poznansky, Pres./Sci.Dir.

Desc: Stroke and aging, heart disease, and immunology, including studies on juvenile diabetes, multiple sclerosis, transplantation and organ rejection, Alzheimer's disease, and the neurobiology of aging. Conducts clinical trials and examines new and existing treatments, including a study on stroke prevention surgery. *Type:* Research center.

John P. Robarts Research Institute

Imaging Research Laboratories

100 Perth Dr.   Ph: (519)663-3833
PO Box 5015   Fax: (519)663-3900
London, ON, Canada N6A 5K8
E-mail: afenster@irus.rri.uwo.ca
URL: http://www.laus.rri.uwo.ca
Contact: Dr. Aaron Fenster, Dir.

Desc: Medical imaging systems and techniques, including diagnostic X-rays, computed tomography, ultrasound, and magnetic resonance imaging. Develops new diagnostic imaging systems and techniques focusing on vascular imaging research, three dimensional image processing and display, multimodality display, image guided surgery and therapy, prostate and breast cancer. *Type:* Research center.

Johns Hopkins Magazine

Johns Hopkins University
3400 N. Charles St.   Ph: (410)516-8514
Baltimore, MD 21218   Fax: (410)516-5251
Contact: Sue De Pasquale, Editor.

Desc: Alumni magazine featuring general interest articles and medical updates. *Type:* Periodical.

Johns Hopkins University

Biomedical Instrumentation Laboratory

School of Medicine   Ph: (410)955-3131
Department of Biomedical   Fax: (410)955-0549
    Engineering
720 Rutland Ave.
Baltimore, MD 21205
E-mail: nthakor@eureka.wbme.jhu.edu
URL: http://www.bme.jhu.edu/~nthakor/Lab/
Contact: Nitish V. Thakor, PhD, Contact.

Desc: Medical instrumentation, signal analysis, and computer modeling and simulation to develop novel diagnostic and therapeutic technologies for cardiovascular diseases and neurological injury. *Type:* Research center.

Johns Hopkins University

Center for Computational Medicine and Biology

School of Medicine   Ph: (410)955-3131
Department of Biomedical   Fax: (410)955-0549
    Engineering
720 Rutland Ave.
Baltimore, MD 21205
E-mail: rwinslow@bme.jhu.edu
URL: http://www.bme.jhu.edu/ccmb/
Contact: Prof. Raimond L. Winslow, Co-Dir.

Desc: Understanding the integrative function in biological systems, including human, through development and application of computational models, and the application of these models to the design of novel therapeutics. *Type:* Research center.

Johns Hopkins University

Center for Epidemiology and Policy

615 N. Wolfe St., Ste. W6041   Ph: (410)614-4714
Baltimore, MD 21205   Fax: (410)955-0863
E-mail: lgordis@jhsph.edu
URL: http://www.med.jhu.edu/cep/
Contact: Dr. Jonathan M. Samet, Co-Dir.

Desc: Use of epidemiologic evidence in the development of public policy. *Type:* Research center.

Johns Hopkins University

Center for Injury Research and Policy

Department of Health Policy &   Ph: (410)955-2636
    Mgmt.   Fax: (410)614-2797
Sch. of Public Health
624 N. Broadway
Baltimore, MD 21205
E-mail: sogaitis@jhsph.edu
URL: http://www.sph.jhu/research/centers/cirp/
Contact: Susanne Ogaitis, Asst.Dir. for Ext.Aff.

Desc: Adolescent drowning and poisoning, alcohol related injuries, aviation safety, childhood injuries, fall injuries in nursing homes, financing trauma care and rehabilitation, homicide and suicide, injuries from firearms, injuries in developing countries, injury sequelae and rehabilitation, injury severity scoring, injury surveillance systems, mathematical models of response to impact, motor vehicle related injuries, occupational injuries, and elderly and highway safety. Develops injury interventions, evaluates legal interventions, examines preventive measures, and evaluates trauma care. *Type:* Research center.

Johns Hopkins University

Center for VDT and Health Research

Sch. of Hygiene and Public   Ph: (410)955-7820
    Health   Fax: (410)955-0792
615 N. Wolfe St., Rm. 4028
Baltimore, MD 21205
E-mail: rgray@jhsph.edu
Contact: Dr. Ronald H. Gray, Dir.

Desc: Health effects of video display terminal (VDT) use, focusing on methodologies for the measurement of electromagnetic field (EMF) exposures associated with VDTs, and the contribution of VDTs to total field exposures; the association between, VDT use and reproductive health problems; the moderating influence of psychosocial stress on VDT use and reproductive health problems or risks of neoplasia; the measurement of physical stresses/forces associated with VDT use and the effects on cumulative trauma disorders (CTDs); and the biological effects of electromagnetic fields at the cellular or subcellular level. *Type:* Research center.

Johns Hopkins University
Division of Comparative Medicine
720 Rutland Ave. Ph: (410)955-3273
Baltimore, MD 21205 Fax: (410)502-5068
E-mail: jstrand@welchlink.welch.jhu.edu
Contact: Dr. John D. Strandberg, Dir.
Desc: Comparative pathology, laboratory animal medicine, retrovirus biology, transgenic biology, infectious diseases, and oncology. Research activities focus on naturally occurring diseases of animals as models of human disease, molecular biology and pathogenesis of lentiviral infections, aquatic toxicology, and benign prostatic hyperplasia. *Type:* Research center.

Johns Hopkins University
Health Services Research and Development Center
624 N. Broadway, Rm.482 Ph: (410)955-3625
Baltimore, MD 21205-1996 Fax: (410)955-0470
E-mail: hsrdc.center@phnet.sph.jhu.edu
Contact: Dr. Donald M. Steinwachs, Dir.
Desc: Conducts health services research, including studies on the following: determinants of health outcomes; the impacts of alternative health care systems on cost and quality; effective strategies for health promotion and disease prevention; and methods of meeting the needs of high risk populations such as the poor, elderly, mentally ill, disabled, and children. Research is conducted using experimental (randomized controlled trials) or nonexperimental methods, and relies to varying degrees on primary data sources obtained through interviews and observation and secondary data sources obtained from management information systems, financial reports, and existing regional and national data sources and surveys. *Type:* Research center.

Johns Hopkins University
Johns Hopkins Hospital Sexual Disorders Clinic
104 E. Biddle St. Ph: (410)955-4150
Baltimore, MD 21202 Fax: (410)539-1664
E-mail: berlinf@aol.com
Contact: Dr. Fred S. Berlin, Dir.
Desc: Biological correlates and treatment of sexual disorders, including pedophilia, sadism, transvestism, voyeurism, exhibitionism, compulsive rape, and other psychosexual disorders. Analyzes and evaluates antiandrogenic and counseling treatment of sex offenders, including the effects of the synthetic progestin, Depo-Provera. *Type:* Research center.

Johns Hopkins University
Medical Imaging Laboratory
School of Medicine Ph: (410)502-6958
Departments of Biomedical Fax: (410)955-0549
  Engineering and Radiology
425 Traylor Bldg.
720 Rutland Ave.
Baltimore, MD 21205
E-mail: emcveigh@mri.jhu.edu
URL: http://prospero.bme-mri.jhu.edu/
Contact: Elliot McVeigh, PhD, Dir.
Desc: Development of new imaging techniques and advanced applications of existing techniques to solve problems in medicine and biology. *Type:* Research center.

Johns Hopkins University
Middle Atlantic Mass Spectrometry Laboratory
725 N. Wolfe St. Ph: (410)955-3022
Baltimore, MD 21205 Fax: (410)955-3420
E-mail: rcotter@welchlink.welch.jhu.edu
Contact: Prof. Robert J. Cotter, Dir.
Desc: Kratos CONCEPT 1H high resolution mass spectrometer, a UV-laser desorption mass spectrometer and a Bio-Ion plasma desorption mass spectrometer as a collaborative resource for researchers from the University, from other academic institutions, or from industry and government laboratories who have need of special instrumentation and assistance in mass spectral measurement, sample preparation, chemical derivatization, and interpretation of spectra. The facility emphasizes analysis of ions of high mass (greater than 2,000 amu) and analysis of nonvolatile compounds. *Type:* Research center.

Johns Hopkins University
Office of Psychohormonal Research
1235 E. Monument St., Ste. Ph: (410)955-3740
  LL20
Baltimore, MD 21202
E-mail: jmoney@welchlink.welch.jhu.edu
Contact: Dr. John Money, Dir.
Desc: Longitudinal psychohormonal research studies of patients with diverse endocrine, genital, and sexological syndromes, related to clinical psychoendocrinology, clinical sexology, gender identity/role (G-I/R), abuse-dwarfism (Kaspar Hauser syndrome), and Munchausen syndrome by proxy. *Type:* Research center.

Johns Hopkins University
Outpatient General Clinical Research Center
Johns Hopkins Hospital Ph: (410)955-5888
Carnegie 313, Ste. C Fax: (410)614-1828
Baltimore, MD 21287
E-mail: gcrc@welchlink.welch.jhu.edu
URL: http://www.gcrc.com
Contact: Christopher Saudek, MD, Dir.
Desc: Funds 125-150 clinical research projects, involving 200-250 investigators, covering a wide variety of medical interests. *Type:* Research center.

Johns Hopkins University
Retinal Vascular Center
Wilmer Ophthalmological Ph: (410)955-7411
  Institute Fax: (410)614-1683
Maumenee Bldg., Rm. 711
601 N. Wolfe St.
Baltimore, MD 21287-9275
E-mail: aschachat@jhmi.edu
URL: http://www.wilmer.jhu.edu
Contact: Dr. Andrew Schachat, Dir.
Desc: Focuses on halting the progression of a variety of retinal-damaging disorders, including macular degeneration, diabetic retinopathy, and eye tumors. Studies the use of lasers in treating retinal, vascular, and macular disorders and explores the underlying causes of retinal, blood vessel, pigment epithelial, and photoreceptor diseases. *Type:* Research center.

Johns Hopkins University
STD Research Group
School of Medicine Ph: (410)955-7636
Ross 1165 Fax: (410)614-9775
720 Rutland Ave.
Baltimore, MD 21205
E-mail: jzenilma@jhmi
URL: http://www.med.jhu.edu/jhustd/stdpage2.htm
Contact: Jonathan M. Zenilman, MD, Dir.
Desc: Edidemiology, prevention and behavioral aspects of sexually transmitted diseases (STDs), and establishing rapid and reliable testing and diagnoses of STDs. *Type:* Research center.

Johns Hopkins University
Welch Center for Prevention, Epidemiology, and Clinical Research
2024 E. Monument St., Ste. Ph: (410)955-6953
  2-600 Fax: (410)955-0476
Baltimore, MD 21205-2223
E-mail: npowe@jhsph.edu
URL: http://www..jhu.edu/~welchc/
Contact: Neil R. Powe, MD, Dir.
Desc: Etiology of disease and disability in populations, through observational epidemiology, randomized controlled trials, and effectiveness outcomes research. Also responsible for the generation and dissemination of knowledge required for prevention of disease and disability. *Type:* Research center.

Joint Division of Newborn Medicine
Creighton Univ. - Univ. of Ph: (402)559-6750
  Nebraska Fax: (402)559-7341
Med. Ctr.
600 S. 42nd St.
Omaha, NE 68198-1205
E-mail: pleuschen@unmc.edu
Contact: M. Patricia Leuschen, PhD, Res.Dir.
Desc: Cell and molecular basis of cerebral ischemia, ontogency of C3 complement in human lung, and physiologic and pharmacodynamic evaluation of infants on ECMO therapy. Conducts clinical trials of two types of high frequency ventilation. *Type:* Research center.

Joslin Diabetes Center
1 Joslin Place Ph: (617)732-2400
Boston, MA 02215 Fax: (617)732-2487
URL: http://www.joslin.harvard.edu/
Contact: Dr. Kenneth E. Quickel, Jr., Pres.
Desc: Diabetes mellitus, including investigations on chemical composition of basement membrane, physiological control of glucose metabolism, neonatal and fetal growth and metabolism, cellular and molecular mechanisms of insulin action, vascular cell biology, ultrastructure of beta cell, pancreatic islets, muscle perfusion, experimental diabetes in animals, immunologic aspects of diabetes, diabetic eye disease, and epidemiology of diabetes. Conducts clinical studies of early stages of diabetic state, treatment, and prevention of diabetes and its complications, especially of a vascular nature, with emphasis on diabetic retinopathy. *Type:* Research center.

The Journal of Critical Illness
Cliggott Publishing Co.
55 Holly Hill Ln. Ph: (203)661-0600
PO Box 4010 Fax: (203)661-8163
Greenwich, CT 06831-0010
Contact: Susan K. Lotstein, Editor; Maria Conforti, Advertising Coord.; Frank T. Iorio, Group Publisher; Ana Santiso Conlan, Publisher; Jonathan L. Bigelow, Chief Operating Officer; Stephen K. Lotstein, Editor; Sarah Williams, Ph.D., Managing Editor.
Desc: Professional journal presenting practical and authoritative information on the diagnosis and management of clinical problems in patients who have, are at risk for, are recovering from serious illness. *Type:* Periodical.

The Journal of Musculoskeletal Medicine
Cliggott Publishing Co.
55 Holly Hill Ln. Ph: (203)661-0600
PO Box 4010 Fax: (203)661-8163
Greenwich, CT 06831-0010
Contact: Leo Cristofar, Editor; Kenneth D. Watkins, Publisher; Diane Carpenteri, Advertising Sales Rep.
Desc: Professional journal combining practical and authoritative information on diagnosis and management of a wide variety of common musculoskeletal disorders. *Type:* Periodical.

The Journal of Respiratory Diseases

Cliggott Publishing Co.
55 Holly Hill Ln.   Ph: (203)661-0600
PO Box 4010   Fax: (203)661-8163
Greenwich, CT 06831-0010
Contact: Craig Borders, Editor; Molly K. Sawyer, Publisher; Andrea Perchak, Advertising Coordinator.

Desc: Journal providing practical information about diagnosis and treatment pertaining to the respiratory system, both as the site of primary disease and as a complication of other clinical problems. *Type:* Periodical.

Journal Watch

Massachusetts Medical Society
Publishing Division
1440 Main St.   Ph: (617)893-3800
Waltham, MA 02254
E-mail: jwatch@world.std.com
URL: http://www.jwatch.org

Desc: Contains citations, with abstracts, to clinical studies reported in about 50 major medical journals and other biomedical literature. Abstracts, prepared by physician editors, provide non-technical summaries of the study question and design, results, conclusions, and significance of the research. *Available:* Ovid Technologies, Inc.; Massachusetts Medical Society, Publishing Division. *Type:* Database.

Kaiser Permanente Center for Health Research

3800 N. Kaiser Center Dr.   Ph: (503)335-2400
Portland, OR 97227-1098   Fax: (503)335-2424
E-mail: durhamma@chr.mts.kpnw.org
URL: http://www.kpuw.org/chr/chr.html
Contact: Mary L. Durham, PhD, Dir.

Desc: Determinants of medical care utilization; organization, financing, costs and quality of medical care in an HMO; health behavior and intervention; physician practice patterns and outcomes; innovation demonstrations in health care organization and financing; epidemiology; effectiveness of alternative therapies and services; and biometry and research methods. Research programs include health services research, social and economic studies, and epidemiology and disease prevention, including behavior intervention and health promotion. *Type:* Research center.

Kaiser Permanente Medical Care Program

Division of Research

3505 Broadway   Ph: (510)450-2000
Oakland, CA 94611-5714   Fax: (510)450-2073
E-mail: jvs@dor.kaiser.org
Contact: Dr. Gary D. Friedman, Dir.

Desc: Epidemiology, biometrics and biostatistics, technology assessment, health services research, and health education research and evaluation. Supports clinical research in medical centers. *Type:* Research center.

Karen M. Engberg M.D.

2329 Oak Park Ln.   Ph: (805)682-8844
Santa Barbara, CA 93105   Fax: (805)682-6499
Contact: Karen M. Engberg, Bureau Chief.
Alt. Contact: 2329 Oak Park Ln., Santa Barbara, CA 93105; telephone: (805)682-8844; fax: (805)682-6499. *Type:* Periodical.

Kuzell Institute for Arthritis and Infectious Diseases

California Pacific Med. Ctr.   Ph: (415)561-1734
2200 Webster St., 3rd Fl.   Fax: (415)441-8548
San Francisco, CA 94115
E-mail: kiaid@cooper.cpmc.org
Contact: Dr. Lowell S. Young, Dir.

Desc: Arthritis and related diseases and infectious diseases. In the area of arthritis, the Institute conducts fundamental investigations on the biology, biochemistry, and pharmacology of tissues and cellular inflammatory reactions, and studies of autoimmune diseases, including systematic lupus erythymatosus (SLE), the biology of neutrophils, replacement of joints, and pharmacology of steroidal and nonsteroidal anti-inflammatory agents. *Type:* Research center.

Lahey Clinic Foundation

41 Mall Rd.   Ph: (781)273-5100
Burlington, MA 01805   Fax: (781)273-8999
Contact: Nancy L. Rizzo, V.Pres., Ambulatory Oper.

Desc: Medical, surgical, and radiological techniques, with special emphasis on clinical applications, including studies on high and mega voltage radiation, treatment of cancer with drugs and immunotherapy, cancer cell kinetics, electronic measurement of bacterial growth, pancreatic and renal transplantation, cardiac surgery, diagnostic radiology, amino acid absorption, treatment of pancreatitis, and hospital and prolonged storage by freezing of blood for transfusion. Maintains a clinic for patient care and application of research results and an educational division for postgraduate medical training and residency, both at the clinic and at local hospitals and medical schools. *Type:* Research center.

Lamaze International

1200 19th St. NW, No. 300   Ph: (202)857-1128
Washington, DC 20036-2422   Free: 800-368-4404
                                     Fax: (202)857-1102
E-mail: lamaze@dc.sba.com
URL: http://www.lamaze-childbirth.com

Contact: Linda Harmon, Exec.Dir.

Desc: Physicians, nurses, nurse-midwives, certified teachers of psychoprophylatic (Lamaze) method of childbirth, other professionals, parents, and others interested in Lamaze childbirth preparation and family-centered maternity care. Disseminates information about the theory and practical application of psychoprophylaxis in obstetrics; administers teacher training courses and certifies qualified Lamaze teachers; provides educational lectures, public forums, films, and written materials; maintains national and local teacher and physician referral service. Also presents materials to prospective parents concerning the demands of childrearing. *Type:* Association.

Lancaster Cleft Palate Clinic

223 N. Lime St.   Ph: (717)396-7415
Lancaster, PA 17602   Fax: (717)396-7409
Contact: Kathlyn C. McElliott, PhD, Pres./CEO.

Desc: Plastic surgery, dentistry, orthodontics, prosthodontics, craniofacial morphology, speech, hearing, otolaryngology, genetics, and behavioral science, particularly in regard to children with craniofacial anomalies. Conducts interdisciplinary study of problems of oral/facial growth, orthognathic surgery, and communicative disorders. *Type:* Research center.

The Laryngoscope—Directory of Otolaryngologic Societies Issue

American Laryngological, Rhinological and
Otological Society, Inc.
c/o Boy's Town National   Ph: (402)498-6666
  Research Hospital   Fax: (402)498-6662
555 N. 30th St.
Omaha, NE 68131

Contact: Byron Bailey, M.D., Editor.

Desc: List of more than 35 international otolaryngologic societies. *Type:* Directory.

Laval University

Infectious Disease Research Centre

2705, blvd. Laurier   Ph: (418)654-2705
Ste. Foy, PQ, Canada G1V 4G2   Fax: (418)654-2715
E-mail: michel.g.bergeron@crchul.ulaval.ca

Contact: Michel G. Bergeron, Dir.

Desc: Molecular basis of action of antimicrobial agents and the mechanisms involved in the microbial resistance against these agents. Develops new transportation vehicles of antimicrobials in bacteria, parasites, and viruses; works on metabolic particularities of parasites; develops new diagnostic kits for quick detection of bacterial and viral infections; and works on new vaccines. *Type:* Research center.

Laval University

Medical Ethics Research Group

Philosophy Dept.   Ph: (418)656-2244
Pavillon Felix Antoine Savard   Fax: (418)656-7267
Quebec, PQ, Canada G1K 7P4
E-mail: marie-helene.parlzeau@fp.ulaval.ca

Contact: Marie-Helene Parizeau, Dir.

Desc: Bioethics, human experimentation, ethical committees, education in ehtics for health professionals. *Type:* Research center.

Laval University

Medical Research Centre

2705, boulevard Laurier   Ph: (418)654-2129
Ste. Foy, PQ, Canada G1V 4G2   Fax: (418)654-2714
E-mail: sec.drs@crchul.ulaval.ca

Contact: Dr. Fernand Labrie, Dir.

Desc: Family medicine, rheumatology and immunology, infectious diseases, health and environment, genetics and molecular medicine, ontogeny and reproduction, molecular endocrinology, hypertension, diabetes, lipids, ophthalmology, pediatrics, hormonal bioregulation, and public health. *Type:* Research center.

Laval University

Medical Research Centre

Diabetes Research Group

2705, boulevard Laurier   Ph: (418)654-2741
Ste. Foy, PQ, Canada G1V 4G2   Fax: (418)654-2792
E-mail: andre.nadeau@crchul.ulaval.ca

Contact: Andre Nadeau, Dir.

Desc: The relationship between physical activity and diabetes, and the identification of factors responsible for the increased level of cardiac mortality in diabetes patients. *Type:* Research center.

Laval University

Medical Research Centre

Family Medicine Research Group

2705, Boulevard Laurier   Ph: (418)654-2701
Ste. Foy, PQ, Canada G1V 4G2   Fax: (418)654-2138
E-mail: pierre.fremont@crchul.ulaval.ca

Contact: Lucie Baillargeon, Dir.

Desc: Causes of, and therapeutic alternatives to, overuse of hypnotic and anxiolytic drugs; family physicians treatment of patients who are facing domestic violence; evaluation of validity of international prostatic symptoms scale; physicians knowledge of diabetic retinopathy; risk of severe perineal tears in relation to median episiotomy; clinical trials on antibiotherapy for various infectious diseases; and smoking cessation. *Type:* Research center.

Laval University

Medical Research Centre

Hormonal Bioregulation Research Group

2705, boulevard Laurier, Rm.   Ph: (418)654-2733
T3-67   Fax: (418)654-2279
Ste. Foy, PQ, Canada G1V 4G2
E-mail: roland.r.tremblay@crchul.ulaval.ca

Contact: Roland R. Tremblay, Dir.

Desc: Functional role of new kallikreins in human prostate; influences of serine proteases in reproductive biology. *Type:* Research center.

Laval University

Saint-Francois-d'Assise Hospital Research Centre

10, rue de l'Espinay   Ph: (418)525-4461
Quebec, PQ, Canada G1L 3L5   Fax: (418)525-4481
E-mail: Jean-Marie.Moutquin@crsfa.ulaval.ca
URL: http://www.crsfa.ulaval.ca

Contact: Dr. Jean-Marie Moutquin, Dir.

Desc: Reproductive endocrinology, perinatalogy, human genetics, biomaterials, magnetic resonance, and biotechnology. *Type:* Research center.

Laval University

Saint-Francois-d'Assise Hospital Research Centre

Reproductive Endocrinology Unit

10, rue de l'Espinay   Ph: (418)525-4461
Quebec, PQ, Canada G1L 3L5   Fax: (418)525-4481
E-mail: jean-marie.moutquin@crffa.ulaval.ca

Contact: Dr. Jean-Marie Moutquin, Dir.

Desc: Treatment and diagnosis of endometriosis, new diagnosis methods, new medical and surgical methods, new modalities of hormonal replacement therapy for menopause, and basic research on growth and immune factors implicated in endometriosis and breast cancer. *Type:* Research center.

Laval University

Saint-Sacrement Hospital Research Centre

1050, chemin Ste-Foy   Ph: (418)682-7838
Quebec, PQ, Canada G1S 4L8   Fax: (418)682-7949

Contact: Pierre Durend, Dir.

Desc: Epidemiology and public health, experimental organogenesis, hematology, and clinical research in gynecology, obstetrics, respiratory diseases, and breast cancer. *Type:* Research center.

Laval University

Saint-Sacrement Hospital Research Centre

Epidemiology Research Group

1050, chemin Ste-Foy   Ph: (418)682-7390
Quebec, PQ, Canada G1S 4L8   Fax: (418)682-7949
E-mail: sylvie.marcoux@gre.ulaval.ca

Contact: Sylvie Marcoux, MD, Dir.

Desc: Population health research, cancer, palliative care, maternal and child health, infectious diseases, environmental and work related diseases, biostatistics, and mathematical modelling. Research programs include clinical trials and cohort and case-control studies. *Type:* Research center.

Lawson Research Institute

University of Western Ontario   Ph: (519)646-6000
St. Joseph's Health Centre   Fax: (519)646-6110
268 Grosvenor St.
London, ON, Canada N6A 4V2
E-mail: dhill@lri.stjosephs.london.on.ca
URL: http://www.stjoseph.london.on.ca/

Contact: Dr. David J. Hill, Sci.Dir.,VP,Res.

Desc: Pregnancy and perinatology, including fetal endocrinology, fetal physiology, fetal neonatal growth, and fetal neonatal and infant health; endocrinology and metabolism, including diabetes and steroid metabolism; neurology and diagnostic imaging, including heart disease, cognitive neurology, development of new diagnostic imaging techniques and approaches, and magnetic resonance (MR) spectroscopy; cell biology, including hemostasis, thrombosis, and lung biology; gastroenterology; musculoskeletal research; GI surgery; and clinical research. *Type:* Research center.

Le Sommaire

ORDRE Professionnel des Technologistes Medicaux du Quebec

1150 Boul. St.-Joseph Est,   Ph: (514)527-9811
Bureau 300   Free: 800-567-PROF
Montreal, PQ, Canada H2J 1L5   Fax: (514)527-7314

Type: Newsletter.

The Learning Center for Interactive Technology-Cognitive Science Branch

U.S. National Library of Medicine - Cognitive Science Branch - Educational Technology

8600 Rockville Pike   Ph: (301)496-6280
Bldg. 38A, Rm. B1N-28   Fax: (301)480-3035
Bethesda, MD 20894-6075
URL: http://wwwetb.nlm.nih.gov/tlc/index.html

Desc: The Learning Center for Interactive Technology Home Page contains information pertaining to educational technology in the health professions. This site offers access to the Learning Center Courseware Database, various tutorials, contact information, research data, monographs and research on authoring systems, data on the Digital Microscopy System Project, and more. *Type:* Database.

Lexington Clinic Foundation for Medical Education and Research Inc.

1221 S. Broadway St.   Ph: (606)258-4000
Lexington, KY 40504-2701   Fax: (606)258-4795

Contact: James W. Bard, MD, Pres.

Desc: Cancer therapy, muscle physiology and athletic injury, diabetes, and cardiac surgery. *Type:* Research center.

Lighthouse Research Institute

111 E. 59th St.   Ph: (212)821-9500
New York, NY 10022   Fax: (212)751-9667
E-mail: aries@play.lighthouse.org
URL: http://www.lighthouse.org

Contact: Aries Arditi, PhD, Dir., Vision Res.

Desc: Physical, functional, and psychological consequences of vision impairment. Vision research areas include helping individuals with low vision maximize their remaining vision, understanding how best to assess visual function, and devising ways of modifying environments for the safety and comfort of people who are visually impaired. *Type:* Research center.

Loeb Health Research Institute

1053 Carling Ave.   Ph: (613)761-4395
Ottawa, ON, Canada K1Y 4E9   Fax: (613)761-4920
E-mail: mchretien@lri.ca
URL: http://www.lri.ca

Contact: Dr. Michel Chretien, CEO/Sci.Dir.

Desc: Neurosciences, clinical epidemiology, growth hormone development, diabetes, cancer, genetics, thyroid disease, molecular medicine, and diseases of ageing. *Type:* Research center.

Long Term Care Monitor

MPL Communications Inc.

133 Richmond St., Ste. 700   Ph: (416)869-1177
Toronto, ON, Canada M5H   Fax: (416)869-0616
3M8

Contact: John Hobel, Editor.

Desc: Features articles on programs, management techniques, and news concerning long term care. Recurring features include news of research, a calendar of events, and notices of publications available. *Type:* Newsletter.

Loose Connections

Ehlers-Danlos National Foundation (EDNF)

6399 Wilshire Blvd., Ste. 510   Ph: (323)651-3038
Los Angeles, CA 90048   Fax: (323)651-1366
E-mail: ednfboard@aol.com; loosejoint@aol.com.

Contact: Linda Newmann-Potash, Editor.

Desc: Provides updated information about Ehlers-Danlos Syndrome (EDS), a hereditary connective tissue disorder. Recurring features include Personal stories, letters to the editor, interviews, news of research, reports of meetings, notices of publications available and articles on relevant topics from members of the medical profession. *Type:* Newsletter.

Los Amigos Research and Education Institute, Inc.

PO Box 3500   Ph: (562)401-8111
Los Amigos Sta.   Fax: (562)803-5569
Downey, CA 90242

Contact: Julia F. LaPlount, Admin.Off.

Desc: Clinical medicine, including multidisciplinary study of severe chronic disabilities in pulmonary and respiratory functions, cardiology, spinal cord injury, orthopedic disabilities, environmental health, stroke, pathokinesiology, liver disease, neuromuscular stimulation and control, rehabilitation of severely disabled persons, cerebral palsy, problem amputations, arthritis, and diabetes. Treats effects of atmospheric pollutants on human lung function, investigates possible causes of Alzheimer's disease, and explores new methods and procedures for care and treatment of gerontology patients. *Type:* Research center.

Louisiana Health and Hospitals Department

Research and Development

PO Box 629   Ph: (504)342-2964
Baton Rouge, LA 70821-0629   Fax: (504)342-9508

Contact: Carolyn Maggio, Dir.

Desc: Health, hospitals. *Type:* Research center.

Lovelace Respiratory Research Institute

2425 Ridgecrest Dr. SE   Ph: (505)262-7044
Albuquerque, NM 87108-5127   Fax: (505)262-7043
E-mail: rrubin@lrri.org
URL: http://www.lrri.org

Contact: Dr. Robert W. Rubin, Pres./CEO.

Desc: Respiratory disease (primarily asthma and cancer), respiratory pharmaceuticals, inhalation drug delivery, inhalation toxicology, aerosol science, animal models of human respiratory disease, and health risks from inhaled materials in the workplace, home, and general environment. *Type:* Research center.

Lupus Beacon

L.E. Support Club

8039 Nova Ct.   Ph: (843)764-1769
North Charleston, SC 29420   Fax: (843)572-9909
URL: http://www.galaxymall.com/commerce/lupus

Contact: Harriet Bey Mesic, Editor, hmesic@awod.com.

Desc: Provides medical information, personal stories, and coping tips on Lupus. *Type:* Newsletter.

LUPUS CONNECTION
Lupus Network, Inc.
230 Ranch Dr.   Ph: (203)372-5795
Bridgeport, CT 06606-1747
Contact: Linda J. Rosinsky, President.
Desc: Provides educational (both orthodox and alternative) information on Lupus for patients and medical professionals. Recurring features include letters to the editor, book reviews, personal stories, and coping hints. *Type:* Newsletter.

Lupus Views and News
Ozarks Chapter, Inc.
Lupus Foundation of America, Inc.
1238 S. Belcrest   Ph: (417)887-1560
Springfield, MO 65804
Contact: Debra Collinge, Editor, debkcollinge@prodigy.net.
Desc: Reports on Chapter meetings and member activities. Contains articles on various aspects of lupus erythematosus, a chronic inflammatory disease that affects connective tissue. *Type:* Newsletter.

The MA Report
Allergy and Asthma Network/Mothers of Asthmatics, Inc.
3554 Chain Bridge Rd., Ste.   Ph: (703)385-4403
200   Free: 800-878-4403
Fairfax, VA 22030   Fax: (703)352-4354
E-mail: aanma@aol.com
Contact: Nancy Sander, Editor.
Desc: Presents educational, medical, and resource information on asthma and allergies. Recurring features include news of research, a calendar of events, news of educational opportunities, and notices of publications available. *Type:* Newsletter.

MADRE
121 W. 27th St., Rm. 301   Ph: (212)627-0444
New York, NY 10001   Fax: (212)675-3704
E-mail: madre@igc.apc.org
URL: http://www.madre.org
Contact: Vivian Stromberg, Exec.Dir.
Desc: Seeks to further the possibilities for peace through a women's human rights agenda in the U.S. *Type:* Association.

Maine Medical Center Research Institute
125 John Roberts Rd.   Ph: (207)761-9090
South Portland, ME 04106   Fax: (207)761-2130
E-mail: lovete@mail.mmc.org
URL: http://zappa.mmcri.mmc.org
Contact: Edmund J. Lovett, III, Assoc.VP, Res.Dir.
Desc: Laboratory, clinical, and epidemiologic research on molecular genetics, hematology, infectious diseases, endocrinology, cardiology and nephrology. *Type:* Research center.

Maisonneuve-Rosemont Hospital Research Centre
5415 de l'Assomption Blvd.   Ph: (514)252-3557
Montreal, PQ, Canada H1T   Fax: (514)252-3430
2M4
E-mail: yleroux@hme.qc.ca
Contact: Claude Perreault, MD, Dir.
Desc: Reproductive biology, including epididymal maturation, acrosome reaction, fertilization, and implantation; immunology, including bone marrow transplantation, transplantation of encapsulated cells, DNA repair, lymphocyte function and ontogeny, immunogenetics, and cytokines; hypertension, including angiotensinogen gene; calcium metabolism; kidney physiology; cancer, including prostate and leukemias; nuclear medicine; and neurology, including cerebrovascular diseases and aphasia. *Type:* Research center.

Mallory Institute of Pathology Foundation
784 Massachusetts Ave.   Ph: (617)534-5314
Boston, MA 02118   Fax: (617)534-5315
Contact: Dr. Leonard S. Gottlieb, Dir.
Desc: Experimental medicine and pathology, with particular reference to cardiovascular diseases, gastrointestinal diseases, liver and kidney diseases, pulmonary diseases, hematopathology, nutritional pathology, immunopathology, environmental pathology, and oncology. *Type:* Research center.

MAMRT Newsletter
Manitoba Association of Medical Radiation Technologists
215 - 819 Sargent   Ph: (204)774-5346
Winnipeg, MB, Canada R3E   Fax: (204)774-5346
0B9
Desc: Contains announcements of conferences and other events of interest to radiation technologists and therapists in Manitoba. Recurring features include messages from some officers and committees and birth/death notices. *Type:* Newsletter.

Managed Care
Stezzi Communications, Inc.
301 Oxford Valley Rd., No.   Ph: (215)321-6663
1105-A   Fax: (215)321-6670
Yardley, PA 19067
E-mail: editors@managedcaremag.com.
URL: http://www.managedcaremag.com.
Contact: John Marcille, Editor; Tim Search, Publisher.
Desc: Professional journal covering healthcare management issues for physicians and managed care executives. *Type:* Periodical.

Managed Care Week
Atlantic Information Services, Inc.
1100 17th St. NW, No. 300   Ph: (202)775-9008
Washington, DC 20036   Free: 800-521-4323
    Fax: (202)331-9542
Contact: Phoebe Eliopoulos, Managing Editor.
Desc: Provides the news on innovative managed care arrangements and the business affairs and compliance strategies of HMOs, PPOs, and POS plans. Recurring features include inserts. *Type:* Newsletter.

MAP International
PO Box 215000   Ph: (912)265-6010
Brunswick, GA 31521-5000   Free: 800-225-8550
    Fax: (912)265-6170
E-mail: mapus@map.org
URL: http://www.map.org
Contact: Paul B. Thompson, Pres./CEO.
Desc: Non-profit Christian relief and development organization that promotes the health of people living in the world's poorest communities. Works with partners in the areas of community health development, disease prevention and eradication, relief and rehabilitation and global health advocacy. Promotes access to health services and essential medicines in more than 100 countries each year. *Type:* Association.

Marshfield Medical Research and Education Foundation
1000 N. Oak Ave.   Ph: (715)387-5241
Marshfield, WI 54449-5790   Fax: (715)389-3131
E-mail: gundersp@mfldclin.edu
URL: http://www.marshmed.org
Contact: Paul D. Gunderson, PhD, Dir.
Desc: Diagnosis and treatment of human disease, including basic and/or applied studies on respitory diseaese, cancer clonogenic testing, plasma proteinase inhibitors in diabetes, human angiotensinogen and renin in hypertension, estrogen receptors in breast cancer, infertility, human genome mapping, epidemiology and biostatistics, and clinical drug trials. Provides research service for area physicians. *Type:* Research center.

Maryland Medical Research Institute
600 Wyndhurst Ave.   Ph: (410)435-4200
Baltimore, MD 21210   Fax: (410)323-8622
E-mail: postmaster@mmri.org
URL: http://www.mmri.org
Contact: Dr. Genell L. Knatterud, Pres.
Desc: Data gathering, analysis, and design for large-scale clinical trials and epidemiological studies in medical areas such as heart disease, cancer, blood disease, septicemia, AIDS, surgical treatment and laser therapy, and in retinal diseases, and the effects of diet on health status. *Type:* Research center.

Massachusetts General Hospital
Reproductive Endocrine Unit
Bartlett Hall Extension 511   Ph: (617)726-8433
Boston, MA 02114   Fax: (617)726-5357
URL: http://www.mgh.harvard.edu
Contact: Alan Schneyer, PhD, Dir., R&D Lab.
Desc: Reproductive endocrinology, focusing on local regulators of gonadal physiology and characterization and regulation of posttransitional processing of inhibin subunits using a variety of techniques, including protein purification and characterization and molecular biology. *Type:* Research center.

Massachusetts Health Research Institute, Inc.
18 Tremont St.   Ph: (617)523-6565
Boston, MA 02108   Fax: (617)523-2070
Contact: Jonathan Spack, Exec.Dir.
Desc: Public health and human services. Sponsors interorganizational demonstration projects in the areas of infant mortality, violence prevention, genetics, and intervention strategies with substance abusers. *Type:* Research center.

Massachusetts Institute of Technology
Center for Biomedical Engineering Administration
Whitaker Coll. of Hea. Sci. &   Ph: (617)258-7026
Tech.
545 Technology Sq.
Cambridge, MA 02139
URL: http://web.mit.edu/cbe/www/goals.html
Contact: Prof. Douglas A. Lauffenburger, Dir.
Desc: Molecular medicine, including molecular engineering, cell and tissue engineering, and physiological systems engineering. *Type:* Research center.

Massachusetts Institute of Technology
Clinical Research Center
50 Ames St., Bldg. E17, Rm.   Ph: (617)253-3091
445   Fax: (617)253-6882
Cambridge, MA 02139
E-mail: dick@mit.edu
Contact: Dr. Richard J. Wurtman, MD, Prog.Dir.
Desc: Normal human metabolism, physiology, and behavior, including studies on hormones (melatonin and sleep), fates of deuterated amino acids, behavioral and neuroendocrine effect of foods (carbohydrate, protein, and caffeine), effects of drugs on memory and other behaviors, and endocrine and metabolic effects on aging. Also studies human diseases such as obesity, Alzheimer's disease, brain injury, Parkinson's disease, seasonal depression, use of brain imaging techniques to follow metabolic events, and facilitation of smoking withdrawal by psychopharmacologic agents. *Type:* Research center.

Mayo Clinic Proceedings
Dowden Publishing Co., Inc.
110 Summit Ave.   Ph: (201)391-9100
Montvale, NJ 07645   Fax: (201)391-2778
E-mail: mayo5738@aol.com.
Contact: Dr. U.B.S. Prakash, Editor, (507)284-2094; Pamela M. Poppalardo, Publisher.

Desc: Medical journal. *Alt. Contact:* Mayo Foundation for Medical Education and Research, 200 1st St. S.W., Rochester, MN 55905; telephone: (507)284-2154; fax: (507)284-0252. *Type:* Periodical.

Mayo Foundation

General Clinical Research Center

St. Mary's Hospital   Ph: (507)255-6122
1216 2nd St. SW   Fax: (507)255-7445
Rochester, MN 55902
E-mail: andresen@mayo.edu
URL: http://www.mayo.edu
Contact: Lawrence Riggs, Dir.

Desc: Allergy, endocrinology, gastrointestinal disease, lipid disorders, osteoporosis, pediatrics, pharmacology, renal disease, surgery, cardiovascular disease, oncology, neurology, hypertension, and nutrition. *Type:* Research center.

McGill University

Anaesthesia Research Department

McIntyre Med. Sci. Bldg.   Ph: (514)398-6001
3655 Drummond St.   Fax: (514)398-4376
Montreal, PQ, Canada H3G
   1Y6
E-mail: krnjevic@medcor.mcgill.ca
Contact: Dr. K. Krnjevic, Dir.

Desc: Physiology, neurochemistry, and pharmacology of synaptic mechanisms and effects of anoxia and anaesthetic drugs in the central nervous system. *Type:* Research center.

McGill University

Artificial Cells and Organs Research Centre

3655 Drummond St.   Ph: (514)398-3512
Montreal, PQ, Canada H3G   Fax: (514)398-4983
   1Y6
E-mail: artcell@physio.mcgill.ca
URL: http://www.physio.mcgill.ca/artcell
Contact: Prof. T.M.S. Chang, Dir.

Desc: Interdisciplinary research using biotechnology, biochemistry, chemical engineering, medicine, enzyme engineering, and chemistry on projects concerning artificial cells, blood substitutes from crosslinked hemoglobin and encapsulated hemoglobin, artificial kidney, artificial liver, detoxifier, immobilized enzymes, cells, including genetically engineered cells, hemoperfusion, microencapsulation, nanoencapsulation, enzyme replacement therapy, drug carriers, and biomaterials. *Type:* Research center.

McGill University

Centre for Medicine, Ethics, and Law

3690 Peel St.   Ph: (514)398-7400
Montreal, PQ, Canada H3A   Fax: (514)398-4668
   1W9
Contact: Dr. B. Robaire, Exec.Dir.

Desc: Social and policy issues which have medical, ethical, and legal dimensions, including medical research, reproductive technology, aging, population, AIDS, euthanasia, genetics, and biotechnology. *Type:* Research center.

McGill University

Centre for Nonlinear Dynamics in Physiology and Medicine

McIntyre Medical Science Bldg.   Ph: (514)398-4336
3655 Drummond St.   Fax: (514)398-7452
Montreal, PQ, Canada H3G
   1Y6
E-mail: mackey@cnd.mcgill.ca
URL: http://www.cnd.mcgill.ca
Contact: Michael C. Mackey, Dir.

Desc: Understanding the origin of dynamic behavior in health and disease, focusing on cyclical hematopoiesis, neurological tremor, and cardiac arrythmias. *Type:* Research center.

McGill University

Institute of Parasitology

Macdonald Campus   Ph: (514)398-7722
21111 Lakeshore Rd.   Fax: (514)398-7857
Ste. Anne de Bellevue, PQ,
   Canada H9X 3V9
E-mail: marilyn@parasit.lan.mcgill.ca
URL: http://www.parasitology.mcgill.ca/
Contact: Dr. Marilyn E. Scott, Dir.

Desc: Epidemiology, ecology, biochemistry, neurophysiology, immunology, population and molecular genetics and molecular biology of parasites. Research includes experimental studies on the relationships and interactions between parasite and host. *Type:* Research center.

McGill University

Lady Davis Institute for Medical Research

3755 Chemin de la Cote-Sainte-   Ph: (514)340-8260
   Catherine   Fax: (514)340-7502
Montreal, PQ, Canada H3T
   1E2
E-mail: sfreedma@ldi.jgh.mcgill.ca
URL: http://www.mcgill.ca/jgh/ldi.htm
Contact: Samuel O. Freedman, MD, Dir.

Desc: AIDS, Aging, Cognitive Neuroscience, Molecular Oncology, Pharmacology of Cancer, Perinatal Pharmacology, Endocrinology and Intermediary Metabolism, Human Genetics, Iron Metabolism, Cardiovascular Diseases, Nephrology and Urology, Clinical Epidemiology, Health Services Research, Psychosocial Aspects of Illness. *Type:* Research center.

McGill University

McGill Centre for Endocrine Studies

Royal Victoria Hospital   Ph: (514)842-1231
Fraser Labs, Rm. M3-15   Fax: (514)849-3681
687 Pine Ave. W.
Montreal, PQ, Canada H3A
   1A1
E-mail: patel@rvhmed.lan.mcgill.ca
Contact: Dr. Yogesh C. Patel, Dir.

Desc: Endocrinology; molecular biology of peptide hormones and their receptors; molecular pharmacology of G protein coupled receptors; proliferative and anti-proliferative cell signaling; apoptosis; neuropeptides in brain, gut, pancreas, and immune system; peptide hormones and development; prostaglandins and metabolites of arachedonic acid. *Type:* Research center.

McGill University

McGill Centre for the Study of Reproduction

Department of Physiology   Ph: (514)398-4316
McIntyre Med. Sci. Bldg.   Fax: (514)398-7452
3655 Drummond St.
Montreal, PQ, Canada H3G
   1Y6
E-mail: riaz@rvhobz.lan.mcgill.ca
Contact: Dr. Riaz Farookhi, Dir.

Desc: Reproduction, including fetal development, pregnancy, parturition, and structure and function of the brain/pituitary/ovarian axis and brain/pituitary/testicular/epididymal axis. Activities include studies of polycystic ovarian disease and follicular atresia, environmental influences on reproductive function, physiological basis of premenstrual tension, the regulation of epididymal enzymes, fetal-placental endocrinology, normal and abnormal development and teratology, reproductive aging, and the effects of gonadal steriods on the brain-pituitary axis and hypothalamic structure. *Type:* Research center.

McGill University

McGill Centre for Tropical Diseases

Montreal General Hospital, Rm.   Ph: (514)934-8049
   D7-153   Fax: (514)933-9385
1650 Cedar Ave.
Montreal, PQ, Canada H3G
   1A4
E-mail: md10@musica.mcgill.ca
Contact: Dr. J. Dick MacLean, Dir.

Desc: Tropical medicine and clinical parasitology, including studies of giardiases, toxocara, toxoplasma, ciguatera, trichinosis, and the epidemiology of medical problems in refugees and travelers. Maintains surveillance of Canadians traveling to, living in, or emigrating from the tropics. *Type:* Research center.

McGill University

Meakins-Christie Laboratories

3626 St. Urbain St.   Ph: (514)398-3864
Montreal, PQ, Canada H2X   Fax: (514)398-7483
   2P2
E-mail: jmartin@meakins.lan.mcgill.ca
URL: http://www.meakins.mcgill.ca
Contact: Dr. James G. Martin, Dir.

Desc: Respiratory physiology and physiopathology, including studies on control of breathing, respiratory mechanics, respiratory muscle fatigue, electromyography, lung morphology and biochemistry, airway dynamics, smooth muscle growth and contractive signalling, eicosanoids, T-lymphocytes, allergic inflammation. *Type:* Research center.

McGill University

Montreal Chest Institute Research Centre

3650 St. Urbain St.   Ph: (514)849-5201
Montreal, PQ, Canada H2X   Fax: (514)843-2095
   2P4
E-mail: wendy@meakins.lan.mcgill.ca
URL: http://www.meakins.mcgill.ca/mci
Contact: Dr. James G. Martin, Dir.

Desc: Respiratory medicine, focusing on chronic obstructive pulmonary diseases (COPD). Research also includes structure-function, physiology, pharmacology, rehabilitation, environment, body surface motion, asthma, cystic fibrosis, and airway hyperresponsiveness. *Type:* Research center.

McGill University

Montreal General Hospital Research Institute

1650 Cedar Ave.   Ph: (514)937-6011
Montreal, PQ, Canada H3G   Fax: (514)934-8261
   1A4
E-mail: mcsr@musica.mcgill.ca
Contact: Dr. Joseph Shuster, Dir.

Desc: Neurosciences, immunology and infectious deseases, cardiac and cardiovascular diseases, rheology, rheumatology, clinical epidemiology, health care economics, cancer, molecular biology, genetics and orthopedics. *Type:* Research center.

McGill University

Neuromuscular Research Group

3801 University St.   Ph: (514)398-8528
Montreal, PQ, Canada H3A   Fax: (514)398-8310
   2B4
E-mail: mcgk@musica.mcgill.ca
Contact: Dr. George Karpati, Coord.

Desc: Neuromuscular research, including molecular genetics, muscle biochemistry, muscle metabolism, neurotoxicology, neuropathology, neurophysiology, cytochemistry, and magnetic resonance spectroscopy. Research focuses on gene therapy for muscle and motor neurons, coordinated expression of genes coding for myofibrillar molecules during differentiation and denervation, use of transgenic mice, cell adhesion molecules and molecular mechanisms of myoblast fusion in vitro, molecular biology of muscle mitochondria (especially in mitochondrial diseases), microscopic and biochemical cytoskeletal alterations in neurons pertaining to diseases such as amyotrophic lateral sclerosis and toxic neuropathies, in vivo magnetic resonance spectroscopy of neuromuscular diseases, comprehensive multidisciplinary investigation of complex neuromuscular diseases, and gene therapy for dystrophin deficiency states. *Type:* Research center.

McLaughlin Research Institute for Biomedical Sciences
1520 23rd St. S.   Ph: (406)452-6208
Great Falls, MT 59405-4900   Fax: (406)454-6019
E-mail: davec@po.mri.montana.edu
Contact: Dr. George A. Carlson, Dir.

Desc: Genetics, immunogenetics, and cancer immunology, including studies of mouse histocompatibility genes and antigens, immunoregulatory gene family diversity and divergence, genetic basis of susceptibility to transmissible neurodegenerative disease, and mitotic recombination in mammalian cells. *Type:* Research center.

McMaster University
Electron Microscopy Central Facility
HSC-2N18   Ph: (905)525-9140
1200 Main St. W., Rm. 3N29   Fax: (905)577-0198
Hamilton, ON, Canada L8S 4J9
E-mail: alalab@whcat.on.ca
URL: http://www.mcmaster.ca
Contact: Dr. Larry Arsenault, MD, Dir.

Desc: Neurosciences, cardiovascular system, mineralization, confocal microscopy, and analytical electron microscopy. Facility is used by many research groups. *Type:* Research center.

McMaster University
Institute for Molecular Biology and Biotechnology
Life Sci. Bldg., Rm. 425   Ph: (905)525-9140
1280 Main St. W.   Fax: (905)521-2955
Hamilton, ON, Canada L8S 4K1
E-mail: hassell@mcmail.cis.mcmaster.ca
URL: http://www.mcmaster.ca
Contact: Dr. John A. Hassell, Dir.

Desc: Molecular biology and biotechnology focusing on genetic engineering, including studies in gene cloning, recombinant DNA, monoclonal antibody analysis, and gene sequencing. Also performs custom synthesis of deoxoligonucleotides and peptides. *Type:* Research center.

MCP Hahnemann University of the Health Sciences
The Allegheny Orthopaedic Institute
221 N. Broad St.   Ph: (215)762-8500
Philadelphia, PA 19107   Fax: (215)564-2825
Contact: Dr. Arnold T. Berman, Dir.
Desc: Arthritis. *Type:* Research center.

MCP Hahnemann University of the Health Sciences
Institute for Cellular Therapeutics
Broad & Vine, Mail Stop 490   Ph: (215)762-3800
Philadelphia, PA 19102
URL: http://www.mcphu.edu/institutes/ict/index.html
Contact: Suzanne T. Ildstad, MD, Dir.
Desc: Stem cell biology and bone marrow transplantation to fight disease. *Type:* Research center.

MCP Hahnemann University of the Health Sciences
Institute for Women's Health
3300 Henry Ave.   Ph: (215)842-7142
Philadelphia, PA 19129   Fax: (215)849-7168
E-mail: bowmans@auhs.edu
URL: http://www.auhs.edu
Contact: Bonita Falkner, MD, Actg.Dir.
Desc: Osteoporosis, mammography, urinary incontinence, menopause, and hypertension. *Type:* Research center.

MCP Hahnemann University of the Health Sciences
Krancer Center for Inflammatory Bowel Disease Research
Broad & Vine Sts.   Ph: (215)762-8101
Philadelphia, PA 19102   Fax: (215)246-5432
E-mail: reynoldj@.auhs.edu
Contact: James C. Reynolds, MD, Dir.
Desc: Cause and treatment of ulcerative colitis and Crohn's disease. *Type:* Research center.

Med/Rec Automation
United Communications Group
11300 Rockville Pike, Ste. 1100   Ph: (301)287-2700
Rockville, MD 20852-3030   Free: 800-929-4824
   Fax: (301)287-2049
E-mail: customer@ucg.com
Contact: Robert Long, Sr. Editor.
Type: Newsletter.

Medi-Scripts/Prescription Pads-U.S.
Medi Promotions Inc.
1050 Wall St. W., Ste. 620   Ph: (201)933-8200
Lyndhurst, NJ 07071   Fax: (201)933-8866
Contact: S. Altman, Publisher.
Desc: Periodical serving the medical profession. *Type:* Periodical.

Medical Benefits
Aspen Law & Business/Panel Publishers
1185 Avenue of the Americas,   Ph: (212)597-0200
37th Fl.   Free: 800-447-1777
New York, NY 10036   Fax: (212)597-0338
Contact: Margaret Mucklo, Editor.
Desc: Focuses on key developments, statistics, and studies relating to the health care system. Covers eight major topic areas: cost containment, employee benefits, employee health/wellness, quality of care, delivery systems, government in health care, legal issues, and health care expenditure data. *Type:* Newsletter.

Medical College of Wisconsin
Center for the Study of Bioethics
8701 Watertown Plank Rd.   Ph: (414)456-8498
Milwaukee, WI 53226   Fax: (414)456-6511
E-mail: rshapiro@its.mcw.edu
URL: http://www.mcw.edu/bioethics/
Contact: Robyn Shapiro, Dir.
Desc: Ethics studies, with special emphasis on AIDS, abortion, drug testing, euthanasia, fetal rights, genetics, technology assessment and allocation of resources, and multicultural approaches to bioethics. *Type:* Research center.

Medical College of Wisconsin
Clinical Research Center
9200 W. Wisconsin Ave.   Ph: (414)257-6819
Milwaukee, WI 53226   Fax: (414)259-1529
Contact: Ahmed H. Kissebah, MD, Dir.
Desc: Physiology and pathophysiology of disease in areas of metabolism, endocrinology, gastroenterology, kidney, central nervous system, connective tissues, hematopietic system, and bone, respiratory, and cardiovascular disorders. *Type:* Research center.

Medical Community Digest
RAMA Group of Companies, Inc.
25 Boxwood Ln.   Ph: (716)668-5223
PO Box 211
Cheektowaga, NY 14227
Contact: Paula A. Gapik, Editor; Richard A. Mausser, Publisher; Joseph Ciffa, Advertising Mgr.
Desc: Newspaper covering the health care and hospital field. *Type:* Periodical.

Medical Device Approval Letter
Washington Information Source
6506 Old Stage Rd., Ste. 100   Ph: (301)770-5553
Rockville, MD 20852-4326   Fax: (301)468-0475
E-mail: wis@fdainfo.com
URL: http://www.FDAinfo.com.
Contact: Kenneth Reid, Editor.
Desc: Lists monthly 510(k) and approved PMA applications for medical devices. Carries articles on topics of related interest. *Type:* Newsletter.

Medical Device Register
Medical Economics Co.
5 Paragon Dr.   Ph: (201)358-7500
Montvale, NJ 07645-1725   Free: 800-223-0581
   Fax: (201)358-7260
E-mail: customer.service@medec.com; mdr@medec.com.
Contact: Thomas B. Young, Editor, (201)258-7920.
Desc: More than 12,000 U.S. manufacturers of medical devices and clinical laboratory products; includes OEM manufacturers. *Type:* Directory.

Medical Economics
Medical Economics Co.
5 Paragon Dr.   Ph: (201)358-7500
Montvale, NJ 07645-1725   Free: 800-223-0581
   Fax: (201)358-7260
E-mail: customer.service@medec.com; jeff.forster@medec.com.
URL: http://www.medc.com; http://www.memag.com.
Contact: Jeff Forster, Editor; Frank Lederer, Publisher, frank.lederer@medec.com; Kevin Bollum, National Sales Director, kevin.bolum@medec.com.
Desc: Magazine covering physicians practice management, professional relations, and financial affairs. *Alt. Contact:* NJ; telephone: (201)358-7340; fax: (201)722-2688; toll-free: 800-526-4870. *Type:* Periodical.

Medical and Health Research Association of New York City, Inc.
40 Worth St., Ste. 720   Ph: (212)285-0220
New York, NY 10013-2988   Fax: (212)385-0565
URL: http://www.mhra.org
Desc: Obstetrics, gynecology, midwifery, nursing, prenatal care and diagnoses, maternity care, infant care, infant mortality, pediatric care, family planning, childhood immunizations, health and HIV education, and nutrition for persons living in New York City. *Type:* Research center.

Medical Insurance Claims Inc.
Kinnelon Professional Complex   Ph: (201)492-2828
170 Kinnelon Rd.   Fax: (201)492-9068
Ste. 10
Kinnelon, NJ 07405
Desc: Distributes Understanding Your Health Insurance. *Alt. Contact:* Kinnelon Professional Complex, 170 Kinnelon Rd., Ste. 10, Kinnelon, NJ 07405; telephone: (201)492-2828; fax: (201)492-9068. *Type:* Periodical.

Medical Malpractice Lawsuit Filings

*Medical Malpractice Verdicts, Settlements &
Experts*

901 Church St.   Ph: (615)255-6288
Nashville, TN 37203-3411
E-mail: llaska@verdictslaska.com

Contact: Lorenda Patterson, Editorial Assistant, (615)255-
6288, fax: (615)255-6289, llaska@verdictslaska.com.

Desc: Contains summaries of more than 37,000 medical
malpractice lawsuits filed in all U.S. District Courts and
51 state courts. *Available:* West Group, WESTLAW.
Type: Database.

Medical Management Network

COR Healthcare Resources

PO Box 40959   Ph: (805)564-2177
Santa Barbara, CA 93140-0959   Fax: (805)564-2146
E-mail: corinfo@corhealth.com
URL: http://www.mmnomume.com.

Contact: Marilyn Lang, RN, Editor.

Desc: Provides summaries of articles about patient care
management from an array of over 150 publications. *Type:*
Newsletter.

Medical Materials Update

Business Communications Co., Inc.

25 Van Zant St.   Ph: (203)853-4266
Norwalk, CT 06855-1781   Fax: (203)853-0348
E-mail: buscom2@aol.com
URL: http://www.buscom.com; http://www.buscom.
com/.

Contact: Diana Milloy, Editor.

Desc: Reports on materials used to make medical devices
such as catheters and shunts, as well as applications like
implants, filters, tubing, and prostheses. Identifies regulatory trends, examines investment possibilities, and evaluates data. *Type:* Newsletter.

Medical Network Strategy Report

COR Healthcare Resources

PO Box 40959   Ph: (805)564-2177
Santa Barbara, CA 93140-0959   Fax: (805)564-2146
E-mail: corinfo@corhealth.com

Contact: Mark Hagland, Editor.

Desc: Provides coverage of hospital-physician integration
models and medical network development. *Type:* Newsletter.

Medical Records Institute

567 Walnut St.   Ph: (617)964-3923
PO Box 600770   Fax: (617)964-3926
Newton, MA 02460
E-mail: cust_service@medrecinst.com
URL: http://www.medrecinst.com

Contact: C. Peter Waegemann, Exec.Dir.

Desc: Conducts research and education in the fields of
medical documentation and computerization of patient
information. *Type:* Association.

Medical Research Council of Canada

Protein Structure and Function Group

University of Alberta   Ph: (780)492-5460
Department of Biochemistry   Fax: (780)492-0886
Edmonton, AB, Canada T6G
    2H7
E-mail: brian.sykes@ualberta.ca
URL: http://www.dradem.biochem.ualberta.ca/mrc

Contact: Dr. Brian D. Sykes, Dir.

Desc: Muscle protein structure and function, enzyme
structure and function, protein-nucleic acid interactions,
and phosphorylation-dephosphorylation of proteins. Performs X-ray diffraction, CD, flourescence, amino acid
analysis and sequence analysis, peptide synthesis, nuclear
magnetic resonance (NMR) and molecular biology. *Type:*
Research center.

Medical Research Institute of Worcester, Inc.

70 Southbridge St., Unit 612   Ph: (508)755-3714
Worcester, MA 01608-2048

Contact: Eugenia Rosemberg, MD, Res.Dir.

Desc: Reproductive endocrinology, with special emphasis
in pituitary gonadal relationships, including purification
and biological and immunological characterization of
human gonadotropins, development of techniques for immunoassay of protein and steroid hormones, characterization of normal ovarian and testicular function,
characterization of specific types of male and female infertility, and use of pituitary hormones for treatment of specific cases of male and female infertility. *Type:* Research
center.

Medical Staff Briefing

Opus Communications

100 Hoods Ln.   Ph: (781)639-1872
PO Box 1168   Free: 800-650-6787
Marblehead, MA 01945   Fax: (781)639-2982
E-mail: customer_service@opuscomm.com
URL: http://www.opuscomm.com

Contact: Jay Kumar, Exec. Editor.

Desc: Seeks to inform medical staff services professionals
and elected physician leaders on credentialing, including
peer review, and legalities. Recurring features include interviews, news of research, book reviews, notices of publications available, and columns titled In Brief, I'd Like to
Know.., Briefings on Publications, and Facts, Forms, and
Formats. *Type:* Newsletter.

Medical Subject Headings Vocabulary File

U.S. National Library of Medicine (NLM)
MEDLARS Management Section

8600 Rockville Pike   Ph: (301)496-3147
Bethesda, MD 20894
URL: http://www.sis.nlm.nih.gov/dirline

Desc: Contains the controlled medical subject headings
and vocabulary thesaurus terms used in compiling the
databases of the National Library of Medicine. Includes
16,000 medical subject headings and 54,000 chemical
substances headings. *Available:* The Dialog Corporation,
DataStar; The Dialog Corporation, DataStar; U.S. National Library of Medicine (NLM), TOXNET. *Type:*
Database.

Medical Technology and Practice Patterns Institute, Inc.

4733 Bethesda Ave., Ste. 510   Ph: (202)333-8841
Bethesda, MD 20814   Fax: (202)333-5586
E-mail: inquiry@mtppi.org
URL: http://www.mtppi.org

Contact: Dennis J. Cotter, Pres.

Desc: New and emerging health-care technologies and
their implications for local, national, and international
policy. Research efforts fall into three broad areas: Health
Services Research, encompassing patient outcomes, phar-
macoeconomics, quality-of-life assessments, and cost-
effectiveness analyses; International Activities, including
conducting surveys of health technology assessment activities worldwide technology assessment modeling, and
sponsorship of workshops and seminars on health policy
issues; and Special Programs, encompassing health-facility
planning, vaccine research and development, and educational outreach. *Type:* Research center.

Medical University of South Carolina

Arthritis Clinical and Research Center

171 Ashley Ave.   Ph: (803)792-3484
Charleston, SC 29425   Fax: (803)792-7121
E-mail: silverr@musc.edu
URL: http://www.musc.edu/rheumatology

Contact: Richard M. Silver, MD, Dir.

Desc: Molecular mechanisms of connective tissue diseases,
microvascular investigations, alterations in gene expression
in fibroblasts, adhesion and nonadhesion molecular interactions in cell behavior, rheumatic disorders, immunologic investigations in rheumatic disease (such as the function
of T-cell subsets), cell culture, and other clinical investigations, especially in Raynaud's, scleroderma, undifferentiat-
ed connective tissue syndromes (UCTS) and SLE.
Research is undertaken in an effort to investigate the underlying mechanisms and the nature of rheumatic and
connective tissue diseases, to expand education and training opportunities in the management of musculoskeletal
diseases, and to develop patient care and community programs which increase the awareness of arthritis and improve access to quality rheumatologic care. *Type:* Research
center.

Medical Utilization Management

Faulkner & Gray, Inc.

11 Penn Plaza, 17th Fl.   Ph: (212)967-7000
New York, NY 10001-2006   Free: 800-535-8403
                                        Fax: (212)967-7180
E-mail: order@faulknergray.com

Contact: Kenneth Moss, Editor.

Desc: Monitors developments related to cost containment,
data disclosure, private standards, PPOs, and Medicare/
Medicaid. Includes coverage of congressional action and
that of federal agencies. *Type:* Newsletter.

The Medicare Advisor

Shannon Publications, Inc.

6380 Lyndon B. Johnson Fwy.,   Ph: (972)789-1476
    No. 286   Free: 800-578-4888
Dallas, TX 75240   Fax: (972)503-9760

Contact: Ellen Bradley, Owner/President, ellenb1@
airmail.net.

Desc: Designed to provide accurate and authoritative information on Medicare. Covers resource materials, training information, new forms, Medicare billing, policy
changes, coding information, patient and employee rights,
and technology issues. *Type:* Newsletter.

The Medicare Manager

Shannon Publications, Inc.

6380 Lyndon B. Johnson Fwy.,   Ph: (972)789-1476
    No. 286   Free: 800-578-4888
Dallas, TX 75240   Fax: (972)503-9760

Contact: Ellen Bradley, Owner/President, ellenb1@
airmail.net.

Desc: Designed to provide accurate and authoritative information on Medicare "Part B." Covers Medicare's billing and coding information, policies, services, resources,
and reimbursements. Recurring features include news of
research, reports of meetings, news of educational opportunities, book resources, and notices of publications available. *Type:* Newsletter.

The Medicare Review

Shannon Publications, Inc.

6380 Lyndon B. Johnson Fwy.,   Ph: (972)789-1476
    No. 286   Free: 800-578-4888
Dallas, TX 75240   Fax: (972)503-9760

Contact: Ellen Bradley, Owner/President, ellenb1@
airmail.net.

Desc: Designed to provide accurate and authoritative information on Medicare. Recurring features include news
of research, reports of meetings, news of educational opportunities, book listings, and notices of publications
available. *Type:* Newsletter.

MEDLARS Name Authority File

U.S. National Library of Medicine (NLM)
MEDLARS Management Section
8600 Rockville Pike   Ph: (301)496-3147
Bethesda, MD 20894
URL: http://www.sis.nlm.nih.gov/dirline

Desc: Contains an authority list of personal names, corporate names, and classification decisions used in compiling the databases of the National Library of Medicine. *Available:* U.S. National Library of Medicine (NLM), TOXNET. *Type:* Database.

MEDLINE

U.S. National Library of Medicine (NLM)
MEDLARS Management Section
8600 Rockville Pike   Ph: (301)496-3147
Bethesda, MD 20894
URL: http://www.sis.nlm.nih.gov/dirline

Desc: Contains approximately 10 million citations to the world's journal literature covering biomedicine, including research, clinical practice, administration, policy issues, and health care services. Author abstracts are available for approximately 60 percent of the citations; English-language abstracts are provided when possible. *Available:* Ovid Technologies, Inc.; Ovid Technologies, Inc.; The Dialog Corporation, DataStar; The Dialog Corporation, DIALOG; The Dialog Corporation, DIALOG; CompuServe Information Service, Knowledge Index; Japan Information Center of Science and Technology (JICST), JICST Online Information System (JOIS); Karolinska Institute Library and Information Center/ Karolinska Institutets Bibliotek och Informationscentral (KIBIC), Medical Information Center (MIC); DIMDI (Deutsches Institut fuer Medizinische Dokumentation und Information); DIMDI (Deutsches Institut fuer Medizinische Dokumentation und Information); U.S. National Library of Medicine (NLM), TOXNET; PaperChase; STN International; STN International; Questel • Orbit; OCLC Online Computer Library Center, Inc., OCLC EPIC; OCLC Online Computer Library Center, Inc., OCLC FirstSearch Catalog; Pan American Health Organization (PAHO), BIREME - Centro Latino-Americano e do Caribe de Informacao em Ciencias da Saude; LEXIS-NEXIS; NIFTY Corporation, NIFTY-SERVE. *Type:* Database.

Meharry Medical College

Center on Tropical Diseases

Div. of Microbiology   Ph: (615)327-6193
1005 D.B. Todd Blvd.   Fax: (615)327-5621
Nashville, TN 37208
E-mail: gchill@ccvax.mmc.edu

Contact: Dr. George Hillnzuela, Contact.

Desc: Molecular, biochemical, and immunological aspects of tropical disease. Specific research includes studies on African trypanosomiasis, Chagas' disease, schistosomiasis, malaria, and leprosy. *Type:* Research center.

Meharry Medical College

Clinical Research Center

1005 D.B. Todd Blvd.   Ph: (615)327-6353
Nashville, TN 37208   Fax: (615)327-5835

Contact: Joseph Hinds, MD, Dir.

Desc: Clinical research, including pulmonary studies, AIDS, sickle cell disease, hypertension, body composition, coronary artery disease, infectious diseases, and oncology. *Type:* Research center.

Methodist Hospital

Sid W. Richardson Institute for Preventive Medicine

6550 Fannin St., SM1423   Ph: (713)793-7417
Houston, TX 77030   Fax: (713)793-1080
E-mail: cdacsor@bcm.tmc.edu

URL: http://www.bcm.tmc.edu

Contact: Clifford Dacso, MD, Med.Dir.

Desc: Analyzes health insurance claims and employee absentee data to evaluate various preventive medicine programs, evaluates the effect of smoking cessation on the occurrence of chronic lung disease, compares different program approaches taken in cardiac rehabilitation (exercise versus comprehensive approaches), and studies depression in patients with heart disease and their spouses. *Type:* Research center.

Methodist Research Institute

1701 N. Senate Blvd.   Ph: (317)929-8861
PO Box 1367   Fax: (317)929-5954
Indianapolis, IN 46206
E-mail: rkovacs@clarian.com

Contact: Dr. Richard Kovacs, Med.Dir.

Desc: Pharmaceutical and device clinical trials, experimental cell research, cell signalling, ion channel physiology, immunology. Other research involves heart, kidney, lung, pancreas, and liver transplants; biliary and renal extracorporeal shock wave lithotripsy; and clot lysis programs. *Type:* Research center.

MGM Update

Medical Group Management Association
104 Inverness Terr. E.   Ph: (303)799-1111
Englewood, CO 80112-5306   Free: 888-608-5601
    Fax: (303)397-1824

Contact: Brenda Hull, Editor.

Desc: Reports on Association news, activities, and services for managers and the medical groups they represent. Covers legislative developments and discusses health-care delivery in the medical field. *Type:* Newsletter.

Michigan State University

Institute of International Health

West Fee Hall, B-301   Ph: (517)353-8992
East Lansing, MI 48824-1315   Fax: (517)355-1894
URL: http://www.msu.edu/unit/ich

Contact: Dr. Evangelos A. Petropoulos, Dir.

Desc: Promotes, supports and coordinates research on world health problems, including overseas health studies. Specific projects include: the Training and research om Environmental and Occupational Health in the Balkans project focusing on Bulgaria, the Cerebral Malaria in Children Project, which conducts studies in tropical medicine in Malawi; Medical Anthropology Program, which conducts health research projects in Asia, Africa, and Latin America on problems related to nutrition, childbirth, infant mortality, traditional health care delivery, and migrant worker health; and the High Blood Pressure Research Project, which conducts conducts collaborative projetcs in Zimbabwe. *Type:* Research center.

Michigan State University

Office of Medical Education Research and Development

College of Human Med.   Ph: (517)353-7791
E. Fee Hall, Rm. A-217   Fax: (517)353-8926
East Lansing, MI 48824
E-mail: ander113@pilot.msu.edu
URL: http://omeradl.chm.msu.edu/users/@tldomerad/

Contact: William A. Anderson, PhD, Dir.

Desc: Medical education evaluation and research including evaluation of innovative educational programs, measures of physician competence, health policy forums, and faculty development. Utilizes an interdisciplinary faculty representing the fields of psychology, anthropology, statistics, and education. *Type:* Research center.

Midwest Biomedical Research Foundation

4801 E. Linwood Blvd., Ste.   Ph: (816)921-8311
   104   Fax: (816)861-1110
Kansas City, MO 64128-2226
Contact: Jeaneatte Evans-Hamilton, Dir.
Desc: Clinical studies, focusing on improving treatments and cures of health problems prevalent among veteran patients and the general population. *Type:* Research center.

Milton Helpern Institute of Forensic Medicine

520 1st Ave.   Ph: (212)447-2343
New York, NY 10016   Fax: (212)447-2744
Contact: Dr. Charles S. Hirsch, Dir.
Desc: Promotes medical-legal research, particularly the problems arising out of the official investigation of sudden, suspicious, violent, and unusual deaths, including those occuring in legal custody. Serves as a repository for material and a reference source in legal medicine, including medical-legal books, journals, and films. *Type:* Research center.

Minneapolis Medical Research Foundation

600 HFA Bldg.   Ph: (612)347-5099
914 S. 8th St.   Fax: (612)337-7189
Minneapolis, MN 55404
URL: http://www.mmrfweb.org
Contact: Phillip Peterson, MD, Pres.
Desc: Medicine, surgery, pediatrics, neurology, urology, renal transplant, endocrinology, nephrology, dialysis, anesthesia, hyperbaric medicine, program evaluation and outcomes research, addiction, AIDS, Alzheimer's disease, trauma, and health care policy. *Type:* Research center.

Minnesota Center for Health Care Ethics

601 25th Ave. S   Ph: (612)690-7895
Minneapolis, MN 55454   Fax: (612)690-7774
E-mail: jarobbins@stkate.edu
Contact: Karen G. Gervais, PhD, Dir.
Desc: Cultural diversity, medical futility, ethics and managed care, autologous bone marrow transplants, living donor studies for tissue and organs, and fetal tissue transplants for Parkinson's disease recipients. Current projects include development of a uniform medical futility policy for Minnesota; approaches to end-of-life issues within the Hmong culture, creation of cultural sensitivity among Western healthcare practitioners; and the attempt to create a casebook for HMO's and healthcare institutions outlining an "ethic of care" that will allow the best treatment of individuals within the guidelines presented by their HMO's. *Type:* Research center.

Modern Medicine

Advanstar Communications
270 Madison Ave.   Ph: (212)951-6708
New York, NY 10016-0695   Fax: (212)686-4841
E-mail: modmed@en.com.
URL: http://www.modernmedicine.com.
Contact: Maura Griffin, Editor, mgriffin@advanstar.com; Michelle Janin, Publisher, mjanin@advanstar.com.
Desc: Publication covering the diagnosis, treatment, and prevention of diseases in primary-care practice. *Type:* Periodical.

The Moisture Seekers Newsletter

Sjogren's Syndrome Foundation
333 N. Broadway, Ste. 2000   Ph: (516)933-6365
Jericho, NY 11753
URL: http://www.sjogrens.com.
Contact: Alexis Skeeman, Editor.
Desc: Educates patients, their families, and health professionals about Sjogren's Syndrome, a disorder marked by dryness of all mucous membranes resulting from deficient secretion of the glands. Allows patients to share information on coping with the syndrome and notifies them of opportunities to participate in clinical investigative programs. *Type:* Newsletter.

Montefiore University Hospital
General Clinical Research Center
8N MUH   Ph: (412)648-6691
200 Lothrop St.   Fax: (412)648-6697
Pittsburgh, PA 15261
E-mail: branch@medl.dept-med.pitt.edu
URL: http://www.pitt.edu/~rks2
Contact: Robert A. Branch, MD, Prog.Dir.
Desc: Cardiology, connective tissue disease, diabetes, endocrinology, hematology and oncology, hypertension, infectious disease, pulmonary physiology, nephrology, transplantation, and behavioral medicine. *Type:* Research center.

Mount Sinai Hospital
Samuel Lunenfeld Research Institute
600 University Ave.   Ph: (416)586-8273
Toronto, ON, Canada M5G   Fax: (416)586-8844
1X5
E-mail: bernstein@mslri.on.ca
URL: http://www.mshri.on.ca
Contact: Dr. Alan Bernstein, Dir.
Desc: Cancer biology, cell biology, clinical epidemiology, endocrinology, hemopoiesis, musculoskeletal diseases, bone mineral metabolism, genetics, developmental biology, immunology, perinatology, neurobiology, physiology, molecular biology, bioinformatics, proteomics, biochemistry, gastroenterology, respiratory research, and hearing research. *Type:* Research center.

Mt. Sinai Medical Center
Cell Imaging Laboratory
Box 1218   Ph: (212)241-6536
Mt. Sinai Medical Center   Fax: (212)860-3369
New York, NY 10029
E-mail: jeisinger@smtplink.mss.edu
Contact: Josef Eisinger, PhD, Dir.
Desc: Applies photophysical concepts and techniques to problems in cell physiology, using instrumentation designed for low-light level, quantitative fluroscence imaging. Current research includes: high-resolution three-dimensional fluorescence imaging of chromosomes and cells, using non-confocal optical sectioning and novel deconvolution and image reconstruction algorithms, and extraction of spatially-resolved dynamic information from two (or more) images acquired at different emission wavelengths or emission polarization conditions. *Type:* Research center.

Mount Sinai School of Medicine of City University of New York
General Clinical Research Center
1184 5th Ave.   Ph: (212)241-6045
Box 1027   Fax: (212)348-5811
New York, NY 10029
E-mail: rdesnick@smtplinf.mssm.edu
URL: http://www.mssm.edu/crc/home-page.html
Contact: Dr. Robert Desnick, Dir.
Desc: Nature and treatment of human diseases through clinical investigation, including studies on Gaucher disease, Parkinson's disease, Fabry's disease, Alzheimer's disease, nutrition, energy expenditure, AIDS, lipid metabolism, peptide and steroid hormones, and lead poisoning. *Type:* Research center.

MRC Communique
Medical Research Council of Canada
Holland Cross   Ph: (613)946-0927
1600 Scott St., PL 3105A   Fax: (613)954-6653
Ottawa, ON, Canada K1A 0W9
URL: http://wwwmrc.hc-sc.gc.ca.
Desc: Provides information of interest to Canadian Medical Research Council funded researchers and partners in health science research. Recurring features include interviews, news of research, a calendar of events, and news of industry partners. *Type:* Newsletter.

MS Ontario
Multiple Sclerosis Society of Canada
250 Bloor St. E., Ste. 1000   Ph: (416)922-6065
Toronto, ON, Canada M4W   Fax: (416)922-7538
3P9
E-mail: info@mssoc.ca
URL: http://www.mssoc.ca/on.
Desc: Provides information about research, services, social action, and activities of the Multiple Sclerosis Society of Ontario. Recurring features include news of research, a calendar of events, reports of meetings, and news of educational opportunities. *Type:* Newsletter.

Multiple Sclerosis Association of America
706 Haddonfield Rd.   Ph: (609)488-4500
Cherry Hill, NJ 08002-2652   Free: 800-LEARN
MS
Fax: (609)661-9797
E-mail: msaa@msaa.com
URL: http://www.msaa.com
Contact: Douglas Franklin, Exec.Dir.
Desc: Works to fulfill the daily needs of multiple sclerosis patients. *Type:* Association.

NAMES News Today
National Association for Medical Equipment Services (NAMES)
625 Slaters Ln., Ste. 200   Ph: (703)836-6263
Alexandria, VA 22314   Fax: (703)836-6730
E-mail: info@names.org
URL: http://www.names.org.
Contact: Jennifer Gisin, Editor, jennig@names.org.
Desc: Informs members of developments in government agencies, state legislatures, and on Capitol Hill, as well as any other pertinent information that affects the home medical equipment services industry. Remarks: Available in print, e-mail, or fax format. *Type:* Newsletter.

Nashville Research Institute, Inc.
1310 24th Ave. S.   Ph: (615)327-0938
Nashville, TN 37212-2637
Desc: Medical clinical trials. *Type:* Research center.

National Association for Holistic Aromatherapy
836 Hanley Industrial Court   Free: 888-ASK-
St. Louis, MO 63144   NAHA
Fax: (314)963-4454
E-mail: info@naha.org
URL: http://www.naha.org/
Contact: Jeanne Rose, Pres.
Desc: Seeks to establish and promote the art and science of aromatherapy as a health care alternative. *Type:* Association.

National Association of Managed Care Physicians
4435 Waterfront Dr., Ste. 101   Ph: (804)527-1905
PO Box 4765   Free: 800-722-0376
Glen Allen, VA 23058-4765   Fax: (804)747-5316
E-mail: sreed@namcp.com
URL: http://www.namcp.com
Contact: Richard Romeis, Pres.
Desc: Licensed physicians and allied health professionals working in managed health care programs; medical residents and students interested in managed health care; corporations or agencies providing services or goods to the industry; interested others. Enhances the ability of practicing physicians to proactively participate within the managed health care arena through research, communication, and education. *Type:* Association.

National Association of Residents and Interns
350 Fairway Dr., Ste. 200   Free: 800-221-2168
Deerfield Beach, FL 33441-1854   Fax: (954)571-8582
E-mail: ppsone@msn.com
URL: http://www.nari-assn.com
Contact: Joseph P. Santoli, Jr., Manager, Membership Services.
Desc: Medical and dental students, interns, residents, and fellows. Contributes to the economic welfare of members through unsecured loan plans, affordable group insurance, group purchase discounts, physician search service, and continuing medical education programs. *Type:* Association.

National Board of Medical Examiners
3750 Market St.   Ph: (215)590-9500
Philadelphia, PA 19104   Fax: (215)590-9555
URL: http://www.usmle.org
Contact: L. Thompson Bowles, M.D., Ph.D, Pres.
Desc: Purposes are: to prepare and administer qualifying examinations either independently or in conjunction with other organizations, of such high quality that legal agencies governing the practice of medicine within each state may, in their discretion, grant a license without further examination for those who have successfully completed such examinations; to cooperate with and, where appropriate, to make its specialized services available to the examining boards of the states, specialty boards, and other organizations concerned with the education and qualification of personnel in the fields of health; to assist medical schools, hospitals and related organizations and institutions in evaluation of the effectiveness of their educational programs; to initiate, develop, and participate in research designed to evaluate the effectiveness of educational programs and techniques, and to assess ever more precisely the knowledge, competence, and qualification of professionals in public health care; to provide educational opportunities for professional personnel in the methods, techniques, and values of testing methods related to knowledge and competence in the broad field of medicine. *Type:* Association.

National Center for Infectious Diseases
Division of Vector-Borne Infectious Diseases
Arbovirus Diseases Branch
PO Box 2087   Ph: (970)221-6442
Fort Collins, CO 80522-2087   Fax: (970)221-6476
Contact: John T. Roehrig, Dir.
Desc: Epidemiology of mosquito and tick-borne viral diseases. Provides consultation and on-site investigations for local, state, national, and international health agencies during arthropod-borne viral disease outbreaks. *Type:* Research center.

National Center for Infectious Diseases
Division of Vector-Borne Infectious Diseases
Bacterial Zoonosis Branch
Plague Section
PO Box 2087   Ph: (303)221-6450
Fort Collins, CO 80522-2087   Fax: (303)221-6476
Contact: Dr. Kenneth Gage, Chf.
Desc: Diagnosis, therapy, epidemiology, and control of bubonic plague; maintains a surveillance system in collaboration with state and federal health agencies to detect fluctuations of infection in animal populations; and serves as a WHO Reference Center for plague diagnosis and control. *Type:* Research center.

National Center for the Study of Wilson's Disease
432 W. 58th St., Ste. 614   Ph: (212)523-8717
New York, NY 10019   Fax: (212)523-8708
Contact: I. Herbert Scheinberg, MD, Contact.
Desc: Wilson's disease and Menkes' disease, focusing on the genetic control of copper balance and the biochemical

regulatory mechanism that prevents the lethal copper deficiency of Menkes' disease and lethal copper toxicity of Wilson's disease. *Type:* Research center.

National Certification Agency for Medical Lab Personnel

PO Box 15945-289   Ph: (913)438-5110
Shawnee Mission, KS 66285   Fax: (913)541-0156
Contact: Michelle Cheney, Assn.Mgr.
Desc: Persons who direct, educate, supervise, or practice in clinical laboratory science. To assure the public and employers of the competence of clinical laboratory personnel; to provide a mechanism for individuals demonstrating competency in the field to achieve career mobility. Develops and administers competency-based examinations for certification of clinical laboratory personnel; provides for periodic recertification by examination or through documentation of continuing education. *Type:* Association.

National Council Against Health Fraud

PO Box 1276   Ph: (909)928-4595
Loma Linda, CA 92354-1276   Fax: (909)928-4995
E-mail: drrenner@msn.com
URL: http://www.ncahf.org
Contact: Dr. William Jarvis, Exec.Dir.
Desc: Evaluates claims made for health products and services, including advertising and labeling practices. *Type:* Research center.

National Directory of Brain Injury Rehabilitation Services

Brain Injury Association
105 N. Alfred St.   Ph: (703)236-6000
Alexandria, VA 22314   Free: 800-444-6443
    Fax: (703)236-6001
E-mail: marketing@biausa.org
URL: http://www.biausa.org.
Contact: Monique Marino, Editor; John Nidhiry, Editor.
Desc: Over 600 providers of services to people with traumatic brain injury, including rehabilitation programs and individual service providers (physicians, rehabilitation professionals, attorneys, etc.) *Type:* Directory.

National Disease Research Interchange

1880 John F. Kennedy Blvd.,   Ph: (215)557-7361
6th Fl.   Free: 800-222-6374
Philadelphia, PA 19103   Fax: (215)557-7154
E-mail: ndri@aol.com
URL: http://www.ndri.com
Contact: Lee Ducat, Pres.
Desc: Procurement, preservation, and distribution of over 100 types of human tissues and organs for medical research. Also coordinates retrieval of pancreatic tissue for the clinical trials of islet cell transplants, a treatment being investigated for insulin-dependent diabetics. *Type:* Research center.

National Foundation for Research in Medicine

2296-83 Caminito Pajarito   Ph: (619)224-2813
San Diego, CA 92107
Contact: Jeanette Baptiste, Contact.
Desc: Independent medical research investigation. *Type:* Research center.

National Heart Foundation Update

American Health Assistance Foundation
15825 Shady Grove Rd., Ste.   Ph: (301)948-3244
140   Free: 800-437-2423
Rockville, MD 20850   Fax: (301)258-9454
Desc: Highlights work of researchers studying heart disease and stroke. Provides tips for preventing and dealing with these disorders. *Type:* Newsletter.

National Jewish Medical and Research Center

1400 Jackson St.   Ph: (303)388-4461
Denver, CO 80206   Free: 800-222-LUNG
    Fax: (303)270-2165
E-mail: lungline@njc.org
URL: http://www.njc.org
Contact: Lynn Taussig, Pres.
Desc: Devoted to treatment, research, and education in chronic respiratory diseases and immunological disorders such as asthma, tuberculosis, cystic fibrosis, chronic bronchitis, emphysema, interstitial lung disease, and systemic lupus erythematosus. Accepts non-sectarian patients of all ages. Disseminates information to the public. *Type:* Association.

National Managed Care Observer

National Managed Care Observer
PO Box 11392
Detroit, MI 48202
Contact: JoAnne S. Wolff, Editor.
Desc: Concerned with quality medical care for African Americans. Also analyzes health- maintenance organizations. *Type:* Newsletter.

National Marfan Foundation

382 Main St.   Ph: (516)883-8712
Port Washington, NY 11050   Free: 800-862-7326
    Fax: (516)883-8040
E-mail: staff@marfan.org
URL: http://www.marfan.org
Contact: Carolyn Levering, Exec.Dir.
Desc: Persons affected with the Marfan syndrome and related connective tissue disorders; families of affected persons; genetic counselors; cardiologists, ophthalmologists, orthopedists, and other medical professionals. (Marfan syndrome is a heritable disorder of the connective tissue affecting the skeleton, lungs, eyes, heart, and blood vessels.). Objectives are to: disseminate accurate and timely information on Marfan syndrome; act as support network and provide a means for patients and relatives to share experiences; improve medical care. *Type:* Association.

National Medical Association

1012 10th St. NW   Ph: (202)347-1895
Washington, DC 20001   Fax: (202)842-3293
URL: http://www.nmanet.org
Contact: Lorraine Cole, PhD, Exec.Dir.
Desc: Professional society of black physicians. Maintains 24 scientific sections representing major specialties of medicine. Plans to establish library. *Type:* Association.

National Organization for Albinism and Hypopigmentation

1530 Locust St., No. 29   Ph: (215)545-2322
Philadelphia, PA 19102-4415   Free: 800-473-2310
    Fax: (609)858-4337
E-mail: noah@albinism.org
URL: http://www.albinism.org
Contact: Charla McMillan, Pres.
Desc: Individuals with albinism and their families; health care professionals; others interested in learning more about albinism. (Albinism is an inherited metabolic disorder that results in reduced pigment in the hair, eyes, and/or skin of those it affects; people with albinism also have impaired eye function including decreased visual acuity, involuntary eye movements, and increased sensitivity to light.) Seeks to educate teachers, health care professionals, and the public about albinism. Provides support to individuals with albinism and their families. *Type:* Association.

National Organization for Rare Disorders

PO Box 8923   Ph: (203)746-6518
New Fairfield, CT 06812-8923   Free: 800-999-6673
    Fax: (203)746-6481
E-mail: orphan@rarediseases.org
URL: http://www.nord-rdb.com/~orphan
Contact: Abbey S. Meyers, Pres.
Desc: Doctors, professionals, academics, voluntary health organizations, and individuals interested in rare disorders. Serves as a clearinghouse for information concerning rare disorders. *Type:* Association.

National Phlebotomy Association

1901 Brightseat Rd.   Ph: (301)386-4200
Landover, MD 20785   Fax: (301)386-4203
URL: http://www.scpt.comNPA.htm
Contact: Diane Crawford, CEO.
Desc: Offers educational programs for phlebotomists; to accredit phlebotomy programs; to give national certification examinations in phlebotomy at the request of approved program. (Phlebotomy is the collection of a blood specimen for analysis in the treatment of disease.) Conducts regional workshops and educational programs. Compiles statistics. *Type:* Association.

National Rare Blood Club

Associated Health Foundation   Ph: (212)889-8245
99 Madison Ave.   Fax: (212)448-1811
New York, NY 10016
Contact: Edward Birnbaum, Pres.
Desc: Persons ages 18-65 with rare blood types who are physically able to donate blood. Operates as a voluntary community service with no fees or dues involved. *Type:* Association.

National Report on Subacute Care

Harling Communications, Inc.
18-2 E. Dundee Rd., Ste. 200   Ph: (847)304-1011
Barrington, IL 60010   Free: 800-894-8786
    Fax: (847)304-1035
E-mail: postacute@aol.com; nrsc@caglonet.com.
Contact: Marjorie Lellis, Editor, (410)326-9796.
Desc: Concerned with all aspects of the industry of subacute care, which is transitional care of less intensity than acute care but more than is provided in a typical nursing home. *Type:* Newsletter.

National Reye's Syndrome Foundation

426 N. Lewis   Ph: (419)636-2679
PO Box 829   Free: 800-233-7393
Bryan, OH 43506   Fax: (419)636-3366
E-mail: reyessyn@mail.bright.net
URL: http://www.right.net/~reyessyn
Contact: Susan Landversicht, Office Mgr.
Desc: Families of children who have had Reye's Syndrome; doctors, scientists, nurses, and other health professionals and concerned individuals. (Reye's Syndrome is a disease affecting the liver and brain. Cause and cure unknown, its mortality rate is over 57 percent). *Type:* Association.

National Stroke Association

96 Inverness Dr. E   Ph: (303)649-9299
Ste. I   Free: 800-STR-OKES
Englewood, CO 80112-5112   Fax: (303)649-1328
E-mail: info@stroke.org
URL: http://www.stroke.org
Contact: Harold W. Todd, Pres.
Desc: Stroke survivors and their families; health care professionals and institutions; the lay community. Seeks to reduce the incidence and impact of stroke by promoting research, educating the public, and providing a network for stroke survivors and concerned persons. Serves as an information referral clearinghouse on stroke; makes available educational materials on stroke prevention, treatment, rehabilitation, resocialization, and research. *Type:* Association.

National Wellness Institute, Inc.

1300 College Court Ph: (715)342-2969
PO Box 827 Fax: (715)342-2979
Stevens Point, WI 54481
E-mail: nwi@wellnessnwi.org
URL: http://www.wellnessnwi.org/
Contact: Dr. Linda Chapin, DDS,MS, Dir.
Desc: Health promotion in large organizations and topics in preventive medicine such as stress reduction, nutrition counseling, weight monitoring, and substance abuse control. *Type:* Research center.

Needle Tips & the Hepatitis B Coalition News

Immunization Action Coalition
1573 Selby, Ste. 234 Ph: (651)647-9009
Saint Paul, MN 55104-6293 Fax: (651)647-9131
E-mail: admin@immunize.org
URL: http://www.immunize.org.
Contact: Deborah Wexler, MD, Editor.
Desc: Provides information about vaccine-preventable diseases. Recurring features include letters to the editor and notices of publications available. *Type:* Newsletter.

Nemours Foundation

Nemours Research Programs

PO Box 269 Ph: (302)651-6819
Wilmington, DE 19899 Fax: (302)651-6810
E-mail: chartzell@nemours.org
URL: http://www.nemours.org
Contact: Charles R. Hartzell, PhD, Dir. of Res.
Desc: Programs are composed of two research departments: the Department of Applied Science and Engineering, which applies technology to the development of communication, mobility, robotic, and therapeutic interactive devices to aid in independent living, education, and employment of disabled children; the Department of Clinical Science conducts medical research in the various fields of basic science as well as physician-directed projects with direct clinical applications. *Type:* Research center.

Neuro Immuno Therapeutic Research Foundation

1092 Boiling Springs Rd. Ph: (864)591-0944
Spartanburg, SC 29303 Fax: (864)591-0622
E-mail: nitrf@aol.com
URL: http://members.aol.com/nitrf
Contact: Dr. H. Hugh Fudenberg, Dir.
Desc: Immunology, Alzheimer's disease, AIDS, autism, and chronic fatigue syndrome. *Type:* Research center.

New Brunswick Health Records Association—Newsbreak

New Brunswick Health Records Association
Chaleur Regional Hospital Ph: (506)548-8961
1750 Sunset Dr. Fax: (506)548-8961
Bathurst, NB, Canada E2A 4L7
Contact: Lise Raiche, Editor.
Desc: Covers Association activities and developments in the health care records field. Recurring features include news of research, a calendar of events, reports of meetings, news of educational opportunities, and job listings. *Type:* Newsletter.

New Directions

National Jewish Medical & Research Center
1400 Jackson St. Ph: (303)398-1080
Denver, CO 80206 Free: 800-423-8891
  Fax: (303)398-1125
Contact: L. Gwatkin, Editor.
Desc: Provides updates on research and clinical progress at the Center. *Type:* Newsletter.

The New England Journal of Medicine

The New England Journal of Medicine
1440 Main St. Ph: (617)843-6356
Waltham, MA 02154-1649 Fax: (617)893-3800
E-mail: nejmcust@mms.org.
URL: http://www.nejm.org.
Contact: Jerome P. Kassirer, M.D., Editor-in-Chief; Robert D. Boverschulte, VP Publishing.
Desc: Journal for the medical profession. *Alt. Contact:* 10 Shattuck St., Boston, MA 02115-6094; telephone: (617)893-3000; fax: (617)893-0413; toll-free: 800-843-6356. *Type:* Periodical.

The New England Journal of Medicine

Massachusetts Medical Society
Publishing Division
1440 Main St. Ph: (617)893-3800
Waltham, MA 02254
E-mail: jwatch@world.std.com
URL: http://www.jwatch.org
Desc: Contains the complete text of the The New England Journal of Medicine (NEJM), including all reports, case records, and correspondence. Provides coverage of research and other developments in all fields of medicine. *Available:* Ovid Technologies, Inc.; The Dialog Corporation, DIALOG; LEXIS-NEXIS, NEXIS; The Dialog Corporation, DataStar. *Type:* Database.

New England Medical Center Hospitals, Inc.

Division of Clinical Care Research

750 Washington St. Ph: (617)636-5065
Box 63 Fax: (617)636-8023
Boston, MA 02111
E-mail: cseidel@es.nemc.org
URL: http://www.nemc.org/medicine/ccr/ccr.htm
Contact: Harry P. Selker, MD, Ch.
Desc: Ongoing research programs in clinical trials in emergency room based cardiovascular health services research, mathematical modeling and statistics, meta-analysis and other evidence-based research methodologies. *Type:* Research center.

New England Medical Center Hospitals, Inc.

General Clinical Research Center

750 Washington Ave. Ph: (617)348-5500
Box 268
Boston, MA 02111
Contact: Dr. Aubrey E. Boyd, III, Prog.Dir.
Desc: Biomedicine, including endocrinology and metabolism, hematology, neurology, nutrition, oncology, immunology, and infectious disease. *Type:* Research center.

New Jersey Institute of Technology

Center for Biomedical Engineering

323 King Blvd. Ph: (973)596-3527
Newark, NJ 07102 Fax: (973)596-5680
E-mail: reisman@njit.edu
URL: http://www.njit.edu
Contact: Stanley Reisman, Dir.
Desc: Design of prosthetic devices (including knee joints, hip joints, and voice prostheses), measurement of fatigue using EMG signal processing, heart rate variability studies, echo cardiography, visual-evoked response, noninvasive measurement of burn areas, cardiac assist devices, intracranial pressure sensing, design and testing of prosthetic heart valves, modelling of circadian rhythm, rehabilitation engineering, modelling of the cardiovascular system, assessment of lower back pain, gait analysis, and modelling of acetylcholinesterase. *Type:* Research center.

New Mexico Clinical Research and Osteoporosis Center

4700 Jefferson NE Ph: (505)855-5505
Albuquerque, NM 87109 Fax: (505)855-5506
E-mail: medsitenm@aol.com
Contact: Lance Rudolph, MD, Dir.
Desc: Health care quality, health promotion, clinical research, and continuing medical education. *Type:* Research center.

New York Blood Center, Inc.

Lindsley F. Kimball Research Center

310 E. 67th St. Ph: (212)570-3000
New York, NY 10021 Fax: (212)570-3195
URL: http://www.nybloodcenter.org
Contact: Robert L. Jones, MD, Pres.
Desc: Immunogenetics and immunohematology, epidemiology and virology of AIDS and hepatitis viruses, molecular and cell biology of red blood cells and developing erythroid cells, platelet interactions with coagulation proteins, human genetics, and hematopoietic growth factors. Performs studies of plasma proteins and seeks to develop new plasma derivatives for therapeutic use. *Type:* Research center.

New York University

General Clinical Research Center

NYU Med. Ctr. Ph: (212)263-7900
550 1st Ave., New Bellevue 8E, Fax: (212)263-8501
  Rm. 36
New York, NY 10016
E-mail: rom01@mcgc16.med.nyu.edu
URL: http://www.med.nyu.edu/gcrc/homepage.html
Contact: Dr. William N. Rom, Dir.
Desc: The unit is a hospital within a hospital that allows investigators to observe patients for extended lengths of time. Projects include studies in endocrinology and metabolism, rheumatology, immunology, genetics, hypertension, hematology, neurology, neurosurgery, respiratory medicine, and infectious diseases. *Type:* Research center.

Newsline

Leukemia Society of America, Inc.
600 3rd Ave. Ph: (212)573-8484
New York, NY 10016 Free: 800-955-4LSA
  Fax: (212)856-9686
URL: http://www.leukemia.org.
Contact: Julie Farin, Editor.
Desc: Publicizes activities of the Society, including fundraising and Society-supported research. Provides information about advances in the research into leukemia and other related cancers. *Type:* Newsletter.

NHF's Handi Resource Update

National Hemophilia Foundation
116 W. 32nd St., 11th Fl. Ph: (212)219-8180
New York, NY 10001-3212 Free: 888-INFO-NHF
Contact: Steven Humes, Editor; Jodie Corngold, Supervising Ed.
Desc: Provides a listing of new resources available to individuals seeking information on bleeding disorders. *Type:* Newsletter.

Nicaragua Medical Aid

2560 9th St., Ste. 213 B Ph: (510)841-1644
Berkeley, CA 94709 Fax: (510)644-2923
Contact: Dr. Paul Kranz, Exec.Dir.
Desc: Supports community-based health care organizations in Nicaragua. *Type:* Association.

North American Primary Care Research Group
PO Box 8729   Free: 800-274-2237
Kansas City, MO 64111   Fax: (816)333-9700
E-mail: napcrg@stfm.org
Contact: Maria Neu, Contact.
Desc: Primary health care. *Type:* Research center.

Northwestern University

Center for Circadian Biology and Medicine
Department of Neurobiology   Ph: (847)491-2865
Evanston, IL 60208
E-mail: fturek@nwu.edu
URL: http://nuinfo.nwu.edu/ccbm/purpose.html
Contact: Fred W. Turek, Dir.
Desc: Circadian rhythms and sleep, including the elucidation of the fundamental mechanisms that underlie circadian dysfunctional for human health, safety and productivity and development of treatments to alleviate symptons of circadian dysfunctions. *Type:* Research center.

Northwestern University

Center for Reproductive Sciences
2-171 Hogan Hall   Ph: (847)491-4464
2153 N. Campus Dr.   Fax: (847)491-5211
Evanston, IL 60208-3520
E-mail: s-hall4@nwu.edu
URL: http://x.biochem.nwu.edu/CRS
Contact: Susan Hall-Perdomo, Contact.
Desc: Reproductive biology, focusing on the regulation of ovarian synthesis and secretion of steroid and peptide hormones on the metabolic pathways and messengers within ovarian structures; regulation of testicular development, secretion of spermatogenesis, and the regulation of synthesis and secretion of the pituitary gonadotropic hormones and prolactin, as well as their actions on the brain, gonads, and breast tissue; and interactions of neural tissue in the brain and spinal cord with the pituitary-gonadal axis. *Type:* Research center.

Northwestern University

Multipurpose Arthritis and Musculoskeletal Diseases Center
303 E. Chicago Ave.   Ph: (312)503-8197
Chicago, IL 60611   Fax: (312)503-0994
E-mail: rmp158@lulu.acns.nwu.edu
Contact: Dr. Richard M. Pope, Dir.
Desc: Biomedical, educational, and health services research in the musculoskeletal diseases. *Type:* Research center.

Northwestern University

Program for Applied Research on Fertility Regulation
680 N. Lakeshore Dr., Ste.   Ph: (312)908-6558
   1000   Fax: (312)908-0014
Chicago, IL 60611
Contact: Gerald I. Zatuchni, MD, Dir.
Desc: Scientific and technical assistance to U.S. institutions for applied research in the field of fertility regulation. *Type:* Research center.

Northwestern University

Samuel Sackett Research Laboratory
680 N. Lakeshore Dr.   Ph: (312)908-9137
Chicago, IL 60611   Fax: (312)908-5820
Contact: Dr. John P. Phair, Dir.
Desc: Cellular and humoral resistance to infection, viral central nervous system infections, pharmacology of antimicrobial agents, investigation of infectious diarrhea, and natural history of infectious diseases. *Type:* Research center.

NPA Bulletin
National Perinatal Association (NPA)
3500 E. Fletcher Ave., Ste. 209   Ph: (813)971-1008
Tampa, FL 33613   Fax: (813)971-9306
E-mail: npaonline@aol.com
Contact: Judith D. Burke, Editor.
Desc: Provides member information. Updates association activities. *Type:* Newsletter.

Nuclear Medicine Technology Certification Board
2970 Clairmont Rd., Ste. 935   Ph: (404)315-1739
Atlanta, GA 30329   Fax: (404)315-6502
E-mail: board@nmtcb.org
URL: http://www.nmtcb.org
Contact: James E. Greene, Jr., PhD. Exec.Dir.
Desc: Purposes are to provide for the certification of nuclear medical technologists and to develop, assess, and administer an examination relevant to nuclear medicine technology. Compiles statistics. *Type:* Association.

Ohio State University

Center for Retrovirus Research
1925 Coffey Rd.   Ph: (614)292-7317
Columbus, OH 43210-1291   Fax: (614)292-6473
E-mail: mathes.2@osu.edu
Contact: Dr. Lawrence Mathes, Dir.
Desc: Animal and human retroviruses, including HIV in humans, feline immunodeficiency virus, equine infectious anemia, and leukemia virus of cats. *Type:* Research center.

Ohio State University

Clinical Research Center
200 Meiling Hall   Ph: (614)292-7755
370 W. 9th Ave.   Fax: (614)688-3282
Columbus, OH 43210
Contact: Manuel Tzagournis, VP.
Desc: Provides facilities and financial support for most inpatient and outpatient clinical investigations of the College, including studies on diabetes, heart disease, endocrine and metabolic disorders, nutrition, neuroendocrine tumors, osteoporosis, cancer, eating disorders, affective disorders and depression, and renal disease. The Center's core laboratory performs high pressure liquid chromatography assays and radioimmunoassays for 17 different peptides and hormones, and PCR determinations. *Type:* Research center.

Ohio State University

Division of Infectious Diseases
410 W. 10th Ave.   Ph: (614)293-8732
Columbus, OH 43210   Fax: (614)293-5240
URL: http://www.osu.edu
Contact: Dr. Robert J. Fass, Dir.
Desc: Pathogenesis, prophylaxis, therapy, pathology, serology of infectious diseases (including Legionnaire's disease, herpes infections, acquired immune deficiency syndrome, and other opportunistic infections), and extensive in vitro and clinical evaluations of antimicrobial agents. *Type:* Research center.

Ohio Valley Tissue and Skin Center
2939 Vernon Pl.   Ph: (513)558-6400
Cincinnati, OH 45219-2430   Free: 800-558-5004
                                                       Fax: (513)558-6440
Contact: Edward C. Robb, Exec. Dir.
Desc: Human tissue, skin and bones. *Type:* Research center.

Oklahoma Medical Research Foundation

Arthritis/Immunology Research Program
825 NE 13th St.   Ph: (405)271-7766
Oklahoma City, OK 73104   Free: 800-522-0211
                                                       Fax: (405)271-4110
E-mail: Moms-Reichlin@OMRS.ouhsc.edu
Contact: Morris Reichlin, MD, Ch.
Desc: Molecular aspects of systemic autoimmunity. *Type:* Research center.

Oklahoma State Medical Association—Medical Directory
Oklahoma State Medical Association
601 W. I-44 Service Rd.   Ph: (405)843-9571
Oklahoma City, OK 73118   Free: 800-522-9452
                                                       Fax: (405)842-1834
E-mail: osma@osmaonline.org
Desc: Approximately 5,500 member physicians in the state of Oklahoma. *Type:* Directory.

Olive View-UCLA Education and Research Institute, Inc.
14445 Olive View Dr., Rm. 218   Ph: (818)364-3434
   Lab.   Fax: (818)364-3465
Sylmar, CA 91342-1438
E-mail: ovmceri@ix.netcom.com
Contact: Denise Tritt, Bus.Mgr.
Desc: Perinatal issues, popamine and alcoholics, neurology, head injury, pulmonary complication in AIDS patence study, clincal studies, and genetics counseling. *Type:* Research center.

On the Beam
Lowe Syndrome Association (LSA)
222 Lincoln St.   Ph: (765)743-3634
West Lafayette, IN 47906
E-mail: LSA@medhelp.org
Contact: Kathy Schroerlucke, Editor.
Desc: Aims to foster communication between families affected by Lowe Syndrome and other interested persons, to provide medical and educational information, and to report news of the Association and its members. Recurring features include letters from parents and pictures of their children, news of research, and listings of resources. *Type:* Newsletter.

The Only Remedy Is a Cure Update Newsletter
Juvenile Diabetes Foundation Canada (JDFC)
89 Granton Dr.   Ph: (905)889-4171
Richmond Hill, ON, Canada   Free: 800-668-0274
   L4B 2N5   Fax: (905)889-4209
Contact: Elizabeth Braden, Canadian Contact, ejbraden@jdfc.ca.
Desc: Informs of the latest developments of the Diabetes Interdisciplinary Research Program Conference. Also reports on volunteers, contributions, and The Only Remedy Is a Cure campaign. *Type:* Newsletter.

Operation Smile International
6435 Tidewater Dr.   Ph: (757)321-7645
Norfolk, VA 23509-1600   Fax: (757)321-7660
E-mail: rfishkin@operationsmile.org
URL: http://www.operationsmile.org
Contact: Thomas Fox, Ph.D, CEO.
Desc: Operation Smile is the not-for-profit, volunteer medical services organization providing free reconstructive surgery to children suffering from facial deformities. Based in Norfolk, Virginia, since its founding in 1982, Operation Smile's volunteers have cared for more than 45,000 children in 16 developing countries and across the United States. Operation Smile emphasizes medical training and educational exchanges during international missions to build long-term self-sufficiency. *Type:* Association.

Oregon Health Sciences University

General Clinical Research Center

3181 SW Sam Jackson Park   Ph: (503)494-7601
Rd., CR107   Fax: (503)494-0165
Portland, OR 97201-3098
E-mail: fallowse@ohsu.edu
URL: http://www.ohsu.edu/gcrc
Contact: Eric Orwoll, MD, Prog.Dir.
Desc: Cardiovascular disease, collagen vascular disease and immunology, endocrinology, hematology, hypertension, metabolism, neurology, oncology, pediatric nephrology, pharmacology, psychiatry, renal disease, and rheumatology. Testing services include steroid receptor analysis, membrane receptor analysis, radioimmunoassay, and spectrophotometric analyses. Type: Research center.

Oregon Tinnitus Data Archive

Oregon Health Sciences University
NeuroSensory Research Center   Ph: (503)494-8032
478   Fax: (503)494-5656
Mail Code NRC04
3181 SW Sam Jackson Park Rd.
Portland, OR 97201-3098
E-mail: ohrc@ohsu.edu
URL: http://www.ohsu.edu/ohrc-otda/
Desc: This database contains medical information on tinnitus, a clinically significant disorder involving ringing or other noises in the ears or head. Tinnitus is not an inconvenience; it is medically impairing and a significant disorder. Type: Database.

Otosclerosis Study Group

5020 E. 68th St.   Ph: (918)494-3636
Tulsa, OK 74136   Fax: (918)494-8915
Contact: Linda Slinkard, MD, Dir.
Desc: Otosclerosis, focusing on the ear and its diseases. Type: Research center.

Pacific Health Research Institute

Thomas Sq. Centre   Ph: (808)524-4411
846 S. Hotel St., Ste. 303   Fax: (808)524-5559
Honolulu, HI 96813
E-mail: vshamba@hhp.hawaii-health.com
Contact: Dr. J. David Curb, Med.Dir.
Desc: Health services and clinical research, including breast cancer, hypertension, osteoporosis, diabetes, heart attacks, drug studies, effects of chemical exposure, and cost-effectiveness analysis. Specific studies focus on risk factors associated with breast cancer, methods of delaying or preventing postmenopausal osteoporosis, isolated systolic hypertension among the elderly, outcomes research, leprosy, interactive videodiscs, geriatrics, and prostate, lung, colorectal, and ovarian cancer screening. Type: Research center.

Paget Foundation for Paget's Disease of Bone and Related Disorders

120 Wall St., Ste. 1602   Ph: (212)509-5335
New York, NY 10005-4001   Free: 800-23-PAGET
   Fax: (212)509-8492
E-mail: pagetfdn@aol.com
Contact: Charlene Waldman, Exec.Dir.
Desc: Patients and their families and friends; physicians; paramedical professionals interested in improving health care of persons suffering from Paget's disease, a chronic disorder which may result in enlarged, deformed, and fragile bones in one or more regions of the skeleton, fibrous dysplasia, and primary hyperparathyroidism (PHPT). Also addresses related bone disorders such as fibrous dysplasia and osteopetrosis. Conducts educational programs for patients, health care professionals, and the public; provides patient assistance and research advocacy; maintains referral service for patients seeking physicians who specialize in treating Paget's disease and PHPT. Type: Association.

Palo Alto Center for Pulmonary Disease Prevention

PO Box 60249   Ph: (415)614-0592
Palo Alto, CA 94306-0249   Fax: (415)614-0591
Contact: Dr. David P.L. Sachs, Dir.
Desc: Smoking cessation, focusing on nicotine replacement pharmaceuticals and non-nicotine replacement cessation trials. Type: Research center.

Pan American Health and Education Foundation

525 23rd St. NW   Ph: (202)974-3416
Washington, DC 20037   Fax: (202)974-3658
E-mail: marksric@paho.org
Contact: Richard Marks, Exec.Sec.
Desc: Seeks to mobilize financial and human resources for the improvement of health and education, particularly in Latin America; to advance the objectives of the Pan American Health Organization and World Health Organization. Cosponsors Program for Textbooks and Instructional Materials, which makes needed items available for the training of health personnel at all levels, including professional, technical, and auxiliary. Works cooperatively with organizations and governmental bodies which share the same objectives. Type: Association.

Parkinson Network

The Parkinson Foundation of Canada
390 Bay St., No. 710   Ph: (416)336-0099
Toronto, ON, Canada M5H   Free: 800-565-3000
2Y2   Fax: (416)366-9190
Contact: Trevor Williams, CEO.
Desc: Dedicated to "raising funds for research into the cause and treatment of Parkinson's, to providing a wide range of services which support Parkinsonians and their families, and to disseminating information to individuals and organizations across Canada." Also covers synopses of grants awarded. Type: Newsletter.

Parkinson Report

National Parkinson Foundation, Inc.
1501 NW 9th Ave.   Ph: (305)547-6666
Miami, FL 33136-1407   Free: 800-327-4545
   Fax: (305)548-4403
E-mail: mailbox@npf.med.miami.edu
URL: http://www.parkinson.org.
Contact: Julian L. Pearson, Editor.
Desc: Carries news of the programs of the Foundation, which is involved in the diagnosis, treatment, care, and rehabilitation of victims of Parkinson's Disease. Provides research updates from around the country, human interest stories, and articles on drugs and medication, neuroscience, and physical medicine and rehabilitation. Type: Newsletter.

Parkinsonian Speak-Out

Robert Bernen
55 Merrick St.   Ph: (401)435-3179
Rumford, RI 02916-2520
Contact: Robert Bernen, Editor.
Desc: Discusses the importance of active participation of therapy for Parkinson Disease patients. Recurring features include letters to the editor, interviews, reports of meetings, and book reviews. Type: Newsletter.

Parkinson's Disease Foundation Newsletter

Parkinson's Disease Foundation
Neurological Institute, 3rd Fl.   Ph: (212)923-4700
710 W. 168th St.   Free: 800-457-6676
New York, NY 10032   Fax: (212)923-4778
Contact: Dinah T. Orr, Editor.
Desc: Educates the public about treatments, ongoing medical research, drug therapies, support groups, and educational programs for Parkinson's Disease. Contains news of fundraising events and publicity programs, helpful suggestions for patients, and success stories about persons with Parkinson's Disease. Type: Newsletter.

Patient Care

Medical Economics Co.
5 Paragon Dr.   Ph: (201)358-7500
Montvale, NJ 07645-1725   Free: 800-223-0581
   Fax: (201)358-7260
E-mail: customer.service@medec.com
Contact: Deborah Kaplan, Editor, (201)358-7244; Dominic Barone, Publisher, (201)358-7332.
Type: Periodical.

Patient Focused Care and Satisfaction

American Health Consultants, Inc.
3525 Piedmont Rd., Bldg. 6,   Ph: (404)262-7436
Ste. 400   Free: 800-688-2421
Atlanta, GA 30305   Fax: (404)262-7837
E-mail: customerservice@ahcpub.com
Contact: Paula Stephens, Managing Editor, (404)262-5521.
Desc: Provides information on reengineering and redesign in the health care arena. Includes guidelines on staffing issues, training, technology, and other aspects of the restructuring process. Type: Newsletter.

PDQ (Physician Data Query)

International Cancer Information Center
National Cancer Institute
National Institutes of Health (NIH)
9030 Old Georgetown Rd.   Ph: (301)496-4907
Bethesda, MD 20892   Fax: (301)480-8105
E-mail: market1@icic.nci.nih.gov
URL: http://www.cancernet.nci.nih.gov.
Contact: Susan M. Hubbard, Editor.
Desc: Records of 22,000 cancer therapy physicians, 300 cancer genetics service providers, 3,000 treatment facilities, and 6,000 accredited mammography screening facilities. Type: Directory.

Pennsylvania State University

Department of Health Evaluation Sciences

Milton S. Hershey Med. Ctr.   Ph: (717)531-7178
PO Box 850   Fax: (717)531-5779
Hershey, PA 17033
E-mail: vchinchi@hes.hmc.psghs.edu
URL: http://www.collmed.psu.edu/hes
Contact: Vernon M. Chinchilli, PhD, V.Ch.
Desc: Biostatistics and epidemiology, health services, and a Data Coordinating Center for multi-state clinical trials. Type: Research center.

Pennsylvania State University

Doctors Kienle Center for Humanistic Medicine

Hershey Med. Ctr.   Ph: (717)531-8037
PO Box 850   Fax: (717)531-3894
Hershey, PA 17033-0850
E-mail: dhufford@psu.edu
URL: http://www.psu.edu
Contact: David J. Hufford, PhD, Dir.
Desc: Developing programs in humanistic medicine, including medical curriculum concerning the patients experience of care, phenomonology of care, and human diversity and medicine. Type: Research center.

People's Medical Society Newsletter

People's Medical Society
462 Walnut St.   Ph: (610)770-1670
Allentown, PA 18102   Free: 800-624-8773
   Fax: (610)770-0607
URL: http://www.peoplesmed.org.
Contact: Jennifer Haywood, Editor, jrh1@peoplesmed.org.
Desc: Promotes the Society's goals of giving people access to medical information previously not available outside

the profession and of compelling our health care system to make reforms so that it can better serve everyone. Discusses policy issues affecting the quality and cost of health care, and profiles individuals who have fought "organized medicine." Recurring features include news about successful reform projects, editorials, and letters to the editor. *Type:* Newsletter.

Perinatal Research Institute

231 Bethesda Ave.   Ph: (513)558-0543
Cincinnati, OH 45267-0541   Fax: (513)558-7770

Desc: Developmental perinatology, including molecular genetics and cell regulation; perinatal nutrition, metabolism, and endocrinology; fetal and neonatal physiology; and perinatal bioengineering and computer engineering. Long-term projects include studies of diabetes in pregnancy and intrauterine growth retardation. *Type:* Research center.

Physical Therapy

American Physical Therapy Association
1111 N. Fairfax St.   Ph: (703)684-2782
Alexandria, VA 22314   Free: 800-999-2782
    Fax: (703)703-3169

E-mail: ptjourn@apta.org.
URL: http://www.apta.org/pt_journal/index.html.

Contact: Jules M. Rothstein, Ph.D., Editor; Jan Reynolds, Managing Editor, (703)706-3182, jreynolds@apta.org; Julie Hilgenberg, Advertising Mgr., (703)706-3183, jhigenberg@apta.org.

Desc: Journal of the American Physical Therapy Association. *Type:* Periodical.

Physician Practice Compliance Report

Opus Communications
100 Hoods Ln.   Ph: (781)639-1872
PO Box 1168   Free: 800-650-6787
Marblehead, MA 01945   Fax: (781)639-2982
E-mail: customer_service@opuscomm.com
URL: http://www.opuscomm.com

Desc: Contains information on how to develop a corporate compliance program, government guidelines for compliance, and practices that have been penalized and fined for fraud and abuse. *Type:* Newsletter.

Physician Profiling and Behavior Change Report

National Health Information, L.L.C.
PO Box 15429   Ph: (404)607-9500
Atlanta, GA 30333-0429   Free: 800-597-6300
    Fax: (404)607-0095
URL: http://www.nhionline.net.

Desc: Contains information on how to cut utilization and costs and improve quality and outcomes. Includes news on physician profiling, compensation and incentive plans, physician education on managed care, data strategies to change behavior, and clinical guidelines. *Type:* Newsletter.

The Physician and Sportsmedicine

McGraw-Hill Healthcare Information Group
4530 W. 77th St.   Ph: (612)835-3222
Minneapolis, MN 55435   Fax: (612)835-3460
URL: http://www.physsportsmed.com.

Contact: Gretchen Drasner, Senior Marketing Mgr.; Janis Cohen, Assoc. Group Publisher; M. James Dougherty, Group VP; Susan Hawthorne, Executive Editor, susan_hawthor@mcgraw-hill.com.

Desc: A peer-reviewed journal on the medical aspects of sports, exercise, and fitness. *Type:* Periodical.

Physicians and Computers

Physicians and Computers
810 S. Waukegan Rd., Suite   Ph: (847)615-8333
200
Lake Forest, IL 60045
Contact: Tom Moorehead, Publisher; Rogers Piercy, Sr. Editor; Michael Moorhead, Production Mgr.

Desc: Journal containing information about computer application to medical practice, including office management. *Type:* Periodical.

Physician's Managed Care Report

American Health Consultants, Inc.
3525 Piedmont Rd., Bldg. 6,   Ph: (404)262-7436
Ste. 400   Free: 800-688-2421
Atlanta, GA 30305   Fax: (404)262-7837
E-mail: 75057.1533@compuserve.com; custserv@ahcpub.com

Contact: Francine Wilson, Editor.

Desc: Provides managed care strategies for physician practices. Recurring features include interviews, a calendar of events, and reports of meetings. *Type:* Newsletter.

Physician's Marketing & Management

American Health Consultants, Inc.
3525 Piedmont Rd., Bldg. 6,   Ph: (404)262-7436
Ste. 400   Free: 800-688-2421
Atlanta, GA 30305   Fax: (404)262-7837
E-mail: customerservice@ahcpub.com

Contact: Francine Wilson, Managing Editor.

Desc: Discusses medical practice issues of physician liability, insurance tracking, practice profitability, personnel issues, Medicare concerns, and marketing medical practices. Remarks: Subscription includes bimonthly supplement, Practice Personnel Bulletin. *Type:* Newsletter.

Physician's Payment Update

American Health Consultants, Inc.
3525 Piedmont Rd., Bldg. 6,   Ph: (404)262-7436
Ste. 400   Free: 800-688-2421
Atlanta, GA 30305   Fax: (404)262-7837
E-mail: customerservice@ahcpub.com

Contact: Richard Jarvis, Managing Editor.

Desc: Devoted entirely to all the payment and reimbursement issues affecting physicians in solo and group practices. Includes Physician's Coding Strategist, a four-page pull-out guide to real-life coding challenges. *Type:* Newsletter.

Physician's Practice Digest

Magazine Works, Inc.
100 S Charles St., 13th Fl.   Ph: (410)539-3100
Baltimore, MD 21201   Free: 800-781-2211
    Fax: (410)539-3188
URL: http://www.ppdnet.com.

Contact: Scott Weber, Publisher; Gerry Hartung, Publisher; Cathy Canning, Editor; Abigail Green, Asst. Editor; Jeffrey Furniss, VP, Sales & Mktg.; Karen Lind, Traffic/Production Mgr.

Desc: Professional magazine covering practice management for physicians. *Type:* Periodical.

Polyclinic Associates

22401 Foster-Winter Dr.   Ph: (248)423-1481
Southfield, MI 48075   Fax: (248)423-1482
Contact: Dr. Claude Oster, CEO.

Desc: Epidemiology of musculoskeletal pain, especially its neurochemical and metabolic and biochemical causes. Examines stress and other psychiatric components of pain, tests experimental groups for certain metabolic disorders such as porphyria and hypoglycemia, and conducts longitudinal studies for occupational hazards. *Type:* Research center.

Population Council

1 Dag Hammarskjold Plz.   Ph: (212)339-0500
New York, NY 10017   Fax: (212)755-6052
E-mail: pubinfo@popcouncil.org
URL: http://www.popcouncil.org
Contact: Linda G. Martin, Pres.

Desc: Biomedical, social science, and public health research. Analyzes demographic trends; conducts biomedical rsearch to understand human reproductive physiology more fully, leading to development of new contraceptives and reproductive health products; works with public and private agencies to promote client-centered reproductive health services of high quality; helps governments design and implement just and sustainable population and development policies; communicates the results of research in the population field; and helps build research capacities in developing countries. *Type:* Research center.

Portland VA Research Foundation, Inc.

PO Box 69539   Ph: (503)273-5228
Portland, OR 97201-0539   Fax: (503)273-5367
E-mail: hickam.david@portland
Contact: David Hickana, MD, Pres.

Desc: Medicine and medical research. *Type:* Research center.

Postacute Data Report

National Health Information, L.L.C.
PO Box 15429   Ph: (404)607-9500
Atlanta, GA 30333-0429   Free: 800-597-6300
    Fax: (404)607-0095
URL: http://www.nhionline.net.

Desc: Provides information on managed care contracts, utilization, and improving the quality of managed care. *Type:* Newsletter.

Postgraduate Medicine

McGraw-Hill Healthcare Information Group
4530 W. 77th St.   Ph: (612)835-3222
Minneapolis, MN 55435   Fax: (612)835-3460
URL: http://www.postgradmed.com.

Contact: M. James Dougherty, Group Vice President, jdougher@mcgraw-hill.com; Peter A. Setness, MD, Editor-in-Chief, psetness@mcgraw-hill.com; Patricia Flynn, Executive Editor, flynn@mcgraw-hill.com.

Desc: Magazine for primary care physicians; presents original clinical articles stressing diagnosis and treatment of practical problems encountered in general medical practice. *Type:* Periodical.

PRA Newsletter

Physician Recruiter's Association (PRA)
Prime National Publishing Corporation
470 Boston Post Rd.   Ph: (617)899-2702
Weston, MA 02193   Free: 800-869-2700
    Fax: (617)899-4900
E-mail: 76150.1602@compuserve.com
Contact: R. Patrick Gates, Editor.

Desc: Reports the news of the Association; provides how-to articles on recruiting. Recurring features include news briefs and Recruiter Billboard (job listings). *Type:* Newsletter.

The Practice Builder Newsletter

The Practice Builder Association
18351 Jamboree Rd.   Ph: (949)253-7900
Irvine, CA 92612-1011   Fax: (949)252-1002
Contact: Alan Bernstein, Publisher; Sam Jones, Editor.

Desc: Offers marketing strategies to small health care practices. *Type:* Newsletter.

Prader-Willi Perspectives

Visible Ink Inc.

40 Holly Ln.   Ph: (516)621-2445
Roslyn Heights, NY 11577   Free: 800-358-0632
                  Fax: (516)484-7154
E-mail: perspectives@sprintmail.com.
URL: http://www.visink.com.
Contact: Sheldon L. Tarkan, Editor.
Desc: Contains articles written by medical and other health professionals about Prader-Willi Syndrome (PWS), a rare genetic disorder. Recurring features include articles written by parents of children with PWS, educators, and others involved with the Syndrome and its management, news of research, reports of meetings, book reviews, notices of publications available, a calendar of events, directories of summer camps and international PWS organizations, and a column titled Parent Perspectives. *Type:* Newsletter.

Preventive Medicine Institute

428 E. 72nd St.   Ph: (212)794-4900
New York, NY 10021-4601   Fax: (212)794-4959
E-mail: mosborne@strang.org
Contact: Dr. Michael P. Osborne, Dir.
Desc: Breast and other cancers and nutrition. *Type:* Research center.

Preventive Medicine Research Institute

900 Bridgeway, Ste. 1   Ph: (415)332-2525
Sausalito, CA 94965   Fax: (415)332-5730
URL: http://www.ornish.com
Contact: Dean Ornish, MD, Pres.
Desc: Prevention and treatment of heart disease through modification of diet, exercise, and relaxation techniques such as yoga, meditation, and visualization. *Type:* Research center.

Productive Rehabilitation Institute of Dallas for Ergonomics

5701 Maple, Ste. 100   Ph: (214)351-6600
Dallas, TX 75235   Fax: (214)351-6453
Contact: Pat Estes, Dir. of Supv. Svcs.
Desc: Ergonomics. Projects focus on utilizing physical exercise for rehabilitating chronic back problems. *Type:* Research center.

The Project

The Miami Project to Cure Paralysis

1611 NW 12th Ave., R-48   Ph: (305)243-6001
Miami, FL 33136   Free: 800-782-6387
                  Fax: (305)243-6017
E-mail: mpinfo@miamiproj.med.miami.edu
URL: http://gsni.com/mia-proj.
Contact: Naomi Kleitman, Editor, (305)243-6226, fax: (305)243-4427.
Desc: Reports on news from the Miami Project to Cure Paralysis. *Type:* Newsletter.

Providence Ambulatory Center

5050 NE Hoyt St., Ste. 540   Ph: (503)215-6600
Portland, OR 97213   Fax: (503)215-7751
E-mail: david_gilbert_md@phsor.org
Contact: David N. Gilbert, MD, Dir.
Desc: Clinical and basic investigations in cancer immunology, cardiovascular diseases, infectious diseases, and diabetes and metabolism. *Type:* Research center.

Public Health Research Institute

455 1st Ave.   Ph: (212)578-0800
New York, NY 10016   Fax: (212)578-0804
E-mail: lmw@phri.org
URL: http://www.phri.org
Contact: Lewis M. Weinstein, Pres.
Desc: Biomedical research with a focus on infectious diseases and public health issues. *Type:* Research center.

Public Responsibility in Medicine and Research

132 Boylston St., 4th Fl.   Ph: (617)423-4112
Boston, MA 02116   Fax: (617)423-1185
E-mail: prmr@aol.com
URL: http://www.aamc.org/research/primr
Contact: Joan Rachlin, Contact.
Desc: Medical research, focusing on education of public responsibility and regulation of research. *Type:* Research center.

Rare Disease Database

The National Organization for Rare Disorders, Inc.

PO Box 8923   Ph: (203)746-6518
New Fairfield, CT 06812-8923 Free: 800-999-6673
                  Fax: (203)746-6481
E-mail: orphan@rarediseases.org
URL: http://www.stepstn.com/nord/db/dbsearch/search.htm
Desc: This database lets you search for information on hundreds of rare diseases. Search by keyword or browse an extensive list of the rare diseases housed in the database. *Type:* Database.

Rehabilitation, Teaching and Research Centre

M.D.S. Lab. Svcs.   Ph: (416)213-4218
100 International Blvd.   Fax: (416)675-4693
Etobicoke, ON, Canada M9W
  6J6
Contact: Dr. A.W. Peter Van Nostrand, Dir.
Desc: Investigates osteoporosis, menopause, sleep, thyroid function, tracheotomy procedures, bones and minerals, brain damage, stroke and depression, and Alzheimer's Disease. *Type:* Research center.

Report on Medicare Compliance

Atlantic Information Services, Inc.

1100 17th St. NW, No. 300   Ph: (202)775-9008
Washington, DC 20036   Free: 800-521-4323
                  Fax: (202)331-9542
Contact: Nina Younstrom, Editor.
Desc: Provides information on Medicare. *Type:* Newsletter.

Research! America

908 King St. No. 400E   Free: 800-366-CURE
Alexandria, VA 22314-3067
E-mail: researcham@aol.com
URL: http://www.researchamerica.org
Contact: Mary Woolley, Pres. & CEO.
Desc: Academia, voluntary health organizations, professional and scientific societies, colleges and universities, businesses and industries, and foundations and philanthropists. Works to increase public awareness of the benefits to humankind of medical research and to build a strong base of citizen support for research into the cure, treatment, and prevention of physical and mental disorders. *Type:* Association.

Research Institute of Acupuncture and Chinese Medicine

66 Skyline Dr.   Ph: (203)758-9900
Middlebury, CT 06762   Fax: (203)758-2758
Contact: Dr. Sung J. Liao, Pres.
Desc: Thermography as an objective measurement of chronic pain and the measurement of acupuncture in the management of chronic pain; clinical investigation of acupuncture as an alternative healing modality. *Type:* Research center.

Research Institute of Palo Alto Medical Foundation

860 Bryant St.   Ph: (650)326-8120
Palo Alto, CA 94301   Fax: (650)329-9114
E-mail: kroberts@pamfri.org
URL: http://www.pamf.org
Contact: Dr. Allen D. Cooper, Dir.
Desc: Clinical and general medical sciences, including immunology, infectious diseases, health services research, cardiac physiology, metabolism, atherosclerosis, and cancer cell biology. *Type:* Research center.

Respiratory Care Manager

Opus Communications

100 Hoods Ln.   Ph: (781)639-1872
PO Box 1168   Free: 800-650-6787
Marblehead, MA 01945   Fax: (781)639-2982
E-mail: customer_service@opuscomm.com
URL: http://www.opuscomm.com
Contact: Paul Nash, Assoc. Editor; Cathy Rossi, Editor.
Desc: Covers topics related to cardiopulmonary and respiratory care management. Recurring features include interviews and news of research. *Type:* Newsletter.

Respiratory Pathogens Research Unit

Dept. of Microbiology and   Ph: (713)798-4474
  Immunology   Fax: (713)798-7375
1 Baylor Plaza
Houston, TX 77030
Contact: Robert B. Couch, MD, Dir.
Desc: Multidisciplinary studies of acute respiratory diseases in humans and animals, including bacteriologic, virologic, and immunologic studies and vaccine and evaluations. *Type:* Research center.

Rockefeller University

Clinical Research Center

Rockefeller Univ. Hospital   Ph: (212)327-8000
1230 York Ave.   Fax: (212)327-7157
New York, NY 10021-6399
E-mail: druegej@rockvax.rockefeller.edu
Contact: James G. Krueger, MD, Dir.
Desc: Chronic immune disorders, dermatology, gastrointestinal motility, lipid metabolism, metabolic disorders, medical biochemistry, cystic fibrostic, AIDS, tuberculosis, neurological disorders, and obesity and nutrition. *Type:* Research center.

Rockefeller University

Laboratory of Electronics

1230 York Ave.   Ph: (212)327-8613
New York, NY 10021   Fax: (212)327-7974
E-mail: ros@rockvax.rockefeller.edu
Contact: Paul Rosen, Mgr.
Desc: Applies computer engineering capabilities (microprocessor-based technology combined with programming methodology and software tools) to biomedicine, including medical diagnosis, prosthesis, and rehabilitation medicine. Conducts with biomedical investigators collaborative experiments involving computer-based measurements of activity: food and drink ingestion, heart rate, nerve and muscle activity, spectral analysis and stimulus patterning in nerve and muscle recording, neurophysiological and psychological experiments, control and data acquisition in analytical chemistry and mass spectrometry, and visual, postural, and neuromuscular research. *Type:* Research center.

Rocky Mountain Research Institute

1304 S. College Ave.   Ph: (970)493-0312
Fort Collins, CO 80524-4114
Contact: Maury Albertson, PhD, Contact.
Desc: Alternative health issues, amalgam mercury toxicity, mental health, and physiology. *Type:* Research center.

Roger Wyburn-Mason and Jack M. Blount Foundation for the Eradication of Rheumatoid Disease

7111 Sweetgum Dr., SW No. A   Ph: (615)799-1002
Fairview, TN 37062-9384   Fax: (615)799-1002
E-mail: administration@arthritistrust.org
URL: http://www.arthritistrust.org

Contact: Perry A. Chapdelaine, Exec.Dir. & Sec.

Desc: Seeks to eradicate rheumatoid disease. Promotes professional university research and supplies free information to physicians and disease victims on Dr. Roger Wyburn-Mason's treatment protocol as modified by other physicians. *Type:* Association.

Rolf Institute of Structural Integration

205 Canyon Blvd.   Ph: (303)449-5903
Boulder, CO 80302   Free: 800-530-8875
   Fax: (303)449-5978
E-mail: rolfinst@aol.com
URL: http://www.rolf.org

Contact: Gary Wolfe, Dir.

Desc: Rolfing (registered trademark) technique of connective tissue manipulation and its effect on integration of human physical structure and physical, emotional, and psychological functioning, including studies on human imbalance and its correction and/or improvement by a technique for reordering of the body to bring its major segments, head, shoulders, thorax, pelvis, and legs, toward a vertical alignment. *Type:* Research center.

Royal College of Physicians and Surgeons of Canada

McLaughlin Centre for Evaluation

774 Echo Dr.   Ph: (613)730-6209
Ottawa, ON, Canada K1S 5N8   Free: 800-668-3740
   Fax: (613)730-8262
E-mail: nadia.mikhael@rcpsc.edu
URL: http://rcpsc.medical.org

Contact: Dr. Nadia Mikhael, Dir.

Desc: Research and development in methods of evaluation for certification in the health professions at the undergraduate, postgraduate, and continuing education levels. Includes in-training evaluation systems; written, oral, and comprehensive examinations; and meta-evaluation. *Type:* Research center.

Royal College of Physicians and Surgeons (of United States of America)

16126 E. Warren   Ph: (313)882-0641
PO Box 24224   Fax: (313)882-0979
Detroit, MI 48224

Contact: Ben Allie, M.D., Exec. Officer.

Desc: Physicians and allied health professionals interested in tropical medicine. Provides postgraduate continuing medical education; confers certificates and diplomas. Maintains speakers' bureau and hall of fame and provides placement services. *Type:* Association.

Rush Primary Care Institute

Center for Health Services Research

Rush-Presbyterian-St. Luke's   Ph: (312)942-3576
Med. Ctr.   Fax: (312)432-1915
1653 W. Congress Pky.
Chicago, IL 60612
URL: http://www.rpci.rush.edu

Contact: Dr. Whitney Addington, Dir.

Desc: Primary care, education, and community outreach. *Type:* Research center.

Rush University

Center for SIDS Research and Disorders of Respiratory Control in Infancy and Childhood

Rush-Presbyterian-St. Luke's   Ph: (312)942-2723
Med. Ctr.   Fax: (312)942-3087
1653 W. Congress Pky.
Chicago, IL 60612
E-mail: dweese@rush.edu

Contact: Dr. Debra E. Weese-Mayer, Dir.

Desc: Sudden infant death syndrome (SIDS) research, including monitoring high-risk infants for apnea, physilogic response to exercise in children with congenital central hypoventilation syndrome, genetic characterization of congenital central hypoventilation syndrome, and the effect of prenatal cocaine (throughout gestation) on postnatal cartoid body response to hypoxia in newborn rats. *Type:* Research center.

Rush University

Office of Research Administration

Rush-Presbyterian-St. Luke's   Ph: (312)942-5498
Med. Ctr.   Fax: (312)942-2874
1653 W. Congress Pkwy.
Chicago, IL 60612
E-mail: pjezek@is.rpslmc.edu

Contact: Leo M. Henikoff, MD, Pres.

Desc: Medical sciences including, surgical sciences, nursing, and health sciences. *Type:* Research center.

Rush University

Rush Arthritis and Orthopedics Institute

1725 W. Harrison St., Ste. 1055   Ph: (312)563-2420
Chicago, IL 60612   Fax: (312)243-7707
E-mail: arth-orth-institute@rush.edu
URL: http://www.rush.edu/Med/AOINS/institute.html

Contact: Dr. Jorge O. Galante, Dir.

Desc: Osteoarthritis and cartilage physiology, inflammatory joint disease, joint replacement, low back pain, orthopedic oncology (musculoskeletal tumors), sports medicine, and scoliosis. *Type:* Research center.

Rush University

Rush Arthritis and Orthopedics Institute

Center for Clinical Studies

1725 W. Harrison St., Ste. 1055   Ph: (312)563-2420
Chicago, IL 60612-3824   Fax: (312)243-7707
E-mail: arth-orth-institute@rush.edu
URL: http://www.rush.edu/Med/AOINS/institute.html

Contact: Dr. Paul Glickman, Dir.

Desc: Evaluating new treatments and therapies for arthritis and related conditions, including problems associated with wound healing. *Type:* Research center.

Rush University

Rush Arthritis and Orthopedics Institute

Sports Medicine Program

1725 W. Harrison St., Ste. 1055   Ph: (312)563-2420
Chicago, IL 60612-3824   Fax: (312)243-7077
E-mail: arth-orth-institute@rush.edu
URL: http://www.rush.edu/Med/AOINS/institute.html

Contact: Dr. Bernard Bach, Jr., Dir.

Desc: Gait analysis, the anterior cruciate ligament, immunomodulatory drugs for treatment of rheumatoid arthritis, the effects of medications aimed at preventing and treating the abnormal thinning of bone that osteoporosis patients exhibit, how patients walk with mild to moderate osteoarthritis of the knee, and the effects of oral medications on their gait. *Type:* Research center.

Rush University

Steroid Research Laboratory

1653 W. Congress Pkwy.   Ph: (312)942-6165
Chicago, IL 60612

Contact: Dr. Ludwig Kornel, Dir.

Desc: The role of mineralocorticoids and glucocorticoids in the molecular mechanism of hypertension; role of insulin in the mechanism of essential hypertension; and autocrine regulation of intracellular cortisol concentrations by enzymes metabolizing cortisol. *Type:* Research center.

Rutgers University

Institute for Health, Health Care Policy, and Aging Research

30 College Ave.   Ph: (732)932-8413
New Brunswick, NJ 08903   Fax: (732)932-6872
E-mail: caboyer@rci.rutgers.edu
URL: http://www.ihhcpar.rutgers.edu/

Contact: Dr. David Mechanic, Dir.

Desc: Research divisions include and focus on the following activities: the Division of Health studies the impact of stress on emotional states and health and risk behaviors and how these latter factors influence the immune system and morbidity and mortality, studies how stress and emotional states affect symptom appraisal and the decision to use health care, and sponsors a Center for Promoting Health Among Elderly Black Americans; the Division of Health Care Policy analyzes the health and cost outcomes of the current allocation of health and resources, with emphasis on preventive care and children's health; analyses the evolution of managed care and its impact on patient outcomes, medical professions and utilization of services; examines trust relationships among consumers and physicians and managed care organizations; the Division on Aging measures income inequality, investigates the role of instrumental and social support as buffers against stress, and identifies predictors of chronic pain and poor self-assessments of health among the elderly; the AIDS Policy Research Group measures health care utilization and cost among patients with HIV illness; the Center for Research on the Organization and Financing of Care for the Severely Mentally Ill provides a structure for interdisciplinary research and training on mental health services and policy for persons with severe and persistent mental illness and examines the human services and family support systems that shape

St. Anthony's Physician Resources Alert

Saint Anthony Publishing Inc.
11410 Isaac Newton Sq.   Ph: (703)904-3900
Reston, VA 20190   Free: 800-632-0123
   Fax: (703)707-5700

Contact: Julia Stitely, Editor.

Desc: Provides information for physicians concerning coding and reimbursement. *Type:* Newsletter.

St. Boniface General Hospital Research Centre

351 Tache Ave.   Ph: (204)235-3206
Winnipeg, MB, Canada R2H   Fax: (204)235-0793
2A6
E-mail: harrys@sbrc.umanitoba.ca
URL: http://www.sbrc.umanitoba.ca

Contact: Harry Schultz, Dir.

Desc: Cardiovascular sciences, magnetic resonance imaging, and degenerative disorders associated with aging, including surgical research, sleep apnea, nursing, microbiology/infectious diseases, psychiatry, epidemiology, anesthesia, nephrology, health care economics, and pharmaceutics. *Type:* Research center.

St. Louis University

Center for Health Care Ethics

Health Science Center   Ph: (314)577-8195
1402 S. Grand Blvd.   Fax: (314)268-5150
St. Louis, MO 63104
E-mail: orourke@wpogate.slu.edu
Contact: Fr. Kevin O'Rourke, Dir.

Desc: Issues in health care ethics, including the influence of physicians in decision making by the parents of newborn babies and the influence of for-profit hospital corporations on the cost of quality health care. Other interests include ethical considerations of the dying patient, defective newborns, genetic engineering, use of life-extending technology, sexual abuse of children, organ transplantation, health care financing, and informed consent. *Type:* Research center.

Sansum Medical Research Institute

2219 Bath St.   Ph: (805)682-7638
Santa Barbara, CA 93105   Fax: (805)682-3332
E-mail: lois@sansum.org
URL: http://www.sansum.org
Contact: Lois Jovanovic, MD, Dir.

Desc: Diabetes mellitus, immunology, cancer, gastrointestinal disorders and physiology. *Type:* Research center.

Schepens Eye Research Institute

20 Staniford St.   Ph: (617)912-0100
Boston, MA 02114-2500   Fax: (617)912-0101
E-mail: geninfo@vision.eri.harvard.edu
URL: http://www.eri.harvard.edu
Contact: Dr. J. Wayne Streilein, Pres. & Dir. of Res.

Desc: Retina, vitreous, cornea, glaucoma, immunology, neuroscience, transplantation, physiological optics, biomedical physics, oculartumors, and pharmacology with strong collaboration between clinic and laboratory studies on diseases of the retina and cornea, and on glaucoma. Develops ophthalmic instruments and devices for diagnosis and treatment of eye disease, and for low vision aids. *Type:* Research center.

Scleroderma Foundation

89 Newbury St., Ste. 201   Ph: (508)535-6600
Danvers, MA 01923-1075   Free: 800-422-1113
    Fax: (508)535-6696
E-mail: sclerofed@aol.com
URL: http://www.scleroderma.org
Contact: Karl Kastorf, Exec.Dir.

Desc: Scleroderma organizations. Promotes medical research to find a cure for scleroderma, a chronic systemic disease affecting all organs resulting from uncontrolled growth of connective tissue. *Type:* Association.

Scripps Clinic and Research Foundation

General Clinical Research Center

Scripps Research Institute   Ph: (619)554-8925
10666 N. Torrey Pines Rd.   Fax: (619)554-6230
La Jolla, CA 92037
E-mail: bieger@scripps.edu
URL: http://www.scripps.edu
Contact: Francis V. Chisari, MD, Dir.

Desc: Develops and evaluates new and experimental therapeutic procedures, including therapies for cancer, vascular disease, thrombotic disease, sleep disorders, multiple sclerosis, hepatitis, inflammatory bowel disease, asthma, alcoholism and depression, and autoimmune diseases such as rheumatoid arthritis and systemic lupus erythematosus. *Type:* Research center.

Scripps Research Institute

10550 N. Torrey Pines Rd.   Ph: (619)784-1000
La Jolla, CA 92037
URL: http://www.scripps.edu

Contact: Richard A. Lerner, MD, Pres.

Desc: Immunology and immunopathology, biochemistry, cell biology, molecular biology, structural biology, oncology, autoimmune diseases, cardiopulmonary diseases, hematology, diabetes and endocrinology, virology, preclinical neuroscience, neuropharmacology, vascular biology, synthetic bioorganic chemistry, biocatalysis and protein design, plant biology, and synthetic and vaccine development. *Type:* Research center.

Secondwind

Manitoba Lung Association
629 McDermot Ave.   Ph: (204)774-5501
Winnipeg, MB, Canada R3A   Fax: (204)772-5083
    1P6

Desc: Provides information concerning lung health. Focuses on asthma and chronic obstructive pulminary disease. *Type:* Newsletter.

Serendipity Association for Research and Implementation of Holistic Health and World Peace

3605 S. Granada   Ph: (619)455-9052
Spring Valley, CA 91977
Contact: Dr. Doug Hemstreet, Contact.

Desc: Holistic health care, focusing on promoting herbs, natural healing systems, and energy medicine for healing problems such as cancer and AIDS. Research also focuses on world peace, including reofrming the educational systems and stopping government misinformation and cover-ups in the health, agriculture, education, defense, and waste industries. *Type:* Research center.

Serological Research Institute

3053 Research Dr.   Ph: (510)223-7374
Richmond, CA 94806-5206   Fax: (510)222-8887
E-mail: bwraxall@serolggical.com
Contact: Brian Wraxall, Exec.Dir.

Desc: Analyzing blood and other body fluids encountered as evidence in criminal and civil matters, including genetic marker typing in blood and other bodily fluid stains and new or improved methods of analysis of serological evidence. *Type:* Research center.

Sherbrooke University

Cellular Mechanisms of Action and Ontogenesis Research Group

Faculte de medecine   Ph: (819)564-5282
Sherbrooke, PQ, Canada J1H   Fax: (819)564-5340
    5N4
E-mail: j.lehoux@courrier.usherb.ca
Contact: Jean-Guy Lehoux, Contact.

Desc: Control of aldosterone secretion, gene expression in adrenal glands, and paracrine control of hormonal synthesis in placenta; regulation and development of hormone receptors in embryo; role of angiotensin II and calcium; study of chitosan and hypocholesterolemia and of ANF and gene expression in adrenal glands; and characterization of an androgen-independent prostate tumor cell line. *Type:* Research center.

Shriners Burns Institute

815 Market St.   Ph: (409)770-6731
Galveston, TX 77550-2725   Fax: (409)770-6919
E-mail: dherndon@sbi.utmb.edu
Contact: David N. Herndon, MD, Chf.

Desc: Thermal injuries, wound healing, and scar formation, including treatment of burned children, cardiopulmonary complications, microcirculatory changes, nutritional and metabolic status, epidemiology and ideology of burn injuries, host responsiveness to secondary infections, lung injuries, and long term outcomes. *Type:* Research center.

Shriners Hospital for Children (Boston, MA)

Shriners Burns Institute

51 Blossom St.   Ph: (617)722-3000
Boston, MA 02114   Fax: (617)523-1684
URL: http://www.shq.org
Contact: Robert Bories, Admin.

Desc: Prevention of scar formation, burned childrens' reactions to drugs, nutrition, lung function after burn injuries, infections in burns, and development of artificial skin. Specializes in treating children with acute, fresh burns; children needing plastic reconstructive or restorative surgery as a result of healed burns; and children with severe scarring, resulting in contractures or interference of proper mobility of the limbs, and deformity of the face. *Type:* Research center.

Shriners Hospital for Children (Portland, OR)

Research Unit

3101 SW Sam Jackson Park Rd.   Ph: (503)221-1537
Portland, OR 97201   Fax: (503)221-3451
E-mail: wah@shcc.org
URL: http://shcc.org
Contact: Dr. William A. Horton, MD, Dir. of Res.

Desc: Connective tissues. *Type:* Research center.

Shute Medical Clinic

367 Princess Ave.   Ph: (519)432-1884
London, ON, Canada N6B 2A7   Fax: (519)432-1886
Contact: Dr. Edward Desaulniers, Med.Dir.

Desc: Total approach to patient care, vitamin dosage response, use of vitamin E for burn treatment, and medicinal use of d-alpha tocopheryl in diabetes, stroke, angina, coronary artery diseases, and intermittent claudication and phlebitis. *Type:* Research center.

Sidelines National Support Network

PO Box 1808   Ph: (949)497-2265
Laguna Beach, CA 92652   Fax: (949)497-5598
E-mail: sidelines@sidelines.org
URL: http://www.sidelines.org
Contact: Candace Hurley, Exec.Dir.

Desc: Former high-risk mothers dedicated to supporting women and their families experiencing a complicated or high-risk pregnancy. A pregnancy is termed "complicated" when the life or health of the mother and/or baby may be at risk. Committed to helping women overcome the risks of preterm birth, low birthweight, and other serious consequences of high risk pregnancies. *Type:* Association.

SIGBIO Newsletter

Special Interest Group on Programming Languages (SIGPLAN)
Association for Computing Machinery
1515 Broadway   Ph: (212)869-7440
New York, NY 10036   Free: 800-342-6626
    Fax: (212)302-5826
E-mail: acmhelp@acm.org
URL: http://www.acm.org/sig_hp/sigbio.html.
Contact: Edward Lamie, Editor.

Desc: Provides information for individuals interested in the potential use of digital and analog computers in biomedical computing. Represents SIGBIO in its efforts to encourage and facilitate communication and exchange of information "concerning problem areas, computer routines, techniques, and activities between individuals and laboratories involved in biomedical research applications." Occasionally includes SIGBIO symposium proceedings. *Type:* Newsletter.

Smithsonian Institution

National Museum of American History

Department of the History of Science and Technology

Science, Medicine, and Society Division

14th St. & Constitution Ave.   Ph: (202)357-2700
NW   Fax: (202)347-7757
Washington, DC 20560

Desc: Division is concerned with the history of public health and pharmacy, 17th-20th century history of medical and dental technology, and 20th century health sciences. *Type:* Government agency, office, or program.

Society of Critical Care Medicine

8101 E. Kaiser Blvd., 3rd Fl.   Ph: (714)282-6000
Anaheim, CA 92808-2259   Fax: (714)282-6050
E-mail: info@sccm.org
URL: http://www.sccm.org
Contact: Steven V. Seekins, Exec. VP & CEO.

Desc: Physicians, nurses, scientists, technicians, respiratory therapists, engineers, pharmacists, and physicians assistants involved in the field of critical care medicine. Purposes are: to improve care for acute life-threatening illnesses and injuries; to promote development of optimal care facilities; to guarantee high educational standards in critical care medicine. SCCM has initiated self-assessment testing program in an effort to establish core curriculum and assist physicians in self-evaluation. *Type:* Association.

Society of Diagnostic Medical Sonographers

12770 Coit Rd., Ste. 708   Ph: (972)239-7367
Dallas, TX 75251   Free: 800-229-9506
   Fax: (972)239-7378
E-mail: alysdale@sdms.org
URL: http://www.sdms/org
Contact: Gwen Grim, Exec.Dir.

Desc: Sonographers, physician sonologists, and those in medical specialties utilizing high frequency sound for diagnostic purposes. Works to advance the science of diagnostic medical sonography to establish and maintain high standards of education, to provide an identity and sense of direction for members. *Type:* Association.

Society for Epidemiologic Research

Department of Family &   Ph: (801)581-7234
   Preventive Medicine   Fax: (801)585-9805
50 N. Medicine Dr., 1C26
Salt Lake City, UT 84132
E-mail: jlyon@dfpm.utah.edu
URL: http://phweb.sph.jhu.edu/pubs/jepi
Contact: Dr. Joseph L. Lyon, Treas.

Desc: Epidemiology, focusing on research and education. *Type:* Research center.

Society of Gastroenterology Nurses and Associates

401 N. Michigan Ave.   Ph: (312)321-5165
Chicago, IL 60611   Free: 800-245-7462
   Fax: (312)321-5194
E-mail: sgna@sba.com
URL: http://www.sgna.org
Contact: Margaret M. Crevey, Exec.Dir.

Desc: To unite personnel engaged in the field of gastroenterology/endoscopy in order to promote the highest professional standards for gastroenterology nurses and associates. Conducts national and regional educational courses and research programs. Cooperates with other professional associations, hospitals, universities, industries, technical societies, research organizations, and governmental agencies. *Type:* Association.

Society for Menstrual Cycle Research

10559 N. 104th Pl.   Ph: (602)451-9731
Scottsdale, AZ 85258
URL: http://www.wilpaterson.edu/wpcpages/icip/smcr/
Contact: Mary Anna Friederich, MD, Contact.

Desc: Women's menstrual cycles, including endocrinology, genetics, physiology, psychology, medicine, sociology, and research, focusing on menstrual cycle networking and the health needs of women. *Type:* Research center.

Society of Nuclear Medicine

1850 Samuel Morse Dr.   Ph: (703)708-9000
Reston, VA 20190-5316   Fax: (703)708-9777
E-mail: jchilds@snm.org
URL: http://www.snm.org

Desc: Professional society of physicians, physicists, chemists, radiopharmacists, nuclear medicine technologists, and others interested in nuclear medicine, nuclear magnetic resonance, and the use of radioactive isotopes in clinical practice, research, and teaching. Disseminates information concerning the utilization of nuclear phenomena in the diagnosis and treatment of disease. Oversees the Technologist Section of the Society of Nuclear Medicine. *Type:* Association.

Society for Progressive Supranuclear Palsy

Johns Hopkins Outpatient   Ph: (410)486-3330
   Center   Free: 800-457-4777
601 N. Caroline St., Ste. 5065   Fax: (410)486-4283
Baltimore, MD 21287
E-mail: epkatz@erols.com
URL: http://www.psp.org
Contact: Ellen Katz, Dir.

Desc: Works to provide help and support to persons with progressive supranuclear palsy (PSP), a degenerative brain disorder related to Parkinson's Disease. *Type:* Association.

Society for the Study of Reproduction

1603 Monroe St.   Ph: (608)256-2777
Madison, WI 53711-2021   Fax: (608)256-4610
E-mail: ssr@ssr.org
URL: http://www.ssr.org
Contact: Judith Jansen, Exec.Sec.

Desc: Reproduction, focusing on interdisciplinary communication within the science. *Type:* Research center.

South Carolina Health and Environmental Control Department

Health Services Division

Laboratories Bureau

Analytical Chemistry Division

8231 Parklane Rd,   Ph: (803)734-5000
Columbia, SC 29223   Fax: (803)734-4777
E-mail: hickeytm@columb68.dhsc.state.us.sc
Contact: Thomas Hickey, PhD, Dir.

Desc: Health issues. *Type:* Research center.

South Carolina Health and Environmental Control Department

Health Services Division

Laboratories Bureau

Division of Laboratories

2600 Bull St.   Ph: (803)935-7000
Columbia, SC 29201   Fax: (803)935-7357
URL: http://www.state.sc.us/dhec/hslab.htm
Contact: Harold Dowda, PhD, Dir.

Desc: Health issues. *Type:* Research center.

South Carolina Health and Environmental Control Department

Health Services Division

Laboratories Bureau

Virology/Serology Division

2600 Bull Street   Ph: (843)734-5000
Columbia, SC 29210   Fax: (843)734-4777
E-mail: parkerek@columb68.dhec.state.sc.us
URL: http://www.state.sc.us:80/dhea/division.htm
Contact: Elizabeth Parker, MPH, Dir.

Desc: Viruses and immune systems. *Type:* Research center.

Spine Letter

Lippincott-Raven Publishers
12107 Insurance Way   Ph: (301)714-2300
Hagerstown, MD 21740   Free: 800-638-3030
   Fax: (301)714-2398
Contact: James N. Weinstein, Editor; Gretchen Henkel, Editor.

Desc: Covers clinical issues relating to spine treatment and care. *Type:* Newsletter.

Stanford University

Center for Biomedical Ethics

701 A Welch Rd., Ste. 1105   Ph: (650)723-5760
Palo Alto, CA 94304   Fax: (650)725-6131
E-mail: BKoenig@stanford.edu
URL: http://www.stanford/edu/dpt/scbe
Contact: Dr. Barbara Koenig, Exec.Dir.

Desc: Scientific and biomedical ethics, focusing on applying ethical reasoning to actual moral problems in the practice of medicine and science; contributing to the national and international discussion of biomedical and scientific issues through research, with a focus on empirical bioethics studies; convening scholars, professionals, and policymakers to debate and propose policy solutions regarding biomedical and scientific ethical issues; and serving as a scholarly resource for the University and the community. *Type:* Research center.

Stanford University

Center for Narcolepsy

1201 Welch Rd., Rm. P-112   Ph: (650)725-6517
Stanford, CA 94305   Fax: (650)498-7761
E-mail: mignot@leland.stanford.edu
URL: http://www-med.stanford.edu/school/psychiatry/narcolepsy/#diagnosis
Contact: Dr. Emmanuel Mignot, Dir.

Desc: All aspects of narcolepsy, from pharmacological treatments for patients to isolating the genes. *Type:* Research center.

Stanford University

Center for Research in Disease Prevention

Sch. of Med.   Ph: (650)723-6145
1000 Welch Rd.   Fax: (650)725-6906
Palo Alto, CA 94304-1825
E-mail: fortmann@stanford.edu
URL: http://scrdp.stanford.edu/
Contact: Stephen P. Fortmann, MD, Dir.

Desc: Prevention and control of chronic disease, alcohol and drug abuse, adolescent pregancy, and injury and death. Stresses a public health or community approach to disease prevention and health promotion and seeks methods to improve the overall level of community health by favorably modifying the environmental and personal factors known to influence chronic disease incidence, including blood pressure, blood cholesterol, cigarette use, obesity, physical activity, and stress. *Type:* Research center.

Stanford University

Gastroenterology Clinic

750 Welch Rd., Ste. 210 Ph: (650)725-3360
Palo Alto, CA 94304-1509 Fax: (650)498-5692
E-mail: hatchel@stanford.edu
Contact: Dr. Gabriel Garcia, Dir.
Desc: Gastroenterology, focusing on treatment of viral hepatitis. *Type:* Research center.

Stanford University

General Clinical Research Center

300 Pasteur Dr., Unit H1 Ph: (650)723-7496
Palo Alto, CA 94305-5251 Fax: (650)725-6698
E-mail: mv.bis@forsythe.stanford.edu
URL: http://www.leland.stanford.edu/dept/gcrc
Contact: Branimir I. Sikic, MD, Prog.Dir.
Desc: Clinical research on nutrition, diabetes, growth hormone deficiencies and growth hormone therapies, oncology, monoclonal antibodies, lupus nephritis, epidermolysis bullosa, pharmokinetics of drugs, interferon, infectious diseases, human immunodeficiency virus (HIV), and sleep disorders; physiological and pathophysiological adaptations of prematurely born infants, critically ill term infants, and normal infants. Also focuses on computer modelling of pressure-limited mechanical ventilation, infant heme catabolism, modulation of circadian rhythmicity in preterm infants, treatment of perinatal infectious diseases such as neonatal herpes simplex infection and AIDS, markers of basement membrane disruption, late pulmonary sequelae of BPD, treatment of newborn skin, cystic fibrosis, and extra corporeal membrane oxygenation (ECMO). *Type:* Research center.

Stanford University

Stanford Arthritis Center

1000 Welch Rd., Ste 203 Ph: (650)723-5907
Palo Alto, CA 94304-5755 Fax: (650)723-9656
E-mail: holman@dbn.stanford.edu
Contact: Dr. Halsted Holman, Dir.
Desc: Arthritis, including epidemiology, health policy, community education, measurement of patient outcomes, comparison of health care systems, and testing of novel treatments resulting from recent biomedical advances. *Type:* Research center.

State Health Monitor

Atlantic Information Services, Inc.
1100 17th St. NW, No. 300 Ph: (202)775-9008
Washington, DC 20036 Free: 800-521-4323
Fax: (202)331-9542
URL: http://www.aispub.com.
Contact: Chad Hudnall, Editor, chudnall@aispub.com; David Mlawsky, Managing Editor.
Desc: Reports on federal developments in Medicare, Medicaid, and health care coverage and payment policy. Publishes news stories on Congress and health care financing administration. *Type:* Newsletter.

State University of New York Health Science Center at Brooklyn

Ambulatory Surgery Unit

450 Clarkson Ave. Ph: (718)780-1350
Box 6 Fax: (718)780-1358
Brooklyn, NY 11203-2012
E-mail: twersky@pipeline.com
Contact: Rebecca S. Twersky, MD, Dir.
Desc: Comparison of clinical experiences and outcomes with remifentanil vs. hypnotic/inhalation based anesthesia; recovery after general anestesia with remifentenanil vs. hypnotic-based fentanyl in patients undergoing outpatient larascopic gynecologic surgery; and pain assessment in the mentally-challenged patient undergoing ambulatory surgical procedures. *Type:* Research center.

State University of New York Health Science Center at Brooklyn

Diabetes Diagnostic and Research Center

445 Lennox Rd. Ph: (718)270-1698
Box 123 Fax: (718)270-1534
Brooklyn, NY 11203
Contact: Harold E. Lebovitz, MD, Prog.Dir.
Desc: Diabetes, endocrinology, immunology and metabolism, nephrology, and carcinoid syndrome. *Type:* Research center.

State University of New York Health Science Center at Stony Brook

Center for Photographic Images of Medicine and HTH Care

Health Sci. Ctr. Ph: (516)444-3228
Media Services, Rm. 044 Fax: (516)444-6172
PO Box 9051
Stony Brook, NY 11794-8030
E-mail: jneville@upo.hsc.sunysb.edu
Contact: Kathleen Gebhart, Dir.
Desc: Houses 3,000 photographic images of medical practices. Activities include searching historical records and archives for additional photographs. *Type:* Research center.

State University of New York Health Science Center at Syracuse

Clinical Research Center

Univ. Hospital Ph: (315)464-9000
750 E. Adams St., Rm. 8602 Fax: (315)464-9002
Syracuse, NY 13210
E-mail: mosesa@mailbox.hscsyr.edu
URL: http://www.hscsyr.edu
Contact: Arnold M. Moses, MD, Prog.Dir.
Desc: Endocrinology, gastroenterology, metabolism, nephrology, oncology, nutrition, and neurology. *Type:* Research center.

Strategy

Canadian Medical Association
1867 Alta Vista Dr. Ph: (613)731-4552
Ottawa, ON, Canada K1G 3Y6 Free: 800-663-7336
Fax: (613)736-5367
E-mail: pubs@cma.ca
Contact: Matthew Bonsall, Editor-in-Chief.
Desc: Focuses on the financial interests of physicians. Discusses topics on financial planning, investment strategies, taxes, legal issues, and practice management. *Type:* Newsletter.

Stroke Clubs, International

805 12th St. Ph: (409)762-1022
Galveston, TX 77550
E-mail: strokeclub@aol.com
Contact: Ellis Williamson, Pres.
Desc: Active members are stroke victims; associate members are individuals interested in the problems of stroke victims. To unite stroke victims for the purpose of aiding each other; to instruct them and their families regarding the nature of stroke and the means for overcoming the resulting handicaps; to aid them in finding employment; and to give the stroke victim hope and encouragement. At monthly meetings, qualified speakers discuss the medical aspects of strokes and member stroke victims discuss their progress and problems. *Type:* Association.

The Supplement

Menuco Corp.
350 Fifth Ave., Ste. 7509 Free: 800-636-8261
New York, NY 10118
Desc: Promotes the ENADA supplement, the oral form of stabilized NADH. Discusses research conducted to discover ENADA's ability to lower blood pressure. *Type:* Newsletter.

TEL-MED—News

TEL-MED
24769 Redlands Blvd., Ste. L Ph: (909)825-6034
Loma Linda, CA 92354
E-mail: telmed@ix.netcom.com
URL: http://www.tel-med.com.
Contact: Michael Carpenter, President.
Desc: Carries general organizational news for licensees of this health and medical telephone information service which operates throughout the U.S., Canada, South America, and Saudi Arabia. Recurring features include news briefs, lists of new licensees, and a message update column. *Type:* Newsletter.

Telco Business Report

Telecom Publishing Group
Warren Publishing, Inc.
2115 Ward Ct. NW Ph: (202)872-9200
Washington, DC 20037 Fax: (202)293-3435
Contact: Jennifer Park, Editor.
Desc: Provides analyses of U.S. telephone company strategies at home and abroad. *Type:* Newsletter.

Telemedicine Business Newsletter

Miller Freeman, Inc.
525 Market St., Ste. 500 Ph: (415)538-3828
San Francisco, CA 94105 Free: 800-289-0969
Fax: (415)278-5371
E-mail: subserv@mfi.com
Contact: Brian Casey, Editor.
Desc: Covers developments in the fast growing industry of telemedicine, including new products and applications, regulatory, legal and ethical issues. *Type:* Newsletter.

Temple University

General Clinical Research Center

3401 N. Broad St. Ph: (215)707-3086
Philadelphia, PA 19140 Fax: (215)707-1560
E-mail: gcrc@vm.temple.edu
Contact: Guenther Boden, MD, Prog.Dir.
Desc: Gastroenterology, cardiology, metabolism, nephrology, neurology, AIDS, pulmonary research, and social phobias. *Type:* Research center.

Temple University

Motility Laboratory/Gastroenterology

H5C Health Sci. Ctr. Campus Ph: (215)707-3433
Sch. of Med. Fax: (215)707-2684
3400 N. Broad St.
Philadelphia, PA 19140
E-mail: krevsky@vm.temple.edu
Contact: Dr. Robert Fisher, Dir.
Desc: Neurohumoral control of gastrointestinal motility, including mechanical properties and neuropeptide receptor characteristics of gastrointestinal tract smooth muscle and neurohormonal interactions in gastrointestinal motility; applied clinical research. *Type:* Research center.

Tennessee Valley Authority

Vice President of Human Resources

Health Services

20 E 11th St., EB 8A Ph: (423)751-2091
Chattanooga, TN 37402-2801
Type: Government agency, office, or program.

Texas A&M University

Laboratory for Protein and Amino Acid Analysis

Department of Animal Science Ph: (409)845-5064
Kleberg Center, Rm. 212 Fax: (409)845-5292
College Station, TX 77843-2471
URL: http://agweb.tamu.edu/ansc/flynn/labhome.htm

Contact: Dr. Guoyao Wu, Hd.

Desc: Analysis of amino acids and how they relate to various biochemical systems in fetal and neonatal systems, including Arginine metabolism and its crucial role in nitric oxide synthesis. *Type:* Research center.

Texas Medical Association
401 W. 15th St.　　　　　　Ph: (512)370-1300
Austin, TX 78701　　　　　　Fax: (512)370-1633
E-mail: tmainfo@texmed.org
URL: http://www.texmed.org
Contact: Louis J. Goodman, PHD, Exec.VP/CEO.
Desc: Promotes the medical profession. Provides lobbying and representation. *Type:* Association.

Thomas Jefferson University
Center for Research in Medical Education and Health Care
Jefferson Med. College　　　Ph: (215)955-8907
1025 Walnut St., Rm. 119　　Fax: (215)923-6939
　College
Philadelphia, PA 19107-5083
E-mail: louisd@jefflin.tju.edu
Contact: Joseph S. Gonnella, MD, Dir.
Desc: Medical education process and factors affecting the quality of cost of health care. Medical education research focuses on the following areas: measurement of physician competence; long-term follow-up study of graduates; program evaluation; specialty choice; and refinement of evaluation methods. *Type:* Research center.

Thomas Jefferson University
Lupus Study Center
1015 Chestnut St., Ste. 1520　Ph: (215)955-8430
Philadelphia, PA 19107　　　Fax: (215)923-5828
Contact: Raphael J. DeHoratius, MD, Dir.
Desc: Systemic lupus erthematosus and autoimmune diseases, including reproductive immunology. *Type:* Research center.

Thomas Jefferson University
Malignant Hyperthermia Research Center
Jefferson Med. Coll.　　　　Ph: (215)955-1858
Dept. of Anesthesiology　　Fax: (215)923-5507
8490 Gibbon
111 S. 11th St.
Philadelphia, PA 19107
E-mail: henry.rosenberg@mail.tju.edu
Contact: Dr. Henry Rosenberg, Dir.
Desc: Malignant hyperthermia, neuromuscular blocking agents, and general anesthetic agents. Studies focus on diagnosis of malignant hyperthermia susceptibility and basic research in mechanisms underlying malignant hyperthermia, anesthetic action, and drug mechanisms. *Type:* Research center.

Thomas Jefferson University
Scleroderma and Arthritis Research Center
233 S. 10th St.　　　　　　Ph: (215)503-5042
Philadelphia, PA 19107　　　Fax: (215)923-4649
E-mail: sergio.jimenez@mail.tju.edu
Contact: Dr. Sergio A. Jimenez, Dir.
Desc: Molecular biology and biochemistry of the connective tissue, pathogenesis of scleroderma and other fibrotic diseases, biological functions of the immune system in health and disease, molecular biology of articular cartilage matrix and heritable diseases of articular cartilage, and identification of gene mutations in human connective tissue diseases and animal models of disease. *Type:* Research center.

Thyroid Foundation of America
Ruth Sleeper Hall, RSL 350　　Ph: (617)726-8500
40 Parkman St.　　　　　　　Free: 800-832-8321
Boston, MA 02114-2698　　　Fax: (617)726-4136
E-mail: info@tsh.org
URL: http://www.tsh.org
Contact: Dr. Lawrence C. Wood, Pres.
Desc: Individuals with thyroid conditions; health professionals. Provides education and support for thyroid patients and health professionals; promotes public awareness of thyroid problems. Sponsors fundraising to support thyroid research; conducts educational programs. *Type:* Association.

Totts Gap Medical Research Laboratories, Inc.
1430 Totts Gap Rd.　　　　Ph: (610)588-0572
Bangor, PA 18013　　　　　Fax: (610)588-8452
E-mail: tottsgap@epix.net
Contact: Stewart Wolf, MD, Dir.
Desc: Neural regulation of visceral function, emphasizing current focus on the cardiovascular system. Specific projects involve the study of the mechanisms of cardiac arrhythmia and sudden death and other aspects of neurocardiology. *Type:* Research center.

UAPD Report
Union of American Physicians and Dentists (UAPD)
1330 Broadway, No. 730　　Ph: (510)839-0193
Oakland, CA 94612-2506　　Fax: (510)763-8756
Desc: Reports on the successful handling of physicians' grievances, negotiations, and collective bargaining. Offers financial reports, election news, and insurance news concerning members of the Union. *Type:* Newsletter.

United Cerebral Palsy Associations
1660 L St. NW, Ste. 700　　Ph: (202)776-0406
Washington, DC 20036　　　Free: 800-USA-5UCP
　　　　　　　　　　　　　Fax: (202)776-0414
Contact: Jeanette Harvey, Exec.Dir.
Desc: Voluntary national federation of state and local affiliates aiding persons with cerebral palsy and other disabilities, and their families. Goals are to prevent cerebral palsy, minimize its effects, and improve the quality of life for persons with cerebral palsy and other disabilities, and their families. Supports research and traineeships for medical and allied personnel; sponsors professional and public education in the prevention and management of cerebral palsy; cooperates with governmental and other agencies concerned with the welfare of persons with disabilities; acts as an advocate on the federal, state, and local levels for the civil rights of people with cerebral palsy and other disabilities, and their families. *Type:* Association.

United Cerebral Palsy Research and Educational Foundation
1660 L St. NW, Ste. 700　　Ph: (202)973-7140
Washington, DC 20036-5602　Free: 800-872-5827
　　　　　　　　　　　　　Fax: (202)776-0414
E-mail: ucpnatl@ucpa.org
URL: http://www.ucpa.org
Contact: Murray Goldstein, D.O., Med.Dir.
Desc: Provides research grants to prevent cerebral palsy and to improve the quality of life for persons with cerebral palsy. Offers clinical fellowships for medical and dental specialists in cerebral palsy. *Type:* Association.

United Ostomy Association
19772 MacArthur Blvd., Ste.　Free: 800-826-0826
　200
Irvine, CA 92612-2405
URL: http://www.uoa.org
Contact: Darlene Smith, Exec.Dir.
Desc: Individuals who have lost the normal function of their bowel or bladder necessitating colostomy, ileostomy, ileal conduit, or ureterostomy surgery, known as ostomy. Aids in rehabilitation of these persons through mutual aid, moral support, and exchange of practical information in managing the stoma and its necessary prosthetic appliances; sponsors visiting program allowing patients to ask non-medical questions of individuals who have experienced a similar condition. *Type:* Association.

United Scleroderma Foundation
89 Newbury St., Ste. 201　　Ph: (978)750-4499
Danvers, MA 01923-1075　　Free: 800-722-HOPE
　　　　　　　　　　　　　Fax: (978)750-9902

E-mail: sclerofed@aol.com
URL: http://www.scleroderma.com
Contact: Karl Kastorf, Exec.Dir.
Desc: Provides educational and emotional support to persons with scleroderma and their families. Stimulates and supports research designed to identify the cause and cure of scleroderma, as well as improve methods of treatment. Enhances the public's awareness of this disease. *Type:* Association.

U.S. Department of the Air Force
Wilford Hall USAF Medical Center
Clinical Investigation Facility
ATTN: WHMC/MSR　　　　Ph: (210)292-7141
1255 Wilford Hall Loop　　Fax: (210)292-6053
Lackland AFB, TX 78236-5319
E-mail: cody@whmc-lafb.af.mil
Contact: Lt.Col. John T. Cody, Dir.
Desc: Medical research includes biological, behavioral, and psychological studies. Investigative efforts have contributed to improved disease prevention, diagnosis, and treatment modalities, including: advances in the application of hyperbaric oxygen therapy in a variety of conditions; better biochemical characterization of disease leading to enhanced understanding of underlying mechanisms in a spectrum of non-cancer diseases; improved procedures for cancer chemo-, immuno-, radiotherapy, and surgical techniques; pioneer development of extra-corporeal membrane oxygenation, high frequency ventilation, and organ transplantation techniques; and selection of improved dental procedures through critical evaluation of safety and effectiveness. *Type:* Research center.

U.S. Department of Defense
Wilford Hall USAF Medical Center
Lackland AFB, TX 78236　　Ph: (210)292-7051
　　　　　　　　　　　　　Fax: (210)292-6053

Contact: Gen. P.K. Carlton, Comdr.
Desc: Central point for all research conducted within Wilford Hall Medical Center (WHMC); and directly or indirectly supports the readiness, education, and patient care missions of WHMC. Activities include research, one-time emergency therapeutic uses of investigational drugs, and training. *Type:* Research center.

U.S. Department of Health and Human Services
200 Independence Ave. SW　Ph: (202)619-0257
Washington, DC 20201
URL: http://www.dhhs.gov/
Contact: Donna E. Shalala, Secretary.
Desc: The Department of Health and Human Services is the cabinet-level department of the federal executive branch most concerned with people and most involved with the nation's human concerns. The Secretary of HHS advises the President on health, welfare, and income security plans, policies, and programs of the federal government. *Type:* Government agency, office, or program.

U.S. Department of Health and Human Services

Administration for Children and Families

370 L'Enfant Promenade SW   Ph: (202)401-9200
Washington, DC 20447

Contact: Olivia A. Golden, Assistant Secretary.

Desc: The Administration for Children and Families provides national leadership and direction to plan, manage, and coordinate comprehensive support services for vulnerable children and families, Native Americans, people with disabilities, refugees and legalized aliens. The mission of ACF is to promote stability, economic security, responsibility and self-sufficiency. *Type:* Government agency, office, or program.

U.S. Department of Health and Human Services

Administration for Children and Families

Administration on Children, Youth and Families

370 L'Enfant Promenade SW   Ph: (202)205-8347
Washington, DC 20024

Desc: The Administration for Children, Youth, and Families advises on matters relating to sound development of children, youth, and families. It oversees and finances a broad range of programs to help children and families develop and grow toward more independent and self-reliant lives. *Type:* Government agency, office, or program.

U.S. Department of Health and Human Services

Administration for Children and Families

Administration for Native Americans

370 L'Enfant Promenade   Ph: (202)690-7776
Washington, DC 20447

Desc: The Administration for Native Americans represents the concerns of American Indians, Alaska Natives, Native Hawaiians, and other Native American Pacific Islanders (including American Samoan Natives) and advises the Assistant Secretary for Human Development Services on their behalf. ANA has primary responsibility for the social and economic development and self-sufficiency of Native Americans; serves as departmental liaison with other federal agencies on Native American affairs; administers a grant program to promote the social and economic development of Native Americans; and explores new program concepts and methods. *Type:* Government agency, office, or program.

U.S. Department of Health and Human Services

Agency for Health Care Policy and Research

Center for General Health Services Intramural Research

Statistics and Research Methodology Division

East-West Towers   Ph: (301)594-1406
4330 East-West Hwy.   Fax: (301)594-2166
Bethesda, MD 20814

Contact: Steven B. Cohen, Dir.

Desc: Complex survey design; sampling techniques; estimation; and reduction of sources of sampling and nonsampling error. Responsible for the statistical design and analysis of the National Medical Expenditure Survey (NMES). *Type:* Research center.

U.S. Department of Health and Human Services

Agency for Health Care Policy and Research

Center for Outcomes and Effectiveness Research

2101 E. Jefferson St., Ste. 605   Ph: (301)594-1485
Rockville, MD 20852   Fax: (301)594-3211

Contact: Carolyn Clancy, MD, Dir.

Desc: Awards grants and contracts for patient outcomes research and studies on practice variations, outcomes research methodologies, and other medical effectiveness research topics. Monitors the work of patient outcomes research teams and the MEDTEP research centers on minority populations. *Type:* Research center.

U.S. Department of Health and Human Services

Agency for Health Care Policy and Research

Office of Management

Grants Management Branch

Executive Office Center   Ph: (301)594-1447
2101 E. Jefferson   Fax: (301)594-3210
Rockville, MD 20852

Contact: Mable L. Lam, Chf.

Desc: Manages the awarding of grants for health care research and programs that have been approved for payment. *Type:* Research center.

U.S. Department of Health and Human Services

Agency for Health Care Policy and Research

Office of Scientific Affairs

Exec. Office Center   Ph: (301)594-1398
2101 E. Jefferson St., Ste 400   Fax: (301)594-0154
Rockville, MD 20852

Contact: Dr. Linda Demloo, Dir.

Desc: Emphasizes three major areas: the Providers Studies Program examines how competition, reimbursement systems, and various types of regulation influence the use and cost of medical care; National Medical Care Expenditures Study uses information from a large national survey to examine the ways in which Americans use and pay for health care services; Long-Term Care Studies Program evaluates the impact of different reimbursement approaches on the admission practices and services of nursing homes, the feasibility of private, long-term care insurance, and the contribution of informal support systems for the elderly. *Type:* Research center.

U.S. Department of Health and Human Services

Agency for Toxic Substances and Disease Registry

Division of Health Studies

1600 Clifton Rd., NE   Ph: (404)639-6200
Mail Stop E-31   Fax: (404)639-6220
Atlanta, GA 30333

Contact: Jeffrey A. Lybarger, Dir.

Desc: Epidemiology and other human health studies, evaluating the relationship between exposure to hazardous substances at waste sites and adverse health effects. Conducts health studies, surveillance programs, and registries. *Type:* Research center.

U.S. Department of Health and Human Services

Centers for Disease Control and Prevention

1600 Clifton Rd., N.E.   Ph: (404)639-3311
Atlanta, GA 30333   Fax: (404)639-7111
E-mail: netinfo@cdc.gov
URL: http://www.cdc.gov

Contact: Jeffrey P. Kaplan, MD, Dir.

Desc: Responsible for protecting the public health of the nation by preventing disease, disability, and premature death and promoting healthy lifestyles for all Americans. Specifically, CDC research focuses on the prevention of infectious diseases, chronic diseases, injury or disease associated with environmental, home, and workplace hazards, and controllable risk factors such as poor nutrition, smoking, lack of exercise, high blood pressure, stress, and drug misuse. *Type:* Research center.

U.S. Department of Health and Human Services

Centers for Disease Control and Prevention

Epidemiology Program Office

Bldg. 1, Rm. 5009   Ph: (404)639-3661
1600 Clifton Rd., N.E.   Fax: (404)639-4088
Atlanta, GA 30333

Contact: Stephen B. Thacker, Dir.

Desc: Public health surveillance, epidemiologic training and research, and consultation in statistical and epidemiologic methods. *Type:* Research center.

U.S. Department of Health and Human Services

Centers for Disease Control and Prevention

Epidemiology Program Office

Division of Prevention Research and Analytic Methods

Mail Stop D-01   Ph: (404)639-4455
1600 Clifton Rd.   Fax: (404)639-4463
Atlanta, GA 30333
E-mail: SMT1.@EPO.EM.CDC.GOV

Contact: Steven Teutsch, Dir.

Desc: Methods for assessing the effectiveness of prevention strategies. *Type:* Research center.

U.S. Department of Health and Human Services

Centers for Disease Control and Prevention

International Health Program Office

1600 Clifton Rd. NE   Ph: (404)639-3311
Atlanta, GA 30333
URL: http://www.cdc.gov/

Contact: Steve Blount, Director.

Type: Government agency, office, or program.

U.S. Department of Health and Human Services

Centers for Disease Control and Prevention

National Center for Chronic Disease Prevention and Health Promotion

1600 Clifton Rd. NE   Ph: (404)639-3311
Atlanta, GA 30333
URL: http://www.cdc.gov/

Contact: James S. Marks, Director.

Type: Government agency, office, or program.

U.S. Department of Health and Human Services

Centers for Disease Control and Prevention

National Center for Infectious Diseases

1600 Clifton Rd. NE   Ph: (404)639-3311
Atlanta, GA 30333   Fax: (404)639-3039
URL: http://www.cdc.gov/

Contact: James M. Hughes, Director.

Desc: The Center for Infectious Diseases coordinates a national program to improve the identification, investigation, diagnosis, prevention, and control of infectious diseases. It maintains programs dealing with AIDS, hospital infections, sexually transmitted diseases, bacterial diseases, host factors, mycotic diseases, parasitic diseases, viral diseases, and vector-borne viral diseases. *Type:* Government agency, office, or program.

U.S. Department of Health and Human Services

Centers for Disease Control and Prevention

National Center for Injury Prevention and Control

1600 Clifton Rd. NE   Ph: (404)639-3311
Atlanta, GA 30333
URL: http://www.cdc.gov/

Contact: Mark L. Rosenberg, Director.

Type: Government agency, office, or program.

U.S. Department of Health and Human Services

Food and Drug Administration

Center for Drug Evaluation and Research

Office of Drug Standards

Mail Code HFD-040   Ph: (301)827-2828
5600 Fishers Ln.   Fax: (301)594-6759
Rockville, MD 20857
URL: http://www.fda.gov/cder/ddmac/index.htm

Contact: Nancy M. Ostrore, PhD, Chf.

Desc: Industry-wide marketing practices of the pharmaceutical industry and improvement of drug communications between FDA, health professionals, and the public. Specific research areas include prescription drugs, marketing practices, and health communications. *Type:* Research center.

U.S. Department of Health and Human Services

Food and Drug Administration

Center for Drug Evaluation and Research

Office of Epidemiology and Biostatistics

Mail Code HFD-737   Ph: (301)443-6414
5600 Fishers Ln.
Rockville, MD 20857

Contact: George Armstrong, Jr., Chf.

Desc: Receives, processes, and maintains data for the Adverse Drug and Biological Product Reaction Database, a compilation of data from adverse reaction reports submitted to the Food and Drug Administration primarily by drug manufacturers, physicians, pharmacists, other health professionals, and consumers. These data are used by the Epidemiology and Surveillance Division to generate alerts and to monitor and support special studies on adverse reactions to drugs and biological products. *Type:* Research center.

U.S. Department of Health and Human Services

Food and Drug Administration

Center for Drug Evaluation and Research

Office of Epidemiology and Biostatistics

Mail Code HFD-713   Ph: (301)443-4594
5600 Fishers Ln., Rm. 18B45   Fax: (301)443-9279
Rockville, MD 20857
E-mail: DUBEY@FDACD.BITNET

Contact: Dr. Satya D. Dubey, Chf.

Desc: Clinical trials for assessing the efficacy and safety of pharmaceuticals; and conducts research in statistical methodologies involving applications of computers in improving review, evaluation, and research methods. *Type:* Research center.

U.S. Department of Health and Human Services

Food and Drug Administration

Center for Drug Evaluation and Research

Office of Epidemiology and Biostatistics

Mail Code HFD-700   Ph: (301)827-3209
5600 Fishers Ln., Rm. 15B45   Fax: (301)480-2825
Rockville, MD 20857
E-mail: FAIRWEATHER@CDER.FDA.GOV

Contact: Dr. William R. Fairweather, Chf.

Desc: Provides statistical and computational support for the Center for Drug Evaluation and Research. Areas of interest are statistics and drug safety, efficacy and quality. *Type:* Research center.

U.S. Department of Health and Human Services

Food and Drug Administration

Office of Planning and Evaluation

Evaluation and Analysis Staff

Mail Code HFP-10   Ph: (301)827-5252
5600 Fishers Ln., Rm. 1064   Fax: (301)827-5260
Rockville, MD 20857
E-mail: kmcevoy@oc.fda.gov
URL: http://www.fda.gov

Contact: Kate McEvoy, Dir.

Desc: In-house analytical consulting services to the FDA Commissioner and program managers. Activities involve evaluation, data collection, and analysis for all program policies and operations administered by the FDA, including pre-market review of drugs and medical devices. *Type:* Research center.

U.S. Department of Health and Human Services

Health Care Financing Administration

Bureau of Data Management and Strategy

Office of Health Care Information Systems

7500 Security Blvd.   Ph: (410)786-1951
N-3-13-15   Fax: (410)786-1783
Baltimore, MD 21244-1850
URL: http://www.hcfa.gov

Contact: Joe Broseker, Dir.

Desc: Development and implementation of pl ans and policies for the classification, standardization, identification, development, and security of data, procedures, and standards to meet the Health Care Financing Administration's information requirements and to provide health care data for research purposes. *Type:* Research center.

U.S. Department of Health and Human Services

Health Care Financing Administration

Center for Medicaid and State Operations

200 Independence Ave. SW   Ph: (202)690-6726
Washington, DC 20201
URL: http://www.hcfa.gov/

Contact: Sally Richardson, Director.

Type: Government agency, office, or program.

U.S. Department of Health and Human Services

Health Management Operations

Office of Resource Management

Grants Policy Branch

Parklawn Bldg.   Ph: (301)443-1832
5600 Fisher Ln.   Fax: (301)594-6133
Rockville, MD 20857

Contact: Stuart Feldsott, Chf.

Desc: Develops and coordinates all grants policies for the Public Health Service. Manages data systems that contain grant information from the Public Health Service. *Type:* Research center.

U.S. Department of Health and Human Services

Health Resources and Services Administration

Bureau of Health Professions

5600 Fishers Ln.   Ph: (301)443-1590
Rockville, MD 20857
URL: http://www.dhhs.gov/hrsa/

Contact: Neil Sampson, Director.

Desc: The Bureau provides national leadership in coordinating, evaluating, and supporting the development and utilization of the nation's health personnel. To accomplish this goal, the Bureau provides financial aid and support for students and research; supports mutidisciplinary training networks; supports increasing representation in the health professions of underserved minorities and other disadvantaged groups; trains primary care medical providers and public health workers in short medical supply in the United States; and conducts AIDS programs designed to increase the number of health care providers who are effectively educated and motivated to counsel, diagnose, treat, and manage persons with HIV infections. *Type:* Government agency, office, or program.

U.S. Department of Health and Human Services

Health Resources and Services Administration

Bureau of Health Professions

Office of Policy and Research

5600 Fishers Ln., Rm. 8808   Ph: (301)443-1355
Park Lawn Bldg.   Fax: (301)443-4414
Rockville, MD 20857

Contact: Art Smith, Chf.

Desc: Provides health and health-related data available at the county level; compatible and consistent health-related data in a variety of forms in order to be of use to the broadest possible range of users; and flexible analytical capabilities for analysis of health and health-related data. *Type:* Research center.

U.S. Department of Health and Human Services

Health Resources and Services Administration

Bureau of Health Resources Development

5600 Fishers Ln.   Ph: (301)443-6652
Rockville, MD 20857   Fax: (301)443-0791
URL: http://www.dhhs.gov/hrsa/

Contact: Joseph F. O'Neill, MD, Director.

Type: Government agency, office, or program.

U.S. Department of Health and Human Services

Health Resources and Services Administration

Bureau of Primary Health Care

5600 Fishers Ln.   Ph: (301)443-2086
Rockville, MD 20857
URL: http://www.dhhs.gov/hrsa/

Contact: Marilyn H. Gaston, MD, Director.

Desc: The mission of the BPHC is to increase access to comprehensive primary and preventative health care and to improve the health status of underserved and vulnerable populations. This mission is achieved through the development and support of systems and providers of high-quality, community-based, culturally-competent services. *Type:* Government agency, office, or program.

U.S. Department of Health and Human Services

Health Resources and Services Administration

Division of Immigration Health Services

5600 Fishers Ln.   Ph: (301)594-4148
Rockville, MD 20857
URL: http://www.dhhs.gov/hrsa

Desc: The Division serves as the primary focal point for planning, management, policy formulation, program coordination, direction, and liaison for all health matters pertaining to aliens detained by the Immigration and Naturalization Service. *Type:* Government agency, office, or program.

U.S. Department of Health and Human Services

Health Resources and Services Administration

Gillis W. Long Hansen's Disease Center

5445 Pointe Clair Rd.   Ph: (504)642-4740
Carville, LA 70721-9607   Fax: (504)642-4728

Contact: Robert R. Jacobson, Dir.

Desc: Care and rehabilitation of patients with Hansen's disease (leprosy) and for basic and applied research related to all aspects of the disease. In addition, Center provides a training facility for professionals and paraprofessionals involved with the diagnosis and treatment of Hansen's disease, both within the United States and abroad. *Type:* Research center.

U.S. Department of Health and Human Services

Health Resources and Services Administration

Maternal and Child Health Bureau

5600 Fishers Ln.   Ph: (301)443-0205
Rockville, MD 20857
URL: http://www.dhhs.gov/hrsa/

Contact: Audrey H. Nora, Director.

Desc: The Bureau develops, administers, directs, coordinates, monitors, and supports federal policy and programs pertaining to health and related-care systems for the nation's mothers and children. *Type:* Government agency, office, or program.

U.S. Department of Health and Human Services

Health Resources and Services Administration

Office of Minority Health

5600 Fishers Ln.   Ph: (301)443-2086
Rockville, MD 20857
URL: http://www.dhhs.gov/hrsa/

Contact: Ileana C. Herrell, Director.
Type: Government agency, office, or program.

U.S. Department of Health and Human Services

Health Resources and Services Administration

Office of Rural Health Policy

5600 Fishers Ln.   Ph: (301)443-2086
Rockville, MD 20857
URL: http://www.dhhs.gov/hrsa/
Contact: Dena Puskin, Director.
Type: Government agency, office, or program.

U.S. Department of Health and Human Services

Indian Health Service

5600 Fishers Ln.   Ph: (301)443-1083
Rockville, MD 20857
URL: http://www.tucson.ihs.gov/
Contact: Michael H. Trujillo, MD, Director.
Desc: The Indian Health Service assures a comprehensive health services delivery system for American Indians and Alaska Natives, with sufficient options to provide for maximum tribal involvement in meeting their health needs. The goal of the Service is to raise the health level of the Indian and Alaska Native people to the highest possible level. *Type:* Government agency, office, or program.

U.S. Department of Health and Human Services

Indian Health Service

Office of Planning, Evaluation, and Legislation

Division of Program Statistics

Twinbrook Metro Plaza   Ph: (301)443-1180
12300 Twinbrook Pkwy., Ste.   Fax: (301)443-1522
450
Rockville, MD 20852
E-mail: adangelo@hqe.ihs.gov
URL: http://www.ihs.gov
Contact: Anthony J. D'Angelo, Dir.
Desc: Main function is to satisfy the American Indian and Alaska Native health statistics information needs of its clients. The Division manages a number of information systems that provide data for measuring the health status of the American Indian and Alaska Native population and appraising IHS program activities. *Type:* Research center.

U.S. Department of Health and Human Services

National Center for Chronic Disease Prevention and Health Promotion

Mail Stop K40   Ph: (770)488-5401
4770 Buford Hwy., NE   Fax: (770)488-5971
Atlanta, GA 30341-3717
Contact: Dr. James S. Marks, Dir.
Desc: Prevention of chronic diseases such as cardiovascular disease, diabetes, and cancer. Translates research findings into community programs and healthier lifestyles. *Type:* Research center.

U.S. Department of Health and Human Services

National Center for Chronic Disease Prevention and Health Promotion

Chronic Disease Control and Community Intervention Division

1600 Clifton Rd. NE   Ph: (770)488-5269
Atlanta, GA 30333   Fax: (770)488-5971
E-mail: dvm0@cdc.gov
Contact: David McQueen, Dir.
Desc: Chronic diseases, including maternal and child health, breast and cervical cancer, diabetes, smoking, adolescents and school health, AIDS and women, and reproductive health. *Type:* Research center.

U.S. Department of Health and Human Services

National Center for Chronic Disease Prevention and Health Promotion

Diabetes Translation Division

Epidemiology and Statistics Branch

4770 Buford Hwy., NE, MSC   Ph: (404)639-3311
K-10   Fax: (404)488-5966
Atlanta, GA 30341-3724
Contact: Dr. Michael Engelgau, Chf.
Desc: Epidemiologic research related to preventing diabetes and its complications. Conducts national surveys on the incidence of diabetes and its complications. *Type:* Research center.

U.S. Department of Health and Human Services

National Center for Health Statistics

6525 Belcrest Rd.   Ph: (301)436-8500
Hyattsville, MD 20782
URL: http://www.cdc.gov/nchswww
Contact: Edward Sondik, Dir.
Desc: National health statistics; conduct research in survey and statistical methodology; provide specialized training programs and technical assistance; and coordinate cooperative programs with state, national, and international organizations. Principal components include the Office of Analysis and Epidemiology, Office of Research and Methodology, and Office of Vital and Health Statistics Systems (Health Care Statistics Division, Health Examination Statistics Division, Health Interview Statistics Division, and Vital Statistics Division). *Type:* Research center.

U.S. Department of Health and Human Services

National Center for Health Statistics

Office of Research and Methodology

Presidential Bldg., Rm. 915   Ph: (301)436-7110
6525 Belcrest Rd.   Fax: (301)436-7955
Hyattsville, MD 20782
Contact: Dr. Lester Curtin, Acting Assoc.Dir.
Desc: Participates in the development of policy, long-range plans, and programs of the National Center for Health Statistics (NCHS); coordinates the Center's applied and basic research program in mathematical statistics and survey design and methodology; formulates statistical standards regarding the survey design, data collection, coding, data analysis, data presentation, and statistical computing for all NCHS data systems and coordinates activities directed at the implementation and maintenance of these standards; serves as the Center's consultant in the fields of mathematical statistics, survey design and methodology, and statistical methodology; consults and collaborates on statistical research projects with Public Health Service agencies and other federal organizations, state and local governments, universities, private research organizations, and international health agencies; and reviews, for statistical merit, research contracts and intramural projects as well as research projects undertaken through contracts, interagency agreements, or intramural activities. *Type:* Research center.

U.S. Department of Health and Human Services

National Center for Health Statistics

Office of Vital and Health Statistics Systems

Health Care Statistics Division

Presidential Bldg., Rm. 952   Ph: (301)436-8522
6525 Belcrest Rd.   Fax: (301)436-7955
Hyattsville, MD 20782
E-mail: ttml@cdc.gov
URL: http://www.cdc.gov/nchswww/nchshome.htm
Contact: Thomas McLemore, Dep.Dir.
Desc: Division's data collection and analysis program administers provider-based health care surveys, which monitor the nation's use of health care resources (including hospitals, nursing homes, and physicians). Specific areas of interest are health statistics, epidemiology, and health services research. *Type:* Research center.

U.S. Department of Health and Human Services

National Center for Health Statistics

Office of Vital and Health Statistics Systems

Health Examination Statistics Division

6525 Belcrest Rd., Rm. 1000   Ph: (301)436-7068
Hyattsville, MD 20782   Fax: (301)436-5431
E-mail: clj1@mch09a.em.cdc.gov
Contact: Clifford Johnson, Contact.
Desc: Nutritional status for adults and children, growth and development of children, nominative or descriptive physiological data for children and adults, chronic disease in adults, and some environmental exposures. *Type:* Research center.

U.S. Department of Health and Human Services

National Center for Health Statistics

Office of Vital and Health Statistics Systems

Health Interview Statistics Division

6525 Belcrest Rd., Rm. 850   Ph: (301)436-7085
Hyattsville, MD 20782   Fax: (301)436-3484
E-mail: amhl.@cdc.gov
Contact: Ann Hardy, Actg.Dir.
Desc: Conducts the National Health Interview Survey (NHIS), a major data collection program of the National Center for Health Statistics. In accordance with the National Health Survey Act of 1956, NHIS provides continuing survey and special follow-up studies on major current health issues affecting the civilian noninstitutionalized population of the United States. *Type:* Research center.

U.S. Department of Health and Human Services

National Center for Infectious Diseases

1600 Clifton Rd. NE, MSC-   Ph: (404)639-3401
C12   Fax: (404)639-3039
Atlanta, GA 30333
E-mail: jmh2@cdc.gov
URL: http://www.cdc.gov/ncdid/ncid.htm
Contact: James M. Hughes, MD, Dir.
Desc: Coordinates a national program to improve the identification, investigation, diagnosis, prevention, and control of infectious diseases. Principal Center components include: Arctic Investigations Program; Bacterial and Mycotic Diseases Division; Hospital Infections Program; Division of AIDS, STD, DTB Lab Research; Division of Parisitic Diseases; Vector-Borne Infectious Diseases Division; and Division of Viral and Rickettsial Diseases; Division of Quarantine; and Scientific Resources Program. *Type:* Research center.

U.S. Department of Health and Human Services

National Center for Infectious Diseases

Arctic Investigations Program

4055 Tud or Centre Dr.   Ph: (907)729-3400
Anchorage, AK 99508   Fax: (907)729-3429
E-mail: jcb3@cdc.gov
URL: http://www.cdc.gov/ncidod/aip/aip.htm
Contact: Dr. Jay C. Butler, Dir.
Desc: Mission is to prevent infectious diseases and improve the quality of life of people living in the arctic and subarctic through: investigation of the causes of infectious diseases; evaluation of methods for disease prevention and control; dissemination of information; provision of epidemiologic, statistical, and laboratory consultation and technical assistance; and assistance in training of personnel to perform studies of conditions that impact health. Activities focus on studies of conditions that occur at high incidence, are unique to, or may be of potential benefit to populations in (and outside of) the arctic and subarctic. *Type:* Research center.

U.S. Department of Health and Human Services

National Center for Infectious Diseases

Division of Bacterial and Mycotic Diseases

Emerging Bacterial and Mycotic Diseases Branch

1600 Clifton Rd. NE   Ph: (404)639-1280
Bldg. 7, Rm. SSB5   Fax: (404)639-1287
MS G35
Atlanta, GA 30333
E-mail: tms1@cdc.gov

Contact: Dr. Tim Shinnick, Ch.

Desc: Tuberculosis and other mycobacterial diseases, emphasizing etiologic agents of tuberculosis, leprosy, and other mycobacterioses; surveillance of the incidence of these diseases; and diagnostic procedures for rapid identification and drug resistance patterns. Principal research interest are moleuclar biology, rapid diagnostic procedures, subtyping mechanisms, immunology, genetics, drug development, virulence factors, and taxonomy. *Type:* Research center.

U.S. Department of Health and Human Services

National Center for Infectious Diseases

Division of Bacterial and Mycotic Diseases

Emerging Bacterial and Mycotic Diseases Branch

1600 Clifton Rd., NE   Ph: (404)639-3150
Mail Stop C09   Fax: (404)639-3970
Atlanta, GA 30333

Desc: Control of emerging, reemerging, and opportunistic bacterial, mycobacterial, fungal, and actinomycotic diseases; provides reference and diagnostic activities for agents causing these diseases of unknown bacterial, fungal, and actinomycotic isolates associated with human disease; performs studies to determine host-parasite factors related to human diseases caused by emerging, reemerging, and opportunistic bacterial, mycobacterial, fungal, and actinomycotic agents; coordinates and collaborates in national and international studies and surveillance for bacterial, mycobacterial, fungal, and actinomycotic diseases; collaborates with the National Center for Prevention Services on studies of tuberculosis; develops and evaluates methods for the diagnosis of emerging, reemerging, and opportunistic bacterial, mycobacterial, fungal, and actinomycotic diseases; and develops, implements, and evaluates prevention strategies for these diseases. *Type:* Research center.

U.S. Department of Health and Human Services

National Center for Infectious Diseases

Division of Parasitic Diseases

4770 Buford Hwy., MS F22   Ph: (770)488-7750
Atlanta, GA 30341-3724   Fax: (770)488-7794
E-mail: dxc6@cdc.gov

Contact: Dr. Daniel G. Colley, Dir.

Desc: Parasitic diseases to define disease etiology, mode of transmission, and populations at risk; works to develop effective methods for diagnosis, prevention, and control; participates in clinical, field, and laboratory research to develop, evaluate, and improve laboratory methodologies and materials and therapeutic practices used for rapid and accurate diagnosis and treatment of parasitic diseases; and sponsors laboratory studies of selected parasitic infections, with emphasis on animal invitro model systems for parasitic relationships, chemotherapy, and immunology, in order to develop effective methods for diagnosis, prevention, and control. *Type:* Research center.

U.S. Department of Health and Human Services

National Center for Infectious Diseases

Division of Parasitic Diseases

Biology and Diagnostics Branch

4770 Buford Hwy., MS F13   Ph: (404)488-4419
Atlanta, GA 30341-3724   Fax: (404)488-4253
E-mail: mle1@ciddpd2.em.cdc.gov

Contact: Mark Eberhard, Chf.

Desc: Etiology, biology, ecology, populations at risk, host-parasite relationships, chemotherapy, and diagnosis of parasitic diseases; offers advice, assistance, and training on the diagnosis, control, and prevention of parasitic diseases; provides reference/diagnostic services for parasitic diseases. *Type:* Research center.

U.S. Department of Health and Human Services

National Center for Infectious Diseases

Division of Parasitic Diseases

Epidemiology Branch

4770 Buford Hwy., MS F22   Ph: (770)488-7789
Atlanta, GA 30341-3724   Fax: (770)488-7761

Contact: Trent Ruebush, Chf.

Desc: Malaria in the U.S. and among U.S. citizens abroad; monitors the efficacy and safety of antimalarial drugs for chemoprophylaxis and chemotherapy; and provides clinical advice and epidemiologic assistance on the treatment, control, and prevention of malaria in the U.S. and abroad. *Type:* Research center.

U.S. Department of Health and Human Services

National Center for Infectious Diseases

Division of Parasitic Diseases

Epidemiology Branch

4770 Buford Hwy., MS F22   Ph: (404)488-7760
Atlanta, GA 30341-3724   Fax: (404)488-7761

Contact: Dennis Juranek, Chf.

Desc: Surveillance and epidemiologic investigations of parasitic diseases, other than malaria, in the U.S. and abroad. *Type:* Research center.

U.S. Department of Health and Human Services

National Center for Infectious Diseases

Division of Parasitic Diseases

Epidemiology Branch

4770 Buford Hwy., MS F22   Ph: (404)488-7760
Atlanta, GA 30341-3724   Fax: (404)488-7761
E-mail: trn1@cdc.gov

Contact: Thomas Navin, Chf.

Desc: Parasitic diseases in the U.S. and abroad; monitors the efficacy and safety of antiparasitic drugs; provides clinical advice and epidemiologic assistance to state and local health departments, other federal agencies, and national and international health organizations, on the diagnosis, treatment, control, and prevention of parasitic diseases. *Type:* Research center.

U.S. Department of Health and Human Services

National Center for Infectious Diseases

Division of Parasitic Diseases

Immunology Branch

4770 Buford Hwy., MS F13   Ph: (770)488-4056
Atlanta, GA 30341-3724   Fax: (770)488-4109
E-mail: vct1@cdc.gov

Contact: Victor Tsang, Chf.

Desc: Efficacious antigens relevant to detection and immunization for the control and prevention of parasitic diseases; develops, improves, and implements technologies useful in the detection, control, and prevention of parasitic diseases, with an emphasis on field-applicable molecular detection assays. *Type:* Research center.

U.S. Department of Health and Human Services

National Center for Infectious Diseases

Division of Parasitic Diseases

Immunology Branch

4770 Buford Hwy., MS F13   Ph: (770)488-4047
Atlanta, GA 30341-3724   Fax: (770)488-4454

Contact: Lataf Lal, Chf.

Desc: Development of transmission blocking vaccines for human malarias and uses a number of malaria species to: identify antigens; clone the genes expressing these antigens; identify appropriate expression systems for recombinant proteins and affective adjuvants where necessary to enhance immunogenecity, with emphases on the sexual stages of the parasite critical for transmission to humans through the mosquito vector. *Type:* Research center.

U.S. Department of Health and Human Services

National Center for Infectious Diseases

Division of Parasitic Diseases

Immunology Branch

4770 Buford Hwy., MS F13   Ph: (770)488-4056
Atlanta, GA 30341-3724   Fax: (770)488-4109

Contact: Victor Tsang, Chf.

Desc: Immunologic events in parasitic infections; identifies, characterizes, and defines, based on immunologic interactions between host and parasite, possible intervention strategies for the control and prevention of parasitic infections. *Type:* Research center.

U.S. Department of Health and Human Services

National Center for Infectious Diseases

Division of Parasitic Diseases

Immunology Branch

4770 Buford Hwy., MS F13   Ph: (770)488-4054
Atlanta, GA 30341-3724   Fax: (770)488-4108
E-mail: pjl1@cdc.gov

Contact: Patrick Lammie, Chf.

Desc: Immunology of the host-parasite relationship with the aim of developing new strategies for immunologic intervention in parasitic and other infectious diseases; also researches new principles concerning the function and regulation of the immune system. *Type:* Research center.

U.S. Department of Health and Human Services

National Center for Infectious Diseases

Division of Parastici Diseases

Entomology Branch

5770 Buford Hwy., MS F12   Ph: (770)488-4240
Atlanta, GA 30341-3724   Fax: (770)488-4108

Contact: Robert Wirtz, Chf.

Desc: Vector control strategies; sponsors molecular, biochemical, and genetic research to develop new vector-based control strategies; develops and applies microanalytical methods assay of pesticides in the environment and to support biochemical studies of pesticide resistance; and evaluates and applies methods to assay antiparasitic drugs in pharmaceutical products and such drugs and their metabolies in body fluids and tissues of humans and other animals. *Type:* Research center.

U.S. Department of Health and Human Services

National Center for Infectious Diseases

Division of Vector-Borne Infectious Diseases

Arbovirus Diseases Branch

PO Box 2087   Ph: (970)221-6442
Fort Collins, CO 80522-2087   Fax: (970)221-6476

Contact: John T. Roehrig, Dir.

Desc: Epidemiology of mosquito and tick-borne viral diseases. Provides consultation and on-site investigations for local, state, national, and international health agencies during arthropod-borne viral disease outbreaks. *Type:* Research center.

U.S. Department of Health and Human Services

National Center for Infectious Diseases

Division of Vector-Borne Infectious Diseases

Bacterial Zoonosis Branch

PO Box 2087   Ph: (303)221-6450
Fort Collins, CO 80522-2087   Fax: (303)221-6476
Contact: Dr. Kenneth Gage, Chf.

Desc: Diagnosis, therapy, epidemiology, and control of bubonic plague; maintains a surveillance system in collaboration with state and federal health agencies to detect fluctuations of infection in animal populations; and serves as a WHO Reference Center for plague diagnosis and control. *Type:* Research center.

U.S. Department of Health and Human Services

National Center for Infectious Diseases

Division of Vector-Borne Infectious Diseases

Dengue Branch

2 Calle Casia   Ph: (787)766-5181
San Juan, PR 00921-3200   Fax: (787)766-6596
E-mail: ggc1@cdc.gov
Contact: Gary G. Clark, Chf.

Desc: Study of dengue, a viral disease spread by mosquitoes. Research includes investigation of vectors, reservoirs of disease, viruses that cause disease, and methods for surveillance prevention and control. *Type:* Research center.

U.S. Department of Health and Human Services

National Center for Infectious Diseases

Division of Viral and Rickettsial Diseases

1600 Clifton Rd., N.E. (MS   Ph: (404)639-3574
A-30)   Fax: (404)639-3163
Atlanta, GA 30333
URL: http://www.cdc.gov/ncidod/dvrd
Contact: Brian W.J. Mahy, Dir.

Desc: Viral and rickettsial diseases of national and international importance. The Division addresses significant disease problems by the integrated application of modern virologic and epidemiologic methodologies--from molecular biologic methodologies (including nucleic acid and protein biochemistry) to immunologic and pathophysiologic methodologies to epidemiologic and statistical methodologies. *Type:* Research center.

U.S. Department of Health and Human Services

National Center for Infectious Diseases

Division of Viral and Rickettsial Diseases

Hepatitis Branch

1600 Clifton Rd., N.E.   Ph: (404)639-2339
Atlanta, GA 30333   Fax: (404)639-1563
E-mail: HSM1@CDC.GOV
URL: http://www.cdc.gov//ncidod//diseases//hepatitis//hepatitis.htm
Contact: Harold S. Margolis, MD, Chf.

Desc: Hepatitis A, B, C, D, and E. Works to implement hepatitis B and hepatitis A immunization programs nationally and internationally. *Type:* Research center.

U.S. Department of Health and Human Services

National Center for Infectious Diseases

Division of Viral and Rickettsial Diseases

Influenza Branch

1600 Clifton Rd., N.E.   Ph: (404)639-3591
Atlanta, GA 30333   Fax: (404)639-2334
E-mail: NJC1@CIDDVD3.EM.CDC.GOV
Contact: Nancy Cox, Chf.

Desc: Focal point within CDC for studies pertaining to influenza viruses, their variation and occurrence in populations, and their control. *Type:* Research center.

U.S. Department of Health and Human Services

National Center for Infectious Diseases

Division of Viral and Rickettsial Diseases

Respiratory and Enteric Virus Branch

1600 Clifton Rd., N.E.   Ph: (404)639-3596
Atlanta, GA 30333   Fax: (404)639-1307
Contact: Larry Anderson, Chf.

Desc: Respiratory viruses such as adenoviruses and respiratory syncytial virus, polio and other enteroviruses, and viruses causing gastroenteritis. *Type:* Research center.

U.S. Department of Health and Human Services

National Center for Infectious Diseases

Division of Viral and Rickettsial Diseases

Viral Exanthems and Herpesvirus Branch

1600 Clifton Rd., N.E.   Ph: (404)639-3532
Atlanta, GA 30333   Fax: (404)639-3163
Contact: Dr. William Reeves, Chf.

Desc: Herpesviruses, poxviruses, rubella and measles viruses, and papillomaviruses as the cause of exanthematous, congenital, perinatal diseases, and cancer. Branch is responsible for the CDC's Chronic Fatigue Syndrome Research Program. *Type:* Research center.

U.S. Department of Health and Human Services

National Center for Infectious Diseases

Division of Viral and Rickettsial Diseases

Viral and Rickettsial Zoonoses Branch

Epidemiology Section   Ph: (404)639-1075
1600 Clifton Rd., N.E.   Fax: (404)639-4436
Atlanta, GA 30333
E-mail: jgoo@cdc.gov
Contact: Dr. James Olson, Supervisory Research Microbiologist.

Desc: Rickettsial agents (such as those of Rocky Mountain spotted fever and Q fever). *Type:* Research center.

U.S. Department of Health and Human Services

National Center for Infectious Diseases

Hospital Infections Program

1600 Clifton Rd. NE   Ph: (404)639-6400
Mail Stop E-69   Fax: (404)639-6459
Atlanta, GA 30333
E-mail: wrj1c@cdc.gov
URL: http://www.cdc.gov/ncidod/hip/hip.htm
Contact: Dr. William Jarvis, Chf., IPB, HiP, Col.

Desc: Hospital-associated infections. The Program serves as the focal point within the National Center for Infectious Diseases for the issuance of recommendations and guidelines on prevention and control of hospital infections. *Type:* Research center.

U.S. Department of Health and Human Services

National Center for Infectious Diseases

Hospital Infections Program

Hospital Environment Laboratory Branch

1600 Clifton Rd. N.E.   Ph: (404)639-3821
Mail Stop C-16   Fax: (404)639-3822
Atlanta, GA 30333
E-mail: jmm8@cdc.gov
Contact: J. Michael Miller, Chf.

Desc: Environmental microbiology, disinfection and sterilization, AIDS, hospital acquired infection, dialysis associated diseases, and endotoxema and control, biofilms, diagnostic microbiology methods. *Type:* Research center.

U.S. Department of Health and Human Services

National Center for Infectious Diseases

Scientific Resources Program

1600 Clifton Rd., NE   Ph: (404)639-3466
Atlanta, GA 30333   Fax: (404)639-3199
E-mail: bzm9@cdc.gov
URL: http://www.srp.cdc.gov

Contact: Dr. William J. Martin, Dir.

Desc: Procures, manages, and distributes the resources required by CDC investigators for research and service activities; conducts protocol reviews for research and diagnostic activities involving laboratory animals, and produces cell cultures, cell culture media, and microbiologic media, using modern methods and exhaustive quality assurance testing; maintains an active applied research program in cell biology, and conducts research leading to the development of new cell culture systems and cell lines; procures, prepares, and distributes sterile glassware and plasticware, and provides packing, shipping, and receiving services for etiologic agents, diagnostic specimens, and reagents from the CDC catalog; and provides services for maintaining and developing laboratory equipment; provides to the NCID research environments the instrumentation and expertise required to develop, refine, and apply modern technologies pertinent to the prevention and control of infectious, autoimmune, neoplastic, and hemotolgic diseases. *Type:* Research center.

U.S. Department of Health and Human Services

National Center for Injury Prevention and Control

4770 Buford Hwy. NE, MS   Ph: (404)488-1475
KO2   Fax: (404)488-1670
Atlanta, GA 30341-3724
E-mail: mlr3@cipcod1.em.cdc.gov
URL: http://www.cdc.gov.ncipc.ncipchm.htm

Contact: Mark L. Rosenberg, MD, MPP, Dir.

Desc: Specific injury control research designed to: yield results directly applicable to identifying interventions to prevent injury occurrence or minimize disability; apply and evaluate the effect of known interventions on injury morbidity, mortality, disability, and costs; or elucidate the etiology and mechanisms of injuries. *Type:* Research center.

U.S. Department of Health and Human Services

National Center for Prevention Services

1600 Clifton Rd., N.E.   Ph: (404)639-4499
Atlanta, GA 30333   Fax: (404)639-2196

Contact: Alan R. Hinman, Sr. Advisor.

Desc: Assists states in the prevention and control of HIV infection, sexually transmitted diseases, tuberculosis, and dental diseases. Also protects the nation from the introduction of diseases from other countries. *Type:* Research center.

U.S. Department of Health and Human Services

National Center for Prevention Services

Division of Tuberculosis Elimination

Surveillance and Epidemiologic Investigations Branch

1600 Clifton Rd., N.E.   Ph: (404)639-8116
Atlanta, GA 30333   Fax: (404)639-8604

Contact: Ida Onorato, MD, Chf.

Desc: Epidemiology of tuberculosis, HIV virus, and drug-resistant tuberculosis. *Type:* Research center.

U.S. Department of Health and Human Services

National Center for Prevention Services

Sexually Transmitted Disease / HIV Prevention Division

Behavioral and Prevention Research Branch

Mail Stop E-44   Ph: (404)639-0829
1600 Clifton Rd., N.E.   Fax: (404)639-0868
Atlanta, GA 30333
E-mail: ROC4@CPSSTD3.EM.CDC.GOV

Contact: Ronald Fichtner, Actg.Chf.

Desc: Individual and group behavior patterns as they affect STD and HIV occurrence and transmission. Undertakes studies to evaluate new methods of prevention and intervention of HIV and STDs, and conducts surveys, studies, and methodological research on the prevalence of sexual and drug-using behavior with increased risks of STDs and HIV. *Type:* Research center.

U.S. Department of Health and Human Services

National Center for Research Resource

Clinical Research Area

One Rockledge Centre, Ste.   Ph: (301)435-0790
  6030   Fax: (301)480-3661
6705 Rockledge Dr.
MSC 7965
Bethesda, MD 20892-7965
E-mail: ospio@ep.ncrr.nih.gov

Desc: Etiology, progression, prevention, control, and cure of human disease. *Type:* Research center.

U.S. Department of Health and Human Services

National Center for Research Resources

General Clinical Research Centers Program

NIH One Rockledge Centre   Ph: (301)435-0790
  Rm. 6030   Fax: (301)480-3661
6705 Rockledge Dr. MSC 7965
Bethesda, MD 20892-7965
E-mail: ineseb@ep.ncrr.nih.gov

Contact: Dr. Inese Beitins, Dir.

Desc: Supports centers that serve as clinical research sites for the investigation of the pathological factors causing disease and for development and testing of innovative diagnostic and treatment techniques aimed at minimizing disease and its debilitating and painful effects. Each general clinical research center is a self-contained unit and can accommodate both outpatients and inpatients. *Type:* Research center.

U.S. Department of Health and Human Services

National Heart, Lung, and Blood Institute

Division of Intramural Research

Pulmonary-Critical Care Medicine Branch

NIH Bldg. 10, Rm. 6D03   Ph: (301)496-1597
10 Center Dr. MSC-1590   Fax: (301)496-2363
Bethesda, MD 20892-1590

Contact: Joel Moss, Chf.

Desc: Structure and function of the lung in health and disease through cellular and biochemical methods. Both laboratory and clinical investigations are conducted and techniques of protein chemistry, molecular biology, tissue culture, and immunology are used. *Type:* Research center.

U.S. Department of Health and Human Services

National Heart, Lung, and Blood Institute

Division of Lung Diseases

Two Rockledge Ctr., Ste. 10018   Ph: (301)435-0233
6701 Rockledge Dr. MSC 7952   Fax: (301)480-3547
Bethesda, MD 20892-7952
E-mail: hurds@gwgate.nhlbi.nih.gov
URL: http://www.nhlbi.nih.gov/nhlbi/nhlbi.htm

Contact: Dr. Suzanne S. Hurd, Dir.

Desc: Focal point for planning and coordinating research and research training programs for all diseases of the respiratory system, including chronic obstructive pulmonary diseases; pediatric pulmonary diseases; occupational and immunologic lung diseases; pulmonary vascular diseases; acute lung injury; asthma; critical care; cystic fibrosis; lung cell biology; respiratory neurobiology and sleep; and pulmonary complications of AIDS. *Type:* Research center.

U.S. Department of Health and Human Services

National Heart, Lung, and Blood Institute

Division of Lung Diseases

Airways Diseases Branch

Westwood Bldg., Rm. 6A15   Ph: (301)594-7443
5333 Westbard Ave.   Fax: (301)594-7487
Bethesda, MD 20892

Contact: Dr. James Kiley, Chf.

Desc: Cause and prevention of airways diseases, with particular interest in the delay or reversal of the progression of airways diseases through greater knowledge of their pathogenesis; and the amelioration of their effects through improved early diagnosis and more effective management. Principal areas of research interest include: chronic obstructive lung diseases, asthma, cystic fibrosis, respiratory neurobiology, and sleep. *Type:* Research center.

U.S. Department of Health and Human Services

National Heart, Lung, and Blood Institute

Division of Lung Diseases

Cell and Developmental Biology Branch

2 Rockledge Center, Ste. 10122   Ph: (301)435-0222
6701 Rockledge Dr., MSC 7952   Fax: (301)480-3557
Bethesda, MD 20892-7952
URL: http://www.nhlbi.nih.gov

Contact: Dr. Dorothy Gail, Dir.

Desc: Pediatric pulmonary diseases, lung cell biology, acute lung injury, interstitial lung disease, pulmonary immunology, AIDS-related lung disease, and tuberculosis. *Type:* Research center.

U.S. Department of Health and Human Services

National Heart, Lung, and Blood Institute

Division of Lung Diseases

Prevention, Education, and Research Training Branch

6701 Rockledge Dr., Ste.   Ph: (301)435-0222
  10018, MSC 7952   Fax: (301)435-3557
Bethesda, MD 20892

Contact: Mary S. Reilly, M.S., Contact.

Desc: Programs in research training development; and programs in prevention, control, and education in lung diseases. *Type:* Research center.

U.S. Department of Health and Human Services

National Institute of Allergy and Infectious Diseases

Division of Microbiology and Infectious Diseases

Sexually Transmitted Diseases Branch

Solar Bldg., Rm. 3A24   Ph: (301)402-0443
Bethesda, MD 20892   Fax: (301)402-1456
E-mail: ph22k@nih.gov

Contact: Dr. Penelope Hitchcock, Chf.

Desc: Sexually transmitted research encompasses basic biomedical, epidemiologic, clinical, and behavioral approaches. *Type:* Research center.

U.S. Department of Health and Human Services

National Institute of Allergy and Infectious Diseases

Division of Mirobiology and Infectious Diseases

Virology Branch

Solar Bldg.   Ph: (301)496-7453
6003 Executive Blvd., Rm.   Fax: (301)402-6059
  3A16
Rockville, MD 20852
E-mail: CL28R@NIH.GOV

Contact: Dr. Catherine Laughlin, Chf.

Desc: Supports grant and contract research on viral infections other than HIV and on prevention and treatment of these infections. *Type:* Research center.

U.S. Department of Health and Human Services

National Institute of Allergy and Infectious Diseases

Laboratory of Infectious Diseases

NIH Bldg. 7, Rm. 100 MSC   Ph: (301)496-2024
  0720   Fax: (301)496-8312
9000 Rockville Pike
Bethesda, MD 20892

Contact: Robert M. Chanock, MD, Chf.

Desc: Defines the cause and epidemiology of medically important viral diseases and develops means for their control. Activities range from identification and antigenic characterization of viruses that cause acute disease of the respiratory and gastrointestinal tracts and liver to basic molecular studies of viral structure, function, and genome organization. *Type:* Research center.

U.S. Department of Health and Human Services

National Institute of Allergy and Infectious Diseases

Laboratory of Microbial Structure and Function

Rocky Mountain Laboratories   Ph: (406)363-3211
903 S. 4th St.   Fax: (406)363-9204
Hamilton, MT 59840

Contact: Tom Schwan, Actg. Chf.

Desc: Structural and functional elements of pathogenic bacterial surface components involved in pathogenesis and/or virulence of selected organisms or in genesis of host immunological responses to infections by these agents. Studies involve itNeissera gonorrhoeae/it, itBorellia burgdorferi/it, and others; both protein and nonprotein components of these gram-negative organism outer membrane are prime study candidates as mediators of interactions between bacterium and host and as likely vaccine components. *Type:* Research center.

U.S. Department of Health and Human Services

National Institute of Allergy and Infectious Diseases

Laboratory of Molecular Microbiology

NIH Bldg. 4, Rm. 315   Ph: (301)496-4012
4 Center Dr., MSC 0460   Fax: (301)402-0226
Bethesda, MD 20892-0460

Contact: Dr. Malcolm A. Martin, Chf.

Desc: Microorganisms and their capacity to produce disease in vertebrate hosts. Of prime importance in this effort is the biochemical characterization of viral genomes and the detailed analyses of gene products regulating expression or giving rise to mature structural proteins. *Type:* Research center.

U.S. Department of Health and Human Services

National Institute of Allergy and Infectious Diseases

Laboratory of Parasitic Diseases

NIH Bldg. 4, Rm. 126   Ph: (301)402-1274
9000 Rockville Pike   Fax: (301)402-2201
Bethesda, MD 20892

Contact: Dr. Louis Miller, MD, Chf.

Desc: Parasitic diseases of humans. A variety of protozoan (malaria, trypanosomes, giardia, leishmania) and helminth (schistosomes, filaria, and strongyloides) parasites are used for experimental work. *Type:* Research center.

U.S. Department of Health and Human Services

National Institute of Allergy and Infectious Diseases

Laboratory of Persistent Viral Diseases

Rocky Mountain Laboratories   Ph: (406)363-9354
903 S. 4th St.   Fax: (406)363-9286
Hamilton, MT 59840
E-mail: bchesebro@nih.gov

Contact: Bruce Chesebro, MD, Chf.

Desc: Virus-host interaction, with the primary aim of elucidating mechanisms involved in establishment, maintenance, and elimination of persistent viral infections. Particular emphasis is placed on persistent viral infections involving cells of the hemopoietic and lymphoid systems and the central nervous system. *Type:* Research center.

U.S. Department of Health and Human Services

National Institute of Allergy and Infectious Diseases

Laboratory of Viral Diseases

NIH Bldg. 4, Rm. 229A   Ph: (301)496-9869
4 Center Dr., MSC0445   Fax: (301)480-1147
Bethesda, MD 20892-0445
E-mail: bmoss@nih.gov

Contact: Dr. Bernard Moss, Chf.

Desc: Genetic organization, expression, replication, assembly, and pathogenicity of viruses. Live recombinant viruses are genetically engineered for use as immunological tools and as vaccines against a variety of infectious agents. *Type:* Research center.

U.S. Department of Health and Human Services

National Institute of Allergy and Infectious Diseases

Microscopy Branch

Rocky Mountain Laboratories   Ph: (406)363-9228
903 S. 4th St.   Fax: (406)363-9371
Hamilton, MT 59840
E-mail: claude_garon@nih.gov

Contact: Dr. Claude F. Garon, Chf.

Desc: Basic biology, biochemistry, immunology, electron microscopy, laser confocal microscopy, and molecular biology concentrating on molecular cloning and pathogenesis. Study emphasis also includes characterizing features of the host-pathogen interaction and identifying and exploiting specific microbial bioproducts for improved diagnostics and/or vaccines. *Type:* Research center.

U.S. Department of Health and Human Services

National Institute of Arthritis and Musculoskeletal and Skin Diseases

NIH Bldg. 31, Rm. 4C32   Ph: (301)496-4353
31 Center Dr., MSC 2350   Fax: (301)480-6069
Bethesda, MD 20892
URL: http://www.nih.gov/niams

Contact: Dr. Stephen I. Katz, PhD, Dir.

Desc: Large number of diverse diseases, including rheumatoid arthritis, osteoarthritis, systemic lupus erythematosus,

muscle diseases, osteoporosis, Paget's disease, back disorders, osteogenesis imperfecta, psoriasis, acne, ichthyosis, epidermolysis bullosa, and vitiligo. The Institute's Intramural Research Program conducts basic research studies in immunology, biophysics, biochemistry, molecular biology, structural biology, pathology and histochemistry, and pharmacology. *Type:* Research center.

U.S. Department of Health and Human Services

National Institute of Arthritis and Musculoskeletal and Skin Diseases

Extramural Activities Program

Bone Biology and Bone Diseases Branch

Natcher Bldg. Rm 5AS-43E   Ph: (301)594-5055
45 Center Dr.   Fax: (301)480-4543
Bethesda, MD 20892
E-mail: mcgowanj@ep.niams.nih.gov

Contact: Joan A. McGowan, Dir.

Desc: Manages a portfolio of extramural grant awards in the areas of basic bone biology including: mineralization; bone cell physiology; genetics; and the epidemiology and clinical applications of bone diseases. *Type:* Research center.

U.S. Department of Health and Human Services

National Institute of Arthritis and Musculoskeletal and Skin Diseases

Extramural Activities Program

Centers Program

45 Center Dr., MSC 6500   Ph: (301)594-5052
Bethesda, MD 20892   Fax: (301)480-4543
E-mail: freemanb@exchange.nih.gov
URL: http://www.nih.gov/niams/grants/ep7.htm

Contact: Julia B. Freeman, PhD, Dir.

Desc: Sponsors Multipurpose Arthritis and Musculoskeletal Diseases centers across the U.S. Activities at these centers include basic and clinical research in the causes of arthritis; developmental and feasibility studies; education research; epidemiologic research and health services research. *Type:* Research center.

U.S. Department of Health and Human Services

National Institute of Arthritis and Musculoskeletal and Skin Diseases

Extramural Activities Program

Muscle Biology Program

Natcher Bldg., Rm 5A5-49E   Ph: (301)594-5128
45 Center Dr., MSC 6500   Fax: (301)480-4543
Bethesda, MD 20892-6500
URL: http://www.nih.gov/niams/grants/ep4.htm

Contact: Richard W. Lymn, PhD, Dir.

Desc: Skeletal muscle development and function in normal disease conditions, including studies on the structure and function of muscle, development and regeneration of muscle, normal and abnormal muscle metabolism, and selected diseases and disorders of skeletal muscle. *Type:* Research center.

U.S. Department of Health and Human Services

National Institute of Arthritis and Musculoskeletal and Skin Diseases

Extramural Activities Program

Musculoskeletal Diseases Branch

MPN1 Rm. 161   Ph: (301)594-4977
7520 Standish Pl., HFD-095   Fax: (301)594-1122
Rockville, MD 20855

Contact: Stephen L. Gordon, PhD, Dir.

Desc: Understanding of the structure, function, formation, metabolism, and biomechanics of bones, joints, and skeletal support structures. Research activity focuses on: osteoporosis and other metabolic diseases; joint replacement methods and materials; developmental disorders, including scoliosis, bone immunology, and transplantation; inherited connective tissue disorders; back disorders; and exercise pathophysiology. *Type:* Research center.

U.S. Department of Health and Human Services

National Institute of Arthritis and Musculoskeletal and Skin Diseases

Intramural Research Program

Arthritis and Rheumatism Branch

NIH Bldg. 10, Rm. 9N228   Ph: (301)496-2612
9000 Rockville Pike   Fax: (301)402-0012
Bethesda, MD 20892
E-mail: pplotz@box-p.nih.gov
URL: http://www.nih.gov/niams/about/irp/arbiutro.htm

Contact: Dr. Paul Plotz, Chf.

Desc: Arthritis, connective tissue diseases, and related areas, including immunology. Activities involve: disease-related studies on the etiology, pathology, and therapy of connective tissue disorders, with special emphasis on systemic lupus erythematosus, polymyositis, and rheumatoid arthritis (both human disease and animal models of these diseases are studied); and fundamental studies on immune regulation, with special emphasis on autoimmunity and mechanisms of immune responses at the cellular and molecular level. *Type:* Research center.

U.S. Department of Health and Human Services

National Institute of Arthritis and Musculoskeletal and Skin Diseases

Intramural Research Program

Laboratory of Physical Biology

NIH Bldg. 6, Rm. 114   Ph: (301)496-5880
6 Center Dr., MSC 2755   Fax: (301)402-0009
Bethesda, MD 20892-2755
E-mail: lcyu@helix.nih.gov

Contact: Leepo C. Yu, PhD, Dir.

Desc: Mechanism of muscle contraction in intact cells and simplified preparations using time-resolved X-ray diffraction in conjunction with mechanochemical techniques. Electron microscopy is used with a wide variety of preparations, and digital image processing techniques are used to enhance resolution. *Type:* Research center.

U.S. Department of Health and Human Services

National Institute of Diabetes and Digestive and Kidney Diseases

NIH Bldg. 31   Ph: (301)496-5877
31 Center Dr. MSC 2560   Fax: (301)402-2125
Bethesda, MD 20892-2560
E-mail: kranzfeldk@hq.niddk.nih.gov
URL: http://www.niddk.nih.gov

Contact: Phillip Gorden, Dir.

Desc: Serious diseases affecting public health. The Institute supports clinical research on the diseases of internal medicine and related subspecialty fields as well as in many basic science disciplines. *Type:* Research center.

U.S. Department of Health and Human Services

National Institute of Diabetes and Digestive and Kidney Diseases

Clinical Nutrition Research Units Program

45 Center Dr.   Ph: (301)594-8883
MSC 6600   Fax: (301)480-8300
Bethesda, MD 20892-6600

Contact: Dr. Van S. Hubbard, Prog.Dir.

Desc: Integrated array of research, educational, and service activities focused on human nutrition in health and disease. Each unit serves as the focal point for an interdisciplinary approach to clinical nutrition research and for the stimulation of research in areas such as improved nutritional support of acutely and chronically ill persons, assessment of nutritional status, effects of disease states on nutrient needs, and effects of changes in nutritional status on disease. *Type:* Research center.

U.S. Department of Health and Human Services
National Institute of Diabetes and Digestive
and Kidney Diseases
Division of Diabetes, Endocrinology, and
Metabolic Diseases

NIH Bldg. 31, Rm. 9A16   Ph: (301)496-7348
31 Center Dr. MSC 2560   Fax: (301)480-6792
Bethesda, MD 20892-2560
E-mail: eastmand@extra.niddk.nih.gov
Contact: Richard C. Eastman, MD, Dir.

Desc: Diabetes mellitus (both insulin dependent and non-insulin dependent diabetes); endocrinological diseases and disorders; and metabolic diseases, including research on the etiology, pathogenesis, and treatment of acquired or inborn errors of metabolism and cystic fibrosis. Support for basic and clinical biomedical research as well as epidemiologic and behavioral studies and clinical trials is provided through investigator-initiated research grants, new investigator awards, program project and center grants, and cooperative agreements. *Type:* Research center.

U.S. Department of Health and Human Services
National Institute of Diabetes and Digestive
and Kidney Diseases
Division of Diabetes, Endocrinology, and
Metabolic Diseases
Cystic Fibrosis Research Program

Natcher Bldg   Ph: (301)594-7567
45 Center Dr. MSC 6600   Fax: (301)480-3503
Bethesda, MD 20892
E-mail: McKeonC@ep.niddk.nih.gov
URL: http://niddk.nih.gov
Contact: Dr. Catherine McKeon, Dir.

Desc: Supports investigator-initiated research projects related to the etiology, pathogenesis, diagnosis, and treatment of cystic fibrosis (CF). In addition, the Program supports a cystic fibrosis research centers and small Business Innovation Research Grants. *Type:* Research center.

U.S. Department of Health and Human Services
National Institute of Diabetes and Digestive
and Kidney Diseases
Division of Diabetes, Endocrinology, and
Metabolic Diseases
Diabetes Center Program

45 Center Dr. MSC 6600   Ph: (301)594-8803
Bethesda, MD 20892-6600   Fax: (301)480-3503
E-mail: GARFIELDS@EP.NLOOK.NIH.GOV
Contact: Dr. Sanford A. Garfield, Prog.Dir.

Desc: Administers two types of center awards: the Diabetes-Endocrinology Research Centers (DERC) and the Diabetes Research and Training Centers (DRTC). The DERC is exclusively oriented toward biomedical research goals, while the DRTCs include training and translation components in addition to biomedical research. *Type:* Research center.

U.S. Department of Health and Human Services
National Institute of Diabetes and Digestive
and Kidney Diseases
Division of Diabetes, Endocrinology, and
Metabolic Diseases
Diabetes Clinical Trials Program

31 Center Dr. MSC 2560   Ph: (301)594-8803
Bethesda, MD 20892-2560   Fax: (301)480-3503
E-mail: garfields@extra.niddk.nih.gov
Contact: Sanford Garfield, PhD, Proj.Coord.

Desc: Supports a multicenter randomized clinical trial to determine whether interventions in high risk individuals can prevent the onset of type-2 diabetes. Participating in this study are 25 medical centers, a data coordinating center, and other supporting institutions that provide centralized technical and biochemical services. *Type:* Research center.

U.S. Department of Health and Human Services
National Institute of Diabetes and Digestive
and Kidney Diseases
Division of Diabetes, Endocrinology, and
Metabolic Diseases
Diabetes Program Branch

45 Center Dr. MSC 6600   Ph: (301)594-8814
Bethesda, MD 20892-2560   Fax: (301)480-3503
E-mail: fradkinj@ep.niddk.nih.gov
Contact: Dr. Judith Fradkin, Actg.Chf.

Desc: Major aims are to define the disease fully in terms of its causes and many complications and to find improved methods for the diagnosis, treatment, cure, and prevention of both the disease and its chronic complications. The Program provides support for basic and clinical studies related to the etiology, pathogenesis, prevention, diagnosis, treatment, and cure of diabetes mellitus, as well as for investigations related to pancreas and islet transplantation, automated insulin delivery systems, and glucose sensors. *Type:* Research center.

U.S. Department of Health and Human Services
National Institute of Diabetes and Digestive
and Kidney Diseases
Division of Diabetes, Endocrinology, and
Metabolic Diseases
Diabetes Research Section

45 Center Dr. MSC 6600   Ph: (301)594-8808
Bethesda, MD 20892-2560   Fax: (301)480-3503
Contact: Dr. Joan Harmon, Dir.

Desc: Provides grant support for investigator-initiated studies covering a wide range of fundamental and clinical studies related to the etiology, pathogenesis, prevention, diagnosis, treatment, and cure of diabetes mellitus and its complications. Specific areas of research interest encompass the structure/function of the pancreatic hormones and related peptides and enzymes; carbohydrate, lipid, and protein metabolism; and nutritional interrelationships, including obesity. *Type:* Research center.

U.S. Department of Health and Human Services
National Institute of Diabetes and Digestive
Kidney Diseases
Division of Diabetes, Endocrinology, and
Metabolic Diseases
Endocrinology and Metabolic Diseases
Research Programs Branch

45 Center Dr. MSC 6600   Ph: (301)594-7567
Bethesda, MD 20892-2560   Fax: (301)480-3503
E-mail: fradkinj@ep.niddk.nih.gov
Contact: Dr. Judith Fradkin, Chf.

Desc: Componets are Cystic Fibrosis Research Program, Endocrinology Research Programs Section, Bone and Mineral Research Program, Metabolism and Structural Biology Research Program, Metabolic Diseases and Gene Therapy Research Program, Pituitary and Neuroendocrinology Research Program, and Growth Factors Research Program. *Type:* Research center.

U.S. Department of Health and Human Services
National Institute of Diabetes and Digestive
and Kidney Diseases
Division of Diabetes, Endocrinology, and
Metabolic Diseases
Endocrinology Research Section

45 Center Dr. MSC 6600   Ph: (301)594-8819
Bethesda, MD 20892-6600   Fax: (301)480-3503
Contact: Dr. Ronald N. Margolis, Chf.

Desc: Supports (through research grants) investigator-initiated basic and clinical studies of normal and abnormal function of the pituitary, thyroid, parathyroid, adrenal, pineal, and thymus glands. Studies of the mode of action of hormones, their biosynthesis, secretion, and metabolism as well as their binding to protein carriers, subsequent release, and the kinetics of binding represent a major component of the Program. *Type:* Research center.

U.S. Department of Health and Human Services
National Institute of Diabetes and Digestive
and Kidney Diseases
Division of Diabetes, Endocrinology, and
Metabolic Diseases
Metabolic Diseases and Gene Therapy
Research Program

45 Center Dr. MSC 6600   Ph: (301)594-8810
Bethesda, MD 20892-2560   Fax: (301)480-3503
E-mail: fradkinj@ep.niddk.nih.gov
Contact: Catherine McKeon, PhD, Dir.

Desc: The primary objective is to support investigator-initiated basic studies on fundamental metabolic processes of diseases within NIDDK. A major goal is support of basic and clinical metabolic studies on a significant number of inherited metabolic disorders. *Type:* Research center.

U.S. Department of Health and Human Services
National Institute of Diabetes and Digestive
and Kidney Diseases
Division of Diabetes, Endocrinology, and
Metabolic Diseases
National Diabetes Data Group

45 Center Dr. MSC 6600   Ph: (301)594-8801
Bethesda, MD 20892-6600   Fax: (301)480-3503
Contact: Dr. Maureen I. Harris, Dir.

Desc: Serves as the major federal focus for the collection, analysis, and dissemination of data on diabetes and its complications. Drawing upon the expertise of the research, medical, and lay communities, the Data Group initiates efforts to: define the data needed to address the scientific and public health issues in diabetes; foster and coordinate the collection of these data from multiple sources; promote the timely availability of reliable data to pertinent scientific, medical, and public organizations; modify data reporting systems to identify and categorize more appropriately the medical and socio-economic impact of diabetes; and promote the standardization of data collection and terminology in clinical and epidemiologic research. *Type:* Research center.

U.S. Department of Health and Human Services
National Institute of Diabetes and Digestive
and Kidney Diseases
Division of Diabetes, Endocrinology, and
Metabolic Diseases
Special Program Branch

5333 Westbard Ave., Rm. 620   Ph: (301)594-7590
Bethesda, MD 20892

Desc: Responsible for all of the Division-related research career development and training awards. These include individual and institutional National Research Service Awards (NRSA), Physician Scientist Awards (PSA), Clinical Investigator Awards (CIA), and Research Career Development Awards (RCDA). *Type:* Research center.

U.S. Department of Health and Human Services
National Institute of Diabetes and Digestive
and Kidney Diseases
Division of Diabetes, Endocrinology, and
Metaolic Diseases
Research Career Development Program

45 Center Dr. MSC 6600   Ph: (301)594-8819
Bethesda, MD 20892-6600   Fax: (301)480-3503
Contact: Dr. Ron Margolis, Dir.

Desc: Administers a variety of research training and career development awards that span the full range of research programs falling within the Division. Prospective applicants are encouraged to contact the Research Career Development Program office regarding any questions about eligibility or provisions of the awards and to obtain current instructions for preparing applications. *Type:* Research center.

U.S. Department of Health and Human Services
National Institute of Diabetes and Digestive
and Kidney Diseases
Division of Digestive Diseases and Nutrition
NIH Bldg. 31, Rm. 9A23   Ph: (301)496-1333
9000 Rockville Pike   Fax: (301)496-2830
Bethesda, MD 20892
E-mail: hoofnaglej@hq.niddk.nih.gov
Contact: Jay H. Hoofnagle, Dir.
Desc: Fundamental and clinical studies of the normal functions of the digestive tract (esophagus, stomach, intestines)
and changes associated with diseases of the liver, gallbladder, biliary tract, and exocrine pancreas; and basic nutrition, nutritional requirements, trace minerals, dietary
fiber, obesity, and clinical nutrition. Principal Division
components include the Digestive Diseases Branch, Nutritional Sciences Branch, and Special Programs Branch.
Type: Research center.

U.S. Department of Health and Human Services
National Institute of Diabetes and Digestive
and Kidney Diseases
Division of Digestive Diseases and Nutrition
Digestive Diseases Programs Branch
Natcher Bldg 45 Rm. 6AN12B   Ph: (301)594-8877
45 Center Dr. MSC 6600   Fax: (301)480-8300
Bethesda, MD 20892-6600
Contact: Dr. Frank A. Hamilton, Prog.Dir.
Desc: Basic and clinical studies on normal and abnormal
function of the enteric nervous system and the central nervous system elements that control the enteric nervous system. Neuroendocrine studies supported include:
histochemistry and neurochemistry, electrical properties of
enteric ganglion cells, chemical neurotransmission, neural
control of effector function, and extrinsic nervous input.
Type: Research center.

U.S. Department of Health and Human Services
National Institute of Diabetes and Digestive
and Kidney Diseases
Division of Digestive Diseases and Nutrition
Digestive Diseases Programs Branch
Rm. 6AN-12A, Bldg. 45   Ph: (301)594-8871
Bethesda, MD 20892   Fax: (301)480-8300
E-mail: tk13v@nih.gov
Contact: Thomas F. Kresina, PhD, Dir.
Desc: Normal function and the diseases of the liver and biliary tract. Areas of basic research include studies on: factors initiating and maintaining hepatic regeneration;
factors leading to liver cell injury, fibrosis, and death; basic
and applied studies on liver transplantation, including
techniques of preservation and storage; metabolism of bile
acids and bilirubin; physiology of bile formation; factors
controlling cholesterol levels in bile; and gallbladder and
bile duct function. *Type:* Research center.

U.S. Department of Health and Human Services
National Institute of Diabetes and Digestive
and Kidney Diseases
Division of Digestive Diseases and Nutrition
Digestive Diseases Programs Branch
5333 Westbard Ave., Rm.   Ph: (301)594-8879
  3A16A   Fax: (301)594-7504
Bethesda, MD 20892
Contact: Dr. Frank A. Hamilton, Prog.Dir.
Desc: Structure of gastrointestinal muscle, the biochemistry of contractile processes and mechanochemical energy
conversion relations between metabolism and contractility
in smooth muscle, extrinsic control of digestive tract motility, and the fluid mechanics of gastrointestinal flow.
Other studies and areas of interest include the actions of
drugs on gastrointestinal motility, intestinal obstruction,
and diseases such as irritable bowel syndrome (functional
digestive disorders), colonic diverticular disease, swallowing disorders, and gastroesophageal reflux. *Type:* Research
center.

U.S. Department of Health and Human Services
National Institute of Diabetes and Digestive
and Kidney Diseases
Division of Digestive Diseases and Nutrition
Digestive Diseases Programs Branch
Natcher Bldg. 4S Rm. 6/AN12B   Ph: (301)594-8877
45 Center Dr. MSC-6600   Fax: (301)480-8300
Bethesda, MD 20892-6600

Contact: Dr. Frank A. Hamilton, Prog.Dir.

Desc: Intestinal immunity and inflammation. Areas of interest include: ontogeny and differentiation of gut-
associated lymphoid tissue; migratory pathways of intestinal lymphoid cells; humoral antibody responses; cell-
mediated cytotoxic reactions and the role of cytotoxic
effector cells in chronic intestinal inflammation; genetic
control of the immune response at mucosal surfaces; immune response to enteric antigens in both intestinal and
extraintestinal sites; granulomatous inflammation; lymphokines and cellular immune regulation; leukotrienes/
prostaglandin effects on intestinal immune responses; T-
cell mediated intestinal tissue injury; the intestinal mast
cell and its role in intestinal inflammation; approaches to
optimal mucosal immunoprophylaxis, including viral,
bacterial, and parasitic diseases; and diseases such as gluten
sensitive, enteropathy, inflammatory bowel disease, and
gastritis. *Type:* Research center.

U.S. Department of Health and Human Services
National Institute of Diabetes and Digestive
and Kidney Diseases
Division of Digestive Diseases and Nutrition
Digestive Diseases Programs Branch
5333 Westbard Ave.   Ph: (301)594-8877
Bethesda, MD 20892   Fax: (301)594-7504

Contact: Dr. Frank Hamilton, Prog.Dir.

Desc: Diabetes, digestive, and kidney dieseases. *Type:* Research center.

U.S. Department of Health and Human Services
National Institute of Diabetes and Digestive
and Kidney Diseases
Division of Digestive Diseases and Nutrition
Epidemiology and Clinical Trails Branch
31 Center Dr., Ste. 9A23   Ph: (301)496-1333
Bethesda, MD 20892

Contact: Dr. Jay Hoofnagle, Dir.

Desc: Comprises the: Epidemiology and Digestive Diseases
Database System, Small Business Innovation Research
Program, and Training Career Development Program.
The Epidemiology and Digestive Diseases Data Base System serves as the major federal focus for the collection,
analysis, and dissemination of data on digestive diseases
and their complications. *Type:* Research center.

U.S. Department of Health and Human Services
National Institute of Diabetes and Digestive
and Kidney Diseases
Division of Digestive Diseases and Nutrition
Epidemiology and Clinical Trials Branch
NIH   Ph: (301)594-8879
Bldg. 45, Rm. 6AN-12K   Fax: (301)480-8300
Bethesda, MD 20892

Contact: Ms. Tommie Tralka, Dir.

Desc: Administers multi- and single center clinical trials in
digestive and nutritional diseases and disorders. *Type:* Research center.

U.S. Department of Health and Human Services
National Institute of Diabetes and Digestive
and Kidney Diseases
Division of Digestive Diseases and Nutrition
Nutritional Sciences Branch
Natcher Bldg. Rm. 6AN-18U   Ph: (301)496-7823
45 Center Dr. MSC 6600   Fax: (301)480-8300
Bethesda, MD 20892
Contact: Dr. Ken May, Prog.Dir.
Desc: Basic and clinical studies related to the requirement,
bioavailability, and metabolism of nutrients and other dietary components at the organ, cellular, and subcellular levels in normal and diseased states. Specific areas of research
interest include: the physiological function and mechanism of action/interaction of nutrients within the body;
the effects of environment, heredity, stress, drug use, toxicants, and physical activity on problems of nutrient imbalance and nutrient requirements in health and disease; and
specific metabolic considerations relating to alternative
forms of nutrient delivery and use, such as total parenteral
nutrition. *Type:* Research center.

U.S. Department of Health and Human Services
National Institute of Diabetes and Digestive
and Kidney Diseases
Division of Digestive Diseases and Nutrition
Obesity and Eating Disorders Program
Bldg. 45, Rm. 6AN-18   Ph: (301)594-8880
Bethesda, MD 20892-6699   Fax: (301)480-8300
Contact: Dr. Susan Yanovski, Dir.
Desc: Biomedical and behavioral aspects of obesity, an-
orexia nervosa, bulimia, and other eating disorders. Goals
are to establish a clear understanding of the etiology, pre-
vention, and treatment of these multifaceted conditions.
Type: Research center.

U.S. Department of Health and Human Services
National Institute of Diabetes and Digestive
and Kidney Diseases
Division of Digestive Diseases and Nutrition
Pancreas Program
Room 6AN-12A, Bldg. 45   Ph: (301)594-8871
45 Centre Dr., MSC 6600   Fax: (301)480-8300
Bethesda, MD 20892
E-mail: tk13v@nih.gov
URL: http://www.nih.gov
Contact: Thomas F. Kresina, PhD, Dir.
Desc: Structure, function, and diseases (excluding cancer
and cystic fibrosis) of the exocrine pancreas. Areas of research interest include: hormonal and neural regulation of
electrolyte, fluid, and enzyme secretion; receptors for se-
cretagogs; stimulus-secretion coupling mechanisms; gut-
islet-acinar interrelations; organization and expression of
pancreatic genes; protein synthesis and export; tissue injury, repair, and regeneration; physiology and pathology of
trophic responses; neural innervention; transcapillary solute and fluid exchange; pancreatic tissue culture and storage, and preservation; imaging of the pancreas; pancreatic
insufficiency; and acute and chronic pancreatitis and relevant experimental models. *Type:* Research center.

U.S. Department of Health and Human Services
National Institute of Diabetes and Digestive
and Kidney Diseases
Division of Intramural Research
NIH Bldg. 10, Rm. 9M222   Ph: (301)496-4128
9000 Rockville Pike   Fax: (301)496-9943
Bethesda, MD 20892-1818
Contact: Allen M. Spiegel, MD, Dir.
Desc: Metabolic diseases such as diabetes, other inborn errors of metabolism, endocrine disorders, mineral metabolism, digestive diseases, nutrition, urology and renal
disease, and hematology. Basic research includes studies in
biochemistry; nutrition; pathology; histochemistry; chemistry; physical, chemical, and molecular biology; pharmacology; and toxicology. *Type:* Research center.

U.S. Department of Health and Human Services
National Institute of Diabetes and Digestive and Kidney Diseases
Division of Intramural Research
Diabetes Branch
NIH Bldg. 10, 8S239   Ph: (301)496-4658
9000 Rockville Pike   Fax: (301)402-0573
Bethesda, MD 20892
Contact: Dr. Simeon Taylor, Chf.

Desc: Receptors for peptide hormones, especially insulin, insulin-like growth factors, and growth hormone. Current projects are focused on the role of receptors in disease states, receptor antibodies, and genetic disorders of glucose metabolism, isolation and characterization of receptor components, the role of receptors in hormone and drug action at the target cell, morphologic correlates of hormone binding to receptor (electron microscopy and immunocytochemistry), and receptors on circulating cells and cells in tissue culture. *Type:* Research center.

U.S. Department of Health and Human Services
National Institute of Diabetes and Digestive and Kidney Diseases
Division of Intramural Research
Digestive Diseases Branch
NIH Bldg. 10, Rm. 9C-103   Ph: (301)496-4201
9000 Rockville Pike   Fax: (301)402-0600
Bethesda, MD 20892
Contact: Dr. Robert T. Jensen, Chf.

Desc: Diseases and disorders of the digestive tract, including the physiology, biochemistry, and etiology of diseases of the gastrointestinal tract and the liver, enzymes and metabolic pathways, disturbances in gastrointestinal tract function, and the effect of various treatments and therapies. Activities are carried out in sections for gastroenterology and liver diseases. *Type:* Research center.

U.S. Department of Health and Human Services
National Institute of Diabetes and Digestive and Kidney Diseases
Division of Intramural Research
Mathematical Research Branch
BSA Bldg.   Ph: (301)496-4325
9190 Wisconsin Ave, Ste. 350   Fax: (301)402-0535
Bethesda, MD 20892-2690
E-mail: asherman@nih.gov
URL: http://mrb.niddk.nih.gov
Contact: Dr. Arthur S. Sherman, Chf.

Desc: Mathematical and theoretical aspects of biological problems and the development of analytical and numerical methodology underlying such an approach. The research programs are designed to provide a formal basis and theoretical apparatus for the rational analysis and quantitative interpretation of biological phenomena. *Type:* Research center.

U.S. Department of Health and Human Services
National Institute of Diabetes and Digestive and Kidney Diseases
Division of Intramural Research
Metabolic Diseases Branch
NIH Bldg. 10 /Rm. 9C-101   Ph: (301)496-5051
9000 Rockville Pike   Fax: (301)496-0200
Bethesda, MD 20892
Contact: Dr. Allan Spiegel, Chf.

Desc: Physiology and nature of metabolic diseases and disorders, with emphasis on the physiology, biochemistry, and mechanism of action of hormones controlling calcium metabolism. Investigations are directed at hormone-receptor interactions, regulation and characterization of adenylate cyclase, and cellular responses to hormones, particularly parathyroid hormone, calcitonin, and parathyroid related peptide. *Type:* Research center.

U.S. Department of Health and Human Services
National Institute of Diabetes and Digestive and Kidney Diseases
Division of Intramural Research
Molecular, Cellular, and Nutritional Endocrinology Branch
NIH Bldg. 10, Rm. 8D14   Ph: (301)496-1540
9000 Rockville Pike   Fax: (301)496-1649
Bethesda, MD 20892
Contact: Dr. Bruce D. Weintraub, Chf.

Desc: Neuroendocrinology; experimental diabetes, metabolism, and nutrition; and growth and development. Research in neuroendocrinology includes basic and clinical investigations on the regulation of hypothalamic, pituitary, and placental polypeptide hormones. *Type:* Research center.

U.S. Department of Health and Human Services
National Institute of Diabetes and Digestive and Kidney Diseases
Division of Intramural Research
Phoenix Epidemiology and Clinical Research Branch
1550 E. Indian School Rd.   Ph: (602)200-5200
Phoenix, AZ 85014   Fax: (602)200-5225
Contact: Dr. Peter H. Bennett, Chf.

Desc: Epidemiological and clinical aspects of diabetes, obesity, and arthritis in the Pima Indians of Arizona. This includes clinical studies on whole-body insulin resistance, nutrition-induced alterations in metabolism, lipid and lipoprotein metabolism, and dietary and exercise therapy in the treatment of diabetic patients. *Type:* Research center.

U.S. Department of Health and Human Services
National Institute of Environmental Health Sciences
Division of Intramural Researh
Laboratory of Pulmonary Pathobiology
Niehs Mail Drop D201   Ph: (919)541-3540
PO Box 12233   Fax: (919)541-4133
Research Triangle Park, NC
    27709
E-mail: Nettesheim@Niehs.nih.gov
URL: http://www.niehs.nih.gov/junction
Contact: Dr. Paul Nettesheim, Chf.

Desc: Elucidate biochemical and molecular mechanisms of differentiation of airway epithelium; elucidate the role of growth factors in regulation of growth of normal and neoplastically transformed airway cells; explore pathogenetic mechanisms of inflammatory processes of the lung, particularly the cellular and biochemical basis of fibrogenesis; and elucidate the mechanisms of regulation of surfactant biosynthesis. *Type:* Research center.

U.S. Department of Health and Human Services
National Institute of General Medical Sciences
Diagnostic Laboratory
1230 York Ave.   Ph: (212)327-8522
Box 2   Fax: (212)327-8536
New York, NY 10021
Contact: Michael D. Hayre, DVM, Dir.

Desc: Provides diagnostic services and prospective and retrospective clinical studies in conjunction with disease screening and laboratory animal diagnostics at Rockefeller University. Research includes: transgenic animal technology; PCR; macrophage biology; and clinical case reviews. *Type:* Research center.

U.S. Department of Health and Human Services
National Institute of Mental Health
5600 Fishers Ln., Rm. 17-99   Ph: (301)443-3673
Rockville, MD 20857   Fax: (301)443-2578
Contact: Steven E. Hyman, MD, Dir.

Desc: Brain, mental illness, and mental health, particularly the causes, prevention, diagnosis, and treatment of mental illnesses. Principal components are: the Divisions of Neuroscience and Behavioral Science, Clinical and Treatment Research, Epidemiology and Services Research, Extramural Activities, and Intramural Research Programs; Offices of Prevention, Equal Employment Opportunity, Rural Mental Health Research, Legislative Analysis and Coordination, Scientific Information, Resource Management, and Science Policy and Program Planning; Office for Special Populations; and Office on AIDS. *Type:* Research center.

U.S. Department of Health and Human Services
National Institutes of Health
1 Center Dr., MSC 0148   Ph: (301)496-4000
Bethesda, MD 20892-0148
Contact: Harold Varmus, Dir.

Desc: Principal medical research arm of the federal government, with a mission to improve the health of the nation by increasing understanding of the processes underlying human health and by acquiring new knowledge to help prevent, detect, diagnose, and treat disease. NIH accomplishes this mission by: supporting research in universities, medical schools, hospitals, and research institutions in this country and abroad; conducting research in its own laboratories and clinics; supporting training for promising young researchers; helping to develop and maintain research resources; identifying research findings that can be applied to the care of patients and helping to transfer such advances to the health care system; promoting effective ways to communicate biomedical information to scientists, health practitioners, and the public; and developing and recommending policies related to the conduct and support of biomedical research. *Type:* Research center.

U.S. Department of Health and Human Services
National Institutes of Health
9000 Rockville Pike   Ph: (301)496-4000
Bethesda, MD 20892
URL: http://www.nih.gov/
Contact: Harold E. Varmus, Director.

Desc: The National Institutes of Health is the principal biomedical research arm of the federal government. Its programs are oriented primarily toward basic and applied scientific studies on the causes, diagnosis, prevention, treatment, and rehabilitation of human diseases and disabilities; the fundamental biological process of growth, development, and aging; and the biological effects of the environment. *Type:* Government agency, office, or program.

U.S. Department of Health and Human Services
National Institutes of Health
Division of Computer Research and Technology
9000 Rockville Pike   Ph: (301)496-5206
Bethesda, MD 20892
URL: http://www.nih.gov/
Contact: William Risso, Director.

Desc: Division conducts an integrated research, developmental, and service program in computer-related physical and life sciences in support of NIH biomedical research programs. *Type:* Government agency, office, or program.

U.S. Department of Health and Human Services
National Institutes of Health
Fogarty International Center
9000 Rockville Pike   Ph: (301)496-2075
Bethesda, MD 20892   Fax: (301)594-1211
URL: http://www.nih.gov/fic/
Contact: Philip E. Schambra, MD, Director.
Desc: The center is dedicated to advancing health of the people of the United States and other nations through international scientific cooperation. *Type:* Government agency, office, or program.

U.S. Department of Health and Human Services
National Institutes of Health
Fogarty International Center for Advanced Study in the Health Sciences
NIH Bldg. 31-B2C08   Ph: (301)496-2075
31 Center Dr., MSC 2220   Fax: (301)594-1211
Bethesda, MD 20892-2220
E-mail: m3p@cu.nih.gov
Contact: Irene Edwards, Contact.
Desc: Promotes international cooperation in biomedical and behavioral research through grants, fellowships, exchange awards, and int ernational agreements. *Type:* Research center.

U.S. Department of Health and Human Services
National Institutes of Health
Fogarty International Center for Advanced Study in the Health Sciences
Division of International Training and Research
NIH 31   Ph: (301)496-1653
9000 Rockville Pike   Fax: (301)402-0779
Bethesda, MD 20892
E-mail: ken_bridbord@nih.gov
URL: http://www.nih.gov/fic
Contact: Kenneth Bridbord, Dir.
Desc: Funds extramural research in order to enhance collaborative projects between U.S. principal investigators and non-U.S. principal investigators and non-U.S. principal investigators through research grants, fellowships, and training grants. *Type:* Research center.

U.S. Department of Health and Human Services
National Institutes of Health
National Center for Research Resources
9000 Rockville Pike   Ph: (301)435-0888
Bethesda, MD 20892
URL: http://www.ncrr.nih.gov/
Contact: Judith L. Vaitukaitis, MD, Director.
Desc: The NCRR creates, develops, and provides a comprehensive range of human, animal, technological and other cost-effective, shared resources. NCRR also funds a variety of investigator-initiated research projects and training and career enhancement programs. *Type:* Government agency, office, or program.

U.S. Department of Health and Human Services
National Institutes of Health
National Eye Institute
9000 Rockville Pike   Ph: (301)496-4583
Bethesda, MD 20892   Fax: (301)496-9970
URL: http://www.nei.nih.gov/
Contact: Carl Kupfer, MD, Director.
Desc: The Institute conducts and supports fundamental studies on the eye and visual system, and on the causes, prevention, diagnosis, and treatment of visual disorders. *Type:* Government agency, office, or program.

U.S. Department of Health and Human Services
National Institutes of Health
National Institute of General Medical Sciences
9000 Rockville Pike   Ph: (301)496-7301
Bethesda, MD 20892   Fax: (301)402-0156
URL: http://www.nih.gov/nigms/
Contact: Marvin Cassman, Director.
Desc: NIGMS supports research and research training in basic biomedical sciences. Institute activities range from cell biology to genetics to pharmacology and systemic response to trauma and anesthesia. *Type:* Government agency, office, or program.

U.S. Department of Health and Human Services
National Institutes of Health
National Institute of General Medical Sciences
45 Center Dr., MSC 6200   Ph: (301)594-2172
Bethesda, MD 20892-6200   Fax: (301)402-0156
E-mail: cassmanm@nih.gov
URL: http://nih.gov/nigms/
Contact: Dr. Marvin Cassman, Dir.
Desc: Non-disease-targeted research and research training in the basic biomedical sciences; maintains no intramural (in-house) research. Program focuses on the areas of cell biology and biophysics; genetics and developmental biology; phamacology, physiology, and biological chemistry; and minority opportunities in research. *Type:* Research center.

U.S. Department of Health and Human Services
National Institutes of Health
National Library of Medicine
9000 Rockville Pike   Ph: (301)496-6308
Bethesda, MD 20892
URL: http://www.nlm.ni.gov/
Contact: Donald A.B. Lindberg, MD, Director.
Desc: The National Library of Medicine serves as the nation's chief medical information source. It is the world's largest research library in a single scientific and professional field. *Type:* Government agency, office, or program.

U.S. Department of Health and Human Services
National Institutes of Health
Office of Administration
Contracts and Grants Division
6100 Executive Blvd.   Ph: (301)496-4487
Rockville, MD 20852   Fax: (301)402-0178
Contact: David W. Snight, Chf.
Desc: Negotiates awards and administers contracts for all NIH institutes that do not have their own contracts office. *Type:* Research center.

U.S. Department of Health and Human Services
National Institutes of Health
Office of Extramural Research
NIH Bldg. 1, Rm. 144   Ph: (301)496-1096
1 Center Dr., Mail Stop 0152   Fax: (301)402-3469
Bethesda, MD 20892
E-mail: wendy_baldwin@nih.gov
URL: http://www.nih.gov/grants/oer.htm
Contact: Wendy Baldwin, PhD, Dep.Dir.
Desc: Adminsters the development and coordination of NIH policies and procedures for awarding funds in support of biomedical research, including policies for the conduct of biomedical and behavioral research involving human subjects or vertebrate animals; and provides policy guidance for the Research Grants Division. *Type:* Research center.

U.S. Department of Health and Human Services
National Institutes of Health
Office of Medical Applications of Research
Bldg. 31, Rm. 1B03   Ph: (301)496-1143
31 Center Dr., MSC-2082   Free: 888-644-2667
Bethesda, MD 20892   Fax: (301)402-0420
E-mail: jferg@helix.nih.gov
URL: http://consensus.nih.gov
Contact: John H. Ferguson, MD, Dir.
Desc: Translation of results of biomedical research pertinent to health care into knowledge that can effectively be employed in the practice of medicine and public health. The Office facilitates and coordinates technical consensus development activities at the National Institutes of Health through the implementation of consensus conferences. *Type:* Research center.

U.S. Department of Health and Human Services
National Institutes of Health
Office for Protection from Research Risks
6100 Executive Blvd. Ste. 3B-01   Ph: (301)496-7005
Rockville, MD 20852   Fax: (301)402-0527
E-mail: G6E@CU.NIH.GOV
Contact: Dr. Gary B. Ellis, Dir.
Desc: Negotiates and implements compliance with the regulations and policies of the Department of Health and Human Services for the protection of human and animal subjects in research. *Type:* Research center.

U.S. Department of Health and Human Services
National Library of Medicine
Bldg. 38, 2S15   Ph: (301)496-6308
8600 Rockville Pike   Fax: (301)496-4450
Bethesda, MD 20894
E-mail: publicinfo@nlm.nih.gov
URL: http://www.nlm.nih.gov
Contact: Donald A.B. Lindberg, Dir.
Desc: World's largest research library in a single scientific and professional field. The Library collects materials in all major areas of the health sciences and, to a lesser degree, in chemistry, physics, botany, and zoology. *Type:* Research center.

U.S. Department of Health and Human Services
National Library of Medicine
Extramural Programs Division
6705 Rockledge Dr., Ste. 301   Ph: (301)496-4621
Bethesda, MD 20892   Fax: (301)402-2952
Contact: Dr. Milton Corn, Assoc.Dir.
Desc: Administers the National Library of Medicine's program of grants fo r support of fundamental and applied work in the organization, representation, utilization, and dissemination of health knowledge, with special interest in medical informatics and biotechnology information. Grants are generally awarded in three main categories: Research, Development, and Demonstration awards are investigator-initiated projects that address problems of health information access, retrieval, and utilization. *Type:* Research center.

U.S. Department of Health and Human Services
National Library of Medicine
Office of Computer and Communications Systems
Special Assistant for Research and Development
Bldg. 38A, Rm. 9F904   Ph: (301)496-9300
8600 Rockville Pike   Fax: (301)496-0673
Bethesda, MD 20894
Contact: Dr. Tamas E. Doszkocs, Computer Sci.
Desc: Information processing, including information retrieval, ergonomics, natural language processing, artificial intelligence, and database management. *Type:* Research center.

U.S. Department of Health and Human Services

Office of Assistant Secretary for Health

Office Of Research Integrity

Rockwall Bldg. 2   Ph: (301)443-3400
5515 Security Ln., Ste. 700   Fax: (301)443-5351
Rockville, MD 20852
E-mail: cpascal@osophs.dhhs.gov
URL: http://ori.dhhs.gov
Contact: Chris Pascal, Actg.Dir.
Desc: Responds to any allegations of scientific misconduct occurring in research supported by the Public Health Service. *Type:* Research center.

U.S. Department of Health and Human Services

Office of Assistant Secretary for Health

Office of Research Integrity

Research Investigations Division

Rockwall Bldg. 2   Ph: (301)443-5330
5515 Security Ln., Ste. 700   Fax: (301)594-0039
Rockville, MD 20852
E-mail: DMACFARLANE@OSOPHS.DHHS.GOV
URL: http://ori.dhhs.gov
Contact: Dorothy K. Macfarlane, Dir.
Desc: Responds to allegations of scientific misconduct occurring in research supported by the Public Health Service. *Type:* Research center.

U.S. Department of Health and Human Services

Office of Disease Prevention and Health Promotion

200 Independence Ave. SW,   Ph: (202)401-6295
   Rm. 738G   Fax: (202)205-9478
Washington, DC 20201
URL: http://nhic-nt.health.org
Contact: Linda Meyers, Actg.Dir.
Desc: Develops and manages the National Health Goals and Objectives (known as Healthy People 2000) for the National Health Information Center. Coordinates policy and program for the Public Health Service. *Type:* Research center.

U.S. Department of Health and Human Services

Public Health Service

Agency for Health Care Policy and Research

2101 E. Jefferson St., Rm. 600   Ph: (301)594-6662
Rockville, MD 20852   Free: 800-358-9295
                     Fax: (301)594-2168
E-mail: info@ahcpr.gov
URL: http://www.ahcpr.gov
Contact: Dr. John Eisenberg, Admin.
Desc: Develops and disseminates research-based information to increase the scientific knowledge needed to enhance consumer and clinical decisionmaking, improve health care quality, and promote efficiency in the organization of public and private systems of health care delivery. Its programs evaluate the effectiveness of medical treatments and other health services and improve access to new scientific and technical information for health care practitioners, policymakers, administrators, insurers, researchers, educators, and consumers. *Type:* Research center.

U.S. Department of Health and Human Services

Public Health Service

Agency for Health Care Policy and Research

Center for General Health Services Extramural Research

Executive Office Center, Rm.   Ph: (301)594-1349
   502   Fax: (301)594-2155
Rockville, MD 20852-4993
Contact: Linda Demlo, Actg.Dir.

Desc: Delivery of health care service in rural areas and frontier areas; and the health of low-income groups, minority groups, and the elderly. Emphasizes the effectiveness, efficiency, and quality of health care services; the outcomes of health care services and procedures; clinical practice, including primary care and practice-oriented research; health care technologies, facilities, and equipment; health care costs, productivity, and market forces; health promotion and disease prevention; health statistics and epidemiology; and medical liability. *Type:* Research center.

U.S. Department of Health and Human Services

Public Health Service

Office of Adolescent Pregnancy Programs

4350 East-West Hwy., ste.   Ph: (301)594-4004
   200W   Fax: (301)594-5980
Bethesda, MD 20814
E-mail: psheeran@osoph.dhhs.gov
URL: http://www.dhhs.gov/progorg/opa/oapp.html
Contact: Patrick J. Sheeran, Actg.Dir.
Desc: Supports care demonstration projects to help pregnant teenagers and their children and families; and prevention demonstration projects to reach teenagers before they become sexually active. Programs include the award of research and evaluation grants and contracts for studies on the causes and consequences of adolescent sexual behavior, contraceptive use, and early childbearing; and evaluation of service delivery. *Type:* Research center.

U.S. Department of Health and Human Services

Public Health Service

Office of Family Planning

Family Planning Program (Service Delivery Improvement Research)

Office of Population Affairs   Ph: (301)594-4008
West Bldg. 4350 East West   Fax: (301)594-4008
   Hwy.
Ste 200
Bethesda, MD 20814
E-mail: opa@osophs.dhhs.gov
URL: http://www.os.dhhs.gov/progorg/opa
Contact: Eugenia Eckard, Prog.Dir.
Desc: Improvement of family planning services delivery for low-income women and others in need of such services. Two types of grants are awarded: individual research project grants and New Investigator Research Awards. *Type:* Research center.

U.S. Department of Health and Human Services

Social Security Administration

Office of Research and Statistics

Division of RSDI Research Statistics

Rm. 4-C 16, Operations Bldg.   Ph: (410)965-0156
6401 Security Blvd.   Fax: (410)966-4071
Baltimore, MD 21235
Contact: Barbara Lingg, Dir.
Desc: Preparation of statistical and analytical data pertaining to RSDI claims and benefit provisions of Title II of the Social Security Act. *Type:* Research center.

U.S. Department of Health and Human Services

Warren Grant Magnuson Clinical Center

NIH Bldg. 10   Ph: (301)496-2563
9000 Rockville Pike   Fax: (301)402-2984
Rm. 2C6-146
Bethesda, MD 20892
E-mail: occc@nih.gov
URL: http://www.cc.nih.gov
Contact: John I. Gallin, M.D., Dir.
Desc: Designed to place patient care facilities close to research laboratories to promote the quick transfer of new

findings of basic and clinical scientists to the treatment of patients. The Center provides high-quality patient care necessary for intramural clinical research conducted at the National Institutes of Health; performs research on methods and systems involved in patient care and study; disseminates information to professionals and to the public relevant to clinical investigation; develops and maintains training programs in the techniques and ethics of biomedical and clinical research; and interacts with scientists and physicians, nationally and internationally, on such mutual problems of clinical research as policy, education, ethics, and priorities. *Type:* Research center.

U.S. Department of Justice

Bureau of Prisons

Health Services Division

320 1st St. NW   Ph: (202)307-3198
Washington, DC 20534
Contact: Kathleen M. Hawk, Director.
Desc: The Health Services Division has oversight responsibility for all medical and psychiatric programs; environmental and occupational health services; food and nutrition services; and farm operations. *Type:* Government agency, office, or program.

U.S. Department of State

Under Secretary for Management

Office of Medical Services

2201 C St. NW   Ph: (202)647-3617
Washington, DC 20520   Fax: (202)663-1613
URL: http://www.state.gov/
Desc: The Office develops, manages, and staffs a worldwide primary health care system for U.S. citizen employees, and their eligible dependents, residing abroad. *Type:* Government agency, office, or program.

U.S. Department of Transportation

Coast Guard

Office of Health and Safety

Coast Guard Bldg.   Ph: (202)267-4512
2100 2nd St. SW   Fax: (202)267-4512
Washington, DC 20590
Contact: R.Adm. Joyce M. Johnson, Chf.
Desc: Provides health-related guidance and policy in support of Coast Guard missions. *Type:* Research center.

United States Sports Academy

Academy Medical Center

1 Academy Dr.   Ph: (334)626-3303
Daphne, AL 36526-9552   Fax: (334)621-2527
E-mail: academy@ussa.sport.ussa.edu
URL: http://www.sport.ussa.edu
Contact: Dr. William Carroll, EdD, Ch.
Desc: Basic exercise physiology and preventive medicine for disease, emphasizing analysis of cardiovascular disease risk factor and life-style change intervention; biomechanical research in gait analysis, sports skills, and structural anomalies; sports medicine research in injury prevention, treatment, and diagnosis; and drug abuse in sports. *Type:* Research center.

University of Alabama at Birmingham

Center for Health Promotion

Sch. of Public Health   Ph: (205)934-6020
1665 University Blvd., Ste. 227   Fax: (205)934-9325
   Royals
Birmingham, AL 35294
E-mail: jrac@uab.edu
URL: http://www.hb.soph.uab.edu
Contact: Dr. Jim Raczynski, Dir.
Desc: Health promotion and disease prevention for underserved population. The center is divided into several com-

ponents, including the Community Care, Project Assessment Care, Survey Research Unit, Surveillance Data Unit, Behavioral Assessment and Intervention Care, Health Communications Unit, and Biopsychosocial Laboratory. *Type:* Research center.

University of Alabama at Birmingham
General Clinical Research Center

3 W. Jefferson Tower   Ph: (205)934-4852
UAB Sta.   Fax: (205)975-6616
Birmingham, AL 35294-6909

Contact: John J. Curtis, MD, Prog.Dir.

Desc: Patient care and laboratory support of clinical investigations for all departments and divisions of the Medical Center, including the Schools of Medicine and Dentistry. Studies are conducted on metabolism, cardiology, hematology, rheumatology, infectious diseases, virology, immunology, pulmonary medicine, renal medicine, gastroenterology, oncology, neurosurgery, AIDS, and the mechanisms of disease. *Type:* Research center.

University of Alabama at Birmingham
Injury Control Research Center

933 19th St. S., Ste. 403   Ph: (205)934-1448
CHSB-19   Fax: (205)975-8143
Birmingham, AL 35294-2041
E-mail: rfine@uab.edu
URL: http://www.uab.edu/icrc/icrc.htm

Contact: Philip R. Fine, PhD, Dir.

Desc: Rehabilitation and occupationally-related injuries, especially burns, intra-articular fractures of the lower extremities, spinal cord injuries, and traumatic brain injuries, focusing on improving rehabilitation practices and processes to help persons with injuries achieve maximum rehabilitation potential; stimulating local faculty development of prevention, acute-care, rehabilitation, epidemiology, and biomechanics research projects; training health care workers and other practitioners, scientists, and students in the discipline of injury prevention and control; providing technical assistance and disseminate information in support of the nation's injury control agenda; and promoting the explicit incorporation of injury prevention initiatives targeting high-risk populations. Center also conducts multidisciplinary research involving faculty from other areas of the University. *Type:* Research center.

University of Alabama at Birmingham
Laboratory of Exocrine Physiology

Univ. Sta.   Ph: (205)934-4588
Birmingham, AL 35294

Desc: Physiology of exocrine glands, focusing on clarifying mechanisms of regulation of glandular growth, development, and secretion, and principal mechanisms by which electrolytes are secreted. Collaborates with scientists in Thailand, Egypt, and Hungary. *Type:* Research center.

University of Alabama at Birmingham
Multipurpose Arthritis and Musculoskeletal Diseases Center

Tinsley Harrison Tower, Rm.   Ph: (205)934-5306
  429   Fax: (205)934-1564
Birmingham, AL 35294-0012
E-mail: Robert.Kimberly@ccc.uab.edu
URL: http://www.dom.uab.edu

Contact: Dr. Robert P. Kimberly, Dir.

Desc: Arthritis and related rheumatic disorders, including investigations into cause, diagnosis, control, and treatment of arthritis and complications resulting from arthritis and related musculoskeletal disorders. *Type:* Research center.

University of Alabama at Birmingham
Ob/Gyn Infectious Disease Research Laboratory

Department of Ob/Gyn   Ph: (205)934-5271
618 20th St. S.   Fax: (205)975-4375
Birmingham, AL 35233-7333
E-mail: bandrews@uab.campus.mci.net

Contact: Dr. William W. Andrews, Dir.

Desc: Infectious etiologies of preterm labor, premature rupture of membranes, markers for preterm birth, new antimicrobial therapies for postpartum endometritis, the relationship between maternal infection and subsequent neonatal sepsis, and sexually transmitted diseases. *Type:* Research center.

University of Alberta
Centre for the Cross-Cultural Study of Health and Healing

Department of Anthropology   Ph: (403)492-0135
Henry Marshall Tory Bldg.,   Fax: (403)492-5273
  B-57
Edmonton, AB, Canada T6G
  2H4
E-mail: crossctr@gpu.srv.ualberta.ca
URL: http://www.ualberta.ca/~crossctr/home.html

Desc: Multicultural health issues, including healing practices and efficacy of traditional healers, and developing a cross-cultural model for understanding similarities and differences among traditional healers; documentation and assessment of alternative healing practices; how societies deal with relationships among traditional, alternative and modern biomedicine; and programs which can best meet the needs of all Canadians, including aboriginals, established ethnic groups, and new immigrants. *Type:* Research center.

University of Alberta
Centre for Studies in Clinical Education

Fac. of Rehabilitation Med.   Ph: (403)492-0841
3-48 Corbett Hall   Fax: (403)492-1626
Edmonton, AB, Canada T6G
  2G4
E-mail: paul.hagler@ualberta.ca
URL: http://www.ualberta.ca/~rehabmed/centers/csce/
csce.html

Contact: Paul Hagler, PhD, Dir.

Desc: Clinical education, including selection procedures for the quota programs, supervisor effectiveness, training and supervision of support personnel, and cost-benefit analysis of student training in clinical service facilities. *Type:* Research center.

University of Alberta
Muttart Diabetes Research and Training Centre

458 Heritage Med. Res. Centre Ph: (403)492-6855
Edmonton, AB, Canada T6G   Fax: (403)492-4666
  2S2
E-mail: Alex.Rubinovitch@ualberta.ca

Contact: A. Rabinovitch, MD, Co-Dir.

Desc: Causes, treatment, and prevention of diabetes mellitus in humans and experimental animals. Provides core research laboratory support services. *Type:* Research center.

University of Arizona
Advanced Biotechnology Laboratory

Department of Anesthesiology   Ph: (520)626-2116
1501 N. Campbell   Fax: (520)626-2689
Tucson, AZ 85724-5114
E-mail: rcw@ccit.arizona.edu

Contact: Richard Watt, Dir.

Desc: Implementation of advanced technology to anesthesia, including utilization of computers for automation of

monitoring and data collection, development of improved anesthesia delivery and monitoring equipment, basic research and development of new monitoring parameters, and ergonomic approaches to anesthesia tasks. Pharmacologic research is also conducted with emphasis on molecular mechanisms of anesthetics. *Type:* Research center.

University of Arizona
Native American Research and Training Center

1642 E. Helen   Ph: (520)621-5075
Tucson, AZ 85719   Fax: (520)621-9802
E-mail: nanderso@u.arizona.edu
URL: http://www.ahsc.arizona.edu/fcm/nartc.html

Contact: Jennie R. Joe, PhD, Dir.

Desc: Health and rehabilitation of disabled and chronically ill Native Americans. Core areas include the following: needs assessment, service delivery, and evaluation as determined by or in cooperation with the disabled; empowerment that is sensitive to Indian values and needs; and vocational rehabilitation, including preventive, restorative, and occupational processes for the disabled that lead to self-sufficiency. *Type:* Research center.

University of British Columbia
Biomedical Research Centre

2222 Health Sci. Mall   Ph: (604)822-7813
Vancouver, BC, Canada V6T   Fax: (604)822-7815
  1Z3
E-mail: john@brc.ubc.ca
URL: http://www.brc.ubc.ca/

Contact: Dr. John W. Schrader, Dir.

Desc: Structure and function of genes and proteins involved in regulation of the growth and differentiation of cells of the immune system, including growth factors or cytokines, their cell surface receptors, and the intracellular enzymes and other proteins that control cellular growth and function. Research activities lie in the general areas of immunology, cancer, ontogeny, and technology development. *Type:* Research center.

University of British Columbia
G.F. Strong Research Laboratory for Medical Research

Division of Infectious Diseases Ph: (604)875-4588
2733 Heather St., Rm. 452, 'D'   Fax: (604)875-4013
  Fl.
Vancouver, BC, Canada V5Z
  3J5
E-mail: ethan@interchange.ubc.ca

Contact: Dr. Reiner, Dir.

Desc: Infectious diseases, immunology, toxic shock syndrome, HIV/AIDS, host defense, macrophage cell regulation, tuberculosis, and leishmaniasis. *Type:* Research center.

University of British Columbia
Jack Bell Research Centre

Vancouver Hospital & Health   Ph: (604)875-4810
  Sciences Centre   Fax: (604)875-4497
2660 Oak St.
Vancouver, BC, Canada V6H
  3Z6
E-mail: dmclean@vanhosp.bc.ca
URL: http://www.research.vhhsc.ubc.ca

Contact: Dr. David McLean, VP, Res.

Desc: Steroid hormone receptors, cancer chemotherapy, inmunogenetics, kinases, micro-surgical procedures for repairing the bladder and uretha after an injury, and lung hazards in the work place and their effects on workers. Research also focuses on improving patient care, determining causes and treatments of diseases, detecting cancer at an early stage, and improving facilities for specialized surgery. *Type:* Research center.

University of Calgary
Department of Community Health Sciences

3330 Hospital Dr. NW   Ph: (403)220-7181
Calgary, AB, Canada T2N 4N1   Fax: (403)270-7307
URL: http://www.bio.health.ucalgary.ca/chs
Contact: Dr. L.R. Sutherland, Hd.

Desc: Biostatistics; epidemiology of acute and chronic disease; interdisciplinary studies on organization and delivery of health care services, emphasizing on utilization and evaluation of such services in maternal and child health; occupational health and public health; and geriatrics. *Type:* Research center.

University of Calgary
Endocrine Research Group

3330 Hospital Dr. NW   Ph: (403)220-3037
Calgary, AB, Canada T2N 4N1   Fax: (403)270-0979
E-mail: dahanley@acs.ucalgary.ca
Contact: Dr. David A. Hanley, Chm.

Desc: Experimental and clinical endocrinology, neurochemistry, histochemistry, synthesis, pharmacology, and receptor mechanisms of peptide and steroid hormones (calcium-regulating hormones, vasoactive peptides, thyroid hormones, neurohypophysical hormones, insulin, and growth factors.). *Type:* Research center.

University of Calgary
Gastrointestinal Research Group

Health Sci. Centre   Ph: (403)220-8457
3330 Hospital Dr. NW   Fax: (403)220-0995
Calgary, AB, Canada T2N 4N1
E-mail: samlee@acs.ucalgary.caca
URL: http://www.gi.ucalgary.ca
Contact: Sam Lee, Ch.

Desc: Neuroendocrine control of gastrointestinal (GI) function, secretory functions in the GI tract, motility of the biliary tract and intestine, intestinal absorption, membrane physiology, immunology of the GI tract, intestinal inflammation, inflammatory bowel disease, developmental physiology, hepatobiliary disease, hepatic receptors, malnutrition, satiety and appetite control, intestinal adaptation, gut hormone, and splanchnic blood flow. *Type:* Research center.

University of Calgary
Infectious Disease Research Group

3300 Hospital Dr. NW   Ph: (403)220-4572
Calgary, AB, Canada T2N 4N1   Fax: (403)270-2772
E-mail: dhart@asc.ucalgary.ca
URL: http://www.ucalgary.ca
Contact: Dr. David Hart, Contact.

Desc: Antimicrobial agents-transport and action, mechanisms of resistance, pharmacology, in vivo activity, pathogenesis-genetic regulation of virulence, chronic pulmonary infections due to pseudomonas aeruginosa, structure and function of reovirus attachment protein and receptors, rapid diagnostic methods, viral and immunological factors in the etiology of diabetes mellitus, anti-herpes virus chemotherapy, molecular biology of interferon, pathogenesis of urinary tract infections, and viral epidemiology. *Type:* Research center.

University of Calgary
Joint Injury and Arthritis Research Group

436 Heritage Medical Research   Ph: (403)220-4244
   Bldg.   Fax: (403)270-0617
3330 Hospital Dr. NW
Calgary, AB, Canada T2N 4N1
URL: http://www.ucalgary.ca/uofc/faculties/med/surgery/mccaig.html
Contact: Dr. R. Bray, Ch.

Desc: Biological and nonbiological transplants of joints and ligaments and electrical stimulation of injured tissues,

including studies of joint reconstruction, gait analysis, sports medicine and athletic injuries, inherited connective tissue diseases, osteoarthritis and rheumatism. *Type:* Research center.

University of Calgary
Julia McFarlane Diabetes Research Centre

Health Science Bldg.   Ph: (403)220-3011
3330 Hospital Dr. NW   Fax: (403)270-7526
Calgary, AB, Canada T2N 4N1
E-mail: yoon@acs.ucalgary.ca
Contact: Dr. Yoon, Dir.

Desc: Cause, cure and prevention of type I and type II diabetes from molecular, cellular and clinical approaches. Participates in national and international collaborative research projects. *Type:* Research center.

University of Calgary
Protein Sequencing Facility

Health Sci. Centre   Ph: (403)220-4479
3330 Hospital Dr. NW
Calgary, AB, Canada T2N 4N1
E-mail: mckayd@ucalgary.ca
Contact: Dr. D.J. McKay, Dir.

Desc: Provides amino acid analysis and protein sequencing to investigators. *Type:* Research center.

University of Calgary
Respiratory Research Group

3330 Hospital Dr. NW, Rm.   Ph: (403)220-7045
   223   Fax: (403)270-8928
Calgary, AB, Canada T2N 4N1
Contact: Dr. Paul A. Easton, Co-Chm.

Desc: Normal and diseased respiratory systems, including mechanics of the respiratory system, muscles of respiration, neural control of breathing, membrane biophysics of smooth muscle cells of the airway and their response to provocative agents in asthma, lung pathology and occupational lung disease, neonatal lung development and disease, sudden infant death syndrome, surface properties of the alveoli of the lung, and blood flow to, from, and through the lungs. *Type:* Research center.

University of California, Irvine
Medical Physics Department

Department of Physics and   Ph: (714)824-6911
   Astronomy
4129 Physical Sci. II
Irvine, CA 92697-4575
URL: http://www.ps.uci.edu/physics/dept.html
Contact: Jon Lawrence, Dept.Chm.

Desc: Medical physics, focusing on human physiology, the effect of physical agents on living tissue, understanding and use of diagnostic and therapeutic techniques, etc. *Type:* Research center.

University of California, Irvine
UCI Diabetes Research Program

Department of Med.   Ph: (714)824-7110
Med Sci I C264   Fax: (714)824-2200
Irvine, CA 92697
Contact: Dr. M. Arthur Charles, Dir.

Desc: Diabetes, including studies in islet transplantation; diabetes remission, induction, and prevention studies; immunology of diabetes; programmable insulin delivery implant systems; aldose reductose inhibitors in humans; hypertension and oral hypoglycerric agent and insulin studies; and studies of growth factors for treatment of diabetic foot ulcers. *Type:* Research center.

University of California, Los Angeles
Bone Research Laboratory

1000 Veteran Ave., Rm. A3-34   Ph: (310)825-6521
Los Angeles, CA 90024-1790   Fax: (310)206-3980
E-mail: murist@ucla.edu
Contact: Dr. Marshall R. Urist, Dir.

Desc: Bone morphogenesis in health and disease, including fundamental and clinical studies in bone biochemistry and physiology. The UCLA group discovered the inductive response of adult connective tissue cells to bone morphogenetic protein. *Type:* Research center.

University of California, Los Angeles
CURE: Digestive Diseases Research Center

WLA VAMC   Ph: (310)312-9284
Bldg. 115, Rm. 115   Fax: (310)268-4963
Los Angeles, CA 90073-1792
E-mail: jwalsh@ucla.edu
URL: http://www.med.ucla.edu/cure
Contact: Dr. John H. Walsh, Dir.

Desc: Peptic ulcer disease, relationship of Helicobacter pylori infection to ulcers. Etiology and treatment of functional bowel disease, cell proliferation, gastrointestinal neoplasm, and nutritional intestinal absorption. *Type:* Research center.

University of California, Los Angeles
General Clinical Research Center

Ctr. for Health Sci.   Ph: (310)825-7117
27-066CHS   Fax: (310)206-9440
10833 Le Conte Ave.
Los Angeles, CA 90095-1697
E-mail: isalusky@ucla.edu
Contact: Isidro B. Salusky, MD, Prog.Dir.

Desc: Cardiovascular system, dermatology, endocrinology and metabolism, gastroenterology, genetic disease, gynecology, hematology, immunology and rheumatology, nephrology, neurology, oncology, and pulmonary physiology. *Type:* Research center.

University of California, Los Angeles
Harbor-UCLA Medical Center
Center for the Study of Inflammatory Bowel Disease

1124 W. Carson St., N-21   Ph: (310)222-2475
Torrance, CA 90502   Fax: (310)212-7837
E-mail: eysselein@humc.edu
Contact: Viktor E. Eysselein, MD, Ch.

Desc: Inflammatory bowel disease, particularly the origin, causes, and treatment of ulcerative colitis and Crohn's disease. Conducts related studies in molecular biology, cell biology, and immunology. *Type:* Research center.

University of California, Los Angeles
Harbor-UCLA Medical Center
Collaborative Center for Reproduction

Walter Martin Research Bldg.,   Ph: (310)222-1867
   RB-1   Fax: (310)533-0627
1124 W. Carson St.
Torrance, CA 90509
E-mail: swerdloff@harbor2.humc.edu
Contact: Dr. Ronald S. Swerdloff, Dir.

Desc: Clinical investigations of overpopulation and infertility through analysis of endocrinology, physiology, pathology, and molecular biology of the reproductive system. *Type:* Research center.

University of California, Los Angeles

Harbor-UCLA Medical Center

General Clinical Research Center

1000 W. Carson St.   Ph: (310)222-2503
Box 16   Fax: (310)533-6972
Torrance, CA 90509-2910
E-mail: wang@harbor6.humc.edu

Contact: Christina Wang, MD, Prog.Dir.

Desc: Biomedicine, endocrinology, reproductive physiology, gastroenterology, genetics, immunology and infectious disease, nephrology, obstetrics and gynecology, labor and delivery, diabetes, metabolism, oncology, pediatrics, nutrition, psychiatry, neurology, AIDS research and neonatology. *Type:* Research center.

University of California, Los Angeles

Southern California Injury Prevention Research Center

UCLA School of Public Health   Ph: (310)206-4115
10833 Le Conte Ave., Room   Fax: (310)794-7989
  76-078 CHS
Los Angeles, CA 90095-1772
E-mail: jfkraus@ucla.edu
URL: http://www.ph.ucla.edu/sciprc/sciprc1.htm

Contact: Jess F. Kraus, PhD, Dir.

Desc: Intentional and unintentional injuries in the socioeconomically disadvantaged, underserved, and ethnically diverse populations in the Southern California region. Research projects include: work-related injuries in high-risk occupations; risk of motor vehicle crash; injuries to children; injuries and deaths; injuries in the elderly; worksite intervention to reduce work-related assault; earthquake injury and preparedness; expanding methods in injury epidemiology; long-term consequences of brain and spinal cord injuries; multiple organ failure from trauma; violence in contemporary American film; evaluation of the 1992 California Helmet Law; back supports in material handlers; marital; and youth violence. *Type:* Research center.

University of California, San Diego

Center for Population Research

Dept. of Reproductive Med.,   Ph: (619)534-8930
  0633   Fax: (619)534-8856
9500 Gilman Dr.
La Jolla, CA 92093
E-mail: dnye@ucsd.edu
URL: http://www.orpheus.ucsd.edu/Repromed/
Reproend

Contact: Prof. Samuel S. Yen, Dir.

Desc: Hypothalamic control of the pituitary and gonadal function in human and animal models, focusing on issues related to neuroendicrine metabolic dysfunction in the aging population. *Type:* Research center.

University of California, San Diego

General Clinical Research Center

UCSD Med. Ctr., 8203   Ph: (619)543-6180
200 W. Arbor Dr.   Fax: (619)543-5536
San Diego, CA 92103-8203
E-mail: mziegler@ucsd.edu
URL: http://euclid.ucsd.edu:80/~gcrc/

Contact: Michael G. Ziegler, MD, Dir.

Desc: Cardiovascular disease, endocrinology, gastroenterology, genetic disease, immunology, infectious disease, metabolism, neurological disease, oncology, pulmonary medicine, renal disease, reproductive endocrinology, rheumatology, hypertension, and gene therapy. *Type:* Research center.

University of California, San Diego

Multipurpose Arthritis and Musculoskeletal Diseases Center

Department of Med.   Ph: (619)534-5393
9500 Gilman Dr.   Fax: (619)534-5475
La Jolla, CA 92093-0664
E-mail: hbluestein@ucsd.edu

Contact: Harry G. Bluestein, Dir.

Desc: Causes and treatment of arthritis. *Type:* Research center.

University of California, San Francisco

Cardiovascular Research Institute

San Francisco, CA 94143-0130   Ph: (415)476-6174
                               Fax: (415)476-2283
E-mail: shaun_couglin@quickmail.ucsf.edu
URL: http://www.medicine.ucsf.edu/cvri/cvri.html

Contact: Dr. Shaun R. Coughlin, Dir.

Desc: Physiology, biochemistry, pharmacology, cell biology, molecular biology, and immunology of the cardiovascular, pulmonary, respiratory, and renal systems; circulation, respiration, lung development, and metabolism of the fetus and newborn; membrane transduction systems; lipoprotein metabolism; growth factors and atherosclerosis; water and electrolyte transport; physical chemistry of contraction/relaxation of muscle; lung injury and repair; myocardial growth and development; macromolecular conformation; and mathematical analysis of biological systems. *Type:* Research center.

University of California, San Francisco

General Clinical Research Center

San Francisco General Hospital   Ph: (415)206-5820
Box 1353   Fax: (415)826-3381
San Francisco, CA 94143-1353
E-mail: debgcrc@itsa.ucsf.edu

Contact: Morris Schambelan, MD, Dir.

Desc: Human disorders, including interdisciplinary clinical studies of aldosterone and renin activity in hypertension and chronic renal insufficiency. Investigates the effect of diet in patients with lipid disorders. *Type:* Research center.

University of California, San Francisco

General Clinical Research Center--Adults

1202 Moffitt Hospital   Ph: (415)476-1241
San Francisco, CA 94143-0126   Fax: (415)476-0986
E-mail: tierneyc@gcrc.uscf.edu

Contact: Joel Palefsky, MD, Prog.Dir.

Desc: Cardiovascular disease, hypertension, clinical pharmacology, lipid metabolism, nephrology, nutrition, oncology, acid-base physiology, dermatology, infectious diseases, reproductive endocrinology, AIDS, potassium metabolism, osteoporosis, recombinant human hemoglobin, liver disease, aging, psychopharmacology, hereditary fructose intolerance, gene theraphy, and wound healing. *Type:* Research center.

University of California, San Francisco

George Williams Hooper Foundation

513 Parnassus Ave., HSW1501   Ph: (415)476-5157
San Francisco, CA 94143-0552   Fax: (415)476-6185

Contact: Dr. J. Michael Bishop, Dir.

Desc: Cancer biology; genetics and physiology of mammalian cells and organisms; animal models resembling human cancers; and cell biology, immunology and the pathogenesis of infectious diseases. *Type:* Research center.

University of California, San Francisco

Hormone Research Institute

Box 0534   Ph: (415)476-2624
San Francisco, CA 94143-0534   Fax: (415)731-3612
E-mail: kelly@cgl.ucsf.edu

Contact: Regis B. Kelly, Dir.

Desc: Research comprises several investigators focusing on hormone receptors, gene regulation in endocrine tissue, mechanisms of regulated secretion, glutamic acid decarboxylase in juvenile diabetes, and the development of the endocrine pancreas. *Type:* Research center.

University of California, San Francisco

Liver Transplant Services

Department of Surgery, Rm.   Ph: (415)476-8028
  M896   Fax: (415)502-4354
PO Box 0780
San Francisco, CA 94143
E-mail: aschern@surgery.ucsf.edu

Contact: Nancy Ascher, MD, Dir.

Desc: Molecular and immunological mechanisms of allograft rejection, with emphasis on regulation and manipulation of the allospecific immune response and on the manipulation of the tumor specific immune response against hepatocellular carcinoma. *Type:* Research center.

University of California, San Francisco

Metabolic Research Unit

513 Parnassus Ave., Rm. HSW   Ph: (415)476-1364
  1117   Fax: (415)476-1660
San Francisco, CA 94143-0540
E-mail: baxter@metabolic.ucsf.edu

Contact: Dr. John D. Baxter, Dir.

Desc: Investigations of metabolic and endocrine diseases, hormone action, hormone receptors, regulation of insulin release, and hormone genes, control of their expression, and their applications to medical problems such as diabetes and hypertension. Conducts a continuing program of basic and clinical research using biochemical, biophysical, physiological, and recombinant DNA methods. *Type:* Research center.

University of California, San Francisco

Reproductive Endocrinology Center

505 Parnassus Ave., HSW 1656   Ph: (415)476-4295
San Francisco, CA 94143   Fax: (415)502-7866
E-mail: robert_jaffe@quickmail.ucsf.edu

Contact: Dr. Robert B. Jaffe, Dir.

Desc: Hormonal regulation of reproductive events at the subcellular, cellular, tissular, and organismic levels. Research projects utilize a variety of species, including domestic and laboratory animals, subhuman primates, and humans. *Type:* Research center.

University of California, San Francisco

Rosalind Russell Medical Research Center for Arthritis

350 Parnassus Ave., Ste. 600   Ph: (415)476-1141
San Francisco, CA 94117   Fax: (415)476-3526
E-mail: ephraim@itsa.ucsf.edu
URL: http://medicine.ucsf.edu/divisions/rheum/

Contact: Ephraim P. Engleman, MD, Dir.

Desc: Arthritis and its probable causes, focusing on on immunology, immunogenetics, and inflammation. Examines health services and policy and educational approaches and methods for arthritis patients and health professionals. *Type:* Research center.

University of California, San Francisco

San Francisco Injury Center for Research and Prevention

San Francisco General Hospital   Ph: (415)206-4623
Department of Surgery, Ward   Fax: (415)206-5950
   3A, Box 0807
1001 Potrero Ave.
San Francisco, CA 94110
E-mail: pknudson@sfghsurg.ucsf.edu
URL: http://itsa.ucsf.edu/~sfic/index.html

Contact: M. Margaret Knudson, MD, Dir.

Desc: Expansion of knowledge in the areas of acute care for trauma victims. Current research includes studies of: cellular pathophysiology in trauma and prospective clinical trials in trauma patients. *Type:* Research center.

University of Chicago

Center for Clinical Medical Ethics

Department of Med.   Ph: (773)702-1453
5841 S. Maryland Ave.   Fax: (773)702-0090
MC 6098
Chicago, IL 60637
E-mail: mcoliner@medicine.bsd.uchicago.edu
URL: http://ccme-mac4.bsd.uchicago.edu/CCME.html

Contact: Mark Siegler, MD, Dir.

Desc: Clinical medical ethics, bioethics, technology assessment, and medical outcomes research. *Type:* Research center.

University of Chicago

Diabetes Research and Training Center

5841 S. Maryland   Ph: (773)702-6217
MC 1027   Fax: (773)834-0486
Chicago, IL 60637
E-mail: polonsky@medicine.bsd.uchicago.edu

Contact: Dr. Kenneth Polonsky, MD, Contact.

Desc: Etiology and pathogenesis of diabetes mellitus and improvement of care of diabetic patients, including studies on isolation and properties of proinsulin, proglucagon and amylin, isolation and characterization of beta cell plasma membranes, regulation of insulin biosynthesis and secretion, hyperlipidemia in diabetes, tissue culture of islet cells and cell tumors, mechanism of enzymatic conversion of proinsulin to insulin, insulin binding, degradation and action, particularly involving glucose transporters in various cells, serum proinsulin and C-peptide levels in normal and diabetic subjects, including studies of insulin of secretion and metabolism. Encourages new endeavors and provides a framework and stimulus for additional collaborative research programs among investigators of different disciplines and backgrounds. *Type:* Research center.

University of Chicago

General Clinical Research Center

5841 S. Maryland Ave.   Ph: (773)702-6980
MC 1027   Fax: (773)702-6952
Chicago, IL 60637
E-mail: vwald@medicine.bsd.uchicago.edu
URL: http://med-www.bsd.uchicago.edu/~gcrc-www/

Contact: Murray J. Favus, Dir.

Desc: Endocrinology, including insulin metabolism in health and disease, evaluation and treatment of hormonal disorders of growth and puberty, and polycystic ovary syndrome; psychiatry, including substance abuse; pharmacology; oncological research chemotherapies in the treatment of malignancies; investigations into human circadian rhythms; and genetics of diabetes, osteoporosis, and asthma. *Type:* Research center.

University of Chicago

Gwen Knapp Center for Lupus and Immunology Research

924 E. 57th St.   Ph: (773)702-4360
Chicago, IL 60637   Fax: (773)702-1576
URL: http://bsd.uchicago.edu/~gwen-knapp/
Contact: Dr. Craig Thompson, Contact.
Desc: Immunological and molecular biological research on the cause and treatment of systemic lupus erythematosus. *Type:* Research center.

University of Chicago

Inflammatory Bowel Disease Research Center

Department of Medicine   Ph: (773)702-6458
5841 S. Maryland Ave., MC   Fax: (773)702-2281
   6084
MC 6084
Chicago, IL 60637
E-mail: echang@medicine.bsd.uchicago.edu
Contact: Dr. Eugene B. Chang, Dir.
Desc: Pathophysiology and treatment of inflammatory bowel diseases, including molecular and cellular immunology, epithelial cell biology, human genetics, inflammation, therapeutic clinical trials, and clinical epidemiology. *Type:* Research center.

University of Chicago

Joseph B. Kirsner Center for the Study of Digestive Diseases

5841 S. Maryland Ave.   Ph: (773)702-9790
Chicago, IL 60637   Fax: (773)702-2182
E-mail: bhunt@medicine.bsd.uchicago.edu
Contact: Dr. Thomas Brasitus, Dir.
Desc: Gastroenterology, including colon cancer, inflammatory bowel disease, irritable bowel syndrome, disorders of the esophagus, and pancreatic cancer. *Type:* Research center.

University of Chicago

Liver Study Unit

5841 S. Maryland   Ph: (773)702-6145
MC 4076   Fax: (773)834-1288
Chicago, IL 60637
Contact: Dr. Alfred L. Baker, Dir.
Desc: Role of nutrition in avoiding or managing liver diseases and new therapeutic approaches for treatment of specific liver diseases. Provides comprehensive care for patients with liver diseases, including assessment of severity using noninvasion methods and management of chronic hepatitis patients. *Type:* Research center.

University of Chicago

Perinatal Center

5841 S. Maryland Ave.   Ph: (773)702-3733
MC 2001, Rm. B-130   Fax: (773)702-1085
Chicago, IL 60637
E-mail: amoawad@babies.bsd.uchicago.edu
Contact: Atef H. Moawad, MD, Co-Dir.
Desc: Fetal-maternal medicine, neonatology, and morbidity and mortality within perinatal medicine. *Type:* Research center.

University of Cincinnati

Cincinnati Rheumatic Disease Study Group

231 Bethesda Ave., ML 563   Ph: (513)558-4701
Cincinnati, OH 45267   Fax: (513)558-3799
Contact: Fred Finkelman, Dir.
Desc: Rheumatic and allergic diseases, including abnormalities in systemic lupus erythematosus, immunogenetics of connective tissue disease, mechanisms of tolerance and immunomodulation, and asthma pathogenesis autoimmune disease. *Type:* Research center.

University of Cincinnati

Division of Epidemiology and Biostatistics

PO Box 670183   Ph: (513)558-1410
Cincinnati, OH 45267-0183   Fax: (513)558-4838
E-mail: charles.buncher@uc.edu
URL: http://www.uc.edu
Contact: Dr. C.R. Buncher, Hd.
Desc: Epidemiologic and biostatistical research, especially in environmental, occupational, and medical fields. *Type:* Research center.

University of Cincinnati

Noyes-Giannestres Biomechanics Laboratories

College of Engineering   Ph: (513)556-4171
PO Box 210048   Fax: (513)556-4162
Cincinnati, OH 45221-0048
E-mail: ed.grood@uc.edu
Contact: Dr. Edward S. Grood, Dir.
Desc: Promotes graduate student involvement in biomechanics research, including human body dynamics, joint mechanics and kinematics, soft tissue mechanics, robotics, ergonomics, mechanical stresses in the work place, and sports medicine. *Type:* Research center.

University of Colorado

General Clinical Research Center--Adults

Health Sci. Ctr.   Ph: (303)372-8879
4200 E. 9th Ave., B-141   Fax: (303)372-8819
Denver, CO 80262
E-mail: manyikt@woolf.uhcolorado.edu
URL: http://www.uchsc.edu/ctrsinst/gcrc
Contact: Robert H. Eckel, MD, Prog.Dir.
Desc: Cardiovascular disease, connective tissue disease, dermatology, endocrinology, gastroenterology, hematology, immunology, metabolism and nutrition, nephrology, neurology, oncology, psychiatry, and pulmonary disease. *Type:* Research center.

University of Connecticut

Contraceptive Development Center

Department of Physiology   Ph: (860)679-2239
MC-3505   Fax: (860)679-1269
Farmington, CT 06030
Contact: Dr. Paul Primakoff, Contact.
Desc: The development of a birth control vaccine using sperm adhesion proteins. Also analyzing molecular mechanisms in mammalian fertilization. *Type:* Research center.

University of Florida

Center for Transplantation Biology

College of Med.   Ph: (352)392-5793
Box 100-275   Fax: (352)392-6249
Gainesville, FL 32610
Desc: Transplantation biology, including graft rejection, and immunological tolerance and disease. *Type:* Research center.

University of Florida

Craniofacial Center

JHMHC, Box 100424   Ph: (352)846-0801
Gainesville, FL 32610   Fax: (352)846-1539
E-mail: williams@dental.ufl.edu
Contact: Dr. W.N. Williams, Dir.
Desc: Studies the efficacy of specific surgical, prosthetic, and health-related professional management and therapy procedures in the early treatment of cleft palate and related craniofacial anomalies; prevention of communicative disorders in children from birth to three years; relationship between craniofacial abnormalities, speech, and hearing disorders; studies on craniofacial, cleft lip, and palate surgery; facial growth and disfigurement; psychological effects of craniofacial disfigurement; and the efficacy of a coordinated, interdisciplinary, team approach in health care delivery. Maintains records on clinical research and graduate or professional education within the three colleges. *Type:* Research center.

University of Florida

General Clinical Research Center

JHMHC, Box 100322　　　　　Ph: (352)395-0032
Gainesville, FL 32610　　　　Fax: (352)338-9843
E-mail: stacpool@gcrc.ufl.edu

Contact: Dr. Peter W. Stacpoole, Prog.Dir.

Desc: Allergy, immunology, rheumatology, cardiology, endocrinology, gastroenterology, hematology, metabolism, obstetrics and gynecology, oncology, and surgery. *Type:* Research center.

University of Florida

Health Science Center-Jacksonville

Office for Research Affairs

653 1 W. 8th St.　　　　　　Ph: (904)549-6693
Jacksonville, FL 32209　　　Fax: (904)549-6844
E-mail: paula.fuqua@jax.ufl.edu

Contact: Paul S. Fuqua, Dir.

Desc: Clinical medicine, including cardiology, obstetrics and gynecology, pediatrics, and fetal medicine. *Type:* Research center.

University Hospital of Quebec

Pavilion CHUL Research Centre

Rheumatology and Immunology Research Centre

2705, boulevard Laurier, Rm. T　Ph: (418)654-2772
1-49　　　　　　　　　　　　Fax: (418)654-2765
Ste. Foy, PQ, Canada G1V 4G2
E-mail: sec.crri@crchul.ulaval.ca

Contact: Pierre Borgeat, Dir.

Desc: Tissue damage in rheumatoid arthritis, regulation of leukotriene synthesis, arachidonic acid metabolism, regulation of antibody production, identification of major surface antigens, molecular mechanisms of neutrophil activation, effects of virus-leukocyte interactions on cell functional responses, regulation of apaptosis, MHC class II-mediated cell signaling, and importance of cellular compatibility. *Type:* Research center.

University of Houston

Biological Clocks Program

Department of Biology and　　Ph: (713)743-2652
　Biochemistry　　　　　　　Fax: (713)743-2636
Houston, TX 77204-5513
E-mail: phardin@dna.bchs.uh.edu
URL: http://www.bchs.uh.edu/research/clocks/

Contact: Prof. Paul Hardin, Contact.

Desc: Cellular and molecular clock mechanisms in animal nervous systems, including behavioral, physiological, biochemical, genetic, and molecular studies of invertebrates and vertebrates. *Type:* Research center.

University of Illinois

Health Systems Research

College of Med.　　　　　　Ph: (815)395-5639
1601 Parkview Ave.　　　　　Fax: (815)395-5602
Rockford, IL 61107
E-mail: joelc@uic.edu
URL: http://www.rockford.uic.edu/hsr.htm

Contact: Joel B. Cowen, Asst. Dean.

Desc: Community health, including primary care, public health, geriatrics, substance abuse, evaluation of delivery of health services, survey research, focus groups, demographic studies, health care planning, program evaluation, and feasibility studies. *Type:* Research center.

University of Illinois at Chicago

Center for Health Services Research

2121 W. Taylor, Rm. 211　　Ph: (312)996-1047
M/C 922　　　　　　　　　Fax: (312)996-0065
Chicago, IL 60612-7260

Contact: Judith A. Cooksey, Dir.

Desc: New health care tehnologies, medical informatics, health manpower, observation unit medicine in the hospital emergency room, and performance of preventive through tertiary healthcare delivery at the systems, program, and specific intervention levels. Studies focus on access, appropriateness, acceptibility, cost, safety, availability, effectiveness, benefits, and overall quality of healthcare. *Type:* Research center.

University of Illinois at Chicago

Craniofacial Center

811 S. Paulina, 1st Fl.　　　Ph: (312)996-7546
Chicago, IL 60612-7308　　Fax: (312)413-1157
E-mail: jwp@uic.edu

Contact: Dr. John W. Polley, Dir.

Desc: Craniofacial biology, growth, and genetics, including mechanisms of cleft palate and psychological and speech development of children with cleft palate and other craniofacial anamolies. *Type:* Research center.

University of Iowa

Center for International Rural and Environmental Health

350 International Ctr.　　　Ph: (319)335-1443
Iowa City, IA 52242　　　　Fax: (319)335-0280
E-mail: burton-kross@uiowa.edu
URL: http://www.cireh.pmeh.uiowa.edu

Contact: Dr. Burton Kross, Dir.

Desc: International rural and environmental health, including occupational exposures to pesticides, groundwater and surface water, contamination by agrichemicals, impact of occupational and social conditions on health, agricultural respiratory disease, medical and environmental health surveillance, air pollution assessment and health effects, birth defects and adverse reproductive outcomes, women's health and development, injury epidemiology and prevention, AIDS and other infectious disease epidemiology, environmental and health assessment of contaminated grain, health care delivery models and systems and location of medical and dental services in rural areas, rural aging epidemiology and care models, and the history of medicine science and public health. *Type:* Research center.

University of Iowa

Diabetes and Endocrinology Research Center

3E19 VA Hospital　　　　　Ph: (319)339-7147
Iowa City, IA 52240　　　　Fax: (319)339-7025
E-mail: rbar@icva.gov
URL: http://uiderc.icva.gov

Contact: Robert S. Bar, MD, Dir.

Desc: Mechanism of action of insulin and related hormones at the cellular level and eucaryotic gene regulation. *Type:* Research center.

University of Kentucky

Center for Reproductive Medicine

Coll. of Med.　　　　　　　Ph: (606)323-5410
Department of OB/GYN　　Fax: (606)323-1931
800 Rose St.
Lexington, KY 40536
E-mail: tecurry@pop.uky.edu

Contact: Prof. Thomas Curry, Dir.

Desc: Reproductive medicine, including artificial insemination; in-vitro fertilization; interfallopian tube transfer; ovulation; and follicular development. *Type:* Research center.

University of Lethbridge

Regional Centre for Health Promotion and Community Studies

TH322-4401 University Dr.　Ph: (403)382-7152
Lethbridge, AB, Canada T1K　Fax: (403)329-2668
　3M4
E-mail: rchpcs@uleth.ca
URL: http://home.uleth.ca/chp

Contact: Judith Kulig, Dir.

Desc: Health promotion. *Type:* Research center.

University of Louisville

Health Promotion and Wellness Center

102 C. Carmichael　　　　　Ph: (502)852-6645
Louisville, KY 40292　　　　Fax: (502)852-5711

Contact: Bryant A. Stamford, PhD, Dir.

Desc: Performs fitness analyses for county police departments, fire fighters, and commonwealth police. Also studies exercise routines. *Type:* Research center.

University of Manitoba

Diabetes Research & Treatment Centre

730 William Ave., Rm. 435　Ph: (204)789-3697
Winnipeg, MB, Canada R3E　Fax: (204)774-7751
　3J7
E-mail: ljmurph@ms.umanitoba.ca
URL:　　http://www.umanitoba.ca/faculties/medicine/
DRTC/

Contact: Dr. Liam Murphy, Dir.

Desc: Diabetes, its treatment and awareness. *Type:* Research center.

University of Manitoba

Northern Health Research Unit

Department of Community　　Ph: (204)789-3250
　Health Sciences　　　　　Fax: (204)789-3905
750 Bannatyne Ave.
Winnipeg, MB, Canada R3E
　0W3
E-mail: nhru@cc.umanitoba.ca
URL: http://www.umanitoba.ca/faculties/medicine/nhru/

Contact: John D. O'Neil, Dir.

Desc: Problems relevant to the health of Aboriginal and northern peoples in Canada. *Type:* Research center.

University of Manitoba

Rheumatic Disease Unit Research Laboratory

Health Sci. Centre, RR014　Ph: (204)787-4020
800 Sherbrook St.　　　　　Fax: (204)787-2420
Winnipeg, MB, Canada R3A
　1M4
E-mail: jawilkin@ccu.umanitoba.ca

Contact: Dr. J.A. Wilkins, Dir.

Desc: Immunoregulatory abnormalities and inflammation in rheumatic diseases. *Type:* Research center.

University of Maryland

Obesity and Diabetes Research Center

Sch. of Med.　　　　　　　Ph: (410)706-3168
10 S. Pine St., 6-00MSTF　Fax: (410)706-7540
Baltimore, MD 21201
E-mail: bchansen@aol.com

Contact: Dr. Barbara Hansen, Dir.

Desc: Basic and applied research focusing on the mechanisms underlying the metabolic and endocrine disorders associated with obesity and diabetes. Also studies hypertriglyceridemia, low HDL-cholesterol, hypertension, nephropathy, neuropathy, and therapeutic agents for treatment of diabetes. *Type:* Research center.

University of Maryland at Baltimore

Center for Studies in Reproduction

Bressler Res. Lab., Rm. 11-019   Ph: (410)706-3391
655 W. Baltimore St.   Fax: (410)706-5747
Baltimore, MD 21201
E-mail: ealbrech@umaryland.edu
URL: http://csr.umaryland.edu/

Contact: Dr. Eugene D. Albrecht, Dir.

Desc: Reproductive biology, including reproductive neuroendocrinology and cellular reproductive endocrinology, cellular endocrinology, perinatal endocrinology, fetal-placental development, uterine and ovarian physiology and biochemistry, steroid regulation of cancer, ovarian embryology and physiology, neuroendocrine regulation of peptidergic neurons, neuroendocrinology of prolactin secretion, neuroendocrinology of aging, and cancer research. *Type:* Research center.

University of Massachusetts at Worcester

Diabetes-Endocrinology Research Center

Med. Sch.   Ph: (508)856-3047
Department of Biochemistry   Fax: (508)856-6231
55 Lake Ave. N.
Worcester, MA 01655
E-mail: thomas.miller@ummed.edu

Contact: Dr. Thomas B. Miller, Jr., Dir.

Desc: Diabetes, including autoimmunity of diabetic rats (Biobreeding/Worcester variety), renin secretion of kidney, lipid metabolism, lipid and growth factor receptors, neurotensin calcium metabolism and bone disease steroid action, and steroid receptors. *Type:* Research center.

University of Medicine and Dentistry of New Jersey

Lyme Disease Center

Med. Education Bldg. 484   Ph: (732)235-7702
1 Robert Wood Johnson's Pl.   Fax: (732)235-7238
New Brunswick, NJ 08901
E-mail: sigallh@umdnj.edu

Contact: Leonard H. Sigal, MD, Dir.

Desc: Lyme disease, including epidemiology and clinical manifestations, immunopathogenesis, and the molecular biology of neurologic manifestations. *Type:* Research center.

University of Medicine and Dentistry of New Jersey

Robert Wood Johnson Medical School Clinical Research Center

1 Robert Wood Johnson Place -   Ph: (732)418-8461
   CN19   Fax: (732)418-8480
New Brunswick, NJ 08903-
   0019
E-mail: gottlieb@umdnj.edu

Contact: Alice B. Gottlieb, Contact.

Desc: Clinical and basic research in various areas of medicine. *Type:* Research center.

University of Miami

Center for Tropical and Parasitic Diseases

Med. Sch., Bldg. A   Ph: (305)243-3116
1600 NW 10th Ave.   Fax: (305)243-3117
Miami, FL 33136

Contact: Dr. Arba Ager, Dir.

Desc: All aspects of malaria, including malaria drug testing in rodents. Also conducts nutritional and chemotherapy research. *Type:* Research center.

University of Miami

Diabetes Research Institute

School of Medicine   Ph: (305)547-6657
PO Box 016960   Fax: (305)243-4404
Miami, FL 33101
URL: http://drinet.med.miami.edu

Contact: Camillo Ricordi, MD, Sci.Dir.

Desc: Etiology, pathogenesis, and treatment of diabetes mellitus, emphasizing the fundamental nature of diabetes, particularly the nature of the immunoregulatory defects that result in the destruction of the pancreatic beta cell as well as the transplantation of allogeneic and/or xenogeneic of pancreatic islets cells in insulin-deficient diabetic animals and humans. Clinical investigations include new intervention studies to prevent progression of latent insulin-dependent diabetes to clinical diseases, and studies of new insulin analogues and evaluation of procedures to quantitate high standards for care of patients with diabetes in community-based studies. *Type:* Research center.

University of Miami

Marine and Freshwater Biomedical Sciences Center

Rosenstiel Sch. of Marine &   Ph: (305)361-4738
   Atmospheric Sci.   Fax: (305)361-4001
4600 Rickenbacker Cswy.
Miami, FL 33149-1098
E-mail: dbaden@rsmas.miami.edu
URL: http://www.rsmas.miami.edu/groups/niehs.html

Contact: Daniel G. Baden, PhD, Dir.

Desc: Neurotoxicology, potent marine metabolites present in seafood, a description of a piscine model for human neurofibromatosis, environmental toxicants, fisheries models for hepatic metabolism, and development of sentinel species for xenobiotic evaluation. *Type:* Research center.

University of Michigan

Biochemical Engineering Laboratory

Dept. of Chemical Engg.   Ph: (734)763-5659
Bldg. 3324 HHDOW   Fax: (734)763-0459
Ann Arbor, MI 48109-2136
E-mail: hywang@engin.umich.edu

Contact: Dr. Henry Y. Wang, Dir.

Desc: Biochemistry and biochemical engineering, including cell culture engineering and scale-up of genetically engineered microbial products and their bioseparation. *Type:* Research center.

University of Michigan

Diabetes Research and Training Center

3920 Taubman Ctr., Box 0354   Ph: (734)936-5504
1500 E. Medical Center Dr.   Fax: (734)936-9240
Ann Arbor, MI 48109-0354

Contact: Douglas A. Greene, MD, Dir.

Desc: Diabetes, including studies on thematic foci of islet hormone secretion and action and complications of diabetes. *Type:* Research center.

University of Michigan

Endocrine Laboratory

6428 Medical Science 1   Ph: (734)764-8142
1301 Catherine   Fax: (734)936-8617
Ann Arbor, MI 48109-0617
E-mail: kmjmenon@umich.edu

Contact: Dr. K.M.J. Menon, Dir.

Desc: Problems of endocrinology, especially as it pertains to female reproduction, and development of endocrine parameters for assessing welfare of mother and fetus. *Type:* Research center.

University of Michigan

General Clinical Research Center

Univ. Hospital   Ph: (734)936-8080
A7119 Box 0108   Fax: (734)936-4024
Ann Arbor, MI 48109-0108
E-mail: pwatkins@umich.edu

Contact: Dr. Paul B. Watkins, Dir.

Desc: Multicategorical research program geared to research on humans in support of clinical studies at department or subspecialty sectional level throughout the Medical School and the Hospital. *Type:* Research center.

University of Michigan

Laboratories for Biorestoration of Oral Tissues

3310 School of Dentistry, Rm.   Ph: (734)763-3388
   3310   Fax: (734)763-5503
1101 N. University Ave.
Ann Arbor, MI 48109-1078
E-mail: ppglab@umich.edu

Contact: Martha Somerman, Contact.

Desc: Connective tissue formation and repair, focusing on identifying and characterizing proteins and genes and establishing their function during development, wound healing, and aging; the role of stem cells to bone cell function and the role of bone environment in cell metastasis. *Type:* Research center.

University of Michigan

Michigan Bone Health Study

Sch. of Public Health   Ph: (734)936-3892
Department of Epidemiology   Fax: (734)763-4552
Ann Arbor, MI 48109-2029
E-mail: mfsowers@umich.edu

Contact: Mary Fran Sowers, PhD, Chm.

Desc: Epidemiology of health and disease, including investigation of origins, nature, and interrelations of major chronic disorders, particularly cardiovascular diseases, diabetes, arthritis, chronic respiratory diseases, and cancer. Also studies biological, social, and physical variables of chronic disease, including environmental factors and stresses as observed in families, households, and other subgroups of the population. *Type:* Research center.

University of Michigan

Michigan Gastrointestinal Peptide Research Center

6520 MSRB I   Ph: (734)647-2942
1150 W. Medical Dr.   Fax: (734)763-2535
Ann Arbor, MI 48109-0682
E-mail: svigo@umich.edu
URL: http://www.med.umich.edu/mgpc

Contact: Chung Owyang, MD, Dir.

Desc: Gastroenterology, including chemistry and biology of gut hormones as they relate to the physiology and pathology of the digestive tract, liver cell differentiation, effect of nutrients on pancreatic endocrine and exocrine secretions, and neuroendocrine modulation of smooth muscle cell function and gut motility. *Type:* Research center.

University of Michigan

Multipurpose Arthritis Center

3918 Taubman Ctr.   Ph: (734)936-9539
Ann Arbor, MI 48109-0358   Fax: (734)763-1253
E-mail: nelias@umich.edu
URL: http://www.med.umich.edu/rheum

Contact: Norma S. Elias, MD, Contact.

Desc: Arthritis pilot projects include studies on ligand recognition by anti-DNA autoantibodies, function and regulation of BLC-2 proto-oncogene in T cell development, crystallographic analysis of the tyrosine phosphatase domains from a CD45-related receptor, and peptide inhibition of T cell adhesion to endothelium and extracellular matrix. Collaborates with Education, Community, and Health Services Research Division on the following research projects: problem-based ambulatory care training for primary care house officers; musculoskeletal work injury: epidemiology and disability; bone mass, body composition, and predicting osteoarthritis; musculoskeletal and physical functioning in older adults; and work injury and disability, with focus on gender, health care, and outcomes. *Type:* Research center.

University of Michigan
Orthopaedic Research Laboratories
400 N. Ingalls Bldg.   Ph: (734)763-9674
Ann Arbor, MI 48109-0486   Fax: (734)647-0003
URL: http://www.orl.med.umich.edu/orl/orl.html
Contact: Dr. S.A. Goldstein, Dir.

Desc: Applies principles of engineering to understand the musculoskeletal system, investigates orthopedic clinical problems, and develops prosthetic devices for treatment of arthritis. *Type:* Research center.

University of Michigan
Protein Folding and Stability Research Laboratory
Institute of Gerontology   Ph: (734)936-7685
300 N. Ingalls St., Rm. 947   Fax: (734)936-2116
Ann Arbor, MI 48109-2007
E-mail: arigafni@umich.edu
URL: http://www.umich.edu/~protein/
Contact: Dr. Ari Gafni, Prin. Investigator.

Desc: Mechanisms of protein folding and stability. *Type:* Research center.

University of Michigan
Pulmonary and Critical Care Medicine Division
Univ. Hospital   Ph: (734)936-5010
3916 Taubman Ctr.   Fax: (734)936-5048
Ann Arbor, MI 48109-0360
E-mail: gtoews@umich.edu
Contact: Dr. Galen B. Toews, Dir.

Desc: Pulmonary diseases and critical care, including cell biology, immunology, and biochemistry of lung and heart. *Type:* Research center.

University of Michigan
Rackham Arthritis Research Unit
Univ. of Michigan Med. Ctr.   Ph: (734)936-5566
3918 Taubman Ctr.   Fax: (734)763-1253
Ann Arbor, MI 48109-0358
E-mail: nelias@umich.edu
Contact: Norma S. Elias, MD, Contact.

Desc: Fundamental concepts of arthritis, including clinical, biochemical, and immunological aspects of various rheumatic diseases, and evaluation of therapeutic agents and surgical procedures. Studies metabolic and physiologic aspects of connective tissue, infectious agents as related to etiology and pathogenesis of connective tissues disease, biochemistry of hyperuricemia and gout, patients with other rheumatic disorders, molecular analysis of genetic bases for specific rheumatic diseases, and development of approaches to gene therapy. *Type:* Research center.

University of Michigan
Reproductive Sciences Program
300 N. Ingalls Bldg., Rm. 1123   Ph: (734)763-0248
NW   Fax: (734)936-8620
Ann Arbor, MI 48109-0404
E-mail: rmidgley@umich.edu
URL: http://www.umich.edu/~rspwww/
Contact: A. Rees Midgley, Dir.

Desc: Biological and behavioral aspects of reproduction, including clinical medicine relating to endocrinological disorders; neuroendocrine regulation of reproduction; morphological and functional studies on the hypothalmic-pituitary-gonadal axis; development of novel, nonradioactive analytical techniques; biosensors and on-line feedback control systems; biological signalling and chronobiology; neuroendocrine physiology and psychology; biochemical endrocrinology relevant to steroidogenesis and hormone action; molecular biology and gene expression; reproductive pharmacology; neurophysiological and sensory regulation of behavior; growth regulation; physical activity and its relationship to neuroendocrine function; biochemical, biological, and behavioral correlates of pregnancy; chemistry and immunology of hormones; synthesis, processing, and secretion of cellular products, including gonadotropins and extracellular matrix; calcium/calmodulin actions; and infertility research. *Type:* Research center.

University of Michigan
Specialized Center of Research in Rheumatoid Arthritis
1150 W. Medical Center Dr.   Ph: (734)763-0308
5520 DMSRB1   Fax: (734)763-8974
Ann Arbor, MI 48109-0681
E-mail: scor@medmail.umich.edu

Contact: Joseph Holoshitz, MD, Contact.

Desc: Rheumatoid arthritis, including studies in cellular and molecular biology and immunology. *Type:* Research center.

University of Michigan
Trauma Burn Center
1500 E. Medical Center Dr.   Ph: (734)936-9666
Ann Arbor, MI 48109-0033   Fax: (734)936-9657

Contact: David J. Dries, Dir.

Desc: Clinical research, standards review, and vaccine and plasma preparation to combat growth of gram negative organisms in burns. *Type:* Research center.

University of Michigan--Flint
Physical Therapy Laboratory for Cumulative Trauma Disorders
Rm. 101 LSA   Ph: (810)762-3373
Physical Therapy Dept.   Fax: (810)766-6668
Sch. of Health Professions and Studies
Flint, MI 48502-2186
E-mail: cpfalzer@umich.edu
URL: http://www.flint.umich.edu
Contact: Lucinda Pfalzer, PhD, Contact.

Desc: Cumulative Trauma Disorders (CTD's) in the workplace, particularly carpal tunnel syndrome. Also studies the biomechanical, lifestyle, psychosocial and economic factors involved in injury prevention in the work place. *Type:* Research center.

University of Minnesota
Clinical Research Center
420 Delaware St. SE   Ph: (612)626-0476
Box 504   Fax: (612)626-2456
Minneapolis, MN 55455

Contact: Dr. David M. Brown, Prog.Dir.

Desc: Human disease, including normal and abnormal physiology and biochemistry in the human being, AIDS, cystic fibrosis, organ transplantation, human growth, carbohydrate metabolism, and a broad range of other medical areas. *Type:* Research center.

University of Minnesota
Coordinating Centers for Biometric Research
Div. of Biostatistics/University   Ph: (612)626-8887
of Minnesota   Fax: (612)626-9054
2221 University Ave. SE, Ste. 200
Minneapolis, MN 55414-3080
E-mail: biostat@gopher.ccbr.umn.edu
URL: http://www.biostat.umn.edu

Contact: Thomas A. Louis, Div.Hd.

Desc: Cancer, AIDS, chronic obstructive pulmonary disease, coronary heart disease, otitis media (ear infection), and hypertension. Research activities include developing new statistical methodology; collaborating on applied projects that influence clinical, public health, and public policy; and applied and methodological research. *Type:* Research center.

University of Missouri--Columbia
Arthritis Center
MA427 Health Science Center   Ph: (573)882-8730
1 Hospital Dr.   Fax: (573)882-1380
Columbia, MO 65212
E-mail: hoffmanr@health.missouri.edu
URL: http://www.hsc.missouri.edu/arthritis
Contact: Robert W. Hoffman, DO, Dir.

Desc: Arthritis, including rheumatic disease rehabilitation, small nuclear ribonucleoprotein characterization and reactivity, depression and arthritis, genetic associations with autoantibodies in Mixed Connective Tissue Disease (MCTD) and SLE, arthritis pain, personalized exercise programs via computer for elderly, pediatric rheumatology, murine models of autoimmune disease, continuing rheumatology education for non-arthritis specialist health care providers, use of state agencies for arthritis education, use of a computerized educational videodisc to teach medical students, residents, and allied health professionals about arthritis, depression, coping strategies and stress management in rheumatoid arthritis, conditioning exercise in combination with medication for fibromyalgia. *Type:* Research center.

University of Missouri--Columbia
Cosmopolitan International Diabetes Center
Columbia, MO 65212   Ph: (573)882-3818
   Fax: (573)884-4609
E-mail: medgtg@mizzou1.missouri.edu

Contact: Dr. George Griffing, MDFAC, Interim Dir.

Desc: Hormonal control of lipolysis, glycosylated proteins, and the effect of diabetic control on vascular complications of diabetes. *Type:* Research center.

University of Missouri--Columbia
Missouri Arthritis Rehabilitation Research and Training Center
Department of Medicine   Ph: (573)882-8096
1 Hospital Dr., DC330.00   Fax: (573)884-5689
Columbia, MO 65212
E-mail: val_baker@pmr.missouri.edu
URL: http://www.hsc.missouri.edu/arthritis/

Contact: V. Baker, Contact.

Desc: Arthritis and arthritis rehabilitation, including management of depression and disability in rheumatoid arthritis. *Type:* Research center.

University of Montreal
Liver Research Group
Centre de Recherche Clinique   Ph: (514)281-2444
   Andre-Viallet   Fax: (514)281-2492
Pavillon St.-Luc
264 est, Rene-Levesque Blvd.
Montreal, PQ, Canada H2X
   1P1
E-mail: huetpm.crcav@sympatico.ca
Contact: Dr. Pierre-Michel Huet, Hd.
Desc: Physiology and physiopathology of the liver, including effects of chronic ingestion of alcohol, hepatic microcirculation in cirrhosis, drug metabolism in cirrhosis, treatment of portal hypertension, hepatic metabolism of vitamin D, liver regeneration and transplantation. *Type:* Research center.

University of Montreal
Research Centre, Hospital du Sacre-Coeur
5400, boulevard Gouin Ouest   Ph: (514)338-2172
Montreal, PQ, Canada H4J 1C5   Fax: (514)338-2694
URL: http://www.crhsc.umontreal.ca
Contact: Louis-Conrad Pelletier, Dir.
Desc: Biomedical modelling, pharmacology, and clinical studies of cardiac arrhythmias, with the aim of describing the spatial distribution of cardiac arrhythmias, their relationship to the nervous system, and their treatment by pharmacologic and noninvasive surgical methods. Centre also studies occupational respiratory diseases, biology of asthma, sleep disorders and neuropsychobiology, and molecular genetics of kidney diseases. *Type:* Research center.

University of Montreal
Sainte-Justine Hospital Research Centre
3175, chemin de la Cote-Sainte-   Ph: (514)345-4691
   Catherine   Fax: (514)345-4698
Montreal, PQ, Canada H3T
   1C5
E-mail: levye@ere.umontreal.ca
Contact: Emile Levy, Dir.
Desc: Basic and clinical research in the field of diseases of the mother and child, including cardiology and pulmonary medicine, endocrinology, biology of reproduction and development, experimental cardiovascular surgery, and gastroenterology and nutrition. Studies also include hematology-oncology, immunology, microbiology, virology, medical genetics, nephrology, and obstetrics. *Type:* Research center.

University of New Mexico
General Clinical Research Center
2211 Lomas Blvd. NE   Ph: (505)272-2366
5 E. Wing, UNMH   Fax: (505)272-0266
Albuquerque, NM 87106
E-mail: lori@gcrcds.unm.edu
Contact: Katherine M. Legoza, Prog.Mgr.
Desc: Diabetes, renal diseases, arthritis, premature infants, asthma, depression, hypertension, and pituitary tumors. Provides inpatient, outpatient, and neonatal facilities (including laboratory, dietary, and nursing support) in support of clinical research. *Type:* Research center.

University of North Carolina at Chapel Hill
Center for Health Promotion and Disease Prevention
255 Rosenau Hall   Ph: (919)966-6039
Campus Box 7400   Fax: (919)966-6264
Chapel Hill, NC 27599-7400
E-mail: across@unc.edu
Contact: Dr. Alan W. Cross, Dir.
Desc: Health promotion and disease prevention at state, regional, and national levels, focusing on cardiovascular disease, cancer, low birth weight prevention, public health and safety, health of minority youth, and health promotion in the workplace. *Type:* Research center.

University of North Carolina at Chapel Hill
General Clinical Research Center
UNC Hospital   Ph: (919)966-1435
101 Manning Dr.   Fax: (919)966-1576
CB 7600
Chapel Hill, NC 27599-7600
E-mail: epo@med.unc.edu
URL: http://www.med.unc.edu
Contact: Eugene P. Orringer, MD, Dir.
Desc: Human physiology and pharmacology, including research on growth hormone and somatomedin-C physiology, hemophilia, AIDS and other sexually transmitted diseases, stress and cardiovascular physiology, cystic fibrosis, drug metabolism and disposition in patients with hepatic and renal dysfunction, glomerular diseases, the neuropsychopharmacologic correlates of depression and other mental illnesses, cancer chemotherapy and immunotherapy, sickle cell anemia and related red blood cell diseases, and cardiac diseases such as congestive failure and arrhythmias. *Type:* Research center.

University of North Carolina at Chapel Hill
Injury Prevention Research Center
Chase Hall   Ph: (919)966-2251
Campus Box 7505   Fax: (919)966-0466
Chapel Hill, NC 27599-7505
E-mail: iprc@unc.edu
URL: http://www.sph.unc.edu/iprc/
Contact: Carol W. Runyan, PhD, Dir.
Desc: Studies the epidemiology, prevention, acute care, and rehabilitation aspects of injuries, including workplace injury, road safety, violence, childhood injury, and program development and evaluation. *Type:* Research center.

University of North Carolina at Chapel Hill
Thurston Arthritis Research Center
CB 7280, Rm. 3330   Ph: (919)966-4191
Thurston Bldg.   Fax: (919)966-1739
Chapel Hill, NC 27514-7280
E-mail: donna_knighten@med.unc.edu
URL: http://www.med.unc.edu/wrkunits/3ctrpgm/mac.we/came.htmhome
Contact: John B. Winfield, MD, Dir.
Desc: Arthritis and autoimmune disease. Laboratory research focuses on immunogenetics, immunoregulation, molecular biology, animal models, and complement studies. *Type:* Research center.

University of North Texas Health Science Center at Fort Worth
Center for Osteoporosis Prevention and Treatment
3500 Camp Bowie Blvd.   Ph: (817)735-2661
Fort Worth, TX 76107-2699   Fax: (817)735-0205
E-mail: brubin@hsc.unt.edu
Contact: Prof. Bernard Rubin, DO, Contact.
Desc: Treatment and prevention of postmenopausal osteoporosis, treatment of steroid-induced osteoporosis, and epidemiology of osteoporosis among various ethnic groups. *Type:* Research center.

University of North Texas Health Science Center at Fort Worth
Institute of Forensic Medicine
3500 Camp Bowie Blvd.   Ph: (817)735-2429
Fort Worth, TX 76107-2699   Fax: (817)735-2424
E-mail: lnancy@hsc.unt.com
Contact: Stephen L. Putthoff, DO, Dir.
Desc: Sudden death due to cardiovascular disease, sudden infant death syndrome, gunshot wounds, blunt and sharp force injuries, and forensic aspects of mass disasters. *Type:* Research center.

University of North Texas Health Science Center at Fort Worth
Wound Healing Research Institute
3500 Camp Bowie Blvd.   Ph: (817)735-2125
Fort Worth, TX 76107-2699   Fax: (817)735-2113
E-mail: ddimitri@hsc.unt.edu
Contact: S. Dan Dimitrijevich, PhD, Actg.Dir.
Desc: Biochemical, biological, physiological, and clinical aspects of tissue repair in humans and the effects of aging on wound healing. Studies include the development and character of in vitro models of human tissue (normal and pathological); the effects of hyperbaric oxygen on wound healing; the effects of aging on growth factor expression; and the role of growth factors on wound healing, cutaneous, ocular, and vascular tissues. *Type:* Research center.

University of Pennsylvania
Center for Clinical Epidemiology and Biostatistics
Sch. of Med.   Ph: (215)898-2368
824 Blockley Hall   Fax: (215)573-5315
423 Guardian Dr.
Philadelphia, PA 19104-6021
E-mail: strom@cceb.upenn.edu
URL: http://cceb.med.upenn.edu
Contact: Dr. Brian L. Strom, Dir.
Desc: Epidemiology of disease and risk factors of clinical importance, especially pharamacoepidemiology, molecular epidemiology, cancer, cardiovascular disease, renal disease, women's health, reproductive epidemiology, emergency medicine, injury, and aging. *Type:* Research center.

University of Pennsylvania
Center for Human Appearance
Medical Center   Free: 800-234-7366
Penn Tower Hotel, 10th Fl.   Fax: (215)349-5895
3400 Spruce St.
Philadelphia, PA 19104
Contact: Dr. Linton A. Whitaker, MD, Dir.
Desc: Treatment of appearance-related problems, including reconstructive and cosmetic procedures to correct aesthetic and functional problems of the face, body, and extremities resulting from birth defects, traumatic injury, and diseases such as cancer and other tumors. The Center is divided into six patient treatment sections: craniofacial, to correct severe deformities of facial areas above the jaws; dentofacial, to correct dental and bone abnormalities of the lower portion of the face; interface, to improve variations in normal facial form; aging, to correct facial, body, and skin changes caused by the aging process; body contour, to improve the appearance of various areas of the body for both medical and cosmetic reasons; and self-image, to counsel patients with body image problems. *Type:* Research center.

University of Pennsylvania
Diabetes Research Center
501 Stemmler Hall   Ph: (215)898-4365
36th & Hamilton Walk   Fax: (215)898-2178
Philadelphia, PA 19104-6015
E-mail: Pharaoh@mail.med.upenn.edu
Contact: Franz M. Matschinsky, MD, Dir.
Desc: Diabetes. Conducts basic studies on both pancreatic islet cell function and insulin action; evaluates new methods to detect and measure early signs of diabetes affecting the nervous systems, the retina, the vascular system, the heart, and the kidney; performs controlled clinical trials of new diets, drugs, and insulin-administration techniques; defines the nature of genetic susceptibility to diabetes; studies factors that increase the risk of complications in diabetes; and reevaluates the long-term benefits of kidney and pancreas transplants in diabetics. *Type:* Research center.

University of Pennsylvania

General Clinical Research Center

160 Dulles Bldg.　　　　　　　Ph: (215)662-2641
3400 Spruce St.　　　　　　　Fax: (215)662-2643
Philadelphia, PA 19104-4283
E-mail: garret@spirit.gcrc.upenn.edu
URL: http://www.gcrc.upenn.edu/
Contact: Garret A. FitzGerald, MD, Dir.
Desc: AIDS, cardiovascular research, chemical senses, chronobiology and sleep, dermatology, endocrinology, gene therapy, metabolism, neonatal medicine, neurology, oncology, psychiatry, and women and minority health issues. *Type:* Research center.

University of Pennsylvania

Pennsylvania Muscle Institute

School of Medicine　　　　　　Ph: (215)898-4017
D700 Richards Bldg.　　　　　Fax: (215)898-2653
3700 Hamelton Walk
Philadelphia, PA 19104-6083
E-mail: goldmany@mail.med.upenn.edu
URL: http://www.med.upenn.edu/~pmi
Contact: Dr. Yale E. Goldman, Dir.
Desc: Studies muscle tissue as it relates to heart disease using specialized techniques developed by the Institute, including rapid spectroscopic methods for measurement of cytoplasmic ions, electron energy loss analysis, and electron probe X-ray analysis for obtaining compositional information about cells. Serves as a regional interdisciplinary center for collaborative studies on development, molecular organization, and function of contractile and regulatory proteins and on mechanics, energetics, excitation/contraction coupling mechanism, and intracellular ion movements in cardiac, smooth, and skeletal muscle. *Type:* Research center.

University of Pittsburgh

Center for Health Law and Bioethics

Medical Arts Bldg., Ste. 300　　Ph: (412)647-5700
3708 Fifth Ave.　　　　　　　Fax: (412)647-5877
Pittsburgh, PA 15213
E-mail: bioethic@pitt.edu
URL: http://www.law.pitt.edu/mdethics
Contact: Dr. Alan Meisel, JD, Dir.
Desc: Theoretical and clinical analysis of the complex ethical issues surrounding the health care process from a multidisciplinary perspective. Research areas include ethical issues surrounding the recruitment of patients to cancer chemotherapy clinical trials, effectiveness of required request laws and policies for organ and tissue donation, quality of nursing care provided to patients with AIDS, doctor-patient communication regarding advance directives, doctor-family communication in an intensive care unit, coercion in management of psychiatric patients, and comparison of ethical issues in engineering with medical ethics issues. *Type:* Research center.

University of Pittsburgh

Cleft Palate-Craniofacial Center

School of Dental Medicine　　Ph: (412)648-8400
Pittsburgh, PA 15261　　　　Free: 800-408-7390
　　　　　　　　　　　　　　Fax: (412)648-8404
E-mail: mlm3@vms.cis.pitt.edu
URL: http://www.pitt.edu/~cleftweb
Contact: Dr. Mary L. Marazita, Dir.
Desc: Cleft palate, cleft lip, and craniofacial anomalies, including interdisciplinary, basic, clinical, genetic, embryological, and teratology studies. Also studies ear diseases, velopharyngeal valving, laryngeal characteristics and motor control for speech, computer reconstruction of nasal capsule, and anatomy of pharyngeal walls. *Type:* Research center.

University of Pittsburgh

Nutrition Biochemistry Laboratory

Grad. Sch. of Public Health　　Ph: (412)624-2020
Department of Epidemiology　　Fax: (412)624-3120
505 Parran Hall
Pittsburgh, PA 15261
E-mail: rwe2@vms.cis.pitt.edu
URL: http://www.pitt.edu/~jreii/lab
Contact: Dr. Rhobert Evans, Dir.
Desc: Etiology and treatment of chronic diseases, including study of lipids, lipoproteins, osteoporsis, diabetes, hypertension, cancer, and aging. *Type:* Research center.

University of Pittsburgh

Protein Research Laboratory

A1224 Scaife Hall　　　　　　Ph: (412)648-9632
Pittsburgh, PA 15261　　　　Fax: (412)648-2117
E-mail: fmf@pitt.edu
Contact: Dr. Frances M. Finn, Dir.
Desc: Endocrinology, including the application of avidin-biotin technology to the isolation of hormone receptors. Seeks to characterize functional domains of the insulin receptor and to identify, isolate, and characterize the receptors for the adrenocorticotrophic hormone ACTH and the hypertensive peptide angiotensin II. *Type:* Research center.

University of Puerto Rico

Arthritis Research Unit

Med. Res. Unit　　　　　　　Ph: (787)764-6839
PO Box 365067　　　　　　　Fax: (787)764-6839
San Juan, PR 00936-5067
E-mail: E_Gonzalez@rcmaca.upr.clu.edu
Contact: Dr. Esther N. Gonzalez-Pares, Dir.
Desc: Immunologic studies of collagen diseases, mainly systemic lupus erythematosus. *Type:* Research center.

University of Puerto Rico

Outpatient Unit for Clinical Research

Univ. District Hospital　　　　Ph: (787)758-2525
Puerto Rico Med. Ctr.　　　　Fax: (787)751-6242
San Juan, PR 00936
Contact: Dr. Reynold Lopez, Dir.
Desc: Parasitic and renal diseases, nutritional deficiencies, and malabsorption. Maintains a 6-bed unit where patients and subjects can be hospitalized for observation under ideal conditions for multidisciplinary clinical studies by faculty members of various departments of the School. *Type:* Research center.

University of Quebec

National Institute for Scientific Research

Armand-Frappier Institute

531 Blvd. des Prairies　　　　Ph: (450)687-5010
Case Postale 100　　　　　　Fax: (450)686-5501
Laval, PQ, Canada H7V 1B7
E-mail: michel_trudel@iaf.uquebec.ca
URL: http://198.168.44.12/
Desc: Human and animal health, including prevention of infectious diseases, virology, immunology, and applied microbiology; environmental health, including cancer epidemiology, biodegradation, professional diseases, and electromagnetism and cancer. *Type:* Research center.

University of Quebec

National Institute for Scientific Research

Armand-Frappier Institute

Epidemiology and Biostatistics Unit

531, blvd. des Prairies　　　　Ph: (514)687-5010
Laval-des-Rapides, PQ, Canada　Fax: (514)686-5501
　H7V 1B7
E-mail: Jack_Siemiatycki@iaf.uquebec.ca

Contact: Dr. Jack Siemiatycki, Dir.

Desc: Epidemiological studies on cancer and other chronic diseases. Research focuses on occupational and environmental risk factors for cancer and juvenile onset diabetes mellitus II, water quality and gastrointestinal illness, air pollution and human health, and data collection and methodological issues in statistical analysis. *Type:* Research center.

University of Quebec

National Institute for Scientific Research

Human Health Division

531, blvd. des Prairies　　　　Ph: (450)687-5010
Laval, PQ, Canada H7V 1B7　Fax: (450)686-5501
E-mail: Pierre.Talbot@iaf.uquebec.ca
URL: http://www.iaf.uquebec.ca

Contact: Dr. Pierre Talbot, Dir.

Desc: Microbiology and immunity, environmental health (epidemiology, toxicology), and molecular pharmacochemistry. *Type:* Research center.

University of Rochester

Clinical Research Center

601 Elmwood Ave.　　　　　Ph: (716)275-5295
Box MED　　　　　　　　　Fax: (716)461-4737
Rochester, NY 14642
E-mail: 74364.2371@compuserve.com
URL:　http://www.urmc.rochester.edu/smd/crc/crcweb.
html

Contact: John E. Gerich, MD, Prog.Dir.

Desc: Studies of normal and deranged tissue and organ function in humans, including endocrinology, metabolism, neurology, gastroenterology, immunology, pulmonary disease, cardiology, hematology, psychiatry, dermatology, infectious disease, oncology, and pediatrics. Functions as a resource for Medical Center faculty. *Type:* Research center.

University of Saskatchewan

Centre for Agricultural Medicine

Royal Univ. Hospital, Wing 3E　Ph: (306)966-8286
Saskatoon, SK, Canada S7N　Fax: (306)966-8799
　0W8
E-mail: dosman@sask.usask.ca
URL: http://www.usask.ca/medicine/agmedicine

Contact: James A. Dosman, MD, Dir.

Desc: Agricultural health problems, including farm accidents, lung disease, cancer, stress, skin problems, and hearing loss. *Type:* Research center.

University of Saskatchewan

Reproductive Biology Research Unit

College of Med.　　　　　　Ph: (306)966-8033
Department of Obstetrics &　Fax: (306)966-8040
　Gynecology
Royal Univ. Hospital
103 Hospital Dr.
Saskatoon, SK, Canada S7N
　0W8
E-mail: pierson@erato.usask.ca

Contact: Dr. Roger A. Pierson, Dir.

Desc: Mammalian reproduction, emphasizing human reproductive biology, fertility, infertility, contraception, and embryo transfer. Emphasizes basic and applied ovarian physiology, including superovulation. *Type:* Research center.

University of South Dakota

Department of Internal Medicine Clinical Research Office

School of Medicine   Ph: (605)333-5245
1100 S. Euclid, Ste. M427   Fax: (605)333-3175
Sioux Falls, SD 57117-5039
Contact: Edward T. Zawada, MD, Dir.

Desc: Oncology, endocrinology, hypertension, muscle disease, microbiology/virology, trace minerals, fertility, nephrology, gastroenterology, cardiology, pulmonary, critical care, geriatrics, rheumatology, and women's health. *Type:* Research center.

University of Southern California

Clinical Research Center

1975 Zonal Ave., Rm. GNH-   Ph: (213)226-4632
6602   Fax: (213)226-2796
Los Angeles, CA 90033
URL: http://www.usc.edu/hsc/gcrc/idex/html
Contact: Dr. Thomas Buchanan, Prog.Dir.

Desc: Clinical endocrinology, infectious diseases, cancer, cardiology, rheumatology, neurology, obstetrics and gynecology, surgery, pediatrics, psychiatry, and radiology, including studies on thyroid hormone metabolism, reproductive endocrinology, role of aldosterone and renin in system, growth hormone metabolism, calcium and bone metabolism, water and electrolyte metabolism, androgen metabolism, obesity, hypertension, diabetes, fasting, and neuromuscular disease. Specific research includes a study on the mechanism by which smoking and contraceptive pills combine to produce cardiovascular disease in women, and the thyroid function, association of obesity, diabetics, and hypertension in fasting and nonthyroidal illnesses. *Type:* Research center.

University of Southern California

Infectious Disease Research Laboratories

LAC-USC Medical Center   Ph: (213)226-3825
General Researcg Lab Bldg.,   Fax: (213)226-3827
   Rm. 2G4
1801 E. Marengo
Los Angeles, CA 90033
E-mail: holtom@hsc.usc.edu
Contact: Dr. Paul Holtom, Dir.

Desc: Infectious diseases, bacteriology, and miscellaneous antibiotic trials. *Type:* Research center.

University of Southern California

Institute for Health Promotion and Disease Prevention Research

1540 Alcazar St.   Ph: (213)342-2600
CHP 207   Fax: (213)342-2601
Los Angeles, CA 90033
E-mail: carljohn@hsc.usc.edu
URL: http://www.usc.edu/go/ipr
Contact: C. Anderson Johnson, PhD, Dir.

Desc: Chronic disease prevention, behavioral epidemiology, patient compliance, HIV/AIDS, and tobacco, alcohol, and other and drug abuse. Activities focus on research in health promotion and disease prevention, with young people as the principal target. *Type:* Research center.

University of Southern California

International Twin Study

1441 E. Lake Ave.   Ph: (213)764-0445
PO Box 33800   Fax: (213)764-0141
Los Angeles, CA 90033
Contact: Dr. Thomas Mack, Dir.

Desc: Epidemiologic investigation of the etiology of various chronic diseases in twins, including cancers (breast, gastrointestinal tract, and melanoma), multiple sclerosis, diabetes, and other chronic diseases. *Type:* Research center.

University of Southern California

Liver Office

7601 E. Imperial Hwy.   Ph: (562)401-8961
Downey, CA 90242   Fax: (562)401-7615
Contact: Dr. Allan G. Redeker, Chf.

Desc: Liver diseases, including both clinical and basic biochemical and virologic studies of cirrhosis and viral hepatitis. *Type:* Research center.

University of Southern California

Neonatology Research Units

1240 Mission Rd., Rm. L919   Ph: (213)226-3408
Los Angeles, CA 90033   Fax: (213)226-3440
E-mail: ramanath@hsc.usc.edu
Contact: Dr. Rangasamy Ramanathan, MD, Dir.

Desc: Clinical problems of the newborn and premature infant, including studies on neonatal jaundice, phototherapy, nutrition and energy metabolism, body composition, renal function, pulmonary function and assisted ventilation, circulation, Sudden Infant Death Syndrome, biophysical monitoring of neonates, and follow-up of motor/mental performance of high risk infants. Operates in conjunction with the Hospital's newborn service, which delivers and cares for 18,000 infants yearly; investigation of research problems is integrated with clinical care of infants and training program for physicians. *Type:* Research center.

University of Tennessee

Clinical Research Center

951 Court Ave., Rm. 326B   Ph: (901)448-5802
Memphis, TN 38163   Fax: (901)448-7608
E-mail: wapplegate@utmem.edu
Contact: William Applegate, MD, Prog.Dir.

Desc: Provides general clinical research facilities for controlled inpatient and outpatient studies on human subjects with various disorders, including sickle cell anemia, diabetes mellitus, hyperandrogenism and other endocrine disorders, kidney disease, liver disorders, hypertension, brain tumors, muscular dystrophy, obesity, metabolic bone diseases, psychiatric disorders, osteoporosis, Reye's syndrome, hirsutism, sexual disorders, reproduction problems, thyroid disorders, breast cancer, and leukemia. Also studies the physiology of hypertension and the metabolic effect of exercise. *Type:* Research center.

University of Tennessee

Division of Reproductive Endocrinology

956 Court Ave., Rm. D328   Ph: (901)448-5859
Memphis, TN 38163   Fax: (901)448-8782
E-mail: wkutteh@utmem1.utmtm.edu
Contact: Dr. William H. Kutteh, MD,PhD, Dir.

Desc: Recurrent pregnancy loss, autoimmune associated infertility, antisperm antibodies, embryonic macromanipulation, pre-implantation diagnosis, menopausal studies, human genetic biology, ectopic pregnancies, and studies of endometriosis. *Type:* Research center.

University of Texas at Arlington

Human Performance Institute

PO Box 19180   Ph: (817)273-2335
Arlington, TX 76019-0180   Fax: (817)273-2548
E-mail: gvk@hpi.uta.edu
URL: http://www-ee.uta.edu/~hpi/hpihome.html
Contact: Dr. George Kondraske, Dir.

Desc: Methods of measurement of human performance, including performance theory, human performance conceptual framework, and specialized instrumentation; studies have broad applications in the fields of space, rehabilitation, the military, and industry. Fundamental focus is on the human system-task interface. *Type:* Research center.

University of Texas at Austin

Institute of Reproductive Biology

Zoology Dept.   Ph: (512)471-3807
Patterson 28   Fax: (512)471-9651
Austin, TX 78712
Contact: Prof. Frank H. Bronson, Dir.

Desc: Studies domestic and wild animal stocks to develop fundamental principles on how environmental factors affect the nervous and endocrine systems and regulate reproduction and sexual behavior. *Type:* Research center.

University of Texas Health Science Center at San Antonio

General Clinical Research Center

7703 Floyd Curl Dr.   Ph: (210)567-4632
San Antonio, TX 78284-7877   Fax: (210)567-4651
E-mail: mundy@uthscsa.edu
URL: http://www.uthscsca.edu
Contact: Gregory R. Mundy, MD, Prog.Dir.

Desc: Metabolic disorders, oncology, endocrinology, epidemiology, infectious disease, neurology, and pharmacology. *Type:* Research center.

University of Texas--Houston Health Science Center

Center for Health Promotion Research & Development

PO Box 20186   Ph: (713)500-9601
Houston, TX 77225   Fax: (713)500-9602
E-mail: guy@utsph.sph.uth.tmc.edu
URL: http://www.utsph.sph.uth.tmc.edu/www/utsph/chprd.home.htm
Contact: Dr. Guy S. Parcel, Dir.

Desc: Health promotion research and development, with emphasis on institutional settings (worksites, medical care facilities, schools, and communities). Studies include the interaction of educational, economic, and environmental influences on health promotion, testing interventions directed toward institutions and individuals, and the innovation, diffusion, and maintenance of health promotion programs. *Type:* Research center.

University of Texas Medical Branch at Galveston

General Clinical Research Center

301 University Blvd., Rte. C31   Ph: (409)772-1950
Galveston, TX 77555-0331   Fax: (409)772-8097
E-mail: charles.stuart@utmb.edu
URL: http://www.gcrc.utmb.edu
Contact: Charles A. Stuart, MD, Prog.Dir.

Desc: Research is performed in disease-related areas including studies of sleep apnea and respiratory control; insulin action in endocrine disorders and other altered metabolic states; extensive stable isotope technology-based studies of the regulation of substrate utilization and energy expenditure in normal and diseased states; endocrinology of the gastrointestinal tract, growth disorders, regulation of hypertension, depression, and appetite control; renal function in diabetes; regulators of asthmatic responses; absorption and lipid abnormalities in cholestatic disorders; and aplastic anemia. *Type:* Research center.

University of Texas Southwestern Medical Center at Dallas

Cecil H. and Ida Green Center for Reproductive Biology Sciences

5323 Harry Hines Blvd.   Ph: (214)648-3260
Dallas, TX 75235-9051   Fax: (214)648-8683
E-mail: restab@mcdnet.swmed.edu
URL: http://www.swmed.edu/home_pages/greenctr/home.html
Contact: Dr. M. Linette Casey, Assoc.Dir.

Desc: Reproductive biology and immunology, including immigration of lymphoid cells into the uterus during the ovarian cycle and pregnancy, as well as the influences of lymphoid cell populations on placental growth and pregnancy success in rodent model systems. *Type:* Research center.

University of Texas Southwestern Medical Center at Dallas

General Clinical Research Center

5323 Harry Hines Blvd.   Ph: (214)590-7783
Dallas, TX 75235-8891   Fax: (214)590-4091
E-mail: khashayar.sakhaee@email.swmed.edu
URL: http://crcdec.swmed.edu
Contact: Khashayar Sakhaee, MD, Prog.Dir.
Desc: Calcium metabolism, cardiopulmonary system, endocrinology, liver diseases, lipid disorders, nephrology, neurology, oncology, and pharmacology. *Type:* Research center.

University of Texas Southwestern Medical Center at Dallas

Harold C. Simmons Arthritis Research Center

5323 Harry Hines Blvd.   Ph: (214)648-9110
Dallas, TX 75235-8884   Fax: (214)648-7995
E-mail: peter.lipsky@email.SWMed.edu
URL: http://www.swmed.edu/home
Contact: Peter E. Lipsky, MD, Dir.
Desc: Inflammatory arthritis. Acts as a resource facility for ankylosing spondylitis-related research. *Type:* Research center.

University of Toronto

Bone and Mineral Group

Faculty of Dentistry   Ph: (416)979-4921
124 Edward St.   Fax: (416)979-4936
Toronto, ON, Canada M5G
 1G6
E-mail: jheersche@dental.utoronto.ca
Contact: Prof. Johan N.M. Heersche, Dir.
Desc: Bone and bone mineral metabolism, focusing on age-related osteoporosis. *Type:* Research center.

University of Toronto

Centre for Health Promotion

Banting Institute   Ph: (416)978-1809
100 College St., Rm. 207   Fax: (416)971-1365
Toronto, ON, Canada M5G
 1L5
E-mail: centre.healthpromotion@utoronto.ca
URL: http://www.utoronto.ca/chp/
Contact: Dr. Irving Rootman, Dir.
Desc: Health, including tobacco research, quality of life issues, and health communication. *Type:* Research center.

University of Toronto

Centre for Health Promotion

Quality of Life Research Unit

100 College St., Ste. 511   Ph: (416)978-1102
Toronto, ON, Canada M5G   Fax: (416)946-3680
 1L5
E-mail: quality.oflife@utoronto.ca
URL: http://www.utoronto.ca/qol/unit.htm
Contact: Dennis Raphael, Co-Dir.
Desc: Quality of life, defined as factors that make living both meaningful and enjoyable, for seniors, adolescents, people with developmental disabilities, persons with physical disabilities, and adults in the general population. *Type:* Research center.

University of Toronto

Institute of Medical Science

Med. Sci. Bldg., Rm. 7213   Ph: (416)978-8886
1 King's College Circle   Fax: (416)971-2253
Toronto, ON, Canada M5S
 1A8
E-mail: dir.medscience@utoronto.ca
URL: http://library.utoronto.ca/www/ims/index.htm
Contact: Dr. Mel Silverman, Dir.
Desc: Multidisciplinary research in clinical and basic medical science and related fields. Research is focused in three distinct areas: molecular; clinical investigation of whole organ integrative biology, and clinical investigation of quantitative methodological approaches to health outcomes. *Type:* Research center.

University of Toronto

Research Services Unit

Department of Public Health   Ph: (416)978-5351
 Sciences   Fax: (416)978-8299
Toronto, ON, Canada M5S
 1A8
E-mail: vartouhi@utstat.utoronto.ca
Contact: H. Skinner, Ch.
Desc: Design and analysis of clinical trials and epidemiological studies, including biostatistics, demography, and data management and analysis. *Type:* Research center.

University of Utah

Clinical Research Center

50 N. Medicine Dr.   Ph: (801)581-6736
Salt Lake City, UT 84132   Fax: (801)581-5393
E-mail: blasalle@crc_gw.med.utah.edu
URL: http://www.crc-gw.med.utah.edu
Contact: James P. Kushner, MD, Prog.Dir.
Desc: Provides facilities for School of Medicine faculty conducting clinical investigations in the areas of renal and cardiac failure, cardiac transplantation, genetic diseases, nutrition and cancer, atherosclerosis, diabetes and obesity, psychiatric and neuromuscular disorders, disorders of intermediary metabolism (porphyrins, carbohydrates, lipids, trace elements), diseases of the endocrine system (adrenal, pituitary, gonad, thyroid, and pancreas), infectious disease, and drug therapy of human diseases. *Type:* Research center.

University of Vermont

Medical Biostatistics/Biometry Facility

27 Hills Science Bldg.   Ph: (802)656-2526
Burlington, VT 05405   Fax: (802)656-0632
E-mail: tashikag@zoo.uvm.edu
Contact: Taka Ashikaga, PhD, Dir.
Desc: Survey research of health behaviors; epidemiologic surveys for respiratory disease, cancer, and lower back pain; clinical trials; and evaluative research in the areas of public education, school health education, patient education, and health professional education. Also performs psychiatric patient follow-up studies, cancer mortality studies, studies on genetic-based disease factors, and studies of impact of acid rain on forest ecosystems. *Type:* Research center.

University of Vermont

Office of Health Promotion Research

1 S. Prospect St.   Ph: (802)656-4187
Burlington, VT 05401   Fax: (802)656-8826
E-mail: rsecktvw@zoo.uvm.edu
URL: http://www.uvm.edu/~ohpr
Contact: Roger H. Secker-Walker, MD, Dir.
Desc: Interdisciplinary research focusing on health education, smoking prevention (primarily with youth and in schools), smoking cessation, particularly in primary care physician's offices and whole communities; breast screening promotion, breast self-exam education, AIDS prevention, diabetes prevention, behavioral/lifestyle change, community-based projects, and alcohol prevention in adolescents using mass media. *Type:* Research center.

University of Virginia

Center for Research in Reproduction

UVa Health Sciences Center,   Ph: (804)924-1807
 No. 391
Charlottesville, VA 22908
URL: http://www.med.virginia.edu/medcntr/centers/crr/
Contact: Dr. John C. Marshall, Dir.
Desc: Human reproduction. *Type:* Research center.

University of Virginia

General Clinical Research Center

Sch. of Medicine   Ph: (804)982-3160
Box 410   Fax: (804)924-9960
Charlottesville, VA 22908
E-mail: pfs2h@virginia.edu
URL: http://www.gcrc.med.virginia.edu
Contact: Dr. Johannes D. Veldhuis, Dir.
Desc: Endocrinology, neurology, surgery, gastroenterology, ophthalmology, cardiology, obstetrics/gynecology, immunology, renal diseases, and ear, nose, and throat studies. Special interests include neuroendocrinology, hypertension, vascular disease, juvenile diabetes mellitus, genetic disorders, fertility disorders, digestive and growth disorders, sleep disorders, asthma and pulmonary disorders, congestive heart failure, arrhythmias, and epilepsy. *Type:* Research center.

University of Washington

Children's Hospital and Medical Center

Exstrophy of Excellence

4800 Sand Point Way NE   Ph: (206)526-2509
PO Box 5371/CH-78   Fax: (206)526-2131
Seattle, WA 98105
E-mail: mmitch@chmc.org
URL: http://www.chmc.org/departmt/surgery/exstroph/center.htm
Contact: Michael Mitchell, MD, Dir.
Desc: Cloacal or bladder exstrophy in children. *Type:* Research center.

University of Washington

Clinical Research Center

Box 356178   Ph: (206)548-4700
Seattle, WA 98195-6178   Fax: (206)548-2890
E-mail: gcrc@u.washington.edu
URL: http://www.crc.washington.edu
Contact: John D. Brunzell, MD, Prog.Dir.
Desc: Conducts a diversified research program designed to make possible precise, laboratory-type measurements of patients' disease states and their progress under various types of treatment. *Type:* Research center.

University of Washington

Diabetes Endocrinology Research Center

VA Medical Center, 358285   Ph: (206)764-2688
1660 S. Columbian Way   Fax: (206)764-2693
Seattle, WA 98108
URL: http://www.washington.edu/medical/som/som_departments/medicine/medicinepages/diabetes_index.html
Contact: Jerry P. Palmer, MD, Dir.
Desc: Diabetes Mellitus and its complications. Provides biomedical research facilities and services that are not readily available to individual investigators, including light and electron microscopy, recruitment of patient volunteers, radioimmunoassays, skin fibroblast and other cultures. *Type:* Research center.

University of Washington

Harborview Injury Prevention and Research Center

325 9th Ave., Box 359960   Ph: (206)521-1520
Seattle, WA 98104   Fax: (206)521-1562
E-mail: fpr@u.washington.edu
URL: http://weber.washington.edu/~hiprc

Contact: Frederick P. Rivara, MD, Dir.

Desc: Injury prevention and the causes and effects of injuries, including studies in epidemiology, health education, and psychology. *Type:* Research center.

University of Wisconsin--Madison

Endocrinology-Reproductive Physiology Program

R121 Animal Health &   Ph: (608)262-3222
   Biomedical Sciences Bldg.   Fax: (608)262-7420
1655 Linden Dr.
Madison, WI 53706
E-mail: erp@ahabs.wisc.edu
URL: http://www.ahabs.wisc.edu/programs/erpuw/main.html

Contact: Dr. Barry Bavister, Prog.Dir.

Desc: Reproductive biology, including ovarian function, examination of pregnancy, postpartum recovery period, regulation of testicular function as it relates to the gametogenic process, the effect of the female reproductive tract environment on the male gamete and its gametogenic process, the role of the sperm in fertilization and embryo loss, the neural, endocrinological, and related mechanisms of the sexual cycle, and cellular and molecular aspects of hormonal synthesis and action. *Type:* Research center.

University of Wisconsin--Madison

Laboratory of Genetics

445 Henry Mall   Ph: (608)262-3112
Madison, WI 53706   Fax: (608)262-2976
E-mail: mrculber@facstaff.wisc.edu
URL: http://www.wisc.edu/genetics/

Contact: Prof. Michael Culbertson, Chm.

Desc: Genetics, including molecular, human, nematode, population, microbial, behavioral, and plant genetics, cytogenetics, yeast genetics, somatic cells, immunogenetics, genetic engineering, and other areas ranging from theoretical genetics to agricultural and medical genetics. *Type:* Research center.

University of Wisconsin--Madison

Office of International Health Affairs

1760 MSC   Ph: (608)263-4150
1300 University Ave.   Fax: (608)262-2327
Madison, WI 53706
E-mail: jlladins@facstaff.wisc.edu

Contact: Dr. Judith L. Ladinsky, Dir.

Desc: Conducts and coordinates international health research, teaching, and other activities for medical students, staff, and international agencies. *Type:* Research center.

University of Wisconsin--Madison

Pulmonary and Critical Care Medicine Section

Department of Medicine   Ph: (608)263-3035
600 Highland Ave., H6/380   Fax: (608)263-3746
Madison, WI 53792-3240

Contact: Dr. James Skatrud, Section Hd.

Desc: Pulmonary physiology, occupational lung disease, and mechanisms of acute lung injury. *Type:* Research center.

University of Wisconsin--Madison

Radioimmunoassay Laboratory

Sch. of Vet. Med.   Ph: (608)263-5863
2015 Linden Dr. W   Fax: (608)263-3926
Madison, WI 53706
E-mail: brownfield@svmk.vetmed.wicwisc.edu

Contact: Prof. Mark S. Brownfield, Dir.

Desc: Performs peptide iodinations and radioimmunoassay tests of endocrinologic samples, including antiserum development and immunocytochemistry, with the potential for development of peptide and protein hormone antisera and purification and labeling of antisera. *Type:* Research center.

University of Wisconsin--Madison

State Laboratory of Hygiene

General Bacteriology Unit

465 Henry Mall, Rm. 326   Ph: (608)262-1616
Madison, WI 53706   Free: 800-442-4618
   Fax: (608)262-3257

E-mail: wjk@slh.wisc.edu
URL: http://www.slh.wisc.edu

Contact: Dr. R.H. Laessig, Dir.

Desc: Antimicrobial susceptibility studies, enteric serotyping, and culture and identification of fastidious and unusual pathogens. Provides bacteriology laboratory support for outbreak management. *Type:* Research center.

Utah Health Department

Epidemiology and Laboratory Services Division

46 Medical Dr.   Ph: (801)584-8401
Salt Lake City, UT 84112   Fax: (801)584-8486
E-mail: cbrokopp@state.ut.us
URL: http://161.119.100.19

Contact: Charles Brokopp, Dir.

Desc: Epidemiology. *Type:* Research center.

Vanderbilt Bill Wilkerson Center

1114 - 19th Ave. S.   Ph: (615)936-5000
Nashville, TN 37212   Fax: (615)936-5013
E-mail: d.wesley.grantham@vanderbilt.edu
URL: http://www.vanderbilt.edu/billwilkersoncenter/bwchome/htm/

Contact: Dr. Fred H. Bess, Dir.

Desc: Hearing science, speech science, and language science, including psychoacoustics, speech perception and production, and child language acquisition and development. Conducts clinical studies of communication disorders dealing with hearing, speech, and language in children and adults, and child language development and its assessment. *Type:* Research center.

Vanderbilt University

Clinical Research Center

21st Ave. S.   Ph: (615)343-6499
Nashville, TN 37232-2195   Fax: (615)343-8649
E-mail: david.robertson@mcmail.vanderbilt.edu
URL: http://www.mc.vanderbilt.edu/gcrc/

Contact: Dr. David Robertson, Dir.

Desc: Human physiology and diseases, including studies in medicine, neuroscience, molecular biology, pharmacology, hematology, cardiovascular diseases, genetics, obstetrics and gynecology, pediatrics, psychiatry, surgery, and psychology. Activities focus on hypertension, hypotension, arrhythmias, carcinoid syndrome, and disorders of the autonomic nervous system. *Type:* Research center.

Vanderbilt University

Diabetes Research and Training Center

Vanderbilt University Medical   Ph: (615)322-7004
   Center   Fax: (615)322-7236
707 Light Hall
Nashville, TN 37232-0615
E-mail: daryl.granner@mcmail.vanderbilt.edu
URL: http://www.vanderbilt.edu/vumc/centers/drtc

Contact: Dr. Daryl K. Granner, MD, Contact.

Desc: Strengthens and extends interdisciplinary diabetes research already under way in basic science and clinical departments at the University, including demonstration and education units for improving diabetes treatment. *Type:* Research center.

Venice Family Clinic

Venice Family Clinic
604 Rose Ave.   Ph: (310)392-8630
Venice, CA 90291

Contact: Gail Margolis, President.

Desc: Reports on news, events, programs, and activities of the Venice Family Clinic in California whose mission is "to provide affordable, accessible health care to those persons who have no other access to such care." Spotlights donors, volunteers, staff members, and others. *Type:* Newsletter.

Veterans Affairs Medical Center (Danville, IL)

Research and Development Service

1900 E. Main St.   Ph: (217)442-8000
Danville, IL 61832   Fax: (217)477-4836
E-mail: prabhudesai.mukund_m@vamcdanville.va.gov

Contact: Mukund Prabhudesai, MD, R&D Coord.

Desc: Alcoholism, rehabilitation, psychology, drugs, and nutrition. Also studies health care management and psychiatry. *Type:* Research center.

Veterans Affairs Medical Center (Martinez, CA)

Research Administration Office

150 Muir Rd.   Ph: (925)372-2000
Martinez, CA 94553   Fax: (925)372-2020
URL: http://www.va.gov

Contact: Robert Efron, MD, Assoc.Chf.

Desc: Basic and clinical biomedical research. *Type:* Research center.

Veterans Affairs Medical Center (Minneapolis, MN)

1 Veterans Dr.   Ph: (612)725-2033
Minneapolis, MN 55417-2300   Fax: (612)725-2093

Contact: Michael D. Levitt, MD, Dir.

Desc: Health services, including cooperative clinical trials, psychiatry, prostate cancer, and kidney disease. *Type:* Research center.

Veterans Affairs Medical Center (Omaha, NE)

Research and Development Service

4101 Woolworth Ave.   Ph: (402)346-8800
Omaha, NE 68105   Fax: (402)449-0604
E-mail: nowling.stephan_d@omaha.va.gov

Contact: Lynell W. Klassen, MD, Assoc.Chf.

Desc: Immunology, infectious disease, oncology, liver disease, diabetes, orthopedics, pulmonary disease, gastroenterology, and endocrinology. Utilizes rats, mice, guinea pigs, rabbits, and dogs as animal models. *Type:* Research center.

Veterans Affairs Medical Center (Palo Alto, CA)
Center for Health Care Evaluation
VA HSR&D Field Program

VA Medical Center (152)   Ph: (415)858-3996
3801 Miranda Ave.   Fax: (415)852-3420
Palo Alto, CA 94304
Contact: Dr. Rudolf Moos, Dir.

Desc: Organization and delivery of health care services; diagnostic assessment, screening, and clinical decision making; evaluation of treatments for substance abuse and psychiatric disorders; health services research methodology. Current projects involve improving diabetes outpatient care; estimating the demand for VA health care; improving HIV screening policies; developing practice guidelines for the prevention of sudden cardiac death; evaluating the effectiveness and cost-effectiveness of interventions for alcohol abuse, drug abuse, and depression. *Type:* Research center.

Veterans Affairs Medical Center (Reno, NV)
Research Service

1000 Locust St.   Ph: (702)328-1486
Reno, NV 89520   Fax: (702)328-1816
Contact: Aaron Smith, PhD, Dir. of Res.

Desc: Alzheimer's disease, bone marrow transplantation, cancer, clinical trials of investigational drugs, diabetes, geriatric rehabilitation, in utero transplantation of blood-forming cells, stress in employment, health services, and surgery. *Type:* Research center.

Veterans Affairs Medical Center (Salt Lake City, UT)
Research Service

500 Foothill Dr.   Ph: (801)584-1271
Salt Lake City, UT 84148   Fax: (801)583-9624
E-mail: straight.richard_c@salt-lake.va.gov
Contact: Richard C. Straight, PhD, Contact.

Desc: Diabetes, cancer, arthritis, aging and alcoholism, stroke and rehabilitation, dermatitis, neuroimmunological diseases, myasthenia gravis, tumors, dementia, laser medicine and surgery, herpes, genetics, cardiology, immunology, basic science, molecular biology, national cooperative drug studies, and rehabilitation research and development of artificial limbs, and clinical outcomes research. *Type:* Research center.

Veterans Affairs Medical Center (West Los Angeles, CA)
Intervention for Severe Mental Health

LA VA Med. Ctr. (116AR)   Ph: (310)794-2638
11301 Wilshire Blvd.   Fax: (310)268-4781
Los Angeles, CA 90073
URL: http://yates.coph.usf.edu/~chb/acpr.html
Contact: Dr. Robert P. Liberman, Dir.

Desc: Clinical research to improve understanding of the etiology and course of schizophrenia and treatment methods for intervention and rehabilitation of individuals diagnosed with schizophrenic disorders. Research is conducted in core laboratories, units, and projects united by a common vulnerability/stress conception of schizophrenia and guided by a multilevel study of environmental, psychological, and biological variables. *Type:* Research center.

Veterans Affairs Pittsburgh Health Care System
Research Service

University Dr. C   Ph: (412)688-6104
Pittsburgh, PA 15240   Fax: (412)688-6945
E-mail: sax.martin@pittsburgh.va.gov
Contact: Martin Sax, Res.Dir.

Desc: Oncogene expression in colon cancer, immunochemical targeting of tumors, dermatology, vascular surgery, three-dimensional structure of bacterial toxins, and transplantation. Neurosciences studies focus on epilepsy, hypertension, and schizophrenia and rehabilitation. *Type:* Research center.

Via Christi Research, Inc.

1100 N. St. Francis, Ste. 100   Ph: (316)291-4900
Wichita, KS 67214-2878   Fax: (316)291-7704
E-mail: pcgardne@via-christi.org
URL: http://www.via-christi.org
Contact: Dr. Peggy C. Gardner, Pres.

Desc: Psychiatry; phase I, II, and III clinical drug studies; orthopedic research; biomedical device and materials research and development; heart, lung, and vascular drug and device development and evaluation; technology transfer and product development; hospital operations research; and pharmacoeconomic research. *Type:* Research center.

Vincent Times

Saint Vincent
232 W. 25 St.   Ph: (814)452-5706
Erie, PA 16544
Contact: Carole W. Wunner, Editor.

Desc: Provides "up-to-date information on health care topics to residents of northwestern Pennsylvania and adjacent areas." *Type:* Newsletter.

Virginia Commonwealth University
General Clinical Research Center

Box 980155   Ph: (804)828-9228
Richmond, VA 23298   Fax: (804)828-5002
E-mail: clore@crcl.crc.vcu.edu
Contact: John N. Clore, MD, Prog.Dir.

Desc: Endocrinology, gastroenterology, infectious disease, metabolism, neurology, pediatrics, pharmacology, psychiatry, pulmonary physiology, and surgery. *Type:* Research center.

Virginia Commonwealth University
Liver Program Project

Box 980711   Ph: (804)828-5396
Richmond, VA 23298-0711   Fax: (804)828-0676
Contact: Dr. Z. Reno Vlahcevic, Proj.Dir.

Desc: Regulation of bile acid synthesis. *Type:* Research center.

Virginia Health and Human Resources Secretariat
Health Department
Epidemiology Office

1500 E. Main St.   Ph: (804)786-6029
Richmond, VA 23219   Fax: (804)786-1076
URL: http://www.vdh.state.va.us
Contact: Dr. Suzanne R. Jenkins, Act.Dir.

Desc: Epidemiology. *Type:* Research center.

Virginia Mason Research Center

1000 Seneca St.   Ph: (206)583-6525
Seattle, WA 98101-2744   Fax: (206)223-7543
URL: http://www.vmn.org/vmrc/vmrc.html
Contact: Dr. Gerald T. Nepom, Dir.

Desc: Immunology, diabetes and clinical research. *Type:* Research center.

Wake Forest University
Comparative Medicine Clinical Research Center

Sch. of Med.   Ph: (336)716-1570
Department of Comparative   Fax: (336)716-1515
  Med.
Med. Ctr. Blvd.
Winston Salem, NC 27157-
  1040
E-mail: tclarkson@cpm.bgsm.edu
URL: http://www.bgsm.edu
Contact: Prof. Thomas B. Clarkson, Contact.

Desc: Animal models of human disease studies, including research in heart disease, osteoporosis, women's health, and arteriosclerosis. Also studies relationship between aggression and low cholesterol levels. *Type:* Research center.

Wake Forest University
Pigeon Resource

Department of Comparative   Ph: (336)716-2135
  Med.   Fax: (336)716-6279
Bowman Gray Sch. of Med.
Medical Center Blvd.
Winston Salem, NC 27157-
  1040
E-mail: wwagner@bgsm.edu
Contact: Dr. W.D. Wagner, Invest.

Desc: Produces, monitors health of, and supplies pigeons for research. *Type:* Research center.

Washington University in St. Louis
General Clinical Research Center

School of Medicine   Ph: (314)362-7617
Campus Box 8071   Fax: (314)362-7989
660 S. Euclid
St. Louis, MO 63110
E-mail: cryer@visar.wustl.edu
Contact: Dr. Philip E. Cryer, Dir.

Desc: Provides clinical research facilities for faculty members of the School. *Type:* Research center.

Wayne State University
Center for Health Research

College of Nursing   Ph: (313)577-4134
5557 Cass Ave.   Fax: (313)577-5777
Detroit, MI 48202
E-mail: ajacox@cms.cc.wayne.edu
URL: http://www.comm.wayne.edu/nursing/nursing.
html
Contact: Dr. Ada Jacox, Assoc. Dean, Res.

Desc: Nursing, urban health, pain reduction in hospitalized children, adolescent health, teen pregnancy, aging, chronicity, health education and promotion (e.g. smoking cessation), community health, psychosocial oncology, health behavior, self care, stress and coping, parent/child health, family health, caregivers of aged individuals, drug use, violence and abuse, sleep patterns, risk-taking with respect to teen pregnancy and sexually transmitted diseases (including HIV), and transcultural nursing. *Type:* Research center.

Weekly Briefings on Subacute Care Regulations & Reimbursement

Opus Communications
100 Hoods Ln.   Ph: (781)639-1872
PO Box 1168   Free: 800-650-6787
Marblehead, MA 01945   Fax: (781)639-2982
E-mail: customer_service@opuscomm.com
URL: http://www.opuscomm.com; http://www.
opuscomm.com.
Contact: Suzanne Perney, Executive Editor; Margaret Dragon, Managing Editor, margaret_dragon@opuscomm.com; Jennifer I. Cofer, Publisher.

Desc: Concerned with subacute care, a type of transitional care that is less intense than acute care but more than what is available in a typical nursing home. *Type:* Newsletter.

Wesley Medical Research Institutes

3306 E. Central   Ph: (316)686-7172
Wichita, KS 67208   Fax: (316)687-0033
Contact: Dr. Sechin Cho, MD, Sci.Dir.

Desc: Maternal and fetal medicine, respiratory distress syndrome in neonates, obstetrical and gynecologic oncology, infant nutrition, genetics, sickle cell anemia, heart disease, cancer, birth defects, infertility, and hypertension. *Type:* Research center.

West Virginia University

Institute of Occupational and Environmental Health

WVU School of Medicine Ph: (304)293-3693
3801 HSC Fax: (304)293-2629
PO Box 9190
Morgantown, WV 26506-9190
E-mail: aducatma@wvu.edu
URL: http://www.hsc.wvu.edu/ioeh
Contact: Ed Doyle, MD, Dir.
Desc: Occupational and environmental health, including occupational medicine and environmental toxicology. *Type:* Research center.

The Western Pennsylvania Hospital Foundation

4818 Liberty Ave. Ph: (412)578-5153
Pittsburgh, PA 15224 Fax: (412)578-4428
E-mail: bbeisgen@msn.com
URL: http://www.WestPennHospital.com
Contact: Arlene Apfel Snyder, Pres.
Desc: Oncology, infertility, cardiology, genetics, geriatrics, pharmaceutical studies, and other health research. *Type:* Research center.

What's New in Medicine

1143 Chamberlain Hwy. Ph: (203)828-5016
Kensington, CT 06037
Contact: L.A. Chotkowski, Author/Owner.
Desc: Distributes weekly medical column containing health news and commentary. *Alt. Contact:* 1143 Chamberlain Hwy., Kensington, CT 06037; telephone: (203)828-5016. *Type:* Periodical.

Whittier Institute for Diabetes

9894 Genesee Ave. Ph: (619)450-1280
La Jolla, CA 92037 Fax: (619)535-0894
Contact: John Engle, Exec.Dir.
Desc: Diabetes and endocrinology research, including islet transplantation, CNS and pituitary function, reproductive biology, growth factor biochemistry, and angiogenesis. *Type:* Research center.

Will Rogers Pulmonary Research Laboratory

1640 Marengo St., Ste. 406 Free: 888-994-3863
Los Angeles, CA 90033-1036
E-mail: wr1@ni.net
URL: http://www.wrinstitute.org
Contact: Dr. Ronald Crystal, Dir.
Desc: Control of pulmonary circulation as it relates to gas exchange in disease and pulmonary hypoxic vasoconstriction. *Type:* Research center.

World Research Foundation

41 Bell Rock Plz. Ph: (520)284-3300
Sedona, AZ 86351-8804 Fax: (520)284-3530
E-mail: information@wrf.org
URL: http://wrf.org
Contact: Steven Ross, PhD, Pres.
Desc: Encourages and supports scientific research to evaluate the phenomenon of healing as it occurs beyond the boundaries of traditional medicine. Projects at major universities funded by the Center have included the following: the existence of a measurable healing energy, the healing potential of lucid dreaming, the positive effects of self-help groups for persons suffering from catastrophic illness, the therapeutic effects of meditation and imagery as stress reducing factors in elementary school children, suggestion and psychic healing in human surgical patients, good humor and good health, and behavioral approaches to reduce pain and nausea of cancer treatments. *Type:* Research center.

Wright State University

Cox Institute

3525 Southern Blvd. Ph: (513)873-5300
Kettering, OH 45429
Contact: D. Diane Myers, Oper.Mgr.
Desc: Myocardial infarction in coronary arteries, biomedical/biochemical applications of nuclear magnetic resonance spectroscopy and imaging, in vivo evaluation of catheter materials thrombogenicity, cerebral edema, cardiac arrest, childhood epilepsy, and cerebral ischemia. *Type:* Research center.

Yale University

Yale Liver Center

Department of Med. Ph: (203)785-4138
Internal Med. Fax: (203)785-7273
PO Box 208019
New Haven, CT 06520-8019
E-mail: James.boyer@yale.edu
URL: http://info.med.yale.edu/intmed/digdis/otherpages/livcntr.html
Contact: Dr. James Boyer, Dir.
Desc: Studies of liver structure, function, and disease; and molecular biology studies in expression of cloning of membrane transport proteins. *Type:* Research center.

Yeshiva University

Diabetes Research and Training Center

Albert Einstein College of Med. Ph: (718)430-4096
1300 Morris Park Ave. Fax: (718)430-8557
Bronx, NY 10461
E-mail: diabetes@aecom.yu.edu
URL: http://medicine.aecom.yu.edu/dc.htm
Contact: Norman Fleischer, MD, Dir.
Desc: Development and assessment of interventions focused on both primary and secondary prevention of complications of diabetes. Evaluation of innovative health professional educational materials and research instruments. *Type:* Research center.

Yeshiva University

Marion Bessin Liver Research Center

Albert Einstein College of Med. Ph: (718)430-2098
Ullman Bldg., Room 625 Fax: (718)430-8975
1300 Morris Park Ave.
Bronx, NY 10461
E-mail: shafritz@aecom.yu.edu
URL: http://www.leperl.ca.aecom.yu.edu/liver
Contact: Dr. David A. Shafritz, Dir.
Desc: Mechanisms of liver cell injury and repair, gene regulation, membrane structure/function, cirrhosis, genetic diseases, heavy metal toxicity, cellular growth control, liver progenitor cells, livery cell transplanation, somatic gene therapy, hepatitis virus infection, chronic liver diseases, and hepatic carcinogenesis. *Type:* Research center.

Medical Administration

American Academy of Medical Administrators

Research and Educational Foundation, Inc.

30555 Southfield Rd., Ste. 150 Ph: (248)540-4310
Southfield, MI 48076 Fax: (248)645-0590
E-mail: info@aameda.org
URL: http://www.aameda.org
Contact: Thomas R. O'Donovan, PhD, Contact.
Desc: Healthcare, focusing on research, education, and professional development. *Type:* Research center.

American Academy of Medical Directors

1 Urban Centre, Ste. 648 Ph: (813)287-2000
Tampa, FL 33609
Contact: Michael B. Guthrie, M.D., Pres.
Desc: Physicians with full- or part-time administrative, management, or leadership responsibilities. Acts as an educational forum exclusively for physicians to aid them in preparing for positions of organizational leadership. Serves as placement service for members seeking new locations or career opportunities. *Type:* Association.

American College of Physician Executives

4890 W. Kennedy Blvd., Ste. Ph: (813)287-2000
200 Free: 800-562-8088
Tampa, FL 33609 Fax: (813)287-8993
URL: http://www.acpe.org
Contact: Roger S. Schenke, Exec.VP.
Desc: Physicians whose primary professional responsibility is the management of health care organizations. Provides for continuing education and certification of the physician executive and the advancement and recognition of the physician executive and the profession. Offers specialized career planning, counseling, recruitment and placement services, and research and information data on physician managers. *Type:* Association.

American Medical Association

Center for Health Policy Research

515 N. State St. Ph: (312)464-5000
Chicago, IL 60610 Fax: (312)464-5849
URL: http://www.ama-assn.org
Contact: James F. Rodgers, PhD, Dir.
Desc: Research in health-related areas such as international health systems, physician payment, Medicare reform, health system reform, physician workforce, access to health care, medical practice costs, professional liability, and practice arrangements. *Type:* Research center.

Arizona State University

Western Network for Education in Health Administration

Center for Health Management Research

School of Health Administration Ph: (602)965-7778
and Policy Fax: (602)965-6654
College of Business
Tempe, AZ 85287-4506
Contact: Eugene Schneider, PhD, Dir.
Desc: New ways to organize and manage patient care, physical-organization relations, and implementation of new approaches to managing quality. *Type:* Research center.

Association of Healthcare Internal Auditors

900 Fox Valley Dr., Ste. 204 Ph: (202)429-5134
Longwood, FL 32779-2552 Fax: (202)223-4579
URL: http://www.ahia.org
Contact: Thomas A. Monahan, CAE, Exec.Dir.
Desc: Health care internal auditors and other interested individuals. Promotes cost containment and increased productivity in health care institutions through internal auditing. *Type:* Association.

Association for Health Services Research

1130 Connecticut Ave. NW, Ph: (202)223-2477
Ste. 700 Fax: (202)835-8972
Washington, DC 20036
E-mail: info@ahsr.org
URL: http://www.ahsr.org
Desc: Healthcare services, focusing on education, improvements, cooperation, funding, and development and implementation of national legislative and administrative policies. *Type:* Research center.

Baylor College of Medicine
Medical Ethics/Health Policy
1 Baylor Plaza Ph: (713)798-6290
Houston, TX 77030 Fax: (713)798-5678
E-mail: bbrody@bcm.tmc.edu
URL: http://www.tmc.edu/ethics/
Contact: Dr. Baruch Brody, Dir.
Desc: Priorities for health care services, methods of funding health care services, and social controls on health care service, including studies on ethics in clinical decision making and value issues in controlling the cost of medicine. *Type:* Research center.

Brandeis University
Institute for Health Policy
Heller Grad. Sch. Ph: (617)736-3900
415 South St. Fax: (617)736-3905
Mail Stop 035
Waltham, MA 02254-9110
E-mail: wallack2@binah.cc.brandeis.edu
URL: http://www.brandeis.edu/heller/ihp/ihp.html
Contact: Stanley S. Wallack, PhD, Exec.Dir.
Desc: Health services research and policy analysis, focusing on the design, development, implementation, and evaluation of innovative financing and delivery systems. Specific areas of research include establishing and implementing national health care expenditure limits, all-payer payment systems, an Alcohol and Drug Services Survey, the changing trends of substance abuse, financing and reimbursement of drug abuse treatment programs, and long-term care for the elderly, including home care services for the disabled elderly and cost effective models and standards for assisted living. *Type:* Research center.

Canadian Health Care Management
MPL Communications Inc.
133 Richmond St., Ste. 700 Ph: (416)869-1177
Toronto, ON, Canada M5H Fax: (416)869-0616
3M8
Contact: John Hobel, Editor.
Desc: Provides current information for health care administrators. *Type:* Newsletter.

Capitation Management Report
National Health Information, L.L.C.
PO Box 15429 Ph: (404)607-9500
Atlanta, GA 30333-0429 Free: 800-597-6300
 Fax: (404)607-0095
URL: http://www.nhionline.net.
Desc: Contains case studies, advice, and management information pertaining to capitation. *Type:* Newsletter.

Capitation Rates and Data
National Health Information, L.L.C.
PO Box 15429 Ph: (404)607-9500
Atlanta, GA 30333-0429 Free: 800-597-6300
 Fax: (404)607-0095
URL: http://www.nhionline.net.
Desc: Provides capitation rates and benchmark data pertaining to risk contracting decisions. Includes PMPM rates and performance benchmarks. *Type:* Newsletter.

Case Management Society of America
Jeanne Boling
8201 Cantrell Rd., Ste. 230 Ph: (501)225-2229
Little Rock, AR 72227-2448 Fax: (501)221-9068
E-mail: cmsa@cmsa.org
URL: http://www.cmsa.org
Contact: Jeanne Boling, Exec.Dir.
Desc: Case management and allied healthcare professionals. Offers members a voice in the future through opportunities for professional leadership and networking opportunities, case management legislative impact and visibility, publications, educational workshops, seminars, conferences, recognition and fellowship opportunities. *Type:* Association.

CCH Monitor—The Newsletter of Managed Care
CCH Inc.
2700 Lake Cook Rd. Ph: (847)267-7000
Riverwoods, IL 60015 Free: 800-449-8114
 Fax: (847)224-8299
URL: http://www.cch.com; http://www.cch.com; http://health.cch.com.
Contact: Jeffrey F. Ghent, Managing Editor; Robert Urbanek, Editor.
Desc: Provides coverage of issues facing managed care providers, with practical advice on managed care plans, including "how to" tips on compliance, coverage, and certification requirements, and analysis of legal developments affecting managed care systems. Recurring features include a calendar of events and reports of meetings. *Type:* Newsletter.

CCH State Pulse Newsletter
CCH Inc.
2700 Lake Cook Rd. Ph: (847)267-7000
Riverwoods, IL 60015 Free: 800-449-8114
 Fax: (847)224-8299
URL: http://www.cch.com
Contact: Jennifer M. Grow, Editor; Paul T. Clark, Assistant Editor.
Desc: Provides information about state health care systems. Recurring features include columns titled State Notes. *Type:* Newsletter.

Center for Research in Ambulatory Health Care Administration
104 Inverness Terr. E. Ph: (303)397-7879
Englewood, CO 80112-5306 Fax: (303)397-1827
E-mail: npiland@mgma.com
URL: http://www.mgma.com/crahca
Contact: Dr. Neill F. Piland, Res.Dir.
Desc: Health services, health economics, new management technologies, tools for effective and efficient administration of healthcare organizations, and outcomes research. *Type:* Research center.

Center for Research in Ambulatory Health Care Administration
104 Inverness Ter. E. Ph: (303)397-7879
Englewood, CO 80112-5306 Fax: (303)397-1827
E-mail: bgreen@mgma.com
URL: http://www.mgma.com
Contact: Barry R. Greene, Ph.D., VP.
Desc: Seeks to advance the art and science of medical group practice management to improve the health of our communities. Vision is to be the source of excellence and innovation as the leading association in providing quality and timely services and resources for medical practice management and leadership. Develops and advances research-based knowledge in the field of ambulatory health care by improving education, management technology, publications, and database services. *Type:* Association.

Columbia University
Center for the Study of Society and Medicine
College of Physicians & Ph: (212)305-4184
 Surgeons Fax: (212)305-6416
630 W. 168th St.
New York, NY 10032
E-mail: cssm@columbia.edu
URL: http://cpmcnet.columbia.edu/dept/cssm
Contact: Dr. David J. Rothman, Dir.
Desc: Conducts interdisciplinary research on issues that arise in clinical and research settings, including studies in bioethics and health policy. Projects include law, bioethics and medical decision making, social policy, analyses of the social history of patienthood. *Type:* Research center.

Connecticut Hospital Association
110 Barnes Rd. Ph: (203)265-7611
PO Box 90 Fax: (203)284-9318
Wallingford, CT 06492
E-mail: lynch@chime.org
URL: http://www.chime.org
Contact: Dennis May, Pres.
Desc: Hospital industry, including hospital administration, manpower development and training, quality of care, shared services and facilities, financial reimbursement, ancillary service utilization, and mental health planning. *Type:* Research center.

Cornell University
Health Benefits Research Unit
225 E. 64th St., Ste. 202 Ph: (212)888-5811
New York, NY 10021-6660 Fax: (212)888-5663
Contact: Dr. Eugene G. McCarthy, Dir.
Desc: Health benefits, including a study on whether physicians offering a second opinion concurred with the original recommendation for elective surgery and a program to identify and direct patients to ambulatory surgical facilities. Arranges appointments between patients and approximately 28,000 board certified surgeons throughout the U.S. *Type:* Research center.

Cost Control Strategies for Health Care Providers
Siefer Consultants, Inc.
PO Box 1384 Ph: (712)732-7340
Storm Lake, IA 50588 Free: 800-747-7342
E-mail: siefer@ncn.net
Contact: Steve Herron, Editor.
Desc: Designed to help heath care providers reduce costs. Discusses various topics, such as reducing facility and equipment expenses, payroll reduction ideas, purchasing efficiencies, effective management information systems, outsourcing, worker safety, quality control strategies, regulatory compliance, and improving collections. *Type:* Newsletter.

Cost Reengineering Report
National Health Information, L.L.C.
PO Box 15429 Ph: (404)607-9500
Atlanta, GA 30333-0429 Free: 800-597-6300
 Fax: (404)607-0095
URL: http://www.nhionline.net.
Desc: Contains ideas in cutting clinical and operational costs in managed care facilities. *Type:* Newsletter.

Dartmouth College
Center for Evaluative Clinical Sciences
7251 Strasenburgh Ph: (603)650-1684
Dartmouth Med. Sch. Fax: (603)650-1225
Hanover, NH 03755-3863
URL: http://www.dartmouth.edu/dms/cecs/
Contact: John E. Wennberg, Dir.
Desc: Evaluative clinical science and health care delivery, including medical care epidemiology, health policy, health behavior, efficacy of medical procedures, quality of medical and surgical care, distribution of health care resources, medical interventions and consequences for patients, care at the end of life, distribution of health care resources across hospital market areas, geriatric health, and sociology of medical organizations. *Type:* Research center.

Data Strategies and Benchmarks
National Health Information, L.L.C.
PO Box 15429 Ph: (404)607-9500
Atlanta, GA 30333-0429 Free: 800-597-6300
 Fax: (404)607-0095
URL: http://www.nhionline.net.
Desc: Provides information on how to evaluate managed care contracts, cut utilization and costs, improve quality and outcomes, and compare performance with established benchmarks. Includes clinical and financial data. *Type:* Newsletter.

Executive Solutions for Healthcare Management

Capitol Publications, Inc.
1101 King St., Ste. 444   Ph: (703)683-4100
Alexandria, VA 22314   Free: 800-655-5597
   Fax: (703)739-6517
URL: http://www.healthcarenet.com.
Contact: Amy Beth Miller, Exec.Ed.; Jeff Bukowski, Editor; Allan Fine, Senior Ed.
Desc: Provides strategies and information to assist healthcare and manged care executives. *Type:* Newsletter.

Harvard University

Division of Health Policy Research and Education

180 Longwood Ave.   Ph: (617)432-1325
Boston, MA 02115   Fax: (617)432-0173
E-mail: newhouse@hcp.med.harvard.edu
Contact: Dr. Joseph Newhouse, Dir.
Desc: Coordinates health policy resources throughout the University, including suggestion of new research initiatives, stimulation of educational activities, coordination of research and educational efforts, promotion of multidisciplinary analysis of complex health policy issues, and dissemination of health policy findings. *Type:* Research center.

Healthcare Financial Management Association

2 Westbrook Corporate   Free: 800-531-HFMA
   Financial Center, Ste. 700   Fax: (708)531-0032
Westchester, IL 60154-5700
E-mail: tarya@hfma.org
URL: http://www.hfma.org
Desc: Financial management professionals employed by hospitals and long-term care facilities, public accounting and consulting firms, insurance companies, medical groups, managed care organizations, government agencies, and other organizations. *Type:* Association.

The Health Care M&A Monthly

Irving Levin Associates, Inc.
72 Park St.   Ph: (203)966-4343
New Canaan, CT 06840   Free: 800-248-1668
   Fax: (203)966-8510
E-mail: levin@nai.net
Contact: Stephen M. Monroe, Senior Editor; Sanford B. Steerer, Editor.
Desc: Details merger activities in subsectors of the health care industry. *Type:* Newsletter.

Health Care Price Index

Price Index Communications
131 E. Anderson, Ste. B   Ph: (406)585-8111
Bozeman, MT 59715   Fax: (406)585-8247
Contact: Nicholas Zelver, Editor, nickz70718@aol.com.
Desc: Updates price changes for professional health care, hospital care, and medical drugs and equipment. *Type:* Newsletter.

Health Care Strategic Management

The Business Word
5350 S. Roslyn St., Ste. 400   Ph: (303)967-0130
Englewood, CO 80111-2125   Free: 800-328-3211
   Fax: (303)290-9025
E-mail: hcsm@businessword.com.
Contact: Donald E.L. Johnson, Publisher; Ed Egger, Managing Editor, ed.egger@businessword.com; Joel Gregg, Sales Mgr.
Desc: Discusses health care planning. *Type:* Newsletter.

Health Research Institute

3538 Torino Way   Ph: (510)676-2320
Concord, CA 94518   Fax: (510)676-2342
Contact: William E. Hembree, Dir.
Desc: Health care financing and delivery, attitudinal studies, and feasibility studies on alternative funding arrangements such as self-insuring and in-house administration, alternative delivery systems, preferred provider organizations, incentive-based medical expense accounts, and prospective-based payment systems. *Type:* Research center.

Healthcare Association of Southern California—News Briefs

Healthcare Association of Southern California (HASC)
515 S. Figueroa St., Ste. 1300   Ph: (213)538-0700
Los Angeles, CA 90071-3322   Fax: (213)629-4272
E-mail: membership@hasc.org.
Contact: Susan Schodeman, Editor.
Desc: Seeks to keep health care executives apprised of important and timely industry-related topics covered by national and local print media, covers health care trends, discusses area hospital financial matters. *Type:* Newsletter.

Healthcare Demand and Disease Management

National Health Information, L.L.C.
PO Box 15429   Ph: (404)607-9500
Atlanta, GA 30333-0429   Free: 800-597-6300
   Fax: (404)607-0095
URL: http://www.nhionline.net.
Desc: Provides in-depth case studies, practical advice, and how-to information needed to implement effective demand and disease management strategies. *Type:* Newsletter.

Healthcare Leadership Review

COR Healthcare Resources
PO Box 40959   Ph: (805)564-2177
Santa Barbara, CA 93140-0959   Fax: (805)564-2146
E-mail: corinfo@corhealth.com
Contact: Dean H. Anderson, Executive Editor.
Desc: Contains summaries of articles on health care management selected from more than 140 publications. *Type:* Newsletter.

Healthcare Management Team Letter

Health Resources Publishing
1913 Atlantic Ave., Ste. F4   Free: 800-516-4343
Manasquan, NJ 08736
E-mail: hrp@healthrespubs.com
URL: http://www.healthrespubs.com.
Contact: Robert K. Jenkins, Editor.
Desc: Alerts management teams or department heads to information that may help them in their roles as decision makers. *Type:* Newsletter.

Healthcare Practice Management News

Business Information Services, Inc.
12811 North Point Ln.   Ph: (301)604-4001
Laurel, MD 20708   Free: 800-559-8550
   Fax: (301)604-5126
E-mail: businfosvc@aol.com
Contact: James Gutman, Publisher; Russ Jackson, Editor, (310)289-8742, fax: (310)289-9628, rajla@aol.com.
Desc: Business and financial news and analysis on practice management requisitions, startups, contracts, alliances, market strategies, financing/investing, technology, and other developments. *Type:* Newsletter.

HIMSS News

Healthcare Information and Management Systems Society (HIMSS)
230 E. Ohio St., Ste. 500   Ph: (312)664-4467
Chicago, IL 60611   Fax: (312)664-6143
E-mail: himss@himss.org.
Contact: Julie Foreman, Editor; David Gabriel, Assistant editor.
Desc: Tracks developments in the health care information and management systems field. Provides latest management trends in information systems, management engineering, and telecommunications. *Type:* Newsletter.

Homecare Administrative HORIZONS

Beacon Health Corp.
12308 N. Corporate Pkwy., Ste.   Ph: (414)243-6100
   100   Free: 800-553-2041
Mequon, WI 53092-3380   Fax: (414)243-1207
E-mail: info@beaconhealth.org
Contact: Diane J. Omdahl, RN, MS, Editor-in-Chief; Susie Cadwallader, Editor.
Desc: Provides homecare agency management information on all kinds of business and personnel topics. Incorporates comprehensive how-to information, current regulatory requirements, and documentation strategies. *Type:* Newsletter.

Homecare DIRECTION

Beacon Health Corp.
12308 N. Corporate Pkwy., Ste.   Ph: (414)243-6100
   100   Free: 800-553-2041
Mequon, WI 53092-3380   Fax: (414)243-1207
E-mail: info@beaconhealth.org
Contact: Diane J. Omdahl, RN, MS, Editor-in-Chief; Susie Cadwallader, Contributing Editor.
Desc: Delivers timely regulatory information with how-to elements to apply to everyday care delivery. Equips agency patient care personnel with knowledge they need to deliver quality care and comply with medicare certification and reimbursement requirements. *Type:* Newsletter.

Hospital Case Management

American Health Consultants, Inc.
3525 Piedmont Rd., Bldg. 6,   Ph: (404)262-7436
   Ste. 400   Free: 800-688-2421
Atlanta, GA 30305   Fax: (404)262-7837
E-mail: customerservice@ahcpub.com
Desc: Provides coverage of hospital-based care planning and critical paths. Offers advice on meeting quality standards, decreasing length of stay, and controlling possible care in a facility. *Type:* Newsletter.

Hospital Payment and Information Management

American Health Consultants, Inc.
3525 Piedmont Rd., Bldg. 6,   Ph: (404)262-7436
   Ste. 400   Free: 800-688-2421
Atlanta, GA 30305   Fax: (404)262-7837
E-mail: customerservice@ahcpub.com
Contact: Kevin New, Editor, kevin.new@medec.com.
Desc: Presents information on how to cope with the DRG system, patient records issues, use of data, information systems, and medicine changes. *Type:* Newsletter.

Inside PPMCs

Atlantic Information Services, Inc.
1100 17th St. NW, No. 300   Ph: (202)775-9008
Washington, DC 20036   Free: 800-521-4323
   Fax: (202)331-9542
Contact: David McGuire, Editor.
Desc: Contains information on health issues and health industry. *Type:* Newsletter.

Institute of Pharmaco-Economics

10665 Jasper Ave., No. 710 Ph: (403)448-4881
Edmonton, AB, Canada T5J Fax: (403)448-0018
 3S9
E-mail: publications@ipe.ab.ca
URL: http://www.ipe.ab.ca/
Contact: Dr. Devidas Menon, Exec.Dir./CEO.
Desc: Results of the use of pharmaceutical products and other health care interventions as they relate to economic decision making in health care. *Type:* Research center.

Jenks Healthcare Business Report

Strafford Publications, Inc.
590 Dutch Valley Rd., NE Ph: (404)881-1141
PO Drawer 13729 Free: 800-926-7926
Atlanta, GA 30324-0729 Fax: (404)881-0074
E-mail: custserv@staffordpub.com
Contact: Jon McKenna, Executive Editor.
Desc: Previews growth strategies of managed care providers, hospitals, drug companies, and medical device manufacturers along with the latest deals in the healthcare sector and how healthcare companies are doing on Wall Street. *Type:* Newsletter.

Jenks Subacute Business Report

Strafford Publications, Inc.
590 Dutch Valley Rd., NE Ph: (404)881-1141
PO Drawer 13729 Free: 800-926-7926
Atlanta, GA 30324-0729 Fax: (404)881-0074
E-mail: custserv@staffordpub.com
Contact: Alan Jenks, Managing Editor.
Desc: Previews growth strategies of both big and small subacute providers, along with the latest deals in the subacute sector and how subacute companies are doing on Wall Street. *Type:* Newsletter.

Johns Hopkins University

Primary Care Policy Center for Underserved Populations

Department of Health Policy Ph: (410)614-2062
 and Management
451 Hampton House
624 N. Broadway
Baltimore, MD 21205
E-mail: rhurd@jhsph.edu
URL: http://www.jhsph.edu/hao/pcpc/
Contact: Dr. Barbara Starfield, Dir.
Desc: Organization, financing, and mode of delivery for primary care to underserved and vulnerable populations. *Type:* Research center.

Medical Group Management Association

104 Inverness Terr. E. Ph: (303)799-1111
Englewood, CO 80112-5306 Free: 888-608-5601
  Fax: (303)643-4439
URL: http://www.mgma.com
Contact: Thomas Adams, CAE, Contact.
Desc: Persons actively engaged in the business management of medical groups consisting of three or more physicians in medical practice with centralized business functions. *Type:* Association.

Medical Office Manager

Ardmore Publishing Company
1800 Peachtree St. NW, Ste. Ph: (404)367-1991
 335 Fax: (404)367-1995
Atlanta, GA 30355
E-mail: ardmore@mindspring.com
Contact: Susan Crawford, Editor.
Desc: Covers medical practice management, including staff management, coding, Medicare, finance, malpractice issues, marketing, and managed care. Recurring features include Interviews, news of research, notices of publications available, and columns titled ICD-9-CM and CPT Coding Update. *Type:* Newsletter.

Medical Records Briefing

Opus Communications
100 Hoods Ln. Ph: (781)639-1872
PO Box 1168 Free: 800-650-6787
Marblehead, MA 01945 Fax: (781)639-2982
E-mail: customer_service@opuscomm.com
URL: http://www.opuscomm.com
Contact: Jennifer I. Cofer, Contact, jennifer_cofer@opuscomm.com; Claudia Hoffacker, Editor, claudia_hoffacker@opuscomm.com.
Desc: Provides news and advice of interest to medical records professionals, including reimbursement, coding, legalities, regulations, and reviews. Recurring features include interviews, book reviews, and columns titled Computer Chronicle, Focus on JCAHO, Benchmarking Report, In Brief, and This Month's Idea. *Type:* Newsletter.

Medical Research Modernization Committee

3200 Morley Rd. Ph: (216)283-6702
Shaker Heights, OH 44122
E-mail: stkaufman@pol.net
URL: http://www.mrmcmed.org
Contact: Stephen R. Kaufman, MD, Contact.
Desc: Research modalities, focusing on their medical and scientific merits in order to identify outdated research methods and promote reliable and efficient methods. *Type:* Research center.

Meharry Medical College

Institute on Health Care for the Poor and Underserved

1005 D.B. Todd Blvd. Ph: (615)327-6819
Nashville, TN 37208 Free: 800-669-1267
  Fax: (615)327-6362
Contact: Dr. Amy Cato, Dir.
Desc: National and local health policies that affect the poor, including: cost of health care; federal, state, and local laws; service delivery and access thereto; bureaucratic regulations and procedures; and individual and group attitudes and behaviors. Specific topics of study include health care for the uninsured, Medicare and Medicaid reform, maternal and infant health care, economic viability of hospitals and their accessiblity by the poor, oral health care in underservedcommunities, AIDS and other debilitating diseases, and innovations in adolescent pregnancy prevention programs. *Type:* Research center.

National Association for Healthcare Recruitment

PO Box 5769 Ph: (216)867-3088
Akron, OH 44372
Contact: Karen A. Hart, Exec.Dir.
Desc: Individuals employed directly by hospitals and other health care organizations which are involved in the practice of professional health care recruitment. Promotes sound principles of professional health care recruitment. Provides financial assistance to aid members in planning and implementing regional educational programs. *Type:* Association.

National Association Medical Staff Services

631 E Butterfield, Ste. 311 Ph: (630)271-9814
Lombard, IL 60148 Fax: (630)271-0295
E-mail: namss@namss.org
URL: http://www.namss.org
Desc: Individuals involved in the management and administration of healthcare provider services. Seeks to: enhance the knowledge and experience of medical staff services professionals; promote the certification of those involved in the profession. *Type:* Association.

Northeastern University

Center for Medical Economics Studies

67 Eastern Point Blvd. Ph: (978)281-4766
Gloucester, MA 01930 Fax: (978)281-4767
E-mail: dolly321@aol.com
Contact: Dr. Harold M. Goldstein, Dir.
Desc: Health manpower, national health insurance, unionization of health workers, computerization of medical records, medical malpractice, and life care plans. *Type:* Research center.

Northport Medical Research Foundation, Inc.

PO Box 1 Ph: (516)281-1846
Middle Island, NY 11953-0001 Fax: (516)281-1846
Contact: Gerard Verbiar, Pres.
Desc: Medical research administration and investigation, cost control, and research proposal preparations, including proposal design, methodology, statistical analysis, budget preparations, scientific review, typing, duplication, final assembly, and delivery to the appropriate funding agency. *Type:* Research center.

Northwestern University

Institute for Health Services Research and Policy Studies

629 Noyes St. Ph: (847)491-5643
Evanston, IL 60208-4170 Fax: (847)491-2202
E-mail: jme352@nwu.edu
URL: http://www.nwu.edu/ihsrps
Contact: Dr. Peter P. Budetti, Dir.
Desc: Health services research and policy analysis focusing on the relationship between health care delivery systems and health outcomes, health economics, organization behavior in health, competition in the delivery of health services, physician and institutional incentives. *Type:* Research center.

Olive View-UCLA Medical Center Foundation

14445 Olive View Dr. Ph: (818)364-3686
North Annex Fax: (818)364-4584
Sylmar, CA 91342-1495
E-mail: bfroelich@aol.com
Contact: Beverly Froelich, Dir.
Desc: Community based needs assessments. *Type:* Research center.

Outpatient Reimbursement Management

American Health Consultants, Inc.
3525 Piedmont Rd., Bldg. 6, Ph: (404)262-7436
 Ste. 400 Free: 800-688-2421
Atlanta, GA 30305 Fax: (404)262-7837
E-mail: customerservice@ahcpub.com
URL: http://www.ahcpub.com.
Contact: Howard Kim, Editor.
Desc: Covers issues concerning outpatient reimbursement, including topics such as managed care, Medicare, benchmarking, APGs, billing, coding, ASCs, HCPCs, CPT-4, and ICD9-CMs. Recurring features include columns titled Sources and News Briefs. *Type:* Newsletter.

Physician Manager

Atlantic Information Services, Inc.
1100 17th St. NW, No. 300 Ph: (202)775-9008
Washington, DC 20036 Free: 800-521-4323
  Fax: (202)331-9542
Contact: Mike Carbine, Editor.
Desc: Provides management and administrative information on and for the medical/health industry. *Type:* Newsletter.

Physician Relations Advisor

American Health Consultants, Inc.

3525 Piedmont Rd., Bldg. 6,   Ph: (404)262-7436
Ste. 400   Free: 800-688-2421
Atlanta, GA 30305   Fax: (404)262-7837
E-mail: customerservice@ahcpub.com

Contact: Glen Harris.

Desc: Offers tips on such topics as promoting loyalty and goodwill to physicians, gain a competitive edge in the marketplace, recruit and retain top-notch doctors, steer clear of medical staff conflicts and related liability, and comply with regulations governing hospital-physician ties. *Type:* Newsletter.

QRC Advisor

Aspen Publishers, Inc.

200 Orchard Ridge Dr., No.   Ph: (301)417-7500
200   Free: 800-638-8437
Gaithersburg, MD 20878   Fax: (301)417-7650
E-mail: customer.service@aspenpubl.com
URL: http://www.aspenpub.com

Contact: Barbara J. Youngberg, RN, JD, Editor.

Desc: Features information on health care facilities, their patients, average costs, income loss from operations, and net income losses. *Type:* Newsletter.

Rockburn Institute

6581 Belmont Woods Rd.   Ph: (410)796-4554
Elkridge, MD 21075   Fax: (410)796-3173

Contact: Dale N. Schumacher, MD, Pres.

Desc: Health care services and effective and efficient management of health care institutions. *Type:* Research center.

Rush University

Center for Health Management Studies

Rush-Presbyterian-St. Luke's   Ph: (312)942-5402
Med. Ctr.   Fax: (312)942-4957
1653 W. Congress Pkwy.
Chicago, IL 60612-3833
E-mail: gglandon@rushu.rush.edu
URL: http://www.rushu.rush.edu

Contact: Gerald Glandon, Dir.

Desc: Health care organizations, including studies in organization and administration, organizational behavior, research design and statistics, cost containment, health economics, health care financial management, quantitative methods and epidemiology, long-term care, and information systems. *Type:* Research center.

Russ Coile's Health Trends

Aspen Publishers, Inc.

200 Orchard Ridge Dr., No.   Ph: (301)417-7500
200   Free: 800-638-8437
Gaithersburg, MD 20878   Fax: (301)417-7650
E-mail: customer.service@aspenpubl.com
URL: http://www.aspenpub.com

Contact: Allan Fine, Editor.

Desc: Provides news and information for hospital administrators seeking to negotiate contracts with HMOs, PPOs, and other managed care organizations. *Type:* Newsletter.

St. Anthony's Healthcare Resources Alert

Saint Anthony Publishing Inc.

11410 Isaac Newton Sq.   Ph: (703)904-3900
Reston, VA 20190   Free: 800-632-0123
                               Fax: (703)707-5700

Contact: Julia Stitely, Editor.

Desc: Provides information on medical records and reimbursement in the health care industry. *Type:* Newsletter.

SERVO

Association of Hospital Auxiliaries of the Province of Quebec

505, Maisonneuve W., Ste. 400 Ph: (514)282-4264
Montreal, PQ, Canada H3A   Fax: (514)282-4289
3C2

Contact: Jacqueline Boiteau, Editor; Helen Munson, Editor.

Desc: Provides news on the activities of the Association. Recurring features include President's message, a calendar of events, reports of meetings, and notices of publications available. *Type:* Newsletter.

Southern Illinois University at Carbondale

Center for Rural Health and Social Service Development

Off. of Econ. & Reg. Devel.   Ph: (618)453-1262
Mailcode 6892   Fax: (618)453-5040
Carbondale, IL 62901-6892
E-mail: psarvela@siu.edu
URL: http://www.siu.edu/~crhssd/

Contact: Paul D. Sarvela, PhD, Dir.

Desc: Health care and social service issues that impact the lives and productivity of the citizens in the state and nation, including alternative service delivery systems and policy alternatives. Studies include rural primary health care, rural safety and health promotion, and rural environmental health. *Type:* Research center.

State University of New York at Stony Brook

Center for Health Policy and Management

Stony Brook, NY 11794-8402   Ph: (516)444-3423
                               Fax: (516)444-2509
E-mail: joan.broderick@sunysb.edu
URL: http://www.uhmc.sunysb.edu/healthpol/mission.htm

Contact: Dr. Stan Altman, Dir.

Desc: Social policy regarding health care, access to care, cost efficiency of care, effectiveness of health care, health education and manpower planning and the assessment and testing of treatment protocols in New York. Same specific projects include a quality and standards analysis of information available to consumers of healthcare information in New York, including assessment of complementary and alternative medicine utilization; efficiency analyses of hospitals and nursing homes operating in New York as well as the University Hospital Department of Medicine. *Type:* Research center.

Texas A&M University

Center for Health Systems and Technology

College of Med.   Ph: (409)776-8655
Joe H. Reynolds Bldg.
College Station, TX 77843-1114

Contact: Robert Stone, MD, Dir.

Desc: Effect of technology on health care organization and economics. Also studies independent living for the elderly. *Type:* Research center.

Tulane University

Center for International Resource Development

Sch. of Public Health &   Ph: (504)584-3655
Tropical Med.   Fax: (504)584-3653
1440 Canal St., Ste. 2200
New Orleans, LA 70112
E-mail: mock@mailhost.tcs.tulane.edu
URL: http://www.tulane.edu/~sphtm/new/

Contact: Nancy Mock, Dir.

Desc: Research and evaluation of international health and development. Center conducts family planning and reproductive health projects in Africa and South and Central America, nutritional epidemiology, family planning impact evaluations worldwide, and health and human resources analysis for Africa. *Type:* Research center.

U.S. Department of Health and Human Services

Agency for Health Care Policy and Research

Office of Health Technology Assessment

6000 Exec. Blvd., Ste. 309   Ph: (301)594-4023
Rockville, MD 20852   Fax: (301)594-4030

Contact: Dr. Douglas Kanerow, Actg.Dir.

Desc: Technologies and develops Public Health Service recommendations in response to requests from agencies administering federally financed health programs such as the Health Care Financing Administration and the Civilian Health and Medical Program of the Uniformed Services (CHAMPUS). *Type:* Research center.

U.S. Department of Health and Human Services

Health Care Financing Administration

200 Independence Ave. SW   Ph: (202)690-6726
Washington, DC 20201   Fax: (202)690-6262
URL: http://www.hcfa.gov/

Contact: Nancy-Ann Min DeParle, Dir of Admin.

Desc: The Health Care Financing Administration oversees the Medicare program, a federal health insurance program for persons over 65 years of age and certain disabled persons; the Medicaid program, which supplies grants to states to provide medical services to the needy; and related federal medical care quality control staffs. *Type:* Government agency, office, or program.

U.S. Department of Health and Human Services

Health Care Financing Administration

Bureau of Program Operations

200 Independence Ave. SW   Ph: (202)690-6726
Washington, DC 20201
URL: http://www.hcfa.gov/

Contact: Steven Pelovitz, Director.

Desc: Bureau manages contractual issues with Medicare intermediaries and carriers and with the state Medicaid agencies. It approves or disapproves state Medicaid plans and establishes performance standards for contractors. *Type:* Government agency, office, or program.

U.S. Department of Health and Human Services

Health Care Financing Administration

Office of Clinical Standards and Quality

200 Independence Ave. SW   Ph: (202)690-6726
Washington, DC 20201
URL: http://www.hcfa.gov/

Contact: Peter Bouxsein, Director.

Desc: Bureau is responsible for seeing that Medicare and Medicaid beneficiaries receive the most appropriate and highest quality care available, and that it is delivered in a cost-effective manner. HCFA's regional offices monitor the states' survey and certification procedures and standards enforcement. *Type:* Government agency, office, or program.

U.S. Department of Health and Human Services

Health Care Financing Administration

Office of Delivery and Financing Research and Demonstration

Program Studies Division

2502 Oak Meadows Bldg.   Ph: (410)966-7703
6325 Security Blvd.
Baltimore, MD 21207

Contact: Carl Josephson, Dir.

Desc: Program studies. *Type:* Research center.

U.S. Department of Health and Human Services

Health Care Financing Administration

Office of Research and Demonstrations

7500 Security Blvd., Rm. C3- Ph: (410)786-6507
20-11 Fax: (410)786-6511
Baltimore, MD 21244-1850
URL: http://www.hcfa.gov/ordhp1.htm
Contact: Barbara Cooper, Dir.
Desc: Conducts and supports data collection efforts and research on health care providers, reimbursement, beneficiary behavior, and health care utilization. Comprises four groups: Research and Evaluation; Information and Methods; Planning and Policy Analysis; and Systems/Technical/Analytic Resources. *Type:* Research center.

U.S. Department of Health and Human Services

Health Care Financing Administration

Office of Research and Demonstrations

Office of State Health Reform Demonstrations

7500 Security Blvd. Ph: (410)786-6660
Mailstop C3-18-26A Fax: (410)966-5515
Baltimore, MD 21244
Contact: Sidney Trieger, Dir.
Desc: Supports, monitors, and evaluates state demonstration programs (through grants and contracts) involving the Medicare and Medicaid programs. Principal areas of research interest are Health Maintenance Organizations (HMOs), end-stage renal disease, preventive services, uninsured, state health reform, and Medicaid and Medicare reimbursement. *Type:* Research center.

U.S. Department of Health and Human Services

Health Resources and Services Administration

5600 Fishers Ln. Ph: (301)443-2086
Rockville, MD 20857
URL: http://www.dhhs.gov/hrsa/
Contact: Claude E. Fox, MD, Director.
Desc: HRSA is the principle primary health care service agency of the federal government. Its mission is to make essential primary care services accessible to the poor, uninsured, and geographically isolated--populations severely underserved by the private health care system. *Type:* Government agency, office, or program.

U.S. Department of Health and Human Services

Office of Health Policy

Economic Analysis Division

U.S. Department of Health and Ph: (202)245-1870
Human Services Fax: (202)245-6518
200 Independence Ave., S.W.,
Rm. 442E
Washington, DC 20201
Desc: Policy research and analyzes various health financing issu es, including Medicaid, Medicare and employer-sponsored health insurance. *Type:* Research center.

U.S. Department of Health and Human Services

Office of Research and Demonstrations

Beneficiary Studies Division

Research and Evaluation Group

C3-19-07 Ph: (410)786-6507
7500 Security Blvd.
Baltimore, MD 21244
Contact: Paul Eggars, Ph.D., Dir.
Desc: Designs and conducts research and evaluations to study the impacts of CHFA and other health care programs, focusing particularly on beneficiary issues. Designs and conducts general studies related to beneficiaries. *Type:* Research center.

U.S. Department of Health and Human Services

Office of Research and Demonstrations

Office of Delivery and Financing Research and Demonstration

Division of Payment Research

C3-19-26 Ph: (410)786-6588
7500 Security Blvd. Fax: (410)786-5515
Baltimore, MD 21244-1850
Contact: Leslie Greenwald, Dir.
Desc: Designs and conducts research and evaluations to study the impacts of HCFA and other health care programs, focusing particularly on payment development and refinement issues. Designs and conducts general studies related to provider payment. *Type:* Research center.

U.S. Department of Health and Human Services

Office of Research and Demonstrations

Office of Demonstrations and Evaluations

Long-Term Care Experimentation Division

C3-20-17 Ph: (410)966-6505
7500 Security Blvd. Fax: (410)966-6551
Baltimore, MD 21244
Contact: James Lubitz, Dir.
Desc: Designs and conducts research and evaluations to study the impacts of HCFA and other health care programs; Designs and conducts general studies related to health care systems; Evaluates demonstration projects, pilot projects and other innovations in HCFA programs; Designs demonstration projects, particularly related to innovative delivery systems, models for long term care and dually-eligible beneficiaries; Develops databases and evaluation methods/tools to evaluate the impact of HCFA programs; Provides technical research and evaluation related support to HCFA, HHS, and others. *Type:* Research center.

U.S. Department of Health and Human Services

Office of Research and Demonstrations

Office of Demonstrations and Evaluations

Research and Evaluation Group

C3-21-28 Ph: (410)786-6500
7500 Security Blvd. Fax: (410)786-5515
Baltimore, MD 21244
Contact: Al Esposito, Dir.
Desc: Research and Evaluation Group provides leadership and executive direction within HCFA for a wide range of health care financing research and demonstration activities. Designs and conducts research and evaluation of the health care delivery system including HCFA and other health care programs. *Type:* Research center.

U.S. Social Security Administration

6401 Security Blvd. Ph: (410)965-1234
Baltimore, MD 21235 Fax: (410)966-1463
URL: http://www.ssa.gov/
Contact: Kenneth S. Apfel, Contact.
Desc: The Social Security Administration administers a national program of contributory social insurance whereby employees, employers, and the self-employed pay contributions which are pooled in special trust funds. When earnings stop or are reduced because the worker retires, dies, or becomes disabled, monthly cash benefits are paid to partially replace the earnings that the family has lost. *Type:* Government agency, office, or program.

University of Alabama at Birmingham

Lister Hill Center for Health Policy

1665 University Blvd. Ph: (205)975-8966
330 Ryals Public Health Bldg. Fax: (205)934-3347
Birmingham, AL 35294-0022
E-mail: morrisey@uab.edu

URL: http://lhcwww.soph.uab.edu
Contact: Michael A. Morrisey, PhD, Dir.
Desc: Health policy research, focusing on health care markets and managed care, maternal and child health, management in public health organizations, and outcomes research. *Type:* Research center.

University of California, Los Angeles

Center for Health Policy Research

650 Charles E. Young Dr. S. Ph: (310)825-5491
PO Box 951772 Rm. 21-293 Fax: (310)825-5960
Los Angeles, CA 90095-1772
E-mail: chpr@admin.ph.ucla.edu
URL: http://www.healthpolicy.ucla.edu
Contact: E. Richard Brown, PhD, Dir.
Desc: Cost-effectiveness of health programs and services and their effects on health of communities and consumers; policy analysis and develops policy tools that address issues of health promotion and disease prevention. *Type:* Research center.

University of California, San Francisco

Institute for Health Policy Studies

1388 Sutter St., 11th Fl. Ph: (415)476-4921
San Francisco, CA 94109 Fax: (415)476-0705
E-mail: hluft@itsa.ucsf.edu
Contact: Harold S. Luft, Dir.
Desc: Health policy and health services. *Type:* Research center.

University of Colorado--Denver

Center for Human Investment Policy

1445 Market St., Ste. 350 Ph: (303)820-5639
Denver, CO 80202 Fax: (303)820-5656
E-mail: hn4463@hamsnet.org
Contact: Donna Garnett, Proj.Dir.
Desc: Ethical and policy issues in health care, including health care for the medically indigent, cost of care, rural health care, medical malpractice costs, prenatal care, public health, euthanasia, and the role of public opinion in policy formation. *Type:* Research center.

University of Florida

Institute for Health Policy Research

Health Science Center Ph: (352)395-8035
JHMHC, Box 100177 Fax: (352)395-8047
Gainesville, FL 32610-0177
E-mail: admin@hpe.ufl.edu
URL: http://www.hpe.ufl.edu
Contact: Prof. Michael K. Miller, Dir.
Desc: Policy research and evaluations of long-term care and aging, hospital cost controls, regulatory and administrative methods in the health sector, health economics and financing, maternal and child health, HIV/AIDS, community epidemiology, outcomes research. *Type:* Research center.

University of Kentucky

Center for Rural Health

100 Airport Gardens Rd., Ste. Ph: (606)439-3557
10 Fax: (606)436-8833
Hazard, KY 41701-9500
E-mail: ltkepfe@pop.uky.edu
URL: http://www2.mccs.uky.edu/ruralhealth
Contact: Loyd Kepferle, Interim Dir.
Desc: Rural health in Kentucky, focusing on health manpower needs, health care delivery, health care policy, and health problems unique to rural populations. Specific areas of study include assessments of new health policy, legislation, and regulation and their impact on rural health delivery, health problems among rural low-income persons and rural population needs in the areas of mental health, substance abuse and prevention. *Type:* Research center.

University of Memphis

Center for Health Services Research

437 Clement Hall   Ph: (901)678-2794
Department of Political Sci.   Fax: (901)678-2983
Memphis, TN 38152

Contact: Winsor C. Schmidt, LLM, Dir.

Desc: Health services research, including health administration, health utilization and access, health finance, health policy and law, guardianship, medical malpractice, mental health policy and law, health ethics, research methodology in health services research, and health decision making. Specific research activities focus on the differential economic impact of infectious diseases among children in various child care settings, physician and incident-specific characteristics that predict medical malpractice claims and lawsuits, and the impact of statutory criteria on civil commitment. *Type:* Research center.

University of Minnesota

Division of Health Services Research and Policy

Box 729 Mayo   Ph: (612)624-6151
420 Delaware St. SE   Fax: (612)624-2196
Minneapolis, MN 55455
E-mail: krale001@maroon.tc.umn.edu
URL: http://www.hsr.umn.edu

Contact: Dr. John E. Kralewski, Div.Hd.

Desc: Long-term care, health insurance, managed health care, patient care outcomes, rural health services, and health policy analysis. *Type:* Research center.

University of Missouri--Kansas City

National Center for Managed Health Care Administration

Bloch 214   Ph: (816)235-1489
5100 Rockhill Rd.   Fax: (816)235-2351
Kansas City, MO 64110-2499
URL: http://www.umkc.edu/mhc

Contact: Michael Wood, Contact.

Desc: Management training for the managed health care industry in the United States and abroad. *Type:* Research center.

University of Texas--Houston Health Science Center

Health Policy Institute

1200 Hermann Pressler, Ste.   Ph: (713)500-9485
901   Fax: (713)500-9493
PO Box 20186
Houston, TX 77225
E-mail: dlow@admin4.hsc.uth.tmc.edu
URL: http://www.sph.uth.tmc.edu/ctr/hpi/hpi.htm

Contact: Dr. M. David Low, Pres.

Desc: Health policy issues at the local, state, national, and international level, including cost, access, and quality of health care. *Type:* Research center.

University of Virginia

Virginia Health Policy Center

Health Sciences Center   Ph: (804)979-6122
Box 413   Fax: (804)979-3830
Charlottesville, VA 22908
E-mail: sar4n@virginia.edu
URL: http://www.virginia.edu/~vhpc/home.html

Contact: Stevenson Richardson, Admin.

Desc: A multidisciplinary, university-wide center devoted to the study of policy and values issues in contemporary health care. *Type:* Research center.

University of Waterloo

Centre for Applied Health Research

Faculty of Applied Health   Ph: (519)885-1211
Science   Fax: (519)885-2694
Burt Matthews Hall
Waterloo, ON, Canada N2L
3G1
E-mail: cahr@healthy.uwaterloo.ca
URL: http://www.ahs.uwaterloo.ca

Contact: Dr. Michael Sharratt, Dir.

Desc: Research conducted through several centers: Murray Alzheimer Research and Education Program; Health Behaviour Research Group; Functional Independence for Seniors; Program Training and Consultation Centre; and Ergonomics and Safety Consulting Services. *Type:* Research center.

University of Wisconsin--Madison

Center for Health Systems Research and Analysis

WARF Bldg., Rm. 1163   Ph: (608)263-4875
610 Walnut St.   Fax: (608)263-4523
Madison, WI 53705-2397
E-mail: davidz@chsra.wic.edu
URL: http://www.chsra.wisc.edu

Contact: Dr. David R. Zimmerman, Dir.

Desc: Five major research areas: quality assessment and improvement, long term care, public health policy and program evaluation, consumer decision making, and patient education and support. *Type:* Research center.

University of Wisconsin--Madison

Wisconsin Network for Health Policy Research

610 Walnut St.
Madison, WI 53705
E-mail: jaknutso@facstaff.wisc.edu
URL: http://www.biostat.wisc.edu/prevmed/network

Contact: David A. Kindig, MD, Dir.

Desc: Health policy. *Type:* Research center.

Vantage Point

Clinical Laboratory Management Association
989 Old Eagle School Rd., Ste.   Ph: (610)995-9580
815   Free: 800-247-9580
Wayne, PA 19087-1704   Fax: (610)995-9568
URL: http://www.clma.org.

Contact: Beth Barrow, Editor, bbarrow@clma.org.

Desc: Features general, health care, and laboratory management tips, trends, and legislative news. Recurring features include news of educational opportunities, job listings, and columns titled Manager's Workshop, Healthcare Management Briefs, Career Corner, Online Update and Legislative Update. *Type:* Newsletter.

West Virginia University

Office of Health Services Research

Health Sci. S.   Ph: (304)293-2601
PO Box 9145   Fax: (304)293-6685
Morgantown, WV 26506-9145
E-mail: cpollard@wvu.edu

Contact: Cecil Pollard, Dir.

Desc: Health services research, manpower studies, resource allocation, demography, and computer technology support. *Type:* Research center.

Your Health Style

Your HealthStyle, Inc.
2525 NW Expressway St., Ste.   Ph: (405)843-4310
202   Free: 800-214-1156
Oklahoma City, OK 73112-   Fax: (405)843-1265
7200
E-mail: yhs@oklahoma.net

Contact: Cindy Sheffield, Editor.

Desc: Discusses health and wellness issues. Designed to promote positive changes resulting in healthier lifestyles. *Type:* Newsletter.

Medical Education

Accreditation Council for Graduate Medical Education

515 N. State St., Ste. 2000   Ph: (312)464-4920
Chicago, IL 60610   Fax: (312)464-4098
URL: http://www.acgme.org

Contact: David C. Leach, M.D., Exec. Dir.

Desc: Representatives from the American Board of Medical Specialties, American Hospital Association, American Medical Association, Association of American Medical Colleges, and Council of Medical Specialty Societies . Accredits postgraduate medical education programs; recommends and conducts studies aimed at improving programs in postgraduate medical education; reviews and approves proposals for new programs in graduate medical education; provides information to the public and government relating to the evaluation and accreditation of graduate medical education programs. Maintains 25 residency review committees including: Allergy and Immunology; Anesthesiology; Colon and Rectal Surgery; Dermatology. *Type:* Association.

American Medical Student Association

1902 Association Dr.   Ph: (703)620-6600
Reston, VA 20191   Free: 800-767-2266
   Fax: (703)620-5873
URL: http://www.amsa.org

Contact: Paul R. Wright, Exec.Dir.

Desc: Medical students; local, state, and national organizations; premedical students, interns, and residents. Seeks to improve medical education by making it relevant to today's needs and by making the process by which physicians are trained more humanistic. Contributes to the improvement of health care of all people; involves its members in the social, moral, and ethical obligations of the profession of medicine. *Type:* Association.

Association of American Medical Colleges

2450 N St. NW   Ph: (202)828-0400
Washington, DC 20037   Fax: (202)828-1125
E-mail: amcas@aamc.org
URL: http://www.aamc.org

Contact: Jordan J. Cohen, M.D., Pres.

Desc: Medical schools, graduate affiliate medical colleges, academic societies, teaching hospitals, and individuals interested in the advancement of medical education, biomedical research, and healthcare. Provides centralized application service. Offers management education program for medical school deans, teaching hospital directors, department chairmen, and service chiefs of affiliated hospitals. *Type:* Association.

Association of University Programs in Health Administration

1110 Vermont Ave., NW, Ste.   Ph: (703)524-5500
220   Fax: (703)525-4791
Washington, DC 20005-3500

Contact: Henry Fernandez, CEO.

Desc: Universities offering graduate and undergraduate study in health services and hospital administration. To improve the quality of education in health services administration. *Type:* Association.

Health Occupations Students of America

6021 Morriss Rd., Ste. 110   Free: 800-321-HOSA
Flower Mound, TX 75028-3762   Fax: (972)506-9919

Contact: Dr. Jim Koeninger, Exec.Dir.

Desc: Secondary and postsecondary students enrolled in health occupations education programs; health professionals and others interested in assisting and supporting the activities of HOSA; alumni of health occupations education programs and individuals who have made significant contributions to the field. Primary aim is to improve the quality of healthcare for all Americans by urging members to develop self-improvement skills. *Type:* Association.

National Association for Practical Nurse Education and Service

1400 Spring St., Ste. 330	Ph: (301)588-2491
Silver Spring, MD 20910	Fax: (301)588-2839

E-mail: napnes@bellatlantic.net

Contact: John H. Word, Exec.Dir.

Desc: Licensed practical/vocational nurses, registered nurses, physicians, hospital and nursing home administrators, and interested others. Provides consultation service to advise schools wishing to develop a practical/vocational nursing program on facilities, equipment, policies, curriculum, and staffing. Promotes recruitment of students through preparation and distribution of recruitment materials. *Type:* Association.

National Student Nurses' Association

555 W. 57th St., Ste. 1327	Ph: (212)581-2211
New York, NY 10019	Fax: (212)581-2368

E-mail: nsna@nsna.org

URL: http://www.nsna.org

Contact: Diane J. Mancino, Ed.D., RN CAE, Exec. Dir.

Desc: Students enrolled in state-approved schools for the preparation of registered nurses. Seeks to aid in the development of the individual nursing student and to urge students of nursing, as future health professionals, to be aware of and to contribute to improving the health care of all people. *Type:* Association.

Society of Teachers of Family Medicine

8880 Ward Pky.	Ph: (816)333-9700
Kansas City, MO 64114	Free: 800-274-2237
	Fax: (816)333-3884

E-mail: admstaff@stfm.org

URL: http://www.stfm.org

Contact: Roger A. Sherwood, CAE, Exec.Dir.

Desc: Physicians involved in teaching or promoting family medicine; individuals in related fields. Organized to promote public welfare by maintaining and improving standards and practices of medical service, especially in the field of family medicine. *Type:* Association.

Medical Technology

Association for the Advancement of Medical Instrumentation—Membership Directory

Association for the Advancement of Medical Instrumentation

3330 Washington Blvd., Ste.	Ph: (703)525-4890
400	Free: 800-332-2264
Arlington, VA 22201-4598	Fax: (703)276-0793

E-mail: publications@aami.org; membership@aami.org.

URL: http://www.aami.org.

Desc: 6,500 physicians, clinical engineers, biomedical engineers and technicians, nurses, researchers, and medical equipment manufacturers. *Type:* Directory.

Directory of Medical Computer Systems

ComputerTalk Associates, Inc.

492 Norristown Rd., Ste. 160	Ph: (610)825-7686
Blue Bell, PA 19422-2355	Fax: (610)825-7641

URL: http://www.computertalk.com.

Contact: Neil R. Bauman, Editor, nb@computertalk.com.

Desc: About 100 medical office data processing system suppliers. All listings are paid. *Type:* Directory.

Medicine

Alpha Epsilon Delta

Office of Career Planning and Placement

University of Virginia	Ph: (804)924-0311
Garrett Hall of Medicine	Fax: (804)924-8907
McCormick Rd.	
Charlottesville, VA 22903	

Contact: Dr. Thomas Pearce, Pres.

Desc: Honor society of men and women in the field of pre-medical study. *Type:* Association.

Alpha Omega Alpha Honor Medical Society

525 Middlefield Rd., Ste. 130	Ph: (650)329-0291
Menlo Park, CA 94025	Fax: (650)329-1618

E-mail: eharris@alphaomegaalpha.org

URL: http://www.pharos.org

Contact: Edward D. Harris, Jr., Exec.Sec.

Desc: Honor society for men and women studying medicine at graduate and postgraduate levels. Sponsors "Leaders in American Medicine" videotape series; underwrites visiting professorships. *Type:* Association.

Barron's Guide to Medical and Dental Schools

Barron's Educational Series, Inc.

250 Wireless Blvd.	Ph: (516)434-3311
Hauppauge, NY 11788	Free: 800-645-3476
	Fax: (516)434-3723

E-mail: info@barronseduc.com; barrons269@aol.com.

URL: http://www.barronseduc.com

Contact: Max Reed, Editor.

Desc: About 220 medical, osteopathic, and dental schools. *Type:* Directory.

Canadian Journal of Herbalism

Ontario Herbalists Association

11 Winthrop Pl.	Ph: (905)536-1509
Stoney Creek, ON, Canada L8G	Fax: (905)664-1567
3M3	

Contact: Keith Stelling, Editor.

Desc: Covers applications of herbalism, plant constituents, the therapeutic value of herbal agents, indigenous Ontario plant identification, events listings, and the full practice of herbalism. Includes articles on growing and cooking with herbs. *Type:* Newsletter.

ED Management

American Health Consultants, Inc.

3525 Piedmont Rd., Bldg. 6,	Ph: (404)262-7436
Ste. 400	Free: 800-688-2421
Atlanta, GA 30305	Fax: (404)262-7837

E-mail: customerservice@ahcpub.com

Contact: Larry Mellick, MD, Editor.

Desc: Tracks developments in the business and management of emergency medical care. *Type:* Newsletter.

Happy Herbaling from Annette

Annette Wheeler

PO Box 740	Ph: (901)686-0154
Ridgetop, TN 37152	

Contact: Annette Wheeler, Editor.

Desc: Discusses the historical uses of herbs and natural remedies. Recurring features include letters to the editor and news of research. *Type:* Newsletter.

Health & Medical Industry Directory

infoUSA

5711 S. 86th Circle	Ph: (402)593-4600
PO Box 27347	Free: 800-555-6124
Omaha, NE 68127	Fax: (402)331-5481

E-mail: internet@infousa.com

URL: http://www.abii.com.

Desc: CD-ROM. Lists over 1.1 million physicians and surgeons, dentists, clinics, health clubs, and other health-related businesses in the U.S. *Type:* Directory.

Herbalgram

American Botanical Council

PO Box 201660	Ph: (512)331-8868
Austin, TX 78720	Free: 800-373-7105
	Fax: (512)331-1924

E-mail: amebotoncl@aol.com

Contact: Mark Blumenthal, Editor.

Desc: Disseminates information on medicinal plants and herbal products and provides coverage of the latest news in the herb industry. Recurring features include lists of recent books and publications, notices of articles in the popular press, market reports, legal and regulatory updates, news of research, and a calendar of events. *Type:* Newsletter.

Jin Shin Do Acupressure Newsletter

Jin Shin Do Foundation

1084 G San Miguel Cyn. Rd.	Ph: (408)763-7702
Watsonville, CA 95076	

Contact: Iona Marsaa Teeguarden, Editor.

Desc: Provides information on bodymind acupressure, news, and main contacts in the U.S., Canada, and Europe. Features a product catalog, a class catalog and articles. *Type:* Newsletter.

The Joint Letter

Lippincott-Raven Publishers

12107 Insurance Way	Ph: (301)714-2300
Hagerstown, MD 21740	Free: 800-638-3030
	Fax: (301)714-2398

Contact: Joseph D. Zuckerman, MD, Editor; Colin Nelson, Editor; Mark L. Schoene.

Desc: Covers joint function, injury and disease. *Type:* Newsletter.

Medical Ultrasound Technology

Lippincott Williams & Wilkins

227 E. Washington Sq.	Ph: (215)238-4200
Philadelphia, PA 19106-3780	Free: 800-777-2295
	Fax: (215)238-4227

URL: http://www.lrpub.com

Contact: Tim Baker, Editor; Linda G. Huang, Editor.

Desc: Serves the entire medical ultrasound community. *Type:* Newsletter.

Medicine & Health

Faulkner & Gray, Inc.

11 Penn Plaza, 17th Fl.	Ph: (212)967-7000
New York, NY 10001-2006	Free: 800-535-8403
	Fax: (212)967-7180

E-mail: order@faulknergray.com

Contact: Paul Cotton, Editor.

Desc: Monitors actions of legislators, regulators, and industry personnel who shape health policy. Reports on legislation, budgets, regulations, court decisions, and debates. *Type:* Newsletter.

Michigan Peer Review Organization

40600 Ann Arbor Rd., No. 200	Ph: (313)459-0900
Plymouth, MI 48170	

Contact: Gary G. Horvat, CEO.

Desc: Allopathic and osteopathic physicians licensed and practicing in Michigan. Conducts medical peer review on quality and propriety of medical services provided to Medicare and Medicaid beneficiaries; provides medical quality and utilization review services to hospitals and insurance agencies. *Type:* Association.

The Official ABMS Directory of Board Certified Medical Specialists

Marquis Who's Who
Reed Elsevier
121 Chanlon Rd.　　　　Ph: (908)464-6800
New Providence, NJ 07974　Free: 800-521-8110
　　　　　　　　　　　　Fax: (908)771-8645
E-mail: info@marquiswhoswho.com
URL: http://www.marquiswhoswho.com.
Contact: Fred Marks, Editor.
Desc: More than 496,000 board-certified specialists in 25 areas of medical practice from allergy to urology. Prior to 1997, all 25 areas were covered in separate publications. *Type:* Directory.

Phi Chi Medical Fraternity

1201 E. Spring St.　　　Ph: (812)948-0581
New Albany, IN 47150　　Free: 800-800-7442
　　　　　　　　　　　　Fax: (812)941-8850
Contact: Daniel H. Cannon, M.D., Chm., Exec. Trustees.
Desc: Professional fraternity - medicine. Maintains Phi Chi Welfare Association, which accepts voluntary contributions to a student loan fund and other services. *Type:* Association.

Phi Delta Epsilon Medical Fraternity

11595 N. Meridian St., Ste. 300　Free: 800-347-3713
Carmel, IN 46032-6950
Contact: Michelle Lee, Exec.Dir.
Desc: Professional fraternity - medicine. *Type:* Association.

Phi Rho Sigma Medical Society

PO Box 90264　　　　　Ph: (317)255-4379
Indianapolis, IN 46290　Fax: (317)253-5067
E-mail: hrodenbe@wpo.iupui.edu
Contact: Martin B. Wice, M.D., Sec.-Treas.
Desc: Professional society - medicine. *Type:* Association.

Red Book

Medical Economics Co.
5 Paragon Dr.　　　　　Ph: (201)358-7500
Montvale, NJ 07645-1725　Free: 800-223-0581
　　　　　　　　　　　　Fax: (201)358-7260
E-mail: customer.service@medec.com
Contact: Cy Caine, Editor.
Desc: Product and manufacturer listings for prescription drugs, over-the-counter medications, and other drug store items. *Type:* Directory.

Touch for Health Education Newsletter

Touch for Health Education Newsletter
6162 La Gloria Dr.　　　Ph: (310)589-5269
Malibu, CA 90265　　　　Fax: (310)589-5369
E-mail: thie@touch4health.com
URL: http://www.touch4health.com.
Contact: John F. Thie, Editor.
Desc: Provides holistic health information, with an emphasis on touch healing. Recurring features include news of research, case histories and testimonials, and Dr. *Type:* Newsletter.

Meeting Planners

Annual Trade Show Directory

Forum Publishing Co.
383 E. Main St.　　　　Ph: (516)574-5000
Centerport, NY 11721　Fax: (516)754-0630
E-mail: forum123@juno.com
URL: http://www.forum123.com
Contact: Martin Stevens, Editor.
Desc: Over 1,800 merchandise trade shows throughout the United States and Canada. *Type:* Directory.

ConventionSouth—Meeting Sites in the South Directory Issue

ConventionSouth Newspaper
PO Box 2267　　　　　Ph: (205)968-5300
Gulf Shores, AL 36547　Fax: (205)968-4532
E-mail: info@conventionsouth.com
Contact: J. Talty O'Connor, Editor.
Desc: List of over 2,000 hotels and resorts in the southern U.S. with facilities for meetings, conferences, and conventions. *Type:* Directory.

Directory of Conventions Regional Editions

Bill Communications, Inc.
355 Park Ave. S.　　　Ph: (212)592-6200
New York, NY 10010-1789　Free: 800-266-4712
　　　　　　　　　　　　Fax: (212)592-6339
Contact: Jean L. Jaworek, Editor, jjaworek@billcom.com.
Desc: Over 14,000 meetings of North American national, regional, and state and local organizations. *Type:* Directory.

Exhibit Builder—Source Book Directory

Exhibit Builder, Inc.
22900 Ventura Blvd No. 245　Ph: (818)225-0100
PO Box 4144　　　　　Free: 800-356-4451
Woodland Hills, CA 91365　Fax: (818)225-0138
E-mail: JillB@xbuilder.com.
Contact: Judy Pomerantz, Editor.
Desc: Manufacturers and suppliers and products and services for the trade show and museum exhibit industries. *Type:* Directory.

Meetings and Conventions—Gavel International Directory Issue

Reed Travel Group
500 Plaza Dr.　　　　　Ph: (201)902-1600
Secaucus, NJ 07094-3626　Free: 800-334-2811
　　　　　　　　　　　　Fax: (201)319-1628
Contact: Alina Dalmau, Editor.
Desc: Lists of over 4,000 convention halls and hotels, primarily in the United States, suitable for meetings; convention bureaus; hotel chains and representatives; industry associations. *Type:* Directory.

Mind the Meetings Index

Interdok Corp.
173 Halstead Ave.　　　Ph: (914)835-3506
Box 326　　　　　　　　Fax: (914)835-6757
Harrison, NY 10528
Contact: Yvette Roper McCutcheon, Editor.
Desc: National and international conferences, seminars, workshops, congresses, institutes and courses, and other meetings in science, engineering, medicine, and technology; covers about 2,500 meetings per year scheduled to occur one month to two years in advance of publication date. *Type:* Directory.

Seminars Directory

Gale Group Inc.
27500 Drake Rd.　　　Ph: (248)699-4253
Farmington Hills, MI 48331-　Free: 800-877-GALE
3535　　　　　　　　　Fax: (248)699-8070
E-mail: galeord@galegroup.com
URL: http://www.galegroup.com.; http://www.gale.com.
Desc: About 8,000 seminars offered by 2,000 organizations. *Type:* Directory.

Successful Meetings—Sourcebook

Bill Communications, Inc.
355 Park Ave. S.　　　Ph: (212)592-6200
New York, NY 10010-1789　Free: 800-266-4712
　　　　　　　　　　　　Fax: (212)592-6339
Contact: Mary Gundermann, Editor, mgunderman@succcssmtgs.com.

Desc: More than 5,000 hotels, convention centers, and convention bureaus. *Type:* Directory.

Trade Opportunity

U.S. International Trade Administration
14th St. & Constitution Ave.　Ph: (202)482-3251
NW　　　　　　　　　　Fax: (202)482-5819
USDOC/ITA, Rm. 3418
Washington, DC 20230
Contact: Helen Simpson-Davis, Editor.
Desc: Leads to export opportunities for United States businesses. *Type:* Directory.

Trade Shows Worldwide

Gale Group Inc.
27500 Drake Rd.　　　Ph: (248)699-4253
Farmington Hills, MI 48331-　Free: 800-877-GALE
3535　　　　　　　　　Fax: (248)699-8070
E-mail: galeord@galegroup.com
URL: http://www.galegroup.com.; http://www.gale.com.
Contact: Kim Hunt, Editor.
Desc: Over 9,700 trade shows and exhibitions, including those held at conferences, conventions, meetings, trade and industrial events, merchandise marts, and national expositions; 6,169 trade show sponsors and organizers; of trade show facilities, services, and information sources, including 1,387 conference and convention centers, 583 visitor and convention bureaus, 334 World Trade Centers; sources of information for the trade show industry, including professional associations, consulting organizations, and publications; and 1,004 trade show industry service suppliers. *Type:* Directory.

The Tradeshow Week Calendar

Tradeshow Week, Inc.
5700 Wilshire Blvd., Ste. 120　Ph: (323)965-5300
Los Angeles, CA 90036-5804　Fax: (323)965-5304
URL: http://www.tradeshowweek.com.
Contact: Darlene Gudea, Editor, dgudea@tsweek.com; Carri Jensen, Editor, cjensen@tsweek.com.
Desc: About 100 major North American trade shows and expositions for a one-week period six months from the date of the issue and one year from date of the issue; overseas trade shows and expositions for a one-week period eight months from the date of the issue. *Type:* Directory.

Tradeshow Week Data Book

Tradeshow Week, Inc.
5700 Wilshire Blvd., Ste. 120　Ph: (323)965-5300
Los Angeles, CA 90036-5804　Fax: (323)965-5304
Contact: Beverley McDonough, Editor.
Desc: Over 4,000 public and trade shows over 50 booths in size scheduled in the United States and Canada up to five years from publication date. *Type:* Directory.

Tradeshow Week Tradeshow 200

Tradeshow Week, Inc.
5700 Wilshire Blvd., Ste. 120　Ph: (323)965-5300
Los Angeles, CA 90036-5804　Fax: (323)965-5304
URL: http://www.tradeshowweek.com.
Contact: Darlene Gudea, Editor, dgudea@tsweek.com; Carri Jensen, Editor, cjensen@tsweek.com.
Desc: 200 largest tradeshows in the United States based on net square feet of paid exhibit space occupied; also lists 50 largest tradeshows in Canada. *Type:* Directory.

Tradeshow Week's Major Exhibit Hall Directory

Tradeshow Week, Inc.
5700 Wilshire Blvd., Ste. 120　Ph: (323)965-5300
Los Angeles, CA 90036-5804　Fax: (323)965-5304
URL: http://www.tradeshowweek.com.
Contact: Darlene Gudea, Editor, dgudea@tsweek.com; Carri Jensen, Editor.

Desc: Exhibit areas of at least 25,000 square feet in convention centers, hotels, auditoriums, arenas, and other facilities in the United States and Canada. *Type:* Directory.

Tradeshow Week's Tradeshow Services Directory
Tradeshow Week, Inc.
5700 Wilshire Blvd., Ste. 120   Ph: (323)965-5300
Los Angeles, CA 90036-5804   Fax: (323)965-5304
Contact: Darlene Gudea, Editor.
Desc: Exhibit designers, builders, carriers, decorators, registration systems, security firms, show managers, convention bureaus, and other types of firms concerned with the management of trade shows; also associations, publications; list of trade show industry meetings. *Type:* Directory.

TradeShows & Exhibits Schedule
Bill Communications, Inc.
355 Park Ave. S.   Ph: (212)592-6200
New York, NY 10010-1789   Free: 800-266-4712
   Fax: (212)592-6339
Contact: Jean L. Jaworek, Editor, jjaworek@billcom.com.
Desc: Trade, industrial, and public shows in North America; international coverage. *Type:* Directory.

TRAINING Marketplace Directory: Off-Site Meeting Facilities
Lakewood Publications, Inc.
50 S. 9th St.   Ph: (612)333-0471
Minneapolis, MN 55402   Free: 800-328-4329
   Fax: (612)333-6521
E-mail: justask@lakewoodpub.com
URL: http://www.trainingsupersite.com.
Contact: Rebecca Ganzel, Editor; Michele Mills, Editor, mmills@lakewoodpub.com.
Desc: List of meetings & facilities specifically geared for off-site training sessions. *Type:* Directory.

Virginia Group Tour & Meeting Planners Directory
Virginia Tourism Corp.
901 E. Byrd St.   Ph: (804)786-2051
Richmond, VA 23219-4048   Free: 800-759-0886
   Fax: (804)786-1919
E-mail: vainfo@vedp.state.va.us
URL: http://www.virginia.org; http://www.virginia.org.
Contact: Barbara Ramos, Editor, bramos@vedp.state.va.us.
Desc: Attractions, accommodations, tours, bus companies, meeting facilities, and other tourist-related organizations in Virginia. *Type:* Directory.

Western Association News—Convention Centers Directory Issue
Schneider Publishing Co.
13274 Fiji Way, 4th Fl.   Ph: (310)577-3700
Marina del Rey, CA 90292   Fax: (310)577-3715
E-mail: info@schneiderpublishing.com; sandi@schneiderpublishing.com; jennifer@schneiderpublishing.com; ann@schneiderpublishing.com.
Contact: Timothy Schneider, Editor.
Desc: List of convention centers in the western United States, including Hawaii and Alaska, Texas, and Canada; listings are paid. *Type:* Directory.

Western Association News—Convention and Visitor's Bureau Directory Issue
Schneider Publishing Co.
13274 Fiji Way, 4th Fl.   Ph: (310)577-3700
Marina del Rey, CA 90292   Fax: (310)577-3715
E-mail: info@schneiderpublishing.com; sandi@schneiderpublishing.com; jennifer@schneiderpublishing.com; ann@schneiderpublishing.com.

Contact: Timothy Schneider, Editor.
Desc: List of convention and visitor's bureaus in the western United States, including Hawaii and Alaska, Texas, and Canada; listings are paid. *Type:* Directory.

Western Association News—Hotels and Meetings Facilities Directory Issue
Schneider Publishing Co.
13274 Fiji Way, 4th Fl.   Ph: (310)577-3700
Marina del Rey, CA 90292   Fax: (310)577-3715
E-mail: info@schneiderpublishing.com; sandi@schneiderpublishing.com; jennifer@schneiderpublishing.com; ann@schneiderpublishing.com.
Contact: Timothy Schneider, Editor.
Desc: List of hotels and meetings facilities in the western United States, including Hawaii, Texas, Alaska, and Canada; listings are paid. *Type:* Directory.

Western Association News—Meetings Suppliers and Services Directory Issue
Schneider Publishing Co.
13274 Fiji Way, 4th Fl.   Ph: (310)577-3700
Marina del Rey, CA 90292   Fax: (310)577-3715
E-mail: info@schneiderpublishing.com; sandi@schneiderpublishing.com; jennifer@schneiderpublishing.com; ann@schneiderpublishing.com.
Contact: Timothy Schneider, Editor.
Desc: List of companies providing supplies and services for meetings and meeting planners in the western United States, including Hawaii and Alaska, Texas, and Canada; listings are paid. *Type:* Directory.

Western Association News—Space Available Hotline Directory Issue
Western Association News, Inc.
13274 Fiji Way, No.416   Ph: (310)577-3700
Marina Del Rey, CA 90292-   Fax: (310)577-3715
7090
E-mail: sandi@schneiderpublishing.com; jennifer@schneiderpublishing.com; ann@schneiderpublishing.com.
Contact: Timothy Schneider, Editor.
Desc: List of near-term meeting space availabilities in the western U.S., including Hawaii and Alaska, Texas, and Canada; listings are paid. *Type:* Directory.

World Meetings—United States and Canada
Macmillan Publishing Co.
Macmillan Library Reference Group
PO Box 159   Free: 800-257-5157
Thorndike, ME 04986
Contact: Peter Jaskowiak, Editor, peter_jaskowiak@prenhall.com.
Desc: Approximately 1,000 upcoming meetings, conventions, seminars, and exhibitions regarding science, medicine, and technology in the United States and Canada. *Type:* Directory.

Mennonite

Council of Mennonite Colleges
400 S. Jefferson   Ph: (316)947-3121
Tabor College   Free: 800-822-6799
Hillsboro, KS 67063   Fax: (316)947-2607
E-mail: webmaster@tabor.edu
URL: http://www.tabor.edu
Contact: Dr. David Brandt, Pres.
Desc: Mennonite Brethren institutions offering two or more years of college work. Promotes understanding and cooperation among member institutions. *Type:* Association.

Mennonite Central Committee
21 S. 12th St.   Ph: (717)859-1151
PO Box 500   Fax: (717)859-2171
Akron, PA 17501-0500
E-mail: mailbox@mcc.org
URL: http://www.mennonitecc.ca/mcc/
Contact: Ronald J.R. Mathies, Exec.Dir.
Desc: Relief and service agency of North American Mennonite and Brethren in Christ churches. Administers and participates in programs of agricultural and economic development, education, health, employment development, relief, peace, and disaster service. 841 workers serve in some 50 countries in Africa, Asia, Europe, and South, Central, and North America. *Type:* Association.

Mennonite Economic Development Associates
1821 Oregon Pike, Ste. 201   Ph: (717)560-6546
Lancaster, PA 17601-6466   Free: 800-665-7026
   Fax: (717)560-6549
E-mail: 72633.3677@compuserve.com
URL: http://www.meda.org
Contact: Ben Sprunger, Pres.
Desc: Business and professional people of the Mennonite faith who want to express their Christian beliefs through their work, in their community, and through international aid. Goals are to: assist members in discovering ways to apply biblical principles to everyday situations in the marketplace; promote community services; invest human and financial resources abroad to contribute to the creation of business and employment opportunities in less developed countries. *Type:* Association.

Mennonite Women
722 Main, Box 347   Ph: (316)283-5100
Newton, KS 67114   Fax: (316)283-0454
Contact: Lara Hall-Blosser, Co-Exec.Coor.
Desc: Encourages Mennonite women to nurture their life in Christ, study the Bible, utilize their gifts, hear each other and engage in mission and service. *Type:* Association.

Rosedale Mennonite Missions
9920 Rosedale-Milford Center   Ph: (614)857-1366
Rd.   Fax: (614)857-1605
Irwin, OH 43029
E-mail: 104677.2661@compuserve.com
Contact: Nathan Miller, Pres.
Desc: Establishes churches and conducts evangelical activities worldwide. Operates development and relief projects in Nicaragua, Costa Rica, and Ecuador. Maintains medical clinics; distributes food and clothing; provides agricultural advice and assistance. *Type:* Association.

Ten Thousand Villages
704 Main St.   Ph: (717)859-8100
PO Box 500   Fax: (717)859-2622
Akron, PA 17501-0500
E-mail: inquiries@villages-mcc.org
URL: http://www.villages.ca
Contact: Paul Myers, Dir.
Desc: Assists over 30,000 artisans and craftspeople in developing countries by marketing their products in North America through wholesale distribution, retail sales, and church displays. A program of Mennonite Central Committee. *Type:* Association.

Mental Health

Ackerman Institute for the Family
149 E. 78th St.   Ph: (212)879-4900
New York, NY 10021   Fax: (212)744-0206
E-mail: psteinglass@ackerman.org
URL: http://www.ackerman.org
Contact: Peter Steinglass, MD, Exec.Dir.

Desc: Cancer and other chronic illnesses, catastrophic illness, AIDS/AIDS-Related Complex (ARC), school problems, women's issues, family violence, stressful life events, family life cycle issues, family factors in psychiatric disorders, alcoholism, and drug abuse. *Type:* Research center.

Addiction and Mental Health Services Corp.
Clarke Institute of Psychiatry Division
33 Russell St.   Ph: (416)595-6000
Toronto, ON, Canada M5S 2S1   Fax: (416)595-5017
E-mail: mcatz@arf.org
URL: http://www.arf.org
Contact: Dr. Paul Garfinkel, Pres/CEO.
Desc: Addiction and mental health. Studies include use and effects of alcohol, tobacco, and other drugs, with concentration in proevention and health promotion, drug and alcoholism treatment; socio-behavioral, medical, biobehavioral, and biochemical research; and program evaluation. *Type:* Research center.

Advocate
NAMI Rhode Island
1255 N. Main St.   Ph: (401)331-3060
Providence, RI 02904-1867   Free: 800-749-3197
     Fax: (401)274-3020
E-mail: amiofri@aol.com
Contact: Nick Sahlin, Ph.D., Exec. Dir., nicknami@aol.com.
Desc: Focuses on the mentally ill in Rhode Island. Provides news on functions of the Alliance as well as news features articles, news, and legislation on mental health. *Type:* Newsletter.

Allan Memorial Institute
1025 Pine Ave. W   Ph: (514)842-1231
Montreal, PQ, Canada H3A   Fax: (514)843-1644
   1A1
Contact: Paul Beaudry, MD, Dir.
Desc: Clinical and field investigation in the areas of clinical psychopharmacology, mood disorders, child and adolescent psychiatry, family studies (including family therapy), and consultation-liaison psychiatry cognitive therapy. *Type:* Research center.

Alliance for the Mentally Ill
200 N. Glebe Rd., Ste. 1015   Ph: (703)524-7600
Arlington, VA 22203-3754   Fax: (703)524-9094
URL: http://www.nami.org
Contact: Laurie Flynn, Contact.
Desc: Mentally ill persons and their families. Works to inform the public about mental illness and enhance the lives of people who are mentally ill. *Type:* Association.

American Psychological Foundation
American Psychological Association
750 1st St. NE   Ph: (202)336-5500
Washington, DC 20002-4242   Free: 800-374-2721
     Fax: (202)336-5568
E-mail: webmaster@apa.org
Desc: Provides information on the grants, awards, and other activities of the American Psychological Foundation, a nonprofit organization established to promote psychology and help extend its benefits to the public. *Type:* Newsletter.

AMI Quebec Newsletter
Alliance for the Mentally Ill (AMI)
5253 Decarie Blvd., Ste. 150   Ph: (514)486-1448
Montreal, PQ, Canada H3W   Fax: (514)486-6157
   3C3
E-mail: amique@dsuper.net
Contact: Ella Amir, Editor, ellaamv@asuper.net.
Desc: Provides notices and reports of meetings, lectures, and seminars. Provides news and schedules of AMI-Quebec. *Type:* Newsletter.

Anxiety Disorders Association of America
11900 Parklawn Dr., Ste. 100   Ph: (301)231-9350
Rockville, MD 20852-2624   Fax: (301)231-7392
E-mail: anxdis@aol.com
URL: http://www.adaa.org
Contact: Ivey Farber, Administrative Dir.
Desc: Health professionals involved in the research and treatment of anxiety disorders, including phobias, panic disorders, and obsessive/compulsive disorders; families of those suffering from an anxiety disorder; interested others. Purpose is to aid sufferers of such conditions and their families through educational and informational services and to facilitate research, progress in treatment, and public and professional education. Does not recommend any one approach to treatment, but believes numerous treatments need to be developed and made available and encourages individuals seeking treatment to learn about treatment options. *Type:* Association.

APA Division Dialog
American Psychological Association
750 1st St. NE   Ph: (202)336-5500
Washington, DC 20002-4242   Free: 800-374-2721
     Fax: (202)336-5568
E-mail: webmaster@apa.org
Contact: Sarah K. Jordan, Editor.
Desc: Contains news on APA divisions and information of interest to members and officers of APA divisions. *Type:* Newsletter.

Aultman Hospital Community Health Research Institute
2600 6th St. SW   Ph: (216)452-9911
Canton, OH 44710   Fax: (216)438-6356
E-mail: jboyer@aultman.com
Contact: Jere M. Boyer, PhD, Dir.
Desc: Clinical and health services, hypertension, and human papilloma virus testing and epidemiology. Also conducts cancer and perinatal research. *Type:* Research center.

Autism Research Institute
4182 Adams Ave.   Ph: (619)281-7165
San Diego, CA 92116   Fax: (619)563-6840
URL: http://www.autism.com/ari/
Contact: Dr. Bernard Rimland, Dir.
Desc: Causes and treatment of severe behavior disorders in children, particularly autism. Conducts computerized analyses of its diagnostic reports on individual children with severe behavior disorders, and studies the relationship between nutrition and learning and behavior disorders. *Type:* Research center.

Behavioral Health OUTCOMES
Manisses Communications Group, Inc.
208 Governor St.   Ph: (401)831-6020
Providence, RI 02906-3246   Free: 800-333-7771
     Fax: (401)861-6370
E-mail: manissescs@manisses.com
Contact: Michael G. Goldstein, M.D., Editor; Anne Marshall Christener, Ph.D., Managing Editor.
Desc: Provides news and research digests about behavioral health outcomes research. *Type:* Newsletter.

Behavorial Health Treatment
Manisses Communications Group, Inc.
208 Governor St.   Ph: (401)831-6020
Providence, RI 02906-3246   Free: 800-333-7771
     Fax: (401)861-6370
E-mail: manissescs@manisses.com
Contact: Melissa Demed, Managing Editor; Linda Watts Jackim, Managing Editor, lindawjackim@manisses.com.
Desc: News and analysis on the delivery, funding, and management of behavioral health treatment services. *Type:* Newsletter.

Calgary WHO Centre for Research and Training in Mental Health
Peter Lougheed Centre   Ph: (403)291-8545
3645, 3500 26th Ave. NE   Fax: (403)219-3520
Calgary, AB, Canada T1Y 6J4
E-mail: arboledj@acs.ucalgary.ca
Contact: Dr. J. Arboleda-Florez, Dir.
Desc: Forensic psychiatry, psychiatric epidemiology, psychopharmacology, and occupational therapy and rehabilitation. *Type:* Research center.

Center for Attitudinal Healing
33 Buchanan Dr.   Ph: (415)331-6161
Sausalito, CA 94965   Fax: (415)331-4545
E-mail: cah@well.com
URL: http://www.healingcenter.org
Contact: Don Goewey, Exec.Dir.
Desc: Nonsectarian organization established to supplement traditional health care by offering free services in attitudinal healing for both children and adults with life-threatening illnesses, loss, or other crises. (The concept of attitudinal healing is based on the belief that it is possible to choose peace rather than conflict, and love rather than fear; the center defines health as inner peace and healing as the process of letting go of fear.) Offers support groups and arranges home and hospital visits for children, youth, and adults. Offers volunteer training program. *Type:* Association.

Center for Research Service for Severe Mental Illness
Hampton House   Ph: (410)955-3625
624 N. Broadway 482   Fax: (410)955-0470
Baltimore, MD 21205-1996
E-mail: dsteinwa@jhsph.edu
Contact: Dr. Donald M. Steinwachs, Dir.
Desc: Mental health care services, including cost effectiveness of alternative treatments, financial support, and alternative organizational and system methods. *Type:* Research center.

Center for the Research and Treatment of Anorexia Nervosa
10921 Wilshire Blvd., Ste. 702   Ph: (213)824-5881
Los Angeles, CA 90024
Contact: Dr. Burt Crausman, PhD, Dir.
Desc: Anorexia nervosa and other eating disorders, including research into their causes, detection, and treatment. *Type:* Research center.

Chestnut Lodge Hospital
500 W. Montgomery Ave.   Ph: (301)424-8300
Rockville, MD 20850   Fax: (301)762-2050
URL: http://www.chestnutlodge.com
Contact: Steven Goldstein, MD, Dir.
Desc: Psychopharmacology, schizophrenia, mental health services, hospital care, and forms of treatment course and outcome of major mental disorders. *Type:* Research center.

Children's Psychopharmacology Unit
New York Univ. Med. Ctr.   Ph: (212)263-6206
Psychiatry Dept.   Fax: (212)263-6216
550 1st Ave.
New York, NY 10016
Desc: Children and psychopharmacology, psychopharmacology in autism, and aggression. *Type:* Research center.

Clinician's Research Digest
American Psychological Association
750 1st St. NE   Ph: (202)336-5500
Washington, DC 20002-4242   Free: 800-374-2721
     Fax: (202)336-5568
E-mail: webmaster@apa.org

Contact: Douglas K. Snyder, Editor.

Desc: Contains selections and summaries of articles from clinical research journals. *Type:* Newsletter.

Communique

American Psychological Association

750 1st St. NE   Ph: (202)336-5500
Washington, DC 20002-4242   Free: 800-374-2721
    Fax: (202)336-5568
E-mail: webmaster@apa.org

Desc: Contains news and articles on the activities of APA's Office of Ethnic Minority Affairs as well as other information of interest to ethnic minorities in psychology. *Type:* Newsletter.

Concordia University (Montreal, PQ, Canada)

Centre for Research in Human Development

7141 Sherbrooke St. West   Ph: (514)848-2240
PY 170   Fax: (514)848-2815
Montreal, PQ, Canada H4B
    1R6
E-mail: lserbin@vax2.concordia.ca
URL: http://www-psych.concordia.ca/CRDH/
Contact: Dr. Lisa Serbin, Dir.

Desc: Psychological development across the human lifespan, focusing on normal social and cognitive development; atypical developmental patterns; and the study of competence in elderly populations. Specific fields of study include developmental, clinical, cognitive and social psychology; education; applied statistics; medicine; pediatrics; and gerontology. *Type:* Research center.

Currents

Louis de la Parte Florida Mental Health Institute

University of South Florida

13301 Bruce B. Downs Blvd.   Ph: (813)974-1991
Tampa, FL 33612-3899
URL: http://www.fmhi.usf.edu/currents.html.
Contact: Patricia Cleveland, Editor, clevelan@hal.fmhi.usf.edu.

Desc: Covers programs, events, research, and staff of the Institute. *Type:* Newsletter.

Dave Garroway Laboratory for the Study of Depression

Pennsylvania Hospital,   Ph: (215)829-7314
    Mezzanine Fl.   Fax: (215)829-7315
210 W. Washington Sq.
Philadelphia, PA 19107
Contact: Howard S. Sudak, MD, Dir.

Desc: Longitudinal studies of depression, including recurring depression, anxiety, and personality disorders in individuals with major depression. Examines predictors of recurrence, objective and subjective measures of symptom severity, and patient vulnerability. *Type:* Research center.

Douglas Hospital Research Centre

6875 La Salle Blvd.   Ph: (514)762-3048
Verdun, PQ, Canada H4H 1R3   Fax: (514)762-3034
E-mail: mcou@musica.mcgill.ca
URL: http://www.mcgill.ca/douglas
Contact: Dr. Rémi Quirion, PhD, Sci.Dir.

Desc: Mental health, including aging, psychoneuroendocrinology, cognitive measurements, and behavior; Alzheimer's disease, incorporating animal models, neurochemistry, and trials of nootropic drugs; depression and its biological markers, with clinical trials of new antidepressants; schizophrenia and alcoholism, including neurochemical studies and new treatment methods; violence neurobiological studies and new treatment methods; social psychiatry and epidemiology; and eating disorders. *Type:* Research center.

Duke University

Anxiety and Traumatic Stress Program

Med. Ctr.   Ph: (252)684-2880
Box 3812   Fax: (252)684-8866
Durham, NC 27710
E-mail: tolme@acpub.duke.edu
Contact: Dr. Jonathan Davidson, Prog.Dir.

Desc: Activities focus on diagnosis and treatment of anxiety disorders, including panic disorder, agoraphobia, social phobias, Post-Traumatic Stress Disorder (PTSD), obsessive-compulsive disorder (OCD), and generalized anxiety, as well as complementary and alteractive medicine. *Type:* Research center.

Duke University

Behavioral Medicine Research Center

Duke Med. Ctr.   Ph: (252)684-3863
PO Box 3926   Fax: (252)681-8960
Durham, NC 27710
E-mail: rbw@bmrc.mc.duke.edu
Contact: Dr. Redford Williams, MD, Dir.

Desc: Behavior, including emotional stress and personality factors as they affect physical diseases with emphasis on coronary disease and cancer. Uses epidemiological and experimental approaches. *Type:* Research center.

Duke University

Occupational Mental Health Programs

Duke Univ. Med. Ctr.   Ph: (919)286-1244
Box 3834   Free: 800-336-3853
Durham, NC 27712   Fax: (919)286-1121
E-mail: stenb001@mc.duke.edu
Contact: Craig Stenberg, Dir.

Desc: Occupational mental health, including managed mental health care, employee assistance programs, and mental health outcome research. *Type:* Research center.

Eastern Washington University

Behavioral Medicine Laboratory

Mail Stop 94   Ph: (509)359-7041
526 5th St.   Fax: (509)359-6927
Cheney, WA 99004-2431
E-mail: wgreene@ewu.edu
Contact: William A. Greene, PhD, Dir.

Desc: Psychophysiology and behavioral medicine, including physiological profiles of Type A personality, hypochondriasis, and fitness and stress control. *Type:* Research center.

Eunice Kennedy Shriver Center for Mental Retardation, Inc.

200 Trapelo Rd.   Ph: (781)642-0001
Waltham, MA 02154-6319   Fax: (781)893-5340
E-mail: preilly@shriver.org
Contact: Dr. Philip Reilly, Dir.

Desc: Interdisciplinary studies in mental retardation conducted through five research departments: Biomedical Sciences Department; Behavioral Sciences Department; Medical Genetics Department; Social Sciences, Ethics, and Law Department; and Developmental Neurobiology Department. *Type:* Research center.

The Florida Psychological Association—News Update

Florida Psychological Association

408 Office Plaza Dr.   Ph: (850)656-2222
Tallahassee, FL 32301-2757   Fax: (850)942-4586
Contact: Tondra McLendon, Office & Board Admin.

Desc: Provides information of interest to psychologists residing in Florida. Recurring features include book reviews, news of research, and news of educational opportunities. *Type:* Newsletter.

Fountain House, Inc.

Van Ameringen Center for Education and Research

425 W. 47th St.   Ph: (212)582-0340
New York, NY 10036   Fax: (212)397-1649
E-mail: 75702,1725@compuserve
URL: http://www.fountainhouse.org
Contact: Cathaleene Macias, PhD, Res.Dir.

Desc: Rehabilitation, symptomatology, and stigma of serious mental illness with a focus on member self-determination in recovery. Evaluates the effectiveness of clubhouse model programs of psychiatric rehabilitation in facilitating post-hospital community adjustment and evaluates the effectiveness of transitional employment and other employment models. *Type:* Research center.

Habilitative Mental Healthcare Newsletter

Psych-Media, Inc.

PO Box 57   Ph: (910)581-3700
Bear Creek, NC 27207   Fax: (910)581-3766

Desc: Publishes articles concerning the diagnosis and treatment of psychological disturbances in individuals with developmental disabilities. Recurring features include news of research and a collection. *Type:* Newsletter.

HIV Center for Clinical and Behavioral Studies

New York State Psychiatric   Ph: (212)543-5969
    Institute   Fax: (212)543-6003
1051 Riverside Dr., Unit 15
New York, NY 10032
E-mail: ehrharda@child.ctmc.columbia.edu
URL: http://www.hivcenternyc.org
Contact: Anke A. Ehrhardt, PhD, Dir. & Prin. Invt.

Desc: Investigates high risk sexual behaviors leading to HIV infection among heterosexual adults (especially women), adolescents, and gay men. Studies include prevention among depressed adolescent girls and gay and lesbian adolescents, development of interventions aimed at heterosexual women and men, serodiscordant male couples, and homeless mentally ill men and women. *Type:* Research center.

Institute for Psychoanalysis

122 S. Michigan, Ste. 1300   Ph: (312)922-7474
Chicago, IL 60603-6107   Fax: (312)922-5656
Contact: Dr. Thomas Pappadis, Dir.

Desc: Psychoanalysis, psychosomatic medicine, psychiatry, and related behavioral sciences. Topics of interest include parent loss, mourning, and stuttering. *Type:* Research center.

Inter-University Group for Research in Ethnopsychiatry and Medical Anthropology

Univ. of Montreal   Ph: (514)343-5832
PO Box 6128, Sta. Centre-Ville   Fax: (514)343-2494
Montreal, PQ, Canada H3C 3J7
Contact: Gilles Bibeau, PhD, Chm.

Desc: Coordinates research in ethnopsychiatry and medical anthropology conducted by individual members at the affiliated institutions. *Type:* Research center.

Johns Hopkins University

Bipolar Pedigree Collection

600 N. Wolfe St., Meyer 3-181   Ph: (410)955-5212
Baltimore, MD 21287   Fax: (410)955-0152
URL: http://www.med.jhu.edu/bipolar/webdoc1.htm
Contact: Dr. J. Raymond DePaulo, Jr., Prin. Investigator.

Desc: Genetics of bipolar disorder (manic-depressive illness), involving families in which someone is suffering from this condition. *Type:* Research center.

The Key

National Mental Health Consumers Self-Help Clearinghouse

1211 Chestnut St., Ste. 1000   Ph: (215)751-1810
Philadelphia, PA 19107   Free: 800-553-4539
   Fax: (215)636-6310

E-mail: info@mhselfhelp.org
URL: http://libertynet.org/-mha/cl_house.html.
Contact: CeCe Lentini, Editor; Violet Phillips, Editor.
Desc: Provides information for consumers of mental health services/psychiatric survivors on mental health issues, including advocacy and alternative mental health services. *Type:* Newsletter.

Lapeer County Community Mental Health Association

1570 Suncrest Dr.   Ph: (810)667-0500
Lapeer, MI 48446   Fax: (810)664-8728
Contact: Richard I. Berman, Ph.D., Exec.Dir.
Desc: Promotes mental health. *Type:* Association.

Laval University

Robert Giffard Research Center

2601, chemin de la Canardiere   Ph: (418)663-5741
Beauport, PQ, Canada G1J 2G3   Fax: (418)663-9540
E-mail: michel.maziade@psa.ulaval.ca
Contact: Michel Maziade, Dir.
Desc: Mental disorders, including Alzheimer's disease, bipolar disorders, and autism. Center searches for diagnostics and treatments for neurological and psychiatric disorders, and works to identify susceptible genes by identifying and characterizing a linkage marker. *Type:* Research center.

Margaret S. Mahler Psychiatric Research Foundation

254 Kent Rd.   Ph: (610)645-5524
Wynnewood, PA 19096   Fax: (610)645-5524
Contact: Dr. William M. Singleton, Pres.
Desc: Issues related to child development, education for parenting, and prevention and early intervention. *Type:* Research center.

MCP Hahnemann University of the Health Sciences

Eastern Pennsylvania Psychiatric Institute

3200 Henry Ave.   Ph: (215)842-4100
Philadelphia, PA 19129   Fax: (215)843-9672
Contact: Kathleen Quigley, V.Pres.
Desc: Neurosciences, mental health, and pharmacology, including basic, clinical, and applied studies on etiology and treatment modalities in mental disability, mental health of normal children, and prevention of mental disorders. Provides residency training programs and training for psychologists, social service workers, student nurses, and occupational therapists at both undergraduate and graduate levels. *Type:* Research center.

Menninger Clinic

Department of Research

Box 829   Ph: (785)350-5357
Topeka, KS 66601-0829   Fax: (785)350-5392
E-mail: sargenj@menninger.edu
URL: http://www.menninger.edu
Contact: John Sargent, MD, Res.Dir.
Desc: Mental health and illness from an interdisciplinary perspective, presently focused on three major content areas: developmental psychopathology, clinical applications of attachment theory, and treatment outcome research. *Type:* Research center.

Mental Health Abstracts

IFI/Plenum Data Corporation

3202 Kirkwood Highway Ste.   Ph: (302)998-0478
203
Wilmington, DE 19808
E-mail: ifiplenum@aol.com
Contact: Jim Brown, Customer Service, (302)998-0478, fax: (302)998-0733.
Desc: Contains more than 500,000 citations, with abstracts, to worldwide literature on mental health. Covers the biomedical, behavioral, and social aspects of the development and maintenance of "normal" behavior and emotional well-being and the etiology, diagnosis, treatment, prevention, and socio-legal implications of mental illness. *Available:* The Dialog Corporation, DIALOG. *Type:* Database.

Mental Health News Alert

CD Publications

8204 Fenton St.   Ph: (301)588-6380
Silver Spring, MD 20910   Free: 800-666-6380
   Fax: (301)588-6385

E-mail: cdpubs@clark.net
Contact: Joseph Lovece.
Desc: Reports on news affecting mental health services, including model programs, healthcare reform, federal and private grants. Also includes updates on managed care opportunities. *Type:* Newsletter.

Mental Health Policy Resource Center

1555 Connecticut Ave. NW,   Ph: (202)462-9600
Ste. 200   Fax: (202)462-9043
Washington, DC 20036-3101
E-mail: pie@pie.org
Contact: Dr. Thomas E. Brian, Exec.Dir.
Desc: Promotes informed policy making on mental health issues at the state and national level. *Type:* Association.

Mental Health Special Interest Section Quarterly

American Occupational Therapy Association, Inc. (AOTA)

PO Box 31220   Ph: (301)652-2682
Bethesda, MD 20824-1220   Free: 800-877-1383
   Fax: (301)652-7711

E-mail: ajotsis@aota.org.
Contact: Betty Cox.
Desc: Focuses on the clinical management of patients requiring mental health services. Publishes articles relevant to occupational therapy practice, including such topics as evaluation protocols, treatment approaches, and program administration. *Type:* Newsletter.

Michael Reese Hospital and Medical Center

Singer Pavillion   Ph: (312)791-3800
2959 South Cottage Grove   Fax: (312)791-8060
Chicago, IL 60616
Contact: Dr. Andrew Martorana, Chf. of Svcs.
Desc: Mental health and mental illness, its etiology, treatment, and prevention, including psychiatry, psychophysiology, clinical psychology, and neurophysiology. Studies ego functions, schizophrenia, the modal adolescent, normal and disturbed adolescents, family dynamics, and comparison of scales of manifest anxiety. *Type:* Research center.

Mid-Missouri Mental Health Center

3 Hospital Dr.   Ph: (573)884-1300
Columbia, MO 65201   Fax: (573)884-1010
Contact: Mark Stansberry, Supt.
Desc: Mental health issues among children and adolescents, including epidemiology of psychiatric disorders, family violence, violence among adolescents, and outcome studies. *Type:* Research center.

NAMI Advocate

National Alliance for the Mentally Ill (NAMI)

200 N. Glebe Rd., Ste. 1015   Ph: (703)524-7600
Arlington, VA 22203-3754   Fax: (703)524-9094
URL: http://www.nami.org.
Contact: Frieda Eastman, Editor, frieda@nami.org.
Desc: Provides information on latest research, treatment, and medications for brain disorders. Reviews status major policy and legislation at federal, state, and local levels. *Type:* Newsletter.

NAMI Rhode Island Update

NAMI Rhode Island

1255 N. Main St.   Ph: (401)331-3060
Providence, RI 02904-1867   Free: 800-749-3197
   Fax: (401)274-3020

E-mail: amiofri@aol.com
Contact: Nick Sahlin, Ph.D., Director, nicknami@aol.com.
Desc: Provides information pertaining to the Alliance for the Mentally Ill of Rhode Island. Recurring features include a calendar of events and news of members. *Type:* Newsletter.

Nathan S. Kline Institute for Psychiatric Research

140 Old Orangeburg Rd., Bldg.   Ph: (914)365-2000
37   Fax: (914)359-7029
Orangeburg, NY 10962
Contact: Robert Cancro, MD, Dir.
Desc: Mental illness, including multidisciplinary studies on its etiology, epidemiology, treatment, and control; computer sciences, emphasizing clinical and administrative services; and biochemical, genetic, physiological, neurochemical, and psychopharmacological research. Collaborates in research with investigators from other institutions and many countries. *Type:* Research center.

National Alliance for the Mentally Ill

200 N. Glebe Rd., No. 1015   Ph: (703)524-7600
Arlington, VA 22203-3754   Free: 800-950-NAMI
   Fax: (703)524-9094

URL: http://www.NAMI.ORG
Contact: Laurie M. Flynn, Exec.Dir.
Desc: Alliance of selfhelp/advocacy groups concerned with severe and chronic mentally ill individuals. Objectives are to provide emotional support and practical guidance to families, and to educate and inform the public about mental illness. Conducts consumer advocacy activities at the local, state, and national levels to enact legislation and to promote funding for institutional and community-based settings for the seriously mentally ill. *Type:* Association.

National Alliance for Research on Schizophrenia and Depression

60 Cutter Mill Rd., Ste. 404   Ph: (516)829-0091
Great Neck, NY 11021   Fax: (516)487-6930
URL: http://www.mhsource.com/narsad.html
Contact: Constance E. Lieber, Pres.
Desc: Raises funds for research on schizophrenia, depression, and other mental illnesses. *Type:* Association.

National Alliance for Research on Schizophrenia and Depression

Grants Office   Ph: (312)641-1666
208 S. LaSalle St., Ste. 1431   Fax: (312)641-3483
Chicago, IL 60604-1003
URL: http://www.mhsource.com/narsad.html
Contact: Brenda Berman, Grants Admin.
Desc: Causes, cure, treatments, and prevention of severe mental illnesses, primarily schizophrenia and depression. Emphasizes biomedical studies of brain diseases. *Type:* Research center.

National Association of State Mental Health Program Directors Research Institute, Inc.
66 Canal Ctr. Plz., Ste. 302
Alexandria, VA 22314-1591
Ph: (703)739-9333
Fax: (703)548-9517
E-mail: noel.mazade@nasmhpd.org
URL: http://www.nasmhpd.org/NRI
Contact: Dr. Noel A. Mazade, Exec.Dir.
Desc: Mental health services and management of state mental health programs. Also compiles data and conducts research activities on various aspects of state mental health agencies financing, staffing, clinical services, and mental health service systems. *Type:* Research center.

National Center for Infants, Toddlers and Families
734 15th St. NW, Ste. 1000
Washington, DC 20005-1013
Ph: (202)638-1144
Fax: (202)638-0851
Contact: Matthew E. Melmed, Exec.Dir.
Desc: Professionals and researchers in the health care industry, policymakers, and parents working to improve the healthy physical, cognitive and social development of infants, toddlers, and their families. *Type:* Association.

National Council for Community Behavioral Healthcare
12300 Twinbrook Pkwy., No. 320
Rockville, MD 20852
Ph: (301)984-6200
Fax: (301)881-7159
E-mail: admin@nccbh.org
URL: http://www.nccbh.org
Contact: Charles Ray, Contact.
Type: Association.

National Council News
National Council for Community Behavioral Healthcare
12300 Twinbrook Pkwy., Ste. 320
Rockville, MD 20854
Ph: (301)984-6200
Fax: (301)881-7159
URL: http://www.nccbh.org.
Contact: Susan Lapetina, Consulting Ed.
Desc: Dedicated to increasing the quality and accessibility of community mental health services. Recurring features include interviews, a calendar of events, news of educational opportunities, book reviews, marketplace news, and job listings. *Type:* Newsletter.

National Depressive and Manic Depressive Association
730 N. Franklin, Ste. 501
Chicago, IL 60610-3526
Ph: (312)642-0049
Free: 800-826-3632
Fax: (312)642-7243
URL: http://www.ndmda.org
Contact: Lydia Lewis, Exec. Dir.
Desc: Seeks to educate patients, families, professionals, and the public concerning the nature of depressive and manic-depressive illnesses as treatable medical diseases; to foster self-help for patients and families; to eliminate discrimination and stigma; to improve access to care; and to advocate for research toward the elimination of these illnesses. *Type:* Association.

National Mental Health Association
1021 Prince St.
Alexandria, VA 22314-2971
Ph: (703)684-7722
Free: 800-969-NMHA
Fax: (703)684-5968
E-mail: nmhainfo@aol.com
URL: http://www.nmha.org
Contact: Michael Faenza, CEO/Pres.
Desc: Addresses all aspects of mental health and mental illness and is dedicated to improving mental health, preventing mental disorders, and achieving victory over mental illnesses. NMHA, in partnership with more than 330 affiliates across the country, accomplishes its mission through advocacy, public education, research, and service. *Type:* Association.

Neurotics Anonymous International Liaison
11140 Bainbridge Dr.
Little Rock, AR 72212
Ph: (501)221-2809
Fax: (501)221-2809
Contact: Grover Boydston, Chm.
Desc: Individuals suffering or recovering from an emotional illness who use the techniques of Neurotics Anonymous to aid and maintain their recovery. Organization has adapted the Twelve Steps of Alcoholics Anonymous and applies them to the problems of mentally and emotionally disturbed (neurotic) individuals. *Type:* Association.

New York Institute for Medical Research, Inc.
150 White Plains Rd.
Tarrytown, NY 10591
Ph: (914)631-8998
Fax: (914)631-8816
Contact: Aileen Kunitz, Exec.Admin.
Desc: Behavioral, psychophysiological, and psychopharmacological research. Topics of interest include depression in young and elderly patients, dementia, anxiety neurosis, behavior and sleep disorders, and phase I studies on healthy volunteers. *Type:* Research center.

New York Mental Health Office
Office of the Chief Medical Officer
Research Division
722 W. 168th St.
New York, NY 10032
Ph: (212)960-2300
Contact: Lynne Wechseler, Res.Admin.
Desc: Mental health. *Type:* Research center.

New York State Psychiatric Institute
1051 Riverside Dr.
New York, NY 10032
Ph: (212)543-5000
Fax: (212)543-6012
E-mail: jmo2@columbia.edu
URL: http://www.nyspi.cpmc.columbia.edu/
Contact: Dr. John Oldham, Dir.
Desc: Psychiatry and neurosciences, including basic and clinical studies in biochemistry, psychoneuropharmacology, neuroendocrinology, neurotoxicology, psychosocial sciences, research and clinical psychology, genetics, nosology, psychophysiology, developmental psychobiology, sociology, epidemiology, communication sciences and psychoanalysis. *Type:* Research center.

New York University
Mental Health Clinical Research Center
Millhauser Laboratories
NYU Sch. of Med.
560 1st Ave., HN 323
New York, NY 10016
Ph: (212)263-5717
Fax: (212)263-7513
E-mail: arnold.friedhoff@ccmail.med.nyu.edu
URL: http://www.med.nyu.edu
Contact: Dr. Arnold J. Friedhoff, Dir.
Desc: Psychiatry. *Type:* Research center.

Newsline
American Psychological Association
750 1st St. NE
Washington, DC 20002-4242
Ph: (202)336-5500
Free: 800-374-2721
Fax: (202)336-5568
E-mail: webmaster@apa.org
Desc: Contains information on books and journals published by APA, including new releases. *Type:* Newsletter.

Nutrition & Mental Health
Canadian Schizophrenia Foundation
16 Florence Ave.
North York, ON, Canada M2N 1E9
Ph: (416)733-2117
Fax: (416)733-2352
E-mail: centre@orthomed.org
URL: http://www.healthy.net.
Contact: Steven Carter, Managing Editor.
Desc: Acquaints readers with the effects of nutrition on mental health, with on emphasis on schizophrenia. *Type:* Newsletter.

Obsessive-Compulsive Anonymous
PO Box 215
New Hyde Park, NY 11040
Ph: (516)741-4901
Fax: (212)768-4679
Contact: Roy C., Contact.
Desc: Individuals suffering from obsessive-compulsive disorders. (OCD is characterized by recurrent unpleasant thoughts and/or repetitive, irrational mannerisms the sufferer feels compelled to perform.) Follows the 12-step method originated by Alcoholics Anonymous World Services to assist members in their recovery. *Type:* Association.

Obsessive-Compulsive Foundation
PO Box 70
Milford, CT 06460-0070
Ph: (203)878-5669
Fax: (203)874-2826
E-mail: info@ocfoundation.org
URL: http://www.ocfoundation.org
Contact: Thomas Styron, Exec. Dir.
Desc: Individuals with obsessive-compulsive disorders and their families and friends; professionals involved in the treatment of OCD. (OCD is often chronic and characterized by recurrent unpleasant thoughts and/or repetitive behaviors that the person feels driven to perform. Individuals with OCD realize their obsessions and compulsions are irrational or excessive, yet find they have no control over them. Individuals with OCD often become demoralized, depressed, and anxious.). Seeks to control and find a cure for OCD while improving the welfare of its individuals with OCD. *Type:* Association.

Ohio State University
Laboratory of Psychobiology
Townsend Hall, Rm. 48
1885 Neil Ave.
Columbus, OH 43210
Ph: (614)292-1749
Fax: (614)292-4537
E-mail: berntson.2@osu.edu
URL: http://www.osu.edu
Contact: Dr. Gary G. Berntson, Contact.
Desc: Psychobiology and comparative psychology, including studies on recovery of function after brain damage, psychopharmacology, psychophysiology, developmental processes, and animal cognition. *Type:* Research center.

On Location
Staten Island Mental Health Society, Inc.
669 Castleton Ave.
Staten Island, NY 10301
Ph: (718)442-2225
Fax: (718)442-2289
E-mail: 103510.552@compuserve.com
Contact: Joan Gerstel, Editor.
Desc: Highlights recent and future Agency events. Diseminates information on upcoming projects. *Type:* Newsletter.

Ontario Ministry of Community and Social Services
Children's Psychiatric Research Institute
Univ. of Western Ontario
600 Sanatorium Rd.
London, ON, Canada N6H 3W7
Ph: (519)471-2540
Fax: (519)641-1922
E-mail: sorinee@epo.gov.on.ca
Contact: E.M. Sorin, Admin.
Desc: Prevention, treatment, and management of the mentally retarded, including studies in cytogenetics, biochemistry, psychology, pediatrics, psychiatry, sociology of mental retardation, delinquency, childhood psychosis, and other abnormal child development. It also provides diagnostic and treatment service to persons with suspected mental retardation, emotional disturbance, and learning disabilities in conjunction with the University's Health Sciences Faculties. *Type:* Research center.

Open Minds

Behavioral Health Industry News, Inc.
10 York St., Ste. 200   Ph: (717)334-1329
Gettysburg, PA 17325   Fax: (717)334-0538
E-mail: openmind88@aol.com.
URL: http://www.openminds.com.
Contact: Monica E. Oss, Editor.
Desc: Provides information on marketing, financial, and legal trends in the delivery of mental health and chemical dependency benefits and services. Recurring features include interviews, news of research, a calendar of events, job listings, book reviews, notices of publications available, and industry statistics. *Type:* Newsletter.

Outcomes and Accountability Alert

Manisses Communications Group, Inc.
208 Governor St.   Ph: (401)831-6020
Providence, RI 02906-3246   Free: 800-333-7771
   Fax: (401)861-6370
E-mail: manissescs@manisses.com
Contact: Linda Watts Jackim, Ph.D., Managing Editor, lwjackim@manisses.com.
Desc: Discusses matters pertaining to behavioral health for those responsible for evaluations. *Type:* Newsletter.

Practitioner Focus

American Psychological Association
750 1st St. NE   Ph: (202)336-5500
Washington, DC 20002-4242   Free: 800-374-2721
   Fax: (202)336-5568
E-mail: webmaster@apa.org
Contact: Paul L. Herndon, Editor.
Desc: Provides legislative and research news and information on the practice of psychology, the delivery of psychological services, and the availability of mental health care. *Type:* Newsletter.

Practitioner Update

American Psychological Association
750 1st St. NE   Ph: (202)336-5500
Washington, DC 20002-4242   Free: 800-374-2721
   Fax: (202)336-5568
E-mail: webmaster@apa.org
Contact: Paul L. Herndon, Editor.
Desc: Provides legislative and research news and information on the practice of psychology, the delivery of psychological services, and the availability of mental health care. *Type:* Newsletter.

Psychiatric Research Institute & Center for Phase I Studies

1100 N. St. Francis, Ste. 200   Ph: (316)291-4774
Wichita, KS 67214   Fax: (316)291-7975
E-mail: dhorst@via-christi-org
URL: http://www.via-christi.org/pri
Contact: Dr. Sheldon H. Preskorn, Dir.
Desc: Clinical drug testing for depression in adults and children, Alzheimer's disease, schizophrenia (inpatient and outpatient), centralized anxiety disorder, panic disorder, antiobesity, and pharmacokinetic drug testing. *Type:* Research center.

Psychology and AIDS Exchange

American Psychological Association
750 1st St. NE   Ph: (202)336-5500
Washington, DC 20002-4242   Free: 800-374-2721
   Fax: (202)336-5568
E-mail: webmaster@apa.org
Contact: Ann Rutherford, Editor.
Desc: Contains AIDS-related research news for practitioners, APA advocacy and legislative efforts in Washington, and other activities of the APA Office on AIDS. *Type:* Newsletter.

Psychology International

American Psychological Association
750 1st St. NE   Ph: (202)336-5500
Washington, DC 20002-4242   Free: 800-374-2721
   Fax: (202)336-5568
E-mail: webmaster@apa.org
Contact: Marian Wood, Editor.
Desc: Contains news on APA's international activities as well as other information on international psychology. *Type:* Newsletter.

PsycINFO®

American Psychological Association (APA) PsycINFO
750 1st St., NE   Ph: (202)336-5650
Washington, DC 20002-4242
E-mail: psycinfo@apa.org
URL: http://www.apa.org/psycinfo
Contact: PsycINFO User Services.
Desc: Contains more than 1,087,000 citations, with abstracts, to the worldwide literature dealing with psychology and the behavioral sciences. Covers both human and animal aspects in most of these fields: animal psychology; applied psychology; communication and language; cultural influences and social issues; developmental psychology; education; neurology and physiology; perception and motor performance; personality; physical and psychological disorders; psychometrics and statistics; treatment and prevention; and personnel and professional issues. *Available:* Ovid Technologies, Inc.; The Dialog Corporation, DataStar; The Dialog Corporation, DIALOG; CompuServe Information Service, Knowledge Index; DIMDI (Deutsches Institut fuer Medizinische Dokumentation und Information); OCLC Online Computer Library Center, Inc., OCLC EPIC; OCLC Online Computer Library Center, Inc., OCLC FirstSearch Catalog; CompuServe Information Service; HeathGate Data Corporation; EBSCOhost; The Gale Group, InfoTrac Web. *Type:* Database.

PsycINFO News

American Psychological Association
750 1st St. NE   Ph: (202)336-5500
Washington, DC 20002-4242   Free: 800-374-2721
   Fax: (202)336-5568
E-mail: webmaster@apa.org
Contact: William C. Hayward, Editor.
Desc: Contains information on PsycINFO databases, products, services, and search techniques. *Type:* Newsletter.

Research and Training Center on Vocational Rehabilitation Services for Persons with Mental Illness

6008 Wayne Ave.   Ph: (215)438-8200
Philadelphia, PA 19144
URL: http://www.matrixresearch.org
Desc: Employment needs of persons with serious psychiatric disabilities, specifically improving access to the Social Security Work Incentives; evaluating alternatives to rehabilitation systems; improving access to employment services; women and work; a multicultural perspective on rehabilitation; the nature of the employer/employee relationship; long-term career paths of persons with serious mental illness; costs of employment services; and the impact of managed care on employment services. *Type:* Research center.

Rockefeller University

Laboratory of Human Behavior and Metabolism

Rockefeller University Hospital   Ph: (212)327-8426
1230 York Ave., Box 310   Fax: (212)327-7150
New York, NY 10021-6399
E-mail: hirsch@rockvax.rockefeller.edu

Contact: Prof. Jules Hirsch, MD, Hd.
Desc: The biology of weight regulation changes in systematic energetics which result from weight changes. *Type:* Research center.

Rural Health Bulletin

American Psychological Association
750 1st St. NE   Ph: (202)336-5500
Washington, DC 20002-4242   Free: 800-374-2721
   Fax: (202)336-5568
E-mail: webmaster@apa.org
Contact: Scotty Hargrove, Editor.
Desc: Provides information on mental health care in rural areas. *Type:* Newsletter.

Rush University

Center for Suicide Research and Prevention

Rush-Presbyterian-St. Luke's   Ph: (312)942-7208
   Med. Ctr.   Fax: (312)942-2177
1725 W. Harrison St., Ste. 955
Chicago, IL 60612
E-mail: DaveAtRush@aol.com
Contact: David C. Clark, PhD, Dir.
Desc: Suicidal behavior, including epidemiological and prevention research. *Type:* Research center.

Rush University

Rush Institute for Mental Well-Being

1725 W. Harrison, Ste. 955   Ph: (312)942-5372
Chicago, IL 60612   Fax: (312)942-2177
Contact: Dr. Jan Fawcett, MD, Dir.
Desc: Clinical treatment of depression and related disorders, including alcoholism, anxiety disorders, and psychoses; treatment for damages caused by such disorders, including social and work impairment, recurrent episodes, and suicides; methods for prevention of depression and related disorders; and stress management techniques. *Type:* Research center.

Rutgers University

Center for Research on the Organization and Financing of Care for the Severely Mentally Ill

30 College Ave.   Ph: (732)932-8415
New Brunswick, NJ 08903   Fax: (732)932-6872
E-mail: mechanic@rci.rutgers.edu
URL: http://www.ihhcpar.rutgers.edu/
Contact: Dr. David Mechanic, Dir.
Desc: Research on mental health services and policy in the state and nationally. Research agenda includes aging caretakers of the mentally ill; barriers to successful patient outcomes following hospitalization; economic consequences of mental illness; facilitating appropriate housing for the severely mentally ill; insurance coverage for young mentally ill adults; improving general medical care for the severely mentally ill; impact of mental health services under managed care; mental health aspects of the AIDS epidemic; psychiatric care in general hospitals; relationships between the general medical and the specialty psychiatric sectors; relationships between minority families and the public mental health system; service elements and the quality of functioning among the chronically mentally ill; study of post-World War II mental health policy; and using managed care to improve mental health services; improving compliance to antipsychotic medications; and impact of the deinstitutionalization on communities. *Type:* Research center.

St. Louis University

Department of Psychiatry

1221 S. Grand Blvd.   Ph: (314)577-8721
St. Louis, MO 63104   Fax: (314)664-7248
E-mail: waldmans@wpogate.slu.edu

URL: http://www.slucare.edu/clinical/psychiatry

Contact: George T. Grossberg, MD, Chm.

Desc: Adult and child psychiatry, geriatric psychiatry, psychopharmacology, psychology, and behavioral medicine, including psychophysiologic reactions in pyschotherapeutic relationships, personality profiles in a general hospital population, emotional response to cardiovascular surgery, emotional responses of children to chronic illness, factors influencing career choice in medicine, and impact of direct entry into psychiatric training on residents and their training programs. *Type:* Research center.

Scion Natural Science Association Inc.

PO Box 457   Ph: (516)862-6651
St. James, NY 11780   Fax: (516)862-8604
E-mail: fink@lij.edu

Contact: Dr. Max Fink, Exec.Dir.

Desc: Psychiatric investigation, including clinical studies on effects of drugs and seizures on human behavior. Supports ongoing studies at different laboratories, usually on a collaborative basis between institutions and Association personnel. *Type:* Research center.

Social Psychiatry Research Institute

150 E. 69th St.   Ph: (212)628-4800
New York, NY 10021   Fax: (212)249-8546
E-mail: niss-33@aol.com

Contact: Dr. Ari Kiev, Pres.

Desc: Mental health and psychiatry, including psychopharmacological studies of antidepressant, anti-anxiety, and Alzheimer's medications. Conducts clinical drug trials. *Type:* Research center.

Spiritual Emergence Network

PO Box 1464   Ph: (408)426-0902
Santa Cruz, CA 95061-1464   Fax: (408)429-1614
E-mail: sen@cruzio.com
URL: http://www.elfi.com/sen

Contact: Craig Turek, Dir.

Desc: Seeks to develop an expanded model of mental health care to help people in crisis by using scientific and spiritual assistance. *Type:* Association.

State University of New York Health Science Center at Brooklyn

Psychophysiological Laboratory

Department of Psychiatry   Ph: (718)270-2022
450 Clarkson Ave., Box 1203   Fax: (718)245-2526
Brooklyn, NY 11203

Desc: Monitors and records heart rate, skin resistance, skin potential, respiration, peripheral blood flow, EEG, and eyeblink response. Applies the orienting response construct to the processes of attention, stimulus-input, and stimulus-processing in response to stimuli of varying intensity, complexity, duration, significance, and modality. *Type:* Research center.

State University of New York Health Science Center at Brooklyn

Psychosomatic Research Program

450 Clarkson Ave.   Ph: (718)270-2352
Box 1203   Fax: (718)270-3887
Brooklyn, NY 11203

Contact: Dr. R. Viswanathan, Dir.

Desc: Clinical research, including the following psychosomatic studies: psychological observance of patients with terminal renal disease before and after their acceptance for kidney transplantation or for maintenance (home) hemodialysis; exploration of the affective state of patients with sickle cell anemia before the onset of sickle cell crises; and psychoendrocrinological study of patients in treatment in the Psychiatric Crisis Clinic through the use of dexamethasone suppression. *Type:* Research center.

State University of New York Health Science Center at Stony Brook

Institute for Mental Health Research

Department of Psychiatry &   Ph: (516)444-2990
   Behavioral Sci.   Fax: (516)444-7534
Stony Brook, NY 11794-8101
E-mail: msedler@mail.psychiatry.sunysb.edu

Contact: Mark J. Sedler, MD, Actg.Chm.

Desc: Seeks to determine neurobiological factors in mental illnesses that can be used to aid in the development of improved treatments. Conducts basic neurobiological research and applied clinical studies. *Type:* Research center.

Timberlawn Psychiatric Research Foundation

2750 Grove Hill Rd.   Ph: (214)388-0451
PO Box 270789   Fax: (214)381-1377
Dallas, TX 75227

Contact: John T. Gossett, PhD, Dir.

Desc: Mental health, including studies in family development, healthy families, and program evaluation. *Type:* Research center.

Today

Mental Health Association of Erie County

999 Delaware Ave.   Ph: (716)886-1242
Buffalo, NY 14209-1805   Fax: (716)881-6428
E-mail: mhaec@localnet.com

Contact: Sandra Majewski, Editor.

Desc: Provides information on mental health issues and industry. *Type:* Newsletter.

U.S. Department of Health and Human Services
National Institute of Mental Health
Division of Clinical and Treatment Research

5600 Fishers Ln., Rm. 17C-20   Ph: (301)443-3683
Rockville, MD 20857   Fax: (301)443-7264

Contact: David Shore, MD, Actg.Dir.

Desc: Service delivery and health economics at the clinical, institutional, and systems levels; the understanding, treatment, and prevention of antisocial and violent behavior and their effects, including law and mental health interaction; and the prevention, control, and treatment of rape, other sexual assault, and their effects. The Division consists of: the Child and Family Support Branch, Services Research Branch, Statistical Research Branch, and Systems Development and Community Support Branch. *Type:* Research center.

U.S. Department of Health and Human Services
National Institute of Mental Health
Division of Clinical and Treatment Research
Child and Adolescent Disorders Research Branch

5600 Fishers Ln., Rm. 18C-17   Ph: (301)443-5944
Rockville, MD 20857   Fax: (301)480-4415
E-mail: dkoretz@mail.nih.gov

Contact: Doreen Koretz, PhD, Chf.

Desc: Child and adolescent disorders, including attention deficit disorder, depression, conduct disorders, and autism. Also investigates suicide among children and adolescents. *Type:* Research center.

U.S. Department of Health and Human Services
National Institute of Mental Health
Division of Clinical and Treatment Research
Mental Disorders of the Aging Research Branch

5600 Fishers Ln., Rm. 10-75   Ph: (301)443-1185
Rockville, MD 20857   Fax: (301)594-6784

Contact: Dr. Barry Lebowitz, Chf.

Desc: Mental health and illness implications of the aging process and old age. This includes studies on: causes, treatment, and prevention of Alzheimer's disease, senile dementia, and related disorders, with emphasis on differential diagnosis, test of memory-enhancing agents, and issues of coexisting illness and excess ability; causes, treatment, and prevention of depression in older persons (including investigations of the relationship of depression to dementing disorders, suicide, alcoholism, medical disease, and other behavioral disorders); causes, treatment, and prevention of behavioral disturbance and dysfunction, with special reference to agitation, assaultive/aggressive behavior, confusion, disorientation, and other behavioral problems; development and refinement of pharmacologic and psychosocial treatments, with special attention to efficacy, safety, side-effects, mechanisms of action, and drug/drug interaction; behavioral medicine and the interface of physical illness and mental disorders in later life; chronically mentally ill elderly, with special attention to treatment and management of schizophrenia and to psychosocial and behavioral approaches to quality of life; design and refinement of methods for treatment intervention, clinical trials, and service delivery models for the elderly; mental illness in nursing homes; effects of families, support systems, and self-help groups on the care of older persons with significant mental disorders.

U.S. Department of Health and Human Services
National Institute of Mental Health
Division of Clinical and Treatment Research
Mood, Anxiety and Personality Disorders Research Branch

5600 Fishers Ln., Rm. 10C16   Ph: (301)443-4524
Rockville, MD 20857   Fax: (301)443-6000

Contact: Mary C. Blehar, PhD, Actg.Chf.

Desc: Anxiety, somatoform, ancertain personality disorders. This includes research on the nature, etiology, diagnosis, classification, course, and treatment of these disorders. *Type:* Research center.

U.S. Department of Health and Human Services
National Institute of Mental Health
Division of Clinical and Treatment Research
Schizophrenia Research Branch

5600 Fishers Ln., Rm. 18C14   Ph: (301)443-3524
Rockville, MD 20857   Fax: (301)443-6000

Contact: John Hsiao, Contact.

Desc: Classification, assessment, etiology, genetics, clinical course, outcome, and pharmacologic, somatic, and psychosocial treatment and rehabilitation of schizophrenia and related disorders. *Type:* Research center.

U.S. Department of Health and Human Services
National Institute of Mental Health
Division of Extramural Activities

5600 Fishers Ln., Rm. 9-105   Ph: (301)443-3367
Rockville, MD 20857   Fax: (301)443-4720
E-mail: jsteinbe@nih.gov
URL: http://www.nimh.nih.gov

Contact: Jane Steinberg, Actg.Dir.

Desc: Provides leadership and advice in developing, implementing, and coordinating extramural programs and policies; represents the Institute on extramural program and policy issues within the Department and with outside organizations; provides scientific and technical review of applications for grants, cooperative agreements, and contracts; and oversees National Advisory Mental Health Council activities. The Division consists of the Office of the Director and the following branches: Clinical, Epidemiological, and Services Review Branch; Neuroscience and Behavioral Science Review Branch; Research Development and Special Projects Review Branch; and Extramural Policy Branch. *Type:* Research center.

U.S. Department of Health and Human Services

National Institute of Mental Health

Division of State and Community Systems Development

Survey and Analysis Branch

5600 Fishers Ln. Ph: (301)443-3343
Parklawn, Rm. 15C-04 Fax: (301)443-7926
Rockville, MD 20857
E-mail: rmanders@samhsa.gov
URL: http://www.mentalhealth.org
Contact: Ronald W. Manderscheid, Chf.

Desc: Statistics on the major characteristics of the nation's mental health service systems, their resources, staffing, utilization patterns, costs, and financing; develops methodology for statistical data collection and demography; and conducts ecological and demographic studies on the need and demand for mental health services. In addition, Branch provides consultation to state and local mental health agencies on statistical methodology, mental health information systems, and the use of data. *Type:* Research center.

U.S. Department of Health and Human Services

National Institute of Mental Health

Epidemiology and Services Research Division

5600 Fishers Ln., Rm. 10-105 Ph: (301)443-3648
Rockville, MD 20857 Fax: (301)443-4045
E-mail: gnorquis@nih.gov
URL: http://www.nimh.nih.gov
Contact: Dr. Grayson Norquist, Dir.

Desc: Epidemiology, psychopathology, classification, assessment, etiology, genetics, clinical course, outcome, treatment, and prevention of mental disorders, with special emphasis on schizophrenic disorders, affective and anxiety disorders, and mental disorders of children and adolescents and of the elderly. Division also reviews and assesses the performance of such programs and collaborates with other federal agencies and with outside organizations. *Type:* Research center.

U.S. Department of Health and Human Services

National Institute of Mental Health

Epidemiology and Services Research Division

Basic Prevention and Behavioral Medicine Research Branch

5600 Fishers Ln., Rm. 10-85 Ph: (301)443-4337
Rockville, MD 20857 Fax: (301)443-4045
Contact: Dr. Fred Altman, Actg.Chf.

Desc: Basic behavioral, biological, genetic, and social factors and psychological processes that impact on physical health and the maintenance of emotional well being. The Branch includes three program areas: Prevention and Behavior Change, Population and Risk, and Behavioral Medicine. *Type:* Research center.

U.S. Department of Health and Human Services

National Institute of Mental Health

Epidemiology and Services Research Division

Epidemiology and Psychopathology Research Branch

60001 Executive Blvd., Rm. Ph: (301)443-3774
7219 Fax: (301)443-7895
MSC-9649
Bethesda, MD 20892-9649
Contact: Charles T. Kaelber, MD, Actg.Chf.

Desc: Assessing mental health/mental illness status of populations in terms of incidence and prevalence; describing the natural history of disorders and identifying illness syndromes in the community as well as in clinical patient populations; developing new epidemiologic, statistical, de-

mographic, and other quantitatively oriented methodologies for assessing the mental illness/health of a population; conducting epidemiologic studies to identify etiologic factors of mental health/mental disorder in different groups in terms of inheritance, experience, behavior, biologic factors, and environment in community or patient populations; conducting case-control studies to test the efficacy of some positive action of intervention; and conducting clinical research in the classification, assessment, etiology, genetics, clinical course, outcome, and treatment of general psychopathology and other mental outcome and treatment of general psychopathology and other mental disorders. Support is provided through research grants, conference grants, small grants, specifically announced cooperative agreements, and institutional research training grants, as well as Research Scientist Development, Research Scientist, Clinical Scientist, and Physician Scientist Awards, and pre- and postdoctoral individual fellowships. *Type:* Research center.

U.S. Department of Health and Human Services

National Institute of Mental Health

Epidemiology and Services Research Division

Prevention Research Branch

5600 Fishers Ln., Rm. 10C09 Ph: (301)443-4283
Rockville, MD 20857 Fax: (301)443-4045
Contact: Eve K. Moscicki, Chf.

Desc: Prevention of mental disorders and behavioral dysfunctions and the promotion of mental health, including preventing socio-emotional problems among infants and young children at risk; preventing conduct and other behavioral disorders in school-aged children; preventing anxiety and depressive disorders in children and adults; promoting mental health through the enhancement of protective factors, including coping mechanisms; preventing suicide and suicidality in preclinical populations; and preventing affective and anxiety disorders in HIV-infected individuals, people at high-risk for infection, their families, caretakers, and loved ones. *Type:* Research center.

U.S. Department of Health and Human Services

National Institute of Mental Health

Epidemiology and Services Research Division

Services Research Branch

5600 Fishers Ln., Rm. 10C-06 Ph: (301)443-3364
Rockville, MD 20857 Fax: (301)443-4045
Contact: Katherine Magruder, Actg.Chf.

Desc: Services delivery and health economics at the clinical, institutional, and systems levels in specialty mental health and health settings; and evaluates interventions to improve diagnosis and clinical practice. *Type:* Research center.

U.S. Department of Health and Human Services

National Institute of Mental Health

Epidemiology and Services Research Division

Violence and Traumatic Stress Research Branch

5600 Fishers Ln., Parklawn, Ph: (301)443-1636
18C-14 Fax: (301)443-4611
Rockville, MD 20857
Contact: Koretz Doreen, PhD, Contact.

Desc: Support research and research training concerned with the development and prevention of adult psychopathology and mental disorders. Included within the Branch are studies aimed at the major brain disorders (e.g., schizophrenia, bipolar disorder, major depression), antisocial and other personality disorders, and co-morbid physical and mental disorders, as well as cross cutting epidemiological studies and studies that examine traumatic stress and victimization as a risk factor for psychopathology. *Type:* Research center.

U.S. Department of Health and Human Services

National Institute of Mental Health

Intramural Research Programs Division

NIH Bldg. 10, Rm. 4N-222 Ph: (301)496-3501
9000 Rockville Pike Fax: (301)480-8348
10 Central Dr.
Bethesda, MD 20892
URL: http://www.intramural.nimh.nih.gov/
Contact: Robert Desimone, Ph.D., Contact.

Desc: Clinical and behavioral, biological, and special research dealing with the causes, diagnosis, treatment, and prevention of mental disorders and the biological and psychosocial factors that determine human behavior and development; provides a focus for national attention in the area of mental health research; and provides technical support through development and maintenance of electronic and mechanical instrumentation and equipment. *Type:* Research center.

U.S. Department of Health and Human Services

National Institute of Mental Health

Intramural Research Programs Division

Social and Behavioral Research Center for Rural Health

2625 N. Loop Dr., Ste. 500 Ph: (515)294-2788
Ames, IA 50010-1190 Fax: (515)294-3613
Contact: Rand Conger, Dir.

Desc: Physical and emotional consequences associated with rapid socioeconomic changes in rural areas, particularly factors that promote tobacco, alcohol, and illicit drug use; and identifies new procedures for effectively delivering illness-prevention and self-help programs to rural people. Developing a coordinated research program on farm safety, focusing on livestock confinement operations, machinery use, grain handling, and chemicals. *Type:* Research center.

U.S. Department of Health and Human Services

National Institute of Mental Health

Intramural Research Programs Division

Socio-Environmental Studies Laboratory

Federal Bldg., Rm. B1A-14 Ph: (301)496-3383
7550 Wisconsin Ave. Fax: (301)402-0621
Bethesda, MD 20892
E-mail: CYS@IRP.NIMH.NIH.GOV
Contact: Carmi Schooler, PhD, Actg.Chf.

Desc: Social structure and personality, and cognition, including studies on basic cognitive and interpersonal processes in normal and schizophrenic individuals throughout the life span. *Type:* Research center.

U.S. Department of Health and Human Services

National Institute of Mental Health

Intramural Research Programs Division (Clinical Research)

Biological Psychiatry Branch

NIH Bldg. 10, Rm. 3N-212 Ph: (301)496-4805
12 Center Dr. Fax: (301)402-0052
Bethesda, MD 20892-1272
Contact: Dr. Robert Post, Chf.

Desc: Clinical psychiatric problems, including manic-depressive and schizo-affective illness, recurrent depression, and panic-anxiety disorders. The Branch's goal is to develop programs to investigate psychologic, biochemical, and neuroanatomic contributions to the study of manic-depressive illness, anxiety disorders, and related symptoms. *Type:* Research center.

U.S. Department of Health and Human Services

National Institute of Mental Health

Intramural Research Programs Division (Clinical Research)

Clinical Psychobiology Branch

NIH Bldg. 10, Rm. 4S-239   Ph: (301)496-2141
10 Center Dr., MSC 1390   Fax: (301)496-5439
Bethesda, MD 20892-1390

Contact: Thomas A. Wehr, MD, Chf.

Desc: Clinical psychiatric and psychobiological research. Research interest includes sleep physiology and biological rythmns, seasonal affective disorder, (SAD) and light treatment. *Type:* Research center.

U.S. Department of Health and Human Services

National Institute of Mental Health

Intramural Research Programs Division (Clinical Research)

Laboratory of Clinical Science

NIH Bldg. 10, Rm. 3D41   Ph: (301)496-2757
10 Center Dr., MSC 1264   Fax: (301)402-0188
Bethesda, MD 20892-1264

Contact: Dennis L. Murphy, MD, Chf.

Desc: Medical research related to mental health. Principal components include the Analytical Biochemistry Section, Pharmacology Section, Geriatric Psychiatry Section, Histopharmacology Section, and Clinical Neuropharmacology Section. *Type:* Research center.

U.S. Department of Health and Human Services

National Institute of Mental Health

Intramural Research Programs Division (Clinical Research)

Psychology and Psychopathology Laboratory

NIH Bldg. 15K, Rm. 101A   Ph: (301)496-2551
15 North Dr.   Fax: (301)402-1218
Bethesda, MD 20892-2668

Contact: Mary La Padula, Contact.

Desc: Genetic and neurobehavioral factors in psychopathology, and on normal cognition, emphasizing the pathology of attention. *Type:* Research center.

U.S. Department of Health and Human Services

National Institute of Mental Health

Intramural Research Programs Division (Neuropsychiatric Research at St. Elizabeth's Hospital)

Clinical and Services Branch

Clinical Brain Disorders Branch   Ph: (202)373-6097
Bldg. 10 Center Dr., Rm. 45-   Fax: (202)373-6252
241
MSC1377
Bethesda, MD 20814-9692
E-mail: eganm@intra.nimh.nih.gov

Contact: Michael Egan, MD, Actg.Dir.

Desc: Schizophrenia, focusing on molecular genetic and epidemiological studies of the new physiological alternatives associated with schizophrenia using patients and their families. *Type:* Research center.

U.S. Department of Health and Human Services

National Institute of Mental Health

Neuroscience and Behavioral Science Division

5600 Fishers Ln., Rm. 11-103   Ph: (301)443-3563
Rockville, MD 20857   Fax: (301)443-1731
E-mail: sfoote@helix.nih.gov
URL: http://www.nimh.nih.gov

Contact: Stephen L. Foote, Ph.D., Acting Dir.

Desc: Programs of research, research training, and resource development in basic and clinical neuroscience; reviews

and assesses the performance of such programs; collaborates with other federal agencies and with outside organizations. The Division consists of the Behavioral and Integrative Neuroscience Research Branch, Molecular and Cellular Neuroscience Research Branch, Genetics Research Branch, Preclinical and Clinical Therapeutics Research Branch, the Research Training and Research Development Program, and the Translational Research and Scientific Technology Program. *Type:* Research center.

U.S. Department of Health and Human Services

National Institute of Mental Health

Neuroscience and Behavioral Science Division

Behavioral, Cognitive, and Social Science Research Branch

5600 Fishers Ln.   Ph: (301)443-3942
Rockville, MD 20857   Fax: (301)443-9876

Contact: Dr. Mary Ellen Oliveri, Chf.

Desc: Programs of research, research training, and resource development in the behavioral sciences to increase understanding of psychological, psychosocial, emotional, and cognitive factors influencing behavior. *Type:* Research center.

U.S. Department of Health and Human Services

National Institute of Mental Health

Neuroscience and Behavioral Science Division

Behavioral and Integrative Neuroscience Research Branch

5600 Fishers Ln., Rm. 11-C-16   Ph: (301)443-1576
Parklawn Bldg.   Fax: (301)443-4822
Rockville, MD 20857
E-mail: SFOOTE@helix.nih.gov

Contact: Stephen Foote, PhD, Chf.

Desc: Brain mechanisms underlying behavior in functional organisms or through theoretical models, with a view to understanding how behavior develops, how it is maintained, and how it is regulated. Branch comprises four programs: Cognitive Neuroscience, including the higher mental activities of thinking, perceiving, feeling, understanding, reasoning, communicating, and remembering; Systems Neuroscience, including functional neural systems, homeostasis, social and survival behaviors, aggression, sexual and reproductive behavior, motivation and reward systems, sleep, and stress; Theoretical and Computational Neuroscience, including models of neural mechanisms; and Clinical Neuroscience, including systems-level studies of schizophrenia, mood and other affective disorders. *Type:* Research center.

U.S. Department of Health and Human Services

National Institute of Mental Health

Office of Scientific Information

5600 Fishers Ln., Rm. 7C-02,   Ph: (301)443-4513
  MSC 8030   Fax: (301)443-4279
Bethesda, MD 20892-8030
E-mail: nimhpubs@nih.gov
URL: http://www.nimh.nih.gov

Contact: Clarissa Wittenberg, Dir.

Desc: Administers the Institute's public communication, scientific information dissemination, and media relations activities. Prepares materials based on current research developments for professionals and the general public. *Type:* Research center.

U.S. Department of Health and Human Services

National Institute for Occupational Safety and Health

Biomedical and Behavioral Science Division

Applied Psychology and Ergonomics Branch

Robert A. Taft Laboratories   Ph: (513)533-8291
4676 Columbia Pkwy.   Fax: (513)533-8596
Cincinnati, OH 45226-1998

Contact: Steve Sauter, Chf.

Desc: Occupational stress and ergonomics. *Type:* Research center.

U.S. Department of Health and Human Services

National Institutes of Health

National Institute of Mental Health

9000 Rockville Pike   Ph: (301)443-3673
Bethesda, MD 20892   Fax: (301)443-0008
URL: http://www.nimh.nih.gov/

Contact: Steven E. Hyman, MD, Director.

Desc: The Institute provides leadership for a national program to increase knowledge and advance effective strategies to deal with problems and issues in the promotion of mental health, and the prevention and treatment of mental illness. *Type:* Government agency, office, or program.

University of California

Center for Mental Health Services Research

2020 Milvia St., Ste. 405, No.   Ph: (510)643-3555
  5610   Fax: (510)643-3522
Berkeley, CA 94720-5610
URL: http://socrates.berkeley.edu/~cmhsr/main.html

Contact: Lonnie Snowden, Ch.

Desc: Organization and financing of care for severely mentally ill persons, including financing and economics, organization of services and systems, and methods and measurement. *Type:* Research center.

University of California, Los Angeles

Harbor-UCLA Medical Center

Research and Education Institute

1124 W. Carson St., B-4 South   Ph: (310)222-4266
Torrance, CA 90502   Fax: (310)222-4264
E-mail: linkeh@harbor2.humc.edu
URL: http://www.humc.edu/rei

Contact: Prof. Keh-Ming Lin, MD, Dir.

Desc: Role of ethnicity (including culture) and biological variables in the mental health of ethnic minority populations. Conducts studies using pharmacokinetic, pharmacodynamic, and pharmacogenetic research techniques to examine ethnic and individual differences in responses to psychotropic drugs. *Type:* Research center.

University of California, Los Angeles

Neuropsychiatric Institute

760 Westwood Plz.   Ph: (310)206-1233
Los Angeles, CA 90024   Fax: (310)825-3942
URL: http://www.npi.ucla.edu

Contact: Dr. Peter C. Whybrow, Dir.

Desc: Psychiatry; neurology; mental retardation; developmental disabilities; and behavioral sciences, including anthropology, biochemistry, neurophysiology, psychology, social and preventive psychiatry, psychopharmacology, and sociology. *Type:* Research center.

University of California, Los Angeles

Program on Psychosocial Adaptation and the Future

Neuropsychiatric Institute Ph: (310)825-0463
760 Westwood Plz. Fax: (310)825-3002
Los Angeles, CA 90024-1759
E-mail: preadapt@ucla.edu
Contact: Dr. Roderic Gorney, Dir.

Desc: Studies psychosocial and cultural determinants of behavior, including impact of television on adults and the clinical role of the sense of the future in mental illness. *Type:* Research center.

University of California, San Francisco

Langley Porter Psychiatric Institute

401 Parnassus Ave. Free: 800-723-7140
San Francisco, CA 94143 Fax: (415)476-7320
URL: http://www.ucsf.edu
Contact: Craig Van Dyke, MD, Dir.

Desc: Clinical studies of psychiatric disorders and psychotherapy and basic research studies in psychopharmacology, neurobiology, cellular and molecular biology, behavioral biology, and social sciences. *Type:* Research center.

University of Cincinnati

Central Psychiatric Clinic

Research and Evaluation Division

Univ. Hospital Ph: (513)558-5944
3259 Elland Ave. Fax: (513)558-3880
Cincinnati, OH 45229
Contact: Mary C. Grace, Dir. of Res.

Desc: Evaluates the Clinic's treatment programs for psychiatric problems of both adults and children, including evaluation of psychotropic medication and prediction of psychotherapy outcome. *Type:* Research center.

University of Colorado

National Center for American Indian and Alaska Native Mental Health Research

Department of Psychiatry Ph: (303)315-9232
University North Pavilion Fax: (303)315-9579
4455 E. 12th Ave., A011-13
Denver, CO 80220
E-mail: spero.manson@uchsc.edu
URL: http://www.uchsc.edu/sm/ncaianmhr/
Contact: Dr. Spero Manson, Dir.

Desc: Center formulates, designs, conducts, and reports studies within four areas of inquiry: determining and improving the performance characteristics of self-report measures of serious psychological dysfunction and diagnostic interviews for assessing alcohol, drug, and mental (ADM) disorders; establishing the prevalence and incidence of ADM disorders and related risk factors through descriptive and experimental epidemiological investigations; developing and evaluating methods for detecting and managing ADM disorders presented in human service settings; and examining the effectiveness of interventions for preventing ADM disorders and promoting well-being. Ongoing studies include the American Indian Vietnam Veterans Project, which studies post-traumatic stress disorder and other psychological problems of Vietnam war veterans in readjusting to civilian life; Flower of Two Soils Reinterview Project, which studies emotional disorders in Native American adolescents; the Health Survey of Indian Boarding Students, which seeks to establish the prevalence and incidence of symptoms of depression, anxiety, suicidal behavior, and substance abuse, and to clarify relative contributions of stressful life events, coping strategies, social support, mastery, and self-esteem; the Foundations of Indian Teens Project, which develops more reliable and valid measures of psychopathology among Indian adolescents, with special emphasis on trauma; and the Voices of Indian Teens Project.

University of Florida

Center for Ambulatory Studies

930 NW 8th Ave. Ph: (352)375-0607
Gainesville, FL 32601 Fax: (352)375-6111
URL: http://www.mammacare.com
Contact: Dr. Mark Kane Goldstein, Dir.

Desc: Behavioral and biomedical engineering, including remote monitoring of ambulatory patients and behavioral aspects of chronically ill outpatients, precision measurement of health-related behaviors, and study of simulated breast with lumps for training in breast self-examination for cancer detection. *Type:* Research center.

University of Illinois at Chicago

National Research and Training Center on Psychiatric Disability

104 S. Michigan Ave., Ste. 900 Ph: (312)422-8180
Chicago, IL 60603 Fax: (312)422-0740
E-mail: jcook@psych.uic.edu
URL: http://www.psych.uic.edu/~rtc/
Contact: Judith A. Cook, PhD, Dir.

Desc: Psychiatric disabilities, including crisis management and prevention of hospitalization; employment, housing, and education; the needs of women and those with diverse cultural backgrounds; familial experiences; and systems integration. *Type:* Research center.

University of Illinois at Chicago

Psychiatric Clinical Research Center

1601 W. Taylor Ph: (312)355-1654
Chicago, IL 60612 Fax: (312)433-8454
E-mail: pjanicak@psych.uic.edu
Contact: Dr. Philip G. Janicak, Dir.

Desc: Psychological and biological factors associated with schizophrenia and major depression and mania, drug trials, brain imaging (PET, MRI, EEG, and ERP), genetic vulnerability, neurotransmitter receptor studies, and information processing studies. Prior to assignment to a research protocol, patients may undergo a drug-free washout period lasting from 3 to 14 days. *Type:* Research center.

University of Iowa

Affective Disorders Research Unit

Department of Psychiatry Ph: (319)353-4434
Psychiatry Research - MEB Fax: (319)353-3003
Iowa City, IA 52242-1000
E-mail: william-coryell@uiowa.edu
Contact: Dr. William H. Coryell, Hd.

Desc: Affective disorders, including clinical symptoms and genetics. Evaluates and follows approximately 200 patients suffering from affective disorders, 600 of their first-degree relatives, and 120 control subjects. *Type:* Research center.

University of Iowa

Department of Psychiatry

Univ. of Iowa Hospitals & Ph: (319)356-4720
Clinics Fax: (319)353-8300
200 Hawkins Dr., Rm. 2911
JPP
Iowa City, IA 52242-1057
E-mail: nancy-andreasen@uiowa.edu
URL: http://data-entry.psychiatry.uiowa.edu/mhcrc/
Contact: Dr. Nancy C. Andreasen, Dir.

Desc: Schizophrenia and other cognitive disorders, utilizing brain imaging modalities and neuropsychological testing to explore cognitive and neural deficits in schizophrenia. Also conducts family and genetic studies in schizophrenia, longitudinal follow-up studies, treatment-response studies, and drug trials. *Type:* Research center.

University of Kentucky

Behavioral Physiology Laboratory

Department of Behavioral Sci. Ph: (606)323-7263
College of Med. Office Bldg. Fax: (606)323-5350
Lexington, KY 40536-0086
E-mail: pwadhwa@pop.uky.edu
Contact: Pathik D. Wadhwa, MD,PhD, Dir.

Desc: Basic and clinical psychophysiology, including cardiovascular risk, ambulatory blood pressure monitoring, psychoneuroendocrinology, blood biochemistry, psychopharmacology, stress-testing, human performance, and experimental behavioral therapeutics. *Type:* Research center.

University of Maryland

Institute of Psychiatry and Human Behavior

701 W. Prat. St., No. 388 Ph: (410)328-6735
Baltimore, MD 21201 Fax: (410)328-3693
E-mail: jtalbott@umpsu.ad.umd.edu
Contact: John Talbott, MD, Dir.

Desc: Psychiatry, neurophysiology and behavioral sciences, including alcoholism and drug abuse, psycholinguistics, violent behavior, human development, interpersonal relations, and psychotic disorders. Focuses on chronic mental illness, mental health care financing, and organization of mental health services. *Type:* Research center.

University of Maryland

Maryland Psychiatric Research Center

PO Box 21247 Ph: (410)455-7101
Catonsville, MD 21228 Fax: (410)788-3837
Contact: Dr. William T. Carpenter, Jr., Dir.

Desc: Etiology and treatment of chronic schizophrenia and including assessment of therapeutic efficacy of treatment, design of safer approaches to antipsychotic and other drug treatments, definition of subgroups of patients to permit clinicians to match patients and treatments, design and implementation of experimental treatments. Neuroscience program studies brain mechanisms involved in the causes, manifestations, and treatment of mental illness. *Type:* Research center.

University of Michigan

Mental Health Research Institute

205 Zina Pitcher Pl. Ph: (734)764-4235
Ann Arbor, MI 48109-0720 Fax: (734)647-4130
E-mail: rpfreed@umich.edu
URL: http://www.med.umich.edu/mhri
Contact: Ruth P. Freedman, Admin.

Desc: Biological and behavioral studies relevant to normal and pathological human behavior and treatment of mental illness. Conducts studies on basic biological mechanisms relevant to normal and pathological behavior. *Type:* Research center.

University of Missouri--Columbia

Missouri Institute of Mental Health

5400 Arsenal St. Ph: (314)644-8851
St. Louis, MO 63139-1494 Fax: (314)644-8834
E-mail: mimhdw@showme.missouri.edu
URL: http://www.mimh.edu
Contact: Danny Wedding, PhD, Dir.

Desc: Mental health policy and ethics, mental health information systems, computer applications for the assessment and treatment of the mentally retarded and mentally ill, outcomes assessments, and mental health program evaluation research. *Type:* Research center.

University of Montreal

Riviere-des-Prairies Hospital Research Centre

7070, blvd. Perras   Ph: (514)323-7260
Montreal, PQ, Canada H1E   Fax: (514)323-4163
1A4
E-mail: jbreton@can.org
Contact: Dr. Jean-Jacques Breton, Dir.
Desc: Validation of measures for evaluating the mental health problems in children and adolescents. *Type:* Research center.

University of Pennsylvania

Center for Cognitive Therapy

Sch. of Med.   Ph: (215)898-4102
The Sci. Ctr., Rm. 754   Fax: (215)573-3717
3600 Market St.
Philadelphia, PA 19104-2648
E-mail: beck@landru.cpr.upenn.edu
Contact: Aaron T. Beck, MD, Dir.
Desc: Psychiatric outpatient clinic, engaged in developing different assessment instruments to measure constructs of cognitive theory, extending the cognitive approach to anxiety and other psychiatric disorders, assessing and predicting suicidal risks, studying outpatient populations, and assessing different training models for cognitive therapists. *Type:* Research center.

University of Pennsylvania

Center for Mental Health Policy and Services Research

3600 Market St., 7th Fl.   Ph: (215)662-2886
Philadelphia, PA 19104   Fax: (215)349-8715
E-mail: trevor@cmhpsr.upenn.edu
URL: http://www.med.upenn.edu/~cmhpsr/
Contact: Trevor Hadley, PhD, Dir.
Desc: Mental health policy and services. *Type:* Research center.

University of Pennsylvania

Depression Research Unit

University City Science Center   Ph: (215)662-3462
3600 Market St., 8th Fl.   Fax: (215)662-6443
Philadelphia, PA 19104-2649
E-mail: amsterdam@mail.psypharm.upenn.edu
Contact: Jay D. Amsterdam, MD, Dir.
Desc: Affective disorders. Research areas include psychopharmacology, particularly development of new antidepressant drugs; clinical neuroendocrinology; and the biochemical causes of major depression. *Type:* Research center.

University of Pennsylvania

Mood and Anxiety Disorders Section

3600 Market St., Ste. 872   Ph: (215)898-4301
Philadelphia, PA 19104-2649   Fax: (215)898-0509
E-mail: schweizer@mail.psypharm.upenn.edu
Contact: Dr. Edward E. Schweizer, Dir.
Desc: Psychopharmacology, including short- and long-term clinical trials on the effects of antidepressive and antianxiety medications. *Type:* Research center.

University of Pennsylvania

Weight and Eating Disorders Program

Department of Psychiatry   Ph: (215)898-7314
3600 Market St., Ste. 738   Fax: (215)898-2878
Philadelphia, PA 19104-2648
E-mail: wadden@mail.med.upenn.edu
URL: http://www.med.upenn.edu/~weight
Contact: Dr. Thomas Wadden, Dir.
Desc: Obesity, binge eating disorder, bulimia (including behavioral treatments for all). body image, metabolic rate and body fat measures, and predictors of adiposity in infancy. *Type:* Research center.

University of Pittsburgh Medical Center

Western Psychiatric Institute and Clinic

W. Psych.   Ph: (412)624-0750
3811 O'Hara St.   Fax: (412)624-8015
Pittsburgh, PA 15213
E-mail: molinarone@msx.upmc.edu
URL: http://www.wpic.pitt.edu
Contact: Nicole Molinaro, Contact.
Desc: Advancement of basic and clinical knowledge in psychological, biological, environmental, and social interactions related to mental health and psychiatric care. Conducts research on psychiatric disorders, including depression, manic-depression, schizophrenia, anorexia nervosa, Alzheimer's disease, autism, anxiety, obsessive-compulsive disorders, and borderline disorders. *Type:* Research center.

University of South Florida

Louis de la Parte Florida Mental Health Institute

13301 Bruce B. Downs Blvd.   Ph: (813)974-4602
Tampa, FL 33612-3807   Fax: (813)974-4699
E-mail: probinso@hal.fmhi.usf.edu
URL: http://www.fmhi.usf.edu
Contact: Dr. David Shern, Dean.
Desc: Mental health care, including aging and mental health, child and family studies, community mental health, and mental health law and policy. *Type:* Research center.

University of Texas--Houston Health Science Center

Mental Sciences Institute

1300 Moursund Ave.   Ph: (713)500-2500
Houston, TX 77030   Fax: (713)500-2553
E-mail: rguynn@msi.uth.tmc.edu
URL: http://www.uth.tmc.edu/med/msi/index.htm
Contact: Dr. Robert Guynn, Dir.
Desc: Biochemical and behavioral aspects of psychiatric diseases, particularly physiopathology and pharmacology of alcohol and drug addiction, and affective and anxiety disorders. Performs basic and clinical studies in neuroendocrinology, metabolism, behavioral science, disorders, mental retardation, neurochemistry, psychophysiology, biochemistry, crime and delinquency, and gerontology. *Type:* Research center.

University of Virginia

Southeastern Rural Mental Health Research Center

Health Sci. Ctr., Box 393   Ph: (804)982-3298
Charlottesville, VA 22908   Fax: (804)982-3275
E-mail: jm8h@virginia.edu
Contact: Jeanne Fox, Dir.
Desc: Rural mental health, focusing African-Americans and impoverished mentally ill individuals and their families. Specific area of study include the incidence and prevalence of mental disorders and co-occurring physical health problems, informal and formal care networks and interventions accessed and utilized by rural high risk populations in need of mental health and health service, and the cost and effectiveness of outreach and alternative models linking mental health, social service, and health care providers in the delivery of services to seriously mentally ill adults, the elderly, women, and children. *Type:* Research center.

University of Wisconsin--Madison

Health Emotions Research Institute

6001 Research Park Blvd.   Ph: (608)263-6161
Madison, WI 53719-1176   Fax: (608)263-9340
E-mail: shattuck@facstaff.wisc.edu
URL: http://www.healthemotions.org
Contact: Ned H. Kalin, MD, Dir.
Desc: Relationships between positive emotions, physiological systems, and health. *Type:* Research center.

Vanderbilt University

Center for Mental Health Policy

1207 18th Ave. S.   Ph: (615)322-8694
Nashville, TN 37212   Fax: (615)322-7049
E-mail: bickman@home.com
URL: http://www.vanderbilt.edu/vipps/cmhp/cmhphome.html
Contact: Leonard Bickman, Dir.
Desc: Evaluation of homeless family programs, effects of family empowerment on children's mental health, patterns of psychiatric hospitalization of children, and evaluation of school mental health services. *Type:* Research center.

Vanderbilt University

Center for Psychotherapy Research

Nashville, TN 37240   Ph: (615)322-0058
Contact: Hans H. Strupp, PhD, Dir.
Desc: Time-limited dynamic psychotherapy. *Type:* Research center.

Veterans Affairs Medical Center (Palo Alto, CA)

NIMH Mental Health Clinical Research Center

MC 116A   Ph: (650)493-2234
3801 Miranda Ave.   Fax: (650)493-4901
Palo Alto, CA 94304
Contact: Adolf Pfefferbaum, MD, Dir.
Desc: Mental illness, focusing on clinical, physiological, and neuropsychological factors, with special emphasis on neuroimaging studies of brain structure and function. Areas include schizophrenia and neurological disorders with psychotic symptoms. *Type:* Research center.

Washington Institute for Mental Illness Research and Training

Eastern Branch   Ph: (509)299-4501
PO Box A   Fax: (509)299-4664
Medical Lake, WA 99022-0045
E-mail: dyck@wsu.edu
Contact: Dennis G. Dyck, PhD, Dir.
Desc: Mental health clinical and services research for persons with severe and persistent mental illness; family and patient psychoeducation and support; and immune function and mental illness. *Type:* Research center.

Washington University in St. Louis

Diabetes Research and Training Center

660 S. Euclid Ave., Box 8212   Ph: (314)362-8290
St. Louis, MO 63110   Fax: (314)362-8265
E-mail: mpuhar@imgate.wustl.edu
URL: http://www.medicine.wustl.edu/drtc
Contact: M. Alan Permutt, MD, Contact.
Desc: Diabetes research, including the causes of diabetes, insulin action, growth factors, and diabetic complications. Promotes biomedical and psychosocial studies of diabetes mellitus by operating core facilities to support established investigators. *Type:* Research center.

World Federation for Mental Health Newsletter

World Federation for Mental Health
1021 Prince St.   Ph: (410)938-3180
Alexandria, VA 22314-2971   Fax: (410)938-3183
E-mail: wfmh@erols.com
URL: http://ssw.ab.umd.edu/wfmh.html; http://www.wfmh.com.
Contact: Elena Berger, Editor.
Desc: Reports activities of member organizations and individual members. Includes news of preparations for World Mental Health Day, an annual event held in October. *Type:* Newsletter.

Yale University
Center for Biocognitive Studies
Yale Psychiatric Institute　　Ph: (203)785-7200
184 Liberty St.　　Fax: (203)785-7855
New Haven, CT 06519
Contact: Dr. Thomas McGlashan, Med.Dir.
Desc: Study of the cognitive, linguistic, psychophysiological, and neuropsychological bases of psychopathology. *Type:* Research center.

Yale University
Ribicoff Research Facilities of the Connecticut Mental Health Center
34 Park St.　　Ph: (203)974-7725
New Haven, CT 06508　　Fax: (203)974-7724
E-mail: eric.nestler@yale.edu
URL:　　http://info.med.yale.edu/psych/org/cmhc/molecular
Contact: Dr. Eric J. Nestler, Dir.
Desc: Preclinical and clinical studies of the neurobiological basis of severe mental disorders, including depression, anxiety, schizophrenia, and drug addiction. Conducts basic research programs in molecular, biochemical, neurophysiological, neuropharmacological, and behavioral fields. *Type:* Research center.

Yeshiva University
Sound View-Throgs Neck Community Mental Health Center
2527 Glebe Ave.　　Ph: (718)904-4400
Bronx, NY 10461　　Fax: (718)931-7307
Contact: Dr. Betzler, Dir.
Desc: Mental health, mental illness, and recovery from mental illness. *Type:* Research center.

Mentally Disabled

American Association on Mental Retardation
444 N. Capitol St. NW, Ste.　　Ph: (202)387-1968
846　　Free: 800-424-3688
Washington, DC 20001-1512　　Fax: (202)387-2193
E-mail: aamr@access.digex.net
URL: http://www.aamr.org
Contact: Ms. M. Doreen Croser, Exec.Dir.
Desc: Physicians, educators, administrators, social workers, psychologists, psychiatrists, students, and others interested in the general welfare of persons with mental retardation and the study of the cause, treatment, and prevention of mental retardation. Maintains 17 divisions and subdivisions. *Type:* Association.

ARC/Mercer
231 Lawrenceville Rd.　　Ph: (609)278-1211
Lawrenceville, NJ 08648　　Fax: (609)278-9291
E-mail: arcmercer@aol.com
Contact: Joseph N. Gousie, Sr., Exec.Dir.
Desc: Parents of, and professionals interested in, mentally retarded citizens. Sponsors day program for infants and adults, residential programs for adults, sheltered workshops, community job placement, supportive employment, and recreation and respite services. *Type:* Association.

The ARC of Monmouth
1158 Wayside Rd.　　Ph: (732)493-1919
Tinton Falls, NJ 07712　　Fax: (732)493-3604
Contact: Deborah Trub Wehrlen, Exec.Dir.
Desc: Provides programs and services for people with mental retardation. *Type:* Association.

The ARC of Monroe County
1000 Elmwood Ave.　　Ph: (716)271-0660
Rochester, NY 14620　　Fax: (716)442-1911
URL: http://www.arcmonroe.org
Contact: James G. Mroczek, Pres.
Desc: Business, community, and family volunteers working to enhance the quality of life for people with developmental disabilities. *Type:* Association.

Association for Children with Down Syndrome
2616 Martin Ave.　　Ph: (516)221-4700
Bellmore, NY 11710　　Fax: (516)221-5867
E-mail: Info@acds.org
URL: http://www.acds.org
Contact: Sam Nussbaum, C.S.W., Exec.Dir.
Desc: Administers infant, toddler, and preschool programs in New York state and sibling programs. Offer recreational and socialization programs and support groups for childres over 5 years of age through adulthood. Parents of children with Down Syndrome; health and educational professionals. Acts as resource and information center about Down Syndrome. *Type:* Association.

Association for the Help of Retarded Children
200 Park Ave. S., Ste. 1201
New York, NY 10003
Contact: Shirley Berenstein, Dir.
Desc: Developmentally disabled children and adults; their families; interested individuals. *Type:* Association.

Bergen-Passaic ARC
James E. Seath
223 Moore St.　　Ph: (201)343-0322
Hackensack, NJ 07601-7402　　Fax: (201)343-0401
URL: http://www.arcbergenpassaic.org
Contact: James E. Seath, Exec.Dir.
Desc: Provides advocacy, services and supports to individuals with disabilities and to their families as well. Programs include early intervention, vocational residential, recreation and family support. *Type:* Association.

Best Buddies International
100 SE Second St., Ste. 1990　　Ph: (305)374-2233
Miami, FL 33131　　Fax: (305)374-5305
E-mail: bestbuddies@juno.com
URL: http://www.bestbuddies.org
Contact: Tracey Herard, Chf.Oper.Off.
Desc: Individuals interested in the social well-being of people with mental retardation. Promotes establishment of friendships between people with mental retardation and other members of the community. *Type:* Association.

Bethesda Lutheran Homes and Services
700 Hoffman Dr.　　Ph: (920)261-3050
Watertown, WI 53094　　Free: 800-369-INFO
　　Fax: (920)261-8441
E-mail: blhsncrc@execpc.com
URL: http://www.bethesdainfo.org
Contact: Kevin Keller, Coord.
Desc: Provides religious education, habilitation services, therapeutic services, vocational training, and residential care for 700 persons with mental retardation in Florida, Illinois, Indiana, Kansas, Maryland, Michigan, Missouri, Ohio, Texas and Wisconsin. *Type:* Association.

Brown County Association for Retarded Citizens
Virginia Baeten
PO Box 12770　　Ph: (920)498-2599
1673 Dousman St.　　Fax: (920)498-2652
Green Bay, WI 54307
Contact: Virginia Baeten, Exec.Dir.
Desc: Parents, professionals, and other interested individuals organized to promote services, research, public understanding, and legislation for individuals with mental retardation and their families. Conducts charitable activities. *Type:* Association.

Charles River Association for Retarded Citizens
989 Central Ave.　　Ph: (781)444-4347
Needham, MA 02192　　Fax: (781)444-5146
E-mail: PMerritt@crarc.org
Contact: Paul Merritt, Pres.
Desc: Support group for retarded persons and their families in the Needham, MA area. Advocates and assists with problems related to retardation. *Type:* Association.

JARC
28366 Franklin Rd.　　Ph: (248)352-5272
Southfield, MI 48034　　Fax: (248)352-5279
E-mail: jarc@speedlink.net
URL: http://www.jaru.org
Contact: Joyce Keller, Exec.Dir.
Desc: Jewish association providing residential care and support services to developmentally disabled adults. Operates 16 group homes that provide access to Jewish services, maintain kosher kitchens, and 4 independent living programs. Provides support to families with children with any disability including respite care, case management, and social activities. *Type:* Association.

New York State Association of Retarded Citizens
393 Delaware Ave.　　Ph: (518)439-8311
Delmar, NY 12054　　Fax: (518)439-1893
E-mail: nysarc@crisny.org
URL: http://www.crisny.org/~nysarc
Contact: Marc N. Brandt, Exec.Dir.
Desc: A not-for-profit, family-based organization working with and for people with mental retardation and other developmental disabilities. *Type:* Association.

Opportunities Unlimited of Niagara
1555 Factory Outlet Blvd.　　Ph: (716)297-6400
LPO Box 360　　Fax: (716)297-7522
Niagara Falls, NY 14304-0360
Contact: Bruce Shields, Pres. & CEO.
Desc: Services for families of and people with developmental disabilities. *Type:* Association.

Springfield Association for Retarded Citizens
One SPARCenter Plaza　　Ph: (217)793-2100
Springfield, IL 62702　　Free: 800-800-6401
　　Fax: (217)793-2127
E-mail: sparc@aol.com
Contact: Carlissa Puckett, Exec.Dir.
Desc: Helps individuals with developmental disabilities improve the quality of their lives. *Type:* Association.

Metallurgy
Aluminum Industry Abstracts
Cambridge Scientific Abstracts (CSA)
7200 Wisconsin Ave., Ste. 601　　Ph: (301)961-6700
Bethesda, MD 20814-4823
E-mail: sales@csa.com
URL: http://www.csa.com
Desc: Contains more than 160,000 citations, with abstracts, to the world's technical and business literature dealing with aluminum production, properties, processing, and applications. Sources include more than 2500 scientific journals and business publications as well as patents, government reports, conference proceedings, translations, dissertations, books, and press releases. *Available:* Cambridge Scientific Abstracts (CSA). *Type:* Database.

Metallurgy

ASM International

9639 Kinsman
Materials Park, OH 44073
Ph: (440)338-5151
Free: 800-336-5152
Fax: (440)338-4634
E-mail: memserv@po.asm-intl.org
URL: http://www.asm-intl.org
Contact: Dr. Michael J. DeHaemer, Mng.Dir.
Desc: Metallurgists, materials engineers, executives in materials producing and consuming industries; teachers and students. Disseminates technical information about the manufacture, use, and treatment of engineered materials. Offers in-plant, home study, and intensive courses through Materials Engineering Institute. *Type:* Association.

Association of Iron and Steel Engineers

3 Gateway Center, Ste. 1900
Pittsburgh, PA 15222
Ph: (412)281-6323
Fax: (412)281-4657
URL: http://www.aise.org
Contact: Lawrence G. Maloney, Mng.Dir.
Desc: Engineers and operators in the basic steel industry; suppliers to the industry. To advance the technical and engineering phases of the production and processing of iron and steel. Develops technical reports for the industry; conducts studies. *Type:* Association.

International Brotherhood of Boilermakers, Iron Ship Builders, Blacksmiths, Forgers and Helpers

753 State Ave., Ste. 570
New Brotherhood
Kansas City, KS 66101
Ph: (913)371-2640
Fax: (913)281-8101
URL: http://www.boilermakers.org
Contact: Charles W. Jones, International Pres.
Desc: AFL-CIO. *Type:* Association.

International Copper Association

260 Madison Ave.
New York, NY 10016
Ph: (212)251-7240
Fax: (212)251-7245
URL: http://www.copper.org
Contact: Jan A. Smolders, Pres.
Desc: Copper producing and fabricating companies. Conducts market development and research on uses for copper through contracts with commercial, institutional, and university organizations. *Type:* Association.

International Lead Zinc Research Organization

2525 Meridian Pky.
PO Box 12036
Research Triangle Park, NC 27709
Ph: (919)361-4647
Fax: (919)361-1957
E-mail: jcole@ilzro.org
URL: http://www.ilzro.org
Contact: Jerome F. Cole, Pres.
Desc: Research organization sponsored by major producers, smelters, and refiners of lead and/or zinc from 15 countries. Seeks to develop new applications for lead and zinc. Seeks to improve current uses of lead and zinc; compiles technical information on these metals. *Type:* Association.

Iron and Steel Society

410 Commonwealth Dr.
Warrendale, PA 15086-7512
Ph: (724)776-1535
Fax: (724)776-0430
E-mail: mailbag@issource.org
URL: http://www.issource.org
Contact: David L. Kanagy, CAE, Exec.Dir.
Desc: Member society of the American Institute of Mining, Metallurgical and Petroleum Engineers. Individuals in the field of iron and steel processing and technology. Seeks to provide a medium of communication and cooperation among those interested in any phase of ferrous metallurgy and materials science and technology. *Type:* Association.

METADEX®

Cambridge Scientific Abstracts (CSA)
7200 Wisconsin Ave., Ste. 601
Bethesda, MD 20814-4823
Ph: (301)961-6700
E-mail: sales@csa.com
URL: http://www.csa.com
Desc: Contains more than 950,000 citations, with abstracts (from 1979), to the worldwide technical literature on the science and practice of metallurgy. Sources include journal articles, conference papers, technical reports, books, dissertations, patents (U.S., British, and European Patent Office), and government reports. *Available:* France Ministry of Defense, Delegation Generale pour l'Armement, Centre de Documentation de l'Armement (CEDOCAR); The Dialog Corporation, DataStar; The Dialog Corporation, DIALOG; FIZ Technik (Fachinformationszentrum Technik e.V.); Questel • Orbit; STN International; European Information Network Services (EINS). *Type:* Database.

Metals Datafile®

Cambridge Scientific Abstracts (CSA)
7200 Wisconsin Ave., Ste. 601
Bethesda, MD 20814-4823
Ph: (301)961-6700
E-mail: sales@csa.com
URL: http://www.csa.com
Contact: Erica Omorogieva, Electronic Information Specialist, (301)941-2509, fax: (301)961-6720, erica@csa.com.
Desc: Contains more than 46,000 records providing designation and specification numbers for ferrous and nonferrous metals and alloys. Includes element concentrations, mechanical and physical properties, including tensile strength, yield point, shear and impact strength, hardness, fatigue life, density, specific heat, melting temperature, and conductivity; uses; manufacturers; and forms. *Available:* STN International; European Information Network Services (EINS). *Type:* Database.

Metalworking Digest

Cahners Business Information
New Product Information Division
301 Gibraltar Dr.
Morris Plains, NJ 07950
Ph: (973)292-5100
Fax: (973)539-3476
Contact: Richard Stevancsecz, Editor; David Esola, Publisher; Peter Hernandez, Advertising Mgr.
Desc: Tabloid for metalworking plant managers, manufacturing engineers, and product design engineers responsible for selecting and specifying machine tools, cutting tools, inspection, measurement devices, fabricating, allied equipment, and supplies. *Type:* Periodical.

Metalworking Technology Guide

Gardner Publications, Inc.
6915 Valley Ave.
Cincinnati, OH 45244-3029
Ph: (513)527-8800
Free: 800-950-8800
Fax: (513)527-8801
URL: http://www.gardnerweb.com
Contact: Tom Beard, Editor-in-Chief, tbeard@gardnerweb.com.
Desc: Supplemental magazine to Modern Machine Shop, covering metalworking technology. *Type:* Periodical.

Metlfax

Adams Business Media
29100 Aurora Rd., Ste. 200
Solon, OH 44139-1855
Ph: (440)248-1125
Fax: (440)248-0187
Contact: Gregory A. Jones, Publisher; James D. Destefani, Editor-in-Chief.
Desc: Metalworking magazine. *Type:* Periodical.

Minerals, Metals, and Materials Society

184 Thorn Hill Rd.
Warrendale, PA 15086-7528
Ph: (724)776-9000
Free: 800-759-4867
Fax: (724)776-3770
E-mail: tmsgeneral@tms.org
URL: http://www.tms.org
Contact: Alexander R. Scott, Exec.Dir.
Desc: A member society of American Institute of Mining, Metallurgical and Petroleum Engineers. Professional society of metallurgists, metallurgical engineers, and materials scientists. Maintains 35 committees. *Type:* Association.

Modern Applications News (MAN)

Nelson Publishing, Inc.
2500 Tamiami Tr. N.
Nokomis, FL 34275-3482
Ph: (941)966-9521
Fax: (941)966-2590
E-mail: nelpub@ix.netcom.com
URL: http://www.mansite.com.
Contact: A.V. Nelson, Group Publisher, (941)966-9521, fax: (941)966-2590; Bob Olree, Associate Publisher, (941)966-9521, fax: (941)966-2590; Larry Olson, Editor, (941)966-9521, fax: (941)966-2590, larry@mansite.com.
Desc: Trade magazine covering metalworking engineering, design, and manufacturing. *Type:* Periodical.

Modern Machine Shop

Gardner Publications, Inc.
6915 Valley Ave.
Cincinnati, OH 45244-3029
Ph: (513)527-8800
Free: 800-950-8800
Fax: (513)527-8801
URL: http://www.gardnerweb.com
Contact: Tom Beard, Editor-in-Chief, tbeard@gardnerweb.com.
Desc: Magazine on metalworking. *Type:* Periodical.

Steelabor

United Steelworkers of America
5 Gateway Ctr.
Pittsburgh, PA 15222
Ph: (412)562-2442
Fax: (412)562-2445
Contact: Charles Robideau, Editor.
Desc: Labor magazine. *Type:* Periodical.

Tooling & Production

Adams Business Media
29100 Aurora Rd., Ste. 200
Solon, OH 44139-1855
Ph: (440)248-1125
Fax: (440)248-0187
E-mail: tooling@toolingandproduction.com.
URL: http://www.toolingandproduction.com.
Contact: James Lorincz, Editor; Stanley J. Modic, Publisher/ Editor-in-chief.
Desc: Magazine concerning metalworking. *Type:* Periodical.

Wire Association International

1570 Boston Post Rd.
PO Box 578
Guilford, CT 06437
Ph: (203)453-2777
Fax: (203)453-8384
E-mail: jcoer@wirenet.org
URL: http://www.wirenet.org
Contact: Paul Casteran, Exec.Dir.
Desc: Society of operating executives, plant superintendents, engineers, chemists, metallurgists, and others in 57 countries concerned with production in wire mills and insulated wire plants that make bars, rods, strip, wire, wire products, fastners, fiberoptic, and electrical wire and cable. Promotes industry contacts. Studies production methods, new materials, and applications for existing materials; provides advisory service on technical and operating problems. *Type:* Association.

Metals

AAASD (Aluminum Association Aluminum Standards and Data)
Aluminum Association
900 19th St. NW   Ph: (202)862-5100
Washington, DC 20006
URL: http://www.aluminum.org
Desc: Contains the nominal composition and composition limits, typical mechanical and physical properties, and tensile properties limits for most U.S. wrought aluminum alloys in commercial use. *Available:* STN International. *Type:* Database.

Aluminum Association
900 19th St. NW, Ste. 300   Ph: (202)862-5100
Washington, DC 20006   Fax: (202)862-5164
URL: http://www.aluminum.org
Contact: J. Stephen Larkin, Pres.
Desc: Producers of aluminum and manufacturers of semifabricated aluminum products. Represents members' interests in legislative activity. Conducts seminars and workshops. *Type:* Association.

American Institute for International Steel Newsletter
*American Institute for International Steel, Inc. -
Pacific Chapter
c/o ANCON*
1010 Cabrillo   Ph: (310)548-8300
San Pedro, CA 90731-4067   Fax: (310)548-8357
Contact: Pat Penney, Editor.
Desc: Carries news of the metal importing industry. Discusses quotas, taxes, customs regulations, and relevant legislation. *Type:* Newsletter.

American Iron and Steel Institute
1101 17th St. NW, 13th Fl.   Ph: (202)452-7100
Washington, DC 20036-4700   Fax: (202)463-6573
URL: http://www.steel.org
Contact: Andrew G. Sharkey, Pres. and CEO.
Desc: Basic manufacturers and individuals in the steel industry. Members operate steel mills, blast furnaces, finishing mills, and iron ore mines. Products include pig iron, steel ingots, sheets, plates, bars, shapes, strips, tin plate, nails, pipe and tubes, railroad rails, wire products, and other basic forms of ferrous metals. *Type:* Association.

American Machinist
Thomas Grasson
1100 Superior Ave.   Ph: (216)696-7000
Cleveland, OH 44114-2543   Fax: (216)696-0177
Contact: Joseph Fristik, Group Publisher, (216)931-9522, jfrlstic@penton.com; T. Grasson, Senior Editor, (216)931-9700, tgrasson@penton.com.
Desc: Magazine. *Type:* Periodical.

American Machinist—Buyers' Guide Issue
Penton Media Inc.
1100 Superior Ave.   Ph: (216)696-7000
Cleveland, OH 44114-2543   Fax: (216)931-9524
E-mail: corpcomm@penton.com
Contact: Lee Teschler, Managing Editor; Diane Hallum, Exec. Editor; Paul Dvorak, Sr. Editor.
Desc: Guide to over 2,600 manufacturers of products and services used by metalworking industries. *Type:* Directory.

American Machinist—Metalworking Buyer's Guide Issue
Penton Media Inc.
1100 Superior Ave.   Ph: (216)696-7000
Cleveland, OH 44114-2543   Fax: (216)931-9524
E-mail: corpcomm@penton.com; ameditor@penton.com; directories@penton.com.

URL: http://pentrax.hsix.com; http://www.penton.com/am.
Contact: Tom Grasson, Editor; Patricia Smith, Editor; Bridget Black, Editor; Allison Venner, Assistant Editor; Chuck Bates, Associate Editor.
Desc: Lists manufacturers of manufacturing equipment, computers and controls, tooling, components, materials and/or services to the durable goods/metalworking industries. *Type:* Directory.

American Welding Society
550 NW Le Jeune Rd.   Ph: (305)443-9353
Miami, FL 33126   Free: 800-443-9353
    Fax: (305)443-7559
E-mail: info@aws.org
URL: http://www.aws.org
Contact: Dr. Frank G. DeLaurier, Exec.Dir.
Desc: One of several sponsors of the Welding Research Council and the Materials Properties Council. Professional engineering society in the field of welding. Sponsors seminars. *Type:* Association.

Blacksmithing Today
Nebraska Blacksmiths, Weldors and Machininsts Association
c/o Phillip Runyan   Ph: (308)728-7887
Rte. 1, Box 105A
Ord, NE 68862
Contact: Phillip Runyan, Editor.
Desc: Covers developments in the art of being a modern smithy as well as Association news. *Type:* Newsletter.

Canadian Resources & PennyMines Analyst
MPL Communications Inc.
133 Richmond St., Ste. 700   Ph: (416)869-1177
Toronto, ON, Canada M5H   Fax: (416)869-0616
   3M8
Desc: Evaluates junior and senior Canadian companies involved in oil and gas, mining, and forestry. Provides recommendations to assist in sound investment decisions. *Type:* Newsletter.

CBSA Capsules
Copper and Brass Servicenter Association (CBSA)
994 Old Eagle School Rd., Ste.   Ph: (610)265-6658
   1019
Wayne, PA 19087-1802
Contact: Franklin Brown, Jr., Editor.
Desc: Features news of the copper and brass industry. Includes reports on legislative and governmental actions and covers member and Association activities. *Type:* Newsletter.

CMP Update
*The EPRI Center for Materials Production (CMP)
Carnegie Mellon Research Institute*
3 Parkway Center E., Rm. 335   Ph: (412)351-4060
Ardmore Blvd.   Fax: (412)351-4207
Pittsburgh, PA 15221
Contact: John Kollar, Editor.
Desc: Furnishes information on the Center's electrotechnology research and development projects, which are aimed at improving the productivity and energy efficiency in materials production. Reviews trends in the metals industry. *Type:* Newsletter.

DRI Steel Forecast
*Standard & Poor's DRI
Data Products Division*
24 Hartwell Ave.   Ph: (781)863-5100
Lexington, MA 02421
E-mail: client_services@dri.mcgraw-hill.com

URL: http://www.dri.mcgraw-hill.com
Contact: Client Services, (617)860-6527, fax: (617)860-6416.
Desc: Contains approximately 500 quarterly and annual forecasts on production, shipment, and consumption of raw steel and steel products in the United States Covers consumption and prices for raw materials, raw steel production, shipments by product and market, imports, exports, inventory, and prices, and consumption by end market and product. Data are reported in terms of quantity or value. *Available:* Standard & Poor's DRI, Data Products Division. *Type:* Database.

Dun and Bradstreet's Industrial Guide: the Metalworking Directory
Dun & Bradstreet
3 Sylvan Way   Ph: (973)605-6442
Parsippany, NJ 07054-3896   Free: 800-526-0651
    Fax: (973)605-6911
E-mail: dnbmdd@dnb.com
Desc: Over 75,000 original equipment manufacturers, metal distributors, and machine tools/metalworking machinery distributors. *Type:* Directory.

Edison Welding Institute
1250 Arthur E. Adams Dr.   Ph: (614)688-5000
Columbus, OH 43221   Fax: (614)688-5001
URL: http://www.ewi.org
Contact: Dr. Karl Graff, Exec.Dir.
Desc: Dedicated to advancing and applying materials joining technology to benefit industry. *Type:* Association.

The FABRICATOR's Literature Directory
*The Croydon Group, Ltd.
Fabricators & Manufacturers Association, International*
833 Featherstone Rd.   Ph: (815)399-8700
Rockford, IL 61107-6302   Fax: (815)399-7279
E-mail: info@fmametalfab.org
URL: http://www.fmametalfab.org.
Contact: Theresa Houck, Editor; Clayton Baznik, Editor.
Desc: Publications, brochures, catalogs, videotapes, and web sites available from companies concerning metal fabricating and forming products, equipment, and services available to the industry. *Type:* Directory.

International Association of Bridge, Structural, Ornamental amd Reinforcing Iron Workers
1750 New York Ave. NW   Ph: (202)383-4810
Washington, DC 20006   Fax: (202)638-4856
Contact: Jake West, Gen.Pres.
Desc: AFL-CIO. *Type:* Association.

International Lead and Zinc
The WEFA Group
1110 Vermont Ave., NW   Ph: (202)775-0610
Washington, DC 20005
URL: http://www.fdic.gov
Desc: Contains approximately 1400 monthly, quarterly, and annual time series on lead and zinc. Covers metal consumption, mine production, metal production, principal end uses, stocks, recovery of secondary lead and zinc, and trade with Socialist countries. *Available:* The WEFA Group. *Type:* Database.

Iron and Steel
The WEFA Group
1110 Vermont Ave., NW   Ph: (202)775-0610
Washington, DC 20005
URL: http://www.fdic.gov
Desc: Contains more than 2000 weekly, monthly, quarterly, and annual historical time series on supply, demand, and trade for the U.S. and worldwide iron and steel industry. *Available:* The WEFA Group. *Type:* Database.

Lead Industries Association

13 Main St. Ph: (973)726-LEAD
Sparta, NJ 07871 Fax: (973)726-4484
E-mail: miller@leadinfo.com
URL: http://www.leadinfo.com
Contact: Jeffrey T. Miller, Exec.Dir.
Desc: Mining companies, smelters, and recyclers; manufacturers of lead products or products of which lead is a component. *Type:* Association.

Magnesium

International Magnesium Association
1303 Vincent Pl., Ste. 1
Mc Lean, VA 22101 Ph: (703)442-8888
 Fax: (703)821-1824
E-mail: ima@bellatlantic.net
URL: http://www.intlmag.org
Contact: Byron Clow, Editor-in-Chief; Janet Ayala, Editor.
Desc: Discusses events and trends in the metallic magnesium industry. Recurring features include a calendar of events, reports of meetings, news of educational opportunities, and notices of publications available. *Type:* Newsletter.

Materials Business File™

Cambridge Scientific Abstracts (CSA)
7200 Wisconsin Ave., Ste. 601 Ph: (301)961-6700
Bethesda, MD 20814-4823
E-mail: sales@csa.com
URL: http://www.csa.com
Desc: Contains more than 90,000 citations, with abstracts, to worldwide literature on technical and commercial aspects of iron and steel, nonferrous metals, and relevant nonmetallic materials such as polymers, ceramics, and composites. Sources include more than 2000 technical journals, trade magazines, newspapers, news briefs, books, conference proceedings, and announcements worldwide. *Available:* The Dialog Corporation, DataStar; The Dialog Corporation, DIALOG; Questel • Orbit; STN International; France Ministry of Defense, Delegation Generale pour l'Armement, Centre de Documentation de l'Armement (CEDOCAR); FIZ Technik (Fachinformationszentrum Technik e.V.). *Type:* Database.

Metal Construction News—Metal Architecture Building Systems Product File and Directory Issue

Modern Trade Communications, Inc.
7450 N. Skokie Blvd. Ph: (847)674-2200
Skokie, IL 60077 Fax: (847)674-3676
E-mail: mtci@moderntrade.com
URL: http://www.moderntrade.com.
Contact: Shawn Zuver, Editor.
Desc: List of more than 990 manufacturers and suppliers of building components and accessories, insulation, doors and frames, mechanical products, cranes, manufacturing and construction equipment; nearly 90 steel erectors; and about 35 industry associations. *Type:* Directory.

Metal Polishers, Buffers, Platers and Allied Workers International Union

PO Box 4055
Kokomo, IN 46904-4055
Contact: Glenn L. Holt, Pres. & Sec.-Treas.
Desc: AFL-CIO. *Type:* Association.

Metal Powder Industries Federation

105 College Rd. E. Ph: (609)452-7700
Princeton, NJ 08540-6692 Fax: (609)987-8523
E-mail: info@mpif.org
URL: http://www.mpif.org
Contact: Donald G. White, Exec.Dir.
Desc: Manufacturers of metal powders, powder metallurgy processing equipment and tools, powder metallurgy prod-
ucts, and refractory and reactive metals. Member associations are: Metal Injection Molding Association; Metal Powder Producers Association; Metal Powder Technology Association; Powder Metallurgy Equipment Association; Powder Metallurgy Parts Association; Refractory Metals Association. Promotes the science and industry of powder metallurgy and metal powder application through: sponsorship of technical meetings, seminars, and exhibits; establishment of standards; compilation of statistics; public relations; publications. *Type:* Association.

Metals Week

McGraw-Hill Companies, Inc.
148 Princeton-Hightstown Rd. Ph: (609)426-5000
Hightstown, NJ 08520
E-mail: 13957 (DIALMAIL)
Contact: Michael Maddox, (617)863-5100.
Desc: Provides daily, weekly, monthly, and annual time series for buyers, sellers, or investors in approximately 60 nonferrous metals, ferroalloys, and metal companies. Includes price quotations with foreign exchange rates provided in pound sterling, German marks, yen, and the Malaysian dollar. *Available:* Standard & Poor's DRI, Data Products Division; Interactive Data Corporation; LEXIS-NEXIS, NEXIS; The Dialog Corporation, DIALOG; Dow Jones Interactive Publishing. *Type:* Database.

Monetary Digest

Certified Mint, Inc.
3550 N. Central Ave., Ste, 705 Free: 800-528-1380
Phoenix, AZ 85012
Contact: William N. Haynes, Editor.
Desc: Published as a service to customers of Certified Mint, Inc., a broker of precious metals. Reviews economic, monetary and political developments affecting the prices of gold and silver. *Type:* Newsletter.

MoneyWorld

Strategic Communications USA
1801 Lee Rd., Ste. 301 Free: 800-333-5697
Winter Park, FL 32789
Desc: Offers investment advice on stocks, bonds, precious metals, and personal finance. *Type:* Newsletter.

NFFS Directory of Non-Ferrous Foundries

Non-Ferrous Founders Society
455 State St., Ste. 100 Ph: (847)299-0950
Des Plaines, IL 60016 Fax: (847)299-3598
E-mail: staff@nffs.org
URL: http://www.nffs.org.
Desc: Member and nonmember foundries producing nonferrous castings. *Type:* Directory.

Pavco Talks

Pavco, Inc.
4450 Cranwood Pkwy. Ph: (216)231-5600
Cleveland, OH 44128-4004 Fax: (216)231-6044
Contact: James V. Pavlish, Editor.
Desc: Provides industry information, including news of zinc plating systems, product developments, and market trends. Recurring features include columns titled Equipment, Product Information, and Quarterly Quotes. *Type:* Newsletter.

Platt's Metals Week

McGraw-Hill, Inc.
2 Penn Plaza Ph: (212)904-2000
New York, NY 10121 Free: 800-223-6180
 Fax: (212)904-6068
URL: http://www.mcgraw-hill.com
Contact: Andy Blamey, Editor.
Desc: Provides the necessary information for those who buy, sell, or invest in nonferrous metals and metal companies. Discusses the effects of price while providing insight into variations of supply and demand. *Type:* Newsletter.

Precious Metals Digest

Soundview Publications Inc.
1350 Center Dr., Ste. 100 Ph: (404)668-0432
Dunwoody, GA 30338 Free: 800-728-2288
Contact: Dennis Wheeler, Editor.
Desc: Intended to "track and digest the voluminous information published each month on gold, silver, and platinum." *Type:* Newsletter.

Precious Metals News and Review

International Precious Metals Institute
4400 Bayou Blvd., Ste. 18 Ph: (850)476-1156
Pensacola, FL 32502-1908 Fax: (850)476-1548
E-mail: ipmi@pond.com
URL: http://www.ipmi.org.
Contact: Larry Manziek, Ph.D, Executive Dir.
Desc: Concerned with developments in the precious metals industries. Covers the areas of production, recycling, processing, applications, and environmental effects. *Type:* Newsletter.

Precision Metalforming Association

6363 Oak Tree Blvd. Ph: (440)585-8800
Cleveland, OH 44131-2556 Fax: (440)585-3126
E-mail: pma@pma.org
URL: http://www.metalforming.com
Contact: Jon E. Jenson, CAE, Pres.
Desc: Manufacturers of metal stampings, precision metal fabrications, and metal spinnings, and their suppliers. Provides information and technical services to members. Conducts educational programs; offers placement service; compiles statistics. *Type:* Association.

Repairing Metalware

Institute of Metal Repair
1558 S. Redwood Ph: (619)747-5978
Escondido, CA 92025
Contact: James R. Walker, Editor.
Desc: Provides technical and trade information on repairing, restoring, and preserving metal objects. Acts as a network publication for metalworkers. *Type:* Newsletter.

Resistance Welder Manufacturers' Association (RWMA) News

Resistance Welder Manufacturers' Association
1900 Arch St. Ph: (215)564-3484
Philadelphia, PA 19103-1498 Fax: (215)963-9785
E-mail: rwma@fernley.com
Desc: Provides information about resistance welding. Recurring features include news of research, a calendar of events, reports of meetings, news of educational opportunities, and member news. *Type:* Newsletter.

The Scroll

National Ornamental and Miscellaneous Metals Association
804 Main St., Ste. F Ph: (404)363-4009
Forest Park, GA 30297 Fax: (404)366-1852
E-mail: nomma2@aol.com
Contact: J. Todd Daniel, Editor.
Desc: Provides information about ornamental metalworks. Recurring features include reports of meetings, news of educational opportunities, chapter reports, and standards and code information. *Type:* Newsletter.

Sheet Metal Forming

Engineering Research Center for Net Shape Manufacturing, Ohio State University
339 Baker Systems/1971 Neil Ave. Ph: (614)292-5063
 Fax: (614)292-7219
Columbus, OH 43210
URL: http://www.nsmwww.eng.ohio.state.edu.
Contact: Sabine Toennesmann, Editor; M. A. Ahmetoglu, Editor.

Desc: Covers net shape manufacturing of sheet metal forming project descriptions and plans. Recurring features include news of research and notices of publications available. *Type:* Newsletter.

Sheet Metal Workers' International Association

1750 New York Ave. NW   Ph: (202)783-5880
Washington, DC 20006   Free: 800-457-7694
    Fax: (202)662-0894

Contact: Arthur Moore, Gen.Pres.
Desc: AFL-CIO. *Type:* Association.

SMACNEWS

Sheet Metal and Air Conditioning Contractors' National Association, Inc.
PO Box 221230   Ph: (703)803-2980
Chantilly, VA 20153-1230   Fax: (703)803-3732
E-mail: info@smacna.org
URL: http://www.smacra.org; http://www.smacna.org.
Contact: Rosalind P. Raymond, Editor.
Desc: Provides information on the sheet metal industry. Covers labor, legislative, and governmental actions affecting the industry. *Type:* Newsletter.

The Stabilizer

Lincoln Electric Company
22801 St. Clair Ave.   Ph: (216)481-8100
Cleveland, OH 44117   Fax: (216)486-1751
URL: http://www.lincolnelectric.com.
Contact: Randy Glassburn, Editor.
Desc: Features companies that have become successful by utilizing arc welding. Recurring features include letters to the editor, interviews, news of research, a calendar of events, news of educational opportunities, safety tips, and features titled How I Did it, How I Fixed it, Award Winner, Welding Safety, Arc Welding Instruction, and Who's New at Lincoln Electric. *Type:* Newsletter.

Steel Digest

Intersteel Technology, Inc.
PO Box 560786   Ph: (704)549-4177
Charlotte, NC 28256-0786   Fax: (704)549-4178
Contact: John A. Vallomy, Editor.
Desc: Highlights new technologies, new equipment, and innovative concepts in the iron and steel industry. Discusses technology pertinent to blast furnaces, oxygen converters, electric arc furnaces, ladle metallury, continuous casting, and general steelmaking. *Type:* Newsletter.

Steel Tank Institute

570 Oakwood Rd.   Ph: (847)438-8265
Lake Zurich, IL 60047   Fax: (847)438-8766
URL: http://www.steeltank.com
Contact: Wayne Geyer, Exec. VP.
Desc: Trade association for manufacturers of steel underground and above ground storage tanks. Develops fabrication standards for secondary containment, corrosion control and thermal insulation. *Type:* Association.

U.S. Pipeline

U.S. Pipe and Foundry Co.
PO Box 10406   Ph: (205)254-7162
Birmingham, AL 35202-0406   Fax: (205)254-7165
E-mail: marketing@uspipe.com
Contact: George J. Bogs, Sales Promotion Manager.
Desc: Contains news of personnel and feature articles of the company. *Type:* Newsletter.

United Steelworkers of America

5 Gateway Center   Ph: (412)562-2400
Pittsburgh, PA 15222   Fax: (412)562-2445
Contact: George Becker, Pres.
Desc: AFL-CIO. *Type:* Association.

Meteorology

Accu-Weather Inc.

619 W. College Ave.   Ph: (814)234-9601–
State College, PA 16801   Fax: (814)238-1339
Contact: Dr. Joel N. Myers, President; Barry Lee Myers, Exec. VP; Elliot Abrams, Sr. VP; Joseph Sobel, Sr. VP; Evan E. Myers, Sr. VP; Michael E. Steinberg, Sr. VP; Sheldon Levine, Dir. of Sales; Andrew Hoover, Mgr. Sales & Mktg.
Alt. Contact: 619 W. College Ave., State College, PA 16801; telephone: (814)234-9601; fax: (814)238-1339.
Type: Periodical.

American Meteorological Society

45 Beacon St.   Ph: (617)227-2425
Boston, MA 02108-3693   Fax: (617)742-8718
E-mail: webadmin@ametsoc.org
URL: http://www.ametsoc.org/AMS
Contact: Richard E. Hallgren, Exec.Dir.
Desc: Professional meteorologists, oceanographers, and hydrologists; interested students and nonprofessionals. Develops and disseminates information on the atmospheric and related oceanic and hydrospheric sciences; seeks to advance professional applications. Activities include guidance service, scholarship programs, career information, certification of consulting meteorologists, and a seal of approval program to recognize competence in radio and television weathercasting. *Type:* Association.

The FIFE Information System: The First ISLSCP Field Experiment

Versar ESM Operations
9200 Rumsey Rd.   Ph: (410)964-9200
Columbia, MD 21045-1934   Fax: (410)964-5156
URL: http://www.versar.com/fife/fifehome.htm
Contact: Donald E. Strebel, Curator, strebeldon@versar.com.
Desc: The First ISLSCP Field Experiment Project (FIFE) was a local-scale climatology project set in the prairies of central Kansas during 1987-1989. It was designed to study the flows of heat and moisture between the land surface and the atmosphere over a region 15x15 km in size. *Type:* Database.

Meteorological and Geoastrophysical Abstracts

MGA, Inc.
25 Porter Rd.   Ph: (978)952-7357
Littleton, MA 01460
URL: http://mganet.org
Contact: Irwin Abrams, Publications Manager, amspubs@aip.org.
Desc: Contains more than 210,000 citations (with abstracts for most years) to the worldwide literature on significant research in meteorology and geoastrophysics. Sources include more than 700 journals and series. *Available:* MGA, Inc. *Type:* Database.

The Ohio State University Atmospheric Sciences Program Home Page

Ohio State University - Department of Geography - Atmospheric Sciences Program
1049 Derby Hall   Ph: (614)292-1957
154 N. Oval Mall   Fax: (614)292-6213
Columbus, OH 43210
URL: http://asp1.sbs.ohio-state.edu
Contact: aspweb@geography.ohio-state.edu.
Desc: The Ohio State University Atmospheric Sciences Program (OSUASP) Home Page provides links to weather forecasts, weather images, satellite images, forecast models, and information about Atmospheric and Climatic Studies at Ohio State. Also housed with the OSUASP is the Office of the State Climatologist for the State of Ohio; web pages also pertain to activities affiliated with that office and also link to the National Climatic Data Center. *Type:* Database.

WXP: The Weather Processor WWW Server

Purdue University - Department of Earth and Atmospheric Sciences
West Lafayette, IN 47907   Ph: (317)494-3292
    Fax: (317)496-1210
URL: http://wxp.atms.purdue.edu/main.html
Contact: Daniel Vietor, Senior Project Specialist, WXP Developer, devo@eas.purdue.edu.
Desc: WXP: The Weather Processor is a software package developed at Purdue University which is a general purpose weather visualization tool for current, forecasted and archived meteorological data. *Type:* Database.

Methodist

General Board of Church and Society of the United Methodist Church

100 Maryland Ave. NE   Ph: (202)488-5600
Washington, DC 20002   Fax: (202)488-5619
E-mail: babeywickrama@umc-gbcs.org
URL: http://www.umc-gbcs.org
Contact: Thom White Wolf Fassett, Gen.Sec.
Desc: Conducts programs of research, education, and action in areas including alcohol and drug use and abuse, delinquency and crime, health care, world peace and arms control, immigration, population, civil liberties, race relations, economic justice, hunger, and environment agriculture. About 15,000 local churches maintain commissions engaged in this work. *Type:* Association.

General Commission on Archives and History of the United Methodist Church

PO Box 127   Ph: (973)408-3189
Madison, NJ 07940   Fax: (973)408-3909
E-mail: cyrigoyen@gcah.org
URL: http://www.gcah.org
Contact: Dr. Charles Yrigoyen, Jr., Gen.Sec.
Desc: Seeks to gather and preserve historical data, records, books, archives, and other property related to the origin and development of the United Methodist Church; to stimulate and encourage historical research and appreciation. Provides genealogical service. Operates museum on the Methodist Church, the Evangelical United Brethren Church, and their antecedents. *Type:* Association.

Methodist Federation for Social Action

212 E. Capitol St., NE   Ph: (202)546-8806
Washington, DC 20003   Fax: (202)546-6811
Contact: Rev. Kathryn J. Johnson, Exec.Dir.
Desc: Independent organization of clergy and laity of the United Methodist church. Provides witness to the Gospel of Jesus Christ to the world; works to eliminate war and abolish nuclear arms; promotes democratic social-economic planning to develop a society without discrimination. *Type:* Association.

National Youth Ministry Organization

PO Box 840   Ph: (615)340-7184
Nashville, TN 37202-0840   Fax: (615)340-7565
E-mail: nymo@aol.com
URL: http://www.umc.org/nymo
Contact: Angela Gay Kinkead, Exec.Dir.
Desc: Youth members elected from among representatives of annual conferences (United Methodist regional groupings); adult members are elected from jurisdictional caucuses/conferences or staff representatives of United Methodist boards and agencies with an interest in youth ministry. Initiates and supports special plans and projects at the national level of the church which are of interest to youth; provides for free expression of the conviction of the church's youth on issues vital to them; cooperates with other church agencies in making recommendations regarding the youth ministry of the church; requests suggestions from annual conference youth groups and makes recommendations to general board nominating committees of youth for board membership. *Type:* Association.

United Methodist Committee on Relief

475 Riverside Dr., Rm. 350   Ph: (212)870-3816
New York, NY 10115   Free: 800-841-1235
   Fax: (212)870-3624
Contact: Paul Dirdak, Jr., Deputy Gen. Sec.
Desc: Service organization of the United Methodist church, with a supervising and policy body of 28 persons who represent the national church membership. *Type:* Association.

Women's Division of the Board of Global Ministries of the United Methodist Church

475 Riverside Dr., Rm. 1504   Ph: (212)870-3752
New York, NY 10115   Fax: (212)870-3736
E-mail: unw@gbgm-umc.org
URL: http://www.gbgm-umc.org/womens-division/
Contact: Joyce D. Sohl, Exec. Officer.
Desc: Women members of the United Methodist Church united to promote spiritual growth and leadership development among women worldwide. Makes available financial support to ministries and social programs benefitting women, children, and youth. *Type:* Association.

Women's Missionary Council of the Christian Methodist Episcopal Church

623 San Fernando Ave.
Berkeley, CA 94707
Contact: Dr. Sylvia Faulk, Pres.
Desc: Women members of the Christian Methodist Episcopal church. Seeks to: discover and share the mission of the church; promote cooperation, fellowship, and mutual counsel concerning the spiritual life and religious activities of the church; encourage Bible study and assist in spreading the Gospel; research and answer society's needs in order to develop programs and resources that will respond to that need. Awards Helena B. *Type:* Association.

World Federation of Methodist and Uniting Church Women - USA

Mrs. Khushnud Azariah
1048 Easthills Dr.
West Covina, CA 91791
Contact: Khushnud Azariah, World Pres.
Desc: Methodist women in 70 countries. Promotes peace among nations, the establishment of human rights, and the elimination of discrimination against women in all countries. Fosters spiritual growth; participates in educational and social outreach programs. *Type:* Association.

World Methodist Council

575 Lakeshore Dr.   Ph: (828)456-9432
PO Box 518   Fax: (828)456-9433
Lake Junaluska, NC 28745
Contact: Joe Hale, Gen.Sec.
Desc: Fraternal and cooperative association of Methodist, Wesleyan, and other related united churches. Seeks to "draw the branches of the Wesleyan Movement closer together in fellowship and devotion to their mutual heritage and to promote among them evangelistic, educational, historical, and other cooperative movements." Exercises no legislative power over separate denomination members but gives focus and leadership to mutually agreed upon goals and programs. Maintains World Methodist Museum of rare books, records, paintings, sculptures, and other materials pertaining to John Wesley and the beginnings of early Methodism. *Type:* Association.

Middle East

Americans for a Safe Israel

1623 3rd Ave., Ste. 205   Ph: (212)828-2424
New York, NY 10128   Fax: (212)828-1717
Contact: Herbert Zweibon, Chm.

Desc: Purpose is to provide and disseminate information to concerned American citizens regarding the nature of the conflict in the Middle East, "based on the belief that a strong Israel is vital to American security interests." Holds frequent seminars and press conferences. Is involved in research regarding the Middle East conflict and relevant issues in other parts of the world. Maintains speakers' bureau. *Type:* Association.

AMIDEAST

1730 M St. NW, Ste. 1100   Ph: (202)776-9600
Washington, DC 20036-4505   Fax: (202)776-7000
E-mail: inquiries@amideast.org
URL: http://www.amideast.org
Contact: Hon. William A. Rugh, Pres. and CEO.
Desc: Dedicated to improving understanding between Americans and the people of the Middle East and North Africa through education, information and development programs. *Type:* Association.

Catholic Near East Welfare Association

1011 1st Ave.   Ph: (212)826-1480
New York, NY 10022-4195   Free: 800-442-6392
   Fax: (212)838-1344
E-mail: bad@cnewa.org
Contact: Msgr. Robert L. Stern, Sec.Gen.
Desc: Catholic organization of individuals and unrelated groups. Raises funds to assist humanitarian projects in 28 countries, primarily in the Near and Middle East; pays costs of education for native priests and sisters and provides money for chapels and rectories, orphanages, convents, and schools. Sponsors health care programs and maintains clinics. *Type:* Association.

Committee for Accuracy in Middle East Reporting in America

PO Box 428   Ph: (617)789-3672
Boston, MA 02456-0428   Fax: (617)787-7853
E-mail: mail@camera.org
URL: http://www.camera.org
Contact: Alex Safian, Assoc.Dir.
Desc: Promotes accurate and balanced coverage of Israel and the Middle East. Works to ensure more "balanced reports in the future by providing information to journalists, publishing monographs on Middle East topics of media interest". *Type:* Association.

Mid-East Commission

PO Drawer 1787   Ph: (252)946-8043
Washington, NC 27889   Fax: (252)946-5489
E-mail: bpaciocco@mideastcom.org
URL: http://mideastcom.org
Contact: Robert J. Paciocco, Exec. Dir.
Desc: Serves as a forum for discussion of regional issues. Assists local governments by administering state and federal programs and grants. *Type:* Association.

National PAC

600 Pennsylvania Ave. SE, Ste.   Ph: (202)879-7710
207   Fax: (202)879-7728
Washington, DC 20003
Contact: Charles D. Brooks, Exec.Dir.
Desc: Encourages support for improved U.S.-Israel relations. Supports Congressional candidates who view Israel as a strategic asset and valuable ally in the Middle East. Works against political anti-Semitism. *Type:* Association.

Near East Foundation

342 Madison Ave., Ste. 1030   Ph: (212)867-0064
New York, NY 10173   Fax: (212)867-0169
Contact: Richard C. Robarts, Pres.
Desc: Works in the Middle East and Africa on projects to increase food production, with related activities in rural and community development and primary health care; provides start-up funds for projects until support is available from local sources. *Type:* Association.

Military

Air Force Association

1501 Lee Hwy.   Ph: (703)247-5800
Arlington, VA 22209   Fax: (703)247-5853
Contact: John Schaud, Exec.Dir.
Desc: U.S. citizens, both civilian and military, united to address the responsibilities imposed by the impact of aerospace technology on modern society. Supports armed strength adequate to maintain the security and peace of the United States and the Free World; promotes public education about the development of adequate aerospace power. *Type:* Association.

Air Force Magazine

Air Force Association
1501 Lee Hwy.   Ph: (703)247-5836
Arlington, VA 22209-1198   Fax: (703)247-5855
E-mail: asmag@afa.org.
URL: http://www.osa.org.
Contact: John T. Correll, Editor; Charles E. Cruze, Publisher.
Desc: Magazine for personnel of United States Air Force, government agencies, and aerospace industry. *Type:* Periodical.

Air Force Sergeants Association

PO Box 50   Ph: (301)899-3500
Temple Hills, MD 20757   Fax: (301)899-8136
Contact: James Staton, Exec.Dir.
Desc: Any enlisted man or woman, active or retired, in the Air Force, Air National Guard, Air Force Reserve, Army Air Corps, or Army Air Forces; ladies auxiliaries. Works to: promote, preserve, and uphold fair and equitable legislation as it pertains to the welfare of the airmen who served and are serving in the U.S.A.F.; maintain the highest professional standards and integrity among members; promote the interests of members, the U.S., and the rest of the "free world"; promote religious, educational, and recreational activities among members, in order to develop a better understanding and mutual respect. Sponsors educational seminars, Air Force training, JOBCAP - a job placement service, and programs for retired members. *Type:* Association.

Airman

U.S. Air Force
Air Force News Service
Kelly Air Force Base, TX
   78241-6105
E-mail: editor@afnews.af.mil.
URL: http://www.af.mil.
Contact: Jerry Stringer, Editor, (210)925-7757, fax: (210)925-7219.
Desc: Official trade magazine of the U.S. Air Force. *Type:* Periodical.

American Legion

Public Relations Division
700 N. Pennsylvania St.   Ph: (317)630-1200
Indianapolis, IN 46204   Free: 800-433-3318
   Fax: (317)630-1368
E-mail: ia@legion.org
URL: http://www.legion.org
Contact: Robert W. Spanogle, Nat. Adjutant.
Desc: Honorably discharged wartime veterans, both male and female, of the U.S. armed forces. Provides a unified voice for veterans. *Type:* Association.

American Legion Auxiliary

777 N. Meridian St., 3rd Fl.   Ph: (317)635-6291
Indianapolis, IN 46204   Fax: (317)636-5590
E-mail: alahq@legion-aux.org

URL: http://www.legion.org/auxil.htm

Contact: Peggy Sappenfield, National Secretary.

Desc: Mothers, wives, sisters, daughters, grandmothers, granddaughters, and great granddaughters of members of the American Legion or of men and women who were in the U.S. Armed Forces during World War I or II, the Korean War, the Vietnam War, Grenada/Lebanon, Panama, or Persian Gulf and lost their lives in war service or died after honorable discharge; women who served in the armed forces during these periods of hostility. *Type:* Association.

American Logistics Association

1133 15th St. NW, Ste. 640   Ph: (202)466-2520
Washington, DC 20005   Fax: (202)296-4419
URL: http://www.ala-national.org

Contact: Alan Barton, Pres.

Desc: Armed forces purchasing agencies and commercial firms. Promotes cooperation among the Defense Department and the industries with which it conducts business. *Type:* Association.

American Military Society

1101 Mercantile Ln., Ste. 100   Free: 800-379-6128
Springdale, MD 20774   Fax: (301)925-1429

Contact: Doug Russell, Pres.

Desc: Active or retired members of the armed services (Army, Navy, Air Force, Marine Corps, and Coast Guard). Develops and supports activities which promote the general well-being of the members; upholds and defends the Constitution; supports national defense; and preserves the memories and traditions of the Armed Forces. *Type:* Association.

American Society of Military Comptrollers

225 Reinekers Ln., Ste. 250   Ph: (703)549-0360
Alexandria, VA 22314   Free: 800-462-5637
   Fax: (703)549-3181

Contact: James F. McCall, Exec.Dir.

Desc: Civilians and military personnel who are now or who have been involved in the overall field of military comptrollership; other interested individuals. *Type:* Association.

Armed Forces Communications and Electronics Association

4400 Fair Lakes Ct.   Ph: (703)631-6100
Fairfax, VA 22033   Free: 800-336-4583
   Fax: (703)631-4693

Contact: Lawrence Pierce, Acting VP.

Desc: Industrial organizations and citizens of the United States and other nations of the Free World. To maintain and improve cooperation among the armed forces, industry, and government concerning design, production, maintenance, and operation of communications, electronics, command and control, computers, intelligence systems, and imagery. Fosters the development of scientific and engineering skills in these areas. *Type:* Association.

Armed Forces Institute of Pathology

6825 16th St. NW   Ph: (202)782-2100
Washington, DC 20306-6000   Fax: (202)782-9376
URL: http://www.afip.org/

Contact: Col. Michael J. Dickerson, Dir.

Desc: Chartered by the Department of Defense to: maintain a consultation service for the diagnosis of pathologic material; conduct experimental, statistical, and morphological research in pathology; provide instruction in advanced pathology and related subjects; prepare, procure, and duplicate teaching aids; operate the AFIP Repository and Research Services; maintain the National Museum of Health and Medicine of the AFIP and a Visual Information Service for the collection, preparation, duplication, reference, and filing of medical illustrative material. Sponsors a series of courses. *Type:* Association.

Army Aviation Association of America

49 Richmondville Ave.   Ph: (203)226-8184
Westport, CT 06880-2000   Fax: (203)222-9863

Contact: William R. Harris, Jr., Exec.Dir.

Desc: Commissioned officers, warrant officers, and enlisted personnel serving in U.S. Army aviation assignments in the active U.S. Army, Army National Guard, and Army Reserve; Department of Army civilian personnel and industry representatives affiliated with army aviation. *Type:* Association.

Army Distaff Foundation

6200 Oregon Ave. NW   Ph: (202)541-0105
Washington, DC 20015   Fax: (202)364-2856

Contact: Maj.Gen. Calvert Benedict, USA, Exec.Dir.

Desc: Provides retirement housing and health care services to active and retired military officers, and their relatives. Operates Knollwood, a military retirement community with independent apartment, as well as assisted living and nursing care. *Type:* Association.

Army Families

Army Family Liaison Office, Department of the Army
DAIM-ZAF, Rm. 2D665   Ph: (703)695-7714
Washington, DC 20310-0600   Fax: (703)693-2587

Contact: Joe Wasserman, Editor, wasserman@pentagon-brace.army.mil.

Desc: Directed toward army families and provides tips and policy on jobs, benefits, education, finances, and government programs. Recurring features include news of educational opportunities and book reviews. *Type:* Newsletter.

ARMY Magazine

Association of the U.S. Army (AUSA)
Box 1560   Ph: (703)841-4300
Arlington, VA 22210   Free: 800-336-4570
   Fax: (703)841-3505

Contact: Mary French, Editor.

Desc: Magazine for Regular Army officers, noncommissioned officers, warrant officers, and senior enlisted personnel; industrialists; civilians with an interest in national defense; and members of the Army National Guard and Reserve. *Type:* Periodical.

Army Medical Research and Materiel Command

Walter Reed Army Institute of Research

Department of Applied Biochemistry

Washington, DC 20307-5100   Ph: (202)782-6361
   Fax: (202)782-7651
E-mail: biochem@wrair-emhl.army.mil

Contact: Peter Chiang, Chf.

Desc: Develops novel drugs to treat military diseases or threats and to elucidate the attendant biochemical pharmacology. Focus areas include pharmacology of Anatoxin-A; medical countermeasures for Botulinum Toxin; nerve agent countermeasures advanced anticonvulsants; prevention of military HIV infection; medical countermeasures for physiologically active compounds; and medical countermeasures for Ricin. *Type:* Research center.

Army Reserve Magazine

U.S. Army Reserve
1421 Jefferson Davis Hwy.   Ph: (703)601-0854
Arlington, VA 22202-3259   Fax: (703)601-0836
E-mail: usarmag@ocar.army.pentagon.mil.
URL: http://www.army.mil/usar.

Desc: Military magazine. *Type:* Periodical.

Army Times

Army Times Publishing Co.
6883 Commercial Dr.   Ph: (703)750-9000
Springfield, VA 22159-0001   Fax: (703)750-8622

Contact: Nat Kornfeld, Editor; Donna Peterson, Editor.

Desc: U.S. Army periodical. *Type:* Periodical.

Association of Graduates

U.S. Military Academy   Ph: (914)938-4600
West Point, NY 10996   Free: 800-232-GRAD
   Fax: (914)446-5751
E-mail: aog@aog.usma.edu
URL: http://www.aog.usma.edu

Contact: Col. Seth F. Hudgins, Jr., Pres.

Desc: Graduates of the United States Military Academy (West Point); membership currently includes all graduates still living. Promotes the welfare of, and raises money for the academy; helps to improve the education and training of the cadets by providing funds beyond the minimum normal appropriations. *Type:* Association.

Association of Graduates of the United States Air Force Academy

3116 Academy Dr.   Ph: (719)472-0300
USAF Academy, CO 80840-4475   Fax: (719)333-4194
E-mail: aog@aog-usafa.org
URL: http://www.aog-usafa.org

Contact: Lt.Col. R. Coppock, USAF, (Ret.) Pres. & CEO.

Desc: Graduates and friends of the U.S. Air Force Academy. Promotes interest in and dedication to the mission, ideals, objectives, activities, and history of the Academy; encourages young people to attend the Academy; encourages and supports fundraising for the Academy. *Type:* Association.

Association of Military Surgeons of the U.S.

9320 Old Georgetown Rd.   Ph: (301)897-8800
Bethesda, MD 20814   Free: 800-761-9320
   Fax: (301)530-5446
E-mail: amsus@amsus.org
URL: http://www.amsus.org

Contact: RADM Frederic G. Sanford, MC, USN Ret.

Desc: Physicians, dentists, veterinarians, nurses, pharmacists, dietitians, therapists, and others of commissioned rank (or grades E5 through E9) or equivalent in the Army, Navy, Air Force, Public Health Service, and Veterans Administration; Reserve and National Guard officers are also eligible for membership. Advances all phases of federal medicine and allied sciences related to federal health services. Provides group insurance. *Type:* Association.

Association of Naval Aviation

2550 Huntington Ave., Ste. 201   Ph: (703)960-2490
Alexandria, VA 22303   Fax: (703)960-4490
E-mail: anahq@ix.netcom.com

Contact: Richard C. Allen, Pres.

Desc: Active or former officers and enlisted men of the aeronautical organizations of the U.S. Navy, Marines, Coast Guard, or other service personnel and civilians; industrial associates. Objectives are to stimulate and extend appreciation of naval aviation; to help the active and reserve military establishment; to merge the various diverse elements of the military, particularly in relation to problems associated with maritime aviation; to promote greater communication among the military, academic, and business communities on issues of maritime aviation. *Type:* Association.

Association of the United States Army

2425 Wilson Blvd.
Arlington, VA 22201-3385

Ph: (703)841-4300
Free: 800-336-4570
Fax: (703)525-9039

E-mail: ausainfo@ausa.org
URL: http://www.ausa.org
Contact: Gen. Gordon R. Sullivan, Pres.
Desc: Professional society of: active, retired, and reserve military personnel; West Point and Army ROTC cadets; civilians interested in national defense. Seeks to advance the security of the United States and consolidate the efforts of all who support the United States Army as an indispensable instrument of national security. *Type:* Association.

Boilermaker Reporter

International Brotherhood of Boilermakers, Iron Shipbuilders, Blacksmiths, Forgers, and Helpers
753 State Ave., No. 570
Kansas City, KS 66101-2511

Ph: (913)371-2640

Contact: Donald Caswell, Managing Editor.
Desc: Newspaper covering trade and union membership news. *Type:* Periodical.

Catholic War Veterans Auxiliary of the U.S.A.

441 N. Lee St.
Alexandria, VA 22314

Ph: (703)549-3622
Fax: (703)684-5196

Contact: Linda M. Torreyson, Exec. Asst.
Desc: Mothers, widows, sisters, daughters, granddaughters, and nieces of living and deceased members of the Catholic War Veterans of the U.S.A. *Type:* Association.

Citizen Airman

Air Force Reserve Command
HQ AFRC/PA
Warner Robins, GA 31098-1635

Ph: (912)327-1773
Fax: (912)327-0878

E-mail: citamn@tecnet2.jcte.jcs.mil.
URL: http://www.afres.af.mil/hq/citamn/default.htm.
Contact: Cliff Tyler, Editor, (912)327-1770, cliff.tyler@afres.af.mil.
Type: Periodical.

Command Information Package

Chief of Public Affairs
Command Information Unit
1500 Army Pentagon 2D622
Washington, DC 20310-1500

Ph: (703)697-0050
Fax: (703)697-5746

E-mail: papaorg@meade-emh2.ftmeade.army.mil
Contact: Willard K. Morris, Editor, morriwk@hgda.army.mil.
Desc: Publication covering information of interest to Army officers, NCOs, and enlisted soldiers. Includes articles on aspects of Army life including professional development and personal affairs. *Type:* Periodical.

DefenseLINK

OASD(PA)/DPC
1400 Defense Pentagon, Rm. 1E757
Washington, DC 20301-1400

Ph: (703)697-5737

E-mail: dpcintrn@osd.pentagon.mil
URL: http://www.dtic.mil/defenselink
Desc: The DefenseLINK Department of Defense (DOD) public affairs online information database contains timely DOD information concerning policies, functions, operations, and organizations. Data include news releases, memoranda for correspondents, press advisories, daily public schedules for the Secretary and Deputy Secretary of Defense, transcripts of DOD news and background briefings, other DOD public affairs documents, and more. *Type:* Database.

Eighth Air Force Historical Society

PO Box 7215
St. Paul, MN 55107

Free: 800-833-1942
Fax: (612)222-7781

Contact: Edward A. Kueppers, Jr., Dir. of Information.
Desc: Veterans of the Eighth Air Force united to perpetuate the history of the Eighth Air Force and encourage units to organize. Maintains the Eighth Air Force Dayton Memorial at the Air Force Museum in Dayton, OH, to provide a permanent commemoration of the more than 46,000 Eighth Air Force men who were casualties in service in World War II. Helps veterans contact their units. *Type:* Association.

Enlisted Association of National Guard of the United States

1219 Prince St.
Alexandria, VA 22314

Ph: (703)519-3846
Free: 800-234-3264

E-mail: natloffc@eangus.org
URL: http://www.eangus.org
Contact: Michael P. Cline, Exec. Dir./CEO.
Desc: Active and retired members of the U.S. National Guard. *Type:* Association.

Family

VFW Magazine
242 W. 27th St., Lobby 1B
New York, NY 10001-5926

Ph: (212)929-1300
Fax: (212)929-9574

Contact: Mary Jane Ryan, Editor; Joseph A. Mugnai, Publisher; Joseph Araneo, Advertising Mgr.
Desc: Magazine focusing on the military family. *Type:* Periodical.

1st Marine Division Association

14325 Willard Rd., Ste. 107
Chantilly, VA 20151

Ph: (703)803-3195
Fax: (703)803-7114

E-mail: oldbreed@aol.com
URL: http://www.erols.com/oldbreed/
Contact: Col. Jerry Brown, USMC, Chief Administrative Officer.
Desc: Veterans who have served in the 1st Marine Division; personnel who served with attached or supporting units. Provides an opportunity for members to reestablish and/or maintain contact with their fellow servicemen. *Type:* Association.

Forty and Eight

777 N. Meridian St.
Rm. 204
Indianapolis, IN 46204

Ph: (317)634-1804
Fax: (317)632-9365

Contact: Robert L. Low, Sec.
Desc: Fraternal organization of veterans who are also members of the American Legion. Contributes aid to underprivileged children. *Type:* Association.

Gold Star Wives of America

Joanne Danna
1964 E. Oak Rd., Unit I-4
Vineland, NJ 08360

Ph: (703)998-0064
Free: 888-479-9788
Fax: (703)998-0064

E-mail: gswives@aol.com
Contact: Joanne Danna, Pres.
Desc: Widows of servicemen who died while on active duty or from service-connected disabilities. Promotes patriotism. *Type:* Association.

Gulf War Health Database

Walter Reed Army Medical Center
The Gulf War Health Center
Bldg. 2, WD 64
6900 16th St.
Washington, DC 20307-5001

Ph: (202)782-6563
Fax: (202)782-3539

E-mail: GULFWAR@wramc1-amedd.army.mil
URL: http://www.wramc.amedd.army.mil/cgi-win/gulfwar.exe

Desc: Dedicated to providing information on the health effects of the Persian Gulf War, this database contains abstracts of journal articles, medical books, and other medical resources. You can search by keyword or via a menu of relevant journals. *Type:* Database.

Henry M. Jackson Foundation for the Advancement of Military Medicine

1401 Rockville Pike, Ste. 600
Rockville, MD 20852

Ph: (301)424-0800
Fax: (301)424-5771

URL: http://www.hjf.org1
Contact: John W. Lowe, Pres.
Desc: Infectious diseases, immunology, wound healing, sepsis, shock and traumatic injury, telemedicine, prostate cancer, cardiovascular disease, addiction medicine, pediatrics and preventive medicine, HIV research, emergency medical training, diagnostic radiology, head injury, and occupational health. Coordinates clinical trials sponsored by private industry. *Type:* Research center.

Korean War Project KIA/MIA/WIA Database

Korean War Project
PO Box 180190
Dallas, TX 75218-0190

URL: http://www.koreanwar.org/
Desc: This database from the Korean War Project lets you find biographical and statistical information on casualties from the Korean War. Search by name, unit, state, city and county, and race. *Type:* Database.

Leatherneck

Marine Corps Association
Box 1775
Quantico, VA 22134

Ph: (703)640-6161
Free: 800-336-0291
Fax: (703)640-0823

E-mail: leatherneck@illuminet.net.
Contact: William V.H. White, Editor; Lt. Gen. Anthony Lukeman, USMC R, Publisher.
Desc: Magazine covering worldwide activities of the U.S. Marine Corps--Marines of today and battles fought. *Type:* Periodical.

LEXIS® Military Justice Library

LEXIS-NEXIS
9443 Springboro Pike
PO Box 933
Dayton, OH 45401-0933

Ph: (937)865-6800

URL: http://www.lex-nexis.com
Desc: Focuses on military justice, veterans, military contracts, and defense publications. *Available:* LEXIS-NEXIS, LEXIS. *Type:* Database.

Marine Corps Association

Box 1775, Marine Corps Base
Quantico, VA 22134-0775

Ph: (703)640-6161
Free: 800-336-0291
Fax: (703)640-0823

Contact: Maj.Gen. Leslie M. Palm, Exec.Dir.
Desc: Comprised of active duty, reserve, retired, Fleet Reserve, honorably discharged Marines, and members of other services who have served with Marine Corps units. Disseminates information about the military arts and sciences to members; assists members' professional advancement; fosters the spirit and works to preserve the traditions of the United States Marine Corps. Maintains discount book service and group insurance plan for members. *Type:* Association.

Marine Corps League

8626 Lee Highway Ste 201
Fairfax, VA 22031-0047

Ph: (703)207-9588
Fax: (703)207-0047

Contact: William Corley, Jr., Exec.Dir.
Desc: Men and women who have served or are serving in the United States Marine Corps. Maintains charitable program. *Type:* Association.

Military Benefit Association

14605 Avion Pkwy.
Chantilly, VA 20151

Ph: (703)968-6200
Free: 800-336-0100
Fax: (703)968-6423

E-mail: mbabarnum@aol.com
URL: http://www.militarybenefit.org
Contact: G.A. Barnum, Pres.
Desc: Active reserve and retired U.S. military personnel and U.S. government civilian personnel. Provides group life insurance and other benefits. *Type:* Association.

Military Order of the World Wars

435 N. Lee St.
Alexandria, VA 22314

Ph: (703)683-4911
Fax: (703)683-4501

E-mail: mowwhq@aol.com
URL: http://www.moww.org
Contact: MG George G. Kundahl, Chief of Staff.
Desc: Commissioned officers and warrant officers who served in the active or reserve components of any of the uniformed services. Promotes patriotic education in schools. *Type:* Association.

Military and Police Uniform Association

PO Box 69A04, Dept. NET
West Hollywood, CA 90069

Ph: (213)650-5112

E-mail: gayboylaca@hotmail.com
URL: http://www.members.tripod.com/~mpua/
Contact: Louis Wendruck, Pres.
Desc: Gay men interseted in military & policy uniforms. Promotes interest in uniforms from the World War II era and social activities between members. Distributes erotic videos of marines & World War II history. Please send a self-addressed stamp envelope for info. *Type:* Association.

Military in Transition Database

MILITRAN, Inc.
PO Box 490
Southeastern, PA 19399-0490

Ph: (610)687-3900

Desc: Contains approximately 30,000 resumes of enlisted personnel, warrant officers, and commissioned officers entering the civilian work force after service in the U.S. military. *Available:* MILITRAN, Inc. *Type:* Database.

Military Update

PO Box 1230
Centreville, VA 20122-8230

Ph: (703)830-6863

E-mail: milupdate@aol.com.
Contact: Tom Philpott, Self-Syndicator.
Alt. Contact: PO Box 1230, Centreville, VA 20122-8230; telephone: (703)830-6863. *Type:* Periodical.

National Association for Uniformed Services

5535 Hempstead Way
Springfield, VA 22151

Ph: (703)750-1342
Free: 800-842-3451
Fax: (703)354-4380

E-mail: naus@ix.netcom.com
URL: http://www.naus.org
Contact: Maj.Gen. Richard D. Murray, Pres.
Desc: Members of the uniformed military services, active, retired or reserve, veteran, enlisted and officers, and their spouses or widows. To develop and support legislation that upholds the security of the U.S., sustains the morale of the uniformed services, and provides fair and equitable consideration for all service people. *Type:* Association.

National Committee for Employer Support of the Guard and Reserve

1555 Wilson Blvd., Ste. 200
Arlington, VA 22209-2405

Ph: (703)696-1400
Free: 800-336-4590
Fax: (703)696-1411

E-mail: webncesgr@osd.mil
URL: http://www.ncesgr.osd.mil
Contact: Kenneth V. Jordan, Exec. Dir.

Desc: Promotes cooperation and understanding between reserve component members and their civilian employers and assists in the resolution of conflicts arising from an employee's military commitment. Operates with a network of almost 4,200 volunteers throughout 54 committees located in each state, commonwealth, territory, and the District of Columbia. Operates an ombudsman program to assist in the informal resolution of employer-employee conflicts resulting from employee participation in the National Guard and Reserve. *Type:* Association.

National Council of Industrial Naval Air Stations

23364 NE, 6th Ave.
Lawtey, FL 32058

Ph: (904)782-1347

Contact: Barry K. Adams, Pres.

Desc: Federation of local groups of government civilian employees at Industrial Naval Air Stations. *Type:* Association.

National Defense Industrial Association

2111 Wilson Blvd., No.400
Arlington, VA 22201

Ph: (703)522-1820
Fax: (703)522-1885

E-mail: iskibbie@ndia.org
URL: http://www.adpa.org

Contact: Lawrence F. Skibbie, Pres.

Desc: Concerned citizens, military and government personnel, and defense-related industry workers interested in industrial preparedness for the national defense of the United States. *Type:* Association.

National Guard Association of the United States

1 Massachusetts Ave. NW
Washington, DC 20001

Ph: (202)789-0031
Fax: (202)682-9358

E-mail: ngaus@ngaus.org
URL: http://www.ngaus.org

Contact: Richard C. Alexander, Exec.Dir.

Desc: Active and Retired Officers and Warrant Officers of the Army National Guard and Air National Guard of the States, Commonwealth of Puerto Rico, the District of Columbia, Guam, and the Virgin Islands. Goals include: adequate national security and a strong Army National Guard and Air National Guard of the United States as components of the armed forces. *Type:* Association.

National Ladies Auxiliary to Veterans of World War I of the U.S.A.

3605 N. Evans Ave.
Evansville, IL 47711

Ph: (812)422-9814

Contact: Viola Poggemeier, Natl.Pres.

Desc: Female relatives of Veterans of World War I of U.S.A. Conducts patriotic, historical, and educational programs. *Type:* Association.

National Military Family Association

6000 Stevenson Ave., Ste. 304
Alexandria, VA 22304-3526

Ph: (703)823-6632
Fax: (703)751-4857

E-mail: families@nmfa.org
URL: http://www.nmfa.org

Contact: Marilyn H. Sobke, Pres.

Desc: Military personnel and spouses; active duty and retired; Reserve and National Guard of the Army, Navy, Air Force, Marine Corps, Coast Guard, U.S. Public Health Service, and the National Oceanic and Atmospheric Administration. Serves as an advocate for military families through involvement in policies affecting them. *Type:* Association.

National Society of the Children of the American Revolution

1776 D St. NW
Washington, DC 20006

Ph: (202)638-3153
Fax: (202)737-3162

E-mail: nscar@nscar.org
URL: http://www.nscar.org
Desc: "Lineal descendants of patriots of the American Revolution from birth to 22 years of age." Supports several mountain schools in the South. *Type:* Association.

National Society, Daughters of the American Revolution

1776 D St. NW
Washington, DC 20006-5392

Ph: (202)628-1776
Fax: (202)879-3252

Contact: Mrs. Dale K. Love, Pres.Gen.

Desc: Women descendants of Revolutionary War patriots. Conducts historical, educational, and patriotic activities. *Type:* Association.

National Society of Scabbard and Blade

Col. Douglas O. Dollar
1018 S Lewis St.
Stillwater, OK 74074-4622

Contact: Col. Douglas O. Dollar, Contact.

Desc: Honorary and recognition fraternity - men and women, military; advanced ROTC; and all-Service. *Type:* Association.

National Society, Sons of the American Revolution

1000 S. 4th St.
Louisville, KY 40203

Ph: (502)589-1776
Fax: (502)589-1671

URL: http://www.sar.org

Contact: Wayne Wideman, Exec.Dir.

Desc: Descendants of men and women who served the patriot cause in the Revolutionary War. Sponsors competitions; operates museum. *Type:* Association.

Naval Enlisted Reserve Association

6703 Farragut Ave.
Falls Church, VA 22042

Ph: (703)534-1329
Fax: (703)534-3617

E-mail: nerabob@aol.com
URL: http://www.nera.org/nera
Contact: Robert H. Lyman, Exec. Sec.
Desc: Enlisted personnel of the U.S. Naval Reserve, Marine Corps Reserve, and Coast Guard Reserve on active duty, inactive duty, or retired. Works to promote career enlisted service in the "sea-going" branches of the armed services; concerned with the readiness, training, morale, and well-being of all Reservists; obtains fair and proper recognition of the contributions made by Reservists to the national defense and to obtain protection and extension of benefits and entitlements for those Reservists who are currently serving and for those who have already served satisfactorily and have retired. *Type:* Association.

Naval Reserve Association

1619 King St.
Alexandria, VA 22314

Ph: (703)548-5800
Fax: (703)683-3647

E-mail: info@navy-reserve.org
URL: http://www.navy-reserve.org
Contact: Thomas Hall, Exec.Dir.
Desc: Naval officers on active or inactive duty or retired. *Type:* Association.

Naval Reservist News

Commander Naval Reserve Force
4400 Dauphine St.
New Orleans, LA 70146-5046

Ph: (504)678-6058
Fax: (504)678-5049

E-mail: cnrfpao@cnrf.nola.navy.mil
URL: http://www.navy.mil/navresfor/.
Contact: Patricia S. Antenucci, Editor, (504)678-6058, fax: (504)678-5049, nrnnews@cnrf.nola.navy.mil; Judy Katzwinkel, Editorial Assistant.

Desc: Tabloid newspaper for members of the Naval Reserve. *Type:* Periodical.

Naval Sea Cadet Corps.

2300 Wilson Blvd. Ph: (703)243-6910
Arlington, VA 22201-3308 Fax: (703)243-3985
E-mail: nscch2@aol.com
Contact: Capt. Mike Ford, Exec.Dir.
Desc: Youths aged 11-17 years interested in the Navy, Marine Corps, Coast Guard, and Merchant Marines. Works to instill good citizenship and patriotism in youth. Encourages qualities such as personal neatness, loyalty, obedience, dependability, and responsibility to others. *Type:* Association.

Navy League of the United States

2300 Wilson Blvd. Ph: (703)528-1775
Arlington, VA 22201 Free: 800-356-5760
  Fax: (703)528-2333
URL: http://www.navyleague.org
Contact: Charles L. Robinson, Natl. Exec.Dir.
Desc: Civilian organization that supports U.S. capability to keep the sea lanes open through a strong, viable Navy, Marine Corps, Coast Guard, and Merchant Marine. *Type:* Association.

Navy-Marine Corps Relief Society

801 N. Randolph St., Rm. 1228 Ph: (703)696-4904
Arlington, VA 22203-1978 Fax: (703)696-0144
Contact: Adm. J.L. Johnson, USN, Pres.
Desc: To assist, financially and otherwise, Navy and Marine Corps personnel and their dependents in times of need. Provides: visiting nurses; budget counseling; thrift shops and food lockers; scholarships and loans for post-secondary education; interest-free loans and outright grants. Work is carried on by auxiliaries located at major Naval and Marine Corps stations and branches at minor stations. *Type:* Association.

Navy Times

Army Times Publishing Co.
6883 Commercial Dr. Ph: (703)750-9000
Springfield, VA 22159-0001 Fax: (703)750-8622
E-mail: navydesk@aol.com.
Contact: Tobias Naegele, Editor; Nat Kornfeld, Advertising Mgr.
Desc: Independent newspaper serving Navy, Marine, and Coast Guard personnel. *Type:* Periodical.

Non Commissioned Officers Association of the United States of America

PO Box 33610 Ph: (210)653-6161
San Antonio, TX 78265 Free: 800-662-2620
  Fax: (210)637-3337
URL: http://www.ncoausa.org
Contact: Roger W. Putnam, Pres.&CEO.
Desc: Noncommissioned and petty officers of the United States military serving in grades E1 through E9 from all five branches of the U.S. Armed Forces; includes active duty and retired personnel, members of the Reserve and National Guard components, and associate members who were in pay grades E1 through E9 inclusive at the time of application for membership. Formed for patriotic, fraternal, social, and benevolent purposes. *Type:* Association.

Off Duty

Off Duty Enterprises
3505 Cadillac Ave., Ste. 0-105 Ph: (714)549-7172
Costa Mesa, CA 92626-1434 Fax: (714)549-4222
E-mail: odutyedit@aol.com; wbrdmr@aol.com.
Contact: Gary Burch, Executive Editor; Walter B. Rios, Publisher; Dagmar Rios, Publisher; Chuck Emerson, Advertising Mgr.

Desc: Leisuretime magazine for U.S. military personnel and their families stationed in the United States, Europe and the Pacific. *Type:* Periodical.

The Officer

The Reserve Officers Association
1 Constitution Ave. NE Ph: (202)479-2200
Washington, DC 20002 Fax: (202)479-0416
Contact: Carol Wilson-Bunn, USAF, Acting Editor; Major Gen. Roger W. Sandler, AUS(R), Publisher.

Desc: Magazine for active and reserve officers of all military branches. *Type:* Periodical.

Pearl Harbor Survivors Association

PO Box 99 Ph: (414)251-0787
Menomonee Falls, WI 53052- Fax: (414)251-8035
0099
E-mail: phsasec97@aol.com
URL: http://members.aol.com/phsasecy97/index.html
Contact: Julius A. Finnern, Sec.

Desc: Members of the U.S. Armed Forces stationed on the island of Oahu or offshore within a three-mile limit during the Japanese attack on Pearl Harbor, December 7, 1941. Fraternal and patriotic society to commemorate that "day of infamy" and to honor the memory of those killed in the attack. *Type:* Association.

Proceedings

U.S. Naval Institute
Preble Hall Ph: (410)268-6110
118 Maryland Ave. Fax: (410)269-7940
Annapolis, MD 21402-5035
Contact: Fred H. Rainbow, Editor; James A. Barber, Jr., Publisher; James E. Burke, Advertising Mgr.

Desc: Magazine on naval and maritime news. *Type:* Periodical.

R & R Shopper's News

Executive Business Media, Inc.
825 Old Country Rd. Ph: (516)334-3030
PO Box 1500 Fax: (516)334-3059
Westbury, NY 11590-0812
E-mail: ebmpubs@ix.netcom.com
Contact: Marji Hess, Editor; Ellis F. Anderson, Publisher; Donna Rapuano, Advertising Mgr.

Desc: Military consumer magazine. *Type:* Periodical.

Recorder-Times

Times Publications, Inc.
8603 Botts Ln. Ph: (512)828-3321
PO Box 17947 Fax: (210)828-3787
San Antonio, TX 78217
Contact: Ed Leal, Editor; Lewis F. Fisher, Publisher.

Desc: Military community newspaper. *Type:* Periodical.

Reserve Officers Association of the United States

1 Constitution Ave. NE Ph: (202)479-2200
Washington, DC 20002 Free: 800-809-9448
  Fax: (202)479-0416
E-mail: blauer@rua.org
URL: http://www.rua.org
Contact: Maj.Gen. Roger W. Sandler, Exec.Dir.

Desc: Reserve, regular, retired, and former Army, Navy, Air Force, Marine, Coast Guard, Public Health Service, and National Oceanic and Atmospheric Administration officers and warrant officers on active or inactive duty. Maintains hall of fame. *Type:* Association.

Retired Activities Branch

Navy Personnel Command Ph: (901)874-4307
5720 Integrity Drive Free: 800-255-8950
Millington, TN 38055-6220 Fax: (901)874-2611
E-mail: p622@persnet.navy.mil
URL: http://www.bupers.navy.mil/codes/pers6/pers62/pers622/Firstpage.htm
Contact: Jerry Sturdwient, Assistant Head.
Desc: A program of the U.S. Department of the Navy. Works to educate Fleet about the Survivor Benefit Plan and aid Navy retirees and widowers with problems regarding the securing of full benefits. *Type:* Association.

The Retired Officer Magazine

The Retired Officers Association
201 N. Washington St. Ph: (703)549-2311
Alexandria, VA 22314 Fax: (703)838-8179
E-mail: editor@trom.org.
URL: http://www.troa.org/serv/trom.asp.
Contact: Col. Warren S. Lacy, Editor; Joanne Hodges, Managing Editor; Maj. Dale Robinson, Business Manager/Administration.

Desc: Published for all uniformed service officers and their families. *Type:* Periodical.

Salute

Military Forces Features, Inc.
51 Atlantic Ave., Ste. 200 Ph: (516)616-1930
New York, NY 11001 Fax: (516)616-1936
E-mail: family@familymedia.com; salute@familymedia.com.
Contact: Don Hirst, Editor, (410)719-6968, fax: (410)719-6267; Joseph Mugnai, Publisher, jmugnai@familymedia.com.

Desc: Magazine serving active duty military personnel stationed in the U.S. *Type:* Periodical.

Sea Power

Navy League of the United States
2300 Wilson Blvd. Ph: (703)528-1775
Arlington, VA 22201 Free: 800-356-5760
  Fax: (703)243-8251
E-mail: mail@www.navyleague.org
URL: http://www.navyleague.org.
Contact: James D. Hessman, Editor, jhessman@navyleague.org; William G. Turner, Advertising Dir., (703)528-2068, bturner@navyleague.org.

Desc: Magazine covering America's seapower and the role of the sea services in defense. *Type:* Periodical.

Semper Fidelis

Commandment of the Marine Corps (MMSR-6)
U.S. Marine Corps
2 Navy Annex Ph: (703)614-1031
Washington, DC 20380-1775 Free: 800-336-4649
URL: http://www.hqmc.usmc.mil/hqmc/manpower/mmsr/semfid1/12e.htm
Contact: Tanya Ramey, Editor, rameyt@mq-smtp3.usmc.mil.

Desc: Provides information of interest to retired Marines. *Type:* Newsletter.

Sergeants

Air Force Sergeants Association
PO Box 50 Ph: (301)899-3500
Temple Hills, MD 20757-0050 Free: 800-638-0594
  Fax: (301)899-8136
E-mail: afsahq@internetmci.com
Contact: David L. Barrette, Exec. Editor; James Staton, Publisher.

Desc: Military magazine. *Type:* Periodical.

Soldiers' Scene

Chief of Public Affairs

Command Information Unit   Ph: (703)697-0050
1500 Army Pentagon 2D622   Fax: (703)697-5746
Washington, DC 20310-1500
E-mail: papaorg@meade-emh2.ftmeade.army.mil
Contact: Willard K. Morris, Editor.

Desc: Informs junior enlisted soldiers of the Army's professional development opportunities and encourages soldiers to take advantage of them. "Provides information on careers, pay and benefits, quality of life, and Army modernization." Remarks: Published as part of the Command Information Package. *Type:* Newsletter.

Sons of the American Legion

PO Box 1055   Ph: (317)630-1204
Indianapolis, IN 46206   Fax: (317)630-1369
E-mail: tal@legion.org
URL: http://www.legion.org
Contact: John W. Kerestan, Liaison.

Desc: Male descendants, stepsons, and adopted sons of members of The American Legion or of deceased veterans of wartime military service who were eligible for Legion membership. Supports the principles of the AL and conducts patriotic activities. Operates charitable program. *Type:* Association.

Special Forces Association

PO Box 41436   Ph: (919)485-5433
Fayetteville, NC 28309   Fax: (919)485-1041
URL: http://www.sfahq.aol.com
Contact: James C. Dean, Exec.Sec.

Desc: Active and retired military men who are now, or who have been, assigned or attached to any U.S. Army Special Forces unit or units. Perpetuates the Special Forces traditions and honors Special Forces troop members who have died. *Type:* Association.

Tailhook Association

9696 Businesspark Ave.   Ph: (619)689-9223
San Diego, CA 92131-1643   Free: 800-322-
    HOOK
    Fax: (619)578-8839
E-mail: thookassn@aol.com
URL: http://www.tailhook.org
Contact: J.R. Davis, Exec.Dir.

Desc: Individuals who have been designated as Naval Aviators or Naval Flight Officers and have made carrier landings; other individuals who have made carrier landings or who have the background and interest to support the objectives of the association. *Type:* Association.

United States Coast Guard Auxiliary

Commandant (G-OCX) U.S.   Ph: (202)267-1010
    Coast Guard HQ   Fax: (202)267-4460
2100 2nd St. SW, Rm. 3001
Washington, DC 20593
URL: http://www.cgaux.org
Contact: Capt. Mark S. Kern, Chief Dir.

Desc: Volunteer civilian organization, administered by the U.S. Coast Guard, composed of men and women, U.S. citizens (age 17 and over) who own at least 25 percent of a motorboat, yacht, aircraft, or amateur radio station or have a special skill. Assists the Coast Guard in search and rescue operations on or over the high seas and on navigable waters. *Type:* Association.

United States Coast Guard Chief Petty Officer Association

5520G Hempstead Way   Ph: (703)941-0395
Springfield, VA 22151   Fax: (703)941-0397
E-mail: cgcpoa@aol.com
Contact: T.R. Scaramastro, Exec.Sec.

Desc: U.S. Coast Guard Chief Petty Officers and USCG Enlisted (EG & below) who are active, retired, or reserve. Purposes are to: promote the welfare of Coast Guard enlisted personnel and their dependents; promote social and recreational activities on the local level; foster cooperation with all local civic groups; aid in the interest of handicapped or hospitalized children and other people in need; foster patriotism and a belief in the democratic form of government. *Type:* Association.

U.S. Department of Defense

Army Medical Research and Materiel Command

Ft. Detrick, Bldg. 660   Ph: (301)619-7613
Frederick, MD 21702-5012   Fax: (301)619-2982
Contact: Brig.Gen. Russell Zajtchuk, Comdr.

Desc: Solving medical problems of military importance. The program, which is designed to maintain or restore the health of the individual soldier, involves: assessment, prevention, diagnosis, and treatment of infectious diseases that would hamper military operations; disease vector surveillance; combat casualty care and rapid return to duty of injured soldiers; management of maxillofacial injury; assessment and prevention of oral diseases; research in dental materials; studies on health hazards of military materiel; studies on factors limiting soldier effectiveness; medical countermeasures to chemical warfare agents, including pretreatment and antidote drugs, skin decontamination compounds and medical management of chemical casualties. *Type:* Research center.

U.S. Department of Defense

Army Medical Research and Materiel Command

Army Medical Research Institute of Chemical Defense

Attn: MCMR-UV-RC   Ph: (410)671-3948
Aberdeen Proving Ground, MD   Fax: (410)436-3004
    21010-5400
E-mail: usamricd_pao@ftdetrck-ccmail.army.mil
URL: http://chemdef.apgea.army.mil/
Contact: Col. James S. Little, Comdr.

Desc: Medical defense of chemical warfare (CW). This includes basic research on mechanisms of action of CW agents and antidotes to establish a database from which to devise improved methods for the prevention, resuscitation, treatment, and management of chemical casualties; and assistance in the integration of products into the logistical system, doctrine development, and training of medical and nonmedical personnel in the management and prevention of chemical casualties. *Type:* Research center.

U.S. Department of Defense

Army Medical Research and Materiel Command

Army Medical Research Institute of Infectious Diseases

Ft. Detrick   Ph: (301)619-2833
1425 Porter St.   Fax: (301)619-4625
Frederick, MD 21702-5011
URL: http://www.usamriid.army.mil
Contact: Col. Gerald W. Parker, Comdr.

Desc: USAMRIID develops vaccines, drugs and diagnostics to protect U.S. forces from biological warfare threats and endemic infectious diseases requiring special containment. *Type:* Research center.

U.S. Department of Defense

Army Medical Research and Materiel Command

Army Research Institute of Environmental Medicine

Environmental Pathophysiology Directorate

Bldg. 42   Ph: (508)233-5153
Natick, MA 01760-5007   Fax: (508)233-5298
Contact: Dr. Ralph P. Francesconi, Dir.

Desc: Prevention, diagnosis, and treatment of common illnesses related to the environmental conditions of heat, cold, and high terrestrial altitude. Conducts both human and animal studies to identify the factors that may predispose an individual to environmental injury. *Type:* Research center.

U.S. Department of Defense

Army Medical Research and Materiel Command

Army Research Institute of Environmental Medicine

Military Nutrition and Biochemistry Division

Natick, MA 01760-5007   Ph: (508)233-4194
    Fax: (508)233-4869
E-mail: rfrancesconi@natick-ccmail.army.mil
URL: http://www.sscom.army.mil/usariem
Contact: Ralph P. Francesconi, PhD, Chf.

Desc: Nutrition research, development, testing, evaluation, and engineering support to the Department of Defense Food and Nutrition Research, Development, Test, and Evaluation and Engineering Program; and provides technical assistance to the Surgeon General of the Army on biomedical aspects of nutrition and performance. *Type:* Research center.

U.S. Department of Defense

Army Medical Research and Materiel Command

Army Research Institute of Environmental Medicine

Occupational Health and Performance Directorate

Bldg. 42   Ph: (508)233-4850
Natick, MA 01760-5007   Fax: (508)233-4195
E-mail: msmutok@natick-cemail.army.mil
Contact: Col. Michael Smutok, Dir.

Desc: Interactive effects of environment, nutrition, and the physiologic and psychologic demands of military operations on soldier health and performance. Objectives focus on the identification and quantification of military operational stressors, characterization of dose-response or energy-injury manifestation, development of attenuation or prevention measures, and development of predictive health and performance models. *Type:* Research center.

U.S. Department of Defense

Army Medical Research and Materiel Command

Army Research Institute of Environmental Medicine

Thermal and Mountain Medicine Division

Natick, MA 01760-5007   Ph: (508)233-4832
    Fax: (508)233-5298
E-mail: msawka@natick-ccmail.army.mil
Contact: Michael Sawka, Dir.

Desc: Illnesses, injuries, and physiological performance effects associated with exposure to the environmental extremes of heat, cold, and high altitude. *Type:* Research center.

U.S. Department of Defense

Army Medical Research and Materiel Command

Walter Reed Army Institute of Research

Washington, DC 20307-5100   Ph: (202)782-3551
    Fax: (202)782-3114
Contact: Col. E.T. Takafuji, Commander.

Desc: Biologically-active substances such as bacteria, viruses, biological and chemical threat agents, and toxic environmental contaminants; trauma and high-energy (wound infections, traumatic organ failure, blood substitutes, laser injury, and high-power microwaves); and stress and performance (combat psychiatric casualties, and sustained operations). Maintains permanent subordinate laboratories in Thailand, Brazil, Kenya, and Germany. *Type:* Research center.

U.S. Department of Defense
Army Medical Research and Materiel Command
Walter Reed Army Institute of Research
Biochemistry Division
Washington, DC 20307-5100   Ph: (202)782-3001
                                   Fax: (202)782-6304
E-mail: biochem@wrair-emhl.army.mil
URL: http://wrair.www.army.mil
Contact: Bhupendra P. Doctor, Dir.
Desc: Divisional components include the Departments of Biological Chemistry, Applied Biochemistry and Membrane Biochemistry. The Department of Biological Chemistry investigates the use of biological products, such as exogenous cholinesterases, and pharmaceutical products, such as huperzine, as pretreatment drugs for organophosphate exposure. *Type:* Research center.

U.S. Department of Defense
Army Medical Research and Materiel Command
Walter Reed Army Institute of Research
Medical Audio-Visual Services Division
Washington, DC 20307-5100   Ph: (202)782-7106
                                   Fax: (202)782-2136
Contact: Imre L. Toth, Dir.
Desc: Provides medical scientific illustration, medical research photography, motion picture production, and classroom/auditorium support meetings (held at WRAIR) for WRAIR research activities; serves as production agency for medical training films involving medical and/or paramedical subjects. *Type:* Research center.

U.S. Department of Defense
Army Medical Research and Materiel Command
Walter Reed Army Institute of Research
Medicine Division
Washington, DC 20307-5100   Ph: (202)782-7300
                                   Fax: (202)782-0703
Contact: Col. Charles E. McQueen, Dir.
Desc: Resolving military medical problems that fall within the general domain of the disciplines of internal medicine through study, laboratory experiments, and consultation. Divisional components include departments of Clinical Physiology, Gastroenterology, Hematology, Medical Research Fellowship, Nephrology, and Respiratory Research. *Type:* Research center.

U.S. Department of Defense
Army Medical Research and Materiel Command
Walter Reed Army Institute of Research
Preventive Medicine Division
Washington, DC 20307-5100   Ph: (202)576-3517
Contact: Lt.Col. John F. Rundage, Dir.
Desc: Plans, conducts, and coordinates graduate education programs in the field of military preventive medicine; assists in the production of technical information concerned with this specialty; and designs and conducts epidemiologic studies. Division also provides epidemiologic consultation services. *Type:* Research center.

U.S. Department of Defense
Department of the Air Force
Air Staff
Surgeon General of the Air Force
1670 Air Force Pentagon   Ph: (703)697-6061
Washington, DC 20330-1670
Contact: Charles H. Roadman, II, Surgeon General of the Air Force.
Desc: The Surgeon General is part of the Air Staff, independent of the basic staff structure, providing advisory and support services to both the Chief of Staff and the Air Staff. Operating components are: (1) Assistant Surgeon General for Dental Services, (2) Biomedical Sciences Corps, (3) Congressional and Public Affairs, (4) Health Care Studies and Evaluations, (5) Medical Programs and Resources, (6) Medical Support, and (7) Nursing Services. *Type:* Government agency, office, or program.

U.S. Department of Defense
Department of the Army
Army Medical Command
c/o Department of the Army   Ph: (202)221-6313
The Pentagon
Washington, DC 20310
URL: http://www.army.mil/
Contact: Lt.Gen. Ronald R. Blanck, Director.
Desc: The U.S. Army Medical Command provides direction and planning for the Army Medical Department in conjunction with the Office of the Surgeon General. *Type:* Government agency, office, or program.

U.S. Department of Defense
Department of the Army
Army Staff
Office of the Army Surgeon General
c/o Department of the Army
The Pentagon   Ph: (703)545-6700
Washington, DC 20310   Fax: (703)681-3243
URL: http://www.army.mil/
Contact: Lt.Gen. Ronald R. Blanck, Surgeon General of the Army.
Desc: The office of the Surgeon General manages health services for the Army and, as directed, for other services, agencies, and organizations. Other responsibilities include health standards for Army personnel; health professional education and training; career management for missioned and warrant officer personnel of the Army Medical Department; medical research, material development and test and evaluation; policies concerning health aspects of Army environmental programs and prevention of diseases; and planning, programming, and budgeting for Army-wide health services. *Type:* Government agency, office, or program.

U.S. Department of Defense
Department of the Navy
Bureau of Medicine and Surgery
c/o Department of the Navy   Ph: (202)762-3701
23rd and E Sts. NW   Fax: (202)762-3211
Washington, DC 20372-5120
Contact: H.M. Koenig, Chief, Bureau of Medicine and Surgery.
Desc: The Bureau directs the provision of medical and dental services for Navy and Marine Corps personnel and other persons authorized by law; ensures that health care program policies are optimally executed through the acquisition and effective utilization of financial and manpower resources; provides professional and technical medical and dental services to the Fleet, Fleet Marine Force, and shore activities of the Navy; ensures that assigned activities are able to achieve successful accreditation and recognition by appropriate governmental and civilian agencies ad commissions; and ensures cooperation with civil authorities in matters pertaining to public health disasters and other emergencies, in conjunction with maintaining and safeguarding the health of the Navy and Marine Corps personnel. *Type:* Government agency, office, or program.

U.S. Department of Defense
Department of the Navy
United States Marine Corps
Office of Health Services
c/o United States Marine Corps   Ph: (703)614-2344
Headquarters
Washington, DC 20380-0001
URL: http://www.usmc.mil/
Type: Government agency, office, or program.

U.S. Department of Defense
Office of Assistant Secretary of Defense for Health Affairs
The Pentagon   Ph: (703)545-6700
Washington, DC 20301-1155   Fax: (703)614-3537
URL: http://www.defenselink.mil/
Desc: Office is responsible for Department of Defense health matters, including preventive medicine; medical readiness; health care delivery; drug and alcohol abuse prevention; and procurement, development, and retention of medical personnel. *Type:* Government agency, office, or program.

U.S. Department of Defense
Office of Assistant Secretary of Defense for Health Affairs
TRICARE Management Activity
c/o The Pentagon
Skyline 5, Ste. 810   Ph: (703)681-6909
5111 Leesburg Pike   Fax: (703)681-8706
Falls Church, VA 22041-3206
URL: http://www.defenselink.mil/
Desc: TRICARE was formed from the consolidation of the TRICARE Support Office, the Defense Medical Programs Activity, and the integration of health management program functions formerly located in the Office of the Assistant Secretary of Defense for Health Affairs. The TMA mission is to manage TRICARE; administer and manage the Defense Health Program appropriation; provide operational direction and support to the Uniformed Services in the management and administration of the TRICARE program; and administer CHAMPUS. *Type:* Government agency, office, or program.

U.S. Department of Defense
Uniformed Services University of the Health Sciences
4301 Jones Bridge Rd.   Ph: (301)295-3030
Bethesda, MD 20814-4799   Fax: (301)295-1960
Contact: James A. Zimble, MD, President.
Desc: The Uniformed Services University of the Health Sciences was established to educate career-oriented medical officers for the Military Departments and the Public Health Service. The University currently incorporates the F. *Type:* Government agency, office, or program.

U.S. Department of Veterans Affairs
Great Lakes HSR&D Field Program
Veterans Administration Medical   Ph: (313)930-5100
   Center   Fax: (313)930-5159
PO Box 130170
Ann Arbor, MI 48113-0170
Contact: Elizabeth W. Bates, PhD, Dir.
Desc: Operational efficiency and effectiveness, quality of care, and mental health services research. Current research and policy analysis projects are concerned with operating room planning models, intensive care and admission scheduling/sizing models systems; mental health services use; veteran's use of VA medical centers and non-VA medical center health services; comparative facility case-mix and mortality methods; and correlates of hospital efficiency. *Type:* Research center.

U.S. Department of Veterans Affairs
Hines Veterans Administration Hospital
Midwest Center for Health Services and Policy Research
(151H)   Ph: (708)216-2414
PO Box 5000   Fax: (708)216-2316
Hines, IL 60141
E-mail: f-weaver@nwu.edu
URL: http://research.hines.med.va.gov

Contact: Dr. Frances Weaver, Acting Dir.

Desc: Conduct relevant, high quality health services research; stimulate health services research and provide technical assistance in its development; provide support and consultation to area managers and providers; and inform and educate VA managers and providers about HSR&D. Research objectives focus on accountability of the health care delivery system; health systems research and chronic diseases; health care management and delivery; and special populations. *Type:* Research center.

U.S. Department of Veterans Affairs

Rehabilitation Research and Development Center

VA Medical Center (153)   Ph: (650)493-5000
3801 Miranda Ave.   Fax: (650)852-3474
Palo Alto, CA 94304
E-mail: zajac@roses.stanford.edu
URL: http://www.guide.stanford.edu/
Contact: James Golf, Dir.

Desc: State-of-the-art technological aids and treatments for disabled veterans to improve their independence and quality of life, especially in their mobility. Specific research areas include orthopedic biomechanics, neuromuscular systems, human-machine integration, fracture healing and implant design, skeletal biology and physical activity, coordination of human movement, surgery simulation, neuromuscular diagnosis and repair, robotics, patient-handling, functional assessment, and technology transfer. *Type:* Research center.

U.S. Department of Veterans Affairs

Vermont Medical and Regional Affairs

Department of Medicine

Research Service

White River Junction, VT   Ph: (802)295-5149
05001   Fax: (802)296-5171
URL: http://wrjval.hitchcock.org
Contact: Leo R. Zacharski, .Assoc.Chf. of Staff for Res.

Desc: Biology, immunology, oncology, psychiatry, psychology, and rheumatology, rehabilitation, health services, AIDS research, artificial nerves, nerve reception, surgical simulations, and molecular biology. Merit Review Program, Research Advisory Group Program, and Special Research Initiatives Program. *Type:* Research center.

U.S. Department of Veterans Affairs

Veterans Health Administration

810 Vermont Ave. NW   Ph: (202)273-4900
Washington, DC 20420
URL: http://www.va.gov/

Desc: The Veterans Health Administration (formerly Health Services and Research Administration) provides hospital, nursing home and domiciliary care, and outpatient medical and dental care to eligible veterans of military service in the Armed Forces. It operates medical centers, domiciliaries, clinics, and nursing home units in the U.S., the Commonwealth of Puerto Rico, and the Republic of the Philippines, and provides for similar care under VA auspices in non-VA hospitals and community nursing homes, and for visits by veterans to non-VA physicians and dentists for outpatient treatment. *Type:* Government agency, office, or program.

U.S. Department of Veterans Affairs

Veterans Health Administration

Health Services Research and Development Service

810 Vermont Ave., N.W.   Ph: (202)535-7156
Mail Code 12-B   Fax: (202)535-7737
Washington, DC 20420
Contact: Daniel Deykin, MD, Dir.

Desc: Supports approximately 100 health services research projects annually in Veterans Affairs medical centers. Projects focus on planning, organization, management, delivery, utilization, and evaluation of health care. *Type:* Research center.

U.S. Department of Veterans Affairs

Veterans Health Administration

Office of Research and Development

U.S. Department of Veterans   Ph: (202)273-8284
Affairs   Fax: (202)273-6526
810 Vermont Ave., N.W.
Washington, DC 20420
E-mail: david.thomas@mnil.va.gov
URL: http://www.va.gov/resdev/
Contact: John R. Feussner, MD, Chf.Res.Off.

Desc: Provides funding for intramural research performed by individual investigators at VA medical centers throughout the United States. These investigators are staff at the medical centers (physicians, basic scientists, nurses, dentists, psychologists, etc.) who apply for research funds from the Central Office of Research and Development through the medical centers' research and development committees. *Type:* Research center.

United States Naval Institute

118 Maryland Ave.   Ph: (410)268-6110
Annapolis, MD 21402-5035   Free: 800-233-8764
                       Fax: (410)269-7940
URL: http://www.usni.org
Contact: Capt. James A. Barber, Jr., CEO.

Desc: Regular, reserve, and retired professionals in the Navy, Marine Corps, and Coast Guard; civilians interested in the advancement of the knowledge of sea power and in advancing professional, literary, and scientific knowledge in the naval and maritime services. Conducts oral history and color print program. *Type:* Association.

United States Submarine Veterans of World War II

862 Chatham Ave.   Ph: (630)834-2718
Elmhurst, IL 60126
Contact: H. T. Vande Kerkhoff, Sec.-Treas.

Desc: Persons who served aboard U.S. Navy submarines during World War II. Perpetuates the memory of individuals who gave their lives in submarine warfare. *Type:* Association.

USO World Headquarters

Washington Navy Yard   Ph: (202)610-5700
1008 Eberle Pl. SE, Ste. 301   Free: 800-876-7469
Washington, DC 20374-5096   Fax: (202)610-5701
URL: http://www.uso.org
Contact: Gen. Carl E. Mundy, Jr., Pres.

Desc: Established to serve the social, welfare, spiritual, recreational, and community involvement needs of U.S. service persons and their dependents. Seeks to provide through a voluntary civilian agency, programs, and services that enhance the quality of life and improve morale. *Type:* Association.

Veterans of the Battle of the Bulge

PO Box 11129   Ph: (703)528-4058
Arlington, VA 22210-2129
Contact: Stanley Wojtusik, Pres.

Desc: World War II veterans who were awarded the Ardennes Campaign (Battle of the Bulge) battle star; other veterans, family members of eligible veterans; interested others. Objectives are to: foster international peace and goodwill; promote friendship; perpetuate the memory of sacrifices involved; preserve historical data and sites. The Battle of the Bulge, fought in Belgium and Luxembourg from Dec. *Type:* Association.

Veterans Research Foundation

921 NE 13th St.   Ph: (405)270-5170
Oklahoma City, OK 73104-   Fax: (405)297-5911
5028
Contact: Carol M. Estrella, Dir.

Desc: Biomedical research for veterans. *Type:* Research center.

WESTLAW® Military Law Library

West Group
620 Opperman Dr.   Ph: (651)687-7000
St. Paul, MN 55164-0526
URL: http://www.westgroup.com

Desc: Contains the complete text of U.S. federal court decisions, statutes and regulations, and administrative law, and texts and periodicals dealing with military law, veterans, and the armed forces. *Available:* West Group, WESTLAW. *Type:* Database.

Women in the Military

Women's Research and Education Institute
1700 18th St. NW, Ste. 400   Ph: (202)328-7070
Washington, DC 20009-2506
E-mail: inform-editor@umail.umd.edu
URL: http://www.inform.umd.edu/EdRes/Topic/
WomensStudies/GovernmentPolitics/Military/
Contact: ws-editor@umail.umd.edu.

Desc: The Women in the Military database contains both statistical and full text data about women serving in the U.S. Army, Navy, Air Force, Marine Corps, and Coast Guard. *Type:* Database.

Minerals

Lapidary Journal—Annual Buyers' Directory Issue

Lapidary Journal
60 Chestnut Ave., Ste. 201   Ph: (610)293-1112
Devon, PA 19333-1312   Fax: (610)293-1717
E-mail: LJmagazine@aol.com.
Contact: Merle White, Editor-in-Chief.

Desc: List of 4,000 suppliers and retailers of gem-cutting and jewelry making and mineral collecting equipment, beads, fossils, minerals, and gems; gem and mineral clubs, bead societies, museums, schools, and shops. *Type:* Directory.

Rock & Gem Magazine—Lapidary Equipment Issue

Miller Magazines, Inc.
4880 Market St.   Ph: (805)644-3824
Ventura, CA 93003   Fax: (805)644-3875
E-mail: rockgemmag@aol.com.
Contact: Susan Muilenburg Haverland, Editor.

Desc: List of over 70 manufacturers and distributors of mechanical lapidary equipment and suppliers of other equipment, findings, and mineral and paleontological specimens. *Type:* Directory.

Mining

American Federation of Mineralogical Societies

PO Box 26523   Ph: (405)682-2151
Oklahoma City, OK 73126-
0523
Contact: Dan McLennan, Admin.

Desc: Hobbyists, collectors of minerals, and amateur lapidaries. Promotes popular interest and education in the earth sciences, particularly geology, mineralogy, paleontology, lapidary, and related subjects. *Type:* Association.

American Mining Congress

1920 N St. NW, Ste. 300   Ph: (202)861-2800
Washington, DC 20036-1612   Fax: (202)861-7535
Contact: John A. Knebel, Pres.
Desc: Producers of domestic coal, metals, and industrial and agricultural minerals; manufacturers of mining and mineral processing machinery, equipment, and supplies; engineering/consulting firms; financial institutions that serve the mining industry. Offers tax, communications, and technical workshops and financial seminar. *Type:* Association.

Bituminous Coal Operators' Association

303 World Center Bldg.   Ph: (202)783-3195
918 16th St. NW   Fax: (202)783-4862
Washington, DC 20006
Contact: Charles Perkins, Sec.-Treas.
Desc: Firms engaged in mining bituminous coal. Promotes improved industrial relations among member coal operators and their employees represented by the International Union United Mine Workers of America. *Type:* Association.

Colorado School of Mines Alumni Association Annual Directory

Colorado School of Mines
Alumni Association
1600 Arapahoe St.   Ph: (303)273-3295
Golden, CO 80401   Free: 800-446-9488
   Fax: (303)273-3583
Contact: Maureen Keller, Editor, maureen.keller@oai. mines.edu.
Desc: List of more than 18,500 graduates of the school (founded 1874). *Type:* Directory.

Copper Development Association

260 Madison Ave.   Ph: (212)251-7200
New York, NY 10016   Free: 800-CDA-
   DATA
   Fax: (212)251-7234
URL: http://www.copper.org
Contact: Robert M. Payne, Pres.
Desc: U.S. and foreign copper mining, smelting and refining companies, U.S. fabricating companies such as brass and wire mills, foundries, and ingot makers. *Type:* Association.

Directory of Mineral-Related Organizations

U.S. Geological Survey
989 National Center   Ph: (703)648-4750
Reston, VA 20192   Fax: (703)648-7757
Contact: Scott F. Sibley, Editor, ssibley@usgs.gov.
Desc: Public and private U.S. organizations offering data, guidance, and advice to the minerals industry. *Type:* Directory.

Earth Science Software Directory

Gibbs Associates
PO Box 706   Ph: (303)444-6032
Boulder, CO 80306   Free: 800-378-5089
   Fax: (303)444-6032
URL: http://www.csn.net/~bgibbs; http://www.csn.net/~bgibbs/erthsci.
Contact: Betty L. Gibbs, Editor, bgibbs@csn.org.
Desc: Over 1,000 software programs with applications in the earth sciences; international coverage. *Type:* Directory.

Gold Prospectors Association of America

43445 Business Park Dr., No.   Ph: (909)699-4749
113   Free: 800-551-9707
Temecula, CA 92590   Fax: (909)699-4062
E-mail: info@goldprospectors.org
URL: http://www.goldprospectors.org

Contact: Thomas Massie, Pres.
Desc: Recreational gold prospectors and miners. Seeks to: promote prospecting as an environmentally compatible operation; further knowledge of gold mining; help small miners attain prospecting success. *Type:* Association.

International Union United Mine Workers of America

900 15th St. NW   Ph: (202)842-7200
Washington, DC 20005   Fax: (202)842-7227
URL: http://www.umwa.org
Contact: Cecil E. Roberts, Pres.
Desc: Independent. *Type:* Association.

Kentucky Mining Directory & Buyers Guide

Al Skinner Enterprises
629 Virginia St. W.   Ph: (304)342-4129
Charleston, WV 25302   Free: 800-235-5188
   Fax: (304)343-3124
E-mail: cpm@newwave.net
Contact: Al Skinner, Editor.
Desc: Coal companies in Kentucky. *Type:* Directory.

Mine Safety and Health News

Legal Publication Services
2008 N. Emerson St.   Ph: (703)276-9796
Arlington, VA 22207   Fax: (703)243-3562
E-mail: minesafety@aol.com.
Contact: Melanie Aclander, Editor, (301)277-8882; Ellen Smith, Editor.
Desc: Covers the U.S. Mine Safety and Health Administration and the Federal Mine Safety and Health Review Commission. *Type:* Newsletter.

Mining Incidents/Accidents Minieres

Canadian Centre for Occupational Health and Safety (CCOHS)
250 Main St. E.   Ph: (905)570-8094
Hamilton, ON, Canada L8N
   1H6
E-mail: custserv@ccohs.ca
URL: http://www.ccohs.ca/
Desc: Contains more than 3500 citations to unpublished reports of occupational health and safety incidents in mining. Covers fatalities, lost-time accidents, explosions, fire, equipment accidents, collapse of structures, and electrical failures. *Type:* Database.

Mining Newsletter

National Safety Council
1121 Spring Lake Dr.   Ph: (630)285-1121
Itasca, IL 60143-3201   Free: 800-539-7468
   Fax: (630)285-1315
URL: http://www.nsc.org
Contact: Kathy Henderson, Editor.
Desc: Concerned with industrial and occupational safety in mines. Discusses safe work practices and safety programs and policies. *Type:* Newsletter.

National Mining Association

1130 17th St. NW   Ph: (202)463-2625
Washington, DC 20036-4677   Fax: (202)463-6152
E-mail: rlawson@nma.org
URL: http://www.nma.org
Contact: Richard L. Lawson, Pres. & CEO.
Desc: Producers and sellers of coal, equipment suppliers, other energy suppliers, consultants, utility companies, and coal transporters. Serves as liaison between the industry and federal government agencies. Keeps members informed of legislative and administrative actions. *Type:* Association.

Pit & Quarry—Reference Manual & Buyers' Guide Issue

Advanstar Communications
7500 Old Oak Blvd.   Ph: (440)243-8100
Cleveland, OH 44130-3369   Free: 800-225-4569
   Fax: (440)891-2733
E-mail: directories@advanstar.com; pitquar@en.com.
URL: http://www.advanstar.com.
Contact: Mark Kuhar, Editor, mkuhar@advanstar.com.
Desc: List of approximately 1,000 manufacturers and other suppliers of equipment, products, and services to the non-metallic mining and quarrying industry. *Type:* Directory.

Society for Mining, Metallurgy, and Exploration

PO Box 625002   Ph: (303)973-9550
Littleton, CO 80162-5002   Free: 800-763-3132
   Fax: (303)973-3845
E-mail: sme@smenet.org
URL: http://www.smenet.org
Contact: Gary D. Howell, Exec.Dir.
Desc: A member society of the American Institute of Mining, Metallurgical and Petroleum Engineers. Persons engaged in the finding, exploitation, treatment, and marketing of all classes of minerals (metal ores, industrial minerals, and solid fuels) except petroleum. Promotes the arts and sciences connected with the production of useful minerals and metals. *Type:* Association.

Southwest Contractor—Directory of Active Mines in Arizona, New Mexico, and Nevada

McGraw-Hill, Inc.
3110 N. Central, Ste. 155   Ph: (602)631-3068
Phoenix, AZ 85012   Free: 800-580-3406
   Fax: (602)631-3073
E-mail: swceditor@aol.com.
Contact: Danielle Beaugureau, Editor.
Desc: Lists of mines and sand/gravel operations in Arizona, New Mexico, Nevada, and western Texas. *Type:* Directory.

Mission

Africa Inland Mission International

PO Box 178   Ph: (914)735-4014
Pearl River, NY 10965   Fax: (914)735-1814
E-mail: aim_info@aimint.org
URL: http://www.aim-us.org
Contact: Dr. Ted Barnett, U.S. Dir.
Desc: Missionaries conducting Bible teaching, community development, education, medical work, and evangelization in Angola, Central African Republic, Chad, Comoro Islands, Kenya, Lesotho, Madagascar, Mozambique, Namibia, Democratic Republic of Congo, Seychelles, Sudan, Tanzania, Uganda, and urban centers in the United States. *Type:* Association.

American Missionary Fellowship

672 Conestoga Rd.   Ph: (610)527-4439
PO Box 368   Fax: (610)527-4720
Villanova, PA 19085
E-mail: amfinfo@aol.com
URL: http://www.homezone.com/amf
Contact: Dr. Donald C. Palmer, Gen.Dir.
Desc: Missionary couples and single missionaries of America's oldest independent home mission. Conducts vacation Bible schools, camp programs, and released time classes. Establishes Sunday schools and churches; sponsors specialized and cross-cultural ministries in urban and rural areas, retirement centers, and among migrant workers. *Type:* Association.

AMG International

6815 Shallowford Rd.
Chattanooga, TN 37421

Ph: (423)894-6060
Free: 800-251-7206
Fax: (423)894-6863

E-mail: amginternational@aol.com
URL: http://www.amginternational.org
Contact: Dr. Spiros Zodhiates, Pres.
Desc: Worldwide interdenominational faith mission working to: spread the gospel around the world. *Type:* Association.

Associated Reformed Presbyterian Church, World Witness

1 Cleveland St., Ste. 220
Greenville, SC 29601

Ph: (864)233-5226
Fax: (864)233-5326

E-mail: worldwitness@worldwitness.org
Contact: John E. Mariner, Exec.Dir.
Desc: Missionaries, retired missionaries, and missionary candidates. Works to support missionary work overseas. *Type:* Association.

Bethany Fellowship Missions

6820 Auto Club Rd., Ste. D
Bloomington, MN 55438

Ph: (612)829-2492
Fax: (612)829-2767

E-mail: 105063.2561@compuserve.com
URL: http://www.ourworld.compuserve.com/homepages/bfm
Contact: Tim Freeman, Dir.
Desc: A division of Bethany Fellowship, Inc. Christian missionaries worldwide. Supports evangelism by conducting activities such as Bible school and church-planting programs; disseminates literature. *Type:* Association.

Children International

2000 E. Red Bridge Rd.
Kansas City, MO 64131

Ph: (816)942-2000
Free: 800-888-3089
Fax: (816)942-3714

E-mail: children@cikc.org
URL: http://www.children.org
Contact: James R. Cook, Pres. & CEO.
Desc: Nondenominational charitable organization dedicated to improving the quality of life of needy children, widows, and other needy individuals. Provides food, clothing, medical care, and education to those in need throughout Latin America, Asia, the Holy Land, and the United States. *Type:* Association.

Chinese Christian Mission

PO Box 750759
Petaluma, CA 94975

Ph: (707)762-1314
Fax: (707)762-1713

E-mail: ccmusa@ix.netcom.com
Desc: Serves as an evangelical faith mission dedicated to reaching Chinese people around the world with the gospel of Jesus Christ. *Type:* Association.

Christ for the Nations

PO Box 769000
Dallas, TX 75376

Ph: (214)376-1711
Free: 800-477-CFNI
Fax: (214)302-6228

E-mail: info@cfni.org
URL: http://www.cfni.org
Contact: Dennis Lindsay, Pres./CEO.
Desc: A missions organization which seeks to promote the Gospel and Christian endeavors through an international network of interdenominational Bible schools, a Native church building program, literature distribution, assisting orphanages, and relief projects. *Type:* Association.

Christian Missionary Fellowship

PO Box 501020
Indianapolis, IN 46250-6020

Ph: (317)578-2700
Fax: (317)578-2827

E-mail: 765344.244@compuserve.com
Contact: Doug Priest, Gen.Dir.

Desc: Congregations, auxiliaries, and individual Christians contributing funds to recruit, send, finance, and oversee foreign Christian missionaries. *Type:* Association.

Church of God World Missions

445 25th St.
Cleveland, TN 37320-8016

Ph: (423)478-7190
Free: 800-535-9343
Fax: (423)478-7215

E-mail: kcooper@cogwm.org
URL: http://www.cogwm.org
Contact: Gene D. Rice, Gen.Dir.
Desc: Department of the Church of God. Promotes the dissemination of the beliefs of individuals of the Church of God to countries outside the United States and Canada. *Type:* Association.

Evangelization Society

500 Salem Ln.
Gibsonia, PA 15044

Ph: (724)935-1329
Fax: (724)935-1351

E-mail: shclc@nauticom.net
Contact: David W. Vogel, Gen.Dir.
Desc: Missionaries and Christians interested in evangelism. Witnesses for Christianity and builds missions in countries outside of the U.S. Operates missions in Zaire. *Type:* Association.

Fellowship International Mission

555 S. 24th St.
Allentown, PA 18104

Ph: (610)435-9099
Free: 888-FIM-9099
Fax: (610)435-2641

E-mail: fim@juno.com
Contact: Dr. Richard R. Ruth, Gen.
Desc: Pastors, missionaries, and administrators. Conducts evangelism and other ministries, including church planting, worldwide; cares for the poor in the Sahara; operates a children's home and school in Morocco, video ministry in Australia, and school and program of personal evangelism in Japan; engages in prison ministry in the U.S., and operates a Bible Institute and orphanage in Brazil, Bible training schools in Uganda and Nigeria, and Brazil, and a camp ministry in Australia. *Type:* Association.

Gospel Missionary Union

10000 N. Oak
Kansas City, MO 64155

Ph: (816)734-8500
Fax: (816)734-4601

Contact: Carl McMindes, Pres.
Desc: Interdenominational organization of foreign missionaries working to set up churches around the world for the cause of world evangelism. *Type:* Association.

HCJB World Radio

1065 Garden of the Gods Rd.
Colorado Springs, CO 80907

Ph: (719)590-9800
Fax: (719)590-9801

Contact: Richard D. Jacquin, Dir. of U.S. Ministries.
Desc: Persons engaged in international missionary shortwave broadcasts transmitted from Quito, Ecuador. Operates AM and FM outlets, including HCJB in Ecuador's 2 largest cities. Disseminates information via television, healthcare services, print media, schools, churches, evangelism, correspondence, and training programs. *Type:* Association.

International Missions

PO Box 14866
Reading, PA 19612-4866

Ph: (610)375-0300
Free: 800-755-7955
Fax: (610)375-6862

E-mail: info@imi.org
URL: http://www.intermissions.org
Contact: Dr. Patrick Cate, Pres./Gen.Dir.
Desc: Nondenominational faith mission emphasizing evangelism, Bible teaching, and church planting. Works in Hong Kong, India, Japan, Middle East, North Africa, Mongolia, Far East, the Philippines, Suriname, Pakistan, Albania, and among Asians living in Germany, England, France, Holland, the Commonwealth of Independent States, and Kenya. *Type:* Association.

Latin America Mission

PO Box 52-7900
Miami, FL 33152-7900

Ph: (305)884-8400
Free: 800-275-8410
Fax: (305)885-8649

E-mail: info@lam.org
URL: http://www.lam.org
Contact: Dr. David R. Befus, Pres.
Desc: Men and women who, motivated by "their love for the Lord Jesus Christ and in obedience to His commands," encourage, assist, and participate with the Latin church in the task of building the church of Jesus Christ in the Latin world and beyond. *Type:* Association.

Maryknoll Sisters of St. Dominic

Maryknoll Sisters Center, No. 511
PO Box 311
Maryknoll, NY 10545-0311

Ph: (914)941-7575
Fax: (914)923-0733

E-mail: clt@mksisters.org
URL: http://www.maryknoll.org
Contact: Sr. Helene O'Sullivan, Pres.
Desc: Catholic women missioners. Purpose is to "proclaim the Gospel of Jesus Christ" through life witness, pastoral ministry, communication, and community development, education, health, research, and social service programs. Members live and work in thirty countries of Africa, Asia, the Central Pacific, Latin America, and the United States. *Type:* Association.

Medical Mission Sisters

8400 Pine Rd.
Philadelphia, PA 19111

Ph: (215)742-6100
Fax: (215)342-3948

E-mail: mms@mms-sna.org
URL: http://www.libertynet.org/~mms1
Contact: Elizabeth Koonthanam, MMS, Soc.Coor.
Desc: International women's religious community that combines religious life with practice of full range of health care services. *Type:* Association.

Men for Missions International

Box A
Greenwood, IN 46142

Ph: (317)881-6752
Fax: (317)865-1076

E-mail: mfmi@oms.mhs.compuserve.com
Contact: Warren G. Hardig, Exec.Dir.
Desc: Laymen associated with OMS International , including businessmen, farmers, skilled tradesmen, and others interested in supporting Christian evangelism worldwide. Members adopt projects that provide services to those in need and that match their vocational interests, hobbies, and amount of spare time available. *Type:* Association.

Mennonite Brethren Missions/Services

2-169 Riverton Ave.
Winnipeg, MB, Canada R2L 2E5

Ph: (204)669-6575
Fax: (204)667-0680

Contact: Victor Adrian, Gen.Sec.
Desc: Mennonite brethren united to bring the gospel to the unevangelized worldwide. Conducts orientation training and charitable programs. *Type:* Association.

Mission Aviation Fellowship

PO Box 3202
Redlands, CA 92373-0998

Ph: (909)794-1151
Free: 800-359-7623
Fax: (909)794-3016

E-mail: maf-us@maf.org
URL: http://www.maf.org
Contact: Gary Bishop, Pres., CEO.
Desc: Service agency for more than 150 evangelical Christian mission societies and national churches in 16 foreign countries. Maintains 87 plane fleet, which provides air transportation, including aerial ambulance service, supply lines to remote areas, surveying of unreached areas, and ferrying of missionaries and nationals to increase their area of effective operation. Operates radio communications networks. *Type:* Association.

Missionary Church

3811 Van Guard Dr. Ph: (219)747-2027
PO Box 9127 Fax: (219)747-5331
Fort Wayne, IN 46899-9127
E-mail: mcdenomusa@aol.com
URL: http://www.mcusa.org
Contact: Dr. John Moran, Pres.
Desc: Conducts denominational work, including church planting in the states. Cooperates with the Evangelical Missionary Church of Canada in conducting overseas activities that include church planting, bible translation, correspondence courses, bible schools and extension seminaries, elementary schools, clinics, youth camps and other programs of evangelism carried out by 122 missionaries, in cooperation with other evangelical mission boards and the national churches in Brazil, Cyprus, Ecuador, Haiti, Dominican Republic, France, Jamaica, Nigeria, Portugal, Russia, Spain, Sierra Leone, Thailand, Indonesia, Guinea, Vietnam, Cuba, China, Chad and among Kurds. Also has established indigenous churches in India and Mexico. *Type:* Association.

The Mustard Seed

PO Box 400 Ph: (626)791-5123
Pasadena, CA 91114-7000 Free: 800-943-2484
  Fax: (626)398-2392
E-mail: themustardseed@themustardseed.org
Contact: Rev. Garry O. Parker, Pres.
Desc: An international, interdenominational Christian ministry which provides services to aboriginal/tribal peoples of Pacific rim countries. We currently work in Indonesia, Taiwan, and Papua New Guinea. Service projects include medical clinics, residential homes for children, the handicapped, and the elderly, economic development projects, relief services, and care for unwedmothers. *Type:* Association.

Nazarene World Mission Society

6401 The Paseo Ph: (816)333-7000
Kansas City, MO 64131 Fax: (816)822-8296
E-mail: nwms@nazarene.org
URL: http://www.nazarene.org/nwms
Contact: Nina G. Gunter, Gen.Dir.
Desc: Members of the Church of the Nazarene in 127 countries. Conducts programs for mission education and assists fundraising to carry on the missionary work of the church. Seeks to encourage young people to enter missionary service. *Type:* Association.

New Tribes Mission

1000 E. 1st St. Ph: (407)323-3430
Sanford, FL 32771-1487 Free: 800-321-5375
  Fax: (407)330-0376
URL: http://www.ntm.org
Contact: David S. Calderwood, Contact.
Desc: Ordained and licensed Protestant missionaries and members of the headquarters and missionary training schools staffs. Undertakes evangelical missionary work among indigenous peoples in Latin America, the Far East, and Africa, including teaching of Christian doctrine, Bible translation, research in linguistics, customs and cultures, and literacy programs. Maintains training schools in Wisconsin, Michigan, Kentucky, Pennsylvania, Missouri, Mississippi, Oregon, and Durham, ON, Canada. *Type:* Association.

North American Indian Ministries

PO Box 151 Ph: (604)946-1227
Point Roberts, WA 98281 Fax: (604)946-1465
E-mail: office@naim.ca
URL: http://www.naim.ca
Contact: Ray Badgero, Pres.
Desc: Professionals, such as teachers and engineers, who also have some theological training. Objective is to establish indigenous Native American churches in urban centers and on reservations. Conducts economic, educational, social, and rehabilitation programs. *Type:* Association.

O.C. International

PO Box 36900 Ph: (719)592-9292
Colorado Springs, CO 80936- Fax: (719)592-0693
6900
URL: http://www.oci.org
Contact: Dr. Lawrence E. Keyes, Pres.
Desc: Interdenominational missionary organization specializing in evangelism and Bible teaching service, motivating, training, and mobilizing churches for church planting and discipleship in Argentina, Taiwan, Philippines, Singapore, Indonesia, India, Greece, Germany, Japan, USA, Canada, South Africa, Spain, Swaziland, Brazil, Kenya, Colombia, Romania, Hong Kong, Guatemala, Mexico, and France. *Type:* Association.

OMS International

941 Fry Rd. Ph: (317)881-6751
Greenwood, IN 46142 Fax: (317)888-5275
E-mail: info@omsternational.org
URL: http://www.omsinternational.org
Contact: J. B. Crouse, Jr., Pres.
Desc: Promotes foreign missionary interests and work in the United States and 16 foreign countries, including the establishment and maintenance of Bible training institutions and schools for the education and training of national workers, evangelists, women, and Bible teachers. Works toward the establishment of indigenous churches; circulates Bibles, religious books, papers, pamphlets, tracts, and other publications. Has established primary schools, high schools, and churches. *Type:* Association.

St. Anthony's Guild

Paterson, NJ 07509-2948 Ph: (973)777-3737
  Free: 800-848-4538
  Fax: (212)594-2769
Contact: Fr. Joseph M. Hertel, OFM, Dir.
Desc: Promotes devotion to St. *Type:* Association.

St. Martin De Porres Guild

141 E. 65th St. Ph: (212)744-2410
New York, NY 10021 Free: 800-850-5228
  Fax: (212)737-3875
E-mail: ferrerrev@aol.com
Contact: Rev. Raymond F. Halligan, Dir.
Desc: Roman Catholic organization that raises funds for the support of missionary activity by Dominican priests and brothers. Provides funds through missionaries for local overseas selfhelp projects. The Guild is named in honor of St. *Type:* Association.

South America Mission

5217 S. Military Trl. Ph: (561)965-1833
Lake Worth, FL 33463-6099 Fax: (561)439-8950
Contact: William K. Ogden, Exec.Dir. (CEO).
Desc: Seeks to evangelize the Indians and inhabitants of South America and to establish self-supporting, self-governing, and self-propagating churches. *Type:* Association.

Teen Missions International

885 E. Hall Rd. Ph: (407)453-0350
Merritt Island, FL 32953 Fax: (407)452-7988
E-mail: tmi@cape.net
URL: http://www.teenmissions.org
Contact: Robert M. Bland, Dir.
Desc: Organizes interdenominational evangelical missionary work projects in areas such as agriculture and community development; programs have operated in 60 countries, including Australia, Brazil, Columbia, India, Indonesia, Mexico, South Africa, and Zimbabwe. Trains teen and adult missionaries through camps and conferences; operates placement service. Promotes the Christian gospel through the production of films, videos, printed materials, and media presentations. *Type:* Association.

Trans World Radio

PO Box 8700 Ph: (919)460-3700
Cary, NC 27512-8700 Free: 800-4567-TWR
  Fax: (919)460-3702
E-mail: info@twr.org
URL: http://www.twr.org
Contact: Thomas J. Lowell, Pres.
Desc: Christian missionary organization broadcasting religious, educational, and cultural programs in more than 140 languages from 12 strategic primary stations in Albania, Armenia, Cyprus, Guam, Monaco, Netherlands Antilles, Poland, Russia, Swaziland, Sri Lanka, Uruguay, and Republic of South Africa. Staff includes missionaries who are Bible teachers, technicians, engineers, program production specialists, and other workers. *Type:* Association.

Transport for Christ International

PO Box 303 Fax: (717)721-9351
Denver, PA 17517
E-mail: tfcdenver@juno.com
URL: http://WWW.layover.com
Contact: Scott A. Weidner, Pres.
Desc: Ministers in the United States, Canada, and Russia. Seeks to preach the gospel of Jesus Christ to truckers. Stimulates contact through chaplain services, promotes highway safety by "assisting in the development of spiritual and emotional stability in transport drivers"; cultivates a spirit of goodwill and cooperation within the entire transport industry; extends Christian counsel and friendship to truckers in times of accident, bereavement, or personal and family crisis; establishes chaplaincy programs. *Type:* Association.

United Indian Missions, International

PO Box 3600 Ph: (520)774-0651
Flagstaff, AZ 86003-3600 Fax: (520)779-3052
E-mail: info@uim.org
URL: http://www.uim.org
Contact: Rev. Warren F. Cheek, Gen.Dir.
Desc: Establishes indigenous churches among native peoples of North America built on the Scriptures and functioning within their cultural orientation. *Type:* Association.

United World Mission

PO Box 668767 Ph: (704)357-3355
Charlotte, NC 28266-8767 Fax: (704)357-6389
Contact: Woody Phillips, Pres.
Desc: Evangelical, nondenominational mission society organized to participate in world evangelism through saturation church planting. Draws support from independent denominational churches and individuals. Over 200 missionaries and national church leaders work in 21 countries serving the following ministries: Bible teaching in Bible schools; Christian day Schools, camps, and correspondence and extension courses; evangelism and church planting in urban and rural areas; literature distribution; medical dispensaries; relief aid. *Type:* Association.

The Voice of the Martyrs

PO Box 443 Ph: (918)337-8015
Bartlesville, OK 74005 Free: 800-747-0085
  Fax: (918)338-0189
E-mail: thevoice@vom-usa.org
URL: http://www.persecution.com
Contact: Tom White, Dir.
Desc: Seeks to help Christians who are persecuted for their faith in Christ in Communist, Islamic and other restricted nations around the world. Delivers Bibles, Christian literature and material help to those who are persecuted. *Type:* Association.

The Way International
PO Box 328
5555 Wierwille Rd.
New Knoxville, OH 45871
Ph: (419)753-2523
Fax: (419)753-2903
Contact: Rev. L. Craig Martindale, Pres.

Desc: Nondenominational biblical research, teaching, and fellowship ministry. Researches the Scriptures to understand their "inherent and inerrant accuracy regarding Jesus Christ." Seeks to: make the knowledge of Jesus Christ and the Scriptures available in every community; teach biblical research truths to others and live the principles of the Word. Offers The Way of Abundance and Power education program, classes, and seminars. *Type:* Association.

World Gospel Mission
Box 948
Marion, IN 46952
Ph: (765)664-7331
Fax: (765)664-7669
URL: http://www.wgm.org
Contact: Dr. Thomas H. Hermiz, Pres.

Desc: Interdenominational evangelistic organization conducting mission work in Argentina, Bolivia, Dominica, Haiti, Honduras, India, Japan, Kenya, Mexico, Hungary, New Guinea, Taiwan, Uganda, Paraguay, Tanzania, Ukraine, and the United States. Activities include evangelism, church planting, and theological education. Maintains educational institutions, clinics, hospitals, and agricultural, industrial, and rehabilitation programs. *Type:* Association.

World Impact
2001 S. Vermont Ave.
Los Angeles, CA 90007
Ph: (323)735-1137
Fax: (323)735-2576
E-mail: info@worldimpact.org
URL: http://www.worldimpact.org
Contact: Dr. Keith Phillips, Pres.

Desc: Seeks to evangelize, disciple and plant churches among U.S. urban poor. Provides job training, housing, food, clothing to the poor. *Type:* Association.

World Opportunities International
1415 Cahuenga Blvd.
Hollywood, CA 90028
Ph: (213)466-7187
Fax: (213)871-1546
Contact: Dr. Roy B. McKeown, Pres.

Desc: Charitable organization that organizes and supports religious and charitable ministries throughout the world through distribution of donated goods. Works to help children worldwide. Acquires large volumes of food clothing, medicenes, hygeine items and educational literature, and dispenses it through 30 inner-city distribution centers in the U.S. *Type:* Association.

World Team
1431 Stuckert Rd.
Warrington, PA 18976
Ph: (215)491-4900
Free: 800-967-7109
Fax: (215)491-4910
Contact: Albert Ehmann, Intl.Pres.

Desc: Missionaries engaged in evangelism, church planting, and training national leadership in Peru, the Philippines, Indonesia, Chile, Europe, Carribean, C.I.S., and Africa. *Type:* Association.

World Vision
34834 Weyerhaeuser Way S
Federal Way, WA 98001
Ph: (253)815-1000
Free: 800-423-4200
URL: http://www.worldvision.org
Contact: Richard Stearns, Pres.

Desc: Christian relief and development organization helping established agencies in 102 countries to meet emergency needs, carry out development activities, and provide needed assistance for over 14 million people. Provides food, medicine, education, equipment, personnel, and literature for schools, hospitals, and communities. *Type:* Association.

Worldteam
1431 Stockert Rd.
Warrington, PA 18976
Ph: (215)491-4900
Free: 800-967-7109
Fax: (215)491-4910
Contact: Albert Ehmann, Pres.

Desc: Interdenominational Christian mission serving 16 Caribbean, South American, European and Asian countries. Works to establish clusters of local churches through effective presentation of the Gospel. Fosters national leadership among members and promotes a team approach to urban church planting. *Type:* Association.

Mortuary Services

Casket & Funeral Supply Association of America Newsletter
Casket & Funeral Supply Association of America
8707 Skokie Blvd., Ste. 306
Skokie, IL 60077
Ph: (847)763-1541
Fax: (847)763-1547
Contact: George W. Lemke, Editor.

Desc: Carries news items of interest to the funeral supply industry, including information on annual conventions, Federal Trade Commission regulations and other court rulings, and cost and pricing issues. *Type:* Newsletter.

Cemeteries of the U.S.
Gale Group Inc.
27500 Drake Rd.
Farmington Hills, MI 48331-3535
Ph: (248)699-4253
Free: 800-877-GALE
Fax: (248)699-8070
E-mail: galeord@galegroup.com
URL: http://www.galegroup.com.
Contact: Deborah M. Burek, Editor.

Desc: Over 22,800 operating and closed cemeteries; state and local historical and genealogical associations, agencies, and publications able to provide information on cemeteries and records. *Type:* Directory.

Funeral Directions
Ontario Funeral Service Association (OFSA)
320 N. Queen St., Ste. 130
Etobicoke, ON, Canada M9C 5K4
Ph: (416)695-3434
Free: 800-268-2727
Fax: (416)695-3583
E-mail: ofsa@interware.net
Contact: Laura Hamilton, Editor, laurah@interware.net.

Desc: Offers information on legislative changes and legal concerns of the funeral service industry. Recurring features include a calendar of events, reports of meetings, news of educational opportunities, and issues affecting due profession. *Type:* Newsletter.

Funeral and Memorial Societies of America
PO Box 10
Hinesburg, VT 05461
Ph: (802)482-3437
Free: 800-458-5563
Fax: (802)482-5246
E-mail: famsa@funerals.org
URL: http://www.funerals.org.famsa
Contact: Lisa Carlson, Exec.Dir.

Desc: Monitors the funeral industry for consumers. Works to: promote the affordability, dignity, and simplicity of funeral rites and memorial services; reduce unjustifiable costs of burial and other funeral services; provide every person with the opportunity to choose the type of funeral or memorial service he or she desires; make available information on body or organ donation. Promotes reciprocity of benefits among member societies; informs public on funeral costs and methods of reducing costs; lobbies for reform of funeral regulations at the state and federal levels. *Type:* Association.

Funeral Service "Insider"
United Communications Group
11300 Rockville Pike, Ste. 1100
Rockville, MD 20852-3030
Ph: (301)287-2700
Free: 800-929-4824
Fax: (301)287-2049
E-mail: customer@ucg.com; layers@ucg.com.
Contact: Gabe Hernandez, Editor, (561)641-7811, ndunnam@ucg.com.

Desc: Covers the latest trends in funeral service education, legislation, franchising, marketing, and consumer purchasing. Recurring features include editorials, news of research, letters to the editor, and a calendar of events. *Type:* Newsletter.

International Cemetary & Funeral Association—Membership Directory and Buyers Guide
International Cemetery and Funeral Association
1895 Preston White Dr., No. 220
Reston, VA 20191
Ph: (703)391-8400
Free: 800-645-7700
Fax: (703)391-8416
E-mail: joeb@icfa.org
Contact: Joe Budzinski, Editor, joeb@icfa.org.

Desc: 4,700 funeral homes and cemeteries of all types, except government; individual members of the association; suppliers of products, equipment, and materials to the industry. *Type:* Directory.

Leadership Bulletin
National Funeral Directors Association
13625 Bishop's Dr.
Brookfield, WI 53005
E-mail: nfda@nfda.org
URL: http://www.nfda.org.
Contact: Renee L. Gryzkewicz, Editor, (414)789-1880, fax: (414)789-6977, rgryzkewicz@nfda.org.

Desc: Covers association activities and funeral business management topics. Reports on government regulation, public relations issues, and local developments. *Type:* Newsletter.

National Funeral Directors Association
Michelle Pafford
13625 Bishops Dr.
Brookfield, WI 53005-6600
Ph: (414)541-2500
Free: 800-228-6332
Fax: (414)541-1909
E-mail: nfda@nfda.org
URL: http://www.nfda.org
Contact: Robert E. Harden, Exec.Dir.

Desc: Federation of state funeral directors' associations with individual membership of funeral directors. Seeks to enhance the funeral service profession and promote quality services to the consumers. *Type:* Association.

Telophase Society
7851 Mission Center Ct., Ste. 104
San Diego, CA 92108-1326
Ph: (619)299-0805
Free: 800-520-5146
Fax: (619)299-8417
Contact: Tom Simonson, Pres.

Desc: Provides services for cremation and burial at sea. Counselors offer families assistance with financial arrangements, death certificate needs, and Veteran arrangements for burial or reimbursements after death. *Type:* Association.

Motorcycles

American Motorcyclist
American Motorcycle Association
33 Collegeview Rd.
Westerville, OH 43081-1484
Ph: (614)891-2425
Free: 800-262-5646
Fax: (614)891 5012
E-mail: ama@ama-cycle.org; letters@ama-cycle.org.

URL: http://www.ama-cycle.org.
Contact: Greg Harrison, Editor, harrison@ama-cycle.org; John Holliday, Advertising Dir., fax: (614)899-3783, holliday@ama-cycle.org.
Type: Periodical.

American Motorcyclist Association

13515 Yarmouth Dr.   Ph: (614)856-1900
Pickerington, OH 43147   Fax: (614)856-1920
E-mail: ama@aama-cycle.org
URL: http://www.ama-cycle.org
Contact: Ed Youngblood, Pres.
Desc: Motorcycle enthusiasts. Rulemaking body for motorcycle competition. Promotes highway safety. *Type:* Association.

Antique Motorcycle Club of America

D.K. Wood
14943 York Rd.   Ph: (410)771-4456
Sparks, MD 21152   Fax: (410)771-4456
E-mail: dwood@aol.com
Contact: D. K. Wood, Sec.
Desc: Individuals interested in collecting and restoring antique motorcycles. Holds National Road Rides, National Meets, and Motorcycling Judging. *Type:* Association.

Blue Knights International Law Enforcement Motorcycle Club

38 Alden St.   Ph: (207)947-4600
Bangor, ME 04401   Fax: (207)947-5814
E-mail: dkintl@midmaine.com
Contact: Bessie Small, Mgr.
Desc: Deputy sheriffs, game wardens, local police, parole officers, state troopers, and other law enforcement personnel participating in recreational motorcycling. Purpose is to improve the public image of motorcycle groups. Promotes motorcycle safety and social organization for recreational activities for off-duty police personnel. *Type:* Association.

BMW Motorcycle Owners of America

PO Box 489   Ph: (314)537-5511
Chesterfield, MO 63006-0489 Fax: (314)537-9848
URL: http://www.bmwmoa.org
Contact: Barbara Zingre, Mgr.
Desc: BMW motorcycle owners organized for pleasure, recreation, safety, and dissemination of information concerning BMW motorcycles. *Type:* Association.

Breakdown and Legal Assistance for Motorcyclists

Deni McDonald
5455 Wilshire Blvd., Ste. 1600   Ph: (213)932-1277
Los Angeles, CA 90036   Free: 800-4-BIKERS
                                  Fax: (213)932-1620
URL: http://www.motorcyclelaw.com
Contact: J. Russell Brown, Dir. and Founder.
Desc: Motorcyclists and motorcycling organizations united to reduce the number of motorcycle accidents and fatalities in the U.S. Members provide reciprocal assistance in areas such as emergency repairs, towing, and transportation. *Type:* Association.

Christian Motorcyclists Association

PO Box 9   Ph: (870)389-6196
Hatfield, AR 71945   Fax: (870)389-6199
URL: http://www.cmausa.com
Contact: Herbie Shreve, Pres.
Desc: Goals are to promote Christian fellowship among motorcyclists through public worship, ministry, and Christian evangelistic rallies and to improve the image of those persons engaged in motorcycling sports. Activities include motorcycle games, fellowship services, gospel and other singing events, and worship services. Sponsors evangelistic schools, state rallies, national rallies, and training programs for its members worldwide. *Type:* Association.

Cycle World

Hachette Filipacchi Magazines, Inc.
1633 Broadway, 41st Fl.   Ph: (212)767-6000
New York, NY 10019   Fax: (212)989-4561
Contact: David Edwards, Editor, (714)720-5369; Larry Little, Vice President, (714)720-5337; Paul A. LaBella, Advertising Dir., (714)720-5350.
Desc: Magazine on street, dirt, dual-purpose, and all-terrain motorcylces. Covering tests, aftermarket products, parts and accessories, competition, personalities, travel, and nostalgia. *Alt. Contact:* 1499 Monrovia Ave., Newport Beach, CA 92663; telephone: (714)720-5300; fax: (714)631-0651. *Type:* Periodical.

Dirt Bike Magazine

Hi-Torque Publishing Co., Inc.
25233 Anza Dr.   Ph: (805)295-1910
Box 9502   Free: 800-762-0345
Valencia, CA 91355   Fax: (805)295-1278
Contact: Ron Lawson, Editor; Roland S. Hinz, Publisher; Scott Wallenberg, Advertising Mgr.
Desc: Cycling magazine. *Type:* Periodical.

Dirt Rider

Petersen Publishing Co., L.L.C.
6420 Wilshire Blvd.   Ph: (323)782-2350
Los Angeles, CA 90048-5515 Fax: (323)782-2704
Contact: Richard P. Lague, Publisher; Scott Goodwin, Publisher; Peter Clancey, Sr., Marketing Dir.
Desc: Off-road motorcycle magazine. *Type:* Periodical.

Dirt Wheels

Hi-Torque Publishing Co., Inc.
25233 Anza Dr.   Ph: (805)295-1910
Box 9502   Free: 800-762-0345
Valencia, CA 91355   Fax: (805)295-1278
Contact: Dennis Cox, Editor; Roland Hinz, Publisher; Scott Wallenberg, Advertising Mgr.
Desc: ATV magazine. *Type:* Periodical.

Gold Wing Road Riders Association

PO Box 42450   Ph: (602)581-2500
Phoenix, AZ 85080-2450   Free: 800-843-9460
                           Fax: (602)581-3844
E-mail: gwrra@org
URL: http://www.gwrra.org
Contact: Mike Wright, Exec.Dir.
Desc: Owners of Honda Gold Wing motorcycles; spouses and dependents of owners. Promotes the pleasure and recreational aspects of Gold Wing motorcycle riding. Coordinates common motorcycle efforts and provides for exchange of information. *Type:* Association.

Harley Owners Group

PO Box 453   Ph: (414)342-4680
3700 W. Juneau   Fax: (414)343-4515
Milwaukee, WI 53208
Contact: Mike Keefe, Dir.
Desc: Harley-Davidson motorcycle owners. Provides benefits, services, and programs to members. Conducts social gatherings, including rallies and receptions. *Type:* Association.

In the Wind

Paisano Publications, Inc.
PO Box 3075   Ph: (818)889-8740
Agoura Hills, CA 91376-3075 Fax: (818)889-4726
URL: http://www.easyriders.com.
Contact: Kim Peterson, Editor; Joe Teresi, Publisher; Lizette Hotinger, Advertising Mgr.
Desc: Motorcycle lifestyle magazine. *Alt. Contact:* PO Box 3000, Agoura Hills, CA 91376-3000; telephone: (818)889-8740; fax: (818)889-1252. *Type:* Periodical.

MBN

Parkhurst Publishing Company
1812 Alaska Ave.   Ph: (714)549-2092
Costa Mesa, CA 92626   Fax: (714)547-4032
Contact: Joseph C. Parkhurst, Editor.
Desc: Focuses on the motorcycle industry, discussing new products, marketing and sales trends, legislation, and market shares reports. Recurring features include book reviews, news of research, statistics, and obituaries. *Type:* Newsletter.

Motocross Action

Hi-Torque Publishing Co., Inc.
25233 Anza Dr.   Ph: (805)295-1910
Box 9502   Free: 800-762-0345
Valencia, CA 91355   Fax: (805)295-1278
Contact: Jody Weisel, Editor; Roland S. Hinz, Publisher; Scott Wallenberg, Advertising Mgr.
Desc: Motocross racing magazine. *Type:* Periodical.

Motorcycle Industry Council

2 Jenner St., Ste. 150   Ph: (949)727-4211
Irvine, CA 92618   Fax: (949)727-4217
Contact: Tim Buche, Pres.
Desc: Manufacturers and distributors of motorcycles and allied industries. Maintains liaison with state and federal governments. Operates collection of research documents, federal and state government documents, and trade publications. *Type:* Association.

Motorcyclist

Petersen Publishing Co., L.L.C.
6420 Wilshire Blvd.   Ph: (323)782-2350
Los Angeles, CA 90048-5515 Fax: (323)782-2704
E-mail: mcmail@petersenpub.com.
Contact: Bob Weber, Publisher, (213)782-2801, fax: (213)782-2534; Richard Lague, Vice President, (213)782-2230, fax: (213)782-2483; Peter Clancey, Mkg. Dir.
Desc: Motorcycle magazine. Includes road tests, technical competition. *Type:* Periodical.

Rider Club

3601 Calletecate   Ph: (910)389-0300
Camarillo, CA 93012
Contact: Joe McNeill, Exec.Dir.
Desc: Promotes motorcycle touring as a safe and enjoyable form of recreation and transportation. Conducts charitable programs. *Type:* Association.

Tattoo

Paisano Publications, Inc.
PO Box 3075   Ph: (818)889-8740
Agoura Hills, CA 91376-3075 Fax: (818)889-4726
Contact: Billy Tinney, Editor; Joe Teresi, Publisher; Greg Andes, Advertising Mgr., fax: (818)889-5214.
Desc: Magazine for tattoo enthusiasts. *Type:* Periodical.

WERA Motorcycle Roadracing

4595 Towne Lake Pkwy. 300/   Ph: (770)924-8404
  100
Woodstock, GA 30189
URL: http://www.wera.com
Contact: Evelyne L. Clarke, Pres.
Desc: Amateur and professional motorcycle racers who compete on the same tracks as auto racers rather than on dirt tracks. Promotes and licenses motorcycle road racing as a sport in the U.S., Canada, and Mexico. *Type:* Association.

Municipal Government

Centre Region Council of Governments
131 S. Fraser St., Ste. 4   Ph: (814)231-3077
State College, PA 16801   Fax: (814)231-3088
Contact: James C. Steff, Exec. Dir.
Type: Association.

Denver Regional Council of Governments
2480 W. 26th Ave., Ste. 200-B   Ph: (303)455-1000
Denver, CO 80211   Fax: (303)480-6790
E-mail: drocg@iex.net
URL: http://www.drcog.org
Contact: Robert D. Farley, Exec. Dir.
Desc: Local governments. Formulates and implements transportation plans, develops water andc wastewater treatment plans. *Type:* Association.

FEIAA Newsletter
Federal Executive Institute Alumni Association (FEIAA)
PO Box 1001   Ph: (703)406-0573
Great Falls, VA 22066-1001   Fax: (703)406-9724
E-mail: mainofc@feiaa.org
Contact: Thomas W. Novotny, Editor.
Desc: Concerned with proposed and recently enacted legislation relating to federal personnel and fringe benefits matters, budgets, and executive issues. Reports on congressional views of interest to the federal community and federal retirement news of interest to annuitants. *Type:* Newsletter.

International City/County Management Association
777 N. Capitol St. NE, Ste. 500   Ph: (202)289-4262
Washington, DC 20002-4201   Fax: (202)962-3500
URL: http://www.icma.org
Contact: William Hansell, Exec.Dir.
Desc: International professional and educational organization for appointed administrators and assistant administrators serving cities, counties, districts, and regions. Provides publications, training, and management assistance to help local government professionals improve their skills and increase their knowledge. *Type:* Association.

International Institute of Municipal Clerks
1212 N. San Dimas Canyon   Ph: (909)592-4462
   Rd.   Fax: (909)592-1555
San Dimas, CA 91773-1223
URL: http://www.iimc.com
Contact: John Devine, Exec.Dir.
Desc: County, city, town, township, village, borough, regional, metropolitan, and district clerks, city secretaries, recorders, and clerks of council. Provide education at universities throughout the U.S. Maintains library of 600 volumes on subjects relating to the clerk field. *Type:* Association.

Maricopa Association of Governments
302 N. 1st Ave., Ste. 300   Ph: (602)254-6300
Phoenix, AZ 85003   Fax: (602)254-6490
E-mail: mag@mag.maricopa.gov
URL: http://www.nova.mcdot.maricopa.gov
Contact: James M. Bourey, Exec.Dir.
Desc: Comprised of managers and mayors of cities, towns and Indian communities within Maricopa County. *Type:* Association.

Metropolitan Washington Council of Governments
777 N. Capital St. NE   Ph: (202)962-3200
Washington, DC 20002   Fax: (202)962-3201
E-mail: infocntr@mwcog.org

URL: http://www.mwcog.org
Contact: Michael Rogers, Exec. Dir.
Desc: Through COG, local government members work in partnership with state and federal government agencies to solve regional transportation, environmental, human services, and public safety problems. *Type:* Association.

Mid-America Regional Council
600 Broadway, Ste. 300   Ph: (816)474-4240
Kansas City, MO 64105   Fax: (816)421-7758
URL: http://www.marc.org
Contact: David A. Warm, Exec.Dir.
Desc: City and county governments in the Kansas City, MO area. Works to improve local government services through cooperation. *Type:* Association.

Mid-Willamette Valley Council of Governments
105 High St. SE   Ph: (503)588-6177
Salem, OR 97301   Fax: (503)588-6094
E-mail: mwvcog@open.org
URL: http://www.open.org/cog
Contact: David A. Galati, Exec.Dir.
Desc: Cities (30), counties (3), special districts (8), and an Indian tribe. Provides a forum for exchange of information among members. *Type:* Association.

The Municipal Open Line
The Union of Nova Scotia Municipalities
1809 Barrington St., Ste. 1106   Ph: (902)423-8331
Halifax, NS, Canada B3J 3K8   Fax: (902)425-5592
Contact: Kenneth R.B. Simpson, Editor.
Desc: Gives information on municipal administration. Recurring features include news of research, a calendar of events, reports of meetings, news of educational opportunities, book reviews, and notices of publications available. *Type:* Newsletter.

National Association of Counties
440 1st St. NW, 8th Fl.   Ph: (202)393-6226
Washington, DC 20001   Fax: (202)393-2630
Contact: Larry E. Naake, Exec.Dir.
Desc: Elected and appointed county governing officials at management or policy level. Provides research for county officials and represents them at the national level. Compiles statistics. *Type:* Association.

National Association of Regional Councils
1700 K St. NW, Ste. 1300   Ph: (202)457-0710
Washington, DC 20006   Fax: (202)296-9352
Contact: William R. Dodge, Exec.Dir.
Desc: Active members (200) are regional councils of local governments and governmental agencies; associate members (50) are libraries, businesses, and other agencies and organizations interested in regionalism as an approach to meeting problems that cross local governmental boundaries, including economic development, transportation, environmental management, housing, services to the elderly, and rural development. Through this approach, local governments within a region pool resources to solve mutual problems on an area-wide basis instead of developing separate and duplicate or conflicting answers to problems. Councils vary from voluntary organizations to directly elected multijurisdictional entities. *Type:* Association.

National Association of Towns and Townships
444 N. Capitol St. NW, Ste   Ph: (202)624-3550
   208   Fax: (202)624-3554
Washington, DC 20001
Contact: Tom Halicki, Exec.Dir.
Desc: Federation of state organizations and individual communities. Provides technical assistance, educational services, and public policy support to local government officials of small communities across the country. Conducts research and develops public policy recommendations to help improve the quality of life for people living in small communities. *Type:* Association.

National Civic League
National Headquarters
1445 Market, Ste. 300   Ph: (303)571-4343
Denver, CO 80202-1717   Free: 800-223-6004
   Fax: (303)571-4404
E-mail: ncl@ncl.org
URL: http://www.ncl.org/ncl
Contact: Christopher T. Gates, Pres.
Desc: Community leaders, Civic leaders, educators, public officials, civic organizations, libraries, nonprofits and businesses interested in community building, transforming democratic institutions and developing techniques of citizen action and participation. Serves as a clearinghouse for information on healthy communities, community renewal, local campaign, finance reform, All-American cities, city and county charters, election systems and techniques of citizen participation. *Type:* Association.

National League of Cities
1301 Pennsylvania Ave. NW,   Ph: (202)626-3000
   Ste. 550   Fax: (202)626-3043
Washington, DC 20004-1763
E-mail: pa@nlc.org
URL: http://www.nlc.org
Contact: Donald J. Borut, Exec. Dir.
Desc: Federation of state leagues and cities. Develops and pursues a national municipal policy which can meet the future needs of cities and help cities solve critical problems they have in common. Represents municipalities before Congress and federal agencies. *Type:* Association.

National Urban Coalition
1120 G St., NW, 9th Fl.   Ph: (202)986-1460
Washington, DC 20005
Contact: Ramona H. Edelin, Ph.D., CEO.
Desc: Seeks to improve the quality of life and opportunity for the disadvantaged in urban areas through the combined efforts of leaders among minorities, business, labor, local government, women, youth, and religion. Operates Say Yes to a Youngster's Future program, which works to increase the participation of African Americans, Hispanics, Native Americans, and females in science, math, and computer education. Provides programs for urban children of color in the areas of science and mathematics; operates AIDS education and information demonstration program for teenagers in Washington, DC. *Type:* Association.

Pennsylvania League of Cities and Municipalities
Pennsylvania League of Cities and Municipalities
414 North Second St.   Ph: (717)236-9469
Harrisburg, PA 17101   Fax: (717)236-6716
E-mail: asturges@plcm.org
URL: http://www.plcm.org/
Contact: jgarner@plcm.org.
Desc: List of benefits to members including training, publications, networking support and lobbying activities. There is also a substantial number of service programs offered to individuals and other municipalities. *Type:* Database.

Planning and Development Collaboratives International
1025 Thomas Jefferson St. NW,   Ph: (202)337-2326
   Ste. 170   Fax: (202)944-2351
Washington, DC 20007
E-mail: 518-0899@mcimail.com
Contact: Theresa Park, Contact.
Desc: Seeks to ensure sustainable economic and social development in urban areas worldwide. *Type:* Association.

Puget Sound Regional Council

1011 Western Ave., Ste. 500   Ph: (206)464-7090
Seattle, WA 98104-1035   Fax: (206)587-4825
E-mail: psrc@psrc.org
URL: http://www.psrc.org
Contact: Mary McCumber, Exec. Dir.
Type: Association.

San Joaquin County Council of Governments

6 S. Eldorado St., Ste. 400   Ph: (209)468-3913
Stockton, CA 95202   Fax: (209)468-1084
E-mail: jgreene@co.san-joaquin.ca.us
Contact: Julia E. Greene, Exec.Dir.
Type: Association.

Southeast Michigan Council of Governments

660 Plaza Dr., Ste. 1900   Ph: (313)961-4266
Detroit, MI 48226   Fax: (313)961-4869
E-mail: tait@semcog.org
URL: http://www.semcog.org
Contact: Paul E. Tait, Exec.Dir.
Desc: Regional planning and association of local governments in Livingston, Macomb, Monroe, Oakland, St. Clair, Washtenaw, and Wayne counties in Michigan. *Type:* Association.

Southeastern Wisconsin Regional Planning Commission

916 N. East Ave.   Ph: (414)547-6721
PO Box 1607   Fax: (414)547-1103
Waukesha, WI 53187-1607
E-mail: sewrpc@globaldialog.com
Contact: Philip C. Evenson, Exec.Dir.
Desc: County and local government units interested in land use, transportation, environmental, and economic development planning in a seven-county area of southeastern Wisconsin. Goals are to: collect, analyze, and disseminate information relative to physical development; prepare a comprehensive plan for the development of the region; foster intergovernmental coordination and cooperation. *Type:* Association.

United States Conference of Mayors

1620 Eye St. NW   Ph: (202)293-7330
Washington, DC 20006   Fax: (202)293-2352
E-mail: uscm@cais.com
URL: http://www.usmayors.org
Contact: J. Thomas Cochran, Exec.Dir.
Desc: Cities with populations of over 30,000, represented by their mayors. Promotes improved municipal government by cooperation between cities and the federal government. Provides educational information, technical assistance, and legislative services to cities. *Type:* Association.

Upper Coastal Plain Council of Governments

PO Drawer 2748   Ph: (919)446-0411
Rocky Mount, NC 27802-2748   Fax: (919)446-5651
E-mail: regl@earthlink.net
Contact: Greg Godard, Exec. Dir.
Desc: Region L COG is comprised of county governments and local municipalities and is one of 18 multi-county planning and development regions in NC. It is governed by local public and private sector officials and is a forum for determining priorities for the larger area of which member communities are integral parts. *Type:* Association.

Urban Institute

2100 M St. NW   Ph: (202)833-7200
Washington, DC 20037   Fax: (202)261-5709
E-mail: paffairs@ui.urban.org
Contact: William Gorham, Pres.
Desc: Founded to meet the need for an independent, broadly based, research organization to conduct studies and propose solutions to the nation's social and economic problems. Works closely with government officials and administrators to improve decisions and performance by providing better information and analytic tools. Is linked with economic and social researchers in government, universities, and other research organizations. *Type:* Association.

Museums

American Association of Museums

1575 Eye St., Ste. 400   Ph: (202)289-1818
Washington, DC 20005-1105   Fax: (202)289-6578
E-mail: aaminfo@aam-us.org
URL: http://www.aam-us.org
Contact: Edward H. Able, Pres. & CEO.
Desc: Art, history, and science museums, art associations and centers, historic houses and societies, preservation projects, planetariums, zoos, aquariums, botanical gardens, college and university museums, libraries, and special museums; trustees and professional employees of museums and others interested in the museum field. *Type:* Association.

Art Institute of Chicago—News and Events

Art Institute of Chicago
Graphic Design &   Ph: (312)443-3540
   Communications Services   Fax: (312)443-1334
111 S. Michigan Ave.
Chicago, IL 60603-6110
E-mail: pubsmus@artic.edu
Contact: Virginia Voedisch, Editor, (312)443-3925, gvoedisch@artic.edu.
Desc: Covers institute and school activities, events, acquisitions, exhibitions, member programs, family programs, and travel programs. Recurring features include news of research, a calendar of events, news of educational opportunities, notices of publications available, and museum shop merchandise. *Type:* Newsletter.

Association of Science-Technology Centers

1025 Vermont Ave. NW, Ste.   Ph: (202)783-7200
   500   Fax: (202)783-7207
Washington, DC 20005-3516
E-mail: info@astc.org
URL: http://www.astc.org
Contact: Bonnie VanDorn, Exec.Dir.
Desc: Science centers and related institutions, including zoos, nature centers, aquaria, planetariums and space theaters, and natural history and children's museums. Supports and stimulates excellence and innovation in science museums, and strengthens their capacity to serve as effective community resources in promoting public understanding of science and technology. *Type:* Association.

Cheekwood

Cheekwood Tennessee Botanical Garden and Museum of Art
1200 Forrest Park Dr.   Ph: (615)353-2164
Nashville, TN 37205-4242   Fax: (615)353-2168
Contact: Martha Farabee, Editor.
Desc: Contains botanical garden and museum of art exhibition articles. Recurring features include a calendar of events, news of educational opportunities, and volunteer opportunities. *Type:* Newsletter.

Huntington Calendar

Huntington Library, Art Collections, and Botanical Gardens
1151 Oxford Rd.   Ph: (818)405-2100
San Marino, CA 91108   Fax: (818)405-0225
Contact: Catherine Babcock, Editor.
Desc: Reports news of the Huntington, its services to the public, and activities of its staff and visiting scholars. Highlights recent acquisitions, items of special interest from the collections, and upcoming exhibitions. *Type:* Newsletter.

Museum Archivist

Museum Archives Section
Society of American Archivists
c/o Amon Carter Museum   Ph: (817)738-1933
3501 Camp Bowie Blvd.   Fax: (817)738-4066
Fort Worth, TX 76107-2695
URL: http://www.chin.gc.ca/Resoures/Forum/e_forum.html.
Contact: Paula Stewart, Editor, paula.stewart@cartermuseum.org.
Desc: Provides news of Society and Section activities, meetings, symposia, educational programs, project research, repository reports, notes, and announcements. Recurring features include letters to the editor, news of research, reports of meetings, and news of educational opportunities. *Type:* Newsletter.

Museum Store Magazine

Museum Store Association
4100 E. Mississippi Ave., No.   Fax: (303)329-6139
   800
Denver, CO 80246-3048
Contact: Jenifer F. Merchant, Editor.
Desc: Carries news and information concerning museum store management. Recurring features include new product information, profiles of museum stores, reports of the Association's annual and regional meetings, letters to the editor, a calendar of events, and news of members. *Type:* Newsletter.

Nicola Valley Historical Quarterly

Nicola Valley Museum Archives Association
2202 Jackon Ave.   Ph: (250)378-4145
PO Box 1262   Fax: (250)378-4145
Merritt, BC, Canada V1K 1B8
Contact: Ken Moyes, Editor; Sigurd Teit, Editor; Bette Sulz, Editor; Barb Watson, Editor.
Desc: Covers various subjects related to Nicola Valley, British Columbia. Recurring features include letters to the editor. *Type:* Newsletter.

Official Museum Directory

National Register Publishing Co.
121 Chanlon Rd.   Ph: (908)464-6800
New Providence, NJ 07974   Free: 800-521-8110
      Fax: (908)508-7671
E-mail: info@renp.com
URL: http://www.reedref.com
Contact: Christina Moxley, Editor.
Desc: Approximately 7,850 institutions of art, history, and science in the United States, including general museums, college and university museums, children's and junior museums, company museums, national park and nature center displays, and highly specialized museums. Also includes a separate volume of 2,000 suppliers of services and products to museums. *Type:* Directory.

Smithsonian Magazine

Smithsonian Magazine
900 Jefferson Dr., SW   Ph: (202)786-2900
Washington, DC 20560
E-mail: edletters@aol.com.
Contact: Don Moser, Editor, fax: (202)786-2564, dmoser@simag.si.edu; Ron Walker, Publisher, fax: (202)633-9454, rwalker@simag.si.edu; David Cator, Advertising Dir., (212)916-1313, fax: (212)986-4259.
Desc: General interest magazine. *Type:* Periodical.

Spectra

Museum Computer Network, Inc.
8720 Georgia Ave., Ste. 501   Ph: (301)585-4413
Silver Spring, MD 20910   Fax: (301)495-0810
Contact: Suzanne Quigley, Editor.

Desc: Provides information on computer software to build data or image bases for museums. Reports on conferences, workshops, and exhibits. *Type:* Newsletter.

Music

Alabama Fan Club
101 Glen Blvd. SW   Ph: (256)845-1646
Fort Payne, AL 35967   Fax: (256)845-5650
Contact: Bruce Burnett, Mngr.
Desc: Fans of the southern-rock band Alabama. (Southern-rock is a musical style that includes country-rock and the blues.) Promotes Alabama's music; provides concert and ticket information; makes available Alabama memorabilia. Conducts charitable activities including annual Alabama June Jam, a concert and fair that raises funds for charity. *Type:* Association.

American Accordionists' Association
PO Box 616   Ph: (516)746-3101
Mineola, NY 11501   Fax: (516)746-7085
E-mail: ameracc@aol.com
URL: http://www.ameraccord.com
Contact: Faithe Deffner, CEO, Pres.
Desc: Certified accordion instructors, students, manufacturers and importers of accordions, and publishers and arrangers of accordion music. Promotes the accordion through contests, concerts, granting of scholarships, and commissioning of contemporary American composers to write for the accordion. *Type:* Association.

American Choral Directors Association
PO Box 6310   Ph: (405)355-8161
Lawton, OK 73506   Fax: (405)248-1465
URL: http://www.acdaonline.org
Contact: Dr. Gene Brooks, Exec.Dir.
Desc: Choral directors for elementary and secondary schools, colleges, universities, church, community and industrial organizations, radio, television, the concert stage, and the recording industry; associate members are publishers and dealers in choral music, manufacturers of choral accessories, and interested individuals. Seeks to foster choral singing. Encourages compositions of superior quality through commissions. *Type:* Association.

American College of Musicians
PO Box 1807   Ph: (512)478-5775
Austin, TX 78767   Fax: (512)478-5843
URL: http://www.pianoguild.com
Contact: Richard Allison, Pres.
Desc: Grants diplomas and degrees to members of the National Guild of Piano Teachers and other worthy musicians who have passed examinations administered by a board of examiners. Membership includes guild judges and members whose qualifications make them eligible to judge. Grants high school, collegiate, and artist diploma to teachers who present programs in the National Piano Playing Auditions that meet basic requirements of the guild; serves as an examinations board in adjudicating guild members' pupils in the auditions. *Type:* Association.

American Federation of Jazz Societies
2787 Del Monte St.
West Sacramento, CA 95691
Desc: Helps support and sustain the promotion, performance, preservation, and perpetuation of jazz. *Type:* Association.

American Guild of English Handbell Ringers
1055 E. Centerville Sta.   Ph: (937)438-0085
Dayton, OH 45459-5503   Fax: (937)438-0434
E-mail: theagehr@ad.com
URL: http://www.agehr.org

Contact: Vic Kostenko, Exec.Dir.
Desc: Church and school groups and individual musicians interested in the art of English handbell ringing. Encourages participation in area and national festivals. *Type:* Association.

American Guild of Organists
475 Riverside Dr., Ste. 1260   Ph: (212)870-2310
New York, NY 10115   Free: 800-AGO-5115
                                     Fax: (212)870-2163
E-mail: info@agohq.org
URL: http://www.agohq.org
Contact: James E. Thomashower, Exec. Dir.
Desc: Educational and service organization organized to advance the cause of organ and choral music and to maintain standards of artistic excellence of organists and choral conductors. *Type:* Association.

American Music Center
30 W. 26th St., Ste. 1001   Ph: (212)366-5260
New York, NY 10010-2011   Fax: (212)366-5265
E-mail: center@amc.net
URL: http://www.amc.net/index.html
Contact: Richard Kessler, Exec.Dir.
Desc: Composers, performers, students, and other music professionals. Appointed official U.S. Information Center for American Music in October 1962 by National Music Council. *Type:* Association.

American Music Scholarship Association
441 Vine St., Ste. 1030   Ph: (513)421-5342
Cincinnati, OH 45202   Fax: (513)421-2672
Contact: Gloria Ackerman, Exec.Dir.
Desc: Seeks to expose young pianists, ages five to 30, to the influence of performances by great musicians; strives to foster greater music appreciation through public exposure of talented artists. *Type:* Association.

American Symphony Orchestra League
1156 15th St. NW, Ste. 800   Ph: (202)776-0212
Washington, DC 20005   Fax: (202)776-0224
E-mail: league@symphony.org
URL: http://www.symphony.org
Contact: Charles Olton, CEO.
Desc: Symphony orchestras; associate members include educational institutions, arts councils, public libraries, business firms, orchestra professionals, and individuals interested in symphony orchestras. Engages in extensive research on diverse facets of symphony orchestra operations and development. *Type:* Association.

BAM Magazine
BAM Media, Inc.
3470 Buskirk Ave.   Ph: (925)934-3700
Pleasant Hill, CA 94523-4316   Fax: (925)946-2985
E-mail: sales@bammedia.com
URL: http://www.musicuniverse.com.
Contact: Bill Crandall, Northern California Editor, fax: (510)946-9060, editorial@bammedia.com; Kris Smith, Northern California Advt. Mgr., sales@bammedia.com.
Desc: Regional music magazine. *Alt. Contact:* fax: (925)946-9061. *Type:* Periodical.

Bands of America
526 Pratt Ave. N.   Ph: (847)891-2263
Schaumburg, IL 60193   Free: 800-848-2263
                                     Fax: (847)891-1812
Contact: L. Scott McCormick, Exec.Dir.
Desc: Works to create, support, and serve the experience of the school band; to provide the opportunity for acknowledgement of young participants; and to promote excellence and participation in young people. *Type:* Association.

Beatles Fan Club: Good Day Sunshine
315 Derby Ave.   Ph: (203)891-8131
Orange, CT 06477   Fax: (203)891-8433
E-mail: rosenay@aol.com
Contact: Charles F. Rosenay, Pres.
Desc: Fans of the Beatles (1958-70). Purpose is to disseminate information about the Beatles and their music to fans. Produces Beatles conventions in several cities; charters group tours to "Beatlesland" (London and Liverpool, England); books Beatles sound-alike bands worldwide. *Type:* Association.

Billboard's International Buyer's Guide
Billboard
1515 Broadway   Ph: (212)536-5004
New York, NY 10036   Free: 800-344-7119
                                     Fax: (212)536-5055
URL: http://www.billboard.com.
Contact: Sonja Quinn, Editor.
Desc: Record companies; music publishers; record and tape wholesalers; services and supplies for the music-record-tape-video industry; record and tape dealer accessories, fixtures, and merchandising products; includes United States and over 65 other countries. *Type:* Directory.

Broadcast Music, Inc.
320 W. 57th St.   Ph: (212)586-2000
New York, NY 10019   Fax: (212)956-2059
Contact: Francis W. Preston, CEO & Pres.
Desc: Nonprofit music licensing organization with more than 90,000 writer and 50,000 publisher affiliates. Acts as steward for the performing rights of the works of its affiliates by collecting license fees from music users and making payments to the creators of the music used (based on a published schedule of payments). Maintains reciprocal agreements with 41 sister licensing organizations worldwide. *Type:* Association.

Canadian Association for Music Therapy Newsletter/Bulletin Association de Musicotherapie du Canada
Canadian Association for Music Therapy (CAMT)
Wilfrid Laurier University   Ph: (519)884-1970
75 University Ave. W.   Free: 800-996-CAMT
Waterloo, ON, Canada N2L   Fax: (519)884-8853
3C5
E-mail: camt@musictherapy.ca
Contact: Jennifer Buchanan, Editor, (519)217-8153, fax: (519)246-2093, buchanan@jbmt.net.
Desc: Provides a channel for exchange of ideas on music therapy. Contains regional and university reports. *Type:* Newsletter.

Catgut Acoustical Society
Carleen M. Hitchins
112 Essex Ave.   Fax: (973)744-9197
Montclair, NJ 07042
E-mail: catgutas@msn.com
URL: http://www.marymt.edu/~cas
Contact: Carleen Maley Hutchins, Sec.
Desc: Physicists, engineers, instrument makers, musicians, and others interested in violin acoustics. Congregates for periodic discussions of plate vibrations, varnish, damping factors, tap tones, air resonance, special properties of the slip-stick action of the bowed string, and other aspects of violin construction and sound. Studies factors affecting the quality of old Italian violins and modern instruments. *Type:* Association.

CD Review

Connell Communications Inc.
86 Elm St.   Ph: (603)924-7271
Peterborough, NH 03458-1052   Fax: (603)924-7013
Contact: Lou Warnycia, Editor; Brian Vaillencourt, Advertising Mgr.; Pam Wilder, Circulation Mgr.
Desc: Consumer music review magazine. *Type:* Periodical.

Ceolas Celtic Music Archive

Ceolas
844 Fremont St.   Ph: (415)326-0680
Menlo Park, CA 94025   Fax: (415)858-0170
E-mail: ceolas@celtic.stanford.edu
URL: http://www.ceolas.org/ceolas.html
Contact: Gerard Manning.
Desc: This site is an excellent collection of material on the sometimes sweet, sometimes rowdy Celtic music. Browse this site for an introduction to the world of traditional Celtic music, then explore its many facets via links and data collections on-site. *Type:* Database.

Chamber Music America

305 7th Ave.   Ph: (212)242-2022
New York, NY 10001-6008   Fax: (212)242-7955
E-mail: info@chamber-music.org
URL: http://www.chamber-music.org
Contact: Dean K. Stein, Exec.Dir.
Desc: Professional chamber music ensembles and presenters; organizations, foundations, and individuals actively supporting chamber music performances. Purposes are to: promote the welfare of professional chamber music ensembles in the U.S.; act as advocate and coordinator in developing governmental, corporate, and private funding for these ensembles; promote public interest in and appreciation of chamber music. *Type:* Association.

Christian Music Directory: Printed Music

Resource Publications, Inc.
160 E. Virginia St., Ste. 290   Ph: (408)286-8505
San Jose, CA 95112-5876   Fax: (408)287-8748
E-mail: info@rpinet.com; cmd@rpinet.com.
URL: http://www.rpinet.com/
Contact: Ray Valido, Editor.
Type: Directory.

Christian Music Directory: Recorded Music

Resource Publications, Inc.
160 E. Virginia St., Ste. 290   Ph: (408)286-8505
San Jose, CA 95112-5876   Fax: (408)287-8748
E-mail: info@rpinet.com; cmd@rpinet.com.
URL: http://www.rpinet.com/
Contact: Ray Valido, Editor.
Desc: List of over 200,000 song and album titles from over 600 record companies who serve the religious music field. *Type:* Directory.

Collectors Record Club

1206 Decatur St.   Ph: (504)525-1776
New Orleans, LA 70116   Fax: (504)523-2629
Contact: George H. Buck, Jr., Exec. Officer.
Desc: Persons interested in authentic jazz and big band music. Promotes the circulation of authentic jazz and big band recordings by providing members with the opportunity of purchasing recordings at a discount. Club uses money from recording sales to make more recordings available on the club's Jazzology label. *Type:* Association.

Concert Music Network

100 Park Ave.   Ph: (212)309-9370
New York, NY 10017-5516   Fax: (212)309-9380
Contact: Peter J. Cleary, President; Roy Lindav, Vice President.

Desc: Classical music format. *Alt. Contact:* 100 Park Ave., New York, NY 10017-5516; telephone: (212)309-9370; fax: (212)309-9380. *Type:* Periodical.

Contemporary A Cappella Society of America

1850 Union St., Ste. 1441   Ph: (415)563-5224
San Francisco, CA 94123   Fax: (415)563-5523
E-mail: casa@casa.org
URL: http://www.casa.org
Contact: Deke Sharon, Pres.
Desc: High school, collegiate, professional, and recreational a cappella groups, and interested individuals. Promotes the advancement of a cappella (a singing style without instrumental accompaniment.). *Type:* Association.

Contemporary Musicians

Gale Group Inc.
27500 Drake Rd.   Ph: (248)699-4253
Farmington Hills, MI 48331-   Free: 800-877-GALE
3535   Fax: (248)699-8070
E-mail: galeord@galegroup.com
URL: http://www.galegroup.com.; http://www.gale.com.
Contact: Luann Brennan, Editor, luann.brennan@gale.com.
Desc: More than 80 popular musicians in all genres per volume; set comprises 24 volumes. *Type:* Directory.

Contemporary Record Society News Magazine

Contemporary Record Society
724 Winchester Rd.   Ph: (610)544-5920
Broomall, PA 19008   Fax: (610)544-5921
E-mail: crsnews@erols.com.
URL: http://www.erols.com/crsnews.
Contact: John Perotti, Contact.
Desc: Trade magazine of the Contemporary Record Society covering music and music reviews. *Type:* Periodical.

Country America

Meredith Corp.
1716 Locust St.   Ph: (515)284-3000
Des Moines, IA 50309-3023   Free: 800-678-2674
    Fax: (515)284-3697
Contact: Richard Krumme, Editor-in-Chief, fax: (515)284-3035; Bill Eftink, Managing Editor, fax: (515)284-3035.
Desc: Country America reflects and upholds the values, traditions, activities, and interests of country people who love country music. *Type:* Periodical.

Country Music

Silver Eagle Publishers
1 Turkey Hill Rd. S   Ph: (203)221-4950
Westport, CT 06880   Fax: (203)221-4948
Contact: Russell D. Barnard, Publisher; Leonard Mendelson, Assoc. Publisher/Advertising Dir.; Warren Beardow, Marketing Dir.
Desc: Consumer magazine covering country music. *Type:* Periodical.

Country Music Foundation

4 Music Sq. E.   Ph: (615)256-1639
Nashville, TN 37203   Fax: (615)255-2245
URL: http://www.country.com
Contact: Kyle Young, Dir.
Desc: Educational foundation. Collects, preserves, interprets, displays, and disseminates items, artifacts, and information related to the history and development of country music and encourages scholarly research in the field of country music and related areas. Operates the Country Music Hall of Fame and Museum, a historic recording studio (formerly RCA's Studio B), and Hatch Show Print (one of the South's oldest-known show poster print shop). *Type:* Association.

Country Song and Dance Society

132 Main St.   Ph: (413)268-7426
PO Box 338   Fax: (413)268-7471
Haydenville, MA 01039
Desc: Admirers of Anglo-American folk music and dancing. Promotes appreciation and performance of Anglo-American folk dances and songs. *Type:* Association.

Delta Omicron

57 Orchard Dr.   Ph: (614)436-5258
Worthington, OH 43085   Fax: (614)436-4776
E-mail: doexof@aol.com
Contact: M. Diane Blain, Exec.Sec.
Desc: Professional fraternity - music. *Type:* Association.

Down Beat

Maher Publications, Inc.
102 N. Haven Rd.   Ph: (630)941-2030
Elmhurst, IL 60126   Free: 800-535-7496
    Fax: (630)941-3210
Contact: John Ephland, Managing Editor; Kevin Maher, Publisher; Frank Alkyer, Publisher.
Desc: Magazine edited for the learning musician. *Type:* Periodical.

Drum Corps International

PO Box 548   Ph: (630)495-9866
Lombard, IL 60148-0548   Fax: (630)495-3792
E-mail: dci@dci.org
URL: http://www.dci.org
Contact: Daniel E. Acheson, Dir.
Desc: Drum and bugle corps. Functions as the promotional, educational, and service arm of North American drum and bugle corps activity. *Type:* Association.

Engelbert's Golden Eagles

28554 Wauketa   Ph: (810)751-1369
Warren, MI 48092
Contact: Richard Habel, Pres.
Desc: Fans of singer Engelbert Humperdinck (1936-) united to promote Humperdinck and foster sales of his recordings. *Type:* Association.

Forester Sisters Fan Club

PO Box 1456   Ph: (706)657-7056
Trenton, GA 30752
Desc: Fans of the Forester Sisters, a country music group comprising Christy, June, Kathy, and Kim Forester. Promotes the group's recording and concert career. *Type:* Association.

Friends of Jackie Wilson

PO Box 262
Carteret, NJ 07008-0262
Contact: Billy Wolfe, Founder & Dir.
Desc: Fans and friends of singer Jackie Wilson (1934-85), whose hits included Reet Petite, Lonely Teardrops, and Higher and Higher. Seeks to keep his memory alive with donations to charities in his name. *Type:* Association.

George Strait Fan Club

PO Box 2119   Ph: (615)824-7176
Hendersonville, TN 37077   Fax: (615)822-2527
Contact: Anita O'Brian, Pres.
Desc: Fans of country-western musician and vocalist George Strait (1952-), who was named male vocalist of the year in 1985, 1986, 1989, and 1990 by both the Academy of Country Music and the Country Music Association; and who received the Entertainer of the Year Award in 1989 and 1990. *Type:* Association.

Girl Groups Fan Club
PO Box 69A04, Dept. NET   Ph: (213)650-5112
West Hollywood, CA 90069
E-mail: gayboylaca@hotmail.com
URL: http://www.members.tripod.com/~ggfc/
Contact: Louis Wendruck, Pres.
Desc: Fans of female singers and female singing groups of
the 1960s and 1970s. Operates as a source for rare records,
photos, t-shirts, postcards, video tapes, and back issues of
the Honeycone, the Orlons, Dee Dee Sharp, Martha and
the Vandellas, the Ronettes, the Marvelettes, the Supremes
and other groups and singers. *Type:* Association.

Gospel Music Networking Guide
Gospel Music Association
1205 Division St.   Ph: (615)242-0303
Nashville, TN 37203   Fax: (615)254-9755
E-mail: gmatoday@aol.com
Contact: Holly Zabka, Editor.
Desc: Gospel musicians, composers, and artists; recording
companies, studios, and production companies; booking
agencies; publishers; performing rights organizations; television and radio broadcasting stations; book stores, Bible
supply stores, and other retailers/managers; publications;
ministry organizations. *Type:* Directory.

Gospel Music Workshop of America
3908 W. Warren Ave.   Ph: (313)898-6900
Detroit, MI 48208   Fax: (313)898-4520
E-mail: slpuddie@worldnet.att.net
URL: http://www.ghwa.org
Contact: Sheila Smith, Dir. of Operations.
Desc: Individuals interested in gospel music. Promotes the
enjoyment and performance of gospel and spiritual music.
Offers musical instruction in performance and composi-
tion. *Type:* Association.

Guitar
Cherry Lane Music Co. Inc.
10 Midland Ave.   Ph: (914)935-5200
Port Chester, NY 10573   Fax: (914)937-0614
Contact: Howard Cleff, Publisher, (914)935-5217; Barbara Seerman, Assoc. Publisher and Advertising Dir.,
(914)935-5243; Maria Coyle, Circulation Mgr.,
(914)935-5248; Harvey Newquist, Editor, (914)935-
5222.
Desc: Publication featuring interviews, instructional columns, and transcripts for bass and guitar players. *Type:* Periodical.

Guitar Player
*Miller Freeman, Inc.—Entertainment Technology
Group*
411 Borel Ave., Ste. 100   Ph: (650)358-9500
San Mateo, CA 94402   Fax: (650)358-9966
E-mail: guitplyr@mfi.com.
URL: http://www.guitarplayer.com/.
Contact: Michael Molenda, Editor; Cynthia Smith, Adver-
tising Dir.; Ed Sengstack, Publisher.
Desc: Magazine featuring guitar-related articles. *Type:* Peri-
odical.

Guitar World
Harris Publications, Inc.
1115 Broadway, 8th Fl.   Ph: (212)807-7100
New York, NY 10010-2803   Fax: (212)627-4678
E-mail: gwedit@aol.com.
Contact: Jeff Kitts, Managing Editor, (212)462-9501, fax:
(212)229-1897, jeffkitts@aol.com.
Desc: Publication featuring interviews with rock artists and
lessons for guitar players. *Type:* Periodical.

Hit Parader
Hit Parader Publications, Inc.
40 Violet Ave.   Ph: (914)454-7420
Poughkeepsie, NY 12601-1521   Fax: (914)454-7507
Contact: Andy Secher, Editor; Vic Sierkowski, Advertising
Mgr.
Desc: Magazine covering heavy metal music. *Type:* Periodi-
cal.

International Musician
American Federation of Musicians
1501 Broadway, Ste. 600   Ph: (212)869-1330
New York, NY 10036   Fax: (212)302-4374
E-mail: info@afm.org; intlmus@afm.org.
Contact: Stephen R. Sprague, Publisher; Jim Rubbone,
Advertising Dir.; Jessica Roe, Editor.
Desc: Tabloid for labor union musicians. *Type:* Periodical.

James "Rebel" O'Leary Fan Club
4885 Springfield Dr.   Ph: (717)792-3060
York, PA 17404-6034
Contact: Barbara Hope, Dir.
Desc: Fans of country musician and singer James "Rebel"
O'Leary (1941-). (O'Leary was given the nickname
"Rebel" when he broke with traditional country music
and began to play his music at a faster tempo).). Promotes
O'Leary and his music. *Type:* Association.

Jammie Ann Fan Club
4885 Springfield Dr.   Ph: (717)792-3060
York, PA 17404-6034
Contact: Rosettia Cora, Pres.
Desc: Individuals interested in promoting country-western
singer and musician Jammie Ann O'Leary (1954-). *Type:*
Association.

Jazz Notes
Jazz Journalists Association
PO Box 3008   Ph: (301)588-7498
Silver Spring, MD 20918-3008
E-mail: jazzmandel@aol.com
Contact: W. Royal Stokes, Editor, wrswing@aol.com.
Desc: Explores the "art and craft of being a jazz journalist/
writer/critic." Cover jazz industry news and debate of criti-
cal approaches. Recurring features include "President's
Report," letters to the editor, reports of meetings, book
reviews, and notices of publications available. *Type:* News-
letter.

Jazziz
Jazziz Magazine, Inc.
3620 NW 43rd St.   Ph: (352)375-3705
Gainesville, FL 32606   Fax: (352)375-7268
E-mail: mail@jazziz.com; jazziz@sprintmail.com.
URL: http://www.jazziz.com.
Contact: Larry Blumenfeld, Editor-in-Chief, lblu@aol.
com; Michael Fagien, Publisher, mfagien@jazziz.com;
Lori Fagien, Publisher, lfagien@jazziz.com.
Desc: Music magazine focusing on all aspects of improvisa-
tional and instrumental music for sophisticated listeners.
Comes monthly with audio and multimedia CD featuring
new, classic and exclusive music. *Type:* Periodical.

JazzTimes
Jazz Times
8737 Colesville Rd., 5th Fl.   Ph: (301)588-4114
Silver Spring, MD 20910-3921   Free: 800-866-7664
                                       Fax: (301)588-5531
E-mail: jtimes@aol.com.
URL: http://www.jazzcentralstation.com.
Contact: Mike Joyce, Editor; Glenn Sabin, Publisher; Lee
Mergner, Assoc. Publisher.
Desc: Magazine incorporating all genres of jazz music for
professionals and fans. *Type:* Periodical.

Jerry Jeff Walker Fan Club
Tried and True Music
PO Box 39   Ph: (512)477-0036
Austin, TX 78767   Fax: (512)477-0095
E-mail: jerryjeff@jerryjeff.com
URL: http://www.jerryjeff.com
Contact: Pam Stock, Pres.
Desc: Fans of songwriter and performer Jerry Jeff Walker
(1942-), best known for composing and recording Mr.
Bojangles (1968). Promotes the work and music of Walk-
er; informs members of upcoming activities and events.
Type: Association.

Live Wire
J.Q. Adams Productions, Inc.
28 W. 25th St., 7th Fl.   Ph: (212)647-0222
New York, NY 10010   Free: 800-229-2294
                             Fax: (212)047-0236
Contact: Mike Smith, Editor; Henry McQueeney, Pub-
lisher; Kelly Barbieri, Managing Editor.
Desc: Magazine reports on hard rock musicians. *Type:* Peri-
odical.

Loretta Lynn Fan Club
PO Box 40328   Ph: (615)371-9596
Nashville, TN 37204-0328   Fax: (615)371-9597
Contact: Loudilla Johnson, Co-Pres.
Desc: Fans and supporters of popular country music singer
and songwriter Loretta Lynn (1935-), who has recorded
numerous hit records and also is a recipient of numerous
awards, including Recording Artist of the Decade by the
American Academy of Achievement. Promotes and keeps
members informed of Lynn's activities. *Type:* Association.

**MENC: The National Association for Music
Education**
1806 Robert Fulton Dr.   Ph: (703)860-4000
Reston, VA 20191   Free: 800-336-3768
                          Fax: (703)860-1531
E-mail: marlynnl@menc.org
URL: http://www.menc.org
Contact: John J. Mahlmann, Ed.D., Exec.Dir.
Desc: Professional organization of music educators, admin-
istrators, supervisors, consultants, and music education
majors in colleges. Publishes materials for music educators,
presents conferences, compiles statistics. *Type:* Associa-
tion.

Metropolitan Opera Association
Lincoln Center   Ph: (212)799-3100
New York, NY 10023   Fax: (212)874-2659
Contact: Joseph Volpe, Gen.Mgr.
Desc: Supporters include individuals, foundations, and
corporations. Objectives are to: produce and make available, through tours, radio, and television, fully staged operas at the Metropolitan Opera House in New York City;
increase public understanding and appreciation of opera.
Sponsors seminars, professional training programs, and in-
school programs. *Type:* Association.

Metropolitan Opera Guild
70 Lincoln Center Plz., 6th Fl.   Ph: (212)769-7000
New York, NY 10023   Fax: (212)769-7007
Contact: Rudolph S. Rauch, Mng.Dir.
Desc: Seeks to promote greater interest in opera; further
musical education and appreciation; broaden the base of
support for the Metropolitan Opera. Conducts educational programs including in-school opera program, in-service
teacher courses, evening lecture series, and student performances at Opera House. Operates five retail outlets and
extensive mail order business as well as member travel program. *Type:* Association.

Michael Bolton Official International Fan Club
Fan Emporium
PO Box 679
Branford, CT 06405
E-mail: fnemporium@aol.com
Ph: (203)483-2843
Fax: (203)483-2845
Contact: Joyce Logan, Pres.
Desc: Fans of the singer-songwriter Michael Bolton. *Type:* Association.

MLA Newsletter
Music Library Association (MLA)
PO Box 487
Canton, MA 02021-0487
E-mail: acadsvc@aol.com.
Ph: (781)828-8450
Fax: (781)828-8915
Contact: Linda Hartig, Editor.
Desc: Serves as an information exchange among music librarians. Published to keep members abreast of events, ideas, and trends related to music librarianship. *Type:* Newsletter.

Modern Drummer Magazine
Modern Drummer Publications, Inc.
12 Old Bridge Rd.
Cedar Grove, NJ 07009
URL: http://www.enews.com.
Ph: (973)239-4140
Fax: (973)239-7139
Contact: Ronald L. Spagnardi, Editor and Publisher; Bob Berenson, Advertising Dir.
Desc: Magazine for amateur, semi-professional, and professional drummers. *Type:* Periodical.

Modern Screen's Country Music
Sterling/Macfadden Partnership
233 Park Ave. S.
New York, NY 10003
Ph: (212)780-3500
Fax: (212)780-3555
Contact: Mike Greenblatt, Editor, mgreenblatt@sterlingmacfadden.rom; Allen Tuller, Advertising Dir.; Barbara Seerman, Advertising Representative., (212)780-3515.
Desc: Magazine for country music fans. *Type:* Periodical.

Monkees, Boyce and Hart Photo Fan Club
PO Box 411
Watertown, SD 57201
E-mail: seagal@dailypost.com
Ph: (605)886-3017
Fax: (605)886-5514
Contact: Jodi Hammrich, Co-Editor & Sec.
Desc: Persons interested in the careers of Davy Jones (1945-), Micky Dolenz (1945-), Peter Tork (1942-), Michael Nesmith (1942-), Tommy Boyce (1939-94), and Bobby Hart (1939-). (Jones, Dolenz, Tork, and Nesmith were members of the Monkees, a 1960s pop-rock group; Boyce and Hart wrote many of the Monkees' songs.) Purposes are to: keep fans apprised of the activities and appearances of the Monkees and Boyce and Hart; promote the careers of the Monkees, Boyce, and Hart; provide a means of communication among fans. *Type:* Association.

Mu Phi Epsilon
4202 Atlantic Ave. Ste 202
Long Beach, CA 90807-2826
E-mail: mpeieo@aol.com
Contact: Gerri Flynn, Exec.Sec-Treas.
Desc: Professional fraternity - music. Established Mu Phi Epsilon Foundation to administer fraternity philanthropies. *Type:* Association.

Music Festivals from Bach to Blues: A Traveler's Guide
Visible Ink Press
27500 Drake Rd.
Farmington Hills, MI 48331-3535
E-mail: galeord@gale.com
URL: http://www.gale.com
Ph: (248)699-4253
Free: 800-776-6265
Fax: (248)699-8067

Contact: Tom Clynes, Editor.
Desc: Over 1,000 music festivals in the United States and Canada. *Type:* Directory.

Music Teachers National Association
441 Vine St., Ste. 505
Cincinnati, OH 45202-2814
E-mail: mtnaadmin@aol.com
URL: http://www.mtna.org
Ph: (513)421-1420
Fax: (513)421-2503
Contact: Dr. Gary L. Ingle, Exec.Dir.
Desc: Professional society of independent and collegiate music teachers committed to furthering the art of music through programs that encourage and support teaching, performance, composition, and scholarly research. *Type:* Association.

Music Trades—Purchaser's Guide to the Music Industry Issue
Music Trades Corp.
80 West St.
Englewood, NJ 07631
Ph: (201)871-1965
Free: 800-423-6530
Fax: (201)871-0455
Contact: Brian T. Majeski, Editor.
Desc: List of 2,000 musical instrument manufacturers and wholesalers, publishers of sheet music, and manufacturers of musical accessories; international coverage. *Type:* Directory.

Musical News
Musicians Union Local 6
116 Ninth St.
San Francisco, CA 94103
Ph: (415)575-0777
Fax: (415)863-6173
Contact: Melinda Wagner, Editor; Gretchen Elliott, Editor.
Desc: Contains union news and information of importance to members of the American Federation of Musicians. *Type:* Newsletter.

MusicHound Blues
Visible Ink Press
27500 Drake Rd.
Farmington Hills, MI 48331-3535
E-mail: galeord@gale.com
URL: http://www.gale.com
Ph: (248)699-4253
Free: 800-776-6265
Fax: (248)699-8067
Contact: Leland Rucker, Editor; Gary Graff, Editor.
Desc: Reviews of blues music albums from over 700 blues groups and individual artists and blues music resources including publications, websites, and fan clubs. *Type:* Directory.

MusicHound Country
Visible Ink Press
27500 Drake Rd.
Farmington Hills, MI 48331-3535
E-mail: galeord@gale.com
URL: http://www.gale.com
Ph: (248)699-4253
Free: 800-776-6265
Fax: (248)699-8067
Contact: Brian Mansfield, Editor; Gary Graff, Editor.
Desc: Nearly 1,000 individual country music artists and groups. *Type:* Directory.

MusicHound Rock
Visible Ink Press
27500 Drake Rd.
Farmington Hills, MI 48331-3535
E-mail: galeord@gale.com
URL: http://www.gale.com
Ph: (248)699-4253
Free: 800-776-6265
Fax: (248)699-8067
Contact: Gary Graff, Editor.
Desc: Nearly 2,000 individual rock artists and groups. *Type:* Directory.

Musicopyright Intelligence
E.S. Proteus
1657 The Fairway, Ste. 123
Jenkintown, PA 19046
Ph: (215)885-3154
Free: 800-962-7770
Fax: (215)885-0670
Contact: E.S. Proteus, Publisher; Eric Nemeyer, Editor.
Desc: Provides information about making money by owning copyrights. Includes research and news on music industry finance and marketing ideas. *Type:* Newsletter.

Nashville Songwriters Association International
1701 W End Ave., 3rd Fl.
Nashville, TN 37203-2601
E-mail: nsai@songs.org
URL: http://www.songs.org/nsai
Ph: (615)256-3354
Fax: (615)256-0034
Contact: Bart Herbison, Exec.Dir.
Desc: Professional and amateur songwriters; individuals in the songwriting industry. Works to advance the art of musical composition and promote the growth of creative leadership for artistic, cultural, and educational progress in the field; helps songwriters gain recognition for their work; participates in legislative work for songwriter benefits. *Type:* Association.

National Federation of Music Clubs
1336 N. Delaware St.
Indianapolis, IN 46202
Ph: (317)638-4003
Fax: (317)638-0503
Contact: Melinda Ullrich, Exec.Dir.
Desc: Local music clubs, state associations, and individuals directly or indirectly connected with musical activities, such as amateur opera groups, elementary and high school music departments, and music conservatories. Aids young musicians; encourages the use of stringed instruments; promotes higher television and radio musical standards and legislation to improve status of musicians. Commissions symphonic works; conducts junior festivals, in which entrants have the opportunity to be rated on individual merits and work toward a designated objective with criteria for evaluation. *Type:* Association.

National Guild of Piano Teachers
808 Rio Grande
PO Box 1807
Austin, TX 78767-1807
URL: http://www.pianoguild.com
Ph: (512)478-5775
Fax: (512)478-5843
Contact: Richard Allison, Pres.
Desc: A division of the American College of Musicians. Professional society of piano teachers and music faculty. To promote music education through examinations, auditions, and competitions from coast to coast. *Type:* Association.

National Music Publishers' Association
711 Third Ave.
New York, NY 10017
URL: http://www.nmpa.org
Ph: (212)370-5330
Fax: (212)953-2384
Contact: Edward P. Murphy, Pres.
Desc: Trade organization representing music publishers. *Type:* Association.

Oak Ridge Boys International Fan Club
329 Rockland Rd.
Hendersonville, TN 37075
URL: http://www.oakridgeboys.com
Ph: (615)824-4924
Fax: (615)822-7078
Contact: Linda Kirkpatrick, Dir.
Desc: Individuals interested in the lives and careers of Joe Bonsall (1948-), Duane Allen (1943-), Richard Sterban (1943-), and William Lee Golden (1937-), who make up the country music group The Oak Ridge Boys. *Type:* Association.

Opera America

1156 15th St. NW, No. 810   Ph: (202)293-4466
Washington, DC 20005   Fax: (202)393-0735
URL: http://www.operaam.org

Contact: Marc A. Scorca, CEO.

Desc: Professional opera companies, allied international companies, other producing, presenting, and educational institutions, individual performing and creative artists, arts administrators and consultants, affiliated businesses, libraries, trustees, volunteers, and patrons. Promotes the growth and expansion of the operatic form; assists in the development of resident professional opera companies through provision of cooperative artistic management services; fosters and improve the education, training, and development of operatic composers, singers, and other talented persons; encourages and assists in the improvement of the quality of operatic presentations; encourages greater appreciation and enjoyment of opera by all segments of society. *Type:* Association.

Operafestival Di Roma

1445 Willow Lake Dr.
Charlottesville, VA 22902-7222
URL: http://www.servtech.com/public/blondie/opera/opera.html

Contact: Louisa Panou Takahashi, Sec.

Desc: Educational organization whose purpose is to recruit faculty, students, and professional musicians in the USA interested in furthering their musical education and practical performing experience. Coordinates a one month educational experience in Rome, Italy. *Type:* Association.

Parents Aren't Supposed to Like It

UXL
27500 Drake Rd.   Ph: (248)699-4253
Farmington Hills, MI 48331-   Free: 800-877-GALE
3535   Fax: (248)699-8069
E-mail: galeord@gale.com

Contact: David P. Bianco, Editor.

Desc: 135 rock and pop bands and musicians considered to be influential to the music scene in the 1990s. *Type:* Directory.

Phi Mu Alpha - Sinfonia

10600 Old State Rd.   Ph: (812)867-2433
Evansville, IN 47711   Free: 800-473-2649
   Fax: (812)867-0633

Contact: James P. Morris, Assoc.Dir.

Desc: Professional fraternity - music. Sponsors collegiate musical activities. Conducts 34 biennial provincial workshops. *Type:* Association.

Phil Collins Information

c/o Brad Lentz   Ph: (913)345-2002
PO Box 12250   Fax: (913)345-2940
Overland Park, KS 66212

Contact: Brad Lentz, Exec. Officer.

Desc: Fans of singer Phil Collins (1951-), who is also a member of the rock music group Genesis. *Type:* Association.

Pi Kappa Lambda

Northwestern University   Ph: (847)491-5737
School of Music   Fax: (847)328-7655
711 Elgin Rd.
Evanston, IL 60208-1200

Contact: Lilias C. Circle, Sec.-Treas.

Desc: Honor society-men and women, music. *Type:* Association.

Popular Music

Gale Group Inc.
27500 Drake Rd.   Ph: (248)699-4253
Farmington Hills, MI 48331-   Free: 800-877-GALE
3535   Fax: (248)699-8070
E-mail: galeord@galegroup.com
URL: http://www.galegroup.com.

Contact: Nat Shapiro, Editor; Bruce Pollock, Editor; Barbara Cohen-Stratyner, Editor.

Desc: Directory of publishers (holders of performance rights and copyrights) of music, including show tunes, jazz, country and western, blues, and rock music, from 1900. *Type:* Directory.

Pulse!

Tower Records, Inc.
2500 Del Monte, Bldg. C.   Ph: (916)373-2450
West Sacramento, CA 95691   Free: 800-525-5713
   Fax: (916)373-2480
URL: http://www.towerrecords.com.

Contact: Suzanne Mikesel, Editor; Mike Farrace, Editor and Publisher; Anthony Howerton, Advertising Mgr.

Desc: Magazine (tabloid) presenting qualitative and quantitative coverage of various forms of recorded sound. *Type:* Periodical.

Reba McEntire International Fan Club

Drawer T-Reba   Ph: (615)259-5353
Nashville, TN 37244   Fax: (615)742-5160

Contact: Melanie Herring, Contact.

Desc: Fans of country music performer Reba McEntire. Makes available souvenirs and memorabilia; disseminates information on McEntire's career activities. Operates charitable programs. *Type:* Association.

REQUEST

Request Media Inc.
10400 Yellow Circle Dr.   Ph: (612)931-8740
Minnetonka, MN 55343   Free: 800-325-0075
   Fax: (612)931-8490
E-mail: staff@requestline.com.
URL: http://www.requestline.com.

Contact: Susan Hamre, Editor.

Desc: Music magazine distributed at record stores. *Type:* Periodical.

Rhythm and Blues Rock and Roll Society

PO Box 1949   Ph: (203)924-1079
New Haven, CT 06510

Contact: William J. Nolan, Dir.

Desc: Record collectors, disc jockeys, record dealers, performing artists, and others dedicated to the preservation and promotion of rhythm and blues music and its counterparts (blues, gospel, and jazz) as a part of U.S. cultural heritage. Sponsors benefit concerts for prisoners, fundraising programs for amateur talent, and music concerts and festivals. *Type:* Association.

RIP

L.F.P., Inc.
8484 Wilshire Blvd., Ste. 900   Ph: (323)651-5400
Beverly Hills, CA 90211   Fax: (323)651-2741
E-mail: hustler@lfp.com

Contact: Greg Kennerson, Editor; Michael Mathieson, Advertising.

Desc: Music magazine. *Type:* Periodical.

Rolling Stone

Wenner Media
1290 Avenue of the Americas   Ph: (212)484-1616
New York, NY 10104   Fax: (212)767-8209

Contact: Jann S. Wenner, Editor and Publisher; Bob Love, Managing Editor; Kent Brownridge, General Mgr.; Fred Woodward, Art Dir.; Dana L. Fields, Group Publisher; Jack Rotherham, Advertising Dir.

Desc: Magazine covering contemporary culture, politics, arts, and music. *Type:* Periodical.

Sawyer Brown International Fan Club

5200 Old Harding Rd.   Ph: (615)799-0850
Franklin, TN 37064-9406   Fax: (615)799-9312
E-mail: sawyer@acton.com

Contact: Jackie Combs, Exec. Officer.

Desc: Fans of the country music band Sawyer Brown, whose members include Mark Miller, Duncan Cameron, Jr., Gregg Hubbard, Joe Smyth, and Jim Scholten. Disseminates information on itineraries and merchandise. *Type:* Association.

Sheet Music Magazine

Piano Today
333 Adams St.   Ph: (914)244-8500
Bedford Hills, NY 10507   Fax: (914)244-8560

Contact: Edward Shanaphy, Editor and Publisher; Kirk Miller, Managing Editor, kirkmiller@yestermusic.com.

Desc: Magazine containing sheet music, musical "how to" articles, and information on new keyboard products. *Type:* Periodical.

Sigma Alpha Iota

34 Wall St., No. 515
Asheville, NC 28801-2710

Contact: Ruth E. Sieber, Exec.Sec.

Desc: College students and alumnae (80,250); honorary members and patronesses (7,750) International Music Fraternity. Promotes music creation, performance, and scholarship. *Type:* Association.

The Singing News Magazine

Singing News Inc.
330 University Hall Dr.   Ph: (704)264-3700
PO Box 2810   Fax: (704)264-4621
Boone, NC 28607-2810

Contact: Jerry Kirksey, Editor; Maurice Templeton, Publisher; Pam Slaney, Advertising Dir.; Danny Jones, Managing Editor.

Desc: Magazine. *Type:* Periodical.

Society for the Preservation and Encouragement of Barber Shop Quartet Singing in America

6315 3rd Ave.   Ph: (414)653-8440
Kenosha, WI 53143-5199   Free: 800-876-SING
   Fax: (414)654-4048
E-mail: info@spebsqsa.org
URL: http://www.spebsqsa.org

Contact: Darryl Flinn, Exec. Dir.

Desc: Men interested in barbershop quartet and chorus singing. Seeks to: preserve barbershop harmony, a traditional form of American music culture; provide an outlet for self-expression in song while serving the community; help cultivate music appreciation. Selects international barbershop quartet and chorus champions annually; stages 16 district and 16 international preliminary contests. *Type:* Association.

The Sounds Page

Foothill.net
PO Box 1427   Ph: (916)367-3818
Foresthill, CA 95631   Fax: (916)367-4140
E-mail: webmaster@foothill.net
URL: http://www.marketrends.net/mthome/sounds.html

Contact: Matt Tourtillott, mrt@foothill.net

Desc: Come on over to The Sounds Page and download 'til your sound card starts smokin'. Sound bites from numerous movies and television shows (along with a few cheesy homemade ones) are posted for easy download. *Type:* Database.

The Source

Source Publications, Inc.
215 Park Ave. S., 11th Fl. Ph: (212)253-3700
New York, NY 10003 Fax: (212)253-9344
URL: http://www.thesource.com.
Contact: Selwyn Hinds, Editor; David Mays, Publisher; H. Edward Young, Publisher.
Desc: Magazine profiling the hip-hop music scene. *Type:* Periodical.

SPIN

VIBE/SPIN Ventures, L.L.C.
6 W. 18th St., 11th Fl. Ph: (212)633-8200
New York, NY 10011-4608 Fax: (212)633-2668
E-mail: autsyem@aol.com.
Contact: Michael Hirschorn, Editor-in-Chief; John Rollins, Publisher; Malcolm Campbell, Advertising Dir.; Dana Sacher, Circulation Dir.
Desc: Consumer magazine covering music and youth culture. *Type:* Periodical.

Sweet Adelines International

PO Box 470168 Ph: (918)622-1444
Tulsa, OK 74147-0168 Free: 800-992-7464
  Fax: (918)665-0894
E-mail: admin@sweetadelineintl.org
URL: http://www.sweetadelineintl.org/
Contact: Donna K. Kerley, Interim Exec.Dir.
Desc: Women singers committed to advancing the musical art form of barbershop harmony through education and performances. *Type:* Association.

TECHNICOM

National Association of Professional Band Instrument Repair Technicians
PO Box 51
Normal, IL 61761
Contact: Chuck Hagler, Editor.
Desc: Serves as an exchange of information among band instrument repair technicians, providing news of developments in the field and articles by Association members. Carries updates on Association activities and profiles of industry professionals. *Type:* Newsletter.

Transoniq Hacker

Transoniq Hacker
1402 SW Upland Dr. Ph: (503)227-6848
Portland, OR 97221 Free: 800-548-8925
E-mail: substransportationnsoniq.com.
URL: http://www.transoniq.com/-trnsoniq.
Contact: Jane Tallsman, Editor.
Desc: Covers electronic products for music composition and performance. Recurring features include equipment reviews. *Type:* Newsletter.

TRI-M Music Honor Society

Menc
1806 Robert Fulton Dr. Ph: (703)860-4000
Reston, VA 20191 Free: 800-336-3768
  Fax: (703)860-2652
URL: http://www.menc.org
Desc: A program of the Music Educators National Conference. Seeks to motivate music students in junior and senior high and recognize their effort and honor their accomplishments. *Type:* Association.

University Musical Society

Burton Memorial Tower, No. Ph: (734)764-2538
100 Free: 800-221-1229
Ann Arbor, MI 48109 Fax: (734)647-1171
E-mail: umstix@umich.edu
URL: http://www.ums.org

Contact: Kenneth C. Fischer, Pres.
Desc: Music, dance, and theatre enthusiasts. Sponsors concerts, announcement parties, and social events. *Type:* Association.

Vibe Magazine

Time Ventures
PO Box 59580 Ph: (303)678-8475
Boulder, CO 80322 Free: 800-477-3974
  Fax: (303)661-1181
URL: http://www.vibe.com.
Contact: Jonathan Von Meter, Editor; Susan Cappo, Advertising Mgr.; Brendan Amyot, Circulation Mgr.
Desc: Publication focusing on popular music and culture. *Type:* Periodical.

Native American

Alaska Federation of Natives

1577 C St., Ste. 100 Ph: (907)274-3611
Anchorage, AK 99501 Fax: (907)276-7989
Contact: Julie Kitka, Pres.
Desc: Alaska Natives (Aleut, Eskimo, and Indian) and regional and profit corporations. To act as lobbyist and advocate on behalf of villages, regional profit, and nonprofit native corporations on social, economic, political, and cultural issues; to provide technical assistance to these groups. *Type:* Association.

All Indian Pueblo Council

PO Box 3256 Ph: (505)884-3820
Albuquerque, NM 87190 Fax: (505)883-7682
Contact: Stanley Pino, Chm.
Desc: Indian tribes. Serves as advocate on behalf of 19 Pueblo Indian tribes on education, health, social, and economic issues; lobbies on those issues before state and national legislatures. Activities are centered in New Mexico. *Type:* Association.

American Indian Health Care Association

1550 Larimer St., No. 225
Denver, CO 80202-1602
Contact: Carol Marquez-Baines, Contact.
Desc: Urban Indian health programs; staff and support persons from member programs and other concerned persons. Develops and assists in the implementation of improved management techniques for urban Indian health care centers including quality community education programs and quality health care delivery systems responsive to community needs. *Type:* Association.

American Indian Heritage Foundation

6051 Arlington Blvd. Ph: (202)463-4267
Falls Church, VA 22044 Fax: (703)532-1921
E-mail: aihf@dgsys.com
Contact: Dr. Wil Rose, CEO.
Desc: Informs and educates non-Indians concerning the culture and heritage of the American Indian. *Type:* Association.

American Indian Tribal Directory

American Indian Heritage Foundation
6051 Arlington Blvd. Ph: (202)IND-IANS
Falls Church, VA 22044
E-mail: aihf@dgsys.com
URL: http://www.indians.org/tribes/
Desc: This comprehensive directory contains a list of federally recognized American Indian tribes in the United States. You can browse lists of the entries arranged and sorted by state, both city and state, or tribe name. *Type:* Database.

Association on American Indian Affairs

PO Box 268 Ph: (605)698-3998
Tekakwitha Complex Agency Fax: (605)698-3316
Rd. 7
Sisseton, SD 57262
Contact: Jerry Flute, Exec.Dir.
Desc: Provides legal and technical assistance to Indian tribes throughout the U.S. in health, education, economic development, resource utilization, family defense, and the administration of justice. Maintains American Indian Fund. *Type:* Association.

Cherokee Advocate

Cherokee Nation
PO Box 948 Ph: (918)456-0671
Tahlequah, OK 74465 Free: 800-256-0671
  Fax: (918)458-6136
E-mail: tfiedler@cherokee.
URL: http://www.cherokee.org.
Contact: Lynn Adair, News Bureau Mgr., lyadair@cherokee.org.
Desc: Tribal newspaper. *Type:* Periodical.

Cook Inlet Native Association

1569 S. Bragaw, Ste. 200 Ph: (907)337-1800
Anchorage, AK 99508
Contact: Jane Goldbeck, Exec.Dir.
Desc: Alaskan natives and American Indians dedicated to nurturing pride in the heritage and traditions of the Alaska native and preserving the customs, folklore, and art of the people. Promotes the potentials, opportunities, and physical, economic, and social well-being of Alaskan natives and American Indians. Offers training programs for word processors, clerical workers, bank tellers, and job-seeking techniques. *Type:* Association.

Council of Energy Resource Tribes

695 S. Colorado Blvd. Ste. 10 Ph: (303)282-7576
Denver, CO 80246 Fax: (303)282-7584
Contact: A. David Lester, Exec.Dir.
Desc: American Indian tribes owning energy resources. Promotes the general welfare of members through the protection, conservation, control, and prudent management of their oil, coal, natural gas, uranium, geothermal, oil shale, and other resources. *Type:* Association.

First Nations Development Institute

The Stores Bldg Ph: (540)371-5615
11917 Main St. Fax: (540)371-3505
Fredericksburg, VA 22408
E-mail: info@firstnations.org
Contact: Rebecca Adamson, Pres.
Desc: Aims to help Native American tribes achieve self-sufficiency using culturally appropriate development methods; promotes economic development and commercial enterprises of reservation-based Indian tribes and non-profit organizations through technical assistance, grants and loans. *Type:* Association.

Indigenous People's Network

Desc: Indigenous, human rights, and energy-conscious organizations. Provides communications services and information to people in remote areas that have little access to public media; disseminates information on threats to the existence of indigenous people; seeks to raise the consciousness of people in North America and Western Europe. Activities include: documentation missions; indigenous refugee project, which assists Mayan refugees fleeing the war areas of Central America; the Indigenous People's Radio Network, which features taped interviews with indigenous leaders and community elders. *Type:* Association.

Institute of American Indian Arts

PO Box 20007   Ph: (505)988-6463
Santa Fe, NM 87504   Free: 800-804-6422
    Fax: (505)986-5543
URL: http://www.iaiancad.org
Contact: Della Warrior, Pres.
Desc: Federally chartered private institution. Offers learning opportunities in the arts and crafts to Native American youth (Indian, Eskimo, or Aleut). Emphasis is placed upon Indian traditions as the basis for creative expression in fine arts including painting, sculpture, museum studies, creative writing, printmaking, photography, communications, design, and dance, as well as training in metal crafts, jewelry, ceramics, textiles, and various traditional crafts. *Type:* Association.

Maniilaq Association

PO Box 256   Ph: (907)442-3311
Kotzebue, AK 99752   Fax: (907)442-7678
Contact: Dennis Tiepelman, Pres.
Desc: Tribal organization serving 11 Alaskan Eskimo villages ranging from 60 to 3000 in population. Works to: promote health and social welfare in the Northwest Arctic Borough region of Alaska; preserve and promote the Eskimo customs, arts, and language; advance education in all forms; stimulate economic activity and social understanding between natives and nonnatives. Maintains group home, senior citizen center, nursing wing, social rehabilitation center, and youth camp; manages Maniiaq Medical Center. *Type:* Association.

National Center for American Indian Enterprise Development

953 E. Juanita Ave.   Ph: (480)545-1298
Mesa, AZ 85204   Free: 800-462-2433
    Fax: (480)545-4208
E-mail: ncaied1@aol.com
URL: http://www.ncaied.org
Contact: Ken Robbins, Pres.
Desc: Promotes business and economic development among American Indians and tribes. Offers business training services to American Indians who own or plan to start businesses in fields including manufacturing, service, construction, retailing, and wholesaling. Assists Indians and tribes in: developing management abilities; assessing operating costs; preparing finance proposals; obtaining financing, bonding, and insurance; controlling the business through effective accounting and information systems; negotiating contracts, leases, and purchases; planning for future business growth. *Type:* Association.

National Indian Youth Council

318 Elm St. SE   Ph: (505)247-2251
Albuquerque, NM 87102   Fax: (505)247-4251
Contact: Norman Ration, Exec.Dir.
Desc: Aims to protect Indian natural resources; protect Indian religious freedom and other tribal and individual civil liberties; protect and enhance treaty rights and federal government's trust relationship and responsibilities; improve Indian health and education; preserve the Indian family unit and community. *Type:* Association.

Native American Educational Services College

2838 W. Peterson   Ph: (773)761-5000
Chicago, IL 60659   Fax: (773)761-3808
URL: http://www.naes.indian.com
Contact: Faith Smith, Pres.
Desc: An educational program accredited by the Commission on Institutions of Higher Education of the North Central Association of Colleges and Schools. Offers a B.A. degree to students in four American Indian communities (2 urban, 2 reservations). *Type:* Association.

Native American Rights Fund

1506 Broadway   Ph: (303)447-8760
Boulder, CO 80302   Fax: (303)443-7776
URL: http://www.narf.org
Contact: John E. Echohawk, Dir.
Desc: Represents Indian individuals, organizations and tribes in legal matters of national significance. *Type:* Association.

Native Americans Information Directory

Gale Group Inc.
27500 Drake Rd.   Ph: (248)699-4253
Farmington Hills, MI 48331-   Free: 800-877-GALE
    3535   Fax: (248)699-8070
E-mail: galeord@galegroup.com
URL: http://www.galegroup.com.
Contact: Julia Furtaw, Editor.
Desc: Approximately 4,500 sources of information on aspects of Native American, Aboriginal Canadian, Native Alaskan, and Native Hawaiian life and culture, including federally recognized tribes, national, state, and local organizations; publishers of newspapers, periodicals, newsletters, and other publications and videos; broadcast media; museum collections; federal government agencies; research centers; educational and studies programs; and library collections. *Type:* Directory.

Native North American Almanac

Gale Group Inc.
27500 Drake Rd.   Ph: (248)699-4253
Farmington Hills, MI 48331-   Free: 800-877-GALE
    3535   Fax: (248)699-8070
E-mail: galeord@galegroup.com
URL: http://www.galegroup.com.
Contact: Duane Champagne, Editor.
Desc: Includes essays on issues of interest to Native Americans and Canadian First Peoples, including history, economy, education, religion, culture, arts, language, law and legislation, activism, the environment, health, and media; each chapter includes, as appropriate, directories of tribal communities, organizations, government agencies, schools, and businesses relevant to the topic. *Type:* Directory.

United Indians of All Tribes Foundation

Daybreak Star Arts Center   Ph: (206)285-4425
Discovery Park   Fax: (206)282-3640
PO Box 99100
Seattle, WA 98199
Contact: Bernie Whitebear, Exec.Dir.
Desc: Provides social, cultural, and educational services to the urban Native American Community owns and operates the Daybreak Star Indian Cultural Center which houses the permanent art collection of the foundation. *Type:* Association.

Natural Resources

The Business of Herbs

Northwind Publications
439 Ponderosa Way   Ph: (505)829-3448
Jemez Springs, NM 87025-8036   Fax: (505)829-3449
E-mail: herbbiz@aol.com.
Contact: Paula Oliver, Editor; David Oliver, Editor.
Desc: Designed to improve productivity and profitability of businesses involving the growing, production, or marketing of herbs. Gives advice on growing techniques, effective marketing techniques, and advertising methods. *Type:* Newsletter.

Department of Natural Resources—Focus

Division of Fish and Wildlife
402 W. Washington St., Rm.   Ph: (317)232-4080
    W273   Fax: (317)232-8150
Indianapolis, IN 46204
Contact: Clark D. McCreedy, Editor.
Desc: Reports on the Department's activities in Indiana. *Type:* Newsletter.

DRI Natural Gas Spot Prices

Standard & Poor's DRI
Data Products Division
24 Hartwell Ave.   Ph: (781)863-5100
Lexington, MA 02421
E-mail: client_services@dri.mcgraw-hill.com
URL: http://www.dri.mcgraw-hill.com
Contact: Client Resource Center, (781)860-6527, fax: (781)860-6416.
Desc: Contains weekly and monthly time series on U.S. natural gas spot prices for each major transaction point, including at the wellhead, delivery to pipeline, at the city-gate for local distribution, and at the burner-tip for utilities and industrial users. *Available:* Standard & Poor's DRI, Data Products Division. *Type:* Database.

Great Lakes Commission

400 4th St.   Ph: (313)665-9135
Ann Arbor, MI 48103-4816   Fax: (313)665-4370
E-mail: glc@glc.org
URL: http://www.great.lakes.net
Contact: Dr. Michael J. Donahue, Exec.Dir.
Desc: Interstate Compact Commission. Designated or appointed officials (according to state statutes) in 8 states party to the Great Lakes Basin Compact. Serves as a research, coordinating, advisory, and advocacy agency on the development, use, and protection of the water and related land resources of the Great Lakes Basin. *Type:* Association.

International Joint Commission

1250 23rd St. NW, Ste. 100   Ph: (202)736-9000
Washington, DC 20440   Fax: (202)736-9015
E-mail: commission@washington.ijc.org
URL: http://www.ijc.org
Desc: Joint U.S.-Canada quasi-judicial and advisory tribunal on boundary and transboundary water problems. Established from Boundary Waters Treaty of 1909 to prevent disputes on the use of boundary and transboundary waters and investigate questions arising from transboundary issues. *Type:* Association.

Natural Resources Newsletter

Forestry Department
University of Kentucky   Ph: (606)257-4646
Lexington, KY 40546-0073   Fax: (606)323-1031
Contact: Allan J. Worms, Editor, aworms@ca.uky.edu.
Desc: Dedicated to "improved management and enjoyment of Kentucky's natural resources." *Type:* Newsletter.

Resource Development Newsletter

Agriculture Extension Service
U.S. Department of Agriculture (USDA)
University of Tennessee   Ph: (423)974-7306
PO Box 1071   Fax: (423)974-7448
Knoxville, TN 37901-1071
URL: http://www.funnelweb.utcc.utk.ed/~richben/news.html.
Contact: Alan Barefield, Editor, abarefield@utk.edu.
Desc: Offers information on resource developments, education programs, community involvement, and environmental concerns in Tennessee. *Type:* Newsletter.

Wild Foods Forum

Wild Foods Forum
PO Box 61413   Ph: (757)421-3929
Virginia Beach, VA 23466-1413   Fax: (757)421-3929
E-mail: wildfood@infi.net
URL: http://www.pilot.infi.net/~wildfood.

Contact: Vickie Shufer, Editor.

Desc: Provides information on wild foods, gathering, and preparation techniques and their benefits as food and medicine. Special features include trip reports, book reviews, and a calendar of events. *Type:* Newsletter.

Natural Sciences

Academy of Natural Sciences

1900 Benjamin Franklin Pky.   Ph: (215)299-1000
Philadelphia, PA 19103   Fax: (215)299-1028
URL: http://www.acnatsci.org

Contact: Paul Hanle, Pres.CEO.

Desc: Natural science research institution and museum with extensive historical and scientific collections of shells, insects, fish, birds, fossils, plants, minerals, and microscopic organisms. Conducts research programs and expeditions; serves as consultant to industry and government on aquatic and terrestrial environmental studies, water use, water quality, and pollution problems. Offers educational programs including: museum classes for 130,000 school children; daily nature theater programs; spring, summer, and fall courses; and an in-service science teaching course for Philadelphia, PA, teachers and youth leaders. *Type:* Association.

American Museum of Natural History

Central Park W, at W. 79th St.   Ph: (212)769-5100
New York, NY 10024-5192   Fax: (212)769-5018
URL: http://www.amh.org

Contact: Ellen V. Futter, Pres.

Desc: Persons interested in the natural sciences. Promotes the study of evolutionary biology. Serves as a research, education, and exhibition center for the study of the zoological, anthropological, and mineralogical sciences. *Type:* Association.

BC Naturalist

Federation of B.C. Naturalists
425-1367 W. Broadway   Ph: (604)737-3057
Vancouver, BC, Canada V6H   Fax: (604)738-7173
4A9

Contact: Stephen Gehlbach, Editor, (604)541-1193; Martine Klaassen.

Desc: Provides news and information on all aspects of nature and the environment in British Columbia. *Type:* Newsletter.

Drought Network News

International Drought Information Center/
National Drought Mitigation Center
University of Nebraska, Lincoln
239 L.W. Chase Hall   Ph: (402)472-6707
PO Box 830749   Fax: (402)472-6614
Lincoln, NE 68583-0749
E-mail: ndmc@enso.unl.edu
URL: http://www.enso.unl.edu/ndmc.

Contact: Deborah A. Wood, Editor, dwood1@unl.edu.

Desc: Provides information on drought prediction, monitoring, impact assessment, adjustment and adaptation, and planning and response. *Type:* Newsletter.

Everglades Online Database

Everglades Information Network
Florida International University   Ph: (305)348-3417
Libraries
University Park
Miami, FL 33199
E-mail: glades@fiu.edu
URL: http://www.fcla.edu/cgi-bin/cgiwrap/~fclwlui/
webluis/TIDLWQE/DBIDQE
Desc: Turn to this searchable online database when you're looking for information on the Florida Everglades. You can access electronic versions of traditional printed materials through the Everglades Digital Library. *Type:* Database.

The Sand Paper

Anza-Borrego Desert Natural History Association
PO Box 310 .   Ph: (760)767-3052
Borrego Springs, CA 92004   Fax: (760)767-3099
E-mail: abdnha@mia.net
Contact: Betsy Knaak, Editor.
Desc: Dedicated to educational, scientific, historic and interpretive endeavors that enhance the public understanding of the natural and cultural resources of the Anza-Borrego Desert Region. *Type:* Newsletter.

Southwest Parks and Monuments Association

221 N. Court Ave.   Ph: (520)622-1999
Tucson, AZ 85701   Fax: (520)623-9519
E-mail: mail@spma.org
URL: http://www.spma.org
Contact: T. J. Priehs, Exec.Dir.
Desc: Seeks to aid in the preservation and interpretation of southwestern features of national interest specifically, 54 national parks and monuments in 11 western states. *Type:* Association.

Yosemite Association

PO Box 230   Ph: (209)379-2646
El Portal, CA 95318   Fax: (209)379-2486
URL: http://www.yose.org
Contact: Steve Medley, Pres.
Desc: Educational organization for individuals, families, and corporations interested in Yosemite National Park. Cooperates with the National Park Service. Provides financial support to NPS programs by publishing books for visitors and by furnishing equipment, supplies, and research facilities. *Type:* Association.

Navy

Fleet Reserve Association

125 N. West St.   Ph: (703)683-1400
Alexandria, VA 22314-2754   Free: 800-372-1924
                                     Fax: (703)549-6610
E-mail: news-fra@fra.org
URL: http://www.fra.org
Contact: Charles L. Calkins, Natl. Exec.Dir.
Desc: Active duty enlisted personnel in the U.S. Navy, Marine Corps, Coast Guard, Fleet Reserves of the Navy, and Fleet Marine Corps and Coast Guard; retired members of these services. *Type:* Association.

Tin Can Sailors

PO Box 100   Ph: (508)677-0515
Somerset, MA 02726   Free: 800-345-1477
                                     Fax: (508)676-9740
E-mail: dd719@aol.com
URL: http://www.destroyers.org
Contact: Thomas J. Peltin, Pres.
Desc: Sailors serving or who have served on naval destroyers. Seeks to promote camaraderie among destroyermen. *Type:* Association.

Nephrology

American Kidney Fund

6110 Executive Blvd., Ste. 1010   Ph: (301)881-3052
Rockville, MD 20852   Free: 800-638-8299
                                     Fax: (301)881-0898
E-mail: helpline@akfinc.org
URL: http://www.akfinc.org
Contact: Karen M. Sendelback, CFRE, Exec.Dir.
Desc: Works to alleviate the financial burdens caused by kidney disease; improve the quality of life for kidney patients; promote kidney health care nationwide. Provides direct financial assistance to needy kidney disease victims with costs specific to their treatment. Funds are raised through direct mail from the public. *Type:* Association.

American Nephrology Nurses' Association

Box 56, E. Holly Ave.   Ph: (609)256-2320
Pitman, NJ 08071   Fax: (609)589-7463
E-mail: anna@mail.ajj.com
URL: http://www.inurse.com/~ANNA
Contact: Ronald P. Brady, Exec.Dir.
Desc: Registered nurses; physicians, dietitians, social workers, and technicians. Promotes continuing education of members at national, regional, and local levels. *Type:* Association.

American Society of Nephrology

1200 19th St. NW, Ste. 300   Ph: (202)857-1190
Washington, DC 20036-2422   Fax: (202)429-5140
E-mail: asn@dc.sba.com
URL: http://www.asn-online.com
Contact: Sherri Mara, Exec.Dir.
Desc: Nephrologists united for the exchange of scientific information. Seeks to contribute to the education of members and to improve the quality of patient care. *Type:* Association.

The Kidney Stones Network Newsletter

Four Geez Press
1911 Douglas Blvd., Ste. 85-131   Ph: (916)781-3440
Roseville, CA 95661-3707   Fax: (916)781-3814
Contact: Gail Golomb, Publisher; Grant Gibbs, Editor.
Type: Newsletter.

National Kidney Foundation

30 E. 33rd St., Ste. 1100   Ph: (212)889-2210
New York, NY 10016   Free: 800-488-2277
                                     Fax: (212)779-0068
URL: http://www.kidney.org
Contact: John Davis, Chief Exec. Officer.
Desc: Supports research, patient services, professional and public education, organ and tissue donor program, and community service. Affiliates conduct community and patient services including: drug banks; transportation; early screening; patient seminars. Sponsors symposium for health care professionals. *Type:* Association.

NKF Family Focus

The National Kidney Foundation, Inc.
30 E. 33rd St.   Ph: (212)889-2210
New York, NY 10016   Free: 800-622-9010
                                     Fax: (212)689-9261
E-mail: webmaster@kidney.org
URL: http://www.kidney.org.
Contact: Karren King, Editor.
Desc: Provides news on kidney disease. Includes articles on nutrition, fitness, news of research, and columns titled From the Editor, Patient/Family Network, Patient and Family Corner, Good Nutrition, The More You Know, and Living Well. *Type:* Newsletter.

Neurological Disorders

ALS Forbes Norris Research Center
2324 Sacramento St., Ste. 150   Ph: (415)923-3604
San Francisco, CA 94115   Fax: (415)673-5184
Contact: Robert G. Miller, MD, Contact.
Desc: Neuromuscular diseases, including Amyotrophic Lateral Sclerosis (Lou Gehrig's Disease). *Type:* Research center.

Alzheimer Treatment Research Center
161 N. Dithridge St.   Ph: (412)683-1181
Pittsburgh, PA 15213   Fax: (412)683-1181
Contact: Arthur C. Walsh, MD, Pres.
Desc: Senility, Alzheimer's disease, and hypochondriasis in the elderly, particularly brain dysfunction related to impaired circulation, psychiatric aspects of senility, treatment of chronic schizophrenia, and the effect of anticoagulant therapy. *Type:* Research center.

American Academy of Neurology
1080 Montreal Ave.   Ph: (651)695-1940
St. Paul, MN 55116-2325
E-mail: aan@aan.com
URL: http://www.aan.com
Contact: Jan W. Kolehmainen, Exec.Dir.
Desc: Professional society of medical doctors specializing in brain and nervous system diseases. Maintains placement service. Sponsors research and educational programs. *Type:* Association.

American Association of Electrodiagnostic Medicine
421 1st Ave., SW, Ste. 300 East   Ph: (507)288-0100
Rochester, MN 55902   Fax: (507)288-1225
E-mail: aaem@aol.com
URL: http://www.aaem.com
Contact: Shirlyn A. Adkins, J.D., Exec.Dir.
Desc: M.D.'s and D.O.'s or foreign equivalent degrees who practice or are interested in electrodiagnostic medicine. Objective is to increase and extend knowledge of electomyography and electrodiagnostic medicine, and to improve patient care. *Type:* Association.

American Association for the Study of Headache
19 Mantua Rd.   Ph: (609)423-0043
Mt. Royal, NJ 08061   Fax: (609)423-0082
E-mail: aashhq@talley.com
URL: http://www.aash.org
Contact: Linda McGillicuddy, Contact.
Desc: Headache and head pain. *Type:* Research center.

American Brain Tumor Association
2720 River Rd., Ste. 146   Ph: (847)827-9910
Des Plaines, IL 60018   Free: 800-886-2282
   Fax: (847)827-9918
E-mail: info@abta.org
URL: http://www.abta.org
Contact: Naomi Berkowitz, Exec.Dir.
Desc: Raises and awards funds for brain tumor research nationwide. Offers assistance to brain tumor patients and their families on strategies of coping and publishes and disseminates patient education material, free of charge. *Type:* Research center.

American Parkinson's Disease Association
1250 Hylan Blvd., Ste. 4B   Ph: (718)981-8001
Staten Island, NY 10305   Free: 800-223-2732
   Fax: (718)981-4399
E-mail: apda@admin.con2.com
URL: http://www.apdaparkinson.com
Contact: Joel Gerstel, Exec.Dir.

Desc: Works to find the cure for Parkinson's disease and to alleviate the suffering of its victims by subsidizing information and referral centers and providing funds for research. Offers counseling services to patients and their families. Maintains 51 information and referral centers and more than 800 support groups. *Type:* Association.

Amyotrophic Lateral Sclerosis Association
27001 Aqoura Rd. Suite 150   Ph: (818)880-9007
Calabasas Hills, CA 91301   Free: 800-782-4747
   Fax: (818)880-9006
Contact: Michael W. Havlicek, Exec.VP.
Desc: Patients; relatives and friends of patients; doctors, neurologists, physical therapists, nurses, and professional organizations dedicated to finding the cause, prevention, and cure for amyotrophic lateral sclerosis (ALS). Offers help and information to ALS patients and their families. Funds ALS-specific research at major medical institutions. *Type:* Association.

Amyotrophic Lateral Sclerosis Clinical Research Center
Univ. of Wisconsin Hospital &   Ph: (608)263-9057
  Clinics   Fax: (608)263-0135
H6/563 Clinical Sci. Ctr.
600 Highland Ave.
Madison, WI 53792-5132
E-mail: brooks@neurology.wisc.edu
Contact: Benjamin Rix Brooks, MD, Dir.
Desc: Amyotrophic lateral sclerosis (ALS), including bulbar function, exercise for ALS patients, and neurochemical, therapeutic, and epidemiological case control studies. Serves as operations center for Amyotrophic Lateral Sclerosis Ciliary Neurotrophic Factor Treatment Study Group. *Type:* Research center.

Andrews-Reiter Epilepsy Research Program
550 Doyle Park Dr.   Ph: (707)578-8985
Santa Rosa, CA 95405-4517   Fax: (707)528-1086
E-mail: djandrews@neteze.com
Contact: Donna J. Andrews, PhD, Dir.
Desc: Behavioral approach to self-control of seizures; adjunctive therapy and medications. *Type:* Research center.

Arthur M. Fishberg Research Center in Neurobiology
Mt. Sinai Med. Ctr.   Ph: (212)241-7368
1 Gustave Levy Pl.   Fax: (212)996-9785
Box 1065
New York, NY 10029
E-mail: james_roberts@fishmailserver.mssm.edu
URL: http://www.mssm.edu/neurobio/home-page.html
Contact: James L. Roberts, PhD, Co-Dir.
Desc: Neurobiological systems in humans and mammals, emphasizing aging research. Specific interests include the neuroendocrinology of stress, reproduction and metabolism, the molecular biology of Alzheimer's disease, schizophrenia, and other neurological/psychiatric diseases, and growth factors and growth factor receptor gene expression in the central nervous system. *Type:* Research center.

Association for Research in Nervous and Mental Disease
1 Gustave Levy Pl.   Ph: (212)740-7608
Box 1052   Fax: (212)831-1816
New York, NY 10029
Contact: Ivan Bodis-Wollner, MD, Contact.
Desc: Neurology, neurosurgery, and psychiatry. *Type:* Research center.

Attention Deficit Information Network
Moira Munns
475 Hillside Ave.   Ph: (781)455-9895
Needham, MA 02494   Fax: (781)444-5466
Desc: People with Attention Deficit Disorders (ADD), their families, and other individuals with an interest in ADD. Promotes improved quality of life for people with ADD. *Type:* Association.

Axion Research Foundation, Inc.
100 Deepwood Dr.   Ph: (203)773-9300
Hamden, CT 06517   Fax: (203)776-2893
E-mail: bus.manager@axion.org
Contact: Dr. D.E. Redmond, Jr., Dir.
Desc: Neural transplantation, neural imaging, Parkinson's disease, and primate visual development. *Type:* Research center.

Baltimore Headache Institute
Johns Hopkins at Green Spring   Ph: (410)583-7171
  Stn.   Fax: (410)583-7173
Foxleigh Bldg., Ste. 165
2330 W. Joppa Rd.
Lutherville, MD 21093
E-mail: bmondell@jhmi.edu
Contact: Dr. Brian Mondell, Med.Dir.
Desc: Treatment of migraine, muscle contraction, and cluster headaches. *Type:* Research center.

Barbara Davis Center for Childhood Diabetes
4200 E. 9th Ave.   Ph: (303)315-8796
Box B140   Fax: (303)315-4124
Denver, CO 80262
URL: http://www.ushc.edu/misc/diabetes/bdc.html
Contact: Dr. H. Peter Chase, Clin.Dir.
Desc: Diabetes in children, including immunopathology, islet cell transplantation, and clinical trials of free radical scavengers in new onset type-I diabetes. Maintains clinical records of 2,000 diabetic children and young adults. *Type:* Research center.

Barrow Neurological Institute
350 W. Thomas Rd.   Ph: (602)406-3196
Phoenix, AZ 85013
URL: http://www.chw.edu/bni
Contact: Michael Holt, Contact.
Desc: Neurosciences. *Type:* Research center.

Baylor College of Medicine
Epilepsy Research Center
One Baylor Plz.   Ph: (713)790-3109
Houston, TX 77030   Fax: (713)793-1574
Contact: Dr. Peter Kellaway, Dir.
Desc: Epilepsy research (as related to human patients) in the following areas: clinical research on neurophysiological, pharmacological, and ontogenetic aspects of epilepsy; design and application of computer-based systems to improve EEG detection, characterization, and quantification of the epileptic process in the brain; fundamental studies employing in-vitro brain slice technique to the elucidation of membrane and synaptic mechanisms in epileptogenesis and the mechanisms of action of anticonvulsant and convulsant agents; and developmental neurogenetics of epilepsy. *Type:* Research center.

Baylor College of Medicine
Jerry Lewis Neuromuscular Disease Research Center
6501 Fannin, Ste. B302   Ph: (713)798-4073
Houston, TX 77030   Fax: (713)798-3853
E-mail: sappel@bcm.tmc.edu
Contact: Stanley H. Appel, MD, Co-Dir.

Desc: Biochemistry, molecular genetics, and physiology of skeletal muscle and motor nerves, including biochemical, physiological, morphological, and genetic techniques to define and compare basic properties of skeletal muscle and neuromuscular disorders. Applies these approaches to animal models of human neuromuscular disease and to cultured muscle and nerve cells from normal and affected people. *Type:* Research center.

Baylor College of Medicine

Sleep Disorders and Research Center

One Baylor Plaza   Ph: (713)798-4886
MS 711 D   Fax: (713)798-4099
Houston, TX 77030
E-mail: cmoore@bcm.tmc.eiw
Contact: Constance A. Moore, Dir.
Desc: Neuropsychopharmacology of sleep and sexual dysfunction in males. *Type:* Research center.

Bernard W. Gimbel Multiple Sclerosis Comprehensive Care Center

Holy Name Hosp.   Ph: (201)837-0727
718 Teaneck Rd.   Fax: (201)837-8504
Teaneck, NJ 07666
E-mail: jhalpel@aol.com
Contact: Mary Ann Picone, MD, Dir.
Desc: Treatment and modalities for the relief of symptoms associated with multiple sclerosis, as well as improvement in overall functioning, prevention of worsening of the disease, and promotion of maximal independence. *Type:* Research center.

Boston University

Electrophysiology Laboratory

Neuromuscular Res. Ctr.   Ph: (617)353-9633
44 Cummington St.   Fax: (617)353-5737
Boston, MA 02215
E-mail: sroy@bu.edu
URL: http://nmrc.bu.edu
Contact: Dr. Serge Roy, Supv.
Desc: In vitro studies of isolated muscles of rats to compare muscle physiology/morphology to the electrical signals produced during muscle contraction. Aims to further the development of surface electromyography (EMG) as a means of assessing human muscle function and fatigue. *Type:* Research center.

Boston University

Harold Goodless Aphasia Research Center

Sch. of Med.   Ph: (617)232-9500
Boston VA Med. Ctr.   Fax: (617)522-4786
150 S. Huntington Ave.
Boston, MA 02130
E-mail: malbert@bu.edu
Contact: Dr. Martin L. Albert, MD,PhD, Dir.
Desc: Cognitive and language impairment following brain damage and closely related topics in psycholinguistics, cognitive science, and behavioral neuroscience. *Type:* Research center.

Boston University

Laboratory of Neuropsychology

715 Albany St.   Ph: (617)638-4803
M-9   Fax: (617)638-4806
Boston, MA 02118
E-mail: hcr@acs.bu.edu
Contact: Marlene Oscar Berman, PhD, Prof. & Ch.
Desc: Alcoholism, aphasia, apraxia, dementia, memory disorders, autism, schizophrenia, dyslexia, normal brain function and behavior, and psychopharmacology. Projects emphasize the relationship between brain structure and brain function, especially as related to human neurological disorders. *Type:* Research center.

Boston University

Motor Unit Laboratory

Neuromuscular Res. Ctr.   Ph: (617)353-9634
44 Cummington St.   Fax: (617)353-5737
Boston, MA 02215
URL: http://www.nmrc.bu.edu
Contact: Dr. Carlo J. De Luca, Supv.
Desc: Investigates how the brain and spinal cord control the activation of muscle cells to produce muscle force. Seeks to examine muscle fiber discharge history in detail, to better understand the physiological rules that regulate muscle contractions, and to improve the ability of the neurologist to categorize and quantify neurological dysfunction. *Type:* Research center.

Boston University

Muscle Fatigue Laboratory

Neuromuscular Reserch Ctr.   Ph: (617)353-9633
44 Cummington St.   Fax: (617)353-5737
Boston, MA 02215
E-mail: sroy@bu.edu
URL: http://nmrc.bu.edu
Contact: Dr. Serge Roy, Supv.
Desc: Development and implementation of surface electromyographic techniques to measure muscle fatigue, including the fatigue process of lower back muscles, measurement of forearm and hand fatigue related to the use of pressurized gloves, and investigation of physiological correlates of muscle fatigue using NMR spectroscopy combined with electromyography. *Type:* Research center.

Boston University

Neuromuscular Research Center

44 Cummington St.   Ph: (617)353-9757
Boston, MA 02215   Fax: (617)353-5737
E-mail: cjd@bu.edu
URL: http://nmrc.bu.edu
Contact: Dr. Carlo J. De Luca, Dir.
Desc: Motor control, including motor unit firing during sustained isometric contractions, synchronization evaluation, synchronization across muscles, and modeling of force production in the muscle; low back pain, including normative database study of back muscle function, EMG parameters of lumbar back muscles, development of test protocols related to the befavior of back mucles, and muscle performance in the back analysis system compared to lifting tasks; posture and movement, etc. The center is organized into the following components: Motor Unit Lab, Muscle Fatigue Lab, Injury Analysis and Prevention Lab, Motion Analysis Lab, Motor Control Lab, and Electrophysiology Lab. *Type:* Research center.

Boston University

Neuromuscular Research Center Design Laboratory

44 Cummington St.   Ph: (617)353-9637
Boston, MA 02215   Fax: (617)353-5737
E-mail: dgilmore@bu.edu
Contact: L. Donald Gilmore, Supv.
Desc: Develops instrumentation for other NMRC laboratories. Provides researchers with electronic hardware and software technologies used to investigate neuromuscular performance in both the lab and clinical environment. *Type:* Research center.

Boston University

Neuromuscular Research Center Motion Analysis Laboratory

44 Cummington St.   Ph: (617)353-9635
Boston, MA 02215   Fax: (617)353-5737
Contact: Dr. Serge Roy, Supv.
Desc: Explores the full range of human movement, including dynamics and kinematics, with emphasis on the neural control and biomechanics of posture and locomotion. *Type:* Research center.

Brain Injury Update

H.D.I. Publishers

PO Box 131401   Ph: (713)526-6900
Houston, TX 77219-1401   Free: 800-321-7037
    Fax: (713)526-7787
E-mail: hdijch@aol.com
Contact: L. Don Lehmkuhl, Ph.D., Editor.
Desc: Provides information on brain injury, rehabilitation, and research. Reviews current literature. *Type:* Newsletter.

Brain Research Foundation

208 S. LaSalle St.   Ph: (312)782-4311
Chicago, IL 60604-1102   Fax: (312)782-6437
Contact: Anne Roosevelt, Exec.Dir.
Desc: Provides support for research projects, new equipment, and scientific education in neurology, psychiatry, neurobiology, neurosurgery, and pharmacology/physiology at the Brain Research Institute of the University of Chicago. *Type:* Research center.

Brain Sciences Center

Veterans Aff. Med. Ctr., 11B   Ph: (612)725-2282
1 Veterans Dr.   Fax: (612)725-2291
Minneapolis, MN 55417
E-mail: omega@maroon.tc.umn.edu
Contact: Apostolos P. Georgopoulos, MD, Dir.
Desc: Brain physiology, cognitive psychology, and motor control. *Type:* Research center.

Brigham and Women's Hospital

Center for Neurologic Diseases

77th Ave. Louis Pasteur HIM   Ph: (617)525-5300
730   Fax: (617)525-5252
Boston, MA 02115-5817
E-mail: weiner@cnd.bwh.harvard.edu
Contact: Dr. Howard L. Weiner, Co-Dir.
Desc: Human autoimmune diseases, including T-cell immunology, T-cell interactions and regulations by cytokines. Also studies immunoregulatory T-cell abnormalities in multiple sclerosis and other autoimmune diseases, and investigations of mechanisms of immunologic tolerance in humans. *Type:* Research center.

Brown University

Center for Neural Sciences

Department of Neurosciences   Ph: (401)863-3548
PO Box 1953   Fax: (401)863-1074
Providence, RI 02912
Contact: Mary Ellen Flinn, Admin.Asst.
Desc: Brain and cerebral cortex, including models and mechanisms of learning, memory, and plasticity. *Type:* Research center.

Carleton University

Centre for Memory Assessment and Research

B531 Loeb   Ph: (613)520-2659
1125 Colonel By Dr.
Ottawa, ON, Canada K1S 5B6
E-mail: tom_tombaugh@carleton.ca
URL: http://gsro.carleton.ca/ors/oru/s75.html
Contact: Tommy N. Tombaugh, Dir.
Desc: Testing and assessment for anyone experiencing memory problems due to illness, aging, injury, or neurological damage; encourages and facilitates research, as well as develops tests for assessing memory and intellectual abilities; and serves as an educational facility and research center focusing on memory illnesses and cognitive rehabilitation. *Type:* Research center.

Case Western Reserve University

Applied Neural Control Laboratory

Charles B. Bolton Bldg., Rm.   Ph: (216)368-2960
   3480   Fax: (216)368-4872
Cleveland, OH 44106-4912
Contact: J. Thomas Mortimer, PhD, Dir.

Desc: Development of technology based on the electrical excitability of nerve tissue for use in electrically controlling bodily organs or systems. Applications include restoration of paralyzed upper and lower extremities, restoration of diaphragm and bladder function, and stimulation of the central nervous system in epilepsy treatment. *Type:* Research center.

Center for Applied Neuropsychology

100 1st Ave., 900a   Ph: (412)391-4570
Pittsburgh, PA 15222-1507   Fax: (412)391-7255
E-mail: mmccue@pitt.edu
URL: http://www1.pitt.edu/~bna1/can/index.html
Contact: Michael McCue, PhD, Dir.

Desc: Neuropsychological and ecological assessment. *Type:* Research center.

Center for Neurochemistry

Nathan S. Kline Institute for   Ph: (914)398-5530
  Psychiatric Res.   Fax: (914)398-5531
140 Old Orangeburg Rd.
Orangeburg, NY 10962
E-mail: Lajtha@kni.rfmh.org
URL: http://www.rfmh.ni.org
Contact: Laura Berlanga, Contact.

Desc: Brain protein and peptide metabolism, chronic drug effects, properties of brain receptors, blood-brain barrier, and effects of addictive drugs. *Type:* Research center.

Center for Neurodevelopmental Studies, Inc.

5430 W. Glenn Dr.   Ph: (602)915-0345
Glendale, AZ 85301   Fax: (602)937-5425
E-mail: cns@netwrx.net
URL: http://www.cirs.org/homepage/cns
Contact: Lorna Jean King, Dir.

Desc: Effective treatment methods for autism and developmental disabilities and standardizing measures for evaluating adult sensory/motor functions (the Stepping Test, Vertical Writing Test, and Object Manipulation Speed Test). Collects data on specific responses of developmentally delayed children to various types of sensory stimulation. *Type:* Research center.

Center for Neurologic Study

9850 Genesee ave., Ste. 320   Ph: (619)455-5463
La Jolla, CA 92037   Fax: (619)455-1713
E-mail: cns@cts.com
URL: http://www.cnsonline.org
Contact: Richard A. Smith, MD, Dir.

Desc: Neuropharmacology and experimental treatment of neurologic diseases. *Type:* Research center.

Cerebral Blood Flow Laboratories

Veterans Admin. Med. Ctr.   Ph: (713)795-5807
  151A   Fax: (713)794-7583
Bldg. 110, Rm. 225
2002 Holcombe Blvd.
Houston, TX 77030
E-mail: jmeyer@bcm.tmc.edu
Contact: John S. Meyer, MD, Dir.

Desc: Measurement of CT morphological changes and cerebral blood flow; cerebrovascular disorders; aging, Alzheimer's and ischemic vascular dementias and responses to medical, surgical, pharmacological, and behavioral treatment; prevention, diagnosis, and treatment of stroke and migraine; cerebral blood flow control and cerebral metabolism; neuropharmacology and physiology; aging; dementia; transient ischemic attacks; and risk factors for stroke. *Type:* Research center.

Cerebral Palsy of Massachusetts

105 Adams St.   Ph: (617)479-7443
Quincy, MA 02169   Fax: (617)786-9820
Contact: Thomas Zukauskas, Exec.Dir.

Desc: Parents of the handicapped and interested groups, clubs, and foundations in southeastern Massachusetts. Promotes restorative, educational, and social services for the developmentally disabled. *Type:* Association.

Charcot-Marie-Tooth Association

Crozer Mills Entpr. Center
601 Upland Ave.   Ph: (610)499-7486
Upland, PA 19015   Free: 800-606-CMTA
                Fax: (610)499-7487
E-mail: cmtassoc@aol.com
URL: http://www.charcot-marie-tooth.org
Contact: Pat Dreibelbis, Dir. of Program Services.

Desc: Charcot-Marie-Tooth patients and their families, medical professionals treating the disorder, and interested individuals. (Charcot-Marie-Tooth Disease, also known as peroneal muscular atrophy or hereditary motor sensory neuropathy, is a progressive neurological disorder beginning in childhood or adult life with weakness and muscle wasting in feet, legs, hands, and arms.) Works to inform and educate patients and their families, the medical community, and the public about medical treatment for CMT. Offers support groups for patients and their families; disseminates educational materials; encourages and funds research; sponsors lay and professional symposia. *Type:* Association.

Chicago Institute of Neurosurgery and Neuroresearch

2515 N. Clark, Ste. 800   Ph: (773)883-8585
Chicago, IL 60614   Fax: (773)935-2132
Contact: Joseph R. Moskal, PhD, Dir. of Res.

Desc: Molecular glycobiology of brain tumors, glycosyltransferase, molecular biology, and ddrt-pcr-based gene discovery. *Type:* Research center.

Children and Adults With Attention Deficit Disorder

499 NW 70th Ave., Ste. 101   Ph: (954)587-3700
Plantation, FL 33317   Free: 800-233-4050
                Fax: (954)587-4599
E-mail: national@chadd.org
URL: http://www.chadd.org
Desc: Parents, adults, and professionals with an interest in attention-deficit disorders. (ADD is a neurologically-based disorder which affects an individual's behavior and learning. The disorder is characterized by deficits in attention span and impulse control, and is often accompanied by hyperactivity.) Goals are to: maintain a support group for parents of children with ADD; provide a forum for continuing education for parents and professionals about ADD; act as a resource for information about ADD; assure that the best educational opportunities are available to children with ADD so that their specific difficulties will be recognized and appropriately managed within educational settings. *Type:* Association.

City of Hope Beckman Research Institute

Division of Neurosciences

1450 E. Duarte Rd.   Ph: (626)357-2484
Duarte, CA 91010   Fax: (626)301-8470
E-mail: jvaughn@coh.org
URL: http://bricoh.coh.org
Contact: Dr. James E. Vaughn, Ch.

Desc: The Division is composed of 12 research sections studying cell biology, cellular neurochemistry, cellular neurophysiology, developmental neurobiology, membrane biochemistry, molecular biology and genetics, neuroanatomy and ultrastructure, neurobiochemistry, neuroen-

docrinology, neuropharmacology, neurophysiology, and receptor physiology. Specific studies include the embryonic development of spinal cord neurons; identification, localization, and functions of neuroactive peptides; molecular and functional studies of transmembrane ion channels; the functional relationship between molecular chemical events and electrical excitability of neuronal elements; interactions between neurotransmitter receptor molecules of the membrane with synaptic proteins; developmental and molecular biological processes involved in the function of cholinergic neurons in normal and animal models of Alzheimer's disease; mechanisms of solute transport localized membranes and the effect of lipid components on operation of transport systems; developmental specificity of the formation of neuronal connections; and molecular genetic studies of Alzheimer's disease, schizophrenia, and manic depressive disorder. *Type:* Research center.

College of Staten Island of City University of New York

Program in Neuroscience

2800 Victory Blvd., 6S229   Ph: (718)982-3950
Staten Island, NY 10314   Fax: (718)982-3953

Contact: Ekkehart Trenkner, Mng.Dir.

Desc: Developmental neurobiology and neurochemistry, and synaptic plasticity, focusing on the regulation and adaptation of neural function, utilizing brain slices, neural cell lines, primary CNS neurons grown in culture, aging and development and neuropathological proceses (Alzheimer's and genetic diseases). *Type:* Research center.

Colorado State University

Program in Molecular, Cellular, and Integrative Neurosciences

Anatomy and Neurobiology   Ph: (970)491-0425
  Dept. 1670   Fax: (970)491-7907
Anatomy/Zoology Bldg.
Fort Collins, CO 80523-1670
E-mail: kbeam@vines.colostate.edu
URL: http://cvmbs.colostate.edu/mcin

Contact: Dr. Kurt G. Beam, Dir.

Desc: Cellular, molecular and integrative approaches to neuroscience, focusing on basic components of the nervous system's development repair, and function largely through studies of cultured neurons, brain slices, and animals. Also investigation of the role of amino acid neurotransmitters in development and aging, structure and function of voltage and ligand gated ion channels, mechanisms of taste reception, basis of circadian rhythms, mechanisms of synaptic function, and regulation of gene expression in early development. *Type:* Research center.

Columbia-Presbyterian Medical Center

Neurological Institute

710 W. 168th St.   Ph: (212)305-8551
New York, NY 10032-3784   Fax: (212)305-6978
E-mail: tap2@columbia.edu

Contact: Timothy A. Pedley, MD, Dir. of Neurology Svc.

Desc: Neurology, neuropathology, neurophysiology, neurological surgery, dystonia, Parkinson's and Alzheimer's diseases, muscular dystrophy, amyotrophic lateral sclerosis (Lou Gehrig's disease), multiple sclerosis, and epilepsy, including basic and clinical studies on function and disease of the nervous system and treatment of nervous diseases and surgical conditions of brain and nervous system. *Type:* Research center.

Columbia University

Alzheimer's Disease Research Center

Department of Pathology   Ph: (212)305-6553
College of Physicians &   Fax: (212)305-4614
  Surgeons
630 W. 168th St.
New York, NY 10032
E-mail: MLS7@columbia.edu
URL: http://156.111.205.100/Ahome.html
Contact: Michael L. Shelanski, Dir.

Desc: Alzheimer's disease and elderly care. Serves as a resource for tissue, cells, and DNA from Alzheimer's disease and control patients. *Type:* Research center.

Columbia University

Center for Parkinson's Disease and Other Movement Disorders

Neurological Inst.   Ph: (212)305-5779
710 W. 168th St.   Fax: (212)305-1304
New York, NY 10032
E-mail: fahn@movdis.cis.columbia.edu
Contact: Stanley Fahn, MD, Dir.

Desc: Phenomenology, pharmacology, treatment, and genetics of Parkinson's disease and other movement disorders. Research activities focus on dystonia, Parkinsonism, tremor, dyskinesia, chorea and tics. *Type:* Research center.

Columbia University

Clinical Research Center for Muscular Dystrophy

College of Physicians &   Ph: (212)305-1664
  Surgeons   Fax: (212)305-3986
Dept. of Neurology, 4-420
630 W. 168th St.
New York, NY 10032
E-mail: sd12@columbia.edu
URL: http://www.columbia.edu
Contact: Salvatore DiMauro, MD, Co-Dir.

Desc: Molecular genetics and hereditary neuromuscular diseases, particularly metabolic myopathies. Conducts molecular genetic, biochemical, and morphological studies of muscle. *Type:* Research center.

Concordia University (Montreal, PQ, Canada)

Centre for Studies in Behavioral Neurobiology

Dept. of Psychology   Ph: (514)848-2200
1455 de Maisonneuve Blvd. W.   Fax: (514)848-2817
Montreal, PQ, Canada H3G
  1M8
E-mail: info@csbn.concordia.ca
URL: http://www-psychology.concordia.ca
Contact: Peter Shizgal, PhD, Dir.

Desc: Neurobiology of motivated, volitional, goal-directed behavior focusing on mechanisms of brain stimulation, psychomotor stimulant, opiate, ethanol, and food rewards. Also studies hormonal effects on motivated behavior and effects of stress and stress hormones on behavior. *Type:* Research center.

Cornell University

Aitken Neuroscience Center

523 E. 72nd St., 8th Fl.   Ph: (212)746-2396
New York, NY 10021   Fax: (212)772-0357
URL: http://www.aitken.org

Desc: Investigates the pathophysiology of traumatic brain injury, uses an in vitro human glial cell culture model of injury to study brain derived inflammatory mediators, and performs ventricular cerebrospinal fluid analysis in human patients. Established physiological model for post traumatic raised intracranial preserve analysis. *Type:* Research center.

Cornell University

Winifred Masterson Burke Medical Research Institute, Inc.

Dementia Research Service

785 Mamaroneck Ave.   Ph: (914)597-2359
White Plains, NY 10605   Fax: (914)597-2757
E-mail: jpblass@mail.med.cosnell.edu
Contact: Dr. John P. Blass, Dir.

Desc: Clinical and basic studies in metabolic and nutritional aspects of degenerative diseases of the nervous system, especially Alzheimer's disease. *Type:* Research center.

Crawford Research Institute at Shepherd Center

2020 Peachtree Rd. NW   Ph: (404)350-7595
Atlanta, GA 30309   Fax: (404)350-7596
E-mail: mike_jones@shepherd.org
URL: http://www.shepherd.org
Contact: Michael L. Jones, PhD, Dir.

Desc: Clinical health services and outcomes, acquired brain injury, spinal cord injury, and multiple sclerosis. *Type:* Research center.

Dartmouth College

Sleep Disorders Center

Dartmouth Hitchcock Medical   Ph: (603)650-7534
  Center   Fax: (603)650-7820
1 Medical Center Dr.
Lebanon, NH 03756
E-mail: michael.j.sateia@dartmouth.edu
Contact: Dr. Michael Sateia, Dir.

Desc: Sleep disorders, sleep apnea due to obesity, hypersomnolence, parasomnias, and insomnia. *Type:* Research center.

Directorate for Biological Sciences

Division of Molecular and Cellular Biosciences

Center for Biological Timing

Univ. of Virginia   Ph: (804)982-4500
Gilmer Hall   Fax: (804)982-4505
Charlottesville, VA 22903
E-mail: clock@virginia.edu
URL: http://www.cbt.virginia.edu
Contact: Dr. Gene D. Block, Dir.

Desc: Problems of biological timing within the nervous and endocrine systems. Specific studies include cellular mechanisms within the neuroendocrine system, environmental control of reproductive cycles, neural basis of rhythmic motor behaviors, and circadian rhythmicity. *Type:* Research center.

Drexel University

Imaging and Computer Vision Center

Computer Vision Center for Vertebrate Brain Mapping

32nd & Market Sts.   Ph: (215)895-1381
Philadelphia, PA 19104   Fax: (215)895-4987
E-mail: oleh_tretaik@coe.drexel.edu
URL: http://coe.drexel.edu/ICVC
Contact: Dr. Oleh John Tretaik, Dir.

Desc: Algorithms for use in basic biological research with emphasis on the methodological needs of nurobiology, with the overall emphasis on quantitative imaging. Current research projects include artificial intelligence techniques for pattern recognition and automated parcellation of brain structures; quantificaion techniques for analysis of microautoradiograms; correction methods for the differential H-3 quenching between white- and gray-matter; and development of new quantitative descriptors of distribution. *Type:* Research center.

Duke University

Duke Center for the Advanced Study of Epilepsy

401 Bryan Res. Bldg.   Ph: (919)684-4241
Research Dr.   Fax: (919)684-8219
Box 3676
Durham, NC 27710
Contact: Dr. James O. McNamara, Dir.

Desc: Clinical and experimental approaches to limbic epilepsy. Current projects include studies of early gene expression in the kindling model of epilepsy, mechanisms of development of Ammon's horn sclerosis, microphysiology of limbic seizures, and role of excitatory amino acids and their receptors in limbic epilepsy. *Type:* Research center.

Duke University

Preuss Laboratory for Brain Tumor Research

Duke Medical center   Ph: (919)684-5018
research Dr., 177 MSRB   Fax: (919)684-6458
Box 3156
Durham, NC 27710
E-mail: bigne001@mc.duke.edu
Contact: Dr. Darell Bigner, Dir.

Desc: Brain tumors. *Type:* Research center.

Duluth Clinic Education and Research Foundation

400 E. 3rd St.   Ph: (218)725-3139
Duluth, MN 55805-1951   Fax: (218)727-7258
E-mail: jdwyer@smdc.org
URL: http://www.smdc.org
Contact: James M. Dwyer, Dir.

Desc: Parkinson's disease, cancer, heart, stroke, and other medical issues. *Type:* Research center.

Dystonia Medical Research Foundation

1 E. Wacker Dr., Ste. 2430   Ph: (312)755-0198
Chicago, IL 60601-1905   Fax: (312)803-0138
E-mail: dystonia@dystonia-foundation.org
URL: http://www.dystonia-foundation.org/
Contact: Dr. Mahlon R. DeLong, Sci.Dir.

Desc: Causes and treatment of generalized dystonia, spasmodic torticollis, writer's cramp, blepharospasm, oromandibular dystonia, Meige's disease, and laryngeal dystonia. *Type:* Research center.

Dystonia Medical Research Foundation

1 E. Wacker Dr., Ste. 2430   Ph: (312)755-0198
Chicago, IL 60601-2001   Free: 800-377-DYST
    Fax: (312)803-0138
E-mail: dystfndt@aol.com
Contact: Valerie F. Levitin, PhD., Exec.Dir.

Desc: Dystonia patients and their families; medical personnel; health agencies; interested individuals. Promotes and funds research and encourages increased public awareness of dystonia, a neurologic muscular disorder causing muscles to jerk and contract into abnormal positions. Disseminates information concerning dystonia. *Type:* Association.

Emory University

Sleep Research Laboratory

1256 Briarcliffe Rd.   Ph: (404)874-4238
Atlanta, GA 30306   Fax: (404)853-4792
URL: http://www.emory.edu
Contact: Dr. Gerald Vogel, Dir.

Desc: Neurophysiological studies of sleep. *Type:* Research center.

Epilepsy Foundation

4351 Garden City Dr. Ph: (301)459-3700
Landover, MD 20785 Free: 800-EFA-1000
Fax: (301)577-2684

E-mail: postmaster@efa.org
URL: http://www.efa.org
Contact: Jeanne A. Carpenter, Pres.

Desc: Supports research into the causes and treatment of epilepsy, pediatrics and epilepsy, and behavioral science applications. Also supports training of research and clinical fellows in epilepsy. *Type:* Research center.

Florida Atlantic University

Center for Complex Systems and Brain Sciences

777 Glades Rd. Ph: (561)297-2230
Boca Raton, FL 33431 Fax: (561)297-3634
E-mail: kelso@walt.ccs.fau.edu
URL: http://www.ccs.fau.edu
Contact: J.A.S. Kelso, Contact.

Desc: Multidisciplinary studies of complex biological systems, focusing on coordination between neural processes and their resultant behaviors on cognitive, neural, and biophysical levels. Contains four major laboratories: Human Brain and Behavior Laboratory; Computational Laboratory for Scientific Visualization; Neuroscience Research Laboratory, which includes neural growth and development, neurophysiology, neuroanatomy, and cellular biophysics; Coordination Dynamics Laboratory. *Type:* Research center.

Georgetown University

Sleep Disorders Center

3800 Reservoir Rd. NW Ph: (202)784-3610
Washington, DC 20007 Fax: (202)784-2920
Contact: Dr. Richard Waldhorn, Jr., Dir.

Desc: Treatment techniques for sleep apnea using nasal continuous positive airway pressure, evaluation of people with nocturnal hypoxia and possible correlates to memory impairment, sleep disturbances in geriatric populations, and psychiatric studies dealing with the presence of depression in people with schizophrenia. Other concentrations include monitoring of epilepsy patients and studies of sudden infant death syndrome. *Type:* Research center.

Guardians of Hydrocephalus Research Foundation

2618 Ave. Z Ph: (718)743-4473
Brooklyn, NY 11235-2023 Free: 800-458-8655
Fax: (718)743-1171

E-mail: guardians1@aol.com
Contact: Michael Fischetti, Founder/Chmn. of Board.

Desc: Hydrocephalics and their families, health care professionals, and other concerned individuals. Seeks to find the cause and cure of hydrocephalus which is the buildup of cerebrospinal fluid in the brain cavity, and can cause brain damage or death if untreated. *Type:* Research center.

Guillain-Barre Syndrome Foundation International

PO Box 262 Ph: (610)667-0131
Wynnewood, PA 19096 Fax: (610)667-7036
E-mail: gbint@ix.netcom.com
URL: http://www.webmast.com/gbs/
Contact: Robert and Estelle Benson, Founders.

Desc: Individuals concerned with Guillain-Barre syndrome (Acute Idiopathic Polyneuritis), a rare, paralyzing, potentially catastrophic disorder of the peripheral nerves. Objectives are to: educate the public and medical community about the availability of support groups and maintain their awareness of the disorder; foster research on cause, prevention, and treatment; encourage financial support for research; develop nationwide support groups. *Type:* Association.

Harvard Brain Tissue Resource Center

McLean Hospital Ph: (617)855-2400
115 Mill St. Free: 800-272-4622
Belmont, MA 02178-9983 Fax: (617)855-3199
E-mail: btrc@mclean.org
URL: http://www.brainbank.mclean.org:8080
Contact: Francine M. Benes, MD, Dir.

Desc: Provides tissues to the neuroscience community for studies of movement disorders, major psychoses, and dementia. *Type:* Research center.

Harvard Medical School

Circadian Neuroendocrine and Sleep Disorders Section

Department of Med. Ph: (617)732-4013
Brigham & Women's Hospital Fax: (617)732-4015
221 Longwood Ave.
Boston, MA 02115
E-mail: caczeisler@gcrc.buh.harvard.edu
Contact: Dr. Charles A. Czeisler, Dir.

Desc: Sleep medicine, circadian aspects of hormone release, circulation and homeostotic regulation of sleep. *Type:* Research center.

Harvey W. Peters Research Center for the Study of Parkinson's Disease and Disorders of the Central Nervous System

Virginia Polytechnic Institute Ph: (540)231-8200
and State University Fax: (540)231-8890
Department of Chemistry
3103 Hahn Hall
Blacksburg, VA 24061-0212
E-mail: ncastagnoli@chemserver.chem.vt.edu
Contact: Prof. James F. Wolfe, Co-Dir.

Desc: Molecular mechanisms of xenobiotic metabolism, and chemically-induced neurodegenerative processes, focusing on Parkinson's disease and epileptic disorders. *Type:* Research center.

Helen Hayes Hospital

Neurology Research Center

Rte. 9W Ph: (914)947-3000
West Haverstraw, NY 10993- Fax: (914)786-4875
1195
E-mail: hes5@columbia.edu
Contact: Helen E. Scharfman, PhD, Supvr.

Desc: Epilepsy, brain injury, and neuroendocrinology. Degenerative neurological disorders such as Huntington's and Alzheimer's diseases are also investigated. *Type:* Research center.

Huntington Medical Research Institutes

734 Fairmount Ave. Ph: (626)397-5436
Pasadena, CA 91105 Fax: (626)397-3330
E-mail: opelw@hmri.org
URL: http://www.hmri.org
Contact: William Opel, PhD, Exec.Dir.

Desc: Electronic neural prosthetic device development; biology of vascular endothelium; cerebrovascular and cardiovascular physiology; early stroke intervention; prostate and breast cancer; cell biology; molecular genetics; proteomics; drug development; and medical applications of magnetic resonance using protons, phosphorous, fluorine, and nitrogen. *Type:* Research center.

Huntington's Disease Center Without Walls

Massachusetts General Hospital Ph: (617)726-5724
Molecular Neurogenetics Unit Fax: (617)726-5735
13th St., Bldg. 149, Rm. 6214
Charlestown, MA 02129
E-mail: gusella@helix.mgh.harvard.edu
Contact: Dr. James F. Gusella, Prog.Dir.

Desc: Huntington's Disease (HD), including protein abnormalities in the HD brain and their relationship to neu-

ronal loss, neuropathological examination of autopsy brain sections, location and measurement of chemical messengers in the brain, neuropsychological tests evaluating deficits in memory and cognitive functioning, social and psychological impact of HD on families, medications increasing levels of chemical messengers in the brain, DNA studies to determine the HD gene, and peptide localization in the nerve cells. *Type:* Research center.

Huntington's Disease Society of America

158 W 29th St., 7th Fl. Ph: (212)242-1968
New York, NY 10001-5300 Free: 800-345-4372
Fax: (212)239-3430

E-mail: curehd@idt.net
URL: http://www.hdsa.org
Contact: Barbara Boyle, Exec.Dir.

Desc: Individuals and groups of volunteers concerned with Huntington's disease, an inherited and terminal neurological condition causing progressive brain and nerve deterioration. Goals are to: identify HD families; educate the public and professionals, with emphasis on increasing consumer awareness of HD; promote and support basic and clinical research into the causes and cure of HD; maintain patient services program, coordinated with various community services, to assist families in meeting the social, economic, and emotional problems resulting from HD. Is working to change the attitude of the working community toward the HD patient, enhance the HD patient's lifestyle, and promote better health care and treatment, both in the community and in facilities. *Type:* Association.

Illinois Institute of Technology

Pritzker Institute of Medical Engineering

10 W. 32nd St. Ph: (312)567-5324
Chicago, IL 60616 Fax: (312)567-5707
E-mail: arzbaecher@charlie.cns.iit.edu
Contact: Dr. Robert Arzbaecher, Dir.

Desc: Neuromuscular studies, implantable systems for detection and control of cardiac arrhythmias, and closed-loop drug infusion systems, including a neuromuscular engineering program for re-enabling paralyzed muscle. *Type:* Research center.

Illinois Institute of Technology

Research Laboratory in Human Biomechanics

Chicago, IL 60616-3793 Ph: (312)567-3926
URL: http://www.iit.edu/colleges/grad/riitcent.html
Contact: Dr. Robert J. Jaeger, Dir.

Desc: Computer-aided biomechanical engineering and lower extremity neuromuscular engineering, including the use of force transducer arrays. *Type:* Research center.

Indiana University

Alzheimer Disease Center and Related Neuropsychiatric Disorders

CG 265 Ph: (317)274-4333
Indianapolis, IN 46202 Fax: (317)274-1497
E-mail: jwillia2@iupui.edu
URL: http://www.indiana.edu/~rugs/ctrdir/cadrnd.html
Contact: Hugh C. Hendrie, MD, Co-Dir.

Desc: Alzheimer Disease and related neuropsychiatric disorders characterized by memory loss and mood disorders in the older adult. *Type:* Research center.

Indiana University

Neuropsychology Research Section

702 Barnhill Dr., Rm. 3751 Ph: (317)274-7327
Indianapolis, IN 46202 Fax: (317)274-1337
E-mail: dkareken@iupui.edu
Contact: Dr. David A. Kareken, Dir.

Desc: Brain-behavior relationships as measured by functional brain imaging and neuropsychological measurement and as affected by neurologic disease and pharmacologic therapies. *Type:* Research center.

Indiana University Bloomington

Institute for Neural Systems and Plasticity

Psychology, Rm. 361   Ph: (812)855-4832
Bloomington, IN 47405
URL: http://www.indiana.edu/~rugs/ctrdir/insp.html
Contact: George V. Rebec, Dir.
Desc: Underlying mechanisms and plasticity in neural systems. *Type:* Research center.

Institute for Research in Behavioral Neuroscience

66 E. 79th St.   Ph: (212)288-6010
New York, NY 10021   Fax: (212)288-6024
Contact: Jason W. Brown, MD, Pres.
Desc: Neuropsychology and aphasia. *Type:* Research center.

Institutes for Achievement of Human Potential

8801 Stenton Ave.   Ph: (215)233-2050
Wyndmoor, PA 19038-8397   Fax: (215)233-9312
E-mail: ChipM@Earthlink.net
URL: http://www.iahp.org
Contact: Janet Doman, Dir.
Desc: Methods of treating severely brain-injured children, including investigations of effects of programs of sensory inputs individually designed according to each child's growth, as well as functional gains and effects of nutrition in enhancing children's response to therapeutic programs. Studies effects of applying similar environmental enrichment and neurological organization programs to non-disabled children of preschool age. *Type:* Research center.

International Association for the Study of Pain

909 NE 43rd St., Ste. 306   Ph: (206)547-6409
Seattle, WA 98105-6020   Fax: (206)547-1703
E-mail: lasp@locke.hs.washington.edu
URL: http://www.halcyon.com/iasp
Contact: Louisa E. Jones, Exec.Off.
Desc: Pain mechanisms and syndromes, focusing on patients with acute and chronic pain. *Type:* Research center.

International Research Council of Neuromuscular Disorders

1434 Pleasantville Rd.   Ph: (614)653-1098
Lancaster, OH 43130   Fax: (614)687-5003
Contact: James R. Grilliot, DC, Contact.
Desc: Neuromuscular diseases, focusing on cure, prevention, causes, effects, and occurrences. *Type:* Research center.

International Tremor Foundation

833 W. Washington Blvd.   Ph: (312)733-1893
Chicago, IL 60607   Fax: (312)733-1896
E-mail: upf_itf@msn.com
Contact: Judy Rosner, Exec.Dir.
Desc: Individuals suffering from tremors, their families and friends and health care professionals. (Tremor is a common symptom of neurologic disease and may be due to trauma, tumor, stroke or degenerative disease. The hands and head are most often affected). *Type:* Association.

John P. Robarts Research Institute

Stroke and Aging Group

Neurodegeneration Research Group

100 Perth Dr.   Ph: (519)663-5777
PO Box 5015   Fax: (519)663-3789
London, ON, Canada N6A 5K8
URL: http://www.rri.on.ca
Contact: Dr. Vladimir Hachinski, Dir.
Desc: Stroke and aging. Investigates new treatments and preventive measures for stroke, including efficacy of ticlopidine (antiplatelet formulation drug) and use of low-density artificial blood compounds to reach parts of brain previously inaccessible due to blood vessel blockage. *Type:* Research center.

Johns Hopkins University

Alzheimer's Disease Research Center

558 Ross Research Bldg.   Ph: (410)955-5632
720 Rutland Ave.   Fax: (410)955-9777
Baltimore, MD 21205-2196
E-mail: adrc@welchlink.welch.jhu.edu
Contact: Dr. Donald L. Price, Dir.
Desc: Alzheimer's disease, including basic and applied studies of symptoms and psychiatric problems. *Type:* Research center.

Johns Hopkins University

Baltimore Huntington's Disease Center

Johns Hopkins Hospital   Ph: (410)955-2398
Meyer 2-181   Fax: (410)955-8233
600 N. Wolfe St.
Baltimore, MD 21287
URL: http://www.med.jhu.edu/bhdc/huntington/html
Contact: Dr. Christopher A. Ross, Contact.
Desc: Huntington's Disease (HD), a hereditary brain disorder and the gene which carries it. Research is conducted by faculty from Johns Hopkins Medical Institutions, Departments of Psychiatry, Neurology, Neuroradiology, Pharmacology, Neuroscience, Biostatistics, and Genetics. *Type:* Research center.

Johns Hopkins University

Laboratory for Human Motor Learning

School of Medicine   Ph: (410)955-7093
Department of Biomedical   Fax: (410)955-0549
Engineering
720 Rutland Ave.
Baltimore, MD 21205
E-mail: nthakor@bme.jhu.edu
URL: http://www.bme.jhu.edu/~nthakor
Contact: Nitish V. Thakor, PhD, Dir.
Desc: The brain and how it controls movements of the arm, particularly how does the brain learn this control; how is the information represented; what parts of the brain are involved in storing the representation and does this change with time; and can damage to the brain affect the ability to learn control. *Type:* Research center.

Johns Hopkins University

Neuropathology Laboratory

558 Ross Research Bldg.   Ph: (410)955-5632
720 Rutland Ave.   Fax: (410)955-9777
Baltimore, MD 21205-2196
E-mail: adrc@welchlink.welch.jhu.edu
Contact: Dr. Donald L. Price, Dir.
Desc: Investigates molecular mechanisms of neurodegenerative diseases. *Type:* Research center.

Johns Hopkins University

Research and Training Center for Hearing and Balance

Auditory Neurophysiology Laboratory

School of Medicine   Ph: (410)614-4547
Department of Biomedical   Fax: (410)614-9599
Engineering
Ross Research Bldg., Rm. 424
720 Rutland Ave.
Baltimore, MD 21205
E-mail: xwang@bme.jhu.edu
URL: http://www.bme.jhu.edu/labs/chb/labs/aud_neurophys.html
Contact: Xiaoqin Wang, PhD, Prin. Investigator.
Desc: Auditory neurophysiology. *Type:* Research center.

Johns Hopkins University

Research and Training Center for Hearing and Balance

Laboratory of Vestibular Neurophysiology

PO Box 41402   Ph: (410)955-3403
Baltimore, MD 21203-6402   Fax: (410)955-0035
E-mail: lminor@welchlink.welch.jhu.edu
URL: http://www.bme.jhu.edu/labs/chb/labs/neurophys.html
Contact: Dr. Lloyd B. Minor, Dir.
Desc: Neurophysiological mechanisms that control vestibulo-ocular reflexes; development of new diagnostic and treatment modalities applicable to patients with vestibular disorders. *Type:* Research center.

Johns Hopkins University

Sleep Disorders Center

Johns Hopkins Bayview Med.   Ph: (410)550-0571
Ctr.   Fax: (410)550-2612
Asthma & Allergy Ctr.
5501 Hopkins Bayview Circle
Baltimore, MD 21224
E-mail: p.l.smith@welchlink.welch.jhu.edu
Contact: Philip L. Smith, MD, Dir.
Desc: Sleep-related disorders. Studies focus on disorders of daytime hypersomnolence, including narcolepsy, periodic leg movements, psychiatric illness, and sleep apnea; disorder-causing insomnia, psychiatric illness, shift work, and sleep apnea; and disruptive sleep patterns, loud snoring, nocturnal seizures, nocturnal terrors, and sleep walking. *Type:* Research center.

Johns Hopkins University

Zanvyl Krieger Mind/Brain Institute

Krieger 338   Ph: (410)516-8640
Baltimore, MD 21218   Fax: (410)516-8648
Contact: Dr. Guy McKhann, MD, Dir.
Desc: Fundamental activities of the human mind, including learning and the use of language, initiation of action and perception, and nervous system plasticity and regeneration. Attempts to address the basic questions of how consciousness is possible and how mind and brain are related. *Type:* Research center.

Kennedy Krieger Research Institute

Blood-Brain Barrier Laboratory

707 N. Broadway   Ph: (410)502-9483
Baltimore, MD 21205   Fax: (410)502-9524
E-mail: goldstein@kennedykrieger.org
URL: http://www.kennedy.org
Contact: Dr. Gary W. Goldstein, Dir.
Desc: Molecular aspects of brain microvessel differentiation, cell-cell signaling, second messengers, and transport systems. Investigates the effects of lead poisoning. *Type:* Research center.

Laboratory for Research on the Neuroscience of Autism

8110 La Jolla Shores Dr., Ste.   Ph: (619)551-7925
200B   Fax: (619)551-7931
La Jolla, CA 92037
URL: http://nodulus.extern.ucsd.edu/ab06000.html
Contact: Eric Courchesne, PhD, Dir.
Desc: Neurophysiological and neuroanatomical basis for autism, including the functional role of the cerebellum in cognition, the brain bases of selective attention, and the neuropsychological consequences of stroke. *Type:* Research center.

Laval University
Neurobiology Research Centre
Hopital de l'Enfant-Jesus Ph: (418)649-5593
1401, 18e Rue Fax: (418)649-5910
Quebec, PQ, Canada G1J 1Z4
E-mail: drcotem@cha.quebec.qc.ca
Contact: Dr. Pierre Durand, Res.Dir.

Desc: Nervous system including development and regeneration, cell biology, synaptic transmission, neurotransmitters and receptors, motor system, neural basis of behavior, Parkinson's disease, and muscular dystrophy. *Type:* Research center.

Loma Linda University
Sleep Disorders Center
Med. Services Ctr. Ph: (909)422-3130
VA Hospital Fax: (909)777-3214
11201 Benton St., 111P
Loma Linda, CA 92357
Contact: Dr. Ralph Downey, III, Dir.

Desc: Sleep disorders, including sleep apnea, insomnia, and narcolepsy. *Type:* Research center.

Louisiana State University Medical Center
Neuroscience Center of Excellence
2020 Gravier St., Ste. D Ph: (504)599-0832
New Orleans, LA 70112 Fax: (504)568-5801
E-mail: nbazan@lsumc.edu
URL: http://www.neuroscience.lsumc.edu
Contact: Dr. Nicolas G. Bazan, Dir.

Desc: Interdisciplinary unit studying clinical and basic neuroscience. *Type:* Research center.

Loyola University Chicago
Neuroscience and Aging Institute
Bldg. No. 117, Rm. 29 Ph: (708)216-6755
2160 S. 1st Ave. Fax: (708)216-6823
Maywood, IL 60153
E-mail: pgriffi@luc.edu
URL: http://www.meddean.luc.edu/lumen/deptwebs/nsai/index.htm
Contact: Israel Hanin, PhD, Dir.

Desc: Neurodegenerative diseases such as Alzheimer's disease, neurodevelopment, neuropeptide receptor systems, neuroendocrinology, neuroimmunology, neurotoxicity, sensory neuroscience, and neuro-oncology. *Type:* Research center.

Mailman Research Center
115 Mill St. Ph: (617)855-3227
Belmont, MA 02178 Fax: (617)855-3479
E-mail: cohenb@mckan.org(mclean.org)
URL: http://www.McLeanHospital.org
Contact: Bruce M. Cohen, Contact.

Desc: Neuropharmacology, neurochemistry, neuropathology, molecular neurogenetics, neuroregeneration, and molecular neurobiology with emphasis on psychiatric neurosciences. *Type:* Research center.

Massachusetts Alzheimer's Disease Research Center
Massachusetts General Hospital Ph: (617)726-1728
ACC, Ste. 830 Fax: (617)726-7718
15 Parkman St.
Boston, MA 02114
E-mail: growdon@helix.mgh.edu
URL: http://neuro.www3mgh.harvard.edu/ADRC/main.html
Contact: John H. Growdon, MD, Dir.

Desc: Coordinates research on Alzheimer's disease, including memory loss, dementia, neuropathology, neuropsy-chology, neurochemistry, and investigational drug studies. Projects focus on biochemical studies on the abnormal proteins that accumulate in the brains of Alzheimer's patients, possible genetic markers or familial traits, anatomical and neurotransmitter abnormalities, and clinical studies of behavior and neuropharmacology. *Type:* Research center.

Massachusetts Institute of Technology
Center for Biological and Computational Learning
Department of Brain & Ph: (617)253-5230
 Cognitive Science
45 Carleton St.
Cambridge, MA 02142
E-mail: tp@ai.mit.edu
URL: http://www.web.mit.edu/cbcl/
Contact: Tomaso Poggio, PhD, Co-Dir.

Desc: Investigates mechanisms of biological information processing using artificial intelligence models of psychophysics, anatomy, and physiology. Studies focus on machine and human learning, vision, and language and motor control. *Type:* Research center.

Massachusetts Institute of Technology
Laboratory of Neuroendocrine Regulation
Bldg. E25-604 Ph: (617)253-6731
Cambridge, MA 02139 Fax: (617)253-6882
E-mail: dick@mit.edu
Contact: Dr. Richard J. Wurtman, MD, Dir.

Desc: Pineal gland and effects of drugs, nutrients, and hormones on brain neurotransmitters and behavior. Specific studies include utilization of choline for acetylcholine and membrane phosphatidylcholine synthesis in cultured neuroblastoma cells and in rat brain; neurotransmitter receptors and second messengers that modulate these two syntheses; interactions of precursor availability (tyrosine and tryptophan) and firing frequency in controlling neurotransmitter (catecholamines and serotonin) release from superfused rat brain slices; effects of tyrosine on catecholamine release from isolated retina; effects of supplemental tyrosine on capacity to withstand stress, sustain motor activity, and perform complex tasks; control of melatonin secretion in rats; mechanisms by which melatonin acts on neurons and induces sleep; aberrant patterns of melatonin secretion in aging and human diseases; effects of macronutrients (carbohydrates and proteins) on brain serotonin synthesis; involvement of serotoninergic neurons in appetite, mood, pain sensitivity, and various appetitive diseases; selective effects of serotoninergic drugs on nutrient selection; Alzheimer's disease; control of APP metabolism by neurotransmitters; and brain phospholipid synthesis; production and maintenance of sleep in humans by melatonin; use of CDP-Choline to treat brain injury or stroke. *Type:* Research center.

McGill University
Centre for Research in Neuroscience
Montreal General Hospital Res. Ph: (514)934-8060
 Institute Fax: (514)934-8265
1650 Cedar Ave.
Montreal, PQ, Canada H3G
 1A4
E-mail: mc10@musica.mcgill.ca
URL: http://www.musica.mcgill.ca
Contact: Dr. Albert J. Aguayo, Dir.

Desc: Studies in neuroscience, particularly in cellular and molecular approaches to the nervous system with emphasis on neural development, regeneration, and neuroendocrine function. Research methodologies include recombinant DNA and classical neuroanatomical and electrophysiological techniques. *Type:* Research center.

McGill University
Laboratory of Molecular Neurogenetics
3801 University St. Ph: (514)398-8523
Montreal, PQ, Canada H3A Fax: (514)398-1509
 2B4
E-mail: eric@ericpc.mmi.mcgill.ca
Contact: Dr. Eric Shoubridge, Dir.

Desc: Genetics and expression of mitochondrial DNA (mtDNA) mutations in human disease. Current research includes investigations of the relationship between mtDNA genotype and biochemical phenotype in primary myoblast cultures and of immortal cybrid cells; studies of the transmission of mtDNA in mammalian systems, specifically segregation of heteroplasmic mtDNA populations in early mouse embryos; in vitro and in vivo mutagenesis of mtDNA, development of techniques to introduce mtDNA mutants into functional mitochondria in model cell systems; and cloning of genes for respiratory chain defects by functional complementation. *Type:* Research center.

McGill University
Laboratory of Neuropathology
3801 University St., Rm. 622 Ph: (514)398-5324
Montreal, PQ, Canada H3A Fax: (514)398-5825
 2B4
E-mail: johnr@mni.lan.mcgill.ca
Contact: Dr. John Richardson, Dir.

Desc: Neuropathology and Alzheimer's disease. *Type:* Research center.

McGill University
Laboratory of Neurotoxicology
Montreal Neurological Institute Ph: (514)398-8509
3801 University St. Fax: (514)398-1509
Montreal, PQ, Canada H3A
 2B4
E-mail: mddm@musica.mcgill.ca
Contact: Dr. Heather Durham, Contact.

Desc: Neurodegenerative diseases, neurotoxicology, and neurobiology; the biological basis of motor neuron diseases; cell culture models of motor neuron diseases, including amyotrophic lateral sclerosis and toxic neuropathies; and therapy of motor neuron diseases. *Type:* Research center.

McGill University
McConnell Brain Imaging Centre
3801 University St. Ph: (514)398-8926
Montreal, PQ, Canada H3A Fax: (514)398-8948
 2B4
E-mail: alan@bic.mni.mcgill.ca
URL: http://www.bic.mni.mcgill.ca
Contact: Alan C. Evans, PhD, Coord.

Desc: Investigates cerebral function using positron emission tomography (PET) and magnetic resonance imaging (MRI) on healthy volunteers and patients with brain tumors, epilepsy, movement disorders, and other acute and chronic neurological illnesses. Research areas include radiochemistry, imaging physics, mapping of cognitive functions in the brain, kinetic analysis, and modeling of biological systems. *Type:* Research center.

McGill University
Montreal Neurological Institute
3801 University St., Rm. 636 Ph: (514)398-1903
Montreal, PQ, Canada H3A Fax: (514)398-8248
 2B4
E-mail: director@mni.lan.mcgill.ca
URL: http://www.mcgill.ca/mni
Contact: Dr. Richard Murphy, Dir.

Desc: Organic aspects of the nervous system, including studies in molecular neurobiology, neuroanatomy, cerebrovascular disease, neurochemistry, epilepsy, neurogenetics, neuroimaging, neuro-immunology, movement disorders, neuromuscular research, neuro-oncology, neuropharmacology, and neuropsychology. *Type:* Research center.

McGill University
Montreal Neurological Institute
Complex Neural Systems
3801 University St.   Ph: (514)398-1913
Montreal, PQ, Canada H3A   Fax: (514)398-5871
  2B4
Contact: Dr. B.E. Jones, Coord.
Desc: Neurobiology. *Type:* Research center.

McGill University
Montreal Neurological Institute
Neuro-Immunology Laboratory
3801 University St.   Ph: (514)398-8531
Montreal, PQ, Canada H3A   Fax: (514)398-7371
  2B4
E-mail: mdan@musica.mcgill.ca
Contact: Dr. Jack Antel, Contact.
Desc: Neuroimmunology, including multiple sclerosis and related disorders. *Type:* Research center.

McGill University
Montreal Neurological Institute
Neuro-Isotope Laboratory
3801 University, Rm. 688   Ph: (514)398-8515
Montreal, PQ, Canada H3A   Fax: (514)398-8540
  2B4
Contact: Dr. Mirko Diksik, Contact.
Desc: Brain cancer, including metabolic characteristics, pharmacokinetics of antitumor agents, and neurotoxicity of antitumor agents. Uses multitracer autoradiographic methods and positron emission tomography (PET) to study brain tumors and cerebral ischemia. *Type:* Research center.

MCP Hahnemann University of the Health Sciences
Center for Neurovirology and Neurooncology
Broad & Vine, Mail Stop 406   Ph: (215)762-3221
Philadelphia, PA 19102-1192
URL: http://www.auhs.edu/medschool/centers/
ctrnvnonc.html
Contact: Kamel Khalili, PhD, Dir.
Desc: Neurologic disorders. *Type:* Research center.

MCP Hahnemann University of the Health Sciences
Center for Neurovirology and Neurooncology
Laboratory of Molecular Neurobiology
Broad & Vine, Mail Stop 406   Ph: (215)762-3221
Philadelphia, PA 19102-1192
URL: http://www.auhs.edu/medschool/centers/
ctrnvnonc.html
Contact: Ellen Meier, PhD, Dir.
Desc: Molecular determinants of pathogenesis in viral and genetic diseases. *Type:* Research center.

MCP Hahnemann University of the Health Sciences
Center for Neurovirology and Neurooncology
Laboratory of Molecular Neurovirology
Broad & Vine, Mail Stop 406   Ph: (215)762-3221
Philadelphia, PA 19102-1192
URL: http://www.auhs.edu/medschool/centers/
ctrnvnonc.html

Contact: Kamel Khalili, PhD, Dir.

Desc: Molecular pathogenesis of viral-induced neurological disorders, molecular mechanisms involved in the formation and progression of brain tumors, and development of a viral vector for gene delivery in the brain. *Type:* Research center.

MCP Hahnemann University of the Health Sciences
Center for Neurovirology and Neurooncology
Laboratory of Molecular Retrovirology
Broad & Vine, Mail Stop 406   Ph: (215)762-3221
Philadelphia, PA 19102-1192
URL: http://www.auhs.edu/medschool/centers/
ctrnvnonc.html

Contact: Prof. Shohreh Amini, MD, Dir.

Desc: Molecular retrovirology with an emphasis on regulation of HIV-1 gene expression in central nervous system cells and the mechanism of cytokine regulation by HIV-1 regulatory proteins. *Type:* Research center.

MCP Hahnemann University of the Health Sciences
Center for Neurovirology and Neurooncology
Laboratory of Molecular Therapeutics
Broad & Vine, Mail Stop 406   Ph: (215)762-6050
Philadelphia, PA 19102-1192   Fax: (215)762-3241
E-mail: rappaportj@auhs.edu
URL: http://www.auhs.edu/medschool/centers/
ctrnvnonc.html

Contact: Jay F. Rappaport, PhD, Dir.

Desc: Treatment of viral-induced neurological disorders and brain tumors using a molecular therapeutic strategy featuring RNA and DNA molecules; the molecular pathogenesis of HIV-1 induced neurological disorders with an emphasis on the study of chemokines and their receptors in the neuropathogenesis of AIDS; and HIV vaccine development. *Type:* Research center.

MCP Hahnemann University of the Health Sciences
Center for Neurovirology and Neurooncology
Laboratory of Neuro-AIDS
Broad & Vine, Mail Stop 406   Ph: (215)762-3221
Philadelphia, PA 19102-1192
URL: http://www.auhs.edu/medschool/centers/
ctrnvnonc.html

Contact: Danuta Kozbor, PhD, Dir.

Desc: Human immunodeficiency virus (HIV) bacterial antigens. *Type:* Research center.

MCP Hahnemann University of the Health Sciences
Center for Neurovirology and Neurooncology
Laboratory of Neuro-Immunology
Broad & Vine, Mail Stop 406   Ph: (215)762-3221
Philadelphia, PA 19102-1192   Fax: (215)762-1898
E-mail: kalmanb@auhs.edu
URL: http://www.auhs.edu/medschool/centers/
ctrnvnonc.html

Contact: Dr. Bernadette Kalman, PhD, Dir.

Desc: Molecular pathogenesis of multiple sclerosis. *Type:* Research center.

MCP Hahnemann University of the Health Sciences
Center for Neurovirology and Neurooncology
Laboratory of Neuropathology
Broad & Vine, Mail Stop 406   Ph: (215)762-3221
Philadelphia, PA 19102-1192   Fax: (215)246-5918
URL: http://www.auhs.edu/medschool/centers/
ctrnvnonc.html

Contact: Sidney Croul, MD, Dir. of Neuropathology.

Desc: Viral infection of the brain and the effect of pathobiological alternatives. *Type:* Research center.

MCP Hahnemann University of the Health Sciences
Center for Neurovirology and Neurooncology
Laboratory of Neurovirology
Broad & Vine, Mail Stop 406   Ph: (215)762-3221
Philadelphia, PA 19102-1192
URL: http://www.auhs.edu/medschool/centers/
ctrnvnonc.html

Contact: Jaymohan Joseph, PhD, Dir.

Desc: Molecular basis for the involvement of the blood-brain barrier in trafficking of inflammatory cells and neurotropic viruses (HIV-1, MHV-4) in the central nervous system, and identification of central nervous system endothelial specific compounds mediating viral infection of the brain. *Type:* Research center.

MCP Hahnemann University of the Health Sciences
Clinical Neuroscience Research Unit
3200 Henry Ave.   Ph: (215)842-4208
Philadelphia, PA 19129   Fax: (215)842-4321

Contact: Dr. Emil F. Coccaro, Dir.

Desc: Nervous system development, regeneration, and repair following injury; and the biology of contractile systems, including muscle and other cells. *Type:* Research center.

MCP Hahnemann University of the Health Sciences
Mid Atlantic Regional Epilepsy Center
3300 Henry Ave.   Ph: (215)842-7706
Philadelphia, PA 19129   Fax: (215)848-2035
E-mail: jacobson@auhs.edu

Contact: Dr. Mercedes Jacobson, Dir.

Desc: Epileptic seizure detection, including seizure detection apparatus studies. *Type:* Research center.

MCP Hahnemann University of the Health Sciences
Movement Disorders Center
1427 Vine St., 1st Fl.   Ph: (215)762-6891
Philadelphia, PA 19102   Fax: (215)246-5043
E-mail: azizi@allegheny.edu
URL: http://www.allegheny.edu

Contact: Dr. Azizi, Med. Advisor.

Desc: Huntington's disease (HD), a hereditary brain disorder, including neuropsychological and electrophysiological studies, psychological problems in HD families, cultured fibroblasts in HD, and miscellaneous chemical studies in HD. Acts as a focal point for the development and support of various regional research projects concerned with Huntington's disease and other genetically determined disorders of the nervous system. *Type:* Research center.

Medical College of Georgia

Alzheimer's Research Center for Clinical and Basic Research
Department of Pharmacology & Ph: (706)721-6355
Toxicology Fax: (706)721-9861
Augusta, GA 30912-2300
E-mail: jbuccafu@mail.mcg.edu
URL: http://www.mcg.edu/centers/alz
Contact: Dr. Jerry J. Buccafusco, Coord.
Desc: Multidisciplinary research on all aspects of Alzheimer's disease, including new therapeutic approaches, diagnostic procedures, and basic studies of etiology. Type: Research center.

Monell Chemical Senses Center
3500 Market St. Ph: (215)898-8878
Philadelphia, PA 19104-3308 Fax: (215)898-2084
E-mail: beauchamp@monell.org
URL: http://www.monell.org
Contact: Dr. Gary K. Beauchamp, Dir.
Desc: Mechanisms and functions of the chemical senses (taste, smell) and chemesthesis, chemical irritation, including studies in the areas of biochemistry, biophysics, endocrinology, physiology, ethology, neurology, behavior, genetics, psychophysics, nutrition, organic chemistry, chemical ecology, and zoology. Research relates to solutions of problems in nutrition, environmental odors, reproduction, disease diagnosis, expansion of world food supply, and alternative means of vertebrate pest control. Type: Research center.

Monell-Jefferson Taste and Smell Research Center
925 Chestnut St., 6th Fl. Ph: (215)955-5652
Philadelphia, PA 19107 Fax: (215)923-4532
E-mail: info@monell.org
URL: http://www.monell.org
Contact: Beverly J. Cowart, PhD, Clin.Dir.
Desc: Smell and taste disorders using a multidisciplinary approach (psychophysical, biophysical, medical, and dental). Type: Research center.

Mount Sinai School of Medicine of City University of New York

Alzheimer's Disease Research Center
Department of Psychiatry Ph: (212)824-7008
1425 Madison Ave. Fax: (212)860-3945
New York, NY 10029
E-mail: kdavis@smtplink.mssm.edu
Contact: Dr. Kenneth L. Davis, Contact.
Desc: Etiology, diagnosis, and treatment of Alzheimer's disease and related dementias. Clinical studies include trials of new drugs and biological markers and longitudinal follow-up studies. Type: Research center.

Multiple Sclerosis Foundation
6350 N. Andrews Ave. Ph: (954)776-6805
Fort Lauderdale, FL 33309-2130 Free: 800-441-7055
Fax: (305)938-8708
E-mail: mssupport@msfacts.org
URL: http://www.msfacts.org
Contact: Jules Kuperberg, Contact.
Desc: Provides funding toward research into the cause, prevention, treatment, and cure of multiple sclerosis. Type: Association.

Muscular Dystrophy Association
3300 E. Sunrise Dr. Ph: (520)529-2000
Tucson, AZ 85718 Fax: (520)529-5300
E-mail: mda@mdausa.org
URL: http://www.mdausa.org
Contact: Robert Ross, Sr. VP & Exec.Dir.

Desc: National voluntary health agency fostering research into the cause and cure of neuromuscular diseases in the following 8 categories. Type: Association.

Myasthenia Gravis Foundation of America
123 W. Madison, Ste. 800 Ph: (312)853-0522
Chicago, IL 60602-4503 Free: 800-541-5454
Fax: (312)853-0523
E-mail: myastheniagravis@msn.com
URL: http://www.myasthenia.org
Contact: Edward S. Trainer, Exec.Dir.
Desc: Persons suffering from myasthenia gravis; their families, doctors, and nurses; others dedicated to the detection, treatment, and cure of MG. Raises funds for research and for professional and public education programs. Provides literature. Type: Association.

National Coalition for Research in Neurological Disorders
1250 24th St. NW, Ste. 300 Ph: (202)293-5453
Washington, DC 20037 Fax: (202)466-0585
E-mail: morgdowney@aol.com
URL: http://www.brainnet.org
Contact: Morgan Downey, Contact.
Desc: Neurological research, focusing on funding. Also lobbies for increased funding for training and research. Type: Research center.

National Multiple Sclerosis Society
733 3rd Ave. Ph: (212)986-3240
New York, NY 10017 Free: 800-FIGHT-MS
Fax: (212)986-7981
E-mail: nat@nmss.org
URL: http://www.nmss.org
Contact: Gen. Michael Dugan, Pres. & CEO.
Desc: Stimulates, supports, and coordinates research into the cause, treatment, and cure of multiple sclerosis; provides services for persons with MS and related diseases and their families; aids in establishing MS clinics and therapy centers. Conducts Creative Will, biennial competition for artists with MS. Maintains numerous committees including international and research and medical programs, and services. Type: Association.

National Multiple Sclerosis Society - Georgia Chapter
12 Perimeter Center E., Ste. Free: 800-822-3379
1200 Fax: (770)984-9352
Atlanta, GA 30346
E-mail: gamssociety@mmdspring.com
URL: http://www.nmss.org
Contact: Terri Pendergast, Pres.
Desc: Coordinates multiple sclerosis research. Type: Association.

National Multiple Sclerosis Society, Greater North Jersey Chapter
1 Kalisa Way, Ste. 310 Ph: (201)967-5599
Paramus, NJ 07652-3550 Free: 800-833-0087
Fax: (201)967-7085
E-mail: chapter@njb.nmss.org
Contact: Nancy P. Lorenzi, Pres.
Desc: Coordinates multiple sclerosis programs and services in northern New Jersey area. Type: Association.

National Neurofibromatosis Foundation
95 Pine St., 16th Fl. Ph: (212)344-6633
New York, NY 10005 Free: 800-323-7938
Fax: (212)747-0004
E-mail: nnf@nf.org
URL: http://www.nf.org/
Contact: Peter Bellermann, Pres.
Desc: Persons with neurofibromatosis and their families. (Neurofibromatosis is the most common neurological disorder caused by a single gene.). Sponsors scientific research to find treatments and a cure for neurofibromatosis. Type: Association.

National Parkinson Foundation
1501 NW 9th Ave. Ph: (305)547-6666
Bob Hope Parkinson's Research Free: 800-327-4545
Center Fax: (305)548-4403
Miami, FL 33136
E-mail: mailbox@npf.med.miami.edu
URL: http://www.parkinson.org
Contact: Nathan Slewett, Chairperson.
Desc: Doctors, nurses, scientists, pharmacologists, and therapists who research, diagnose, and treat Parkinsonism. Supports basic and clinical research for Parkinsonism and related neurological disorders and provides physical, speech, and occupational therapy. NPF is associated with the University of Miami School of Medicine, and supports the National Parkinson Institute, which provides diagnosis, treatment, care, and rehabilitation. Type: Association.

National Science Foundation
Directorate for Biological Sciences
Division of Integrative Biology and Neuroscience
Developmental Neuroscience Program
4201 Wilson Blvd., Rm. 685 Ph: (703)306-1423
Arlington, VA 22230 Fax: (703)306-0349
E-mail: lkromer@nsf.gov
URL: http://www.nsf.gov
Contact: Lawrence Kromer, Dir.
Desc: Supports research on the factors that influence the formation, growth, and aging of the nervous system; how neurons and glia differentiate and regenerate; how connections between neurons are formed and maintained; and the interactions of environmental and genetic factors in neural development. Type: Research center.

National Science Foundation
Directorate for Biological Sciences
Division of Integrative Biology and Neuroscience
Neuroscience Program
4201 Wilson Blvd., Rm. 685 Ph: (703)306-1423
Arlington, VA 22230 Fax: (703)306-0349
Contact: Dr. Bruce Umminger, Dir.
Desc: Neuroscience. Type: Research center.

National Science Foundation
Directorate for Biological Sciences
Division of Integrative Biology and Neuroscience
Sensory Systems Program
4201 Wilson Blvd., Rm. 685 Ph: (703)306-1416
Arlington, VA 22230 Fax: (703)306-0349
E-mail: cplatt@nsf.gov
Contact: Christopher Platt, Prog.Off.
Desc: Sensory systems. Type: Research center.

National Spasmodic Torticollis Association
PO Box 424 Ph: (715)516-1824
Mukwonago, WI 53149 Free: 800-HUR-TFUL
Fax: (715)516-1824
Contact: Patricia Murray, Exec.Dir.
Desc: Persons afflicted with spasmodic torticollis (ST), a syndrome in which the muscles on one side of the neck contract and pull the head to the side, sometimes pushing the chin up or down. ST usually occurs in adults and can sometimes be treated successfully with medication and physical therapy. Educates the public on ST so that persons with early symptoms know to seek proper medical help from a neurologist or neurosurgeon. Type: Association.

National Tuberous Sclerosis Association

8181 Professional Place, Ste. 110 — Ph: (301)459-9888
Landover, MD 20785 — Free: 800-225-6872
E-mail: ntsa@capcon.net — Fax: (301)459-0394
URL: http://www.ntsa.org
Contact: Barbara K. Witten, Pres.

Desc: Encourages and provides grants for research into the diagnosis, cause, management, and cure of tuberous sclerosis. (Tuberous sclerosis is a genetic disease characterized by one or more of the following: epileptic seizures, mental retardation, behavioral problems, tumors, or skin lesions.) Provides support to families affected by the disease through a nationwide network of volunteer area representatives and the distribution of informational packets. Conducts educational programs for medical and allied professionals. Type: Association.

Neuropsychiatric Research Institute

PO Box 1415 — Ph: (701)293-1335
Fargo, ND 58107-1415 — Fax: (701)293-3226
E-mail: email@nrifargo.comm
URL: http://www.arifargo.com
Contact: James E. Mitchell, MD, Pres.

Desc: Basic and clinical studies of the central nervous system. Specific applications include eating disorders and stroke. Type: Research center.

NeuroScience Network

Administrative Office — Ph: (514)934-8290
1650 Cedar Ave., Rm. L7-132 — Fax: (514)934-8216
Montreal, PQ, Canada H3G 1A4
E-mail: nsnet@is.mgh.mcgill.ca
URL: http://www.cns.ucalgary.ca/nce
Contact: Warren C. Bull, Exec.Dir.

Desc: Concentrates on development of gene technology; enhancement of neuronal survival; promotion of sprouting and regeneration; identification and use of neurotrophic factors; restitution of motor function; and identification of molecules that inhibit regeneration. Type: Research center.

The Neurosciences Institute

10640 John Jay Hopkins Dr. — Ph: (619)626-2000
San Diego, CA 92121 — Fax: (619)626-2099
E-mail: info@nsi.edu
URL: http://www.nsi.edu
Contact: W. Einar Gall, Res.Dir.

Desc: Promotes conceptual and theoretical progress in understanding the function of the nervous system at all levels, particularly higher functions of the brain (perception, memory, sensation) and their implications in understanding human behavior. A research program for resident Institute Fellows in theoretical neurobiology provides training in methods used to construct neural theories and develops theoretical models of neural systems that are biologically sound and experimentally testable at synaptic, cellular, and network levels. Type: Research center.

New England Medical Center Hospitals, Inc.

Electromyography Laboratory

750 Washington Ave. — Ph: (617)636-7580
Neurology Department EMG. — Fax: (617)636-9124
Box 314
Boston, MA 02111
E-mail: william.brown@es.nemc.org
Contact: Dr. William Brown, Dir.

Desc: Electrical studies of nerves and muscles to aid in the research and diagnosis of muscular dystrophy, amyotrophic lateral sclerosis, and other polyneuropathies. Type: Research center.

New York University

Center for Neural Science

4 Washington Pl., Rm. 809 — Ph: (212)998-7780
New York, NY 10003 — Fax: (212)995-4011
E-mail: cns@nyu.edu
URL: http://www.cns.nyu.edu

Contact: Prof. J. Anthony Movshon, Dir.

Desc: Neural science studies, ranging from molecular and cellular aspects to fully integrated systems and cognitive approaches. Specific research includes cell biological mechanisms underlying plasticity and stability of neurons; new sprout formation by adult mammalian neurons; drive and hedonic mechanisms in the brain and how they interact; use of image analysis procedures to study the functional anatomy of sensorimotor integration in the rat brain; neural processes that generate movements; genetic and molecular manipulations in the fruit fly to study the interplay between plasticity and programming in the nervous system; amino acid regulation of dopamine utilization under basal and stress conditions using a variety of techniques, including in vivo microdialysis; individual neurons in visual perception; magnetic fields accompanying the flow of currents within the brain's neurons; effects of developmental visual disorders on the structure and function of the visual system; problems of color vision using both psychophysical and electrophysical techniques; modeling of the human visual system; identification of the neural systems and cellular mechanisms used by the brain to assign emotional significance to sensory stimuli; the acquisition of color information, fusion of visual information from multiple sources, signal detection theory, and visual calibration; analysis of functional properties of neurons; and mathematical and computational models of complex behaviors.

New York University

Jerry Lewis Neuromuscular Disease Center

Department of Rehabilitation — Ph: (212)263-6350
Med. — Fax: (212)263-5499
400 E. 34th St., Rm. RG 29
New York, NY 10016

Contact: Dr. Mathew Lee, Prof. & Chm.

Desc: Diagnosis and clinical care of patients disabled by neuromuscular disease. Type: Research center.

New York University

Medical Center Head Trauma Program

660 1st Ave. — Ph: (212)263-6806
New York, NY 10010 — Fax: (212)263-6807
E-mail: yehuda.ben-yishay@ccmail.med.nyc.edu

Contact: Dr. Yehuda Ben-Yishay, Dir.

Desc: Young adults suffering from head injuries. Conducts systematic remedial training in attention and concentration, various aspects of perception, perceptual-motor integration (eye-hand integration), and logical reasoning and interpersonal skills. Type: Research center.

New York University Medical Center

Millhauser Laboratories

550 1st Ave. — Ph: (212)263-5717
New York, NY 10016 — Fax: (212)263-7513
E-mail: afriedhoff@ingen.com

Contact: Dr. Arnold J. Friedhoff, Dir.

Desc: Basic and clinical neurobiological approaches to adaptive mechanisms in brain, including molecular biology and neuropharmacology. Type: Research center.

New York University Medical Center

Nathan Kline Institute for Psychiatric Research

Center for Alzheimer's Disease Research

140 Old Orangeburg Rd. — Ph: (914)398-5423
Orangeburg, NY 10962 — Fax: (914)398-5422
E-mail: nixon@nki.rfmh.org
URL: http://www.rfmh.org/nki
Contact: Dr. Ralph Nixon, Dir.

Desc: Molecular neuroscience and aging, including molecular neurobiology of proteases, signal transduction, neurodegenerative disease, protein/peptide analytical techniques, molecular genetics, vesicle biology, transgenic modeling. Type: Research center.

North American Spine Society

6300 N. River Rd., Ste. 500 — Ph: (847)698-1630
Rosemont, IL 60018-4231 — Fax: (847)823-8668
URL: http://www.spine.org
Contact: Eric J. Muehlbauer, Exec.Dir.

Desc: Educational organization of physicians, osteopaths, orthopedists, neurosurgeons, physiatrists, radiologists, and other professionals interested in the human spine. Works to improve the quality of scientific practice in spinal disorders; exchange ideas and disseminate scientific information about clinical techniques; investigate and propagate methods by which malfunction of the spine can be corrected. Type: Association.

Northwestern University

Institute for Neuroscience

320 E. Superior St. — Ph: (312)503-4300
Chicago, IL 60611 — Fax: (312)503-7345
E-mail: e-mugnaini@nwu.edu
URL: http://www.nwu.edu/nuin/
Contact: Dr. Enrico Mugnaini, Dir.

Desc: Sensory neurobiology and psychophysics, neuroendocrinology, biological rhythms, neural development and plasticity, electrophysiology and pharmacology of excitable membranes, and neuroimmunology and virology. Type: Research center.

Northwestern University

Spinal Cord Injury Center

250 E. Superior, Rm. 619 — Ph: (312)908-3425
Chicago, IL 60611 — Fax: (312)908-1819
E-mail: dfelten@nwu.edu
URL: http://www.nwu.edu/spine
Contact: Dr. Paul R. Meyer, Jr., Prog.Dir.

Desc: Health services for the spinal cord injured, including studies on cost-effectiveness of systematic care and the feasibility of expanding and improving community resources. Seeks to develop a multidisciplinary continuous system of comprehensive health services that meet the wide range of needs of persons severely disabled by a spinal cord injury: from point of injury requiring emergency treatment and evacuation, through acute care, rehabilitation, vocational and educational preparation, community job placement, and long-term follow-up. Type: Research center.

Ohio State University

Neuroscience Program

3082 Graves Hall — Ph: (614)292-4769
333 W. 10th Ave. — Fax: (614)292-0490
Columbus, OH 43210
E-mail: hinkle.3@osu.edu
URL: http://www.med.ohiostate.edu/neuro/neurohome.html
Contact: Dr. James S. King, Ch.

Desc: Spinal cord injury, tumor biology, neuromuscular disease, epilepsy, Parkinson Disease, multiple sclerosis, stroke, neural development, regeneration, plasticity, regeneration, molecular neurobiology, and neuroimmunology. Type: Research center.

Ohio State University
Sleep Disorders Center

Rhodes Hall, Rm. S1039   Ph: (614)293-8260
410 W. 10th   Fax: (614)293-4506
Columbus, OH 43210
URL: http://www.osu.edu

Contact: Dr. Charles Pollak, Dir.

Desc: Diagnosis of impotence, applications of pharmaceutical agents in depression and other psychiatric disorders in adults, and disorders of sleep and arousal. Techniques include psychometric laboratory evaluation, monitoring sleep/awake disorders by all-night polysomnographic recordings, penile tumescence studies, multiple sleep latency studies, and electronic pupillometry. *Type:* Research center.

Ohio State University
Spinal Cord Injury Research Center

403 Hamilton Hall   Ph: (614)292-4953
1645 Neil Ave.   Fax: (614)292-0577
Columbus, OH 43210
E-mail: stokes.1@osu.edu

Contact: Bradford T. Stokes, PhD, Dir.

Desc: Mechanical and histological parameters of cord injury, mechanisms of membrane injury, microenvironment of spinal cord tissues after impact injury, gangliosides metabolism in traumatized nerve, reorganization of sensory mechanisms after spinal lesions, effects of nerve on limb regeneration, and ontogeny and remodeling of spinal systems in the opossum. Examines sequelae of spinal cord injury in terms of cellular and molecular mechanisms of degeneration and regeneration, which are understood through study of the developing nervous system. *Type:* Research center.

Oregon Health Sciences University
Neurological Sciences Institute

1120 NW 20th Ave.   Ph: (503)413-7217
Portland, OR 97209-1595   Fax: (503)413-7229

Contact: Paul J. Cordo, PhD, Ch.

Desc: Research goal is to increase the knowledge and understanding of the structure and function of the nervous system, from the level of the molecule to the level of the brain and sensory organs. Examines the function of the nervous and sensory systems in the following five areas: dizziness and balance disorders; pain and other somatosensory disorders; visual disorders; neuronal development and regeneration; and movement control disorders. *Type:* Research center.

Paralyzed Veterans of America
Spinal Cord Research Foundation

801 18th St. NW   Ph: (202)416-7659
Washington, DC 20006-3517   Free: 800-424-8200
    Fax: (202)416-7641
E-mail: tracys@pva.org
URL: http://www.pva.org

Desc: Clinical, psychosocial, and technological aspects of spinal cord injury or dysfunction. *Type:* Research center.

Parkinson's Disease Foundation

710 West 168th St.   Ph: (212)923-4700
3rd Fl.   Free: 800-457-6676
New York, NY 10032   Fax: (212)923-4778

Contact: Robin Elliott, Exec.Dir.

Desc: Raises funds for support of scientific research into causes, prevention, and cure of Parkinson's disease. *Type:* Association.

Princeton University
Cutaneous Communication Laboratory

Psychology Dept.   Ph: (609)258-5277
Green Hall   Fax: (609)258-1113
Princeton, NJ 08544-1010
E-mail: rcholewi@princeton.edu
URL: http://www.princeton.edu/~pucclabs
Contact: Dr. Roger W. Cholewiak, Prin.Invest.

Desc: Sensory psychophysiology and experimental psychology, including experimental investigations in all phases of cutaneous sensitivity with special reference to utilization of data in communication systems, under conditions of sensory handicap, or when other sensory modalities are overloaded. Research includes studies of pattern recognition and discrimination with psychophysical procedures and scaling techniques, including multidimensional designs; more elementary dimensions of tactile experience; and the interrelations of various dimensions of touch. *Type:* Research center.

Rehabilitation Institute of Toronto
Sleep Research Laboratory

550 University Ave.   Ph: (416)597-3078
Toronto, ON, Canada M5G   Fax: (416)597-8959
2A2
Contact: Dr. T. Douglas Bradley, Dir.

Desc: Disturbances of breathing during sleep, including the mechanisms underlying sleep apnea disorders and possible treatments. Projects include research on breathing and oxygenation during sleep in patients with congestive heart failure in whom heart failure may be related to, or aggravated by, nocturnal ventilatory disturbances. *Type:* Research center.

Rehabilitation Institute of Toronto
Stroke Rehabilitation Unit

550 University Ave.   Ph: (416)597-5111
Toronto, ON, Canada M5G   Fax: (416)597-1977
2A2
E-mail: hajek@sprint.ca
Contact: Dr. V.E. Hajek, Contact.

Desc: Monitors and evaluates aspects of the rehabilitation experience on the Stroke Unit, including patients' response and progress to different therapies and treatments, and to orthotic devices and aids. Also participates in a study of mood disorders and cognitive impairment resulting from stroke. *Type:* Research center.

Research and Training Center on Community Integration of Individuals With Traumatic Brain Injury

Mount Sinai Medical Center   Ph: (212)241-7917
1 Gustave L. Levy Pl., Box 1240
New York, NY 10029
URL: http://academic.mssm.edu/tbinet/content.htm
Contact: Naomi Tyler Lloyds, Contact.

Desc: Community integration of traumatic brain injury (TBI) survivors, including increasing understanding of how TBI affects community integration, developing new models of community integration, and treating cognitive/behavioral disorders that most affect the TBI survivor's functioning within the community. *Type:* Research center.

Rockefeller University
Laboratory of Neuroendocrinology

1230 York Ave.   Ph: (212)327-8624
Box 165   Fax: (212)327-8634
New York, NY 10021-6399
E-mail: mcewen@rockvax.rockefeller.edu
Contact: Bruce S. McEwen, Hd.

Desc: Seeks to locate brain sites and understand the mechanisms by which hormones promote neural plasticity and thereby alter endocrine function, behavior, neurological states, and mood. Also studies the influence of gonadal and adrenal hormones on aging in the brain. *Type:* Research center.

Rush University
Biological Rhythms Research Laboratory

Rush-Presbyterian-St. Luke's   Ph: (312)942-8328
   Med.Ctr.   Fax: (312)942-6050
1653 W. Congress Pkwy.
Chicago, IL 60612
E-mail: ceastman@rush.edu

Contact: Charmane Eastman, PhD, Dir.

Desc: Human circadian rhythms, focusing on the use of bright light, melatonin and exercise for adaptation to night shift work. *Type:* Research center.

Rush University
Multiple Sclerosis Center

1725 W. Harrison St., Ste. 309   Ph: (312)942-8011
Chicago, IL 60612   Fax: (312)942-2253

Contact: Floyd A. Davis, MD, Dir.

Desc: Multiple sclerosis, including understanding of nerve impulse conduction in both normal and pathologic states and pathophysiology of conduction in multiple sclerosis and allied demyelinating conditions, improving conduction in diseased nerves by pharmacologic therapy, and development of a detailed molecular model of the organization of the ion-specific channels of the nerve membrane. Patient studies include programs in neuroactive drugs, thermolability phenomena, analysis of individual's psychological stresses and the resulting coping mechanisms, and the effect of disease on children of patients and the overall family unit. *Type:* Research center.

Rush University
Rush Alzheimer's Disease Center

710 S. Paulina   Ph: (312)942-4463
8 North   Fax: (312)942-4154
Chicago, IL 60612
URL: http://www.rush.edu

Contact: Dr. Jacob H. Fox, Co-Dir.

Desc: Alzheimer's disease, including causes, treatment, and cure. Conducts clinical trials of new drug treatments and analyzes potential risk factors in the development of Alzheimer's disease. *Type:* Research center.

Rush University
Rush Neuroscience Institute

Rush-Presbyterian-St. Luke's   Ph: (312)942-8729
   Med. Ctr.   Fax: (312)942-2380
1653 W. Congress Pky.
Chicago, IL 60612
E-mail: jfox@neuro.rush.edu

Contact: Dr. Jacob H. Fox, Co-Dir.

Desc: Alzheimer's disease, Parkinson's disease, and stroke, including community-based studies, clinical investigations, and laboratory investigations using brain tissue and animal experimentation. Studies also focus on development of new drugs to improve symptoms of multiple sclerosis. *Type:* Research center.

Rutgers University
Center for Molecular and Behavioral Neuroscience

197 University Ave.   Ph: (973)353-1080
Newark, NJ 07102   Fax: (973)353-1760
E-mail: tallal@axon.rutgers.edu
URL: http://www.cmbn.rutgers.edu

Contact: Dr. Paula Tallal, Co-Dir.

Desc: Molecular and behavioral neuroscience research for applications to behavioral dysfunctions in humans. Serves as a technology transfer unit between the University and industry. *Type:* Research center.

Scripps Research Institute

Department of Neuropharmacology

10550 N. Torrey Pines Rd.
La Jolla, CA 92037
Ph: (619)784-9730
Fax: (619)784-8851
E-mail: fbloom@scripps.edu

Contact: Dr. Floyd E. Bloom, Dir.

Desc: Mechanisms of cellular communication in the nervous and endocrine systems. Primary areas of research include: the molecular identification of chemical messengers (neurotransmitters and hormones) and characterization of the structure and function of the cells that secrete them; establishing the role of these substances in normal physiological regulation; establishing the possible pathophysiological roles in clinical disorders of the brain and endocrine system; employing molecular genetic methods to detect virus-selected pathologic mechanisms; interactions between neurotransmitters, cytokines, neurons, glia, and brain macrophages in virus or neurodegenerative disorders; and mechanisms of actions of addictive drugs. *Type:* Research center.

Society for Neuroscience

11 Dupont Cir. NW, Ste. 500
Washington, DC 20036
Ph: (202)462-6688
URL: http://www.sfn.org

Contact: Nancy Beang, Exec.Dir.

Desc: Scientists engaged in research relating to the nervous system. Seeks to advance understanding of nervous systems, including their relation to behavior, by bringing together scientists of various backgrounds and by facilitating research at all levels of biological organization. Maintains central source of information on interdisciplinary curricula and training programs in the neurosciences. *Type:* Association.

Solomon Park Research Institute

12815 NE 124th St., Ste. I
Kirkland, WA 98034-8313
Ph: (425)821-7005
Fax: (425)821-5508
E-mail: spri@solomon.org
URL: http://www.solomon.edu

Contact: Patric A. Clapshaw, PhD, Dir.

Desc: Amyotrophic lateral sclerosis (ALS), also known as Lou Gehrig's Disease, including androgenic determinants and viral causes. *Type:* Research center.

Southern California Neuropsychiatric Institute

6794 La Jolla Blvd.
La Jolla, CA 92037
Ph: (619)454-2102
Fax: (619)454-2104
E-mail: asialangscngpi@general.com

Contact: Dr. Sydney Walker, III, Dir.

Desc: Sleep disorders, post-concussion syndrome, and hyperactivity. *Type:* Research center.

Stanford University

Center for Research on Sleep and Circadian Rhythm

701 Welch Rd., Ste. 2226
Palo Alto, CA 94304
Ph: (650)723-8134
Fax: (650)725-7341
E-mail: dement@leland.stanford.edu

Contact: Dr. William C. Dement, Dir.

Desc: Sleep, including brain mechanisms which control transitions between sleep and wakefulness, transitions between sleep states, and the circadian timing between those various states. *Type:* Research center.

Stanford University

Stanford Pain Management Service

Med. Ctr.
300 Pasteur Dr., Rm. 408A
Stanford, CA 94305
Ph: (650)723-6238
Fax: (650)725-7743

Contact: Raymond Gaeta, MD, Dir.

Desc: Pain mechanisms, actions of analgesic substances, and pharmacokinetic and pharmacodynamic modeling. *Type:* Research center.

State University of New York Health Science Center at Brooklyn

Neurodynamic Laboratory

Department of Psychiatry
450 Clarkson Ave., Box 1203
Brooklyn, NY 11203
Ph: (718)270-2024
Fax: (718)270-4081
E-mail: hb@sv2.neurodyn.hscbklyn.edu

Contact: Henri Begleiter, Dir.

Desc: Use of evoked brain potentials to assess central nervous system changes due to alcoholism and drug addiction. *Type:* Research center.

Sun Health Research Institute

Alzheimer's Center

PO Box 1278
Sun City, AZ 85372
Ph: (602)876-5466
Fax: (602)876-5461
URL: http://www.sunhealth.org

Contact: Dr. Joseph Rogers, Pres.

Desc: Alzheimer's disease causes and prevention. *Type:* Research center.

Sun Health Research Institute

Christopher Parkinson's Research Center

10515 W. Santa fe
PO Box 1278
Sun City, AZ 85372
Ph: (602)876-5439
Fax: (602)876-5695
E-mail: jjoyce@sunhealth.org

Contact: Jeffrey N. Joyce, PhD, Sr.Sci.

Desc: Parkinson's disease, focusing on treatment strategies and basic research on causes. *Type:* Research center.

Syracuse University

Institute for Sensory Research

Merrill Lane
Syracuse, NY 13244-5290
Ph: (315)443-4164
Fax: (315)443-1184
E-mail: bob_smith@isr.syr.edu
URL: http://128.230.6.180/inst.html

Contact: Dr. Robert L. Smith, Dir.

Desc: Sensory processes (hearing, vision, and touch) and orofacial biomechanics, using an interdisciplinary approach, including psychophysics, neurophysiology, neurochemistry, anatomy, cell biology, physiology, and biosimulation. Basic and applied research and development projects. *Type:* Research center.

Texas Tech University

Tarbox Parkinson's Disease Institute

Health Science Center
3601 4th St., Rm. 4A112
Lubbock, TX 79430
Ph: (806)743-2800
Fax: (806)743-1866
URL: http://www.ttuhsc.edu/pages/neuro/neurol.html

Desc: Neurophysical and neuropharmacological studies of the central nervous system of vertebrates as they relate to Parkinson's disease and other neurological disorders. *Type:* Research center.

Thomas Jefferson University

Neurosurgery Research Laboratories

1015 Chestnut St., 14th Fl.
Philadelphia, PA 19107
Ph: (215)955-6744
Fax: (215)923-8071

Contact: Frederick A. Simeone, MD, Ch.

Desc: Basic mechanisms involved in stroke and trauma including cytokine production, adhesion molecules, infartt size and edema formatiom in vitro and in vivo. Clinical influence of circadian rhythms and identification of hibernation triggers. *Type:* Research center.

Thomas Jefferson University

Regional Spinal Cord Injury Center of Delaware Valley

375 Main Bldg.
132 S. 10th St.
Philadelphia, PA 19107-5099
Ph: (215)955-6579
Fax: (215)955-5152
E-mail: ditunno1@jeflin.tju.edu
URL: http://jefline.tju.edu/spinalcord

Contact: Dr. John F. Ditunno, Jr., Proj.Dir.

Desc: Acute care and rehabilitation for individuals disabled by spinal cord injury. Collaborative research studies with other centers are conducted in the areas of quality of life, parenting with spinal cord injury, and program evaluation. *Type:* Research center.

Thomas Jefferson University

Sleep Disorders Center

Jefferson Med. Coll.
1025 Walnut St., Ste. 313
Philadelphia, PA 19107
Ph: (215)955-6175
Fax: (215)955-9783
E-mail: karl.doghramji@mail.tju.edu
URL: http://www.tju.edu

Contact: Karl Doghramji, MD, Dir.

Desc: Sleep/wake disorders or disorders which may have characteristic sleep markers. Also studies seasonal affective disorder; phototherapy for circadian rhythm disorders; and human sexuality, particularly erectile impotence; sleep apnea syndrome, narcolepsy insomnia, and daytime hypersomnia. *Type:* Research center.

Tourette Syndrome Association

42-40 Bell Blvd.
Bayside, NY 11361
Ph: (718)224-2999
Free: 800-237-0717
Fax: (718)279-9596
E-mail: tourette@ix.netcom.com

Contact: Judit Ungar, Exec.Dir.

Desc: People with Tourette Syndrome (TS) and their families and friends; physicians, nurses, teachers, psychologists, social workers, and other professionals; organizations such as mental health agencies. (TS is characterized by involuntary muscular movements and utterances of sounds or words, and is often undiagnosed or misdiagnosed.). Develops and disseminates educational materials to families, professionals, and agencies involved in health care, education, and governments. *Type:* Association.

Traumatic Brain Injury Update

University of Washington
Rehabilitation Medicine RJ-30
Seattle, WA 98195
Ph: (206)685-3999

Desc: Publishes abstracts of current world literature concerning diagnosis and management of individuals with brain injuries. Recurring features include news of research. *Type:* Newsletter.

Tufts-New England Medical Center

Brain Tumor Center

750 Washington St., Box 178
Boston, MA 02111
Ph: (617)636-5858
Fax: (617)636-7587
E-mail: julian.wu@es.nemc.org
URL: http://www.nemc.org/home/departments/adult/neurosur.htm

Contact: Dr. Julian Wu, Dir.

Desc: Treatment of brain tumors. Combines standard radiation treatment or chemotherapy with advanced neurosurgery and radiotherapy to control or shrink malignant gliomas. *Type:* Research center.

Tulane University

U.S.-Japan Biomedical Research Laboratories

| Hebert Res. Ctr. | Ph: (504)394-7199 |
| Belle Chasse, LA 70037 | Fax: (504)394-7169 |

E-mail: arimura@mailhist.tcs.tulane.edu

URL: http://www.mcl.tulans.edu

Contact: Dr. Akira Arimura, Dir.

Desc: Neuroendocrinology and neuroscience, particularly in the areas of neuropeptides and immune-neuroendocrine interactions. Studies include physiology of hypothalamic neurohormones with emphasis on isolation and characterization of novel hypophysiotrophic hormones and the role of cytokines in trophic brain function following injury. *Type:* Research center.

United Cerebral Palsy Association of Western New York

7 Community Dr.	Ph: (716)894-0130
Buffalo, NY 14225	Free: 800-390-8272
	Fax: (716)894-8257

Contact: Virginia Purcell, Exec.Dir.

Desc: Individuals in Erie, Cattaragus, Chautaugua, and Allegany counties, NY united to provide comprehensive services and programs to persons with cerebral palsy and similar disabilities. *Type:* Association.

United Parkinson Foundation

| 833 W. Washington Blvd. | Ph: (312)733-1893 |
| Chicago, IL 60607 | Fax: (312)733-1896 |

E-mail: upf_itf@msn.com

Contact: Judy Rosner, Exec.Dir.

Desc: Patients, family members, medical personnel and other interested persons. Assembles and publishes reliable information about symptoms, medications and therapy helpful to sufferers of Parkinson's disease and related illnesses. *Type:* Association.

U.S. Department of Defense

Army Medical Research and Materiel Command

Walter Reed Army Institute of Research

Division of Neurosciences

| Washington, DC 20307-5100 | Ph: (202)782-3037 |
| | Fax: (202)782-6910 |

Contact: Dr. G. Jean Kant, Dir.

Desc: Pertinent aspects of military medicine that involve the central nervous system. Research is performed to improve neuroprotection and treatment for combat casualty care, operational stress, infectious disease, and defense against biological and chemical threats. *Type:* Research center.

U.S. Department of Health and Human Services

National Institute on Aging

Laboratory of Neurosciences

NIH Bldg. 10, Rm. 6C103	Ph: (301)496-1765
10 Center Dr., MSC 1582	Fax: (301)402-0074
Bethesda, MD 20892-1582	

E-mail: sir@helix.nih.gov

Contact: Dr. Stanley Rapoport, Chf.

Desc: Function, structure, physiology, biochemistry, and pharmacology of the central and peripheral nervous system. Laboratory also examines changes that take place in these systems during development and aging in animal models and humans. *Type:* Research center.

U.S. Department of Health and Human Services

National Institute on Aging

Neuroscience and Neuropsychology of Aging Program

NIH Gateway Bldg., Ste. 3C307	Ph: (301)496-9350
7201 Wisconsin Ave. MSC9205	Fax: (301)496-1494
Bethesda, MD 20892-9205	

Desc: Normal and pathological aging of the nervous system and its behavioral consequences. Etiology or pathogenesis of Alzheimer's disease, improve diagnosis, and eventually provide a sound basis for effective therapy. *Type:* Research center.

U.S. Department of Health and Human Services

National Institute on Alcohol Abuse and Alcoholism

Basic Research Division

Neurosciences and Behavioral Research Branch

| 6000 Executive Blvd. | Ph: (301)443-4223 |
| Bethesda, MD 20892-7003 | Fax: (301)594-0673 |

E-mail: whunt@willco.niaaa.nih.gov

URL: http://www.niaaa.nih.gov

Contact: Walter A. Hunt, PhD, Chf.

Desc: Effect of alcohol on the brain and behavior. *Type:* Research center.

U.S. Department of Health and Human Services

National Institute of Diabetes and Digestive and Kidney Diseases

Laboratory of Neuroscience

NIH Bldg. 8	Ph: (301)496-8100
9000 Rockville Pike	Fax: (301)402-2872
Bethesda, MD 20892	

Contact: Dr. Phil Skolnick, Chf.

Desc: Neurosciences. *Type:* Research center.

U.S. Department of Health and Human Services

National Institute of Mental Health

Intramural Research Programs Division

Experimental Therapeutic Branch

NIH Bldg. 10, Rm. 4F-229A	Ph: (301)496-4303
10 Center Dr., MSC 1380	Fax: (301)480-5135
Bethesda, MD 20892-1380	

Contact: David Pickar, MD, Chf. of Expmt. Therapeutics.

Desc: Basic and clinical neuroscience and attempts to integrate data on the biochemistry and pharmacology of the central nervous system with an understanding of the pathogenesis and treatment of major psychiatric diseases. Branch comprises the Clinical and Pharmacology Section, Clinical Studies Section, Molecular Neurogenetics Section, and Molecular Pharmacology Section. *Type:* Research center.

U.S. Department of Health and Human Services

National Institute of Mental Health

Intramural Research Programs Division (Basic Research)

Cerebral Metabolism Laboratory

NIH Bldg. 36, Rm. 1A-05	Ph: (301)496-1371
9000 Rockville Pike	Fax: (301)480-1668
Bethesda, MD 20892	

E-mail: louis@siloh.nimh.nih.gov

Contact: Louis Sokoloff, MD, Chf.

Desc: Neurochemistry and neurophysiology using biochemical methods for measuring local cerebral glucose utilization, local cerebral blood flow, and local cerebral protein synthesis in vivo. Laboratory comprises sections on clinical brain imaging and developmental neurochemistry. *Type:* Research center.

U.S. Department of Health and Human Services

National Institute of Mental Health

Intramural Research Programs Division (Basic Research)

Neurochemistry Laboratory

NIH Bldg. 36, Rm. 3D-30	Ph: (301)496-3579
36 Convent Dr. MSC 4096	Fax: (301)480-9284
Bethesda, MD 20892	

E-mail: kaufman@codon.nih.gov

Contact: Seymour Kaufman, PhD, Chf.

Desc: Fundamental physical and chemical mechanisms of the nervous system as they relate to mental health. Subjects of recent interest include research in phenylketonuria and regulation of neurotransmitter biosynthesis; studies on nitric oxide synthase. *Type:* Research center.

U.S. Department of Health and Human Services

National Institute of Mental Health

Intramural Research Programs Division (Clinical Research)

Clinical Neuroendocrinology Branch

NIH Bldg. 10, Rm. 2D-46	Ph: (301)496-6884
10 Center Dr.	Fax: (301)402-1561
Bethesda, MD 20892-1284	

Contact: Philip W. Gold, MD, Chf.

Desc: Physiological organization of neuroendocrine systems and on the relevance of alterations in neuroendocrine function to the pathophysiology and etiology of major psychiatric disorders. *Type:* Research center.

U.S. Department of Health and Human Services

National Institute of Mental Health

Intramural Research Programs Division (Clinical Research)

Neurophsiology Laboratory

| NIHAC Bldg. 110, Rm. 119 | Ph: (301)496-1201 |
| Poolesville, MD 20837 | Fax: (301)402-0236 |

Contact: Charles Gerfen, Actg.Chf.

Desc: Neurophysiology. *Type:* Research center.

U.S. Department of Health and Human Services

National Institute of Mental Health

Intramural Research Programs Division (Clinical Research)

Neuropsychology Laboratory

NIH Bldg. 49, Rm. 1B80	Ph: (301)496-5625
49 Convent Dr., MSC 4415	Fax: (301)402-0046
Bethesda, MD 20892-4415	

E-mail: mm@nimh.nih.gov

Contact: Dr. Robert Desimore, Dir.

Desc: Relationships between neural structures and behavior in nonhuman primates using a multidisciplinary approach to study cognitive functions such as perception, attention, memory, and emotion in Old World monkeys. *Type:* Research center.

U.S. Department of Health and Human Services

National Institute of Mental Health

Intramural Research Programs Division (Neuropsychiatric Research at St. Elizabeth's Hospital)

Biochemical Genetics Laboratory

Bldg. 10, Rm. 2D54	Ph: (301)435-3583
9000 Rockville Pike	Fax: (301)480-9862
Bethesda, MD 20892	

E-mail: merrilc@helix.nih.gov

Contact: Carl R. Merril, MD, Chf.

Desc: Affects of aging on the central nervous system; and molecular neurobiology, focusing on proteins and nucleic acids in normal and disease states. *Type:* Research center.

U.S. Department of Health and Human Services
National Institute of Mental Health
Intramural Research Programs Division
(Neuropsychiatric Research at St. Elizabeth's Hospital)
Clinical Brain Disorders Branch

2700 Martin Luther King Ave., Ph: (202)373-6225
S.E. Fax: (202)373-6214
Washington, DC 20032

Contact: Daniel R. Weinberger, MD, Chf.

Desc: Neuropsychiatric disorders, with emphasis on schizophrenia, dementias, movement disorders, and suicide. Principal fields of research interest are pharmacology and neuropsychology, neuroimaging, and neuropathology. *Type:* Research center.

U.S. Department of Health and Human Services
National Institute of Mental Health
Intramural Research Programs Division
(Neuropsychiatric Research at St. Elizabeth's Hospital)
Neuropsychiatry Branch

2700 Martin Luther King Ave., Ph: (202)373-6233
S.E. Fax: (202)373-6244
Washington, DC 20032
E-mail: wyattr@dirpc.nimh.nih.gov

Contact: Richard J. Wyatt, MD, Chf.

Desc: Biomedical and clinical studies, focusing on biochemistry of schizophrenia, aging, regeneration, pharmacology, neuropsychiatry, drug abuse and tardive dyskinesia. Activities are carried out in the Aging Section, Clinical Neuropsychiatry Section, Molecular Neuropsychiatry Section, and Preclinical Neuroscience Section. *Type:* Research center.

U.S. Department of Health and Human Services
National Institute of Mental Health
Neuroscience and Behavioral Sciences Division
Molecular and Cellular Neuroscience Research Branch

NeuroScience Ctr. Bldg. Ph: (301)443-1504
6001 Executive Blvd. Fax: (301)443-4822
Rockville, MD 20857

Contact: Dr. Stephen Zalcman, Chf.

Desc: Behavior and brain function in order to develop knowledge of basic biological/molecular mechanisms underlying mental disorders and to understand the basic processes involved in the action of psychoactive drugs. Activities involve biobehavioral research, neurobiological research, and psychopharmacological research, which includes support for clinical and preclinical studies on the physiological sites and mechanisms of actions of psychoactive drugs. *Type:* Research center.

U.S. Department of Health and Human Services
National Institute of Neurological Disorders and Stroke

Bldg. 31, Rm. 8-A52 Ph: (301)496-9746
Bethesda, MD 20892-2540 Fax: (301)496-0296
URL: http://www.ninds.nih.gov

Contact: Gerald D. Fischbach, M.D., Dir.

Desc: Causes, prevention, diagnosis, and treatment of neurological disorders and stroke. The Institute conducts, fosters, and supports research and research training in neurological and muscle disorders through: intramural, collaborative, and field research in its own laboratories, branches, and clinics, and through contracts; research grants to scientific institutions and to individuals; individual and institutional research training awards to increase trained professional research manpower in neurological fields; and cooperation with various agencies in collecting and disseminating educational and informational material related to neurological disorders and stroke. *Type:* Research center.

U.S. Department of Health and Human Services
National Institute of Neurological Disorders and Stroke
Division of Convulsive, Infectious and Immune Disorders

Federal Bldg., Rm. 5A12 Ph: (301)496-6541
7550 Wisconsin Ave. Fax: (301)402-0302
Bethesda, MD 20892

Contact: F.J. Brinley, Jr., Dir.

Desc: Convulsive and paroxysmal disorders; neuromuscular disorders, the peripheral neuropathies; and pain, neurotoxicology, neuroendocrinology, and MS, ALS, neuroimmunology; neurourology, AIDS. Division comprises branches for Epilepsy. *Type:* Research center.

U.S. Department of Health and Human Services
National Institute of Neurological Disorders and Stroke
Division of Convulsive, Infectious and Immune Disorders
Developmental Neurology Branch

7550 Wisconsin Ave. Ph: (301)496-6701
Bethesda, MD 20892 Fax: (301)402-8887

Contact: Dr. Philip Sheridan, Chf.

Desc: Birth defects and genetic and developmental disorders, neuromuscular disorders, neonatal brain disorders, neural tube defects (spina bifida and related disorders), the neurophysiology of learning disorders, the phakomatoses (tuberous sclerosis, neurofibromatosis, and related disorders), and autism and related behavioral disorders; and supports centers of neurogenetic disorders of infants and children. *Type:* Research center.

U.S. Department of Health and Human Services
National Institute of Neurological Disorders and Stroke
Division of Convulsive, Infectious and Immune Disorders
Epilepsy Branch

7550 Wisconsin Ave., Rm. 516 Ph: (301)496-1917
Bethesda, MD 20892 Fax: (301)496-9916
E-mail: ps59i@nih.gov
URL: http://www.ninds.nih.gov

Contact: Dr. Philip H. Sheridan, Chf.

Desc: Epilepsy research. Goals are to promote research into the basic mechanisms, etiologies, prevention, diagnosis, and treatment of epilepsies. *Type:* Research center.

U.S. Department of Health and Human Services
National Institute of Neurological Disorders and Stroke
Division of Demyelinating, Atrophic, and Dementing Disorders

Federal Bldg., Rm. 810 Ph: (301)496-5679
7550 Wisconsin Ave. Fax: (301)480-1080
Bethesda, MD 20892

Contact: Dr. Michael D. Walker, MD, Dir.

Desc: Understanding, diagnosis, treatment, and prevention of a broad scope of neurological disorders of adults and the aged. These diseases include Alzheimer's disease and other dementias, Parkinson's disease, Huntington's disease, and amyotrophic lateral sclerosis, as well as demyelinating disorders such as multiple sclerosis. *Type:* Research center.

U.S. Department of Health and Human Services
National Institute of Neurological Disorders and Stroke
Division of Demyelinating, Atrophic, and Dementing Disorders
Huntington's Disease Research Roster

Department of Medical Ph: (317)274-2245
Genetics, Medical Research Fax: (317)274-2387
and Library
Indiana University Medical
Center
975 W. Walnut St.
Indianapolis, IN 46202-5251
URL: http://medgen.iupui.edu

Contact: Dr. P. Michael Conneally, Prin.Invest.

Desc: To compile a registry of families with, or at risk for, Huntington's Disease (HD) that can be used as a resource for HD research. The Roster contains 113,055 records of individuals in 2340 families located in all 50 states as well as in other countries. *Type:* Research center.

U.S. Department of Health and Human Services
National Institute of Neurological Disorders and Stroke
Division of Extramural Activities

7550 Wisconsin Ave. Ph: (301)402-9248
Bethesda, MD 20892 Fax: (301)402-4370
E-mail: CUA@CUNIH.GOV
URL: http://www.ninds.nih.gov/grntcnhp.htm

Contact: Contance W. Atwell, PhD, Dir.

Desc: Provides administrative support and coordination for the Institute's research grant, research training, and research contract activities. Division directs and carries out scientific and technical merit review of proposals for research contracts, program projects, clinical research centers, special research grants such as multi-institutional clinical trials, and career development and research training. *Type:* Research center.

U.S. Department of Health and Human Services
National Institute of Neurological Disorders and Stroke
Division of Intramual Research (Clinical Neurosciences Program)
Biometry and Field Studies Branch

7550 Wisconsin Ave., Rm. Ph: (301)496-4106
7A12 Fax: (301)496-3444
Bethesda, MD 20892

Contact: Dr. James Dambrosia, Actg.Chf.

Desc: Statistics and related disciplines to design, conduct, and analyze collaborative studies involving the etiology, natural history, prevention, treatment, incidence, and prevalence of neurological disorders. Branch also provides consultation in biostatistics, demography, and survey design to NINDS and other neuroscientists. *Type:* Research center.

U.S. Department of Health and Human Services
National Institute of Neurological Disorders and Stroke
Division of Intramural Research

Bldg. 36, Rm. 4-D20 Ph: (301)496-4297
9000 Rockville Pike Fax: (301)402-2818
Bethesda, MD 20892
E-mail: kopin@helix.nih.gov

Contact: Harold Gainer, PhD, Actg.Dir.

Desc: Neurological sciences and relevant disciplines, including drug therapies for debilitating neurological diseases such as Parkinsonism, new techniques to help scientists better understand how the brain and nervous system function, and major research advances in neurovirology, neurochemistry, and other fields. Current interests include central nervous system disorders, such as Creutzfeldt-Jakob disease, that appear to be slow infections caused by transmissible virus-like agents; Inherited disorders of lipid metabolism, such as Gaucher's disease, Niemann-Pick disease, Fabry's disease, Krabbe's disease, and Tay-Sachs disease. *Type:* Research center.

U.S. Department of Health and Human Services

National Institute of Neurological Disorders and Stroke

Division of Intramural Research (Basic Neurosciences Program)

Bldg. 36, Rm. 4-D20   Ph: (301)496-5468
9000 Rockville Pike   Fax: (301)402-1566
Bethesda, MD 20892
E-mail: hgatnih@codon.nih.gov
URL: http://intra.ninds.nih.gov

Contact: Dr. Harold Gainer, PhD, Dir.

Desc: Comprises laboratories for: Adaptive Systems, Central Nervous System Studies, Experimental Neuropathology, Molecular Biology, Molecular and Cellular Neurobiology, Molecular Medicine and Neuroscience, Neural Control, Neurobiology, Neurochemistry, Neurophysiology, and Viral and Molecular Pathogenesis and sections for Neurogenetics and Synaptic Mechanisms. *Type:* Research center.

U.S. Department of Health and Human Services

National Institute of Neurological Disorders and Stroke

Division of Intramural Research (Basic Neurosciences Program)

Laboratory of Central Nervous System Studies

NIH Bldg. 36, Rm. 4A-05   Ph: (301)496-4821
36 Convent Dr., MSC4122   Fax: (301)496-9946
Bethesda, MD 20892
E-mail: gibbs@codon.nih.gov

Contact: Dr. Clarence J. Gibbs, Jr., Chf.

Desc: Medical surveillance of disease patterns in many primitive and isolated populations; slow, latent, and temperate virus infections, particularly chronic degenerative neurologic diseases and their pathogenesis and mechanisms of virus persistence. Also studies configuration and change resulting in conversion of normal host precursors to infectious proteins in the transmissible amyloidoses of the brain. *Type:* Research center.

U.S. Department of Health and Human Services

National Institute of Neurological Disorders and Stroke

Division of Intramural Research (Basic Neurosciences Program)

Laboratory of Developmental Neurogenetics

NIH Bldg. 36, Rm. 5D06   Ph: (301)496-9106
9000 Rockville Pike   Fax: (301)496-0899
Bethesda, MD 20892

Contact: Dr. Lynn Hudson, Actg.Chf.

Desc: Molecular events that occur in the replication and expression of genetic materials in mammalian cells and their viruses. Genetic, biochemical, and recombinant DNA techniques are used to study gene replication and transcription. *Type:* Research center.

U.S. Department of Health and Human Services

National Institute of Neurological Disorders and Stroke

Division of Intramural Research (Basic Neurosciences Program)

Laboratory of Experimental Neuropathology

NIH Bldg. 36, Rm. 4A29   Ph: (301)496-4747
9000 Rockville Pike   Fax: (301)402-1030
Bethesda, MD 20892
E-mail: hwebster@codon.nih.gov

Contact: Dr. Henry Webster, Chf.

Desc: Cellular organization of the developing and adult nervous system; investigates cellular and subcellular abnormalities that cause or are associated with neurological diseases and experimental lesions in the nervous system. Laboratory develops and coordinates electron-microscopic, immunocytochemical, virological, immunological, and biochemical methods to explore cellular mechanisms of myelin formation, breakdown, and regeneration, especially those relevant to multiple sclerosis and other demyelinating diseases. *Type:* Research center.

U.S. Department of Health and Human Services

National Institute of Neurological Disorders and Stroke

Division of Intramural Research (Basic Neurosciences Program)

Laboratory of Molecular Biology

Bldg. 5829   Ph: (301)496-6574
9000 Rockville Pike   Fax: (301)496-4276
Bethesda, MD 20892-4157

Contact: Dr. Ronald McKay, Actg.Chf.

Desc: Investigation of the mechanism controlling the initiation and control of cell differentiation by physiological and genetic engineering methods and the synthesis and function of neuroreceptors. These studies contribute to the understanding of genetic and developmental disorders and have demonstrated how some of the disorders can be avoided by the careful use of drugs and proper nutrition during pregnancy. *Type:* Research center.

U.S. Department of Health and Human Services

National Institute of Neurological Disorders and Stroke

Division of Intramural Research (Basic Neurosciences Program)

Laboratory of Molecular and Cellular Neurobiology

9000 Rockville Pike, Bldg. 49,   Ph: (301)496-6647
Rm. 2A10   Fax: (301)496-8244
Bethesda, MD 20892
E-mail: RQUARLES@POPGERVER.NIH.GOV

Contact: Dr. Richard Quarles, Chf.

Desc: Molecular and cellular neurobiology, myelination, and cell surface receptors. *Type:* Research center.

U.S. Department of Health and Human Services

National Institute of Neurological Disorders and Stroke

Division of Intramural Research (Basic Neurosciences Program)

Laboratory of Neural Control

NIH Bldg. 49, Rm. 3A50   Ph: (301)496-4305
9000 Rockville Pike   Fax: (301)402-4836
Bethesda, MD 20892
E-mail: REBURKE@HELIX.NIH.GOV
URL: http://intra.ninds.nih.gov/lncon/index.html

Contact: Dr. Robert Burke, Chf.

Desc: Properties of mammalian nerve cells and on the organization of the mammalian central nervous system, with particular reference to studies of the control of movement. Current experimental studies involve five main areas: the neurobiology of spinal cord motorneurons and motor units; the organization of interneuron circuits in the spinal cord; the development of motor systems in the avian spinal cord; and the generation of respiratory rhythms. *Type:* Research center.

U.S. Department of Health and Human Services

National Institute of Neurological Disorders and Stroke

Division of Intramural Research (Basic Neurosciences Program)

Laboratory of Neurobiology

NIH Bldg. 36, Rm. 2A21   Ph: (301)496-1354
9000 Rockville Pike   Fax: (301)480-1485
Bethesda, MD 20892
E-mail: TSR@codon.nih.gov
URL: http://intra.ininds.nih.gov

Contact: Dr. Thomas S. Reese, Chf.

Desc: Structural research on the organization of the nervous system. Specific areas of interest are: synaptic transmission, neural membranes, the intracellular sequestration of ions, the blood-brain barrier, and axonal transport. *Type:* Research center.

U.S. Department of Health and Human Services

National Institute of Neurological Disorders and Stroke

Division of Intramural Research (Basic Neurosciences Program)

Laboratory of Neurochemistry

NIH Bldg. 36, Rm. 4D-20   Ph: (301)496-1671
9000 Rockville Pike   Fax: (301)496-1339
Bethesda, MD 20892-4130
E-mail: hgatnih@codon.nib.gov

Contact: Dr. Harold Gainer, Chf.

Desc: Molecular events that underlie both the normal functioning of the developing and mature nervous system and the derangements that occur in neurological disease. Areas of study include: mechanisms of active ion transport, protein phosphorylaton, neuronal development and regeneration, gene expression of neuropeptides and their receptors, and neuronal cytoskeletal proteins. *Type:* Research center.

U.S. Department of Health and Human Services

National Institute of Neurological Disorders and Stroke

Division of Intramural Research (Basic Neurosciences Program)

Laboratory of Neurophysiology

NIH Bldg. 36, Rm. 2C-02   Ph: (301)496-2414
9000 Rockville Pike   Fax: (301)402-1565
Bethesda, MD 20892
E-mail: jlbarker@codon.nih.gov
URL: http://intra.ninds.nih.gov/lnp/index.html

Contact: Jeffery Barker, MD, Chf.

Desc: Receptor biology, including studies in molecular biology, biochemistry, anatomy, and physiology. All of the Laboratory's projects involve multidisciplinary analysis of the physiological properties of vertebrate central neurons studied in vitro. *Type:* Research center.

U.S. Department of Health and Human Services

National Institute of Neurological Disorders and Stroke

Division of Intramural Research (Basic Neurosciences Program)

Neuroepidemiology Branch

Federal Building Rm. 714	Ph: (301)496-1714
7550 Wisconsin Ave.	Fax: (301)496-2358
Bethesda, MD 20814	

Contact: Cecilia Blutstein, Contact.

Desc: Neuroepidemiology, the epidemiologic investigation of neurologic disorders, which requires a thorough knowledge of both clinical neurology and epidemiologic methods. The program focuses on research, education, and consultation in neuroepidemiology. *Type:* Research center.

U.S. Department of Health and Human Services

National Institute of Neurological Disorders and Stroke

Division of Intramural Research (Clinical Neurosciences Program)

NIH Bldg. 10, Rm. 5N226	Ph: (301)496-1561
10 Center Dr., MSC 1428	Fax: (301)402-1007
Bethesda, MD 20892-1428	

E-mail: HALLETT@CODON.NIH.GOV

URL: http://intra.ninds.nih.gov/

Contact: Mark Hallett, MD, Dir.

Desc: Problems important in Clinical Neurology and Neurosurgery. The Office of the Clinical Director provides clinical neurological services to investigators within the Institute and other NIH institutes. *Type:* Research center.

U.S. Department of Health and Human Services

National Institute of Neurological Disorders and Stroke

Division of Intramural Research (Clinical Neurosciences Program)

Basic Neuroscience Branch

NIH Bldg. 36, Rm. 5A25	Ph: (301)496-3206
9000 Rockville Pike	Fax: (301)496-8765
Bethesda, MD 20892	

E-mail: gerry@helix.nih.gov

Contact: Dr. Gerald Ehrenstein, Chf.

Desc: Molecular and cellular mechanisms responsible for excitation, membrane potentials, the generation of the nerve impulse, and synaptic activity. Research includes the use of physical and chemical techniques, online and offline digital computers, and a variety of applied mathematical methods. *Type:* Research center.

U.S. Department of Health and Human Services

National Institute of Neurological Disorders and Stroke

Division of Intramural Research (Clinical Neurosciences Program)

Clinical Neurosciences Branch

NIH Bldg. 10, Rm. 6N252	Ph: (301)496-4297
9000 Rockville Pike	Fax: (301)402-0180
Bethesda, MD 20892	

Contact: Irwin J. Kopin, Chf.

Desc: Neurosciences. *Type:* Research center.

U.S. Department of Health and Human Services

National Institute of Neurological Disorders and Stroke

Division of Intramural Research (Clinical Neurosciences Program)

Developmental and Metabolic Neurology Branch

NIH Bldg. 10, Rm. 3D04	Ph: (301)496-3285
10 Center Dr. MSC 1260	Fax: (301)496-9480
Bethesda, MD 20892-1260	

E-mail: robrady@codon.nih.gov

URL: http://www.ninds.nih.gov/neurosci/clinical/dmnb/dmnb.htm

Contact: Dr. Roscoe O. Brady, Chf.

Desc: Genetic disorders of metabolism, demyelinating disorders, biochemistry of cell membranes, and signal transduction mechanisms in normal and neoplastic tissues. Principal areas of interest are biochemistry, genetics, neurochemistry, neuroimmunology, molecular genetics, and adult and pediatric neurology. *Type:* Research center.

U.S. Department of Health and Human Services

National Institute of Neurological Disorders and Stroke

Division of Intramural Research (Clinical Neurosciences Program)

Experimental Therapeutics Branch

NIH Bldg. 10, Rm. 5C103	Ph: (301)496-7993
10 Center Dr., MSC 1406	Fax: (301)496-6609
Bethesda, MD 20892-1406	

Contact: Dr. Thomas N. Chase, Chf.

Desc: Improved pharmacotherapies for neurologic disease. The Branch operates a vertically integrated program of research, extending from basic molecular biology to clinical trials, focusing on neurodegenerative diseases such as Alzheimer's disease and Parkinson's disease. *Type:* Research center.

U.S. Department of Health and Human Services

National Institute of Neurological Disorders and Stroke

Division of Intramural Research (Clinical Neurosciences Program)

Laboratory of Molecular Medicine and Neuroscience

NIH 36	Ph: (301)496-1635
36 Convent Dr.	Fax: (301)594-5799
Bethesda, MD 20892-4164	

E-mail: eomajor@codon.nih.gob

Contact: Eugene Major, Chf.

Desc: Neurologic diseases at the clinical, biological, and molecular levels. Experimental emphasis is on the pathogenesis of diseases involving cellular dysfunctions caused by neurotropic viruses, toxic cytokines, or possible genetic alterations. *Type:* Research center.

U.S. Department of Health and Human Services

National Institute of Neurological Disorders and Stroke

Division of Intramural Research (Clinical Neurosciences Program)

Medical Neurology Branch

NIH Bldg. 10, Rm. 5N234	Ph: (301)496-9526
10 Center Dr., MSC 1430	Fax: (301)402-1007
Bethesda, MD 20892-1430	

E-mail: hallett@codon.nih.gov

URL: http://www.intra.ninds.nih.gov/

Contact: Mark Hallett, MD, Chf.

Desc: Basic and clinical aspects of a variety of neurologic disorders, including: pathophysiological mechanisms and treatment of movement disorders; pathophysiology of neuromuscular diseases; and cognitive neuropsychology. *Type:* Research center.

U.S. Department of Health and Human Services

National Institute of Neurological Disorders and Stroke

Division of Intramural Research (Clinical Neurosciences Program)

Neuroimmunology Branch

NIH Bldg. 10, Rm. 5B-16	Ph: (301)496-1801
10 Center Dr., MSC 1400	Fax: (301)402-0373
Bethesda, MD 20892-1400	

Contact: Dr. Henry F. McFarland, Chf.

Desc: Activities of the Neuroimmunology Branch include basic and clinical investigations related to multiple sclerosis (MS) and other possible immunological-based diseases. Studies focus on examining basic or fundamental immunological questions, including a study of experimental animal models and the cellular immune response to potential antigens in the nervous system. *Type:* Research center.

U.S. Department of Health and Human Services

National Institute of Neurological Disorders and Stroke

Division of Intramural Research (Clinical Neurosciences Program)

Surgical Neurology Branch

NIH Bldg. 10, Rm. 5D37	Ph: (301)496-5728
10 Center Dr., MSC 1414	Fax: (301)402-0380
Bethesda, MD 20892-1414	

E-mail: oldfield@box-o.nih.gov

Contact: Dr. Edward H. Oldfield, Chf.

Desc: Current areas of research, most of which integrate basic science, applied laboratory science, animal experimentation, and human studies include new therapeutic approaches (genetically-engineered immunotoxins, genetically-engineered viral vectors, new drug delivery techniques) for brain tumors and pituitary tumors, mechanisms of brain edema associated with brain tumors, mechanisms of tumor-associated angiogenesis, mechanisms of the beneficial recovery after cerebral implants or neurotrophic factors for Parkinson's disease, studies of certain types of cerebrovascular disease (vasospasm, regulation of cerebral blood flow, spinal arteriovenous malformations), von Hippel-Lindau syndrome, and functional neurosurgery (seizure surgery, development of implanted prosthesis for blindness). *Type:* Research center.

U.S. Department of Health and Human Services

National Institute of Neurological Disorders and Stroke

Division of Stroke, Trauma and Neurodegenerative Disorders

7550 Wisconsin Ave.	Ph: (301)496-2581
Federal Bldg., 810	Fax: (301)480-1080
Bethesda, MD 20892	

Contact: Dr. Michael Walker, Dir.

Desc: Stroke and central nervous system trauma, including support for basic, applied, and clinical research. This includes support for multidisciplinary cerebrovascular clinical research centers, a comprehensive stroke center program, spinal cord injury centers, a comprehensive CNS trauma center program, and head injury centers, as well as larger numbers of individual, investigator-initiated research grants. *Type:* Research center.

U.S. Department of Health and Human Services
National Institute of Neurological Disorders and Stroke
Division of Stroke, Trauma, and Neurodegenerative Disorders
Neural Prosthesis Program
7550 Wisconsin Ave., Rm. 916   Ph: (301)496-5746
Bethesda, MD 20892   Fax: (301)402-1501
E-mail: fh2@cu.nih.gov
Contact: Dr. Frederick Terry Hambrecht, Hd.
Desc: Development of aids for the neurologically disabled based on direct interfaces with neural tissue. Principal areas of research interest are cochlear implants and cochlear nucleus implants for the deaf; visual prostheses for the blind; and motor prostheses for the paralyzed. *Type:* Research center.

U.S. Department of Health and Human Services
National Institute of Neurological Disorders and Stroke
Small Business Innovation Research Program
Federal Bldg. 1016   Ph: (301)496-4188
Bethesda, MD 20892   Fax: (301)402-4370
URL: http://www.ninds.nih.gov
Contact: Sonny Kreitman, Dir.
Desc: Comprises awards for three phases of research: the objective of Phase I is to establish the technical merit and feasibility of proposed research efforts that may ultimately lead to commercial products or services; the objective of Phase II is to continue the research and development efforts initiated in Phase I that are likely to result in commercial products or services; and the objective of Phase III, where appropriate, is for the small business to pursue, with non-federal funds, the commercialization of the results of the research and development funded in Phases I and II. Recent areas of interest include: development of novel antiepileptic drugs; devices for automated seizure detection; research and development of magnetoencephalography (MEG); development of applications for evoked potentials; development of a portable EEG device; and development of instrumentation for monitoring autonomic nervous system (ANS) function. *Type:* Research center.

U.S. Department of Health and Human Services
National Institutes of Health
National Institute of Neurological Disorders and Stroke
9000 Rockville Pike   Ph: (301)496-5751
Bethesda, MD 20892
URL: http://www.ninds.nih.gov/
Contact: Audrey S. Penn, Acting Director.
Desc: NINDS conducts and supports fundamental and applied research on human neurological disorders, such as Parkinson's disease, epilepsy, multiple sclerosis, muscular dystrophy, head and spinal cord injuries, and stroke. It also conducts and supports research on the development and function of the normal brain and nervous system in order to better understand normal processes relating to disease states. *Type:* Government agency, office, or program.

U.S. Department of Veterans Affairs
Rehabilitation Research and Development Center
Design Development
Laboratory of Neuromuscular Biomechanics
VA Medical Center   Ph: (650)493-5000
3801 Miranda Ave.   Fax: (650)852-3228
Palo Alto, CA 94304-1200
Contact: Maurice LeBlanc, Dir.
Desc: Supports research on coordination of human lower extremity muscles during functional activities, such as standing, walking, and pedaling in able-bodied and disabled persons. *Type:* Research center.

U.S. Department of Veterans Affairs
Rehabilitation Research and Development Center
Design Development
Laboratory of Neuromuscular Electrophysiology
3801 Miranda Ave.   Ph: (650)493-5000
Palo Alto, CA 94304-1200
Contact: Maurice LeBlanc, Dir.
Desc: Human neuromuscular electrophysiology data. Laboratory activities center around devices used to stimulate and record from both nerve and muscle tissue, and the associated computer peripheral devices to collect, analyze, and record this data. *Type:* Research center.

University of Alabama at Birmingham
Brain Resource Program
Sparks Ctr., Rm. 843   Ph: (205)934-7359
Univ. Sta.   Fax: (205)975-6356
Birmingham, AL 35294-0017
E-mail: dismukes@path.uab.edu
Contact: Dr. Steven L. Carroll, Dir.
Desc: Collects donated brains from deceased elderly patients with brain disorders, mainly schizophrenia and Alzheimer's, for studies in the causes and treatments of mental disorders. In brain tissues donated by deceased Alzheimer's disease patients, research focuses on nerve cell damage that occurs in the temporal lobe and the hippocampus, the gatekeeper for the memory. *Type:* Research center.

University of Alabama at Birmingham
Center for Neuroimmunology
Department of Neurology   Ph: (205)934-2402
625 19th St. S.   Fax: (205)975-6030
Birmingham, AL 35233
E-mail: jwhitaker@email.neuro.uab.edu
URL: http://www.neuro.uab.edu:80/MS.html
Contact: John Whitaker, MD, Chm.
Desc: Multiple sclerosis, myasthenia gravis, glia, paraneoplastic syndromes, and idiotypes. *Type:* Research center.

University of Alabama at Birmingham
Kirklin Pain Treatment Center
UAB Med. Ctr.   Ph: (205)801-8250
2000 6th Ave. S, 3rd Fl.   Fax: (205)801-8253
Birmingham, AL 35233
Contact: Dr. Judy McDanal, Med.Dir.
Desc: Chronic pain and the management of chronic pain from benign or malignant sources. Also conducts studies on the effectiveness of group outpatient therapy for pain patients and their families and prior physical and/or sexual trauma and its relation to pain. *Type:* Research center.

University of Alabama at Birmingham
Neurobiology Research Department
CIRC 516   Ph: (205)934-0100
1719 6th Ave. S.   Fax: (205)934-6571
Birmingham, AL 35294-0021
E-mail: mjf@nrc.uab.edu
URL: http://www.uab.edu
Contact: Prof. Michael J. Friedlander, Dir.
Desc: Basic biology of the brain, including studies of cellular and molecular biology, high resolution 3-dimensional imaging of nerve cells, neurophysiology, biochemistry, biophysics, computer simulation of the nervous system and individual nerve cells, and electrophysiology. Special interests include developmental neurobiology, synaptic transmission, signal transduction, control of coordinated movement, vision physiology, receptor and ion channel development, mechanisms of seizures, sensorimotor integration, neuroembryology, and pharmacological studies. *Type:* Research center.

University of Alabama at Birmingham
Parkinson's Disease Center
Jefferson Tower, Rm. 1225   Ph: (205)934-9100
Birmingham, AL 35294   Fax: (205)934-0928
E-mail: tony@email.neuro.uab.edu
URL: http://www.neuro.uab.edu/pd%20center/pdmain.html
Contact: Paul Atchison, MD, Co-Dir.
Desc: Investigates Parkinson's disease, catecholamine receptors, genetics, and basal ganglion; and conducts related drug studies. *Type:* Research center.

University of Alberta
Neurochemical Research Unit
MacKenzie Centre   Ph: (403)492-7604
Department of Psychiatry   Fax: (403)492-6841
Edmonton, AB, Canada T6G 2B7
E-mail: glen.baker@ualberta.ca
Contact: Prof. G.B. Baker, Co-Dir.
Desc: Biochemical bases of depression, panic disorder, schizophrenia and neurodegenerative disorders. Also studies the modes of action of drugs used to treat these psychiatric disorders, such as the effects of antidepressants and neuroleptics on levels of biogenic amines and metabolites and on receptors in the brain; the function of trace amines in the brain; synthesis and pharmacological testing of potential antidepressant, neuroleptic and neuroprotective drugs; measurements of biogenic amines and amino acids in body fluids; and drug-drug interactions involving cytochrome P450 isozymes. *Type:* Research center.

University of Arizona
Center for Complex Systems
Physics Dept.   Ph: (520)621-4190
Tucson, AZ 85721   Fax: (520)621-4721
E-mail: dis@physics.arizona.edu
URL: http://www.physics.arizona.edu/~dls
Contact: Daniel Stein, Dir.
Desc: Complex systems in neurobiology, physics, and other areas. *Type:* Research center.

University of Arizona
Sleep Disorders Center
College of Med.   Ph: (520)694-6112
Univ. Med. Ctr., Rm. 1338   Fax: (520)694-2515
Tucson, AZ 85724
E-mail: squan@sneeze.resp-sci.arizona.edu
Contact: Stuart F. Quan, MD, Dir.
Desc: Sleep disorders guided by studies in neurology, psychology, pulmonology, and pediatrics. Research efforts concentrate on sleep apnea, sudden infant death syndrome, nocturnal penile tumescence, male sexual dysfunction, seizure disorders, insomnia, narcolepsy, and restless leg syndrome. *Type:* Research center.

University of British Columbia
Kinsmen Laboratory of Neurological Research
2255 Wesbrook Mall   Ph: (604)822-7018
Vancouver, BC, Canada V6T 1Z3   Fax: (604)822-7981
Contact: Dr. Steven Vincent, PhD, Hd.
Desc: Neurological sciences, including studies on behavioral effects of specific brain lesions and/or drugs, central nervous system histochemistry and electron microscopy, Parkinsonism, epilepsy, Alzheimer's disease, dystonia, neurotransmitter systems and behavior, chorea, muscular dystrophy, psychopharmacology, and in vivo brain microdialysis and voltammetry. *Type:* Research center.

University of British Columbia
Laboratories of Neurophysiology
Copp Bldg.   Ph: (604)822-2671
Department of Physiology   Fax: (604)822-6048
2146 Health Sci. Mall
Vancouver, BC, Canada V6T
    1Z3
E-mail: baim@unixg.ubc.ca
URL: http://www.physiology.ubc.ca
Contact: Dr. Kenneth Baimbridge, Dir.
Desc: Neurophysiology, including studies of basal ganglia, limbic forebrain, spinal cord, mechanisms of synaptic transmission in central nervous system, and amino acids. Type: Research center.

University of Calgary
Neuroscience Research Group
3330 Hospital Dr. NW   Ph: (403)220-4601
Calgary, AB, Canada T2N 4N1   Fax: (403)283-2700
E-mail: Ksharkey@acs.ucalgary.ca
URL: http://www.ucalgary.ca/~neuro/
Contact: Dr. Keith Sharkey, Chm.
Desc: Multidisciplinary group of independently funded researchers investigating various aspects of the nervous system, including hypothalamic mechanisms of thermoregulation, endocrine and autonomic control, axonal transport, nerve regeneration, actions of anesthetics, developmental neurobiology, synaptic circuitry, molluscan neurobiology, neurotransmitter/peptide pharmacology, structure and function of visual system, neuropathological disorders, molecular neurobiology, molecular biology of neurodegenerative disorders, sensory and motor physiology, cerebellar structure and function, and restorative neurology. Type: Research center.

University of California, Davis
Rehabilitation Research and Training Center in Neuromuscular Disease
Sch. of Med.   Ph: (530)752-2903
Department of Physical Med. &   Fax: (530)752-3468
    Rehabilitation
1 Shields Ave.
TB 191
Davis, CA 95616
E-mail: kdevereaux@ucdavis.edu
URL: http://disability.ucdavis.edu
Contact: Mark A. Wineinger, RTC Dir.
Desc: Addresses the needs of individuals who are affected by chronically disabling neuromuscular diseases. Research is directed to physical performance and nutritional status; evaluation and treatment of swallowing disorders, dyspnea, respiratory control, and rehabilitation therapeutics; employment opportunities and vocational rehabilitation; the educational mainstreaming of children and young adults; and strategies to improve the quality of life and community integration. Type: Research center.

University of California, Irvine
Herklotz Research Facility
Center for the Neurobiology of Learning and Memory
320 Qureshey Res. Lab.   Ph: (949)824-5193
Irvine, CA 92697-3800   Fax: (949)824-8481
E-mail: jlmcgaug@uci.edu
URL: http://www.memory.uci.edu
Contact: Dr. James L. McGaugh, Dir.
Desc: Neurobiology of learning and memory, including biochemical mechanisms, systems neurophysiology, modulation of memory, cognitive neuropsychology, and neural modeling. Type: Research center.

University of California, Irvine
Memory Disorders Clinic
Department of Neurology   Ph: (949)824-6088
Irvine, CA 92697   Fax: (949)824-2132
E-mail: astarr@ucl.edu
Contact: Arnold Starr, MD, Dir.
Desc: Multidisciplinary approach to diagnosis and treatment of memory disorders, including the development and testing of memory enhancement programs. Type: Research center.

University of California, Los Angeles
Brain Research Institute
Gonda Goldschmied   Ph: (310)825-5061
    Neuroscience and Genetics Fax: (310)206-5855
    Research Center
Los Angeles, CA 90095-1761
E-mail: lmaninge@bri.medsch.ucla.edu
URL: http://www.medsch.ucla.edu/som/bri/
Contact: Allan Tobin, Dir.
Desc: Brain and central nervous system, including interdisciplinary studies in developmental neurobiology, molecular neurobiology, neuroanatomy, neurobiophysics, neurochemistry, neurocytology, neuroendocrinology, neuroimaging, neuromuscular physiology, neuropathology, neuropharmacology, neurophysiology, behavior, neuroimmunology, and experimental epilepsy. Also conducts research on aging, Alzheimer's Disease, alcohol effects on the central nervous system, cellular neurobiology, neuroendocrinology, and neuromuscular plasticity. Type: Research center.

University of California, Los Angeles
Jerry Lewis Neuromuscular Research Center
School of Medicine   Ph: (310)825-3734
Los Angeles, CA 90024   Fax: (310)206-5052
E-mail: adg@jlnrc.medsch.ucla.edu
Contact: Dr. A.D. Grinnell, Dir.
Desc: Structure, function, and interaction of nerve and muscle, both in normal and diseased tissue. Studies concentrate on membrane biophysics, cell physiology, biochemistry, immunology, and their relation to neuromuscular disease. Type: Research center.

University of California, Los Angeles
Reed Neurological Research Center
710 Westwood Plaza, Rm.   Ph: (310)206-2101
    4-238   Fax: (310)206-5518
Los Angeles, CA 90095
E-mail: toga@loni.ucla.edu
URL: http://www.loni.ucla.edu
Contact: Dr. Arthur W. Toga, Contact.
Desc: Neuroanatomy, neuroimaging, neurophysiology, and neurological diseases. Type: Research center.

University of California, San Diego
Alzheimer's Disease Research Center
9500 Gilman Dr.   Ph: (619)622-5800
La Jolla, CA 92093-0948   Fax: (619)622-1017
Contact: Dr. Leon Thal, Prin.Invest.
Desc: Longitudinal research on the clinical and cognitive changes associated with Alzheimer's disease and other dementing illnesses by obtaining epidemiological data, medical histories, analysis of blood and sera, administration of batteries of neuropsychological tests, and neurological examinations of patients. Performs clinical drug trials, research on electrophysiology and neuroimaging studies, evaluations of the effects of caregiving stress on the caregivers, studies of memory and language dysfunction, and the possibility of a genetic or metabolic basis for Alzheimer's disease. Type: Research center.

University of California, San Francisco
CNS Injury and Edema Research Center
C-224   Ph: (415)476-2987
521 Parnassus   Fax: (415)476-9650
San Francisco, CA 94143-0651
Contact: Prof. Pak H. Chan, Contact.
Desc: Brain edema and central nervous system injury; molecular biology of central nervous system. Type: Research center.

University of California, San Francisco
Keck Center for Integrative Neurosciences
UCSF   Ph: (415)476-1062
Box 0444   Fax: (415)502-4848
San Francisco, CA 94143
URL: http://www.keck.ucsf.edu
Contact: Dr. Steve Lisberger, Dir.
Desc: Neurochemistry of pain modulatory systems in the brainstem and spinal cord, using in vivo microdialysis, cytochemistry and high pressure liquid chromotography. Type: Research center.

University of California, San Francisco
Laboratory for CNS Injury and Disease
521 Parnassus Ave.   Ph: (415)476-4850
San Francisco, CA 94143   Fax: (415)476-5634
E-mail: noblelj@itsa.ucsf.edu
Contact: Linda J. Noble, PhD, Dir.
Desc: Models of traumatic brain injury, focal cerebral ischemia, and traumatic spinal cord and their treatment. Examines mechanisms of progressive cellular injury, in vivo and in vitro, and evaluates possible methods of cell protection. Type: Research center.

University of Chicago
Brain Research Institute
Department of Surgery, Box   Ph: (773)702-2123
    MC 3026   Fax: (773)702-3518
5841 S. Maryland
Chicago, IL 60637
E-mail: dtorrey@surgery.bsd.uchicago.edu
Contact: Bryce Weir, MD, Dir.
Desc: Alzheimer's disease, amyotrophic lateral sclerosis, myasthenia gravis, AIDS, sleep and sleep disorders, dyslexia, hyperkinesia, epilepsy and epileptoid disorders, mental retardation, mental illness, and brain and nervous system disorders such as multiple sclerosis, muscular dystrophy, cerebral palsy, encephalitis, Parkinson's disease, stroke, cerebral hemorrhage, aneurysm tumor, head injury, and intractable pain. Conducts basic research in neurophysiology, neuropharmacology, neuroanatomy, molecular biology, neuroimmunology, and virology. Type: Research center.

University of Cincinnati
Headache Center
Aring Neurology Dept.   Ph: (513)475-8730
222 Piedmont Ave.   Fax: (513)475-8033
Cincinnati, OH 45219
E-mail: ramadanm@email.uc.edu
URL: http://www.uc.edu
Contact: Dr. M. Ramadan, Dir.
Desc: Migraine headaches. Type: Research center.

University of Colorado--Denver
Rocky Mountain Taste and Smell Center
4200 E. 9th Ave.   Ph: (303)315-6600
Box B-205   Fax: (303)315-8787
Denver, CO 80262-0205
E-mail: bruce.jafek@uchsc.edu
Contact: Bruce W. Jafek, MD, Med.Dir.
Desc: Taste and smell dysfunction, using animal and human models, including ultrastructural change in the sense of smell during post viral states, head trauma, aging and taste dysfunction due to radiation therapy, and drugs. Type: Research center.

University of Connecticut
Center for Neurological Sciences
Univ. of Connecticut Health   Ph: (860)679-4678
Ctr.   Fax: (860)679-1274
263 Farmington Ave., Rm. L4071
Farmington, CT 06030-3405
E-mail: nsinfo@neuron.uchc.edu
URL: http://www3.uchc.edu/nsinfo
Contact: D. Kent Morest, MD, Dir.
Desc: An interdisciplinary approach to understanding the normal functions and disorders of the nervous system. Programs encompass experimental approaches ranging from the molecular to the systems level including cellular, molecular, and developmental neurobiology, neuroanatomy, neurophysiology, neur ochemistry, neuroendocrinology, neuroimmunology, neuropharmacology, and neuropathology. *Type:* Research center.

University of Connecticut
Connecticut Chemosensory Clinical Research Center
Health Ctr.   Ph: (860)679-1000
Farmington, CT 06030   Fax: (860)679-2910
Contact: Dr. Marion E. Frank, Prin.Invest.
Desc: Taste and smell disorders of various etiologies, plus independent research projects studying chemosensory function. *Type:* Research center.

University of Florida
Brain Institute
J.H.M. Health Sci. Ctr.   Ph: (352)392-0490
PO Box 100244   Fax: (352)846-0185
Gainesville, FL 32610-0244
E-mail: ufbi@cortex.health.ufl.edu
URL: http://www.ufbi.ufl.edu
Contact: William G. Luttge, PhD, Dir.
Desc: Peripheral Nerve Trauma Research Program, including biomaterials research, peripheral nerve regeneration, and mechanisms and control of pain associated with peripheral nerve trauma; Head Injury Research Program, including injury- and/or stroke-induced problems with memory, language, attention, emotion, motor skills, and epilepsy; molecular, cellular, and immunological mechanisms involved in nerve cell death and injury following stroke or closed head injury; Neurodegenerative Diseases Program, including molecular biologic studies of genetic bases of a variety of neurologic dysfunctions, including neurodegenerative movement disorders, cell biological studies on Batten's disease, and cell biological and MRI studies of laboratory animal models of multiple sclerosis. Additional studies include the underlying causes of Alzheimer's disease; the neurobiological consequences of alcohol and cocaine abuse in both adults and fetuses; and the molecular and cellular mechanisms and the behavioral and neurologic consequences of such viral-induced neurodegenerative diseases as AIDS, polio, and measles. *Type:* Research center.

University of Florida
Center for Neurobiological Sciences
Med. Sci. Bldg., Box 100244   Ph: (352)392-3383
Gainesville, FL 32610   Fax: (352)392-8347
E-mail: vierck@ufbi.ufl.edu
Contact: Dr. Charles Vierck, Jr., Dir.
Desc: Neurobiological sciences, including neuroanatomy, neurology, neuropsychology, neurophysiology, neurochemistry, neuropharmacology, and neuroendocrinology. Centralizes interdisciplinary communication and research training in neurobiological sciences and coordinates graduate student, postdoctoral, and faculty research in this area at the University. *Type:* Research center.

University Hospital of Cleveland
University Alzheimer Center
12200 Fairhill Rd.   Ph: (216)844-7360
Cleveland, OH 44120   Fax: (216)844-7239
E-mail: pjw3@po.cwru.edu
URL: http://www.cwru.edu/affil/adsc/intro.html
Contact: Karl Herrup, PhD, Int.Dir.
Desc: Long term studies of persons with memory problems, Alzheimer's disease, caregiver studies, and clinical studies to develop effective treatments for memory disorders. *Type:* Research center.

University of Illinois at Chicago
Consultation Clinic for Epilepsy
912 S. Wood St., Rm. 156   Ph: (312)996-7360
Chicago, IL 60612   Fax: (312)413-7704
E-mail: neuro@uic.edu
URL: http://www.uic.edu/depts/mcne
Contact: Dr. Daniel B. Hier, Dir.
Desc: Neurophysiology and neuropharmacology in the convulsive state, including studies on surgery for intractable psychomotor epilepsy, epidemiology of epilepsy, and side effects of various anticonvulsants. Also evaluates various new anticonvulsants. *Type:* Research center.

University of Illinois at Chicago
Electroencephalography Laboratory
Department of Neurology, M/C   Ph: (312)996-3865
722   Fax: (312)413-8540
1740 W. Taylor, 2nd Fl., Rm. 2171
Chicago, IL 60612
Contact: Dr. John R. Hughes, Hd.
Desc: Psychophysiology, including studies on clinical correlates of electroencephalic abnormalities, epilepsy, and organic brain disease. *Type:* Research center.

University of Iowa
Alzheimer's Disease Research Center
College of Med.   Ph: (319)356-2571
Department of Neurology   Fax: (319)356-4505
200 Hawkins Dr.
Iowa City, IA 52242
E-mail: antonio_damasio@uiowa.edu
Contact: Antonio Damasio, Dir.
Desc: Alzheimer's disease and related conditions. Departments with participating specialists include anatomy, radiology, pathology, ophthalmology and psychology. *Type:* Research center.

University of Kansas
Center for Neurobiology and Immunology Research
Higuchi Biosciences Ctr.   Ph: (785)864-5183
2099 Constant Ave.   Fax: (785)864-3578
Lawrence, KS 66047-3729
E-mail: ekm@smissman.hbc.ukans.edu
URL: http://www.hbc.ukans.edu
Contact: Dr. Elias K. Michaelis, Dir.
Desc: Neurobiology and immunology, focusing on the problems of chronic, neurodegenerative diseases and immunological disorders. Specific interests include the development of new analytical methods for monitoring nerve cell activity in the brain, exploratory research in the mechanisms of neurodegeneration and the development of new therapeutic strategies based on the use of proteins or oligonucleotides as drug treatments, studies of the regulation of antibody production by immune system cells and the development of new screening procedures for immunotherapeutic agents, designing of new peptide drugs for the control of immune rejection reactions, and new molecular biological tools for recombinant DNA research. *Type:* Research center.

University of Kansas
Neurobiology Research Laboratory
VA Med. Ctr.   Ph: (816)861-4700
4801 Linwood Blvd.   Fax: (816)922-3375
Kansas City, MO 64128
E-mail: serpin@kuhub.cc.ukans.edu
URL: http://www.kumc.edu/kcbamc/research/nbrl
Contact: Barry W. Festoff, MD, Dir.
Desc: Development, plasticity, and diseases of the nervous system. Studies focus on synaptic formation and metabolism; roles of serine proteases and inhibitors (serpins); regulation of amyloid precursor protein processing in Alzheimer's disease; and biological markers in head injuries. *Type:* Research center.

University of Kentucky
Alzheimer's Disease Research Center
101 Sanders-Brown Bldg.   Ph: (606)323-6040
Lexington, KY 40536-0230   Fax: (606)323-2866
E-mail: wmarkesbery@aging.coa.uky.edu
URL: http://www.cua.uky.edu
Contact: William R. Markesbery, MD, Dir.
Desc: Alzheimer's disease, focusing on the cause, treatment, and eventual cure. *Type:* Research center.

University of Louisville
Center for Research in the Special Senses
Myers Hall   Ph: (502)852-0340
Louisville, KY 40292   Fax: (502)852-0865
E-mail: snbarno1@ulkyum.louisville.edu
Contact: Susan Barnett, Res.Admin.
Desc: Sensory research, including deterioration through aging. Investigates the effects of chronic sinusitis, loss of balance, and diabetes on the senses. *Type:* Research center.

University of Manitoba
Spinal Cord Research Centre
Fac. of Med.   Ph: (204)789-3761
730 William Ave.   Fax: (204)789-3930
Winnipeg, MB, Canada R3E 3J7
E-mail: info@scrc.umanitoba.ca
URL: http://www.scrc.umanitoba.ca
Contact: Prof. Larry M. Jordan, PhD, Co-Dir.
Desc: Mechanisms controlling major functional systems in the brain and spinal cord and development of clinical tools for the treatment of injury and diseases affecting these systems. *Type:* Research center.

University of Maryland
Center for the Study of Cerebrovascular Disease and Stroke
22 S. Green St.   Ph: (410)328-5080
Baltimore, MD 21201   Fax: (410)328-1409
E-mail: tprice@umab.umd.edu
Contact: Thomas R. Price, MD, Prin. Investigator.
Desc: Cerebrovascular disease, including stroke, computer modelling of stroke, use of artificial intelligence in stroke patient care, aphasia recovery in stroke patients, and development of prognostics for stroke patient care, criteria of diagnosis of embolic stroke, drug use/abuse as a cause of stroke, stroke in the young, and progressing ischemic stroke. Activities are carried out through the Stroke Epidemiology Unit, Systolic Hypertension in the Elderly Project, Cardiovascular Health Study. *Type:* Research center.

University of Maryland

Multiple Sclerosis Clinical Center

Neurology Dept., N4W46   Ph: (410)328-5605
22 S. Greene St.   Fax: (410)328-5899
Baltimore, MD 21201
E-mail: kjohnson@neurologyl.ab.umd.edu
Contact: Kenneth P. Johnson, MD, Chm.
Desc: Immunologic and virologic research in multiple sclerosis. Also conducts clinical trials of new treatment for multiple sclerosis. *Type:* Research center.

University of Maryland at College Park

Neuroscience and Cognitive Science Program

College of Life Sci.   Ph: (301)405-8910
College Park, MD 20742   Fax: (301)314-9358
E-mail: sd136@umail.umd.edu
URL: http://www.inform.umd.edu
Contact: Dr. Arthur Popper, Dir.
Desc: Coordinates and integrates neurosciences and cognitive studies. *Type:* Research center.

University of Medicine and Dentistry of New Jersey

Institute for Disability Prevention ans Wellness

1 Medical Center Dr., Ste. 146   Ph: (609)566-6247
Stratford, NJ 08084   Fax: (609)566-6397
E-mail: findletw@umdnj.edu
Contact: Prof. Thomas W. Findley, MD, Dir.
Desc: Rehabilitation and neuromuscular disorders and wellness. *Type:* Research center.

University of Memphis

Neuropsychology Laboratory

Psychology Dept.   Ph: (901)678-2821
Memphis, TN 38152   Fax: (901)678-2579
E-mail: clong@cc.memphis.edu
URL: http://neuro.psyc.memphis.edu
Contact: Dr. Charles J. Long, Dir.
Desc: Evaluation and development of assessment and treatment procedures for neurologically impaired patients. Specific studies focus on head trauma and chronic pain. *Type:* Research center.

University of Miami

Center for Neurological Diseases

1501 NW 9th Ave.   Ph: (305)243-6732
PO Box 016960   Free: 800-707-5589
Miami, FL 33136   Fax: (305)243-4678
Contact: Noble David, MD, Contact.
Desc: Neuroscience, including physiological, neurochemical, anatomical, metabolic, neuropharmacological and vascular mechanisms that account for normal brain function, and the changes in these which underlie neurological diseases such as stroke, senile dementia, epilepsy, Parkinson's syndrome, Alzheimer's disease, multiple sclerosis, amyotrophic lateral sclerosis (ALS), and other neurological dysfunctions. *Type:* Research center.

University of Miami

Cerebral Vascular Disease Research Center

Department of Neurology,   Ph: (305)243-6449
(D4-5)   Fax: (305)547-5830
PO Box 016960
Miami, FL 33101
Contact: Dr. Myron D. Ginsberg, Hd.
Desc: Cerebrovascular physiology, brain metabolism, and pathophysiology of cerebral ischemia/hypoxia, focusing on animal models of focal and global ischemia. *Type:* Research center.

University of Miami

Miami Project to Cure Paralysis

PO Box 016960, Mail Locator   Ph: (305)243-6226
R-48   Free: 800-782-6387
Miami, FL 33101   Fax: (305)243-4427
E-mail: mpinfo@miamiproject.med.miami.edu
URL: http://www.miamiproject.miami.edu

Contact: W. Dalton Dietrich, PhD, Sci.Dir.

Desc: Basic, clinical, and rehabilitative studies of spinal cord injury (SCI), emphasizing characterization of SCI (magnetic resonance imaging, electron microscopy, experimental models, and electrophysiology); design of effective treatments (molecular neurobiology, cell therapy, and tissue transplantation); and maximization of function (functional electrical stimulation, male fertility, and motor-evoked potentials). *Type:* Research center.

University of Miami

Touch Research Institute

Department of Pediatrics   Ph: (305)243-6781
Medical School   Fax: (305)243-6488
PO Box 016820
Miami, FL 33101
E-mail: tfield@mednet.med.miami.edu
URL: http://www.miami.edu/touch-research

Contact: Tiffany M. Field, PhD, Dir.

Desc: Sense of touch, including the biology of touch in health and development, and the role of touch therapy in medicine and the treatment of disease. Specific research areas include the use of massage in enhancing immune function in AIDS and cancer patients, massage effects on growth in premature infants, underlying mechanism responsible for the relationship between touch and physical growth and emotional development in infants and children, the role of massage in sports medicine and wound healing, the effects of touch therapy on addictive personalities, pain reduction during invasive medical procedures, and alleviation of skin disorders such as eczema and psoriasis. *Type:* Research center.

University of Michigan

Center for Neural Communication Technology

4112 Elecl. Engg. & Cmpt. Sci.   Ph: (734)764-5417
Ann Arbor, MI 48109   Fax: (734)763-8041
E-mail: dja@eecs.umich.edu
URL: http://www.engin.umich.edu/facilty/cnct/

Contact: Prof. David J. Anderson, PhD, Dir.

Desc: Neural circuits, including extensions of micromachined microelectrode, biological neural networks, histological visualization and assesment. *Type:* Research center.

University of Michigan

Neurobiology Laboratory

6223 School of Dentistry   Ph: (734)763-1080
1101 N. University Ave.   Fax: (734)764-7406
Ann Arbor, MI 48109-1078
E-mail: rmbrad@umich.edu
URL: http://www.umich.edu

Contact: Robert M. Bradley, Dir.

Desc: Sensory and motor circuits, taste sensation, and associated reflexes, including salivation. Specific areas of study include the sense of taste, focusing on the cellular factors that regulate functional differentiation of salt taste pathways; interrelations between afferent taste input and brainstem control of salivary gland reflexes; and regeneration of peripheral taste nerves through micro-electrode arrays to develop a system from chronic, in vivo study of regenerated sensory nerve fibers. *Type:* Research center.

University of Michigan

Neurosurgery Laboratory

Kresge Med. Res. Bldg.   Ph: (734)764-1207
Ann Arbor, MI 48109   Fax: (734)763-7322
Contact: Dr. J.T. Hoff, Dir.
Desc: Cerebral ischemia, edema, structure and function of central nervous system and its ability to sustain trauma, vascular insufficiency, and brain tumor oncogenesis. *Type:* Research center.

University of Michigan

Stomatognathic Physiology Laboratory

3218 School of Dentistry   Ph: (734)764-7149
1011 N. University Ave.   Fax: (734)764-7406
Ann Arbor, MI 48109-1078
E-mail: csto@umich.edu
Contact: Christian S. Stohler, Dir.
Desc: Central nervous system adaptations to pain, focusing on the effect of muscle pain on motor function. Also investigates the significance of experimental pain models for various types of human pathology. *Type:* Research center.

University of Minnesota

Positron Emission Tomography Center

Minneapolis VA Medical Center   Ph: (612)725-2230
1 Veterans Dr.   Fax: (612)725-2068
Minneapolis, MN 55417
E-mail: webmaster@pet.med.va.gov
URL: http://pet.med.va.gov:8080/
Contact: David Rottenberg, Dir.
Desc: Clinically-oriented research in cardiology, neurology and psychiatry. *Type:* Research center.

University of Montreal

Experimental Neuropsychology Research Group

C.P. 6128, Succursale Centre-   Ph: (514)343-6111
Ville   Fax: (514)343-5787
Montreal, PQ, Canada H3C 3J7
E-mail: leporef@ere.umontreal.ca
URL: http://www.fas.umontreal.ca/psy/grplabs/grene/index.htm
Contact: Dr. Franco Lepore, Dir.
Desc: Neural substrates of sensory-motor integration in animals and humans, focusing on the anatomical and physiological organization of sensory systems (vision, somesthesis, audition) in several animal species, especially monkeys and cats. Also conducts behavioral evaluation of humans with normal sensory-motor function (visual perception, visuomotor functions, somesthesis, audition) and humans with congenital or acquired cerebral damage (agenesis of the corpus callosum, callosotomies, hemispherectomies, and occipital lobe damage). *Type:* Research center.

University of Montreal

Neurological Sciences Research Centre

Faculty of Med.   Ph: (514)343-6366
PO Box 6128, Sta. Centre-ville   Fax: (514)343-6113
Montreal, PQ, Canada H3C 3J7
E-mail: crsn@ere.umontreal.ca
URL: http://www.cam.org/~cyrd/crsn/
Contact: Dr. Serge Rossignol, Dir.
Desc: Functions of the nervous system, including sensory motor functions, and the cortical and subcortical control of rhythmical movements of the limbs and voluntary movements of the arm and the hand; the sensory motor system; sensory mechanisms concerning pain and plasticity; functional properties and localization of cell ensembles defined by their neurotransmitter in various regions of the brain; and functions of sleep, speech, and aging. *Type:* Research center.

University of Montreal

Research Group on the Autonomic Nervous System

Department of Physiology/   Ph: (514)343-7562
   Faculty of Med.   Fax: (514)343-2257
2900 boulevard Edouard-
   Montpetit
CP 6128, Succursale Centre-ville
Montreal, PQ, Canada H3C 3J7
E-mail: grsna@ere.umontreal.ca
Contact: Dr. Jacques de Champlain, Dir.

Desc: Studies of the autonomic nervous system, focusing on cell and molecular biology of sympathetic neurotransmission, receptors, second messengers, cardiovascular regulation, and clinical research projects in hypertension and cardiac dysfunctions. *Type:* Research center.

University of North Carolina at Chapel Hill

Neuroscience Center

CB 7250   Ph: (919)966-2405
Chapel Hill, NC 27599-7250   Fax: (919)966-1322
E-mail: kuni@css.unc.edu
URL: http://www.neuroscience.unc.edu
Contact: Kunihiko Suzuki, MD, Dir.

Desc: Prevention, diagnosis, and treatment of mental retardation and related aspects of human development utilizing a single disciplinary or interdisciplinary approach. Basic research is targeted at obtaining new knowledge of structure and function of the developing nervous system to be applied to other neurological and psychiatric illness. *Type:* Research center.

University of Oregon

Institute of Neuroscience

Huestis Hall   Ph: (541)686-4556
Eugene, OR 97403   Fax: (541)686-4548
E-mail: morrow@uoneuro.uoregon.edu
URL: http://www.neuro.uoregon.edu
Contact: Dr. William Roberts, Dir.

Desc: Interdisciplinary approaches to basic questions in neuroscience, with particular emphasis on behavior, neurochemistry, neurophysiology, developmental neurobiology, and sensory systems. The Institute is composed of faculty members from the Departments of Biology, Computer Science, Psychology, and Physical Education. *Type:* Research center.

University of Ottawa

Neurosciences Research Institute

451 Smyth Rd.   Ph: (613)562-5461
Ottawa, ON, Canada K1H   Fax: (613)562-5403
   8M5
E-mail: plajeune@danis.med.uottawa.ca
URL: http://www.nri.on.ca
Contact: Dr. Antoine Hakim, Dir.

Desc: Neuroprotection, neuronal regeneration and recovery, mechanisms of cell injury, stroke, depression, schizophrenia, and axotomy. *Type:* Research center.

University of Pennsylvania

Brain Behavior Laboratory

Department of Neuropsychiatry   Ph: (215)662-2826
Gates Bldg., 10th Fl.   Fax: (215)662-7903
3400 Spruce St.
Philadelphia, PA 19104-4283
E-mail: gur@bbl.psycha.upenn.edu
URL: http://www.med.upenn.edu/bbl/BBL_home.shtml
Contact: Ruben Gur, PhD, Dir.

Desc: New techniques for measuring regional brain function in relationship to behavior including cerebral blood flow, and metabolism using positron emmission tomogra-

phy (PET); and functional MRI (FMRI); anatomic measures using magnetic resonance imaging (MRI), and neuropsychological testing for studying brain behavior relationships. Populations studied include normals (average and talented), psychiatric (schizophrenic, major depression, anxiety disorders, and dementia), and neurologic (stroke or cerebrovascular disease, epilepsy and parkinsonism). *Type:* Research center.

University of Pennsylvania

Cerebrovascular Research Center

Johnson Pavilion, Rm. 429   Ph: (215)662-2632
3610 Hamilton Walk   Fax: (215)349-5629
Philadelphia, PA 19104
E-mail: reivich@cvrc.med.upenn.edu
Contact: Dr. Martin Reivich, Dir.

Desc: Cerebrovascular research with an emphasis on cerebral circulation and metabolism. Conducts PET, SPECT, MRI, neuropsychologic, and neurologic studies on various brain disorders, including acute stroke, brain tumor, epilepsy, dementia, Parkinson's disease, and schizophrenia. *Type:* Research center.

University of Pennsylvania

David Mahoney Institute of Neurological Sciences

Stemmler Hall, Rm. 467   Ph: (215)898-8754
Philadelphia, PA 19104-6074   Fax: (215)573-2015
E-mail: dichter@mail.med.upenn.edu
URL: http://www.med.upenn.edu/ins/
Contact: Prof. Marc A. Dichter, MD,PhD, Dir.

Desc: Nervous system, including multidisciplinary basic studies in neuroanatomy, neurobiology, neurochemistry, neuroembryology, neurophysiology, neuropharmacology, physiological psychology, computational neuroscience, pathophysiology of neurological, and psychiatric diseases. *Type:* Research center.

University of Pennsylvania

Smell and Taste Center

5 Ravdin Bldg.   Ph: (215)662-6580
3400 Spruce St.   Fax: (215)349-5266
Philadelphia, PA 19104
E-mail: doty@mail.med.upenn.edu
Contact: Dr. Richard L. Doty, Dir.

Desc: Identifies and treats disorders of taste and smell. Develops clinical smell and taste tests, investigates nasal airflow parameters, examines gustatory glucose sensitivity in diabetes and depression, studies MRI-based measures of brain volume changes in olfactory disorders, studies neuroendocrine relations with chemosensory function, conducts behavioral and neurophysiological studies of olfactory and trigeminal function, and studies the pathophysiology of oral sensory abnormalities. *Type:* Research center.

University of Pittsburgh

Center for Neuroscience

Biomedical Science Tower,   Ph: (412)624-5043
   E1440   Fax: (412)648-1441
Pittsburgh, PA 15261
Contact: Pat Levitt, Co-Dir.

Desc: Neuroscience and neural diseases. *Type:* Research center.

University of Puerto Rico

Institute of Neurobiology

Med. Sci. Campus   Ph: (787)721-4149
Blvd. del Valle 201   Fax: (787)725-3804
Viejo San Juan, PR 00901
E-mail: a_selverston@rcmaca.upr.clu.edu
Contact: Allen I. Selverston, PhD, Dir.

Desc: Neurophysiology, neuroanatomy, neurochemistry, and neuropharmacology, primarily in relation to tropical marine invertebrates and lower vertebrates, including cell electrophysiology, and biochemical and immunological studies. *Type:* Research center.

University of Quebec at Montreal

Cognitive Neuroscience Laboratory

PB 8888, Succ. Centre-Ville   Ph: (514)987-7002
Montreal, PQ, Canada H3C   Fax: (514)987-8952
   3P8
E-mail: lnc@uqam.ca
Contact: Francois Richer, PhD, Dir.

Desc: Cognitive neuroscience, including frontal dysfunction, movement disorders and cerebral bases of speech, language, attention, and memory. Also performs fMRi, evoked potential modeling and quantitative speech analysis. *Type:* Research center.

University of Rochester

Center for Visual Science

Rochester, NY 14627   Ph: (716)275-2459
   Fax: (716)271-3043
E-mail: david@cvs.rochester.edu
URL: http://www.cvs.rochester.edu/
Contact: Dr. David Williams, Dir.

Desc: Optical, physiological, perceptual, and computational aspects of visual science. Encourages research in vision in Departments of Brain and Cognitive Sciences, Optics, Neurology, Neurobiology and Anatomy, Ophthalmology, and Computer Science. *Type:* Research center.

University of Tennessee at Memphis

Center for Neuroscience

875 Monroe Ave.   Ph: (901)448-5956
Memphis, TN 38163-2194   Fax: (901)448-8098
E-mail: skitai@utmem1.edu
URL: http://cns.utmem.edu/home.html
Contact: Dr. Stephen T. Kitai, Dir.

Desc: General neurosciences, including epilepsy studies; movement disorders (Parkinson's disease, Huntington's disease, and muscular dystrophy); vision studies (retinal disease and central visual pathways malfunction); developmental neurobiology (tissue culture and transplant in the basal ganglia, development of neural circuitry in the central visual system, neurological mutants and chimeras, development of cerebral and cerebellar cortical cytoarchitechtonics, and development of synapses in the retina); neuroendocrinology (control of brain neurotransmitters, temperature regulation in host defense response to infectious agents, and hormonal regulation of neuroeffector mechanisms); neurotransmitter action in the brain (biochemical analysis of neurotransmitters and hormone action, second messenger systems and effect of psychiatric medicine on these systems, and neuropeptide systems involved in pain and stress); and central nervous system control of the cardiovascular system (hypertension and temperature regulation); and sleep mechanisms. *Type:* Research center.

University of Texas at Austin

Laboratory for Artificial Neural Systems

ENS 516   Ph: (512)471-8980
Austin, TX 78712-1084   Fax: (512)471-5907
E-mail: ghosh@pine.ece.utexas.edu
URL: http://www.lans.ece.utexas.edu/
Contact: Prof. Joydeep Ghosh, Dir.

Desc: Artificial neural systems. *Type:* Research center.

University of Texas at Dallas

Sleep Study Unit

Southwestern Med. Ctr.	Ph: (214)648-8758
Department of Psychiatry	Fax: (214)648-5444
5323 Harry Hines Blvd.	
Dallas, TX 75235-9070	

Contact: Roseanne Armitage, PhD, Dir.

Desc: Sleep/wake studies, including insomnia, depression, narcolepsy, schizophrenia and normal sleep, as well as basic sleep neurophysiology. *Type:* Research center.

University of Texas Southwestern Medical Center at Dallas

Alzheimer's Disease Center

Department of Psychiatry	Ph: (214)648-3886
5323 Harry Hines Blvd.	Fax: (214)648-2450
Dallas, TX 75235-8898	

E-mail: mcullu@mednet.swmed.edu

Contact: Dr. Munro Cullum, Dir., Neuropsychology.

Desc: Alzheimer's diseasee and aging in the brain, focusing on loss of cognitive functions and test measurements including IQ, problem solving, abstract thinking, spatial and dexterity skills, attention and concentration, language function, and memory. *Type:* Research center.

University of Texas Southwestern Medical Center at Dallas

Neuromuscular Treatment Center

Department of Neurology	Ph: (214)648-6419
5323 Harry Hines Blvd.	Fax: (214)648-9311
Dallas, TX 75235-8897	

E-mail: wbryan@mednet.swmed.edu

Contact: Wilson Bryan, MD, Contact.

Desc: Immune-mediated neuromuscular disorders, including myasthenia gravis, amyotrophic Lateral Sclerosis (Lou Gehnig's Disease), Spinal Muscullar Atrophy, and inflammatory polyneuropathy. Activities include clinical therapeutic trials. *Type:* Research center.

University of Toronto

Centre for Research in Neurodegenerative Diseases

Tanz Neuroscience Bldg.	Ph: (416)978-7461
6 Queen's Park Crescent W.	Fax: (416)978-1878
Toronto, ON, Canada M5S 3H2	

Contact: Dr. Peter St. George-Hyslop, Int.Dir.

Desc: Neurodegenerative diseases of the human brain, focusing on the causes of Alzheimer's disease, Amyotrophic Lateral Sclerosis, and other nerve cell defects, the development of effective treatment for patient care, and clinical trials. Specific areas of study include genetic mutation of chromosome 21, protein degeneration of synapses and synaptic vesicles, identification and characterization of the molecular development of the nervous systems, collaborative studies on the aluminum hypothesis for Alzheimer's disease, and the study of motor control and the mechanisms that result in nerve cell degeneration in both the brain and the spinal cord. *Type:* Research center.

University of Toronto

Neurochemistry Laboratory

6368 Med. Sci. Bldg.	Ph: (416)978-8971
Toronto, ON, Canada M5S 1A8	Fax: (416)971-2112

E-mail: j.wherrett@utoronto.va

Contact: Dr. John R. Wherrett, Co-Dir.

Desc: Neurochemistry, including studies on chemical pathology of nervous system, phospholipids, lipid metabolism in subcellular membranes, and animal models of stroke. *Type:* Research center.

University of Toronto

Toronto Hospital Research Institute

Playfair Neuroscience Unit

399 Bathurst St.	Ph: (416)603-5030
Toronto, ON, Canada M5T 2S8	Fax: (416)603-5745

E-mail: carlen@playfair.utoronto.ca

Contact: Dr. P.L. Carlen, Dir.

Desc: Cell and membrane neurobiology, molecular neurobiology, neuroprotection, cognitive and neurophysiological aspects of normal and abnormal limb movement control, normal and pathological eye movement control and visual processing, neuropharmacology, spinal cord injury, neuro-oncology, epilepsy and cerebrovascular disease. *Type:* Research center.

University of Virginia

Neuromuscular Center

UVA Med. Ctr.	Ph: (804)924-5304
Department of Neurology, Box 394	Free: 800-251-3627
	Fax: (804)924-9068
Charlottesville, VA 22908	

E-mail: lhp3n@virginia.edu

URL: http://www.virginia.edu

Contact: Dr. Larry H. Phillips, II, Co-Dir.

Desc: Electrophysiology of dystrophy skeletal muscle fibers, biochemical studies of the properties of normal and dystrophic cells in culture, structure and chromosome linkage of human muscle genes, genetic heterogeneity among the hereditary motor sensory neuropathies, long chain fatty acids in Olivo-Ponto-cerebellar atrophy, the axonal cytoskeleton following IDPN administration, biochemical differences in shrimp claw muscle protein, membrane enzymes involved in muscle regulation, safety margin of neuromuscular transmission in normal and diseased muscle, and the humoral hypothesis in the Eaton-Lambert syndrome. Also conducts clinical research in such neuromuscular diseases as myasthenia gravis, Eaton-Lambert syndrome, Charcot-Marie-tooth disease, and diabetic polyneuropathy. *Type:* Research center.

University of Washington

Alzheimer Research Center

4225 Roosevelt Way, NE No. 301	Ph: (206)543-6761
	Fax: (206)543-8791
Seattle, WA 98105-6099	

E-mail: walters@chinook.alz.washington.edu

URL: http://www.weber.u.washington.edu/~adrcweb/

Contact: Marie Walters, Admin.

Desc: Basic mechanisms underlying the development of adult dementing disorders, with particular attention to heritable susceptibility factors underlying Alzheimer's disease. *Type:* Research center.

University of Wisconsin--Madison

Neuropsychology Laboratory

600 N. Highland Ave.	Ph: (608)263-5430
Madison, WI 53792-6180	Fax: (608)265-0172

E-mail: hermann@neurology.wisc.edu

Contact: Dr. Bruce Hermann, Dir.

Desc: Clinical neuropsychology in neuropsychological correlates of epilepsy, cognitive and affective changes in aging, and differential diagnosis of dementia with a view toward cognitive and memory remediation. *Type:* Research center.

Veterans Affairs Medical Center (West Los Angeles, CA)

National Neurological Research Specimen Bank (W 127A)

W. Los Angeles VA Med. Ctr.	Ph: (310)268-3536
11301 Wilshire Blvd.	Fax: (310)268-4768
Los Angeles, CA 90073	

E-mail: wtourtel@ucla.edu

URL: http://www.loni.ucla.edu/~nnrsb/nnrsb

Contact: Dr. W.W. Tourtellotte, Dir.

Desc: Serves as a resource bank for cryopreserved human brain, spinal fluid, serum, and other tissue. Provides specimens to research community, particularly in the area of neurological and psychiatric diseases, including Huntington's disease, Alzheimer's disease, Down's syndrome, multiple sclerosis, and epilepsy. *Type:* Research center.

Wake Forest University

Cerebrovascular Research Center

Bowman Gray Sch. of Med.	Ph: (336)716-2336
Department of Neurology	Fax: (336)716-5477
Med. Ctr. Blvd.	
Winston Salem, NC 27157-1068	

E-mail: kneedham@wfusm.edu

Contact: Dr. James F. Toole, Dir.

Desc: Cerebrovascular research, including ultrasound, neurological diseases, coronary studies, biostatistics, transient ischemic attack (TIA), comparative medicine in atherosclerosis, neuropsychological evaluation, cerebral circulation, and anatomy/physiology. *Type:* Research center.

Wake Forest University

Epilepsy Education Center

Medical Center Blvd.	Ph: (336)716-2321
Winston Salem, NC 27157-1078	Free: 800-642-0500
	Fax: (336)716-9489

E-mail: pgibson@bgsm.edu

Contact: Dr. Patricia Gibson, Dir.

Desc: Social and psychological aspects of epilepsy and clinical trials of anti-epileptic medication. *Type:* Research center.

Wakefulness Sleep Education and Research Foundation, Inc.

1442 Santa Luisa Dr.	Ph: (619)457-4233
Solana Beach, CA 92075	Fax: (619)657-0559

E-mail: mitter@scripps.edu

Contact: Merrill M. Mitler, PhD, Dir.

Desc: Clinical sleep studies including narcolepsy, drug development, and sleep apnea. *Type:* Research center.

Wayne State University

Laura S. Nye Surgical Research Fund for Desmoid Tumors

Department of Surgery	Ph: (313)745-8778
Harper Hosp.	Fax: (313)745-1873
3990 John R.	
Detroit, MI 48201	

E-mail: dfsurg@aol.com

Contact: David Fromm, MD, Ch.

Desc: Desmoid tumor treatment, including photodynamic therapy after excision of tumor. *Type:* Research center.

William T. Gossett Parkinson's Disease Center

Henry Ford Hospital	Ph: (313)876-2585
Department of Neurology	Fax: (313)876-3014
2799 W. Grand Blvd.	
Detroit, MI 48202	

E-mail: gorell@neuro.hfh.edu

Contact: Jay M. Gorell, MD, Dir.

Desc: Parkinson's disease and its causes and treatments, including risk factors, cognitive and motor deficits, new medication trials, animal nerve cell investigations, and disordered brain chemistry measurements. *Type:* Research center.

Yale University

PVA/EPVA Center for Neuroscience and Regeneration Research

VA Med. Ctr.   Ph: (203)937-3802
Bldg. 34, 127A   Fax: (203)937-3801
West Haven, CT 06516
E-mail: stephen_waxman@qm.yale.edu
Contact: Dr. Stephen G. Waxman, Dir.
Desc: Basic mechanisms of central nervous system development, function, injury, and functional recovery with a major emphasis on spinal cord dysfunction. Concerns include molecular basis for neurological disorders, nerve cell growth and regeneration, pathophysiology of conduction in injured nerve fibers, regeneration of the central nervous system in mammalian species, and multiple sclerosis as a model for understanding how demyelinated nerve fibers regain their ability to effectively transmit electrical impulses. *Type:* Research center.

Nuclear Energy

Nuclear Power Plants Worldwide

Gale Group Inc.
27500 Drake Rd.   Ph: (248)699-4253
Farmington Hills, MI 48331-   Free: 800-877-GALE
  3535   Fax: (248)699-8070
E-mail: galeord@galegroup.com
URL: http://www.galegroup.com.
Contact: Peter Dresser, Editor.
Desc: Approximately 740 operable and nonoperable (planned, on order, under construction, shut down, cancelled, indefinitely deferred, or decommissioned) nuclear power plants in 39 countries. *Type:* Directory.

Nuclear Regulatory Commission

11555 Rockville Pike   Ph: (301)415-7000
Washington, DC 20555-0001
URL: http://www.nrc.gov/
Contact: Shirley Ann Jackson, Chairman of the Board.
Desc: The Nuclear Regulatory Commission licenses and regulates the civilian uses of nuclear energy to protect public health and safety and the environment. *Type:* Government agency, office, or program.

Nuclear War and Weapons

American Nuclear Energy Council

410 1st St. SE   Ph: (202)484-2670
Washington, DC 20003
Contact: Edward M. Davis, Pres.
Desc: Organizations having an interest in any facet of the peaceful application of nuclear energy, including uranium suppliers, utilities, engineer/contractors, and equipment manufacturers. Purposes are to: support the development of nuclear power as an energy source; coordinate and project the interests of the American nuclear industry to Congress and the Executive Branch; relate congressional and Executive Branch actions affecting nuclear energy issues to member companies. *Type:* Association.

American Nuclear Society

555 N. Kensington Ave.   Ph: (708)352-6611
La Grange Park, IL 60526   Fax: (708)352-0499
URL: http://www.ans.org
Contact: Harry A. Bradley, Exec.Dir.
Desc: Physicists, chemists, educators, mathematicians, life scientists, engineers, metallurgists, managers, and administrators with professional experience in nuclear science or nuclear engineering. Works to advance science and engineering in the nuclear industry. Disseminates information; promotes research; conducts meetings devoted to scientific and technical papers; works with government agencies, educational institutions, and other organizations dealing with nuclear issues. *Type:* Association.

Campaign to Boycott SDI

c/o John B. Kogut   Ph: (217)333-1060
1110 W. Green St.   Fax: (217)333-4990
University of Illinois
Urbana, IL 61801
Contact: John B. Kogut, Co-Founder.
Desc: Scientists and engineers in applied physics, astronomy, chemistry, computer science, engineering, mathematics, and physics departments at universities, who affirm that they will not accept government contracts to perform research on the Strategic Defense Initiative, known colloquially as Star Wars. Believes that it is not possible to build a reliable SDI system; that building the SDI system will spur the arms race, prevent meaningful arms control negotiations, and violate existing arms control agreements; and that the SDI system will encourage nuclear war. Seeks to curtail the development of the SDI system; educates the scientific community on the role it has been asked to play in increasing support for the SDI system. *Type:* Association.

INFACT

256 Hanover St., 3rd Fl.   Ph: (617)742-4583
Boston, MA 02113   Fax: (617)367-0191
URL: http://www.infact.com
Contact: Kathryn Mulvey, Dir.
Desc: Works to stop life-threatening activities of transnational corporations and increase their accountability to people around the world. Builds strategic campaigns to forge change. Best known for its two successful international consumer boycotts: the first from 1977-1984 of Nestle, successfully improved Nestle's unethical marketing of infant formula in developing countries; the second from 1986-1993 of General Electric, succeeded in removing GE from its leadership role in the production and promotion of nuclear weapons. *Type:* Association.

Institute of Nuclear Power Operations

700 Galleria Pky.   Ph: (770)644-8000
Atlanta, GA 30339-5957   Fax: (770)644-8549
Contact: Ken Strahm, Pres.
Desc: Electric utilities operating nuclear power plants. Aids in the evaluation of plant operations and develops criteria. Operates the National Academy for Nuclear Training. *Type:* Association.

International Physicians for the Prevention of Nuclear War

727 Massachusetts Ave., 2nd Fl. Ph: (617)868-5050
Cambridge, MA 02139-3323   Fax: (617)868-2560
E-mail: ippnwbos@igc.apc.org
URL: http://www.healthnet.org/ippnw/
Contact: Michael Christ, Exec.Dir.
Desc: Federation of national physicians' organizations representing 200,000 physicians in 60 countries dedicated to mobilizing the influence of the medical profession against the threat of war and its weapons. Seeks to focus international attention on the medical consequences of nuclear or conventional war. Works to delegitimize, and therefore abolish, all forms of nuclear weaponry. *Type:* Association.

National Nuclear Data Center (NNDC)

Brookhaven National Laboratory - Department of Advanced Technology National Nuclear Data Center
PO Box 5000   Ph: (516)344-5084
Upton, NY 11973-5000
E-mail: services@bnlnd2.dne.bnl.gov
URL: http://www.nndc.bnl.gov
Contact: Thomas W. Burrows, nndctb@bnl.gov.
Desc: The NNDC Online Data Service contains several national nuclear databases, including: CINDA; CSISRS (EXFOR); ENSDF; ENDF; MIRD; NUDAT; NSR and XRAY. Also included are newsletters and data citation guidelines. *Type:* Database.

Nuclear Control Institute

Nuclear Control Institute
1000 Connecticut Ave. NW,   Ph: (202)822-8444
  Ste. 804   Fax: (202)452-0892
Washington, DC 20036
E-mail: nci@access.digex.net
URL: http://www.nci.org/nci/index.htm
Contact: Steven Dolley, Research Director.
Desc: Site contains information on NCI related activities and links to many nuclear-related WWW sites. All the details about current world nuclear hotspots are covered such as China, India/Pakistan, and Iraq. *Type:* Database.

Nuclear Science Abstracts

U.S. Department of Energy
Office of Scientific and Technical Information (OSTI)
PO Box 62   Ph: (423)574-1000
Oak Ridge, TN 37831
E-mail: ostiwebmaster@apollo.osti.gov
URL: http://www.osti.gov
Desc: Contains more than 947,000 citations to worldwide literature on nuclear science and technology. *Available:* The Dialog Corporation, DIALOG. *Type:* Database.

Physicians for Social Responsibility

1101 14th St., 7th Fl.   Ph: (202)898-0150
Washington, DC 20005   Fax: (202)898-0172
Contact: Robert K. Musil, Ph.D., Exec. Dir.
Desc: Medical professionals and others with doctoral degrees and medical students concerned with the threat of nuclear war, environmental degradation, and violence in our society; others supporting the work of PSR. Educates the public on the medical effects of nuclear war and nuclear weapons and on the implications of national policy and legislative actions on arms control and environmental issues. *Type:* Association.

Union of Concerned Scientists

2 Brattle Square   Ph: (617)547-5552
Cambridge, MA 02238-9105   Fax: (617)864-9405
Contact: Howard C. Ris, Jr., Exec.Dir.
Desc: Advocacy organization concerned about the impact of advanced technology on society. Conducts research on energy policy, global environmental problems, transportation, biotechnology, and arms control. Disseminates research results to the public and assists members and the public in presenting their views before administrative agencies and the courts. *Type:* Association.

The U.S. Nuclear Weapons Cost Study Project

U.S. Nuclear Weapons Cost Study Project
The Brookings Institution   Ph: (202)797-6000
1775 Massachusetts Ave. NW   Fax: (202)797-6004
Washington, DC 20036-2188
E-mail: brookinfo@brook.edu
URL: http://www.brook.edu/fp/projects/nucwcost/weapons.htm
Contact: Stephen I. Schwartz, Director, sschwartz@brook.edu.
Desc: Excerpts from some of the official and expansive reports and studies about the U.S. nuclear program. *Type:* Database.

Utility Nuclear Waste and Transportation Program

Desc: Electric utilities united to promote solutions to the problem of radioactive waste management. Seeks to monitor high-level and low-level nuclear waste management programs. Maintains task forces and working groups for specific problems. *Type:* Association.

Women's Action for New Directions

691 Massachusetts Ave. Ph: (617)643-6740
Arlington, MA 02476 Free: 800-444-
                      WAND
                      Fax: (617)643-6744
E-mail: info@wand.org
URL: http://www.wand.org
Contact: Susan Shaer, Exec.Dir.

Desc: Women's initiative uniting women and men in an effort to halt and reverse the nuclear arms race and redirect spending to meet human and environmental needs. Objectives are: to empower women to act politically; to raise public awareness about nuclear issues; to support grass roots organizing for educational and political activities across the country; to monitor legislative activities that have an impact on nuclear weapons policy; to organize congressional district lobbying networks to be mobilized before key nuclear weapons votes. Compiles statistics. *Type:* Association.

World Peacemakers

11427 Scottsbury Ter. Ph: (301)916-0442
Germantown, MD 20876 Fax: (301)916-5335
E-mail: worldpeacemakers@compuserve.com
URL: http://www.nonviolence.org/
Contact: Bill Price, Dir.

Desc: Promotes an understanding of what true security is and how to move toward it. Emphasizes the ethical, spiritual, economic, and political dimensions of the "growing threat of nuclear war and the overall degradation of our security as the arms race continues." Works to increase public understanding of the "unprecedented dangers" facing mankind and publicize the need for the U.S. to stop the arms race and concentrate on solving global problems such as unemployment and the protection of cities and rural communities. *Type:* Association.

Nursing

Advances in Nursing Science

Aspen Publishers, Inc.
200 Orchard Ridge Dr., No. Ph: (301)417-7500
  200 Free: 800-638-8437
Gaithersburg, MD 20878 Fax: (301)417-7650
E-mail: customer.service@aspenpubl.com
URL: http://www.aspenpub.com; http://www.aspenpub.com.
Contact: Peggy Chinn, Editor.

Desc: Academic medical journal. *Alt. Contact:* 200 Orchard Ridge Dr., Ste. 200, Gaithersburg, MD 20878; telephone: (301)417-7500; fax: (301)417-7550. *Type:* Periodical.

Alaska Nurse

Alaska Nurses Association
237 E. 3rd Ave., Ste. 3 Ph: (907)274-0827
Anchorage, AK 99501 Fax: (907)272-0292
E-mail: aknurse@ptialaska.net
URL: http://www.aknurse.org.
Contact: Kathy North, Editor.

Desc: Provides information on nursing and health. *Type:* Newsletter.

American Academy of Nurse Practitioners

National Administrative Office Ph: (512)442-4262
PO Box 12846 Fax: (512)442-6469
Austin, TX 78711
E-mail: admin@aanp.org
URL: http://www.aanp.org
Contact: Zo DeMarchi, Dir. of Association Services.

Desc: Promotes high standards of health care delivered by nurse practitioners. Acts as a forum to enhance the identity and continuity of nurse practitioners. Addresses national and state legislative issues that affect members; acts as a resource center on legislative activity. *Type:* Association.

American Assembly for Men in Nursing—Interaction

American Assembly for Men in Nursing
437 Twin Bay Dr. Fax: (904)484-8762
Pensacola, FL 32534-1350

Desc: Aimed at male nurses and male nursing students. Contains information on Assembly officers, events, and activities. *Type:* Newsletter.

American Association of Neuroscience Nurses

224 N. Des Plaines, No. 601 Ph: (312)993-0043
Chicago, IL 60661 Fax: (312)993-0362
E-mail: assnneuro@aol.com
URL: http://www.aann.org

Contact: Shelly Johnson, Exec.Dir.

Desc: Registered nurses engaged in or primarily interested in neurosurgical or neurological nursing. Objectives are to: foster interest, education, and high standards of practice in the field of neuroscience nursing; encourage continuing growth in the field; provide a medium for communication among neuroscience nurses in the U.S. *Type:* Association.

American Association of Nurse Anesthetists

222 S. Prospect Ph: (847)692-7050
Park Ridge, IL 60068-4001 Fax: (847)692-6968
E-mail: info@aana.com
URL: http://www.aana.com

Contact: John F. Garde, Exec.Dir.

Desc: Active registered professional nurses who have successfully completed an accredited program in nurse anesthesia and passed a national examination for certification. Advances the art and science of anesthesiology; promotes research in anesthesia; develops educational standards and techniques for the administration of anesthesia. Sponsors continuing education; promotes biennial recertification. *Type:* Association.

American Association of Occupational Health Nurses

2920 Brandy Wine Rd., Ste. Ph: (770)455-7757
  100 Fax: (770)455-7271
Atlanta, GA 30341
E-mail: aaohn@aaohn.org
URL: http://www.aaohn.org

Contact: Ann Cox, CAE, Exec.Dir.

Desc: Registered professional nurses employed by business and industrial firms; nurse educators, nurse editors, nurse writers, and others interested in occupational health nursing. Promotes and sets standards for the profession. Provides and approves continuing education; maintains governmental affairs program; offers placement service. *Type:* Association.

American College of Nurse-Midwives

818 Connecticut Ave., Ste. 900 Ph: (202)728-9860
Washington, DC 20006 Fax: (202)289-9897
E-mail: info@acnm.org
URL: http://www.midwife.org

Contact: Helen Marieskind.

Desc: Seeks to develop and support the profession of certified nurse-midwives in order to promote the health and well-being of women and infants within their families and communities. A CNM is a licensed health care practitioner educated in the two disciplines of nursing and midwifery. Provides gynecological services and care of mothers and babies throughout the maternity cycle; members have completed an ACNM accredited program of study and clinical experience in midwifery and passed a national certification exam. *Type:* Association.

American Journal of Critical Care

American Association of Critical-Care Nurses (AACN)
101 Columbia Ph: (949)362-2000
Aliso Viejo, CA 92656 Free: 800-809-2273
                       Fax: (949)362-2049
E-mail: aacninfo@aacn.org; ajcc@aol.com.
URL: http://www.aacn.org

Contact: Michelle Hopkins, Managing Editor, michelle.hopkins@aacn.org; Bob Vrooman, Advertising Dir., bob.vrooman@aacn.org.

Desc: Professional journal covering nursing. *Type:* Periodical.

American Journal of Nursing

American Journal of Nursing Co.
345 Hudson St. Ph: (212)886-1200
New York, NY 10014 Free: 800-627-0484
                    Fax: (212)886-1209

Contact: Martin DiCarlantonio, Editor; James Nagle, Advertising Mgr.

Desc: Journal for staff nurses, nurse managers, and clinical nurse specialists. Focuses on patient care in hospitals, hospital ICUs and homes. Provides news coverage of health care from the nursing perspective. *Type:* Periodical.

The American Nurse

American Nurses Association
600 Maryland Ave. SW, Ste. Ph: (202)651-7024
  100 W. Free: 800-274-4262
Washington, DC 20024-2571 Fax: (202)651-7005
Contact: Connie Helmlinger, Editor, taneditor@ana.org; Elizabeth MoNamara, Advertising/Sales.

Desc: Newspaper (tabloid) for the nursing profession. *Type:* Periodical.

American Nurses Association

600 Maryland Ave. SW, Ste. Ph: (202)651-7000
  100 W. Free: 800-637-0323
Washington, DC 20024-2571 Fax: (202)651-7001
URL: http://www.nursingworld.org
Contact: Beverly L. Malone, PhD,RN, Pres.

Desc: Member associations representing registered nurses. Sponsors American Nurses Foundation (for research), American Academy of Nursing, Center for Ethics and Human Rights, International Nursing Center, and American Nurses Credentialing Center. Maintains hall of fame. *Type:* Association.

American Organization of Nurse Executives

One N. Franklin, 34th Fl. Ph: (312)422-2800
Chicago, IL 60606 Fax: (312)422-4504
Contact: Marjorie Beyers, RN, Exec.Dir.

Desc: Provides leadership, professional development, advocacy, and research to advance nursing practice and patient care, promote nursing leadership and excellence, and shape healthcare public policy. Supports and enhances the management, leadership, educational, and professional development of nursing leaders. Offers placement service through Career Development and Referral Center. *Type:* Association.

American Society of PeriAnesthesia Nurses

6900 Grove Rd. Ph: (609)845-5557
Thorofare, NJ 08086 Fax: (609)848-1881
URL: http://www.aspan.org/index.htm
Contact: Terry R. McLean, RN, CP, Pres.

Desc: Nurses practicing in all phases of ambulatory surgery, preanesthesia and post anesthesia care. Promotes quality and cost effective care for patients, their families, and the community through public and professional education, research and standards of practice. Offers continuing education programs. *Type:* Association.

American Society of Post Anesthesia Nurses
11512 Allecingie Pkwy.   Ph: (804)379-5516
Richmond, VA 23235
Contact: Keven Dill, Dir.
Desc: Postanesthesia nurses. Promotes upgrading of standards of postanesthesia patient care and the professional growth of licensed nurses involved in the care of patients in the immediate postanesthesia period. Provides forum for exchange of knowledge and ideas on patient care; facilitates cooperation among postanesthesia nurses and physicians and other medical personnel; encourages specialization and research in the field. *Type:* Association.

AONE Updates
American Organization of Nurse Executives (AONE)
1 N. Franklin, 34th Fl.   Ph: (312)422-2800
Chicago, IL 60606   Fax: (312)422-4504
Contact: Laura Kroll, Dir. of Operations.
Desc: Provides updates for nurses in executive practice on health care and nursing related initiatives, legislation, research, and education. *Type:* Newsletter.

Arizona Nurse
Arizona Nurses Association
1850 E. Southern Ave., Ste. 1   Ph: (602)831-0404
Tempe, AZ 85282   Fax: (602)839-4780
Contact: Ela-Joy Lehrman, Editor.
Desc: Provides news and information of interest to Arizona nurses. *Type:* Newsletter.

Aspen's Advisor for Nurse Executives
Aspen Publishers, Inc.
200 Orchard Ridge Dr., No.   Ph: (301)417-7500
  200   Free: 800-638-8437
Gaithersburg, MD 20878   Fax: (301)417-7650
E-mail: customer.service@aspenpubl.com
URL: http://www.aspenpub.com
Contact: Cathleen K. Wilson, Ph.D., R.N., Editor.
Desc: Focuses on leadership roles in the nursing field. Offers information on bridging the gender gap in nursing, education, patient care teams, and leadership strategies. *Type:* Newsletter.

Association of Operating Room Nurses
2170 S. Parker Rd.   Ph: (303)755-6300
Ste. 300   Free: 800-755-2676
Denver, CO 80231-5711   Fax: (303)750-3212
URL: http://www.aorn.org/
Contact: Lola M. Fehr, R.N.,, Exec.Dir.
Desc: Professional perioperative (operating room) nurses. *Type:* Association.

Association of Pediatric Oncology Nurses
4700 W. Lake Ave.   Ph: (708)375-4724
Glenview, IL 60025-1485   Fax: (708)375-4777
E-mail: apon@amctec.com
URL: http://www.apon.org/
Contact: M. Kathleen Klaeser, CAE, Exec.Dir.
Desc: Scientific and educational association seeking to establish lines of communication among nurses caring for children and adolescents with cancer. Encourages updating of literature and development of standards of care for children with cancer. *Type:* Association.

Association of Rehabilitation Nurses
4700 W. Lake Ave.   Ph: (847)375-4710
Glenview, IL 60025-1485   Free: 800-229-7530
                                     Fax: (847)375-4777
E-mail: info@rehabnursc.org
URL: http://www.rehabnurse.org
Contact: Anne Cordes, R.N.,, Exec.Dir.
Desc: Registered nurses concerned with or actively engaged in the practice of rehabilitation nursing; others interested in rehabilitation. Works to advance the quality of rehabilitation nursing practice through educational opportunities and to facilitate the exchange of ideas. *Type:* Association.

Association of Women's Health, Obstetric and Neonatal Nurses
2000 L St. Nw, Ste. 740   Ph: (202)261-2400
Washington, DC 20036
E-mail: lisad@awhonn.org
URL: http://www.awhonn.org
Contact: Gail Kincaide, Exec.Dir.
Desc: Members are registered nurses; associate members are allied health workers with an interest in obstetric, women's health, and neonatal (OGN) nursing. Promotes and establishes the highest standards of OGN nursing practice, education, and research; cooperates with all members of the health team; stimulates interest in OGN nursing. Sponsors educational meetings, audiovisual programs, and continuing education courses. *Type:* Association.

Beginnings
American Holistic Nurses Association
PO Box 2130   Ph: (520)526-2196
Flagstaff, AZ 86003   Free: 800-278-2462
                                     Fax: (520)526-2752
E-mail: ahna-flag@flaglink.com
Contact: Marie Fasano-Ramos, Editor, (805)643-4943.
Desc: Functions as the official newsletter of the Association, which seeks to "renew and enhance the art of nurturing and caring for the whole person." Offers educational information on holistic nursing and healing modalities, and provides news of the Association. Recurring features include editorials, news of research, letters to the editor, news of members, book reviews, a social and ethical column, and a calendar of events. *Type:* Newsletter.

The BRN Report
California Board of Registered Nursing (BRN)
PO Box 944210   Ph: (916)322-3350
Sacramento, CA 94244-2100   Fax: (906)327-4402
Contact: Katherine Weinkam, MS,RN, Editor.
Desc: Supplies information on various subjects of interest to California registered nurses. Recurring features include news of board members, news of research, coverage of enforcement and diversion issues, and a calendar of meetings. *Type:* Newsletter.

Canadian Health Care Guild—Pulse
Canadian Health Care Guild (CHCG)
17410 107th Ave., No. 200   Ph: (403)483-8126
Edmonton, AB, Canada T5S   Free: 800-252-7984
  1E9   Fax: (403)484-3341
Contact: Mark Fitton, Editor.
Desc: Provides members with updates on opportunities for continuing professional education and employment as well as updates on union activities to promote effective and compassionate health care for patients. Recurring features include a calendar of events, meeting reports, articles, a financial column, and columns titled Pulse Beat, Just for the Health of It, and Let's Talk Labour. *Type:* Newsletter.

Canadian Nurse (L'Infirmiere Canadienne)
Canadian Nurses Association
50 Driveway   Ph: (613)237-2133
Ottawa, ON, Canada K2P 1E2   Free: 800-361-8404
                                     Fax: (613)237-3520
E-mail: cnj@cna-nurses.ca.
URL: http://www.cna-nurses_ca
Contact: Judith Haines, Editor-in-Chief, editor@cna-nurses.ca.
Desc: Professional journal for nurses (English and French). *Type:* Periodical.

Canadian Nursing Management
MPL Communications Inc.
133 Richmond St., Ste. 700   Ph: (416)869-1177
Toronto, ON, Canada M5H   Fax: (416)869-0616
  3M8
Contact: Ruth Featherstone, Editor.
Desc: Provides news for nurse managers. *Type:* Newsletter.

CardSearch
CardTrak of America
PO Box 1700   Ph: (301)695-4660
Frederick, MD 21702   Free: 800-344-7714
                                     Fax: (301)695-0160
E-mail: cardtrak@ramresearh.com; staff@ramresearch.com.
URL: http://www.ramresearch.com.
Contact: Robert B. McKinley, Editor.
Desc: Publishes a comprehensive guide to bank credit cards in regard to pricing, low interest rates, no annual fees, benefits, and gold and secured cards. *Type:* Newsletter.

Caring
Manitoba Association of Licensed Practical Nurses
200-1601 Regent Ave. W   Ph: (204)663-1212
Winnipeg, MB, Canada R2C   Free: 877-663-1212
  3B3   Fax: (204)663-1207
Contact: Verna Holgate, Editor, veh@sympatico.ca.
Desc: Contains educational articles, reports, and surveys pertinent to the nursing profession. Recurring features include letters to the editor, a calendar of events, reports of meetings, news of educational opportunities, board meeting highlights, and a licensed practical nurse (LPN) page. *Type:* Newsletter.

Chicago Nurse
Chicago Nurses Association
203 N. Wabash Ave., Ste. 1507   Ph: (312)263-2708
Chicago, IL 60601   Fax: (312)263-2710
Desc: Contains general information and news relating to Association activities and health articles written by the membership. *Type:* Newsletter.

City of Hope National Medical Center
Department of Nursing Research and Education
1500 E. Duarte Rd.   Ph: (818)301-2346
Duarte, CA 91010   Fax: (818)301-8941
E-mail: mgrant@smtplink.coh.org
Contact: Marcia Grant, Dir.
Desc: Clinical nursing, including nursing administration, nursing education, delivery of nursing services, nursing organization, and the relationship of patient problems to nursing. Research focuses on quality of life, pain and symptom management, improving nursing attitudes and skills in caring for patients and their families, and reducing complications and side effects of therapy and patient psychological distresses associated with therapeutic and diagnostic procedures. *Type:* Research center.

Connecticut Nursing News
Connecticut Nurses' Association
377 Research Pkwy., Ste. 2D   Ph: (203)238-1207
Meriden, CT 06450   Fax: (203)238-3437
E-mail: ct_nurses_assoc@compuserve.com
Contact: Frances Feldsine.
Desc: Focuses on the nursing profession. Aims to advance the nursing practice through promoting high standards of education while assuring quality health care. *Type:* Newsletter.

Critical Care Choices

Springhouse Corp.
1111 Bethlehem Pike
PO Box 908
Spring House, PA 19477
URL: http://www.springnet.com; http://www.springnet.com.

Ph: (215)646-8700
Free: 800-346-7844
Fax: (215)646-4399

Contact: Jan Corwin Enger, Editor, (215)646-8700, fax: (215)653-0826, jan.enger@springnet.com.

Desc: 2-part clinical and career directory for critical care nurses. Non-profit and investor-owned hospitals and departments of the United States government that hire critical care nurses. Does not report specific positions available. *Type:* Directory.

Critical Care Nurse

Critical Care Nurse
101 Columbia
Aliso Viejo, CA 92656

Ph: (949)362-2000
Free: 800-899-1712
Fax: (949)362-2049

E-mail: ccn@aol.com.

Contact: JoAnn Alspach, R.N., Editor; Bonnie J. Horrigan, Director, bonnie.horrigan@aacn.org; Michael Villaire, Managing Editor, michael.villaire@aacn.org.

Desc: Nursing journal. *Type:* Periodical.

Cumulative Index to Nursing and Allied Health Literature

CINAHL Information Systems
1509 Wilson Terrace
Glendale, CA 91206
E-mail: cinahl@cinhal.com
URL: http://www.cinahl.com

Ph: (818)409-8005

Contact: June Levy.

Desc: Contains more than 282,000 citations, with abstracts, to articles published in more than 800 English-language nursing and 17 allied health journals. Also covers relevant materials from biomedicine, management, health sciences librarianship, education, and consumer health journals. *Available:* The Dialog Corporation, DataStar; PaperChase; CARL Corporation; CINAHL Information Systems; OCLC Online Computer Library Center, Inc., OCLC FirstSearch Catalog; OCLC Online Computer Library Center, Inc., OCLC EPIC; Aries Systems Corporation; EBSCOhost. *Type:* Database.

District 6 News and Views

Kansas State Nurses Association, District 6
PO Box 2786
Wichita, KS 67201

Contact: Kay Bacaus, Editor.

Desc: Disseminates information on nursing. *Type:* Newsletter.

DNA Focus

Dermatology Nurses Association (DNA)
East Holly Ave., Box 56
Pitman, NJ 08071-0056

Ph: (609)256-2330
Fax: (609)589-7463

Contact: Edna Atwater, Editor.

Desc: Covers member and chapter information, letters, regional reports, upcoming seminars, conventions, and healthcare updates. Recurring features include letters to the editor, a calendar of events, reports of meetings, and news of educational opportunities. *Type:* Newsletter.

East Carolina University

Office of Research & Evaluation

School of Nursing
Rivers Bldg., Room 127
Greenville, NC 27858-4353
E-mail: koldjeskid@mail.ecu.edu
URL: http://www.ecu.edu

Ph: (919)328-4325
Fax: (919)328-2168

Contact: Dr. Dixie Koldjeski, PhD, Assoc. Dean, Res. & Eval.

Desc: Basic and applied nursing research, including symptom management, women's health care, rural health, and family health. *Type:* Research center.

The Exchange

Education Enterprises
56 McArthur Ave.
Staten Island, NY 10312
E-mail: nnba2000@aol.com.

Free: 800-331-6534
Fax: (718)317-0858

Desc: Provides news and information of interest to nurse entrepreneurs. *Type:* Newsletter.

The Florida Nurse

Florida Nurses Association
PO Box 536985
Orlando, FL 32853-6985
E-mail: theflnurse@aol.com

Ph: (407)896-3261
Fax: (407)896-9042

Contact: Willa Fuller, Editor, (407)896-3261.

Desc: Brings news of interest to nurses in Florida. Recurring features include news of research, a calendar of events, reports of meetings, and news of educational opportunities. *Type:* Newsletter.

Frontier Nursing Service

132 FNS Dr.
Wendover, KY 41775
URL: http://www.barefoot.com/fns

Ph: (606)672-2317
Fax: (606)672-3022

Contact: Deanna Severance, Dir.

Desc: Provides health care to persons in approximately 1000 square miles of eastern Kentucky using a 40-bed hospital, two primary care centers, three rural health clinics, and a home health agency. Operates Frontier School of Midwifery and Family Nursing. Provides social and ancillary services; conducts research on health services; compiles statistics; offers educational programs. *Type:* Association.

Hand in Hand

Saskatchewan Association of Licensed Practical Nurses (SALPN)
2310 Smith St.
Regina, SK, Canada S4P 2P6

Ph: (306)525-1436
Free: 888-257-2576
Fax: (306)347-7784

E-mail: salpn@dlcwest.com

Contact: Ede Leeson, Editor.

Desc: Provides the Association members with information of topical interest. *Type:* Newsletter.

Healthwire

Federation of Nurses and Health Professionals
American Federation of Teachers
555 New Jersey Ave. NW
Washington, DC 20001
URL: http://www.aft.org.

Ph: (202)879-4491
Fax: (202)879-4597

Contact: Priscilla M. Nemeth, Editor.

Desc: Explores national news and issues affecting health care workers. Discusses general union developments as well as labor and union concerns specific to the health care field. *Type:* Newsletter.

IMAGE

Sigma Theta Tau Intl.
550 W. North St.
Indianapolis, IN 46202

Ph: (317)634-8171
Free: 800-634-7575
Fax: (317)634-8188

E-mail: stti@stti-sun.iupui.com

Contact: Beverly Henry, R.N., Editor, (312)996-0103, fax: (312)996-0680, imagebh@uic.edu; Nancy Dickenson-Hazard, R.N., Publisher.

Desc: Scholarly, peer-reviewed articles on nursing. *Alt. Contact:* UIC School of Nursing 845 S. Damen Ave., Chicago, IL 60612; telephone: (312)996-0103; fax: (312)996-0680. *Type:* Periodical.

ISNA Bulletin

Indiana State Nurses Association (ISNA)
2915 N. High School Rd.
Indianapolis, IN 46224-2969

Ph: (317)299-4575
Fax: (317)297-3525

Contact: Naomi Patchin, Editor.

Desc: Covers current events of nursing issues in Indiana. Recurring features include letters to the editor, a calendar of events, and reports of meetings. *Type:* Newsletter.

Kent County Visiting Nurse Association

51 Health Ln.
Warwick, RI 02886

Ph: (401)737-6050
Free: 800-348-6417
Fax: (401)738-0247

Contact: Nancy Roberts, CEO.

Desc: Provides skilled nursing and rehabilitation services to patients in their homes. Sponsors health promotion activities; conducts hospice program. *Type:* Association.

Legislative Network for Nurses

Business Publishers, Inc.
8737 Colesville Rd., Ste. 1100
Silver Spring, MD 20910

Ph: (301)589-5103
Free: 800-274-6737
Fax: (301)587-4530

E-mail: bpinews@bpinews.com

Contact: Sarah Spencer, Editor, (301)587-6300, sspencer@bpinews.com.

Desc: Covers Washington and other news of interest to nurses, including health care funding, labor relations, occupational safety, and health. *Type:* Newsletter.

Maryland Nurse

Maryland Nurses Association
849 International Dr., Ste. 255
Linthicum Heights, MD 21090

Ph: (410)859-3000
Fax: (410)859-3001

Contact: Kathryn V. Hall, Contact.

Desc: Membership newsletter of the Maryland Nurses Association. Recurring features include news of members, news of research, and news of educational opportunities. *Type:* Newsletter.

Medical College of Georgia

Center for Nursing Research

Sch. of Nursing
Jennings Wing, EB-202
Augusta, GA 30912
E-mail: vkemp@mail.mcg.edu
URL: http://www.mcg.edu

Ph: (706)721-3162
Fax: (706)721-0655

Contact: Virginia Kemp, PhD, Assoc. Dean for Grad. Prog. & Research.

Desc: Cognitive functioning and control in institutionalized elderly; asthma; family, health risk, and lifestyle change; learning with computer-aided education (CAE) equipment, and computer-aided instruction (CAI); and cancer and rehabilitation nursing, rural health, self-esteem, and abuse and homeless issues. *Type:* Research center.

Minority Nurse Newsletter

Tucker Publications, Inc.
PO Box 580
Lisle, IL 60532-0580
E-mail: sallen@tuckerpub.com.

Ph: (630)969-3809
Fax: (630)969-3895

Contact: Dr. Mary Branch, Editor, (773)995-3910; Mary Anderson, Editor; Clay Allen, Advertising Mgr., callen@tuckerpub.com.

Desc: Provides health care information of interest to minority nursing faculty. *Type:* Newsletter.

MNA Accent

Minnesota Nurses' Association (MNA)
1295 Bandana Blvd., No. 140   Ph: (651)646-4807
St. Paul, MN 55108   Free: 800-536-4662
                                  Fax: (651)647-5301
Contact: Marilyn Cunningham, Editor; Jan Rabbers, Editor.
Desc: Provides news of developments and legal issues affecting the nursing field in Minnesota. Reports on arbitration, resolutions, and community activities involving nurses. *Type:* Newsletter.

NASN Newsletter

Health Information Publications, Inc.
1719 Rte. 10   Ph: (201)267-8938
Parsippany, NJ 07054
Contact: Debbie Ilardi, Managing Editor.
Desc: Covers recent activity regarding school nursing. *Type:* Newsletter.

National Alliance of Nurse Practitioners

325 Pennsylvania Ave. SE   Ph: (202)675-6350
Washington, DC 20003-1100
Contact: Judith Dempster, DNSC, Chairperson.
Desc: Nurse practitioners. Seeks to emphasize the role of Nurse Practitioners in efficient and cost-effective health care services. Promotes continuing education for all health care professionals. *Type:* Association.

National Association of Neonatal Nurses

701 Lee St., Ste. 450   Ph: (847)299-NANN
Des Plaines, IL 60016   Free: 800-451-3795
                                  Fax: (847)297-6768
URL: http://www.nann.org
Contact: Barbara Morrison, Exec.Dir.
Desc: Nurses currently working in neonatal intensive care units. Promotes professional development of members. *Type:* Association.

National Association of Orthopaedic Nurses

E. Holly Ave.   Ph: (609)256-2310
Box 56   Fax: (609)589-7463
Pitman, NJ 08071-0056
E-mail: naon@mail.ajj.com
URL: http://www.inurse.com/~naon
Contact: Pat Reichart, Exec. Sec.
Desc: Registered, licensed practical, or licensed vocational nurses involved or knowledgeable in orthopedic nursing. Enhances the personal and professional growth of orthopedic nurses through continuing education programs. *Type:* Association.

National Association of School Nurses

PO Box 1300   Ph: (207)883-2117
Scarborough, ME 04070-1300   Fax: (207)883-2683
E-mail: nasnweb@aol.com
URL: http://www.VRmedia.com/nurses/
Contact: Beverly Farquhar, Exec. Dir.
Desc: School nurses who conduct comprehensive school health programs in public and private schools. Objectives are: to provide national leadership in the promotion of health services for schoolchildren; to promote school health interests to the nursing and health community and the public; to monitor legislation pertaining to school nursing. *Type:* Association.

National Association of Traveling Nurses

PO Box 35189   Ph: (708)453-0080
Chicago, IL 60707-0189   Fax: (708)453-0083
Contact: L. David Stoller, Chm.
Desc: Members of the medical profession. Provides travel information. *Type:* Association.

National Certification Corporation for the Obstetric, Gynecologic and Neonatal Nursing Specialties

645 N. Michigan Ave., Ste. 900   Ph: (312)951-0207
Chicago, IL 60611
URL: http://www.nccnet.org
Contact: Betty Burns, CAE, Exec.Dir.
Desc: Promotes quality nursing care by encouraging nurses to demonstrate special knowledge by participating in a voluntary national certification program for obstetric/gynecologic nurse practitioners, inpatient obstetric nurses, neonatal intensive care nurses, neonatal nurse practitioners, low-risk neonatal nurses, electronic fetal monitoring, breastfeeding, menopause, and maternal newborn nurses. *Type:* Association.

National League for Nursing

61 Broadway, 33rd Fl.   Ph: (212)989-9393
New York, NY 10006-2701   Free: 800-669-9656
                                  Fax: (212)989-2272
URL: http://www.nln.org
Contact: Dr. Sheila Ryan, Pres.
Desc: Individuals and leaders in nursing and other health professions, and community members interested in solving health care problems (9,000); agencies, nursing educational institutions, departments of nursing in hospitals and related facilities, and home and community health agencies (1800). Works to assess nursing needs, improve organized nursing services and nursing education, and foster collaboration between nursing and other health and community services. Provides tests used in selection of applicants to schools of nursing; also prepares tests for evaluating nursing student progress and nursing service tests. *Type:* Association.

New York State Nurses' Association

46 Cornell Rd.   Ph: (518)782-9400
Latham, NY 12110   Fax: (518)782-9530
E-mail: info@nysna.org
Contact: Martha L. Orr, Exec.Dir.
Desc: Professional society for registered nurses in New York. *Type:* Association.

Nurse to Nurse

Registered Nurses Association of Nova Scotia (RNANS)
Barrington Tower, Scotia Sq.   Ph: (902)491-9744
1894 Barrington St., Ste. 600   Free: 800-565-9744
Halifax, NS, Canada B3J 2A8   Fax: (902)491-9510
E-mail: info@rnans.ns.ca
URL: http://www.rnans.ns.ca.
Contact: Marie Dauphinee-Booth, Editor, mdaupinee-booth@rnans.ns.ca.
Desc: Informs members of the activities and achievements of the Association. Provides a forum for the exchange of ideas, information, research, and concerns relevant to regulation and nursing practice. *Type:* Newsletter.

Nurses Organization of Veterans Affairs

1726 M St. NW, Ste. 1101   Ph: (202)296-0888
Washington, DC 20036   Fax: (202)833-1577
E-mail: nova@nanurse.org
Contact: Deborah Beck, Exec.Dir.
Desc: Voluntary, nonprofit professional society of Department of Veterans Affairs registered nurses. Objective is to provide VA nurses with the opportunity to preserve and improve quality care and professionalism through legislative influence. *Type:* Association.

Nurseweek

Nurseweek Publishing
1156 Aster Ave., Ste. C   Ph: (408)249-5877
Sunnyvale, CA 94086-6810   Free: 800-859-2691
                                  Fax: (408)249-8204
E-mail: nurseweek@nurseweek.com; editor@nurseweek.com.
URL: http://www.nurseweek.com.
Contact: Whitney Wood, Managing Editor, fax: (408)249-3767, whitneyw@nurseweek.com; Andrew Baldwin, Publisher, fax: (408)249-8670, andyb@nurseweek.com; Ray Riordan, National Advertising Dir., fax: (972)488-8300, rayr@dhc.net; Barbara Bronson Gray, Editor-in-Chief, fax: (818)889-2929, bbgray@ibm.net.
Desc: Magazine (tabloid) featuring articles for R.N.'s. *Type:* Periodical.

Nursing Archives Newsletter

Nursing Archives
Department of Special Collections
Boston University
771 Commonwealth Ave.   Ph: (617)353-3696
Boston, MA 02215   Fax: (617)353-2838
Contact: Helen Sherwin, Editor.
Desc: Covers activities and information relating to the Nursing Archives. *Type:* Newsletter.

Nursing Management

Spring House
434 W Downer Pl.   Free: 800-950-0879
Aurora, IL 60506
Contact: Leah Curtin, Editor; John H. Harling, Publisher.
Desc: Magazine focusing on nursing management. *Type:* Periodical.

Nursing News

Nurses Association of the Counties of Long Island
99 Tulip Ave., Ste. 404   Ph: (516)352-0717
Floral Park, NY 11001   Fax: (516)352-4993
E-mail: mack@worldnet.att.net
Contact: Eileen Wild, Editor.
Desc: Covers topics related to nursing care. Reports news and activities of the Association. *Type:* Newsletter.

Nursing 96

Springhouse Corp.
1111 Bethlehem Pike   Ph: (215)646-8700
PO Box 908   Free: 800-346-7844
Spring House, PA 19477   Fax: (215)646-4399
E-mail: nursing@springnet.com.
URL: http://www.springnet.com
Contact: Jeff Berman, Publisher; Patricia Nornhold, RN, Executive Dir.
Desc: Practical journal for nurses. Includes special sections for hospital critical-care and home health. *Type:* Periodical.

ONA News

Ontario Nurses Association (ONA)
85 Grenville St., Ste. 400   Ph: (416)964-8833
Toronto, ON, Canada M5S   Fax: (416)964-8891
   3A2
Contact: Melanie Pottins, Editor.
Desc: Highlights labor, education, and practice issues affecting the nursing profession. *Type:* Newsletter.

Oncology Nursing Society

501 Holiday Dr.   Ph: (412)921-7373
Pittsburgh, PA 15220   Fax: (412)921-6565
E-mail: member@ons.org
URL: http://www.ons.org
Contact: Pearl Moore, CEO.

Desc: Registered nurses interested in oncology. Seeks to: promote high professional standards in oncology nursing; provide a network for the exchange of information, resources, and peer support; encourage nurses to specialize in oncology; promote and develop educational programs in oncology nursing extending through the graduate level; identify, encourage, and foster nursing research in improving the quality of patient care. *Type:* Association.

OR Manager

OR Manager, Inc.
PO Box 5303   Free: 800-442-9918
Santa Fe, NM 87502-5303   Fax: (505)983-0790
E-mail: 75467.1545@compuserve.com

Contact: Elimor S. Schrader, Publisher; Pat Patterson, Editor.

Desc: Provides information for nurses in decision-making positions in the operating room. Includes news related to management of the operating room, ambulatory and outpatient surgery, management strategies, business planning, implications of health care policy, new technology, and updates of techniques. *Type:* Newsletter.

Prairie Rose

North Dakota Nurses Association
549 Airport Rd.   Ph: (701)223-1385
Bismarck, ND 58504-6107   Fax: (701)223-0575

Contact: Sharon Moos, Editor.

Desc: Covers nursing and health care issues in North Dakota. *Type:* Newsletter.

Quickening

American College of Nurse-Midwives
818 Connecticut Ave., NW, Ste.   Ph: (202)728-9860
   900   Fax: (202)728-9897
Washington, DC 20006
E-mail: info@acnm.org; quick@acnm.org.
URL: http://www.midwife.org; http://www.acnm.org;
http://www.midwife.org.

Contact: Kimberly J.P. Patamia, Editor.

Desc: Promotes the training and certification of nurse-midwives. Recurring features include membership, board and convention news, announcements of relevant meetings and workshops, help-wanted items, and lists of significant publications. *Type:* Newsletter.

Recruitment Directions

National Association for Health Care Recruitment
PO Box 531107
Orlando, FL 32853-1107

Contact: Karen Hart, Editor.

Desc: Concerned with recruitment and retention of nurses, allied health, and other professionals in the health care industry. Includes regional news, recruitment resources, and a column titled Presidential Perspectives. *Type:* Newsletter.

Reflections

Sigma Theta Tau International
550 W. North St.   Ph: (317)634-8171
Indianapolis, IN 46202   Free: 888-634-7575
                                Fax: (317)634-8188
E-mail: stti@stti-sun.iupui.edu

Contact: Julie Goldsmith, Editor.

Desc: Highlights the meetings, conferences, seminars, and national and international events of this honor society. Contains news relating to the nursing profession and feature stories on nurses. *Type:* Newsletter.

RN

Medical Economics Co.
5 Paragon Dr.   Ph: (201)358-7500
Montvale, NJ 07645-1725   Free: 800-223-0581
                                Fax: (201)358-7260
E-mail: customer.service@medec.com; rn@medec.com.
Contact: Marianne Dekker Mattera, Editor, (201)358-7470; Terrence Meacock, Publisher; Wendy Raupers, National Sales Mgr., (201)358-7471.
Desc: Clinical journal for registered nurses. *Alt. Contact:* telephone: (201)358-7314; fax: (201)358-7450; toll-free: 800-526-4870. *Type:* Periodical.

Sigma Theta Tau International

550 W. North St.   Ph: (317)634-8171
Indianapolis, IN 46202   Free: 888-634-7575
                                Fax: (317)634-8188
E-mail: stti@stti.iupui.edu
URL: http://www.iupui.edu
Contact: Nancy Dickenson-Hazard, Exec. Officer.
Desc: Honor society - nursing. *Type:* Association.

Tar Heel Nurse

North Carolina Nurses Association
PO Box 12025   Ph: (919)821-4250
Raleigh, NC 27605-2025   Fax: (919)829-5807
Contact: Sindy Barker, Editor, sinbarker@aol.com.
Desc: Covers news and activities of the Association. Recurring features include a calendar of events, reports of meetings, news of educational opportunities, and a column titled President's Message. *Type:* Newsletter.

UNA Newsbulletin

United Nurses of Alberta (UNA)
10611 98th Ave., Ste. 900   Ph: (780)425-1025
Edmonton, AB, Canada T5K   Free: 800-252-9394
   2P7   Fax: (780)426-2093
E-mail: nurses@una.ab.ca
URL: http://www.una.ab.ca.
Desc: Offers educational information for nurses regarding bargaining, organizing, labor legislation, health and safety, and grievance and arbitration. Recurring features include letters to the editor, news of research, a calendar of events, reports of meetings, and news of educational opportunities. *Type:* Newsletter.

U.S. Department of Health and Human Services
National Institute of Nursing Research

NIH Bldg. 31, Rm. 5B-03   Ph: (301)496-8230
9000 Rockville Pike   Fax: (301)480-4969
Bethesda, MD 20892
Contact: Dr. Patricia A. Grady, Dir.
Desc: Basic and clinical nursing research, training, and other programs in patient care research and information dissemination. The research programs of the Institute address actual and potential health problems. *Type:* Research center.

U.S. Department of Health and Human Services
National Institute of Nursing Research
Division of Extramural Activities

Bldg. 45, Rm. 3AN12   Ph: (301)594-5963
Bethesda, MD 20892-6300   Fax: (301)480-8260
E-mail: mary_leveck@ep.ninr.nih.gov
URL: http://www.nih.gov/ninr/
Contact: Dr. Mary D. Leveck, Acting Dir.
Desc: Human responses to illness and disability throughout the life span. Focus is on the biological, behavioral, and psychosocial factors that contribute to these conditions and on methods to improve responses or alleviate the effects of the illness or disease. *Type:* Research center.

U.S. Department of Health and Human Services
National Institute of Nursing Research
Division of Extramural Activities
Nursing Systems Branch

Bldg. 45, Rm. 3AN-12   Ph: (301)594-5966
45 Center Dr., MSC 6300   Fax: (301)480-8260
Bethesda, MD 20892-6300
E-mail: pmoritz@ep.ninr.nih.gov
Contact: Dr. Patricia Moritz, Chf.
Desc: Inquiry into the delivery of health care which includes the study of the structural, organizational, and economic context of clinical practice and the processes of care delivery in relation to the assessment of clinical endpoints of appropriate care which encompass quality, efficacy, and effectiveness. Reflecting the NINR focus on patient care research, the Branch includes research on approaches to nursing management and patient care delivery. *Type:* Research center.

U.S. Department of Health and Human Services
National Institute of Nursing Research
Intramural Research Division
Clinical Therapeutics Laboratory

Bldg. 10, Rm. 10C 103   Ph: (301)402-1833
   (MSC1851)   Fax: (301)496-7184
9000 Rockville Pike
Bethesda, MD 20892-1851
Contact: Christine Grady, Chf.
Desc: Symptom management with emphasis on two primary groups: HIV-infected adults and the elderly. *Type:* Research center.

U.S. Department of Health and Human Services
National Institute of Nursing Research
Intramural Research Division
Laboratory for the Study of Human Responses to Health and Illness

NIH 31   Ph: (301)402-3583
9000 Rockville Pike   Fax: (301)435-3435
Bethesda, MD 20892
Contact: Annette B. Wysocki, PhD, Sci.Dir.
Desc: Research in wound healing. *Type:* Research center.

U.S. Department of Health and Human Services
National Institutes of Health
National Institute of Nursing Research

9000 Rockville Pike   Ph: (301)496-0207
Bethesda, MD 20892
URL: http://www.nih.gov.ninr/
Contact: Patricia A. Grady, Director.
Desc: The Institute provides leadership for nursing research, supports and conducts research and training, and disseminates information to build a scientific base for nursing practice and patient care and to promote health and ameliorate the effects of illness on the American people. *Type:* Government agency, office, or program.

University of Akron
Center for Nursing

209 Caroll St.   Ph: (330)972-6968
Akron, OH 44325   Fax: (330)972-5883
E-mail: ekinion@uakron.edu
URL: http://www.uakron.edu/nursing/facility/tour2.htm
Contact: Dr. Elizabeth Kinion, Dir.
Desc: Nursing outcomes, education and research and the relationship between family influences and health behaviors. Offers health care services to vulnerable individuals and families and provides a clinical laboratory for faculty and students to address patient care and response to care. *Type:* Research center.

University of Manitoba

Manitoba Nursing Research Institute

Winnipeg, MB, Canada R3T
2N2

Ph: (204)474-9080
Fax: (204)474-7683

URL: http://www.umanitoba.ca/faculties/nursing/mnri/mnri.htm

Contact: Prof. Lorna Guse, PhD, Dir.

Desc: Nursing economics, health outcomes, and health policy. *Type:* Research center.

University of Miami

Institute for the Study of Culture and Nursing

School of Nursing
5801 Red Rd.
Coral Gables, FL 33143

Ph: (305)284-1553
Fax: (305)284-5686

E-mail: swalsh@miami.edu

URL: http://www.miami.edu/nur

Contact: Dr. S. Walsh, Dir.

Desc: Clinical nursing, focusing on serving multicultural populations and managing multicultural organizations. *Type:* Research center.

University of Michigan

Center for Nursing Research

400 N. Ingalls, Rm. 4236
Ann Arbor, MI 48109-0482

Ph: (734)764-9554
Fax: (734)936-3644

E-mail: npender@umich.edu

Contact: Dr. Nola Pender, Dir.

Desc: Facilitates faculty research by providing consultation on design and data analysis and by assisting in the development of proposals. *Type:* Research center.

University of Texas at Arlington

Center for Nursing Research

PO Box 19407
Arlington, TX 76019

Ph: (817)272-2776
Fax: (817)272-5006

E-mail: clcason@uta.edu

URL: http://www.uta.edu/nursing

Contact: Dr. Carolyn L. Cason, Dir.

Desc: Hispanic health needs, health promotion and prevention of illness, palliative care, rural health care, nursing care outcomes, and economics of health care delivery. *Type:* Research center.

Visiting Nurse Association of Hampshire County

395 Pleasent St.
Northampton, MA 01060-3914

URL: http://www.valinet.com/~hampvna/

Contact: Lisa Woolery, Interim CEO.

Desc: Individuals in Hampshire County, MA. Seeks to provide quality home health care and environmental support services to residents. *Type:* Association.

VNAB Newsletter

Visiting Nurse Association of Brooklyn (VNAB)
Public Relations Department
138 S. Oxford St.
Brooklyn, NY 11217

Ph: (718)230-6927
Fax: (718)636-7572

Desc: Presents information of home care and visiting nursing issues. *Type:* Newsletter.

Von Canada Report

Von Canada Report
5 Blackburn Ave.
Ottawa, ON, Canada K1N 8A2

Ph: (613)233-5694
Fax: (613)230-4376

E-mail: comm@von.ca

Contact: Richard Marritt, Editor-in-Chief; Marie Belanger, Editor.

Desc: Reports on the Victorian Order of Nurses. *Type:* Newsletter.

Wound, Ostomy and Continence Nurses Society: An Association of E.T. Nurses

1550 S. Coast Hwy., Ste. 200
Laguna Beach, CA 92651

Free: 888-224-9626
Fax: (714)376-3456

E-mail: membership@wocn.org

URL: http://www.wocn.org

Contact: Maria Garces, Exec.Dir.

Desc: Seeks to support ET, wound, ostomy, and continence, nurses by promoting educational, clinical, and research opportunities and to guide the delivery of expert health care to individuals with wounds, ostomies, and incontinence. *Type:* Association.

Your Union Matters

Nova Scotia Nurses' Union
65 Queen St.
Dartmouth, NS, Canada B2Y
1G4

Ph: (902)469-1474
Fax: (902)466-6935

E-mail: nsnu@fox.nsfn.ca

Contact: Jean Candy, Editor.

Desc: Provides news of Union activities and nursing issues in Nova Scotia. *Type:* Newsletter.

Nutrition

American Dietetic Association

216 W. Jackson Blvd., Ste. 800
Chicago, IL 60606-6995

Ph: (312)899-0040
Fax: (312)899-1979

URL: http://www.eatright.org

Contact: Beverly Bajus, COO.

Desc: Dietetic professionals, registered dietitians and dietetic technicians serving the public through promotion of optimal nutrition, health and well being. Seeks to shape the food choices and impact the nutritional status of the public in hospitals, colleges, universities, schools, day care centers, research, business and industry. *Type:* Association.

American Society for Parenteral and Enteral Nutrition

8630 Fenton Ste., No. 412
Silver Spring, MD 20910-3805

Ph: (301)587-6315
Fax: (301)587-2365

E-mail: aspen@nutr.org

URL: http://www.clinnutr.org

Contact: Barney Sellers, Exec.Dir.

Desc: Physicians, dietitians, nurses, pharmacists, and members of the industry. Works to promote quality patient care, education, and research in the field of nutrition and metabolic support in all health care settings. Educates health care professionals. *Type:* Association.

Better Nutrition Magazine

Intertec Publishing
5 Penn Plaza, 13th Fl.
New York, NY 10001-1810

Ph: (212)613-9700
Fax: (212)613-9749

Contact: James J. Gormley, Editor, (212)613-9757; Ted Lotz, Publisher, (770)618-0316, fax: (770)618-0343.

Desc: Magazine focusing on 'all-natural dietary and lifestyle approaches to optimal nutrition and health.' *Type:* Periodical.

CAB: Human Nutrition

CAB International
CABI Publishing
10 E. 40th St., Ste. 3203
New York, NY 10016

Ph: (212)481-7018

E-mail: cabi-nao@cabi.org

URL: http://www.cabi.org

Contact: Tania Fisher, Product Manager.

Desc: Contains more than 315,000 citations, with abstracts, to current periodical and other published literature relating to human nutrition and metabolism and allied topics. Corresponds to Nutrition Abstracts and Reviews, Series A: Human and Experimental and in part to the online CAB ABSTRACTS, CAB HUMAN, and CAB NUTRITION databases. *Available:* The Dialog Corporation, DataStar. *Type:* Database.

Center for Endocrinology, Metabolism and Molecular Medicine

15-709 Tarry
303 Chicago Ave.
Chicago, IL 60611

Ph: (312)503-0139
Fax: (312)908-9032

E-mail: ljameson@nwu.edu

URL: http://www.medicine.nwu.edu/endocrine/

Contact: Dr. Larry Jameson, Ch.

Desc: Endocrinology, metabolism, and nutrition, including diabetes, growth hormones, obesity and hypertension, and catecholamines. *Type:* Research center.

Columbia University

Institute of Human Nutrition

College of Physicians &
Surgeons
630 W. 168th St.
PH 15E, Rm. 1512
New York, NY 10032

Ph: (212)305-4808
Fax: (212)305-3079

E-mail: rjd20@columbia.edu

Contact: Richard J. Deckelbaum, MD, Dir.

Desc: Atherosclerosis, lipoprotein-receptor-cell interaction; lipid emulsion metabolism; free fatty acids and cell lipid metabolism; basic retinoid and vitamin A physiology, biochemistry, and molecular biology; food and nutrition policy and law; intestinal ion transport mechanisms; enteric nervous system; human lipoprotein metabolism; lipolytic enzymes and endothelial cell biology; atherosclerosis; mineral metabolism and toxicology; carbohydrate and lipid metabolism, obesity, diabetes mellitus, food intake regulation; calcium metabolism; vascular cell biology; pathogenesis of thrombosis; regulation of intracellular cholesterol metabolism; endocytic pathways in macrophages; cholestryl ester transfer; protein structure/function and mutagenesis; regulation of gene expression; molecular nutrition; molecular mechanisms of carcinogenesis. *Type:* Research center.

Council for Responsible Nutrition

1875 Eye St. NW, Ste. 400
Washington, DC 20036-5409

Ph: (202)872-1488
Fax: (202)872-9594

E-mail: webmaster@crnusa.org

URL: http://www.crnusa.org

Contact: John Cordaro, Pres.

Desc: Manufacturers, distributors, and other companies involved in the production and sale of nutritional supplements, including vitamins and minerals. Seeks an improvement in the general health of the U.S. *Type:* Association.

Dietary Managers Association

406 Surrey Woods Drive
St. Charles, IL 60174

Ph: (630)587-6336
Free: 800-323-1908
Fax: (630)587-6308

URL: http://www.dmaonline.org

Contact: William S. St. John, Exec.Dir.

Desc: Dietary managers united to maintain a high level of competency and quality in dietary departments through continuing education. Provides educational programs and placement service. *Type:* Association.

Dr. Betty Kamen's Underground Online Nutrition Newsletter

Nutrition Encounter
61 Bahama Reef
PO Box 5847
Novato, CA 94948

Ph: (415)883-5154
Fax: (415)883-9051

E-mail: sikam@earthlink.net

URL: http://www.bettykamen.com.

Contact: Betty Kamen, PhD, Editor.

Desc: Provides online information about new nutritional therapies. *Type:* Newsletter.

Environmental Nutrition

Environmental Nutrition, Inc.
52 Riverside Dr., 15A   Ph: (212)362-0424
New York, NY 10024   Fax: (212)362-2066
E-mail: 76521.2250@compuserve.com
Contact: Susan Male Smith, Editor.
Desc: Keeps readers abreast of new findings and breakthroughs in nutrition and diet. Discusses nutrition in connection with food additives, food fads and diets, pharmaceuticals and vitamins, and disease prevention. *Type:* Newsletter.

Feingold Association of the United States

127 East Main St., Ste. 106   Ph: (516)369-9340
Riverhead, NY 11901   Fax: (516)369-2988
E-mail: membership@feingold.org
URL: http://www.feingold.org
Contact: Jane Hersey, Dir.
Desc: Individuals who believe overactivity, aggression, Attention Deficit Disorder, sleep disturbances, and learning disabilities are often alleviated by adherence to a program developed by Ben F. Feingold, M.D. which eliminates synthetic colors, synthetic flavors, and BHA, BHT, and TBHQ (preservatives) from the diet. Goals are: to support the dietary management schedule known as the Feingold Program; to gather and disseminate information on food supply and to support public availability of such information. *Type:* Association.

Food and Nutrition Board

2101 Constitution Ave. NW   Ph: (202)334-1732
Washington, DC 20418   Fax: (202)334-2316
E-mail: fnb@nas.edu
Contact: Carol Suitor, Acting Dir.
Desc: Evaluates and offers advice to the federal government concerning the relationship between food consumption, nutritional status, and public health. *Type:* Association.

Health Bites

Health Bites
PO Box 641037
Beverly Hills, CA 34465-1037
Contact: Kimberly Bush, Editor.
Desc: Directed toward diabetic and/or heart patients. Contains recipes that are primarily sugar-free, low-fat, low-cholesterol, and low-sodium. *Type:* Newsletter.

Health Diet & Nutrition

Publishing and Business Consultants
4427 W. Slauson Ave.
Los Angeles, CA 90043-2717
Contact: Atia Napoleon, Editor and Publisher.
Desc: Magazine featuring basic dietary habits, nutritional information and personal health care. *Type:* Periodical.

HealthWatchers System

Health Watchers System
13402 N. Scottsdale Rd., Ste. B.   Free: 800-321-6917
150   Fax: (602)948-8150
Scottsdale, AZ 85254-4054
E-mail: info@healthwatchers.com
URL: http://www.healthwatchers.com.
Contact: Gary A. Martin, Editor, drmartin@healthwatchers.com.
Desc: Discusses the merits of various "natural health products" (mainly dietary supplements) available from Health-Watchers System. Also provides information on studies and research relating to health problems brought on by vitamin deficiencies. *Type:* Newsletter.

Indiana University-Purdue University at Indianapolis

Mead Johnson Mass Spectrometry Laboratory

RR 208   Ph: (317)274-4715
Indianapolis, IN 46202   Fax: (317)274-2065
E-mail: sdenne@iupui.edu
URL: http://www.indiana.edu/~rugs/ctrdir/mjmsl.html
Contact: Scott C. Denne, MD, Dir.
Desc: Nutrition and metabolism, including fetal, neonatal, and adult protein and glucose metabolism; infant and adult energy expenditure and body composition; human muscle metabolism and exercise; and diabetes. *Type:* Research center.

International Life Sciences Institute - North America

1126 16th St. NW, No. 300   Ph: (202)659-0074
Washington, DC 20036   Fax: (202)659-3859
Contact: George E. Hardy, Jr., Exec.Dir.
Desc: Promotes basic research and education in the areas of nutrition toxicology through support of research, scientific symposia, workshops, and monographs. *Type:* Association.

Johns Hopkins University

Center for Human Nutrition

School of Hygiene and Public   Ph: (410)614-4070
    Health   Fax: (410)955-0196
615 N. Wolfe St.
Baltimore, MD 21205
E-mail: bcaballe@jhsph.edu
URL: http://www.sph.jhu.edu/research/centers/nutrition/navibar.html
Contact: Dr. Benjamin Caballero, Dir.
Desc: The role of nutrition in health and disease and the development of new ways to apply that knowledge to improve the health of people, including maternal and child nutrition, obesity and chronic diseases, micronutrient deficiencies, and nutrient metabolism. *Type:* Research center.

King James Medical Laboratory/Omegatech

24700 Center Ridge Rd.   Ph: (440)835-2150
Cleveland, OH 44145   Fax: (440)835-2177
URL: http://www.kingjamesomegatech-lab.com
Contact: Dr. Raymond J. Shamberger, Dir.
Desc: Nutrition and trace elements, including role of dietary thiamine, serum enzyme activities, synthesis and utilization of creatine, effect of zinc supplement, and sorption from the gut. *Type:* Research center.

Laval University

Human Nutrition Research Group

Department of Human   Ph: (418)656-2131
    Nutrition   Fax: (418)656-3353
Quebec, PQ, Canada G1K 7P4
E-mail: helene.jacques@aln.ulaval.ca
Contact: Helene Jacques, Dir.
Desc: Nutrient bioavailability: mechanisms and metabolic impact. *Type:* Research center.

Laval University

Joseph Rheaume Laboratory

Pavillon Paul-Comtois   Ph: (418)656-2315
Quebec, PQ, Canada G1K 7P4   Fax: (418)656-3353
E-mail: laurent.savoie@aln.ulaval.ca
Contact: Laurent Savoie, Dir.
Desc: Nutrient bioavailability, the effect of food proteins on mineral bioavailability in vitro and in vivo, and kinetics and forms of amino acids at various levels of blood circulation. *Type:* Research center.

LifelineLetter

Oley Foundation for Home Parenteral & Enteral Nutrition
Albany Medical Center   Ph: (518)262-5079
214 Hun Memorial, A-23   Free: 800-776-6539
Albany, NY 12208   Fax: (518)262-5528
E-mail: joan_bishop@ccgateway.amc.edu
Contact: Roslyn Scheib Dahl, Editor.
Desc: Explains the home use of specialized nutritional therapies(homePEN: Home Parenteral and Enteral Nutrition): enteral (tube) nutrition, for those who cannot eat but have at least a partially-functioning intestinal tract; and parenteral (intravenous) nutrition, for those who cannot absorb nutrients into their systems because of a damaged or removed intestinal tract. Fosters patient-to-patient communication for those on homePEN nutritional support. *Type:* Newsletter.

McGill University

McGill Nutrition and Food Science Centre

Royal Victoria Hospital   Ph: (514)843-1665
687 Pine Ave. W., Room H6.61   Fax: (514)843-1706
Montreal, PQ, Canada H3A
    1A1
E-mail: emarliss@rvhmed.lan.mcgill.ca
Contact: Dr. Errol B. Marliss, Dir.
Desc: Promotes clinical and basic research in nutrition and food science. *Type:* Research center.

Memorial Sloan-Kettering Cancer Center

Nutrition Information Center

515 E. 71st St., Rm. 202   Ph: (212)746-1617
New York, NY 10021   Fax: (212)746-8310
E-mail: mswhite@mail.ned.cornell.edu
Contact: Dr. Barbara Levine, Dir.
Desc: Nutritional education of physicians. Serves as a resource in clinical nutrition, nutritional research, and general nutrition. *Type:* Research center.

Nutrition Action Healthletter

Center for Science in the Public Interest
1875 Connecticut Ave. NW,   Ph: (202)332-9110
    Ste. 300   Fax: (202)265-4954
Washington, DC 20009
E-mail: circ@cspinet.org; nah@essential.org.
URL: http://www.cspinet.org; http://www.cspinet.org.
Contact: Stephen Schmidt, Editor.
Desc: Covers food and nutrition, the food industry, and relevant government regulations and legislation. Focuses on the connections among diet, lifestyle, and disease. *Type:* Newsletter.

Nutrition Health Review

Vegetus Publications
Box 406   Ph: (610)896-1853
Haverford, PA 19041   Fax: (610)896-1857
Contact: Frank Ray Rifkin, Editor.
Desc: Aims to educate the public about nutrition and health. Covers developments in areas including medical care, psychology, childraising, and geriatrics. *Type:* Newsletter.

Nutrition Health Review

Nutrition Health Review
Box No. 406   Ph: (610)896-1853
Haverford, PA 19041   Fax: (610)896-1857
Contact: Frank R. Rifkin, Editor; Andrew Rifkin, Publisher; Noreen Branigan, Circulation Mgr.
Desc: Health magazine (tabloid). *Alt. Contact:* Box No. 406, Haverford, PA 19041. *Type:* Periodical.

Nutrition Notes

American Society for Nutrition Sciences
9650 Rockville Pike   Ph: (301)530-7050
Bethesda, MD 20814-3990   Fax: (301)571-1892
Desc: Contains updates on nutrition legislation, public affairs, and public information policies. Reviews the results of nutritional research conducted by members of the Institute, which is comprised of nutrition scientists from universities, government, and industry. *Type:* Newsletter.

On Your Mark

The Sugar Association, Inc.
1101 15th St. NW, Ste. 600   Ph: (202)785-1122
Washington, DC 20005   Fax: (202)785-5019
E-mail: sugar@sugar.org
Contact: Michelle Plaut, Editor.
Desc: Presents news and information on nutrition and fitness, especially carbohydrate issues. *Type:* Newsletter.

St. Joseph's University

Food Nutrition and Health Research Institute

Ctr. for Food Marketing   Ph: (610)660-1617
5600 City Ave.   Fax: (610)660-1604
Philadelphia, PA 19131
E-mail: dkeast@sju.edu
Contact: Debra Rose Keast, Dir.
Desc: Conducts surveys on health and nutritional lifestyles. Seeks to develop products and marketing communications which encourage sound nutrition and promote good health. *Type:* Research center.

Tiffin Topics

Food & Nutrition Services
New Hampshire State Department of Education
State Office Park South   Ph: (603)271-3646
101 Pleasant St.   Fax: (603)271-1953
Concord, NH 03301
Contact: Elaine Vandyke, Editor.
Desc: Provides nutritional information of interest to school food service directors. Reports on changes in federal regulations and new state sanitary food codes. *Type:* Newsletter.

Tufts University Health & Nutrition Letter

Tufts University
50 Broadway, Ste. 1504   Ph: (212)668-0411
New York, NY 10004   Fax: (212)668-0421
E-mail: tuftshnltr@aol.com.
Contact: Stanley Gershoff, Editor; Lawrence Lindner, Exec. Editor, fax: (617)350-7974; Gail Zyla, Senior Editor.
Desc: Addresses the medical and health aspects of nutrition and exercise. Offers nutrition-related advice in nontechnical language. *Type:* Newsletter.

U.S. Department of Agriculture

Center for Nutrition Policy and Promotion

1120 20th St. NW, Ste. 200   Ph: (202)418-2312
Washington, DC 20036-3406   Fax: (202)208-2321
URL: http://www.usda.gov/fns/cnpp.htm
Desc: The Center for Nutrition Policy and Promotion coordinates nutrition policy in the USDA and provides overall leadership in nutrition education for the American public. It also coordinates with the Department of Health and Human Services in the review, revision, and dissemination of the *Dietary Guidelines for Americans,* the federal government's statement of nutrition policy formed by a consensus of scientific and medical professionals. *Type:* Government agency, office, or program.

U.S. Department of Agriculture

Food and Nutrition Service

3101 Park Center Dr.   Ph: (703)305-2286
Alexandria, VA 22302   Fax: (703)305-2420
URL: http://www.usda.gov/fns.htm
Desc: The Food and Nutrition Service, operated in cooperation with states and local governments, administers programs to make food assistance available to people in need. In particular, the service administers Special Nutrition Programs designed to improve the nutrition of children, particularly those from low income families. *Type:* Government agency, office, or program.

U.S. Department of Health and Human Services

Food and Drug Administration

Center for Food Safety and Applied Nurtition

Office of Cosemetics and Colors

Mail Code HFS-100   Ph: (202)245-4530
200 C St., S.W.   Fax: (202)205-5219
Washington, DC 20204
Contact: Dr. John Bailey, Actg.Dir.
Desc: Development of methods for the identification and determination of colors, color residues and contaminants, cosmetics, and fragrances. *Type:* Research center.

U.S. Department of Health and Human Services

Food and Drug Administration

Center for Food Safety and Applied Nutrition

200 C St., S.W.   Ph: (202)205-4850
Washington, DC 20204   Fax: (202)205-5025
E-mail: jlevih@bangate.fds.gov
Contact: Joseph Levitt, Dir.
Desc: Principal goals are to gather, analyze, and monitor published and unpublished information pertinent to the consumption, quality, and safety of foods and cosmetics; determine the nutritional needs of various population groups and develop strategies to improve the nutritional status of those at risk; isolate, purify, and identify potentially hazardous food and cosmetic constituents and adulterants, including biological, microbial, and chemical contaminants; develop, validate, and apply quantitative methods of analysis for potentially hazardous constituents, adulterants, and contaminants of foods and cosmetics, including environmental contaminants, animal drugs, and metabolites of microbial origin; develop, improve, and validate biological tests for various forms of human toxicity, including chronic toxicity, fetal and neonatal toxicity, behavioral and immunotoxicity, and dermal and ocular toxicity; apply toxicity tests and epidemiological studies to determine the adverse effects (hazards) of food constituents and contaminants and of cosmetics ingredients, singly or in combination; improve the accuracy of methods used to assess potential risks to human health associated with the constituents and contaminants of foods and cosmetics; develop practical control technologies necessary to detect or prevent hazards resulting from the storage or processing of foods or cosmetics; and assess social, economic, and environmental determinants and impacts of Center actions.

U.S. Department of Health and Human Services

Food and Drug Administration

Center for Food Safety and Applied Nutrition

c/o Food and Drug   Free: 800-332-4010
  Administration
5600 Fishers Ln.
Rockville, MD 20857
URL: http://www.fda.gov/
Contact: Joe Levitt, Director.
Desc: The Center conducts research and develops standards on the composition, quality, nutrition, and safety of foods, food additives, colors, and cosmetics; conducts re-

search designed to improve the detection, prevention, and control of contamination that may be responsible for illness or injury conveyed by foods, colors, and cosmetics; coordinates and evaluates FDA's surveillance and compliance programs relating to foods, color, and cosmetics; reviews industry petitions and develops regulations for food standards to permit the safe use of color additives and food additives; collects and interprets data on nutrition, food additives, and environmental factors affecting the total chemical result posed by food additives; and maintains a nutritional data bank. *Type:* Government agency, office, or program.

U.S. Department of Health and Human Services

Food and Drug Administration

Center for Food Safety and Applied Nutrition

Office of Plant and Diary Foods and Beverages

Rm. 4827, HFS-300   Ph: (202)205-4064
200 C St. SW   Fax: (202)205-4422
Washington, DC 20204-0001
E-mail: jev@fdacf.ssw.dhhs.gov
URL: http://vm.cfsan.fda.gov/list.html

Contact: Dr. John E. Vanderveen, Dir.

Desc: Safety and quality of foods derived from plants, milk, eggs, and game foods, including studies on detection of inorganic and organic contaminants, pesticides and natural toxins; identification of virulence factors associated with foodborne pathogens; impact of foodborne pathogens on immune response; natural product chemistry of herbal products; and food processing and packaging; and risk assessment of harmful substances in foods. *Type:* Research center.

U.S. Department of Health and Human Services

National Institute of Diabetes and Digestive and Kidney Diseases

Division of Digestive Diseases and Nutrition

Nutritional Sciences Branch

45 Center Dr. MSC 6600   Ph: (301)594-8883
Bethesda, MD 20892-6600   Fax: (301)480-8300

Contact: Dr. Van S. Hubbard, Dir.

Desc: Basic, clinical, and behavioral research and training directed toward the improvement of human health. Priority areas of research are: human nutrition requirements, including environmental and host factors that may affect requirements, such as nutrient imbalance, drugs, disease, stress, and activity levels; physiological function of essential nutrients in health and disease, with emphasis on amino acids, calcium, magnesium, trace elements, and vitamins; and significance of proportion and amount of macronutrients (dietary proteins, fats, and carbohydrates) in metabolism. *Type:* Research center.

U.S. Department of Health and Human Services

National Institute of Diabetes and Digestive and Kidney Diseases

U.S.-Japan Malnutrition Panel

5333 Westbard Ave., Rm.   Ph: (301)594-7573
  3A18B   Fax: (301)594-7504
Bethesda, MD 20892

Contact: Dr. Van S. Hubbard, Prog.Dir.

Desc: Mission is to foster and support investigator-initiated research to help alleviate the serious problem of malnutrition. The increasing westernization of the Japanese diet and the increasing affluence among the Japanese people may play a role in the changes seen in nutritional status and incidence of nutritionally related diseases in that country. *Type:* Research center.

University of California, Berkeley, Wellness Letter

University of California, Berkeley School of Public Health

632 Broadway, 11th Fl. Ph: (212)505-2255
New York, NY 10012 Fax: (212)505-5462

Contact: Dr. Sheldon Margen, Chairman, Editorial Board.

Desc: Gives latest medical findings and practical information on achieving a healthier lifestyle. *Type:* Newsletter.

University of California, Davis

Clinical Nutrition Research Unit

Division of Clinical Nutrition & Ph: (530)752-6778
    Metabolism Fax: (530)752-3470
Sch. of Med., TB-156
Davis, CA 95616
E-mail: chhalsted@ucdavis.edu

Contact: Charles Halsted, MD, Dir.

Desc: Human nutrition in health and disease. Studies focus on the relationship of diet to disease, energy metabolism, and development. *Type:* Research center.

University of California, Davis

Gastroenterology and Nutrition Center

Pediatric GI Ph: (916)734-3750
UCD Med. Ctr. Fax: (916)456-2236
2516 Stockton Blvd.
Sacramento, CA 95817
E-mail: michael.haight@ucdmc.ucdavis.edu
URL: http://www.ucdmc.ucdavis.edu

Contact: Dr. Michael Haight, Chf., Pediatric Gastroenterology.

Desc: Pediatric nutritional support, and feeding problems in children, Pediatric Short Bowel Syndrome, outcomes and lactation. *Type:* Research center.

University of Chicago

Clinical Nutrition Research Unit

5841 S. Maryland Ave., Box Ph: (773)702-6741
    MC4080 Fax: (773)702-6972
Chicago, IL 60637
E-mail: msitrin@medicine.bsd.uchicago.edu

Contact: Michael D. Sitrin, MD, Dir.

Desc: Human and clinical nutritional biology, particularly in relation to pregnancy, growth retardation, digestive and cardiovascular diseases, diabetes, and cancer. Conducts vitamin metabolism, lipoprotein, lipid, stable isotope, trace metal, and radioimmunoassay analyses. *Type:* Research center.

University of Maryland

Nutrition Laboratory

Department of Human Ecology Ph: (410)651-6056
Henson Ctr., Rm. 2101 Fax: (410)651-6207
Princess Anne, MD 21853
E-mail: bblakely@umes-bird.umd.edu

Contact: Dr. Bettie Blakely, Contact.

Desc: Nutrition and metabolism. *Type:* Research center.

University of Nevada, Reno

Nutrition Education & Research Program

Sch. of Med. Ph: (702)784-4474
Redfield Bldg., No. 153 Fax: (702)784-4468
Reno, NV 89557
E-mail: sach@unr.edu

Contact: Dr. Sachiko T. St. Jeor, Dir.

Desc: Clinical nutrition. *Type:* Research center.

University of Texas Southwestern Medical Center at Dallas

Center for Human Nutrition

5323 Harry Hines Blvd. Ph: (214)648-3111
Dallas, TX 75235-9052 Fax: (214)648-4837
E-mail: sgrund@mcdnet.swmed.edu

Contact: Dr. Scott M. Grundy, Dir.

Desc: Human nutrition. Investigates the preventive effects of vitamins C and E on atherosclerosis. *Type:* Research center.

University of Washington

Clinical Nutrition Research Unit

Department of Med. Ph: (206)543-6166
Division of Metabolism, Box Fax: (206)685-3781
    356426
Seattle, WA 98195

Contact: Prof. Alan Chait, MD, Prin.Invest.

Desc: Human nutrition in health and disease, including nutritional health maintenance, improved nutritional support of the acutely and chronically ill, assessment of nutritional status, effects of diseased states on nutritional needs, and effects of nutrition on disease states. Conducts research with human subjects and populations. *Type:* Research center.

USDA Agricultural Research Service

Grand Forks Human Nutrition Research Center

2420 2nd Ave. N. Ph: (701)795-8353
PO Box 9034, State Univ. Sta. Fax: (701)795-8395
Grand Forks, ND 58202-9034
E-mail: i:fnielsen@gfhnrc.ars.usda.gov
URL: http://www.gfhnrc.ars.usda.gov

Contact: Forrest Nielsen, PhD, Dir.

Desc: Role of mineral elements (including magnesium, copper, manganese, iron, boron, selenium, chromium and zinc) in nutrition; bone, cardiovascular, and brain development, maintenance, and function; body composition; and neurological response; and other mechanisms by which these elements sustain life and promote growth in humans. *Type:* Research center.

USDA Nutrient Database

Agricultural Research Service

Nutrient Data Laboratory Ph: (301)734-8491
Beltsville Human Nutrition Fax: (301)734-5643
    Research Center
4700 River Rd., Unit 89
Riverdale, MD 20737
E-mail: ndlinfo@rbhnrc.usda.gov
URL: http://www.nal.usda.gov/fnic/cgi-bin/nut_search.pl

Desc: This database provides basic nutritional information on a wide variety of foodstuffs consumed by humans - even fast-food cheeseburgers. Enter a term to search for and the database will return a list of items that match that term or parts of it. *Type:* Database.

Vanderbilt University

Clinical Nutrition Research Unit

C2104 Med. Ctr. North Ph: (615)343-4747
21st and Garland Ave. Fax: (615)343-6229
Nashville, TN 37232-2279
E-mail: raymond.burk@mcmail.vanderbilt.edu

Contact: Raymond F. Burk, MD, Contact.

Desc: Mechanisms of body weight and regulation, focusing on exercise and energy expenditure. Metabolism of amino acids, carbohydrates, lipids, minerals, and trace metals. *Type:* Research center.

Your Health

International Academy of Nutrition & Preventive Medicine

34 Wall St., Ste. 405 Ph: (704)258-3243
Asheville, NC 28801 Fax: (704)253-7781

Contact: Elizabeth Pavka, M.S., Editor.

Desc: Contains a variety of perspectives on using nutrition and preventive medicine. Recurring features include interviews and a calendar of events. *Type:* Newsletter.

Nuts

Almond Board of California

1150 9th St. Ph: (209)549-8262
Ste. 1500 Fax: (209)549-8267
Modesto, CA 95354
URL: http://www.almondsarein.com

Contact: Rodger Wasson, Exec. Officer.

Desc: Participants are almond packers and growers. Purpose is to administer the federal marketing order for almonds regarding the production research, quality control, and supply allocation of almonds. *Type:* Association.

Blue Diamond Growers

PO Box 1768 Ph: (916)442-0771
Sacramento, CA 95812 Fax: (916)325-2880

Contact: Walter Payne, Pres. & CEO.

Desc: California almond growers. Processes and markets Blue Diamond almonds, hazelnuts, macadamias, and pistachios for members on a cooperative basis. *Type:* Association.

California Pistachio Commission

1318 E. Shaw Ave., Ste. 420 Ph: (209)221-8294
Fresno, CA 93710 Fax: (209)221-8044
E-mail: info@capistachiocomm.org
URL: http://www.pistachio.org

Contact: Karen Reinecke, Pres.

Desc: Eight commission members and eight alternate members elected by the 520 pistachio producers in California. Purposes are to develop domestic and international markets for California pistachios through promotion and public relations; conduct production and marketing research; and improve communication among growers. *Type:* Association.

California Pistachio Commission

1318 E. Shaw Ave., Ste. 420 Ph: (209)221-8294
Fresno, CA 93710 Fax: (209)221-8044
E-mail: info@capistachiocomm.org
URL: http://www.pistachios.org

Contact: Karen Reinecke, Pres.

Desc: Eight commission members selected by the 500 pistachio producers in California. Purposes are to: develop domestic and international markets through advertising, promotion, and public relations; conduct production and marketing research; improve communications among growers. *Type:* Association.

Georgia Peanut Commission

110 E. 4th St. Ph: (912)386-3470
PO Box 967 Free: 800-346-4993
Tifton, GA 31793 Fax: (912)386-3501
E-mail: growpeanuts@aol.com
URL: http://www.peanutbutterlovers.com

Contact: Don Koehler, Exec.Dir.

Desc: Peanut farmers whose goals are to research, disseminate information on, and promote Georgia's peanut crop. *Type:* Association.

In a Nutshell

National Pecan Shellers Association
5775 Peachtree-Dunwoody Rd.,   Ph: (404)252-3663
Ste., 500G   Fax: (404)252-0774
Atlanta, GA 30342
E-mail: npsa@assnhq.com

Contact: Larry Davenport, Editor; Sue Taylor, Editor.

Desc: Compiles information on the pecan industry. Recurring features include calendar of events. *Type:* Newsletter.

The Nut Kernel

Pennsylvania Nut Growers Association (PNGA)
654 Beinhower Rd.   Ph: (717)938-6090
Etters, PA 17319-9774   Fax: (717)938-6090

Contact: Tucker Hill, Editor, tuckerh@mail.microserve.net.

Desc: Features information for amateur and expert nut growers on cultural practices, new developments in propagation, and knowledge of new and better cultivars and where to get them. Contains supplements of reports on the latest practices, experiments in progress, and storage of nuts. *Type:* Newsletter.

The Nutshell

Northern Nut Growers Association (NNGA)
654 Beinhower Rd.   Ph: (717)938-6090
Etters, PA 17319-9774   Fax: (717)938-6090

Contact: Tucker Hill, Editor, tuckerh@mail.microserve.net.

Desc: Brings information to amateur and expert nut growers on cultural practices, new developments in propagation, and knowledge of new and better cultivars and where to get them. Contains supplements of reports on the latest practices, experiments in progress, and storage of nuts. *Type:* Newsletter.

P-Nutty News and Notes

Virginia-Carolina Peanut Promotions
PO Box 8   Ph: (919)459-9977
Nashville, NC 27856-0008   Fax: (919)459-7396
URL: http://www.aboutpeanuts.com.

Contact: Betsy Owens, Editor, betsy@aboutpeanuts.com.

Desc: Provides nutritional information, recipes, ideas for economical use, and storage suggestions for peanuts and peanut foods. Educates the public and promotes the edible consumption of peanuts grown in North Carolina and Virginia. *Type:* Newsletter.

Peanut Advisory Board

500 Sugar Mill Rd., Ste. 105-A   Ph: (770)998-7311
Atlanta, GA 30350   Fax: (770)998-5962
E-mail: pabnuts@aol.com
URL: http://www.peanutbutterlovers.com

Contact: Mitch Head, Exec.Dir.

Desc: Represents 10,000 peanut farmers in Georgia, Alabama, and Florida. *Type:* Association.

Peanut Report

Federal-State Market News
PO Box 1447   Ph: (912)228-1208
State Farmers Market-Stall No.   Fax: (912)225-1516
   39
Thomasville, GA 31792

Desc: Provides information on shelled and unshelled peanuts as well as peanut oil and peanut meals in the Southeast. Includes "Free on Board" (F.O.B.) shipping point prices, crop reports, export data, stock updates, and processing and marketing information. *Type:* Newsletter.

Peanut Research

American Peanut Research and Education Society
Oklahoma State University   Ph: (405)744-9634
376 Agriculture Hall   Fax: (405)744-5269
Stillwater, OK 74078
E-mail: jrs@soilwater.agr.okstate.edu.

Contact: John P. Beasley, Jr., Editor.

Desc: Keeps members of the Society up to date on current research affecting the peanut industry, with reports on specific research projects, programs, seminars, conferences, publications, and persons involved. Recurring features include literature citations, annual meeting information, and obituaries. *Type:* Newsletter.

Peanut and Tree Nut Processors Association— Bulletin

Peanut and Tree Processors Association
9005 Congressional Ct.   Ph: (301)365-4080
Potomac, MD 20854

Contact: Russell E. Barker, Editor.

Desc: Contains news items on the Association and on member companies, who are manufacturers of peanut butter and packaged nuts and suppliers of goods and services to the industry. Also reports on industry trends. *Type:* Newsletter.

Pecan-E-Gram

Southeastern Pecan Growers Association
c/o Sally W. Beshears   Ph: (904)997-3458
Rt. 4, Box 4188
Monticello, FL 32344

Desc: Describes the Association's work to improve methods of fertilization, disease and insect control, marketing, grading, and storage of pecans. Supplies updates on agricultural, economic, and industry developments affecting the market for pecans. *Type:* Newsletter.

Pecan Report

Federal-State Market News
PO Box 1447   Ph: (912)228-1208
State Farmers Market-Stall No.   Fax: (912)225-1516
   39
Thomasville, GA 31792

Desc: Designed to report on prices paid to growers in the major pecan producing states. Carries industry information from such sources as crop production and cold storage reports, whole terminal market prices, export data, and import data including daily pecan crosings from Mexico. *Type:* Newsletter.

Pecan Shellers Update

National Pecan Shellers Association
5775 Peachtree-Dunwoody Rd.,   Ph: (404)252-3663
Ste., 500G   Fax: (404)252-0774
Atlanta, GA 30342
E-mail: npsa@assnhq.com

Contact: Larry Davenport, Editor; Sue Taylor, Editor.

Desc: Compiles information on the pecan industry. *Type:* Newsletter.

SONG News

Society of Ontario Nut Growers (SONG)
RR 1   Ph: (905)262-4927
Niagara on the Lake, ON,
   Canada L0S 1J0

Contact: Douglas Campbell, Editor.

Desc: Promotes all aspects of nut growing. Discusses scientific research concerning breeding and cultivation. *Type:* Newsletter.

Oceanography

Calypso Log

The Cousteau Society
870 Greenbrier Cir., Ste. 402   Ph: (757)523-9335
Chesapeake, VA 23320   Free: 800-441-4395
                                   Fax: (757)523-2747
E-mail: cousteau@infi.net

Contact: Isabelle Erard, Editor-in-Chief; Gregoire Koulbanis, Scientific Supervisor; Francine Cousteau, Editorial Dir.; Lisa Rao, American Section Editor, cousteauny@aol.com.

Desc: Magazine containing articles on environmental issues, ecology, and the ocean. *Type:* Periodical.

Coral Health and Monitoring Program

National Oceanic and Atmospheric Administration - Atlantic Oceanographic and Meteorological Laboratory
Ocean Chemistry Division   Ph: (305)361-4396
4301 Rickenbacker Causeway
Miami, FL 33149-1026
E-mail: hendee@aoml.noaa.gov
URL: http://coral.aoml.noaa.gov

Desc: The Coral Health and Monitoring Program's mission is to provide services to help improve and sustain coral reef health throughout the world. Site resources include a historical database, document listings on member nation activities, a mailing list, a directory of the world's coral researchers, and more. *Type:* Database.

Index to Marine Geological Samples

U.S. National Geophysical Data Center
NOAA/NGDC Mail Code   Ph: (303)497-6339
   E/GC3   Fax: (303)497-6513
325 Broadway
Boulder, CO 80303
URL: http://www.ngdc.noaa.gov/mgg/curator/curator.html

Contact: Carla Moore, cmoore@ngdc.noaa.gov.

Desc: The Curators' Database contains a listing of more than 91,000 cores, grabs, and dredges from the seafloor archived at participating institutions worldwide. It contains inventory and standardized lithology, texture, and age information for samples archived by oceanographic institutions and government agencies. *Type:* Database.

Oceanic Abstracts

Cambridge Scientific Abstracts (CSA)
7200 Wisconsin Ave., Ste. 601   Ph: (301)961-6700
Bethesda, MD 20814-4823
E-mail: sales@csa.com
URL: http://www.csa.com

Desc: Contains more than 187,000 citations to the worldwide literature on oceanography and marine-related aspects of other sciences. Includes biology, geology and geophysics, meteorology, acoustics and optics, desalination, pollution, resources, engineering, mining, ships and shipping, submersibles and buoys, and government laws and regulations. *Available:* The Dialog Corporation, DIALOG; STN International; European Information Network Services (EINS); Cambridge Scientific Abstracts (CSA), Internet Database Service. *Type:* Database.

Oceanic Society

218 D St. SE   Ph: (202)544-2600
Washington, DC 20003

Contact: Clifton Curtis, Pres.

Desc: A special project of Friends of the Earth . Dedicated to the protection and wise use of the oceans and the marine environment through public education and awareness programs and conservation activities. Sponsors public policy, policy analysis, and conferences. *Type:* Association.

University of Hawaii Satellite Oceanography Laboratory

University of Hawaii, Manoa - Department of Oceanography - Satellite Oeanography Laboratory
1000 Pope Rd.   Ph: (808)956-7633
Honolulu, HI 96822
E-mail: flament@satftp.soest.hawaii.edu
URL: http://satftp.soest.hawaii.edu/satlab/
Desc: This site is funded by the Virtual Hawaii Project which provides access to Earth and space science data on Hawaii. The Satellite Oceanography Laboratory focuses on meteorological and geophysical information about the Pacific, including satellite data and images, oceanographic experiments data, refereed papers published by members of the Satellite Oceanography Laboratory group, catalogs of the lab's raw data holdings, space shuttle radar images, and a collection of hurricane images. *Type:* Database.

Odd Fellows

Grand United Order of Odd Fellows
262 S. 12th St.   Ph: (215)735-8774
Philadelphia, PA 19107   Fax: (215)735-2422
Desc: Individuals united for social and charitable purposes. Conducts seminars and professional training. Sponsors charitable and educational programs; provides children's services; maintains library. *Type:* Association.

Independent Order of Odd Fellows
422 Trade St.   Ph: (336)725-5955
Winston-Salem, NC 27101-   Fax: (336)722-7317
2830
E-mail: ioofsgl@aol.com
URL: http://www.ioof.org
Contact: Terry L. Barrett, Sovereign Grand Sec.
Desc: Fraternal beneficiary society. Maintains research program at Johns Hopkins University, Baltimore, MD; sponsors Education Foundation for financial assistance to students beyond the high school level. Maintains museum. *Type:* Association.

International Association of Rebekah Assemblies, IOOF
422 N. Trade St.   Ph: (336)725-6037
Winston-Salem, NC 27101   Fax: (336)773-1066
E-mail: iarasec@aol.com
Contact: Janet Simmonds, Sec.
Desc: Women's auxiliary to the Independent Order of Odd Fellows. *Type:* Association.

Office Equipment

BTA Hotline
Business Technology Association
12411 Wornall Rd.   Ph: (816)941-3100
Kansas City, MO 64145   Free: 800-366-6950
                                 Fax: (816)941-8034
E-mail: btapubs@aol.com
Contact: Brent Hoskins, Editor; Mike Coleman, Associate Editor.
Desc: Supports the Association's efforts to provide retailers of business equipment with current information relating to management, service, and business systems. Reports information regarding the Association of interest to retailers of business equipment. *Type:* Newsletter.

Business Consumer Guide
Beacon Research Group, Inc.
125 Walnut St.   Ph: (617)924-0044
Watertown, MA 02172   Fax: (617)924-0055
URL: http://www.buysmart.com
Contact: Mie-Yun Lee, Editor.

Desc: Directed toward evaluating office products and services for the business community. Recurring features include letters to the editor and news of research. *Type:* Newsletter.

Business Consumer's Advisor
Buyers Laboratory Inc.
20 Railroad Ave.   Ph: (201)488-0404
Hackensack, NJ 07601   Fax: (201)488-0461
E-mail: info@buyers-lab.com
Contact: Daria Hoffman, Editor.

Desc: Focusses on office equipment and supplies, offering purchasing advice and exploring methods of increasing office productivity through appropriate management of the equipment and its operators. Offers readers a chance to share their experiences, evaluate products and equipment, and gives results of Buyers Laboratory's testing. *Type:* Newsletter.

Business Technology Association
12411 Wornall   Ph: (816)941-3100
Kansas City, MO 64145   Free: 800-247-2176
                                 Fax: (816)941-2829
E-mail: info@btanet.org
URL: http://www.bta.org
Contact: Michael R. Wvkitsch, Exec.Dir.

Desc: Resellers of office equipment and networking products and services. Offers 60 seminars on management, service, technology, and business systems. Conducts research; provides buiness-supporting services and benefits, including insurance, and legal counsel. *Type:* Association.

Copier Review
Buyers Laboratory Inc.
20 Railroad Ave.   Ph: (201)488-0404
Hackensack, NJ 07601   Fax: (201)488-0461
E-mail: info@buyers-lab.com
Contact: Daria Hoffman, Editor.

Desc: Covers copiers and developments in the copier industry. Offers product reviews, Buyers Laboratory preliminary test findings, test reports on copiers, and fact sheets on copiers. *Type:* Newsletter.

Facilities Design & Management—Directory of Consultants & Service Firms Issue
Miller Freeman, Inc.
1 Penn Plaza, 10th Fl.   Ph: (212)714-1300
New York, NY 10119-1198   Fax: (212)643-5612
E-mail: lannunziato@mfi.com.
Contact: Eileen McMorrow, Editor.

Desc: Listing of firms offering products, services, and consulting services to facilities designers and managers. *Type:* Directory.

FAXreporter
Buyers Laboratory Inc.
20 Railroad Ave.   Ph: (201)488-0404
Hackensack, NJ 07601   Fax: (201)488-0461
E-mail: info@buyers-lab.com
Contact: Peter Davidson, Editor.

Desc: Features "news of the fax industry—in-depth analysis of new equipment, the effects of yen/dollar exchange rates, new pricing plans, new features, the latest in fax applications, and insider interviews." Remarks: Subscription includes facsimile test reports and fact sheets. *Type:* Newsletter.

Industry Report
The Business Products Industry Association (BPIA)
301 N. Fairfax St.   Ph: (703)549-9040
Alexandria, VA 22314   Free: 800-542-6672
                                 Fax: (703)683-7552
E-mail: communications@bpia.org
Contact: Max Busetti, Associate Editor.
Desc: Provides news and information on business products, furnishings, and machines industry. Recurring features include news of Association activities, news of members, a comment page, statistics, obituaries, and special interest columns. *Type:* Newsletter.

Matrix Minutes
Facility Matrix Group
PO Box 7620   Ph: (810)767-5790
Flint, MI 48507-0620   Free: 800-527-5360
Contact: Monte Harper, Editor.
Desc: Offers information on trends in the business interiors industry. Recurring features include columns titled President's Message and customer focus. *Type:* Newsletter.

Office Products Analyst
Louis E. Slawetsky
50 Chestnut St.   Ph: (716)232-5320
Rochester, NY 14604   Fax: (716)454-5760
E-mail: theopa00l@aol.com
Contact: Kathy Dwyer, (973)227-8699, fax: (973)227-3644.
Desc: Addresses user reliability studies and industry trend analysis for copiers, printers, facsimiles, computers, and supplies. *Type:* Newsletter.

Office Products Manufacturers Alliance
BPIA
301 N. Fairfax St.   Ph: (703)549-9040
Alexandria, VA 22314-2696   Free: 800-542-6672
                                 Fax: (703)683-7552
E-mail: rhorshok@bpia.com
URL: http://www.bpia.org
Contact: Randy Horshok, Exec.VP.
Desc: Manufacturers of commercial and retail office products. Promotes performance and cooperation among members and enhances relationships with other branches of the industry. Conducts information programs; compiles statistics; provides industry specific services. *Type:* Association.

Open Information Systems
Patricia Seybold Group
85 Devonshire St., 5th Fl.   Ph: (617)742-5200
Boston, MA 02109-3504   Free: 800-826-2424
                                 Fax: (617)742-1028
Contact: Susan E. Alrich, Editor in Chief, saldrich@psgroup.com.
Desc: Covers trends, products, technologies, and standards surrounding key open systems issues facing management, including operating systems, platforms, and systems management tools for Unix, Windows/NT, and other open systems; migration strategies; client/server development tools; open DBMS; OLTP and transaction monitors; middleware, PC and open systems integration; and open systems standards and consortia. *Type:* Newsletter.

School and Home Office Products Association
3055 Kettering Blvd, Ste. 401   Ph: (937)297-2250
Dayton, OH 45439   Free: 800-854-7467
                                 Fax: (937)297-2254
E-mail: info@shopa.org
URL: http://www.shopa.org
Contact: Steve Jacober, Pres.
Desc: Manufacturers, wholesaler and service merchandisers, importers, retailers, commercial/contract stationers,

manufacturers representatives, and associated individuals. Promotes the advancement of the school, office, and home office product industry through an annual trade show, research initiations and other benefits and services. *Type:* Association.

SIGOIS Newsletter
Special Interest Group on Programming Languages (SIGPLAN)
Association for Computing Machinery
1515 Broadway   Ph: (212)869-7440
New York, NY 10036   Free: 800-342-6626
                               Fax: (212)302-5826
E-mail: acmhelp@acm.org
Contact: Simon Gibbs, Editor.
Desc: Discusses all aspects of the application of computing techniques to office activities. Contains methodological and technical articles, surveys, proposed office automation standards, and specification and evaluations from actual case studies. *Type:* Newsletter.

Striking Home
Dvorak International
Box 44   Ph: (802)287-2343
Poultney, VT 05764-0044
E-mail: dvorakint@aol.com
Contact: Steve Ingram, Editor.
Desc: Contains news, reviews, and information on Dvorak keyboard layout. *Type:* Newsletter.

Uncommon Sense
Practice Performance Publishing Inc.
2508 E. Willow, Ste. 302   Ph: (310)595-1728
Long Beach, CA 90806   Fax: (310)595-0023
Contact: Jeffrey J. Denning, Editor; Judy Bee, Publisher.
Desc: Provides purchasing information for office products. *Type:* Newsletter.

Oils and Fats

Render—National Renderers Association Directory Issue
National Renderers Association
PO Box 529   Ph: (530)644-8428
Camino, CA 95709   Fax: (530)644-8429
E-mail: editors@rendermagazine.com
Contact: Tina M. Caparella, Editor.
Desc: List of member producers, brokers, and suppliers of animal fats and proteins; equipment manufacturers and firms serving the rendering industry; coverage includes overseas members. *Type:* Directory.

U.S. Offshore Oil Company Contact List
Offshore Data Services, Inc.
PO Box 19909   Ph: (713)781-2713
Houston, TX 77224-1909   Fax: (713)781-9594
E-mail: editors@offshore-data.com
URL: http://www.offshore-data.com
Contact: Marie Sheffer, Editor.
Desc: Approximately 265 oil companies with U.S. offshore leases. *Type:* Directory.

Washington Correspondence
National Institute of Oilseed Products
1101 15th St., NW, Ste. 202   Ph: (202)785-8450
Washington, DC 20005   Fax: (202)223-9741
E-mail: niop@assnhq.com
Contact: Richard E. Cristol, Editor; Belva W. Jones, Editor.
Desc: Publishes information on vegetable oilseeds, vegetable oils and meals, animal fats, fish oils and meals. Includes statistics and reports on legislation, world trade, supply and demand, and transportation. *Type:* Newsletter.

Ophthalmology

American Academy of Ophthalmology
655 Beach St.   Ph: (415)561-8500
San Francisco, CA 94109   Fax: (415)561-8533
URL: http://www.eyenet.org
Contact: H. Dunbar Hoskins, M.D., Exec.VP.
Desc: Ophthalmologists concerned with high-quality eye care and the continuing education of members. *Type:* Association.

American Society of Cataract and Refractive Surgery
4000 Legato Rd. No., 850   Ph: (703)591-2220
Fairfax, VA 22033   Fax: (703)591-0614
E-mail: ascrs@ascrs.org
URL: http://www.ascrs.org
Contact: David A. Karcher, Exec.Dir.
Desc: Ophthalmologists interested in anterior segment surgery and refractive corneal surgery. Offers continuing medical education to ophthalmologists on cataract and refractive surgery techniques, intraocular lens designs, and related research areas; assists allied health care professionals in ophthalmology on medical and surgical care of pseudophakic (lens implant) patients. Works to improve public education in the field of eye care. *Type:* Association.

Association for Research in Vision and Ophthalmology
9650 Rockville Pike   Ph: (301)571-1844
Bethesda, MD 20814-3998   Fax: (301)571-8311
E-mail: mem@arvo.arvo.org
URL: http://www.faseb.org/arvo/
Contact: Joanne G. Angle, Exec.Dir.
Desc: Professional society of researchers in vision and ophthalmology. To encourage ophthalmic research in the field of blinding eye disease. *Type:* Association.

Columbia University
Edward S. Harkness Eye Institute
Columbia-Presbyterian Med.   Ph: (212)305-2725
  Ctr.   Fax: (212)305-5962
635 W. 165th St., Rm. 218
New York, NY 10032-3784
E-mail: stanley.chang@columbia.edu
URL: http://www.cpmcnet.cpmc.columbia.edu/dept/eye
Contact: Stanley Chang, MD, Dir.
Desc: Ophthalmology, including excimer lasers, new pulsed infrared lasers, patholophysiology and surgical management of orbitopathy, topical and depot corticosteriods in the treatment of post-cataract cystoid macular edema, glaucoma, endothelial growth factors for wound healing in animal models, and effects of diabetes mellitus upon the retinal microvasculature. *Type:* Research center.

Columbia University
Eye Radiation and Environmental Research Laboratory
Columbia-Presbyterian Med.   Ph: (212)305-6748
  Ctr.   Fax: (212)305-6749
630 W. 168th St., Rm. 212
New York, NY 10032-3784
E-mail: bvw1@columbia.edu
URL: http://cpmcnet.columbia.edu/dept/eye/rad
Contact: Dr. Basil Worgul, Dir.
Desc: Cellular mechanisms of radiation cataract, cataractogenesis, the effects of heavy particles on ocular tissue, and potential risks to the eyes of astronauts during extended manned flight in the hostile radiational environment of space. Also conducting Ukrainian/American Chernobyl ocular study. *Type:* Research center.

Columbia University
Retina Research Laboratory
Columbia-Presbyterian Med.   Ph: (212)305-5688
  Ctr.   Fax: (212)305-9087
635 W. 165th St.
New York, NY 10032-3784
E-mail: pg10@columbia.edu
URL: http://cpmcnetcolumbia.edu/dept/eye/retina
Contact: Peter Gouras, MD, Dir.
Desc: Retinal transplantation, biochemical markers for vitamin A metabolism in cultured human retinal epithelial cells, and gene insertion technology. *Type:* Research center.

Detroit Institute of Ophthalmology
15415 E. Jefferson Ave.   Ph: (313)824-4710
Grosse Pointe Park, MI 48230-1328
Contact: Dr. Philip C. Hessburg, Dir.
Desc: Ophthalmology, low vision rehabilitation, and studies related to the relationship between vision and the operation of motorized vehicles. *Type:* Research center.

Diabetes Treatment and Research Center
50 Staniford St., Ste. 340   Ph: (617)726-1847
Boston, MA 02114-2517   Fax: (617)726-1871
E-mail: nathan@gcrc.mgit.harvard.edu
URL: http://www.mgh.harvard.edu
Contact: Dr. David Nathan, Dir.
Desc: Diabetes research, including a ten-yer study of diabetics and studies of implantable pumps. *Type:* Research center.

Eye Care
1412 28th NW   Ph: (202)628-3816
Washington, DC 20007-3145   Fax: (703)904-3945
Contact: Donna A. Fujiwara, Dir.
Desc: Serves the visually neglected by bringing up-to-date ophthalmic care to people who would otherwise have little or no access to professional help for eye injuries or eye diseases. Maintains seven clinics, a paraprofessional ophthalmic assistants training program, three ophthalmic operating suites, and a rehabilitation program in Haiti. Sponsors an educational exhibit about eyes in the Children's Museum in Washington, DC. *Type:* Association.

Eye Research Foundation of Central New York, Inc.
3107 E. Genesee St.   Ph: (315)445-2220
Syracuse, NY 13224
Contact: Carol Richman Wandner, Exec.Dir.
Desc: Cause, cure, and prevention of eye diseases, including diabetic retinopathy, macular degeneration, and retinal detachment; and eye injuries, including children's eye injuries caused by BB guns and toys, and sporting, industrial, and other accidents. *Type:* Research center.

Florida Ophthalmic Institute
7106 NW 11th Pl., Ste. B   Ph: (352)331-2020
Gainesville, FL 32605-3192   Fax: (352)331-2019
Contact: Norman S. Levy, MD, Dir.
Desc: Understanding and treatment of human ocular diseases, including glaucoma and external ocular pathology. *Type:* Research center.

Foundation for Education and Research in Vision
University of Houston   Ph: (713)743-2255
College of Optometry   Fax: (713)743-2053
4901 Calhoun Rd.
Houston, TX 77204
Contact: Marilyn Levi, Contact.
Desc: Optometry, focusing on the study of human vision. Also provides financial assistance for relevant research projects. *Type:* Research center.

Georgetown University
Center for Sight
Med. Ctr.   Ph: (202)687-4448
3800 Reservoir Rd. NW   Fax: (202)687-4978
Washington, DC 20007
E-mail: cupplesh@gunet.georgetown.edu
Contact: Dr. Howard Cuplex, Contact.
Desc: Effectiveness, outcomes, and utilization of eye care; epidemiology of eye care delivery; functional status and utility assessment. Research includes outcomes of cataract, glaucoma, diabetic eye disease, and barrier reduction related to eye care use. *Type:* Research center.

Glaser Murphy Retina Treatment Center
901 Dulaney Valley Rd., Ste.   Ph: (410)337-4500
  200   Fax: (410)337-3975
Towson, MD 21204
E-mail: retina@digex.net
URL: http://www.access.digex.net/~retina
Contact: Dr. Bert Glaser, Dir.
Desc: Abnormal events in the retina and vitreous that result from diabetes, sickle cell anemia, injury, and retinal detachment. *Type:* Research center.

Glaucoma Foundation
John W. Corwin
33 Maiden Ln.   Ph: (212)504-1901
New York, NY 10038   Free: 800-GLAUCOMA
     Fax: (212)504-1933
E-mail: glaucomafdn@mindspring.com
URL: http://www.glaucoma-foundation.org/info
Contact: John W. Corwin, Exec.Dir.
Desc: Individuals who have been affected by glaucoma and interested others. Works to increase public awareness and to provide research funding. *Type:* Association.

Glaucoma Research Foundation
200 Pine St., Ste. 200   Ph: (415)986-3162
San Francisco, CA 94104-2712   Free: 800-826-6693
     Fax: (415)986-3763
E-mail: info@glaucoma.org
URL: http://www.glaucoma.org
Contact: Tara Steele, Exec.Dir.
Desc: Clinical and laboratory studies of glaucoma. Sponsors the Normal Tension Glaucoma Study, a collaborative 25 center study; the Glaucoma Research Catalyst Program; and the Glaucoma Research Eye Donor Network, which provides laboratory scientists access to glaucomatous eye tissue. *Type:* Research center.

Glaucoma Research Foundation
200 Pine St., Ste. 200   Ph: (415)986-3162
San Francisco, CA 94104-2712   Free: 800-826-6693
     Fax: (415)986-3763
E-mail: info@glaucoma.org
URL: http://www.glaucoma.org
Contact: Tara L. Steele, Exec.Dir.
Desc: Dedicated to protecting the sight and independence of individuals with glaucoma through research and education, with the ultimate goal of finding a cure. Funds several research programs including Shaffer International Fellowship, Clinician-Scientist Fellowship and project grants. *Type:* Association.

Harvard University
Howe Laboratory of Ophthalmology
Massachusetts Eye & Ear   Ph: (617)573-3963
  Infirmary   Fax: (617)573-4290
243 Charles St.
Boston, MA 02114
E-mail: mapplebury@meei.harvard.edu

Contact: Meredithe L. Applebury, PhD, Dir.
Desc: Programs to study development, structure, function, and malfunction of the mammalian, visual system. Current investigations focus on mechanisms of retinal functioning, development, and degeneration; ocular tumors; glaucoma; corneal wound healing; and ocular inflammatory diseases. *Type:* Research center.

Indiana University Bloomington
Borish Center for Ophthalmic Research
OPT, 2nd Fl.   Ph: (812)855-4093
Bloomington, IN 47405
E-mail: sonip@indiana.edu
URL: http://www.opt.indiana.edu/bcor/bcor.html
Contact: P. Sarita Soni, Co-Dir.
Desc: Visual disorders, ocular pathologies, and systemic disease that affect the eye and its adnexia. Recent studies include contact lens comparison trials, extended wear contact lens trial, and decreasing dryness in contact lenses, collaborative longitudinal evaluation of keratoconus, teens and contact lenses, and development of confocal microscopy. *Type:* Research center.

Indiana University Bloomington
Cornea Contact Lens Research Laboratory
OPT, 2nd Fl.   Ph: (812)855-4093
Bloomington, IN 47405
URL: http://www.indiana.edu/~rugs/ctrdir/cclrl.html
Contact: P. Sarita Soni, Dir.
Desc: Corneal topography, physiology, and pathology. *Type:* Research center.

Institute for Visual Sciences, Inc.
1 E. 71st St.   Ph: (212)305-2919
New York, NY 10021
Contact: Melissa Mount, Exec.Dir.
Desc: Ophthalmology, with emphasis on the development of diagnostic and therapeutic techniques for the care of the eye using existing physical sciences technology such as optical imagery (cameras, lasers, video scanning, holography) and ultrasonography. Studies focus on the applications of liquid dye, carbon dioxide, and neodymium-YAG lasers to the treatment of eye diseases and conditions that threaten sight, including glaucoma, macular degeneration, cataract, and diabetic retinopathy. *Type:* Research center.

International Eye Foundation
7801 Norfolk Ave., Ste. 200   Ph: (301)986-1830
Bethesda, MD 20814   Fax: (301)986-1876
E-mail: info@ief.permanet.org
Contact: Victoria M. Sheffield, Exec.Dir.
Desc: Qualified ophthalmologists who are members of the Society of Eye Surgeons . Promotes the prevention of blindness worldwide. Disseminates information to ophthalmologists on recent advances in eye surgery and trains physicians, nurses, paramedical personnel, and technicians in the care and treatment of eye patients. *Type:* Association.

Johns Hopkins University
Biomedical Optics Laboratory
School of Medicine   Ph: (410)614-2528
Department of Biomedical   Fax: (410)955-0549
  Engineering
Ross Research Bldg., Rm. 724
720 Rutland Ave.
Baltimore, MD 21205
E-mail: skuo@bme.jhu.edu
URL: http://www.bme.jhu.edu/~skuo/Lab/
Contact: Scot C. Kuo, Prin. Investigator.
Desc: Optical tools (optical tweezers, optical rheometry, video-enhanced optical microscopy, fluorescence micros-

copy, digital image processing); cell mechanics (non-invasive, real-time monitoring of cell mechanics during chemotaxis, cell crawling, granule secretion, and mitosis); microtubule-based motility (kinesin force generation, single-molecule assays, genetic engineering, organelle transport, chromosome movement); and collaborations (electromotility of outer hair cells, chromosome movement, biological rheology, and mechanics of biological materials). *Type:* Research center.

Johns Hopkins University
Dana Center for Preventive Ophthalmology
Wilmer Ophthalmological   Ph: (410)955-2777
  Institute   Fax: (410)955-2542
Wilmer, Rm. 120
600 N. Wolfe St.
Baltimore, MD 21287-9019
E-mail: HQuigley@welchlink.welch.jhu.edu
URL: http://www.wilmer.jhu.edu
Contact: Harry A. Quigley, MD, Dir.
Desc: Aims to identify eye disorders amenable to intervention and to develop intervention strategies. Studies concentrate on cataract and glaucoma, including the role of ultraviolet light in the development of cataract, evaluation of new techniques for diagnosing glaucoma at its earlier stages, and why black Americans develop glaucoma nine times more frequently than white Americans. *Type:* Research center.

Johns Hopkins University
Lions Vision Research and Rehabilitation Center
Wilmer Low Vision   Ph: (410)955-0580
  Rehabilitation Service   Fax: (410)955-1829
550 N. Broadway, 6th Fl.
Baltimore, MD 21205
E-mail: rmassof@lions.med.jhu.edu
Contact: Dr. Robert Massof, Dir.
Desc: Development and refinement of devices and procedures for rehabilitating visual function using psychophysics, optics, computer-assisted video enhancement, and electrophysiology; mechanisms and progression of diseases of the retina, optic nerve, and visual pathways in the brain; glaucoma, optic ne uritis, and other neurologic disorders; and diseases primarily limited to the retina such as retinitis pigmentosa, diabetic retinopathy, and age-related macular degeneration. *Type:* Research center.

Johns Hopkins University
Ocular Immunology Laboratory
Wilmer Ophthalmological   Ph: (410)955-3524
  Institute   Fax: (410)614-1114
Woods Research, Rm. 457
600 N. Wolfe St.
Baltimore, MD 21287-9142
E-mail: rprender@welchlink.welch.jhu.edu
Contact: Dr. Robert A. Prendergast, Dir.
Desc: Cause, detection, treatment, and prevention of immunogenic and other inflammatory diseases of the eye, rejection of corneal grafts, and pathogenesis of autoimmune ocular disease. *Type:* Research center.

Johns Hopkins University
Retinal Degenerations Research Center
Wilmer Ophthalmological   Ph: (410)955-7589
  Institute   Fax: (410)955-0749
Maumenee Res. Bldg., Rm. 519
600 N. Wolfe St.
Baltimore, MD 21287-9257
E-mail: radler@ishtar.med.jhu.edu
URL: http://www.wilmer.jhu.edu
Contact: Dr. Ruben Adler, Dir.
Desc: Biochemistry of essential constituents of the retina and its adjacent tissues and potential interactions among them as related to retinitis pigmentosa and other retinal degenerations. *Type:* Research center.

Johns Hopkins University

Wilmer Ophthalmological Institute

600 N. Wolfe St.　　　　　Ph: (410)955-6846
Baltimore, MD 21287-9278　　Fax: (410)955-0675
E-mail: mgoldbrg@gwgatel.jhmi.jhu.edu
URL: http://www.wilmer.jhu.edu

Contact: Morton F. Goldberg, MD, Chm.

Desc: Ophthalmology, including studies of macular degeneration, diabetic retinopathy, cataracts and the cornea, ocular immunology, uveitis (inflammatory eye diseases), retinal-damaging disorders, retinal degenerations, glaucoma, preventive ophthalmology, strabismus (misaligned or crossed eyes), double vision, amblyopia (reduced vision in one eye), hereditary eye diseases, neuroophthalmology, oculomotor functions, correlation of changes in the structure and form of eye tissue with symptoms of illness, development of new technology and techniques to study visual function disorders, development of new optical aids for the visually handicapped, immunohistochemical analysis of the blood retina barrier, retinal gene expression, genetics of eye diseases, molecular biology of eye development, molecular biology of glaucoma, and retinal pigment epithelium (RPE). *Type:* Research center.

Joint Commission on Allied Health Personnel in Ophthalmology

2025 Woodlane Dr.　　　　　Ph: (612)731-2944
St. Paul, MN 55125-2995　　　Free: 800-284-3937
　　　　　　　　　　　　　　Fax: (612)731-0410

E-mail: jcahpo@jcahpo.org
URL: http://www.jcahpo.org

Contact: Lynn D. Anderson, Exec.Dir.

Desc: A certifying agency for allied health personnel. Objectives are: to encourage the establishment of medically oriented programs for training allied health personnel in ophthalmology; to develop standards of education and training in the field; to examine, certify, and recertify ophthalmic medical personnel, and encourage their continued occupational development. Conducts national certifying examinations. *Type:* Association.

Laval University

Medical Research Centre

Ophthalmology Research Group

2705, boulevard Laurier　　　Ph: (418)654-2105
Ste. Foy, PQ, Canada G1V 4G2　Fax: (418)654-2131
E-mail: groupe.ophtalmo@crchul.ulaval.ca

Contact: Dr. Alain Rousseau, Dir.

Desc: Viscoelastics, laser corneal surgery, ocular melanoma, corneal wound healing and corneal transplantation, genetics in melanoma and glaucoma. *Type:* Research center.

Louisiana State University

Eye Center

2020 Gravier St., Ste. B　　　Ph: (504)568-6700
New Orleans, LA 70112　　　　Fax: (504)568-4210
URL: http://www.lsu.edy.edu

Contact: Dr. Herbert Kaufman, Dir.

Desc: Ophthalmology, including a study linking hazy peripheral vision with colored contact lenses, lasers in ophthalmology, ocular surgery techniques, biomaterials and drug delivery, graft rejection, neurobiology and neurochemisty, and viral infection, latency, and treatment. *Type:* Research center.

Macula Foundation, Inc.

210 E. 64th St.　　　　　　　Ph: (212)605-3777
New York, NY 10021　　　　　Free: 800-622-8524
　　　　　　　　　　　　　　Fax: (212)605-3795

Contact: Lawrence A. Yannuzzi, MD, Dir.

Desc: Macular diseases, including epidemiologic, immunologic, biochemical, and clinical therapeutic studies. *Type:* Research center.

MCP Hahnemann University of the Health Sciences

Center for the Preservation of Vision

Div. of Ophthalmology　　　　Free: 888-898-4746
3300 Henry Ave.　　　　　　　Fax: (610)664-2599
Philadelphia, PA 19129
E-mail: visioncenter@auhs.edu
URL: http://www.auhs.edu/medschool/centers/ctrpresvis.html

Contact: Dr. Jay L. Federman, Dir.

Desc: Laser applications in the treatment of eye diseases, development of a vision sensing device capable of transmitting light impulses to the brain. *Type:* Research center.

Medical College of Wisconsin

Eye Institute

925 N. 87th St.　　　　　　　Ph: (414)456-7915
Milwaukee, WI 53226　　　　　Fax: (414)456-6300
URL: http://www.mcw.edu/ophthalmology

Contact: Dr. Dale Hueer, MD, Dir.

Desc: Ophthalmology, including pediatric ophthalmology, neuro-ophthalmology, orbital and ophthalmic reconstructive surgery, anterior segment studies, corneal diseases, cataracts, retinal detachment, diabetic retinopathy, glaucoma, and laser treatment. *Type:* Research center.

Medical University of South Carolina

Storm Eye Institute

167 Ashley Ave.　　　　　　　Ph: (843)792-3206
Charleston, SC 29403　　　　　Fax: (843)792-1723
E-mail: magill@musc.edu

Contact: David J. Apple, Dir. of Res.

Desc: Metabolism of vitamin A in the eye, toxicity of oxygen in lens and cornea, ocular parasites, and photoreceptor electrophysiology. *Type:* Research center.

Mississippi State University

Rehabilitation Research and Training Center on Blindness and Low Vision

PO Drawer 6189　　　　　　　Ph: (601)325-2001
Mississippi State, MS 39762　　Free: 800-675-7782
　　　　　　　　　　　　　　Fax: (601)325-8989

E-mail: rrtc@ra.msstate.edu
URL: http://www.msstate.edu/Dept/RRTC/blind.html

Contact: Dr. J. Elton Moore, Dir.

Desc: Career development intervention strategies for people who are blind or severely visually impaired; employment aspects of blindness and low vision. *Type:* Research center.

Mount Sinai School of Medicine of City University of New York

Vision Research Center in Ophthalmology

1 Gustave Levy Pl.　　　　　　Ph: (212)241-6249
Box 1183　　　　　　　　　　Fax: (212)289-5945
New York, NY 10029
E-mail: oscarc@worldnet.att.net
URL: http://www.mssm.edu/ophth/

Contact: Dr. Oscar A. Candia, Dir.

Desc: Ophthalmology. *Type:* Research center.

Myopia International Research Foundation

1265 Broadway, Rm. 608　　　Ph: (212)684-2777
New York, NY 10001　　　　　Fax: (212)684-2888

Contact: Joel Weintraub, MD, Pres.

Desc: Myopia, focusing on causes, prevention, treatment, and research. *Type:* Research center.

National Eye Research Foundation

910 Skokie Blvd., No. 207A　　Ph: (847)564-4652
Northbrook, IL 60062　　　　　Free: 800-621-2258
　　　　　　　　　　　　　　Fax: (847)564-0807

E-mail: NERF1955@aol.com
URL: http://www.nerf.org

Contact: Andrew Kim, Contact.

Desc: Vision, focusing on better eye care. Also promotes education relating to the eye care and contact lenses. *Type:* Research center.

National Eye Research Foundation Newsletter

National Eye Research Foundation

910 Skokie Blvd., Ste. 207 A　　Ph: (847)564-4641
Northbrook, IL 60062　　　　　Fax: (847)564-0807

Contact: Dr. Newton K. Wesley, Editor.

Desc: Reports on issues related to eye health care. Provides information on subjects such as devices for correcting vision, resource material for the visually handicapped, and eye research. *Type:* Newsletter.

National Glaucoma Research Report

American Health Assistance Foundation

15825 Shady Grove Rd., Ste.　　Ph: (301)948-3244
140　　　　　　　　　　　　Free: 800-437-2423
Rockville, MD 20850　　　　　Fax: (301)258-9454

Desc: Highlights the work of glaucoma researchers and provides tips for individuals with glaucoma. Recurring features include news of research and columns titled From the Presidents and Ask the Experts. *Type:* Newsletter.

New England College of Optometry

Myopia Research Center

424 Beacon St.　　　　　　　Ph: (617)369-0180
Boston, MA 02115　　　　　　Fax: (617)369-0174
E-mail: heldr@iserver.ne-optometry.edu
URL: http://www.ne-optometry.edu

Contact: Richard Held, PhD, Res.Dir.

Desc: Human and animal studies on the development of myopia, resolution limits of human eye, and autoimmune response in diabetes. *Type:* Research center.

Oakland University

Eye Research Institute

422 Dodge Hall　　　　　　　Ph: (248)370-2391
Rochester, MI 48309-4480　　　Fax: (248)370-2006
E-mail: blanks@oakland.edu

Contact: Dr. Janet C. Blanks, Dir.

Desc: Biochemistry, biophysics, cell biology, physiology, pharmacology, and photobiology. Research focuses on ocular tissues and includes the following topics of interest: molecular genetics of lens proteins, ion transport and radiation damage of the cornea, light damage of the retina, signal transduction in photoreceptors, ocular drug metabolism and detoxification, and experimental models of proliferative vitreoretinopathy, uveoretinitis, cataracts (radiation and oxidation and calcium), and diabetic complications of the eye. *Type:* Research center.

Ohio Wesleyan University

Eye Research Projects

Delaware, OH 43015　　　　　Ph: (740)368-3801
　　　　　　　　　　　　　　Fax: (740)368-3299

E-mail: dorobbin@cc.owu.edu
URL: http://www.owu.edu/~ps/psych.html

Contact: David O. Robbins, PhD, Dir.

Desc: Visual psychophysics and electrophysiology, color vision, and effects of laser irradiation on retinal morphology and function. *Type:* Research center.

Ophthalmic Research Institute

6110 Executive Blvd., Ste. 506   Ph: (301)984-4735
Rockville, MD 20852   Fax: (301)984-4737
E-mail: vickis@aaoptom.org
Contact: Victoria Singer, Asst.Dir.
Desc: Vision research, instumentation and procedure evaluation, and new treatment methods. *Type:* Research center.

Ophthalmic Research Laboratory and Eye Institute

Swedish Med. Ctr.-Seattle   Ph: (206)386-6000
747 Broadway Ave.   Fax: (206)384-2767
Seattle, WA 98122
URL: http://www.swedish.org
Contact: Richard Peterson, Dir.
Desc: Color vision physiology; demyelinating disease, especially vision loss from multiple sclerosis; and laser surgery technology. *Type:* Research center.

ORBIS International

330 W. 42nd St., Ste. 1900   Ph: (212)244-2525
New York, NY 10036   Free: 800-ORBIS-US
  Fax: (212)244-2744
E-mail: executive@ny.orbis.org
URL: http://www.orbis.org
Contact: Pina Taormina, Pres. and Exec.Dir.
Desc: Dedicated to fighting blindness worldwide through medical education and hands-on training for ophthalmologists, nurses, anesthesiologists, biomedical technicians, and community health care workers. *Type:* Association.

Oregon Health Sciences University

Elks' Children's Eye Clinic

Casey Eye Institute   Ph: (503)494-7675
3375 SW Terwilliger Blvd.   Fax: (503)494-5347
Portland, OR 97201-4197
E-mail: palmere@ohsu.edu
URL: http://www.ohsu.edu/~cei/casey.html
Contact: Earl A. Palmer, MD, Contact.
Desc: Pediatric ophthalmology with particular reference to abnormalities of binocular vision. Studies in strabismus, infantile and congenital glaucoma, retinopathy in premature infants, toxicology, congenital cataract, and genetic diseases. *Type:* Research center.

Pan-American Association of Ophthalmology

1301 S. Bowen Rd., Ste. 365   Ph: (817)265-2831
Arlington, TX 76013   Fax: (817)275-3961
E-mail: paao@flash.net
URL: http://www.flash.net/~paao
Contact: Teresa J. Bradshaw, Admin.
Desc: Ophthalmologists throughout the Western Hemisphere. Seeks to improve the treatment of eye diseases and prevention of blindness in the Americas through the exchange of ideas and treatments. *Type:* Association.

Pennsylvania College of Optometry

Cornea and Specialty Contact Lens Service

1200 W. Godfrey Ave.   Ph: (215)276-6100
Philadelphia, PA 19141   Fax: (215)276-1329
E-mail: joel@pco.edu
URL: http://www.pco.edu/research.htm
Contact: Joel A. Silbert, OD, Prin. Investigator.
Desc: Progression of the corneal warpage syndrome known as keratoconus; cornea and contact lenses studies, including testing lenses and lens care products for various manufacturers. The study on keratoconus, known as the Collaborative Longitudinal Evaluation of Keratoconus, is funded by the National Eye Institute. *Type:* Research center.

Pennsylvania College of Optometry

Corneal Refractive Surgery Research

1200 W. Godfrey Ave.   Ph: (215)276-6000
Philadelphia, PA 19141
E-mail: dgubman@pco.edu
URL: http://www.pco.edu/research.htm
Contact: Dr. David T. Gubman, Res.Dir.
Desc: Corneal refractive surgery. *Type:* Research center.

Pennsylvania College of Optometry

Glaucoma Research Center

1200 W. Godfrey Ave.   Ph: (215)276-6000
Philadelphia, PA 19141
E-mail: glaucdoc@aol.com
URL: http://www.pco.edu/research.htm
Contact: G. Richard Bennett, OD, Dir.
Desc: Determining whether patients with ocular hypertension (elevated eye pressure but without glaucoma) benefit over the longer term from medical management of their pressure. This study, known as the Ocular Hypertension Treatment Study, is funded by the National Eye Institute for eight years. *Type:* Research center.

Pennsylvania College of Optometry

Hafter Family Light and Laser Institute

Old York Rd. & Township Line   Ph: (215)780-1427
Rd.   Fax: (215)780-1424
Elkins Park, PA 19027
E-mail: felix@pco.edu
URL: http://www.pco.edu/research.htm
Contact: Dr. Felix M. Barker, Dir.
Desc: Corneal and retinal light damage effects, especially from short wavelength energy sources; ocular photosensitization; laser effects; excimer laser studies, including corneal wound healing in normal and diabetic individuals; Glaucoma; myopia; kerato conus. *Type:* Research center.

Pennsylvania College of Optometry

Institute for the Visually Impaired

8360 Old York Rd.   Ph: (215)276-6000
Elkins Park, PA 19027
E-mail: felix@pco.edu
URL: http://www.pco.edu/research.htm
Contact: Dr. Felix M. Barker, Dir.
Desc: Partial sight or low vision, including rehabilitation teaching, and low vision rehabilitation, orientation, and mobility. *Type:* Research center.

Research to Prevent Blindness

645 Madison Ave., 21st Fl.   Ph: (212)752-4333
New York, NY 10022-1010   Free: 800-621-0026
  Fax: (212)688-6231
E-mail: tfurlong@rpbusa.org
URL: http://www.rpbusa.org
Contact: Diane S. Swift, Contact.
Desc: Blinding eye-diseases, focusing on causes, prevention, and treatment. *Type:* Research center.

Sensory Electrophysiology Research Unit

Touro Infirmary   Ph: (504)897-8179
1401 Foucher St.   Fax: (504)897-7637
New Orleans, LA 70115
Contact: David A. Newsome, MD, Dir.
Desc: Mechanisms, causes, and treatment of retinal dystrophies and diseases, including transplantation of retinal cells. Multidisciplinary studies focus on cell biology, molecular biology, biochemistry, immunohistology, and clinical trials. *Type:* Research center.

Smith-Kettlewell Eye Research Institute

2232 Webster St.   Ph: (415)561-1620
San Francisco, CA 94115   Fax: (415)561-1610
E-mail: abs@skivs.ski.org
URL: http://www.ski.org
Contact: Alan B. Scott, MD, Dir.
Desc: Visual sciences, oculomotor functioning, and rehabilitation engineering, including long-term study of the surgical and pharmacological treatment of strabismus; development of diagnostic tests for glaucoma, retinitis pigmentosa, diabetic retinopathy, and senile macular degeneration; research on the physiological basis of eye movements and retinal development; studies in motion detection, pattern perception, and stereopsis; and development and evaluation of sensory aids and devices for the deaf, blind, deaf/blind, and sensory-impaired individuals. *Type:* Research center.

Smith-Kettlewell Eye Research Institute

Rehabilitation Engineering Research Center

2232 Webster St.   Ph: (415)561-1619
San Francisco, CA 94115   Fax: (415)561-1610
E-mail: ruth@kivs.ski.org
URL: http://www.ski.org
Contact: Dr. John A. Brabyn, Contact.
Desc: Technology for blindness, visual impairment, and multi-sensory loss. *Type:* Research center.

Texas A&M University

Institute of Ocular Pharmacology

College of Medicine   Ph: (409)845-2817
College Station, TX 77843-1114   Fax: (409)845-0699
Contact: Dr. George C.Y. Chiou, Dir.
Desc: Ocular pharmacology (the use of drugs for treating eye disease), including glaucoma, ocular inflamation, retinal degeneration, myopia, and cataract treatment. *Type:* Research center.

U.S. Department of Health and Human Services

National Eye Institute

Division of Biometry and Epidemiology

NIH Bldg. 31, Rm. 6A52   Ph: (301)496-1331
31 Center Dr. MSC 2510   Fax: (301)496-2297
Bethesda, MD 20892-2510
E-mail: flf@1.nei.nih.gov
URL: http://www.nei.nih.gov
Contact: Fredrick Ferris, MD, Dir.
Desc: Plan, develop, and conduct human population studies concerned with the cause, prevention, and treatment of eye disease and vision disorders, with emphasis on the major causes of blindness. This includes studies of incidence and prevalencein defined populations, prospective and retrospective studies of risk factors, natural history studies, clinical trials, genetic studies, and studies to evaluate diagnostic procedures. *Type:* Research center.

U.S. Department of Health and Human Services

National Eye Institute

Division of Biometry and Epidemiology

Clinical Trials Branch

NIH Bldg. 31, Rm. 6A52   Ph: (301)496-6583
31 Center Dr. MSC 2510   Fax: (301)496-2297
Bethesda, MD 20892
E-mail: flf@1.nei.nih.gov
URL: http://www.nei.nih.gov
Contact: Frederick L. Ferris, Chf.
Desc: Plan, develop, and conduct human population studies concerned with the cause, prevention, and treatment of eye disease and vision disorders, with emphasis on the major causes of blindness. This includes studies of incidence and prevalence on defined populations, prospective and retrospective studies of risk factors, natural history studies, clinical trials, genetic studies, and studies to evaluate diagnostic procedures. *Type:* Research center.

U.S. Department of Health and Human Services

National Eye Institute

Extramural Research

NIH EPS, Ste. 350   Ph: (301)496-5301

6120 Executive Blvd., MSC   Fax: (301)402-0528
7164

Bethesda, MD 20892-7164

E-mail: rh27v@nih.gov

URL: http://www.nei.nih.gov/

Contact: Dr. Ralph Helmsen, Res.Rsrcs.Off.

Desc: Improving the prevention, diagnosis, and treatment of visual disorders. This support includes the award of grants, cooperative agreements, fellowships, and contracts for research in retinal and choroidal diseases, corneal diseases, cataract, glaucoma, strabismus, amblyopia, visual processing, and low vision. *Type:* Research center.

U.S. Department of Health and Human Services

National Eye Institute

Extramural Research

Corneal Diseases Program

NIH Bldg. EPS, Rm. 350   Ph: (301)496-5301

6120 Executive Blvd.   Fax: (301)402-0528

Rockville, MD 20852

E-mail: loreanne.mcnicol@nei.nih.gov

URL: http://www.nei.nih.gov

Contact: Lore Anne McNicol, PhD, Dir.

Desc: Ophthalmic research relating to corneal diseases and focusing on diseases of the cornea and the external ocular structures, including the conjunctiva and eyelids; corneal transplantation and wound healing; and contact lenses and surgical correction of refractive problems. *Type:* Research center.

U.S. Department of Health and Human Services

National Eye Institute

Extramural Research

Retinal Diseases Program

Executive Plz., South, Ste. 350   Ph: (301)496-0484

6120 Executive Blvd., MSC-   Fax: (301)402-0528
7164

Bethesda, MD 20892-7164

E-mail: pad@.nei.nih.gov

URL: http://www.nei.nih.gov

Contact: Peter A. Dudley, PhD, Contact.

Desc: Structure and function of the retina and choroid in health and disease. NEI-fostered investigations include studies of the structure and metabolism of photoreceptor cells and their relationship to the underlying pigment epithelium; the retina's response to light and the initial processing of visual information transmitted to the visual centers of the brain; inflammation of the uveal tract (the iris, choroid, and ciliary body); and of the vitreous gel that fills the center of the eye. *Type:* Research center.

U.S. Department of Health and Human Services

National Eye Institute

Extramural Research

Strabismus, Amblyopia, Visual Processing, and Low Vision

NIH   Ph: (301)496-5301

Executive Plaza S., Ste. 350   Fax: (301)402-0528

6120 Executive Blvd., MSC
7164

Bethesda, MD 20892-7164

E-mail: oberdorfer@nei.nih.gov

URL: http://www.nei.nih.gov/

Contact: Michael D. Oberdorfer, PhD, Prog.Dir.

Desc: Contact person for extramural support for basic and clinical research on a broad range of studies concerned with the development and function of the neural pathways from the eye to the brain, the central processing of visual information, visual perception, optical properties of the eye, oculomotor function, functioning of the pupil, and control of the ocular muscles. A large number of congenital, developmental, and degenerative abnormalities affect the visual sensorimotor system, but two disorders are of primary concern--strabismus and amblyopia. *Type:* Research center.

U.S. Department of Health and Human Services

National Eye Institute

Intramural Research Program

NIH Bldg. 10, Rm. 10N202   Ph: (301)496-3123

9000 Rockville Pike   Fax: (301)402-0485

Bethesda, MD 20892-1858

E-mail: rnq@helix.nih.gov

Contact: Dr. Robert B. Nussenblatt, Actg.Dir.

Desc: In-house research aimed at improving the prevention, diagnosis, and treatment of visual disorders. Major subject of research include retinal and choroidal diseases, corneal diseases, cataract, glaucoma, and sensory and motor disorders of vision. *Type:* Research center.

U.S. Department of Health and Human Services

National Eye Institute

Intramural Research Program

Laboratory of Immunology

NIH Bldg. 10, Rm. 10N202   Ph: (301)496-3123

9000 Rockville Pike   Fax: (301)402-0485

Bethesda, MD 20892

E-mail: RNQ@HELIX.NIH.GOV

Contact: Dr. Robert B. Nussenblatt, Sci.Dir.

Desc: Clinical research into the causes, preventions, diagnosis, and treatment of visual system disorders. It translates laboratory research results into clinical application, directs and administers the Institute's clinical care program, and assures functioning of the eye ward and clinic in the NIH Clinical Center. *Type:* Research center.

U.S. Department of Health and Human Services

National Eye Institute

Laboratory on Mechanisms of Ocular Diseases

NIH Bldg. 6, Rm. 237   Ph: (301)496-6669

9000 Rockville Pike   Fax: (301)496-1759

Bethesda, MD 20892

Contact: J. Samuel Zigler, Actg.Chf.

Desc: Mechanisms involved in cataract formation, pharmacologic and pathophysiologic aspects of aldose reductase in diabetic complications, molecular biology of a retinal dystrophy, and cataract caused by an enzyme deficiency. Laboratory also provides training opportunities in related diabetes and cataract research. *Type:* Research center.

U.S. Department of Health and Human Services

National Eye Institute

Laboratory of Molecular and Developmental Biology

NIH Bldg. 6   Ph: (301)496-9467

Rm. 201   Fax: (301)402-0781

6 Center Dr., MSC-2730

Bethesda, MD 20892

E-mail: joramp@intna.nei.nih.gov

Contact: Dr. Joram Piatigorsky, Chf.

Desc: Cellular and molecular biology, with emphasis on molecular and developmental genetics. The research is designed to elucidate both normal and disease processes, and particular attention is given to hereditary diseases that can be studied at the gene level. *Type:* Research center.

U.S. Department of Health and Human Services

National Eye Institute

Laboratory of Retinal Cell and Molecular Biology

NIH Bldg. 6, Rm. 310   Ph: (301)496-3447

6 Center Dr. MSC 2740   Fax: (301)402-1883

Bethesda, MD 20892-2740

E-mail: bnwigg@helix.nih.gov

URL: http://www.nei.nih.gov/intramural/lrcmb.htm

Contact: Dr. Barbara N. Wiggert, Actg. Chf.

Desc: Biochemistry, molecular biology, and neurobiology of the retina. *Type:* Research center.

U.S. Department of Health and Human Services

National Eye Institute

Laboratory of Sensorimotor Research

NIH Bldg. 49, Rm. 2A50   Ph: (301)496-9375

49 Convent Dr. MSC 4435   Fax: (301)402-0511

Bethesda, MD 20892-4435

Contact: Dr. Robert H. Wurtz, Chf.

Desc: Sensorimotor organization of the primate visual and oculomotor systems using a multidisciplinary approach that includes physiological, behavioral, psychophysical, and anatomical methods. Principal areas of research interest are: vision and oculomotor research, visuomotor integration, neuro-ophthalmologic mechanisms, and oculomotor control. *Type:* Research center.

U.S. Department of Health and Human Services

National Eye Institute

Office of International Program Activities

NIH Bldg. 31, Rm. 6A-06   Ph: (301)496-4876

9000 Rockville Pike   Fax: (301)480-3246

Bethesda, MD 20892-2510

Contact: Terrence Gillen, MA,MBA, Dir., OIPA.

Desc: Research and data collection and analysis. *Type:* Research center.

U.S. Department of Health and Human Services

National Institutes of Health

National Eye Institute

NIH Bldg. 31, Rm. 6A03   Ph: (301)496-2234

31 Center Drive, MSC 2510   Fax: (301)496-9970

Bethesda, MD 20892

URL: http://www.nei.nih.gov/

Contact: Dr. Carl Kupfer, Dir.

Desc: Improving prevention, diagnosis, and treatment of visual disorders. Specifically, the Institute: supports research and research training through grants, fellowships, and contracts to medical schools and research institutions; conducts laboratory and clinical research in its own facilities and fosters statistical and epidemiological studies of visual disorders in human populations; fosters research on rehabilitation of the visually handicapped; encourages the application of research findings to clinical practice; heightens public awareness of vision problems; and cooperates with voluntary organizations that engage in related activities. *Type:* Research center.

University of British Columbia

VGH/UBC Eye Care Centre

Department of Ophthalmology   Ph: (604)875-4199

2550 Willow St.   Fax: (604)875-4663

Vancouver, BC, Canada V5Z
3N9

Contact: Dr. Jack Rootman, Hd.

Desc: Effects of diabetes on the eye with specific emphasis on circulation, electroneurophysiology of the retina, glaucoma epidemiology, visual perception, ocular therapeutics, color vision in ocular diseases, ocular oncology, orbital disease, thyroid orbitopathy, congenital glaucoma, neurophysiology and neuropharmacology of cortical vision, experimental pathology, central nervous system development, neural mechanisms underlying amblyopia and strabismus, computational vision, anatomical connections of the central visual system, molecular biological studies of neurotransmitters, receptors, and growth factors in the visual system. *Type:* Research center.

University of Calgary

Lions Sight Centre

Department of Anatomy   Ph: (403)220-7501
3330 Hospital Dr. NW   Fax: (403)283-2700
Calgary, AB, Canada T2N 4N1
E-mail: wstell@acs.ucalgary.ca
Contact: Dr. William K. Stell, Dir.

Desc: Structure, function, molecular genetics, chemistry, and development of vertebrate photoreceptors (rods and cones) and neural retina. Also studies retinal development and regeneration; myopia and regulation of ocular growth; diabetic retinopathy; and molecular genetics of human vision disorders. *Type:* Research center.

University of California, Los Angeles

Jules Stein Eye Institute

100 Stein Plaza   Ph: (310)825-5053
Los Angeles, CA 90095-7000   Fax: (310)206-7488
E-mail: mondino@jsei.ucla.edu
URL: http://www.medsch.ucla.edu/som/jsei
Contact: Bartly J. Mondino, MD, Dir.

Desc: Research and study in sciences related to vision, care of patients with eye disease, and education in ophthalmology. *Type:* Research center.

University of California, San Francisco

Francis I. Proctor Foundation for Research in Ophthalmology

95 Kirkham St.   Ph: (415)476-1442
San Francisco, CA 94143-0944   Fax: (415)502-2521
Contact: John P. Whitcher, MD, Dir.

Desc: Infectious and inflammatory diseases of the eye with particular emphasis on chlamydial infections, trachoma, herpetic eye infections, dry eye conditions, and uveitis. *Type:* Research center.

University of California, San Francisco

Ocular Oncology Research Unit

Beckman Vision Center-   Ph: (415)476-0779
   Department of   Fax: (415)502-3230
   Ophthalmology
10 Kirkham St.
Box 730
San Francisco, CA 94143
Contact: Joan M. O'Brien, MD, Dir.

Desc: Molecular biology and immunology of intracolar tumors, new treatment protocols, genetic testing and therapy. *Type:* Research center.

University of Chicago

Visual Sciences Center

939 E. 57th St.   Ph: (773)702-8888
Chicago, IL 60637   Fax: (773)702-8094
E-mail: jernest@midway.uchicago.edu
URL: http://bsd.uchicago.edu/oph/Index.html
Contact: Dr. J. Terry Ernest, Dir.

Desc: Ophthalmology, visual physiology and function of the retina, color vision, evoked occipital response, laser and xenon photocoagulation for retinal disease, and pharmacology of the retinal pigment epithelium. Also conducts electron microscopy and visual molecular biology studies. *Type:* Research center.

University Eye Research Foundation, Inc.

University of Nebraska Medical   Ph: (402)559-4276
   Center   Fax: (402)559-5514
600 S. 42nd St.
Omaha, NE 68198-5540
E-mail: myablons@unmc.edu
Contact: Dr. Michael E. Yablonski, Hd.

Desc: Ophthalmology, focusing on glaucoma (clinical and laboratory studies testing the efficacy of various drug treatments), the retina (formulation of method and procedures to begin transplantation of retinal pigment epithelial cells), the cornea, infectious diseases, ocular pharmacology, molecular biology, and biochemistry. *Type:* Research center.

University of Florida

Center for Vision Research

JHMHC, Box 100284   Ph: (352)846-2100
Gainesville, FL 32610   Fax: (352)392-8554
E-mail: sherwood@exe1.eye.ufl.edu
URL: http://www.eye.ufl.edu
Contact: Mark B. Sherwood, MD, Dir.

Desc: Electrophysiology of the retina and biochemistry, immunology, molecular genetics, and oncology of ocular diseases. *Type:* Research center.

University of Illinois at Chicago

Lions of Illinois Eye Research Institute

UIC Eye Ctr.   Ph: (312)996-6590
1855 W. Taylor St.   Fax: (312)996-7770
Chicago, IL 60612
E-mail: josepuli@uic.edu
URL: http://www.uic.edu/com/eye/
Contact: Prof. Jose S. Pulido, Hd.

Desc: Diabetic retinopathy, glaucoma, cataracts, macular degeneration, herpes keratitis, retinitis pigmentosa, corneal biochemistry, molecular biology, and retinal photoreceptors. Houses the clinical trials of the UIC Department of Ophthalmology and Visual Sciences, including the Advanced Glaucoma Intervention Study, Collaborative Ocular Melanoma Study, Herpetic Eye Disease Study, and Retinopathy of Prematurity; research studies of the Applied Physics Laboratory, Lens Biochemistry Laboratory, Ophthalmic Pathology Laboratory, Ocular Molecular Biology Laboratories, Ocular Biochemistry Laboratory, Photoreceptor Research Laboratory, Laboratory of Retinal Physiology and Neurobiology, and Retinal Cell Biology Laboratory. *Type:* Research center.

University of Illinois at Chicago

Low Vision Rehabilitation Laboratory

Department of Ophthalmology   Ph: (312)996-7179
1855 W. Taylor St.   Fax: (312)996-7770
Chicago, IL 60612
Contact: Janet Szlyk, Dir.

Desc: Physiology of normal and pathologic retinas utilizing computer analyzed digitized images. *Type:* Research center.

University of Louisville

Kentucky Lions Eye Center

301 E. Muhammad Ali Blvd.   Ph: (502)852-5460
Louisville, KY 40202   Fax: (502)852-7446
E-mail: capateo1@ulkyvm.louisville.edu
URL: http://www.louisville.edu/medschool/ophthalmology
Contact: Dr. Christopher A. Paterson, Res.Dir.

Desc: Visual sciences and eye diseases. *Type:* Research center.

University of Miami

Bascom Palmer Eye Institute

Department of Ophthalmology   Ph: (305)326-6031
1638 NW 10th Ave.   Fax: (305)326-6306
Miami, FL 33136
URL: http://www.bpei.med.miami.edu
Contact: Dr. Richard Parrish, Ch.

Desc: Glaucoma, infectious and external corneal diseases, molecular biology and genetics, neurophysiology, ocular virology, ocular immunology, hereditary retinal diseases with special emphasis on Retinitis Pigmentosa, and ophthalmic applications of lasers and polymers. Also conducts studies to improve the techniques and technology related to patient care and the prevention of blindness. *Type:* Research center.

University of Miami

Bascom Palmer Eye Institute

Ophthalmic Biophysics Center

Department of Ophthalmology   Ph: (305)326-6069
PO Box 016880   Fax: (305)326-6139
B
Miami, FL 33101
E-mail: jmparel@bpei.med.miami.edu
Contact: Prof. Jean-Marie Parel, Dir.

Desc: Research activities involve the development and refinement of ophthalmic devices, including testing and design of the Phaco-Ersatz, a lens substitute for intraocular lenses commonly used after cataract surgery, and the development of an implant to permit the sustained release of small amounts of medication over an extended period of time, as well as several glaucoma shunt-valves devices, a controlled iontophoresis system designed to non-invasively transfer drugs into the eye to avoid systemic side effects, and an artificial cornea. Additional research includes selection of individual lasers for ophthalmic use and testing of two high speed laser cutting systems designed to offer new precision and beam control for delicate surgeries. *Type:* Research center.

University of Miami

Bascom Palmer Eye Institute

Retinis Pigmentosa Center

School of Medicine   Ph: (305)243-6545
Department of Ophthalmology   Fax: (305)243-4888
PO Box 016880
Miami, FL 33101
E-mail: jclarkso@med.net.med.miami.edu
URL: http://www.miami.edu
Contact: Dr. John G. Clarkson, Dean, School of Medicine.

Desc: Treatment and prevention of retinis pigmentosa, a group of disorders that cause degeneration of the retina's light-sensing cells (photoreeptors) responsible for sending visual information to the brain. Areas of specialization include diagnostics, retinal photochemistry and physiology, and molecular and cell biology. *Type:* Research center.

University of Michigan

W.K. Kellogg Eye Center

Department of Ophthalmology   Ph: (734)763-1415
1000 Wall St.   Fax: (734)936-8633
Ann Arbor, MI 48105-1994
E-mail: plichter@umich.edu
URL: http://www.med.umich.edu/KEC
Contact: Prof. Paul R. Lichter, Chm.

Desc: Basic and clinical eye research, focusing on medical and molecular genetics and molecular biology of opthalmic disease, retinal physiology, corneal wound healing, diabetic retinopathy, eye diseases in children and adults, laser research, patient and physician education, and genetic screening on a research basis. *Type:* Research center.

University of Minnesota

Minnesota Laboratory for Low-Vision Research

504 Elliott Hall   Ph: (612)625-4516
75 E. River Rd.   Fax: (612)626-2079
Minneapolis, MN 55455
E-mail: info@vision.psych.umn.edu
URL: http://vision.psych.umn.edu/www/legge-lab
Contact: Gordon E. Legge, PhD, Dir.

Desc: Reading difficulties and other visual problems encountered by people of low vision, improved tests of reading, and new technology for aiding in reading. *Type:* Research center.

University of Missouri--St. Louis

Center for Corneal and Contact Lens Research

Sch. of Optometry   Ph: (314)516-5606
8001 Natural Bridge   Fax: (314)516-5150
St. Louis, MO 63121
E-mail: swgbach@umslvma.umsl.edu
URL: http://www.optometry.com
Contact: Gary Bachman, OD, Interim Dir.

Desc: Clinical research in contact lens design, materials, and applications; and basic ocular studies relating to the effects of contact lens. Conducts research on excimer laser corneal reshaping and biomedical materials. *Type:* Research center.

University of North Texas Health Science Center at Fort Worth

North Texas Eye Research Institute

3500 Camp Bowie Blvd.   Ph: (817)735-2048
Fort Worth, TX 76107-2699   Fax: (817)735-2610
E-mail: jturner@molly.hsc.unt.edu
URL: http://www.hsc.unt.edu/research/eye.htm
Contact: James E. Turner, PhD, Dir.

Desc: Eye diseases, including studies on the retina, RPE cells, trophic factors, ocular diabetes, autoimmune diseases, optic nerve regeneration, glaucoma, corneal wound healing, cell death, and aging. *Type:* Research center.

University of Pennsylvania

Vision Research Center

School of Medicine   Ph: (215)898-6917
143 Anatomy Chemistry   Fax: (215)898-4217
36th & Hamilton Walk
Philadelphia, PA 19104
E-mail: liebmanp@mail.med.upenn.upenn.edu
URL: http://vrc.med.upenn.edu/
Contact: Dr. Paul Liebman, Prin.Invest.

Desc: Serves as a branch of the National Eye Institute of the National Institutes of Health to fund eye research projects at the University. Studies concentrate on mechanisms of normal and defective vision, including their molecular, genetic, developmental, electrophysiological, neural, and cognitive aspects. *Type:* Research center.

University of Texas--Houston Health Science Center

Hermann Eye Center

Department of Ophthalmology   Ph: (713)704-1777
  & Visual Science   Fax: (713)500-0682
6431 Fannin St., Rm. 7024
7 Jones
Houston, TX 77030
URL: http://eye.med.uth.tmc.edu
Contact: Richard S. Ruiz, MD, Chm.

Desc: Cataracts, corneal disease, glaucoma, neuroophthalmology, ophthalmic surgery, pediatric ophthalmology, strabismus, and retinal disease. Additional studies include ocular melanoma, retinitis pigmentosa, diabetes, retinal pigment epithelial transplantation, ischemic optic neuropathy decompression, and pattern electrogram in Alzheimer's disease. *Type:* Research center.

University of Toronto

Eye Bank Laboratory

1 Spadina Crescent   Ph: (416)978-7355
Toronto, ON, Canada M5S 2J5   Fax: (416)978-1522
E-mail: eye.bank@utoronto.ca
Contact: Dr. David S. Rootman, Contact.

Desc: Donor corneal and scleral tissue preservation and sterilization, preparation of fascia lata suture, and toxicology related to donor eye. *Type:* Research center.

University of Waterloo

Centre for Contact Lens Research

Sch. of Optometry   Ph: (519)888-4742
Waterloo, ON, Canada N2L   Fax: (519)884-8769
  3G1
E-mail: dfonn@sciborg.uwaterloo.ca
URL: http://www.optometry.uwaterloo.ca/~cclr/
Contact: Dr. Desmond Fonn, Dir.

Desc: All areas related to contact lenses in order to monitor and understand the effects of contact lenses on the eye, the development of methods for evaluating and measuring the reactions to contact lens wear, and the safety and efficacy of pre and post market release of new lens materials and related products. *Type:* Research center.

Wayne State University

Kresge Eye Institute

4717 St. Antoine   Ph: (313)577-1320
Detroit, MI 48201   Fax: (313)577-5482
URL: http://www.med.wayne.edu/kresgeeye
Contact: Gary Abrams, Contact.

Desc: Cellular and molecular biology, electron microscopy, electrophysiology, neuro-ophthalmology, ophthalmic pathology, orthoptics, biochemistry of phototransduction in the vertebrate retina, cornea, glaucoma, vitreoretinal, and biochemistry and immunology of the eye. *Type:* Research center.

Wills Eye Hospital

Research Division

900 Walnut St.   Ph: (215)928-3268
Philadelphia, PA 19107   Fax: (215)592-4628
Contact: Larry A. Donoso, Co-Dir.

Desc: Vitreoretinal surgery, and vitreoretinal disease management and research. Develops new instrumentation and surgical techniques and ocular application of various laser wavelengths in the various ophthalmic subspecialties in addition to vitreoretinal diseases. *Type:* Research center.

Yale University

Vision Research Center

Boardman Bldg., Box 208061   Ph: (203)785-4282
330 Cedar St.   Fax: (203)737-7401
New Haven, CT 06520-8061
E-mail: colin.barnstable@yale.edu
URL: http://info.med.yale.edu/ophtha/
Contact: Colin J. Barnstable, Prin.Invest.

Desc: Vision including studies on transduction, transport, myopia, neurobiology of growth and development, glaucoma, and diabetic retinopathy. *Type:* Research center.

York University

Centre for Vision Research

103 Farquharson Bldg.   Ph: (416)736-5659
4700 Keele St.   Fax: (416)736-5857
North York, ON, Canada M3J
  1P3
E-mail: i.howard@hpl.ista.ca
URL: http://www.yorku.ca/research/vision/
Contact: Ian P. Howard, Dir.

Desc: Human and animal vision using psychophysical, physiological and computational procedures, focusing on spatial vision as applied to work in aviation, medicine, and space research. *Type:* Research center.

Optometry

AAO News

Alberta Association of Optometrists (AAO)
11830 Kingsway Ave., Ste. 902   Ph: (403)451-6824
Edmonton, AB, Canada T5G   Free: 800-272-8843
  0X5   Fax: (403)452-9918
Contact: Gerald Schram, Editor.

Desc: Covers news of interest in the field of optometry in Canada. *Type:* Newsletter.

American Board of Opticianry

10337 Democracy Ln.   Ph: (703)691-8356
Fairfax, VA 22030   Fax: (703)691-4152
URL: http://www.adl.org
Contact: Candace Prudum, Dir.

Desc: Provides uniform standards for dispensing opticians by administering the National Opticianry Competency Examination and by issuing the Certified Optician Certificate to those passing the exam. Also administers the Master in Ophthalmic Optics Examination and issues certificates to opticians at the advanced level passing the exam. Maintains records of persons certified for competency in eyeglass dispensing. *Type:* Association.

American Optometric Association

243 N. Lindbergh Blvd.   Ph: (314)991-4100
St. Louis, MO 63141   Fax: (314)991-4101
URL: http://www.aoanet.org/
Contact: Jeffrey Mays, Exec.Dir.

Desc: Professional association of optometrists, students of optometry, and paraoptometric assistants and technicians. Purposes are: to improve the quality, availability, and accessibility of eye and vision care; to represent the optometric profession; to help members conduct their practices; to promote the highest standards of patient care. *Type:* Association.

Eyewitness

Contact Lens Society of America
441 Carlisle Dr.   Ph: (703)437-5100
Herndon, VA 22070-4802
E-mail: clsa@huskynet.com
Contact: Patrick Goughary, Editor.

Desc: Informs members of developments in the contact lens industry. Also reports on related educational information and technical papers. *Type:* Newsletter.

National Association of Optometrists and Opticians

PO Box 479   Ph: (419)798-4071
Marblehead, OH 43440   Fax: (419)798-5548
Contact: Franklin D. Rozak, Sec./Treas.

Desc: Licensed optometrists, opticians, and corporations. Conducts public affairs programs of mutual importance to members; serves as an organizational center for special purpose programs; acts as a clearinghouse for information affecting the retail optical industry. *Type:* Association.

National Board of Examiners in Optometry

4340 E. West Hwy., Ste. 1010   Ph: (301)652-5192
Bethesda, MD 20814   Free: 800-969-EXAM
      Fax: (301)907-0013
E-mail: nbeo@optometry.org
URL: http://www.optometry.org
Contact: Dr. Norman E. Wallis, Exec.Dir.

Desc: Administers entry-level criterion-referenced credentialing examinations to students and graduates of accredited schools and colleges of optometry for use by individual state licensing boards. Provides other evaluation, assessment, and survey services to the profession. *Type:* Association.

Optical Society of America

2010 Massachusetts Ave. NW   Ph: (202)223-8130
Washington, DC 20036   Fax: (202)223-1096

Contact: John Thorner, Exec.Dir.

Desc: Persons interested in any branch of optics: research, instruction, optical applications, manufacture, distribution of optical equipment, and physiological optics. Sponsors topical meetings. *Type:* Association.

Opticians Association of America

10341 Democracy Ln.   Ph: (703)691-8355
Fairfax, VA 22030   Fax: (703)691-3929

Contact: Jackie Fairbarns, Contact.

Desc: Retail dispensing opticians who fill prescriptions for glasses or contact lenses written by a vision care specialist. Works to advance the science of ophthalmic optics. *Type:* Association.

The Optometrist's Patient Newsletter

Newsletters Ink
1866 Colonial Village Ln.   Ph: (717)393-1010
PO Box 11177   Free: 800-822-1858
Lancaster, PA 17605-1177

Contact: Ann Mead Ash, Editor, amash@classroom.net.

Desc: Carries patient-oriented articles on vision and eye health topics such as prevention and detection of eye disease, new vision products and technologies, and eye safety. Remarks: May be customized to include the name of the optometrist or practice on the masthead; space is available for articles written by the subscribing practice. *Type:* Newsletter.

Organizations

Associations Unlimited

Gale Group Inc.
27500 Drake Rd.   Ph: (248)699-4253
Farmington Hills, MI 48331-   Free: 800-877-GALE
    3535   Fax: (248)699-8070
E-mail: galeord@galegroup.com

URL: http://www.galegroup.com.; http://www.gale.com/ gale/galenet/gnetcont.html; http://www.gale.com.

Desc: More than 440,000 associations and organizations worldwide. *Type:* Directory.

Associations Yellow Book

Leadership Directories, Inc.
104 5th Ave.   Ph: (212)627-4140
New York, NY 10011   Fax: (212)645-0931
E-mail: info@leadershipdirectories.com; associations@ leadershipdirectories.com.

URL: http://www.leadershipdirectories.com; http://www. leadershipdirectories.com.

Contact: Christiane M. Muntone, Editor.

Desc: Over 43,000 officers, executives, professional staff, and directors at over 1,100 trade and professional associations in the U.S. with budgets over $2 million. *Type:* Directory.

CyberHound's Guide to Associations and Nonprofit Organizations on the Internet

Gale Group Inc.
27500 Drake Rd.   Ph: (248)699-4253
Farmington Hills, MI 48331-   Free: 800-877-GALE
    3535   Fax: (248)699-8070
E-mail: galeord@galegroup.com

URL: http://www.galegroup.com.; http://www. cyberhound.com/.

Desc: Approximately 2,500 Internet sites of membership associations and nonprofit organizations. *Type:* Directory.

Directory of International Organizations

Georgetown University
413 Leavey Center   Ph: (202)687-6780
Washington, DC 20057-1066   Fax: (202)687-6763

Contact: Hans-Albrecht Schraepler, Editor.

Desc: International organizations. *Type:* Directory.

Encyclopedia of Associations: International Organizations

Gale Group Inc.
27500 Drake Rd.   Ph: (248)699-4253
Farmington Hills, MI 48331-   Free: 800-877-GALE
    3535   Fax: (248)699-8070
E-mail: galeord@galegroup.com

URL: http://www.galegroup.com.; http://www.gale.com.

Contact: Tara Sheets, Editor; Christine Maurer, Editor.

Desc: Over 20,800 international nonprofit membership organizations, including multinational, binational, and national organizations based throughout the world covering all subjects and a variety of activities. *Type:* Directory.

Encyclopedia of Associations: National Organizations of the U.S.

Gale Group Inc.
27500 Drake Rd.   Ph: (248)699-4253
Farmington Hills, MI 48331-   Free: 800-877-GALE
    3535   Fax: (248)699-8070
E-mail: galeord@galegroup.com

URL: http://www.galegroup.com.; http://www.gale.com.

Contact: Tara Sheets, Editor; Christine Maurer, Editor.

Desc: Approximately 23,000 nonprofit U.S. membership organizations of national scope divided into 18 classifications: trade, business, and commercial; environmental and agricultural; legal, governmental, public administration, and military; engineering, technicological, and natural and social science; educational; cultural; social welfare; health and medical; public affairs; fraternal, nationality, and ethnic; religious organizations; veterans, hereditary, and patriotic; hobby and avocational; athletic and sports; labor unions, associations, and federations; chambers of commerce and trade and tourism; Greek and non-Greek letter societies, associations, and federations; fan clubs. *Type:* Directory.

Encyclopedia of Associations: Regional, State, and Local Organizations

Gale Group Inc.
27500 Drake Rd.   Ph: (248)699-4253
Farmington Hills, MI 48331-   Free: 800-877-GALE
    3535   Fax: (248)699-8070
E-mail: galeord@galegroup.com

URL: http://www.galegroup.com.; http://www.gale.com.

Contact: Tyra Phillips, Editor.

Desc: Series of five volumes, each containing approximately 20,000 listings for American associations limited in activity to regional, state, and local levels. Does not duplicate entries in "Encyclopedia of Associations," which covers national organizations. *Type:* Directory.

Greater Washington Society of Association Executives

1426 21st St. NW, Ste. 200   Ph: (202)429-9370
Washington, DC 20036-5901   Fax: (202)833-1129
URL: http://www.gwsae.org

Contact: Susan Sarfati, CAE, Pres./CEO.

Desc: Works to maximize the power and performance of association professionals, one person at a time. *Type:* Association.

National Directory of Nonprofit Organizations

The Taft Group
27500 Drake Rd.   Ph: (248)699-4253
Farmington Hills, MI 48331-   Free: 800-347-GALE
    3535   Fax: (248)699-8097
E-mail: galeord@gale.com

URL: http://www.gale.com/taft/

Contact: Ned Burels, Editor.

Desc: Over 260,000 nonprofit organizations; volume 1 covers organizations with annual incomes of over $100,000; volume 2 covers organizations with incomes between $25,000 and $99,999. *Type:* Directory.

Orinthology

American Birding Association

PO Box 6599   Ph: (719)578-1614
Colorado Springs, CO 80934-   Free: 800-850-2473
    6599   Fax: (719)578-1480

URL: http://www.americanbirding.org

Contact: Paul Gregn, Acting Exec.Dir.

Desc: Purposes are: to promote the hobby of birding; to educate the public in the appreciation of birds and their contribution to the environment; to contribute to the study of birds in their natural habitat; to contribute to the development of improved methods of population studies of birds. *Type:* Association.

Bird Watcher's Digest

Bird Watcher's Digest Press
149 Acme St.   Ph: (740)373-5285
Marietta, OH 45750   Free: 800-879-2473
        Fax: (740)373-8443

E-mail: editor@birdwatchersdigest.com

URL: http://www.birdwatchersdigest.com; http://www. birdwatchersdigest.com.

Contact: Wm. H. Thompson, III, Editor, editor@ birdwatchersdigest.com; Elsa Thompson, Publisher; William H. Thompson, Publisher; Andrew M. Thompson, Advertising Dir./Contact, amt@birdwatchersdigest.com.

Desc: Magazine devoted to birds and bird watchers. *Type:* Periodical.

Cornell Laboratory of Ornithology

PO Box 11   Ph: (607)254-2425
Ithaca, NY 14851   Free: 800-843-2425
        Fax: (607)254-2415

URL: http://www.ornith.cornell.edu/

Contact: John Fitzpatrick, Dir.

Desc: Center for the study, conservation, and appreciation of birds. Acts as educational liaison between the professional ornithologist and the public. Encourages volunteer participation in bird observation and data collection. *Type:* Association.

Orthopedics

American Academy of Orthopaedic Surgeons

6300 N. River Rd.   Ph: (847)823-7186
Rosemont, IL 60018-4262   Free: 800-346-AAOS
        Fax: (847)823-8125

E-mail: webhelp@aaos.org

URL: http://www.aaos.org

Contact: Dr. William Tipton, Exec.VP.

Desc: Professional society of orthopedic surgeons certified by the American Board of Orthopedic Surgery to practice orthopedic (bone and joint) surgery. *Type:* Association.

American Orthopaedic Foot and Ankle Society

1216 Pine St., Ste. 201   Ph: (206)223-1120
Seattle, WA 98101-1944   Free: 800-235-4855
                              Fax: (206)223-1178

E-mail: aofas@aofas.org
URL: http://www.aofas.org

Contact: Richard Cantrall, Exec.Dir.

Desc: Members of American Academy of Orthopaedic Surgeons interested in research on, education in, and care of the foot and ankle. *Type:* Association.

Anderson Orthopaedic Research Institute

PO Box 7088   Ph: (703)619-4411
Alexandria, VA 22307   Fax: (703)799-5982
E-mail: research@aori.org
URL: http://www.aori.org

Contact: Dr. Charles A. Engh, Sr., Med.Dir.

Desc: Orthopaedics, focusing on total joint replacements. *Type:* Research center.

Arthroscopy Association of North America

6300 N. River Rd., Ste. 104   Ph: (847)292-2262
Rosemont, IL 60018   Fax: (847)292-2268
E-mail: moreinfo@aana.org
URL: http://www.aana.org

Contact: Edward A. Goss, Exec.Dir.

Desc: Orthopedic surgeons. To advance arthroscopy, a diagnostic or surgical procedure in which an arthroscope, is inserted into a joint. The surgeon can either look directly into the arthroscope or observe on a screen the view projected by the arthroscope. *Type:* Association.

Conservative Orthopedics International Association

2547 Monroe St.   Ph: (313)563-0360
Dearborn, MI 48124   Fax: (248)669-0636

Contact: Dr. Stephen R. Castor, Pres.

Desc: Medical doctors, osteopaths, chiropractors, orthopedists, psychiatrists, and physical therapists. Promotes continuing education, research, and practice of conservative orthopedics. (Conservative orthopedics concentrates on nonoperative, nonradical, preventive and rehabilitive treatment of musculoskeletal disorders.) Seeks to advance the science and art of conservative orthopedics as they relate to the whole person. *Type:* Association.

Foundation for Hand Research and Education

PO Box 80434   Ph: (317)471-4340
8501 Harcourt Rd.   Fax: (317)876-0462
Indianapolis, IN 46280-0434
E-mail: fdnhand@inetdirect.net
URL: http://www.indianahandcenter.com

Contact: Elaine Skopelja, Dir.

Desc: Upper extremity surgery and rehabilitation. *Type:* Research center.

Hospital for Joint Diseases
Orthopaedic Institute
Cartilage and Bone Research Center

301 E. 17th St.   Ph: (212)598-6000
New York, NY 10003
URL: http://www.hjd.edu/Orthopaedics/Cartilage.html

Contact: Paul Di Cesare, MD, Dir.

Desc: Role of noncollagenous matrix in human rheumatoid and osteoarthritis and the role of the inflammatory phase in demineralized bone osteoinduction. *Type:* Research center.

Hospital for Joint Diseases
Orthopaedic Institute
Geriatric Hip Fracture Research Group

301 E. 17th St.   Ph: (212)598-6106
New York, NY 10003   Fax: (212)598-6793
E-mail: gina.aharonoff@cc.med.nyu.edu
URL: http://www.hjd.edu/Orthopaedics/GHFRG.html

Contact: Joseph D. Zuckerman, MD, Dir.

Desc: Hip fracture patients and their recovery after surgery. *Type:* Research center.

Hospital for Joint Diseases
Orthopaedic Institute
Shoulder Institute and Research Group

301 E. 17th St.   Ph: (212)598-6129
New York, NY 10003   Fax: (212)598-6581
URL: http://www.hjd.edu/Orthopaedics/ShoulderInst.html

Contact: Frances Cuomo, MD, Dir.

Desc: Shoulder disorders, including the effect of osteoarthritis and instability on proprioceptive ability, strength recovery following rotator cuff repair, operative vs. nonoperative treatment of type II distal clavicle fractures, and recovery of strength and propriaception after two different capsulorrhaphy procedures. *Type:* Research center.

Hospital for Special Surgery
Research Division
Laboratory for Soft Tissues Research

535 E. 70th St.
New York, NY 10021
URL: http://hss.hss.edu/research/soft_tiss.htm

Contact: Russell F. Warren, MD, Sect.Hd.

Desc: Connective soft tissues related to orthopedics and rheumatology. *Type:* Research center.

Institute for Spine and Biomedical Research

6300 W. Parker Rd., Ste. 100   Ph: (972)608-5150
Plano, TX 75093-7916   Fax: (972)608-5183
E-mail: tf@isbr.org

Contact: Dr. Thomas D. Franklin, Jr., Pres./CEO.

Desc: Spinal issues, biomechanical engineering, clinical trials and orthopedics. *Type:* Research center.

Johns Hopkins University
Orthopaedic Research Laboratories

Johns Hopkins Hospital   Ph: (410)502-6416
Ross Bldg., 2nd Fl., Rm. 225   Fax: (410)502-6414
720 Rutland Ave.
Baltimore, MD 21205
E-mail: ahr@welchlink.welch.jhu.edu

Contact: R.N. Stauffer, MD, Orthopaedic Dept.Chm.

Desc: Bone morphogenetic proteins, tissue engineering, cartilage repair, nerve repair, biomechanics, and bioengineering. *Type:* Research center.

Little People's Research Fund, Inc.

80 Sister Pierre Dr.   Ph: (410)494-0055
Towson, MD 21204-7534   Free: 800-232-5773
                            Fax: (410)494-0062

Contact: Dr. Steven Kopits, Med.Dir.

Desc: Orthopedic disabilities associated with skeletal dysplasia (also known as dwarfism), including child development from adolescence and into adulthood and new surgical procedures. *Type:* Research center.

National Orthotic and Prosthetic Research Institute

PO Box 491   Ph: (212)755-3366
New York, NY 10021

Contact: Ralph Florio, Contact.

Desc: Fabrication of aluminum into canes, crutches, and walkers. *Type:* Research center.

National Osteoporosis Foundation

1232 22nd St., NW   Ph: (202)223-2226
Washington, DC 20037   Fax: (202)223-2237
E-mail: nofmail@nof.org
URL: http://www.nof.org

Contact: Sandra C. Raymond, Exec.Dir.

Desc: Seeks to: increase public awareness and knowledge about osteoporosis; provide information about osteoporosis to sufferers and their families; educate physicians and allied health professionals; advocate for increased governmental support for research on osteoporosis; and support basic biomedical, epidemiological, clinical, behavioral, and social research and research training. *Type:* Association.

Northwestern University
Prosthetics Research Laboratory

345 E. Superior St., Rm. 1441   Ph: (312)908-8560
Chicago, IL 60611-4496   Fax: (312)908-6526
E-mail: d-childress@nwu.edu
URL: http://pele.repoc.nwu.edu/repocalt.shtml

Contact: Dudley S. Childress, Dir.

Desc: Improvement of prostheses and orthoses, improved fitting and manufacturing processes for prothesis/orthosis systems, and improved basic understanding of human interactions with these systems. *Type:* Research center.

Northwestern University
Rehabilitation Engineering Research Program

345 E. Superior St., Rm. 1441   Ph: (312)908-8560
Chicago, IL 60611-4496   Fax: (312)908-6526
E-mail: d-childress@nwu.edu
URL: http://pele.repoc.nwu.edu/repocalt.shtml

Contact: Dudley S. Childress, Dir.

Desc: Improvement of prosthesis and orthoses, fitting and manufacturing processes for such devices, and basic understanding of human interactions with systems of these types. *Type:* Research center.

Orthopaedic Research Institute

929 N. St. Francis   Ph: (316)268-8674
Wichita, KS 67214-3882   Free: 800-362-0070
                            Fax: (316)291-7799

Contact: Dr. Francis Cooke, Dir.

Desc: Design, development, and testing of orthopaedic implants, materials, and instruments. Specific areas of research include artificial replacement joints, absorbable pins and rods for surgically stabilizing bone fractures, devices for the fusion of severely compromised knees, applying a metal foam to orthopaedic implants for tissue attachment, improving external frames for controlling grossly unstable fractures of the pelvis, and combining absorbable glass fibers and plastics for composite implants in the human body. *Type:* Research center.

Orthopaedics Overseas

PO Box 65157, Washington   Ph: (202)296-0928
    Sta.   Fax: (202)296-8018
Washington, DC 20035-5157
E-mail: hvo@aol.com

Contact: Nancy Kelly, Exec.Dir.

Desc: Orthopedic surgeons interested in volunteering as consultants in developing countries. Trains physicians in developing countries in diagnostic, conservative, and operative management techniques. *Type:* Association.

Orthopedic Biomechanics Institute

5848 S. 300 East   Ph: (801)269-4030
Salt Lake City, UT 84107-6121   Fax: (801)269-4015

Contact: E. Paul France, PhD, Dir.

Desc: Orthopedic biomechanics and sports injuries. *Type:* Research center.

Orthopedic Research Society

6300 N. River Rd., Ste. 727   Ph: (847)698-1625
Rosemont, IL 60018-4262   Fax: (847)823-0536
E-mail: ors@aaos.org
URL: http://www.ors.org
Contact: Colette Hohimer, Dir.
Desc: Orthopedic surgery and research. *Type:* Research center.

Pennsylvania State University

Center for Locomotion Studies

Recreation Bldg., Rm. 29   Ph: (814)865-1972
University Park, PA 16802-2002   Fax: (814)863-4755
E-mail: prc@psu.edu
URL: http://www.celos.psu.edu
Contact: Peter R. Cavanagh, PhD, Dir.
Desc: Gait analysis and foot mechanics with particular emphasis on diabetic patients and the elderly. Conducts research on the nature and causes of locomotor pathologies, space flight-induced osteoporosis, foot pressure profiles, posture and balance, and effects of alcohol on gait and posture. *Type:* Research center.

Ranawat Orthopedic Research Foundation, Inc.

Lenox Hill Hosp.   Ph: (212)434-4700
130 E. 77th St.   Fax: (212)628-4782
New York, NY 10021-1803
E-mail: csranawat@mindspring.com
URL: http://www.totaljoint.com
Contact: Chitranjan S. Ranawat, MD, Dir.
Desc: Materials and methods related to total hip and knee replacement surgery. *Type:* Research center.

U.S. Department of Veterans Affairs

Rehabilitation Research and Development Center

Orthopaedic Biomechanics Section

3801 Miranda Ave.   Ph: (650)493-5000
Palo Alto, CA 94304-1200
Contact: Dr. Gary Beaupre, Dir.
Desc: Implant design, including the role of mechanical stresses in the growth, development, and degeneration of the skeleton; mechanical properties of bone; bone fracture healing and remodeling; and relationships between in vivo stress and tissue physiology. Applied research includes a study of orthopaedic implants, such as total joint replacement and fracture fixation plates. *Type:* Research center.

Wayne State University

Bioengineering Center

818 W. Hancock St.   Ph: (313)577-1344
Detroit, MI 48202   Fax: (313)577-8333
E-mail: king@rrb.eng.wayne.edu
URL: http://www.ttb.eng.wayne.edu
Contact: Dr. Albert I. King, Dir.
Desc: Automotive and aircraft safety, injury mechanisms, and spinal function, including lower back pain, orthopedic biomechanics, and head injury. *Type:* Research center.

Osteopathic Medicine

American Association of Colleges of Osteopathic Medicine

5550 Friendship Blvd., Ste. 310   Ph: (301)968-4100
Chevy Chase, MD 20815-7231   Fax: (301)968-4101
Contact: Dr. Douglas H. Wood, D.O., Ph.D., Pres.
Desc: Osteopathic medical colleges. Operates centralized application service; monitors and works with Congress and other government agencies in the planning of health care programs. Gathers statistics on osteopathic medical students, faculty, and diplomates. *Type:* Association.

American Association of Physician Specialists, Inc.

2296 Henderson Mill Rd., Ste.   Ph: (770)939-8555
206   Free: 800-447-9397
Atlanta, GA 30345
URL: http://www.aapsga.com
Contact: William J. Carbone, Exec. Dir.
Desc: Osteopathic and allopathic physicians. Formed for the benevolent, scientific, and educational purposes of improving the practice of the specialty disciplines. Promotes the study and education of specialty disciplines and high intellectual, moral, and ethical standards in specialty practice. *Type:* Association.

American College of Osteopathic Family Physicians

330 E. Algonquin, Ste. 1   Ph: (847)228-6090
Arlington Heights, IL 60005   Free: 800-323-0794
   Fax: (847)228-9755
Contact: George Nyhart, Exec.Dir.
Desc: Doctors of osteopathic medicine in family practice. To advance standards of family practice by encouraging and increasing educational opportunities; to promote general understanding of the scope of family physician and establish a department of family practice in hospitals. Maintains collection of medical tapes and cross references of available libraries owned by individual physicians; keeps complete records of members and their training. *Type:* Association.

American Osteopathic Association

142 E. Ontario St.   Ph: (312)202-8000
Chicago, IL 60611   Free: 800-621-1773
   Fax: (312)202-8200
Contact: John B. Crosby, Exec.Dir.
Desc: Osteopathic physicians, surgeons, and graduates of approved colleges of osteopathic medicine. Associate members include teaching, research, administrative, and executive employees of approved colleges, hospitals, divisional societies, and affiliated organizations. Forms (with its affiliates) an officially recognized structure of the osteopathic profession. *Type:* Association.

Outdoor Recreation

American Camping Association

5000 State Rd. 67 N.   Ph: (765)342-8456
Martinsville, IN 46151-7902   Fax: (765)342-2065
E-mail: aca@camps.org
URL: http://www.acacamps.org
Contact: Peg L. Smith, Exec.Dir.
Desc: Camp owners, directors, program directors, businesses, and students interested in resident and daycamp programming for youth and adults. Conducts camp standards. Offers educational programs in areas of administration, staffing, child development, promotion, and programming. *Type:* Association.

Bassin'

NatCom Inc.
5300 CityPlex Tower   Ph: (918)491-6100
2448 E. 81st St.   Fax: (918)491-9424
Tulsa, OK 74137-4207
E-mail: 73172.2054@compuserve.com.
Contact: Gerald W. Pope, Publisher; Gordon Sprouse, VP Marketing; Jeff Gibson, Contact; Mark Chestnut, Editor-in-Chief.
Desc: Bass fishing magazine featuring articles on equipment, techniques, and locations; as well as profiles of successful bass fishermen. *Type:* Periodical.

Canoe and Kayak Magazine

Canoe America Associates
PO Box 3146   Ph: (206)827-6363
Kirkland, WA 98083   Free: 800-692-2663
   Fax: (206)827-1893
E-mail: ads@canoekayak.com
URL: http://www.canoekayak.com/canoekay.
Contact: Jan Nesset, Editor; Glen Bernard, Assoc. Pub.; Peter R. Becker, Adv. Rep.
Desc: Magazine on canoeing, kayaking, camping, and other outdoor recreation activities. *Type:* Periodical.

Christian Camping International/U.S.A.

PO Box 62189   Ph: (719)260-9400
Colorado Springs, CO 80962-   Fax: (719)260-6398
2189
E-mail: cciusa@cciusa.org
URL: http://www.cciusa.org
Contact: Robert Kobielush, Contact.
Desc: Works to equip those who "shape lives through Christian camps and conference centers" by providing ongoing encouragement, professional training, and timely resources. *Type:* Association.

Deer & Deer Hunting

Krause Publications, Inc.
700 E. State St.   Ph: (715)445-2214
Iola, WI 54990   Free: 800-258-0929
   Fax: (715)445-4087
E-mail: info@krause.com; krause@krause.com
URL: http://www.krause.com
Contact: Patrick Durkin, Editor, durkinp@krause.com; Debbie Knauer, Publisher, knauerd@krause.com.
Desc: Magazine devoted to the hunting of white-tailed deer focusing on techniques, deer biology, behavior and management. *Type:* Periodical.

Family Campers and RVers

4804 Transit Rd., Bldg. 2   Ph: (716)668-6242
Depew, NY 14043   Fax: (716)668-6242
Contact: Fran Opela, Office Mgr.
Desc: Family campers and hikers; others interested in outdoor activities. Promotes and enchances the experience of "family" style camping/RVing. *Type:* Association.

Field & Stream

Times Mirror Magazines, Inc.
2 Park Ave.   Ph: (212)779-5000
New York, NY 10016-5601   Fax: (212)779-5522
E-mail: fsmagazine@aol.com.
URL: http://fieldandstream.com.
Contact: Slaton L. White, Editor, fax: (212)725-3836; Jeff Paro, Publisher; Steve Clow, National Sales Mgr.
Desc: Magazine focusing on hunting and fishing. Also covers camping, shooting sports, boating, and sportsmen's dogs. *Type:* Periodical.

Fishing and Hunting News

Outdoor Empire Publishing, Inc.
511 Eastlake Ave. E.   Ph: (206)624-3845
Seattle, WA 98109   Free: 800-645-5489
   Fax: (206)695-8512
E-mail: oeppubs@mail.nwlink.com; staff@fhnews.com.
URL: http://fhnews.com.
Contact: Patrick McGann, Editor; William Farden, Publisher; Kathryn Schultz, Advertising Mgr.; Del Sachwitz, Circulation Mgr.
Desc: Hunting and fishing magazine. *Type:* Periodical.

Florida Sportsman
Wickstrom Publishers
5901 SW 74th St., Ste. 310   Ph: (305)661-4222
Miami, FL 33143   Fax: (305)284-0277
E-mail: editor@flsportsman.com.
URL: http://www.flsportsman.com.
Contact: Glenn Law, Editor; Karl Wickstrom, Publisher; Robert L. Mitchell, Advertising Mgr.
Desc: Boating, fishing, camping, hunting, and conservation magazine. *Type:* Periodical.

FUR-FISH-GAME
A.R. Harding Publishing Co.
2878 E. Main St.   Ph: (614)231-9585
Columbus, OH 43209
Contact: Mitch Cox, Editor; Jeff Kirn, Publisher; Eric Schweinhagen, Advertising Mgr.
Desc: Magazine featuring hunting, trapping, fishing, dogs, and conservation. *Type:* Periodical.

Knives Illustrated
McMullen Argus Publishing, Inc.
774 S. Placentia Ave.   Ph: (714)939-2400
Placentia, CA 92870   Fax: (714)572-1864
Contact: Bud Lang, Editor; Chris Yee, Publisher; Eric Suter, Advertising Mgr.; Cynthia MacFarlane, Circulation Mgr.
Desc: Magazine on the development, design, and manufacture of bladed instruments; for people interested in bladed instruments for both everyday use and as collectible works of art. *Type:* Periodical.

Ontario Out of Doors
Maclean Hunter Ltd.
777 Bay St., 6th Fl.   Ph: (416)596-5000
Toronto, ON, Canada M5W   Fax: (416)596-5552
1A7
Contact: Burton J. Myers, Editor; Ronald C. Goodman, Publisher; Lynda Watson, Advertising Mgr.
Desc: Fishing and hunting magazine. *Alt. Contact:* 227 Front St. E., Ste. 100, Toronto, ON, Canada M5A 1A7; telephone: (416)386-0185; fax: (416)941-9113. *Type:* Periodical.

Outdoor Life
Times Mirror Magazines, Inc.
2 Park Ave.   Ph: (212)779-5000
New York, NY 10016-5601   Fax: (212)779-5522
Contact: Vin Sparano, Editor; Brendan Banahan, Publisher; Robert C. Hanna, Advertising Mgr.
Desc: Outdoor sports magazine. *Type:* Periodical.

Outdoor World
Outdoor World
300 W. 3rd St.   Ph: (817)921-9300
Fort Worth, TX 76102-2905   Fax: (817)921-9313
Contact: Hal Brown, Publisher; Eddie Lee Rider, Jr., Editor; George Agoglia, Circulation Mgr.
Desc: Magazine catering to outdoor enthusiasts. *Type:* Periodical.

Outside
Mariah Media, Inc.
Outside Plaza 400 Market St.   Ph: (505)989-7100
Santa Fe, NM 87501   Fax: (505)989-4700
E-mail: editor@outsidemag.com.
URL: http://www.outside.starwave.com.
Contact: Lawrence J. Burke, Chm.; Mark Bryant, Editor; Greg Cliburn, Executive Editor; Scott Parmelee, Publisher; Chris Czmyrid, Marketing Director; Anne Mollo-Christensen, V.P., Business Development.
Desc: Magazine covering outdoor sports (hiking, climbing, kayaking, camping, cycling) travel, people, politics, art, and literature of the world outside. *Type:* Periodical.

Outward Bound
100 Mystery Point Rd.   Ph: (914)424-4000
Garrison, NY 10524   Free: 800-243-8520
   Fax: (914)424-4280
E-mail: national@outwardbound.org
URL: http://www.outwardbound.org
Contact: John J. Bierwirth, Pres.
Desc: Operates 5 wilderness schools and 10 urban centers in the U.S. to help young people and adults discover and extend their own resources and abilities by confronting them with a series of increasingly difficult challenges. Programs operate in 22 states and other areas including the Rocky Mountains of Colorado, the Superior-Quetico Wilderness area of northern Minnesota, Hurricane Island off the coast of Maine, Oregon's Cascade range, Pisgah National Forest in North Carolina, New York City, Nepal, and Costa Rica. *Type:* Association.

Petersen's Hunting
Petersen Publishing Co., L.L.C.
6420 Wilshire Blvd.   Ph: (323)782-2350
Los Angeles, CA 90048-5515   Fax: (323)782-2704
Contact: Jeff Young, Publisher; Ken Elliott, Publisher; Peter Clancey, Senior Vice President.
Desc: Sport hunting magazine. *Type:* Periodical.

Pheasants Forever
Pheasants Forever, Inc.
1783 Buerkle Circle   Ph: (651)773-2000
St. Paul, MN 55110   Fax: (651)773-5500
E-mail: pf@pheasantsforever.org.
URL: http://www.pheasantsforever.org.
Contact: Jeffrey S. Finden, CEO; Mark Herwig, Editor.
Desc: Magazine for conservationist pheasant hunters. *Type:* Periodical.

Range Magazine
Range Magazine
PO Box 639   Ph: (702)884-2200
Carson City, NV 89702-0639   Free: 800-RAN-GE4U
   Fax: (702)884-2213
Contact: C. J. Hadley, Editor and Publisher, cj@range.carson-city.nv.us.
Desc: Consumer magazine covering cowboys, sheepherders, and other people who work the land in the Western U.S. *Type:* Periodical.

Slat Water Sportsman
Times Mirror Magazines, Inc.
2 Park Ave.   Ph: (212)779-5000
New York, NY 10016-5601   Fax: (212)779-5522
E-mail: swsfish@ultranet.com.
URL: http://www.saltwatersportsman.com.
Contact: Colin M. Cunningham, Jr., Editor-in-Chief/Publisher; Barry Gibson, Editor; Jaye McAuliffe, Assoc. Pub.
Desc: Magazine on salt water fishing and boating *Alt. Contact:* 77 Franklin St., 10th Fl., Boston, MA 02110; telephone: (617)338-2300; fax: (617)338-2309. *Type:* Periodical.

SnoWest
Harris Publishing, Inc.
520 Park Ave.   Ph: (208)524-7000
Idaho Falls, ID 83402   Fax: (208)522-5241
E-mail: richard@potatogrower.com; info@snowest.com.
Contact: Steve Janes, Publisher, janes@snowest.com; Greg Manwaring, Sales Mgr., greggm@snowest.com; Lane Lindstrom, Editor, lindstm@snowest.com.
Desc: Magazine for snowmobilers. *Type:* Periodical.

Trailblazer
Thousand Trails, Inc.
2711 Lyndon B. Johnson Fwy.,   Ph: (972)243-2228
No. 200   Free: 800-328-6226
Dallas, TX 75234-7317   Fax: (972)488-5024
E-mail: trailblazer@airmail.net.
Contact: Karen Palmer, Assoc. Publisher/Art Dir.; Rebecca Williams, Ad sales, (501)464-4655, rebecca@airkanssas.net; John Powers, Editor-in-Chief, (501)464-4663; Kelly Howard, Ad. Sales, (972)488-4854.
Desc: Recreational lifestyle magazine for members of Thousand Trails and Naco. *Type:* Periodical.

Turkey and Turkey Hunting
Krause Publications, Inc.
700 E. State St.   Ph: (715)445-2214
Iola, WI 54990   Free: 800-258-0929
   Fax: (715)445-4087
E-mail: info@krause.com; krause@krause.com
URL: http://www.krause.com
Contact: Brad Rucks, Advertising Mgr.; Brian Lovett, Editor; Debbie Knauer, Publisher.
Desc: Sportsmen magazine featuring turkey hunting. *Type:* Periodical.

Western Outdoors
Western Outdoors Publications
3197-E Airport Loop Dr.   Ph: (714)546-4370
Costa Mesa, CA 92626   Fax: (714)662-3486
E-mail: woutdoors@aol.com.
Contact: Jack Brown, Editor; Robert Twilegar, Publisher.
Desc: Fishing and boating magazine. *Alt. Contact:* PO Box 2027, Newport Beach, CA 92659-1027; telephone: (714)546-4370; fax: (714)662-3486. *Type:* Periodical.

Packaging

Activities Reports
Research & Development Associates for Military Food & Packaging Systems, Inc.
16607 Blanco Rd., Ste. 1506   Ph: (210)493-8024
San Antonio, TX 78232   Fax: (210)493-8036
E-mail: rda50@flash.net
URL: http://www.militaryfood.org
Contact: Marygene I. Fagan, Editor.
Desc: Contains news items on military food and packaging systems. Reports member and meeting news. *Type:* Newsletter.

Board Converting News
N.V. Business Publishers Corp.
43 Main St.   Ph: (732)502-0500
Avon by the Sea, NJ 07717   Free: 800-962-3001
   Fax: (732)502-9606
E-mail: editorbcn@aol.com.
URL: http://www.pin.co.uk.
Contact: Ted Vilardi, Jr., President; Jim Curley, Editor; Howard Neft, Group Publisher; Tom Vilardi, Publisher.
Desc: Covers current industry news, and provides articles on marketing techniques, price and shipment information, and supplier products. Recurring features include editorials, current industry news, letters to the editor, news of members, and a calendar of events. *Type:* Newsletter.

Can Manufacturers Institute—Executive Focus
Can Manufacturers Institute
1625 Massachusetts Ave. NW,   Ph: (202)232-4677
No. 500   Fax: (202)232-5756
Washington, DC 20036
Contact: Dana Rissland, Editor.
Desc: Highlights the activities of the association and reports on developments of concern to member manufacturers, producers, sellers, and distributors of tin, aluminum, and composite cans. Recurring features include legislative regulatory updates, news of members, and reports of meetings. *Type:* Newsletter.

Federal/State Review

Can Manufacturers Institute
1625 Massachusetts Ave. NW,   Ph: (202)232-4677
  No. 500   Fax: (202)232-5756
Washington, DC 20036

Contact: Theresa M. Termine, Editor.

Desc: Reviews federal and state legislative and regulatory activities affecting the can manufacturing industry. Covers developments in areas including mandatory deposits, restrictive packaging, environmental protection, and taxation. *Type:* Newsletter.

Flexible Packaging Association

1090 Vermont Ave. NW, Ste.   Ph: (202)842-3880
  500   Fax: (202)842-3841
Washington, DC 20005-4960
E-mail: fpa@flexpack.org

Contact: Glenn Braswell, Pres.

Desc: Converters of paper, foil, and plastic packaging materials. Associate members are industry suppliers. Promotes the welfare of the flexible packaging industry by: communicating with federal and state governments and the public on subjects of concern to the industry; promoting the use of flexible packaging; conducting technical, manufacturing, and statistical programs; establishing standards and specifications. *Type:* Association.

Flexible Packaging Association Update

Flexible Packaging Association (FPA)
1090 Vermont Ave., Ste. 500   Ph: (202)842-3880
Washington, DC 20005-4960   Fax: (202)842-3841

Contact: Tim Reitz, Editor.

Desc: Reviews legislative, regulatory, marketing, and public relations issues in the flexible packaging industry. Reports Association initiatives. *Type:* Newsletter.

Food, Cosmetics & Drug Packaging

Elsevier Science Inc.
655 Avenue of the Americas   Ph: (212)989-5800
New York, NY 10010   Fax: (212)633-3990
E-mail: usinfo@elsevier.com
URL: http://www.elsevier.com

Desc: Examines regulatory and technical developments involving food, cosmetics, and drug packaging. *Type:* Newsletter.

Good Packaging Magazine—Western Packaging Directory

Pacific Trade Journals
1315 E. Julian St., Bldg. 1   Ph: (408)286-1661
San Jose, CA 95116-1011   Fax: (408)298-6757

Desc: List of over 1,000 manufacturers of packaging machinery, materials handling equipment, and services. *Type:* Directory.

Institute of Packaging Professionals

481 Carlisle Dr.   Ph: (703)318-8970
Herndon, VA 20170   Free: 800-432-4085
                                 Fax: (703)814-4961

E-mail: iopp@pkgmatters.com
URL: http://www.iopp.org

Contact: William C. Pflaum, Exec.Dir.

Desc: Practicing professionals in the fields of packaging and handling. Holds annual Packaging Design Competition. Offers professional certification and continuing education programs; has 10 standing technical committees and several technical task force groups; maintains speakers' bureau and bookstore. *Type:* Association.

Lookout Foods

Marketing Intelligence Service, Ltd.
6473-D State Rte. 64   Ph: (716)374-6326
Naples, NY 14512-9726   Free: 800-836-5710
                                 Fax: (716)374-5217

E-mail: mi@productscan.com
URL: http://www.productscan.com.

Contact: Daniel Smith, Publications Mgr.; Chris Sharman, Editor; Tom Vierhile, Exec. Editor.

Desc: Carries photographs and detailed descriptions of the most innovative products, package design, line extensions, and marketing background in consumer goods categories. Also copies advertising support. *Type:* Newsletter.

Lookout Nonfoods

Marketing Intelligence Service, Ltd.
6473-D State Rte. 64   Ph: (716)374-6326
Naples, NY 14512-9726   Free: 800-836-5710
                                 Fax: (716)374-5217

E-mail: mi@productscan.com
URL: http://www.productscan.com.

Contact: Daniel Smith, Editor.

Desc: Carries photographs and detailed descriptions of the most innovative products, package design, line extensions, and marketing background in consumer goods categories. Covers nonprescription drugs, cosmetics and toiletries, and miscellaneous household items. *Type:* Newsletter.

Official Board Markets

Advanstar Communications
312 W. Randolph St., Ste. 600   Ph: (312)553-8900
Chicago, IL 60606-1721   Fax: (312)553-8926
E-mail: abmpbp@en.com.

Contact: Mark Arzoumanian, Editor.

Desc: Carries news of current business developments in the converting, paper, and packaging industries. Recurring features include paperboard and recovered paper prices. *Type:* Newsletter.

Official Container Directory

Advanstar Communications
7500 Old Oak Blvd.   Ph: (440)243-8100
Cleveland, OH 44130-3369   Free: 800-225-4569
                                 Fax: (440)891-2733

E-mail: directories@advanstar.com

Contact: Karen Eagle, Editor, fax: (440)891-2727, keagle@advanstar.com.

Desc: About 3,000 manufacturers of corrugated and solid fiber containers, folding cartons, rigid boxes, fiber cans and tubes, and fiber drums. Includes a buyers' guide of approximately 1,000 suppliers of equipment, materials, and services for the industry, a packaging and shipping machinery guide; and another packaging products guide. Coverage includes Canada. *Type:* Directory.

Pack Info

Institute of Packaging Professionals Press
481 Carlisle Dr.   Ph: (703)318-8970
Herndon, VA 20170-4823   Free: 800-432-4085
                                 Fax: (703)814-4961

E-mail: iopp@pkgmatters.com
URL: http://www.packinfo-world.org/

Contact: William C. Pflavin, Editor.

Desc: Functions as one of the informational services of PI/USA and serves as a "pipeline to the packaging world." Contains both committee and chapter news. Recurring features include a calendar of events, profiles, notices of relevant publications, and articles on packaging topics ranging from environmental issues to new products. *Type:* Newsletter.

Packaging

Cahners Business Information
1350 E. Touhy Ave.   Ph: (847)635-8800
Des Plaines, IL 60018   Free: 800-446-6551
                                 Fax: (847)635-6856

E-mail: bkinross@cahners.com
Contact: Greg Erickson, Editor; John Blatnik, Publisher.
Desc: Business trade magazine for the packaging field. *Type:* Periodical.

Packaging Sourcebook

North American Publishing Co.
401 N. Broad St.   Ph: (215)238-5300
Philadelphia, PA 19108   Free: 800-777-8074
                                 Fax: (215)238-5270

URL: http://www.napco.com
Contact: Lisa A. Denshuick, Editor, (215)238-5335, fax: (215)238-5099, LDenshuick@napco.com.
Desc: Packaging buyers, package printers and converters, forms and label printers, consultants, designers, contractors, and materials and equipment/machinery manufacturers, distributors, and suppliers. Also includes research and development firms, testing facilities, shippers/carriers, associations/exhibition companies, educational facilities, environmental controls and services, and die cutters, makers and suppliers. *Type:* Directory.

Packaging Strategies

Packaging Strategies, Inc.
122 S. Church St.   Ph: (610)436-4220
West Chester, PA 19382-3223   Fax: (610)436-6277
E-mail: packinfo@packstrat.com
URL: http://www.packstrat.com.
Contact: William H. LeMaire, Editorial Dir./Publisher, editors@packstrat.com.
Desc: Focuses on emerging trends, technologies, and business issues pertaining to the packaging industry. Reports on new packaging materials, containers, equipment, and technology, and business concerns. *Type:* Newsletter.

Packaging World

Summit Publishing Co.
One IBM Plaza, Ste. 3131   Ph: (312)751-1616
330 Wabash Ave.   Free: 800-355-5595
Chicago, IL 60611   Fax: (312)222-1310
E-mail: editorial@packworld.com.
URL: http://www.packworld.com.
Contact: Arnie Orloski, Jr, Editor; Joseph Angel, Publisher.
Desc: Packaging trade journal. *Type:* Periodical.

The Packet

National Paperbox Association
801 N. Fairfax St., No. 211   Ph: (703)684-2212
Alexandria, VA 22314   Fax: (703)683-6920
E-mail: boxmaker@paperbox.org
URL: http://www.paperbox.org; http://www.paperbox.org.
Contact: Scott Miller, Editor.
Desc: Spotlights Association news and related items of interest to carton manufacturers. Recurring features include news of research, a calendar of events, news of educational opportunities, and notices of publications available. *Type:* Newsletter.

Paperboard Packaging Council

201 N. Union St., Ste. 200   Ph: (703)836-3300
Alexandria, VA 22314   Fax: (703)836-3290
E-mail: ppcmail@erols.com
URL: http://www.ppcnet.org
Contact: Marla Donahue, Contact.
Desc: Manufacturers of paperboard packaging. Sponsors public relations activities, occasional safety programs, and annual technical seminar. Conducts overall industry statistical studies, marketing surveys, product reviews, and labor relations and bargaining agreement studies. *Type:* Association.

PHL Bulletin

National Institute of Packaging, Handling, and Logistic Engineers
6902 Lyle St.   Ph: (301)459-9105
Lanham, MD 20706-3454   Fax: (301)459-4925

Desc: Discusses developments in the fields of packaging, handling, and logistics. Focuses on important government and industry research and on the latest government standards and specifications for packaging materials, processes, and equipment. *Type:* Newsletter.

SMT Trends

New Insights
304 Vallejo St.   Ph: (510)787-2273
Crockett, CA 94525   Fax: (510)787-2273

Desc: Covers news of developments in surface mount technology (SMT), printed circuit board manufacturing, component packaging, RCB inspection and testing, industry trends, markets, and issues such as ISO 9000 standards and elimination of toxics. *Type:* Newsletter.

Spray Technology & Marketing

Industry Publications, Inc.
3621 Hill Rd.   Ph: (201)227-5151
Parsippany, NJ 07054   Fax: (201)227-9219

Contact: Michael L. SanGiovanni, Editor.

Desc: Lists of about 775 custom fillers of spray products and suppliers of spray packaging components, chemicals, machinery, and related services; international coverage. *Type:* Directory.

TechPak

The McGraw-Hill Companies
Aviation Week Group
1200 G St. NW, Ste. 200   Ph: (202)383-2403
Washington, DC 20005-3802   Free: 800-752-4959
    Fax: (202)383-7956

E-mail: awgnews@mcgraw-hill.com

Contact: Robert Martino, Editor.

Desc: Focuses on food, beverage, and consumer product packaging. Discusses technological innovations, regulatory and legislation activities, company movements, processing strategies, and environmental issues. *Type:* Newsletter.

VSLI Assembly and Packaging Update

Semiconductor Equipment & Materials International (SEMI)
805 E. Middlefield Rd.   Ph: (650)964-5111
Mountain View, CA 94043   Fax: (650)967-5375
E-mail: semihq@semi.org; newsletters@semi.org.
URL: http://www.semi.org; http://www.semi.org.

Desc: Topics inluce "developments in the industry, packaging trends, Europe and Far East news, conferences, training seminars, equipment review, new designs, and materials." Delivered by electronic mail. *Type:* Newsletter.

Paper

American Forest and Paper Association

1111 19th St. NW   Ph: (202)463-2700
Washington, DC 20036   Free: 800-878-8878

Contact: Red Cavaney, Pres.

Desc: U.S. manufacturers of pulp, paper, and paperboard. Gathers, compiles, and disseminates information; conducts research on scientific and technical problems. *Type:* Association.

Canadian Paper Analyst

JDR Publications
PO Box 300   Ph: (514)933-8749
Victoria Sta.   Fax: (514)849-8367
Westmount, PQ, Canada H3Z
   2V5

Contact: Jim Rowland, Editor, rowland@accent.net.

Desc: Analyzes trends in the Canadian pulp, paper, and paperboard industry. *Type:* Newsletter.

Document Management Industries Association

433 E. Monroe Ave.   Ph: (703)836-6232
Alexandria, VA 22301-1693   Free: 800-336-4641
    Fax: (703)836-2241

E-mail: editor@formmag.com
URL: http://www.dmia.org

Contact: Peter L. Colaianni, CAE, Exec.VP.

Desc: Independent distributors, manufacturers, and suppliers of forms, business printing and document management services. Sponsors educational and training programs. Compiles statistics. *Type:* Association.

ESMA News Letter

Engraved Stationery Manufacturers Association (ESMA)
305 Plus Park Blvd.   Ph: (615)366-1094
Nashville, TN 37217-1005   Fax: (615)366-4192

Contact: Donald G. Pake, Editor.

Desc: Reports on happenings both within and affecting the engraved stationery industry. Carries articles on selling, tax incentive programs, management, and developments in labor and employment law. *Type:* Newsletter.

IBFI, The International Association

100 Daingerfield Rd.   Ph: (703)841-9191
Alexandria, VA 22314-2886   Fax: (703)522-5750

Contact: Thomas Playford, Pres.

Desc: Manufacturers of business forms and providers of forms and systems automation solutions; associate members are suppliers to business forms industry including manufacturers of paper and press equipment. Promotes high standards of production, marketing, financial, and managerial activities; provides a vehicle for the solution of common industry problems in an effective and efficient manner; fosters anticipation and awareness of change in economic, social, and technological environments and positive reaction to these forces. Offers seminars and training courses with certification. *Type:* Association.

Institute of Paper Chemistry

1043 E. South River St.   Ph: (414)734-9251
Appleton, WI 54912

Contact: Harry A. Posner, Jr., Pres.

Desc: Member companies are manufacturers of pulp paper or paperboard. Educational and research center affiliated with Lawrence University, Appleton, WI. *Type:* Association.

Institute of Paper Science and Technology

500 10th St. NW   Ph: (404)894-5700
Atlanta, GA 30318   Free: 800-558-6611
    Fax: (404)894-4778

E-mail: bob.patterson@ipst.edu
URL: http://www.ipst.edu

Contact: Dr. James L. Ferris, Contact.

Desc: Corporations engaged in the manufacture of paper products. Seeks to advance the science and technology of paper making. *Type:* Association.

Monthly Newsprint Statistics

Canadian Pulp & Paper Association
Sun Life Bldg., 19th Fl.   Ph: (514)866-6621
1155 Metcalfe St.   Fax: (514)866-3035
Montreal, PQ, Canada H3B
   4T6

E-mail: cppacda@ibm.net

Desc: Updates information on the pulp and paper industry of Canada. Remarks: Also available in French. *Type:* Newsletter.

National Council of the Paper Industry for Air and Stream Improvement

PO Box 13318   Ph: (919)558-1999
Research Triangle Park, NC   Fax: (919)558-1998
   27709-3318

E-mail: mmcreynolds@ncasi.org
URL: http://www.ncasi.org

Contact: Dr. Ronald Yeske, Pres.

Desc: Conducts research on environmental problems related to industrial forestry and the manufacture of pulp, paper, and wood products. *Type:* Association.

News Paper

Maine Pulp & Paper Association
PO Box 5670   Ph: (207)622-3166
Augusta, ME 04332-5670

Contact: Mary E. LeBlanc, Editor.

Desc: Presents the news and views of the Maine paper industry trade association, including legislative information. Discusses the industry's positions on business in Maine. *Type:* Newsletter.

Paper Industry Management Association

1699 Wall St., Ste. 212   Ph: (847)956-0250
Mount Prospect, IL 60056-5782   Fax: (847)956-0520

Contact: Scott A. Baumruck, Exec.Dir.

Desc: Professional organization of pulp, paper mill, and paper converting production executives. *Type:* Association.

Paper Recycler

Miller Freeman, Inc.
525 Market St., Ste. 500   Ph: (415)538-3828
San Francisco, CA 94105   Free: 800-289-0969
    Fax: (415)278-5371

E-mail: subserv@mfi.com

Contact: Debbie Garcia, Editor.

Desc: Forecasts changes in supply, demand, and price for grades in all wastepaper categories. Covers news of legislation, technology, transportation, grade profiles, recycled projects, and wastepaper markets. *Type:* Newsletter.

Paper Stock Report

McEntee Media Corp.
13727 Holland Rd.   Ph: (216)362-7979
Brook Park, OH 44142   Fax: (216)362-6553

Contact: Ken McEntee, Editor, ken@recycle.cc; Rick Downing, Advertising Mgr.; Carol Garbo, Advertising Rep.

Desc: Describes news and trends in the market for recovered paper, includes current market prices for wastepaper. *Type:* Newsletter.

PAPERCHEM

Institute of Paper Science and Technology
500 Tenth St., N.W.   Ph: (404)894-5700
Atlanta, GA 30318

Desc: Contains more than 460,000 citations, most with abstracts, to the worldwide scientific and technical literature and patents on theories, resources, products, and processes of the pulp, paper, and board industries. Both manufacturing and use aspects are covered. *Available:* The Dialog Corporation, DIALOG; The Dialog Corporation, DIALOG; STN International; STN International. *Type:* Database.

The Paperworker

United Paperworkers International Union
3340 Perimeter Hill Dr.   Ph: (615)834-8590
PO Box 1475   Fax: (615)333-6667
Nashville, TN 37211
Contact: Richard T. Blin, Editor.
Desc: Labor newspaper (tabloid). *Type:* Periodical.

Pulp & Paper Forecaster

Miller Freeman, Inc.
525 Market St., Ste. 500   Ph: (415)538-3828
San Francisco, CA 94105   Free: 800-289-0969
        Fax: (415)278-5371
E-mail: subserv@mfi.com
Contact: Harold Cody, Editor, (415)538-3801.
Desc: Forecasts production, capacity, and operating rates
for six major paper grades. Includes two years each of his-
torical, forecast, and current year data. *Type:* Newsletter.

Pulp & Paper Project Report

Miller Freeman, Inc.
525 Market St., Ste. 500   Ph: (415)538-3828
San Francisco, CA 94105   Free: 800-289-0969
        Fax: (415)278-5371
E-mail: subserv@mfi.com
Contact: Harold Cody, Editor.
Desc: Reports on expansion and modernization, new mills
and machines, and capital spending programs in the paper
and pulp industry. Includes statistical information on mill
capacity and paper grades. *Type:* Newsletter.

Pulp & Paper Week

Miller Freeman, Inc.
525 Market St., Ste. 500   Ph: (415)538-3828
San Francisco, CA 94105   Free: 800-289-0969
        Fax: (415)278-5371
E-mail: subserv@mfi.com
Contact: Joyce Routson, Editor, (415)538-3819.
Desc: Reports business and financial news concerning the
paper and pulp industry. Compiles price and production
figures and discusses market conditions, industry mergers,
expansions, labor developments, international trade, and
other topics of interest. *Type:* Newsletter.

Recycling Markets

N.V. Business Publishers Corp.
43 Main St.   Ph: (732)502-0500
Avon by the Sea, NJ 07717   Free: 800-962-3001
        Fax: (732)502-9606
E-mail: nvrecycle@aol.com.
URL: http://www.pin.co.uk.
Contact: Tom Vilardi, Publisher; Ted Vilardi, Jr., Presi-
dent; Jim Curley, Editor; Amy Snell, Managing Editor;
Howard Neft, Group Publisher.
Desc: Covers aspects of the waste paper industry and metal
recycle products. Includes editorials, information on sup-
plier products, and waste paper prices. *Type:* Newsletter.

TAPPI

Technology Park/Atlanta   Ph: (770)446-1400
PO Box 105113   Free: 800-332-8686
Atlanta, GA 30348-5113   Fax: (770)446-6947
E-mail: serviceline@tappi.org
URL: http://www.tappi.org
Contact: Wayne Gross, Exec.Dir.
Desc: Executives, managers, engineers, research scientists,
superintendents, and technologists in the pulp, packaging,
converting, paper, nonwovens, and allied industries. Conducts conferences on coating, pulp manufacturing, engineering, nonwovens, process and product quality,
polymers, laminations and coatings, paper and board
manufacturing, corrugated containers, packaging, forest
biology, printing, research and development, environment, finishing, and converting. Develops testing methods
for laboratory analyses and process control. *Type:* Association.

Walden's Fiber & Board Report

Walden-Mott Corporation
225 N. Franklin Tpke.   Ph: (201)818-8630
Ramsey, NJ 07446-1600   Free: 888-292-5336
        Fax: (201)818-8720
E-mail: walden@walden-mott.com
Contact: Gregg B. Fales, Editor.
Desc: Offers news and analysis on markets in linerboard,
corrugated, newsprint, box board, market pulp, and sec-
ondary fiber. Presents trends, prices, North American and
European reports, pulp inventories, and industry produc-
tion data. *Type:* Newsletter.

Walden's Paper Report

Walden-Mott Corporation
225 N. Franklin Tpke.   Ph: (201)818-8630
Ramsey, NJ 07446-1600   Free: 888-292-5336
        Fax: (201)818-8720
E-mail: walden@walden-mott.com
Contact: Sylvia P. Peremes, Editor.
Desc: Covers marketing trends on the North American
paper industry. Reviews price movements, inventory ad-
justments, sales, company expansion, mergers, acquisi-
tions, and general financial rates of manufacturers. *Type:*
Newsletter.

Parents

Adoptive Families of America

2309 Como Ave.   Ph: (612)645-9955
St. Paul, MN 55108   Free: 800-372-3300
        Fax: (612)645-0055
E-mail: afmag@ibm.net
Contact: Thomas M. Richards, Exec. V.P.
Desc: Adoptive and prospective adoptive families; acts as
an umbrella organization for adoptive parent support
groups. Provides support, assistance, and information to
adoptive parents. Seeks to create opportunities for successful adoptive placement; promotes the health and welfare
of children without permanent homes. *Type:* Association.

Atlanta Baby

Atlanta Baby
4330 Georgetown Sq. II, No.   Ph: (770)454-7599
506   Fax: (770)454-7699
Atlanta, GA 30338-6217
E-mail: atlparnt@family.com
Contact: Liz White, Publisher; Peggy Middendorf, Editor.
Desc: Consumer magazine covering family issues. *Type:*
Periodical.

Baby Magazine

Baby Magazine
124 E. 40th St., Rm. 1101   Ph: (212)986-1422
New York, NY 10016-1723   Fax: (212)338-9011
Contact: Jeanne Muchnick, Editor; Suzanne Robotti, Pub-
lisher; Dina Kaliko, Production/Circulation Mgr.; John
Knecht, National Advertising Mgr.
Desc: Consumer publication covering pre- and postnatal
care through the baby's first year. *Type:* Periodical.

Best Wishes Magazine

Family Communications Inc.
37 Hanna Ave., Unit 1   Ph: (416)537-2604
Toronto, ON, Canada M6K   Fax: (416)538-1794
1W9
E-mail: info@todaysbride.ca
Contact: Bettie Bradley, Editor; Tracy Hitchcock, Assoc.
Editor.
Desc: Magazine for new parents. *Type:* Periodical.

Chicago Parent Magazine

Wednesday Journal, Inc.
141 S. Oak Park Ave.   Ph: (708)386-5555
Oak Park, IL 60302   Fax: (708)524-0447
E-mail: chiparent@aol.com.
Contact: Sharon Bloyd-Peshkin, Editor; Kit Olah, Sales
Mgr.
Desc: Tabloid featuring child-related articles and compre-
henseive calendar of events, programs, and activities for
the greater Chicago area. *Type:* Periodical.

CHILD

G J USA Publishing
375 Lexington Ave.   Ph: (212)499-2010
New York, NY 10017   Fax: (212)499-2038
E-mail: childmail@childmagazine.com
Contact: Pamela Abrams, Editor; Susan Summer, Publish-
er.
Desc: Magazine for parents with children from newborn
to 12 years old. *Type:* Periodical.

City Parent

City Parent
467 Speers Rd.   Ph: (905)815-0017
Oakville, ON, Canada L6K 3S4   Free: 800-387-7682
        Fax: (905)815-0511
E-mail: city.parent@ocna.org.
Contact: Liz Campbell, Editor; Cathryn Oliver, Advertising Dir.; Jane Muller, Editor-in-Chief.
Desc: Magazine serving as parents' guide to upcoming
events and activities in and around Toronto for children
under twelve. *Type:* Periodical.

Expecting

Family Communications Inc.
37 Hanna Ave., Unit 1   Ph: (416)537-2604
Toronto, ON, Canada M6K   Fax: (416)538-1794
1W9
E-mail: info@todaysbride.ca
Contact: Donald G. Swinburne, Publisher; Bettie Bradley,
Corporate Editor; Tracy Hitchcock, Editor; Roberta Lee,
Art Dir.; Monique Jacobe, Production Mgr.; Monique Ja-
cobs, Production Mgr.; Donna Enman, Distribution
Mgr.; Karen Nicol, Circulation Supervisor.
Desc: Publication for expectant women. *Type:* Periodical.

Family Life

Hachette Filipacchi Magazines, Inc.
1633 Broadway, 41st Fl.   Ph: (212)767-6000
New York, NY 10019   Fax: (212)989-4561
E-mail: familylife@aol.com.
Contact: Peter Herbst, Editor-in-Chief.
Desc: Magazine for parents of children ages 3-12 years.
Type: Periodical.

Girl Scout Leader

Girl Scouts of U.S.A.
420 5th Ave.   Ph: (212)852-8000
New York, NY 10018-2798   Fax: (212)852-6511
Desc: Magazine with information and news of interest to
Girl Scout adult volunteers and staff. *Type:* Periodical.

Great Expectations

Today's Parent Group
269 Richmond St. W   Ph: (416)596-8680
Toronto, ON, Canada M5V   Fax: (416)596-1991
1X1
Contact: Fran Fearnley, Editor-in-Chief; Holly Bennett,
Editor; Christopher Emery, Director.
Desc: Magazine for expectant and new parents. *Type:* Peri-
odical.

Helping Other Parents in Normal Grieving
1215 E. Michigan Ave.   Ph: (517)483-3873
PO Box 30480   Fax: (517)351-1404
Lansing, MI 48909
Contact: Carolyn R. Wickham, Hospital Coord.
Desc: Medical professionals, social service workers, and clergy; parents who have experienced a miscarriage, stillbirth, or the death of an infant. Provides support to newly bereaved parents through trained parents who have suffered a similar loss and resolved their grief. Promotes community education regarding the effect that a miscarriage, stillbirth, or neonatal death has on parents. *Type:* Association.

L.A. Parent
L.A. Parent
PO Box 3204   Ph: (818)846-0400
Burbank, CA 91504   Fax: (818)841-4300
Contact: Christine Elston, Editor, fax: (818)841-4380; Kay Mount, General Mgr., fax: (818)841-4380.
Desc: Magazine for parents. *Type:* Periodical.

Lamaze Parents' Magazine
Lamaze Institute for Family Education
9 Old Kings Hwy. S.   Ph: (203)656-3600
Darien, CT 06820   Fax: (203)656-2221
E-mail: lamaze@lamaze.com
Contact: Carole Sherwood, VP of Editorial and Production.
Desc: Magazine on childbirth and third trimester of pregnancy. *Type:* Periodical.

Lamazebaby
Lamaze Institute for Family Education
9 Old Kings Hwy. S.   Ph: (203)656-3600
Darien, CT 06820   Fax: (203)656-2221
E-mail: lamaze@lamaze.com
Contact: Carole Sherwood, VP of Editorial and Production.
Desc: Magazine covering an infant's first year of life. *Type:* Periodical.

Living
Shalom Foundation, Inc.
Rte. 2, Box 656   Ph: (540)249-3177
Grottoes, VA 24441   Free: 888-833-3333
                           Fax: (540)249-3177
E-mail: tgether@aol.com.
Contact: Richard Benner, Director; Melodie Davis, Editor.
Desc: Family magazine. *Type:* Periodical.

Mothers at Home
8310-A Old Courthouse Rd. Ph: (703)827-5903
Vienna, VA 22182   Free: 800-783-4666
                           Fax: (703)790-8587
E-mail: mah@netrail.net
URL: http://www.mah.org
Contact: Betty Walter, Exec.Dir.
Desc: Dedicated to the support of mothers who choose to stay at home to raise their children. Serves as a forum for the exchange of information among mothers. Provides information at congressional hearings. *Type:* Association.

MUMS National Parent-to-Parent Network
Julie Gordon
150 Custer Ct.   Ph: (920)336-5333
Green Bay, WI 54301-1243   Fax: (920)339-0995
E-mail: mums@netnet.net
Contact: Julie Gordon, Pres.
Desc: Parents or care providers of a child with any disability, rare disorder, chromosomal abnormality or health condition. Seeks to provide support to parents in the form of a networking system that matches parents with other parents whose children have the same or similar condition, including rare disorders. *Type:* Association.

National Organization of Circumcision Information Resource Centers
PO Box 2512   Ph: (415)488-9883
San Anselmo, CA 94979   Fax: (415)488-9660
E-mail: nocirc@concentric.net
URL: http://www.nocirc.org
Contact: Marilyn Fayre Milos, R.N., Exec.Dir.
Desc: Serves as an umbrella organization for circumcision information centers internationally; seeks to educate professionals and the public about routine infant male circumcision and the practice of female genital mutilation; defending the body integrity rights of infants and children. Maintains mailing list of 20,000 hospitals, planned parenthood clinics, expectant parents, and individual professionals in fields related to health care, law and ethics. Conducts continuing education courses for registered nurses. *Type:* Association.

National Organization of Mothers of Twins Clubs
PO Box 23188   Ph: (505)275-0955
Albuquerque, NM 87192-1188   Free: 800-243-2276
URL: http://www.nomotc.org
Contact: Lois Gallmeyer, Exec.Sec.
Desc: Twin clubs seeking to broaden the understanding of those aspects of child development and rearing which relate especially to twins through the interchange of information among parents, educators, doctors, and others. Goals are: to make information about twins available to the public; to increase awareness of the individuality of each twin; to assist in medical research. Operates speakers' bureau; maintains bibliography of books on twin care. *Type:* Association.

National Organization of Restoring Men
R. Wayne Griffiths
3205 Northwood Dr., Ste. 209   Ph: (510)827-4077
Concord, CA 94520   Fax: (510)827-4119
E-mail: waynerobb@aol.com
URL: http://www.norm.org
Contact: R. Wayne Griffiths, Exec.Dir.
Desc: Provides support for men who desire to restore their foreskin after circumcision. Acts as a forum for exchange of information on methods and techniques of foreskin restoration. Helps men to "regain a sense of wholeness and self-directedness". *Type:* Association.

National PTA - National Congress of Parents and Teachers
330 N. Wabash Ave., Ste. 2100   Ph: (312)670-6782
Chicago, IL 60611-3690   Free: 800-307-4PTA
                                Fax: (312)670-6783
E-mail: info@pta.org
URL: http://www.PTA.org
Contact: Lois Jean White, Pres.
Desc: Parents, teachers, students, principals, administrators, and others interested in uniting the forces of home, school, and community on behalf of children and youth. Works for legislation benefitting children and youth through its Washington, DC office. Maintains resource center. *Type:* Association.

New Mother
Today's Parent Group
269 Richmond St. W   Ph: (416)596-8680
Toronto, ON, Canada M5V Fax: (416)596-1991
1X1
Desc: Magazine for new mothers. *Type:* Periodical.

Non-Circumcision Educational Foundation
PO Box 251   Ph: (717)529-2561
Oxford, PA 19363
Contact: James E. Peron, Exec.Dir.

Desc: Parents, childbirth educators, nurse-midwives, nurses, doctors, and other interested individuals. Seeks to: stop routine infant circumcision; provide medical information regarding such surgery. Opposes what it calls the unnecessary surgery of baby boys, use of silver nitrate in eyes, and other medical treatments which violate the physical and emotional well-being of the newborn. *Type:* Association.

Owl Canadian Family
Multi-Vision Publishing, Inc.
655 Bay St., Ste. 1100
Toronto, ON, Canada M5G
2K4
E-mail: owlfamily@m-v-p.com.
Contact: Kristin Jenkins, Editor; Heather McArdle, Managing Editor; Susan Thornburrow, Advertising Dir.
Desc: Family activity magazine for parents. *Type:* Periodical.

Parenting
Parenting
PO Box 3204   Ph: (818)846-0400
Burbank, CA 91504   Fax: (818)841-4300
URL: http://family.com.
Contact: Christine Elston, Editor, fax: (818)841-4380; Kay Mount, General Mgr., fax: (818)841-4380.
Desc: Newspaper. *Type:* Periodical.

Parenting Magazine
Parenting Magazine
1325 Avenue of the Americas,   Ph: (212)522-8989
27th Fl.   Fax: (212)522-8699
New York, NY 10019
URL: http://www.parenttime.com.
Contact: Diane Oshin, Publisher.
Desc: Magazine for contemporary parents. *Type:* Periodical.

Parents Baby
Gruner & Jahr USA Publishing
375 Lexington Ave., 10th Fl.   Ph: (212)499-2000
New York, NY 10017-4024   Free: 800-599-8489
                               Fax: (212)499-2159
Contact: Jane Traulsen, Editor, (212)499-2084, fax: (212)499-2159, jtraulse@gjusa.com; Sue Rapier, Advertising Dir., (212)499-2122, srapier@gjusa.com; Alison Kase, Publications Mgr., (212)499-2118, akase@gjusa.com; Molly Ingram, (212)499-2094, fax: (212)499-2097, mingram@gjusa.com.
Desc: Consumer magazine for new parents. *Type:* Periodical.

Parents' Choice
Parents' Choice Foundation
1935 Beacon St.   Ph: (617)965-5913
Waban, MA 02168-1461   Fax: (617)965-4516
Contact: Diana Huss Green, Editor.
Type: Periodical.

Parents Expecting
Gruner & Jahr USA Publishing
375 Lexington Ave., 10th Fl.   Ph: (212)499-2000
New York, NY 10017-4024   Free: 800-599-8489
                               Fax: (212)499-2159
Contact: Jane Traulsen, Contact, (212)499-2084; Sharon Summer, Group Publisher, (212)499-2123; Sue Rapier, Advertising Dir.; Alison Kase, Publications Mgr., (212)499-2118, akase@gjusa.com; Molly Ingram, Contact, (212)499-2094, fax: (212)499-2097, mingram@gjusa.com.
Desc: Magazine for expectant mothers. *Type:* Periodical.

Parents Helping Parents

3041 Olcott St.   Ph: (408)727-5775
Santa Clara, CA 95054-3222   Fax: (408)727-0182
URL: http://www.php.com.
Contact: Mary Helen Peterson, M.A., Exec.Dir.
Desc: Parents, professionals, lay counselors, families, and friends committed to alleviating the problems, hardships, and concerns of families with children having special needs, such as physical, mental, emotional, or learning disabilities; intensive nursery care; preemies; long-term, chronic, or terminal illness due to accident, birth defect, or illness. Helps children with special needs receive the care, services, education, love, hope, respect, and acceptance they deserve. Offers education, support, information, and training for parents to decrease isolation and increase a sense of personal control. *Type:* Association.

Parents Magazine

Gruner & Jahr USA Publishing
375 Lexington Ave., 10th Fl.   Ph: (212)499-2000
New York, NY 10017-4024   Free: 800-599-8489
                 Fax: (212)499-2159
Contact: Ann Pleshette Murphy, Editor; John G. Hahn, Publisher.
Desc: Magazine covering children, health, marriage, and family life. *Type:* Periodical.

Parents of Murdered Children

100 E. 8th St., B-41   Ph: (513)721-5683
Cincinnati, OH 45202   Free: 888-818-POMC
                 Fax: (513)345-4489
E-mail: natlpomc@aol.com
URL: http://www.pomc.com
Contact: Nancy Ruhe, Exec.Dir.
Desc: Self help organization for anyone who has had a friend or family member murdered. Offers support and friendship to those who have experienced the violent death of a family member or friend; fosters their physical and emotional health; works to heighten society's awareness of the problems faced by those who survive a homicide victim. *Type:* Association.

Parents Pregnancy Frequently Asked Questions

Gruner & Jahr USA Publishing
375 Lexington Ave., 10th Fl.   Ph: (212)499-2000
New York, NY 10017-4024   Free: 800-599-8489
                 Fax: (212)499-2159
Contact: Jane Traulsene, Editor, (212)499-2084, fax: (212)499-2097; Sue Rapier, Advertising Dir., (212)499-2122, srapier@gjusa.com; Alison Kase, Publications Mgr., (212)499-2118, akase@gjusa.com; Molly Ingram, (212)499-2094, fax: (212)499-2097.
Desc: Consumer magazine for expectant parents. *Type:* Periodical.

Parents' Press

Parents' Press
1454 6th St.   Ph: (510)524-1602
Berkeley, CA 94710-1431   Fax: (510)524-0912
E-mail: parentsprs@aol.com.
Contact: Dixie Jordan, Editor.
Desc: Local consumer magazine covering parenting. *Type:* Periodical.

Parents Without Partners

401 N. Michigan Ave.   Ph: (312)644-6610
Chicago, IL 60611-4267   Free: 800-637-7974
                 Fax: (312)321-5194
E-mail: pwp@sba.com
URL: http://www.parentswithoutpartners.org
Contact: K.M. Bell, Exec.Dir.
Desc: Custodial and noncustodial parents who are single by reason of widowhood, divorce, separation, or otherwise. To alleviate the problems of single parents in relation to the welfare and upbringing of their children and the acceptance into the general social order of single parents and their children. *Type:* Association.

San Diego Parent

San Diego Parent
PO Box 3204   Ph: (818)846-0400
Burbank, CA 91504   Fax: (818)841-4300
Contact: Christine Elston, Editor; Kay Mount, General Mgr.
Desc: Newspaper. *Type:* Periodical.

Scouting

Boy Scouts of America
1325 W. Walnut Hill Ln.   Ph: (972)580-2000
PO Box 152079   Fax: (972)580-2079
Irving, TX 75015-2079
URL: http://www.bsa.scouting.org.
Contact: Jon Halter, Editor; Warren Young, Publisher.
Desc: Magazine for adult Scout leaders. *Type:* Periodical.

SHARE-Pregnancy and Infant Loss Support

St. Joseph's Health Center   Ph: (314)947-6164
300 1st Capitol Dr.   Free: 800-821-6819
St. Charles, MO 63301   Fax: (314)947-7486
E-mail: share@nationalshareoffice.com
URL: http://www.nationalshareoffice.com
Contact: Catherine Lammert, RN, Exec.Dir.
Desc: Participants are parents who have suffered the loss of a child through miscarriage, stillbirth, or early infant death; supporters. Purposes are: to provide comfort and support to the bereaved parents; to continue reassurance and care beyond the hospital stay; to encourage the physical and emotional health of the parents and siblings. Makes presentations accompanied by films. *Type:* Association.

South Florida Parenting

South Florida Parenting, Inc.
5555 Nob Hill Rd.   Ph: (954)747-3050
Sunrise, FL 33351   Free: 800-244-8447
                 Fax: (954)747-3055
E-mail: kbochi@tribune.com.
Contact: Lisa Goodlin, Advertising and Marketing Dir., (954)747-3051, lgoodlin@tribune.com.
Desc: Parenting magazine. *Type:* Periodical.

Successful Black Parenting

Successful Black Parenting
PO Box 6359   Ph: (215)476-7660
Philadelphia, PA 19139-6359   Fax: (215)476-1664
E-mail: blkparent@aol.com.
URL: http://www.netnoir.com/sbp/index.html.
Contact: Useni Eugene Perkins, Editor-in-Chief; Janice Robinson, Publisher; Marta Sanchez-Speer, Publisher, mspeer87@aol.com.
Desc: Magazine for black parents and extended family. Designed to support the black family in raising children. *Alt. Contact:* 2325 W. Ainslie, 2nd Fl., Chicago, IL 60625; telephone: (773)769-8422, (773)769-8423. *Type:* Periodical.

Today's Parent

Today's Parent Group
269 Richmond St. W   Ph: (416)596-8680
Toronto, ON, Canada M5V   Fax: (416)596-1991
  1X1
URL: http://www.todaysparent.com.
Contact: Beverly Topping, Pres./CEO; Mitchell B. Dent, Publisher/COO; Fran Fearnley, Editor-in-Chief.
Desc: Magazine for parents of children from birth to 12 with special emphasis on children newborn to three years old. *Type:* Periodical.

Toughlove International

PO Box 1069   Ph: (215)348-7090
Doylestown, PA 18901   Free: 800-333-1069
                 Fax: (215)348-9874
E-mail: tlove@netcarrier.com
URL: http://www.toughlove.org
Contact: Julene Burch, Exec.Dir.
Desc: A network of over 800 support groups for parents of children aged 8-50 with problems. Encourages parents to work together in the community to initiate and maintain positive behavior changes for children in trouble. Local support groups meet weekly; members volunteer to help other parents and kids with active support such as tutoring, driving to counseling, and negotiating living arrangements. *Type:* Association.

Triplet Connection

PO Box 99571   Ph: (209)474-0885
Stockton, CA 95209   Fax: (209)474-2233
E-mail: tc@tripletconnection.org
URL: http://www.tripletconnection.org
Contact: Janet L. Bleyl, Pres.
Desc: Parents and expectant parents of triplets or larger multiple births. Works to help families prepare and deal with high-risk multiple pregnancy and birth, and aftermath of such births. *Type:* Association.

United Bronx Parents

773 Prospect Ave.   Ph: (718)991-7100
Bronx, NY 10455   Fax: (718)991-7643
Contact: Lorraine Montenegro, Exec. Officer.
Desc: Community based organization. *Type:* Association.

Washington Families

Washington Families
462 Herdon Pkwy., Ste. 206   Ph: (703)318-1385
Herndon, VA 20170   Fax: (703)318-8509
E-mail: washfmly@family.com
URL: http://www.washingtonfamilies.com.
Contact: Brenda Mills Hyde, Publisher.
Desc: Consumer magazine covering parenting for families. *Type:* Periodical.

Parks and Recreation

American Land Rights Association

PO Box 400   Ph: (206)687-3087
Battle Ground, WA 98604   Fax: (206)687-2973
E-mail: alra@pacifier.com
URL: http://www.landrights.org
Contact: Charles S. Cushman, Exec.Dir.
Desc: Individuals holding property, equity interest, grazing permits, leases, mining claims, or real estate in or adjacent to federally managed areas such as national parks, forests, and other federal lands. Also includes people affected by the Endangered Species Act and the Clean Water Act. Seeks to ensure that members are treated fairly and consistently. *Type:* Association.

American Zoo and Aquariums Association

AZA Executive Offices   Ph: (301)562-0777
8403 Colesville Rd.   Fax: (301)562-0888
Ste. 710
Silver Spring, MD 20910-3314
E-mail: sbutler@aza.org
URL: http://www.aza.org
Contact: Syd Butler, Exec.Dir.
Desc: Zoological park and aquarium personnel; individuals interested in promoting zoos and aquariums for educational and scientific interpretation of nature and animal conservation and for public recreation and cultural pursuits. *Type:* Association.

Foreign Affairs Recreation Association

Department of State Bldg., Rm. Ph: (202)530-5657
2928 Fax: (202)530-5752
320 21st St. NW
Washington, DC 20520

Contact: Edwin Leffler, Gen.Mgr.

Desc: Employees of Action, the Agency for International Development, the Arms Control and Disarmament Agency, the United States Information Agency, the State Department, and the Peace Corps; associate members are employees of other government agencies; affiliate members are other interested individuals. Offers members a program of cultural, social, and physical activities. Programs include housing, barber shop, retail, film, and mail-order stores, service center for discount ticket sales, business cards, and valet shop. *Type:* Association.

Friends of the National Zoo

National Zoological Park Ph: (202)673-4950
Washington, DC 20008 Fax: (202)673-4738

URL: http://www.fonz.org

Contact: Clinton A. Fields, Exec.Dir.

Desc: Dedicated to providing biological education, to protecting the environment, and to serving the needs of visitors and the community for high quality recreational experiences. *Type:* Association.

Government Product News—Buyers Guide for Park and Recreation Equipment Issue

Penton Media Inc.

1100 Superior Ave. Ph: (216)696-7000
Cleveland, OH 44114-2543 Fax: (216)931-9524

E-mail: corpcomm@penton.com

Contact: Leslie Drahos, Editor.

Desc: List of over 1,100 manufacturers of park and recreation products and equipment. *Type:* Directory.

International Association of Amusement Parks and Attractions

1448 Duke St. Ph: (703)836-4800
Alexandria, VA 22314 Fax: (703)836-4801

URL: http://www.iaapa.org

Contact: John R. Graff, Pres. & CEO.

Desc: Operators of amusement parks, tourist attractions, water parks, miniature golf courses, and family entertainment centers; manufacturers and suppliers of amusement equipment and services. *Type:* Association.

National Parks and Conservation Association

1776 Massachusetts Ave. NW, Ph: (202)223-6722
Ste. 200 Free: 800-NAT-PARK
Washington, DC 20036 Fax: (202)659-0650

E-mail: npca@npca.org

URL: http://www.npca.org

Contact: Carol Aten, Exec.VP.

Desc: Seeks to protect, preserve, and enhance the U.S. National Park System. *Type:* Association.

Species in Parks: Flora and Fauna Database

University of California, Davis - Information Center for the Environment

Division of Environmental Ph: (916)752-8027
Studies Fax: (916)752-3350
Davis, CA 95616

E-mail: info@ice.ucdavis.edu

URL: http://ice.ucdavis.edu/nps/

Contact: Dr. James F. Quinn, jfquinn@ucdavis.edu.

Desc: The NP Flora and Fauna databases allow users to efficiently access, edit, and retrieve information contained in Park vertebrate animal and vascular plant survey databases. NP Flora and NP Fauna are tools to manage species lists and related metadata. *Type:* Database.

Waters

Vancouver Aquarium Marine Science Centre

PO Box 3232 Ph: (604)659-3474
Vancouver, BC, Canada V6B Fax: (604)659-3515
3X8

Contact: Sheila Hill, Editor, (604)659-3402, hills@vanaqua.org.

Desc: Recurring features include a calendar of events, news of educational opportunities, and articles of marine interest. *Type:* Newsletter.

Pathology

American Registry of Pathology

c/o Armed Forces Institute of Ph: (202)782-2143
Pathology Fax: (202)782-4567
14th St. & Alaska Ave. NW
Washington, DC 20306-6000

Contact: Donald West King, M.D., Exec.Dir.

Desc: Engages in cooperative enterprises in medical research and education with the Armed Forces Institute of Pathology . Functions as a fiscal agent in the management of research grants and monies derived from tuition fees publications and contributions. Serves as a link between, and encourages cooperation among, the military and civilian medical, dental, and veterinary communities for the mutual benefit of military and civilian medicine. *Type:* Association.

American Society of Clinical Pathologists

2100 W. Harrison Ph: (312)738-1336
Chicago, IL 60612 Free: 800-621-4142
  Fax: (312)738-1619

Contact: Robert C. Rock, M.D., Exec.VP.

Desc: Works to promote public health and safety by the appropriate application of pathology and laboratory medicine. *Type:* Association.

Case Western Reserve University

Institute of Pathology

2085 Adelbert Rd. Ph: (216)368-5172
Cleveland, OH 44106 Fax: (216)368-0494

E-mail: mel@po.cwru.edu

URL: http://www.cwru.edu/med/pathology

Contact: Dr. Michael E. Lamm, Dir.

Desc: Immunology, immunopathology, aging, cell biology, neurodegenerative disease, and oncology. *Type:* Research center.

College of American Pathologists

325 Waukegan Rd. Ph: (847)832-7000
Northfield, IL 60093-2750 Free: 800-323-4040
  Fax: (847)832-8000

Contact: Lee VanBremen, Ph.D.,, Exec.VP.

Desc: Physicians practicing the specialty of pathology (diagnosis, treatment, observation, and understanding of the progress of disease or medical condition) obtained by morphologic, microscopic, chemical, microbiologic, serologic, or any other type of laboratory examination made on the patient. Fosters improvement of education, research, and medical laboratory service to physicians, hospitals, and the public. Provides job placement information for members. *Type:* Association.

International Academy of Pathology

Florabel G. Mullick

Armed Forces Institute of Ph: (202)782-2550
Pathology Fax: (202)782-7166
Center for Advanced Pathology
14th St. & Alaska Ave. NW
Washington, DC 20306-6000

Contact: Ms. Leslie Middleton, M.D., Sec.

Desc: Professional society of pathologists and medical scientists. Aim is to improve methods of teaching pathology.

Coordinates anatomical pathology, pathologic physiology, and comparative pathology; promotes research in pathology in medical schools, laboratories, hospitals, and medical museums. *Type:* Association.

Pathweb - Virtual Pathology Museum

University of Connecticut Health Center

Farmington, CT 06030 Ph: (860)679-2000

E-mail: pathweb@www2.uchc.edu

URL: http://pathweb.uchc.edu/

Contact: T.V. Rajan, Ph.D., Chairman, rajan@neuron.uchc.edu.

Desc: An impressively diverse collection of medical information, Pathweb provides an in-depth collection of images, information, and clinical data on pathology and related issues. Browse the database by organs, general disease process, or organ and process. *Type:* Database.

South Carolina Health and Environmental Control Department

Health Services Division

Laboratories Bureau

Division of Clinical Cytology

ED231 Parklane Rd. Ph: (843)734-5000
Columbia, SC 29223 Fax: (843)935-7357

Contact: Marc S. Busnardo, MD, Dir.

Desc: Nature of diseases and the changes caused by them. *Type:* Research center.

U.S. Armed Forces Institute of Pathology

Registry of Comparative Pathology

Washington, DC 20306-6000 Ph: (202)782-2440
  Fax: (202)782-9150

E-mail: org@email.afip.osd.mil

URL: http://www.afig.org/rcp

Contact: Dr. Timothy O'Niel, Dir.

Desc: Comparative pathology, histopathology, and animal models of human disease. Serves as a national resource center for consultation in comparative pathology. *Type:* Research center.

United States and Canadian Academy of Pathology

3643 Walton Way Extension Ph: (706)733-7550
Augusta, GA 30909 Fax: (706)733-8033

E-mail: iap@uscap.usa.com

Contact: Fred Silva, M.D., Sec.-Treas.

Desc: Works for the advancement of pathology teaching, practice, and research. *Type:* Association.

U.S. Department of Health and Human Services

National Cancer Institute

Laboratory of Pathology

NIH Bldg. 10, Rm. 2A33 Ph: (301)496-3185
10 Center Dr. MSC 1500 Fax: (301)402-0043
Bethesda, MD 20892-1500

Contact: Dr. Lance Liotta, Chf.

Desc: Surgical pathology and autopsy services at the Clinical Center of the NIH. Offers diagnostic electron microscopy studies and cytopathologic services, including exfoliative and fine needle aspiration; provides all types of histological services and staining procedures for National Cancer Institute scientists; and conducts research programs in various areas of experimental cancer research. *Type:* Research center.

U.S. Department of Health and Human Services

National Institute of Allergy and Infectious Diseases

Laboratory of Immunopathology

NIH Bldg. 7, Rm. 304   Ph: (301)496-1150
7 Center Dr., MSC 0760   Fax: (301)402-0077
Bethesda, MD 20892-0760

Contact: Dr. Herbert C. Morse III, Chf.

Desc: Mechanisms by which retroviruses and adenoviruses induce disease. Activities involve: evaluation of the genetic organization of viruses in relation to their pathogenic properties; definition of the characteristics of normal target cell population and the effects of viruses on these cells; and identification of host characteristics that influence the outcome of virus infections. *Type:* Research center.

U.S. Department of Health and Human Services

National Institute of Environmental Health Sciences

Division of Intramural Research

Pathology Branch

PO Box 12233   Ph: (919)541-5716
Research Triangle Park, NC Fax: (919)541-4714
    27709
E-mail: boorman@niehs.nih.gov
URL: http://jeeves.niehs.nih.gov/
Contact: Dr. Gary Boorman, Chf.

Desc: Histology, toxicological pathology, rodent pathology, anatomic pathology, alternate animal models, oncogene expression in rodent tumors, and air toxics. Also conducts long-term rodent and drinking water disinfection bi-products research studies. *Type:* Research center.

Universities Associated for Research and Education in Pathology, Inc.

9650 Rockville Pke.   Ph: (301)571-1880
Bethesda, MD 20814-3993   Fax: (301)571-1879
E-mail: uarep@pathol.faseb.org
Contact: Frances A. Pitlick, PhD, Exec.Off.

Desc: Administers and coordinates educational and research activities in human pathology, including studies on environmental factors in human diseases, environmental pathology, safety of food additives, health effects attributed to unregulated toxic waste disposal sites, accident and forensic pathology, and environmental health policies. Provides core material for pathology instruction to medical students and residents. *Type:* Research center.

University of Southern California

Lung Disease, Cancer, and Environmental Pathobiology

2011 Zonal Ave., HMR 201   Ph: (213)342-1165
Los Angeles, CA 90033   Fax: (213)342-3049
E-mail: rsherwin@hsc.usc.edu
Contact: Dr. Russell P. Sherwin, Hd.

Desc: Environmental and oncologic pathology, lung disease, cancer, lymphocytes, macrophages, air toxicants, general pathobiology, histochemistry, histopathology, radioisotopes, tissue culture, and electron microscopy, including studies on pathogenesis of lung and breast cancer, pathogenesis and pathologic diagnosis of pulmonary emphysema, biologic effects of air pollution, and computer-assisted image analysis. *Type:* Research center.

Peace

Baptist Peace Fellowship of North America

4800 Wedgewood Dr.   Ph: (704)521-6051
Charlotte, NC 28209   Fax: (704)521-6053
URL: http://www.bpfna.org
Contact: Ken Sehested, Exec.Dir.

Desc: Baptists from various conventions interested in focusing attention on peace and justice issues. Conducts educational and charitable programs; maintains speakers' bureau; offers children's programs. *Type:* Association.

Buddhist Peace Fellowship

Dept. E   Ph: (510)655-6169
PO Box 4650   Fax: (510)655-1369
Berkeley, CA 94704
E-mail: bpf@bpf.org
URL: http://www.bpf.org/
Contact: Alan Senauke, Dir.

Desc: Devoted to the cultivation of world wide peace, social justice, nonviolence, and environmental activism. Objectives include witnessing to the Buddhist commitment to nonviolence as a means of social change, and promoting national and international Buddhist peace projects. BPF members work in disarmament and environmental campaigns, and provide support for homeless people and Buddhist prisoners. *Type:* Association.

Clergy and Laity Concerned

340 Mead Rd.
Decatur, GA 30030
Contact: Marian Willingham, Co-Chair.

Desc: Individuals of different races, religions, ages, ethnic and economic backgrounds. Seeks "to bring moral, ethical, and religious values to bear on issues of human rights, racial and gender justice, militarism, and economic justice at home and abroad." *Type:* Association.

Council for a Livable World

110 Maryland Ave. NE, Ste.   Ph: (202)543-4100
    409   Fax: (202)543-6297
Washington, DC 20002
E-mail: clw@clw.org
URL: http://www.clw.org
Contact: John Isaacs, Pres./Exec. Dir.

Desc: Endorses and raises funds for Senate candidates who support arms control and reduced military spending. Concentrates efforts on the U.S. Senate, "which has unique powers in foreign affairs and military spending." *Type:* Association.

Disarm Education Fund

36 E. 12th St., 6th Fl.   Ph: (212)475-3232
New York, NY 10003   Fax: (212)979-1583
E-mail: disarm@igc.apc.org
Contact: Robert Schwartz, Exec.Dir.

Desc: Promotes international peace, social justice, and self-determination through opposition to military intervention and nuclear arms. Supports a demilitarized foreign policy and believes that freedom from war is a fundamental human right. *Type:* Association.

Fellowship of Reconciliation

PO Box 271   Ph: (914)358-4601
Nyack, NY 10960   Fax: (914)358-4924
E-mail: for@forusa.org
URL: http://www.nonviolence.org/for
Contact: Virginia Baron, Exec.Dir.

Desc: Interfaith organization. Committed to creating peace and justice, locally and globally, using education, training, coalition-building, and nonviolent action. *Type:* Association.

International Association of Educators for World Peace

PO Box 3282, Mastin Lake Sta.   Ph: (256)534-5501
Huntsville, AL 35810   Fax: (256)536-1018
E-mail: mercieca@hiwaay.net
Contact: Charles Mercieca, Ph.D., Exec.VP.

Desc: Teachers, students, attorneys, medical doctors, social workers, clergy, businesspeople, and other individuals united to achieve world peace and better international relations through education. Promotes improved curriculum and methods of instruction in schools and seeks to implement the United Nations Universal Declaration of Human Rights. Cooperates with programs organized by the United Nations Educational, Scientific, and Cultural Organization . *Type:* Association.

International Peace Academy

777 United Nations Plz., 4th Fl.   Ph: (212)687-4300
New York, NY 10017   Fax: (212)983-8246
E-mail: ipa@ipacademy.org
URL: http://www.ipacademy.org
Contact: David Malone, Pres.

Desc: Private postgraduate educational institute for professional training in skills of conflict management. All meetings and programs of the academy are by invitation only and not open to the public. Conducts international training seminars in the Middle East, Europe, Africa, Latin and North America, and Asia. *Type:* Association.

National Peace Corps Association

1900 L St. NW, Ste. 205   Ph: (202)293-7728
Washington, DC 20036   Fax: (202)293-7554
URL: http://www.rpcv..org
Contact: Charles F. Dambach, Pres.

Desc: Former Peace Corps staff and Peace Corps volunteers who have returned to the U.S. from duty overseas; associate members are interested individuals who have not served in the Peace Corps. *Type:* Association.

National Peace Foundation

1819 H St. NW, Ste. 1200   Ph: (202)223-1770
Washington, DC 20006   Free: 800-23-PEACE
                            Fax: (202)223-1718
E-mail: ntlpeace@aol.com
URL: http://www.nationalpeace.org
Contact: Stephen P. Strickland, Pres. & Bd.Chm.

Desc: Individuals and organizations seeking to advance conflict resoultion and peace education; supports the efforts of the U.S. Institute of Peace . Provides information and education regarding the management and resolution of conflict. *Type:* Association.

Pax Christi - U.S.A.

532 W. 8th St.   Ph: (814)453-4955
Erie, PA 16502   Fax: (814)452-4784
E-mail: info@paxchristiusa.org
URL: http://www.nonviolence.org/pcusa
Contact: Nancy Small, Natl. Coord.

Desc: Roman Catholics and others committed to the Christian ideal of nonviolence. Works for disarmament and demilitarization, economic and interracial justice, human rights and global restoration, education for peace, and alternatives to violence. *Type:* Association.

Peace Action

1819 H St. NW, No. 420
Washington, DC 20006
E-mail: gclark@peace-action.org
URL: http://www.webcom.com/peaceact/
Contact: Phyllis Gagnier, Exec. Officer.

Desc: Works through national and grassroots citizens' action to promote global nuclear disarmament, cut military spending, and end the international arms trade. *Type:* Association.

Peace Corps

1111 20th St., NW   Ph: (202)692-2100
Washington, DC 20526   Free: 800-424-8580
                           Fax: (202)692-2109
URL: http://www.peacecorps.gov
Contact: Mark Gearan, Dir.

Desc: Independent federal government agency; area offices, recruitment centers, and overseas operations. Seeks to: promote world peace and friendship; help people in other countries meet trained manpower needs; further mutual understanding among Americans and people from other countries. Volunteers are trained in language, technical, and cross-cultural skills. *Type:* Association.

Peace Pac—Congressional Update

Peace Pac
110 Maryland Ave. NE   Ph: (202)543-4100
Washington, DC 20002   Fax: (202)543-6297

Contact: Suzanne Kerr, Editor, skerr@ciw.org.

Desc: Profiles congressional candidates and their position on nuclear arms control. Reviews congressional races and endorses specific candidates. *Type:* Newsletter.

Quest for Peace

c/o Quixote Center   Ph: (301)699-0042
PO Box 5206   Fax: (301)864-2182
Hyattsville, MD 20782
E-mail: quixote@quixute.org
URL: http://www.igc.apc.org/quixote

Contact: Dolores Pomerleau, Co-Dir.

Desc: A project of the Quixote Center. Religious, human rights, and social justice organizations and individuals interested in providing development and humanitarian aid to the people of Nicaragua and Haiti, including items such as vegetable seeds, clothing, and school supplies. Provides packing and shipping services for groups interested in sending humanitarian aid to Nicaragua. *Type:* Association.

Sri Chinmoy Oneness-Home Peace Run

c/o Peace Runs International   Ph: (718)760-0250
61-20 Grand Central Pky., Ste.   Fax: (718)592-1696
B-408
Forest Hills, NY 11375
E-mail: pri@peacerun.com
URL: http://www.peacerun.com

Contact: Neil Vineberg, Exec.Dir.

Desc: Organizes biennial international relay run, featuring a lighted torch in the Olympic tradition, to support world peace and to demonstrate the power of individuals working together toward a common goal. Maintains speakers' bureau; sponsors educational programs. *Type:* Association.

U.S. Institute of Peace

1200 17th St. Nw, Ste. 200   Ph: (202)457-1700
Washington, DC 20036-3011   Fax: (202)429-6063
E-mail: usip_requests@usip.org
URL: http://www.usip.org

Contact: Richard H. Solomon, Pres.

Desc: Federally funded institute created by the U.S. Congress; directors are appointed by the U.S. president with Senate approval. *Type:* Association.

Witness for Peace

1229 15th St. NW   Ph: (202)588-1472
Washington, DC 20005   Fax: (202)588-1572
E-mail: witness@witnessforpeace.org
URL: http://www.witnessforpeace.org

Contact: Steven Bennett, Exec.Dir.

Desc: Grass roots movement working through nonviolent action to change those U.S. foreign and economic policies that lead to poverty and oppression in Latin American and the Carribean, and to offer just alternatives. Activists and volunteers engage in direct action to affect positive policy Changes. *Type:* Association.

Women's International League for Peace and Freedom, U.S. Section

1213 Race St.   Ph: (215)563-7110
Philadelphia, PA 19107-1691   Fax: (215)563-5527
E-mail: wilpf@wilpf.org
URL: http://www.wilpf.org

Contact: Betty Burkes, Pres.

Desc: Women working, through nonviolent means, to: eliminate U.S. economic and military intervention abroad, discrimination on any basis, and governmental surveillance and repression; establish total universal disarmament and unconditional amnesty for war resisters; improve and ensure civil rights; promote peace education in schools and communities; establish "an economy that puts people before profits." Sponsors committee of educators and parents studying ways to teach peaceful attitudes in social relationships. Conducts research and seminar/training programs. *Type:* Association.

World Conference on Religion and Peace

777 United Nations Plz.   Ph: (212)687-2163
New York, NY 10017   Fax: (212)983-0566

Contact: Dr. William F. Vendley, Sec.Gen.

Desc: Leadership and institutions from major world religions. Develops effective international, multireligious cooperation in peace efforts. Works for a just international economic order, nuclear and conventional arms limitation, human rights, conservation of natural resources, conflict resolution, child issues and education for peace. *Type:* Association.

World Peace Prayer Society

800 3rd Ave., 37th Fl.   Ph: (212)755-4755
New York, NY 10022   Fax: (212)935-1389
E-mail: peacepal@worldpeace.org
URL: http://www.worldpeace.org

Contact: Mrs. Masami Saionji, Chairperson.

Desc: Persons advocating world peace. Purpose is to spread the message and prayer: "May Peace Prevail on Earth." Plants peace poles, 4-sided pillars with the message of peace inscribed on every side. Performs the World Peace Prayer Ceremony worldwide. *Type:* Association.

Pediatrics

American Academy of Pediatrics

141 Northwest Point Blvd.   Ph: (847)228-5005
Elk Grove Village, IL 60009-   Fax: (847)228-5097
0927
E-mail: kidsdocs@aap.org
URL: http://www.aap.org

Contact: Joe M. Sanders, Jr., Exec.Dir.

Desc: Professional medical society of pediatricians and pediatric subspecialists. Operates small member library of books and journals on pediatric medicine, office practice, and child health care policy. Maintains 48 committees, councils, and tasks forces including: Accident and Poison Prevention; Early Childhood, Adoption and Dependent Care; Infectious Diseases. *Type:* Association.

National Pediculosis Association—Progress

National Pediculosis Association
PO Box 610189   Ph: (617)449-6487
Newton, MA 02161   Free: 800-446-4NPA
          Fax: (617)449-8129

Contact: Deborah Z. Altschuler, Editor; Linda Menditto, Editor.

Desc: Provides new information on the diagnosis, treatment, prevention, and management of pediculosis (head lice), as well as other entomological diseases affecting children. *Type:* Newsletter.

Pediatrics

American Academy of Pediatrics
141 N.W. Point Blvd.   Ph: (847)228-5005
P.O. Box 927
Elk Grove Village, IL 60009-
0927
E-mail: journals@aap.org
URL: http://www.aap.org

Desc: Contains the complete text of Pediatrics, a monthly journal published by the American Academy of Pediatrics. Includes all images, tables, and figures from the original articles. *Available:* LEXIS-NEXIS, NEXIS; Ovid Technologies, Inc. *Type:* Database.

Pediatrics for Parents

Pediatrics for Parents, Inc.
PO Box 1069   Fax: (207)947-3134
Bangor, ME 04402-1069
E-mail: pediatricsforparents@pobox.com

Contact: Richard J. Sagall, Editor.

Desc: Provides information on children's health care and child safety. Carries original articles and abstracts on such topics as poison prevention, food labeling, and various childhood diseases and medical problems. *Type:* Newsletter.

Performing Arts

Actors' Equity Association

165 W. 46th St.   Ph: (212)869-8530
New York, NY 10036   Fax: (212)719-9815
E-mail: aeisenberg@actorsequity.org
URL: http://www.actorsequity.org

Contact: Alan Eisenberg, Exec.Dir.

Desc: AFL-CIO. Represents professional actors and stage managers. *Type:* Association.

American Federation of Musicians of the United States and Canada

1501 Broadway, Ste. 600   Ph: (212)869-1330
New York, NY 10036   Fax: (212)764-6134
E-mail: info@afm.org
URL: http://www.afm.org

Contact: Steve Young, Pres.

Desc: AFL-CIO. Musicians. Seeks to improve the wages and working conditions of members. *Type:* Association.

American Guild of Musical Artists

1727 Broadway   Ph: (212)265-3687
New York, NY 10019   Fax: (212)262-9088

Contact: Louise J. Gilmore, Exec.Sec.

Desc: AFL-CIO. Opera and classical concert singers, classical ballet and modern dance performers, and affiliated stage directors, stage managers and choreographers. *Type:* Association.

ArtSEARCH

Theatre Communications Group
355 Lexington Ave.   Ph: (212)697-5230
New York, NY 10017   Fax: (212)983-4847
E-mail: tcg@tcg.org; artsrch@tcg.org.

Contact: Carol Van Keuren, Dir. of Advertising, fax: (212)986-3432, ads@tcg.org.

Desc: Publishes classified listings for job opportunities in the arts, especially theatre, dance, music, and educational institutions. Listings include opportunities in administration, artistic, education, production, and career development. *Type:* Newsletter.

Association of Performing Arts Presenters

1112 16th St. NW, Ste. 400   Ph: (202)833-2787
Washington, DC 20036   Fax: (202)833-1543
E-mail: artspres@artspresenters.org
URL: http://www.artspresenters.org
Contact: Susan Farr, Exec.Dir.

Desc: Arts organizations involved in presentation of the professional performing arts; artists and artist management companies. Explores the roles, responsibilities, and opportunities for presenters, artists' managers, and artists, in order "to enable and celebrate the rich and diverse presenting field in its service to the public." *Type:* Association.

ENCORE

Encore Publishing, Inc.
87 Wall St.   Ph: (206)443-0445
Seattle, WA 98121   Fax: (206)443-1246
E-mail: adsales@encore.wa.com.
Contact: Paul P. Heppner, Publisher; Harry Oesterreicher, Executive Asst. to the Publisher.

Desc: Official program publisher for Seattle Opera, Seattle Symphony, Seattle Repertory Theatre, Pacific Northwest Ballet, A Contemporary Theatre (Seattle), Broadway Center for the Performing Arts (Tacoma, WA), Tacoma Actors Guild, Seattle Children's Theatre, Intiman Theatre, and The Paramount. *Type:* Periodical.

International Alliance of Theatrical Stage Employees, Motion Picture Technicians, Artists and Allied Crafts of the U.S. and Canada

1515 Broadway, Ste. 601   Ph: (212)730-1770
New York, NY 10036   Fax: (212)921-7699
Contact: Thomas C. Short, International Pres.

Desc: AFL-CIO; Canadian Labour Congress. *Type:* Association.

Opera News

Metropolitan Opera Guild, Inc.
70 Lincoln Center Plaza   Ph: (212)769-7080
New York, NY 10023   Fax: (212)769-8500
E-mail: info@metguild.org; info@operanews.com.
URL: http://www.operanews.com.
Contact: Rudolph S. Rauch, Editor and Publisher; Brian Kellow, Managing Editor; Jeffrey Hildt, Assoc. Publisher; Elaine Kones, Advertising Dir.; Anella Pereira, Circulation Mgr.

Desc: Opera magazine presenting news, reviews, and features. *Type:* Periodical.

Performing Arts Career Directory

Gale Group Inc.
27500 Drake Rd.   Ph: (248)699-4253
Farmington Hills, MI 48331-   Free: 800-877-GALE
3535   Fax: (248)699-8070
E-mail: galeord@galegroup.com
URL: http://www.galegroup.com.
Contact: Bradley J. Morgan, Editor; Joseph M. Palmisano, Editor.

Desc: Over 360 organizations in the performing arts offering entry-level positions and internships, including commercial and nonprofit performing arts centers, companies, and festivals; Broadway, Off-Broadway, regional and community theater companies; music ensembles; dance companies and troupes; and theater production companies. Also lists sources of help-wanted ads, professional associations, producers of videos, databases, career guides, and professional guides and handbooks. *Type:* Directory.

Screen Actors Guild

5757 Wilshire Blvd.   Ph: (213)954-1600
Los Angeles, CA 90036-3635
URL: http://www.sag.com
Contact: Ken Orsatti, Exec.Dir.

Desc: AFL-CIO. Compiles statistics. *Type:* Association.

Show Biz News & Model News

Show Biz News & Model News
244 Madison Ave., Ste. 393   Ph: (212)969-8715
New York, NY 10016   Fax: (212)969-8715
Contact: John King, Publisher.

Desc: Model and show business news magazine. *Alt. Contact:* telephone: (516)763-7499. *Type:* Periodical.

Wolf Trap Foundation for the Performing Arts

1624 Trap Rd.   Ph: (703)255-1920
Vienna, VA 22182   Fax: (703)255-1905
E-mail: wolftrap@wolf-trap.org
URL: http://www.wolf-trap.org
Contact: Terrence D. Jones, Jr., Pres. & CEO.

Desc: Established at the request of the Secretary of the Interior to fund and contract programs at Wolf Trap Farm Park for the Performing Arts. Created by an Act of Congress in 1966, Wolf Trap Farm Park is the first National Park dedicated to the performing arts. Presents opera, musical comedy, ballet, theater, modern dance, and classical and pop concerts in the Filene Center, the park's 7000 person capacity outdoor theater, and in The Barns of Wolf Trap, a 350-seat theater with performances year-round. *Type:* Association.

Petroleum

Advanced Recovery Week

Pasha Publications, Inc.
1600 Wilson Blvd., Ste. 600   Ph: (703)528-1244
Arlington, VA 22209
E-mail: superfnd@psha.com
URL: http://www.207.197.196.194
Desc: Contains the complete text of Advanced Recovery Week, a weekly newsletter on tertiary oil recovery. Provides technical and economic analyses of current recovery projects. *Type:* Database.

American Association of Professional Landmen

4100 Fossil Creek Blvd.   Ph: (817)847-7700
Fort Worth, TX 76137-2791   Fax: (817)847-7704
E-mail: aapl@landman.org
URL: http://www.landman.org
Contact: Robin Forte', Dir. of Education.

Desc: Professional society of petroleum landmen, independent lease brokers, oil operators, and company exploration managers. Supports a four-year college curriculum developed by AAPL and a trust fund granting scholarships to students. Sponsors annual local and national institutes; approves industry forms. *Type:* Association.

American Petroleum Institute

1220 L St. NW   Ph: (202)682-8000
Washington, DC 20005   Fax: (202)682-8029
URL: http://www.ati.org
Contact: Red Cavaney, Pres. & CEO.

Desc: Corporations in the petroleum and allied industries, including producers, refiners, marketers, and transporters of crude oil, lubricating oil, gasoline, and natural gas. Provides public policy development, advocacy, research, and technical services to enhance the ability of the petroleum industry to fulfill its mission: meeting the nation's energy needs; enhancing the environmental, health, and safety performance of the industry; conducting research to advance petroleum technology, equipment, and standards. *Type:* Association.

CASI Report

Convenient Automotive Services Institute (CASI)
PO Box 7010   Ph: (301)588-9077
Silver Spring, MD 20907
Contact: Larry Northrup, Editor.

Desc: Reports on current activities in the quick oil change market, including trends, regulatory news, and business ideas. Recurring features include letters to the editor, interviews, news of research, a calendar of events, reports of meetings, news of educational opportunities, notices of publications available, and columns titled Washington Report, Industry News, and Management Matters. *Type:* Newsletter.

Compoundings

Independent Lubricant Manufacturers Association
651 S. Washington St.   Ph: (703)684-5574
Alexandria, VA 22314-4109   Fax: (703)836-8503
E-mail: ilma@ilma.org
URL: http://www.ilma.org; http://www.compoundings.org.
Contact: Michael Cannizzaro, Editor, editor@ilma.org.

Desc: Presents timely technical and marketing news about the lubricant manufacturing industry. Covers trends, new products, legislative, and regulatory information. *Type:* Newsletter.

DRI World Oil Forecast

Standard & Poor's DRI
Data Products Division
24 Hartwell Ave.   Ph: (781)863-5100
Lexington, MA 02421
E-mail: client_services@dri.mcgraw-hill.com
URL: http://www.dri.mcgraw-hill.com
Contact: Client Resource Center, (781)860-6527, fax: (781)860-6416.

Desc: Contains approximately 250 quarterly and annual forecasts of production, stocks, consumption, and prices of crude oil worldwide. Covers 7 major industrial countries (Canada, Germany, France, Italy, Japan, United Kingdom, and United States), Organization of Petroleum Exporting Countries (OPEC), Mexico, other less-developed countries (LDC's), Communist countries, and non-Communist countries. *Available:* Standard & Poor's DRI, Data Products Division. *Type:* Database.

Energy Detente

Tele-Drop Inc.
PO Box 6002   Ph: (805)383-2400
Camarillo, CA 93011-6002   Fax: (805)383-2424
Contact: Trilby Lundberg, Editor and Publisher.

Desc: Provides petroleum statistics for western and eastern hemisphere. Includes refining netback pricing series, fuel price/tax series, and national petroleum end user prices in US dollars worldwide. *Type:* Newsletter.

Field Reports

Workover/Well Servicing Publications, Inc.
6060 N. Central Expwy., Ste.   Ph: (214)692-0771
428   Free: 800-692-0771
Dallas, TX 75206   Fax: (214)692-0162
Contact: Kristin Van Veen, Editor, kvaneen@aesc.net.

Desc: Covers industry news, legislative and regulatory issues concerning the energy services and business operations. Recurring features include columns titled Washington Update, Chapter Chat, and Rig Activity Report. *Type:* Newsletter.

Gas Research Institute

8600 W. Bryn Mawr Ave.   Ph: (773)399-8100
Chicago, IL 60631   Fax: (773)399-8170
URL: http://www.gri.org
Contact: Stephen D. Ban, Pres. & CEO.

Desc: Plans and manages research and technology development related to supply of natural gas, efficient gas-fueled appliances and equipment, distribution, safety and environmental impacts, and basic research. *Type:* Association.

Hart's Midcontinent Petroleum Directory

Hart Publications

1201 Seven Locks Rd., Ste. 300 Ph: (301)424-3338
Potomac, MD 20854 Free: 800-897-4278
  Fax: (301)309-9473

E-mail: hartinfo@phillips.com
URL: http://www.hartpub.com
Contact: Pauline Brown, Editor.
Desc: Nearly 10,000 firms involved in the petroleum industry in Oklahoma, Missouri, Arkansas, Kansas, Nebraska, Colorado, and the Texas Panhandle, including the Dallas-Ft. Worth area. *Type:* Directory.

Hart's Rocky Mountain Petroleum Directory

Hart Publications

1201 Seven Locks Rd., Ste. 300 Ph: (301)424-3338
Potomac, MD 20854 Free: 800-897-4278
  Fax: (301)309-9473

E-mail: hartinfo@phillips.com
URL: http://www.hartpub.com
Contact: Pauline Brown, Editor, pbrown@phillips.com.
Desc: About 10,000 petroleum companys, associations, and agencies in Arizona, Colorado, Idaho, Montana, Nebraska, Nevada, New Mexico, North Dakota, South Dakota, Utah, and Wyoming. *Type:* Directory.

Herold's Comparative Appraisal Reports

John S. Herold, Inc.

333 Ludlow St., Ste. 2 Ph: (203)359-4339
Stamford, CT 06902-6987 Fax: (203)359-0773
E-mail: tfrangione@herold.com.
Contact: Robert E. Gillon, Editor.
Desc: Supplies appraisals of the present value of oil, gas reserves, and other tangible assets of more than 120 oil companies (approximately 10-12 companies per issue). Utilizes the discounted cash flow method to help investors make "sound, safe and profitable investments." Recurring features include news of research. *Type:* Newsletter.

Houston/Texas Oil Directory

Atlantic Communications

1635 W. Alabama Ph: (713)529-1616
Houston, TX 77006-4196 Free: 800-654-1480
  Fax: (713)523-7804
E-mail: ac@oilonline.com
URL: http://www.oilonline.com/atcom.html.
Contact: Joey Villarreal, Editor; Sheila Renfro, Editor; Roland Martinez, Editor.
Desc: Nearly 11,000 Texas businesses involved in the oil industry. *Type:* Directory.

International Federation of Petroleum and Chemical Workers

435 S. Newport Way Ph: (303)333-7605
Denver, CO 80224
Contact: Curtis J. Hogan, Gen.Sec.
Desc: Workers in the petroleum and chemical industries. Fosters cooperation among members. Is currently undergoing reorganization. *Type:* Association.

International Petroleum Finance

Petroleum Intelligence Weekly

575 Broadway Ph: (212)941-5500
New York, NY 10012 Fax: (212)941-5508
Contact: Dillard P. Spriggs, Editor.
Desc: Analyzes the profits, finances, and management strategies of publicly and nationally owned companies in the oil industry. Includes OPEC financial developments, loans, borrowing, spending by oil companies, and statistics on stocks, drilling operations, and production. *Type:* Newsletter.

International Pipe Line and Offshore Contractors Directory

Energy Communications, Inc.

PO Box 50089 Ph: (214)954-0124
Dallas, TX 75250 Fax: (214)954-0129
E-mail: info@iplocadirectory.com
URL: http://iplocadirectory.com.
Contact: Abbott Sparks, Editor; Rita Aves, Assoc. Publisher; Janell Fowler, Publication Mgr.; Janell Fowler, Editor.
Desc: Over 220 pipeline and offshore contractors and suppliers in 128 countries. *Type:* Directory.

IUPIW Views

International Union of Petroleum & Industrial Workers, (IUPIW)

8131 E. Rosecranes Ph: (562)630-6232
Paramount, CA 90723 Free: 800-624-5842
  Fax: (562)408-1073

Contact: Robert Davidson, Editor.
Desc: Presents labor, safety, and consumer news for petroleum and industrial workers. Recurring features include obituaries, a schedule of activities, editorials, news of research, letters to the editor, news of members, and a calendar of events. *Type:* Newsletter.

National Petrochemical and Refiners Association

1899 L St. NW, Ste. 1000 Ph: (202)457-0480
Washington, DC 20036 Fax: (202)457-0486
URL: http://www.npradc.org
Contact: Urvan R. Sternfels, Pres.
Desc: Petroleum, refining and petrochemical manufacturers. *Type:* Association.

Nozzle Chatter

Association of Diesel Specialists

9140 Ward Pkwy. Ph: (816)444-3500
Kansas City, MO 64114-3313
E-mail: adshq@aol.com
Contact: Robert G. Stewart, Editor.
Desc: Provides news of the Association and the diesel industry. Recurring features include letters to the editor, news of research, a calendar of events, news of educational opportunities, and notices of publications available. *Type:* Newsletter.

OFFSHORE

PennWell Publishing Co.

1421 S. Sheridan Ph: (918)832-9346
Tulsa, OK 74112
E-mail: sandram@pennwell.com
Contact: Susan Anderson, Pennwell Directories Publisher, (800)544-7390.
Desc: Contains the complete text of Offshore, a magazine covering developments in offshore oil and gas exploration and production. Covers exploration, drilling, production, processing, and transportation; rig design and maintenance; and support operations. *Available:* LEXIS-NEXIS, NEXIS. *Type:* Database.

Oil/Energy Statistics Bulletin

Oil Statistics Company, Inc.

PO Box 189 Ph: (617)447-6407
Whitman, MA 02382 Fax: (617)447-3977
Contact: John J. McGilvray, Editor.
Desc: Provides company analyses for stock market recommendations on the investment merits of oil, gas, and competitive energy stocks, covering U.S., Canadian, and international oil producers and explorers. Discusses events "that have a bearing on the merits of investing in their shares." Recurring features include stock recommendations and follow-up advice. *Type:* Newsletter.

Oil Express

United Communications Group

11300 Rockville Pike, Ste. 1100 Ph: (301)287-2700
Rockville, MD 20852-3030 Free: 800-929-4824
  Fax: (301)287-2049
E-mail: customer@ucg.com
Contact: Andy Spitzler, Editor.
Desc: Provides news on independent marketing programs of major oil companies and instructional material on gasoline marketing. Includes news and guidance on convenience store operations and diversification ideas for petroleum marketers. *Type:* Newsletter.

Oil & Gas Journal

PennWell Publishing Co.

1421 S. Sheridan Ph: (918)832-9346
Tulsa, OK 74112
E-mail: sandram@pennwell.com
Contact: Susan Anderson, Pennwell Directories Publisher, (713)621-9720.
Desc: Contains the complete text of Oil & Gas Journal, a magazine covering oil and gas production, exploration, drilling, processing, marketing, and transportation. Provides legal and regulatory news, demand and supply forecasts, commentary on issues affecting the energy industry, and statistics covering rig counts, refinery production, and stocks and imports. *Available:* LEXIS-NEXIS, NEXIS; PennWell Publishing Co. *Type:* Database.

OPIS Petroleum Supply Europe

OPIS Directories

1255 Route 70, Ste. 32-N Ph: (732)901-8800
Lakewood, NJ 08701 Free: 800-275-0950
  Fax: (732)363-4271
URL: http://www.opisnet.com.
Contact: Nancy Menke, Editor, nmenke@opisnet.com; Michael Bailey, Editor.
Desc: 2,286 companies and 7,000 persons in petroleum supply in Europe, Africa, the Far East, and the Middle East. *Type:* Directory.

OPIS Petroleum Terminal Encyclopedia

OPIS Directories

1255 Route 70, Ste. 32-N Ph: (732)901-8800
Lakewood, NJ 08701 Free: 800-275-0950
  Fax: (732)363-4271
URL: http://www.opisnet.com.
Contact: Nancy Menke, Editor, nmenke@opisnet.com; Michael Bailey, Editor.
Desc: About 2,500 corporate and independently owned oil terminals capable of storing refined and crude oil products, natural gas liquids, petrochemicals, asphalt, or lube oil; coverage includes Canada and Europe. *Type:* Directory.

PESA News

Petroleum Equipment Suppliers Association

9225 Katy Fwy., Ste. 401
Houston, TX 77024
Contact: Ted Venker, Editor.
Desc: Reports news concerning oilfield tool manufacturers, service, and supply companies. Covers the activities of the Association, the oil industry, and related legislation. *Type:* Newsletter.

Petroleum Equipment Institute

PO Box 2380 Ph: (918)494-9696
Tulsa, OK 74101 Fax: (918)491-9895
E-mail: pei@peinet.org
URL: http://www.pei.org
Contact: Robert N. Renkes, Exec.VP.
Desc: Distributors and manufacturers of equipment used in service stations, bulk plants, and other petroleum marketing operations. *Type:* Association.

Petroleum Newsletter

National Safety Council
1121 Spring Lake Dr.   Ph: (630)285-1121
Itasca, IL 60143-3201   Free: 800-539-7468
    Fax: (630)285-1315
URL: http://www.nsc.org
Contact: Kathy Henderson, Editor.
Desc: Serves as a medium for the exchange of accident pre-vention information and techniques for personnel in occu-pations involving petroleum. Promotes safety awareness, safe practices, and safe products at home, on the road, and on the job. *Type:* Newsletter.

Petroleum Outlook

John S. Herold, Inc.
333 Ludlow St., Ste. 4
Stamford, CT 06902-6987   Ph: (203)869-2585
Contact: Randy S. Rose, Editor.
Desc: Reports on and analyzes the latest petroleum indus-try developments for energy investors. Supplies statistics on finding costs, reserves, and prices for a "universe of 50 small oil companies," alternating monthly with similar in-formation on 50 larger companies. *Type:* Newsletter.

Platt's Oil Export/Import Report

McGraw-Hill, Inc.
1221 Avenue of the Americas   Ph: (212)512-6410
New York, NY 10020
Desc: Covers movements of key crudes and petroleum products in the United States. Includes import and export statistics. *Available:* McGraw-Hill, Inc., Electronic Mar-kets and Information Systems (EMIS). *Type:* Database.

Platt's Oilgram News

McGraw-Hill, Inc.
1221 Avenue of the Americas   Ph: (212)512-6410
New York, NY 10020
Desc: Contains the complete text of Platt's Oilgram News, a newsletter on the oil and gas industry worldwide. *Avail-able:* The Dialog Corporation, DIALOG; LEXIS-NEXIS, NEXIS; Dow Jones Interactive Publishing. *Type:* Data-base.

Platt's Oilgram Price Report

McGraw-Hill, Inc.
1221 Avenue of the Americas   Ph: (212)512-6410
New York, NY 10020
Desc: Contains the complete text of Platt's Oilgram Price Report, a newsletter on the world oil and gas supply and prices. Covers crude oil markets, petroleum product prices and futures trading, supply and demand trends, techno-logical advances, and news of events that affect the oil and gas industry. *Available:* The Dialog Corporation, DIA-LOG; LEXIS-NEXIS, NEXIS; Dow Jones Interactive Publishing. *Type:* Database.

Platt's Oilgram Price Report

Standard & Poor's Platts
1221 Avenue of the Americas   Ph: (212)512-3320
New York, NY 10020   Fax: (212)512-3272
E-mail: feedback@platts.com
Contact: Shirley S. Savage, Editor, (212)512-2937, fax: (212)512-3272, ssava@platts.com.
Desc: Provides price information for crude and refined oil products. *Type:* Newsletter.

Platt's Petrochemical Report

McGraw-Hill, Inc.
1221 Avenue of the Americas   Ph: (212)512-6410
New York, NY 10020
Desc: Contains the complete text of Platt's International Petrochemical Report, a newsletter on the petrochemical industry worldwide. Covers supply and demand trends, company acquisitions, plant startups and shutdowns, con-tract awards, environmental issues, and legislation and reg-ulations. *Available:* The Dialog Corporation, DIALOG; Dow Jones Interactive Publishing; LEXIS-NEXIS. *Type:* Database.

Platt's Week

McGraw-Hill, Inc.
1221 Avenue of the Americas   Ph: (212)512-6410
New York, NY 10020
Desc: Reports forecasting developments in the petroleum industry. Provides market information, industry statistics, and interviews with industry figures. *Available:* McGraw-Hill, Inc., Electronic Markets and Information Systems (EMIS). *Type:* Database.

Service Station Dealers of America

9420 Annapolis Rd., No. 311   Ph: (301)577-4956
Lanham, MD 20706   Fax: (301)731-0039
Contact: Roy Littlefield, Exec.VP.
Desc: Service station operators and affiliated state and local associations. *Type:* Association.

SGA Directory

Oildom Publishing Co. of Texas, Inc.
14515 Briarhills Pkwy., No. 208   Ph: (281)558-6930
Houston, TX 77077   Fax: (281)558-7029
Type: Directory.

Society of Independent Gasoline Marketers of America

11911 Freedom Dr., Ste. 590   Ph: (703)709-7000
Reston, VA 20190   Fax: (703)709-7007
Contact: Kenneth A. Doyle, Exec.VP.
Desc: Chain gasoline marketers, wholesale and retail. In-forms members of current governmental and legislative ac-tivities; represents the marketers' interests before government and legislative and regulatory agencies; pro-vides statistical data on industry. *Type:* Association.

Society of Petroleum Engineers

222 Palisades Creek Dr.   Ph: (972)952-9393
Richardson, TX 75080   Fax: (972)952-9435
E-mail: spedal@spelink.spe.org
URL: http://www.spe.org
Contact: Georgeann Bilich, Contact.
Desc: Worldwide professional society of engineers in the field of petroleum engineering. *Type:* Association.

Society of Professional Well Log Analysts

8866 Gulf Fwy., Ste. 320   Ph: (713)947-8727
Houston, TX 77017   Fax: (713)947-7181
E-mail: vicki@spwla.org
URL: http://www.spwla.org
Contact: Vicki J. King, Exec.Dir.
Desc: Engineers and geologists who evaluate sedimentary beds by electrical, nuclear, acoustic, lithological, or other means to determine the presence of gas, oil, and other nat-urally occurring substances. Works to investigate new log-ging tools and interpretation techniques and promote research in the field. *Type:* Association.

TulsaLetter

Petroleum Equipment Institute
PO Box 2380   Ph: (918)494-9696
Tulsa, OK 74101   Fax: (918)491-9895
E-mail: pei@peinet.org
Contact: Robert N. Renkes, Editor, rrenkes@peinet.org.
Desc: "Contains authoritative information on state and federal regulations, industry specifications, new products, management techniques, personnel changes and other in-formation" of special concern to the petroleum marketing equipment industry. Carries summaries of new Environ-mental Protection Agency (EPA) and Occupational Safety and Health Administration (OSHA) regulations covering gasoline and fuel oil marketing; legal advisories; informa-tion on industry trends; membership applications; and in-dustry personnel changes. *Type:* Newsletter.

Pets

American Pet Products Manufacturers Association

255 Glenville Rd.   Ph: (203)532-3602
Greenwich, CT 06831   Free: 800-452-1225
    Fax: (203)532-0551
E-mail: aferrante@appma.org
URL: http://www.appma.org
Contact: William Schoolman, Exec. VP.
Desc: U.S. Manufacturers and importers of pet products. Provides public relations program to promote pet owner-ship and pet care. *Type:* Association.

The Pet Companion

The Pet Companion
3871 Piedmont Ave., No. 305   Ph: (510)533-7777
Oakland, CA 94611-5351   Fax: (510)533-7571
E-mail: petcom@earthlink.net
Contact: Grace Neufeld, Editor and Publisher.
Desc: Newspaper covering pet care and animal topics. *Type:* Periodical.

Petlife

Magnolia Media Group
300 W. 3rd St.   Ph: (817)215-9125
Fort Worth, TX 76102-2905   Fax: (817)215-9015
E-mail: lsimpson@mmqweb.com
Contact: C. C. Risenhoover, Publisher, crisenhoover@mmqweb.com.
Desc: Magazine for pet lovers, covering dogs, cats, horses. *Type:* Periodical.

World Wide Pet Supply Association

406 S. 1st Ave.   Ph: (626)447-2222
Arcadia, CA 91006-3829   Fax: (626)447-8350
E-mail: info@wwpsa.com
Contact: Doug Poindexter, Exec.VP.
Desc: Manufacturers, retailers, and distributors of pet food and services and of avian, aquarium, and companion ani-mal care products, equipment, and services. Seeks to ad-vance the economic interests of members; promotes responsible pet ownership. Conducts trade shows, certifi-cate training courses, and seminars for pet shop retailers, grooming establishments, and veterinary clinics. *Type:* As-sociation.

Pharmaceuticals

AHCA Notes

American Health Care Association
1201 L St. NW   Ph: (202)842-4444
Washington, DC 20005   Fax: (202)842-3860
URL: http://www.ahca.org.
Contact: Audrey Haar, Editor.
Desc: Presents information on nursing homes, assisted liv-ing, and residential care facilities. Covers legislation on prescription drug prices, nurse assistant training, certifica-tion enforcement, Medicare/Medicaid and long term care requirements, and legal activities. *Type:* Newsletter.

American Association of Pharmaceutical Scientists

1650 King St., Ste. 200   Ph: (703)548-3000
Alexandria, VA 22314-2747   Fax: (703)684-7349
E-mail: aaps@aaps.org
URL: http://www.aaps.org
Contact: John B. Cox, CAE, Exec.Dir.
Desc: Pharmaceutical scientists. Provides a forum for exchange of scientific information; serves as a resource in forming public policies to regulate pharmaceutical sciences and related issues of public concern. Promotes pharmaceutical sciences and provides for recognition of individual achievement; works to foster career growth and the development of members. *Type:* Association.

Consumer Health Product Association

1150 Connecticut Ave. NW   Ph: (202)429-9260
Washington, DC 20036   Fax: (202)233-6835
URL: http://www.chpa_info.org
Contact: James D. Cope, Pres.
Desc: Marketers (70) of nonprescription drugs, which are packaged, over-the-counter medicines; associate members (150) include suppliers, advertising agencies, and advertising media. *Type:* Association.

Drug Information Fulltext

American Society of Health-System Pharmacists (ASHP)
7272 Wisconsin Ave.   Ph: (301)657-3000
Bethesda, MD 20814
E-mail: kgibbons@ashp.org
Desc: Contains the complete text of approximately 1500 monographs covering more than 50,000 commercially available and experimental drugs in the United States. Covers uses, interactions, pharmacokinetics, dosage, administration, chemistry, stability, adverse reactions, and preparation information. *Available:* Ovid Technologies, Inc.; Oxford Molecular Group, Chemical Information Systems; The Dialog Corporation, DIALOG; CompuServe Information Service, Knowledge Index; The Dialog Corporation, DataStar; LEXIS-NEXIS. *Type:* Database.

Drug Topics

Medical Economics Co.
5 Paragon Dr.   Ph: (201)358-7500
Montvale, NJ 07645-1725   Free: 800-223-0581
    Fax: (201)358-7260
E-mail: customer.service@medec.com; drug_topics@medec.com.
Contact: Valentine Cardinale, Editor; Lee A. Maniscalco, Group Publisher; Harold E. Cohen, R. Ph., Publisher.
Desc: Newsmagazine for pharmacists. *Type:* Periodical.

First DataBank Blue Book

Hearst Corp.
645 Stewart Ave.   Ph: (212)969-7568
Garden City, NY 11530   Fax: (212)969-7564
Contact: Ed Edelstein, Editor.
Desc: List of manufacturers of prescription and over-the-counter drugs, sold in retail drug stores. *Type:* Directory.

Generic Pharmaceutical Industry Association

1620 Eye St. NW, Ste. 800   Ph: (202)833-9070
Washington, DC 20006-4005   Fax: (202)833-9612
E-mail: info@gpia.org
URL: http://www.gpia.org
Contact: Dr. Alice Till, Pres.
Desc: Manufacturers and distributors of generic medicines and providers of technical services and goods. Members are dedicated to providing quality pharmaceuticals to consumers at affordable prices. *Type:* Association.

Global Cosmetic Industry Catalog

Advanstar Communications
131 W. First St.   Free: 800-346-0085
Duluth, MN 55802
E-mail: fulfill@superfil.com
Contact: Karen Hoppe, Editor.
Desc: Over 1,400 manufacturers and suppliers of packaging, packaging equipment, private formulas, manufacturing equipment, aerosols, and raw materials used in drug and cosmetic manufacturing; industry associations and periodicals. *Type:* Directory.

Hayes Independent Druggist Guide

Edward N. Hayes, Publisher
PO Box 3436
Mission Viejo, CA 92690-1436
Contact: Jay Douglas Hayes, Editor.
Desc: Approximately 28,000 independent U.S. drug stores (those with 5 or fewer affiliate stores). *Type:* Directory.

International Pharmaceutical Abstracts

American Society of Health-System Pharmacists (ASHP)
7272 Wisconsin Ave.   Ph: (301)657-3000
Bethesda, MD 20814
E-mail: kgibbons@ashp.org
Contact: Kate Gibbons, Database Coordinator, (301)657-3000, fax: (301)657-1641, Kgibbons@ashp.org.
Desc: Contains more than 250,000 citations, with abstracts, to the world's literature dealing with the development and use of drugs or the clinical, practical, theoretical, scientific, economic, and ethical aspects of professional pharmaceutical practice. Covers pharmaceutical research, development and technology; adverse drug reactions and toxicity; drug evaluations, analyses, and interactions; pharmaceutical chemistry; and information processing for the pharmaceutical industry. *Available:* Ovid Technologies, Inc.; The Dialog Corporation, DataStar; The Dialog Corporation, DIALOG; STN International; DIMDI (Deutsches Institut fuer Medizinische Dokumentation und Information); EBSCO Publishing; U.S. National Library of Medicine (NLM), TOXNET; American Society of Health-System Pharmacists (ASHP). *Type:* Database.

International Society for Pharmaceutical Engineering

3816 W. Linebaugh Ave., No.   Ph: (813)960-2105
412   Fax: (813)264-2816
Tampa, FL 33624
Contact: Robert P. Best, Pres./CEO.
Desc: Pharmaceutical, biotechnological, medical device, diagnostic, and cosmetic engineers and technicians in 60 countries who are responsible for designing, supervising, and maintaining process equipment, systems, and instrumentation in health care materials manufacturing facilities. Promotes information exchange between members and regulatory agencies; enhances productivity. Gathers and disseminates information; sponsors continuing education programs and seminars. *Type:* Association.

Monthly Prescribing Reference

Prescribing Reference, Inc.
170 Broadway, Ste. 1612   Ph: (212)766-7200
New York, NY 10038   Fax: (212)732-2360
Contact: Jeanette Murphy, R.Ph., Editor; Mark E. Bugni, Publisher.
Desc: Drug reference digest providing physicians with information on widely prescribed, OTC & FDA approved drugs. *Type:* Periodical.

NACDS Executive Newsletter

National Association of Chain Drug Stores
413 N. Lee St.   Ph: (703)549-3001
Alexandria, VA 22313
Contact: John Covert, Editor, jcovert@nacds.org.
Desc: Reports information for operators of chain drug stores, including industry concerns, government actions, activities of the Association, executive appointments and promotions, and obituaries. *Type:* Newsletter.

National Pharmaceutical Council

1894 Preston White Dr.   Ph: (703)620-6390
Reston, VA 20191   Fax: (703)476-0904
Contact: Karren Williams, Pres./CEO.
Desc: Pharmaceutical manufacturers producing high quality prescription medication and other pharmaceutical products. Generates research; conducts specialized educational programs, and forums. *Type:* Association.

Parenteral Drug Association

7500 Old Georgetown Rd., Ste.   Ph: (301)986-0293
620   Fax: (301)986-0296
Bethesda, MD 20814
E-mail: info@pda.org
URL: http://www.pda.org
Contact: Edmund M. Fry, Pres.
Desc: Individuals working in the research, development, or manufacture of parenteral (injectable) drugs and sterile products. Promotes the advance of parenteral science and technology in the interest of public health. *Type:* Association.

Pharmaceutical Manufacturers Association— State Capital Report

Pharmaceutical Manufacturers Association
1100 15th St. NW, Ste. 900   Ph: (202)835-3400
Washington, DC 20005
Contact: Ellen J. Franklin, Editor.
Desc: Reports state legislative and regulatory activities affecting the prescription drug industry. Provides synopses of new bills introduced in different states and updates of legislative actions in process. *Type:* Newsletter.

Pharmaceutical Ventures

Scitec Services, Inc.
5324 Sinclair Rd.   Ph: (614)433-0648
Columbus, OH 43229-5002   Fax: (614)433-0432
E-mail: bxnj14a@prodigy.com.
Contact: Frank McKim, Editor.
Desc: Covers emerging and development-stage pharmaceutical and biotechnology companies from an investor perspective. *Type:* Newsletter.

Pharmacy Today

American Pharmaceutical Association
2215 Constitution Ave., NW   Ph: (202)429-7557
Washington, DC 20037   Free: 800-237-2742
    Fax: (202)628-5425
E-mail: pharmtoday@mail.aphanet.org
URL: http://www.aphanet.org
Contact: Rick Harding, Dir. of Editorial; Mark R. Vogel, Managing Editor.
Desc: Reports news and opinions of interest to pharmacists. Includes comprehensive coverage of pharmacotherapeutic, legislative, and socioeconomic news of every segment of the pharmacy profession. *Type:* Newsletter.

Pharmacy Today

American Pharmaceutical Association
2215 Constitution Ave., NW   Ph: (202)429-7557
Washington, DC 20037   Free: 800-237-2742
    Fax: (202)628-5425
URL: http://www.aphanet.org

Contact: William J. Reynolds, Advertising Dir., (202)429-7582, fax: (202)628-5425, pharmtoday@mail.aphanet.org; Rick Harding, Dir. of Periodicals, (202)429-7557.
Desc: Reports on current news and opinions for pharmacists. *Type:* Periodical.

Physicians' Desk Reference
Medical Economics Co.
5 Paragon Dr.   Ph: (201)358-7500
Montvale, NJ 07645-1725   Free: 800-223-0581
                                  Fax: (201)358-7260
E-mail: customer.service@medec.com
Desc: List of 250 manufacturers of more than 4,000 commonly prescribed drug products. *Type:* Directory.

The Representative
NAGMR Consumer Products Brokers
401 N. Michigan Ave.   Ph: (312)644-6610
Chicago, IL 60611-4267   Fax: (312)321-5158
E-mail: nagmr@sba.com
URL: http://www.nagmr.org.
Contact: Jack M. Springer, Editor.
Desc: Contains Association, industry, and tax information for consumer product brokers who specialize in selling drug, health, and non-food products and beauty aids to food and drug chains and mass merchandisers. Recurring features include news of members, a calendar of events. *Type:* Newsletter.

Toiletries, Fragrances and Skin Care—The Rose Sheet
F-D-C Reports, Inc.
5550 Friendship Blvd., Ste. 1   Ph: (301)657-9830
Chevy Chase, MD 20815   Free: 800-332-2181
                                  Fax: (301)656-3094
E-mail: fdcr@clarknet.com
URL: http://www.fdcreports.com.
Contact: Catherine Heinze, Editor; Holly Mead, Editor; Carrie Weissenberg, Editor.
Desc: Covers the cosmetics industry, including regulatory and legal issues, scientific developments, testing methodologies, mergers and acquisitions, Europe 1992 factors, marketing strategies, new product launches, and advertising and retail promotions. Recurring features include columns titled In Brief, Marketing in Briefs, and Trademark Review. *Type:* Newsletter.

Tufts CSDD Newsletter
Tufts Center for the Study of Drug Development
192 South St., Ste. 550   Ph: (617)636-2185
Boston, MA 02111   Fax: (617)636-2425
E-mail: tuft_csdd@infonet.tufts.edu
Contact: Joseph A. DiMasi, PhD, Editor, (617)636-2116, jdimasi@infonet.Tufts.edu.
Desc: Provides information regarding economic and regulatory aspects of drug development. Recurring features include announcements of publications and news of staff activities. *Type:* Newsletter.

Pharmacy
Academy of Pharmaceutical Research and Science
American Pharmaceutical Assoc.   Ph: (202)628-4410
2215 Constitution Ave. NW   Free: 800-237-2742
Washington, DC 20037   Fax: (202)628-0443
E-mail: ssa@mail.aphanet.org
URL: http://www.aphanet.org
Contact: Scott S. Antall, Contact.
Desc: Pharmaceuticals, focusing on quality measurement, development of practice-based research, and outcomes research in the broadcast sense. *Type:* Research center.

Academy of Students of Pharmacy
2215 Constitution Ave., NW   Ph: (202)628-4410
Washington, DC 20037   Free: 800-237-APHA
                                  Fax: (202)783-2351
E-mail: apha-asp@mail.aphanet.org
URL: http://www.aphanet.org
Contact: Eloise D. Thibault, Asso. Dir., Student Dev.
Desc: A program of the American Pharmaceutical Association . Professional society of pharmacy students. Keeps members informed of the affairs of the APhA and the profession. *Type:* Association.

Alpha Zeta Omega
4422 Porpoise Dr.
Tampa, FL 33617
Contact: Bruce Strell, Dir.
Desc: Professional fraternity - men and women, pharmacy. Sponsors scholarships, grants-in-aid, and visiting lectureships at colleges where a chapter of AZO is maintained. Raises funds for the "City of Hope" in Los Angeles, CA, the Arthritis Foundation, and the Hebrew University of Pharmacy in Israel. *Type:* Association.

American Association of Colleges of Pharmacy
1426 Prince St.   Ph: (703)739-2330
Alexandria, VA 22314   Fax: (703)836-8982
E-mail: lalsop@aacp.org
URL: http://www.aacp.org
Contact: Richard P. Penna, Exec.VP.
Desc: College of pharmacy programs accredited by American Council on Pharmaceutical Education ; corporations and individuals. Compiles statistics. *Type:* Association.

American College of Apothecaries
Research and Education Foundation
PO Box 341266   Ph: (901)383-8119
Memphis, TN 38184   Fax: (901)383-8882
E-mail: acainfo@acaresourcecenter.org
URL: http://www.acaresourcecenter.org
Contact: D.C. Huffman, Jr., Exec.Dir.
Desc: Three-fold objective of the Foundation is to promote public welfare through development of services in institutions providing health care, encourage and conduct research to improve health care and education, and encourage health care practitioners to improve the quality and availability of their services. *Type:* Research center.

American Pharmaceutical Association - Academy of Pharmacy Practice and Management
Susan C. Winckler
2215 Constitution Ave. NW   Ph: (202)628-4410
Washington, DC 20037-2985   Free: 800-237-APHA
                                  Fax: (202)783-2351
E-mail: apha-appm@mail.aphanet.org
URL: http://www.aphanet.org
Contact: Janet N. Edwards, Assoc.Dir., Practice Development.
Desc: Pharmacists concerned with rendering professional services directly to the public, without regard for status of employment or environment of practice. Purposes are to provide a forum and mechanism whereby pharmacists may meet to discuss and implement programs and activities relevant and helpful to the practitioner of pharmacy; to recommend programs and courses of action which should be undertaken or implemented by the profession; to coordinate academy efforts so as to be an asset to the progress of the profession. Provides and cosponsors continuing education meetings, seminars, and workshops; produces audiovisual materials. *Type:* Association.

American Society of Consultant Pharmacists
1321 Duke St.   Ph: (703)739-1300
Alexandria, VA 22314-3563   Fax: (703)739-1321
E-mail: info@ascp.com
URL: http://www.ascp.com
Contact: R. Timothy Webster, Exec.Dir.
Desc: Registered pharmacists and educators who are largely concerned with pharmaceutical procedures within nursing homes and related health facilities. Works to: improve consultant pharmacist services to nursing homes and other long-term care facilities; define professional standards and to promote the certification of the profession; exchange information; sponsor and encourage the development of educational facilities and courses for the advancement of the profession; promote wider public information efforts; represent the interests of the profession before legislative and administrative branches of government; sponsor group service programs; promote public health and welfare. *Type:* Association.

American Society of Health System Pharmacists
7272 Wisconsin Ave.   Ph: (301)657-3000
Bethesda, MD 20814   Fax: (301)657-1251
Contact: Kate Gibbons.
Desc: Professional society of pharmacists employed by hospitals, HMOs, clinics, and other health systems. Provides personnel placement service for members; sponsors professional and personal liability program. Conducts educational and exhibit programs. *Type:* Association.

Animal Health Institute
501 Wythe St.   Ph: (703)684-0011
PO Box 1417-D50   Fax: (703)684-0125
Alexandria, VA 22313-1480
E-mail: webmaster@ahi.org
URL: http://www.ahi.org
Contact: Alexander S. Mathews, Pres. CEO.
Desc: Represents manufacturers of animal health products (vaccines, pharmaceuticals, and feed additives used in modern food production; and medicines for household pets). *Type:* Association.

BioTech Market News & Strategies
Conmar Enterprises, Inc.
PO Box 11155   Ph: (954)522-4344
Ft. Lauderdale, FL 33339   Fax: (954)522-7750
E-mail: biotek2000@aol.com.
Contact: Edward J. Chandler, Jr., Editor.
Desc: Offers market data and product development strategies to corporate executives in the biotechnology and pharmaceutical fields. Covers "new marketable applications in biotechnology, emerging competition worldwide," and "current market assessments and future projections including changing market segments, demographics, and characteristics." Features summaries of lawsuits related to biotechnology, patents, and environmental regulations. *Type:* Newsletter.

Center for Imaging and Pharmaceutical Research
Massachusetts General Hospital   Ph: (617)726-7832
East   Fax: (617)726-7830
Bldg. 149, 13th St.
Charlestown, MA 02129-2060
URL: http://cipr.mgh.harvard.edu
Contact: Dr. Gerald Wolf, Dir.
Desc: Use of modern imaging technology in drug development, including investigation of radiologic imaging approaches that more accurately measure local drug concentrations, drug activity, and drug-induced alterations in tissue perfusion and tissue metabolism. Specific activities include. *Type:* Research center.

Chain Drug Marketing Association

James Devine
43157 W Nine Mile Rd.   Ph: (248)449-9300
Novi, MI 48376   Free: 800-935-2362
      Fax: (248)449-9396
E-mail: cdma1@aol.com
URL: http://www.chaindrug.com
Contact: James Devine, Pres.
Desc: Drug store chains located throughout the world. Represents members in the market for merchandise; keeps them abreast of trends in relevant fields. *Type:* Association.

Consumer Pharmacist

ELBA Medical Foundation Inc.
1818 N. Trunbull Dr.   Ph: (504)833-3600
Metairie, LA 70004-1403
Contact: John F. DiMaggio, Editor.
Desc: Features letters to the editor, interviews, news of research, reports of meetings, book reviews, and columns titled Infobits, New Drugs, and OTC Preparations. *Type:* Newsletter.

Cooper Cardiology

3 Cooper Plz., Ste. 311   Ph: (609)342-2054
Camden, NJ 08103-1438   Fax: (609)342-6608
Contact: Barbara O'Connor, Dir.
Desc: Cardiological drugs, focusing on development and testing studies. *Type:* Research center.

Drug Information Association

501 Office Center Dr., Ste. 450   Ph: (215)628-2288
Fort Washington, PA 19034-   Fax: (215)641-1229
3211
E-mail: dia@diahome.org
URL: http://www.diahome.org
Contact: Joseph R. Assenzo, PhD, Exec.Dir.
Desc: Persons who handle drug information in government, industry, the medical and pharmaceutical professions, and allied fields. Seeks to provide mutual instruction on the technology of drug information processing in all areas, including collecting, selecting, abstracting, indexing, coding, vocabulary building, terminology standardizing, computerizing data storage and retrieval, tabulating, correlating, computing, evaluating, writing, editing, reporting, and publishing. Conducts workshops, symposia, and seminars. *Type:* Association.

DRUGDEX® System

MICROMEDEX®, Inc.
6200 Syracuse Way South, Ste.   Ph: (303)486-6400
300
Englewood, CO 80111-4740
E-mail: info@mdx.com
URL: http://www.micromedex.com
Contact: Customer Support.
Desc: Contains information on drugs. Comprises the following 3 files: • Drug Evaluations--contains about 775 monographs on drugs. *Type:* Database.

Florida A&M University

Center for Anti-Inflammatory Research

201 Dyson Pharmacy   Ph: (904)559-3310
Tallahassee, FL 32307   Fax: (904)599-3347
Contact: Henry J. Lee, Dir.
Desc: Anti-inflammatory steroids, including development of organic extraction procedures for pharmacokinetic studies. *Type:* Research center.

Galichia Research Institute

551 N. Hillside St., Ste. 340   Ph: (316)689-4198
Wichita, KS 67214-4923   Fax: (316)684-2738
E-mail: atunstall@galichia.com

URL: http://www.ks.research.com
Contact: Ann C. Tunstall, PhD, Dir.
Desc: Pharmaceutic drug and device studies. *Type:* Research center.

The Green Sheet

FDC Reports, Inc.
5550 Friendship Blvd., Suite 1   Ph: (301)657-9830
Chevy Chase, MD 20815
E-mail: fdcr@clark.net
URL: http://www.fdcreports.com
Desc: Provides news and information on the pharmacy profession and the pharmaceutical distribution system. *Available:* LEXIS-NEXIS, LEXIS. *Type:* Database.

Henry Ford Hospital

Sleep Disorders Center

2799 W. Grand Blvd., CFP3   Ph: (313)876-4417
Detroit, MI 48202   Fax: (313)664-3567
Contact: Thomas Roth, PhD, Dir.
Desc: Psychopharmacology of sleep, daytime sleepiness, and sleep disorders, including sleep-related apnea. *Type:* Research center.

Hospital Pharmacy Director's Monthly Management Series

Rx-Data-Pac Service
8907 Terwilliger's Trail
Cincinnati, OH 45249
Contact: Dr. I.H. Goodman, Editor.
Desc: Serves as a "guide to successful hospital pharmacy management." Offers ideas and strategies to improve decision making and curb absenteeism. *Type:* Newsletter.

IDENTIDEX® System

MICROMEDEX®, Inc.
6200 Syracuse Way South, Ste.   Ph: (303)486-6400
300
Englewood, CO 80111-4740
E-mail: info@mdx.com
URL: http://www.micromedex.com
Contact: Customer Support.
Desc: Contains identification information on more than 40,000 pharmaceuticals including prescription and OTC, trademarked, and generic drugs, "look-alike" stimulants, and street drugs, in tablet and capsule form. Users can search by manufacturer imprint code. *Type:* Database.

IDIS Drug File

University of Iowa
College of Pharmacy
Iowa Drug Information Service (IDIS)
100 Oakdale Campus, N330   Ph: (319)335-4800
OH
Iowa City, IA 52242-5000
E-mail: idis@uiowa.edu
URL: http://www.uiowa.edu/~idis
Contact: Donna Brus, (319)3354800, idis@uiowa.edu.
Desc: Contains more than 350,000 citations to worldwide English-language literature on human drug therapy. Each record identifies the article type (e.g., case report, clinical study) and covers population age, drug administration techniques, pharmacokinetics, toxicology, drug interactions, and side effects. *Available:* University of Iowa, College of Pharmacy, Iowa Drug Information Service (IDIS); The Dialog Corporation, DataStar; Ovid Technologies, Inc. *Type:* Database.

Indiana University-Purdue University at Indianapolis

Pharmacology Research Laboratory

Sch. of Med.   Ph: (317)274-7844
635 Barnhill Dr.   Fax: (317)274-7714
Indianapolis, IN 46202-5120
E-mail: besch@indiana.edu
Contact: Dr. Henry R. Besch, Jr., Chm.
Desc: Cardiovascular pharmacology, molecular toxicology, drug metabolism, cyclic AMP, membrane biophysics, cancer chemotherapy and cardiac glycosides, and antiarrythmics, including studies on metabolism of transplanted tumors, structure activity relations of cardiac glycosides, and tyanodine analogs. *Type:* Research center.

Institute for Clinical Science, Inc.

1833 Delancey Pl.   Ph: (215)829-7068
Philadelphia, PA 19103   Fax: (215)829-3094
E-mail: 104657,346@compuserve.com
Contact: Dr. F. William Sunderman, Pres./Dir.
Desc: Anatomic and clinical pathology, including studies in metal carcinogenesis and toxicology. *Type:* Research center.

Institute for Drug Development

14960 Omicron   Ph: (210)677-3800
San Antonio, TX 78245-3217   Fax: (210)677-0058
E-mail: dvonhoff@saci.org
URL: http://www.ctrc.saci.org
Contact: Daniel D. Von Hoff, MD, Dir.
Desc: Anticancer drug development. Research activities in the Discovery Research Section include functions of extrachromosomal DNA fragments in tumor cells; tumor progression (oncogenesis); differentiation of human tumors; amplified oncogenes and drug resistance genes on extrachromosomal DNA fragments; chromosomal rearrangement and mechanism of repair of broken chromosomes in mammalian cells; mapping of human chromosome 3; mapping on the short arm of human chromosome 17; and transgenic mouse models for various types of cancer. *Type:* Research center.

John P. Robarts Research Institute

Clinical Pharmacology Group

100 Perth Dr.   Ph: (519)663-5777
PO Box 5015   Fax: (519)663-3789
London, ON, Canada N6A 5K8
E-mail: feldmanr@lhsc.on.ca
Contact: Dr. Feldman, Dir.
Desc: Studies cardiovasular and immunosuppressive agents, both in vivo and in vitro, and drug analysis and pharmacokinetic and pharmacodynamic studies, as well as in vitro determinations of mechanisms of adverse drug reactions. *Type:* Research center.

Kappa Psi

Kappa Psi Central Office
University of Oklahoma HSC   Ph: (405)271-6942
College of Pharmacy   Fax: (405)271-3830
1110 N. Stonewall
Oklahoma City, OK 73190
E-mail: robert-magarian@ouhsc.edu
URL: http://www.kappa-psi.org
Contact: Robert A. Magarian, Ph.D., Exec.Dir.
Desc: Professional fraternity - pharmacy. *Type:* Association.

Lambda Kappa Sigma

2565-A U.S. 23   Free: 800-LKS-1913
Alpena, MI 49707
URL: http://www.lks.org
Contact: Karae Steinke, Exec. Dir.
Desc: Professional fraternity - pharmacy. *Type:* Association.

Laval University

Research Unit on Renal and Cardiovascular Pharmacology

Hotel-Dieu de Quebec Res. Ph: (418)691-5561
  Centre Fax: (418)691-5562
11, cote ju Palais
Quebec, PQ, Canada G1R 2J6
E-mail: elizabeth.lemay@crhdq.ulaval.ca
URL: http://www.crhdq.ulaval.ca

Contact: Dr. Marcol Lebel, Dir.

Desc: Pathogenesis of cardiovascular disorders, including high blood pressure, ischemic vascular diseases, and renal or cardiac therapies. *Type:* Research center.

Long Island University

Pharmaceutical Study Center

Schwartz College of Pharmacy Ph: (718)488-1234
1 University Plz. Fax: (718)488-0628
75 DeKalb Ave.
Brooklyn, NY 11201
E-mail: ayalan@hornet.liunet.edu

Contact: Alisa Yalan, Media Dir.

Desc: Pharmacy, pharmacology, pharmacy administration, drug information, and hospital pharmacy. *Type:* Research center.

Massachusetts Institute of Technology

Program on the Pharmaceutical Industry

Sloan Sch. of Mgt. Ph: (617)253-5194
38 Memorial Dr., E56-390 Fax: (617)253-3033
Cambridge, MA 02139-4307
E-mail: popi-www@mit.edu
URL: http://web.mit.edu/popi/

Contact: Stan N. Finkelstein, MD, Dir.

Desc: Competitiveness, performance, and productivity in the pharmaceutical field. *Type:* Research center.

MCP Hahnemann University of the Health Sciences

Laboratory of Human Pharmacology

Dept. of Pharmacology Ph: (215)762-8237
Sch. of Med. Fax: (215)762-3722
Broad & Vine Sts.
Philadelphia, PA 19102

Contact: Benjamin Calesnick, MD, Dir.

Desc: Using such analytical methods as chromatography, colorimetry, and spectrometry, the Laboratory studies the metabolism, potentiation, and toxicity of drugs, including antibiotics, ataractics, pesticides, sedatives, solvents, stimulants, aerosols, fumes, and radioactive chemicals. Also examines the induction or inhibition of microsomal metabolizing systems, and pollutants. *Type:* Research center.

Meadowbrook Medical Education and Research Foundation, Inc.

2201 Hempstead Tpke. Ph: (516)572-6724
East Meadow, NY 11554-1859 Fax: (516)572-5791

Contact: Alan F. King, Exec.Sec./Treas.

Desc: Clinical drugs studies. *Type:* Research center.

Medical Care and Research Foundation

1420 Ogden Ph: (303)831-0267
Denver, CO 80218-1910 Fax: (303)831-4079

Contact: Frank B. McGlone, MD, Exec.Dir.

Desc: Drug studies. *Type:* Research center.

The Medical Letter

Medical Letter Inc.
1000 Main St. Ph: (914)235-0500
New Rochelle, NY 10801 Free: 800-211-2769
  Fax: (914)576-3377
URL: http://www.medletter.com.

Contact: Mark Abramowicz, Editor.

Desc: Appraises new drugs in terms of their effectiveness, side effects, and possible alternative medications. Reviews other developments in medicine, including nondrug therapy and new diagnostic aids. *Type:* Newsletter.

Medical University of South Carolina

Interdisciplinary Program in Cell and Molecular Pharmacology and Experimental Therapeutics

171 Ashley Ave. Ph: (843)792-2471
Charleston, SC 29425 Fax: (843)792-2475
URL: http://www2.musc.edu/pharm/pharm.html

Contact: Dr. Harry Margolius, Chm.

Desc: Pharmacology, toxicology, molecular genetics and structural biology, including structure-function studies of proteins for primary sequence, posttranslational modifications, and characterization of the binding site of ligands; investigations of molecular design; and studies on cellular and molecular processes that control systemic arterial pressure, especially arachidonate metabolism, neurotransmitters, drug disposition and drug toxicity. Conducts studies of excitation-contraction coupling, excitation-secretion coupling, and water transport and regulation in cells and membrane mechanisms by norepinephrine, arachidonic acid metabolites, kallikrein-kinins, atrial peptides, and antihypertensive drugs. *Type:* Research center.

NAPM News Bulletin

National Association of Pharmaceutical Manufacturers (NAPM)
320 Old Country Rd. Ph: (516)741-3699
Garden City, NY 11530 Fax: (516)741-3696
E-mail: napmgenrx@aol.com; napmgenrx@aol.com.

Contact: Robert S. Milanese, Editor.

Desc: Focuses on the regulatory, legal, and technical aspects of the generic pharmaceutical industry. Covers legislative developments and changes in government regulations. *Type:* Newsletter.

National Association of Boards of Pharmacy

700 Busse Hwy. Ph: (847)698-6227
Park Ridge, IL 60068 Fax: (847)698-0124
URL: http://www.nabp.net

Contact: Carmen A. Catizone, Exec.Dir.

Desc: Pharmacy boards of several states, District of Columbia, Puerto Rico, Virgin Islands, several Canadian provinces, and the states of Victoria, Australia, and New South Wales. Provides for inter-state reciprocity in pharmaceutic licensure based upon a uniform minimum standard of pharmaceutic education and uniform legislation; improves the standards of pharmaceutical education licensure and practice. *Type:* Association.

National Association of Chain Drug Stores

Ronald L. Ziegler
413 N. Lee St. Ph: (703)549-3001
PO Box 1417-D49 Fax: (703)836-4869
Alexandria, VA 22313
URL: http://www.nacds.org

Contact: Ronald L. Ziegler, Pres. & CEO.

Desc: Chain drug members (130); associate members (1400) and (80) international members include manufacturers, suppliers, manufacturer's representatives, publishers, and advertising agencies. Interprets actions by government agencies in such areas as drugs, public health, federal trade, labor, and excise taxes. Sponsors meetings and pharmacy student recruitment program. *Type:* Association.

National Community Pharmacists Association

205 Daingerfield Rd. Ph: (703)683-8200
Alexandria, VA 22314-2885 Free: 800-544-7447
  Fax: (703)683-3619
E-mail: calvin.anthony@ncpanet.org
URL: http://www.ncpanet.org

Contact: Calvin J. Anthony, Exec.VP.

Desc: Owners and managers of independent drugstores and pharmacists employed in retail drugstores offering pharmacy service. Provides support for undergraduate pharmacy education through National Association of Retail Druggists Foundation. *Type:* Association.

National Council for Prescription Drug Programs

4201 N. 24th St., Ste. 365 Ph: (602)957-9105
Phoenix, AZ 85016 Fax: (602)955-0749
E-mail: ncpdp@ncpdp.org
URL: http://www.ncpdp.org

Contact: Lee Ann C. Stember, Pres.

Desc: Works to create and promote data interchange and processing standards to the pharmacy services sector of the health care industry; and to provide a continuing source of accurate and reliable information that supports the diverse needs of its membership. *Type:* Association.

National Wholesale Druggists' Association

1821 Michael Faraday Dr., Ste. Ph: (703)787-0000
  400 Fax: (703)787-6930
Reston, VA 20190
URL: http://www.nwda.org

Contact: Ronald J. Streck, Pres. and CEO.

Desc: Wholesalers and manufacturers of drug and health care products and industry service providers. Compiles statistics; sponsors research and specialized education programs. Has on-line e-mail bulletin service. *Type:* Association.

NWDA Executive Newsletter

National Wholesale Druggists' Association
1821 Michael Faraday Dr., Ste. Ph: (703)787-0000
  400 Fax: (703)787-6930
Reston, VA 20190

Contact: Lauren Asplen, Editor.

Desc: Reports trends and changes in the wholesale drug industry. Covers promotions within member companies, instructional and promotional material available, and Association activities. *Type:* Newsletter.

Ohio State University

Clinical Pharmacology Division

College of Med. Ph: (614)292-8600
Graves Hall, Rm. 5084 Fax: (614)292-4253
333 W. 10th Ave.
Columbus, OH 43210-1239
E-mail: gerber.2@osu.edu
URL: http://www.ohio-state.edu

Contact: Dr. Nicholas Gerber, Dir.

Desc: Clinical drug studies. *Type:* Research center.

Oregon Health Sciences University

DMSO Research Laboratory and Clinic

3181 SW Sam Jackson Park Ph: (503)494-8474
  Rd., L225 Fax: (503)494-5352
Portland, OR 97201
E-mail: whortonj@ohsu.edu
URL: http://www.dmso.org

Contact: Stanley W. Jacob, MD, Hd.

Desc: Pharmacological properties of dimethyl sulfoxide (DMSO). Provides staff consultants in clinical and basic research relevant to pharmacological activity of dimethyl sulfoxide. *Type:* Research center.

Pharmaceutical Care Management Association

2300 9th St. S., Ste. 210
Arlington, VA 22204-2320

Ph: (703)920-8480
Free: 888-SAY-PCMA
Fax: (703)920-8491

E-mail: pcma@pcmanet.org
URL: http://www.pcmanet.org
Contact: Delbert D. Konnor, Pres. & CEO.

Desc: Represents managed care pharmacy and its health-care partners in pharmaceutical care: managed healthcare organizations, PBMs, HMOs, PPOs, third party administrators, healthcare insurance companies, drug wholesalers, pharmaceutical manufacturers, and community pharmacy networks. Serves its members and America's healthcare system by promoting education, legislation, practice standards, and research that foster quality, affordable pharmaceutical care. PCMA members serve more than 150 million enrolled lives. *Type:* Association.

Pharmaceutical News Index®

Bell & Howell Information and Learning
300 N. Zeeb Rd.
PO Box 1346
Ann Arbor, MI 48106-1346

Ph: (734)761-4700

E-mail: info@umi.com
URL: http://www.umi.com
Contact: Paula McCoy, Associate Editor.

Desc: Contains more than 637,000 citations to business, legislative, and product news items reported in some major pharmaceutical and medical device newsletters: FDC Reports (Pink Sheet), 1974 to date; Drug Research Reports (Blue Sheet), December 1985 to date; Pharma Japan, 1983 to date; Clinica World Medical Devices News, 1983 to date; Medical Devices, December 1977 to date; Diagnostics and Instrumentation Reports (Gray Sheet), December 1977 to date; Quality Control Reports (Gold Sheet), December 1977 to date; Weekly Pharmacy Reports (Green Sheet), December 1977 to date; SCRIP World Pharmaceutical News, 1980 to date; FDC Reports (Rose Sheet), December 1984 to date; Technology Reimbursement Reports (Beige Sheet), early 1985 to date; Animal Pharm World Animal Health News, December 1984 to date; Applied Genetics News; Biomedical Business International, December 1984 to date; Biomedical Safety and Standards, December 1987 to date; Biomedical Technology Information Service, December 1987 to date; Clinical Lab Letter, December 1987 to date; Radiology and Imaging Letter, December 1987 to date; Health Devices, December 1984 to date; Health Business, 1989 to date; Health Legislation & Regulation, 1989 to date; and Medicine & Health, 1989 to date. Also covers Washington Drug and Device Letter and PMA Newsletter from December 1975 to November 1977. *Available:* Ovid Technologies, Inc.; Ovid Technologies, Inc.; OCLC Online Computer Library Center, Inc., OCLC EPIC.

Pharmacy Times

Romaine Pierson Publishers, Inc.
1065 Old Country Rd., Ste. 213
Westbury, NY 11590

Ph: (516)997-0377
Fax: (516)997-0344

E-mail: pharmtimes@aol.com.
Contact: Mary Jane Garvey, R.Ph., Publisher; Bruce Buckley, Editor-in-Chief.

Desc: Journal providing information on health items (including prescription and over-the-counter drugs and surgical supplies) to independent, chain, and hospital pharmacists. *Type:* Periodical.

Phi Delta Chi

PO Box 1883
Athens, GA 30603-1883

Ph: (706)613-0300
Fax: (706)613-0200

E-mail: phidexnatl@aol.com
URL: http://www.umich.edu/~jbonasso/pdcnew/home.htm

Contact: Anthony D. Chaffee, Exec.Dir.
Desc: Professional fraternity - pharmacy. *Type:* Association.

The Pink Sheet

FDC Reports, Inc.
5550 Friendship Blvd., Suite 1
Chevy Chase, MD 20815

Ph: (301)657-9830

E-mail: fdcr@clark.net
URL: http://www.fdcreports.com

Desc: Provides news and analysis of developments affecting prescription and over-the-counter drugs. Includes updates on regulatory policies and actions by the Food and Drug Administration (FDA), the Federal Trade Commission (FTC), Congress, the courts, and other federal and state agencies. *Available:* LEXIS-NEXIS, LEXIS; The Dialog Corporation, DIALOG; The Dialog Corporation, DIALOG; The Dialog Corporation, DataStar; Ovid Technologies, Inc.; Ovid Technologies, Inc. *Type:* Database.

The Pink Sheet

F-D-C Reports, Inc.
5550 Friendship Blvd., Ste. 1
Chevy Chase, MD 20815

Ph: (301)657-9830
Free: 800-332-2181
Fax: (301)656-3094

E-mail: fdcr@clarknet.com
URL: http://www.fdcreports.com.
Contact: Michael McCaughan, Editor, (301)664-7145, fax: (301)656-3094, mmccaugh@elsvier.com.

Desc: Provides in-depth news and analysis about developments affecting prescription medicines, including FDA, FTC, and HCFA policies and actions, as well as federal and state legislation affecting the drug industry. Coverage includes FDA recalls and seizures, mergers and acquisitions, biotechnology startups, new product activity, and company research and development. *Type:* Newsletter.

POISINDEX® System

MICROMEDEX®, Inc.
6200 Syracuse Way South, Ste. 300
Englewood, CO 80111-4740

Ph: (303)486-6400

E-mail: info@mdx.com
URL: http://www.micromedex.com
Contact: Customer Support.

Desc: Contains toxicological information on more than one million commercial, pharmaceutical, and biological substances. Covers commonly used household products, industrial chemicals and products, pharmaceutical products (prescription, generic, and over-the-counter (OTC)), and biological entities (botanic, zoologic, and food poisoning). *Type:* Database.

Reproductive Toxicology Center

Columbia Hospital for Women
2440 M St. NW, Ste. 217
Washington, DC 20037-1404

Ph: (202)293-5137
Fax: (202)778-6199

Contact: Anthony Scialli, MD, Dir.

Desc: Effects of the chemical and physical environment on human fertility, pregnancy, and development. *Type:* Research center.

Rho Chi

Duquesne University
School of Pharmacy
Pittsburgh, PA 15282

Ph: (412)396-6361
Fax: (412)396-5130

E-mail: bricker@duq2.cc.duq.edu
URL: http://www.duq.edu/pharmacy/rhochi.html
Contact: J. Douglas Bricker, National Sec.

Desc: Honor society - men and women, pharmacy. Presents annual Rho Chi Lecture. *Type:* Association.

Rockefeller University

Laboratory of Metabolism-Pharmacology

1230 York Ave.
New York, NY 10021-6399

Ph: (212)327-8494
Fax: (212)327-8690

Contact: Attallah Kappas, Hd.

Desc: Regulation of heme biosynthesis and heme catabolism as affected by those genetic and environmental factors that have major influences on the oxidative metabolism of drugs, hormones, and environmental chemicals in liver and other tissues. *Type:* Research center.

Rutgers University

Controlled Drug-Delivery Research Center

College of Pharmacy
41 Gordon Rd., Ste. D
Piscataway, NJ 08854

Ph: (732)445-6180
Fax: (732)445-6175

Contact: Prof. Yie W. Chien, Dir.

Desc: Transdermal controlled and enhanced drug delivery, noninvasive and modulated delivery of peptide/protein drugs, targeting drug delivery, and transmucosal controlled drug administration, as applied to the development of novel drug delivery systems. *Type:* Research center.

St. Jude Children's Research Hospital

Department of Molecular Pharmacology

332 N. Lauderdale
Memphis, TN 38105-2729

Ph: (901)495-3456
Fax: (901)521-1668

URL: http://www.stjude.org
Contact: Dr. Peter Houghton, Dir.

Desc: Human tumor xenografts, experimental chemotherapy, selectivity of drug action in in vivo, cytostasis and cytotoxicity, colon carcinoma and rhabdomyosarcoma, thymidylate synthase, molecular events controlling cell death, and relationships between genes involved in cell cycle control and sensitivity to chemotherapy. *Type:* Research center.

Sherbrooke University

Institute of Pharmacology of Sherbrooke

Departement de Pharmacologie
Faculte de medecine
3001, 12e Ave. Nord
Sherbrooke, PQ, Canada J1H 5N4

Ph: (819)564-5239
Fax: (819)564-5400

E-mail: p.sirois@courrier.usherb.ca
URL: http://www.crc.cuse.usherb.ca/ips/ips.html
Contact: Prof. Pierre Sirois, Dir.

Desc: Cardiovascular and pulmonary pharmacology, including peptides and lipids, prostaglandins, leukotrienes, angiotensin, bradykinin, and related compounds. *Type:* Research center.

Stanford University

Laboratory for Transplantation Immunology

Department of Cardiothoracic Surgery
300 Pasteur Dr.
Palo Alto, CA 94305-5407

Ph: (650)723-5641
Fax: (650)725-3846

E-mail: rem@leland.stanford.edu
URL: http://www.med.stanford.edu/
Contact: Dr. Randall E. Morris, Dir.

Desc: Develops compounds to reduce rejection of transplanted organs. Studies focus on molecules, monoclonal antibodies, and naturally occurring substances. *Type:* Research center.

State University of New York at Buffalo

Clinical Pharmacokinetics Laboratory

Millard Fillmore Hospital
3 Gates Circle
Buffalo, NY 14209

Ph: (716)887-4704
Fax: (716)887-4566

E-mail: jschenta@mfhs.edu

URL: http://www.wings.buffalo.edu/academic/department/pharmacy/cpl/

Contact: Dr. Jerome J. Schentag, Dir.

Desc: Pharmacokinetics and pharmacodynamics of drugs in volunteers and hospitalized patients. Major emphasis on geriatric patients, pharmacology, nutrition, cancer, cardiology, metabolism, and infectious disease states. *Type:* Research center.

The Tan Sheet

F-D-C Reports, Inc.
5550 Friendship Blvd., Ste. 1   Ph: (301)657-9830
Chevy Chase, MD 20815   Free: 800-332-2181
                                  Fax: (301)656-3094
E-mail: fdcr@clarknet.com
Contact: Karl Vhlendorf, Editor.

Desc: Provides "in-depth coverage of nonprescription pharmaceuticals and dietary supplement/nutritionals." Topics include congressional hearings and legislation, business and marketing news, FDA recalls and seizures, regular listing of product trademarks, and activities of FTC, CPSC, and FDA. *Type:* Newsletter.

Tufts Center for the Study of Drug Development

Tufts University   Ph: (617)636-0070
192 South St., Ste. 550   Fax: (617)636-8425
Boston, MA 02111
URL: http://www.tufts.edu/med/research/csdd
Contact: Kenneth I. Kaitin, PhD, Dir.

Desc: Public policy on worldwide drug development and its trends, including study of the impact of drug regulation on pharmaceutical innovation; survey of pharmaceutical firms to determine origin, flow, and fate of new chemical entities (NCEs) and biopharmaceuticals; evaluation of therapeutic significance of marketed drugs; economic analysis of drug development costs; and legal and regulatory issues in drug development. *Type:* Research center.

U.S. Department of Health and Human Services

Agency for Toxic Substances and Disease Registry

Division of Toxicology

1600 Clifton Rd., NE   Ph: (404)639-6300
Mail Stop E-29   Fax: (404)639-6315
Atlanta, GA 30333
Contact: Dr. Christopher DeRosa, Dir.

Desc: Priority hazardous substances. Sets priorities for research, initiates programs, and identifies data needs for publication of itToxicological Profiles/it. *Type:* Research center.

U.S. Department of Health and Human Services

Food and Drug Administration

Center for Biologics Evaluation and Research

Molecular Pharmacology Staff

8800 Rockville Pike   Ph: (301)496-2205
Bldg. 29, Rm. 419   Fax: (301)480-5527
Bethesda, MD 20892
E-mail: Nakhasi@A1.CBER.FDA.GOV
Contact: Hira L. Nakhasi, Chf.

Desc: Molecular mechanisms of viral and parasitic infections. Seeks to develop therapeutic agents using chemical synthesis of oligonucleotide analogues complementary to viral genes. *Type:* Research center.

U.S. Department of Health and Human Services

Food and Drug Administration

Center for Drug Evaluation and Research

1451 Rockville Pike, Rm. 6027   Ph: (301)594-5400
Rockville, MD 20852   Fax: (301)594-6197
Contact: Janet Woodcock, Dir.

Desc: Develops FDA policy with regard to the safety, effectiveness, and labeling of all drugs for human use; reviews and evaluates new drug applications and notices of claimed investigational exemption of new drugs; develops and implements standards for the safety and effectiveness of all over-the-counter drugs; monitors the quality of marketed drugs through product testing, surveillance, and compliance programs; develops guidelines on current Good Manufacturing Practices for use by the drug industry; develops and disseminates information and educational material on drugs to the medical community and the public; conducts research and develops scientific standards on the composition, quality, safety, and efficacy of human drugs; collects and evaluates information on the effects and use trends of marketed drugs; monitors prescription drug advertising and promotional labeling to assure their accuracy and integrity; analyzes data on accidental poisonings; and disseminates toxicity and treatment information on medicines. Principal Center components are the Office of Compliance, Office of Drug Evaluation I, Office of Drug Evaluation II, Office of Drug Standards, Office of Epidemiology and Biostatistics, and Office of Research Resources. *Type:* Research center.

U.S. Department of Health and Human Services

Food and Drug Administration

Center for Drug Evaluation and Research

Division of Over-the-Counter Drug Products

9201 Corporate Blvd.   Ph: (301)827-2222
Rockville, MD 20850   Fax: (301)827-2316
URL: http://fda.gov/cder/otc/index.htm
Contact: Dr. Debra L. Bowen, MD, Dir.

Desc: Reviews over-the-counter (OTC) medications marketed in the United States. *Type:* Research center.

U.S. Department of Health and Human Services

Food and Drug Administration

Center for Drug Evaluation and Research

Office of Generic Drugs

Metro Park North   Ph: (301)443-1544
7500 Standish Pl.   Fax: (301)594-0181
Rockville, MD 20855
Contact: James Chaney, Dir.

Desc: Bioequivalence and dissolution testing data submitted by pharmaceutical firms in support of abbreviated new drug applications. Principal fields of research include biopharmaceutics, pharmacokinetics, and analytical methods. *Type:* Research center.

U.S. Department of Health and Human Services

Food and Drug Administration

Center for Drug Evaluation and Research

Office of Research Resources

Mail Code HFD-420   Ph: (301)443-1223
5600 Fishers Ln., Rm. 13B06
Rockville, MD 20857
Contact: Dr. Henry Malinowski, Dep.Dir.

Desc: Development of biopharmaceutic studies, including in vivo studies of drug pharmaceutics; development of dissolution methodology; and development of specifications for drug approval. *Type:* Research center.

U.S. Department of Health and Human Services

Food and Drug Administration

Center for Drug Evaluation and Research

Office of Testing and Research

Parklawn Bldg.   Ph: (301)594-0510
5600 Fishers Ln., Rm. 13B06   Fax: (301)827-3787
Rockville, MD 20857
Contact: Dr. Charles K. Greishaber, Actg.Dir.

Desc: Provides expert advice to units of the Center on matters involving the pharmacology, toxicology, microbiolo-

gy, and bioanalysis of drugs, antibiotics, and hormones, including insulin. Division also plans and conducts research in a wide variety of pharmacological, toxicological, microbiological, and analytical problems; performs bioassays to determine drug potency (including testing insulin for certification); and appraises and approves current and proposed standards and specifications for drugs requiring bioanalysis and validates such analytical methodology. *Type:* Research center.

U.S. Department of Health and Human Services

Food and Drug Administration

Center for Drug Evaluation and Research

Office of Testing and Research

1114 Market St., Rm. 1002   Ph: (314)539-2134
St. Louis, MO 63101   Fax: (314)539-2011
URL: http://www.fda.gov/cder/dtaad

Contact: Thomas P. Layloff, Jr., Dir.

Desc: Conducts method validation for new drug applications and analyzes drug substances for abbreviated new drug applications; serves as the FDA collaborating laboratory for the acceptance of reference standards for the United States Pharmacopeia; assists in monitoring the quality of marketed drugs through surveillance and compliance actions; conducts research to establish official laboratory techniques or methods to test drugs for compliance with standards of identity, strength, and purity; develops analytical methods, particularly automated methods adapted to large volumes of samples; and collects data to support bioavailability and bioequivalence reviews of drugs. Laboratory operations include long-range research activities related to analytical methods and analyses related to the FDA's surveillance programs and other aspects of drug monitoring. *Type:* Research center.

U.S. Department of Health and Human Services

Food and Drug Administration

National Center for Toxicological Research

Biometry Staff

County Rd. 3   Ph: (870)543-7001
Jefferson, AR 72079   Fax: (870)543-7576
E-mail: dgaylor@nctr.fda.gov

Contact: Dr. David Gaylor, Dir.

Desc: Statistical design and analysis of toxicological experime nts. Principal area of research interest is biostatistics in toxicology, including survival analysis, time to tumor estimation and testing, and extrapolation of effects from high to low doses, and dose-response modeling for developmental defects. *Type:* Research center.

U.S. Department of Health and Human Services

Food and Drug Administration

Office of Orphan Products Development

5600 Fishers Ln.   Ph: (301)827-3666
HF-35   Fax: (301)443-4915
Rockville, MD 20857
E-mail: mhaffner@bangate.fda.gov
URL: http://www.fda.gov/orphan

Contact: Marlene E. Haffner, Dir.

Desc: Availability of orphan products. Orphan products are defined as drugs, biologics, medical devices, and foods for medical purposes which are indicated for a rare disease or condition (i.e., one affecting fewer than 200,000 people in the U.S.). *Type:* Research center.

U.S. Department of Health and Human Services

National Cancer Institute

Division of Cancer Treatment, Diagnosis and Centers

Developmental Therapeutics Program

Executive Plaza N., Ste. 831   Ph: (301)496-8795
6130 Executive Blvd.   Fax: (301)480-4817
Bethesda, MD 20892-7448
Contact: Dr. Ven Narayanan, Chf.

Desc: Acquiring and managing the flow of unique synthetic compounds for evaluation as potential anticancer agents. *Type:* Research center.

U.S. Department of Health and Human Services

National Cancer Institute

Division of Clinical Sciences

Cancer Therapy Evaluation Program

Exec. Plaza N., Rm. 715   Ph: (301)496-5223
6130 Executive Blvd.   Fax: (301)402-0428
Rockville, MD 20852
Contact: Dr. Mario Senol, Actg.Ch.

Desc: Develops new investigational drugs by sponsoring clinical trials to evaluate their pharmacology, toxicities, and efficacy. Activities focus on: obtaining Investigational New Drug exemption (IND) authorization from the Food and Drug Administration; managing and monitoring Phase I trials of new agents developed by the Division of Cancer Treatment ; developing and implementing a plan for Phase II trials in specific tumor types and monitoring the results of these clinical trials; developing and implementing, in collaboration with the Clinical Investigations Branch of CTEP, Phase III trials in selected areas of promising activity observed in Phase II; meeting FDA regulatory requirements for all active INDs in collaboration with CTEP's Regulatory Affairs Branch; and distributing investigational new drugs. *Type:* Research center.

U.S. Department of Health and Human Services

National Cancer Institute

Laboratory of Molecular Pharmacology

NIH Bldg. 37, Rm. 5D02   Ph: (301)496-5944
37 Convent Dr. MSC 4255   Fax: (301)402-0752
Bethesda, MD 20892-4255
Contact: Dr. Yves Sommier, Chf.

Desc: Mechanisms of action of anticancer agents are studied in culture and subcellular systems, with particular attention to effects involving DNA and nuclear proteins. Investigations focus on the relation between drug-induced macromolecular damage (and its repair) and cell survival. *Type:* Research center.

U.S. Department of Health and Human Services

National Center for Infectious Diseases

Division of Parasitic Diseases

Entomology Branch

4770 Buford Hwy., MS F12   Ph: (770)488-4240
Atlanta, GA 30341-3724   Fax: (770)488-4108
URL: http://bew5@ciddpd2.em.cdc.gov
Contact: Robert A. Wirtz, Chf.

Desc: Vector control strategies and disseminates the results; conducts research on vector biology and the molecular and biochemical mechanisms for insecticide resistance; develops biochemical and bioassay field tests to assess vector insecticide susceptibility; develops and validates chemical tests for the detection of parasitic disease drugs and their metabolites in body fluids and tissues, and determines the pharmacologic response to such drugs; develops chemical procedures to detect new and existing pesticides in various formulations. *Type:* Research center.

U.S. Department of Health and Human Services

National Heart, Lung, and Blood Institute

Laboratory of Chemical Pharmacology

NIH Bldg. 10, Rm. 8N117   Ph: (301)496-2593
9000 Rockville Pike   Fax: (301)402-0171
Bethesda, MD 20892

Contact: Dr. James R. Gillette, Chf.

Desc: Drug metabolism; mechanisms of allergic responses; and mechanisms of drug-induced cellular damage. *Type:* Research center.

U.S. Department of Health and Human Services

National Institute of Diabetes and Digestive and Kidney Diseases

Laboratory of Biochemical Pharmacology

NIH Bldg. 8, Rm. 223   Ph: (301)496-4193
9000 Rockville Pike   Fax: (301)402-0240
Bethesda, MD 20892

Contact: Herbert Tabor, Chf.

Desc: Biochemical, genetic, and molecular biological investigations. Included are studies on polyamine synthesis and action, nucleic acid and protein biosynthesis, tryptophan biosynthesis, and yeast and it*Escherichia coli*/it genetics. *Type:* Research center.

U.S. Department of Health and Human Services

National Institute of Diabetes and Digestive and Kidney Diseases

Laboratory of Bioorganic Chemistry

NIH Bldg. 8A, Rm. 1A17   Ph: (301)496-4024
9000 Rockville Pike   Fax: (301)402-0008
Bethesda, MD 20892

Contact: John W. Daly, Chf.

Desc: Mission is to elucidate the mechanism of interaction of pharmacologically active substances with biological systems. Research is designed to develop new chemical agents as tools for the study of membrane and cytosol functions of cells. *Type:* Research center.

U.S. Department of Health and Human Services

National Institute on Drug Abuse

Medications Development Division

Clinical Trials Branch

Parklawn Bldg.   Ph: (301)443-3318
5600 Fishers Ln.   Fax: (301)443-2599
Rockville, MD 20857

Contact: Peter Bridge, Chf.

Desc: Pharmacotherapy of substance abuse and HIV risk reduction for new and marketed medications. *Type:* Research center.

U.S. Department of Health and Human Services

National Institute on Drug Abuse

Medications Development Division

Pharmacology and Toxicology Branch

Parklawn Bldg.   Ph: (301)443-6270
5600 Fishers Ln.   Fax: (301)443-2599
Rockville, MD 20857

Contact: David McCann, Chf.

Desc: Discovery and non-clinical evaluation of pharmacotherapies for cocaine, opiate and methamphetamine dependence. *Type:* Research center.

U.S. Department of Health and Human Services

National Institute of Environmental Health Sciences

Division of Intramural Research

Laboratory of Cellular and Molecular Pharmacology

PO Box 12233   Ph: (919)541-3332
Research Triangle Park, NC 27709
Contact: Dr. J.W. Putney, Chf.

Desc: Biological effects of environmental factors; species differences in mechanism of dose- and time-response for the actions of selected environmental hazards; mechanisms for disposition of xenobiotics, including biotransformation, and biological transport and elimination; and cellular signal transduction systems, as known, or potential sites for pathological interaction with environmental agents. *Type:* Research center.

U.S. Department of Health and Human Services

National Institute of General Medical Sciences

Pharmacology and Biorelated Chemistry Program

45 Center Dr., MSC 6200   Ph: (301)594-7808
Bethesda, MD 20892-6200   Fax: (301)594-7728
E-mail: rogersm@nigms.nih.gov
URL: http://www.nih.gov/nigms/
Contact: Dr. Michael E. Rogers, Dir.

Desc: Supports research and research training aimed at improving the molecular-level understanding of fundamental biological processes and discovering approaches to their control. Research supported by the Division takes multifaceted approaches to problems in pharmacology, physiology, biochemistry, and biorelated chemistry that are either very basic in nature or that have implications for more than one disease area. *Type:* Research center.

U.S. Department of Health and Human Services

National Institute of General Medical Sciences

Pharmacology Research Associate Program

5333 Westbard Ave.   Ph: (301)496-7707
Bethesda, MD 20892   Fax: (301)402-0019
Contact: Christine K. Carrico, PhD, Dir.

Desc: Developing leaders in pharmacological research for key positions in academic, industrial, and government research laboratories. Each year 11 recently trained scientists are selected for a two-year period of postdoctoral research in laboratories of the National Institutes of Health and Alcohol, Drug Abuse, and Mental Health Administration. *Type:* Research center.

U.S. Pharmacist

Jobson Publishing Corp.

100 Avenue of the Americas   Ph: (212)274-7000
New York, NY 10013-1678   Fax: (212)431-0500
URL: http://www.uspharmicist.com.
Contact: Angele D'Angelo, Editor-in-Chief.

Desc: National pharmacy publication which includes views on prescription and over-the-counter drugs, for the purpose of clinical application education. *Type:* Periodical.

United States Pharmacopeial Convention

12601 Twinbrook Pky.   Ph: (301)881-0666
Rockville, MD 20852   Free: 800-822-8772
   Fax: (301)816-8148

E-mail: webmaster@usp.org
URL: http://www.usp.org
Contact: Jerome A. Halperin, Exec.VP & CEO.

Desc: Dedicated to promoting the public health by establishing and disseminating officially recognized standards of quality and authoritive information for the use of medicines and other health care technologies by health professionals, patients and consumers. *Type:* Association.

University of Arizona

Center for Pharmaceutical Economics

College of Pharmacy   Ph: (520)626-4450
Tucson, AZ 85721   Fax: (520)626-2023
E-mail: coons@pharmacy.arizona.edu
URL: http://www.pharmacy.arizona.edu
Contact: Stephen Joel Coons, PhD, Dir.

Desc: Assessment of outcomes associated with the use of pharmaceuticals, including quality of life assessment and pharmacoeconomic analysis (cost-effectiveness and cost-utility analysis). Also focuses on the development and assessment of disease intervention models and disease management programs. *Type:* Research center.

University of California, San Francisco

Immunogenetics and Transplantation Laboratory

Davies Medical Center   Ph: (415)476-3883
Main Hospital, Level B   Fax: (415)476-0379
45 Castro St.
San Francisco, CA 94114
URL: http://itl-2.ucsf.edu/
Contact: Dolly Tayn, PhD, Interim Dir.

Desc: Immunogenetics and transplantation, including immunopharmacology of immunosuppressive agents. *Type:* Research center.

University of Cincinnati

Cincinnati Medical Heritage Center

121 Wherry Hall   Ph: (513)558-5120
Eden & Bethesda Aves.   Fax: (513)558-0472
Cincinnati, OH 45267-0574
E-mail: billie.broaddus@uc.edu
URL: http://aitl.uc.edu/cmhc/coverpage.htm
Contact: Billie Broaddus, Dir.

Desc: History of medicine and pharmacy. *Type:* Research center.

University of Florida

Center for Drug Discovery

College of Pharmacy   Ph: (352)392-8186
Pharmaceutics Dept.   Fax: (352)392-8589
Box 100497, J. Hillis Miller
    Health Center
Gainesville, FL 32610-0497
E-mail: bodor@cop.health.ufl.edu
URL: http://www.cop.ufl.edu/centers/CDD/cdd.htm
Contact: Prof. Nicholas Bodor, PhD, Exec.Dir.

Desc: Pharmaceutical research embracing a variety of topics from computer-aided drug design and medicinal chemistry to analytical, pharmacokinetic and pharmacodynamic programs, drug stability and formulation development, and drug metabolism and toxicity. Current projects focus on retrometabolic drug design. *Type:* Research center.

University of Georgia

College of Pharmacy

Research and Graduate Studies Programs

Athens, GA 30602   Ph: (706)542-1911
    Fax: (706)542-5269
E-mail: sfeldman@rx.uga.edu
URL: http://www.rx.uga.edu/
Contact: Dr. Stuart Feldman, Dean.

Desc: Medicinal chemistry, pharmaceutics, pharmacology, toxicology, and pharmacy administration, including studies of synthetic antimalarials, antineoplastics, anti-AIDS compounds, microencapsulation of drugs, drug induced enzyme induction, dietary influences on drug metabolism, analytical chemistry, hypertension and anti-hypertension drug action, drug utilization studies, drug abuse, pharmacy manpower, marketing of drug products, and socioeconomics of pharmacy practice. *Type:* Research center.

University of Houston

Center for the Pharmaceutical Care of the Elderly

College of Pharmacy   Ph: (713)795-8377
1441 Moursund, Ste. 316   Fax: (713)795-8383
Houston, TX
E-mail: dnewell@bayou.uh.edu
URL: http://www.pharmacy.uh.edu/centers/centerelderly.html
Contact: Debra Newell, Coord.

Desc: Aging and its impact on pharmaceutical care, including understanding and utilization of medications in the elderly. *Type:* Research center.

University of Illinois at Chicago

Center for Pharmaceutical Biotechnology

College of Pharmacy   Ph: (312)996-0796
833 S. Wood St. - M/C 874   Fax: (312)996-9303
Chicago, IL 60612-7231
E-mail: mjohnson@uic.edu
URL: http://www.uic.edu/pharmacy/research/cphb
Contact: Dr. Michael E. Johnson, Dir.

Desc: Structural and molecular biology focusing on pharmaceutical applications. *Type:* Research center.

University of Iowa

Center for Health Effects of Environmental Contamination

100 Oakdale Campus No. N202   Ph: (319)335-4550
    OH   Fax: (319)335-4747
Iowa City, IA 52242-5000
E-mail: cheec@uiowa.edu

Contact: Pete Weyer, Contact.

Desc: Fate and transport of toxic substances in the environment, radon and indoor air contaminants, nonpoint source chemical contamination of water supplies, and epidemiologic studies that relate the occurrence of diseases to contaminant exposure. *Type:* Research center.

University of Iowa

Pharmaceutical Service Division

College of Pharmacy   Ph: (319)335-8674
115 S. Grand Ave.   Fax: (319)335-9418
Iowa City, IA 52242
E-mail: rolland-poust@uiowa.edu
URL: http://www.uiowa.edu/~pharmser/
Contact: Rolland I. Poust, Dir.

Desc: Drug delivery systems for pharmaceutical investigations, including parenterals, capsules, tablets, liquids, lyophilized products, and dermatologicals, for human clinical trials. *Type:* Research center.

University of Kansas

Center for Drug Delivery Research

Department of Pharmaceutical   Ph: (785)864-3755
    Chem.   Fax: (785)865-5738
2095 Constant Ave.
Lawrence, KS 66047
E-mail: stella@smissman.hbc.ukans.edu
URL: http://www.hbc.ukan.edu
Contact: Valentino Stella, PhD, Dir.

Desc: Basic and applied research on chemically-driven drug delivery systems; physiochemical and biological factors that affect delivery systems; and unstable and insoluble drugs such as anticancer agents, peptides, and proteins. *Type:* Research center.

University of Kansas

Higuchi Biosciences Center

2099 Constant Ave.   Ph: (785)864-5183
Lawrence, KS 66047-2535   Fax: (785)864-3738
E-mail: ekm@smissman.hbc.ukans.edu
URL: http://www.hbc.ukans.edu
Contact: Dr. Elias K. Michaelis, Dir.

Desc: Pharmaceutical chemistry, bioanalytical chemistry, drug design, drug delivery systems, neurological sciences, immunology, and related technology, focusing on the discovery, analysis, formulation, delivery, toxicology, and pharmacology of drugs. *Type:* Research center.

University of Kentucky

Pharmaceutical Science and Technology Center

College of Pharmacy, Rm. 309   Ph: (606)257-5288
907 Rose St.   Fax: (606)323-5985
Lexington, KY 40536-0082
E-mail: jay@pop.uky.edu
URL: http://www.uky.edu/pharmacy/research/epst.html
Contact: Dr. Michael Jay, Dir.

Desc: Drug product development and evaluation. Provides industrial support through the development and preparation of clinical supplies of drug products under government regulations. *Type:* Research center.

University of Maryland

Center on Drugs and Public Policy

School of Pharmacy   Ph: (410)706-4044
100 N. Greene St., 6th Fl.   Fax: (410)706-5394
Baltimore, MD 21201-1563
E-mail: pmckerch@pharmacy.ab.umd.edu
Contact: Dr. McKercher, PhD, Dir.

Desc: Drug utilization review, outpatient drug benefits under the OBRA 90, cost effective drug therapies, pharmaceutical care services, health outcomes related to drug therapy, pharmacoepidemiology, pharmacy manpower, the pharmaceutical industry, impact of changes in the organization and financing of health care services, and patient compliance with prescribed drug regimen. *Type:* Research center.

University of Michigan

Antiviral Laboratory

4222 Sch. of Dentistry   Ph: (734)763-5481
1011 N. University Ave.   Fax: (734)764-7406
Ann Arbor, MI 48109
E-mail: jcdrach@umich.edu
URL: http://www.umich.edu/~websvcs/doughb/bms/people/drach.html
Contact: Dr. John C. Drach, PhD, Hd.

Desc: Antiviral and antineoplastic drugs, including the discovery of new antiviral drugs, how such drugs act at the genetic, cellular and biochemical level, and how they are metabolized in uninfected and virus-infected cells. Areas of research include viruses, herpes, and AIDS. *Type:* Research center.

University of Michigan

Upjohn Center for Clinical Pharmacology

3709 Upjohn Ctr.   Ph: (734)764-9121
School of Medicine   Fax: (734)763-3438
Ann Arbor, MI 48109-0504
Contact: Dr. William D. Ensminger, Dir.

Desc: Clinical pharmacology. *Type:* Research center.

University of Mississippi

Pharmaceutical Marketing and Management Research Program

Waller Lab Complex, Rm. 101   Ph: (228)232-5948
University, MS 38677   Fax: (228)232-5262
E-mail: ribfb@olemiss.edu

URL: http://www.olemiss.edu/depts/rips/pmmrp/

Contact: Dr. Benjamin F. Banahan, Div.Coord.

Desc: Proprietary and inhouse marketing and management studies relating to pharmaceutical products, including formulary decision factors, generic substitution, reimbursement issues, medication compliance and consumer preferences. Conducts mail surveys, telephone interviews, focus groups, internet surveys, consumer reaction panels, and surveys of professionals at national and state meetings. *Type:* Research center.

University of Mississippi

Research Institute of Pharmaceutical Sciences

Sch. of Pharmacy   Ph: (228)232-7132
University, MS 38677   Fax: (228)232-5118
E-mail: kroberts@olemiss.edu
URL: http://olemiss.edu/depts/rips

Contact: Dr. Kenneth B. Roberts, Exec.Dir.

Desc: Health services, focusing on rural health, biological sciences, toxicology studies on the fate and effects of environmental chemicals, pharmaceutical marketing and management, as well as natural products. *Type:* Research center.

University of Missouri--Kansas City

Drug Information Service

2411 Holmes, MG-200   Ph: (816)235-5490
Kansas City, MO 64108   Fax: (816)235-5491
E-mail: pjbryant@cctr.umkc.edu

Contact: Dr. Patrick J. Bryant, Dir.

Desc: Literature research, evaluation of clinically-related drug problems, questions from health care professionals and consumers and competitive technical intelligence-related questions. *Type:* Research center.

University of Montreal

Fernand Sequin Research Centre

Hopital Louis-H.-Lafontaine   Ph: (514)251-4015
7331, rue Hochelaga   Fax: (514)251-2617
Montreal, PQ, Canada H1N
  3V2
E-mail: hugues.cormier@umontreal.ca

Contact: Dr. Hugues Cormier, Dir.

Desc: Neurochemistry, including drug mechanisms of action; psychopharmacology, including pharmacodynamics and pharmacokinetics of psychoactive drugs; and psychosocial behavioral and clinical evaluations, including the development of psychotherapeutic methods, evaluation of programs, and societal problems. *Type:* Research center.

University of Southern California

Laboratory of Applied Pharmacokinetics

USC Sch. of Med.   Ph: (213)342-1300
Clinical Science Center, Rm.   Fax: (213)342-1302
  134-B
2250 Alcazar St.
Los Angeles, CA 90033
E-mail: jelliffe@hsc.usc.edu
URL: http://www.usc.edu/hsc/lab_apk

Contact: Roger W. Jelliffe, MD, Dir.

Desc: Designing systems for pharmacokinetic studies and strategies for optimal therapeutic drug monitoring in patients and optimal adaptive control of drug dosage regimens for patients. Activities include development and testing of computer programs for simulation, parameter identification, and optimal adaptive control of drug dosage regimens and pharmacokinetic systems in clinical settings; investigation of process and measurement noise in the clinical therapeutic environment; development of software for making population pharmacokinetic models; software for stochastic adaptive control of drug dosage regimens; and development of clinically reliable interfaces and intelligent automated apparatus for delivering complex drug regimens. *Type:* Research center.

University of Tennessee

Drug Information Center

875 Monroe, Ste. 109   Ph: (901)448-5555
Memphis, TN 38163   Fax: (901)448-5419
E-mail: utdic@utmem1.utmem.edu

Contact: Dr. Peter A. Chyka, Dir.

Desc: Therapeutic and pharmaceutical drugs. Provides therapeutic and pharmaceutic drug information to health care professionals. *Type:* Research center.

University of Texas at Austin

Drug Dynamics Institute

College of Pharmacy   Ph: (512)471-4841
Austin, TX 78712-1074   Fax: (512)471-2746
E-mail: cjmcclelland@mail.utexas.edu

Contact: James W. McGinity, Dir.

Desc: Pharmaceutical research, development, and testing, including discovery of new medicinal agents, improvement of drug therapy, mechanisms of drug action, and re-evaluation of marketed products. *Type:* Research center.

University of Utah

Center for Controlled Chemical Delivery

Room 205, BPRB   Ph: (801)581-6654
Univ. of Utah   Fax: (801)581-7848
Salt Lake City, UT 84112

Contact: Dr. Sung Wan Kim, Dir.

Desc: Controlled drug delivery systems. Specific studies include the following: hydrogel and polymer synthesis, including water-soluble, bioactive, and biodegradable polymers; transdermal drug delivery, including skin immunoreaction and sensitization, irritation mechanism, drug interaction with stratum corneum membranes, physicochemical analysis of drug permeation mechanisms, and design of optimum delivery of matrix or rate-controlling membranes; functional polymers for gastrointestinal drug delivery; polymeric prodrugs and chemical modification of drugs for specific organ targeting or long-term delivery of therapeutic agents; and delivery of peptides and protein drugs. *Type:* Research center.

University of Wisconsin--Madison

Sonderegger Research Center

Sch. of Pharmacy   Ph: (608)263-9664
425 N. Charter St.   Fax: (608)263-9664
Madison, WI 53706

Contact: Betty Chewning, PhD, Dir.

Desc: Interdisciplinary health care research, including quality of health care in nursing homes, economic issues in delivery and reimbursement of pharmacy services, health care provider-patient communication, legal aspects of pharmacy practice, use of computerized education and decision-making programs for consumers, and impact of federal and state policy/regulation in pharmacy prescribing and practice. *Type:* Research center.

University of Wisconsin--Milwaukee

Marine and Freshwater Biomedical Sciences Center

PO Box 413   Ph: (414)382-1735
Milwaukee, WI 53201   Fax: (414)229-5530
E-mail: petering@scd.uwm.edu
URL: http://www.scd.uwm.edu

Contact: Dr. David Petering, Dir.

Desc: Aquatic models in biomedicine and comparative toxicology. Studies transformation and metabolism of toxic organic chemicals and metals and investigates genetic, neurobehavioral, and immunological responses of organisms to such chemicals. *Type:* Research center.

University of Wisconsin--Milwaukee

Medicinal Chemistry Group

Department of Chemistry   Ph: (414)229-5856
PO Box 413   Fax: (414)229-5530
Milwaukee, WI 53201
E-mail: capncook@alpha1.csd.uwm.edu

Contact: Prof. James M. Cook, Dir.

Desc: Drugs, including studies of valium receptors in the brain; drugs that do not sedate patients, including anticonvulsant agents, sedative/hypnotic agents, and muscle relaxants; and antimalarial agents, barbiturate antagonists, antagonists of alcohol/barbituate overdoses, and cardiovascular agents. Activities focus on synthesis of compounds to reduce drug addiction and control illness. *Type:* Research center.

Vanderbilt University

Center for Clinical Pharmacology

532 Med. Res. Bldg. 1   Ph: (615)322-3304
Nashville, TN 37232-6602   Fax: (615)322-4707
E-mail: dan.roden@mcmail.vanderbilt.edu
URL: http://www.mc.vanderbilt.edu

Contact: Dr. Dan M. Roden, Dir.

Desc: Interdisciplinary research in drug actions, especially in humans. Specific research includes xenobiotic disposition, ion channel physiology and pharmacology, hypertension and the autonomic nervous system, and eicosanoid biology. *Type:* Research center.

West Side Institute for Science and Education

2030 W. Taylor St.
Chicago, IL 60612-4223

Contact: E.M. Hubach, Dir.

Desc: Drug company studies and clinical trials. *Type:* Research center.

World Life Research Institute

23000 Grand Terr. Rd.   Ph: (909)825-4773
Colton, CA 92324   Fax: (909)783-3477

Contact: Bruce W. Halstead, MD, Dir.

Desc: Toxicology, medical research, poisonous and venomous marine animals, drugs from the sea, chronic degenerative diseases, marine biotoxicology, and ethnobotany and terrestrial phytochemistry in a search for new drugs from natural resources, especially organic chemical agents derived from plants or animals having application to therapeutic medicine and human nutrition. Maintains extensive foreign contacts in 6,000 regions of the world, particularly underdeveloped areas in Asia and Latin America, in search of new drugs. *Type:* Research center.

Yeshiva University

Biotechnology Resource in Pulsed EPR Spectroscopy

Albert Einstein College of   Ph: (718)430-2175
  Medicine   Fax: (718)430-8935
Department of Molecular
  Pharmacology
1300 Morris Park Ave.
Bronx, NY 10461
E-mail: nikaloi@spin.aecom.yu.edu

Contact: Dr. Nikaloi Avdievich, Lab.Mgr.

Desc: Electron spin echo (ESE) modulation and ENDOR studies of metalloproteins, metal-drug complexes, transition metal model complexes and radical species of biological importance. Questions being addressed include ligation structures surrounding paramagnetic metal centers in these systems and the effects of various substrates or inhibitors. *Type:* Research center.

Philanthropy

America's New Foundations
The Taft Group
27500 Drake Rd.   Ph: (248)699-4253
Farmington Hills, MI 48331-   Free: 800-347-GALE
3535   Fax: (248)699-8097
E-mail: galeord@gale.com
URL: http://www.gale.com/taft/; http://www.taftgroup.com.
Contact: Bodhan Romaniuk, Editor.
Desc: Over 3,000 private, corporate, and community foundations created since 1990 with annual incomes or annual giving of at least $100,000. *Type:* Directory.

Amnesty Action
Amnesty International USA
322 8th Ave.   Ph: (212)807-8400
New York, NY 10001   Free: 800-266-3789
                         Fax: (212)627-1451
E-mail: lberg@aiusa.org
URL: http://www.amnesty-usa.org
Contact: Ron Lajoie, Editor; Tim Ledwith, Membership Communications Dir.
Desc: Magazine focusing on worldwide human rights issues. *Type:* Periodical.

Catholic Campaign for Human Development
U.S. Catholic Conference
3211 4th St. NE   Ph: (202)541-3000
Washington, DC 20017   Free: 800-946-4CHD
                         Fax: (202)541-3329
URL: http://www.nccbuscc.org/chd
Contact: Rev. Robert Vitillo, Exec.Dir.
Desc: A program of the United States Catholic Conference. Goals are: to raise money through a collection in Catholic churches, and to allocate these funds to self-help projects sponsored by groups of poor and low-income persons; to educate the nonpoor community about causes of poverty and injustice. *Type:* Association.

Combined Health Appeal of America
1745 Old Springhouse Ln., Ste.   Ph: (770)936-0362
413   Free: 800-242-2911
Atlanta, GA 30338   Fax: (770)936-0725
E-mail: chaa@worldnet.att.net
Contact: Edward Godshall, Pres.
Desc: Our mission is to foster the development and growth of combined Health Appeals throughout the United States, to conduct cost-effective workplace giving campaigns, and to raise needed funds for medical research, education, and patient services on behalf of our member health agencies. *Type:* Association.

Corporate Giving Yellow Pages
The Taft Group
27500 Drake Rd.   Ph: (248)699-4253
Farmington Hills, MI 48331-   Free: 800-347-GALE
3535   Fax: (248)699-8097
E-mail: galeord@gale.com
URL: http://www.gale.com/taft/
Contact: Lori Schoenenberger, Editor, lori.schoenenberger@gale.com.
Desc: More than 3,500 corporate contact persons with information on corporate charitable giving. *Type:* Directory.

Directory of Corporate and Foundation Givers
The Taft Group
27500 Drake Rd.   Ph: (248)699-4253
Farmington Hills, MI 48331-   Free: 800-347-GALE
3535   Fax: (248)699-8097
E-mail: galeord@gale.com
URL: http://www.gale.com/taft/; http://www.taftgroup.com.

Contact: Matthew Brisloois, Editor.
Desc: 8,000 private foundations, corporate foundations, and companies that give money to nonprofit organizations. *Type:* Directory.

Directory of International Corporate Giving in America and Abroad
The Taft Group
27500 Drake Rd.   Ph: (248)699-4253
Farmington Hills, MI 48331-   Free: 800-347-GALE
3535   Fax: (248)699-8097
E-mail: galeord@gale.com
URL: http://www.gale.com/taft/; http://www.taftgroup.com.
Contact: Monica Hubbard, Editor.
Desc: 443 foreign-owned companies that support nonprofit organizations in the U.S., and 170 U.S. companies that support organizations overseas. *Type:* Directory.

Directory of Research Grants
Oryx Press
4041 N. Central Ave., Ste. 700   Ph: (602)265-2651
Phoenix, AZ 85012-3397   Free: 800-279-6799
                         Fax: 800-279-4663
E-mail: info@oryxpress.com
URL: http://www.oryxpress.com;   http://www.higheredconnect.com/grantselect.
Contact: Millie Hannum, Editor.
Desc: Most current and complete information on nearly 6,000 research funding sources. *Type:* Directory.

FC Search: Foundation Center's Database on CD-ROM
Foundation Center
79 5th Ave.   Ph: (212)620-4230
New York, NY 10003-3076 Free: 800-424-9836
                         Fax: (212)807-3677
Desc: 45,000 grant makers in the United States; 200,000 recently awarded grants. *Type:* Directory.

Foundation Directory
The Foundation Center
79 Fifth Ave.   Ph: (212)620-4230
New York, NY 10003-3050
URL: http://www.fdncenter.org
Desc: Contains descriptions of more than 34,500 currently active grantmaking foundations. Covers private grantmaking, community, and operating foundations, and direct corporate giving. *Available:* The Dialog Corporation, DIALOG; The Dialog Corporation, DIALOG. *Type:* Database.

Foundation Grants Index
The Foundation Center
79 Fifth Ave.   Ph: (212)620-4230
New York, NY 10003-3050
URL: http://www.fdncenter.org
Desc: Contains descriptions of more than 300,000 grants of $10,000 or more ($5000 or more for 1984-1988) awarded to non-profit organizations worldwide by more than 830 major U.S. philanthropic foundations. *Available:* The Dialog Corporation, DIALOG; The Dialog Corporation, DIALOG. *Type:* Database.

The Foundation Reporter
The Taft Group
27500 Drake Rd.   Ph: (248)699-4253
Farmington Hills, MI 48331-   Free: 800-347-GALE
3535   Fax: (248)699-8097
E-mail: galeord@gale.com
URL: http://www.gale.com/taft/; http://www.taftgroup.com.
Contact: Bohdan Romaniuk, Editor, bob.romaniuk@gale.com.

Desc: More than 1,000 private philanthropic foundations with at least $10 million in assets or $500,000 in annual giving. *Type:* Directory.

Fund Raiser's Guide to Religious Philanthropy
The Taft Group
27500 Drake Rd.   Ph: (248)699-4253
Farmington Hills, MI 48331-   Free: 800-347-GALE
3535   Fax: (248)699-8097
E-mail: galeord@gale.com
URL: http://www.gale.com/taft/; http://www.taftgroup.com.
Contact: Bob Romaniuk, Editor.
Desc: Over 1000 private foundations that dispense funds to religious organizations. *Type:* Directory.

Gifts In Kind International
333 N. Fairfax St., Ste. 100   Ph: (703)836-2121
Alexandria, VA 22314   Fax: (703)549-1481
Contact: Susan Corrigan, Pres.
Desc: Encourages and assists businesses in donating products to voluntary human services and environmental organizations and arts and education programs. Promotes in-kind gift giving as an effective means for donors to manage inventory levels, increase productivity, lower storage costs, and receive tax credits. Identifies and selects recipients; administers details involving taxes and transportation to facilitate donating. *Type:* Association.

GRANTS
Oryx Press
4041 N. Central Ave., Ste. 700   Ph: (602)265-2651
Phoenix, AZ 85012-3397
E-mail: info@oryxpress.com
Contact: Jennifer Ashley, Senior Editor, (602)265-2651, fax: (602)265-6250, info@oryxpress.com.
Desc: Contains descriptions of more than 9000 grants offered by U.S. federal, state, and local governments; commercial organizations; professional associations; private and community foundations; the Canadian government; and private organizations. *Available:* The Dialog Corporation, DIALOG; OCLC Online Computer Library Center, Inc., OCLC FirstSearch Catalog; Knowledge Express Data Systems, Knowledge Express. *Type:* Database.

Grants on Disc
The Taft Group
27500 Drake Rd.   Ph: (248)699-4253
Farmington Hills, MI 48331-   Free: 800-347-GALE
3535   Fax: (248)699-8097
E-mail: galeord@gale.com
URL: http://www.gale.com/taft/
Desc: Lists 390,00 grants with an additional 30,000 grants added quarterly. Provides access to thousands of grants through name, location, amount, year, and category searches. *Type:* Directory.

Guide to Grantmakers in the Rochester Area
Rochester Grantmakers Forum
55 St. Paul St.   Ph: (716)232-2380
Rochester, NY 14604   Fax: (716)232-8413
E-mail: rgf@frontiernet.net
Contact: Jane Ellen, Editor.
Desc: Approximately 165 sources of funding grants for non-profit organizations, primarily in upstate New York; includes foundations, corporations, trusts, and other philanthropic programs. *Type:* Directory.

Independent Charities of America
21 Tamal Vista Blvd., No. 209   Ph: (415)924-1108
Corte Madera, CA 94925   Free: 800-477-0733
                         Fax: (415)924-1379
E-mail: info@independentcharities.org

URL: http://www.independentcharities.org/

Contact: Michael Howland, Pres.

Desc: Represents 414 charitable organizations in the U.S. Coordinates workplace fund drives. *Type:* Association.

Independent Sector

1200 18th St. NW, Ste. 200   Ph: (202)467-6100
Washington, DC 20036   Fax: (202)416-0580

Contact: Sara E. Melendez, Pres.

Desc: Corporations, foundations, and national voluntary organizations. Purposes are to "preserve and enhance our national tradition of giving, volunteering and not-for-profit initiative"; to educate the public about the role of the independent nonprofit sector; to conduct research on the independent nonprofit sector and its usefulness to society. Engages in government relations in order to assure the continuance of a healthy independent nonprofit sector and encourages effective management of philanthropic and voluntary organizations. *Type:* Association.

National Society of Fund Raising Executives

1101 King St., Ste. 700   Ph: (703)684-0410
Alexandria, VA 22314   Free: 800-666-FUND
    Fax: (703)684-0540

E-mail: nsfre@nsfre.org
URL: http://www.nsfre.org

Contact: Paulette Maehara, CFRE, Pres./CEO.

Desc: Fundraising executives who work for nonprofit and philanthropic organizations. Purposes are: to foster the development and growth of professional fundraising executives committed to the philanthropic process; to establish professional ethical standards and to require its members to adhere to those standards; to provide guidance and assistance to philanthropic institutions and agencies with fundraising programs; to offer continuing professional education and career enhancement services for philanthropic fundraising professionals. Maintains speakers' bureau. *Type:* Association.

National Voluntary Health Agencies

1925 K St. NW, Ste. 510   Ph: (202)467-5913
Washington, DC 20006   Free: 800-654-0845
    Fax: (202)467-4280

URL: http://www.nvha.org

Contact: Daniel Snare, Exec.Dir.

Desc: Nonprofit corporation of national health agencies. Generates funds thru workplace charitable solicitation and distributes them to member agencies. *Type:* Association.

990-PF Desktop Document Service

The Taft Group
27500 Drake Rd.   Ph: (248)699-4253
Farmington Hills, MI 48331-   Free: 800-347-GALE
3535   Fax: (248)699-8097

E-mail: galeord@gale.com
URL: http://www.gale.com/taft/

Desc: Over 10,000 foundations' 990-PFs. *Type:* Directory.

Practical Guide to Planned Giving

The Taft Group
27500 Drake Rd.   Ph: (248)699-4253
Farmington Hills, MI 48331-   Free: 800-347-GALE
3535   Fax: (248)699-8097

E-mail: galeord@gale.com
URL: http://www.gale.com/taft/

Contact: Laurie Fundukian, laurie.fundukian@gale.com.

Desc: Lists resources for fund raisers, along with additional sources of information, such as books, magazines, seminars, publishers, software programs. Principal content of publication is an explanation of various aspects of planned giving for nonprofit professionals. *Type:* Directory.

Prospector's Choice

The Taft Group
27500 Drake Rd.   Ph: (248)699-4253
Farmington Hills, MI 48331-   Free: 800-347-GALE
3535   Fax: (248)699-8097

E-mail: galeord@gale.com
URL: http://www.gale.com/taft/

Desc: 10,000 detailed funder profiles on top private foundation and corporate direct giving programs. *Type:* Directory.

United Way of America

701 N. Fairfax St.   Ph: (703)836-7100
Alexandria, VA 22314   Fax: (703)683-7840

Contact: Betty Beene, Pres.

Desc: Local United Way organizations in the U.S. Provides national, regional, and local program support and consulting to United Ways in the areas of fundraising, budgeting, management, fund distribution, planning, and communications. *Type:* Association.

United Way International

701 N. Fairfax St.   Ph: (703)519-0092
Alexandria, VA 22314   Fax: (703)519-0097

E-mail: uwi@unitedway.org

Contact: Robert M. Beggan, Pres./CEO.

Desc: Provides technical assistance to members. Offers information exchange, training for volunteers and professionals, and charitable programs. Helps with start-up of United Way type organizations in counties without one. *Type:* Association.

Who's Wealthy in America

The Taft Group
27500 Drake Rd.   Ph: (248)699-4253
Farmington Hills, MI 48331-   Free: 800-347-GALE
3535   Fax: (248)699-8097

E-mail: galeord@gale.com
URL: http://www.gale.com/taft/

Contact: Bob Romaniuk, Editor.

Desc: Over 100,000 persons in the U.S. with an inferred net worth of at least $1 million. *Type:* Directory.

Philately

Linn's Stamp News—North American Stamp Store Directory Issue

Linn's Stamp News
911 Vandemark Rd.   Ph: (513)498-0801
PO Box 29   Free: 800-448-7293
Sidney, OH 45365   Fax: 800-340-9501
E-mail: linns@linns.com

Desc: List of retail stamp stores throughout North America. *Type:* Directory.

Yellow Pages for Stamp Collectors

Linn's Stamp News
911 Vandemark Rd.   Ph: (513)498-0801
PO Box 29   Free: 800-448-7293
Sidney, OH 45365   Fax: 800-340-9501
E-mail: linns@linns.com; bjones@linns.com; lhoman@linns.com.

Contact: Michael Laurence, Editor.

Desc: Associations carrying products/services for stamp collectors. *Type:* Directory.

Philosophy

American Philosophical Association

Eric Hoffman
University of Delaware   Ph: (302)831-1112
Newark, DE 19716   Fax: (302)831-8690

E-mail: apaonline@udel.edu
URL: http://www.udel.edu/apa

Contact: Eric Hoffman, Exec.Dir.

Desc: College and university teachers of philosophy and others with an interest in philosophy. Facilitates exchange of ideas in philosophy, encourages creative and scholarly activity in philosophy, and fosters the professional work of teachers of philosophy. *Type:* Association.

Ayn Rand Institute

PO Box 6099   Ph: (310)306-9232
Inglewood, CA 90312   Fax: (310)306-4925

E-mail: essay@aynrand.org
URL: http://www.aynrand.org/contests

Contact: Dr. Michael S. Berliner, Exec.Dir.

Desc: Purpose is to promote increased awareness and understanding of Objectivism as defined by philosopher, essayist, and novelist Ayn Rand (1905-82), author of *The Fountainhead, Atlas Shrugged,* and other books. (Rand's philosophy of Objectivism upholds the supremacy of individual rights through advocacy of reason as the ultimate source of knowledge, self-interest as the proper code of ethics, and laissez-faire capitalism as the ideal political-economic system.) Group believes that "historical trends are the inescapable product of philosophy." Seeks to change current political and economic trends in the U.S. by changing underlying philosophies, primarily by introducing Rand's Objectivism into university courses and classrooms. *Type:* Association.

Center for Philosophy, Law, Citizenship

SUNY   Ph: (516)420-2047
Knapp Hall 15   Fax: (516)420-2698
Farmingdale, NY 11735

Contact: Prof. James P. Friel, Pres. & Dir.

Desc: Students, faculty, instructors, and other interested individuals. Seeks recognition of the person as the focus of the community. *Type:* Association.

Give But Give Wisely

Council of Better Business Bureaus, Inc.
4200 Wilson Blvd., No. 800   Ph: (703)276-0100
Arlington, VA 22203-1838   Fax: (703)525-8277

Contact: Bennett Weiner, Vice President.

Desc: Helps individuals make informed giving decisions to charities. Lists national charities generating the most inquiries to the Council of Better Business Bureaus. *Type:* Newsletter.

Phi Sigma Tau

Department. of Philosophy   Ph: (414)288-6857
Marquette University   Fax: (414)288-3300
Milwaukee, WI 53201-1881

Contact: Lee C. Rice, Exec.Sec.

Desc: Honor society - men and women, philosophy. *Type:* Association.

Philosopher's Index

Bowling Green State University
Philosophy Documentation Center
1616 E. Wooster St.   Ph: (419)372-2419
Bowling Green, OH 43403-0189

E-mail: leaman@bgnet.bgsu.edu

Desc: Contains more than 200,000 citations, with abstracts, to periodical articles and other published literature on philosophy and such related topics as aesthetics, epistemology, ethics, history of philosophy, logic, metaphysics, and social and political philosophy, as well as the philosophy of related interdisciplinary fields such as education, history, law, religion, and science. Covers English-language journals and books since 1940 and major philosophy journals in other languages published since 1967. *Available:* The Dialog Corporation, DIALOG; CompuServe Information Service, Knowledge Index. *Type:* Database.

Philosophy and Computers

American Philological Association (APA)
Holy Cross College   Ph: (508)793-2203
Department of Classics
Worcester, MA 01610
URL: http://www.udel.edu/apa.

Contact: Jon Dorbolo, Editor, dorboloj@ucs.orst.edu; John Long, Contact, (302)831-2895, johnlong@udel.edu.

Desc: Provides updates on activities and issues of the Committee. Recurring features include letters to the editor. *Type:* Newsletter.

Rosicrucian Digest

Rosicrucian Order, AMORC
Rosicrucian Park   Ph: (408)947-3600
1342 Naglee Ave.   Fax: (408)947-3677
San Jose, CA 95191

Contact: Robin Thompson, Editor.

Desc: Magazine covering mysticism, science, and philosophy. *Type:* Periodical.

Word Trade

Word Trade
207 S. Elliot Rd., Ste. 210   Ph: (919)384-0083
Chapel Hill, SC 27514   Fax: (919)968-2557
E-mail: wordtrade@wordtrade.com
URL: http://www.wordtrade.com.

Contact: Paul Nagy, Managing Editor, pnagy@wordtrade.com; Gilbert Hershey, Review Editor, ghershey@wordtrade.com.

Desc: Reviews new books; specializes in general trade titles, religious studies, and philosophy. Recurring features include editorials on publishing trends, and a column titled Views of the News. *Type:* Newsletter.

Photography

American Photo

Hachette Filipacchi Magazines, Inc.
1633 Broadway, 41st Fl.   Ph: (212)767-6000
New York, NY 10019   Fax: (212)989-4561

Contact: David Schonauer, Editor, (212)767-6273, fax: (212)333-2439, dschon1@aol.com; Richard Rabinowitz, Publisher, (212)767-6058, fax: (212)489-4217; Michael Citron, Advertising Dir.

Desc: Photography magazine. *Type:* Periodical.

American Society of Media Photographers

14 Washington Rd., Ste. 502   Ph: (609)799-8300
Princeton Junction, NJ 08550-   Fax: (609)799-2233
1033
URL: http://www.asmp.org

Contact: Richard Weisgrau, Exec.Dir.

Desc: Professional society of freelance photographers. Works to evolve trade practices for photographers in communications fields. *Type:* Association.

American Society of Media Photographers Bulletin

American Society of Media Photographers (ASMP)
14 Washington Rd., Ste. 502   Ph: (609)799-8300
Princeton Junction, NJ 08550-   Fax: (609)799-2233
1033
E-mail: info@asmp.org

Contact: Peter Skinner, Editor.

Desc: Association newsletter for members of the American Society of Media Photographers. *Type:* Newsletter.

Archive Photos

530 W. 25th St.   Ph: (212)675-0115
New York, NY 10001   Fax: (212)675-0379
E-mail: 102264.534@compuserve.com.
URL: http://www.archivephotos.com.

Contact: Patrick Montgomery, President; Eric Rachlis, VP Sales.

Alt. Contact: 530 W. 25th St., New York, NY 10001; telephone: (212)675-0115; fax: (212)675-0379. *Type:* Periodical.

ASMP Bulletin

American Society of Media Photographers (ASMP)
PO Box 652   Ph: (360)293-7959
Anacortes, WA 98221   Fax: (360)293-8912
E-mail: info@asmp.org; bulletin@asmp.org.
URL: http://www.asmp.org.

Contact: Peter Skinner, Editor, skinner@asmp.org.

Desc: Features articles on professional photography, copyright laws, and photographic techniques. Recurring features include interviews and news of research. *Type:* Newsletter.

Contemporary Photographers

St. James Press, Inc.
27500 Drake Rd.   Ph: (248)699-4253
Farmington Hills, MI 48331-   Free: 800-877-4253
3535   Fax: (248)699-8069
E-mail: galeord@gale.com

Contact: Martin Marix Evans, Editor, ( )44 01 327 858380.

Desc: About 750 living photographers and outstanding deceased photographers from the recent past; international coverage. *Type:* Directory.

Electronic Photography News

Photofinishing News, Inc.
10915 Bonita Beach Rd., No.   Ph: (941)992-4421
1091   Fax: (941)992-6328
Bonita Springs, FL 34135-9049
URL: http://www.photo-news.com; http://www.photo-news.com.

Contact: Don Franz, Editor, dfranz@photo-news.com; John Larish, Editor.

Desc: Provides information on "marketing and technical developments in electron/digital age captive, manipulation, and printing for the graphic arts and photography matter." *Type:* Newsletter.

Feature Photo Service Inc.

62 W. 45th St.   Ph: (212)944-7744
New York, NY 10036   Fax: (212)944-9536
E-mail: fpsphoto@aol.com.
URL: http://www.featurephoto.com.

Contact: Bob Goldberg, President; Richard Horwitz, Vice President.

Desc: Distributes business feature photos. *Alt. Contact:* 62 W. 45th St., New York, NY 10036; telephone: (212)944-7744; fax: (212)944-9536. *Type:* Periodical.

Gamma-Liaison Photos Inc.

11 E. 26th St.   Ph: (212)779-6300
New York, NY 10010   Fax: (212)779-6334

Contact: Michel G. Bernard, President; Jennifer B. Coley, Exec. VP; Donnamarie Barnes, Prod. Ed.

Desc: Distributes stock photography. *Alt. Contact:* 11 E. 26th St., New York, NY 10010; telephone: (212)779-6300; fax: (212)779-6334. *Type:* Periodical.

Globe Photos Inc.

275 7th Ave.   Ph: (212)645-9292
New York, NY 10001   Fax: (212)627-8932

Contact: Mary Beth Whelan, President; Raymond D. Whelan, Vice President; Dick Denuet, Bureau Chief; Raymond F. Whelan, Assignment Ed.

Desc: Distributes celebrity/personality photos, light news, general stock. *Alt. Contact:* 275 7th Ave., New York, NY 10001; telephone: (212)645-9292; fax: (212)627-8932. *Type:* Periodical.

Imaging Products & Services Directory

Photo Imaging Entrepreneur
2627 Grimsley St.   Ph: (336)854-8088
Greensboro, NC 27403   Free: 800-854-4119
    Fax: (336)854-8566
E-mail: imagingent@aol.com

Contact: Frank Elliott, Editor, elliott@photoent.com.

Desc: About 900 manufacturers, distributors, and suppliers of photofinishing products and services; international coverage. *Type:* Directory.

Impact Visuals Photo & Graphics Inc.

24 W. 25th St.   Ph: (212)807-6622
12th Fl.   Fax: (212)807-6644
New York, NY 10010
E-mail: impact@igc.apc.org.

Contact: Martin Vega, General Mgr.; Karen Berman, Picture Ed.; Jane Welna, Sales Mgr.

Desc: Distributes documentary photojournalism for editorial and advertising use. *Alt. Contact:* 24 W. 25th St., 12th Fl., New York, NY 10010; telephone: (212)807-6622; fax: (212)807-6644. *Type:* Periodical.

International Center of Photography

1130 5th Ave.   Ph: (212)860-1777
New York, NY 10128   Fax: (212)360-6490
URL: http://www.icp.org

Contact: Willis Hartshorn, Dir.

Desc: Professional and amateur photographers, corporations, and interested individuals. Teaches and promotes the appreciation and understanding of photography (and its extension to film and videotape) as an artistic, scientific, literary, and educational endeavor. Houses a permanent collection of prints and audiovisual tapes. *Type:* Association.

International Fire Photographers Association Journal

International Fire Photographers Association (IFPA)
PO Box 366   Ph: (503)838-0899
Independence, OR 97351-0366   Fax: (503)838-4335

Contact: Penny Turpen James, Contributing Editor; Gert Zoutendijk, Contributing Editor, gertzout@open.org.

Desc: Offers technical information on fire photography as well as news of Association events and reports from directors. Recurring features include editorials, letters to the editor, news of members, a calendar of events, and a column titled President's Message. *Type:* Newsletter.

International Photo News
226 S. B St.   Ph: (407)582-6038
Lake Worth, FL 33460   Fax: (407)585-5434
Contact: Elliott S. Kravetz, Bureau Chief; Jay N. Kravetz, Asst. Bureau Chief.
Desc: Distributes celebrity interviews, entertainment column, movie reviews, singles' column, You and Your Health, and You and Your Law. *Alt. Contact:* 226 S. B St., Lake Worth, FL 33460; telephone: (407)582-6038; fax: (407)585-5434. *Type:* Periodical.

National Free Lance Photographers Association
Box 406
Solebury, PA 18963
Contact: H. Jeffrey Valentine, Pres.
Desc: Amateur and professional photographers throughout the world; affiliate members include photographic schools, laboratories, stores, clubs, repair stations, and studios. Assists and cooperates with news media in obtaining photographs when regular coverage is not available. Maintains photographic file from members for industry; registers members' equipment in case of theft or loss. *Type:* Association.

National Press Photographers Association
3200 Croasdaile Dr., Ste. 306   Ph: (919)383-7246
Durham, NC 27705   Fax: (919)383-7261
Contact: Charles H. Cooper, Exec.Dir.
Desc: Professional news photographers and others whose occupation has a direct professional relationship with photojournalism, the art of news communication by photographic image through publication, television film, or theater screen. *Type:* Association.

Petersen's Photographic Magazine
Petersen Publishing Co., L.L.C.
6420 Wilshire Blvd.   Ph: (323)782-2350
Los Angeles, CA 90048-5515   Fax: (323)782-2704
Contact: Jackie Augustine, Publisher.
Desc: Photography magazine. *Type:* Periodical.

Photo International/Photo Associates News Service
7010 Brookfield Plz.   Ph: (703)451-9204
No. 806   Fax: (703)451-0332
Springfield, VA 22150-2914
Contact: Peter Heimsath, Bureau Mgr.
Desc: Distributes photo journalism pieces. *Alt. Contact:* 7010 Brookfield Plz., No. 806, Springfield, VA 22150-2914; telephone: (703)451-9204; fax: (703)451-0332. *Type:* Periodical.

PhotoBulletin-Weekly
PhotoSource International
Pine Lake Farm   Ph: (715)248-3800
1910 35th Rd.   Free: 800-624-0266
Osceola, WI 54020   Fax: (715)248-7394
E-mail: info@photosource.com
URL: http://www.photosource.com; http://www.photosource.com.
Contact: Angela Dober, Managing Editor; Rohn Engh, Publisher, psi2@photosource.com.
Desc: Announces current photograph needs of book and magazine publishers, corporations, government, and advertising agencies. Includes specific information on deadlines and prices. *Type:* Newsletter.

PhotoDaily
PhotoSource International
Pine Lake Farm   Ph: (715)248-3800
1910 35th Rd.   Free: 800-624-0266
Osceola, WI 54020   Fax: (715)248-7394
E-mail: info@photosource.com

URL: http://www.photosource.com; http://www.photosource.com.
Contact: Deb Koehler, Editor, eds@photosource.com; Rohn Engh, Editor, psi2@photosource.com.
Desc: Announces current photograph needs of book and magazine publishers, corporations, government, and advertising agencies. Provides specific information on deadlines and prices. *Type:* Newsletter.

Photographic Society of America
3000 United Founders Blvd.,   Ph: (405)843-1437
  Ste. 103   Fax: (405)843-1438
Oklahoma City, OK 73112
Contact: Jacki Noel, Operations Mgr.
Desc: Camera clubs; amateur, advanced amateur, and professional photographers. *Type:* Association.

The PhotoLetter
PhotoSource International
Pine Lake Farm   Ph: (715)248-3800
1910 35th Rd.   Free: 800-624-0266
Osceola, WI 54020   Fax: (715)248-7394
E-mail: info@photosource.com
URL: http://www.photosource.com; http://www.photosource.com.
Contact: Deb Koehler, Editor, eds@photosource.com; Rohn Engh, Publisher, psi2@photosource.com.
Desc: Informs photographers of a large network of publishers, art directors, and photo editors who currently need material for textbooks, magazines, and encyclopedias. *Type:* Newsletter.

Photo Marketing Association International
3000 Picture Pl.   Ph: (517)788-8100
Jackson, MI 49201   Fax: (517)788-8371
Contact: Roy S. Pung, Exec.Dir.
Desc: Retailers of photo and video equipment, film, and supplies; firms developing and printing film. *Type:* Association.

Photoreporters Inc.
875 Avenue of the Americas   Ph: (212)736-7602
Ste. 1003   Fax: (212)465-0651
New York, NY
E-mail: photoreps@earthlink.com.
Contact: Bruce Pomerantz, President.
Alt. Contact: 875 Avenue of the Americas, Ste. 1003, New York, NY; telephone: (212)736-7602; fax: (212)465-0651. *Type:* Periodical.

PhotoStock Notes/Plus
PhotoSource International
Pine Lake Farm   Ph: (715)248-3800
1910 35th Rd.   Free: 800-624-0266
Osceola, WI 54020   Fax: (715)248-7394
E-mail: info@photosource.com
URL: http://www.photosource.com; http://www.photosource.com.
Desc: Provides information for stock photographers and suggests equipment and materials for photobuyers. Recurring features include news of educational opportunities, a calendar of events, and book reviews. *Type:* Newsletter.

PhotoStockNotes
PhotoSource International
Pine Lake Farm   Ph: (715)248-3800
1910 35th Rd.   Free: 800-624-0266
Osceola, WI 54020   Fax: (715)248-7394
E-mail: info@photosource.com
URL: http://www.photosource.com; http://www.photosource.com.
Contact: Angela Dober, Managing Editor.
Desc: Features information on marketing of and trends involved with stock photos for such publications as textbooks, magazines, and encyclopedias. *Type:* Newsletter.

Popular Photography
Hachette Filipacchi Magazines, Inc.
1633 Broadway, 41st Fl.   Ph: (212)767-6000
New York, NY 10019   Fax: (212)989-4561
E-mail: popeditor@aol.com
Contact: Jason Schneider, Editor, (212)767-6924; Richard Rabinowitz, Publisher, (212)767-6161, fax: (212)482-4217; Michael Citron, Advertising Dir., (212)767-6162.
Desc: Photography magazine. *Type:* Periodical.

Professional Photographers of America
229 Peachtree St. NE, Ste. 2200 Ph: (404)522-8600
Atlanta, GA 30303   Free: 800-786-6277
                                 Fax: (404)614-6404
URL: http://www.ppa-world.org
Contact: Donna R. McMahon, Exec.Dir.
Desc: Professional society of portrait, wedding, commercial, and industrial, and specialized photographers. *Type:* Association.

School Photographer
Professional School Photographers of America
c/o Photo Marketing Association Ph: (517)788-8100
  International   Fax: (517)788-8371
3000 Picture Pl.
Jackson, MI 49201
E-mail: amcilrec@pmai.org.
URL: http://www.pmai.org.
Contact: Anne McIlree, Editor.
Desc: Provides news and information on school photography. Recurring features include news of market research, a calendar of events, and news of educational opportunities. *Type:* Newsletter.

Shutterbug
Patch Communications
5211 S. Washington Ave.   Ph: (407)268-5010
Titusville, FL 32780-7315   Fax: (407)267-1894
Contact: Bob Shell, Editor; Bonnie Paulk, Editorial Director; Don Welk, Publisher.
Desc: Photography magazine. *Type:* Periodical.

Stereo Photographers, Collectors and Enthusiasts Club
PO Box 2368   Ph: (310)837-2368
Culver City, CA 90231   Fax: (310)558-1653
URL: http://www.stereoscopy.com/reel3d
Contact: David Starkman, Tech.Dir.
Desc: Stereo photographers, collectors, and enthusiasts. Furthers interest in three-dimensional photography by pooling information sources, resources, and ideas. *Type:* Association.

Today's Photographer Magazine
American Image Inc.
6495 Shallowford Rd.   Ph: (336)945-9867
Lewisville, NC 27023   Free: 800-654-9557
                                 Fax: (336)945-3711
URL: http://www.aipress.com.
Contact: Vonda H. Blackburn, Editor/Contact; Jack M. Gallimore, Publisher; Sarah Hinshaw, Associate Publisher.
Desc: Photography magazine. *Alt. Contact:* PO Box 777, Lewisville, NC 27023. *Type:* Periodical.

Wagner International Photos Inc.
62 W. 45th St.   Ph: (212)944-7744
6th Fl.   Fax: (212)944-9536
New York, NY 10036-4208
Contact: Larry Lettera, President; Patrick Callahan, Chief Photographer.
Alt. Contact: 62 W. 45th St., 6th Fl., New York, NY 10036-4208; telephone: (212)944-7744; fax: (212)944-9536. *Type:* Periodical.

Wieck Photo Database Inc.
13500 Midway Rd.   Ph: (972)392-0888
Ste. 500   Fax: (972)934-8848
Dallas, TX 75244
E-mail: desk@wieckphoto.com.
Contact: Travis Hughs, Chm./CEO; Jim Wieck, Pres./ Chief Oper. Officer; Tim Roberts, VP-Systems; Marge Boatright, VP-Sales; Jere Cox, Dir.-Mktg.
Desc: Distributes news and PR photos. *Alt. Contact:* 13500 Midway Rd., Ste. 500, Dallas, TX 75244; telephone: (972)392-0888; fax: (972)934-8848. *Type:* Periodical.

The Zebras
44 Horseshoe Ln., N.   Ph: (716)734-0294
Henrietta, NY 14467   Fax: (716)344-4765
Contact: R. D. Zakia, Contact.
Desc: Photographers. Promotes the practice of silver-based writing with light, known as black and white photography. *Type:* Association.

Physical Fitness

Aerobics and Fitness Association of America
15250 Ventura Blvd., Ste. 200   Ph: (818)905-0040
Sherman Oaks, CA 91403   Free: 800-446-AFAA
    Fax: (818)990-5468
URL: http://www.afaa.com
Contact: Linda D. Pfeffer, R.N., Exec. Officer.
Desc: Professional association that promotes safety and excellence in exercise instruction throughout the world. *Type:* Association.

American Alliance for Health, Physical Education, Recreation and Dance
1900 Association Dr.   Ph: (703)476-3400
Reston, VA 20191   Free: 800-213-7193
    Fax: (703)476-9527
E-mail: evp@aahperd.org
URL: http://www.aahperd.org
Contact: Michael G. Davis, Exec.VP.
Desc: Students and educators in physical education, dance, health, athletics, safety education, recreation, and outdoor education. Purpose is to improve its fields of education at all levels through such services as consultation, periodicals and special publications, leadership development, determination of standards, and research. *Type:* Association.

American Running and Fitness Association
4405 East-West Hwy., Ste. 405   Ph: (301)913-9517
Bethesda, MD 20814   Free: 800-776-ARFA
    Fax: (301)913-9520
E-mail: arfarun@aol.com
URL: http://www.arfa.org
Contact: Susan Kalish, Exec.Dir.
Desc: Individual runners, exercise enthusiasts, and sports medicine professionals. Promotes running and other aerobic activities; fosters the preventive maintenance concept in health preservation. Serves as repository for data on running and fitness. *Type:* Association.

Atlanta Sports & Fitness Magazine
Atlanta Sports & Fitness Magazine, Inc.
359 E. Paces Ferry Rd. NE, Ste.   Ph: (404)842-0359
101   Fax: (404)816-5215
Atlanta, GA 30305
E-mail: asfmag1@aol.com
Contact: Jim Robinson, Publisher; Laura Weldon, Editor; Sherri Adair, Executive Director; Suzanne Klarer, Director of Events; Kris Burnett, Business Mgr.
Desc: General interest sports, health, and fitness journal. Journal includes a feature called Atlanta Health and Beauty every month. *Type:* Periodical.

Coaching Management
College Athletic Administrator
438 W. State St.   Ph: (607)272-0265
Ithaca, NY 14850   Fax: (607)272-2015
E-mail: maginc@aol.com.
Contact: Eleanor Frankel, Editor; Mark Goldberg, Publisher.
Desc: Magazine for high school and college head coaches for football, basketball, baseball and volleyball. *Type:* Periodical.

Delta Psi Kappa
PO Box 90264   Ph: (317)255-4379
Indianapolis, IN 46290   Fax: (317)253-5067
Contact: Harriet Rodenberg, Exec.Dir.
Desc: Professional fraternity - health, physical education, recreation, and dance. *Type:* Association.

Exercise Safety Association
10151 University Blvd., No.
138
Orlando, FL 32817-1981
E-mail: askesa@aol.com
Contact: Sharon Foy, Dir.
Desc: Fitness instructors, personal trainers, health spas, YMCAs, community recreation departments, and hospital wellness programs. Purposes are: to improve the qualifications of exercise instructors; to train instructors to develop safe exercise routines that will help people avoid injury while exercising; to prepare instructors for national certification. Offers training in aerobics and exercise and on the physiological aspects of exercise. *Type:* Association.

Fit Magazine
Goodman Media Group, Inc.
1700 Broadway, 34th Fl.   Ph: (212)541-7100
New York, NY 10019   Fax: (212)245-1241
Contact: Lisa Klugman, Editor; Jason Goodman, Publisher; John Damboragian, Advertising Mgr.
Desc: Health, fitness, lifestyles for women on the go. *Type:* Periodical.

Flex Magazines
Weider Publications
21100 Erwin St.   Ph: (818)884-6800
Woodland Hills, CA 91367-   Free: 800-423-5590
3712   Fax: (818)704-5734
E-mail: jweider@weiderpub.com
Contact: Jerry Kindela, Editor-in-Chief; George DePirro, Managing Editor; Bob Washburn, Publisher; GreggLoria, Advertising Mgr.
Desc: Men's and women's competitive body building magazine. *Type:* Periodical.

Health and Fitness News Service
Times Mirror Sq.   Ph: (213)237-7987
Los Angeles, CA 90053
Contact: Karin Hsiao, Editor.
Desc: Distributes health and fitness news and features. *Alt. Contact:* Times Mirror Sq., Los Angeles, CA 90053; telephone: (213)237-7987. *Type:* Periodical.

IDEA, The Health and Fitness Source
6190 Cornerstone Ct. E., Ste.   Ph: (619)535-8979
204   Free: 800-999-IDEA
San Diego, CA 92121   Fax: (619)535-8234
E-mail: member@ideafit.com
URL: http://www.ideafit.com
Contact: Kathie Davis, Exec.Dir.
Desc: Provides continuing education for fitness professionals including; fitness instructors, personal trainers, program directors, and club/studio owners. *Type:* Association.

Institute for Aerobics Research
12330 Preston Rd.   Ph: (972)341-3200
Dallas, TX 75230   Free: 800-635-7050
    Fax: (972)341-3224
Contact: Mark Donovan, Controller.
Desc: Goals are to promote understanding of the relationship between living habits and health, to provide leadership in enhancing the physical and emotional well-being of individuals, and to promote participation in aerobics. Seeks to increase the quality and quantity of fitness programs within major institutions. Conducts innovative studies on health and living habits and methods of facilitating changes in living habits; promotes the awareness and skills needed to develop a positive life-style. *Type:* Association.

International Health, Racquet and Sportsclub Association
263 Summer St.   Ph: (617)951-0055
Boston, MA 02210   Free: 800-228-4772
    Fax: (617)951-0056
E-mail: info@ihrsa.org
URL: http://www.ihrsa.org
Contact: John McCarthy, Exec.Dir.
Desc: Health, racquet, and sport clubs (2400); racquet sports manufacturers and suppliers (350). Promotes the continued growth of the health, racquet, and sports club industry in 35 countries. *Type:* Association.

Living Fit
Weider Publications
21100 Erwin St.   Ph: (818)884-6800
Woodland Hills, CA 91367-   Free: 800-423-5590
3712   Fax: (818)704-5734
E-mail: jweider@weiderpub.com
Desc: A newstand-only publication for health and fitness fans. *Type:* Periodical.

Muscle & Fitness
Weider Publications
21100 Erwin St.   Ph: (818)884-6800
Woodland Hills, CA 91367-   Free: 800-423-5590
3712   Fax: (818)704-5734
E-mail: jweider@weiderpub.com
URL: http://www.muscle-fitness.com.
Contact: Joe Weider, Publisher; Tom Deters, D.C., Editor-in-Chief, fax: (818)595-0427.
Desc: Physical fitness and lifestyle magazine. *Alt. Contact:* telephone: (818)595-0427; fax: (818)595-0463. *Type:* Periodical.

Muscular Development
Advanced Research Press, Inc.
2120 Smithtown Ave.   Ph: (516)467-3140
Ronkonkoma, NY 11779   Free: 800-645-5626
    Fax: (516)467-1241
Contact: Steve Blechman, Editor-in-Chief; Roy Ulin, Business Mgr.; Angela Frizalone, Advertising and Sales Controlled.
Desc: Bodybuilding and physical fitness magazine. *Type:* Periodical.

National Association for Sport and Physical Education
1900 Association Dr.   Ph: (703)476-3410
Reston, VA 20191   Free: 800-213-7193
    Fax: (703)476-8316
E-mail: naspe@aahperd.org
URL: http://www.aahperd.org/naspe.html
Contact: Dr. Judith C. Young, Exec.Dir.
Desc: Men and women professionally involved with physical activity and sports. Seeks to improve the total sport and physical activity experience in America. Conducts research and education programs in such areas as sport psychology, curriculum development, kinesiology, history, philosophy, sport sociology, and the biological and behavioral basis of human activity. *Type:* Association.

National Athletic Trainers Association

2952 Stemmons Fwy., Ste. 200   Ph: (214)637-6282
Dallas, TX 75247-6103   Free: 800-879-6282
    Fax: (214)637-2206
URL: http://www.nata.org

Contact: Eve Becker-Doyle, CAE, Contact.

Desc: Athletic trainers from universities, colleges, and junior colleges; professional football, baseball, basketball, and ice hockey; high schools, preparatory schools, military establishments, sports medicine clinics, and business/industrial health programs. *Type:* Association.

National Dance-Exercise Instructor's Training Association

1503 S. Washington Ave., Ste.   Ph: (612)340-1306
    208   Free: 800-237-6242
Minneapolis, MN 55454   Fax: (612)340-1619

Contact: Michael Wollman, Exec.Dir.

Desc: Fitness and aerobic exercise instructors. Seeks to provide standardized training and certification to aerobic exercise and fitness instructors. Produces choreography and dance-exercise program curricula; administers certification examinations. *Type:* Association.

National Federation of Professional Trainers

PO Box 4579   Ph: (317)447-3296
Lafayette, IN 47903   Free: 800-SAY-NFPT
    Fax: (317)447-3648
E-mail: nfpt@nfpt.com
URL: http://www.nfpt.com/nfpt

Contact: Ron Clark, Pres.

Desc: Seeks to provide affordable, convenient, comprehensive, and applicable information; offer organizational certification credentials for consumer recognition of competence; provide certified affiliates with ongoing education; establish a network of support, and provide professional products and services to trainers and consumers', and facilitate and encourage the exchange of ideas, knowledge, business experiences, and financial opportunities between all fitness administrators internationally. *Type:* Association.

National Strength and Conditioning Association

1955 N Union Blvd.   Ph: (719)632-6722
Colorado Springs, CO 80909-   Fax: (719)632-6367
    2229
E-mail: nsca@usa.net
URL: http://www.nsca lift.org

Contact: Harvey Newton, Exec.Dir.

Desc: Professionals in the sports science, athletic, and fitness industries. Promotes the total conditioning of athletes to a level of optimum performance, with the belief that a better conditioned athlete not only performs better but is less prone to injury. Gathers and disseminates information on strength and conditioning techniques and benefits. *Type:* Association.

Shape

Weider Publications
21100 Erwin St.   Ph: (818)884-6800
Woodland Hills, CA 91367-   Free: 800-423-5590
    3712   Fax: (818)704-5734
E-mail: jweider@weiderpub.com
URL: http://www.shapemag.com.

Contact: Barbara S. Harris, Editor, (818)595-0593; Joe Weider, Publisher.

Desc: Magazine for women covering nutrition, weight control, physical fitness, psychology, fashion, beauty and travel. *Type:* Periodical.

3HO Foundation

PO Box 351149   Ph: (310)552-3416
Los Angeles, CA 90035   Fax: (310)557-8414

Contact: Shakti Parwha Kaur Khalsa, Exec.Sec.

Desc: Students and teachers of Kundalini Yoga, which includes all types of Yoga, who practice the "Healthy, Happy, Holy way of life" as taught by Yogi Bhajan. Operates 108 centers in the U.S., Canada, Japan, Puerto Rico, South America, Australia, Europe, and Mexico. Provides nursery school education; sponsors teacher training courses. *Type:* Association.

Walking

Reader's Digest Publications
28 W. 23rd   Ph: (212)366-8853
New York, NY 10010-5204   Free: 800-937-9241
    Fax: (212)633-4699
E-mail: walkingmag@aol.comp.

Contact: Seth Bauer, Editor.

Desc: Magazine for recreational and fitness walkers; includes articles on health, fitness, nutrition, travel, gear and equipment, and events. *Alt. Contact:* 9-11 Horcourt Street, Boston, MA 02116; telephone: (617)266-3322, (617)226-7373. *Type:* Periodical.

Physics

American Association of Physicists in Medicine

One Physics Ellipse   Ph: (301)209-3350
College Park, MD 20740-3846   Fax: (301)209-0862
E-mail: aapm@aapm.org
URL: http://www.aapm.org

Contact: Sal Trofi, Jr., Exec.Dir.

Desc: Persons professionally engaged in application of physics to medicine and biology in medical research and educational institutions. encourages interest and training in medical physics and related fields; promotes high professional standards; disseminates technical information. *Type:* Association.

American Association of Physics Teachers

1 Physics Ellipse   Ph: (301)209-3300
College Park, MD 20740-3842   Fax: (301)209-0845
URL: http://www.aapt.org

Contact: Dr. Bernard V. Khoury, Exec. Officer.

Desc: Professional society of teachers of physics in colleges, universities, and secondary schools; undergraduates and graduates with major interest in physics. *Type:* Association.

American Institute of Physics

1 Physics Ellipsc   Ph: (301)209-3100
College Park, MD 20740-3843   Fax: (301)209-0843
URL: http://www.aip.org

Contact: Dr. Marc H. Brodsky, Exec.Dir. & CEO.

Desc: Corporation of ten national societies in the fields of physics, astronomy and related disciplines with a total of 100,000 members, 17 affiliated societies, 68 corporate associates, and 7500 student members. Seeks to assist in the advancement and diffusion of the knowledge of physics and its application to human welfare. To this end the institute publishes scientific journals devoted to physics and related sciences; provides secondary information services; provides online electronic journals serves the public by making available to the press and other channels of public information reliable communications on physics and its progress; carries on extensive career services activities; maintains projects directed toward providing information about physics education to students, physics teachers, and physics departments; encourages and assists in the documentation and study of the history of recent physics; cooperates with local, national, and international organizations devoted to physics; and fosters the relations of the science of physics to other sciences and to the arts and industry. *Type:* Association.

American Physical Society

1 Physics Ellipse   Ph: (301)209-3200
College Park, MD 20740-3844   Fax: (301)209-0865
E-mail: exoffice@aps.org
URL: http://www.aps.org

Contact: Judy R. Franz, Exec. Officer.

Desc: Scientists worldwide, dedicated to the advancement and the diffusion of the knowledge of physics. Publishes some of the leading international physics journals, organizes major scientific meetings, and provides strong outreach programs in physics education and in international and public affairs. *Type:* Association.

JILA

Box 440   Ph: (303)492-7789
Boulder, CO 80309-0440   Fax: (303)492-5235

Contact: W. Patrick McInerny, Exec. Officer.

Desc: Interdisciplinary institute for research and graduate education in the physical sciences. Located on the main campus of th University of Colorado (CU) in Boulder, JILA is operated jointly by CU and the National Institute of Standards and Technology (NIST). Special interests include: ultra-low-temperature atomic collisions, including Bose Einstein condensation; the chemistry of small molecules; laser physics and precision measurements; spectroscopy and spectral line broadening; solar physics; and astrophysical observation and measurements. *Type:* Association.

Physicians Financial News

PFN Publishing, Inc.
One Harmon Meadow Blvd.   Ph: (201)864-2400
Secaucus, NJ 07094   Fax: (201)864-3626

Contact: Noreen Perrotta, Editor; Irene Stewart, Advertising Dir.; Patricia Quilty, Advertising Mgr.; Jeannette Brandofino, Co-Publisher.

Desc: Tabloid for primary-care physicians, covering personal finance, health care delivery, professional liability, and practice management. *Alt. Contact:* 19 W. 34th St., Suite 1010, New York, NY 10001; telephone: (212)643-0991; fax: (212)643-1079. *Type:* Periodical.

Physics Today

American Institute of Physics
1 Physics Ellipse   Ph: (301)209-3070
College Park, MD 20740-3843   Fax: (301)209-0843
E-mail: aipinfo@aip.org

Contact: Stephen G. Benka, Editor; Richard T. Kobel, Advertising Mgr.

Desc: Journal covering news of physics research and activities that affect physics. *Alt. Contact:* One Physics Ellipse, College Park, MD 20740; telephone: (301)209-2440, (301)209-0842; fax: (301)209-0842. *Type:* Periodical.

Searchable Physics Information Notices

American Institute of Physics (AIP)
500 Sunnyside Blvd.   Ph: (516)576-2265
Woodbury, NY 11797-2999
E-mail: aipinfo@aip.org
URL: http://www.aip.org/pt/guide/

Contact: Tim Ingoldsby, Director of Product Development, (516)576-2265, fax: (516)576-2499, timgoldsby@aip.org.

Desc: Contains approximately 750,000 citations, with author-prepared abstracts, from over 80 U.S., Russian, and Chinese translation journals and U.S. conference proceedings in physics and astronomy that have been published by the American Institute of Physics and its member societies. *Available:* The Dialog Corporation, DIALOG; American Institute of Physics (AIP), PINET Plus (Physics INformation NETwork); EBSCOhost. *Type:* Database.

Sigma Pi Sigma

1 Physics Ellipse   Ph: (301)209-3007
College Park, MD 20740   Fax: (301)209-0839
E-mail: sps@aip.org
Contact: Dr. Dwight E. Neuenschwander, Exec.Dir.
Desc: Honor society - men and women, physics. Recognizes and encourages the attainment of high scholarship and potential achievement in physics among outstanding students. *Type:* Association.

Solid State and Superconductivity Abstracts

Cambridge Scientific Abstracts (CSA)
7200 Wisconsin Ave., Ste. 601   Ph: (301)961-6700
Bethesda, MD 20814-4823
E-mail: sales@csa.com
URL: http://www.csa.com
Contact: Erica Omorogieva, Electronic Information Specialist, (301)941-2509, fax: (301)961-6720, erica@csa.com.
Desc: Contains more than 149,000 citations, with abstracts, to the worldwide theoretical and applied literature on solid state studies. Covers chemistry, physics, metallurgy, resonance, materials, measurement, and superconductivity theories, applications, and problem areas. *Available:* STN International; Cambridge Scientific Abstracts (CSA), Internet Database Service. *Type:* Database.

Physiology

The Dream Encyclopedia

Gale Group Inc.
27500 Drake Rd.   Ph: (248)699-4253
Farmington Hills, MI 48331-   Free: 800-877-GALE
3535   Fax: (248)699-8070
E-mail: galeord@galegroup.com
URL: http://www.galegroup.com.
Desc: Organizations involved in the study of dreams, including sleep research centers and laboratories. Principal content of publication is 250 dream topics, along with possible symbol interpretations. *Type:* Directory.

Plastics

Modern Plastics Encyclopedia

McGraw-Hill, Inc.
2 Penn Plaza   Ph: (212)904-2000
New York, NY 10121   Free: 800-223-6180
                     Fax: (212)904-6068
URL: http://www.mcgraw-hill.com
Contact: William A. Kaplan, Editor.
Desc: List of about 5,000 suppliers of over 350 types of products and services to the plastics industry in the United States and Canada (Buyers' Guide); Trade Names Directory; Guide to world-wide Plastics Associations. *Type:* Directory.

PLASNEWS (PLASPEC Daily News)

D & S Data Resources, Inc.
218 East Bridge St.   Ph: (215)428-1060
Morrisville, PA 19067
E-mail: plaspec.com
Contact: Abbe Scheiner, Vice President.
Desc: Contains prices and critical plastics industry news. Reports the latest developments in the plastics industry, including plant start-ups and closings, market demand, new materials and technologies, new markets, corporate mergers and takeovers, environmental and other governmental regulatory actions, price news, and recycling. *Available:* STN International; D & S Data Resources, Inc. *Type:* Database.

PLASPEC Materials Selection Database

D & S Data Resources, Inc.
218 East Bridge St.   Ph: (215)428-1060
Morrisville, PA 19067
Contact: Abbe Scheiner, Vice President, (215)428-1060, fax: (215)428-1069.
Desc: Contains detailed specifications and pricing details on more than 13,000 grades of commercially available plastics materials for the plastics industry. Selectable by more than 100 physical and performance characteristics, including new grades. *Available:* The Dialog Corporation, DIALOG; STN International. *Type:* Database.

Plastics Business News

Market Search Inc.
2727 Holland Sylvania Rd., Ste.   Ph: (419)535-7899
A
Toledo, OH 43615
Contact: James R. Best, Editor.
Desc: Examines significant developments in the top markets for plastics and plastics products. Predicts price trends and reviews and forecasts major indexes that affect the plastics industry. *Type:* Newsletter.

Plastics Compounding Redbook

Advanstar Communications
7500 Old Oak Blvd.   Ph: (440)243-8100
Cleveland, OH 44130-3369   Free: 800-225-4569
                     Fax: (440)891-2733
E-mail: directories@advanstar.com
URL: http://www.advanstar.com.
Contact: Laverne Leonard, Editor.
Desc: Over 1,000 suppliers of resins, additives, fillers and other materials, compounding equipment, and services to the plastics compounding industry. *Type:* Directory.

Plastics Focus

Plastics Connection, Inc.
21 A Pray St.   Ph: (413)549-5020
PO Box 814   Fax: (413)549-9955
Amherst, MA 01004
Contact: Michael L. Berins, Editor.
Desc: Provides news and interpretation of events affecting the plastics industry, including changes and trends in resin pricing, applications and markets for plastics, growth opportunities in existing markets, machinery and processing developments, international competition and opportunities, and new polymers, blends, and alloys. *Type:* Newsletter.

Plastics Technology Processing Handbook and Buyers' Guide

Bill Communications, Inc.
355 Park Ave. S.   Ph: (212)592-6200
New York, NY 10010-1789   Free: 800-266-4712
                     Fax: (212)592-6339
URL: http://www.plasticstechnology.com.
Contact: Matthew H. Naitove, Editor, mnaitove@plasticstechnology.com; Louis Bell, Editor, lbell@plasticstechnology.com; Sherri Fuchs, Editor, (212)592-6566, sfuchs@plasticstechnology.com.
Desc: Over 4,000 manufacturers of plastics processing equipment and materials, including injection molding, blow molding and extrusion machinery; auxiliary and secondary equipment including decorating and assembly products thermoplastic and thermoset resins; chemicals and additives. *Type:* Directory.

plasticsBRIEFS—Design and Materials Newsletter

Market Search Inc.
2727 Holland Sylvania Rd., Ste.   Ph: (419)535-7899
A
Toledo, OH 43615
Contact: James R. Best, Editor.
Desc: Publishes news affecting successful design with plastics. Recurring features include news of research. *Type:* Newsletter.

plasticsBRIEFS—Extrusion and Blow Molding Newsletter

Market Search Inc.
2727 Holland Sylvania Rd., Ste.   Ph: (419)535-7899
A
Toledo, OH 43615
Contact: James R. Best, Editor.
Desc: Provides news on extrusion and blow molding that affects sales, profits, and product quality of the industry. Recurring features include news of research. *Type:* Newsletter.

plasticsBRIEFS—Injection Molding Newsletter

Market Search Inc.
2727 Holland Sylvania Rd., Ste.   Ph: (419)535-7899
A
Toledo, OH 43615
Contact: James R. Best, Editor.
Desc: Provides news on injection molding that affects sales, profits, and product quality of the industry. Recurring features include news of research. *Type:* Newsletter.

plasticsBRIEFS—Reinforced Plastics Newsletter

Market Search Inc.
2727 Holland Sylvania Rd., Ste.   Ph: (419)535-7899
A
Toledo, OH 43615
Contact: James R. Best, Editor.
Desc: Features information on new sales opportunities, quality improvements, technology and innovation, competition, and pricing in the plastics industry. *Type:* Newsletter.

plasticsBRIEFS—Thermoplastics Marketing Newsletter

Market Search Inc.
2727 Holland Sylvania Rd., Ste.   Ph: (419)535-7899
A
Toledo, OH 43615
Contact: James R. Best, Editor.
Desc: Focuses on news affecting thermoplastics sales and market developments. Covers trends, opportunities, technology, innovation, and competition. *Type:* Newsletter.

Polymer Blends, Alloys and IPNs Abstracts

Technomic Publishing Co., Inc.
851 New Holland Ave.   Ph: (717)291-5609
Box 3535   Free: 800-233-9936
Lancaster, PA 17604-3535   Fax: (717)295-4538
E-mail: customer@techpub.com
URL: http://www.techpub.com
Contact: John W. deGroot, Editor.
Desc: Summarizes the growing literature and patents on plastics technology. Includes new information on chemistry, properties and performance, testing, processing, and applications. *Type:* Newsletter.

Polyurethane Division, Society of the Plastics Industry
1801 K St. NW, Ste. 600k   Ph: (202)974-5364
Washington, DC 20006-1300   Fax: (202)296-7005
URL: http://www.polyurethane.org
Contact: Fran W. Lichtenberg, Exec.Dir.
Desc: Manufacturers of chemicals used in the manufacture of polyurethane foam and foam products such as furniture cushions, bedding, and building insulation; equipment manufacturers. *Type:* Association.

Polyurethane News
Polyurethane Division
Society of the Plastics Industry
1801 K St. NW, Ste. 600K   Ph: (202)974-5200
Washington, DC 20006   Fax: (202)822-8481
URL: http://www.polyurethane.org.
Contact: Fran W. Lichtenberg, Editor.
Desc: Offers information on new publications, conferences, and legislation and regulation affecting the polyurethane industry. *Type:* Newsletter.

Regulatory Update
Weisfeld Associates
1 Franklin Town Blvd., No.   Ph: (215)567-7235
1204   Fax: (215)567-7235
Philadelphia, PA 19103
URL: http://www.polymers.com; http://www.regup.plastics.com/.
Contact: Lewis B. Weisfeld, Editor, lweisfeld@aol.com.
Desc: Covers proposed and final government regulatory developments related to health, safety, and the environment pertaining to the plastics industry. Contains media and industry comment and reaction. *Type:* Newsletter.

Society of Plastics Engineers
14 Fairfield Dr.   Ph: (203)775-0471
Brookfield, CT 06804-0403   Fax: (203)775-8490
E-mail: 4spemail@4spe.org
URL: http://www.4spe.org
Contact: Michael R. Cappelletti, Exec.Dir.
Desc: Professional society of plastics scientists, engineers, sales professionals, educators, students, and others interested in the design, development, producti on, and utilization of plastics materials, products, and equipment. Conducts seminars. Maintains 92 sections. *Type:* Association.

Society of the Plastics Industry
1801 K St. NW, Ste. 600K   Ph: (202)974-5200
Washington, DC 20006   Fax: (202)296-7005
E-mail: feedback@socplas.org
URL: http://www.socplas.org
Contact: Larry L. Thomas, Pres.
Desc: Manufacturers and processors of molded, extruded, fabricated, laminated, calendered, and reinforced plastics; manufacturers of raw materials, machinery, tools, dies, and molds; testing laboratories; consultants. Supports research; proposes standards for plastics products. Compiles statistics. *Type:* Association.

Urethane Abstracts
Technomic Publishing Co., Inc.
851 New Holland Ave.   Ph: (717)291-5609
Box 3535   Free: 800-233-9936
Lancaster, PA 17604-3535   Fax: (717)295-4538
E-mail: customer@techpub.com
URL: http://www.techpub.com
Contact: John W. deGroot, Editor.
Desc: Contains current international literature and U.S. patents on polyurethanes and polyisocyanurates. *Type:* Newsletter.

Urethane Plastics and Products
Technomic Publishing Co., Inc.
851 New Holland Ave.   Ph: (717)291-5609
Box 3535   Free: 800-233-9936
Lancaster, PA 17604-3535   Fax: (717)295-4538
E-mail: customer@techpub.com
URL: http://www.techpub.com
Contact: Jerry S. Pool, Editor.
Desc: Features marketing, technology, and applications of urethane plastics and products. Describes the success of specific products, tests, and research. *Type:* Newsletter.

Plumbing

American Supply Association
222 Merchandise Mart, Ste.   Ph: (312)464-0090
1360   Fax: (312)464-0091
Chicago, IL 60654
E-mail: asaemail@interserv.com
URL: http://www.asa.net/tech
Contact: Inge Calderon, Exec.VP.
Desc: National association of wholesale, distributors, and manufacturers of plumbing and heating, cooling, pipes, valves, and fittings. Compiles statistics on operating costs and makes occasional studies of compensation, fringe benefits, wages, and salaries. Conducts research studies and forecasting surveys. *Type:* Association.

ASA News
American Supply Association (ASA)
222 Merchandise Mart, Ste.   Ph: (312)464-0090
1360   Fax: (312)464-0091
Chicago, IL 60654-1202
E-mail: asaemail@interserv.com
URL: http://www.asa.net.
Contact: Mary Jo Martin, Chief Editor, maryjomartin@earthlink.net.
Desc: Provides "thought-provoking" editorial coverage of distributors and manufacturers in the plumbing and piping industry, regional and national industry events, and it ems of interest. *Type:* Newsletter.

National Certified Pipe Welding Bureau— Membership Directory
National Certified Pipe Welding Bureau
1385 Piccard Dr.   Ph: (301)869-5800
Rockville, MD 20850   Fax: (301)990-9690
Contact: Jack Hansmann, Editor.
Desc: About 600 mechanical contractors regularly engaged in the fabrication or erecting of piping systems, who employ certified pipe welders. *Type:* Directory.

PHC Profit Report
Business News Publishing Co.
3150 River Rd., Ste. 101   Ph: (847)297-3714
Des Plaines, IL 60018   Fax: (847)297-8371
Contact: Jim Dlsltynski, Editor and Publisher.
Desc: Provides information on marketing, financial management, employee relations, and news and commentary on the plumbing-heating-cooling industry. *Type:* Newsletter.

United Association of Journeymen and Apprentices of the Plumbing and Pipe Fitting Industry of the U.S. and Canada
PO Box 37800   Ph: (202)628-5823
Washington, DC 20013   Fax: (202)628-5024
Contact: Martin Maddaloni, Gen.Pres.
Desc: AFL-CIO. *Type:* Association.

Podiatry

American Academy of Podiatric Practice Management Newsletter
American Academy of Podiatric Practice Management
2737 E. Oakland Park Blvd.   Ph: (305)561-3338
Ft. Lauderdale, FL 33306
Contact: Robert C. Purdy, D.P.M., Editor.
Desc: Supplies management information for Academy members. Covers such subjects as investments, advertising and marketing, and tax planning. *Type:* Newsletter.

American Board of Podiatric Surgery
3330 Mission St.   Ph: (415)826-3200
San Francisco, CA 94110-5009   Fax: (415)826-4640
E-mail: jlamb@abps.org
URL: http://www.abps.org
Contact: James A. Lamb, Exec.Dir.
Desc: Podiatrists certified as diplomates. Objectives are: to protect and improve public health by advancing the science of foot surgery and by encouraging the study and evaluation of standards of foot surgery; to act upon application for certification of legally licensed podiatrists to ascertain their competency in foot surgery; to grant certificates to candidates who have met all qualifications. *Type:* Association.

American College of Foot and Ankle Surgeons
515 Busse Hwy.   Ph: (847)292-2237
Park Ridge, IL 60068   Free: 800-421-2237
    Fax: (847)292-2022
E-mail: acfas@pop.mbsi.net
Contact: Thomas R. Schedler, CAE, Exec.Dir.
Desc: Objectives are to: promote and disseminate information on podiatric surgery among the public, podiatric surgeons, and other health professionals; encourage and publish research findings and related literature; provide intensive programs for clinical and experimental research to improve podiatric surgery. *Type:* Association.

American Podiatric Medical Association
9312 Old Georgetown Rd.   Ph: (301)571-9200
Bethesda, MD 20814   Fax: (301)530-2752
E-mail: askapma@apma.org
URL: http://www.apma.org
Contact: Glenn B. Gastwirth, DPM.
Desc: Professional society of podiatrists and doctors of podiatric medicine. *Type:* Association.

Temple University School of Podiatric Medicine Gait Study Center
8th & Race Sts.   Ph: (215)629-0300
Philadelphia, PA 19107   Free: 800-220-FEET
E-mail: hhillstrom@pcpm.edu
URL: http://www.temple.edu/podiatry
Contact: Dr. Howard Hillstrom, PhD, Dir.
Desc: Posture and locomotion studies, focusing on the causes of abnormal gait conditions. Conducts basic and clinical research in biomechanics and biomedical engineering with special emphasis on the lower extremities. *Type:* Research center.

Poetry

Academy of American Poets
584 Broadway, Ste. 1208   Ph: (212)274-0343
New York, NY 10012   Fax: (212)274-9427
E-mail: poets@artswire.org
URL: http://www.poets.org
Contact: William Wadsworth, Contact.
Desc: Seeks to encourage, stimulate, and foster the appreciation of American poetry. *Type:* Association.

Poets and Writers

72 Spring St.   Ph: (212)226-3586
New York, NY 10012   Fax: (212)226-3963
E-mail: ef@pwonline.com
Contact: Elliot Figman, Exec.Dir.

Desc: Serves as an information clearinghouse for the literary community; works to increase the audience for contemporary literature. Maintains information center; sponsors readings and workshops. Conducts research programs; compiles statistics. *Type:* Association.

Poland/Polish

Alliance of Poles of America

6966 Broadway   Ph: (216)883-3131
Cleveland, OH 44105   Fax: (216)883-3172
Contact: John Borkowski, Pres.

Desc: Fraternal benefit life insurance society. *Type:* Association.

American Federation of Polish Jews

136 E. 39th St.   Ph: (212)689-4930
New York, NY 10016
Contact: Dr. Solomon Goldman, Sec.

Desc: Seeks to preserve the memory and the history of Polish Jewry through the establishment of an institute to study 1000 years of Jewish Life in Poland at Tel Aviv University in Israel. Participates in negotiations with Polish officials aimed at obtaining compensation for the Jewish schools, hospitals, and other public buildings which were confiscated by the Polish government. *Type:* Association.

Polish Air Force Veterans Association

351 NW Richmond Beach Rd.,
   Apt. 317
Seattle, WA 98177-3154
Contact: Tadeusz Maj, Pres.

Desc: International organization of Polish Air Force veterans of World War II. Established to maintain comradeships formed during the War. Objectives are to: aid hospitals and schools; assist widows, orphans, and other dependents of Polish Air Force personnel; cooperate with other organizations devoted to the cultural welfare of ex-service persons. *Type:* Association.

Polish Beneficial Association

2595 Orthodox   Ph: (215)535-2626
Philadelphia, PA 19137   Fax: (215)535-0169
Contact: Theodore S. Drejski, Pres.

Desc: Fraternal benefit insurance society for persons of Slavic or Polish descent and of the Greek Orthodox or Roman Catholic faith. Actively engages in patriotic, religious, social, and fraternal activities. *Type:* Association.

Polish Falcons of America

615 Iron City Dr.   Ph: (412)922-2244
Pittsburgh, PA 15205   Free: 800-535-2071
                  Fax: (412)922-5029
URL: http://www.polishfalcons.org
Contact: Wallace Zielinski, Pres.

Desc: Fraternal benefit insurance society for persons of Polish or Slavic descent and their spouses or any individual who is judged supportive of the purpose and ethnic heritage of the Polish Falcons of America. Promotes social, educational, and physical fitness activities. Conducts track and field meets. *Type:* Association.

Polish Legion of American Veterans, U.S.A., Ladies Auxiliary

2141 Vernon   Ph: (734)675-1354
Trenton, MI 48183
Contact: Wanda Swiecki, Treas.

Desc: Women related to veterans of Polish descent who have served in the U.S. armed forces. Presents annual scholarships to graduating high school seniors. *Type:* Association.

Polish National Alliance of the United States of North America

6100 N. Cicero   Ph: (773)286-0500
Chicago, IL 60646   Free: 800-621-3723
                  Fax: (773)286-9148
Contact: Edward J. Moskal, Pres.

Desc: Fraternal benefit life insurance society. Men, women, and children of Polish, Lithuanian, Ruthenian, or Slovak descent or affiliation and spouses of members. Sponsors fraternal, educational, charitable, and life insurance programs. *Type:* Association.

Polish National Union of America

1002 Pittston Ave.   Ph: (717)344-1513
Scranton, PA 18505   Fax: (717)961-5961
Contact: Edmund Kotula, Pres.

Desc: Fraternal benefit life insurance society. *Type:* Association.

Polish Roman Catholic Union of America

984 Milwaukee Ave.   Ph: (773)278-3210
Chicago, IL 60622   Free: 800-772-8632
                  Fax: (773)278-4595
Contact: Josephine Szarowicz, Sec.Treas.

Desc: Fraternal benefit life insurance society. Sponsors sports and youth activities and children's social and recreation programs. Conducts language school and dance programs. *Type:* Association.

Polish Union of the United States of North America

PO Box 660   Ph: (717)823-1611
Wilkes Barre, PA 18703-0660   Fax: (717)829-7849
Contact: Charlotte L. Androckitis, Gen.Sec.

Desc: Fraternal benefit life insurance society. *Type:* Association.

Polish Women's Alliance of America

205 S. Northwest Hwy.   Ph: (847)384-1200
Park Ridge, IL 60068   Free: 888-522-1898
                  Fax: (847)384-1222
E-mail: pres@pwaa.org
URL: http://www.pwaa.org.
Contact: Delphine Lytell, Pres.

Desc: Fraternal benefit life insurance society administered by women. Supports and contributes to charitable and relief foundations in the U.S. and abroad. *Type:* Association.

Political Action

AIDS Action Council

1875 Connecticut Ave. NW,   Ph: (202)986-1300
   Ste. 700   Free: 800-644-AIDS
Washington, DC 20009   Fax: (202)986-1345
E-mail: aidsaction@aidsaction.org
URL: http://www.aidsaction.org
Contact: Daniel Zingale, Exec.Dir.

Desc: Serves as a representative in Washington, DC, of more than 1400 community-based AIDS service organizations. Advocates, at the federal level, for more effective AIDS policy, legislation, and funding. Works collaboratively with AIDS Action Foundation, a national public policy research organization. *Type:* Association.

American Medical Political Action Committee

c/o American Medical   Ph: (202)789-7400
   Association   Fax: (202)789-7469
1101 Vermont Ave. NW
Washington, DC 20005
Contact: Kevin Walker, Exec. Dir.

Desc: Physicians, their spouses, and others interested in political action and participation in public affairs. Seeks to further political knowledge of its members and to provide them with means for concerted political action. *Type:* Association.

Business-Industry Political Action Committee

888 Sixteenth St., NW   Ph: (202)833-1880
Washington, DC 20006   Fax: (202)833-2338
URL: http://www.bipac.org
Contact: Gregory S. Casey, Pres. & CEO.

Desc: Businesspeople who support "pro-market" candidates for Congress. Describes itself as the political action arm of the business community. Not affiliated with any political party. *Type:* Association.

Campaign California

926 J St., No. 1400   Ph: (916)447-8950
Sacramento, CA 95814
Contact: Karl Ory, Chief Adm. Officer.

Desc: State organization that attempts to introduce new issues into the political arena such as: rebuilding the Democratic party; controlling toxic wastes; developing affordable and better child care; stopping environmental cancer; achieving low-cost housing and tenants' rights. Works to elect progressive candidates to office in California. *Type:* Association.

Citizen Action Fund

1730 Rhode Island Ave. NW,   Ph: (202)775-1580
   Ste. 403   Fax: (202)296-4054
Washington, DC 20036
Contact: Ira Arlook, Exec.Dir.

Desc: Citizens working for economic democracy and social justice. Goal is to make the concerns of the majority of Americans felt in economic, environmental, and political decision-making. Seeks more jobs, safe and affordable energy, fair taxes, equal voting rights, and a safe and healthy community and workplace, free of toxic hazards. *Type:* Association.

CIVICUS: World Alliance for Citizen Participation

919 18th St. NW, 3rd Fl.   Ph: (202)331-8518
Washington, DC 20006   Fax: (202)331-8774
E-mail: info@civicus.org
URL: http://www.civicus.org
Contact: Angela Lane, Communications Officer.

Desc: Strengthens citizen action and civil society throughout the world. *Type:* Association.

Common Cause

1250 Connecticut Ave., NW   Ph: (202)833-1200
Washington, DC 20036   Fax: (202)659-3716
E-mail: grassroots@commoncause.org
URL: http://www.commoncause.org
Contact: Ann McBride, Pres.

Desc: Nonpartisan citizens' lobby. Dedicated to fighting for open, honest, and accountable government at the national, state, and local levels. Gathers and disseminates information on the effects of money in politics; lobbies for political finance and other campaign reforms. *Type:* Association.

Common Cause/Kentucky

2100 Gardiner Ln., No. 104B   Ph: (502)458-7065
Louisville, KY 40205-2947   Fax: (502)458-7065
E-mail: cmncause@venus.net
URL: http://www.nonprofit.venus.net/cmncause/
Contact: Ivonne Rovira, Exec. Dir.

Desc: Advocates government accessibility, ethics, campaign, finance reform and other good government issues. *Type:* Association.

Common Cause of New Hampshire

4 Park St., 215   Ph: (603)228-1881
Concord, NH 03301-6313   Free: 800-926-1064
                  Fax: (603)226-3408
E-mail: ccnh@totalnetnh.net

URL: http://www.commoncause.org/states/newhampshire

Contact: Nancy E. Snow, Exec.Dir.

Desc: Nonpartisan Citizens' Lobby Organization which monitors governmental process to insure fairness. Works on right to know, corporate welfare, campaign finance reform, ethics, and lobbyist disclosure. *Type:* Association.

Free Congress Research and Education Foundation

717 2nd St. NE   Ph: (202)546-3000
Washington, DC 20002   Fax: (202)543-5605
E-mail: gblake@fcref.org
URL: http://www.freecongress.org

Contact: Paul M. Weyrich, Pres.

Desc: Brings messages of traditional values, conservative government, an institutional reform to America. Projects include Judicial Selection Monitoring Project, "Taking Back Our Constitution" seminar services and the Center for Technology Policy's privacy papers. Through publications and TV programs on America's Voice networkbrings messages of traditional values, conservative government, an institutional reform to America. *Type:* Association.

Pay for Schools by Regulating Cannabis

PO Box 86741   Ph: (503)235-4606
Portland, OR 97286   Fax: (503)295-0883
E-mail: treefreeeco@igc.pac.org

Contact: D. Paul Stanford, Dir.

Desc: Concerned citizens who believe in hemp's environmental benefits. Seeks to regulate cannabis sales in state liquor stores to fund education and drug treatment programs. *Type:* Association.

Political Federations

Council of Volunteer Americans

Jack Clayton
PO Box 1222   Ph: (703)379-9188
Sterling, VA 20167
URL: http://www.impeachclinton.org

Contact: Jack Clayton, V.Pres.

Desc: Individuals opposed to the policies of President Bill Clinton. Seeks to "hold the Clinton White House accountable" for what the group believes are "numerous improprieties and wrongdoings." *Type:* Association.

U.S. Term Limits Foundation

1125 15th St. NW, Ste. 501   Ph: (202)463-3200
Washington, DC 20005   Free: 800-733-6440
    Fax: (202)463-3210
E-mail: admin@ustermlimits.org

Contact: Dave Mohel, Contact.

Desc: Individuals and organizations. Seeks to "restore citizen control of government by rallying Americans to limit congressional, state, and local terms." *Type:* Association.

Political Parties

CENDATA™

U.S. Bureau of the Census
Suitland Federal Center   Ph: (301)457-4100
Washington, DC 20233-8300
URL: http://www.census.gov

Desc: Contains selected text and numeric data from Census Bureau economic and demographic reports, press releases, and new product announcements. Economic and demographic reports cover agriculture, business, construction and housing, foreign trade, government, manufacturing, and selected data from Current Population Reports, and the 1990 U.S. Census of Population and Housing. *Available:* CompuServe Information Service. *Type:* Database.

Conservative Party

486 78th St.   Ph: (718)921-2158
Brooklyn, NY 11209   Fax: (718)921-5268

Contact: Michael R. Long, State Chm.

Desc: Political organization in New York State dedicated to "individual liberty, limited constitutional government, and defense of the Republic against its enemies." Seeks to "restore respect for individual responsibility and individual effort as the key feature of our national system." Its platform calls for: reduction in federal controls and expenditures; a balanced federal budget and reduction of the federal debt; revision of tax laws and reduction of personal and corporate income tax rates; legislation to curb coercive practices by unions; elimination of rent control and opposition to government control of prices or wages; reciprocal reduction of tariffs and elimination of import quotas; reliance on private institutions, programs, and physicians to meet nation's medical needs; passage of a constitutional amendment to permit nonsectarian, noncoercive prayer in public schools; limitation of American foreign aid and military and technical assistance to nations opposing communism; elimination of the communist government in Cuba; repeal of laws permitting abortion; opposition to the Equal Rights Amendment. *Type:* Association.

Guyana Republican Party

PO Box 260185   Ph: (973)484-3431
Brooklyn, NY 11226-0185   Free: 800-577-7468
    Fax: (973)484-1615
E-mail: 103203.652@compuserve.com

Contact: Leslie F. Prince, Exec.Chm. & Founder.

Desc: Workds to assist the Guyanese community, socially, politically and economically. Conducts lobbying activities in the United States. Seeks to maintain stability within the Caribbean. *Type:* Association.

International Green Party

461 N Lake, No. 209
Aurora, IL 60506

Contact: Randall Toler, Chm.

Desc: Ecologists, social democrats, anti-nuclear and peace activists. Objectives are to strengthen international environmental and anti-nuclear movements and promote election of Green party candidates to Congress and parliaments in the world. *Type:* Association.

Iowa Democratic Party

5661 Fleur Dr.
Des Moines, IA 50321-2841
URL: http://www.netins.net/showcase/democrat

Contact: Mike Peterson, Chm.

Desc: Works to elect Democrats to local, state, and national office. Provides: software development and other computer services, layout and design; mailing services. *Type:* Association.

Libertarian National Committee

2600 Virginia Ave. NW, Ste.   Ph: (202)333-0008
100   Free: 800-682-1776
Washington, DC 20037   Fax: (202)333-0072
E-mail: lphq@digex.net
URL: http://www.lp.org.

Contact: Steve Dasbach, Dir.

Desc: Political party formed to bring Libertarian ideas to the American public via political campaigns, to elect Libertarians to office and to pressure major-party candidates into taking more Libertarian stands. *Type:* Association.

National Socialist Union Green Political Party

Ti Huit
1564 Indiana Ave.   Ph: (801)972-3902
Salt Lake City, UT 84104

Contact: Ti Huit, Founder.

Desc: Rebuild America into a Spiritual Military Republic, Nationalizing the major industries to save to USA & the environment. *Type:* Association.

Nebraska Republican State Central Committee

421 S. 9th St., Ste. 233   Ph: (402)475-2122
Lincoln, NE 68508   Free: 800-829-3459
    Fax: (402)475-3541
E-mail: negop@aol.com

Contact: Beth Smith, Exec.Dir.

Desc: Works to elect Republicans to local, state, and national office. *Type:* Association.

New Party

2380 Ave., 3rd Fl.   Ph: (718)246-3713
Brooklyn, NY 11217   Free: 800-220-1294
    Fax: (718)246-3718
E-mail: natint@newparty.org

Contact: Adam Glickman, Communications Dir.

Desc: A progressive, independent political party working at the grassroots level. *Type:* Association.

Peace and Freedom Party

PO Box 422644   Ph: (415)861-0870
San Francisco, CA 94142   Fax: (415)864-3389

Contact: Paul Kangas, Contact.

Desc: Union members, professionals, students, environmental activists, women, teenagers, minorities, gays, and other activists who work for world socialism; also includes former church members and former members of such groups as La Raza Unida Party, Christic Institute, National Rainbow Coalition, Students for a Democratic Society, and the Black Panther Party. Objectives are to: provide safe, natural, affordable, health care to all people; release the Nixon Watergate tape, jail George Bush for the J.F.K. assassination, reduce the Pentagon budget by 50 percent; establish a 4 day work week; cancel the national debt by a 50% capital tax on the 1000 richest families; end poverty, racism, and sexism; fight organized crime; abolish individual taxes and the IRS; lower present voting age to 13 "so kids can vote before they're drafted"; provide chiropractic adjustments to all addicted to tobacco, alcohol and drugs to cure addictions; distribute condoms to youths as a disease-prevention measure; promote the French abortion pill RU-486; create a free education system; free all political prisoners, especially Sirhan Sirhan. *Type:* Association.

POPLINE

U.S. National Library of Medicine (NLM)
MEDLARS Management Section
8600 Rockville Pike   Ph: (301)496-3147
Bethesda, MD 20894
URL: http://www.sis.nlm.nih.gov/dirline

Desc: Contains approximately 251,000 citations, with abstracts, to the worldwide literature on family planning and population. Includes research in human fertility, contraceptive methods, maternal and child health care, family planning services, AIDS in developing countries, program operations and evaluations, community issues, demography, censuses, vital statistics, and related health, law, and policy issues. *Available:* U.S. National Library of Medicine (NLM), TOXNET; National Information Services Corporation (NISC), BiblioLine. *Type:* Database.

Population Reference Bureau

1875 Connecticut Ave. NW,   Ph: (202)483-1100
Ste. 520   Free: 800-877-9881
Washington, DC 20009   Fax: (202)328-3937
E-mail: popref@prb.org
URL: http://www.prb.org

Contact: Peter Donaldson, Pres.

Desc: Private, nonprofit educational organization that gathers, interprets, and disseminates information on the facts and implications of national and world population trends. Maintains Population Information Service. *Type:* Association.

Populist Party of America

PO Box 426   Ph: (412)443-7300
Allison Park, PA 15101-0426   Fax: (412)443-4240
Contact: Donald B. Wassall, Chm.

Desc: Political party espousing the idea that "values and beliefs of the middle class majority should rule, rather than special interests and minority pressure groups." Objective is to become an alternative choice for Americans. Believes in the nationalist philosophy of "America First." Operates speakers' bureau. *Type:* Association.

The Right Site

Easy Analytic Software, Inc.
891 East Oak Rd.   Ph: (609)691-9253
PO Box 363   Fax: (609)696-2130
Vineland, NJ 08360
E-mail: howeasi@msn.com
URL: http://www.easidemographics.com/

Desc: Boasting of "1,000,000 pages of FREE easy-to-use Demographic Reports," the Easy Analytic Software site contains a large database of demographic and census information suitable for demographic researchers, marketers, and other concerns. Accessed via progressive navigation through increasingly focused lists of criteria, you can search several different geographical ranges by such criteria as ZIP codes, metropolitan areas, TV centers, counties, cities, area codes, and regions. *Type:* Database.

United Nations Population Information Network

United Nations, Social Development and Poverty Elimination Division
One UN Plaza, DC-1, 20th Fl.   Ph: (212)906-5046
New York, NY 10017   Fax: (212)906-5313
E-mail: khannas@un.org
URL: http://www.undp.org/popin/popin.htm

Desc: The United Nations Population Information Network (POPIN) coordinates a wealth of information including statistics, publications, conferences, lists, databases, and other resources from around the world. The POPIN Electronic library contains bibliographies and bibliographic databases, indexes, journals, newsletters, maps, software, glossaries, directories, and registers. *Type:* Database.

U.S.English

1747 Pennsylvania Ave., NW,   Ph: (202)833-0100
   Ste. 1100   Fax: (202)833-0108
Washington, DC 20006
E-mail: info@us-english.org
URL: http://www.us-english.org
Contact: Mr. Mauro E. Mujica, Chm. and CEO.

Desc: Leading national citizens action group dedicated to preserving our common bond by making English the official language of government in the U.S. *Type:* Association.

Political Science

Almanac of American Politics

National Journal Inc.
1501 M St., NW, Ste. 300   Ph: (202)739-8400
Washington, DC 20005
E-mail: eevans@njdc.com
URL: http://www.cloakroom.com

Desc: Contains the complete text of The Almanac of American Politics, providing descriptions and analyses of persons and events in American politics. Descriptions include biographical profiles, political histories of states and districts, names of governors, and members of Congress. *Available:* LEXIS-NEXIS, NEXIS; Legi-Slate, Inc. *Type:* Database.

American Political Science Association

1527 New Hampshire Ave. NW   Ph: (202)483-2512
Washington, DC 20036-1206   Fax: (202)483-2657
E-mail: apsa@apsanet.org
URL: http://www.apsanet.org
Contact: Catherine E. Rudder, Exec.Dir.

Desc: College and university teachers of political science, public officials, research workers, and businessmen. "Encourages the impartial study and promotes the development of the art and science of government." Develops research projects of public interest and educational programs for political scientists and journalists; seeks to improve the knowledge of and increase citizen participation in political and governmental affairs. Serves as clearinghouse for teaching and research positions in colleges, universities, and research bureaus in the U.S. *Type:* Association.

AP Alert/Political

The Associated Press (AP)
50 Rockefeller Plaza   Ph: (212)621-1585
New York, NY 10020
URL: http://www.ap.org

Desc: Covers local, state, and national political news and statistics. Emphasis is on political campaigns and elections. *Available:* Bell & Howell Information and Learning. *Type:* Database.

Country Report Services

IBC USA Licensing Inc.
The PRS Group
6320 Fly Rd., Suite 102   Ph: (315)431-0511
P.O. Box 248
East Syracuse, NY 13057-0248
E-mail: custserv@prsgroup.com
Contact: Mary Lou Walsh, Managing Director.

Desc: Contains the complete text of reports covering economic and political conditions for 100 countries worldwide. *Available:* LEXIS-NEXIS, NEXIS; The Gale Group, InfoTrac Web; Thomson Financial Securities Data (TFSD). *Type:* Database.

Inter-University Consortium for Political and Social Research

PO Box 1248   Ph: (734)998-9900
University of Michigan Institute   Fax: (734)998-9889
   for Social Research
Ann Arbor, MI 48106-1248
E-mail: netmail@icpsr.umich.edu
URL: http://www.icpsr.umich.edu
Contact: Richard Rockwell, Exec.Dir.

Desc: Cooperative partnership between institutions of higher education represented by departments of political science, history, sociology, and related disciplines concerned with the systematic study of political and social behavior. Seeks to facilitate research in the social sciences by: developing a major data repository providing access to basic research materials; conducting an advanced training program providing formal course work in methodology, research techniques, and substantive fields for advanced graduate students and faculty; stimulating new research projects; consulting in computer support needs. *Type:* Association.

Joint Center for Political and Economic Studies

1090 Vermont Ave. NW, Ste.   Ph: (202)789-3500
   1100   Fax: (202)789-6390
Washington, DC 20005
Contact: Eddie N. Williams, Pres.

Desc: Funded in part by the Ford Foundation. Organized to provide, on a nonpartisan basis, research, public policy analysis, and information programs for black and other minority elected and appointed public officials. Collects and analyzes data on all aspects of black political participation. *Type:* Association.

Pi Sigma Alpha

1527 New Hampshire Ave. NW   Ph: (202)483-2512
Washington, DC 20036   Fax: (202)483-2657
E-mail: pisigmaa@erols.com
URL: http://www.apsanet.org/~psa
Contact: James I. Lengle, Exec.Dir.

Desc: Honor society - men and women, political science. *Type:* Association.

Politics

ADA Today

Americans for Democratic Action (ADA)
1625 K St. NW, Ste. 210   Ph: (202)785-5980
Washington, DC 20006   Fax: (202)785-5969
E-mail: adaction@ix.netcom.com
Contact: Valerie Dulk-Jacobs, Editor.

Desc: Reports on the organization's legislative advocacy and political action in domestic, foreign, military, economic, social and environmental policy areas as well as chapter activities. *Type:* Newsletter.

The American Spectator

The American Spectator
2020 N. 14th St., Ste. 750   Ph: (703)243-3733
Arlington, VA 22201   Free: 800-524-3469
    Fax: (703)243-6814

E-mail: amspec@ix.netcom.com
URL: http://www.spectator.org.
Contact: Wladyslaw Pleszczynski, Exec. Editor; R. Emmett Tyrrell, Jr., Editor; Terry Eastland, Publisher; John Funk, Advertising Mgr.; Joseph P. Whistler, Director.

Desc: A national opinion magazine covering politics, culture and current events. *Alt. Contact:* fax: (703)243-9582. *Type:* Periodical.

Americans for Democratic Action

1625 K St. NW, Ste. 210   Ph: (202)785-5980
Washington, DC 20006   Free: 800-787-2734
    Fax: (202)785-5969
E-mail: adaction@ix.netcom.com
URL: http://www.adaction.org
Contact: Amy Isaacs, Dir.

Desc: Professionals and businesspersons, labor leaders, educators, students, political leaders, and other individuals interested in liberal political ideas. To formulate liberal domestic and foreign policies based on the changing needs of American democracy, enlist public understanding and support of these policies, and put them into effect through the political process. *Type:* Association.

Americans United for Separation of Church and State

1816 Jefferson Pl. NW   Ph: (202)466-3234
Washington, DC 20036   Free: 800-875-3707
    Fax: (202)466-2587

E-mail: americansunited@au.org
URL: http://www.au.org
Contact: Barry W. Lynn, Contact.

Desc: Educates the American people about the vital role separation of church and state plays in safeguarding religious freedom. Opposes efforts to bridge the gap between church and state by Religious Right groups. *Type:* Association.

The Associate

The Nation
33 Irving Pl., 8th Fl.   Ph: (212)209-5400
New York, NY 10003   Free: 800-333-8536
    Fax: (212)982-9000

E-mail: info@thenation.com
Contact: Peggy Randall, Editor.

Desc: In-house newsletter of The Nation Magazine. Recurring features include interviews, news of research, a calendar of events, reports of meetings, and notices of publications available. *Type:* Newsletter.

Association of Community Organizations for Reform Now

1024 Elysian Fields Ave.   Ph: (504)943-0044
New Orleans, LA 70117   Fax: (504)944-7078
E-mail: acorn@acorn.org
Contact: Wade Rathke, Chief Organizer.
Desc: Families of low and moderate income advocating a stronger local neighborhood voice in and power over the economic, political, and social institutions that dominate their lives. Advocates the concept of a "majority constituency" (defined by ACORN as individuals of low to moderate income who are shut out of the power structure in this country). Supports group involvement in electoral politics. *Type:* Association.

Capital Connections

1698 32nd St. NW   Ph: (202)337-2044
Washington, DC 20007   Fax: (202)338-4750
E-mail: btwm32a@prodigy.com.
URL: http://www.iapps.com/capitalconnections.
Contact: Karen Feld, Columnist; Sharon Berry, Ed. Asst.
Desc: Distributes political and social columns. *Alt. Contact:* 1698 32nd St. NW, Washington, DC 20007; telephone: (202)337-2044; fax: (202)338-4750. *Type:* Periodical.

Captive Nations Committee

PO Box 540, Gracie Sta.   Ph: (718)439-8044
New York, NY 10028-0005   Fax: (718)439-8044
Contact: Horst Adolf Uhlich, Pres.
Desc: Ethnic groups and concerned individuals organized to carry out activities that support their anti-communist beliefs. Supports freedom for all the captive nations; promotes boycott of merchandise from communist nations. Sponsors annual parade and seven-day educational program in New York City during Captive Nations Week. *Type:* Association.

Cardinal Mindszenty Foundation

PO Box 11321   Ph: (314)727-6279
St. Louis, MO 63105   Fax: (314)727-5897
E-mail: info@mindszenty.org
URL: http://www.mindszenty.org
Contact: Eleanor Schlafly, Pres.
Desc: Conducts educational and research activities concerning Communist objectives, tactics, and propaganda through study groups, lectures, radio programs, and conferences. *Type:* Association.

Center for the Study of Democratic Institutions

10951 W. Pico Blvd., 3rd Fl.   Ph: (310)474-0011
Los Angeles, CA 90064   Free: 800-336-1007
    Fax: (310)474-8061
Contact: Nathan Gardels, Exec. Officer.
Desc: Educational corporation. Investigates critical issues confronting the world today. Publishes New Perspectives Quarterly (NPQ) on social and political issues. *Type:* Association.

Center for Voting and Democracy

PO Box 60037   Ph: (301)270-4616
Washington, DC 20039   Fax: (301)270-4133
E-mail: fairvote@compuser.com
URL: http://www.igc.org/cvd/
Contact: John Anderson, Pres.
Desc: Individuals and groups interested in democratic alternatives to "winner-take-all" voting systems. Focuses on the system of proportional representation (PR). *Type:* Association.

Christopher News Notes

The Christophers, Inc.
12 E. 48th St.   Ph: (212)759-4050
New York, NY 10017   Fax: (212)838-5073
E-mail: tci@idt.net
URL: http://www.christophers.org.
Contact: Stephanie Raha, Editor-in-Chief, ( )-, fax: (212)838-5073; Margaret O'Connell, Sr. Research Editor.
Desc: Each issue addresses one topic of current interest in light of Christophers' motto, "It is better to light one candle than to curse the darkness." Shows how people took personal responsibility and initiative to bring constructive change to society by addressing this issue of contemporary concern. *Type:* Newsletter.

Congressional Quarterly Inc.

1414 22nd St. NW   Ph: (202)887-8500
Washington, DC 20037   Fax: (202)728-1863
URL: http://voter96.cqalert.com.
Contact: Neil Skene, Pub./Pres.; Robert Merry, Exec. Ed./VP; LuAnne Slagle, Dir. Mktg.; Jeanne Jennings, Media Mktg. Mgr., jjennings@cqalert.com.
Desc: Distributes congressional features. *Alt. Contact:* 1414 22nd St. NW, Washington, DC 20037; telephone: (202)887-8500; fax: (202)728-1863. *Type:* Periodical.

Continental Newstime

Continental Features/Continental News Service
501 W. Broadway, Ste. 265,   Ph: (619)492-8696
  Plaza A
San Diego, CA 92101
E-mail: newstime@hotbot.com; newstime@hotbot.com.
Contact: Gary P. Salamone.
Desc: Provides news and commentary on national and international affairs. Recurring features include Video reviews. *Type:* Newsletter.

Council on Foreign Relations

58 E. 68th St.   Ph: (212)434-9400
New York, NY 10021   Fax: (212)861-2504
URL: http://www.foreignrelations.org
Contact: Leslie H. Gelb, Pres.
Desc: Individuals with specialized knowledge of and interest in international affairs. Studies the international aspects of American political, economic, and strategic problems. *Type:* Association.

Crusade Against Corruption

PO Box 4063
Marietta, GA 30061
Contact: J. B. Stoner, Chm.
Desc: White persons with non-Jewish ancestry. Promotes the formation of a totally white "Christian" America through complete racial separation, the outlawing of interracial marriages, and exclusive white Christian immigration. Believes that "affirmative action is a corruption" and promotes the "repeal of all corrupt laws and policies that discriminate against the White race." Advocates jobs for white persons, "America First" foreign and trade policies, the expulsion of communists, and an end to detente and trade between the former Soviet Union and the U.S. *Type:* Association.

Cuba Solidarity Web Site

Institute for Global Communications
Presidio Bldg. 1012, First Fl.   Ph: (415)561-6100
Torney Ave.   Fax: (415)561-6101
San Francisco, CA 94129-0904
E-mail: webweaver@igc.org
URL: http://www.igc.apc.org/cubasoli/
Contact: Dana Simon, dsimon@igc.apc.org.
Desc: This fascinating Web site works on multiple levels. Project InfoMed, one of the sponsors of this site, is an ambitious undertaking designed to improve the quality of health services in Cuba. *Type:* Database.

Democratic Socialists of America

180 Varick St., 12th Fl.   Ph: (212)727-8610
New York, NY 10014   Fax: (212)727-8616
E-mail: dsa@dsausa.org
URL: http://www.dsausa.org/dsa
Contact: Alan Charney, National Dir.
Desc: Individuals who believe "the realization of the potential of humankind requires many important basic institutional changes, among which are the social ownership and democratic control of the decisive means of production and distribution." Dedicated to "building a society at the service of human needs" and seeks to create a foreign policy "dedicated to the peaceful extension of democratic rule for all the peoples of the world." Works to protect and expand civil liberties, encourage democratic social planning, and distribute the nation's wealth and income more equitably. Maintains youth groups on 40 campuses. *Type:* Association.

Facts on File

Facts On File, Inc.
11 Penn Plz.   Ph: (212)967-8800
New York, NY 10001-2006   Free: 800-322-8755
    Fax: (212)967-9196
E-mail: lmilberg@factsonfile.com
URL: http://www.factsonfile.com
Contact: Thomas E. Hitchings, Editor-in-Chief.
Desc: Distills all major news of the U.S. and the world in a detailed and weekly format. *Type:* Newsletter.

Facts on File World News Digest

Facts On File News Services
Division of PRIMEDIA Reference Corporation
11 Penn Plaza, 15th Fl.   Ph: (212)290-8090
New York, NY 10001-2006   Free: 800-363-7976
    Fax: (212)967-9051
E-mail: info@facts.com
URL: http://www.facts.com.
Contact: Marion Farrier, Managing Editor.
Desc: Provides worldwide coverage of current events. Addresses politics, foreign affairs, business, finance, government, justice, the environment, culture, personalities, sports, and more. *Type:* Newsletter.

The Final Call

The Final Call
734 W. 79th St.   Ph: (312)602-1230
Chicago, IL 60620   Fax: (312)602-1013
URL: http://www.aol.org.
Contact: James Muhammad, Editor-in-Chief; Richard Muhammed, Managing Editor; Fontaine Muhammed, General Mgr.
Desc: Newspaper serving the black community. *Type:* Periodical.

FREE World Government, Earthbank

PO Box 331228   Ph: (305)584-6679
Coconut Grove, FL 33133-1228
E-mail: do17629c@dcfreenet.seflin.lib.us
Contact: Wendell Sharman Phillips, Global Facilitator.
Desc: Promotes international peace through the establishment of a global democratic plebiscites (government). (FREE stands for Federated Republics of Earth and its Environs.) Areas of concern include population control, nuclear disarmament, world hunger, human rights, creative conflict resolution, abolition of war, soil remineralization, and alternative energy technology. Offers interest-free lifetime loans and grants to organic, solar agricultural and conservation projects to individuals and community centers worldwide. *Type:* Association.

Freedom House

1319 18th St., NW
Washington, DC 20036
Ph: (202)296-5101
Fax: (202)296-5078
E-mail: fh@freedomhouse.org
URL: http://www.freedomhouse.org
Contact: Jim Denton, Exec.Dir.
Desc: Promotes political rights and civil liberties world-wide. *Type:* Association.

Freedoms Foundation at Valley Forge

PO Box 706, 1601 Valley Forge
Rd.
Valley Forge, PA 19482-0706
Ph: (610)933-8825
Free: 800-896-5488
Fax: (610)935-0522
E-mail: ffvf@ffvf.org
URL: http://www.ffvf.org
Contact: RADM Richard C. Ustick, USN, Ret. Pres.
Desc: Dedicated to promoting responsible citizenship. Promotes responsibilities as the key to good citizenship and essential to the protection and preservation of rights. *Type:* Association.

Fund for an Open Society

311 S. Juniper St., Ste. 400
Philadelphia, PA 19107
Ph: (215)735-6915
Fax: (215)735-2507
E-mail: 102400.733@compuserve.com
Contact: Don DeMarco, Exec.Dir.
Desc: Mortgage fund established to provide an economic incentive in the form of financially advantageous loans to persons making housing moves that decrease segregation, that is, moves by a minority family to a white neighborhood or by a white family to a predominantly minority or well-integrated neighborhood. Purposes are to: help neighborhoods become interracial; help existing interracial neighborhoods maintain stability; help prevent displacement in gentrifying neighborhoods; strengthen neighborhoods by facilitating the purchase and rehabilitation of abandoned homes; help solve the problem of segregated schools by breaking down walls of residential segregation. Actively seeks the support of local institutions, businesses, and community groups. *Type:* Association.

Habitat World

Habitat for Humanity International, Inc.
121 Habitat St.
Americus, GA 31709-3498
Ph: (912)924-6935
Fax: (912)924-6541
Contact: Milana McLead, Editor.
Desc: Newspaper covering the activities of the Habitat for Humanity. *Type:* Periodical.

Hemisfile

Institute of the Americas
10111 N. Torrey Pines Rd.
La Jolla, CA 92037
Ph: (619)453-5560
Fax: (619)453-2165
URL: http://www.ioa.ucsd.
Contact: Jeffrey Carmel, Editor.
Desc: Provides political and economic information on North and South America. *Type:* Newsletter.

HOTLINE

American Political Network, Inc.
APN/Access
3129 Mount Vernon Ave.
Alexandria, VA 22305-2640
Ph: (703)518-8704
E-mail: info@apn.com
URL: http://www.cloakroom.com
Contact: Chris Parente, chris@apn.com.
Desc: Contains news and information on U.S. national, state, and local political campaigns and issues. *Available:* American Political Network, Inc., APN/Access; American Political Network, Inc., APN/Access; LEXIS-NEXIS, NEXIS; West Group, WESTLAW. *Type:* Database.

Imprimis

Center for Constructive Alternatives
Hillsdale College
33 E. College St.
Hillsdale, MI 49242
Ph: (517)437-0190
Free: 800-437-2268
Fax: (517)437-0654
Contact: Ronald Trowbridge, Executive Editor; Lissa Roche, Managing Editor, lissa.roche@ac.hillsdale.edu.
Desc: Hillsdale Colleges award-winning monthly speech digest offers timely observations by some of the nation's leading figures who have spoken before the college's audiences. *Type:* Newsletter.

Institute for the Future

2744 Sand Hill Rd.
Menlo Park, CA 94025-7020
Contact: Robert Johansen, Pres.
Desc: Assists organizations, businesses, industry, and the government in conducting long-term futures research. Promotes practical application of information techniques for improved management and productivity. Services include consultation, forecasting and strategic planning, teleconferencing and office systems, videotex, home information assistance, and health care. *Type:* Association.

International Private Power Quarterly

The McGraw-Hill Companies
1221 Avenue of the Americas,
36th Fl.
New York, NY 10020
Ph: (212)512-6410
Free: 800-223-6180
Fax: (212)512-2723
E-mail: gsafos@mhenergy.com
Contact: Peter Maloney, Editor, (212)904-2541, pmaloney@mhenergy.com.
Desc: Provides a country-by-country review of emerging power markets in Asia, the Pacific Rim, Latin America, Western and Eastern Europe, and key republics of the former Soviet Union. Each country profile details project proposals, the generation and fuel picture, and the political and business climate. *Type:* Newsletter.

International Republican Institute

1212 New York Ave. NW, Ste.
900
Washington, DC 20005-6107
Ph: (202)408-9450
Fax: (202)408-9462
E-mail: web@iri.org
URL: http://www.iri.org
Contact: Lorne Craner, Pres.
Desc: Conducts programs outside the United States to promote democracy and strengthen free-markets, and the rule-of-law. Conducts programs in Albania, Angola, Azerbaijan, Belarus, Bulgaria, Burma, Cambodia, China, Cuba, El Salvador, Georgia, Guatemala, Haiti, Indonesia, Liberia, Macedonia, Mexico, Moldove, Mongolia, Morocco, Nicaragua, POland, Romania, Russia, Serbia, Slovakia, South Africa, Turkey, Thailand, Ukraine, Venezuela, Vietnam, West Bank and Gaza Strip, Western Sahara, and Zimbabwe. *Type:* Association.

Issues and Controversies on File

Facts On File News Services
Division of PRIMEDIA Reference Corporation
11 Penn Plaza, 15th Fl.
New York, NY 10001-2006
Ph: (212)290-8090
Free: 800-363-7976
Fax: (212)967-9051
E-mail: info@facts.com
URL: http://www.facts.com.
Contact: Jeff Hoover, Managing Editor.
Desc: Provides factual information on current issues and controversies. Each article provides background information, pros and cons, statistics, historical background, bibliographies, and sources of internet information pertaining to a particular issue. *Type:* Newsletter.

Joint Action in Community Service

5225 Wisconsin Ave. NW, Ste.
404
Washington, DC 20015
Ph: (202)537-0996
Fax: (202)363-0239
Contact: William Harvey Wise, Exec.Dir.
Desc: Formed by leaders of national Protestant, Catholic, and Jewish associations. Has developed a local-level network of 5000 volunteers who are available on-call to assist male students formerly in the Job Corps program in dealing with the problems they face in the areas of housing, employment, education, transportation, budget planning, legal and medical aid, training opportunities, and citizenship information. Main focus of program is the availability of a committed and trained volunteer who will work on a one-to-one basis with an individual who has needs and help that individual meet them. *Type:* Association.

Laborers Political League

905 16th St. NW
Washington, DC 20006
Ph: (202)638-5753
Fax: (202)737-2754
Contact: Donald Kaniewski, Dir.
Desc: Seeks to inform the laborers of the U.S. of the need to exercise their right to vote; supports candidates for office who demonstrate concern for the working person and for the aims and objectives of the trade union movement; works for the passage of favorable legislation and the repeal of unfavorable legislation; conducts a program of education about such laws and their opponents and supporters. *Type:* Association.

League of Conservation Voters

1707 L St. NW, Ste. 750
Washington, DC 20036
Ph: (202)785-8683
Fax: (202)835-0491
E-mail: lcv@lcv.org
URL: http://www.lcv.org
Contact: Deb Callahan, Pres.
Desc: Seeks to protect the environment through political action, by helping to elect pro-conservation candidates to Congress and holding members accountable for their actions. *Type:* Association.

League of National Defense

PO Box 292
Brooklyn, NY 11237
Ph: (718)381-3804
Contact: Constantin Burlacu, Chm.
Desc: Fights against communist and neo-communist dictatorships in Romania and promotes nationalism, liberty and human rights. *Type:* Association.

League of Women Voters of the United States

1730 M St. NW
Washington, DC 20036
Ph: (202)429-1965
Fax: (202)429-0854
E-mail: lwv@lwv.org
URL: http://www.lwv.org
Contact: Natalie Testa, Exec.Asst.
Desc: Voluntary organization of citizens (men and women) 18 years old or over. Promotes political responsibility through informed and active participation of citizens in government and acts on selected governmental issues. *Type:* Association.

Left Business Observer

Left Business Observer
250 W. 85th St.
New York, NY 10024-3217
Ph: (212)874-4020
Fax: (212)874-3137
URL: gopher:csf.colorado.edu; http://www.panix.com/~dhenwood/LBO_home.html.
Contact: Doug Henwood, Editor, dhenwood@pnnix.wm.
Desc: Provides news and analysis of international politics from a leftist point of view. Contains information on central banks and financial markets. *Type:* Newsletter.

The Liberal

The Liberal

9350 Yonge St.　　　　　　Ph: (905)881-3373
PO Box 390　　　　　　　　Free: 800-565-6357
Richmond Hill, ON, Canada　Fax: (905)881-9924
　L4C 4Y6
E-mail: newsroom@yorkregion.com
URL: http://www.rhliberal.net.
Contact: Debora Kelly, Editor, dkelly@yorkregion.com;
Ian Proudfoot, Publisher; Gord Paolucci, Advertising
Mgr.
Desc: Community newspaper. *Type:* Periodical.

Movement for an Independent and Democratic Cuba

10020 SW 37th Ter.　　　　Ph: (305)551-8484
Miami, FL 33165
Contact: Cmdr. Huber Matos, Sec.Gen.
Desc: Political scientists, educators, economists, and other
interested individuals. Organized to "denounce the aggressive nature of Castro's satellite government, and to establish the need for a joint strategy which will prevent the
large majorities of the peoples of the Americas from suc-
cumbing to minority groups directed from Havana and
Moscow." Objectives are defined by the movement's five
"ideological-programmatical points": national independence; political democracy; economic democracy; social
justice; Latin American integration. Maintains that at the
"end of Soviet occupation and the Castro dictatorship we
will see the rebirth of Cuban democracy." Urges support
from other democratic forces of the continent and the
western world. *Type:* Association.

NAE Washington Insight

National Association of Evangelicals (NAE)

1001 Connecticut Ave., NW,　Ph: (202)789-1011
　Ste. 522　　　　　　　　　Fax: (202)842-0392
Washington, DC 20036
E-mail: naeopadc@aol.com; insight@nae.net.
Desc: Covers government activities and political develop-
ments from the viewpoint of religion. *Type:* Newsletter.

National Association for Neighborhood Schools

Joyce Haws

Communications Office　　Ph: (216)398-4667
3905 Muriel Ave.
Cleveland, OH 44109
E-mail: rhaws@aol.com
URL: http://www.nans.org
Contact: William D'Onofrio, Pres.
Desc: Organizations, and activists in 38 states opposed to
forced busing for racial balance or other diversity goals in
public schools. Seeks to "bring an end to racial control and
forced busing of school children and to oppose harmful
federal interference in the schools" by encouraging Congress to use its power under the Constitution to challenge
the authority of the judiciary and the bureaucracy. *Type:*
Association.

National Committee for Independent Political Action

PO Box 170610　　　　　　Ph: (718)643-9603
Brooklyn, NY 11217
Contact: Ted Glick, Coord.
Desc: Individuals who are members of community organizations, civil rights groups, women's organizations, peace
groups, and other progressive political groups. Purpose is
to bring together grass roots progressive movements into
one organized framework in order to represent the political interests of groups not represented by either major political party and to allow independent activists to share
strategy and ideas. Goal is to develop independent political
and electoral activity aimed at changing society to bring
about economic and political democracy. *Type:* Association.

National Endowment for Democracy

1101 15th St. NW, Ste. 700　Ph: (202)293-9072
Washington, DC 20005　　　Fax: (202)223-6042
URL: http://www.ned.org
Contact: Carl Gershman, Pres.
Desc: A private, grant-making, government-financed effort
promoting worldwide development of democratic values
and human rights and freedoms through private sector initiatives. Provides the opportunity for exchange between
democratic groups abroad and U.S. private sector groups
such as the two major political parties, labor, and business.
Type: Association.

National Neighbors

Desc: Federation of interracial neighborhoods. Fosters and
encourages successful multiracial neighborhoods. Seeks to
strengthen interracial neighborhoods and promote open
housing through technical assistance and consultant visits
in the areas of real estate, open housing, education, and
neighborhood safety training. *Type:* Association.

National Review

National Review

215 Lexington Ave., 4th Fl.　Ph: (212)679-7330
New York, NY 10016　　　　Fax: (212)849-2835
E-mail: nronline@ix.netcom.com.
URL: http://www.nationalreview.com.
Contact: Rich Laury, Editor; Edward A. Capano, Publish-
er; Thomas L. Rhodes, President; William F. Buckley, Jr.,
Editor-at-Large.
Desc: Magazine reporting on national and international
facts and politics. *Type:* Periodical.

National Socialist Movement

PO Box 580669　　　　　　Ph: (651)659-6307
Minneapolis, MN 55458-0669
URL: http://www.nsm88.com
Contact: Jeff Schoep, Commander.
Desc: White Americans of non-Jewish descent. Primary
objective is "National Socialist control of all white home-
lands, including the U.S., through national self-
determination." *Type:* Association.

The National Voter

*League of Women Voters of the United States
(LWVUS)*

1730 M St. NW, Ste. 1000　Ph: (202)429-1965
Washington, DC 20036-4508　Fax: (202)429-0854
E-mail: lwv@lwv.org
URL: http://www.lwv.org.
Contact: Meg S. Duskin, Editor, megd@lwv.org.
Desc: Official journal of the League of Women Voters en-
couraging active citizen involvement in goverment. *Type:*
Periodical.

National Write Your Congressman

9696 Skillman, Ste. 170　　Ph: (214)342-0299
Dallas, TX 75243-8253　　　Fax: (214)342-9186
Contact: Roger L. Adamson, Pres. & CEO.
Desc: Encourages and assists individuals in writing public
officials. Provides research and tools needed to correspond
with officials. Offers pro and con issue information and
voting records of members' legislators; conducts monthly
polls on timely issues and reports results to its members,
to Congress and to the President; offers research service
whereby members may request information on specific issues before Congress. *Type:* Association.

NETWORK

801 Pennsylvania Ave. SE, Ste.　Ph: (202)547-5556
　460　　　　　　　　　　　　Fax: (202)547-5510
Washington, DC 20003-2167
E-mail: network@igc.apc.org

Contact: Kathy Thornton, RSM, National Coord.
Desc: Lay and religious women and men who lobby to influence public policy in Washington. Goals are to secure
just access to economic resources, reordering federal budget priorities, and global economic justice. *Type:* Association.

NotiSur: South American Affairs

*University of New Mexico
Latin American Institute
Latin America Data Base (LADB)*

801 Yale, NE　　　　　　　Ph: (505)277-6839
Albuquerque, NM 87131-1016
E-mail: info@ladb.unm.edu
URL: http://ladb.unm.edu
Contact: Rebecca Reynolds Bannister.
Desc: Contains the complete text of NotiSur: South Amer-
ican Affairs, a weekly newsletter reporting news on diverse
political and economic issues and conflicts such as political
party platforms and election results, rebel activities and
peace talks, military influence and funding, and interna-
tional conflicts and agreements. *Available:* LEXIS-NEXIS,
NEXIS; Latin America Data Base; LEXIS-NEXIS. *Type:*
Database.

NYPIRG Agenda

New York Public Interest Research Group, Inc.

9 Murray St.　　　　　　　Ph: (212)349-6460
New York, NY 10007　　　　Fax: (212)349-1366
Contact: Tracy Peel, Editor.
Desc: Concerned with the ways in which average citizens
can work for social reform. Reports on energy, environment, taxes, government and corporate accountability,
and other issues of current importance. *Type:* Newsletter.

Park Ridge Center

211 E. Ontario, Ste. 800　　Ph: (312)266-2222
Chicago, IL 60611-3215　　　Fax: (312)266-6086
URL: http://www.prchfe.org
Contact: Laurence O'Connell, Pres. & CEO.
Desc: Physicians and other health care professionals, theo-
logians, ethicists, clergy, and pastoral counselors. Interreli-
gious, multidisciplinary institute for the study of health,
faith, and ethics. Seeks to fill what the center perceives as
a worldwide need for the study of religious aspects of
human well-being, especially as they relate to prevention
and treatment of disease, interpretation of illness and
health, and similar concerns. *Type:* Association.

Pi Alpha Alpha

1120 G St. NW, Ste. 730　　Ph: (202)628-8965
Washington, DC 20005　　　Fax: (202)626-4978
E-mail: paa@naspaa.org
Contact: Michael A. Brintnall, Natl.Dir.
Desc: Individuals who demonstrate academic achievement
in public affairs and administration programs in member
schools of the National Association of Schools of Public
Affairs and Administration. Encourages and recognizes
outstanding scholarship and accomplishment in public affairs and administration; fosters integrity, professionalism,
and creative performance in the conduct of governmental
and related public service activities. *Type:* Association.

Political Database of the Americas

*Georgetown University - Center for Latin
American Studies*

Washington, DC 20057-1002
URL:　http://www.georgetown.edu/LatAmerPolitical/
home.html
Desc: A scholarly database covering the political and governmental structure of the Americas, this vast repository
of information brings together documents and statistics on

politics and democratic processes in North, Central, and South America and the Caribbean. Here you can find information on governmental structure, constitutions, electoral laws, political parties, national flags and symbols, and other political and public policy information. *Type:* Database.

Political Resource Directory

Political Resources, Inc.
PO Box 3177   Ph: (802)660-2869
Burlington, VT 05401   Free: 800-423-2677
     Fax: (802)864-9502
E-mail: polresinc@aol.com
URL: http://politicalresources.com;   http://politicalresources.com.
Contact: Carol Hess, Editor.
Desc: 4,700 professionals at 3,500 organizations in the field of politics, including national, state, and local consultants, pollsters, researchers, press and public relations staff, television and radio commercial producers, speech and communications advisors, and suppliers of voting lists, fundraising lists, computer software, and advertising goods and services. Also includes lists of Republican and Democratic party organizations; list of members of the American Association of Political Consultants; and political dates. *Type:* Directory.

Political Risk Letter

IBC USA Licensing Inc.
The PRS Group
6320 Fly Rd., Suite 102   Ph: (315)431-0511
P.O. Box 248
East Syracuse, NY 13057-0248
E-mail: custserv@prsgroup.com
Contact: Mary Lou Walsh, Managing Director., (315)431-0511, fax: (315)431-0200, mlw@polrisk.com.
Desc: Contains the complete text of Political Risk Letter, a monthly newsletter covering political and economic conditions in 100 countries. Provides risk ratings for export, financial transfer, and direct investment based on estimated probabilities for political, economic, and social stability. *Available:* Chamber World Network, Asia Intelligence Wire; LEXIS-NEXIS. *Type:* Database.

Post-Soviet Media Law & Policy Newsletter

Benjamin N. Cardozo School of Law
55 5th Ave.
New York, NY 10003
URL: http://www.vii.org/monroe
Contact: Monroe Price, price@ymail.yu.edu.
Desc: The Post-Soviet Media Law & Policy Newsletter is a monthly newsletter following media law and policy developments in the former Soviet Union, East & Central Europe, and some coverage in transition societies worldwide. Intelligently written articles are in each issue, with some issues containing special supplements, on things like the Baltics or the Russian election. *Type:* Database.

Progressive Review Home Page

Progressive Review
1739 Connecticut Ave. NW   Ph: (202)232-5544
Washington, DC 20009   Fax: (202)234-6222
URL: http://emporium.turnpike.net/P/ProRev/index.htm
Contact: Sam Smith, Editor, ssmith@igc.org.
Desc: The site provides a unique perspective on Washington politics; or, in it's own words: "Telling it like it is since 1966." It contains statistics and articles about specific issues and a library a user can search for information about many hot topics. *Type:* Database.

Public Advocate of the U.S.

5613 Leesburg Pike, Ste. 17   Ph: (202)546-3224
Falls Church, VA 22041
Contact: Eugene Delgaudio, Exec.Dir.
Desc: Advocates limited federal government. *Type:* Association.

The Republican Woman

National Federation of Republican Women
124 N. Alfred St.   Ph: (703)548-9688
Alexandria, VA 22314   Fax: (703)548-9836
E-mail: nfrw@worldweb.net
URL: http://www.nfrw.org
Contact: Amy McKinley, Editor.
Desc: Trade magazine covering politics and women for members. *Type:* Periodical.

Republicans for Choice

2760 Eisenhower Ave, Ste. 260   Ph: (703)960-9882
Alexandria, VA 22314-5223   Fax: (703)960-9885
E-mail: gop4choice@erols.com
URL: http://www.rfc-pac.org
Contact: Ann Stone, Chm.
Desc: Republicans who support a woman's right to choose abortion. Seeks to change the Republican party platform to reflect the views of pro-choice party members. Supports pro-choice Republican candidates at all levels in primaries and general elections. *Type:* Association.

Reuter Transcript Report

Reuters Information Services Inc.
1700 Broadway   Ph: (212)603-3300
New York, NY 10019
Desc: Provides a word-for-word record of White House, United States federal agency, and Capitol Hill press briefings and news conferences; presidential speeches and related events; interviews with foreign leaders; major television interview programs; and other Washington, D.C. political events. *Available:* Reuters Ltd.; Congressional Quarterly Inc. (CQ); LEXIS-NEXIS, NEXIS. *Type:* Database.

Reuter Washington Report

Reuters Information Services Inc.
1700 Broadway   Ph: (212)603-3300
New York, NY 10019
Desc: Provides coverage of events in Washington, D.C., including press conferences, government hearings, speeches, demonstrations, the President's schedule, Congressional schedules, diplomatic events, and financial items. *Available:* Reuters Ltd.; LEXIS-NEXIS, NEXIS. *Type:* Database.

The Right-To-Know Network

RTK NET
1742 Connecticut Ave. NW   Ph: (202)234-8494
Washington, DC 20009   Fax: (202)234-8584
E-mail: webmaster@rtk.net
URL: http://www.rtk.net/
Desc: This site is an excellent source for access to governmental information on the environment, on housing issues, and on campaign financing. The Right-to-Know Network makes several government databases on these issues freely available. *Type:* Database.

SCLC National Magazine

Southern Christian Leadership Conference (SCLC)
334 Auburn Ave. NE   Ph: (404)522-1420
Atlanta, GA 30303   Free: 800-421-0472
     Fax: (404)524-7957
Contact: Dr. Steven W. Blood, Sr., Publisher; Mike Dejoie, Editor; Marcia Nobler, Advertising Dir.; Janet Walz, Office Mgr.

Desc: Publication directed toward black and Civil Rights communities. *Type:* Periodical.

Selous Foundation

325 Pennsylvania Ave. SE   Ph: (202)547-6963
Washington, DC 20003
Contact: Morgan Norval, Chm.
Desc: Dedicated to the study of conflict and providing for a strong national defense. *Type:* Association.

Sonoma County Free Press Newsletter

Sonoma County Free Press
PO Box 296   Ph: (707)874-2248
Occidental, CA 95465-0296
URL: http://www.sonomacountyfreepress.org/.
Contact: Mary Moore, Editor.
Desc: Provides a forum for the diversity of viewpoints on social and political issues of Sonoma County. Recurring features include letters to the editor, interviews, news of research, reports of meetings, book reviews, and columns titled Grandma Nudge, My Body Is Mine, Nuke Notes, Pesticides, Issues of Racism, Sexism, Classism, Prisons. *Type:* Newsletter.

Starthrowers

PO Box 192   Ph: (318)828-2375
615 Trowbridge St.   Fax: (318)828-4039
Franklin, LA 70538
Contact: Bernard Broussard, Exec. Officer.
Desc: Individuals advocating peace, social justice, human rights, anti abortion and euthanasia, relations, and the denouncement of the death penalty. Organizes boycotts and petition drives to promote legislative support. Offers home study courses in peace, justice, and environmental spirituality. *Type:* Association.

SunONE Newszine

Interactive Media Lab
Box 118400   Ph: (352)846-0171
Gainesville, FL 32611   Fax: (352)846-0172
URL: http://iml.jou.ufl.edu/sunone/
Desc: This joint project of the Gainesville Sun and the University of Florida, Interactive Media Lab is a weekly online magazine serving Gainesville, Florida. The site provides online news, entertainment, features on such topical subjects as technology, health and science. *Type:* Database.

Trend Letter

The Global Network
1101 30th St. NW, Ste. 130   Ph: (202)337-5960
Washington, DC 20007   Free: 800-368-0115
     Fax: (202)337-9189
E-mail: tl@gphinc.com.
Contact: Leah Thayer, Editor, editors@gphinc.com.
Desc: Highlights "megatrends" in the U.S. Examines developments in areas of government, management, human resources, communication and technology, education, energy, the environment, financial services, entrepreneurs, food and agriculture, health, housing and development, marketing, social relations, transportation and travel, global economy, business and industry, the women's movement, and consumer affairs. *Type:* Newsletter.

20/20 Vision National Project

1828 Jefferson Pl. NW   Ph: (202)833-2020
Washington, DC 20036   Free: 800-669-1782
     Fax: (202)833-5307
E-mail: vision@2020vision.org
URL: http://www.2020vision.org
Contact: James Wyerman, Exec. Dir.
Desc: Promotes citizen involvement in influencing public policies that endorse protection of the environment, an in-

crease in national and global security, reduction of military spending, and the support of individual economic and social needs. Encourages individual political activism by providing convenient, simple, effective activities designed to take less than 20 minutes to complete. Organization name is derived from the belief that an individual's contribution of 20 minutes a month and $20 a year can have a significant impact on public policy. *Type:* Association.

Vaughan Liberal

The Liberal
9350 Yonge St. Ph: (905)881-3373
PO Box 390 Free: 800-565-6357
Richmond Hill, ON, Canada Fax: (905)881-9924
 L4C 4Y6
E-mail: newsroom@yorkregion.com; news.room@rhliberal.net.
URL: http://www.yorkregion.com.
Contact: Debora Kelly, Editor, dkelly@yorkregion.com; Ian Proudfoot, Publisher; Gord Paolucci, Advertising Mgr.
Desc: Community newspaper. *Alt. Contact:* PO Box 390, Richmond Hill, ON, Canada L4C 4Y6; telephone: (905)881-3373; fax: (905)881-9924; toll-free: 800-565-6357. *Type:* Periodical.

Visions Foundation

2201 S St. NW Ph: (202)462-1779
Washington, DC 20008-4013 Fax: (202)462-3997
Contact: Gary A. Puckrein, Exec.Dir.
Desc: African Americans. To promote understanding of the Afro-American culture. *Type:* Association.

The Voice of the Martyrs

The Voice of the Martyrs, Inc.
PO Box 443 Ph: (918)337-8015
Bartlesville, OK 74005-0443 Free: 800-747-0085
 Fax: (918)338-0189
E-mail: thevoice@vom-usa.org; communications@vom-usa.org.
Contact: Tom White, Editor; Cheryl Odden, Editor, fax: (918)338-8832.
Desc: Concerned with bringing aid to Christian families living in Communist countries, former Communist countries, and Muslim areas. Reports news of mission work. *Type:* Newsletter.

Votelink

Votelink
1655 Walnut St., Ste. 200 Ph: (303)444-1383
Boulder, CO 80302 Fax: (303)444-1346
E-mail: editor@votelink.com
URL: http://www.votelink.com
Contact: webmaster@sterinfo.com.
Desc: Votelink's e-democracy voting pages offer free voting and online discussion of today's hottest news. Topics change on a weekly basis and range from the right to free speech and the conflict between your favorite politicians to teenage drinking licenses and castration of sex offenders. *Type:* Database.

Washington G2 Reports

1111 14th St. NW Ph: (202)789-1034
Ste. 711
Washington, DC 20005
Contact: Dennis Weissman, Pres./Pub.; D.J. Curren, Editor.
Desc: Distributes information for clinical laboratories and hospitals. *Alt. Contact:* 1111 14th St. NW, Ste. 711, Washington, DC 20005; telephone: (202)789-1034. *Type:* Periodical.

The Washington Monthly Co.

1611 Connecticut Ave. NW Ph: (202)462-0128
Washington, DC 20009 Fax: (202)332-8413
Contact: Casandra Tate, PUB; Charles Peters, Editor-in-Chief; Amy Waldman, Editor.
Desc: Distributes political news. *Alt. Contact:* 1611 Connecticut Ave. NW, Washington, DC 20009; telephone: (202)462-0128; fax: (202)332-8413. *Type:* Periodical.

The Weekly Standard

The Weekly Standard
1150 17th St. NW, No. 505 Ph: (202)293-4900
Washington, DC 20036 Fax: (202)293-4901
Contact: William Kristol, Editor and Publisher; David Bass, Deputy Publisher; Jennifer Felten, Business Mgr.
Desc: Consumer magazine covering political issues. *Type:* Periodical.

Whistle Stop

Harry S. Truman Library Institute
U.S. Hwy. 24 & Delaware St. Ph: (816)833-0425
Independence, MO 64050-1798 Free: 800-769-8561
 Fax: (816)833-2715
E-mail: library@truman.nara.gov
Contact: Lenore K. Bradley, Editor.
Desc: Contains articles pertaining to U.S. 33rd President, Harry S. *Type:* Newsletter.

Women Proutists

PO Box 56466 Ph: (202)829-2278
Washington, DC 20040 Fax: (202)829-0462
E-mail: proutwdc@prout.org
Contact: A. Dyuti Maya, Sec.
Desc: Purpose is to enhance the dignity of women through economic independence, cultural renaissance, and lasting social change based on neo-humanism and a universal spiritual outlook. *Type:* Association.

World Federalist Association

PO Box 15250 Ph: (202)546-3950
Washington, DC 20003 Free: 800-WFA-0123
 Fax: (202)546-3749
E-mail: wfa@wfa.org
URL: http://www.wfa.org
Contact: Tim Barner, Dir.
Desc: Educational organization working to transform the United Nations into a "democratic world federation capable of ensuring peace, economic progress, and environmental protection." Seeks to institute international environmental controls and effective arms control and establish world institutions to handle problems, including pollution, terrorism, and the population explosion. *Type:* Association.

World Future Society

7910 Woodmont Ave., Ste. 450 Ph: (301)656-8274
Bethesda, MD 20814 Free: 800-989-8274
 Fax: (301)951-0394
E-mail: wfsinfo@wfs.org
URL: http://www.wfs.org/wfs
Contact: Edward S. Cornish, Pres.
Desc: Individuals interested in forecasts and ideas about the future. Seeks to "contribute to a reasoned awareness of the future and the importance of its study, without advocating particular ideologies or engaging in political activities; to advance responsible and serious investigation of the future and to promote development of methods for the study of the future; to facilitate communication among groups and individuals interested in studying or planning for the future." *Type:* Association.

Pollution

Air and Waste Management Association

1 Gateway Ctr., 3rd Fl. Ph: (412)232-3444
Pittsburgh, PA 15222 Free: 800-270-3444
 Fax: (412)232-3450
E-mail: info@awma.org
URL: http://www.awma.org
Contact: John Thorner, Exec.Dir.
Desc: Seeks to provide a neutral forum for the exchange of technical information on a wide variety of environmental topics. *Type:* Association.

Center for Clean Air Policy

750 First St., Ste. 1140 Ph: (202)408-9260
Washington, DC 20002 Fax: (202)408-8896
E-mail: general@ccap.org
Contact: Edward A. Helme, Exec.Dir.
Desc: Participants are U.S. state governors and corporate, academic, and public interest leaders. Develops and analyzes approaches to resolving environmental and energy issues. *Type:* Association.

Citizens for a Better Environment

3255 Hennepin Ave. S Ph: (612)824-8637
No. 60 Fax: (612)824-0506
Minneapolis, MN 55408
E-mail: cbemn@igc.apc.org
URL: http://www.cbemn.org
Contact: Tim Rudnicki, Exec.Dir.
Desc: Works to reduce exposure to toxic substances in air, water, and land. Focuses on research, public information, and advocacy, including formal and informal interaction with policy-making bodies on a state, regional, and national level. A trained staff of scientists, researchers, and policy analysts evaluate specific problems, testify at legislative and regulatory hearings, and file suits in state and federal courts. *Type:* Association.

Clean Water Action

4455 Connecticut Ave. NW, Ph: (202)895-0420
 Ste. A300 Fax: (202)895-0438
Washington, DC 20008-2328
E-mail: cwa@essential.org
URL: http://www.cleanwateraction.org
Contact: David Zwick, Pres.
Desc: Works locally, statewide, and nationally for clean, safe, and affordable water. Seeks to: prevent health-threatening pollution; create environmentally safe jobs and businesses; empower people to make democracy work. Organizes grassroots groups, coalitions, and campaigns to protect the environment, economic well-being, and quality of life. *Type:* Association.

Clean Water Fund

c/o David Zwick Ph: (202)895-0432
4455 Connecticut Ave. NW, Fax: (202)895-0438
 Ste. A300-16
Washington, DC 20008-2328
E-mail: cleanwater@essential.org
URL: http://www.essential.org/cwa
Contact: David Zwick, Exec.Dir.
Desc: Research and educational organization promoting public interest and involvement in issues related to water, toxic materials, and natural resources. Participants include scientific and policy experts, writers of environmental legislation, politicians, and grass roots organizers. Works to improve the effectiveness of local environmental groups. *Type:* Association.

Pollution Abstracts

Cambridge Scientific Abstracts (CSA)
7200 Wisconsin Ave., Ste. 601   Ph: (301)961-6700
Bethesda, MD 20814-4823
E-mail: sales@csa.com
URL: http://www.csa.com
Desc: Contains more than 225,000 abstracts to the worldwide technical and non-technical literature on pollution research, sources, and controls. Covers air, water, land, thermal, noise, and radiological pollution; pesticides; sewage and waste treatment; environmental action; and toxicology and health. *Available:* The Dialog Corporation, DataStar; The Dialog Corporation, DIALOG; CompuServe Information Service, Knowledge Index; STN International; European Information Network Services (EINS); Cambridge Scientific Abstracts (CSA), Internet Database Service. *Type:* Database.

Wastewater Technology Buyers Guide

Water Environment Federation
601 Wythe St.   Ph: (703)684-2400
Alexandria, VA 22314-1994   Free: 800-666-0206
    Fax: (703)684-2492
E-mail: msc@wef.org
URL: http://www.wef.org
Contact: Thomas Wolfe, Editor.
Desc: Listings of the Water Environment Federation (WEF) associate members, municipal/industrial products. *Type:* Directory.

Water Environment Federation

601 Wythe St.   Ph: (703)684-2400
Alexandria, VA 22314-1994   Free: 800-666-0206
    Fax: (703)684-2492
URL: http://www.wef.org
Contact: Dr. Quincalee Brown, Exec.Dir.
Desc: Technical societies representing chemists, biologists, ecologists, geologists, operators, educational and research personnel, industrial wastewater engineers, consultant engineers, municipal officials, equipment manufacturers, and university professors and students dedicated to the enhancement and preservation of water quality and resources. Seeks to advance fundamental and practical knowledge concerning the nature, collection, treatment, and disposal of domestic and industrial wastewaters, and the design, construction, operation, and management of facilities for these purposes. Disseminates technical information; promotes good public relations and regulations that improve water quality and the status of individuals working in this field. *Type:* Association.

Population

Center for Communication Programs

111 Market Pl., Ste. 310   Ph: (410)659-6300
Johns Hopkins University   Fax: (410)659-6266
Baltimore, MD 21202
E-mail: ccp@jhuccp.org
URL: http://www.jhuccp.org
Contact: Phyllis Tilson Piotrow, Ph.D., Dir.
Desc: Promotes and develops public awareness of family planning, AIDS prevention, and maternal and child health primarily in developing countries. Seeks to increase knowledge of health education through research and technology; implement health communication in worldwide settings; develop innovative mass media programs, interpersonal communication, national campaigns, and training workshops; apply new concepts and technology in evaluating health communication projects. Admininisters Population Communication Services (founded in 1982), providing technical and financial assistance for information, education, and communication projects to promote family planning and health in developing countries, and Population Information Program (founded in 1972), which maintains the largest computerized bibliographic population data base. *Type:* Association.

Growth Strategies

Growth Strategies
2118 Wilshire Blvd., Ste. 826   Ph: (310)451-2990
Santa Monica, CA 90403   Fax: (310)828-0427
Contact: Roger Selbert, Editor.
Desc: Explores economic, social, political, technological, demographic, lifestyle, consumer, business, management, and marketing trends. *Type:* Newsletter.

Monthly Product Announcement

U.S. Department of Commerce
Customer Service
Bureau of the Census
Washington, DC 20233   Ph: (301)457-4501
    Fax: (301)457-4714
E-mail: majordomo@scensus.gov.
URL: http://www.census.gov/mp/www/mpa.htmlmpa.
Contact: Mary Kilbride, Editor.
Desc: Provides listings of all new Census Bureau products, primarily publications and data files, and includes ordering information and order forms. Covers demographic, geographic, and economic subjects derived from census and survey information, and estimates and projections programs. *Type:* Newsletter.

Negative Population Growth

1608 20th St., NW, Ste. 200   Ph: (202)667-8950
Washington, DC 20009   Fax: (202)667-8950
E-mail: npg@npg.org
URL: http://www.npg.org
Contact: Donald Mann, Pres.
Desc: Individuals who believe that "a drastic reduction in total population size represents the only viable option consistent with human survival." Promotes a 50% reduction in U.S. and total world population size over the next 90-100 years. Advocates that the birth rate be lowered by voluntary measures such as national population control programs, financial and tax incentives, and public education. *Type:* Association.

Population Action International

1120 19th St. NW, Ste. 550   Ph: (202)659-1833
Washington, DC 20036   Fax: (202)293-1795
URL: http://www.populationaction.org
Contact: Amy Coen, Pres.
Desc: PAI is dedicated to advancing policies and programs that slow population growth in order to enhance the quality of life for all pages PAI advocates expansion of voluntary family planning, other reproductive health services, and educational and economic opportunities for girls and women. *Type:* Association.

Population Communications International

777 United Nations Plz., Ste.   Ph: (212)687-3366
7C   Fax: (212)661-4188
New York, NY 10017-3521
E-mail: pciny@population.org
URL: http://www.population.org
Contact: David O. Poindexter, Pres.
Desc: Works worldwide in the fields of population, environment and development. Develops motivational communication campaigns on family planning and other population-related topics for use in countries with the highest population growth rates. Promotes increased individual understanding of the relationships between family size, the environment, and the health, happiness, and prosperity of individuals, families, and communities. *Type:* Association.

Population Council

1 Dag Hammarskjold Plz.   Ph: (212)339-0500
New York, NY 10017   Fax: (212)755-6052
E-mail: pubinfo@popcouncil.org

URL: http://www.popcouncil.org
Contact: Linda G. Martin, Pres.
Desc: Aims to improve reproductive health and achieve a balance between people and resources. Analyzes demographic trends; conducts biomedical research to develop new contraceptives; works with public and private agencies to improve the quality of family planning and reproductive health services. Helps governments design and implement just and sustainable population and development policies; communicates the results of research in the population field to a broad audience; and helps build research capacities in developing countries. *Type:* Association.

Population-Environment Balance

2000 P St. NW, Ste. 210   Ph: (202)955-5700
Washington, DC 20036   Fax: (202)955-6161
E-mail: uspop@balance.org
URL: http://www.balance.org
Contact: Maria L. Sepulveda, Exec.Dir.
Desc: Works to educate and impress upon the American public and policymakers the "adverse effects" of population growth on the environment. Advocates population stabilization in the U.S.; seeks reform to U.S. immigration policy. *Type:* Association.

Population Institute

107 2nd St. NE   Ph: (202)544-3300
Washington, DC 20002   Free: 800-787-0038
    Fax: (202)544-0068
E-mail: web@populationinstitute.org
URL: http://www.populationinstitute.org
Contact: Werner Fornos, Pres.
Desc: U.S. members (25,000) are doctors, lawyers, businessmen, educators, religious leaders, and other concerned individuals. Overseas members (7000) are those influential in their country's leadership structure and those working directly in the population/family planning field. *Type:* Association.

State Data Center Newsletter

Tennessee State Data Center
University of Tennessee at Knoxville
Center for Business and   Ph: (615)974-5441
  Economic Research
Glocker Business Bldg., Ste. 100
Knoxville, TN 37996-4170
Contact: Betty B. Vickers, Editor.
Desc: Informs data users on surveys, censuses, and publications of the U.S. Department of Commerce and Bureau of the Census. *Type:* Newsletter.

Zero Population Growth - Seattle Chapter

4426 Burke Ave N   Ph: (206)548-0152
Seattle, WA 98103   Free: 800-767-1956
    Fax: (206)548-0152
E-mail: zpgseattle@earthlink.net
URL: http://www.cn.org/zpg
Contact: Peter Kostmayer, Exec.Dir.
Desc: Works to educate and motivate Americans to help meet global population challenge, and to mobilize support for the adoption of policies and programs necessary to stop global population growth. Participates in coalitions, influences governmental policies on the international, national, state, and local levels; works with the media; engages in teacher training and public education programs. Conducts research, interprets and applies the research of others. *Type:* Association.

Postal Service

The American Postal Worker

American Postal Workers Union, AFL-CIO
1300 L St. NW   Ph: (202)842-4200
Washington, DC 20005   Fax: (202)842-4297
Contact: Moe Biller, Editor.
Desc: AFL-CIO postal labor. *Type:* Periodical.

Bar Avion

Harry L. Baisden
3523 Slade Run Dr.   Ph: (703)538-6416
Falls Church, VA 22042
E-mail: hbaisden@erol.com
Contact: Harry L. Baisden, Editor.
Desc: Covers international issues affecting postal companies, administrations, delivery companies, and major international mailers. Recurring features include a calendar of events. *Type:* Newsletter.

Branch 3 Buzz

Branch No. 3 N. A. L. C.
4845 Union Rd.   Ph: (716)631-3940
Buffalo, NY 14225
Contact: Gary Marzolf, Editor.
Desc: Covers news, events, and useful information of interest to letter carriers of the Buffalo region who are members of the Association. Recurring features include colorado From Your Editor, Vice- President's Report, and Secretary-Treasurer's Report. *Type:* Newsletter.

Business Mailers Review

Business Mailers Review
5604 N. 24th St.   Ph: (703)237-7962
Arlington, VA 22205   Fax: (703)538-6841
E-mail: mailer@pasha.com.
Contact: Kate Phelan Muth, Editor, muth@erols.com.
Desc: Concerned with the monitoring of the U.S. Postal Service, private carriers, and suppliers. *Type:* Newsletter.

Memo to Mailers

U.S. Postal Service
National Customer Support Center
Unites States Postal Service
6060 Primacy Pkwy., Ste. 101   Free: 800-238-3150
Memphis, TN 38188-0001   Fax: (901)767-8853
E-mail: mmailers@usps.gov.
URL: http://www.usps.gov.
Contact: Jim Quirk, Editor.
Desc: Reports changes in postal regulations and rates and offers information on how to use mail effectively. *Type:* Newsletter.

National Association of Postmasters of the United States

8 Herbert St.   Ph: (703)683-9027
Alexandria, VA 22305-2600   Fax: (703)683-6820
E-mail: napus@napus.org
Contact: Tea Carrico, Nat.Pres.
Desc: Serves the professional interests of postmasters and promotes cooperation and interchange of ideas between members and officials of the U.S. Postal Service. *Type:* Association.

National Postal Arts Association

PO Box 182   Ph: (207)666-8453
Bowdoinham, ME 04008-0182
Contact: Carlo Pittore, Liaison.
Desc: Artists utilizing correspondence to encourage mail art. Sponsors exhibitions. Compiles statistics. *Type:* Association.

The National Rural Letter Carrier

National Rural Letter Carriers' Association
1630 Duke St., 4th Fl.   Ph: (703)684-5545
Alexandria, VA 22314-3465   Fax: (703)548-8735
Contact: Dale Holton, Editor; Kathleen O'Connor, Managing Editor.
Desc: Magazine covering postal service issues for members. *Type:* Periodical.

Postal Record

National Association of Letter Carriers
100 Indiana Ave. NW   Ph: (202)393-4695
Washington, DC 20001-2144   Fax: (202)737-1540
Contact: Vincent R. Sombrotto, Editor.
Desc: Magazine for active and retired letter carriers. *Type:* Periodical.

Postal World

United Communications Group
11300 Rockville Pike, Ste. 1100   Ph: (301)287-2700
Rockville, MD 20852-3030   Free: 800-929-4824
                                 Fax: (301)287-2049
E-mail: customer@ucg.com; postlwld@ucg.com.
Contact: Marcus J. Smith, President.
Desc: Disseminates information to help readers run a more efficient mail operation. "Discusses how to trim postage costs, speed delivery, improve mailroom productivity, and plan for rate increases." Recurring features include an annual salary survey and periodic special reports. *Type:* Newsletter.

Postmasters Advocate Express

National League of Postmasters of the United States
1023 N. Royal St.   Ph: (703)548-5922
Alexandria, VA 22314-1569   Fax: (703)836-8937
Desc: Monitors the advocacy activities of the League, which sponsors the Postmasters Benefit Plan and represents postmasters before Congress and provides liaison to USPS. Covers pertinent legislative developments and postal issues. *Type:* Newsletter.

Postal Workers

American Postal Workers Union

1300 L St. NW   Ph: (202)842-4200
Washington, DC 20005   Fax: (202)842-4297
Contact: Moe Biller, Pres.
Desc: AFL-CIO. *Type:* Association.

National Alliance of Postal and Federal Employees

1628 11th St. NW   Ph: (202)939-6325
Washington, DC 20001   Fax: (202)939-6389
Contact: James M. McGee, Pres.
Desc: Independent. Works to eliminate employment discrimination. *Type:* Association.

National Association of Letter Carriers of the U. S.A.

100 Indiana Ave. NW   Ph: (202)393-4695
Washington, DC 20001   Fax: (202)737-1540
URL: http://www.nalc.org
Contact: Vincent R. Sombrotto, Pres.
Desc: AFL-CIO. Provides Collective Bargaining representation for city delivery letter carriers employed by the U.S. Postal Service. *Type:* Association.

National Association of Postal Supervisors

1727 King St., Ste. 400   Ph: (703)836-9660
Alexandria, VA 22314-2753   Fax: (703)836-9665
E mail: napsweb@naps.org

URL: http://www.naps.org
Contact: Vincent Palladino, Pres.
Desc: Independent. *Type:* Association.

National League of Postmasters of the United States

1023 N. Royal St.   Ph: (703)548-5922
Alexandria, VA 22314-1569   Fax: (703)836-8937
Contact: Joseph W. Cinads, Pres.
Desc: Independent. Sponsors the Postmasters Benefit Plan, an insurance program operated under the Federal Employees Health Benefit Program (FEHBP). Represents postmasters and other federal employees before Congress. *Type:* Association.

National Postal Mail Handlers Union

1101 Conn. Ave., NW, Ste. 500   Ph: (202)833-9095
Washington, DC 20036-4303   Fax: (202)833-0008
Contact: William Quinn, Pres.
Desc: AFL-CIO. Operates as a division of Laborers' International Union of North America. *Type:* Association.

National Rural Letter Carriers' Association

1630 Duke St., 4th Fl.   Ph: (703)684-5545
Alexandria, VA 22314-3465   Fax: (703)548-8735
URL: http://www.nrlca.org/
Contact: Clifford D. Dailing, Sec.Treas.
Desc: Independent. *Type:* Association.

Poverty

Center for Community Change

1000 Wisconsin Ave. NW   Ph: (202)342-0519
Washington, DC 20007   Fax: (202)342-1132
Contact: Andrew Mott, Dir.
Desc: Assists community groups of urban and rural poor in making positive changes in their communities. Designs and delivers technical assistance to these community organizations, focuses attention on national issues dealing with human poverty, and works to make government more responsive to the needs of the poor. Sponsors workshops. *Type:* Association.

Food for the Poor

James J. Cavnar
550 SW 12th Ave., Bldg. 4   Ph: (954)427-2222
Deerfield Beach, FL 33442   Fax: (954)570-7654
Contact: Ferdinand Mahfood, Founder/Dir.
Desc: Works to improve the health, economic, spiritual, and social conditions of the poor, primarily in the Caribbean and Latin America. *Type:* Association.

Free Store/Food Bank

112 E. Liberty   Ph: (513)241-1064
Cincinnati, OH 45210   Fax: (513)357 4683
Contact: Stephen Gibbs, Exec. Officer.
Desc: Seeks to help those in need, including poor people and victims of disasters and emergencies. Supplies food, clothing, beds, blankets, stoves, refrigerators, and space heaters to the needy. Attempts to raise levels of fixed income programs for the poor; monitors food stamp legislation; offers advocacy services on behalf of the poor. *Type:* Association.

Homeless Archives

University of Colorado at Boulder
Communications for a
    Sustainable Future
Boulder, CO 80309
URL: http://csf.colorado.edu/homeless/
Contact: Dee Southard, southard@oregon.uoregon.edu.
Desc: This site contains research reports, FAQs, bibliographies, program and shelter descriptions, conference and funding announcements, and statistical information on homelessness. IT also contains graphical information (including photographs), missing persons postings, fund raising ideas, teaching files, and a global news service with text from several homeless newspapers. *Type:* Database.

Mercy Corps International

3030 SW 1st Ave.   Ph: (503)796-6800
Portland, OR 97201-4796   Free: 800-292-3355
    Fax: (503)796-6844
E-mail: programs@mercycorps.org
Contact: Neal Keny-Guyer, CEO.
Desc: Assists poverty-stricken communities throughout the world to achieve self-reliance, productivity, and human dignity. *Type:* Association.

National Coalition for the Homeless

ARInternet Corp.
8201 Corporate Dr., Ste. 1100
Landover, MD 20785
E-mail: nch@ari.net
URL: http://nch.ari.net
Desc: The National Coalition for the Homeless (NCH) Homepage describes the NCH and its mission, provides legislation information, directories, publications data, and more. *Type:* Database.

National Coalition for the Homeless

1012 14th St., NW   Ph: (202)737-6444
No. 600   Fax: (202)737-6445
Washington, DC 20005-3406
E-mail: nch@ari.net
URL: http://www.nch.ari.net
Contact: Mary Ann Gleason, Exec.Dir.
Desc: Serves as a clearinghouse of information for social service and legal agencies, church organizations, private charities, community groups, and individuals interested in helping the homeless. Exchanges information, strategies, and resources; lobbies and educates the public on housing/homelessness problems. Seeks to expand America's supply of low-income housing. *Type:* Association.

Plan News

Foster Parents Plan of Canada
95 St. Clair Ave. W.   Ph: (416)920-1654
Toronto, ON, Canada M4V   Free: 800-268-7174
    3B5   Fax: (416)920-9942
Contact: Colleen Scott, Editor.
Desc: Updates current sponsors on changes, projects, and special events in Foster Parents Plan programs worldwide. Focuses on program areas in the developing world. *Type:* Newsletter.

Synergos Institute

100 E. 85th St.   Ph: (212)517-4900
New York, NY 10028   Fax: (212)517-4815
URL: http://www.people2people.org
Contact: S. Bruce Schearer, Pres. & CEO.
Desc: A private, non-governemntal, non-profit organization funded by grants from foundations, corporations, international agencies, and individual contributors. Works with voluntary organizations and other groups in supporting local communities to develop effective, sustainable solutions to poverty problems. Also works closely with Associates and a dozen partner organizations in 18 countries. *Type:* Association.

Union Settlement Association

237 E. 104th St.   Ph: (212)360-8823
New York, NY 10029   Fax: (212)360-8835
Contact: Ramon J. Rodriguez, Exec.Dir.
Desc: Privately sponsored social service agency that assists individuals of all ages in low income neighborhoods in East Harlem, NY. Has served as a pioneer and innovator in neighborhood social action. Maintains a community center providing adult and senior citizen programs, a summer day camp, and recreational, educational, and counseling programs for families and youth; an adolescent resource center and a community garden; a teen drug prevention model program, teen parenting and pregnancy prevention; four senior centers offering hot meals and recreational and social services to residents in one of the first violence prevention program city-sponsored apartment houses for older citizens; and the James Weldon Johnson Family and Children's Counseling Center providing complete psychiatric and psychological services and AIDS services. *Type:* Association.

Women in Community Service

1900 N. Beauregard St., Ste.   Ph: (703)671-0500
    103   Free: 800-442-WICS
Alexandria, VA 22311   Fax: (703)671-4489
E-mail: wicsnatl@aol.com
Contact: Ruth C. Herman, Exec.Dir.
Desc: Women in Community Service (WICS), a national nonprofit organization founded in 1964, reduces the number of young women living in poverty by promoting self-reliance and economic independence. WICS addresses issues surrounding employment, job training, welfare reform, poverty and cultural diversity. Each year, WICS volunteers and staff help more than 150,000 low-income women and young adults by providing support services, mentoring and workforce preparation programs nationwide. *Type:* Association.

World Concern

PO Box 33000   Ph: (206)546-7201
19303 Fremont Ave. N.   Fax: (206)546-7269
Seattle, WA 98133
Contact: Paul Kennel, Exec.Dir.
Desc: Christians working to empower refugees and poor people through relief and self help development strategies. Seeks to bring hope to the poor through programs which restore health, enable families to attain self-sufficiency, ensure basic education, prevent diseases, protect livestock, and improve the environment. Programs include: refugee resettlement; primary health care; community planning; housing; small business development; veterinary training; reforestation; farming assistance. *Type:* Association.

Psychiatry

American Academy of Child and Adolescent Psychiatry

3615 Wisconsin Ave. NW   Ph: (202)966-7300
Washington, DC 20016-3007   Free: 800-333-7636
    Fax: (202)966-2891
E-mail: executive@aacap.org
URL: http://www.aacap.org
Contact: Virginia Q. Anthony, Exec.Dir.
Desc: Professional society of degreed physicians who have completed an additional five years of residency in child and adolescent psychiatry. Seeks to stimulate and advance medical contributions to the knowledge and treatment of psychiatric illnesses of children and adolescents. *Type:* Association.

American Association for Geriatric Psychiatry

7910 Woodmont Ave., Ste.   Ph: (301)654-7850
    1050   Fax: (301)654-4137
Bethesda, MD 20814
E-mail: main@aagpgpa.org
URL: http://www.aagpgpa.org
Contact: Janet L. Pailet, J.D., Exec.Dir.
Desc: Psychiatrists interested in promoting better mental health care for the elderly. Maintains placement service and speakers' bureau. *Type:* Association.

American Psychiatric Association

1400 K St. NW   Ph: (202)682-6000
Washington, DC 20005   Fax: (202)682-6114
E-mail: apa@psych.org
URL: http://www.psych.org
Contact: Steven Mirin, M.D., Med.Dir.
Desc: Psychiatrists. Seeks to further the study of the nature, treatment, and prevention of mental disorders. *Type:* Association.

Association for Ambulatory Behavioral Healthcare

301 N. Fairfax St., Ste. 109   Ph: (703)836-2274
Alexandria, VA 22314   Fax: (703)836-0083
E-mail: aabh@aabh.org
URL: http://www.aabh.org
Contact: Mark A. Knight, MSW, Exec. Officer.
Desc: Individuals interested in the development and improvement of partial hospitalization within the continuum of psychiatric treatment. To support, encourage, and stimulate the expansion of partial hospitalization services. Sponsors educational discussions on partial hospitalization, including clinical research and administrative issues. *Type:* Association.

Maryland Association of Psychiatric Support Services

109 Melrose Ave., Ste. C   Ph: (301)788-1865
Catonsville, MD 21228   Fax: (410)788-1768
E-mail: mdmapss@aol.com
Contact: Herbert S. Cromwell, Jr., Exec.Dir.
Desc: Promotes community based psychiatric programs for indivduals with long-term mental illnesses. *Type:* Association.

National Association of Psychiatric Health Systems

1317 F St. NW, Ste. 301   Ph: (202)393-6700
Washington, DC 20004-1105   Fax: (202)783-6041
E-mail: naphs@naphs.org
URL: http://www.naphs.org
Contact: Mark Covall, Exec.Dir.
Desc: Represents behavioral healthcare systems that are committed to the delivery of responsive, accountable, and clinically effective treatment and prevention programs for people with mental and substance abuse disorders. *Type:* Association.

World Association for Social Psychiatry

656 Romero Cannon Rd.   Ph: (805)969-1376
Santa Barbara, CA 93108   Fax: (805)969-1376
Contact: John L. Carleton, M.D., Honorary Pres.
Desc: Professionals, contributors, and interested individuals active in allied fields of social psychiatry including anthropology, social work, nursing, or occupational therapy. Objectives are to: study the nature of man and his surrounding culture; research methods to prevent and treat internal changes and behaviorial disorders; advance the physical, social, and philosophic well-being of mankind. Fosters collaboration among members and distributes theoretical and practical information. *Type:* Association.

Psychology

Adult Children Anonymous, Region 8

PO Box 150331   Ph: (817)478-3191
Arlington, TX 76015
E-mail: jestes@arlington.net
URL: http://www.adultchildren.org
Contact: Josie Estes, Contact.
Desc: Selfhelp support group for adult children of alcoholic and dysfunctional families. *Type:* Association.

American Counseling Association

5999 Stevenson Ave.   Ph: (703)823-9800
Alexandria, VA 22304-3300   Free: 800-347-6647
   Fax: (703)823-0252

URL: http://www.counseling.org
Contact: John Jaco, Exec.Dir.
Desc: Counseling professionals in elementary and secondary schools, higher education, community agencies and organizations, rehabilitation programs, government, industry, business, private practice, career counseling, and mental health counseling. Conducts professional development institutes and provides liability insurance. Maintains Counseling and Human Development Foundation to fund counseling projects. *Type:* Association.

American Psychological Association

750 First St. NE   Ph: (202)336-5500
Washington, DC 20002-4242   Free: 800-374-2721
URL: http://www.apa.org/
Contact: Raymond D. Fowler, PhD, CEO.
Desc: Scientific and professional society of psychologists. Students participate as affiliates. Works to advance psychology as a science, a profession, and as a means of promoting human welfare. *Type:* Association.

American Psychological Society

1010 Vermont Ave. NW, Ste.   Ph: (202)783-2077
1100   Fax: (202)783-2083
Washington, DC 20005-4907
E-mail: aps@aps.washington.dc.us
URL: http://www.psychologicalscience.org
Contact: Alan G. Kraut, Contact.
Desc: Scientists and academics. Works for the advancement of the discipline of psychology and the promotion of human welfare through research and application. *Type:* Association.

American Psychologist

American Psychological Association
750 1st St. NE   Ph: (202)336-5500
Washington, DC 20002-4242   Free: 800-374-2721
   Fax: (202)336-5568
E-mail: webmaster@apa.org
Contact: Raymond D. Fowler, Editor; Susan Knapp, Exec. Editor; Jodi Ashcraft, Advertising Mgr.; Juanita Brodie, Circulation Mgr.; Terri Pilkerton, Advertising Sales Rep.
Desc: Official journal of the Association. Publishes empirical, theoretical, and professional articles. *Type:* Periodical.

Anorexia Nervosa and Related Eating Disorders

PO Box 5102   Ph: (541)344-1144
Eugene, OR 97405
E-mail: jarinor@rio.com
URL: http://www.anred.com
Contact: Dr. J. Bradley Rubel, Pres.
Desc: Anorectics and bulimics; families and friends of anorectics and bulimics; medical and mental health professionals, school personnel, pastors, and community youth workers involved with anorectics and bulimics. Collects and disseminates information on anorexia nervosa, bulimia, and other eating disorders. *Type:* Association.

APA Monitor

American Psychological Association
750 1st St. NE   Ph: (202)336-5500
Washington, DC 20002-4242   Free: 800-374-2721
   Fax: (202)336-5568
E-mail: webmaster@apa.org
Contact: Rhea K. Farberman, Executive editor; Jodi Ashcraft, Advertising Mgr.; Tyrone Ingram, Advertising Sales Rep.
Desc: Official newspaper of the APA. Reports on the science, profession, and social responsibility of psychology, including latest legislative developments affecting mental health, education, and research support. *Type:* Periodical.

APAGS Newsletter

American Psychological Association
750 1st St. NE   Ph: (202)336-5500
Washington, DC 20002-4242   Free: 800-374-2721
   Fax: (202)336-5568
E-mail: webmaster@apa.org; apags@apa.org.
Contact: Susan Lillich, Editor; Deborah Fletcher, Editor; Cory Fitzpatrick, Editor; Ron E. Wilder, Editor.
Desc: Provides information of relevance to psychology graduate students. *Type:* Newsletter.

Association for Research and Enlightenment

PO Box 595   Ph: (757)428-3588
Virginia Beach, VA 23451   Free: 800-333-4499
   Fax: (757)422-6921
E-mail: are@are-cayce.com
URL: http://www.are-cayce.com
Contact: Charles Thomas Cayce, Ph.D., Pres.
Desc: Seeks to give physical, mental, and spiritual help through investigation of the 14,305 "readings" left by Edgar Cayce (1877-1945), a clairvoyant diagnostician who is said to have "possessed an ability to diagnose, in a kind of self-imposed hypnotic sleep, medical problems in individuals whom he had never seen." With regard to medical data from the Cayce readings, ARE recommends that, except for noncritical home remedies, all medical information should be used under supervision of a licensed physician. *Type:* Association.

Bottom Line/Personal

Boardroom, Inc.
55 Railroad Ave.   Ph: (203)625-5900
PO Box 2614   Fax: (203)861-7057
Greenwich, CT 06836
Contact: Martin Edelston, Editor.
Desc: Publishes "expert advice on how to live longer, better, richer, and wiser." Covers topical issues with a personal slant aimed at helping those involved with careers handle their personal lives more successfully. Features articles on tax issues, money information, traveling, family, friends, and general health and happiness. *Type:* Newsletter.

CenterPiece

Center for Psychology and Social Change
1493 Cambridge St.   Ph: (617)497-1553
Cambridge, MA 02139   Fax: (617)497-0122
Contact: Mary Ellen Hynes, Editor.
Desc: Features articles on Center research projects, and educational programs, focusing on psychosocial issues relating to peace and ecology. *Type:* Newsletter.

Co-Dependents Anonymous

PO Box 33577   Ph: (602)277-7991
Phoenix, AZ 85067-3577
URL: http://www.codependents.org
Desc: Selfhelp group based on an adaptation of the 12-step program of Alcoholics Anonymous World Services . Conducts recovery program for co-dependents. *Type:* Association.

Common Ground

Common Ground
305 San Anselmo Ave.   Ph: (415)459-4900
San Anselmo, CA 94960   Free: 800-442-4922
   Fax: (415)459-4974
E-mail: comngrnd@ix.netcom.com
URL: http://www.comngrnd.com.
Contact: Baha Uddin Alpine, Editor and Publisher, (415)455-1644.
Desc: Magazine (tabloid) listing over 1000 organizations and individuals offering resources for personal transformation including art, yoga, psychology, psychic arts, spiritual practices, and more in the San Francisco Bay area. *Type:* Periodical.

Council for the National Register of Health Service Providers in Psychology

1120 G St. NW, Ste. 330   Ph: (202)783-7663
Washington, DC 20005   Fax: (202)347-0550
URL: http://www.nationalregister.org
Contact: Judy E. Hall, Ph.D., Contact.
Desc: Psychologists who are licensed or certified by a state/provincial board of examiners of psychology and who have met council criteria as health service providers in psychology. *Type:* Association.

Employee Assistance Program Management Letter

American Business Publishing
PO Box 456   Ph: (732)292-1100
Allenwood, NJ 08720   Free: 800-516-4343
   Fax: (732)292-1111
E-mail: hrp@healthrespubs.com; eap@healthrespubs.com.
Contact: Beth-Ann Kerber, Editor.
Desc: Discusses issues encompassing the employee assistance program (EAP). *Type:* Newsletter.

Encyclopedia of Occultism and Parapsychology

Gale Group Inc.
27500 Drake Rd.   Ph: (248)699-4253
Farmington Hills, MI 48331-   Free: 800-877-GALE
3535   Fax: (248)699-8070
E-mail: galeord@galegroup.com
URL: http://www.galegroup.com.
Contact: J. Gordon Melton, Editor.
Desc: Primarily an encyclopedia; however, publication includes numerous listings for contemporary cults, organizations, periodicals, and individuals. *Type:* Directory.

Focal Point

Research and Training Center on Family Support and Children's Mental Health
Regional Research Institute
Portland State University
PO Box 751   Ph: (503)725-4170
Portland, OR 97207-0751   Free: 800-628-1696
   Fax: (503)725-4180
URL: http://www.rtc.pdx.edu.
Contact: Elizabeth Caplan, Editor, caplane@rri.pdx.edu.
Desc: Features information on support groups, organizations, strategies, and conferences to aid families that have children with emotional, mental, and/or behavioral disorders. Recurring features include news of research, reports of meetings, and notices of publications available. *Type:* Newsletter.

The Gale Encyclopedia of Psychology

Gale Group Inc.
27500 Drake Rd.   Ph: (248)699-4253
Farmington Hills, MI 48331-   Free: 800-877-GALE
3535   Fax: (248)699-8070
E-mail: galeord@galegroup.com
URL: http://www.galegroup.com.
Contact: Susan Gall, Editor.
Desc: Lists organizations relevant to psychology, including psychology associations and information clearinghouses. Principal content of publication is 400 articles covering a broad range of psychology topics. *Type:* Directory.

Health and Psychosocial Instruments

Behavioral Measurement Database Services
PO Box 110287   Ph: (412)687-6850
Pittsburgh, PA 15232-0787
Contact: Dr. Evelyn Perloff, Director, (412)687-6850, fax: (412)687-6850, bmdshapi@aol.com.
Desc: Contains descriptions of information on instruments of use in assessing the health and behavior of infants, chil-

dren, adolescents, adults, and the elderly. Topics covered include public health, communication, psychology, nursing, organizational behavior, medicine, sociology, physical education, psychiatry, human resources, gerontology, and dental medicine. *Available:* Ovid Technologies, Inc. *Type:* Database.

Hypnotherapy Today
American Association of Professional Hypnotherapists
2443 Ash St., Ste. D
Palo Alto, CA 94306-1858
Contact: William S. Brink, Editor.
Desc: Serves as a forum for the exchange of information and experience among professionals who use hypnosis in clinical therapy and education. Features discussions of theories, methods, and ideas. *Type:* Newsletter.

Journal of Counseling & Development
American Association for Counseling and Development
5999 Stevenson Ave.   Ph: (703)823-9800
Alexandria, VA 22304-3300   Free: 800-347-6647
                              Fax: (703)823-0252
Contact: Edwin L. Herr, Editor.
Desc: Publishes archival and current news of the Association. Reports on advances in research and in techniques or innovations. *Type:* Newsletter.

National Association of School Psychologists
4340 East West Hwy., Ste. 402   Ph: (301)657-0270
Bethesda, MD 20814-4411   Fax: (301)657-0275
E-mail: ahyman@naspweb.org
URL: http://www.naspweb.org
Contact: Susan Gorin, Exec.Dir.
Desc: School psychologists. Serves the mental health and educational needs of all children and youth. *Type:* Association.

National Board for Certified Counselors
3 Terrace Way, Ste. D   Ph: (336)547-0607
Greensboro, NC 27403-3660   Free: 800-398-5389
                              Fax: (336)547-0017
E-mail: nbcc@nbcc.org
URL: http://www.nbcc.org
Contact: Thomas W. Clawson, Exec.Dir.
Desc: Establishes and monitors professional credentialing standards for counselors. *Type:* Association.

Overachievers Anonymous
1766 Union St. Ste. C   Ph: (415)928-3600
San Francisco, CA 94123
Contact: Carol Orsborn, Founder.
Desc: A self-help group for overachieving women and men. The organization's motto is "Enough is Enough." Sponsors no meetings or fundraisers and elects no officers. *Type:* Association.

Overeaters Anonymous
6075 Zenith Ct. NE   Ph: (505)891-2664
Rio Rancho, NM 87124-6424   Fax: (505)891-4320
E-mail: overeatr@technet.nm.org
URL: http://www.overeatersAnonymous.org
Contact: Jorge N. Sever, Exec.Dir.
Desc: Individuals who have a desire to stop eating compulsively. A twelve-step self-help fellowship patterned after that of Alcoholics Anonymous. *Type:* Association.

The PS Quarterly
Psychology Society
100 Beekman St.   Ph: (212)285-1872
New York, NY 10038-1810   Fax: (212)285-1872
Contact: Pierre C. Haber, Editor.

Desc: Seeks to propagate and analyze news developments and research in the treatment of patients. Monitors current issues in psychology, facilities for treatment, and foreign meetings. *Type:* Newsletter.

Psi Beta
1027 Westbridge   Ph: (423)265-6555
PO Box 4838   Free: 888-PSI-BETA
Chattanooga, TN 37405   Fax: (423)265-0033
E-mail: psibetainc@aol.com
URL: http://www.ivc.cc.ca.us/PSIBETA
Contact: Carol Tracy, Exec.Dir.
Desc: Honor society - community, and junior college psychology students. Participates in psychology conventions. Provides means for contact with professors in students' areas of interest. *Type:* Association.

Psi Chi, National Honor Society in Psychology
407 E. 5th St., Ste. B   Ph: (423)756-2044
Chattanooga, TN 37403   Fax: (423)265-1529
E-mail: psichi@psichi.org
URL: http://www.psichi.org
Contact: Kay Wilson, Exec. Officer.
Desc: Honor society - men and women, psychology. *Type:* Association.

Psychology Today
Sussex Publishers, Inc.
49 21st St., 11th Fl.   Ph: (212)260-7210
New York, NY 10010-6213   Fax: (212)260-7566
E-mail: psychtoday@aol.com
Contact: Anastasia Toufexis, Exec. Dir., fax: (212)260-7445.
Desc: Magazine covering psychology for the layman. *Type:* Periodical.

Relationships Today
Romantic Lifelines
1224 NW 9th Ave.
Gainesville, FL 32601-4942
Contact: Lyle Benjamin, Editor and Publisher.
Desc: Magazine teaching people how to improve the quality of their relationships. *Type:* Periodical.

Sexaholics Anonymous
PO Box 111910   Ph: (615)331-6230
Nashville, TN 37222   Fax: (615)331-6901
E-mail: saico@sa.org
URL: http://www.sa.org
Contact: Kay Shotwell, Office Mgr.
Desc: Individuals wishing to stop their sexually self-destructive thinking and behavior such as fantasy, pornography, adultery, masturbation, incest, or criminal sexual activity. Group believes that the sexaholic is addicted to lust and sex as others are to alcohol or drugs; this behavior is often followed by guilt, remorse, and depression, and may damage relationships with family and peers. *Type:* Association.

Shanti
1546 Market St.   Ph: (415)864-2273
San Francisco, CA 94102-6007 Fax: (415)864-6584
URL: http://www.shanti.org
Contact: Robert A. Rybicki, Exec.Dir.
Desc: Volunteer counseling service offering ongoing support to individuals who face a diagnosis of acquired immune deficiency syndrome (AIDS) and their loved ones in the San Francisco, CA, area. Shanti is a Sanskrit word meaning "inner peace." Provides peer counseling, and practical assistance, including van service, to people with AIDS. Conducts psychosocial training programs for health care professionals, clergy, and laypeople. *Type:* Association.

Subconsciously Speaking
Harriman Publishing Company
Infinity Institute International, Inc.
4110 Edgeland, Ste. 800   Ph: (248)549-5594
Royal Oak, MI 48073-2285   Free: 800-257-5467
                              Fax: (248)549-5421
URL: http://www.infinityinst.com.
Contact: Anne H. Spencer, Editor, aspencer@infinityinst.com.
Desc: Contains information on aspects of hypnosis, imagery, or suggestibility. Serves to "elevate the consciousness of all who read these pages through the publishing of important and timely information as well as advice and ideas from knowledgeable experts." Recurring features include news of research, a calendar of events, reports of meetings, news of educational opportunities, book reviews, notices of publications available, and a column titled Founder's Message. *Type:* Newsletter.

Tests: A Comprehensive Reference for Assessments in Psychology, Education and Business
PRO-ED, Inc.
8700 Shoal Creek Blvd.   Ph: (512)451-3246
Austin, TX 78757   Free: 800-897-3202
                              Fax: (512)302-9129
E-mail: proedrd2@aol.com
URL: http://www.proedinc.com; http://proedinc.com.
Contact: Taddy Maddox, Editor.
Desc: Nearly 500 publishers of over 3,000 psychological, educational, aptitude, and other tests. *Type:* Directory.

Psychotherapy

American Association for Marriage and Family Therapy
1133 15th St. NW, Ste. 300   Ph: (202)452-0109
Washington, DC 20005   Fax: (202)223-2329
E-mail: central@aamft.org
URL: http://www.aamft.org
Contact: Michael Bowers, Exec.Dir.
Desc: Professional society of marriage and family therapists. Assumes a major role in developing & maintaining the highest standards of excellence in this field. *Type:* Association.

American Group Psychotherapy Association
25 E. 21st St., 6th Fl.   Ph: (212)477-2677
New York, NY 10010   Fax: (212)979-6627
E-mail: groupsinc@aol.com
Contact: Marsha Block, CEO.
Desc: Psychiatrists, psychologists, social workers, psychiatric nurses, and other mental health professionals who meet specific educational and professional requirements. Sponsors educational and research programs. *Type:* Association.

The Bridge
248 W. 108th St.   Ph: (212)663-3000
New York, NY 10025   Fax: (212)663-3181
E-mail: bridgeinfo@aol.com
Contact: Murray Itzkowitz, DSW, Exec.Dir.
Desc: A mental health and rehabilitation center for chronic mentally disabled adults suffering serious emotional difficulties and homeless mentally disabled adults. Provides community residence housing, daily programs, evening and weekend programs, and vocational training and placement. *Type:* Association.

Common Boundary
7005 Florida St.   Ph: (301)652-9495
Chevy Chase, MD 20815   Free: 800-548-8737
                              Fax: (301)652-0579
E-mail: connect@commonboundary.org

URL: http://www.commonboundary.org

Contact: Mariann Payne, Ph.D., Exec.Dir.

Desc: Mental health professionals and others concerned with the relationship between spirituality, psychotherapy, and creativity. *Type:* Association.

Family Therapy Network

7705 13th St. NW   Ph: (202)829-2452
Washington, DC 20012   Fax: (202)726-7983
E-mail: ftnetwork@aol.com

Contact: Richard Simon, Dir.

Desc: Promotes the exchange of ideas and information among psychotherapists. *Type:* Association.

Karen Horney Clinic

329 E. 62nd St.   Ph: (212)838-4333
New York, NY 10021   Fax: (212)838-7158

Contact: Henry A. Paul, M.D., Exec.Dir.

Desc: To promote the psychoanalytic and psychotherapeutic treatment of individuals and groups focusing on the special problems of children, adolescents, victims of violent crimes, adult survivors of childhood sexual abuse, and persons with psychoneurotic and emotional problems. Named for Karen Horney (1885-1952), German/American psychoanalyst and author of several books on neurosis, psychoanalysis, and related topics. Conducts children's services. *Type:* Association.

Postgraduate Center for Mental Health

124 E. 28th St.   Ph: (212)576-4168
New York, NY 10016   Fax: (212)576-4198
URL: http://www.pcmh-institute.org/

Contact: Richard Hlavacek, Pres. & CEO.

Desc: Provides: therapy for individuals, groups, couples, and families; training; psychiatric day and evening care program; community services and public educational programs. Conducts research. Maintains: social rehabilitation clinic; child/adolescent and family clinic; adult clinic; employee support service; group residence for the mentally ill preparing for independent living. *Type:* Association.

Primal Institute Newsletter

Primal Institute
10379 W. Pico Blvd.   Ph: (310)785-9456
Los Angeles, CA 90064   Free: 800-228-5777
                Fax: (310)785-9481
E-mail: primal-@ix.netcom.com

Contact: Vivian Janov, Editor.

Desc: Focuses on developments and research in primal therapy in regard to science, medicine, society, and culture. Emphasizes how health, child care, and human relationships relate to primal therapy. *Type:* Newsletter.

Psychotherapy Bulletin

Division of Psychotherapy
American Psychological Association
3900 E. Camelback Rd., Ste. Ph: (602)912-5329
  200   Fax: (602)957-4828
Phoenix, AZ 85018
E-mail: div29@theadmin-com.

Contact: Linda Campbell, Editor.

Desc: Recurring features include letters to the editor, news of research, reports of meetings, news of educational opportunities, committee reports, legislative issues, and columns titled Washington Scene, Finance, Marketing, Professional Liability, Medical Psychology Update, and Substance Abuse. *Type:* Newsletter.

Recovery

802 N. Dearborn St.   Ph: (312)337-5661
Chicago, IL 60610   Fax: (312)337-5756
URL: http://www.recovery-inc.com

Contact: Shirley Sachs, Exec.Dir.

Desc: Community mental health organization offering a self-help method developed by the neuropsychiatrist Dr. Abraham A. Low at the Psychiatric Institute of the University of Illinois Medical School. *Type:* Association.

Public Policy

American Enterprise Institute for Public Policy Research

1150 17th St. NW   Ph: (202)862-5914
Washington, DC 20036   Fax: (202)862-7178

Contact: Christopher C. DeMuth, Pres.

Desc: Private research group which seeks to preserve and improve: open and competitive enterprise; limited and public-oriented government; defense and foreign policies; cultural and political values. Conducts research on domestic and international economic policy; foreign and defense policy; social and political studies. Conducts annual public policy week in December, AEI World Forum in June, Election Watch, during National election years. *Type:* Association.

American Legislative Exchange Council

910 17th St., NW, 5th Fl. Ph: (202)466-3800
Washington, DC 20006   Fax: (202)466-3801
E-mail: caron@alec.org
URL: http://www.alec.org

Contact: Duane Parde, Exec.Dir.

Desc: State legislators (3000); business organizations and foundations (600). Nonpartisan public affairs and research organization supporting the preservation of "individual liberties, basic American values and institutions, productive free enterprise, private property rights and limited representative government." Through legislative conferences, brings elected representatives together with experts in fields of national interest to share thoughts and legislative proposals in all areas of public policy, with emphasis on sound, imaginative ideas for promoting fiscal responsibility, lowering taxes, encouraging economic growth, safeguarding individual liberties, and fostering federalism. *Type:* Association.

Atlas Economic Research Foundation— Highlights

Atlas Economic Research Foundation
4084 University Dr., Ste. 103 Ph: (703)934-6969
Fairfax, VA 22030   Fax: (703)352-7530
E-mail: atlas@atlas-fdn.org
URL: http://www.his.com/~atlas/hi-lites/highlite.htm;
http://www.atlas-fdn.org.

Contact: Jo Kwong, Editor, jkwong@osf1.gmu.edu; jo.kwong@atlas-fdn.org.

Desc: Contains news on public policy institutes, research, publications, and programs. Recurring features include news of research, reports of meetings, and notices of publications available. *Type:* Newsletter.

Brookings Institution

1775 Massachusetts Ave. NW Ph: (202)797-6000
Washington, DC 20036   Fax: (202)797-6004
E-mail: brookinfo@brook.edu
URL: http://www.brook.edu/

Contact: Michael H. Armacost, Pres.

Desc: Independent organization devoted to nonpartisan research, education, and publication in the fields of economics, government, and foreign policy. Conducts numerous conferences, forums, and seminars. *Type:* Association.

Cato Institute

1000 Massachusetts Ave. NW Ph: (202)842-0200
Washington, DC 20001-5403 Fax: (202)842-3490
E-mail: cato@cato.org
URL: http://www.cato.org

Contact: Edward H. Crane, III, Pres.

Desc: A public policy research foundation dedicated to increasing policy debate to allow consideration of more options the institute believes are consistent with traditional American principles of limited government, individual liberty, and peace. Conducts research; operates speakers' bureau. Holds policy forums. *Type:* Association.

Center for National Policy

1 Massachusetts Ave. NW, Ste. Ph: (202)682-1800
  333   Fax: (202)682-1818
Washington, DC 20001-1401

Contact: Maureen S. Steinbruner, Pres.

Desc: Promotes open discussion of the fundamentals of American public policy, including understanding of the substance of issues, determination of individual and common interests, and assessment of the attitudes, values and opinions of the public. *Type:* Association.

Center for Policy Alternatives

1875 Conneticut Ave. NW, Ste. Ph: (202)387-6030
  710   Free: 800-935-0699
Washington, DC 20009   Fax: (202)986-2539
E-mail: info@cfpa.org
URL: http://www.cfpa.org

Contact: Linda Tarr-Whelan, Pres. & CEO.

Desc: State and local government officials and community activists interested in restructuring public policies on the state and local level. Acts as national clearinghouse and forum for ideas on progressive public policy. Offers technical assistance to groups and individuals in developing model legislation. *Type:* Association.

Ethics and Public Policy Center

1015 15th St. NW   Ph: (202)682-1200
Washington, DC 20005   Fax: (202)408-0632
E-mail: ethics@eppc.org
URL: http://www.eppc.org

Contact: Elliott Abrams, Pres.

Desc: Conducts a program of research, writing, publication, and conferences "to encourage reflective debate on major domestic and foreign policy problems." Focuses on the role of organized religion in the public policy arena. Addresses current issues in light of enduring concepts and values. Attempts to clarify the relationship "between the specific and the general, and between political necessity and moral principle." Conducts educational seminars. *Type:* Association.

Foundation for National Progress

731 Market St.   Ph: (415)665-6637
San Francisco, CA 94103 Fax: (415)665-6696
E-mail: harris@motherjones.com
URL: http://www.motherjones.com

Contact: Jay Harris, Treas.

Desc: Conducts studies and research concerning problems related to the political and economic progress of American civilization; holds seminars. *Type:* Association.

Hudson Institute

Herman Kahn Center   Ph: (317)545-1000
5395 Emerson Way   Free: 800-
PO Box 26-919   HUDSON-0
Indianapolis, IN 46226   Fax: (317)545-9639
E-mail: info@hudson.org
URL: http://www.hudson.org

Contact: Herb London, Pres.

Desc: Not an association. Members of this research center are elected from academic, governmental, and business/industrial sectors. Studies public policy issues in areas of national security, international and domestic economics, education and employment, energy and technology, agriculture and environment, and future studies. *Type:* Association.

The Independent Institute

100 Swan Way   Ph: (510)632-1366
Oakland, CA 94621-1428   Fax: (510)568-6040
E-mail: info@independent.org
URL: http://www.independent.org
Contact: David J. Theroux, Pres.
Desc: Research and educational organization conducting studies on the political economy of social and economic problems. Encourages innovative thought to redefine debate over public issues and promote new directions for government reform. *Type:* Association.

League of Women Voters Education Fund

1730 M St. NW, Ste. 1000   Ph: (202)429-1965
Washington, DC 20036   Fax: (202)429-0854
E-mail: lwv@lwv.org
URL: http://www.lwv.org
Contact: Elizabeth Kraft, Asst.Dir.
Desc: Educational arm of the League of Women Voters of the United States. *Type:* Association.

National Center for Public Policy Research

777 N. Capitol St., NE, No.   Ph: (202)371-1400
803   Fax: (202)408-7773
Washington, DC 20002
E-mail: info@nationalcenter.org
URL: http://www.nationalcenter.org
Contact: Amy Moritz Ridenour, Pres.
Desc: Educates the public about public policy issues. Conducts research; distributes national policy analysis papers, memorandums, brochures, newsletters, article reprints, and other materials to the public, libraries, and the media. *Type:* Association.

National Defense Council Foundation

1220 King St.   Ph: (703)836-3443
Alexandria, VA 22314   Fax: (703)836-5402
E-mail: ndcf@erols.com
URL: http://www.ndcf.org
Contact: Maj. F. Andy Messing, Jr., Exec.Dir.
Desc: Works to: conduct studies on what the group calls low-intensity conflicts (such as those in Angola and Colombia); aid those in the area of conflict; organize fact-finding missions to these conflict areas for congressmen; combat drug trafficking through research and legislation; coordinate studies on energy and the environment. *Type:* Association.

Organization Trends

Capital Research Center
1513 16th St. NW   Ph: (202)483-6900
Washington, DC 20036   Fax: (202)483-6902
E-mail: crc@capitalresearch.org
URL: http://www.capitalresearch.org.
Contact: Patrick J. Reilly, Editor, preilly@capitalresearch.org.
Desc: Analyzes public policy organizations. *Type:* Newsletter.

Pacific Research Institute for Public Policy

755 Sansome, Ste. 450   Ph: (415)989-0833
San Francisco, CA 94111   Fax: (415)989-2411
URL: http://www.pacificresearch.org
Contact: Sally C. Pipes, Pres.
Desc: Goal is to inform the public about issues that affect the free enterprise system and the rights of individuals. Studies public policy issues. Maintains speakers' bureau. *Type:* Association.

Public Agenda

6 E. 39th St., 9th Fl.   Ph: (212)686-6610
New York, NY 10016   Fax: (212)889-3461
E-mail: paresearch@aol.com
URL: http://www.publicagenda.org
Contact: Daniel Yankelovich, Pres.
Desc: Works to help citizens better understand critical policy issues and to help the nations leaders better understand the public's point of view. *Type:* Association.

Reason Foundation

3415 S. Sepulveda Blvd., Ste.   Ph: (310)391-2245
400   Fax: (310)391-4395
Los Angeles, CA 90034
E-mail: gpassantino@reason.org
URL: http://www.reason.com
Contact: George Passantino, Jr., Public Affairs Dir.
Desc: Executives, public officials, media, and other interested individuals. Provides a better understanding of the intellectual basis of a free society and develops new ideas in public policy. *Type:* Association.

Roosevelt Center for American Policy Studies

316 Pennsylvania Ave. SE, Ste.   Ph: (202)547-7227
500
Washington, DC 20003
Contact: Michael Higgins, Exec.VP.
Desc: Scholars and policymakers. Purpose is to provide the public with unbiased information on major public policy issues in an effort to create a bridge between the public and policymakers and to develop constructive choices concerning the nation's future. Works toward improved decision-making in a nonpartisan manner; does not lobby or advocate any particular policy outcome. *Type:* Association.

Twentieth Century Fund

41 E. 70th St.   Ph: (212)535-4441
New York, NY 10021   Fax: (212)879-9197
Contact: Richard C. Leone, Pres.
Desc: A research foundation that sponsors and supervises timely analyses of economic policy, foreign affairs, political and governance, and media issues. Endowment was provided by its founder, Edward A. Filene, a Boston merchant and civic leader. *Type:* Association.

U.S. Public Interest Research Group

218 D. St. SE   Ph: (202)546-9707
Washington, DC 20003   Fax: (202)546-2461
E-mail: pirg@pirg.org
URL: http://www.pirg.org
Contact: Gene Karpinski, Exec.Dir.
Desc: Individuals who contribute time, effort, or funds toward public interest research and advocacy. Conducts research, monitors corporate and government actions, and lobbies for reforms on consumer, environmental, energy, and governmental issues. Current efforts include support for: laws to protect consumers from unsafe products and unfair banking practices; laws to reduce the use of toxic chemicals; strengthening of the Clean Air Act; efforts to reduce global warming and ozone depletion; energy conservation and use of safe, renewable energy sources. *Type:* Association.

Public Relations

Bulldog Reporter—Eastern Edition

Infocom Group
5900 Hollis St., Ste. R2   Ph: (510)596-9300
Emeryville, CA 94608   Free: 800-959-1059
     Fax: (510)596-9331
E-mail: bulldogrep@aol.com.
Contact: Jim Welte, Editor.
Desc: Features information on effective ways to place stories in newspapers, magazines, and radio and/or television programs. Recurring features include interviews, media contact listings, and media personnel changes. *Type:* Newsletter.

Bulldog Reporter: West

Infocom Group
5900 Hollis St., Ste. R2   Ph: (510)596-9300
Emeryville, CA 94608   Free: 800-959-1059
     Fax: (510)596-9331
E-mail: bulldog@infocomgroup.com.
Contact: Aimee Grove, Editor, agrove@infocomgroup.com.
Desc: Covers U.S. news media for public relations professionals. *Type:* Newsletter.

Communication Briefings

Briefings Publishing Group
1101 King St., Ste. 110   Ph: (703)548-3800
Alexandria, VA 22314   Free: 800-888-2084
     Fax: (703)684-2136
E-mail: tloomis@briefings.com; customerserve@briefings.com.
Contact: Jack Gillespie, Editor; Joe McGavin, Exec. Editor; Isabelle Bruder Smith, Managing Editor.
Desc: Provides communication ideas and techniques for a wide variety of areas, including public relations, advertising, fund raising, speeches, media relations, human resources, and employee/manager relations. Carries interviews with top communicators, business leaders, university experts, and research specialists. *Type:* Newsletter.

The Community Relations Report

Joe Williams Communications
300 SE 4th St.   Ph: (918)336-2267
PO Box 924   Free: 800-833-5946
Bartlesville, OK 74005   Fax: (918)336-2733
E-mail: joewmscomm@aol.com; staff@jwcom.com.
Contact: Joe Williams, Editor.
Desc: Reports on innovative and creative corporate community relations activities throughout the country. Covers different techniques of improving community relations such as programs, activities, cultural events, and philanthropy grants. *Type:* Newsletter.

Corporate Community Relations Letter

The Boston College Center for Corporate Community Relations
36 College Rd.   Ph: (617)552-4545
Chestnut Hill, MA 02167   Fax: (617)552-8499
E-mail: cccr@bc.edu
Contact: Susan Thomas, Editor.
Desc: Reports on the significant news, information, and research that impacts the corporation and its relationship with the community. Covers identification of emerging trends; anticipation of new issues; useful reports, books, and studies; activities of prominent community organizations; and information on the development of effective corporate programs. *Type:* Newsletter.

Corporate Public Issues and Their Management

Issue Action Publications, Inc.
207 Loudoun St. SE   Ph: (703)777-8450
Leesburg, VA 20175-3115
Contact: Teresa Yancey Crane, Editor.
Desc: Covers the evolving field of issue management, the executive's systems approach to policy formulation and profit. Recurring features include profiles of corporate and association issue management programs, case histories, reports on seminars, and references to enhance issue management effectiveness. *Type:* Newsletter.

Customers First

The Dartnell Corp.
360 Hiatt Dr.   Free: 800-621-5463
Palm Beach Gardens, FL 33418   Fax: (561)622-2423
E-mail: dartnell@dartnellcorp.com
URL: http://www.dartnellcorp.com

Contact: Molly Miller, Editor.

Desc: Provides training and advice on customer service issues, including such topics as communication, dealing with difficult customers, and overall service improvement. Recurring features include columns titled What Would You Do?, Problem Clinic, and Testing Yourself. *Type:* Newsletter.

The Gauge

The Delahaye Group
117 Bow St.　　　　　Ph: (603)431-0111
Portsmouth, NH 03801　Free: 800-926-0028
　　　　　　　　　　　Fax: (603)431-0669
Contact: Katharine Delahaye Paine, Publisher, kpaine@delahaye.com; William Teunis Paarlberg, Editor, wpaarlberg@aol.com; Ellen Northrop, Exec.Ed.

Desc: Provides information on and evaluates marketing communications activities of companies. Recurring features include interviews, news of research, and a calendar of events. *Type:* Newsletter.

Jack O'Dwyer's Newsletter

J.R. O'Dwyer Company, Inc.
271 Madison Ave.　　　Ph: (212)679-2471
New York, NY 10016　　Fax: (212)683-2750
Contact: Jack O'Dwyer, Editor.

Desc: Provides nationwide coverage of the public relations industry. Reports on executive and account changes, new public relations firms, and honors won in the field. *Type:* Newsletter.

Lifestyle Media-Relations Reporter

Infocom Group
5900 Hollis St., Ste. R2　Ph: (510)596-9300
Emeryville, CA 94608　　Free: 800-959-1059
　　　　　　　　　　　Fax: (510)596-9331
Contact: Amy Graff, Editor.

Desc: Covers lifestyle/consumer media for public relations professionals. Recurring features include interviews. *Type:* Newsletter.

MediaQuest

MediaQuest Publishing
PO Box 9222　　　　　Ph: (617)536-5353
Boston, MA 02114　　　Fax: (617)367-9151
Contact: Barbara Kalunian, Editor and Publisher.

Desc: Provides information on media placement for public relations professionals. Includes interviews with broadcast and print journalists. *Type:* Newsletter.

O'Dwyer's Directory of Corporate Communications

J. R. O'Dwyer Co., Inc.
271 Madison Ave.　　　Ph: (212)679-2471
New York, NY 10016　　Fax: (212)683-2750
Contact: Jack O'Dwyer, Publisher, jackodwyer@aol.com.

Desc: Public relations departments of approximately 4,450 major United States companies (listed on the New York Stock Exchange and in the "Fortune" list of 1,000 largest firms); also includes similar information on over 1,300 large trade associations and foreign embassies in the United States. *Type:* Directory.

O'Dwyer's Directory of Public Relations Executives

J. R. O'Dwyer Co., Inc.
271 Madison Ave.　　　Ph: (212)679-2471
New York, NY 10016　　Fax: (212)683-2750
Contact: Jack O'Dwyer, Editor, jackodwyer@aol.com.

Desc: About 9,300 corporation and public relations agency executives and private counselors. *Type:* Directory.

Partyline Newsletter

Partyline Publishing Company
35 Sutton Pl.　　　　　Ph: (212)755-3487
New York, NY 10022　　Fax: (212)755-4859
URL: http://www.partylinepublishing.com.
Contact: Morton Yarmon, Editor and Publisher, byarmon@ix.netcom.com.

Desc: Disseminates information about media placement opportunities for public relations professionals. *Type:* Newsletter.

PR Marcom Jobs East

Rachel PR Services
208 E. 51st St., No. 1600
New York, NY 10022
Contact: Janis Brett-Elspas, Editor.

Desc: Provides news of job openings in public relations, marketing, journalism, communications, public relations agencies and corporations, and freelance and temporary writing positions. Focuses on the New York City, Washington, D.C., Boston, and surrounding states. *Type:* Newsletter.

PR Marcom Jobs Mid-America

Rachel P.R. Services
1650 S. Pacific Coast Hwy., Ste. 200-C
Redondo Beach, CA 90277
Contact: Janis Brett-Elspas, Editor.

Desc: Provides news of job openings in public relations, marketing, communications, journalism, public relations agencies and corporations, as well as freelance and temporary writing positions. Focuses on the midwest, south, southeast, mid-altantic, rocky mountains and southwestern U.S. *Type:* Newsletter.

PR Marcom Jobs West: Northern California/Pacific Northwest

Rachel P.R. Services
1650 S. Pacific Coast Hwy., Ste. 200-C
Redondo Beach, CA 90277
Contact: Janis Brett-Elspas, Editor.

Desc: Provides information concerning job openings in public relations, journalism, marketing, communications, public relations agencies and corporations, and freelance and temporary writing positions. Focuses on opportunities in the Northern California and Pacific Northwest areas. *Type:* Newsletter.

PR Marcom Jobs West: Southern California

Rachel P.R. Services
1650 S. Pacific Coast Hwy., Ste. 200-C
Redondo Beach, CA 90277
Contact: Janis Brett-Elspas, Editor.

Desc: Provides news of job openings in public relations, marketing, communications, journalism, public relations agencies and corporations, and freelance and temporary writing positions. Focuses on opportunities in Southern California. *Type:* Newsletter.

PR News

Phillips Business Information, Inc.
1201 Seven Locks Rd., Ste. 300　Ph: (301)340-1520
Potomac, MD 20854　　　Free: 888-707-5809
　　　　　　　　　　　Fax: (301)340-3847
E-mail: clientservices.pbi@phillips.com
Contact: Debra Zimmerman Murphey, Editor.

Desc: Carries public relations news and information of interest to high-level executives. Offers a two-page case study in each issue on an aspect of public relations within business, industry, and government. *Type:* Newsletter.

PR Reporter

PR Publishing Company, Inc.
Dudley House　　　　　Ph: (603)778-0514
PO Box 600　　　　　　Fax: (603)778-1741
Exeter, NH 03833-0600
E-mail: prr@nh.ultranet.com.
Contact: Patrick Jackson, Editor.

Desc: Gives news of developments, trends, and research in the field of public relations. Provides alternating supplements: Tips and Tactics, Managing the Human Climate, Purview (summarizing pertinent articles and books relating to social science) and plain talk. *Type:* Newsletter.

PR Watch

Center for Media & Democracy, Inc.
3318 Gregory　　　　　Ph: (608)233-3346
Madison, WI 53711-1725　Fax: (608)238-2236
E-mail: 74250.735@compuserve.com
URL: http://www.prwatch.org.
Contact: John Stauber, Editor.

Desc: Features original investigative exposes of the public affairs industry. Recurring features include book reviews and notices of publications available. *Type:* Newsletter.

Public Relations Career Directory

Gale Group Inc.
27500 Drake Rd.　　　Ph: (248)699-4253
Farmington Hills, MI 48331-　Free: 800-877-GALE
　3535　　　　　　　　Fax: (248)699-8070
E-mail: galeord@galegroup.com
URL: http://www.galegroup.com.
Contact: Bradley J. Morgan, Editor.

Desc: Approximately 125 companies offering job opportunities, internships, and training possibilities for those seeking a career in public relations; sources of help-wanted ads, professional associations, videos, databases, career guides, and professional guides and handbooks. *Type:* Directory.

Public Relations Career Opportunities

Public Relations Career Opportunities
1575 Eye St. NW, Ste. 1190　Ph: (202)408-7904
Washington, DC 20005　　Fax: (202)408-7907
E-mail: prsacareer@aol.com.
Contact: James Zaniello, Managing Director.

Desc: Provides information about positions available in the fields of public affairs and public relations. *Type:* Newsletter.

Public Relations Society of America

33 Irving Pl., 3rd Fl.　　Ph: (212)995-2230
New York, NY 10003-2376　Free: 800-WER-PRSA
　　　　　　　　　　　Fax: (212)995-0757
URL: http://www.prsa.org
Contact: Ray Gaulke, COO.

Desc: Professional society of public relations practitioners in business and industry, counseling firms, government, associations, hospitals, schools, and nonprofit organizations. Conducts professional development programs. Maintains Professional Practice Center. *Type:* Association.

Public Relations Society of America, Chicago Chapter—Membership Directory

Public Relations Society of America, Chicago Chapter
30 N. Michigan Ave., Ste. 508　Ph: (312)372-7744
Chicago, IL 60602

Desc: About 550 individuals engaged in public relations and related occupations in Chicago. *Type:* Directory.

The Publicity Hound

The Summit Group, LLC

3930 Hwy. O

Saukville, WI 53080

Ph: (414)284-7451

Fax: (414)284-1737

Contact: Joan Stewart, Publisher, jstewart@execpc.com.

Desc: Provides techniques and strategies on self-promotion and inexpensive publicity. Recurring features include letters to the editor, interviews, news of research, book reviews, news of educational opportunities, notices of publications available, and columns titled Advice From Media People, Seasonal Story Ideas, Resource Page, Success Stories, and Media Insider Secrets. *Type:* Newsletter.

The Ragan Report

Lawrence Ragan Communications, Inc.

212 W. Superior St., Ste. 200

Chicago, IL 60610

Ph: (312)335-0037

Free: 800-878-5331

Fax: (312)573-3730

Contact: Steve Crescenzo, Editor.

Desc: Offers ideas and techniques for communications executives, especially the organizational press. Provides commentary; "how-to" advice on writing, photography, and design; plus examples of outstanding work in the field. *Type:* Newsletter.

Society of Consumer Affairs Professionals in Business

801 N. Fairfax St., Ste. 404

Alexandria, VA 22314

Ph: (703)519-3700

Fax: (703)549-4886

E-mail: socap@aol.com

URL: http://www.socap.org

Contact: Louis Garcia, CAE, Exec.Dir.

Desc: Individuals engaged in the management of consumer affairs/customer service divisions of businesses. Purposes are: to foster the integrity of business in its dealings with consumers; to promote harmonious relationships among business, government, and consumers; to advance the consumer affairs profession. *Type:* Association.

Public Speaking

Burt Dubin Professional Speakers Profit Letter

Personal Achievement Institute

1 Speaking Success Rd.

Kingman, AZ 86402-6543

Ph: (520)753-7546

Free: 800-321-1225

Fax: (520)753-7554

E-mail: bdubinspkr@aol.com.

Contact: Burt Dubin, President, burt@dubinspeak.com.

Desc: Identifies steps to take to increase profitability in areas of professional speaking, marketing, and business. Recurring features include news of research. *Type:* Newsletter.

International Training in Communication

2519 Woodland Dr.

Anaheim, CA 92801

Ph: (714)995-3660

Fax: (714)995-6974

E-mail: itcmb@aol.com

URL: http://www.escape.ca/.~itcintl

Contact: Muriel Bryant, Exec.Dir.

Desc: Individuals interested in speech improvement, communication, lexicology, leadership training, and skill in organizational techniques and self-development. Maintains speakers' bureau. *Type:* Association.

National Catholic Forensic League

Richard Gaudette

21 Nancy Rd.

Milford, MA 01757

Ph: (508)473-0438

Fax: (508)473-0438

URL: http://www.web.ncfl.org

Contact: Richard Gaudette, Sec.-Treas.

Desc: Schools promoting curricular and extracurricular speech and debate in public, parochial, and private secondary schools. *Type:* Association.

National Forensic League

125 Watson St.

PO Box 38

Ripon, WI 54971-0038

Ph: (920)748-6206

Fax: (920)748-9478

E-mail: nfl@mail.wiscnet.net

URL: http://www.debate.uvm.edu/nfl.html

Contact: James M. Copeland, Exec.Sec.

Desc: High school honor society. Promotes the art of debate, oratory, interpretation, and extemporaneous speaking. Conducts educational programs; maintains speakers' bureau; sponsors competitions; maintains hall of fame; compiles statistics, publishes magazine, conducts outreach programs, provides education audio, video and print material, provides awards. *Type:* Association.

National Speakers Association

1500 S. Priest Dr.

Tempe, AZ 85281

Ph: (602)968-2552

Fax: (602)968-0911

E-mail: information@nsaspeaker.org

URL: http://www.nsaspeaker.org

Contact: Beverly Babb, Dir.

Desc: Professional speakers. Works to increase public awareness of the speaking profession, advance the integrity and visibility of professional speakers, and provide a learning and communication vehicle to professional speakers. *Type:* Association.

Tips

Toastmasters International, Inc.

23182 Arroy Vista

Rancho Santa Margarita, CA 92688

Ph: (714)858-8255

Fax: (714)858-1207

Contact: Beth Curtis, Assoc. Editor; Suzanne Frey, Editor.

Desc: Contains leadership tips, organization, and club programming suggestions. Recurring features include a calendar of events and news of speech competitions and awards. *Type:* Newsletter.

The Toastmaster

Toastmasters International, Inc.

23182 Arroy Vista

Rancho Santa Margarita, CA 92688

Ph: (714)858-8255

Fax: (714)858-1207

Contact: Suzanne Frey, Editor, sfrey@toastmasters.org.

Desc: Magazine covering leadership, communication and public speaking. *Alt. Contact:* PO Box 9052, Mission Viejo, CA 92690; telephone: (714)858-8255; fax: (714)858-1207; toll-free: 800-993-7732. *Type:* Periodical.

Toastmasters International

PO Box 9052

Mission Viejo, CA 92690

Ph: (949)858-8255

Fax: (949)858-1207

E-mail: tminfo@toastmasters.org

URL: http://www.toastmasters.org

Contact: Terrence J. McCann, Exec.Dir.

Desc: Men and women who wish to improve their communication and leadership skills. Sponsors clubs in corporate, government, and military facilities, as well as local communities in over 70 countries. Sponsors annual World Championship of Public Speaking. *Type:* Association.

Publishing

AAP Monthly Report

Association of American Publishers, Inc. (AAP)

1718 Connecticut Ave.

Washington, DC 20009

Ph: (202)232-3335

Fax: (202)745-0694

URL: http://www.publishers.org.

Contact: Judith Platt, Editor, jplatt@publishers.org.

Desc: Examines subjects of interest to publishers, including copyright issues, First Amendment issues, Washington legislation, and programs and activities of the Association. Recurring features include reports of meetings, and notices of publications available. *Type:* Newsletter.

ABA Bookselling This Week

American Booksellers Association (ABA)

828 S. Broadway

Tarrytown, NY 10591

Ph: (914)591-2665

Free: 800-637-0037

Fax: (914)631-8391

E-mail: info@bookweb.org

Contact: Gabrielle Quaranta, Editor.

Desc: Author personal appearances and other activities related to promotion of new books. *Type:* Directory.

AbraCadaBrA

Alliance for Contemporary Book Arts

PO Box 24415

Los Angeles, CA 90024

Ph: (310)821-8269

Contact: Gerald Lange, Editor.

Desc: Communicates information on the promotion and preservation of creative work in the book arts in the Southern California region. *Type:* Newsletter.

ABVS Launch Pad

Audit Bureau of Circulations

900 N Meacham Rd.

Schaumburg, IL 60173-4968

Ph: (847)605-0909

Fax: (847)605-0483

URL: http://www.accessabvs.com.

Contact: Marye Metzger, Editor.

Desc: Provides information on the activities and services of the Audit Bureau of Verification Services, Inc. Includes sections devoted to the three divisions of ABVS—ABC Interactive, ABC Expomark and New Media. *Type:* Newsletter.

AEJMC Viewpoints

Visual Communication Division

Association for Education in Journalism & Mass Communication (AEJMC)

c/o Paul Lester, School of Communications

California State University

Fullerton, CA 92834

Contact: Bill Ryan, Editor.

Desc: Concerned with items of interest to photography, graphics, desktop publishing, and visual communication educators. *Type:* Newsletter.

American Association of Dental Editors Newsletter

American Association of Dental Editors

22W054 Stratford Pl.

Glen Ellyn, IL 60137-6809

Ph: (708)354-2982

Fax: (708)354-2914

E-mail: iadde.dent@syslink.mes.com.

Contact: Joanna Carey, Editor.

Desc: Carries information on writing articles for dental publications. Presents a glossary of terms and news of members. *Type:* Newsletter.

American Business Press

675 3rd Ave., Ste. 415

New York, NY 10017

Ph: (212)661-6360

Fax: (212)370-0736

E-mail: abp2@aol.com

Contact: Gordon T. Hughes, II, Pres.

Desc: Business, technical, scientific, trade, and marketing periodicals with audited circulation and independent ownership. *Type:* Association.

American Typecasting Fellowship Newsletter

American Typecasting Fellowship

PO Box 263

Terra Alta, WV 26764

Ph: (304)789-2455

Contact: Richard L. Hopkins, Editor.

Desc: Devoted to conveying information on the preservation of equipment and technology related to metal typecasting. Covers type founding, type design, matrix making, and letterpress printing. *Type:* Newsletter.

Ancillary Profits Newsletter
SIMBA Information Inc.
11 River Bend Dr. S Ph: (203)358-4100
PO Box 4234 Free: 800-307-2529
Stamford, CT 06907-0234 Fax: (203)358-5824
E-mail: simbainfo@simbanet.com
Contact: Jane Zarem, Editor.
Desc: Investigates ways business publishers can boost their magazine's, newsletter's, or newspaper's profits through directories, conferences, merchandise sales, and videos and 83 other businesses. *Type:* Newsletter.

ASBPE National Newshound
American Society of Business Press Editors (ASBPE)
376 E. Saint Charles Rd. Ph: (630)889-4141
Lombard, IL 60148-2361 Fax: (630)889-4140
URL: http://www.ASBPE.org.
Contact: Peggy Smedley, Editor.
Desc: Provides news about the Association and the business publishing. Recurring features include calendar of events, reports of meetings, and news of educational opportunities. *Type:* Newsletter.

Association of American Publishers
71 5th Ave. Ph: (212)255-0200
New York, NY 10003-3004 Fax: (212)255-7007
URL: http://www.publishers.org
Contact: Pat Schroeder, Pres. & CEO.
Desc: Trade association representing producers of: hardbound and softbound general, educational, trade, reference, religious, scientific, technical, and medical books; instructional materials; classroom periodicals; maps, globes, tests, and software. *Type:* Association.

Bacon's Media Calendars
Bacon's Information Inc.
332 S. Michigan Ave., Ste. 900 Ph: (312)922-2400
Chicago, IL 60604 Free: 800-621-0561
 Fax: (312)987-9773
E-mail: directories@baconsinfo.com
URL: http://www.baconsinfo.com; http://www.edcals.com.
Desc: Publishers of over 3,000 magazines and over 200 major daily newspapers. *Type:* Directory.

Book Marketing Update
Bradley Communications Corp.
PO Box 1206 Ph: (610)259-1070
Lansdowne, PA 19050 Fax: (610)284-3704
E-mail: info@bookmarket.com.
URL: http://www.bookmarket.com/bmu.
Contact: John Kremer, Editor, johnkremer@bookmarket.com.
Desc: Surveys resources for publishers interested in marketing their books to bookstores, libraries, wholesalers, catalogs, book clubs, and other special markets. *Type:* Newsletter.

Book Newsletter
International Publishers Co., Inc.
239 W. 23rd St., 5th Fl. Ph: (212)366-9816
New York, NY 10011 Fax: (212)366-9820
E-mail: service@intpubny.com
URL: http://www.intpubnyc.com
Contact: Betty Smith, Managing Editor.
Desc: Announces and describes new titles being released by International Publishers in the subject areas of general nonfiction, politics, religion, and classic and contemporary Marxism-Leninism. Also reprints reviews which have appeared in various publications concerning titles from International Publishers' backlist. *Type:* Newsletter.

Book Publishing Report
SIMBA Information Inc.
11 River Bend Dr. S Ph: (203)358-4100
PO Box 4234 Free: 800-307-2529
Stamford, CT 06907-0234 Fax: (203)358-5824
E-mail: simbainfo@simbanet.com
Contact: Peter Breen, Managing Editor.
Desc: Provides information on book publishing trends, developments, and trade. Analyzes mergers, acquisitions, financial reports, sales agreements, market segment data, distribution, the international front of publishing, industry events, and personnel changes. *Type:* Newsletter.

Books in Print
R. R. Bowker
A Unit of Cahners Business Information
121 Chanlon Rd. Ph: (908)464-6800
New Providence, NJ 07974 Free: 888-269-5372
 Fax: (908)771-7704
E-mail: info@bowker.com
URL: http://www.bowker.com.
Contact: Doreen Gravesande, Editor; Barbara Holton, Editor.
Desc: "Books in Print" is the basic source of information concerning books currently or formerly offered for sale by publishers and distributors in the United States. It includes an extensive list of United States book publishers (over 50,000), along with bibliographical information on over 1.7 million books. *Type:* Directory.

BookWire
Individual, Inc. - BookWire, Inc.
8 New England Executive Park Free: 800-226-6594
W.
Burlington, MA 01803
E-mail: www@bookwire.com
URL: http://www.bookwire.com:80
Desc: BookWire is the book industry's most comprehensive and thorough online information source. Data ranges from bestseller lists and reviews to news and literary events. *Type:* Database.

The Bookwoman
Women's National Book Association
160 Fifth Ave. Ph: (212)675-7805
New York, NY 10010
Contact: Lynn Page Whittaker, Editor; Donna Jonte, Editor.
Desc: Covers major topics of interest to publishers, librarians, educators, writers, and agents in the book world. Recurring features include editorials, letters to the editor, book reviews, and news of members, articles, essays, profiles of woman-owned presses, and news of the bookworld and WNBA chapters. *Type:* Newsletter.

Bowker/Whitaker Global Books in Print Plus
R. R. Bowker
A Unit of Cahners Business Information
121 Chanlon Rd. Ph: (908)464-6800
New Providence, NJ 07974 Free: 888-269-5372
 Fax: (908)771-7704
E-mail: info@bowker.com
URL: http://www.bowker.com.
Desc: CD-ROM. Approximately 2 million English-language books published worldwide. Represents listings found in "Books in Print," "Whitaker's BookBank," "International Books in Print," "Canadian Telebook," "Australian Books in Print," and "New Zealand Books in Print". *Type:* Directory.

The Business Publisher
JK Publishing, Inc.
PO Box 71020 Ph: (414)332-1625
Milwaukee, WI 53211 Fax: (414)332-0916
Contact: John Kenney, Editor.
Desc: Focuses on the business publishing industry. Studies the effects of new technologies, opportunities, and the emergence of unexpected competitors of traditional print publishers. *Type:* Newsletter.

The Business Reader
The Business Reader Review
PO Box 3627 Ph: (757)258-4746
Williamsburg, VA 23187 Fax: (757)258-3398
E-mail: bizbooks@gte.net; bizbooks@gte.net.
Contact: Theodore Kinni, Editor.
Desc: Provides information on new business books. Recurring features include book reviews. *Type:* Newsletter.

Capell's Circulation Report
Gruppo, Levey, & Company
60 E. 42nd, Ste. 3810 Ph: (212)697-5753
New York, NY 10165-0006 Fax: (212)949-7294
Contact: Dan Capell, Editor.
Desc: Provides news, information, ideas, and analysis of trends and happenings in magazine circulation, advertising sales, and management. Contains guides to creative services, list managers, newsstand distributors, subscription agents, and fulfillment companies. *Type:* Newsletter.

Card News
Greeting Card Association
1030 15th St., NW, Ste. 870 Ph: (202)393-1778
Washington, DC 20005 Fax: (202)393-0336
E-mail: gca@rgminc.com
Contact: Marianne McDermott, Exec. Dir.
Desc: Provides greeting card publishers with industry updates, news of pertinent Washington issues, new products, and business opportunities available. Features articles on industry and Association topics. *Type:* Newsletter.

CATLINE
U.S. National Library of Medicine (NLM)
MEDLARS Management Section
8600 Rockville Pike Ph: (301)496-3147
Bethesda, MD 20894
URL: http://www.sis.nlm.nih.gov/dirline
Desc: Contains full bibliographic descriptions of more than 673,000 books and serials cataloged at the U.S. National Library of Medicine. *Available:* DIMDI (Deutsches Institut fuer Medizinische Dokumentation und Information). *Type:* Database.

CD-ROMs in Print
Gale Group Inc.
27500 Drake Rd. Ph: (248)699-4253
Farmington Hills, MI 48331- Free: 800-877-GALE
3535 Fax: (248)699-8070
E-mail: galeord@galegroup.com
URL: http://www.galegroup.com.; http://www.gale.com.
Contact: Jeff Sumner, Editor, jeff.sumner@galegroup.com.
Desc: CD-ROM products, publishers, compilers, and distributors. *Type:* Directory.

Children's Books in Print
R. R. Bowker
A Unit of Cahners Business Information
121 Chanlon Rd. Ph: (908)464-6800
New Providence, NJ 07974 Free: 888-269-5372
 Fax: (908)771-7704
E-mail: info@bowker.com
Contact: Doreen Gravesande, Editor; Barbara Holton, Editor.

Desc: List of over 8,000 publishers of children's books (other than textbooks) and over 127,000 titles for all age levels through senior high school. *Type:* Directory.

CLMPages

Council of Literary Magazines and Presses (CLMP)
154 Christopher St., Ste. 3-C   Ph: (212)741-9110
New York, NY 10014-2839   Fax: (212)741-9112
E-mail: clmpnyc@aol.com
Contact: Celia O'Donnell, Editor.
Desc: Provides information on CLMP's activities and its constituency of literary presses and magazines. *Type:* Newsletter.

CMPA Newsletter

Canadian Magazine Publishers Association (CMPA)
130 Spadina Ave. No. 202   Ph: (416)504-0274
Toronto, ON, Canada M5V   Fax: (416)504-0437
2L4
E-mail: cmpainfo@cmpa.ca; cmpamtrig@cmpa.ca.
URL: http://www.cmpa.ca.
Contact: Emily Sinkins, Editor.
Desc: Reports on the magazine publishing industry in Canada, including lobbying efforts, pertinent government legislation, and activities and concerns of the Association and its members. Recurring features include news of research, a calendar of events, reports of meetings, description of new member magazines, news of educational opportunities, notices of publications available, and a column titled Source. *Type:* Newsletter.

Complete Directory of Large Print Books and Serials

R. R. Bowker
A Unit of Cahners Business Information
121 Chanlon Rd.   Ph: (908)464-6800
New Providence, NJ 07974   Free: 888-269-5372
   Fax: (908)771-7704
E-mail: info@bowker.com
URL: http://www.bowker.com.
Contact: R. Crego, Editor; D. Gravesande.
Desc: List of over 700 publishers and distributors of more than 14,000 books and 120 periodicals printed in at least 14-point type. *Type:* Directory.

Computer Publishing & Advertising Report

SIMBA Information Inc.
11 Riverbend Dr. S.   Ph: (203)358-4100
PO Box 4234   Free: 800-307-2529
Stamford, CT 06907-0234   Fax: (203)358-5824
E-mail: info@simbanet.com
URL: http://www.simbanet.com; http://www.simbanet.com.
Contact: Linda Kopp, Sr. Managing Editor, (203)358-4285, linda_kopp@simbanet.com; Matt Boyle, Assoc. Ed.
Desc: Tracks the $4 billion-plus computer publishing and advertising industries. Features tabulations of advertising linage in 40 leading computer magazines; data on computer ad spending in the general business press, newspapers, television, radio, and the Internet. *Type:* Newsletter.

Copy Source Quarterly

Bureau of Business Practice
24 Rope Ferry Rd.   Ph: (860)442-4365
Waterford, CT 06386   Free: 800-243-0876
   Fax: (860)437-3555
URL: http://www.bbpnews.com
Contact: Kathleen Cipriani, Editor, kathleen_cipriani@prenhall.com.
Desc: Provides information for company newsletter editors. Includes articles, cartoons, and quotations covering customer service, finance, health, leadership and teamwork, personal and professional development, safety, sales, and word games. *Type:* Newsletter.

The Cornerstone

RR Bowker
121 Chanlon Rd.   Fax: (908)665-3528
New Providence, NJ 07974
E-mail: info@bowker.com
Contact: Valerie Berk, Editor.
Desc: Provides updates on information technology, serials publishing, and new products and programs from R.R. Bowker. *Type:* Newsletter.

The Cowles/SIMBA Report on Directory Publishing

SIMBA Information Inc.
11 River Bend Dr. S   Ph: (203)358-4100
PO Box 4234   Free: 800-307-2529
Stamford, CT 06907-0234   Fax: (203)358-5824
E-mail: simbainfo@simbanet.com
Contact: Victor Rubell, Editor.
Desc: Reports on news and trends in the directory and yellow pages publishing industry. Announces publication start-ups and corporate acquisitions; follows legislative developments and other trends pertaining to directory publishing. *Type:* Newsletter.

CyberHound's Guide to Publications on the Internet

Gale Group Inc.
27500 Drake Rd.   Ph: (248)699-4253
Farmington Hills, MI 48331-   Free: 800-877-GALE
3535   Fax: (248)699-8070
E-mail: galeord@galegroup.com
URL: http://www.galegroup.com.; http://www.cyberhound.com/.
Desc: More than 3,700 newspapers, journals, magazines, newsletters, and news services on the Internet. *Type:* Directory.

The Daily Free Press

Net One
729 Boylston St., Ste. 206   Ph: (617)437-7668
Boston, MA 02116   Fax: (617)437-7697
URL: http://www.dfpress.com/
Contact: webmaster@dfpress.com.
Desc: The Daily Free Press is an independent student paper serving Boston University. The paper covers campus and city news, sports, and provides a forum for opinions. *Type:* Database.

Data Conversion Update

Data Conversion Laboratory
184-13 Horace Harding Exp.   Ph: (718)357-8700
Fresh Meadows, NY 11365   Fax: (718)357-8776
E-mail: convert@dclb.com
URL: http://www.dclab.com.
Contact: Don Zirilli, Editor.
Desc: Provides news of electronic data transfer, OCR, imaging, electronic publishing, CDROM, and SGML. Also publishes case studies. *Type:* Newsletter.

Demko Publishing

21946 Pine Trace   Ph: (407)482-6271
Boca Raton, FL 33428
E-mail: trendnews@demko.com.
URL: http://www.demko.com.
Contact: David J. Demko, Ed.-in-Chief Aging America News Net; Marie Mentzer, Author Health Care & Housing; Elizabeth Rupich, Author Arts & Entertainment; Dorothy Harris, Author Education.
Desc: Distributes lifestyle columns on aging. *Alt. Contact:* 21946 Pine Trace, Boca Raton, FL 33428; telephone: (407)482-6271. *Type:* Periodical.

Desktop for Profit

National Association of Printers & Lithographers
75 W. Century Rd.   Ph: (201)634-9600
Paramus, NJ 07652   Free: 800-642-6215
   Fax: (201)634-0324
E-mail: publications@napl.org
URL: http://www.napl.org.
Contact: Cynthia L. Shaw, Editor.
Desc: Supplies information on how to get the most out of your investment in digital prepress equipment written by "noted industry expert Patrick White of White & Associates." *Type:* Newsletter.

Directories in Print

Gale Group Inc.
27500 Drake Rd.   Ph: (248)699-4253
Farmington Hills, MI 48331-   Free: 800-877-GALE
3535   Fax: (248)699-8070
E-mail: galeord@galegroup.com
URL: http://www.galegroup.com.; http://www.gale.com/; http://www.gale.com.
Contact: Dawn Conzett DesJardins, Editor, dawn.desjardins@gale.com.
Desc: Approximately 15,100 business and industrial directories, professional and scientific rosters, biographical dictionaries, directory databases, directory issues of periodicals, and other lists and guides of all kinds. Includes directories published in the U.S. and having local, state, regional, or national coverage as well as directories published outside the U.S. An interedition supplement supplies approximately 710 newly discovered directories. Directories published outside the U.S. were formerly covered in International Directories in Print. *Type:* Directory.

Directory Marketplace

Todd Publications
PO Box 635   Ph: (914)358-6213
Nyack, NY 10960   Free: 800-747-1056
   Fax: (914)358-1059
E-mail: toddpub@aol.com
URL: http://www.toddpublications.com; http://www.toddpublication.com.
Contact: Barry T. Klein, Editor.
Desc: Serves as a means for directory and reference book publishers to advertise their publications. Offers reference book publishing news, including notices of mergers and acquisitions, title and address changes, and other news items from the directories publishing arena. *Type:* Newsletter.

Directory of United Nations Databases and Information Systems

Bernan Associates
4611-F Assembly Dr.   Ph: (301)459-2255
Lanham, MD 20706-4391   Free: 800-274-4447
   Fax: (301)459-0056
E-mail: query@bernan.com
URL: http://www.bernan.com
Desc: 615 selected information services, information systems, and databases operated by or in association with the 38 organizations of the United Nations systems. Also covers indexing services, abstracting services, statistical services, library services, documentation services, clearinghouses, referral centers, and information analysis services. *Type:* Directory.

Directory World Source Book

SIMBA Information Inc.
11 River Bend Dr. S   Ph: (203)358-4100
PO Box 4234   Free: 800-307-2529
Stamford, CT 06907-0234   Fax: (203)358-5824
E-mail: simbainfo@simbanet.com; dwedit@cowlesbiz.com.

Contact: Kathleen M. Joyce, Editor.

Desc: Over 250 publishers of classified yellow pages telephone directories; 750 suppliers of products and services to the industry, including advertising agencies, sales representatives, and printers; 2,500 industry executives. *Type:* Directory.

Directory World's Source Book

SIMBA Information Inc.

11 River Bend Dr. S   Ph: (203)358-4100
PO Box 4234   Free: 800-307-2529
Stamford, CT 06907-0234   Fax: (203)358-5824
E-mail: simbainfo@simbanet.com

Desc: 800 directory and Yellow Pages publishers, CMR's/agencies, industry suppliers, service providers, and printers and 2,000 industry contacts. *Type:* Directory.

The Dorset House Quarterly

Dorset House Publishing Co., Inc.

353 W. 12th St.   Ph: (212)620-4053
New York, NY 10014   Free: 800-342-6657
                          Fax: (212)727-1044
E-mail: dhpubco@aol.com; dhqmail@aol.com.
URL: http://www.dorsethouse.com

Contact: David McClintock, Editor.

Desc: Provides news and discounts of books, as well as author profiles. Recurring features include book reviews and interviews. *Type:* Newsletter.

Editor & Publisher/Free Paper Publisher—Community, Specialty, & Free Publications Year Book

Editor & Publisher Co., Inc.

11 W. 19th St.   Ph: (212)675-4380
New York, NY 10011-4234   Fax: (212)691-6939
E-mail: edpub@mediainfo.com
URL: http://mediainfo.com; http://www.mediainfo.com.

Desc: Community paid and non-paid weeklies, shoppers, and total market coverage. *Type:* Directory.

Editor & Publisher International Year Book

Editor & Publisher Co., Inc.

11 W. 19th St.   Ph: (212)675-4380
New York, NY 10011-4234   Fax: (212)691-6939
E-mail: edpub@mediainfo.com
URL: http://mediainfo.com; http://www.mediainfo.com.

Contact: David Maddux, Editor, davidm@mediainfo.com.

Desc: Daily and Sunday newspapers in the United States and Canada; weekly newspapers; foreign daily newspapers; special service newspapers; newspaper syndicates; news services; journalism schools; foreign language and Black newspapers in the United States; news, picture, and press services; feature and news syndicates; comic and magazine services; advertising clubs; trade associations; clipping bureaus; house organs; journalism awards; also lists manufacturers of equipment and supplies. *Type:* Directory.

The Editorial Eye

EEI Press

66 Canal Center Plaza, Ste. 200   Ph: (703)683-0683
Alexandria, VA 22314   Free: 800-683-8380
                                  Fax: (703)683-4915
E-mail: info@eeicom.com; eye@eeicom.com.
URL: http://www.eeicom.com/eye/.

Contact: Linda B. Jorgensen, Editor.

Desc: Contains articles, tests, and columns that treat the full range of editorial questions, including editing, writing, and style. *Type:* Newsletter.

The Editors' Exchange

American Society of Newspaper Editors Foundation

11690 Sunrise Valley Dr., No.   Ph: (703)453-1122
B   Fax: (703)453-1133
Reston, VA 20190
E-mail: asne@asne.org
URL: http://www.asne.org; http://www.asne.org/ideas.
Contact: Craig Branson, Editor, cbranson@asne.org.

Desc: Presents information and ideas on daily newspaper newsroom innovations. *Type:* Newsletter.

Editors Round Table

Editors Round Table

1419 E. Marietta Ave.
Spokane, WI 99207-5026
Contact: Elinor Nuxoll, Editor.

Desc: Designed for editors of special interest publications, including pen pal, year club, and family directories. Provides information on various publications and editors. *Type:* Newsletter.

Electric Pages

International Informatics Institute

405 4th St.   Ph: (718)499-1884
Brooklyn, NY 11215   Fax: (718)499-1970
URL: http://www.in3.org.
Contact: Jack Powers, Editor, jpowers@in3.org.

Desc: Covers new publishing and media technologies from a publisher's perspective. Discusses such topics as digital printing, fax publishing, CD-ROM audiotex, videotex, electronic advertising, telecommunications, multimedia, and other interactive publishing tools. *Type:* Newsletter.

European Specialist Publishers Directory

Gale Group Inc.

27500 Drake Rd.   Ph: (248)699-4253
Farmington Hills, MI 48331-   Free: 800-877-GALE
3535   Fax: (248)699-8070
E-mail: galeord@galegroup.com
URL: http://www.galegroup.com.

Desc: Nearly 4,000 publishers in Europe that specialize in a limited range of subjects or in two or more separate areas where there is little or no overlap. *Type:* Directory.

Fillers for Publications

Pat Johnston

7015 Prospect Pl. NE   Ph: (505)884-7636
Albuquerque, NM 87110-4311   Fax: (505)888-0477
Contact: John Raydell, Editor; Pat Johnston, Editor.

Desc: Supplies brief items for editors with a space on the page to fill: tips, quips, anecdotes, rhymes, aphorisms, resolutions, games, historical items, editorials, safety and consumer advice, and jokes. Recurring features include a profile of an admirable American, a recipe, holiday features, and columns titled Brainstorming (supplies headlines, layouts, story assignments, and ideas for a publication) and Comprehensive Column Stretchers. *Type:* Newsletter.

Fit to Print

Morgan Printing

Books & Publications

900 Old Koenig Ln., No. 135   Ph: (512)459-5194
Austin, TX 78756   Fax: (512)451-0755
E-mail: morgan@flash.net

Desc: Provides information about Morgan Printing. Includes employee profiles, publishing advice, and a calendar of events. *Type:* Newsletter.

Folio

Cowles Business Media, a Division of Intertec Publishing

PO Box 4949   Ph: (203)358-9900
Stamford, CT 06907   Free: 800-795-5445
                          Fax: (203)358-5812
Contact: Neil Cassidy, Editor; Eric Charlesworth, Editor.

Desc: Provides news and intelligence in the magazine industry through faxes. Monitors deals, dealmakers, policies, winners, and losers. *Type:* Newsletter.

Four Geez Press

1911 Douglas Blvd.   Ph: (916)781-3440
Ste. 85   Fax: (916)781-6837
Roseville, CA 95661
E-mail: ggolomb@ns.net.

Desc: Distributes health and lifestyle column. *Alt. Contact:* 1911 Douglas Blvd., Ste. 85, Roseville, CA 95661; telephone: (916)781-3440; fax: (916)781-6837. *Type:* Periodical.

Freelance

Saskatchewan Writers Guild

1925 7th Ave.   Ph: (306)757-6310
PO Box 3986   Free: 800-667-6788
Regina, SK, Canada S4P 3R9   Fax: (306)565-8554
E-mail: swg@sk.sympatico.ca
URL: http://www.skwriter.ca
Contact: April Davies, Editor.

Desc: Covers news of the Guild, literary issues, the business and craft of writing, etc. *Type:* Newsletter.

The Freelancer

Editorial Freelancers Association, Inc. (EFA)

71 W. 23rd St., Ste. 1910   Ph: (212)929-5400
New York, NY 10010   Fax: (212)929-5439
E-mail: info@the-efa.org
Contact: Mary Ratcliffe, Editor; Louise Weiss, Editor; Georgia Maas, Editor.

Desc: Publishes news of the concerns and activities of EFA, whose members "provide freelance editorial services to the publishing and communications industries." Recurring features include letters to the editor, news of members, book reviews, a calendar of events, columns on usage and business, and columns titled Reports on General Meetings, Bulletin Board, Bloopers, and Grammatical Gleanings. *Type:* Newsletter.

Gale Database of Publications and Broadcast Media

The Gale Group

27500 Drake Rd.   Ph: (248)699-4253
Farmington Hills, MI 48331-
3535
URL: http://www.galegroup.com
Contact: Customer Service. Toll-free: 800-877-GALE.

Desc: Provides descriptive and contact information on nearly 64,000 newsletters, magazines, directories, radio and television stations, and cable companies. Corresponds to the following three publications: • Directories in Print, covering more than 16,000 directories at the international, national, and selected regional, state, and city levels in all subject areas published worldwide. *Available:* The Dialog Corporation, DIALOG; The Gale Group, GaleNet. *Type:* Database.

Gale Directory of Publications and Broadcast Media

Gale Group Inc.

27500 Drake Rd.   Ph: (248)699-4253
Farmington Hills, MI 48331-   Free: 800-877-GALE
3535   Fax: (248)699-8070
E-mail: galeord@galegroup.com

Publishing

URL: http://www.galegroup.com.; http://www.gale.com.
Contact: Kristin Mallegg, Editor, kristin.mallegg@gale.com.
Desc: Approximately 35,000 publications and broadcasting stations, including newspapers, magazines, journals, radio stations, television stations, and cable systems in the U.S. and Canada. Newsletters and directories are excluded. *Type:* Directory.

Glasserfield Directory

10240 Camarillo St. Ph: (818)769-4774
Ste. 210
Toluca Lake, CA 91602
Contact: Selma Glasser, Pres./Ed.
Alt. Contact: 10240 Camarillo St., Ste. 210, Toluca Lake, CA 91602; telephone: (818)769-4774. *Type:* Periodical.

Graphic Communications World

Green Sheet Communication Inc.
PO Box 727 Ph: (914)472-3051
Hartsdale, NY 10530-0727 Fax: (914)472-3880
Contact: John R. Werner, Editor.
Desc: Provides information about the printing and publishing industries and monitors industry trends. Recurring features include announcements of technology developments, financial reports, news from within the industry, and a Bimonthly calendar of events. *Type:* Newsletter.

Graphic News

Printing Industry of Minnesota, Inc. (PIM)
2829 University Ave. S.E., Ste. Ph: (612)379-3360
  750 Free: 800-448-7566
Minneapolis, MN 55414-3222 Fax: (612)379-6030
Contact: Elizabeth Miller, Editor.
Desc: Discusses management topics related to the printing industry. *Type:* Newsletter.

Grids

Society of Publication Designers
60 E. 42nd St., No. 721 Ph: (212)983-8585
New York, NY 10165-0015 Fax: (212)983-6043
E-mail: spdnyc@aol.com
URL: http://www.spd.org.
Contact: Bride M. Whelan, Editor.
Desc: Intended for art directors, designers, editors, production managers, and others concerned with layout and design of consumer, business, and professional publications and newspapers. Promotes excellence in design, illustration, and photography. *Type:* Newsletter.

Guide to American Directories

B. Klein Publications
PO Box 6578 Ph: (407)496-3316
Delray Beach, FL 33482 Fax: (407)496-5546
Contact: Barry T. Klein, Editor.
Desc: Approximately 8,000 trade, professional, and other directories, bibliographies, statistical compilations, federal and state agency publication catalogs, filmographies and discographies, dictionaries, handbooks, etc. *Type:* Directory.

Guide to Country Information in International Governmental Organization Publications

Congressional Information Service, Inc.
4520 East-West Hwy., Ste. 800 Ph: (301)654-1550
Bethesda, MD 20814-3389 Free: 800-638-8380
  Fax: (301)654-4033
E-mail: cisinfo@lexis-nexis.com
URL: http://www.cispubs.com; http://www.cispubs.com.
Desc: Publications concerning nations of the world issued by international government organizations (IGOs). *Type:* Directory.

Guide to Microforms in Print

Meckler Publishing
20 Ketchum St Ph: (203)226-6967
Westport, CT 06880 Free: 800-632-5597
  Fax: (203)454-5840
E-mail: info@mecklermedia.com
Desc: 100,000 international bibliographic listings of microform titles. *Type:* Directory.

Guide to Official Publications of Foreign Countries

Congressional Information Service, Inc.
4520 East-West Hwy., Ste. 800 Ph: (301)654-1550
Bethesda, MD 20814-3389 Free: 800-638-8380
  Fax: (301)654-4033
E-mail: cisinfo@lexis-nexis.com
URL: http://www.cispubs.com; http://www.cispubs.com.
Desc: Publications recommended for U.S. depository libraries. *Type:* Directory.

The Heliocentric Network

Three-Stones Publications Ltd.
539 181st St. SW Ph: (206)242-7670
PO Box 68817 Fax: (206)243-2882
Seattle, WA 98168-0817
Contact: Lisa Jean Bothell, Editor.
Desc: Provides information about the publishing industry. Includes information on writers, editors, publishers, artists, and publishing opportunities. *Type:* Newsletter.

HomeStyles Publishing and Marketing Inc.

275 Market St. Ph: (612)338-8155
Ste. 521 Free: 800-547-5570
Minneapolis, MN 55405 Fax: (612)338-5866
Contact: Roger Heegaard, Publisher; Jeff Heegaard, President; Craig Bryan, Mktg. Dir.
Desc: Distributes blueprints for houses. *Alt. Contact:* 275 Market St., Ste. 521, Minneapolis, MN 55405; telephone: (612)338-8155; fax: (612)338-5866; toll-free: 800-547-5570. *Type:* Periodical.

How To Be Your Own Publisher Update

Bibliotheca Press
c/o Prosperity & Profits Unltd. Ph: (303)575-5676
PO Box 416
Denver, CO 80201-0416
Contact: A. Doyle, Editor.
Desc: Acts as a reference for self publishers. Distributed by Prosperity & Profits Unlimited Distribution Services, PO Box 416, Denver, CO, 80201. *Type:* Newsletter.

The Huenefeld Report

Huenefeld Company, Inc.
PO Box 665 Ph: (781)275-1070
Bedford, MA 01730-0665 Fax: (781)275-1713
Contact: John Huenefeld, Editor.
Desc: Concerned with management techniques and organizational development in small book-publishing houses. Issues focus on a single aspect of the business. *Type:* Newsletter.

IASC Bulletin

Indexing and Abstracting Society of Canada (IASC)
PO Box 744, Sta. F
Toronto, ON, Canada M4Y
  2N6
Contact: James Turner, Editor, turner@ere.umontreal.ca.
Desc: Features information of interest to professional indexers and abstractors. Recurring features include letters to the editor, a calendar of events, reports of meetings, news of educational opportunities, job listings, book reviews, and notices of publications available. *Type:* Newsletter.

Ideas

International Newspaper Marketing Association
12770 Merit Dr., Ste. 330 Ph: (972)991-5900
Dallas, TX 75251-1212 Fax: (972)991-3151
Contact: Dawn McMullan, Editor.
Desc: Tracks current trends in newspaper marketing and successful marketing stories from newspaper around the world. *Type:* Newsletter.

Ideas Unlimited for Editors

Newsletter Services, Inc.
9700 Philadelphia Ct. Ph: (301)731-5200
Lanham, MD 20706-4405 Free: 800-345-2611
  Fax: (301)731-5201
E-mail: parenas@nsi.tm
Desc: Contains pre-formatted editorial fillers and camera-ready art for editors of company publications. *Type:* Newsletter.

IDG Books Worldwide, Inc.

IDG Books Worldwide, Inc.
919 E. Hillsdale Blvd., Ste. 400 Ph: (415)655-3000
Foster City, CA 94404-2112 Fax: (415)655-3299
E-mail: feedback@www.idgbooks.com
URL: http://www.idgbooks.com
Desc: IDG Books Worldwide, Inc., is a global knowledge company with best-selling technology, business, and self-help books and computer-based training tools designed to make learning accessible and fun. They are the publishers of the ever present "For Dummies" series. IDG maintains its user-friendly reputation in this superbly crafted web site, filled with information about its make-it-simple-for-me books, including what their names are, where to buy them, how to write them, which sell best, and so on. *Type:* Database.

Interactive Content

Jupiter Communications
627 Broadway, 2nd Fl. Ph: (212)780-6060
New York, NY 10012-2612 Free: 800-488-4345
  Fax: (212)780-6075
URL: http://www.jup.com.
Contact: Mark Moridian, Group Director, Content.
Desc: Features "entry strategies for mainstream media, including how to port your interactive programs to online services and the latest information on the hottest CD-Rom products." Topics include digital mapping, news on demand, and interactive TV. Also contains intellegience information on major media corporations. *Type:* Newsletter.

Interactive PR & Marketing News

Phillips Business Information, Inc.
1201 Seven Locks Rd., Ste. 300 Ph: (301)340-1520
Potomac, MD 20854 Free: 888-707-5809
  Fax: (301)340-3847
E-mail: clientservices.pbi@phillips.com
Contact: Diane Schwartz, Managing Editor; Roger Friedman, Editor, rfriedman@phillips.com.
Desc: Reports in each issue on a selected subject in management for executives of periodical publishing companies. Written in a symposium format. *Type:* Newsletter.

International Directory of Little Magazines and Small Presses

Dustbooks
PO Box 100 Ph: (530)887-6110
Paradise, CA 95967 Free: 800-477-6110
  Fax: (530)877-0222
E-mail: dustbooks@telis.org
Contact: Len Fulton, Editor, len@dustbooks.telis.org.
Desc: Over 6,000 small, independent magazines, presses, and papers. *Type:* Directory.

International Literary Market Place

R. R. Bowker
A Unit of Cahners Business Information
121 Chanlon Rd.   Ph: (908)464-6800
New Providence, NJ 07974   Free: 888-269-5372
                               Fax: (908)771-7704
E-mail: info@bowker.com
URL: http://www.bowker.com.
Contact: Caroline Buckley, Editor.
Desc: More than 10,370 publishers in over 180 countries outside the United States and Canada, and about 1,150 trade and professional organizations related to publishing abroad; includes major printers, binders, typesetters, book manufacturers, book dealers, libraries, literary agencies, translators, book clubs, reference books and journals, periodicals, prizes, and international reference section. *Type:* Directory.

Ironwood Publications

PO Box 974   Ph: (217)345-5592
Charleston, IL 61920
E-mail: cfaws@eiu.edu
Contact: Allen W. Smith, Self-Syndicator.
Desc: Distributes Contemplating Life, an inspirational/philosophical column that focuses on the individual and daily life. *Alt. Contact:* PO Box 974, Charleston, IL 61920; telephone: (217)345-5592. *Type:* Periodical.

ISWNE Newsletter

International Society of Weekly Newspaper Editors
Department of Journalism   Ph: (605)688-4171
PO Box 2235   Fax: (605)688-4271
South Dakota State University
Brookings, SD 57007-0596
Contact: Richard W. Lee, Editor, leer@ur.sdstate.edu.
Desc: Concentrates on news related to the editorial content of weekly newspapers. Provides examples from member papers. *Type:* Newsletter.

The Jokesmith

Edward C. McManus
44 Queen's View Rd.   Ph: (508)481-0979
Marlborough, MA 01752   Fax: (508)481-0979
Contact: Edward C. McManus, Editor.
Desc: Provides comedy material for business and professional speakers. Contains roast lines, presentation remarks, speaker skits, and "anecdotal jokes to make a point." Recurring features include reports of meetings, book reviews, and notices of publications available. *Type:* Newsletter.

The Kleper Report on Digital Publishing

Graphic Dimensions
134 Caversham Woods   Ph: (716)381-3428
PO Box 20075
Pittsford, NY 14534
E-mail: mkleper@printerport.com; info@printerport.com.
URL: http://www.printerport.com/kdp; http://www.printerport.com.
Contact: Michael Kleper, Editor.
Desc: Reviews software program packages for desktop publishing, imaging, multimedia, and web publishing. *Type:* Newsletter.

Koob Stra

Center for Book Arts
626 Broadway   Ph: (212)460-9768
New York, NY 10012   Fax: (212)673-4635
E-mail: bookarts@pipeline.com
Contact: Peter Smith, Editor.
Desc: Promotes the arts of the book: printing, bookbinding, papermaking, calligraphy, and preservation. Composed of international calendar of readings, workshops, and exhibitions; news of educational programs sponsored by the Center; news of small presses; and book arts suppliers information. *Type:* Newsletter.

Laughing Bear Newsletter

Laughing Bear Press
PO Box 613322   Ph: (817)858-9515
Dallas, TX 75261-3322
E-mail: editor@laughingbear.com
URL: http://www.laughingbear.com.
Contact: Tom Person, Editor, editor@laughingbear.com.
Desc: Reviews small press and business publications; provides information and resources on publishing, designs, and planning techniques for self-published books. Contains news and commentary on independent publishing and related services. *Type:* Newsletter.

Laughter Works—The Newsletter

Laughter Works
PO Box 1076   Ph: (916)863-1592
Fair Oaks, CA 95628   Free: 800-626-5233
                                Fax: (916)863-5072
E-mail: laftrworks@aol.com
Contact: Jim Pelley, Editor.
Desc: Offers information on the application of humor and laughter in the business and health care fields. Recurring features include interviews, news of research, a calendar of events, reports of meetings, news of educational opportunities, and book reviews. *Type:* Newsletter.

LIFE

Time Inc.
Time-Life Bldg.   Ph: (212)522-1212
New York, NY 10020
URL: http://www.pathfinder.com/time
Desc: Contains the complete text of Life, a monthly magazine covering current events and lifestyle trends. Includes interviews with famous or interesting local, national, or international personalities, as well as photographic views of people, places, and events. *Available:* LEXIS-NEXIS, NEXIS. *Type:* Database.

Literary Market Place

R. R. Bowker
A Unit of Cahners Business Information
121 Chanlon Rd.   Ph: (908)464-6800
New Providence, NJ 07974   Free: 888-269-5372
                               Fax: (908)771-7704
E-mail: info@bowker.com
Contact: Karen Hallard, Managing Editor.
Desc: Over 16,000 firms or organizations offering services related to the publishing industry, including 3,800 book publishers in the United States and Canada who issued three or more books during the preceding year, plus a small press section of publishers who publish less than three titles per year or those who are self-published. Also included: book printers and binders; book clubs; book trade and literary associations; selected syndicates, newspapers, periodicals, and radio and TV programs that use book reviews or book publishing news; translators and literary agents. *Type:* Directory.

Magazine Publishers of America

919 3rd Ave., 22nd Fl.   Ph: (212)872-3700
New York, NY 10022   Fax: (212)888-4217
E-mail: infocenter@magazine.org
URL: http://www.magazine.org
Contact: Donald D. Kummerfeld, Pres.
Desc: Publishers of more than 1000 consumer and other magazines issued not less than four times a year. Activities include: Advertising Marketing Department to promote magazines as an advertising medium; Washington office to report on federal legislation and postal rates and regulations; Consumer Marketing Department to provide information services and assistance to members in all areas of circulation marketing. Conducts member surveys on magazine finance, paper usage, and compensation. *Type:* Association.

Magazines for Libraries

R. R. Bowker
A Unit of Cahners Business Information
121 Chanlon Rd.   Ph: (908)464-6800
New Providence, NJ 07974   Free: 888-269-5372
                               Fax: (908)771-7704
E-mail: info@bowker.com
URL: http://www.rcedref.com.
Contact: Judy Salk, Editor.
Desc: About 7,300 periodicals, nearly 1,300 new entries. *Type:* Directory.

Maine in Print

Paul Doiron
12 Pleasant St.   Ph: (207)729-6333
Brunswick, ME 04011   Fax: (207)725-1014
Contact: Lisa Holbrook, Editor.
Desc: Serves the Maine Writers & Publishers Alliance, providing information about writers, contests, and grant information. Recurring features include a calendar of events and book reviews and submissions page. *Type:* Newsletter.

Manuscript Society—News

The Manuscript Society
350 N. Niagara St.
Burbank, CA 91505
E-mail: manuscrip@aol.com
Contact: S.L. Carson, Editor.
Desc: Examines news regarding location and collection of handwritten documents, letters, and autographs of historic value. Carries news on preservation, thefts, forgeries, exhibits, and discoveries. *Type:* Newsletter.

MediaINFO Links

Editor & Publisher Co.
11 West 19th St.   Ph: (212)675-4380
New York, NY 10011-4234   Fax: (212)929-1894
E-mail: edpub@mediainfo.com
URL: http://www.mediainfo.com/emedia/
Desc: An exceptional resource from Editor & Publisher, this database is a directory of media outlets worldwide. Listed here are newspapers, TV and radio stations, city directories, associations, and more. *Type:* Database.

Mid-America Publishers Association Newsletter

Mid-America Publishers Association
PO Box 376   Free: 800-421-1321
Ada, MI 49301
E-mail: midampa@aol.com
Contact: Chris Roerden, Editor.
Desc: Contains Association news and information of interest to small and medium-sized publishers. Recurring features include letters to the editor, interviews, a calendar of events, reports of meetings, news of educational opportunities, book reviews, and notices of publications available. *Type:* Newsletter.

MSRRT Newsletter

Minnesota Library Association, Social Responsibilities Round Table (MSRRT)
4645 Columbus Ave. S.
Minneapolis, MN 55407
URL: http://www.cs.unca.edu/~davidson/msrrt.
Contact: Chris Dodge, Editor, cdodge@sun.hennepin.lib.mn.us.
Desc: Contains news and commentary on libraries, media, and cultural issues. Annotates independent, noncommercial, and politically-oriented alternative periodicals. *Type:* Newsletter.

Multimedia Publisher

Worldwide Videotex
PO Box 3273   Ph: (561)738-2276
Boynton Beach, FL 33424-3273
E-mail: markedit@gnn.com; markedit@juno.com.
URL: http://www.wvpubs.com.
Desc: Examines news and trends in the multimedia publishing industry. Reports on marketing strategies, available media, and information and entertainment products. *Type:* Newsletter.

NAQP News

PrintImage International
401 N. Michigan Ave., Ste.   Ph: (312)321-6886
    2100   Free: 800-234-0040
Chicago, IL 60611-4267   Fax: (312)527-6789
E-mail: printimage@printimage.org
Desc: Features information on the newest technologies in electronic publishing, color copying, mailing services, and computer hardware and software. Includes association news, advice on management and marketing methods, government issues affecting the industry, and an ideas exchange forum. *Type:* Newsletter.

National Directory of Magazines

Oxbridge Communications Inc.
150 5th Ave., Ste. 302   Ph: (212)741-0231
New York, NY 10011   Free: 800-955-0231
                                     Fax: (212)633-2938
E-mail: info@mediafinder.com
URL: http://www.mediafinder.com.
Contact: Joy Goldstein, Editor; Savita Ali, Editor.
Desc: Over 25,000 magazines; coverage includes Canada. *Type:* Directory.

New Media Week

Phillips Business Information, Inc.
1201 Seven Locks Rd., Ste. 300   Ph: (301)340-1520
Potomac, MD 20854   Free: 888-707-5809
                                     Fax: (301)340-3847
E-mail: clientservices.pbi@phillips.com
Contact: Kismet Gould, Publisher; Christine Stavem, Editor.
Desc: Advises on distribution, pricing, and marketing of electronic content, including CDROMs and online publishing. *Type:* Newsletter.

New York Newspaper Publishers Association

600 Broadway   Ph: (518)449-1667
Albany, NY 12207   Fax: (518)449-5053
URL: http://www.nynpa.com
Contact: Diane Kennedy, Pres.
Desc: Daily newspapers; newspaper executives. Lobbies on behalf of daily newspapers. *Type:* Association.

The News-Times

Ottaway Newspapers Inc.
333 Main St.   Ph: (203)744-5100
Danbury, CT 06810
URL: http://www.newstimes.com/
Contact: webmaster@newstimes.com.
Desc: The News-Times is a local newspaper from Danbury, CT, and covers a wide variety of topics, including international and national news. *Type:* Database.

NewsBulletin

Audit Bureau of Circulations
900 N Meacham Rd.   Ph: (847)605-0909
Schaumburg, IL 60173-4968   Fax: (847)605-0483
URL: http://www.accessabc.com.
Contact: Marybeth Meils, Editor.
Desc: Provides information on the Audit Bureau of Circulations activities, rules, and services. *Type:* Newsletter.

NewsInc.

SIMBA Information Inc.
11 River Bend Dr. S   Ph: (203)358-4100
PO Box 4234   Free: 800-307-2529
Stamford, CT 06907-0234   Fax: (203)358-5824
E-mail: simbainfo@simbanet.com
URL: http://www.simbanet.com.
Contact: Carl Mercurio, Editorial Director.
Desc: Covers the newspaper industry, including advertising and online information. Includes articles on related industries, including cable and telecommunications. *Type:* Newsletter.

Newsletter Communications

The Newsletter Factory
1830 Water Pl., Ste. 120   Ph: (770)955-1600
Atlanta, GA 30342   Free: 800-788-9550
                                     Fax: (770)955-3313
E-mail: nlf@mindspring.com.
Contact: Elizabeth Stankiewicz, Editor; G.W. Hall, Editor; Thom Hartmann, Editor.
Desc: Provides news and information to help professionals use newsletters for effective communications. Scope includes creating, enhancing, and/or improving newsletters of varying types, sizes, and purposes. *Type:* Newsletter.

The Newsletter Consultant

Laughing Bear Press
PO Box 613322   Ph: (817)858-9515
Dallas, TX 75261-3322
E-mail: editor@laughingbear.com
Contact: Tom Person, Editor.
Desc: Advises on using newsletters for promotion and customer service. Subscription includes individual consulting services by mail or e-mail. *Type:* Newsletter.

Newsletter Database™

The Gale Group
27500 Drake Rd.   Ph: (248)699-4253
Farmington Hills, MI 48331-
    3535
URL: http://www.galegroup.com
Contact: (650)378-5000, fax: (800)676-2345.
Desc: Provides the complete text of more than 500 newsletters published by more than 165 publishers worldwide which track strategic and competitive developments affecting business and industry. Provides information on company developments; ventures and activities; new products and applied technologies; market and industry trends and conditions; government policies; funding, regulation, and legislation; international trade opportunities; and global eco-political activities, including events in the United States, Canada, Europe, Japan, Latin America, the Middle East, and the Pacific Rim. *Available:* The Dialog Corporation, DataStar; The Dialog Corporation, DIALOG; Dow Jones Interactive Publishing; STN International; Bell & Howell Information and Learning; FT PROFILE; CompuServe Information Service; Thomson Financial Services, Inc., I/PLUS Direct; European Information Network Services (EINS); The Gale Group, InfoTrac Web. *Type:* Database.

Newsletter Design

Newsletter Clearinghouse
44 W. Market St.   Ph: (914)876-2081
PO Box 311   Free: 800-572-3451
Rhinebeck, NY 12572   Fax: (914)876-2561
Contact: Howard Penn Hudson, Editor-in-Chief, hphudson@aol.com.
Desc: Reviews and evaluates newsletters by discussing layout, illustration, paper stock, type style, and color. Explores innovations in newsletter design, including desktop publishing, software, and design trends. *Type:* Newsletter.

Newsletter Nameplate

Ruddle Creative
111 N. Market St., Ste. 715   Ph: (408)297-3000
San Jose, CA 95113   Free: 800-7RU-
                                          DDLE
                                     Fax: (408)287-0540
E-mail: nameplate@ruddle.com.
URL: http://www.ruddle.com.
Contact: Henry Ruddle, fax: (ED), henry@ruddle.com.
Desc: Designed to provide information of interest to editors, writers, and others involved in the media industry. Includes tips on how to produce quality writing and graphics. *Type:* Newsletter.

The Newsletter on Newsletters

Newsletter Clearinghouse
44 W. Market St.   Ph: (914)876-2081
PO Box 311   Free: 800-572-3451
Rhinebeck, NY 12572   Fax: (914)876-2561
Contact: Howard Penn Hudson, Editor, hphusdon@aol.com.
Desc: Informs readers about all aspects of the newsletter industry. Profiles new newsletters, offers information on resources for newsletter publishers, and reports on newsletter acquisitions and industry personnel. *Type:* Newsletter.

Newsletter Publishers Association—Hotline

Newsletter Publishers Association
1501 Wilson Blvd., Ste. 509   Ph: (703)527-2333
Arlington, VA 22209   Free: 800-356-9302
                                     Fax: (703)841-0629
E-mail: npa@newsletters.org
Contact: Rebecca E. Milstien, Dir. of Communications; Patricia M. Wysocki, Exec. Dir.
Desc: Covers the commercial newsletter publishing industry, including trends, regulations, U.S. Postal Service developments, marketing techniques, editorial problems and solutions, and newsletter publishers in the news. *Type:* Newsletter.

Newsletter on Serials Pricing Issues

University of North Carolina at Chapel Hill
Office of Information Technology
215 Flemington Rd.   Ph: (919)929-3513
Chapel Hill, NC 27514-5637   Fax: (919)960-0847
URL: http://www.lib.unc.edu/prices.
Contact: Marcia Tuttle, Editor, tuttle@email.unc.edu.
Desc: Concerned with the pricing of library serials. Includes examples of titles considered to be overpriced, strategies for coping with price increases, actions to keep prices down, librarians' evaluation and cancellation policies and procedures, and announcements of relevant meetings. *Type:* Newsletter.

Newsletters in Print

The Gale Group
27500 Drake Rd.   Ph: (248)699-4253
Farmington Hills, MI 48331-
    3535
URL: http://www.galegroup.com
Contact: Customer Service. Toll-free: 800-877-GALE.
Desc: Provides descriptions of more than 11,000 subscription, membership, and free newsletters, bulletins, digests, updates, and similar serial publications issued by U.S. and Canadian public and private organizations, including agencies, trade and professional associations, and companies. *Type:* Database.

Newsletters in Print

Gale Group Inc.
27500 Drake Rd.   Ph: (248)699-4253
Farmington Hills, MI 48331-   Free: 800-877-GALE
3535   Fax: (248)699-8070
E-mail: galeord@galegroup.com
URL: http://www.galegroup.com.; http://www.gale.com.
Contact: Jeff Sumner, Editor, jeff.sumner@galegroup.com.
Desc: More than 11,000 periodicals of newsletter format
issued on a regular basis by both commercial and noncommercial publishers. *Type:* Directory.

Newspaper Association of American

1921 Gallows Rd., Ste. 600   Ph: (703)902-1600
Vienna, VA 22182   Fax: (703)917-0636
E-mail: naainfo@naa.org
URL: http://www.naa.org
Contact: John F. Sturm, Pres. & CEO.
Desc: Promotes the interests of the newspaper business.
Type: Association.

Newspapers Career Directory

Gale Group Inc.
27500 Drake Rd.   Ph: (248)699-4253
Farmington Hills, MI 48331-   Free: 800-877-GALE
3535   Fax: (248)699-8070
E-mail: galeord@galegroup.com
URL: http://www.galegroup.com.
Contact: Bradley J. Morgan, Editor.
Desc: About 300 companies offering job opportunities, internships, and training possibilities for those seeking a career in newspapers; sources of help-wanted ads, professional associations, videos, databases, career guides, and professional guides and handbooks. *Type:* Directory.

Oregon Newspaper Publishers Association

7150 SW Hampton, No. 111   Ph: (503)624-6397
Portland, OR 97223   Fax: (503)639-9009
E-mail: onpa@orenews.com
URL: http://www.orenews.com
Contact: J. Leroy Yorgason, Exec.Dir.
Desc: Publishers of Oregon newspapers. Promotes the
highest quality in newpaper publishing. *Type:* Association.

People & Product

Newspaper Association of America
1921 Gallows Rd., Ste. 600   Ph: (703)902-1600
Vienna, VA 22182-3900   Fax: (703)917-0636
Contact: Ronn Levine, Editor, levir@naa.org.
Desc: Function as the newspaper industry's vehicle to discuss, develop, and promote the practices within the industry that address the changing marketplace and reflect the changing workforce. Successor to Minorities in the Newspaper Business. *Type:* Newsletter.

Periodical Abstracts

Bell & Howell Information and Learning
300 N. Zeeb Rd.   Ph: (734)761-4700
PO Box 1346
Ann Arbor, MI 48106-1346
E-mail: info@umi.com
URL: http://www.umi.com
Contact: Maria Keller, (502)583-4111, fax: (502)589-
9159, mkeller@umi.com.
Desc: Contains citations, with abstracts, to more than
1600 general-interest periodicals plus the current six
months of the Wall Street Journal and The New York
Times. Available in four editions: • Periodical Abstracts
Library--covers 500 titles. *Available:* Ameritech Library
Services, Vista; OCLC Online Computer Library Center,
Inc., OCLC FirstSearch Catalog. *Type:* Database.

Perspectives

International Publishing Management Association
1205 W. College St.   Ph: (816)781-1111
Liberty, MO 64068-3733   Fax: (816)781-2790
E-mail: ipmainfo@ipma.org
URL: http://www.ipma.org.
Contact: Jeff Langford, Editor.
Desc: Provides new, activities, and events concerning the
International Publishing Management Association. Recurring features include news of research, a calendar of events,
reports of meetings, news of educational opportunities,
book reviews, conference information, and a column titled
Executive Insight. *Type:* Newsletter.

PMA Newsletter

Publishers Marketing Association (PMA)
627 Aviation Way   Ph: (310)372-2732
Manhattan Beach, CA 90266   Fax: (310)374-3342
E-mail: pmaonline@aol.com
URL: http://www.pma-online.org; http://www.pma-
online.org.
Contact: Jan Nathan, Editor.
Desc: Informs member entrepreneurial book publishers
about upcoming marketing programs and other Association activities aimed at helping independent publishers
succeed. Also carries articles on topics such as desktop
publishing and typesetting systems. *Type:* Newsletter.

PNPA Press

Pennsylvania Newspaper Association (PNA)
3899 N. Front St.   Ph: (717)234-4067
Harrisburg, PA 17110-1221   Fax: (717)234-0746
Contact: Amy Smith, Editor, amys@staff.pnpa.com.
Desc: Focuses on the newspaper industry in Pennsylvania.
Follows current trends, member news, and association
events. *Type:* Newsletter.

@press

Port City Press Inc.
1323 Greenwood Rd.   Ph: (410)486-3000
Baltimore, MD 21208-3692   Free: 800-858-PORT
                                 Fax: (410)486-0706
Contact: Melissa Emery, Editor.
Desc: Covers news and developments of interest to Port
City Press customers. *Type:* Newsletter.

Printing and Publishing Newsletter

National Safety Council
1121 Spring Lake Dr.   Ph: (630)285-1121
Itasca, IL 60143-3201   Free: 800-539-7468
                                 Fax: (630)285-1315
URL: http://www.nsc.org
Contact: Kathy Henderson, Editor.
Desc: Carries special reports and information concerning
accident prevention and safety in printing and publishing
establishments. Discusses products and processes, contaminants and attitudes, conditions, regulations, and laws affecting safety. *Type:* Newsletter.

Professional Publishing Report

SIMBA Information Inc.
11 Riverbend Dr. S.   Ph: (203)358-4100
PO Box 4234   Free: 800-307-2529
Stamford, CT 06907-0234   Fax: (203)358-5824
E-mail: info@simbanet; info@simbanet.com.
URL: http://www.simbanet.com; http://www.simbanet.
com.
Contact: Linda Kopp, Senior Managing Editor, (203)358-
4285; Megan St. John, VP and General Manager,
(203)358-4261; Matthew Bechard, Associate Editor,
(203)358-4346.
Desc: Features news on the publishing industry, including
company figures, mergers, industry trends, revenue comparisons, and more. *Type:* Newsletter.

Publications Update

World Bank
1818 H St., NW   Ph: (202)473-1010
Rm. F4K-256   Fax: (202)522-2125
Washington, DC 20433
E-mail: books@worldbank.org
URL: http://www.worldbank.org.
Contact: Brett Kitchen, Editor.
Desc: Lists and describes all new titles published by the
World Bank. Topics include education, information technology, management, trade, and taxation. *Type:* Newsletter.

Publishers' Auxiliary—Syndication Issue

Publishers' Auxiliary
1010 N. Glebe Rd., Ste. 450   Ph: (703)907-7900
Arlington, VA 22201   Free: 800-829-4662
                                 Fax: (703)907-7901
E-mail: pubaux@nna.org
URL: http://www.nna.org.
Contact: Stan Schwartz, Editor, stan@nna.org.
Desc: List of over 200 companies and individuals offering
syndicated articles, columns, and other material to newspapers. *Type:* Directory.

Publishers Directory

Gale Group Inc.
27500 Drake Rd.   Ph: (248)699-4253
Farmington Hills, MI 48331-   Free: 800-877-GALE
3535   Fax: (248)699-8070
E-mail: galeord@galegroup.com
URL: http://www.galegroup.com.; http://www.gale.com.
Contact: Louise Gagne, Editor, louise_gagne@gale.com.
Desc: Over 19,400 new and established, commercial and
nonprofit, private and alternative, corporate and association, government and institution publishing programs and
their distributors; includes producers of books, classroom
materials, prints, reports, and databases. *Type:* Directory.

Publishers, Distributors, and Wholesalers of the United States

R. R. Bowker
A Unit of Cahners Business Information
121 Chanlon Rd.   Ph: (908)464-6800
New Providence, NJ 07974   Free: 888-269-5372
                                 Fax: (908)771-7704
E-mail: info@bowker.com
URL: http://www.bowker.com.
Contact: Barbara Holton, Editor; D. Gravesande, Editor.
Desc: Over 86,000 publishers, distributors, and wholesalers; includes associations, museums, software producers
and manufacturers, and others not included in "Books in
Print". *Type:* Directory.

Publishers, Distributors, and Wholesalers of the U.S.

R.R. Bowker
121 Chanlon Rd.   Ph: (908)464-6800
New Providence, NJ 07974
URL: http://www.bowker.com
Contact: Yvette Berthel, Tape/Online Services, yvette.
berthel@bowker.com.
Desc: Contains information on more than 95,000 publishing companies and organizations. Provides name, address,
telephone number, International Standard Book Number
(ISBN) prefix, Standard Address Number (SAN), acronym or abbreviation, imprints, discount schedules, and return policies. *Available:* The Dialog Corporation,
DIALOG; LEXIS-NEXIS, NEXIS. *Type:* Database.

Publishers' News You Can Use

Twin Peaks Press
PO Box 129　　　　　　　　Ph: (360)694-2462
Vancouver, WA 98666-0129　　Fax: (360)696-3210
E-mail: twinpeak@pacifier.com
URL: http://www.pacifier.com/~twinpeak/press/; http://www.pacifier.com/~twinpeak/press/.
Contact: Helen Hecker, Editor and Publisher.
Desc: Publishes money-making and cost-saving ways for publishers to market their products. Topics include marketing, trade secrets, tips for professionals, and electronic and World Wide Web news. *Type:* Newsletter.

Publisher's Report

National Association of Independent Publishers
PO Box 430　　　　　　　　Ph: (941)648-4420
Highland City, FL 33846　　Fax: (941)648-4420
E-mail: naip@aol.com
Contact: Betsy Lampe, Editor.
Desc: Concerned with book publishing, primarily from the viewpoint of small publishers and self-publishers. Includes information on production, marketing, distribution, sales, promotion and more. *Type:* Newsletter.

Publishers Weekly—Calendar Roundup Issue

Cahners Publishing Co.
245 W. 17th St.　　　　　　Ph: (212)463-6828
New York, NY 10014　　　　Free: 800-523-9654
　　　　　　　　　　　　Fax: (212)463-6530
URL: http://www.bookwire.com.
Contact: John Mutter, Editor.
Desc: Listing of more than 100 publishers of calendars and engagement books. *Type:* Directory.

Publishing Poynters

Para Publishing
PO Box 8206-239　　　　　　Ph: (805)968-7277
Santa Barbara, CA 93118-8206　Free: 800-PAR-APUB
　　　　　　　　　　　　Fax: (805)968-1379
E-mail: orders@parapublishing.com
URL: http://www.parapublishing.com; http://www.parapublishing.com.
Contact: Dan Poynter, Editor.
Desc: Contains publishing industry news as well as management and marketing suggestions. Recurring features include news of research, news of educational opportunities, book reviews, and notices of publications available. *Type:* Newsletter.

Readers' Guide to Periodical Literature

H.W. Wilson Company
950 University Ave.　　　　Ph: (718)588-8400
Bronx, NY 10452
E-mail: custserv@hwwilson.com
URL: http://www.hwwilson.com
Contact: Technical Support Department., techmail@info.hwwilson.com.
Desc: Contains citations to articles appearing in approximately 240 of the most popular English-language general interest periodicals published in the United States and Canada. Includes coverage of The New York Times. *Available:* OCLC Online Computer Library Center, Inc.; OCLC EPIC; OCLC Online Computer Library Center, Inc., OCLC FirstSearch Catalog; Ovid Technologies, Inc.; SilverPlatter Information, Inc.; H.W. Wilson Company, WilsonWeb. *Type:* Database.

The Russ von Hoelscher Direct Response Profit Report

Publishers Media
PO Box 1295　　　　　　　Ph: (619)282-5822
El Cajon, CA 92022-1295　　Fax: (619)588-9103
E-mail: onlinemedia@access1.com

Contact: Russ von Hoelscher, Editor.
Desc: Provides marketing advice for independent publishers and small presses, with special emphasis given to the non-bookstore market. Recurring features include letters to the editor, interviews, news of research, and book reviews. *Type:* Newsletter.

Self Publishing Update

Update Publicare Co.
c/o Prosperity & Profits　　Ph: (303)575-5676
　Unlimited
PO Box 416
Denver, CO 80201
Contact: A. Doyle, Editor.
Desc: Features information on self publishing for non-profit organizations, institutes, small businesses, and writers. *Type:* Newsletter.

The Seybold Report on Publishing Systems

Seybold Publications, Inc.
PO Box 644　　　　　　　　Ph: (215)565-2480
Media, PA 19063　　　　　　Free: 800-325-3830
　　　　　　　　　　　　Fax: (215)565-4659
Contact: Stephen Edwards, Editor, sedwards@seyboldpubs.com.
Desc: Covers editorial electronics, text editing, typesetting and industry news. Provides in-depth reviews of equipment used in the publishing industry and reports of trade shows and conferences. *Type:* Newsletter.

Shannon Knows DEC

Terry C. Shannon
135 Leland Farm Rd.　　　　Ph: (508)881-5563
Ashland, MA 01721　　　　　Fax: (508)881-5563
Contact: Terry C. Shannon, Editor, shannon@world.std.com.
Desc: Analyzes Digital Equipment Corporation products and business strategies. Furnishes intelligence and other I.T. *Type:* Newsletter.

Small Press Notes & Reviews

Dry Bones Press
PO Box 640345　　　　　　　Ph: (415)292-7371
San Francisco, CA 94164　　Fax: (415)292-7371
E-mail: webmaster@drybones.com
URL: http://www.drybones.com; http://www.drybones.com/.
Contact: Steven Babitsky, Editor.
Desc: Publishes reviews of small press titles, as well as some book excerpts. *Type:* Newsletter.

The Small Press Review

Dustbooks
PO Box 100　　　　　　　　Ph: (530)887-6110
Paradise, CA 95967　　　　　Free: 800-477-6110
　　　　　　　　　　　　Fax: (530)877-0222
E-mail: dustbooks@telis.org
Contact: Len Fulton, Editor, len@dustbooks.com.
Desc: Publishes information and reviews of small press books and literary magazines. *Type:* Newsletter.

SNAPShot

Society of National Association Publications
1650 Tysons Blvd., Ste. 200　Ph: (703)506-3285
Mc Lean, VA 22102　　　　　Fax: (703)506-3266
URL: http://www.snaponline.org
Contact: Allison Parker, Editor.
Desc: Seeks to "represent, promote and advance the common interests of publications owned or controlled by voluntary associations or societies." Reports on postal news affecting second- and third-class mail, tax matters, Society programs and activities, and publishing information and events. Recurring features include news of members, notices of employment opportunities and editorial awards presented, reports on the annual conference, and information on publications of interest. *Type:* Newsletter.

Soundview Executive Book Summaries

Soundview Executive Book Summaries
723 Pond Ln.　　　　　　　Ph: (802)388-8910
Middlebury, VT 05753-1164　Free: 800-521-1227
　　　　　　　　　　　　Fax: (802)388-8939
E-mail: sales@summary.com
URL: http://www.summary.com.
Contact: Roger M. Griffith, Sr. Editor, editor@summary.com; Chris Murray, Editor, editor@summary.com; Anita Warren, Editor, awarren@sover.net.
Desc: Summarizes thirty business books per year by leading American publishers. *Type:* Newsletter.

Span Connection

Small Publishers Association of North America
425 Cedar St.　　　　　　　Ph: (719)395-4790
PO Box 1306　　　　　　　　Fax: (719)395-8374
Buena Vista, CO 81211-1306
E-mail: span@spannet.org
Contact: Marilyn Ross, Editor.
Desc: Provides information about and for independent and small publishers. Recurring features include columns titled Fiction Corner, Bits 'n Bytes, News You Can Use, and National Publicity Roundup. *Type:* Newsletter.

SPEX

Bay Area Independent Publishers Association (BAIPA)
PO Box E　　　　　　　　　Ph: (415)257-8275
Corte Madera, CA 94976
URL: http://www.baipa.org.
Desc: Discusses opportunities and changes in the field of publishing. Reviews members' books. *Type:* Newsletter.

Standard Periodical Directory

Oxbridge Communications Inc.
150 5th Ave., Ste. 302　　　Ph: (212)741-0231
New York, NY 10011　　　　Free: 800-955-0231
　　　　　　　　　　　　Fax: (212)633-2938
E-mail: info@mediafinder.com
URL: http://www.mediafinder.com.
Contact: Deborah Striplin, Editorial Director, (212)741-0231 X212; Joy Goldstein, Sr. Editor; Craig Schwartzberg, Editor.
Desc: 85,000 magazines, journals, newsletters, directories, house organs, association publications, etc., in the United States and Canada. *Type:* Directory.

tech Comments

Society for Technical Communication, Southeastern Michigan Chapter
PO Box 1289　　　　　　　Ph: (313)944-0358
Ann Arbor, MI 48106　　　　Fax: (313)995-1114
URL: http://stc.org/region4/smc.
Contact: Kathleen A. Young, Editor.
Desc: Keeps chapter members informed of events and shares information about the work of technical communicators. Recurring features include letters to the editor, a calendar of events, reports of meetings, news of educational opportunities, job listings, book reviews, notices of publications available, and messages from chapter president and regional director. *Type:* Newsletter.

Tel-aire Publications Inc.

3105 E. Carpenter Fwy.　　Free: 800-749-1841
Irving, TX 75062　　　　　　Fax: (214)579-7483
Contact: David A. McGee, President; Richard Stein, Natl. Sales Mgr.
Desc: Distributes TV listings TV and video feature packages. *Alt. Contact:* 3105 E. Carpenter Fwy., Irving, TX 75062; fax: (214)579-7483; toll-free: 800-749-1841. *Type:* Periodical.

Trialogue
Yankee Book Peddler, Inc.
999 Maple St.   Ph: (603)746-3102
Contoocook, NH 03229   Free: 800-258-3774
          Fax: (603)746-5628
E-mail: service@ybp.com; trialogue@ybp.com.
URL: http://www.ybp.com.
Contact: Jennifer B. Goodrich, Managing Editor.
Desc: Contains information from the book publishing industry pertinent to librarians. Recurring features include a column titled Digest of Publishing/Trade News. *Type:* Newsletter.

Ulrich's International Periodicals Directory
R. R. Bowker
A Unit of Cahners Business Information
121 Chanlon Rd.   Ph: (908)464-6800
New Providence, NJ 07974   Free: 888-269-5372
          Fax: (908)771-7704
E-mail: info@bowker.com; ulrichs@bowker.com.
Contact: Judy Salk, Editor, (908)665-2847, fax: (908)508-7695, judy.salk@bowker.com; Edvika Popilskis, Editor.
Desc: Nearly 165,000 current periodicals and newspapers published worldwide. *Type:* Directory.

Ulrich's International Periodicals Directory
R.R. Bowker
121 Chanlon Rd.   Ph: (908)464-6800
New Providence, NJ 07974
URL: http://www.bowker.com
Contact: Yvette Berthel, Tape/Online Services, (908)665-2854, fax: (908)771-7756, yvette.berthel@bowker.com.
Desc: Contains bibliographic descriptions, subject classification, and ordering information for approximately 220,000 serial publications, including international magazines, newsletters, academic and scholarly journals, and general-interest publications published regularly as well as annuals, continuations, conference proceedings, and other serial publications that are published at least once every 3 years. Includes information of more than 100,000 publication cessations since 1979, former names of publications, former ISSNs, as well as ordering information, names, addresses, and phone numbers for 90,000 publishers in 200 countries. *Available:* The Dialog Corporation, DIALOG; Ovid Technologies, Inc.; LEXIS-NEXIS, NEXIS. *Type:* Database.

VCH Library News
VCH Publishers, Inc.
605 3rd Ave.   Ph: (212)850-6000
New York, NY 10158   Free: 800-367-8249
          Fax: (212)850-6088
Contact: Pete Jansic, Editor.
Desc: Lists and describes new VCH publications, monographs, and reference sets in the fields of chemistry and chemical engineering, food science, materials science, physics, and life sciences. *Type:* Newsletter.

Vertical File Index
H.W. Wilson Company
950 University Ave.   Ph: (718)588-8400
Bronx, NY 10452
E-mail: custserv@hwwilson.com
URL: http://www.hwwilson.com
Contact: Technical Support Department., techmail@info.hwwilson.com.
Desc: Contains more than 29,000 citations to English-language non-book materials of general interest, including charts and posters, booklets, pamphlets, museum catalogs, exhibition bulletins, and government and university publications. Covers agriculture, art, business, careers, current events, energy conservation, food and nutrition, geography, history, hobbies, home repair, law, medicine and health, personal finance, and travel. *Available:* H.W. Wilson Company, WilsonWeb. *Type:* Database.

Wilson Journal Directory
H.W. Wilson Company
950 University Ave.   Ph: (718)588-8400
Bronx, NY 10452
E-mail: custserv@hwwilson.com
URL: http://www.hwwilson.com
Contact: Technical Support Department., techmail@info.hwwilson.com.
Desc: Contains information on more than 4300 periodicals cited in databases and publications of The H.W. Wilson Company. *Available:* H.W. Wilson Company, WilsonWeb. *Type:* Database.

Wilson Journal Directory
H. W. Wilson Co.
950 University Ave.   Ph: (718)588-8400
Bronx, NY 10452   Free: 800-367-6770
          Fax: (718)590-1617
E-mail: custserv@hwwilson.com
Contact: Barbara Chen, Editor.
Desc: Over 4,700 periodicals cited in H. W. Wilson publications and databases; international coverage. *Type:* Directory.

Wilson Publishers Directory
H. W. Wilson Co.
950 University Ave.   Ph: (718)588-8400
Bronx, NY 10452   Free: 800-367-6770
          Fax: (718)590-1617
E-mail: custserv@hwwilson.com
Desc: Over 34,000 publishers and distributors cited in the Wilson databases. *Type:* Directory.

Wilson Publishers Directory
H.W. Wilson Company
950 University Ave.   Ph: (718)588-8400
Bronx, NY 10452
E-mail: custserv@hwwilson.com
URL: http://www.hwwilson.com
Contact: Technical Support Department., techmail@info.hwwilson.com.
Desc: Contains information on more than 30,000 publishers cited in Cumulative Book Index, Book Review Digest, Essay and General Literature Index, Short Story Index, and the standard catalogs. Includes publisher name, mailing address, International Standard Book Number prefix, and names and addresses of subsidiaries, agents, and distributors. *Available:* H.W. Wilson Company, WilsonWeb. *Type:* Database.

Words on Cassette
R. R. Bowker
A Unit of Cahners Business Information
121 Chanlon Rd.   Ph: (908)464-6800
New Providence, NJ 07974   Free: 888-269-5372
          Fax: (908)771-7704
E-mail: info@bowker.com
URL: http://www.bowker.com.
Contact: D. Gravesande, Editor; Barbara Holton, Editor.
Desc: List of producers and distributors of spoken word cassettes in literature, radio shows, seminars, interviews, plays, speeches. *Type:* Directory.

Worldwide Graphics
Reebius Research Labs, Inc.
3952 N. Southport   Ph: (312)935-2135
Box 143   Fax: (312)935-2146
Chicago, IL 60613-2699
E-mail: wwgraph@suba.com.
URL: http://www.suba.com/~wwgraph/.
Contact: Rod Piechowski, Editor.
Desc: Reports on printing and publishing trends worldwide. Covers news on publishers' and printers' mergers, acquisitions, technology, and financial information. *Type:* Newsletter.

The Writer—"Special Market Lists" Section
The Writer, Inc.
120 Boylston St.   Ph: (617)423-3157
Boston, MA 02116   Fax: (617)423-2168
E-mail: writer@user1.channel1.com.
URL: http://www.channel1.com/thewriter/; http://www.channel1.com/thewriter.
Contact: Ann-Margaret Hemings Caljouw, Editor.
Desc: Section on markets for freelance writers, with focus on a different type of market each month. Included is a short description of the particular market and its general editorial requirements, followed by a list of publications in that market. *Type:* Directory.

Yellow Pages Publishers Association
3773 Cherry Creek North Dr.   Ph: (303)333-9772
Ste. 920   Fax: (303)320-6999
Denver, CO 80209
URL: http://www.yppa.org
Contact: James C. Logan, Jr., Pres.
Desc: Publishing companies producing Yellow Pages telephone directories. Purposes are to facilitate the buying and selling of Yellow Pages advertising; encourage the use of Yellow Pages by consumers and advertisers and to establish and promote a cooperative advertising program. Represents members before other bodies; acts as a forum for discussion and resolution of members' common problems. *Type:* Association.

Purchasing

Buying Strategy Forecast
Purchasing Magazine
Cahners Publishing Company
275 Washington St.   Ph: (617)558-4650
Newton, MA 02158   Fax: (617)558-4327
Contact: Tom Stundza, Editor, stundza@cahner.com.
Desc: Provides purchasing managers with price and supply forecasts, industrial commodity market analyses, manufacturing outlooks, and buying strategies to cut costs and increase company profits. Alerts readers to spot shortages, favorably priced items, and product changes. *Type:* Newsletter.

Caveat Emptor
Ontario Public Buyers Association
111 4th Ave., Ste. 361   Ph: (905)682-2644
Ridley Sq.   Fax: (905)682-2644
St. Catharines, ON, Canada L2S 3P5
URL: http://vaxxine.com/opba/
Contact: C.B. Bott, Editor; J.O. Bott, Editor.
Desc: Contains information of interest to anyone who spends public funds. Recurring features include updates on OPBA's Internet Bid Document Advertising System and internal databank and articles dealing with new technology, management issues, and methodology related to the expenditure of public funds. *Type:* Newsletter.

NAEB Bulletin
National Association of Educational Buyers, Inc. (NAEB)
450 Wireless Blvd.   Ph: (516)273-2600
Hauppauge, NY 11788   Fax: (516)952-3660
E-mail: jfox@naeb.org.
Contact: Joan S. Fox, CAE, Editor.
Desc: Features information on institutional purchasing and news of the Association. Recurring features include a calendar of events, reports of meetings, news of educational opportunities, job listings, book reviews, notices of publications available, and columns titled Professional Perspective, Market Index, and Roamin' With Yeoman. *Type:* Newsletter.

NASPO Newsletter
National Association of State Purchasing Officials
167 W. Main St., Ste. 600   Ph: (606)231-1877
Lexington, KY 40507   Fax: (606)231-1928
URL: http://www.naspo.org; http://www.naspo.org.
Contact: Leslie Scott, Editor, lflynn@iglov.rom.
Desc: Covers Association activities and purchasing innovations in state governments. Reports on developments in energy efficiency and recycling. *Type:* Newsletter.

National Association of Purchasing Management
2055 E. Centennial Cir.   Ph: (602)752-6276
PO Box 22160   Free: 800-888-6276
Tempe, AZ 85285-2160   Fax: (602)752-7890
URL: http://www.napm.org
Contact: Paul Novak, Exec. VP.
Desc: Purchasing and materials managers for industrial, commercial, and utility firms; educational institutions and government agencies. Disseminates information on procurement. *Type:* Association.

National Institute of Governmental Purchasing
151 Spring St.   Free: 800-FOR-NIGP
Herndon, VA 20170
URL: http://www.nigp.org
Contact: Rick Grimm, CPPO, Contact.
Desc: Federal, state, provincial, county, and local government buying agencies; hospital, school, prison, and public utility purchasing agencies in the U.S. and Canada. Develops standards and specifications for governmental buying; promotes uniform purchasing laws and procedures; conducts specialized education and research programs. *Type:* Association.

New England Purchaser
Purchasing Management Association of Boston, Inc. (PMAB)
200 Baker Ave., No. 306   Ph: (508)371-2522
Concord, MA 01742-2108
Contact: Christiane Loup, Editor.
Desc: Reports organization news. Recurring features include membership notes, list of CPM certification recipients, book reviews, and a column titled The President's Messages. *Type:* Newsletter.

Professional Purchasing
American Purchasing Society
430 W. Downer Pl.
Aurora, IL 60506-5035
E-mail: propurch@aol.com.
Contact: Harry E. Hough, Editor.
Desc: Provides information on policies, procedures, methods, and prices of purchasing. Features price indexes. *Type:* Newsletter.

Progressive Purchasing
Purchasing Management Association of Canada (PMAC)
2 Carlton St., Ste. 1414   Ph: (416)977-7111
Toronto, ON, Canada M5B 1J3   Free: 888-799-0877
   Fax: (416)977-8886
E-mail: info@pmac.ca
Contact: A. Marshall, Editor, amarshall@pmac.ca.
Desc: Presents news on the association's C.P.P. Accreditation program, new developments in purchasing, industry trends, and profiles of membership. *Type:* Newsletter.

Purchasing Magazine
Cahners Business Information
275 Washington St.   Ph: (617)964-3030
Newton, MA 02458   Fax: (617)558-4470
URL: http://www.purchasing.com.

Contact: Kevin Fitzgerald, Editor, (617)558-4224, fax: (617)558-4327, kevinf@cahners.com; John F. O'Connor, Publisher, jo'connor@cahners.com.
Desc: Magazine for buying professionals. *Type:* Periodical.

Purchasing Manager's Bulletin
Bureau of Business Practice
24 Rope Ferry Rd.   Ph: (860)442-4365
Waterford, CT 06386   Free: 800-243-0876
   Fax: (860)437-3555
URL: http://www.bbpnews.com
Contact: Wayne Muller, Editor, wayne_muller@prenhall.com.
Desc: Profiles the practices of successful purchasing operations in manufacturing and service companies and organizations. Features advice from purchasing executives and managers on controlling costs, improving quality and assuring optimum supplier performance. *Type:* Newsletter.

Southern Purchasor—Buyer's Guide Issue
National Association of Purchasing Management-Carolinas-Virginia, Inc.
5601 Roanne Way, Ste. 305   Ph: (336)292-9228
Greensboro, NC 27409-2932   Fax: (336)292-8415
Contact: B.A. Hempstead, Editor.
Desc: 695 purchasing companies in the Carolinas and Virginia. *Type:* Directory.

Supplier Selection and Management Report
Institute of Management & Administration, Inc.
29 W. 35th St., 5th Fl.   Ph: (212)244-0360
New York, NY 10001-2299   Fax: (212)564-0465
E-mail: subserve@ioma.com
URL: http://www.ioma.com
Contact: Joe Mazel, Editor, jmazel@ioma.com; Perry Patterson, Publisher, ppatterson@ioma.com.
Desc: Provides information for supply managers. Remarks: Also available via e-mail in Adobe Acrobat. *Type:* Newsletter.

Radio

ABC Radio Networks
125 West End Ave.   Ph: (212)456-1000
New York, NY 10023-6298
Contact: Robert F. Callahan, Jr., President; Derek Berghuis, Programming and Affiliate Mktg. Sr. VP; Stuart Krane, VP/Group Dir.; Corinne L. Baldassano, Programming VP.
Desc: Format comprises ABC Contemporary; ABC Direction; ABC Entertainment; ABC FM; ABC AM; ABC Information; ABC Rock; and Satellite Music. *Alt. Contact:* 125 West End Ave., New York, NY 10023-6298; telephone: (212)456-1000; Capital Cities/ABC Inc.; 2040 Avenue of the Stars, Century City, CA 90067; telephone: (310)557-7777. *Type:* Periodical.

ABN Radio
1515 W. Lane Ave.   Ph: (614)486-9577
Columbus, OH 43221   Fax: (614)487-8205
Contact: Ed Johnson, President; Randy Helt, General Sales Mgr.; Grant Neilley, Dir. of Operations.
Desc: Ohio agricultural radio format. *Alt. Contact:* 1515 W. Lane Ave., Columbus, OH 43221; telephone: (614)486-9577; fax: (614)487-8205. *Type:* Periodical.

American Forum Radio
5025 Centennial Blvd.   Ph: (719)528-7040
Colorado Springs, CO 80919   Fax: (719)528-6544
Contact: Skip Joeckdel, Vice President; Dave Rose, Vice President.
Alt. Contact: 5025 Centennial Blvd., Colorado Springs, CO 80919; telephone: (719)528-7040; fax: (719)528-6544. *Type:* Periodical.

American Radio Relay League
225 Main St.   Ph: (860)594-0200
Newington, CT 06111   Fax: (860)594-0259
E-mail: hq@arrl.org
URL: http://www.arrl.org
Contact: David Sumner, Exec.VP.
Desc: Licensed amateur radio operators in the U.S. and others interested in amateur radio communication and experimentation. Operates a nationwide message handling network, the National Traffic System, with members serving as official relay stations, observers, emergency coordinators, and bulletin stations. *Type:* Association.

American Urban Radio Networks
463 7th Ave.   Ph: (212)714-1000
New York, NY 10018   Fax: (212)714-2349
Contact: Ronald R. Davenport, Co-Chairman; Sydney L. Small, Co-Chairman; Jack Bryant, Co-President; E.J. Williams, Co-President.
Desc: Comprises SBN Sports Network; SPM Radio Network; STRZ Entertainment Network. *Alt. Contact:* 463 7th Ave., New York, NY 10018; telephone: (212)714-1000; fax: (212)714-2349. *Type:* Periodical.

The AMSAT Journal
Radio Amateur Satellite Corporation (AMSAT)
PO Box 27   Ph: (301)589-6062
Washington, DC 20044   Fax: (301)608-3410
Contact: Russ Tillman, Editor.
Desc: Carries news of the organization, items on small satellites, calls for papers, and notices of upcoming conferences. *Type:* Newsletter.

Arkansas Radio Network
PO Box 4189   Ph: (501)661-7550
Little Rock, AR 72214   Fax: (501)661-7620
Contact: Neal Gladner, General Mgr.; Dennis Kelly, News Dir.
Desc: Talk radio and news format. *Alt. Contact:* PO Box 4189, Little Rock, AR 72214; telephone: (501)661-7550; fax: (501)661-7620. *Type:* Periodical.

Business Radio Network
5025 Centennial Blvd.   Ph: (719)528-7040
Colorado Springs, CO 80919   Fax: (719)528-5170
Contact: Pat McCrummen, VP-Affiliate Services; Dave Rose, VP-Programming.
Alt. Contact: 5025 Centennial Blvd., Colorado Springs, CO 80919; telephone: (719)528-7040; fax: (719)528-5170. *Type:* Periodical.

CBS Radio Networks
51 W. 52nd St.   Ph: (212)975-4321
New York, NY 10019   Fax: (212)975-1519
Contact: Nancy C. Widmann, President.
Alt. Contact: 51 W. 52nd St., New York, NY 10019; telephone: (212)975-4321; fax: (212)975-1519; CBS Inc.; 7800 Beverly Blvd., Los Angeles, CA 90036; telephone: (213)852-2345. *Type:* Periodical.

Children's Syndicated Radio Network
Box 294   Ph: (517)663-8442
Eaton Rapids, MI 48827
Alt. Contact: Box 294, Eaton Rapids, MI 48827; telephone: (517)663-8442. *Type:* Periodical.

CNN Radio Network
One Center   Ph: (404)827-1500
Box 105366
Atlanta, GA 30348-5366
Contact: Len King, GM.
Alt. Contact: One Center, Box 105366, Atlanta, GA 30348-5366; telephone: (404)827-1500. *Type:* Periodical.

Community Radio News

National Federation of Community Broadcasters (NFCB)
Fort Mason Center, Bldg. D   Ph: (415)771-1160
San Francisco, CA 94123
E-mail: nfcb@aol.com

Contact: Pam Kulik, Editor.

Desc: Serves as a medium of communication for independent, community-licensed radio stations. Contains brief articles and news items on such topics as public broadcasting and programming, legislative developments, activities of the Federal Communications Commission, and local stations. *Type:* Newsletter.

CQ Amateur Radio

CQ Communications
25 Newbridge Rd.   Ph: (516)681-2922
Hicksville, NY 11801   Fax: (516)681-2926
E-mail: cqmagazine@aol.com.

Contact: Alan A. Dorhoffer, Editor; Richard A. Ross, Publisher; Arnie Sposato, Advertising Mgr.

Desc: Services information to the radio amateur. *Type:* Periodical.

CRC Radio Network Cadena Radio Centro

1645 N. Vine St.   Ph: (213)463-3800
Ste. 220   Fax: (213)463-3800
Hollywood, CA 90028

Contact: Carlos J. Aguirre, Vice Chm.; Barrett L. Alley, President; William Cherry, General Mgr.

Desc: Spanish radio format. *Alt. Contact:* 1645 N. Vine St., Ste. 220, Hollywood, CA 90028; telephone: (214)463-3800; fax: (213)463-3800; Lotus Hispanic Reps 50 E. 42nd St., Ste. 2301, New York, NY 10017; telephone: (212)697-7601. *Type:* Periodical.

Creative Radio Network

PO Box 7749   Ph: (818)991-3892
Thousand Oaks, CA 91359   Fax: (818)991-3894

Contact: Darwin Lamm, President.

Alt. Contact: PO Box 7749, Thousand Oaks, CA 91359; telephone: (818)991-3892; fax: (818)991-3894. *Type:* Periodical.

CRN International Inc.

1 Circular Ave.   Ph: (203)288-2002
Hamden, CT 06514   Fax: (203)281-3291

Contact: Barry Berman, President; S. Richard Kalt, Sr. VP; Gary E. Zenobia, Network Operations Dir.; Lucille Fortunado, Affiliate Relations Dir.

Desc: News, sports, and weather format. *Alt. Contact:* 1 Circular Ave., Hamden, CT 06514; telephone: (203)288-2002; fax: (203)281-3291. *Type:* Periodical.

Dow Jones Radio Network

200 Liberty St.   Ph: (212)416-2381
14th Fl.   Fax: (212)416-4195
New York, NY 10281

Contact: Peggy Belden, Dir. Broadcast Services; Debra Adamski, Affiliate Relations Coordinator.

Alt. Contact: 200 Liberty St., 14th Fl., New York, NY 10281; telephone: (212)416-2381; fax: (212)416-4195. *Type:* Periodical.

DX Monitor

International Radio Club of America
6059 Essex St.   Ph: (909)687-5910
Riverside, CA 92504-1599
E-mail: jhon9@juno.com

Contact: Donald E. Erickson, Editor, erickson@csnsys.com.

Desc: Publishes information pertaining to broadcast band DXing (long-distance radio reception). Reports on domestic and foreign stations that have been received by members, and on the quality of the reception. *Type:* Newsletter.

Eastern Public Radio Network

301 N. Beauregard St.   Ph: (703)658-4851
No. 1417   Fax: (703)658-1742
Alexandria, VA 22312-2914

Contact: Marion van den Bosch, Exec. Dir.

Desc: Public radio format. *Alt. Contact:* 301 N. Beauregard St., No. 1417, Alexandria, VA 22312-2914; telephone: (703)658-4851; fax: (703)658-1742. *Type:* Periodical.

ESPN Radio, Inc.

ESPN Plaza   Ph: (203)585-2000
935 Middle St.
Bristol, CT 06010

Alt. Contact: ESPN Plaza, 935 Middle St., Bristol, CT 06010; telephone: (203)585-2000. *Type:* Periodical.

The 50 MHz DX Bulletin

Victor Frank Publishing
12450 Skyline Blvd.   Ph: (415)851-7031
Woodside, CA 94062-4554

Contact: Victor R. Frank, Editor, frank@horizon.sri.com.

Desc: "Dedicated to the understanding and utilization of long distance propagation in the 6meter Amateur band." Includes circulation and DX reports. *Type:* Newsletter.

Inside Radio

Inside Radio, Inc.
1930 E. Marlton Pike, Ste. S-93   Ph: (609)424-6800
Cherry Hill, NJ 08003   Fax: (609)424-2301

Contact: Jerry Del Polliano, Editor and Publisher.

Desc: Offers news on the radio trade industry. *Type:* Newsletter.

Interstate Radio Network, Inc.

435 N. Michigan Ave.   Ph: (312)222-4784
Chicago, IL 60611   Fax: (312)222-3476

Contact: John Cowan, Contact; Nancy Torres, Contact.

Desc: Country music format. *Alt. Contact:* 435 N. Michigan Ave., Chicago, IL 60611; telephone: (312)222-4784; fax: (312)222-3476. *Type:* Periodical.

Jon Sullivan's Radio Promotion Bulletin

Sullivan Company
5350 Pine Cliff   Ph: (281)855-2964
Houston, TX 77084-3140   Fax: (281)855-2964
E-mail: radiobul@compassnet.com.

Contact: Jon Sullivan, Publisher.

Desc: Explores promotion ideas for innovative broadcasters. Features articles pertaining to client sales promotions and station marketing. *Type:* Newsletter.

Jones Satellite Networks

8250 S. Akron   Free: 800-784-8700
Ste. 205   Fax: (303)799-0551
Englewood, CO 80112

Contact: Eric Hauenstein, VP/Gen. Mgr.; Phil Barry, Programming and Operations VP.

Desc: Format comprises adult Hit Radio; Good Time Oldies; Soft Hits; Z Spanish; U.S. Country; CD Country; NAC; and Rock Alternative all 24 hour. *Alt. Contact:* 8250 S. Akron, Ste. 205, Englewood, CO 80112; fax: (303)799-0551; toll-free: 800-784-8700. *Type:* Periodical.

Journal of College Radio

Intercollegiate Broadcasting System, Inc.
367 Windsor Highway   Fax: (914)565-7446
New Windsor, NY 12553-7900
E-mail: ibshq@aol.com

Contact: Fritz Kass, Editor.

Desc: Provides informational and educational materials related to the establishment, operation, programming, and development of school and college radio stations. Recurring features include editorials, letters to the editor, news of members, book reviews, and a calendar of events. *Type:* Newsletter.

Longhorn Radio Network

Univ. of Texas at Austin   Ph: (512)471-1631
Communication Bldg. B   Fax: (512)471-3700
Austin, TX 78712-1090

Contact: John L. Hanson, Jr., Exec. Producer; William F. Grimes, Distribution Mgr.

Alt. Contact: Univ. of Texas at Austin, Communication Bldg. B, Austin, TX 78712-1090; telephone: (512)471-1631; fax: (512)471-3700. *Type:* Periodical.

The M Street Journal

M Street Corporation
54 Music Sqr. E., Ste. 201   Ph: (615)251-1525
Nashville, TN 37203   Free: 800-248-4242
          Fax: (615)251-8798

Contact: Robert Unmacht, Editor, robertu@tapscan.com.

Desc: Reports on "radio station regulatory applications, actions, and filings; construction permit activity; format changes; and other U.S. and Canadian radio news of interest to the broadcast industry." Covers all radio markets, large and small. *Type:* Newsletter.

M Street Radio Directory

M Street Corporation
54 Music Sqr. E., Ste. 201   Ph: (615)251-1525
Nashville, TN 37203   Free: 800-248-4242
          Fax: (615)251-8798

Contact: Robert Unmacht, Editor.

Desc: Approximately 14,000 AM and FM radio stations in the U.S. and Canada. *Type:* Directory.

MRN Motor Racing Network Radio

1801 International Speedway   Ph: (904)947-6400
   Blvd.
Daytona Beach, FL 32114

Contact: John McMullin, Pres./GM; Cheryl Knight-Marzello, Dir. of Affiliates.

Desc: Sports format including NASCAR stock car racing and related programming. *Alt. Contact:* 1801 International Speedway Blvd., Daytona Beach, FL 32114; telephone: (904)947-6400. *Type:* Periodical.

NAB RadioWeek

National Association of Broadcasters
1771 N St. NW   Ph: (202)429-5477
Washington, DC 20036-2891   Free: 800-368-5644
          Fax: (202)775-3515
E-mail: nabpubs@nab.org; sbloomqu@nab.org.

Contact: Tom Butts, Editor, tbutts@nab.org.

Desc: Covers radio broadcasting from legislative, regulatory, political, technical, management, and sales/marketing perspectives. Contains pertinent industry news, promotions of NAB conferences, product announcements, and coverage of awards competitions. *Type:* Newsletter.

National Public Radio NPR

635 Massachusetts Ave. NW
Washington, DC 20001

Contact: Delano E. Lewis, President; F. Kim Hodgson, Chm.

Alt. Contact: 635 Massachusetts Ave. NW, Washington, DC 20001. *Type:* Periodical.

One to One II

CreeYadio Services
PO Box 9787
Fresno, CA 93794

Desc: Provides topical bits, jokes, and record-liners for radio broadcasters. Remarks: Published as a supplement to the newsletter, One to One. *Type:* Newsletter.

Pacifica Foundation

3729 Cahuenga Blvd., West   Ph: (818)985-8800
North Hollywood, CA 91604
Contact: Patricia Scott, Exec.Dir.

Desc: Nonprofit educational corporation owned and operated by the Pacifica National Board of Directors and chartered by the state of California. Operates six noncommercial, listener-supported FM radio stations in five metropolitan areas (KPFA and KPFB, Berkeley, CA; KPFK, Los Angeles, CA; WBAI, New York City; KPFT, Houston, TX; WPFW, Washington, DC). *Type:* Association.

Peach State Public Radio Network

1540 Stewart Ave. SW   Ph: (404)756-4730
Atlanta, GA 30310   Fax: (404)756-4088
Contact: Richard Ottinger, Exec. Dir; Van Joyner, Director; Bill Bergeron, Program Dir.
Alt. Contact: 1540 Stewart Ave. SW, Atlanta, GA 30310; telephone: (404)756-4730; fax: (404)756-4088. *Type:* Periodical.

PIA Radio Sports

680 N. Lake Shore Dr.   Ph: (312)943-8888
Ste. 1230   Fax: (312)943-5464
Chicago, IL 60611
Contact: Brad Saul, CEO; Chuck Kellner, Vice President.
Alt. Contact: 680 N. Lake Shore Dr., Ste. 1230, Chicago, IL 60611; telephone: (312)943-8888; fax: (312)943-5464. *Type:* Periodical.

Public Radio International

100 N. 6th St.   Ph: (612)338-5000
Suite 900A   Fax: (612)330-9222
Minneapolis, MN 55403
URL: http://www.pri.org.
Contact: Stephen L. Salyer, Pres./CEO; Bruce Theriault, Sr. VP Network Operations; Melinda Ward, Sr. VP Programming; Timothy Engel, VP Finance & Administration; Doug Eichten, VP Development; Janet de Acevedo, Dir. National Promotion & Media Relation.

Desc: Format comprises news/Information; Classical Music; Contemporary Music; and Comedy/Variety. *Alt. Contact:* 100 N. 6th St., Suite 900A, Minneapolis, MN 55403; telephone: (612)338-5000; fax: (612)330-9222. *Type:* Periodical.

QCWA Hotline Report

Quarter Century Wireless Association, Inc. (QCWA)
159 E. 16th St.   Ph: (541)683-0987
Eugene, OR 97401   Fax: (541)683-4181
Contact: Jim Walsh, Editor, jwalsh@teleport.com.

Desc: Provides news of the Association, which promotes an interest in amateur radio communications and in the advancement of electronics. Recurring features include information on pertinent legislation and regulation, news of members, and announcements of Association activities. *Type:* Newsletter.

QCWA News

Quarter Century Wireless Association, Inc. (QCWA)
159 E. 16th St.   Ph: (541)683-0987
Eugene, OR 97401   Fax: (541)683-4181
Contact: Gerry Wentz, Editor; Jim Walsh, General Mgr., jwalsh@teleport.com.

Desc: Provides information of interest to amateur radio operators, such as historical items, semi-technical material, and book reviews. Recurring features include editorials, letters to the editor, news of members, and columns titled QCWA Computing, Operating Practices, and A Quarter Century in Space. *Type:* Newsletter.

Quarter Century Wireless Association

Jim Walsh
159 E. 16th St.   Ph: (541)683-0987
Eugene, OR 97401   Fax: (541)683-4181
E-mail: jwalsh@teleport.com
URL: http://www.qcwa.org
Contact: Jim Walsh, Gen.Mgr.

Desc: Amateur radio (wireless) operators throughout the world who were licensed for operation at least 25 years ago. To encourage friendship and cooperation among members; to promote interest in amateur radio communications and in the advancement of electronics; to use the knowledge and experience of members for the benefit of all radio amateurs. *Type:* Association.

Radio Iowa

2700 Grand Ave.   Ph: (515)282-1984
Ste. 103
Des Moines, IA 50312
Contact: Clyde G. Lear, Owner; Steve Mays, General Mgr.; Charles Peters, Chief Engineer; O. Kay Henderson, News Dir.

Desc: News state radio format. *Alt. Contact:* 2700 Grand Ave., Ste. 103, Des Moines, IA 50312; telephone: (515)282-1984; Learfield Communications. *Type:* Periodical.

Radio Pennsylvania Inc.

1982 Locust Ln.   Ph: (717)232-8400
PO Box 2954   Fax: (717)232-7612
Harrisburg, PA 17105
Contact: Douglas F. Easter, General Mgr.; Craig Rhodes, News Dir.; Mark O'Neill, Sports Dir.
Alt. Contact: 1982 Locust Ln., PO Box 2954, Harrisburg, PA 17105; telephone: (717)232-8400; fax: (717)232-7612. *Type:* Periodical.

Radio & Records Digital Guide

Radio and Records, Inc.
10100 Santa Monica Blvd., 5th   Ph: (310)553-4330
Fl.   Fax: (310)203-8727
Los Angeles, CA 90067-4004
E-mail: mailroom@rronline.com
Contact: Ron Rodrigues, Editor.

Desc: 50 companies working in the digital broadcasting industry. *Type:* Directory.

Radio & Records Program Supplier Guide

Radio and Records, Inc.
10100 Santa Monica Blvd., 5th   Ph: (310)553-4330
Fl.   Fax: (310)203-8727
Los Angeles, CA 90067-4004
E-mail: mailroom@rronline.com
Contact: Ron Rodrigues, Editor.

Desc: More than 1,200 listings with profiles of regular and special programs, details on full-time formats, and information about production services. *Type:* Directory.

Radiomutuel Inc.

1717 boul. Rene-Levesque est   Ph: (514)529-3210
Montreal, PQ, Canada H2L   Fax: (514)529-3219
4E8
Contact: Normand Beauchamp, CEO.

Alt. Contact: 1717 boul. Rene-Levesque est, Montreal, PQ, Canada H2L 4E8; telephone: (514)529-3210; fax: (514)529-3219. *Type:* Periodical.

Ray Sports Radio Network

PO Box 3810   Ph: (919)480-1576
Kill Devil Hills, NC 27948-   Fax: (919)480-4655
3810
Contact: Bill Ray, President; Gem Megers, Sports Dir.
Alt. Contact: PO Box 3810, Kill Devil Hills, NC 27948-3810; telephone: (919)480-1576; fax: (919)480-4655. *Type:* Periodical.

The REACTer

React International Inc.
5210 Auth Rd., No. 403
Suitland, MD 20746-4330
E-mail: react@wichila.fn.net
Contact: Lynda Stafford, Office Mgr.

Desc: Concerns the organization's efforts to assist with highway safety and emergency assistance by establishing citizen communication networks with public safety agencies, disaster services, and other groups. Recurring features include editorials, letters to the editor, news of members, and a calendar of events. *Type:* Newsletter.

SBS Network Inc.

26 W. 56th St.   Ph: (212)541-6700
New York, NY 10019   Fax: (212)541-8535
Alt. Contact: 26 W. 56th St., New York, NY 10019; telephone: (212)541-6700; fax: (212)541-8535. *Type:* Periodical.

The Source

1755 S. Jefferson Davis Hwy.   Ph: (703)413-8300
Arlington, VA 22202   Fax: (703)413-8445
Desc: News and talk radio format. *Alt. Contact:* 1755 S. Jefferson Davis Hwy., Arlington, VA 22202; telephone: (703)413-8300; fax: (703)413-8445; NBC Radio Network. *Type:* Periodical.

South Carolina Network

3710 Landmark Dr.   Ph: (803)790-4300
Ste. 100   Fax: (803)790-4309
Columbia, SC 29204
Contact: Stacy Long, Sales Mgr.; Nancy Fletcher, Affiliate Relations; John Winfield, Operations Mgr.; Tracy Best, Sales Rep.; Phil Kornblut, Sports Dir.; Lana Cox, News Dir.; Claudia Mauldin, Traffic Mgr.; William Christopher, News Reporter; Theresa Riley, News Reporter.

Desc: Sports and news format. *Alt. Contact:* 3710 Landmark Dr., Ste. 100, Columbia, SC 29204; telephone: (803)790-4300; fax: (803)790-4309. *Type:* Periodical.

Spark GAP Times

Old Old Timers Club
3191 Darvany Dr.   Ph: (214)352-4743
Dallas, TX 75220-1611
E-mail: ootc@ticnet.com
Contact: Milbert A. Wells, Editor.

Desc: Concerns the activities and reminiscences of Club members, all of whom have been operating their own radio transmitters since the early days of radio. Recurring features include editorials, letters to the editor, a calendar of events, and columns titled Silent Key, New Members, and President's Message. *Type:* Newsletter.

SPERDVAC Radiogram

Society to Preserve and Encourage Radio Drama, Variety and Comedy (SPERDVAC)
PO Box 7177   Ph: (310)947-9800
Van Nuys, CA 91409
Contact: Dan Haefele, Editor.

Desc: Publishes news of the Society, which is concerned with early and contemporary radio broadcasting, performers from early radio, and programs broadcast during the early Golden Age of Radio. Recurring features include record and book reviews, news of research, obituaries, and a column titled McGee's Closet. *Type:* Newsletter.

Superadio Network

56 Central St.   Ph: (508)608-2000
Southborough, MA 01745
Contact: John Garabedian, President; Rich O'Brien, VP Sales; Mike Ortolano, Dir. Programming.

Desc: Open House Party Network; and Prime FM formats. *Alt. Contact:* 56 Central St., Southborough, MA 01745; telephone: (508)608-2000. *Type:* Periodical.

SWL

American Shortwave Listeners Club (ASWLC)
16182 Ballad Ln.   Ph: (714)846-1685
Huntington Beach, CA 92649-
    2272
E-mail: wdx6aa@aol.com.
Contact: Stewart H. MacKenzie, Editor.
Desc: Focuses on the hobby of long distance radio listening. Lists loggings from radio stations throughout the world, including time and date of reception, frequency, and format type. *Type:* Newsletter.

Telecom Exchange

Industrial Telecommunication Association, Inc. (ITA)
1110 N. Glebe Rd., Ste. 500   Ph: (703)528-5115
Arlington, VA 22201   Fax: (703)524-1074
URL: http://www.ita-relay.com.
Contact: J. Sharpe Smith, Editor, sharpe@ita-rela.com.
Desc: Contains news and information on the industrial use of two-way radio. Reports on governmental regulatory actions, usage trends, and the activities of the Association. *Type:* Newsletter.

Radiology

American College of Radiology

1891 Preston White Dr.   Ph: (703)648-8900
Reston, VA 20191   Free: 800-ACR-LINE
    Fax: (703)648-9176
URL: http://www.acr.org
Contact: John J. Curry, Exec.Dir.
Desc: Principal organization serving radiologists with programs which focus on the practice of radiology and the delivery of comprehensive radiological health services. These programs in medical sciences, education, and in practice management, serve the public interest and the interests of the medical community in which radiologists serve in both diagnostic and therapeutic roles. Seeks to "advance the science of radiology, improve radiologic service to the patient, study the economic aspects of the practice of radiology, and encourage imroved and continuing education for radiologists and allied professional fields". *Type:* Association.

American Healthcare Radiology Administrators

PO Box 334   Ph: (978)443-7591
Sudbury, MA 01776   Free: 800-443-AHRA
    Fax: (978)443-8046
E-mail: info@ahraonline.org
URL: http://www.ahraonline.org
Contact: Mary S. Reitter, Exec.Dir.
Desc: Radiology and healthcare managers. Works to improve management of radiology departments in hospitals, physician practices, and other health care facilities; to provide a forum for publication of educational, scientific, and professional materials. *Type:* Association.

American Roentgen Ray Society

c/o Paul R. Fullagar   Ph: (703)648-8992
1891 Preston White Dr.   Free: 800-438-2777
Reston, VA 20191   Fax: (703)264-8863
URL: http://www.arrs.org
Contact: Paul R. Fullagar, Exec.Dir.
Desc: Trade association for board certified radiologists. *Type:* Association.

American Society for Therapeutic Radiology and Oncology

1891 Preston White Dr.   Ph: (703)295-6760
Reston, VA 20191   Free: 800-962-7876
    Fax: (703)476-8167
URL: http://www.astro.org

Contact: Gregg Robinson, COO.
Desc: Physicians who limit their practice to radiation therapy; associate members are scientists and health care personnel who have a major interest "in furthering the aims of the society"; junior members are residents who have completed one year of training in radiation therapy. Aim is "to extend the benefits of radiation therapy to patients with cancer or other disorders, to advance its scientific basis, and to provide for the education and professional fellowship of its members." *Type:* Association.

Baylor College of Medicine

Herbert J. Frensley Center for Imaging Research

1 Baylor Plz.   Ph: (713)798-5146
Houston, TX 77030   Fax: (713)798-5745
E-mail: lhayman@bcm.tmc.edu
URL: http://www.bcm.tmc.edu/imaging/
Contact: Dr. L. Anne Hayman, MD, Dir.
Desc: Magnetic resonance imaging and spectroscopy of brain and muscle in normal and altered states (human experimental animal models, excised samples), the development of novel diagnostic imaging applications, and functional magnetic resonance imaging of normal cognitive function following brain injury in psychiatric conditions. *Type:* Research center.

Baylor College of Medicine

NMR Spectroscopy Laboratories

1 Baylor Plaza, Ste. 130H   Ph: (713)798-8980
Houston, TX 77030   Fax: (713)798-4283
E-mail: mchari@bcm.tmc.edu
Contact: Dr. M. Chari, Dir.
Desc: Nuclear magnetic resonance imaging and spectroscopy, including development of software and hardware and applications to biological and clinical conditions. Concentrates on in vivo spectroscopy. *Type:* Research center.

Columbia University

Center for Radiological Research

630 W. 168th St.   Ph: (212)305-5660
VC 11-230   Fax: (212)305-3229
New York, NY 10032
E-mail: halleri@cpmail-am.cis.columbia.edu
Contact: Dr. Eric J. Hall, Dir.
Desc: Human and rodent cell transformation assay systems at the cellular and molecular levels. *Type:* Research center.

Conference of Radiation Control Program Directors

205 Capital Ave.   Ph: (502)227-4543
Frankfort, KY 40601-2832   Fax: (502)227-7862
URL: http://www.crcpd.org
Contact: Charles M. Hardin, Exec.Dir.
Desc: State and local radiological program directors; individuals from related federal protection agencies. Serves as a forum for the interchange of experience, concerns, developments, and recommendations among radiation control programs and related agencies. Encourages cooperation between enforcement programs and agencies at state and federal levels. *Type:* Association.

Edmonton Radiopharmaceutical Centre

11560 University Ave.   Ph: (403)432-8970
Edmonton, AB, Canada T6G   Fax: (403)432-8411
    1Z2
E-mail: john.scott@cancerboard.ab.ca
Contact: J.R. Scott, Dir.
Desc: Radiopharmaceutical development, including brain blood flow tracers and tumor markers. *Type:* Research center.

Joint Center for Radiation Therapy

330 Brookline Ave., 5th Fl.   Ph: (617)667-9550
Boston, MA 02215   Fax: (617)667-9551
URL: http://www.jcrt.harvard.edu/jcrt/
Contact: C. Norman Coleman, Chm.
Desc: Tumor cell biology, focusing on microenvironments and molecular biology techniques and radiation induced processes. *Type:* Research center.

Kettering Medical Center

Nuclear Medicine Department

Wright State Univ. Sch. of Med.   Ph: (937)296-7211
Section of Nuclear Med.   Fax: (937)296-4265
3535 Southern Blvd.
Kettering, OH 45429
Contact: Dr. Joseph C. Mantil, Dir.
Desc: Clinical studies of dementia, deep venous thrombosis, pulmonary response to radiation exposure, utility of thallium scans (SPECT), and In-111 labeled white cells in evaluation of microscopic changes in infectious disease and malignancy; positron emission tomography (PET) studie s of cardiac, neurologic, and oncologic cases; serotonin receptor studies; and PET studies of chemo- and radiation therapy responses. Clinical activities include serial lung scans of radiation therapy patients, retrospective reviews of radionuclide venograms, cisternograms, and thallium scans. *Type:* Research center.

Lawrence Berkeley National Laboratory

Center for Functional Imaging

1 Cyclotron Rd.   Ph: (510)486-5435
Mail Stop 55-121   Fax: (510)486-4768
Berkeley, CA 94720
URL: http://www.cfi.ibl.gov
Contact: Dr. Thomas F. Budinger, Hd.
Desc: Research medicine and radiation biophysics, emphasizing imaging instrument and radiopharmaceuticals development, and the diagnosis and treatment of human diseases using charged particle irradiation therapy. Develops imaging instrumentation and computer programs for the study of brain and heart disease in conjunction with new pharmaceuticals. *Type:* Research center.

Long Island Jewish Medical Center

Nuclear Medicine Division

270-05 76th Ave.   Ph: (718)470-7080
New Hyde Park, NY 11040   Fax: (718)470-9247
Contact: Christopher Palestro, MD, Dir.
Desc: Applications of radioisotopes to clinical medicine. The Division is especially concerned with research on new applications, including instrumentation, and in use of isotopes in study of metabolic processes and infection. *Type:* Research center.

Massachusetts Institute of Technology

Biotechnology Resource Center for Research in Lasers and Medicine

NCRR   Ph: (617)253-5377
Bldg. 6, Rm. 014   Fax: (617)253-4513
77 Massachusetts Ave.
Cambridge, MA 02139-4307
Contact: Dr. Ramachandra R. Dasari, Contact.
Desc: Spectral diagnostics for tissue types, which can lead to real-time diagnosis of diseased tissue; and studies laser tissue damage and ablation, as a function of wavelength and the dependence on the optical and thermal properties of the tissue. Research includes development of the portable spectrometer for laser-induced fluorescence studies for use in a clinical setting and use of Raman spectroscopy techniques for diagnosing tissue characteristics. *Type:* Research center.

Massachusetts Institute of Technology
Center for Magnetic Resonance
Francis Bitter Magnet Laboratory

170 Albany St.   Ph: (617)253-5478
NW 14-3218   Fax: (617)253-5405
Cambridge, MA 02139

Contact: Elisabeth Shortsleeve, Contact.

Desc: Makes available high-field Nuclear Magnetic Resonance (NMR) spectrometers to study biological molecules (liquid- or solid-state), viral particles, cells, intact tissues, and small animals under conditions of maximal spectral dispersion (resolution) with enhanced sensitivity. Current research includes: natural and model membrane structure, dynamics, function, phase diagrams, phase transitions, and solid-state studies of amino acids, peptides, and bone; protein conformation and interactions, e.g., insulin, NMR microscopy; dynamics of energy metabolism in tumors, skeletal muscle, cells, animal brain and heart, and human eye lens; and DNA structure and dynamics. *Type:* Research center.

Massachusetts Institute of Technology
Laser Biomedical Research Center

77 Massachusetts Ave.   Ph: (617)253-7700
Cambridge, MA 02139   Fax: (617)253-4513
E-mail: msfeld@mit.edu
URL: http://web.mit.edu/spectroscopy/www/staff/msfeld.html

Contact: Dr. Michael S. Feld, Dir.

Desc: Lasers and medicine. Uses a tunable laser facility for measuring optical properties of tissue and studying tissue ablation mechanisms; develops new methods for real-time spectroscopic identification of tissue types and conditions; performs laser fluorescence studies in single cells; investigates UV Raman and resonance Raman applications in biology and medicine; and conducts time-resolved picosecond studies in tissue and other biological systems. *Type:* Research center.

Mayo Biomedical Imaging Resource

Mayo Clinic   Ph: (507)284-4937
200 1st St. SW   Fax: (507)284-1632
Rochester, MN 55905
E-mail: rar@mayo.edu
URL: http://www.mayo.edu/bir

Contact: Richard A. Robb, PhD, Dir.

Desc: Provides expertise and technology related to biomedical imaging, scientific visualization, computer graphics, computer workstations, and computer networks. Through professional consultation, advanced software and hardware systems, and technical support, investigators use the Resource for ongoing research studies, ad hoc projects, feasibility testing, and/or development of applications and systems to be subsequently installed in the user's library. *Type:* Research center.

McGill University
Medical Physics Unit

Montreal General Hospital   Ph: (514)934-8052
1650 Cedar Ave., Rm. L5-109 Fax: (514)934-8229
Montreal, PQ, Canada H3G
    1A4
E-mail: epodgorsak@medphys.mgh.mcgill.ca
URL: http://www.medphys.mgh.mcgill.ca
Contact: Prof. Ervin B. Podgorsak, Dir.

Desc: Medical imaging, including resonant cavity imaging, filter functions (computer tomography), positron-emission tomography, nuclear magnetic resonance imaging, and electronic processing. Other studies include physical aspects of radiation oncology and radiation dosimetry, radiosurgery, radiation hazards and protection, physical aspects of nuclear cardiology, and dosimetry in diagnostic radiology. *Type:* Research center.

Medical College of Wisconsin
Biophysics Research Institute

8701 Watertown Plank Rd.   Ph: (414)456-4000
Milwaukee, WI 53226   Fax: (414)456-6512
E-mail: balvama@mcw.edu
URL: http://www.biophysics.mcw.edu/
Contact: B. Kalyanraman, PhD, Interim Dir.

Desc: Biophysics, with emphasis on functional magnetic resonance imaging and electron spin resonance. *Type:* Research center.

National Council on Radiation Protection and Measurements

7910 Woodmont Ave., Ste. 800   Ph: (301)657-2652
Bethesda, MD 20814   Free: 800-229-2652
                               Fax: (301)907-8768
E-mail: ncrp@ncrp.com
URL: http://www.ncrp.com
Contact: William M. Beckner, Exec.Dir.

Desc: Organization of nationally recognized scientists who share the belief that significant advances in radiation protection and measurement can be achieved through cooperative effort. Conducts research focusing on safe occupational exposure levels and disseminates information. *Type:* Association.

New York University
Laboratory of Cancer and Radiobiological Research

754 Brown Bldg.   Ph: (212)263-5349
Washington Sq.   Fax: (212)998-8200
New York, NY 10003
Contact: Dr. Anna Goldfeder, Dir.

Desc: Cancer and radiobiology, including basic studies on biological and structural properties of both normal and cancer cells and their relation to radiosensitivity and involvement of oncogenic viruses and chemical agents in neoplasia. Studies interactions of ionizing radiation, microwave-induced hyperthermia, and chemotherapy, including their effects on tumor regression in mice. *Type:* Research center.

Radiation Oncology Research and Development Center

4201 St. Antoine   Ph: (313)745-9207
Detroit, MI 48201   Fax: (313)745-2314
E-mail: don@urop.com
URL: http://www.roc.wayne.edu
Contact: Arthur T. Porter, MD, Pres.

Desc: Radiation therapy, cancer research, medical information systems, three-dimensional imaging, neutron therapy, radiosurgery, brachytherapy, clinical protocols, and unsealed source therapy. *Type:* Research center.

Radiological Society of North America

820 Jorie Blvd.   Ph: (630)571-2670
Oak Brook, IL 60523-2251   Fax: (630)571-7837
URL: http://www.rsna.org
Contact: Delmar J. Stauffer, Exec.Dir.

Desc: Radiologists and scientists in fields closely related to radiology. Promotes study and practical application of radiology, radium, electricity, and other branches of physics related to medical science. *Type:* Association.

San Jose State University
Institute for Biopsychological Studies of Color, Light, Radiation, Health

Department of Psychology   Ph: (408)924-5614
San Jose, CA 95192-0120   Fax: (408)924-5605
Contact: Dr. Robert J. Pellegrini, Dir.

Desc: Organismic effects of electromagnetic energy, particularly studies of physical health and behavior as affected by environmental color and lighting in institutional settings and toxic radiation exposure. *Type:* Research center.

Sherbrooke University
MRC Group in the Radiation Sciences

Faculty of Med.   Ph: (819)346-1110
Sherbrooke, PQ, Canada J1H   Fax: (819)564-5442
    5N4
E-mail: lsanche@courrier.usherb.ca
URL: http://www.mednuc.usherb.ca

Contact: Dr. Léon Sanche, Dir.

Desc: The complex sequences of events initiated by the absorption of energy from ionizing radiation in biological material (which ultimately result in transformations at the cellular level), and the development of new types of drugs to enhance the therapeutic and diagnostic efficiency of radiation for the purpose of improving the treatment of human cancer with radio- and phototherapy. *Type:* Research center.

U.S. Department of Health and Human Services
Food and Drug Administration
Center for Devices and Radiological Health

9200 Corporate Blvd., Rm. 100   Ph: (301)443-4690
Rockville, MD 20850   Fax: (301)594-1320
E-mail: DBB@FDADR.CDRH.FDA.GOV

Contact: D. Bruce Burlington, MD, Dir.

Desc: Develops and carries out a national program designed to control unnecessary exposures of humans to and assure the safe and efficacious use of ionizing and non-ionizing radiation-emitting electronic products; and develops and carries out a national program to assure the safety, effectiveness, and proper labeling of medical devices for human use. *Type:* Research center.

U.S. Department of Health and Human Services
Food and Drug Administration
Center for Devices and Radiological Health
Biometric Sciences Division

Mail Code HFZ-540   Ph: (301)443-7120
5600 Fishers Ln.   Fax: (301)443-0097
Rockville, MD 20857

Contact: Dr. Richard P. Chiacchierini, Dir.

Desc: Statistical and epidemiologic review; medical devices evaluation, including risk assessment of post marketing long- and intermediate-term epidemiological effects; and review of pre-market approvals and post-market surveillance studies. Activities primarily involve epidemiological and experimental data collection, analysis, and interpretation; statistical methodology development; and statistical modeling of risk/benefit. *Type:* Research center.

U.S. Department of Health and Human Services
Food and Drug Administration
Center for Devices and Radiological Health
Office of Device Evaluation

9200 Corporate Blvd.   Ph: (301)594-2022
Rockville, MD 20850   Fax: (301)594-2510
URL: http://www.fda.gov

Contact: Susan Alpert, Dir.

Desc: Responsible for the evaluation of clinical and non-clinical data to establish the safety and effectiveness of medical devices and their marketability in the U.S.; and regulatory control of clinical trials involving medical devices. Principal areas of interest are health and physical sciences. *Type:* Research center.

U.S. Department of Health and Human Services
Food and Drug Administration
Center for Devices and Radiological Health
Office of Science and Technology
9200 Corporate Blvd.   Ph: (301)827-4777
HFZ-100   Fax: (301)827-4787
Rockville, MD 20857
E-mail: dem@cdrh.fda.gov
Contact: Donald Marlowe, Dir.

Desc: Pysical, life, and engineering sciences. Specific activities involve: conducting research on the human health effects of radiation and medical devices and on existing and emerging health technologies; providing the Center and other units with laboratory support; and managing the research, development, and product testing engineering programs of the Center. *Type:* Research center.

U.S. Department of Health and Human Services
Food and Drug Administration
Center for Devices and Radiological Health
Office of Surveillance and Biometrics
Mail Code HFZ-542   Ph: (301)594-0616
5600 Fishers Ln.   Fax: (301)443-8559
Rockville, MD 20857
E-mail: gxc@cdrh.fda.gov
Contact: Gregory Campbell, PhD, Dir.

Desc: Statistical aspects of clinical trials submitted to the Center for Devices and Radiological Health (CDRH) as medical device applications. The division also performs statistical research and risk/benefit analyses on the safety, effectiveness, and use of medical devices and the risks of radiation. *Type:* Research center.

U.S. Department of Health and Human Services
National Cancer Institute
Division of Cancer Treatment, Diagnosis and Centers
Clinical Oncology Program
NIH Bldg. 10, Rm. B3B69   Ph: (301)496-5457
9000 Rockville Pike   Fax: (301)480-5439
Bethesda, MD 20892
Contact: Dr. Paul Okunieff, Chf.

Desc: Clinical investigation of cancer treatment using X-ray technology; and laboratory investigation of radiobiology of human tumor cell lines, mechanisms of action of various compounds and their effects on radiosensitization/radioprotection, and phototherapy and radioimmunoglobulin for prescriptions. Emphasis is on radiation sensitizing compounds, radioprotecting compounds, intraoperative irradiation, and atypical fractionation schemes. *Type:* Research center.

U.S. Department of Health and Human Services
National Cancer Institute
Division of Cancer Treatment, Diagnosis and Centers
Radiation Research Program
Executive Plaza N. 800   Ph: (301)496-6111
6130 Executive Blvd., MSC   Fax: (301)480-5785
7440
Bethesda, MD 20892-7440
E-mail: mansfield@tpepn.nci.nih.gov
Contact: Dr. Richard Cumberlin, Actg.Dir.

Desc: Diagnosis, staging, treatment, and post-treatmen t evaluation for the cancer patient for whom radiation and related forms of energy are used. It is an extramural radiation research program which establishes program priorities, allocates resources, maintains project integration, evaluates program effectiveness, and represents the program area in the management and scientific decision-making processes of the National Cancer Institute. *Type:* Research center.

University of California, Irvine
Beckman Laser Institute and Medical Clinic
1002 Health Science Rd. E.   Ph: (949)824-4713
Irvine, CA 92612   Fax: (949)824-8413
E-mail: mberns@bli.uci.edu
URL: http://www.bli.uci.edu
Contact: Dr. Michael W. Berns, Dir.

Desc: Basic research includes genetics, cell biology, spectroscopy, and biophysics. Conducts basic laser studies of cellular functions, including genetic expression, cell motility, and cell membrane behavior; and biophysical studies of thermal, fluorescence, acoustic/mechanical, photochemical, and ionization effects of radiation on biological material. *Type:* Research center.

University of California, Irvine
Brain Imaging Center
College of Medicine   Ph: (949)824-7872
182 Irvine Hall   Fax: (949)824-2230
Irvine, CA 92697-3960
E-mail: jcwu@uci.edu
URL: http://brains.bic.uci.edu
Contact: Joseph C. Wu, MD, Clinical Dir.

Desc: PET scan analysis of brain functions focusing on mental illness, brain tumors, Alzheimer's disease, near drowning, traumatic brain injury, and aberrant behavior. *Type:* Research center.

University of California, Irvine
Laser Microbeam and Medical Program
1002 Health Science Rd. E.   Ph: (949)824-8367
Irvine, CA 92697   Fax: (949)824-8413
E-mail: tromberg@bli.uci.edu
URL: http://www.bli.uci.edu
Contact: Dr. Bruce J. Tromberg, Dir.

Desc: Combines sophisticated methods of microscopy, computational methods, and laser spectroscopy to investigate cellular, genetic, and developmental problems that are related to cancer, heart disease, neurobiology, and other health problems. Focuses on basic and translational research, particularly in the areas of laser-tissue interactions, tissue optics, photodynamic therapy, and functional imaging. *Type:* Research center.

University of California, Los Angeles
Leo G. Rigler Center for Radiological Research
UCLA Med. Ctr.   Ph: (310)825-6561
Department of Radiology
Ctr. for Health Sci., Rm. BV-135
Los Angeles, CA 90024
Contact: John Robert, Res.Assoc.

Desc: Radiological science and its application to diagnosis and treatment of catastrophic diseases, involving such techniques as magnetic resonance imaging (MRI), internal radiation management of carcinomatous lesions, vascular occlusion with ferrosilicone in tumor management, and cobalt source gamma irradiation of brain tumors. *Type:* Research center.

University of California, Los Angeles
UCLA-DOE Laboratory of Structural Biology and Molecular Medicine
201 Molecular Biology Institute
Los Angeles, CA 90095-1570
E-mail: david@mbi.ucla.edu
URL: http://www.doe-mbi.ucla.edu
Contact: Dr. David Eisenberg, Dir.

Desc: Structural biology and nuclear medicine, including supporting fields of physics, engineering and radiopharmacology. *Type:* Research center.

University of California, San Francisco
Radiation Oncology Research Laboratory
1855 Folsom, Rm. MCB 200   Ph: (415)476-2461
San Francisco, CA 94103   Fax: (415)476-9069
E-mail: dewey@rorl.ucsf.edu
Contact: Dr. Wm. Dewey, Prof.

Desc: Effects of ionizing radiation and hyperthermia in killing mammalian cells and interfering with cell cycle progression, with emphasis on applying basic concepts to radiation oncology. *Type:* Research center.

University of Chicago
Franklin McLean Memorial Research Institute
5841 S. Maryland Ave.   Ph: (773)702-6271
MC 1037   Fax: (773)702-5986
Chicago, IL 60637
E-mail: rnbk@midway.uchicago.edu
Contact: Prof. Robert N. Beck, Dir.

Desc: Application of various forms of radiant energy in treatment of cancerous and other neoplastic growth, including the biological aspects of radioactive elements and penetrating radiations in normal and diseased human beings, use of radioisotopes both as therapeutic measures and as diagnostic tools for research on cancer and fundamental life processes, and related topics in biology, metabolism, and biochemistry in vivo and in vitro. *Type:* Research center.

University of Iowa
Radiation Research Laboratory
Medical Laboratories, Rm. B180   Ph: (319)335-8019
Iowa City, IA 52242   Fax: (319)335-8039
E-mail: mrobbins@blue.weeg.uiowa.edu
URL: http://everest.radiology.uiowa.edu/~rad/rad.home.html
Contact: M.E.C. Robbins, PhD, Dir., Res.

Desc: Radiation biology, free radical biology, antioxidant enzymes, gene expression, and gene therapy. *Type:* Research center.

University of Kentucky
Radiation Therapy Oncology Center
Med. Ctr.   Ph: (606)323-6486
800 Rose St.   Fax: (606)257-4931
Lexington, KY 40536
E-mail: mohmohi@pop.uky.edu
Contact: Mohammed Mohiuddin, MD, Dir.

Desc: Radiation oncology research, participates in national cooperative group studies, RTOG, SWOG, NSABP, and GOG. Studies brain, bowel, head and neck cancer, and chemotherapy. *Type:* Research center.

University of Michigan
Division of Nuclear Medicine
Univ. Hospital   Ph: (734)936-5388
1500 E. Medical Center Dr.   Fax: (734)936-8182
B1G412
Ann Arbor, MI 48109-0028
E-mail: dkuhl@umich.edu
Contact: Dr. David E. Kuhl, Contact.

Desc: Diagnosis and treatment of disease using radionuclides and radionuclide-labeled compounds. Develops methods of nuclear medicine procedures. *Type:* Research center.

University of Missouri--Columbia
Radiation Oncology Program
Ellis Fischel Cancer Ctr.   Ph: (573)882-8644
115 Bus. Loop 70 W.   Fax: (573)882-8817
Columbia, MO 65203
E-mail: westgates@health.missouri.edu
Contact: Steven Westgate, Contact.

Desc: Clinical protocols; national multi-institutional studies for cancer problems. *Type:* Research center.

University of Pennsylvania

Metabolic Magnetic Resonance Research and Computing Center

Department of Radiology   Ph: (215)898-2044
B1, Stellar-Chance Labs   Fax: (215)573-2113
Philadelphia, PA 19104-6100
E-mail: jack@mail.mmrrcc.upenn.edu
URL: http://www.mmrrcc.upenn.edu

Contact: John S. Leigh, PhD, Dir.

Desc: Performs in vivo monitoring of specific metabolites in localized regions of tissues and organs in humans utilizing multinuclear magnetic resonance spectroscopy and metabolic imaging; develops targeted magnetite-based contrast agents for gene therapy and diagnosis; and develops techniques for near infrared optical imaging and spectroscopy in humans. *Type:* Research center.

University of Pennsylvania

Pendergrass Diagnostic Radiology Laboratories

Sch. of Med.   Ph: (215)662-6630
Department of Radiology   Fax: (215)349-5115
3400 Spruce St.
Philadelphia, PA 19104-6086

Contact: Harold L. Kundel, MD, Dir.

Desc: Diagnostic imaging, emphasizing digital computers, computed tomography, ultrasound, radiography, and nuclear magnetic resononce (NMR). The Laboratories study radiologic/physiologic correlation interventional procedures and the basic biology of NMR imaging. *Type:* Research center.

University of Pittsburgh

Pittsburgh NMR Institute

Med. Ctr. at Presbyterian Univ.   Ph: (412)647-3018
   Hospital   Fax: (412)647-6512
Desoto & O'Hara St
Pittsburgh, PA 15213

Contact: Loretta Hanwell, Dir.

Desc: Human disease studies using magnetic resonance imaging (MRI) and spectroscopy. Develops new contrast agents to enhance tissue specificity or measure organ function with magnetic resonance, as well as new techniques for studying animals and patients with magnetic resonance. *Type:* Research center.

University of Rochester

Rochester Center for Biomedical Ultrasound

203 Hopeman Engineering   Ph: (716)275-9542
   Bldg., Box 270126   Fax: (716)473-0486
Rochester, NY 14627-0126
E-mail: rcbu@ece.rochester.edu
URL: http://www.ece.rochester.edu/users/rcbu/

Contact: Prof. Kevin J. Parker, Dir.

Desc: Ultrasonic diagnosis, including imaging and Doppler ultrasound; ultrasonic treatment, including diathermy and the treatment of glaucoma and kidney and gall stones ultrasonic biophysics, including acoustic cavitation, generation and detection of ultrasound, tissue characterization, attenuation and scattering, shock fields, and nonlinear sound propagation; and biological effects of ultrasound. Also conducts research to establish safety limits for the use of ultrasound and to discover new applications, including new contrast agents. *Type:* Research center.

University of Texas Health Science Center at San Antonio

Center for Environmental Radiation Toxicology

7703 Floyd Curl Dr.   Ph: (210)567-5560
San Antonio, TX 78284-7800   Fax: (210)567-3446
E-mail: meltz@uthscsa.edu

Contact: Martin Meltz, PhD, Dir.

Desc: Effects of individual and combined exposures to microwave radiation, ionizing radiation, UV light and chemicals on biological systems. Current investigations focus on a variety of normal and cancerous in vitro cell lines, and human peripheral blood lymphocytes. *Type:* Research center.

University of Texas Southwestern Medical Center at Dallas

Mary Nell and Ralph B. Rogers Magnetic Resonance Center

5801 Forest Park Rd.   Ph: (214)648-5886
Dallas, TX 75235-9085   Fax: (214)648-5881
E-mail: cmallo@mednet.swmed.edu
URL: http://www.mednet.swmed.edu/home_pages/rogersmr

Contact: Dr. Craig R. Malloy, Dir.

Desc: Nuclear magnetic resonance (NMR) spectroscopy and imaging for the analysis of metabolism in various small animal and tissue culture models, including high energy phosphate metabolism, intracellular cations, intermediary metabolism, and perfusion. *Type:* Research center.

University of Texas Southwestern Medical Center at Dallas

Mary Nell and Ralph B. Rogers Magnetic Resonance Center

Southwestern Magnetic Resonance Facility

5801 Forest Park Dr., MC-9085   Ph: (214)648-5886
Dallas, TX 75235-9085   Fax: (214)648-5881
E-mail: cmallo@mednet.swmed.edu
URL: http://www.swmed.edu/home_pages/rogersmr

Contact: Dr. Craig R. Malloy, Contact.

Desc: Magnetic resonance imaging and spectroscopy of analytical samples, perfused organs, and small animals. *Type:* Research center.

University of Utah

Dixon Laser Institute

155 S. 1452 E., No. 220   Ph: (801)581-8201
Salt Lake City, UT 84112-8906   Fax: (801)585-3098
E-mail: werner@mailutah.edu

Contact: R. Kim Davis, MD, Dir.

Desc: Laser research, including applications of lasers in medicine, industry, and the military. Biomedical studies focus on gastroenterology, cardiology, otolaryngology, obstetrics-gynecology, urology, genetics, microsurgery, dentistry, and photodynamic therapy. *Type:* Research center.

University of Washington

Diagnostic Imaging Sciences Center

Department of Radiology   Ph: (206)543-0873
Box 357115   Fax: (206)543-3495
Seattle, WA 98195-7115
E-mail: jimnel@u.washington.edu

Contact: James Nelson, MD, Dir.

Desc: Diagnostic imaging, including PET, NMR spectroscopy and imaging, nucle ar medicine imaging and therapy, x-ray physics, ultrasound imaging, physiology, including angio-intervention techniques, image processing, and contrast media testing. *Type:* Research center.

University of Wisconsin--Madison

National Magnetic Resonance Facility

Department of Biochemistry   Ph: (608)262-3173
Room 171, Biochemistry   Fax: (608)262-3759
   Addition Bldg.
433 Babcock Drive
Madison, WI 53706-1544
E-mail: markley@nmrfam.wisc.edu
URL: http://www.nmrfam.wisc.edu

Contact: John L. Markley, Hd.

Desc: Structural and conformational analysis of proteins, nucleic acids, carbohydrates, lipids, and other biomolecules; structure-function studies of macromolecular assemblies; noninvasive analysis of the biochemistry or intact cells, tissue, or organs; in vivo investigations of the biochemistry of rats or other small animals; nuclear magnetic resonance (NMR) imaging of small objects. Current core and collaborative projects include: strategies for assigning NMR spectra of proteins; determination of three dimensional (3-D) structures of small proteins and nucleic acids from NMR data; preparation of stable-isotope labeled amino acids and proteins; uses of stable isotopes in multi-dimensional (NMR) studies of proteins; applications of NMR to protein engineering; elucidation of enzyme mechanisms and protein-ligand interactions; application of 2-D and 3-D NMR methodology to the study of cellular biochemistry; computer-aided design of NMR experiments; post-acquisition processing of NMR data; and semi-automated analysis of NMR data from proteins. *Type:* Research center.

Washington University in St. Louis

Mallinckrodt Institute of Radiology

510 S. Kingshighway Blvd.   Ph: (314)362-8436
St. Louis, MO 63110   Fax: (314)362-8399
E-mail: welch@mirlink.wustl.edu
URL: http://www.mir.wustl.edu/

Contact: Dr. Michael Welch, Chf.

Desc: Radiological diagnostic, treatment, research, and training center including nuclear medicine, radiation oncology, radiation sciences, and diagnostic radiology. The diagnostic radiology division is comprised of seven sections: abdominal, cardiac, chest, computer, musculoskeletal, pediatric, and neuroradiology. *Type:* Research center.

Washington University in St. Louis

Mallinckrodt Institute of Radiology

Hyperthermia Service

Radiation Oncology Ctr.   Ph: (314)362-8503
4939 Children's Pl., Ste. 5500   Fax: (314)362-8521
Box 8224
St. Louis, MO 63110
E-mail: moros_eg@rophys.wustl.edu

Contact: Robert J. Myerson, MD, Ch.

Desc: Hyperthermia treatment of cancer, simultaneous thermoradiotherapy, and bioassay of predictors of hyperthermic response. *Type:* Research center.

Wayne State University

MR Center

Harper Hospital   Ph: (313)745-1395
3990 John R Rd.   Fax: (313)993-0233
Detroit, MI 48201
E-mail: evelhoch@mednet.wayne.edu

Contact: Dr. Jeffrey L. Evelhoch, Dir.

Desc: Evaluates the potential for NMR (nuclear magnetic resonance) spectroscopy and imaging to provide predictors of response to chemotherapeutic drugs. *Type:* Research center.

Railroads

American Short Line and Regional Railroad Association

1120 G St. NW, Ste. 520   Ph: (202)628-4500
Washington, DC 20005   Fax: (202)628-6430
E-mail: aslrra@aslrra.org
URL: http://www.alsrra.org
Contact: Frank Turner, Pres.
Desc: Independently owned short line (usually less than 100 miles) railroads. *Type:* Association.

Association of American Railroads

50 F St. NW   Ph: (202)639-2100
Washington, DC 20001   Fax: (202)639-2156
URL: http://www.aar.org
Contact: Mr. Edward Hamberger, Jr., Pres./CEO.
Desc: Coordinating and research agency of the American freight railway industry. Fields of interest include railroad operation and maintenance, statistics, research, public relations, communications, signals, car exchange rules, safety, police and security matters, and testing and standards of railroad equipment. *Type:* Association.

Brotherhood of Locomotive Engineers, International

1370 Ontario St., Mezzanine   Ph: (216)241-2630
Cleveland, OH 44113-1701   Fax: (216)241-6516
Contact: Clarence Monin, Int.Pres.
Desc: Independent. Offers regional educational seminars. Compiles statistics. *Type:* Association.

Brotherhood of Maintenance of Way Employees

26555 Evergreen Rd., Ste. 200   Ph: (248)948-1010
Southfield, MI 48076-4225   Fax: (248)948-7150
Contact: M. A. Fleming, Pres.
Desc: AFL-CIO; Canadian Labour Congress. *Type:* Association.

Brotherhood of Railroad Signalmen

601 W. Golf Rd.   Ph: (847)439-3732
Box U   Fax: (847)439-3743
Mount Prospect, IL 60056
Contact: W. D. Pickett, Pres.
Desc: AFL-CIO. *Type:* Association.

Brotherhood Railway Carmen Division/ Transportation Communications Union

3 Research Pl.   Ph: (301)948-4910
Rockville, MD 20850   Fax: (301)948-1369
Contact: Richard A. Johnson, Gen.Pres.
Desc: AFL-CIO. A division of the Transportation Communications International Union. *Type:* Association.

DRI Freight Transportation Forecast

Standard & Poor's DRI
Data Products Division
24 Hartwell Ave.   Ph: (781)863-5100
Lexington, MA 02421
E-mail: client_services@dri.mcgraw-hill.com
URL: http://www.dri.mcgraw-hill.com
Contact: Client Services, (617)860-6527, fax: (617)860-6416.
Desc: Contains monthly, quarterly, and annual forecasts for U.S. surface freight transportation. *Available:* Standard & Poor's DRI, Data Products Division. *Type:* Database.

Eastern Railroad Association

1250 Broadway, Ste. 1100   Ph: (212)340-8810
New York, NY 10001
Contact: Henry J. Positano, Gen.Mgr.
Desc: Railroads located in the Eastern Territory. Publishes rates; maintains library of tariff publications. *Type:* Association.

National Association of Railroad Passengers

900 2nd St. NE, Ste. 308   Ph: (202)408-8362
Washington, DC 20002   Fax: (202)408-8287
E-mail: narp@narprail.org
URL: http://www.narprail.org
Contact: Ross Capon, Exec.Dir.
Desc: Users of rail passenger service, other concerned individuals, and organizations wishing to improve and expand rail passenger service. Seeks to increase public awareness and understanding of rail passenger service and its benefits. *Type:* Association.

National Association of Retired and Veteran Railway Employees

300 Cedar Blvd., Ste. 201-A   Ph: (412)563-5611
Pittsburgh, PA 15228-1155   Fax: (412)563-5612
E-mail: NARVRE@compuserve.com
URL: http://www.ourworld.compuserve.com/homepages/NARVRE
Contact: A. W. Westphal, Pres.
Desc: Active and retired railroad men and women with at least 10 years of service; widows and widowers of railroad personnel; individuals with less than 10 years of service are associate members. United to advance the rights of members, primarily through legislative action. Works to retain pension benefits for railway employees and their families under the revised Railroad Retirement Act of 1974. *Type:* Association.

National Railway Historical Society

PO Box 58547   Ph: (215)557-6606
Philadelphia, PA 19102-8547   Fax: (215)557-6740
E-mail: nrhs@compuserve.com
URL: http://www.rrhistorical.com/nrhs
Contact: Lynn Burshtin, Off.Mgr.
Desc: Persons interested in North American rail transportation. Preserves historical information on railroad subjects and sponsors railroad inspection trips to points of interest. Conducts research on railroads. *Type:* Association.

National Railway Labor Conference

1901 L St. NW, Ste. 500   Ph: (202)862-7200
Washington, DC 20036   Fax: (202)862-7230
Contact: Robert F. Allen, Chm.
Desc: Railroads and switching and terminal companies. Serves as a management collective bargaining agency for the railroad industry. Conducts bargaining with unions on a national level in connection with rates of pay, rules, and working conditions. *Type:* Association.

Transportation Communications International Union

3 Research Pl.   Ph: (301)948-4910
Rockville, MD 20850   Fax: (301)948-1369
Contact: Robert Scardelletti, Pres.
Desc: AFL-CIO; Canadian Labour Congress. Maintains research and educational programs. Maintains Responsible Citizens Political League as politicial action arm. *Type:* Association.

U.S. Rail News

Business Publishers, Inc. (BPI)
951 Pershing Dr.   Ph: (301)587-6300
Silver Spring, MD 20910-4464
URL: http://www.bpinews.com
Desc: Contains the complete text of U.S. Rail News, a newsletter on the freight and passenger rail transportation industry. *Type:* Database.

United Transportation Union

14600 Detroit Ave.   Ph: (216)228-9400
Lakewood, OH 44107-4250   Fax: (216)228-5755
Contact: Charles Little, Pres.
Desc: Promotes the interests of people who work in the transportation industry. *Type:* Association.

Western Railroad Association

151 Ellis St. NE, Ste. 200
Atlanta, GA 30303-2400
Contact: James N. Baker, Pres.
Desc: Compiles and distributes regu lated tariff matter. Maintains 200 volume library on tariffs, tariff supplements, and division sheets. *Type:* Association.

Western Railroad Traffic Association

151 Ellis St., NE, Ste. 200
Atlanta, GA 30303-2400
Contact: R.C. Becker, Chm.
Desc: A division of the Western Railroad Association . Railroads operating in the western U.S. Processes regulated rates and rate quotation services. *Type:* Association.

Reading

Center for Rehabilitation Technology—News Update

Center for Rehabilitation Technology (CRT)
Georgia Institute of Technology
College of Agriculture
490 10th St.   Ph: (404)894-4960
Atlanta, GA 30332-0156   Free: 800-726-9119
   Fax: (404)894-9320
Contact: Robert L. Todd, Editor.
Desc: Informs the public on Center activities and products, upcoming conferences, and new technology in the market for persons with disabilities. *Type:* Newsletter.

Dallas Rehabilitation Institute

9713 Harry Hines Blvd.   Ph: (214)904-6799
Dallas, TX 75220-5441   Fax: (214)904-6119
Contact: Rob Smart, CEO.
Desc: Provides treatment and assesses physical disabilities, including those associated with spinal cord injury, head injury, stroke, arthritis, amputations, spinal pain, and other orthopedic or neuromuscular problems. Conducts cooperative studies on a human performance measurement system designed to assess 500 aspects of human performance. *Type:* Research center.

Georgia Institute of Technology

Center for Rehabilitation Technology

490 10th St.   Ph: (404)894-4960
Atlanta, GA 30332-0156   Free: 800-726-9119
   Fax: (404)894-9320
E-mail: zena.rubin@arch.gatech.edu
URL: http://www.arch.gatech.edu/crt/
Contact: Joe Koncelik, Dir.
Desc: Develops equipment and procedures to help persons with disabilities. Maintains design and development laboratories and a national information center for the collection and dissemination of information on all aspects of rehabilitation technology. *Type:* Research center.

Real Estate

Adventist Development and Relief Agency International

12501 Old Columbia Pike   Ph: (301)680-6380
Silver Spring, MD 20904   Free: 800-424-2372
   Fax: (301)680-6370
Contact: Ralph S. Watts, Jr., Pres.

Desc: A nonsectarian relief and development agency of the Seventh-day Adventist Church serving developing countries. Sponsors institutional and community development, preventive health care, agricultural, and nutrition programs in Africa, Asia, the Pacific region, and Latin America. Teaches AIDS awareness and prevention. *Type:* Association.

American Industrial Real Estate Association

700 S. Flower, Ste. 600   Ph: (213)687-8777
Los Angeles, CA 90017   Fax: (213)687-8616
E-mail: rsurace@airea.com
URL: http://www.airea.com
Contact: Ronald J. Surace, COO.
Desc: Real estate men and women specializing in industrial and commercial properties; affiliate members are title companies, mortgage loan companies, public utilities, and developers. Membership concentrated in southern California. Encourages high professional standards. /alx Sponsors a course on industrial real estate, in cooperation with the University of California. Has developed industrial multiple listing system and standard lease forms. Supports the Industrial Multiple, a subsidiary of AIR which serves as a clearinghouse for information on industrial listings. Maintains a computerized multiple listing system. *Type:* Association.

American Institute of Certified Planners

1776 Massachusetts Ave. NW,   Ph: (202)872-0611
   Ste. 400   Free: 800-954-1669
Washington, DC 20036   Fax: (202)872-0643
E-mail: aicp@planning.org
URL: http://www.planning.org
Contact: Frank So, Exec.Dir.
Desc: Members of the APA who have met the requirements of education, practice, and examination established for the professional practice of public planning. *Type:* Association.

American Jewish World Service

989 Ave. of the Americas, Fl. 10   Ph: (212)736-2597
New York, NY 10018-5410   Fax: (212)736-3463
E-mail: jws@jws.org
URL: http://www.ajws.org
Contact: Stepanie Fingeroth, Asst. to Pres.
Desc: A Jewish-sponsored humanitarian and relief organization working on an exclusively non-sectarian basis in the developing world. AJWS' aim is to provide the means for disadvantaged people particularly women and children and threatened minorities, to move toward self-sufficiency. *Type:* Association.

American Land Title Association

1828 L St. NW, Ste. 705   Ph: (202)296-3671
Washington, DC 20036   Free: 800-787-ALTA
             Fax: (202)223-5843
E-mail: service@alta.org
URL: http://www.alta.org
Contact: James R. Maher, Exec.VP.
Desc: Abstracters, title insurance companies, and attorneys specializing in real property law. *Type:* Association.

American Planning Association

122 S. Michigan Ave., Ste. 1600   Ph: (312)431-9100
Chicago, IL 60603-6107   Fax: (312)431-9985
Contact: Frank So, Pres.
Desc: Public and private planning agency officials, professional planners, planning educators, elected and appointed officials, and other persons involved in urban and rural development. Works to foster the best techniques and decisions for the planned development of communities and regions. Provides extensive professional services and publications to professionals and laypeople in planning and related fields; serves as a clearinghouse for information. *Type:* Association.

American Resort Development Association

1220 L St. NW, Ste. 500   Ph: (202)371-6700
Washington, DC 20005   Fax: (202)289-8544
E-mail: webmaster@arda.org
URL: http://www.arda.org/arda
Contact: Cynthia Huheey, Pres.
Desc: Developers of retirement, residential, resort, and recreational communities, and timesharing and outdoor resorts; suppliers to the resort development industries. Offers seminars; conducts research and surveys. *Type:* Association.

Apartment Management Newsletter

Helene Mandelbaum
2095 Broadway, No. 404   Ph: (212)787-6931
New York, NY 10123
Contact: Helene Mandelbaum, Editor.
Desc: Covers topics of concern to apartment managers and owners, such as renting and marketing apartments, operating economics, resident relations, maintenance, and legal updates. *Type:* Newsletter.

The Appraiser

The Appraisal Institute of American, Inc.
386 Park Ave. S., Ste. 2000   Ph: (212)889-5404
New York, NY 10016   Fax: (212)889-5503
E-mail: appraisersassn@compuserve.com
Contact: Hermine Chivian-Cobb, Editor.
Desc: Covers topics of interest to personal property appraisers. Recurring features include a calendar of events, book reviews, and news of educational opportunities. *Type:* Newsletter.

Appraiser Gram

National Association of Independent Fee Appraisers
7501 Murdoch Ave.   Ph: (314)781-6688
St. Louis, MO 63119   Fax: (314)781-2872
E-mail: info@naifa.com
Contact: Donna J. Walter, Editor.
Desc: Publishes information of interest to real estate appraisers, including news of Association activities. *Type:* Newsletter.

Armenian Relief Society of Eastern USA

80 Bigelow Ave.   Ph: (617)926-3801
Watertown, MA 02472
Contact: Ms. Maral Orchanian, Exec.Sec.
Desc: Armenian women and men throughout the world; includes 3200 members in the U.S. and Canada. Raises and distributes money for relief of Armenian people and for advancement of educational and cultural activities. *Type:* Association.

Black's Guide: Dallas/Fort Worth

Black's Guide, Inc.
16415 Addison Rd., Ste. 316   Ph: (972)931-1299
Addison, TX 75001   Free: 800-861-4755
             Fax: (972)931-1224
E-mail: gmeyers@sprynet.com.
URL: http://www.blacksguide.com.
Contact: Fran Piegari, Editor.
Desc: Office space available in multi-tenanted buildings and developments over 15,000 square feet in size in the Dallas/Fort Worth area. *Type:* Directory.

Building Owners and Managers Association International

1201 New York Ave. NW, Ste.   Ph: (202)408-2662
   300   Fax: (202)371-0181
Washington, DC 20005
E-mail: soppen@boma.org
URL: http://www.boma.org

Contact: Robert Angle, Exec. Officer.
Desc: Building owners, managers, developers, leasing professionals, facility managers, asset managers and the providers of goods and services. Represents all facets of the commercial real estate industry. *Type:* Association.

Business Opportunities Journal

Business Service Corp.
868 Rosecrans   Ph: (619)224-2695
San Diego, CA 92106   Fax: (619)224-2696
E-mail: boj@boj.com; boj@boj.com.
URL: http://www.boj.com.
Contact: Wayne Wakefield, President.
Desc: Newspaper covering business, real estate, and franchises. *Alt. Contact:* PO Box 60762, San Diego, CA 92166; telephone: (619)223-5615; fax: (619)223-1705; toll-free: 800-854-6570. *Type:* Periodical.

Buying, Selling & Owning Your Home

ECV LP
333 Sylvan Ave., Ste. 400   Ph: (201)568-4600
Englewood Cliffs, NJ 07632   Fax: (201)568-3646
Contact: Oliver Brown, Editor; William Fried, Co-Founder.
Desc: Homebuyer's guide. *Type:* Periodical.

California Real Estate Magazine

California Association of Realtors
525 S. Virgil Ave.   Ph: (213)739-8320
Los Angeles, CA 90020-1406   Fax: (213)480-7724
Contact: Stacy Katzin, Advertising Mgr., (213)739-8321, stacey-katzin@car.org; Anne Framroze, Editor and Publisher.
Desc: Magazine promoting professionalism and skills of real estate brokers and agents. "Offers in depth news and information focusing on California's real estate issues and trends." *Type:* Periodical.

Campgroundata

Campground Data Resource
225 E. Stuart Ave.   Ph: (941)676-0009
Lake Wales, FL 33853   Free: 800-889-0355
             Fax: (941)676-0009
E-mail: 71072.2342@compuserve.com
Contact: Dale S. Bourdette, Editor, dale_bourdette@worldnet.att.net.
Desc: Provides information for campground buyers and sellers to help them make informed buy or sell decisions. *Type:* Newsletter.

The Clayton-Fillmore Report

Clayton-Fillmore Ltd.
125 Dorset Ct.   Ph: (303)663-0606
Castle Rock, CO 80104-9285   Fax: (303)663-1616
Contact: Howard Treibitz, Editor.
Desc: Features articles on various aspects of the national real estate industry. Profiles three American cities per issue in terms of their demographics, economics, housing, office, retail, and industrial real estate markets. *Type:* Newsletter.

Commercial Investment Real Estate Institute

430 N. Michigan Ave.   Ph: (312)321-4460
Chicago, IL 60611   Free: 800-621-7027
             Fax: (312)321-4530
URL: http://www.ccim.com
Contact: Susan Groeneveld, CAE, Exec. VP.
Desc: Commercial investment real estate brokers, developers, asset managers, and others involved in commercial investment properties. Seeks to enhance the professional competence of commercial real estate practitioners. *Type:* Association.

Commercial Lease Law Insider

Brownstone Publishers, Inc.
149 Fifth Ave., 16th Fl.   Ph: (212)473-8200
New York, NY 10010-6801   Free: 800-643-8095
                           Fax: (212)473-8786
E-mail: comlease@aol.com; omnh@ouwww.ou.edu.
Contact: Nicole R. Lefton, Esq., Editor.
Desc: Reviews national legal developments and leasing techniques for real estate professionals. Provides "how to" advice for structuring commercial property leases, including sample lease language and methods for attracting new tenants and keeping old ones. *Type:* Newsletter.

Commercial Mortgage Alert

Harrison Scott Publications, Inc.
5 Marine View Plaza, Ste. 301   Ph: (201)659-1700
Hoboken, NJ 07030   Free: 800-283-9363
                                Fax: (201)659-4141
E-mail: hsp@bellatlantic.net
Contact: Andrew Albert, Publisher; Thomas J. Ferris, Editor.
Desc: Covers the commercial mortgage market. Recurring features include a calendar of events and a column titled The Grapevine. *Type:* Newsletter.

Crittenden Report Real Estate Financing

Crittenden Research, Inc.
45 Leveroni Ct., Ste. 204   Ph: (415)382-2485
PO Box 1150   Free: 800-421-3483
Novato, CA 94948   Fax: (415)382-2476
E-mail: webmaster@crittendenonline.com
Contact: John Goodwin, Editor.
Desc: Disseminates information about the real estate finance industry. Discusses loans, mortgages, profitability and bank terms. *Type:* Newsletter.

The Dealmakers

TKO Real Estate Advisory Group, Inc.
PO Box 2630   Ph: (609)587-6200
Mercerville, NJ 08690   Free: 800-732-5856
                            Fax: (609)587-3511
E-mail: deal.makers@dealmakers.net; ted.kraus@
dealmakers.net.
URL: http://www.property.com.
Contact: Chris Gesualdi, Editor, chrisges@dealmakers.net.
Desc: Offers listings and "in-depth reporting" on various aspects of retail real estate: shopping center vacancies, shopping centers for sale, retail conversions, retailers seeking new locations, and management of retail property. Examines various real estate services, such as brokers, investors, consultants, and management companies. *Type:* Newsletter.

Directory of Professional Appraisers

American Society of Appraisers
PO Box 17265   Ph: (202)478-2228
Washington, DC 20041   Free: 800-ASA-VALU
                            Fax: (202)742-8471
E-mail: asainfo@appraisers.org
URL: http://www.appraisers.org; http://www.appraisers.org.
Contact: Rebecca Ewing, Editor.
Desc: Approximately 3,500 appraisers of businesses, real property, personal property, machinery, equipment, gems and jewelry, and all other types of property; limited international coverage. *Type:* Directory.

District of Columbia Real Estate Reporter

Land Development Institute, Ltd.
1300 N St. NW   Ph: (202)232-2144
Washington, DC 20005   Fax: (202)232-8924
Contact: Steve Sullivan, Editor.
Desc: Covers zoning and rental housing commissions, the Court of Appeals, the City Council, and government agencies dealing with real estate issues in Washington D.C. Recurring features include a list of current and pending legislation. *Type:* Newsletter.

FDIC—Investment Properties Publication

Federal Deposit Insurance Corp.
550 17th St. NW   Ph: (202)393-8400
Washington, DC 20429   Free: 800-834-8400
                           Fax: (202)898-3543
URL: http://www.fdic.gov; http://www.fdic.gov.
Desc: Properties owned by the Federal Deposit Insurance Corporation, including land, commercial real estate, multifamily dwellings, hotels, motels, and resorts, with an asking price of $5,000 or more. *Type:* Directory.

First Tuesday

Realty Publications Inc.
1485 Spruce, Ste. H   Ph: (909)781-7300
PO Box 20068   Fax: (909)781-4721
Riverside, CA 92507
Contact: Fred Crane, Editor and Publisher; Pat Radcliffe, Advertising Mgr.
Desc: Magazine for real estate professionals. *Type:* Periodical.

Flight Lines

Real Estate Aviation Chapter
5440 St. Charles Rd.   Ph: (708)547-7100
Berkeley, IL 60163-1287   Fax: (708)547-8000
Contact: W.J. Haeger, Editor.
Desc: Advises the real estate industry on airport and aviation development and expansion as it affects real estate values. Discusses ideas and problems involved with aviation and land ownership. *Type:* Newsletter.

Florida Real Estate

Florida Real Estate Magazine, L.P.
PO Box 4258
Vero Beach, FL 32964
Desc: Trade magazine for realtors. *Type:* Periodical.

Greater Tampa Realtor News

Greater Tampa Association of Realtors
2918 W. Kennedy Blvd.   Ph: (813)879-7010
Tampa, FL 33609   Fax: (813)879-8977
Contact: Brenda Raggitt, Editor.
Desc: Provides news of Association activities and educational programs. Spotlights local, state, and national issues of interest to real estate professionals. *Type:* Newsletter.

Habitabec Plus

Habitabec PLUS
8620 Berri St.   Ph: (514)389-5944
Montreal, PQ, Canada H2P   Free: 800-465-1913
  2G4   Fax: (514)385-5982
Contact: Jacques Dery, Publisher; Chantal Dery, National Representative.
Desc: Consumer housing and real estate tabloid (French and English). *Type:* Periodical.

Homes Magazine

Homes Publishing Group
178 Main St.   Ph: (905)479-4663
Unionville, ON, Canada L3R   Free: 800-363-4663
  2G9   Fax: (905)479-4482
URL: http://www.homesmag.com/.
Contact: Patrick Tiuy, Editor; Michael Rosset, Publisher, rosset@homesmag.com; Hope McLarnon, V.P. of Sales; Lisa Kelly, Production Mgr.; Dianne MacKenzie, Art Director.
Desc: Magazine covering real estate, decor, and homes. *Type:* Periodical.

Honolulu Board of Realtors

1136 12th Ave., Ste. 200   Ph: (808)732-3000
Honolulu, HI 96816-3796   Fax: (808)732-3055
E-mail: hbradmin@hbr.com

URL: http://www.hbr.com
Contact: Peggy Comeau, Exec.V.Pres.
Desc: Promotes education, high professional standards, and modern techniques in specialized real estate work. *Type:* Association.

Hotel Motel Brokers of America

10220 N. Executive Hills Blvd.,   Ph: (816)891-7070
  Ste. 610   Free: 800-821-5191
Kansas City, MO 64153   Fax: (816)891-7071
URL: http://www.hmba.com
Contact: Robert Kralicek, Exec.VP.
Desc: Real estate brokers specializing in sales of and investments in hotel and motel properties. Members cooperate in the interchange of listings and data by computer, so the buying public will have information concerning all hotels available through the members of the association. *Type:* Association.

Illinois Real Estate Letter

Office of Real Estate Research (ORER)
University of Illinois
304 David Kinley Hall   Ph: (217)244-0951
1407 W. Gregory Dr.   Fax: (217)244-9867
Urbana, IL 61801
E-mail: orer@uiuc.edu
Contact: Peter F. Colwell, Editor; Joseph W. Trefzger, Editor.
Desc: Provides news and analysis of developments in real estate research. *Type:* Newsletter.

Innside Issues

HMBA: America's Hotel Broker
10220 N. Executive Hills Blvd.,   Ph: (816)891-7070
  Ste. 610   Free: 800-821-5191
Kansas City, MO 64153   Fax: (816)891-7071
Contact: Robert Kralicek, Publisher; Sharon Lemon, Editor, sharon@hmba.com.
Desc: Focuses on investment opportunities in the lodging industry. *Type:* Newsletter.

Institute of Real Estate Management

430 N. Michigan Ave.   Ph: (312)329-6000
Chicago, IL 60611-4090   Free: 800-837-0706
                            Fax: (312)410-7960
E-mail: swinn@irem.org
URL: http://www.irem.org
Contact: Ronald Vukas, Exec.VP.
Desc: Professional organization of real property and asset managers. Awards professional designation Certified Property Manager (CPM) to qualifying individuals and Accredited Management Organization (AMO) to qualifying management firms. Also awards Accredited Residential Manager service award which recognizes outstanding residential site managers. *Type:* Association.

International Accrediting Commission for Real Estate and Appraisal Education and Training

Robert G. Johnson
1224 N Nokomis NE   Ph: (320)763-7626
Alexandria, MN 56308-5072   Fax: (320)763-9290
Contact: Robert G. Johnson, Exec.Dir.
Desc: Real estate and appraisal training programs and institutions. Promotes advancement of real estate and appraisal education and training. *Type:* Association.

International Medical Corps

11500 W Olympic Blvd., No.   Ph: (310)826-7800
  565   Free: 800-481-4IMC
Los Angeles, CA 90064-1524   Fax: (310)442-6622
E-mail: imc@imc-la.com
URL: http://www.imc-la.org
Contact: Nancy A. Aossey, Pres. & CEO.

Real Estate

Desc: Staff and volunteers include physicians, surgeons, nurses, physician assistants and persons with expertise in administration, management, logistics and finances. Seeks to save lives, relieve suffering and improve the quality of life through health interventions and related activities that build local capacity in areas worldwide where few organizations dare to serve. Offers medical training and healthcare to local populations and medical assistance to people at highest risk, and with the flexibility to respond rapidly to emergency situations. *Type:* Association.

International Real Estate Newsletter
International Real Estate Institute
1224 N. Nokomis, NE   Ph: (320)763-4648
Alexandria, MN 56308   Fax: (320)763-9290

Contact: Robert G. Johnson, Editor.

Desc: Recurring features include a column titled Cultural Considerations. *Type:* Newsletter.

Investment Property and Real Estate Capital Markets Report
Institutional Real Estate, Inc.
1475 N. Broadway, Ste. 300   Ph: (925)933-4040
Walnut Creek, CA 94596   Fax: (925)934-4099
E-mail: irei@irei.com

Contact: Geoffrey Dohrmann, Editor and Publisher; Larry Gray, Managing Editor.

Desc: Covers commercial real estate transaction marketplace. *Type:* Newsletter.

ISA Professional Appraisers Information Exchange
International Society of Appraisers
16040 Christensen Rd., Ste. 102   Ph: (206)241-0359
Seattle, WA 98188-2965   Free: 888-472-5762
                                  Fax: (206)241-0436
E-mail: isa_hq@compuserve.com

Contact: Alice L. Coleman, Editor.

Desc: News, events, and articles on personal property appraising and the International Society of Appraisers. *Type:* Newsletter.

Land Owner
Professional Farmers of America, Inc.
219 Parkade   Ph: (319)277-1278
PO Box 6   Fax: (319)277-7896
Cedar Falls, IA 50613
URL: http://www.profarmer.com.

Contact: Jerry Carlson, Editor.

Desc: Contains information for farmland owners. Covers land management, regional price trends, buyer and seller attitudes, and government farm programs and their impact on the land market. *Type:* Newsletter.

Letter of the Law
Real Estate Center
Texas A&M University
College Station, TX 77843-2115   Ph: (409)845-2031
                                  Free: 800-244-2144
                                  Fax: (409)845-0460
E-mail: info@recenter.tamu.edu
URL: http://www.recenter.tamu.edu.

Contact: David S. Jones, Editor; Jennifer V. Hofmann, Editor.

Desc: Provides news and information on current case law, and new statutes and regulations that affect real estate. *Type:* Newsletter.

Mr. Landlord
Home Rental Publishing
PO Box 64442   Ph: (757)424-7997
Virginia Beach, VA 23467   Free: 800-950-2250
                          Fax: (757)467-1427
E-mail: customerservice@mrlandlord.com
URL: http://www.mrlandlord.com.

Contact: Jeffrey E. Taylor, Editor.

Desc: Covers all aspects of management of small rental properties. *Type:* Newsletter.

Montana Land Magazine
Real Estate Publications, Inc.
PO Box 30516   Ph: (406)259-3534
Billings, MT 59107-0516   Fax: (406)259-1676
E-mail: bigsky@montanalandmagazine.com

Contact: G.L. (Gordy) Dangerfield, Advertising Mgr.

Desc: Real estate magazine. *Type:* Periodical.

The Mortgage and Real Estate Executives Report
Warren, Gorham & Lamont R.I.A. Group
90 Fifth Ave., 10th Fl.   Ph: (212)807-2193
New York, NY 10011   Free: 800-950-1216
                           Fax: (212)337-4183

Contact: Alvin L. Arnold, Editor.

Desc: Provides comprehensive information on real estate financing and investment, covering market strategies, tax angles and developments, and mortgage lending and financing techniques. Carries updates on important real estate events and trends, government regulations and rulings, and federal aids to real estate financing. *Type:* Newsletter.

Moving and Relocation Sourcebook and Directory
Omnigraphics Inc.
2500 Penobscot Bldg.   Ph: (313)961-1340
Detroit, MI 48226   Free: 800-234-1340
                        Fax: (313)961-1383
E-mail: info@omnigraphics.com
URL: http://www.omnigraphics.com; http://www.omnigraphics.com.

Contact: Diane Barlow, Editor; Nancy V. Kniskern, Editor.

Desc: Areas of interest in 100 of the largest metropolitan areas in the U.S., including educational institutions, medical and health care facilities, arts organizations, sports and recreation venues, newspapers and other media, public libraries, public safety organizations, churches and synagogues. *Type:* Directory.

Nacore International
440 Columbia Dr., Ste. 100   Ph: (561)683-8111
West Palm Beach, FL 33409   Free: 800-726-8111
                               Fax: (561)697-4853
E-mail: nacore@nacore.com
URL: http://www.nacore.com

Contact: H. Gordon Wyllie, MCR, Exec.Dir./CEO.

Desc: Executives, attorneys, real estate department heads, architects, engineers, analysts, researchers, and anyone responsible for the management, administration, and operation of national and regional real estate departments of national and international corporations. Provides a meeting ground for the exchange of ideas, experience, and problems among members; encourages professionalism within corporate real estate through education and communication; protects the interests of corporate realty in dealing with adversaries, public or private; maintains contact with other real estate organizations; publicizes the availability of fully qualified members to the job market. Maintains Institute for Corporate Real Estate as educational arm. *Type:* Association.

NAIOP, the Forum for Commercial Real Estate—Membership Directory
NAIOP
Woodland Park   Ph: (703)904-7100
2201 Cooperative Way, 3rd Fl.   Fax: (703)904-7942
Herndon, VA 20171
E-mail: feedback@naiop.org
URL: http://www.naiop.org/.

Contact: Thomas J. Bisacquino, Editor.

Desc: Over 5,000 member firms involved in the development of industrial and office properties. *Type:* Directory.

Naples Guide
Naples Guide
947 4th Ave. S   Ph: (941)262-6524
Naples, FL 34102   Fax: (941)262-3468
E-mail: stugrang@aol.com.

Contact: Alyce Mathias, Editor and Publisher.

Desc: Magazine covering arts, entertainment, shopping, dining, beauty, health, home and garden, and real estate in Naples, FL, and the surrounding areas. *Type:* Periodical.

National Apartment Association
201 N. Union St., Ste. 200   Ph: (703)518-6141
Alexandria, VA 22314   Fax: (703)518-6191
E-mail: membership@naahq.com
URL: http://www.naahq.org

Contact: Amy Dozier, Exec.VP.

Desc: Federation of 155 state and local associations of industry professionals engaged in all aspects of the multifamily housing industry, including owners, builders, investors, developers, managers, and allied service representatives. Provides education and certification for property management executives, on-site property managers, maintenance personnel, property supervisors, and leasing agents. *Type:* Association.

National Association of Industrial and Office Properties
2201 Cooperative Way   Ph: (703)904-7100
Herndon, VA 20171   Free: 800-666-6780
                        Fax: (703)904-7942
E-mail: naiop@naiop.org
URL: http://www.naicp.org

Contact: Thomas J. Bisacquino, Pres.

Desc: Owners and developers of industrial, office, and related properties; others interested in commercial and industrial real estate are admitted as associate members. Seeks to stimulate the growth of the commercial real estate industry and to help improve prospects and profits of members. Promotes exchange of information; speaks on behalf of members concerning legislation and taxation problems affecting the industry; fosters establishment and maintenance of standards for the operation of industrial/office properties; seeks liaison and cooperation with other groups. *Type:* Association.

National Association of Realtors
430 N. Michigan Ave.   Free: 800-874-6500
Chicago, IL 60611   Fax: (312)329-5962
URL: http://www.realtor.com

Contact: Terrence McDermott, Exec.VP.

Desc: Federation of 54 state and territory associations and 1860 local real estate boards whose members are real estate brokers and agents. Terms are registered by the association in the U.S. Patent and Trademark Office and in the states. *Type:* Association.

National Association of Review Appraisers and Mortgage Underwriters
1224 N. Nokomis, NE   Ph: (320)763-6870
Alexandria, MN 56308-5072   Fax: (320)763-9290
E-mail: nara@iami.org

URL: http://www.iami.org/nara.html

Contact: Robert G. Johnson, Exec.Dir.

Desc: Real estate professionals and mortgage underwriters who aid in determining value of property. Acts as umbrella group for real estate appraisers. *Type:* Association.

National Delinquency Survey

Mortgage Bankers Association of America
1125 15th St. NW   Free: 800-793-MBAA
Washington, DC 20005

Contact: David Lereah, Editor.

Desc: Carries information on residential mortgage delinquency and foreclosure rates at national, regional, and state levels. Reports delinquency rates by length of time and type of loan. *Type:* Newsletter.

National Directory of Exchange Groups

Creative Real Estate Magazine
Drawer L   Ph: (619)756-1441
Rancho Santa Fe, CA 92067   Fax: (619)756-1111

Contact: A. D. Kessler, Editor; J. S. McNary, Editor.

Desc: Over 125 professional real estate marketing groups practicing tax-deferred real estate exchanging; over 200 real estate investors associations nationwide. *Type:* Directory.

National Multi Housing Council

1850 M St. NW, Ste. 540   Ph: (202)974-2300
Washington, DC 20036   Fax: (202)775-0112
E-mail: info@nmhc.org
URL: http://www.nmhc.org

Contact: Jonathan L. Kempner, Pres.

Desc: Builders, developers, owners, financers, and managers of multifamily housing and condominium developments, and interested multifamily housing organizations. Monitors and responds to federal legislative and regulatory actions and issues affecting multifamily housing. Serves as clearinghouse and coordinator for other associations. *Type:* Association.

National Realty Committee

1420 New York Ave. NW, Ste.   Ph: (202)639-8400
    1100   Fax: (202)639-8442
Washington, DC 20005
E-mail: email@nrc.org

Contact: Jeffrey DeBoer, Pres. & COO.

Desc: Commercial Real estate owners, advisors, builders, investors, lenders, and managers. Serves as an advocate for national tax, finance, technology, and environmental policy issues of concern to income-producing real estate. *Type:* Association.

New Homes Magazine

MDM Publications
3151 Airway Ave., Ste. C-3   Ph: (714)751-5813
Costa Mesa, CA 92626   Fax: (714)755-5500

Contact: Daniel B. Ciauri, Publisher.

Desc: New real estate magazine. *Alt. Contact:* 3151 Airway Ave., Ste. C-3, Costa Mesa, CA 92626. *Type:* Periodical.

Office Guide

Greater Dallas Chamber
1201 Elm St., Ste. 2000   Ph: (214)746-6704
Dallas, TX 75270   Fax: (214)746-6799
E-mail: mchapman@dallaschamber.org.

Contact: Laura Brumley, Editor.

Desc: Office buildings in the greater Dallas area. *Type:* Directory.

Ontra Update

Ontra, Inc.
816 Congress Ave., Ste. 2000   Ph: (512)478-9455
Austin, TX 78701

Contact: Gloria Souhami, Editor.

Desc: Covers the residential market of real estate in the U.S., as well as commercial leasing. Recurring features include news of research, a calendar of events, reports of meetings, news of educational opportunities, and notices of publications available. *Type:* Newsletter.

Professional Report of Industrial and Office Real Estate

Society of Industrial and Office Realtors
700 11th St. NW, Ste. 510   Ph: (202)737-1150
Washington, DC 20001-4511   Free: 888-891-7467
                                   Fax: (202)737-8796
URL: http://www.sior.com; http://www.sior.com.

Contact: Linda P. Nasvaderani, Editor, (202)737-8783, lnasvaderani@mail.sior.com.

Desc: Dedicated to corporate real estate brokerage, development, and management. Recurring features include news of members and the Society, news of educational programs sponsored by the Society, book reviews, news of research, and statistics. *Type:* Newsletter.

Property Management Association—Bulletin

Property Management Association
7900 Wisconsin Ave., Ste. 204   Ph: (301)907-9326
Bethesda, MD 20814
E-mail: pma@erols.com
URL: http://www.reji.com/reji/associations/pma/nonmember/data.

Contact: Linda LeBaron, Managing Editor.

Desc: Reports market trends and other information related to property management. Contains information on the Association and tips for members. *Type:* Newsletter.

The Property Professional

National Property Management Association
1108 Pinehurst Rd.   Ph: (813)736-3788
Dunedin, FL 34698   Fax: (813)736-6707
E-mail: npma@gate.net

Contact: Sara Helmick-Weaver, Editor.

Desc: Provides information on government/contractor property asset management. Carries news of courses, seminars, personalities in the field, and the activities of the Association and its chapters. *Type:* Newsletter.

Public Lands Council

1301 Pennsylvania Ave. NW,   Ph: (202)347-5355
    Ste. 300   Fax: (202)737-4086
Washington, DC 20004
URL: http://www.nca.org

Contact: Lance Kotschwar, Exec.Dir.

Desc: Ranchers who hold permits and leases for grazing livestock (cattle and sheep) on public lands in 14 western states. Represents the interests of public land ranchers before the U.S. Congress and the Executive Branch. *Type:* Association.

Real Estate Alert

Harrison Scott Publications, Inc.
5 Marine View Plaza, Ste. 301   Ph: (201)659-1700
Hoboken, NJ 07030   Free: 800-283-9363
                                   Fax: (201)659-4141
E-mail: hsp@bellatlantic.net

Contact: Andrew Albert, Publisher; Thomas J. Ferris, Editor.

Desc: Provides information on current sales of assets of liquidated financial Industry. Includes a calendar of events. *Type:* Newsletter.

Real Estate Brokerage Managers Council

430 N. Michigan Ave.   Ph: (312)321-4400
Chicago, IL 60611-4092   Fax: (312)329-8882
URL: http://www.crb.com

Contact: Bonnie Cobean, Exec. VP.

Desc: Managers and individuals in management-related real estate jobs. Aids members in improving their abilities and increasing the profitability of their firms. *Type:* Association.

Real Estate Broker's Insider

Alexander Research & Communications, Inc.
215 Park Ave. S, Ste. 1301   Ph: (212)228-0246
New York, NY 10003   Fax: (212)228-0376

Contact: Jean DeSapio, Editor; Michael Schau, Editor.

Desc: Provides up-to-date information concerning trends and developments in the residential and commercial property markets, mortgage financing, housing starts, consumer spending, new sales and business management ideas, and franchised real estate networks. Contains news of mergers, tax changes, interest rates, sales volume, real estate office automation, and convention news. *Type:* Newsletter.

Real Estate Center Trends

Real Estate Center
Texas A&M University
College Station, TX 77843-2115   Ph: (409)845-2031
                                   Free: 800-244-2144
                                   Fax: (409)845-0460
E-mail: info@recenter.tamu.edu
URL: http://www.recenter.tamu.edu.

Contact: David S. Jones, Editor.

Desc: Supplies statistics on 50 major Texas real estate markets, including single-family/multi-family building permits, listings, sales, inventory, median and average home prices, price distribution, and office/retail/commercial building permits. *Type:* Newsletter.

Real Estate Investors Classified

Ted Kraus
PO Box 2630   Ph: (609)587-6200
Mercerville, NJ 08690   Fax: (609)587-3511
E-mail: deal.makers@dealmakers.net; reic@dealmakers.net.
URL: http://www.property.com.

Contact: Ann O'Neal, Editor.

Desc: Provides information on commercial real estate for sale, acquisition requirements, and financing sources. Recurring features include news of research, and notices of publications available. *Type:* Newsletter.

Real Estate Investor's Monthly

John T. Reed Publishing
342 Bryan Dr.   Ph: (925)820-6292
Alamo, CA 94507   Fax: (925)820-1259
URL: http://www.johntreed.com/reim.html.

Contact: John T. Reed, Editor, johnreed@johntreed.com.

Desc: Tracks real estate investment by individual sole proprietors. Includes book reviews. *Type:* Newsletter.

Real Estate Marketing Management Alert

Damarka Enterprises Inc.
8215 Sutton Pl., N.   Ph: (904)733-0881
Jacksonville, FL 32217   Fax: (904)636-5448
E-mail: realtorjax@aol.com.

Contact: Robert H. Bossen, Editor.

Desc: Offers ideas and strategies in marketing and management to increase productivity and improve service. Recurring features include letters to the editor, interviews, book reviews, and notices of publications available. *Type:* Newsletter.

Real Estate Matters Syndicate

395 Dundee Rd. Ph: (847)835-3450
Glencoe, IL 60022 Fax: (847)835-3451

Contact: Ilyce R. Glink, Publisher, ilyceglink@aol.com; Samuel J. Tamkin, Editor.

Desc: Distributes columns about real estate matters. *Alt. Contact:* 395 Dundee Rd., Glencoe, IL 60022; telephone: (847)835-3450; fax: (847)835-3451. *Type:* Periodical.

Real Estate Mortgage Advisory Ltd.

5555 DTC Pkwy. Ph: (303)779-0663
Ste. 3200-C Fax: (303)779-4157
Englewood, CO 80111

Contact: Sandy Perkins, Vice President.

Desc: Distributes real estate information. *Alt. Contact:* 5555 DTC Pkwy., Ste. 3200-C, Englewood, CO 80111; telephone: (303)779-0663; fax: (303)779-4157. *Type:* Periodical.

Real Estate Newsletter

Phoenix Ventures Inc.
320 Valley Ph: (319)752-5415
Burlington, IA 52601 Fax: (319)752-3421

Contact: Barbara Boeding, Editor.

Desc: Carries information on various real estate trends, including news of design, remodeling, and new industry trends. *Remarks:* Mastheads can be imprinted with company logos; design of custom mastheads is available. *Type:* Newsletter.

Real Estate Tax Digest

Matthew Bender & Company
Two Park Ave. Ph: (212)448-2118
New York, NY 10016 Free: 800-252-9257
 Fax: (212)448-2749

Contact: Raymond Camiscioli, Senior Tax Editor, raymond.p.camiscioli@bender.com.

Desc: Features articles on and analyses of legislation, Treasury regulations, federal court and Tax Court decisions, Revenue Rulings, Revenue Procedures, and selected Letter Rulings of the Internal Revenue Service pertaining to federal taxation affecting real estate activities. Includes columns titled Special Topics, New Developments, Practitioner's Corner, and Inside Washington. *Type:* Newsletter.

Real Estate Tax Ideas

Warren, Gorham & Lamont, Inc.
RIA Group
PO Box 6159 Free: 800-950-1216
Carol Stream, IL 60197

Contact: Gerald J. Robinson, Editor; Stephen L. Owen, Editor.

Desc: "Plants real estate tax ideas so as to obtain the most favorable tax treatment in real estate transactions." Alerts readers to important legislative, regulatory, and tax developments affecting real estate taxation and outlines legitimate techniques of tax avoidance. *Type:* Newsletter.

Real Estate Today

National Association of Realtors
430 N. Michigan Ave. Ph: (312)329-8458
Chicago, IL 60611-4087 Free: 800-374-6500
 Fax: (312)329-5978

Contact: Maureen Glass, Publisher.

Desc: Applications-oriented magazine featuring how-to approach to aspects of residential real estate sales, brokerage management, and commercial real estate. *Type:* Periodical.

Realtor News

National Association of Realtors
700 11th St. NW Ph: (202)383-1193
Washington, DC 20001-4507 Fax: (202)383-1231
E-mail: narpubs.nar@notes.compuserve.com

Contact: Marjorie Green, Publisher; William Adkinson, Publisher.

Desc: Real estate magazine *Type:* Periodical.

Realtors Land Institute Newsletter

Realtors Land Institute
430 N. Michigan Ave. Ph: (312)329-8440
Chicago, IL 60611 Free: 800-441-LAND
 Fax: (312)329-8633
E-mail: rli@realtors.org
URL: http://www.rliland.com.

Contact: Belinda Carter, Editor, belindarli@aol.com.

Desc: Contains articles of interest to realtors dealing with farm and land real estate. Recurring features include news of the Institute and tax information. *Type:* Newsletter.

The Recruiting Pipeline

The Recruiting Network, Inc.
PO Box 68366 Ph: (847)524-8487
Schaumburg, IL 60168-0366 Free: 800-562-6593
E-mail: rpipeline@aol.com

Contact: Carol W. Johnson, Editor, (847)356-9601, fax: (847)524-9926, carolwj@aol.com.

Desc: Dedicated "to providing the latest and most accurate recruiting and retention information available in the real estate industry." Recurring features include news of research and column titled Carol's Corner. *Type:* Newsletter.

Residential Sales Council

430 N. Michigan Ave., Ste. 300 Ph: (312)321-4400
Chicago, IL 60611 Fax: (312)329-8886
E-mail: info@rscouncil.com
URL: http://www.rscouncil.com

Contact: Nina Cottrell, Exec.VP.

Desc: A council of the Realtors National Marketing Institute. To enhance the professional competence of those engaged in residential real estate sales. Conducts courses and seminars; awards Certified Residential Specialist designation. *Type:* Association.

Resolution Trust Reporter

Dorset Group, Inc.
11 Penn Plaza Fax: (212)695-8172
New York, NY 10001

Contact: John Gynn, Publisher; Stan Strachan, Editor; Stephan Potter, Production Mgr.; Brian Quasitrock, Advertising Dir.; Ralph Wegs, Promotions Dir.

Desc: Monitors the activities of the Resolution Trust Corporation, especially on assets, thrifts, and real estate. *Type:* Newsletter.

SHARE: Building a New El Salvador Today

PO Box 192825 Ph: (415)882-1530
San Francisco, CA 94119 Fax: (415)882-1540
E-mail: share@igc.apc.org
URL: http://www.igc.org/share/

Contact: Jose Artiga, Exec.Dir.

Desc: Individuals, churches, religious orders, Central American refugee groups, and other organizations concerned about the effects of the conflict in El Salvador on its people. Provides moral and financial support and technical assistance to rural and urban poor of El Salvador. Emphasizes community development and self-sufficiency. *Type:* Association.

SNL REIT Weekly

SNL Securities
321 E. Main St. Ph: (804)977-1600
PO Box 2124 Fax: (804)977-4466
Charlottesville, VA 22902
E-mail: subscriptions@snl.com; feedback@snl.com.
URL: http://www.snl.com.

Contact: Keith E. Pomroy, Editor, (804)977-1888, fax: (804)984-8030, kpomroy@snl.

Desc: Communicates by fax the previous week's activity involving REITs. Includes comprehensive articles on current industry trends, condensed news stories, recent capital offerings and the latest market information. *Type:* Newsletter.

Society of Industrial and Office Realtors

700 11th St. NW, Ste. 510 Ph: (202)737-1150
Washington, DC 20001-4511 Fax: (202)737-8796

Contact: Pam Hinton, Sr. VP.

Desc: Real estate brokers specializing in industrial and office properties; representatives of railroads, utilities, financial institutions, corporations, and industrial park developments. Conducts studies of special problems of industrial development, development of sale-lease back techniques, surveys of plants or site locations, and availability. *Type:* Association.

Tennessee Realtor

Tennessee Association of Realtors
1910 Adelicia St. Ph: (615)321-0515
PO Box 121149 Fax: (615)320-0452
Nashville, TN 37212-1149

Contact: Stephen Harding, Editor.

Desc: Provides news of interest on real estate. *Type:* Newsletter.

Tierra Grande

Real Estate Center
Texas A&M University
College Station, TX 77843-2115 Ph: (409)845-2031
 Free: 800-244-2144
 Fax: (409)845-0460
E-mail: info@recenter.tamu.edu
URL: http://recenter.tamu.edu.

Contact: David S. Jones, Editor, (409)845-0369, djones@recenter.tamu.edu.

Desc: Journal covering real estate research. *Type:* Periodical.

Today's Realtor

National Association of Realtors
700 11th St. NW Ph: (202)383-1193
Washington, DC 20001-4507 Fax: (202)383-1231
E-mail: narpubs.nar@notes.compuserve.com
URL: http://www.judds.com/tr.htm.

Contact: Pamela Geurds Kabati, Editorial Dir.; Annette Cohen, Publisher.

Desc: Real estate magazine. *Type:* Periodical.

Urban Land Institute

1025 Thomas Jefferson St. NW, Ph: (202)624-7000
 Ste. 500W Free: 800-321-5011
Washington, DC 20007-5201 Fax: (202)624-7140
E-mail: joinuli@uli.org
URL: http://www.uli.org

Contact: Joseph C. Canizaro, Pres.

Desc: Real estate developers, planners, architects, engineers, academicians, government officials and financiers. Encourages effective urban planning and development through research and education. *Type:* Association.

Vacation Ownership Council

Desc: A membership council of the American Resort and Residential Development Association. Developers of time-sharing resorts and professionals who provide goods or services to developers. Conducts public relations campaign to educate consumers, financial institutions, regulators, legislators, real estate brokers, travel agents, and other industries on the advantages of timesharing. *Type:* Association.

Valuation Insights & Perspectives

Appraisal Institute
875 N. Michigan Ave., Ste.   Ph: (312)335-4100
  2400   Fax: (312)335-4400
Chicago, IL 60611-1980
Contact: Debbie Katz, Editor.
Desc: Covers current news and trends in the real estate appraisal field. *Type:* Newsletter.

The Voice

Metropolitan Indianapolis Board of Realtors, Inc.
1912 N. Meridian St.   Ph: (317)956-1912
Indianapolis, IN 46202   Fax: (317)956-5050
E-mail: thevoice@mibor.net.
Contact: Leslie Haney, Editor.
Desc: Discusses topics that relate to the real estate industry. Covers financial news, political decisions, educational seminars, local topics of concern, national member recognition, and community involvement. *Type:* Newsletter.

Washington Office Guide & Buildout Directory

Real Estate Washington, Inc.
1400 I St., NW, Ste. 400   Ph: (202)789-8889
Washington, DC 20007   Free: (202)789-4147
Contact: Michael Pretzer, Editor.
Desc: List of about 1,800 office buildings in Washington, D.C. area that have space available. *Type:* Directory.

WCR Communique

Women's Council of Realtors (WCR)
National Association of Realtors
430 N. Michigan Ave.   Ph: (312)329-8483
Chicago, IL 60611   Fax: (312)329-3290
Contact: Gwen Dillman, Editor.
Desc: Carries articles on personal and career growth topics relating to women in real estate. Includes council news. *Type:* Newsletter.

WESTLAW® Real Property Library

West Group
620 Opperman Dr.   Ph: (651)687-7000
St. Paul, MN 55164-0526
URL: http://www.westgroup.com
Desc: Contains the complete text of U.S. state court decisions from all 50 states and the District of Columbia and related legal sources, law reviews, texts, and bar association journals dealing with property rights and real estate transactions and such related topics as condominium and cooperative ownership, eminent domain, estates in real property, and restrictive covenants. *Available:* West Group, WESTLAW. *Type:* Database.

Women's Council of Realtors

430 N. Michigan Ave.   Ph: (312)329-8483
Chicago, IL 60611   Fax: (312)329-3290
E-mail: wcr@wcr.org
URL: http://www.wcr.org
Desc: Women and men real estate brokers and salespeople. Provides opportunity for real estate professionals to participate at local, state, and national levels. Makes programs available for personal and career growth. *Type:* Association.

Recreation

American Association for Nude Recreation

1703 N. Main St.   Ph: (407)933-2064
Kissimmee, FL 34744   Free: 800-879-6833
                                  Fax: (407)933-7577
E-mail: aanr@magicnet.net
Contact: Roslyn Scheer, Exec.Dir.
Desc: Mission Statement: Promote, enhance and protect, in appropriate settings, nude recreation and nude living in the Americas. *Type:* Association.

Auctioneer—Directory Issue

National Auctioneers Association
8880 Ballentine   Ph: (913)541-8084
Overland Park, KS 66214   Fax: (913)894-5281
E-mail: naahq@aol.com
Contact: Holly Neuman, Editor, naahqholly@aol.com.
Desc: List of about 6,000 auctioneers. *Type:* Directory.

Club Med

PO Box 347258   Ph: (305)925-9000
Coral Gables, FL 33234-7258   Free: 800-CLUB-
                                       MED
                                  Fax: (305)443-0562
Contact: Kamal Shah, Pres.
Desc: Based in Paris, France, the club maintains more than 120 low-cost vacation villages in 35 countries on 5 continents. *Type:* Association.

Directory of North American Fairs, Festivals, and Expositions

Amusement Business
PO Box 24970   Ph: (615)321-4250
Nashville, TN 37202   Free: 800-999-3322
                                  Fax: (615)327-1575
URL: http://www.amusementbusiness.com; http://www.
amusementbusiness.com.
Contact: Karen Oertley, Editor.
Desc: Almost 5,000 state and county fairs, festivals, and public expositions that run three days or longer; coverage includes Canada. *Type:* Directory.

Georgia National Fair

Georgia Natl. Fairgrounds and Agricenter
401 Larry Walker Pkwy.   Ph: (912)987-3247
PO Box 1367   Fax: (912)987-7218
Perry, GA 31069-1367
E-mail: mtreptow@alltel.com
URL: http://GNFA.com
Contact: Michael A. Froehlich, Exec.Dir.
Type: Association.

Hostelling International-American Youth Hostels

733 15th St. NW, No. 840   Ph: (202)783-6161
Washington, DC 20005   Fax: (202)783-6171
E-mail: hiayhserv@hiayh.org
URL: http://www.hiayh.org .
Contact: Richard Martyr, Ph.D., Exec.Dir.
Desc: Provides inexpensive, educational, and environmentally respectful travel opportunities for all ages, especially for youth; promotes appreciation for cultural values of all societies. *Type:* Association.

International Amusement Industry Buyers Guide

Amusement Business
PO Box 24970   Ph: (615)321-4250
Nashville, TN 37202   Free: 800-999-3322
                                  Fax: (615)327-1575
URL: http://www.amusementbusiness.com; http://www.
amusementbusiness.com.
Contact: Karen Oertley, Editor.

Desc: Manufacturers, importers, and suppliers of amusement rides, games, and merchandise as well as food and drink equipment and supplies. *Type:* Directory.

International Association of Amusement Parks and Attractions—International Directory and Buyer's Guide

International Association of Amusement Parks and Attractions (IAAPA)
1448 Duke St.   Ph: (703)836-4800
Alexandria, VA 22314   Fax: (703)836-4801
URL: http://www.iaapa.org.
Contact: Bill Stevenson, Publisher, bstevens@iaapa.org.
Desc: Over 1,800 member amusement parks and attractions; 3,600 suppliers of products and services to the amusement industry; over 600 individuals and concessionaires; international coverage. *Type:* Directory.

International Association of Fairs and Expositions

PO Box 985   Ph: (417)862-5771
Springfield, MO 65801   Free: 800-516-0313
                                  Fax: (417)862-0156
E-mail: iafg@iafenet.org
Contact: Lewis Miller, Exec.VP.
Desc: State associations of fairs representing 3200 state, district, and county agricultural fairs. Membership also includes 1300 individual fairs. *Type:* Association.

Iowa State Fair

Statehouse   Ph: (515)262-3111
Des Moines, IA 50319   Free: 800-545-FAIR
                                  Fax: (515)262-6906
URL: http://www.iowastatefair.org
Contact: Marion Lucas, Gen.Mgr.
Type: Association.

Leisure Industry Report

Leisure Industry/Recreation News
PO Box 43563   Ph: (202)232-7107
Washington, DC 20010-9563
Contact: Marj Jensen, Editor.
Desc: Reports on trends and the outlook for leisure and discretionary spending in such markets as travel, music, theater, sports, gaming, advertising and publishing, television and movies, and theme parks. *Type:* Newsletter.

Massachusetts Association for Recreation and Employee Services

214 Rocky Hill Rd   Ph: (508)252-4197
Rehoboth, MA 02769   Fax: (508)252-4199
E-mail: maresadmin@aol.com
URL: http://www.mares.org
Contact: Debby Casna, Pres.
Desc: Companies in Massachusetts and throughout New England. Promotes improved recreation and employee service programs and activities. *Type:* Association.

National Employee Services and Recreation Association—Keynotes

National Employee Services and Recreation Association
2211 York Rd., Ste. 207   Ph: (630)368-1280
Oak Brook, IL 60523-2371   Fax: (630)368-1286
E-mail: nesrahq@nesra.org
Contact: Renee M. Mula, Editor, reneemula@nesra.org.
Desc: Provides programming and administration ideas for employee services and recreation managers. Recurring features include new techniques, survey findings, news briefs, management tips, programming ideas, and Association news. *Type:* Newsletter.

National Recreation and Park Association

22377 Belmont Ridge Rd.　　Ph: (703)820-4940
Ashburn, VA 20148　　　　　Free: 800-626-6772
　　　　　　　　　　　　　　Fax: (703)671-6772

Contact: R. Dean Tice, Exec.Dir.

Desc: Public interest organization dedicated to improving the human environment through improved park, recreation, and leisure opportunities. Activities include: programs for the development and upgrading of professional and citizen leadership in the park, recreation, and leisure field; dissemination of innovations and research results; technical assistance to affiliated organizations, local communities, and members; providing information on public policy; public education; extensive publications program. Maintains 3000 volume library. *Type:* Association.

National Spa and Pool Institute

2111 Eisenhower Ave.　　Ph: (703)838-0083
Alexandria, VA 22314　　Fax: (703)549-0493
E-mail: rgalvin@nspi.org
URL: http://www.nspi.org

Contact: Roger Galvin, CEO.

Desc: Builders, dealers, designers, service companies, retail stores, engineers, manufacturers, distributors, public officials, suppliers, and service persons concerned with public and residential swimming pools, spas, and hot tubs. Goals are to: raise spa and pool industry standards; expand interest and use of swimming pools, spas, and hot tubs; achieve uniformity in federal, state, and local regulations affecting swimming pool, spa, and hot tub operations. *Type:* Association.

The Naturist Society

PO Box 132　　　　　　Ph: (920)426-5009
Oshkosh, WI 54902　　Fax: (920)426-5184
E-mail: naturist@naturist.com
URL: http://www.naturist.com

Contact: Lee Baxandall, Pres.

Desc: Provides communication and coordination for the clothes-optional recreation movement as a natural solution to many problems of modern living. Maintains "body acceptance is the idea, nude recreation is the way". Conducts research programs, speakers' bureau, and specialized education. *Type:* Association.

Premier Dining

Cendant
Comp-U-Card Division
40 Oakview Dr.　　　Ph: (203)365-2000
Trumbull, CT 06611
URL: http://www.cendant.com

Contact: Lew Bednarczuk, Product Manager, Interactive Services.

Desc: Contains descriptions and discount offers for more than 10,000 restaurants in more than 45 major U.S. cities. *Available:* Prodigy Services Company, PRODIGY; CompuServe Information Service; America Online, Inc. *Type:* Database.

Recreation Resources—Buyer's Guide Issue

Adams/Recreation Publishing, Inc.
2101 S Arlington Heights Rd.,
　　No. 150
Arlington Heights, IL 60005-
　　4142

Contact: Galynn Nordstrom, Editor.

Desc: Directory of 1,000 suppliers of products and services to the managed recreation industry, including manufacturers of sports equipment, clothing, park and playground equipment, pool chemicals, etc. *Type:* Directory.

Roller Coasters: An Illustrated Guide to the Rides in the United States and Canada

McFarland & Co., Inc., Publishers
960 Hwy. 88 W　　　Ph: (336)246-4460
Box 611　　　　　　Free: 800-253-2187
Jefferson, NC 28640　Fax: (336)246-5018
E-mail: mcfarland@skybest.com
URL: http://www.mcfarlandpub.com

Contact: Todd H. Throgmorton, Editor.

Desc: About 200 roller coasters in the U.S. and Canada. *Type:* Directory.

RSA Today

Roller Skating Association
6905 Corporate Dr.　　　Ph: (317)875-3390
Indianapolis, IN 46278-1927
E-mail: rsa@oninternet.com

Contact: Susan Davis, Editor; Tina Massa, Editor.

Desc: Focuses on the concerns of commercial roller skating rink operators. "Zeros in on rink problems and advice, news, music, promotions, legal issues." Carries Association news, notes on insurance and purchasing programs, reprints, and convention information. *Type:* Newsletter.

RWorld

The Orange County Register
625 N. Grand Ave.　　　Ph: (714)835-1234
Santa Ana, CA 92701
E-mail: ocregister@link.freedom.com
URL: http://www.ocregister.com/

Desc: The OCRegister.com online newspaper boasts a marvelous computer section called Connect, which is part of the Sunday print version. There are also personals ads, news, and features. *Type:* Database.

Tenting Directory

Woodall Publishing Co.
13975 W. Polo Trail Dr.　　Ph: (847)362-6700
Lake Forest, IL 60045-5000　Free: 800-323-9076
　　　　　　　　　　　　　　Fax: (847)362-8776
E-mail: emd@woodallpub.com
URL: http://www.woodalls.com; http://www.woodalls.com.

Contact: Deborah Spriggs, Publisher.

Desc: Campgrounds in the U.S. and Canada that have tent sites and tent rentals. *Type:* Directory.

Workamper News

Debbie Robus
201 Hiram Rd.　　　　Ph: (501)362-2637
Heber Springs, AR 72543
E-mail: workamper@arkansas.net.

Contact: Greg Robus, Editor.

Desc: Provides a list of information on seasonal and full-time job openings at campgrounds, forests, and public and private resort areas. *Type:* Newsletter.

Recreational Vehicles

Blue Ribbon Coalition

1540 N Arthur Ave.　　　Ph: (208)233-6570
Pocatello, ID 83202　　　Free: 800-BLUE-RIB
　　　　　　　　　　　　　Fax: (208)233-8906
E-mail: brclark@sharetrails.org
URL: http://www.sharetrails.org

Contact: Clark L. Collins, Exec.Dir.

Desc: Individuals and organizations involved in off highway recreation such as snowmobiles, motorcycles, mountain bikes, and ATVs, hiking, equestrian riders, 4x4's, skiers and boaters; small business owners and recreation organizations. Seeks to preserve access for off highway recreation; promotes conservation of natural resources; encourages cooperation among members and government land managers. *Type:* Association.

Escapees

c/o Joe Peterson　　　Ph: (409)327-8873
100 Rainbow Dr.　　　Free: 888-757-2582
Livingston, TX 77351　Fax: (409)327-4388
E-mail: club.business@mail.escapees.com
URL: http://www.escapees.com

Contact: Joe Peterson, Founder & Pres.

Desc: Support network for RVers who travel for extensive periods. *Type:* Association.

Family Motor Coach Association

8291 Clough Pike　　　Free: 800-543-3622
Cincinnati, OH 45244　Fax: (513)474-2332

Contact: Charlie Atkinson, Pres.

Desc: Owners of motor homes used for recreation, travel, and camping. Qualifying vehicles must be self-propelled and self-contained, including all the conveniences of a home (cooking, sleeping, and sanitary facilities), and in which the driver's seat is accessible in a walking position from the living quarters. Aids local chapters and members with information on safety, product analysis, special activities, and news of other members. *Type:* Association.

Good Sam Recreational Vehicle Club

2575 Vista Del Mar　　Ph: (805)667-4100
Ventura, CA 93001　　Free: 800-765-6080
　　　　　　　　　　　Fax: (805)667-4454

E-mail: goodsam@tl.com
URL: http://www.goodsamclub.com/

Contact: Susan Bray, Exec.Dir.

Desc: Recreational vehicle enthusiasts who act as "Good Samaritans" on the road by aiding members in distress. Offers free benefits to members, including credit card loss protection, trip routing service, and mail forwarding. Provides comprehensive discount programs on camping fees, RV financing and insurance, tour programs, emergency road service and magazine subscriptions for members. *Type:* Association.

Holiday Rambler Recreational Vehicle Club

PO Box 587　　　　　Ph: (219)862-7330
Wakarusa, IN 46573　Fax: (219)862-7390

Contact: Paul Barbour, C.O.O.

Desc: Owners of recreational vehicles manufactured by Holiday Rambler Corp. Sponsors social and recreational activities such as rallies, caravans, and tour groups. Offers a scholarship program and children's services; sponsor competitions. *Type:* Association.

Wally Byam Caravan Club International

803 E. Pike St.　　　　Ph: (937)596-5211
Jackson Center, OH 45334　Fax: (937)596-5542

Contact: Cindy Reed, Dir.

Desc: Owners of classic Airstream travel trailers and motor homes. Objectives are to: provide a satisfying and meaningful travel experience; promote international goodwill; encourage development of outdoor recreational vehicle facilities. Maintains code of ethics for trailer traveling; sponsors unit, regional, national, and international rallies. *Type:* Association.

Winnebago-Itasca Travelers

PO Box 268　　　　　Ph: (515)582-6874
Forest City, IA 50436　Free: 800-643-4892
　　　　　　　　　　　Fax: (515)582-6703
E-mail: wit@winnebagoind.com
URL: http://www.winnebagoind.com

Contact: Mike Anderson, Gen.Mgr.

Desc: Owners of recreational vehicles manufactured by Winnebago Industries, Inc. United for the mutual enjoyment of their vehicles, travel opportunities, new friendships, and activities. Conducts caravans; operates store. *Type:* Association.

Refugees

American Near East Refugee Aid

1522 K St. NW, Ste. 202   Ph: (202)347-2558
Washington, DC 20005   Fax: (202)682-1637
E-mail: anera@anera.org

Contact: Dr. Peter Gubser, Pres.

Desc: Organizations associated with economic development and refugee relief; interested individuals. Established to provide assistance to Palestinian refugees, Lebanese, and other needy individuals in the Middle East and to further American understanding of the Middle East. Sponsors rural and urban development projects through local institutions, and social projects in health and education; helps support agricultural cooperatives; provides donations of medical supplies; offers scholarship program; helps to provide education and skills training for Palestinian children; sponsors literacy classes and job-training programs for adults. *Type:* Association.

American Refugee Committee

2344 Nicollet Ave. S., Ste. 350   Ph: (612)872-7060
Minneapolis, MN 55404-3305   Fax: (612)872-4309
E-mail: archq@archq.org
URL: http://www.interaction.org

Contact: Liz Menapace, Recruitment Asst.

Desc: Works for the survival, health and well-being of refugees, displaced persons and those at risk. ARC staff and volunteers, provide primary health care, training and other health related services to more than one million people in Asia, Africa, Europe, and Central America. *Type:* Association.

International Rescue Committee

122 E. 42nd St.   Ph: (212)551-3000
New York, NY 10168   Fax: (212)551-3180
E-mail: bode@intrescom.org

Contact: Renold Levy, Pres.

Desc: Nonsectarian, nonpartisan, voluntary agency founded by Albert Einstein and supported by individuals, foundations, corporations, unions, and civic, educational, human rights, and community groups. Assists refugee victims of religious, political, and racial persecution, civil strife, famine, and war. Current programs are located in Africa, Asia, Central America, Europe, North America, and the Middle East. *Type:* Association.

Lutheran Immigration and Refugee Service

390 Park Ave. S, 7th Fl.   Ph: (212)532-6350
New York, NY 10016-8803   Fax: (212)683-1329

Contact: Ralston H. Deffenbaugh, Jr., Dir.

Desc: Acts as advocate for immigrants and refugees; trains and encourages Lutheran groups in advocacy processes. *Type:* Association.

United States Committee for Refugees

1717 Massachusetts Ave. NW,   Ph: (202)347-3507
Ste. 200   Fax: (202)347-3418
Washington, DC 20036
E-mail: uscr@irsa-uscr.org
URL: http://www.refugees.org

Contact: Roger P. Winter, Dir.

Desc: Serves as an information and advocacy center seeking to communicate the plight of the world's millions of refugees to the American people and to provide a nongovernmental focal point for humanitarian concern in meeting the needs of a changing world refugee situation. Consults with national and international leaders. Maintains close liaison with voluntary organizations and supports specialized UN agencies working to alleviate refugee problems. *Type:* Association.

Rehabilitation

The AAF Newsletter

American Amputee Foundation
PO Box 250218   Ph: (501)666-2523
Hillcrest Sta.   Fax: (501)666-8367
Little Rock, AR 72225

Contact: C.J. McCaleb, Editor.

Desc: Communicates information on health issues and events for Foundation members. Covers rehabilitation, counseling, product information, and financial assistance. *Type:* Newsletter.

ABLEDATA

U.S. National Institute on Disability and Rehabilitation Research (NIDRR)
ABLEDATA
8455 Colesville Rd., Ste. 935   Ph: (301)608-8998
Silver Spring, MD 20910-3319
E-mail: abledata@macroint.com
URL: http://www.abledata.com

Contact: Katherine Belknap, Assistant Project Director, (301)589-8998, fax: (301)608-8958, abledata@macroint.com.

Desc: Contains descriptions of more than 24,000 products and equipment made available by nearly 3000 manufacturers for use by persons with disabilities. Covers rehabilitative aids and equipment for personal care, home management, mobility, communication, therapeutic, sensory, educational, vocational, and transportation needs. *Available:* U.S. National Institute on Disability and Rehabilitation Research (NIDRR), ABLEDATA. *Type:* Database.

Alamo Institute of Research

8122 Datapoint, Ste. 1200   Ph: (210)696-8534
San Antonio, TX 78229   Fax: (210)614-7270

Contact: James W. Simmons, MD, Dir.

Desc: Sports medicine and rehabilitation. Conducts cooperative research in the area of human performance measurement for therapy and rehabilitation, and clinical and surgical studies for the spine and musculoskeletal system. *Type:* Research center.

American Academy of Physical Medicine and Rehabilitation

1 IBM Plz., Ste. 2500   Ph: (312)464-9700
Chicago, IL 60611-3604   Fax: (312)464-0227
E-mail: aapmr1@aapmr.org
URL: http://www.aapmr.org

Contact: Ronald A. Henrichs, CAE, Exec.Dir.

Desc: National medical specialty society of physical medicine and rehabilitation physicians whose patients include people with physical disabilities and chronic, disabling illnesses. Mission is to maximize quality of life, minimize the incidence and prevalence of impairments, disability, and handicaps, promote societal health, and enhance the understanding and development of physiatry. *Type:* Association.

American Therapeutic Recreation Association

1414 Prince St., Ste. 204   Ph: (703)683-9420
Alexandria, VA 22314   Fax: (703)683-9431
E-mail: national@atra-tr.org
URL: http://www.atra-tr.org

Contact: Ann D. Huston, Exec.Dir.

Desc: Therapeutic recreation professionals and students; interested others. (Therapeutic recreation is often referred to as recreational therapy and uses treatment modalities to improve the physical, mental, and emotional functions of persons with illnesses or disabling conditions.). Promotes the use of therapeutic recreation in hospitals, mental rehabilitation centers, physical rehabilitation centers, senior citizen treatment centers, and other public health facilities. *Type:* Association.

CARF, The Rehabilitation Accreditation Commission

4891 E. Grant Rd.   Ph: (520)325-1044
Tucson, AZ 85712   Fax: (520)318-1129
E-mail: webmaster@carf.org
URL: http://www.carf.org

Contact: Donald E. Galvin, PhD, Pres./CEO.

Desc: Sponsored by rehabilitation organizations. The commission is the standard setting and accrediting authority for organizations providing rehabilitation services. Encourages development and improvement of uniformly high standards of performance for all organizations serving individuals with developmental, physical, or emotional disabilities. *Type:* Association.

Courage News

Courage Center
3915 Golden Valley Rd.   Ph: (612)520-0520
Golden Valley, MN 55422   Fax: (612)520-0355

Contact: Katie Knips, Editor.

Desc: Publishes news of Courage Center, a nonprofit organization providing rehabilitation and independent living services for people with physical disabilities and speech, hearing, and vision impairments. Recurring features include profiles of clients, donors, volunteers, programs and services offered by Courage Center, and up coming events. *Type:* Newsletter.

Directory of Medical Rehabilitation Facilities

HCIA Inc.
300 E. Lombard St., Ste. 1700   Ph: (410)576-9600
Baltimore, MD 21202
E-mail: info@hcia.com
URL: http://www2.hcia.com

Contact: Shawn Nocher, Project Manager/Writer, snoch@hcia.com.

Desc: Provides information on more than 1800 physical rehabilitation facilities and programs in the United States for persons disabled due to injury or debilitating disease. Covers programs offered by hospital-sponsored rehabilitation departments, private hospitals, and free-standing clinics. *Type:* Database.

ICD - International Center for the Disabled

340 E. 24th St.   Ph: (212)679-0100
New York, NY 10010

Contact: John B. Wingate, Exec.Dir.

Desc: Not an association. Outpatient rehabilitation center for persons with physical and combined physical and emotional disabilities. Services include: medical diagnostic/evaluation and treatment; occupational therapy; physical therapy; sensory feedback therapy; behavioral medicine; speech and hearing therapy; vocational evaluation; job training and placement; outpatient chemical dependency services; special programs for the confused and disoriented elderly and head-injured adolescent and adults. *Type:* Association.

The Institute for Rehabilitation and Research

1333 Moursund Ave.   Ph: (713)799-5000
Houston, TX 77030   Fax: (713)799-7095
URL: http://www.tirr.org

Contact: Louisa F. Adelung, Pres.

Desc: Clinical neurophysiologic, neuroendocrinologic, psychoccologic, and exercise tolerance studies of patients with severe spinal cord injuries; development and assessment of mechanical and electronic assistive devices for neurologically impaired individuals; research and technical developments concerned with the effects of pressure on human tissue; provision of personal assistance for persons with severe physical disabilities; and program evaluations to improve services for persons with head injury, amputation, or spinal cord injury. *Type:* Research center.

Jimmie Heuga Center

PO Box 491   Ph: (970)926-1290
27 Main St., Ste. 303   Free: 800-367-3101
Edwards, CO 81632-0491   Fax: (970)926-1295
Contact: Richard W. Hicks, PhD, Dir., Res. & Educ.
Desc: Conducts and coordinates studies aimed at improving the quality of life for those with multiple sclerosis (MS) and other potentially debilitating neurological disorders. Focuses on the effects of goal-oriented exercise on the fitness of those with MS. *Type:* Research center.

Kennedy Krieger Research Institute

707 N. Broadway   Ph: (410)502-9483
Baltimore, MD 21205   Fax: (410)502-9524
E-mail: goldstein@kennedykrieger.org
URL: http://www.kennedykrieger.org
Contact: Dr. Gary W. Goldstein, Pres.
Desc: Pediatric rehabilitation evaluation, treatment, and research, including interdisciplinary studies in genetics, biochemistry, toxicology, neurochemistry, metabolic diseases, speech and hearing, pharmacology, behavioral sciences, and special education. Major emphasis is placed on physical rehabilitation, effectiveness of drug support, behavior modification, evaluation of neurological disorders in children, and developing and testing training techniques. *Type:* Research center.

Louisiana Tech University

Center for Biomedical Engineering and Rehabilitation Science

PO Box 3185   Ph: (318)257-4562
Ruston, LA 71272   Fax: (318)255-4175
E-mail: phale@coes.latech.edu
URL: http://www.latech.edu
Contact: Dr. Paul N. Hale, Jr., Dir.
Desc: Studies conditions leading to disabilities (systems physiology), develops and applies technology to assist disabled people, and develops expert systems in systems physiology and rehabilitation services. *Type:* Research center.

Massachusetts Institute of Technology

Eric P. and Evelyn E. Newman Laboratory for Biomechanics and Human Rehabilitation

77 Massachusetts Ave., Rm.   Ph: (617)253-2277
   3-146   Fax: (617)258-7018
Cambridge, MA 02139
E-mail: neville@mit.edu
Contact: Prof. Neville Hogan, Contact.
Desc: Amputation prostheses, normal and pathological human neuromuscular systems, and diagnosis and therapy of muscular, skeletal, and joint malfunctions using an engineering approach. Studies include cybernetic limb and sensory prostheses, mobility aids for the blind, suppression of tremor, functional electrical stimulation, instrumentation for and kinematic studies of human movement, synovial joint mechanics, pathogenesis of osteoarthritis, biomechanics of the hip, knee, and ankle, musculoskeletal models for pathological diagnosis, and computer-aided surgical simulation. *Type:* Research center.

McGill University

Centre for the Study of Host Resistance

Montreal General Hospital   Ph: (514)934-8038
1650 Cedar Ave., Rm. A-6149   Fax: (514)933-7146
Montreal, PQ, Canada H3G
   1A4
E-mail: md88@musica.mcgill.ca
Contact: Dr. Emil Skamere, Dir.
Desc: Genetic regulation of host susceptibility and resistance in diseases of adulthood, including cancer, tuberculosis, malaria, and other infectious diseases. *Type:* Research center.

National Institute for Rehabilitation Engineering

Box T   Ph: (973)853-6585
Hewitt, NJ 07421   Free: 800-736-2216
E-mail: dons@warwick.net
URL: http://www.members.warwick.net/nire
Contact: Donald Selwyn, Dir.
Desc: Invention, design, construction, fitting, and servicing of special devices for individuals with any specific physical disability or combination of disabilities; time/motion analyses; job modification engineering; task-performance mobility; driver training; computer software adapted for people with handicapping conditions. *Type:* Research center.

National Rehabilitation Association

633 S. Washington St.   Ph: (703)836-0850
Alexandria, VA 22314   Fax: (703)836-0848
E-mail: info@nationalrehab.org
Contact: Michelle Vaughan, Exec.Dir.
Desc: Mission is providing opportunities through knowledge and diversity for professionals in the fields of rehabilitation of people with disabilities. *Type:* Association.

New York University

Medical Rehabilitation Research and Training Center

400 E. 34th St.   Ph: (212)998-4636
New York, NY 10016   Fax: (212)263-8815
E-mail: Mathew.Lee@mcrks.med.nyu.edu
Contact: Dr. Mathew Lee, Actg.Chm.
Desc: Rehabilitation for brain trauma and stroke victims and comprehensive management of neuromuscular disease. Seeks to identify and validate specific treatment modalities applied to persons disabled by neuromuscular disorders, develop and improve new and existing treatment modalities, and quantify and standardize methods of evaluating disease activity and remission. *Type:* Research center.

Newsletter of the Rehabilitation Research and Training Center at Virginia Commonwealth University

Rehabilitation Research and Training Center on Supported Employment
PO Box 842011   Ph: (804)828-1851
Richmond, VA 23284-2011   Fax: (804)828-2193
E-mail: tcblanke@saturn.vcu.edu.
URL: http://www.vcu.edu/rrtcweb.
Contact: Katherine J. Inge, Editor.
Desc: Reports on "the supported employment of people with developmental and other disabilities." Publishes original research, new resources, and human interest features. *Type:* Newsletter.

Oregon Stroke Association Newsletter

Oregon Stroke Association
1015 NW 22nd Ave.   Ph: (503)229-7124
Portland, OR 97210-5198   Free: 800-780-8996
Contact: Betty Hooter, Editor.
Desc: Disseminates information on the causes of strokes and recovery; provides news of Club gatherings. Recurring features include a calendar of events and a column titled Stroke Clubs in Oregon. *Type:* Newsletter.

Packard Children's Hospital at Stanford

Rehabilitation Engineering Center

1010 Corporation Way   Ph: (650)237-9200
Palo Alto, CA 94304   Fax: (650)919-1486
E-mail: re.nzo@LPch.stanford.edu
URL: http://www-med.stanford.edu/lpch/rec/
Contact: Hugh O'Neill, Actg. Dir.
Desc: Rehabilitation technology, emphasizing speech aids, prosthetics, orthotics, seating, mobility, and worksite accommodation for people with disabilities. *Type:* Research center.

Physical Therapy Reimbursement News

American Physical Therapy Association
1111 N. Fairfax St.   Ph: (703)684-2782
Alexandria, VA 22314   Free: 800-999-2782
           Fax: (703)703-3169
Contact: Jim Nugent, Editor.
Desc: Tracks reimbursement trends in the medical field of physical therapy. *Type:* Newsletter.

Rancho Rehabilitation Engineering Program

Los Amigos Research &   Ph: (562)401-7994
   Education Institute, Inc.   Fax: (562)803-6117
Bonita Hall
7503 Bonita St.
Downey, CA 90242
E-mail: mcneal@hsc.usc.edu
URL: http://www.ranchorep.org
Contact: Don McNeal, PhD, Dir.
Desc: Develops appropriate technology and assessment procedures in the field of orthopedic rehabilitation and assures their availability to children with physical disabilities. Other projects include identifying the changing needs for worksite accommodation as employees with disabilities grow older. *Type:* Research center.

Rehab Continuum Report

American Health Consultants, Inc.
3525 Piedmont Rd., Bldg. 6,   Ph: (404)262-7436
   Ste. 400   Free: 800-688-2421
Atlanta, GA 30305   Fax: (404)262-7837
E-mail: customerservice@ahcpub.com
Contact: Francine Wilson, Editor, (404)231-0618; Valerie Loner, Managing Editor.
Desc: Offers practical guidance and case studies on the successful management of rehabilitation programs. Includes articles on maximizing reimbursement from all sources; staying ahead of proposed policy changes; planning for and complying with agency standards such as Commission on Accreditation of Rehabilitation Facilities (CARF), Health Care Financing Administration (HCFA), and the Joint Commission; ensuring coordinated and quality patient care; and procudures on administrative matters. *Type:* Newsletter.

REHABDATA

U.S. National Institute on Disability and Rehabilitation Research (NIDRR)
National Rehabilitation Information Center (NARIC)
8455 Colesville Rd., Suite 935   Ph: (301)588-9284
Silver Spring, MD 20910-3319
URL: http://www.naric.com/naric
Contact: Bill Schutz, Manager, Public Inquiries.
Desc: Contains more than 50,000 citations and abstracts to both print and audiovisual materials relating to the rehabilitation of persons with physical or mental disabilities. Includes reports from projects funded by the National Institute of Disability and Rehabilitation Research (NIDRR) and the Rehabilitation Services Administration (RSA), as well as journal articles, audiovisual materials, directories, and commercial publications. *Available:* U.S. National Institute on Disability and Rehabilitation Research (NIDRR), ABLEDATA; National Rehabilitation Information Center (NARIC). *Type:* Database.

Rehabilitation Institute of Chicago

345 E. Superior, Ste. 1406   Ph: (312)908-3381
Chicago, IL 60611   Fax: (312)908-2208
E-mail: zevric@casbah.acns.nwu.edu
Contact: Dr. W. Zev Rymer, Dir. of Res.
Desc: Rehabilitation medicine, brain trauma, stroke, atherosclerosis, neuromuscular diseases, applied neurophysiology, deep venous thrombosis, spinal cord injury, arthritis, prosthetics/orthotics, rehabilitation nursing, allied health, and communicative disorders. *Type:* Research center.

Rehabilitation Institute of Michigan
261 Mack Blvd.   Ph: (313)745-9731
Detroit, MI 48201   Fax: (313)745-9863
E-mail: mdijkers@med.wayne.edu
Contact: Dr. Marcel Dijkers, Dir. of Res.
Desc: Physical medicine and rehabilitation medicine, including electromyography, rehabilitation engineering, neuropsychology, measures of rehabilitation outcome, and methods of evaluation and treatment of patients with closed head injuries, spinal cord injuries, cerebrovascular accidents, and other diagnoses. *Type:* Research center.

Roosevelt Warm Springs Institute for Rehabilitation
PO Box 1000   Ph: (706)655-5633
Warm Springs, GA 31830-0268   Fax: (706)655-5630
E-mail: paulamer@gomail.doas.state.ga.us
URL: http://www.rooseveltrehab.org
Contact: Paula Merchant, Contact.
Desc: Clinical aspects of rehabilitation, marketing, administration, and product development. *Type:* Research center.

San Diego State University

Interwork Institute

Rehabilitation Research and Training Center of the Pacific
5850 Hardy Ave., Ste. 112   Ph: (619)594-0139
San Diego, CA 92182-5313   Fax: (619)594-4208
E-mail: guerrero@interwork.sdsu.edu
URL: http://interwork.sdsu.edu/projects/rrtcp/
Contact: Fred R. McFarlane, PhD, Dir.
Desc: Improvement of the quality of rehabilitation services for persons with disabilities, especially to assure culturally relevant rehabilitation systems; to expand capacity building through research and training activities; to expand, improve and implement effective use of rehabilitation database systems; and to promote assistive technology. Research focuses on meeting the needs of Pacific Islanders with disabilities in Hawaii, Palau, Micronesia, the Marshall Islands, Guam, the Northern Marianas, and American Samoa. *Type:* Research center.

Sister Kenny Institute
800 E. 28th St. at Chicago Ave.   Ph: (612)863-4005
Minneapolis, MN 55407   Fax: (612)863-2833
E-mail: canine@allina.com
URL: http://www.ski-rehab.org
Contact: Dr. Kent Canine, Dir./Res. & Educ.
Desc: Physical medicine and rehabilitation. Aims to improve the quality, effectiveness, and efficiency of rehabilitation patient care. *Type:* Research center.

Sister Kenny Institute
800 E. 28th St. at Chicago Ave.   Ph: (612)863-4457
Minneapolis, MN 55407   Fax: (612)863-2591
Contact: Mark Dixon, Exec.Dir.
Desc: To investigate, evaluate, promote, and support projects in rehabilitation and provide rehabilitative patient care. *Type:* Association.

Stanford University

Stanford Cardiac Rehabilitation Program
780 Welch Rd., Ste. 106   Ph: (650)723-6463
Palo Alto, CA 94304-5735   Fax: (650)723-6798
E-mail: Lynda@scrp.stanford.edu
Contact: Robert F. DeBusk, MD, Dir.
Desc: Recovery from heart attack and coronary heart surgery, systems to facilitate risk factor modification in healthy individuals and patients with heart disease, and systems to enhance the cost-effectiveness of care provided to patients with heart disease. Coordinates random clinical trials in Kaiser foundation hospitals. *Type:* Research center.

Tufts University

Research and Training Center in Rehabilitation and Childhood Trauma
New England Med. Ctr.   Ph: (617)636-5031
750 Washington St.,   Fax: (617)636-5513
   Department 750 K-R
Boston, MA 02111-1901
URL: http://www.nemc.org/rehab/homepage.htm
Contact: Carla Vi Di Scala, MD, Dir.
Desc: Impact of rehabilitation on children with traumatic injury. Projects include: National Pediatric Trauma Registry; outcome of injuries to children with preexisting medical conditions; impact of medical insurance and local rehabilitation resources on injured children; causes and costs of severe injuries to children that occur at school; study of head injuries to children while bicycling and during informal recreation; natural history of injury recovery in children; evaluation of early rehabilitation interventions to decrease complications in children; and family-centered service coordination for educational and vocational needs. *Type:* Research center.

U.S. Department of Veterans Affairs

Rehabilitation Technology Assessment Section
103 S. Gay St., 6th Fl.   Ph: (410)962-3934
Baltimore, MD 21202   Fax: (410)962-9670
Desc: Rehabilitation technology to the Department of Veterans Affairs; evaluates commercially-available rehabilitation systems, products, and devices; develops product safety and performance standards for products used by disabled veterans; establishes procedures for assessment of disabled veterans in hospitals, homes, and work sites; provides guidance to researchers, developers, and manufacturers through consultation and brief analyses of prototypes of preproduction items; collects and disseminates information on rehabilitation technology and new products to VA rehabilitation organizations, facilities, clinicians, and end users; and conducts product design and development to provide systems, products, and devices to meet veterans' needs. *Type:* Research center.

University of Alabama at Birmingham

Rehabilitation Research and Training Center in Secondary Complications in Spinal Cord Injury
Department of Physical   Ph: (205)934-3283
   Medicine & Rehabilitation   Fax: (205)975-4691
Spain Rehabilitation Center
1717 6th Ave. S., Rm. 506
Birmingham, AL 35233-7330
E-mail: richards@sun.rehabm.uab.edu
URL: http://www.spinalcord.uab.edu/docs/rrtchome.htm
Contact: J. Scott Richards, PhD, Res.Dir.
Desc: Prevention and treatment of secondary conditions of spinal cord injury (SCI), including urologic, respiratory and pulmonary complications; pain; psycho-social conditions; nutrition; and assessment of secondary conditions. *Type:* Research center.

University of Alabama at Birmingham

Spinal Cord Injury Care System
Spain Rehab Ctr.   Ph: (205)934-3330
1717 6th. Ave S   Fax: (205)975-9754
Birmingham, AL 35233-7330
E-mail: jackson@sun.rehab.uab.edu
URL: http://www.sci.rehabm.uab.edu/docs/modeluab.htm
Contact: Amie Jackson, MD, Proj.Dir. & Ch.
Desc: Rehabilitation needs of those with spinal cord injury (SCI), including urological studies. System objectives include: to deliver and improve comprehensive medical, vocational, and psychosocial rehabilitation services for individuals with SCI; to evaluate both the effectiveness of

services and their costs and benefits; to produce new and useful information; to demonstrate and evaluate the application of improved methods and equipment; and to participate in national studies of the benefits of a spinal cord injury service system. *Type:* Research center.

University of Alabama at Birmingham

Spinal Cord Injury Care System

National Spinal Cord Injury Statistical Center
Spain Rehabilitation Ctr.   Ph: (205)934-3320
1717 6th Ave. S.   Fax: (205)934-2709
Birmingham, AL 35233-7330
E-mail: nscisc@sun.rehabm.uab.edu
Contact: Amie Jackson, MD, Ch.
Desc: Data collection, storage, and analyses of national spinal cord injury statistics, submitted by 18 federally sponsored Spinal Cord Injury Care Systems. *Type:* Research center.

University of California, San Diego

Hyperbaric Medicine Center
Med. Ctr.   Ph: (619)543-5222
200 W. Arbor Dr.   Fax: (619)543-3122
San Diego, CA 92103-8688
E-mail: tneuman@ucsd.edu
Contact: Dr. Tom Neuman, Dir.
Desc: Hyperbaric oxygen therapy, including application in burns, infectious diseases, wound healing, and diving medicine. *Type:* Research center.

University of Michigan

Center for Occupational Rehabilitation and Health
Williamsburg Office Complex   Ph: (734)998-7676
400 E. Eisenhower Pkwy., Ste.   Fax: (734)998-7990
   E
Ann Arbor, MI 48104
URL: http://www.med.umich.edu/pmr/spine
Contact: Lynette Rasussen, Dir.
Desc: Evaluates and recommends efficient and safe work environments to enhance health and minimize injury. Other activities include assessing physical and cognitive functions relating to endurance, speed, and accuracy; identifying and addressing primary and secondary limitations; assessing and specifying home and work-site accessibility; providing case management services; and analyzing the work site to integrate the individual's physical, cognitive, and social abilities into the specific job setting. *Type:* Research center.

University of Montana

Research and Training Center on Rural Rehabilitation Services
52 Corbin Hall   Ph: (406)243-5467
Missoula, MT 59812   Free: 888-268-2743
                                  Fax: (406)243-4730
E-mail: ruraldoc@selway.umt.edu
URL: http://ruralinstitute.umt.edu
Contact: Tom Seekins, PhD, Dir.
Desc: Employment and vocational rehabilitation service needs of people with disabilities in rural areas; intervention development to improve employment outcomes; rural supported employment models; rural independent living; improvement of transportation, health care, housing, and accessibility; rural models for prevention of secondary disabilities; disability legislation and American Indian Tribes; and alternative models of delivery of rural rehabilitation services. *Type:* Research center.

University of Montreal

Montreal Research Centre

Rehabilitation Institute

6300, ave. Darlington   Ph: (514)340-2078
Montreal, PQ, Canada H3S 2J4   Fax: (514)340-2154
E-mail: levin@ere.umontreal.ca
URL: http://ireadapt.qc.ca

Contact: Mindy Levin, Sci.Dir.

Desc: Biomedical research, focusing on rehabilitation of patients suffering from spinal cord injury, amputation, stroke, and traumatic head injuries; behavioral research, including studies of the physical, psychological, and occupational obstacles that prevent brain-injured persons from being reintegrated into society; and rehabilitation engineering for upper- and lower-limb amputees. *Type:* Research center.

University of Vermont

Vermont Back Research Center

1 S. Prospect St.   Ph: (802)656-4582
Burlington, VT 05401   Free: 800-527-7320
    Fax: (802)660-9243
E-mail: backtalk@salus.med.uvm.edu
URL: http://salus.med.uvm.edu/~backtalk

Contact: Martin Krag, MD, Dir.

Desc: Prevention, assessment, and rehabilitation of low back pain, injury, and disability. Past projects have focused on disability prediction and prevention; development and testing of tools and techniques for evaluating intervertebral motion; lifting capacity and effort; effects of exercise; orthotic devices; effects of posture, seating, and vibration; and work demands. *Type:* Research center.

West Virginia University

University Affiliated Center for Developmental Disabilities

955 Hartman Run Rd.   Ph: (304)293-4692
Morgantown, WV 26505   Fax: (304)293-7294

Contact: Ashok S. Dey, Dir.

Desc: Developmental disabilities, mental retardation (all ages), nutrition, under nutrition, brain development, speech and language development, medical aspects of developmental disabilities, high-risk families, and program evaluation. Graduate research assistants come from various University disciplines to participate in applied research activities. *Type:* Research center.

Western Michigan University

Occupational Therapy Teaching Research Clinic

Occupational Therapy Dept.   Ph: (616)387-3850
1201 Oliver St.   Fax: (616)387-3845
Kalamazoo, MI 49008
E-mail: berit.miller@.wmich.edu
URL: http://www.wmich.edu

Contact: Berit Miller, Coord.

Desc: Occupational therapy and clinical research on developmental disabilities and learning disabilities. *Type:* Research center.

Wichita State University

National Rehabilitation Engineering Center

Wichita, KS 67260-0044   Ph: (316)978-6314
    Fax: (316)978-3853
E-mail: e.hoyer@ee.twsu.edu

Contact: Elmer Hoyer, PhD, Dir.

Desc: Employment for handicapped adults. *Type:* Research center.

Relief

Air Serv International

1902 Orange Tree Ln., Ste. 200   Ph: (909)793-2627
PO Box 3041   Fax: (909)793-0226
Redlands, CA 92373-0993
E-mail: asi@xc.org
URL: http://www.airserv.org

Contact: Kenneth W. Frizzell, Pres.

Desc: Provides air transport of relief and development personnel, medicines, and cargo to countries devastated by war or natural disaters. *Type:* Association.

American Red Cross National Headquarters

1621 N. Kent St.   Ph: (703)248-4219
Arlington, VA 22209
URL: http://www.redcross.org

Contact: Steve Bullock, Pres.

Desc: Operating under congressional charter and fulfilling America's obligations under certain international treaties, the American Red Cross serves members of the armed forces and veterans and their families, aids disaster victims, and assists other Red Cross societies in times of emergency. Other activities include: blood services; training of volunteers for chapters, hospitals, and other community agencies; community services; international activities; service opportunities for youth. Maintains 46 regional blood centers. *Type:* Association.

American Red Magen David for Israel

888 7th Ave., Ste. 403   Ph: (212)757-1627
New York, NY 10106   Fax: (212)757-4662
E-mail: armdi@juno.com

Contact: Benjamin Saxe, Exec.VP.

Desc: U.S. support arm for Magen David Adom (MDA), Israel's equivalent of the Red Cross Society. Supports the MDA emergency medical, ambulance, blood, and disaster services which benefit Israel's entire population. *Type:* Association.

Americares Foundation

161 Cherry St.   Ph: (203)972-5500
New Canaan, CT 06840   Free: 800-486-HELP
    Fax: (203)966-6028
E-mail: info@americares.org
URL: http://www.americares.org

Contact: Robert C. Macauley, CEO.

Desc: Private relief organization dedicated to saving lives and fulfilling emergency medical needs worldwide. Sponsors airlifts and sea shipments of food, medicine, and medical supplies to provide immediate relief whenever and wherever needed. Responds to disasters caused by earthquakes, famines, floods, political upheavals, and wars. *Type:* Association.

The Brother's Brother Foundation

1501 Reedsdale St., Ste. 3005   Ph: (412)321-3160
Pittsburgh, PA 15233-2341   Fax: (412)321-3325
E-mail: bbfound@aol.com
URL: http://www.brothersbrother.com

Contact: Luke L. Hingson, Pres.

Desc: Delivers surplus goods including pharmaceuticals and other medical supplies, food, books, seeds, tools, intraocular lenses, used eyeglasses, and other gifts-in-kind to 35 developing nations. Maintains speakers' bureau. *Type:* Association.

CARE

151 Ellis St. NE   Ph: (404)681-2552
Atlanta, GA 30303-2439   Free: 800-521-CARE
    Fax: (404)577-9418

Contact: Peter D. Bell, CEO/Pres.

Desc: International aid and development organization providing disaster aid and self help development programs overseas. *Type:* Association.

CARE World Report

CARE

151 Ellis St. NE   Ph: (404)681-2552
Atlanta, GA 30303-2439

Contact: Erin Blair, Editor.

Desc: Contains news of current CARE services in 61 developing nations overseas and describes CARE's programs. Recurring features include news of emergencies and items on donors to CARE's programs and projects. *Type:* Newsletter.

Church World Service

475 Riverside Dr., Ste. 678   Ph: (212)870-2257
New York, NY 10115   Fax: (212)870-3523
URL: http://www.nccusa.org

Contact: Rodney Page, Dir.

Desc: Cooperative agency of 32 Protestant and Orthodox communions of the National Council of the Churches of Christ in the U.S.A. . Local community hunger education and fundraising events coordinated by regional offices. *Type:* Association.

Church World Service and Witness

475 Riverside Dr., Rm. 678   Ph: (212)870-2061
New York, NY 10115-0050   Free: 800-456-1310
    Fax: (212)870-3523
E-mail: rondah@cws.ncccusa.org

Contact: Rodney I. Page, Exec.Dir.

Desc: Division of the National Council of Churches of Christ in the U.S.A. providing worldwide development and emergency aid to the poor in east and southern Asia, Africa, Latin America, Middle East, and Eastern Europe. Engages in works of Christian compassion, relief, technical assistance, reconstruction, interchurch aid, and ministering to the victims of war and other emergencies such as famines and floods. *Type:* Association.

Cityteam Ministries

2302 Zanker Rd.   Ph: (408)232-5600
San Jose, CA 95131-1137   Fax: (408)428-9505

Contact: Patrick J. Robertson, Pres.

Desc: Works to provide disadvantaged people in the inner city with emergency services and spirtual guidance. *Type:* Association.

Doctors Without Borders

6 East 39th St., 8th Floor   Ph: (212)679-6800
New York, NY 10016   Free: 888-392-0392
    Fax: (212)679-7016
URL: http://www.dwb.org

Contact: Joelle Tanguy, Exec.Dir.

Desc: Medical and non-medical professionals. Provides assistance to victims of war, natural and man-made disasters, and epidemics, and to others who lack access to health care. Each year more than 2,000 volunteers provide relief in more than 80 countries. *Type:* Association.

Northwest Medical Teams International

PO Box 10   Ph: (503)624-1000
Portland, OR 97207   Fax: (503)624-1001

Contact: Ron Post, Pres.

Desc: Provides disaster relief and medical assistance to vulnerable individuals affected by war, epidemics, poverty, physical deformities and illnesses, and natural disasters. *Type:* Association.

Presiding Bishop's Fund for World Relief

PO Box 12043   Ph: (212)922-5129
Newark, NJ 07101   Free: 800-334-7626
    Fax: (212)983-6377
E-mail: pbfwr@dfms.org
URL: http://www.pbfwr.org

Contact: Angela Cappiello, CMP, CAE, Dir. of Grants.

Desc: Relief and development arm of the Episcopal church. Purpose is to provide relief of worldwide human suffering. Responds to natural disasters and other emergencies; communicates appeals for financial aid at times of emergencies; makes grants for relief, rehabilitation, and development. *Type:* Association.

Tibetan Aid Project

2910 San Pablo Ave.   Ph: (510)848-4238
Berkeley, CA 94702   Free: 800-33T-IBET
                             Fax: (510)548-2230

E-mail: tap@dnai.com
URL: http://www.nyingma.org

Contact: Tarthang Tulku, Pres.

Desc: A project of the Tibetan Nyingma Relief Foundation. Offers assistance to individuals in Tibet and Tibetan refugees in India, Nepal, Bhutan, and Sikkim. Conducts Tibetan Student Support Program; sponsors relief distribution to monasteries and schools for support of religious and community activities. *Type:* Association.

U.S. Federal Emergency Management Agency

Federal Emergency Management Agency - Office of Emergency Information
500 C St. SW
Washington, DC 20472
E-mail: webmaster@fema.gov
URL: http://www.fema.gov

Desc: The FEMA WWW server provides information about the agency and access to its services. The full text of several publications can be found here, as well as and press releases, regional office data, information concerning disaster assistance, and more. *Type:* Database.

World Emergency Relief

2075 Corte Del Norgal Ste. S   Ph: (760)930-8001
Carlsbad, CA 92009   Free: 888-HUG-4-
                                        KID
                                Fax: (760)930-9085

URL: http://www.wer-us.org

Contact: Rev. Joel MacCollam, Pres.

Desc: Promotes micro-economic development and institutional advancement for Native Americans and underdeveloped countries. *Type:* Association.

World Mercy Fund

PO Box 227
Waterford, VA 20197-0227

Contact: Fr. Patrick Leonard, Pres. & CEO.

Desc: Builds hospitals and provides medical facilities and water for less fortunate peoples of the world, particularly those in Africa. Has built hospitals and clinics in Africa that are equipped with mobile units. Has initiated projects to bring fresh water to places where it is most urgently needed. *Type:* Association.

Religion

Associated Church Press Directory

Associated Church Press
PO Box 21749
Washington, DC 20009-1749

Contact: Joe Roos, Editor, jroos@erols.com.

Desc: About 200 periodicals issued by member religious organizations of Christian denominations and their publishing houses; some Christian independent publishers are also included. *Type:* Directory.

Directory of Departments and Programs of Religious Studies in North America

Council of Societies for the Study of Religion (CSSR)
Valparaiso University   Ph: (219)464-5515
Valparaiso, IN 46383-6493   Free: 888-422-2777
                              Fax: (219)464-6714

E-mail: cssr@valpo.edu
URL: http://www.cssr.org.

Contact: David G. Truemper, Editor, david.truemper@valpo.edu.

Desc: Approximately 400 departments of religious studies or theology and schools of theology, described in detail; also lists about 1,200 other departments, programs, and schools of religion and theology. *Type:* Directory.

Directory of Religious Organizations in the United States

Gale Group Inc.
27500 Drake Rd.   Ph: (248)699-4253
Farmington Hills, MI 48331- Free: 800-877-GALE
    3535   Fax: (248)699-8070
E-mail: galeord@galegroup.com
URL: http://www.galegroup.com.; http://www.gale.com.

Contact: J. Gordon Melton, Editor; Amy Lucas, Editor.

Desc: About 2,500 organizations that provide services for, information on, support to, or act to influence churches, sects, cults, and other primary religious bodies in the United States; includes associations, publishers, broadcasters, social service organizations, consultants, missionary groups and missions, electronic services providers, research organizations, and educational groups. *Type:* Directory.

Encyclopedia of Afterlife Beliefs and Phenomena

Gale Group Inc.
27500 Drake Rd.   Ph: (248)699-4253
Farmington Hills, MI 48331- Free: 800-877-GALE
    3535   Fax: (248)699-8070
E-mail: galeord@galegroup.com
URL: http://www.galegroup.com.

Contact: James Lewis, Editor.

Desc: Lists organizations associated with the belief of an afterlife and related phenomena. Principal content of publication is 250 entries about the nonmedical aspects of the afterlife and death. *Type:* Directory.

Encyclopedia of American Religions

Gale Group Inc.
27500 Drake Rd.   Ph: (248)699-4253
Farmington Hills, MI 48331- Free: 800-877-GALE
    3535   Fax: (248)699-8070
E-mail: galeord@galegroup.com
URL: http://www.galegroup.com.; http://www.gale.com.

Contact: J. Gordon Melton, Editor.

Desc: Approximately 2,300 religious and spiritual groups in the United States and Canada, including Roman Catholic, Judaic, Protestant, Eastern, and Middle Eastern religions, and other beliefs and practices, such as occultism, magick, Satanism, and communes. Contains an essay on the development of religion in the U.S. and Canada; historical essays discussing the development of the 24 major religious families and traditions; and directory sections listing individual churches and groups constituting the religious families discussed in the historical essays (with two additional sections for churches and groups not belonging to one of the religious families). *Type:* Directory.

National Directory of Churches, Synagogues, and Other Houses of Worship

Gale Group Inc.
27500 Drake Rd.   Ph: (248)699-4253
Farmington Hills, MI 48331- Free: 800-877-GALE
    3535   Fax: (248)699-8070
E-mail: galeord@galegroup.com
URL: http://www.galegroup.com.

Contact: J. Gordon Melton, Editor; John Krol, Editor.

Desc: More than 350,000 churches, synagogues, and other places of worship in the United States. Published in four regional volumes. *Type:* Directory.

New Community Living Magazine

MEMCO Publications
2155 Dumas St.   Ph: (407)453-0572
Merritt Island, FL 32952   Free: 800-805-5565
                           Fax: (407)452-9042

E-mail: memco@scci.net

Contact: Ernie Mello, Editor; Maggie Mello, Editor.

Desc: Help and information to Civic & Religious Organization Community information in Florida. *Type:* Directory.

Religious Bodies in the United States

Garland Publishing, Inc.
19 Union Square W.   Ph: (212)414-0650
New York, NY 10003   Free: 800-627-6273
                           Fax: (212)414-0659

E-mail: info@garland.com
URL: http://www.garlandpub.com;   http://www.garlandpub.com.

Contact: J. Gordon Melton, Editor.

Desc: Religious bodies, interfaith organizations, denominations, and publications. *Type:* Directory.

Renting and Leasing

American Rental Association

1900 19th St.   Ph: (309)764-2475
Moline, IL 61265   Free: 800-334-2177
                           Fax: (309)764-2747

E-mail: ara@ararental.org
Contact: James R. Irish, Exec.VP.

Desc: Firms engaged in the rental of banquet and party equipment, tools, machinery, and other products; includes independent, franchised, and chain store operators. Associates are suppliers of equipment, merchandise, and other items. Seeks to: develop a standard of ethics; foster better business methods; promote study of economic trends in the rental industry. *Type:* Association.

ARA Inside Track

American Rental Association
1900 19th St.   Ph: (309)764-2475
Moline, IL 61265   Free: 800-334-2177
                           Fax: (309)764-1533

E-mail: ara@ararental.org
Contact: Sandy Howell, Editor, sandy.howell@ararental.rog.

Desc: Provides updates on the Association, which is devoted to the development of a standard of ethics and better business practice in the rental industry. Reports on the efforts of the Association to study economic trends in the industry. *Type:* Newsletter.

ARA Washington News

American Rental Association
1900 19th St.   Ph: (309)764-2475
Moline, IL 61265   Free: 800-334-2177
                           Fax: (309)764-1533

E-mail: ara@ararental.org

Contact: Sandy Howell, Editor, sandy.howell@ararental.org.

Desc: Carries legislative news pertinent to the rental equipment industry. Covers action on Capitol Hill and reviews government publications. *Type:* Newsletter.

Association of Progressive Rental Organizations

9015 Mountain Ridge Dr., Ste.   Ph: (512)794-0095
220   Free: 800-204-2776
Austin, TX 78759   Fax: (512)794-0097
URL: http://www.apro-rto.com
Contact: Bill Keese, Exec.Dir.

Desc: Dealer and industry suppliers. Trade association serving rental dealers in the home appliance, furniture, and consumer electronics industry who market their products with a rental-purchase plan. Purposes are to: foster trade and commerce; collect and disseminate information; represent members before legislative committees, government bureaus, and other bodies in matters affecting the industry. *Type:* Association.

Commercial Leasing Law and Strategy

Leader Publications
New York Law Publishing Company
345 Park Ave., South   Ph: (212)545-6170
New York, NY 10010   Free: 800-888-8300
   Fax: (212)696-1848
E-mail: leader@ljextra.com; poguelman@lsextra.com.
Contact: Stephanie McEvily, Editor.

Desc: Discusses the legalities and financial aspects of commercial leasing. *Type:* Newsletter.

Equipment Leasing Association

4301 N. Fairfax Dr.   Ph: (703)527-8655
Ste. 550   Fax: (703)527-2649
Arlington, VA 22203
E-mail: ela@elamail.com
URL: http://www.elaonline.com
Contact: Michael J. Fleming, Pres.

Desc: Companies, divisions, or subsidiaries whose principal activity is the leasing of equipment to other commercial users. *Type:* Association.

Leader's Equipment Leasing Newsletter

Leader Publications
New York Law Publishing Company
345 Park Ave., South   Ph: (212)545-6170
New York, NY 10010   Free: 800-888-8300
   Fax: (212)696-1848
E-mail: leader@ljextra.com; leader@ljextra.com.
Contact: Adam Schlagman, Editor.

Desc: Provides information on lender and lessor equipment companies. Includes judicial rulings, international market outlook, and Environmental Protection Agency (EPA) proposals pertaining to the leasing industry. *Type:* Newsletter.

Rental Management—Who's Who in the Rental Industry Issue

American Rental Association
1900 19th St.   Ph: (309)764-2475
Moline, IL 61265   Free: 800-334-2177
   Fax: (309)764-1533
E-mail: ara@ararental.org
Contact: Brian Alm, Editor, brian.alm@ararental.org.
Desc: Lists of about 7,200 member rental companies, branch locations, services, and suppliers to the rental industry in the United States, limited international coverage; also lists association officers, other associations in the industry, and ARA state and local groups. *Type:* Directory.

Textile Rental Services Association of America

1130 E. Beach Blvd., Ste. B   Ph: (954)457-7555
PO Box 1283   Free: 800-868-TRSA
Hallandale, FL 33008   Fax: (954)457-3890
URL: http://www.trsa.org
Contact: J. Burton Eller, Exec.Dir.

Desc: Industrial laundering, linen supply, dust control, commercial laundering, and other for-profit textile maintenance and rental services, and allied companies. Conducts seminars in customer contracts, customer service and retention, delivery management, energy conservation, health care laundering, industrial marketing, laundering technology, management development, marketing, preventive maintenance, production management, profitability analysis, sales, strategic planning, supervisory training, and textile management. Compiles statistics. *Type:* Association.

Truck Renting and Leasing Association

1725 Duke St., Ste. 600   Ph: (703)299-9120
Alexandria, VA 22314   Fax: (703)299-9115
E-mail: jmpayne@trala.org
URL: http://www.trala.org
Contact: J. Michael Payne, Pres. & CEO.

Desc: Truck and trailer rental and leasing companies and systems; suppliers to the industry. Seeks to encourage and promote a favorable climate and sound environment conducive to the renting and leasing of trucks, tractors, and trailers, and dedicated contract carriage. *Type:* Association.

Reproductive Rights

Planned Parenthood of the Rocky Mountains

Gary Jamieson
950 Broadway   Ph: (303)321-PLAN
Denver, CO 80203   Fax: (303)861-0268
URL: http://www.plannedparenthood.org
Contact: Gary Jamieson, Senior VP/CFO.
Type: Association.

Republican Party

Arizona Republican Party

3501 N. 24th St.   Ph: (602)957-7770
Phoenix, AZ 85016   Fax: (602)224-0932
E-mail: info@azgop.org
Contact: Jane P. Lynch, Exec.Dir.

Desc: Individuals united to promote the Republican Party platform, elect Republican candidates to public office, and register new voters. *Type:* Association.

College Republican National Committee

600 Pennsylvania Ave., S.E., Ste.   Ph: (202)608-1411
301   Free: 888-765-3564
Washington, DC 20003   Fax: (202)608-1429
URL: http://www.crnc.org
Contact: Laura Dove, Exec.Dir.

Desc: College students representing 1100 American campuses. Aims toward the furtherance of the beliefs of the Republican Party on the campus, educating young people in the realm of politics. Sponsors lectures, debates, and seminars in practical politics. *Type:* Association.

Log Cabin Republicans

1633 Q St. NW, No. 210   Ph: (202)347-5306
Washington, DC 20009   Fax: (202)347-5224
E-mail: lcrnat@aol.com
URL: http://www.lcr.org
Contact: Rich Tafel, Exec.Dir.

Desc: Partisan organization representing gay and lesbian individuals. Operates at the grass roots level by supporting Republican candidates. Maintains a Washington office with staff devoted to lobbying, candidate tracking, and policy development. *Type:* Association.

National Congressional Club

100-C Hunters Ln.
PO Box 18848
Youngsville, NC 27596-9789
Contact: Carter Wrenn, Exec.Dir.

Desc: Political action committee that raises funds on behalf of Republican Senator Jesse Helms of North Carolina. *Type:* Association.

National Federation of Republican Women

124 N. Alfred St.   Ph: (703)548-9688
Alexandria, VA 22314   Fax: (703)548-9836
E-mail: nfrw@worldweb.net
URL: http://www.nfrw.org
Contact: Christine Oster, Contact.

Desc: Purposes are: to provide an organization through which women who share the principles of the Republican Party can join in Republican activities; to distribute political educational materials; to recruit and support qualified and electable Republican candidates; to encourage more women to seek public office and to provide them with campaign expertise through NFRW-sponsored Campaign Management Schools across the country; to provide research material and legislative information to federation members. *Type:* Association.

National Teen Age Republican Headquarters

10260 Crestwood Dr.   Ph: (703)368-4214
Manassas, VA 20108   Fax: (703)368-0830
Contact: Barbara Wells, Dir.

Desc: High school students. Promotes involvement of teenagers in the U.S. political process. *Type:* Association.

Prostitutes Anonymous

11225 Magnolia Blvd.
Box 181
North Hollywood, CA 91601
Contact: Jody Williams, Contact.

Desc: Men and women who have been involved in prostitution, phone sex, nude dancing, pornography, mistressing, or any other form of commercial sex activities. Members use a 12-step program for recovery from prostitution. Provides support for members by discussing experiences and problems in person, through the mail, or over the phone. *Type:* Association.

Republican Mainstream Committee

236 Massachusetts Ave. NE, Ste.   Ph: (202)546-8070
410   Fax: (202)546-2370
Washington, DC 20002
E-mail: kenruberg@mainstream.org
URL: http://www.mainstream.org
Contact: Ken Ruberg, Exec.Dir.

Desc: Centrist Republican political committee. Encourages grass roots outreach and organization by moderate and progressive Republicans. Maintains speakers' bureau and placement service. *Type:* Association.

Republican National Committee

310 1st St. SE   Ph: (202)863-8500
Washington, DC 20003   Fax: (202)863-8820
E-mail: info@rnc.org
URL: http://www.rnc.org/
Contact: Jim Nichelson, Chm.

Desc: Authorized and recreated every four years by the Republican National Nominating Convention. Under the direction of the Chairman, RNC provides support activities to Republican administrations, members of Congress, governors, state and local office holders, and Republican campaigns at all levels. Operates a field staff to advise state and local party organizations and campaigns; conducts research on current issues; assists the states in their own research and computer operations; seeks to facilitate the drawing of equitable lines in the redistricting and reapportionment process resulting from the decennial census. *Type:* Association.

Republican National Hispanic Assembly of the United States

600 Pennsylvania Ave. SE, Ste. 300   Ph: (202)608-1400
Washington, DC 20003-4316
E-mail: rnha1@aol.com
URL: http://www.rnha.org
Contact: Jose Rivera, Chairman.

Desc: Republicans of Hispanic descent. Goals are to: educate Hispanics about the political process in the U.S.; register voters; recruit Hispanics for the Republican party. *Type:* Association.

Republicans Abroad International

310 1st St. SE   Ph: (202)608-1423
Washington, DC 20003   Fax: (202)608-1431
E-mail: republicansai@mindspring.com
URL: http://www.republicansabroad.org/
Contact: Michael J. Jones, Dir.

Desc: To Americans living abroad, their spouses, and their dependents. Objectives are to: promote active participation of nonresident Americans in Republican political activities; facilitate voter registration and absentee voting; represent the Republican Party and its supporters abroad. Disseminates information concerning the Republican Party and its candidates. *Type:* Association.

Ripon Society

501 Capitol Court, NE, Ste. 300   Ph: (202)546-1292
   Free: 800-98-RIPON
Washington, DC 20002   Fax: (202)547-6560
E-mail: riponsoc@aol.com
Contact: Michael Gill, Exec.Dir.

Desc: Moderate Republicans primarily from business, professional, and academic communities. Urges the Republican Party to: adopt a moderate, middle of the road course "since it offers the greatest possibility for constructive achievement"; take a lead in forging a more flexible American foreign policy; develop new initiatives and programs to solve the nation's domestic and urban crises; promote individual civil liberties and equal rights for all under the law; encourage economic opportunity through the expansion of the free enterprise system. Formulates and disseminates Republican positions on domestic and foreign political issues; prepares research papers. *Type:* Association.

Young Republican National Federation

600 Pennsylvania Ave. SE, Ste. 302   Ph: (202)608-1417
   Fax: (202)608-1430
Washington, DC 20003
E-mail: yrnfink@aol.com
URL: http://www.yrnf.org
Contact: J. Mance Bowden, III, Exec.Dir.

Desc: Men and women between the ages of 18 and 40. Provides the opportunity for young people who are interested in good government under Constitutional principles to become engaged in an active political program. Seeks to further the aims of the Republican Party among young people and to train future candidates, party leaders, and citizens. *Type:* Association.

Research

American Educational Research Association

1230 17th St. NW   Ph: (202)223-9485
Washington, DC 20036   Fax: (202)775-1824
URL: http://www.aera.net
Contact: William J. Russell, Exec. Officer.

Desc: Educators and behavioral scientists interested in the development, application, and improvement of educational research. Members include professors, state and local school system research directors, research specialists, graduate students of education, and educators in foreign countries. *Type:* Association.

American National Standards Institute

11 W. 42nd St., 13th Fl.   Ph: (212)642-4900
New York, NY 10036   Fax: (212)398-0023
Contact: Sergio Mazza, Pres.

Desc: Industrial firms, trade associations, technical societies, labor organizations, consumer organizations, and government agencies. Serves as clearinghouse for nationally coordinated voluntary standards for fields ranging from information technology to building construction. *Type:* Association.

American Society for Testing and Materials

100 Barr Harbor Dr.   Ph: (610)832-9500
West Conshohocken, PA 19428   Fax: (610)832-9555
E-mail: service@astm.org
URL: http://www.astm.org
Contact: Carla J. Falco, PR Manager.

Desc: Engineers, scientists, managers, professionals, academicians, consumers, and skilled technicians holding membership as individuals in or representatives of business firms, government agencies, educational institutions, and laboratories. Establishes standards for materials, products, systems, and services. Has 130 technical committees (each having five to 50 subcommittees). *Type:* Association.

Animal Behavior Abstracts

Cambridge Scientific Abstracts (CSA)

7200 Wisconsin Ave., Ste. 601   Ph: (301)961-6700
Bethesda, MD 20814-4823
E-mail: sales@csa.com
URL: http://www.csa.com

Desc: Contains more than 60,000 citations, with abstracts, to the worldwide literature on ethology, the study of animal behavior. Covers neurophysiology, behavioral ecology, biochemical, anatomical, and neurophysiological correlates, sleep, brain stimulation, drug studies, hormones, habituation, reinforcement, avoidance, discrimination, complex learning, memory, theoretical models, communication, aggression, social spacing, and dominance in animals. *Available:* Cambridge Scientific Abstracts (CSA), Internet Database Service. *Type:* Database.

The Animal Research Data Base

University of Georgia - The College of Family and Consumer Sciences

Athens, GA 30602
E-mail: mhulsey@fcs.uga.edu
URL: http://www.fcs.uga.edu/~mhulsey/GDB.html
Contact: Greg Popken, Itsmine@med.unc.edu.

Desc: As distasteful a thought as it may be for animal lovers (and most of us are), few medical advancements in our lifetime would have been possible without animal experimentation. Drawing from a number of sources, Greg Popken has done a great deal to dispel some of the myths and horror stories about animal experimentation done by medical researchers. *Type:* Database.

APA Research Funding Bulletin

American Psychological Association

750 1st St. NE   Ph: (202)336-5500
Washington, DC 20002-4242   Free: 800-374-2721
   Fax: (202)336-5568
E-mail: webmaster@apa.org
URL: http://www.apa.org/science.
Contact: Catherine Robertson, Editor.

Desc: Comprises an index of funding announcements from private and public agencies. Includes a complete summary of the Request for Proposal or Request for Application, deadline date, sponsoring institution, amount of funding available, and contact person. *Type:* Newsletter.

Association of Professional Researchers for Advancement

414 Plaza Dr., Ste. 209   Ph: (630)655-0177
Westmont, IL 60559   Fax: (630)655-0391
E-mail: apra@adminsys.com
URL: http://www.weber.u.washington.edu/~d/amb/apra/apra.html
Contact: Judith Keel, Exec.Dir.

Desc: Individuals involved in educational, medical, cultural, and religious organizations; fundraising consultants. Facilitates education and dissemination of information about prospect research; encourages professional development and cooperative relationships among members. (Prospect research is aimed at securing gifts, grants, and charitable donations for nonprofit organizations.). *Type:* Association.

Battelle Memorial Institute

505 King Ave.   Ph: (614)424-6424
Columbus, OH 43201
Contact: Dr. Ronald S. Paul, CEO, Pres.

Desc: Nonprofit, public purpose organization. Conducts scientific research on a contract basis for industrial firms and government agencies in chemistry, biochemistry, metallurgy, physics, energy, computer technology, electronics, nucleonics, ceramics, transportation, education and training, environmental quality, medical engineering, urban problems, mechanical engineering, and other fields. Maintains research centers in :Geneva, Switzerland; Frankfurt/Main, West Germany; Richland, WA; and Columbus, OH. *Type:* Association.

Canadian Research Index

Micromedia Ltd.

20 Victoria St.   Ph: (416)362-5211
Toronto, ON, Canada M5C 2N8
E-mail: info@micromedia.on.ca
URL: http://www.micromedia.on.ca
Contact: Gail Dykstra, gdykstra@mmltd.com.

Desc: Contains approximately 140,000 citations, with abstracts to Canadian research and report literature in all subject fields. Covers monographs, annual reports, and reports in series issued in English or French by the following types of organizations: all levels of government in Canada, research institutions, universities, laboratories, professional societies, corporations, consultants, and associations. *Available:* Micromedia Ltd. *Type:* Database.

Carnegie Institution of Washington

1530 P St. NW   Ph: (202)387-6400
Washington, DC 20005-1910   Fax: (202)387-8092
URL: http://www.ciw.edu
Contact: Maxine F. Singer, Pres.

Desc: Conducts fundamental research and predoctoral and postdoctoral training in the physical and biological sciences at: the Observatories, Pasadena, CA; Las Campanas Observatory, Chile; Geophysical Laboratory, Washington, DC; Department of Terrestrial Magnetism, Washington, DC; Department of Plant Biology, Stanford, CA; and Department of Embryology, Baltimore, MD. *Type:* Association.

Computer Retrieval of Information on Scientific Projects

U.S. National Institutes of Health
Division of Research Grants
Research Documentation Section

6701 Rockledge Dr., Rm. 3210   Ph: (301)435-0656
Bethesda, MD 20892
E-mail: drt2atscu.nih.gov
URL: http://www.nih.gov
Contact: Dorrette Worrell, Chief, RDS, (301)435-0656, drt@drgpo.drg.nih.gov.

Desc: Contains descriptions of more than 65,000 biomedical research projects that are currently in progress or recently completed and supported by the U.S. Public Health Services. *Available:* Ovid Technologies, Inc. *Type:* Database.

The Cyberskeptic's Guide to Internet Research
BiblioData
PO Box 61   Ph: (781)444-1154
Needham Heights, MA 02494   Fax: (781)449-4584
E-mail: ina@bibliodata.com
Contact: Ruth Orenstein, Editor, ruth@bibliodata.com.
Desc: Provides information on using the Internet for practical research. Targets users who are familiar with other services such as DIALOG and NEXIS so comparisons can be made. *Type:* Newsletter.

Directory of American Research and Technology
R. R. Bowker
A Unit of Cahners Business Information
121 Chanlon Rd.   Ph: (908)464-6800
New Providence, NJ 07974   Free: 888-269-5372
                                              Fax: (908)771-7704
E-mail: info@bowker.com
Contact: Beverley McDonough, Managing Editor.
Desc: Over 13,000 nongovernmental facilities active in research with commercial applications. *Type:* Directory.

Federal Research in Progress
U.S. National Technical Information Service (NTIS)
5285 Port Royal Rd.   Ph: (703)605-6515
Springfield, VA 22161
URL: http://www.fedworld.gov/ntis/ntishome.html
Desc: Contains descriptions of more than 165,000 research projects in progress and recently completed research sponsored primarily by federal government agencies. Covers basic and applied research in all areas of the life, physical, social, behavioral, and engineering sciences. *Available:* The Dialog Corporation, DIALOG; The Dialog Corporation, DIALOG; Knowledge Express Data Systems, Knowledge Express. *Type:* Database.

The Frame
Survey Sampling, Inc.
1 Post Rd.   Ph: (203)255-4200
Fairfield, CT 06430   Fax: (203)254-0372
E-mail: info@ssisamples.com
URL: http://www.worldopinion.com.
Contact: Diane Urso, Editor.
Desc: Provides information on the survey research industry regarding sampling methodologies and technologies. Recurring features include letters to the editor, interviews, news of research, and reports of meetings. *Type:* Newsletter.

Industrial R & D Alert
Technical Insights
John Wiley and Sons, Inc.
32 N. Dean St.   Ph: (201)568-4744
Englewood, NJ 07631
E-mail: TIInf@wiley.com
URL: http://www.wiley.comm/technicalinsights
Contact: Mark Roberts, Director of Computer Operations, (201)568-6764, irdinfo@insights.com.
Desc: Contains the complete text of Industrial R&D Alert, a weekly newsletter on developments with industrial potential available for licensing. Covers chemistry, electronics, materials engineering, instrumentation, biotechnology, robotics, and emerging technologies. *Available:* CompuServe Information Service. *Type:* Database.

Industrial Research Institute
1550 M St. NW, Ste. 1100   Ph: (202)296-8811
Washington, DC 20005-1712   Fax: (202)776-0756
Contact: Charles F. Larson, Exec.Dir.
Desc: Manufacturers and industrial firms maintaining industrial research laboratories. Identifies and promotes effective techniques for the organization and management of research, development, and engineering in support of technological innovation. *Type:* Association.

Institute for Creation Research
10946 Woodside Ave. N   Ph: (619)448-0900
Santee, CA 92071   Fax: (619)448-3469
URL: http://www.icr.org
Contact: John D. Morris, Ph.D., Pres.
Desc: Asserts "the inerrancy of scripture through the abundant evidence in science." *Type:* Association.

International Research Centers Directory
Gale Group Inc.
27500 Drake Rd.   Ph: (248)699-4253
Farmington Hills, MI 48331-   Free: 800-877-GALE
    3535   Fax: (248)699-8070
E-mail: galeord@galegroup.com
URL: http://www.galegroup.com.; http://www.gale.com.
Contact: Michelle E. Eads, Editor, michelle.eads@gale.com.
Desc: Over 8,500 research and development facilities maintained outside the United States by governments, universities, or independent organizations, and concerned with all areas of physical, social, and life sciences, technology, business, military science, public policy, and the humanities. *Type:* Directory.

Laboratory Equipment
Cahners Business Information
New Product Information Division
301 Gibraltar Dr.   Ph: (973)292-5100
Morris Plains, NJ 07950   Fax: (973)539-3476
URL: http://www.labequipmag.com.
Contact: Helen Robinson, Editor; Wayne Curtis, Publisher, wcurtis@gordon.cahners.com.
Desc: Magazine (tabloid) covering research, development, and industrial laboratories news. *Type:* Periodical.

Laboratory Medicine
American Society of Clinical Pathologists
2100 W. Harrison St.   Ph: (312)738-1336
Chicago, IL 60612   Fax: (312)738-0101
URL: http://www.asep.org.
Contact: Lynn Olson, Managing Editor; Joseph Dingee, Ad. Sales Asst.
Desc: Professional journal covering medical technology and pathology. *Type:* Periodical.

Laboratory Regulation Manual Newsletter
Aspen Publishers, Inc.
200 Orchard Ridge Dr., No.   Ph: (301)417-7500
    200   Free: 800-638-8437
Gaithersburg, MD 20878   Fax: (301)417-7650
E-mail: customer.service@aspenpubl.com
URL: http://www.aspenpub.com
Contact: Patricia Younger, Editor; Cynthia Conner, Editor.
Desc: Provides news of events relating to laboratory regulations. Updates the Laboratory Regulation Manual. *Type:* Newsletter.

National Technology Transfer Center Home Page
U.S. National Technology Transfer Center
316 Washington Ave.   Ph: (304)243-2128
Wheeling, WV 26003   Free: 800-678-6882
                                              Fax: (304)243-4386
URL: http://iridium.nttc.edu/nttc.html
Contact: Chuck Monfradi, webmaster@nttc.edu.
Desc: The National Technology Transfer Center Home Page contains information on new technologies and business opportunities resulting from federally-sponsored research and development, including a directory of federal laboratories and technology resources, new federally-sponsored technologies available for licensing, NTTC research and technology reports, and current SBIR and STTR solicitations. *Type:* Database.

Northwest Regional Educational Laboratory
c/o Robert R. Rath   Ph: (503)275-9500
101 SW Main St., Ste. 500   Fax: (503)275-9489
Portland, OR 97204
Contact: Robert R. Rath, Exec.Dir.
Desc: Educational institutions. Provides research and development assistance to schools and communities to improve educational programs. Disseminates research, development, training, and technical assistance information. *Type:* Association.

Research Centers Directory
Gale Group Inc.
27500 Drake Rd.   Ph: (248)699-4253
Farmington Hills, MI 48331-   Free: 800-877-GALE
    3535   Fax: (248)699-8070
E-mail: galeord@galegroup.com
URL: http://www.galegroup.com.; http://www.gale.com.
Contact: Donna Wood, Editor, donna.wood@gale.com.
Desc: Over 14,200 university, government, and other nonprofit research organizations established on a permanent basis to carry on continuing research programs in all areas of study; includes research institutes, laboratories, experiment stations, research parks, technology transfer centers, and other facilities and activities; coverage includes Canada. *Type:* Directory.

Research Centers and Services Directories
The Gale Group
27500 Drake Rd.   Ph: (248)699-4253
Farmington Hills, MI 48331-
    3535
URL: http://www.galegroup.com
Contact: Customer Service. Toll-free: 800-877-GALE.
Desc: Contains descriptions of more than 27,000 organizations conducting research worldwide. For each facility, provides organization name, director or officer name, address, telephone and FAX numbers, affiliated institutions, publications and services, and research description. *Available:* The Dialog Corporation, DIALOG; The Gale Group, GaleNet. *Type:* Database.

Research News
Bureau of Business Research
Graduate School of Business
University of Texas at Austin
PO Box 7459   Ph: (512)471-1616
Austin, TX 78713   Free: 888-212-4386
                                              Fax: (512)471-1063
E-mail: bbr@uts.cc.utexas.edu; res.news@mail.utexas.edu.
URL: http://www.utexas.edu/depts/bbr/rnews/.
Contact: Mary La Motte, Editor, (512)475-7810, mlamotte@mail.utexas.edu.
Desc: Reports on funding opportunities for business, economic, and faculty research and publication achievements at the University of Texas at Austin. Recurring features include interviews, news of research, calendar of events, reports of meetings, faculty and Center's news, and colloquia. *Type:* Newsletter.

Research Services Directory

Grey House Publishing
Pocket Knife Square   Ph: (860)435-0868
Lakeville, CT 06039   Free: 800-562-2139
   Fax: (860)435-0867
E-mail: books@li.com
URL: http://www.greyhouse.com
Desc: More than 4,500 commercial laboratories, consultants, firms, data collection and analysis centers, individuals, and facilities in the private sector that conduct contractual or proprietary research in all areas of business, government, humanities, social science, and science and technology. *Type:* Directory.

Tinnitus Today

American Tinnitus Association (ATA)
PO Box 5   Ph: (503)248-9985
Portland, OR 97207   Free: 800-634-8978
   Fax: (503)248-0024
E-mail: tinnitus@ata.org.
URL: http://www.ata.org.
Desc: Magazine focusing on developments in the field of tinnitus research and management strategies. *Type:* Periodical.

Restaurants

Bay Sports Review—Directory of Bay Area Sports Bars and Restaurants

Bay Sports Review
PO Box 4520   Ph: (925)934-7647
Berkeley, CA 94704   Fax: (925)934-7650
Contact: Paul Matson, Editor.
Desc: List of over 300 bars and restaurants in the San Francisco Bay area with multiple televisions, pool tables, dart boards, large screen televisions, interactive video, video games, jukeboxes, sports games, satellite dishes, and other amenities that cater to sports fans. *Type:* Directory.

Retailing

AGSA News

Art Glass Suppliers Association
1100-H Brandywine Blvd.   Ph: (740)452-4541
PO Box 3388   Fax: (740)452-2552
Zanesville, OH 43702-3388
E-mail: agsa.info@offinger.com
Contact: Tricia Kidd, Editor, trkidd@offinger.com.
Desc: Seeks to inform buinesses involved in the decorative glass and art glass supply industry. Provides retail tips, trade show and association news, news of members, and a calendar of events. *Type:* Newsletter.

American Luggage Dealers Cooperative

610 Anacapa St., Ste. G   Ph: (805)966-6909
Santa Barbara, CA 93101   Fax: (805)966-5710
E-mail: mjalda@aol.com
URL: http://www.luggagedealers.com
Contact: Marion L. Jones, Exec.Dir.
Desc: Retail luggage stores united to develop progressive merchandising programs and provide merchandising opportunities that benefit both the customer and retailer. Commissions buying power surveys. *Type:* Association.

American Truck Stop Owners Association

PO Box 4949   Ph: (910)744-5555
Winston-Salem, NC 27115-4949   Fax: (910)744-1184
Contact: Lloyd L. Golding, Pres.
Desc: Truck stop operators and suppliers united to promote and improve the truck stop industry. *Type:* Association.

ARA Newsletter

Apparel Retailers of America (ARA)
325 7th St., Ste. 1000   Ph: (202)347-1932
Washington, DC 20004-2801
Contact: Suzanne Kilgore, Editor.
Desc: Reports business and industry news to owners and operators of apparel specialty stores. Supplies discussion and suggestions about subjects such as store credit, community promotional campaigns, store design and construction, and sales policy. *Type:* Newsletter.

ARSC Newsletter

Association for Recorded Sound Collections, Inc. (ARSC)
PO Box 543   Ph: (410)757-0488
Annapolis, MD 21404-0543   Fax: (410)349-0175
E-mail: peters@umd5.umd.edu.
Contact: Mike Devecka, Editor.
Desc: Covers the Association's activities and the aspects of recordings and recorded sound. Recurring features include a calendar of events, reports of meeting, and notices of publications available. *Type:* Newsletter.

Association Sales and Marketing Companies

2100 Reston Pky., Ste. 400   Ph: (703)758-7790
Reston, VA 20191-1218   Fax: (703)758-7787
E-mail: info@asmc.org
URL: http://www.asmc.org
Contact: Robert C. Schwarze, Pres. & CEO.
Desc: Sales Agencies and manufacturers who use agencies to go to market. Strives to maintain a highly respectable position in those industries served by its members. *Type:* Association.

Barnard's Retail Trend Report

Barnard Enterprises, Inc.
17 Kenneth Rd.   Ph: (908)561-2300
Upper Montclair, NJ 07043-2541
Contact: Kurt Barnard, Editor.
Desc: Forecasts predictions, analyzes, explains, and identifies trends and events affecting retail operations. Recurring features include market statistics and news of research. *Type:* Newsletter.

The Bedroom Industry Newsletter

Specialty Sleep Association
236 Rte. 38 West, Ste. 100   Ph: (609)231-8500
Moorestown, NJ 08057   Free: 800-336-7322
   Fax: (609)231-4664
E-mail: ssa@ahint.com
Contact: Linda Lauer, Editor.
Desc: Provides Association news and covers government regulations affecting the bedding industry and related topics in labor and employee relations. Carries news of people, places, and products in the industry. *Type:* Newsletter.

BISON Franchise Search

Cell Group, Inc./BISON
3419 NW Evangeline Thruway   Ph: (318)896-8360
Carencro, LA 70520-9000   Fax: (318)896-8736
E-mail: cell@iamerica.net
URL: http://www.bison1.com/BisonFranch1.html
Desc: Wondering what it would take to set up a franchise restaurant operation? Stop by this site and do a little exploring to find out what - and how much - might be involved in buying, setting up, and operating a franchise. Search the database for over 1,500 franchises in 90 different business categories, from the hamburger restaurants we all know (and maybe love) to the brand-name transmission shops, insurance agencies, and photocopy services. *Type:* Database.

Carlson Report for Shopping Center Management

Carlson Report, Inc.
PO Box 502830   Ph: (317)576-9889
Indianapolis, IN 46250-7830   Free: 800-546-9889
   Fax: (317)576-0441
E-mail: ravencom@prodigy.net.
Contact: William R. Wilburn, Editor.
Desc: Serves as a forum for ideas on improving shopping center management. Concerned with leasing, sales analysis, landscaping, maintenance, security, and marketing. *Type:* Newsletter.

Category Reports

Marketing Intelligence Service, Ltd.
6473-D State Rte. 64   Ph: (716)374-6326
Naples, NY 14512-9726   Free: 800-836-5710
   Fax: (716)374-5217
E-mail: mi@productscan.com
URL: http://www.productscan.com.
Contact: Kim Cruise, Editor.
Desc: Provides product reporting services in the following areas: foods, beverages, snacks, health and beauty aids, household, and pets. *Type:* Newsletter.

Clothing Manufacturers Association—News Bulletin

Clothing Manufacturers Association of the U.S.A.
730 Broadway, 9th Fl.   Ph: (212)529-0823
New York, NY 10003   Fax: (212)529-1739
Contact: Robert A. Kaplan, Editor.
Desc: Disseminates information for the Association relating to developments in or affecting the manufacturing of men's and boy's tailored clothing in the U.S. Contains statistics on sales, production, size, and industry earnings. *Type:* Newsletter.

The Crafts Report

Crafts Report
300 Water St.   Ph: (302)656-2209
Wilmington, DE 19801   Free: 800-777-7098
   Fax: (302)656-4894
URL: http://www.craftsreport.com/.
Contact: Bernadette Finnerty, Editor.
Desc: Reports marketing and financial news for the professional craftsperson. Discusses selling techniques, buying supplies wholesale, saving on taxes, and pricing craftwork. *Type:* Newsletter.

CTDA Tile News & Views

Ceramic Tile Distributors Association (CTDA)
800 Roosevelt Rd., Bldg. C, Ste. 20   Ph: (630)545-9415
Glen Ellyn, IL 60137   Free: 800-938-CTDA
   Fax: (630)790-3095
Desc: Presents information and news of interest to the tile industry. Recurring features include news of research, reports of meetings, news of educational opportunities, editorials, and a column titled President's Corner. *Type:* Newsletter.

Data Link

Independent Cash Register Dealers Association (ICRDA)
1900 Cross Beam Dr.   Ph: (704)357-3124
Charlotte, NC 28217   Fax: (704)357-3127
E-mail: icrda@ix.netcom.com
Contact: Casey A. Neel, Editor.
Desc: Provides information about the point-of-sale industry. *Type:* Newsletter.

Davis Database

Herbert W. Davis and Company
1 Executive Dr., Ste. 280   Ph: (201)944-5580
Fort Lee, NJ 07024-3311   Fax: (201)944-2044
Desc: Discusses current topics in physical distribution and customer service and provides ideas to improve customer service and increase productivity. Offers results of service performance and cost surveys by industry. *Type:* Newsletter.

Denver Merchandise Mart Directory

Denver Merchandise Mart
451 E. 58th Ave.   Ph: (303)292-6278
Denver, CO 80216   Free: 800-289-6278
   Fax: (303)297-8473
Contact: Davene L. Coutts, Editor.
Desc: About 4,000 manufacturers, importers, and wholesale distributors of men's, women's, and children's clothing, western apparel, shoes, gifts, gourmet items, bath accessories, jewelry, resort merchandise, and home furnishings who are represented in the Denver Merchandise Mart. *Type:* Directory.

Fabric Marketing Research

Fabric Marketing Research
234 5th Ave.   Ph: (212)686-2345
New York, NY 10001   Fax: (212)532-2626
E-mail: feedback@fabricmarketing.com
URL: http://www.fabricmarketing.com/
Desc: The Fabric Marketing Research database lets you search for manufacturers, producers, wholesalers, and others in the apparel, textile, and soft goods industries. The database can be searched without charge online, and additional information services are available on a fee basis. *Type:* Database.

Fastener Industry News

Fastener Industry News
2009 NE 16th Ave.   Ph: (503)335-0183
Portland, OR 97212-4430   Fax: (503)335-3451
E-mail: fin@fastenernews.com
Contact: John Wolz, Editor.
Desc: Covers business activities of the companies comprising the fastener industry. Reports on mergers, expansions, restructurings, marketing shifts, management appointments, and new company start-ups. *Type:* Newsletter.

FCICA Update

Floor Covering Installation Contractors Association (FCICA)
PO Box 948   Ph: (706)226-5488
Dalton, GA 30722-0948
Desc: Features articles on members and conferences in the floor covering installation industry. Recurring features include interviews, news of research, and a calendar of events. *Type:* Newsletter.

FIA Executive Digest

Footwear Industries of America
1420 K St., Ste. 600   Ph: (202)789-1420
Washington, DC 20005   Free: 800-688-SOLE
   Fax: (202)789-4058
E-mail: info@fia.org
URL: http://www.fia.org; http://www.fia.org.
Contact: Barbara Singer, Editor.
Desc: Publishes Association activities in the areas of footwear technology, finance and management, national affairs, and marketing. Provides current industry statistics. *Type:* Newsletter.

Food Marketing Institute

800 Connecticut Ave. NW   Ph: (202)452-8444
Washington, DC 20006   Fax: (202)429-4519
E-mail: fmi@fmi.org
URL: http://www.fm.org
Contact: Timothy M. Hammonds, Pres.
Desc: Grocery retailers and wholesalers. Maintains liaison with government and consumers. *Type:* Association.

Footwear Industries of America

1420 K St. NW, Ste. 600   Ph: (202)789-1420
Washington, DC 20005   Fax: (202)789-4058
E-mail: info@fia.org
URL: http://www.fia.org
Contact: Fawn Evenson, Pres.
Desc: American manufacturers of footwear and their suppliers, importers, and distributors. Provides information on all aspects of the industry including marketing, technology, finance, management, statistics, and national affairs. *Type:* Association.

Formalwords

International Formalwear Association
401 N. Michigan Ave.   Ph: (312)644-6610
Chicago, IL 60611   Fax: (312)321-5144
Contact: Annette Claussen, Editor.
Desc: Concerned with the promotion of the formalwear industry, providing specialized information on profit strategies, marketing, merchandising, advertising, sales, and other areas of interest. Includes Association news and columns titled President's Message, and Member Profile. *Type:* Newsletter.

Franchise Annual

Todd Publications
PO Box 635   Ph: (914)358-6213
Nyack, NY 10960   Free: 800-747-1056
   Fax: (914)358-1059
E-mail: toddpub@aol.com
URL: http://www.toddpublications.com
Desc: Approximately 5,000 franchises, distributors, licensors and franchise consultants with U.S. or Canadian headquarters, as well as 465 overseas listings. *Type:* Directory.

The Guide to Canadian Retailers & Distributors

Chain Store Guide Information Services
3922 Coconut Palm Dr.   Ph: (813)627-6800
Tampa, FL 33619   Free: 800-927-9292
   Fax: (813)627-6882
E-mail: info@csgis.com
Contact: Nikki Flenon, Editor; Joe Pielech, Editor.
Desc: More than 2,400 companies and 8,900 key executives and buying personnel are profiled in industries such as apparel specialty, food distribution, home furnishings, restaurants, grocery and more. *Type:* Directory.

Independent Bookselling Today

Paz & Associates
c/o Donna Paz   Ph: (615)298-2303
2106 20th Ave. So.   Free: 800-260-8605
Nashville, TN 37212-4312   Fax: (615)298-9864
E-mail: dpaz@pazbookbiz.com.
Contact: Mark Kaufman, Editor, mkaufman@pazbookbiz.com.
Desc: Offers business ideas and advice to independent retail booksellers for developing a profitable store. Presents strategies to help create "shopping experiences that set independent retail booksellers apart from discounters and mass merchants." Takes a business management angle of independent bookselling; features a specific topic per issue. *Type:* Newsletter.

Independent Cash Register Dealers Association—Membership Directory

Independent Cash Register Dealers Association (ICRDA)
1900 Cross Beam Dr.   Ph: (704)357-3124
Charlotte, NC 28217   Fax: (704)357-3127
E-mail: icrda@ix.netcom.com
URL: http://www.icrda.org.
Contact: Casey A. Neel, Editor.
Desc: About 545 member manufacturers, dealers, and suppliers of cash register and point-of-sale systems. *Type:* Directory.

Inside Retailing

Lebhar-Friedman, Inc.
425 Park Ave.   Ph: (212)756-5228
New York, NY 10022-3556   Free: 800-453-2427
   Fax: (212)756-5120
Contact: David Mahler, Editor, dmiou@aol.com.
Desc: Provides up-to-date information on what is happening in the retail industry and how current economic conditions affect retailing. Summarizes actions, acquisitions, and policies of major retail chains across the U.S. *Type:* Newsletter.

Insider

Trade Dimensions
45 Danbury Rd.   Ph: (203)563-3000
Wilton, CT 06897   Fax: (203)563-3131
E-mail: info@tradedimensions.com
URL: http://www.tradedimensions.com
Contact: Brian Thomas, Editor, (203)563-3045.
Desc: Features news of expanding retail chains and their key leasing contacts; shopping center projects, including expansions, renovations, and new centers; acquisitions of shopping center properties; legal cases and decisions; financing news; and news of industry personalities. Includes columns titled Shop Talk, Developments, Acquisitions, The Law, and People. *Type:* Newsletter.

International Council of Shopping Centers

665 5th Ave.   Ph: (212)421-8181
New York, NY 10022   Fax: (212)486-0849
E-mail: icsc@icsc.org
URL: http://www.icsc.org/
Contact: John Riordan, Pres.
Desc: Owners, developers, retailers, and managers of shopping centers; architects, engineers, contractors, leasing brokers, promotion agencies, and others who provide services and products for shopping center owners, shopping center merchant associations, retailers, and public and academic organizations. Promotes professional standards of performance in the development, construction, financing, leasing, management, and operation of shopping centers throughout the world. *Type:* Association.

International Mass Retail Association

1700 N. Moore St. Ste. 2250   Ph: (703)841-2300
Arlington, VA 22209   Fax: (703)841-1184
URL: http://www.imra.org
Contact: Robert J. Verdisco, Pres.
Desc: Mass discount retailing chains; associate members are manufacturers, accounting firms, banks, and service organizations. Purpose is to conduct research and educational programs on every phase of mass retailing. *Type:* Association.

International Product Alert

Marketing Intelligence Service, Ltd.
6473-D State Rte. 64   Ph: (716)374-6326
Naples, NY 14512-9726   Free: 800-836-5710
   Fax: (716)374-5217
E-mail: mi@productscan.com

URL: http://www.productscan.com.

Contact: Sherie Meeker-Barton, Editor.

Desc: Provides concise reports on new products in 18 countries outside of the U.S. and Canada. *Type:* Newsletter.

International Sanitary Supply Association

7373 N. Lincoln Ave.   Ph: (847)982-0800
Lincolnwood, IL 60646   Free: 800-225-4772
    Fax: (847)982-1012

E-mail: info@issa.com

URL: http://www.issa.com

Contact: John Garfinkel, Exec. Dir.

Desc: Manufacturers, distributors manufacturer representatives, and associate members of cleaning and maintenance supplies, chemicals, and equipment used by janitors, custodians, and maintenance workers in all types of industrial, commercial, and institutional buildings. Represents members in 65 countries. Produces films and other educational materials. *Type:* Association.

Jim Lahm's Video Specialist New Technology

J. Lahm Consultants, Inc.

1025 Stanford Ave.   Ph: (714)738-8422
Fullerton, CA 92831-2809   Free: 800-835-9060
    Fax: (714)738-4860

E-mail: vidspecnt@aol.com.

Contact: Jim Lahm, Editor.

Desc: Reports, advises, and analyzes products, services, and developments of home video technologies and video dispensing machines. *Type:* Newsletter.

Lee Howard's U.S.A. Wholesale Sources Directory

Selective Books, Inc.

PO Box 984   Ph: (813)891-6451
Oldsmar, FL 34677   Fax: (813)855-5791

E-mail: sbooks@mindspring.com

Contact: C. Cusack, Publisher.

Desc: Suppliers of consumer merchandise that is available at wholesale prices, for dealers only. *Type:* Directory.

Loeb Retail Letter

Loeb Associates Inc.

PO Box 1155   Ph: (212)596-4034
New York, NY 10018   Fax: (212)596-4642

E-mail: loeb@idt.net

URL: http://www.loebassociates.com.

Contact: Walter F. Loeb, Editor, loeb@mail.idt.net.

Desc: Publishes articles on the retail industry. Recurring features include news of research. *Type:* Newsletter.

Marketers Forum Magazine

Forum Publishing Co.

383 E. Main St.   Ph: (516)574-5000
Centerport, NY 11721   Fax: (516)754-0630

E-mail: forum123@juno.com

URL: http://www.forum123.com

Contact: Martin Stevens, Editor.

Desc: Over 1,000 suppliers of products suitable for retail stores and flea markets. *Type:* Directory.

Michigan Retailers Association

221 N. Pine St.   Ph: (517)372-5656
Lansing, MI 48933   Free: 800-366-3699
    Fax: (517)372-1303

E-mail: lmeyer@retailers.com

URL: http://www.retailers.com

Contact: Larry Meyer, CEO.

Desc: Retail stores and outlets. Promotes the interests of members through legislative and educational activities. *Type:* Association.

Monday Report on Retailers

Maclean Hunter Business Publications

Maclean Hunter Bldg.   Ph: (416)596-5000
777 Bay St., 5th Fl.
Toronto, ON, Canada M5W
    1A7

E-mail: dbenmergui@mhpublishing.com.

Contact: Don Douloff, Editor, (416)596-5910, ddouloff@mhpublishing.com; Gloria Gallagher, Publisher; Cheryl Treliving, Circulation Mgr.

Desc: Provides information on the Canadian retail industry. *Type:* Newsletter.

Multimedia Monitor

Phillips Business Information, Inc.

1201 Seven Locks Rd., Ste. 300   Ph: (301)340-1520
Potomac, MD 20854   Free: 888-707-5809
    Fax: (301)340-3847

E-mail: clientservices.pbi@phillips.com

Contact: Rockley Miller, Editor; Vicki L. Reeve, Editor; Craig Webb, Editor.

Desc: Provides news and analysis covering application, innovation, and technology within multimedia, interactive video, compact disc, and related fields. *Type:* Newsletter.

NACS

National Association of Convenience Stores (NACS)

1605 King St.   Ph: (703)684-3600
Alexandria, VA 22314   Fax: (703)836-4564

URL: http://www.cstorecentral.com.

Contact: Stewart Small, Editor, ssmall@cstorecentral.com; Lindsay Hutter, Editor.

Desc: Reports on key industry trends and innovative practices of convenience store companies. Recurring features include news of research, a calendar of events, reports of meetings, news of educational opportunities, and notices of publications available. *Type:* Newsletter.

NAMM PlayBack

National Association of Music Merchants (NAMM)

5790 Armada Dr.   Ph: (760)438-8001
Carlsbad, CA 92008   Fax: (760)438-7327

E-mail: namm@namm.com

Contact: John Maher, Editor.

Desc: Published to keep member retailers and manufacturers of musical instruments apprised of industry news and Association trade shows. Also publicizes the Association's educational services and membership benefits. *Type:* Newsletter.

NAMSB News

National Association of Men's Sportswear Buyers, Inc. (NAMSB)

60 E. 42nd St., Rm. 2430   Ph: (212)856-9644
New York, NY 10165-2430   Fax: (212)856-0825

E-mail: info@NAMSB-SHOW.com

Contact: Jack Herschlag, Editor.

Desc: Contains information on men's fashion trends and NAMSB services and programs. Recurring features include a column titled Memo to Members. *Type:* Newsletter.

National-American Wholesale Grocers' Association

201 Park Washington Ct.   Ph: (703)532-9400
Falls Church, VA 22046   Fax: (703)538-4673

Contact: John R. Block, Pres.

Desc: Wholesale grocers and foodservice distributors. Provides technical assistance, research, and educational services in areas such as warehousing, transportation, information technology, financial management, and human resources. Represents members in industry councils, regulatory agencies, and Congress. *Type:* Association.

National Association of College Stores

500 E. Lorain St.   Ph: (440)775-7777
Oberlin, OH 44074   Free: 800-622-7498
    Fax: (216)775-4769

E-mail: info@nacs.org

URL: http://www.nacs.org

Contact: Brian Cartier, CAE, Exec.Dir.

Desc: Institutional, private, leased, and cooperative college stores (3200) selling books, supplies, and other merchandise to college students, faculty, and staff; associate members include publishers and suppliers (1200). Seeks to effectively serve higher education by providing educational opportunities, services, and products to college stores and their suppliers. *Type:* Association.

National Association of Floor Covering Distributors—News and Views

National Association of Floor Covering Distributors

401 N. Michigan Ave.   Ph: (312)321-6836
Chicago, IL 60611-4205   Fax: (312)245-1085

E-mail: info@nafcd.org

Contact: Tina Gonsalues, Editor.

Desc: Provides news of the Association and the floor covering industry. Recurring features include news of members, notices of publications available, news of educational opportunities, reports of meetings, and a calendar of events. *Type:* Newsletter.

National Association of Recording Merchandisers

9 Eves Dr., Ste. 120   Ph: (609)596-2221
Marlton, NJ 08053   Fax: (609)596-3268

URL: http://www.narm.com

Contact: Pamela Horovitz, Pres.

Desc: NARM serves the music and other prerecorded entertainment software industry as the pre-eminent forum for insight and dialogue. Its members include retailers, wholesalers, distributors, entertainment software suppliers, and suppliers of related products and services. *Type:* Association.

National Association of Retail Dealers of America

10 E. 22nd St., Ste. 310   Ph: (630)953-8950
Lombard, IL 60148   Fax: (630)953-8957

Contact: Elly Valas, Exec.Dir.

Desc: Retailers of appliances, home electronics, computers, furniture, and audio components; associate members include manufacturers, utilities, distributors of appliances and consumer electronics, and financial institutions. Works to create more profitable dealerships. Services include management consulting, sales training, advertising workshops, computer service bureau, School of Service Management, Institute of Management, surveys, credit union, bank card program, and management training. *Type:* Association.

National Association of Wholesaler-Distributors

1725 K St. NW   Ph: (202)872-0885
Washington, DC 20006   Fax: (202)785-0586

Contact: Dirk Van Dongen, Pres.

Desc: Federation of national, state, and regional associations, and individual wholesaler-distributor firms. Represents industry's views to the federal government. Analyzes current and proposed legislation and government regulations affecting the industry. *Type:* Association.

National Automatic Merchandising Association

20 N. Wacker Dr., Ste. 350   Ph: (312)346-0370
Chicago, IL 60606   Fax: (312)704-4140

URL: http://www.vending.org

Contact: Richard M. Geerdes, Pres./CEO.

Desc: Manufacturing and operating companies in the automatic vending machine industry; food service management firms; office coffee machine operators; suppliers of products and services. *Type:* Association.

National Grocers Association

1825 Samuel Morse Dr.   Ph: (703)437-5300
Reston, VA 20190   Fax: (703)437-7768
URL: http://www.nationalgrocers.org
Contact: Thomas K. Zaucha, Pres.
Desc: Independent food retailers (2000); wholesale food distributors (60) servicing 29,000 food stores. Promotes industry interests and works to advance understanding, trade, and cooperation among all sectors of the food industry. *Type:* Association.

National Nutritional Foods Association

3931 MacArthur Blvd., No. 101   Ph: (949)622-6272
Newport Beach, CA 92660-   Fax: (949)622-6266
   3021
E-mail: nnfa@aol.com
URL: http://www.nnfa.org
Contact: Michael Q. Ford, Exec.Dir.
Desc: Retailers, wholesalers, brokers, distributors and manufacturers of natural, nutritional, dietetic foods, supplements, and natural body care products. *Type:* Association.

NATSO, Representing the Travel Plaza and Truckstop Industry

1199 N. Fairfax St., Ste. 801   Ph: (703)549-2100
Alexandria, VA 22314   Fax: (703)684-4525
E-mail: feedback@natso.com
URL: http://www.natso.com
Contact: W. Dewey Clower, Pres.
Desc: Owners and operators of travel plazas and truck stops that can facilitate professional truckers and all highway travelers; allied members include oil companies and other product and service vendors. Seeks to elevate the image of the industry by encouraging superior service and facilities. *Type:* Association.

The NSPI Business Owners Journal

National Spa and Pool Institute (NSPI)
2111 Eisenhower Ave.   Ph: (703)838-0083
Alexandria, VA 22314   Fax: (703)549-0493
Contact: Barbara Brady, Editor, bbrady@nspi.org.
Desc: News of the Institute and member activities in the series of briefs. *Type:* Newsletter.

The Outlet Retail Directory

Value Retail News
A Unit of The International Council of Shopping Centers
29399 US Hwy. 19, N., Ste.   Ph: (727)781-9717
   130   Fax: (727)781-7551
Clearwater, FL 33761-2137
E-mail: vrn@ix.netcom.com
URL: http://www.icsc.org.
Contact: Fred J. Filer, Publisher.
Desc: More than 525 outlet retail chains. *Type:* Directory.

Paint and Decorating Retailers Association —Register

Paint and Decorating Retailers Association
403 Axminster Dr.   Ph: (314)326-2636
Fenton, MO 63026   Free: 800-737-0107
   Fax: (314)326-1823
E-mail: info@pdra.org
Contact: Diane Capuano, Editor.
Desc: Presents information on the paint and decorating industry, including news of governmental and legislative actions, business trends, retailing tips, association activities, marketing and management tips, and special feature stories. *Type:* Newsletter.

The Peter Berlin Report on Shrinkage Control— Executive Edition

Peter Berlin Retail Consulting Group, Inc.
380 N. Broadway, Ste. 306   Ph: (516)932-0450
Jericho, NY 11753   Fax: (516)932-9393
E-mail: sainc@sprintmail.com
Contact: Peter D. Berlin, Editor.
Desc: Provides information on current trends, tools, and techniques for reducing inventory losses in retail stores from shoplifting, employee theft, and paperwork error. Features include news of research, new products, and reports of surveys. *Type:* Newsletter.

PRC News

Corbell Publishing Co.
4676 Admiralty Way, Ste. 300   Ph: (310)574-5337
Marina del Rey, CA 90292   Fax: (310)574-5383
URL: http://www.corbell.com.
Contact: Deborah Rolfe, Editor; Maureen A. Healy, President/Publisher, mhealy8136@aol.com.
Desc: Covers video software, blank video tape, VCRs, video industry business information, new video releases, and promotions of video industry personnel. Recurring features include industry statistics, a calendar of events, reports of meetings, research information, and available publications. *Type:* Newsletter.

The Pricing Advisor

Eric Mitchell
3277 Roswell Rd., Ste. 620   Ph: (770)509-9933
Atlanta, GA 30305   Fax: (770)509-1963
E-mail: info@pricing-advisor_com.
Contact: Eric Mitchell, Editor and Publisher, mitchell@pricing-advisor.com.
Desc: Provides information and advice about pricing. *Type:* Newsletter.

Product Alert

Marketing Intelligence Service, Ltd.
6473-D State Rte. 64   Ph: (716)374-6326
Naples, NY 14512-9726   Free: 800-836-5710
   Fax: (716)374-5217
E-mail: mi@productscan.com
URL: http://www.productscan.com.
Contact: Diane Beach, Editor.
Desc: Reports on new consumer goods launched in American retailing, including foods and beverages, nonprescription drugs, cosmetics and toiletries, and miscellaneous household items. Lists products that are an extension of an existing product line, package changes, and marketing plans. *Type:* Newsletter.

PRODUCTSCAN

Marketing Intelligence Service Ltd.
6473D Route 64   Ph: (716)374-6326
Naples, NY 14512-9726
E-mail: mktgintelsvc@cis.compuserve.com
URL: http://ourworld.compuserve.com/homepages/mktgintelsvc
Contact: Janet Mansfield, Manager.
Desc: Includes more than 160,000 new product reports detailing new food, beverage, health and beauty aids, household, tobacco and pet products worldwide from 1980 to the present. Productscan Online offers detailed descriptions of these new consumer packaged goods. *Available:* Marketing Intelligence Service Ltd. *Type:* Database.

The Purdue Retailer

Retail Institute
Purdue University
1262 Matthews Hall, Rm. 318   Ph: (317)494-8301
West Lafayette, IN 47907-1262   Fax: (317)494-0869
Contact: Dr. Holly Schrank, Editor, schrankh@purdue.edu.

Desc: Supplies research information and practical suggestions to large and small business owners who have direct consumer contact. *Type:* Newsletter.

Recognition Review

Awards and Recognition Association
35 E. Wacker Dr., Ste. 500   Ph: (312)782-5252
Chicago, IL 60601   Fax: (312)236-1140
URL: http://www.ara.org.
Contact: Sara Geimer, Editor.
Desc: Covers news and general information on the awards and engraving industry. Focuses on the association's trade shows, product developments and additions, Association business, and industry success stories. *Type:* Newsletter.

The Retail Challenge

International Council of Shopping Centers
665 5th Ave.   Ph: (212)421-8181
New York, NY 10022-5370   Fax: (212)486-0849
Desc: Covers "the nuts and bolts of retailing and provides the industry know-how to boost your merchant's productivity." Features how-to information on selling techniques, customer service, motivation, operations, advertising, promotion, and marketing. *Type:* Newsletter.

Retail Notes

The Quick Study
PO Box 577069   Ph: (312)666-0866
Chicago, IL 60657   Fax: (312)666-0320
Contact: Melissa King, Owner.
Desc: Summarizes news affecting retail with focus on the largest retailers, including Walmart, Sears, and Kmart. Includes trends of the industry. *Type:* Newsletter.

Retail Performance Monitor

CSM Communications Company Inc.
205 Regency Executive Park   Ph: (704)523-8511
   Dr., Ste. 105   Fax: (704)523-7919
Charlotte, NC 28217-3989
Contact: Ralph H. Sullivan, Editor.
Desc: Monitors sales, earnings, bankruptcies, liquidations, mergers, acquisitions, corporate management changes, economic influences, regulatory strategic planning, consolidations, and store performances of the retail industry. Recurring features include news of research. *Type:* Newsletter.

Retail Systems Alert

Ardeh Research Corporation
PO Box 332   Ph: (617)527-4626
Newton, MA 02464   Fax: (617)527-8102
URL: http://www.retailsystems.com.
Contact: Thomas H. Friedman, Editor, tfriedman@retailsytems.com; Eric L. Olson, Managing Editor.
Desc: Provides information on various automated systems, including those monitoring distribution, merchandise planning, labor scheduling, credit and payment, and inventory. Contains a calendar of events. *Type:* Newsletter.

Retail, Wholesale and Department Store Union

30 E. 29th St.   Ph: (212)684-5300
New York, NY 10016   Fax: (212)779-2809
Contact: Lenore Miller, Pres.
Desc: AFL-CIO. *Type:* Association.

Retailing Today

Robert Kahn and Associates
PO Box 249   Ph: (925)254-4434
Lafayette, CA 94549   Fax: (925)284-5612
Contact: Robert Kahn, Editor.
Desc: Focuses on general merchandise, apparel, furniture, hardware, automotive, and food retailing. *Type:* Newsletter.

SDA Newsletter
Soap and Detergent Association (SDA)
475 Park Ave. S.   Ph: (212)725-1262
New York, NY 10016   Fax: (212)213-0685
Contact: Janet Donohue, Editor.
Desc: Presents brief news items on the soap and detergent industry. Covers news of government and legislative developments, research and technical developments, and activities of the Association and its divisions. *Type:* Newsletter.

Sheldon's Retail
Todd Publications
PO Box 635   Ph: (914)358-6213
Nyack, NY 10960   Free: 800-747-1056
                          Fax: (914)358-1059
E-mail: toddpub@aol.com
URL: http://www.toddpublications.com
Contact: Massar, Editor.
Desc: Executives, merchandise managers, and buyers in 1,350 major department stores, 450 chain headquarters, 550 major women's stores plus 500 chains. *Type:* Directory.

Shoe Retailing Today
National Shoe Retailers Association
9861 Broken Land Pkwy., Ste.   Ph: (410)381-8282
  255   Free: 800-673-8446
Columbia, MD 21046-1151
Contact: Carol Blank, Editor.
Desc: Provides news of regional Chapter activities, developments in independent shoe retailing, Recurring features include news of members, calendar of events, and a four-page How-To on a topic of interest to independent shoe retailers. *Type:* Newsletter.

The Shopper - Your Guide to Shopping Online Malls and Stores
Internet Shopping Directory, Inc.
865 Tahoe Blvd., Ste. 211   Ph: (702)831-2251
Incline Village, NV 89451   Fax: (702)831-3925
E-mail: kerry@shoppingdirect.com
URL: http://www.shoppingdirect.com/
Contact: Patrick Gannon, President and CEO, patrick@shoppingdirect.com.
Desc: The explosive growth of electronic and Internet commerce makes it difficult to keep pace with all the stores popping up online, but The Shopper can help you find your way through the maze. This site is a directory of over 1,000 shopping sites on the Web, all of which are independently rated and reviewed. *Type:* Database.

Shopping Center Digest
JOMURPA Publishing, Inc.
20 N. Broadway   Ph: (914)348-7000
Nyack, NY 10960   Free: 800-211-6958
                          Fax: (914)426-0802
E-mail: scdigest@shoppingcenters.com; scdigest@ucs.net.
URL: http://www.shoppingcenters.com; http://www.shoppingcenters.com.
Contact: Murray Shor, Editor.
Desc: Reports on new and expanding shopping centers throughout Canada and the U.S. and on expansion plans of retail chains. *Type:* Newsletter.

Shopping Center News
Maclean Hunter Ltd.
777 Bay St., 6th Fl.   Ph: (416)596-5000
Toronto, ON, Canada M5W   Fax: (416)596-5552
  1A7
E-mail: dbenmergui@mhpublishing.com.
Contact: Don Douloff, Editor, (416)596-5910, ddouloff@mhpublishing.com.
Desc: Contains news on shopping mall and retail space development, expansion, and renovation. Covers management and leasing issues. *Type:* Newsletter.

Shopping Center Newsletter
Phoenix Ventures Inc.
320 Valley   Ph: (319)752-5415
Burlington, IA 52601   Fax: (319)752-3421
Contact: Teresa Levinson, Editor.
Desc: Covers ideas for seasonal promotions for shopping centers. Recurring features include a calendar of events. *Type:* Newsletter.

Shopping Centers Today
International Council of Shopping Centers
665 5th Ave.   Ph: (212)421-8181
New York, NY 10022-5370   Fax: (212)486-0849
Contact: Debra Hazel, Editor.
Desc: Presents news of the shopping center industry, including "the development of new shopping centers and the expansion and rehabilitation of existing ones, along with the leasing programs of retail tenants." Covers shopping center design, construction, management, and marketing. Recurring features include news of industry meetings and reports on legislative and regulatory actions. *Type:* Newsletter.

The Source
PGA Services, Inc.
1913 Guernsey Ave.   Ph: (215)884-6006
Abington, PA 19001-3701   Fax: (215)884-6007
Contact: John McNelis, Editor.
Desc: Offers coupon, new product, and other information related to retail grocers, pharmacies, and department stores. *Type:* Newsletter.

The Sourcebook of Franchise Opportunities
Irwin Professional Publishing
1333 Burr Ridge Pkwy   Ph: (708)789-4000
Burr Ridge, IL 60521   Free: 800-634-3966
                          Fax: (708)798-6933
Contact: Robert E. Bond, Editor; Jeffrey M. Bond, Editor.
Desc: Over 3,000 franchising opportunities. *Type:* Directory.

Southern Lawnmower Dealer's Newsletter
Roger R. Stewart
PO Box 6426   Ph: (423)983-1477
Maryville, TN 37802   Fax: (423)984-9902
Contact: Roger R. Stewart, Editor, rogst@aol.com.
Desc: Carries trade information about the lawnmower industry in the southeastern United States. *Type:* Newsletter.

Sunglass Association of America—Industry News
Sunglass Association of America (SAA)
49 East Ave.   Ph: (203)845-9015
Norwalk, CT 06851   Fax: (203)847-1304
E-mail: info@sunglassassociation.com
Desc: Covers news from the sunglass industry. *Type:* Newsletter.

Supermarket Strategic Alert
Pollack Associates
PO Box 331   Ph: (212)734-0753
New York, NY 10021
E-mail: info@supermarketalert.com.
Contact: Mary Pollack, Editor and Publisher.
Desc: Provides information for grocery store suppliers. *Type:* Newsletter.

T-Shirt Business Info Mapping Newsletter
Prosperity & Profits Unlimited, Distribution Services
PO Box 416   Ph: (303)575-5676
Denver, CO 80201-0416
Contact: A.C. Doyle, Editor and Publisher.
Desc: Provides business information for the t-shirt industry. *Type:* Newsletter.

Throwing Power
Ion Publishing
500 W. 32nd St.   Ph: (612)824-1456
Minneapolis, MN 55408   Fax: (612)824-3431
Contact: Matthew Knopp, Editor.
Desc: Provides information on electrocoat paint, organic electrodeposition, organic metal finishing, and waterbome paint. Recurring features include news of research, a calendar of events, notices of publications available, and a column titled E-Coat Solutions. *Type:* Newsletter.

Tile News
Italian Trade Commission
499 Park Ave.   Ph: (212)980-1500
New York, NY 10022   Fax: (212)758-1050
E-mail: newyork@italtrade.com; tileinfo@italtrade.com.
URL: http://www.italytile.com; http://www.italtrade.com.
Contact: Jacqueline Greaves, Editor, greaves@italtrade.com.
Desc: Announces Italian tile products available in the U.S. Discusses developments in the tile industry. *Type:* Newsletter.

Today's Hospital Gift Shop Business
Nason & Associates
PO Box 8204   Ph: (828)298-1322
Asheville, NC 28814-8204 Fax: (828)298-1312
Contact: Marilyn Nason, Editor.
Desc: Directed toward hospital gift shop business operations. Profiles new products, events, conferences, seminars, workshops and shows relating to hospital gift shops. *Type:* Newsletter.

Two/Ten International Footwear Foundation
56 Main St.   Ph: (617)923-4500
Watertown, MA 02472   Free: 800-FIND-210
                          Fax: (617)926-6037
Contact: Michael M. Appell, Pres.
Desc: Workers in the shoe, leather, and allied industries. (Foundation derives its name from its previous location, 210 Lincoln St., which was known as the leather and shoe center in Boston, MA.) Objectives are to provide assistance to people in the footwear, leather, and allied trades who may be in financial need; promote the general welfare of those engaged in the shoe industry. Operates gerontology services program for shoepeople 55 years and over. *Type:* Association.

Video Week
Warren Publishing, Inc.
2115 Ward Ct. NW   Ph: (202)872-9200
Washington, DC 20037   Fax: (202)296-4397
E-mail: warrenpub@mindspring.com
URL: http://www.telecommunications.com
Contact: Cindy Spielvogel, Editor, (212)686-5410, fax: (212)889-5097.
Desc: Focuses on areas such as home video programming, piracy, legislation and regulation, costs and prices, and cable services. Publishes trade show news, interviews, news of research, and personnel updates. *Type:* Newsletter.

Voice Coil

Audio Amateur Publications
PO Box 876   Ph: (603)924-9464
Peterborough, NH 03458-0876   Free: 888-924-9465
   Fax: (603)924-9467
E-mail: custserv@audioXpress.com
Contact: Vance Dickason, Editor.
Desc: Provides information, industry news, and software and test equipment reviews relevant to the loudspeaker industry. Recurring features include news of research, a calendar of events, reports of meetings, news of educational opportunities, job listings, and notices of publications available. *Type:* Newsletter.

Weekly Comments

Johnson Redbook Service
345 Hudson St., 15th Fl.
New York, NY 10014
Contact: Edward F. Johnson, Editor.
Desc: Forecasts and tracks consumer trends and their effects on the sales and earnings of the retail, apparel, textile, and chemical industries. Updates forecasts quarterly. *Type:* Newsletter.

Western-English Industry Report

Western English Retailers Association
451 E. 58th Ave., Ste. 4781   Ph: (303)298-7882
Denver, CO 80216   Fax: (303)292-8468
E-mail: wera@frii.com
URL: http://www.wera.org.
Contact: Susan Leach, Exec. Editor; Sushil Dulai Wenholz, Copy Editor.
Desc: Disseminates information on trends, markets, business techniques, and issues on the nation's retailers of Western and English apparel, tack, and equipment. *Type:* Newsletter.

Windham Hill Records Catalog & Occasional

Windham Hill Records Catalog & Occasional
PO Box 5501   Ph: (415)329-0647
Beverly Hills, CA 90209-5501   Free: 800-888-8544
E-mail: whinfo@windham.com
URL: http://www.windham.com.
Contact: Allison Cayo, Editor; Roy Gattinella, Editor; Gina Rayfield, Editor; Jill Santos, Editor.
Desc: Features general artist updates, new release , and other news. Recurring features include a calendar of events and catalog listings for Windham Hill and subsidiary labels. *Type:* Newsletter.

World Floor Covering Association

2211 E. Howell Ave.   Ph: (714)978-6440
Anaheim, CA 92806-6033   Free: 800-624-6880
   Fax: (714)978-6066
E-mail: wfca@wfca.org
URL: http://www.wfca.org
Contact: D. Christopher Davis, CEO.
Desc: Retail floorcovering store owners and managers; floorcovering distributors and manufacturers. Provides liaison, through a Washington, DC lobbyist, between the membership and government organizations that affect the business. Maintains Industry Education Foundation and a Group Insurance Trust. *Type:* Association.

Worldwide Franchise Directory

Gale Group Inc.
27500 Drake Rd.   Ph: (248)699-4253
Farmington Hills, MI 48331-   Free: 800-877-GALE
3535   Fax: (248)699-8070
E-mail: galeord@galegroup.com
URL: http://www.galegroup.com.
Contact: Susan Boyles Martin, Editor.
Desc: Franchise background, start-up, agreement, and foreign outlet contact information for over 1,500 business franchises worldwide. *Type:* Directory.

Xpressions

Xpres Corporation
111 Cloverleaf Dr.   Ph: (910)768-7400
Winston-Salem, NC 27103   Free: 800-334-0425
   Fax: (910)768-4629
Contact: Nikki Kates, Editor.
Desc: Recurring features include interviews, a calendar of events, news of research, new products, technical tips. *Type:* Newsletter.

Retirement

AARP Bulletin

American Association of Retired Persons (AARP)
601 E St. NW   Ph: (202)434-2277
Washington, DC 20049   Fax: (202)434-6451
E-mail: aarp1@aol.com; bulletin@aarp.org.
URL: http://www.aarp.org.
Contact: Elliot Carlson, Editor, (202)434-3340.
Desc: Monitors issues and events affecting Americans aged 50 and over. Covers medical benefits and other services of interest. *Type:* Newsletter.

The AARP Pharmacy Service Enjoying Good Health Newsletter

Retired Persons Services, Inc.
500 Montgomery St.   Ph: (703)684-0245
Alexandria, VA 22314   Fax: (703)836-2947
E-mail: www.rpsrx.com
URL: http://www.rpspharmacy.com/nl.
Contact: Joan M. Zimmerman, Editor, jzimmerman@ rpsrx.com.
Desc: Offers health information and medical tips on topics relevant for the elderly. Recurring features include notices of publications available. *Type:* Newsletter.

American Association of Retired Persons

601 E St. NW   Ph: (202)434-2277
Washington, DC 20049   Free: 800-424-3410
   Fax: (202)434-2320
URL: http://www.aarp.org/
Contact: Horace B. Deets, Exec.Dir.
Desc: Persons 50 years of age or older, working or retired. Seeks to improve every aspect of living for older people. Has targeted four areas of immediate concern: health care, women's initiative, worker equity, and minority affairs. *Type:* Association.

American Association of Retired Persons, Ohio Office

1 S. High St.   Ph: (614)224-9800
Columbus, OH 43215   Free: 800-424-3410
   Fax: (614)224-9801
Contact: Ryan Redlingshafer, Ohio Rep.
Type: Association.

American Association of Retired Persons Webplace

American Association of Retired Persons
601 E St. NW   Free: 800-424-3410
Washington, DC 20049
E-mail: member@aarp.org
URL: http://www.aarp.org/
Desc: One of the most powerful lobbies in the country, AARP represents millions of Americans over the age of 50, many of whom still have 10 or more years to work before retiring. However, one thing all members have in common is a concern that all the benefits and privileges of retirement will be there when the time comes. *Type:* Database.

Association of Retired Americans

6505 E. 82nd St., 130   Free: 800-806-6160
Indianapolis, IN 46260   Fax: (317)915-2510
URL: http://www.ara-usa.org
Contact: Earl E. Heath, Pres.
Desc: Senior Americans, age 45 or more interested in enhancing their lives through group benefits. Purpose is to offer a program of high quality, low-cost benefits and services to members. *Type:* Association.

The Consumer's Directory of Continuing Care Retirement Communities

American Association of Homes and Services
901 E St. NW, Ste. 500   Ph: (202)783-2242
Washington, DC 20004-2037   Fax: (202)783-2255
Desc: 500 retirement communities providing an integrated continuum of short-term and long-term care, including health care, housing, and home and community-based services. *Type:* Directory.

The Directory of Retirement Facilities

HCIA Inc.
300 E. Lombard St.   Ph: (410)576-9600
Baltimore, MD 21202   Free: 800-568-3282
   Fax: (410)752-6309
E-mail: pubs@hcia.com; info@hcia.com
Contact: Beth Christ, Editor.
Desc: Over 18,000 assisted living, congregate care, independent living and continuing care facilities in the United States. *Type:* Directory.

Estate & Retirement Planning Letter

Lombardi Publishing Co.
51 Toro Rd.   Ph: (416)633-1600
North York, ON, Canada M3J   Fax: (416)633-6188
2A4
Contact: Marisha Roman, Editor.
Desc: Provides advice on estate and retirement planning, including trusts, wills, powers of attorney, RRSPs, Section 8s, estate freezes, RRIFs, and other retirement issues. Offers recommendations for a self-directed RRSP. *Type:* Newsletter.

Maine State Retirement News

Maine State Retirement System for Members and Retirees
46 State House Sta.   Ph: (207)287-3461
Augusta, ME 04333-0046   Free: 800-451-9800
   Fax: (207)287-1032
Contact: Jane Torres, Editor, jtorres@msrs.org.
Desc: Provides news of interest to retirees and members of the MSRS. Recurring features include news of legislation and benefit changes. *Type:* Newsletter.

Maine State Retirement Report

Maine State Retirement System for Employers
46 State House Sta.   Ph: (207)287-3461
Augusta, ME 04333-0046
Contact: Susan E. Cottle, Editor.
Desc: Provides news and information to those employers affected by the Maine State Retirement System. Recurring features include news of pertinent legislation. *Type:* Newsletter.

National Association for Retired Credit Union People

PO Box 391   Ph: (608)231-7188
Madison, WI 53701-0391   Free: 800-937-2644
   Fax: (608)231-7229
Contact: Philip A. Tschudy, Exec.Dir.
Desc: Organized by retired credit union leaders to help senior (over age 50) and retired credit union members ob-

tain financial services for retirement planning and management, and to extend the benefits of credit union membership to retirees. Services include: consumer information; mail order discount pharmacy services; travel discounts; accidental death an dismemberment insurance; eye wear discount program, retail pharmacy discount, quarterly PRIME TIMES magazine, full - service travel agency. *Type:* Association.

National Retired Teachers Association, Division of AARP

601 E St. NW Ph: (202)434-2277
Washington, DC 20049 Fax: (202)434-2320

Contact: Horace B. Deets, Exec.Dir.

Desc: Active and retired teachers and educators age 50 and older. Became a division of the American Association of Retired Persons in 1982. *Type:* Association.

Older Americans Almanac

Gale Group Inc.
27500 Drake Rd. Ph: (248)699-4253
Farmington Hills, MI 48331- Free: 800-877-GALE
3535 Fax: (248)699-8070
E-mail: galeord@galegroup.com
URL: http://www.galegroup.com.

Contact: Ronald J. Manheimer, Editor.

Desc: Lists personal names and organizations related to topics on older Americans. Principal content of publication is essays on aging-related topics. *Type:* Directory.

Older Americans Information Directory

Grey House Publishing
Pocket Knife Square Ph: (860)435-0868
Lakeville, CT 06039 Free: 800-562-2139
 Fax: (860)435-0867
E-mail: books@li.com
URL: http://www.greyhouse.com

Desc: About 5,600 organizations, agencies, and publications of interest to senior citizens in the U.S., including associations, libraries and information centers, continuing education programs, research centers, federal, state, and local government agencies, hotlines, legal resources, periodicals, newsletters, directories, book publishers, syndicated radio and television programs, videos, electronic databases, and discount programs. *Type:* Directory.

The Pension Actuary

American Society of Pension Actuaries
4350 N. Fairfax Dr., Ste. 820 Ph: (703)516-9300
Arlington, VA 22203-1619 Fax: (703)516-9308

Contact: Chester Salkind, Editor; Pam Means, Editor-in-Chief.

Desc: Covers current topics of significance to actuaries and consultants in the field of pensions. *Type:* Newsletter.

Railroad Retirement Board

844 N Rush St. Ph: (312)751-4776
Chicago, IL 60611-2092 Fax: (312)751-7154
URL: http://www.rrb.gov/

Contact: Cherryl T. Thomas, Chairman of the Board.

Desc: The Railroad Retirement Board administers comprehensive retirement-survivor and unemployment-sickness benefit programs for the nation's railroad workers and their families under the Railroad Retirement and Railroad Unemployment Insurance Acts. In connection with the retirement program, the Board has administrative responsibilities under the Social Security Act for certain benefit payments and railroad workers' Medicare coverage. *Type:* Government agency, office, or program.

Resources

FISI-Madison Financial
PO Box 40726 Ph: (615)371-2400
Nashville, TN 37204
Contact: Melany Klinck, Editor.

Desc: Provides information on consumer issues, retirement, leisure activities, travel, and second careers. *Type:* Newsletter.

The Retirement Letter

Phillips Publishing International, Inc.
7811 Montrose Rd. Ph: (301)340-2100
Potomac, MD 20854 Fax: (301)424-0245
Contact: Peter A. Dickinson, Editor; Philip A. Springer, Editor, philandpete@phillips.com.

Desc: Offers advice to retired persons and those approaching retirement on making, and saving money. Provides articles on investments, taxes, insurance, travel, health care, and housing. *Type:* Newsletter.

Retirement News

Arizona State Retirement System
330 N. Central Ave., 12th Fl. Ph: (602)240-2000
Phoenix, AZ 85012 Free: 800-621-3778
Contact: Kim Kaan, Editor, (602)240-2048.

Desc: Provides new of interest to retired and active members of Arizona State Retirement System. Features news on legislation and benefit changes. *Type:* Newsletter.

Retirement Planning Advisor

Hearst Business Communications, Inc.
645 Stewart Ave. Ph: (516)229-3601
Garden City, NY 11530 Free: 800-659-9878
 Fax: (516)229-3636
E-mail: raionline@hearst.com
Contact: Beth Helfont, Editor, bhelfont@raionline.com.

Desc: Directed toward pre-retirees planning for retirement. Provides understandable and helpful information on a variety of subjects, including finances, insurance, health, relationships and social issues. *Type:* Newsletter.

Retirement Plans Report

Western League of Savings Institutions
9841 Airport Blvd., Ste. 418 Ph: (310)414-8300
Los Angeles, CA 90045-5416
Contact: Gloria Sewell-Hacko, Editor; Connie C. Gonzales, Editor.

Desc: Reports on tax reform laws affecting retirement plan benefits. Covers IRAs (Individual Retirement Accounts) as well as the Basic Plan. *Type:* Newsletter.

Senior Citizens Services

Gale Group Inc.
27500 Drake Rd. Ph: (248)699-4253
Farmington Hills, MI 48331- Free: 800-877-GALE
3535 Fax: (248)699-8070
E-mail: galeord@galegroup.com
URL: http://www.galegroup.com.

Desc: 15,000 organizations from the private sector that provide senior services, 57 State Agencies on Aging, 670 Area Agencies on Aging. Separated into four volumes each available separately: Northeastern States, Southern and Mid-Atlantic States, Midwestern States, and Western States. *Type:* Directory.

Southern California Senior Life

Senior Media, Inc.
6022 W. Pico Blvd., Ste. 7 Ph: (323)933-9228
Los Angeles, CA 90035 Fax: (323)933-9261
E-mail: seniorlife@aol.com.
URL: http://www.seniornews.com.
Contact: Jerry Beigel, Editor.

Desc: Covers issues of interest to senior citizens living in southern California, including health, nutrition, travel, leisure, entertainment, and sports. Also contains information on financial affairs, legal matters, housing, employment, and political issues. *Type:* Newsletter.

The Steelworkers Oldtimer

The Steelworkers Oldtimer
200 White Hampton Ln., Apt. Ph: (412)833-4761
116
Pittsburgh, PA 15236-1546
Contact: Raymond W. Pasnick, Editor.

Desc: Serves retired members of the United Steelworkers of America by providing articles and news items on subjects of concern to the elderly: retirees club news, developments in social security, retirement problems, and pertinent legislative activities. Recurring features include news of Foundation activities, profiles of members, poems, cartoons, obituaries, and columns titled Senior Trading Post and Oldtimers Mail Bag. *Type:* Newsletter.

TIAA-CREF

730 Third Ave. Ph: (212)490-9000
New York, NY 10017-3206 Free: 800-842-2733
 Fax: (212)972-7533
URL: http://www.tiaacref.org
Contact: John H. Biggs, Chm., Pres. and CEO.

Desc: Provides a nationwide portable pension system for over 2 million employees of some 8,000 colleges, universities, independent schools, and related nonprofit educational and research institutions. *Type:* Association.

Wasatch Letter

Wasatch Planning and Publishing Corporation
3495 S. Medford Dr. Ph: (801)292-4378
Bountiful, UT 84010 Fax: (801)292-6927
Contact: Mary Flood, Editor.

Desc: Advises subscribers on developing an individual retirement plan. Discusses planning and choices among conservative, average, and aggressive investments, emphasizing mutual funds. *Type:* Newsletter.

WBF in Action

Workmen's Benefit Fund of the U.S.A.
99 N. Broadway Ph: (516)936-6060
Hicksville, NY 11801-2905 Fax: (516)938-6882
Contact: Charles L. Grossman, Editor.

Desc: Reports on matters of concern to retired workers: social security, inflation, insurance, health, the arts, and leisure activities. Recurring features include news of the Fund's activities. *Type:* Newsletter.

Right to Life

American Life League

PO Box 1350 Ph: (540)659-4171
Stafford, VA 22555 Free: 888-546-2580
 Fax: (540)659-2586
E-mail: jbrown@all.org
URL: http://www.all.org
Contact: Judie Brown, Pres.

Desc: Serves as a pro-life service organization providing educational materials, books, flyers, and programs for local, state, and national pro-life, pro-family organizations. Sponsors national pro-life meetings, training sessions, and seminars. Special fields of interest: abortion; euthanasia; organ transplantation; population; world hunger. *Type:* Association.

American Life League

PO Box 1350 Ph: (703)659-4171
Stafford, VA 22555 Fax: (703)659-2586
Contact: Judie Brown, Pres.

Desc: Pro-life individuals opposed to abortion. Primary goal is to secure passage of a Human Life Amendment to the U.S. Constitution that would effect legal recognition of the "personhood" of the unborn, and secure constitutional protection of human beings from the moment of fertilization. *Type:* Association.

American Pro Life Council

1612 S. Prospect Ave.
Park Ridge, IL 60068
Contact: John de Paul Hansen, Pres.
Desc: Provides right-to-life activists with insurance, credit union, and other programs containing pro-life provisions. Has established American Family Society and a general insurance agency, and uses profits to fund pro-life causes. *Type:* Association.

Christian Americans for Life

PO Box 977   Ph: (918)438-4234
Tulsa, OK 74102   Fax: (918)438-4235
Contact: Dr. Billy James Hargis, CEO.
Desc: Campaigns against abortion. Maintains program to support adoption instead of abortion. Compiles statistics, mails letters, and conducts research programs. *Type:* Association.

Convenience Store News

Macfadden Trade Publishing
355 Park Ave. S.   Ph: (917)256-2491
New York, NY 10010   Fax: (212)592-6616
Contact: Maureen Azzato, Editor; Joan Toth, Publisher.
Desc: Trade magazine on convenience store and petroleum marketing. *Type:* Periodical.

Eternal Life

PO Box 787   Ph: (502)348-3963
Bardstown, KY 40004   Fax: (502)348-2224
Contact: William J. Smith, Contact.
Desc: Orthodox, lay Catholics. Seeks to organize a Catholic response to "exploitive and sinful sexual behaviors and attitudes" such as abortion, fetal experimentation, euthanasia, sterilization, premarital sex, homosexuality, divorce, pornography, artificial insemination, and contraception. Promotes family-centered sexuality and spirituality by bringing the perspective of Catholic teachings into the prolife movement. *Type:* Association.

National Organization of Episcopalians for Life

405 Frederick Ave.   Ph: (412)749-0455
Sewickley, PA 15143-1522   Free: 800-707-6635
    Fax: (412)749-0422
E-mail: noelife@aol.com
URL: http://www.episcopalian.org/noel
Contact: Georgette Forney, Exec.Dir.
Desc: Episcopalians organized to reaffirm their faith and reestablish moral responsibility in the Christian response to human life issues. Focuses on issues concerning the protection and enhancement of human existence in accordance with God's laws. *Type:* Association.

Pro-Life Action League

6160 N. Cicero, No. 600   Ph: (773)777-2900
Chicago, IL 60646   Fax: (773)777-3061
E-mail: scheidler@ibm.net
URL: http://www.prolifeaction.org
Contact: Joseph M. Scheidler, Exec.Dir.
Desc: Individuals, including doctors, lawyers, business leaders, and students, who are pro-life. *Type:* Association.

Women Exploited by Abortion

PO Box 279   Ph: (817)578-1681
Dawson, TX 76639-0279   Fax: (817)578-1681
Contact: Kathy Walker, Pres.

Desc: Christian-oriented organization of women who have had abortions and regret their action; associate members are concerned individuals who have not had abortions. Provides support and counseling for women and men who suffer from emotional and physical problems as a result of their abortions. Offers counseling to pregnant women considering abortion; refers women who decide to have their babies to other groups that assist needy expectant mothers. *Type:* Association.

Rubber

Rubber Manufacturers Association

1400 K St. NW, Ste. 900
Washington, DC 20005
Contact: Donald Shea, Pres.
Desc: Manufacturers of tires, tubes, mechanical and industrial products, roofing, sporting goods, and other rubber products. *Type:* Association.

United Steel Workers of America, Rubber/Plastics Industry Conference

570 White Pond Dr.   Ph: (330)869-0320
Akron, OH 44320-1156   Fax: (330)869-5627
Contact: John Sellers, Contact.
Desc: AFL-CIO, Canadian Labour Congress. *Type:* Association.

Russia

All Moscow Information Yearbook

Shapolsky Publishers, Inc.
136 W. 22nd St.   Ph: (212)633-2023
New York, NY 10011   Fax: (212)633-2123
Contact: G. Broido, Editor.
Desc: Organizations, government agencies, companies, cooperatives, and other entities involved or interested in international trade. *Type:* Directory.

Carroll's Russian Government Directory

Carroll Publishing
4701 Sangamore Rd., No. S155   Ph: (301)263-9800
Bethesda, MD 20816   Free: 800-336-4240
    Fax: (301)263-9801
E-mail: custsvc@carrollpub.com
URL: http://www.carrolpub.com
Desc: More than 10,000 Russian leaders, including Parliament, Administration of the President, Academy of Sciences, ministries, agencies, local and regional governments, associations, foundations, banks, commodity exchanges, Chambers of Commerce, and embassies. *Type:* Directory.

Russian and Eurasia Facts & Figures Annual

Academic International Press
PO Box 1111   Fax: (850)934-0953
Gulf Breeze, FL 32562-1111
E-mail: aipress@aol.com
URL: http://sites.gulf.net/aip/; http://www.ai-press.com.
Contact: Lawrence R. Robertson, Editor, robertson@umiami.ir.miami.edu.
Desc: List of government agencies and officials in the former Soviet Union, including leading organizations, corporations, and institutions in the military, foreign affairs, political affairs, and economy, including industrial and agricultural production, energy, foreign trade, communications, transportation, population, international relations, foreign aid, finance, science, technology and space, law, cultural life, health, education, and welfare. Each annual volume supplements and updates previous volumes. *Type:* Directory.

Safety

AAA Foundation for Traffic Safety

1440 New York Ave. NW, Ste.   Ph: (202)638-5944
201   Free: 800-305-7233
Washington, DC 20005   Fax: (202)638-5943
E-mail: steph@aaafts.org
URL: http://www.aaafts.org
Contact: David K. Willis, Pres./CEO.
Desc: Dedicated to saving lives and reducing injuries by preventing traffic crashes. *Type:* Association.

ABIH/BCSP Joint Committee

208 Burwash Ave.   Ph: (217)359-2686
Savoy, IL 61874   Fax: (217)359-0055
E-mail: bcsp@bcsp.com
URL: http://www.bcsp.org
Contact: Roger L. Brauer, Ph.D., Exec.Dir.
Desc: Grants the Occupational Health and Safety Technologist, Construction Health and Safety Technician, and Safety Trained Supervisor in Contruction to individuals involed in the field of safety who pass an exam and meet other criteria. Conducts research in the evaluation of competency for those involved in many areas of safety practice. *Type:* Association.

American Highway Users Alliance

1776 Massachusetts Ave. NW   Ph: (202)857-1200
Washington, DC 20036   Fax: (202)857-1220
E-mail: gohighway@aol.com
URL: http://www.highways.org
Contact: William D. Fay, Pres./CEO.
Desc: Organizations and associations representing major industry and highway-user groups. To promote highway safety and encourage sound highway transportation development on a national basis by cooperating with private and public organizations active in these areas. *Type:* Association.

American Rape Prevention Association

50 Muth Dr.   Ph: (510)254-0963
Orinda, CA 94563
Contact: Joseph Eugene Spott, Co-CEO.
Desc: Men, women, and children dedicated to preventing rape, incest, domestic violence and rape, sexual harassment, and kidnap/rape/murder (RIDS). Trains women and girls to respond to assault by using weapons against attackers, whom the association refers to as RIDS predators. ARPA believes that a female trained in RIDS prevention is "aggressive and offensive, forcing the RIDS predator to be defensive and try to escape from her." Asserts that rape crisis and battered women's programs encourage women to be dependent on law enforcement and social agencies for protection and discourage women from taking preventive measures in the event of an attack. *Type:* Association.

American Society of Safety Engineers

1800 E. Oakton St.   Ph: (847)699-2929
Des Plaines, IL 60018-2187   Fax: (847)296-3769
Desc: Professional society of safety engineers, safety directors, and others concerned with accident prevention, environmental protection and safety and health programs. Sponsors National Safety Month conducts research and educational programs. Develops/publishes ANSI safety-related standatds & other technical literature. *Type:* Association.

American Traffic Safety Services Association

15 Riverside Pkwy., Ste. 100   Ph: (540)368-1701
Fredericksburg, VA 22406-1022   Fax: (540)368-1717
E-mail: general@atssa.com
URL: http://www.atssa.com
Contact: Roger A. Wentz, Exec.Dir.

Desc: Individuals and firms engaged in the renting, leasing, and/or selling of highway signs, pavement markings, and traffic control devices for construction and repair areas; suppliers to the industry. Distributes technical information; promotes safety; compiles statistics; promotes uniform use of lights, signs, pavement markings, and barricades. Sponsors training courses for Worksite Traffic Supervisors and Pavement Marking technicians annually. *Type:* Association.

Association of Public-Safety Communications Officials - International

2040 S. Ridgewood Ave.   Ph: (904)322-2500
Daytona Beach, FL 32119   Free: 888-APCO-911
    Fax: (904)322-2501
E-mail: apco@apcointl.org
URL: http://www.apcointl.org
Contact: Chris Bevevino, Exec.Dir.

Desc: Employees of municipal, county, state, and federal public safety agencies such as 911 emergency phone line, fire, police, highway maintenance, forestry-conservation, civil defense, special emergency, and local government; individuals who sell public safety communication products. Objectives are to: foster the development and progress of the art of public safety communications; ensure greater cooperation in the correlation of the work and activities of the several town, county, state, and federal agencies; promote cooperation between these agencies and the Federal Communications Commission. Conducts surveys, management and training seminars, and grant-in-aid projects with federal funding agencies. *Type:* Association.

Being Well

Society for Professional Well-Being
21 W. Colony Pl., Ste. 150   Ph: (919)489-9167
Durham, NC 27705
E-mail: profwellbe@aol.com

Desc: Covers Society activities. Provides information on coping skills, networking, and stress reduction. *Type:* Newsletter.

BNA Occupational Safety & Health Daily

The Bureau of National Affairs, Inc. (BNA)
1231 25th St. NW   Ph: (202)452-4200
Washington, DC 20037
E-mail: bnaplus@bna.com
URL: http://bna.com/mkt/hrl/hrlwdec.htm

Desc: Contains current information on legislative, regulatory, and judicial activities that affect occupational safety and health. *Available:* LEXIS-NEXIS, LEXIS; West Group, WESTLAW. *Type:* Database.

BNA's SafetyNet

Bureau of National Affairs, Inc. (BNA)
1231 25th St. NW   Ph: (202)452-4323
Washington, DC 20037   Free: 800-372-1033
    Fax: (202)452-7773
E-mail: bnaplus@bna.com
Contact: Stanley S. Pond, Managing Editor, spond@bna.com.

Desc: Designed to help employers deal with occupational safety and health regulations, policies, standards, and practices, and to understand the effects of compliance on employee relations. Covers the establishment, management, evaluation, maintenance, and administration of health and safety programs. *Type:* Newsletter.

Briefings on Hospital Safety

Opus Communications
100 Hoods Ln.   Ph: (781)639-1872
PO Box 1168   Free: 800-650-6787
Marblehead, MA 01945   Fax: (781)639-2982
E-mail: customer_service@opuscomm.com
URL: http://www.opuscomm.com

Contact: Steve Zisson, Editor.

Desc: Targets safety committees. Reports on current issues, regulators, and Joint Commission on Accreditation of Healthcare Organizations (JCAHO) compliance and standards guidelines. *Type:* Newsletter.

Cal-OSHA Reporter

Commanon Corporation
PO Box 1100   Ph: (530)470-7500
Grass Valley, CA 95945-1100   Fax: (530)470-7600
E-mail: helpdesk@cal-osha.com; help@cal-osha.com
URL: http://www.cal-osha.com.
Contact: Anne Bell, Editor.

Desc: Reports on laws, regulations, court cases, and other issues of interest to occupational safety and health professionals. Recurring features include a calendar of events, reports of meetings, news of educational opportunities, job listings, and notices of publications available. *Type:* Newsletter.

California Safety and Health Law Monitor

M. Lee Smith Publishers LLC
5201 Virginia Way   Ph: (615)373-7517
PO Box 5094   Free: 800-274-6774
Brentwood, TN 37024-5094   Fax: 800-785-9212
E-mail: custserv@mleesmith.com
URL: http://www.mleesmith.com.
Contact: Jeffrey Tanenbaum, Editor.

Desc: Covers state and local job safety and health developments and related workplace developments. *Type:* Newsletter.

Canadian Occupational Health & Safety News

Southam, Inc.
PO Box 603   Ph: (317)297-5500
Indianapolis, IN 46206   Free: 800-827-7468
    Fax: (317)299-1356
Contact: Angela Stelmakowich, Editor.

Desc: Aims to help subscribers "develop their occupational health and safety knowledge and skills and reduce accident and illness rates in their workplaces." Provides occupational health and safety professionals with information on new legal requirements, approaches to reducing hazards, training and education alternatives, and news of upcoming events. Recurring features include Research Reports, Legislative Update, notices of publications available, and a calendar of events. *Type:* Newsletter.

Canadian Studies/Etudes Canadiennes

Canadian Centre for Occupational Health and Safety (CCOHS)
250 Main St. E.   Ph: (905)570-8094
Hamilton, ON, Canada L8N 1H6
E-mail: custserv@ccohs.ca
URL: http://www.ccohs.ca/
Contact: Eleanor Irwin.

Desc: Contains citations to current or recently completed studies in occupational health and safety by Canadians or about the Canadian workplace. For each study, provides title, description, status (e.g., start/end, grant year), performing organization and investigators, funding body, and publications resulting from the study. *Type:* Database.

Case Law/Jurisprudence

Canadian Centre for Occupational Health and Safety (CCOHS)
250 Main St. E.   Ph: (905)570-8094
Hamilton, ON, Canada L8N 1H6
E-mail: custserv@ccohs.ca
URL: http://www.ccohs.ca/
Desc: Provides summaries of cases and decisions related to occupational safety and health for jurisdictions across Canada. For each case, provides date, jurisdiction, and decision-making forum. *Type:* Database.

CCINFOdisc: MSDS (A1)

Canadian Centre for Occupational Health and Safety (CCOHS)
250 Main St. E.   Ph: (905)570-8094
Hamilton, ON, Canada L8N 1H6
E-mail: custserv@ccohs.ca
URL: http://www.ccohs.ca/
Contact: Eleanor Irwin.

Desc: Contains the complete text of more than 70,000 current English-language Material Safety Data Sheets and related technical information on chemicals. Comprises the following 2 files: • Material Safety Data Sheets (MSDS)--contains Material Safety Data Sheets for more than 70,000 commercially available chemical substances used in a variety of workplace settings. *Available:* Canadian Centre for Occupational Health and Safety (CCOHS). *Type:* Database.

Center for Auto Safety

2001 S St. NW, Ste. 410   Ph: (202)328-7700
Washington, DC 20009-1160
URL: http://www.autosafety.org
Contact: Clarence M. Ditlow, III, Dir.

Desc: Independent nonprofit organization founded by Ralph Nader and Consumers Union of United States. Seeks to "reduce the human and economic losses wrought by the automobile and the auto industry." As an auto and highway safety advocate, the center monitors government agencies charged with regulation of the industry, supports safety standards, participates in the rule-making procedures of the National Highway Traffic Safety Administration and the Federal Highway Administration, and occasionally institutes legal action. Collects literature and statistics on automobile safety and analyzes developments in the field. *Type:* Association.

CHEMINFO

Canadian Centre for Occupational Health and Safety (CCOHS)
250 Main St. E.   Ph: (905)570-8094
Hamilton, ON, Canada L8N 1H6
E-mail: custserv@ccohs.ca
URL: http://www.ccohs.ca/
Contact: Eleanor Irwin.

Desc: Contains descriptive, health, and precautionary data on pure chemicals, natural substances, and chemical mixtures resulting from or used in industrial processes. For each chemical, provides substance identification, including name, synonyms, Chemical Abstracts Service (CAS) Registry Number, and molecular and structural formula, as well as information about its uses and occurrences, physical properties, appearance, reactivity, warning properties (e.g., odors, irritation), animal toxicity data, proposed Workplace Hazardous Materials Information System (WHMIS) classification, fire and explosion hazards, and human health effects from acute or chronic exposure. *Available:* Canadian Centre for Occupational Health and Safety (CCOHS). *Type:* Database.

Crisis Management Reporter

Remy Publishing Company
401 N. Franklin St., 3rd Fl.   Ph: (312)464-0300
Chicago, IL 60610   Free: 800-542-6670
    Fax: (312)464-0166
Contact: Gerald Muray, Editor.

Desc: Presents crisis situations and action-oriented analyses in the airline, bank, chemical and drug manufacturers, and oil industries. Assists these industries in preparation and prevention of real-life crises. *Type:* Newsletter.

Directory of Safety Consultants and Rehabilitation Management Providers

Business Insurance
740 N. Rush St.
Chicago, IL 60611-2590

Ph: (312)649-5279
Fax: (312)280-3174

Contact: Sandra L. Budde, Editor.
Desc: List of more than 150 employee safety consultants and over 70 employee rehabilitation management providers. *Type:* Directory.

Employment Safety and Health Guide— Summary

CCH Inc.
2700 Lake Cook Rd.
Riverwoods, IL 60015

Ph: (847)267-7000
Free: 800-449-8114
Fax: (847)224-8299

URL: http://www.cch.com; http://www.health.cch.com; http://www.cch.com.
Contact: Diane Ward, Editor.
Desc: A summary that provides a quick insight into the week's developments on decision rules, regulations and other developments. *Type:* Newsletter.

Family Safety & Health

National Safety Council
1121 Spring Lake Dr.
Itasca, IL 60143-3201

Ph: (630)285-1121
Free: 800-539-7468
Fax: (630)285-1315

URL: http://www.nsc.org; http://www.nsc.org/pubs/fsh.htm.
Contact: Laura Coyne, Editor, (630)775-2276; Sharon Lewis, Assoc. Editor; John Kennedy, Publisher.
Desc: Magazine aimed at preventing accidents at home and on the road and promoting health and fitness. *Alt. Contact:* 1121 Spring Lake Dr., Itasca, IL 60143-3201; telephone: (630)775-2286, (630)775-2276; fax: (630)775-2285; toll-free: 800-621-7615. *Type:* Periodical.

Fatality Reports

Canadian Centre for Occupational Health and Safety (CCOHS)
250 Main St. E.
Hamilton, ON, Canada L8N 1H6

Ph: (905)570-8094

E-mail: custserv@ccohs.ca
URL: http://www.ccohs.ca/
Desc: Contains information about the circumstances surrounding occupationally related fatalities in Canada. Includes date and place of inquiry, date and place of accident, name and occupation of deceased, industrial sector, cause of death, manner of death (e.g., accidental, preventable), accident description, and recommendations of the reviewing agency. *Type:* Database.

Federal Mine Safety and Health Review Commission

1730 K St. NW
Washington, DC 20006-3867

Ph: (202)653-5625
Fax: (202)653-5030

E-mail: info@fmshrc.gov
Contact: Mary Lu Jordan, Chairman of the Board.
Desc: The Commission, and its Office of Administrative Law Judges are charged with deciding cases brought pursuant to the Federal Mine Safety and Health Act of 1977 by the Mine Safety and Health Administration, mine operators, and miners or their representatives. These cases generally involve review of the Administration's enforcement actions including citations, mine closure orders, and proposals for civil penalties issued for violations of the act or the mandatory safety and health standards promulgated by the Secretary of Labor. *Type:* Government agency, office, or program.

Federation of American Scientists

Federation of American Scientists
307 Massachusetts Ave. NE
Washington, DC 20002

Ph: (202)546-3300
Fax: (202)675-1010

E-mail: fas@fas.org
URL: http://www.fas.org/
Contact: Michael Panetta.
Desc: This Federation of American Scientists is provided to assist in analysis and advocacy on science, technology and public policy for global security. Included is information on nuclear weapons, arms sales, biological hazards and space policy. *Type:* Database.

Ground Water Monitor

Business Publishers, Inc. (BPI)
951 Pershing Dr.
Silver Spring, MD 20910-4464

Ph: (301)587-6300

URL: http://www.bpinews.com
Desc: Contains the complete text of Ground Water Monitor, a biweekly newsletter on legal and regulatory developments affecting the protection of ground water resources. Provides news of state and federal legislation, hearings on rules proposed by the United States Environmental Protection Agency (EPA) or state health agencies, and decisions before state and federal courts on hazardous waste disposal and ground water protection. *Type:* Database.

Hazardous Substances Resource Guide

Gale Group Inc.
27500 Drake Rd.
Farmington Hills, MI 48331-3535

Ph: (248)699-4253
Free: 800-877-GALE
Fax: (248)699-8070

E-mail: galeord@galegroup.com
URL: http://www.galegroup.com.
Contact: Richard Pohanish, Editor; Stanley A. Greene, Editor.
Desc: Organizations and research centers involved with hazardous substances treatment. Principal content of publication is a guide to approximately 1,200 hazardous materials and their handling, use, disposal, and health risks. *Type:* Directory.

Health and Safety Science Abstracts

Cambridge Scientific Abstracts (CSA)
7200 Wisconsin Ave., Ste. 601
Bethesda, MD 20814-4823

Ph: (301)961-6700

E-mail: sales@csa.com
URL: http://www.csa.com
Desc: Contains more than 64,000 citations, with abstracts, to the worldwide literature on safety science and hazard control, with an emphasis on the identification, evaluation, and elimination or control of hazards. Includes coverage of issues related to liability. *Available:* STN International; Cambridge Scientific Abstracts (CSA), Internet Database Service. *Type:* Database.

Health in the Workplace

MPL Communications Inc.
133 Richmond St., Ste. 700
Toronto, ON, Canada M5H 3M8

Ph: (416)869-1177
Fax: (416)869-0616

Contact: Laurie Blake, Editor.
Desc: Provides information about workplace health and safety. Topics include safety audits, ergonomics, and stress. *Type:* Newsletter.

Indoor Air Quality Update

Cutter Information Corporation
37 Broadway, Ste. 1
Arlington, MA 02174-5552

Ph: (781)648-8702
Free: 800-325-3717
Fax: (781)648-1950

E-mail: klovering@cutter.com
Contact: Carlton Vogt, Editor.

Desc: Focuses on the prevention and control of indoor air pollution from various industry perspectives. Reports on controlling potential pollutant sources, HVAC operation, and legislation. *Type:* Newsletter.

Inside OSHA

Inside Washington Publishers
PO Box 7167
Ben Franklin Sta.
Washington, DC 20044-7167

Ph: (703)416-8500
Free: 800-424-9068

E-mail: iwp@iwpnews.com
Contact: Bob Cusack, Managing Editor; Dugie Standeford, Associate Editor; Debbie Rieck, Associate Editor.
Desc: Reports on news of the Occupational Safety and Health Administration. *Type:* Newsletter.

Integrated Risk Information System

U.S. Environmental Protection Agency (EPA)
Office of Pollution, Prevention, and Toxics
401 M St., SW
Washington, DC 20460

Ph: (202)554-1404

URL: http://www.epa.gov
Desc: Contains information on the health risk assessment of 700 hazardous substances. Covers toxicity, carcinogenicity, chemical and physical properties, and applicable regulations. *Available:* U.S. National Library of Medicine (NLM), TOXNET. *Type:* Database.

International Product Safety News

Product Safety International
PO Box 1561 - GR
Middletown, CT 06457-1561

Ph: (860)344-1651

E-mail: gr.psi@safetylink.com; gr.ipsn@safetylink.com.
URL: http://www.safetylink.com.
Contact: Arthur E. Michael, Editor.
Desc: Features news, information, and resources concerning International Safety Agency approvals such as Canadian Standards Association (CSA), International Electrotechnical Commission (IEC), Technischer Uberwachungs-Verein (TUV), Verband Deutscher Electrotechniker (VDE), Underwriters Laboratories (UL), and National Recognized Testing Laboratories (NRTL). Recurring features include columns titled EC92 & Beyond, Technotes, and Question & Answer column. *Type:* Newsletter.

Job Safety Consultant

Business & Legal Reports, Inc.
39 Academy St.
Madison, CT 06443

Ph: (203)318-0000
Free: 800-727-5257
Fax: (203)245-2559

E-mail: service@blr.com
Contact: Marcia Wagshol, Editor.
Desc: Covers industrial safety and health, Occupational Safety and Health Administration (OSHA) and company safety strategies. Recurring features include columns titled Editor's Corner, Updates & Alerts, Safety in Action, Technical Tips, and Safety Talks. *Type:* Newsletter.

Job Safety and Health

The Bureau of National Affairs, Inc. (BNA)
1231 25th St. NW
Washington, DC 20037

Ph: (202)452-4200

E-mail: bnaplus@bna.com
URL: http://bna.com/mkt/hrl/hrlwdec.htm
Desc: Contains the complete text of Job Safety and Health, a newsletter that summarizes new industrial safety practices and trends in industry; examines difficult safety problems and their solutions; provides information on setting up and maintaining safety and health programs; and explains significant changes in the law, court and agency decisions, and important arbitration awards. *Type:* Database.

Job Safety and Health Quarterly

Occupational Safety and Health Administration (OSHA)

U.S. Department of Labor

200 Constitution Ave. NW, N 3647 Washington, DC 20210

Ph: (202)219-8615

Contact: Anne Cyr, Editor.

Desc: Informs readers of changes, developments, and new rulings made by the Occupational Safety and Health Administration (OSHA). *Type:* Newsletter.

Keller's Industrial Safety Report

J.J. Keller & Associates Inc.

3003 W. Breezewood Ln. PO Box 368 Neenah, WI 54957-0368

Ph: (414)722-2848

Contact: Julie A. Nussbaum, Editor.

Desc: Concerned with activities of the Occupational Safety and Health Administration (OSHA) and all aspects of safety in an industrial setting. Recurring features include includes sections titles OSHA Activity, Safety Issues, and State Activity. *Type:* Newsletter.

Keller's OSHA Safety Training Newsletter

J. J. Keller & Associates, Inc.

3003 W. Breezewood Ln. PO Box 368 Neenah, WI 54957-0368

Ph: (920)722-2848 Free: 800-327-6868 Fax: 800-727-7516

E-mail: sales@jjkeller.com URL: http://www.jjkeller.com

Contact: Judie Smithers, Editor; Webb A. Shaw, Editorial Mgr.

Desc: Provides information on training, techniques, and guidelines to promote safe work practices and a safe work environment. Recurring features include case studies and columns titled Safety Selections and Q&A. *Type:* Newsletter.

Labor Division Newsletter

National Safety Council

1121 Spring Lake Dr. Itasca, IL 60143-3201

Ph: (630)285-1121 Free: 800-539-7468 Fax: (630)285-1315

URL: http://www.nsc.org; http://www.nsc.org.

Contact: Kathy Henderson, Editor.

Desc: Concerned with industrial and occupational safety, safe work practices, and products. Covers industrial safety programs and relevant legislation and regulations. *Type:* Newsletter.

Living Safety Magazine

Canada Safety Council

1020 Thomas Spratt Place Ottawa, ON, Canada K1G 5L5

Ph: (613)739-1535 Fax: (613)739-1566

E-mail: csc@safety-council.org

Contact: Jack Smith, Editor, jsmith@safety-council.org.

Desc: Magazine on off-the-job safety in the areas of traffic, recreation, and the home. *Type:* Periodical.

Medical Environment Update Newsletter

Medical Environment, Inc.

5721 Arapahoe Rd., Ste. 2B Boulder, CO 80303

Ph: (303)442-5300 Free: 800-788-6240 Fax: (303)440-9897

Contact: George W. Hunt, Editor and Publisher; Matthew Ostrowski, Editor.

Desc: Provides news and items of interest to medical facilities. Covers government mandated policies and standards, as well as training materials designed to make work easier for the facility's safety officer. *Type:* Newsletter.

MiOSHA News

Michigan Department of Consumer Industry Services

Division of Occupational Health

3423 N. Martin Luther King Jr. Blvd. PO Box 30649 Lansing, MI 48909-8149

Ph: (517)335-8250 Fax: (517)335-8761

Contact: Gregg Grubb, Editor.

Desc: Contains information relevant to occupational safety and health in relation to Michigan's employers and employees. *Type:* Newsletter.

Mothers Against Drunk Driving

511 E. John Carpenter Fwy., No. 700 Irving, TX 75062

Ph: (972)744-6233 Free: 800-GET-MADD Fax: (972)869-2206

E-mail: info@madd.org URL: http://www.madd.org/

Contact: Dean Wilkerson, Exec.Dir.

Desc: Victims of drunk driving crashes; concerned citizens. Encourages citizen participation in working towards reform of the drunk driving problem and the prevention of underage drinking acts as the voice of victims of drunk driving crashes by speaking on their behalf to communities, businesses, and educational groups and providing materials for use in medical facilities, and health and driver education programs. *Type:* Association.

Motorcycle Safety Foundation

2 Jenner St., Ste. 150 Irvine, CA 92618-3800

Ph: (714)727-3227 Free: 800-446-9227 Fax: (714)727-4217

URL: http://www.msf-usa.org

Contact: Tim Buche, Pres.

Desc: Leading motorcycle manufacturers in the U.S. united to reduce motorcycle accidents and injuries through operator education, licensing improvement and public information. Conducts Motorcycle Safety Education Instructor Preparation Workshops and various other seminars and training sessions. *Type:* Association.

MSDS

Canadian Centre for Occupational Health and Safety (CCOHS)

250 Main St. E. Hamilton, ON, Canada L8N 1H6

Ph: (905)570-8094

E-mail: custserv@ccohs.ca URL: http://www.ccohs.ca/

Desc: Contains complete text of approximately 100,000 current English-language Material Safety Data Sheets (MSDS) on chemical products exactly as contributed by over 600 manufacturers and suppliers. Each MSDS provides information on product hazards, emergency response, first aid measures, and safe working procedures. *Type:* Database.

National Association of Women Highway Safety Leaders

7206 Robinhood Dr. Upper Marlboro, MD 20772

Ph: (301)868-7583 Fax: (301)868-1892

Contact: Agnes Barton, Contact.

Desc: Women and representatives of women's organizations with interests in traffic safety. Objectives are to reduce traffic crashes, injuries, and deaths by: supporting and implementing the National Highway Safety Standards in communities and states, and nationwide; encouraging each political subdivision to assume its responsibility for highway safety; aiming at more uniformity in traffic safety programs and regulations within the 50 states, the District of Columbia, and Puerto Rico, St. Thomas, St. *Type:* Association.

National Center for Assault Prevention

606 Delsea Dr. Sewell, NJ 08080

Ph: (609)582-7000 Free: 800-258-3189 Fax: (609)582-3588

E-mail: pstanislaksi@msn.com URL: http://www.ncap.org

Contact: Pat Stanislaski, Exec.Dir.

Desc: Purpose is to prevent interpersonal violence against vulnerable populations through education, prevention training, and research. Provides services to children aged two and one half years through adolescence, children and adults with mental retardation and developmental disabilities, and older citizens. Conducts research on the causes, consequences, and prevention of interpersonal violence. *Type:* Association.

National Fire Protection Association

1 Batterymarch Park PO Box 9101 Quincy, MA 02269-9101

Ph: (617)770-3000 Fax: (617)770-0700

E-mail: library@nfpa.org URL: http://www.nfpa.org

Contact: George D. Miller, Pres.

Desc: Membership drawn from the fire service, business and industry, health care, educational and other institutions, and individuals in the fields of insurance, government, architecture, and engineering. Develops, publishes, and disseminates standards, prepared by approximately 250 technical committees, intended to minimize the possibility and effects of fire and explosion; conducts fire safety education programs for the general public. Provides information on fire protection, prevention, and suppression; compiles annual statistics on causes and occupancies of fires, large-loss fires (over $1,000,000), fire deaths, and fire fighter casualties. *Type:* Association.

National Fire Sprinkler Association

Robin Hill Corporate Park Rte. 22, Box 1000 Patterson, NY 12563

Ph: (914)878-4200 Fax: (914)878-4215

E-mail: vandeyar@nfsa.org URL: http://www.NFSA.org

Contact: John A. Viniello, Pres.

Desc: Manufacturers, suppliers, contractors, and installers of fire sprinklers and related products and services. Conducts Labor negotiations for the industry with 19 Local unions. Conducts educational programs to promote the concept of automatic fire sprinkler protection. *Type:* Association.

National Safety Council

1121 Spring Lake Dr. Itasca, IL 60143-3201

Ph: (630)285-1121 Fax: (630)285-1315

URL: http://www.nsc.org

Contact: G. Scannell, Pres.

Desc: A voluntary nongovernmental organization. Promotes injury reduction by providing a forum for the exchange of safety and health ideas, techniques, and experiences and the discussion of injury prevention methods. Offers courses in first aid, occupational safety and traffic safety. *Type:* Association.

NCOSH Safety & Health News

North Carolina Occupational Safety & Health Project (NCOSH)

PO Box 2514 Durham, NC 27715

Ph: (919)286-9249 Fax: (919)286-4857

E-mail: ncosh@igc.org

Contact: Betsy Barton, Editor.

Desc: Reports on the Project's labor union and safety and health activities in North Carolina. Covers such topics as toxic substances, Right to Know campaigns, worker's compensation, and medical clinics and surveys. *Type:* Newsletter.

Safety

NFPA Journal—Buyers' Guide

National Fire Protection Association (NFPA)
1 Batterymarch Park   Ph: (617)770-3000
Quincy, MA 02269-9101   Free: 800-344-3555
     Fax: (617)770-0700
URL: http://www.nfpa.org; http://www.nfpa.org.
Contact: Kathleen Robinson, Publisher.
Desc: List of manufacturers and consultants of fire protection, fire safety, and fire service products. *Type:* Directory.

NIOSHTIC

U.S. National Institute for Occupational Safety and Health (NIOSH)
Education and Information Division
Information Resources Branch
4676 Columbia Pkwy.   Ph: (513)533-8359
Cincinnati, OH 45226
Contact: Fred Blosser.
Desc: Contains more than 200,000 citations, with abstracts, to literature on occupational safety and health from more than 400 core journals, as well as monographs and technical reports. Includes Chemical Abstracts Service (CAS) Registry Numbers. *Available:* Canadian Centre for Occupational Health and Safety (CCOHS); The Dialog Corporation, DIALOG; Karolinska Institute Library and Information Center/ Karolinska Institutets Bibliotek och Informationscentral (KIBIC), Medical Information Center (MIC); European Information Network Services (EINS); STN International; National Information Services Corporation (NISC), BiblioLine. *Type:* Database.

Occupational Hazards—Annual Directory Issue

Penton Media Inc.
1100 Superior Ave.   Ph: (216)696-7000
Cleveland, OH 44114-2543   Fax: (216)931-9524
E-mail: corpcomm@penton.com
Contact: Stephen G. Minter, Editor.
Desc: List of about 1,900 manufacturers of equipment and products, and suppliers of services for industrial safety, health, hygiene, hazardous material control, and plant protection. *Type:* Directory.

Occupational Health Management

American Health Consultants, Inc.
3525 Piedmont Rd., Bldg. 6,   Ph: (404)262-7436
   Ste. 400   Free: 800-688-2421
Atlanta, GA 30305   Fax: (404)262-7837
E-mail: customerservice@ahcpub.com
Contact: Greg Freeman, Editor.
Desc: Provides news of research, advice to employers, and columns titled Industry Spotlight and Workers' Comp Update. *Type:* Newsletter.

Occupational Health & Safety

Stevens Publishing Corp.
5151 Belt Line Road, Ste. 1010   Ph: (972)687-6700
Dallas, TX 75240   Fax: (972)687-6799
E-mail: jlaws@stevenspublishing.com.
Contact: Craig S. Stevens, Publisher; Jerry Laws, Editor, jlaws@cmpu.net; Dana Cornett, Group Publisher.
Desc: Magazine covering federal and state regulation of occupational health and safety. *Type:* Periodical.

Occupational Health & Safety Letter

Business Publishers, Inc.
8737 Colesville Rd., Ste. 1100   Ph: (301)589-5103
Silver Spring, MD 20910   Free: 800-274-6737
   Fax: (301)587-4530
E-mail: bpinews@bpinews.com
URL: http://www.bpinews.com.
Contact: Pat Phibbs, Editor.
Desc: Covers federal and state legislation, standards, regulations, research activities, and enforcement cases concerning safety and health in the workplace environment. Concerned particularly with the Occupational Safety and Health Act (OSHA) of 1970. *Type:* Newsletter.

Occupational Safety & Health Reporter

Bureau of National Affairs, Inc. (BNA)
1231 25th St. NW   Ph: (202)452-4323
Washington, DC 20037   Free: 800-372-1033
   Fax: (202)452-7773
E-mail: bnaplus@bna.com
URL: http://www.bna.com.
Contact: Stanley S. Pond, Editor, spond@bna.com.
Desc: Provides a notification and reference service covering federal and state regulation of occupational safety and health, standards, legislation, enforcement activities, research, and legal decisions. Recurring features include a calendar of meetings and seminars and the full text of selected administrative rulings, proposed standards, criteria documents, variance notices, and compliance manuals. *Type:* Newsletter.

Occupational Safety & Health Reporter

The Bureau of National Affairs, Inc. (BNA)
1231 25th St. NW   Ph: (202)452-4200
Washington, DC 20037
E-mail: bnaplus@bna.com
URL: http://bna.com/mkt/hrl/hrlwdec.htm
Desc: Contains the complete text of Occupational Safety & Health Reporter, a newsletter covering legislative, regulatory, and judicial developments involving worker safety and health. Covers proposed and final standards and regulations of the Occupational Safety and Health Administration (OSHA), enforcement activities, legal activities of the courts and the Occupational Safety and Health Review Commission, investigations, congressional hearings, petitions for variances from OSHA standards, announcements of grants or denials, news about worker safety and health conferences, and worker right-to-know laws at the state and federal levels. *Available:* LEXIS-NEXIS, LEXIS. *Type:* Database.

Occupational Safety and Health Review Commission

1120 20th St. NW   Ph: (202)606-5100
Washington, DC 20036-3419   Fax: (202)606-5050
URL: http://www.oshrc.gov/
Contact: Stuart E. Weisberg, Chairman of the Board.
Desc: The Occupational Safety and Health Review Commission is charged with ruling on cases forwarded to it by the Department of Labor when disagreements arise over the results of safety and health inspections performed by the Department's Occupational Safety and Health Administration. *Type:* Government agency, office, or program.

Ontario Occupational Health and Safety Law Report

MPL Communications Inc.
133 Richmond St., Ste. 700   Ph: (416)869-1177
Toronto, ON, Canada M5H   Fax: (416)869-0616
   3M8
Contact: Susan Stanton, Editor.
Desc: Provides information about Ontario, Canada's, health and safety laws. *Type:* Newsletter.

OSHA Compliance Advisor

Business & Legal Reports, Inc.
39 Academy St.   Ph: (203)318-0000
Madison, CT 06443   Free: 800-727-5257
   Fax: (203)245-2559
E-mail: service@blr.com
Contact: John F. Brady, Editor-in-Chief.
Desc: Provides information on employee safety issues, Occupational Safety and Health Act (OSHA), programs, accident incidents, and job hazards. Recurring features include columns titled Compliance Report, Federal Register Digest, From the States, Washington Watch, News Roundup. *Type:* Newsletter.

OSHA Regulations - Standards 29 CFR

U.S. Department of Labor - Occupational Safety and Health Administration
200 Constitution Ave.   Free: 800-321-6742
Washington, DC 20210
URL: http://www.osha-slc.gov/OshStd_toc/OSHA_Std_toc.html
Desc: No doubt you've heard the comments: "We have to follow OSHA standards" or "OSHA's gonna shut the place down if this keeps up." So what exactly are the OSHA standards, and what kind of violations would make them close a facility? This web site has that information, and helps take some of the mystery out of the mission of the Occupational Safety and Health Administration. Here you can search among the complete collection of OSHA regulations (from the Code of Federal Regulations). *Type:* Database.

OSHA Required Training for Supervisors

Business & Legal Reports, Inc.
39 Academy St.   Ph: (203)318-0000
Madison, CT 06443   Free: 800-727-5257
   Fax: (203)245-2559
E-mail: service@blr.com
Contact: John F. Brady, Editor.
Desc: Profiles training information on occupational hazard violations, electrical safety, protective equipment, chemical splashes, and court decisions. *Type:* Newsletter.

OSHANEWS

Merritt Publishing
6133 Bristol Pkwy., Ste. 140   Ph: (310)450-7234
Culver City, CA 90230-6613   Free: 800-638-7597
   Fax: (310)396-4563
E-mail: merritt2@interserve.com; connien@merrittpub.com.
Contact: Connie Nitzschner, Editor; Amy Gordon, Assistant Editor.
Desc: Examines regulations and standards of the Occupational Safety & Health Administration (OSHA). Spotlights safety and health issues, risk management, and accident prevention. *Type:* Newsletter.

OSHAWeek

Stevens Publishing Corp.
5151 Belt Line Road, Ste. 1010   Ph: (972)687-6700
Dallas, TX 75240   Fax: (972)687-6799
Contact: Ralph Jensen, Editor-in-Chief; Katie Hooten, Editor.
Desc: Reports on news and updates on safety issues. Recurring features include news of research and a calendar of events. *Type:* Newsletter.

Repetitive Stress Injury Litigation Reporter

Andrews Publications
175 Strafford Ave., Bldg. 4, Ste.   Ph: (610)225-0510
   140   Free: 800-345-1101
Wayne, PA 19087   Fax: (610)225-0501
Contact: Barbara Pizzirani, Editor.
Type: Newsletter.

Resources

Canadian Centre for Occupational Health and Safety (CCOHS)
250 Main St. E.   Ph: (905)570-8094
Hamilton, ON, Canada L8N
   1H6
E-mail: custserv@ccohs.ca
URL: http://www.ccohs.ca/
Desc: Contains more than 2800 references to Canadian organizations, people, and agencies in the field of occupational health and safety. For each organization, includes name, location, working language, areas of responsibility, and subject area of activity. *Type:* Database.

Safety Compliance Alert
Progressive Business Publications
370 Technology Dr.   Ph: (610)695-8600
Malvern, PA 19355   Free: 800-220-5000
                             Fax: (610)651-2981
URL: http://www.pbp.com.
Contact: Maureen Hennessy, Editor.
Desc: Presents real world examples to help safety professionals avoid accidents and fires, reduce costs, and comply with changing OSHA rules. Recurring features include news of research, a calendar of events, news of educational opportunities, and a column titled Sharpen Your Judgment. *Type:* Newsletter.

Safety Compliance Letter
Bureau of Business Practice
24 Rope Ferry Rd.   Ph: (860)442-4365
Waterford, CT 06386   Free: 800-243-0876
                             Fax: (860)437-3555
URL: http://www.bbpnews.com
Contact: Michele Rubin, Editor, michele_rubin@prenhall.com.
Desc: Features interviews with safety professionals detailing their successful safety programs. Recurring features include interviews and advice from Occupational Safety and Health Administration (OSHA) personnel, OSHA news in brief, and tips on how to comply with OSHA regulations. *Type:* Newsletter.

Safety Focus
National Safety Council
1121 Spring Lake Dr.   Ph: (630)285-1121
Itasca, IL 60143-3201   Free: 800-539-7468
                             Fax: (630)285-1315
URL: http://www.nsc.org
Contact: Laura Coyne, Editor, (630)775-2776, fax: (630)775-2285.
Desc: Concerned with occupational safety, safety products, hazard control, and accident prevention in the following industries and sectors: chemical, metals, heath care, marine, air transport, public employment, rubber/plastics, laboratories/emerging technology, and retail trades and services. Recurring features include news of research and announcements of related conferences. *Type:* Newsletter.

Safety, Health, and Environmental Resource Center International
Homphreys Bldg., Ste. 201   Ph: (816)543-4744
Warrensburg, MO 64093   Fax: (816)543-4959
E-mail: sherici@cmsuvmb.cmsu.edu
Contact: Dr. Robert L. Baldwin, Pres.
Desc: Cooperating organizations united to advance safety, health, and the environment worldwide. *Type:* Association.

Safety Management
Bureau of Business Practice
24 Rope Ferry Rd.   Ph: (860)442-4365
Waterford, CT 06386   Free: 800-243-0876
                             Fax: (860)437-3555
URL: http://www.bbpnews.com
Contact: Jane Winkler, Editor, jane_winkler@prenhall.com.
Desc: Discusses successful safety programs and legal issues pertinent to safety management. *Type:* Newsletter.

Safety Now
Bureau of Business Practice
24 Rope Ferry Rd.   Ph: (860)442-4365
Waterford, CT 06386   Free: 800-243-0876
                             Fax: (860)437-3555
URL: http://www.bbpnews.com
Contact: Jane Winkler, Managing Editor, jane_winkler@prehall.com; Joyce Anne Grabel, Managing Editor.

Desc: Provides safety information and training skills for front-line supervisors to put safety policy into practice. Recurring features include interviews. *Type:* Newsletter.

Safety Signals
Industrial Safety Equipment Association
1901 N. Moore St.   Ph: (703)525-1695
Arlington, VA 22209   Fax: (703)528-2148
E-mail: isea@safetycentral.org
Contact: Bruce R. Clash, Editor, brclash@safetycentral.org.
Desc: Contains information about the safety equipment industry, ISEA member companies, Association activities, and upcoming meetings and events. *Type:* Newsletter.

Safety and the Supervisor
Clement Communications, Inc.
Concord Industrial Park   Ph: (610)459-1700
10 LaCrue Ave.   Free: 800-345-8101
Concordville, PA 19331   Fax: (610)459-0936
Contact: Eric C. Blomfelt, Senior Contributing Ed.; Maureen L. Solon, Exec. Editor; George Y. Clement, Publisher.
Desc: Provides supervisors and managers with safety techniques and information to improve the work environment. *Type:* Newsletter.

Safeworker
National Safety Council
1121 Spring Lake Dr.   Ph: (630)285-1121
Itasca, IL 60143-3201   Free: 800-539-7468
                             Fax: (630)285-1315
URL: http://www.nsc.org
Contact: Laura Coyne, Editor, (630)775-2276, fax: (630)775-2285, coynel@nsc.org; Kathleen Misovic, Assoc. Editor, (630)775-2288, misovick@nsc.org; John Kennedy, Publisher, (630)775-2103, kennedyj@nsc.org.
Desc: Trade magazine covering safety tips to workers on various topics. *Type:* Periodical.

Tennessee Valley Authority
Labor Relations and Safety
Occupational Health and Safety Division
400 W Summit Hill Dr.   Ph: (615)632-2101
Knoxville, TN 37902-1499
Type: Government agency, office, or program.

Texas A&M University
Occupational Health and Safety Institute
Department of Nuclear   Ph: (409)862-4409
  Engineering   Fax: (409)845-6443
College Station, TX 77843-3133
E-mail: j-rock@tamu.edu
Contact: Dr. James C. Rock, Dir.
Desc: Occupational health and safety, with a goal of safe use and disposal of essential hazardous materials and processes. Areas of study include industrial hygiene, health physics, safety engineering, aerosol science, occupational epidemiology, fire protection engineering, product safety engineering, occupational exposure assessment, industrial ventilation, indoor air quality, noise and vibration control, material substitution, electrofiltration, separation sciences, indoor bioaerosols, electrostatic separation for hazardous waste streams, and low toxicity product substitution. *Type:* Research center.

TOMES Plus® System
MICROMEDEX®, Inc.
6200 Syracuse Way South, Ste.   Ph: (303)486-6400
  300
Englewood, CO 80111-4740
E-mail: info@mdx.com

URL: http://www.micromedex.com
Contact: Customer Support.
Desc: Contains chemical, medical, and toxicological information for the industrial and occupational medicine markets. Covers clinical effects, range of toxicity, workplace standards, kinetics, and physiochemical standards. *Available:* MICROMEDEX®, Inc. *Type:* Database.

Underwriters Laboratories
333 Pfingsten Rd.   Ph: (847)272-8800
Northbrook, IL 60062   Fax: (847)272-8129
Contact: Tom Castino, Pres.
Desc: A product safety certification laboratory with additional laboratories in Melville, NY Santa Clara, CA and Research Triangle Park, NC. Establishes and operates product safety certification programs to ascertain that items produced under the service are safeguarded against reasonably foreseeable risks. Maintains a worldwide network of field representatives who make unannounced visits to factories to countercheck products bearing the UL Mark. *Type:* Association.

U.S. Department of Commerce
National Institute of Standards and Technology
Office of the Director of Administration
Occupational Health and Safety Division
c/o Department of Commerce   Ph: (301)975-3058
14th St. between Constitution Fax: (301)926-1630
  & Pennsylvania Aves. NW
Washington, DC 20230
E-mail: inquiries@nist.gov
URL: http://www.nist.gov/
Type: Government agency, office, or program.

U.S. Department of Health and Human Services
Centers for Disease Control and Prevention
National Institute for Occupational Safety and Health
1600 Clifton Rd. NE   Ph: (404)639-3311
Atlanta, GA 30333
URL: http://www.cdc.gov/
Contact: Linda Rosenstock, Director.
Desc: NIOSH is the primary federal agency engaged in research to eliminate on-the-job hazards to health and safety. Institute is responsible for identifying occupational safety and health hazards, for determining methods to control them, and for recommending federal standards to limit the hazards. *Type:* Government agency, office, or program.

U.S. Department of Health and Human Services
National Institute for Occupational Safety and Health
Centers for Disease Control and   Ph: (202)401-6997
  Prevention   Free: 800-356-4674
200 Independence Ave. SW   Fax: (202)205-2207
Rm. 715 H, Humphrey Bg
Washington, DC 20201
E-mail: pubstaff@cdc.gov
URL: http://www.cdc.gov/niosh/homepage.html
Contact: Linda Rosenstock, MDM, Dir.
Desc: Research to eliminate on-the-job hazards to health and safety. Institute is responsible for identifying occupational safety and health hazards, for determining methods to control them, and for recommending federal standards to limit the hazards. *Type:* Research center.

U.S. Department of Health and Human Services
National Institute for Occupational Safety and Health
Appalachian Laboratory for Occupational Safety and Health

1095 Willowdale Rd.	Ph: (304)285-5704
Morgantown, WV 26505-2888	Fax: (304)285-5820

Contact: Charlotte Dalton, Management Oper.Off.

Desc: Occupational safety and health, focusing on safe working environments, occupational-related respiratory diseases, cross-sectional prospective morbidity and mortality studies, and performance records of respirators and hazard measuring instruments. Maintains a national surveillance data system for the early detection and monitoring of occupational accidents and injuries, and NIOSHTIC database and microfiche collection. *Type:* Research center.

U.S. Department of Health and Human Services
National Institute for Occupational Safety and Health
Safety Research Division

Appalachian Laboratory for	Ph: (304)284-5700
Occup. Safety & Health	Fax: (304)284-5876
944 Chestnut Ridge Rd.	
Morgantown, WV 26505-2888	

Contact: Dr. Thomas R. Bender, Dir.

Desc: Occupational traumatic injuries and deaths; musculoskeletal injuries; worker protection technology, particularly the study of respirator and chemical protective clothing characteristics and performance; related hazard sensing, measuring, and monitoring technologies; and physiological effects of work and protective ensemble use. The Division is mandated to investigate ways to reduce the incidence of occupational injuries and deaths and to administer the federal respirator testing and certification program. *Type:* Research center.

U.S. Department of Labor
Bureau of Labor Statistics
Office of Compensation and Working Conditions
Office of Safety, Health, and Working Conditions

2 Massachusetts Ave. NE	Ph: (202)606-5900
Washington, DC 20212	

Desc: Office compiles occupational safety and health statistics; and makes grants to states and other local agencies to assist in the development and administration of programs dealing with occupational safety and health statistics. Office maintains the nationwide employer record keeping system on job-related injuries and illnesses, conducts the annual survey based on these records, analyzes the results, and compiles supplementary statistics from other sources. *Type:* Government agency, office, or program.

U.S. Department of Labor
Mine Safety and Health Administration

4015 Wilson Blvd., Ste. 601	Ph: (703)235-1452
Arlington, VA 22203	Fax: (703)235-1563

Desc: The Mine Safety and Health Administration develops and promulgates mandatory safety and health standards; ensures compliance with such standards; assesses civil penalties for violations; investigates accidents; cooperates with and provides assistance to the states in the development of effective state mine safety and health programs; improves and expands training programs in cooperation with the states and the mining industry; and in coordination with the Department of Health and Human Services and the Department of the Interior, contributes to the improvement and expansion of mine safety and health research and development. All of these activities are aimed at preventing and reducing mine accidents and occupational diseases in the mining industry. *Type:* Government agency, office, or program.

U.S. Department of Labor
Occupational Safety and Health Administration

200 Constitution Ave. NW	Ph: (202)219-8151
Washington, DC 20210	

Desc: The Occupational Safety and Health Administration develops and promulgates occupational safety and health standards; develops and issues regulations; conducts investigations and inspections to determine the status of compliance with safety and health standards and regulations; and issues citations and proposes penalties for noncompliance with safety and health standards and regulations. *Type:* Government agency, office, or program.

Wisconsin Safety & Health
Wisconsin Council of Safety Division
Wisconsin Manufacturers & Commerce Foundation

501 E. Washington Ave.	Ph: (608)258-3400
PO Box 352	Free: 800-236-3400
Madison, WI 53701	Fax: (608)258-3413

E-mail: wcs@wmc.org

Contact: Bryan M. Roessler, Editor.

Desc: Concerned with industrial safety. Carries Occupational Safety and Health Administration (OSHA) information and news of the Wisconsin Council of Safety. *Type:* Newsletter.

Workplace Violence Prevention Reporter
James Publishing, Inc.

PO Box 25202	Ph: (714)755-5450
Santa Ana, CA 92799-5202	Free: 800-601-6535
	Fax: (714)751-2709

Contact: I. Perrin Weston, Editor.

Desc: Provides federal and state news on violence in the workplace. Includes information on prevention and training techniques to keep the work environment and employees safe. *Type:* Newsletter.

Sales

Alert
General Services Administration (DK)

18th & F Sts. NW, Rm. 6215	Ph: (202)501-1426
Washington, DC 20405	

Desc: Deals with selling to the U.S. government. *Type:* Newsletter.

ARW Counterline
Air-Conditioning and Refrigeration Wholesalers Association

1650 S. Dixie Hwy., 5th Fl.	Ph: (305)755-7000
Boca Raton, FL 33432-7462	Fax: (305)491-8100

E-mail: e-mail@arwi.org

Contact: James S. McMullen, Editor.

Desc: Carries informational and motivational articles to help inside and counter sales personnel generate customer loyalty, handle customer complaints, and to increase sales. *Type:* Newsletter.

Brian Jeffrey's SalesTalk
Salesforce Training & Consulting Inc.

1451 Donald Munro Dr.	Ph: (613)839-7355
Carp, ON, Canada K0A 1L0	Free: 800-461-7355
	Fax: (613)839-1842

E-mail: info@salesforcetraining.com; salestalk@salesforcetraining.on.ca.

URL: http://www.salesforcetraining.com

Contact: Lorraine Jeffrey, Editor.

Desc: Provides sales professionals with information on developments and improvements within the marketing, sales, and advertsing industries. Recurring features include columns titled Publishers Podium, Guest Column, Hints-Tips-Ideas, and Sales Manager's Corner. *Type:* Newsletter.

Bureau of Wholesale Sales Representatives

1100 Spring St. NW, Ste. 700	Ph: (404)870-7600
Atlanta, GA 30309	Free: 800-877-1808
	Fax: (404)870-7601

URL: http://www.bwsr.com

Contact: Michael Wolyn, CEO.

Desc: Salesmen of wholesale women's, men's, and children's apparel and accessories, shoes, toys, and western wear and equipment. *Type:* Association.

Canadian Professional Sales Association—Contact
Canadian Professional Sales Association

145 Wellington St. W., Ste. 310	Ph: (416)408-2685
Toronto, ON, Canada M5J 1H8	Fax: (416)408-2684

E-mail: contact@cpsa.com

Contact: Corinne Radake, Editor.

Desc: Informs members of new developments, research, and events within the Association and sales industry. Contains interviews and feature articles of interest to members. *Type:* Newsletter.

C.S.T. Focus
C.S.T. Consultants, Inc.

600-240 Duncan Mill Rd.	Ph: (416)445-7377
Don Mills, ON, Canada M3B 3P1	Free: 877-333-7377
	Fax: (416)445-1708

E-mail: cstplan@cst.org

Contact: Lennox Toppin, Editor, fax: (416)445-0387, ltoppin@cst.org.

Desc: Directed toward CST sales representatives across Canada and Bermuda. *Type:* Newsletter.

The Direct Response Specialist
Galen Stilson

PO Box 1075	Ph: (813)786-1411
Tarpon Springs, FL 34688-1075	Fax: (813)785-7049

Contact: Galen Stilson, Editor, gstilson@mindspring.com.

Desc: Offers successful response/profit tips, tricks, and techniques for achieving direct mail goals. Considers all subjects directly relating to increasing mail marketing response and profits, including copywriting, mailing lists, fulfillment, results analysis, image development, and media evaluation. *Type:* Newsletter.

Direct Selling Association

1666 K St. NW, Ste. 1010	Ph: (202)293-5760
Washington, DC 20006-2808	Fax: (202)463-4569

E-mail: info@dsa.org

URL: http://www.dsa.org

Contact: Neil H. Offen, Pres.

Desc: Manufacturers and distributors selling consumer products door-to-door, by appointment, and through home-party plans. Products include food, gifts, housewares, dietary supplements, cosmetics, apparel, jewelry, decorative accessories, reference books, water treatment units, security systems, and vacuum cleaners. Offers specialized education; conducts research programs; compiles statistics. *Type:* Association.

Issues & Answers in Sales Management
Clement Communications, Inc.

Concord Industrial Park	Ph: (610)459-1700
10 LaCrue Ave.	Free: 800-345-8101
Concordville, PA 19331	Fax: (610)459-0936

E-mail: editor@clement.com.

Contact: Ellen Brandt, Sr.Ed.; Robi Miller, Managing Editor; George Clement, Publisher.

Desc: Provides sales managers and supervisors with techniques and strategies to improve customer service and profits. Includes topics such as the Internet, tradeshow tips, and cold-calling hints. *Type:* Newsletter.

Master Salesmanship

Clement Communications, Inc.
Concord Industrial Park Ph: (610)459-1700
10 LaCrue Ave. Free: 800-345-8101
Concordville, PA 19331 Fax: (610)459-0936
Desc: Designed to help sales managers motivate, train, and inform their salespeople. Offers pointers on improving old sales skills and developing new ones. *Type:* Newsletter.

NAW Report

National Association of Wholesaler-Distributors (NAW)
1725 K St. NW Ph: (202)872-0885
Washington, DC 20006
Contact: Kimberley Morgan, Editor; Jane Lilly, Assistant Editor.
Desc: Publishes information on government issues and actions affecting wholesaler-distributors specifically and the business community generally. Recurring features include reports on federal legislative and regulatory developments; legal and insurance trends; industry research and statistics; and business services offered through the association's group purchasing program. *Type:* Newsletter.

Net Profit

Meg Dalen
4533 MacArthur Blvd., No. 232
Newport Beach, GA 92660
Contact: Meg Dalen, Editor.
Desc: Provides ideas and encouragement to sales people, particularly those working through the Internet. Recurring features include letters to the editor, interviews, news of research, and book reviews. *Type:* Newsletter.

New Account Selling

The Dartnell Corp.
360 Hiatt Dr. Free: 800-621-5463
Palm Beach Gardens, FL 33418 Fax: (561)622-2423
E-mail: dartnell@dartnellcorp.com
URL: http://www.dartnellcorp.com
Contact: Terry Breen, Editor.
Desc: Offers ideas and inspiration related to selling to new accounts. Covers "cold calling," prospecting, and techniques for maintaining new customers. *Type:* Newsletter.

News of the World

World Floor Covering Association
2211 E. Howell Ave. Ph: (714)978-6440
Anaheim, CA 92806 Free: 800-624-6880
Fax: (714)978-6066
URL: http://www.wfca.org.
Contact: D. Christopher Davis, Editor.
Desc: Covers news of members, activities, and programs of the Association. Focuses on the floor covering industry. *Type:* Newsletter.

Overcoming Objections

The Dartnell Corp.
360 Hiatt Dr. Free: 800-621-5463
Palm Beach Gardens, FL 33418 Fax: (561)622-2423
E-mail: dartnell@dartnellcorp.com
URL: http://www.dartnellcorp.com
Contact: Chris Heide, Editor, heide@dartnellcorp.com.
Desc: Offers ideas and inspiration to salespeople, with a focus on techniques for overcoming objections. Recurring features include interviews, news of research, and book reviews. *Type:* Newsletter.

PMC Newsletter

Premium Marketing Club of New York
244 Broad St. Ph: (732)842-5070
Red Bank, NJ 07701 Fax: (732)219-1938
E-mail: pmc@pmc-ny.com

URL: http://www.pmc-ny.com.
Contact: Karen Kircher, Editor.
Desc: Reports incentive marketing news as well as news of club activities. *Type:* Newsletter.

Professional Selling

Bureau of Business Practice
24 Rope Ferry Rd. Ph: (860)442-4365
Waterford, CT 06386 Free: 800-243-0876
Fax: (860)437-3555
URL: http://www.bbpnews.com
Contact: Karen Barretta, Editor, karen_barretta@prenhall.com.
Desc: "Presents practical solutions to everyday sales problems." *Type:* Newsletter.

Sales and Marketing Executive Report

The Dartnell Corp.
360 Hiatt Dr. Free: 800-621-5463
Palm Beach Gardens, FL 33418 Fax: (561)622-2423
E-mail: dartnell@dartnellcorp.com
URL: http://www.dartnellcorp.com
Contact: Christen P. Heide, Editor, cheide@dartnellcorp.com.
Desc: Discusses topics of interest to managers, including motivating and training sales personnel, executive self-improvement, and advertising and public relations strategies. Recurring features include news of research, letters to the editor, book reviews, a calendar of events, and columns titled Sales/Marketing Briefs and Special Report. *Type:* Newsletter.

Sales and Marketing Executives International

5500 Interstate North Pkwy., Ph: (770)661-8500
No. 545 Fax: (770)661-8512
Atlanta, GA 30328
E-mail: smeihq@smei.org
URL: http://www.smei.org
Contact: Michael Price, Exec.Dir.
Desc: Executives concerned with sales and marketing management, research, training, and other managerial aspects of distribution. Members control activities of 3,000,000 salespersons. Undertakes studies in the field of selling and sales management; sponsors sales workshops, rallies, clinics, and seminars. *Type:* Association.

Sales & Marketing Report

Lawrence Ragan Communications, Inc.
316 N. Michigan Ave., Ste. 300 Ph: (312)960-4100
Chicago, IL 60601 Free: 800-878-5331
Fax: (312)960-4105
E-mail: cservice@ragan.com
Contact: Steve Crescenzo, Editor; Mark Ragan, Publisher; Carol Jackson, Managing Editor; Dan Oswald, President.
Desc: Provides information about strategic sales coaching, building a high performance sales team, boosting morale and productivity, and managing time more effectively. *Type:* Newsletter.

Sales and Marketing Success

Printing Industries of America, Inc.
100 Daingerfield Rd. Ph: (703)519-8100
Alexandria, VA 22314 Fax: (703)548-3227
Contact: Cliff Weiss, Editor.
Desc: Provides management information to graphic arts companies for marketing products and improving sales techniques. *Type:* Newsletter.

Sales Mastermind

The Economic Press, Inc.
12 Daniel Rd. Ph: (973)227-1224
Fairfield, NJ 07004-2565 Free: 800-526-2554
Fax: (973)227-8360
E-mail: order@epinc.com
Contact: Jeffrey Gitoner, Editor, edit@epinc.com.
Desc: Offers sales tips, skill imrpovement and attitude techniques for salespeople. Discusses how to get more business from existing customers, expanding the buyers' circle, and keeping customers. *Type:* Newsletter.

The Sales Rep's Advisor

Alexander Research & Communications, Inc.
215 Park Ave. S, Ste. 1301 Ph: (212)228-0246
New York, NY 10003 Fax: (212)228-0376
Contact: Laurence Alexander, Editor.
Desc: Provides strategies to run a business better and more profitably. Focuses on preventive legal and business matters, rather than selling techniques, covering such topics as taxes, law, business management, and personal finance. *Type:* Newsletter.

Salesmanship

The Dartnell Corp.
360 Hiatt Dr. Free: 800-621-5463
Palm Beach Gardens, FL 33418 Fax: (561)622-2423
E-mail: dartnell@dartnellcorp.com
URL: http://www.dartnellcorp.com
Contact: Terry Breen, Editor.
Desc: Offers sales ideas and inspiration, profiles of top-producing salespeople, and articles on topics related to sales success. *Type:* Newsletter.

The Selling Advantage

Progressive Business Publications
370 Technology Dr. Ph: (610)695-8600
Malvern, PA 19355 Free: 800-220-5000
Fax: (610)651-2981
URL: http://www.pbp.com.
Contact: Phil Ahr, Editor.
Desc: Explores new strategies and proven techniques to improve sales performance. Recurring features include book reviews and a column titled Tale of the Sale. *Type:* Newsletter.

Selling Power

Personal Selling Power
PO Box 5467 Ph: (703)752-7000
Fredericksburg, VA 22403-0467 Free: 800-752-7355
Fax: (703)752-7001
E-mail: sellngpow@aol.com.
URL: http://www.sellingpower.com
Contact: Gerhard Gschwandtner, Publisher.
Desc: Magazine presenting motivational and sales skills and techniques for sales and marketing executives. *Type:* Periodical.

Spare Time

Kipen Publishing Corp.
5810 W. Oklahoma Ave. Ph: (414)543-8110
Milwaukee, WI 53219-4300 Fax: (414)543-9767
E-mail: publisher@spare-time.com; ads@spare-time.com.
URL: http://www.spare-time.com.
Contact: Peter Abbott, Editor, editor@spare-time.com; Dennis K. Wilk, Publisher, publisher@spare-time.com; Deborah Roan, Marketing, marketing@spare-time.com; Sandie Ross, Reader Services, readers@spare-time.com; Gary Dorn, Advertising Prod., ads@spare-time.com.
Desc: Magazine featuring articles on business start-up and money-making opportunities. *Type:* Periodical.

Strategic Sales Management

Bureau of Business Practice
24 Rope Ferry Rd.   Ph: (860)442-4365
Waterford, CT 06386   Free: 800-243-0876
         Fax: (860)437-3555
URL: http://www.bbpnews.com
Contact: Karen Barretta, Editor, karen_baretta@prenhall.
com.
Desc: Reports on what people in the sales management
field are doing to produce measurable sales profits. Focuses
on sales hiring, training, managing, motivation, and results. *Type:* Newsletter.

Successful Closing Technique

The Dartnell Corp.
360 Hiatt Dr.   Free: 800-621-5463
Palm Beach Gardens, FL 33418   Fax: (561)622-2423
E-mail: dartnell@dartnellcorp.com
URL: http://www.dartnellcorp.com
Contact: Terry Breen, Editor.
Desc: Provides information about improving sales and deal
closings. *Type:* Newsletter.

Trade Show Ideas

Trade Show Exhibitors Association
5501 Backlick Rd., Ste. 105   Ph: (703)941-3725
Springfield, VA 22151-3940   Fax: (703)941-8275
E-mail: tsea@tsea.org; iea@eabbs.org.
URL: http://www.tsea.org
Contact: Sharon E. McDonagh, CPS, Mgr. of Publications
and Design.
Desc: Supplies news and information of interest to exhibit
managers and their suppliers. Carries case studies, "how-
to" items, checklists, and industry data. *Type:* Newsletter.

Tradeshow Week

Darlene Gudea
5700 Wilshire Blvd., Ste. 120   Ph: (213)965-5300
Los Angeles, CA 90036-5804   Fax: (213)965-5330
Contact: Darlene Gudea, VP/Pub/Editor, dgudea@
tsweek.com.
Desc: Provides coverage of tradeshows, facilities, labor conditions, new exhibit ideas, people, and a comprehensive
show calendar. *Type:* Newsletter.

What's Working in Sales Management

Progressive Business Publications
370 Technology Dr.   Ph: (610)695-8600
Malvern, PA 19355   Free: 800-220-5000
         Fax: (610)651-2981
URL: http://www.pbp.com.
Contact: Leah Rapposelli, Editor.
Desc: Acts as a time-saving resource for busy sales managers. Recurring features include interviews, news of research, a calendar of events, and news of educational
opportunities. *Type:* Newsletter.

Science

American Association for the Advancement of Science

1200 New York Ave., NW   Ph: (202)326-6400
Washington, DC 20005
URL: http://www.aaas.org
Contact: Richard S. Nicholson, Exec. Officer.
Desc: The largest general scientific organization representing all fields of science. Membership includes more than
143,000 individuals and 296 scientific societies, professional organizations, and state and city academies (many
of which sponsor junior academies of science). Objectives
are to further the work of scientists to facilitate cooperation among them, to foster scientific freedom and responsibility, to improve the effectiveness of science in the
promotion of human welfare, to advance education in science, and to increase public understanding and appreciation of the importance and promise of the methods of
science in human progress. *Type:* Association.

American Association for Crystal Growth— Directory

*American Association for Crystal Growth
(AACG)*
PO Box 3233   Ph: (805)492-7047
Thousand Oaks, CA 91359-   Fax: (805)492-4062
   0233
E-mail: aacg@lafn.org
Contact: Patricia Morris Hotsenpiller, Editor, (302)695-
2153, fax: (302)695-1664, morrispa@esvax.dnet.dupont.
com.
Desc: 600 physical scientists (chemists, physicists, cera-
mists, chemical and electrical engineers, etc.) concerned
with crystal growth theory and practice. *Type:* Directory.

American Association for Laboratory Accreditation

5301 Buckeystown Pike., Ste.   Ph: (301)644-3200
   350   Fax: (301)662-2974
Frederick, MD 21704-8307
E-mail: punger@a2la.org
URL: http://www.a2la.org
Contact: Peter S. Unger, Pres.
Desc: Individuals, associations, corporations, universities,
laboratories, research institutes, and government agencies
interested in improving the quality of laboratories. Accredits testing laboratories certifies laboratory reference materials, and registers quality systems. *Type:* Association.

American Association for Laboratory Animal Science

9190 Crestwyn Hills Dr.   Ph: (901)754-8620
Memphis, TN 38125   Fax: (901)753-0046
E-mail: info@aalas.org
URL: http://www.aalas.org
Contact: Michael R. Sondag, Exec.Dir.
Desc: Persons and institutions professionally concerned
with the production, use, care, and study of laboratory animals. Serves as clearinghouse for collection and exchange
of information on all phases of laboratory animal care and
management and on the care, use, and procurement of
laboratory animals used in biomedical research. *Type:* Association.

American Association of Stratigraphic Palynologists

Dr. Thomas d. Demchuk
600 N. Dairy Ashford   Ph: (281)366-5399
Box 2197   Fax: (281)366-3195
Houston, TX 77252-2197
E-mail: dtpocknall@aol.com
URL: http://www.geology.utoronto.ca/AASP
Contact: Dr. David Packnall, Sec.-Treas.
Desc: Persons engaged or interested in research in all aspects of palynology (the branch of science dealing with
pollen, spores, and other organic-walled microfossils); institutions and companies that sponsor research in palynology. Promotes the science of palynology as related to
stratigraphic applications, paleoecology, paleoclimatology,
and biostratigraphy. *Type:* Association.

American College of Forensic Examiners

611 E. Wells St.   Ph: (414)881-3818
Milwaukee, WI 53202   Free: 800-A-EXPERT
         Fax: (414)881-4702
E-mail: webmaster@acfe.com
URL: http://www.acfe.com
Contact: Sally Kolf, Contact.
Desc: Professionals in the field of forensic examination, including the following disciplines: accident reconstruction,
criminology, hypnosis, all medical fields, physics, psychiatry, psychology, and toxicology. Works to advance the
profession of forensic examination through education,
training, and certification. *Type:* Association.

American Institutes for Research in the Behavioral Sciences

3333 K St. NW, Ste. 300   Ph: (202)342-5000
Washington, DC 20007   Fax: (202)342-5033
URL: http://www.air-dc.org
Contact: Dr. David A. Goslin, Pres. & CEO.
Desc: Scientific and educational research organization.
Conducts behavioral and social science research in fields
of education, social program evaluation, healthcare,
human performance, usability engineering, human factors, problems of the specially challenged, education finance, and document design. Supported by contracts and
grants from industry, foundations, and government agencies. *Type:* Association.

American Laboratory News

International Scientific Communications, Inc.
30 Controls Dr.   Ph: (203)926-9300
PO Box 870   Fax: (203)926-9310
Shelton, CT 06484-0870
E-mail: iscpubs@iscpubs.com
URL: http://www.iscpubs.com
Contact: William Wham, Publisher; Brian Howard, Edi-
tor; Maureen Jezierny, Production Mgr.; Susan Messinger,
Managing Editor.
Desc: Trade magazine for scientists. *Type:* Periodical.

American Men and Women of Science

R. R. Bowker
A Unit of Cahners Business Information
121 Chanlon Rd.   Ph: (908)464-6800
New Providence, NJ 07974   Free: 888-269-5372
         Fax: (908)771-7704
E-mail: info@bowker.com
Contact: Richard Lanam, Editor.
Desc: Over 119,600 U.S. and Canadian scientists active in
the physical, biological, mathematical, computer science,
and engineering fields; includes references to previous edition for deceased scientists and nonrespondents. *Type:* Directory.

American Men and Women of Science

R.R. Bowker
121 Chanlon Rd.   Ph: (908)464-6800
New Providence, NJ 07974
URL: http://www.bowker.com
Contact: Yvette Berthel, Tape/Online Services.
Desc: Contains biographical information on more than
119,600 U.S. and Canadian engineers and scientists in the
biological and physical sciences. *Available:* LEXIS-NEXIS,
NEXIS; The Dialog Corporation, DIALOG. *Type:* Data-
base.

American Scientist

Sigma Xi, The Scientific Research Society
PO Box 13975   Ph: (919)549-0097
Research Triangle Park, NC   Free: 800-282-0444
   27709-3975   Fax: (919)549-0090
E-mail: editors@amsci.org; ads@amsci.org; subs@amsci.
org.
Contact: Rosalind Reid, Editor; David Schoonmaker,
Managing Editor; Kate Miller, Assoc. Publisher.
Desc: Scientific magazine. *Type:* Periodical.

American Society for Cell Biology—Directory

American Society for Cell Biology
9650 Rockville Pike   Ph: (301)530-7153
Bethesda, MD 20814   Fax: (301)530-7139
E-mail: ascbinfo@ascb.org
Contact: Elizabeth Marincola, Editor.
Desc: 8,500 scientists with research experience in cell biol-
ogy or an allied field. *Type:* Directory.

American Society for Nondestructive Testing

1711 Arlingate Ln.   Ph: (614)274-6003
PO Box 28518   Free: 800-222-2768
Columbus, OH 43228-0518   Fax: (614)274-6899
URL: http://www.asnt.org
Contact: Donald Embinder, Mkt. Mng.

Desc: Metallurgists, quality control specialists, welding engineers, industrial management personnel, technicians, educators, and suppliers of equipment and services. Promotes education and techniques in methods of nondestructive testing utilizing penetrating radiations, magnetics, electricity, sound, heat, penetrants and visual-optics for the aerospace, airframe, automotive, marine, railroad, chemical, petroleum, electronics, nuclear, materials-joining, ordnance, and utilities industries. *Type:* Association.

American Society for Photogrammetry and Remote Sensing

5410 Grosvenor Ln., Ste. 210   Ph: (301)493-0290
Bethesda, MD 20814-2160   Fax: (301)493-0208
E-mail: asprs@asprs.org
URL: http://www.asprs.org
Contact: James Plasker, CAE, Exec.Dir.

Desc: Firms, individuals, government employees, and academicians engaged in photogrammetry, photointerpretation, remote sensing, and geographic information systems and their application to such fields as archaeology, geographic information systems, military reconnaissance, urban planning, engineering, traffic surveys, meteorological observations, medicine, geology, forestry, agriculture, construction, and topographic mapping. *Type:* Association.

Annual Reviews

4139 El Camino Way   Ph: (415)493-4400
PO Box 10139   Free: 800-523-8635
Palo Alto, CA 94303-0139   Fax: (415)855-9815
E-mail: science@annurev.org
URL: http://www.annurev.org
Contact: Samuel Gubins, Pres.-Editor-in-Chief.

Desc: Fosters advancement of the sciences through publication of original *Annual Reviews* in fields of study including anthropology, astronomy and astrophysics, biochemistry, biophysics and biomolecular structure, chemistry, earth and planetary sciences, ecology and systematics, energy and the environment, entomology, fluid mechanics, genetics, immunology, materials science, medicine, microbiology, neuroscience, nuclear and particle science, nutrition, pharmacology and toxicology, physical chemistry, physiology, phytopathology, plant physiology and plant molecular biology, political science, psychology, public health, and sociology. *Type:* Association.

The Antarctica Project

PO Box 76920   Ph: (202)544-0236
Washington, DC 20013   Fax: (202)544-8483
E-mail: antarctic@igc.org
URL: http://www.asoc.org
Contact: Beth Clark, Dir.

Desc: Works to preserve Antarctica by monitoring all activities to ensure minimal environment impact, and consulting with key users of Antarctica, including scientists, tourists, governments. *Type:* Association.

Applied Science & Technology Index

H.W. Wilson Company
950 University Ave.   Ph: (718)588-8400
Bronx, NY 10452
E-mail: custserv@hwwilson.com
URL: http://www.hwwilson.com
Contact: Technical Support Department., techmail@info.hwwilson.com.

Desc: Contains citations to articles, book reviews, interviews, new product reviews, and selected editorials and letters to the editor in 411 English-language trade and industrial publications. Covers aeronautics and space science, chemistry, computer science, construction industry, electric and electronics industry, energy resources and research, fire and fire prevention, food industry, geology, machinery, mathematics, mineralology, metallurgy, oceanography, physics, plastics, textiles, transportation, and the following engineering fields: chemical, civil, electrical, environmental, industrial, mechanical, mining, nuclear, and telecommunications. *Available:* H.W. Wilson Company, WilsonWeb; Ovid Technologies, Inc.; OCLC Online Computer Library Center, Inc., OCLC EPIC; OCLC Online Computer Library Center, Inc., OCLC FirstSearch Catalog; SilverPlatter Information, Inc. *Type:* Database.

Armenian Engineers and Scientists of America

1616 S. Victory Blvd. 205   Ph: (818)574-3372
Glendale, CA 91201   Fax: (818)574-3372
URL: http://www.aesa.org
Contact: Vazgen Ghoogassian, Pres.

Desc: Armenian scientists and engineers living in the United States. Promotes advancement of science and engineering and related disciplines and technologies in Armenia. *Type:* Association.

Association for Assessment and Accreditation of Laboratory Animal Care International

11300 Rockville Pike, Ste. 1211   Ph: (301)231-5353
Rockville, MD 20852-3035   Free: 800-926-0066
                                     Fax: (301)231-8282
E-mail: accredit@aaalac.org
URL: http://www.aaalac.org
Contact: John G. Miller, DVM, Exec.Dir.

Desc: Promotes the humane treatment of animals in science though a voluntary accreation program. More than 600 institutions around the world have earned AAALAC International accreditation, demonstrating their commitment to responsible animal care and use. *Type:* Association.

The Aurora Page

Michigan Technological University - Department of Geological Engineering and Sciences
1400 Townsend Dr.   Ph: (906)487-2531
Houghton, MI 49931-1295   Fax: (906)487-3371
E-mail: tjbornho@mtu.edu
URL: http://www.geo.mtu.edu/weather/aurora/
Contact: Michael Dolan, System Admin., Dept. of Geology, mtdolan@mtu.edu.

Desc: The Aurora Page database provides forecasts and warnings, geomagnetic disturbances, images, and sighting reports about the 'Northern Lights.' Much of the data are updated hourly. Numerous links to related sites are also available. *Type:* Database.

Beta Kappa Chi

Dupont Hall, Rm. 204
Hampton University
Hampton, VA 23668
Contact: Dr. Elaine T. Eatman, Exec.Sec.

Desc: Honor society - men and women, science and mathematics. *Type:* Association.

Bio-Rad

Bio-Rad Laboratories
Life Science Group   Free: 800-424-6723
2000 Alfred Nobel Dr.
Hercules, CA 94547
Contact: Anne Stevens, Editor.

Desc: Carries information about chromatography, electrophoresis, HPLC, molecular biology, and immunochemistry. *Type:* Newsletter.

BioScan: The Worldwide Biotech Industry Reporting Service

Oryx Press
4041 N. Central Ave., Ste. 700   Ph: (602)265-2651
Phoenix, AZ 85012-3397   Free: 800-279-6799
                                     Fax: 800-279-4663
E-mail: info@oryxpress.com
URL: http://www.oryxpress.com
Contact: Janet Woolum, Editor.

Desc: Over 1,000 companies currently doing product research and development in food processing, agriculture, medicine, and other fields in the biotechnology industry. *Type:* Directory.

Biotechnology Software

Mary Ann Liebert, Inc. Publishers
2 Madison Ave.   Ph: (914)834-3100
Larchmont, NY 10538   Fax: (914)834-3771
E-mail: info@liebertpub.com
Contact: Dr. Kevin Alern, Editor.

Desc: Reviews scientific software and hardware. Recurring features include letters to the editor, news of research, a calendar of events, job listings, and book reviews. *Type:* Newsletter.

Calcium and Calcified Tissue Abstracts

Cambridge Scientific Abstracts (CSA)
7200 Wisconsin Ave., Ste. 601   Ph: (301)961-6700
Bethesda, MD 20814-4823
E-mail: sales@csa.com
URL: http://www.csa.com
Desc: Contains more than 37,000 citations, with abstracts, to the worldwide literature on the metabolism of calcium and related minerals. Covers intestinal absorption of calcium, phosphorus, and magnesium; osteoporosis, osteomalacia, and other bone diseases; and effects of pregnancy, menopause, aging, and metabolism on bone structure and calcium metabolism. *Type:* Database.

Canada Centre for Remote Sensing

Canada Centre for Remote Sensing
588 Booth St.   Ph: (613)947-1272
Ottawa, ON, Canada K1A 0Y7   Fax: (613)947-1408
E-mail: info@ccrs.nrcan.gc.ca
URL: http://www.ccrs.nrcan.gc.ca/ccrs/homepg.pl?e
Desc: The Canada Centre for Remote Sensing web site contains data center links, CCRS image inventory (from thousands of satellite photos/images), CCRS bulletin board, and directory and product information for the remote sensing community in Canada. Also included is an extensive bibliographic database, a glossary of terms, background and specific data for CCRS, research and technical specs, a guided tour of Canada from space, and more. *Type:* Database.

Carolina Tips

Carolina Biological Supply Co.
2700 York Rd.   Ph: (919)584-0381
Burlington, NC 27215   Free: 800-334-5551
E-mail: caroscipub@aol.com
URL: http://www.carosci.com; http://www.gene.com/ae.
Contact: Dr. Phillip Owens, Editor.

Desc: Contains articles of interest to science teachers from the elementary to college levels. Remarks: Free to science teachers requesting on school letterhead and health professionals. *Type:* Newsletter.

Chemoreception Abstracts

Cambridge Scientific Abstracts (CSA)
7200 Wisconsin Ave., Ste. 601   Ph: (301)961-6700
Bethesda, MD 20814-4823
E-mail: sales@csa.com
URL: http://www.csa.com

Desc: Contains more than 25,000 citations, with abstracts, to the worldwide literature on taste, smell, internal chemoreception, chemotaxis, and associated forms of sensitivity. Sources include specialist literature such as journals, books, conference proceedings, and reports. *Type:* Database.

Chi Beta Phi

Department of Natural Sciences   Ph: (703)665-4547
1460 University Dr.
Winchester, VA 22601
Desc: Honorary society - men and women, scientific. *Type:* Association.

Conference Papers Index

Cambridge Scientific Abstracts (CSA)
7200 Wisconsin Ave., Ste. 601   Ph: (301)961-6700
Bethesda, MD 20814-4823
E-mail: sales@csa.com
URL: http://www.csa.com
Contact: Cheryl Droffner, Editor.
Desc: Contains approximately 1.4 million citations to scientific and technical papers presented at regional, national, and international meetings. Covers current research and development activities, primarily in the life sciences, medicine, chemistry, physical sciences, and engineering. *Available:* The Dialog Corporation, DIALOG; STN International. *Type:* Database.

Current Contents Search®

Institute for Scientific Information (ISI)
3501 Market St.   Ph: (215)386-0100
Philadelphia, PA 19104
E-mail: isiorder@isinet.com
URL: http://www.isinet.com
Desc: Provides complete bibliographic coverage, with abstracts, to articles listed in the tables of contents of approximately 7500 leading journals in the sciences, social sciences, and arts and humanities. Covers clinical medicine (CLIN); life sciences (LIFE); arts and humanities (ARTS); engineering, technology, and applied sciences (TECH); social and behavioral sciences (BEHA); agriculture, biology, and environmental sciences (AGRI); and physical, chemical, and earth sciences (PHYS). *Available:* Ovid Technologies, Inc.; Ovid Technologies, Inc.; The Dialog Corporation, DIALOG; The Dialog Corporation, DIALOG; The Dialog Corporation, DataStar; DIMDI (Deutsches Institut fuer Medizinische Dokumentation und Information); The Gale Group, InfoTrac Web; The Gale Group, InfoTrac Web. *Type:* Database.

Current Science

Weekly Reader Corp.
200 First Stamford Pl.   Ph: (203)705-3500
PO Box 120023   Fax: (203)705-1661
Stamford, CT 06912-0023
E-mail: science@weeklyreader.com.
Contact: Dan Hogan, Managing Editor; Richard J. LeBrasseur, Publisher; Eric Ecker, Editor.
Desc: Science magazine for junior and senior high school students. *Type:* Periodical.

Discover

Disney Publishing
500 S. Buena Vista   Ph: (818)567-5739
Burbank, CA 91521   Fax: (818)566-9870
URL: http://www.enews.com/magazines/discover.
Contact: Paul Hoffman, President; Marc Zabludoff, Editor; Margaret Foley, Managing Editor; Lee Rosenbaum, Publisher; Jim Keplesky, Assoc. Publisher, Adv.; Thomas Slater, Circulation Dir.; Karen Render, Director; Rus Dev, Director.
Desc: Magazine focusing on science, from astronomy to zoology. *Alt. Contact:* 114 5th Ave., New York, NY 10011; fax: (212)633-4817. *Type:* Periodical.

DTIC Research and Technology Work Unit Information System

U.S. Defense Technical Information Center (DTIC)
8725 John J. Kingman Rd., Ste   Ph: (703)767-8224
0944
Fort Belvoir, VA 22060-6218
E-mail: jlewis@dtic.mil
URL: http://www.dtic.mil

Contact: Wade Cook, Division Chief, AIS Management, (703)767-8000, fax: (703)767-7033, wcook@dtic.mil.

Desc: Contains more than 268,000 summaries of completed and in-progress defense-related projects in the areas of science and technology. *Available:* U.S. Defense Technical Information Center (DTIC), Defense RDT&E OnLine System (DROLS). *Type:* Database.

Encyclopedia of Physical Sciences and Engineering Information Sources

Gale Group Inc.
27500 Drake Rd.   Ph: (248)699-4253
Farmington Hills, MI 48331-   Free: 800-877-GALE
3535   Fax: (248)699-8070
E-mail: galeord@galegroup.com
URL: http://www.galegroup.com.

Contact: Steven Wasserman, Editor; Martin A. Smith, Editor; David Wilt, Editor; Judy Erickson, Editor.

Desc: Nearly 16,000 organizations, publications, online databases, and other sources of live and print information in the physical sciences and engineering fields. *Type:* Directory.

Encyclopedia of Strange and Unexplained Physical Phenomena

Gale Group Inc.
27500 Drake Rd.   Ph: (248)699-4253
Farmington Hills, MI 48331-   Free: 800-877-GALE
3535   Fax: (248)699-8070
E-mail: galeord@galegroup.com
URL: http://www.galegroup.com.

Desc: Organizations and publications associated with unexplained physical phenomena. Principal content of publication is 200 reports on these occurrences and related scientists, investigators, witnesses, theories, beliefs, and hoaxes. *Type:* Directory.

Entomological Society of America

9301 Annapolis Rd.   Ph: (301)731-4535
Lanham, MD 20706   Fax: (301)731-4538
E-mail: esa@entsoc.org
URL: http://www.entsoc.org

Contact: Kathryn Meckley, Dir. of Srvcs.

Type: Association.

Entomology Abstracts

Cambridge Scientific Abstracts (CSA)
7200 Wisconsin Ave., Ste. 601   Ph: (301)961-6700
Bethesda, MD 20814-4823
E-mail: sales@csa.com
URL: http://www.csa.com

Desc: Contains more than 181,000 citations, with abstracts, to the worldwide literature on insects, arachnids, myriapods, onychophorans, and terrestrial isopods. Sources include specialist literature such as journals, books, conference proceedings, and reports. *Available:* National Information Services Corporation (NISC), BiblioLine. *Type:* Database.

Federation of Societies for Coatings Technology—Year Book and Membership Directory

Federation of Societies for Coatings Technology
492 Norristown Rd.   Ph: (610)940-0777
Blue Bell, PA 19422-2350   Fax: (610)940-0292
E-mail: publications@coatingstech.org; fsct@coatingstech.org.
Contact: Patricia D. Ziegler, Editor; Patricia D. Ziegler, Editor.
Desc: About 7,500 chemists, technicians, and supervisory production personnel in the decorative and protective coatings industry who are members of the 27 constituent societies of the federation. *Type:* Directory.

General Science Index

H.W. Wilson Company
950 University Ave.   Ph: (718)588-8400
Bronx, NY 10452
E-mail: custserv@hwwilson.com
URL: http://www.hwwilson.com
Contact: Technical Support Department., techmail@info.hwwilson.com.
Desc: Contains citations to articles and book reviews in 167 English-language periodicals in the general sciences. Coverage ranges from general interest magazines such as Discover and Sierra, to the specialized, such as Journal of the American Chemical Society--starting with May 1984. *Available:* H.W. Wilson Company, WilsonWeb; H.W. Wilson Company, WilsonWeb; Ovid Technologies, Inc.; OCLC Online Computer Library Center, Inc., OCLC EPIC; OCLC Online Computer Library Center, Inc., OCLC FirstSearch Catalog; Ameritech Library Services, Vista; NlightN. *Type:* Database.

General Systems Bulletin

International Society for the Systems Sciences (ISSS)
PO Box 6808   Ph: (502)899-3332
Louisville, KY 40206-0808
Contact: Jennifer Wilby, Editor.
Desc: Contains editorials, correspondence, planning of annual meetings, and reports on systems science and database development. Recurring features include letters to the editor, a calendar of events, reports of meetings, book reviews, and notices of publications available. *Type:* Newsletter.

Global Change Master Directory

U.S. National Aeronautics and Space Administration - Goddard Space Flight Center - Global Change Data Center
Greenbelt, MD 20771   Ph: (301)441-4202
   Fax: (301)441-9486
E-mail: gcmduso@gcmd.gsfc.nasa.gov
URL: http://gcmd.gsfc.nasa.gov
Contact: Lola Olsen, olsen@gcmd.gsfc.nasa.gov.
Desc: The Global Change Master Directory (GCMD) contains information on Earth science, environmental, biosphere, climate, and global change data holdings. Conference information is also available here and DIF text and web editors are also provided for download. *Type:* Database.

Guide to American Scientific and Technical Directories

Todd Publications
PO Box 635   Ph: (914)358-6213
Nyack, NY 10960   Free: 800-747-1056
   Fax: (914)358-1059
E-mail: toddpub@aol.com
URL: http://www.toddpublications.com
Contact: Barry Klein, Editor.

Desc: Approximately 3,500 directories that focus primarily on topics in science and technology. *Type:* Directory.

Human Resources Research Organization

66 Canal Center Pl., Ste. 400   Ph: (703)549-3611
Alexandria, VA 22314   Fax: (703)549-9025
Contact: Lauress C. Wise, Pres.
Desc: Behavioral and social science researchers seeking to improve human performance, particularly in organizational settings, through behavioral and social science research, development, consultation and instruction. Promotes research and development to solve specific problems in: training and education; development, refinement, and instruction in the technology of training and education; studies and development of techniques to improve the motivation of personnel in training and on the job; research of leadership and management, and development of leadership programs; criterion development, individual assessment, and program evaluation in training and operating systems; measurement and evaluation of human performance under varying circumstances; organizational development studies, including performance counseling, group decision-making, and factors that affect organizational competence; development of manpower information systems and the application of management science on personnel systems. Encourages use of high technology for instructional purposes by means of computer assisted instruction, interactive video, and computer literacy. *Type:* Association.

Innovation and Ideas

Publishing and Business Consultants
4427 W. Slauson Ave.
Los Angeles, CA 90043-2717
Contact: Atia Napoleon, Editor and Publisher.
Desc: Magazine featuring breakthroughs in science and high technology. *Type:* Periodical.

Institute of Medicine

2101 Constitution Ave. NW   Ph: (202)334-2169
Washington, DC 20418   Fax: (202)334-1412
URL: http://www2.nas.edu/iom
Contact: Kenneth I. Shine, Pres.
Desc: Identifies, studies, and reports on the nation's major problems in medicine and the health sciences; recognizes outstanding achievements in the field. Operated under the auspices of the National Academy of Sciences. *Type:* Association.

Institutes for Behavior Resources

2437 15th St. NW   Ph: (202)328-1550
Washington, DC 20009   Fax: (202)234-1592
Contact: Joseph V. Brady, Ph.D., Pres.
Desc: Personnel with backgrounds in psychology, education, sociology, social services, and law. Conducts basic and applied research in behavioral psychology; investigates human performance, law and behavior, and social problems. Plans, develops, and evaluates educational, training, and management systems. *Type:* Association.

Intelligence

Edward Rosenfeld
PO Box 20008   Ph: (212)222-1123
New York, NY 10025-1510   Free: 800-638-7257
   Fax: (212)222-1123
E-mail: i@eintelligence.com
URL: http://eintelligence.com.
Contact: Edward Rosenfeld, Editor.
Desc: Covers technologies that affect the future of computing and offers viewpoints. Concentrates on business, research and government activities in neural networks, parallel processing, pattern recognition, natural language interfaces, voice and speech technologies, and art and graphics. *Type:* Newsletter.

ISTP&B Search®

Institute for Scientific Information (ISI)
3501 Market St.   Ph: (215)386-0100
Philadelphia, PA 19104
E-mail: isiorder@isinet.com
URL: http://www.isinet.com
Contact: Technical Help Desk Rep., custserv@isinet.com.
Desc: Contains bibliographic data, indexing approximately 4100 published scientific and technical proceedings each year and more than 160,000 individual papers covering all disciplines of the sciences. Also provides bibliographic data on the individual chapters of the world's most recently published mult-authored scientific and technical books and single-authored books that are part of a multi-authored series. *Available:* DIMDI (Deutsches Institut fuer Medizinische Dokumentation und Information). *Type:* Database.

LC-GC—Buyers' Guide Issue

Advanstar Communications
859 Willamette St.   Ph: (541)343-1200
Eugene, OR 97401-6806   Fax: (541)344-3514
E-mail: lcgcedit@lcgcmag.com.
URL: http://www.lcgcmag.com.
Contact: Jeffrey Schier, Editor.
Desc: List of approximately 900 manufacturers of liquid, gas, and other chromatography instrumentation, chemicals, and supplies for the separations sciences. *Type:* Directory.

Life Science Laboratory Reference

Cahners Business Information
New Product Information Division
301 Gibraltar Dr.   Ph: (973)292-5100
Morris Plains, NJ 07950   Fax: (973)539-3476
E-mail: bioprodmag.com.
Contact: Stephen C. Ernst, Editor.
Desc: Listing of manufacturers of antibodies, antiseras, and other related products. *Type:* Directory.

Life Sciences Organizations and Agencies Directory

Gale Group Inc.
27500 Drake Rd.   Ph: (248)699-4253
Farmington Hills, MI 48331-   Free: 800-877-GALE
3535   Fax: (248)699-8070
E-mail: galeord@galegroup.com
URL: http://www.galegroup.com.
Contact: Brigitte T. Darnay, Editor; Margaret Labash Young, Editor.
Desc: About 7,500 associations, government agencies, research centers, educational institutions, libraries and information centers, museums, consultants, electronic information services, and other organizations and agencies active in agriculture, biology, ecology, forestry, marine science, nutrition, wildlife and animal sciences, and other natural and life sciences. *Type:* Directory.

Measurements and Control/Measurement and Control News

Measurements and Data Corp.
2994 W. Liberty Ave.   Ph: (412)343-9666
Pittsburgh, PA 15216   Fax: (412)343-9685
E-mail: editor@mac-med.com.
Contact: H. Saluja, Managing Editor, hsaluja@mac-med.com; Milton H. Aronson, Editor and Publisher.
Desc: Magazine covering measurements and control instrumentation field. *Type:* Periodical.

Microbiology Abstracts, Section A: Industrial and Applied Microbiology

Cambridge Scientific Abstracts (CSA)
7200 Wisconsin Ave., Ste. 601   Ph: (301)961-6700
Bethesda, MD 20814-4823
E-mail: sales@csa.com
URL: http://www.csa.com
Desc: Contains more than 100,000 citations, with abstracts, to international periodical and other literature covering industrial and applied microbiology. Sources include specialist literature such as journals, books, conference proceedings, and reports. *Type:* Database.

Microbiology Abstracts, Section B: Bacteriology

Cambridge Scientific Abstracts (CSA)
7200 Wisconsin Ave., Ste. 601   Ph: (301)961-6700
Bethesda, MD 20814-4823
E-mail: sales@csa.com
URL: http://www.csa.com
Contact: Anthea Gotto, Manager of Electronic Services, (301)961-6795, fax: (301)961-6720, anthea@csa.com.
Desc: Contains more than 150,000 citations, with abstracts, to international periodical and other literature covering bacteriology, especially as related to medicine and related areas. Sources include specialist literature sources such as journals, books, conference proceedings, and reports. *Type:* Database.

Microbiology Abstracts, Section C: Algology, Mycology & Protozoology

Cambridge Scientific Abstracts (CSA)
7200 Wisconsin Ave., Ste. 601   Ph: (301)961-6700
Bethesda, MD 20814-4823
E-mail: sales@csa.com
URL: http://www.csa.com
Desc: Contains more than 115,000 citations, with abstracts, to international periodical and other literature covering algology, mycology, and protozoology. Sources include specialist literature such as journals, books, conference proceedings, and reports. *Type:* Database.

National Center for Appropriate Technology

PO Box 3838   Ph: (406)494-4572
Butte, MT 59702   Free: 800-275-6228
   Fax: (406)494-2905
URL: http://www.ncat.org
Contact: Kathleen Hadley, Exec. Officer.
Desc: Seeks to develop, apply, research, and transfer applications of appropriate technologies that meet long-term human needs for energy, shelter, environment, and sustainable agriculture, particularly the needs of low-income individuals. *Type:* Association.

National Center for Improving Science Education

2000 L St. NW, Ste. 616   Ph: (202)467-0652
Washington, DC 20036   Fax: (202)467-0659
E-mail: info@ncise.org
Contact: Senta A. Raizen, Dir.
Desc: Promotes changes in state and local policies and practices in science curriculum, teaching, and assessment. *Type:* Association.

National Congress of Inventors Organizations

Intervention Services International Corporation
PO Box 93669   Ph: (213)878-6925
Los Angeles, CA 90093-6690
Contact: Cordell Lundahl, Contact.
Desc: Inventors' groups. Coordinates information relating to inventor education and programs such as wanted and available inventions and credible organizations offering development and marketing assistance. Offers children's services and educational programs. *Type:* Association.

National Earth Science Teachers Association

2000 Florida Ave. NW   Ph: (202)462-6900
Washington, DC 20009   Free: 800-966-2481
         Fax: (202)328-0566
E-mail: fireton@kosmos.agu.org
Contact: M. Frank Watt Ireton, Ph.D., Exec. Advisor.
Desc: Earth science teachers and individuals interested in precollege earth science education. Promotes the advancement and improvement of the field. Provides materials and information sessions at national and regional conferences. *Type:* Association.

National Institute of Standards and Technology

U.S. Department of Commerce - National Institute of Standards and Technology
Gaithersburg, MD 20899-0001   Ph: (301)975-6478
E-mail: inquiries@nist.gov
URL: http://www.nist.gov/
Desc: The National Institute of Standards and Technology (NIST) database provides organizational information such as press releases, current Nobel Prize and Baldrige Award winners, and tours of NIST programs. Other topics include employment opportunities, newsletters, budget updates, congressional testimony, descriptions of major NIST programs, reference materials, recent photos and graphics illustrating NIST's major programs, and staff listings. *Type:* Database.

National Inventors Foundation

403 S. Central Ave.   Ph: (818)246-6546
Glendale, CA 91204-1601   Fax: (818)244-1882
E-mail: rustyr@earthlink.net
URL: http://www.inventions.org
Contact: Ted DeBoer, Exec.Dir.
Desc: Independent inventors united to educate individuals regarding the protection and promotion of inventions and new products. Instructs potential inventors on patent laws and how to protect their inventions through methods developed by the foundation. *Type:* Association.

National Research Council

2101 Constitution Ave. NW   Ph: (202)334-2000
Washington, DC 20418
URL: http://www.nas.edu
Contact: E. William Colglazier, Exec. Officer.
Desc: Scientists, engineers, and other professionals serving pro bono on approximately 900 study committees. Serves as an independent adviser to the federal government on scientific and technical questions of national importance; is jointly administered by the National Academy of Sciences, National Academy of Engineering, and Institute of Medicine . Carries out objectives through conferences, technical committees, surveys, collection and analysis of scientific and technical data, and administration of public and private funds for research projects and fellowships. *Type:* Association.

National Science Foundation

4201 Wilson Blvd.   Ph: (703)306-1234
Arlington, VA 22230   Free: 800-877-8339
         Fax: (703)306-0157
E-mail: info@nsf.gov
URL: http://www.nsf.gov
Contact: Neal F. Lane, Dir.
Desc: Independent agency in the Executive Branch concerned primarily with the support of basic and applied research and education in the sciences and engineering. Funds scientific research in mathematical, physical, biological, computer, engineering, social and other sciences, including unclassified research activities in matters relating to international cooperation; fosters the interchange of scientific information; supports the development and use of computers and other scientific methods and technologies. *Type:* Association.

National Science Teachers Association

1840 Wilson Blvd.   Ph: (703)243-7100
Arlington, VA 22201-3000   Fax: (703)243-7177
E-mail: publicinfo@NSTA.org
URL: http://www.nsta.org
Contact: Gerry Wheeler, Exec.Dir.
Desc: Teachers seeking to foster excellence in science teaching. Studies students and how they learn, the curriculum of science, the teacher and his/her preparation, the procedures used in classroom and laboratory, the facilities for teaching science, and the evaluation procedures used. *Type:* Association.

National Speleological Society

2813 Cave Ave.   Ph: (256)852-1300
Huntsville, AL 35810-4431   Fax: (256)851-9241
E-mail: nss@caves.org
URL: http://www.caves.org
Contact: Camille Mueller, Operations Mgr.
Desc: Biologists, geologists, geophysicists, mineralogists, and other scientists whose fields are related to: the study of caves and related phenomena; persons interested in caves and their exploration; libraries and scientific educational organizations; commercial caves. Investigates, collects, compiles, preserves, and publishes information on caves and their contents. *Type:* Association.

New York Academy of Sciences

2 E. 63rd St.   Ph: (212)838-0230
New York, NY 10021   Free: 800-843-6927
         Fax: (212)753-3479
Contact: Rodney W. Nichols, Pres. and CEO.
Desc: Individuals holding advanced degrees in scientific disciplines; interested individuals, corporations, associations, and nongovernmental institutions. Represents the interests of members and the advancement of scientific disciplines by disseminating information, educating scientists and the public on scientific issues, and promoting the role of science in human welfare concerns. *Type:* Association.

NSTA Supplement Directory of Science Education Suppliers

National Science Teachers Association
1840 Wilson Blvd.   Ph: (703)312-9209
Arlington, VA 22201-3000   Free: 800-722-6782
         Fax: (703)243-7177
URL: http://www.nsta.org.
Contact: Gerry Wheeler, Editor.
Desc: Over 900 publishers of science books, manufacturers and distributors of audio-visual materials, computers and software, suppliers of scientific equipment and laboratory supplies, and suppliers of educational services. *Type:* Directory.

NTIS Bibliographic Database

U.S. National Technical Information Service (NTIS)
5285 Port Royal Rd.   Ph: (703)605-6515
Springfield, VA 22161
URL: http://www.fedworld.gov/ntis/ntishome.html
Desc: Contains bibliographic descriptions for over 2.5 million items including unrestricted technical reports from U.S. and non-U.S. government-sponsored research, development, and engineering analyses. The unpublished U.S. reports are prepared by federal, state, and local agencies and their contractors or grantees. Major areas of coverage include the biological, social, and physical sciences; mathematics; engineering; and business information. *Available:* France Ministry of Defense, Delegation Generale pour l'Armement, Centre de Documentation de l'Armement (CEDOCAR); The Dialog Corporation, DataStar; The Dialog Corporation, DIALOG; The Dialog Corporation,

DIALOG; CompuServe Information Service, Knowledge Index; Questel • Orbit; Questel • Orbit; STN International; NIFTY Corporation, NIFTY-SERVE; Ovid Technologies, Inc.; Ovid Technologies, Inc.; European Information Network Services (EINS). *Type:* Database.

Oak Ridge Associated Universities

PO Box 117   Ph: (423)576-3000
130 Badger Ave.   Fax: (423)576-3643
Oak Ridge, TN 37831-0117
E-mail: townsenr@orav.org
URL: http://www.orau.org
Contact: Ronald Townsend, Pres.
Desc: Private, not-for-profit corporation and a consortium of 87 doctoral-granting colleges and universities. ORAU serves the government, academia, and the private sector in important areas of science and technology. *Type:* Association.

Omni

Omni Publications International Ltd.
277 Park Ave.   Ph: (212)702-6000
New York, NY 10172   Fax: (212)702-6262
Contact: Keith Ferrell, Editor; Bob Guccione, Publisher.
Desc: Magazine of science, fact, fiction, and prediction. Covers space, science, health, high technology, environment, and the arts. *Type:* Periodical.

Organization for Tropical Studies

North American Office   Ph: (919)684-5774
Box 90630   Fax: (919)684-5661
Durham, NC 27708-0630
E-mail: nao@acpub.duke.edu
URL: http://www.ots.duke.edu
Contact: Gary S. Hartshorn, Exec.Dir.
Desc: Universities with established graduate-level programs in tropical studies and research institutions with tropical focus. Seeks to promote understanding of tropical environments and to provide a basis for intelligent use and conservation of the tropics. Offers field-oriented graduate-level courses in areas such as tropical ecology and agroforestry. *Type:* Association.

PIR International Protein Sequence Database

National Biomedical Research Foundation (NBRF)
Protein Information Resource (PIR)
3900 Reservoir Rd., N.W.   Ph: (202)687-2121
Washington, DC 20007
E-mail: PIRMAIL@NBRF.GEORGETOWN.EDU
URL: http://www-nbrf.georgetown.edu/pir
Contact: Desiree D. Groins, Project Supoort Specialist, PIRMAIL@NBRF.GEORGETOWN.EDU.
Desc: Contains descriptions of more than 100,000 partial and whole protein sequences representing more than 25 million amino acids that were isolated or inferred from the gene sequences. Descriptions include function of protein, taxonomy, sequence features of biological interest, how sequence was experimentally determined, unambiguously determined residues within the sequence, and citations to relevant literature. *Available:* National Biomedical Research Foundation (NBRF), Protein Information Resource (PIR); IntelliGenetics, Inc., BIONET On-line Service. *Type:* Database.

Popular Science

Times Mirror Magazines, Inc.
2 Park Ave.   Ph: (212)779-5000
New York, NY 10016-5601   Fax: (212)779-5522
Contact: Fred Abatemarco, Editor-in-Chief, abatemarco@popsi.com; John Crawley, Publisher; Michele Folman, Director; Cecelia Wessner, Editor, wessner@popsci.com.
Desc: General interest science magazine. *Type:* Periodical.

Reasons to Believe

PO Box 5978
Pasadena, CA 91117

Ph: (626)335-1480
Free: 800-482-7836
Fax: (626)852-0178

E-mail: reasons@reasons.org
URL: http://www.reasons.org/

Contact: Hugh Ross, Pres.

Desc: Seeks to explain the theory of creation in a Biblically sound and scientifically valid manner, in an effort to remove the doubts of skeptics and strengthen the faith of Christians. *Type:* Association.

Refractory News

The Refractories Institute
650 Smithfield St., Ste. 1160
Pittsburgh, PA 15222-3907

Ph: (412)281-6787
Fax: (412)281-6881

E-mail: triassn@aol.com

Contact: Florence R. Story, Editor, frstory@aol.com.

Desc: Provides producers of fire brick and other refractory materials, and suppliers of refractory raw materials and production equipment, with news of research, industry trends and developments, and items of general interest to membership. Also contains notices of Institute events, programs, and activities. *Type:* Newsletter.

SAMA Group of Associations

225 Reinekers, Ste. 625
Alexandria, VA 22314

Ph: (703)836-1360
Fax: (703)836-6644

Desc: Umbrella organization of trade associations including the Analytical Life Science Systems Association, the Laboratory Products Association, and the Opto-Precision Instruments Association. Member companies include manufacturers and distributors of analytical, biomolecular, and optical instrumentation, laboratory equipment, and related products and services. *Type:* Association.

Science

American Association for the Advancement of Science
1200 New York Ave., NW
Washington, DC 20005

Ph: (202)326-6626
Fax: (202)289-4950

URL: htpp://www.sciencemag.org.

Contact: Floyd Bloom, Editor; Richard S. Nicholson, Publisher; Beth Rosner, Associate Publisher; Susan Meredith, Advertising Mgr.; Janis Crowley, Recruitment Advertising Mgr.

Desc: Magazine devoted to science, scientific research, and public policy. *Type:* Periodical.

Science-By-Mail

Museum of Science
Science Park
Boston, MA 02114-1099

Ph: (617)589-0437
Free: 800-729-3300
Fax: (617)589-0474

E-mail: sbm@mos.org
URL: http://www.mos.org/mos/sbm/sciencemail.html

Contact: Melissa Cotter Dempsey, Program Dir.

Desc: Promotes correspondence between scientists of various disciplines and children in order to increase children's knowledge of scientists and the nature of their work. *Type:* Association.

Science Illustrated

Science Illustrated, L.P.
8428 Holly Leaf Dr.
Mc Lean, VA 22102

Ph: (703)356-1688
Fax: (703)356-1688

Contact: Jane Alexander, Editor; Tod Herbers, Publisher.

Desc: Magazine for physicians containing general science information. *Type:* Periodical.

The Science and Mathematics Initiative (SAMI) Database

The Annenberg/CPB Projects
Attn: Learner Online
901 E. St. NW
Washington, DC 20004

Ph: (202)879-9600

E-mail: info@learner.org
URL: http://www.learner.org/sami/sami.html

Desc: The Science and Mathematics Initiatives (SAMI) database is a compendium of online educational resources for teachers, administrators, and educators. In this searchable database you will find material such as lesson plans and classroom projects for all levels of students, grant and funding sources, rural resources, computer software resources, and math and science curriculum resources. *Type:* Database.

Science News

Science Service, Inc.
1719 N St. NW
Washington, DC 20036

Ph: (202)785-2255
Fax: (202)785-1243

E-mail: sciedu@sciserv.org

Contact: Julie Ann Miller, Editor, fax: (202)659-0365; Donald Harless, Publisher.

Desc: Reports on new findings in physical, biological and behavioral sciences. *Type:* Periodical.

Science Service

1719 N St. NW
Washington, DC 20036

Ph: (202)785-2255

Contact: Alfred McLaren, Publisher; Laura Jackson Vaughan, Managing Editor; Patrick Young, Editor.
Desc: Distributes science media news. *Alt. Contact:* 1719 N St. NW, Washington, DC 20036; telephone: (202)785-2255. *Type:* Periodical.

Science World

Scholastic, Inc.
555 Broadway
New York, NY 10012

Ph: (212)343-6100
Free: 800-724-6527
Fax: (212)343-4535

E-mail: custserv@scholastic.com
URL: http://www.scholastic.com

Contact: Mark Bregman, Editor; G. Estabrook Kindred, Advertising Mgr.

Desc: Science magazine for students in grades 7-10. *Type:* Periodical.

Science Writers

National Association of Science Writers, Inc.
7310 Broxburn Ct.
Bethesda, MD 20817

Ph: (301)229-6770

E-mail: sciwriters@aol.com.
URL: http://nasw.org.

Contact: Howard J. Lewis, Editor.

Desc: Covers the preparation and interpretation of science news for the public. Recurring features include editorials, letters to the editor, and news of members. *Type:* Newsletter.

Scientific American

Scientific American Magazine
415 Madison Ave.
New York, NY 10017

Ph: (212)754-0550
Fax: (212)355-6245

Contact: John Rennie, Editor-in-Chief; Joachim P. Roster, Publisher; Kate Dobson, Advertising Dir.

Desc: Magazine for technical managers and professionals covering a broad range of physical, life, and social sciences and their applications to industry, the professions, and public policy. *Type:* Periodical.

Scientific and Technical Organizations and Agencies Directory

Gale Group Inc.
27500 Drake Rd.
Farmington Hills, MI 48331-3535

Ph: (248)699-4253
Free: 800-877-GALE
Fax: (248)699-8070

E-mail: galeord@galegroup.com
URL: http://www.galegroup.com.

Desc: Over 25,600 national and international organizations and agencies concerned with the physical and applied sciences, engineering, and technology, including associations, computer information services, consulting firms, educational institutions, foundations, government advisory organizations, federal government agencies, general grant and assistance programs, libraries and information centers, patent sources and services, research and development centers, scholarships, fellowships, and loans, science-technology centers, standards organizations, state academies of science, and state government agencies in the fields of aeronautics and space sciences, chemistry, computer science specialties, electronics, geography, geology, machinery, mathematics, metallurgy, meteorology, mineralogy, nuclear science, petroleum and gas, physics, plastics, transportation, water resources, and other areas. *Type:* Directory.

SciSearch®

Institute for Scientific Information (ISI)
3501 Market St.
Philadelphia, PA 19104

Ph: (215)386-0100

E-mail: isiorder@isinet.com
URL: http://www.isinet.com

Desc: Provides complete bibliographic data plus citations to worldwide literature across a wide range of scientific and technological disciplines. Covers approximately 4600 journals. *Available:* The Dialog Corporation, DataStar; The Dialog Corporation, DIALOG; The Dialog Corporation, DIALOG; DIMDI (Deutsches Institut fuer Medizinische Dokumentation und Information); DIMDI (Deutsches Institut fuer Medizinische Dokumentation und Information); STN International; STN International. *Type:* Database.

The SETI Institute - Search for Extraterrestrial Intelligence

SETI Institute
2035 Landings Dr.
Mountain View, CA 94043

Ph: (650)961-6633
Fax: (650)961-7099

E-mail: info@hertz.seti-inst.edu
URL: http://www.seti-inst.edu/

Desc: Its mission is to find who's out there. Stop by this site if you want to know more about SETI - the Search for Extraterrestrial Intelligence. *Type:* Database.

Sigma Xi, Scientific Research Society

99 Alexander Dr.
PO Box 13975
Research Triangle Park, NC 27709

Ph: (919)549-4691
Free: 800-243-6534
Fax: (919)549-0090

E-mail: pblair@sigmaxi.org
URL: http://www.sigmaxi.org

Contact: Dr. Peter D. Blair, Exec.Dir.

Desc: Honorary society for men and women in scientific research. Offers grants-in-aid research; sponsors national lecturers panel and national forums. *Type:* Association.

Sigma Zeta

Millard B. Niver
Malone College
Canton, OH 44709

Ph: (330)471-8177
Fax: (330)454-6977

Contact: Millard B. Niver, Sec.-Treas.

Desc: Honor society of men and women in science and mathematics. *Type:* Association.

SIRS Researcher®

SIRS, Inc.
PO Box 2348   Ph: (561)994-0079
Boca Raton, FL 33427-2348
E-mail: custserve@sirs.com
URL: http://www.sirs.com
Contact: Dana Fieni Lewis, Public Relations and Project Coordinator.
Desc: Contains the complete text of articles and graphics from more than 1200 domestic and international publications. Provides current and historical information on social issues, health, the sciences, business, and global events. *Available:* Ameritech Library Services, Vista; OCLC Online Computer Library Center, Inc., OCLC FirstSearch Catalog; The Gale Group, InfoTrac Web; CARL Corporation. *Type:* Database.

Skeptics Society

2761 N. Marengo Ave.   Ph: (626)794-3119
Altadena, CA 91001   Fax: (626)794-1301
E-mail: skepticmag@aol.com
Contact: Dr. Michael Shermer, Exec. Officer.
Desc: Scholars, scientists, and historians. Promotes the use of scientific methods to scrutinize such non-scientific traditions as religion, myth, superstition, mysticism, new age beliefs, and cults. *Type:* Association.

Society of Automotive Engineers

400 Commonwealth Dr.   Ph: (412)776-4841
Warrendale, PA 15096-0001   Fax: (412)776-5944
E-mail: sae@sae.org
URL: http://www.sae.org
Contact: Max E. Rumbaugh, Jr., Contact.
Desc: Engineers, business executives, educators, and students from more than 80 countries who come together to share information and exchange ideas for advancing the engineering of mobility systems. SAE is the major source of technical information and expertise used in designing, building, maintaining and operating self-propelled vehicles, whether land-, sea-, air-, or space-based. Collection, organization, storage and dissemination of information on cars, trucks, aircraft, space vehicles, off-highway vehicles, marine equipment, and engines of all types. *Type:* Association.

SPIE-The international Society for Optical Engineering

PO Box 10   Ph: (360)676-3290
Bellingham, WA 98227-0010   Fax: (360)647-1445
E-mail: spie@spie.org
URL: http://www.spie.org
Contact: James E. Pearson, Exec.Dir.
Desc: Seeks to advance the profession of Optical Engineering and to promote the engineering, scientific, and commerical development and application of optical, photonic, imaging, and optoelectronic technologies through its meetings, publications, education, and communications programs. *Type:* Association.

Today's Science on File

Facts On File News Services
Division of PRIMEDIA Reference Corporation
11 Penn Plaza, 15th Fl.   Ph: (212)290-8090
New York, NY 10001-2006   Free: 800-363-7976
     Fax: (212)967-9051
E-mail: info@facts.com
URL: http://www.facts.com.
Contact: Josh Ulick, Managing Editor.
Desc: Delivers news in science, technology, medicine, and the environment. *Type:* Newsletter.

Triangle

120 S Center St.
Plainfield, IN 46168-1214
Contact: Robert M. Hamlett, Exec.Dir.
Desc: Social fraternity - architecture, engineering, and sciences. *Type:* Association.

Triangle Coalition for Science and Technology Education

1201 New York Ave., NW Ste.   Ph: (202)289-2911
700   Free: 800-582-0115
Washington, DC 20005-3917   Fax: (202)289-1303
E-mail: tricoal@aol.com
URL: http://www.triangle-coalition.org
Contact: Walter L. Purdy, Exec.Dir.
Desc: A consortium of national organizations representing the business sector, scientific and engineering societies, and educational associations. Goal is to improve the quality of science and technology education for all students. Collects, organizes, and disseminates information on problems and identifies solutions that will improve science and technology education. *Type:* Association.

WESTLAW® Science and Technology Library

West Group
620 Opperman Dr.   Ph: (651)687-7000
St. Paul, MN 55164-0526
URL: http://www.westgroup.com
Desc: Provides access to information relating to the fields of biology, chemistry, and physical and computer science technologies. Includes the complete text of the McGraw-Hill Encyclopedia of Science and Technoloy and more than 70 databases accessible from Knight-Ridder Information Services, Inc., DIALOG via WESTLAW. *Available:* West Group, WESTLAW. *Type:* Database.

Who's Who in Technology

The Gale Group
27500 Drake Rd.   Ph: (248)699-4253
Farmington Hills, MI 48331-3535
URL: http://www.galegroup.com
Contact: Customer Service. Toll-free: 800-877-GALE.
Desc: Contains biographies of approximately 25,000 contemporary American scientists and engineers. Covers individuals in biotechnology, chemistry, civil and mechanical engineering, computer science, earth sciences, electronics, energy, materials science, and physics and optics. *Available:* Questel • Orbit. *Type:* Database.

Wilson Applied Science & Technology Abstracts

H.W. Wilson Company
950 University Ave.   Ph: (718)588-8400
Bronx, NY 10452
E-mail: custserv@hwwilson.com
URL: http://www.hwwilson.com
Desc: Contains more than one million abstracts to all articles cited in the Applied Science & Technology Index from March 1993 to date. Includes an index of non-English-language periodicals if English abstracts are provided. *Available:* H.W. Wilson Company, WilsonWeb; H.W. Wilson Company, WilsonWeb; SilverPlatter Information, Inc.; SilverPlatter Information, Inc.; OCLC Online Computer Library Center, Inc., OCLC EPIC; The Dialog Corporation, DIALOG; The Dialog Corporation, DIALOG; Ovid Technologies, Inc.; Ovid Technologies, Inc. *Type:* Database.

World Databases in Science

National Register Publishing Co.
121 Chanlon Rd.   Ph: (908)464-6800
New Providence, NJ 07974   Free: 800-521-8110
     Fax: (908)508-7671
E-mail: info@renp.com
URL: http://www.reedref.com
Contact: C.J. Armstrong, Editor.
Desc: Science information on databases, including CD-ROM, magnetic tape, diskette, online, fax, or databroadcast worldwide. *Type:* Directory.

Young Scientist Program

Washington University School of Medicine
Campus Box 8226   Ph: (314)362-4841
660 S. Euclid Ave.   Free: 800-852-9074
St. Louis, MO 63110   Fax: (314)362-3369
E-mail: sotog@medicine.wustl.edu
URL: http://medinfo.wustl.edu/~ysp/
Contact: Monica Simpson, ysp@medicine.wustl.edu.
Desc: The Young Scientist Program was created to attract disadvantaged high school students, in the St. Louis area, into the sciences. *Type:* Database.

Science Fiction

Affaire de Coeur

Brandywyne Books
3976 Oak Hill Rd.   Ph: (510)569-5675
Oakland, CA 94605   Fax: (510)632-8868
URL: http://www.sseven.
Contact: Louise Snead, Publisher.
Desc: Magazine for romantic readers and writers. *Type:* Periodical.

Alfred Hitchcock's Mystery Magazine

Dell Magazines
475 Park Ave. S, 11th Fl.   Ph: (212)686-7188
New York, NY 10016   Fax: (212)686-7414
Contact: Cathleen Jordan, Editor; Bruce Schwartz, Circulation Mgr.
Desc: Magazine for mystery enthusiasts. *Type:* Periodical.

Ellery Queen's Mystery Magazine

Dell Magazines
475 Park Ave. S, 11th Fl.   Ph: (212)686-7188
New York, NY 10016   Fax: (212)686-7414
E-mail: eqmysmag@aol.com.
Contact: Janet Hutchling, Editor.
Desc: Consumer magazine covering short story mysteries. *Type:* Periodical.

Romantic Times

Romantic Times Publishing Group
55 Bergen St.   Ph: (718)237-1097
Brooklyn, NY 11201   Free: 800-989-8816
     Fax: (718)624-2526
E-mail: rtmag1@aol.com.
URL: http://www.romantictimes.com.
Contact: Carol Stacy, Publisher, fax: (718)624-4231.
Desc: Magazine containing romance book reviews and author profiles and romance industry news. *Type:* Periodical.

Soldier of Fortune

Omega Group
Box 693   Ph: (303)449-3750
Boulder, CO 80306   Free: 800-800-7630
     Fax: (303)444-5617
E-mail: editor@sofmag.com.
URL: http://www.sofmag.com.
Contact: Robert K. Brown, Editor and Publisher; Dwight Swift, Managing Editor; John Walker, Advertising Dir.; Greg Peterson, CFO.

Desc: Monthly publication of military adventure and foreign intrigue. *Alt. Contact:* 5735 Arapahoe Ave., Boulder, CO 80303-1340; telephone: (303)449-3750; fax: (303)444-5617. *Type:* Periodical.

Star Trek: The Official Fan Club

PO Box 111000   Ph: (303)574-0907
Aurora, CO 80042   Free: 800-TRUE-FAN
    Fax: (303)574-9442

Contact: Daniel H. Madsen, Pres.

Desc: Fans of the syndicated science fiction television series Star Trek, which aired from 1966-69 and the current series, Star Trek: The Next Generation as well as StarTrek: Deep Space Nine and StarTrek: Voyager. Keeps members informed about the program, cast members, and movie spinoffs. *Type:* Association.

Star Trek Welcommittee

PO Drawer 12
Saranac, MI 48881

Contact: Shirley S. Maiewski, Chm.

Desc: Central information center whose volunteer workers answer fans' questions about Star Trek and provide new fans with complete information about Star Trek "fandom." (Star Trek is a science fiction television series.). *Type:* Association.

Star Wars Fan Club

PO Box 111000   Ph: (303)574-0907
Aurora, CO 80042   Free: 800-TRUE-FAN
    Fax: (303)574-9442

Contact: Daniel H. Madsen, Contact.

Desc: Promotes the films and career of George Lucas. *Type:* Association.

Starlog

Starlog Group, Inc.
475 Park Ave. S.   Ph: (212)689-2830
New York, NY 10016   Fax: (212)889-7933

Contact: David McDonnell, Editor.

Desc: Magazine about science fiction. *Type:* Periodical.

True Experience

Sterling/Macfadden Partnership
233 Park Ave. S.   Ph: (212)780-3500
New York, NY 10003   Fax: (212)780-3555

Contact: Rose Bernstein, Editor; Allen Tullner, Publisher; Lisa Rabidoux Finn, Editorial Director.

Desc: Romance magazine. *Type:* Periodical.

True Love

Sterling/Macfadden Partnership
233 Park Ave. S.   Ph: (212)780-3500
New York, NY 10003   Fax: (212)780-3555

Contact: Alison Way, Editor, (212)979-4895; Andrea Potochniak, Assoc. Editor.

Desc: Romance magazine. *Type:* Periodical.

UFO Contact Center International

3001 S. 288th St., No. 304   Ph: (206)946-2248
Federal Way, WA 98003   Fax: (206)946-2531

Contact: Aileen Garoutte, Dir.

Desc: Individuals who have had UFO experiences. Offers group therapy and regressive hypnosis to assist in recovering memory of experience. Conducts research on UFO's and UFO abductions. *Type:* Association.

United Federation of Planets

6201 Revere St.
Philadelphia, PA 19149

Contact: Michael R. Marinelli, Pres.

Desc: Fans of the science fiction television series Star Trek. Promotes ideals presented and upheld by characters of the show, including respect for all life forms, a concept referred to by the group as "infinite diversity through infinite combinations." Maintains community services including reading programs and aid to the homeless. Maintains small museum. *Type:* Association.

World Science Fiction Society

c/o Southern California Inst. for   Ph: (818)366-3827
    Fan Interests   Fax: (818)366-7987
PO Box 8442
Van Nuys, CA 91409
E-mail: bep@deltanet.com

Contact: Carl G. Brandon, Exec.Sec.

Desc: Professionals and amateurs involved in all aspects of science fiction (books, magazines, movies, and radio-television) united to sustain interest in science fiction. *Type:* Association.

Scouting

Boy Scouts of America

1325 W. Walnut Hill Ln.   Ph: (972)580-2000
PO Box 152079   Fax: (972)580-2502
Irving, TX 75015-2079
URL: http://www.bsa.scouting.org

Contact: Jere B. Ratcliffe, Chief Scout Exec.

Desc: Tiger Cubs (age six); Cub Scouts (ages seven-ten); Boy Scouts (ages 11-18); Venturers (male and female, age 15-20); Lone Scouts; male and female adult leaders and volunteer workers. Educational program geared toward the character development, citizenship training, and mental and physical fitness of boys and young adults. Conducts studies on problems and needs of youth. *Type:* Association.

Girl Scouts of the U.S.A.

420 5th Ave.   Ph: (212)852-8000
New York, NY 10018-2798   Free: 800-GSU-SA4U
    Fax: (212)852-0639
E-mail: misc@gsusa.org
URL: http://www.girlscouts.org

Contact: Marsha Johnson Evans, Natl.Exec.Dir.

Desc: Daisy Girl Scouts (ages 5-6 or grades K-1); Brownie Girl Scouts (ages 6-8 or grades 1-3); Junior Girl Scouts (ages 8-11 or grades 3-6); Cadette Girl Scouts (ages 11-14 or grades 6-9); Senior Girl Scouts (ages 14-17 or grades 9-12). Membership includes girls, adult volunteers, and professional workers. Purpose is to meet the special needs and interest of girls and help them to share their abilities as citizens in their homes, their communities, their country and the world. *Type:* Association.

National Boy Scouts of America

9190 Wisconsin Ave.   Ph: (301)214-9110
Bethesda, MD 20814   Fax: (301)564-3648

Contact: Ron L. Carroll, Exec. Officer.

Desc: Boys aged six to 20. Promotes citizenship training, character development, and personal fitness. *Type:* Association.

National Catholic Committee on Scouting

c/o Boy Scouts of America   Ph: (972)580-2109
1325 Walnut Hill Ln.   Fax: (972)580-7870
PO Box 152079
Irving, TX 75015-2079

Contact: Eleanore Starr, Admin.Sec.

Desc: Functions on national and diocesan levels to advise national and local Boy Scouts of America councils on principles and practices of the Catholic Church as they apply to the 11,000 Scout units in Catholic parishes. Promotes integration of Catholic teachings and practices in the program of scouting for Catholic youth and adults. Compiles statistics on scouting under Catholic auspices. *Type:* Association.

National Eagle Scout Association

Boy Scouts of America
1325 W. Walnut Hill   Ph: (972)580-2000
PO Box 152079   Fax: (972)580-2502
Irving, TX 75038

Contact: Melvin D. Hunter, Exec. Officer.

Desc: Boy Scouts, Venturers, and adults who have attained the Eagle Scout rank and wish to give continued service to the Boy Scout movement and local communities. Emphasizes high ideals and standards of personal conduct; promotes leadership, fellowship, citizenship, and a spirit of service among all Scouts; encourages Scout advancement. *Type:* Association.

Order of the Arrow

1325 W. Walnut Hill Ln.   Ph: (972)580-2438
PO Box 152079   Fax: (972)580-2502
Irving, TX 75015-2079

Contact: Clyde M. Mayer, Dir.

Desc: Boy Scouts, Varsity Scouts, and adult scout leaders who are qualified as first class scouts and campers (15 or more days and nights of camping) and elected as honor campers by members of their own units. Promotes scout camping and serves local councils in the camping program (known as the Brotherhood of Cheerful Service), Indian lore ceremonies, and use of Indian costumes and terminology. Provides for youth and young adult leadership development. *Type:* Association.

Securities

American Stock Exchange

86 Trinity Pl.   Ph: (212)306-1000
New York, NY 10006   Fax: (212)306-1218

Contact: Richard Syron, Chm. CEO.

Desc: A domestic and international equities and derivative securities market. Provides an auction marketplace that integrates service and information programs for its listed companies. *Type:* Association.

Asset-Backed Alert

Harrison Scott Publications, Inc.
5 Marine View Plaza, Ste. 301   Ph: (201)659-1700
Hoboken, NJ 07030   Free: 800-283-9363
    Fax: (201)659-4141
E-mail: hsp@bellatlantic.net

Contact: Thomas J. Ferris, Editor; Andrew Albert, Publisher.

Desc: Provides information about non-mortgage receivables, such as outstanding loans. *Type:* Newsletter.

Asset Sales Report

American Banker/Bond Buyer Inc.
International Thomson Publishing Corp.
1 State St. Plaza   Ph: (212)803-8200
New York, NY 10004   Free: 800-362-3807
    Fax: (212)843-9612

Contact: Michael Sisk, Editor.

Desc: Covers all aspects of the asset-backed securitization market, including weekly deals, legal and regulatory developments, and people moves. *Type:* Newsletter.

Bond Market Association

40 Broad St., 12th Fl.   Ph: (212)809-7000
New York, NY 10004-2373   Fax: (212)440-5260
URL: http://www.bondmarkets.com

Contact: Heather L. Ruth, Pres.

Desc: Represents securities firms and banks that underwrite, trade and sell debt securities, both domestically and internationally. *Type:* Association.

Chicago Board Options Exchange
400 S. LaSalle   Ph: (312)786-5600
Chicago, IL 60605   Free: 800-OPT-IONS
     Fax: (312)786-7409
Contact: William J. Brodsky, CEO & Chm.
Desc: Individuals and firms engaged in the buying and selling of listed options. CBOE lists options on more than 680 stocks and on the two most actively traded indices in the world, the S&P 100 and the S&P 500, as well as on the Nasdaq 100 Index, the S&P SmallCap 600 Index, the Russell 2000 Index and fourteen sector indices. Options on the CBOE Mexico Index, the Latin 15 Index, the Nikkei 300 Index, the CBOE Isreal Index and the FT-SE 100 Index comprise CBOE's foreign index-option complex. *Type:* Association.

Emerging Markets Traders Association
63 Wall St., 20th Fl.   Ph: (212)908-5000
New York, NY 10005
URL: http://www.emta.org
Contact: Michael Chamberlin, Exec.Dir.
Desc: Dedicated to promoting the orderly development of fair, efficient and transparent trading market for emerging market instruments and to helping integrate the emerging markets into the global financial market place. *Type:* Association.

International Securities Regulation Report
LRP Publications
747 Dresher Rd.   Ph: (215)784-0941
PO Box 980   Free: 800-341-7874
Horsham, PA 19044-0980   Fax: (215)784-0870
E-mail: custserve@lrp.com
Contact: Stephen Ackerman, Editor.
Desc: Deals with regulation of international securities trading, new trading links among markets, and cooperation among governments in enforcing securities laws. *Type:* Newsletter.

Investment Company Institute
1401 H St. NW, 12th Fl.   Ph: (202)326-5800
Washington, DC 20005-2148   Fax: (202)326-8309
E-mail: info@ici.com
URL: http://www.ici.org
Contact: Matthew Fink, Pres.
Desc: Represents open-end and closed-end investment companies registered under Investment Company Act of 1940; investment advisers to, and underwriters of, such companies; unit investment trust sponsors; interested others. *Type:* Association.

Mortgage-Backed Securities Letter
Securities Data Publishing
Circulation Dept.   Ph: (212)432-0045
40 W. 57th St., 11th Fl.
New York, NY 10019
E-mail: mbs@iddis.com.
Contact: Mark Kollar, Editor.
Desc: Covers developments in the structured finance markets. Analyzes transactions and their collateral; follows litigation, refinancing opportunities, and market conditions. *Type:* Newsletter.

NASD Notices to Members
National Association of Securities Dealers, Inc.
1735 K St. NW   Ph: (202)728-6900
Washington, DC 20006   Fax: (202)728-8882
Contact: Claire McIntyre, Writer/Editor.
Desc: Informs of the Association's regulations and developments. Presents news of the Board of Governors meetings. *Type:* Newsletter.

National Association of Bond Lawyers
1761 S. Naperville Rd., Ste. 105   Ph: (630)690-1135
Wheaton, IL 60187   Fax: (630)690-1685
E-mail: nabl@ntsource.com
Contact: Patricia F. Appelhans, Exec.Dir.
Desc: Lawyers whose law practices deal with obligations issued by or on behalf of: a state, territory, or possession of the United States; a political subdivision; the District of Columbia. This includes the rendering of legal opinions in connection with the delivery of such obligations. Aids in educating members and others in the law relating to state and municipal obligations. *Type:* Association.

National Association of Securities Dealers
1735 K St. NW   Ph: (202)728-8000
Washington, DC 20006-1506   Fax: (202)293-6260
Contact: Frank Zarb, CEO & Pres.
Desc: Securities firms doing business with the public. Serves as a self-regulatory organization for for NASDAQ (National Association of Securities Dealers Automated Quotations) and over-the-counter markets, operating under the oversight of the Federal Securities and Exchange Commission. *Type:* Association.

New York Society of Security Analysts
1 World Trade Center, Ste.   Ph: (212)912-9249
  4447   Free: 800-248-0108
New York, NY 10048   Fax: (212)912-9310
E-mail: staff@nyssa.org
URL: http://www.nyssa.org
Contact: T. Wayne Whipple, Exec.Dir.
Desc: Security analysts and portfolio managers employed primarily in New York by brokerage houses, banks, insurance companies, mutual funds, and other financial institutions. *Type:* Association.

Pacific Stock Exchange
301 Pine St.   Ph: (415)393-4000
San Francisco, CA 94104   Free: 800-TALK-PSE
     Fax: (415)393-4041
URL: http://www.pacificex.com
Contact: Robert Greber, CEO & Chm.
Desc: Maintains markets in nearly 1800 equity issues and 300 options in San Francisco and Los Angeles, CA. *Type:* Association.

Private Placement Report
American Banker/Bond Buyer Inc.
International Thomson Publishing Corp.
1 State St. Plaza   Ph: (212)803-8200
New York, NY 10004   Free: 800-362-3807
     Fax: (212)843-9612
Contact: David Gaffen, Editor.
Desc: Reports on unregistered securities buying, selling, and trading. Provides information on purchasers, deal structures, pricing, and the effects of Rule 144A. *Type:* Newsletter.

Regulatory & Compliance Alert
National Association of Securities Dealers, Inc.
1735 K St. NW   Ph: (202)728-6900
Washington, DC 20006-1506   Fax: (202)728-8882
URL: http://www.nasdr.com.
Contact: Rosa A. Maymi, Regulatory Communications Services, (202)728-8981, maymir@nasd.com.
Desc: Provides information on the Association's federal and state compliance developments, regulatory policies, and disciplinary actions taken by the Association against member firms and individuals. *Type:* Newsletter.

SEC No-Action Letter Weekly
Washington Service Bureau, Inc.
655 15th St. NW   Ph: (202)508-0600
Washington, DC 20005   Free: 800-955-5219
     Fax: (202)508-0694
Contact: Hugh Kennedy, Editor.
Desc: Publishes abstracts of all no-action letters issued by the Securities and Exchange Commission. Includes applicable regulations. *Type:* Newsletter.

Securities and Commodities Litigation Reporter
Andrews Publications
175 Strafford Ave., Bldg. 4, Ste.   Ph: (610)225-0510
  140   Free: 800-345-1101
Wayne, PA 19087   Fax: (610)225-0501
Contact: Robert W. McSherry, Editor.
Desc: Publishes "clear summaries and the full texts of key court opinions, briefs, responses and complaints" filled by "key attorneys" in the area of securities and commodities litigation. *Type:* Newsletter.

Securities Industry Association
120 Broadway   Ph: (212)608-1500
New York, NY 10271   Fax: (212)608-1604
E-mail: info@sia.com
URL: http://www.sia.com
Contact: Marc E. Lackritz, Pres.
Desc: Investment bankers, securities underwriters, and dealers in stocks and bonds. To represent and serve all segments of the securities industry and provide a unified voice in legislation, regulation, and public information. Conducts studies and compiles statistics on investment, securities markets, and related matters. *Type:* Association.

Securities Week
McGraw-Hill Financial Services, Co.
25 Broadway   Ph: (212)208-8377
New York, NY 10004   Fax: (212)509-8994
Contact: Michael Ocrant, Editor.
Desc: Acts as a trade publication for Wall Street executives, publishing news stories on pertinent events and developments within the industry including those related to legislative and regulatory activity, major stock exchanges, investment banking and retail firms, institutional trading, and new products. Recurring features include reports on research departments and a column titled Financial Futures/Commodities Report. *Type:* Newsletter.

Security Investing
John Charles Mallon & Associates
305 Madison Ave., Ste. 1166   Ph: (212)697-0028
New York, NY 10165   Fax: (212)697-1576
Contact: John Charles Mallon, Editor.
Desc: Reports on investing in the global security (protection) industry. *Type:* Newsletter.

Trading Systems Technology
Waters Information Services, Inc.
PO Box 2248   Ph: (607)770-9242
Binghamton, NY 13902-2248   Free: 800-947-7947
E-mail: kmiller@watersinfo.com.
Contact: Peter Harris, Editorial Director.
Desc: Covers technology applications in the financial markets, including trader workstations, trading room data processing and communications technology, analytical software and expert systems, and automation of global market infrastructure. Remarks: Alternate fax: (607) 770-9435. *Type:* Newsletter.

Security

American Security Council

5545 Security Cir.   Ph: (540)547-1776
Boston, VA 22713   Fax: (540)547-9737
Contact: John F. Fisher, CEO.

Desc: Individuals, companies, colleges, labor unions, and others supporting a national research and information center on national security. Maintains Washington bureau. Organizes and serves as program secretariat for Coalition for Peace Through Strength. *Type:* Association.

ASIS Dynamics

American Society for Industrial Security
1625 Prince St.   Ph: (703)519-6200
Alexandria, VA 22314   Free: 800-777-5006
    Fax: (703)519-1518
Contact: Ann Longmore-Etheridge, Editor.

Desc: Provides news concerning Society activities. Recurring features include a calendar of events, reports of meetings, and columns titled Information Central Station, Portfolio, Chapter News, ASIS Foundation, CPP Closeup, Committee Briefs, and ASIS Events. *Type:* Newsletter.

ASIS International

1625 Prince St.   Ph: (703)519-6200
Alexandria, VA 22314-2818   Fax: (703)519-6299
URL: http://www.asisonline.org
Contact: Michael J. Stack, Exec.Dir.

Desc: Security professionals responsible for loss prevention and security for businesses, government, or public organizations and institutions. *Type:* Association.

Association of Certified Fraud Examiners

716 West Ave.   Ph: (512)478-9070
Austin, TX 78701   Free: 800-245-3321
    Fax: (512)478-9297
E-mail: acfe@cfenet.com
URL: http://www.cfenet.com
Contact: Joseph T. Wells, Founder and Chairman.

Desc: Corporate managers, executives, auditors, trainers, security directors, and others employed in financial institutions; business, law enforcement, and social science professionals. Works to classify and examine financial crimes such as white-collar embezzlement, forgery, and fraud as well as their frequency and methodology to develop effective preventive plans and policies for businesses. Provides lectures on topics including fraud prevention, detection, auditing, security, and management awareness. *Type:* Association.

Business Executives for National Security

1717 Pennsylvania Ave. NW,   Ph: (202)296-2125
    Ste. 350   Fax: (202)296-2490
Washington, DC 20006
E-mail: bens@bens.org
URL: http://www.bens.org
Contact: Stanley A. Weiss, Chm.

Desc: A nonpartisan, nonideological organization of America's professional and business leaders. Believes that genuine national security is a product of economic strength coupled with an effective, affordable defense. Also believes that the employment of proven business practices improves national security. *Type:* Association.

Business Executives for National Security Education Fund

1615 L St. NW, Ste. 330   Ph: (202)296-2125
Washington, DC 20036   Fax: (202)296-2490
Contact: Dr. Tyrus W. Cobb, Pres.

Desc: Promotes the objectives of Business Executives for National Security. Raises public awareness of what the group feels the U.S. must do to achieve genuine national security: manage a capable defense; promote economic strength through growth; prevent the use of nuclear weapons. *Type:* Association.

Computer Security Digest

Computer Protection Systems, Inc.
PO Box 6121   Ph: (313)459-8787
Plymouth, MI 48170
Contact: Jack Bologna, Editor.

Desc: Provides information on computer security; company lawsuits; software viruses, failures, and piracy; and international privacy protection. *Type:* Newsletter.

Institute for Defense Analyses

1801 N. Beauregard   Ph: (703)845-2300
Alexandria, VA 22311   Fax: (703)845-2588
Contact: Gen. Larry D. Welch, USAF, Ret. Pres.

Desc: Trustees are drawn from the entire university community and from the public at large. Seeks to provide "an independent and objective source of analyses, evaluations and advice for the United States Government." Originally formed to meet the needs of the Department of Defense, IDA works primarily for the Office of the Secretary of Defense and the Joint Chiefs of Staff; also conducts research, systems evaluation and policy analysis for other Department of Defense offices as well as other agencies. *Type:* Association.

International Security Officer's Police and Guard Union

321 86th St.   Ph: (718)836-3508
Brooklyn, NY 11209   Fax: (718)836-6757
Contact: Frank Mancini, Pres.
Desc: Independent. *Type:* Association.

International Union of Security Officers

2404 Merced St.   Ph: (510)895-9905
San Leandro, CA 94577   Fax: (510)895-6974
Contact: Robert Ulrich, Pres.

Desc: Independent. Guards and security officers. Seeks to improve wages, hours, and working conditions for security officers and guards. *Type:* Association.

International Union, United Plant Guard Workers of America

25510 Kelly Rd.   Ph: (810)772-7250
Roseville, MI 48066   Free: 800-228-7492
    Fax: (810)772-9644
Contact: Eugene P. McConville, Pres.
Desc: Independent. *Type:* Association.

KingAlarm Review

KingAlarm Distributors, Inc.
35 Green St.   Ph: (201)488-4990
Hackensack, NJ 07601-4003
Desc: Offers classified advertising space to security alarm dealers and installers who wish to sell used equipment. *Type:* Newsletter.

Link-Letter

Chain Link Fence Manufacturers Institute
1776 Massachusetts Ave. NW,   Ph: (202)659-3537
No. 500   Fax: (202)857-1220
Washington, DC 20036
Contact: Mark Levin, Editor.

Desc: Provides information on metalworking and related subjects of significance to chain link fence manufacturers, including import and supply data. Supplies association and membership news. *Type:* Newsletter.

National Burglar and Fire Alarm Association

7101 Wisconsin Ave., Ste. 901   Ph: (301)907-3202
Bethesda, MD 20814   Fax: (301)907-7897
E-mail: staff@alarm.org
URL: http://www.alarm.org
Contact: Brad Shipp, Exec.Dir.

Desc: Dealers and installers of electrical burglar and fire alarm equipment. *Type:* Association.

National Security Industrial Association

1025 Connecticut Ave. NW,
    Ste. 300
Washington, DC 20036
Contact: Thomas C. Richards, Pres.

Desc: More than 320 small, medium-sized, and large industrial, research, legal, and educational organizations, which constitute a substantial part of our national security technology infrastructure. Fosters a close working relationship and effective two-way communication between government (primarily defense-related issues) and industry. *Type:* Association.

The Peter Berlin Report on Shrinkage Control— Store Manager Edition

Peter Berlin Retail Consulting Group, Inc.
380 N. Broadway, Ste. 306   Ph: (516)932-0450
Jericho, NY 11753   Fax: (516)932-9393
E-mail: sainc@sprintmail.com

Contact: Peter D. Berlin, Editor.

Desc: Provides information on current trends, tools, and techniques for reducing inventory losses in retail stores from shoplifting, employee theft, and paperwork error. Features include news of research, products, and reports of surveys. *Type:* Newsletter.

Search for Common Ground

1601 Connecticut Ave., Ste. 200   Ph: (202)265-4300
Washington, DC 20009   Fax: (202)232-6718
E-mail: search@sfcg.org
URL: http://www.sfcg.org
Contact: John Marks, Pres.

Desc: Purpose is to bring about a fundamental shift in the way nations act so that international security is assured. Purpose is based on the assumptions that: all people, regardless of their political views, want to feel secure; common ground exists and can be expanded among individuals and nations; a fundamental shift in the way nations act is possible; the means are emerging to catalyze this shift; a safe world is possible. Organizes workshops and other meetings to bring together participants representing diverse political views in an effort to find common ground and to discover new approaches to questions of international security; produces television series; conducts programs in the middle east, former Soviet Union, Macedonia, Buundi, South Africa and domestically. *Type:* Association.

Secure Signals

National Cable Television Association
1724 Massachusetts Ave. NW   Ph: (202)775-3550
Washington, DC 20036   Fax: (202)775-3675
URL: http://www.ncta.com
Contact: Jim Allen, Editor.

Desc: Provides educational and informative pieces on security issues in cable television and communications. *Type:* Newsletter.

Security Management Bulletin

Bureau of Business Practice
24 Rope Ferry Rd.   Ph: (860)442-4365
Waterford, CT 06386   Free: 800-243-0876
    Fax: (860)437-3555
URL: http://www.bbpnews.com
Contact: Rick Dann, Editor, richard_dann@prenhall.com.

Desc: Focuses on such topics as preventing employee theft, access control, fire protection, computer security, trade secret protection, training and supervision of uniformed security officers, protection of employees, and emergency preparedness. *Type:* Newsletter.

Seed

Seed World—Seed Trade Buyers Guide

Scranton Gillette Communications, Inc.
380 E. Northwest Hwy., Ste.   Ph: (847)391-1000
    200   Fax: (847)390-0408
Des Plaines, IL 60016-2282
E-mail: seedworld@aol.com.
URL: http://www.seedworld.com.
Contact: Beth Meneghini, Editor.
Desc: List of suppliers of products and services for the seed industry and related businesses. *Type:* Directory.

Seismology

National Information Service for Earthquake Engineering

University of California, Berkeley
Earthquake Engineering   Ph: (510)231-9461
    Abstracts Database   Fax: (510)231-9403
1301 S. 46th St.
Richmond, CA 94804-4698
E-mail: info@nisee.ce.berkeley.edu
URL: http://www.eerc.berkeley.edu/
Contact: Chuck James, Earthquake Engineering Librarian, cjames@eerc.berkeley.edu.
Desc: The scope of the Earthquake Engineering Abstracts Database is all the world's literature on earthquake engineering and earthquake hazards reduction. The database contains citations and abstracts for more than 76,000 items published since 1971. *Type:* Database.

Volcanoes Page

Michigan Technological University - Department of Geological Engineering and Sciences
1400 Townsend Dr.   Ph: (906)487-2531
Houghton, MI 49931-1295   Fax: (906)487-3371
E-mail: tjbornho@mtu.edu
URL: http://www.geo.mtu.edu/volcanoes/
Contact: Michael Dolan, System Admin., Dept. of Geology, mtdolan@mtu.edu.
Desc: The Volcanoes Page contains information on several active volcanoes, as well as image maps, definitions of terms, satellite imagery, a bibliography, historical data, related research, and much more. The ultimate goal is to work towards a new edition of the Catalog of Active Volcanoes of the World, a project of the International Association of Volcanology and Chemistry of the Earth's Interior (IAVCEI). *Type:* Database.

Service

Association for Services Management International

1342 Colonial Blvd., Ste. 25   Ph: (941)275-7887
Fort Myers, FL 33907   Fax: (941)275-0794
E-mail: afsmi@afsmi.org
URL: http://www.afsmi.org
Contact: David Henault, CEO.
Desc: Promotes and develops services management as a professional discipline. *Type:* Association.

The Customer Communicator

The Customer Service Group
215 Park Ave. S., Ste. 1301   Ph: (212)228-0246
New York, NY 10003   Fax: (212)228-0376
URL: http://www.CustomerServiceGroup.com.
Contact: Susan Hash, Executive Editor; Anita Rosepka, Editorial Dir.; Margaret DeWitt, Publisher.
Desc: Serves as a guideline for customer relations skills while it "boosts morale." Covers customer representative skills and provides tipson customer contact, handling complaints, checklists, and promotional contests. Remarks: a monthly training module. *Type:* Newsletter.

Customer Service Manager's Letter

Bureau of Business Practice
24 Rope Ferry Rd.   Ph: (860)442-4365
Waterford, CT 06386   Free: 800-243-0876
    Fax: (860)437-3555
URL: http://www.bbpnews.com
Contact: Anna M. Trusky, Editor, anna-trusky@prenhall.com.
Desc: Offers tips on customer service techniques and skills and features interview-based articles. *Type:* Newsletter.

The Customer Service Professional

Kaset International
8875 Hidden River Pkwy., Ste.   Ph: (813)977-8875
    400   Fax: (813)971-3511
Tampa, FL 33637
Contact: John Gutierrez, Editor; Linda Hines, Publisher, lhines@kaset.com.
Desc: Provides information for customer service professionals. *Type:* Newsletter.

Distribution Center Management

Alexander Research & Communications, Inc.
215 Park Ave. S., Ste. 1301   Ph: (212)228-0246
New York, NY 10003   Fax: (212)228-0376
Contact: Anita Rosepka, Editor.
Desc: Focuses on personnel and operational related issues of manufacturing firms. *Type:* Newsletter.

Doing Right Things Right

Doing Right Things Right Co.
5 Commercial Circle, No. 204   Ph: (617)332-0534
Dedham, MA 02026-2636
E-mail: drtr95@aol.com.
Contact: Donald Caplin, Editor.
Desc: Provides information about customer satisfaction and quality work. *Type:* Newsletter.

EASA Currents

Electrical Apparatus Service Association, Inc. (EASA)
1331 Baur Blvd.   Ph: (314)993-2220
St. Louis, MO 63132   Fax: (314)993-1269
Contact: Carl Fields, Editor; Linda Raynes, Editor.
Desc: Provides news of the electric motor sales and repair industry and related topics, including safety, financial management, and market trends. Recurring features include articles by the staff engineers and committees, chapter news, and news of members. *Type:* Newsletter.

Executive Report on Customer Retention

Alexander Research & Communications, Inc.
215 Park Ave. S, Ste. 1301   Ph: (212)228-0246
New York, NY 10003   Fax: (212)228-0376
Contact: Susan Hash, Editor.
Desc: Serves as a guideline for customer satisfaction strategies. *Type:* Newsletter.

First-Rate Customer Service

Economics Press, Inc.
12 Daniel Rd.   Ph: (973)227-1224
Fairfield, NJ 07004-2565   Free: 800-526-2554
    Fax: (973)526-2554
E-mail: info@epinc.com; order@epinc.com
URL: http://www.epinc.com
Contact: John McDonnel, Editor, edit@epinc.com.
Desc: Offers customer contact personnel advice on enthusiasm and a service-oriented attitude on the job. Recurring features include feature titled A Case in Point. *Type:* Newsletter.

Hair International News

Hair International
PO Box 273   Ph: (717)838-0795
Palmyra, PA 17078   Fax: (717)838-0796
E-mail: hairint@nbn.net
Desc: Covers the barber and cosmetology business. Publishes feature articles and current news. *Type:* Newsletter.

How to Double Your Income

E. Kenneth Lange
7112 N. 15 Pl.   Free: 800-486-3033
Phoenix, AZ 85020-5416   Fax: (602)395-9624
Contact: E. Kenneth Lange, Editor.
Desc: Covers income opportunities for hairstylists. *Type:* Newsletter.

ICA Update

International Carwash Association (ICA)
401 N. Michigan Ave.   Ph: (312)321-5199
Chicago, IL 60611-4212   Free: 888-ICA-8422
    Fax: (312)245-1083
E-mail: ica@sba.com
URL: http://www.carwash.org.
Contact: Pete Nettesheim, Editor.
Desc: Aims to supply professional car wash and detail operators with information that will help them provide better customer service and keep abreast of developments affecting their businesses. Presents Association news as well as results of relevant studies. *Type:* Newsletter.

Illinois Services Directory

Manufacturers' News, Inc.
1633 Central St.   Ph: (847)864-7000
Evanston, IL 60201   Free: 888-752-5200
    Fax: (847)332-1100
E-mail: info@mninfo.com; sales@mninfo.com
URL: http://www.mninfo.com; http://www.manufacturersnews.com.
Contact: Louise M. West, Editor.
Desc: Over 28,241 wholesalers, jobbers, contractors, retailers, services, etc. in Illinois. *Type:* Directory.

International Carwash Association

401 N. Michigan Ave.   Ph: (312)321-5199
Chicago, IL 60611-4267   Fax: (312)245-1085
E-mail: ica@sba.com
URL: http://www.carwash.org
Contact: Mark O. Thorsby, Exec.Dir.
Desc: Membership consists of car wash & detail operators, manufacturers, and suppliers distributors. The ICA Promotes the car wash industry by providing educational opportunities to members and gathering information on the industry and its customer. *Type:* Association.

International Civil Service Commission

2 United Nations Plz., DC2-   Ph: (212)963-8466
    1060   Fax: (212)963-0159
New York, NY 10017
Contact: Prakash Ranadive, Exec.Sec.
Desc: Recommends and establishes terms and conditions of employment for approximately 50,000 United Nations system staff. *Type:* Association.

National School Supply and Equipment Association

8300 Colesville Rd., Ste. 250   Ph: (301)495-0240
Silver Spring, MD 20910   Free: 800-395-5550
    Fax: (301)495-3330
E-mail: nssea@aol.com
URL: http://www.nssea.org
Contact: Tim Holt, Pres.
Desc: Manufacturers, dealers, retailers, and independent manufacturers' representatives of school equipment, instructional materials, and supplies. *Type:* Association.

Quality Quips Newsletter

QP Publishing

PO Box 237   Ph: (724)348-8949
Finleyville, PA 15332-0237   Fax: (724)348-8949

Contact: Nancy Sue Swoger, Editor, swogerdl@usaor.net.

Desc: Provides information about providing quality customer service. Recurring features include book reviews. *Type:* Newsletter.

Self-Storage Now

MiniCo, Inc.

2531 W. Dunlap, No. 201   Ph: (602)870-1711
Phoenix, AZ 85021   Free: 800-824-6864
                                              Fax: (602)861-1094

E-mail: publishing@minico.com; ssnow@minico.com.

URL: http://www.mimco.com.

Contact: Bill Marks, Editor.

Desc: Deals with operating information for the self storage industry. Recurring features include interviews and calendar of events. *Type:* Newsletter.

SERLINE

U.S. National Library of Medicine (NLM)

MEDLARS Management Section

8600 Rockville Pike   Ph: (301)496-3147
Bethesda, MD 20894

URL: http://www.sis.nlm.nih.gov/dirline

Contact: Toby Port, Librarian, (301)496-8235.

Desc: Contains citations to approximately 86,000 serial titles, including all serials and numbered congresses that are on order, in process, or currently received at the National Library of Medicine (NLM). Many records contain locator information for about 165 major biomedical libraries in the Regional Medical Library Network that have the publications. *Available:* The Dialog Corporation, Data-Star; DIMDI (Deutsches Institut fuer Medizinische Dokumentation und Information). *Type:* Database.

Service Employees International Union

1313 L St. NW   Ph: (202)898-3200
Washington, DC 20005   Fax: (202)898-3402

URL: http://www.seiu.org/

Contact: Andrew Stern, Pres.

Desc: AFL-CIO; Canadian Labour Congress. *Type:* Association.

Sweeping

National Chimney Sweep Guild

16021 Industrial Dr., Ste. 8   Ph: (301)963-5600
Gaithersburg, MD 20877   Free: 800-536-0118
                                              Fax: (301)963-0838

E-mail: sweeping1@aol.com.

Contact: Calli Schmidt, Editor.

Desc: Provides an opportunity for professional chimney sweeps to share ideas and to become acquainted with new products and techniques. Disseminates technical information on the venting and chimney service industry. *Type:* Newsletter.

Tom Peters Fast Forward

TPG Communications

555 Hamilton Ave.   Ph: (415)326-4496
Palo Alto, CA 94301   Free: 800-333-8878
                                              Fax: (415)326-7065

Desc: Presents information on how to improve an organization by providing top customer service, researching competition, implementing technology, comparing target users and buyers, and granting power to employees. Recurring features include news of research. *Type:* Newsletter.

Service Clubs

Altrusa International

332 S. Michigan Ave., No. 1123   Ph: (312)427-4410
Chicago, IL 60604   Fax: (312)427-8521

E-mail: altrusa@mcimail.com

Contact: William H. Jepson, Exec.Dir.

Desc: Executives and professionals organized to "help resolve civic and social welfare problems within the community and the world and promote international understanding." Designs and implements community service projects such as Action for Literacy. Supports the AI Foundation, which sponsors the Literacy and Community Service of local clubs. *Type:* Association.

Association of Junior Leagues International

660 1st Ave.   Ph: (212)683-1515
New York, NY 10016   Fax: (212)481-7196

Contact: Holly Sloan, Exec. Officer.

Desc: Women committed to promoting voluntarism and to improving the community through effective action and leadership of trained volunteers. *Type:* Association.

Circle K International

3636 Woodview Trace   Ph: (317)875-8755
Indianapolis, IN 46268-3196   Free: 800-549-2647
                                              Fax: (317)879-0204

E-mail: cki@kiwanis.org

URL: http://www.kiwanis.org/circlek

Contact: Krista Zizzo, Admin.

Desc: Organized by Kiwanis International . College students worldwide interested in serving others and developing friendships and leadership skills. Provides an opportunity for responsible student action in meeting the needs of the campus and community. *Type:* Association.

Civitan International

1 Civitan Pl.   Ph: (205)591-8910
Birmingham, AL 35213-1983   Free: 800-CIV-ITAN
                                              Fax: (205)592-6307

E-mail: civitan@civitan.org

URL: http://www.civitan.org

Contact: W. John Rynearson, CAE, Exec.VP.

Desc: Service organization of business and professional men and women in 20 countries interested in promoting good citizenship on local, national, and international levels. Sponsors Civitan International Research Center at University of Alabama at Birmingham. *Type:* Association.

Good Bears of the World

PO Box 13097   Ph: (419)531-5365
Toledo, OH 43613   Fax: (419)531-5365

Contact: Terrie Stong, Chm.

Desc: Promoters and collectors of teddy bears in 10 countries. *Type:* Association.

Junior Chamber International

400 University Dr.   Ph: (305)446-7608
Coral Gables, FL 33134   Fax: (305)442-0041

Contact: Benny L. Ellerbe, Sec.Gen.

Desc: National Jaycee organizations representing 400,000 individuals between the ages of 18 and 40 dedicated to the principles of leadership training through community development. Sponsors a course on individual development; conducts charitable programs; sponsors competitions. Maintains program information library. *Type:* Association.

Junior Optimist Octagon International

4494 Lindell Blvd.   Ph: (314)371-6000
St. Louis, MO 63108   Fax: (314)371-6006

E-mail: youthclubs@optimist.org

Contact: Teri Flotron, Prog.Mgr.

Desc: Boys and girls in grades six through nine throughout North America. Sponsored by Optimist International and local Optimist Clubs in North America. Fosters adult/youth relationships. *Type:* Association.

Key Club International

3636 Woodview Trace   Ph: (317)875-8755
Indianapolis, IN 46268-3196   Fax: (317)879-0204

E-mail: keyclub@kiwanis.org

URL: http://www.keyclub.org

Contact: Stan D. Soderstrom, Admin.

Desc: Clubs for secondary school students interested in service for others, good citizenship, and leadership training. Sponsored by Kiwanis International. *Type:* Association.

Kiwanis International

3636 Woodview Trace   Ph: (317)875-8755
Indianapolis, IN 46268   Free: 800-549-2647
                                              Fax: (317)879-0204

E-mail: kiwanismail@kiwanis.org

URL: http://www.kiwanis.org

Contact: A.G. Terry Shaffer, Intl.Sec.

Desc: Local clubs representing business and professional individuals in 83 countries and geographic regions. Seeks to: provide assistance to the young and elderly; develop community facilities; foster international understanding and goodwill. Sponsors Young Children: Priority One, a service program to benefit children up to age five. *Type:* Association.

Lions Clubs International

300 22nd St.   Ph: (630)571-5466
Oak Brook, IL 60523   Fax: (630)571-8890

E-mail: lions@lionsclubs.org

URL: http://www.lionsclubs.org

Contact: Win Hamilton, Exec.Admin.

Desc: Local clubs representing business and professional men and women in 185 countries and geographic areas. Provides community service in order to increase international understanding and cooperation. Fosters awareness of environmental, social, and health related problems. *Type:* Association.

National Assistance League

5627 Fernwood Ave.   Ph: (213)469-5897
Los Angeles, CA 90028   Fax: (323)469-0669

Contact: Carolyn Gordon, Pres.

Desc: "To act as a friend at any and all times to men, women and children in need of care, guidance and assistance, spiritually, materially and physically." Each chapter controls and administers at least one self-sustaining philanthropic project. Projects include boys' clubs, children's theatre guilds, clothing centers, day nurseries, dental centers, family services, geriatric programs, girls' clubs, centers for the hearing-, visually-, and speech-impaired, homemaker service, hospital equipment bank, toy loans, volunteer bureaus, well-baby clinics, and youth employment service. *Type:* Association.

National Association of Colored Women's Clubs

5808 16th St. NW   Ph: (202)726-2044
Washington, DC 20011   Fax: (202)726-0023

Contact: Carole A. Early, Hdqtrs.Sec.

Desc: Federation of black women's clubs. Carries on program of civic service, education, social service, and philanthropy. Sponsors National Association of Youth Clubs. *Type:* Association.

National Association of Junior Auxiliaries

PO Box 1873   Ph: (601)332-3000
Greenville, MS 38702-1873   Fax: (601)332-3076

E-mail: najanet@tecinfo.com

URL: http://www.techinfo.com/~najanet

Contact: Norma N. DeLong, Exec.Dir.

Desc: Women over 21 years of age. Encourages women to become active and constructive participants in their communities, assume responsible leadership in meeting community problems, render charitable services which are beneficial to the general public, and cooperate with other organizations performing similar services. Offers children's services. *Type:* Association.

National Association of Negro Business and Professional Women's Clubs
1806 New Hampshire Ave. NW   Ph: (202)483-4206
Washington, DC 20009   Fax: (202)462-7253
URL: http://www.nanbpwc.com
Contact: Glo Ivory, Exec.Dir.
Desc: Women actively engaged in a business or a profession who are committed to rendering service through club programs and activities. Seeks to direct the interest of business and professional women toward united action for improved social and civic conditions, and to provide enriching and ennobling experiences that will encourage freedom, dignity, self-respect, and self-reliance. Offers information and help regarding education, employment, health, housing, legislation, and problems of the aged and the disabled. *Type:* Association.

National Exchange Club
3050 Central Ave.   Ph: (419)535-3232
Toledo, OH 43606-1700   Free: 800-924-2643
   Fax: (419)535-1989
E-mail: nechq@aol.com
URL: http://www.nationalexchangeclub.com
Contact: David A. Nershi, CAE, Exec. VP.
Desc: Business and professional men's and women's service clubs involved in child abuse prevention, crime prevention, good citizenship, youth, and community service. *Type:* Association.

NGA
1007 B Street Rd.   Ph: (215)322-5759
Southampton, PA 18966   Fax: (215)322-6078
Contact: Maryanna Trembath, Exec.Dir.
Desc: Contributors of new clothing, household linens and basic personal care items (toiletries) distributed locally to those in need, through recognized community organizations and agencies which register with our national organization and agree to give our gifts to needy people. *Type:* Association.

Optimist International
4494 Lindell Blvd.   Ph: (314)371-6000
St. Louis, MO 63108   Fax: (314)371-6006
E-mail: headquarters@optimist.org
URL: http://www.optimist.org
Contact: Stephen P. Lawson, Exec.Dir.
Desc: Volunteer Service clubs dedicated to youth and community service. *Type:* Association.

Pilot International and Pilot International FND
244 College St.   Ph: (912)743-7403
PO Box 4844   Fax: (912)743-2173
Macon, GA 31213-0599
URL: http://www.pilotinternational.org
Contact: Cynthia Mills, Exec.Dir.
Desc: Civic service organization with clubs for executives and professionals in 6 countries. Local groups seek to improve civic, social, and commercial welfare of their communities. *Type:* Association.

Rotary International
1 Rotary Center   Ph: (847)866-3000
1560 Sherman Ave.   Fax: (847)328-8554
Evanston, IL 60201-3698
URL: http://www.rotary.org/
Contact: Aaron Hyatt, Gen.Sec.
Desc: Business and professional executives in 150 countries and additional 34 geographical regions. Undertakes community development programs; promotes high ethical standards in business and professions; fosters "international understanding, goodwill, and peace." Supports polio immunization campaigns. Maintains Rotary Foundation which offers scholarships to outstanding men and women, enabling them to study or teach in other countries. *Type:* Association.

Ruritan National
Ruritan Rd.   Ph: (703)674-5431
PO Box 487   Fax: (703)674-2304
Dublin, VA 24084
Contact: Richard Ely, Exec.Dir.
Desc: Nonpartisan, non-sectarian community service organization. Goals are: to create better understanding between rural and urban people, communities, and business; to aid in charitable work and disaster relief efforts; to promote industrial and agricultural growth and economic development. Funds the Ruritan National Foundation, a trust for the encouragement, promotion, and financing of charitable, educational, and benevolent activities. *Type:* Association.

Sertoma International
1912 E. Meyer Blvd.   Ph: (816)333-8300
Kansas City, MO 64132-1174   Free: 800-593-5646
   Fax: (816)333-4320
E-mail: infosertoma@sertoma.org
URL: http://www.sertoma.org
Contact: Gene Homn, CAE, Exec.Dir.
Desc: Civic service club of business and professional men and women in Canada, Mexico, and the United States. Motto is to render "service to mankind" (phrase from which group's name is derived). Sponsors: Sertoma Foundation, which provides service to persons with communicative disorders; Hearing and Speech Services; Serteen and Collegiate Sertoma clubs. *Type:* Association.

Soroptimist International of the Americas
2 Penn Center Plaza, Ste. 1000   Ph: (215)557-9300
Philadelphia, PA 19102   Free: 800-942-4629
   Fax: (215)568-5200
E-mail: siang@soroptimist.org
Contact: Leigh Wintz, Exec.Dir.
Desc: Executive and professional women in 21 countries in North and South America and Asia. Areas of activity include economic and social development, education, environment, health, human rights, the status of women, and international understanding. Sponsors "S" Clubs (high school service clubs), Sigma Societies and Venture Clubs of the Americas. *Type:* Association.

Zonta International
557 W. Randolph St.   Ph: (312)930-5848
Chicago, IL 60661-2206   Fax: (312)930-0951
URL: http://www.zonta.org
Contact: Janet Halstead, Exec.Dir.
Desc: Business and professional executives worldwide "working together to advance the status of women." Coordinates service projects that provide health, and income-generation, including cooperative projects with U.N. agencies. Conducts program to assist young women in the fields of public affairs and policy-making. *Type:* Association.

Service Fraternities

Alpha Phi Alpha Fraternity
2313 St. Paul St.   Ph: (410)554-0040
Baltimore, MD 21218   Fax: (410)554-0054
Contact: Ronald Anderson, Exec.Dir.
Desc: Service fraternity founded for people of African descent; the organization has been interracial since 1945. *Type:* Association.

Alpha Phi Omega
14901 E. 42nd St.   Ph: (816)373-8667
Independence, MO 64055   Fax: (816)373-5975
E-mail: aponed@aol.com
URL: http://www.apo.org
Contact: Patrick W. Burke, Exec.Dir.

Desc: Works to help campus, community, state, and nation. *Type:* Association.

Columbia
Knights of Columbus
1 Columbus Plaza   Ph: (203)772-2130
New Haven, CT 06510-3326   Fax: (203)772-1923
Contact: Richard McMunn, Editor.
Desc: International Catholic family magazine (French, Spanish, and English). *Type:* Periodical.

Grand Aerie, Fraternal Order of Eagles
PO Box 25916   Ph: (414)781-7585
Milwaukee, WI 53225-0916
Contact: D.R. "Jim" West, GrandWorthy Pres.
Desc: Fraternal society. Provides grants; maintains hall of fame; conducts charitable program. *Type:* Association.

Phi Delta Kappan
Phi Delta Kappa International
408 N. Union   Ph: (812)339-1156
PO Box 789   Free: 800-766-1156
Bloomington, IN 47402-0789   Fax: (812)339-0018
E-mail: headquarters@pdkintl.org; kappan@pdkintl.org.
URL: http://www.pdkintl.org; http://www.kiva.net/ ~pdicintl/.
Contact: Pauline B. Gough, Editor; Carol Bucheri, Advertising Dir.
Desc: Magazine for professional educators. *Type:* Periodical.

Service Sororities
Alpha Kappa Alpha
5656 S. Stony Island Ave.   Ph: (773)684-1282
Chicago, IL 60637   Fax: (773)288-8251
Contact: Alison Harris Alexander, Exec.Dir.
Desc: Service sorority. Provides community services; compiles statistics. *Type:* Association.

Beta Sigma Phi
1800 W. 91st Pl.   Ph: (816)444-6800
Box 8500   Free: 800-821-3989
Kansas City, MO 64114   Fax: (816)333-6206
Contact: John J. Ross, Pres.
Desc: Social, service, and cultural society - business and professional women and housewives, over age 18. Operates charitable program. *Type:* Association.

Delta Sigma Theta
1707 New Hampshire Ave. NW   Ph: (202)986-2400
Washington, DC 20009   Fax: (202)986-2513
Contact: Roseline McKinney, Exec.Dir.
Desc: Public service sorority of Black women. Maintains Delta Research and Educational Foundation. *Type:* Association.

Epsilon Sigma Alpha
363 W. Drake Rd.   Ph: (970)223-2824
Fort Collins, CO 80526   Fax: (970)223-4456
E-mail: esainfo@esaintl.com
URL: http://www.esaintl.com
Contact: B. J. Clark, Exec.Dir.
Desc: Leadership service sorority. *Type:* Association.

Zeta Phi Beta
1734 New Hampshire Ave. NW   Ph: (202)387-3103
Washington, DC 20009   Fax: (202)232-4593
Contact: Vickie L. Robinson, Deputy Exec.Dir.
Desc: Service and social sorority. Maintains Zeta Phi Beta Sorority Educational Foundation. *Type:* Association.

Sexual Abuse

Giarretto Institute
232 E. Gish Rd., 1st Fl. Ph: (408)453-7611
San Jose, CA 95112 Fax: (408)453-9064
E-mail: giarretto@earthlink.net
URL: http://www.giarretto.org
Contact: Brian Abbott, Ph.D., Exec.Dir.
Desc: Purpose is to offer therapy and guided self-help support to sexually abused children and their families, and to men and women unable to cope with the trauma of having been sexually abused as children. *Type:* Association.

Society's League Against Molestation
c/o Women Against Rape/ Ph: (609)858-7800
  Childwatch Free: 800-491-
PO Box 346 WATCH
Collingswood, NJ 08108 Fax: (609)858-7063
E-mail: jcsun@juno.com
Contact: Judy Yeh, Deputy Dir.
Desc: Works to: prevent sexual abuse and exploitation of children; educate the public through media programs and speeches about child molestation; date rape; sexual harrassment; counsel and assist victims and their families. Researches the social, psychological, and legal aspects of child molestation; monitors court cases and verdicts and suggests introduction of stricter legislation. Offers tips for prevention and awareness of child molestation. *Type:* Association.

Survivors of Incest Anonymous
PO Box 21817 Ph: (410)282-3400
Baltimore, MD 21222-6817 Fax: (410)282-3400
URL: http://www.siawso.org
Contact: Linda L. Davis, Public Info. Officer.
Desc: Serves as a support group and selfhelp recovery program for any adult who was a victim of sexual abuse as a child. *Type:* Association.

Shipping

American Bureau of Shipping
2 World Trade Ctr., 106th Fl. Ph: (212)839-5000
New York, NY 10048 Fax: (212)839-5130
URL: http://www.eagle.org
Contact: Robert D. Somerville, Pres.
Desc: Shipowners, shipbuilders, naval architects, marine underwriters, and others associated with the international marine industry. International classification society concerned with determining mechanical and structural fitness of vessels, drilling units, and other marine structures for intended services. Establishes universal standards by which ships, mobile off-shore drilling units, and other marine structures are designed, built, and maintained. *Type:* Association.

American Moving and Storage Association
John Brewer
1611 Duke St. Ph: (703)683-7410
Alexandria, VA 22314 Fax: (703)683-7527
URL: http://www.amconf.org
Contact: Joseph M. Harrison, Pres.
Desc: Local, intrastate, interstate, and international movers who transport household goods, office and institutional equipment, and high-value products. *Type:* Association.

American Shipper—Southern Trade & Logistics Issue
Howard Publications, Inc.
300 W. Adams St., Ste. 600 Ph: (904)355-2601
Jacksonville, FL 32202-5304 Free: 800-874-6422
  Fax: (904)791-8836
Contact: Gary G. Burrows, Editor, gburrows@shippers.com.

Desc: Steamship, towing, transportation companies, forwarders, brokers, ship builders, dry dock facilities, warehouses, marine sales and service companies, banks, and other firms engaged in shipping and world trade in the coastal and river ports of North Carolina, South Carolina, Tennessee, Georgia, Alabama, Louisiana, Mississippi and Florida; also lists related government agencies and industrial parks. *Type:* Directory.

Bureau of Explosives
Association of American Railroads
50 F St. NW Ph: (202)639-2222
Washington, DC 20001
Contact: Charles L. Keller, Dir.
Desc: Established by the Association of American Railroads to assist carriers, chemical and container manufacturers, explosives producers, government facilities, and all others operating under the U.S. Department of Transportation's hazardous materials regulations. Acts as agent for railroads, motor carriers, and steamship companies. *Type:* Association.

DRI/TBS World Sea Trade Forecast
Standard & Poor's DRI
Data Products Division
24 Hartwell Ave. Ph: (781)863-5100
Lexington, MA 02421
E-mail: client_services@dri.mcgraw-hill.com
URL: http://www.dri.mcgraw-hill.com
Contact: Client Services, (617)860-6527, fax: (617)860-6416.
Desc: Contains more than 3 million historical and forecast time series on worldwide waterborne trade. Covers 205 major trading routes. *Available:* Standard & Poor's DRI, Data Products Division. *Type:* Database.

Drop Shipping Marketing Methods
Drop Shipping News
Box 7838 Ph: (212)688-8797
New York, NY 10150
URL: http://www.drop-shipping-news.com.
Contact: Nicholas T. Scheel, Editor, nscheel@drop-shipping-news.com.
Desc: Covers all aspects of drop shipping. *Type:* Newsletter.

The Handbook for International Trade
Geyer-McAllister Publications, Inc.
51 Madison Ave. Ph: (212)689-4411
New York, NY 10010-1603 Fax: (212)683-7929
Contact: Maria Reines Weiskott, Editor.
Desc: Lists more than 600 shipping lines and agents, in addition to foreign freight forwarders and maritime associations. *Type:* Directory.

Hazardous Materials Advisory Council
1101 Vermont Ave. NW, Ste. Ph: (202)289-4550
  301 Fax: (202)289-4074
Washington, DC 20005
E-mail: hmacinfo@hmac.org
URL: http://www.hmac.org
Contact: Jonathan Collom, Pres.
Desc: Shippers, carriers, and container manufacturers of hazardous materials, substances, and wastes; shipper and carrier associations. Works to promote safe transportation of these materials; provides assistance in answering regulatory questions, guidance to appropriate governmental resources, and advice in establishing corporate compliance and safety programs. Conducts seminars on domestic and international hazardous materials packaging and transporting; sponsors educational programs. *Type:* Association.

Inter-American Freight Conference
806 Plaza 2 Ph: (201)451-0001
Harborside Financial Center Fax: (201)451-4470
Jersey City, NJ 07311-3980
Contact: John L. Morris, Exec. Officer.
Desc: Shipping lines operating between U.S. Atlantic and Gulf ports and Argentina, Brazil, Paraguay, and Uruguay. Encourages cooperation in the promotion and development of international trade between Argentina, Brazil, Paraguay, and Uruguay and the U.S. *Type:* Association.

LEXIS® Admiralty Library
LEXIS-NEXIS
9443 Springboro Pike Ph: (937)865-6800
PO Box 933
Dayton, OH 45401-0933
URL: http://www.lex-nexis.com
Desc: Provides a comprehensive collection of domestic and British case law, statutory and regulatory materials, as well as a variety of relevant secondary legal and non-legal research resources that are essential to admiralty and maritime practitioners. *Available:* LEXIS-NEXIS, LEXIS. *Type:* Database.

Logistics Management and Distribution Report
Logistics Management & Distribution Report
275 Washington St. Ph: (617)558-4473
Newton, MA 02458 Fax: (617)558-4327
E-mail: lm@cahners.com.
URL: http://www.logisticsmgmt.
Contact: Peter Bradley, Editor and Publisher.
Desc: Publication covering the areas of logistics, transportation, and supply-chain management. *Type:* Periodical.

National Cargo Bureau
30 Vesey St. Ph: (212)571-5000
New York, NY 10007 Fax: (212)571-5005
E-mail: ncbnyk@natcargo.org
Contact: James J. McNamara, Pres.
Desc: Representatives of the maritime industry, marine underwriters, and government departments closely associated with the maritime industry. Recommends regulations to the government for the safe and uniform stowage of dangerous cargo and grain in bulk. *Type:* Association.

National FOB Report
U.S. Department of Agriculture
Agricultural Marketing Service
Fruit and Vegetable Market News
2202 Monterey St., Ste. 104-A Ph: (559)487-5178
Fresno, CA 93721-3129 Free: 800-487-8796
  Fax: (559)487-5199
URL: http://www.ams.usda.gov/marketnews.htm.
Contact: Kevin Morris, Officer-in-Charge.
Desc: Deals with fruits. Covers the major growing areas, rail and truck shipment information, and FOB shipping point prices. *Type:* Newsletter.

National FOB Review
U.S. Department of Agriculture
Agricultural Marketing Service
Fruit and Vegetable Market News
2202 Monterey St., Ste. 104-A Ph: (559)487-5178
Fresno, CA 93721-3129 Free: 800-487-8796
  Fax: (559)487-5199
URL: http://www.ams.usda.gov/marketnews.htm.
Contact: Kevin Morris, Officer-in-Charge.
Desc: Each issue contains the FOB Shipping point price reports issued nationwide by Market News on that day. *Type:* Newsletter.

National Motor Freight Traffic Association

2200 Mill Rd.   Ph: (703)838-1810
Alexandria, VA 22314   Fax: (703)683-1094
E-mail: nmfta@erols.com
URL: http://www.erols.com/nmfta

Contact: Martin E. Foley, Exec.Dir.

Desc: Motor common carriers of general commodities. Represents interests of membership before the Surface Transportation Board, the congress, the courts and state regulatory agencies. *Type:* Association.

National Shipping Point Trends Report

U.S. Department of Agriculture
Agricultural Marketing Service
Fruit and Vegetable Market News
2202 Monterey St., Ste. 104-A   Ph: (559)487-5178
Fresno, CA 93721-3129   Free: 800-487-8796
                                 Fax: (559)487-5199
URL: http://www.ams.usda.gov/marketnews.htm.

Contact: Kevin Morris, Officer-in-Charge.

Desc: Summarizes movement, demand, and price for each fruit and vegetable commodity at each of the nation's shipping points. *Type:* Newsletter.

Northwest Ships & Shipping Database

Tacoma Public Library
1102 Tacoma Ave. S.   Ph: (253)591-5666
Tacoma, WA 98402   Fax: (253)627-1693
URL: http://www.tpl.lib.wa.us/nwr/shipscgi.htm

Desc: A database for mariners and those who long to go to sea, this searchable index contains information on more than 13,000 ships, including full-text records on over 1,000 of them. Here you'll find ship names (including former names), information on builders, careers, disposition, and history. *Type:* Database.

Pacific Maritime Association

PO Box 7861   Ph: (415)576-3200
San Francisco, CA 94120   Fax: (415)989-1425
E-mail: darwin@pmanet.org
URL: http://www.pmanet.org

Contact: Joe Miniace, Pres.

Desc: Provides industrial relations services for the shipping industry on the West Coast. *Type:* Association.

Propeller Club of the U.S.

3927 Old Lee Hwy., No. 101A   Ph: (703)691-2777
Fairfax, VA 22030   Fax: (703)691-4173
E-mail: propclubhq@aol.com

Contact: J. Daniel Smith, Exec.VP.

Desc: Promotes and supports the American Merchant Marine and aids in the development of Great Lakes, inland waterway, and harbor improvement. Activities include: National Maritime Essay Contests; Adopt-a-Ship Plan, Student Port Program. *Type:* Association.

Seaports Infopages

Compass North America, Inc.
1825 Ponce de Leon Blvd., Ste.   Ph: (305)667-8175
  330   Fax: (305)662-4868
Coral Gables, FL 33134
E-mail: webmaster@seaportsinfo.com
URL: http://www.seaportsinfo.com/

Desc: This site provides a wide range of information about world seaports, with a special focus on seaports of the western hemisphere. Included is tonnage by bulk category, primary inbound and outbound cargo, and main channel depths. *Type:* Database.

Transportation Telephone Tickler

The Journal of Commerce
454 Marshall St.   Ph: (908)859-1300
Phillipsburg, NJ 08865   Free: 800-222-0356
                                 Fax: (908)454-6507

E-mail: tttickler@aol.com.

Contact: Linda M. Kasza, Operations Mgr.

Desc: 25,000 companies and agents in North American port districts which provide transportation services ranging from air freight forwarding to warehousing. Published in a four-volume national edition and 7 regional editions. *Type:* Directory.

Shooting

Amateur Trapshooting Association

601 W. National Rd.   Ph: (937)898-4638
Vandalia, OH 45377   Fax: (937)898-5472
E-mail: shootata@bright.net
URL: http://www.shootata.com

Contact: David D. Bopp, Exec.Dir.

Desc: Persons who participate or are interested in the sport of trapshooting. Sanctions and determines rules governing shoots held by local, state, provincial, and worldwide trapshooting associations. *Type:* Association.

American Single Shot Rifle Association

John Gary Staup
709 Carolyn Dr.   Ph: (419)692-3866
Delphos, OH 45833   Fax: (419)695-3756
E-mail: rprusok@nmu.edu

Contact: John Gary Staup, Contact.

Desc: Individuals who have an interest in the collection, use, preservation, and study of single shot rifles and their accessories. Devoted to the development and organization of activities that involve the classic single shot rifles in the German-American Schuetzen and Creedmoor tradition. Opposes legislative curtailment of the right to possess and use arms "by decent and peaceful persons as shooters, collectors, and sportsmen"; cooperates with law enforcement agencies in the prevention of illegal or abusive use of arms; provides the public with accurate information on the subject of arms and their accessories. *Type:* Association.

International Handgun Metallic Silhouette Association

PO Box 368   Ph: (319)752-9623
Burlington, IA 52601   Fax: (319)753-1312
E-mail: fscotto121@aol.com

Contact: J.R. Wythe, Pres.

Desc: Handgun enthusiasts who shoot at metallic silhouettes of chickens, pigs, turkeys, and rams at ranges of 50, 100, 150, and 200 meters, respectively. Sanctions tournaments. *Type:* Association.

National Muzzle Loading Rifle Association

PO Box 67   Ph: (812)667-5131
Friendship, IN 47021
URL: http://www.nmlrr.org

Contact: John Miller, Exec.VP.

Desc: Persons interested in black powder shooting. Seeks to preserve the heritage of black powder shooting and to promote safety in the use of arms. Maintains national range located at Friendship, IN. *Type:* Association.

National Rifle Association of America

11250 Waples Mill Rd.   Ph: (703)267-1000
Fairfax, VA 22030   Free: 800-672-3888
                                 Fax: (703)267-3989

E-mail: comm@nrahq.org
URL: http://www.nra.org/

Contact: Wayne R. LaPierre, Jr., Exec.VP.

Desc: Target shooters, hunters, gun collectors, gunsmiths, police officers, and others interested in firearms. Promotes rifle, pistol, and shotgun shooting, hunting, gun collecting, home firearm safety, and wildlife conservation. Encourages civilian marksmanship. *Type:* Association.

National Shooting Sports Foundation

Flintlock Ridge Office Ctr.   Ph: (203)426-1320
11 Mile Hill Rd.   Fax: (203)426-1087
Newtown, CT 06470-2359

Contact: Robert T. Delfay, Pres./CEO.

Desc: Supported by manufacturers of firearms and ammunition, accessories, components, gun sights, hunting clothes, and other reputable firms that make a profit from hunting and shooting; includes outdoor and gun magazine publishers. To foster a better understanding and more active participation in the shooting sports. *Type:* Association.

National Skeet Shooting Association

5931 Roft Rd.   Ph: (210)688-3371
San Antonio, TX 78253   Free: 800-877-5338
                                 Fax: (512)688-3014

E-mail: nssa@nssa-nsca.com
URL: http://www.nssa-nsca.com

Contact: Mike Hampton, Exec.Dir.

Desc: Amateur skeet shooters. Registers competitive shoots and supervises them through formulation and enforcement of rules. Honors outstanding individuals whose shooting achievements and contributions to the sport of skeet qualify them for a position of honor in the Skeet Shooting Hall of Fame. *Type:* Association.

National Sporting Clays Association

5931 Roft Rd.   Ph: (210)688-3371
San Antonio, TX 78253-9261   Free: 800-877-5338
                                 Fax: (210)688-3014

URL: http://www.nssa-nsca.com

Contact: Mike Hampton, Exec.Dir.

Desc: Promotion of shooting sports. *Type:* Association.

Skating

United States Amateur Confederation of Roller Skating

PO Box 6579   Ph: (402)483-7551
Lincoln, NE 68506   Fax: (402)483-1465

Contact: George Pickard, Exec.Sec.

Desc: Amateur organization sponsoring competitive roller skating that includes inline skates. *Type:* Association.

United States Figure Skating Association

20 1st St.   Ph: (719)635-5200
Colorado Springs, CO 80906   Fax: (719)635-9548
E-mail: usfsa1@aol.com
URL: http://www.usfsa.org

Contact: John LeFevre, Exec.Dir.

Desc: Member clubs with over 142,000 registered members. National governing body for the sport of figure skating in the U.S. *Type:* Association.

USA Roller Skating

4730 South St.   Ph: (402)483-7551
PO Box 6579   Fax: (402)483-1465
Lincoln, NE 68506
E-mail: usacrs@usacrs.com
URL: http://www.usacrs.com

Contact: George Pickard, Exec.Dir.

Desc: Amateur roller skaters and inline skaters. Serves as governing body for competitive roller skating, artistic skating, hockey, and speed skating in the U.S. *Type:* Association.

Skiing

Cross Country Skier

Collins Chase Publications
PO Box 50120   Ph: (612)377-0312
Minneapolis, MN 55405   Free: 800-827-0607
    Fax: (612)381-9182
URL: http://www.crosscountryskier.com/.
Desc: Magazine emphasizing touring, destinations, and technique in cross-country skiing. *Type:* Periodical.

Mountain Sports & Living

Miller Publishing Group
810 7th Ave., 4th Fl.   Ph: (212)636-2700
New York, NY 10019   Fax: (212)636-2710
Contact: Carol Smith, President/CEO.
Desc: Magazine of mountain sports and living. *Type:* Periodical.

National Brotherhood of Skiers

1525 E. 53rd St., Ste. 408   Ph: (773)955-4100
Chicago, IL 60615
Contact: Samuel E. Lawler, Pres.
Desc: Minority ski clubs. Promotes winter sports among minorities, with emphasis on youth. Seeks to locate and develop talented ski racers through local, regional, and national competitions. *Type:* Association.

National Ski Patrol System

Ski Patrol Bldg., Ste. 100   Ph: (303)988-1111
133 S. Van Gordon St.   Fax: (303)988-3005
Lakewood, CO 80228
E-mail: nsp@nsp.org
URL: http://www.nsp.org
Contact: Stephen Over, Exec.Dir.
Desc: Promotes ski safety and handling of injuries at ski areas. *Type:* Association.

New England Skiers' Guide

Ski Racing International, Inc.
6971 Main St., Ste. 1   Ph: (802)496-7700
PO Box 1125   Free: 800-552-1558
Waitsfield, VT 05673   Fax: (802)496-7704
E-mail: sracing@skiracing.com
Contact: Tim Etchells, Editor.
Desc: Several hundred downhill ski resorts and sites, and cross-country ski areas and trails in New England. *Type:* Directory.

POWDER

POWDER
PO Box 1028   Ph: (714)496-5922
Dana Point, CA 92629   Free: 800-289-8983
    Fax: (714)496-7849
E-mail: powdermag@aol.com.
Contact: Steve Casimiro, Managing Editor; Brent Diamond, Publisher; Ben Warrer, Advertising Dir.
Desc: Magazine for ski enthusiasts (advanced and intermediate). *Type:* Periodical.

Professional Ski Instructors of America

133 S. Van Gordon St., Ste.   Ph: (303)987-9390
101   Fax: (303)988-3005
Lakewood, CO 80228
Contact: Stephen Over, Exec.Dir.
Desc: Professional-certified Alpine and Nordic ski teachers. Promotes ski instruction by professional teachers. Developed American Teaching Method (ATM), which has received international recognition. *Type:* Association.

Seventy Plus Ski Club

c/o Lloyd T. Lambert
1633 Albany St.
Schenectady, NY 12304-2905
Contact: Lloyd T. Lambert, Founder.
Desc: Active downhill skiers 70 years old and older; members must show proof of legal age. Provides members with information regarding areas where they can ski free or at discount. Conducts trips and special meetings worldwide. *Type:* Association.

Ski

Times Mirror Magazines, Inc.
2 Park Ave.   Ph: (212)779-5000
New York, NY 10016-5601   Fax: (212)779-5522
URL: http://www.skinet.com.
Contact: Andrew W. Bigford, Editor, awbig@kincf.com; Andrew W. Clurman, Publisher.
Desc: Magazine devoted to skiing. *Alt. Contact:* 929 Pearl St., Ste. 200, Boulder, CO 80302; telephone: (303)448-7600; fax: (303)448-7612. *Type:* Periodical.

Ski America

Ski America
PO Box 737   Ph: (413)637-9810
Lenox, MA 01240   Fax: (413)637-9873
Contact: Barry Hollister, Editor and Publisher; B. Robert Wadsworth, Senior Vice Pres. Advertising.
Desc: Magazine on skiing. *Type:* Periodical.

Ski Europe: A Comprehensive Guide to Europe's Best Resorts

World-Leisure Corp.
177 Paris St.   Ph: (617)569-1966
Boston, MA 02128   Free: 800-292-1966
    Fax: (617)561-7654
E-mail: wleisure@aol.com
URL: http://www.worldleisure.com
Contact: Charles Leocha, Editor.
Desc: Over 80 ski resorts in Switzerland, Austria, Italy, France, Germany. *Type:* Directory.

The Ski Industry Letter

Skiletter, Inc.
115 Lilly Pond Ln.   Ph: (914)232-5094
Katonah, NY 10536
Desc: Discusses the ski industry and related professionals, specifically the areas of marketing and other statistics. *Type:* Newsletter.

Ski Presse

Skier International Inc.
C.P. 143   Ph: (514)464-3121
Beloeil, PQ, Canada J3G 4T1   Fax: (514)464-9210
E-mail: skipresse@videothom.net.
Desc: Journal publishing information on the skiing industry. *Alt. Contact:* 850 Bernard Pilon, McMasterville, PQ, Canada J3G 5X7. *Type:* Periodical.

Skiing

Times Mirror Magazines, Inc.
2 Park Ave.   Ph: (212)779-5000
New York, NY 10016-5601   Fax: (212)779-5522
E-mail: skiing@shinet.com.
URL: http://www.skinet.com/skiing.
Contact: Rick Kahl, Editor; Andrew W. Clurman, VP/Publisher.
Desc: Skiing magazine. *Alt. Contact:* 929 Pearl St., Ste. 200, Boulder, CO 80302; telephone: (303)448-7600; fax: (303)448-7612. *Type:* Periodical.

Student Ski Association

26 Sagamore Rd.   Ph: (508)336-8775
Seekonk, MA 02771   Fax: (508)336-8775
Contact: Richard Sorel, Pres.
Desc: Membership entitles college and graduate students to reduced rates on lift tickets, ski lessons, and rentals at 150 ski areas nationwide. Members are also eligible for low-cost ski and beach trips to Stowe and Stratton, VT, Bermuda, and Ft. Lauderdale, Winter Park, and Daytona Beach, FL. *Type:* Association.

United States Ski Association

PO Box 100   Ph: (435)649-9090
Park City, UT 84060   Fax: (435)649-3613
Contact: Bill Marolt, Pres.
Desc: Colleges throughout the U.S. fielding Nordic and Alpine ski teams in regional and national competitions; colleges sponsoring recreational ski clubs. Purpose is to encourage educational, recreational, and competitive ski programs. *Type:* Association.

U.S. Ski and Snowboard Association

PO Box 100   Ph: (435)649-9090
Park City, UT 84060   Fax: (435)649-3613
Contact: Bill Marolt, CEO.
Desc: Chartered as the official governing body for skiing in the U.S. *Type:* Association.

World Ski Association

393 S Harlan St., Ste. 120   Ph: (303)936-6348
Lakewood, CO 80226   Free: 800-525-SNOW
    Fax: (303)936-6375
E-mail: worldski@aol.com
URL: http://www.worldski.com
Contact: Cheryl Nerney, Pres.
Desc: Recreational skiers and snowboarders. Arranges skiing excursions and travel for members. Provides members with wholesale travel service utilizing commercial airlines. *Type:* Association.

Small Business

American Association for Consumer Benefits

PO Box 100279   Ph: 800-872-8896
Fort Worth, TX 76185   Free: 800-872-8896
    Fax: (817)377-5633
E-mail: info@aacb.org
URL: http://www.aacb.org
Contact: James Redmond, Contact.
Desc: Small business owners and employees. Promotes the availability of medical and other benefits to small business owners, their families, and employees. *Type:* Association.

American Association of Franchisees and Dealers

3636 4th Ave., Ste. 310   Ph: (619)209-3775
San Diego, CA 92103-4237   Free: 800-733-9858
    Fax: (619)209-3777
E-mail: benefits@aafd.org
URL: http://www.aafd.org
Contact: Robert L. Purvin, Jr., Chm.
Desc: Franchise business owners. Represents the interests of franchise business owners. *Type:* Association.

American Home Business Association

4505 S. Wasatch Blvd.   Free: 800-556-9150
Salt Lake City, UT 84124   Fax: (801)273-2399
E-mail: info@homebusinessworks.com
URL: http://www.homebusinessworks.com
Contact: Larry Brickman, Pres. & CEO.
Desc: Individuals operating home-based businesses. Works to assist persons in operating a profitable home-based business. Distributes information on taxes, equipment, and other topics. *Type:* Association.

American Small Businesses Association

206 E. College St.
Grapevine, TX 76051-5364
Contact: Vernon Castle, Exec.Dir.
Desc: Small business owners. Supports legislation favorable to the small business enterprise; organizes members to collectively oppose unfavorable legislation. Informs members of proposed legislation affecting small businesses; conducts business education programs. *Type:* Association.

Art of Self Promotion

Creative Marketing and Management
PO Box 23   Ph: (201)653-0783
Hoboken, NJ 07030-0023   Free: 800-737-0783
                             Fax: (201)222-2494
E-mail: info@artofselfpromotion.com
Contact: Ilise Benun, Editor and Publisher.
Desc: Provides marketing information for small business owners. *Type:* Newsletter.

BEST Employers Association

2515 McCabe Way   Ph: (714)756-1000
Irvine, CA 92614   Free: 800-854-7417
                             Fax: (714)553-1232
E-mail: bestplans@bestplans.com
Contact: Donald R. Lawrenz, Exec.Sec.
Desc: Provides small independent businesses with managerial, economic, financial, and sales information helpful for business improvement. *Type:* Association.

Bootstrappin' Entrepreneur

Research Done Write!
8726 S. Sepulveda Blvd., Ste.   Ph: (310)568-9861
  B261-NIP
Los Angeles, CA 90045
E-mail: Ibootstrap@aol.com.
Contact: Kimberly Stansell, Editor, kbmberlynla@aol.com.
Desc: Helps people run a business on a shoestring budget with survival strategies and business building tips. Companion to book, Bootstrapper's Succes Secrets: 151 Tactics for Building Your Business on a Shoestring Budget (Career Press). *Type:* Newsletter.

Bulletproof Marketing for Small Businesses

Franklin-Sarrett Publishers
3761 Vineyard Trace   Ph: (770)578-9410
Marietta, GA 30062   Fax: (770)973-4243
E-mail: info@franklin-sarrett.com
URL: http://www.franklin-sarrett.
Contact: Kay Borden, Editor and Publisher, kborden@mindspring.com.
Desc: Provides publicity information for small businesses. *Type:* Newsletter.

Business Franchise Guide

CCH Inc.
2700 Lake Cook Rd.   Ph: (847)267-7000
Riverwoods, IL 60015   Free: 800-449-8114
                             Fax: (847)224-8299
URL: http://www.cch.com
Contact: James Rooney, Editor; Joan Goode, Advertising Dir.
Desc: Directed toward all aspects of franchising, including rules, developments, laws, and state disclosure. *Type:* Newsletter.

Business Market Association

4131 N. Central Expy., Ste. 720
Dallas, TX 75204
Contact: R. Mark King, Pres.
Desc: Small- and medium-sized businesses. Works to bring large corporate lobbying and benefits to companies who do not have the workforce to achieve those benefits. *Type:* Association.

CIBC Small Business Edge

Ariad Custom Publishing
119 Spadina Ave., No. 1005   Ph: (416)971-9294
Toronto, ON, Canada M5V   Free: 800-668-1990
  2L1   Fax: (416)971-9292
Contact: Regina daSilva, Editor.
Desc: Newsletter for small buisness clients of Candian Imperial Bank of Commerce. Recurring features include letters to the editor, interviews, news of educational opportunities, job listings, a calendar of events, book reviews, and notices of publications available. *Type:* Newsletter.

Cleveland Small Business News

Small Business News, Inc.
14725 Detroit Ave. No. 300   Ph: (216)228-6397
Cleveland, OH 44107   Free: 800-988-4726
                             Fax: (216)529-8924
E-mail: 74631.3631@compuserve.com.
Contact: Fred Koury, Publisher.
Desc: Monthly publication. Primary focus is to provide decision makers with solutions to the daily challenges of business growth. *Type:* Periodical.

CommonWealth Letters

National Capital Corporation
PO Box 21172   Free: 800-889-2020
Tampa, FL 33622
Contact: D.D Miller, Editor.
Desc: Provides information and insight to starting entrepreneurships. *Type:* Newsletter.

Dividend$

Florida Small Business Development Centers
University of West Florida
State Director's Office   Ph: (850)595-6060
19 West Garden St., Ste. 300 Free: 800-644-SBDC
Pensacola, FL 32501   Fax: (850)595-6070
E-mail: fsbdc@uuf.edu
URL: http://www.floridasbdc.com.
Contact: Kelly McLeod, Editor.
Desc: Provides information concerning the support services available to small businesses, such as management development, technical information, and marketing assistance. Discusses current legislation, recent developments in the business world, and other issues of concern to small business operators. *Type:* Newsletter.

EduQuest Connections

Mejia & Associates, Inc.
1047 E. 29th St.   Ph: (718)253-5113
Brooklyn, NY 11210   Fax: (718)253-1434
E-mail: EduQuest@ix.netcom.com.
Contact: Aimee Mejia, Publisher; Danette Green, Editor.
Desc: Provides information written and compiled by business owners, business educators, consultants, and journalists for small and home-based business owners. Addresses links between education and business, training, investments, health issues, telecommunications, and technological trends. *Type:* Newsletter.

Family Business Advisor

Business Owner Resources
PO Box 4356   Ph: (770)425-6673
Marietta, GA 30061-0633   Free: 800-551-0633
                             Fax: (770)425-1776
E-mail: busownres@aol.com.
URL: http://www.fbop.com.
Contact: Craig E. Aronoff, Ph.D., Editor.
Desc: Covers business management, family relations, and asset protection. Addresses succession planning, estate planning, conflict management, compensation, family meetings, strategic planning, and board composition. *Type:* Newsletter.

Family Business Professional

Harcourt Brace Professional Publishing
525 B St., No. 1900   Ph: (619)699-6716
San Diego, CA 92101-4495   Free: 800-831-7799
                             Fax: (619)699-6716
URL: http://www.hbpp.com; http://www.hbpp.com.
Desc: Advises on strategies and information to develop and maintain a family-owned business. *Type:* Newsletter.

Franchise News

Franchise News
3820 Premier Ave.   Ph: (901)368-3333
Memphis, TN 38118   Fax: (901)368-1144
E-mail: franmark@msn.com; franmark@msn.com.
Contact: R. C. Richey, Editor.
Desc: Provides information about franchising. Recurring features include letters to the editor, interviews, news of research, a calendar of events, news of educational opportunities, reports of meetings, notices of publications available, and legal and global franchising news. *Type:* Newsletter.

Franchising in Canada

Canadian Franchisors Association
5054 Orbitor Dr., Bldg. 12,   Ph: (416)625-2896
  Unit 201
Mississaqua, ON, Canada L4W
  4Y4
Contact: Margaret Guerrier, Publisher; Gordon Green, Editor.
Desc: Focuses on news about Canadian franchises. *Type:* Newsletter.

Govcon

GovCon, Inc
1445 Research Blvd.   Ph: (301)545-6868
5th Floor   Fax: (301)545-6899
Rockville, MD 20850
E-mail: raj@govcon.com
URL: http://www.govcon.com/
Contact: Raj Khera, raj@govcon.com.
Desc: GovCon is a site dedicated to helping contractors with U.S. Federal Government contracts. *Type:* Database.

The Home Business Advocate

Alternate Press
RR 1   Ph: (519)448-4001
St. George, ON, Canada N0E   Fax: (519)448-4411
  1N0
E-mail: natural@life.ca
URL: http://www.life.ca
Contact: Wendy Priesnitz, Editor and Publisher.
Desc: Discusses business topics of interest to home-based business owners. *Type:* Newsletter.

Home Business Idea Possibility Newsletter

Prosperity & Profits Unlimited, Distribution Services
PO Box 416   Ph: (303)575-5676
Denver, CO 80201-0416
Contact: A. Doyle, Publisher.
Desc: Offers ideas for home businesses. *Type:* Newsletter.

The Home Business Report

The Kerner Group, Inc.
PO Box 19
Martins Creek, PA 18063-0019
Contact: Rick Kerner, Editor.
Desc: Provides information on how to operate a home-based business or work from home. Features real life success stories, "how-to" articles on marketing, and strategies to keep focused on goals. *Type:* Newsletter.

Home Income Reporter

Red Hot Publishing Co.

PO Box 7423   Ph: (609)835-2347
Trenton, NJ 08628-0423   Fax: (609)835-2324

Contact: Ed Durham, Editor and Publisher; F. Henderson, Circulation Mgr.

Desc: Furnishes information on how to start up and run a home-based business. Recurring features include book reviews and profiles of successful home-based businesses. *Type:* Newsletter.

Home Treasures Newsletter

Home Treasures
1250 Clark Mill Rd.
Sweet Home, OR 97386-3014

Desc: Publishes information on successful home-based businesses. *Type:* Newsletter.

The Home Workplace

The Worksteaders Club
1126 Glengrove Ave. W.
North York, ON, Canada M6B
    2K4

Contact: Maurice Boychuk, Editor.

Desc: Provides information on 700 Canadian companies that utilize services of home based workers, freelance professionals, and entrepreneuers. *Type:* Newsletter.

Homebased

Joyce E. Francis
450 Lexington Ave.
Grand Central PO Box 2614
New York, NY 10163-2614

Contact: Joyce E. Francis, Editor and Publisher.

Desc: Profiles successful home-based businesses and offers advice to those who would like to operate their own home-based business. *Type:* Newsletter.

HomeWorking

Essence Communications, Inc.
1500 Broadway, 6th Fl.   Ph: (212)642-0600
New York, NY 10036   Free: 800-274-9398
    Fax: (212)921-5173

Desc: Provides information on how to start and run a home-based business. *Type:* Newsletter.

I'm Too Busy to Read Marketing Report Service

Win-Win Marketing
16501 Franklin Rd.   Ph: (408)247-0122
Fort Bragg, CA 95437-8714   Fax: (408)249-5754
E-mail: towin@aol.com

Contact: Oran Kangas, Editor; Frankie Kangas, Publisher.

Desc: Provides marketing information for small businesses. *Type:* Newsletter.

Independent Operations

American Financial Services Association (AFSA)
Government Affairs Department   Ph: (202)296-5544
919 18th St. NW   Fax: (202)223-0321
Washington, DC 20006
E-mail: afsa@afsamail.com
URL: http://www.americanfinsvcs.com.

Contact: Thomas L. Thomas, Editor.

Desc: Furnishes members with news of the financial services industry, small business, and other areas of concern to the members of the Association's Section on Independent Operations. Provides news of current legislation, regulations, and individual/company profiles. *Type:* Newsletter.

International Association of Business

701 Highlander Blvd., Ste. 110   Ph: (817)465-2922
Arlington, TX 76015-4325   Fax: (817)467-5940

Contact: Paula Rainey, Pres.

Desc: Small business owners. Keeps members informed of trends in the business industry. *Type:* Association.

International Franchise Association

1350 New York Ave. NW, Ste.   Ph: (202)628-8000
    900   Fax: (202)628-0812
Washington, DC 20005
E-mail: ifa@franchise.org
URL: http://www.franchise.org

Contact: Don J. DeBolt, Pres.

Desc: Firms in 100 countries utilizing the franchise method of distribution for goods and services in all industries. *Type:* Association.

International Gay and Lesbian Franchise Association

2765 N Scottsdale Rd., Ste.
    104D
Scottsdale, AZ 85257
E-mail: gayfranch@aol.com

Contact: Thomas R. Cutler, Pres.

Desc: Gay and lesbian potential franchisee owners; franchisors. Works to insure that gay and lesbian people are not discriminated against in the granting of franchise businesses. *Type:* Association.

Making Money at Home

Summit Productions, Inc.
461 Loyside Dr., Ste. 105
Winchester, VA 22602

Contact: Ed Helvey, Editor.

Desc: Designed for people working part or full time from their homes, whether for a company, government agency, or self-employed. Offers business, management, marketing and sales tips. *Type:* Newsletter.

More Business

Settel Associates, Inc.
11 Wimbledon Court   Ph: (516)681-1505
Jericho, NY 11753

Contact: Trudy Settel, Editor.

Desc: Provides information and ideas of interest to small business owners. Carries marketing advice, management tips, and success stories. *Type:* Newsletter.

Most Likely to Succeed

Richard Siedlecki Consulting, Inc.
4767 Lake Forrest Dr. NE   Ph: (404)303-9900
Atlanta, GA 30342-2539
E-mail: sied@mindspring.com

Desc: Provides tips, techniques, and insights on managing and marketing small and growing businesses. Recurring features include interviews, news of research, book reviews, and notices of publications available. *Type:* Newsletter.

NASBIC News

National Association of Small Business Investment Companies (NASBIC)
666 11th St. NW, No. 750   Ph: (202)628-5055
Washington, DC 20001   Fax: (202)628-5080
E-mail: nasbic@nasbic.org
URL: http://www.nasbic.org.

Contact: Jeanette D. Paschal, Editor, jpaschal@nasbic.org.

Desc: Provides information about firms licensed as small business investment companies (SBICs) under the Small Business Investment Act of 1958. Covers new or proposed regulations and legislation, executive branch developments, and Small Business Administration funding. *Type:* Newsletter.

National Association for the Cottage Industry

PO Box 14850   Ph: (773)472-8116
Chicago, IL 60614   Fax: (773)472-8117
E-mail: corlaee@worldnet.att.net

Contact: Coralee Smith Kern, Contact.

Desc: People who work in their homes (known as "worksteaders"), either producing merchandise, providing services, or using a flexible work site, such as a computer terminal in the home connected to a main system elsewhere. Acts as an advocacy group for cottage workers; provides access to information on business organizational methods, marketing, promotion, and financial and family assistance; builds and develops a database of information from areas such as zoning, taxing, and licensing requirements, government reports, profiles on successful home-based businesses, accounting procedures, and legal questions. Develops solutions to deal with the unique problems connected with the cottage industry, such as worker isolation. *Type:* Association.

National Association for the Self-Employed

PO Box 612067   Free: 800-232-NASE
Dallas, TX 75261-2067   Fax: 800-551-4446
URL: http://www.nase.org

Contact: Bennie Thayer, Pres. & CEO.

Desc: Self-employed and small independent businesspersons. Acts as an advocate at the state and federal levels for self-employed people. *Type:* Association.

National Association of Small Business Investment Companies

666 11th St. NW, No. 750   Ph: (202)628-5055
Washington, DC 20001   Fax: (202)628-5080
E-mail: nasbic@nasbic.org
URL: http://www.nasbic.org

Contact: Lee W. Mercer, Pres.

Desc: Firms licensed as small business investment companies (SBICs) under the Small Business Investment Act of 1958. *Type:* Association.

National Business Association

PO Box 700728   Ph: (214)458-0900
Dallas, TX 75370   Free: 800-456-0440
    Fax: (214)960-9149
E-mail: nbal2@airmail.net
URL: http://www.nationalbusiness.org

Contact: Robert G. Allen, Pres.

Desc: Employed owners of small businesses. Promotes and assists the growth and development of small businesses. *Type:* Association.

National Business Owners Association

820 Gibbon St. Ste. 204   Ph: (202)737-6501
Alexandria, VA 22314   Free: 888-713-NBOA
    Fax: (703)838-0149
E-mail: mikenboa@erols.com
URL: http://www.nboa.com

Contact: Thomas Rumfelt, Chm.

Desc: Small business owners. Promotes the interests of small business. *Type:* Association.

National Federation of Independent Business

53 Century Blvd., Ste. 250   Ph: (615)872-5800
Nashville, TN 37214   Fax: (615)872-5353
URL: http://www.nfibonline.com

Contact: Fred Holladay, VP & CFO.

Desc: Independent business and professional people. Presents opinions of small and independent business to state and national legislative bodies. *Type:* Association.

National Small Business United

1156 15th St. NW, Ste. 1100   Ph: (202)293-8830
Washington, DC 20005   Free: 800-345-6728
    Fax: (202)872-8543
E-mail: nsbu@nsbu.org
URL: http://www.nsbu.org
Contact: Todd McCraken, Pres.
Desc: Small businesses including manufacturing, wholesale, retail, service, and other firms. Purposes are to advocate at the federal level on behalf of smaller businesses. *Type:* Association.

NBIA Review

National Business Incubation Association (NBIA)
20 Circle Dr., Ste. 190   Ph: (740)593-4331
Athens, OH 45701-3211   Fax: (740)593-1996
E-mail: info@nbia.org; shayhow@nbia.org.
URL: http://www.nbia.org.
Contact: Sally Hayhow, Editor, shayhow@nbia.org.
Desc: Serves as an information exchange and network for individuals interested in business incubation. (Incubators are facilities that provide low-cost space, shared office services, and management and technical consulting to new and fledging firms.) *Type:* Newsletter.

New York State Small Business Development Center

State University of New York   Ph: (518)443-5398
SUNY Central Pl., S-523   Fax: (518)465-4992
Albany, NY 12246
E-mail: kingjl@sbdc.suny.edu
URL: http://www.smallbiz.suny.edu/nysbdc.htm
Contact: James L. King, State Dir.
Desc: Regional centers providing information and assistance to small businesses. Makes available training and counseling services. *Type:* Association.

On Target

William Hartsman & Associates
PO Box 784   Ph: (513)339-0336
Troy, OH 45373-0784
Contact: William Hortsman, Editor and Publisher.
Desc: Presents strategic planning and marketing concepts geared toward small and midsize companies. *Type:* Newsletter.

Our Place

Home-Based Working Moms
PO Box 500164   Ph: (512)266-0900
Austin, TX 78750-0164   Fax: (512)918-1471
E-mail: hbwm@hbwm.com
URL: http://www.hbwm.com.
Contact: Lesley Spencer, Editor, lesley@hbwm.com.
Desc: Advocates home employment and home businesses to allow parents more time with their children. Offers ideas, marketing tips, member profiles to promote successful employment at home. *Type:* Newsletter.

Penny-Pinchers Periodical

CD Kloek & Associates
843 E. Main St., Suite 100   Fax: (503)776-3429
Medford, OR 97504-7137
Contact: Chris Kloek, Publisher.
Desc: Offers advice on profit making and saving money for small businesses. *Type:* Newsletter.

Perspectives on Family Business

Newkirk Products
15 Corporate Dr.   Ph: (518)452-1000
Albany, NY 12203-5154
Desc: Directed toward family businesses. *Type:* Newsletter.

The Pick & Shovel Marketing Report

Beyond Marketing Group, Inc.
PO Box 11344   Ph: (910)924-9443
Winston-Salem, NC 27116-   Fax: (910)924-0062
1344
Contact: Lynette Hawkins, President.
Desc: Provides marketing ideas for small businesses on how to increase sales without spending significant amounts of money. Includes ideas on promotion, advertising, and image building. *Type:* Newsletter.

Profit - The Bottom Line in Greater New Haven Business

Greater New Haven Chamber of Commerce
900 Chapel St., 10th Fl.   Ph: (203)782-4300
New Haven, CT 06510-2865   Fax: (203)782-4729
E-mail: gnhcc@connix.com; info@gnhcc.com
URL: http://www.newhavenchamber.com.
Contact: Thomas R. Violante, Editor.
Desc: Provides the latest news on issues affecting businesses in the New Haven area. Discusses transportation and environmental topics, the workforce, and retail and economic developments. *Type:* Newsletter.

Profits

Small Business Development Center
Howard University
2600 Sixth St., NW, Rm. 125   Ph: (202)806-1550
Washington, DC 20059-0001
Contact: Mary Merchant, Editor.
Desc: Discusses ways to increase profits for small businesses. *Type:* Newsletter.

Quick-Solutions

Vincent Shelton
PO Box 1266
Upper Marlboro, MD 20773-
1266
Contact: B.L. Chancey, Editor.
Desc: Publishes news and information of interest to small businesses. Also provides computer articles. *Type:* Newsletter.

Safe Money Report

Weiss Publishing & Marketing
4176 Burns Rd.   Ph: (561)684-3300
West Palm Beach, FL 33410   Free: 800-289-9222
Desc: Provides financial business news for both small and large businesses. *Type:* Newsletter.

SBANE Enterprise

Smaller Business Association of New England (SBANE)
204 2nd Ave.   Ph: (781)890-9070
Waltham, MA 02451   Free: 800-366-6803
    Fax: (781)890-4567
E-mail: info@sbane.org
URL: http://www.pbane.org
Contact: Julie Scofield, Editor.
Desc: Reports on matters of concern to those who are engaged in small businesses in the New England area. Includes news of government actions and legislation and economic trends. *Type:* Newsletter.

SBDC News

Sponsor-Iowa Small Business Development Centers
Iowa State University   Ph: (515)292-6351
137 Lynn
Ames, IA 50010-7126
Contact: Jan DeYoung, Publisher.
Desc: Explores assistance and reports services available to small businesses in Iowa. *Type:* Newsletter.

SCOR Report

SCOR Report
PO Box 781992   Ph: (972)620-2489
Dallas, TX 75378-1992   Fax: (972)406-0213
Contact: Tom Stewart-Gordon, Editor, tsg@scor-report.com.
Desc: Deals with capital formation alternatives for small companies with emphasis on public offerings using the Small Corporate Offering Registration Exemption found under Regulations A and D of the Securities Acts of 1933 as amended. Aims to help small companies, their lawyers, accountants and advisors raise capital by keeping them up to date on changes in state and federal laws, regulations and programs. *Type:* Newsletter.

Score Association

Service Corps of Retired Executives Association
409 3rd St. SW, 4th Fl.   Ph: (202)205-6762
Washington, DC 20024   Free: 800-634-0245
    Fax: (202)205-7636
URL: http://www.score.org
Contact: W. Kenneth Yancey, Jr., Exec.Dir.
Desc: Volunteer program sponsored by U.S. Small Business Administration in which active and retired business management professionals provide free management assistance to men and women who are considering starting a small business, encountering problems with their business, or expanding their business. SCORE offers free one-on-one counseling and low cost workshops on a variety of business topics. *Type:* Association.

Self Employment Update

Update Publicare Co.
c/o Prosperity & Profits   Ph: (303)575-5676
Unlimited
PO Box 416
Denver, CO 80201
Contact: A.C. Doyle, Editor.
Desc: Introduces readers to the broad interest of self-employment. Carries news of relevant books. *Type:* Newsletter.

The Small Business Advisor

Small Business Advisors, Inc.
PO Box 436   Ph: (516)295-1387
Woodmere, NY 11598   Free: 800-669-0773
E-mail: smalbusadv@aol.com
Contact: Joseph Gelb, Publisher; Ann Liss, Editor.
Desc: Seeks to help emerging growth companies increase profits. Considers small business issues, including marketing sales, finance, taxes, organizing, competition, management, and human resources. *Type:* Newsletter.

The Small Business Advocate

Office of Advocacy
U.S. Small Business Administration
409 3rd St. SW   Ph: (202)205-6531
Washington, DC 20416   Fax: (202)205-6928
URL: http://www.sba.gov/advo/news.
Contact: John Ward, Managing Editor.
Desc: Provides updates on activities and issues of the Office of Advocacy, which examines the impact of legislative proposals and other public policy issues on small businesses. *Type:* Newsletter.

Small Business Assistance Center

554 Main St.   Ph: (508)756-3513
PO Box 15014   Fax: (508)770-0528
Worcester, MA 01615-0014
Contact: Francis R. Carroll, Pres.
Desc: A division of the Small Business Service Bureau. Businesses with less than 100 employees. Offers planning and strategy programs to aid businesspersons in starting, improving, or expanding small businesses. *Type:* Association.

Small Business Builder
MarketLine
824 S. Main St.   Ph: (815)356-8800
Crystal Lake, IL 60014   Fax: (815)356-8804
Contact: John Cummata, Editor and Publisher; Lois Cummata, Circulation Director; Michael DiFrisco, Art Director.
Desc: Focuses on management, marketing, and profits for small businesses. *Type:* Newsletter.

Small Business Chronicle
Philadelphia Small Business Chronicle, Inc.
3012 Butler Pike
Conshohocken, PA 19428-2115
Contact: Libby Barland, Publisher; Greg Matusky, Editor.
Desc: Publishes items of interest to small businesses. *Type:* Newsletter.

Small Business Computing
SBE Reports
6 Stumpbridge Rd.   Ph: (215)355-6084
PO Box 6   Fax: (215)364-2212
Southampton, PA 18966
Contact: C. Moore, Editor.
Desc: Provides information to small business executives. *Type:* Newsletter.

Small Business Council of America—Alert
Small Business Council of America, Inc.
4800 Hampden Ln., 7th Fl.   Ph: (301)656-7603
Bethesda, MD 20814   Fax: (301)654-7354
Contact: Alan P. Cleveland, Editor.
Desc: Monitors federal tax legislation affecting small business. Reports on the Council's advocacy in support of legislation creating economic incentives for small businesses. *Type:* Newsletter.

Small Business Digest
Costar Enterprises
PO Box 1620
Pineville, WV 24874-1620
Contact: Nigel Maxey, Editor.
Desc: Publishes news items and topics of interest to small businesses. *Type:* Newsletter.

Small Business Economic Trends
National Federation of Independent Business Education Foundation
600 Maryland Ave. SW, Ste.   Ph: (202)554-9000
770   Fax: (202)554-5572
Washington, DC 20024-2520
Desc: Analyzes economic trends for small businesses. *Type:* Newsletter.

Small Business Executive Report
Charles Moore Associates, Inc.
Box 6, Stump Rd.   Ph: (215)355-6084
Southampton, PA 18966-0006   Fax: (215)364-2212
Desc: Covers economic and commercial trends and other information related to small businesses. *Type:* Newsletter.

Small Business News Report
Home Office Management Services
1151 NE Todd George Rd.   Ph: (816)525-4484
Lees Summit, MO 64086-5332   Fax: (816)525-4484
Contact: Beth Smith, Editor, bob-bethsmith@att.net.
Desc: Directed toward persons working from home or would like to be a homebaser. Recurring features include news of educational opportunities, book reviews, and notices of publications available and start-up tips. *Type:* Newsletter.

Small Business Opportunities
Harris Publications, Inc.
1115 Broadway, 8th Fl.   Ph: (212)807-7100
New York, NY 10010-2803   Fax: (212)627-4678
E-mail: smallbizop@harris-pub.com.
Contact: Stanley Harris, Publisher; Susan Rakowski, Editor, (212)462-9567; Arlene Jaffee, Advertising Mgr., (212)462-9544.
Desc: How-to magazine for small business owners. *Type:* Periodical.

Small Business Service Bureau
554 Main St.   Ph: (508)756-3513
PO Box 15014   Fax: (508)770-0528
Worcester, MA 01615-0014
Contact: Francis R. Carroll, Pres.
Desc: Businesses employing fewer than 100 individuals. Provides national assistance concerning small business group insurance, cash flow, taxes, and management problems. Offers legislative advocacy, group benefit services, group insurance, and group health plans. *Type:* Association.

Small Business Systems
Charles Moore Associates, Inc.
Box 6, Stump Rd.   Ph: (215)355-6084
Southampton, PA 18966-0006   Fax: (215)364-2212
Type: Newsletter.

The Small Business Tax Review
A/N Group, Inc.
17 Scott Dr.   Ph: (516)549-4090
PO Box 895
Melville, NY 11747
E-mail: angroup@pb.net
URL: http://www.smbiz.com; http://www.smbiz.com.
Contact: Steven A. Hopfenmuller, Editor.
Desc: Reports tax news on such topics as new laws, court cases, IRS rulings, fringe benefits, and business and individual taxes, with emphasis on smaller businesses. Advises on financial planning and technical aspects of small business management. *Type:* Newsletter.

Small Business Taxes and Management
A/N Group, Inc.
17 Scott Dr.   Ph: (516)549-4090
PO Box 895
Melville, NY 11747
E-mail: angroup@pb.net
URL: http://www.smbiz.com; http://www.smbiz.com.
Contact: Steven A. Hopfenmuller, Publisher.
Desc: Offers current tax news, reviews of recent cases, tax saving tips, and personal financial planning for small business owners. Includes articles on issues such as finance and management. *Type:* Newsletter.

Small Business-USA
National Small Business United
1156 15th St. NW, Ste. 1100   Free: 800-243-7232
Washington, DC 20005   Fax: (202)872-8543
URL: http://www.nsbu.org
Contact: Tara Lytle, Editor-in-Chief.
Desc: Reports on activities of the Association on behalf of small businesses in the Washington, DC, area. *Type:* Newsletter.

Small Business Wealth Builder
Enterprise Publishing
6069 Crown Royal Cir.
Alexandria, VA 22310-1744
Contact: Ted Nicholas, Publisher; Ann Faccenda, Editor.
Desc: Discusses ways for small businesses to increase their profitibility. *Type:* Newsletter.

Small Business Wire
Business Communications Co., Inc.
25 Van Zant St.   Ph: (203)853-4266
Norwalk, CT 06855-1781   Fax: (203)853-0348
E-mail: buscom2@aol.com
URL: http://www.buscom.com
Contact: Robert Ward, Editor.
Desc: Reports on business news from the Council. *Type:* Newsletter.

Small Corporation Update
Harcourt Brace & Company
525 B St., Ste. 1900   Ph: (619)231-6616
San Diego, CA 92101-4495   Free: 800-831-7799
   Fax: (619)699-6593
E-mail: propub@harcourtbrace.com; newsletters@hbpp.com.
Contact: John L. Springer, Editor and Publisher.
Desc: Provides information and advice for small corporations. Includes tax and management information. *Type:* Newsletter.

Visions of Success
Business-By-The-Book
PO Box 290284   Ph: (612)924-2442
Minneapolis, MN 55429   Fax: (612)305-4600
Contact: Tami Athens, Editor.
Desc: Provides tips and information to help entrepreneurs succeed in business. Topics include sales/marketing, communication, leadership, training, and a listing of support organizations, training opportunities, and business products. *Type:* Newsletter.

Winning Ways
Winning Ways
PO Box 39412   Ph: (612)835-5647
Minneapolis, MN 55439
Contact: Barbara J. Winter, Editor.
Desc: Provides information and ideas for the self-employed. *Type:* Newsletter.

Soccer

American Youth Soccer Organization
12501 S. Isis   Ph: (310)643-6455
Hawthorne, CA 90250   Free: 800-USA-AYSO
   Fax: (310)640-5310
URL: http://www.soccer.org
Contact: Dick Wilson, Exec.Dir.
Desc: Individuals dedicated to the development of children in America through youth soccer. In process of developing a library. *Type:* Association.

National Soccer Coaches Association of America
6700 Squibb Rd., Ste. 215   Ph: (913)362-1747
Mission, KS 66202-3252   Free: 800-458-0678
   Fax: (913)362-3439
E-mail: mmcfarl104@aol.com
URL: http://www.nscaa.com
Contact: James Sheldon, Contact.
Desc: Soccer coaches and interested individuals. *Type:* Association.

Soccer America-Yellow Pages
Soccer America
1235 10th St.   Ph: (510)528-5000
Berkeley, CA 94710   Free: 800-997-6223
   Fax: (510)528-5177
URL: http://www.socceramerica.com.
Contact: Julie Lauer, Editor.
Desc: List of over 5,000 youth and adult soccer clubs, organizations, and leagues; suppliers of soccer products and services; sponsors of soccer tournaments; directory of national soccer organizations, professional teams, European teams, and complete list of FIFA offices, continental and national offices. *Type:* Directory.

Soccer Association for Youth

4050 Executive Park Dr., Ste. 100
Cincinnati, OH 45241
Ph: (513)769-3800
Free: 800-233-7291
Fax: (513)769-0500
E-mail: sayusa@saysoccer.org
URL: http://www.saysoccer.org
Contact: Sheila A. Shay, Dir. of Operations.
Desc: Children ages four through 18 who are interested in soccer. Supported by a network of coaches, administrators, and sponsors. Seeks to assure maximum participation with even competition at various age levels and to offer equal opportunity regardless of ability or sex. *Type:* Association.

South Texas Youth Soccer Association

PO Box 1370
Georgetown, TX 78627-1370
Ph: (512)863-4969
Fax: (512)869-4785
E-mail: marilynt@igg-tx.net
Contact: Bill Forest, Pres.
Desc: Soccer players between the ages of five and 19. Seeks to develop and promote the game of soccer for young people. *Type:* Association.

Touchline

Soccer Association for Youth U.S.A.
4050 Executive Park Dr., Ste. 100
Cincinnati, OH 45241
Ph: (513)769-3800
Free: 800-233-7291
Fax: (513)769-0500
E-mail: sayusa@saysoccer.org
URL: http://sayusa@saysoccer.org
Contact: Janine Sullivan, Editor, jsullivan@saysoccer.org.
Desc: Provides information and instruction for soccer coaches and parents of children who play soccer. Recurring features include reports of meetings. *Type:* Newsletter.

United States Youth Soccer Association

899 Presidential Dr., Ste. 117
Richardson, TX 75081
Ph: (972)235-4499
Free: 800-467-2237
Fax: (214)235-4480
URL: http://www.usysa.org/index2.htm
Contact: Al Abeson, Dir. of Operations.
Desc: The youth division of United States Soccer Federation. Soccer players between the ages of five and 19. Seeks to develop and promote the game of soccer for young people. *Type:* Association.

Virginia Youth Soccer Association

2239G Tacketts Mill Dr.
Woodbridge, VA 22192-3024
Ph: (703)494-0030
Fax: (703)551-4114
E-mail: vysa@aol.com
URL: http://www.vysa.com
Contact: Julie Caramanica, State Admin.
Desc: Soccer coaches, administrators, players, and volunteers. Promotes and develops soccer for youths under age 19 in Virginia and the District of Columbia. *Type:* Association.

Social Clubs

The Associated Clubs

1 Townsite Plz., Ste. 315
Topeka, KS 66603
Ph: (785)232-0892
Fax: (785)232-0892
Contact: Ben B. Franklin, Pres.
Desc: Husband and wife social dinner clubs seeking to facilitate an exchange of ideas between local and national leaders in business, public affairs, and the professions, regardless of other club, party, or religious affiliations. Works to keep the public informed on problems of government, business, industry, finance, and the professions through addresses by national leaders. *Type:* Association.

Bald-Headed Men of America

102 Bald Dr.
Morehead City, NC 28557
Ph: (919)726-1855
Fax: (919)726-6061
E-mail: jcapps4102@aol.com
URL: http://members.aol.com/baldusa
Contact: John T. Capps, III, Founder.
Desc: Bald-headed men who agree with the philosophy "Bald is beautiful." Dedicated to the belief that bald-headed men (whether chrome-dome, balding pate, or bald spot) have extra individual character. Strives to cultivate a sense of pride for all bald-headed men and to eliminate the loss of self-esteem associated with the loss of hair. Promotes National Rub a Bald Head Week. *Type:* Association.

DeMolay International

10200 N. Executive Hills Blvd.
Kansas City, MO 64153-1367
Ph: (816)891-8333
Fax: (816)891-9062
E-mail: demolay@demolay.org
URL: http://www.demolay.org
Contact: Jeff Speaker, Exec.Dir.
Desc: Fraternal organization for young men between the ages of 13 (or 12 years if completed 7th grade) and 21. Seeks to build character and develop leadership abilities in young men. *Type:* Association.

International Brotherhood of Old Bastards

2330 S. Brentwood Blvd., Ste. 666
St. Louis, MO 63144-2096
Ph: (314)544-3311
Fax: (314)961-9828
Contact: Bro. Cozen P. Bantling, Supreme Archbastard.
Desc: Fraternal organization that offers members "no committees, no assessments, no responsibilities, no annual dues - a lifetime membership card and the opportunity to prove you're a real bastard." Conducts 10 symposia/year. *Type:* Association.

International Directory of Swing Clubs, Publications, and Events

North American Swing Club Association (NASCA)
PO Box 7128
Buena Park, CA 90622-7128
Ph: (714)229-4870
Fax: (714)821-9919
E-mail: nasca@nasca.com
URL: http://www.nasca.com.
Contact: Robert McGinley, PhD, Editor.
Desc: Over 600 heterosexual swing clubs (recreational social sex), conventions, publications, computer services, organizations, tours, and special events; limited international coverage. *Type:* Directory.

Lefthanders International

PO Box 8249
Topeka, KS 66608
Ph: (785)234-2177
Fax: (785)232-3999
Contact: Dean R. Campbell, Publisher & Pres.
Desc: Individuals who are lefthanded. Serves the needs and interests of lefthanders worldwide; addresses issues of discrimination and scarcity of products; recognizes lefthanders' accomplishments in areas of sports, entertainment, the arts, and the work world. Offers a complete line of mail order products designed specifically for lefthanders. *Type:* Association.

Mikes of America

PO Box 580075
Minneapolis, MN 55458
Ph: (612)722-4704
Contact: Michael D. Nelson, Pres.
Desc: A nationwide promotional campaign to unite all of the "Mikes" in America. To solidify the nominative bond and promote the heritage of the name that has existed "since the time of the Archangels." *Type:* Association.

National Association of Single People

380 E. Yale Loop
Irvine, CA 92614
Ph: (949)654-0040
Fax: (602)994-9700
Contact: Richard Baron, Contact.
Desc: Promotes improvement of benefits and representation for single community. *Type:* Association.

Procrastinators' Club of America

Box 712
Bryn Athyn, PA 19009
Ph: (215)947-9020
Fax: (215)947-7007
Contact: Les Waas, Pres.
Desc: Individuals who promote the philosophy of relaxation through putting off until later those things that needn't be done today. Activities include a Christmas party in June and a Fourth of July picnic in January, plus various unusual and offbeat events that publicize the art of procrastination. Honors "Be Late for Something Day," Sept. *Type:* Association.

Redheads International

537 Newport Center Dr.
Newport Beach, CA 92660
Ph: (949)249-4411
Free: 800-247-6553
E-mail: redking@earthlink.net
URL: http://www.redheadclub.com
Contact: Stephen Douglas, Pres. & Founder.
Desc: Redheads in 30 countries. United to promote an attractive and positive image of redheads. *Type:* Association.

Social Fraternities

Acacia

8777 Purdue Rd., Ste. 130
Indianapolis, IN 46268
Ph: (317)872-8210
Fax: (317)872-8213
E-mail: acacianat@aol.com
URL: http://www.acacia.org
Contact: Darold W. Larson, Exec.Dir.
Desc: Social fraternity. Sponsors Shriner's Burns Institute for Children. *Type:* Association.

Alpha Chi Rho

109 Oxford Way
Neptune, NJ 07753
Ph: (732)869-1895
Fax: (732)988-5357
E-mail: axprbhq@aol.com
Contact: Mr. D. Matthew Jenkins, Exec.Dir.
Desc: Social fraternity. Maintains AXP Educational Foundation. *Type:* Association.

Alpha Delta Phi

6126 Lincoln Ave.
Morton Grove, IL 60053
Ph: (847)965-1832
Fax: (847)965-1871
Contact: Terri Eastmade, Asst.Dir.
Desc: Social fraternity. Sponsors literary competitions; maintains placement service, biographical archives, and museum. Conducts educational programs. *Type:* Association.

Alpha Delta Pi

1386 Ponce de Leon Ave. NE
Atlanta, GA 30306
Ph: (404)378-3164
Contact: Lorie Brown, Exec.Dir.
Desc: Social sorority. *Type:* Association.

Alpha Epsilon Pi

8815 Wesleyan Rd.
Indianapolis, IN 46268-1171
Ph: (317)876-1913
Fax: (317)876-1057
E-mail: aepihq@indy.net
URL: http://www.aepi.org
Contact: Sidney N. Dunn, Exec.VP.
Desc: Social fraternity. Maintains Alpha Epsilon Pi Foundation as philanthropic arm that awards scholarships, loans, and grants. *Type:* Association.

Alpha Kappa Lambda

2902 N. Meridian   Ph: (317)924-4265
Indianapolis, IN 46208   Fax: (317)924-4271
Contact: R. Keith Gilchrist, Exec.Dir.
Desc: Social fraternity. Sponsors The Alpha Kappa Lambda Educational Foundation. Maintains small library; compiles statistics. *Type:* Association.

Alpha Phi Delta

236 N. Governors Ave.
Dover, DE 19904-3116
E-mail: centralo@dmv.com
Contact: Jim Lentini, Exec.Sec.
Desc: Men's social fraternity. *Type:* Association.

Alpha Sigma Phi

8645 Guion Rd., Ste. J   Ph: (317)870-1911
Indianapolis, IN 46268-3028   Fax: (317)872-8272
E-mail: alpha.sigs@iquest.net
Contact: Thomas R. Hinkley, Exec.VP.
Desc: General fraternity. *Type:* Association.

Alpha Tau Omega

One North Pennsylvania St.   Ph: (317)684-1865
12th Fl.   Fax: (317)684-1862
Indianapolis, IN 46204
URL: http://www.ato.org
Contact: Wynn R. Smiley, Exec.Dir.
Desc: Social and leadership development fraternity. *Type:* Association.

Beta Theta Pi

PO Box 6277   Ph: (513)523-7591
5134 Bonham Rd.   Free: 800-800-2382
Oxford, OH 45056   Fax: (513)523-2381
E-mail: sbecker@wooglin.com
URL: http://www.BetaThetaPi.org
Contact: Stephen B. Becker, Adm.Sec.
Desc: Social fraternity. *Type:* Association.

The Caduceus

Kappa Sigma Fraternity
PO Box 5066   Ph: (804)295-3193
Charlottesville, VA 22905   Fax: (804)296-9557
E-mail: mailbox@imh.kappasigma.org
URL: http://www.kappasigma.org.
Contact: W. Len Rayburn, Editor, lrayburn@kappasigma.org.
Desc: Kappa Sigma fraternity magazine. *Type:* Periodical.

Chi Psi

20180 Governors Hwy., Ste.   Ph: (708)283-1480
303   Fax: (708)283-1490
Olympia Fields, IL 60461
URL: http://www.chipsi.org
Contact: Don Kreger, Exec.Dir.
Desc: Social fraternity. Maintains Chi Psi Educational Trust. Conducts leadership institutes and self-development programs. *Type:* Association.

Degree of Pocahontas, Improved Order of Red Men

4521 Speight Ave.   Ph: (817)756-1221
Waco, TX 76711-1708   Fax: (817)756-4828
E-mail: redman@texasinternet.com
URL: http://www.redmen.org
Contact: Robert E. Davis, Sec.
Desc: A degree of the Great Council of U.S. Improved Order of Red Men for Red Men and their female relatives and friends. Goals are "freedom, friendship and charity." Maintains museum. *Type:* Association.

Delta Kappa Epsilon

35 McKinley Pl.   Ph: (313)886-2400
Grosse Pointe Farms, MI 48236   Free: 800-560-3353
    Fax: (313)886-2227
E-mail: deke@home.com
URL: http://www.dke.org
Contact: David K. Easlick, Jr., Exec.Dir.
Desc: Social fraternity. Provides counseling and advice to undergraduate and alumni groups on chapter operation and management. *Type:* Association.

Delta Sigma Phi

330 S. Oxford Ave.   Ph: (513)523-1907
Oxford, OH 45056-0230   Fax: (513)523-7292
E-mail: centraloffice@dspnet.org
URL: http://www.dspnet.org
Contact: John Hockman, Exec.Dir.
Desc: Social fraternity. *Type:* Association.

Delta Upsilon

8705 Founders Rd.   Ph: (317)875-8900
PO Box 68942   Fax: (317)876-1629
Indianapolis, IN 46268
E-mail: ihq@deltau.org
URL: http://www.deltau.org
Contact: Abraham L. Cross, Exec.Dir.
Desc: General men's fraternity. Provides educational programming, service opportunities, social activities, and life skills training. Operates biographical achives and museum. *Type:* Association.

Dramatic Order Knights of Khorassan

110 N. Wabash Ave.   Ph: (317)664-7925
Marion, IN 46952-2614   Fax: (317)664-7925
E-mail: mfk46952@comteck.com
Contact: Martin Koehler, Imperial Sec.
Desc: Fraternal order auxiliary of the Supreme Lodge Knights of Pythias. Sponsors humanitarian activities. Offers student loans for children of members. *Type:* Association.

Epsilon Sigma Phi

PO Box 626   Ph: (218)864-8678
Battle Lake, MN 56515   Fax: (218)864-8064
E-mail: jscarlson@aol.com
URL: http://www.llcsp-nat.tamu.edu
Contact: Judith S. Carlson, Exec.Dir.
Desc: Honorary fraternity - extension professionals in the Land Grant University Extension Service and United States Department of Agriculture Extension Program. *Type:* Association.

Farmhouse

11020 NW Ambassador Dr.,   Ph: (816)891-9445
Ste. 330   Fax: (816)891-0838
Kansas City, MO 64153
Desc: Social fraternity. *Type:* Association.

Fraternal Order of Orioles

Raymond N. Martzall
1 Synder St.   Ph: (717)336-7653
Denver, PA 17517
Contact: Raymond N. Martzall, Exec. Officer.
Desc: Men's fraternal society with auxiliaries. *Type:* Association.

Great Council of U.S. Improved Order of Red Men

4521 Speight Ave.   Ph: (817)756-1221
Waco, TX 76711-1708   Fax: (817)756-4828
E-mail: redmen@iamerica.com
URL: http://www.members.xoom.com/redmen/

Contact: Robert E. Davis, Sec.
Desc: Fraternal society of American citizens. Contributes to local charities. Maintains museum. *Type:* Association.

Junior Order, Knights of Pythias

1495 Hancock St.   Ph: (617)472-8800
Quincy, MA 02169   Fax: (617)376-0363
E-mail: kop@earthlink.net
Contact: Alfred A. Saltzman, Supreme Sec.
Desc: Young men's auxilary of the Supreme Lodge Knights of Pythias. Promotes the ideals of fraternity, patriotism, health, and character for boys between the ages of 12 and 17. Conducts educational and charitable programs. *Type:* Association.

Kappa Alpha Order

PO Box 1865   Ph: (540)463-1865
Lexington, VA 24450   Fax: (540)463-2140
E-mail: kaohdq@aol.com
URL: http://www.ka-order.org
Contact: Larry S. Wiese, Exec.Dir.
Desc: Social fraternity. Compiles statistics; maintains biographical records archives and museum. Conducts drug and alcohol awareness programs; operates speakers' bureau. *Type:* Association.

Kappa Alpha Psi

2322-24 N. Broad St.   Ph: (215)228-7184
Philadelphia, PA 19132   Fax: (215)228-7181
Contact: Richard Lee Snow, Exec.Dir.
Desc: Social fraternity. Sponsors charitable and educational programs and children's services. Maintains speakers' bureau and placement service; compiles statistics. *Type:* Association.

Kappa Delta Rho

331 S. Main St.   Ph: (724)838-7100
Greensburg, PA 15601   Fax: (724)838-7101
E-mail: kdr@kdr.com
Contact: Shawn M. Hoke, Exec.Dir.
Desc: Strives for promotion of Greek life and/or the fraternity. *Type:* Association.

Kappa Sigma

PO Box 5066   Ph: (804)295-3193
Charlottesville, VA 22905   Fax: (804)296-9557
E-mail: kscaduceus@aol.com
URL: http://www.kappasigma.org
Contact: Mitchell B. Wilson, Exec.Dir.
Desc: Social fraternity. *Type:* Association.

The Key Reporter

Phi Beta Kappa Society
1785 Massachusetts Ave., NW,   Ph: (202)265-3808
4th Fl.   Fax: (202)265-0083
Washington, DC 20036
E-mail: scholar@pbk.org
Contact: Priscilla S. Taylor, Editor.
Desc: Functions as an official publication of Phi Beta Kappa, a liberal arts and sciences honorary society for men and women college graduates. Recurring features include news of members, articles of general interest, and book reviews. *Type:* Newsletter.

Kiwanis Magazine

Kiwanis International
3636 Woodview Trace   Ph: (317)875-8755
Indianapolis, IN 46268-3196   Free: 800-549-2647
    Fax: (317)879-0204
E-mail: kiwanismail@kiwanis.org
Contact: Charles M. Jonak, Managing Editor, cjonak@kiwanis.org; Patrick A. Hatcher, Advertising Dir., phatcher@kiwanis.org.

Desc: Magazine covering business, professional, and topics of general interest to Kiwanis. *Alt. Contact:* 3636 Woodview Trace, Indianapolis, IN 46268; toll-free: 800-549-2647. *Type:* Periodical.

Lambda Chi Alpha

8741 Founders Rd. Ph: (317)872-8000
Indianapolis, IN 46268 Fax: (317)875-3828
E-mail: headquarters@lambdachi.org
URL: http://www.lambdachi.org
Contact: Thomas A. Helmbock, Exec.VP.
Desc: General Fraternity. Maintains hall of fame and museum. Founder of the North American Food Drive, which raises more than 1 million pounds of food each year for the needy. *Type:* Association.

Legionarios del Trabajo in America

Grand Lodge Ph: (209)463-6516
2154 S. San Joaquin St. Fax: (209)463-6516
Stockton, CA 95206
Contact: Gloria Villarta, Sec.
Desc: Fraternal organization. Provides specialized education; holds seminars. Operates charitable program; plans to establish a library. *Type:* Association.

The Lion Magazine

Lions Clubs International
300 W. 22nd St. Ph: (630)571-5466
Oak Brook, IL 60523-8815 Fax: (630)571-8890
Contact: Robert Kleinfelder, Editor, (630)571-5466; Mary Kay Rietz, Advertising & Production Manager, (630)571-5466.
Desc: Magazine containing club news for service minded men and women. *Type:* Periodical.

Mooseheart, International

Rte. 31 Ph: (630)859-2000
Mooseheart, IL 60539 Fax: (630)859-6616
URL: http://www.mooseintl.org
Contact: Frank A. Sarnecki, Dir.Gen.
Desc: Fraternal organization comprising of a men's component (Loyal Order of Moose) and a women's component (Women of the Moose). *Type:* Association.

National Beta Club

151 W. Lee St. Ph: (864)583-4553
Spartanburg, SC 29306-3012 Free: 800-845-8281
  Fax: (864)542-9300
E-mail: betaclub@betaclub.org
URL: http://www.betaclub.org
Contact: George W. Lockamy, Exec.Dir.
Desc: Academic-Leadership-service organization for students. Junior Beta Club includes fifth through ninth grade students; Senior Beta Club includes ninth through 12 grades. Activities and meetings focus on leadership, character development and community service. *Type:* Association.

Omega Gamma Delta

89 Longview Rd. Ph: (516)883-2897
Port Washington, NY 11050- Fax: (516)883-7460
  3039
Contact: Robert S. Tarleton, Sec.
Desc: High school men's social fraternity and associated alumni organization. Conducts charitable programs. *Type:* Association.

Omega Psi Phi

3951 Snapfinger Pkwy. Ph: (404)284-5533
Decatur, GA 30035 Fax: (404)284-0333
Contact: Alonza Bennett, Dir.
Desc: Social fraternity. *Type:* Association.

Phi Beta Sigma Frat

145 Kennedy St. NW Ph: (202)726-5424
Washington, DC 20011-5294 Fax: (202)882-1681
Contact: Dr. Lawrence E. Miller, Exec.Dir.
Desc: Seeks to develop and translate into functional realities the ideals of brotherhood, service, and scholarship. *Type:* Association.

Phi Delta Theta

2 S. Campus Ave. Ph: (513)523-6345
Oxford, OH 45056 Fax: (513)523-9200
E-mail: ghq@phidelt-ghq.com
URL: http://www.PhiDelt-GHQ.com/
Contact: Robert A. Biggs, Exec.VP.
Desc: General fraternity. Conducts educational programs. Maintains museum. *Type:* Association.

Phi Gamma Delta

1201 Red Mile Rd. Ph: (606)255-1848
PO Box 4599 Fax: (606)253-0779
Lexington, KY 40544-4599
Contact: William A. Martin, III, Exec.Dir.
Desc: Men's college fraternity. *Type:* Association.

The Phi Gamma Delta

Phi Gamma Delta Fraternity
PO Box 4599 Ph: (606)255-1848
Lexington, KY 40544-4599 Fax: (606)253-0779
E-mail: phigam@mis.net.
Contact: William A. Martin, III, Editor; Suzanne Cox, Publications Coord.
Desc: Fraternity magazine. *Type:* Periodical.

Phi Kappa Sigma

2 Timber Dr. Ph: (610)469-3232
Chester Springs, PA 19425 Fax: (610)469-3286
Contact: Robert Miller.
Desc: Social fraternity. Conducts educational and charitable programs. *Type:* Association.

Phi Kappa Tau

15 N. Campus Ave. Ph: (513)523-4193
Oxford, OH 45056 Fax: (513)523-9325
E-mail: john@phikappatau.org
URL: http://www.phikappatau.org
Contact: John M. Green, Exec. Dir.
Desc: Social fraternity. Conducts educational and scholarship programs. Sponsors competitions. *Type:* Association.

Phi Kappa Theta National

3901 W. 86th St., Ste. 125 Ph: (317)872-9934
Indianapolis, IN 46268 Fax: (317)879-1889
E-mail: phikapexec@aol.com
URL: http://www.phikaps.org
Contact: Mark T. McSweeney, Exec.Dir.
Desc: Social fraternity. Maintains membership data. Provides leadership development opportunities. *Type:* Association.

Phi Mu Delta

PO Box 296 Ph: (814)234-0626
State College, PA 16804 Fax: (814)237-4296
E-mail: pmd@shas.com
Contact: Jane Weaver, Adm.Asst.
Desc: Social fraternity. Maintains data banks and archives. *Type:* Association.

Phi Sigma Kappa

2925 E. 96th St. Ph: (317)573-5420
Indianapolis, IN 46240 Fax: (317)573-5430
Contact: Thomas E. Recker, Exec.VP.
Desc: Social fraternity. Grants foundation scholarships. Maintains library; conducts educational programs. *Type:* Association.

Pi Beta Phi

7730 Carondelet, Ste. 333 Ph: (314)727-7338
St. Louis, MO 63105 Fax: (314)727-8049
E-mail: pibetaphi@compuserve.com
URL: http://www.pibetaphi.org
Contact: Renee R. Mercer, Exec.Dir.
Desc: Social fraternity. *Type:* Association.

Pi Kappa Alpha

8347 W. Range Cove Ph: (901)748-1868
Memphis, TN 38125 Fax: (901)748-3100
URL: http://www.pka.com
Contact: Raymond L. Orians, Exec.VP.
Desc: Social fraternity. Compiles statistics; promotes philanthropic activities. *Type:* Association.

Pi Kappa Phi

PO Box 240526 Ph: (704)504-0888
Charlotte, NC 28224 Fax: (704)521-8962
URL: http://www.pikapp.org
Contact: Mark E. Timmes, CEO.
Desc: Social fraternity. *Type:* Association.

Pi Lambda Phi

98 Millplain Rd., Ste. 3-C Ph: (203)794-9003
Danbury, CT 06811 Fax: (203)794-9057
Contact: Alan V. Wunsch, Contact.
Desc: Social fraternity. *Type:* Association.

Psi Upsilon

3003 E. 96th St. Ph: (317)571-1833
Indianapolis, IN 46240-1307 Fax: (317)844-5170
URL: http://www.psiu.org
Contact: Mark A. Williams, Exec.Dir.
Desc: General fraternity. Provides educational programming. *Type:* Association.

Rosicrucian Order, AMORC English Grand Lodge

1342 Naglee Ave. Ph: (408)947-3600
Rosicrucian Park Fax: (408)947-3677
San Jose, CA 95191
URL: http://www.rosicrucian.org
Contact: Kristie Knutson, Pres.
Desc: International fraternal order. Maintains Rose-Croix University International; the Rosicrucian Egyptian Museum, housing thousands of exhibits on ancient civilizations and an art gallery; the Rosicrucian Planetarium; research library. *Type:* Association.

The ROTARIAN

Rotary International
One Rotary Center Ph: (847)866-3000
1560 Sherman Ave. Fax: (847)866-9732
Evanston, IL 60201
E-mail: 75457.3577@compuserve.com.
Contact: Willmon L. White, Editor-in-Chief, (847)866-3046; Edward A. Schimmelpfennig, Advertising Mgr., (847)866-3195, schimme@riorc.mhs.compuserve.c; Charles W. Pratt, Editor, (847)866-3205, prattc@riotc.mhs.compuserve.com.
Desc: General interest magazine on community service and international understanding. *Type:* Periodical.

The Royal Neighbor

Royal Neighbors of America
230 16th St. Ph: (309)788-4561
Rock Island, IL 61201 Free: 800-627-4762
  Fax: (309)788-9234
E-mail: rnafield@ix.netcom.com; rnafields@ix.netcom.com.
Contact: Kathy Teel, APR, Sr. Mgr., Public Relations/Printing.

Desc: Fraternal magazine. *Type:* Periodical.

The Sample Case
The Order of United Commercial Travelers of America
632 N. Park St.   Ph: (614)228-3276
PO Box 159019   Free: 800-848-0123
Columbus, OH 43215-8619   Fax: (614)228-1898
Contact: Megan Woitovich, Editor; David Knapp, Art Dir.
Desc: Fraternal magazine. *Type:* Periodical.

Shield & Diamond
Pi Kappa Alpha Fraternity
8347 W. Range Cove   Ph: (901)748-1868
Memphis, TN 38125   Fax: (901)748-3100
E-mail: pka@wspi.wspice.com
URL: http://www.pka.com.
Contact: Kevin E. Virta, Editor; Barbara E. Perkins, Managing Editor.
Desc: College fraternity magazine. *Type:* Periodical.

Sigma Alpha Epsilon
PO Box 1856   Ph: (847)475-1856
Evanston, IL 60204   Free: 800-233-1856
                                      Fax: (847)475-2250
E-mail: saenational@msn.com
Contact: Richard L. Lies, Exec.Dir.
Desc: Social fraternity. *Type:* Association.

Sigma Alpha Mu
651 N. Range Line Rd.   Ph: (317)846-0600
Carmel, IN 46032   Fax: (317)846-9462
E-mail: samhq@aol.com
URL: http://www.sam.org
Contact: Aaron M. Girson, Exec.Dir.
Desc: Social fraternity. Operates charitable program. *Type:* Association.

Sigma Chi Corporation
1714 Hinman Ave.   Ph: (847)869-3655
Evanston, IL 60204
URL: http://www.sigmachihq.org
Contact: Mark Anderson, Exec. Officer.
Desc: Social fraternity. *Type:* Association.

Sigma Nu
PO Box 1869   Ph: (703)463-1869
Lexington, VA 24450   Fax: (703)463-1669
Contact: R. Bradley Beacham, Dir. of Prog.Svcs.
Desc: Social fraternity. Sponsors professional training. Operates hall of fame and museum. *Type:* Association.

Sigma Phi Epsilon
310 S. Boulevard   Ph: (804)353-1901
PO Box 1901   Fax: (804)359-8160
Richmond, VA 23218-1901
URL: http://www.ngesigephq.org
Contact: Jacques Vauclain, Exec.Dir.
Desc: Social fraternity. Maintains Sigma Phi Epsilon Educational Foundation and National Housing Corporation. *Type:* Association.

Sigma Phi Epsilon Journal
Sigma Phi Epsilon Fraternity, Inc.
Box 1901   Ph: (804)353-1901
Richmond, VA 23218   Fax: (804)359-8160
E-mail: hq@sigephq.org; journal@sigephq.org.
URL: http://www.sigep.org/periodic.
Contact: Nathan E. Gamble, Editor/Publication Dir., gamble@sigephq.org.
Desc: Sigma Phi Epsilon national fraternal magazine. *Type:* Periodical.

Sigma Pi Fraternity, International
PO Box 1897   Ph: (812)882-1897
Vincennes, IN 47591   Free: 800-FEB-1897
                                      Fax: (812)726-4602
E-mail: sigmapihq@aol.com
URL: http://www.sigmapi.org/
Contact: Mark S. Briscoe, Jr., Exec.Dir.
Desc: Social fraternity. *Type:* Association.

Sigma Tau Gamma
101 Ming St.   Ph: (660)747-2222
PO Box 54   Fax: (816)747-9599
Warrensburg, MO 64093
E-mail: stghq@iland.net
Contact: William P. Bernier, Exec.VP.
Desc: Social fraternity. *Type:* Association.

Supreme Grove, United Ancient Order of Druids
Daniel R. Arndts
4040 Merrimac Ave.   Ph: (937)276-5672
Dayton, OH 45405
E-mail: danatlowrider@netscape.net
Contact: Daniel R. Arndts, Supreme Sec.-Treas.
Desc: Men and women who believe in the principles of "Unity, Peace, and Concord" as well as a Supreme Being and are "United to Assist". *Type:* Association.

Supreme Lodge Knights of Pythias
1495 Hancock St.   Ph: (617)472-8800
Quincy, MA 02169   Fax: (617)376-0363
E-mail: kop@earthlink.net
URL: http://www.pythias.org
Contact: Alfred A. Saltzman, Supreme Sec.
Desc: Seeks to follow the example of the story of Damon and Pythias and encourage brotherly love. *Type:* Association.

Tau Epsilon Phi
120 West Merchant Street   Ph: (609)573-9575
Audubon, NJ 08106   Fax: (609)573-9441
E-mail: tep@pipeline.com
URL: http://www.tep.org
Contact: George Hasenberg, Pres.
Desc: Social and educational fraternity. Operates hall of fame and museum; conducts charitable program. Maintains Tau Epsilon Phi Foundation to provide scholarships and student aid funds. *Type:* Association.

Tau Kappa Epsilon
8645 Founders Rd.   Ph: (317)872-6533
Indianapolis, IN 46268   Fax: (317)875-8353
E-mail: tkeogc@tkehq.org
URL: http://www.tlcehq.org
Contact: Timothy J. Murphy, CEO & Exec.VP.
Desc: Social fraternity. Maintains charitable program; conducts educational programs on leadership and character development. *Type:* Association.

Theta Chi
3330 Founders Rd.
Indianapolis, IN 46268
Contact: David L. Westol, Exec.Dir.
Desc: Social fraternity. Maintains museum. Compiles statistics. *Type:* Association.

Theta Delta Chi
135 Bay State Rd.   Ph: (617)262-2815
Boston, MA 02215-1708   Free: 800-999-1847
                                      Fax: (617)262-3798
E-mail: tdxcfo@aol.com
Contact: Todd Daniels, Dir. of Operations.
Desc: Social fraternity. Conducts charitable and educational programs. Sponsors Theta Delta Chi Educational Foundation and Theta Delta Chi Founder's Corporation. *Type:* Association.

Theta Nu Epsilon Society
3538 Central Ave., Ste. 2A Ph: (909)684-6778
Riverside, CA 92506   Free: 800-TNE-1870
E-mail: notnes@pe.net
URL: http://www.pe.net/notnes
Contact: John L. Louderback, Contact.
Desc: Sophomores, juniors, seniors, and alumni of universities. Cultivates leadership ability and "a sense of manhood." *Type:* Association.

Theta Xi
9974 Old Olive Street Rd.   Ph: (314)993-6294
St. Louis, MO 63141   Fax: (314)993-6608
E-mail: TXHQ@ThetaXiHQ.org
URL: http://www.thetaxihq.org
Contact: Alan L. Gardner, Exec.Dir.
Desc: College social fraternity. *Type:* Association.

The Trident of Delta Delta Delta
Delta Delta Delta
PO Box 5987   Ph: (817)633-8001
Arlington, TX 76005-5987   Fax: (817)652-0212
E-mail: trideltaeo.org@trideltaeo.org; trident@trideltaeo.org.
Desc: Women's fraternity magazine. *Type:* Periodical.

Ukrainian Fraternal Association
440 Wyoming Ave.   Ph: (717)342-0937
Scranton, PA 18503   Fax: (717)347-5649
Contact: Ivan Oleksyn, Pres.
Desc: Fraternal benefit life insurance society. *Type:* Association.

Zeta Beta Tau
5905 Vincennes Rd., Ste. 101 Ph: (317)334-1898
Indianapolis, IN 46268-3025
E-mail: zbtnational@zbt.org
Contact: Jonathon I. Yulish, Exec.Dir.
Desc: Social fraternity. *Type:* Association.

Zeta Psi Fraternity of North America
15 S. Henry St.   Ph: (914)735-1847
Pearl River, NY 10965   Fax: (914)735-1989
Contact: Gregory J. Plezia, Exec.Dir.
Desc: Social fraternity. Sponsors Leadership Training Institute, providing professional training and seminars. Maintains Zeta Psi Educational Foundation and Zeta Psi Foundation of Canada. *Type:* Association.

Social Sciences

Heritage
Southern California Library for Social Studies and Research
6120 S. Vermont Ave.   Ph: (323)759-6063
Los Angeles, CA 90044   Fax: (323)759-2252
E-mail: archives@sociallib.org
Desc: Reports news of the Library, "a leading resource center specializing in radical, progressive, labor and minorities literature." Provides information on Library-sponsored conferences and programs, new collections, research services, issues of social history, and plans for future development. Recurring features include news of research and a calendar of events. *Type:* Newsletter.

Inform
120 Wall St.   Ph: (212)361-2400
New York, NY 10005-4001   Fax: (212)361-2412
E-mail: inform@informinc.org
URL: http://www.informinc.org
Contact: Joanna Underwood, Pres.
Desc: Examines business practices that harm the environment and endanger public health and report on practical actions that can be taken to prevent or alleviate these problems. *Type:* Association.

Institute for Social Research

University of Michigan   Ph: (734)764-8363
426 Thompson St.   Fax: (734)764-2377
Ann Arbor, MI 48104-2321
E-mail: isr@mail.isr.umich.edu
URL: http://www.isr.umich.edu
Contact: David L. Featherman.
Desc: Social science research professionals and supportive
staff engaged in social science research on a national and
an international basis. Conducts research on a broad range
of subjects utilizing four constituent research centers: Survey Research Center is concerned primarily with the study
of large populations, organizations, and special segments
of society and generally utilizes interview surveys; Research
Center for Group Dynamics is concerned with the development of the basic science of behavior in groups, as well
as social factors in human cognition, perception, and development; Center for Political Studies investigates a variety of political behavior, focusing on national politics in
many countries, and maintains a data archive with a collection of election and other social science data. Other activities and services include: intercenter programs and
special projects; international research, education, and
consultation. *Type:* Association.

National Council for the Social Studies

3501 Newark St. NW   Ph: (202)966-7840
Washington, DC 20016-3167   Fax: (202)966-2061
E-mail: ncss@ncss.org
URL: http://www.ncss.org
Contact: Martharose Laffey, Exec.Dir.
Desc: Teachers of elementary and secondary social studies,
including instructors of civics, geography, history, law,
economics, political science, psychology, sociology, and
anthropology; interested others. Promotes the teaching of
social studies to the best advantage of the student. *Type:*
Association.

Pi Gamma Mu

1001 Millington St., Ste. B   Ph: (316)221-3128
Winfield, KS 67156   Fax: (316)221-7124
E-mail: pgm@jinx.sckans.edu
URL: http://www.sckans.edu/~pgm
Contact: Sue Watters, Exec.Dir.
Desc: Honor society - social science. *Type:* Association.

Social Sciences Index

H.W. Wilson Company
950 University Ave.   Ph: (718)588-8400
Bronx, NY 10452
E-mail: custserv@hwwilson.com
URL: http://www.hwwilson.com
Contact: Technical Support Department.
Desc: Contains citations to articles and book reviews in
some 415 English-language periodicals (starting in February 1983) in the social sciences. Covers anthropology, economics, environmental sciences, geography, law and
criminology, planning and public administration, political
science, psychology, social aspects of medicine, sociology,
international relations, and related subjects. *Available:*
Ovid Technologies, Inc.; OCLC Online Computer Library Center, Inc., OCLC EPIC; OCLC Online Computer Library Center, Inc., OCLC FirstSearch Catalog;
Ameritech Library Services, Vista; SilverPlatter Information, Inc.; H.W. Wilson Company, WilsonWeb. *Type:*
Database.

Social SciSearch®

Institute for Scientific Information (ISI)
3501 Market St.   Ph: (215)386-0100
Philadelphia, PA 19104
E-mail: isiorder@isinet.com
URL: http://www.isinet.com

Desc: Contains complete bibliographic data plus citations
to significant articles from the 1500 most important social
sciences journals worldwide and social sciences articles
from 3200 journals in the natural, physical, and biomedical sciences. Corresponds to the Social Sciences Citation
Index publication and the online Social SciSearch® database. *Available:* The Dialog Corporation, DataStar; The
Dialog Corporation, DIALOG; The Dialog Corporation,
DIALOG; DIMDI (Deutsches Institut fuer Medizinische
Dokumentation und Information); DIMDI (Deutsches
Institut fuer Medizinische Dokumentation und Information). *Type:* Database.

Social Sororities

Alpha Chi Omega

5939 Castle Creek Pky. N Dr.   Ph: (317)579-5050
Indianapolis, IN 46250   Fax: (317)579-5051
URL: http://www.alphachiomega.org
Contact: Nancy Leonard, Exec.Dir.
Desc: Social sorority. Sponsors Alpha Chi Omega Founda-
tion. *Type:* Association.

Alpha Epsilon Phi

111 Prospect St., No. 2
Stamford, CT 06901-1208
Contact: Bonnie Rubenstein, Exec.Dir.
Desc: Social sorority. *Type:* Association.

Alpha Gamma Delta

8701 Founders Rd.   Ph: (317)872-2655
Indianapolis, IN 46268   Fax: (317)875-5824
Contact: Julie Cretin, Exec.Dir.
Desc: Social sorority. *Type:* Association.

Alpha Omicron Pi

9025 Overlook Blvd.   Ph: (615)370-0920
Brentwood, TN 37027   Fax: (615)371-9736
E-mail: aoiihq@alphaomicronpi.org
URL: http://www.alphaomicronpi.org
Contact: Melanie Doyle, Exec.Dir.
Desc: Social sorority. *Type:* Association.

Alpha Phi International Fraternity

4301 Sherman Ave.   Ph: (847)475-0663
Evanston, IL 60201   Fax: (847)475-6820
E-mail: fraternity@alphaphi.org
URL: http://www.alphaphi.org
Contact: Catherine M. Collins, Exec.Dir.
Desc: Social sorority. *Type:* Association.

Alpha Sigma Alpha

9001 Weslyan Rd., Ste. 200   Ph: (317)871-2920
Indianapolis, IN 46268   Fax: (317)871-2924
E-mail: asa@pcis.net
URL: http://www.alphasigmaalpha.org
Contact: Lisa Tait Longo, Exec.Dir.
Desc: General sorority. *Type:* Association.

Alpha Sigma Tau

1929 Canyon Rd.   Ph: (205)978-2179
Birmingham, AL 35216   Fax: (205)978-2182
URL: http://www.alphasigmatau.org
Contact: Lenore Seibel King, Dir.
Desc: Social sorority. *Type:* Association.

Alpha Xi Delta Women's Fraternity

8702 Founders Rd.   Ph: (317)872-3500
Indianapolis, IN 46268   Fax: (317)872-2947
E-mail: fhq@alphaxidelta.org
URL: http://www.alphaxidelta.org
Contact: Virginia B. Carroll, Exec.Dir.

Desc: Social sorority. *Type:* Association.

Chi Omega

3395 Players Club Pky.   Ph: (901)748-8600
Memphis, TN 38125   Fax: (901)748-8686
Contact: Lissa Morgan, Exec.Dir.
Desc: Social sorority. *Type:* Association.

Delta Delta Delta

2313 Brookhollow Plaza Dr.   Ph: (817)633-8001
PO Box 76005   Fax: (817)652-0212
Arlington, TX 76006
Contact: Cari Cook, Exec.Dir.
Desc: Social sorority. *Type:* Association.

Delta Gamma

3250 Riverside Dr.   Ph: (614)481-8169
PO Box 21397   Fax: (614)481-0133
Columbus, OH 43221-0397
Contact: Margaret Hess Watkins, Exec.Dir.
Desc: Social sorority. Delta Gamma Foundation serves as
channel for philanthropic activities. Sponsors annual semi-
nar for alumnae advisers to collegiate chapters and rush
seminar for collegiate officers. *Type:* Association.

Delta Phi Epsilon

734 W. Port Plz., Ste. 271   Ph: (314)275-2626
St. Louis, MO 63146   Fax: (314)275-2655
E-mail: info@dphie.org
URL: http://www.dphie.org
Contact: Ellen Alper, Exec.Dir.
Desc: Social sorority. *Type:* Association.

Delta Zeta

202 E. Church St.   Ph: (513)523-7597
Oxford, OH 45056   Fax: (513)523-1921
Contact: Cynthia W. Menges, Exec.Dir.
Desc: Social sorority. *Type:* Association.

Gamma Phi Beta

12737 E. Euclid Dr.   Ph: (303)799-1874
Englewood, CO 80111-6445   Fax: (303)799-1876
E-mail: execdir@gammaphibeta.com
Contact: Alison W. Maguire, Exec.Dir.
Desc: Social sorority. Operates networking service for
members who are traveling or moving. Maintains girls
camp. *Type:* Association.

Kappa Alpha Theta

8740 Founders Rd.   Ph: (317)876-1870
Indianapolis, IN 46268   Fax: (317)876-1925
Contact: Elizabeth Sierk, Exec.Dir.
Desc: Social sorority. Conducts educational programs.
Type: Association.

Kappa Delta

3205 Players Ln.   Ph: (901)748-1897
Memphis, TN 38125   Free: 800-536-1897
    Fax: (901)748-0949
Contact: Elisabeth Wibker, Nat'l. Pres.
Desc: Social sorority. *Type:* Association.

Kappa Kappa Gamma

530 E. Town St.   Ph: (614)228-6515
Box 38   Fax: (614)228-7809
Columbus, OH 43216
Contact: J. Dale Brubeck, Exec.Dir.
Desc: Social sorority. Serves as a network for career infor-
mation; offers placement service. Maintains Heritage Mu-
seum with exhibits pertaining to the history of women and
sorority memorabilia. *Type:* Association.

Phi Mu
3558 Habersham at Northlake   Ph: (770)496-5582
Tucker, GA 30084   Fax: (770)496-0833
Contact: Lana Lewis, Exec.Dir.
Desc: Social sorority sponsors charitable and educational activities; offers placement service. Conducts competitions. *Type:* Association.

Phi Sigma Sigma
23123 State Rd. 7, Ste. 250   Ph: (561)451-4415
Boca Raton, FL 33428   Fax: (561)451-4576
Contact: Dianne Macey, Exec. Officer.
Desc: Social sorority. *Type:* Association.

Sigma Delta Tau
111 Congressional Blvd. Ste 110   Free: 800-745-1917
Carmel, IN 46032-5651
Contact: Ann Stringer Braly, Exec.Dir.
Desc: Social sorority. Presents awards and scholarships. Offers career networking for alumnae, placement services, and educational loans. *Type:* Association.

Sigma Kappa
8733 Founders Rd.   Ph: (317)872-3275
Indianapolis, IN 46268   Fax: (317)872-0716
Contact: Dr. Tisa Mason, Exec.Dir.
Desc: Social sorority. *Type:* Association.

Sigma Sigma Sigma
Box 466   Ph: (540)459-4212
Woodstock, VA 22664   Fax: (540)459-2361
Contact: Paula Geary, CAE, Contact.
Desc: Social sorority. *Type:* Association.

Supreme Temple Order Pythian Sisters
Wenonah Jones
PO Box 1257   Ph: (406)563-6433
Anaconda, MT 59711
Contact: Wenonah Jones, Supreme Sec.
Desc: Women's auxiliary of the Supreme Lodge Knights of Pythias. Donates to many projects benefitting blood drives, retarded citizens, and patients suffering from cancer, cystic fibrosis, polio, cerebral palsy, and heart and kidney ailments. *Type:* Association.

Theta Phi Alpha
27025 Knickerbocker Rd.
Bay Village, OH 44140-2343
URL: http://members.aol.com/TPAweb
Contact: Tammy Lenhart, Contact.
Desc: Social sorority. Sponsors annual Founders Day; conducts fundraising projects for charitable organizations. *Type:* Association.

Zeta Tau Alpha
3450 Founders Rd.   Ph: (317)872-0540
Indianapolis, IN 46268   Fax: (317)876-3948
Contact: Deb Ensor, Exec.Dir.
Desc: Social sorority. *Type:* Association.

Social Welfare

Focus: HOPE
1355 Oakman Blvd.   Ph: (313)494-5500
Detroit, MI 48238   Fax: (313)494-4340
E-mail: jackson@novell.focushope.edu
Contact: Eleanor Josaitis, Dir.
Desc: Civil and human rights organization serving the Detroit, MI tri-county area. Sponsors food program for the elderly, and mothers and their children. *Type:* Association.

Kitsap Community Resources
802 7th St.   Ph: (360)478-2301
Bremerton, WA 98337-1512   Fax: (360)415-2706
E-mail: mikeb@kcr.org
URL: http://www.kcr.org
Contact: Larry Eyer, Exec.Dir.
Desc: Operates social service programs in Kitsap County, WA. *Type:* Association.

Tressler Lutheran Services
960 Century Dr.   Ph: (717)795-0300
Mechanicsburg, PA 17055   Fax: (717)795-0353
E-mail: bill_swanger/tls@tressler.org
URL: http://www.tressler.org
Contact: Thomas W. Hurlocker, Pres./CEO.
Desc: Provides health and social services in Pennsylvania, Delaware, and Maryland. *Type:* Association.

Social Work

ADL on the FRONTLINE
Anti-Defamation League of B'nai B'rith
823 United Nations Plaza   Ph: (212)490-2525
New York, NY 10017   Fax: (212)867-0779
Contact: Jane R. Ornauer, Editor.
Desc: Features articles on the League's programs and activities. Recurring features include letters to the editor, interviews, news of research, reports of meetings, news of educational opportunities, book reviews, and notices of publications available. *Type:* Newsletter.

American Association of State Social Work Boards
400 S. Ridge Pky., Ste. B   Ph: (540)829-6880
Culpeper, VA 22701   Free: 800-225-6880
    Fax: (540)829-0142
E-mail: info@aasswb.org
URL: http://www.aasswb.org
Contact: Donna DeAngelis, Exec.Dir.
Desc: State boards and authorities empowered to regulate the practice of social work within their own jurisdictions. Seeks to protect the recipient of social work service and promote confidence in and accountability of the social work profession by establishing national regulatory standards for the practice of professional social work. *Type:* Association.

American Friends Service Committee
1501 Cherry St.   Ph: (215)241-7000
Philadelphia, PA 19102   Free: 800-558-AFSC
    Fax: (215)241-7247
E-mail: afscinfo@afsc.org
URL: http://www.afsc.org
Contact: Kara Newell, Exec.Dir.
Desc: Founded by and related to the Religious Society of Friends (Quakers); supported and staffed by individuals sharing basic values regardless of religious affiliation. Attempts to relieve human suffering and find new approaches to world peace and social justice through nonviolence. Work in 22 countries and 43 areas of the United States includes development and refugee relief, peace education, and community organizing. *Type:* Association.

American Humane Association
63 Inverness Dr. E   Ph: (303)792-9900
Englewood, CO 80112   Fax: (303)792-5333
URL: http://www.americanhumane.org
Contact: Robert F.X. Hart, Pres.
Desc: Organization representing agencies and individuals seeking to prevent cruelty to children and animals. Provides materials on animal care and child abuse and neglect. Offers training for animal care/control agencies and to child protective services personnel. *Type:* Association.

American Public Human Services Association
810 1st St. NE, Ste. 500   Ph: (202)682-0100
Washington, DC 20002-4267   Fax: (202)289-6555
URL: http://www.apwa.org
Contact: A. Sidney Johnson, III, Exec.Dir.
Desc: Public human service agencies, their professional staff members, and others interested in public human services. *Type:* Association.

Catholic Charities USA
1731 King St., Ste. 200   Ph: (703)549-1390
Alexandria, VA 22314   Fax: (703)549-1656
E-mail: info@catholiccharitiesusa.org
URL: http://www.catholiccharitiesusa.org
Contact: Rev. Fred Kammer, SJ, Pres.
Desc: Local Catholic agencies in the U.S. Maintains consulting and information service; promotes research; maintains interest in broad social problems including welfare, teen pregnancy, child hunger and care for the elderly; coordinates Catholic response to disasters in the United States. *Type:* Association.

Center for Human Services
7200 Wisconsin Ave., Ste. 600   Ph: (301)654-8338
Bethesda, MD 20814   Fax: (301)941-8427
URL: http://www.urc-chs.com
Contact: David D. Nicholas, M.D., Dir.
Desc: Provides technical assistance to government, industry, and human service agencies in areas of training, human resource management, leadership and management development, health education, quality assurance, communications, and international development. Assists organizations in enhancing productivity and competitiveness by developing bias-free selection tests, performance appraisals, certification procedures, and job design and redesign. Makes available development services including organizational diagnosis, systems analysis and intervention, change and total quality management, strategic planning, team building, and management coaching and counseling. *Type:* Association.

Christian Foundation for Children and Aging
1 Elmwood Ave.   Ph: (913)384-6500
Kansas City, KS 66103-3719   Free: 800-875-6564
    Fax: (913)384-2211
E-mail: cfca@sky.net
URL: http://www.cfcausa.org
Contact: Louis Finocchario, Exec.Dir.
Desc: Seeks to advance the physical, mental, spiritual, and social welfare of the economically disadvantaged, especially children and aging persons in developing countries U.S. Sponsors provide financial support and correspond with individuals in need; volunteers help provide social services, including medical, educational, and nutritional programs. Provides Christian education and guidance Conducts orientation program for volunteers and Mission Awareness trips to Mexico and Central America. *Type:* Association.

Clinical Social Work Federation
PO Box 3740   Ph: (703)522-3866
Arlington, VA 22203   Free: 800-270-9739
    Fax: (703)522-9441
URL: http://www.cswf.org
Contact: Linda B. O'Leary, Adm. Coord.
Desc: State societies of clinical social work united to provide a vehicle for states and/or regional societies to share concerns common to clinical social work, develop consensual solutions to problems beyond the jurisdiction of any single society, and carry out appropriate courses of action. *Type:* Association.

Council on Accreditation of Services for Families and Children

120 Wall St., Fl. 11   Ph: (212)797-3000
New York, NY 10005-3902   Fax: (212)797-1428
E-mail: coanet@aol.com
URL: http://www.coanet.org
Contact: Jean K. Elder, PhD, VP-Marketing and Business Development.
Desc: Seeks to strengthen and actively promote the quality of social and mental health services that support and improve the lives of children, adults, and families and the well-being of society through nationally recognized standards of best practice for behavioral healthcare organizations. *Type:* Association.

CRISTA Ministries

19303 Fremont Ave. N.   Ph: (206)546-7200
PO Box 330303   Fax: (206)546-7484
Seattle, WA 98133-9703
Contact: James A. Gwinn, Pres.
Desc: Offers services and programs for youth, the elderly, the impoverished, and the troubled. *Type:* Association.

Cuban American National Council

300 SW 12th Ave., 3rd Fl.   Ph: (305)642-3484
Miami, FL 33130   Fax: (305)642-7463
E-mail: info@cnc.org
URL: http://www.cnc.org
Contact: Guarione M. Diaz, Pres. & Exec.Dir.
Desc: Aims to identify the socioeconomic needs of the Cuban population in the U.S. and to promote needed human services. Services the needy through research and human services while advocating on behalf of Hispanics and other minority groups. *Type:* Association.

Employee Assistance Professionals Association

2101 Wilson Blvd., Ste. 500   Ph: (703)522-6272
Arlington, VA 22201-3062   Fax: (703)522-4585
E-mail: eapamain@aol.com
URL: http://www.eap-association.com
Contact: Sylvia Straub, Ph.D., CAE.
Desc: Persons employed in the development or operation of employee assistance programs (EAPs) and/or services as administrators, consultants, or motivational advisors; persons with an interest in the field; individuals enrolled in courses leading to degrees in employee assistance-related disciplines; firms, institutions, and associations. Encourages the systematic development of employee assistance programs. Serves as an advocate with the public and private sectors for the support and development of the EAP movement. *Type:* Association.

Ladies of Charity of the United States of America

PO Box 31697   Ph: (816)942-5622
St. Louis, MO 63131
Contact: Charleen M. Brain, Pres.
Desc: Local autonomous associations operating under the auspices of the Roman Catholic church. Purpose is to give personal service and pastoral care to the poor, the sick, the elderly, and youth wherever and whenever necessary. Conducts national and regional workshops. *Type:* Association.

NASW News

National Association of Social Workers
750 1st St. NE, Ste. 700   Ph: (202)408-8600
Washington, DC 20002-4241   Free: 800-638-8799
    Fax: (202)336-8312
E-mail: naswnews@naswdc.org.
URL: http://www.naswpress.org.
Contact: John O'Neil, MSW, (202)336-8241, joneill@naswdc.org.
Desc: Recurring features include letters to the editor, job listings, notices of publications available, and columns titled From the President, Moving Forward , and Special Work in the Public Eye. *Type:* Newsletter.

National Association of Social Workers

750 First St. NE, Ste. 700   Ph: (202)408-8600
Washington, DC 20002-4241   Free: 800-638-8799
    Fax: (202)336-8312
E-mail: info@naswdc.org
URL: http://www.naswdc.org
Contact: Dr. Josephine Nieves, Exec.Dir.
Desc: Regular members are persons who hold a minimum of a baccalaureate degree in social work. Associate members are persons engaged in social work who have a baccalaureate degree in another field. Student members are persons enrolled in accredited (by the Council on Social Work Education) graduate or undergraduate social work programs. *Type:* Association.

National Benevolent Association of the Christian Church

Ron Hollon
11780 Borman Dr.   Ph: (314)993-9000
St. Louis, MO 63146-4157   Fax: (314)993-9018
URL: http://www.nbacares.org
Contact: Cindy R. Dougherty, Pres.
Desc: Division of Social and Health Services of the Christian Church (Disciples of Christ). Cares for older adults, children, youth, families, children and adults with mental retardation, and individuals who are chronically mentally ill. Services are provided through over 71 facilities or programs in 21 states offering residential living and independent retirement living, nursing care, treatment centers for children who are emotionally disturbed, crisis intervention centers for children, foster care and adoption, single parent training programs, sheltered workshops, group homes for persons who are chronically mentally ill, and day-care centers. *Type:* Association.

National Coalition of Hispanic Health and Human Services Organizations

1501 16th St. NW   Ph: (202)387-5000
Washington, DC 20036   Fax: (202)797-4353
Contact: Jane L. Delgado, Ph.D., Pres.-CEO.
Desc: National coalition of health, mental health, and human service agencies and organizations and professional individuals serving Hispanics. Primary mission is to improve health and human services to Hispanic communities throughout the United States, including Puerto Rico. Works to help Hispanic community-based organizations to develop new model programs, strengthen local infrastructures, and conduct studies. *Type:* Association.

National Council of U.S. Society of St. Vincent de Paul

58 Progress Pky.   Ph: (314)576-3993
Maryland Heights, MO 63043   Fax: (314)576-6755
E-mail: svdpus@aol.com
URL: http://www.svdpuscouncil.org
Contact: Paulette Carron, Communications Dir.
Desc: Catholic laity engaged in personal service, primarily on the parish level. Promotes and practices charity by providing: financial assistance to the poor; counseling services; volunteer and professional social services; summer camps; salvage bureaus; drop-in centers for homeless and aged; personal visitation. *Type:* Association.

Operation PUSH

930 E. 50th St.   Ph: (773)373-3366
Chicago, IL 60615   Fax: (773)373-3571
Contact: Rev. Jessie Jackson, Pres./CEO.
Desc: Seeks to create an ethical atmosphere; encourages self and community motivation and social responsibility. *Type:* Association.

Partnership for the Homeless

305 7th Ave., 13th Fl.   Ph: (212)645-3444
New York, NY 10001-3274   Free: 800-438-0005
    Fax: (212)477-HOME
E-mail: tpfth@aol.com
Contact: Joel Sesser, Pres.
Desc: Provides emergency food and shelter for homeless individuals in the New York City area. Offers selfhelp, job training, counseling, furniture, and other assistance programs aimed at helping the homeless become self-sufficient. *Type:* Association.

Presbyterian Health, Education and Welfare Association

Presbyterian Center, Rm. 3B-   Ph: (502)569-5794
    3041   Fax: (502)569-8034
100 Witherspoon St.
Louisville, KY 40202
Contact: Rev. Helen Locklear, Exec.Dir.
Desc: Health, education, and welfare agencies and programs related to the Presbyterian Church, U.S.A.; individuals with a variety of professional skills who are concerned about issues in the health, education, and welfare fields. Among member agencies are children's homes and services, hospital and health services, homes and services for the aging, community centers, and neighborhood houses. Coordinates HEW programming; establishes standards for the effectiveness of services; organizes social action and research; provides consultative services to community ministries; prepares and distributes materials on critical issues. *Type:* Association.

The Salvation Army

615 Slaters Ln.   Ph: (703)684-5500
PO Box 269   Fax: (703)684-3478
Alexandria, VA 22313
Contact: Commissioner Robert A. Watson, Natl.Cmdr.
Desc: Commissioned officers are ordained ministers devoting full time to religious and social welfare activities; members of local church or corps community centers are known as soldiers. An international Christian religious and charitable movement, organized on a paramilitary pattern, dedicated to meeting the physical, spiritual, and emotional needs of mankind. Work is carried out through local centers of operation which include adult rehabilitation centers, clinics, outpatient programs for unwed mothers, recreation centers, camping programs for children and adults, senior and children's day care, senior housing and activity centers, and emergency feeding and shelter stations; and through service extension units located in communities not supporting a full Salvation Army program, which extend aid in emergencies. *Type:* Association.

Social Work Abstracts

National Association of Social Workers (NASW)
750 First St., NE, Ste. 700   Ph: (202)336-8277
Washington, DC 20002-4241
E-mail: apayne@naswdc.org
Contact: Alfredda H. Payne, Managing Editor, (202)336-8277, fax: (202)336-8311, apayne@naswdc.org.
Desc: Contains more than 36,000 citations, with abstracts, to journal articles, doctoral dissertations, and other materials on social work and related fields. Also contains the complete text of the 1997 Register of Clinical Social Workers. *Available:* National Association of Social Workers (NASW). *Type:* Database.

Unitarian Universalist Association of Congregations - Washington Office for Faith in Action

2026 P St. NW   Ph: (202)296-4672
Washington, DC 20036-6907   Fax: (202)296-4673
E-mail: uuawo@aol.com

URL: http://www.uua.org

Contact: Rev. Meg Riley, Dir.

Desc: A section of the Unitarian Universalist Association Department for Faith in Action. Seeks to apply the insights of humanistic ethics and liberal religion to public policy and the formulation of legislation. Special priority concerns include: reproductive rights, affirmative action, a comprehensive nuclear test ban treaty, racial justice, civil rights, and religious liberties. *Type:* Association.

Volunteers of America

110 S. Union St. Ph: (703)548-2288
Alexandria, VA 22314 Free: 800-899-0089
 Fax: (703)684-1972

Contact: Charles Gould, Pres.

Desc: A Christian human services organization offering over 400 programs in 300 communities across the U.S. for the elderly, youth, families, alcoholics, drug abusers, and the disabled. Compiles statistics; maintains speakers' bureau. *Type:* Association.

Welfare Research, Inc.

112 State St., Ste. 1020 Ph: (518)432-2563
Albany, NY 12207 Fax: (518)432-2564
E-mail: 103353.3003@compuserve.com

Contact: Rebecca McBride, Contact.

Desc: A consulting organization aimed at improving social service agencies operations and services. Provides research, evaluation, training, and technical and management assistance to the human services community. Conducts policy studies in child welfare, adolescent health, teen pregnancy, employment for welfare recipients, and service needs of refugees. *Type:* Association.

Sociology

Alpha Kappa Delta

c/o Al Short Ph: (512)245-2384
Southwest Texas State
 University
Department of Sociology
San Marcos, TX 78666

Contact: Al Short, Contact.

Desc: Honorary society - men and women, sociology. *Type:* Association.

American Sociological Association

1722 N St. NW Ph: (202)833-3410
Washington, DC 20036 Fax: (202)785-0146

Contact: Dr. Felice Levine, Exec. Officer.

Desc: Sociologists, social scientists, and others interested in research, teaching, and application of sociology; graduate and undergraduate sociology students. Compiles statistics. Operates the ASA Teaching Resources Center, which develops a variety of materials useful in teaching sociology. *Type:* Association.

Hastings Center

The Hastings Center Ph: (914)424-4040
Garrison, NY 10524-5555 Fax: (914)424-4545
E-mail: mail@thehastingscenter.org
URL: http://www.thehastingcenter.org

Contact: Thomas Murray, Pres.

Desc: Individuals concerned with medical, professional, and environmental ethics including physicians, nurses, lawyers, administrators, public policymakers, and other academic and health care professionals. Conducts research on issues relevant to ethics. Offers consulting services. *Type:* Association.

Institute for Research in Social Science Public Opinion Poll Question Database

University of North Carolina - Institute for Research in Social Science
Chapel Hill, NC 27599 Ph: (919)962-2211
E-mail: data_archives@irss.unc.edu
URL: http://www.irss.unc.edu/data_archive/pollsearch.html

Desc: The IRSS Data Archive maintains a catalog of the more than 2,800 studies and series in its data holdings, and is one of the oldest and largest archives of machine-readable data in the United States. This site allows users to search the Public Opinion Poll Question Database via a form that allows a wide variety of permutations; this allows for extremely narrow or extremely broad searching. *Type:* Database.

Social Science Research Council

810 7th Ave., Fl. 31 Ph: (212)377-2700
New York, NY 10019-5818 Fax: (212)377-2727
E-mail: lastname@ssrc.org
URL: http://www.ssrc.org

Contact: Orville Gilbert Brim, Interim Pres.

Desc: Social scientists. Promotes the advancement of interdisciplinary research in the social sciences. Encourages the development of new research methods, confronts theoretical controversies, and identifies promising topics and issues for new empirical investigation. *Type:* Association.

Social Work

National Association of Social Workers
750 1st St. NE, Ste. 700 Ph: (202)408-8600
Washington, DC 20002-4241 Free: 800-638-8799
 Fax: (202)336-8312
E-mail: press@naswda.org

Contact: Paula Delo, Executive Editor, pdelo@naswdc.org.

Desc: Magazine for social workers. *Type:* Periodical.

sociofile

Sociological Abstracts, Inc.
Cambridge Scientific Abstracts
PO Box 22206 Ph: (619)695-8803
San Diego, CA 92192-0206
E-mail: socio@cerfnet.com

Contact: Terry M. Owen, Electronics Product Manager.

Desc: Provides more than 445,000 citations and abstracts from the following 2 files: • Sociological Abstracts--contains abstracts of articles from more than 2500 journals and serial publications in the field of sociology and related disciplines in the social and behavioral sciences. Covers original research, monographic publications, conference papers, and dissertations from Dissertation Abstracts International. *Available:* Ovid Technologies, Inc.; EBSCOhost. *Type:* Database.

Sociological Abstracts

Sociological Abstracts, Inc.
Cambridge Scientific Abstracts
PO Box 22206 Ph: (619)695-8803
San Diego, CA 92192-0206
E-mail: socio@cerfnet.com

Contact: Terry M. Owen, Electronic Products Manager, (619)695-8803, fax: (619)695-0416, socio@cerf.net.

Desc: Contains information on sociology and social policy from 1963 to the present. Comprises the following 2 files: • Social Planning, Policy & Development Abstracts (SOPODA)--contains citations, with abstracts, to articles from more than 2500 journals and serials covering the social sciences, including social welfare, planning and policy, and development, as applied to specific settings and situations. *Available:* Ovid Technologies, Inc.; The Dialog

Corporation, DIALOG; DIMDI (Deutsches Institut fuer Medizinische Dokumentation und Information); OCLC Online Computer Library Center, Inc., OCLC FirstSearch Catalog; The Gale Group, InfoTrac Web. *Type:* Database.

Sociology of Death and Dying

Trinity College
715 Stadium Dr. Ph: (210)736-7011
San Antonio, TX 78212
E-mail: sjones@trinity.edu
URL: http://www.trinity.edu/~mkearl/death.html

Desc: An exceptional collection of sociology resources on the issues of death and dying, this site presents a well-organized and easily accessible collection to the web-browsing public. Examine such aspects of this subject death in the arts; death across cultures and time; ghosts and alleged contact with the dead; Americans' belief in the Devil; death and consumerism; and much, much more. *Type:* Database.

Softball

Amateur Softball Association of America

2801 NE 50th St. Ph: (405)424-5266
Oklahoma City, OK 73111- Fax: (405)424-3855
 7203
URL: http://www.softball.org

Contact: Ron Radigonda, Exec.Dir.

Desc: National Governing body for amateur softball in the U.S.; regulates 56,000 umpires and more than 260,000 teams. Programs include National Softball Hall of Fame, a Junior Olympic youth softball and clinics and coaching schools. *Type:* Association.

National Softball Association

PO Box 7 Ph: (606)887-4114
Nicholasville, KY 40340 Fax: (606)887-4874
E-mail: nsahdqtrs@aol.com

Contact: Hugh Cantrell, Exec.Dir.

Desc: Promotes participation in and enjoyment of amateur softball. Maintains hall of fame. *Type:* Association.

United States Specialty Sports Association

3935 S. Crater Rd. Ph: (804)732-4099
Petersburg, VA 23805 Fax: (804)732-1704

Contact: Don Bedonatis, Exec.Dir.

Desc: Teams, umpires, and directors. Promotes amateur slo-pitch softball. State programs involve divisional and world championships. *Type:* Association.

USA Softball

Amateur Softball Association of America (ASA)
2801 NE 50th St. Ph: (405)424-5266
Oklahoma City, OK 73111 Fax: (405)424-3855

Contact: Ronald Babb, Editor.

Desc: Reports on fast, slow, and modified pitch softball activities across the nation and world. Recurring features include tournament listings, player and team profiles, hall of fame information, and international competitions. *Type:* Newsletter.

Spain/Spanish

Sigma Delta Pi

PO Box 55125 Ph: (909)684-4340
Riverside, CA 92517

Contact: Ignacio R. M. Galbis, Exec.Sec.-Treas.

Desc: Honorary society - men and women, Spanish language and literature. *Type:* Association.

Spanish Speaking Unity Council
1900 Fruitvale Ave., Ste. 2A Ph: (510)535-6900
Oakland, CA 94601 Fax: (510)534-7771
URL: http://www.unitycouncil.org
Contact: Arabella Martinez, CEO.
Desc: Works to improve the quality of life in low income community of Oakland, CA. Devises economic development strategies complemented by social services, housing, child care, and other community services. *Type:* Association.

Speech and Hearing

Adelphi University

Hy Weinberg Center for Communication Disorders
PO Box 701 Ph: (516)877-4850
Garden City, NY 11530-4299 Free: 800-ADE-LPHI
Fax: (516)877-4783
E-mail: soman@adlibv.adelphi.edu
Contact: Dr. Bonnie Soman, Dir.
Desc: Speech-language pathology and audiology, and speech and hearing disorders. *Type:* Research center.

American Ear Association for Research
c/o Dr. Paul Yanick, Jr. Ph: (717)296-6316
PO Box 24 Free: 888-ANTIAGE
Saugerties, NY 12477-0024
Contact: Dr. Paul Yanick, Jr., Exec. Officer.
Desc: Objectives are: to aid hearing-impaired children and adults who suffer from tinnitus and hearing-related problems; to offer a coordinated approach to the provision of rehabilitation services; to further technology and promote research in the field of hearing problems. (Tinnitus is a purely subjective sensation of noise, as when an individual complains of a ringing or roaring in his or her ears.) Disseminates information about hearing loss and problematic tinnitus conditions; conducts research and reviews findings on effects of stress, diet, malnutrition, and lack of exercise on human hearing and tinnitus problems; sponsors competitions, seminars, and training programs for physicians and the public. Maintains library; offers children's services. *Type:* Association.

American Hearing Research Foundation
55 E. Washington St., Ste. 2022 Ph: (312)726-9670
Chicago, IL 60602 Fax: (312)726-9695
Contact: William L. Lederer, Contact.
Desc: Deafness and hearing disorders, focusing on medical research, education, and public information. *Type:* Research center.

American Speech-Language-Hearing Association
10801 Rockville Pke. Ph: (301)897-5700
Rockville, MD 20852 Free: 800-638-8255
Fax: (301)897-7348
E-mail: actioncenter@asha.org
URL: http://www.asha.org
Contact: Frederick T. Spahr, Ph.D., Exec.Dir.
Desc: Professional association for speech-language pathologists, audiologists, and speech language and hearing scientists. Acts as an accrediting agency for college and university graduate school programs and clinic and hospital programs and as a certifying body for professionals providing speech, language, and hearing services to the public. Offers career information, listing of university training programs, and certification requirements. *Type:* Association.

American Tinnitus Association
PO Box 5 Ph: (503)248-9985
Portland, OR 97207-0005 Free: 800-634-8978
Fax: (503)248-0024
E-mail: Tinnitus@ata.org
URL: http://www.ata.org
Contact: Gloria E. Reich, Exec.Dir.
Desc: Physicians, audiologists, hearing aid dispensers, and individuals who suffer from tinnitus (noises in the head or ears). Disseminates information about tinnitus; provides regional lists of service providers to patients seeking help; supports research into causes of tinnitus. Sponsors workshops on the testing, evaluating, and management of tinnitus patients and encourages and supports selfhelp groups for tinnitus patients. *Type:* Association.

Asha
American Speech-Language-Hearing Association
10801 Rockville Pike Ph: (301)897-5700
Rockville, MD 20852 Fax: (301)571-0457
URL: http://www.asha.org/asha/.
Contact: Joanne Jessen, Ph.D., Managing Editor; Pamela J. Leppin, Advertising Mgr.
Desc: Magazine on hearing, language, and speech. *Type:* Periodical.

Association for Research in Otolaryngology, Inc.
19 Mantua Rd. Ph: (609)423-0041
Mt. Royal, NJ 08061 Fax: (609)423-3420
E-mail: headquarters@aro.org
URL: http://www.aro.org
Contact: Susan Whitehouse, Exec.Dir.
Desc: Basic science and clinical problems associated with hearing, speech, the sense of balance, smell, taste, and diseases of the head and neck. *Type:* Research center.

Baylor College of Medicine

Stuttering Center and Speech Motor Control Laboratory
6501 Fannin, Ste. NB302 Ph: (713)798-7415
Houston, TX 77030 Fax: (713)798-6417
E-mail: davidr@bcm.tmc.edu
Contact: Dr. David Rosenfield, Dir.
Desc: Speech motor control system, including stuttering, voice problems, motor control, and digital signal and acoustic processing. *Type:* Research center.

Brooklyn College of City University of New York

Speech and Hearing Center
Boylan Hall Ph: (718)951-5186
Rm. 4400 Fax: (718)951-4363
Brooklyn, NY 11210
Contact: Dr. Grale Gurland, Dir.
Desc: Normal communications and communication disorders, including studies of speech, language, and hearing. *Type:* Research center.

Center for the Study and Treatment of Dyslexia
610 West College St., Ste. 120
Murfreesboro, TN 37130
E-mail: dyslexia@frank.mtsu.edu
URL: http://www.mtsu.edu/academic/dyslexia/index.html
Contact: Diane J. Sawyer, PhD, Dir.
Desc: Dyslexia, focusing on diagnostic services and monitoring the progress of students with dyslexia who are receiving intervention in their schools. *Type:* Research center.

City University of New York

Center for Research in Speech and Hearing Sciences
33 W. 42nd St. Ph: (212)642-2352
New York, NY 10036 Fax: (212)642-2379
E-mail: hochberg@mailhub.gc.cuny.edu
Contact: Dr. Irving Hochberg, Dir.
Desc: Programmable digital hearing aids, nonauditory sensory aids, speech perception of hearing impaired, rehabilitation strategies for the deaf, rehabilitation of cochlear implant patients, acoustic analysis of speech, electrophysiology, neurolinguistics of bilingualism, aging and dementia, child language disorders, and developmental psycholinguistics. *Type:* Research center.

Cleveland Hearing and Speech Center
11206 Euclid Ave. Ph: (216)231-8787
Cleveland, OH 44106 Fax: (216)231-7141
URL: http://www.commercepark.com/chsc
Contact: Bernard P. Henri, PhD, Exec.Dir.
Desc: Speech, language, and hearing disorders, Alzheimer's Disease, and slow progressive aphasia. *Type:* Research center.

Deafness Research Foundation
15 W. 39th St., 6th Fl. Ph: (212)768-1181
New York, NY 10018-3806 Free: 800-535-DEAF
Fax: (212)768-1782
E-mail: drfl@village.ios.com
URL: http://village.ios.com/~drfl
Contact: Jane Fortune, Ch.
Desc: Causes, treatment, and prevention of deafness and other serious ear disorders, including studies of implants, deafness in the young and the elderly, middle ear infections, Meniere's disease, tinnitus (ringing in the ears), excessive noise, hair cell regeneration, genetics, and otoacoustic emissions. *Type:* Research center.

Delta Sigma Rho - Tau Kappa Alpha
Frank Thompson
University of Alabama Ph: (205)348-8077
Communications College Fax: (205)348-8080
PO Box 87012
Tuscaloosa, AL 35487-0172
Contact: Frank Thompson, Sec.
Desc: Honorary society - men and women, forensics. Sponsors national debate and individual event competitions. *Type:* Association.

Ear Research Foundation
1901 Floyd St. Ph: (941)366-1148
Sarasota, FL 34239-2909 Fax: (941)953-3205
E-mail: earsinus@aol.com
URL: http://www.ear-sinusctr.com
Contact: Dr. Herbert Silverstein, Pres.
Desc: Meniere's disease, acoustic neuroma, benign positional vertigo, laser-assisted otological surgery for inner- and middle-ear disorders, cholesteatoma in children, cochlear implants, and vestibular rehabilitation. *Type:* Research center.

Eaton-Peabody Laboratory of Auditory Physiology
Massachusetts Eye & Ear Ph: (617)573-3745
Infirmary Fax: (617)720-4408
243 Charles St.
Boston, MA 02114
E-mail: mcl@epl.meei.harvard.edu
Contact: M. Charles Liberman, PhD, Actg.Dir.
Desc: Vertebrate auditory system and auditory information processing, including feedback control systems in normal and pathologic hearing. Approaches include anatomical, physiological, functional imaging, pharmacological, chemical and molecular biological studies of animal models as well as human subjects. *Type:* Research center.

Florida State University

Communication

College of Communication
432 Diffenbaugh
Tallahassee, FL 32306-1531
E-mail: jmayo@garnet.acns.fsu.edu
Ph: (850)644-8459
Fax: (850)644-8994

Contact: Dr. John Mayo, Dean.

Desc: Speech acoustics, speech physiology, speech disorders, acoustic forensics, and psychoacoustics. *Type:* Research center.

Haskins Laboratories

270 Crown St.
New Haven, CT 06511
E-mail: haskins@haskins.yale.edu
URL: http://www.haskins.yale.edu
Ph: (203)865-6163
Fax: (203)865-8963

Contact: Dr. Carol A. Fowler, Pres.

Desc: Speech production and perception by humans and computers, motor control, and reading. *Type:* Research center.

Hollins Communications Research Institute

PO Box 9737
Roanoke, VA 24020-1737
E-mail: adm-hcri@rbnet.com
URL: http://www.stuttering.org
Ph: (540)265-5650
Fax: (540)265-0386

Contact: Ronald L. Webster, PhD, Dir.

Desc: Basic features of stuttering, behaviorally-based stuttering therapy, and variables that modify speech fluency in people who stutter and fluent speakers. *Type:* Research center.

House Ear Institute

2100 W. 3rd St.
Los Angeles, CA 90057
E-mail: webmaster@hei.org
URL: http://www.hei.org
Ph: (213)483-4431
Fax: (213)483-8789

Contact: James Boswell, CEO.

Desc: Develops conceptual and technically feasible approaches to resolving hearing and balance disorders through applied research. Conducts research on subjects including hearing aids, auditory implants, aging ear, brain mapping, nearoanatomy, infant hearing diagnosis, and acoustic tumor. Offers seminars and classes for senior residents and practicing physicians. *Type:* Association.

Houston Ear Research Foundation

7737 Southwest Fwy., Ste. 630
Houston, TX 77074
Ph: (713)771-9966
Free: 800-843-0807
Fax: (713)771-0546

E-mail: jangil@hern.org

Contact: Jan Gilden, Exec.Dir.

Desc: Aims to improve health care and education for deaf and hearing-impaired children. Provides funds for follow-up testing for recipients of cochlear implants. *Type:* Research center.

Indiana University-Purdue University at Indianapolis

De Vault Otologic Research Laboratory

702 Bamhill Dr., Rm. 44
Indianapolis, IN 46202
URL: http://www.indiana.edu/~rugs/ctrdir/dvorl.html
Ph: (317)274-4915

Contact: Karen Iler Kirk, Dir.

Desc: Benefit of different sensory aids to hearing-impaired children, specifically changes in speech production, speech perception, language, cognitive skills after cochlear implants. *Type:* Research center.

International Center for Hearing and Speech Research

52 Lomb Memorial Dr.
Rochester, NY 14623
E-mail: rxf1389@ritvax.isc.rit.edu
Ph: (716)475-6403
Fax: (716)475-6677

Contact: Dr. Robert Frisina, Sr., Dir.

Desc: Prevention, early detection, diagnosis, and treatment of people with hearing and speech impairments. *Type:* Research center.

Johns Hopkins University

Center for Hearing and Balance

Auditory Anatomy and Physiology Laboratory

School of Medicine
Traylor 510
720 Rutland Ave.
Baltimore, MD 21205
E-mail: dryugo@bme.jhu.edu
URL: http://www.bme.jhu.edu/labs/chb/labs/ap_aud.html
Ph: (410)955-4543
Fax: (410)614-4748

Contact: David K. Ryugo, Prin. Investigator.

Desc: Identified cell populations, their synaptic connections, and revealing features of their signaling capabilities. *Type:* Research center.

Johns Hopkins University

Research and Training Center for Hearing and Balance

In Vitro Auditory Physiology Laboratory

School of Medicine
420 Ross Research Bldg.
720 Rutland Ave.
Baltimore, MD 21205
E-mail: pmanis@bme.jhu.edu
URL: http://www.bme.jhu.edu/labs/chb/labs/iv_aud.html
Ph: (410)955-6978
Fax: (410)955-1299

Contact: Paul B. Manis, PhD, Prin. Investigator.

Desc: Mechanisms of information processing in the cochlear nucleus. *Type:* Research center.

Johns Hopkins University

Research and Training Center for Hearing and Balance

Neural Encoding Laboratory

School of Medicine
505 Traylor Bldg.
720 Rutland Ave.
Baltimore, MD 21205
E-mail: eyoung@bme.jhu.edu
URL: http://www.bme.jhu.edu/labs/chb/labs/neural_enc.html
Ph: (410)955-3162
Fax: (410)955-1299

Contact: Eric D. Young, PhD, Prin. Investigator.

Desc: Representation and processing of complex stimuli in the auditory system. *Type:* Research center.

Kent State University

Speech and Hearing Clinic

A104 Music and Speech Bldg.
Kent, OH 44242
E-mail: msinglet@phoenix.kent.edu
URL: http://www.educ.kent.edu/elsa/clinic/clinic.html
Ph: (330)672-2672
Fax: (330)672-2643

Contact: Mary Eleise Jones-Singletary, PhD, Contact.

Desc: Speech pathology and audiology, including staff specialties in infant, children's, and adult languages, stuttering, phonology, aural rehabilitation, and hearing aids. *Type:* Research center.

Louisiana State University

Kresge Hearing Research Laboratory of the South

2020 Gravier St., Ste. A
New Orleans, LA 70112
E-mail: cberli@lsumc.edu
URL: http://www.lsumc.edu
Ph: (504)568-4785
Fax: (504)568-4460

Contact: Dr. Charles I. Berlin, Dir.

Desc: Auditory research, pharmacology, anatomy, psychophysics, molecular genetics, and audiology, including studies on cochlear implants, auditory evoked potentials, ultra-high frequency hearing, effects of hearing impairments on brain structure, temporal order in hearing, auditory processing of frequency-varying signals, perceptual skills in learning-disabled children, speech perception, cochlear emissions, and the role of chemical elements in hearing. *Type:* Research center.

Loyola University Chicago

Parmly Hearing Institute

6525 N. Sheridan Rd.
Chicago, IL 60626
E-mail: wyost@luc.edu
URL: http://www.parmly.luc.edu
Ph: (773)508-2710
Fax: (773)508-2719

Contact: Dr. William A. Yost, Dir.

Desc: Psychophysics, physiology, and anatomy of audition and investigation of sensory/perceptual processes, including studies on relations among sense/organ action, anatomy and physiology of afferent nervous system, cerebral sensory mechanisms, psychophysical characteristics of auditory system, application of theory of signal detectability to psychophysics, and detection and recognition of auditory signals in noise. *Type:* Research center.

Midwest Ear Institute, Inc.

2940 Baltimore Ave., Ste. 300
Kansas City, MO 64108-3405
Ph: (816)531-0003
Fax: (816)751-4616

Contact: Elaine Leander, Dir.

Desc: Auditory prostheses. *Type:* Research center.

National Communication Association Directory

National Communication Association

5105 Backlick Rd., No. E
Annandale, VA 22003
E-mail: members@natcom.org
Ph: (703)750-0533
Fax: (703)914-9471

Contact: James L. Gaudino, Editor.

Desc: About 7,000 higher education and secondary teachers and students in the field of communication (interpersonal, public speaking, mass media, rhetoric, etc.); speech communication journals; state speech associations; affiliated national and regional associations; practitioners in government, business, and industry; limited international coverage. Includes list of institutions with undergraduate and graduate communication departments. *Type:* Directory.

National Student Speech Language Hearing Association

10801 Rockville Pike
Rockville, MD 20852
URL: http://www.asha.org
Ph: (301)897-5700
Fax: (301)897-7350

Contact: Frederick Spahr, Ph.D., Chief Admin./Fin. Officer.

Desc: Preprofessional organization for undergraduate and graduate students in speech-language pathology, speech and hearing sciences, and audiology. *Type:* Association.

New York Foundation for Otologic Research

920 Park Ave.
New York, NY 10028
Ph: (212)988-3100
Fax: (212)517-8699

Contact: Dr. Alan Austin Scheer, Dir.

Desc: Unsolved hearing problems, including otosclerosis, nerve deafness, Menieres disease, and other associated problems of dizziness and head noises. Analyzes electrical patterns of sound conduction and studies conduction of sound through the skin and dental nerves. *Type:* Research center.

Ohio State University
Division of Otologic Research
4331 Univ. Hospitals Clinic   Ph: (614)293-8103
456 W. 10th Ave.   Fax: (614)293-5506
Columbus, OH 43210
E-mail: tdemaria@pop.service.ohio-state.edu
Contact: Dr. Thomas F. DeMaria, Dir.

Desc: Otology, including animal models for otitis media, acoustic trauma, morphological studies on the inner ear, and immunologic investigations of the middle and inner ear. Also studies the development of animal models for studying middle ear infection using microbiological, immunologic, morphologic and molecular biological methods, temporal bone histopathology (human and animal), electron microscopy of auditory and vestibular systems, pathogenesis of otitis media, and sensory transduction mechanism. *Type:* Research center.

Oregon Health Sciences University
Oregon Hearing Research Center
3181 SW Sam Jackson Park Rd.   Ph: (503)494-8032
NRCO4   Fax: (503)494-5656
Portland, OR 97201-3098
E-mail: nuttal@ohsu.edu
URL: http://www.ohsu.edu/ohrc/
Contact: Alfred L. Nuttall, PhD, Dir.

Desc: Hearing problems, including clinical studies of ototoxicity, vestibular physiology, noise damage, anatomy of the ear, tinnitus, and interactions between various insults to the ear, through a multiple attack utilizing electrophysiological measures, behavioral measures, histological evaluations, and human psychophysics. *Type:* Research center.

Phonetician—Directory Issue
International Society of Phonetic Sciences
PO Box 12323   Ph: (904)377-8622
University Sta.   Fax: (904)392-6170
Gainesville, FL 32604
Contact: Patricia Hollien, Editor, hollien@ufcc.ufl.edu.

Desc: Nearly 1,500 voting member phoneticians, phonologists, linguists, engineers, communication scientists, language teachers, speech pathologists, phoniatrists, logopedists, and national phonetic sciences organizations, worldwide. Entries include: Name, affiliation, address. *Type:* Directory.

Pi Kappa Delta
Dr. Robert Littlefield
Box 5075, University Sta.   Ph: (701)231-7783
North Dakota State University   Fax: (701)231-7784
Fargo, ND 58105-5075
E-mail: rlittlef@badlands.nodak.edu
Contact: Dr. Robert Littlefield, Sec.Treas.

Desc: Recognition fraternity - men and women, forensics. Maintains hall of fame; compiles statistics; sponsors competitions. *Type:* Association.

Queens College of City University of New York
Augmentative Communication Center
Linguistics & Com. Disorders   Ph: (718)997-2940
Dept.   Fax: (718)997-2873
65-30 Kissena Blvd.
Flushing, NY 11367-1597
Contact: Dr. Arlene Kraat, Dir.

Desc: Severe speech and language disabilities, including treatment methods of augmentative and alternative communication (AAC) modes. AAC enhances communication through the use of signs, symbolic gestures, language boards, and computerized communication devices. *Type:* Research center.

Queens College of City University of New York
Speech and Hearing Center
65-30 Kissena Blvd.   Ph: (718)997-2930
GERTZ Bldg.   Fax: (718)997-2935
Flushing, NY 11367-1597
Contact: Dr. Joel Stark, Dir.

Desc: Communicative disorders in children and adults, focusing on audiological testing and treatment. *Type:* Research center.

Speech Simulation Research Foundation
PO Box 824   Ph: (757)442-2755
Nassawadox, VA 23413
Contact: Susan Penney, Dir.

Desc: Human communication development related to tactile speech reception for people who are deaf or hard of hearing. *Type:* Research center.

State University of New York at Buffalo
Center for Hearing and Deafness
215 Parker Hall   Ph: (716)829-2001
Buffalo, NY 14214   Fax: (716)829-2980
E-mail: salvi@acsu.buffalo.edu
URL: http://wings.buffalo.edu/faculty/research/chd/
Contact: Dr. Richard J. Salvi, Hd.

Desc: Restoring the hearing of the deaf, hearing loss due to loud noises, medication, or age, middle ear infections in children, hearing loss in infants. Studies include hair cell regeneration, drug therapy and otoxic drugs, noise-induced hearing loss, middle ear disease, infant hearing assessment, auditory plasticity, mechanical transduction, age-related hearing loss, and central auditory processing. *Type:* Research center.

State University of New York at Buffalo
Hearing Research Laboratory
215 Parker Hall   Ph: (716)829-2001
Buffalo, NY 14214   Fax: (716)829-2980
E-mail: salvi@acsu.buffalo.edu
URL: http://wings.buffalo.edu/faculty/CHD/
Contact: Dr. Richard J. Salvi, Co-Dir.

Desc: Hearing, including effects of noise, effects of ototoxic drugs, and basic auditory processes. *Type:* Research center.

State University of New York at Buffalo
Speech-Language and Hearing Clinic
130 Park Hall   Ph: (716)645-3410
Buffalo, NY 14260   Fax: (716)645-2216
E-mail: smundier@acsu.buffalo.edu
Contact: Gary J. Rentschler, PhD, Dir.

Desc: Audiology, speech and hearing sciences, speech/language pathology, speech perception and acoustics, and augmentative communication. *Type:* Research center.

State University of New York College at Fredonia
Youngerman Center for Communications Disorders
Thompson Hall   Ph: (716)673-3203
Fredonia, NY 14063   Fax: (716)673-3235
E-mail: perez@fredonia.edu
URL: http://www.fredonia.edu
Contact: Dr. Dennis M. Perez, Dir.

Desc: Community clinic and student training center for speech/language pathology and audiology. Provides facilities and data for faculty engaged in research projects in the areas of audiology, voice and speech science, and language. *Type:* Research center.

State University of New York College at Plattsburgh
Auditory Research Laboratory
107 Beaumont Hall   Ph: (518)564-7701
101 Broad St.   Fax: (518)564-7827
Plattsburgh, NY 12901
E-mail: hamernrp@splava.cc.plattsburgh.edu
URL: http://www.plattsburgh.edu/arl/
Contact: Dr. Roger P. Hamernik, Dir.

Desc: Pathology of hearing associated with noise, drugs, congenital birth defects, and disease processes. *Type:* Research center.

State University of New York Health Science Center at Brooklyn
Research Unit on Communicative Processes
450 Clarkson Ave.   Ph: (718)270-3078
Box 88   Fax: (718)270-3017
Brooklyn, NY 11203
Contact: Dr. Norbert Freedman, Dir.

Desc: Communicative issues in psychiatric treatment, including doctor-patient interaction, the clinical interview, the psychotherapeutic interview, and the psychoanalytic interview. Objective studies of communicative behavior are also conducted through analysis of language, kinesics, and cognitive processes. *Type:* Research center.

Temple University
Communication Sciences
13th & Cecil B. Moore Ave.   Ph: (215)204-7543
Philadelphia, PA 19122   Fax: (215)204-5954
E-mail: iglesias@vm.temple.edu
Contact: Dr. Aquiles Iglesias, Ch.

Desc: Speech and hearing science, including investigation of clinical functions of speech pathology and therapy. Conducts research in normal speech, language, and hearing, as well as studies of disordered speech, fluency, voice, language, and hearing. *Type:* Research center.

Temple University
Section of Audiology and Auditory Research
Kresge W. Bldg., Rm. 302   Ph: (215)707-3661
3440 N. Broad St.   Fax: (215)707-3650
Philadelphia, PA 19140
E-mail: florence@flower.aud.temple.edu
Contact: Florence Petersen, PhD, Dir.

Desc: Psychological and physiological acoustics, clinical research in audiology, clinical and basic research in evoked potentials, auditory and vestibular functioning, and human and animal experimentation in otology. *Type:* Research center.

U.S. Department of Health and Human Services
National Institute on Deafness and Other Communication Disorders
NIH Bldg. 31, Rm. 3C02   Ph: (301)402-0900
9000 Rockville Pike   Fax: (301)402-1590
Bethesda, MD 20892-2320
Contact: James F. Buttey, Jr., MD,PhD, Dir.

Desc: Biomedical and behavioral research and research training on normal processes and disorders of hearing, balance, smell, taste, voice, speech, and language, including hearing and deafness, hearing loss, hearing impairment, tinnitus, presbycusis, Waardenburg syndrome, Usher syndrome, dizziness, Meniere's disease, vestibular system, smell and taste disorders, voice disorders, spasmodic dysphonia, vocal cord paralysis, stuttering, speech disorders, language disorders, and aphasia. *Type:* Research center.

U.S. Department of Health and Human Services

National Institute on Deafness and Other Communication Disorders

Division Extramural Activities

6120 Executive Blvd., 400C   Ph: (301)496-8693
Bethesda, MD 20892   Fax: (301)402-6250
URL: http://www.nih.gov/nidcd/

Contact: Craig A. Jordan, PhD, Actg.Dir.

Desc: Communication sciences and disorders. *Type:* Research center.

U.S. Department of Health and Human Services

National Institute on Deafness and Other Communication Disorders

Division of Human Communications

Executive Plaza S., Rm. 400C   Ph: (301)496-1804
6120 Executive Blvd.   Fax: (301)402-6251
MSC 7180
Rockville, MD 20852-7180
URL: http://www.nih.gov

Contact: Judith Cooper, Actg.Dir.

Desc: Administers grants, contracts, and national research service awards for extramural research on hearing, balance, smell, taste, voice, speech, and language. Areas of research interest include diagnosis, treatment, and prevention of communication disorders, including the prevention and early diagnosis of hearing impairments that may result from exposure to noise or ototoxic drugs; the causes and treatment of tinnitus; the normal function of the central nervous system and the relationship of the taste, smell, and touch senses to the early detection of systemic disease; disorders such as stuttering, misarticulation, delayed language development, and phonatory disorders. *Type:* Research center.

U.S. Department of Health and Human Services

National Institute on Deafness and Other Communication Disorders

Division of Intramural Research

Bldg. 10, Rm. 5055   Ph: (301)402-4216
10 Center Drive   Fax: (301)402-1140
Bethesda, MD 20892
E-mail: vanwaesc@nidcd.nih.gov

Contact: Dr. Carter Van Waes, Actg.Clin.Dir.

Desc: Genetic and immune pathogenesis of head and neck neoplasms affecting human communication. *Type:* Research center.

U.S. Department of Health and Human Services

National Institute on Deafness and Other Communication Disorders

Division of Intramural Research

Audiology Unit

NIH Bldg. 10, Rm. 5C-306   Ph: (301)496-5368
9000 Rockville Pk.   Fax: (301)402-0409
Bethesda, MD 20892
E-mail: PI6@CU.NIH.GOV

Contact: Anita Pikus, Chf.

Desc: Hearing and auditory function in various genetic, immunologic, or acquired conditions, including type 2 neurofibromatosis, Waardenburg syndrome, inherited metabolic degenerative disorders and non-syndromic hereditary hearing loss, and von-Hippel Lindau disease. *Type:* Research center.

U.S. Department of Health and Human Services

National Institute on Deafness and Other Communication Disorders

Division of Intramural Research

Voice and Speech Section

NIH Bldg. 10, Rm. 5D38   Ph: (301)496-9365
10 Center Dr., MSC 1416   Fax: (301)480-0803
Bethesda, MD 20892-1416
E-mail: cludlow@pop.nidcd.nih.gov
Contact: Christy L. Ludlow, PhD, Chf.
Desc: Speech and voice studies, including the neurophysiological and biomechanical bases of normal speech and voice production, pathophysiology of idiopathic speech and voice disorders such as spasmodic dysphonia and stuttering, and medical and surgical approaches to treatment of these disorders. Investigates sensorimotor regulation of the laryngeal musculature; motion and electromyographic analyses of laryngeal functioning during speech, respiration, and swallowing; magnetic and electrical stimulation of the central and peripheral laryngeal nervous system; and new treatment approaches including botulinum toxin, medication trials in patients with stuttering disorders, and phonosurgery for voice disorders. *Type:* Research center.

University of Alabama

Speech and Hearing Center

Department of Communicative   Ph: (205)348-7131
   Disorders   Fax: (205)348-1845
Box 870242
Tuscaloosa, AL 35487-0242
E-mail: gculton@woodsquad.as.ua.edu
Contact: Dr. Gerald L. Culton, Chm.
Desc: Communication disorders, including clinical studies associated with graduate training in speech-language pathology and audiology. *Type:* Research center.

University of Alabama at Birmingham

Speech and Hearing Sciences Department

Spain Rehab. Center   Ph: (205)934-4814
Birmingham, AL 35233   Fax: (205)934-7420
E-mail: flegeje.dept.rehab_sciences@uab.edu
URL: http://www.uab.edu
Contact: James Emil Flege, Hd.
Desc: Physiology, aerodynamics, acoustics, and perception of speech. Activities focus on basic physiology and acoustic studies of normal and abnormal speech learning. *Type:* Research center.

University of Arkansas at Little Rock

Rehabilitation Research and Training Center for Persons Who Are Deaf or Hard of Hearing

4601 W. Markham   Ph: (501)686-9691
Little Rock, AR 72205   Fax: (501)686-9698
E-mail: DWatson@comp.uark.edu
URL: http://www.uark.edu/depts/rehabres
Contact: Dr. Douglas Watson, Dir.
Desc: Rehabilitation of individuals who are deaf or hard of hearing, focusing on improving career preparation, entry, retention, and advancement of these individuals in the workplace. *Type:* Research center.

University of Chicago

Temporal Bone Laboratory for Ear Research

5841 S. Maryland Ave., MC   Ph: (773)702-6686
   1035   Fax: (773)702-6809
Chicago, IL 60637
E-mail: rhinojos@surgery.bsd.uchicago.edu
Contact: Dr. Raul Hinojosa, Dir.
Desc: Pathological basis for impairment of hearing and deafness and animal research on auditory and vestibular systems. *Type:* Research center.

University of Colorado at Boulder

Speech, Language, and Hearing Center

CB 409   Ph: (303)492-5375
Boulder, CO 80309   Fax: (303)492-3274
Contact: Susan M. Moore, Dir.
Desc: Evaluation and treatment of speech, language, learning, and hearing disorders. *Type:* Research center.

University of Maine

Conley Speech and Hearing Center

L-5 N. Stevens Hall   Ph: (207)581-2006
5754 N. Stevens Hall   Fax: (207)581-1953
Orono, ME 04469
E-mail: mboyd@maine.maine.edu
URL: http://www.umaine.edu
Contact: Dr. Kimbrough Oller, Contact.
Desc: Speech and language disorders of adults and children, including aphasia, voice disorders, acquisition of language by children, stuttering, articulation disorders, apraxia, and interpersonal skills in clinical processes. *Type:* Research center.

University of Memphis

Center for Research Initiatives and Strategies for the Communicatively Impaired

807 Jefferson Ave.   Ph: (901)678-5800
Memphis, TN 38105   Fax: (901)525-1282
E-mail: mmendel@cc.umemphis.edu
Contact: Maurice I. Mendel, Dir.
Desc: Speech and hearing, especially high technology applications to habilitation and rehabilitation of the communicatively impaired. Contributes to master's and doctoral programs in speech and hearing sciences. *Type:* Research center.

University of Michigan

Kresge Hearing Research Institute

1301 E. Ann St., Rm. 5032   Ph: (734)764-8111
Ann Arbor, MI 48109-0506   Fax: (734)764-0014
E-mail: carolet@umich.edu
URL: http://www.med.umich.edu/khri/
Contact: Dr. Josef Miller, Dir.
Desc: Auditory physiology and pathology, including studies on the reception, coding and processing of complex speech signals by the auditory system, transduction processes of the inner ear, cochlear blood flow and inner ear metabolism, development of cochlear prostheses and appropriate speech processor schemes, immune mediated hearing loss, the effects of age and environmental stress factors on hearing, biochemistry and motility of hair cells, afferent and efferent transmitters of the inner ear, psychophysics of hearing in normal individuals, immunology and immune systems related to squamous cell carcinoma, mechanisms of sound, localization, molecular biology and genetics of the inner ear, and human genetics (limkage studies). *Type:* Research center.

University of Michigan

Kresge Hearing Research Institute

Auditory Anatomy Laboratory

1301 E. Ann St.   Ph: (734)763-0060
Ann Arbor, MI 48109-0506   Fax: (734)764-0014
E-mail: shuler@umich.edu
URL: http://www.med.umich.edu/khri/audanat
Contact: Dr. Richard Altschuler, Dir.
Desc: Structure of the damaged ear and damage to the auditory structures of the brain due to noise, drugs, or disease. Evaluates the risks of new otologic treatments, surgeries, and devices, including the cochlear prosthesis; identifies neurotransmitters in the cochlea and auditory brainstem; and examines auditory pathways. *Type:* Research center.

University of Michigan

Kresge Hearing Research Institute

Auditory Prosthesis Animal Psychophysics Laboratory

Box 0506 Ph: (734)763-2292
Ann Arbor, MI 48109 Fax: (734)764-0014
Contact: Dr. Bryan Pfingst, Dir.

Desc: Restoration of hearing in profoundly deaf persons. Studies the processing of speech in the brain and encoding of speech in the auditory system, and uses hearing tests with rhesus monkeys, humans, and other animals to design and develop bionic ear implants, also called cochlear prostheses. *Type:* Research center.

University of Michigan

Kresge Hearing Research Institute

Biochemistry Laboratory

1301 E. Ann St. Ph: (734)763-3572
Ann Arbor, MI 48109-0506 Fax: (734)764-0014
E-mail: schacht@umich.edu
URL: http://www.med.umich.edu/khri/biochem/
Contact: Dr. Jochen Schacht, Dir.

Desc: Cellular and molecular mechanisms of hearing and deafness. Investigates the normal biochemical events that occur in cells of the inner ear when hearing and that are impaired in hearing disorders such as those induced by noise and certain drugs. *Type:* Research center.

University of Michigan

Kresge Hearing Research Institute

Electrophysiology Laboratory

1301 E. Ann St. Ph: (734)764-8110
Ann Arbor, MI 48109-0506 Fax: (734)764-0014
E-mail: ddolan@umich.edu
Contact: David F. Dolan, PhD, Dir.

Desc: Electrical responses to sound in the inner ear. Studies the response of individual receptor cells, or hair cells, of one ear while the other ear is acoustically or electrically stimulated. *Type:* Research center.

University of Michigan

Kresge Hearing Research Institute

Neurophysiology and Biophysics Laboratory

1301 E. Ann St. Ph: (734)764-8110
Ann Arbor, MI 48109 Fax: (734)764-0014
E-mail: josef@umich.edu
URL: http://www.med.umich.edu/khri/
Contact: Dr. Josef Miller, Dir.

Desc: Neural and electrical encoding of various auditory stimuli in the brain to determine how the brain aids in hearing. Projects include synthesis of artificial speech and other signals, computer analysis of electrically recorded neural signals, and histological preparations of sections. *Type:* Research center.

University of Michigan

Kresge Hearing Research Institute

Pharmacology Laboratory

1301 E. Ann St. Ph: (734)764-8111
Ann Arbor, MI 48109-0506 Fax: (734)764-0014
E-mail: sbledsoe@umich.edu
Contact: Dr. Sanford Bledsoe, Contact.

Desc: Studies the chemical substances (transmitters), used in intercellular communication which mediate the transduction and encoding of sounds from the inner ear to the auditory structures of the brain. Also studies auditory physiology, psychophysics, molecular biology and genetics, clinical investigations of auditory function. *Type:* Research center.

University of Montreal

Acoustics Group

Faculte de medecine Ph: (514)343-7301
Ecole d'orthophonie et Fax: (514)343-5740
 d'audiologie
C.P. 6128, Succursale Centre-
 ville
Montreal, PQ, Canada H3C 3J7
E-mail: gettyl@ere.umontreal.ca
Contact: Louise Getty, Dir.

Desc: Noise and its effect on health and safety, effects of occupational hearing loss, occupational and psychosocial rehabilitation of individuals with hearing loss, audiological rehabilitation of individuals with acquired hearing loss, noise as a nuisance, cultural aspects of acquired hearing loss, and sound warning signal recognition in industrial rooms. *Type:* Research center.

University of Nebraska--Lincoln

Barkley Memorial Center

Barkley Ctr. 301 Ph: (402)472-2145
Lincoln, NE 68583-0738 Fax: (402)472-7697
E-mail: bernthal@unlinfo.unl.edu
URL: http://www.unl.edu//barkley
Contact: John Bernthal, Dir.

Desc: Communication deficiency and disorder research, including study of brain stem audiometry; fluency, motor speech disorders, phonological, acquisition of sign language, speech perception, language and learning disorders; behavioral impairment; and hearing impairment; augmentative and alternative communication; and use of paraprofessionals in special education. *Type:* Research center.

University of North Carolina at Chapel Hill

Division of Speech and Hearing Sciences

Med. Sch., Wing D Ph: (919)966-1006
CB 7190 Fax: (919)966-0100
Chapel Hill, NC 27599-7190
E-mail: jroush@css.unc.edu
Contact: Dr. Jackson Roush, Dir.

Desc: Speech and hearing as part of the overall training, research, and clinical services missions of the Division. *Type:* Research center.

University of Oklahoma

Keys Speech and Hearing Center

PO Box 26901 Ph: (405)271-4214
Oklahoma City, OK 73190 Fax: (405)271-3360
Contact: Dr. Richard Talbott, PhD, Dir.

Desc: Loudness and acoustic reflex, temporal integration and acoustic reflex, critical bands measured with pulsation pattern psychophysical technique, sensory scaling, absolute thresholds for frequency modulated signals, bone conduction vibrator calibration, bone conduction speech audiometry, intelligibility of distorted speech, electrocochleography, brain stem auditory-evoked responses, acoustic correlates of abnormal vocal quality, aerodynamics of voice production, phonemic and morphologic studies of language of the communicatively impaired, and assessment of receptive and expressive language abilities. *Type:* Research center.

University of Texas at Dallas

Callier Center for Communication Disorders

1966 Inwood Rd. Ph: (214)905-3000
Dallas, TX 75235-7298 Fax: (214)905-3022
E-mail: roeser@callier.utdallas.edu
URL: http://www.utdallas.edu/dept/hd/cc/
Contact: Dr. Ross J. Roeser, Dir.

Desc: Behavioral, electrophysiological, and anatomical studies of audition; behavioral and electrophysiological studies of normal and disordered speech production and perception; evoked potential and brain mapping; the linguistic and cognitive abilities of persons with aphasia and other neurogenic speech and language impairments; language development of children with chronic otitis media; development and assessment of communicative abilities in children with multiple handicaps; vibrotactile aids; and aural rehabilitation. *Type:* Research center.

University of Texas Southwestern Medical Center at Dallas

Division of Communicative and Vestibular Disorders

Department of Ph: (214)648-2018
 Otorhinolaryngology Fax: (214)648-9122
5323 Harry Hines Blvd.
Dallas, TX 75235-9035
E-mail: ashoup@mednet.swmed.edu
URL: http://www.swmed.edu

Contact: Angela Shoup, Ph.D., CCC-A, Dir.

Desc: Dizziness, vertigo, gait and balance disorders, inner ear fluid disorders, auditory perception, and auditory neurophysiology. *Type:* Research center.

University of Tulsa

Mary K. Chapman Center for Communicative Disorders

600 S. College Ave. Ph: (918)631-2504
Tulsa, OK 74104-3189 Fax: (918)631-3668
E-mail: christenjm@centum.utulsa.edu
URL: http://www.utulsa.edu/

Contact: John M. Christensen, PhD, Ch.

Desc: Communication disorders, including laryngectomy and speech, and language and hearing problems. Also conducts aid tests. *Type:* Research center.

University of Virginia

Communication Disorders Program

Speech Language Hearing Ctr. Ph: (804)982-2323
Colony Plaza Fax: (804)924-4621
2205 Fountain Ave., Ste. 202
Charlottesville, VA 22903
E-mail: ren3f@virginia.edu
URL: http://www.cutty@school.virginia.edu/curry/dept/
edhs/cohdis/prepro.html

Contact: Dr. Robert E. Novak, Dir.

Desc: Speech and language pathology, audiology, early detection in infant speech/language/hearing disorders, education of the deaf, and speech and hearing science, including computer applications to communications disorders treatment. Supervises doctoral research in these fields and sponsors meetings of interest to speech and language pathologists, audiologists, and educators of the hearing impaired. *Type:* Research center.

University of Wisconsin

Auditory Physiology Center

Department of Physiology Ph: (608)262-0818
MSI Rm. 127 Fax: (608)265-3500
1300 University Ave.
Madison, WI 53706-1532
E-mail: rlmoss@physiology.wisc.edu
URL: http://www.neurophys.wisc.edu/neurophys/

Contact: Richard L. Moss, Dir.

Desc: Auditory research at the systems, cellular, and molecular levels. *Type:* Research center.

University of Wisconsin--Madison
Trace Research and Development Center
Waisman Ctr., S-151   Ph: (608)262-6966
1500 Highland Ave.   Fax: (608)262-8848
Madison, WI 53705
E-mail: info@trace.wisc.edu
URL: http://www.trace.wisc.edu
Contact: Gregg Vanderheiden, PhD, Dir.

Desc: Computer access by disabled individuals and augmentative communication and control for speech impaired individuals; research directed toward individuals with language and physical disabilities caused by stroke, head trauma, cerebral palsy, multiple sclerosis, muscular dystrophy, and other disorders. *Type:* Research center.

Virginia Lions Hearing Foundation & Research Center, Inc.
University of Virginia Health   Ph: (804)296-5466
   Sci. Ctr.   Free: 800-251-3627
Box 477   Fax: (804)243-6732
Charlottesville, VA 22908
E-mail: jmt35@virginia.edu
URL: http://www.lions24b.org/vlhf/vlhf.htm
Contact: Paul R. Lambert, MD, Med.Dir.

Desc: Cochlear implants, newborn hearing screening, implantable hearing aids, hair cell regeneration in the cochlea, ototoxicity (drug damage), noise damage, electrical stimulation of auditory nerves. *Type:* Research center.

Yeshiva University
Institute of Communication Disorders
c/o Montefiore Med. Ctr.   Ph: (718)920-2991
Department ENT, 3rd Fl.   Fax: (718)405-9014
   Green Pav
3400 Bainbridge Ave.
Bronx, NY 10467
E-mail: ruben@aecom.yu.edu
Contact: Robert J. Ruben, MD, Chm.

Desc: Communicative disorders, including hearing, listening, voice, speech, and language studies; molecular developmental biology; molecular genetics; the synergy of culture and disease; morbidity; genetic studies; and genetics of communication disorders. *Type:* Research center.

Sporting Goods
American Recreational Racket Sports Association
PO Box 35189   Ph: (708)453-0080
Chicago, IL 60707-0189   Fax: (708)453-0083
Contact: L. David Stoller, Chm.

Desc: Evaluates tennis and other racket sport equipment for the sporting goods industry and offers equipment certification program. *Type:* Association.

American Sportfishing Association
1033 N. Fairfax St., Ste. 200   Ph: (703)519-9691
Alexandria, VA 22314   Fax: (703)519-1872
URL: http://www.asafishing.org
Contact: Mike Horak, Dir. of Comm,.

Desc: Manufacturers and importers of fishing tackle and allied products. Promotes fishing for children and adults. Compiles statistics. *Type:* Association.

BSR on Fitness
Bay Sports Review
PO Box 4520   Ph: (925)934-7647
Berkeley, CA 94704   Fax: (925)934-7650
Contact: Christopher Weills, Publisher.

Desc: Directed toward health and fitness industry personnel. Acts as a vehicle to communicate their message to decision makers with authority to purchase products for their business. *Type:* Newsletter.

Camping Magazine—Buyer's Guide Issue
American Camping Association
5000 State Rd. 67 N.   Ph: (765)342-8456
Martinsville, IN 46151   Free: 800-428-CAMP
   Fax: (765)342-2065
E-mail: bookstore@aca-camps.org
URL: http://www.acacamps.org
Contact: Sandy Cameron, Editor.

Desc: List of over 200 firms providing sporting equipment, food, infirmary supplies, etc. for children's and other organized camps. *Type:* Directory.

Canoe & Kayak Magazine—Buyer's Guide Issue
Canoe America Associates
PO Box 3146   Ph: (206)827-6363
Kirkland, WA 98083   Free: 800-692-2663
   Fax: (206)827-1893
E-mail: ads@canoekayak.com
Contact: Dennis Stuhaug, Editor.

Desc: Lists of about 300 manufacturers of over 2,500 canoes, kayaks, inflatable boats, paddles, and personal flotation devices in the United States and Canada. *Type:* Directory.

Dealernews—Buyers Guide
Advanstar Communications
201 Sandpointe Ave., Ste. 600   Ph: (714)513-8400
Santa Ana, CA 92707   Free: 800-854-3112
   Fax: (714)513-8680
URL: http://www.advanstar.com; http://www.dealernews.com.
Contact: Robin Hartfiel, Editor, rhartfiel@advanstar.com.

Desc: List of manufacturers, distributors, OEMs, and service organizations serving the motorcycle, all-terrain vehicle, and watercraft industries. *Type:* Directory.

Diving Equipment and Marketing Association
2050 S. Santa Cruz St., Ste.   Ph: (714)939-6399
   1000   Free: 800-TM2-DIVE
Anaheim, CA 92805   Fax: (714)939-6398
E-mail: dema110@aol.com
URL: http://www.dema.org
Contact: Regina Franklin, Exec.Dir.

Desc: International sport diving (scuba) organizations and associations promoting or reporting diving activities individuals or organizations providing educational, travel, or other services in the field. Purposes are to promote advancement within the diving equipment industry, to encourage the growth of diving activities, and to enhance public enjoyment of recreational diving. *Type:* Association.

Ehlert's Powersports Business—Guide to Suppliers Issue
Ehlert Publishing Group, Inc.
6420 Sycamore Ln.   Ph: (612)476-2200
Maple Grove, MN 55369   Free: 800-848-6247
   Fax: (612)476-8065
Contact: Joe Delmont, Editor, joe-d@mail.epginc.com.

Desc: Lists of 250 manufacturers of products related to the snowmobile industry and approximately 150 independent distributors. *Type:* Directory.

NSSRA Newsletter
National Ski & Snowboard Retailers Association
1699 Wall St.   Ph: (847)439-4293
Mount Prospect, IL 60056   Fax: (847)439-0111
Contact: Thomas B. Doyle, President.

Desc: Informs ski and snowboard retail stores on critical industry issues such as guidelines and litigation exposure and marketing. *Type:* Newsletter.

SGMA Today
Sporting Goods Manufacturers Association (SGMA)
200 Castlewood Dr.   Ph: (561)842-4100
North Palm Beach, FL 33408   Fax: (561)863-8984
Contact: Carol Feder, Editor, (561)840-1107, fax: (561)840-1130, cfsgma@aol.com.

Desc: Covers news of the sporting goods industry, including news of trade shows, legislation, international trade, and industry events. Reports on the activities of member associations. *Type:* Newsletter.

Shooting Industry—Buyers Guide Issue
Publishers Development Corp.
591 Camino de la Reina, Ste.   Ph: (619)297-8520
   200   Free: 800-633-8001
San Diego, CA 92108   Fax: (619)297-5353
Contact: Russ Thurman, Editor.

Desc: Manufacturers, wholesalers, and importers of guns and related equipment and supplies. *Type:* Directory.

SIA Retailer & Rep Advisor
Ski Industries America (SIA)
8377B Greensboro Dr.   Ph: (703)556-9020
Mc Lean, VA 22102-3587   Fax: (703)821-8276
E-mail: siamail@ix.netcom.com
Contact: Jennifer Smyers Burt, Editor.

Desc: Reports on the association's trade shows, marketing programs, retail publications and videos, and other on-snow industry news. Remarks: Incorporates the former USIA Ski Retailer and Rep Newsletter. *Type:* Newsletter.

Sporting Goods Manufacturers Association
200 Castlewood Dr.   Ph: (561)842-4100
North Palm Beach, FL 33408   Fax: (561)863-8984
E-mail: sgma@ix.netcom.com
URL: http://www.sportlink.com
Contact: John D. Riddle, CEO & Pres.

Desc: Manufacturers of athletic clothing, footwear, and sporting goods. Seeks to increase sports participation and create growth in the sporting goods industry. *Type:* Association.

The Super Show Official Show Directory and Sports Product Guide
The Super Show
1450 NE 123 St.   Ph: (305)893-8771
North Miami, FL 33161   Free: 800-327-3736
   Fax: (305)893-8783
E-mail: supershow@aol.com; laura@csmp.com.
Contact: Hardy Katz, Editor.

Desc: Sporting goods manufacturers worldwide. *Type:* Directory.

Sports
Access Fund
PO Box 17010   Ph: (303)545-6772
Boulder, CO 80308   Free: 888-863-6237
   Fax: (303)545-6774
E-mail: info@accessfund.org
URL: http://www.accessfund.org
Contact: Sally Moser, Exec.Dir.

Desc: Dedicated to supporting climber's interests while preserving diverse climbing resources. *Type:* Association.

Adelphi University
Human Performance Laboratory
Woodruff Hall   Ph: (516)877-4270
Garden City, NY 11530   Fax: (516)877-4258
E-mail: otto@adlibu.adelphi.edu
Contact: Dr. Robert Otto, Dir.

Desc: Human performance as it relates to exercise. *Type:* Research center.

Amateur Athletic Union

c/o The Walt Disney World
Resort
PO Box 10000
Lake Buena Vista, FL 32830-
1000
E-mail: pam@aausports.org
URL: http://www.aausports.org

Ph: (407)934-7200
Free: 800-AAU-4USA
Fax: (407)934-7242

Contact: Bobby Dodd, Pres.

Desc: Seeks to establish, develop, and implement a comprehensive youth sports program for athletes ages three to 19. Offers activities in 34 sports and conducts local, association (by state divisions), regional, and national championships. Bestows more than 300,000 awards. *Type:* Association.

American Double Dutch League

PO Box 776
Bronx, NY 10451

Ph: (212)865-9606

Contact: David A. Walker, Pres.

Desc: Individuals promoting the sport of Double Dutch rope jumping. (Double Dutch is a style of rope jumping in which two turners swing two ropes in opposite directions allowing them to touch the ground alternately, eggbeater style, while one or more participants jump through the ropes doing tricks.) Benefits of Double Dutch rope jumping include teamwork, cooperation, healthy competition, physical fitness, leadership, and creativity. The sport can be played by youngsters of all ages and requires only two ropes. Sponsors annual citywide, regional, and worldwide competitive events. *Type:* Association.

American Hockey Magazine

The Publishing Group, Inc.
1775 Bob Johnson Rd.
Colorado Springs, CO 80906-
4026

Ph: (719)599-5500
Fax: (719)599-5994

Contact: Darryl Seibel, Editor-in-Chief; Kris Pleimann, Editor.

Desc: U.S.A. Hockey (sports association) magazine. *Type:* Periodical.

American Hunter

National Rifle Association of America
11250 Waples Mill Rd.
Fairfax, VA 22030-9400

Ph: (703)267-1300
Free: 800-672-3888
Fax: (703)267-3971

URL: http://www.nra.org.

Contact: John Zent, Editor, (703)267-1332, fax: (703)267-3971; Diane Senesac, Advertising Dir., (703)267-1316, fax: (703)267-3800.

Desc: Hunting magazine emphasizing technique, sportsmanship, and safety. *Type:* Periodical.

American Professional Surfing Association

Surf House
Box 2174
Palm Beach, FL 33480

Ph: (305)832-4420

Contact: Dr. Gary F. R. Filosa, II, Pres.

Desc: Professional surfers competing in 16 events in the sport of surfing, bodyboarding, bodysurfing, kneeboarding, paddleboarding, sailsurfing, snowsurfing, standup shortboard surfing, standup longboard, surfskiing, and tandem surfing, and in the surfing Triathlon, Pentathlon, and Decathlon. Purpose is to govern all 16 events of professional surfing. *Type:* Association.

American Racing Pigeon Union

PO Box 18465
Oklahoma City, OK 73154-
0465
URL: http://www.pigeon.org

Ph: (405)478-2240
Free: 800-755-ARPU
Fax: (405)670-4748

Contact: Rick Phalen, Exec.Dir.

Desc: Persons interested in racing homing pigeons. *Type:* Association.

American Sports

American Sports Network, Inc.
PO Box 6100
Rosemead, CA 91770

Ph: (626)292-2222
Fax: (626)292-2221

Contact: Sam Sandler, Editor; Louis Zwick, Publisher; Steve Lowenstein, Advertising Mgr.

Desc: Sports magazine. *Type:* Periodical.

American Surfing Association

Surf House
Box 2174
Palm Beach, FL 33480

Ph: (305)832-4420

Contact: Dr. Winston Holt, Exec.Dir.

Desc: Competitive athletes. Purposes are: to make surfing an Olympic event; to standardize rules and regulations for the conduct and judging of surfing competitions; to represent the interests of the public in surfing; to promote surfing as an amateur sport; to formulate and maintain an informed national policy for amateur surfing; to guide governmental and nongovernmental groups in their respective areas of activity; to provide leadership in all aspects of American amateur surfing. Holds annual All-American Surfing Championships. *Type:* Association.

American Turners

1127 E. Kentucky St.
PO Box 4216
Louisville, KY 40204

Ph: (502)636-2395
Fax: (502)636-2395

Contact: Shirley Luckhardt, Sec.

Desc: Promotes health and physical education for the family through gymnastics, swimming, games, bowling, and cultural education through classes in music, painting, and handicrafts. Holds annual national tournaments in gymnastics, volleyball, basketball, softball, swimming, bowling, and cultural activities. *Type:* Association.

American Water Ski Association

799 Overlook Dr.
Winter Haven, FL 33884

Ph: (941)324-4341
Free: 800-533-AWSA
Fax: (941)325-8259

URL: http://www.usawaterski.org

Contact: Steve McDermeit, Exec.Dir.

Desc: Promotes competitive and recreational water skiing in the U.S. Authorizes and establishes rules for competition and certifies performance records in water skiing. Conducts water ski skills program and clinics for instructors and tournament officials. *Type:* Association.

Aqua-Field Turkey Hunting Guide

Aqua-Field Publishing Company, Inc.
66 W. Gilbert St., Ste. FL-2
Red Bank, NJ 07701

Ph: (908)935-1222
Fax: (908)935-9846

Contact: Edward Montague, Editor; Steve Ferber, Publisher.

Desc: Magazine on hunting methods, tactics, and equipment. *Type:* Periodical.

Arizona State University
Exercise and Sport Research Institute

Exercise Sci. & Physical
Education Dept.
Tempe, AZ 85287-0404
E-mail: philip.martin@asu.edu
URL: http://www.asu.edu/clas/espe/

Ph: (602)965-3913
Fax: (602)965-8108

Contact: Dr. Philip E. Martin, Dir.

Desc: Exercise and sport, including exercise physiology, sports psychology, exercise biochemistry, biomechanics, and motor behavior of various populations (children, athletes, elderly, adults). Provides exercise testing and exercise programs for research purposes. *Type:* Research center.

Aurora Mental Health Research Institute

14301 E. Hampden Ave.
Aurora, CO 80014
E-mail: 76570,2177@compuserve.com

Ph: (303)617-2300
Fax: (303)617-2397

Contact: Dr. Randy C. Stith, Dir. of Res.

Desc: Community-based mental health services and the support systems they require. Provides technical assistance to private and public agencies with special emphasis on person-machine issues relating to microcomputer and mainframe computers. *Type:* Research center.

Backpacker Magazine

Rodale Books
400 S. 10th St.
Emmaus, PA 18098-0099

Ph: (610)967-5171
Fax: (610)967-7722

E-mail: ddonche1@rodalepress.com; backpackdm@aol.com.
URL: http://www.rodalepress.com; http://www.bpbasecamp.com.

Contact: John Viehmann, Publisher; Thom Hogan, Exec. Editor, (610)967-8540, fax: (610)967-8181, thogan1@vodalepress.com; Nicholas Friedman, Assoc. Publisher, (610)967-7544, nfriedm1@rodalepress.com.

Desc: Magazine on self-propelled off road wilderness travel. *Type:* Periodical.

Bay Sports Review—Directory of Reno/Lake Tahoe Sports Book Casinos

Bay Sports Review
PO Box 4520
Berkeley, CA 94704
E-mail: baysport@aol.com.

Ph: (925)934-7647
Fax: (925)934-7650

Contact: Paul Matson, Editor.

Desc: List of major casinos in Reno and Lake Tahoe, Nevada that offer sports book facilities for legal wagers on professional and collegiate sporting events. *Type:* Directory.

Baylor Sports Science Lab

411 N. Washington, Ste. 3000
Dallas, TX 75246
E-mail: dg.mcbrayer@baylordallas.edu

Ph: (214)820-1513
Fax: (214)820-1682

Contact: Darvin G. McBrayer, Coord.

Desc: Sports/Fitness science, including exercise physiology and nutrition. *Type:* Research center.

Beckett Sports Collectibles and Autographs

Statabase, Inc.
15850 Dallas Parkway
Dallas, TX 75248
URL: http://www.beckett.com.

Ph: (972)991-6657
Fax: (972)991-8930

Contact: Dr. James Beckett, Editor and Publisher; Len Shelton, Editor, lshelton@beckett.com; Jeff Anthony, Advertising Mgr.

Desc: Sports magazine highlighting future NBA, NFL, and major league baseball stars. *Type:* Periodical.

Billiard Congress of America

910 23rd Ave.
Coralville, IA 52241-1221
E-mail: bca@netins.net
URL: http://www.bca-pool.com

Ph: (319)351-2112
Fax: (319)351-7767

Contact: Bruce D. Cottew, Exec.Dir.

Desc: Develops rules for billiards and pocket billiards. *Type:* Association.

Black College Sports Review

Winston-Salem Chronicle
617 N. Liberty St.   Ph: (336)722-8624
PO Box 1636   Fax: (336)723-9173
Winston-Salem, NC 27101-
    2912
Contact: Ernest H. Pitt, Publisher, fax: (336)748-0006.
Desc: Magazine covering black college sports; insert to black newspaper. *Type:* Periodical.

Blackpowder Hunter

Aqua-Field Publishing Company, Inc.
66 W. Gilbert St., Ste. FL-2   Ph: (908)935-1222
Red Bank, NJ 07701   Fax: (908)935-9846
Contact: Edward Montague, Editor; Steve Ferber, Publisher.
Desc: Magazine on hunting. *Type:* Periodical.

Bow and Arrow Hunting

Y-Visionary Publishing, LP
265 S Anita Dr., Ste. 120   Ph: (714)939-9991
Orange, CA 92868-3310   Fax: (714)939-9901
Contact: Bob Torres, Editor, (914)989-9991, fax: (714)939-9901; Chris Antoniardis, Advertising Mgr.
Desc: Magazine for bow hunters and archery enthusiasts. *Type:* Periodical.

Bowhunter Magazine

Cowles Enthusiast Media
4 High Ridge Park   Ph: (203)322-2400
Stamford, CT 06905   Fax: (203)322-1966
Contact: M.R. James, Editor, (406)756-9340, fax: (406)756-1754; Fred Wallace, Advertising Dir., (502)773-3737, fax: (502)773-3738; Richard Cochran, Editorial Director, (717)540-6717, fax: (717)657-9552.
Desc: The magazine is dedicated to the sport of Bowhunting *Type:* Periodical.

Bowhunting

Aqua-Field Publishing Company, Inc.
66 W. Gilbert St., Ste. FL-2   Ph: (908)935-1222
Red Bank, NJ 07701   Fax: (908)935-9846
Contact: Edward Montague, Editor; Steve Ferber, Publisher.
Desc: Magazine on bowhunting. *Type:* Periodical.

Bowhunting World

Ehlert Publishing Group, Inc.
6420 Sycamore Ln.   Ph: (612)476-2200
Maple Grove, MN 55369   Free: 800-848-6247
    Fax: (612)476-8065
Contact: Mike Strandlund, Editor; Dave Clayton, Sr. Sales Representative; Patty Brady, Sr. Sales Rep.
Desc: Magazine for all-season bowhunters and competitive archers. *Type:* Periodical.

Bowling-Golfing News

Master Associates
131 Winthrop Ave.   Ph: (914)292-9114
Liberty, NY 12754-1219   Fax: (914)292-9114
E-mail: bowlgolf@catskill.net.
Contact: E.C. Townsend, Editor.
Desc: Provides news and information on bowling and golf. *Type:* Newsletter.

Bridgewater State College

Human Performance Lab
Bridgewater, MA 02325   Ph: (508)697-1200
    Fax: (508)697-1717
E-mail: rhaslam@bridgew.edu
Contact: Dr. Robert Haslam, Dir.
Desc: Exercise physiology, including metabolic responses to exercise, blood flow responses to exercise, prediction of athlete success, and police and fire fighter fitness. *Type:* Research center.

Brigham Young University

Human Performance Research Center
Provo, UT 84602   Ph: (801)378-3981
Contact: A. Garth Fisher, PhD, Dir.
Desc: Exercise physiology, including studies of cardiovascular changes due to exercise, energy cost of various types of exercise, and body composition changes due to exercise. *Type:* Research center.

Cincinnati Sports Medicine Research and Education Foundation
Deaconess Hospital   Ph: (513)559-2818
311 Straight St.   Fax: (513)475-5263
Cincinnati, OH 45219
E-mail: sankerjuls@aol.com
URL: http://www.cincinnatisportsmed.com
Contact: Frank R. Noyes, MD, Dir.
Desc: Orthopedic and sports medicine with emphasis on clinical problems and surgical treatment. Areas of interest include rehabilitation protocols, use of allografts and autografts to replace knee ligaments, meniscal allografts, biomechanics of the knee and shoulder, and gait analysis. *Type:* Research center.

City Sports

City Sports, Inc.
214 S. Cedros Ave.   Ph: (619)793-2711
Solana Beach, CA 92075   Fax: (619)793-2710
Contact: Lois Schwartz, Editor; Bob Babbitt; John Smith.
Desc: Regional magazine (tabloid) promoting an active lifestyle. Includes articles on participation sports such as cycling, skiing, running, inline skating, and outdoor adventure. *Alt. Contact:* 214 S. Cedros Ave., Solana Beach, CA 92075; telephone: (619)793-2711; fax: (619)793-2710. *Type:* Periodical.

Clell Wade Coaches Directory

Clell Wade Coaches Directory, Inc.
PO Box 177   Ph: (417)847-2783
Cassville, MO 65625   Fax: (417)847-5920
E-mail: coadir@getonthe.net
Contact: Kay Elliott, Owner.
Desc: Published in 50 state and/or regional editions as well as 10 Canadian province editions, this series covers high school and college athletic programs and their personnel. *Type:* Directory.

Club E: The Dale Earnhardt Fan Club
4707 E. Baseline Rd.   Ph: 888-332-5823
Phoenix, AZ 85040   Free: 888-332-5823
    Fax: (602)337-3760
URL: http://www.earnhardtfan.com
Contact: Trisha Reilly, Mgr.
Desc: Fans of the race car driver Dale Earnhardt. *Type:* Association.

Colorado State University

Human Performance Laboratory
Department of Exercise & Sport   Ph: (970)491-7436
    Science   Fax: (970)491-0445
Fort Collins, CO 80523
E-mail: israel@cahs.colostate.edu
URL: http://www.colostate.edu
Contact: Dr. Richard Gay Israel, Exec.Dir.
Desc: Human performance, body composition, metabolism, nutrition and sports performance, and exercise physiology. *Type:* Research center.

CricInfo: The Home of Cricket on the Internet
SportsLine USA, Inc.
6340 NW 5th Way   Ph: (954)351-2120
Fort Lauderdale, FL 33309   Free: 800-771-4616
    Fax: (954)776-4745
E-mail: support@sportsline.com
URL: http://www.usa.cricket.org/
Desc: The CricInfo Cricket Database contains open-access information of interest to Cricket enthusiasts. Articles include those on old and new scorecards, schedules, statistics, humor, tour itineraries, match summaries, and information (back to 1791), and profiles of grounds and players, among others. *Type:* Database.

Deer Hunting North America

Aqua-Field Publishing Company, Inc.
66 W. Gilbert St., Ste. FL-2   Ph: (908)935-1222
Red Bank, NJ 07701   Fax: (908)935-9846
Contact: Edward Montague, Editor; Steve Ferber, Publisher.
Desc: Magazine on deer hunting. *Type:* Periodical.

Deer and Turkey Show Previews

Target Communications Corp.
7626 W. Donges Bay Rd.   Ph: (414)242-3990
Mequon, WI 53097   Free: 800-324-3337
    Fax: (414)242-7391
E-mail: targcomm@execpc.com
URL: http://www.deerinfo.com
Contact: Glenn Helgeland, Editor; Cheryl Keller, Sales Mgr.
Desc: Six magazines on 6 deer and turkey hunting shows. *Type:* Periodical.

Delaware All-Sports Research
1601 Milltown Rd., Ste. 24   Ph: (302)998-0178
Wilmington, DE 19808   Fax: (302)999-0700
Contact: Dr. J.P. Contompasis, Dir.
Desc: Sports medicine, including clinical and biomechanics research and etiology, treatment, and prevention of sports injuries. Biomechanics research is primarily concerned with lower extremity functions and pathomechanics. *Type:* Research center.

Divers Alert Network
Peter B. Bennett Center   Ph: (919)684-2948
6 W. Colony Place   Free: 800-446-2671
Durham, NC 27705   Fax: (919)490-6630
E-mail: shust001@mc.duke.edu
URL: http://www.diversalertnetwork.org
Contact: Peter Bennett, PhD, Exec.Dir.
Desc: Promotes recreational scuba diving safety and health. Develops emergency oxygen equipment and training. *Type:* Association.

Eastern Surfing Association
PO Box 207   Ph: (410)213-0515
Ocean City, MD 21842   Free: 800-WE-
    SHRED
    Fax: (410)213-2397
E-mail: centralhq@surfesa.org
URL: http://www.surfesa.org
Contact: Kathlyn B. Phillips, Exec.Dir.
Desc: Promotes the sport of surfing through amateur competitions; works to protect public beaches. *Type:* Association.

ESPNet SportsZone

Starwave Corporation
13810 SE Eastgate Way   Ph: (206)957-2000
Bellevue, WA 98005   Fax: (206)957-2009
URL: http://espnet.sportszone.com/
Desc: ESPNet's SportsZone provides the latest scores, statistics, and latest sports news free; subscribers get in-depth

analysis, expert columnists, player profiles, video highlights, live audio (NBA and NFL); the Zone Store; chatrooms, and more. There are also links to other major sports such as NASCAR online and the NBA.com. *Type:* Database.

Florida Sports Magazine

Florida Sports Inc.
PO Box 558090   Ph: (305)265-0060
Miami, FL 33255   Free: 800-932-2118
    Fax: (305)265-0906
URL: http://www.floridasports.com.
Contact: Jim Woodman, Jr., Editor and Publisher, jwoodman@floridasports.com.
Desc: Newspaper (tabloid) covering Florida's participatory sports; featuring sports profiles, event coverage, training suggestions, nutrition, sports medicine, travel, and sports calendar. *Type:* Periodical.

Football Digest

Century Publishing Co.
990 Grove St.   Ph: (847)491-6440
Evanston, IL 60201-4370   Fax: (847)491-0459
E-mail: century@wwa.com
Contact: Norman Jacobs, Publisher; Dale Jacobs, Production Dir.
Desc: Pro football magazine. *Type:* Periodical.

Football News

Football News, Inc.
8033 NW 36 St.   Ph: (305)594-0508
Miami, FL 33166   Free: 800-334-4005
    Fax: (305)594-0518
Contact: Tom Curtis, Publisher; Andy Cohen, General Mgr.
Desc: Sports magazine covering college and professional football. *Type:* Periodical.

Fred Bear Sports Club

RR 4   Ph: (352)376-2411
4600 SW 41st Blvd.   Fax: (352)376-6115
Gainesville, FL 32608-4999
Contact: Frank Scott, Contact.
Desc: Bowhunters and others dedicated to the protection of outdoor ecology and proper wildlife management of North American woods, fields, and waters. Encourages compliance with the rules of fair chase and state game and fish laws. Conducts demographic research on bowhunters. *Type:* Association.

Grand Valley State University

Human Performance Laboratory

132 Fieldhouse   Ph: (616)895-3228
Allendale, MI 49401   Fax: (616)895-3232
E-mail: scottj@gvsu.edu
Contact: James R. Scott, Coord.
Desc: Human performance studies, including elite athlete performance profiles (wrestlers), functional electrostimulation exercise with quadriplegic participants, and faculty/staff fitness and lifestyle assessments. *Type:* Research center.

Guide to Yoga Teachers & Classes

Yoga International
RR 1, Box 407   Ph: (570)253-4929
Honesdale, PA 18431   Free: 800-253-6243
    Fax: (570)253-6360
E-mail: yimag@yimag.com
URL: http://www.yimag.com.
Contact: Deborah Willoughby, Editor.
Desc: Regional, national, and international listings of yoga programs, as well as yoga teacher certification programs. *Type:* Directory.

Guns&Gear

B.A.S.S. Inc.
5845 Carmichael Rd.   Ph: (334)272-9530
Montgomery, AL 36117-2329   Fax: (334)279-7148
E-mail: bassinc@mindspring.com; gunsgear@mindspring.com.
Contact: Colin Moore, Editor; Helen Sevier, Publisher; Mike Swain, Adv./Sales Mgr.; Celeste McCaleb, Promotions Coord.; Stephen Mitchell, Adv. Director.
Desc: Hunting and shooting related news and product reviews. *Alt. Contact:* PO Box 17900, Montgomery, AL 36141; telephone: (334)272-9530. *Type:* Periodical.

Handicapping Monthly

Handicapping Monthly
Box 539
Medinah, IL 60157
Contact: Roger Bruce, Editor.
Desc: Gives information on how horse racing handicapping is treated like a business. Recurring features include news of research. *Type:* Newsletter.

Harmon Football Forecast

PO Box 994   Ph: (516)432-6376
Long Beach, NY 11561
Contact: James M. Harmon, Editor and Publisher.
Desc: Distributes weekly college and NFL forecasts. *Alt. Contact:* PO Box 994, Long Beach, NY 11561; telephone: (516)432-6376. *Type:* Periodical.

High Technology Fitness Research Institute

2434 N. Greenview, Ste. 305   Ph: (773)528-1000
Chicago, IL 60614   Fax: (773)929-5733
E-mail: bgoldman@worldheath.net
URL: http://www.worldhealth.net
Contact: Dr. Bob Goldman, Dir.
Desc: Effects of drugs and ergogenetics on human performance and analysis of health and fitness products and programs on the market, including fitness technology applications in the treatment and prevention of lifestyle-induced pathologies. Programs include training methods for athletes, the development of protocols and standards for fitness technology evaluation, drug dependency, longevity, and aids to conventional physical therapy for patients with chronic back pain. *Type:* Research center.

Hockey Digest

Century Publishing Co.
990 Grove St.   Ph: (847)491-6440
Evanston, IL 60201-4370   Fax: (847)491-0459
E-mail: century@wwa.com
Contact: Norman Jacobs, Publisher; Kenneth Leiker, Senior Editor; Dale Jacobs, Production Dir.; James O'Connor, Managing Editor.
Desc: Magazine covering professional hockey. *Type:* Periodical.

Hockey North America

11501 Sunset Hills Rd., 4th Fl.   Ph: (703)471-0400
Reston, VA 20190   Free: 800-446-2539
    Fax: (703)904-7160
Contact: Elliott Root, C.O.O.
Desc: Hockey league. *Type:* Association.

Hoosier Outdoors

Recreation Vehicle Indiana Council (RVIC)
3210 Rand Rd.   Ph: (317)247-6258
Indianapolis, IN 46241   Free: 800-837-7842
    Fax: (317)243-9174
E-mail: imharvic@ix.netcom.com
Desc: Recreation vehicle lifestyle magazine and Indiana campground directory. *Type:* Periodical.

Human Performance International

3127 W. International Speedway   Ph: (904)248-1402
Blvd.   Fax: (904)248-1403
Daytona Beach, FL 32124-1070
E-mail: hpi19@idt.net
Contact: Dr. Dan Q. Marisi, Dir.
Desc: Biomechanical, physiological, and psychological and medical factors affecting human performance during competitive racing and other athletic activities, such as the influence of body heat on cardiovascular stress. *Type:* Research center.

Ice Skating Institute

17120 Dallas Pkwy., Ste. 140   Ph: (972)735-8800
Dallas, TX 75248   Fax: (972)735-8815
E-mail: isi@skateisi.com
URL: http://www.skateisi.com
Desc: Ice rink owners and managers; builders and suppliers for the industry; skaters; ice skating instructors. Seeks to educate ice rink owners, operators, and instructors and to increase public interest in ice skating. *Type:* Association.

Interbike Directory

Miller Freeman, Inc.
502 W. Cordova Rd.   Ph: (505)988-7224
Santa Fe, NM 87501   Free: 800-486-2701
    Fax: (505)988-5099
E-mail: brin2@aol.com
Contact: John Crenshaw, Editor.
Desc: Approximately 1,850 manufacturers and distributors of bicycle products and related organizations and events; international coverage. *Type:* Directory.

International Center for Aquatic Research

1 Olympic Plaza   Ph: (719)578-4578
Colorado Springs, CO 80909   Fax: (719)578-4669
URL: http://www.usswim.org
Contact: Steve Roush, Contact.
Desc: Human performance studies, including training methodology, exercise biochemistry, physiology of performance, muscle strength/power and conditioning, motion and computer analysis, and sports technology. *Type:* Research center.

International Cheerleading Foundation

10660 Barkley   Ph: (913)649-3666
Overland Park, KS 66212   Free: 800-255-0296
    Fax: (913)341-6031
Contact: Randy Neil, Pres.
Desc: Cheerleaders, drill teams, mascots, pep clubs, and faculty coaches from youth leagues, junior and senior high schools, and colleges in the United States, Europe, Canada, and Central and South America. Conducts summer camps, national cheerleading championships, and home camps; develops educational publications, videotapes, and computer programs for cheerleaders. *Type:* Association.

International Council of Motor Sport Sciences

3905 Vincennes Rd., Ste. 303   Ph: (317)471-3596
Indianapolis, IN 46268   Fax: (317)471-3508
Contact: Jon Potter, Bus.Admin.
Desc: Enhancement of performance and safety in automobile racing, including the physical and psychological aspects of race performance as well as the role of diet, exercise, and mental preparation in performance. *Type:* Research center.

International Jet Sports Boating Association

1239 E. Warner Ave.   Ph: (714)751-4277
Santa Ana, CA 92705   Free: 800-949-1462
    Fax: (714)751-8418
Contact: Jay Gillogly, VP.
Desc: Owners, competitors, dealers, performance product manufacturers, and individuals supporting the sport of

personal watercraft. Promotes the recreational and competitive use of certain single- and double-rider motorized watercraft; serves as the major sanctioning body for the sport of personal watercraft. *Type:* Association.

International Racquetball Federation

1685 W. Uintah   Ph: (719)635-5396
Colorado Springs, CO 80904-   Fax: (719)635-0685
2921
E-mail: usrapr@webaccess.net
URL: http://www.racqmag.com
Contact: Luke St. Onge, Sec.Gen.

Desc: International sports federations representing over 14 million members. Fosters the promotion, development, and improvement of racquetball throughout the world. Seeks to increase interest and participation in the sport. *Type:* Association.

International Soap Box Derby

PO Box 7225   Ph: (330)733-8723
Akron, OH 44306   Fax: (330)733-1370
E-mail: 2077607@mcimail.com
Contact: Jeff Iula, Gen.Mgr.

Desc: Youth racing program sponsored by civic clubs, service organizations, business firms, interested groups, and individuals. Franchises Soap Box Derby programs throughout the U.S. and in several foreign countries. *Type:* Association.

Junior Bowhunter Program

National Field Archery Association
31407 Outer I-10
Redlands, CA 92373
Contact: Pam Shilling, Exec.Sec.

Desc: A division of the National Field Archery Association. Youth compound bow enthusiasts. Provides clubs and programs for youth interested in archery. *Type:* Association.

Kansas-Oklahoma Sports Guide of High Schools and Colleges Coaches Directory

Craftsman Publications, Inc./Western Sports Guides
3984 Donipman Dr.   Ph: (915)584-7791
PO Box 12476   Fax: (915)584-7791
El Paso, TX 79913
Contact: Carol Coynor, Editor; Cynthia L. Smith, Editor.

Desc: Covers about 1,070 schools and colleges in Kansas and Oklahoma; types of personnel included, kinds of information provided, etc., are same as in "Arizona-Nevada-New Mexico Sports Guide" *Type:* Directory.

Kent State University

Exercise Physiology Lab

Sch. of Exercise, Leisure &   Ph: (330)672-2857
Sport   Fax: (330)672-4106
162 MACC Annex
Kent, OH 44242
E-mail: wsinning@kentvm.kent.edu
Contact: Dr. Wayne E. Sinning, Contact.

Desc: Exercise physiology, body composition, and physical fitness, including studies of protein metabolism and exercise, cardiovascular/respiratory responses during exercise in heat and cold, an neuromuscular integration/biomechanics, and psychosocial reactivity to behavioral stressors. *Type:* Research center.

Laban/Bartenieff Institute of Movement Studies, Inc.

11 E. 4th St.   Ph: (212)477-4299
New York, NY 10003   Fax: (212)477-3702
E-mail: Lims@info.erds.com
Contact: Lucy Rumack, Dir. of Certificate Prog.

Desc: Perception, description, and analysis of human movement for applications in dance and theater, physical therapy, psychotherapy, nonverbal communication, management consulting, anthropology, and fitness and sports training. The Institute's mission is to further the studies of the principles of movement formulated by Rudolf Laban (1879-1958), an Austro-Hungarian dancer, choreographer, and philosopher, and Irmgard Bartenieff (1900-1981), who applied her Laban training to physical therapy, dance therapy, anthropology, and dance. *Type:* Research center.

Laval University

Physical Activity Sciences Laboratory

Pavillon de l'education physique   Ph: (418)656-5174
et des sports   Fax: (418)656-3044
Quebec, PQ, Canada G1K 7P4
E-mail: claude.bouchard@kin.msp.ulaval.ca
Contact: Claude Bouchard, Dir.

Desc: Genetic and molecular basis of adaptation to exercise and nutritional stresses by obese individuals and highly active or sedentary individuals and their relatives. Research focuses on lipid and lipoprotein metabolism, adipose tissue and skeletal muscle metabolism, fat distribution, and the role of genetic polymorphism. *Type:* Research center.

Maccabi USA/Sports for Israel

1926 Arch St., Ste. 4R   Ph: (215)561-6900
Philadelphia, PA 19103   Fax: (215)561-5470
E-mail: maccabi@maccabiusa.com
URL: http://www.maccabiusa.com
Contact: Barbara G. Lissy, Exec. Dir.

Desc: Individuals, groups, and foundations interested in encouraging a program of participation by Jewish youth in sports, physical fitness, and physical education. Sponsors United States Maccabiah Games Team, Israel Sports Center for the Disabled, and the Wingate Institute for Physical Education in Israel. Develops, promotes, and supports international, national and regional based athletic activities. *Type:* Association.

Media Sports Business

Paul Kagan Associates, Inc.
126 Clock Tower Pl.   Ph: (831)624-1536
Carmel, CA 93923   Fax: (831)625-3225
E-mail: info@kagan.com
Contact: George Niesen, Editor.

Desc: Discusses the economics of national and regional cable and pay TV sports. Includes semiannual census of cable and pay sports channels, coverage of values of sports media rights, and news of other developments in the field. *Type:* Newsletter.

Melpomene Institute for Women's Health Research

1010 University Ave.   Ph: (612)642-1951
St. Paul, MN 55104   Fax: (612)642-1871
E-mail: melpomen@skypoint.com
URL: http://www.melpomene.org
Contact: Judy Mahle Lutter, Pres.

Desc: Physically active women and girls, including effects of exercise on menstruation, pregnancy, adolescent girls, self-esteem and physical activity, menopause, body image, osteoporosis, stress and aging, children's introduction to physical activity, and disabled women and exercise. *Type:* Research center.

Men's Fitness

Weider Publications
21100 Erwin St.   Ph: (818)884-6800
Woodland Hills, CA 91367-   Free: 800-423-5590
3712   Fax: (818)704-5734
E-mail: jweider@weiderpub.com

URL: http://www.mensfitness.com.
Contact: Joe Weider, Publisher.

Desc: Magazine devoted to health, nutrition, fitness and general lifestyle. *Type:* Periodical.

NASCAR Winston Cup Scene

Street & Smith's Sports Group
First Citizen Plaza   Ph: (704)375-7404
128 S. Tryon St., Ste. 2200   Free: 800-704-3757
Charlotte, NC   Fax: (704)371-3299
Contact: Steve Waid, Vice President, (704)371-3966, fax: (704)371-3990, shwaid@ix.netcom.com.

Desc: Trade paper covering the NASCAR Winston Cup and Busch Series circuits. *Type:* Periodical.

National Association of African-American Sportswriters and Broadcasters

308 Deer Park Ave.   Ph: (516)462-3933
Dix Hills, NY 11746
Contact: Clyde Davis, Pres.

Desc: African-American men and women involved in the sports industry. Provides job information in the areas of sports medicine, sports law, and sports management. *Type:* Association.

National Association of Sports Officials

2017 Lathrop Ave.   Ph: (414)632-5448
Racine, WI 53405   Fax: (414)632-5460
E-mail: naso@naso.com
Contact: Barry Mano, Pres.

Desc: Active sports officials, umpires, companies, and individuals interested in sports. Develops programs to assist in the education of sports officials; engages in programs to instruct fans, coaches, players, and the media on the role of sports officials. Conducts clinics and camps; sponsors public service ads. *Type:* Association.

National Association of Underwater

9942 Currie Davis Dr., Ste. H   Ph: (909)621-5801
Tampa, FL 33619-2667   Fax: (909)621-6405
Contact: Jim Bram, Pres.

Desc: Encourages all levels of divers and nondivers to continue their education about the underwater environment. *Type:* Association.

National Association of Underwater Instructors

9942 Currie Daves Dr., Ste. H   Ph: (813)628-6284
Tampa, FL 33619-2667   Free: 800-553-6284
     Fax: (813)628-8253
E-mail: nauihq@nauiww.org
URL: http://www.naui.org/
Contact: James Bram, Pres.

Desc: Certified instructors of basic, advanced, and specialized courses in underwater diving. *Type:* Association.

National Collegiate Athletic Association

6201 College Blvd.   Ph: (913)339-1906
Overland Park, KS 66211   Fax: (913)339-0030
URL: http://www.ncaa.org
Contact: Cedric W. Dempsey, Exec.Dir.

Desc: Universities, colleges, and allied educational athletics associations devoted to the administration of intercollegiate athletics. Operates statistics service for college football and baseball; women's softball; men's and women's basketball; publishing service; film production service. Maintains 42 sports committees including: Baseball; Ice Hockey; Men's and Women's Basketball Rules; Men's Football; Men's and Women's Fencing; Men's and Women's Golf; Men's and Women's Gymnastics; Men's and Women's Lacrosse; Men's and Women's Rifle; Men's and Women's Skiing; Men's and Women's Swimming; Men's and Women's Track and Field; Men's and Women's Volleyball; Men's Wrestling; Women's Softball. *Type:* Association.

National Federation Interscholastic Officials Association

11724 NW Plaza Cir.   Ph: (816)464-5400
PO Box 20630   Fax: (816)464-5571
Kansas City, MO 64195
URL: http://www.nfhs.org
Contact: Don Sparks, Dir.

Desc: High school, youth league, and college sports officials. Objective is to promote the professional growth and image of interscholastic sports officials. Provides a forum for officials to make suggestions on rules and procedures in high school sports in the U.S. *Type:* Association.

National Federation of State High School Associations

11724 NW Plaza Cir.   Ph: (816)464-5400
PO Box 20626   Fax: (816)464-5571
Kansas City, MO 64195-0626
URL: http://www.nfhs.org
Contact: Robert F. Kanaby, Exec.Dir.

Desc: Federation of high school athletic/activities associations from the 50 U.S. states, the District of Columbia, Virgin Islands, 11 Canadian provinces, Bermuda, and Guam representing more than 20,400 high schools. Seeks to protect and supervise the interstate athletic, musical, and speech and debate interests of high schools and coordinate the activities of state associations. *Type:* Association.

National Federation of State High School Associations—NFHS News

National Federation of State High School Associations
11724 NW Plaza Circle   Ph: (816)464-5400
Kansas City, MO 64153-1158   Fax: (816)464-5571
Contact: Bruce L. Howard, Editor.

Desc: Covers NFHS news, national high school athletic/activities rules and regulations, sportsmanship, sports medicine and psychology, athletic administration, and healthy lifestyles. Recurring features include columns titled Around the Nation, Music and Speech and Debate, Where Are They Now?, and Ideas That Work. *Type:* Newsletter.

National Field Archery Association

31407 Outer I-10   Ph: (909)794-2133
Redlands, CA 92373   Free: 800-811-2331
                             Fax: (909)794-8512
URL: http://www.smart.net/~stimsonr/nfaa.html
Contact: Marihelen Rogers, Exec.Sec.

Desc: Field archers and bowhunters. Sponsors field archery schools, three national tournaments, and 16 sectional tournaments; works toward conservation of game and its natural habitat. *Type:* Association.

National High School Rodeo Association

11178 N. Huron, Ste. 7   Ph: (303)452-0820
Denver, CO 80234   Free: 800-46-NHSRA
                             Fax: (303)452-0912
E-mail: info@nhsra.org
Contact: Kent Sturman, Gen. Mgr.

Desc: Sponsors and promotes high school rodeo; organization hosts the NHSRA Finals, which is believed to be the world's largest rodeo featuring 1500 state and provincial champions competing in a week-long, 13-performance rodeo. *Type:* Association.

National Horseshoe Pitchers Association of America

Dick Hansen
3085 76th St.   Ph: (414)835-9108
Franksville, WI 53126
Contact: Dick Hansen, Sec.-Treas.

Desc: Fosters, develops, and promotes the sport of horseshoe pitching on all levels, both as recreational pastime and competitive sport. Has established a unified code of rules, equipment, and playing procedures. Makes available game-related items including official shoes, trophies, scoresheets, and ringer charts. *Type:* Association.

National Institute for Fitness and Sport

250 University Blvd.   Ph: (317)274-3432
Indianapolis, IN 46202-5192 Fax: (317)274-7408
URL: http://www.nifs.org
Contact: Jerry Taylor, Pres.

Desc: Exercise physiology, sports medicine, and health and fitness education. *Type:* Research center.

National Pocket Billiard Association

PO BOX 340245   Ph: (414)328-3693
Milwaukee, WI 53234-0245
Contact: Arthur J. Manske, Pres.

Desc: Pool players (8-ball); foosball players; taverns; pool parlors. Sanctions league and tournament competition; standardizes rules and procedures; processes data and, through use of computers, ensures fair competition. Maintains charitable program and hall of fame. *Type:* Association.

National Shuffleboard Association

Howard J. Rayle
1415 Main St. Lot 267
Dunedin, FL 34698-6225
Contact: Howard J. Rayle, Pres.

Desc: Federation of state shuffleboard associations. Promotes and supervises tournaments, including national championship tournaments; establishes official rules of play; organizes and assists state shuffleboard associations; operates museum and Hall of Fame containing trophies and articles of historical interest. Promotes International Shuffleboard, which is composed of competing teams from the U.S., Australia, Canada, and Japan. *Type:* Association.

National Speed Sport News

National Speed Sport News
6509 Hudspeth Rd.   Ph: (704)455-2531
PO Box 1210   Fax: (704)455-2605
Harrisburg, NC 28075
E-mail: access@mountainmessenger.com
Contact: Chris Economaki, Editor and Publisher; Corinne Economaki, Publisher.

Desc: Newspaper featuring auto racing, sport cars, and motors. *Type:* Periodical.

New York Road Runners Club

9 E. 89th St.   Ph: (212)860-4455
New York, NY 10128   Fax: (212)860-9754
Contact: Allan Steinfeld, Pres.

Desc: Runners united to promote running for fitness and competition. Sponsors 150 races throughout the year, including New York City Marathon and Triathlon. Conducts classes and clinics for beginning, intermediate, and advanced runners. *Type:* Association.

News/Retrieval Sports Report

Dow Jones & Company, Inc.
P.O. Box 300   Ph: (609)520-4000
Princeton, NJ 08543-0300
URL: http://www.dj.com
Desc: Contains the complete text of sports news stories and statistics from the SportsTicker news service. Includes game scores, league standings, team schedules, and sports transactions. *Available:* Dow Jones & Company, Inc. *Type:* Database.

Nicholas Institute of Sports Medicine and Athletic Trauma

130 E. 77th St.   Ph: (212)434-2700
New York, NY 10021   Fax: (212)434-2687
URL: http://www.nismat.org
Contact: Dr. Stephen J. Nicholas, Dir.

Desc: Sports medicine in the areas of orthopedics and trauma, fluid and electrolyte balance, nutrition, endocrinology and physical therapy, cardiology, and biomechanics. *Type:* Research center.

North American Hunter

North American Outdoor Group, Inc.
12301 Whitewater Dr., Ste. 260 Ph: (612)988-7117
Minnetonka, MN 55343   Free: 800-688-7611
                             Fax: (612)936-9169
E-mail: addept@naoginc.com
URL: http://www.huntingclub.com.
Contact: Gregg Gutschow, Editor, (612)988-7225; Tom Perrier, Publisher; Russell M. Nolan, Group Publisher.

Desc: Hunting magazine. *Type:* Periodical.

North American Hunting Club

12301 Whitewater Dr.   Ph: (612)936-9333
PO Box 3401   Fax: (612)936-9755
Minnetonka, MN 55343
Contact: Steven F. Burke, Pres.

Desc: Hunters of game animals and birds of North America. Seeks to improve the hunting skills of members and promote the enjoyment of the sport. *Type:* Association.

The Olympian

U.S. Olympic Committee
One Olympic Plaza   Ph: (719)578-4529
Colorado Springs, CO 80909   Fax: (719)578-4677
E-mail: olympian.magazine@usoc.org.
URL: http://www.olympic-usa.org.
Contact: Bob Condron, Editor; H.O. Zimman, Publisher, (781)598-9230, fax: (781)599-4018; David Zimman, Advertising Mgr.

Desc: Magazine reporting the activities of the U.S. Olympic Committee. *Type:* Periodical.

The Olympic Factbook

The Gale Group
27500 Drake Rd.   Ph: (248)699-4253
Farmington Hills, MI 48331-3535
URL: http://www.galegroup.com
Desc: A guide to the winter and summer Olympic games, covering traditional, new, and demonstration sports. For each sport, provides history and highlights, rules and procedures, a list of winners, and biographical profiles of past winners and this year's hopefuls, as well a schedule of events. *Available:* LEXIS-NEXIS, NEXIS. *Type:* Database.

Pennsylvania State University Biomechanics Laboratory

39 Rec. Hall   Ph: (814)865-3445
University Park, PA 16802   Fax: (814)865-2440
E-mail: vxz1@psu.edu
URL: http://www.psu.edu/dept/biomechanics
Contact: Dr. Vladimir Zatisiorsky, Dir.

Desc: Human movement, including scientific study and analysis of human motion as observed in sports, industry, and activities of daily living. Analyzes gymnastics, diving, cross-country skiing, swimming, and other sports through use of high-speed video, force measuring devices, and on-line computer techniques. *Type:* Research center.

Pennsylvania State University

Center for Sports Medicine

1850 E. Park Ave., Ste. 112   Ph: (814)865-3566
University Park, PA 16802   Fax: (814)865-7803

Contact: Dr. Wayne Sebastianelli, Dir.

Desc: Physiology of human performance, sports conditioning, and the role of exercise in the prevention and rehabilitation of sports injuries. Areas of investigation include molecular biology, physiology, biomechanics, locomotion studies, nutrition, bioengineering, and epidemiology. *Type:* Research center.

Pennsylvania State University

Noll Physiological Research Center

129 Noll Laboratory Bldg.   Ph: (814)865-3453
University Park, PA 16802   Fax: (814)865-4602
E-mail: paf4@psu.edu
URL: http://www.noll.psu.edu/

Contact: Dr. Peter A. Farrell, Dir.

Desc: Metabolic adaptations to stress, biology of aging, and environmental and exercise physiology. Studies the effects of aging, physical activity, nutritional status, and heat, cold, and altitude stress on muscle metabolism and function, thermoregulation and cardiovascular control, immune function, and carbohydrate, insulin, and protein metabolism. *Type:* Research center.

People-to-People Sports Committee

71 S. Orange Ave., No. 207   Ph: (516)482-5158
South Orange, NJ 07079-1715   Fax: (516)482-3239

Contact: Dr. Rand P. Milton, Pres.

Desc: Persons prominent in the promotion of sports, particularly on an international level; national sports organizations. Promotes international sports exchanges to increase international goodwill and understanding. Makes donations of sports equipment and provides coaches to developing countries of the world. *Type:* Association.

Polo—Winter Polo Directory Issue

Westchester Media

8214 Westchester Dr.   Fax: (214)750-4522
Dallas, TX 75225

Desc: List of 20 polo clubs with winter seasons. *Type:* Directory.

Pop Warner Football

586 Middletown Blvd., Ste.   Ph: (215)752-2691
C-100   Fax: (215)752-2879
Langhorne, PA 19047
E-mail: pwlsreg@aol.com
URL: http://www.dickbutkus.com/popwarner

Contact: Jon C. Butler, Exec.Dir.

Desc: Youths ages 5 to 16 organized into approximately 5,000 teams playing tackle and flag football under safety-first rules. Affiliated local groups must enforce strict safety rules, equipment standards, and age and weight limitations. *Type:* Association.

Pro-Am Sports Service/Mile Square Publisher

PO Box 24072   Ph: (317)632-1984
Indianapolis, IN 46224   Fax: (317)630-0111

Contact: David C. Sassman, Editor and Publisher.

Desc: Distributes sports, features, alternative religion, music and book reviews. *Alt. Contact:* PO Box 24072, Indianapolis, IN 46224; telephone: (317)632-1984; fax: (317)630-0111. *Type:* Periodical.

Professional Association of Diving Instructors

30151 Tomas   Ph: (714)540-7234
Rancho Santa Margarita, CA   Free: 800-729-7234
92688-2125   Fax: (714)540-2609
URL: http://www.padi.com

Contact: Brian Cronin, VP.

Desc: Educates and certifies underwater scuba instructors. *Type:* Association.

Professional Billiards Tour

4412 Commercial Way   Ph: (352)596-7808
Spring Hill, FL 34606-1966   Free: 888-PRO-POOL
    Fax: (352)596-7441

Contact: Don Mackey, CEO.

Desc: Interested individuals united to promote the sport of professional billiards. Seeks to get television air play and commercial sponsors for the sport. *Type:* Association.

Professional Rodeo Cowboys Association

101 Prorodeo Dr.   Ph: (719)593-8840
Colorado Springs, CO 80919   Fax: (719)548-4876

Contact: Steve Hatchell, Commissioner.

Desc: Rodeos (800); contestants, stock contractors, and contract performers (5760) in the sport of professional rodeo. Acts as rule-making and governing body for professional rodeo; grants approval to and provides leadership for rodeos sponsored by local community groups. Produces annual National Finals Rodeo through the National Finals Rodeo Committee. *Type:* Association.

The Record

USA Track & Field (USATF)

PO Box 120   Ph: (317)261-0500
Indianapolis, IN 46206   Fax: (317)261-0481
URL: http://www.usatf.org.

Contact: Mark Springer, Editor.

Desc: Covers developments and events in track and field, long distance running, and race walking. Carries information on athletic rules, competitions, and training camps. *Type:* Newsletter.

Road Runners Club of America

Henley Gabeau

1150 S. Washington St., Ste.   Ph: (703)836-0558
250   Fax: (703)836-4430
Alexandria, VA 22314
E-mail: office@rrca.org
URL: http://www.rrca.org/~rrca/

Contact: Henley Gabeau, Exec.Dir.

Desc: Active long-distance runners and other persons who are interested in promoting long-distance running on an amateur basis in the U.S. Works to encourage running, especially road running, by sponsoring championships and other races on the road, track, and cross-country; also sponsors time trials, social runs, jogging, lectures, and demonstrations. *Type:* Association.

Rodale's SCUBA Diving

Rodale Books

400 S. 10th St.   Ph: (610)967-5171
Emmaus, PA 18098-0099   Fax: (610)967-7722
E-mail: ddonche1@rodalepress.com
URL: http://www.rodalepress.com

Contact: Dave McAfee, Publisher; Dane Farnum, Advertising Dir.

Desc: Magazine on scuba diving. *Alt. Contact:* 6600 Abercom St., Ste. 208, Savannah, GA 31405-5840; telephone: (912)351-0855; fax: (912)351-0890. *Type:* Periodical.

Roller Skating Association International

6905 Corporate Dr.   Ph: (317)347-2626
Indianapolis, IN 46278-1927   Fax: (317)347-2636
E-mail: rsa@rollerskating.org
URL: http://www.rollerskating.org

Contact: Katherine Mandusic McDonell, Exec.Dir.

Desc: Independent roller skating rink operators; associate members are rink managers, teachers, and suppliers and manufacturers. Promotes the business and recreational sport of roller skating. *Type:* Association.

Runner's World

Rodale Books

400 S. 10th St.   Ph: (610)967-5171
Emmaus, PA 18098-0099   Fax: (610)967-7722
E-mail: ddonche1@rodalepress.com; rwedit@rodalepress.com
URL: http://www.rodalepress.com; http://www.runnersworld.com.

Contact: Amby Burfoot, Editor; George A. Hirsch, Publisher, (212)682-2237; Claudia Malley, Asst. Pub.

Desc: Running, jogging, and health magazine. *Type:* Periodical.

Running Times—Marathon Guide Column

Fitness Publishing, Inc.

213 Danbury Rd.   Ph: (203)761-1113
Wilton, CT 06897   Fax: (203)761-9933

Contact: Janet Newman, Editor.

Desc: Calendar of about 200 marathons and half marathons to take place during the coming six-month period. *Type:* Directory.

Running Times—Road Race Calendar Column

Fitness Publishing, Inc.

213 Danbury Rd.   Ph: (203)761-1113
Wilton, CT 06897   Fax: (203)761-9933

Contact: Janet Newman, Editor.

Desc: List of running events in the United States and worldwide. *Type:* Directory.

Shotgun Sports

Shotgun Sports, Inc.

PO Box 6810   Ph: (916)889-2220
Auburn, CA 95604   Free: 800-676-8920
    Fax: (916)889-9106
E-mail: shotsports@aol.com; shotgunsports@mcocnoxies.org; shotgun_sports@macnexus.org.
URL: http://www.shotgun_sports.com.

Contact: Frank Kodl, Editor and Publisher.

Desc: Magazine for clay target shooting and hunting. *Type:* Periodical.

Skin Diver

Petersen Publishing Co., L.L.C.

6420 Wilshire Blvd.   Ph: (323)782-2350
Los Angeles, CA 90048-5515   Fax: (323)782-2704

Contact: Bill Gleason, Editor and Publisher; Peter Clancey, Senior Vice President.

Desc: Magazine covers diving, underwater photography, and diving education. *Type:* Periodical.

Snow Goer

Camar Publications Ltd.

210-340 Ferrier St.   Ph: (905)475-8440
Markham, ON, Canada L3R   Fax: (905)475-9246
2Z5
URL: http://www.snowgoermagazine.com.

Contact: Jacqueline Howe, Publisher, jacquelinehowe@camarpublications.com; Chris Knowles, Editor, sgeditorial@sympatico.ca; John King, Sales Mgr., johnking@camarpublications.com.

Desc: Magazine for Canadian snowmobilers. *Type:* Periodical.

Snow Sports Industries America

8377-B Greensboro Dr.   Ph: (703)556-9020
Mc Lean, VA 22102-3587   Fax: (703)821-8276
E-mail: siamail@snowsports.com
URL: http://www.snowlink.com

Contact: David Ingemie, Pres.

Desc: Manufacturers, distributors, and suppliers of ski, snowboard, on-snow, and outdoor action sports apparel, equipment, footwear, and accessories. To encourage friendly trade and social relationships in the on-snow industry. *Type:* Association.

Soccer Jr.

Triplepoint Inc.
27 Unquowa Rd.   Ph: (203)259-5766
Fairfield, CT 06430   Fax: (203)256-1119
E-mail: soccerjrol@aol.com.
Contact: Joe Provey, Editor; Tom Mindrum, Publisher.
Desc: Magazine about soccer. *Type:* Periodical.

Splash

McMullen Argus Publishing, Inc.
774 S. Placentia Ave.   Ph: (714)939-2400
Placentia, CA 92870   Fax: (714)572-1864
Contact: Rob Hallstrom, Editor, (714)572-6887, fax:
(714)572-4265; Greg Gill, VP of Advertising.
Desc: Magazine for personal watercraft sports enthusiasts.
Type: Periodical.

Sport Magazine

Petersen Publishing Co., L.L.C.
6420 Wilshire Blvd.   Ph: (323)782-2350
Los Angeles, CA 90048-5515 Fax: (323)782-2704
Contact: Norb Garrett, Editor; Polly Perkins, President.
Desc: Magazine on major spectator sports. *Alt. Contact:*
110 Fifth Fl., 3rd Fl., New York, NY 10011; telephone:
(212)886-3600; fax: (212)229-4838. *Type:* Periodical.

SPORTDiscus

Sport Information Resource Centre (SIRC)
1600 James Naismith Dr.   Ph: (613)748-5658
Gloucester, ON, Canada K1B
  5N4
E-mail: moreinfo@sirc.ca
URL: http://www.sirc.ca/
Contact: SIRC Reference Services.
Desc: Contains more than 500,000 bibliographic citations,
some with abstracts, to the worldwide scientific and practical literature (articles, monographs, dissertations, conference proceedings, research reports, audiovisual material)
for individual and team sports, sports medicine, physical
fitness, physical education and related areas. Covers the literature on practice, strategy, technique, training, equipment, sport psychology, biomechanics, exercise
physiology, teaching, coaching, and officiating. *Available:*
Ovid Technologies, Inc.; The Dialog Corporation, Data-
Star; The Dialog Corporation, DIALOG. *Type:* Database.

The Sporting News

The Sporting News Publishing Co.
10176 Corporate Square Dr., Ph: (314)997-7111
  Ste. 200   Free: 800-325-4081
St. Louis, MO 63132   Fax: (314)993-7726
E-mail: tsnmail@aol.com.
URL: http://www.sportingnews.com
Contact: John Rawlings, Editor; Fran Farrell, Publisher.
Desc: Sports magazine (tabloid). *Type:* Periodical.

Sports Adviser Features

1323 S. 6th St.   Ph: (630)377-6676
PO Box 891   Fax: (630)513-5438
St. Charles, IL 60174
Contact: P. Andrew Andersen, President.
Alt. Contact: 1323 S. 6th St., PO Box 891, St. Charles,
IL 60174; telephone: (630)377-6676; fax: (630)513-
5438. *Type:* Periodical.

Sports Afield

Hearst Magazines
959 8th Ave.   Ph: (212)649-2000
New York, NY 10019-5905
E-mail: saletters@hearst.com.
URL: http://sportsafield.com.
Contact: John Atwood, Editor; Mike Wade, Publisher.

Desc: Outdoor sports magazine. *Alt. Contact:* 250 W. 55th
St., New York, NY 10019; telephone: (212)649-4000;
fax: (212)581-3923. *Type:* Periodical.

Sports Biofile & Bio-Toons

71 Dockerty Hollow Rd.   Ph: (201)728-0591
West Milford, NJ 07480   Fax: (201)728-0591
URL: http://espnet.sportszone.com/editors/zoned/
biofiles.
Contact: Mark Malinowski, Editor; Bud Boccone, Artist.
Alt. Contact: 71 Dockerty Hollow Rd., West Milford, NJ
07480; telephone: (201)728-0591; fax: (201)728-0591.
Type: Periodical.

Sports Card Review & Value Line

William Paul Publishing, Inc.
PO Box 267   Ph: (414)246-7236
Sussex, WI 53089-0267   Fax: (414)246-9074
Contact: Jon Brecka, Editor and Publisher.
Desc: Magazine offering insider information. *Type:* Period-
ical.

Sports Fan's Connection

Gale Group Inc.
27500 Drake Rd.   Ph: (248)699-4253
Farmington Hills, MI 48331- Free: 800-877-GALE
  3535   Fax: (248)699-8070
E-mail: galeord@galegroup.com
URL: http://www.galegroup.com.
Contact: Bradley J. Morgan, Editor.
Desc: Sports leagues, associations, teams, conferences, services, fantasy camps, tournaments, bowl games, halls of
fame, radio and tv stations, videos, books, magazines,
newsletters, and newspapers dealing with professional, collegiate, and Olympic sports in the U.S. and Canada. Also
lists international Olympic committees worldwide. *Type:*
Directory.

Sports Illustrated

Time Inc.
Time-Life Bldg.   Ph: (212)522-1212
New York, NY 10020
URL: http://www.pathfinder.com/time
Desc: Contains the complete text of Sports Illustrated, a
weekly magazine covering current sports events and trends
in leisure and recreation. Includes news and analyses of
collegiate and professional teams, predictions of winners
and losers in major sporting events, interviews with sports
personalities, and recommendations on purchasing sports
equipment or learning particular sports. *Available:* LEXIS-
NEXIS, NEXIS; CompuServe Information Service. *Type:*
Database.

Sports Illustrated

Time Inc.
Time-Life Bldg., Rockefeller Ph: (212)522-1212
  Center   Fax: (212)522-0315
1271 Avenue of the Americas
New York, NY 10020
Contact: Mark Malvoy, Editor; Donald J. Barr, Publisher;
Thomas Hickey, Advertising Mgr.
Desc: Sports magazine. *Type:* Periodical.

Sports Market Place

Franklin Covey Sports Division
350 E. Elliot Rd.   Ph: (480)539-3800
Chandler, AZ 85225   Free: 800-776-7877
                            Fax: (480)539-3811
E-mail: fcsports@timemanagement.com;   smp@
timemanagement.com.
Contact: Richard A. Lipsey, Editor.
Desc: Manufacturers, organizations, professional sports
teams, broadcasting networks, sports arenas, syndicators,

publications, trade shows, marketing services, corporate
sports sponsors, and other groups concerned with the
business and promotional aspects of sports generally and
with air sports, arm wrestling, auto sports, badminton,
baseball, basketball, biathlon, bowling, boxing, curling,
equestrian, exercise, fencing, field hockey, football, golf,
gymnastics, ice hockey, lacrosse, martial arts, paddleball,
paddle tennis, platform tennis, pentathlon, racquetball,
rowing, rugby, running/jogging, skiing, soccer, softball,
squash, swimming, table tennis, tennis, track and field,
volleyball, water sports, weightlifting, and wrestling. *Type:*
Directory.

Sports by Voort

255 Main St.   Ph: (201)593-0563
Ste. C-2   Fax: (201)593-0563
Madison, NJ 07940
Alt. Contact: 255 Main St., Ste. C-2, Madison, NJ 07940;
telephone: (201)593-0563; fax: (201)593-0563. *Type:* Pe-
riodical.

Sportsbuff Features

PO Box 197   Ph: (508)468-2632
Hamilton, MA 01936
Contact: Steve Ollove, Editor; Ken Wagner, Assoc. Ed.
Desc: Distributes weekly sports crossword puzzle. *Alt. Con-
tact:* PO Box 197, Hamilton, MA 01936; telephone:
(508)468-2632. *Type:* Periodical.

SportsLine USA

SportsLine USA
6340 NW 5th Way   Ph: (954)351-2120
Fort Lauderdale, FL 33309   Free: 800-771-4616
                            Fax: (954)776-4745
E-mail: feedback@sportsline.com
URL: http://www.sportsline.com
Desc: Definitely the place for the sports fanatic. Want to
see the boxscore for yesterday's game between Norwich
and Bowie in the Eastern League? You can find it here,
along with a cornucopia of equally esoteric statistics. *Type:*
Database.

Supertrax International Magazine

Supertrax Publishing LLC
3432 Hwy. 101   Ph: (612)473-7870
Minnetonka, MN 55345   Free: 800-905-8729
                            Fax: (612)473-7805
E-mail: trax@ican.net; supertrax@aol.com.
Contact: C.J. Ramstad, Publisher.
Desc: Magazine for snowmobilers. *Type:* Periodical.

SURFER Magazine

Surfer Publications, Inc.
Box 1028   Ph: (714)496-5922
Dana Point, CA 92629   Fax: (714)496-7849
URL: http://www.surfermag.com.
Contact: Steve Hawk, Editor; Doug Palladini, Publisher;
Laurie Smith, Advertising Coordinator.
Desc: Magazine about the sport of surfing. *Type:* Periodi-
cal.

Surfing Magazine

McMullen Argus Publishing, Inc.
774 S. Placentia Ave.   Ph: (714)939-2400
Placentia, CA 92870   Fax: (714)572-1864
E-mail: surfing@netcom.com.
Contact: Jamie Brisick, Editor, jamieb@mcmullenargus.
com; Robert Mignogna, Publisher, bobmi@
mcmullenargus.com; Bob Graff, Sales Mgr.; James Lynch,
Advertising Sales Mgr., jamesl@mcmullenargus.com.
Desc: Surfing magazine. *Alt. Contact:* 950 Calle Amanecer,
No. C, San Clemente, CA 92673; telephone: (714)492-
7873; fax: (714)498-6485. *Type:* Periodical.

Surfrider Foundation

122 S. El Camino Real, No. 67   Ph: (949)492-8170
San Clemente, CA 92672   Free: 800-743-7873
  Fax: (949)492-8142
E-mail: surfrider@aol.com
URL: http://www.surfrider.org
Contact: Dr. Pierce J. Flynn, Exec.Dir.

Desc: Individuals interested in coastal conservation and ocean wave recreation, especially surfing. Works to: preserve and enhance beach environments and coastal ecologies; promote water safety and recreational beach activity; protect such resources, when necessary, through local activism, education, conservation and research. Represented by 37 national chapters and affiliates in Australia, France, Brazil, and Japan. *Type:* Association.

Temple University

Biokinetics Research Laboratory

Pearson Hall   Ph: (215)204-8753
Philadelphia, PA 19122   Fax: (215)204-4662
Contact: Dr. Zebulon Kendricks, Dir.

Desc: Exercise physiology, biomechanics, and motor learning, including studies on biochemical adaptations to exercise, muscular strength and endurance, longitudinal effects of regular vigorous physical activity, environmental influences on physical work, metabolism, and perceptual motor behavior. *Type:* Research center.

Temple University

Center for Sports Medicine and Science

Health Sci. Ctr. Campus   Ph: (215)707-2111
3400 N. Broad St.   Fax: (215)707-2324
Philadelphia, PA 19140
Contact: Michael Clancy, Chm.

Desc: Post-operative knee surgery follow-up, post-operative arthroscopic shoulder surgery follow-up, and development of instrument for arthroscopic knee reconstruction. *Type:* Research center.

Texas A&M University

Human Performance Laboratories

Department of Health &   Ph: (409)845-4802
  Kinesiology   Fax: (409)847-8987
College Station, TX 77843-4243
E-mail: jwilmore@tamu.edu
URL: http://hlknweb.tamu.edu
Contact: Dr. Jack H. Wilmore, PhD, Contact.

Desc: Human performance, including exercise physiology, motor learning/control/development, and biomechanics. *Type:* Research center.

Texas A&M University

Hyperbaric Laboratories

College Station, TX 77843-1264   Ph: (409)845-5031
  Fax: (409)845-8913
Contact: Dr. William P. Fife, Dir.

Desc: Hyperbaric medicine, diving medicine, and clinical medicine. Specific studies include migraine headaches, post-polio syndrome, cystoid macular edema, chronic fatigue syndrome, and closed head injuries. *Type:* Research center.

Touchdown Illustrated

Touchdown Publications, Inc.
2815 Mitchell Dr., No. 202   Ph: (510)933-0230
Walnut Creek, CA 94598   Fax: (510)933-0371
E-mail: craiger@interport.net.
Contact: Peggy Keganey; Robert Fulton.

Desc: Magazine on college football. *Alt. Contact:* Touchdown/PSP, 355 Lexington Ave., New York, NY 10017; telephone: (212)697-1460; fax: (212)286-8154. *Type:* Periodical.

TRACKS

California Department of Fish and Game
1416 Ninth St.   Ph: (916)653-7203
Sacramento, CA 95814   Fax: (916)653-1019
URL: http://www.dfg.ca.gov.
Contact: Lorna Bernard, Editor, (916)653-0991, lbernard@hq.dfg.ca.gov.

Desc: Features up-to-date surveys on herd compositions, hunting results, articles concerning deer management, and statistics on license sales and articles on state's other big game species. *Type:* Newsletter.

TransWorld Skateboarding Magazine

TransWorld Media
353 Airport Rd.   Ph: (619)722-7777
Oceanside, CA 92054   Fax: (619)722-0653
E-mail: twsnow@twsnet.com.
URL: http://www.twsnow.com.
Contact: Peggy Cousins, Publisher; Larry Bauma, Publisher.

Desc: Magazine for skateboarders. *Type:* Periodical.

TransWorld Snowboarding Magazine

TransWorld Media
353 Airport Rd.   Ph: (619)722-7777
Oceanside, CA 92054   Fax: (619)722-0653
Contact: Peggy Cousins, Publisher; Larry Bauma, Publisher.

Desc: Magazine for the snowboarding industry. *Type:* Periodical.

Underwater Society of America

PO Box 628   Ph: (650)583-8492
Daly City, CA 94017   Fax: (650)583-0614
E-mail: croseusoac@aol.com
Contact: Carol Rose, Pres.

Desc: Those who participate in and support the sports of skin diving, spearfishing, scuba diving, underwater photography, underwater hockey, and fin swimming. The society is interested in the advancement of underwater exploration, engineering, and science. Sponsors national skin diving, scuba diving, underwater photography, hockey, underwater rugby, and fin swimming competitions. *Type:* Association.

United States Amateur Racquetball Association

1685 W. Uintah   Ph: (719)635-5396
Colorado Springs, CO 80904-2921   Fax: (719)635-0685
E-mail: kvicroy@usra.org
URL: http://www.usra.org
Contact: Luke St. Onge, Exec.Dir.

Desc: Racquetball players and enthusiasts. Promotes racquetball as a sport; organizes racquetball to be a self-governing sport of, by, and for the players; encourages building of facilities for the sport; conducts racquetball events including annual national and international tournaments. Maintains hall of fame, children's services, and charitable programs. *Type:* Association.

United States Curling Association

c/o David Garber   Ph: (715)344-1199
1100 Center Point Dr.   Free: 888-CUR-LERS
Box 866   Fax: (715)344-2279
Stevens Point, WI 54481
E-mail: usacurl@coredcs.com
URL: http://www.usacurl.org
Contact: David Garber, Exec.Dir.

Desc: Federation of regional curling associations and their member clubs. (Curling is a game in which curling stones are delivered along ice to a mark.) Promotes curling in the U.S. by sponsoring national curling championships. *Type:* Association.

United States Diving

Pan American Plz.   Ph: (317)237-5252
201 S. Capitol Ave., Ste. 430   Fax: (317)237-5257
Indianapolis, IN 46225
E-mail: usdiving@aol.com
URL: http://www.usdiving.org
Contact: Todd B. Smith, Exec.Dir.

Desc: Athletes, coaches, officials, and interested individuals. Promotes diving as a sport; conducts diving programs at all levels of competitive ability from beginner to Olympic. Conducts research in sports sciences; compiles statistics. *Type:* Association.

United States Fencing Association

1 Olympic Plaza   Ph: (719)578-4511
Colorado Springs, CO 80909-5744   Fax: (719)632-5737
E-mail: usfencing@aol.com
URL: http://www.usfa.org
Contact: Michael Massik, Exec.Dir.

Desc: Amateur fencers. Conducts local, national, and international fencing competitions and selects Pan American, World University, World Championship, and Olympic teams. Conducts junior training camps, regional coaches seminars, and annual national coaches' college. *Type:* Association.

U.S. Field Hockey Association

1 Olympic Plz.   Ph: (719)578-4567
Colorado Springs, CO 80909   Fax: (719)632-0979
E-mail: usfha@usfieldhockey.com
URL: http://www.usfieldhockey.com
Contact: Jane Betts, Exec.Dir.

Desc: Clubs, schools, and colleges where men and women and boys and girls play field hockey; umpires and interested individuals. National governing body for men's and women's field hockey recognized by the United States Olympic Committee. Seeks to: promote interest in the sport of field hockey through exhibition games, coaching clinics, and technical materials; develop a quality youth sport program for children ages 6 to 13; sponsor annual national tournaments for members; enable national teams to compete internationally; certify and train coaches. *Type:* Association.

U.S. Flag and Touch Football League

7709 Ohio St.   Ph: (440)974-8735
Mentor, OH 44060   Fax: (440)974-8441
E-mail: usftl@interax.com
URL: http://www.e-sports.com/usftl
Contact: Michael Cihon, Exec.Dir. & Pres.

Desc: Players of flag and touch football and officials. (Flag and touch football are modified versions of standard football in which touching or deflagging is substituted for tackling.). Provides rule books, educational materials, and video tapes to members. *Type:* Association.

United States Judo Federation

Desc: People interested in the sport of judo. Supervises the technical aspects of the sport such as refereeing, judging, testing of ranks, conducting tournaments, and sponsoring tours. Sponsors teacher's institute; conducts regional and national clinics. *Type:* Association.

U.S. Lacrosse and the Lacrosse Museum and National Hall of Fame

113 W. University Pky.   Ph: (410)235-6882
Baltimore, MD 21210   Fax: (410)366-6735
E-mail: sstenersen@lacrosse.org
URL: http://www.lacrosse.org
Contact: Steve Stenersen, Exec.Dir.

Desc: Service organization dedicated to the promotion and expansion of men's and women's lacrosse. Maintains lacrosse museum and hall of fame. Sponsors annual Hall of Fame Classic. *Type:* Association.

United States Luge Association

35 Church St.   Ph: (518)523-2071
Lake Placid, NY 12946   Fax: (518)523-4106
E-mail: usaluge@usaluge.org
URL: http://www.usaluge.org
Contact: Ronald Rossi, Exec.Dir.
Desc: Luge athletes and interested individuals. Selects qualified athletes for the U.S. Olympic Luge Team. *Type:* Association.

United States Masters Swimming

PO Box 185   Ph: (603)537-0203
Londonderry, NH 03053   Fax: (603)537-0204
E-mail: usms@usms.org
URL: http://www.usms.org
Contact: Tracy Grilli, Exec.Sec.
Desc: Adults aged 19 years and over. interested in participating in swimming for fun, fitness, and competition. *Type:* Association.

United States Olympic Committee

1 Olympic Plz.   Ph: (719)632-5551
Colorado Springs, CO 80909-   Fax: (719)578-4677
5760
Contact: William J. Hybl, Pres.
Desc: Federation of sports governing bodies constituting the governing body in the representation of the U.S. in the competitions and events of the Olympic and Pan American games. Works to coordinate, organize, select, finance, equip, transport, house, and feed team members. *Type:* Association.

U.S. Paddle Tennis Association

189 Seeley St.   Ph: (718)788-2094
Brooklyn, NY 11218
Contact: Mike Corbett, Pres.
Desc: Paddle tennis enthusiasts, clubs, and regional associations. Works to increase the popularity of paddle tennis. *Type:* Association.

United States Parachute Association

1440 Duke St.   Ph: (703)836-3495
Alexandria, VA 22314   Fax: (703)836-2843
E-mail: uspa@uspa.org
URL: http://www.uspa.org
Contact: Christopher J. Needels, Exec.Dir.
Desc: Promotes safety in skydiving. *Type:* Association.

United States Rowing Association

201 S. Capitol Ave., Ste. 400   Ph: (317)237-5656
Indianapolis, IN 46225   Free: 800-314-4769
    Fax: (317)237-5646
Contact: Frank J. Coyle, Exec.Dir.
Desc: Universities, colleges, prep schools, high schools, and rowing clubs; individuals who are competing rowers, former rowers, and rowing enthusiasts. Promotes, fosters, and governs amateur rowing in the U.S. Promulgates rules and regulations governing the sport. *Type:* Association.

United States Rugby Football Union

3595 E. Fountain Blvd.   Ph: (719)637-1022
Colorado Springs, CO 80910   Free: 800-280-6302
    Fax: (719)637-1315
E-mail: usarugby@rmii.com
URL: http://www.usarugby.org
Contact: Jen Pope, Membership Communications.
Desc: Federation comprising the Midwest Rugby Football Union, South Rugby Union, Pacific Coast Rugby Union, Western Rugby Union of the United States, Southern California Rugby Union, Northeast Rugby Union, Mid-Atlantic Rugby Union, and representing 60,000 rugby players. To promote the sport of rugby in the U.S.; to establish and administer policies; to represent the U.S. in international rugby affairs. *Type:* Association.

United States Sports Academy

1 Academy Dr.   Ph: (334)626-3303
Daphne, AL 36526   Fax: (334)626-1149
E-mail: academy@ussa-sport.ussa.edu
URL: http://www.sport.ussa.edu
Contact: Dr. Cynthia E. Ryder, VP, Inst.Res.
Desc: Sport and sport education in an effort to upgrade sports medicine, sport coaching, sport management, and fitness management, including studies of athletic injuries, body composition of adults, motor performance of youth, physical fitness of adults, ECG abnormalities and changes due to exercise, biomechanical analysis of gross motor skills and three-dimensional gait analysis, product and equipment evaluation and drug use/abuse in sports evaluation and analysis. Research is carried on with local high school athletes, members of the USSA student body, youth involved in the Academy's overseas projects, and selected off-campus program participants. *Type:* Research center.

United States Squash Racquets Association

PO Box 1216   Ph: (610)667-4006
23 Cynwyd Rd.   Fax: (610)667-6539
Bala Cynwyd, PA 19004
E-mail: exec.dir@us-squash.org
URL: http://www.us-squash.org/squash/
Contact: Craig W. Brand, Exec.Dir.
Desc: Member of United States Olympic Committee . To establish and enforce uniformity in the rules of the game, standardize court specifications and schedules, and conduct tournaments. *Type:* Association.

United States Swimming

1 Olympic Plaza   Ph: (719)578-4578
Colorado Springs, CO 80909   Fax: (719)578-4669
Contact: Chuck Wielgus, Exec.Dir.
Desc: Swimmers, former swimmers, coaches, officials, administrators, and athletic associations. National governing body for competitive amateur swimming. Selects teams for various international competitions including the Olympics. *Type:* Association.

United States Volleyball Association

3595 E. Fountain Blvd.   Ph: (719)637-8300
Colorado Springs, CO 80910-   Fax: (719)597-6307
1740
Contact: Kerry Klostermann, Exec. Dir.
Desc: National governing body for the sport of volleyball. *Type:* Association.

United States Water Polo

1685 W Uintah   Ph: (719)634-0699
Colorado Springs, CO 80904   Fax: (719)634-0866
E-mail: uswp@uswp.org
URL: http://www.uswp.org
Contact: Brett Bernard, Pres.
Desc: Athletes, administrators, officials, and coaches. Promotes the sport of water polo in the U.S. *Type:* Association.

University of British Columbia

Allan McGavin Sports Medicine Centre

3055 Wesbrook Mall   Ph: (604)822-4045
Vancouver, BC, Canada V6T   Fax: (604)822-9058
1Z3
E-mail: dclement@unixg.ubc.ca
URL: http://courses.cstudies.ubc.ca/sports-med/
Contact: Douglas B. Clement, MD, Co-Dir.
Desc: Iron metabolism in exercise, growth hormone and exercise, biomechanics of running and use of foot orthotic devices, anaerobic threshold in runners, overuse injuries in running, and overuse injuries in aerobic fitness classes. The unit also functions as a clinical service and education center. *Type:* Research center.

University of Calgary

Human Performance Laboratory

Faculty of Kinesiology   Ph: (403)220-3436
2500 University Dr. NW   Fax: (403)284-3553
Calgary, AB, Canada T2N 1N4
E-mail: croberts@kin.ucalgary.ca
URL: http://www.kin.ucalgary.ca
Contact: Dr. Benno M. Nigg, Dir.
Desc: Mobility and longevity; biomechanics, including load on the musculoskeletal system, basic muscle mechanics, joint mechanics, lower back biomechanics, orthoses, sport shoes, and sports equipment; exercise physiology, including muscle physiology, limiting factors in performance and biochemistry of high performance; and neuromotor psychology, including studies involving ice hockey video discs and studies of eye movement in sports. *Type:* Research center.

University of Calgary

Sport Medicine Centre

2500 University Dr. NW   Ph: (403)220-8232
Calgary, AB, Canada T2N 1N4   Fax: (403)282-6170
E-mail: maitland@acs.ucalgary.ca
URL: http://www.kin.ucalgary.ca/SMC/html/index.html
Contact: Prof. Murray Maitland, Dir.
Desc: Human movement and sport, including anthropometry, athletic therapy, biochemistry, biomechanics, epidemiology, growth and development, nutrition, orthopedics, orthotics, physiology, physiotherapy, and sport medicine. *Type:* Research center.

University of Central Florida

Exercise Physiology and Wellness

College of Education ED214   Ph: (407)823-2598
Department of Exceptional &   Fax: (407)823-3859
    Physical Education
Orlando, FL 32816
URL: http://www.pegafus.cc.ucf.edu/~excpel
Contact: Dr. Gerald Geraley, Dir.
Desc: The human body's responses and adaptations to exercise. Studies include coronary heart disease prevention, rehabilitation, and stress testing, aerobic and anerobic testing and training of elite athletes, development of elite women athletes, exercise and fitness of preschool children, exercise and aging, and obesity as it relates to exercise and nutrition. *Type:* Research center.

University of Delaware

Sports Science Laboratory

S. College Ave.   Ph: (302)831-8006
Newark, DE 19716   Fax: (302)831-3693
Contact: Michelle Provost-Craig, PhD, Co-Dir.
Desc: Sports science, biomechanics, excercise physiology, bone density, and elite skaters. *Type:* Research center.

University of Florida

Center for Exercise Science

27 Florida Gym   Ph: (352)392-9575
Gainesville, FL 32611   Fax: (352)392-0316
E-mail: spowers@hhp.ufl.edu
Contact: Scott Powers, PhD, Dir.
Desc: Fitness as it relates to athletic performance, as well as the general population, including research on biomechanics and skill acquisition; health risk factors; exercise and the lumbar and cervical spine, sports, aging, menopause, diabetes, and athletic performance. *Type:* Research center.

University of Illinois at Urbana-Champaign

Athletic Training Research Lab

906 S. Goodwin   Ph: (217)333-7699
Urbana, IL 61801   Fax: (217)244-7322
E-mail: g-bell@uiuc.edu
URL: http://www.kines.uiuc.edu/atcentral/

Contact: Prof. Gerald W. Bell, Dir.

Desc: Therapeutic affects of exercise on musculoskeletal injuries, medical supervision of sports programs, response of wheelchair athletes to exercise and training programs, and epidemiological of sports injuries for high school participants, intramural sports participants, and dance students. *Type:* Research center.

University of Illinois at Urbana-Champaign

Biomechanics Research Laboratory of Illinois

Department of Kinesiology   Ph: (217)333-2461
906 S. Goodwin   Fax: (217)244-7322
Freer Hall
Urbana, IL 61801
E-mail: j-chow1@uiuc.edu
URL: http://www.uiuc.edu

Contact: Dr. J. Chow, Contact.

Desc: Sports biomechanics (tennis, fencing, athletics, volleyball, and rope jumping), biomechanics of sports safety and injury potential, force production, occupational biomechanics (firefighting tasks), movement patterns of the elderly, and strength training. *Type:* Research center.

University of Manitoba

Health, Leisure, and Human Performance Research Institute

303 Max Bell Centre   Ph: (204)474-7087
Winnipeg, MB, Canada R3T   Fax: (204)261-4802
  2N2
E-mail: mahon@ms.umanitoba.ca
URL: http://www.umanitoba.ca/faculties/physed/research/

Contact: Dr. Michael J. Mahon, Dir.

Desc: Exercise and environmental medicine, exercise physiology, leisure and tourism, biomechanics, and life span and disability. *Type:* Research center.

University of Miami

Human Performance Laboratory

PO Box 248065   Ph: (305)284-3024
Coral Gables, FL 33124   Fax: (305)284-5168
E-mail: aperry@jaguar.ir.miami.edu
URL: http://www.education.miami.edu

Contact: Dr. A. Perry, Dir.

Desc: Kinesiology, muscle cell and cardiovascular physiology, sports nutrition, obesity, electromyography, lipid physiology, exercise biochemistry, and athlete's evaluation. *Type:* Research center.

University of Michigan

Health Management Research Center

1027 E. Huron St.   Ph: (734)763-2462
Ann Arbor, MI 48104-1688   Fax: (734)763-2206
E-mail: dwe@umich.edu
URL: http://www.umich.edu/~hmrc

Contact: Dr. D.W. Edington, Dir.

Desc: Examines the relationships between lifestyle behaviors, quality of life, organizational productivity, and health care costs. *Type:* Research center.

University of Missouri--Columbia

Exercise Physiology

Department of Nutritional   Ph: (573)882-0062
  Sciences   Fax: (573)884-6992
38 Rothwell Gymnasium
Columbia, MO 65211
URL: http://www.missouri.edu/~nutsci/exphy.htm

Contact: Tom Thomas, PhD, Dir.

Desc: Exercise physiology, including calorie expenditure and different modes of exercise; exercise and blood lipoproteins. *Type:* Research center.

University of Nevada, Las Vegas

Exercise Physiology Laboratory

4505 Maryland Pkwy.   Ph: (702)895-3766
Box 3034   Fax: (702)895-4191
Las Vegas, NV 89154-3034
E-mail: golding@ccmail.nevada.edu

Contact: Dr. Lawrence A. Golding, Dir.

Desc: Primary function and research emphasis is the study of the biology of exercise. Studies include the physiological effect of both the immediate effect of exercise and the long range effect of physical training, the effect of the environment on physical performance (heat, humidity, cold, altitude, and pollution), the effect of aging on physical performance, and the impact of exercise on the older adult, the effects of drug use and diet supplement on physical performance, and a longitudinal study on the effect of regular exercise on coronary risk factors and aging. *Type:* Research center.

University of North Carolina at Chapel Hill

National Center for Catastrophic Sports Injury Research

311 Woollen Gymnasium   Ph: (919)962-2021
CB 8605   Fax: (919)962-0489
Chapel Hill, NC 27599-8605
E-mail: mueller@emil.unc.edu

Contact: Dr. Frederick O. Mueller, Dir.

Desc: Fatality and permanent injury in sports, especially football. *Type:* Research center.

University of Oregon

International Institute for Sport and Human Performance

1243 University of Oregon   Ph: (541)346-4114
Eugene, OR 97403-1243   Fax: (541)346-0935
E-mail: hheiny@oregon.uoregon.edu
URL: http://darkwing.uoregon.edu/~iishp/

Contact: Henriette Heiny, PhD, Dir.

Desc: Sport and exercise sciences, sports medicine health, general wellness, and sport issues in the humanities and arts. *Type:* Research center.

University of Pittsburgh

Center for Exercise and Health-Fitness Research

A149B Trees Hall   Ph: (412)648-8251
Pittsburgh, PA 15261   Fax: (412)648-7092

Contact: Dr. Robert J. Robertson, Dir.

Desc: Physiology of exercise and work, perception of physical exertion, cardiac rehabilitation, and ergogenic aids, including studies conducted by full-time faculty members and graduate students of the University. *Type:* Research center.

University of Rhode Island

Exercise Science Laboratories

25 W. Independence Sq.   Ph: (401)874-5631
Kingston, RI 02881   Fax: (401)874-5630
E-mail: manfredi@uriacc.uri.edu

Contact: Thomas Manfredi, PhD, Co-Dir.

Desc: Physiological profiles of athletic populations, diet and weight loss, aging and exercise. *Type:* Research center.

University of Utah

Human Performance Research Laboratory

300 South 1850 East, Rm.   Ph: (801)585-6172
  230E   Fax: (801)585-3992
Salt Lake City, UT 84112

Contact: Dr. Andrea T. White, Dir.

Desc: Effects of exercise and environment on muscular, cardiovascular, respiratory, nervous, and thermoregulatory systems of the human body. Programs are conducted on exercise and multiple sclerosis patients, women at risk for osteoporosis, exercise and functional abilities and health benefits. *Type:* Research center.

University of Wisconsin--La Crosse

Human Performance Laboratory

Mitchell Hall   Ph: (608)785-8685
1725 State St.
La Crosse, WI 54601
E-mail: nkbutts@uwlax.edu

Contact: N.K. Butts, Dir.

Desc: Provides facilities for research fellows and graduate students to perform short-term and long-term medical and paramedical research in areas of exercise and cardiovascular diseases. Conducts body composition testing (hydrostatic weighing), cardiovascular and pulmonary testing, and blood chemistry testing for faculty, students, and members of the public. *Type:* Research center.

U.S.A. Gymnastics

201 S. Capitol, Ste. 300   Ph: (317)237-5050
Indianapolis, IN 46225   Fax: (317)237-5069
URL: http://www.usa-gymnastics.org

Contact: Robert V. Colarossi, Pres.

Desc: National associations or organizations concerned with amateur sports, particularly gymnastics. Conducts national program in gymnastics for Junior Olympics and Junior, Senior, and Elite International level gymnasts. Selects teams for World Championships, World Cup, Pan American Games, Olympic Games, and other international events. *Type:* Association.

U.S.A. Hockey

1775 Bob Johnson Dr.
Colorado Springs, CO 80906-
  4090

Contact: David Ogrean, Exec.Dir.

Desc: Promotes the growth of ice hockey in America by encouraging, developing, advancing all participants and administering the sport. *Type:* Association.

Vanderbilt University

Energy Balance Laboratory

Clinical Research Center   Ph: (615)343-8497
21st Ave. S.   Fax: (615)343-8915
Nashville, TN 37232-2195
E-mail: kong.chen@mcmail.vanderbilt.edu

Contact: Dr. Kong Chen, Dir.

Desc: Use of indirect calorimetry to measure energy expenditure, and metabolic rate and physical activities under a variety of conditions, including exercise, dietary intake, and environmental changes. Emphasis is on the identification of determinants of energy expenditure and body weight regulation. *Type:* Research center.

Waterski Magazine

World Publications, Inc.

330 W. Canton Ave.   Ph: (407)628-4802
Winter Park, FL 32789   Fax: (407)628-7061
E-mail: waterski@worldzine.com.

Contact: Terry L. Snow, Publisher; John McEver, Jr., Advertising Dir.; Pierce Hoover, Editor.

Desc: Magazine on waterskiing. *Type:* Periodical.

Western States College Sports Guide

Craftsman Publications, Inc./Western Sports Guides

3984 Donipman Dr.	Ph: (915)584-7791
PO Box 12476	Fax: (915)584-7791
El Paso, TX 79913	

Contact: Carol Coynor, Editor; Cynthia L. Smith, Editor.

Desc: Athletic coaches and other athletics-related staff at junior colleges and universities in Alaska, Arizona, California, Colorado, Idaho, Kansas, Montana, Nevada, New Mexico, Oklahoma, Oregon, Texas, Utah, Washington, and Wyoming. *Type:* Directory.

Windy City Sports Magazine

Windy City Publishing, Inc.

1450 W. Randolph	Ph: (312)421-1551
Chicago, IL 60607	Fax: (312)421-1454
E-mail: wcpublish@aol.com	
URL: http://www.windycitysportsmag.com.	

Contact: Jeff Banowetz, Editor; Doug Kaplan, Publisher.

Desc: Magazine covering amateur sports in the Chicago area. *Type:* Periodical.

Women's Sports & Fitness

Sports & Fitness, Inc.

2025 Pearl St.	Ph: (303)440-5111
Boulder, CO 80302	Fax: (303)440-3313
E-mail: kaasfp@aol.com.	

Contact: Dagny Scott, Editor; Daemon Filson, Publisher.

Desc: Magazine covering women's sports, fitness, nutrition, and health. *Type:* Periodical.

Women's Sports Foundation

Eisenhower Park	Ph: (516)542-4700
East Meadow, NY 11554	Free: 800-227-3988
	Fax: (516)542-4716
E-mail: wosport@aol.com	
URL: http://www.lifetimetv.com/wosport	

Contact: Dr. Donna Lopiano, Exec.Dir.

Desc: Encourages and supports the participation of women in sports activities for their health, enjoyment, and mental development; educates the public about athletic opportunities and the value of sports for women. Develops educational guides, provides travel and training grants and internship program, and supports the enforcement of the Title IX amendments of the 1972 Equal Education Act and the Amateur Sports Act. Sponsors an information and resource clearinghouse on women's sports and fitness. *Type:* Association.

World Footbag Association

PO Box 775208	Ph: (970)870-9898
Steamboat Springs, CO 80477	Free: 800-878-8797
	Fax: (970)870-2846
E-mail: wfa@worldfootbag.com	
URL: http://www.worldfootbag.com	

Contact: Bruce Guettich, Pres.

Desc: Footbag enthusiasts and players of organized footbag games. (A footbag, sometimes known by the brand name Hacky Sack, is a palm-sized bag weighing a little more than one ounce that players attempt to keep in the air using their feet and knees.). Promotes: interest in footbags and cooperative and competitive footbag games; fitness and skill development through seminars, workshops, clinics, and national training camps. *Type:* Association.

World Wide Web of Sports

Massachusetts Institute of Technology - Laboratory for Computer Science

Telemedia, Networks, and	Ph: (617)253-6005
Systems Group	Fax: (617)253-2673
545 Technology Sq., Rm. 510	
Cambridge, MA 02139	
E-mail: sportsmaster@tns.lcs.mit.edu	
URL: http://www.tns.lcs.mit.edu/cgi-bin/sports	

Desc: The World Wide Web of Sports site contains links to information on practically every sport in existence. Topics include team home pages, publications, access to related Usenet groups, and a variety of related information. *Type:* Database.

Standards

International Standards Desk Reference

AMACOM

1601 Broadway	Ph: (212)586-8100
New York, NY 10019-7420	Free: 800-262-9699
	Fax: (212)903-8168
E-mail: cust_serv@amanet.com	
URL: http://www.amanet.org	

Contact: Amy Zuckerman, Editor.

Desc: Appendixes listing organizations and agencies involved in aspects of standards such as quality assurance, health and safety, and product standards. *Type:* Directory.

State Government

Alabama Government Manual

Alabama Law Institute

Box 861425	Ph: (205)348-7411
Tuscaloosa, AL 35486	Fax: (205)348-8411
Contact: Dr. Richard Thigpen, Editor.	

Desc: Over 200 state executive and regulatory agencies and staff functions, and offices in the legislative and judicial branches. *Type:* Directory.

American City & County Municipal Index—The Purchasing Guide for City, Township, County Officials and Consulting Engineers

Intertec Publishing
A Primedia Co.

6151 Powers Ferry Rd. NW	Ph: (770)995-2500
Atlanta, GA 30339-2941	Fax: (770)618-0476
URL: http://www.localgov.com.	

Contact: Janet Ward, Editor.

Desc: Directory of municipal and county governments with populations of 10,000 or more and their officials concerned with the purchasing of materials, equipment, and services; separate listing of suppliers of these products and services. *Type:* Directory.

Arizona Tax Research Association Newsletter

Arizona Tax Research Foundation

1814 W. Washington St.	Ph: (602)253-9121
Phoenix, AZ 85007	Fax: (602)253-6719

Desc: Covers state and local government spending in Arizona. Seeks to "promote efficiency and economy in Arizona government and reductions at all levels." Recurring features include news of research, reports of meetings, and notices of publications available. *Type:* Newsletter.

California Journal Roster and Government Guide

Information for Public Affairs, Inc.

2101 K. St.	Ph: (916)444-2840
Sacramento, CA 95816	Fax: (916)446-5369
Contact: A.G. Block, Editor, agb@statenet.com.	

Desc: State agencies; independent boards, commissions, and departments; congressional delegation; legislators; constitutional officers and governor's staff. *Type:* Directory.

Carroll's State Directory

Carroll Publishing

4701 Sangamore Rd., No. S155	Ph: (301)263-9800
Bethesda, MD 20816	Free: 800-336-4240
	Fax: (301)263-9801
E-mail: custsvc@carrollpub.com	
URL: http://www.carrolpub.com; http://www.carrollpub.com.	

Contact: Mary Forschler, Editor.

Desc: About 43,000 state government officials in all branches of government; officers, committees and members of state legislatures; managers of boards and authorities. *Type:* Directory.

Civil Service Bulletin

Michigan State Department of Civil Service

400 S. Pine St.	Ph: (517)373-8604
PO Box 30002	Fax: (517)335-2884
Lansing, MI 48909	

Contact: Karen Semrav, Editor.

Desc: Publishes information of interest to classified employees in the state of Michigan. Concerned with pay and fringe benefits in civil service, employee relations actions, and issues determined by the Civil Service Commission. *Type:* Newsletter.

Connecticut State Register and Manual

Connecticut Secretary of State

30 Trinity St.	Ph: (860)509-6230
Hartford, CT 06106	Fax: (860)509-6140
E-mail: miles.rapoport@po.state.ct.us	
URL: http://www.state.ct.us/sots/.	

Contact: Peter J. Bartucca, Editor, peter.bartucca@po.state.ct.us.

Desc: State departments, agencies, institutions, boards, commissions, legislators, judiciary; elected and appointed officials and board members of towns, cities, and boroughs; political party officials; school superintendents, historical societies, general museums, libraries, and presses. *Type:* Directory.

Council of State Governments

Phyllis Santos

2760 Research Park Dr.	Ph: (606)244-8000
PO Box 11910	Free: 800-800-1910
Lexington, KY 40578-1910	Fax: (606)244-8001
E-mail: info@csg.org	
URL: http://www.csg.org	

Contact: Daniel M. Sprague, Exec.Dir.

Desc: Acts as the catalyst for state leaders to network, identify solutions, and share ideas. Serves all three branches of state government in all states and U.S. jurisdictions by providing leadership education, research and information services. *Type:* Association.

Delaware Legislative Roster

Delaware State Chamber of Commerce

PO Box 671	Ph: (302)655-7221
Wilmington, DE 19899-0671	Fax: (302)654-0691
E-mail: dscc@inet.net	

Contact: Andrew D. Stayton, Editor, staytona@inet.net; Suzanne Moore, Editor.

Desc: Principal state officials and members of the legislature. County officials, City of Wilmington Government staff and cabinet. *Type:* Directory.

Gold Coast News

Gold Coast News

PO Box 3637	Ph: (305)674-9746
Miami Beach, FL 33140	Fax: (305)674-1439

Contact: Charles Hesser, Editor.

Desc: Reports on events occuring in Southeast Florida from Palm Beach to Key West. *Type:* Newsletter.

Government Finance Officers Association Newsletter

Government Finance Officers Association
180 N. Michigan Ave., Ste. 800   Ph: (312)977-9700
Chicago, IL 60601-7401   Fax: (312)977-4806
Contact: Karen Utterback, Editor.
Desc: Provides updates on current events, innovations, and federal legislation affecting public finance management for state and local government finance officers. Covers cash management, budgeting, accounting, auditing, and financial reporting, public employee retirement administration, and related issues. *Type:* Newsletter.

Home Page Washington

Washington Interactive Technologies
710 Sleater-Kinney Rd. SE, Ste.   Ph: (360)902-3570
Q
Lacey, WA 98503
E-mail: HomePageWA@dis.wa.gov
URL: http://www.wa.gov/home.htm
Desc: While conceived as a site featuring state government, Home Page Washington indexes just about every facet of state and local organizations. More, site designers have remembered that the internet is supposed to be fun, too. *Type:* Database.

The Leader Online

Jefferson County Leader
PO Box 552   Ph: (360)385-2900
Port Townsend, WA 98368   Fax: (360)385-3422
E-mail: news@ptleader.com
URL: http://www.olympus.net/biz/leader/
Desc: The Leader Online is a community newspaper serving Washington state's east Olympic Peninsula. The site's features include local news, sports, business, and visitor's information. *Type:* Database.

Legislature, Senate, and House Registers, State of Maine

Clerk of the House
Maine State Legislature
2 State House Station   Ph: (207)287-1400
Augusta, ME 04333-0002   Fax: (207)287-1456
Contact: Joseph W. Mayo, Editor.
Desc: Principal Maine state officials, members of the legislature, and legislative employees. *Type:* Directory.

LEXIS® Liens Library

LEXIS-NEXIS
9443 Springboro Pike   Ph: (937)865-6800
PO Box 933
Dayton, OH 45401-0933
URL: http://www.lex-nexis.com
Desc: Provides access to current information extracted from Uniform Commercial Code Article 9 filings on personal property in all 50 states and the District of Columbia. Includes judgements and liens filed in the county clerk's office for 35 states and Philadelphia County. *Available:* LEXIS-NEXIS, LEXIS. *Type:* Database.

LEXIS® State Law Library

LEXIS-NEXIS
9443 Springboro Pike   Ph: (937)865-6800
PO Box 933
Dayton, OH 45401-0933
URL: http://www.lex-nexis.com
Desc: Contains decisions, orders, and opinions from the highest courts and intermediate courts for the 50 U.S. states and the District of Columbia. *Available:* LEXIS-NEXIS, LEXIS. *Type:* Database.

LEXIS® States Library

LEXIS-NEXIS
9443 Springboro Pike   Ph: (937)865-6800
PO Box 933
Dayton, OH 45401-0933
URL: http://www.lex-nexis.com
Desc: Offers many of the case law, code, and agency materials found in the 53 individual state libraries (50 states plus the District of Columbia, Puerto Rico, and the Virgin Islands). Features many large group files which allow several individual files to be accessed in the same search. *Available:* LEXIS-NEXIS, LEXIS. *Type:* Database.

List of State Officers, Members of U.S. Congress, State Senators and State Representatives

Connecticut Secretary of State
30 Trinity St.   Ph: (860)509-6230
Hartford, CT 06106   Fax: (860)509-6140
E-mail: miles.rapoport@po.state.ct.us
Contact: Peter J. Bartucca, Editor.
Desc: Principal state officials, Connecticut congressional delegation, and legislators. *Type:* Directory.

List of State Water Pollution Control Administrators

Association of State and Interstate Water Pollution Control Administrators (ASIWPCA)
750 1st St. NE, Ste. 1010   Ph: (202)898-0905
Washington, DC 20002   Fax: (202)898-0929
E-mail: admin1@asiwpca.org
URL: http://www.asiwpca.org; http://www.asiwpca.org.
Contact: Roberta Savage, Editor.
Desc: About 65 member administrators. *Type:* Directory.

The Main Street Stationer

Mijo Lithographing Company, Inc.
304 S. Main St.   Ph: (601)746-4693
PO Box 1104   Fax: (601)746-4390
Yazoo City, MS 39194
Contact: Mary M. Jones, Editor.
Desc: Features local news and events of interest to Yazoo City, Mississippi residents. *Type:* Newsletter.

Moody's Municipal & Government Manual

Financial Information Services (FIS)
60 Madison Ave., 6th Fl.   Ph: (212)413-7601
New York, NY 10010   Free: 800-342-5647
    Fax: (212)413-7777
E-mail: fis@fisonline.com
URL: http://www.fisonline.com.
Contact: MaryRose Carosia, Editor.
Desc: About 16,000 municipalities, counties, school districts, and other local taxing units with long-term debt of more than $5,000,000, plus state governments and institutions, federal government and agencies, and foreign governments with Moody ratings. *Type:* Directory.

National Association of Attorneys General

750 First St. NE, Ste. 1100   Ph: (202)326-6000
Washington, DC 20002   Fax: (202)408-7014
URL: http://www.naag.org
Contact: Christine T. Milliken, Exec.Dir.
Desc: Attorneys general of the 50 states, District of Columbia, American Samoa, Guam, Puerto Rico, Virgin Islands, and Northern Mariana Islands. Sponsors legal education seminars on consumer protection, environmental protection, antitrust, corrections, insurance, charitable trusts and solicitations, and Supreme Court practice. *Type:* Association.

National Association of State Information Resource Executives

National Association of State Information Resource Executives
167 W. Main St., Ste. 600   Ph: (606)231-1885
Lexington, KY 40507-1324   Fax: (606)231-1928
E-mail: nasire@iglou.com
URL: http://www.nasire.org/
Desc: This site offers news and events about the association, which encompasses the United States (including territories). It offers general information about the association and its work, and provides lists of their published materials, which can be ordered online. *Type:* Database.

National Conference of State Legislatures

1560 Broadway, Ste. 700   Ph: (303)830-2200
Denver, CO 80202   Fax: (303)863-8003
URL: http://www.ncsl.org
Contact: William T. Pound, Exec.Dir.
Desc: National organization of state legislators and legislative staff. Aims are: to improve the quality and effectiveness of state legislatures; to ensure states a strong, cohesive voice in the federal decision-making process; to foster interstate communication and cooperation. Compiles research data. *Type:* Association.

National Governors' Association

Hall of States   Ph: (202)624-5300
444 N. Capitol St. NW, Ste.   Fax: (202)624-5313
267
Washington, DC 20001
Contact: Raymond C. Scheppach, Exec.Dir.
Desc: Governors of the 50 states, Guam, American Samoa, the Virgin Islands, the Northern Mariana Islands, and Puerto Rico. Serves as vehicle through which governors influence the development and implementation of national policy and apply creative leadership to state problems. *Type:* Association.

North Carolina DataNet

Institute for Research in Social Science (IRSS)
University of North Carolina at Chapel Hill
Manning Hall   Ph: (919)962-3062
Chapel Hill, NC 27599-3355
URL: http://www.unc.edu/depts/irss/datanet.htm.
Contact: Jenifer Drolet, Editor, jdrolet.irss@mhs.unc.edu.
Desc: Provides statewide data for members of the Network and others. *Type:* Newsletter.

Ohio Government Directory

Ohio Trucking Association
50 W. Broad St., Ste. 1111   Ph: (614)221-5375
Columbus, OH 43215   Fax: (614)221-3717
E-mail: ohtrukassn@aol.com
Contact: David F. Bartosic, Editor.
Desc: Members of all houses of the Ohio legislature, Ohio's representatives and senators in Washington, D.C., and elected and some appointed officials. *Type:* Directory.

State Government Research Directory

Gale Group Inc.
27500 Drake Rd.   Ph: (248)699-4253
Farmington Hills, MI 48331-   Free: 800-877-GALE
3535   Fax: (248)699-8070
E-mail: galeord@galegroup.com
URL: http://www.galegroup.com.
Contact: Kay Gill, Editor; Susan E. Tufts, Editor.
Desc: About 850 state government-sponsored research programs, institutes, test centers, and facilities. *Type:* Directory.

States News

Council of State Governments
2760 Research Park Dr.　　　Ph: (606)244-8000
PO Box 11910　　　　　　　Fax: (606)244-8001
Lexington, KY 40578-1910
E-mail: info@csg.org
URL: http://www.csg.org/
Contact: Sarah Whitmire, Electronic Products Coordinator, swhitmire@csg.org.
Desc: This site provides information about membership, activities of the council, and resources available to members. *Type:* Database.

Who's Who in Government of Hawaii

Chamber of Commerce of Hawaii
1132 Bishop St., Ste. 402　　Ph: (808)545-4300
Honolulu, HI 96813　　　　　Fax: (808)545-4309
E-mail: info@cochawaii.org
Contact: Sam Powell, Editor.
Desc: Elected and appointed senior military, judiciary, federal, state, and county officials. *Type:* Directory.

Women in Government

Joy N. Newton
2600 Virginia Ave. NW., Ste.　　Ph: (202)333-0825
709　　　　　　　　　　　　Fax: (202)333-0875
Washington, DC 20037-1905
Contact: Joy N. Newton, Exec.Dir.
Desc: Coalition of elected women in state, national, and international governments. Promotes dialogue between the public and private sectors. Serves as an information clearinghouse. *Type:* Association.

Statistics

American Statistical Association

1429 Duke St.　　　　　　　Ph: (703)684-1221
Alexandria, VA 22314-3415　Fax: (703)684-2037
E-mail: asainfo@amstat.org
URL: http://www.amstat.org
Contact: Ray A. Waller, Exec.Dir.
Desc: Professional society of persons interested in the theory, methodology, and application of statistics to all fields of human endeavor. *Type:* Association.

American Statistics Index

Congressional Information Service, Inc. (CIS)
4520 East-West Hwy., Suite　Ph: (301)654-1550
800
Bethesda, MD 20814-3389
E-mail: 12425 (DIALMAIL)
URL: http://www.cispubs.com
Desc: Contains more than 142,000 citations, with abstracts, to publications containing social, economic, demographic, and other statistical data collected and analyzed by the U.S. government. *Available:* The Dialog Corporation, DIALOG. *Type:* Database.

The Chance Database

The Chance Project
Dartmouth College -
　Mathematics Department
Hanover, NH 03755
URL: http://www.dartmouth.edu/~chance/
Contact: J. Laurie Snell, jlsnell@Dartmouth.EDU.
Desc: This database is an educator's tool for use in designing and teaching a course in chance, or in introductory probability and statistics. Information is available here on basic concepts of probability, articles on chance, statistical data, and other teaching aids and associated material on the subject of probability and chance. *Type:* Database.

Infonation

United Nations Publications
2 UN Plaza, Rm. DC2-853　　Ph: (212)963-8302
New York, NY 10017　　　　Free: 800-253-9646
　　　　　　　　　　　　　Fax: (212)963-3489
E-mail: publications@un.org
URL:　　　http://www.un.org/Pubs/CyberSchoolBus/
infonation/e_infonation.htm
Contact: globalschoolbus@un.org.
Desc: From United Nations Publications comes this data-packed site that should be of particular interest to students of comparative economics and geography. The visitor may select up to seven nations from among the member countries of the United Nations. *Type:* Database.

Institute for Econometric Research

2200 SW 10th St.　　　　　Ph: (954)421-1000
Deerfield Beach, FL 33442　Free: 800-499-0066
　　　　　　　　　　　　　Fax: (954)570-8200
URL: http://www.mfmag.com
Contact: Norman G. Fosback, Pres.
Desc: Fosters scientific research into stock markets and related financial phenomenon. Compiles statistics. *Type:* Association.

International Biometric Society

1444 I St. NW, Ste. 700　　Ph: (202)712-9049
Washington, DC 20005-2210　Fax: (202)216-9646
E-mail: ibs@bostromdc.com
URL: http://www.tibs.org
Contact: Charles McGrath, CAE, Exec.Dir.
Desc: Biologists, statisticians, and others interested in applying statistical techniques to research data. Works to advance subject-matter sciences through the development of quantitative theories and the development, application, and dissemination of effective mathematical and statistical techniques. *Type:* Association.

International Vital Records Handbook

Genealogical Publishing Co., Inc.
1001 N. Calvert St.　　　　Ph: (410)037-8271
Baltimore, MD 21202　　　Free: 800-296-6687
　　　　　　　　　　　　　Fax: (410)752-8492
E-mail: orders@genealogical.com
Contact: Thomas Jay Kemp, Editor.
Desc: Vital records offices for 67 countries and territories in North America, the British Isles and other English-speaking countries, and Europe. *Type:* Directory.

NSFNET Backbone Statistics Page

Georgia Institute of Technology - College of Computing, Graphics, Visuulization, and Usability Center
801 Atlantic Dr.　　　　　Ph: (404)894-3152
Atlanta, GA 30332-0280　Fax: (404)894-9846
URL:　　http://www.cc.gatech.edu/gvu/stats/NSF/merit.
html
Contact: James Pitkow, pitkow@cc.gatech.edu.
Desc: The NSFNET Backbone Statistics Page offers access to the data provided by Merit NIC Services. Statistics represent traffic, broken down by service, during the one-month reporting period. *Type:* Database.

STAT-USA/Internet

U.S. Department of Commerce - Economics and Statistics Administration
STAT-USA　　　　　　　　Ph: (202)482-1986
HCHB Rm. 4885　　　　　Free: 800-STA-TUSA
Washington, DC 20230　　Fax: (202)482-2164
E-mail: stat-usa@doc.gov
URL: http://www.stat-usa.gov/
Desc: STAT-USA/Internet is the online source for business and economic information produced by the federal gov-

ernment. This easy to navigate site contains timely business and economic information from more than 50 federal agencies and distributes it from a central source, and provides quick and easy access to thousands of files, including trade statistics, overseas contacts, market research reports, daily economic releases, and procurement information. *Type:* Database.

State and Local Statistics Sources

Gale Group Inc.
27500 Drake Rd.　　　　　Ph: (248)699-4253
Farmington Hills, MI 48331-　Free: 800-877-GALE
3535　　　　　　　　　　Fax: (248)699-8070
E-mail: galeord@galegroup.com
URL: http://www.galegroup.com.
Contact: M. Balachandran, Editor; Sarojini Balachandran, Editor.
Desc: Over 60,000 citations to publications issued by state government agencies, local and national associations, universities, commercial producers, federal government agencies, and other organizations that provide statistical information at a regional, state, or local level in subject areas such as accidents, agriculture, cost of living, economics, elections, environment, finance, foreign trade, health, income, insurance, labor force, livestock, minorities, population, professions, revenue sharing, salaries and wages, travel and tourism, taxation, and water supply. *Type:* Directory.

Statistics Sources

Gale Group Inc.
27500 Drake Rd.　　　　　Ph: (248)699-4253
Farmington Hills, MI 48331-　Free: 800-877-GALE
3535　　　　　　　　　　Fax: (248)699-8070
E-mail: galeord@galegroup.com
URL: http://www.galegroup.com.
Contact: Jacqueline Wasserman O'Brien, Editor; Steven R. Wasserman, Editor, (410)956-6855, fax: (410)626-2031.
Desc: Provides over 100,000 citations to publications and organizations that make published and unpublished statistical data available on over 20,000 specific subjects. Citations are classified by subject, and include organization or publisher name, address, and title of publication or information service. *Type:* Directory.

StatLib

Carnegie Mellon University
5000 Forbes Ave.　　　　Ph: (412)268-2000
Pittsburgh, PA 15213
E-mail: statlib@lib.stat.cmu.edu
URL: http://lib.stat.cmu.edu
Contact: Pantelis Vlachos, Dept. of Statistics, vlachos@stat.cmu.edu.
Desc: StatLib is an archive containing software, datasets, multivariate analyses, datasets, algorithms, and a variety of other specific and general information for statisticians. Contributions by statisticians and other users welcomed. *Type:* Database.

Vassarstats: Statistical Computation Website

Vassar College - Department of Psychology
124 Raymond Ave.
Poughkeepsie, NY 12604-0396
URL: http://faculty.vassar.edu/~lowry/VassarStats.html
Contact: Richard Lowry, lowry@vassar.edu.
Desc: This site will easily become a cherished treasure for students, researchers, and others who have to do statistics calculations regularly. This interactive site will perform statistical calculations in several different areas such as probability, proportions, correlation and regression, t-tests, analysis of variance and covariance, and others. *Type:* Database.

Substance Abuse

Addiction Research and Treatment Corporation
22 Chapel St.   Ph: (718)260-2900
Brooklyn, NY 11201   Fax: (718)260-8276
Contact: Dr. Beny J. Primm, Exec.Dir.
Desc: Operates a multi-modality drug treatment program with six ambulatory treatment clinics and a Skills Training Center. Funded by the state of New York Substance Abuse Services and Medicaid reimbursements. Treatments employed are primarily detoxification, methadone maintenance, and drug-free services. *Type:* Association.

Addiction Research and Treatment Corporation
22 Chapel St.   Ph: (718)260-2917
Brooklyn, NY 11201   Fax: (718)522-3186
E-mail: artbrown@aol.com
Contact: Dr. Lawrence S. Brown, Jr., Sr.V.Pres.
Desc: Alcohol and drug addiction, including studies on alcoholism among those addicted to opiates, immunological parameters of drug abuse, stress among patients and staff, and the relationship of patterns of drug abuse and sexual practices to the frequency of human immunodeficiency virus (HIV) infection (exposure to AIDS virus). Conducts clinical trials of drugs for drug abuse and the treatment of HIV disease. *Type:* Research center.

Addictions RX
4794 NE 17th Ave.   Ph: (305)491-5368
Ft. Lauderdale, FL 33334-5610   Fax: (305)491-8481
Contact: James Strawbridge, Writer.
Desc: Distributes questions and answers related to all addictions, including workaholics and heroin. *Alt. Contact:* 4794 NE 17th Ave., Ft. Lauderdale, FL 33334-5610; telephone: (305)491-5368; fax: (305)491-8481. *Type:* Periodical.

Al-Anon Family Group Headquarters, World Service Office
1600 Corporate Landing Pkwy.   Ph: (757)563-1600
Virginia Beach, VA 23454-5617   Free: 888-4AL-
                                   ANON
                                   Fax: (757)563-1655
E-mail: wso@al-anon.org
URL: http://www.al-anon.alateen.org
Contact: Carole Kuney, Contact.
Desc: Relatives and friends of individuals with an alcohol problem. Operates Alateen for members 12-20 years of age whose lives have been adversely affected by someone else's drinking problem, usually a parent's. *Type:* Association.

Alateen
1600 Corporate Landing Pkwy.   Ph: (757)563-1600
Virginia Beach, VA 23454-5617   Free: 888-4AL-
                                   ANON
                                   Fax: (757)563-1655
E-mail: wso@al-anon.org
URL: http://www.alateen.org
Contact: Ric Buchanan, Exec.Dir.
Desc: Individuals ages 12-19 who have been adversely affected by a relative or friend with an alcohol problem. *Type:* Association.

Alcohol and Alcohol Problems Science Database
U.S. National Institute on Alcohol Abuse and Alcoholism (NIAAA)
Scientific Communications Branch
6000 Executive Blvd., Suite 409   Ph: (301)443-3860
Willco Bldg.
Bethesda, MD 20892-7003
URL: http://www.niaaa.nih.gov
Contact: Kathleen Mullen, Information Services Manager., (202)842-7600, fax: (202)842-0418.

Desc: Contains approximately 100,000 citations, with abstracts, to worldwide literature on alcoholism research. Sources include periodicals, monographs, conference proceedings, reports, and dissertation abstracts. *Available:* Ovid Technologies, Inc. *Type:* Database.

Alcohol Information for Clinicians and Educators Database
Dartmouth Medical School
Project CORK Institute
Vermont Department of Health
Office of Alcohol & Drug Abuse
    Programs
108 Cherry St., Box 70
Burlington, VT 05402
E-mail: linda.vanwart@dartmouth.edu
URL: http://www.cit.state.vt.us/adap/cork/cork1.htm
Desc: Contains more than 26,000 citations, with abstracts, to published biomedical, social science, and social policy literature covering all aspects of alcohol and other drug use and abuse. Covers the resource collection of Project CORK Institute, which was founded to develop a curriculum on alcoholism for medical professionals. *Available:* Dartmouth College Libraries, Library Online System. *Type:* Database.

Alcoholism and Drug Addiction Research Foundation
Clinical Research and Treatment Institute
33 Russell St.   Ph: (416)595-6106
Toronto, ON, Canada M5S 2S1   Fax: (416)595-6619
Contact: Dr. E.M. Sellers, VP.
Desc: Alcohol and drug abuse. Studies are carried out in six treatment areas: pre-clinical research (molecular, pharmacologic, and behavioural); human experimental studies; brief interventions; moderate-severe dependence (including relapse prevention); mental health and comorbidity; and Health Recovery Services in the Community. *Type:* Research center.

American Society of Addiction Medicine
4601 N. Park Ave., Arcade Ste.   Ph: (301)656-3920
   101   Fax: (301)656-3815
Chevy Chase, MD 20815
E-mail: usamoffice@aol.com
URL: http://www.asam.org
Contact: James F. Callahan, D.P.A., Exec.VP/CEO.
Desc: Physicians with special interest and experience in the field of alcoholism and other drug dependencies and who wish to share this experience with other professionals in order to extend their knowledge of addictive diseases; promote dissemination of that knowledge; enlighten the public regarding these problems; advance education and research in the field of addiction. Holds annual Ruth Fox Course for Physicians, annual Medical-Scientific Conference and five other conferences/courses. *Type:* Association.

Arkansas Health Department
Alcohol and Drug Abuse Prevention Bureau
5800 W. 10th, Ste 907   Ph: (501)280-4500
Little Rock, AR 72204   Fax: (501)280-4532
E-mail: rstephen@mail.doh.state.ar.us
URL: http://health.state.ar.us/
Contact: Ray L. Stephens, Assoc.Bur.Dir.
Desc: Substance abuse prevention. *Type:* Research center.

BACCHUS and Gamma Peer Education Network
National Headquarters   Ph: (303)871-0901
PO Box 100430   Fax: (303)871-0907
Denver, CO 80250
E-mail: bacgin@aol.com
Contact: Drew Hunter, Exec.Dir.
Desc: Students, advisors, faculty, and staff of colleges and universities in the U.S., Canada, and Mexico. Primary mission is to deliver alcohol abuse prevention and health education to college students and their communities. *Type:* Association.

Behavioral Disease Management Report
Manisses Communications Group, Inc.
208 Governor St.   Ph: (401)831-6020
Providence, RI 02906-3246   Free: 800-333-7771
                                   Fax: (401)861-6370
E-mail: manissescs@manisses.com
Desc: Reports on strategies to improve programs and contain costs in delivering substance abuse and mental health services. *Type:* Newsletter.

Brown University
Center for Alcohol and Addiction Studies
Box G-BH   Ph: (401)444-1818
Providence, RI 02912   Fax: (401)444-1850
E-mail: david_lewis@brown.edu
URL: http://www.caas.brown.edu
Contact: David C. Lewis, MD, Dir.
Desc: Alcohol and addiction studies, including an individual's relationship to alcohol and the effectiveness of community reinforcement on treatment, the relationship between smoking and drinking among alcoholics, matching treatment focus to dysfunction, social skills treatment of cocaine abusers, cue exposure and social skills treatment for alcoholics, deterring preadolescent drug and AIDS-risky behavior, time dynamics of alcohol treatment outcome, treatment research validation and extension program, substance abuse prevention program for Native American youth, hospital intervention services, and healthcare policy. *Type:* Research center.

The Brown University Digest of Addiction Theory and Application
Manisses Communications Group, Inc.
208 Governor St.   Ph: (401)831-6020
Providence, RI 02906-3246   Free: 800-333-7771
                                   Fax: (401)861-6370
E-mail: manissescs@manisses.com; lwjackim@manisses.com.
Contact: David C. Lewis, Editor.
Desc: Digests and abstracts articles on alcoholism and drug dependencies. Draws articles from more than 80 international scholarly journals. *Type:* Newsletter.

Cocaine Anonymous World Services
PO Box 2000   Ph: (310)559-5833
Los Angeles, CA 90049-8000   Free: 800-347-8998
                                   Fax: (310)559-2554
E-mail: cawso@ca.org
URL: http://www.ca.org
Contact: K.D. Zager, Dir. of Operations.
Desc: Fellowship of men and women who share their experience, strength, and hope with each other. that they may solve their common problem and help others to recover from addiction and remain free from cocaine and all other mind-altering drugs. *Type:* Association.

Drug & Alcohol Abuse Education
Editorial Resources, Inc.
PO Box 21129   Ph: (202)783-2929
Washington, DC 20009
Contact: Bob Swierczek, Editor.
Desc: Addresses drug abuse education, prevention, and treatment. Focuses on Washington, D.C.-based events. *Type:* Newsletter.

Drug, Alcohol, and Other Addictions
Oryx Press
4041 N. Central Ave., Ste. 700   Ph: (602)265-2651
Phoenix, AZ 85012-3397   Free: 800-279-6799
                                   Fax: 800-279-4663
E-mail: info@oryxpress.com
URL: http://www.oryxpress.com
Desc: Nearly 12,000 federal, state, and local addiction treatment programs including public and private centers. *Type:* Directory.

Drug Detection Report

Business Publishers, Inc.

8737 Colesville Rd., Ste. 1100   Ph: (301)589-5103

Silver Spring, MD 20910   Free: 800-274-6737

   Fax: (301)587-4530

E-mail: bpinews@bpinews.com

Contact: Donald E. Viraska, Editor.

Desc: Reports on drug testing in the workplace, including regulations, legislation, and scientific developments. Discusses such topics as random testing, "reasonable suspicion" testing, and federal regulation of drug testing laboratories. *Type:* Newsletter.

Friends Research Institute

505 Baltimore Ave.   Ph: (410)823-5116

PO Box 10676   Fax: (410)823-5131

Baltimore, MD 21285

E-mail: friendsres@aol.com

URL: http://www.friendsresearch.org

Contact: Patrick F. Bogan, Exec.Dir.

Desc: Studies narcotic addiction to provide statistical documentation of its relation to crime, effectiveness of addiction treatment programs, and HIV as a result of lifestyle. Also conducts pharmaceutical and medical device research. *Type:* Research center.

The HIP Report

Help for Incontinent People, Inc. (HIP)

PO Box 8310   Ph: (803)579-7900

Spartanburg, SC 29305-8310   Free: 800-272-3337

   Fax: (803)579-7902

Contact: Katherine F. Jeter, Editor.

Desc: Furnishes information on the causes, prevention, diagnosis, treatments, and management alternatives of incontinence. Recurring features include letters to the editor, news of research, reports of meetings, news of educational opportunities, book reviews, and notices of publications available. *Type:* Newsletter.

ICPA Reporter

International Commission for the Prevention of Alcoholism and Drug Dependency

12501 Old Columbia Pike   Ph: (301)680-6719

Silver Spring, MD 20904   Fax: (301)680-6090

E-mail: 74617.1663@compuserve.com; pettitb@gc.adventist.org

Contact: Thomas R. Neslund, Editor.

Desc: Reports on activities of the Commission worldwide, which seeks to prevent alcoholism and drug dependency. Recurring features include a calendar of events and notices of publications available. *Type:* Newsletter.

Johns Hopkins University

Behavioral Pharmacology Research Unit

Johns Hopkins Bayview Campus   Ph: (410)550-0035

5510 Nathan Shock Dr.   Fax: (410)550-0030

Baltimore, MD 21224-6823

E-mail: bigelow@welchlink.welch.jhu.edu

Contact: George E. Bigelow, PhD, Sci.Dir.

Desc: Human behavioral pharmacology of substance abuse and dependence, including clinical studies on abuse liability assessment, performance effects, and applied treatment interventions for opioids (analgesics) and narcotics, sedatives, anxiolytics, tobacco, nicotine, caffeine, and cocaine. *Type:* Research center.

Mothers Against Drunk Driving

MADD

511 E. John Carpenter Fwy., 700

Irving, TX 75062

E-mail: Info@madd.org

URL: http://www.madd.org

Desc: The MADD Home Page provides information about the Mothers Against Drunk Driving, including the history and goals of the organization. There are valuable statistics and reports on the progress and accomplishments of the organization. *Type:* Database.

Mount Sinai School of Medicine of City University of New York

Alcohol Research and Treatment Center

VA Medical Center   Ph: (718)579-1646

130 W. Kingsbridge Rd.   Fax: (718)733-6257

Bronx, NY 10468

E-mail: liebercs@aol.com

Contact: Dr. Charles S. Lieber, Dir.

Desc: Disease control strategy for alcoholism and its medical complications, including a public health approach with emphasis on early detection of alcoholism and early diagnosis of its medical complications and the focus of major therapeutic efforts on susceptible subgroups. Specific areas of research include the effects of ethanol on microsomal P450 enzymes, biochemical markers of alcohol consumption, acetaldehyde metabolism and toxicity, pathogenesis of alcohol-liver injury (prevention and treatment), effects of ethanol on hepatic lipids and prostaglandin metabolism, ethanol-nutrient interactions, ethanol and cancer, and ethanol and the gastrointestinal tract. *Type:* Research center.

Narcotics Anonymous

PO Box 9999   Ph: (818)773-9999

Van Nuys, CA 91409   Fax: (818)700-0700

E-mail: jeffg@na.org

URL: http://www.na.org

Contact: Jeff Gershoff, Fellowship Svcs.

Desc: Recovering addicts throughout the world meet to offer help to fellow addicts seeking recovery. *Type:* Association.

National Alliance of Methadone Advocates

435 2nd Ave.   Ph: (212)595-6262

New York, NY 10010   Fax: (212)595-6262

E-mail: nama@interport.net

URL: http://www.methadone.org/

Contact: Joycelyn Woods, Exec.VP.

Desc: Methadone maintenance patients and supporters of methadone maintenance treatment. Promotes quality methadone maintenance treatment as the most effective modality for the treatment of heroin addiction. *Type:* Association.

National Association of Alcoholism and Drug Abuse Counselors

1911 Fort Myer Dr., Ste. 900   Ph: (703)741-7686

Arlington, VA 22209   Free: 800-548-0497

   Fax: (703)741-7698

E-mail: naadac@well.com

URL: http://www.naadac.org

Contact: Linda Kaplan, Exec.Dir.

Desc: Counselors in alcoholism and drug abuse treatment. Objective is to provide national representation for counselors as well as for their training and education. Works to gain public recognition of alcoholism as a disease. *Type:* Association.

National Association on Drug Abuse Problems

355 Lexington Ave.   Ph: (212)986-1170

New York, NY 10017   Fax: (212)697-2939

Contact: John Darin, Pres.

Desc: Sponsored by business and labor organizations. Serves as an information clearinghouse and referral bureau for corporations and local communities interested in prevention of substance abuse and treatment of substance abusers. Provides: resources to local communities seeking to combat drug and alcohol abuse; corporate services for employers interested in creating a drug-free workplace. *Type:* Association.

National Association of State Alcohol and Drug Abuse Directors

808 17th St. NW, Ste. 410   Ph: (202)293-0090

Washington, DC 20006   Fax: (202)293-1250

E-mail: dcoffice@nasadad.org

URL: http://www.nasadad.org

Contact: John S. Gustafson, Exec.Dir.

Desc: Purposes are: to represent the interests of state alcohol and drug abuse directors and their agencies before Congress and federal agencies; to foster development of comprehensive alcohol and drug abuse programs on state resources/services, alcohol and drug issues related to AIDS, drunk driving, and criminal justice activities in each state. Operates Project for Addiction Counselor Training, AIDS Policy Project, Criminal Justice Programs, Methadone Treatment Quality Assurance System project, and the National Prevention Network (NPN). Serves as an information clearinghouse. *Type:* Association.

National Development and Research Institutes, Inc.

2 World Trade Center 16th Fl.   Ph: (212)845-4400

New York, NY 10048-0203   Fax: (212)845-4696

E-mail: john.baumann@ndri.org

URL: http://www.ndri.org

Contact: Dr. Fred Streit, Exec.Dir.

Desc: Drug abuse, including evaluations of treatment and prevention programs; AIDS research as it relates to substance abuse; epidemiology of drug abuse; drugs and crime; drug abuse and the criminal justice system; street studies of drug sales, use, and prevention; evaluation and enhancement of AIDS outreach; and intervention services for high-risk adolescents. *Type:* Research center.

National Good Templar

National Council of the U.S., I.O.G.T.

1106 E. Oakland Ave.   Ph: (517)485-9900

Lansing, MI 48906   Fax: (517)485-1928

Contact: Robert Hammond, Editor.

Desc: Aims to educate members of the IOGT on the effects of alcohol and drugs. Recurring features include news of research and memorials. *Type:* Newsletter.

New York State Office of Alcoholism and Substance Abuse Services

Research Institute on Addictions

1021 Main St.   Ph: (716)887-2566

Buffalo, NY 14203-1016   Fax: (716)887-2252

E-mail: connors@ria.org

URL: http://www.ria.org/

Contact: Gerard J. Connors, PhD, Dir.

Desc: Etiology, course, treatment, and prevention of alcoholism and substance abuse. Studies the following six aspects of substance abuse: normative patterns; biochemical, physiological, psychological, and social antecedents and consequences; biopsychosocial aspects of consumption in early and middle adulthood; family aspects; alcohol-drug interactions; and treatment and prevention strategies. *Type:* Research center.

Ontario Tobacco Research Unit

33 Russell St.   Ph: (416)595-6888

Toronto, ON, Canada M5S 2S1   Fax: (416)595-6068

E-mail: otru@arf.org

URL: http://www.arf.org/otru

Contact: Roberta Ferrence, Dir.

Desc: Tobacco control, including epidemiology, tobacco use and cessation, tobacco and youth, gender issues in tobacco use, ethnicity and tobacco use, economic factors in tobacco use, tobacco policy attitudes, policy and program evaluation, community interventions, and enviromental tobacco smoke. *Type:* Research center.

Pacific Institute for Research and Evaluation

Prevention Research Center

2150 Shattuck Ave., Ste. 900   Ph: (510)486-1111
Berkeley, CA 94704   Fax: (510)644-0594
E-mail: holder@prev.org

Contact: Harold D. Holder, PhD, Dir.

Desc: Environmental approaches to the prevention of alcohol-related problems. Projects include studies of individual and environmental factors within the worksite associated with alcohol problems, peer influences and the influences of prime time television on adolescent values and attitudes about drinking, risk factors associated with alcohol-impaired driving, beverage server training to reduce intoxication among customers, the structure and function of alcohol beverage control agencies, legal issues and legislation, drinking and alcohol problems among Mexican-Americans, computer simulation to determine regional alcohol use and abuse, and community trial prevention projects to seek innovative and effective strategies to reduce alcohol-involved injury and deaths, and postdoctoral and multidisciplinary health service research training programs. *Type:* Research center.

Phoenix House Foundation

164 W. 74th St.   Ph: (212)595-5810
New York, NY 10023   Fax: (212)496-6035

Contact: Mitchell S. Rosenthal, M.D., Pres.

Desc: Provides drug abuse treatment, vocational and educational services through individual, group and family counseling, and self help rehabilitation programs. Operates 20 facilities for adolescents and adults in New York, New Jersey and California and Texas. Operates extensive range of drug-free treatment programs including: Phoenix Academy (Board of Education certified, residential high school for adolescents); Step One (Board of Education certified day-school); IMPACT (outpatient intervention for teenagers and their parents); long-term residential treatment for adults; short-term out-patient and in-patient adult drug treatment. *Type:* Association.

PrevLine: Prevention Online

U.S. National Clearinghouse for Alcohol and Drug Information
PO Box 2345   Ph: (301)468-2600
Rockville, MD 20847-2345   Free: 800-729-6686
   Fax: (301)468-6433

URL: http://www.health.org

Contact: webmaster@health.org.

Desc: National Clearinghouse for Alcohol and Drug Information PrevLine database provides information dealing with many aspects of drug abuse, prevention, and health, such as scientific findings, prevention programs and materials, field experts, Federal grants, and market research. The material is tailored to policymakers, opinion leaders, media, parents, teachers, young people. *Type:* Database.

Project Renewal

200 Varick St., 9th Fl.   Ph: (212)620-0340
New York, NY 10014   Fax: (212)243-4868

Contact: Edward I. Geffner, Exec.Dir.

Desc: Provides care for homeless adults in New York City. Funded by the New York City Department of Mental Health, Mental Retardation and Alcoholism Services, the U.S. Department of Housing and Urban Development, the New York State Office of Mental Health, the New York City Department of Homeless Services, the New York City Human Resources Administrative Divison of AIDS Service, the New York State Office of Alcoholism and Substance Abuse Services, private individuals, and corporations and foundations. *Type:* Association.

Recovery Resources

3950 Chester Ave   Ph: (216)431-4131
Cleveland, OH 44114-4625   Fax: (216)431-4133
Contact: Myrtle I. Muntz, Pres.

Desc: Works for the prevention and treatment of alcoholism and other drug dependence through programs of public and professional education, community service, treatment, and the promotion of alcoholism research. Provides employee assistance program in drug free workplace assistance. *Type:* Association.

Rockefeller University

Laboratory of the Biology of Addictive Diseases

1230 York Ave.   Ph: (212)327-8247
New York, NY 10021-6399   Fax: (212)327-8574
E-mail: sudulj@rockvax.rockefeller.edu
URL: http://www.rockefeller.edu
Contact: Dr. Mary Jeanne Kreek, Hd.Prof.

Desc: Biological basis of opiate, alcohol, and cocaine addiction; the biological correlates of addictive disease, including the physiological and pharmacological effects of chronic drug use; and the medical complications of drug use, especially hepatitis B, hepatitis delta, and human immunodeficiency viral infections. Other areas include molecular neurobiology of the addictive diseases with special attention on the role of the endogenous opioid system in these disorders, including cocaine dependency and alcoholism, as well as opiate addition; and the role of the endogenous opioids and the specific opioid receptors in the addictive diseases and in normal and abnormal physiology of the neuroendocrine and gastrointestinal systems. *Type:* Research center.

Rubicon

1300 MacTavish Ave.   Ph: (804)359-3255
Richmond, VA 23230   Fax: (804)359-5137
Contact: Van Watley, Exec.Dir.

Desc: A substance abuse rehabilitation and treatment program. Maintains one outpatient, one intensive outpatient, two specific male residential, and one specific female residential treatment facilities, and a detoxification unit. Attempts to teach program participants an alternate lifestyle, using many different approaches for each individual and making extensive use of: individual, family, and group therapy; education; cultural and career development programs; correctional intervention. *Type:* Association.

Rutgers University

Center of Alcohol Studies

607 Allison Rd.   Ph: (908)445-2190
Piscataway, NJ 08854-8001   Fax: (908)445-3500
E-mail: cas2@rci.rutgers.edu
URL: http://www.rci.rutgers.edu/~cas2
Contact: Robert J. Pandina, PhD, Dir.

Desc: Causes and treatment of alcoholism and drug abuse, diverse actions of alcohol and other drugs on the body, means to prevent alcohol and other drug misuse, and the incidence and prevalence of normal and problem alcohol consumption in the U.S. and the world, including human enzyme systems important in alcohol metabolism, development of tolerance and physical dependence on alcohol, and hormonal changes. *Type:* Research center.

SAMHSA News

Substance Abuse and Mental Health Services Administration
Office of Applied Studies
5600 Fishers Ln.   Ph: (301)443-0525
Rm. 16-105   Fax: (301)443-9847
Rockville, MD 20857
URL: http://www.samhsa.gov.
Contact: Peggy Adams, Editor; Deborah Goodman, Editor.

Desc: Provides news on prevention and treatment of mental health and substance abuse disorders from the agency's Centers for Substance Abuse Treatment, Substance Abuse Prevention, and Mental Health Services. Recurring features include information on grant opportunities and news of research. *Type:* Newsletter.

Secular Organizations for Sobriety

5521 Grosvenor Blvd.   Ph: (310)821-8430
Los Angeles, CA 90066   Fax: (310)821-2610
Contact: James R. Christopher, Founder.

Desc: Recovering alcoholics and drug addicts; families and friends of alcoholics or drug addicts. Serves as a support system free of any religious or spiritual undercurrent; believes sobriety is a process of personal responsibility. Espouses "a healthy skepticism" and encourages self-reliance and free thought. *Type:* Association.

Southern California Research Institute

11914 W. Washington Blvd.   Ph: (310)390-8481
Los Angeles, CA 90066   Fax: (310)398-6651
E-mail: mburns5573@aol.com
Contact: Dr. Marcelline Burns, Dir.

Desc: Effects of alcohol and drugs on behavior, including effects of alcohol and drugs on driving. *Type:* Research center.

STRAIGHT, Inc.

1430 Kristina Way   Ph: (757)499-9111
Chesapeake, VA 23320-8917   Free: 800-333-8929
Contact: Bernadine Braithwaite, Exec.Dir.

Desc: Trained personnel, adolescent drug users and their families, and rehabilitated drug users. Objective is to treat drug-using adolescents through the use of an intensive, highly structured, progressive therapeutic process; the program takes nine to 12 months to complete and involves the drug user as well as his/her family. The program works to retrain adolescents in the values and rules of their culture and help them to relinquish the values of the drug subculture. *Type:* Association.

U.S. Department of Health and Human Services

National Institute on Alcohol Abuse and Alcoholism

Willco Bldg., Ste. 400   Ph: (301)443-3885
6000 Executive Blvd.   Fax: (301)443-7043
Bethesda, MD 20892-7003
URL: http://www.niaaa.nih.gov
Contact: Enoch Gordis, Dir.

Desc: Prevention and treatment of alcohol-related problems and alcoholism. Seeks to develop new scientific knowledge that will reduce the incidence and prevalence of alcohol abuse and alcoholism and the associated morbidity and mortality. *Type:* Research center.

U.S. Department of Health and Human Services

National Institute on Alcohol Abuse and Alcoholism

Basic Research Division

Willco Bldg., Rm. 402   Ph: (301)443-0799
6000 Exec. Blvd.   Fax: (301)594-0673
Bethesda, MD 20892
E-mail: sz14w@nih.gov
URL: http://www.niaaa.nih.gov
Contact: Samir Zakhari, Dir.

Desc: Multiple determinants and processes of alcoholism and other alcohol-related problems; on the prevention of alcohol abuse; and on the diagnosis, treatment, and rehabilitation of persons who abuse alcohol. Division administers the Institute's National Alcohol Research Centers Program as well as its research scientists development and training programs. *Type:* Research center.

U.S. Department of Health and Human Services
National Institute on Alcohol Abuse and
Alcoholism
Basic Research Division
Biomedical Research Branch

Willco Bldg., St. 402   Ph: (301)443-4224
6000 Executive Blvd., MSC   Fax: (301)594-0673
  7003
Bethesda, MD 20892-7003
Contact: Dr. Sam Zakhari, Chf.

Desc: Supports and administers NIAAA extramural research grants and training programs on the effects of alcohol abuse and alcoholism as related to the central nervous system, the fetal alcohol syndrome, and neuroendocrine and pathological conditions. Research is aimed at reduction of morbidity and mortality associated with alcoholism and alcohol abuse and includes research in the areas of etiology, pathogenesis, identification, treatment, and prevention as well as in the development of basic research tools and methodologies. *Type:* Research center.

U.S. Department of Health and Human Services
National Institute on Alcohol Abuse and
Alcoholism
Basic Research Division
National Centers and Special Programs

6000 Executive Blvd.   Ph: (301)443-2531
Rm. 402   Fax: (301)594-0673
Bethesda, MD 20892
E-mail: tvanderv@willco.niaaa.nih.gov
URL: http://www.niaaa.nih.gov
Contact: Dr. Ernestine Vanderveen, Assoc.Dir.

Desc: Provides grant support for Alcohol Research Centers to conduct interdisciplinary research on alcoholism and problems related to alcohol abuse. These grants are typically for a five-year period and are intended to encourage research by providing stable, long term support of research on the nature, causes, diagnosis, treatment, control, prevention, and consequences of alcohol abuse and alcoholism. *Type:* Research center.

U.S. Department of Health and Human Services
National Institute on Alcohol Abuse and
Alcoholism
Biometry and Epidemiology Division

6000 Executive Blvd., MSC   Ph: (301)443-3306
  7003   Fax: (301)443-8614
Bethesda, MD 20892-7003
Contact: Mary Dufor, MD, Actg.Dir.

Desc: Incidence and prevalence of alcohol abuse and alcoholism (both nationally and in specific population groups); conducts national surveillance activities to collect and analyze alcohol-related program data through various information systems; and develops and maintains information systems to collect and analyze alcohol-related data. Division also collaborates with other organizations engaged in alcohol data collection activities, such as state-based information systems, in order to exchange pertinent data and to utilize existing data systems where appropriate. *Type:* Research center.

U.S. Department of Health and Human Services
National Institute on Alcohol Abuse and
Alcoholism
Division of Clinical and Prevention Research

6000 Executive Blvd.   Ph: (301)443-1206
Willco Bldg., St. 505   Fax: (301)443-8774
Bethesda, MD 20892-7003
URL: http://www.niaaa.nih.gov
Contact: Richard K. Fuller, MD, Dir.

Desc: Supports alcohol abuse and alcoholism treatment, prevention, and health services research through grants and cooperative agreements. Principal Division components are the Prevention Research Branch, the Treatment Research Branch, and the Health Services Research Program. *Type:* Research center.

U.S. Department of Health and Human Services
National Institute on Alcohol Abuse and
Alcoholism
Intramural Clinical and Biological Research
Division

NIH Bldg. 10, Rm. 3C103   Ph: (301)496-8996
9000 Rockville Pike   Fax: (301)402-0445
Bethesda, MD 20892
Contact: Dr. Markku Linnoila, Dir.

Desc: Multiple determinants and processes of alcoholism and other alcohol-related problems and on prevention, diagnosis, treatment, and rehabilitation. It also provides in-house research scientist training in a variety of disciplines for work in alcohol-related research and collaborates with other agencies, universities, and scientific organizations. *Type:* Research center.

U.S. Department of Health and Human Services
National Institute on Alcohol Abuse and
Alcoholism
Intramural Clinical and Biological Research
Division
Clinical Studies Laboratory

NIH Bldg. 10, Rm. 3C114   Ph: (301)496-5353
9000 Rockville Pike   Fax: (301)402-0445
Bethesda, MD 20892
Contact: Paul Andreas, Contact.

Desc: Neuroscience, clinical pharmacology, analytical biochemistry, internal medicine, and psychiatry, all as related to alcoholism. *Type:* Research center.

U.S. Department of Health and Human Services
National Institute on Alcohol Abuse and
Alcoholism
Intramural Clinical and Biological Research
Division
Laboratory of Molecular and Cellular
Neurobiology

Park Bldg., Rm. 158   Ph: (301)443-1234
Bethesda, MD 20892-8115   Fax: (301)480-6882
Contact: Dr. Forrest Weight, Chf.

Desc: Alcohol and alcoholism, physiology, and pharmacology. *Type:* Research center.

U.S. Department of Health and Human Services
National Institute on Alcohol Abuse and
Alcoholism
Prevention Research Center

Pacific Institute for Research and   Ph: (510)486-1111
  Evaluation   Fax: (510)644-0594
2150 Shattuck Ave., Ste. 900
Berkeley, CA 94704
E-mail: holder@prev.org
Contact: Harold D. Holder, PhD, Dir.

Desc: Prevention of alcohol-related problems. Research focuses on better understanding the social and physical environment that influences individual behavior and problems relating to alcohol abuse. *Type:* Research center.

U.S. Department of Health and Human Services
National Institutes of Health
National Institute on Alcohol Abuse and
Alcoholism

9000 Rockville Pike   Ph: (301)443-3885
Bethesda, MD 20892
URL: http://www.niaaa.nih.gov/
Contact: Enoch Gordis, MD, Director.

Desc: The Institute conducts and supports biomedical and behavioral research, health services research, research training, and health information dissemination with respect to the prevention and treatment of alcohol abuse and alcoholism, and provides a national focus for the Federal effort to increase knowledge and promote effective strategies to deal with health problems and issues associated with alcohol abuse and alcoholism. *Type:* Government agency, office, or program.

U.S. Department of Health and Human Services
National Institutes of Health
National Institute on Drug Abuse

9000 Rockville Pike   Ph: (301)443-6480
Bethesda, MD 20892
URL: http://www.nida.nih.gov/
Contact: Alan I. Leshner, Director.

Desc: The Institute's mission is to lead the Nation in bringing the power of science to bear on drug abuse and addiction, through the strategic support and conduct of research across a broad range of disciplines, and the rapid and effective dissemination and use of the results of that research to significantly improve drug abuse and addiction prevention, treatment, and policy. *Type:* Government agency, office, or program.

U.S. Department of Health and Human Services
Substance Abuse and Mental Health Services
Administration

5600 Fishers Ln.   Ph: (301)443-4797
Rockville, MD 20857
URL: http://www.samhsa.gov/
Contact: Nelba Chavez, Director.

Desc: The mission of SAMHSA is to ensure that knowledge, based on science and state-of-the-art practice is effectively used for the prevention and treatment of addictive and mental disorders. Major components include: Center for Substance Abuse, Center for Substance Abuse Treatment, Center for Mental Health Services, and Office of Management, Planning, and Communications. *Type:* Government agency, office, or program.

University of California, Los Angeles
Alcohol Research Center

Neuropsychiatric Inst.   Ph: (310)825-1891
760 Westwood Plaza   Fax: (310)206-7309
Los Angeles, CA 90024
Contact: Dr. Ernest P. Noble, Dir.

Desc: Causes of alcoholism, including genetic predisposition. *Type:* Research center.

University of California, San Francisco
Ernest Gallo Clinic and Research Center

San Francisco General Hospital   Ph: (415)648-7111
Bldg. 1, Rm. 101   Fax: (415)648-7116
1001 Potrero Ave.
San Francisco, CA 94110
E-mail: diamond@itsa.ucsf.edu
URL: http://egcrc.ucsf.edu
Contact: Dr. Ivan Diamond, Contact.

Desc: Alcoholism, with special emphasis on cellular and molecular mechanisms of alcohol dependence and genetic differences between cells of alcoholics and cells of non-alcoholics. *Type:* Research center.

University of Colorado--Denver
Alcohol Research Center

4200 E. 9th Ave.   Ph: (303)315-8609
Denver, CO 80262   Fax: (303)315-7499
E-mail: adron.harris@uchsc.edu
URL: http://www.hsc.colorado.edu/ctrsinst/alcrc/indaex.html
Contact: Dr. R. Adron Harris, Sci.Dir.

Desc: Mechanism of the action of alcohol to determine the ways in which alcohol affects the brain during both acute and chronic periods of intake, including studies on alcohol as a stimulus, different responses elicited by alcohol, and the products of alcohol metabolism. Uses genetic manipulation in animal models to define the acute and chronic affects of alcohol in relation to heredity. *Type:* Research center.

University of Connecticut

Alcohol Research Center

263 Farmington Ave. Ph: (860)679-3423
Farmington, CT 06030-1410 Fax: (860)679-1296
E-mail: hesselbrock@psych.uchc.edu

Contact: Victor Hesselbrock, PhD, Sci.Dir.Prod.

Desc: Genetic, psychiatric, biological, behavioral, and cross-cultural aspects of alcoholism, including alcoholic typologies, treatment matching, familial alcoholism, alcohol dependence syndrome, and early intervention. Activities focus on clinical trials of new psychotherapies and pharmacotherapies, biological responses to alcohol-related stimuli, diagnosis of alcohol dependence, animal studies of neurobiological correlates of alcohol consumption, ASP and family history variables as risk factors in the development of alcohol dependence, and research on treatment services for alcoholics. *Type:* Research center.

University of Kentucky

Center on Drug and Alcohol Research

209W Medical Center, Annex 4 Ph: (606)257-2355
Lexington, KY 40536-0226 Fax: (606)323-1193
E-mail: cleukef@pop.uky.edu
URL: http://www.uky.edu/rhs/cdar/cdar2.htm

Contact: Dr. Carl G. Leukefeld, Dir.

Desc: Biological, social, and psychological aspects of alcohol and drug abuse; and HIV/AIDS. Conducts household and other surveys. *Type:* Research center.

University of Manitoba

Alcohol and Tobacco Research Unit

Department of Community Ph: (204)787-4686
    Health Sciences
750 Bannatyne Ave.
Winnipeg, MB, Canada R3E
    0W3
URL: http://www.umanitoba.ca/faculties/medicine/chs/alcohol.htm

Desc: Health, behavioral, social and economic correlates and consequences of the use of alcohol, tobacco and other drugs consumed for non-therapeutic purposes. *Type:* Research center.

University of Michigan

Alcohol Research Center

Bldg. 2, Ste. A Ph: (734)998-7952
400 E. Eisenhower Pkwy. Fax: (734)998-7994
Ann Arbor, MI 48108
E-mail: zuckerra@umich.edu
URL: http://www.med.umich.edu/psych/sub/index.html

Contact: Dr. Robert Zucker, Dir.

Desc: Alcohol problems among the elderly, etiology and treatment of alcoholism and health services. *Type:* Research center.

University of North Carolina at Chapel Hill

Center for Alcohol Studies

Thurston-Bowles Bldg. Ph: (919)966-5678
CB No. 7178 Fax: (919)966-5679
Chapel Hill, NC 27599-7178
E-mail: ftcrews@med.unc.edu
URL: http://www.med.unc.edu/alcohol/

Contact: Fulton T. Crews, PhD, Dir.

Desc: Broad range of studies on alcohol effects on brain, liver and fetus. *Type:* Research center.

University of Pennsylvania

Substance Abuse Treatment Unit

VA Medical Center Ph: (215)823-5141
Bldg. 7, 116-D Fax: (215)823-4690
University & Woodland Aves.
Philadelphia, PA 19104
E-mail: woody@research.trc.upenn.edu

Contact: George Woody, MD, Dir.

Desc: Alcohol and drug dependence, including research on psychotherapy, endocrine system, alcoholism and schizophrenia, methadone-maintained cocaine abusers, and outpatient versus inpatient detoxification. *Type:* Research center.

University of Washington

Alcohol and Drug Abuse Institute

3937 15th Ave. NE Ph: (206)543-0937
Box 351415 Fax: (206)543-5473
Seattle, WA 98105-6696
E-mail: ddonovan@u.washington.edu
URL: http://weber.u.washington.edu/~adai

Contact: Dennis M. Donovan, PhD, Dir.

Desc: Social, clinical, and psychological aspects of alcohol and drug abuse. *Type:* Research center.

University of Wisconsin--Madison

Center for Addiction Research and Education

777 S. Mills St. Ph: (608)263-1076
Madison, WI 53715 Fax: (608)263-5813
E-mail: lmanwell@fammed.wisc.edu
URL: http://www.fammed.wisc.edu/care

Contact: Dr. Michael Fleming, Dir.

Desc: Alcoholism and drug addiction, including prevention, diagnosis, and treatment. *Type:* Research center.

Veterans Affairs Medical Center (Portland, OR)

Research Service

3710 SW Veterans Hospital Rd. Ph: (503)273-5125
PO Box 1034 Fax: (503)273-5351
Portland, OR 97201

Contact: Dr. Michael P. Davey, Assoc.Chf., Res.

Desc: Genetics of alcoholism and substance abuse, osteoporosis in men, virology (CMV, HIV), immunology, diabetes, multiple sclerosis, hematology-oncology, spinal cord regeneration, tardive dyskinesia, health services research, hypertension, dermatology (malignant melanoma), etiology of rheumatoid arthritis, Alzheimer's disease, audiology, and colon cancer. *Type:* Research center.

Wayne State University

Fetal Alcohol Research Center

C.S. Mott Ctr. Ph: (313)577-1485
275 E. Hancock Fax: (313)577-8554
Detroit, MI 48201
E-mail: rjsokol@moose.mad.wayne.edu

Contact: Dr. Robert J. Sokol, Dir.

Desc: Consequences of prenatal alcohol and drug exposure in animals and humans. Investigates methods for medical professionals to identify pregnancies at risk for alcohol-related birth defects. *Type:* Research center.

Wright State University

Rehabilitation Research and Training Center on Drugs and Disability

School of Medicine Ph: (937)259-1384
PO Box 927 Fax: (937)259-1395
Dayton, OH 45401-0927
E-mail: sardi@wright.edu
URL: http://www.med.wright.edu/SOM/SARDI/

Contact: Dennis Moore, EdD, Dir.

Desc: Substance abuse issues among individuals qualifying for vocational rehabilitation services. *Type:* Research center.

Youth Power

300 Lakeside Dr. Ph: (510)451-6666
Ste. 1340 Free: 800-258-2766
Oakland, CA 94612 Fax: (510)451-9360
E-mail: youth@youthpower.org
URL: http://www.youthpower.org

Contact: Elliot Levin, Exec.Dir.

Desc: Local clubs comprised of children aged 5-18. Develops, promotes, and evaluates the work of member and affiliate clubs. Conducts research-based programs in youth development and primary prevention including tobacco, alcohol, and illegal substance abuse, dropouts, and teenage pregnancy programs. *Type:* Association.

Surgery

AAOMS Surgical Update

American Association of Oral and Maxillofacial Surgeons (AAOMS)
9700 W. Bryn Mawr Ave. Ph: (847)678-6200
Rosemont, IL 60018-5701 Free: 800-822-6637
    Fax: (847)678-6286
E-mail: ahuizinga@aaoms.org.

Desc: Provides "the dental profession and others with current information on the speciality of oral and maxillofacial surgery and patient care." *Type:* Newsletter.

Agnes Barr Chase Surgical Research Foundation

Temple Univ. Hospital Ph: (215)707-5080
Parkinson Pavilion, 4th Fl. Fax: (215)707-1915
Broad & Ontario Sts.
Philadelphia, PA 19140
E-mail: jrudy@vm.temple.edu

Contact: Dr. Stuart I. Meyers, MD, Chm., Dept. of Surgery.

Desc: Provides support for research in the Department of Surgery, with emphasis on the specialities of gastrointestinal, vascular, and cardio-thoracic surgery. *Type:* Research center.

American Academy of Facial Plastic and Reconstructive Surgery

310 S. Henry St. Ph: (703)299-9291
Alexandria, VA 22314 Free: 800-332-FACE
    Fax: (703)299-8898
E-mail: info@aafprs.org
URL: http://www.facial-plastic-surgery.org

Contact: Stephen C. Duffy, V.President.

Desc: Physicians specializing in facial plastic surgery. Promotes research and study in the field. Maintains speakers' bureau. *Type:* Association.

American Association of Neurological Surgeons

22 S. Washington St. Ph: (847)692-9500
Park Ridge, IL 60068-4287 Fax: (847)692-2589
E-mail: info@aans.org
URL: http://www.aans.org

Contact: Robert E. Draba, Ph.D., Exec.Dir.

Desc: Neurological surgeons united to promote excellence in neurological surgery and its related sciences. Provides funding to foster research in the neurosciences. *Type:* Association.

American Association of Oral and Maxillofacial Surgeons

9700 W. Bryn Mawr Ph: (847)678-6200
Rosemont, IL 60018-5701 Free: 800-822-6637
    Fax: (847)678-6286

Contact: Dr. Robert Rinaldi, Asst.Exec.Dir.

Desc: Dentists specializing in disease diagnosis and surgical, adjunctive, and esthetic treatment of diseases, injuries, and defects of the oral and maxillofacial region (jaw deformities, dental implants, infections, and oral cancer). *Type:* Association.

American College of Surgeons

633 N. Saint Clair St. Ph: (312)202-5000
Chicago, IL 60611-3211 Fax: (312)202-5001
E-mail: postmaster@facs.org
URL: http://www.facs.org

Contact: Samuel A. Wells, M.D., Dir.

Desc: Professional association of surgeons worldwide organized primarily to improve the quality of care for surgical patients by elevating the standards of surgical education and practice. Type: Association.

American Society for Aesthetic Plastic Surgery

11081 Winners Cir., No. 200
Los Alamitos, CA 90720-2813

Contact: Robert G. Stanton, Exec.Dir.

Desc: Board-certified plastic surgeons. Provides continuing education to members in the area of aesthetic plastic surgery, through presentation of papers, study sessions, and scientific sessions. Operates grant program. Type: Association.

American Society of Plastic and Reconstructive Surgeons

444 E. Algonquin Rd. Ph: (847)228-9900
Arlington Heights, IL 60005 Fax: (847)228-9131
URL: http://www.plasticsurgery.org

Contact: Dave Fellers, Exec.Dir., CAE.

Desc: Professional society of plastic surgeons. Works in cooperation with the Plastic Surgery Educational Foundation to promote optimal care for plastic surgery patients through research, service, and education activities. Sponsors public/patient education program, clinical symposia, and professional development workshops. Type: Association.

American Society for Surgery of the Hand

6300 N. River Rd., Ste. 600 Ph: (847)384-8300
Rosemont, IL 60018-4256 Fax: (847)384-1435
E-mail: info@hand-surg.org
URL: http://www.hand-surg.org

Contact: Jeryl Hough, Exec.Dir.

Desc: Surgeons specializing in surgery of the hand. Promotes contributions and funds research in the field of hand surgery. Type: Association.

American Society of Transplant Physicians

6900 Grove Rd. Ph: (609)848-6205
Thorofare, NJ 08086 Fax: (609)848-4016
E-mail: ast@slackinc.com
URL: http://www.astp.org/

Contact: Susan Nelson, Exec.Dir.

Desc: Promotes and encourages education and research with respect to transplantation medicine and immunology; provides a forum for exchange of scientific information related to transplantation across solid organ specialties. Type: Association.

Center for Hip and Knee Surgery

Orthopaedic Res. Foundation, Ph: (317)831-2273
Inc. Fax: (317)831-9347
1199 Hadley Rd.
Mooresville, IN 46158
E-mail: mjalbohm@aol.com
URL: http://www.hipandkneesurgery.com

Contact: Marjorie J. Albohm, Dir.

Desc: Total joint replacement surgery, arthritis surgery, reconstructive joint surgery, sports medicine, physical therapy, and foot, ankle, and shoulder surgery. Type: Research center.

Christine M. Kleinert Institute for Hand and Microsurgery, Inc.

225 Abraham Flexner Way., Ste. Ph: (502)562-0305
850 Fax: (502)562-0326
Louisville, KY 40202
E-mail: gcrain@kkahand.com
URL: http://www.cmki.org

Contact: Thomas Wolff, MD, Pres.

Desc: Upper extremity care, including nerve compression conditions and carpal tunnel syndrome; nerve regeneration; biomechanical studies; replanted and transplanted tissue and the most effective ways of increasing survival and function; and hand and microsurgery techniques, including anatomical studies. Type: Research center.

Duke University
Plastic Surgery Research Laboratories

Med. Ctr. Ph: (252)684-3929
Box 3906 Fax: (252)681-2670
Durham, NC 27710
E-mail: klitz@duke.edu
URL: http://www.duke.edu/~klitz

Contact: Prof. Bruce Klitzman, Dir.

Desc: Microvascular physiology, plastic surgery, including wound healing, monitoring tissue viability, thrombolytic therapy, preservation of organs, and biocompatibility of synthetic vascular grafts (prostheses). Also conducts studies on microcirculation, skin cancer, and aging skin. Type: Research center.

Edward Dana Mitchell Surgical Research Laboratory

Univ. of Tennessee Dept. of Ph: (901)448-8370
Surgery Fax: (901)448-7306
956 Court., E228
Memphis, TN 38163

Contact: Dr. Kenneth Kudsk, Dir.

Desc: Surgery, transplantation, sepsis, shock, nutrition, hepatic dysfunction, and gut immunology. Type: Research center.

Georgetown University
Division of Comparative Medicine

3950 Reservoir Rd. NW, Rm. Ph: (202)687-2488
G05 Fax: (202)687-6256
Washington, DC 20007

Contact: Stephen P. Schiffer, DVM, Dir.

Desc: Medical sciences, with particular reference to surgical aspects, including basic studies of tissue transplantation, neuroscience, techniques of extracorporeal circulation, magnetic resonance imaging (MRI) techniques, and technique of perfusion of orbital artery and heart/lung transplantation. Also designs and develops valvular devices and other cardiac instrumentation and evaluates vascular prosthetic devices. Type: Research center.

Institute for Applied Laser Surgery

2 Bala Plz., Ste. PL-13 Ph: (610)667-4080
Bala Cynwyd, PA 19004 Fax: (610)667-2748

Contact: Dr. Ronald A. Kirschner, Dir.

Desc: Surgical applications of lasers and laser-related accessory development. Activities include development of new procedures in cardiovascular, peripheral vascular, cutaneour, plastic, urologic, gynocologic, orthopedic surgery, and endoscopic surgery. Type: Research center.

International College of Surgeons

1516 N. Lake Shore Dr. Ph: (312)642-3555
Chicago, IL 60610 Fax: (312)787-1624
E-mail: info@icsglobal.org
URL: http://www.icsglobal.org

Contact: Max Downham, Exec.Dir.

Desc: General surgeons and surgical specialists in 110 countries maintaining official relations with the World

Health Organization . Promotes the universal teaching and advancement of surgery and its allied sciences. Maintains International Museum of Surgical Sciences containing specialty rooms showing the growth and perfection of many surgical specialties. Type: Association.

International Federation of Societies for Surgery of the Hand

c/o Miguel A. Vargas Busquets, Ph: (809)833-3248
M.D. Fax: (809)831-4400
165 E. Mendez Vigo St.
Mayaguez, PR 00680

Contact: Miguel A. Vargas Busquets, M.D., Sec.Gen.

Desc: Individuals involved in hand surgery. Coordinates activities by maintaining liaison among member societies; promotes the exchange of information; attempts to improve opportunities for study and observation on an international level. Establishes and recommends standards of nomenclature, classification of malformations, and disability evaluation; promotes a bibliography of world literature on surgery of the hand. Type: Association.

International Society for Heart and Lung Transplantation

14673 Midway Rd., Ste. 108 Ph: (972)490-9495
Addison, TX 75001 Fax: (972)490-9499
E-mail: ishlt@aol.com
URL: http://www.infi.et/~ishlt

Contact: Amanda W. Rowe, Exec.Dir.

Desc: Medical doctors, Ph.D.s, nurses, researchers, and others interested in artificial hearts and in heart and heart-lung failure and transplantation. Provides a center for discussion, exchange of information, and activities that promote the interests of heart and lung transplantation. Seeks to heighten awareness of public and governmental agencies regarding developments in the field. Type: Association.

Interplast

300-B Pioneer Way Ph: (650)962-0123
Mountain View, CA 94041- Fax: (650)962-1619
1506
E-mail: interplast@worldaccessnet.com
URL: http://www.interplast.org

Contact: Susan W. Hayes, Pres./CEO.

Desc: Sends volunteer teams of medical professionals to developing countries to perform free reconstructive surgery on patients with birth defects, burns, and other crippling deformities. Type: Association.

McGill University
Department of Surgery
Division of Surgical Research

Donner Bldg. Ph: (514)398-3290
740 Docteur Penfield Ave. Fax: (514)398-8361
Montreal, PQ, Canada H3A
1A4

Contact: Dr. Julius Gordon, Dir.

Desc: Cancer research and immunology. Type: Research center.

Microsurgical Transplantation Research Foundation

Davies Medical Center Ph: (415)565-6136
Mob Annex 140 Fax: (415)864-1654
45 Castro St.
San Francisco, CA 94114
E-mail: pps@the-buncke-clinic.com
URL: http://www.buncke.org

Contact: Dr. Harry J. Buncke, Dir.

Desc: Physiological and technical outcomes of microvascular replantation and transplantation; reconstructive microsurgery, and hand surgery; cryopreservation of tissues; hyperbaric oxygen therapy; and tissue oximetry with ischemia/perfusion injury. Type: Research center.

National Foundation for Transplants

1102 Brookfield, Ste. 200   Ph: (901)684-1697
Memphis, TN 38119   Free: 800-489-3863
   Fax: (901)684-1128
E-mail: natfoundtx@aol.com
URL: http://www.transplants.org
Contact: Gary McMahan, Dir.
Desc: Works to guide and assist fundraising for transplant patients and their families. *Type:* Association.

National Institute of Transplantation

2200 W. 3rd St., Ste. 100   Ph: (213)413-2779
Los Angeles, CA 90057-1922   Fax: (213)484-6652
E-mail: SalehAswad@Earthlink.net
URL: http://www.transplantation.com
Contact: Robert Mendez, MD, Dir.
Desc: Kidney and pancreas transplantation and new approaches to organ transplantation and avoiding organ rejection. *Type:* Research center.

New York University

Institute of Reconstructive Plastic Surgery

560 1st Ave.   Ph: (212)263-5209
New York, NY 10016   Fax: (212)263-5400
Contact: Joseph G. McCarthy, MD, Dir.
Desc: Etiology and treatment of craniofacial anomalies, bone physiology, including distraction, computer graphics, microvascular surgery, and wound healing, including studies of cleft lip and cleft palate, jaw deformities, ear malformations, hand injuries, and allied problems. *Type:* Research center.

Plastic Surgery Research Council

444 E. Algonquin Rd.   Ph: (847)228-8375
Arlington Heights, IL 60005   Fax: (847)228-6409
E-mail: ch@plasticsurgery.org
Contact: Cathy Hay, Contact.
Desc: Plastic surgery. *Type:* Research center.

Plastic Surgery Research Council

Univ. of Pittsburgh Med. Ctr.   Ph: (412)648-8100
Scaife Hall 676   Fax: (412)648-1987
3550 Terrace St.
Pittsburgh, PA 15261
E-mail: pcj@nauticom.net
URL: http://www.pittsburgh-tissue.net
Contact: Peter Johnson, MD, Contact.
Desc: Tissue engineering. *Type:* Research center.

St. Louis University

Theodore Cooper Surgical Research Institute

1402 S. Grand   Ph: (314)577-8000
St. Louis, MO 63104   Fax: (314)268-5180
E-mail: smith@nimue.hood.edu
Contact: Dr. Gregory S. Smith, PhD, Dir.
Desc: Gastrointestinal and hepatic physiology, bioartificial liver, myocardial revascularization, drug metabolism, pharmacokinetics, toxicokinetics, organ transplantation and preservation, cardiac assist and replacement, myocardial preservation and pulmonary function, islet cell transplantation, immunology/nutrition, shock and multiple organ failure, neuropharmacology, transplantation immunogenetics, image guided surgery, and molecular biology. *Type:* Research center.

Surgical Products

Cahners Business Information
New Product Information Division
301 Morris Gibraltar Dr.   Ph: (973)292-5100
Morris Plains, NJ 07950   Fax: (973)539-3476
URL: http://www.surgprodmag.com.
Contact: Colleen Purtell, Editor, cpurtell@cahners.com; Darrell White, Publisher, darrellwhite@cahners.com.

Desc: Magazine on products, technology, equipment, and supplies for operating rooms, intensive care/coronary care units, central supply (in hospitals), and surgicenters. *Type:* Periodical.

United Network for Organ Sharing

1100 Boulders Pky., Ste. 500   Ph: (804)330-8500
PO Box 13770   Fax: (804)330-8517
Richmond, VA 23225
URL: http://www.unos.org

Contact: Walter K. Graham, Exec.Dir.

Desc: Transplant and organ procurement centers, tissue-typing labs, and health care professionals engaged in organ transplant operations. Administers the National Organ Procurement and Transplantation Network and the U.S. Scientific Registry for Organ Transplantation. *Type:* Association.

U.S. Department of Defense

Army Medical Research and Materiel Command

Army Institute of Surgical Research

Ft. Sam Houston, Bldg. 3611   Ph: (210)916-2720
3400 Rawley E. Chambers Ave.   Fax: (210)227-8502
San Antonio, TX 78234-6315

Contact: Col. Cleon W. Goodwin, Comdr./Dir.

Desc: Investigation of problems of mechanical and thermal injuries; care of patients with such injuries; education and training of physicians and ancillary medical personnel in the principles of management of injured patients; and investigative studies at both the basic and clinical levels. Principal subject of research (basic and applied) is burn care, including studies in fluid resuscitation, host resistance, metabolic response, nutrition, leukocyte dysfunction, thyroid hormone kinetics, wound care, surgical infection, inhalation injury, surgical critical care, skin substitutes, and mechanical trauma. *Type:* Research center.

U.S. Department of Defense

Army Medical Research and Materiel Command

Walter Reed Army Institute of Research

Surgery Division

Washington, DC 20307-5100   Ph: (202)782-3796
   Fax: (202)782-0617

Contact: Frederick Pearce, Dir.

Desc: Military medical problems of combat injury, shock, wounding, and resuscitation (singly or in combination) in order to establish optimal prophylactic and therapeutic care of severely injured patients. Division also develops adjuncts for the diagnosis and management of blast-induced injury to the lung and/or gastrointestinal tract; and develops and provides laboratory models for biomedical assessment of medical material systems. *Type:* Research center.

U.S. Department of Health and Human Services

National Cancer Institute

Division of Clinical Sciences

Surgery Branch

NIH Bldg. 10, Rm. 2B42   Ph: (301)496-4164
9000 Rockville Pike   Fax: (301)402-1738
Bethesda, MD 20892

Contact: Dr. Steven Rosenberg, Chf.

Desc: Treatment of solid tumors and a broad program of laboratory research in cancer. A wide variety of malignancies are studied, including melanomas, sarcomas, rectal cancer, breast carcinoma, pancreatic cancers, and head and neck cancers. *Type:* Research center.

University of Alberta

Surgical-Medical Research Institute

1074 Dentistry Pharmacy Bldg.   Ph: (403)492-3386
Edmonton, AB, Canada T6G   Fax: (403)492-1627
2N8
E-mail: rrajotte@gpu.srv.ualberta.ca
Contact: Dr. Ray V. Rajotte, Dir.
Desc: Institute is composed of multidisciplinary teams carrying out biomedical research. Principal fields of study include: islet transplantation, the immunology of diabetes, glucose regulation studies, experiments for extending the application of laparoscopic surgery and including a minimal access laboratory, and metabolic aspects of organ preservation (liver, heart, small bowel). *Type:* Research center.

University of Manitoba

Health Sciences Centre

Surgical Research Office

Department of Surgery   Ph: (204)787-3791
GE 611-820 Sherbrook St.   Fax: (204)787-1342
Winnipeg, MB, Canada R3A
1R9
E-mail: hunruh@hsc.mb.ca
Contact: Dr. Helmut Unruh, Res.Dir.
Desc: Orthopedics, oncology, gastrointestinal surgery, neurosurgery, respirology, urology, cardiology, and pediatric and general surgery. *Type:* Research center.

University of Michigan

Pediatric Surgery Research Laboratories

F3970 Mott Children's Hospital   Ph: (734)764-4151
Ann Arbor, MI 48109-0245   Fax: (734)936-9784
E-mail: acoran@umich.edu
URL: http://www.umich.edu/surg/peds
Contact: Arnold G. Coran, MD, Dir.
Desc: Pediatric surgery, including physiological and biochemical changes during septic and hemorrhagic shock in puppies, physiology and metabolism of patients receiving total parenteral nutrition, physiology of endorectal pull-through operations for Hirschprung's disease in dogs, determination of trace element levels in infants receiving oral feedings or total parenteral nutritional solutions, and bacterial translocation in newborn babies. *Type:* Research center.

University of Michigan

Thoracic Surgery Research Lab

B560 MSRB II, Box 0686   Ph: (734)936-5800
Univ. Med. Ctr.
Ann Arbor, MI 48109
Contact: Dr. Mark Orringer, Dir.
Desc: Cardiovascular and pulmonary physiology and transplantations, cellular and molecular aspects of allograft rejection and tolerance, molecular genetics of human lung and esophageal cancer, regional ventricular function (using sonomicrometry measurements) in conditions of ischemia, infarction, and reperfusion, neonatal myocardial performance and protection of the neonatal heart during ischemia, and role of cytokines in cardiac and pulmonary injury. *Type:* Research center.

University of Michigan

Transplantation Research Laboratories

Medical School   Ph: (734)747-4485
Division of Transplantation   Fax: (734)936-7234
Department of Surgery
A560 Medical Science Research
Bldg. II
Ann Arbor, MI 48109-0654
E-mail: merionb@umich.edu
URL: http://www.med.umich.edu/trans/public/trl/
Contact: Dr. Robert M. Merion, Ch.

Desc: Transplantation, including the immunological mechanisms of allograft rejection and tolerance in a variety of models. *Type:* Research center.

University of Pennsylvania

Harrison Department of Surgical Research

313 Stemmler Hall   Ph: (215)898-8081
Margarett M. Clark Laboratories   Fax: (215)573-2001
Philadelphia, PA 19104-6070
Contact: Clyde F. Barker, MD, Dir.

Desc: Cancer, cardiovascular disease, gastrointestinal physiology, shock and surgical bacteriology, nutrition of surgical patients, and surgical specialities, including studies of stomach and duodenum, pancreas, colon, liver, blood flow, hypertension, equilibrium tissue oxygen requirements, tissue oxygen, oxygen supply in shock and shock-like states, chemotherapy, patient antitumor agents, immunology, ultraviolet light in protection against wound infection, transplantation of tissues and organs, and role of electronics in surgical research. *Type:* Research center.

Vanderbilt University

S.R. Light Laboratory for Surgical Research

MCN, Rm. CC-2307   Ph: (615)322-2096
Nashville, TN 37232   Fax: (615)343-1355
Contact: Phillip E. Williams, Dir.

Desc: All phases of medicine involving use of experimental animals. Specific research includes studies of metabolism, particularly mechanisms of stress-related changes in glucose and amino acids; cardiothoracic study of pathophysiology of ischemic myocardium; and renovascular physiology. *Type:* Research center.

Taxation

American Society of Chartered Life Underwriters and Chartered Financial Consultants—Assets

American Society of Chartered Life Underwriters and Chartered Financial Consultants
270 Bryn Mawr Ave.   Ph: (215)526-2500
Bryn Mawr, PA 19010
Contact: Roslyn Myers, Editor.

Desc: Discusses "making the most astute judgments in response to the changing financial scene." Covers estate planning, pensions, life and health insurance, tax, retirement, and financial planning, and employee benefits. *Type:* Newsletter.

Americans for Tax Reform

1320 18th St. NW, Ste. 200   Ph: (202)785-0266
Washington, DC 20036   Fax: (202)785-0261
URL: http://www.atr.org
Contact: Grover Norquist, Pres.

Desc: Corporations (60); trade organizations (150) and taxpayer groups (1500). Sponsors the Taxpayer Protection Pledge, a covenant made by incumbents and other candidates for national office who promise to oppose all income tax increases. Bestows awards. *Type:* Association.

Aura Wealth Newsletter

Aura Publishing Company
Post Office Box 1367   Ph: (914)834-2322
Scarsdale, NY 10583   Free: 800-878-3703
                   Fax: (914)833-0930
E-mail: wealth@aura.com.
URL: http://www.aura.com/wealth.
Contact: Dr. Richard A. Sandell, Editor.

Desc: Warns of overt and covert taxation in developed and developing countries meant to diminish personal wealth; and of governmental policies directed towards increasing dependence of individuals and reduction of free enterprise for the accumulation of wealth. Offers advice on protecting and increasing personal wealth. *Type:* Newsletter.

BNA Tax Updates

The Bureau of National Affairs, Inc. (BNA)
1231 25th St. NW   Ph: (202)452-4200
Washington, DC 20037
E-mail: bnaplus@bna.com
URL: http://bna.com/mkt/hrl/hrlwdec.htm

Desc: Contains news and information on developments in federal tax legislation. Includes Congressional bill action (e.g., status on floor and in conference), private-sector reaction to legislation, Senate investigation reports, Circuit and Supreme Court opinions, and Internal Revenue Service determinations. *Available:* LEXIS-NEXIS, LEXIS; West Group, WESTLAW. *Type:* Database.

Business Organizations with Tax Planning

Matthew Bender & Company, Inc.
1275 Broadway   Free: 800-223-1940
Albany, NY 12204   Fax: 800-544-6572
URL: http://www.bender.com.
Contact: D. Schneider, Editor.

Desc: Covers tax planning for corporations, partnerships, and joint ventures. *Type:* Newsletter.

Cal-Tax Digest

California Taxpayers' Association
921 11th St., Ste. 800   Ph: (916)441-0490
Sacramento, CA 95814-2821   Fax: (916)441-1619
Contact: Ron Roach, Editor, (916)930-3104, ron@calfax.org.

Desc: Concerned with efficiency and economy in government and issues affecting taxes. *Type:* Newsletter.

Canadian Tax Planners Newsletter

Canadian Tax Planners Ltd.
30 Mapleton Pl.   Ph: (519)641-1015
London, ON, Canada N6K 4A5   Fax: (519)641-0322
Contact: D.C. Pollock, Editor, don.pollock@sympatico.ca; Karen Pollock, Circulation Mgr.

Desc: Reviews Canadian income tax. *Type:* Newsletter.

The Canadian Taxpayer

Carswell
Thomson Professional Publishing
One Corporate Plaza
2075 Kennedy Rd.   Ph: (416)609-3800
Scarborough, ON, Canada M1T   Free: 800-387-5164
   3V4   Fax: (416)298-5082
E-mail: orders@carswell.com
Contact: Arthur B.C. Drache, Editor.

Desc: Provides "analyses of tax trends, political appointments, tax policies and landmark cases." *Type:* Newsletter.

Capital Ideas

NTU Foundation
108 N. Alfred St.   Ph: (703)683-5700
Alexandria, VA 22314   Fax: (703)683-5722
URL: http://www.ntu.org.
Contact: Peter J. Sepp, Editor.

Desc: Contains information on workings of the Union, which attempts to limit and reduce government taxation and spending. Recurring features include a column titled Outrage of the Month. *Type:* Newsletter.

CCH Federal Tax Weekly

CCH Inc.
2700 Lake Cook Rd.   Ph: (847)267-7000
Riverwoods, IL 60015   Free: 800-449-8114
                   Fax: (847)224-8299
URL: http://www.cch.com
Contact: George Jones, Product Group Leader.

Desc: Provides information about tax code changes and updates, information on the IRS, and tax advice. Recurring features include columns titled Practitioners' Corner, Washington Report, and Briefly Noted. *Type:* Newsletter.

CCH Tax Day: State

CCH Incorporated
4025 W. Peterson Ave.   Ph: (773)583-8500
Chicago, IL 60646
URL: http://www.cch.com

Desc: Contains summaries of recent tax developments in all 50 states and the District of Columbia. Includes major new and pending legislation, administrative rulings, judicial decisions, governors' messages, and news of meetings and conventions. *Available:* LEXIS-NEXIS, LEXIS; West Group, WESTLAW; PricewaterhouseCoopers LLP, Tax News Network. *Type:* Database.

Citizens for an Alternative Tax System

10600-A Crestwood Dr.   Ph: (703)368-6113
Manassas, VA 20109   Free: 800-767-7577
                   Fax: (703)368-5843
E-mail: 73414.150@compuserve.com
URL: http://www.nrst.org
Contact: Victor Krohn, CEO, Natl. Chmn.

Desc: Individuals, businesses, and corporations in search of a viable alternative to the present income tax system. Promotes the use of a national sales tax as a replacement for income tax. Conducts lobbying activities. *Type:* Association.

Clinical Toxicology of Commercial Products

Oxford Molecular Group
Chemical Information Systems
810 Gleneagles St., Ste. 300   Ph: (410)321-8440
Towson, MD 21286
E-mail: cissupport@oxmol.com
Contact: fax: (410)296-0712.

Desc: A database system that contains chemical and toxicological information on approximately 20,000 commercial products (excluding food products) derived from 3000 chemicals. Records can be retrieved by manufacturer, trade name, manufacturer's approved usage, date of most recent change in chemical formulation, chemical names of ingredients, and Chemical Abstracts Service Registry Number. *Type:* Database.

Committee on State Taxation

Douglas Lindholm
122 C St. NW, Ste. 330   Ph: (202)484-5222
Washington, DC 20001   Fax: (202)484-5229
E-mail: dlindholm@statetax.org
URL: http://www.statetax.org/schedule.html
Contact: J. William McArthur, Jr., Pres. & Exec.Dir.

Desc: Multistate corporate taxpayers. Promotes adoption of taxation policies beneficial to members. *Type:* Association.

Commodity Tax News

Canadian Institute of Chartered Accountants
277 Wellington St. W.   Ph: (416)977-3222
Toronto, ON, Canada M5V   Free: 800-268-3793
   3H2   Fax: (416)977-8585
URL: http://www.cica.ca
Contact: Peter H. Wood, Editor.

Desc: Monitors legislation, administrative developments, and commentary on recent case law concerning commodity tax. *Type:* Newsletter.

CPA Client Tax Letter

The American Institute of Certified Public Accountants
Harborside Financial Ctr.   Ph: (201)938-3287
201 Plaza 3   Free: 800-TOA-ICPA
Jersey City, NJ 07311-3881   Fax: (201)398-3741
Contact: Maria Luzarraga Albanese, Editor.

Desc: Covers tax planning, including laws and legislation. *Type:* Newsletter.

Daily Tax Report

The Bureau of National Affairs, Inc. (BNA)
1231 25th St. NW   Ph: (202)452-4200
Washington, DC 20037
E-mail: bnaplus@bna.com
URL: http://bna.com/mkt/hrl/hrlwdec.htm
Contact: BNA PLUS, (202)452-4323, fax: (202)822-8092, bnaplus@bna.com.
Desc: Contains the complete text of the Daily Tax Report. *Available:* LEXIS-NEXIS, LEXIS; West Group, WESTLAW; PricewaterhouseCoopers LLP, Tax News Network. *Type:* Database.

Daily Tax Report

Bureau of National Affairs, Inc. (BNA)
1231 25th St. NW   Ph: (202)452-4323
Washington, DC 20037   Free: 800-372-1033
    Fax: (202)452-7773
E-mail: bnaplus@bna.com; dtr@bna.com.
URL: http://www.bna.com.
Contact: Rebecca McCracken, Managing Editor, (202)452-4590, fax: (202)452-7504, rmccracken@bna.com.
Desc: Summarizes and analyzes national legislative, regulatory, judicial, and policy developments of interest to accountants and tax lawyers. Covers Internal Revenue Service private letter rulings, court decisions, administrative regulations and rulings, and accounting standards. *Type:* Newsletter.

Dollars & Sense

National Taxpayers Union
108 N. Alfred St.   Ph: (703)683-5700
Alexandria, VA 22314   Fax: (703)683-5722
E-mail: ntu@ntu
URL: http://www.ntu.org.
Contact: Peter J. Sepp, Editor.
Desc: Examines wasteful government spending, regulation of the economy, taxation, and problems of local governments. Reports the organization's efforts to limit and reduce government taxation and spending. *Type:* Newsletter.

The Fair Tax

11015 Cumpston St.   Ph: (818)763-1000
North Hollywood, CA 91601   Free: 800-FAIR-TAX
    Fax: (818)769-7358
Contact: Boris Isaacson, Pres. & Founder.
Desc: Corporation and individual taxpayers, and interested individuals united to sponsor a national initiative which would replace all federal, state, county, and city taxes and fees with a one percent trade charge on all purchases. *Type:* Association.

Foreign Tax Law Bi-Weekly Bulletin

Foreign Tax Law, Inc.
PO Box 2189   Ph: (904)253-5785
Ormond Beach, FL 32175-2189   Fax: (904)257-3003
E-mail: ftlp@foreignlaw.com
URL: http://www.foreignlaw.com/
Contact: Sondra Yanaura, Editor.
Desc: Includes articles on current tax rates, proposed new tax and commercial laws, translations, of selected tax and commercial legislation, investment laws, primers on the conduct of business, digests of recently passed tax and commercial laws, labor laws, digests on double taxation conventions, banking laws, and trade laws, in countries throughout the world. Emphasis is given to full-text translations of tax and commercial amendment laws. *Type:* Newsletter.

IAAO Opportunities

International Association of Assessing Officers
130 E. Randolph, Ste. 850   Ph: (312)819-6100
Chicago, IL 60601-6217   Fax: (312)819-6149
E-mail: webmaster@iaao.org
URL: http://www.iaao.org
Contact: Hediye Kerman, Editor.
Desc: Reports on the educational programs and activities of the Association, which is concerned with assessment administration and property tax. Recurring features include news of members, job opportunities, letters to the editor, legislative news, announcements of meetings, news of research, and a calendar of events. *Type:* Newsletter.

Incentive Taxation

Center for the Study of Economics
8775 Cloudleap Ct.   Ph: (410)740-1177
Columbia, MD 21045
E-mail: hgeorge@smart.net
URL: http://www.smart.net/~hgeorge.
Contact: Steven Cord, Editor, (410)740-1111, fax: (410)740-3279; Joshua Vincent, Assoc. Ed., fax: (410)740-3279.
Desc: Covers property rate tax reform and land value taxation. Recurring features include book reviews. *Type:* Newsletter.

Institute for Professionals in Taxation

3350 Peachtree Rd., NE, Ste.   Ph: (404)240-2300
   280   Fax: (404)240-2315
Atlanta, GA 30326
URL: http://www.ipt.org
Contact: Billy D. Cook, Exec.Dir.
Desc: Corporate property and sales tax representatives; attorneys, appraisers, consultants, and accountants who represent corporate taxpayers. Seeks to foster the education of members; promote study in property and sales taxation; encourage the interchange of ideas and assistance among members; facilitate cooperation with governmental authorities in solving problems of ad valorem (imposed at a rate percent of value) and sales tax administration. Strives for high standards of competence and efficiency in corporate property and sales tax management. *Type:* Association.

Internal Revenue Bulletin

Research Institute of America
PO Box 5159   Free: 800-431-9025
Carol Stream, IL 60197
Desc: Presents new treasury and IRS releases in full official text. Contains rulings and decisions, releases on treaties, tax legislation, administrative and procedural releases, disbarment and suspensions. *Type:* Newsletter.

International Assignment Review

Price Waterhouse LLP
300 Atlantic St., 6th Fl.   Ph: (203)363-1815
Stamford, CT 06901   Fax: (203)969-2115
Contact: Michael Budnick, Editor-in-Chief; Judith McMillan, Sr. Editor, judith_mcmillan@notes.pw.com; Laura K. Gourlay, Editor.
Desc: Informs readers of recent developments in taxation, human resources, and software issues that affect the assignment of personnel to international locations. *Type:* Newsletter.

International Association of Assessing Officers

130 E. Randolph St., Ste. 850   Ph: (312)819-6100
Chicago, IL 60601   Fax: (312)819-6149
URL: http://www.iaao.org
Contact: Eugene Jackson, Exec.Dir.
Desc: State and local officials concerned with valuation of property for ad valorem property tax purposes. Works to improve standards and conduct research on tax assessment. Offers educational programs and seminars; awards professional designations; makes available research and consulting services. *Type:* Association.

International Tax Report

Donoghue Organization
IBC USA, Inc.
290 Eliot   Ph: (508)881-2800
Ashland, MA 01721   Free: 800-343-5413
Contact: Richard Casna, Editor.
Desc: Covers the interplay of double taxation treaties, offshore companies and tax havens, pricing standards in inter-company transactions, dealing with tax authority investigations, tax incentives for foreign employees, year-end tax planning, host country taxation of foreign joint ventures, trusts. withholding tax, and tax disclosure laws. *Type:* Newsletter.

IRS Practice and Procedures

Mark A. Stephens, Ltd.
10018 Colesville Rd.   Ph: (301)593-0443
Silver Spring, MD 20901   Fax: (301)593-1978
Contact: LaVaughn T. Davis, Editor.
Desc: Summarizes latest developments involving taxes and the Internal Revenue Service. Covers court decisions, legislative actions, changes in IRS policy, and audit procedures. *Type:* Newsletter.

The Jacobs Report on Asset Protection Strategies

Research Press, Inc.
4500 W. 72nd Terrace   Ph: (913)362-9667
Box 8137   Fax: (913)362-9667
Prairie Village, KS 66208
E-mail: rpi@rpifs.com; rpi@sky.net
URL: http://www.rpifs.com.
Contact: Vernon K. Jacobs, Editor.
Desc: Provides an in-depth critique on confusing or complex financial strategy such as limited partnerships, living trusts, insurance solvency, or offshore trusts. *Type:* Newsletter.

The Kiplinger Tax Letter

Kiplinger Washington Editors, Inc.
1729 H St. NW   Ph: (202)887-6491
Washington, DC 20006   Free: 800-544-0155
    Fax: (202)887-6542
Contact: Steven Ivins, Editor.
Desc: Reports new tax regulations, changes, decisions, and pending legislation. Includes coverage of the House Ways and Means and Senate Committees, federal monetary and fiscal policy, securities, finance, and social security. *Type:* Newsletter.

LEXIS® Federal Tax Library

LEXIS-NEXIS
9443 Springboro Pike   Ph: (937)865-6800
PO Box 933
Dayton, OH 45401-0933
URL: http://www.lex-nexis.com
Desc: Contains a comprehensive, up-to-date collection of tax-related materials. Includes federal and state tax case law, Internal Revenue Service rulings and releases, state tax administrative decisions and rulings, the Internal Revenue Code, federal tax regulations, international news and treaties, tax looseleaf services, tax periodicals, tax law reviews, tax dailies, pending state legislation, and state property records. *Available:* LEXIS-NEXIS, LEXIS. *Type:* Database.

LEXIS® State Tax Library

LEXIS-NEXIS
9443 Springboro Pike   Ph: (937)865-6800
PO Box 933
Dayton, OH 45401-0933
URL: http://www.lex-nexis.com
Desc: Contains a collection of state tax materials which includes case law, pending legislation, administrative decisions and rulings, code material, property record information, and daily news. *Available:* LEXIS-NEXIS, LEXIS. *Type:* Database.

Limited Liability Companies Advisor

CCH Inc.
2700 Lake Cook Rd.   Ph: (847)267-7000
Riverwoods, IL 60015   Free: 800-449-8114
    Fax: (847)224-8299
E-mail: llcadvisor@cch.com.
URL: http://www.cch.com; http://www.tax.cch.com.
Contact: Laura Lowe, JD, Editor, (847)267-2492, lowel@
cch.com; Maurice Cashin, JD, Editor, (847)267-2373,
cashinm@cch.com; Sheri Miller, JD, Editor, (847)267-
2748, millers@cch.com.
Desc: Provides federal tax, state tax, and business news and
developments impacting limited liability companies. Recurring features include interviews, reports of meetings on
limited liability corporations, IRS audit reports, state legislation and rules, and state by state updates. *Type:* Newsletter.

Multistate Tax Commission

444 N. Capitol St. NW, Ste.   Ph: (202)624-8699
    425   Fax: (202)624-8819
Washington, DC 20001
Contact: Dan R. Bucks, Exec.Dir.
Desc: States that have enacted the Multistate Tax Compact
into law; states whose governors have requested associate
membership or which have enacted the Compact legislation conditional upon congressional approval. Purposes
are to: facilitate proper determination of state and local tax
liability of multistate taxpayers, including the equitable
apportionment of tax bases and settlement of apportionment disputes; promote uniformity or compatibility in
significant components of tax systems; facilitate taxpayer
convenience and compliance in the filing of tax returns
and in other phases of tax administration; to avoid dupli-
cative taxation. Performs corporate income tax audits,
sales and use tax audits, and property tax audits in the
form of a joint audit. *Type:* Association.

National Association of Enrolled Agents

200 Orchard Ridge Rd., No.   Ph: (301)212-9608
    302   Free: 800-424-4339
Gaithersburg, MD 20878   Fax: (301)990-1611
E-mail: naea1@aol.com
URL: http://www.naea.org
Contact: Janet B. Bray, Exec.VP.
Desc: Individuals who have gained Enrolled Agent status
and are thus qualified to represent all classes of taxpayers
at any administrative level of the Internal Revenue Service.
Promotes ethical representation of the financial position
of taxpayers before government agencies. *Type:* Associa-
tion.

National Association of Tax Practitioners

720 Association Dr.   Ph: (920)749-1040
Appleton, WI 54914   Fax: (920)749-1062
URL: http://www.natptax.com
Contact: Alan Prahl, Exec.Dir.
Desc: Persons engaged in the practice of preparing federal
or state tax returns including tax preparers, enrolled
agents, certified public accountants, licensed public accountants, public accountants, and attorneys. Purposes
are: to foster high standards in the tax preparation profession; to promote and protect the interest of tax practitioners. Provides and promotes continuing tax educational
seminars for tax preparers. *Type:* Association.

National Coalition of IRS Whistleblowers

PO Box 65471   Ph: (202)546-5345
Washington, DC 20035   Free: 800-IRS-1913
    Fax: (202)543-6484
Contact: Paul J. DesFosses, Pres.
Desc: Current and former employees of the U.S. Internal
Revenue Service; concerned Americans. Identifies, re-

searches, and debates and advocates on issues concerning
the policies and operations of the IRS, with particular emphasis on those policies and operations which the coalition
feels intrude unreasonably into the lives of private citizens.
Type: Association.

National Tax-Limitation Committee

151 N. Sunrise Ave., Ste. 901   Ph: (916)786-9400
Roseville, CA 95661
Contact: Lewis K. Uhler, Pres.
Desc: Campaigns for federal and state constitutional
amendments which would limit government spending and
taxation. Promotes education and research on methods of
limiting taxation. Actively supports Tax Limitation/
Balanced Budget Constitutional Amendment. *Type:* Association.

National Taxpayers Union

108 N. Alfred St.   Ph: (703)683-5700
Alexandria, VA 22314   Free: 800-829-4258
    Fax: (703)683-5722
URL: http://www.ntu.org
Contact: Pete Sepp, VP of Communications.
Desc: Seeks to: reduce government spending; cut taxes;
protect the rights of taxpayers. *Type:* Association.

The Outlook

Wakeman/Walworth, Inc.
300 N. Washington St.   Ph: (703)549-8606
Alexandria, VA 22314   Free: 800-876-2545
URL: http://newsletters@statecapitals.com.
Contact: Keyes Walworth, Editor.
Desc: Covers trends in state law making and developments
in all areas of state government action that may be indicators of changes in public policy, including those affecting
taxes and revenues, economic development, drug abuse,
abortion, environmental issues, and teacher salaries. *Type:*
Newsletter.

Payroll Administration Guide

Bureau of National Affairs, Inc. (BNA)
1231 25th St. NW   Ph: (202)452-4323
Washington, DC 20037   Free: 800-372-1033
    Fax: (202)452-7773
E-mail: bnaplus@bna.com
Contact: Michael Baer, Managing Editor, mbaer@bna.
com.
Desc: Concerned with federal and state employment tax,
and wage-hour and wage-payment laws. *Type:* Newsletter.

Personal Property Section News

International Association of Assessing Officers
130 E. Randolph, Ste. 850   Ph: (312)819-6100
Chicago, IL 60601-6217   Fax: (312)819-6149
E-mail: webmaster@iaao.org
URL: http://www.iaao.org
Contact: Hediye Kerman, Editor.
Desc: Offers news and information of interest to government employees responsible for valuing personal property
for ad valorem tax purposes. Recurring features include reprints of significant articles and notices of upcoming seminars. *Type:* Newsletter.

The Research Institute's New Jersey Tax Notebook

*Public Affairs Research Institute of New Jersey,
Inc.*
212 Carnegie Center, Ste. 100   Ph: (609)452-0220
Princeton, NJ 08540-6212   Fax: (609)452-1788
E-mail: parinj@aol.com
URL: http://www.nj.com/pari.
Desc: Covers legislative proposals, tax legislative hearings,
summaries of studies and reports on New Jersey tax issues,
detailed information on regulatory activity, the work of
state commissions, and related matters. Updates important court decisions on taxation. *Type:* Newsletter.

Sales Tax Newsletter

*New York State Department of Taxation &
Finance, Technical Service Bureau, State
Campus*
State Campus
Albany, NY 12227
Desc: Focuses on the application of sales tax to specific
types of transactions. Recurring features include news of
recent legislation and regulations. *Type:* Newsletter.

Sales & Use Tax Alert

State Taxation Institute
PO Box 81143   Ph: (404)457-1000
Atlanta, GA 30366   Free: 800-846-2202
E-mail: newsltrs@pronews.com
Contact: Deirdre Gregg, Editor.
Desc: Covers corporate sales and use tax issues. Reports on
pending legislation, legal developments nationwide, and
potential sales and use tax problems faced by corporations
during audits. *Type:* Newsletter.

Single Persons for Tax Equality Association

Desc: Unmarried men and women who would like to see
federal income taxes for individuals based on one tax table.
Maintains speakers' bureau; conducts research program;
compiles statistics. *Type:* Association.

Small Business Tax Control

Inside Mortgage Finance Publications
PO Box 42518   Ph: (301)951-1240
Washington, DC 20015   Fax: (301)656-1709
URL: http://www.imfpubs.com.
Contact: David Cooper, Editor.
Desc: Alerts readers to changes in tax laws. Provides tax-
saving ideas for small business owners and managers. *Type:*
Newsletter.

Southeastern Tax Alert

State Taxation Institute
PO Box 81143   Ph: (404)457-1000
Atlanta, GA 30366   Free: 800-846-2202
E-mail: newsltrs@pronews.com
Contact: Deirdre Gregg, Editor.
Desc: Covers income taxes, sales taxes, and property taxes
in Alabama, Florida, and Georgia. Covers potential tax
traps and how to avoid them. *Type:* Newsletter.

Spidell's California Taxletter

Spidell Publishing, Inc.
PO Box 61044   Ph: (714)776-7850
Anaheim, CA 92803-6144   Fax: (714)776-9906
Contact: Robert A. Spidell, Editor.
Desc: Reports on developments in California taxes, includ-
ing legislative changes, court cases, appeals and audit activ-
ity, administrative action, and ballot proposition. Focuses
on how tax developments affect California taxpayers. *Type:*
Newsletter.

The Stanger Report

Robert A. Stanger & Co., Inc.
PO Box 7490   Ph: (732)389-3600
Shrewsbury, NJ 07702   Fax: (732)544-0779
Contact: Robert A. Stanger, Publisher; Keith D. Allaire,
Exec. Editor; Nancy Schabel Mahon, Editor-in-Chief.
Desc: Provides objective analysis for investing in oil and
gas, real estate, equipment leasing, and other areas of investment. Reports new trends, partnership sales prices, secondary market prices, partnership performance, and
provides updates on tax and regulatory developments affecting investment decisions. *Type:* Newsletter.

State Tax Review

CCH Inc.
2700 Lake Cook Rd.　　　Ph: (847)267-7000
Riverwoods, IL 60015　　Free: 800-449-8114
　　　　　　　　　　　　Fax: (847)224-8299

URL: http://www.cch.com; http://www.cch.com.

Contact: CCH Tax Law Editors, Editor.

Desc: Includes digests of legislation, regulations, court decisions, administrative rulings, and all-state surveys. Remarks: Electronic version is called CCH Tax Day: State (updated daily). *Type:* Newsletter.

Stop Taxes on Food Committee

Mark A. Gibson
17 S High St., Ste. 1070
Columbus, OH 43215-3419　Ph: (614)228-7107

Contact: Mark A. Gibson, Treas.

Desc: Fosters and promotes issues about food tax. *Type:* Association.

Tax Accountant's Communique

Peyron Associates, Inc.
3212 Preston St.　　　　Ph: (502)637-7483
Louisville, KY 40213
E-mail: 71744.2032@compuserve.com
URL: http://www.smartbiz.com.

Contact: Dan Peyron, Editor.

Desc: Offers tax-savings tips for tax practitioners, preparers, and accountants. Recurring features include updates on IRS policies and procedures, and court rulings. *Type:* Newsletter.

Tax Administration News

Carswell
Thomson Professional Publishing
One Corporate Plaza
2075 Kennedy Rd.　　　Ph: (416)609-3800
Scarborough, ON, Canada M1T　Free: 800-387-5164
　　3V4　　　　　　　　Fax: (416)298-5082
E-mail: orders@carswell.com

Contact: Samuel Slutsky, Editor.

Desc: Lists the Interpretation Bulletins and Advance Tax Rulings covered in Tax Administration Reports. Summarizes the content in detail and highlights contentious matters and policy statements. *Type:* Newsletter.

Tax Administrators News

Federation of Tax Administrators
Hall of the States　　　Ph: (202)624-5890
444 N. Capitol St. NW, Ste.
　　348
Washington, DC 20001

Contact: Audrey Maynard, Editor.

Desc: Focuses on state tax legislation and administration. Covers research results and federal legislation that affects state taxation. *Type:* Newsletter.

Tax-Advantaged Securities Law Report

WestGroup
375 Hudson St.　　　　Ph: (212)929-7500
New York, NY 10014　　Free: 800-422-2101
　　　　　　　　　　　　Fax: (212)807-6209

Contact: Robert J. Haft, Editor; Peter M. Fass, Contact.

Desc: Devotes each issue to one or two articles on federal or major state law concerning tax-advantaged securities. Presents explanation and analysis of new decisions, laws, rulings, and regulations. *Type:* Newsletter.

Tax Analysts

6830 N. Fairfax Dr.　　　Ph: (703)533-4400
Arlington, VA 22213　　Free: 800-955-3444
　　　　　　　　　　　　Fax: (703)533-4444

E-mail: webmaster@tax.org
URL: http://www.tax.org

Contact: Thomas F. Field, Exec.Dir.

Desc: Comprehensively reviews all federal tax law developments; compiles statistics. *Type:* Association.

Tax Executives Institute

1200 G St., NW, No. 300　　Ph: (202)638-5601
Washington, DC 20005-3814　Fax: (202)638-5607
URL: http://www.TEI.org

Contact: Michael J. Murphy, Exec.Dir.

Desc: Professional society of executives administering and directing tax affairs for corporations and businesses. Maintains TEI Education Fund. *Type:* Association.

Tax Fax

Tax Analysts
6830 N. Fairfax Dr.　　　Ph: (703)533-4400
Arlington, VA 22213　　Free: 800-955-3444
　　　　　　　　　　　　Fax: (703)533-4444

E-mail: cservice@tax.org

Contact: Scott Antonides, Editor.

Desc: Faxes information on all developments in the tax field, including congressional, IRS, courts, state, and international news. Provides an online database service containing full text document retrieval. *Type:* Newsletter.

Tax Features

Tax Foundation, Inc.
1250 H St. NW, No. 750　　Ph: (202)783-2760
Washington, DC 20005-3908
E-mail: tf@taxfoundation.org
URL: http://www.taxfoundation.org.

Contact: William Ahern, Editor, (202)661-4224, ahern@taxfoundation.org.

Desc: Presents brief summaries of foundation studies and analyses. *Type:* Newsletter.

Tax Haven Report

Lombardi Publishing Co.
51 Toro Rd.　　　　　　Ph: (416)633-1600
North York, ON, Canada M3J　Fax: (416)633-6188
　　2A4

Desc: Offers offshore investing advice for tax purposes. Analyzes one offshore tax haven per issue. *Type:* Newsletter.

Tax Information Service

National Accounting and Finance Council
2200 Mill Rd.　　　　　Ph: (703)838-1915
Alexandria, VA 22314

Contact: Neal Castles.

Desc: Provides comprehensive coverage on tax news affecting the motor carrier industry. Reports on federal, state, and local tax court rulings; newly enacted federal and state tax laws; and IRS rulings, regulations, and revenue proceedings. *Type:* Newsletter.

Tax Letter & Social Security Report

Peyron Associates, Inc.
3212 Preston St.　　　　Ph: (502)637-7483
Louisville, KY 40213
E-mail: 71744.2032@compuserve.com
URL: http://www.smartbiz.com.

Contact: Dan Peyron, Editor.

Desc: Offers tax-savings tips, with an emphasis on social security. Includes updates on IRS policies and procedures, and court rulings. *Type:* Newsletter.

Tax Management Estates, Gifts, and Trusts Journal

Tax Management Inc.
Bureau of National Affairs, Inc.
1250 23rd St. NW　　　Ph: (202)833-7240
Washington, DC 20037　　Free: 800-372-1033
URL: http://taxmanagement.bna.com.

Contact: Glenn B. Davis, Managing Editor.

Desc: Provides practical guidance information on and reviews recent developments in estates, gifts, and trusts. Recurring features include sections titled Detailed Analysis, Working Papers, How-To-Do-It, and Bibliography and Reference. *Type:* Newsletter.

Tax Management Financial Planning Journal

Tax Management Inc.
Bureau of National Affairs, Inc.
1250 23rd St. NW　　　Ph: (202)833-7240
Washington, DC 20037　　Free: 800-372-1033
URL: http://taxmanagement.bna.com.

Contact: Glenn B. Davis, Managing Editor.

Desc: Covers topics in financial planning, including memoranda on current financial and tax planning strategies. *Type:* Newsletter.

Tax Management Foreign Income Portfolios

Tax Management Inc.
Bureau of National Affairs, Inc.
1250 23rd St. NW　　　Ph: (202)833-7240
Washington, DC 20037　　Free: 800-372-1033
URL: http://taxmanagement.bna.com.

Contact: Glenn B. Davis, Managing Editor.

Desc: Exists as a self-contained section of Tax Management Portfolio Series. Includes more than 60 portfolios covering problems arising from foreign taxation of U.S. companies abroad, U.S. taxation of foreign operations, and the conduct of business operations in other countries. *Type:* Newsletter.

Tax Management IRS Practice and Policy

Tax Management Inc.
Bureau of National Affairs, Inc.
1250 23rd St. NW　　　Ph: (202)833-7240
Washington, DC 20037　　Free: 800-372-1033
URL: http://taxmanagement.bna.com.

Contact: Glenn B. Davis, Managing Editor.

Desc: Reviews rulings, cases, policies, and procedures affecting practice before the IRS. *Type:* Newsletter.

Tax Management Memorandum

Tax Management Inc.
Bureau of National Affairs, Inc.
1250 23rd St. NW　　　Ph: (202)833-7240
Washington, DC 20037　　Free: 800-372-1033
URL: http://taxmanagement.bna.com.

Contact: Glenn B. Davis, Managing Editor.

Desc: Carries analyses of tax development. Recurring features include in-depth coverage of a single tax development in each issue. *Type:* Newsletter.

Tax Management Portfolio Series: Compensation Planning

Tax Management Inc.
1250 23rd St., N.W.　　Ph: (202)833-7240
Washington, DC 20037-1166
E-mail: tm@bna.com
URL: http://www.taxmanagement.bna.com

Contact: Glenn Davis, Managing Editor.

Desc: Contains a series of portfolios, each analyzing topics relating to pension, employee benefits, and deferred compensation planning. Portfolios include detailed analyses, working papers, and bibliographies and references. *Available:* West Group, WESTLAW; LEXIS-NEXIS, LEXIS. *Type:* Database.

Tax Management Portfolio Series: Estates, Gifts, and Trusts

Tax Management Inc.
1250 23rd St., N.W.   Ph: (202)833-7240
Washington, DC 20037-1166
E-mail: tm@bna.com
URL: http://www.taxmanagement.bna.com
Contact: Glenn Davis, Managing Editor.
Desc: Contains analyses of U.S. estate, gift, and trust tax issues prepared by tax attorneys and accountants. *Available:* West Group, WESTLAW; LEXIS-NEXIS, LEXIS. *Type:* Database.

Tax Management Portfolio Series: Foreign Income

Tax Management Inc.
1250 23rd St., N.W.   Ph: (202)833-7240
Washington, DC 20037-1166
E-mail: tm@bna.com
URL: http://www.taxmanagement.bna.com
Contact: Glenn Davis, Managing Editor.
Desc: Contains analyses of U.S. foreign income tax issues prepared by tax attorneys and accountants. *Available:* West Group, WESTLAW; LEXIS-NEXIS, LEXIS. *Type:* Database.

Tax Management Portfolio Series: Real Estate

Tax Management Inc.
1250 23rd St., N.W.   Ph: (202)833-7240
Washington, DC 20037-1166
E-mail: tm@bna.com
URL: http://www.taxmanagement.bna.com
Contact: Glenn Davis, Managing Editor.
Desc: Contains a series of potfolios, each treating specific aspects of taxation that affect real estate transactions. Portfolios include detailed analyses, working papers, and bibliographies and references. *Available:* West Group, WESTLAW; LEXIS-NEXIS, LEXIS. *Type:* Database.

Tax Management Tax Practice Series Bulletin

Tax Management Inc.
Bureau of National Affairs, Inc.
1250 23rd St. NW   Ph: (202)833-7240
Washington, DC 20037   Free: 800-372-1033
Contact: Glenn B. Davis, Managing Editor.
Desc: Answers most of the common questions tax professionals face in daily practice, with analyses by expert practitioners. Includes the weekly Tax Practice Bulletin. *Type:* Newsletter.

Tax Management U.S. Income

Tax Management Inc.
Bureau of National Affairs, Inc.
1250 23rd St. NW   Ph: (202)833-7240
Washington, DC 20037   Free: 800-372-1033
URL: http://taxmanagement.bna.com.
Contact: Glenn B. Davis, Editor.
Desc: Covers tax planning problems involving federal taxation of domestic income. Recurring features include sections titled Detailed Analysis, Working Papers, and Bibliography. *Type:* Newsletter.

Tax Management—Washington Tax Review

Tax Management Inc.
Bureau of National Affairs, Inc.
1250 23rd St. NW   Ph: (202)833-7240
Washington, DC 20037   Free: 800-372-1033
URL: http://taxmanagement.bna.com.
Contact: Glenn Davis, Editor.
Desc: Reviews legislative activities and anticipates legislative action. Carries briefs and in-depth articles on tax issues pending at the executive, legislative, and judicial levels. *Type:* Newsletter.

Tax Management Weekly Report

Tax Management Inc.
Bureau of National Affairs, Inc.
1250 23rd St. NW   Ph: (202)833-7240
Washington, DC 20037   Free: 800-372-1033
URL: http://taxmanagement.bna.com.
Contact: Glenn B. Davis, Managing Editor.
Desc: Covers developments affecting taxation and the tax aspects of accounting. Includes summaries of federal cases. *Type:* Newsletter.

Tax Management Weekly Report

Tax Management Inc.
1250 23rd St., N.W.   Ph: (202)833-7240
Washington, DC 20037-1166
E-mail: tm@bna.com
URL: http://www.taxmanagement.bna.com
Contact: Glenn Davis, Managing Editor.
Desc: Contains the complete text of Tax Management Weekly Report, a newsletter covering legislative, regulatory, judicial, and policy actions related to taxation and accounting. Provides summaries of selected cases, Internal Revenue Service (IRS) rulings and procedures, private letter rulings by code section, and general counsel and technical memoranda. *Available:* LEXIS-NEXIS, LEXIS; West Group, WESTLAW. *Type:* Database.

Tax Notes

Tax Analysts
6830 N. Fairfax Dr.   Ph: (703)533-4600
Arlington, VA 22213
E-mail: twells@tax.org@internet
URL: http://www.tax.org
Contact: Bert Hubinger, Copywriter, (703)533-4610, cbergin@tax.org@internet.
Desc: Contains the complete text of Tax Notes Magazine, dating from 1982 through 1997. *Available:* LEXIS-NEXIS, LEXIS. *Type:* Database.

Tax Notes Today

Tax Analysts
6830 N. Fairfax Dr.   Ph: (703)533-4600
Arlington, VA 22213
E-mail: twells@tax.org@internet
URL: http://www.tax.org
Desc: Provides daily tax news coverage, including the complete text of items to be published in Tax Notes. Includes news items and feature articles on tax developments, tax policy issues, and congressional developments. *Available:* The Dialog Corporation, DIALOG; LEXIS-NEXIS, LEXIS; PricewaterhouseCoopers LLP, Tax News Network. *Type:* Database.

Tax Practice Bulletin

Tax Management Inc.
Bureau of National Affairs, Inc.
1250 23rd St. NW   Ph: (202)833-7240
Washington, DC 20037   Free: 800-372-1033
URL: http://taxmanagement.bna.com.
Contact: Glenn B. Davis, Editor.
Desc: Answers most of the common questions tax professionals face in daily practice. Provides analyses by expert practitioners. *Type:* Newsletter.

Tax Savings Report

National Taxpayers Union
108 N. Alfred St.   Ph: (703)683-5700
Alexandria, VA 22314   Fax: (703)683-5722
E-mail: ntu@ntu
URL: http://www.ntu.org.
Contact: Ellen M. Katz, Editor.
Desc: Imparts tax savings tips and ideas on how to best use IRS regulations to the taxpayer's advantage. Discusses such topics as expense deductions, tax planning for senior citizens, job hunting expense deductions, and child care tax credit. *Type:* Newsletter.

Tax Talk

Tax Talk
1562 1st Ave.
New York, NY 10028
Desc: Aims to help individuals save money by reducing taxes written in everyday language for the layman. Covers legal loopholes, tax law changes, tax traps, and planning techniques. *Type:* Newsletter.

Tax Times

Carswell
Thomson Professional Publishing
One Corporate Plaza
2075 Kennedy Rd.   Ph: (416)609-3800
Scarborough, ON, Canada M1T   Free: 800-387-5164
     3V4   Fax: (416)298-5082
E-mail: orders@carswell.com
Desc: Summarizes "the latest developments affecting taxation including tax cases in the Federal Court, the Tax Court of Canada, and the occasional Provincial Court." Remarks: Bulk subscription rates are available. *Type:* Newsletter.

Tax Update for Business Owners

Harcourt Brace & Company
525 B St., Ste. 1900   Ph: (619)231-6616
San Diego, CA 92101-4495   Free: 800-831-7799
          Fax: (619)699-6593
E-mail: propub@harcourtbrace.com; newsletters@hbpp.com.
Contact: John Springer, Publisher; Karen Sanders, Editor; Helen Faulkner, Circulation Mgr.
Desc: Supplies tax information for small businesses. *Type:* Newsletter.

Tax Week

CCH Inc.
2700 Lake Cook Rd.   Ph: (847)267-7000
Riverwoods, IL 60015   Free: 800-449-8114
          Fax: (847)224-8299
URL: http://www.cch.com
Contact: Jerry Nestor, JD, Managing Editor; Mildred Carter, JD, Editor; David Jaffe, JD, Editor; Thomas Kabaker, JD, Editor; John Muller, JD, Editor; Marie O'Donnell, JD, Editor; Larry Perlman, JD, Editor; Allen Reibman, JD, Editor; Neil Ringquist, JD, Editor; Jennifer Thalman, JD, Editor.
Desc: Provides information about tax code changes and updates, information on the IRS, and tax advice. Recurring features include columns titled Tax Pointer and Practical Filings. *Type:* Newsletter.

Tax Wise Money

Agora, Inc.
1217 St. Paul St.   Ph: (410)223-2510
Baltimore, MD 21202   Free: 800-433-1528
          Fax: (410)223-2559
E-mail: 75127.1411@compuserve.com
Contact: Robert Carlson, C.P.A., Editor.
Desc: Emphasizes long-term capital gains investments. Discusses growth stocks, tax-managed mutual funds, utilities stocks, bonds, real estate and real estate tax shelters, hard money investments, and incorporation as ways to convert ordinary income to capital gains. *Type:* Newsletter.

Taxation and Revenue Policies

Wakeman/Walworth, Inc.
300 N. Washington St.   Ph: (703)549-8606
Alexandria, VA 22314   Free: 800-876-2545
URL: http://statecapitals.com.
Contact: Keyes Walworth, Editor.
Desc: Covers state revenue-raising programs other than property taxes, including sales taxes; excise taxes; business, occupation, inheritance, gasoline, bank, and capital gains taxes; and lotteries. Reports on court decisions and other regulatory rulings. *Type:* Newsletter.

Taxes on Parade

CCH Inc.
2700 Lake Cook Rd. Ph: (847)267-7000
Riverwoods, IL 60015 Free: 800-449-8114
Fax: (847)224-8299
URL: http://www.cch.com; http://www.cch.com; http://business.ccc.com.
Desc: Review of the week's federal income, excise, estate and gift tax developments. *Type:* Newsletter.

Taxes - Property

Wakeman/Walworth, Inc.
300 N. Washington St. Ph: (703)549-8606
Alexandria, VA 22314 Free: 800-876-2545
E-mail: newsletters@statecapitals.com.
URL: http://statecapitals.com.
Contact: Keyes Walworth, Editor.
Desc: Covers laws and regulations regarding property taxes, including assessment programs, exemptions, incentives, collection methods, court decisions, and other regulatory rulings. Emphasizes school financing, including referenda, state aid formulas, alternative methods, budgetary issues related to teacher pay, class sizes, and drug testing programs. *Type:* Newsletter.

1040 Report

National Association of Tax Practitioners
720 Association Dr. Ph: (920)749-1040
Appleton, WI 54914-1483 Free: 800-558-3402
Fax: (920)749-1062
E-mail: natp@natptax.com
Contact: David L. Mellem, Editor, davidm@natptax.com.
Desc: Helps to communicate the purposes of the Association, which are to foster high standards in the tax preparation profession and to promote and protect the interests of tax practitioners. Includes tax law and regulations, statistics, and news of members. *Type:* Newsletter.

A Weekly Alert

Research Institute of America
PO Box 5159
Carol Stream, IL 60197 Free: 800-431-9025
Desc: Updates federal tax developments. Reports the latest tax events in Congress, the courts, the treasury, and the IRS. *Type:* Newsletter.

WESTLAW® Taxation Library

West Group
620 Opperman Dr. Ph: (651)687-7000
St. Paul, MN 55164-0526
URL: http://www.westgroup.com
Desc: Contains the complete text of U.S. federal and state court decisions, statutes and regulations, administrative law decisions, specialized files, and texts and periodicals dealing with taxation. *Available:* West Group, WESTLAW. *Type:* Database.

Worldwide Tax Daily

Tax Analysts
6830 N. Fairfax Dr. Ph: (703)533-4600
Arlington, VA 22213
E-mail: twells@tax.org@internet
URL: http://www.tax.org
Contact: Bert Hubinger, Copywriter, (404)664-7807, bfernand@tax.org@internet.
Desc: Contains international tax news and a collection of full-text international tax documents, including worldwide treaties. *Available:* LEXIS-NEXIS, LEXIS; The Dialog Corporation, DIALOG; West Group, WESTLAW. *Type:* Database.

Telecommunications

ADSL News

Information Gatekeepers Inc.
214 Harvard Ave. Ph: (617)232-3111
Boston, MA 02134 Free: 800-323-1088
Fax: (617)734-8562
E-mail: info@igigroup.com
URL: http://wwwigigroup.com
Desc: Contains news on worldwide developments in digital subscriber line technologies, including ADSL, RDSL, SDSL, VDSL, and HDSL. *Type:* Newsletter.

Advanced Intelligent Network News

Phillips Business Information, Inc.
1201 Seven Locks Rd., Ste. 300 Ph: (301)340-1520
Potomac, MD 20854 Free: 888-707-5809
Fax: (301)340-3847
E-mail: clientservices.pbi@phillips.com
URL: http://www.phillips.com.
Contact: Andrew Braunbery, Editor.
Desc: Covers the development and applications of advanced intelligent networks (AINs) as well as Regional Bell Operating Company (RBOC) marketing and management strategies. Discusses AIN applications in such areas as signalling system 7 (SS7), open network architecture (ONA), caller identification, wireless private branch exchange (PBX), personal communications network (PIN), and enhanced 800 and 900 services. *Type:* Newsletter.

ALERT!

Cambridge Communications Inc.
MediaMap Ph: (617)374-9300
215 1st St. Fax: (617)374-9346
Cambridge, MA 02142
Contact: Ezra Friedman, Editor; Lynne Yorke LaPlante, Managing Editor.
Desc: Delivers updates on the media through news, articles, and publication profiles. Includes editorial moves and changes and tradeshow information. *Type:* Newsletter.

ASIA PACIFIC

Information Gatekeepers Inc.
214 Harvard Ave. Ph: (617)232-3111
Boston, MA 02134 Free: 800-323-1088
Fax: (617)734-8562
E-mail: info@igigroup.com
URL: http://wwwigigroup.com
Desc: Provides information and news on the telecommunications market in Asia. *Type:* Newsletter.

AT&T National Toll-Free Directory—Business Buyer's Guide

AT&T
340 Mount Kemble Ave., Ste. Ph: (201)993-4414
360 Free: 800-426-8686
Morristown, NJ 07960-6656 Fax: (201)285-3579
URL: http://www.tollfree.att.net.
Desc: Contains over 120,000 toll-free numbers operating in the U.S. The "AT&T National Toll-Free Directory—Business Edition" and the "AT&T National Toll-Free Directory" are distributed to 3,500,000 businesses and consumers. *Type:* Directory.

AT&T National Toll-Free Directory—Shopper's Guide

AT&T
340 Mount Kemble Ave., Ste. Ph: (201)993-4414
360 Free: 800-426-8686
Morristown, NJ 07960-6656 Fax: (201)285-3579
URL: http://www.tollfree.att.net.
Contact: Patricia G. Selden, Publisher.
Desc: Contains over 60,000 toll free 800 and 888 numbers operating in the U.S. The "AT&T National toll free Directory—Consumer Edition" and the "AT&T National toll free Directory—Business Edition" are distributed to 3,500,000 businesses and consumers. *Type:* Directory.

Audiotex News

Audiotex News
2362 Hempstead Tpke., 2nd Fl. Ph: (516)735-3398
East Meadow, NY 11554 Free: 800-735-3398
Fax: (516)735-3682
URL: http://www.audiotexnews.com.
Contact: Carol Morse, Editor & Publisher, carol@audiotex.news.com.
Desc: Covers news, trends, regulations, and information on the 900/800 pay-per-call business. Recurring features include interviews, news of research, calendar of events, reports of meetings, book reviews, and notices of publications available. *Type:* Newsletter.

Audiotex Update

Worldwide Videotex
PO Box 3273 Ph: (561)738-2276
Boynton Beach, FL 33424-3273
URL: http://www.wvpubs.com.
Contact: Mark Wright, Editor, markedit@juno.com.
Desc: Provides the latest news and information on the audiotex industry. Discusses voice processing/information products, services, companies, marketing strategies, and research and development. *Type:* Newsletter.

Auditel Report

Auditel, Inc.
213 Stage Rd. Ph: (603)329-5000
Hampstead, NH 03841 Free: 800-FIX-ISDN
Fax: (603)329-5511
E-mail: info@auditel.com
URL: http://www.auditel.com.
Contact: Joseph J. Scotti, President.
Desc: Provides up-to-date Telecom news to businesses throughout the U.S. Includes topics on voice service, data service, video and internet issues and events. *Type:* Newsletter.

BIB Interactive Sourcebook

North American Publishing Co.
401 N. Broad St. Ph: (215)238-5300
Philadelphia, PA 19108 Free: 800-777-8074
Fax: (215)238-5270
URL: http://www.napco.com
Desc: 50 interactive companies and 5,900 interactive executives at 4,500 interactive organizations. *Type:* Directory.

Brazil Telecom

Information Gatekeepers Inc.
214 Harvard Ave. Ph: (617)232-3111
Boston, MA 02134 Free: 800-323-1088
Fax: (617)734-8562
E-mail: info@igigroup.com
URL: http://wwwigigroup.com
Desc: Covers developments in the telecommunications market in Brazil. *Type:* Newsletter.

The Cable Industry Directory

Phillips Publishing International, Inc.
7811 Montrose Rd. Ph: (301)340-2100
Potomac, MD 20854 Fax: (301)424-0245
Desc: 4,500 contacts at cable MSOs, broadcasters, telecommunication companies in cable, equipment companies, and business and technical services companies serving the cable industry. *Type:* Directory.

Canadian Communications Network Letter

Evert Communications Ltd.
1296 Carling Ave. Ph: (613)728-4621
Ottawa, ON, Canada K1Z 7K8 Fax: (613)728-0385
E-mail: newsdesk@evert.com; services@evert.com
URL: http://www.evert.com.

Telecommunications

Contact: Brant Scott, Editor.

Desc: Offers concise, reliable and authoritative perspectives of the Canadian telecommunications sector, with special emphasis on the performance and integrity of terrestrial and space-based networks. Reports on corporate mergers and acquisitions, new contracts, market developments and trends, and any other items pertinent to the national telecommunications infrastructure. *Type:* Newsletter.

Cellular Experts News

TRM Ltd.
PO Box 1091   Free: 800-382-3446
Stanwood, WA 98292-1091
Contact: Tom Madden, Editor.

Desc: Updates the improvements made in the safety, performance and reliability of cellular telephones. Offers money-saving advice and other information. *Type:* Newsletter.

Cellular Networking Perspectives

Cellular Networking Perspectives Ltd.
2636 Toronto CR NW   Ph: (403)289-6609
Calgary, AB, Canada T2N 3W1 Free: 800-633-5514
                            Fax: (403)289-6658
E-mail: cnpsales@cnp-wireless.com
Contact: David Crowe, Editor, crowed@cnp-wireless.com.

Desc: Provides news and analysis of wireless standards and technology. Includes netowrk standards, such as IS-41, analog, digital, cellular, and PCS radio standards. *Type:* Newsletter.

Cellular Sales & Marketing Newsletter

Creative Communications, Inc.
PO Box 1519-GR   Ph: (703)715-6113
Herndon, VA 20172
E-mail: cellsalesm@aol.com.
Contact: Stuart Crump, Jr., Editor.

Desc: Provides information on cellular telecommunications, marketing, sales promotions and advertising. *Type:* Newsletter.

Cellular Telecommunications Industry Association

1250 Connecticut Ave. NW,   Ph: (202)785-0081
   Ste. 200   Fax: (202)785-0721
Washington, DC 20036
Contact: Thomas E. Wheeler, Pres. & CEO.

Desc: Individuals and organizations actively engaged in cellular radiotelephone communications, including: telephone companies and corporations providing radio communications; lay firms; engineering firms; consultants and manufacturers. (A cellular radiotelephone is a mobile communications device. An area is geographically divided into low frequency cells monitored by a computer that switches callers from one frequency to another as they move from cell to cell.) Objectives are to: promote, educate, and facilitate the professional interests, needs, and concerns of members with respect to the development and commercial applications of cellular technology; provide an opportunity for exchanging experience and concerns; broaden the understanding and importance of cellular communication technology. *Type:* Association.

Chronolog

Knight-Ridder Information, Inc.
11000 Regency Pkwy., No. 10
Cary, NC 27511-8518
Contact: Carol Wilson, Editor.

Desc: Updates information on the company's products, publications, services, and users. Covers related news in Europe, Australia, Canada, and Mexico. *Type:* Newsletter.

Communications Business & Finance

Telecommunications Reports International, Inc.
1333 H St. NW, Ste. 100 E   Ph: (202)842-3006
Washington, DC 20005   Free: 800-822-6338
                            Fax: (202)842-3047
E-mail: customerservice@tr.com
URL: http://www.brp.com; http://www.tr.com.
Contact: Erik Heinicke, Editor, eheinicke@tr.com.

Desc: Provides timely news and in-depth analysis on the financial and investment aspects of the multi billion dollar communications business. Covers opportunities, business actions and reactions, as well as the impact of regulation on the financial health of competing companies. *Type:* Newsletter.

Communications News

Nelson Publishing, Inc.
2500 Tamiami Tr. N.   Ph: (941)966-9521
Nokomis, FL 34275-3482   Fax: (941)966-2590
E-mail: nelpub@ix.netcom.com; info@comnews.com.
URL: http://www.comnews.com.
Contact: Vern Nelson, Group Publisher; Ripley Hotch, Editor, ripley@comnews.com.

Desc: Magazine featuring networking communications technology applications. *Type:* Periodical.

Communications News—Conferencing Directory

Nelson Publishing, Inc.
2500 Tamiami Tr. N.   Ph: (941)966-9521
Nokomis, FL 34275-3482   Fax: (941)966-2590
E-mail: nelpub@ix.netcom.com
URL: http://www.comnews.com.
Contact: Ripley Hotch, Editor.
Type: Directory.

Communications News—Integrated Network Access Directory

Nelson Publishing, Inc.
2500 Tamiami Tr. N.   Ph: (941)966-9521
Nokomis, FL 34275-3482   Fax: (941)966-2590
E-mail: nelpub@ix.netcom.com
URL: http://www.comnews.com.
Contact: Ripley Hotch, Editor.
Type: Directory.

Communications News—Internetworking Directory

Nelson Publishing, Inc.
2500 Tamiami Tr. N.   Ph: (941)966-9521
Nokomis, FL 34275-3482   Fax: (941)966-2590
E-mail: nelpub@ix.netcom.com
URL: http://www.comnews.com.
Contact: Ripley Hotch, Editor.
Type: Directory.

Communications News—Test Equipment Directory

Nelson Publishing, Inc.
2500 Tamiami Tr. N.   Ph: (941)966-9521
Nokomis, FL 34275-3482   Fax: (941)966-2590
E-mail: nelpub@ix.netcom.com
URL: http://www.comnews.com.
Contact: Ripley Hotch, Editor.
Type: Directory.

Communications News—Wireless Directory

Nelson Publishing, Inc.
2500 Tamiami Tr. N.   Ph: (941)966-9521
Nokomis, FL 34275-3482   Fax: (941)966-2590
E-mail: nelpub@ix.netcom.com
URL: http://www.comnews.com.

Contact: Ripley Hotch, Editor.
Type: Directory.

Connections

Ameritech Services, Inc.
2000 W. Ameritech Center Dr.   Ph: (847)248-2000
Hoffman Estates, IL 60192   Fax: (847)248-3992
Contact: Ron Kalich, Editor.

Desc: Present perspectives on the state of capital recovery in telecommunications and updates on recovery areas in the Ameritech region. Recurring features include a calendar of events and columns on life studies, methods and financial analyses, and software support. *Type:* Newsletter.

The Connector Industry Yearbook

Bishop & Associates, Inc.
22118 20th Ave. SE   Ph: (206)485-0572
Bothell, WA 98041   Free: 800-829-0572

Desc: List of 9 connector companies and profiles of key connector industry executives. *Type:* Directory.

Digital Media

Internet/Media Strategie Inc.
Old City Hall   Ph: (253)627-7060
625 Commerce St., Ste. 330 Free: 888-463-7364
Tacoma, WA 98402
URL: www.digmedia.com.

Contact: Mitch Ratcliffe, Editor and Publisher, godsdog@ratcliffe.com; Tricia Chan, Editor.

Desc: Analyzes business opportunities on the Internet and other technologies. Recurring features include book reviews, notices of publications available, and columns titled Focus, Techne, and Flux. *Type:* Newsletter.

Directory of Fiberoptics Installers

KMI Corp.
America's Cup Ave. at 31 Bridge   Ph: (401)849-6771
   St.   Free: 800-343-4035
Newport, RI 02840   Fax: (401)847-5866
E-mail: info@kmicorp.com; jtjones@kmicorp.com.
URL: http://www.kmicorp

Contact: John N. Kessler, Editor.

Desc: Over 250 international fiberoptics installers. *Type:* Directory.

Eastern European & Former Soviet Telecom Report

International Technology Consultants (ITC)
4340 East-West Hwy., Ste. 220   Ph: (301)907-0060
Bethesda, MD 20814-4411   Fax: (301)907-6555

Contact: S. Blake Swensrud, Editor; Justin P. Friedman, Editor; Johanna Arnesson, Editor.

Desc: Covers the telecommunications industry in Eastern Europe. Recurring features include interviews, news of research, a calendar of events, and country reports. *Type:* Newsletter.

Edge

Edge Publishing
1319 Military Cutoff Rd., No.   Ph: (908)852-7217
   207
Wilmington, NC 28405-3634

Contact: Al Lynd, Editor.

Desc: Provides current product and organization changes within AT&T and external developments affecting AT&T. Tracks AT&T product developments, marketing strategies, and results. *Type:* Newsletter.

Effective Telephone Techniques

The Dartnell Corp.
360 Hiatt Dr.   Free: 800-621-5463
Palm Beach Gardens, FL 33418   Fax: (561)622-2423
E-mail: dartnell@dartnellcorp.com
URL: http://www.dartnellcorp.com

Contact: Molly Miller, Editor.

Desc: Provides information and advice on telephone usage, including 800-numbers, answering calls, and transferring calls. Recurring features include columns titled Quick Tips, What Would You Do?, and Problems & Solutions. *Type:* Newsletter.

Electronic Messaging News

Phillips Business Information, Inc.
1201 Seven Locks Rd., Ste. 300   Ph: (301)340-1520
Potomac, MD 20854   Free: 888-707-5809
    Fax: (301)340-3847
E-mail: clientservices.pbi@phillips.com
URL: http://www.phillips.com.

Contact: Lana Sansur, Editor.

Desc: Provides information and analysis on strategic deployment and implementation of electronic messaging technology. Recurring features include case studies and interviews. *Type:* Newsletter.

EMMS

Telecommunications Reports International, Inc.
1333 H St. NW   Ph: (202)842-3022
Washington, DC 20005   Free: 800-822-6338
    Fax: (202)842-1875
E-mail: customerservice@tr.com; customerserice@brp.com.
URL: http://www.tr.com; http://www.tr.com.

Contact: Eric Arnum, Editor.

Desc: 00ES Focuses on developments in the electronic mail and messaging market: online enhanced services, store-and-forward, local area networks and wide area network communicating terminals, and personal computers. Assesses the effects of these technologies on traditional communication carriers. *Type:* Newsletter.

ENTELEC Newsletter

Energy Telecommunications and Electrical Association (ENTELEC)
PO Box 795038   Ph: (214)235-0655
Dallas, TX 75379   Fax: (214)235-0653

Desc: Disseminates information for member individuals and firms involved in the construction, maintenance, and operation of automation systems, communication systems, and electrical power installations. Reprints technical papers that were presented at the most recent annual conference, as well as abstracts of papers to be presented at the next conference. *Type:* Newsletter.

Epigram

Epigraphx LLC
750 Broadway St.   Ph: (650)298-0144
Redwood City, CA 94063-3124   Fax: 800-238-9084
URL: http://www.epigraphx.com.

Contact: Jennifer McCallister, Editor; Scott Edwards, President; Timothy H. O'Connor, Account Exec.

Desc: Describes automated communications such as enhanced fax services for businesses and professionals interested in hightech developments. Recurring features include success stories and descriptions of new services. *Type:* Newsletter.

European Telecom

Information Gatekeepers Inc.
214 Harvard Ave.   Ph: (617)232-3111
Boston, MA 02134   Free: 800-323-1088
    Fax: (617)734-8562
E-mail: info@igigroup.com
URL: http://wwwigigroup.com
Desc: Covers various aspects of telecommunications in Europe. Includes strategic information and market opportunities. *Type:* Newsletter.

Facsimile & Voice Services

Phillips Business Information, Inc.
1201 Seven Locks Rd., Ste. 300   Ph: (301)340-1520
Potomac, MD 20854   Free: 888-707-5809
    Fax: (301)340-3847
E-mail: clientservices.pbi@phillips.com
URL: http://www.phillips.com.
Contact: Jennifer Walsh, Editor.

Desc: Provides information on new technology, business applications, corporate developments, and industry trends. *Type:* Newsletter.

FCC Report

Telecom Publishing Group
Warren Publishing, Inc.
2115 Ward Ct. NW   Ph: (202)872-9200
Washington, DC 20037   Fax: (202)293-3435
Contact: Jennifer Park, Editor.

Desc: Monitors communication regulation and government oversight. Offers synopsis of all regulatory developments in each FCC Bureau, as well as U.S. Courts of Appeal decisions and Capitol Hill oversight of communications issues. *Type:* Newsletter.

Fiber Datacom

Information Gatekeepers Inc.
214 Harvard Ave.   Ph: (617)232-3111
Boston, MA 02134   Free: 800-323-1088
    Fax: (617)734-8562
E-mail: info@igigroup.com
URL: http://wwwigigroup.com
Contact: Paul Polishuk, Editor.

Desc: Covers the applications of fiber optics in buildings, campuses, and companies for telecommunications, including fiber optics, coaxial cables, twisted wire pairs, and radio. Details new products, competition, technology, regulations and standards, contracts and awards, and market trends. *Type:* Newsletter.

Fiber in the Loop

Information Gatekeepers Inc.
214 Harvard Ave.   Ph: (617)232-3111
Boston, MA 02134   Free: 800-323-1088
    Fax: (617)734-8562
E-mail: info@igigroup.com
URL: http://wwwigigroup.com
Contact: Paul Polishuk, Editor.

Desc: Covers developments in fiber and consumer application in the communications industry. *Type:* Newsletter.

Fiber Optics Business Newsletter

Information Gatekeepers Inc.
214 Harvard Ave.   Ph: (617)232-3111
Boston, MA 02134   Free: 800-323-1088
    Fax: (617)734-8562
E-mail: info@igigroup.com
URL: http://wwwigigroup.com
Contact: Paul Polishuk, Editor.

Desc: Provides information on the fiber optics industry, including procurement opportunities, international tenders, major contract awards, cost and market trends, joint ventures, and business conferences and meetings. *Type:* Newsletter.

Fiber Optics Weekly Update

Information Gatekeepers Inc.
214 Harvard Ave.   Ph: (617)232-3111
Boston, MA 02134   Free: 800-323-1088
    Fax: (617)734-8562
E-mail: info@igigroup.com
URL: http://wwwigigroup.com
Contact: Paul Polishuk, Editor.

Desc: Provides market insights into the impact of new developments, products, competition, technology, and standards in the fiber optics industry. *Type:* Newsletter.

411 Newsletter

United Communications Group
11300 Rockville Pike, Suite   Ph: (301)816-8950
1100
Rockville, MD 20852
E-mail: joshcohen@ucg.com
URL: http://www.ucg.com
Contact: Phillip B. Kemelor, Mgr.

Desc: Contains the complete text of 411 Newsletter, providing information for corporate telecommunications managers. Covers selection of local and long-distance services, design and installation of private networks, system maintenance and expansion, and telephone bill auditing. *Available:* The Gale Group; Bell & Howell Information and Learning; Bell & Howell Information and Learning. *Type:* Database.

411 Newsletter

Center for Communications Management Information
11300 Rockville Pike, Ste. 1100   Ph: (301)287-2700
Rockville, MD 20852-3030   Free: 888-275-2264
    Fax: (301)816-8945
E-mail: sales@ccmi.com
Contact: Steve Pastorkovich, Editor.

Desc: Offers "practical, cost-cutting management tips for corporate telecommunications managers." Considers such topics as how to make equipment buys go easier, software programs for telecom managers, and lowering costs of calling. *Type:* Newsletter.

Gigabit News

Information Gatekeepers Inc.
214 Harvard Ave.   Ph: (617)232-3111
Boston, MA 02134   Free: 800-323-1088
    Fax: (617)734-8562
E-mail: info@igigroup.com
URL: http://wwwigigroup.com
Contact: Paul Polishuk, Editor; Nomi Burstein.

Desc: Covers developments, products, competition, technology, and standards in the fiber distributed data interface (FDDI) industry, as well as twisted wire pairs. Recurring features include a calendar of events. *Type:* Newsletter.

IEEE Communications Society

3 Park Ave., Ste. 17A   Ph: (212)705-8900
New York, NY 10016-5902   Fax: (212)705-8999
E-mail: memberservices@ieee.org
URL: http://www.comsoc.org
Contact: John M. Howell, Exec.Dir.

Desc: Industry professionals with a common interest in advancing all communications technologies. Seeks to foster original work in all aspects of communications science, engineering, and technology and encourages the development of applications that use signals to transfer voice, data, image, and/or video information between locations. *Type:* Association.

India Telecom

Information Gatekeepers Inc.
214 Harvard Ave.   Ph: (617)232-3111
Boston, MA 02134   Free: 800-323-1088
                          Fax: (617)734-8562
E-mail: info@igigroup.com
URL: http://wwwigigroup.com
Contact: Nomi Burstein, Managing Editor.
Desc: Provides coverage of the Indian telecommunications market. *Type:* Newsletter.

Industrial Telecommunications Association

1110 N. Glebe Rd., Ste. 500   Ph: (703)528-5115
Arlington, VA 22201   Fax: (703)524-1074
URL: http://www.ita-relay.com
Contact: Mark E. Crosby, Pres. & CEO.
Desc: Private land mobile radio licensees and independent radio sales and service organizations. Represents members before the FCC and U.S. Congress. *Type:* Association.

Industry Pulse

Telecommunications Industry Association
2500 Wilson Blvd., Ste. 300   Ph: (703)907-7721
Arlington, VA 22201-3836   Fax: (703)907-7727
E-mail: tia@tia.eia.org
URL: http://www.tiaonline.org.
Contact: Sharon Grace, Editor, sgrace@tia.eia.org; Vince Hancock, Asst. Ed., (703)907-7975, fax: (703)907-7727, vhancock@tia.eia.org.
Desc: Publishes news of the Association, its members, and its activities. *Type:* Newsletter.

Infotech

Ameritech Services, Inc.
2000 W. Ameritech Center Dr.   Ph: (847)248-2000
Hoffman Estates, IL 60192   Fax: (847)248-3992
Contact: Phil Curtiss, Editor.
Desc: Provides news of Ameritech network disclosures, technical documents, and ordering information. *Type:* Newsletter.

Institute for Global Communications

Bldg. 1012, 1st. Fl.   Ph: (415)561-6100
Tornery Ave.   Fax: (415)561-6101
PO Box 29904
San Francisco, CA 94129-0904
E-mail: outreach@igc.org
URL: http://www.igc.org
Desc: Provides computer networking tools for international communications and information exchange. *Type:* Association.

Interactive Services Association

PO Box 65782   Ph: (301)495-4955
Washington, DC 20035-5782   Fax: (301)495-4959
E-mail: isa@isa.net
URL: http://www.isa.net
Contact: Jeff Richards, Exec.Dir.
Desc: Trade association serving businesses that deliver telecommunications-based interactive services. (Interactive services refers to services that use telecommunications for information exchange, communications, transactions, and entertainment through a computer, videotex terminal, enhanced telephone, or television.) Focuses on personal use of interactive services in the home, office, and public locations. *Type:* Association.

International Communications Association

2735 Villa Creek Dr.   Ph: (972)620-7020
Dallas, TX 75234   Free: 800-ICA-INFO
                                Fax: (972)488-9985
Contact: Robert Harper, Pres.
Desc: Representatives who are responsible for telecommunications services and facilities of major companies, corpo-

rations, and other organizations. Seeks to: exchange ideas and experiences in the communications field. Conducts short courses, technical, educational and research programs, and operates job placement service. *Type:* Association.

International PBX/Telecommunicators Newsletter

International PBX/Telecommunicators
2426 Swan Blvd.   Ph: (414)771-5336
Wauwatosa, WI 53226
Contact: Ila Mae Hora, Editor.
Desc: Furnishes articles and commentary to assist switchboard operators and communication directors to better communicate with customers and government. Recurring features include letters to the editor, interviews, news of research, a calendar of events, reports of meetings, news of educational opportunities, and columns titled President's Message, New Equipment, and Helpful Hints. *Type:* Newsletter.

International Teleconferencing Association

100 Four Falls Corporate   Ph: (610)941-2020
  Center, Ste. 105   Fax: (610)941-2015
West Conshohocken, PA 19428
E-mail: staff@itca.org
URL: http://www.itca.org
Contact: Henry S. Grove, III, Exec.Dir.
Desc: Vendors of teleconferencing equipment or services; users, researchers, and consultants. Seeks to: educate the public about the uses and impacts of teleconferencing technology; encourage the successful use of teleconferencing; foster information exchange; serve as a liaison with international government agencies. Organizes educational programs; compiles statistics. *Type:* Association.

The Internet and Online Industry Sourcebook

Gateway Publishing
1230 Macklind   Ph: (314)647-0600
St. Louis, MO 63110   Fax: (314)647-2422
Desc: 600 internet and online industry companies including content providers, software developers, and access providers. *Type:* Directory.

Internet Telecom

Information Gatekeepers Inc.
214 Harvard Ave.   Ph: (617)232-3111
Boston, MA 02134   Free: 800-323-1088
                                Fax: (617)734-8562
E-mail: info@igigroup.com
URL: http://wwwigigroup.com
Desc: Reports on developments in telecommunications and data services. Includes information on the Internet, new carriers, software suppliers, and equipment manufacturers. *Type:* Newsletter.

Internet Telephone

Information Gatekeepers Inc.
214 Harvard Ave.   Ph: (617)232-3111
Boston, MA 02134   Free: 800-323-1088
                                Fax: (617)734-8562
E-mail: info@igigroup.com
URL: http://wwwigigroup.com
Desc: Provides marketing and technology information on new developments in the telecommunications industry. *Type:* Newsletter.

ISDN News

Phillips Business Information, Inc.
1201 Seven Locks Rd., Ste. 300 Ph: (301)340-1520
Potomac, MD 20854   Free: 888-707-5809
                                Fax: (301)340-3847
E-mail: clientservices.pbi@phillips.com

Contact: Lori Marie Sylvia, Editor.
Desc: Provides information on strategies, marketing, and applications in the ISDN industry. *Type:* Newsletter.

ISDN Newsletter

Information Gatekeepers Inc.
214 Harvard Ave.   Ph: (617)232-3111
Boston, MA 02134   Free: 800-323-1088
                                Fax: (617)734-8562
E-mail: info@igigroup.com
URL: http://wwwigigroup.com
Contact: Paul Polishuk, Editor.
Desc: Covers "worldwide trends in technology, markets, and applications" in the Integrated Service Digital Network (ISDN) industry. Includes information on policy and regulation developments, standards, and new companies in the industry. *Type:* Newsletter.

ISP Business

Information Gatekeepers Inc.
214 Harvard Ave.   Ph: (617)232-3111
Boston, MA 02134   Free: 800-323-1088
                                Fax: (617)734-8562
E-mail: info@igigroup.com
URL: http://wwwigigroup.com
Desc: Covers news of the business aspects of Internet service providers worldwide. Includes information on finances, marketing, mergers and acquisitions, joint ventures, technologies, customer billing and service, new products, and international developments. *Type:* Newsletter.

Japan Telecom

Information Gatekeepers Inc.
214 Harvard Ave.   Ph: (617)232-3111
Boston, MA 02134   Free: 800-323-1088
                                Fax: (617)734-8562
E-mail: info@igigroup.com
URL: http://wwwigigroup.com
Contact: Nomi Burstein, Managing Editor.
Desc: Provides coverage of the telecommunications industry in Japan. *Type:* Newsletter.

Japan Telecommunications Scan

Kyodo News International, Inc.
50 Rockefeller Plaza, Ste. 803 Ph: (212)397-3723
New York, NY 10020   Free: 800-536-3510
Desc: Discusses the Nippon Telegraph & Telephone Public Corporation (NTT) of Japan. Examines NTT's telecommunications role in Japan, including the latest technological developments and marketing in the telecommunications and electronics fields. *Type:* Newsletter.

Land Mobile Radio News

Phillips Business Information, Inc.
1201 Seven Locks Rd., Ste. 300 Ph: (301)340-1520
Potomac, MD 20854   Free: 888-707-5809
                                Fax: (301)340-3847
E-mail: clientservices.pbi@phillips.com
URL: http://www.phillips.com.
Contact: David Toll, Editor, dtoll@phillips.com; Joelle Martin, Publisher.
Desc: Informs readers of new Federal Communications Commission (FCC) rules and regulations regarding mobile radio, and reports on products soon to hit the marketplace. Focuses on cellular dispositions and designations and settlements, FCC microwave spectrum policy, and the latest moves made by mobile radio companies. *Type:* Newsletter.

Latin American Telecom Report

International Technology Consultants (ITC)
4340 East-West Hwy., Ste. 220   Ph: (301)907-0060
Bethesda, MD 20814-4411   Fax: (301)907-6555
Contact: Edward Czarnecki, Editor; Andrea Katz, Editor.
Desc: Covers the telecommunications industry in Latin America. Recurring features include interviews, a calendar of events, market research, and business analyses. *Type:* Newsletter.

Local Competition Report

Telecom Publishing Group
Warren Publishing, Inc.
2115 Ward Ct. NW   Ph: (202)872-9200
Washington, DC 20037   Fax: (202)293-3435
Contact: Jennifer Park, Editor.
Desc: Tracks regulatory decisions, technological breakthroughs, and competitive strategies of competitive local exchange carriers companies. Covers access, CAPs, interconnection, private networks, number portability, shared tenant services, rights-of-way, centrex resale, state regulation, alternative local transport, federal regulation, access parity, wireless alternatives, local unbundling, cable television, telco strategies, new technologies, signalling system 7 (SS7) database access, local resale, rates, pricing, and competitive network integration. *Type:* Newsletter.

Long-Distance Competition Report

Telecom Publishing Group
Warren Publishing, Inc.
2115 Ward Ct. NW   Ph: (202)872-9200
Washington, DC 20037   Fax: (202)293-3435
Contact: Jennifer Park, Editor.
Desc: Provides news of AT&T business strategy, new products and services, internal structure, regulatory matters, competitive analysis, and stock reports. *Type:* Newsletter.

Mexico Telecom

Information Gatekeepers Inc.
214 Harvard Ave.   Ph: (617)232-3111
Boston, MA 02134   Free: 800-323-1088
   Fax: (617)734-8562
E-mail: info@igigroup.com
URL: http://wwwigigroup.com
Contact: Dr. Paul Polishuk, Editor and Publisher; Nomi Burstein, Assistant Editor.
Desc: Covers the telecommunications industry in Mexico, including competition, government regulations, international business and ventures, and market intelligence. *Type:* Newsletter.

MMTAlert

MultiMedia Telecommunications Association
2500 Wilson Blvd., Ste. 300   Ph: (703)907-7470
Arlington, VA 22209   Fax: (703)907-7478
E-mail: info@mmta.org
Contact: Mary Bradshaw, Editor.
Desc: Provides information about telecommunications industry news, law and regulations. Includes actions by the Federal Communications Commission, Department of Justice, and Congress. *Type:* Newsletter.

Mobile Data Report

Telecom Publishing Group
1101 King St., 4th Fl.   Ph: (703)683-4100
Alexandria, VA 22314   Free: 800-327-7205
   Fax: (703)739-6490
URL: http://www.cappubs.com/tpg; http://capitol.cappubs.com/am/.
Contact: Stephen Bouvet, Editor, sboevet@cappubs.com.
Desc: Analyzes the rapidly expanding market for portable data communications. Reports on dedicated specialized mobile radios, alphanumeric radio pagers, land mobile satellites, and electronic messaging. *Type:* Newsletter.

Mobile Satellite News

Phillips Business Information, Inc.
1201 Seven Locks Rd., Ste. 300   Ph: (301)340-1520
Potomac, MD 20854   Free: 888-707-5809
   Fax: (301)340-3847
E-mail: clientservices.pbi@phillips.com
Contact: David Bross, Managing Editor; Clayton Kunz, Asst. Editor.
Desc: Reports on new technology, applications, corporate activities, marketing trends, and competition in the mobile satellite industry. *Type:* Newsletter.

Mobilis: The Mobile Computing Lifestyle Magazine

Mobilis Magazine
1055 Escalon Ave., Ste. 808   Ph: (408)720-1979
PO Box 61329
Sunnyvale, CA 94086
URL: http://www.volksware.com/mobilis/
Desc: Mobilis is a magazine devoted solely to mobile computing. There are articles, product and services reviews, as well as a section where questions may be asked by readers and answered by Ms. *Type:* Database.

Multifunctional Monthly

Buyers Laboratory Inc.
20 Railroad Ave.   Ph: (201)488-0404
Hackensack, NJ 07601   Fax: (201)488-0461
E-mail: info@buyers-lab.com
Contact: Jane Lyons, Contact.
Desc: Contains information on telecommunication products. *Type:* Newsletter.

Multimedia Telecommunication News

Stoneridge Technical Services
PO Box 1891   Ph: (301)424-0114
Rockville, MD 20849   Fax: (301)424-8971
Contact: William W. Creitz, Editor.
Desc: Provides news on multimedia messaging and communication technology involving data, fax, graphics, voice and/or video. Covers new products, technology, applications, markets, and company activities. *Type:* Newsletter.

MultiMedia Telecommunications Association

2500 Wilson Blvd. Ste 300   Ph: (703)907-7472
Arlington, VA 22201-3834   Free: 800-799-MMTA
   Fax: (703)907-7478
E-mail: info@mmta.org
URL: http://www.mmta.org
Contact: Mary Bradshaw, Pres.
Desc: Manufacturers and distributors of communications and computer equipment; suppliers, consultants, and users of voice and data technology; related service and information providers. Provides public relations, research, and membership services. Conducts specialized education and research programs. *Type:* Association.

Municipal Cable TV and Telecommunications News

O'Reilly, Rancilio, Nitz, Andrews and Turnbull P.C.
12900 Hall Rd., Ste. 350   Ph: (810)726-1000
Sterling Heights, MI 48313   Fax: (810)726-1560
URL: http://www.ameritech.net.users/nlehto/index.html.
Contact: Neil J. Lehto, Editor, nlehto@ameritech.net.
Desc: Contains information on telecommunications including cable and digital television and telephone services. *Type:* Newsletter.

NAFTA/Latin America Telecommunications Directory

Counterpart, Inc.
2200 Clarendon Blvd., Ste.   Ph: (703)516-7000
1410   Fax: (703)516-7005
Arlington, VA 22201
Desc: 1,200 telecommunications companies in Latin America. *Type:* Directory.

National E-mail and Fax Directory

Gale Group Inc.
27500 Drake Rd.   Ph: (248)699-4253
Farmington Hills, MI 48331-   Free: 800-877-GALE
3535   Fax: (248)699-8070
E-mail: galeord@galegroup.com
URL: http://www.galegroup.com.; http://www.gale.com.
Contact: Sheila Dow, Editor, dow@gale.com.
Desc: More than 160,000 fax numbers and nearly 50,000 e-mail addresses for businesses, government agencies, and other institutions and organizations. *Type:* Directory.

National Telecommunications and Information Administration

U.S. Department of Commerce - National Telecommunications and Information Administration
Office of Policy Coordination
   and Management
14th and Constitution Ave. NW
Washington, DC 20230
E-mail: webmaster@ntia.doc.gov
URL: http://www.ntia.doc.gov/
Desc: The home of the National Telecommunications and Information Administration contains a wealth of information about the U.S. government's telecommunication policies, the National Information Infrastructure, or general background about the administration. *Type:* Database.

National Telephone Cooperative Association— Washington Report

National Telephone Cooperative Association
2626 Pennsylvania Ave. NW   Ph: (202)298-2300
Washington, DC 20037-1695   Fax: (202)298-2320
E-mail: frs@ntca.org.
Contact: Matthew Green, Editor; Jill O'Rourke, Editor.
Desc: Covers legislative and regulatory developments in telecommunications, such as price-cap regulation, subsidizing, and actions of the Federal Communications Commission (FCC). *Type:* Newsletter.

North American Fax Directory

Dial-A-Fax Directories Corp.
930 Fox Pavilion   Ph: (215)887-5700
Jenkintown, PA 19046   Fax: (215)887-7076
E-mail: berylwolk@aol.com
Contact: Rich Seifert, Editor.
Desc: Approximately 209,000 companies that possess facsimile machines. *Type:* Directory.

North American Telecom NewsWatch

United Communications Group
11300 Rockville Pike, Ste. 1100   Ph: (301)287-2700
Rockville, MD 20852-3030   Free: 800-929-4824
   Fax: (301)287-2049
E-mail: customer@ucg.com
Contact: Fritz McCormick, Editor, mccormick@org.com.
Desc: Disseminates information on telecommunications culled from numerous sources. Organizes material into the following categories: management, marketplace, hardware/software, technologies, mergers and acquisitions, carriers, finance, regulation and legislation, and international developments. *Type:* Newsletter.

1394 Newsletter

Information Gatekeepers Inc.
214 Harvard Ave.   Ph: (617)232-3111
Boston, MA 02134   Free: 800-323-1088
           Fax: (617)734-8562
E-mail: info@igigroup.com
URL: http://wwwigigroup.com
Desc: Covers developments in the telecommunications market, including new technology. *Type:* Newsletter.

The Orbiter

Society of Satellite Professionals International
225 Reinekers Ln.   Ph: (703)549-8696
Alexandria, VA 22314   Fax: (703)549-9728
URL: http://www.sspi.com
Contact: Carol McKibben, Editor, (818)678-2001, fax: (818)775-2906.
Desc: Covers member and chapter activities, developments in commercial satellite communications technology and applications, and activities of corporate sponsors. Recurring features include a calendar of events, reports of meetings, and columns titled Chairman's Corner, Letter from the President, and Corporate Corner. *Type:* Newsletter.

Pacific Telecommunications Council

2454 S. Beretania St., Ste. 302 Ph: (808)941-3789
Honolulu, HI 96826   Fax: (808)944-4874
E-mail: info@ptc.org
URL: http://www.ptc.org/
Contact: Richard J. Barber, Exec.Dir.
Desc: Organizations and professionals involved as providers, users, policymakers, and analysts in telecommunications development in the Americas, Oceania, and Asia. *Type:* Association.

The PCIA Washington Bulletin

Personal Communications Industry Association
500 Montgomery St., Ste. 700 Ph: (703)739-0300
Alexandria, VA 22314-1561 Free: 800-759-0300
          Fax: (703)836-1608
Contact: Shary Denes, Editor.
Desc: Reports on legislative and regulatory news on the personal communication industry. *Type:* Newsletter.

PCS Week

Phillips Business Information, Inc.
1201 Seven Locks Rd., Ste. 300 Ph: (301)340-1520
Potomac, MD 20854   Free: 888-707-5809
          Fax: (301)340-3847
E-mail: clientservices.pbi@phillips.com
URL: http://www.phillips.com; http://www.phillips.com/cgi/catalog/info?PCS.
Contact: John Sullivan, Editor, jsullivan@phillips.com; Joelle Martin, Publisher.
Desc: Covers new technologies and products, corporate activities, international markets, and standards and regulations related to the microcell and personal communication network (PCN). *Type:* Newsletter.

Personal Communication Industry Association

500 Montgomery St. Ste. 700 Ph: (703)739-0300
Alexandria, VA 22314   Free: 800-759-0300
URL: http://www.pcia.com
Contact: Emmett B. Kitchen, Jr., Pres.
Desc: Works to protect, serve, and lead members of the mobile communications industry in their endeavors to effectively provide communications support to the U.S. business community. Acts as the industry advocate in shaping telecommunications policy to protect the mobile communications industry; serves both the industry and the government as a resource for education, information, and spectrum management. *Type:* Association.

Personal Communications Industry Association

500 Montgomery St., No. 700 Ph: (703)739-0300
Alexandria, VA 22314   Fax: (703)836-1608
URL: http://www.pcia.com
Contact: Jay Kitchen, Pres.
Desc: Carriers licensed by the Federal Communications Commission providing Personal Communications Services, paging and cellular services to the public; companies providing products and services to the industry. Promotes development of industry standards; publishes market studies; represents members before Congress, the administration, and the FCC; sponsors an award-winning national public relations campaign on behalf of the industry. Maintains the PCIA Science and Education Foundation including the LifePage Program, which makes pagers available to patients awaiting organ transplants. *Type:* Association.

Phillips Telephone Industry Directory

Phillips Business Information, Inc.
1201 Seven Locks Rd., Ste. 300 Ph: (301)340-1520
Potomac, MD 20854   Free: 888-707-5809
          Fax: (301)340-3847
E-mail: clientservices.pbi@phillips.com
Desc: Approximately 4,600 manufacturers, distributors, suppliers, telecommunication carriers, regulatory agencies, consulting and marketing research agencies, law firms, and trade associations involved in telecommunications. *Type:* Directory.

PhoneDisc New York & New England

PhoneDisc USA Corp.
70 Atlantic Dr.   Ph: (617)639-2900
PO Box 648   Free: 800-284-8353
Marblehead, MA 01945
E-mail: info@phonedisc.com
Desc: CD-Rom. Over 12 million residences and businesses in New York and New England. *Type:* Directory.

PhoneDisc QuickRef

PhoneDisc USA Corp.
70 Atlantic Dr.   Ph: (617)639-2900
PO Box 648   Free: 800-284-8353
Marblehead, MA 01945
E-mail: info@phonedisc.com
Desc: CD-Rom. 100,000 businesses; state, federal, and local governments; libraries; colleges and universities; embassies; law firms; industrial manufacturers; associations; organizations, etc. *Type:* Directory.

PhoneDisc USA Residential and Business

PhoneDisc USA Corp.
70 Atlantic Dr.   Ph: (617)639-2900
PO Box 648   Free: 800-284-8353
Marblehead, MA 01945
E-mail: info@phonedisc.com
Desc: CD-Rom. Nearly 85 million addresses in the United States. *Type:* Directory.

Premise Wiring

Information Gatekeepers Inc.
214 Harvard Ave.   Ph: (617)232-3111
Boston, MA 02134   Free: 800-323-1088
           Fax: (617)734-8562
E-mail: info@igigroup.com
URL: http://wwwigigroup.com
Desc: Contains news and analysis on the markets, technology, and applications of fiber optics for data communications, process control, building and campus wiring, high speed data links such as Fibre Channel, ATM, SCSI, ESCON, HIPPI, and plastic optical fiber. *Type:* Newsletter.

RBOC Update

Worldwide Videotex
PO Box 3273   Ph: (561)738-2276
Boynton Beach, FL 33424-3273
E-mail: markedit@juno.com
URL: http://www.wvpubs.com
Desc: Contains news of the Regional Bell Operating Companies (RBOCs). Covers gate way operations, efforts to offer additional services, videotex trials, marketing strategies, and the operation of new services. *Type:* Newsletter.

Report on Electronic Commerce

Telecommunications Reports International, Inc.
1333 H St. NW   Ph: (202)842-3022
Washington, DC 20005   Free: 800-822-6338
          Fax: (202)842-1875
E-mail: customerservice@tr.com
URL: http://www.tr.com; http://www.tr.com.
Contact: Jerry Ashworth, Editor.
Desc: Offers news, analysis, and practical information on strategies involving transaction processing, interactive advertising, regulations, home-banking and shopping, security, and standards. Recurring features include interviews, news of research, reports of meetings, and book reviews. *Type:* Newsletter.

Report on Wireless

Evert Communications Ltd.
1296 Carling Ave.   Ph: (613)728-4621
Ottawa, ON, Canada K1Z 7K8 Fax: (613)728-0385
E-mail: newsdesk@evert.com; services@evert.com
URL: http://www.evert.com/wireless.
Contact: Carole Jeffrey, Subscriber Services; Debbie Lawes, Senior.Ed.
Desc: Covers information on the wireless communications industry including technology, product development, licensing, manufacturing, distribution, regulation, and public policy, product research, equipment manufacturing and distribution. Recurring features include news of research and a calendar of events. *Type:* Newsletter.

Russian Telecom Newsletter

Information Gatekeepers Inc.
214 Harvard Ave.   Ph: (617)232-3111
Boston, MA 02134   Free: 800-323-1088
           Fax: (617)734-8562
E-mail: info@igigroup.com
URL: http://wwwigigroup.com
Contact: Dr. Paul Polishuk, Publisher; Prof. Sergei L. Galkin, Editor; Prof. Yuri B. Vymorkovl, Editor.
Desc: Covers the telecommunications industry in Russia, including competition, government regulations, international business and ventures, cellular, satellites, and market intelligence. Also features new products and conference reports. *Type:* Newsletter.

Satellite Broadcasting and Communications Association

225 Reinekers Ln., Ste. 600 Ph: (703)549-6990
Alexandria, VA 22314   Free: 800-541-5981
          Fax: (703)549-7640
E-mail: info@sbca.org
URL: http://www.sbca.com
Contact: Charles C. Hewitt, Pres.
Desc: Equipment manufacturers of satellite earth stations; dealers and distributors in satellite earth station equipment; satellite service and software and program providers; other interested individuals. Purposes are to: promote the interest of the public in satellite communications; eliminate misconceptions about the use of satellite earth stations; establish the rights of satellite earth station users to view programs from satellites. *Type:* Association.

Shosteck Cellular Strategies

Church Street Publishing, Inc.
PO Box 6271   Ph: (401)941-6447
Providence, RI 02940-6271   Free: 800-717-5847
E-mail: rluhr@aol.com; jzweig1@aol.com.
Contact: Herschel Shosteck, President.
Desc: Provides analysis of the U.S. and world cellular/wireless industries, based on the market research of Herschel Shosteck Associates. *Type:* Newsletter.

Sidney Allinson's HOTLINE

Sidney Allinson
660 Cairndale Rd.   Ph: (250)478-0457
Victoria, BC, Canada V9C 3L3   Fax: (250)478-0457
E-mail: sid@islandnet.com
Contact: Sidney Allinson, Editor and Publisher, sid@islandnet.com.
Desc: Publishes information of interest to writers, trainers, Internet site managers, seminar leaders, copywriters, business consultants, and executives in business and government. Recurring features include news of research, news of educational opportunities, and book reviews. *Type:* Newsletter.

SONET/SDH/MAN

Information Gatekeepers Inc.
214 Harvard Ave.   Ph: (617)232-3111
Boston, MA 02134   Free: 800-323-1088
                          Fax: (617)734-8562
E-mail: info@igigroup.com
URL: http://wwwigigroup.com
Contact: Paul Polishuk, Editor.
Desc: Covers developments, products, competition, technology, and standards in the metropolitan area network (MAN) market. *Type:* Newsletter.

South American Telecom

Information Gatekeepers Inc.
214 Harvard Ave.   Ph: (617)232-3111
Boston, MA 02134   Free: 800-323-1088
                          Fax: (617)734-8562
E-mail: info@igigroup.com
URL: http://wwwigigroup.com
Contact: Nomi Burstein, Managing Editor.
Desc: Discusses the telecommunications industry in South America. *Type:* Newsletter.

State & Local Communications Report

Telecommunications Reports International, Inc.
1333 H St. NW, Ste. 100 E   Ph: (202)842-3006
Washington, DC 20005   Free: 800-822-6338
                              Fax: (202)842-3047
E-mail: customerservice@tr.com
URL: http://www.brp.com; http://www.tr.com.
Contact: Lynn Stanton, Editor.
Desc: Provides coverage of the U.S. domestic telecommunications industry. *Type:* Newsletter.

State Telephone Regulation Report

Telecom Publishing Group
Warren Publishing, Inc.
2115 Ward Ct. NW   Ph: (202)872-9200
Washington, DC 20037   Fax: (202)293-3435
Contact: Herb Kirchhoff, Editor, (517)726-1401, fax: (517)726-1404, herbkir@mvcc.com.
Desc: Examines state telephone regulatory issues and decisions. Covers major state-level telephone lawsuits and court action, providing complete citations of lawsuits and decisions. *Type:* Newsletter.

Systems & Network Management Report

DataTrends Publications Inc.
PO Box 4460   Ph: (703)779-0574
Leesburg, VA 20177   Free: 800-766-8130
                      Fax: (703)779-2267
E-mail: dtrends@ix.netcom.com
Contact: Jeff Caruso, Editor.
Desc: Covers distributed systems management tools and platforms. *Type:* Newsletter.

Technology Voice

Ottawa Carleton Research Institute (OCRI)
36 Steacte Dr.   Ph: (613)592-8160
Kanata, ON, Canada K2K 2A9   Fax: (613)592-8163
URL: http://www.ocri.ca/ocrinews.html.
Contact: Gerry Turcotte, Editor.
Desc: Promotes the activities and accomplishments of the Ottawa-Carelton research community and the Institute. Focuses on communications, telecommunications, microelectronics, and bioscience. *Type:* Newsletter.

Tele-Service News

Worldwide Videotex
PO Box 3273   Ph: (561)738-2276
Boynton Beach, FL 33424-3273
E-mail: markedit@gnn.com; markedit@juno.com.
URL: http://www.wvpubs.com.
Desc: Reports on the products, services, research, development, and business plans of Regional Bell Operating Companies (RBOCs), long distance carriers, and other telecommunications and telephone industry vendors. Covers electronic data interchange (EDI), cellular service, fiber optics, gateways, and government regulations. *Type:* Newsletter.

Telecom Calendar Newsletter

Information Gatekeepers Inc.
214 Harvard Ave.   Ph: (617)232-3111
Boston, MA 02134   Free: 800-323-1088
                          Fax: (617)734-8562
E-mail: info@igigroup.com
URL: http://wwwigigroup.com
Contact: Paul Polishuk, Editor.
Desc: Acts as a 10-year calendar covering trade shows, conferences, and major seminars worldwide concerned with telecommunications, electronics, Integrated Services Digital Network (ISDN), computers, fiber optics, optoelectronics, and end user applications. *Type:* Newsletter.

Telecom & Network Security Review

Pasha Publications
1600 Wilson Blvd., Ste. 600   Ph: (703)528-1244
Arlington, VA 22209   Free: 800-424-7821
                                Fax: (703)528-4926
E-mail: mailer@pasha.com
Contact: Beth McConnell, Editor and Publisher.
Desc: Spotlights exclusive coverage of toll fraud, network security, and internal phone abuse. Recurring features include letters to the editor. *Type:* Newsletter.

Telecom Perspectives

Gardner Group
56 Top Gallant Rd.   Ph: (203)316-1010
Stamford, CT 06904   Fax: (203)316-1100
Contact: Melanie Posey, Editor, poseyma@mcgraw-hill.com.
Desc: Analyzes competition and strategic developments in the telecommunications industry. Provides insight as to what competitors are doing and how to respond to market developments. *Type:* Newsletter.

Telecom Standards

Information Gatekeepers Inc.
214 Harvard Ave.   Ph: (617)232-3111
Boston, MA 02134   Free: 800-323-1088
                          Fax: (617)734-8562
E-mail: info@igigroup.com
URL: http://wwwigigroup.com
Contact: Paul Polishuk, Editor.
Desc: Communicates on telecommunications standards activities worldwide. Also contains important information on status, availability of standards, and "how to" obtain standards. *Type:* Newsletter.

Telecom Tacity Network Services (TTNS)

Phillips Infotech
1111 Marlkress Rd., Ste. 101   Ph: (609)424-1100
Cherry Hill, NJ 08003   Free: 800-678-4642
                                 Fax: (609)424-1999
E-mail: cborn@phillips.com
URL: http://www.phillips-infotech.com.
Contact: Kathleen Adams, Editor.
Desc: Describes and evaluates communication services available in the U.S. marketplace. *Type:* Newsletter.

Telecom Tactics

Phillips Business Information, Inc.
1201 Seven Locks Rd., Ste. 300   Ph: (301)340-1520
Potomac, MD 20854   Free: 888-707-5809
                                   Fax: (301)340-3847
E-mail: clientservices.pbi@phillips.com
Contact: Larry Feidelman, Associate Publisher.
Desc: Electronic information service that provides competitive intelligence on telecommunications industry leaders and services in 14 different areas from pay telephone services to satellite operators. *Type:* Newsletter.

Telecommunications Act Information Service

Telecommunications Reports International, Inc.
1333 H St. NW   Ph: (202)842-3022
Washington, DC 20005   Free: 800-822-6338
                       Fax: (202)842-1875
E-mail: customerservice@tr.com
URL: http://www.tr.com
Contact: Erma Wehrenburg, Senior Mgr.
Desc: Offers attorneys, business executives, government officials, and researchers convenient access to the entire Telecommunications Act. *Type:* Newsletter.

Telecommunications Alert

United Communications Group
11300 Rockville Pike, Suite   Ph: (301)816-8950
   1100
Rockville, MD 20852
E-mail: joshcohen@ucg.com
URL: http://www.ucg.com
Desc: Contains the complete text of Telecommunications Alert, a newsletter summarizing developments in data, voice, and video communications from more than 200 sources, including Communications Daily, FCC Week, ISDN Strategies, and Personal Computing. Covers regulations and legislation, technical developments, new product announcements, and business news, including mergers, acquisitions, joint ventures, and corporate financial performances. *Available:* The Gale Group; Bell & Howell Information and Learning; Center for Communications Management Information (CCMI), Q-Tell 1000. *Type:* Database.

Telecommunications Directory

Gale Group Inc.
27500 Drake Rd.   Ph: (248)699-4253
Farmington Hills, MI 48331-   Free: 800-877-GALE
    3535   Fax: (248)699-8070
E-mail: galeord@galegroup.com
URL: http://www.galegroup.com.; http://www.gale.com.
Contact: Kim Forster, Editor, Kim.Forster@gale.com.
Desc: Approximately 3,800 national and international voice and data communications networks, electronic mail services, teleconferencing facilities and services, facsimile services, Internet access providers, videotex and teletext operations, transactional services, local area networks, audiotex services, microwave systems/networkers, satellite facilities, and others involved in telecommunications, including related consultants, advertisers/marketers; associations, regulatory bodies, and publishers. *Type:* Directory.

Telecommunications Industry Association

2500 Wilson Blvd., Ste. 300   Ph: (703)907-7700
Arlington, VA 22201-3834   Fax: (703)907-7728
E-mail: mlesso@tia.eia.org
Contact: Matthew J. Flanigan, Pres.
Desc: Companies that manufacture products for or provide services to the telecommunications industry. Promotes the industry. *Type:* Association.

Telecommunications Magazine

Horizon House Publications, Inc.
685 Canton St.   Ph: (781)769-9750
Norwood, MA 02062   Fax: (781)769-9884
E-mail: jed@jedonline.com; tcs@telecoms.mag.com.
URL: http://www.telecoms-mag.com.
Contact: Jack Pazzanese, Assoc. Pub.; Tom Valovic, Editor-in-Chief; William Bazzy, President.
Desc: Magazine on international voice, data, and image networks communications. *Type:* Periodical.

Telecommunications Reports International

Telecommunications Reports International, Inc.
1333 H St. NW   Ph: (202)842-3022
Washington, DC 20005   Free: 800-822-6338
    Fax: (202)842-1875
E-mail: customerservice@tr.com
URL: http://www.tr.com; http://www.tr.com.
Contact: John Alden, Editor, jalden@tr.com.
Desc: Provides a global perspective on telecommunications. Covers "trade battles," industry and government actions, Intelsat and the International Telecommunications Union (ITU), international telecom tariffs and services, financial developments, and privatizations. *Type:* Newsletter.

Telecommunications Reports with TR Daily

Telecommunications Reports International, Inc.
1333 H St. NW   Ph: (202)842-3022
Washington, DC 20005   Free: 800-822-6338
    Fax: (202)842-1875
E-mail: customerservice@tr.com
URL: http://www.tr.com; http://www.tr.com.
Contact: Victoria A. Mason, Editor, vmason@tr.com.
Desc: Documents weekly events in the domestic and international common carrier industry. Focuses on developments in the regulatory, legal, and legislative areas, but also provides news on labor unions, new products and services, personnel changes, and various trade associations. *Type:* Newsletter.

Telecommunications Research and Action Center

PO Box 27279   Ph: (202)263-2950
Washington, DC 20038-7279   Fax: (202)408-1134
E-mail: trac@trac.org

URL: http://www.trac.org
Contact: Sam Simon, Counsel.
Desc: A citizen-supported, nonprofit organization. Improves the quality of electronic media through concerted public action. Conducts projects designed to identify public interest in the area of radio, television, cable television, telephone, and new technologies. *Type:* Association.

TeleCommunicator

Association of Telemessaging Services International
1200 19th St. NW, Ste. 300   Ph: (202)429-5151
Washington, DC 20036-2422   Fax: (202)223-4579
E-mail: atsi@dc.sba.com
Contact: Herta Tucker, Editor.
Desc: Contains news concerning telephone company, legislative and governmental actions, and Association activities. *Type:* Newsletter.

Telecommuting Review

Gil Gordon Associates
10 Donner Ct.   Ph: (732)329-2266
Monmouth Junction, NJ 08852
URL: http://www.gilgordon.com.
Contact: Gil Gordon, Editor.
Desc: Focuses on telecommuting work-at-home applications, products, and services. Describes telecommuting programs at various companies and provides contacts' name and phone numbers for additional information. *Type:* Newsletter.

TeleCompetition Report

Telecommunications Reports International, Inc.
1333 H St. NW   Ph: (202)842-3022
Washington, DC 20005   Free: 800-822-6338
    Fax: (202)842-1875
E-mail: customerservice@tr.com
URL: http://www.tr.com; http://www.tr.com.
Contact: Brian Hammond, Editor.
Desc: Covers the competitive local exchange telecommunications business. Discusses regulatory, legal, financial, strategic, and technological issues. *Type:* Newsletter.

Telemedia News and Views

Opus Research, Inc.
345 Chenery St.   Ph: (415)239-0244
San Francisco, CA 94131   Fax: (415)239-6932
Contact: Daniel N. Miller, Editor/Publisher; Mark A. Plakias, Contributing Editor; Peter Krasilousky, Contributing Editor.
Desc: Serves as "the only source for in-depth analysis and behind-the-scenes coverage of Telemedia markets and trends," covering automated voice services, including Voice Information Services (Audiotex), pay-per-call services, Talking Yellow Pages, and Talking Newspapers, as well as inbound long-distance services which employ 800 or 900 numbers. Recurring features include applications, products, markets, personnel, regulation, and notices of publications available. *Type:* Newsletter.

Telephone IP News

Worldwide Videotex
PO Box 3273   Ph: (561)738-2276
Boynton Beach, FL 33424-3273
E-mail: markedit@gnn.com; markedit@juno.com.
URL: http://www.wvpubs.com.
Desc: Provides information provider (IP) industry news for various telephone services, such as 900, 970, and 976 numbers. Covers new products, public service commission rulings, and marketing strategies. *Type:* Newsletter.

Telephone Pioneers of America

930 15th St., Rm. 1200   Ph: (303)571-1200
Denver, CO 80202   Fax: (303)572-0520
URL: http://www.telephone-pioneers.org/
Contact: Jack Sawka, Exec.Dir.
Desc: Active and retired telecommunications employees. *Type:* Association.

TeleStrategies—Insight

TeleStrategies, Inc.
1355 Beverly Rd., Ste. 110   Ph: (703)734-7050
Mc Lean, VA 22101-3623
URL: http://www.telestrategies.com.
Contact: Rene Banglesdorf, Editor, fax: (703)556-8445, rene@telestragies.com.
Desc: Carries industry analyses. *Type:* Newsletter.

T.I.E. News

Special Interest Group for Telecommunications International Society for Technology in Education (ISTE)
1787 Agate St.   Ph: (541)346-4414
Eugene, OR 97403-1923   Free: 800-336-5191
    Fax: (541)346-5890
E-mail: iste@oregon.uoregon.edu
Contact: Trevor Owen, Editor.
Desc: Addresses the issues of instructional use of telecommunications in the classroom. *Type:* Newsletter.

TR Wireless

Telecommunications Reports International, Inc.
1333 H St. NW, Ste. 100 E   Ph: (202)842-3006
Washington, DC 20005   Free: 800-822-6338
    Fax: (202)842-3047
E-mail: customerservice@tr.com
URL: http://www.brp.com; http://www.tr.com.
Contact: Victoria Mason, Editor-in-Chief; Wilson Dizard, Editor, wdizard@tr.com.
Desc: Covers developments in cellular, personal communications, and other wireless communications areas. Provides information on legislative and government regulatory activities and monitors actions of major telecommunications corporations. *Type:* Newsletter.

TRIO Network

Telecommunications Research Institute of Ontario (TRIO)
340 March Rd., Ste. 400   Ph: (613)592-9211
Kanata, ON, Canada K2K 2E4   Fax: (613)592-8163
E-mail: telecom@trio.ca
URL: http://www.trio.ca/trionet.htm.
Contact: Rob Prebble, Editor.
Desc: Reports telecommunications research activities within the Institute. Profiles graduate students and member companies. *Type:* Newsletter.

UTC, The Telecommunications Association

1140 Connecticut Ave. NW,   Ph: (202)872-0030
    Ste. 1140   Fax: (202)872-1331
Washington, DC 20036
URL: http://www.utc.org
Contact: William R. Moroney, Pres./CEO.
Desc: Electric, gas, water, steam utilities, and gas pipelines. Assists in the development and improvement of telecommunications media used in the operation of energy utilities and gas pipelines; promotes cooperation among energy utilities and gas pipelines in all matters concerning telecommunications; represents member interests before federal and state agencies. *Type:* Association.

Utilities Telecommunications News

Information Gatekeepers Inc.
214 Harvard Ave.
Boston, MA 02134

Ph: (617)232-3111
Free: 800-323-1088
Fax: (617)734-8562

E-mail: info@igigroup.com
URL: http://wwwigigroup.com
Contact: Nomi Burstein, Managing Editor.
Desc: Focuses on the role of utilities in telecommunications. Topics include government and regulations, business, and the Internet. *Type:* Newsletter.

Veteran Wireless Operators Association—News Letter

Veteran Wireless Operators Association, Inc.
46 Murdock St.
Fords, NJ 08863

Ph: (908)225-2539

Contact: Edward F. Pleuler, Jr., Editor.
Desc: Carries articles regarding wireless communications systems aboard merchant/military vessels and reminiscences from member veteran wireless operators. Recurring features include letters to the editor, interviews, book reviews, and notices of publications available. *Type:* Newsletter.

Virtual Office Market & Technology Newsletter

Information Gatekeepers Inc.
214 Harvard Ave.
Boston, MA 02134

Ph: (617)232-3111
Free: 800-323-1088
Fax: (617)734-8562

E-mail: info@igigroup.com
URL: http://wwwigigroup.com
Desc: Covers telecommunications, networking equipment, and services market for the virtual office. Explores new technologies, issues, and trends for companies wanting to provide services, products or people on demand—temporary or virtual workers. *Type:* Newsletter.

Voice Technology and Services News

Phillips Business Information, Inc.
1201 Seven Locks Rd., Ste. 300
Potomac, MD 20854

Ph: (301)340-1520
Free: 888-707-5809
Fax: (301)340-3847

E-mail: clientservices.pbi@phillips.com
Contact: Paige M. Albiniak, Editor, palbiniak@phillips.com.
Desc: Provides comprehensive news and analysis of the voice technology marketplace. Features business strategies, new product developments and enhanced technologies of voice processing and related markets. *Type:* Newsletter.

Washington Telecom News

Phillips Business Information, Inc.
1201 Seven Locks Rd., Ste. 300
Potomac, MD 20854

Ph: (301)340-1520
Free: 888-707-5809
Fax: (301)340-3847

E-mail: clientservices.pbi@phillips.com
Contact: Ray Py, Editor.
Desc: Provides "weekly news and analysis of regulations, legislation, and judicial decisions" affecting the telecommunications industry. Recurring features include columns titled Contracts and The Spectrum Report. *Type:* Newsletter.

Washington Telecom Week

Inside Washington Publishers
PO Box 7167
Ben Franklin Sta.
Washington, DC 20044-7167

Ph: (703)416-8500
Free: 800-424-9068

E-mail: iwp@iwpnews.com
Contact: Joe Burey, Publisher; Jim Rogers, Chief Editor; Heather Weaver, Associate Editor.
Desc: "The Inside Washington look at federal telecommunications policymaking." Covers phone, video, cable and satellite companies. *Type:* Newsletter.

The Washington Weekly Report

Organization for Promotion and Advancement of Small Telecommunications Companies (OPASTCO)
21 Dupont Circle NW, Ste. 700
Washington, DC 20036

Ph: (202)659-5990
Fax: (202)659-4619

E-mail: twwr@opastco.org.
Contact: Jessica Earle, Editor, jme@opastco.org.
Desc: Monitors legislative and regulatory issues and actions affecting telecommunications in rural areas. Includes news of the organization and its members. *Type:* Newsletter.

WDM Newsletter

Information Gatekeepers Inc.
214 Harvard Ave.
Boston, MA 02134

Ph: (617)232-3111
Free: 800-323-1088
Fax: (617)734-8562

E-mail: info@igigroup.com
URL: http://wwwigigroup.com
Desc: Provides worldwide coverage on technology, markets and applications. *Type:* Newsletter.

Wireless Business and Finance

Phillips Business Information, Inc.
1201 Seven Locks Rd., Ste. 300
Potomac, MD 20854

Ph: (301)340-1520
Free: 888-707-5809
Fax: (301)340-3847

E-mail: clientservices.pbi@phillips.com
Contact: Mike Maynard, Senior Editor, mmaynard@phillips.com; Joelle Martin, Publisher.
Desc: Provides news and analysis on investment opportunities and financial activities in the worldwide wireless industry. Includes updates on corporate activities, industry initiatives, and financial backers. *Type:* Newsletter.

Wireless Cellular

Information Gatekeepers Inc.
214 Harvard Ave.
Boston, MA 02134

Ph: (617)232-3111
Free: 800-323-1088
Fax: (617)734-8562

E-mail: info@igigroup.com
URL: http://wwwigigroup.com
Contact: Paul Polishuk, Editor.
Desc: Covers international developments in the wireless telecommunications industry, including new products, market opportunities and forecasts, regulations and standards, procurements, mergers and acquisitions, and applications. *Type:* Newsletter.

Wireless Connections

GTE Telecommunications Services Inc.
201 N. Franklin St., 7th Fl.
Tampa, FL 33602

Ph: (813)273-3939
Fax: (813)273-3280

Contact: Mike Flanagan, Marketing Communications Manager.
Desc: Directed toward GTE Telecommunication Services' customers; aims to provide "thoughtful, relevant information about the wireless industry and GTE's innovative line of more than 20 advanced software services and solutions." Communicates news of products, the wireless communications industry, and upcoming special events. Recurring features include interviews. *Type:* Newsletter.

Wireless Data & Messaging

Paul Kagan Associates, Inc.
126 Clock Tower Pl.
Carmel, CA 93923

Ph: (831)624-1536
Fax: (831)625-3225

E-mail: info@kagan.com
Desc: Contains analysis of private and public values of wireless messaging companies. Includes trends and statistics. *Type:* Newsletter.

Wireless Data News

Phillips Business Information, Inc.
1201 Seven Locks Rd., Ste. 300
Potomac, MD 20854

Ph: (301)340-1520
Free: 888-707-5809
Fax: (301)340-3847

E-mail: clientservices.pbi@phillips.com
Contact: Randy Sukow, Senior Editor, rsukow@phillips.com; Joelle Martin, Publisher & Vice President.
Desc: Provides analysis of technology, applications, marketing, and competition in the mobile communications industry. Scope is international. *Type:* Newsletter.

Wireless Local Loop

Information Gatekeepers Inc.
214 Harvard Ave.
Boston, MA 02134

Ph: (617)232-3111
Free: 800-323-1088
Fax: (617)734-8562

E-mail: info@igigroup.com
URL: http://wwwigigroup.com
Contact: Paul Polishuk, Editor.
Desc: Covers developments in technology, business activity, and regulations for the wireless telecommunications spectrum. *Type:* Newsletter.

Wireless PCS

Information Gatekeepers Inc.
214 Harvard Ave.
Boston, MA 02134

Ph: (617)232-3111
Free: 800-323-1088
Fax: (617)734-8562

E-mail: info@igigroup.com
URL: http://wwwigigroup.com
Contact: Paul Polishuk, Editor.
Desc: Covers developments in the wireless personal communications network (PCN) industry, including new products and technology, standards and regulation, market opportunities and forecasts, procurements, mergers and acquisitions, and applications. *Type:* Newsletter.

Wireless Satellite & Broadcasting

Information Gatekeepers Inc.
214 Harvard Ave.
Boston, MA 02134

Ph: (617)232-3111
Free: 800-323-1088
Fax: (617)734-8562

E-mail: info@igigroup.com
URL: http://wwwigigroup.com
Contact: Paul Polishuk, Editor.
Desc: Covers developments in technology, business activity, and regulation for the statellite and broadcasting telecommunications industry. *Type:* Newsletter.

Wireless Tactics

Phillips Infotech
1111 Marlkress Rd., Ste. 101
Cherry Hill, NJ 08003

Ph: (609)424-1100
Free: 800-678-4642
Fax: (609)424-1999

Contact: Don Stuart, Editor.
Desc: Describes and evaluates wireless communications products and services available in the U.S. marketplace. *Type:* Newsletter.

Wireless Telecom Investor

Paul Kagan Associates, Inc.
126 Clock Tower Pl.
Carmel, CA 93923

Ph: (831)624-1536
Fax: (831)625-3225

E-mail: info@kagan.com
Contact: George Niesen, Editor.
Desc: Provides analysis of private and public values of cellular telephone paging, PCS and other wireless telecom companies. Includes coverage of databases of subscribers, market penetrations, market potential, and industry growth. *Type:* Newsletter.

Wireless Telecommunications Newsletter

Information Gatekeepers Inc.
214 Harvard Ave.   Ph: (617)232-3111
Boston, MA 02134   Free: 800-323-1088
                    Fax: (617)734-8562
E-mail: info@igigroup.com
URL: http://wwwigigroup.com

Contact: Paul Polishuk, Editor.

Desc: Covers developments in the telecommunications industry, including new products and technology, regulations and standards, building applications, market opportunities and forecasts, and procurements. *Type:* Newsletter.

Wiretalk

Underwriters Laboratories, Inc.
333 Pfingsten Rd.   Ph: (847)272-8800
Northbrook, IL 60062-2096   Fax: (847)272-0472
E-mail: northbrook@ul.com
URL: http://www.ul.com/about/wtalk/index.html.

Contact: John Koenig, Managing Editor; Tom Guida, Technical Editor.

Desc: Publishes news and information on wire and cable certification programs. *Type:* Newsletter.

World Communications Directory and Buyers Guide

Counterpart, Inc.
2200 Clarendon Blvd., Ste.   Ph: (703)516-7000
  1410   Fax: (703)516-7005
Arlington, VA 22201

Desc: 15,000 international communications companies. *Type:* Directory.

Worldwide Telecom

Worldwide Videotex
PO Box 3273   Ph: (561)738-2276
Boynton Beach, FL 33424-3273
URL: http://www.wvpubs.com.

Desc: Focuses on activities of U.S. corporations regarding international telecommunications markets and products. *Type:* Newsletter.

Television

The Andy Griffith Show Rerun Watchers Club

9 Music Sq. S, Ste. 146
Nashville, TN 37203-3203
URL: http://www.mayberry.com/tagsrwc

Contact: Jim Clark, Contact.

Desc: Individuals devoted to watching and promoting the airing of reruns of the The Andy Griffith Show. (The show, which originally ran from 1960 to 1968, is aired daily in about 100 television markets nationwide.) Encourages members to write to television stations that air reruns of the show and express their appreciation. Facilitates communication among members on matters relating to the show. *Type:* Association.

The Cable Guide

TVSM, INC.
309 Lakeside Dr.   Ph: (215)443-9300
Horsham, PA 19044   Fax: (215)675-9837
URL: http://www.tottv.com.

Contact: Jay Gissen, Editor; Alan Wragg, Publisher.

Desc: Cable TV program guide. *Type:* Periodical.

Cable Optics Monthly Newsletter

Information Gatekeepers Inc.
214 Harvard Ave.   Ph: (617)232-3111
Boston, MA 02134   Free: 800-323-1088
                    Fax: (617)734-8562
E-mail: info@igigroup.com
URL: http://wwwigigroup.com

Contact: Nomi Burstein, Editor.

Desc: Covers developments, products, competition, technology, and standards for the use of fiber optics in the cable television industry. *Type:* Newsletter.

Cable TV Advertising

Paul Kagan Associates, Inc.
126 Clock Tower Pl.   Ph: (831)624-1536
Carmel, CA 93923   Fax: (831)625-3225
E-mail: info@kagan.com

Contact: Paul Kagan, Editor.

Desc: Reports on commercial-time sales by cable television systems and networks. Covers law and legislation concerning television advertising. *Type:* Newsletter.

Cable TV Finance

Paul Kagan Associates, Inc.
126 Clock Tower Pl.   Ph: (831)624-1536
Carmel, CA 93923   Fax: (831)625-3225
E-mail: info@kagan.com

Contact: George Niesen, Editor.

Desc: Focuses on commercial, insurance, and bank loans to cable operators. Discusses financing activity and trends in the cable television industry. *Type:* Newsletter.

Cable TV Investor

Paul Kagan Associates, Inc.
126 Clock Tower Pl.   Ph: (831)624-1536
Carmel, CA 93923   Fax: (831)625-3225
E-mail: info@kagan.com

Contact: Paul Kagan, Editor.

Desc: Concerns investment in cable television systems and publicly held cable television stocks. Discusses stock performance and announces cable system sales. *Type:* Newsletter.

Cable TV Law Reporter

Paul Kagan Associates, Inc.
126 Clock Tower Pl.   Ph: (831)624-1536
Carmel, CA 93923   Fax: (831)625-3225
E-mail: info@kagan.com

Contact: George Niesen, Editor.

Desc: Reports on law and legislation concerning the cable television industry. Gives summaries of cases recently in court and discusses the case decisions and issues raised by these decisions. *Type:* Newsletter.

Cable TV and New Media Law & Finance

Leader Publications
New York Law Publishing Company
345 Park Ave., South   Ph: (212)545-6170
New York, NY 10010   Free: 800-888-8300
                    Fax: (212)696-1848
E-mail: leader@ljextra.com

Contact: David M. Rice, Editor; Michael Botein, Editor.

Desc: Provides forecasts and analyses of important judicial, legislative, and financial developments affecting cable television and related telecommunications industries. Discusses topics such as franchising and cable company funding. *Type:* Newsletter.

Cable TV Programming

Paul Kagan Associates, Inc.
126 Clock Tower Pl.   Ph: (831)624-1536
Carmel, CA 93923   Fax: (831)625-3225
E-mail: info@kagan.com

Contact: Paul Kagan, Editor.

Desc: Discusses programming on both basic networks and cable television. Contains news of new programming on specific cable networks and analyzes their strategies. *Type:* Newsletter.

Cable TV Regulation

Paul Kagan Associates, Inc.
126 Clock Tower Pl.   Ph: (831)624-1536
Carmel, CA 93923   Fax: (831)625-3225
E-mail: info@kagan.com

Contact: George Niesen, Editor.

Desc: Concerned with cable franchises and renewals; includes news of franchising/renewal laws legislation pertaining to franchising and renewals. *Type:* Newsletter.

Cable TV Technology

Paul Kagan Associates, Inc.
126 Clock Tower Pl.   Ph: (831)624-1536
Carmel, CA 93923   Fax: (831)625-3225
E-mail: info@kagan.com

Contact: Paul Kagan, Editor.

Desc: Concentrates on technical advances in the cable television area. Reports the upgrade and the rebuilding of existing systems. *Type:* Newsletter.

Cabletter

Cabletelevision Advertising Bureau (CAB)
830 3rd Ave., FRNT 2   Ph: (212)508-1200
New York, NY 10022-7522   Fax: (212)832-3268
URL: http://www.cabletvadbureau.com.

Contact: Scott Pesner, Editor.

Desc: Offers information on the Bureau's activities in the cable industry, concentrating on the areas of research, local/national sales, and the value of cable television as an advertising medium. Recurring features include news of research, reports of meetings, and notices of publications available. *Type:* Newsletter.

Computer Audit Update

Elsevier Science Inc.
655 Avenue of the Americas   Ph: (212)989-5800
New York, NY 10010   Fax: (212)633-3990
E-mail: usinfo@elsevier.com
URL: http://www.elsevier.com

Desc: Addresses issues in the auditing of electronic data processing systems. Covers security, disaster recovery, audit methods and types, legislation, and aspects of auditing specific software. *Type:* Newsletter.

Contemporary Theatre, Film, and Television

Gale Group Inc.
27500 Drake Rd.   Ph: (248)699-4253
Farmington Hills, MI 48331-   Free: 800-877-GALE
  3535   Fax: (248)699-8070
E-mail: galeord@galegroup.com
URL: http://www.galegroup.com.; http://www.gale.com.
Contact: Joshua Kondek, Editor, joshua.kondek@gale.com.

Desc: In 23 volumes, more than 7,500 leading and up-and-coming performers, directors, writers, producers, designers, managers, choreographers, technicians, composers, executives, and dancers in the United States, Canada, Great Britain and the world. Each volume includes updated biographies for people listed in previous volumes and in "Who's Who in the Theatre," which this series has superseded. *Type:* Directory.

Dark Shadows Fan Club

PO Box 69104, Sept. NET   Ph: (213)650-5112
West Hollywood, CA 90069
E-mail: gayboylaca@hotmail.com
URL: http://www.members.tripod.com/~dsfc/
Contact: Louis Wendruck, Pres.
Desc: Fans of the gothic television serial Dark Shadows, which aired on the ABC television network from 1966-71. *Type:* Association.

Dark Shadows Official Fan Club

PO Box 92   Ph: (973)762-7208
Maplewood, NJ 07040
Contact: Ann Wilson, Exec.Dir.
Desc: Clubs in three countries that publish newsletters and magazines dedicated to the preservation of the memory of the 1960s television show Dark Shadows and the 1990s revival series. Seeks to keep members informed regarding the lives of cast members. Donates convention proceeds to various charities; Maintains archives of memorabilia issued in relation to the show and the subsequent MGM movies House of Dark Shadows and Night of Dark Shadows. *Type:* Association.

Daytime TV

Sterling/Macfadden Partnership
233 Park Ave. S.   Ph: (212)780-3500
New York, NY 10003   Fax: (212)780-3555
Contact: Lucille Giordano, Editor; Morton Tuller, Publisher; Mel Goldman, Advertising Mgr.
Desc: Magazine featuring daytime television's programs and personalities. *Type:* Periodical.

Digital Television

Paul Kagan Associates, Inc.
126 Clock Tower Pl.   Ph: (831)624-1536
Carmel, CA 93923   Fax: (831)625-3225
E-mail: info@kagan.com
Desc: Provides information on strategies the broadcast, cable, satellite, home video, and computer industries have for implementing digital technology. Includes news on HDTV products and new HDTV programming. *Type:* Newsletter.

Encyclopedia of Television

Fitzroy Dearborn Publishers
919 N. Michigan Ave.   Ph: (312)587-0131
Chicago, IL 60611   Free: 800-850-8102
    Fax: (312)587-1049
E-mail: fitzroyd@aol.com
URL: http://www.fitzroydearborn.com
Contact: Horace Newcomb, Editor.
Desc: English-language television shows, topics, genres, networks, personalities, and institutions. *Type:* Directory.

Interactive Television

Paul Kagan Associates, Inc.
126 Clock Tower Pl.   Ph: (831)624-1536
Carmel, CA 93923   Fax: (831)625-3225
E-mail: info@kagan.com
Desc: Contains information on developments, analysis, and projections on interactive television. Reports on cable, broadcast, computer, satellite, telephone, and wireless technology. *Type:* Newsletter.

ITA:/research

Association for Interactive Media
1301 Connecticut Ave. NW,   Ph: (202)408-0008
   5th Fl.   Fax: (202)408-0111
Washington, DC 20036
E-mail: info@interactivehq.org
Contact: Steven Pastorkovich, Editor.
Desc: Features reports and updates on the latest in new media market research. Offers exposure to the latest findings on the consumer market for interactive television. *Type:* Newsletter.

ITVA

International Television Association (ITVA)
6311 N. O'Connor Rd., Ste.   Ph: (972)869-1112
   230   Fax: (972)869-2980
Irving, TX 75039
E-mail: itvahq@worldnet.att.net
URL: http://www.itva.org; http://www.itva.org.
Contact: Rene Chapin, Dir. of Communications.
Desc: Concerned with the video industry and visual communications. Carries news about industry trends and issues, the Association, members, and the annual conference. *Type:* Newsletter.

Munsters and the Addams Family Fan Club

PO Box 69A04, Dept. NET   Ph: (213)650-5112
West Hollywood, CA 90069
E-mail: gayboylaca@hotmail.com
URL: http://www.members.tripod.com/~mafc/
Contact: Louis Wendruck, Pres.
Desc: Fan club for individuals interested in the Addams Family and the Munsters television shows. Facilitates information exchange. *Type:* Association.

NAB TV Today

National Association of Broadcasters
1771 N St. NW   Ph: (202)429-5477
Washington, DC 20036-2891   Free: 800-368-5644
    Fax: (202)775-3515
E-mail: nabpubs@nab.org; sbloomqu@nab.org.
Contact: Tom Butts, Editor, tbutts@nab.org.
Desc: Covers the television industry from legislative, regulatory, political, technical, and management perspectives. Features pertinent industry news and reports of NAB conferences, products, services, and awards competitions. *Type:* Newsletter.

The Pay TV Newsletter

Paul Kagan Associates, Inc.
126 Clock Tower Pl.   Ph: (831)624-1536
Carmel, CA 93923   Fax: (831)625-3225
E-mail: info@kagan.com
Contact: George Niesen, Editor.
Desc: Carries reports and economic analyses of the pay television industry. Includes an annual cable/pay census issue, 10-year projections for pay cable and pay-per-view (PPV), PPV event analyses, and discussions of the economics of pay TV networks. *Type:* Newsletter.

Pocket Station Listing Guide

Publications Dept.
National Association of Television Program Executives (NATPE International)
2425 Olympic Blvd., Ste. 550E   Ph: (310)453-4440
Santa Monica, CA 90404   Fax: (310)453-5258
Contact: Ron Gold, Editor, rongold@natpe.org; Maria Sussman, Editor.
Desc: 1,500 network-affiliated, independent, and public television stations in the U.S., Canada, and Latin America. *Type:* Directory.

Private Cable Investor

Paul Kagan Associates, Inc.
126 Clock Tower Pl.   Ph: (831)624-1536
Carmel, CA 93923   Fax: (831)625-3225
E-mail: info@kagan.com
Desc: Covers topics on private cable (satellite master antenna) television. Includes information on finance, investment, marketing, and legal issues. *Type:* Newsletter.

Program Guide

Community Communications, Inc.
11510 E. Colonial Dr.   Ph: (407)273-2300
Orlando, FL 32817   Fax: (407)273-1519
Contact: Elena Ahrens, Editor; Wendy McCabe, Executive Editor, wmfe@magicnet.net.
Desc: Provides members with a monthly public television program guide. *Type:* Newsletter.

Satellite TV Week

Fortuna Communications Corp.
180 S. Fortuna Blvd.   Ph: (707)725-6951
PO Box 308   Free: 800-345-8876
Fortuna, CA 95540-0308   Fax: (707)725-4311
E-mail: satellit@humboldt1.com.
Contact: James E. Scott, Editor, fax: (707)725-9639, editor@humboldt1.com; Patrick O'Dell, Publisher; George Bryant, Advertising Dir.
Desc: Magazine listing satellite TV programming and industry related news. *Type:* Periodical.

Soap Opera Digest

Soap Opera Digest
745 5th Ave.   Ph: (212)332-0250
New York, NY 10151   Fax: (212)332-0252
Contact: Lynn Leahey, Editor; Linda Vaughan, Publisher.
Desc: Magazine providing daytime television viewers with a comprehensive look at a particular soap opera theme. *Alt. Contact:* 45 West 25th St., New York, NY 10010; telephone: (212)229-8410; fax: (212)645-0683. *Type:* Periodical.

Soap Opera Magazine

Soap Opera Magazine, Inc.
600 SE Coast Ave.
Lantana, FL 33462
Contact: Joseph PolIcy, Editor.
Desc: Magazine reporting on daytime television soap operas. *Type:* Periodical.

Soap Opera Update

Bauer Publishing Co.
270 Sylvan Ave.   Ph: (201)569-6699
Box 1648   Fax: (201)569-6264
Englewood Cliffs, NJ 07632
Desc: Magazine including show synopses, news, review, indepth invterviews, and games. *Type:* Periodical.

The Sponsors Report

Joyce Julius and Associates, Inc.
3785 Varsity Dr.   Ph: (313)971-1900
Ann Arbor, MI 48108   Fax: (313)971-2059
Contact: Eric Wright, Managing Editor.
Desc: Features statistical analyses of the television exposure received by corporations sponsoring sports and special event, national telecasts. *Type:* Newsletter.

Syndication News

Copley Entertainment Inc.
PO Box 751   Ph: (203)259-0525
Fairfield, CT 06430   Fax: (203)259-3321
E-mail: copley@snet.net
Contact: Paul R. Krumins, Editor.
Desc: Provides analysis of the television industry, including programming trends, ratings, and demographics. Also features business discussion about network, cable, syndication, and new technologies. *Type:* Newsletter.

Telemedium

National Telemedia Council
120 E. Wilson St.   Ph: (608)257-7712
Madison, WI 53703   Fax: (608)257-7714
E-mail: ntelemedia@aol.com
URL: http://danenet.wicip./ntc; http://danenet.wicip.
org/NTC.
Contact: Marieli Rowe, Editor, (608)257-7712, fax:
(608)257-7714.
Desc: Features include information on media literacy, suggested reading lists, trends in the media, a "teacher idea exchange (TIE)" and articles of special interest. Authors include top leaders and educators in the media literacy field. *Type:* Newsletter.

Television & Cable Action Update

Warren Publishing, Inc.
2115 Ward Ct. NW   Ph: (202)872-9200
Washington, DC 20037   Fax: (202)296-4397
E-mail: warrenpub@mindspring.com
URL: http://www.telecommunications.com
Contact: Susan Seiler, Managing Editor.
Desc: Reports on broadcast and cable industry activity. Discusses new stations, systems, franchises and applications, and changes and sales to all listings. *Type:* Newsletter.

Television & Cable Factbook

Warren Publishing, Inc.
2115 Ward Ct. NW   Ph: (202)872-9200
Washington, DC 20037   Fax: (202)296-4397
E-mail: warrenpub@mindspring.com
URL: http://www.telecommunications.com
Contact: Michael C. Taliaferro, Managing Editor.
Desc: Commercial and noncommercial television stations and networks, including educational, low-power and instructional TV stations, and translators; United States cable television systems; cable and television group owners; national sales representatives of television stations; equipment manufacturers and distributors; program and service suppliers; brokerage and financing companies; consulting engineers; brokers; attorneys practicing before the Federal Communications Commission; cable system sales representatives; international coverage. *Type:* Directory.

Television Index

Television Index, Inc.
1515 Broadway, 14th Fl.   Ph: (212)536-5185
Brooklyn, NY 11228   Fax: (212)536-8868
Contact: Jonathan Miller, Editor.
Desc: Covers all commercial network series debuting or returning during the current week, with production credits, and history. Includes all network specials, variety shows, and documentaries, with credits and sponsors. *Type:* Newsletter.

The Toronto Sun

Sun Media Corp.
333 King St. E   Ph: (416)947-2222
Toronto, ON, Canada M5A   Fax: (416)947-2441
  3X5
URL: http://www.canoe.ca.
Contact: Lorrie Goldstein, Editor; Mike Strobel, Managing Editor; Doug Knight, Publisher; Peter Leupen, Advertising Dir.; Peter O'Sullivan, Editor-in-Chief; Julie Kirsh, Manager.
Desc: General newspaper. *Type:* Periodical.

TV Blueprint

Wilen Media Corp.
135 Oval Dr.   Ph: (516)439-5000
Islandia, NY 11722-1406   Fax: (516)439-4536
Contact: John Diaz, EVP; Darrin Wilen, President,
wilen@wilenmedia.com.

Desc: Magazine serving cable television subscribers and companies. *Type:* Periodical.

TV Data

Northway Plaza   Ph: (518)792-9914
Queensbury, NY 12804   Free: 800-338-TVDT
                                  Fax: 800-755-6786
E-mail: tvdata@tvdata.com.
URL: http://www.tvdata.com.
Contact: Arthur Bassin, Pres./CEO; Kathleen F. Wern, VP-Sales; Bill Callahan, Asst. VP-Sales; Kenneth Carter, VP-Bus. Dev./CFO; Roger K. Moore, VP-Operations/ Exec. Ed.; Amy Mann, Managing Editor; Kevin Joyce, Interactive & Online Services Product Mg; Gordon Sacks, Entertainment Features Syndicate Ed.; Al McGarthy, Entertainment Features Syndicate Asst. M; Glenn Teichman, Entertainment Features Syndicate Asst. M.
Desc: Distributes television programming information and entertainment features. *Alt. Contact:* Northway Plaza, Queensbury, NY 12804; telephone: (518)792-9914; fax: 800-755-6786; toll-free: 800-338-TVDT. *Type:* Periodical.

TV Guide

News America Publishing, Inc.
200 Madison Ave.   Ph: (212)293-8500
New York, NY 10016-3903   Fax: (212)633-2938
Contact: Anthea Disney, Editor; Barry Golson, Advertising Mgr.; Roger Youman, Editor; Mary G. Berner, Publisher; Joseph W. Cece, Editor; Wayne P. Campanelli, Advertising Mgr.
Desc: Television entertainment and information magazine. *Type:* Periodical.

TV Host Monthly

TVH, Inc.
3935 Jonestown Rd.   Ph: (717)657-1700
PO Box 1665   Free: 800-922-4678
Harrisburg, PA 17105   Fax: (717)657-2921
E-mail: tvh@tvhost.com
Contact: Dave Stefanic, CEO; Frank Dillahey, VP; Lou Pirnik, Advertising Dir.; Curt Jantz, Pres./Pub.
Desc: Special interest publication serving cable television customers and cable television system companies. *Type:* Periodical.

TV News

Community Publications of America Inc.
80 8th Ave., Ste. 315   Ph: (212)243-6800
New York, NY 10011   Fax: (212)243-7457
Contact: Liz Farkas, Editor; Allan Horwitz, Publisher.
Desc: Magazine covering television, sports, music, concerts, records, books, films, and TV and movie stars. Also includes consumer articles. *Type:* Periodical.

TV & Politics Watch

Peter Donhowe
17 E. University, No. 630   Ph: (217)355-0444
Champaign, IL 61820
Contact: Peter DonHowe, Editor, p.donhowe@uiuc.edu.
Desc: Analyzes politics as represented through television. *Type:* Newsletter.

TV Program Investor

Paul Kagan Associates, Inc.
126 Clock Tower Pl.   Ph: (831)624-1536
Carmel, CA 93923   Fax: (831)625-3225
E-mail: info@kagan.com
Contact: George Niesen, Editor.
Desc: Monitors trends in television program syndication. Reports market data on the monetary value of television programs and networks, as well as the value of public and private companies engaged in the television program business. *Type:* Newsletter.

TV Week Magazine

Canada Wide Magazines & Communications Ltd.
4180 Lougheed Hwy., 4th Fl.   Ph: (604)299-7311
Burnaby, BC, Canada V5C 6A7   Fax: (604)299-9188
E-mail: circulation@canadawide.com
Contact: Robin Roberts, Editor; Peter Legge, Publisher; Harry van Hemmen, Sales Mgr.
Desc: BC's premier television information & entertainment guide. *Type:* Periodical.

Ultimate TV

UltimateTV
15821 Ventura Blvd., Ste. 410   Ph: (818)995-6808
Encino, CA 91436   Fax: (818)379-4747
URL: http://www.ultimatetv.com
Desc: Ultimate TV contains a wealth of information concerning television. *Type:* Database.

Videazimut Clips

Videazimut
3680, rue Jeanne-Mance, bureau   Ph: (514)982-6660
430   Fax: (514)982-6122
Montreal, PQ, Canada H2X
  2K5
E-mail: videaz@web.org
Contact: Sylvia Roy, Editor.
Desc: Promotes audiovisual communication for democracy and development. Publishes in English, French, and Spanish. *Type:* Newsletter.

Video Competition Report

Telecommunications Reports International, Inc.
1333 H St. NW, Ste. 100 E   Ph: (202)842-3006
Washington, DC 20005   Free: 800-822-6338
                                  Fax: (202)842-3047
E-mail: customerservice@tr.com
URL: http://www.brp.com; http://www.tr.com.
Contact: Jeff Williams, Editor.
Desc: Follows cable TV and telecommunication strategies for delivery of video services, technologies and standards, business and financial news, convergence of cable-telco-computer industries, service innovations, market trials, federal and state regulatory developments, and legal actions. *Type:* Newsletter.

Warren's Cable Regulation Monitor

Warren Publishing, Inc.
2115 Ward Ct. NW   Ph: (202)872-9200
Washington, DC 20037   Fax: (202)296-4397
E-mail: warrenpub@mindspring.com
URL: http://www.telecommunications.com
Contact: Patrick Ross, Editor.
Desc: Tracks rate increases by local cable systems, broken down into groups of comparable systems, and all subscriber complaints filed and resulting FCC decisions. Intended to help cable operators and regulators determine whether their proposed rate increases are reasonable in light of the 1992 Cable Act and subsequent rate reduction mandates. *Type:* Newsletter.

The White Dot

The White Dot
PO Box 577257
Chicago, IL 60657-7257
E-mail: info@whitedot.org
URL: http://www.whitedot.org.
Contact: Jean Lotus, Editor, jlotus@whitedot.org.
Desc: Directed toward "TV-free households." Contains testimonials of persons who have eliminated television totally from their homes and offers tips on how to succeed, social benefits of life without the "boob tube", and other related topics. *Type:* Newsletter.

Tennis

American Tennis Association
8100 Cleary Blvd.
Plantation, FL 33324-1370
Contact: Albert A. Tucker, Exec.Dir.
Desc: Persons interested in tennis. Promotes and develops tennis among blacks. Supports training programs to develop Teaching Professionals. *Type:* Association.

Tennis
Golf Digest/Tennis, Inc.
5520 Park Ave.   Ph: (203)373-7000
PO Box 0395   Free: 800-451-2386
Trumbull, CT 06611-0395   Fax: (203)371-2505
URL: http://www.tennis.com.
Contact: Donna Doherty, Editor; Gordon Medenica, Publisher; Rick Beispel, Advertising Mgr.
Desc: Tennis magazine. *Type:* Periodical.

Tennis Industry Association
200 Castlewood Dr.   Ph: (843)686-3036
North Palm Beach, FL 33408   Fax: (843)686-3078
E-mail: tiakurt@aol.com
URL: http://www.sportlink.com
Contact: Kurt Kamperman, Pres.
Desc: Manufacturers of tennis equipment, apparel, and footwear; court builders and architects; accessory manufacturers; suppliers and distributors. To promote and encourage participation in recreational tennis; to work for the betterment of the game. *Type:* Association.

Tennis—Places to Play/Camps & Clinics Issue
Golf Digest/Tennis, Inc.
5520 Park Ave.   Ph: (203)373-7000
PO Box 0395   Free: 800-451-2386
Trumbull, CT 06611-0395   Fax: (203)371-2505
Contact: Donna Doherty, Editor.
Desc: List of over 800 tennis resorts and tennis camps. *Type:* Directory.

Tennis Travelogue Special Advertising Section
Miller Sports Group, LLC
810 Seventh Ave., 4th Fl.   Ph: (212)636-2700
New York, NY 10019
Desc: Guide to hotels and resorts with tennis facilities in North America and the Islands; listings limited to advertisers. *Type:* Directory.

Tennis USTA
New York Times Magazine Group
5 John Clarke Rd.
Newport, RI 02840
Contact: Robert Moseley, Editor; Gordon Medenica, Publisher.
Desc: Magazine for U.S. Tennis Association members. *Alt. Contact:* 5520 Park Ave., Trumbull, CT 06611; telephone: (203)373-7155; fax: (203)371-2199; 5520 Park Ave., Trumbull, CT 06611; telephone: (203)373-7115; fax: (203)371-2199. *Type:* Periodical.

Tennis Week
Tennis Week
341 Madison Ave., Ste.600   Ph: (212)808-4750
New York, NY 10017   Free: 800-800-TENN
                                   Fax: (212)983-6302
E-mail: tennisweek@tennisweek.com.
Contact: Eugene L. Scott, Editor and Publisher; Carole Graebner, Advertising Dir.; Roberta Faig, Advertising Mgr.
Desc: Tennis news publication including features, business and politics of the game, rankings, results, schedules coverage of camps, resorts, and tournaments. *Alt. Contact:* 341 Madison Ave., Ste. 600, New York, NY 10017; telephone: (212)808-4750; fax: (212)983-6302; toll-free: 800-800-TENN. *Type:* Periodical.

United States Professional Tennis Association
1 USPTA Centre   Ph: (713)978-7782
3535 Briarpark Dr.   Free: 800-877-8248
Houston, TX 77042   Fax: (713)978-7780
E-mail: uspta@uspta.org
URL: http://www.uspta.org
Contact: Tim Heckler, CEO.
Desc: Professional tennis instructors, tennis-teaching professionals and college coaches. Seeks to improve tennis instruction in the United States; maintains placement bureau and library. *Type:* Association.

United States Professional Tennis Registry
PO Box 4739   Ph: 800-421-6289
Hilton Head Island, SC 29938   Fax: (803)686-2033
URL: http://www.usptr.org
Contact: Daniel Santorum, Exec.Dir. & CEO.
Desc: Tests, certifies, and registers international tennis teaching professionals. *Type:* Association.

United States Tennis Association
70 W. Red Oak Ln.   Ph: (914)696-7000
White Plains, NY 10604   Fax: (914)696-7167
Contact: Julia A. Levering, Pres.
Desc: Federation of local tennis clubs, educational institutions, recreation departments, and other groups and individuals interested in the promotion of tennis. Works to develop tennis as a means of healthful recreation and physical fitness and maintain high standards of fair play and sportsmanship. *Type:* Association.

United States Tennis Association, Southern Section
3850 Holcomb Bridge Rd., No.   Ph: (770)368-8200
305
Norcross, GA 30092
URL: http://www.usta-sta.com
Contact: John Callen, Exec.Dir.
Desc: Individuals interested in the sport of tennis in the southeastern U.S. Provides education to the public on the benefits of playing tennis. *Type:* Association.

USA Tennis - NJTL
70 W. Red Oak Ln.   Ph: (914)696-7000
White Plains, NY 10604-3602   Fax: (914)696-7029
E-mail: myrick@usta.com
URL: http://www.usta.com
Contact: Jeneise Myrick, Natl.Admin.
Desc: A community-based introductory youth team program designed to provide all youngsters access to tennis. Motivates and maintains youngsters' interest in not only tennis, but in education . The program introduces youngsters to basic strokes, uses a simple scoring method and promotes team play. *Type:* Association.

WTA Tour Players Association
133 1st St. NE   Ph: (813)895-5000
St. Petersburg, FL 33701   Fax: (813)894-1982
Contact: Bart McGuire, CEO & Exec.Dir.
Desc: Professional women tennis players. Purpose is to represent members with regard to professional tournaments. *Type:* Association.

Testing

American College Testing
2201 N. Dodge St.   Ph: (319)337-1000
Box 168   Fax: (319)339-3021
Iowa City, IA 52243
Contact: Richard L. Ferguson, Pres.
Desc: Provides guidance-oriented assessment and research programs for students, schools, colleges, universities, voca-

tional-technical institutes, and scholarship agencies. ACT Assessment Program, which consists of a profile questionnaire, interest inventory, and four 35-60 minute tests in English, mathematics, reading, and scientific reasoning, is completed by more than 1,500,000 students annually. It provides colleges and universities with information used in admission, placement, and advising. *Type:* Association.

The College Board
1560 Sherman Ave., Ste. 1001   Ph: (847)866-1700
Evanston, IL 60201-4805   Fax: (847)866-9280
E-mail: mro@collegeboard.org
URL: http://www.collegeboard.org
Contact: Donald M. Stewart, Pres.
Desc: Public and private institutions and associations of higher education; public and private secondary schools; K-12 school systems and associations serving secondary education. Provides direction, coordination, services, and research in facilitating the transition of students from high school to college. Sponsors a variety of guidance, admissions, and placement examinations throughout the school year. *Type:* Association.

Educational Records Bureau
220 East 42nd St.   Ph: (212)672-9800
New York, NY 10017   Fax: (212)370-4096
URL: http://www.erbtest.org
Contact: Dr. Thomas F. Maguire, Pres.
Desc: Independent and nonpublic schools, international schools, and suburban public schools. Provides student testing services and research to member schools; ability/achievement test, writing assessment, and independent school admissions program. *Type:* Association.

Educational Testing Service
Rosedale Rd.   Ph: (609)921-9000
Princeton, NJ 08541   Fax: (609)734-5410
E-mail: etsinfo@ets.org
URL: http://www.ets.org
Contact: Nancy S. Cole, Pres.
Desc: Educational measurement and research organization, founded by merger of the testing activities of American Council on Education, Carnegie Foundation for the Advancement of Teaching, and The College Board. *Type:* Association.

International Society for Performance Improvement
1300 L St. NW, Ste. 1250   Ph: (202)408-7969
Washington, DC 20005   Fax: (202)408-7972
E-mail: info@ispi.org
URL: http://www.ispi.org
Contact: Richard D. Battaglia, Exec.Dir.
Desc: Leading international association dedicated to improving productivity and performance in the workplace through the application of performance and instructional technologies. Offers education and employment referral service. Publishes books and periodicals. *Type:* Association.

Quality—Buyers Guide for Test, Inspection, Measurement and Evaluation Issue
Cahners Business Information
2000 Clearwater Dr.   Ph: (630)320-7000
Oak Brook, IL 60523   Free: 800-826-6270
                                   Fax: (630)320-7373
URL: http://www.qualitymag.com.
Contact: Gary Parr, Editor.
Desc: List of manufacturers and distributors of quality control equipment for measurement, inspection, data analysis, evaluation, and destructive and nondestructive testing; also lists testing laboratories, consultants, software and training organizations. *Type:* Directory.

Secondary School Admission Test Board

CN 5339   Ph: (609)683-4440
Princeton, NJ 08543   Fax: (609)683-1702
URL: http://www.ssat.org/ssat
Contact: Regan Kenyon, President.
Desc: Administers entrance examinations for 600 independent schools in the U.S. and in foreign countries to 50,000 candidates. The tests are administered at centers throughout the world. *Type:* Association.

TEST Engineering & Management—Annual Buyers' Guide Issue

The Mattingley Publishing Co., Inc.
3756 Grand Ave., Ste. 205   Ph: (510)839-0909
Oakland, CA 94610-1545   Fax: (510)839-2950
E-mail: testmag@crl.com; testmag@mattingley-publ.com.
Contact: Eve Mattingley-Hannigan, Editor.
Desc: List of 200 suppliers of equipment and services for reliability/qualification testing and environmental simulation purposes. *Type:* Directory.

Textiles

Amalgamated Clothing and Textile Workers Union

1710 Broadway   Ph: (212)265-7000
New York, NY 10019   Fax: (212)265-3415
Contact: Jay Mazor, Pres.
Desc: AFL-CIO; Canadian Labour Congress. Sponsors Sidney Hillman Foundation and Rieve-Pollock Foundation. *Type:* Association.

American Association of Textile Chemists and Colorists

PO Box 12215   Ph: (919)549-8141
Research Triangle Park, NC   Fax: (919)549-8933
27709-2215
URL: http://www.aatcc.org
Contact: John Y. Daniels, Exec.Dir.
Desc: Recognized as an authority for test methods including: colorfastness to light, washing, perspiration, and pleating; damage caused by retained chlorine; crease resistance; shrinkage; durable press; water resistance; biological and dyeing properties. *Type:* Association.

American Textile Reporter

International Society of Industrial Fabric Manufacturers
PO Box 1369   Ph: (704)861-2063
Kings Mountain, NC 28086-
1369
Desc: Covers topics of interest about the textile industry. *Type:* Newsletter.

ARTA News

American Reuseable Textile Association (ARTA)
PO Box 801   Ph: (941)644-7477
Mulberry, FL 33860
Contact: William Carrsul, Editor.
Desc: Concerned with applications of reusable textiles. Recurring features include a calendar of events and reports of meetings. *Type:* Newsletter.

California Wool Growers Newsletter

California Wool Growers Association
1225 H. St., No. 101   Ph: (916)444-8122
Sacramento, CA 95814-1910
Contact: Jay Wilson, Editor.
Desc: Provides information and news to California's lamb and wool producers. Recurring features include news of research, a calendar of events, reports of meetings, and news of educational opportunities. *Type:* Newsletter.

Connecticut Magazine

Communications International
35 Nutmeg Dr.   Ph: (203)380-6600
Trumbull, CT 06611   Fax: (203)380-6612
E-mail: ctmag@pcnet.com.
URL: http://www.connecticut.com.
Contact: Charles Monagan, Editor; Michael Mims, Publisher.
Desc: Magazine for Connecticut residents. Includes articles on politics, fashion, business, home interiors, restaurant reviews, the arts, and real estate. *Type:* Periodical.

Cotton Council International

1521 New Hampshire Ave.   Ph: (202)745-7805
Washington, DC 20036   Fax: (202)483-4040
E-mail: cottonusa@cotton.org
URL: http://www.cottonusa.org
Contact: Allen Terhaar, Exec.Dir.
Desc: Representatives of all segments of the U.S. cotton industry. International cotton sales promotion organization cooperating with cotton interests in foreign countries. *Type:* Association.

Cotton's Week

National Cotton Council
PO Box 12285   Ph: (901)274-9030
Memphis, TN 38182   Fax: (901)725-0510
URL: http://www.cotton.org
Contact: Fred W. Middleton, Editor, fmiddleton@cotton.org.
Desc: Reports legislative, administrative, and economic actions and issues affecting the cotton industry from the field to the fabric. Recurring features include news of research and reports of meetings. *Type:* Newsletter.

Council of the United Textile Workers of America

1369 W. Andrew Johnson Hwy   Ph: (423)317-8000
Ste. 200   Fax: (423)317-8003
Morristown, TN 37814
E-mail: cutwa@aol.com
Contact: James Altom, Pres.
Desc: AFL-CIO. *Type:* Association.

Crochet Digest

House of White Birches
306 E. Parr Rd.   Ph: (219)589-4000
Berne, IN 46711   Fax: (219)589-8093
Contact: Carl H. Muselman, Publisher; Arthur K. Muselman, Publisher; John Robinson, President; Vivian Rothe, Director; Laura Scott, Editor.
Desc: Magazine containing crochet patterns for afghans, doilies, toys, clothing, holiday decorations, bazaar items, fashion, children, and home. *Type:* Periodical.

Crochet World

House of White Birches
306 E. Parr Rd.   Ph: (219)589-4000
Berne, IN 46711   Fax: (219)589-8093
URL: http://www.whitebirches.com
Contact: Susan Hankins, Editor; George Hague, Advertising Mgr.; John Robinson, CEO; Vivian Rothe, Editorial Director; Scott Moss, Marketing Director.
Desc: Magazine containing crochet ideas and patterns, including toys, afghans, dolls, doilies, clothing, and household accessories. *Type:* Periodical.

Davison's Gold Book

Davison Publishing Co., Inc.
PO Box 1289   Ph: (704)785-8700
Concord, NC 28026   Free: 800-328-4766
    Fax: (704)785-8701
E-mail: textiles@davisonbluebook.com

URL: http://www.davisonbluebook.com; http://www.davisonbluebook.com.
Contact: Bruce W. Nealy, President.
Desc: Suppliers of equipment, materials, and services for the textile industry. *Type:* Directory.

Fibre Market News

GIE Publishing Co.
4012 Bridge Ave.   Ph: (216)961-4130
Cleveland, OH 44113   Free: 800-456-0707
    Fax: (216)961-0364
Contact: Daniel Sandoval, Editor.
Desc: Focuses on developments affecting the recycled paper industry and current market trends. Recurring features include news of research and educational opportunities, legislative updates, a calendar of events, and meeting reports. *Type:* Newsletter.

Fur Takers of America

7 Garden Ridge   Ph: (812)537-3630
Lawrenceburg, IN 47025
Contact: Marcia Walston, Treas.
Desc: Fur trappers, fur buyers, trapping supply people, hunters, fur dressers, conservationists, and other interested individuals. Seeks to educate trappers in humane methods of trapping and conservation ethics. *Type:* Association.

The Idaho Wool Grower Bulletin

Idaho Wool Growers Association
802 W. Bannock, No. 205   Ph: (208)344-2271
Boise, ID 83702   Fax: (208)336-9447
Contact: Mike Guerry, Publisher; Billie Jean Siddoway, Editor, bsiddowa@agri.state.id.us; Stan Boyd, Editor; Paula St. Jeor, Advertising Mgr.
Desc: Directed towards Idaho wool growers. *Type:* Newsletter.

INDA, Association of the Nonwoven Fabrics Industry

PO Box 1288   Ph: (919)233-1210
Cary, NC 27512   Fax: (919)233-1282
URL: http://www.inda.org
Contact: Ted Wirtz, Pres.
Desc: Primary and secondary manufacturers and marketers of nonwoven fabrics; suppliers of raw materials; institutions and manufacturers of machinery. *Type:* Association.

INDA Communication/Action Network

INDA, Association of the Nonwoven Fabrics Industry
1300 Crescent Green, Ste. 135   Ph: (919)677-0060
Cary, NC 27511   Fax: (919)677-0211
Contact: Peggy Blake, Editor.
Desc: Reports on Association activity in technology, marketing, government relations, and international trade. Remarks: INDA is an acronym for the Association's former name, International Nonwovens and Disposables Association. *Type:* Newsletter.

Industrial Fabrics Association International

1801 County Rd. B W.   Ph: (651)222-2508
Roseville, MN 55113-4061   Free: 800-225-4324
    Fax: (651)631-9334
E-mail: generalinfo@ifai.com
URL: http://www.ifai.com
Contact: Stephen Warner, Pres.
Desc: Fiber producers, weavers, nonwoven producers, coaters, laminators, finishers, and producers and manufacturers of canvas and industrial fabric end products in more than 36 countries. Provides technical, marketing, production, governmental, and public relations services. *Type:* Association.

Inside Textiles

Point Publishing Co., Inc.
PO Box 1309   Ph: (732)295-8258
Point Pleasant, NJ 08742

Contact: Noreen C. Heimbold, Editor.

Desc: Reports on the textile industry worldwide, including data on fiber prices, mill output, and textile use in the apparel industry and elsewhere. Monitors trends, industry earnings, company acquisitions and mergers, and promotions/job changes among industry personnel. *Type:* Newsletter.

Marine Textiles and Upholstery Journal—Buyers Guide Issue

RCM Enterprises, Inc.
2233 University Ave. W., Ste.   Ph: (612)523-0666
410   Fax: (612)523-0665
St. Paul, MN 55114
E-mail: rcmpub@aol.com

Contact: Joe Palowski, Editor.

Desc: Manufacturers and distributors serving the upholstery and marine market with fabric, equipment, and supplies. *Type:* Directory.

The Marker

Natural Colored Wool Growers Association
3012 Sutton Rd.   Ph: (810)797-4155
Lapeer, MI 48446   Fax: (810)797-4155

Contact: Viki Clark, Editor.

Desc: Assists members in the development of colored sheep wool and promotes the usefulness of colored wool products. Discusses such topics as production, sales, and sheep breeding and registration. *Type:* Newsletter.

Miniature Quilts

Chitra Publications
2 Public Ave.   Ph: (717)278-1984
Montrose, PA 18801   Free: 800-628-8244
    Fax: (717)278-2223
E-mail: chitra@epix.net

Contact: Christiane Meunier, Publisher.

Desc: Pattern magazine focusing on miniature quilts. Features techniques and how-to articles. *Type:* Periodical.

National Cotton Council of America

PO Box 820285   Ph: (901)274-9030
Memphis, TN 38182-0285   Fax: (901)725-0510
E-mail: info@cotton.org

Contact: Phillip C. Burnett, Exec.VP.

Desc: Delegates from 19 cotton producing states, named by their respective producer, ginner, warehousemen, merchant, cooperative, textile manufacturer, and cottonseed crusher organizations in each state. Seeks to increase consumption of U.S. cotton and cottonseed products. *Type:* Association.

National Trappers Association

PO Box 3667   Ph: (309)829-2422
Bloomington, IL 61702   Fax: (309)829-7615
E-mail: trappers@aol.com
URL: http://www.nationaltrappers.com

Contact: Craig Spoores, Pres.

Desc: Harvesters of furbearers (muskrat, fox, coyote, mink, beaver, raccoon, bobcat, and others) for the purpose of wildlife management, animal damage control, and outdoor recreation. Promotes sound environmental education programs and conservation of natural resources. *Type:* Association.

National Wool Market Review

Livestock and Seed Division
Agricultural Marketing Service
U.S. Department of Agriculture
711 O St.   Ph: (970)353-9750
Greeley, CO 80631

Contact: Keith Padgett, Editor.

Desc: Provides statistics and other information on the wool industry. Includes reports on wool grades, mill consumption of apparel wool, and price and markets. *Type:* Newsletter.

NAUMD News

National Association of Uniform Manufacturers and Distributors (NAUMD)
1156 Avenue of the Americas   Ph: (212)869-0670
New York, NY 10036   Fax: (212)575-2847
URL: http://www.naumd.com.

Contact: Jackie Rosselli, Editor.

Desc: Reports news that affects the uniform manufacturing and distributing industry. Also discusses Association programs and seminars, committee activities, and governmental trends and regulations. *Type:* Newsletter.

Nonwoven Markets

Miller Freeman, Inc.
600 Harrison St.   Ph: (650)905-2200
San Francisco, CA 94107   Free: 800-227-4675
    Fax: (650)908-6604
E-mail: techlearning_editors@mfi.com
URL: http://www.millerfreeman.com; http://www.nonwovens.com.

Contact: Philip Goldsmith, Exec. Editor, gsmith@mfi.com.

Desc: Covers the international nonwovens industry, including raw material suppliers, converters, and finished product producers. Includes market and company news stories as well as full-length feature Recurring features include reports of meetings, industry prices, and patent news. *Type:* Newsletter.

Quilting Today

Chitra Publications
2 Public Ave.   Ph: (717)278-1984
Montrose, PA 18801   Free: 800-628-8244
    Fax: (717)278-2223
E-mail: chitra@epix.net

Contact: Christiane Meunier, Publisher.

Desc: Magazine featuring original projects and full spectrum of quilts from contemporary art to traditional and antique. *Type:* Periodical.

Rawhide and Leather Braiders Association

Robert D. Stewart
6905 North 2200 West, No.   Ph: (801)649-9481
7-C
Park City, UT 84060-8215

Contact: Robert D. Stewart, Exec. Officer.

Desc: Promotes the rawhide and leather braiding industry. Acts as a forum for the exchange of information between members. Maintains educational programs. *Type:* Association.

Sandy Parker Reports

Sandford Advertising, Inc.
224 W. 30th St.   Ph: (212)947-1144
New York, NY 10001-3904   Fax: (516)791-4751

Contact: Sandy Parker, Publisher.

Desc: Reports on the international fur industry in areas of sales, distribution, retailing, and pricing. *Type:* Newsletter.

Sheep Industry News

American Sheep Industry Association, Inc.
6911 S. Yosemite St.   Ph: (303)771-3500
Englewood, CO 80112-1414   Fax: (303)771-8200
E-mail: info@sheepusa.org
URL: http://www.sheepusa.org.

Contact: Laura Gerhard, Editor/Communications Mgr., lgerhard@sheepusa.org.

Desc: Covers the sheep industry. *Type:* Newsletter.

Textile & Apparel Newsletter

APICS—The Educational Society for Resource Management
5301 Shawnee Rd.   Ph: (703)354-8851
Alexandria, VA 22312   Free: 800-444-2742
    Fax: (703)354-8106
URL: http://www.apics.org.

Contact: David Bowman, Editor, d_bowman@apics-hq.org.

Desc: Covers production, consulting, and manufacturing in the textile and apparel (TA) fields. *Type:* Newsletter.

Textile Processors, Service Trades, Health Care, Professional and Technical Employees International Union

303 E. Wacker Dr., Ste. 1109   Ph: (312)946-0450
Chicago, IL 60601   Fax: (312)946-0453

Contact: Frank A. Scalish, Gen.Pres.
Type: Association.

Textile Technology Digest

Institute of Textile Technology
Roger Milliken Textile Library and Information Services
2551 Ivy Rd.   Ph: (804)296-5511
Charlottesville, VA 22903-4614
E-mail: library@itt.edu

Contact: Adrienne D. Granitz, Director of Library Information Services, (804)296-5511, fax: (804)977-5400, adrienneg@itt.edu.

Desc: Contains approximately 250,000 citations, with abstracts, to worldwide literature of more than 300 journals plus other sources including books, proceedings, and trade literature in the field of textile technology. Covers fibers, yarn production, fabric production, textile finishing, apparel production, methods of testing and measurement, textile mill management, and the textile industry. *Available:* The Dialog Corporation, DIALOG. *Type:* Database.

Traditional Quiltworks

Chitra Publications
2 Public Ave.   Ph: (717)278-1984
Montrose, PA 18801   Free: 800-628-8244
    Fax: (717)278-2223
E-mail: chitra@epix.net

Contact: Christine Meunier, Publisher.

Desc: Offers full-color photos, full-size patterns, and how-to articles on quilting. *Type:* Periodical.

TRI/Princeton

PO Box 625   Ph: (609)924-3150
Princeton, NJ 08542   Fax: (609)683-7836

Contact: Dr. Gale Eaton, Pres.

Desc: Conducts nonproprietary and proprietary scientific research in support of the textile and allied industries. Conducts textile-related education in the physical and engineering sciences at the predoctoral level, in cooperation with Princeton University, and at the postdoctoral level. Disseminates research information through scientific papers, research reports, seminars, technical conferences, and maintenance of a specialized library. *Type:* Association.

Union of Needletrades, Industrial and Textile Employees

1710 Broadway Ph: (212)265-7000
New York, NY 10019 Fax: (212)315-3803
URL: http://www.uniteunion.org
Contact: Jay Mazur, Pres.
Desc: AFL-CIO. *Type:* Association.

United Garment Workers of America

4207 Lebanon Rd. Ph: (615)889-9221
Hermitage, TN 37076 Fax: (615)885-3107
Contact: Dave Johnson, Gen.Pres.
Desc: AFL-CIO. *Type:* Association.

Theater

Alpha Psi Omega

James Fisher
Theater Department Ph: (765)361-6394
Wabash College Fax: (765)361-6341
Crawfordsville, IN 47933
E-mail: fisherj@scholar.wabash.edu
Contact: James Fisher, Exec. Officer.
Desc: Recognition fraternity for men and women in dramatics at four-year colleges and universities. *Type:* Association.

American Conservatory Theater Foundation

30 Grant Ave. Ph: (415)834-3200
San Francisco, CA 94108 Fax: (415)834-3360
Contact: Carey Perloff, Artistic Dir.
Desc: Provides resources for the American Conservatory Theatre which functions as a repertory theatre and accredited acting school, offering a Master of Fine Arts degree. Holds national auditions for the MFA program in Chicago, IL, New York City, and Los Angeles, CA, usually in February. Holds student matinees, school outreach programs, and in-theatre discussions between artist and audiences. *Type:* Association.

Birmingham Children's Theatre

PO Box 1362
Birmingham, AL 35201
E-mail: bct@bct123.org
URL: http://www.bct123.org
Contact: Ms. Theresa Gentle, Pub.Rel.
Desc: Strives to educate, enlighten, and entertain students for pre-school to 12th grade. *Type:* Association.

Contemporary Dramatists

St. James Press, Inc.
27500 Drake Rd. Ph: (248)699-4253
Farmington Hills, MI 48331- Free: 800-877-4253
3535 Fax: (248)699-8069
E-mail: galeord@gale.com
Contact: K. A. Berney, Editor.
Desc: Approximately 450 living dramatists who are writing or have written in the English language. *Type:* Directory.

Delta Psi Omega

James Fisher
Wabash Coll. Ph: (317)361-6394
Theater Department Fax: (765)361-6341
Crawfordsville, IN 47933
E-mail: fisherj@scholar.wabash.edu
Contact: James Fisher, Bus.Mgr.
Desc: Honorary fraternity - men and women, dramatics (junior college). *Type:* Association.

Dramascope

National Association for Drama Therapy
6 Woods Rd. Fax: (203)355-3838
Sherman, CT 06784-1941
E-mail: 103467.1714@compuserve.com
Contact: Nina Strongylou, Editor.
Desc: Publishes news of this Association "founded to establish and uphold high standards of professional competence among drama therapists." Recurring features include reprints of articles, member profiles, a calendar of events, news of research, book reviews, and job listings. Also includes columns titled Board Member Reports and A Letter From the President. *Type:* Newsletter.

Educational Theatre Association

2343 Auburn Ave. Ph: (513)421-3900
Cincinnati, OH 45219-2819 Fax: (513)421-7077
E-mail: info@etassoc.org
URL: http://www.etassoc.org
Contact: Ronald L. Longstreth, Exec.Dir.
Desc: Professional educators, theatre artists working with education, middle school teachers, students, high school teachers and students. Advances theatre arts in high schools. Focuses on strengthening advocacy, student development, and teacher training. *Type:* Association.

Equity News

Actors' Equity Association
165 W. 46th St. Ph: (212)869-8530
New York, NY 10036 Fax: (212)921-8454
Contact: Dick Moore, Editor, (212)719-9570; Helaine Feldman, Editor.
Desc: Covers union meetings and contracts of the Association and supplies other information of significance to professional actors and actresses. Recurring features include letters to the editor, an officer's report, and a pension and health column. *Type:* Newsletter.

Eugene O'Neill Memorial Theater Center

305 Great Neck Rd. Ph: (860)443-5378
Waterford, CT 06385 Fax: (860)443-9653
E-mail: kathyagolio@usa.net
URL: http://www.eugeneoneill.org
Contact: George C. White, Fnd./Chm.
Desc: Persons interested in supporting the center's projects: a museum, theater, library, and school in Waterford, CT; established as a permanent memorial to Eugene O'Neill (1888-1953), U.S. playwright. The Theater Collection includes memorabilia, books, pictures, and reference materials dealing with O'Neill and the American theatre. *Type:* Association.

Friars Club

57 E. 55th St. Ph: (212)751-7272
New York, NY 10022 Fax: (212)355-0217
Contact: Jean Pierre Trebot, Exec.Dir.
Desc: Theatrical writers, movie, television, and radio performers, motion picture and television executives, theatrical agents, and public relations executives. *Type:* Association.

National Association of Theatre Owners

4605 Lankershim Blvd., Ste. Ph: (818)506-1778
340 Fax: (818)506-0269
North Hollywood, CA 91602
E-mail: nato-inc@earthlink.net
Contact: Mary Ann Grasso, Vice Pres. and Exec.Dir.
Desc: Owners, operators, and executives of motion picture theaters. *Type:* Association.

National Collegiate Players

Hamlin University
Department of Theatre and Ph: (651)523-2297
Communication Arts Fax: (651)523-3066
1536 Hewitt Ave.
St. Paul, MN 55104
Contact: Dr. William H. Kimes, Pres.
Desc: Men and women, drama. The emblem of the organization is Pi Epsilon Delta. *Type:* Association.

New England Theatre Conference— Membership Directory and Resource Book

New England Theatre Conference, Inc.
Northeastern University Ph: (617)424-9275
Department of Theatre Fax: (617)424-1057
360 Huntington Ave.
Boston, MA 02115
E-mail: netc@world.std.com
Contact: Corey Boniface, Editor.
Desc: 800 individuals and 100 groups. *Type:* Directory.

Performing Arts

Performing Arts Network
10350 Santa Monica Blvd., No. Ph: (310)839-8000
350 Fax: (310)839-5651
Los Angeles, CA 90025
Contact: Dana Kitaj, Editor; Ed Conn, Publisher; Gilman Kroft, President.
Desc: Edited for theatre and concert-goers in greater Los Angeles, San Francisco and San Diego. The publications supply synopses, scenes and, where appropriate, the musical numbers of plays as well as cast biographies and articles dealing with the background of a particular play and historical/analytical program notes for concerts. It also presents articles of a general nature dealing with music, theatre, film and dance, audio and video. Monthly features include columns on travel, fashion and California real estate. *Alt. Contact:* 10350 Santa Monica Blvd., No. 350, Los Angeles, CA 90025; telephone: (310)839-8000; fax: (310)551-1939. *Type:* Periodical.

Playbill

The Philadelphia Spotlite
3401 N. I St., 5th Fl. Ph: (215)425-2500
Philadelphia, PA 19134 Fax: (215)425-1155
Contact: Joan Alleman, Editor; Ira L. Kamens, Publisher.
Desc: Theater magazine. *Type:* Periodical.

Preview Theater Magazine

Hogan Communications
150 E. Olive Ave., Ste. 208 Ph: (818)848-4876
Burbank, CA 91502 Fax: (818)848-4995
Contact: Michael P. Hogan, Publisher.
Desc: Movie, home video, and music magazine for college students. *Type:* Periodical.

Texas International Theatrical Arts Society

3101 N. Fitzhugh, Ste. 301 Ph: (214)528-6112
Dallas, TX 75204 Fax: (214)528-2617
E-mail: tadams@titas.org
URL: http://www.titas.org
Contact: Tom Adams, Exec. Producer.
Desc: Theatrical agencies working to book entertainers and international acts into all live music venues. Provides placement service; conducts educational seminars. *Type:* Association.

Theatre Communications Group

355 Lexington Ave. Ph: (212)697-5230
New York, NY 10017 Fax: (212)983-4847
Contact: Ben Cameron, Exec.Dir.
Desc: Service organization for nonprofit professional theatres and theatre artists, administrators, and technicians;

associate members include smaller, emerging and educational theatres. Objectives are to: foster cooperation, information sharing, and interaction among members; expand the artistic and administrative capabilities of the professional theatre; develop public awareness and appreciation of the theatre's role in society; act as a resource for the press, funding sources, and government agencies. Operates the National Theatre Artist Residency Program which bestows up to 10 grants of $100,000 annually to nonprofit professional theatres to enable one or more artists to spend substantial time in residence at each grantee institution, as well as other grants and fellowships. *Type:* Association.

Theatre Development Fund
David LeShay
1501 Broadway   Ph: (212)221-0885
New York, NY 10036   Fax: (212)768-1563
Contact: Thomas F. Leahy, Pres.
Desc: A nonprofit corporation founded to stimulate the production of plays of ment in the commercial and not-for-profit theatre. TDF has broadened its scope of activities to provide support for almost every area of professional theatre, dance, and music. Offers low-cost admissions to a wide variety of plays, dance, and musical events for the benefit of those who might otherwise be unable to attend. *Type:* Association.

Theatre Education Association
3368 Central Pky.   Ph: (513)559-1996
Cincinnati, OH 45225   Fax: (513)559-0012
E-mail: info@etassoc.org
Contact: Ronald L. Longstreth, Exec.Dir.
Desc: A branch of the Educational Theatre Association . To champion the cause of the school theatre teacher. Conducts research and educational programs; maintains hall of fame. *Type:* Association.

Theatre Guild
135 Central Pk. W, No. 4-S   Ph: (212)873-0676
New York, NY 10023-2413   Fax: (212)873-5972
Contact: Philip Langner, Pres.
Desc: Theatrical producing organization. Encourages and promotes attendance at dramatic, musical, and theatrical performances "of an artistic character and high standard of excellence." Sponsors American Theatre Society, a national subscription service for major Broadway attractions touring principal cities throughout the United States, and Theatre Guild Abroad, which enables participants to travel on cultural exchange programs. *Type:* Association.

Theta Alpha Phi
242 E. Park St.   Ph: (614)882-3998
Westerville, OH 43081
Contact: Betty J. Stockton, Sec.-Treas.
Desc: Recognition fraternity for men and women involved in college theatre. *Type:* Association.

Wang Theatre
270 Tremont St.   Ph: (617)482-9393
Boston, MA 02116-5603   Fax: (617)451-1436
Contact: Josiah A. Spaulding, Jr., Pres./CEO.
Type: Association.

Theology

Adventist Community Services
12501 Old Columbia Pike   Ph: (301)680-6438
Silver Spring, MD 20904-6600   Free: 800-301-7171
                                Fax: (301)680-6464
URL: http://www.adventist.communityservices.org
Contact: John Gavin, Exec. Dir.
Desc: Service agency of the Seventh-day Adventist Church. Participates in local, regional, and national disaster relief work. Offers basic social services, health screening, literacy tutoring, and prison ministry. *Type:* Association.

Anglican Journal/Journal Anglican
Board of Trustees of the Anglican Church of Canada
600 Jarvis St.   Ph: (416)924-9192
Toronto, ON, Canada M4Y 2J6   Fax: (416)921-4452
E-mail: dharris@national.anglican.ca.
URL: http://www.anglican.ca.
Contact: Carolyn Purden, Editor.
Desc: Religious tabloid. *Type:* Periodical.

The Anthonian
St. Anthony's Guild
Box 2948   Ph: (201)574-6224
Paterson, NJ 07509-2948   Free: 800-848-4538
E-mail: anthonian@aol.com.
Contact: Rev. Cassian A. Miles, O.F.M., Editor.
Desc: Magazine of the Franciscan Order in the Catholic Church. *Type:* Periodical.

Association of Islamic Charitable Projects
4431 Walnut St.   Ph: (215)387-8888
Philadelphia, PA 19104   Fax: (215)387-3815
E-mail: aicp@ix.netcom.com
URL: http://www.aicp.org
Contact: Riad Nachef, Pres.
Desc: Seeks to spread knowledge about Islam. *Type:* Association.

Association of Theological Schools in the United States and Canada
10 Summit Park Dr.   Ph: (412)788-6505
Pittsburgh, PA 15275-1103   Fax: (412)788-6510
E-mail: ats@ats.edu
URL: http://www.ats.edu
Contact: Daniel Aleshire, Exec.Dir.
Desc: Protestant, Roman Catholic, and Orthodox graduate theological schools in the U.S. and Canada. *Type:* Association.

Astara
792 W. Arrow Hwy.   Ph: (909)981-4941
PO Box 5003   Fax: (909)920-9541
Upland, CA 91785-5003
E-mail: theastara@aol.com
URL: http://www.astara.org
Contact: Jeffrey L. Meyer, Contact.
Desc: Non-profit spiritual development provider. Purposes are to publish study material and produce recordings and instructional tapes in the fields of metaphysics and mysticism. *Type:* Association.

ATLA Religion Database
American Theological Library Association (ATLA)
820 Church St., Ste. 400   Ph: (847)869-7788
Evanston, IL 60201-5613
E-mail: atla@atla.com
Contact: ATLA Technical/Search Support, atla@atla.com.
Desc: Contains more than one million citations, with abstracts (journal abstracts for 1975 through 1985 only), to journal articles published in more than 1400 international journals and 14,000 multi-author works annually covering all aspects of world religions, including Buddhism, Christianity and its denominations, Confucianism, Hinduism, Islam, Judaism, and others. *Available:* SilverPlatter Information, Inc.; Ovid Technologies, Inc.; OCLC FirstSearch Electronic Collections Online. *Type:* Database.

The Auditor
American Saint Hill Organization
Church of Scientology
1413 N. Berendo St.   Ph: (213)660-5553
Los Angeles, CA 90027
Contact: Janet Bertinot, Editor.
Desc: Gives news of activities, achievements, and training in Scientology. Recurring features include letters to the editor and interviews. *Type:* Newsletter.

The Baptist Standard
Baptist Standard Publishing Co.
PO Box 660267   Ph: (214)630-4571
Dallas, TX 75266-0267   Free: 800-749-4610
                                Fax: (214)638-8535
E-mail: http://www.bapstand@flash.net; bapstand@flash.net.
URL: baptiststandard.com.
Contact: Marv Knox, Editor.
Desc: Baptist journal. *Type:* Periodical.

Brethren in Christ World Missions
431 Grantham Rd.   Ph: (717)697-2634
PO Box 390   Fax: (717)691-6053
Grantham, PA 17027-0390
E-mail: bicwm@messiah.edu
URL: http://www.nie-church.org/wm/
Contact: Rev. Jack McClane, Exec.Dir.
Desc: Overseas missionaries and Brethren in Christ local congregations in North America. Seeks to foster a fellowship of believers worldwide by offering overseas missionary work and educational and medical activities. Maintains speakers' bureau. *Type:* Association.

Buddhist Churches of America Federation of Buddhist Women's Associations
Buddhist Churches of America
1710 Octavia St.   Ph: (415)776-5600
San Francisco, CA 94109   Fax: (415)771-6293
Contact: Rev. Kodo Umezu, Exec.Dir.
Desc: Women members of Buddhist churches of Jodo Shinshu faith. Promotes American Buddhism through publications, community service, fundraising, and recreational and educational programs. *Type:* Association.

Catholic Update
St. Anthony Messenger Press
1615 Republic St.   Ph: (513)241-5615
Cincinnati, OH 45210   Free: 800-488-0488
                                Fax: (513)241-0399
E-mail: stanthony@americancatholic.org
URL: http://www.americancatholic.org
Contact: Jack Wintz, Editor; John Bookser Feister, Managing Editor.
Desc: Informing Catholics on issues and developments in Catholic thinking and living. *Type:* Newsletter.

The Catholic Voice
The Catholic Voice
3014 Lakeshore Ave.   Ph: (510)893-5339
Oakland, CA 94610-3615   Fax: (510)893-4734
E-mail: cathvoice@aol.com.
Contact: Monica Clark, Editor; John S. Cummins, Publisher.
Desc: Catholic newspaper. *Type:* Periodical.

Charisma
Strang Communications Co.
600 Rinehart Rd.   Ph: (407)333-0600
Lake Mary, FL 32746-4968   Fax: (407)333-7100
E-mail: charisma@strang.com.
URL: http://www.charismamag.com.

Contact: Stephen Strang, Publisher; J. Lee Grady, Editor, grady@strang.com; Jimmy Stewart, Managing Editor, stewart@strang.com; Billy Bruce, News Editor, bruce@strang.com.
Desc: Religious. *Alt. Contact:* 600 Rinehart Rd., Lake Mary, FL 32746; telephone: (407)333-0600; fax: (407)333-7133. *Type:* Periodical.

Church of the Brethren General Board Global Mission Partnership
1451 Dundee Ave.   Ph: (847)742-5100
Elgin, IL 60120   Free: 800-323-8039
                          Fax: (847)742-6103
E-mail: mission_gb@brethern.org
Contact: Mervin Keeney, Contact.
Desc: Mission and service agency of the Church of the Brethren. *Type:* Association.

Church Pension Fund
445 Fifth Ave.   Ph: (212)592-1800
New York, NY 10016   Free: 800-223-6602
                          Fax: (212)779-3370
Contact: Alan F. Blanchard, Pres.
Desc: Administers the clergy pension system of the Episcopal church including life, accident, and health benefits. *Type:* Association.

Church of Scientology of California
1404 N. Catalina   Ph: (213)661-0836
Los Angeles, CA 90027
Contact: Gail Armstrong, Exec. Officer.
Desc: Individuals of all ages, social groups, and religious denominations throughout the world. Scientology is an applied religious philosophy founded and developed by American philosopher and author, L. Ron Hubbard; the church was founded by early Scientologists in Los Angeles. *Type:* Association.

Church Universal and Triumphant
Dept. 793 Box 5000   Free: 800-245-5445
Corwin Springs, MT 59030- Fax: 800-221-8307
5000
E-mail: admin@tsl.org
URL: http://www.tsl.org
Contact: Gilbert Cleirbaut, Pres.
Desc: Conducts religious services and disseminates the teachings of the Ascended Masters as interpreted by Elizabeth Clare Prophet. (The organization defines the Ascended Masters as those individuals throughout human history who have returned to God. Ascended Masters recognized by the group include Gautama Buddha, Confucius, Moses, Jesus Christ, Saint Germain and the Virgin Mary.). *Type:* Association.

Coalition for Religious Freedom
5817 Dawes Ave.
Alexandria, VA 22311-1114
Contact: Dan Holdgreiwe, Exec.Dir.
Desc: Americans of all faiths who are concerned about First Amendment freedoms. Seeks to preserve First Amendment rights protecting the free exercise of religion. Acts as a forum for the religious community of all denominations to effectively deal with the various levels and divisions of government on matters concerning the preservation of religious freedom. *Type:* Association.

Correspondent
Aid Association for Lutherans
4321 N. Ballard Rd.   Ph: (920)734-5721
Appleton, WI 54919   Fax: (920)730-4818
E-mail: aalha:l@aal.org; correspondent@aal.org.
Contact: Pat Millerer, Editor, fax: (920)730-4765, pat_miller@aal.org.

Desc: Magazine for member of the Aid Association for Lutherans. *Type:* Periodical.

The Denver Post
The Denver Post
1560 Broadway   Ph: (303)820-1010
Denver, CO 80202   Free: 800-336-7678
                          Fax: (303)820-1369
URL: http://www.denverpost.com.
Contact: Gil Spencer, Editor; Donald Hunt, Publisher.
Desc: General newspaper. *Type:* Periodical.

Dharma Realm Buddhist Association
Sagely City of 10 Thousand   Ph: (707)462-0939
  Buddhas   Fax: (707)462-0949
PO Box 217
Talmage, CA 95481-0217
Contact: Hsuan Hua, Chm.
Desc: Annual Buddhist events at the City of 10,000 Buddhas include: three-week winter meditation session, three-week spring bowing session, three-week summer Sutra recitation session. *Type:* Association.

Episcopal Synod of America
6300 Ridglea Pl., Ste. 910   Ph: (817)735-1675
Fort Worth, TX 76116   Free: 800-225-3661
                             Fax: (817)735-1351
E-mail: esanhq@compuserve.com
Contact: Rev. Samuel L. Edwards, SSC, Dir.
Desc: Dioceses, parishes, institutions, and societies of laity and clergy of the Episcopal Church of America who "embrace the Gospel of Jesus Christ and uphold the evangelical faith and order, laboring with zeal for the reform and renewal of the church." Promotes the establishment and implementation of cooperative programs. *Type:* Association.

Episcopalians United for Revelation, Renewal, and Reformation
30325 Bainbridge Rd.   Ph: (440)248-0090
Bldg. A, Ste. 1   Free: 800-553-3645
Solon, OH 44139   Fax: (440)248-7176
E-mail: eunited@worldnett.att.net
Contact: Rev. Todd H. Wetzel, Exec.Dir.
Desc: Laypeople working to maintain the traditional doctrine of the Episcopal church. Seeks to influence the structure of the church to more faithfully reflect the teachings of Jesus Christ. Fosters leadership training and education; facilitates communication among members. *Type:* Association.

Faith Alive
PO Box 1987   Ph: (717)848-2137
York, PA 17405   Fax: (717)845-9739
E-mail: faweekend@aol.com
Contact: Thomas G. Riley, Pres.
Desc: Witnessing fellowship within the Episcopal church. Seeks to bring new perspective to vows of baptism and confirmation via weekend programs for adults, teens, and children. *Type:* Association.

Federation of Islamic Associations in the U.S. and Canada
25351 5 Mile & Aubery Rd.
Redford, MI 48239
E-mail: michaol2@jumo.com
Desc: Religious, political, social, and educational organization that acts as an umbrella for Muslim groups in the U.S. and Canada. Objectives are to: defend the human rights of Muslims and all oppressed people through democratic, political means; promote the spirit, ethics, philosophy, and culture of Muslim heritage; answer questions and correct misconceptions about Islam; promote friendly relations between Muslims and non-Muslims of North America. *Type:* Association.

Foursquare World Advance
International Church of the Foursquare Gospel
1910 W. Sunset Blvd., Ste. 200   Ph: (213)989-4234
PO Box 26902   Fax: (213)989-4544
Los Angeles, CA 90026-0176
E-mail: comm@foursquare.org.
Contact: Ron Williams, Editor.
Desc: Magazine containing devotional information, teaching, and experiences. *Type:* Periodical.

The Friend
Church of Jesus Christ of Latter-day Saints
50 E. North Temple St.   Ph: (801)240-2210
Salt Lake City, UT 84150-3226   Fax: (801)240-5997
Contact: Vivian Paulsen, Editor.
Desc: Magazine aimed at children 3-11 years old. Stories focus on character-building. *Alt. Contact:* UT; telephone: (801)240-2210. *Type:* Periodical.

Guideposts Magazine
Guideposts
39 Seminary Hill Rd.   Ph: (914)225-3681
Carmel, NY 10512   Free: 800-431-2344
                          Fax: (914)228-2111
URL: http://www.guideposts.org.
Contact: Fulton Oursler, Jr., Editorial Dir.
Desc: Inspirational interfaith magazine. *Alt. Contact:* 16 East 34 St., New York, NY 10016; telephone: (212)251-8100; fax: (212)684-0679. *Type:* Periodical.

Home Life
Baptist Sunday School Board
127 9th Ave. N.   Ph: (615)251-2271
Nashville, TN 37234   Fax: (615)251-5008
Contact: Jon Walker, Editor.
Desc: Magazine on marriage, parenting, and family relationships. *Type:* Periodical.

International Religious Liberty Association
Dr. John Graz
12501 Old Columbia Pike   Ph: (301)680-6680
Silver Spring, MD 20904-6600   Fax: (301)680-6695
E-mail: 74532.240@compuserve.com
URL: http://www.irla.com
Contact: Dr. John Graz, Sec.Gen.
Desc: Seeks to "publish and proclaim the principles of the universal right to religious liberty, promote respect for the religious rights and freedoms of all humankind, minorities as well as majorities, and secure worldwide recognition of and respect for the basic human right to freedom of conscience and belief." *Type:* Association.

Islamic Mission of America
143 State St.   Ph: (718)875-6607
Brooklyn, NY 11201
Contact: Mohamed Kabbaj, Chm.
Desc: Dedicated to the propagation of the Islamic faith. Prepares students for missionary work. Maintains mosque in Brooklyn, NY and an institute for teaching religion and Arabic. *Type:* Association.

The Islamic Society of North America
PO Box 38   Ph: (317)839-8157
Plainfield, IN 46168   Fax: (317)839-1840
E-mail: membership@isna.net
URL: http://www.isna.net
Contact: Sayyid Muhammad Syeed, Sec.Gen.
Desc: Seeks to serve as an association of Muslim organizations and individuals that serve the diverse needs of Muslims in North America. Aims to provide a uniform platform of expression for Islam, to develop educational, da'wah and social services that translate the teachings of the Qur'an and the Sunnah into everyday living, and to enhance Islamic identity in the society at large. *Type:* Association.

Liguorian

Liguori Publications

1 Liguori Dr.　　　　　　　Ph: (314)464-2500
Liguori, MO 63057　　　　　Free: 800-464-2555
　　　　　　　　　　　　　　Fax: (314)464-8449
E-mail: 104626.1547@compuserve.com.
URL: http://www.liquori.org; http://www.liguori.org.
Contact: Allan Weinert, C.SS.R, Editor.
Desc: Catholic magazine. *Type:* Periodical.

The Lookout

Standard Publishing

8121 Hamilton Ave.　　　　Ph: (513)931-4050
Cincinnati, OH 45231　　　　Fax: (513)931-0950
Contact: David Faust, Editor; Mark A. Taylor, Publisher.
Desc: Christian magazine for adults. *Type:* Periodical.

The Lutheran

Augsburg Fortress, Publishers

100 S. Fifth St., Ste. 700　　Ph: (612)330-3300
PO Box 1209　　　　　　　　Free: 800-426-0115
Minneapolis, MN 55440-1209　Fax: (612)330-3455
E-mail: lutheran@elca.org.
URL: http://www.thelutheran.org.
Contact: Edgar R. Trexler, Editor, etrexler@elca.org; Roger R. Kahle, Managing Editor, rkahle@elca.org; David L. Miller, Sr., Sr. Editor, dmiller@elca.org; Sonia C. Solomonson, Sr. Editor, ssolomon@elca.org; Michael Watson, Art Dir., mwatson@elca.org; Brad Gray, Ad Sales, grayb@augsburg-fortress.org.
Desc: Magazine of the Evangelical Lutheran Church in America. *Alt. Contact:* 8765 W. Higgins Rd., Chicago, IL 60631-4183; telephone: (773)380-2540; fax: (773)380-2751; toll-free: 800-638-3522. *Type:* Periodical.

Makatab Tarighat Oveyssi Shahmaghsoudi

PO Box 5827　　　　　　　　Ph: (202)364-2609
Washington, DC 20016　　　　Free: 800-820-2180
　　　　　　　　　　　　　　Fax: (202)364-2608
E-mail: mtos@cais.com
URL: http://www.mto.shahmaghsoudi.org
Contact: Salaheddin Ali Nader Shah Angha, Contact.
Desc: Individuals who participate in designated religious and educational activities of Makatab Tarighat Oveyssi Shahmaghsoudi. (M.T.O. Shahmaghsoudi maintains that each individual can attain a knowledge of eternal and immutable Truth through a simultaneous process of self-cognition and annihilation of the self in God.). Provides religious instruction; promotes world peace and tranquility on both the interpersonal and international levels. *Type:* Association.

Maryknoll Magazine

Maryknoll Fathers

PO Box 308　　　　　　　　Ph: (914)941-7590
Maryknoll, NY 10545-0308　　Fax: (914)945-0670
E-mail: maryknollmag@igc.apc.org
Contact: Stephen T. DeMott, Publisher, sdemott@igc.apc.org; Rev. Joseph R. Veneroso, Editor, veneroso@igc.apc.org.
Desc: Catholic overseas mission magazine. *Type:* Periodical.

Mission Frontiers

U.S. Center for World Mission

1605 Elizabeth St.　　　　　Ph: (626)398-2241
Pasadena, CA 91104　　　　　Fax: (626)398-2263
E-mail: rickwmf@aol.com.
Contact: Ralph D. Winter, Editor.
Desc: Bulletin of the United States Center for World Mission; editorial on evangelical Frontier Christian missions. *Type:* Periodical.

Moody Magazine

Moody Bible Institute

820 N. LaSalle Blvd.　　　　Ph: (312)329-2150
Chicago, IL 60610　　　　　　Fax: (312)329-2149
E-mail: moodyltrs@moody.edu.
URL: http://www.moody.edu/moodymag.
Contact: Bruce Anderson, General Mgr., (312)329-2157, banderso@moody.edu; Tim Willms, Operations Dir., (312)329-2147, twillms@moody.edu.
Desc: Religious magazine. *Alt. Contact:* 820 N. LaSalle Blvd., Chicago, IL 60610; telephone: (312)329-2164; fax: (312)329-2149. *Type:* Periodical.

National Association of Church Business Administration

7001 Grapevine Hwy., Ste. 324　Ph: (817)284-1732
Fort Worth, TX 76180　　　　Free: 800-898-8085
　　　　　　　　　　　　　　Fax: (817)284-1762
E-mail: info@nacbanet.org
URL: http://www.nacbanet.org
Contact: Simeon May, Exec.Dir.
Desc: Business administrators and managers employed by local churches or institutions of the Christian church. Provides a program of study, service, fellowship, training, information exchange, and problem discussion. *Type:* Association.

National United Church Ushers Association of America

906 Pritchard Pl NE　　　　Ph: (770)971-0799
Marietta, GA 30068
Contact: Raymond Hall, Administrative Assistant.
Desc: Active church ushers. Conducts ushering education and public relations. Maintains ushering school. *Type:* Association.

New Era

Church of Jesus Christ of Latter-day Saints

50 E. North Temple St.　　　Ph: (801)240-2210
Salt Lake City, UT 84150-3226　Fax: (801)240-5997
Contact: Richard M. Romney, Managing Editor.
Desc: Religious magazine for teens. *Alt. Contact:* UT; telephone: (801)240-2951. *Type:* Periodical.

North American Islamic Trust

2622 E. Main St.　　　　　　Ph: (317)839-9248
Plainfield, IN 46168　　　　　Fax: (317)839-2511
E-mail: islamicbookservice@msn.com
Contact: M. Naziruddin Ali, Gen.Mgr.
Desc: Distributes Islamic books and religious supplies. Sponsors children's services and charitable program. *Type:* Association.

Order of the Daughters of the King

PO Box 2196　　　　　　　　Ph: (404)419-8580
Marietta, GA 30061-2196　　　Fax: (404)419-0686
E-mail: dok1885@aol.com
Contact: Sue I. Schlanbusch, Nat. Pres.
Desc: Women in the Episcopal and Roman Catholic church (and churches in communion with the Episcopal church or sharing the historic Episcopate) who have taken vows of prayer and service for the spread of Christ's Kingdom. Supports domestic and overseas missionaries. *Type:* Association.

Orthodox Observer

Greek Orthodox Archdiocese Press

8 E. 79th St.　　　　　　　　Ph: (212)570-3555
New York, NY 10021　　　　　Fax: (212)744-0239
E-mail: goarch@goarch.org; observer@goarch.org.
URL: http://www.goarch.org/goa/observer.
Contact: Stavros Papagermanos, Managing Editor; Jim Golding, Editor; Zoe Gnesoulis, Advertising Mgr., zoe@goarch.org.

Desc: Religious newspaper (English, Greek). *Type:* Periodical.

The Plain Truth

Plain Truth Ministries

Pasadena, CA 91129　　　　　Ph: (626)304-6077
　　　　　　　　　　　　　　Free: 800-309-4466
　　　　　　　　　　　　　　Fax: (626)795-5106
E-mail: monte_wolverton@ptm.org.
URL: http://www.ptm.org.
Contact: Joseph Trach, President; Greg Albrecht, Editor-in-Chief.
Desc: Religious magazine. *Type:* Periodical.

Plus

Peale Center for Christian Living

66 E. Main St.　　　　　　　Ph: (914)855-5000
Pawling, NY 12564　　　　　　Free: 800-938-3322
　　　　　　　　　　　　　　Fax: (914)855-1462
Contact: Ric Cox, Editor.
Desc: General audience Christian magazine. *Type:* Periodical.

Presbyterians Today

Presbyterian Church (U.S.A.)

100 Witherspoon St.　　　　　Ph: (502)569-5000
Louisville, KY 40202-1396　　Free: 800-524-2612
　　　　　　　　　　　　　　Fax: (502)569-5018
E-mail: today@pcusa.org.
Contact: Catherine Cottingham, Managing Editor, (502)569-5634; Eva Stimson, Editor, (502)569-5635.
Desc: Presbyterian magazine. *Alt. Contact:* 100 Witherspoon St., Louisville, KY 40202-1396; telephone: (502)569-5637; fax: (502)569-8632. *Type:* Periodical.

Pulpit Helps

AMG Publishers

6815 Shallowford Rd.　　　　Ph: (423)894-6060
Chattanooga, TN 37421　　　　Free: 800-251-7206
　　　　　　　　　　　　　　Fax: (423)510-8074
E-mail: amgpublisher@aol.com; editor@pulpithelps.com.
URL: http://www.amginternational.org; http://www.pulpithelps.com.
Contact: Spiros Zodhiates, Editor-in-Chief; Ted Kyle, Managing Editor; Bob Dasal, Editor and Publisher.
Desc: Features articles on Bible studies, outlines for scripture themes, and ministry. Recurring features include columns titled Bulletin Inserts, The Pastor's Library, Word Studies, Outlines, Family Helps, Illustrations, Marketplace, and N.E.W.S. *Type:* Newsletter.

Religious Science International

W. 1636 1st Ave.　　　　　　Ph: (509)624-7000
Spokane, WA 99204　　　　　Free: 800-662-1348
　　　　　　　　　　　　　　Fax: (509)624-9322
E-mail: rsiho@aol.com
URL: http://www.rsintl.org
Contact: Art Strassenberg, Gen.Mgr.
Desc: To support the growth and quality of existing churches and encourage and foster the pioneering of new works for the purpose of teaching the Science of Mind and the practice of Spiritual Mind Treatment. *Type:* Association.

Response

United Methodist Board of Global Ministers

475 Riverside Dr., Rm. 1323　Ph: (212)678-6161
New York, NY 10115-0122
Contact: Carol Marie Herb, Editor.
Desc: Religious magazine. *Type:* Periodical.

Rutherford Institute

PO Box 7482
Charlottesville, VA 22906-7482
E-mail: staff@rutherford.org
URL: http://www.rutherford.org
Contact: John W. Whitehead, Pres.
Ph: (804)978-3888
Fax: (804)978-1789

Desc: Provides legal and educational services without charge to individuals whose First Amendment freedoms have been threatened or infringed. Areas of primary concern are: freedom of speech; public, private, and home school related issues; parental rights and the expression of family values; freedom of religious institutions and individuals to abide by their beliefs without government interference; the sanctity of all human life; religious persecution in countries outside the United States. The institute is named for Samuel B. *Type:* Association.

Save Our World

Church of God World Missions

PO Box 8016
Cleveland, TN 37320-8016
Contact: Robert D. McCall, Editor.
Ph: (423)478-7202
Fax: (423)478-7155

Desc: Newspaper (tabloid) containing news items and feature articles about international missions promoting Church of God. *Alt. Contact:* 2490 Keith St. NW, Cleveland, TN 37311; telephone: (423)478-7190. *Type:* Periodical.

Seamen's Church Institute of New York/New Jersey

241 Water St.
New York, NY 10038
E-mail: csr@seamenschurch.org
URL: http://www.seamenschurch.org
Contact: Rev. Peter Larom, Dir.
Ph: (212)349-9090
Fax: (212)349-8709

Desc: Ecumenical agency affiliated with the Protestant Episcopal Diocese of New York to serve the personal counseling material, and spiritual needs of merchant seafarers of all countries in the greater ports of New York/New Jersey. Offers personal counseling services, recreation facilities, education, and legal services. Sponsors ship service and international ship visiting, professional counseling and referral, and credit bureau. *Type:* Association.

Signs of the Times

Pacific Press Publishing Association

PO Box 5353
Nampa, ID 83653-5353
Ph: (208)465-2500
Free: 800-447-7377
Fax: (208)465-2531

URL: http://www.pacificpress.com; http://www.
pacificpress.com/signs.
Contact: Marvin Moore, Editor, mmoore@pacificpress.
com.

Desc: Religious magazine. *Type:* Periodical.

SIMNOW

SIM International

10 Huntingdale Blvd.
Scarborough, ON, Canada
  M1W 2S5
URL: http://www.sim.org.
Contact: David W. Fuller, Editor.
Ph: (416)497-2424
Fax: (416)497-2444

Desc: Journal focusing on missions activity in Africa, Asia, and South America. *Type:* Periodical.

Society of Pragmatic Mysticism

c/o Leonebel Connaway
RR 1, Box 800
Pawlet, VT 05761
E-mail: 104024.1534@compuserve.com
Contact: Leonebel Connaway, Dir.
Ph: (802)325-3107
Fax: (802)325-3107

Desc: Religious organization founded by Mildred Mann (author of numerous books on metaphysical research and

interpretation), which teaches that God dwells within each individual and that each person can, with conscious effort and direction of thought, achieve union with the presence of God. Has over 30,000 students throughout the world, reaching them primarily through subscription series and correspondence. *Type:* Association.

Soka Gakkai International-United States of America

606 Wilshire Blvd.
Santa Monica, CA 90401
E-mail: sgiusa1@aol.com
URL: http://www.sgi-usa.org
Contact: Fred M. Zaitsu, Gen.Dir.
Ph: (310)260-8900
Fax: (310)260-8917

Desc: Addresses the issues facing the individual and humanity as a whole through neighborhood discussion groups, youth activities, educational seminars, and conferences. Fuji Art Museum, the Tokyo Fuji Art Museum, and the Institute of Oriental Philosophy. *Type:* Association.

Spiritual Counterfeits Project

PO Box 4308
Berkeley, CA 94704
E-mail: scp@dnai.com
URL: http://www.scp-inc.org
Contact: Tal Brooke, Pres.
Ph: (510)540-0300
Fax: (510)540-1107

Desc: A Christian think-tank comprised of individuals from top schools who have spent years on various spiritual paths-(from Sai Baba and Rajneesh, to TM and the Course in Miracles)-before leaving them. Examines spiritual phenomena and cultural trends such as Cyberspace, Near Death Experiences, Deep Ecology, Gaia, Witchcraft, and UFOs. Maintains extensive files on cults, the occult, and new religious movements. *Type:* Association.

Supreme Master Ching Hai Meditation Association

PO Box 5662
El Monte, CA 91734

Desc: Individuals of all religious faiths and cultural backgrounds. Works to enable members to elevate their consciousness and develop their inner potential through meditation. Conducts educational progams and lectures. *Type:* Association.

The Tablet

The Tablet Publishing Co.

653 Hicks St.
Brooklyn, NY 11231
Contact: Ed Wilkinson, Editor.
Ph: (718)858-3838
Fax: (718)858-2112

Desc: Catholic newspaper (English). *Type:* Periodical.

Theosophical Society in America

1926 N. Main St.
PO Box 270
Wheaton, IL 60189-0270
E-mail: theos@netcom.com
URL: http://www.theosophical.org
Contact: John Algeo, Pres.
Ph: (630)668-1571
Free: 800-669-1571
Fax: (630)668-4976

Desc: "To form a nucleus of the universal brotherhood of humanity without distinction of race, creed, sex, caste or color; to encourage the comparative study of religion, philosophy, and science; to investigate unexplained laws of nature and the powers latent in humanity." *Type:* Association.

Together

Shalom Foundation, Inc.

Rte. 2, Box 656
Grottoes, VA 24441
Ph: (540)249-3177
Free: 888-833-3333
Fax: (540)249-3177

E-mail: tgether@aol.com.
Contact: Melodie Davis, Editor.

Desc: Religious magazine containing stories describing the way people have been changed by Jesus Christ. *Type:* Periodical.

TV Guide

Telemedia Communications, Inc.

25 Sheppard Ave. W, Ste. 100
North York, ON, Canada M2N
  6S7
E-mail: tvguide@telemedia.org.
URL: http://www.tvguide.com.
Ph: (416)733-7600
Fax: (416)733-7981

Contact: Bill Anderson, Acting Editor, (416)218-3572, fax: (416)733-3568; Cathie Taylor, Advertising Dir., (416)218-3572, fax: (416)218-3635.

Desc: Television entertainment and information magazine. *Type:* Periodical.

Unitarian Universalist Service Committee

130 Prospect St.
Cambridge, MA 02139-1845
E-mail: postmaster@uusc.org
URL: http://www.uusc.org
Contact: Valora Washington, Exec.Dir.
Ph: (617)868-6600
Fax: (617)868-7102

Desc: International human rights organization. Advances human rights through a potent combination of advocacy, education and grassroots partnership. Focuses on civil and political rights, indigenous rights and women's rights. *Type:* Association.

United Methodist Reporter

Newspaper Division United Methodist Communications Council

PO Box 660275
Dallas, TX 75266-0275
Ph: (214)630-6495
Free: 800-947-0207
Fax: (214)630-0079

E-mail: 76113.662@compuserve; webhead@umr.org.
URL: http://www.umr.org.
Contact: Ronald P. Patterson, Publisher.

Desc: Religious newspaper. *Type:* Periodical.

The Upper Room

The Upper Room

1908 Grand Ave.
Nashville, TN 37202
Ph: (615)340-7333
Free: 800-925-6847
Fax: (615)340-7006

URL: http://www.upperroom.org; http://www.
upperroom.org.
Contact: Stephen Bryant, Editor and Publisher; Mary Lou Redding, Managing Editor; Jim Stafford, Assistant Editor; Janice Wooding, Contact.

Desc: Religious publication. *Type:* Periodical.

The Watchtower

Watchtower Bible and Tract Society of New York, Inc.

25 Columbia Heights
Brooklyn, NY 11201
Ph: (718)560-5600
Fax: (914)560-5619

Contact: James N. Pellechia, Contact, (718)560-5600, fax: (718)560-5619, ghawkins@wtbts.org.

Desc: Nonpolitcal journal that "keeps watch on world events as these fulfill Bible prophecy." Available in 130 languages. *Type:* Periodical.

Watchtower Bible and Tract Society of New York

25 Columbia Heights
Brooklyn, NY 11201-2483
URL: http://www.watchtower.org
Contact: Max H. Larson, VP.
Ph: (718)625-3600

Desc: Serves as legal agent for Jehovah's Witnesses who number 5,888,640 worldwide, with 1,040,000 members in the U.S. *Type:* Association.

The World

Unitarian Universalist Association

25 Beacon St.   Ph: (617)742-2100

Boston, MA 02108   Fax: (617)367-3237

E-mail: worldmag@uua.org.

Contact: Amy Hoffman, Editor, ahoffman@uua.org; Myha Nguyen, Advertising Mgr., fax: (617)742-7025, bfrasier@uua.org; Irene Greene, Circulation Mgr., igreene@vva.org.

Desc: Religious news magazine. *Type:* Periodical.

World Vision Magazine

World Vision, Inc.

PO Box 9716   Ph: (253)815-1000

Federal Way, WA 98063-9716   Free: 800-777-5777

    Fax: (253)815-3445

E-mail: worvismag@aol.com.

URL: http://www.worldvision.org.

Contact: Larry Wilson, Sr. Editor, (253)815-2371, lwilson@mary.wuus.org; Don Aylard, Art Dir., (253)815-2025, dayland@mary.wuus.org; Dr. Robert A. Seiple, Publisher, (253)815-2138; Shelley Ngo, Managing Editor, (253)815-2226, sngo@mary.wuus.org.

Desc: Christian humanitarian magazine covering worldwide poverty issues. *Type:* Periodical.

World Vision Today Magazine

World Vision, Inc.

PO Box 9716   Ph: (253)815-1000

Federal Way, WA 98063-9716   Free: 800-777-5777

    Fax: (253)815-3445

E-mail: worvismag@aol.com.

Contact: Dr. Robert A. Seiple, Publisher; Shelly Ngo, Managing Editor.

Desc: Christian humanitarian magazine covering children in poverty stricken and disaster areas of the Third World. *Alt. Contact:* PO Box 9716, Federal Way, WA 98063-9716; telephone: (206)815-1000. *Type:* Periodical.

Worldwide Challenge

Campus Crusade for Christ

100 Sunport Ln.   Ph: (407)826-2390

Orlando, FL 32809   Free: 800-688-4992

    Fax: (407)826-2374

E-mail: wchallenge@aol.com.

URL: http://www.ccci.org/wwwc.

Contact: Sherry M. Cumpstone, Mktg./Circulation, (407)826-2389, cumpstone@cci.org.

Desc: Religion and theology magazine. *Type:* Periodical.

Young Women of the Church of Jesus Christ of Latter-Day Saints

76 N. Main   Ph: (801)240-2141

Salt Lake City, UT 84150   Fax: (801)240-5458

Contact: Margaret D. Nadauld, Pres.

Desc: Girls between the ages of 12 and 18. Seeks to strengthen the spiritual life of young women through Christian values and experiences. Reinforces the values of faith, divine nature, individual worth, knowledge, choice and accountability, good works, and integrity. *Type:* Association.

Youth Worker Update

CCM Communications

107 Kenner Ave.   Ph: (615)386-3011

Nashville, TN 37205-2207   Fax: (615)386-3380

Contact: Dave Urbanski, Editor.

Desc: Keeps professional and volunteer youth workers current with the latest youth-culture trends, research, news and youth ministry resources. *Type:* Newsletter.

Therapy

American Association for Respiratory Care

11030 Ables Ln.   Ph: (972)243-2272

Dallas, TX 75229-4593   Fax: (972)484-2720

E-mail: info@aarc.org

URL: http://www.aarc.org

Contact: Sam P. Giordano, Exec.Dir.

Desc: Allied health society of respiratory therapists and other respiratory caregivers employed by hospitals, skilled nursing facilities, home care companies, group practices, educational institutions, and municipal organizations. Encourages, develops, and provides educational programs for persons interested in the profession of respiratory care; and to advance the science of respiratory care. *Type:* Association.

American Occupational Therapy Association

4720 Montgomery Ln.   Ph: (301)652-2682

PO Box 31220   Free: 800-668-8255

Bethesda, MD 20824-1220   Fax: (301)652-7711

E-mail: praota@aota.org

URL: http://www.aota.org

Contact: Jeanette Bair, Exec.Dir.

Desc: Registered occupational therapists and certified occupational therapy assistants who. provide services to people whose lives have been disrupted by physical injury or illness, developmental problems, the aging process, or social or psychological difficulties. *Type:* Association.

American Physical Therapy Association

1111 N. Fairfax St.   Ph: (703)684-2782

Alexandria, VA 22314   Free: 800-999-2782

    Fax: (703)684-7343

URL: http://www.apta.org

Contact: Francis J. Mallon, Esq, CEO.

Desc: Professional organization of physical therapists and physical therapist assistants and students. Fosters the development and improvement of physical therapy service, education, and research; evaluates the organization and administration of curricula; directs the maintenance of standards and promotes scientific research. *Type:* Association.

Intravenous Nurses Society

10 Fawcett St.   Ph: (617)441-3008

Cambridge, MA 02138-1110   Fax: (617)441-3009

URL: http://www.ins1.org

Contact: Mary Alexander, CEO.

Desc: Registered nurses involved in intravenous (I.V.) therapy; licensed practical nurses and pharmacists. Works to promote the education of individuals practicing intravenous therapy. *Type:* Association.

National Board for Respiratory Care

8310 Nieman Rd.   Ph: (913)599-4200

Lenexa, KS 66214   Fax: (913)541-0156

E-mail: nbrc-info@nbrc.org

URL: http://www.nbrc.org.

Contact: Steven K. Bryant, Exec.Dir.

Desc: Offers credentialing examinations for respiratory therapists, respiratory therapy technicians, pulmonary technologists, and perinatal/pediatric respiratory care specialists. *Type:* Association.

National Council for Therapeutic Recreation Certification

7 Elmwood Dr.   Ph: (914)639-1439

New City, NY 10956   Fax: (914)639-1471

E-mail: nctrc@ix.netcom.com

Contact: Peg Connolly, Ph.D., Exec.Dir.

Desc: Objectives are to: establish national evaluative standards for certification and recertification of individuals who work in the therapeutic recreation field; grant recognition to individuals who voluntarily apply and meet established standards; monitor adherence to standards by certified personnel. *Type:* Association.

Orthopaedic Section, American Physical Therapy Association

2920 E. Ave. S.   Ph: (608)788-3982

Ste. 200

La Crosse, WI 54601-7202

Contact: Terri A. DeFlonan, Exec.Dir.

Desc: Orthopaedic physical therapists and physical therapist assistants who belong to the American Physical Therapy Association ; physical therapy educators and students. Supports the continued growth of the physical therapy profession through education and research; promotes development of a standard certification procedure for the field. *Type:* Association.

Therapy Dogs International

Ursula Kempe

PO Box 517

Mendham, NJ 07945-0517

Contact: Ursula Kempe, Treas.-Admin.

Desc: Owners of registered Therapy Dogs (dogs of various breeds who have had formal obedience training, are under total verbal control, and have a good temperament). Promotes the use of dogs as helpful in the rehabilitation of physical and mental illnesses of patients living in nursing homes, hospitals, and other institutions. Believes that dogs can enhance the quality of life for patients by providing companionship and a diversion from the institutional routine. *Type:* Association.

Thoracic Medicine

American Thoracic Society

1740 Broadway, 14th Fl.   Ph: (212)315-8778

New York, NY 10019-4374   Fax: (212)315-6498

Contact: Carl Booberg, Exec.Dir.

Desc: International Professional and scientific Society for respiratory and critical care medicine. Seeks to prevent and fight respiratory diseases through research, education and advocacy. Also serves as the medical section of the American Lung Association. *Type:* Association.

International Academy of Chest Physicians and Surgeons

American College of Chest Physicians

3300 Dundee Rd.   Ph: (847)498-1400

Northbrook, IL 60062   Fax: (847)698-1791

URL: http://www.chestnet.org

Contact: Alvin Lever, Exec. VP/CEO.

Desc: Aim is to further the continuing education of specialists in chest medicine and surgery. Offers teaching materials at nominal cost to help members stay informed of new developments in chest medicine. Sponsors postgraduate sessions and holds seminars. *Type:* Association.

Research and Education Foundation for Chest Disease

911 Busse Hwy.   Ph: (312)698-2200

Park Ridge, IL 60068

Contact: Alfred Soffer, M.D., Exec.Dir.

Desc: Physicians and surgeons specializing in chest diseases. Supports investigations being conducted in the field of chest medicine. Presents annual Cecile Lehman Mayer Research Award for pulmonary and cardiovascular research. *Type:* Association.

Society of Thoracic Surgeons

401 N. Michigan Ave.   Ph: (312)644-6610

Chicago, IL 60611-4267   Fax: (312)527-6635

Contact: Michael Thompson, Exec. Dir.

Desc: Surgeons who confine their practice to the field of thoracic-cardiovascular surgery. Objectives are: to improve the quality and practice of thoracic and cardiovascular surgery as a specialty; to strengthen and establish basic standards in training programs; to encourage clinical and basic research; to promote the professional development of those surgeons specializing in the field; to represent and sponsor those surgeons who have recently entered the field. *Type:* Association.

Tobacco

ACAS Bulletin

Arizonans Concerned About Smoking (ACAS)
PO Box 13355   Ph: (602)451-4006
Scottsdale, AZ 85267   Fax: (602)451-4006
Contact: Donald N. Morris, Editor.
Desc: Disseminates information on pro-health tobacco control ordinances and legislative bills that support these goals but do not pre-empt local ordinances. Reports on citizen expressed concerns of the health hazards of tobacco products, including chew/spit tobacco use. *Type:* Newsletter.

Americans for Nonsmokers' Rights

2530 San Pablo Ave., Ste. J   Ph: (510)841-3032
Berkeley, CA 94702   Fax: (510)841-3060
E-mail: anr@no-smoke.org
URL: http://www.no-smoke.org
Contact: Julia Carol, Co-Dir.
Desc: Seeks to protect the rights of nonsmokers in the workplace and other public settings. Maintains American Nonsmokers' Rights Foundation, which promotes smoking prevention, educationa programs, and public education about passive smoking. *Type:* Association.

Burley Stabilization Corporation

PO Box 6447   Ph: (423)525-9381
Knoxville, TN 37914   Fax: (423)525-8383
E-mail: bscorp@usit.net
Contact: William O. L. Myers, Mng.Dir.
Desc: Burley tobacco growers' cooperative marketing organization. Coordinates the price support program for burley tobacco in Tennessee, North Carolina, and Virginia under contract with Commodity Credit Corporation. *Type:* Association.

Burley Tobacco Growers Cooperative Association

PO Box 860   Ph: (606)252-3561
Lexington, KY 40588   Fax: (606)231-9804
Contact: Danny McKinney, CEO.
Desc: Producers of burley tobacco in Kentucky, Indiana, Ohio, West Virginia, and Missouri. Administers government price supports on tobacco for the Commodity Credit Corporation in this area. *Type:* Association.

Eastern Dark-Fired Tobacco Growers Association

1109 S. Main St.   Ph: (615)384-4543
PO Box 517   Fax: (615)384-4545
Springfield, TN 37172
Contact: Dan Borthick, Pres.
Desc: Dark tobacco growers. Membership concentrated in Kentucky and Tennessee. *Type:* Association.

Flue-Cured Tobacco Cooperative Stabilization Corporation

1304 Annapolis Dr.   Ph: (919)821-4560
PO Box 12300   Fax: (919)821-4564
Raleigh, NC 27605
Contact: Lionel Edwards, Mgr.
Desc: Flue-cured tobacco producers' marketing cooperative for six southern states. *Type:* Association.

Group Against Smokers' Pollution

PO Box 632   Ph: (301)459-4791
College Park, MD 20741-0632
Contact: Willard K. Morris, Sec.
Desc: Nonsmokers who are adversely affected by tobacco smoke united to promote the rights of nonsmokers, educate the public about the problems of second-hand smoke, and regulate smoking in places where nonsmokers are exposed. Supports the establishment and enforcement of laws and other public policy measures which reduce environmental tobacco smoke. Provides information and referral services; distributes educational literature, buttons, posters, and bumper stickers. *Type:* Association.

SmokeFree Educational Services

PO Box 3316   Ph: (212)912-0960
New York, NY 10008   Fax: (212)488-8911
E-mail: smokefree@usa.net
URL: http://www.smokefree.org
Contact: Joseph Cherner, Pres.
Desc: Mission statement is "to win the right to live and work in a smokefree environment, and to educate people about the unhealthy and socially undesirable consequences of tobacco addiction." Works for: more education for people on the consequences of tobacco addiction; tobacco-free schools; larger health warnings on cigarette ads and cigarette packs; health warnings on cigarettes sold to less developed countries; ending tobacco sponsorship of youth oriented events; eliminating cigarette vending machines; and 100% smokefree public places. *Type:* Association.

Stop Teen-Age Addiction to Tobacco

360 Huntington Ave., No. 241   Ph: (413)732-7828
Boston, MA 02115-5005   Fax: (413)732-4219
Contact: Judy Sopenski, Dir.
Desc: Devoted to reducing the use of tobacco by children and teens through grassroots community projects, policy research, public education, advocacy, communication and counter-advertising. *Type:* Association.

TMA Issues Monitor

Tobacco Merchants Association of the U.S., Inc.
PO Box 8019   Ph: (609)275-4900
Princeton, NJ 08543-8019   Fax: (609)275-8379
E-mail: roberta@tma.org
Contact: Darryl Jayson, Editor.
Desc: Tracks issues and trends affecting the tobacco industry worldwide. Covers import and export news, related legislation, production and marketing information, and statistics. *Type:* Newsletter.

TMA Leaf Bulletin

Tobacco Merchants Association of the U.S., Inc.
PO Box 8019   Ph: (609)275-4900
Princeton, NJ 08543-8019   Fax: (609)275-8379
E-mail: roberta@tma.org
Contact: Darryl Jayson, Editor.
Desc: Reports events and developments affecting leaf tobacco markets. Covers subjects such as export credit sales, price supports, acreage allotments, crop production, and governmental actions. *Type:* Newsletter.

TMA Legislative Bulletin

Tobacco Merchants Association of the U.S., Inc.
PO Box 8019   Ph: (609)275-4900
Princeton, NJ 08543-8019   Fax: (609)275-8379
E-mail: roberta@tma.org
Contact: Kay Carmello, Editor.
Desc: Reports on federal and state legislation and regulations affecting the tobacco industry. *Type:* Newsletter.

TMA Tobacco Barometer

Tobacco Merchants Association of the U.S., Inc.
PO Box 8019   Ph: (609)275-4900
Princeton, NJ 08543-8019   Fax: (609)275-8379
E-mail: roberta@tma.org
Contact: Mark Schoenfeld, Editor.
Desc: Covers manufactured production, taxable removals, and tax-exempt removals for cigarettes, large cigars, little cigars, chewing tobacco, snuff, and pipe tobacco. *Type:* Newsletter.

TMA Tobacco Weekly

Tobacco Merchants Association of the U.S., Inc.
PO Box 8019   Ph: (609)275-4900
Princeton, NJ 08543-8019   Fax: (609)275-8379
E-mail: roberta@tma.org
Contact: David Goldstein, Editor.
Desc: Summarizes key domestic tobacco industry issues as they develop at the federal, state, and local levels. Covers excise taxes, marketing and distribution, corporate finance, leaf and trade, health campaigns, and product liability. *Type:* Newsletter.

TMA Trademark Report

Tobacco Merchants Association of the U.S., Inc.
PO Box 8019   Ph: (609)275-4900
Princeton, NJ 08543-8019   Fax: (609)275-8379
E-mail: roberta@tma.org
Contact: Kathy McCormick, Editor.
Desc: Tracks tobacco product and tobacco accessory trademarks and brand names from test markets through registration. Covers renewals and cancellations. *Type:* Newsletter.

TMA World Alert

Tobacco Merchants Association of the U.S., Inc.
PO Box 8019   Ph: (609)275-4900
Princeton, NJ 08543-8019   Fax: (609)275-8379
E-mail: roberta@tma.org
Contact: Marketa Stoy, Editor.
Desc: Covers tobacco industry and corporate issues worldwide, on a country-by-country basis, including corporate finance, excise taxes, marketing and distribution developments, leaf and trade, and health campaigns. *Type:* Newsletter.

Tobacco Associates

1725 K St. NW, Ste. 512   Ph: (202)828-9144
Washington, DC 20006   Fax: (202)828-9149
Contact: Kirk Wayne, Pres.
Desc: Producers and warehousemen in the flue-cured producing area. Promotes the export market for flue-cured tobacco. *Type:* Association.

Tobacco Barometer: Cigarettes, Cigars, Little Cigars

Tobacco Merchants Association of the U.S., Inc.
PO Box 8019   Ph: (609)275-4900
Princeton, NJ 08543-8019   Fax: (609)275-8379
E-mail: roberta@tma.org
Contact: Mark Schoenfeld, Editor.
Desc: Publishes statistics on production and sales of cigarettes, cigars, little cigars, and smokeless and smoking tobacco. Makes comparisons with the same period during the previous year and analyzes current developments and trends. *Type:* Newsletter.

Tobacco Barometer: Smoking, Chewing, and Snuff

Tobacco Merchants Association of the U.S., Inc.
PO Box 8019   Ph: (609)275-4900
Princeton, NJ 08543-8019   Fax: (609)275-8379
E-mail: roberta@tma.org

Contact: Mark Schoenfeld, Editor.

Desc: Lists statistics on quarterly and cumulative production and sales of smoking tobacco, chewing tobacco, and snuff. Makes comparisons with the same period of the previous year, and has an analysis of current developments and trends. *Type:* Newsletter.

Tobacco and Health Research Institute

Univ. of Kentucky   Ph: (606)257-5798
Cooper & University Drs.   Fax: (606)323-1077
Lexington, KY 40546
E-mail: mdavies@pop.uky.edu
URL: http://www.uky.edu/-thri/homeweb.html
Contact: Dr. H. Maelor Davies, Dir.
Desc: Tobacco production, manufacture of tobacco products, chemistry and physics of tobacco products and smoke, response of nonhuman biological systems to tobacco products, human response to tobacco products, tobacco and cardiovascular and pulmonary diseases, and relationship between tobacco and health. Develops ways to identify and eliminate detrimental compounds. *Type:* Research center.

Tobacco Industry Litigation Reporter

Andrews Publications
175 Strafford Ave., Bldg. 4, Ste.   Ph: (610)225-0510
140   Free: 800-345-1101
Wayne, PA 19087   Fax: (610)225-0501
URL: http://www.andrewspub.com/tobacco.
Contact: Thomas Hennessey, Esq., Editor, fax: (610)225-0501, tomh@andrewspub.com.
Desc: Monitors major litigation brought against the tobacco industry. Reports on discovery, protective orders, and cross-claims in asbestos cases and on the preemption provision of the Federal Cigarette Labeling and Advertising Act. *Type:* Newsletter.

Tobacco Stocks

U.S. Department of Agriculture
Agricultural Marketing Service
Tobacco Programs
Washington, DC 20250   Ph: (202)205-0489
    Fax: (202)205-0099
Desc: Provides information on stocks of leaf tobacco held by grower cooperatives on a reported-weight basis. *Type:* Newsletter.

Tobacco Trade Barometer: Exports

Tobacco Merchants Association of the U.S., Inc.
PO Box 8019   Ph: (609)275-4900
Princeton, NJ 08543-8019   Fax: (609)275-8379
E-mail: roberta@tma.org
Contact: Mark Schoenfeld, Editor.
Desc: Carries statistics on exports of tobacco and tobacco products. Gives listings by country of destination, with quantities and values exported in the current month, in the year to date, and in comparison with previous periods. *Type:* Newsletter.

Tobacco Trade Barometer: Imports

Tobacco Merchants Association of the U.S., Inc.
PO Box 8019   Ph: (609)275-4900
Princeton, NJ 08543-8019   Fax: (609)275-8379
E-mail: roberta@tma.org
Contact: Mark Schoenfeld, Editor.
Desc: Carries statistics on imports of tobacco leaf and tobacco products. Gives tables on type, by country of origin, with quantities being brought in and their values. *Type:* Newsletter.

Tourism

Albuquerque Convention and Visitors Bureau

20 1st Plaza, No. 501   Ph: (505)842-9918
Albuquerque, NM 87102   Free: 800-284-2282
    Fax: (505)848-1176
Contact: Richard Gilliland, Pres.
Desc: Promotes convention business and tourism in Albuquerque, NM. *Type:* Association.

Austrian National Tourist Office

500 5th Ave., Ste. 2009   Ph: (212)575-7723
New York, NY 10110   Fax: (212)730-4568
E-mail: 73410.414@compuserve.com
Contact: Erich Neuhold, Dir.
Desc: Austrian Department of Commerce, Austrian Federal Chamber of Commerce, and state tourism boards in nine Austrian states. Promotes American tourism in Austria. Also maintains offices in 11 other countries. *Type:* Association.

CAB: Leisure, Recreation and Tourism

CAB International
CABI Publishing
10 E. 40th St., Ste. 3203   Ph: (212)481-7018
New York, NY 10016
E-mail: cabi-nao@cabi.org
URL: http://www.cabi.org
Desc: Contains more than 25,000 citations, with abstracts, to current periodical and other published literature relating to leisure, recreation, and tourism activities, facilities, and allied topics. Corresponds to Leisure, Recreation and Tourism Abstracts and the online CAB: Leisure, Recreation and Tourism database, and in part to the online CAB ABSTRACTS database and CAB ABSTRACTS on CD-ROM product. *Available:* DIMDI (Deutsches Institut fuer Medizinische Dokumentation und Information); The Dialog Corporation, DataStar. *Type:* Database.

Denver Metro Convention and Visitors Bureau

1555 California St., Ste 300   Ph: (303)892-1112
Denver, CO 80202-4264   Free: 800-480-2010
    Fax: (303)892-1636
Contact: Eugene Dilbeck, CEO.
Desc: Promotes Denver, CO as a convention and vacation destination. *Type:* Association.

German National Tourist Board

Gen. Mgr.
122 East 42nd St., 52nd Fl.   Ph: (212)661-7200
New York, NY 10168-0072
URL: http://www.germany-tourism.de
Contact: Ursula Schorcher, Chm.
Desc: Encourages and promotes tourism to Germany. *Type:* Association.

Guam Visitors Bureau

PO Box 3520   Ph: (671)646-5278
Agana, GU 96910   Free: 800-024-GUAM
    Fax: (671)646-8861
Desc: Promotes tourism in Guam. Conducts charitable activities. *Type:* Association.

Irish-American Landmarks

Visible Ink Press
27500 Drake Rd.   Ph: (248)699-4253
Farmington Hills, MI 48331-   Free: 800-776-6265
3535   Fax: (248)699-8067
E-mail: galeord@gale.com
URL: http://www.gale.com
Contact: John A. Barnes, Editor.
Desc: Approximately 3,000 sites and memorials of the people of Ireland in America. *Type:* Directory.

Islands

Islands Publishing Co.
PO Box 4728   Ph: (805)745-7100
Santa Barbara, CA 93140-4728   Free: 800-322-1161
    Fax: (805)745-7105
E-mail: islands@islandsmag.com
Contact: Joan Tapper, Editor-in-Chief, (805)745-7110, fax: (805)745-7102, jtapper@islandsmag.com; William Kasch, Publisher, (805)745-1199, fax: (805)745-7105, wkasch@islandsmag.com; Michelle Gamble, Dir., Advertising, (805)745-7150, fax: (805)745-7105, mgamble@islandsmag.com; Rina Viray, Production Mgr., (805)745-7131, fax: (805)745-7102, rviray@idslandsmag.com; Barry Service, Circulation Dir., (805)745-7140, fax: (805)745-7105, bservice@islandsmag.com.
Desc: Publication on islands of the world and traveling. *Type:* Periodical.

Jamaica Tourist Board

801 2nd Ave., 20th Fl.   Ph: (212)856-9727
New York, NY 10017   Free: 800-233-4582
    Fax: (212)856-9730
Contact: Noel Mignott, Deputy Dir.
Desc: Participates in travel trade expositions. *Type:* Association.

New Zealand Tourism Board

501 Santa Monica Blvd., Ste.   Ph: (310)395-7480
300   Free: 800-388-5494
Santa Monica, CA 90401   Fax: (310)395-5453
URL: http://www.nztb.govt.nz
Contact: Annie Dundas, Contact.
Desc: Promotes New Zealand as a desirable site for tourism and international conventions and as a favorable destination for incentive travel programs. Answers inquiries about New Zealand and provides research and source materials. Compiles statistics. *Type:* Association.

San Francisco Convention and Visitors Bureau

John Marks
201 3rd St., Ste. 900   Ph: (415)391-2000
San Francisco, CA 94103-3185   Fax: (415)974-6900
Contact: John Marks, Pres.
Desc: Promotes convention business and tourism in San Francisco, CA. *Type:* Association.

Seattle-King County Convention and Visitors Bureau

520 Pike Tower, No. 1300   Ph: (206)461-5800
Seattle, WA 98101   Fax: (206)461-5855
Contact: Steve Morris, Pres./CEO.
Desc: Promotes King County, WA as an ideal convention site and tourist destination. *Type:* Association.

Tampa/Hillsborough Convention and Visitors Association

400 N. Tampa, Ste. 1010   Ph: (813)223-1111
Tampa, FL 33602   Free: 800-826-8358
    Fax: (813)229-6616
URL: http://www.gotampa.com
Contact: Jim Clark, Pres./CEO.
Desc: Hospitality suppliers who market Hillsborough County and Tampa, FL as a convention and tourist destination. *Type:* Association.

WHERE Toronto

WHERE Toronto
6 Church St., 2nd Fl.   Ph: (416)364-3336
Toronto, ON, Canada M5E   Fax: (416)594-3375
1M1
E-mail: whereedit@aol.com.
Contact: Jacquelyn Waller-Vintar, Editor; Giorgina Bigioni, Publisher, (416)955-4970; Nadine Wallace, Communications Co-ordinator, (416)955-4969; Laurie MacLean, Adv. Sales Mgr., (416)955-4974, lauriemaclean@whcrc-int.com.

Desc: Magazine showcasing what Toronto has to offer: restaurants, shops, attractions, theater, music, art, sports, clubs and pubs. *Type:* Periodical.

Toxicology

Asbestos Victims of America
PO Box 66594   Ph: (408)438-5864
Scotts Valley, CA 95067-6594   Fax: (408)476-3646
E-mail: maurerd@ix.netcom.com

Contact: Heather R. Maurer, CEO.

Desc: Individuals suffering from asbestos-related diseases, families and friends of asbestos victims, and those concerned about the hazards of asbestos. Has been endorsed by union members. Assists asbestos victims and their families in solving related medical, emotional, and financial problems. *Type:* Association.

Black Lung Association
Bill Bailey
Box 872   Ph: (304)252-9654
Crab Orchard, WV 25827

Contact: Bill Bailey, Exec. Officer.

Desc: Working miners, disabled miners, and friends. Objectives are to promote safer working conditions for coal miners and just compensation for disabled miners. Strives for increases in: mine health and safety standards; state and federal benefits for victims of black lung (pneumoconiosis), and other chronic respiratory and pulmonary diseases caused by coal dust; Social Security disability insurance benefits; workmen's compensation; hospitalization and pension benefits for disabled miners and the widows and orphans of miners who have died as a result of their occupation. *Type:* Association.

Canadian Network of Toxicology Centres
Bovey Bldg.   Ph: (519)837-3320
Gordon St.   Fax: (519)837-3861
Guelph, ON, Canada N1G
   2W1
E-mail: lritter@tox.uoguelph.ca
URL: http://www.uoguelph.ca/cntc/

Contact: Dr. Len Ritter, Exec.Dir.

Desc: Toxicology, including risk assessment and epidemiology, environmental concerns, carcinogenesis and genetics, teratology, metabolism and pharmacokinetics, pathology, and analytical chemistry. *Type:* Research center.

Chemical Evaluation Search and Retrieval System
Michigan State Department of Environmental Quality
Surface Water Quality Division
Great Lakes and Environmental Assessment Section
Knapp's Office Centre   Ph: (517)335-4184
P.O. Box 30273
Lansing, MI 48909

Contact: Marjorie Fitch, Librarian.

Desc: Contains toxicological data on approximately 450 chemicals. Each record, representing one chemical, may provide up to 120 data items, covering physical and chemical properties, toxicity, carcinogenicity, mutagenicity, teratogenicity, and, when available, environmental fate. *Available:* Canadian Centre for Occupational Health and Safety (CCOHS); Oxford Molecular Group, Chemical Information Systems. *Type:* Database.

Chemical Industry Institute of Toxicology
6 Davis Dr.   Ph: (919)558-1200
PO Box 12137   Fax: (919)558-1300
Research Triangle Park, NC
   27709
E-mail: ciitinfo@ciit.org
URL: http://www.ciit.org

Contact: Roger O. McClellan, Pres.

Desc: Toxicity data obtained at various levels of biological organization in order to assess exposure-related human health risks. Specific research includes chemical carcinogenesis with investigations in DNA-reactive, mitogenic, cytotoxic, and receptor-mediated agents; risk assessment methodology and extrapolation modeling; respiratory/fiber toxicology; genetic toxicology; neurotoxicology; endocrines and reproductive/developmental toxicology. *Type:* Research center.

Chemical Industry Institute of Toxicology
PO Box 12137   Ph: (919)558-1200
Research Triangle Park, NC Fax: (919)558-1300
   27709
E-mail: ciitinfo@ciit.org
URL: http://www.ciit.org

Contact: Dr. Roger O. McClellan, CEO & Pres.

Desc: Chemical and pharmaceutical companies. Aims to develop the scientific data required for evaluation of the potential health risks of chemicals, pharmaceuticals, and consumer products. Works to: understand human health risk from occupational or environmental exposures; improve species extrapolations used in product safety evaluations; update the existing toxicological testing and investigation of commodity chemicals; develop improved testing methods; train professional toxicologists; serve health and environmental needs of the public through research in toxicology. *Type:* Association.

Colorado State University
Center for Environmental Toxicology and Technology
Foothills Campus   Ph: (970)491-8522
Fort Collins, CO 80523   Fax: (970)491-8304
E-mail: ryang@cvmbs.colostate.edu

Contact: Dr. Raymond S. H. Yang, Dir.

Desc: Hazards associated with environmental exposure to chemical and physical agents, focusing on complex chemical mixtures and chemical-radiation interaction. Also studies growth, reproduction, immune function, physiologically based pharmacokinetics, genetic and molecular markers of disease, and ecotoxicology and bioremediation, focusing on hazardous waste mixtures. *Type:* Research center.

Dermal Absorption
U.S. Environmental Protection Agency (EPA)
Office of Pollution, Prevention, and Toxics
401 M St., SW   Ph: (202)554-1404
Washington, DC 20460
URL: http://www.epa.gov

Desc: Contains more than 3100 records on the qualitative and quantitative health effects of approximately 655 chemical substances administered to humans and test animals via the dermal route. Each record covers a single experiment and includes chemical identification and characteristics; study protocol; description of test organism; summary results; dosage results; detailed absorption, metabolism, distribution, and excretion data; and bibliographic reference. *Available:* Oxford Molecular Group, Chemical Information Systems. *Type:* Database.

Developmental and Reproductive Toxicology
U.S. National Library of Medicine (NLM)
Specialized Information Services Division
8600 Rockville Pike   Ph: (301)496-6531
Bethesda, MD 20894
E-mail: toxmail@toxnetmail.nlm.nih.gov
URL: http://toxnet.nlm.nih.gov

Contact: Dart Representative, (301)496-3147, fax: (301)480-3537, toxmail@tox.nlm.nih.gov.

Desc: Contains more than 37,000 citations, with abstracts, to the worldwide literature on teratology. Includes citations to literature in chemical, physical, or biological agents that may cause birth defects. *Available:* U.S. National Library of Medicine (NLM), TOXNET. *Type:* Database.

Gastrointestinal Absorption Database
U.S. Environmental Protection Agency (EPA)
Office of Pollution, Prevention, and Toxics
401 M St., SW   Ph: (202)554-1404
Washington, DC 20460
URL: http://www.epa.gov

Desc: Contains more than 12,000 citations to worldwide literature on experiments in gastrointestinal absorption, distribution, metabolism, and excretion of orally administered chemical substances. Covers reports on test conditions (e.g., substance tested, test animal) in more than 4900 studies involving approximately 3100 chemical substances administered to laboratory animals or human subjects. *Available:* Oxford Molecular Group, Chemical Information Systems. *Type:* Database.

HAZARDLINE®
MDL Information Systems, Inc.
14600 Catalina St.   Ph: (510)895-1313
San Leandro, CA 94577
E-mail: ohs@mdli.com
URL: http://www.mdli.com

Contact: Richard Cohen, Vice President, (212)789-3653, fax: (212)789-3646.

Desc: Contains regulatory, health, and precautionary data on more than 4,000 commonly used toxic and hazardous substances. It combines data contained in Material Safety Data Sheets (MSDS) with additional details to provide up-to-date information on more than 30 categories such as specific emergency provisions, leak and spill procedures, symptoms, and certifications. *Available:* MDL Information Systems, Inc. *Type:* Database.

Hazardous Substances Data Bank
U.S. National Library of Medicine (NLM)
Specialized Information Services Division
8600 Rockville Pike   Ph: (301)496-6531
Bethesda, MD 20894
E-mail: toxmail@toxnetmail.nlm.nih.gov
URL: http://toxnet.nlm.nih.gov

Contact: HSDB Representative, (301)496-6531, fax: (301)480-3537, toxmail@tox.nlm.nih.gov.

Desc: Contains data on more than 4500 chemical substances that are of known or potential toxicity and to which substantial populations are exposed. Includes 150 data elements grouped into the following 10 classes of information: • Substance Identification Information--includes Chemical Abstracts Service name and Registry number, synonyms, molecular formula, standard transportation number, and EPA hazardous wastes number. *Available:* U.S. National Library of Medicine (NLM), TOXNET; STN International. *Type:* Database.

Inter-University Centre for Toxicology

c/o Department Biological Sciences	Ph: (514)343-7722
UQAM	Fax: (514)343-6120

CP 8888, Succ. Centre-ville
Montreal, PQ, Canada H3C 3P8
E-mail: chevalier.gaston@uqam.ca
Contact: Gaston Chevalier, D.Sc., Dir.
Desc: Biological detection of environmental contaminants in living organisms, characterization of harmful effects of potentially toxic chemicals, and development of diagnostic tests and methods for evaluating toxicity. *Type:* Research center.

Oregon Health Sciences University

Center for Research on Occupational and Environmental Toxicology

3181 SW Sam Jackson Park Rd., L606	Ph: (503)494-4273
	Fax: (503)494-4278

Portland, OR 97201-3098
E-mail: spencer@ohsu.edu
URL: http://www.ohsu.edu/croet
Contact: Dr. Peter S. Spencer, Dir.
Desc: Adverse effects of occupational and environmental chemicals on the human nervous system, exposure to neurotoxic chemicals for behavior, endocrine and neurological function, and the links between neurotoxic chemicals, and degenerative disorders of the nervous system, molecular and cellular mechanisms underlying the adverse effects of chemicals on the nervous system during development, in the adult and in the aged, chronic and delayed actions of chemical substances, the genetic basis for susceptibility to chemical attack, and the role of occupational and environmental chemical agents in triggering developmental defects, neuroendocrine dysfunction, various neurological and psychiatric conditions, and neurodegenerative disorders such as Parkinson and Alzheimer diseases, cancer developmental disorders, and genetic and immune-system dysfunction. Employs epidemiological and other field methods to research relationships between chemical exposures and neurodegenerative disorders such as amyotrophic lateral sclerosisand Parkinson's disease, assessing the validity and reliability of neurobehavioral (and other) screening batteries for the detection of early, reversible abnormalities in brain function. *Type:* Research center.

Society of Toxicology

1767 Business Center Dr., Ste. 302	Ph: (703)438-3115
	Fax: (703)438-3113

Reston, VA 20190-5332
E-mail: sothq@toxicology.org
URL: http://www.toxicology.org
Contact: Shawn Douglas Lamb, Exec.Dir.
Desc: Persons who have conducted and published original investigations in some phase of toxicology and who have a continuing professional interest in this field. (Toxicology is the quantitative study of materials that may or may not adversely affect the health of humans, animals, and/or the environment.) Sponsors placement service at Annual Meeting. *Type:* Association.

Thomas Jefferson University

Occupational and Environmental Health Division

Jefferson Med. College	Ph: (215)955-8381
1020 Locust St., Rm. 314-JAH	Fax: (215)955-2169

Philadelphia, PA 19107
E-mail: simpson1@jeflin.tju.edu
Contact: Dr. Lance Simpson, Dir.
Desc: Mechanisms and actions of toxins at the cellular, subcellular, and molecular levels. *Type:* Research center.

Toxic Chemical Release Inventory

U.S. National Library of Medicine (NLM)
Specialized Information Services Division

8600 Rockville Pike	Ph: (301)496-6531

Bethesda, MD 20894
E-mail: toxmail@toxnetmail.nlm.nih.gov
URL: http://toxnet.nlm.nih.gov
Desc: Contains information on the annual estimated releases of toxic chemicals in the environment, as mandated by Title III of the SUPERFUND Amendments and Reauthorization Act (SARA) of 1986. *Type:* Database.

Toxic Substances Control Act Test Submissions

U.S. Environmental Protection Agency (EPA)
Office of Pollution, Prevention, and Toxics

401 M St., SW	Ph: (202)554-1404

Washington, DC 20460
URL: http://www.epa.gov
Contact: Geraldine Nowak, Technical Information Specialist.
Desc: Contains approximately 100,000 toxicologic studies of chemical substances described in more than 29,000 unpublished health and safety reports submitted by chemical manufacturers, users, and importers to the EPA under the provisions of the Toxic Substances Control Act (TSCA). Approximately 8000 different chemical substances are referenced. *Available:* Oxford Molecular Group, Chemical Information Systems; The Dialog Corporation, DIALOG; STN International; U.S. National Library of Medicine (NLM), TOXNET. *Type:* Database.

U.S. Department of Health and Human Services

Food and Drug Administration

National Center for Toxicological Research

3900 N.C.T.R. Rd.	Ph: (501)543-7000
Jefferson, AR 72079-9502	Fax: (501)543-7576

URL: http://www.fda.gov/
Contact: Bernard A. Schwetz, Director.
Desc: The Center for Toxicological Research conducts research programs to study the biological effects of potentially toxic chemical substances found in the environment, emphasizing the determination of the health effects resulting from long-term, low-level exposure to chemical toxicants, and the basic biological processes for chemical toxicants in animal organisms; develops improved methodologies and test protocols for evaluating the safety of chemical toxicants and the data that will facilitate the extrapolation of toxicological data from laboratory animals to man; and develops Center programs as a natural resource under the National Toxicology Program. *Type:* Government agency, office, or program.

U.S. Department of Health and Human Services

Food and Drug Administration

National Center for Toxicological Research

Biochemical Toxicology Division

HFT-110	Ph: (870)543-7202
3900 NCTR Dr.	Fax: (870)543-7136

Jefferson, AR 72079
Contact: Dr. Frederick A. Beland, Dir.
Desc: Biochemical mechanisms of toxicity and chemical carcinogenesis, including research on the metabolic activation of chemical toxicants; identification of cellular constituents modified by activated chemical toxicants; elucidation of biochemical and other mechanisms by which chemical carcinogenicity and mutagenicity are initiated and expressed; determination of critical detoxification pathways; studies on effects of cellular repair mechanisms on toxic response; and research on metabolism routes and rates. *Type:* Research center.

U.S. Department of Health and Human Services

Food and Drug Administration

National Center for Toxicological Research

Chemistry Division

Bldg. 51, Mail Stop HFT-230	Ph: (501)543-7301
3900 NCTR Rd.	Fax: (501)543-7686

Jefferson, AR 72079
Contact: Harold C. Thompson, Jr., Dir.
Desc: New or improved chemical procedures for the trace analysis of carcinogens, teratogens, mutagens, toxicants, and other biologically-active substrates; state-of-the-art techniques to enhance sensitivity, speed, and accuracy of trace-level analytical chemical determinations; instrument laboratory and conducting studies utilizing highly specialized spectrometric techniques; develops and implements automated chemical data systems; and develops and implements analytical methods to ensure nutritional integrity and absence of deleterious substances in animal diets as they affect bioassay results. Areas of interest also include environmental/occupational surveillance and methods, inductively coupled plasma emission, Fourier transform infrared spectroscopy, and LC-MS and GC-MS. *Type:* Research center.

U.S. Department of Health and Human Services

Food and Drug Administration

National Center for Toxicological Research

Division of Biometry and Risk Assessment

Mail Code HFT-20	Ph: (870)543-7304
3900 NCTR Rd	Fax: (870)543-7720

Jefferson, AR 72079
E-mail: jyoung@nctr.fda.gov
Contact: Dr. John F. Young, PhD, Hd.
Desc: Accesses the human risks from exposure to toxicants, focusing on pharmacokinetics and pharmacodynamics. *Type:* Research center.

U.S. Department of Health and Human Services

Food and Drug Administration

National Center for Toxicological Research

Genetic Toxicology Division

Bldg. 53	Ph: (501)543-7496
3900 NCTR Dr.	Fax: (501)543-7720

Jefferson, AR 72079
E-mail: dcasciano@nctr.fda.gov
URL: http://www.nctr.fda.gov
Contact: Dr. Daniel A. Casciano, Div. Dir.
Desc: Development of in vivo and in vitro genetic toxicology assay systems for use in risk and hazard assessment of potential human carcinogens and mutagens. Areas of research interest include genetics, cell biology, molecular biology, microbiology, and toxicology. *Type:* Research center.

U.S. Department of Health and Human Services

Food and Drug Administration

National Center for Toxicological Research

Office of Research Support

3900 N.C.T.R. Rd.	Ph: (870)543-7130
Jefferson, AR 72079-9502	Fax: (870)543-7576

E-mail: vattwood@nctr.fda.gov
URL: http://www.fda.gov/nctr/index.html
Contact: Victor G. Attwood, Deputy Director for Management.
Desc: Provides support to the NCTR by providing facility maintenance, animal husbandry, computer operations, and pathological services. *Type:* Research center.

U.S. Department of Health and Human Services
Food and Drug Administration
National Center for Toxicological Research
Pathology Associates

PO Box 26   Ph: (870)543-7401
3900 NCTR Rd   Fax: (870)543-7030
Jefferson, AR 72079
Contact: Thomas J. Bucci, Prog.Dir.

Desc: Effects of a number of chemicals and their v arying dosages for different time intervals of treated animals (including making inferences about the potential effect of the same chemicals upon the health of human beings); and studies on the toxicological effects of nerve agents (in co-operation with the Department of Defense), including standard teratology, delayed neuropathy, dominant-lethal, subchronic, and multigenerational protocols. Program also evaluates techniques required to recognize meaningful deviations from normal at earlier times or promise increased specificity in identifying these. *Type:* Research center.

U.S. Department of Health and Human Services
National Institute of Environmental Health
Sciences
division of Intramural Research
Laboratory of Reproductive and Developmental
Toxicology

PO Box 12233   Ph: (919)541-3512
Research Triangle Park, NC   Fax: (919)541-0696
  27709
Contact: Dr. Kenneth S. Korach, Chf.

Desc: Reproductive and developmental biology/toxicology, including gamete biology, developmental endocrinology, pharmacology, germ cell differentiation, genital tract development, ontogeny of hormone response, and developmental regulation of gene expression. *Type:* Research center.

U.S. Department of Health and Human Services
National Institute of Environmental Health
Sciences
Environmental Toxicology Program
Toxicology Branch

Mail Drop A3-02   Ph: (919)541-7992
Research Triangle Park, NC   Fax: (919)541-3647
  27709
E-mail: lucier@niehs.nih.gov
Contact: George Lucier, Dir.

Desc: Activities are carried out in five work groups; the Chemical Dispositon Group studies the absorption, distribution,metabolism, and excretion of a range of chemicals to provide information useful in the design and interpretation of chemical toxicity and carcinogenicity activities; the Developmental and Reproductive Toxicology Group provides an in-house research program, consultation to program toxicologists on the design of special studies, and participation with National Institute for Occupational Safety and Health and National Center for Toxicological Research personnel in the organization, coordination, and long-range planning of the National Toxicology Program's reproductive and developmental toxicology program (in-house research activities include evaluating the reproductive toxicity of environmental and industrial chemicals, providing data on the toxic potential and mechanism of chemicals, and enhancing the development of new and more appropriate testing systems); the Immunologic Toxicology Group selects, refines, and validates a panel of immunology and host resistance procedures to define immunotoxicity and correlating changes in immune function with alterations in host resistance; and the Inhalation Toxicology Group conducts studies on compounds that enter the body primarily by inhalation; and works toward the technologic advancement of gas-vapor inhalation methodologies/facilities. (Further information on a fifth group, the Metal Toxicology Group, was n

U.S. Department of Health and Human Services
National Institute for Occupational Safety and
Health
Biomedical and Behavioral Science Division
Experimental Toxicology Branch

Robert A. Taft Laboratories   Ph: (513)533-8392
Mail Stop C-23   Fax: (513)533-8510
4676 Columbia Pkwy.
Cincinnati, OH 45226
Contact: Dr. Russell Savage, Chf.

Desc: Toxicity of industrial chemicals. Activities involve investigations of carcinogenesis, mutagenesis, toxicity to the male and female reproductive systems, developmental toxicity, cardiovascular disease, pulmonary toxicology, dermatotoxicology, and biological monitoring and metabolism of xenobiotics. *Type:* Research center.

U.S. Department of Health and Human Services
National Toxicology Program

PO Box 12233   Ph: (919)541-3971
Research Triangle Park, NC   Fax: (919)541-0295
  27709
E-mail: hart@niehs.nih.gov
URL: http://ntp-server.niehs.nih.gov/
Contact: Dr. Kenneth Olden, Dir.

Desc: Reliable series of relatively inexpensive short-term tests and protocols useful for the public health regulation of toxic chemicals, including the development of test batteries to assess genetic, neurobehavioral, and immunological toxicities; expand the toxicological profiles of chemicals tested; increase the rate of testing of chemicals for such toxic effects as carcinogenicity, mutagenicity, and reproductive and developmental effects (NTP also examines the chemicals for neurobehavioral, immunological, and other toxic effects where appropriate) within funding limits; and disseminate results of NTP's testing and methods development programs to government research and regulatory agencies, industry, labor, environmental groups, the scientific community, and the public. Chemicals chosen for testing are those that involve widespread or intense human exposure, or those for which existing data on toxic effects are inadequate. *Type:* Research center.

University of Arizona
Arizona Poison and Drug Information Center

College of Pharmacy   Ph: (520)626-6016
Tucson, AZ 85724   Fax: (520)626-2720
E-mail: poisoncenter@elixer.pharm.arizona.edu
URL: http://www.pharmcy.arizona.edu/poison
Contact: Dr. Theodore G. Tong, Contact.

Desc: Toxicology and psychopharmacology, including studies of relative efficacy of certain antidotes in treatment of various poisonings. Conducts research in drug information, including patent information services, post-marketing surveillances, and adverse drug reactions. *Type:* Research center.

University of California, Davis
Institute of Toxicology and Environmental
Health

One Shields Ave.   Ph: (916)752-1340
Old Davis Rd.   Fax: (916)752-5300
Davis, CA 95616
E-mail: pahunter@ucdavis.edu
URL: http://iteh.ucdavis.edu
Contact: Dr. James W. Overstreet, Dir.

Desc: Coordinates interdisciplinary research on biomedical and toxicological problems related to exposure to chemical, physical, and biological toxic agents or to ionizing radiation. Seeks to determine basic mechanisms of toxic effects and to predict human health hazards from continual exposure to realistic levels of toxic substances in the environment or in the workplace. *Type:* Research center.

University of Florida
Center for Environmental and Human
Toxicology

PO Box 110885   Ph: (352)392-4700
Gainesville, FL 32611   Fax: (352)392-4707
E-mail: etox@gnv.ifas.ufl.edu
Contact: Dr. Stephen M. Roberts, Dir.

Desc: Environmental and human toxicology. *Type:* Research center.

University of Montreal
Human Toxicology Research Group

Medecine du travail et d'hygiene   Ph: (514)343-6581
  du milieu   Fax: (514)343-2200
Faculte de medecine
C.P 6128, succursale Centre-
  ville
Montreal, PQ, Canada H3C 3J7
E-mail: krishnak@ere.umontreal.ca
URL: http://alize.ere.umontreal.ca/gris/sp/dmthm
Contact: Kannan Krishnan, Dir.

Desc: Toxicokinetic modeling, biological monitoring, exposure assessment and mofeling, toxicological evaluations, and health risk assessment of pollutants (solvents, metals, organometallics, pesticides). *Type:* Research center.

University of Utah
Center for Human Toxicology

Biomedical Polymers Research   Ph: (801)581-5117
  Bldg., Rm. 490   Fax: (801)581-5034
Salt Lake City, UT 84112
E-mail: drollins@alanine.pharm.utah.edu
Contact: Dr. Douglas E. Rollins, Dir.

Desc: Clinical, forensic, and bioanalytical toxicology, including studies in clinical pharmacology and toxicology, drug metabolism, disposition, adverse interactions, alcohol/drugs and driving, proficiency testing, postmortem toxicology, data interpretation, and new chromatographic and mass spectrometry techniques in toxicology. *Type:* Research center.

University of Wisconsin--Madison
Environmental Toxicology Center

B157 Steenbock Library   Ph: (608)263-4580
550 Babcock Dr.   Fax: (608)262-5245
Madison, WI 53706-1293
E-mail: uwetox@facstaff.wisc.edu
URL: http://www.wisc.edu/etc/
Contact: Prof. Colin R. Jefcoate, Dir.

Desc: Toxicology and problems related to presence of potentially hazardous synthetic and naturally occurring chemicals in the environment, e.g. heavy metals, chlorinated hydrocarbons, pesticides, mycotoxins, and foodborne toxins, including identification, quantification, and toxicologic studies of such chemicals. *Type:* Research center.

Vanderbilt University
Center in Molecular Toxicology

23rd Ave. and Pierce   Ph: (615)322-2261
Nashville, TN 37232-0146   Fax: (615)322-3141
E-mail: info@toxicology.mc.vanderbilt.edu
URL: http://www.toxicology.mc.vanderbilt.edu
Contact: Dr. F. Peter Guengerich, Dir.

Desc: Biochemical and chemical toxicology and carcinogenesis, including enzymatic oxidation and conjugation, oxidative damage, DNA damage and mutagenesis, regulation of gene expression, and environmental pathology. Service core facilities include mass spectrometry, NMR, cell biology, protein chemistry, and moleculer recognition. *Type:* Research center.

Wayne State University
Institute of Chemical Toxicology
2727 2nd Ave., Rm. 4000   Ph: (313)577-0100
Detroit, MI 48201   Fax: (313)577-0082
E-mail: rnovak@cms.cc.wayne.edu
URL: http://www.wayne.edu/ict
Contact: Dr. Raymond F. Novak, Dir.
Desc: Chemical hazards of the environment and industrial workplace, including toxicology of air pollutants, solvents, and heavy metals. Also studies carcinogenesis, metabolic, and hematologic effects resulting from exposure to toxic agents; and molecular and cellular approaches to examine early events in toxicity. *Type:* Research center.

White Lung Association
PO Box 1483   Ph: (410)243-5864
Baltimore, MD 21203-1483   Fax: (410)243-5234
E-mail: whitelung@aol.com
Contact: James Fite, Exec.Dir.
Desc: A selfhelp organization for those with conditions associated with exposure to asbestos. Serves as a clearinghouse providing information on legal and medical assistance to asbestos victims and interested persons. *Type:* Association.

Toys

Creepy Crawlers Fan Club
Box 3940   Ph: (847)352-6565
Schaumburg, IL 60168-3940   Fax: (847)352-9607
Contact: A.J. Marsiglia, Exec. Officer.
Desc: Young children. *Type:* Association.

International Union of Allied Novelty and Production Workers
1950 W. Erie St.   Ph: (312)738-0822
Chicago, IL 60622
Desc: AFL-CIO. *Type:* Association.

Small World—Directory Issue
Earnshaw Publications, Inc.
225 W. 34th St., Rm. 1212   Ph: (212)563-2742
New York, NY 10122   Fax: (212)629-3249
Contact: Michelle Feder, Editor.
Desc: List of more than 200 manufacturers of furniture, wheel goods, toys, and accessories for children and infants. Also lists showrooms, wholesalers, buyers, suppliers, licensors, trade associations, and brand names. *Type:* Directory.

Track and Field

U.S.A. Track and Field
1 RCA Dome Suite 140   Ph: (317)261-0500
Indianapolis, IN 46225   Fax: (317)261-0481
Contact: Craig A. Masback, CEO.
Desc: Athletic clubs, high school and college/university athletic groups, athletic officials, statisticians, and fans. Serves as the national governing body for track and field, long distance running, and race walking. *Type:* Association.

USA Triathlon
3595 E. Fountain Blvd., Ste.   Ph: (719)597-9090
   F-1   Fax: (719)597-2121
Colorado Springs, CO 80910
Contact: Steve Locke, Exec.Dir.
Desc: Triathletes united to sanction safe, fair, and well-managed triathlon and duathlon events. (The triathlon consists of competition in swimming, cycling, and running, and is completed in one day or over a sequence of days.) Coordinates state, regional, national, and international triathlon championships in all official distances; offers athlete and race director insurance and race competitor and club insurance. *Type:* Association.

Trade

Caribbean Exporters, Importers and Business Services Directory
Caribbean Business Development Group, Inc.
67 Wall St., Ste. 2411   Ph: (212)323-7952
New York, NY 10005   Fax: (212)943-2300
Contact: Lloyd Pilgrim Spooner, Editor.
Desc: Over 5,500 exporters, importers, and business service companies in 23 Caribbean countries. *Type:* Directory.

Colorado International Trade Directory
World Trade Center Denver
1625 Broadway, Ste. 680   Ph: (303)592-5760
Denver, CO 80202   Fax: (303)592-5228
E-mail: wtcdenver@worldnet.att.net
Contact: James F. Reis, Editor.
Desc: About 1,200 Colorado importers and exporters, and 400 firms and organizations offering services to Colorado firms involved in international trade. *Type:* Directory.

Directory of North American International Trade Associations
Federation of International Trade Associations
11800 Sunrise Valley Dr., No.   Ph: (703)620-1588
   210   Free: 800-969-FITA
Reston, VA 20191   Fax: (703)391-0159
E-mail: info@fita.org
URL: http://www.fita.org.
Desc: 300 member trade associations in the U.S., Canada, and Mexico. *Type:* Directory.

Exporters' Encyclopedia
Dun & Bradstreet
3 Sylvan Way   Ph: (973)605-6442
Parsippany, NJ 07054-3896   Free: 800-526-0651
   Fax: (973)605-6911
E-mail: dnbmdd@dnb.com
Desc: List of United States and foreign government agencies, international trade associations, and firms specializing in international business and trade research; covers about 180 countries. *Type:* Directory.

Federal Trade Commission
Pennsylvania Ave. at 6th St.   Ph: (202)326-2222
   NW   Fax: (202)326-3676
Washington, DC 20580
URL: http://www.ftc.gov/
Contact: Robert Pitofsky, Chairman of the Board.
Desc: One of the principal functions of the FTC is to safeguard the public by preventing the dissemination of false or deceptive advertisements of consumer products in general; food, drug, cosmetics, and therapeutic devices in particular; as well as other unfair or deceptive practices. *Type:* Government agency, office, or program.

Golden Gate Atlas and World Trade Directory
Marine Exchange of the San Francisco Bay Region
Fort-Mason Center, Bldg. B,   Ph: (415)441-6600
   Ste. 325   Fax: (415)441-3080
San Francisco, CA 94123
E-mail: info@sfmx.org
Contact: Terry Hunter, Editor.
Desc: Ports, shipping firms, dredging firms, customs brokers, freight forwarders, attorneys, consulting engineers, exporters, state and federal government agencies, and maritime unions in the San Francisco Bay region. *Type:* Directory.

Hong Kong Trade Directory
Selective Books, Inc.
PO Box 984   Ph: (813)891-6451
Oldsmar, FL 34677   Fax: (813)855-5791
E-mail: sbooks@mindspring.com
Contact: Lee Howard, Editor.
Desc: Approximately 300 manufacturers of wholesale products and consumer merchandise in Hong Kong. *Type:* Directory.

International Directory of Importers
Interdata
1741 Kekamek NW   Ph: (360)779-1511
Poulsbo, WA 98370   Fax: (360)697-4696
E-mail: interdata@export-leads.com
URL: http://www.export-leads.com.
Desc: A nine-volume series that covers over 150,000 importers and distributors in 156 countries throughout the world. Separate volumes or regional editions: "Asia/Pacific (two volumes)," 30,000 importers in Australia, Bangladesh, China, Hong Kong, India, Indonesia, Kazakhstan, Malaysia, Mauritus, Nepal, New Zealand, Pakistan, Philippines, Singapore, South Korea, South Pacific Islands, Sri Lanka, Taiwan, and Thailand; "Europe" (three volumes), 54,000 importers in Austria, Belgium, Belarus, Bulgaria, Croatia, Czech Republic, Estonia, Denmark, Finland, France, Germany, Greece, Hungary, Iceland, Ireland, Italy, Latvia, Lithuania, Macedonia, Netherlands, Norway, Poland, Portugal, Romania, Russia, Slovakia, Spain, Sweden, Switzerland, Ukraine Republic, and the United Kingdom; "Middle East," 14,000 importers in Bahrain, Egypt, Iran, Israel, Jordan, Kuwait, Lebanon, Malta, Oman, Qatar, Saudi Arabia, Syria, Turkey, United Arab Emirates, and Yemen; "North America," 20,000 United States and Cana *Type:* Directory.

Philippine Trade Directory
Selective Books, Inc.
PO Box 984   Ph: (813)891-6451
Oldsmar, FL 34677   Fax: (813)855-5791
E-mail: sbooks@mindspring.com
Contact: Lee Howard, Editor.
Desc: 300 manufacturers and suppliers of wholesale products and raw materials in the Philippines. *Type:* Directory.

San Diego World Trade Directory
Greater San Diego Chamber of Commerce
402 W. Broadway, Ste. 1000   Ph: (619)544-1300
San Diego, CA 92101-3585   Fax: (619)234-0571
E-mail: info@sdchamber.org
URL: http://www.sdchamber.org
Contact: Laurie Schaffer, Editor.
Desc: About 900 San Diego county companies involved in international trade. *Type:* Directory.

Taiwan Trade Directory
Selective Books, Inc.
PO Box 984   Ph: (813)891-6451
Oldsmar, FL 34677   Fax: (813)855-5791
E-mail: sbooks@mindspring.com
Contact: Lee Howard, Editor.
Desc: About 300 manufacturers and suppliers of wholesale products and consumer products in Taiwan. *Type:* Directory.

United States-Italy Trade Directory
Italy-America Chamber of Commerce
730 5th Ave., Ste. 600   Ph: (212)459-0044
New York, NY 10019   Fax: (212)279-5839
E-mail: info.newyork@italchambers.net
URL: http://www.italchambers.net/newyork.
Contact: Franco De Angelis, Editor.
Desc: More than 4,000 importers and exporters to and from the United States. *Type:* Directory.

WEPZA International Directory of Export Processing Zones and Free Trade Zones
The Flagstaff Institute
PO Box 986   Ph: (520)779-0052
Flagstaff, AZ 86002   Fax: (520)774-8589
E-mail: instflag@aol.com
URL: http://www.wepza.org/world/; http://www.wepza.org/world/.
Desc: More than 800 export processing and free trade zones worldwide. *Type:* Directory.

Trails

Adirondack Mountain Club
814 Goggins Rd.   Ph: (518)668-4447
Lake George, NY 12845-4117   Free: 800-395-8080
                              Fax: (518)668-3746
E-mail: adkinfo@adk.org
URL: http://www.adk.org
Contact: Jo Benton, Exec. Dir.
Desc: Persons interested in mountains, trails, camping, and forest conservation, especially in the Adirondack Mountain region of New York state. Conducts various recreational, conservation, and educational activities. Maintains trails in the Adirondacks and elsewhere; operates two lodges. *Type:* Association.

Appalachian Mountain Club
Communications Assistant
5 Joy St.   Ph: (617)523-0636
Boston, MA 02108   Fax: (617)523-0722
Contact: Andrew Falender, Exec.Dir.
Desc: Objectives are to cultivate public knowledge of the environment and promote enjoyment of the outdoors throughout the northeastern U.S. *Type:* Association.

Appalachian Trail Conference
PO Box 807   Ph: (304)535-6331
Harpers Ferry, WV 25425   Fax: (304)535-2667
E-mail: info@atconf.org
Contact: David N. Startzell, Exec.Dir.
Desc: Federation of trail and hiking clubs and individuals interested in the Appalachian Trail, a 2,160 mile foot trail extending from Maine to Georgia along the crests of Appalachian range. Manages and protects from incompatible land development the trail and approximately 100,000 acres of federally owned land surrounding it. Maintains museum, archive, land trust, and visitor center. *Type:* Association.

The Mountaineers
300 3rd Ave. W.   Ph: (206)284-6310
Seattle, WA 98119   Fax: (206)284-4977
E-mail: clubmail@mountaineers.org
URL: http://www.mountaineers.org/climb
Contact: Sue Weckerly, Exec.Dir.
Desc: Persons of all ages interested in exploring and studying the mountains, forests, and watercourses of the Northwest, preserving the history and traditions of the region, and encouraging protective legislation and other conservation activities. Membership is concentrated in the northwestern U.S. *Type:* Association.

Rails-to-Trails Conservancy
1100 17th St., NW, 10th Fl.   Ph: (202)331-9696
Washington, DC 20036   Fax: (202)331-9680
Contact: David Burwell, Pres.
Desc: Hikers, runners, bicyclists, cross-country skiers, equestrians, state and local park officials, trail enthusiasts, and interested groups or individuals. Promotes the conversion of abandoned railways into trails for public use and wildlife conservation; seeks to build a transcontinental trailway network that will preserve the nation's railroad corridor system. Notifies local groups of upcoming abandonments; assists public and private agencies; publicizes rails-to-trails issues; sponsors short-term land purchases to preserve rail corridors. *Type:* Association.

The Wireless Software Directory
Telecom Publishing Group
1101 King St., 4th Fl.   Ph: (703)683-4100
Alexandria, VA 22314   Free: 800-327-7205
                              Fax: (703)739-6490
Desc: Over 100 companies offering software supporting wireless applications including paging, transportation, mobil office communications, and personal messaging. *Type:* Directory.

Transportation

Amalgamated Transit Union
5025 Wisconsin Ave. NW   Ph: (202)537-1645
Washington, DC 20016   Fax: (202)244-7824
Contact: James La Sala, Pres.
Desc: AFL-CIO; Canadian Labour Congress. *Type:* Association.

American Bus Association
1100 New York Ave. NW, Ste.   Ph: (202)842-1645
  1050   Free: 800-283-2877
Washington, DC 20005-3934   Fax: (202)842-0850
E-mail: abainfo@buses.org
URL: http://www.buses.org
Contact: Peter J. Pantuso, Pres. & CEO.
Desc: Privately owned bus operating firms engaged in intercity, local, charter, and tour service; state associations; motor bus manufacturers; oil, gas and tire distributors and other suppliers; travel/tourism industry destinations, attractions and organizations; others concerned with the operation of bus service and promotion of motorcoach tours. Seeks to promote bus travel, to stimulate the establishment of bus terminals and connecting schedules, and to increase the visibility of buses in travel and tourism. Advocates equitable laws and cooperates with public officials to ensure vehicle, street and highway safety. *Type:* Association.

American Road and Transportation Builders Association
The ARTBA Bldg.   Ph: (202)289-4434
1010 Massachusetts Ave. NW   Fax: (202)289-4435
Washington, DC 20001
E-mail: artba@aol.com
URL: http://www.artba-hq.org
Contact: T. Peter Ruane, Pres. & CEO.
Desc: Highway, bridge, rail and airport contractors; federal, state, county, and municipal engineers and officials; engineers in private practice; manufacturers and distributors of construction equipment; producers and suppliers of materials and services; educators and students of highway engineering; representatives from the traffic safety industry; individuals engaged in other aspects of the design, manufacture, sale, fabrication, installation, and service of devices and materials relating to traffic control during the construction and operation of transportation facilities. Serves as liaison between the industry and government. Sponsors business insurance program, drug testing program, educational and technical workshops. *Type:* Association.

American Trucking Associations
2200 Mill Rd.   Ph: (703)838-1700
Alexandria, VA 22314-4677   Free: 800-ATA-LINE
                             Fax: (703)684-5720
E-mail: ata-infocenter@trucking.org
URL: http://www.trucking.org
Contact: Walter B. McCormick, Jr., CEO & Pres.
Desc: Motor carriers, suppliers, state trucking associations, and national conferences of trucking companies. Works to influence the decisions of federal, state, and local government bodies; promotes increased efficiency, productivity, and competitiveness in the trucking industries; sponsors American Trucking Associations Foundation. *Type:* Association.

APTANet
American Public Transit Association
1201 New York Ave. NW   Ph: (202)898-4000
Washington, DC 20005   Fax: (202)898-4049
E-mail: info@apta.com
URL: http://www.apta.com/
Desc: This site promotes the use of public transportation by providing lots of links to multiple Transit Web Sites. The site is searchable by keyword. *Type:* Database.

Commercial Carrier Journal
Cahners Business Information
201 King of Prussia Rd.   Ph: (610)964-4000
Radnor, PA 19087-5114   Fax: (610)964-2915
E-mail: marketaccess@cahners.com; dirmktg@chilton.net.
Contact: Gerald F. Standley, Editor; Gregory S. Sheremet, Publisher; Haig Dagdigian, Advertising Mgr.
Desc: Magazine containing management, maintenance, and operations information for truck and bus fleets. *Type:* Periodical.

Electronic Data Interchange Association
1800 Diagonal Rd., No. 280
Alexandria, VA 22314-2340
Contact: Gregory B. Harter, CEO & Pres.
Desc: Organizations who use EDI (Electronic Data Interchange). Fosters the development and implementation of EDI. Provides educational and informational support to users of EDI; monitors legislative and regulatory actions. *Type:* Association.

Fleet Owner
Intertec Publishing Corp.
9800 Metcalf Ave.   Ph: (913)341-1300
Overland Park, KS 66212   Free: 800-400-5945
                             Fax: (913)967-1328
URL: http://www.fleetowner.com.
Contact: Thomas L. Moore, Editor, fax: (914)682-0922, tmoore@fleetowner.com; Thomas W. Duncan, Publisher, (914)287-6710, tduncan@fleetowner.com.
Desc: Magazine for managers of commercial motor fleets. *Type:* Periodical.

In Transit
Amalgamated Transit Union, AFL-CIO, CLC
5025 Wisconsin Ave. NW   Ph: (202)537-1645
Washington, DC 20016-4139   Fax: (202)244-7824
Contact: Shawn T. Perry, Editor.
Desc: Amalgamated transit union magazine. *Type:* Periodical.

Independent Truck Owner/Operator Association
PO Box 621   Free: 800-628-4866
Stoughton, MA 02072
Contact: Marshall Siegel, Pres.
Desc: Independent truck owner/operators, merchant vendors, motel chains, equipment manufacturers, truck dealers, motor carriers, fuel stops, and finance organizations. Works to ensure the survival of the small independent truck owner/operator. Seeks to better the business acumen of members through the dissemination of information; lobbies on behalf of the transportation industry. *Type:* Association.

Institute of Transportation Engineers
525 School St. SW, Ste. 410 Ph: (202)554-8050
Washington, DC 20024-2797   Fax: (202)863-5486
URL: http://www.ite.org
Contact: Thomas W. Brahms, Exec.Dir.
Desc: Transportation engineers and professionals. Enables engineers and other professionals with knowledge and

competence in transportation and traffic engineering to contribute individually and collectively toward meeting human needs for mobility and safety. Promotes professional development of members by the support and encouragement of education, stimulation of research, development of public awareness, exchange of professional information, and maintenance of a central point of reference and action. *Type:* Association.

Intermodal Association of North America

7501 Greenway Ctr Dr., Ste.   Ph: (301)982-3400
720   Fax: (301)982-4815
Greenbelt, MD 20770-6705
E-mail: iana@intermodal.org
URL: http://www.intermodal.org

Contact: Joni Casey, Pres.

Desc: Companies involved in intermodal freight transportation domestically and/or internationally within North America, including railroad, ocean carrier/stack train operator, intermodal truck/highway carrier, intermodal marketing, and supplier companies; associate members are companies which have an interest in the well-being and development of the intermodal industry. Mission is to promote the benefits of intermodal freight transportation and encourage its growth through innovation and dialogue. Goals are: to promote the benefits of the shipping community; to provide members a forum to discuss common issues and innovations; to foster members professional development; to participate in governmental proceedings impacting the industry; to inform and educate lawmakers and other government representatives about the industry. *Type:* Association.

International Bridge, Tunnel and Turnpike Association

2120 L St. NW, Ste. 305   Ph: (202)659-4620
Washington, DC 20037   Fax: (202)659-0500
E-mail: ibtta@ibtta.org
URL: http://www.IBTTA.org

Contact: Neil D. Schuster, Exec.Dir.

Desc: Public and private agencies operating toll bridges, tunnels, and turnpikes and companies providing support services and equipment. Monitors and reports on events and legislative action affecting transportation systems worldwide. *Type:* Association.

International Brotherhood of Teamsters

25 Louisiana Ave. NW   Ph: (202)624-6800
Washington, DC 20001   Fax: (202)624-8102
URL: http://www.teamster.org/

Contact: Ron Carey, Gen.Pres.

Desc: Workers, retirees, and their family members in transportation, construction, factories, offices, hospitals, public agencies, airlines, movies, convention centers, warehouses, and many other kinds of work places. Fights for a better future for working families. *Type:* Association.

Land Line

Owner-Operator Independent Drivers Association Inc.
311 R.D. Mize Rd.   Ph: (816)229-5791
Grain Valley, MO 64029   Free: 800-444-5791
   Fax: (816)229-0518

E-mail: ooida@aol.com

Contact: Todd Spencer, Editor and Publisher; Sandi Soendker, Managing Editor.

Desc: Business magazine for professional truckers. *Type:* Periodical.

LEXIS® Transportation Library

LEXIS-NEXIS
9443 Springboro Pike   Ph: (937)865-6800
PO Box 933
Dayton, OH 45401-0933
URL: http://www.lex-nexis.com

Desc: Contains federal transportation case law, statutes and agency decisions. Emphasizes three modes of transportation (aviation, railroad, and trucking) and how these modes are regulated by the federal government. *Available:* LEXIS-NEXIS, LEXIS. *Type:* Database.

Logistics Management and Distribution Report

Cahners Business Information
201 King of Prussia Rd.   Ph: (610)964-4000
Radnor, PA 19087-5114   Fax: (610)964-2915
E-mail: marketaccess@cahners.com

Contact: Peter Bradley, Editor, (617)558-4359; Thomas Esposito, Publisher, (610)964-4383, fax: (610)964-4381.

Desc: Magazine for shippers, carriers, and warehouse personnel. *Type:* Periodical.

Logistics Management & Distribution Report Buyers Guide

Cahners Business Information
275 Washington St.   Ph: (617)964-3030
Newton, MA 02458   Fax: (617)558-4470
E-mail: lm@cahners.com.
URL: http://www.logisticsmgmt.com.

Contact: Peter Bradley, Editor.

Desc: Companies that provide airfreight service, motor carrier service, intermodal service, and steamship service; third-party logistics providers; ports; transportation industry organizations; and logistic technology providers. *Type:* Directory.

The Maintenance Council of the American Trucking Associations

2200 Mill Rd.   Ph: (703)838-1763
Alexandria, VA 22314-5388   Fax: (703)684-4328
E-mail: tmc@trucking.org
URL: http://www.trucking.org/inside_ata/councils/tmc.htm

Contact: Carl T. Kirk, Exec.Dir.

Desc: Dedicated to the improvement of trucking equipment and its maintenance. Cooperates in mutual exchange of information among vehicle designers, manufacturers, users, and equipment and maintenance specialists. Maintains liaison with appropriate federal agencies. *Type:* Association.

Maintenance Matters

The Maintenance Council of the American Trucking Associations
2200 Mill Rd.   Ph: (703)838-1763
Alexandria, VA 22314   Free: 800-ATA-LINE
   Fax: 800-225-8382

E-mail: tmc@trucking.org
URL: http://www.trucking.org

Contact: Marsh Galloway, Editor.

Desc: Features improvement of fleet truck equipment, its maintenance, and maintenance management. Covers product, equipment, and regulation news. *Type:* Newsletter.

Middle Atlantic Conference

PO Box 397   Ph: (301)779-7710
Riverdale, MD 20737   Fax: (301)779-7719

Contact: Dave Holt, Exec.VP.

Desc: Freight rate and tariff agency for motor common carriers operating in northeastern states. *Type:* Association.

Mid-West Truckers Association

2727 N. Dirksen Pky.   Ph: (217)525-0310
Springfield, IL 62702   Fax: (217)525-0342

Contact: Robert L. Jasmon, Exec.VP.

Desc: Owners and operators of trucking companies. Serves as a unified voice for truckers nationwide; conducts lobbying. Sponsors services to members including: mass purchasing program, whereby members may purchase parts at wholesale rates; drug and alcohol testing program; assistance with international registration; license plate procurement; group insurance programs self-funded worker's Compensation Program. *Type:* Association.

Moody's Transportation Manual

Financial Information Services (FIS)
60 Madison Ave., 6th Fl.   Ph: (212)413-7601
New York, NY 10010   Free: 800-342-5647
   Fax: (212)413-7777

E-mail: fis@fisonline.com
URL: http://www.fisonline.com.

Contact: John Ieraci, Editor.

Desc: About 1,000 railroads, airlines, steamship companies, electric railways, bus and truck lines, oil pipelines, bridge and tunnel operators, and automobile and truck leasing companies. *Type:* Directory.

Motor Freight Carriers Association

499 S. Capitol St. SE   Ph: (202)554-3060
Ste. 502A   Fax: (202)554-3160
Washington, DC 20003
URL: http://www.mfca.org

Contact: Timothy P. Lynch, CEO/Pres.

Desc: Motor carriers. united to promote economic interests of unionized motor freight carriers in public policy and collective bargaining arenas. *Type:* Association.

National Industrial Transportation League

1700 N. Moore St., Ste. 1900   Ph: (703)524-5011
Arlington, VA 22209-1904   Fax: (703)524-5017
E-mail: info@nitl.org
URL: http://www.nitl.org

Contact: Edward M. Emmett, Pres.

Desc: Seeks to promote adequate national and international transportation; encourages the exchange of ideas and information concerning traffic and transportation; and cooperates with regulatory agencies and other transportation companies in developing an understanding of legislation. *Type:* Association.

National Motorists Association

402 W. 2nd. St.   Ph: (608)849-6000
Waunakee, WI 53597   Fax: (608)849-8697
E-mail: nma@motorists.org
URL: http://www.motorists.org

Contact: James J. Baxter, Pres.

Desc: Dedicated to protecting the rights of motorists; enhancing personal mobility; implementing rational traffic laws; and improving driver skills and driver courtesy. Supports physical improvements in the highway environment; the return of integrity to user fee taxation and expenditutes; speed limits that are set according to sound engineering principles; and the elimination of "speed traps," arbitrary and abusive insurance company practices and discriminatory traffic regulations. Seeks to find ways to improve driver education and accommodation of the physically impaired. *Type:* Association.

Official Intermodal Guide

Primedia Information Inc.
10 Lake Dr.   Ph: (609)371-7700
Hightstown, NJ 08520-5397   Free: 800-221-5488
   Fax: (609)371-7879

Contact: Kathy Keeney, Editor.

Desc: Intermodal transport services, including railroads, steamship lines, rail and port intermodal terminals and facilities, shippers' agents and associations, drayage carriers, and other common carriers. *Type:* Directory.

Owner-Operator Independent Drivers Association

PO Box L   Ph: (816)229-5791
Grain Valley, MO 64029   Free: 800-444-5791
                                               Fax: (816)229-0518
E-mail: ooida@ooida.com
URL: http://www.ooida.com
Contact: Jim Johnston, Pres.
Desc: Truck owner-operators, small fleet operators, and drivers. Lobbying association seeking to improve owner-operator working conditions. Provides national recognition and a channel for members to voice interests and concerns on changes that affect the trucking business. *Type:* Association.

Safe Driver

National Safety Council
1121 Spring Lake Dr.   Ph: (630)285-1121
Itasca, IL 60143-3201   Free: 800-539-7468
                                               Fax: (630)285-1315
URL: http://www.nsc.org
Contact: Laura Coyne, Editor, (446)30775-2276, fax: (630)775-2285, coyne/@nsc.org; John H. Kennedy, Publisher, (630)775-2103, kennedyj@usc.org; Kathleen Misovic, Assoc. Ed., (630)775-2288, misovick@nsc.org.
Desc: Trade magazine for professional car, bus and truck drivers. *Type:* Periodical.

Teamsters for a Democratic Union

PO Box 10128   Ph: (313)842-2600
Detroit, MI 48210   Fax: (313)842-0227
E-mail: tdudetroit@igc.org
URL: http://www.igc.org/tdu/
Contact: Ken Paff, National Organizer.
Desc: Rank-and-file members of the International Brotherhood of Teamsters working to reform the structure and practices of the union and its leadership. Concerns include health insurance fraud, corruption, weak representation, contract negotiations, concessions, and pensions. Initiates coordinated challenges to entrenched leadership, educating members on local and national elections, and sponsoring legal actions. *Type:* Association.

Thomas Register's Inbound Logistics Guide

Thomas Publishing Co.
5 Penn Plaza   Ph: (212)695-0500
New York, NY 10001   Fax: (212)290-7206
E-mail: ordertr@thomasregister.com
Contact: Tamara Adams, Editor.
Desc: Top transportation companies in 11 categories that provide transportation services for inbound freight. *Type:* Directory.

Transport Workers Union of America

80 West End Ave.   Ph: (212)873-6000
New York, NY 10023   Fax: (212)721-1431
Contact: Sonny Hall, Pres.
Desc: Transit, railroad, and airline workers who are members of the AFL-CIO. *Type:* Association.

Transportation Clubs International

7116 Stinson Ave. No. B-221
Gig Harbor, WA 98335-1100
Contact: James Egbert, Exec.Dir.
Desc: Men and women in the traffic and transportation fields, including railroads, bus lines, trucking firms, and traffic managers of industrial firms. *Type:* Association.

Transportation Research Board

2101 Constitution Ave. NW   Ph: (202)334-2934
Washington, DC 20418   Fax: (202)334-2003
Contact: Robert E. Skinner, Jr., Exec.Dir.
Desc: Encourages research and provides a national clearinghouse and correlation service for research activities and information on transportation technology. *Type:* Association.

TRIS (Transportation Research Information Service)

National Academy of Sciences
National Research Council
Transportation Research Information Services
2101 Constitution Ave., N.W.   Ph: (202)334-3250
Washington, DC 20418
URL: http://www.nas.edu/trb/about/tris.html
Contact: Jerome Maddock, (202)334-2995, fax: (202)334-3495, jmaddock@nas.edu.
Desc: Contains more than 450,000 citations, with abstracts, to literature on transportation, including air, highway, rail, maritime, mass transit, and other transportation modes. Also includes resumes of data from recent or ongoing research projects on transportation-related subjects. *Available:* The Dialog Corporation, DIALOG. *Type:* Database.

Truckload Carriers Association

2200 Mill Rd., 3rd Fl.   Ph: (703)838-1950
Alexandria, VA 22314   Fax: (703)836-6610
E-mail: tca@truckload.org
URL: http://www.truckload.org
Contact: Lana R. Batts, Pres.
Desc: Contract carriers, irregular route common carriers, shippers, and others closely related to the motor carrier industry. Acts as industry spokesman for this segment of the trucking industry; represents the interests of contract and irregular route carriers before Congress, all Federal agencies, and the courts. Conducts charitable programs. *Type:* Association.

Upper Great Plains Transportation Institute

IACC Bldg., Rm. 430   Ph: (701)231-7767
PO Box 5074   Fax: (701)231-1945
Fargo, ND 58105
E-mail: ggriffin@plains.nodak.edu
URL: http://www.ugpti.org
Contact: Gene C. Griffin, Dir.
Type: Association.

Urban Transport News

Business Publishers, Inc. (BPI)
951 Pershing Dr.   Ph: (301)587-6300
Silver Spring, MD 20910-4464
URL: http://www.bpinews.com
Desc: Contains the complete text of Urban Transport News, a newsletter on public transportation issues and developments. Covers relevant activities of the United States Congress, the White House, Department of Transportation (DOT), and state and local transportation agencies, as well as the transportation equipment and service industries. *Type:* Database.

UTU News

United Transportation Union (UTU)
14600 Detroit Ave.   Ph: (216)228-9400
Cleveland, OH 44107   Fax: (216)228-5755
E-mail: utu@compuserve.com
Contact: Eric Eakin, Editor.
Desc: For members of the United Transportation Union. *Type:* Newsletter.

WESTLAW® Transportation Library

West Group
620 Opperman Dr.   Ph: (651)687-7000
St. Paul, MN 55164-0526
URL: http://www.westgroup.com
Desc: Contains the complete text of U.S. federal court decisions, statutes and regulations, administrative law, and texts and periodicals dealing with transportation, including the U.S. federal regulation of surface and air transportation industries (excluding the U.S. Postal Service), the commercial transport of freight and passengers, and injuries related to commercial transportation. *Available:* West Group, WESTLAW. *Type:* Database.

What's Working in Vehicle Management

Progressive Business Publications
370 Technology Dr.   Ph: (610)695-8600
Malvern, PA 19355   Free: 800-220-5000
                                               Fax: (610)651-2981
URL: http://www.pbp.com.
Contact: Leroy Williams, Jr., Editor.
Desc: Helps fleet managers ensure safe operation of vehicles by complying with DOT regulations, as well as hire and retain good drivers. Recurring features include interviews, news of research, a calendar of events, news of educational opportunities, and a column titled Sharpen Your Judgment. *Type:* Newsletter.

Travel

AAA Maryland Motorist

AAA Mid-Atlantic
c/o John Moyer   Ph: (215)864-5455
2040 Market St.   Fax: (215)864-7906
Philadelphia, PA 19103
Contact: John C. Moyer, Editor.
Desc: Auto club publication featuring auto, travel, and insurance stories. *Type:* Periodical.

AAA Mid-Atlantic Motorist Maryland Divsion

AAA Mid-Atlantic
c/o John Moyer   Ph: (215)864-5455
2040 Market St.   Fax: (215)864-7906
Philadelphia, PA 19103
Contact: John C. Moyer, Editor.
Desc: Offers information on automotive and travel subjects (including legislative issues) to AAA members. *Type:* Newsletter.

AAA Motorist

AAA West Penn/West Virginia
5900 Baum Blvd.   Ph: (412)365-7243
Pittsburgh, PA 15206   Fax: (412)362-0926
Contact: Ann Reed Rose, Editor.
Desc: Features motoring and travel news for auto club members. *Type:* Newsletter.

AAA Traveler

AAA New Jersey Automobile Club
1 Hanover Rd.   Ph: (973)377-7200
Florham Park, NJ 07932   Fax: (973)377-2979
E-mail: aaanjacpr@aol.com.
Contact: Pamela S. Fischer, Editor.
Desc: AAA membership newspaper. *Type:* Periodical.

AAA Traveler

AAA East Penn
1020 Hamilton St.   Ph: (610)434-5141
PO Box 1910   Fax: (610)778-3381
Allentown, PA 18105-1910
URL: http://www.aaaeastpenn.com.
Contact: Judith A. Barberich, Editor, (610)778-3301, jab@aaaeastpenn.com.

Desc: Travel and automotive magazine for motorists. *Type:* Periodical.

AAA Traveler

New Jersey Automobile Club
AAA
1 Hanover Rd.   Ph: (973)377-7200
Florham Park, NJ 07932-1899   Fax: (973)377-2979
E-mail: aaanjacpr@aol.com
Contact: Pamela S. Fischer, Editor.
Desc: Considers issues of interest to Club members, including the latest travel, safety, insurance, and motorist/pedestrian information. Covers recent AAA, New Jersey Automobile Club, and Foundation for Safety activities and services along with reports of local and national legislation affecting members. *Type:* Newsletter.

Adventure Road

Amoco Enterprises, Inc.
200 E. Randolph Dr.   Ph: (312)856-2583
Chicago, IL 60601   Fax: (312)856-2379
Contact: M. Holstein, Editor; D.W. Larson, Publisher.
Desc: Travel magazine. *Type:* Periodical.

Adventure West

Adventure Media, Inc.
PO Box 3210   Ph: (702)832-3700
Incline Village, NV 89450 Fax: (702)832-3775
URL: http://www.adventurewest.com.
Contact: Rick Dyes, Publisher; Kristina Scheck, Managing Editor; Dave Mulligan, Managing Editor; Lorelli Gimbry, Editor.
Desc: Nationally distributed consumer magazine, subscription based, adventure travel in western North America. *Alt. Contact:* 924 Incline Way, Ste. M, Incline Village, NV 89451; telephone: (702)832-3730; fax: (702)832-3775. *Type:* Periodical.

Adventures in Travel

Foster Travel Publishing
P.O. Box 5715   Ph: (510)549-2202
Berkeley, CA 94705-0715
E-mail: foster@compuserve.com
Contact: Lee Foster, Owner, (510)549-2202, fax: (510)549-2202, lee@fostertravel.com.
Desc: Contains the complete text of articles for tourists on approximately 250 travel destinations worldwide. Covers culture and history of area, main attractions, suggested side-trips, and sources for further information. *Available:* CompuServe Information Service. *Type:* Database.

Air Traveler's Handbook

Carnegie Mellon University
School of Computer Science   Ph: (412)268-8525
5000 Forbes Ave.   Fax: (412)268-5576
Pittsburgh, PA 15213-3891
E-mail: scs@cs.cmu.edu
URL: http://www.cs.cmu.edu/afs/cs/user/mkant/Public/Travel/airfare.html
Contact: Mark Kantrowitz, mkant@cs.cmu.edu.
Desc: This is the homepage for The Air Traveler's Handbook, the FAQ posting for the rec.travel.air newsgroup. The site claims to have the most comprehensive annotated collection of links to air travel and general travel resources on the Internet. *Type:* Database.

Airline, Ship & Catering—Onboard Services Buyer's Guide & Directory Issue

International Publishing Co. of America
PO Box 470067   Ph: (407)397-0200
Celebration, FL 34747-0067 Free: 800-525-2015
                            Fax: (407)397-2222
E-mail: intlpub@ipca.com; onboard@ipca.org.

Contact: Alex Morton, Managing Editor.
Desc: List of over 6,000 airlines, railroads, ship lines, caterers, and terminal restaurants; duty-free stores; and suppliers of food and beverages, tableware, and onboard entertainment. *Type:* Directory.

American Automobile Touring Alliance

National Automobile Club
1151 E Hillsdale Blvd.   Ph: (415)777-4000
Foster City, CA 94404-1609   Fax: (415)882-2141
Contact: Arthur Hedges, Contact.
Desc: Promotes and facilitates touring between nations. *Type:* Association.

American Cowboy

American Cowboy
PO Box 6630   Ph: (307)672-7171
Sheridan, WY 82801   Free: 800-369-0196
                          Fax: (307)672-7766
E-mail: cowboy@cowboy.com.
URL: http://wwwamericancowboy.com.
Contact: Sandy Bales, fax: (307)672-7676, sbales@cowboy.com.
Desc: Adventurous magazine that portrays the spirit of the West and appeals to the ever-growing number of western enthusiasts. *Type:* Periodical.

American Society of Travel Agents

Dept. 0621   Ph: (703)739-2782
Washington, DC 20073-0621 Fax: (703)838-8467
URL: http://www.astanet.com
Contact: Dick Knodt, CTC, Exec.VP & COO.
Desc: Travel agents; allied members are representatives of carriers, hotels, resorts, sightseeing and car rental companies, official tourist organizations, and other travel interests. Purposes are to: promote and encourage travel among people of all nations; to promote the image and encourage the use of professional travel agents worldwide; serve as an information resource for the travel industry worldwide; promote and represent the views and interests of travel agents to all levels of government and industry; promote professional and ethical conduct in the travel agency industry worldwide; facilitate consumer protection and safety for the traveling public. *Type:* Association.

American Truck Historical Society

300 Office Park Dr., No. 120   Ph: (205)870-0566
Birmingham, AL 35223   Fax: (205)870-3069
Contact: Larry L. Scheef, Mng.Dir.
Desc: Employees of trucking and truck-related companies and organizations, hobbyists, and professors of transportation. Objective is to collect and preserve the history of trucks and trucking and to honor members of the industry. Conducts educational programs. *Type:* Association.

American Way

American Airlines Publishing
4333 Amon Carter Blvd.   Ph: (817)967-1804
MD 5598   Fax: (817)967-1571
Fort Worth, TX 76155-9640
E-mail: 76322.67@compuserve.com.
URL: http://www.americanair.com/away.
Contact: John Clark, Editor, (817)967-04101862; Terrie Lonergan, Advertising Dir., (817)931-9300, terrie_lonergan@amrcorp.com; Rick Morrison, Publisher, (817)967-1787, fax: (817)931-9300, rick_morrison@amrcorp.com.
Desc: In-flight magazine. *Type:* Periodical.

Arizona Highways

Arizona Highways
2039 W. Lewis Ave.   Ph: (602)258-6641
Phoenix, AZ 85009   Free: 800-543-5432
                           Fax: (602)254-4505
URL: http://www.arizhwys.com/.
Contact: Robert J. Early, Editor; Rebecca Mong, Managing Editor; Nina LaFrance, Publisher.
Desc: Travel magazine covering regional history, natural science, folklore, and natural history. *Alt. Contact:* 2039 W. Lewis Ave., Phoenix, AZ 85009. *Type:* Periodical.

Arrigoni Travel Syndication

PO Box 1004   Ph: (415)454-0876
Fairfax, CA 94978   Fax: (415)456-2697
Contact: Patricia Arrigoni, President.
Desc: Distributes destinations and senior travel trips. *Alt. Contact:* PO Box 1004, Fairfax, CA 94978; telephone: (415)454-0876; fax: (415)456-2697. *Type:* Periodical.

Association of Community Travel Clubs

2330 S. Brentwood Blvd.   Ph: (314)961-2300
St. Louis, MO 63144   Fax: (314)961-9828
Contact: George G. White, Sr., VP.
Desc: Community travel clubs that travel regularly as groups. Schedules groups on cruise ships. Manages 13 travel agencies in the Midwest. *Type:* Association.

ASU Travel Guide

Airline Services Unlimited (ASU)
1525 E. Francisco Blvd.   Ph: (415)459-0300
San Rafael, CA 94901   Fax: (415)459-0494
E-mail: ass@asuguide.com
URL: http://asuguide.com.
Contact: Christopher Gil, Editor.
Desc: Over 3,700 airlines, lodgings, tours, car rental companies, and cruise lines, which allow discounts to airline employees worldwide. *Type:* Directory.

Atmosphere

Melaine Communications Group Inc.
3300 Bloor St. W, Ste. 3120   Ph: (416)233-4348
Centre Tower   Fax: (416)233-9367
Etobicoke, ON, Canada M8X
  2X3
E-mail: melaine@inforamp.net
Contact: Susan Melnyk, Editor; Russell Riseley, Asssociate Editor; Nicole Verni, Production, Advertising Sales.
Desc: Consumer magazine for CANADA 3000 Airlines passengers (English and French). *Type:* Periodical.

Bath/Brunswick Visitor's Guide

Chamber of Commerce of the Bath-Brunswick Region
45 Front St.   Ph: (207)443-9751
Bath, ME 04530   Fax: (207)442-0808
E-mail: ccbbr@midcoastmaine.com
URL: http://www.midcoastmaine.com.
Contact: Richard Tetrev, Editor.
Desc: Tourist attractions and accommodations, recreational services, restaurants, banks, campgrounds, festivals, real estate agencies, educational institutions, and other companies and service organizations in Arrowsic, Bath, Brunswick, Georgetown, Phippsburg, Edgecomb, West Bath, Wiscasset, and Woolwich, Topsham, Harpswell, Orr's Island, Bailey Island. *Type:* Directory.

Beautiful British Columbia Magazine

Beautiful British Columbia Magazine
929 Ellery St.   Ph: (250)384-5456
Victoria, BC, Canada V9A 7B4   Free: 800-663-7611
                            Fax: (250)384-2812
E mail: orders@beautifulbc.cq; ed@beautifulbc.cq.

URL: http://www.beautifulbc.com; http://www.beautifulbc.cq.

Contact: Bryan McGill, Editor-in-Chief; Robert Hunt, President, rhunt@beautifulbc.cq.

Desc: Consumer magazine covering geography and travel in British Columbia, Canada. *Type:* Periodical.

Bed & Breakfast Encyclopedia

American Historic Inns, Inc.
PO Box 669   Ph: (714)499-8070
Dana Point, CA 92629-0669   Fax: (714)499-4022
E-mail: generalha@homearts.com
URL: http://homearts.com/affil/ahi/main/ahihome.htm
Desc: This database lets you search for bed and breakfasts and country inns throughout the United States and Canada. Use the InnFinder to sort through thousands of inns and locate lodging by state or region, type of inn, size of inn, and neighboring attractions. *Type:* Database.

Bed and Breakfast and Historic Inns

Minnesota Bed & Breakfast Guild, an affiliate of the Minnesota Hotel & Lodging Association
871 Jefferson Ave.   Ph: (612)222-7401
St. Paul, MN 55102   Fax: (612)222-7347
E-mail: info@hospitalitymn.com
Contact: Sandy Lien, Editor.
Desc: Over 180 bed and breakfast facilities and inns located throughout Minnesota. *Type:* Directory.

Belize First Magazine

Equator Publications
270 Beaverdam Rd.   Ph: (828)665-4466
Candler, NC 28715   Fax: (828)667-1717
E-mail: bzefirst@aol.com.
URL: http://www.turq.com/belizefirst/.
Contact: Lan Sluder, Editor and Publisher.
Desc: Magazine that covers travel and retirement in Belize and other places along the Caribbean Coast of Central America and Mexico. *Type:* Periodical.

Best Read Guide

Best Read Guide
PO Box 1958   Ph: (508)240-1212
Orleans, MA 02653   Fax: (508)240-2912
E-mail: bestread@capecod.com.
URL: http://www.capecod.com.
Contact: Walter Brooks, Publisher; Julie Brooks, Managing Editor.
Desc: Magazine aiding vacationing families in Cape Cod. *Type:* Periodical.

Better Business Traveling

Traveling Times, Inc.
25115 B-130 W. Ave. Stanford   Ph: (661)295-1250
Valencia, CA 91355-3922   Fax: (661)295-8558
Contact: Mirko A. Ilich, Editor.
Desc: Provides news and information of interest to business travelers. *Type:* Newsletter.

Business Travel News

Miller Freeman Publications
600 Harrison St.   Ph: (415)905-2200
San Francisco, CA 94107
URL: http://www.msi.com
Desc: Contains the complete text of Business Travel News, a newspaper covering legal, regulatory, and commercial developments affecting the travel industry, with an emphasis on business-related travel. *Available:* Bell & Howell Information and Learning. *Type:* Database.

California Highway Conditions

Amdahl Corp.
1250 E. Arques Ave.   Ph: (408)746-6000
Sunnyvale, CA 94088-3470   Free: 800-288-0443
E-mail: webmaster@amdahl.com
URL: http://www.amdahl.com/internet/general/travel/ca-highway.html
Desc: This site provides up-to-date information on California's highways conditions, covering road closures, construction, and restrictions. Conditions are updated automatically from the California Department of Transportation. *Type:* Database.

Canadian Geographic

Canadian Geographic Enterprises
39 McArthur Ave.   Ph: (613)745-4629
Vanier, ON, Canada K1L 8L7   Free: 800-267-0824
                             Fax: (613)744-0947
E-mail: editorial@cangeo.ca.
URL: http://www.cangeo.ca/.
Contact: Rick Boychuk, Editor, editorial@canego.ca; John L. Thompson, Publisher.
Desc: Magazine presenting articles exploring Canada's people, cities, wildlife, wilderness, history and beauty. *Type:* Periodical.

Canadian Inflight

Transcontinental Publications, Inc.
777 Bay St., Ste. 2700
Toronto, ON, Canada M5G
    2C8
Contact: Kathleen Hurd, Managing Editor.
Type: Periodical.

Car & Travel Monthly

AAA Automobile Club of New York
1415 Kellum Pl.   Ph: (516)873-2249
Garden City, NY 11530-1690   Fax: (516)873-2355
E-mail: c-and-t@aaany.com.
Contact: Peter Crescenti, Editor; Barbara Crook, Advertising Mgr., (407)444-8545, fax: (407)444-8500, bcrook@national.aaa.com.
Desc: Magazine focusing on motoring and travel. *Type:* Periodical.

Caribbean Hotel Association

1000 Ave. Ponce De Leon   Ph: (787)725-9139
5th Fl.   Fax: (809)725-9108
San Juan, PR 00907
E-mail: jbell@chabotels.com
Contact: John Bell, Exec.VP.
Desc: Hotels and hotel associations throughout the Caribbean region; allied members are companies selling related products and services. Promotes the continuing improvement and expansion of the Caribbean hospitality industry. Maintains Caribbean Hospitality Training Institute, CHA General Agency Corporation, Caribbean Hotel Foundation, CHA Properties, and CHA Reservation Management Service (CHARMS) and Caribbean Culinary Federation. *Type:* Association.

Caribbean Travel and Life

Caribbean Travel and Life, Inc.
330 West Canton Ave.   Ph: (407)628-4802
Winter Park, FL 32789   Fax: (407)628-7061
E-mail: sb3@worldzine.com.
URL: http://www.carib.com.
Contact: Steve Blount, Editor; Sue Gilman, Publisher.
Desc: Magazine covering travel, culture, and leisure in the Caribbean. *Type:* Periodical.

Chevy Outdoors

C. E. Publishing
30400 Van Dyke   Ph: (810)574-9100
Warren, MI 48093-2368   Fax: (810)575-9328
Contact: Steve Wilke, Editor.
Desc: Motorist magazine. *Type:* Periodical.

Community Spirit Magazine (Carmel)

Community Spirit Publications
Box 4628   Ph: (408)625-1557
Carmel, CA 93921   Fax: (408)625-3424
E-mail: mediamanagement@mcimail.com
Contact: Susan Hawthorne, Editor; Sharon Ewing, Advertising.
Desc: Trade magazine covering environmental, technology and travel issues. *Type:* Periodical.

Conde Nast Traveler

Conde Nast Publications, Inc.
140 E. 45th St., 39th Fl.   Ph: (212)880-8800
New York, NY 10017   Free: 800-223-0780
                             Fax: (212)880-8248
E-mail: letters@brides.com
Contact: Harold Evans, Editor-in-Chief; Thomas J. Wallace, Exec. Editor; Ron Galotti, Publisher; Thomas Florio, Advertising Dir.
Desc: Magazine for the frequent traveler. Offers information, advice, and observations on destinations, hotels, transportation, shopping, and dining. *Type:* Periodical.

Consumer Reports Travel Letter

Consumers Union of U.S., Inc.
101 Truman Ave.   Ph: (914)378-2000
Yonkers, NY 10703-1057   Free: 800-234-2188
                             Fax: (914)378-2904
Contact: Laurie Berger, Editor, (415)239-6001, fax: (415)239-4271, lberger@crtl.com.
Desc: Provides travelers with information and advice on travel goods and services. Discusses such topics as air and rail passes, air fare, hotel rates, car rental fees, and techniques for optimizing foreign exchange rates. *Type:* Newsletter.

Country Inns Bed & Breakfast

Country Inns Bed & Breakfast
PO Box 182   Ph: (973)762-7090
South Orange, NJ 07079   Free: 800-289-4667
                             Fax: (973)762-1491
E-mail: countryinn@aol.com.
URL: http://www.innsandouts.com/countryinns/html.
Contact: Gail Rudder Kent, Editor; Susan Ullrich, Advertising.
Desc: Magazine covering travel, interior design, and lifestyle, specifically country inns and bed and breakfasts. *Type:* Periodical.

Craighead's International Business Travel and Relocation Guide to 81 Countries

Gale Group Inc.
27500 Drake Rd.   Ph: (248)699-4253
Farmington Hills, MI 48331- Free: 800-877-GALE
    3535   Fax: (248)699-8070
E-mail: galeord@galegroup.com
URL: http://www.galegroup.com.
Desc: Section dealing with 78 countries throughout the world and giving for each country and its principal cities airport information, hotels, representatives of United States banks, hospitals, schools for foreign residents, etc. Principal content of publication is country profiles for international business travelers; climate information, currency and communications tips, legal documents necessary for living or working in the country, and other information useful to business persons. *Type:* Directory.

Cruise Connoisseur

Traveling Times, Inc.
25115 B-130 W. Ave. Stanford   Ph: (661)295-1250
Valencia, CA 91355-3922   Fax: (661)295-8558

Contact: Mirko A. Ilich, Editor.

Desc: Presents information on cruise destinations. *Type:* Newsletter.

Cruise Travel Magazine

World Publishing Co.
990 Grove St.   Ph: (847)491-6440
Evanston, IL 60201-4370   Fax: (847)491-6462
E-mail: century@wwa.com

Contact: Robert Meyers, Editor; Norman Jacobs, Publisher; Charles Doherty, Managing Editor.

Desc: Magazine covering consumer-oriented cruise-ship vacations. *Type:* Periodical.

Delta Teen-Lift

Delta Sigma Theta Sorority   Ph: (202)986-2400
1707 New Hampshire Ave. NW   Fax: (202)986-2513
Washington, DC 20009

Contact: Ella McNair, Program Dir.

Desc: Sponsored by Delta Sigma Theta to raise the aspirations of disadvantaged teenagers by providing travel experiences which would combine first-hand information on educational opportunities and facilities, contact with persons in diversified occupations, and an opportunity to meet and talk with people who have made outstanding contributions to public and private enterprises. Teen-Lift is an organized tour that takes selected young people on trips to educational, business, and cultural centers in metropolitan areas. Provides financial assistance to cover costs of tours. *Type:* Association.

The Digest

The Blue Ridge Digest Publishing Co., Inc.
PO Box 1758   Ph: (828)667-1607
Asheville, NC 28802-1758   Fax: (828)667-1607
E-mail: brpgsm1@worldnet.att.net
URL: http://www.blueridgedigest.com.

Contact: Ann Buzenberg, M.S.; Tom Hardy, Publisher.

Desc: Blue Ridge Great Smoky Mountains travel guide. *Type:* Periodical.

Diversion (New York)

Hearst Business Communications
1790 Broadway, Ste. 6   Ph: (212)969-7544
New York, NY 10019-1412   Fax: (212)969-7563

Contact: Tom Passavant, Editor; Leslie Dubin, Publisher; William K. Baker, VP/General Mgr.; Aviva Belsky, Sr. Account Mgr.

Desc: Trade magazine covering travel and leisure for physicians. *Type:* Periodical.

Elegant Small Hotels

Lanier Publishing International
PO Box D   Ph: (707)763-0271
Petaluma, CA 94953   Fax: (707)763-5762
E-mail: lanier@travelguides.com; scapernter@travelguides.com.
URL: http://www.travelguides.com; http://www.travelguides.com.

Contact: Pamela Lanier, Editor.

Desc: More than 200 hotels in the U.S., Mexico, and the Caribbean that have acquired high ratings for their accommodations, services, and location; each has between 40 and 200 rooms. *Type:* Directory.

Endless Vacation

Resort Condominiums International, Inc.
3502 Woodview Trace   Ph: (317)876-1692
Indianapolis, IN 46268   Fax: (317)871-9507
E-mail: evletters@rci.com.

Contact: Laurie Borman, Editor-in-Chief; Tom Heine, Art Dir.; Glenn Tourville, Advertising Mgr.; Bob Shenberger, Man., Prod. & Circ.

Desc: Travel magazine. *Type:* Periodical.

Excite Travel

Excite, Inc.
555 Broadway Ave.   Ph: (650)568-6000
Redwood City, CA 94063   Fax: (650)568-6030
URL: http://www.city.net

Desc: Excite Travel by City.Net provides community and tourist information on more than 5,000 world-wide travel destinations. Visitors can access travel information by continent, region, country, or city. *Type:* Database.

Family Motor Coaching—Membership Directory Issue

Family Motor Coach Association
8291 Clough Pike   Ph: (513)474-3622
Cincinnati, OH 45244   Free: 800-543-3622
   Fax: (513)388-5286
E-mail: magazine@fmca.com
Contact: Robbin Gould, Editor.

Desc: List of over 90,000 members; includes lists of motorhome manufacturers, dealers, sources for parts and repairs, dealers in used motorhomes, and motorhome rental agencies. *Type:* Directory.

Federation of American Consumers and Travelers

318 Hillsboro Ave.   Ph: (618)656-0454
PO Box 104   Free: 800-872-3228
Edwardsville, IL 62025
E-mail: gmsfact@aol.com
URL: http://www.fact-org.org
Contact: Barbara Sweet, Natl.Dir.

Desc: Individuals organized to obtain lower prices for merchandise, consumer services, and travel. Disseminates consumer information to members; monitors legislation affecting consumers; conducts educational programs. *Type:* Association.

GO Magazine

AAA Carolinas
6600 AAA Dr.   Ph: (704)569-3600
Charlotte, NC 28212   Fax: (704)569-7815
Contact: Tom Crosby, Editor, (704)569-7733, trcrosby@aaaqa.com.

Desc: Tabloid focusing on motoring and travel. *Type:* Periodical.

Going Places

Canada Wide Magazines & Communications Ltd.
4180 Lougheed Hwy., 4th Fl.   Ph: (604)299-7311
Burnaby, BC, Canada V5C 6A7   Fax: (604)299-9188
E-mail: circulation@canadawide.com
Contact: Pat Price, Editor; Rickr McMorran, Publisher; Tim Nast, Sales Mgr.

Desc: Travel and motorist magazine for members of Manitoba Motor League. *Type:* Periodical.

The Hartford Automobiler

AAA Automobile Club of Hartford
815 Farmington Ave.   Ph: (860)236-3261
West Hartford, CT 06119-1584   Free: 800-842-4320
   Fax: (860)523-1797
Contact: Jennifer Kyle, Editor, (860)570-4318.

Desc: Auto club magazine. *Type:* Periodical.

Hawaii

Fancy Publications
PO Box 6050   Ph: (949)855-8822
Mission Viejo, CA 92690   Free: 800-365-4421
   Fax: (949)855-3045
E-mail: hawaii@fancypubs.com.
Contact: John Hollon, Editor, jhollon@fancypubs.com.

Desc: Magazine about Hawaii for both visitors and residents. *Alt. Contact:* 1210 Auahi St., No. 231, Honolulu, HI 96814; fax: (808)947-0924. *Type:* Periodical.

Hideaways International

15 Goldsmith St.   Ph: (508)486-8955
PO Box 1270   Free: 800-843-4433
Littleton, MA 01460   Fax: (508)486-8525
Contact: Michael F. Thiel, Contact.

Desc: Specialized travel club focusing on "out-of-the-ordinary" vacation sites. Provides villa and condominium rentals, yacht charters, and occupancy at country inns and small resorts; makes available discount airfares, car rentals, and accomodations. *Type:* Association.

Highways

TL Enterprises, Inc.
2575 Vista Del Mar   Ph: (805)667-4100
Ventura, CA 93001   Free: 800-765-1912
   Fax: (805)667-4434
E-mail: goodsam@tl.com.
URL: http://www.goodsamclub.com/highways.
Contact: Susan Bray, Editorial Dir.; Ronald H. Epstein, Editor, reptein@tl.com; Kimberley Winters, Assoc. Editor, kwinters@tl.com; Terry Banister, Asst. Editor/Action Line, tbanister@tl.com; Jeanne Jones, Art Dir.; Bob Livingston, Technical Editor; Diane Fuller, Copy Editor; La Rae Lawson, Copy Editor; Sherman Goldenberg, Midwest Editor; Bruce Barnett, Contributing Editor; Bones Evers, Contributing Editor; Rich Johnson, Contributing Editor; Brenda Hutchinson, Production Mgr.

Desc: Magazine for recreational vehicle owners. *Type:* Periodical.

Historic Festivals: A Traveler's Guide

Visible Ink Press
27500 Drake Rd.   Ph: (248)699-4253
Farmington Hills, MI 48331-3535   Free: 800-776-6265
   Fax: (248)699-8067
E-mail: galeord@gale.com
URL: http://www.gale.com
Contact: George Cantor, Editor.

Desc: Over 300 festivals of historic importance in the United States. *Type:* Directory.

Historic Traveler

Cowles History Group
6405 Flank Dr.   Ph: (203)321-1781
Harrisburg, PA 17112   Fax: (203)322-0302
Contact: Tom Huntington, Editor, tomh@cowles.com; Peter Lenahan, Publisher, peterl@cowles.com; Suzanne Kradel, Advertising Dir.

Desc: Consumer magazine covering travel to historic sites. *Type:* Periodical.

Home and Away

AAA Cincinnati
15 W. Central Pkwy.   Ph: (513)762-3330
Cincinnati, OH 45202
Contact: Merrilee Campbell, Editor.

Desc: Auto club and travel magazine. *Type:* Periodical.

Home & Away

AAA Chicago Motor Club
999 E. Touhy Ave.   Ph: (708)390-9000
Des Plaines, IL 60018   Fax: (708)390-9112
Contact: Brian Nicol, Editor; Lionel Kramer, Publisher; Vern Cornish, Advertising Mgr.
Desc: Official publication for members of AAA-Chicago Motor Club. Features include travel stories and articles on motoring. *Type:* Periodical.

Home & Away

Home & Away Magazine
10703 J St. St.   Ph: (402)592-5000
Omaha, NE 68127   Fax: (402)331-1152
Contact: Brian Nicol, Editor and Publisher; Vern Cornish, Advertising Mgr./Publisher.
Desc: Travel and recreation magazine published for American Automobile Association members in the Midwest. *Type:* Periodical.

Home & Away (Hoosier Edition)

Midwest Magazine Network
PO Box 88505   Ph: (317)923-1500
Indianapolis, IN 46208   Fax: (317)924-4669
Contact: Stephanie Hinds, Regional Editor, (317)923-1500; Terry Farias, Publisher, (317)923-1500; Brian Nicol, Editor and Publisher, (412)390-1000; Vern Cornish, Advertising Mgr., (412)390-1000.
Desc: Magazine for AAA Hoosier Motor Club members in Central Indiana. *Type:* Periodical.

Home & Away (Minnesota Edition)

AAA Minnesota/Iowa
2900 AAA Ct.   Ph: (319)332-3316
Bettendorf, IA 52722   Fax: (319)332-1098
Contact: Sherry K. Freese, Editor/Advertising Mgr., (319)332-3361, sherry.freese@mn-ia.aa.com.
Desc: Travel and motoring magazine. *Type:* Periodical.

Home & Away (Ohio Edition)

Ohio Auto Club
90 E. Wilson Bridge Rd.   Ph: (614)431-7919
Worthington, OH 43085
Contact: William J. Purpura, Editor; Vern Cornish, Advertising Dir., (402)390-1000.
Desc: American Automobile Association travel magazine. *Type:* Periodical.

Hotel & Travel Index—International Edition

Reed Travel Group
500 Plaza Dr.   Ph: (201)902-1600
Secaucus, NJ 07094-3626   Free: 800-334-2811
                          Fax: (201)319-1628
Contact: Lesley Krautheun, Editor.
Desc: Over 45,000 hotels worldwide; reservation offices. *Type:* Directory.

Illinois Travel Guide

Illinois Bureau of Tourism
Illinois Department of Commerce and Community Affairs
100 W. Randolph St., Ste. Ph: (312)814-4732
  3-400   Free: 800-226-6632
Chicago, IL 60601   Fax: (312)814-6175
URL: http://www.enjoyillinois.com.
Contact: Elisa Marcus, Editor.
Desc: Attractions, hotels, motels, and bed and breakfasts in Illinois *Type:* Directory.

Independent Travel Agencies of America Association

5353 N. Federal Hwy., Ste. 300   Ph: (305)772-4660
Fort Lauderdale, FL 33308   Free: 800-950-5440
                                  Fax: (305)772-5797
Contact: David Mueller, Pres.
Desc: Entrepreneurs wishing to open travel agencies. Provides training, testing, certification, oversight, and support in the establishment of travel agencies. Serves as a voice in the travel industry for members. *Type:* Association.

Institute of Certified Travel Agents

148 Linden St.   Ph: (781)237-0280
PO Box 812059   Free: 800-542-4282
Wellesley, MA 02482   Fax: (781)237-3860
Contact: Robert Lepisto, Pres.
Desc: Individuals who have been accredited as Certified Travel Counselors (CTC) after meeting the institute's requirements (5 years' travel industry experience, 5 travel management courses, 4 examinations, an original research project, and a presentation). Seeks to increase the level of competence in the travel industry. Provides continuing education, and examination and certification programs; conducts workshops and professional management seminars. *Type:* Association.

Interactive Travel Report

Garrett Communications
210 N. Adams St., Ste. 1000   Ph: (301)738-7927
Rockville, MD 20850   Free: 888-427-7388
                              Fax: (301)738-7896
E-mail: garrett@radix.net; garretttvl@aol.com; itreport@aol.com.
URL: http://www.garrett-comm.com.
Contact: David B. Kirby, Editor.
Desc: Reports on sales and marketing efforts in the travel and communications industries as travel products are increasingly sold directly and interactively to travelers through the Internet, commercial online services, and other new media. Recurring features include news of interactive marketing efforts, news of research, interviews, reports of meetings, and the column CounterPoint. *Type:* Newsletter.

International Airline Passengers Association

PO Box 700188   Ph: (972)404-9980
Dallas, TX 75370   Free: 800-821-4272
                         Fax: (972)233-5348
E-mail: iapa@iapauia.com
URL: http://www.iapa.com
Contact: Terry A. Evans, Pres.
Desc: Persons who are frequent users of airlines. Represents frequent flyers in matters of safety, comfort, convenience, and economy. Conducts semiannual survey regarding travel preferences and opinions in order to present consumers' viewpoints to airlines and government agencies. *Type:* Association.

International Association of Tour Managers - North American Region

65 Charnes Dr.   Ph: (203)466-0425
East Haven, CT 06513-1225   Fax: (203)787-6384
E-mail: gdomp@callnet.com
Contact: G. Domenic Passarelli, Exec.Dir.
Desc: Travel agents, travel wholesalers, airlines, hotel associations, shipping lines, tourist organizations, restaurants, shops, and entertainment organizations. Works to maintain the highest possible standards of tour management; guarantee excellence of performance; educate the travel world on the role of the tour manager (also referred to as tour director, tour escort, or tour leader) in the successful completion of the tour itinerary and in bringing business to related industries. Represents members in influencing legislation and advising on travel policy. *Type:* Association.

International Family Recreation Association— Official Member Guide Directory

International Family Recreation Association
Pine Forest Rd.   Ph: (850)944-7992
Box 520   Fax: (850)944-0018
Gonzalez, FL 32560-0520
E-mail: nrvockws@spydee.net
Contact: K. W. Stephens, Vice President; David E. Dykes, Editor; K. W. Stephens, Editor.
Desc: 6,800 individuals and companies involved in recreation, conservation of natural resources, and recreation safety. *Type:* Directory.

International Travel Writers and Editors Association

8383 E. Evans Rd.   Ph: (602)998-2000
Scottsdale, AZ 85260-3614   Fax: (602)998-8022
E-mail: ismp@iami.org
URL: http://www.iami.org/ismp.html
Contact: Robert G. Johnson, Contact.
Type: Association.

Ireland of the Welcomes

Ireland of the Welcomes
The Mill   Ph: (203)454-0344
49 Richmondville Ave.   Fax: (203)454-8871
Westport, CT 06880
Contact: Letitia Pollard, Editor; Donal Guilfoyle, Publisher.
Desc: Magazine featuring the heritage, countryside, culture, and people of Ireland. *Type:* Periodical.

Island Visitor

Visitor Publications
1824 Store St.   Ph: (250)388-3676
Victoria, BC, Canada V8T 4R4   Fax: (250)386-2624
E-mail: idenoni@pine.com
Contact: Dave Preston, Editor; Adrian Andrew, Sales Mgr.
Desc: Consumer magazine covering tourism for Victoria and Vancouver Islands. *Type:* Periodical.

Japan Airline Winds

JALIS
3 Park Ave., 28th Fl.   Ph: (212)679-7920
New York, NY 10016   Fax: (212)679-7929
E-mail: jalmedia@aol.com; jaliskikue@worldnet.att.net.
Contact: Gabrielle Ricra, Contact.
Desc: Inflight magazine on Japan Airlines. *Type:* Periodical.

Kentucky Travel Guide

Editorial Services Company
812 South 3rd St.   Ph: (502)584-2720
Louisville, KY 40203   Free: 800-888-0695
                         Fax: (502)584-2722
E-mail: esc@kytravel.com
URL: http://www.kytravel.com.
Contact: Sara N. Reisz, Editor.
Desc: Travel publication focusing on attractions, events and facilities for 169 Kentucky cities. *Type:* Periodical.

Key to the Door. . .Illustrated

Door County Publishing Co.
Box 130   Ph: (920)743-3321
Sturgeon Bay, WI 54235-0130   Fax: (920)743-5817
Desc: Guide for visitors to Door County, Wisconsin. *Type:* Periodical.

Keystone AAA Motorist

AAA Mid-Atlantic

c/o John Moyer Ph: (215)864-5455
2040 Market St. Fax: (215)864-7906
Philadelphia, PA 19103

Contact: J.C. Moyer, Editor.

Desc: Auto club membership newspaper (tabloid) providing information on domestic and international travel and automotive safety. *Type:* Periodical.

Latitudes

Caribbean Travel and Life, Inc.

330 West Canton Ave. Ph: (407)628-4802
Winter Park, FL 32789 Fax: (407)628-7061
E-mail: affcarib@aol.com.
URL: http://www.carib.com.

Contact: Steve Blount, Editor; Jane Mcallister, Publisher.

Desc: In-flight magazine for American Eagle airlines' San Juan, PR, and Miami, FL hubs (English and Spanish). *Type:* Periodical.

Leisure World

Ontario Motorist Publishing Co. Ltd.

1253 Ouellette Ave. Ph: (519)971-3207
Windsor, ON, Canada N8X 1J3 Fax: (519)977-1197
E-mail: doug@ompc.com; ompc@ompc.com
URL: http://www.ompc.com; http://www.ompc.com.

Desc: Consumer magazine covering travel and leisure for members of the Canadian Automobile Association. *Type:* Periodical.

LEISUREWAYS

Canada Wide Magazines & Communications Ltd.

4180 Lougheed Hwy., 4th Fl. Ph: (604)299-7311
Burnaby, BC, Canada V5C 6A7 Fax: (604)299-9188
E-mail: circulation@canadawide.com

Contact: Deborah Milton, Editor, lways@istar.ca; Peter Legge, Publisher; John Tarbat, Advertising Mgr.

Desc: Travel magazine for members of Canadian Automobile Association in Ontario. *Alt. Contact:* 2 Carlton St., No. 801, Toronto, ON, Canada M5B 1J3; telephone: (416)595-5007; fax: (416)924-6308. *Type:* Periodical.

Lonely Planet - Destinations

Lonely Planet Publications

Embarcadero West Ph: (510)893-8555
150 Linden St. Free: 800-275-8555
Oakland, CA 94607-2538 Fax: (510)893-8563
E-mail: info@lonelyplanet.com
URL: http://www.lonelyplanet.com/dest/dest.htm

Desc: A superb resource of travel information for every continent (including Antarctica), Lonely Planet on-line's Destination pages are a rich source of cultural, historical, and geographical material on hundreds of locations worldwide. You can search for locations or begin browsing at a map of the world and click onto the country or continent you're interested in. *Type:* Database.

Map West San Francisco Visitor Map

MAP WEST, Inc.

2161 Union St., Ste. 3 Ph: (415)474-3126
San Francisco, CA 94123-4003 Fax: (415)885-6070
E-mail: bhuber@mapwest.com
URL: http://www.mapwest.com/

Desc: If you don't have relatives in the Bay Area but still want to visit, check out this site for your free copy of the San Francisco Bay Area Map. They offer trip planning and assistance for anyone planning to vacation in the Bay area. *Type:* Database.

Michigan Living

AAA Automobile Club of Michigan

1 Auto Club Dr. Ph: (313)336-1506
Dearborn, MI 48126 Fax: (313)336-1344
E-mail: michliving@aol.com.
URL: http://www.aaamich.com.

Contact: Ronald E. Garbinski, Editor, (248)816-9265, fax: (248)816-2251, regarbo@aol.com; Khristi Zimmeth, Sr. Editor.

Desc: Magazine covering travel, recreation and lifestyle activities in Michigan, the U.S., and around the world. Also reports on highway and home safety. *Type:* Periodical.

Midwest Traveler

AAA Auto Club of Missouri

12901 N. 40 Dr. Ph: (314)523-7350
St. Louis, MO 63141 Free: 800-222-7623
Fax: (314)523-6982

Contact: Michael J. Right, Editor; Debbie Klein, Managing Editor, acmdmk@ibm.net; Dennis R. Heinze, Associate Editor, acmdrh@ibm.net.

Desc: Motor club magazine with an emphasis on travel. *Type:* Periodical.

Mobil Travel Guide

Mobil Oil Corporation

1 Fountain Square Ph: (703)846-2384
11911 Freedom
Reston, VA 20190
URL: http://www.mobil.com

Desc: Contains descriptions and ratings (1 to 5 stars) of 20,000 hotels, motels, resorts, and restaurants in 53 cities in the United States and Canada. Each listing includes name, address, and full description of features and services. *Available:* Prodigy Services Company, PRODIGY. *Type:* Database.

Montana Travel Planner

Travel Montana

Department of Commerce Ph: (406)444-2654
1424 9th Ave. Free: 800-847-4868
Helena, MT 59620 Fax: (406)444-1800
E-mail: webmaster@visitmt.com
URL: http://visitmt.com.

Contact: Donnie Sexton, Editor.

Desc: About 3,000 motels, hotels, bed and breakfast services, ranches, resorts, hostels, hot springs, private and public campgrounds, and licensed outfitters and guiding services in Montana. *Type:* Directory.

Motor News

AAA Auto Club of South Jersey

700 Laurel Oak Rd. Ph: (609)783-4222
PO Box 1953 Fax: (609)627-9025
Voorhees, NJ 08043

Contact: Joel L. Vittori, Pres./CEO & Publisher; Carol A. Scott, Associate Publisher/Editor, cscott@eaasj.com.

Desc: Travel newspaper (tabloid). *Type:* Periodical.

MotorHome

TL Enterprises, Inc.

2575 Vista Del Mar Ph: (805)667-4100
Ventura, CA 93001 Free: 800-765-1912
Fax: (805)667-4434
URL: http://www.tl.com.

Contact: Bill Estes, Publisher; Barbara Leonard, Editorial Dir.; Terry Thompson, Natl. Sales Dir.

Desc: Magazine for motorhome enthusiasts. *Type:* Periodical.

Motorist

AAA Washington

1745-114th Ave. S.W. Ph: (206)462-2222
Bellevue, WA 98004 Fax: (206)646-2193
E-mail: aaawacm@aol.com.

Contact: Janet E. Ray, Publisher; John Powers, Editor.

Desc: Newspaper (tabloid) for auto club members. *Type:* Periodical.

National Business Travel Association

1650 King St., Ste. 401 Ph: (703)684-0836
Alexandria, VA 22314 Fax: (703)684-0263

Contact: Norman Sherlock, Exec. Dir.

Desc: Travel managers and providers. Works to: enhance the educational advancement and image of the profession and membership; enhance the value of the travel manager in meeting corporate travel needs and financial goals; provide education to members about industry matters, issues, and technology; cultivate a positive public image of the corporate travel industry; advocate and protect the interests of members and their corporations on legislative and regulatory matters; promote safety, security, efficiency and quality travel; and enhance professionalism and recognition of the industry and individual members. *Type:* Association.

National Geographic Traveler

National Geographic Society

1145 17th St. NW Ph: (202)857-6112
Washington, DC 20036 Free: 800-638-6400
Fax: (202)775-6141
E-mail: natgeo1@aol.com; traveler@nationalgeographic.com.
URL: http://www.nationalgeographic.com; http://www.nationalgeographic.com.

Contact: Keith Bellows, Editor; Dawn Drew, Advertising Dir.

Desc: Travel magazine emphasizing practical information about U.S. and foreign destinations. *Type:* Periodical.

National Geographic Traveler—Calendar of Events

National Geographic Society

1145 17th St. NW Ph: (202)857-6112
Washington, DC 20036 Free: 800-638-6400
Fax: (202)775-6141
E-mail: natgeo1@aol.com
URL: http://www.nationalgeographic.com

Contact: Kathie Gartrell, Editor.

Desc: Festivals, parades, special exhibits, and other events throughout the U.S. and Canada scheduled for the two months covered in each issue. Also includes some international events. *Type:* Directory.

National Geographic WORLD

National Geographic Society

1145 17th St. NW Ph: (202)857-6112
Washington, DC 20036 Free: 800-638-6400
Fax: (202)775-6141
E-mail: natgeo1@aol.com
URL: http://www.nationalgeographic.com

Contact: Susan Tejada, Editor, (202)828-6651, fax: (202)775-6112, stejada@ngs.org.

Desc: Magazine featuring factual stories on outdoor adventure, natural history, sports, science, and history for children ages 8 through 13. *Type:* Periodical.

Nevada Events and Shows

Nevada Magazine

555 E Washington Ave., No. Ph: (702)486-2433
5600 Free: 800-495-3281
Las Vegas, NV 89101 Fax: (702)486-2789
E-mail: nevmag@aol.com.

Contact: Ann Henderson, Editor, (702)486-2433, nev-mag@aol.com; Richard Moreno, Publisher, (702)687-5416, fax: (702)687-6159; Patty Noll, Advertising Dir. *Desc:* Travel magazine. *Type:* Periodical.

New Mexico Magazine

State of New Mexico

Lew Wallace Bldg.   Ph: (505)827-7447
495 Old Santa Fe Trail   Fax: (505)827-6496
Santa Fe, NM 87503
URL: http://www.state.nm.us/nmag.
Contact: Emily Drabanski, Editor, (505)827-6392; John McMahon, Publisher, (505)827-6346; Patsy Martinez, Advertising Mgr., (505)476-0213.
Desc: Magazine with travel and historical features on New Mexico, southwestern cuisine. Includes photo features, Native American stories. *Type:* Periodical.

Newport Traveler

Traveler Publications, Inc.

174 Bellevue Ave., No. 205   Ph: (401)847-0226
Newport, RI 02840   Free: 800-675-0226
               Fax: (401)847-5267
Contact: Jeffrey C. Hall, Publisher; Judy Rush, Business Mgr.; Kirby Varacalli, Sales Mgr.
Desc: Newspaper for residents and tourists in southern New England. *Type:* Periodical.

North American Indian Landmarks—A Traveler's Guide

Gale Group Inc.

27500 Drake Rd.   Ph: (248)699-4253
Farmington Hills, MI 48331-   Free: 800-877-GALE
   3535   Fax: (248)699-8070
E-mail: galeord@galegroup.com
URL: http://www.galegroup.com.
Contact: George Cantor, Editor.
Desc: Approximately 340 sites in the U.S. and Canada significant to Native North American history, including historical, tribal, and art museums, monuments, plaques, parks, reservations, birthplaces, grave sites, battlefields. *Type:* Directory.

OAG Business Travel Planner

Reed Travel Group—OAG Travel Services Division

2000 Clearwater Dr.   Ph: (630)574-6000
Oak Brook, IL 60521   Free: 800-DIA-LOAG
               Fax: (630)574-6090
E-mail: info@oag.com
URL: http://www.oag.com.
Contact: Richard Manfready, Editor.
Desc: 14,500 destination cities, military installations (U.S. only), and colleges and universities in North America; over 31,500 hotels and motels; calendar of events; city, state or province, and national tourist offices; tour operators; car rental agencies; airlines and charter air taxi firms, and airport limousine services; consulates and missions of foreign countries in North America; United States foreign service offices; hotel and motel systems, and toll free reservations services; airport club locations, frequent flyer and frequent guest information. *Type:* Directory.

OAG Electronic Edition Travel Service

OAG World Wide (OAG)

2000 Clearwater Dr.   Ph: (630)574-6000
Oak Brook, IL 60521
E-mail: info@oag.com
URL: http://www.oag.com
Contact: OAG HelpDesk, info@oag.com.
Desc: Provides up-to-date travel-related information for travelers worldwide. Comprises 18 files, including the following: • OAG Electronic Edition--offers information on current airline flights and fares, flight availability, more than 50,000 hotels worldwide, and an online flight reservation capability. *Available:* OAG World Wide (OAG). *Type:* Database.

OAG Pocket Flight Guide - North American Edition

Official Airline Guides

2000 Clearwater Dr.   Ph: (630)574-6000
Oak Brook, IL 60523-8806   Free: 800-323-3537
               Fax: (630)574-6667
Contact: Richard A. Nelson, Publisher; Barbara J. Comiskey, Editor; Paul B. Beatty, General Mgr.
Desc: Directory containing quick reference airline schedules of nonstop and multi-stop flights on the most frequently traveled routes throughout all 50 United States, Canada, Caribbean, and Mexico. *Type:* Periodical.

Pacific Asia Travel Association

Telesis Tower, Ste. 1000   Ph: (415)986-4646
1 Montgomery St.   Fax: (415)986-3458
San Francisco, CA 94104
E-mail: patahq@pata.org
URL: http://www.pata.org
Contact: Joe McInerney, Pres. & CEO.
Desc: Government tourist bureaus; cruise companies, airlines, railroads, commercial travel bureaus, hotels, tour operators, and hotel associations throughout the world. Conducts marketing program to promote travel to the countries and islands of the Greater Pacific region; works to facilitate and unify entry and exit procedures in members' countries; provides travel information service to the industry disseminates travel news to the press and other media; coordinates market research to determine potential markets and the future impact of overseas travelers. Develops destination development task forces. *Type:* Association.

Physician's Travel & Meeting Guide

Quadrant Health Co.

26 Main St.   Ph: (973)701-8900
Chatham, NJ 07928
E-mail: ptmg@qhc.com.
Contact: Bea Riemschneider, Editor-in-Chief, (973)701-2716, bea.riemschneider@qhc.com; Terrance A. Bean, Publisher, (973)701-2704, terrance.bean@qhc.com.
Desc: Magazine for physicians. *Type:* Periodical.

The Practical Gourmet

Healthy Gourmet, Inc.

Gourmet Bldg.   Ph: (516)924-8555
7 Putter Ln.
PO Box 102
Middle Island, NY 11953-0102
Contact: Gaylen Andrews, R.N., Food & Restaurant Ed.; Dr. Andrew S. Linick, Travel Features Ed., linickgrp@att.net; Barbara J. Deal, M.S., Assoc. Editor.
Desc: Focuses on the "affluent gourmet traveler desiring delicious, healthy worldwide culinary excellence and entertainment." Discusses "upscale" (2-5 star) properties, resorts, destinations, special events, and wine tastings. Provides dining awards (2-5 star) and quality ratings for restaurants. *Type:* Newsletter.

Prince Edward Island Visitors Guide

Government of Prince Edward Island

95 Rochford St.   Ph: (902)368-4400
PO Box 940   Free: 800-463-4PEI
Charlottetown, PE, Canada C1A   Fax: (902)368-4416
   7M5
URL: http://www.gov.pe.ca/vg/
Desc: With festivals all year round, scenic beauty, and some of the warmest water north of the Carolinas, Prince Edward Island is a popular vacation spot for many. Prince Edward Island Visitors Guide on-line provides you with the information about getting to the island, accommodation facilities, restaurants, activities and festivals as well as cultural and historical information. *Type:* Database.

Punch In Travel & Entertainment News Syndicate

400 E. 59th St.   Ph: (212)755-4363
Ste. 9-F
New York, NY 10022
E-mail: punchin@usa.net.
URL: http://inx.net:80/punchin/.
Contact: J. Walman, President; Jerry Preiser, Managing Editor; Nancy Preiser, Managing Editor.
Alt. Contact: 400 E. 59th St., Ste. 9-F, New York, NY 10022; telephone: (212)755-4363. *Type:* Periodical.

Punch in International Travel and Entertainment Magazine

Enterprises Publishing

400 E. 59th St., Ste. 9F   Ph: (212)755-4363
New York, NY 10022
Contact: Nancy Dreiser, Editor.
Desc: Consumer magazine covering lifestyle and business and luxury travel. *Type:* Periodical.

Relax

Advantar Communications

270 Madison Ave.   Ph: (212)951-6708
New York, NY 10016-0695   Fax: (212)686-4841
Contact: Michelle Janin, Publisher; Judi Dash, Editor.
Type: Periodical.

Resorts & Great Hotels

Islands Publishing Co.

PO Box 4728   Ph: (805)745-7100
Santa Barbara, CA 93140-4728   Free: 800-322-1161
               Fax: (805)745-7105
E-mail: islands@islandsmag.com
URL: http://www.resortsandgreathotels.com.
Contact: Dan Fox, Publisher; Annette Burden, Editor; Kelly Foy, Associate Editor; Shoshana Levy, Operations Mgr.; Mindy Sofro, Operations Mgr.
Desc: Magazine covering great resorts and hotels. *Type:* Periodical.

Rocky Mountain News

Scripps Howard

400 W. Colfax Ave.   Ph: (303)892-5000
PO Box 719   Free: 800-933-1990
Denver, CO 80204   Fax: (303)892-5081
URL: http://www.insidedenver.com.
Contact: Jay Ambrose, Editor; Larry D. Strutton, Publisher, President; Vern Mallinen, Advertising Dir.
Desc: General newspaper. *Type:* Periodical.

SEE Beaches

Miles Media Group, Inc.

3675 Clark Rd.   Ph: (941)922-3575
Sarasota, FL 34233-2358   Free: 800-683-0010
               Fax: (941)923-6309
E-mail: mmg@netline.net
Contact: Patti Upton, Publisher, (800)683-1000; Errol Croft, Editorial Dir.
Desc: Consumer travel guides. *Type:* Periodical.

See Florida Keys

Miles Media Group, Inc.

3675 Clark Rd.   Ph: (941)922-3575
Sarasota, FL 34233-2358   Free: 800-683-0010
               Fax: (941)923-6309
E-mail: mmg@netline.net
Contact: Shelley Sisko, Assoc. Publisher; John Criswell, Publisher.
Desc: Tourist magazine for the Florida Keys. *Type:* Periodical.

September Days Club
339 Jefferson Rd.
Parsippany, NJ 07054
Contact: John Bonifield, Contact.
Desc: A nonprofit discount travel organization for people 50 and older, created by Days Inns of America, Inc. Purpose is to encourage travel and attract senior citizens to Days Inns, Hotels, Suites and Daystops through publications and discounts on travel, rooms, food, gifts, and at major tourist attractions. Organizes international and domestic tours. *Type:* Association.

Silver Bird Travel Features
Gate 6 1/2 Berth 4   Ph: (415)331-7700
Sausalito, CA 94965
Contact: Kevin Keating, Author.
Desc: Distributes magazine, newspaper, and TV features. *Alt. Contact:* Gate 6 1/2 Berth 4, Sausalito, CA 94965; telephone: (415)331-7700. *Type:* Periodical.

SKY Magazine--(Delta Air Lines)
Pace Communications, Inc.
1301 Carolina St.   Ph: (336)378-6065
Greensboro, NC 27401-1001   Fax: (336)378-8261
E-mail: skymagads@aol.com; skymag@aol.com.
URL: http://www.delta-sky.com.
Contact: John G. Masters, Publisher, fax: (336)274-2679, skymagads@aol.com; Duncan Christy, Editorial Dir., fax: (336)274-2220; Mickey McLean, Managing Editor, fax: (336)274-2220.
Desc: General interest in-flight magazine. *Type:* Periodical.

Society of Incentive & Travel Executives
21 W. 38th St., 10th Fl.   Ph: (212)575-0910
New York, NY 10018   Fax: (212)575-1838
E-mail: site1@ix.netcom.com
URL: http://www.site-intl.org
Contact: Robert Vitagliano, CITE, Exec.VP & CEO.
Desc: Individuals responsible for the administration or sale of incentive travel including corporate users, incentive travel houses, cruise lines, hotel chains, resort operators, airlines, and tourist boards. Unites individuals in the incentive travel industry and facilitates information exchange and problem solving on a personal and professional basis. Supports expansion of incentive travel through public relations, promotion, and speakers' bureau activities. *Type:* Association.

Southern Living Vacations
Southern Progress
2100 Lakeshore Dr.   Ph: (205)877-6000
Birmingham, AL 35209-6721   Free: 888-737-3529
                              Fax: (205)877-6600
Contact: Karen Lingo, Editor.
Desc: Themed guides covering travel in the South. *Type:* Periodical.

Southwest Spirit
American Airlines Publishing
4333 Amon Carter Blvd.   Ph: (817)967-1804
MD 5598   Fax: (817)967-1571
Fort Worth, TX 76155-9640
Contact: Richelle Thompson, Exec. Editor; Terrie Lonergan, Assoc. Publisher.
Desc: Magazine for customers of Southwest Airlines. Includes book reviews. *Type:* Periodical.

Strand Magazine
Strand Media Group, Inc.
1357-21st Ave. No. Ste. 103   Ph: (843)626-8911
Myrtle Beach, SC 29577   Fax: (843)626-6452
E-mail: strandmag@aol.com; strandmag@aol.com.
Contact: Delores Blount, Publisher.

Desc: Vacation guide. *Type:* Periodical.

The Student Traveller
Canadian Federation of Students-Services
45 Charles St., E., Ste. 100   Ph: (416)966-2887
Toronto, ON, Canada M4Y   Fax: (416)966-4043
1S2
E-mail: mail@travelcuts.com; stutrav@travelcuts.com.
Contact: Ann Klug, Editor; Ann Klug, Advertising Dir.
Desc: Travel magazine for students in Canada. *Type:* Periodical.

Sunset Magazine
Sunset Publishing Corp.
80 Willow Rd.   Ph: (415)321-3600
Menlo Park, CA 94025   Free: 800-227-7346
                             Fax: (415)321-0551
Contact: Rosalie Muller-Wright, Editor; Stephen Seabolt, President; Anthony Glaves, Publisher.
Desc: Magazine covering western homes, gardens, food and travel (5 regional editions). *Type:* Periodical.

Texas Highways
Texas Department of Transportation
Travel & Information Division   Ph: (512)483-3675
PO Box 141009   Free: 800-839-4997
Austin, TX 78714-1009   Fax: (512)483-3672
Contact: Kathy Murphy, Publisher; Jack Lowry, Editor.
Desc: Official travel magazine of Texas; covering scenic, recreational, historical, cultural, and ethnic interests. *Type:* Periodical.

This is Indianapolis
Indianapolis Convention and Visitors Association
One RCA Dome, Ste. 100   Ph: (317)639-4282
Indianapolis, IN 46225   Free: 800-323-INDY
                             Fax: (317)684-2590
E-mail: icva@indianapolis.org
Contact: William R. Hendrickson, Manager, bhendrickson@indianapolis.org; Mary K. Huggard, Vice President, mhuggard@indianapolis.org.
Desc: Hotel inroom Indianapolis visitors guide. *Type:* Periodical.

This Week Kauai
This Week Publications
274 Puuhale Rd., Ste. 200   Ph: (808)845-0572
Honolulu, HI 96819   Fax: (808)852-6350
E-mail: editor@thisweek.com
URL: http://www.thisweek.com.
Contact: Keri Shepherd, Editor; Ron Cruger, Publisher.
Desc: Visitor magazine with maps, coupons, and tourist information. *Type:* Periodical.

Thunder Bay Guest Magazine
Algoma Publishers Ltd.
1126 Roland St.   Ph: (807)623-4424
Thunder Bay, ON, Canada P7B   Fax: (807)622-3140
5M4
URL: http://www.tbsource.com.
Contact: Lorraine Deck, Editor; Elizabeth Dougall, Publisher; Mavis Hoard, Advertising.
Desc: Tourist guide. *Type:* Periodical.

Today in San Diego
Today in San Diego
3600 Mission Blvd.   Ph: (619)488-0357
San Diego, CA 92109   Fax: (619)488-0357
Contact: John B. Moriarty, Editor and Publisher.
Desc: Magazine (tabloid) distributed in hotel rooms, transportation centers, and visitor information areas in San Diego County containing articles and advertising on attractions, activities, shopping, and dining in San Diego, California. *Type:* Periodical.

Trailer Life
TL Enterprises, Inc.
2575 Vista Del Mar   Ph: (805)667-4100
Ventura, CA 93001   Free: 800-765-1912
                             Fax: (805)667-4434
Contact: Bill Estes, Publisher; Barbara Leonard, Editorial Dir.; Janet Van Bibber, Advertising Dir.
Desc: Magazine for recreational vehicle (RV) enthusiasts. *Type:* Periodical.

Travel Holiday
Reader's Digest Publications
28 W. 23rd   Ph: (212)366-8853
New York, NY 10010-5204   Free: 800-937-9241
                             Fax: (212)633-4699
Contact: Margaret Staats Simmons, Editor; Elizabeth Hettich, Advertising Mgr.; Samuel Young, Editor; Lou DiLorenzo, Editor; Pat Haegele, Publisher; Ruth Halpert, Advertising Mgr.
Desc: Magazine for the frequent pleasure traveler. Articles feature off-season, off-the-beaten-path destinations as well as more standard, popular tourist areas--in the U.S. and abroad. *Type:* Periodical.

Travel International
EWA Publications
2446 E. 65th St.   Ph: (718)763-7034
Brooklyn, NY 11234   Fax: (718)763-7035
Contact: Kevin Browne, Editor; Justin Baron, Publisher; Bill Tarrington, Advertising Mgr.
Desc: Community newspaper. *Type:* Periodical.

Travel & Leisure
American Express Publishing Corp.
1120 Avenue of the Americas   Ph: (212)382-5600
New York, NY 10036   Free: 800-333-6569
                             Fax: (212)382-5877
Contact: Ed Kelly, Publisher; Nancy Novogrod, Editor-in-Chief.
Desc: Travel magazine. *Type:* Periodical.

Travel & Leisure
Features 66 Alexander Rd.   Ph: (617)969-4102
Newton, MA 02161
Contact: Eleanor Margolis, Destinations Ed.; Milton Gun, Cruise News; Howard Neal, Travel Away.
Desc: Distributes travel columns. *Alt. Contact:* Features 66 Alexander Rd., Newton, MA 02161; telephone: (617)969-4102. *Type:* Periodical.

Travel Montana
Matthew T. Cohn
1424 9th Ave.   Ph: (406)444-2654
PO Box 200533   Free: 800-VIS-ITMT
Helena, MT 59620   Fax: (406)444-1800
E-mail: webmaster@visitmt.com
URL: http://www.travel.mt.gov
Contact: Matthew T. Cohn, Dir.
Desc: Promotes Montana as a travel destination and as a location for filming of motion pictures and television commercials. *Type:* Association.

Travel National
EWA Publications
2446 E. 65th St.   Ph: (718)763-7034
Brooklyn, NY 11234   Fax: (718)763-7035
Contact: Kevin Browae, Editor; Justin Baron, Publisher; Bill Tarrington, Advertising Mgr.
Desc: Magazine on travel. *Type:* Periodical.

Travel News

Travel Agents International, Inc.
11006 4th St. N., No. 27   Ph: (813)576-8241
St. Petersburg, FL 33716-2945   Fax: (813)579-0529
Contact: Matthew Wiseman, Editor.
Desc: Travel publication. *Type:* Periodical.

Travel & Tourism Executive Report

Leisure Industry/Recreation News
PO Box 43563   Ph: (202)232-7107
Washington, DC 20010-9563
Contact: Marj Jensen, Editor.
Desc: Specializes in presentation of articles on travel marketing campaigns. Covers demographics. *Type:* Newsletter.

TravelAmerica

World Publishing Co.
990 Grove St.   Ph: (847)491-6440
Evanston, IL 60201-4370   Fax: (847)491-6462
E-mail: century@wwa.com
URL: http://www.travelamerica.com.
Contact: Robert Meyers, Editor; Randy Mink, Managing Editor; Norman Jacobs, Publisher, fax: (847)491-0459, normj@wwa.com.
Desc: Consumer travel magazine. *Type:* Periodical.

Travelers Advantage/Travelers Access

Cendant
Comp-U-Card Division
40 Oakview Dr.   Ph: (203)365-2000
Trumbull, CT 06611
URL: http://www.cendant.com
Contact: Lew Bednarczuk, Product Manager, Interactive Services.
Desc: Contains travel information, including airfare, hotels, condominiums, cruises, tours, and car rentals. Packages are offered at discounted prices. *Available:* Prodigy Services Company, PRODIGY; CompuServe Information Service; America Online, Inc.; Cendant, Comp-U-Card Division. *Type:* Database.

TRAVELHOST

Travelhost, Inc.
10701 Stemmons Fwy.   Ph: (214)691-1163
Dallas, TX 75220-2419   Free: 800-527-1782
                                Fax: (214)869-1552
URL: http://www.travelhost.com.
Contact: James E. Buerger, Publisher; Brad Calley, VP/GM Publications, brad@travelhost.com.
Desc: In-room magazine for business and vacation travelers. Regional issues contain features on local dining and entertainment, television listings, maps, and general information. Content and advertising vary by region. *Type:* Periodical.

Traveling Times

Traveling Times, Inc.
25115 B-130 W. Ave. Stanford   Ph: (661)295-1250
Valencia, CA 91355-3922   Fax: (661)295-8558
Contact: Mirko A. Ilich, Editor and Publisher.
Desc: Travel journal. *Type:* Periodical.

Traveling Times

Traveling Times, Inc.
25115 B-130 W. Ave. Stanford   Ph: (661)295-1250
Valencia, CA 91355-3922   Fax: (661)295-8558
Contact: Mirko A. Ilitch, Editor.
Desc: Highlights popular vacation spots around the world. *Type:* Newsletter.

The Traveller

North West Commercial Travellers' Association of Canada
PO Box 336   Ph: (204)957-1442
Winnipeg, MB, Canada R3C   Free: 800-665-6928
  2H6   Fax: (204)957-0115
Contact: Terry Carruthers, Editor.
Desc: Provides news of the Association and its activities. Updates members on discounts available and recommends hotels, car rental companies, and services for cost-conscious commercial travellers. *Type:* Newsletter.

Travelware Suppliers Directory

Business Journals, Inc.
50 Day St.   Ph: (203)853-6015
PO Box 5550   Free: 800-521-0227
Norwalk, CT 06856   Fax: (203)852-8175
Contact: Amanda West, Editor, akanaga@travelwaremag.com.
Desc: 500 manufacturers and importers that supply hardware, leather, fabrics, and other components to the luggage and leather goods industry (SIC 3161). *Type:* Directory.

The United Church Observer

Observer Publications, Inc.
478 Huron St.   Ph: (416)960-8500
Toronto, ON, Canada M5R   Fax: (416)960-8477
  2R3
E-mail: observer@inforamp.net.
Contact: Muriel Duncan, Editor; Ena Norbury, Circulation Supervisor; David Wilson, Assoc. Editor; Fran Oliver, Editorial Asst.
Desc: Religious and general interest magazine. *Type:* Periodical.

United Hemispheres

Pace Communications, Inc.
1301 Carolina St.   Ph: (336)378-6065
Greensboro, NC 27401-1001   Fax: (336)378-8261
Contact: Kate Greer, Editor; Bonnie McElveen-Hunter, Publisher; John Ballantyne, Vice President Sales and Marketing.
Desc: In flight magazine for United Airlines passengers. *Type:* Periodical.

USAir Magazine

NYT Custom Publishing
122 E. 42nd St.   Ph: (212)499-3543
New York, NY 10168   Fax: (212)499-3573
Contact: Catherine Sabino, Editor; Robert Young, Publisher.
Desc: In-flight magazine. *Type:* Periodical.

VACATIONS

Vacation Publications, Inc.
1502 Augusta, Ste. 415   Ph: (713)974-6903
Houston, TX 77057   Fax: (713)974-0445
Contact: R. Alan Fox, Editor and Publisher; Robin Fowler, Managing Editor.
Type: Periodical.

Vermont Green Mountain Guide

Patience & Persistence in Marketing, Inc.
RR No. 1, Box 112, 44   Ph: (802)886-3333
  Country Rd.   Fax: (802)886-3333
North Springfield, VT 05150
Contact: Cindy Thiel, Pres./Pub.
Desc: Tourist publication including dining, attractions, calendar of events, history, editorials, and lodging in Vermont. *Type:* Periodical.

VIA

California State Automobile Association
150 Van Ness Ave.   Ph: (415)565-2454
San Francisco, CA 94102   Free: 800-468-7563
                                Fax: (415)552-5825
Contact: Lynn Ferrin, Editor; Kate MacIntyre, Advertising Mgr., (415)565-2455.
Desc: Magazine covering worldwide and regional travel and recreation, restaurants, cars and car care, motorists issues, and traffic safety. *Type:* Periodical.

Virginia is for Lovers Travel Guide

Virginia Tourism Corp.
901 E. Byrd St.   Ph: (804)786-2051
Richmond, VA 23219-4048   Free: 800-759-0886
                                Fax: (804)786-1919
E-mail: vainfo@vedp.state.va.us
URL: http://www.virginia.org; http://www.virginia.org.
Contact: Pamela Jewell, Editor, (804)371-8168, pjewell@vedp.state.va.us; Julie Grimes, Editor, (804)371-8164, jgrimes@vedp.state.va.us.
Desc: More than 900 museums, historic buildings and villages, recreational parks and facilities, hotels, restaurants, shops, visitors bureaus, and other tourist attractions, sites, and travel services in Virginia; events, fairs, and festivals; Virginia arts commissions. *Type:* Directory.

Vista USA

C. E. Publishing
30400 Van Dyke   Ph: (810)574-9100
Warren, MI 48093-2368   Fax: (810)575-9328
Contact: Martha J. Mendez, Editor.
Desc: Magazine of the Exxon Travel Club. *Type:* Periodical.

West Michigan Winter Fun and Get-Away Guide

West Michigan Tourist Association
1253 Front Ave. NW   Ph: (616)456-8557
Grand Rapids, MI 49504-3216   Free: 800-442-2084
                                Fax: (616)456-8958
E-mail: info@wmta.org
URL: http://www.wmta.org.
Contact: Kristi Kortman, Editor.
Desc: About 60 downhill and cross-country ski areas, 40 snowmobiling areas, lodging and rental facilities in western Michigan; approximately 125 winter events, festivals, races, unique shopping experiences, and romantic getaways. *Type:* Directory.

Westways

Automobile of S. California
3333 Fairview Rd., A327   Ph: (714)885-2376
Costa Mesa, CA 92626   Fax: (714)885-2335
Contact: Susan LaTempa, Editor-in-Chief, (714)885-2406; John Dinkel, Publisher, (714)885-2401; Bob Bradley, Dir. of Advertising, (714)885-2403; Richard Stayton, Managing Editor, (714)885-2359.
Desc: Magazine covering regional, domestic and international travel, recreation, and events. *Type:* Periodical.

Westworld

Canada Wide Magazines & Communications Ltd.
4180 Lougheed Hwy., 4th Fl.   Ph: (604)299-7311
Burnaby, BC, Canada V5C 6A7   Fax: (604)299-9188
E-mail: circulation@canadawide.com
Contact: Robin Roberts, Editor; Peter Legge, Publisher; Neil Soper, Advertising Mgr.; Tim Nast, SM1.
Desc: Magazine for auto club members in British Columbia, Alberta, and Saskatchewan. *Type:* Periodical.

Westworld Alberta

Canada Wide Magazines & Communications Ltd.
4180 Lougheed Hwy., 4th Fl.   Ph: (604)299-7311
Burnaby, BC, Canada V5C 6A7   Fax: (604)299-9188
E-mail: circulation@canadawide.com
Contact: Pete Legge, Publisher; M. Weeks, Circulation Mgr.; Rick McMorran, Sales Mgr.; Pat Price, Editor.
Desc: Magazine for members of the Alberta Motor Association. *Type:* Periodical.

Where Magazine

Where Magazine
475 Park Ave. S., Ste.2100   Ph: (212)725-8100
New York, NY 10016   Fax: (212)725-3412
URL: http://www.wheremags.com.
Contact: Michael Kelly Tucker, Editor; Merrie L. Davis, Publisher.
Desc: Guide for visitors. *Type:* Periodical.

Where Rocky Mountains

RMV Publications Ltd.
One Palliser Sq., Ste. 250   Ph: (403)299-1885
125 Ninth Ave. SE   Fax: (403)299-1899
Calgary, AB, Canada T2G 0P6
URL: http://www.whererockymountains.com.
Contact: Jack Newton, Editor and Publisher, (403)299-1885, jnewton@cadvision.com; Glenn Miles, Advertising Mgr., (403)299-1881, gmiles@cadvision.com.
Desc: Consumer magazine covering visitor information for the Canadian Rocky Mountains. *Type:* Periodical.

WHERE Victoria

Pacific Island Publishers
1001 Wharf St., 3rd Fl.   Ph: (604)388-4324
Victoria, BC, Canada V8W 1T6   Fax: (604)388-6166
E-mail: keypac@islandnet.com.
Contact: Anna Scolnkk, Publisher; Carolyn Camilleri, Editor.
Desc: Visitors travel guide. *Type:* Periodical.

Where Washington

Where Washington
1225 19th St. NW, Ste. 510   Ph: (202)463-4550
Washington, DC 20036   Fax: (202)463-4553
E-mail: wheredc@mindspring.com.
Contact: Rick Mellineaux, Publisher; Jean Cohen, Editor; Kecia Jenkins, Circulation Mgr.; Julie DeVol, Advertising Dir.
Desc: Consumer magazine covering tourist information for Washington, DC. *Type:* Periodical.

Where & When Pennsylvania's Travel Guide

Barash Group
403 S. Allen St.   Ph: (814)238-5051
PO Box 77   Free: 800-326-9584
State College, PA 16804-0077   Fax: (814)237-4327
E-mail: email@barashgroup.com
Contact: Mimi Ungar Coppersmith, Publisher, (800)326-9584, fax: (814)238-3415, mimi@barashgroup.com.
Desc: Guide to travel, events, and activities across Pennsylvania. *Type:* Periodical.

Wild Planet! 1,001 Extraordinary Events for the Inspired Traveler

Visible Ink Press
27500 Drake Rd.   Ph: (248)699-4253
Farmington Hills, MI 48331-   Free: 800-776-6265
3535   Fax: (248)699-8067
E-mail: galeord@gale.com
URL: http://www.gale.com
Desc: 1,001 unique travel destinations and events, worldwide. *Type:* Directory.

Worldwide Travel Information Contact Book

Gale Group Inc.
27500 Drake Rd.   Ph: (248)699-4253
Farmington Hills, MI 48331-   Free: 800-877-GALE
3535   Fax: (248)699-8070
E-mail: galeord@galegroup.com
URL: http://www.galegroup.com.
Contact: Burkhard Herbote, Editor.
Desc: Approximately 45,500 contacts and sources for travel information including: travel agents, associations, tourist authorities, tour operators, lodging associations, and publications. *Type:* Directory.

Yesterday's Island

Yesterday's Island, Inc.
PO Box 626   Ph: (508)228-9165
Nantucket, MA 02554   Fax: (508)228-1348
Contact: Suzanne M. Daub, Editor; Jerry T. Daub, Publisher.
Desc: Tourist guide. *Type:* Periodical.

Trucks

American Motor Carrier Directory

Primedia Information Inc.
10 Lake Dr.   Ph: (609)371-7700
Hightstown, NJ 08520-5397   Free: 800-221-5488
                                  Fax: (609)371-7879
Contact: John G. Capers, III, Editor, jcapers@primediainfo.com.
Desc: Lists of all licensed Less Than Truckload (LTL) general commodity carriers in the United States; includes specialized motor carriers and related services; includes refrigerated carriers, heavy haulers, bulk haulers, riggers, and specified commodity carriers; state and federal regulatory bodies governing the trucking industry; tariff publishing bureaus; freight claim councils; industry associations, etc. *Type:* Directory.

Car & Travel

AAA Southern Pennsylvania
118 E. Market St.   Ph: (717)845-2222
PO Box 2387   Fax: (717)845-5444
York, PA 17405-2387
Contact: Donna Snyder, Editor.
Desc: Travel and motoring magazine for auto club membership. *Type:* Periodical.

Commercial Carrier Journal—Buyers' Guide Issue

Cahners Business Information
201 King of Prussia Rd.   Ph: (610)964-4000
Radnor, PA 19087-5114   Fax: (610)964-2915
E-mail: marketaccess@cahners.com
URL: http://www.ccjmagazine.com/buyers.htm.
Contact: Gerald F. Standley, Editor.
Desc: List of vehicles, components and accessories suppliers for the truck and bus fleet markets. *Type:* Directory.

Commercial Carrier Journal—Top 100 Issue

Cahners Business Information
201 King of Prussia Rd.   Ph: (610)964-4000
Radnor, PA 19087-5114   Fax: (610)964-2915
E-mail: marketaccess@cahners.com
URL: http://www.ccjmagazine.com.
Contact: Gerald F. Standley, Editor, gstandle@chilton.net.
Desc: List of top 100 for-hire motor carriers, ranked by gross revenues; also the next 200 carriers in gross revenue. *Type:* Directory.

The Dixie Trucker

Fastline
4900 Fox Run Rd.   Free: 800-626-6409
PO Box 248   Fax: (502)222-0615
Buckner, KY 40010
E-mail: fastpub@aol.com
Contact: William G. Howard, Publisher.
Desc: Truck trade magazine covering the southern trucking industry. *Type:* Periodical.

Heavy Duty Trucking

Newport Communications
PO Box W   Ph: (714)261-1636
Newport Beach, CA 92658-   Free: 800-233-1911
8910   Fax: (714)261-2904
E-mail: aryder@heavytruck.com.
URL: http://www.heavytruck.com.
Contact: Doug Condra, Editor; George Jacovides, Publisher.
Desc: Magazine serving large, medium and small fleet managers whose firms operate class 6, 7 and 8 trucks in the U.S. *Type:* Periodical.

Heavy Duty Trucking—Council of Fleet Specialists Equipment Buyer's Guide & Services Directory

Newport Communications Div.
HIC Corp.
38 Executive Park, Ste. 300   Ph: (714)261-1636
Irvine, CA 92614-6745   Fax: (714)261-2904
Contact: Doug Condra, Editor.
Desc: 500 Council of Fleet Specialists member manufacturers and wholesalers specializing in heavy-duty truck parts and repairs. *Type:* Directory.

Mid-America Weekly Trucking

Heartland Communications Group, Inc.
1003 Central Ave.   Ph: (515)574-2264
PO Box 1115   Free: 888-247-2000
Fort Dodge, IA 50501   Fax: (515)574-2161
Contact: Beth Buehlar, Editor; Denise McLellan, Publisher; Cindy Youngquist, Advertising Mgr.
Desc: Magazine serving all segments of America's largest regional trucking market. *Type:* Periodical.

NATSO Truckers News

Newport Communications
PO Box W   Ph: (714)261-1636
Newport Beach, CA 92658-   Free: 800-233-1911
8910   Fax: (714)261-2904
URL: http://www.heavytruck.com.
Contact: Steve Sturgess, Editor, ssturgess@heavytruck.com; Deborah Whistler, Managing Editor.
Desc: Magazine (tabloid) for professional truck drivers and owner-operators. Official publication of National Association of Truck Stop Operators. *Type:* Periodical.

Official Motor Carrier Directory

Official Motor Freight Guides, Inc.
1700 W. Cortland St.   Ph: (773)278-2454
Chicago, IL 60622   Free: 800-621-4650
                                  Fax: (773)489-0482
Contact: Edward K. Koch, Editor.
Desc: Approximately 2,100 general and specialized motor carriers and air cargo carriers; federal and state agencies concerned with the trucking industry; tariff publishing bureaus; United States and Canadian port authorities; state associations. *Type:* Directory.

Overdrive

Overdrive Magazine, Inc.
PO Box 3187   Ph: (205)349-2990
Tuscaloosa, AL 35403   Free: 800-633-5953
                               Fax: (205)349-3765
E-mail: editors@overdriveonline.com.
URL: http://www.overdriveonline.com.
Contact: Linda Longton, Editorial Dir., fax: (205)750-8070, longton@overdriveonline.com.
Desc: Business/lifestyle publication for owner-operators.
Type: Periodical.

Owner Operator

Cahners Business Information
201 King of Prussia Rd.   Ph: (610)964-4000
Radnor, PA 19087-5114   Fax: (610)964-2915
E-mail: marketaccess@cahners.com
Contact: Leon E. Witconis, Editor; Gregory S. Sheremet, Publisher; Haig Dagdigian, Advertising Mgr.
Desc: Magazine. *Type:* Periodical.

Through the Gears Trucking Magazine

J. B. Scott Publishing
PO Box 2685   Ph: (256)835-4901
Anniston, AL 36202   Free: 800-240-2130
                               Fax: (256)835-4905
E-mail: jbscottpub.@aol.com
Contact: Eric Larson, Contributing Editor; Jeff Borrelli, Advertising Mgr.; Tammy Borrelli, Business Mgr.
Desc: Trucking magazine. *Type:* Periodical.

Truck Paper

Sandhills Publishing
120 W. Harvest Dr.   Ph: (402)479-2181
PO Box 85310   Free: 800-331-4890
Lincoln, NE 68501-5310   Fax: (402)479-2195
Contact: Lee Chapin, Publisher.
Desc: Tabloid featuring trucks, trailers, and parts for sale. *Alt. Contact:* 120 W. Harvest Dr., PO Box 85010, Lincoln, NE 68521-4408; telephone: (402)479-2140; fax: (402)479-2134; toll-free: 800-247-4868. *Type:* Periodical.

Trucker's Connection

Trucker's Connection, Inc.
5960 Crooked Creek Rd., Ste.   Ph: (770)416-0927
15   Fax: (770)416-1734
Norcross, GA 30092
E-mail: 102400.573@compuserve.com.
Contact: Megan Coleman, Editor-in-Chief, megan_coleman@compuserve.com; Wendell Adcock, Associate Publisher, wendell@truckersconnectioninc.com; Jon Grassi, Circulation Director.
Desc: Trade magazine for over-the-road, long haul truck operators. *Type:* Periodical.

Truckers News

Newport Communications
PO Box W   Ph: (714)261-1636
Newport Beach, CA 92658-   Free: 800-233-1911
8910   Fax: (714)261-2904
E-mail: ssturgess@heavytruck.com.
Contact: Deborah Whistler, Managing Editor; Maria Barnett, Editor; Rick DeMuesy, Advertising Mgr.
Desc: Magazine for patrons of truck stops. *Type:* Periodical.

United Church of Christ

Reformed Church Women

475 Riverside Dr., Rm. 1825
New York, NY 10027
Desc: Women of the Reformed Church in America dedicated to promoting fellowship for spiritual growth among members. Provides opportunities and avenues of service for community involvement in areas of concern such as the homeless and hungry. Encourages theological contemplation. *Type:* Association.

United Nations

Global Policy Forum Home Page

Global Policy Forum
777 UN Plaza, Ste. 76   Ph: (212)557-3161
New York, NY 10017   Fax: (212)557-3165
E-mail: globalpolicy@globalpolicy.org
URL: http://www.igc.apc.org/globalpolicy/

Desc: The site describes United Nations policies and problems and what a user can do to become involved. *Type:* Database.

New York City Commission for the United Nations, Consular Corps, and International Business

2 United Nations Plz., 27th Fl.
New York, NY 10017

Desc: The mayor's official liaison between the city of New York and the international diplomatic and business communities. Responsible for promoting the role of the city as headquarters of the United Nations and as one of the main centers of foreign consulates and foreign businesses. Assists in the total adjustment of the international diplomatic and business communities to the life and culture of the city; provides advice and counseling on landlord-tenant problems, school placement, and general casework. *Type:* Association.

United Nations

United Nations Headquarters   Ph: (212)963-1234
New York, NY 10017   Fax: (212)963-4879
E-mail: inquiries@un.org
URL: http://www.un.org

Contact: Kofi Annan, Sec.Gen.

Desc: Countries around the world representing 98% of the world's population. Established following World War II to: identify and solve international disputes that threaten world peace and security; advocate respect for human rights, the "dignity and worth of the human person, and the equal rights of men and women and of nations large and small;" work to create conditions where justice and respect for treaties and international law can be maintained. Members pledge to live peacefully beside their neighbors, and not to use armed force except in the common interest. *Type:* Association.

United Nations Association of the United States of America

801 2nd Ave.   Ph: (212)907-1300
New York, NY 10017   Fax: (212)682-9185
E-mail: unahq@unausa.org
URL: http://www.unausa.org

Contact: Ambassador Alvin Adams, Pres./CEO.

Desc: Seeks to strengthen the United Nations and the role of the United States in the United Nations to prepare it for the challenges of the future. Carries out research and public education programs on the UN and other multilateral institutions. Promotes annual nationwide observance of UN Day. *Type:* Association.

World Federalist Movement

777 U.N. Plaza, 12th Fl.   Ph: (212)599-1320
New York, NY 10017   Fax: (212)599-1332
E-mail: wfm@igc.apc.org
URL: http://www.igc.apc.org/icc/

Contact: Sir Peter Ustinov, Pres.

Desc: Strives to achieve a just world order by strengthening the United Nations. *Type:* Association.

Urology

American Prostate Society

7188 Ridge Rd.   Ph: (410)859-3735
Hanover, MD 21076   Free: 800-678-1238
                               Fax: (410)850-0818
Contact: Claude Gerard, Chm.
Desc: Works to increase the public's awareness of prostate disease. *Type:* Association.

American Urological Association

1120 N. Charles St.   Ph: (410)727-1100
Baltimore, MD 21201   Fax: (410)223-4370
E-mail: aua@auanet.org
URL: http://www.auanet.org
Contact: G. James Gallagher, Exec.Dir.
Desc: Professional society of physicians specializing in urology. Provides placement service. Conducts educational programs; maintains museum. *Type:* Association.

Columbia University

Molecular Urology Laboratory

Department of Urology   Ph: (212)305-5727
College of Physicians and   Fax: (212)305-1564
   Surgeons
630 W. 168th St.
New York, NY 10032
Contact: Dr. Ralph Buttyan, Dir.
Desc: Molecular biology, focusing on prostate cancer, bladder disease, renal disease, erectile dysfunction, and cell death research. *Type:* Research center.

National Association for Continence

PO Box 8310   Ph: (864)579-7900
Spartanburg, SC 29305-8310   Free: 800-BLA-
                                      DDER
                               Fax: (864)579-7902
URL: http://www.nafc.org
Contact: Liv Osby, Dir. Of Marketing.
Desc: Works to help individuals who have bladder control problems. Acts as a clearinghouse of information and services involving incontinence and assistive devices for consumers and their families as well as medical, nursing, and social service organizations. *Type:* Association.

Polycystic Kidney Research Foundation

4901 Main St., Ste. 200   Ph: (816)931-2600
Kansas City, MO 64112-2634   Free: 800-753-2873
                               Fax: (816)931-8655
E-mail: pkdcure@pkrfoundation.org
URL: http://www.kumc.edu/pkrf/
Contact: Thomas G. Flesch, Chm.
Desc: Conducts, promotes, and supports studies on the cause, treatment, and cure of polycystic kidney disease (PKD). Activities include identification of gene defect responsible for PKD, analysis of abnormal cell and cyst growth, and analysis of kidney function and progressive kidney failure. *Type:* Research center.

Simon Foundation for Continence

Box 815   Ph: (847)864-3913
Wilmette, IL 60091   Free: 800-23-SIMON
                               Fax: (847)864-9758
Contact: Cheryle B. Gartley, Pres.
Desc: Persons with urinary and bowel incontinence; family members, doctors, medical personnel, and others concerned with the condition. Seeks to educate the public on urinary and bowel problems, to provide information to persons with incontinence, and to remove the stigma attached to the condition. Acts as support group. *Type:* Association.

U.S. Department of Health and Human Services

National Heart, Lung, and Blood Institute

Laboratory of Kidney and Electrolyte Metabolism

NIH Bldg. 10, Rm. 6N260   Ph: (301)496-3187
10 Center Dr., MSC 1603   Fax: (301)402-1443
Bethesda, MD 20892
E-mail: maurice_burg@nih.gov
Contact: Dr. Maurice B. Burg, Chf.

Desc: Mechanism and regulation (hormonal and otherwise) of a variety of transport processes in systems, including the intact kidney, isolated perfused segments of renal tubules, and epithelial cell cultures. Emphasis is on electrophysiology, quantitative microscopy, nuclear magnetic resonance, and intermediary metabolism as related to transport. *Type:* Research center.

U.S. Department of Health and Human Services

National Institute of Diabetes and Digestive and Kidney Diseases

Division of Extramural Activities

Natcher Bldg.   Ph: (301)594-8834
45 Center Dr., MSC 6600   Fax: (301)480-3505
Bethesda, MD 20892-6600
URL: http://www.niddk.nih.gov
Contact: Walter S. Stolz, Dir.

Desc: Serves as the service organization to the rest of the extramural division and is comprised of three branches: the review branch which reviews research grant applications; the grants management branch which prepares and issues grant awards; and the contracts and acquisition management branch which prepares and issues contracts. *Type:* Research center.

U.S. Department of Health and Human Services

National Institute of Diabetes and Digestive and Kidney Diseases

Division of Kidney, Urologic, and Hematologic Diseases

NIH Bldg. 31, Rm. 9A17   Ph: (301)496-6325
31 S. Center   Fax: (301)402-4874
MSC 2560
Bethesda, MD 20892-2560
E-mail: briggs@hq.niddk.nih.gov
URL: http://www.niddk.nih.gov
Contact: Josephine P. Briggs, MD, Dir.

Desc: Kidney, urinary, and hematologic disorders, including epidemiologic studies and clinical trials. Offers investigator-initiated research grants and awards, program/project grants, center grants, and cooperative agreements. *Type:* Research center.

U.S. Department of Health and Human Services

National Institute of Diabetes and Digestive and Kidney Diseases

Division of Kidney, Urologic, and Hematologic Diseases

Chronic Renal Diseases Program

DKUHD   Ph: (301)594-7717
Natcher Bldg., Rm. 6A513   Fax: (301)480-3510
45 Center Dr. MSC 6600
Bethesda, MD 20892-6600
E-mail: gladys_hirschman@nih.gov
Contact: Gladys H. Hirschman, MD, Prog.Dir.

Desc: Kidney diseases and develops treatments to prevent their onset and progression. Focuses on pathophysiology (including immunopathogenic mechanisms) of chronic renal diseases such as lupus nephritis, polycystic kidney disease, or interstitial nephritis, IgA nephropathy, and other glomerulopathies/glomerulonephritis; progressive renal disease; renial diseases of congenitial and genetic origins i.e., polycystic kidney disease; kidney disease in children and in minority populations; role of nutrition in renal disease; kidney disease caused by diabetes mellitus, including studies on pathogenic mechanisms, genetic morphologic and functional markers; and natural history of diabetic nephropathy, hypertensive renal disease and all of the above in the pediatric population. *Type:* Research center.

U.S. Department of Health and Human Services

National Institute of Diabetes and Digestive and Kidney Diseases

Division of Kidney, Urologic, and Hematologic Diseases

Renal Physiology / Cell Biology Program

DKUHD   Ph: (301)594-7719
Natcher Bldg   Fax: (301)480-3510
45 Center Dr. MSC 6600
Bethesda, MD 20892-6600
Contact: Dr. James Scherbenske, Prog.Dir.

Desc: Underlying mechanisms of kidney disease. Studies in this program examine the normal structure and function of the kidney, including its biochemistry, metabolism, transport, and fluid-electrolyte dynamics. *Type:* Research center.

U.S. Department of Health and Human Services

National Institute of Diabetes and Digestive and Kidney Diseases

Division of Kidney, Urologic, Hematologic Diseases

Urology and Women's Urological Health Program

NIH/NIDDK/DKUHD   Ph: (301)594-7717
Natcher Bldg Rm. 6AS-19E   Fax: (301)480-3510
Bethesda, MD 20892-6600
E-mail: leroy-nyberg@nih.gov
Contact: Leroy M. Nyberg, Dir.

Desc: Normal and disease states of genitourinary system, including structure and function of the bladder, urethra, and prostate. Program interests include pyelonephritis, interstitial cystitis, urolithiasis, benign prostatic hyperplasia, prostatitis, impotence and sexual dysfunction, and urinary incontinence. *Type:* Research center.

U.S. Department of Health and Human Services

National Institutes of Health

National Institute of Diabetes and Digestive and Kidney Diseases

9000 Rockville Pike   Ph: (301)496-3583
Bethesda, MD 20892
URL: http://www.niddk.nih.gov/
Contact: Phillip Gorden, MD, Director.

Desc: The Institute conducts, fosters, and supports basic and clinical research into the causes, prevention, diagnosis, and treatment of the various metabolic and digestive diseases. It covers the broad areas of diabetes, blood, endocrine, and metabolic diseases; digestive diseases and nutrition; and kidney and urologic diseases. *Type:* Government agency, office, or program.

University of Alabama at Birmingham

Nephrology Research and Training Center

Division of Nephrology   Ph: (205)934-3585
UAB Sta.   Fax: (205)934-1879
1900 University Blvd., Rm. 647
  THT
Birmingham, AL 35233
E-mail: dwarnock@nrtc.dom.uab.edu
URL: http://www.nrtc.uab.edu
Contact: David G. Warnock, MD, Dir.

Desc: Membrane transport, renal tubular transport, acid base physiology, renal hypertension, renal ultrastructure, epithelial ion transport, electron microprobe, erythropoietin, and population studies of genetic factors in hypertension. *Type:* Research center.

University of Alabama at Birmingham

Urological Rehabilitation and Research Center

1717 6th Ave. S.   Ph: (205)934-5359
Birmingham, AL 35233   Fax: (205)934-2709
E-mail: klloyd@urology.uab.edu
URL: http://www.uab.edu
Contact: L. Keith Lloyd, MD, Hd.
Desc: Urological dysfunctions. *Type:* Research center.

University of Kansas

Division of Nephrology and Hypertension

3901 Rainbow Blvd.   Ph: (913)588-6074
Kansas City, KS 66160-7382   Fax: (913)588-3867
E-mail: ddiederi@kumc.edu
Contact: Dennis Diederich, MD, Dir.

Desc: Laboratory and clinical investigations into kidney physiology, polycystic kidney disease, basement membrane structure and function, kidney stones, acute renal failure, and diuretics. Research methods include tubule microperfusion, amino acid analyses, peptide synthesis, and morphometrics. *Type:* Research center.

University of Louisville

Kidney Disease Program

615 S. Preston St.   Ph: (502)852-5757
Louisville, KY 40202-1718   Fax: (502)852-7643
E-mail: graron01@ulkyvm.louisville.edu
URL: http://kdpsparc.kdp-baptist.louisville.edu
Contact: George R. Aronoff, MD, Ch.

Desc: Kidney disease, focusing on the following areas: cellular physiology, second messengers, biological transport, cellular immunology, transplantation, artificial membranes, dialysis, clinical pharmacology, pharmacokinetics, nephrotoxicity, drug metabolism, hypertension, and tissue typing. *Type:* Research center.

University of Medicine and Dentistry of New Jersey

Urology Research Laboratory

185 S. Orange Ave., Rm. H516   Ph: (973)972-4488
Newark, NJ 07103-2714   Fax: (973)972-3892
Contact: Dr. Robert Irwin, MD, Dir.

Desc: Interaction between retinoids and audiogens in the control of prostate cells and its role in prostate cancer. Effects of spinal cord injury on male reproduction and testing regimens to prevent such effects. *Type:* Research center.

University of Rochester

Nephrology Research Program

601 Elmwood Ave., Box 675   Ph: (716)275-4517
Rochester, NY 14642   Fax: (716)442-9201
E-mail: davidbushinsky@urmc.rochester.edu
Contact: Dr. David Bushinsky, Dir.

Desc: Physiological regulation of water and salt excretion, renal potassium handling in vivo and in the isolated perfused kidney, regulation of intrarenal blood flow, fluorescence videomicroscopy studies of inner medullary blood flow, role of nucleosides as regulators of kidney function and hemodynamics, renal microvascular endothelium and epithelial cell cultures, in vivo perfusion of capillaries from the renal microcirculation, pathogenesis of acute renal failure, modulators of renal ischemic injury, and studies of tubular functioning in humans. *Type:* Research center.

University of Southern California
Division of Nephrology
1200 N. State St.   Ph: (213)226-7337
Rm. GNH 4250   Fax: (213)226-5390
Los Angeles, CA 90033
Contact: Dr. Shaul G. Massry, Chf.
Desc: Calcium, phosphorus metabolism, vitamin D metabolism, sympathetic nervous system in hypertension, salt sensitive hypertension and parathyroid hormone toxicity in uremia. Kidney dialysis studies include improved dialysis, immunologic aspects of renal disease, hypertension, and control of salt and water balance, and mechanisms of diabetic complications. *Type:* Research center.

Washington University in St. Louis
Chromalloy American Kidney Center
1 Barnes Hospital Plaza, Box   Ph: (314)362-8231
  8126   Fax: (314)362-7875
St. Louis, MO 63110
E-mail: eslatopol@ingate.wustl.edu
Contact: Dr. Eduardo Slatopolsky, Dir.
Desc: Lipid abnormalities in uremia, muscle protein metabolism in uremia, metabolic bone disease in uremia, parathyroid hormone, and vitamin D and aluminum metabolism. *Type:* Research center.

Utilities

Association of California Water Agencies
Stephen Hall
910 K St., Ste. 250   Ph: (916)441-4545
Sacramento, CA 95814-3577   Fax: (916)441-7893
Contact: Stephen Hall, Exec.Dir.
Desc: Public water agencies and related businesses. Encourages the orderly development of water distribution in California. *Type:* Association.

Communications Supply Service Association
5700 Murray St.   Ph: (501)562-7666
Little Rock, AR 72209   Free: 800-252-2772
    Fax: (501)562-7616
E-mail: mmc@cssa.net
URL: http://www.cssa.net
Contact: Larry W. Hoaglan, Pres.
Desc: Small, independent, cooperative or commercial telephone companies. *Type:* Association.

Competitive Telecommunications Association
1900 M Street NW Ste 800   Ph: (202)296-6650
Washington, DC 20036   Fax: (202)296-7585
E-mail: jferguson@comptel.org
URL: http://www.comptel.org
Contact: Robert Duke, Dir., Business Affairs.
Desc: Long-distance telecommunications service providers. Serves as a voice for the competitive long-distance telephone industry and competitive operator service providers on both the legislative and regulatory levels. *Type:* Association.

Distributor Management Digest
Business Marketing & Publishing, Inc.
PO Box 7457   Ph: (203)834-9959
Wilton, CT 06897
Contact: George B. Young, Editor.
Desc: "Covers business and electrical news of interest to owners, presidents, and sales managers. Brings electrical distributor management electrical industry news and reports." *Type:* Newsletter.

DRI Utility Cost Forecasting
Standard & Poor's DRI
Data Products Division
24 Hartwell Ave.   Ph: (781)863-5100
Lexington, MA 02421
E-mail: client_services@dri.mcgraw-hill.com
URL: http://www.dri.mcgraw-hill.com
Contact: Client Services, (617)860-6527, fax: (617)860-6416, jmothersole@dri.mcgraw-hill.com.
Desc: Contains more than 800 quarterly, semiannual, and annual forecast cost indexes for construction, operation, and maintenance of electric and gas utilities. *Available:* Standard & Poor's DRI, Data Products Division. *Type:* Database.

Edison Electric Institute
701 Pennsylvania Ave., NW   Ph: (202)508-5000
Washington, DC 20004-2696   Fax: (202)508-5360
URL: http://www.eei.org
Contact: Thomas R. Kuhn, Pres.
Desc: Investor-owned electric utility companies operating in the U.S. International affiliates and associates from all over the world. *Type:* Association.

Electric Power Database
Electric Power Research Institute (EPRI)
Technical Information Division
PO Box 10412   Ph: (415)855-2000
Palo Alto, CA 94303
URL: http://www.epri.com
Desc: Contains information on more than 33,000 ongoing and completed research and development projects related to electric power generation, transmission, and distribution. Includes hydroelectric power, fossil fuels, nuclear power, solar power, transmission, economics, advanced power systems, metering, load management, and environmental assessment. *Available:* The Dialog Corporation, DIALOG. *Type:* Database.

Energy Services Marketing Letter
RMI
111 Presidential Blvd.   Ph: (610)667-2160
Bala Cynwyd, PA 19004   Fax: (610)667-5593
E-mail: richard.smithers@bala.synergic.com.
Contact: Zeta Cross, Editor.
Desc: Deals with energy efficiency, demand-side management, and conservation in the electric utility industry. Recurring features include news of research, reports of meetings, news of educational opportunities, and notices of publications available. *Type:* Newsletter.

Handy-Whitman Index
Whitman, Requardt and Associates
2315 St. Paul St.   Ph: (410)235-3450
Baltimore, MD 21218
Contact: Dennis R. Funk, P.E., (410)235-3450, fax: (410)467-7425.
Desc: Contains approximately 2400 annual and semiannual indexes of building costs for construction of public utilities in the United States, aggregated for 6 geographical regions with similar economic characteristics. Covers electric, gas, and water. *Available:* Standard & Poor's DRI, Data Products Division. *Type:* Database.

Human Resources Report
American Public Power Association (APPA)
2301 M St. NW   Ph: (202)467-2900
Washington, DC 20037-1484   Fax: (202)467-2910
Contact: Jeff Tarbert, Editor.
Desc: Reports on public sector labor and personnel issues, especially those concerning the electric utility industry. Summarizes case studies in public labor relations. *Type:* Newsletter.

LEXIS® Public Utilities Law Library
LEXIS-NEXIS
9443 Springboro Pike   Ph: (937)865-6800
PO Box 933
Dayton, OH 45401-0933
URL: http://www.lex-nexis.com
Desc: Contains public utilities-related case decisions from all state supreme courts and most state appellate courts. Includes United States Code Service Titles 16, 30, 42, and 47, and decisions from the Federal Energy Regulatory Commission since 1977, the Federal Power Commission from 1931 to 1977, the Nuclear Regulatory Commission (NRC) since 1975, and state regulatory agencies in about 20 states. *Available:* LEXIS-NEXIS, LEXIS. *Type:* Database.

Maryland Southern Electric Co-op
South MD Electric Cooperative
PO Box 1937   Ph: (301)274-3111
Hughesville, MD 20637   Free: 888-440-3311
    Fax: (301)274-0086
E-mail: info@smleco.com
URL: http://www.smecd.com
Contact: Janice S. Penn, V.Pres.
Type: Association.

National Association of Regulatory Utility Commissioners
PO Box 684   Ph: (202)898-2200
Washington, DC 20044-0684   Fax: (202)898-2213
E-mail: pwelsh@naruc.com
URL: http://www.naruc.com
Contact: Peggy Welsh, Exec.Dir.
Desc: Public utility commissioners having jurisdiction over public utilities in the areas of gas, electricity, telecommunications and water. Goal is to serve the consumer interest by working to improve the quality and effectiveness of regulation of public utilities. Works to: advance commission regulation through examination and discussion of subjects dealing with the operation and supervision of public utilities; promote uniformity of regulation of public utilities; foster coordinated action by regulatory commissions to protect the public interest. *Type:* Association.

National Exchange Carrier Association
100 S. Jefferson Rd.   Ph: (201)884-8000
Whippany, NJ 07981   Free: 800-228-8597
    Fax: (201)884-8469
E-mail: webmaster@neca.org
URL: http://www.neca.org
Contact: Bruce W. Baldwin, Pres.
Desc: All local telephone companies in the continental U.S., Puerto Rico, Virgin Islands, Hawaii, and Alaska. Purpose is to prepare and file interstate access charges and administer revenue pools created by those charges. Compiles statistics. *Type:* Association.

National Telephone Cooperative Association
2626 Pennsylvania Ave. NW   Ph: (202)298-2300
Washington, DC 20037   Fax: (202)298-2320
E-mail: frs@ntca.com
Contact: David Lasher, Pres.
Desc: Nonprofit association representing nearly 500 locally owned and controlled telecommunications cooperatives and companies throughout rural and small-town America. Provides members with aggressive legislative representation on Capital Hill, and regulatory representation at the Federal Communications Commission and in the courts. *Type:* Association.

Northwest Electric Utility Directory

Northwest Public Power Association (NWPPA)
PO Box 4576 Ph: (360)254-0109
Vancouver, WA 98662-0576 Fax: (360)254-5731
E-mail: nwppa@nwppa.org; debbie@nwppa.org.
Contact: Debbie Kuraspediani, Editor.
Desc: Electric utilities in Washington, Oregon, Idaho, Montana, Alaska, British Columbia, Alberta, plus coverage of Nevada, Utah, California, North Dakota, and Wyoming. Also list of over 250 associate members. *Type:* Directory.

NUCA Safety News

National Utility Contractors Association
4301 N. Fairfax Dr., Ste. 360 Ph: (703)358-9300
Arlington, VA 22203 Fax: (703)358-9307
URL: http://www.nuca.com.
Contact: George Kennedy, Editor.
Desc: Provides safety news and articles for underground utility contractors. *Type:* Newsletter.

Public Utilities Reports

Public Utilities Reports
8229 Boone Blvd., Ste. 401 Ph: (703)847-7720
Vienna, VA 22182
URL: http://www.pur.com.
Desc: Contains the complete text of Public Utilities Fortnightly, a magazine covering public utilities and the energy industry. Covers financial news, policy issues, legislation and regulation, power generation, and energy technology. *Available:* West Group, WESTLAW; Public Utilities Reports. *Type:* Database.

Public Utility Financing Tracker

P U F T, Inc.
2408 Durango Ln. Ph: (630)904-3503
Naperville, IL 60564
Desc: Follows and disseminates information on new issue stocks and bonds of public utility companies. *Type:* Newsletter.

United States Telephone Association

1401 H St., Ste. 600 Ph: (202)326-7300
Washington, DC 20005-2136 Fax: (202)326-7333
URL: http://www.usta.org
Contact: Roy Neel, Pres.
Desc: Local operating telephone companies or telephone holding companies. Members represent a total of 114 million access lines. Conducts educational and training programs. *Type:* Association.

Utilities Division Newsletter

National Safety Council
1121 Spring Lake Dr. Ph: (630)285-1121
Itasca, IL 60143-3201 Free: 800-539-7468
 Fax: (630)285-1315
URL: http://www.nsc.org; http://www.nsc.org.
Contact: Laura Coyne, Editor, (630)775-2276, fax: (630)775-2285.
Desc: Focuses on accident prevention and safety awareness among public utilities workers on and off the job. Analyzes accident case reports and discusses trends. *Type:* Newsletter.

Utility & Energy Portfolio

21st Century Publishers
1320 Curt Gowdy Dr. Ph: (307)635-5511
Cheyenne, WY 82009
Contact: Richard J. Maturi, Editor.
Desc: Covers the utility and energy industries with analysis of investment opportunities. Discusses investment topics such as value investing and short selling. *Type:* Newsletter.

Utility Workers Union of America

815 16th St. NW Ph: (202)347-8105
Washington, DC 20006 Fax: (202)347-4872
Contact: Donald E. Wightman, Pres.
Desc: AFL-CIO. Sponsors ten educational conferences each year for local officers. *Type:* Association.

Veterans

American Ex-Prisoners of War

Clydie J. Morgan
3201 E. Pioneer Pky., No. 40 Ph: (817)649-2979
Arlington, TX 76010 Fax: (817)649-0109
E-mail: pow@flash.net
Contact: Clydie J. Morgan, Adjutant.
Desc: Former military prisoners of war and civilian internees. Seeks to: acquaint the public with the needs, problems, and handicaps associated with prisoners of war; promote research in the fields connected with injuries, diseases, and syndromes stemming from imprisonment; advocate and foster complete and effective reconditioning programs for ex-prisoners of war; foster patriotism and civic loyalty; encourage fraternal and historical activities. *Type:* Association.

American GI Forum of United States

3204 Highland Ph: (512)882-7602
Corpus Christi, TX 78405 Fax: (512)882-7602
Contact: Dr. Hector P. Garcia, Founder.
Desc: Veterans of the Armed Forces of the U.S., primarily of Mexican origin, and their families. To "foster and perpetuate the principles of American democracy based on religious and political freedom for the individual and equal opportunity for all." Special programs include: Business Development Center provides assistance in starting or expanding businesses; Hispanic Education Foundation raises funds for scholarships, grants, and research in education relating to the Hispanic; National Veterans Outreach Program; SER-JOBS for Progress . Also works for the advancement of members in the mass media field, and in political representation. *Type:* Association.

American Legion Auxiliary's National News

American Legion Auxiliary's National News
777 N. Meridian, St., 3rd Fl. Ph: (317)635-6291
Indianapolis, IN 46204-1189 Fax: (317)636-5590
E-mail: alahq@iquest.net
Contact: Lauralyn T. Mohr, Editor; Thomas G. Bowman, Advertising Mgr.
Desc: Magazine for Auxiliary members. *Type:* Periodical.

American Legion, Indiana Department

777 N. Meridian St. Ph: (317)630-1300
Indianapolis, IN 46204 Fax: (317)237-9891
Contact: K. Michael Ayers, Chief Administrative Officer.
Desc: Honorably discharged wartime veterans, both male and female, of World Wars I and II, the Korean and Vietnam Wars, and the Grenada, Panama, Lebanon, Bosnia, and Desert Storm conflicts. *Type:* Association.

American Legion Magazine

American Legion National Headquarters
PO Box 1055 Ph: (317)630-1212
Indianapolis, IN 46206 Fax: (317)630-1369
E-mail: tal@legion.org.
URL: http://www.legion.org; http://www.legion.org.
Contact: Dick McNally, Publisher, (317)630-1289.
Desc: General interest magazine for veterans. *Type:* Periodical.

American Legion, Ohio Department

PO Box 14348 Ph: (614)268-7072
Columbus, OH 43214 Fax: (614)268-3048
E-mail: ohlegion@netwalk.com
Contact: Roger Hight, Adjutant.
Desc: Honorably discharged wartime veterans, both male and female, of World Wars I and II, the Korean and Vietnam Wars, Panama, Lebanon, Grenada, and Desert Storm. Sponsors athletic teams, charitable events, Christmas card program, and bowling and trap shooting competitions. *Type:* Association.

American Legion, Pennsylvania State Department

PO Box 2324 Ph: (717)730-9100
Harrisburg, PA 17105 Fax: (717)975-2836
E-mail: palegion@redrose.net
URL: http://www.pa-legion.com
Contact: Stanley W. Reinhard, Jr., Dept.Adjutant.
Desc: Honorably discharged wartime veterans of World Wars I and II, the Korean and Vietnam wars, as well as those who served in Grenada, Lebanon, Beirut, and Desert Storm. Promotes interests of veterans, rehabilitation, national security, and patriotism. *Type:* Association.

American Military Retirees Association

426 US Oval, Suite 1200 Ph: (518)563-9479
Plattsburgh, NY 12903 Free: 800-424-2969
 Fax: (518)563-9479
E-mail: amra1975@aol.com
Contact: Msgt. Robert N. Gerhardt, USAF, Exec.Dir.
Desc: Persons honorably retired for length of service or disability from all branches and grades of the armed forces and their widows or widowers; persons still on active duty. Goals: to maintain "COLA" Program; authorization for CHAMPUS for all military retirees regardless of age; to maintain adequate care at military/VA medical facilities. Works to support or oppose legislation in the best interests of members and to protect the earned privileges and benefits of military retirees. *Type:* Association.

American Veterans Committee

6309 Bannockburn Dr. Ph: (301)320-6490
Bethesda, MD 20817 Fax: (301)320-6490
E-mail: willenzj@mindspring.com
Contact: June A. Willenz, Exec.Dir.
Desc: Veterans of World War I, World War II, the Korean conflict, the Vietnam War, and the Persian Gulf conflict. "To achieve a more democratic and prosperous America and a more stable world." *Type:* Association.

AMVETS (American Veterans of World War II, Korea and Vietnam)

4647 Forbes Blvd. Ph: (301)459-9600
Lanham, MD 20706-4380 Fax: (301)459-7924
E-mail: amvets@amvets.org
URL: http://www.amvets.org
Contact: Robert P. Carbonneau, Exec. Dir.
Desc: Works to promote world peace, preserve the American way of life and help veterans to help themselves. Membership is open to anyone who is currently serving, or who has honorably served in the Armed Forces of the United States-to include the National Guard and Reserves-at anytime after September 15, 1940. Actively follows all veterans legislation on Capitol Hill and plays a key role in its enactment. *Type:* Association.

Army and Navy Union, U.S.A.

1391 Main St. Ph: (330)784-0388
Lakemore, OH 44250
Contact: Norman Henninger, Adjutant.
Desc: Servicemen and veterans of the armed forces during peace or war. Participates in veterans service work of all types. Provides children's services. *Type:* Association.

Badger Legionnaire & American Legion Auxiliary Wisconsin

Wisconsin American Legion
812 E. State St.   Ph: (414)271-1940
Milwaukee, WI 53202   Fax: (414)271-8335
E-mail: wilegion@execpc.com
Contact: Rick Barnett, Editor.
Desc: Magazine for veterans. *Type:* Periodical.

California Legionnaire

The American Legion
Dept. of California   Ph: (415)431-2400
117 Veterans War Memorial   Fax: (415)255-1571
  Bldg.
401 Van Ness Ave.
San Francisco, CA 94102
Contact: E. Paul Terry, Publishing Mgr.; Christopher Woodby, Editor.
Desc: Newspaper (tabloid) for veterans on legislation, the Veterans Administration, health fields, field operations, work of the legion and auxiliary in community affairs, and changes in post, unit, district, and department. *Type:* Periodical.

The California Veteran

Veterans of Foreign Wars of the U.S.
7111 Governors Circle   Ph: (916)424-1684
Sacramento, CA 95823   Fax: (916)424-9049
Contact: Oren D. Robinson, Editor.
Desc: Newspaper (tabloid) for veterans and their families. *Type:* Periodical.

Catholic War Veterans of the U.S.A.

441 N. Lee St.   Ph: (703)549-3622
Alexandria, VA 22314   Fax: (703)684-5196
Contact: Linda M. Torreyson, Exec.Asst.
Desc: American veterans of the Catholic faith. Conducts charitable programs for the welfare and rehabilitation of veterans and their dependents. *Type:* Association.

DAV Magazine

Disabled American Veterans National Headquarters
PO Box 14301   Ph: (513)441-7300
Cincinnati, OH 45250-0301   Fax: (513)442-2090
URL: http://www.dav.org.
Contact: Gary Weaver, Editor, fax: (660)442-2088, gweaver@davmail.org; James A. Chaney, Production Manager, jchancey@davmail.org; David E. Autry, Deputy Nat'l Director of Communications, (202)554-3501, fax: (202)554-3581; Jim Hall, Assistant Nat'l Director of Communicatio, feedback@davmail.org.
Desc: Veterans magazine on disability issues. *Type:* Periodical.

Disabled American Veterans

PO Box 14301   Ph: (606)441-7300
Cincinnati, OH 45250-0301
E-mail: ahdav@one.net
URL: http://www.dav.org
Contact: Arthur H. Wilson, Nat. Adjutant.
Desc: Veterans with service-connected disabilities. Major activity is service to disabled veterans and their families. DAV employs 280 National Service Officers in Department of Veterans Affairs (VA) offices in 49 states and Puerto Rico to act as free-of-charge attorneys-in-fact, counseling and processing veterans' claims for compensation and benefits. *Type:* Association.

Disabled American Veterans Auxiliary

3725 Alexandria Pike   Ph: (606)441-7300
Cold Spring, KY 41076   Fax: (606)442-2095
URL: http://www.dav.org

Contact: Maria Tedrow, Adjutant.
Desc: Women relatives of service-connected disabled veterans, and women eligible in their own right to membership in the Disabled American Veterans. To aid the parent organization (DAV); to serve veterans and their dependents. Programs include: volunteer hospital work, Americanism, community service, child welfare, and legislative activities. *Type:* Association.

82d Airborne Division Association, Inc.

NFCS, PO Box 9308   Ph: (910)822-4534
Fayetteville, NC 28311-7694
Contact: Manuel E. De DeJesus, Exec.Dir.
Desc: Veterans throughout the United States and overseas and active members of the 82d Airborne Division stationed at Ft. Bragg, NC. Dedicated to developing the common bond existing between all men and women who served with the 82d Airborne Division and other airborne units. *Type:* Association.

Federal Employees Veterans Association

PO Box 183
Merion Station, PA 19066
Contact: Lester Harris, III, Exec. Officer.
Desc: Federal government employees who have veterans' preference in federal employment under the G. I. Bill. Works to maintain and increase veterans' preference in federal employment and prevent "the discrimination against the veteran that was rampant in federal agencies in the post-World War II era." *Type:* Association.

Grosse Pointe War Memorial Association

32 Lake Shore Dr.   Ph: (313)881-7511
Grosse Pointe Farms, MI Fax: (313)884-6638
  48236-3784
E-mail: gpwminfo@warmemorial.org
URL: http://www.warmemorial.org
Contact: Mark R. Weber, Ph.D., Pres.
Desc: Works to honor individuals who have served in the armed forces and provide educational, cultural, civic and patriotic activities for citizens. *Type:* Association.

Gulf War Review

Department of Veterans Affairs
Environmental Agents Services -   Ph: (202)273-8580
  131   Fax: (202)273-9080
V.A. Headquarters
810 Vermont Ave. NW
Washington, DC 20420
Contact: Donald J. Rosenblum, Editor.
Desc: Provides information on health concerns of Gulf War veterans and their families. Includes scientific research, legislation, policies, and procedures. *Type:* Newsletter.

The Hoosier Legionnaire

The American Legion, Indiana Dept.
777 N. Meridian St.   Ph: (317)630-1391
Indianapolis, IN 46204   Free: 888-723-7999
                         Fax: (317)237-9891
Contact: K. Michael Ayers, Publisher, (317)630-1263; Maria Gottlieb, Managing Editor, maria4pu@aol.com.
Desc: Newspaper (tabloid) for members of the American Legion in Indiana. *Type:* Periodical.

Iowa Legionnaire

Iowa American Legion
720 Lyon St.   Ph: (515)282-5068
Des Moines, IA 50309-5417   Free: 800-365-8387
                         Fax: (515)282-7583
Contact: James E. Demarest, Editor.
Desc: American Legion magazine. *Type:* Periodical.

Jewish War Veterans of the U.S.A.

1811 R St. NW   Ph: (202)265-6280
Washington, DC 20009   Fax: (202)234-5662
E-mail: jwv@erols.com
URL: http://www.penfed.org/jwv/home.htm
Contact: Herb Rosenbleeth, Exec.Dir.
Desc: American veterans of Jewish faith who served in the wars of the U.S. Works to perpetuate Americanism, fight anti-Semitism, combat bigotry, preserve the memories and records of patriotic American Jews, maintain National Service Offices throughout the country and provide a voice on Capitol Hill for veterans' legislation and issues of concern to the American Jewish community. *Type:* Association.

Jewish War Veterans of the U.S.A. - National Ladies Auxiliary

1811 R St. NW   Ph: (202)667-9061
Washington, DC 20009   Fax: (202)462-3192
Contact: Barbara Greenberg, Nat.Pres.
Desc: Sisters, wives, mothers, daughters, widows, and lineal descendants of Jewish veterans of wars of the United States. Sends gifts to servicemen overseas; conducts youth programs; provides service to hospitalized veterans. Has furnished a surgical wing at Chaim Sheba Medical Center in Israel and has contributed equipment to an amniotic laboratory there. Provides children's services; conducts charitable programs. *Type:* Association.

Korean War Veterans Association

PO Box 10806   Ph: (703)522-9629
Arlington, VA 22210   Fax: (410)282-8498
Contact: Harley Coon, Pres.
Desc: Korean War veterans; families of those listed as killed, missing-in-action, or prisoner-of-war; individuals who served at least 90 days in Korea. Supports what the association considers the "founding ideals" of the U.S.; promotes the pride and dignity of veterans; works toward developing recognition of those who lost their lives in Korea; fosters camaraderie and communication among members; perpetuates the memory of the war in which they fought. Currently working to develop Korean War Memorial Library Museum. *Type:* Association.

Ladies Auxiliary to the Veterans of Foreign Wars of the United States

406 W. 34th St.   Ph: (816)561-8655
Kansas City, MO 64111   Fax: (816)931-4753
E-mail: info@ladiesauxvfw.com
URL: http://www.ladiesauxvfw.com
Contact: Margaret Bergeron, Sec.-Treas.
Desc: Wives, widows, mothers, stepmothers, grandmothers, daughters, foster daughters, stepdaughters, granddaughters, sisters, half sisters, stepsisters, and foster sisters of persons eligible for membership in the VFW. Conducts voluntary hospital and rehabilitation work and sponsors various patriotic, Americanism, and youth activities. Supports VFW National Home, Eaton Rapids, MI. *Type:* Association.

Legion Magazine

Canvet Publications Ltd.
359 Kent St., Ste. 407   Ph: (613)235-8741
Ottawa, ON, Canada K2P 0R6   Fax: (613)233-7159
Contact: Mac Johnston, Editor; Jan Buchanan-Redden, Advertising Coord.
Desc: Magazine for members of the Royal Canadian Legion, and for veterans, ex-service personnel and their families. *Type:* Periodical.

Michigan Overseas Veteran

Department of Michigan Veterans of Foreign Wars

924 N. Washington Ph: (517)485-9456
Lansing, MI 48901 Fax: (517)485-6432
E-mail: webmaster@mivfw.org; barry@mivfw.org.
Contact: Val Cemonceli, Contact.
Desc: Publication reporting on legislation and programs for veterans. *Alt. Contact:* Box 20036, Lansing, MI 48901. *Type:* Periodical.

Military Order of the Purple Heart of the United States of America

5413-B Backlick Rd. Ph: (703)642-5360
Springfield, VA 22151 Fax: (703)642-2054
E-mail: info@purpleheart.org
URL: http://www.purpleheart.org
Contact: John B. Kirby, Adjutant Gen.
Desc: Persons awarded the Purple Heart Medal for wounds received in action while members of the Armed Forces of the U.S. Conducts service and welfare work on behalf of disabled and needy servicemen and veterans and their dependents. *Type:* Association.

Minnesota Legionnaire

Minnesota American Legion Publishing Co.

State Veterans Service Bldg. Ph: (651)291-1800
St. Paul, MN 55155-0001 Fax: (651)291-1057
E-mail: department@mnlegion.org; mnamlegion@landoflakes.com.
Contact: Alan T. Zdon, Editor, azdon@mnlegion.org.
Desc: Membership newspaper. *Type:* Periodical.

Museum News

National Museum of American Jewish Military History

1811 R St. NW Ph: (202)265-6280
Washington, DC 20009 Fax: (202)462-3192
E-mail: jwv@erols.com.
URL: http://www.penfed.org/jwv/home.htm.
Contact: Sandor Cohen, Museum Dir.; Ed Liskey, Asst Curator.
Desc: Reports on the activities and exhibits associated with the memorial and museum commemorating the services of American Jews in the American Armed Forces. *Type:* Newsletter.

The National AMVET

AMVETS

4647 Forbes Blvd. Ph: (301)459-9600
Lanham, MD 20706 Fax: (301)459-7924
E-mail: amvets@amvets.org.
Contact: Richard W. Flanagan, Editor, dflanagan@amvets.org.
Desc: Magazine containing service-related infromation and data for veterans. *Type:* Periodical.

National Association for Black Veterans

PO Box 11432 Ph: (414)265-8940
Milwaukee, WI 53211 Free: 800-842-4597
Fax: (414)332-4627
Contact: Thomas H. Wynn, Sr., Exec. Officer.
Desc: Black and other minority veterans, primarily those who fought in Vietnam. Represents the interests of minority veterans before the Veterans Administration. Operates Metropolitan Veterans Service to obtain honorable discharges for minority and low-income veterans who in the organization's opinion unjustly received a less than honorable discharge. *Type:* Association.

National Museum of American Jewish Military History

1811 R St. NW Ph: (202)265-6280
Washington, DC 20009 Fax: (202)462-3192
E-mail: jwvusa@esols.com
URL: http://www.penfed.org/jwv/museum.htm
Contact: Harvey S. Friedman, Pres.
Desc: Organizations and corporations. United to preserve the records of Jews who served in the U.S. armed forces and educate the public about their contributions to America's freedom. *Type:* Association.

National Veterans Outreach Program

American GI Forum

206 San Pedro, Ste. 200 Ph: (210)223-4096
San Antonio, TX 78205-1100 Fax: (210)223-4970
E-mail: giforum@txdirect.net
Contact: Carlos Martinez, Pres. & CEO.
Desc: Provides services to the economically disadvantaged, recently separated veterans (within the last 48 months), and Vietnam era veterans. *Type:* Association.

Non-Commissioned Officers Association

225 N. Washington St. Ph: (703)549-0311
Alexandria, VA 22314 Fax: (703)549-0245
E-mail: djohn@ncoausa.org
URL: http://www.ncoausa.org
Contact: Richard Johnson, Exec.Dir.
Desc: Veterans association Promotes passage of legislation affecting veterans; address matters of interest to active-duty and retired career military people. *Type:* Association.

Paralyzed Veterans of America

801 18th St. NW Ph: (202)872-1300
Washington, DC 20006 Fax: (202)785-4452
E-mail: info@pva.org
URL: http://www.pva.org
Contact: Gordon Mansfield, Exec.Dir.
Desc: Veterans who have incurred an injury or disease affecting the spinal cord and causing paralysis. Through national service program, assists veterans, dependents, and survivors in obtaining Department of Veterans Affairs benefits due them; works for federal benefits of various kinds. *Type:* Association.

Regular Veterans Association

5200 Wilkinson Blvd. Ph: (704)394-6105
Charlotte, NC 28208-5450 Fax: (704)391-9998
Contact: Archie L. Hargett, Natl.Cmdr.
Desc: Active, retired, disabled, and honorably discharged members of the Armed Forces of the United States who served in peace or war. Provides assistance to veterans, widows, and family members in obtaining government benefits. Sponsors service programs through the Veterans Administration; conducts welfare programs to assist disabled and needy veterans. *Type:* Association.

The Retired Enlisted Association

1111 S. Abilene Ct. Ph: (303)752-0660
Aurora, CO 80012 Free: 800-338-9337
Fax: (303)752-0835
E-mail: editor@trea.org
URL: http://www.trea.org
Contact: John Muench, Natl.Exec.Dir.
Desc: Retirees who have served in the military as enlisted persons; medically retired persons. Associate members are enlisted persons who have been on active duty for at least 10 years; widows/widowers of retired enlisted persons. Supports the rights and benefits of retired enlisted persons and their families. *Type:* Association.

Retired Enlisted Association—Voice

Retired Enlisted Association

1111 S. Abilene Ct. Ph: (303)752-0660
Aurora, CO 80012-4909 Free: 800-338-9337
Fax: (303)752-0835
E-mail: treahq@trea.org; editor@trea.org.
URL: http://www.TREA.org.
Desc: Reports on the rights and benefits of retired enlisted persons and their families. Reviews legislation on cost of living allowances and the use of medical facilities. *Type:* Newsletter.

The Retired Officers Association

201 N. Washington St. Ph: (703)549-2311
Alexandria, VA 22314-2539 Free: 800-245-8762
Fax: (703)838-8173
E-mail: troa@troa.org
URL: http://www.troa.org
Contact: Lt.Gen. Michael A. Nelson, USAF, Pres.
Desc: Men and women who are or have been commissioned or warrant officers in any component of the Army, Navy, Air Force, Marine Corps, Coast Guard, National Oceanic and Atmospheric Administration, and Public Health Service. Supports strong national defense and represents and assists members and their dependents and survivors with retirement issues and benefits. *Type:* Association.

Supreme Pup Tent, Military Order of the Cootie

211 S. Victoria
Iowa Park, TX 76367
Contact: Herman Cook, Contact.
Desc: Honor degree members of the Veterans of Foreign Wars of the U.S.A. serving the VFW. Members visit and entertain hospitalized veterans and support the VFW National Home for Children in Eaton Rapids, MI. *Type:* Association.

TEXAS LEGION TIMES

American Legion, Dept. of Texas

PO Box 789 Ph: (512)472-4138
Austin, TX 78767 Fax: (512)472-0603
Contact: Kerry L. Hall, Editor.
Desc: Newspaper (tabloid) for American Legion veteran organization members. *Type:* Periodical.

Veterans of Foreign Wars of the United States

406 W 34th St. Ph: (816)756-3390
Kansas City, MO 64111 Fax: (816)968-1157
E-mail: vfw@vfwdc.org
URL: http://www.vfw.org
Contact: Larry W. Rivers, Adjutant General.
Desc: Overseas veterans of the Spanish American War, World Wars I and II, the Korean and Vietnam wars, the Persian Gulf War, Grenada, Panama, and Lebanon in which an overseas campaign medal was received. Seeks to: insure the national security through maximum military strength; speed the rehabilitation of the nation's disabled and needy veterans; assist the widows, orphans, and dependents of disabled and needy veterans; promote Americanism through education in patriotism and constructive service to the communities in which we live. *Type:* Association.

VFW Auxiliary

Ladies Auxiliary to the VFW

406 W. 34 St. Ph: (816)561-7663
Kansas City, MO 64111 Fax: (816)931-4753
E-mail: info@ladiesauxvfw.com
URL: http://www.ladiesauxvfw.com.
Contact: Marilyn Ebersole, Editor.
Desc: VFW auxiliary patriotic services magazine. *Alt. Contact:* 406 W. 34th St., Kansas City, MO 64111; telephone: (816)561-8655; fax: (816)931-4753. *Type:* Periodical.

VFW Magazine

VFW Magazine
242 W. 27th St., Lobby 1B   Ph: (212)929-1300
New York, NY 10001-5926   Fax: (212)929-9574
Contact: Rich Kolb, Editor and Publisher; Harry Church, Advertising Dir.
Desc: Magazine for the Veterans of Foreign Wars. *Alt. Contact:* 406 W. 34th St., Kansas City, MO 64111-2736; telephone: (816)756-3390; fax: (816)968-1169. *Type:* Periodical.

Women's Auxiliary to the Military Order of the Cootie

2511 N. 74th St.   Ph: (913)334-3530
Kansas City, KS 66109   Fax: (913)299-6855
E-mail: supermoca@juno.com
Contact: Lynda Wallace, Treas.
Desc: Women who are members of the Ladies Auxiliary to the Veterans of Foreign Wars of the U.S.A. . Activities include: volunteer work in VA hospitals and local hospitals, rest homes, and mental institutions; scholarship program for education of children from VFW National Home. *Type:* Association.

Veterinary

American Animal Hospital Association

PO Box 150899   Ph: (303)986-2800
Denver, CO 80215-0899   Free: 800-252-2242
   Fax: (303)986-1700
E-mail: aahapr@aol.com
URL: http://www.healthypet.com/
Contact: John W. Albers, D.V.M., Exec.Dir.
Desc: Veterinarians engaged in small animal practice who own or staff small animal hospitals. Works for the promotion of excellence in small animal medicine and improvement of hospital facilities. *Type:* Association.

American Association of Equine Practitioners

4075 Iron Works Parkway   Ph: (606)233-0147
Lexington, KY 40511   Free: 800-443-0177
   Fax: (606)233-1968
E-mail: gcarpenter@aacp.org
URL: http://www.aaep.org
Contact: Gary L. Carpenter, Exec.Dir.
Desc: Veterinarians who specialize in equine medicine and surgery. Disseminates the latest scientific information relative to the practice of equine medicine; promotes research on horses. *Type:* Association.

American Veterinary Medical Association

1931 N. Meacham Rd., Ste.   Ph: (847)925-8070
100   Free: 800-248-2862
Schaumburg, IL 60173-4360   Fax: (847)925-1329
URL: http://www.avma.org
Contact: Bruce Little, D.V.M., Contact.
Desc: Professional society of veterinarians. Conducts educational and research programs. Provides placement service. *Type:* Association.

American Veterinary Medical Association— Directory

American Veterinary Medical Association
1931 N. Meacham Rd, Ste. 100   Ph: (847)925-8070
Schaumburg, IL 60173-4360   Fax: (847)925-1329
E-mail: avmainfo@avma.org
Contact: Karen M. Wernette, DVM, Editor.
Desc: 65,000 veterinarians; not limited to AVMA members. *Type:* Directory.

Animal Breeding Abstracts

CAB International
CABI Publishing
10 E. 40th St., Ste. 3203   Ph: (212)481-7018
New York, NY 10016
E-mail: cabi-nao@cabi.org
URL: http://www.cabi.org
Contact: Tania Fisher, Product Manager.
Desc: Contains citations, with abstracts, to current periodical and other published literature relating to animal breeding and allied subjects. Corresponds to Animal Breeding Abstracts and in part to the online CAB ABSTRACTS, CAB ANIMAL PRODUCTION, and CAB: Veterinary Sciences/Medicine databases and the CAB ABSTRACTS on CD-ROM and BEASTCD CD-ROM product. *Type:* Database.

AnimalNews

Morris Animal Foundation
45 Inverness Dr. E.   Ph: (303)790-2345
Englewood, CO 80112   Free: 800-243-2345
   Fax: (303)790-4066
Contact: Jennifer Chavez, Editor.
Desc: Contains reports from foundation-sponsored studies at veterinary colleges. *Type:* Newsletter.

Care for Pets

American Veterinary Medical Association
1931 N Meacham Rd., Ste. 100   Ph: (847)925-8070
Schaumburg, IL 60173   Fax: (847)925-1329
E-mail: AVMAINFO@avma.org
URL: http://www.avma.org/care4pets/default.htm
Desc: This page, sponsored by the AVMA, promotes responsible pet ownership and provides details on a variety of topics, ranging from animal health and safety to choosing or losing a pet. The site also provides statistics by breed in the Selecting a Pet section. *Type:* Database.

Dolphin Research Center

PO Box 522875   Ph: (305)289-1121
Marathon Shores, FL 33052   Fax: (305)743-7627
E-mail: drc-ed@reefnet.com
URL: http://www.dolphins.org
Contact: Jayne Shannon Rogriguez, Pres.
Type: Association.

Harvard University

New England Regional Primate Research Center

1 Pine Hill Dr.   Ph: (508)624-8002
PO Box 9102   Fax: (508)460-0612
Southborough, MA 01772-9102
E-mail: rhunt@warren.med.harvard.edu
URL: http://www.hms.harvard.edu/nerprc/
Contact: Dr. Bertha K. Madras, Ph.D, Acting Dir.
Desc: Conducts biomedical research using simian primates of diseases of simian primates, including clinical and comparative pathology, behavioral biology, immunology, molecular virology, microbiology, viral oncology, nutrition, and primatology. *Type:* Research center.

Helminthological Abstracts

CAB International
CABI Publishing
10 E. 40th St., Ste. 3203   Ph: (212)481-7018
New York, NY 10016
E-mail: cabi-nao@cabi.org
URL: http://www.cabi.org
Contact: Tania Fisher, Product Manager.
Desc: Contains citations, with abstracts, to current periodical and other published literature relating to medical and veterinary helminthology. Corresponds to Helminthological Abstracts and in part to the online CAB ABSTRACTS, CAB: Medical Parasitology and Mycology, CAB: Veterinary and Medical, and CAB: Veterinary Sciences/Medicine databases, and the VETCD CD-ROM and CAB ABSTRACTS on CD-ROM products. *Type:* Database.

Index Veterinarius

CAB International
CABI Publishing
10 E. 40th St., Ste. 3203   Ph: (212)481-7018
New York, NY 10016
E-mail: cabi-nao@cabi.org
URL: http://www.cabi.org
Contact: Tania Fisher, Product Manager.
Desc: Contains citations to the world's periodical and other published literature relating to veterinary science. Animals covered include cattle, horses, sheep, goats, pigs, poultry, cats, dogs, rabbits, cage birds, laboratory animals, wildlife, zoo animals, fish, and other domestic animals. *Type:* Database.

Jackson Laboratory

Mouse Mutant Resource

600 Main St.   Ph: (207)288-6223
Bar Harbor, ME 04609   Fax: (207)288-6149
E-mail: mtd@jax.org
URL: http://www.jax.org/resources/documents/mmr/mmr.homepage.html
Contact: Muriel T. Davisson, PhD, Contact.
Desc: Identifies, characterizes, and genetically maps new inherited endocrine, neurological, immunological, skeletal, and other mutations of the laboratory mouse. *Type:* Research center.

Johns Hopkins University

Center for Alternatives to Animal Testing

Sch. of Public Health   Ph: (410)223-1693
111 Marketplace, Ste. 840   Fax: (410)223-1603
Baltimore, MD 21202-6709
E-mail: caat@caat.jhsph.edu
URL: http://www.sph.jhu.edu/~altweb
Contact: Dr. Alan M. Goldberg, Dir.
Desc: Fosters development of scientifically acceptable in vitro and other alternatives to animal testing for use in development and safety evaluation of commercial and therapeutic products. Catalyzes validation of alternative methods. *Type:* Research center.

MCP Hahnemann University of the Health Sciences

Research Animal Facility

Broad & Vine Sts.   Ph: (215)762-7970
Mailstop 436   Fax: (215)762-7449
Philadelphia, PA 19102
URL: http://www.allegheny.edu
Contact: Dr. Silverman, Asst.VP.
Desc: Supports University biomedical research activities through inspection and reception of all laboratory animals, quarantining of all nonhuman primates and other species depending upon the nature of the study, and long-term housing of nonhuman primates, canines, swine, rats, mice, and other species. Serves as a teaching resource for the Graduate School. *Type:* Research center.

Ohio State University

Laboratory Animal Center

6089 Godown Rd.   Ph: (614)292-3382
Columbus, OH 43235   Fax: (614)457-2107
E-mail: stone.4@osu.edu
URL: http://www.isy.edy

Contact: Douglas Stone, DVM, Assoc.Dir.

Desc: Supports University biomedical research activities through inspection and reception of all laboratory animals, quarantining of all nonhuman primates and other species depending upon the nature of the study, and long-term housing of nonhuman primates, canines, swine, and other species. Serves as a teaching resource for the College of Veterinary Medicine. *Type:* Research center.

Oregon Regional Primate Research Center

505 NW 185th Ave.   Ph: (503)645-1141
Beaverton, OR 97006   Fax: (503)690-5532
E-mail: smithsu@ohsu.edu
URL: http://www.teleport.com/~orprc
Contact: Dr. M. Susan Smith, Dir.

Desc: Seeks to advance biomedical knowledge through basic research with nonhuman primates, including studies on reproductive biology, neuroscience, and experimental pathology. Specific projects include studies on the events that control fertility in primates, causes and control of premature labor, mechanisms of steroid action, and factors affecting neural differentiation, function and plasticity. *Type:* Research center.

Pet Product News Buying Guide Directory

Fancy Publications
PO Box 6050   Ph: (949)855-8822
Mission Viejo, CA 92690   Free: 800-365-4421
    Fax: (949)855-3045
Contact: Jack Sweet, Editor.

Desc: More than 2,000 trade associations, manufacturers and distributors of pet supplies and equipment, manufacturers' representatives, wholesalers of pets, and industry publishers. *Type:* Directory.

Petfood Industry—Directory/Source Book

Watt Publishing Co.
122 S. Wesley Ave.   Ph: (815)734-4171
Mt. Morris, IL 61054-1497   Fax: (815)734-4201
E-mail: schreibre@wattmm.mhs.compuserve.com.
Contact: Tim Phillips, Editor, phillips@wattmm.mhs.compuserve.com.

Desc: List of over 800 suppliers of ingredients, equipment, and other materials to pet food manufacturers; pet food manufactures; industry associations; international coverage (SIC 2047). *Type:* Directory.

Pig News and Information

CAB International
CABI Publishing
10 E. 40th St., Ste. 3203   Ph: (212)481-7018
New York, NY 10016
E-mail: cabi-nao@cabi.org
URL: http://www.cabi.org
Contact: Tania Fisher, Product Manager, t.fisher@cabi.org.

Desc: Contains news items, review articles, and abstracts of journal articles related to pigs. Includes reports highlighting pig production in selected countries. *Type:* Database.

Protozoological Abstracts

CAB International
CABI Publishing
10 E. 40th St., Ste. 3203   Ph: (212)481-7018
New York, NY 10016
E-mail: cabi-nao@cabi.org
URL: http://www.cabi.org
Desc: Contains citations, with abstracts, to current periodical and other published literature relating to protozoan diseases affecting man and animals. Covers malaria, trypanosoma, amoebal, toxoplasma, babesia, coccidia, giardia, leishmania, and AIDS-opportunistic infections. *Type:* Database.

Purdue University
Center for Paralysis Research

Sch. of Vet. Med.   Ph: (765)494-7600
1244 VCPR   Fax: (765)494-7605
West Lafayette, IN 47907-1244
E-mail: cpr@vet.purdue.edu
URL: http://www.vet.purdue.edu/depts/cpr/cpr.html
Contact: Dr. Richard Borgens, Dir.

Desc: Experimental treatments for spinal cord injury, focusing on recruitment of spared pathways in the spinal cord through the use of 4-Aminopyridine (4-AP), reconnection and regeneration of severely damaged nerve pathways through the use of oscillating electrical fields, and replacement of spinal cord using enteric neuron transplantation. *Type:* Research center.

Regional Primate Research Center

Univ. of Washington   Ph: (206)543-1430
Health Sci. Ctr., Box 357330   Fax: (206)685-0305
Seattle, WA 98195
E-mail: bmorton@bart.rprc.washington.edu
Contact: William R. Morton, VMD, Dir.

Desc: Central nervous and cardiovascular systems, immunobiology, virology, behavior, reproduction and perinatal studies, development and application of advanced electronic and mechanical instruments, and data acquisition systems for use in primate research. *Type:* Research center.

Review of Medical and Veterinary Entomology

CAB International
CABI Publishing
10 E. 40th St., Ste. 3203   Ph: (212)481-7018
New York, NY 10016
E-mail: cabi-nao@cabi.org
URL: http://www.cabi.org
Contact: Tania Fisher, Product Manager.

Desc: Contains citations, with abstracts, to current periodical and other published literature relating to medical and veterinary entomology. Covers insects and other arthropods which transmit diseases or are otherwise injurious to man and to animals of significance to man, including blattaria, mallophaga, anoplura, hemiptera, siphonaptera, dipters, acari, and arachnida. *Type:* Database.

Review of Medical and Veterinary Mycology

CAB International
CABI Publishing
10 E. 40th St., Ste. 3203   Ph: (212)481-7018
New York, NY 10016
E-mail: cabi-nao@cabi.org
URL: http://www.cabi.org
Contact: Tania Fisher, Product Manager.

Desc: Contains citations, with abstracts, to current periodical and other published literature relating to medical and veterinary mycology. Covers mycoses of man and domestic, farm, and wild animals as well as allergic disorders associated with fungi and poisoning by fungi or mold-contaminated food. *Type:* Database.

Scientists Center for Animal Welfare

7833 Walker Dr., Ste. 340   Ph: (301)345-3500
Greenbelt, MD 20770   Fax: (301)345-3503
E-mail: scaw@erols.com
URL: http://www.erols.com/scaw/scaw.htm
Contact: Lee Krulisch, Exec.Dir.

Desc: Compiles information and encourages discussion on public accountability, public policy, and the scientist's responsibilities regarding proper standards of animal care and use, particularly in biomedical research, testing, and education. Other areas of interest include agricultural animals and acceptable standards for wildlife research. *Type:* Research center.

State University of New York Health Science Center at Brooklyn
Primate Behavior Laboratory

450 Clarkson Ave., Box 120   Ph: (718)270-1447
Brooklyn, NY 11203   Fax: (718)270-3887
E-mail: lrosenbl@netmail.hscbklyn.edu
Contact: Dr. Leonard A. Rosenblum, Dir.

Desc: Normative and experimental studies of the development of bonnet and pigtail macaques and squirrel monkeys, including the development of mother-infant relations and infant social development, environmental factors and social development, psychosocial factors, nonhuman primate sexual behavior, primate models of psychopathology, and experimental studies of environmental enrichment, learning, and perception with computer-mediated video tasks in individual and group settings. *Type:* Research center.

Tulane University
Tulane Regional Primate Research Center

Covington, LA 70433   Ph: (504)892-2040
    Fax: (504)893-1352
E-mail: gerone@tpc.tulane.edu
URL: http://rhesus.tpc.tulane.edu
Contact: Dr. Peter J. Gerone, Dir.

Desc: Use of nonhuman primates in biomedical research projects in fields of cancer, immunology, infectious diseases, primate medicine, parasitology, primatology, pathology, reproductive physiology, urology, gene therapy and veterinary science. *Type:* Research center.

U.S. Department of Agriculture
Agricultural Research Service
National Agricultural Library

6303 Ivy Ln., Rm. 450   Ph: (301)344-2340
Greenbelt, MD 20770   Fax: (301)504-7042
Desc: The National Agricultural Library provides information services over a broad range of agricultural interests to a wide cross-section of users, from research scientists to the general public. The Library assists users through a variety of specialized information centers. *Type:* Government agency, office, or program.

U.S. Department of Agriculture
Animal and Plant Health Inspection Service
Veterinary Services

14th St. and Independence Ave.   Ph: (202)720-2511
SW
Washington, DC 20250
Desc: Veterinary Services officials are responsible for determining the existence and extent of outbreaks of communicable diseases and pests affecting livestock and poultry. They organize and conduct control and eradication programs in cooperation with state officials, and cooperate with animal health officials in other countries in planning and conducting disease control efforts in those countries. *Type:* Government agency, office, or program.

U.S. Department of Defense
Army Medical Research and Materiel Command
Walter Reed Army Institute of Research
Veterinary Medicine Division

Washington, DC 20307-5100   Ph: (202)295-7000
    Fax: (202)295-7891
Contact: Lt.Col. John Parrish, Dir.

Desc: Advises and provides consultative service to the field on matters pertaining to Veterinary medicine; provides centralized animal resource support to military medical research institutes within or near Washington, DC; conducts basic and applied research on diseases of animals employed in medical research; conducts comprehensive diagnostic surveillance of government-owned animals used in conjunction with direct service activities of medical research programs; provides all experimental animals and related support resources to WRAIR, including development of methods for improvement and standardization of laboratory animals; and conducts specialized training in laboratory animal medicine. Divisional components include departments of Animal Resources, Animal Medicine, and Animal Husbandry. *Type:* Research center.

U.S. Department of Health and Human Services

Food and Drug Administration

Center for Veterinary Medicine

c/o Food and Drug   Ph: (301)594-1755
   Administration   Fax: (301)594-1830
5600 Fishers Ln.
Rockville, MD 20857
URL: http://www.fda.gov/
Contact: Stephen F. Sundlof, Director.
Desc: The Center develops and conducts programs with respect to the safety and efficacy of veterinary preparations and devices; evaluates proposed use of veterinary preparations for animal safety and efficacy; and evaluates FDA's surveillance and compliance programs relating to veterinary drugs and other veterinary medical matters. *Type:* Government agency, office, or program.

U.S. Department of Health and Human Services

Food and Drug Administration

Center for Veterinary Medicine

Toxicology Team

Metro Park North II   Ph: (301)594-1680
7500 Standish Pl.   Fax: (301)594-2297
Rockville, MD 20855
Contact: Tom Mulligan, Ld.
Desc: Determines human food safety of drug residues in animal products in response to the Food, Drug, and Cosmetic Act. Assesses the environmental impact of the approval of new drugs in response to the National Environmental Protection Act. *Type:* Research center.

U.S. Department of Health and Human Services

National Center for Research Resources

Comparative Medicine Program

Laboratory Animal Sciences Program

9000 Rockville Pike   Ph: (301)496-5795
Bldg 12A Rm 4007, MSC5662   Fax: (301)402-0006
Bethesda, MD 20892
Contact: Dr. Judith Vaitukaitis,, Director.
Desc: New animal models, to improve the care and health of animals used in research, and to train veterinarians in laboratory animal medicine. Focus is on the development of improved methods for diagnosing and controlling diseases among laboratory animals; and providing support to special breeding programs to ensure an adequate supply of animals that have been shown to be good models of human diseases or that serve as important research subjects. *Type:* Research center.

University of California, Davis

California Regional Primate Research Center

Davis, CA 95616   Ph: (530)752-0447
      Fax: (530)752-8201
E-mail: aghendrickx@ucdavis.edu
URL: http://www.crprc.ucdavis.edu/crprc/homepage.html
Contact: Dr. Andrew G. Hendrickx, Dir.
Desc: Developmental and reproductive biology, behavioral and neurology, genetics, neurosciences, virology and im-

munology, infectious diseases, pulmonary and respiratory diseases, primate medicine, and primate pathology. Focuses on preventive medicine for humans through the use of nonhuman primates as animal models in such studies as the effects of toxic compounds, developmental toxicology, metabolic diseases, infectious agents, altered environments, and pharmacokinetics of various drugs. *Type:* Research center.

University of Chicago

Animal Resources Center

5841 S. Maryland   Ph: (773)702-9368
MC 1030   Fax: (773)702-9152
Chicago, IL 60637
E-mail: gus@arc_1_bsd.uchicago.edu
Contact: Dr. August Battles, Dir.
Desc: Supports research on animals and animal models. *Type:* Research center.

University of Hawaii at Manoa

Kewalo Marine Laboratory

41 Ahui St.   Ph: (808)539-7300
Honolulu, HI 96813   Fax: (808)599-4817
E-mail: hadfield@uhunix.uhcc.hawaii.edu
URL: http://www.kewalo.hawaii.edu
Contact: Dr. Michael G. Hadfield, Dir.
Desc: Biomedical research, including molecular, cell, and developmental biology using marine animals (primarily invertebrate gametes) as experimental material. *Type:* Research center.

University of Illinois at Chicago

Biologic Resource Laboratory

M/C 533   Ph: (312)996-7040
1840 W. Taylor St.   Fax: (312)996-8065
Chicago, IL 60612
E-mail: btb@uic.edu
Contact: Dr. B. Taylor Bennett, Dir.
Desc: Houses animals and provides research and teaching support involving animal models for Colleges of Medicine, Dentistry, Pharmacy, and Nursing of the University. *Type:* Research center.

University of Kansas

Animal Care Unit

Lawrence, KS 66045
      Ph: (785)864-5587
      Fax: (785)864-5305
E-mail: jbresnahan@labrat.acu.ukans.edu
URL: http://www.ukans.edu/~acu/acu.html
Contact: James F. Bresnahan, DVM, Dir.
Desc: Provides care to animals used in research, teaching, and public education at the Lawrence campus. Provides animal care, diagnostic, treatment, and necropsy services to control disease conditions and monitor health status of animal colonies. *Type:* Research center.

University of Kansas

Laboratory Animal Resources

UK Med. Ctr.   Ph: (913)588-7015
2010 W. 39th St.   Fax: (913)588-7277
Kansas City, KS 66160-7185
E-mail: tdavid@kumc.edu
Contact: Tony David, DVM, Dir.
Desc: Houses and maintains many species of animals required for various facets of biomedical research and for teaching purposes at the University. Supports a wide variety of research projects involving laboratory animals and operates a comprehensive laboratory animal program. *Type:* Research center.

University of Miami

Animal Disease and Investigative Laboratory

Sch. of Med.   Ph: (305)243-6927
Div. of Comparative Pathology   Free: 800-596-7390
PO Box 016960, R-46   Fax: (305)243-5662
Miami, FL 33101
E-mail: naltman@mednet.miami.edu
Contact: Norman H. Altman, VMD, Dir.
Desc: Diagnosis and control of diseases and abnormal physiological conditions in laboratory animals at University of Miami biomedical research facilities. This laboratory performs gross and microscopic pathology, clinical chemistry, hematology, radioimmunoassay, microbiology, parasitology and serology for biomedical research programs. *Type:* Research center.

University of Michigan

Unit for Laboratory Animal Medicine

Animal Res. Facility   Ph: (734)764-0277
Ann Arbor, MI 48109-0614   Fax: (734)936-3235
E-mail: dringler@umich.edu
URL: http://www.drda.umich.edu/ULAM/pages/ulamhome.htm
Contact: Dr. D.H. Ringler, Dir.
Desc: Biomedical sciences including comparative medicine, laboratory animal medicine, animal models for biomedical research, and proper use and care of laboratory animals. Provides veterinary care for all vertebrate animals used in research and education at the University. *Type:* Research center.

University of Missouri--Columbia

Research Animal Diagnostic and Investigative Laboratory

Coll. of Vet. Med.   Ph: (573)882-5983
1600 E. Rollins   Free: 800-669-0825
Columbia, MO 65211   Fax: (573)884-7521
E-mail: vmradil@vetmed.missouri.edu
URL: http://www.hsc.missouri.edu/vetmed/radil
Contact: Dr. Joseph E. Wagner, Dir.
Desc: Human health research through the use of animals. *Type:* Research center.

University of Missouri--Kansas City

Laboratory Animal Center

1015 E. 50th St.   Ph: (816)235-1681
Kansas City, MO 64110   Fax: (816)235-5275
E-mail: petersd@smtpgate.umkc.edu
Contact: David K. Peters, DVM, Dir.
Desc: Physiology, exploratory surgery, and immunology. *Type:* Research center.

University of Montana

Primate Laboratory

Department of Psychology   Ph: (406)243-2091
Missoula, MT 59812   Fax: (406)243-6366
E-mail: py_adp@selway.umt.edu
Contact: Dr. Allen D. Szalda-Petree, Dir.
Desc: Social and learning behaviors of developing monkeys, specifically rhesus monkeys (Macaca mulatta). Also conducts research in the use of computer video tasks to study discrimination learning, foraging behavior, and perceptual motor skills in primates. *Type:* Research center.

University of Oklahoma

Animal Resources

Health Sci. Ctr., BMSB 203   Ph: (405)271-5185
PO Box 26901   Fax: (405)271-2660
Oklahoma City, OK 73190
E-mail: gary-white@ouhsc.edu
URL: http://www.ouhsc.edu

Contact: Gary L. White, DVM, Dir.

Desc: Biomedical studies in general areas of physiology, pathology, microbiology, surgery, and internal medicine. *Type:* Research center.

University of Pennsylvania

Referral Center for Animal Models of Human Genetic Disease

Vet. Hospital   Ph: (215)573-2162
3850 Spruce St.   Fax: (215)898-9923
Philadelphia, PA 19104-6010

Contact: Dr. Donald F. Patterson, Prin. Investigator.

Desc: Identification, characterization, evaluation, and dissemination of animal models of human genetic disease, particularly models that occur in domestic animals, with emphasis on hereditary metabolic diseases, hereditary defects in sexual development, congenital malformations, and hereditary diseases of blood. Activities include characterization of mutant genes at the molecular level. *Type:* Research center.

University of Pittsburgh

Center for Research in Reproductive Physiology

S 330 Biomedical Sci. Tower   Ph: (412)648-9281
Pittsburgh, PA 15261   Fax: (412)383-7159
E-mail: plant1@vms.cis.pitt.edu

Contact: Tony M. Plant, PhD, Dir.

Desc: Neuroendocrine control of reproduction in rhesus monkeys. *Type:* Research center.

University of Puerto Rico

Caribbean Primate Research Center

Med. Sci. Campus   Ph: (787)784-0322
PO Box 1053   Fax: (787)795-6700
Sabana Seca, PR 00952-1053
E-mail: mkessler@coqui.net
URL: http://ourworld.compuserve.com/homepages/oceanpkvete/html

Contact: Dr. Matthew J. Kessler, Dir.

Desc: General primate behavior and biology with emphasis on sociobiology and diseases of nonhuman primates. The nonhuman primate populations and associated genealogical records make possible an evaluation of genetic, ecological, and social influences on the incidence and progress of disorders of adaptation and enable research to be conducted on control of population growth, evolution of social interaction by family selection, inbreeding potential of confined populations, reproductive behavior, positional behaviors and the development of degenerative joint disease, diabetes, obesity, and macular degeneration. *Type:* Research center.

University of South Alabama

Primate Research Laboratory

College of Med.   Ph: (334)460-6293
Department of Comparative   Fax: (334)460-6286
 Med., MSB 992
Mobile, AL 36688-0002

Contact: Bob Ricker, Lab.Supv.

Desc: Primates, especially as animal models of human diseases. *Type:* Research center.

University of Southwestern Louisiana

New Iberia Research Center

4401 W. Admiral Dr.   Ph: (318)482-0225
New Iberia, LA 70560   Fax: (318)482-0308
E-mail: tjr7173@usl.edu

Contact: Dr. Thomas J. Rowell, Dir.

Desc: Human disease research, animal models development, and pharmacology/toxicology research. *Type:* Research center.

University of Texas at Austin

Animal Resources Center

2701 Speedway   Ph: (512)471-7534
Austin, TX 78705   Fax: (512)471-4336
E-mail: jfineg@mail.utexas.edu
URL: http://www.utexas.edu/research/arc/

Contact: Jerry Fineg, DVM, Dir.

Desc: Provides a facility for research and housing of research animals. Also involved in diagnostic and procedural manipulation of the animals used in research and teaching elsewhere in the University. *Type:* Research center.

University of Texas Southwestern Medical Center at Dallas

Animal Resources Center

5232 Harry Hines Blvd.   Ph: (214)648-3340
Dallas, TX 75235-9037   Fax: (214)648-2659

Contact: Dr. William P. Porter, Dir.

Desc: Pathogenesis, control, and prevention of murine mycoplasmosis, genetic susceptibility and resistance to infectious agents, feline immunodeficiency virus infection as a model for HIV infection, and animal models for Lyme disease. *Type:* Research center.

University of Utah

Radiobiology Laboratory

40 N. 2030 E. Front   Ph: (801)581-6600
Salt Lake City, UT 84112-5860   Fax: (801)581-7008
E-mail: scmiller@msscc.med.utah.edu

Contact: Dr. Scott C. Miller, Dir.

Desc: Chemistry, physics, biochemistry, bone sciences, and veterinary aspects and pathology of long-term physiological and biochemical effects of internally deposited radioisotopes. *Type:* Research center.

University of Wisconsin--Madison

Animal Care and Gnotobiotic Division

1300 University Ave., Ste. 601   Ph: (608)262-0456
Madison, WI 53706-1510   Fax: (608)265-6765
E-mail: jtcroft@facstaff.wisc.edu
URL: http://biostat.wisc.edu/cgi-bin/gnotolab/gnotolab.pl

Contact: Dr. Joe Thulin, Dir.

Desc: Host/parasite interactions, implicating immunology, kidney and thymus transplants, caries, bladder cancer, and toxicology; provides investigators with the technology and equipment necessary to carry out their research on animals that are either completely free of viable microorganisms or have a known microbial flora (flora-defined or gnotobiotic); improves methods used in the care of gnotobiotes, the units housing them, and equipment maintaining them; offers germfree foster mothers, rats, and mice, athymic and euthymic, to qualified researchers; performs caesarian derivations for affiliated organizations and commercial suppliers to upgrade the quality of research animals. *Type:* Research center.

University of Wisconsin--Madison

Research Animal Resources Center

396 Enzyme Institute   Ph: (608)262-1238
1710 University Ave.   Fax: (608)265-2698
Madison, WI 53705
E-mail: parks@rarc.wisc.edu

Contact: Christine M. Parks, Dir.

Desc: Laboratory animal diseases. *Type:* Research center.

University of Wisconsin--Madison

Wisconsin Regional Primate Research Center

1220 Capitol Ct.   Ph: (608)263-3500
Madison, WI 53715-1299   Fax: (608)263-4031
E-mail: kemnitz@primate.wisc.edu
URL: http://www.primate.wisc.edu

Contact: Dr. Joseph W. Kemnitz, Dir.

Desc: Reproduction and development, neurobiology, physiological ethology, psychobiology, aging and metabolic diseases, immunogenetics and immunology and virology. Emphasizes biomedical research and studies on captive and wild primate conservation; rhesus colonies for research in aging, AIDS, and developmental biology; and common marmosets, for research in reproduction and aging behavior. *Type:* Research center.

Veterinary Bulletin

CAB International
CABI Publishing
10 E. 40th St., Ste. 3203   Ph: (212)481-7018
New York, NY 10016
E-mail: cabi-nao@cabi.org
URL: http://www.cabi.org

Contact: Tania Fisher, Product Manager.

Desc: Contains citations, with abstracts, to current periodical and other published literature relating to the field of animal health. Animals covered include cattle, horses, sheep, goats, pigs, poultry, cats, dogs, rabbits, cage birds, other small animals, laboratory animals, wildlife, zoo animals, fish, and other domestic animals. *Type:* Database.

Yale University

Resource for the Study of Laboratory Animal Diseases

PO Box 8016   Ph: (203)785-2525
New Haven, CT 06520-8016   Fax: (203)785-7499

Contact: Dr. Robert O. Jacoby, Chm.

Desc: Diagnostic and laboratory animal medicine, including research on animal diseases, research on diseases of laboratory animals, and preliminary studies to determine if a disease is suitable as a model for human disease. Studies include rodent parvoviruses, rodent coronaviruses, animal models of papillomatosis, nantavins infections. *Type:* Research center.

Vietnam

11th Armored Cavalry's Veterans of Vietnam and Cambodia

1602 Lorrie Dr.   Ph: (972)235-6542
Richardson, TX 75080-3409
E-mail: ktrp11acr@aol.com
URL: http://www.11thcavnam.com/11acvvc.html

Contact: Ollie W. Pickral, Pres.

Desc: Those who served with or were affiliated with the 11th Armored Cavalry Regiment in Vietnam and Cambodia from August 1966 to March 1972; wives, parents, and children of those troopers killed in action. Promotes members' physical, mental, and social development. *Type:* Association.

Veterans of the Vietnam War

760 Jumper Rd.   Ph: (570)825-7215
Wilkes Barre, PA 18702-8033   Free: 800-VIE-
                                      TNAM
                                Fax: (570)825-8223

E-mail: vvnwnatl@epix.net
URL: http://www.vvnw.org

Contact: Michael Milne, Natl. Commander.

Desc: Veterans and nonveterans united to aid Vietnam and veterans of all eras. POW/MIAs, United Veterans Beacon House Projects (Homeless Program). Maintains collection of literature on such subjects as Agent Orange, post-traumatic stress syndrome, employment, and incarcerated veterans. *Type:* Association.

Vietnam

Primedia History Group

741 Miller Dr., Ste. D-2   Ph: (703)771-9400
Leesburg, VA 20175   Fax: (703)779-8345
E-mail: vietnam@thehistorynet.com.
URL: http://www.thehistorynet.com.
Contact: Col. Harry G. Summers, Jr., Editor; David Kirk, Publisher.
Desc: Magazine covering personalities, weapons, battles, and history of the Vietnam war while examining America's participation in the conflict. *Type:* Periodical.

Vietnam Helicopter Pilots Association

5530 Birdcage St., Ste. 200   Free: 800-505-VHPA
Citrus Heights, CA 95610
E-mail: hq@vhpa.org
URL: http://www.vhpa.org
Contact: Thomas Payne, Pres.
Desc: All who flew helicopters in Vietnam during the Vietnam conflict (1961-75). Seeks to perpetuate spirit of camaraderie among members. *Type:* Association.

Vietnam Veterans of America

1224 M St. NW   Ph: (202)628-2700
Washington, DC 20005-5783   Free: 800-VVA-1316
    Fax: (202)628-5880
Contact: George Duggins, Pres.
Desc: Congressionally chartered, nationwide veterans service organization formed specifically for Vietnam veterans. Objectives are to work for the employment, education benefits, improved psychological assistance, and health care of Vietnam veterans. *Type:* Association.

Who's Who in Vietnam

Baron's Who's Who

412 N. Coast Hwy., Ste. B110   Ph: (949)497-8615
Laguna Beach, CA 92651   Fax: (949)786-8918
E-mail: info@baronswhoswho.com
URL: http://www.baronswhoswho.com; http://baronswhoswhos.com/vietnam/wwvndet.htm.
Contact: John L. Pellam, Editor.
Desc: 1,133 prominent and influential personalities in Vietnam today. *Type:* Directory.

Vocational Education

American Vocational Association

Association for Career and Technical Education

1410 King St.   Ph: (703)683-3111
Alexandria, VA 22314   Free: 800-826-9972
    Fax: (703)683-7424
E-mail: avahq@avaonline.org
URL: http://www.avaonline.org
Contact: Bret Lovejoy, Exec.Dir.
Desc: Teachers, supervisors, administrators, and others interested in the development and improvement of vocational, technical, and practical arts education. Areas of interest include: secondary, postsecondary, and adult vocational education; education for special population groups; cooperative education. Works with such government agencies as: Bureau of Apprenticeship in Department of Labor; Office of Vocational Rehabilitation in Department of Health and Human Services; Veterans Administration; Office of Vocational and Adult Education of the Department of Education. *Type:* Association.

Business Professionals of America

5454 Cleveland Ave.   Ph: (614)895-7277
Columbus, OH 43231-4021   Free: 800-334-2007
    Fax: (614)895-1165
E-mail: bpa@ix.netcom.com
URL: http://www.bpa.org

Contact: Gary L. Hannah, CEO & Pres.
Desc: High school and postsecondary vocational, business, and office education students. Seeks to develop leadership abilities, interest in the American business system, and competency in office occupations within the framework of vocational education. *Type:* Association.

Career College Association

10 G St. NW, Ste. 750   Ph: (202)336-6700
Washington, DC 20002   Fax: (202)336-6828
E-mail: waltb@career.org
URL: http://www.career.org
Contact: Omer Waddles, Pres.
Desc: Private postsecondary schools providing career education. Seeks to inform members of the accreditation process and regulations affecting vocational education. *Type:* Association.

National Vocational-Technical Honor Society

PO Box 1336   Ph: (828)698-8011
Flat Rock, NC 28731   Free: 800-801-7090
    Fax: (828)698-8564
E-mail: apowell@nvths.org
URL: http://www.nvths.org
Contact: C. Allen Powell, Exec.Dir./Co-Founder.
Desc: Honor students engaged in occupational and vocational-technical programs at secondary, postsecondary, public, or private schools in the U.S. Promotes vocational-technical education, career development, skilled workmanship, and individual qualities such as leadership and honesty. Works to strengthen the link between vocational-technical institutions and business and industry. *Type:* Association.

Voluntarism

Association of Junior Leagues International

660 1st Ave.   Ph: (212)683-1515
New York, NY 10016-3241   Fax: (212)481-7196
Contact: Jane Silverman, Exec.Dir.
Desc: Works to serve the Junior Leagues in developing the potential of women, promoting volunteerism and improving communities. *Type:* Association.

Corporation For National Service - Puerto Rico/Virgin Islands Chapter

U.S. Federal Bldg.   Ph: (809)766-5314
150 Carlos Chardon Ave., Ste.   Fax: (787)766-5189
662
San Juan, PR 00918-1737
Contact: Loretta Phelps De Cordova.
Desc: Promotes and helps fund community-based, self-help volunteer projects for: Americorps, VISTA, and NSSC (Foster Grandparents, Senior Companions, RSVP). *Type:* Association.

HealthFare U.S.A.

9411 Connecticut Ave.   Ph: (301)942-6601
Kensington, MD 20895
Contact: Jack A. Marshall, Pres.
Desc: Volunteer and community groups, corporate and government sponsors, health organizations, and media groups. Purpose is to help implement high quality, comprehensive health education and promotion programs. Organizes health fairs that serve the public by: providing multiple health screenings in convenient locations; promoting self-assessment and health awareness; coordinating and using existing resources; assisting participants in understanding how daily lifestyle choices and habits affect overall health status; and offering referral services. *Type:* Association.

Retired and Senior Volunteer Program

1201 New York Ave., NW   Ph: (202)606-5000
Washington, DC 20525   Free: 800-424-8867
    Fax: (202)565-2743
URL: http://www.cns.gov
Contact: Thomas E. Endres, Dir.
Desc: Not an association. Funded and administered by The Corporation for National Service. Volunteers of at least 55 years of age from all socioeconomic levels and educational backgrounds who are willing and able to perform services on a regular basis. *Type:* Association.

Senior Companion Program

Washington Urban League   Ph: (202)529-8701
2900 Newton St. NE   Fax: (202)832-3127
Washington, DC 20018
Contact: Brenda L. Turner, Dir.
Desc: Administered by ACTION, an independent government agency. Offers volunteer opportunities for low-income persons age 60 and over to establish a one-to-one relationship with other older persons, particularly the frail elderly in their homes, in an effort to delay or prevent institutionalization. Provides services to the elderly in institutions in an attempt to render them capable of returning to community life. *Type:* Association.

Volunteer Services Administration

American Society of Directors of Volunteer Services

American Hospital Association   Ph: (312)422-3939
1 North Franklin   Fax: (312)422-4575
Chicago, IL 60606
Contact: Nancy Brown, Editor; Ilse Almanza, Editor.
Desc: Provides a means of intercommunication for directors of volunteer services within health care institutions. Offers guidance on matters relating to health care volunteer services management in order to maintain professional standards and increase the competence of individual members. *Type:* Newsletter.

Waste

AIDIS-USA Section

601 Wythe St.   Ph: (703)684-2400
Alexandria, VA 22314-1994   Fax: (703)684-2492
E-mail: aidis_usa@compuserve.com
Contact: J. Ellis Turner, Pres.
Desc: Sanitary engineers in government, private business, and educational institutions throughout the Western Hemisphere. Promotes study and solution of sanitary engineering and environmental problems as a necessary condition for economic and social development in the Americas and for advancing understanding; establishes uniform standards for permanent protection of health of all Western Hemisphere inhabitants. Maintains 30 sections. *Type:* Association.

American Public Works Association

2345 Grand Blvd., Ste. 500   Ph: (816)472-6100
Kansas City, MO 64108   Free: 800-595-APWA
    Fax: (816)472-1610
E-mail: atatum@apwa.net
Contact: Pete King, Exec.Dir.
Desc: Chief administrators, commissioners, and directors of public works, city engineers, superintendents, and department heads of transportation, water, waste water, solid waste, equipment services, and buildings and grounds; federal, provincial, and state administrators and engineers; consultants and educators; associate members are equipment manufacturers' representatives, utility company officials, and contractors; student members are engineering and public administration students interested in the theo-

ry and practice of the design, construction, maintenance, administration, and operation of public works facilities and services. Conducts historical research on public works subjects and demonstrates applicability of history to current public works problems and issues through Public Works Historical Society. Sponsors research and education foundations. *Type:* Association.

Association of Metropolitan Sewerage Agencies

1000 Connecticut Ave., NW,   Ph: (202)833-AMSA
  Ste. 410   Fax: (202)833-4657
Washington, DC 20036-5302
E-mail: info@amsa-cleanwater.org
URL: http://www.amsa-cleanwater.org
Contact: Ken Kirk, Exec.Dir.

Desc: Public waste water treatment facilities, consulting firms and other private and public organization. Seeks to advance knowledge in the management of metropolitan sewerage agencies and develop more effective public service by encouraging the establishment of sound sewage collection, treatment and disposal policies. *Type:* Association.

Association of State and Territorial Solid Waste Management Officials

444 N. Capitol St. NW, Ste.   Ph: (202)624-5828
  315   Fax: (202)624-7875
Washington, DC 20001
URL: http://www.astswmo.org
Contact: Thomas J. Kennedy, Exec.Dir.

Desc: Represents state solid and hazardous waste directors. *Type:* Association.

Automotive Recyclers Association

3975 Fair Ridge Dr., Ste. 20   Ph: (703)385-1001
Terrace Level-North   Free: 888-385-1005
Fairfax, VA 22033-2924   Fax: (703)385-1494
E-mail: dove@autorecyc.org
URL: http://www.autorecyc.org
Contact: William P. Steinkuller, Exec.VP.

Desc: Firms selling recycled auto, truck, motorcycle, bus, and farm and construction equipment parts, retail and wholesale; operators of long line (telephone) circuits; firms selling equipment and services to the industry. Seeks to improve business practices and operating techniques through exchange of information via publications and meetings. *Type:* Association.

BNA Toxics Law Daily

The Bureau of National Affairs, Inc. (BNA)
1231 25th St. NW   Ph: (202)452-4200
Washington, DC 20037
E-mail: bnaplus@bna.com
URL: http://bna.com/mkt/hrl/hrlwdec.htm

Desc: Contains analyses of legislative, regulatory, and judicial activities that affect radioactive and toxic waste management and related insurance litigation. *Available:* LEXIS-NEXIS, LEXIS; West Group, WESTLAW. *Type:* Database.

Center For Health, Environment and Justice

PO Box 6806   Ph: (703)237-2249
Falls Church, VA 22040
E-mail: cchw@essential.org
URL: http://www.essential.org/cchw
Contact: Lois Marie Gibbs, Exec.Dir.

Desc: Concerned with the likelihood of adverse physical effects on adults and children from contact with toxic chemicals and other hazardous wastes. *Type:* Association.

CERCLIS Database of Hazardous Waste Sites

U.S. Environmental Protection Agency (EPA)
Office of Emergency and Remedial Response
401 M St., SW, MC 5202G   Ph: 800-424-9346
Washington, DC 20460
URL: http://www.epa.gov/oerrpage/sperfnd/web
Contact: Margret L. Brown, Program Analyst, (703)603-8876, fax: (703)603-9305, brown.margret@epamail.epa.gov.

Desc: Contains information on more than 10,000 releases of hazardous substances reported to the U.S. Environmental Protection Agency (EPA). *Available:* Oxford Molecular Group, Chemical Information Systems; West Group, WESTLAW; U.S. Environmental Protection Agency (EPA), Office of Emergency and Remedial Response. *Type:* Database.

Clean Sites, Inc.

901 N. Washington St., Ste.
  604
Alexandria, VA 22314-1535
Contact: Edwin H. Clark, II, Pres.

Desc: Established by a coalition of environmentalists, industry representatives, and government officials. Works to improve and expedite the process of cleaning up hazardous waste sites. *Type:* Association.

Community Environmental Council

930 Miramonte Dr.   Ph: (805)963-0583
Santa Barbara, CA 93109   Fax: (805)962-9080
Contact: Jon Clark, Dir.

Desc: Individuals and environmental organizations whose prime objective is environmental education, research, and technical assistance. Current focus is on waste management policy and technology, and land-use policy. Operates 4 recycling centers and 3 community gardens. *Type:* Association.

Environmental Manager's Compliance Advisor

Business & Legal Reports, Inc.
39 Academy St.   Ph: (203)318-0000
Madison, CT 06443   Free: 800-727-5257
                  Fax: (203)245-2559
E-mail: service@blr.com
Contact: John F. Brady, Editor.

Desc: Discusses toxic and hazardous substance management, Environmental Protection Agency (EPA) testing, government legislation, and the Department of Transportation's (DOT) rulings on hazardous materials transports. Recurring features include a calendar of events and columns titled News Roundup, Compliance Report, Washington Watch, Hazmat Transportation News, From the States, Federal Register Digest, and Conferences & Seminars. *Type:* Newsletter.

Global Recycling Network

Global Recycling Network
2715A Montauk Hwy.   Ph: (516)286-5580
Brookhaven, NY 11719   Free: 800-8GRN-INC
                  Fax: (516)286-5551
E-mail: grn@grn.com
URL: http://grn.com/grn/
Contact: webmaster@verio.net.

Desc: The Global Recycling Network is an information service to aid businesses worldwide in the recycling of resources, surplus manufactured goods, and outdated or used machinery. To assist businesses in turning inventory losses into new found profits, or to purchase goods at affordable prices, GRN created an Internet-linked database that allows them to make contact with an entirely new, constantly expanding, arena of buyers-sellers throughout the world. *Type:* Database.

Institute of Scrap Recycling Industries

1325 G St. NW, Ste. 1000   Ph: (202)737-1770
Washington, DC 20005   Fax: (202)626-0900
E-mail: isri@isri.org
URL: http://www.isri.org

Contact: Robin Wiener, Exec.Dir.

Desc: Processors, brokers, and consumers engaged in the recycling of ferrous, nonferrous, and nonmetallic scrap; related industry organizations. Conducts specialized education and research programs. *Type:* Association.

Integrated Waste Management

McGraw-Hill, Inc.
1221 Avenue of the Americas   Ph: (212)512-6410
New York, NY 10020

Desc: Contains the complete text of Integrated Waste Management, a newsletter covering trends and developments in the worldwide conversion of agricultural, industrial, municipal, and solid wastes to energy forms. Covers recycling, composting, source reduction, and landfilling. *Type:* Database.

Sludge

Business Publishers, Inc. (BPI)
951 Pershing Dr.   Ph: (301)587-6300
Silver Spring, MD 20910-4464
URL: http://www.bpinews.com

Desc: Contains the complete text of Sludge Newsletter, a newsletter on sludge management, treatment, disposal, generation, and use. Covers sludge management developments of industrial and municipal residuals and by-products of air and water pollution control. *Type:* Database.

Solid Waste Association of North America

1100 Wayne Ave., Ste. 700   Ph: (301)585-2898
PO Box 7219   Fax: (301)589-7068
Silver Spring, MD 20907
E-mail: info@swana.org
URL: http://www.swana.org

Contact: John H. Skinner, Ph.D., Exec.Dir./CEO.

Desc: Public agency officials and private corporate officials, including employees, managers of public solid waste management agencies and their manufacturers, suppliers, consultants, and contractors. Mission is to advance the practice of environmentally and economically sound municipal solid waste management in North America. *Type:* Association.

Weapons Complex Monitor

Exchange/Monitor Publications
1913 I St. NW, 6th Fl.   Ph: (202)296-2814
Washington, DC 20006   Free: 800-776-1314
                  Fax: (202)296-2805
E-mail: excpub@aol.com.
URL: http://www.exchangemonitor.com.

Contact: Edward L. Helminski, Publisher, helminski@exchangemonitor.com; Christopher P. Logan, Editorial Director, logan@exchangemonitor.com; Jamin D. Hegeman, Reporter, hegeman@exchangemonitor.com; Tricia A. Holly, Reporter, holly@exchangemonitor.com.

Desc: Devoted exclusively to providing intelligence and inside information on the largest environmental program in the world--the cleanup of the Department of Energy's nuclear weapons comples. Includes special bi-weekly report on radioactive waste management and nuclear facility cleanup in Russia and the post-Soviet States. *Type:* Newsletter.

Water

AGWSE Newsletter

Association of Ground Water Scientists and Engineers (AGWSE)
National Ground Water Association (NGWA)
601 Dempsey Rd.   Ph: (614)898-7791
Westerville, OH 43081   Free: 800-551-7379
                        Fax: (614)898-7786
E-mail: ngwa@ngwa.org
Contact: Cate Ebling, Editor, ceblin@ngwa.org.
Desc: Reports on the activities of the AGWSE, an association of ground water industry scientists and engineers. *Type:* Newsletter.

American Society of Dowsers

PO Box 24   Ph: (802)684-3417
Brainerd St.   Free: 800-711-9530
Danville, VT 05828   Fax: (802)684-2565
E-mail: asd@dowsers.org
URL: http://www.newhampshire.com/dowsers.org
Contact: Brenda Paquin, Dir.
Desc: Amateur and professional dowsers and others interested in locating water, oil, mineral deposits, and various objects and information with or without the use of forked sticks, pendulums, and rods. Promotes fellowship and the teaching of dowsing skills. Informs the public on the significance and uses of dowsing. *Type:* Association.

American Water Works Association

6666 W. Quincy Ave.   Ph: (303)794-7711
Denver, CO 80235   Free: 800-926-7337
                      Fax: (303)795-1440
URL: http://www.awwa.org
Contact: Jack W. Hoffbuhr, Exec.Dir.
Desc: Water utility managers, superintendents, engineers, chemists, bacteriologists, and other individuals interested in public water supply; municipal- and investor-owned water departments; boards of health; manufacturers of waterworks equipment; government officials and consultants interested in water supply. Develops standards and supports research programs in waterworks design, construction, operation, and management. *Type:* Association.

Association of Ground Water Scientists and Engineers

601 Dempsey Rd.   Ph: (614)898-7791
Westerville, OH 43081 Free: 800-551-7379
                       Fax: (614)898-7786
URL: http://www.h2o-ngwa.org
Contact: Jacqueline Mack, Contact.
Desc: A technical division of the National Ground Water Association. Hydrogeologists, geologists, hydrologists, civil and environmental engineers, geochemists, biologists, and scientists in related fields. Seek to: provide leadership and guidance for scientific, economical, and beneficial groundwater development; promote the use, protection, and management of the world's groundwater resources. *Type:* Association.

EARDC Home Page

Southwest Texas State University - Edwards Aquifer Research and Data Center
Freeman Bldg.   Ph: (512)245-2329
San Marcos, TX 78666   Fax: (512)245-2669
URL: http://eardc.swt.edu
Contact: Bob Ourso, ourso@eardc.swt.edu.
Desc: The Edwards Aquifer Research and Data Center contains information on the Edwards Aquifer, a unique karst aquifer that supplies water to San Antonio and neighboring cities and supports the habitat of at least four endangered species. EARDC information includes maps; aerial photography; National Weather Service and Texas

Natural Resources Information System data on precipitation, evaporation, humidity, solar radiation, and wind speed and direction; species composition, distribution, and dynamics; surface and groundwater data; geologic and soil data; and census data. *Type:* Database.

Environmental Industry Associations

4301 Connecticut Ave., NW,   Ph: (202)244-4700
  Ste. 300   Free: 800-424-2869
Washington, DC 20008   Fax: (202)966-4818
URL: http://www.envasns.org
Contact: Bruce Parker, Pres./CEO.
Type: Association.

Groundwater Management Caucus

PO Box 905   Ph: (785)462-3915
Colby, KS 67701   Fax: (785)462-2693
Contact: Wayne Bossert, Exec.Sec.
Desc: Directors and staff members of water and natural resource districts; members of related institutions and organizations; universities. Objective is to provide a forum for the exchange of information concerning groundwater management and conservation technology and research. *Type:* Association.

Independent Liquid Terminals Association Newsletter

Independent Liquid Terminals Association
1133 15th St. NW, Ste. 650   Ph: (202)659-2301
Washington, DC 20005-2710   Fax: (202)466-4166
E-mail: info@ilta.org
Contact: John Prokop, Editor.
Desc: Contains news of interest to persons who operate aboveground bulk liquid storage tanks and terminals for shippers, users, and carriers of petroleum, chemicals, edibles, and other bulk liquid commodities. Covers federal, state, and local legislation affecting the industry and regional news of the Association. *Type:* Newsletter.

National Association of Water Companies

1725 K St. NW, Ste. 1212   Ph: (202)833-8383
Washington, DC 20006   Fax: (202)331-7442
Contact: Peter L. Cook, Exec.Dir.
Desc: Investor-owned and operated water companies; associate members are individuals with an engineering, scientific, or other professional interest in the association. Conducts research and keeps members informed of economic, legal, and regulatory developments; encourages communication between investor-owned water companies and regulatory agencies; seeks to improve members' service to the public. Works with National Association of Regulatory Utility Commissioners. *Type:* Association.

National Ground Water Association

601 Dempsey Rd.   Ph: (614)898-7791
Westerville, OH 43081 Free: 800-551-7379
                       Fax: (614)898-7786
E-mail: ngwa@ngwa.org
URL: http://www.ngwa.org
Contact: Jacqueline Mack, Contact.
Desc: Ground water drilling contractors; manufacturers and suppliers of drilling equipment; ground water scientists such as geologists, engineers, public health officials, and others interested in the problems of locating, developing, preserving, and using ground water supplies. Conducts seminars, and continuing education programs. Encourages scientific education, research, and the development of standards; offers placement services; compiles market statistics. *Type:* Association.

National Water Conditions

U.S. Geological Survey
419 National Center
Reston, VA 20192
URL: http://h2o.usgs.gov/nwc/
Contact: Krishna Sarma, kvsarma@mailqvarsa.er.usgs.gov.
Desc: The U.S. Geological Survey keeps detailed reports on current water conditions, rainfall totals, and flooding conditions. *Type:* Database.

Passaic River Coalition

246 Madisonville Rd.   Ph: (908)766-7550
Basking Ridge, NJ 07920   Fax: (908)766-7550
E-mail: prcwater@aol.com
Contact: Ella F. Filippone, Exec.Admin.
Desc: Organizations, foundations, corporations, municipalities, and individuals concerned with environmental quality in the Passaic River Watershed. (The Passaic River Watershed is an urban river system in New York and New Jersey that provides water to three and a half million people.) Seeks to resolve the problems of an urban river system focusing on explosive population growth, water pollution, water supply, flood control, sewage and garbage disposal, and urban decay. Conducts research into land use, water quality and supply, wildlife and vegetation, flood control, historic preservation, water testing, and solid waste recovery. *Type:* Association.

Water Quality Association

4151 Naperville Rd.   Ph: (630)505-0160
Lisle, IL 60532   Fax: (630)505-9637
URL: http://www.wqa.org
Contact: Peter J. Censky, Exec.Dir.
Desc: Individuals or firms engaged in the manufacture and/or assembly and distribution and/or retail selling of water treatment equipment, supplies, and services. Promotes the acceptance and use of industry equipment, products, and services. Provides activities, programs, and services designed to improve economy and efficiency within the industry. *Type:* Association.

Water Resources Abstracts

U.S. Geological Survey
Water Resources Scientific Information Center (WRSIC)
425 National Center   Ph: (703)648-6820
Reston, VA 22092
Desc: Contains more than 334,000 citations, with abstracts, to scientific and technical literature on the water resource-related aspects of the physical, social, and life sciences. Covers related engineering and legal aspects of the characteristics, conservation, control, use, and management of water resources. *Available:* The Dialog Corporation, DIALOG; National Information Services Corporation (NISC), BiblioLine. *Type:* Database.

Water Technology Online - The Internet Source for the Water Treatment Industry

National Trade Publications, Inc.
13 Century Hill Dr.   Ph: (518)783-1281
Latham, NY 12110
URL: http://waternet.com/
Desc: You drink it, bathe in it, and are mostly made of it. If you want to know more about water and water treatment, dive into the Water Technology Online site. *Type:* Database.

Water & Wastes Digest

Scranton Gillette Communications, Inc.
380 E. Northwest Hwy., Ste.   Ph: (847)391-1000
  200   Fax: (847)390-0408
Des Plaines, IL 60016-2282
Contact: Gail Hanczar, Editor; Ian Lisk, Exec. Editor; Wesley D. Shoup, Publisher; LaMay Eide, Advertising Mgr.

Desc: Magazine (tabloid) featuring product news for decision makers in the municipal and industrial water and water pollution control industries. *Type:* Periodical.

WATERNET

American Water Works Association (AWWA)
Volunteer & Technical Support
6666 W. Quincy Ave.   Ph: (303)794-7711
Denver, CO 80235
E-mail: hchiacch@awwa.org
URL: http://www.awwa.org
Desc: Contains more than 40,000 citations, with abstracts, to literature on water quality, water utility management, analytical procedures for water quality testing, energy-related economics, water system materials, water and wastewater treatment and reuse, industrial and potable uses of water, and environmental issues related to water. Typical data elements include author name, article title, journal title, publication date, volume and issue numbers, page numbers, availability, ISSN, language, document type, and abstract. *Available:* The Dialog Corporation, DIALOG. *Type:* Database.

WaterWise

N.C. Sea Grant College Program
North Carolina State University
Box 8605   Ph: (919)515-2454
Raleigh, NC 27695-8605   Fax: (919)515-7095
Contact: Barbara Doll, Editor, barbara_doll@ncsu.edu.
Desc: Examines issues, research, and events related to water quality, with one topic covered in depth per issue. *Type:* Newsletter.

Wildlife

American Ostrich Association

PO Box 162627 0   Ph: (817)624-3322
Fort Worth, TX 76161   Fax: (817)624-2047
E-mail: aoa@flash.net
URL: http://www.ostriches.org
Contact: Mac Young, Exec.Dir.
Desc: Supports the American Ostrich Industry through: government and legislative action; promotion of ostrich and ostrich products; information and referral services for breeders and allied businesses; and scientific research conducted in partnership with the American Ostrich Research Foundation. *Type:* Association.

The Electronic Zoo

Washington University
Division of Comparative
    Medicine
Box 8061, 660 S. Euclid Ave.
660 S. Euclid Ave.
St. Louis, MO 63110
URL: http://netvet.wustl.edu/e-zoo.htm
Contact: Ken Boschert, DVM, Associate Director.
Desc: The Electronic Zoo - written and maintained by a practicing veterinarian - is an exhaustive database of electronic resources for persons interested in animals, veterinary medicine, zoos, and related topics. Click on a subject in the Electronic Zoo index and you'll get hundreds of links and references to animal-related resources. *Type:* Database.

Moose Magazine

Moose International
Mooseheart, IL 60539   Ph: (708)859-2000
                              Fax: (708)859-6620
Contact: Kurt N. Wehrmeister, Managing Editor; Frank A. Sarnecki, Publisher.
Desc: News for and about the 1.7 million men and women the Moose Fraternal Organization and its endeavors on behalf of children, seniors and communities. *Type:* Periodical.

National Bird-Feeding Society

PO Box 23   Ph: (847)272-0135
Northbrook, IL 60065-0023
E-mail: birdseye1@aol.com
Contact: Sue Wells, Exec.Dir.
Desc: Individuals interested in improving methods of bird feeding. Conducts public information campaigns. Funds research programs. *Type:* Association.

Society of Parrot Breeders and Exhibitors

PO Box 369   Ph: (603)672-4568
Groton, MA 01450   Fax: (603)672-3120
URL: http://www.upatsix/spbe.com
Contact: Dr. Al E. Decoteau, Bd.Chm.
Desc: Aviculturists; parrot breeders and exhibitors. Seeks to prevent parrot extinction. *Type:* Association.

Wildlife Worldwide

National Information Services Corporation
(NISC)
Wyman Towers   Ph: (410)243-0797
3100 St. Paul St.
Baltimore, MD 21218
E-mail: sales@nisc.com
URL: http://www.nisc.com
Desc: Contains more than 415,000 citations to the world's literature on mammals, birds, reptiles, and amphibians. Comprises the following databases: • Wildlife Review Abstracts--contains citations, with abstracts, to the worldwide literature on mammals, birds, reptiles, and amphibians. *Available:* National Information Services Corporation (NISC), NISC DISCover. *Type:* Database.

Wildlife Conservation

African Wildlife Foundation

1400 16th St. NW, Ste. 120   Ph: (202)939-3333
Washington, DC 20036   Free: 800-344-TUSK
                              Fax: (202)939-3332
E-mail: awfwash@igc.apc.org
URL: http://www.awf.org
Contact: R. Michael Wright, Contact.
Desc: Works to: conduct programs training Africans in wildlife management and ecology; offer technical assistance in park and reserve management. *Type:* Association.

American Horse Protection Association

1000 29th St. NW, T100   Ph: (202)965-0500
Washington, DC 20007
Contact: Robin C. Lohnes, Exec.Dir.
Desc: Individuals interested in the protection and welfare of horses, both wild and domestic. Gained passage of the Horse Protection Act of 1970, which makes illegal the showing of "sored" horses in interstate commerce, and the Wild Horse and Burro Protection Act of 1971 and the Commercial Transportation of Equines for Slaughter Act of 1996. *Type:* Association.

Atlantic Salmon Federation

PO Box 429   Ph: (506)529-4581
St. Andrews, NB, Canada E0G   Fax: (506)529-4438
    2X0
Contact: Bill Taylor, Pres.
Desc: Conservationists, scientists, government personnel, and salmon anglers. Promotes preservation and management of Atlantic salmon stocks. Program includes wide-ranging projects in education, management, research, and international cooperation. *Type:* Association.

Bat Conservation International

PO Box 162603   Ph: (512)327-9721
Austin, TX 78716-2603   Fax: (512)327-9724
E-mail: bbcnon@batcon.org

URL: http://www.batcon.org
Contact: Dr. Merlin D. Tuttle, Exec.Dir.
Desc: Documents the value and conservation needs of bats. *Type:* Association.

Black Bass Foundation

260 Crest Rd.   Ph: (803)637-3100
Edgefield, SC 29824
Contact: Tom Rodgers, Pres.
Desc: Works to protect bass and their habitat. *Type:* Association.

Bounty Wildlife Information Service

4849 E. St. Charles Rd.   Ph: (573)474-6967
Columbia, MO 65201
E-mail: claun01@aol.com
Contact: H. Charles Laun, Dir.
Desc: Individuals interested in the removal of wildlife bounties in the U.S. and Canada. *Type:* Association.

Defenders of Wildlife

1101 14th St., NW, Ste. 1400   Ph: (202)682-9400
Washington, DC 20005   Fax: (202)682-1331
E-mail: defenders@defenders.org
URL: http://www.defenders.org
Contact: Rodger Schlickeisen, Pres.
Desc: Persons interested in wildlife and conservation. Promotes the preservation and protection of wildlife and wildlife habitat through education, litigation, research, and advocacy. Programs focus on habitat preservation for biological diversity, endangered species recovery, international wildlife trade, and wildlife on public lands such as wildlife refuges and national forests. *Type:* Association.

Ducks Unlimited

1 Waterfowl Way   Ph: (901)758-3825
Memphis, TN 38120   Free: 800-753-8257
                          Fax: (901)758-3850
URL: http://www.ducks.org
Contact: Matthew B. Connolly, Jr., Exec.VP.
Desc: Conservationists in the U.S., Canada, Mexico, New Zealand, and Australia interested in migratory waterfowl and wildlife habitat conservation. Works to restore or enhance natural wetland areas for migratory waterfowl in the prairie provinces of Canada, which provide 70 percent of North America's wild geese and ducks, in prime nesting, staging, and wintering areas of the U.S., and in Mexico where millions of waterfowl spend winter. The American group raises funds for construction and rehabilitation work carried on by the field operating organizations. *Type:* Association.

Elsa Clubs of America

PO Box 4572   Ph: (818)761-8387
North Hollywood, CA 91617-
    0572
Contact: A. Peter Rasmussen, Jr., Gen.Mgr.
Desc: Sponsored by Elsa Wild Animal Appeal - U.S.A. Young people up to 18 years of age. *Type:* Association.

Elsa Wild Animal Appeal - U.S.A.

PO Box 348   Ph: (217)897-1086
Mahomet, IL 61853-0348   Fax: (217)897-1086
Contact: Donald A. Rolla, Pres.
Desc: Families and individuals interested in wildlife. Founded by Joy Adamson (1910-80), author of Born Free, and named after Elsa the lioness, subject of the book. Purposes are to: further the conservation of wildlife and wild places, particularly in America; educate children on the values and needs of wildlife and the environment; promote the establishment of protective wildlife reserves and viable wildlife conservation projects. *Type:* Association.

Endangered Species Homepage

U.S. Fish and Wildlife Service - Division of Endangered Species, Washington Office Branch of Information Management

U.S. Dept of the Interior
1849 C St. NW
Washington, DC 20240
E-mail: R9FWE_DES.BIM@mail.fws.gov
URL: http://www.fws.gov/~r9endspp/endspp.html

Desc: The Endangered Species Program database provides the official list of endangered and threatened plants and animals. Users can find a copy of the Endangered Species Act of 1973 as well as the list of endangered wildlife and plants as published in the Federal Register. *Type:* Database.

Hawk Mountain Sanctuary Association

1700 Hawk Mountain Rd.   Ph: (610)756-6961
Kempton, PA 19529   Fax: (610)756-4468
URL: http://www.hawkmountain.org

Contact: Cynthia Lenhart, Exec.Dir.

Desc: Conserves and protects wildlife, especially birds of prey such as eagles, hawks, and falcons. Maintains 2,400-acre wildlife sanctuary through which more than 20,000 birds of prey migrate each fall. Sponsors annual lecture series and research programs; conducts international internship program. *Type:* Association.

International Society for the Protection of Mustangs and Burros

PO Box 14194   Ph: (602)991-0273
Scottsdale, AZ 85267-4194   Fax: (602)991-2920
E-mail: ispmb@compuserve.com
URL: http://www.ourworld.compuserve.com/
homepages/ispmb

Contact: Karen A. Sussman, Pres.

Desc: Persons interested in the protection and preservation of wild horses and burros. Goals are to recognize wild horses and burros as a valuable resource contributing to the biological diversity of the land and enriching the lives of human beings; acknowledge that wild horses and burros are one of the last living symbols of the heritage of many cultures; maintain organizational trust, credibility, and leadership; ensure the enforcement and prevent erosion of existing laws and assist in the development of new laws for the protection and preservation of wild horses and burros and their habitat; encourage and implement research and educational programs that increase appreciation, understanding, and preservation of wild horses, burros, and their hahbitat; promote humane treatment of wild horses and burros worlwide; and foster cooperative efforts with government agencies and other organziations in attaining quality programs relating to wild horses and burros and their habitat. *Type:* Association.

International Union for the Conservation of Nature's Primate Specialist Group

c/o Conservation International   Ph: (202)429-5660
2501 M Street NW, Ste. 200   Free: 800-429-5660
Washington, DC 20037   Fax: (202)887-0192
E-mail: r.mittermeier@conservation.org

Contact: Russell A. Mittermeier, Chmn.

Desc: Primatologists. Advocates the preservation of all current species belonging to the order of primates. Strives to ensure the survival of endangered species through planned breeding in captivity and to provide protection for primates in areas of high primate populations. *Type:* Association.

International Wildlife

National Wildlife Magazine

8925 Leesburg Pike   Ph: (703)790-4524
Vienna, VA 22184   Fax: (703)790-4544
E-mail: info@nwf.org; pubs@nwf.org.

URL: http://www.nwf.org; http://www.nwf.org.

Contact: Bob Strohm, Editor-in-Chief; Jonathan Fisher, Editor.

Desc: Magazine featuring nature, wildlife, and environmental issues from around the world. *Alt. Contact:* telephone: (703)790-4510; fax: (703)790-4544. *Type:* Periodical.

International Wildlife Coalition

70 E. Falmouth Hwy.   Ph: (508)548-8328
East Falmouth, MA 02536   Free: 800-548-8704
                                  Fax: (508)548-8542

E-mail: lwcadopt@ccsnet.com
URL: http://www.iwc.org

Contact: Daniel J. Morast, Pres.

Desc: Works to preserve wildlife and wildlife habitats in United States, Sri Lanka, Brazil, Australia, United Kingdom, and Canada. *Type:* Association.

Missouri Conservationist

Department of Conservation
Public Affairs Division

Box 180   Ph: (573)751-4115
Jefferson City, MO 65102   Fax: (573)751-2260

Contact: Tom Cwyngr, Editor, cwynat@mail.
conservation.state.mo.us.

Desc: Government magazine covering fish, forests, and wildlife. *Type:* Periodical.

Mountain Lion Foundation

PO Box 1896   Ph: (916)442-2666
Sacramento, CA 95812   Fax: (916)442-2871
E-mail: mlf@mountainlion.org
URL: http://www.mountainlion.org/

Contact: Lynn Sadler, Dir.

Desc: Dedicated to the preservation and long-term survival of the mountain lion, other wildlife, and their habitat. *Type:* Association.

National Wild Turkey Federation

PO Box 530   Ph: (803)637-3106
770 Augusta Rd.   Free: 800-THE-
Wild Turkey Ctr.   NWTF
Edgefield, SC 29824   Fax: (803)637-0034
E-mail: nwtf@gabn.net
URL: http://www.nwtf.org

Contact: Rob Keck, Exec.VP/CEO.

Desc: Wild turkey enthusiasts and hunters. Dedicated to the wise conservation and management of the American wild turkey as a valuable natural resource. *Type:* Association.

National Wildlife

National Wildlife Magazine

8925 Leesburg Pike   Ph: (703)790-4524
Vienna, VA 22184   Fax: (703)790-4544
E-mail: info@nwf.org; pubs@nwf.org'.
URL: http://www.nwf.org; http://www.nwf.org.

Contact: Mark Wexler, Editor; Bob Strohm, Editor-in-Chief.

Desc: Magazine focusing on nature, wildlife, and environmental issues. *Type:* Periodical.

North American Wildlife Foundation

PO Box 3128   Ph: (701)222-8857
Bismarck, ND 58502   Free: 888-987-3695
                                  Fax: (701)223-4645

E-mail: delta4duck@aol.com

Contact: Lloyd Jones, V.P.

Desc: To ensure, through financial support, the continuity of effective, practical, and systematic research of manage-

ment practices and techniques, locally, nationally, and internationally, in order to benefit wildlife and other natural resources in the public interest. The foundation works through cooperating agencies, organizations, and institutions and does not serve as an action group. Owns Delta Waterfowl Research Station in Manitoba, Canada. *Type:* Association.

Pelican Man's Bird Sanctuary

1708 Ken Thompson Pky.   Ph: (941)388-4444
Sarasota, FL 34236   Fax: (941)388-3258
E-mail: pelicanma@aol.com
URL: http://www.pelicanman.com

Contact: Dale Shields, Pres. & Founder.

Desc: Individuals and corporations interested in supporting environmental and wildlife preservation. Seeks to promote wildlife protection and rescue. Operates a rehabilitation center for injured pelicans, blue herons, gulls, and other birds and animals. *Type:* Association.

The Peregrine Fund

5666 W. Flying Hawk Ln.   Ph: (208)362-3716
Boise, ID 83709   Fax: (208)362-2376
E-mail: tpf@peregrinefund.org
URL: http://www.peregrinefund.org

Contact: Dr. William Burnham, Pres.

Desc: Science-based organization focusing on birds for the conservation of nature. Seeks to reestablish natural populations of endangered and threatened birds, conserve habitat and biological diversity, and develop infrastructures for in-country conservation. Informs the public of the value and the need for conservation. *Type:* Association.

Pheasants Forever

PO Box 428
Middlefield, OH 44062
E-mail: pf@pheasantsforever.org
URL: http://www.pheasantsforever.org

Contact: Jeffrey S. Finden, CEO.

Desc: Protects and restores the natural habitats of pheasants and other wildlife. Works to: rebuild lost wetlands; re-establish shelterbelts (barriers of trees or shrubs that reduce erosion and provide protection for wildlife); plant nesting cover for pheasants. Encourages legislation that promotes pheasant habitat conservation. *Type:* Association.

Quail Unlimited

PO Box 610   Ph: (803)637-5731
Edgefield, SC 29824   Fax: (803)637-0037
URL: http://www.outdoorsource.com/quail

Contact: Jerry W. Allen, Admin.VP.

Desc: Works for quail and upland bird conservation through its habitat management program and research. *Type:* Association.

Rocky Mountain Elk Foundation

PO Box 8249   Ph: (406)523-4500
Missoula, MT 59807-8249   Free: 800-CALL-ELK
                                  Fax: (406)523-4550

E-mail: rmef@rmef.org
URL: http://www.rmef.org

Contact: Robert W. Munson, Exec.Dir.

Desc: Works to ensure the future of elk and other wildlife by conserving, restoring, and enhancing natural habitats. *Type:* Association.

Ruffed Grouse Society

451 McCormick Rd.   Ph: (412)262-4044
Coraopolis, PA 15108   Free: 888-564-6747
                                  Fax: (412)262-9207

E-mail: rgshq@aol.com
URL: http://www.ruffedgrousesociety.org

Contact: Dr. Samuel R. Pursglove, Jr., Exec.Dir.

Desc: Conservationists dedicated to improving the environment for ruffed grouse, woodcock, and other forest wildlife. Encourages private, industrial, state, county, and federal landowners to manage their woodlands to benefit forest wildlife. *Type:* Association.

Safari Club International

4800 W Gates Pass Rd.   Ph: (520)620-1220
Tucson, AZ 85745

Contact: Rudolph A. Rosen, Admin. Dir.

Desc: Sportsmen united to encourage conservation of wildlife. Promotes hunting as a wildlife management tool; aims to preserve public hunting and protect hunters' rights. Fosters public education concerning conservation; sponsors research. *Type:* Association.

Save the Manatee Club

500 N. Maitland Ave.   Ph: (407)539-0990
Maitland, FL 32751   Free: 800-432-5646
    Fax: (407)539-0871
E-mail: membership@savethemanatee.org
URL: http://www.savethemanatee.org

Contact: Judith Vallee, Exec.Dir.

Desc: Naturalists, students, businessmen, and other individuals. Works to help save and protect the West Indian manatee, an endangered marine mammal, and its habitat. *Type:* Association.

Sea Shepherd Conservation Society

PO Box 628   Ph: (310)301-7325
Venice, CA 90294   Fax: (310)574-3161
E-mail: seashepherd@seashepherd.org
URL: http://www.seashepherd.org

Contact: Lisa Distefano, International Dir.

Desc: International activist conservation society concerned with the protection and conservation of marine mammals. Operates research ships with volunteer crew. Opposes exploitation of all marine life and fights the problem through education, confrontation, and enforcement, although primary involvement is in enforcement of international laws, treaties, and regulations against driftnetting, illegal whaling, and sealing activities. *Type:* Association.

Trout Unlimited

1500 Wilson Blvd., Ste. 310   Ph: (703)522-0200
Arlington, VA 22209-2404   Fax: (703)284-9400
E-mail: trout@tu.org
URL: http://www.tu.org/trout

Contact: Charles F. Gauvin, Pres./CEO.

Desc: Works to conserve, protect, and restore the cold-water habitat of trout, salmon, and steelhead by influencing the activities and programs of governmental agencies, by keeping the public informed on water management problems, and by restoring and maintaining streams and lakes. Emphasizes the sport of fishing. Conducts research and education programs; compiles statistics. *Type:* Association.

Whitetails Unlimited

PO Box 720   Ph: (414)743-6777
Sturgeon Bay, WI 54235-0720   Free: 800-274-5471
    Fax: (414)743-4658

Contact: Peter J. Gerl, Exec.Dir.

Desc: Dedicated to sound deer management. *Type:* Association.

Wild Horse Organized Assistance

PO Box 555   Ph: (775)851-4817
Reno, NV 89504   Fax: (775)851-4817

Contact: Dawn Y. Lappin, Chwm.

Desc: A foundation for the welfare and perpetuation of wild free-roaming horses and burros. (The number of wild horses in the U.S. has diminished from 2,000,000 in 1900 to around 70,000 today). *Type:* Association.

Wildlife Conservation

Wildlife Conservation
2300 Southern Blvd.   Ph: (718)220-5121
Bronx, NY 10460   Fax: (718)584-2625
E-mail: 201438@mci.mail.com.
URL: http://www.wcs.org.

Contact: Joan Downs, Editor, (718)220-5897.

Desc: Magazine dedicated to the conservation of wildlife. *Type:* Periodical.

Wildlife Forever

10365 W. 70th St.   Ph: (612)936-0605
Eden Prairie, MN 55344   Fax: (612)936-0915
E-mail: wildlife_forever@pclink.com
URL: http://www.wildlifeforever.org

Contact: Douglas Grann, Exec.Dir.

Desc: Individuals united to preserve America's wildlife heritage through the conservation and management of habitats, plant life, and wildlife. *Type:* Association.

Wildlife Preservation Trust International

1520 Locust St., Ste. 704   Ph: (215)731-9770
Philadelphia, PA 19102   Fax: (215)731-9766
E-mail: homeoffice@wpti.org
URL: http://www.cc.columbia.edu/cu/cerc/wpti.html

Contact: Mary C. Pearl, Ph.D., Exec.Dir.

Desc: Provides support for the captive breeding of endangered species to save them from extinction. Supports research in areas related to captive breeding of endangered species and the reintroduction to the wild of captive bred animals. Trains students in captive breeding techniques and operates public education programs. *Type:* Association.

The Wildlife Society

5410 Grosvenor Ln.   Ph: (301)897-9770
Bethesda, MD 20814-2197   Fax: (301)530-2471
E-mail: tws@wildlife.org
URL: http://www.wildlife.org/index.html

Contact: Harry E. Hodgdon, Exec.Dir.

Desc: Scientific and educational society of wildlife biologists, research scientists, conservation law enforcement officers, resource managers, and others interested in resource conservation and wildlife management on a sound biological basis. Takes an active role in preventing human-induced environmental degradation; works to increase awareness and appreciation of wildlife values; seeks the highest standards in all activities of the wildlife profession. *Type:* Association.

Wine

American Wine Society—News

American Wine Society
3006 Latta Rd.   Ph: (716)225-7613
Rochester, NY 14612   Fax: (716)225-7613
E-mail: angel910@aol.com
URL: http://www.vicon.net/~aws

Contact: Robert Miller, Editor, (606)624-5621, jrmwine@aol.com.

Desc: Keeps readers abreast of Society activities and affairs on the national, regional, and local levels. *Type:* Newsletter.

Casa Nuestra Journal

Casa Nuestra Vineyards
3473 Silverado Trail, N.   Ph: (707)963-5783
St. Helena, CA 94574-9662

Contact: Gene Kirkham, Editor.

Desc: Highlights news from the winery. Profiles new wine releases and announces awards and honors won. *Type:* Newsletter.

Chandon Club News

Chandon Club
Domaine Chandon
1 California Dr.   Ph: (707)944-8844
Yountville, CA 94599   Free: 800-234-8844
    Fax: (707)944-1123
URL: http://www.dchandon.com/.

Contact: Joy Henderson, Editor.

Desc: Profiles wines at the Domaine Chandon winery in Napa, California. Contains production news, club events, and activities. *Type:* Newsletter.

Connoisseurs' Guide to California Wine

Charles E. Olken and Earl G. Singer
PO Box V   Ph: (510)865-3150
Alameda, CA 94501

Contact: Charles E. Olken, Editor; Earl G. Singer, Editor.

Desc: Presents reviews of and reports about California wines, including information about availability, price, and aging potential. *Type:* Newsletter.

Fine Wine Folio

Holland and Edwards Publishing Inc.
250 Mercer St., No. A203   Ph: (212)673-5773
New York, NY 10012   Fax: (212)995-8956
E-mail: hollandedwards@compuserve.com

Desc: Features one of the world's wine regions in each issue. Includes history, wine descriptions, and a menu created for a particular wine created by a noted restaurant. *Type:* Newsletter.

Frick Winery—Information Letter

Frick Winery
23072 Walling Rd.   Ph: (415)776-7331
Geyserville, CA 95441-9676   Fax: (415)776-7331
E-mail: frick@frickwinery.com

Contact: Bill Frick, Editor.

Desc: Focuses on the wines and operations of the Frick Winery. Recurring features include items on award-winning Frick wines and new releases, recipes, and suggestions for wine/food combinations. *Type:* Newsletter.

The Gomberg-Fredrikson Report

Gomberg, Fredrikson & Associates
703 Market St., Ste. 1602   Ph: (415)957-5071
San Francisco, CA 94103   Fax: (415)957-5804
E-mail: info@gomfred.com

Contact: Jon A. Fredrikson, Editor.

Desc: Provides wine industry statistics by company and group, including both imported and U.S.-produced wines. Presents figures on shipments into trade channels from individual companies on a month-by-month, year-by-year basis, showing various trends. *Type:* Newsletter.

Grower Advocate

Napa Valley Grape Growers Association
811 Jefferson St.   Ph: (707)944-8311
Napa, CA 94559   Fax: (707)224-7836

Contact: Claudia Glade, Program Coordinator, claudia@l-cafe.net.

Desc: Supplies grape commodity and vineyard news. Carries technical information on grape and wine production, legislative updates, news of research, and Association and valley news. *Type:* Newsletter.

Impact Newsletter

M. Shanken Communications, Inc.
387 Park Ave. S., 8th Fl.   Ph: (212)684-4224
New York, NY 10016   Free: 800-866-0775
    Fax: (212)684-5424
E-mail: dfleming@mshanken.com

Contact: Marvin R. Shanken, Editor.

Desc: Provides statistical information for tracking marketing trends of brands, companies, and market segments. Lists the top ten brands of alcoholic beverages. *Type:* Newsletter.

Les Amis du Vin

5015 Glenoak Dr.
Louisville, OH 44641-8831
Contact: Ron Fonte, Pres.
Desc: "Wine lovers devoted to the appreciation of fine wine and the art of leisurely dining." Familiarizes members with the variety, uses, and enjoyment of wine. Sponsors regular group wine tastings and dinners; offers charter flight trips to American and European vineyards. Presents awards; maintains speakers' bureau of world wine and food experts. *Type:* Association.

Napa Valley Vintners Association

PO Box 141   Ph: (707)942-9775
St. Helena, CA 94574   Free: 800-982-1371
    Fax: (707)942-0171
E-mail: napavintners@aol.com
URL: http://www.napavintners.com
Contact: Linda Reiff, Exec.Dir.
Desc: Promotes Napa Valley, CA, wines and wineries; disseminates information about Napa Valley wines to the public. *Type:* Association.

The Quarterly Review of Wines

QRW Publishing
24 Garfield Ave.   Ph: (781)729-7132
Winchester, MA 01890   Fax: (781)721-0572
E-mail: qrwinc@tiac.net.
URL: http://www.qrw.com.
Contact: Richard L. Elia, Editor and Publisher; Beth Hamilton, Sales/Circulation; Jack Lynch, Advertising Mgr.
Desc: Consumer magazine on fine wines and selected spirits. *Type:* Periodical.

Smart Wine's Smart Taste™ Wine Review Database

New World Wine Communications, Inc.
867 W. Napa St.   Ph: (707)939-0822
Sonoma, CA 95476   Fax: (707)939-0833
URL: http://www.wineratings.com/
Contact: Richard Shell, President, richardshell@smartwine.com.
Desc: Wine expert or wine novice will find something of interest at Smart Wine's Wine Review Database. Use the database Power Search to narrow down your wineseeking through a progressive list of menus, from country to winery, vineyard, taste, price, and more. *Type:* Database.

Society of Medical Friends of Wine—Bulletin

Society of Medical Friends of Wine
301 Harbor Light Rd.   Ph: (415)389-8693
Alameda, CA 94501-5965   Fax: (415)389-8905
Contact: Albert Alhadeff, Editor.
Desc: Gives news of the Society and its member physicians and surgeons who advocate the nutritional and therapeutic values of wine. Provides articles on various historical, cultural, and medicinal aspects of wine. *Type:* Newsletter.

Vinotizie Italian Wine Newsletter

Italian Trade Commission
499 Park Ave.   Ph: (212)980-1500
New York, NY 10022   Fax: (212)758-1050
E-mail: newyork@italtrade.com
URL: http://www.italianmade.com.
Contact: Augusto Marchini, Editor, gus@italtrade.com.
Desc: Reviews wines imported from Italy. Discusses developments in the Italian wine industry and market. *Type:* Newsletter.

The Wine Advocate

Robert M. Parker, Jr.
PO Box 311   Ph: (301)329-6477
Monkton, MD 21111
Contact: Robert M. Parker, Jr., Editor.
Desc: Serves as an "independent guide to fine wines." *Type:* Newsletter.

Wine Enthusiast Magazine

Wine Enthusiast Co.
8 Saw Mill River Rd.   Ph: (914)345-8463
Hawthorne, NY 10532   Fax: (914)345-3028
Contact: W.R. Tish, Editor; Adam Strum, Publisher.
Desc: Magazine reporting news on wines and spirits; includes profiles of industry leaders from around the world as well as a consumer wine report. *Type:* Periodical.

Wine Institute

425 Market St., Ste. 1000   Ph: (415)512-0151
San Francisco, CA 94105   Fax: (415)442-0742
URL: http://www.wineinstitute.org
Contact: John A. De Luca, Pres.
Desc: Initiates and advocates state, federal, and international public policy to enhance the environment for the responsible consumption and enjoyment of wine. *Type:* Association.

Wine Letter

Raymond Vineyards
849 Zinfandel Ln.   Ph: (707)963-3141
St. Helena, CA 94574   Free: 800-525-2659
    Fax: (707)963-8498
Contact: Kas McGregor, Editor.
Desc: Provides information on the winery and its products. Recurring features include tasting notes, updates on the winery and vineyard practices, and calendar of events. *Type:* Newsletter.

Wine Spectator

M. Shanken Communications, Inc.
387 Park Ave. S., 8th Fl.   Ph: (212)684-4224
New York, NY 10016   Free: 800-866-0775
    Fax: (212)684-5424
E-mail: dfleming@mshanken.com
URL: http://www.winespectator.com.
Contact: Marvin R. Shanken, Editor and Publisher; Jim Gordon, Managing Editor.
Desc: Lifestyle Magazine for the wine consumer. *Type:* Periodical.

Wine and Spirits Wholesalers of America—Upfront

Wine and Spirits Wholesalers of America, Inc.
805 Fifteenth St. NW, Ste. 430   Ph: (202)371-9792
Washington, DC 20005   Fax: (202)789-2405
Contact: David Dickerson, Editor.
Desc: Provides news and information regarding government actions, anti-abuse efforts, and other news of interest to wholesale distributors of domestic and imported wine and distilled spirits. *Type:* Newsletter.

Winedata Wine Industry Monitors

Gomberg, Fredrikson & Associates
703 Market St., Ste. 1602   Ph: (415)957-5071
San Francisco, CA 94103   Fax: (415)957-5804
E-mail: info@gomfred.com
Contact: Jon A. Fredrikson, Editor.
Type: Newsletter.

Women

AAUW Outlook

American Association of University Women
1111 16th St. NW   Ph: (202)785-7700
Washington, DC 20036   Free: 800-326-AAUW
    Fax: (202)872-1425
E-mail: info@aauw.org
Contact: Jackie Zakrewsky, Editor, (202)785-7734, editor@aauw.org.
Desc: Magazine covering women's concerns including current family, education and legislative issues. *Type:* Periodical.

The Ada Project

Yale University - Computer Science Department
51 Prospect St.   Ph: (203)432-6429
PO Box 208285   Fax: (203)432-0593
New Haven, CT 06520-8285
E-mail: tap-comments@cs.yale.edu
URL: http://www.cs.yale.edu/HTML/YALE/CS/HyPlans/tap/tap.html
Contact: Elisabeth Freeman.
Desc: The Ada Project has been created to serve as a clearinghouse for information and resources relating to women in all types of computing (not just the Internet). Since studies have shown that young female students still often are made to suffer math anxiety or are steered away from science and computing, the importance of this site cannot be overestimated. *Type:* Database.

Aglow International

PO Box 1749   Ph: (425)775-7282
Edmonds, WA 98020-1749   Fax: (425)778-9615
E-mail: aglow@aglow.org
URL: http://www.aglow.org/
Contact: Kay Rogers, Dir.
Desc: Women in approximately 137 countries. Provides support, education, training, and ministry opportunities to "lead women to Jesus Christ and provides opportunity for Christian women to grow in their faith and minister to others." *Type:* Association.

American Association of University Women

1111 16th St. NW   Ph: (202)785-7700
Washington, DC 20036   Free: 800-326-AAUW
    Fax: (202)872-1425
E-mail: info@aauw.org
URL: http://www.aauw.org/index.html
Contact: Amy Swanger, Exec.Dir.
Desc: Graduates of regionally accredited colleges; colleges, universities, and two-year or community colleges. Advocates educational equity for women and girls. *Type:* Association.

American Association of University Women Educational Foundation

1111 16th St. NW   Ph: (202)728-7602
Washington, DC 20036   Fax: (202)463-7169
URL: http://www.aauw.org/index.html
Contact: Janice Weinman, Exec.Dir.
Desc: An arm of the American Association of University Women. Established to: expand AAUW's primary emphasis on educational work; facilitate the building of endowments for fellowships, research, and public service projects; supplement and further specified areas of AAUWEF concern; assume administrative and managerial responsibilities in the AAUW Educational Center. Sponsors conferences; encourages development of the Educational Center in Washington, DC, as a center for women scholars throughout the world; seeks support from other foundations for research and educational projects; also receives contributions from AAUW members. *Type:* Association.

American Woman

Goodman Media Group, Inc.
1700 Broadway, 34th Fl. Ph: (212)541-7100
New York, NY 10019 Fax: (212)245-1241
Contact: Lynn Varacalli, Editor-in-Chief; Charles Goodman, Publisher; Ilona Price, Assoc. Editor; Tracy Grinnell, Asst. Editor.
Desc: Lifestyle magazine for women. *Type:* Periodical.

American Woman Motorscene

American Woman Motorscene
2424 Coolidge Hwy., Ste. 203 Ph: (248)614-0017
Troy, MI 48084 Fax: (248)614-8929
Contact: Courtney Caldwell, Publisher, courtney@americanwoman.com; BJ Killeen, Editor.
Desc: Automotive adventure and lifestyle magazine targeting working and active women *Alt. Contact:* 1510 11th St., Suite 201B, Santa Monica, CA 90401; telephone: (310)260-0192; fax: (310)260-0175. *Type:* Periodical.

The AWC Source

Association for Women in Computing (AWC)
41 Sutter St., Ste. 1006 Ph: (415)905-4663
San Francisco, CA 94104
E-mail: awc@awc-hq.org
Desc: Focuses on issues relevant to the field of computer information technology. Carries information on conferences and regional meetings. *Type:* Newsletter.

Awed in Business

American Woman's Economic Development Corporation
71 Vanderbilt Ave., 3rd Fl.
New York, NY 10169-0005
Desc: Focuses on women in business. *Type:* Newsletter.

AWSCPA Newsletter

American Woman's Society of Certified Public Accountants
401 N. Michigan Ave. Ph: (312)644-6610
Chicago, IL 60611 Free: 800-297-2721
 Fax: (312)321-6869
E-mail: admin@awscpa.org
URL: http://www.awscpa.org.
Desc: Concerned with future developments within the accounting profession for women CPA's. Carries items on new accounting methods, member profiles, and other topics of interest. *Type:* Newsletter.

Bachelor Book Magazine

Bachelor International Enterprises, Inc.
8222 Wiles Rd., Ste. 111 Ph: (954)341-8801
Coral Springs, FL 33067 Fax: (954)341-8982
E-mail: bachlor@msn.com; info@bachelorbook.com.
URL: http://www.bachelorbook.com.
Contact: Mindi F. Rudan, Publisher; Paul Gallota, Publisher; Nina L. Diamond, Managing Editor; Gary Lampner, Food Editor; Anise Hartman, Travel Editor; Arron Barberian, Wine Editor; Parker Lewis, Health Editor; Pam Atertonian, Music Editor; Lisa Hall, New Products Editor; Hank Rudan, Finance Editor; Rick Lesser, Beauty Editor; Hank Rudan, Tech and Computer Editor; Tracy Damus, Fitness Editor; Mindi Rudan, Gardening and Hobby Editor.
Desc: Magazine for women that profiles single, eligible men in the U.S. and Canada. Plus stories and topics geared towards enrichment and empowerment of the lives of single women. *Type:* Periodical.

Business and Professional Women's Foundation

2012 Massachusetts Ave. NW Ph: (202)293-1100
Washington, DC 20036 Fax: (202)861-0298
URL: http://www.bpwusa.org

Contact: Gail Shaffer, Exec.Dir.
Desc: Dedicated to improving the economic status of working women through their integration into all occupations. *Type:* Association.

Chatelaine

Maclean Hunter Ltd.
777 Bay St., 6th Fl. Ph: (416)596-5000
Toronto, ON, Canada M5W Fax: (416)596-5552
 1A7
E-mail: chatcour@maclean.hunter-quebec.qc.ca.
URL: http://www.canoe.ca/chatelaine.
Contact: Rona Maynard, Editor; Lee J. Simpson, Publisher; Bill McDonald, Advertising Sales Dir.
Desc: Magazine for women. *Type:* Periodical.

Church Women United

475 Riverside Dr., Rm. 812 Ph: (212)870-2347
New York, NY 10115-0832 Free: 800-298-5551
 Fax: (212)870-2338
E-mail: cgreer@churchwomen.org
URL: http://www.churchwomen.org
Contact: Dr. Kathleen S. Hurty, Gen.Dir.
Desc: Ecumenical movement uniting Protestant, Roman Catholic, Orthodox, and other Christian church women into one Christian community. Supports peace, human rights, justice, and the empowerment of women. Works to strengthen the presence of ecumenical women in both the national and global arenas through offices in Washington, DC and the United Nations . *Type:* Association.

Complete Woman

Associated Publications, Inc.
875 N. Michigan Ave., Ste. Ph: (312)266-8680
 3434
Chicago, IL 60611-1901
Contact: Bonnie L. Krueger, Editor; James L. Spurlock, Publisher.
Desc: Women's general interest. *Type:* Periodical.

Cosmopolitan

Hearst Magazines
959 8th Ave. Ph: (212)649-2000
New York, NY 10019-5905
Contact: Kate White, Editor; Donna Kalajian, Publisher; Susan Plagemann, Assoc. Publisher.
Desc: Lifestyle magazine for young working women. Includes general interest features, personality profiles, movie, book, and music reviews, and service editorials on beauty, fashion, home decorating, food, nutrition, diet, health, and fitness. *Alt. Contact:* 224 W. 57th St., New York, NY 10019; telephone: (212)649-3570. *Type:* Periodical.

Directory of Women Entrepreneurs

Wind River Publications Inc.
2359 Henderson Mill Ct. Fax: (404)496-5986
Atlanta, GA 30345
Contact: Patricia A. Morrall, Publisher.
Desc: Approximately 3,200 women-owned businesses; companies with minority and women professional development programs, women's groups and organizations, and minority business assistance offices. *Type:* Directory.

The Edge

American Society of Women Accountants
60 Revere Dr., Ste. 500 Ph: (847)205-1029
Northbrook, IL 60062 Free: 800-326-2163
 Fax: (847)480-9282
E-mail: aswa@aswa.org
URL: http://www.aswa.org.
Contact: Allison Conte, Editor.
Desc: Publishes news and information of interest to women accountants. Carries Society news, excerpts from chapter newsletters, and items on professional activities of members. *Type:* Newsletter.

Elegant Bride

Pace Communications, Inc.
1301 Carolina St. Ph: (336)378-6065
Greensboro, NC 27401-1001 Fax: (336)378-8261
E-mail: ebedit@aol.com.
Contact: Linda Stansbury, Exec. Editor; Bonnie McElveen-Hunter, Pres./CEO, fax: (336)273-4808; Edward F. Calfo, Publisher.
Desc: Nationally-distributed bridal publication. *Type:* Periodical.

Elle

Hachette Filipacchi Magazines, Inc.
1633 Broadway, 41st Fl. Ph: (212)767-6000
New York, NY 10019 Fax: (212)989-4561
Contact: Gail Stone, Publisher; Regis Pagniez, Publications Dir.
Desc: Magazine covering fashion, styles, and trends for young women. *Type:* Periodical.

Enrich!

National Chamber of Commerce for Women
10 Waterside Plaza, Ste. 6H
New York, NY 10010
URL: http://womens_chamber.org.
Contact: R. Wright, Editor; M. Finster, Ad.Mgr.
Desc: Strives to assist readers on business-plan, career-path, and pay-comparison goals. *Type:* Newsletter.

The Enterprising Woman

The Enterprising Woman
453 Regal Dr. Ph: (519)451-0059
London, ON, Canada N5Y 1K1 Fax: (519)451-8945
Contact: Gail Garbett, Publisher.
Desc: Designed to provide information of interest to businesswomen. Includes articles on such topics as computers, running a business, investing, advertising, marketing, as well as fitness, makeup, and officewear. *Type:* Newsletter.

Executive Female

National Association for Female Executives
30 Irving Place Ph: (212)477-2200
New York, NY 10003 Fax: (212)477-8125
E-mail: nafe@nafe.com
URL: http://www.nase.com.
Contact: Gay Bryant, Editor; Rebecca Darvin, Publisher; Audrey Weber, Advertising Mgr.
Desc: Magazine covering career and financial management for professional executive and entrepreneurial women. *Type:* Periodical.

Fashion 'n Figure

PO Box 1183 Ph: (216)659-6231
Bath, OH 44210-1183
Contact: Paige Palmer, President.
Desc: Distributes fashion and travel photographs and press releases. *Alt. Contact:* PO Box 1183, Bath, OH 44210-1183; telephone: (216)659-6231. *Type:* Periodical.

Fashion Sense

455 E. 80th St. Ph: (212)861-3779
New York, NY 10021
Contact: Lila Nadell, President.
Alt. Contact: 455 E. 80th St., New York, NY 10021; telephone: (212)861-3779. *Type:* Periodical.

FEW's News and Views

Federally Employed Women, Inc.
1400 Eye St. NW, Ste. 425 Ph: (202)898-0994
Washington, DC 20005 Fax: (202)898-0998
Contact: Michael Varhola, Editor.

Desc: Concerned with women's issues, particularly those involving women in the federal government. Reports on administration actions affecting the status of women and analyzes significant legislation. *Type:* Newsletter.

Financial Woman Today

Financial Women International (FWI)
200 N. Glebe Rd., Ste. 820   Ph: (703)807-2007
Arlington, VA 22203-3728   Fax: (703)807-0111
E-mail: fwistaff@erols.com
Contact: Kathleen S. Robeson, Publications Mgr.
Desc: Features articles of interest to female professionals in the financial services industry, and focuses on issues of interest to working women. *Type:* Newsletter.

First for Women

Bauer Publishing Co.
270 Sylvan Ave.   Ph: (201)569-6699
Box 1648   Fax: (201)569-6264
Englewood Cliffs, NJ 07632
Contact: Dena Vane, Editor-in-Chief.
Desc: Magazine for women featuring articles on fashion, food, decorating, and beauty. *Type:* Periodical.

FLARE

Maclean Hunter Ltd.
777 Bay St., 6th Fl.   Ph: (416)596-5000
Toronto, ON, Canada M5W   Fax: (416)596-5552
1A7
URL: http://www.flare.com.
Contact: Suzanne Boyd, Editor-in-Chief, (416)596-5458, editors@flare.com; David Hamilton, Publisher, (416)596-5079, fax: (416)596-5799; Orietta Minatel, Advertising Dir., (416)596-5464, ominatel@mhpublishing.com.
Desc: Fashion beauty & lifestyle magazine for women. *Alt. Contact:* 777 Bay St., 7th Fl., Toronto, ON, Canada N5W 1A7. *Type:* Periodical.

For the Bride by Demetrios

DJE Publications Ltd.
222 W. 37th St.   Ph: (212)967-0750
New York, NY 10018   Fax: (212)947-7024
Contact: Patricia Daly, Advertising Dir.
Desc: Consumer magazine. *Type:* Periodical.

Future Homemakers of America

1910 Association Dr.   Ph: (703)476-4900
Reston, VA 20191   Fax: (703)860-2713
E-mail: natlhdqtrs@fhahero.org
URL: http://www.fhahero.org
Contact: Alan T. Rains, Jr., Exec.Dir.
Desc: Young men and women studying family and consumer sciences and related occupational courses in public and private schools through grade 12 in the U.S., Puerto Rico, and the Virgin Islands. Youth assume social roles in areas of personal growth, family life, vocational preparation, and community involvement. *Type:* Association.

General Commission on the Status and Role of Women

1200 Davis St.   Ph: (708)869-7330
Evanston, IL 60201   Fax: (708)475-5061
Contact: Ann Sherer, Pres.
Desc: A commission of the United Methodist Church. Laypersons and clergy interested in the status of women in the UMC. Works to protect the rights of women, both lay and clergy, in the UMC. *Type:* Association.

General Federation of Women's Clubs

1734 N St. NW   Ph: (202)347-3168
Washington, DC 20036-2990   Free: 800-443-GFWC
        Fax: (202)835-0246
E-mail: gfwc@gfwc.org

URL: http://www.gfwc.org
Contact: Maxine Scarbro, International Pres.
Desc: International women's volunteer service organization with members from 7500 U.S. clubs. Provides volunteer leadership training and development. *Type:* Association.

Glamour

Conde Nast Publications, Inc.
140 E. 45th St., 39th Fl.   Ph: (212)880-8800
New York, NY 10017   Free: 800-223-0780
        Fax: (212)880-8248
E-mail: letters@brides.com
Contact: Bonnie Fuller, Editor; Mary Bemer, Publisher.
Desc: Fashion, beauty, and health magazine. *Type:* Periodical.

HERS Newsletter

Hysterectomy Educational Resources and Services Foundation (HERS)
422 Bryn Mawr Ave.   Ph: (610)667-7757
Bala Cynwyd, PA 19004   Fax: (610)667-8096
Contact: Nora W. Coffey, Editor; Joanne West, Editor; Helen E. Plotkin, Editor.
Desc: Features articles on information and services concerning hysterectomy and castration. Covers health issues, and chronicles of individual experiences. *Type:* Newsletter.

HOMEmaker's Magazine (Madame au Foyer)

Telemedia Communications, Inc.
25 Sheppard Ave. W, Ste. 100   Ph: (416)733-7600
North York, ON, Canada M2N   Fax: (416)733-7981
6S7
Contact: Sally Armstrong, Editor-in-Chief, (416)440-8352; Barrie Wykes, Vice Pres./Pub., (416)440-8360; T.J. Flynn, Advertising Dir., (416)440-8361.
Desc: Women's magazine (English and French). *Type:* Periodical.

Images

Multi-Vision Publishing, Inc.
655 Bay St., Ste. 1100
Toronto, ON, Canada M5G
2K4
Contact: Mr. Ashley Harvey, Publisher; Ms. Kate MacDonald, Editor.
Desc: Women's magazine covering lifestyle, fashion, beauty, and health. *Type:* Periodical.

International Christian Women's Fellowship

PO Box 1986   Ph: (317)635-3100
Indianapolis, IN 46206   Fax: (317)635-4426
E-mail: efrost@dhm.disciples.org
Contact: Ellen Frost, Sec.-Treas.
Desc: Women who are members of the Christian Church (Disciples of Christ) and others who accept the purpose of the CWF. Administered by The Office of Disciples Women, Division of Homeland Ministries, of the Christian Church (Disciples of Christ) in the U.S. and Canada. "To provide opportunities for spiritual growth, enrichment, education, and creative ministries to enable women to develop a sense of personal responsibility for the whole mission of the Church of Jesus Christ," through a program of study, worship, and service and through preparation of women for fuller participation in the total church life. *Type:* Association.

International Committee for World Day of Prayer

475 Riverside Dr., Rm. 560   Ph: (212)870-3049
New York, NY 10115   Fax: (212)870-3587
Contact: Eileen King, Exec.Dir.
Desc: Christian women united to observe a common day of prayer established on the first Friday in March.

Through World Day of Prayer, which began in 1887, women "affirm their faith in Jesus Christ; share their hopes and fears, their joys and sorrows, their opportunities and needs." Encourages women to "become aware of the whole world and no longer live in isolation; to share the faith experience of Christians in other countries and cultures; to take up the burdens of other people and pray with and for them; to become aware of their talents and use them in the service of society." Affirms "that prayer and action are inseparable and that both have an imponderable influence in the world." *Type:* Association.

International Women's Health Coalition

24 E. 21st St., 5th Fl.   Ph: (212)979-8500
New York, NY 10010   Fax: (212)979-9009
E-mail: info@iwhc.org
URL: http://www.iwhc.org
Contact: Joan B. Dunlop, Pres.
Desc: Seeks to promote and provide high quality reproductive health care for women in the Southern countries. Provides technical assistance, supports innovative health care projects and policy-oriented field research in Africa, Asia and Latin America. Produces public education materials. *Type:* Association.

Ladies' Home Journal

Meredith Corp.
1716 Locust St.   Ph: (515)284-3000
Des Moines, IA 50309-3023   Free: 800-678-2674
        Fax: (515)284-3697
E-mail: lhj@nyc.mdp.com.
URL: http://www.lhj.com.
Contact: Myrna Blyth, Editor; Michael Brownstein, Publisher.
Desc: Women's magazine. *Alt. Contact:* 125 Park Ave., New York, NY 10017; telephone: (212)557-6600; fax: (212)455-1313; toll-free: 800-374-4545. *Type:* Periodical.

Mademoiselle

Conde Nast Publications, Inc.
140 E. 45th St., 39th Fl.   Ph: (212)880-8800
New York, NY 10017   Free: 800-223-0780
        Fax: (212)880-8248
E-mail: letters@brides.com; mllemag@aol.com.
Contact: Elizabeth Crow, Editor-in-Chief; Catherine Viscardi Johnson, Publisher; John Messina, Advertising Dir.
Desc: Young women's magazine. *Type:* Periodical.

Modern Bride

K-III Family Leisure Group
249 W. 17th St.   Ph: (212)462-3400
New York, NY 10011   Fax: (212)367-8335
URL: http://www.modernbride.com.
Contact: Cele Goldsmith Lalli, Editor; Nina Lawrence, Publisher.
Desc: Magazine for brides. *Type:* Periodical.

MOMS in Touch International

PO Box 1120   Free: 800-949-
Poway, CA 92074   MOMS
        Fax: (619)486-5132
E-mail: mitihqtrs@compuserve.com
Contact: Fern Nichols, Pres.
Desc: Encourages mothers and others to meet and to pray for children and schools; to be a positive influence; to support public and private schools; and to pray that schools may be guided by biblical values and high moral standards. *Type:* Association.

Mothering Magazine

Mothering Magazine
PO Box 1690   Ph: (505)984-8116
Santa Fe, NM 87504   Free: 800-984-8116
                                Fax: (505)986-8335
E-mail: mothering.ni.net; mother@ni.net.
URL: http://www.mothering.com.
Contact: Peggy O'Mara, Editor and Publisher, (505)984-6293, peggo@mothering.com; ASHISHA, Managing Editor, (504)984-6298, ashisha@mothering.com.
Desc: Magazine of natural family living including articles on homeschooling, midwifery, alternative family health, family, book reviews, breast-feeding. *Type:* Periodical.

National Black Women's Health Project

175 Trinity Ave SW   Ph: (404)758-9590
Atlanta, GA 30303
Contact: Julia Scott, President.
Desc: Encourages mutual and selfhelp advocacy among women to bring about a reduction in health care problems prevalent among black women. Urges women to communicate with health care providers, seek out available health care resources, become aware of selfhelp approaches, and communicate with other black women to minimize feelings of powerlessness and isolation, and thus realize they have some control over their physical and mental health. Points out the higher incidence of high blood pressure, obesity, breast and cervical cancers, diabetes, kidney disease, arteriosclerosis, and teenage pregnancy among black women than among other racial or socioeconomic groups. *Type:* Association.

National NOW Times

National Organization for Women, Inc.
1000 16th St. NW, Ste. 700   Ph: (202)331-0066
Washington, DC 20036   Fax: (202)785-8576
E-mail: now@now.org; nnt@now.org.
URL: http://www.now.org.
Contact: Patricia Ireland, Editor; Lisa Bennett-Higney, Managing Editor.
Desc: Feminist magazine. *Type:* Periodical.

National Women's Health Network

514 10th St. NW, Ste. 400   Ph: (202)347-1140
Washington, DC 20004   Fax: (202)347-1168
Contact: Cynthia Pearson, Exec.Dir.
Desc: An advocacy organization giving women a greater voice in the health care system in the United States. It is the only such membership organization and has a 20-year history of accomplishments on behalf of all women. Its clearinghouse of women's health information helps women make well-informed decisions. *Type:* Association.

National Women's Mailing List

PO Box 68   Ph: (707)632-5763
Jenner, CA 95450   Fax: (707)632-5589
URL: http://www.electrapages.com
Contact: Jill Lippitt, Dir.
Desc: A project of the Women's Information Exchange. Seeks to utilize information technology to facilitate outreach, communication networking, and resource-sharing among women. Individual women and women's organizations are able to sign up to receive mail in a variety of interest areas, such as politics, health, sports, women's culture, and spirituality. *Type:* Association.

NCJW Journal

National Council of Jewish Women, Inc.
53 W. 23rd St.   Ph: (212)645-4048
New York, NY 10010   Fax: (212)645-7466
E-mail: mail@ncjw.org
URL: http://www.ncjw.org
Contact: Lauren Schwartz Linfield, Editor.

Desc: Periodical reporting social policy issues of interest to NCJW members. *Alt. Contact:* Lauren Schwartz Linfield 6 Trailing Rock Ln., Westport, CT 06880; telephone: (203)256-1370. *Type:* Periodical.

Network News

National Network for Women's Employment
1625 K. St. NW, Ste. 300   Ph: (202)467-6346
Washington, DC 20006   Free: 800-235-2732
                                Fax: (202)467-5366
Contact: Carol Hamilton, Editor.
Desc: Provides information for service providers in women's education and job training programs. Covers regional news from Network state organizations, and other organizational news. *Type:* Newsletter.

New Woman

K-III Magazine Corporation
2 Park Ave.   Ph: (212)545-3500
New York, NY 10016   Fax: (212)545-3590
Contact: Betsy Carter, Editor; Mary Donahue Quinlan, Publisher; Jeannette Benny, Dir. of Editorial Services.
Desc: Magazine covering women's interests including career, relationships, health, money, fitness, fashion, and beauty. Also publishes profiles of pacesetters. *Type:* Periodical.

9 to 5 Newsletter

9 to 5, National Association of Working Women
231 W. Wisconsin Ave., Ste.   Ph: (414)274-0925
  900   Free: 800-522-0925
Milwaukee, WI 53203   Fax: (414)272-2870
E-mail: nat9to5@execpc.com
Desc: Addresses concerns and rights of women office workers, covering such topics as pay equity, job stress, child care, proper use of office technology, and respect among employees and from employers. Reports on the Association's activities, which include legislative publicity, and health and safety campaigns. *Type:* Newsletter.

The Nurturing Network

Campus of Fancisican University   Free: 800-TNN-
University Blvd.   4MOM
Steubenville, OH 43952   Fax: (740)284-4860
Contact: Mary Cunningham Agee, Exec.Dir.
Desc: A nationwide network of volunteers who provide practical support for college and working women facing unplanned pregnancies. Members offer counseling, medical services, nurturing homes, employment, and assistance with financial and educational issues. Makes available referrals for legal assistance, adoption, and support services for over 8,000 mothers and their children. *Type:* Association.

Older Women's League

666 11th St. NW, Ste. 700   Ph: (202)783-6686
Washington, DC 20001   Fax: (202)638-2356
Contact: Deborah Briceland-Betts, Exec.Dir.
Desc: Middle-aged and older women; persons of any age who support issues of concern to mid-life and older women. Primary issues include access to health care insurance, support for family caregivers, reform of social security, access to jobs and pensions for older women, effects of budget cuts on women, and maintaining self-sufficiency throughout life. Operates speakers' bureau; prepares educational materials; compiles statistics. *Type:* Association.

Online

Association for Women in Computing, Twin Cities Chapter
PO Box 131022
Roseville, MN 55113
E-mail: awc@acm.org

Contact: Jennifer D. Wise, Editor.
Desc: Promotes communication, education, and professional development and advancement of women in computing. Publishes news of the Chapter, its members, and its activities. *Type:* Newsletter.

PEO International

3700 Grand Ave.   Ph: (515)255-3153
Des Moines, IA 50312   Fax: (515)255-3820
Contact: Anne Pettygrove, CAO.
Desc: International women's organization seeking to further opportunities for higher education for women. Has established International Peace Scholarship Fund, Educational Loan Fund, Program for Continuing Education, and PEO Scholar Awards. Maintains Cottey Junior College for Women, Nevada, MO. *Type:* Association.

Perspective

Catalyst
120 Wall St.   Ph: (212)777-8900
New York, NY 10005   Fax: (212)477-4252
E-mail: info@catalystwomen.org
Contact: Debra Scheinholtz, Editor.
Desc: Provides business information on such topics as leadership, mentoring, and work/family programs for women in the corporate world. Recurring features include success stories from top American corporations. *Type:* Newsletter.

Redbook Magazine

Hearst Magazines
959 8th Ave.   Ph: (212)649-2000
New York, NY 10019-5905
Contact: Lesley Jane Seymour, Editor-in-Chief; Jayne Jamison, Publisher; Susan Blank, Assoc. Publisher.
Desc: Magazine containing articles and fiction features for young working mothers. *Alt. Contact:* 224 W. 57th St., New York, NY 10019; telephone: (212)649-3450. *Type:* Periodical.

SELF Magazine

Conde Nast Publications, Inc.
140 E. 45th St., 39th Fl.   Ph: (212)880-8800
New York, NY 10017   Free: 800-223-0780
                                Fax: (212)880-8248
E-mail: letters@brides.com
Contact: Rochelle Udell, Editor-in-Chief; Larry Burstein, Publisher; Victoria Lasdon, Advertising Dir.
Desc: Magazine serving as sourcebook for contemporary women. *Type:* Periodical.

Supermodel News

Supermodel News
PO Box 87265   Ph: (770)964-0105
College Park, GA 30337
Contact: Beverly Davis, Editor.
Desc: Deals with the modeling industry. Provides information on modeling opportunities and beauty pageants. *Type:* Newsletter.

Texas Woman's University

Texas Woman's University
Box 425589 TWU Sta.   Ph: (940)898-2000
Denton, TX 76204-3589   Fax: (940)898-3198
E-mail: info@twu.edu
URL: http://www4.twu.edu/
Desc: This site goes into detail about the educational programs available at Texas Woman's University and provides a virtual tour of the campus. Other features include virtual museum exhibitions, course schedules, statistics, a guide to student services, and more. *Type:* Database.

Top Model

Hachette Filipacchi Magazines, Inc.
1633 Broadway, 41st Fl.   Ph: (212)767-6000
New York, NY 10019   Fax: (212)989-4561
Contact: Martine Sicard, Editor.
Desc: Magazine covering the fashion industry, including articles on newest beauty trends and interviews with top models. *Type:* Periodical.

Toronto Life Fashion Magazine

Key Publishers Co. Ltd.
59 Front St. E.   Ph: (416)364-3334
Toronto, ON, Canada M5E   Fax: (416)861-1169
1B3
E-mail: fashion@istar.ca.
URL: http://www.torontolife.com.
Contact: Joan Harting Barham, Editor; Shelagh Tarleton, Publisher.
Desc: Fashion magazine. *Type:* Periodical.

Toronto Women's Health Network Newsletter

Toronto Women's Health Network
c/o L. Spring   Ph: (416)392-0898
1884 Davenport Rd.   Fax: (416)392-0645
Toronto, ON, Canada M6N
4Y2
E-mail: twhn@web.net
URL: http://www.web.net/~twnn.
Contact: L. Spring, Editor, lspring@city.toronto.on.ca.
Desc: Serves as an information exchange on women's health issues and events. Includes reports of monthly meetings. *Type:* Newsletter.

Town & Country

Hearst Magazines
959 8th Ave.   Ph: (212)649-2000
New York, NY 10019-5905
Contact: Pamela Fiori, Editor-in-Chief; Molly Schaefer, Publisher.
Desc: Magazine featuring society, travel, fashion, beauty, home, art/antiques, health, financial, and philanthropy. *Alt. Contact:* 1700 Broadway, 30th Fl., New York, NY 10019; telephone: (212)903-5000; fax: (212)262-7107. *Type:* Periodical.

True Story

Sterling/Macfadden Partnership
233 Park Ave. S.   Ph: (212)780-3500
New York, NY 10003   Fax: (212)780-3555
Contact: Tina Pappalardo, Editor, (212)979-4912; Allen Tuller, Publisher; Lisa Finn, Editorial Dir., (212)979-4915.
Desc: Magazine for young women, containing stories, editorials, and articles about beauty and health, home management, recipes and food, parenting, and personal advice. *Type:* Periodical.

Union of Palestinian Women's Association in North America

3148 W 63rd St.
Chicago, IL 60629-2750
Contact: Maha Jarad, Contact.
Desc: Promotes national and social self-determination and independence for Palestine. Strives toward emancipation and empowerment of Palestinian and Arab women. Encourages unity among Palestinian women; supports the women's movement worldwide. *Type:* Association.

United Order True Sisters

100 State St., No. 1020
Albany, NY 12207-1801
Contact: Dorothy B. Giuriceo, Exec. Admin.
Desc: Charitable organization that offers personal service to indigent persons with cancer or AIDS. *Type:* Association.

Victoria

Hearst Magazines
959 8th Ave.   Ph: (212)649-2000
New York, NY 10019-5905
Contact: Nancy Lindemeyer, Editor-in-Chief, nlindemeyer@hearst.com; Alan M. Waxbenberg, Publisher.
Desc: Lifestyle magazine for women. *Alt. Contact:* 224 W. 57th St., New York, NY 10019; telephone: (212)649-3720. *Type:* Periodical.

Vogue

Conde Nast Publications, Inc.
140 E. 45th St., 39th Fl.   Ph: (212)880-8800
New York, NY 10017   Free: 800-223-0780
Fax: (212)880-8248
E-mail: letters@brides.com
Contact: Anna Wintour, Editor; Anne Fuchs, Publisher; Diane Oshin, Advertising Mgr.
Desc: Women's fashion and beauty magazine. *Type:* Periodical.

WeddingBells Magazine

WeddingBells Inc.
50 Wellington St. E, 2nd Fl.   Ph: (416)862-8479
Toronto, ON, Canada M5E   Free: 800-387-9877
1C8   Fax: (416)862-2184
E-mail: sales@weddingbells.com.
URL: http://weddingbells.com.
Contact: Crys Stewart, Editor-in-Chief; Diane Hall, Publisher.
Desc: Consumer magazine for engaged couples. *Type:* Periodical.

Who's Who of American Women

Marquis Who's Who
Reed Elsevier
121 Chanlon Rd.   Ph: (908)464-6800
New Providence, NJ 07974   Free: 800-521-8110
Fax: (908)771-8645
E-mail: info@marquiswhoswho.com
Contact: Lisa Weissbard, Managing Editor.
Desc: Over 24,000 high-profile women in all fields. *Type:* Directory.

WIT

Northern New England Tradeswomen
189 N Main St., Ste. 9   Ph: (802)476-4040
Barre, VT 05641-4173
Contact: Ruth Durkee, Editor.
Desc: Provides a network of support, information, and skill sharing for women in skilled trades professions. *Type:* Newsletter.

Woman's Day

Hachette Filipacchi Magazines, Inc.
1633 Broadway, 41st Fl.   Ph: (212)767-6000
New York, NY 10019   Fax: (212)989-4561
Contact: Jane Chesnutt, Editor; Jan Studin, Publisher; Laura Klein, Advertising Dir.
Desc: Women's magazine. *Type:* Periodical.

Woman's World

Heinrich Bauer North America Inc.
270 Sylvan Ave.   Ph: (201)569-0006
PO Box 1648   Fax: (201)569-3584
Englewood Cliffs, NJ 07632
E-mail: dearww@aol.com.
Contact: Andrea Florczak, Editor; Konrad Wiederholz, Advertising Mgr.; Todd Selbert, Editor.
Desc: Woman's service and entertainment magazine. *Type:* Periodical.

Women as Managers

The Economic Press, Inc.
12 Daniel Rd.   Ph: (973)227-1224
Fairfield, NJ 07004-2565   Free: 800-526-2554
Fax: (973)227-8360
E-mail: order@epinc.com
Contact: Linda Bullock, Editor, edit@epinc.com.
Desc: Offers suggestions to women in management who seek higher career levels. Discusses career-influencing women's issues. *Type:* Newsletter.

Women's Information Directory

Gale Group Inc.
27500 Drake Rd.   Ph: (248)699-4253
Farmington Hills, MI 48331-   Free: 800-877-GALE
3535   Fax: (248)699-8070
E-mail: galeord@galegroup.com
URL: http://www.galegroup.com.
Contact: Shawn Brennan, Editor.
Desc: Nearly 10,800 sources of information for and about women in the U.S., including national, state, and local organizations; publishers and booksellers of women's materials; newspapers, magazines, newsletters, other directories, and videos; museums; awards, honors, and prizes; government agencies and assistance programs; research centers; women's studies programs at colleges and universities; consultants; scholarships and other financial aids; electronic resources; and library collections. *Type:* Directory.

Women's League Outlook

Women's League for Conservative Judaism
48 E. 74th St.   Ph: (212)628-1600
New York, NY 10021   Free: 800-628-5083
Fax: (212)772-3507
E-mail: wleague74@aol.com
Contact: Maureen Wise, Managing Editor.
Desc: Magazine focusing on issues of concern to contemporary Jewish women and their families. *Type:* Periodical.

Women's Missionary Society, AME Church

1134 11th St. NW   Ph: (202)371-8886
Washington, DC 20001   Fax: (202)371-8820
URL: http://www.amenet.org/wms/main_fr.htm
Contact: Dorothy Adams Peck, Intl. Pres.
Desc: Women members of the African Methodist Episcopal Church. Seeks to: "help each woman and youth grow in the knowledge and experience of God through his son Jesus Christ; seek fellowship with women in other lands; make possible opportunities and resources to meet the changing needs and concerns of women and youth through intensive training, recruitment, and Christian witnessing; offer a fellowship so strong, a message so convincingly interpreted and imparted, and an enthusiasm so contagious, that the Gospel through us will be at work in the world so that we will be able to draw humankind into the fellowship of love." Sponsors administrative retreats, health institutes, health initiatives focusing on Breast Cancer, Prostate Cancer, etc., AIDS, etc., Sojourner Project, international exchanges, missionaries, leadership training programs, and educational programs for religious leaders. Operates womens information bureau; compiles statistics. *Type:* Association.

Women's News

Women's News
PO Box 829   Ph: (914)835-5400
Harrison, NY 10528-0829   Fax: (914)835-5718
E-mail: achiever33@aol.com.
Contact: Merna Popper, Publisher; Jamie Kiffel, Managing Editor; Dennis Bennett, Assoc. Ed.
Desc: Feminist newspaper geared toward women's issues, problems, events, health, and wealth. Features pull-out event calendar, newsbriefs, followups, classifieds, displays, letters, and special issues. *Type:* Periodical.

Women's Wear Daily

7 W. 34th St.   Ph: (212)630-4000
New York, NY 10001   Fax: (212)630-3566
Desc: Distributes items on the fashion industry. *Alt. Contact:* 7 W. 34th St., New York, NY 10001; telephone: (212)630-4000; fax: (212)630-3566. *Type:* Periodical.

Working Mother

Lang Communications, Inc.
230 Park Ave.   Ph: (212)551-9500
New York, NY 10169
URL: http://www.womweb.com.
Contact: Judsen Culbreth, Editor; Susan Sellger, Publisher.
Desc: Magazine for working mothers. *Alt. Contact:* 230 Park Ave., 7th Fl., New York, NY 10169; telephone: (212)551-9407, (212)551-9411; fax: (212)551-9757. *Type:* Periodical.

Working Woman

McDonald Communications Corp.
135 W. 50th St.   Ph: (212)445-6100
New York, NY 10020   Free: 800-234-9675
     Fax: (212)445-6197
E-mail: editors@workingwomanmag.com; wwedit@womweb.com.
URL: http://www.workingwomanmag.com.
Contact: Bernadette Grey, Editor-in-Chief; Laura Goldstein, Exec. Ed.; Nicola Godfrey, Managing Editor.
Desc: Magazine for women in business. *Type:* Periodical.

Wood

American Bamboo Society Newsletter

American Bamboo Society
750 Krumkill Rd.   Ph: (518)458-7618
Albany, NY 12203-5976   Fax: (518)458-7625
URL: http://www.bamboo.org/abs/.
Contact: Michael A. Bartholomew, Editor.
Desc: Promotes interest in the identification, propagation, utilization, culture, and appreciation of bamboos. Provides descriptions of seeds, flowers, and species. *Type:* Newsletter.

American Plywood Association—Management Report

American Plywood Association
PO Box 11700   Ph: (253)565-6600
Tacoma, WA 98411-0700   Fax: (253)565-7265
Contact: Jack Merry, Editor.
Desc: Provides news influencing the use or acceptance of structural panels. Covers subjects including economic outlook, promotional programs and other activities of the Association, and legislative developments. *Type:* Newsletter.

American Woodworker

Rodale Books
400 S. 10th St.   Ph: (610)967-5171
Emmaus, PA 18098-0099   Fax: (610)967-7722
E-mail: ddonche1@rodalepress.com; awletters@aol.com.
URL: http://www.rodalepress.com; http://www.americanwoodworker.com.
Contact: David Sloan, Editor and Publisher, (610)967-8799; Don Schroder, Advertising Dir., (610)967-7871.
Desc: Magazine devoted to helping woodworkers improve their skills. *Alt. Contact:* 22 S. 2nd St., Emmaus, PA 18098; fax: (610)967-7692. *Type:* Periodical.

FDM—The Source—Woodworking Industry Directory

Cahners Business Information
1350 E. Touhy Ave.   Ph: (847)635-8800
Des Plaines, IL 60018   Free: 800-446-6551
     Fax: (847)635-6856
E-mail: bkinross@cahners.com
URL: http://www.fdmmag.com.
Contact: Bruce Plantz, Editor, bplantz@cahners.com.
Desc: List of over 1,800 suppliers to secondary woodworking industry; coverage includes Canada. *Type:* Directory.

Fine Woodworking

Taunton Press
63 S. Main St., Box 5506   Free: 800-926-8776
Newtown, CT 06470-5506   Fax: (203)270-6751
E-mail: jchilds@taunton.com; fww@taunton.com.
URL: http://www.taunton.com; http://www.taunton.com.
Contact: Scott Gibson, Editor; James Chiavelli, Publisher; Dick West, Advertising Mgr.
Desc: Technical magazine for the amateur and professional woodworker. *Alt. Contact:* 191 S. Main St., Newtown, CT 06470; telephone: (203)426-8171; fax: (203)270-6751; toll-free: 800-283-7252. *Type:* Periodical.

Hardwood Plywood and Veneer News

Hardwood Plywood & Veneer Association
PO Box 2789   Ph: (703)435-2900
Reston, VA 20195-0789   Fax: (703)435-2537
E-mail: hpva@hpva.org
URL: http://www.hpva.org; http://www.hpva.org.
Contact: Curt Alt, Editor, calt@hpva.org.
Desc: Supplies information on developments that affect the hardwood plywood and veneer industry. Covers topics related to prefinishing of hardwood plywood. *Type:* Newsletter.

IHPA Newsletter

International Wood Products Association (IHPA)
4214 King St. W   Ph: (703)820-6696
Alexandria, VA 22302   Fax: (703)820-8550
E-mail: info@ihpa.org
URL: http://www.ihpa.org.
Contact: Wendy Baer, Editor.
Desc: Provides news on the wood products industry. Recurring features include news of research, a calendar of events, reports of meetings, and news of educational opportunities. *Type:* Newsletter.

International Woodfiber Report

Miller Freeman, Inc.
525 Market St., Ste. 500   Ph: (415)538-3828
San Francisco, CA 94105   Free: 800-289-0969
     Fax: (415)278-5371
E-mail: subserv@mfi.com
Contact: James McLaren, Editor; Chris Lyddan, Assistant Editor, (804)768-4186; Dale Murphy, Production Editor.
Desc: Provides information about wood fiber. Includes supply, availability, consumption, and harvesting news, environmental standards, timber legislation, and pricing trends. *Type:* Newsletter.

The Modern Woodmen Magazine

Modern Woodmen of America
1701 1st Ave.   Ph: (309)786-6481
PO Box 2005   Fax: (309)786-5603
Rock Island, IL 61204-2005
Contact: Gloria Bergh, Editor; Jill Lain Weaver, Editor, jweaver@modern-woodmen.org.
Desc: Fraternal magazine. *Type:* Periodical.

National Hardwood Lumber Association—News

National Hardwood Lumber Association
PO Box 34518   Ph: (901)382-1818
Memphis, TN 38184-0518   Fax: (901)382-6419
E-mail: nhla@natlhoodwood.org
Contact: Paul Houghland, Jr., Editor.
Desc: Provides news of the hardwood lumber industry and carries articles on hardwood products, business trends, and significant legislative actions. Recurring features include news of conventions, members, and of the Association's promotional activities, and a calendar of events. *Type:* Newsletter.

National Sash and Door Jobbers Association Bulletin

National Sash & Door Jobbers Association (NSDJA)
10225 Robert Trent Jones   Ph: (813)372-3665
  Pkwy.   Fax: (813)372-2879
New Port Richey, FL 34655-4649
Desc: Provides information on the activities of the National Sash and Door Jobbers Association. Promotes wholesale distribution of windows, door, millwork, and related products. *Type:* Newsletter.

National Wooden Pallet and Container Association

1800 N. Kent St., Ste. 911   Ph: (703)527-7667
Arlington, VA 22209-2109   Fax: (703)527-7717
E-mail: palletcomm@aol.com
URL: http://www.nwpca.com
Contact: John J. Healy, CAE, Pres.
Desc: Manufacturers, recyclers, and distributors of pallets, containers, reels, and other unit load bases used in warehousing, distribution, and logistics. Compiles industry information; develops national product standards; conducts market research. *Type:* Association.

Pacific Rim Wood Market Report

Wood Note Publishing
PO Box 918   Ph: (253)858-2646
Gig Harbor, WA 98335   Fax: (253)858-2874
E-mail: wnp@harbornet.com
Contact: Linda K. Barr, Editor and Publisher.
Desc: Provides market information about the Pacific Rim wood industry. Topics include lumber and logging. *Type:* Newsletter.

Random Lengths Locator

Random Lengths Publications, Inc.
450 Country Club Rd., Ste. 240   Ph: (541)686-9925
Eugene, OR 97401   Fax: (541)686-9629
E-mail: rlmail@randomlengths.com
URL: http://www.randomlengths.com
Contact: Jeff Redd, Editor.
Desc: Acts as a clearinghouse for advertising in the forest products industry. Includes black and white graphics. *Type:* Newsletter.

Random Lengths Midweek

Random Lengths Publications, Inc.
450 Country Club Rd., Ste. 240   Ph: (541)686-9925
Eugene, OR 97401   Fax: (541)686-9629
E-mail: rlmail@randomlengths.com
URL: http://www.randomlengths.com; http://www.randomlengths.com.
Contact: B. Elmore, Editor.
Desc: Serves as a price guide for the wood products market, covering dimension lumber, studs, boards, and plywoods. A supplemental service to Random Lengths. *Type:* Newsletter.

The Vital Link

Woodworking Machinery Distributors Association
289 Aberdeen Ave.   Ph: (610)265-6658
Exton, PA 19341-2766   Fax: (610)265-3419
Contact: R. Franklin Brown, Jr., Editor.
Desc: Provides news of the woodworking machinery distribution industry. Contains items on pertinent governmental and legislative actions, Association activities, and business trends. *Type:* Newsletter.

Wood Machining News

Wood Machining Institute
PO Box 476
Berkeley, CA 94701   Ph: (925)943-5240
    Fax: (925)945-0947
Contact: Dr. Ryszard Szymani, Editor, szymani@woodmachining.com.
Desc: Provides news and technical information on the latest worldwide developments in the field of wood machining. Covers equipment and technology of saws and sawing, planing and sanding operations, and the production of veneer and chips. *Type:* Newsletter.

Wood & Wood Products—Red Book Issue

Vance Publishing Corp.
400 Knightsbridge Parkway   Ph: (847)634-2600
Lincolnshire, IL 60069   Free: 800-343-2016
    Fax: (847)634-4379
URL: http://www.iswonline.com.
Contact: Margie Melaniphy, Editor.
Desc: List of approximately 3,000 manufacturers, distributors, and importers of machinery, equipment, and supplies for industrial woodworking applications; related state agencies and trade organizations, wood industry consultants, and lumber producers. Includes some European listings. *Type:* Directory.

WOODMEN Magazine

Woodmen of the World/Omaha Woodmen Life Insurance Society
1700 Farnam St.   Ph: (402)342-1890
Omaha, NE 68102   Free: 800-225-3108
    Fax: (402)271-7269
E-mail: service@woodmen.com
Contact: Billie Jo Foust, Assistant editor, (402)271-7863, fax: (402)271-7269, bfoust@woodmen.com; Scott J. Darling, Managing Editor, (402)271-7211, fax: (402)271-7269.
Desc: Fraternal magazine for Society members and their families. *Type:* Periodical.

Woodsmith

August Home Publishing
2200 Grand Ave.   Ph: (515)282-7000
Des Moines, IA 50312   Free: 800-311-3991
    Fax: (515)283-0447
Contact: Donald Peschke, Publisher; Terry J. Strohman, Contact.
Desc: Magazine for woodworking hobbyists. *Type:* Periodical.

Woodworker's Journal

Rockler Press
4365 Willow Dr.   Ph: (612)478-8232
Medina, MN 55340   Fax: (612)478-8396
URL: http://todayswoodworker.com.
Contact: Rob Johnston, Assoc. Editor, (612)478-8255, editor@woodworkersjournal.com; Nancy Ammend, Managing Editor; Michelle Scribner, Circulation Coordinator, (612)478-8276; J.F. Van Gilder, Co. Publisher's Rep., jimvg@flash.net.
Desc: Magazine featuring projects, tips and techniques for novice and experienced woodworking hobbyists. *Type:* Periodical.

Woodmen

Modern Woodmen of America

1701 1st Ave.   Ph: (309)786-6481
Rock Island, IL 61201   Fax: (309)793-5507
URL: http://www.modern-woodmen.org
Contact: Clyde C. Schoek, Pres.
Desc: Fraternal benefit life insurance society. *Type:* Association.

Woodmen Rangers

1700 Farnam St.   Ph: (402)271-7258
Omaha, NE 68102   Fax: (402)449-7733
Contact: John S. Manna, Mgr.
Desc: Youth organization sponsored by Woodmen of the World Life Insurance Society for boys and girls; active members are 8 to 15 years old participate in programs that enhance leadership training, character, and personal development. Good citizenship and civic responsibility is stressed. Rangers also attend summer camp provided by each marketing area. *Type:* Association.

Woodmen of the World

9777 S. Yosemite St., Ste. 200   Ph: (303)792-9777
Littleton, CO 80124-3115   Fax: (303)792-9793
Contact: David Wilson, Pres.
Desc: Fraternal benefit life insurance society. Members located in 23 states. *Type:* Association.

Woodmen of the World/Omaha Woodmen Life Insurance Society

Woodmen Tower   Ph: (402)342-1890
1700 Farnam St.   Fax: (402)271-7269
Omaha, NE 68102
E-mail: service@woodmen.com
URL: http://www.woodmen.com/
Contact: Scott J. Darling, V.Pres.
Desc: Fraternal benefit life insurance society. Provides charitable program and children's services; maintains museum. *Type:* Association.

World Affairs

Association of World Citizens

55 New Montgomery St., Ste.   Ph: (415)541-9610
224   Fax: (415)227-4878
San Francisco, CA 94105
E-mail: info@worldcitizens.org
URL: http://www.worldcitizens.org
Contact: Douglas Mattern, Pres.
Desc: Individuals united in their concern about the state of the earth and their willingness to accept responsibility as inherent members of the world community. Promotes an end to war and the establishment of a world community; opposes the arms race. Seeks to meet basic human needs, protect the environment, and cooperate with similar groups on human rights issues and other causes. *Type:* Association.

Forum International: International Ecosystems University

91 Gregory Ln., No. 21   Ph: (925)671-2900
Pleasant Hill, CA 94523   Fax: (925)946-1500
E-mail: forum@ix.netcom.com
Contact: Dr. Nicolas D. Hetzer, Dir.
Desc: Works to create a forum for education, research, and action to deal with problems such as environmental deterioration, socioeconomic change, poverty, overpopulation, and lack of educational opportunity. *Type:* Association.

The Fund for Peace

1701 K St. NW, 11th Fl.   Ph: (202)223-7940
Washington, DC 20006   Fax: (202)223-7947
E-mail: comments@fundforpeace.org
URL: http://www.fundforpeace.org
Contact: Pauline H. Baker, Pres.
Desc: Promotes education and research and proposes practical solutions to global problems that threaten human survival. Fosters security through respect for the principles of constitutional democracy. Conducts core activities and nurtures the development of semi-autonomous projects that promote scholarship, education and action for peace, justice and a secure world. *Type:* Association.

Globe

Globe Communications
5401 NW Broken Sound Blvd.   Ph: (561)997-7733
Boca Raton, FL 33487-3587   Free: 800-749-7733
    Fax: (561)241-5689
Contact: Mike Rosenbloom, Publisher; Jack Linder, Advertising Mgr.
Desc: Consumer magazine (tabloid). *Type:* Periodical.

Hoover Institution on War, Revolution and Peace

Stanford University   Ph: (415)723-0603
Stanford, CA 94305-6010   Fax: (415)723-1687
E-mail: info@hoover.stanford.edu
URL: http://www.hoover.stanford.edu
Contact: John Raisian, Ph.D., Dir.
Desc: Devoted to interdisciplinary scholarship and advanced research in the social sciences and public policy on domestic and international affairs. Maintains archives and library on political, economic, and social change in the 20th century. *Type:* Association.

Life Magazine

Time Inc.
Time-Life Bldg., Rockefeller   Ph: (212)522-1212
    Center   Fax: (212)522-0315
1271 Avenue of the Americas
New York, NY 10020
Contact: Patricia Ryan, Editor; Elizabeth P. Valk, Publisher; David L. Long, Advertising Mgr.
Desc: General interest picture magazine focusing on contemporary people and events. *Type:* Periodical.

The Nation

The Nation
33 Irving Pl., 8th Fl.   Ph: (212)209-5400
New York, NY 10003   Free: 800-333-8536
    Fax: (212)982-9000
E-mail: info@thenation.com
URL: http://www.thenation.com.
Contact: Victor Navasky, Publisher & Editorial Dir., (212)242-8400 ext. 208; Katrina vanden Heuvel, Editor, (212)242-8400 ext. 224; Art Winslow, Exec. Editor, (212)242-8400 ext. 225; Perry Janoski, Vice President, Advertising, (212)242-8400 ext. 203; Teresa Stack, Vice President, Circulation, (212)242-8400 ext. 212; Peter Rothberg, Publicity and Special Projects Dir., (212)242-8400 ext. 213; Jack Berkowitz, President, (212)242-8400 ext. 204.
Desc: Current affairs magazine. *Type:* Periodical.

Planetary Citizens

PO Box 1045   Ph: (916)926-3244
Mount Shasta, CA 96067-1045   Fax: (916)926-1245
Contact: Donald Keys, Pres.
Desc: Individuals who promote the concept of "global oneness" and the interdependence of all peoples regardless of national origin. Members register as "planetary citi-

zens." Focuses on interspecies and interdimensional communication. Offers a "Planetary Passport" document reflecting the belief in "One Earth, One Humanity, One Destiny." Advocates expanding the authority of the United Nations to act on behalf of humanity. *Type:* Association.

U.S. News & World Report
U.S. News & World Report
2400 N St. NW | Ph: (202)955-2000
Washington, DC 20037-1196 | Fax: (202)955-2049
URL: http://wwwz.USN.com/usnews/.
Contact: James Fallows, Editor; Pat Hagerty, Advertising Mgr.; Tom Evans, Publisher.
Desc: National and international news magazine. *Type:* Periodical.

U.S.A. Today
U.S.A. Today
99 W. Hawthorne Ave. | Ph: (516)568-9191
Valley Stream, NY 11580-6101
Contact: Robert S. Rothenberg, Managing Editor; Stanley Lehrer, Publisher; Stephen Donenfeld, Advertising Representative.
Desc: Magazine featuring political opinions. *Type:* Periodical.

World Notables

Buffalo Bill Memorial Association
PO Box 1000 | Ph: (307)587-4771
Cody, WY 82414 | Free: 800-533-3838
| Fax: (307)587-5714
URL: http://www.bbhc.org
Contact: B. Byron Price, Exec.Dir.
Desc: Organized for the preservation and exhibition of Western Americana pertaining to the Rocky Mountain and Northern Plains regions, through the Buffalo Bill Museum, Whitney Gallery of Western Art, Plains Indian Museum, and Cody Firearms Museum. *Type:* Association.

International Tesla Society
PO Box 17697 | Ph: (719)475-0918
Colorado Springs, CO 80935- | Free: 800-397-0137
7697 | Fax: (719)475-0582
E-mail: tesla@usa.net
URL: http://www.tesla.org
Contact: J. W. McGinnis, Pres.
Desc: Scientists, engineers, historians, and individuals interested in Nikola Tesla (1857-1943), a Yugoslav-American electrical scientist and inventor. Objectives are to increase public awareness of Tesla and his inventions and to stimulate interest in Tesla's discoveries and theories. Provides forum for voicing new and untested ideas. *Type:* Association.

James Beard Foundation
167 W. 12th St. | Ph: (212)675-4984
New York, NY 10011 | Free: 800-36B-EARD
| Fax: (212)645-1438
E-mail: beardlib@interport.net
URL: http://www.jamesbeard.org
Contact: Len Pickell, Pres.
Desc: Seeks to honor James Beard (1903-85), the "father of fine cooking in America," and advance the recognition and appreciation of the culinary arts in the U.S. To restore Beard's house in New York City for use as a culinary resource space, library, and archive. Activities include: special dinners from around the world; demonstrations and workshops with guest cooking teachers; wine tastings and winemaker dinners; monthly professional networking luncheons; monthly Italian luncheons. *Type:* Association.

Ladies' Hermitage Association
4580 Rachel's Ln. | Ph: (615)889-2941
Hermitage, TN 37076 | Fax: (615)889-9208
Contact: James M. Vaughan, Exec.Dir.
Desc: Individuals interested in Andrew Jackson (1767-1845), 7th President of the U.S., 1829-37, the Jackson family, and preservation of related historic properties. His Tennessee residence is known as The Hermitage. Maintains 650 acre historic Jackson compound including the Hermitage mansion, Tulip Grove mansion, Old Hermitage Church, other historic buildings, and Andrew Jackson Visitors Center. *Type:* Association.

Mount Vernon Ladies' Association
P.O. Box 110 | Ph: (703)780-2000
Mount Vernon, VA 22121-0110 | Fax: (703)799-8698
E-mail: mvinfo@mountvernon.org
URL: http://www.mountvernon.org
Contact: Mr. James C. Rees, Resident Dir.
Desc: Dedicated to the preservation of the home and tomb of George Washington (1732-99), the first President of the U.S. *Type:* Association.

Robert E. Lee Memorial Association
Stratford Hall Plantation | Ph: (804)493-8038
Stratford, VA 22558 | Fax: (804)493-0333
E-mail: sgarner@stratfordhall.org
URL: http://www.stratfordhall.org/relma.htm
Contact: J. R. Fishburne, Exec.Dir.
Desc: Supported by membership and contributions to restore, preserve, and maintain Stratford Hall Plantation as a living memorial to General Robert E. *Type:* Association.

Wrestling

U.S.A. Wrestling
6155 Lehman Dr. | Ph: (719)598-8181
Colorado Springs, CO 80918 | Fax: (719)598-9440
E-mail: usaw@concentric.net
Contact: Jim Scherr, Exec.Dir.
Desc: Amateur wrestlers, coaches, officials, and representatives of major school organizations. Serves as national governing body and member of U.S. Olympic Committee. Seeks to develop, improve, and promote the sport of wrestling. *Type:* Association.

Youth

American Academy of Achievement
PO Box 4089 | Ph: (213)457-8052
Malibu, CA 90265
Contact: Wayne Reynolds, Exec.Dir.
Desc: National sponsors and recipients of Golden Plate Awards. Purpose is to inspire American youth to set high standards for themselves and to excel in their endeavors. Provides a forum for the discussion of career issues between students and adults who have achieved success in business, entertainment, literature, the military, the professions, public service, sports, and the sciences. *Type:* Association.

American Girl
Pleasant Co.
PO Box 620991 | Ph: (608)836-4848
Middleton, WI 53562 | Fax: (608)831-7089
URL: http://www.americangirl.com.
Contact: Julia Prohaska, Contact; Sarah Jane Brian, Editor-in-Chief.
Desc: General interest magazine for girls ages 8-12. *Type:* Periodical.

American Youth Foundation
1315 Ann Ave. | Ph: (314)772-8626
St. Louis, MO 63104 | Fax: (314)772-7542
E-mail: ayfbob@aol.com
Contact: Robert S. MacArthur, Pres.
Desc: Develops leadership in youth and the adults and institutions that serve young people by helping them achieve their personal best, live balanced lives, and serve others. Maintains Miniwanca in Shelby, MI, and Merrowvista Education Center in Tuftonboro, NH. Programs include Youth Leadership Compact, St. *Type:* Association.

Association of Boys and Girls Clubs Professionals
c/o Boys & Girls Clubs of the | Ph: (727)546-1032
Suncoast
5111 66th St N Ste. 200
St. Petersburg, FL 33709
Contact: Nelson Perri, Pres.
Desc: Boys and girls club professionals. Promotes welfare, standards, professionalism, and certification. Sponsors training seminars, professional institutes, and research. *Type:* Association.

Awana
1 E. Bode Rd. | Ph: (708)213-2000
Streamwood, IL 60107 | Fax: (708)213-9301
URL: http://www.awana.org
Contact: David Genn, CEO.
Desc: Missionaries operates an outreach ministry in 80 countries. Complies statistics; provides supplies to local church clubs programs; sponsors leader training and Bible Quiz clubs. *Type:* Association.

Boys' Life
Boy Scouts of America
1325 W. Walnut Hill Ln. | Ph: (972)580-2000
PO Box 152079 | Fax: (972)580-2079
Irving, TX 75015-2079
Contact: J.D. Owen, Editor-in-Chief, (214)580-2366; J. Warren Young, Publisher.
Desc: General service magazine for boys, edited to their interests. *Type:* Periodical.

Breakaway Magazine
Focus on the Family
8605 Explorer Dr. | Ph: (719)531-3400
Colorado Springs, CO 80920- | Free: 800-232-6459
1051 | Fax: (719)548-5860
E-mail: tifeditor@fotf.org; corrdpt@fotf.org.
Contact: Greg Johnson, Editor.
Desc: Christian magazine for teenage boys. *Type:* Periodical.

Camp Fire Boys and Girls
4601 Madison Ave. | Ph: (816)756-1950
Kansas City, MO 64112-1278 | Fax: (816)756-0258
E-mail: info@campfire.org
URL: http://www.campfire.org
Contact: Stewart Smith, Exec.Dir.
Desc: Provides coeducational programming for approximately 667,000 participants annually, through 125 councils in 41 states and the District of Columbia. Provides programs that include mentoring opportunities through community clubs, environmental education, camping, and direct child care services. Other innovative activities include an in-school community-service curriculum, gang peace programs, pregnancy prevention programs and a course that teaches teens to provide respite care for children with disabilities. *Type:* Association.

Careers & Colleges

Careers & Colleges
989 6th Ave., 6th Fl.   Ph: (212)563-4688
New York, NY 10018-5410   Free: 800-964-0763
                             Fax: (212)967-2531
E-mail: ccmagazine@aol.com.
Contact: Sue Macy, Editor-in-Chief; Colleen Smith, Advertising Mgr.; Marie Gentile, V.P. Sales and Marketing.
Desc: Magazine providing career information to high school students throughout the United States. *Type:* Periodical.

Christian Service Brigade

Box 150   Ph: (630)665-0630
Wheaton, IL 60189   Free: 800-815-5573
                             Fax: (630)665-0372
E-mail: brigadecsb@aol.com
URL: http://www.csbministries.org
Contact: David Hall, Pres.
Desc: Boys ages six to 18 (38,000), enrolled in local church units; adult leaders (12,000). Provides local evangelical churches with a "Christ-centered weekday activity and achievement program whose aim is to win boys for Christ, guide them in personal study of the Word of God, and train them in Christian living." Geared to meet the needs of boys for physical, mental, social, and spiritual development through such activities as weekly meetings, devotions, and achievement system. Skills training, leadership opportunities, camping, sports, uniforms, badges, and awards are part of the program, but the emphasis is on religious education and training for Christian leadership. *Type:* Association.

Covenant House

346 W. 17th St.   Ph: (212)727-4000
New York, NY 10011-5002   Fax: (212)989-7586
Contact: Sr. Mary Rose McGeady, D.C., Pres. & CEO.
Desc: Crisis center providing immediate, short-term care for runaway and homeless youth under 21 years of age, including counseling, food, shelter, clothing, medical treatment, and legal assistance. Operates transitional living programs for homeless youth, young mothers and their children. Operates short-term substance abuse intervention program. *Type:* Association.

Current Events

Weekly Reader Corp.
200 First Stamford Pl.   Ph: (203)705-3500
PO Box 120023   Fax: (203)705-1661
Stamford, CT 06912-0023
Contact: Charles Piddock, Editor, (203)638-2619; Richard J. LeBrasseur, Advertising Mgr., (203)638-2667, fax: (203)346-5994; Eric Ecker, Editor, (203)638-2423.
Desc: Newspaper for junior and senior high school students. *Type:* Periodical.

Dallas Metropolitan Young Men's Christian Association

601 N. Akard St.   Ph: (214)880-9622
Dallas, TX 75201   Fax: (214)871-3014
URL: http://www.ymcadallas.org
Contact: J. Ben Casey, Jr., Contact.
Desc: Seeks to develop and improve the spiritual, social, mental, and physical well-being of young people and adults. *Type:* Association.

DECA Dimensions

DECA
1908 Association Dr.   Ph: (703)860-5000
Reston, VA 20191   Fax: (703)860-4013
E-mail: deca_dimensions@deca.org.
URL: http://www.deca.org.
Contact: Carol Lund, Managing Editor, carol_lund@deca.org.

Desc: Membership magazine for DECA student members covering business, management, marketing leadership, and finance topics. *Type:* Periodical.

Direction Sports

600 Wilshire Blvd., No. 320   Ph: (213)627-9861
Los Angeles, CA 90017-3215   Fax: (213)627-9862
Contact: Tulley N. Brown, Exec.Dir.
Desc: Schools, recreation departments, and youth-serving organizations such as YMCAs and Boys Clubs which purchase curriculum, program materials, and training and evaluation systems from DS. Designs, tests, and operates methods of peer-run educational/recreational programming to enhance learning skills, motivation to learn, and self-esteem. *Type:* Association.

Families, 4-H, and Nutrition

Cooperative State Research   Ph: (202)720-2908
   Education and Extension   Fax: (202)690-2469
   Service
Washington, DC 20250-2225
Contact: Alma C. Hobbs, Deputy Admin.
Desc: Youth, primarily nine to 19 years old, in rural and urban areas of 3150 counties in the United States, the District of Columbia, Puerto Rico, Guam, Virgin Islands, American Samoa, Micronesia, and Northern Marianas. Serves as a youth education program of the Cooperative Extension System. *Type:* Association.

Focus on the Family Clubhouse Jr.

Focus on the Family
8605 Explorer Dr.   Ph: (719)531-3400
Colorado Springs, CO 80920- Free: 800-232-6459
   1051   Fax: (719)548-5860
E-mail: tifeditor@fotf.org
Contact: Jesse Florea, Editor; Kim Washburn, Asst. Editor.
Desc: Consumer Christian magazine for children ages 4 to 8 years. *Type:* Periodical.

Fund for American Studies

1526 18th St. NW   Ph: (202)986-0384
Washington, DC 20036   Free: 800-741-6964
                           Fax: (202)986-0390
E-mail: rharts@tfas.org
URL: http://www.dcinternships.org
Contact: Roger R. Ream, Contact.
Desc: Promotes and supports the development of campus leadership through programs designed to encourage and facilitate the preparation of young people, without regard to race, color, national origin, or religious belief, for the assumption of leadership roles. Programs are built upon the concept that students who confront national and international issues with the assistance of accomplished professionals are those who will be the most qualified leaders. The program educates students from Eastern & Central Europe about principles of democratic government and free enterprise. *Type:* Association.

Gates Magazine

Gates Communications
PO Box 5181
Richmond, VA 23220
Contact: C. Mason Gates, Publisher; Stephanie Shweck, Editor.
Desc: Magazine for college students. *Type:* Periodical.

Girls' Life

Monarch Avalon, Inc.
4517 Hartford Rd.   Ph: (410)254-9200
Baltimore, MD 21214   Fax: (410)254-0991
E-mail: publisher@girlslife.com; editorial@girlslife.com.
Contact: Karen Bokram, Publisher, karen@girlslife.com; Jennifer Brown, Advertising Mgr.; Kelly White, Senior Editor; Edward Weiss, Marketing Dir.; Suzanne Long, Circulation Mgr.

Desc: Consumer magazine for girls and Girl Scouts ages 8-14 years. *Type:* Periodical.

Guideposts for Kids

Guideposts
39 Seminary Hill Rd.   Ph: (914)225-3681
Carmel, NY 10512   Free: 800-431-2344
                           Fax: (914)228-2111
Contact: Marylou Carney, Editor, mcarney@gp4k.org; Janine Scolpino, Circulation Dir.
Desc: Consumer magazine covering puzzles, games, and interfaith literature for children. *Alt. Contact:* PO Box 638, Chesterton, IN 46304; telephone: (219)929-4429; fax: (219)926-3839. *Type:* Periodical.

High Adventure

General Council of the Assemblies of God Gospel Publishing House
1445 Boonville Ave.   Ph: (417)862-2781
Springfield, MO 65802-1894 Fax: (417)862-0416
Contact: Ken Hunt, Directory of Publications; Marshall Bruner, Editor.
Desc: Religious and inspirational magazine for boys. *Type:* Periodical.

Hugh O'Brian Youth Foundation Alumni Association

10880 Wilshire Blvd., Rm. 411   Ph: (213)474-4370
Los Angeles, CA 90024
Contact: Judi Powell, Dir.
Desc: Individuals who attended an International Leadership Seminar sponsored by the Hugh O'Brian Youth Foundation organized to support and extend the goals and objectives of the foundation. Seeks to ensure the continual growth and development of the foundation and to provide for continued interaction among former attendees, known as ambassadors. Serves as liaison between the foundation and past ambassadors; represents the foundation before civic and community organizations. *Type:* Association.

Hugh O'Brian Youth Leadership

10880 Wilshire Blvd., Ste. 410   Ph: (310)474-4370
Los Angeles, CA 90024   Fax: (310)475-5426
Contact: Mary Leslie, Pres/CEO.
Desc: Seeks, recognizes, and develops leadership potential in American and international high school sophomores by sponsoring annual state and international leadership seminars. (The group is named for actor Hugh O'Brian, who founded the organization upon returning from a nine-day visit with Dr. Albert Schweitzer). *Type:* Association.

International Leadership Center

1600 2 Turtle Creek Village   Ph: (214)526-2953
Dallas, TX 75219
Desc: Business executives, corporations, an d legal and accounting firms. Works to build a network of leaders. Researches th e leadership structure of American cities and counties; examines the power structure s of government, business, and ethnic groups and the interactions among them. *Type:* Association.

International Youth Foundation

Rick Little
32 South St., Ste. 500   Ph: (410)347-1500
Baltimore, MD 21202   Fax: (410)347-1188
Contact: Bill Reese, COO.
Desc: Dedicated to the positive development of children and youth between the ages of 5 and 20. *Type:* Association.

Junior State of America

60 E. 3rd Ave., Ste. 320
San Mateo, CA 94401

Ph: (650)347-1600
Free: 800-334-5353
Fax: (650)347-7200

E-mail: jsa@jsa.org
URL: http://www.jsa.org

Contact: Richard T. Prosser, Exec.Dir.

Desc: Nonpartisan organization of high school student leaders interested in politics and government. Serves as a student opinion forum stressing the development of leadership skills. *Type:* Association.

Junior Statesmen Foundation

60 E. 3rd Ave., Ste. 320
San Mateo, CA 94401

Ph: (650)347-1600
Free: 800-334-5353
Fax: (650)347-7200

E-mail: jsa@jsa.org
URL: http://www.jsa.org

Contact: Richard T. Prosser, Exec.Dir.

Type: Association.

Keynoter

Keynoter
3636 Woodview Trace
Indianapolis, IN 46268-3196

Ph: (317)875-8755

E-mail: keynoter@kiwanis.org.

Contact: Julie A. Carson, Editor-in-Chief.

Desc: Magazine of the high school service organization Key Club International. *Type:* Periodical.

Kids Internationally Distributed Superstation

935 Morrison Ave.
St. Louis, MO 63104

Contact: Nancy Joyce, Exec.Dir.

Desc: Children, their teachers, and interested parents. Seeks to empower children, teachers, parents, and interested community leaders to influence the future. *Type:* Association.

Know Your World Extra

Weekly Reader Corp.
200 First Stamford Pl.
PO Box 120023
Stamford, CT 06912-0023

Ph: (203)705-3500
Fax: (203)705-1661

Contact: W. Scott Ingram, Editor, (203)638-2441; Richard J. Le Brasseur, Publisher, (203)638-2667, fax: (203)346-5994; Eric Ecker, Vice Pres./Group Product Developer, (203)638-2423.

Desc: Newspaper for junior and senior high school students. *Type:* Periodical.

Leadership Institute

1101 N. Highland St.
Arlington, VA 22201

Ph: (703)247-2000
Free: 800-827-5323
Fax: (703)247-2001

E-mail: todsteward@lead-inst.org
URL: http://www.lead-inst.org

Contact: Morton C. Blackwell, Pres.

Desc: Nonpartisan foundation which conducts educational programs primarily in the areas of conservative leadership identification training and placement. Seminars are conducted by experienced leaders in public policy and consist of lectures, exercises, discussions, and examinations. Sponsors Capitol Hill Training Seminar, Student Publications Seminars, Youth Leadership School, and a job and talent bank which assists seminar graduates and others in finding short-term or permanent employment in activities related to public policy. *Type:* Association.

Link, The College Magazine

Creative Media Generations, Inc.
110 Greene St., Ste. 407
New York, NY 10012

Ph: (212)966-1100
Free: 800-943-LINK
Fax: (212)966-1380

Contact: Ty Wenger, Editor; Robert Aronson, Advertising Dir.

Desc: Publication that examines contemporary issues from a students point of view. *Type:* Periodical.

Metro YMCAs of the Oranges

2 Babcock Place
West Orange, NJ 07052

Ph: (973)325-8881
Fax: (973)325-8771

Contact: W. Daniel McCain, Pres. & CEO.

Desc: Seeks to develop and improve the spiritual, social, mental, and physical life of youth and adults in the NJ area. Provides child care, camping, community health and fitness programs, job exploration, and substance abuse prevention. *Type:* Association.

Michigan State University Extension 4-H Youth Programs

Michigan State University
6H Berkey Hall
East Lansing, MI 48824-1111

Ph: (517)355-0180
Fax: (517)355-6748

E-mail: markc@msue.msu.edu
URL: http://www.msue.msu.edu/msue/cyf/youth/index.html

Contact: Dr. Cynthia B. Mark.

Desc: Youths (204,472) and volunteer leaders (25,026). Provides educational activities designed to promote development of good citizenship, leadership, and self-sufficiency. *Type:* Association.

National 4-H Council

7100 Connecticut Ave.
Chevy Chase, MD 20815-4999

Ph: (301)961-2840
Free: 800-368-7432
Fax: (301)961-2894

E-mail: info@fourhcouncil.edu
URL: http://www.fourhcouncil.edu

Contact: Richard J. Sauer, Pres.

Desc: Works to build community partnerships that value and involve youth in solving issues critical to their lives, their families, and society. *Type:* Association.

North Central Florida YMCA

5201 NW 34th St.
Gainesville, FL 32605

Ph: (352)374-9622
Fax: (352)372-5247

URL: http://gator.net/~ncfymca

Contact: Shawn Patch, CEO.

Desc: Seeks to develop and improve the spiritual, social, mental, and physical well-being of young people and adults. *Type:* Association.

NYC/New Youth Connections

Youth Communication
224 W. 29th St., 2nd Fl.
New York, NY 10001

Ph: (212)242-3270
Fax: (212)242-7057

E-mail: youthcomm@aol.com

Contact: Carol Kelly, Editor; Keith Hefner, Publisher.

Desc: Youth magazine. *Type:* Periodical.

Pioneer Clubs

Box 788
27 W. 130 St. Charles Rd.
Wheaton, IL 60189

Ph: (630)293-1600
Free: 800-694-2582
Fax: (630)293-3053

E-mail: pcinfo@enteract.com
URL: http://www.pioneerclubs.org

Contact: Judy Bryson, Pres.

Desc: Christian movement for children and youth ages 2 to 18 organized in more than 3200 churches of some 70 denominations in the U.S., Canada, and foreign countries.

Seeks "to lead young people to personal experience with Jesus Christ and help them relate their Christian experience to every phase of life." Program includes a weekly club meeting, summer camping, and a system of achievements and special leadership training opportunities. Sponsors educational and training program for adult leaders and volunteers; conducts seminars, workshops, and program research. *Type:* Association.

Play Magazine

Milor Entertainment Group
3620 NW 43rd St.
Gainesville, FL 32606

Ph: (352)375-3705
Fax: (352)375-7268

Contact: Michael Fagien, Editor-in-Chief; Lori Fagien, Publisher.

Desc: Consumer magazine that reviews the latest in music, video, books, multimedia, toy and game technology for children and the family. *Type:* Periodical.

Presidential Classroom

119 Oronoco St.
Alexandria, VA 22314

Ph: (703)683-5400
Free: 800-441-6533
Fax: (703)548-5728

E-mail: prezclass@aol.com
URL: http://www.presidentialclassroom.org

Contact: Jay Wickliff, Exec.Dir.

Desc: High school juniors and seniors. Seeks to provide an in-depth study and an insider's behind-the-scenes look at the U.S. government in Washington, DC, to students; enlighten students by personal involvement in government functions. Promotes a dedication to and a greater understanding of the American system of government. *Type:* Association.

Read

Weekly Reader Corp.
200 First Stamford Pl.
PO Box 120023
Stamford, CT 06912-0023

Ph: (203)705-3500
Fax: (203)705-1661

E-mail: edread@weeklyreader.com.

Contact: Scott Ingram, Managing Editor, (203)705-3479, singram@weeklyreader.com; Kate Davis, Editor, (203)705-3406, kdavis@weeklyreader.com; Ellen Florian, Assoc. Editor, (203)705-3449, eflorian@weeklyreader.com.

Desc: A language arts magazine for junior & senior high school students, featuring award winning youngadult literature, classic adaptations, and history theme issues. *Type:* Periodical.

Seventeen

K-III Magazine Corp.
850 3rd Ave., 9th Fl.
New York, NY 10022

Ph: (212)407-9700
Fax: (212)935-4237

Contact: Merideth Berlin, Editor-in-Chief; Janice Grossman, Publisher.

Desc: Magazine for young women, ages 12-24. *Type:* Periodical.

16 Magazine

16 Magazine, Inc.
233 Park Ave. S.
New York, NY 10003

Ph: (212)979-4932
Fax: (212)979-7342

Contact: Randi Reisfeld, Editorial Dir.; Jackie Jarosz, Associate Editor; Allen Tuller, Publisher; John Garoly, Advertising Mgr.

Desc: Magazine for teens. *Type:* Periodical.

Teen Beat

Sterling/Macfadden Partnership
233 Park Ave. S.
New York, NY 10003

Ph: (212)780-3500
Fax: (212)780-3555

Contact: Karen L. Williams, Editor, (212)979-4882, fax: (212)979-7342.

Desc: Teen entertainment magazine covering teen movie stars, TV stars, music, new products, and fashion. *Type:* Periodical.

Teen Times

Future Homemakers of America
1910 Association Dr.   Ph: (703)476-4900
Reston, VA 20191   Fax: (703)860-2713
E-mail: natlhdqtrs@fhahero.org
Contact: Alan T. Rains, Exec. Dir., arains@fhahero.org; Patti Hopkins, Advertising and Communications Coord., phopkins@fhahero.org.
Desc: Student association magazine reporting organization news and discussing issues of concern to teens. *Type:* Periodical.

THRASHER

High Speed Productions, Inc.
1303 Underwood   Ph: (415)822-3083
San Francisco, CA 94124   Fax: (415)822-8359
Contact: Kevin J. Thatcher, Publisher; Edward H. Riggins, Publisher; Eben Sterling, Advertising.
Desc: Skateboard magazine. *Type:* Periodical.

Tiger Beat Magazine

Sterling/Macfadden Partnership
233 Park Ave. S.   Ph: (212)780-3500
New York, NY 10003   Fax: (212)780-3555
E-mail: tigerbmail@aol.com.
Contact: Louise A. Barile, Editor; John Goroly, Advertising Mgr., (212)922-9320.
Desc: Teenage entertainment magazine. *Type:* Periodical.

What! A Magazine

M2 Communications Inc.
108-93 Lombard Ave.   Ph: (204)985-8160
Winnipeg, MB, Canada R3B   Fax: (204)943-8991
  3B1
E-mail: what@fox.nstn.ca.
Desc: Consumer magazine for teenagers in Canada. *Type:* Periodical.

YM

Gruner & Jahr USA Publishing
375 Lexington Ave., 10th Fl.   Ph: (212)499-2000
New York, NY 10017-4024   Free: 800-599-8489
                                 Fax: (212)499-2159
Contact: Lesley Seymour, Editor, (212)499-1697; Alyce Alston, Publisher, (212)499-1640.
Desc: Magazine for young women aged 12-24. *Type:* Periodical.

YMCA International Branch

71 W. 23 St., Ste. 1904   Ph: (212)727-8800
New York, NY 10010   Fax: (212)727-8814
Contact: Alice L. Mairs, Dir.
Desc: International program run through YMCA of Greater New York, on behalf of the YMCA of the USA. Purpose is to assist international students and sponsored visitors who have come to the U.S. for study or purposeful, short-term travel. *Type:* Association.

YMCA of San Francisco

44 Montgomery St., Ste. 770   Ph: (415)391-9622
San Francisco, CA 94104   Fax: (415)391-1303
Contact: Gregory W. O'Brien, Acting Pres. & CEO.
Desc: Seeks to develop and improve the spiritual, social, mental, and physical well-being of young people and adults. *Type:* Association.

YMCA of the United States of America

101 N. Wacker Dr.   Ph: (312)977-0031
Chicago, IL 60606   Free: 800-872-9622
                                 Fax: (312)977-9063
URL: http://www.ymca.net/
Contact: Richard Clegg, Assoc.Dir.
Desc: A volunteer movement characterized by local program control designed to meet the community needs of people of all ages, races, religions, abilities, and incomes. Focus is on nuturing the healthy development of children, promoting positive behavior in teens, and strengthening families. Provides group activities, facilities for physical and health education and training, youth sports activities, aquatics instruction, camping, parent-child programs, child care, and counseling. *Type:* Association.

Young Life

PO Box 520   Ph: (719)473-4262
Colorado Springs, CO 80901   Fax: (719)381-1750
URL: http://www.younglife.org
Contact: Denny Rydberg, Pres.
Desc: A Christian program for adolescents offering camping during the summer and on winter weekends, and a club program that operates during the school year. *Type:* Association.

Young Men's Christian Association of Central Maryland

20 S. Charles St., Ste. 600   Ph: (410)837-9622
Baltimore, MD 21201   Fax: (410)752-5452
Contact: Lee Jensen, Pres./CEO.
Desc: Seeks to develop and improve the spiritual, social, mental, and physical well-being of young people and adults. *Type:* Association.

Young Men's Christian Association of Greater Cincinnati

1105 Elm St.   Ph: (513)651-2100
Cincinnati, OH 45210
Contact: George H. Edmiston, Pres.
Desc: Seeks to develop and improve the spiritual, social, mental, and physical life of youth and adults in the Hamilton County, OH and northern Kentucky areas. *Type:* Association.

Young Men's Christian Association of Metropolitan Denver

25 East 16th Ave.   Ph: (303)861-2256
Denver, CO 80202   Fax: (303)830-7391
Contact: Kevin McCorry, Dir. of Communications.
Desc: Seeks to put Christian principles into action through programs that build a healthy body, mind, and spirit. *Type:* Association.

Young Men's Christian Association of the Rockies

Schlessman Center Executive   Ph: (970)586-4444
  Offices   Fax: (970)586-6088
Estes Park, CO 80511-2800
E-mail: info@ymcarockies.org
URL: http://www.ymcarockies.org
Contact: E. Eugene Garris, Pres. & CEO.
Desc: Puts Christian principles into practice through programs, staff and facilities in an environment that builds healthy spirit, mind and body for all. It is being accomplished by serving conferences of a religious, educational or recreational nature, providing unifying experiences for families, offering traditional summer camping experiences for boys and girls, and serving the staff with leadership opportunities and productive work experiences. *Type:* Association.

Young Women's Christian Association of Greater Pittsburgh

305 Wood St.   Ph: (412)391-5100
Pittsburgh, PA 15222-1982
Contact: Margaret Tyndall, Ph.D., CEO.
Desc: Seeks to develop and improve the spiritual, social, mental, and physical life of young people and adults. Works to eliminate racism. *Type:* Association.

Young Women's Christian Association of the United States of America

Empire State Bldg.   Ph: (212)755-4500
350 5th Ave., Ste. 301   Fax: (212)273-7806
New York, NY 10118
E-mail: Pmathai'Davis@ywca.org
Contact: Dr. Prema Matillai, Exec.Dir.
Desc: Women and girls over 12 years of age and their families who participate in service programs of health education, recreation, clubs and classes, and counseling and assistance to girls and women in the areas of employment, education, human sexuality, self improvement, voluntarism, citizenship, emotional and physical health, and juvenile justice. Seeks to make contributions to peace, justice, freedom, and dignity for all people; works toward the empowerment of women and the elimination of racism. Conducts international advocacy program on human rights and on peace and development. *Type:* Association.

Youth for Christ/U.S.A.

PO Box 228822   Ph: (303)843-9000
Denver, CO 80222   Fax: (303)843-9002
E-mail: yfc@gospelcom.net
URL: http://www.gospelcom.net/yfc
Contact: Roger Cross, Pres.
Desc: Interdenominational organization for the evangelization and discipling of teenagers. Fights juvenile delinquency through counseling and Youth Guidance programs for youth penal institutions. Carries on projects in 127 countries through Youth for Christ International. *Type:* Association.

YWCA El Paso del Norte Region

1918 Texas Ave.   Ph: (915)533-2311
El Paso, TX 79901   Fax: (915)533-7921
URL: http://rgfn.epcc.edu/users/au238
Contact: Myrna J. Deckert, CEO.
Desc: Seeks to develop and improve the spiritual, social, mental, and physical well-being of young people and adults. Provides health, child care, and cooperative services, services to teen parents, and counseling. *Type:* Association.

Zoology

American Beekeeping Federation—News Letter

American Beekeeping Federation, Inc.
PO Box 1038   Ph: (912)427-4233
Jesup, GA 31598   Fax: (912)427-8447
E-mail: info@abfnet.org
URL: http://abfnet.org.
Contact: Troy H. Fore, Jr., Editor, troyfore@abfnet.org.
Desc: Discusses Federation activities and national problems of the beekeeping industry. Also covers related legislation, regulations, and marketing and production information. *Type:* Newsletter.

Eastern Apicultural Society of North America

Loretta Surprenant
County Home Rd.   Ph: (518)963-7593
Box 300A
Essex, NY 12936
Contact: Loretta Surprenant, Sec.
Desc: Hobbyist beekeepers and producers of honey; supporting members are manufacturers of beekeeping equipment and packers of honey. *Type:* Association.

Entomological Society of America

9301 Annapolis Rd.　　　　Ph: (301)731-4535
Lanham, MD 20706-3115　　Fax: (301)731-4538
E-mail: info@entsoc.org
URL: http://www.entsoc.org

Contact: Douglas M. Kleine, CAE, Exec.Dir.

Desc: Professional society of entomologists and others interested in the study of insects. Operates ESA Certification Program. Conducts specialized education and research programs; maintains placement services. *Type:* Association.

Gorilla Foundation

PO Box 620-530　　　　Ph: (650)851-8505
Woodside, CA 94062　　Free: 800-63G-OAPE
　　　　　　　　　　　Fax: (650)851-0291

E-mail: hanabiko@earthlink.net
URL: http://www.gorilla.org

Contact: Dr. Ronald H. Cohn, VP/Treas.

Desc: Promotes conservation, propagation, and behavioral study of apes, particularly gorillas. *Type:* Association.

Hive Lights

Canadian Honey Council
234-5149 Country Hills Blvd.　Ph: (403)208-7141
　NW, Ste. 236　　　　　　　Fax: (403)547-4317
Calgary, AB, Canada T3A 5K8
E-mail: chc-ccm@telusplanet.net

Contact: Fran Kay, Editor.

Desc: Cover topics related to the beekeeping and honey industry. Recurring features include letters to the editor, news of research, a calendar of events, reports of meetings, news of educational opportunities, and job listings. *Type:* Newsletter.

Jacksonville Zoological Society

8605 Zoo Pkwy.　　　　Ph: (904)757-4463
Jacksonville, FL 32218　　Fax: (904)757-4315
URL: http://www.jaxzoo.org

Contact: C. Douglas Page, DVM, Exec.Dir.

Desc: Zoo support organization. Conducts educational activities. *Type:* Association.

Library News for Zoos and Aquariums

Suzanne K. Braun
Indianapolis Zoo　　　　　Ph: (317)630-5110
1200 W. Washington St.　　Fax: (317)630-5114
Indianapolis, IN 46222
E-mail: sbraun@mail.indyzoo.com

Contact: Suzanne K. Braun, Editor.

Desc: Offers a forum for zoo and aquarium librarians to exchange information, ideas, problems, and experiences in their profession. Informs those institutions without librarians on how to set up functional libraries. *Type:* Newsletter.

Manitoba Beekeeper

Manitoba Beekeepers' Association
Box 1448　　　　　　　Ph: (204)326-3763
Steinbach, MB, Canada R0A　Fax: (204)945-4327
　2A0
E-mail: manbeekr@mb.sympatico.ca

Contact: Ron Rudiak, Editor.

Desc: Furnishes information about beekeeping. Recurring features include news of research, a calendar of events, and reports of meetings. *Type:* Newsletter.

Sydney's Koala Club News

Zoological Society of San Diego, Inc.
PO Box 551　　　　　　Ph: (619)231-1515
San Diego, CA 92112　　Fax: (619)231-1725

Contact: Karen E. Worley, Editor.

Desc: Focuses on the animal and plant collections and activities at the San Diego Zoo and the San Diego Wild Animal Park. Carries profiles and photographs of particular animals, as well as general natural history and conservation articles for children. *Type:* Newsletter.

Zoological Record Online®

BIOSIS
Two Commerce Square　　Ph: (215)587-4800
2001 Market St., Ste. 700
Philadelphia, PA 19103-7095
E-mail: info@mail.biosis.org
URL: http://www.biosis.org

Desc: Contains more than 1.3 million citations to the worldwide literature on zoology, with systematic and taxonomic information for 27 animal groups, including Mammalia, Aves, Reptilia, Amphibia, Pisces, Protochordata, Hemiptera, Insecta, Crustacea, and Protozoa. Topics include taxonomy, physiology, morphology, parasitology, biochemistry, biophysics, evolution, ecology, genetics, behavior, biometrics, communication, disease, habitat, histology, immunology, life cycle and development, locomotion, nomenclature, techniques, and zoogeography. *Available:* The Dialog Corporation, DIALOG. *Type:* Database.

ZOONOOZ

Zoological Society of San Diego, Inc.
PO Box 551　　　　　　Ph: (619)231-1515
San Diego, CA 92112　　Fax: (619)231-1725

Contact: Thomas L. Scharf, Editor.

Desc: Magazine on natural history, animal science, and conservation. *Alt. Contact:* , PO Box 551, San Diego, CA 92112-0551. *Type:* Periodical.

Title and Keyword Index

This index provides an alphabetical listing of all entry names and important keywords within entry names. The number following the index citation refers to the page number(s) for the cited entry.

Title and Keyword Index

Title and Keyword Index

E

Title and Keyword Index

Title and Keyword Index

Title and Keyword Index

Title and Keyword Index

M

Q

S

T

W

Z